THE AUTHORITY SINCE 1868

THE WORLD ALMANAC

AND BOOK OF FACTS

1993

WORLD ALMANAC
AN IMPRINT OF PHAROS BOOKS • A SCRIPPS HOWARD COMPANY
NEW YORK

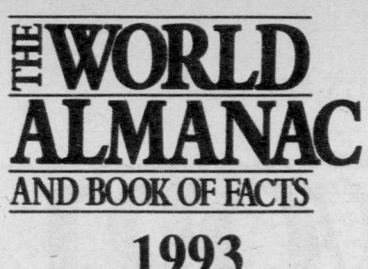

THE WORLD ALMANAC AND BOOK OF FACTS

1993

Editor: Mark S. Hoffman
Senior Editor: June Foley **Senior Assistant Editor:** Thomas McGuire
Chronology & Special Features: Donald Young **Index:** Aris Georgiadis
Editorial Assistant: Michael Northrop

Pharos Books
President: David Hendin
Vice President & Publisher: Phyllis Henrici
Publicity Manager: Joyce H. Stein **Sales Manager:** Patricia Hughes
Director of Manufacturing: Randy Lang **Rights Manager:** Tracey M. Bussell

---

The editors acknowledge with thanks the many letters of helpful comment and criticism from readers of THE WORLD ALMANAC, and invite further suggestions and observations. Because of the volume of mail directed to the editorial offices, it is not possible to reply to each letter writer. However, every communication is read by the editors and all comments and suggestions receive careful attention. Inquiries regarding contents should be sent to: Editor, The World Almanac, 200 Park Avenue, New York, NY 10166.

THE WORLD ALMANAC is published annually in November.

THE WORLD ALMANAC does not decide wagers.

The first edition of THE WORLD ALMANAC, a 120-page volume with 12 pages of advertising, was published by the New York World in 1868, 125 years ago. Annual publication was suspended in 1876. Joseph Pulitzer, publisher of the New York World, revived THE WORLD ALMANAC in 1886 with the goal of making it a "compendium of universal knowledge." It has been published annually since then. In 1931, it was acquired by the Scripps Howard Newspapers; until 1951, it bore the imprint of the New York World-Telegram and thereafter, until 1967, that of the New York World-Telegram and Sun. It is now published in paper and clothbound editions by Pharos Books, a Scripps Howard company.

THE WORLD ALMANAC & BOOK OF FACTS 1993

Library of Congress Catalog Card Number 4-3781
International Standard Serial Number (ISSN) 0084-1382
Pharos Books (softcover) ISBN 0-88687-658-3
Pharos Books (hardcover) ISBN 0-88687-659-1
Microform Edition since 1868: University Microfilms Intl.
Printed in the United States of America
The softcover and hardcover editions are distributed to the trade in the United States by St. Martin's Press.

WORLD ALMANAC
An Imprint of Pharos Books
A Scripps Howard Company
200 Park Avenue, New York, NY 10166

1993 HIGHLIGHTS

GENERAL INDEX

— B —

—J—

—K—

— O —

—P—

Addenda, Late News, Changes

County Seats (p. 442)

The county seat for Baker County, Oregon is Baker City.

Disasters (p. 575)

The death toll from the typhoon that struck the Philippines, Oct. 22, 1952, should be 440.

Nations (pp. 732; 736; 740; 752; 760; 807; 823)

Azerbaijan: Voted against joining the Commonwealth of Independent States, Oct.

Brazil: Itamar Augusto Franco appointed President, Oct. 2.

Canadian voters rejected a complex constitutional package aimed at easing secessionist desires in Quebec and preserving national unity.

Estonia: Lennart Meri elected President, Oct. 7.

Guyana: Cheddi Jagan elected President, Oct. 7.

Ukraine: Leonid Kuchma named President, Oct. 13.

Nobel Prizes (pp. 308-310)

(Each 1992 Nobel Prize included a cash award of about $1.2 million.)

Physiology or Medicine: Two Americans from the Univ. of Washington in Seattle, Edmond H. Fisher and Edwin G. Krebs, won for their discovery of a regulatory mechanism affecting almost all cells.

Memorial Prize in Economic Science: Gary S. Becker, an American at the Univ. of Chicago, won for "having extended the domain of economic theory to aspects of human behavior which had previously been dealt with—if at all—by other social science disciplines such as sociology, demography, and criminology."

Physics: George Charpak, a citizen of France who was born in Poland and works on the French/Swiss border, won. He invented a particle detector used in many discoveries about the ultimate nature of matter.

Chemistry: Rudolph A. Marcus, a Canadian-born scientist at the Calif. Institute of Technology in Pasadena, won by finding a way to predict certain interactions between molecules in solution.

Peace: The award went to Rigoberta Menchú of Guatemala, for her work in "social justice and ethno-cultural reconciliation based on respect for the rights of indigenous peoples."

Literature: Derek Walcott won for poetry of a "melodious and sensitive" style as well as "historical vision, the outcome of a multicultural commitment." Born in St. Lucia, the West Indies, Walcott teaches at Boston University.

Sports (pp. 901; 896)

Boxing: Virgil Hill defeated Frank Tate to win the WBA Light Heavyweight title. Iran Barkley relinquished the title and to defend his IBF Super Middleweight title.

Basketball: Magic Johnson announced his re-retirement, Nov. 2.

Track and Field: Sergei Bubka set a world record in the pole vault, clearing 20 feet 1½ inches, Sept. 20; Sam Bell, Charlie Greene, Jess Mortensen, Charlie Jenkins, and Archie Williams were named to the Track & Field Hall of Fame.

United Nations (p. 824)

The Belgrade Government was expelled from the seat previously occupied by the Yugoslav Federation.

Zip Codes (pp. 410-411; 416)

In Maryland, the correct zip code for Bethesda is 20814, for Kensington 20895, for Laurel 20707, for Riverdale 20737.

In New Jersey, the correct zip code for Fairfield is 07004.

Notable Quotes in 1992

"Would you please shut up and sit down!"

George Bush, to a group of POW-MIA families protesting his campaign speech in Crystal City, Va.

"The defense budget is more than a piggy bank for people who want to get busy beating swords into pork barrels."

George Bush, campaigning at a high-tech robotics plant in Anaheim, Cal.

"When I was in England I experimented with marijuana a time or two, I didn't like it, I didn't inhale it, and never tried it again."

Bill Clinton

"This will probably cause you to faint because you never heard anybody in public life say they made a mistake."

Ross Perot, on his withdrawal from the presidential race.

"The way political campaigns are run is a mess. The people want a new political climate where the system does not attract ego-driven, power-hungry people."

Ross Perot

"That's fine phonetically, but you're missing just a little bit."

Dan Quayle, to Trenton, N.J., sixth grader William Figueroa after the youngster correctly spelled the word "potato," which Quayle thought was spelled "potatoe."

"He seems like an average type of man. He's not smart. I'm not trying to rag on him or anything. But he has the same mentality I have—and I'm in the eighth grade."

Vanessa Martinez, after Dan Quayle visited her high school in Los Angeles.

"I watched that giant masquerade ball up at Madison Square Garden, where 20,000 liberals and radicals came dressed up as moderates and centrists in the greatest single exhibition of cross-dressing in American political history."

Presidential candidate *Patrick Buchanan*

"It is about a socialist, anti-family political movement that encourages women to leave their husbands, kill their children, practice witchcraft, destroy capitalism and become lesbians."

Televangelist *Pat Robertson,* who spoke at the Republican convention, on the proposed equal rights amendment.

"I have never seen a professional baseball game, an episode of 'Dallas' or of Roseanne Barr or of Geraldo Rivera or of the black lady who is alternately fat and thin, I forget her name."

William F. Buckley, countering attacks on George Bush's lack of the common touch.

"I think it's about time we voted for senators with breasts. After all, we've been voting for boobs long enough."

Arizona senatorial candidate *Claire Sargent,* on women candidates.

"We believe he wanted to win in the worst way."

Seminole County, Fla., Sheriff *Don Eslinger* on a state representative challenger charged with attempted murder of his opponent.

"There is no reason for that. I don't think they gave me a lobotomy, because it's not at that end that this happened."

French President *Francois Mitterrand,* on whether he might be forced to resign after surgery for prostate cancer.

"Many, if not all, of my presidential opponents are certifiable idiots."

Philippine presidential candidate *Miriam Defensor Santiago.*

"We now have the opportunity, so fervently pursued for generations, to guarantee a peaceful transition to democracy. America must respond to this challenge, as we have so many times before, through leadership of an international coalition to secure the success of reform in Russia and the other states of the former Soviet Union."

Letter from four living presidents—*Richard Nixon, Gerald Ford, Jimmy Carter, and Ronald Reagan.*

"Tell Bush, come quickly! Tell Bush I spend every day and every night here! Me, an old grandmother! Tell him to come and defend us, please!."

Dzemila Merdan, hiding from mortar and artillery shells in Sarajevo.

"If an employer can cut workers out of a health plan after they become ill, health insurance is just an elaborate shell game."

Thomas B. Stoddard, representing a man who lost his benefits before dying of AIDS.

"Not a day goes by when a hospital emergency room somewhere in America doesn't have a case where some elderly person has been abandoned, usually by the children."

John Meyers of the American Association of Retired Persons.

"To all you mothers out there who are raising your children alone either by choice or necessity, don't let anyone tell you you're not a family."

Diane English, "Murphy Brown" creator, accepting her Emmy.

(continued)

"Religious beliefs and religious expression are too precious to be either proscribed or prescribed by the state."
Justice Anthony M. Kennedy.

"American workers don't work hard enough. They don't work but demand high pay."
Yoshio Sakurauchi, Japanese House speaker.

"Now especially it is time for Japan, an exporting nation, to assume a larger share of the West's common responsibility."
German Chancellor Helmut Kohl.

"People, I just want to say, you know, can we all get along? I mean, we're stuck here for a while. Let's try to work it out."
Rodney King

"Half of the American people never read a newspaper. Half never vote for President. One hopes it is the same half."
Gore Vidal

"People want to know why I do this, why I write such gross stuff. I like to tell them I have the heart of a small boy—and I keep it in a jar on my desk."
Stephen King.

"He wanted to write more, but President Bush made him stop before the book was finished."
Jay Leno on Norman Schwarzkopf's new book.

"Regarding my love for Soon-Yi . . .she's a lovely, intelligent, sensitive woman who has and continues to turn my life around in a wonderfully positive way."
Woody Allen, admitting he is having an affair with the college-age adopted daughter of his longtime companion, actress Mia Farrow.

"I want my name in the press. Why? Because I can make a lot of money. I figure if I'm going through all this pain and suffering, I'm getting a Ferrari."
Amy Fisher, hours before being sentenced in a plea bargin to five to 15 years in jail for shooting her alleged lover's wife.

"It's not Hollywood, this ain't Walt Disney. This is about the state of race relations in the world."
Spike Lee, asking blacks to skip work or school to see his film "Malcolm X."

"They say you have to stop eating when he does. But what if he's having a snack and you're starving? Do you have to eat fast?"
Charles Barkley, on being introduced to Monaco's Prince Rainier.

"I am angry that I was put in the position of having to lie if I wanted to protect my privacy."
Arthur Ashe, announcing he has AIDS.

"The really scary thing is that some of those people work for the government."
Washington Redskins lineman *Joe Jacoby,* on fans who attend games wearing pig snouts.

"These greenies have nice speeches, but in practice they're pigs."
Rio Earth Summit janitor *Manuel DeSoto,* while sweeping up streamers, wrappers and cups near a meeting on waste management.

"Who is she?"
Casey Weldon, Florida State Univ. quarterback, when told he was going to meet Ringo Starr.

"For every step forward in electronic communications we've taken two steps back in humanity. People know how to use a computer and answering machines but have forgotten how to connect with one another."
Letitia Baldrige, authority on etiquette.

"We definitely wanted to start in New York because—as you say—if you can make it there, you can make it anywhere."
Pierre Jeanjean, an executive with the Paris-based JCDecaux company, which installed six experimental automatic public toilets in the Big Apple.

"Your food stamps will be stopped effective March, 1992, because we received notice that you passed away. May God bless you. You may reapply if there is a change in your circumstances."
From a letter to a dead person from the Greenville County (S.C.) Department of Social Services.

Notable Decisions of the U.S. Supreme Court, 1991-92

(For further information, see *Supreme Court, Chronology,* and *Addenda.*)

The Supreme Court issued 107 signed decisions in the 1991-92 term, the lowest number in more than 20 years. Of those decisions, 42 were unanimous, a slight increase from 1990-91. Only 14 cases were decided by 5-4 votes, down from 21 in the previous term and 37 in 1989-90. The decrease in close votes was generally attributed to the strengthening of the court's conservative bloc with the addition of Clarence Thomas. However, three justices who had been considered allied with the court's conservative faction at times formed a center-right coalition that cast the deciding votes in a number of surprisingly liberal rulings. The three justices, David H. Souter, Anthony M. Kennedy, and Sandra Day O'Connor, agreed with one another on 71% of the court's rulings during the 1991-92 term. Although they often joined with Chief Justice William H. Rehnquist and Justices Antonin Scalia and Clarence Thomas in a conservative majority, as the term progressed they increasingly joined the court's more liberal minority to uphold the precedents set by earlier liberal courts on abortion, school prayer, and school desegregation.

Among the most significant decisions, the court:

Upheld, 5-4, most of the provisions of a Pennsylvania law that imposed strict limits on a woman's ability to obtain an abortion. However, the majority also reaffirmed that a woman's basic right to choose an abortion was "a rule of law and a component of liberty we cannot renounce." The provisions upheld included an "informed consent" clause requiring doctors and clinics to present women seeking abortions with state-prepared information on abortions and fetal development; a mandatory 24-hour waiting period between the presentation and the abortion procedure; and a requirement that women under 18 obtain the consent of one parent or a judge before undergoing the abortion. The court struck down a provision that required women to notify their husbands of their intent to obtain an abortion. (June 29)

Ruled, 5-4, that nonsectarian prayers at a public high school graduation violated First Amendment principles separating church and state. (June 24)

125th ANNIVERSARY EDITION

The World Almanac

and Book of Facts for 1993

The Top 10 News Stories

Thoroughly defeating Pres. George Bush and Independent Ross Perot, Bill Clinton was elected the 42nd President of the U.S. Democrats retained control of the House and Senate, as four women won their Senate races, including two in Calif. and the first black woman senator in Ill.

Heading the list of issues in the 1992 presidential campaign was the state of the U.S. economy—the recession, unemployment, taxes, and the budget deficit.

Eruptions of rioting and racial tension swept South-Central Los Angeles after the acquittal of 4 police officers charged with assault and excessive use of force in the arrest of Rodney King.

Reports of massacres and "ethnic cleansing" marked the fighting among the newly formed nations of what once was Yugoslavia.

Entering 1992, the Soviet Union ceased to exist as 15 new nations were formed, including Russia, which moved to reach new agreements with the U.S. on reducing nuclear weapons.

AIDS continued to spread throughout the world; the World Health Organization estimated that by the year 2000, up to 40 million people would be infected.

Destroying life and property, hurricanes Andrew and Iniki struck Florida and Louisiana and the island of Kauai in Hawaii; earthquakes in California and Egypt caused property damage and many deaths.

European nations began efforts to solidify the European Community as they sought to create a single currency and a common foreign and defense policy.

Relief efforts to reduce the death and suffering caused by famine and civil war in Somalia and other African nations were headed by the U.N.

Submitted to the states for ratification in 1789, an amendment to control the timing of pay raises for senators and representatives became the 27th amendment to the U.S. Constitution.

America: Starting Again

By John Chancellor

Sam Ervin, the Senator from North Carolina, used to say that if something went wrong with your life in the United States, you could always move to another part of it and start again. The Senator wasn't talking about running away from the law; he was talking about the chance to make a new start, which he thought was a special and wonderful aspect of life in America. People did it all the time when he was born in 1896; they were doing it when he died 88 years later. Call it renewal, revival, rejuvenation: breaking with the past and starting again is a very American act.

When the first edition of *The World Almanac* was published in 1868, the United States itself was starting anew. It had gone through a terrible Civil War, the assassination of a president, and the impeachment trial of another. The nation had been tested under fearful conditions, but the Constitution had worked. The U.S. had preserved its unique distinction. Alone among the nations of the world, it had invented itself. It had created its own nationality. In the mid-19th century, only Great Britain had reached constitutional maturity. Germany and Italy did not exist in their present form. Russia was ruled by a tsar, France by an emperor, Spain by a king. China slept under the Ch'ing Dynasty.

When the Civil War ended, the United States had grown much but changed little from the time of its declaration of independence. Americans were still rural, agrarian, homespun and horse drawn, mainly of British stock, conservative and plain-spoken.

But change was in the air. The old Jeffersonian model of a pastoral society, based in part on slave labor, had come to an end. The country was beginning an enormous expansion. According to the 1860 census, there were 31,000,000 Americans; 62,000,000 were counted in 1890, and more than 8,000,000 of these new citizens were immigrants. In that time, seven new states were established, adding an area three times the size of France.

Life on the frontier was hard. Indians were treated with appalling cruelty. General Philip Henry Sheridan met a Comanche chief who said, "Me good Indian." Sheridan replied, "The only good Indians I ever saw were dead," which became a popular saying. The government took the Indians' best land, confined them to barren reservations, and outlawed their religion.

Things weren't much better for blacks in the states of the old Confederacy. In 1877, the Republicans in Washington, D.C. brought federal troops home from the south, and Democrats in southern states enacted laws that imposed segregation. Some of those Jim Crow laws would stay on the books for 80 years.

Life in parts of the country was as raw as frontier whiskey. But the coarseness of the United States in those years must be balanced against the accomplishments of the nation, and there were a wide array of those. They included the writings of Mark Twain, Emily Dickinson, Henry James, Edgar Allan Poe, Louisa May Alcott, the paintings of Winslow Homer and Mary Cassatt, the speeches of Frederick Douglass and Ralph Waldo Emerson, the music of Scott Joplin and John Philip Sousa—the whole, wonderful, boisterous panoply of American life in the late 19th Century.

The first edition of *The World Almanac* was printed on a modern press. Its readers could send telegrams, ride in elevators and travel on transatlantic steamships. A patent had been issued for a typewriter. In the next few decades, Bell invented the telephone, Edison the incandescent light and the phonograph, Eastman the Kodak camera, and Gillette the safety razor. The first professional baseball team, the Cincinnati Red Stockings, was founded in 1868. A year later, the first labor union was organized, and the first local female suffrage law was passed. By the end of the century, there were four rail lines spanning the United States and 200,000 miles of track. In 30 years, the U.S. had built a high-technology transportation system able to meet the demands of a new industrial power of continental size.

The country we know today took shape in those headstrong, heedless years. Divisions between rich and poor had never been greater. A class of American multimillionaires was created. Bribery and swindling were commonplace, and bust followed boom. Crime and lawlessness were uncontrollable in parts of northern cities. Politics in New York City was in the corrupt grip of the Tweed Ring. In the years after the Civil War, Republicans tried to equate the Democratic Party with slavery and rebellion; it was called "waving the bloody shirt." Americans today complain about the poor quality of their politicians. It is not a new lament. James Bryce wrote his classic study of the United States, *The American Commonwealth*, in the 1880s. One of its chapters is titled, "The Best Men Do Not Go Into Politics."

In 1898, the nation was hustled into a trumped-up war with Spain by the yellow press of William Randolph Hearst and Joseph Pulitzer. In victory, the U.S. acquired Puerto Rico, Guam, and the Philippines. Cuba became an American protectorate. In 1903, the U.S. took its first step toward building the Panama Canal. Pres. Theodore Roosevelt sent a flotilla of American warships around the world in a three-year display of naval power. What Henry Luce would call "The American Century" was underway.

Roosevelt won the Nobel Peace Prize in 1906 for his accomplishments as an international peacemaker. Twelve years later, American soldiers were in Europe, helping the Allies to win World War I.

When the doughboys came home in 1918, some of the Americans who welcomed them had been born before the Civil War. That year, *The World Almanac* celebrated its 50th birthday. An astonishing amount of achievement and growth had been packed into 50 breathless years.

II

The second transformation of the United States was caused by the Cold War. The victors of World War I committed a series of diplomatic and economic blunders that led to a global depression and, 21 years later, a second world war. When World War II ended, the two most powerful countries were the U.S. and the Soviet Union, and they soon faced each other across a deep ideological divide. World War II, from Germany's attack on Poland to the bursts of nuclear fission over Japan, lasted six years. The Cold War lasted more than 40.

In 1835, Alexis de Tocqueville published *Democracy In America*, in which he made a remarkable prophecy about Russia and America. He wrote, "Their point of departure is different and their paths diverse; nevertheless, each seems called by some secret design of Providence one day to hold in its hands the destinies of half the world." During the Cold War, that seemed to have come true.

On one side was the U.S.S.R., with its vast territory, its iron grip on the countries of Eastern Europe, its ally China, and its friends in the Third World. On the other was the U.S., incomparably richer than any other country, its allies in Western Europe and Asia, and a web of military alliances designed to contain communist expansion: NATO, CENTO, SEATO.

The United States spent, in today's dollars, $100 billion on the Marshall Plan to rebuild Western Europe after the war. This enormous investment was sold to the American people and the Congress as a way of keeping those devastated democracies from turning to communism. Soviet actions made it an easy sale. Stalin was a ruthless dictator running a paranoid regime with expansionist ambitions. A giant Soviet propaganda machine said communism was the wave of the future, which worried a lot of Americans. There was a red scare in America during the Truman administration, and in 1950 Senator Joseph R. McCarthy began his toxic and corrosive anti-communist crusade.

During the Cold War, national defense in the name of anti-communism became a rationale for all kinds of action. When the Soviets put the first space satellite into earth orbit in 1957, Americans worried that their schools were not turning out enough scientists. The Congress put together an aid package for schools, which was called The National Defense Education Act.

So much money was spent on armaments that Pres. Dwight Eisenhower warned against what he called "the military-industrial complex." In his farewell address, Eisenhower said, "This conjunction of an immense military establishment and a large arms industry is new to the American experience. The total influence—economic, political, even spiritual—is felt in every city, every statehouse, every office of the federal government. We recognize the imperative need for this development. Yet we must not fail to comprehend its grave implications."

One of the consequences of the military-industrial complex was a shift of power to states in the south and the west. Large companies with defense contracts built factories in the sunny south, the southwest, and in balmy southern California. These factories created jobs and attracted other companies. The growth in population gave these states more political power. The Cold War gave birth to the Sun Belt. And the Sun Belt has produced every elected president since the death of John F. Kennedy. Texas: Lyndon Johnson and, nominally, George Bush; Georgia: Jimmy Carter; California: Richard Nixon and Ronald Reagan. (Gerald Ford was never elected president.) Of these elected presidents, only Lyndon Johnson is regarded as a liberal; Carter was a conservative Democrat.

The Cold War and its defense industries have had a profound effect on American politics for the last quarter of a century. It kept the draft going in the U.S. for 18 years after the end of World War II; Nixon finally ended it in his second term. The U.S. was drawn into numerous crises and two wars because of communism: the Bay of Pigs debacle in Cuba, the muzzle-to-muzzle confrontation between Russian and American tanks in Berlin, and the Cuban missile crisis of 1962. Pres. Harry Truman sent American troops to defend South Korea in a war that was never declared, and Lyndon Johnson sent American troops to Vietnam in another undeclared war. The Vietnam War was a great tragedy for the United States, and its echoes are heard today. In the 1992 presidential campaign, the Republicans made an issue of service in Vietnam. It was the bloody shirt being waved again, a hundred years later.

The Cold War was a necessity when it began, when the Soviet regime posed a genuine threat to democratic governments. It was a necessity at least until Khruschev put missiles in Cuba in 1962. After that, its own momentum kept the Cold War going until it was stopped by the internal contradictions of the communist system. But while it lasted, life in the U.S. was shaped by it.

The Cold War was won by the west, but there were no victory celebrations, no ticker-tape parades. For Americans, the Cold War didn't have a real ending. It just stopped, like a movie projector that had run out of film.

III

Today, the people of the United States confront the need for a third transformation. That is a strange thing to say about a country so rich. By all standards, the U.S. is the wealthiest country on the planet. The size of its economy, as measured by its Gross National Product, is twice as big as Japan's. American fashions, films, and music are the most influential in the world. American workers enjoy a standard of living higher than almost any others. The U.S. is among the leaders in science, technology, and medical research. Its universities attract the best minds from all over the world.

Yet something appears to have gone seriously wrong. Novelist John Updike says, "The United States seems to be a rich country without any money." Eight out of ten Americans believe the country is on the wrong track.

This widespread pessimism is a new phenomenon in a country which has provided nearly every new generation with a more prosperous life. But by 1973, the American economy began to sour, and despite some ups and downs, things haven't got better since then. And in many ways, things are getting worse. Defense spending during the Cold War was not a primary cause of the problem.

The federal budget is being destroyed by entitlement programs that are out of control but politically untouchable. The U.S. is the world's largest debtor, and the interest payment on the national debt in 1991 was larger than the entire Gross National Product of Mexico. The economy is suffering from anemia caused by a great burden of public and private debt. The war on drugs has not been won, cities are struggling with crime and inadequate budgets, and the number of Americans in jail or prison has doubled in the last eight years, and has increased about 150 percent in the last eleven.

America is losing its competitive edge with the rest of the world. It has fallen behind its competitors in the quality of its roads, bridges, and telecommunications. The American educational system from kindergarten through high school is not producing enough graduates qualified for the high-technology jobs of the future. Unlike its economic rivals, it is still searching for a way to design a comprehensive health care program.

These things are crippling the United States at an extremely dangerous time. A new world order is taking shape that will be commercial and highly competitive. The end of the Cold War and the reduced fear of nuclear war is making superpower rivalries obsolete. The next century will be dominated by economic rivalry between trading blocs, in Europe, North America, along the Pacific Rim, and in the Caribbean Basin. In this new order, winners and losers will be determined by the quality of a country's infrastructure, the stability of its economy, and the health and education of its workers.

The first edition of *The World Almanac* lists postage rates for mail sent abroad to the "Roman States," to the "Kingdom of Naples," to "German States and Free Cities." These seemed like permanent sovereignties in 1868, with their noble families, their sturdy militias, their flags and emblems of statehood. But in a few years they disappeared.

The United States is not going to disappear, but, as we have seen, it can be transformed by the forces of change. Americans invented their government institutions in the 18th Century, created their nationality in the 19th, and became the world's strongest country in the 20th.

Now the 21st Century approaches and with it the inevitability of change. We must wonder if the American people will find renewal and rejuvenation within themselves, will discover again their capacity for innovation and adaptation.

If not, alas, the nation's future will be shaped by sightless forces of history over which Americans will have no control. That would be a pity.

Mr. Chancellor is Senior Commentator for NBC News; he is the author of Peril and Promise, a Commentary on America.

The Economy in 1992

The most important issue for the people in the industrial nations of Europe, Asia, and North America in 1992 was the state of their economies. It was the overriding issue in the U.S. presidential campaign, which featured President Bush blaming the recession and the slow, stagnant recovery on the Congress, which he claimed failed to pass his economic program or to address the budget deficit. The Democratic challenger, Arkansas Governor Bill Clinton, blamed the nation's economic woes on the failed economic policies of the Reagan and Bush administrations.

Growth and Unemployment

The Commerce Department reported that the Gross Domestic Product, the total output of goods and services produced within the borders of the U.S., grew at an inflation-adjusted rate of 1.4 percent in the second quarter of 1992. This figure represented a decline from the 2.9 percent growth rate recorded in the first quarter, and spurred fears that the recession—which began in July 1990 and probably ended sometime in 1991, although no formal designation that it was over had been made—may resume. Since Bush took office in Jan. 1989, the economy showed less than a 0.5 percent average growth rate.

The June unemployment rate reached 7.8 percent, an 8-year high. The number of people filing first-time claims for unemployment benefits was 400,000 the week ending Sept. 5, the Labor Department reported, a sign that there was little improvement in the labor market. There were now 3.2 million people collecting unemployment benefits.

The sharp drop in military spending in 1990 and 1991 was an important reason that the U.S. was having such trouble pulling out of the recession. While critics of military spending argued that the money and manpower could be better used in the civilian sector, the cutbacks eroded an important pillar of the economy.

A forecast by the National Association of Business Economists in August said that the U.S. would experience a slow growth, low-inflation economy for the rest of 1992 and for 1993. The survey of 243 NABE members predicted that the U.S. Gross Domestic Product would grow 2.3 percent in 1992, and 2.8 percent in 1993. Inflation would be 3.2 percent in 1992, 3.5 percent the next year.

Some 50 leading economists met in Aug. at Jackson Hole, Wyo. for a conference, "Policies for Long-Term Economic Growth," which was sponsored by the Federal Reserve Bank of Kansas City. There was no shortage of ideas: Martin Feldstein, president of the National Bureau of Economic Research said Americans should save more. "Our net savings rate is just 2 percent of Gross Domestic Product," he said. "Its off the charts in international comparisons of savings rates."

Several speakers urged the U.S. to subsidize spending on machinery by establishing an investment tax credit. But Lawrence A. Kudlow, a member of the Reagan administration, disagreed, "We would be in great error if we go back to a more planned-economy approach," he said, asserting that faster growth would result from lower taxes, less regulation, and less government intervention in the economy.

The economists did agree in one area: education was a sure way for a nation to increase its output. They stressed the importance of improving "human capital," meaning that a better educated, better trained work force could lift a nation's growth rate.

"Human capital can be important for research and development and for adapting technologies from other countries," said Robert J. Barro, an economics professor at Harvard University.

Business

While many Americans were struggling, U.S. corporations were doing fairly well. The Commerce Dept. reported that second quarter after-tax corporate profits were 5.5 percent of sales. By contrast, in the 1974-75 recession, profit margins bottomed at 2.6 percent, and the 1981-82 recession low was 3.3 percent. The profit figures reflected the fact that companies were doing a better job of controlling costs in the face of weak demand by holding down wage increases and getting along with fewer workers, as well as paying lower interest rates on the money they borrowed. The stagnant economy did not affect the financial markets: on June 1, the Dow Jones Industrial Average broke 3,400 for the first time before falling back slightly later in the year.

Housing starts, often a key to recovery from recession, rose 10.4 percent in August to a seasonally adjusted annual rate of 1.2 million, the Commerce Department reported. However, permits issued for new construction, an indicator of future housing activity, fell in August for the sixth consecutive month.

The Federal Mortage Association reported that interest on fixed-rate 30-year mortages averaged 8.13 percent for the week ending July 10, the lowest rate since July 1973.

Bush Administration

As President Bush ran for reelection, it was clear that by most gauges, the U.S. economy had performed worse under his leadership than under that of any president since World War II. Economic growth was slower, more businesses failed, fewer jobs were created, and the national debt soared to a record high.

Ronald Reagan led the U.S. through its longest period of peacetime economic expansion in the 1980s and his vice president, George Bush, promised to continue to work for strong growth. However, after several months of economic stagnation, the economy fell into recession in the summer of 1990. Later that year, the President agreed to a tax increase as the price for striking a deficit-reduction agreement with Congress. It would be the political turning point of his presidency; his most memorable line from the 1988 convention speech, "Read my lips: no new taxes" would come back to haunt him.

The perception of the President by many people was that he chose to focus on his main interest, foreign affairs, and was indifferent toward economic policy. He appeared slow to recognize that the poor economy was causing many Americans to suffer, and so he was seen by many as indecisive and insensitive.

Bush strongly supported the North American Free Trade Agreement, which would eliminate trade barriers between the U.S., Canada, and Mexico. *(See p. 146 for details).*

Poverty

The number of Americans living in poverty rose by 2.1 million to a total of 35.7 million, and the poverty rate rose to 14.2 percent in 1991, according to the annual report on income and poverty by the Census Bureau. The latest poverty rate was the highest since the recession of the early 1980s, and the number of poor people was the highest since 1964, when Pres. Lyndon Johnson declared his war on poverty. The report also disclosed that median household income, after adjusting for inflation, fell by $1,077 to $30,126. A family of four was classified as poor if it had cash income of less than $13,924 in 1991. The poverty level is updated each year to reflect changes in the Consumer Price Index.

The Census Bureau report said that the poverty rate for white Americans rose to 11.3 percent in 1991, from 10.7 percent in 1990. For blacks, the poverty rate rose to 32.7 percent from 31.9 percent, and for Hispanics, it rose to 28.7 percent from 28.1 percent. The South had the highest poverty rate—16 percent.

The gap between rich and poor did not widen in 1991, but the long-term trend pointed to an increasing inequality of income. The richest fifth of all households got 46.5 percent of all household income in 1991, up from 43.5 percent in 1971, and 44.4 percent in 1981. The poorest fifth got 3.8 percent of all income in 1991, contrasted with 4.1 percent in 1971 and 1981.

Critics claimed that the report exaggerated the extent of income inequity and poverty by ignoring most government assistance to the poor, and that the statistics were not adjusted for the huge increase in the number of one-parent families over the past two decades. The increase in the number of poor families headed by women accounted for nearly two-thirds of the net increase in the number of poor families in 1991. The Census Bureau conceded that if non-cash benefits like food stamps and Medicaid were counted as income, the poverty rate would have been lowered to 11.4 percent in 1991.

U.S. Budget Deficit

Everybody was talking about the expanding U.S. budget deficit in 1992, but nobody was doing much about it. President Bush, Jan. 19, sent to Congress a $1.52 trillion budget proposal for fiscal 1993, which would begin Oct. 1, 1992. The budget contained a projected deficit of about $341 billion, which would be the largest in U.S. history; the fiscal 1992 budget deficit was estimated at $333.5 billion. The president's budget projected a federal deficit each year from 1992 to 1997 totaling $1.5 trillion, increasing U.S. debt to $4.2 trillion in 1997 from $2.7 trillion in 1991.

More than half of the proposed fiscal 1993 budget was consumed by three items—Social Security, defense spending, and interest payments on the national debt.

Neither the White House nor Congress appeared serious about solving the budget deficit problem, which most experts agreed would entail cuts in spending and/or tax increases.

The White House proposed a constitutional amendment that would require balanced federal budgets. The proposal was rejected by Congress, June 11.

Sen. Warren Rudman, a New Hampshire Republican who had long led the fight to hold down the deficit, observed: "The blame for this lies with the Congress and the President, with Democrats and Republicans alike, most all of whom have been unwilling to make the hard choices or to explain to the American people that there is no such thing as a free lunch. In a time when we are at war economically," he continued, "when the security of America is being drained drop by drop, we cannot seem to get it together."

A number of states wrestled with the problem of balancing revenue with expenditures in 1992. The most notable was California, with a budget deficit estimated at $10.7 billion, which included a shortfall in the current fiscal year ending July 1, as well as a projected deficit in the following year. The state's political leaders became deadlocked over how to close the massive deficit, and missed a July 1 budget deadline. This left the state bankrupt and forced it to issue IOU's to pay state workers and creditors. By early August, many banks stopped honoring the IOU's. An agreement was finally reached and a budget was signed by the governor, Sept. 2.

Global Economy

The industrial nations in Europe and Asia also faced economic problems in 1992. Japan's Nikkei stock average fell to 14,768.17 on Aug. 13, its lowest level in six and a half years and a fall of more than 60 percent since peaking at an all-time high in late 1989. The plunge was attributed to a lack of confidence in the government's ability to resuscitate the economy, which was projected to grow at about 2.5 percent through March 1993, significantly less than the spectacular growth rates recorded in the 1980s.

Japan announced, Aug. 28, that it would spend $86 billion, the largest economic rescue package in the nation's history, to try to stimulate growth and strengthen a banking system that had been jeopardized by falling real estate and stock prices. The money would be used to more than double public works spending for the current fiscal year, and to provide new incentives to encourage business investment. The plan also included measures to stabilize banks and other financial institutions by making it easier for them to dispose of bad loans.

Japan was able to use fiscal stimulus, a classic countercyclical tool, because of its sizable budget surplus; it was the only major industrial nation in a position to launch a major expansionary program.

U.S. Pres. George Bush and the chairmen of the Big Three U.S. auto makers visited Japan in January to obtain trade concessions. Japan agreed to a series of conciliatory moves aimed at improving the market for U.S. goods in Japan. Japanese manufacturers pledged to boost the value of U.S.-made auto parts they would buy.

A currency crisis erupted in Europe, Sept. 16, when Britain dropped out of the European Monetary System. Its departure from the monetary system, a cornerstone of greater European unity, left the program of economic coordination in disarray. The crisis was rooted in the high cost of German unification, which drove up German interest rates at a time when other European countries needed lower rates to help them out of their economic slowdown.

The European Monetary System, begun in 1979, was designed to foster currency stability and promote economic policies to reduce inflation throughout Europe. The currencies of the 11 members (before Britain's decision to suspend participation) are linked in trading bands. When a currency hits the bottom or the top of its range, the country's central bank must act to keep it within the trading band. This can be done by intervening in the foreign exchange market to buy or sell the currency or by moving interest rates up or down. In the current crisis, the pound fell through the bottom of their trading range against the German mark.

If action by a central bank does not prevent a breach, a revaluation of the currency is required. The British tried to defend the pound by raising interest rates. When that failed, they in effect unilaterally devalued the pound by suspending their participation in the European Monetary System. The European Monetary System was seen as preceding the move to a single European currency by the end of 1999.

Further turmoil was averted, Sept. 20, when French voters narrowly approved the Maastricht Treaty, the cornerstone of the Economic Community. A French rejection of the treaty would have opened up the region to a period of political uncertainty and ecomomic disarray.

Nations of the former Soviet Union faced a difficult transition from a communist to a capitalist economy in 1992. In Apr., the International Monetary Fund and the World Bank formally offered membership to most of the members of the Commonwealth of Independent States, as well as Estonia, Latvia, and Lithuania.

Russian Pres. Boris Yeltsin addressed the Group of Seven industrial democracies, July 8, and told the Western leaders that there was a "very serious risk" of heightened political unrest in Russia. The leaders endorsed a $24 billion aid package to be provided under the International Monetary Fund, and backed the release of the first $1 billion in aid. *(See Chronology and Index for 1991–92 economic developments.)*

Tom McGuire, Economics Editor

The Economy Under Presidential Administrations, 1945-1992

Source: U.S. Dept. of Labor, Commerce; Bureau of Labor Statistics; Federal Reserve Board; Economic Policy Inst., Council of Economic Advisors; *N.Y. Times*

President	Gross Domestic Product	Jobs	Disposable Income	Industrial Production	Hourly Wage	Misery[1] Index	Inflation	Interest Rate
Truman (1945-52)	25.0%	5.9%	7.5%	35.3%	N.A.	3.8	0.8%	2.8%
Eisenhower (1953-56)	9.4	3.3	10.0	14.6	N.A.	6.7	3.0	3.3
Eisenhower (1957-60)	7.3	3.4	4.7	0.8	N.A.	6.9	1.4	3.9
Kennedy/Johnson (1961-64)	20.4	6.4	12.1	36.6	10.8	6.1	1.0	4.1
Johnson (1965-68)	19.4	9.7	15.5	26.2	12.2	8.1	4.7	5.7
Nixon (1969-72)	12.4	8.3	10.8	14.7	9.8	8.9	3.4	5.9

(continued)

President	Gross Domestic Product	Jobs	Disposable Income	Industrial Production	Hourly Wage	Misery[1] Index	Inflation	Interest Rate
Nixon/Ford (1973-76)	7.6%	8.1%	7.5%	5.2%	5.8	12.5	4.9%	6.7%
Carter (1977-80)	11.5	11.2	7.3	12.8	1.5	18.2	12.5	11.7
Reagan (1981-84)	10.1	6.3	8.5	9.3	1.4	11.4	3.9	11.2
Reagan (1985-88)	14.0	9.8	6.6	15.7	1.3	9.7	4.4	9.1
Bush[2] (1989-92)	2.5	0.7	1.2	−0.4	−1.7	10.5	3.0	7.8

(1) Inflation rate plus unemployment at end of term. (2) Through May 1992. NA = not available.

Bill Clinton, Democratic Nominee for President

Bill Clinton was born William Jefferson Blythe 3rd on Aug. 19, 1946 in Hope, Ark., the son of William and Virginia Blythe. Blythe, a traveling salesman, died in an auto accident before his son was born. His mother married Roger Clinton and several years later, at age 16, Bill Blythe changed his name to Bill Clinton. Clinton attended Georgetown Univ., Oxford Univ. in England as a Rhodes scholar, and Yale Law School.

Clinton worked on George McGovern's 1972 presidential campaign and for the House Judiciary Committee in 1973. He taught at the Univ. of Arkansas, 1974-76, during which time he ran an unsuccessful race for Congress. He was elected Arkansas State Attorney General in 1976.

In 1978, he was elected the nation's youngest governor, but was defeated for reelection in 1980. He successfully ran for governor again in 1982, 1984, 1986, and 1990. He married Hillary Rodham in 1975. She is a successful lawyer and a social activist. They have a daughter, Chelsea, age 12.

Despite personal attacks on his character, he won the majority of the presidential primaries while moving the Democratic Party toward the center, trying to appeal to middle-class suburbanites who had deserted the party during the Reagan era.

In his formal acceptance speech at the Democratic National Convention, Clinton focused on what he called "the forgotten middle class." He said that he would revive the U.S. economy and promised a "New Covenant" that would offer a new approach to government.

H. Ross Perot, Independent Candidate for President

H. Ross Perot was born in Texas in 1930. He graduated from the U.S. Naval Academy. After working as a salesman for IBM, Perot founded Electronic Data Systems in 1962, and sold the company to General Motors in 1984 for $2.4 billion. Perot received public attention in 1979, when he hired commandoes to rescue two of his employees who had been taken hostage in Iran.

Perot's campaign promised to end "government gridlock" and to eliminate the federal budget deficit. In July, even though Perot was leading Pres. Bush and Gov. Clinton in some polls, he dropped his presidential bid. He explained that "it would be disruptive to the country" for him to continue. In late Oct., Perot claimed that he withdrew to avoid a "dirty tricks" campaign aimed at his daughter by the Republicans. On Oct. 1, Perot reactivated his campaign and announced that he would run as an independent candidate for president. In making his announcement just 33 days before the election, Perot said, "I thought that both political parties would address the problems that face the nation. We gave them a chance. They didn't do it."

Miscellaneous Facts

—The average commute to work in the U.S. is 22.4 minutes—up from 21.7 minutes a decade ago—according to the Census Bureau. Workers in the New York metropolitan area endure the longest commute—30.6 minutes. Washington, D.C. is second, and Chicago third.

—The most frequently prescribed drug in 1991, according to a survey published in *American Druggist*, was Amoxil, an antibiotic. The estrogen supplement Premarin was second, and the anti-ulcer Zantac was third.

—*Hudson Hawk* was the worst movie of 1991 according to the Golden Raspberry Award Foundation. Kevin Costner in *Robin Hood* was the worst actor, and Sean Young in *A Kiss Before Dying* was the worst actress.

—Denison Univ. has the best looking students, and Duke Univ. the happiest, according to a 28,000-student survey of *The Student Access Guide to the Best Colleges*. The survey rated the California Inst. of Technology as having the best academics and Sweet Briar College the most interesting teachers. Georgia Tech was plagued with the most boring teachers, State Univ. of New York, Albany the worst food, and Arizona State Univ. had the worst dorms.

—John Steinbeck's *Of Mice and Men* was the book most frequently challenged by school censors during the 1991-92 school year, according to the People for the American Way. Other "challenged" books include *The Catcher in the Rye*, *The Adventures of Huckleberry Finn*, *The Color Purple*, and Steinbeck's *The Grapes of Wrath*.

—Have you been wondering what happened to the Iraqi planes that sought refuge in Iran in the final phase of the Persian Gulf war to escape destruction at the hands of Allied forces? Iran announced, July 30, 1992, that it was keeping the planes as partial payment for over several hundred billion dollars in damages from the Iraq-Iran war of 1980-88.

—At precisely 23 hours, 59 minutes, 60 seconds Coordinated Universal Time on June 30, 1992, one second was added to the world's time in order to keep super-accurate atomic clocks in step with the Earth's rotation. This was the 17th "leap second" that has been inserted into atomic clocks since 1972.

—On any given day, 71 percent of Americans read a newspaper, 38 percent read a book for work or school, 36 percent read a magazine, and 33 percent read a book for pleasure, according to a 1991 Gallup Poll.

—A survey reported in *TV Guide* said that one out of four Americans would not stop watching TV even if they were paid $1 million, and 46 percent would not give up watching it for anything less than $1 million. Gratuitous violence was found offensive by 46 percent of Americans, the survey said, while 24 percent were offended by explicit sex.

—Nearly half of the population of the U.S. moved from one home to another from 1985 to 1989, according to a Census Bureau report. In the nearly 3 decades from 1960 to 1989, more than 91 percent of U.S. households had moved, the report said.

—In a 1991 Gallup Poll, 53 percent of respondents said that they did not have a gun in the house.

—To many people, their cars are like members of their family. Some of the most popular names for cars are: Betsy, Batmobile, Big Bird, My Love, The Beast, The War Pig, and Sherman (after the tank).

—The National Weather Service reports that, based on a 20-year study, the average number of people who die each year from floods and flash floods is 146. Lightning takes the lives of an average of 80 people per year, tornadoes 69, and hurricanes 17.

—Sexual intercourse occurs more than 100 million times daily, resulting in 910,000 conceptions and about 350,000 cases of sexually transmitted disease, according to a report by the World Health Organization.

Bill Clinton Elected President

Democrats Retain Control of Congress

Gov. Bill Clinton of Arkansas, a Democrat, was elected the 42nd president of the United States, Nov. 3. He defeated the Republican incumbent, George Bush, and also turned back a well-financed challenge by an independent candidate, Texas billionaire H. Ross Perot. In achieving a big victory in the Electoral College and a clear plurality in the popular vote, Clinton brought to an end 12 years of Republican control of the White House.

Like the 2 most recent Democratic presidents, Lyndon Johnson of Texas and Jimmy Carter of Georgia, Clinton came from a former Confederate state. His Southern ties and relatively moderate positions on economic and social issues seemed to reassure voters who in recent years had rejected the presidential candidacies of northern Democratic liberals.

Clinton campaigned almost exclusively on opposition to what he termed the trickle-down economic policies of the administrations of Ronald Reagan and Bush. But while arguing that wealthy Americans should bear a greater proportion of the tax burden, he also spoke out against the traditional tax-and-spend philosophy long associated with the Democrats. In fact, Clinton had been the chairman of the Democratic Leadership Council, a subset of national party figures who had sought to moderate the policies of the national party. As the United States struggled through an economic recession and a sluggish recovery in 1992, Clinton's ideas reached a receptive audience.

Bush, for his part, had enjoyed great popularity because of the quick Allied victory over Iraq in the Persian Gulf war in 1991, and because communism had collapsed in Eastern Europe and the Soviet Union during his presidency. But Bush seemed less sure-footed when focusing on a domestic agenda, and the centerpiece of his deficit-reduction policy—a major tax increase negotiated with Democratic leaders in Congress—alienated many in his own party.

Perot had run a hugely successful computer-services company, and his public reputation rested primarily on his decades-long effort to locate American servicemen missing in Southeast Asia after the Vietnam war. He entered the race formally a month before the election, and spent $60 million, much of it on television "programs"—advertisements—to get his message out. He warned of an impending economic crisis triggered by the immense federal budget deficits. He decried the increase in the national debt from $1 trillion to $4 trillion since Reagan became president in 1981, and his draconian plan included deep cuts in the military budget and domestic programs and a 50-cents-a-gallon increase in the gasoline tax. He promised that his plan would erase the deficits in 5 years.

Public-opinion surveys had shown that a majority of Americans were unhappy with Bush's handling of the economy, and the results of the election suggested that a plurality of voters preferred Clinton's rather cautious program, which visualized a 50 percent reduction in the deficit over 4 years combined with "investments" in the private sector to stimulate growth.

Clinton became the first minority president—with clearly less than half of the total popular vote—since 1968. The Democrats continued to control both houses of Congress by large margins.

Presidential Voting

Clinton was victorious in 32 states and the District of Columbia having 370 electoral votes, far more than the 270 majority needed for election. Bush won in 18 states having 168 electoral votes. Perot failed to win any electoral votes. The nationwide popular vote was much closer; Clinton, 43 percent; Bush, 38 percent; and Perot, 19 percent.

With 3 major candidates in the contest, some traditional voting patterns became blurred. Nonetheless, it was apparent that Clinton had made progress in firming up the coalition of voting blocs that had carried Franklin Delano Roosevelt and Harry Truman to victory. Blacks stayed with Clinton even though the governor made few gestures in their direction and got only lukewarm support from civil rights leader Jesse Jackson. The so-called Reagan Democrats, many of whom were blue-collar workers, had begun to drift away from the Republicans in the 1988 election, and many more shifted to Clinton or Perot in 1992.

In recent presidential elections, Democrats had enjoyed greater support among women than among men, and 1992 was no exception. Bush opposed abortion in most cases, while Clinton was pro-choice, and this issue appeared to work somewhat to the Democrat's advantage. Young voters, once a mainstay of the Democrats, had swung to Reagan in the 1980s, but the newest wave of young people went in greater numbers for Clinton and his running mate for vice president, Albert Gore Jr., Democratic senator from Tennessee.

The South, once solid for the Democrats, had become a strong conservative base for Reagan and Bush, but Clinton and Gore chipped away, picking up their home states and also winning Louisiana and Georgia. The Democratic ticket won everywhere in the Northeast and took all the industrial Midwest except Indiana. Bush held the wheat belt. California's big prize of 54 electors, the most ever for any state, went decisively for Clinton in a year of high unemployment and racial tension following riots in Los Angeles in the spring. Clinton also eroded the Republican stronghold in the Rocky Mountain region.

Perot's showing was the best by any independent or 3d-party candidate since Theodore Roosevelt launched a vigorous but unsuccessful comeback attempt in 1912. The billionaire's supporters, determined to shake up the system, stuck with him despite pre-election polls showing that he could not win. In conceding defeat, Perot left open the possibility that he might back a new political movement.

A survey of Americans leaving the voting booths showed that those who had supported Clinton were primarily concerned about the economy and jobs, health care, and education, in that order.

The Senate and House

With one third of the Senate up for election, the Democrats made a net pickup of one seat, for a 58-42 majority. In the House, the Democratic majority shrank slightly from 266-166 to about 260-174 in late returns. One Independent kept his seat.

Although the shift in relative strength of the major parties was small, 1992 was a year of upheaval in Congressional voting. Reapportionment added many seats to the South and West, at the expense of representation in the Midwest and Northeast. Voters were angry because Congress had voted itself a pay hike, and scores of House members had written overdrafts on their accounts in the House bank. Nineteen incumbents lost in the primaries. Others fell in the November voting, but Speaker Thomas Foley (D, Wash.), Majority Leader

Richard Gephardt (D, Mo.), Minority Leader Robert Michel (R, Ill.), and Minority Whip Newt Gingrich (R, Ga.) all came through. Women, blacks, and Hispanic Americans were elected to the House in record numbers.

In the Senate voting, women scored a major breakthrough. Eleven women had won major-party nominations, and 5 of these, all Democrats, won. Carol Moseley Braun, Cook County, Ill., Recorder of Deeds, became the first black woman to be elected to the Senate. Both seats to be filled in California went to women—former San Francisco Mayor Dianne Feinstein and Rep. Barbara Boxer. State Sen. Patty Murray won in Washington state, and Barbara Mikulski was re-elected in Maryland. Sen. Nancy Kassebaum (R, Kan.) was not up for re-election.

Rep. Ben Nighthorse Campbell (D) of Colorado became the second Native American ever to win a seat in the Senate.

Three incumbent senators were defeated. They were John Seymour (R, Cal.), who lost to Feinstein; Bob Kasten (R, Wis.); and Terry Sanford (D, N.C.), who had undergone heart surgery during the campaign.

Sanford lost to Lauch Faircloth, who had switched from the Democratic to the Republican party. The winner in Wisconsin was Russell Feingold, who had previously won in an upset in the Democratic primary after his favored opponents ruined their chances with an exchange of negative attacks. Senate Minority Leader Robert Dole (R, Kan.) was among the incumbents returned to the Senate.

The Governorships

Democrats won 8 of the 12 governorships being contested, increasing their advantage in the nation's statehouses from 28-20 to 30-18. Two governors were independents. In North Carolina, Jim Hunt, a Democrat, reclaimed the governorship that he had once held. In Indiana, Democrat Evan Bayh, at 36 still the nation's youngest governor after 4 years in office, won easily.

Other Ballot Issues

Voters in 14 states approved propositions that would impose limits—usually 12 years—on the length of service by their members of Congress. Supporters of these measures believed that politicians who spent decades in Congress became too preoccupied with power and perquisites, and were more responsive to lobbyists than to the needs of the people.

Oregon voters defeated an amendment to the state constitution that defined homosexuality as perverse and that would have permitted discrimination against homosexuals.

The Primaries and Conventions

From the start, the 1992 presidential campaign was full of surprises. Apparently discouraged by Bush's success in the Gulf war, no Democrats who were well-known nationally tossed their hats into the ring. But even as other Democrats declared their candidacies late in 1991, the recession was taking hold. Pundits installed Clinton, a 12-year governor of Arkansas, as the early favorite, based on his well-organized campaign and endorsements by a number of party leaders. Clinton had been voted the most effective governor in the nation by his fellow governors, and he had succeeded in raising his state's standards in education. As required by law, he had also balanced the state's budget 12 times, and had kept taxes low, but Arkansas remained a poor state, ranking near the bottom in such categories as personal income.

Paul Tsongas, a former senator from Massachusetts, won in New Hampshire, but his pro-business platform and his offhand, almost shy, public persona failed to attract sufficient support around the country, and Tsongas eventually dropped out and endorsed Clinton. Edmund (Jerry) Brown, the former governor of California, stayed in the contest until the convention. His anti-establishment campaign—including his own cap of $100 on contributions—endeared him to many, but other Democrats could not accept his proposal for a flat tax, under which everyone would pay the same rate.

After Clinton had locked up the nomination, he chose Sen. Albert Gore Jr. (Tenn.) as his running mate for vice president. As a ranking authority in the Senate on environmental issues and foreign affairs, Gore nicely balanced Clinton's qualifications. But Clinton and Gore also had much in common. At ages 46 and 44, respectively, they symbolized the "baby boomer" generation, and the nomination of 2 moderate Southerners made it easier for the Democrats to evade the liberal label.

Bush's path to renomination was not without bumps. Pat Buchanan, a conservative television and newspaper commentator, challenged him in the primaries. Bush got only 53 percent of the total vote cast in the the Republican primary in New Hampshire, a state hard hit by the recession. Although Bush won all of the subsequent primaries and caucuses, a large protest vote for Buchanan or uncommitted delegates showed up in many states. Buchanan's extremely conservative views tended to limit his appeal, but his relentless attacks on Bush for abandoning his 1988 pledge not to raise taxes weakened the president for the fall campaign.

Perot, riding a wave of public displeasure with the major parties, said early in 1992 that he would run as an independent if his supporters circulated petitions and put him on the ballot in all 50 states. They ultimately did so, but in the meantime the unpredictable Perot set up a campaign organization, then decided not to run, and, after being branded a quitter, plunged back into the fray.

The Fall Campaign

The final months of the campaign were remarkable for the sharp increase in interest by the American people. Up to 90 million people watched the 3-way presidential debates, and the ratings for Perot's 30-minute commercials topped those of some competing entertainment programs.

Bush promised that in his second term he would expend the effort on domestic affairs that he had devoted to international crises during his first term, and he apologized for raising taxes in 1990. He contended that the economy was in decent shape, arguing that even the high 7.5 percent unemployment rate meant that 93 percent of American workers were employed. And yet, in announcing that James Baker 3d, his effective secretary of state and then his campaign manager, would be his economic czar after the election, Bush also indicated that he would replace his principal economic advisers.

Bush made trust and character major issues. He asserted that Clinton had "waffled" on many issues and that he had not "leveled" with the voters on how he had avoided the draft. Clinton stuck with the economy, relentlessly calling for change and new leadership. During the debates, Clinton seemed far more forceful in laying out his proposals. Polls taken throughout the fall showed Clinton maintaining a lead.

Don Young, Special Features Editor

CHRONOLOGY OF THE YEAR'S EVENTS

Reported Month by Month in 3 Categories: National, International, and General
Oct. 16, 1991 to Oct. 23, 1992

OCTOBER

National

Bush Veto on Jobless Benefits Upheld — The Senate failed, **Oct. 16**, to override a jobless-benefits bill that had been voted by Pres. George Bush. The bill would have provided up to 20 additional weeks of unemployment benefits to workers, depending on the overall level of unemployment in their respective states. Bush said that the provisions of the bill, in adding to the federal deficit, would delay the country's economic recovery. The vote in the Senate to override was 65-35, just 2 votes short of the required two-thirds.

Bush Picks Barr for Attorney General — Pres. George Bush announced, **Oct. 16**, that he would nominate William Barr to serve as attorney general. Barr had been serving as acting attorney general since August, when Richard Thornburgh resigned to seek election to the U.S. Senate. Since then, Barr had overseen a successful rescue of 9 hostages being held by prison inmates in Alabama.

Navy Drops Allegation in Ship Disaster — The U.S. Navy reversed its previous position on the possible cause of an explosion aboard the battleship *Iowa* in 1989 that had caused the death of 47 sailors. After its first investigation, the Navy concluded that Gunner's Mate 2nd Class Clayton Hartwig had "most probably" planted a detonating device among the bags of gunpowder in one of the ship's turrets. Hartwig was killed in the explosion. After an independent investigation raised questions about this conclusion, the Navy resumed its own investigation. Adm. Frank Kelso, chief of naval operations, announced, **Oct. 17**, that the Navy could draw no conclusion about either an accidental explanation or a "wrongful intentional act." The Navy issued an apology to Hartwig's family.

Consumer Prices Jump — The Labor Dept. reported, **Oct. 17**, that consumer prices had risen 0.4 percent in September, an increase large enough to suggest that inflationary pressures might be reviving. The Commerce Dept. said, **Oct. 17**, that the merchandise trade deficit had edged upward to $6.76 billion in August. On Wall Street, the Dow-Jones Industrial Average closed at an all-time high of 3077.15 on **Oct. 18**. The Commerce Dept. reported, **Oct. 29**, that the U.S. gross national product had increased at a 2.4 percent annual rate during the 3rd quarter, after 3 consecutive quarterly declines, evidence that the recession might be ending.

Committee Approves CIA Nominee — Robert Gates, the controversial choice of Pres. George Bush to head the Central Intelligence Agency, cleared a major hurdle, **Oct. 18**, when the Senate Select Committee on Intelligence voted, 11-4, to recommend his nomination to the full Senate. During his confirmation hearings, some witnesses had praised Gates as experienced and well qualified, while others had charged that he had altered intelligence reports to suit the views of his superiors.

Ex-Klansman Gains in Bid for Governor — David Duke, a former Grand Wizard of the Ku Klux Klan, survived the first round of voting, **Oct. 19**, in his campaign to win the governorship of Louisiana. In the nonpartisan primary, Duke polled 32 percent of the vote, trailing former Gov. Edwin Edwards, who received 34 percent. Duke was a Republican, Edwards a Democrat. The incumbent governor, Buddy Roemer, had started the year as a Democrat but had switched to the Republican Party. Even though Pres. George Bush had campaigned in behalf of his re-election, Roemer finished third in the primary with 27 percent, and was thus eliminated from the runoff. Duke, once an advocate of Nazism, said his previous activities had been "youthful indiscretions." In his campaign he called for "equal rights" for white people.

Brown Enters Presidential Race — Edmund G. "Jerry" Brown, a former governor of California, entered the contest for the Democratic presidential nomination, **Oct. 21**. His principal campaign theme was criticism of the political establishment. He denounced politics as corrupt, blamed this on the availability of big sums of money, and said he would accept no campaign contributions larger than $100.

International

Israeli, Arab Leaders Meet in Madrid — Representatives of Israel, the Palestinians, and several Arab countries met in Madrid after a formal invitation of the United States and the Soviet Union. The conference had long been an objective of U.S. diplomacy. Palestinian leaders told Sec. of State James Baker in Jerusalem, **Oct. 18**, that they would send a delegation that Israel could accept. Israel's demands had included the requirement that no delegates have open ties to the Palestine Liberation Organization. Israel and the Soviet Union resumed diplomatic relations on **Oct. 18**. The conference opened at the Spanish Royal Palace in Madrid, **Oct. 30**. Arab countries formally represented were Egypt, Lebanon, Jordan, and Syria. Observers came from other countries. In an address, Pres. George Bush said, "we seek peace, real peace," which he said must include diplomatic and economic relations, trade, investment, and cultural exchange. Soviet Pres. Mikhail Gorbachev also spoke. In his opening statement on **Oct. 31**, Israeli Prime Minister Yitzhak Shamir urged the Arabs to renounce their holy war against Israel. Syrian Foreign Minister Farouk al-Sharaa said, **Oct. 31**, that all Arab land taken by Israel by force must be returned before peace could come. Dr. Haidar Abdel-Shafi, leader of the Palestinian delegation, said, **Oct. 31**, that Palestinians in the territories occupied by Israel could accept a period of limited self-rule before a Palestinian state was established.

8 Soviet Republics Sign Economic Treaty — Pres. Mikhail Gorbachev and the presidents of 8 Soviet republics signed an economic union treaty in Moscow, **Oct. 18**, that declared "private ownership, free enterprise, and competition" to be the "basis for economic recovery." The presidents of 4 other republics—Azerbaijan, Georgia, Moldavia, and Ukraine—boycotted the signing. The Ukrainian parliament voted, **Oct. 22**, to create an independent armed force that would have a strength of at least 400,000. The Ukrainian government announced, **Oct. 23**, that it would henceforth conduct its own economic transactions with other countries.

U.S. Hostage, 15 Arab Prisoners Freed — The process of freeing hostages and prisoners continued in the Middle East. On **Oct. 21**, the Israelis freed 15 Arab prisoners; the Islamic Jihad for the Liberation of Palestine, a Shiite Muslim faction, released Jesse Turner, an American who was a professor of mathematics at Beirut University College, after nearly 5 years of captivity.

Cambodian Factions Sign Peace Treaty — The government of Cambodia and leaders of 3 rebel factions signed a peace treaty in Paris, **Oct. 23**, that gave promise of ending the long armed struggle for control of the Southeast Asian country. Representatives of 18 other nations, including the United States, Soviet Union, and China, also signed the treaty. During an interim period, United Nations personnel, both military and civilian, would oversee a transition during which the factions would largely disarm. Prince Norodom Sihanouk, a former ruler of the country, would serve as provisional leader of Cambodia during the transition. Under the treaty, 350,000 refugees would be repatriated.

General

Gunman Kills 23 in Cafeteria — A man armed with 2 9-mm semiautomatic pistols killed 23 persons in Killeen, Tex., **Oct. 16**, and wounded 20 others. The man, identified as George Hennard of Belton, Tex., drove a pickup truck through a window of Luby's Cafeteria and then began shooting people inside the building. The gunfire continued for about 10 minutes. Twenty-two people were killed instantly and another died later. A policeman shot and wounded the gunman, who went into a rest room, where he apparently shot himself to death. The death toll was the highest from any mass shooting in the United States.

Fires in California Kill 24 — Fires driven by high winds and benefitting from dry conditions swept through residential areas of Oakland and Berkeley, Calif., on **Oct. 20 and 21**, causing the death of at least 24 people and injuries to 148. More than 1,800 houses and 900 apartment units were destroyed. Damage was estimated at $5 billion.

Depletion of Ozone Reported in Spring, Summer — A panel established by the U.N. Environment Program reported, **Oct. 22**, that the Earth's ozone layer was being depleted in temperate latitudes during the spring and summer. Ozone depletion had been considered as essentially a winter phenomenon. The ozone helped block the sun's ultraviolet rays. Its depletion during warm weather could damage crops and cause a sharp increase in the number of skin-cancer cases. The panel urged a quick phaseout of chlorofluorcarbons, regarded as the principal culprits in the ozone depletion. The DuPont company, leading manufacturer of these chemicals, said, **Oct. 22**, it would end their production by 1997.

NOVEMBER

National

Arctic Refuge Controversy Sinks Energy Bill — A national energy bill, containing many provisions supported by the Bush administration, was blocked in the U.S. Senate, **Nov. 1**. The bill, sponsored by Sen. J. Bennett Johnston (D, La.), would have set higher fuel-efficiency standards for cars, eased restrictions on utilities, supported construction of nuclear power plants, and deregulated oil and gas pipelines. It also would have opened the Arctic National Wildlife Refuge in Alaska to drilling for oil, which triggered organized opposition from environmental groups. They supported a filibuster, and with 60 votes required to cut off debate, only 50 senators supported cloture. Advocates of the bill conceded it was dead for the rest of the year.

Economic Indicators Drop — The Commerce Dept. reported, **Nov. 1**, that the index of leading economic indicators fell by 0.1 percent in September, the first decline since January. The Labor Dept. said, **Nov. 1**, that the unemployment rate rose from 6.7 percent to 6.8 percent in October. The department reported, **Nov. 13**, that prices charged by producers for finished goods had jumped 0.7 percent in October, the biggest increase in a year. On **Nov. 14**, the department said, however, that consumer prices had risen only 0.1 percent in October. The U.S. merchandise trade deficit stood at $6.79 billion in September, the Commerce Dept. said on **Nov. 19**.

Jackson Declines to Run for President — Jesse Jackson, who had made strong bids for the Democratic presidential nomination in 1984 and 1988, announced, **Nov. 2**, that he would not seek the presidency in 1992. Jackson was serving as the so-called shadow senator from the District of Columbia. He advised his supporters to remain neutral "free agents" for the time being.

Upset in Pennsylvania Highlights Voting — On **Nov. 5**, election day, both major parties could claim some significant victories, but a surprising result in Pennsylvania drew most attention. The Republican nominee, former Gov. Richard Thornburgh, who had resigned as U.S. attorney general to make the race, was expected to capture a U.S. Senate seat. Sen. Harris Wofford, the Democratic nominee, had been appointed to fill a vacancy earlier in 1991, but he was less well known. Wofford criticized the economic policies of the Bush administration and campaigned for national health insurance. He won 55 percent of the vote. His victory was seen as a signal of public concern about the state of the economy, and on election day Pres. George Bush, who had been criticized for spending too much time abroad, abruptly postponed a trip to Asia and Australia. In Kentucky, Lt. Gov. Brereton Jones was elected governor, keeping the office in Democratic hands. In Mississippi, however, the incumbent governor, Ray Mabus, a Democrat, lost to Kirk Fordice, who would become the first Republican governor of the state since Reconstruction. In New Jersey, where tax increases pushed through by Gov. James Florio, a Democrat, were unpopular, the Republicans won control of the State Legislature. In major contests for mayor decided on **Nov. 5**, incumbents Kurt Schmoke and Raymond Flynn, both Democrats, were re-elected in Baltimore and Boston, respectively. Edward Rendell, a Democrat, was elected mayor in Philadelphia, and U.S. Rep. Steve Bartlett, a Republican, won in Dallas.

Senate Confirms Gates to Head CIA — The U.S. Senate, **Nov. 5**, approved the nomination of Robert Gates to serve as director of central intelligence. The vote was 64-31, with all the opposing votes being cast by Democrats. Sen. Sam Nunn (D, Ga.) supported Gates, though he said he was uncertain he was the right person for the job.

Ex-Klan Leader Loses Louisiana Runoff — Edwin Edwards recaptured his old job, the governorship of Louisiana, defeating David Duke, a former leader of the Ku Klux Klan, in a runoff election. Duke ran as a Republican, but on **Nov. 6**, Pres. George Bush lashed out at what he called Duke's "long record—an ugly record—of racism and bigotry." The supporters of Edwards, a Democrat, said they were worried that Duke's election would set back tourism and economic development by outside investors. In the voting, **Nov. 16**, Edwards won 61 percent of the vote, overall, because he swept almost all of the black vote. Duke won about 55 percent of votes cast by whites.

Bush Signs Job-Discrimination Bill — Pres. George Bush signed a job-discrimination bill that would make it easier for workers to take legal action. Bush had vetoed a bill in September that he called a "quota bill" unduly burdensome to employers. The House, **Nov. 7**, completed Congressional action on the revised bill.

Designed to overturn Supreme Court decisions, the bill required that hiring and promotion be related to job performance. Those claiming discrimination could sue for damages, not just for back pay and lost benefits. Bush said he would sign the new bill. A controversy flared, **Nov. 20**, when the White House circulated a draft of a presidential directive that sought to reverse federal regulations authorizing certain racial preferences in the hiring and promotion of federal employees. The draft directive was widely criticized by civil rights leaders and in Congress on the ground that it would undermine the new legislation, and it was withdrawn by the White House. In signing the bill, **Nov. 21**, Bush declared his opposition to discrimination and his support for affirmative action programs.

Bush's Top Aide Involved in New Dispute — John Sununu, the White House chief of staff, whose conduct had drawn frequent criticism, became involved in a new controversy. In a **Nov. 12** speech, Pres. George Bush suggested that banks lower the interest rates they charged on credit cards. The Senate then considered an amendment to a bill that would cap interest rates on credit cards. Apparently believing that such a cap would have a negative impact on the profitability of banks, Wall Street investors sold stocks heavily on **Nov. 14**, driving the Dow Jones Industrial Average down 120 points. After a newspaper reported, **Nov. 21**, that Sununu had inserted the credit-card recommendation into Bush's speech, Sununu replied, in a television interview broadcast **Nov. 24**, that Bush had ad-libbed the suggestion. The White House denied that Bush had ad-libbed the remark, and Sununu was widely criticized for attempting to shift responsibility to the president.

Senate Confirms Barr as Attórney General — The Senate approved Pres. George Bush's nomination of William Barr to be U.S. attorney general. At his hearings, **Nov. 12** and **13**, before the Senate Judiciary Committee, Barr acknowledged that the Justice Department's investigation of the Bank of Credit and Commerce International had been slow and uncoordinated. He supported overturning Roe v. Wade and said he did not believe that the right of privacy extended to abortion. The committee, **Nov. 15**, approved Barr's nomination unanimously, and the Senate approved him, **Nov. 20**, by voice vote.

Bush Signs Bill to Help Unemployed — A compromise bill providing for additional benefits for unemployed workers was signed by Pres. George Bush. He had vetoed a previous version of the bill in October. The new legislation met his requirement for a funding mechanism. Money would come from high-income workers who paid taxes quarterly and whose incomes had increased. They would pay taxes based on current earnings, not on what they had earned in the previous year. The compromise bill, which Bush signed, **Nov. 15**, would give all unemployed workers at least 6 weeks of additional benefits, and up to 20 additional weeks, depending on the level of unemployment in their state.

Poindexter's Conviction Overturned — A panel of the U.S. Court of Appeals for the District of Columbia, **Nov. 15**, overturned the conviction of John Poindexter in the Iran-contra case. Poindexter had been convicted in 1990 of conspiracy, obstructing Congress, and making false statements to Congress while serving as national security adviser to Pres. Ronald Reagan. He was sentenced to 6 months in prison. The Appeals Court panel held, however, that witnesses who had testified at his trial had been unfairly influenced by testimony Poindexter had given to Congress in 1987. The ruling was 2-1. Another former top Reagan administration official, Elliott Abrams, who had served as assistant secretary of state for inter-American affairs, was sentenced, **Nov. 15**. He had pleaded guilty in October to 2 misdemeanor accounts of withholding information from Congress during the Iran-contra hearings. Abrams was put on probation for 2 years and required to perform 100 hours of community service. Duane Clarridge, a former official of the Central Intelligence Agency, was indicted, **Nov. 26**, on 7 counts of lying to Congress concerning the diversion of money from arms sales to the Nicaraguan contras.

Sen. Cranston Receives Reprimand — Sen. Alan Cranston (D, Cal.) received a formal reprimand on the Senate floor, **Nov. 20**, for having interceded in behalf of Charles Keating in exchange for campaign contributions. Keating had owned the Lincoln Federal Savings and Loan, and its bankruptcy, which was expected to cost the government $2.6 billion, was perhaps the most publicized failure in the S & L debacle. The Senate Ethics Committee, which had approved the reprimand, found that Cranston had acted "without corrupt intent," but it rebuked him for an "impermissible pattern of conduct in which fund-raising and official activities were substantially linked."

International

Yeltsin Initiates Radical Reforms in Russia — The parliament of the Russian republic of the USSR, **Nov. 1**, granted Russian Pres. Boris Yeltsin broad power to initiate radical economic reforms. Yeltsin said he planned to lift most price controls, privatize many state farms and state industries, and cut off Russian financial support to Soviet central ministries and foreign aid. Two Soviet republics, Ukraine and Moldova, signed the Soviet economic-union treaty, **Nov. 6**, after initially declining to do so. Pursuant to another plan supported by Soviet Pres. Mikhail Gorbachev, 7 republics, on **Nov. 14**, reached a preliminary agreement on a loose confederation, a "Union of Sovereign States." From **Nov. 15-17**, Yeltsin issued decrees asserting Russian control over its natural resources. He suspended licenses for oil exports outside Russia, and took control over production of gold and other metals. The Bush administration announced, **Nov. 20**, that $1.25 billion in loan guarantees would be made available for Soviet food purchases. The Group of Seven leading industrial countries agreed, **Nov. 21**, to defer repayments on foreign debts of the Soviet Union. On **Nov. 25**, representatives of 7 republics balked at signing the treaty creating a loose confederation that they had agreed to 11 days earlier. It was reported, **Nov. 27**, that Pres. George Bush would recognize an independent Ukraine if the republic voted for independence in a forthcoming referendum. The Gorbachev government, **Nov. 28**, expressed surprise at what appeared to constitute a shift of U.S. support from the central government of the USSR. After first saying that he would not support another round of deficit spending by the central government, Yeltsin, **Nov. 30**, said he would finance the Soviet payroll for the immediate future.

Middle East Talks Conclude in Madrid — The Middle East peace conference continued in Madrid, as the second round of speeches were delivered, **Nov. 1**. Rebutting criticism of Israel, Prime Minister Yitzhak Shamir called Syria one of the world's most oppressive and tyrannical regimes. Syrian Foreign Minister Farouk al-Sharaa called Shamir a terrorist, displaying a British "wanted" poster for him dating from 1947. Dr. Haidar Abdel-Shafi, head of the Palestinian delegation, pleaded for reconciliation, urging Israel to "abandon mutual fear and mistrust" and to "approach us as equals within a two-state solution." The Israelis met with the Palestinians and Jordanians, **Nov. 3**, and agreed to continue talks on Palestinian self-rule in a meeting that was described as businesslike and cordial. Separate talks between the Israelis and the Syrians made no progress. The conference concluded, **Nov. 4**, without any agreement among the parties on where they would meet next.

Mrs. Marcos Returns to Philippines — Imelda Marcos, widow of Pres. Ferdinand Marcos, returned to the Philippines, **Nov. 4**, after 5 years of exile in the U.S. Several thousand supporters welcomed her at Manila airport. She was arrested, **Nov. 5**, on tax fraud charges related to money allegedly seized during her husband's presidency. Mrs. Marcos was released after posting bail.

Miyazawa Becomes Premier of Japan — Having already been elected president of the ruling Liberal Democratic Party, Kiichi Miyazawa formally became premier of Japan, **Nov. 5**. He succeeded Toshiki Kaifu, who had fallen from favor with party leaders. Miyazawa appointed Michio Watanabe, the runner-up in the election for the LDP presidency, as foreign minister.

NATO Takes a New Approach — Leaders of the member states of the North Atlantic Treaty Organization met in Rome to map a new course of action. In unveiling a new "strategic concept," **Nov. 7**, they concluded that the threat from the Soviet bloc had disappeared. But the statement concluded that political instability in Eastern Europe or the proliferation of weapons of mass destruction could pose problems in the future. Future NATO military forces were projected to be smaller, more mobile, and capable of being built up through utilization of reserves. Pres. George Bush, addressing the summit, **Nov. 7**, said the U.S. would keep forces in Europe. When he added, "If you don't need us any longer, say so," all the other countries urged that U.S. troops remain in Europe. On **Nov. 8**, Bush had an audience with Pope John Paul II.

Two Libyans Indicted in Bombing of Plane — On **Nov. 14**, both the U.S. Justice Dept. and Scottish authorities indicted 2 Libyan intelligence officers in the bombing of a Pan American World Airways plane in 1988 that killed 270 people. The U.S. investigators said one of the Libyans had obtained luggage tags that permitted the other to put a suitcase with a bomb onto the flight. A U.S. State Dept. spokesman called the bombing "a Libyan government operation from start to finish."

Sihanouk Named President of Cambodia — After more than a decade in exile, Prince Norodom Sihanouk returned to Cambodia, **Nov. 14**. Sihanouk had been put on the Cambodian throne by the French in 1941, and had been an influential figure ever since, but he had fled the country when the Vietnamese installed a government in 1979. Under the peace treaty approved by the government and rebel factions in October, Sihanouk was to head an interim government, but after his return he was named president by the government. Sihanouk said, **Nov. 16**, that leaders of the Khmer Rouge, a Communist faction that had run Cambodia in the late 1970s, should be tried in the deaths of some 1 million Cambodians during their rule. Khieu Samphan, a former Khmer Rouge leader, received a far less pleasant welcome, **Nov. 27**, when a mob attacked his house and beat him. Khieu Samphan and several other former Khmer Rouge leaders were evacuated to Thailand. The Khmer Rouge said, **Nov. 28**, that the violent incident would not cause it to abandon its commitment to the peace agreement.

U.S., British Hostages Released — Two more Western hostages were released, **Nov. 18**, by Islamic Jihad, a Shiite Muslim faction in Lebanon. One of the freed men, Terry Waite, had represented the archbishop of Canterbury in the Middle East as a negotiator for the release of hostages until he, as well, was taken hostage in 1987. The other, Thomas M. Sutherland, former dean of agriculture at American University in Beirut, had been held since 1985. Israeli officials said, **Nov. 18** and **19**, that some 300 Lebanese and Palestinian prisoners that they controlled would not be freed until information was provided about 4 Israeli servicemen believed captured in Lebanon.

Egyptian Nominated as U.N. Secretary General — Boutros Ghali, an Egyptian law professor, journalist, and diplomat, was nominated, **Nov. 21**, by the U.N. Security Council to serve as secretary general of the United Nations. Ghali's approval by the General Assembly would be a formality. Ghali, the first Arab and first African to hold the office, would succeed Javier Pérez de Cuéllar of Peru, who was retiring after 10 years as secretary general. Ghali had gained prominence as a peace negotiator between Egypt and Israel in the late 1970s.

General

Publisher's Death Investigated — Robert Maxwell, creator of an international media empire, died in November under mysterious circumstances. Over several decades, the British entrepreneur had acquired holdings, mostly in the U.S. and Britain, that were valued in the billions of dollars. Some of his principal properties were the Mirror Group newspapers in Britain, the Macmillan book-publishing company, and the *New York Daily News*. He had sold off several of his holdings in 1991 to service an immense debt. While cruising off the Canary Islands, **Nov. 5**, Maxwell disappeared from his yacht. His body was found several hours later. While speculation grew that Maxwell, a flamboyant and controversial figure, had met with foul play, Spanish authorities indicated, **Nov. 6**, that he had probably suffered a fatal heart attack and fallen overboard.

Infected by AIDS Virus, Basketball Star Retires — Earvin (Magic) Johnson retired from professional basketball after he tested positive for the HIV virus that causes acquired immune deficiency syndrome. After leading Michigan State to a national college title, Johnson had starred 12 years with the Los Angeles Lakers. He received the league's most valuable player award 3 times, and the Lakers won 5 NBA titles. On **Nov. 7**, Johnson announced that he had become infected with the virus and had retired on advice of his doctors. The AIDS virus had proved fatal to more than 125,000 Americans during the past decade. At this press conference and in subsequent statements, Johnson appealed to young people to practice safe sex or abstain from sex outside marriage. On **Nov. 15**, he accepted an invitation from Pres. George Bush to join the National Commission on AIDS.

Japan to Stop Using Big Fishing Nets — Japan said, **Nov. 26**, that it would stop using huge fishing nets in the northern Pacific. The U.S. had led an effort in the United Nations to impose a moratorium on the nets, which extended up to 40 miles in length and which caused the death of great numbers of fish, birds, whales, and turtles. Japanese fishermen used the nets to catch a species of squid popular in Japan. Though it had argued that the fishing-net ban would put 10,000 people out of work, Japan announced that it would phase out the nets by the end of 1992.

DECEMBER

National

Sununu Resigns as Bush's Chief of Staff — John Sununu, the White House Chief of Staff, offered to resign, **Dec. 3**, and Pres. George Bush accepted his offer the same day. Sununu had been the center of several controversies during his 3 years in the White House, including complaints that he had used government transportation for personal and political trips. Many leaders of the government had said that they found Sununu to be brusque and abrasive in manner. Bush, **Dec. 5**, named Samuel Skinner, the Sec. of Transportation, to succeed Sununu.

White House Says Recession Continues — The Commerce Dept. reported, **Dec. 3**, that the leading economic indicators rose 0.1 percent in October. Although the Labor Dept. reported, **Dec. 6**, that the unemployment rate had held at 6.8 percent in November, it also said that the number of payroll jobs had decreased by 241,000 in the same month. The department reported, **Dec. 13**, that consumer prices had risen 0.4 percent in November. White House spokesman Marlin Fitzwater told reporters, **Dec. 17**, "the recession does continue." Interviewed on television, **Dec. 17**, Pres. George Bush did not use the word recession but acknowledged that the economy was a problem. General Motors Corp. announced, **Dec. 18**, that it would close 21 of its 125 factories in North America and cut 74,000 employees from its payrolls. In 10 years, G.M.'s share of the U.S. vehicle market had declined from 44 percent to 35 percent. The Commerce Dept. said, **Dec. 19**, that the U.S. merchandise trade deficit was $6.73 billion in October. On **Dec. 20**, in the hopes of spurring economic growth, the Federal Reserve Board reduced 2 key interest rates. It cut the rate for loans to member institutions (the discount rate) from 4.5 percent to 3.5 percent, and it dropped the rate for overnight loans between banks (the federal funds rate) from 4.5 percent to 4 percent. The discount rate had not been so low since 1964. Major banks, **Dec. 20**, cut their prime rate to 6.5 percent, the lowest level since 1977. The cut in interest rates spurred a rally on Wall Street, and the Dow Jones Industrial Average closed, **Dec. 31**, at an all-time high of 3168.83. For the year, the Dow was up 20 percent. The Commerce Dept. said, **Dec. 31**, that the leading economic indicators had fallen 0.3 percent in November.

Ex-Chairman of S & L Convicted of Fraud — Charles Keating, one of the most prominent figures in the investigation of the savings and loan debacle, was convicted of 17 counts of securities fraud, **Dec. 4**. Keating had been chairman of the Lincoln Savings & Loan Association in California. In his trial, the prosecution asserted that Keating had defrauded investors by inducing them to buy high-risk Lincoln bonds that were not insured. Some 17,000 persons had invested $250 million in the bonds. When American Continental Corp., Lincoln's parent company, filed for bankruptcy, the investments could not be retrieved. On **Apr. 10**, Keating was sentenced to 10 years in prison and fined $250,000.

Two Challenge Bush in GOP Primaries — David Duke and Patrick Buchanan said that they would challenge Pres. George Bush in presidential primary elections in 1992. Duke, a Louisiana state representative, announced his candidacy, **Dec. 4**. Duke, a former Grand Wizard of the Ku Klux Klan, had just lost a hard-fought campaign for governor of Louisiana, but even in defeat he apparently had attracted a nationwide following. Bush, **Dec. 5**, named his own re-election campaign team, headed by Commerce Secretary Robert Mosbacher, as chairman, and Robert Teeter, a pollster. Mosbacher planned to resign from the cabinet in January. On **Dec. 10**, Buchanan, a columnist and television talk-show host, entered the Republican presidential race. An outspoken conservative, Buchanan had held important positions in the White House under presidents Richard Nixon and Ronald Reagan. Buchanan said that Bush "would put America's wealth and power at the service of some vague 'new world order.' We will put America first." Gov. Mario Cuomo of New York announced, **Dec. 20**, that he would not seek the Democratic presidential nomination. For many weeks Cuomo had said that he was giving serious thought to running. In removing himself from consideration, Cuomo cited the lack of progress in resolving New York State's serious fiscal problems.

Two Big Cities Get New Mayors — Two major mayoralty contests were decided in nonpartisan runoff elections in December. In Houston, **Dec. 7**, Bob Lanier, a developer, defeated state Rep. Sylvester Turner. The incumbent, Kathy Whitmire, the mayor for a decade, had been eliminated in the first round of voting. On **Dec. 10**, in San Francisco, Frank Jordan, a former chief of police, defeated Mayor Art Agnos. Jordan had deplored an increase in crime and panhandlers in the city.

International

Last 3 U.S. Hostages in Lebanon Are Freed — The last 3 Americans being held hostage in Lebanon were set free in December. The exchange of captives, which had gained momentum in recent months, continued, **Dec. 1**, when the Israeli-backed South Lebanon Army freed 25 Arabs. Two Americans, Joseph Cicippio and Alann Steen, were freed, **Dec. 2** and **3**, respectively, by Moslem factions, and it was subsequently learned that they had suffered permanent injuries as a result of mistreatment by their captors. Terry Anderson, a former Associated Press correspondent, was freed by Islamic Jihad, **Dec. 4**, after almost 7 years in captivity. The long and energetic effort by his sister, Peggy Say, to keep the plight of Anderson and the other hostages in the public eye had finally been rewarded. The remains of 2 Americans, U.S. Marine Corps Lt. Col. William Higgins and former CIA officer William Buckley, were found in Beirut, **Dec. 22** and **Dec. 27**, respectively, after anonymous callers had phoned Lebanese authorities. Two German relief workers, seized in 1989, were the only Westerners still held hostage in Lebanon.

Middle East Talks Held in Washington — The Middle East talks were scheduled to reopen in Washington, D.C., **Dec. 4**, but the Israeli delegation was not present because of Israel's objection to the U.S. capital as a site for the talks. The Israelis arrived a few days later, however, and talks were underway by **Dec. 10**. Talks between the Israelis and the joint Jordanian-Palestinian delegation failed to make headway because of the Israelis' refusal to meet separately with the 2 other parties. The Israeli-Syrian talks made little headway. It was agreed, **Dec. 22**, that the talks would resume in Washington in January.

Attack on Pearl Harbor Recalled 50 Years Later — The 50th anniversary of the Japanese attack on the Pearl Harbor naval base in Hawaii was observed in December. Japanese leaders expressed regret over the attack, but the Japanese Diet (parliament) declined to adopt a resolution expressing regret after Pres. George Bush declined to apologize for the atomic-bomb attacks on Hiroshima and Nagasaki. On **Dec. 7**, the aniverary of the attack, Bush led the observance near the place where the battleship *USS Arizona* had been sunk. Some 2,000 veterans who had been at Pearl Harbor attended the observance. In his speech, Bush warned against isolationism and against a protectionist policy in international trade.

European Countries Strengthen Their Ties — Leaders of the 12 European Community countries agreed, **Dec. 11**, to 2 treaties that brought them closer to a full union. They met in Maastricht, the Netherlands. In one treaty, the participating countries agreed to "define and implement a common foreign and security policy." The other treaty would establish a single currency in 1999. It was agreed, however, that the British Parliament would decide, at a later date, if Britain would join the single currency. Both treaties required ratification by individual countries.

North and South Korea Sign Agreement — On **Dec. 13**, in Seoul, South Korea, the premiers of North and South Korea signed an agreement that represented a step back from confrontation. Although the 2 countries had signed an armistice ending the Korean War in 1953, they were still technically at war. Under the new agreement, the countries promised not to interfere in each other's internal affairs and to issue a joint declaration of nonaggression. A formal peace treaty was seen as a future outgrowth of the new agreement. It did not address the question of North Korea's atomic weapons. Pres. Roh Tae Woo of South Korea announced, **Dec. 18**, that all U.S. nuclear weapons had been withdrawn from his country.

U.N. Repeals 'Zionism is Racism' Resolution — The U.N. General Assembly voted to repeal a 1975 resolution that had equated Zionism with racism. The impetus for that resolution had come from the Soviet bloc, the Arab countries, and other 3rd-world countries. Its repudiation, **Dec. 16**, by a vote of 111-25, reflected the change that had occurred in international affairs during the past 2 years. The Soviet Union and the former Communist nations of Eastern Europe voted for repeal. Although no Arab country voted for repeal, some of the more moderate Arab states absented themselves during the vote.

Yugoslavia, Serbia Accept Peace Plan — A year of bloodshed and devastation in Yugoslavia ended on a hopeful note. On **Dec. 19**, Germany said it would recognize Croatia and Slovenia, the republics seeking independence from Yugoslavia. On **Dec. 19** and **20**, respectively, 2 more republics, Macedonia and Bosnia-Herzegovina, petitioned the European community for recognition. The central government and the republic of Serbia, **Dec. 31**, accepted a peace plan proposed by Cyrus Vance, the U.N. special envoy to Yugoslavia. The plan provided that 10,000 U.N. peacekeeping soldiers would be deployed in battered Croatia after a cease-fire went into effect.

Bank Agrees to Give Up $550 Million U.S. Assets — It was announced, **Dec. 19**, that the scandal-plagued Bank of Credit and Commerce International had reached an agreement with the U.S. Justice Dept. and a New York City district attorney to settle criminal charges against the institution. The bank would forfeit all its U.S. assets, some $550 million, which would be used to reimburse BCCI depositors around the world and to give support to 2 U.S. banks that BCCI had acquired and that were in poor financial condition. The settlement did not affect indictments pending against former BCCI officials.

Islamic Party Strong in Algerian Voting — The Islamic Salvation Front ran far ahead in the first round of voting for seats in Algeria's parliament, **Dec. 26**. In the country's first free parliamentary election, the fundamentalist Islamic party won nearly enough seats to control parliament. The rest of the seats would be decided in a runoff election in January. Algeria's ruling party, the National Liberation Front, ran a poor third. The Islamic party sought to establish a state based on a strict legal code derived from the Koran.

General

Maxwell's Private Companies File for Bankruptcy — It was reported, **Dec. 3**, that Spanish pathologists had concluded that Robert Maxwell, the publisher, had suffered a heart attack before he fell off his yacht and died in November. They ruled out foul play. The Mirror Group, a Maxwell property, announced, **Dec. 3**, that it was investigating loans and asset transfers from the company's pension fund to companies that Maxwell controlled. On **Dec. 4**, Britain's Serious Fraud Office began a similar inquiry. On **Dec. 5**, Maxwell's sons, Ian and Kevin, sought bankruptcy protection in Britain for Maxwell's privately owned companies. Also on **Dec. 5**, the *New York Daily News*, another part of the Maxwell empire, filed for bankruptcy in the U.S.

Pan American Ceases Operations — Delta Air Lines, which had been providing financial support to Pan American World Airways, announced, **Dec. 3**, that it would not offer any further assistance. Pan Am then closed operations, **Dec. 4**, ending one of the most important and colorful chapters in aviation history. The year 1991 had also seen the demise of Eastern Airlines and Midway Airlines.

William Kennedy Smith Acquitted of Rape Charge — A member of the Kennedy family was acquitted in a rape case in December. The trial, which was telecast live, attracted wide attention. The man charged, William Kennedy Smith, was a nephew of Sen. Ted Kennedy (D, Mass.), who was among many who testified during the trial. On **Dec. 11**, the jury found Smith not guilty of sexual battery—Florida's legal term for rape. To protect the woman's privacy, her face was not shown on television. In a television interview, broadcast **Dec. 19**, she identified herself publicly as Patricia Bowman.

Suspect in Kahane's Murder Is Acquitted — An Egyptian immigrant who had been charged with the shooting death of the militant Jewish leader Rabbi Meir Kahane was found not guilty. Kahane had been shot at a hotel in New York City in 1990. The jury, **Dec. 21**, also found the accused man, El Sayyid Nosair, not guilty of shooting and wounding a postal policeman, but convicted him of 4 lesser charges. Although many people were present at the time Kahane was shot, no one testified to seeing Nosair commit the crime.

Soviet Union Disbands and Is Replaced by a Commonwealth of Independent States

The Soviet Union was disbanded in December 1991 and replaced by a Commonwealth of Independent States. The commonwealth consisted of 11 of the 12 republics that had remained in the USSR after the 3 Baltic republics became independent earlier in 1991. Having no one left to govern, Soviet Pres. Mikhail Gorbachev resigned, and Russian Pres. Boris Yeltsin became the dominant figure in the commonwealth.

Created in 1922, the Soviet Union had been the world's largest country, geographically, and, since World War II, one of the world's 2 military superpowers. The nation's economy was in ruins, and the fitful transition to free markets had not alleviated the crisis.

Attempts by Gorbachev to create a loose economic and political federation had been making some headway until **Dec. 1.** On that day, the people of the Ukraine, the so-called breadbasket of the Soviet Union, voted overwhelmingly in favor of independence from the USSR. Leonid Kravchuk, who already held the title of president, became the first popularly elected president of the Ukraine. Pres. George Bush, **Dec. 2,** directed Sec. of State James Baker to visit the Ukraine to explore establishing diplomatic relations, and to discuss control of nuclear weapons on its territory.

Gorbachev, **Dec. 3,** renewed his appeal for preservation of the union, but on the same day, Yeltsin recognized the Ukraine as an independent state. Ukraine's parliament, **Dec. 5,** endorsed the results of the independence referendum.

At a meeting on **Dec. 8,** the leaders of the 3 Slavic republics of the USSR signed an agreement to form a Commonwealth of Independent States. The signatories were Yeltsin, Kravchuk, and Stanislav Shushkevich, chairman of the parliament of Belarus. The agreement blamed "short-sighted policies" of the national government for a "deep political and economic crisis" and ethnic conflicts. The 3 leaders agreed that members of the commonwealth would be fully independent and that all Soviet national laws were void in the signatory republics. Other republics of the Soviet Union were invited to join the commonwealth.

The commonwealth would have a central authority in Minsk, the capital of Belarus. The Soviet ruble would be the common currency in the commonwealth. Members would adhere to international agreements signed by the USSR, observe neutrality in international affairs, and work for nuclear disarmament.

Gorbachev, **Dec. 9,** denounced the agreement as illegal and said it "can only intensify the chaos and anarchy in society."

The Ukrainian and Belarus parliaments approved the agreement, **Dec. 10.** Amendments added by the Ukrainians provided for a separate Ukrainian currency and Ukrainian control over conventional armed forces on its soil. The Russian parliament approved the agreement, **Dec. 12.** Kravchuk, **Dec. 12,** declared himself commander of all Soviet armed forces in Ukrainian territory.

On **Dec. 13,** the 5 Central Asian republics—Kazakhstan, Kyrgyzstan, Tajikistan, Turkmenistan, and Uzbekistan—decided to join the commonwealth.

Baker flew to the Soviet Union and met separately, **Dec. 16,** with Gorbachev and Yeltsin. During his trip, Baker got assurances from the leaders of 4 republics—Belarus, Ukraine, Russia, and Kazakhstan—which had nuclear weapons that these weapons would remain under central control. Kravchuk told Baker, **Dec. 18,** that Ukraine would destroy all nuclear weapons on its soil.

Yeltsin directed the Russian government, **Dec. 19,** to take over the Kremlin and the central government, aside from the ministries of defense and atomic energy.

On **Dec. 21,** leaders of 11 republics met in Alma-Ata, capital of Kazakhstan, and signed agreements creating the commonwealth. The leaders reaffirmed that the commonwealth was an alliance of fully independent states, but that commonwealth policy would be set by coordinating bodies.

Georgia was not represented at Alma-Ata because rebels were seeking to overthrow its president, Zviad Gamsakhurdia. The president was under siege in the parliament building in Tbilisi. The power struggle caused the deaths of 50 people in late December.

Gorbachev and Yeltsin met, **Dec. 23,** to arrange for a transfer of power. In an address to the country, **Dec. 25,** Gorbachev announced his resignation, after nearly 7 years in power. He noted that during that time the Cold War had ended, the arms race had stopped, and "This society acquired freedom, liberated itself politically and spiritually." He cited the new era of free elections, freedom of the press, religious freedom, and human rights. Gorbachev also hailed the movement toward a market economy, but said, "The process of renovating this country . . .turned out to be far more complicated than could be expected," and he summed up: "The old system collapsed before the new one had time to begin working."

Bush announced, **Dec. 25,** that the U.S. would recognize the independence of all 12 republics and would establish diplomatic relations with 6 right away. Within the next few days, many countries announced that they would recognize and establish relations with some or all of the former Soviet republics.

Eleven commonwealth leaders, having formed the Council of Heads and State, met, **Dec. 30,** and agreed to put the USSR's long-range nuclear arsenal under a central command. If war came, leaders of the 4 states having such weapons would have to give their approval before they were used. The leaders agreed that any state could have its own armed forces.

In Russia, state subsidies for most goods and services were removed, **Jan. 2.** Milk, bread, medicine, and gasoline were among items exempted. Prices on the exempted items were raised somewhat, and the prices of everything else rose sharply. To counter the impact on average citizens, the government raised the minimum wage and increased the pay of state employees. Belarus (formerly, Byelorussia), Moldova (formerly, Moldavia), and Ukraine also allowed prices to rise.

The seige in Tbilisi ended, **Jan. 6,** when Gamsakhurdia and about 100 supporters fled the Georgian capital. Gamsakhurdia insisted he was still the president, but rebel leaders seized control of the government and promised to turn rule over to civilian parties when possible.

After Kravchuk declared that former Soviet military personnel in the Ukraine must swear allegiance to Ukraine, Yeltsin said, **Jan. 9,** "The Black Sea fleet was, is, and will be Russia's." On **Jan. 11,** the 2 states agreed tentatively that part of the fleet would go to Ukraine.

On **Jan. 14,** Gorbachev began work as chairman of the International Foundation for Social, Economic and Political Research, a think tank based in Moscow.

Some 5,000 former Soviet military officers demanded, **Jan. 17,** that all forces remain under a unified command within the Commonwealth.

Bush, **Jan. 22,** announced $645 million in new U.S. assistance to the Commonwealth, subject to Congressional approval. On **Jan. 23,** at a meeting at which representatives of 47 nations and major international financial institutions sought means of assisting the Commonwealth, Baker announced that the U.S. would begin an emergency airlift of food and medicine.

During his U.N. visit, **Jan. 31,** Yeltsin said that Russia and 3 other new states were setting up a means of controlling strategic land-based missiles on their soil.

Yeltsin met with Bush at Camp David, **Feb. 1.** The leaders pledged to remove "any remnants of Cold War hostility." Their joint declaration also said, "Russia and the United States do not regard each other as potential adversaries."

In Paris, **Feb. 7**, Yeltsin and Pres. François Mitterand signed a treaty of friendship that committed the parties to consult with each other during a crisis and to build "a network of peace and solidarity." They agreed on limits to their nuclear and conventional weaponry.

The emergency airlift of food and medical supplies got underway, **Feb. 10**, from Frankfurt, Germany. Fourteen countries were providing help, with deliveries scheduled for 23 destinations in the Commonwealth.

From **Feb. 11-16**, Baker traveled to Moldova, Armenia, Azerbaijan, Turkmenistan, Tajikistan, and Uzbekistan as part of the process of establishing diplomatic relations.

Meeting in Minsk, **Feb. 14**, leaders of the republics were unable to agree on forming a unified military command—except for strategic nuclear weapons. Ukraine, Moldova, and Azerbaijan said they would form their own armed forces under civilian control.

Baker met with Russian leaders in Moscow, **Feb. 17-18**, to discuss the disarmament of the U.S. and Commonwealth nuclear arsenals. The West had been concerned that unemployed Soviet nuclear weapons experts might be employed by 3rd-world countries. Yeltsin and Baker announced, **Feb. 17**, that Russia, Germany, and the U.S. would establish a program for utilizing the talents of the Soviet experts for "nonmilitary endeavors."

Georgia's ruling Military Council, **Mar. 10**, chose former Soviet Foreign Minister Eduard Shevardnadze to head a newly established State Council. In effect, he succeeded the ousted Gamsakhurdia as head of state. Born in Georgia, Shevardnadze had risen to prominence there in the Communist Party and had gone on to gain international recognition as a leader of the reform movement in the USSR.

Officials from Armenia and Azerbaijan signed a draft truce agreement, **Mar. 15**, following a 6-week period in which the conflict between the 2 former republics had worsened and resulted in the deaths of hundreds of people.

Ten of the 11 presidents of the Commonwealth states met at a summit in Kiev, the Ukrainian capital, **Mar. 20**. To deal with the Armenian-Azerbaijani crisis, the leaders decided to form some sort of peace-keeping force, but no details were worked out. At a press conference of the presidents, Yeltsin and Kravchuk clashed over the issue of the transfer of Ukraine's tactical nuclear weapons to Russia. Kravchuk was concerned that the weapons would be added to Russia's own arsenal.

The International Monetary Fund announced, **Mar. 31**, its endorsement of Russia's economic reform plan. The decision meant that Russia could receive up to $4 billion in IMF aid over a year's time.

On **Apr. 1**, Bush and German Chancellor Helmut Kohl announced that 7 major industrial nations would provide the Russian Federation with $18 billion in financial and humanitarian aid and $6 billion to help stabilize the ruble. Bush warned that if Russia's experiment in democracy failed, the world could become a dangerous place. He called on Congress to provide aid for Russia and the other former Soviet republics.

The Russian parliament was sharply divided over the efficacy of Yeltsin's reform program, and on **Apr. 6**, a majority of the deputies barely beat back a motion of no-confidence in the government. Then, in a shift, the deputies voted, **Apr. 11**, for a resolution calling the reform program unsatisfactory and asking Yeltsin to resign as prime minister (while continuing as president) by the end of July. Partially reversing itself again, **Apr. 15**, the parliament approved a declaration of conditional support for Yeltsin's economic policies.

The IMF, **Apr. 27**, accepted 14 former Soviet republics—all except Azerbaijan—as members.

The nuclear states within the Commonwealth agreed, **Apr. 29**, that the U.S. would negotiate separately with them on control of nuclear weapons. Kravchuk, in Washington, D.C., **May 6**, said Ukraine would cut its nuclear arsenal as required by the Strategic Arms Reduction Treaty (START), which the U.S. and the Soviet Union had signed in 1991. Kravchuk and Bush signed several bilateral agreements. One granted most-favored-nation trade status to Ukraine.

On **May 7**, Yeltsin issued decrees that created armed forces for Russia and named Yeltsin as their commander.

Representatives of 6 Commonwealth countries met in Tashkent, in Uzbekistan, **May 15**, and signed a mutual-security treaty that committed them not to wage war against each other and pledged collective military response should any of them be attacked by any outside country.

After the Crimean parliament voted to declare the Crimea independent of Ukraine, the Russian legislature voted, **May 21**, to nullify a 1954 agreement transferring Crimea from Russia to the Ukraine. Most of Crimea's population consisted of ethnic Russians.

Sec. of State Baker and representatives of the 4 Commonwealth states having nuclear weapons—Belarus, Kazakhstan, Russia, and Ukraine—met in Libson, Portugal, **May 23**, and signed protocols to the START treaty promising compliance with the treaty.

Yeltsin and Kravchuk signed an 18-point agreement, **June 23**, that ended tensions between Russia and Ukraine. The 2 states agreed to divide the ships of the Black Sea fleet and to share and jointly finance their bases. Because the Crimean Peninsula was not discussed, it appeared that Yeltsin was not pressing his claim to that area. The 2 presidents also reached economic and trade agreements.

Early on **June 24**, supporters of former Pres. Gamsakhurdia seized the television and radio center in Tbilisi and called for his return as leader of Georgia. But troops loyal to Shevardnadze, chairman of Georgia's governing State Council, defeated the rebels in a brief fight.

Later on **June 24**, Shevardnadze flew to Sochi on the Black Sea and signed an agreement with Yeltsin aimed at ending rebellious fighting in the Georgian province of South Ossetia, where the majority favored union with Russia. Yeltsin said a peacekeeping force would be sent to the area.

JANUARY

National

Wilder Drops Out of Presidential Race — Gov. L. Douglas Wilder of Virginia became the first of the major contenders for the Democratic presidential nomination to drop out of the race. He said, **Jan. 8**, that he was withdrawing to devote his full attention to governing Virginia. Public-opinion polls indicated that Wilder had not attracted widespread support. Gov. Bill Clinton of Arkansas, another presidential contender, was caught up in controversy after a tabloid newspaper, the *Star*, alleged that he had a number of extramarital affairs. Clinton, in a television interview, **Jan. 26**, acknowledged "wrongdoing" and having caused "pain in my marriage."

U.S. Economy Contracted in 1991 — The government reported that the U.S. economy contracted in 1991, for the first time in 9 years. The Labor Dept. reported, **Jan. 9**, that the producer price index for finished goods had edged downward by 0.1 percent in 1991, the first decline in wholesale prices in 5 years. The department reported, **Jan. 10**, that unemployment stood in December at 7.1 percent, the highest in more than 5 years. The department said, **Jan. 16**, that consumer prices had risen 3.1 percent in 1991, the lowest annual increase since 1986. The Commerce Dept. reported, **Jan. 17**, that the U.S. trade deficit narrowed to $3.57 billion in November, the smallest in 9 years. The U.S. gross domestic product contracted 0.7 percent (adjusting for inflation) in 1991, the department announced, **Jan. 29**, and this was the first decline since 1982. The department reported, **Jan. 31**, that the leading economic indicators fell 0.3 percent in December, to their lowest level since June 1991.

Bush Announces New Initiatives — In his annual State of the Union address, **Jan. 28**, Pres. George Bush announced proposals to reduce nuclear arsenals and to deal with the U.S. economic recession. He called for a reduction in the defense budget of $50 billion over the next 5 years. The president endorsed cancellation of the Midgetman ICBM program, and he proposed to cap the number of MX intercontinental ballistic missiles and B-2 stealth bombers. The plan included an end to production of nuclear warheads for the Trident II submarine-launched missiles. Faced with a sharp decline in popularity as measured in public-opinion polls, the President said that the same courage and common purpose that had brought victory in the Persian Gulf War and that had helped the country face down the communist threat during the Cold War could now be focused on economic problems. To speed economic growth, Bush said he had told federal departments and agencies to impose a 3-month moratorium on new government regulations and that he had ordered the Internal Revenue Service to reduce the amount withheld from the paychecks of employees. The president endorsed a capital-gains tax as low as 15.4 percent and he advocated eliminating 246 programs that "don't deserve federal funding." Bush endorsed a $3,750 health-insurance tax credit for poor families, and he also called for legislation that would provide a tax credit for first-time home buyers and ease rules for withdrawals from individual retirement accounts. He also backed allowing taxpayers to deduct interest paid on education loans. Pres. Bush challenged Congress to pass his economic proposals by Mar. 20. In response to Bush's arms initiatives, Pres. Boris Yeltsin of Russia proposed, **Jan. 29**, that the U.S. and the former Soviet republics each reduce their strategic warheads by at least 2,000 over 5 years.

Bush Submits 1993 Federal Budget — Pres. George Bush, **Jan. 29**, submitted to Congress a budget for the 1993 fiscal year that contained a projected deficit of $351.9 billion. The budget estimated that for the current 1992 fiscal year the deficit would be $399.4 billion, an all-time record. The 1993 budget contained details of proposals Bush had made in his State of the Union message. While proposing to eliminate or cut back hundreds of programs, Bush also called for increased spending on the Head Start pre-school education program, antidrug programs, prisons, highway development, and aid to the newly independent states emerging from the former Soviet Union.

International

Salvadoran Peace Agreement Signed — Representatives of the government of El Salvador and the Farabundo Marti National Liberation Front signed an interim agreement, **Jan. 1**, that would end the country's 12-year civil war. The conflict between the government and the left-wing rebels had taken 75,000 lives. The agreement had been a goal of U.N. Secretary Gen. Javier Pérez de Cuéllar, and it was signed at U.N. headquarters in New York City just as Pérez was scheduled to step down at the end of his term. Under the agreement, the rebels would give up their arms and return to civilian life. They would not share power but would be guaranteed full political freedom. The government would reduce its armed forces and provide land to peasants who had supported the insurrection. A formal treaty was signed in Mexico City, **Jan. 16**, by Pres. Alfredo Cristiani and 5 top rebel leaders. A cease-fire was to go into effect **Feb. 1**.

Bush Promotes Trade During Trip to Far East — During a visit to countries in the Far East and Pacific Rim, Pres. George Bush sought to improve the position of the U.S. in international trade. He was accompanied by 21 business executives, including the chairmen of the "Big 3" U.S. automakers. Those who questioned the wisdom of the trip suggested that Bush was presenting himself as a car salesman. Visits to Australia (**Dec. 31-Jan. 3**), Singapore (**Jan. 3-5**), and South Korea (**Jan. 5-7**) proved relatively uneventful. Bush and his entourage arrived in Japan, **Jan. 7**. Negotiations with Japanese government leaders and business executives were tense because some Japanese had made it known that problems of the U.S. auto industry were of its own making. Comparisons were made in the media between the large incomes of U.S. auto executives and the more modest remuneration of their Japanese counterparts. During discussions, **Jan. 7-9**, major Japanese car companies agreed to increase the sale of U.S.-built automobiles through their dealer outlets in Japan. Japanese manufacturers agreed that over the next few years they would nearly double—to $19 billion—the value of U.S.-made auto parts that they would purchase. The Japanese made other commitments with respect to markets for computers, paper, and glass. Bush, who had maintained a strenuous schedule on his trip, fell ill, **Jan. 8**, during a state dinner at the residence of Prime Minister Kiichi Miyazawa. He vomited and collapsed, but regained consciousness within a few minutes and returned to his suite at the Akasaka Palace. Bush's illness was diagnosed as a 24-hour intestinal flu. The president appeared to recover quickly, and on **Jan. 9**, called the trip a success. Chrysler Chairman Lee Iacocca, back in the U.S., **Jan. 10**, said he was tired of hearing that U.S. auto industry problems were "our own damn fault."

Arabs, Israelis Meet in Washington, Moscow — Talks between Arab and Israeli representatives resumed in Washington, and other meetings took place in Moscow. After a Jewish settler was killed, **Jan. 1**, in the Gaza Strip, the Israeli defense ministry, **Jan. 2**, ordered 12 Palestinian activists deported because of "terrorist activities" and "incitement." Also on **Jan. 2**, the Israeli parliament approved a budget authorizing construction of 5,000 housing units in the occupied territories. Protesting the planned deportations, delegates representing the Palestinians and other Arabs postponed, **Jan. 3** and **4**, their departure for peace talks in Washington. The U.N. Security Council, **Jan. 6**, voted, 15-0, to condemn the deportations as a violation of international law. Arab leaders then indicated they would attend the Washington talks. The 2 sides began their meetings on **Jan. 13**, and on **Jan. 14**, the Palestinians put forth a plan for self-government in the occupied territories that provided for a Palestinian parliament. Israel, **Jan. 15**, rejected the proposal, saying it essentially amounted to full independence. The talks ended, **Jan. 16**, with little apparent progress. Believing, however, that the Israeli stand had not been firm enough, 2 right-wing parties, **Jan. 19**, withdrew from the Israeli government coalition, leaving Prime Minister Yitzhak Shamir without a majority in parliament. Delegates from Israel, 10 Arab nations, and the European Community attended wide-ranging talks in Moscow, **Jan. 28** and **29**. The Palestinians did not participate because of Israeli objections to the composition of their delegation. Some of the Persian Gulf states were negotiating with Israel for the first time. Arms control and economic development were among the regional issues that were discussed.

European Community Recognizes Croatia, Slovenia — Two breakaway Yugoslav republics, Croatia and Slovenia, gained some international recognition, **Jan. 15**. On **Jan. 7**, a Yugoslav air force jet had shot down an unarmed helicopter carrying observers from the European Community, killing all 5 aboard. The Yugoslav defense ministry accepted responsibility for the attack and expressed "deep regret." The European Community and some individual countries recognized the independence of Croatia and Slovenia, and Germany established formal diplomatic relations. A State Department spokeman said the U.S. would not extend any recognition unless the Yugoslav government and the rebellious republics resolved their conflict peacefully and gave assurances that ethnic minorities would be protected.

Results of Algerian Election Voided — The prospect that Algeria might soon become a fundamentalist Islamic state faded in January. The fundamentalists had won the first round of voting for parliament in December. Pres. Chadli Benjedid resigned, **Jan. 11**, and was replaced by a ruling council dominated by the army. The council, **Jan. 12**, canceled the runoff election that would have determined the winners of parliamentary seats where no candidate had had a majority in the first voting. The new council was quickly superceded by a new ruling body, the State Security Panel, which on **Jan. 12** voided the results of the December election. The Islamic Salvation Front, the fundamentalist party, said, **Jan. 17**, that 500 of its members had been arrested. On **Jan. 22**, Algerian police arrested Abdelkader Hachani, acting head of the salvation front, who was reportedly held for inciting the army to mutiny.

Heads of Governments Attend U.N. Summit — Leaders of governments from around the world attended a U.N. Security Council summit meeting in New York City, **Jan. 31**. Those present included the leaders of all 5 permanent members of the Council. Pres. Boris Yeltsin represented Russia, which had replaced the Soviet Union as a permanent member. In an address to the Council, Yeltsin called for deeper cuts in nuclear and conventional arms. He proposed that the U.S. and Russia work together to create a global antimissile shield similar to the U.S. "Star Wars" program. In his address, Pres. George Bush vowed to maintain sanctions against Iraq until Pres. Saddam Hussein was ousted. Premier Li Peng of China emphasized that other countries should stay out of his country's internal affairs. Yeltsin later met privately with U.S. leaders of government and business. Bush and Li Peng conferred with each other in the highest contact between leaders of the 2 countries since the Chinese crushed a pro-democracy movement in 1989.

General

FDA Halts Sale, Use of Breast Implants — The U.S. Food and Drug Administration, **Jan. 6**, obtained a moratorium on the sale and implantation of silicone-gel breast implants. FDA Commissioner David Kessler told of reports that users were experiencing increased incidence of autoimmune and connective-tissue disorders. He indicated the need to determine how often the implants leaked or broke. Some 2 million women had had the implants inserted, mostly for cosmetic reasons, but also for reconstruction of a breast after surgery.

Two Rare Condors Released Into Wild — The long, expensive effort to save the California condor from extinction reached a new phase in January. The majestic birds, with wingspans of 9½ feet, had almost disappeared from their range in the Los Padres National Forest as the result of hunting and the use of pesticides. The last surviving condors had been captured by 1987, and bred in captivity. Their number had risen from 27 to 52. On **Jan. 14**, a male and female were released into the wild as the first step toward restoring the birds to their natural habitat.

Macy's Files for Bankruptcy — R. H. Macy & Co, owner of 251 retail stores in the U.S., filed for bankruptcy, **Jan. 27**. Macy's flagship store in New York City was billed as the world's largest. Macy's purchase, in 1988, of I. Magnin and Bullock's, for $1.1 billion, had burdened the company with a large debt, and the economic recession had adversely affected the 1991 Christmas shopping season.

TWA Files for Bankruptcy — Trans World Airlines Inc., **Jan. 31**, became the latest major U.S. carrier to file for bankruptcy. TWA had been burdened with large debt since its new owner, Carl Icahn, had made it a private company in 1988. Revenues had fallen during the economic recession. TWA was negotiating a restructuring plan with its major creditors.

FEBRUARY

National

Auto Companies Report Big Losses — Huge losses by the Big 3 U.S. automobile makers dominated the economic news. Chrysler reported, **Feb. 6**, that it had lost $795 million in 1991. The Labor Dept. reported, **Feb. 7**, that the unemployment rate had remained at 7.1 percent in January, and that the number of payroll jobs had shrunk by 91,000. Ford Motor Co. said, **Feb. 13**, that it had lost $2.26 billion in 1991, its greatest loss ever in one year. The Labor Dept. said, **Feb. 14**, that prices charged by producers for finished goods had declined 0.3 percent in January. The department reported, **Feb. 19**, that consumer prices had risen 0.1 percent in January. The Commerce Dept. reported, **Feb. 20**, that the merchandise trade deficit stood at $66.20 billion for all of 1991, the lowest gap since 1983. On **Feb. 24**, General Motors announced a loss of $4.45 billion in 1991, the greatest in history for any U.S. company. G.M. named 12 plants it planned to close over 3 years. On Wall Street, the Dow Jones Industrial Average closed, **Feb. 24**, at 3283.32, an all-time high, which analysts attributed to a belief by investors that an economic recovery would soon begin.

Voting Begins in Presidential Contests — The process of choosing the nominees of the Democratic and Republican parties for president began in earnest. On **Feb 6**, the *Wall Street Journal* published an article that raised questions about how Arkansas Gov. Bill Clinton, a candidate for the Democratic nomination, had avoided service in the military during the Vietnam war.

Clinton had made a commitment to enter the Reserve Officers Training Corp at the Univ. of Arkansas, but later decided not to join the ROTC and made himself available for the draft. Col. Eugene Holmes, the ROTC director at Arkansas at that time, told the *Journal* that Clinton "was able to manipulate things" so that he didn't have to serve. Former Pres. Ronald Reagan, **Feb. 9**, endorsed Pres. George Bush for re-election. The voting for president got underway, **Feb. 10**, on the Democratic side when Sen. Tom Harkin of Iowa won the caucuses in his own state by a lopsided margin. On **Feb. 12**, Clinton released the text of a letter he had written to Col. Holmes on Dec. 3, 1969, in which he described his profound opposition to the war in Vietnam, but said he had decided to pass up the ROTC and accept the draft "to maintain my political viability within the system." Two days earlier, on Dec. 1, Clinton had drawn a high number in the draft lottery that made it unlikely that he would ever be drafted. Bush formally announced his candidacy on **Feb. 12**, and predicted that his administration would soon get the economy going at "full speed." He also said, "I believe government is too big, and it costs too much." The first primary, in New Hampshire on **Feb. 18**, was vigorously contested by all the candidates. On the Republican side, Pat Buchanan rebuked Bush for going back on his "no new taxes" pledge, and said the President had spent too much time on foreign affairs while ignoring the U.S. economy. Bush campaigned in New Hampshire, but relied mostly on efforts by others, including Vice Pres. Dan Quayle. The state had been hard hit by the recession, and Bush got only 53 percent of the vote. Buchanan received 37 percent. Among the Democrats, former Sen. Paul Tsongas, from the adjacent state of Massachusetts, received 33 percent. A liberal on social issues, Tsongas also supported pro-business policies and opposed the middle-class tax cut being advocated by Democratic leaders in Congress. Clinton, although apparently damaged by reports in the press about his past, finished second with 25 percent. The other candidates trailed badly, and a write-in effort in behalf of Gov. Mario Cuomo (N.Y.) produced only 4 percent of the vote. Tsongas and former Gov. Jerry Brown (Cal.) ran about even in the Maine caucuses, **Feb. 23**, and Sen. Bob Kerrey (Neb.) won the South Dakota primary, **Feb. 25**. In South Dakota, 31 percent of the Republican voters supported an uncommitted slate, further evidence of Bush's declining popularity.

Reporters Refuse to Name Sources — The controversy over the nomination of Clarence Thomas to serve on the U.S. Supreme Court had an aftermath. The Senate had ordered an inquiry into how sexual-harassment allegations made by Prof. Anita Hill against Thomas had been leaked to the press. The reporters who broke the story, Timothy Phelps of *Newsday* and Nina Totenberg of National Public Radio, were subpoenaed to testify before a Senate special counsel. Phelps, on **Feb. 13**, and Totenberg, on **Feb. 24**, both refused to name their sources, who were believed to be staff members of one of the members of the Senate Judiciary Committee. The reporters cited the constitutional guarantee of freedom of the press. Phelps said the people "had a need and a right to know that serious allegations had been made" against Thomas.

Arts Endowment Chairman Forced to Resign — John Frohnmayer, chairman of the National Endowment for the Arts, was forced to resign. During Frohnmayer's 2½-year tenure, conservatives had criticized as pornographic or blasphemous several projects funded by the endowment. On **Feb. 20**, Pat Buchanan, who was challenging Pres. George Bush for the Republican presidential nomination, called the endowment "the upholstered playpen of the arts and crafts auxiliary of the Eastern liberal establishment." Buchanan indicated he would make the endowment an issue in Southern presidential primaries. On **Feb. 20**, Frohnmayer was asked by the White House to resign.

House Backs Tax Cut for Middle Class — The House, **Feb. 27**, approved a tax bill that would provide a tax credit of up to $400 for middle-income couples and $200 for individuals. The bill would increase the tax rate for high-income Americans from 31 percent to 35 percent, and it provided for a 10 percent surcharge for those with a taxable income of more than $1 million. The vote was 221-209, with only one Republican supporting it, while 46 Democrats opposed it. Although the bill included some of the proposals that Pres. George Bush had made in his State of the Union address, Bush criticized the bill, primarily for its tax-increase features.

International

U.S. Returns Haitians to Homeland — A confrontation between the U.S. government and Haitian refugees reached a conclusion. After the president of Haiti was overthrown in a coup in September 1991, many Haitians fled their country, hoping for refuge in the United States. U.S. ships picked up more than 14,000 at sea, and held most of them at Guantanamo Bay in Cuba, at the U.S. Naval base. Based on interviews, the U.S. Immigration and Naturalization Service determined that about 3,400 had plausible claims for political asylum. A U.S. Supreme Court ruling, **Jan. 31**, opened the way for the U.S. to return the remaining Haitians to their homeland. This process began, **Feb. 1**, and on **Feb. 3**, the first 381 refugees arrived in Port-au-Prince, the capital of Haiti, aboard U.S. Coast Guard cutters.

Japanese Leader Criticizes U.S. Workers — On **Feb. 3**, Prime Minister Kiichi Miyazawa said it appeared that in recent years Americans had been losing their commitment to the work ethic. He said more U.S. college graduates preferred to make big money on Wall Street rather than turn out products of value. The prime minister also said that leveraged buyouts and junk bonds had burdened U.S. companies with great debt.

Rebellion Thwarted in Venezuela — An attempt to overthrow the government of Venezuela failed. The coup attempt was led by mid-level military officers, but did not have the support of top commanders. The rebels attacked the presidential palace in Caracas after midnight, **Feb. 4**. One of their leaders said, early that morning, that their purpose was to set up a junta to deal with the country's economic and social problems. The coup was defeated by loyalist troops by afternoon, and more than 1,000 officers and soldiers who had participated were arrested.

U.N. Takes Action on Yugoslavia — Franjo Tudjman, president of Yugoslavia's breakaway republic of Croatia, said, **Feb. 6**, he would support the deployment of a U.N. peace-keeping force in Croatia. On **Feb. 21**, the U.N. Security Council approved such a force, which would enforce the truce then in effect and protect the minority Serbs living in Croatia. Serbian Pres. Slobodan Milosevic, **Feb. 27**, welcomed the U.N. decision and said it marked the end of the civil war. Voters in another Yugoslav republic, Bosnia-Herzegovina, voted overwhelmingly, **Feb. 29** and **Mar. 1**, in favor of independence.

Israelis Kill Hizballah Leader — On **Feb. 16**, Israeli helicopter gunships attacked a motorcade in southern Lebanon and killed Sheik Abbas al-Musawi, the leader of Hizballah (Party of God), a Lebanese Shiite organization. For a decade, Hizballah had been engaged in kidnappings of Westerners and terrorist attacks on Western and Israeli targets. Musawi had headed Hizballah's ruling council since 1991. The Israeli gunships fired rockets at Musawi's convoy and then the attackers fired automatic weapons at those attempting to escape on foot. Musawi's wife and son and at least 4 of his bodyguards were also killed. Israeli Defense Minister Moshe Arens said, **Feb. 16**, that Musawi had "lots of blood on his hands," and that the attack had been intended as an assassination attempt.

Rabin to Challenge Shamir in Israel — Israel's 2 major parties, approaching a parliamentary election in June, chose their leaders in February. On **Feb. 19**, for the first time, the Labor Party chose its leader by a vote of the party membership. Yitzhak Rabin narrowly ousted Shimon Peres as leader. Although Rabin supported the exchange of some land for peace with the Arabs, he was considered less dovish than Peres. On **Feb. 20**, the central committee of the ruling Likud Party renominated Prime Minister Yitzhak Shamir as leader. In the 3-way contest, however, Shamir received less than 50 percent of the vote.

Loan Guarantees for Israel Debated — The debate over whether the U.S. should grant $10 billion in loan guarantees to Israel took a new turn. Israel had sought the assistance to help it absorb a large number of emigres from the former Soviet Union. Sec. of State James Baker, testifying before a House subcommittee, **Feb. 24**, said the Bush administration would support the guarantees only if Israel stopped its settlement efforts in the occupied territories. He said the administration would object to the construction of houses as well as the clearing of land and the building of new roads and sewers. Israeli and Arab negotiators resumed their peace talks in Washington, **Feb. 24**. Israel offered a self-governing plan that would give Palestinians authority over most local affairs, but it did not provide for an overall administrative body. Israeli forces would not be withdrawn from the territories. Hanan Ashrawi, a Palestinian spokeswoman, rejected the proposal, **Feb. 26**, and likened it to apartheid.

U.N. Confronts Iraq on Weapons — United Nations representatives sought to carry out a U.N. mandate that all Iraqi ballistic missiles and other weapons of mass destruction be destroyed. The elimination of the weapons had been a condition of the cease-fire that had ended the Persian Gulf war. Iraq, **Feb. 26-28**, refused to allow the U.N. team to begin dismantling the Scud missile production plants and other facilities. The U.N. Security Council, **Feb. 28**, issued a statement warning Iraq that it had "no later than the week of 9 March 1992" to respond or face "serious consequences."

General

NASA Reports on Ozone Depletion — The U.S. National Aeronautics and Space Administration reported, **Feb. 3**, on the threat to the ozone layer, the protective canopy in the atmosphere that blocked ultraviolet rays from the sun. The radiation caused skin cancer and blindness. NASA found that chemicals believed harmful to the ozone were at record levels over northern New England and eastern Canada. Therefore, the danger of ozone depletion was greater than previously thought. The Senate voted, 96-0, **Feb. 6**, for a bill providing for a faster phase-out of the chemicals. Pres. George Bush, **Feb. 11**, ordered producers of the chemicals to end their production by 1995. The chemicals were used in air conditioners, refrigerators, computers, and cleaning solvents.

Korean Students Score High in Math, Science — A survey of 175,000 students from around the world showed that South Koreans ranked high in math and science. The survey, whose results were released **Feb. 5**, had been funded by the U.S. Dept. of Education, the National Science Foundation, and the Carnegie Foundation. Nine-year-olds were tested in 10 countries and 13-year-olds in 15 countries. South Koreans ranked first in math and science in both age groups, although 13-year-old Taiwanese tied for first in mathematics. American 9-year-olds placed 9th in math and 3rd in science. American 13-year-olds were 14th in math and 13th in science. High performance was correlated with time spent doing homework or reading rather than watching television.

Ex-Champ Mike Tyson Convicted of Rape — Former heavyweight boxing champion Mike Tyson was convicted of rape in Indianapolis, **Feb. 10**. Tyson had been a celebrity guest at the Miss Black America beauty pageant held in Indianapolis in July 1991. At that time, a contestant in the pageant, Desiree Washington, charged that Tyson had raped her. The jury found Tyson guilty of rape and 2 criminal counts of deviant conduct. On **Mar. 26**, Tyson was sentenced to 6 years in prison and fined $30,000. With good behavior, he could be freed in 3 years.

Killer of 15 Men, Boys Found to Be Sane — Jeffrey Dahmer, who had pleaded guilty to killing 15 young men and boys, was found to be sane by a jury in Milwaukee, **Feb. 15**. Dahmer, who had mutilated his victims and eaten parts of some of them, had pleaded insanity. Ten of the 12 jurors, the minimum required for a verdict, found that Dahmer was sane. On **Feb. 17**, he was sentenced to 15 consecutive life terms in prison.

United Way's President Forced to Resign — William Aramony, president of the United Way of America, was forced to resign, **Feb. 27**, after articles in the press called attention to his salary ($390,000) and other compensation and expenses he had received. United Way consists of some 2,100 local chapters that raise money—$3 billion in 1990—for many different charities. An internal investigation had found questionable record-keeping and accounting practices. Aramony had headed United Way since 1970.

MARCH

National

Senator Retires After Sexual Allegations — Brock Adams (Wash.) announced, **Mar. 1**, that he was dropping his campaign for re-election to the U.S. Senate. His announcement came hours after the *Seattle Times* had published an article in which 8 women, who were not identified, said that Adams had mistreated them sexually. One woman said that Adams had drugged her and raped her. Adams, who had been in public life for 3 decades, said he had never harmed anyone.

Bush, Clinton Lead in Presidential Balloting — Pres. George Bush and Gov. Bill Clinton of Arkansas moved well ahead in the contests for the Republican and Democratic presidential nominations. On the Republican side, the **Mar. 3** Georgia primary was especially hard-fought. The Bush campaign criticized newspaper columnist Pat Buchanan for opposing the Persian Gulf war, and Buchanan rebuked Bush for supporting "pornographic art" financed by the National Endowment for the Arts. Strongly criticized by Buchanan for reneging on his "no new taxes" pledge, Bush said that his 1990 budget deal with Congressional Democrats, containing a tax increase, had been a mistake. In Georgia, as well as in Colorado and Maryland the same day, Bush defeated Buchanan by margins of about 2-1. Among the Democrats, the Georgia primary was seen as critical for Clinton, because it was the first to be held in his home region. Former Sen. Paul Tsongas (Mass.) said Clinton's support for a middle-class tax cut was just a vote-getting ploy, but Clinton said Tsongas cared more about the rich and corporations. Clinton won 57 percent in Georgia, Tsongas 24 percent. Tsongas, however, defeated Clinton in Maryland, and former California Gov. Jerry Brown, stressing anti-nuclear and anti-corruption themes, won in Colorado. Also on **Mar. 3**, Tsongas won a primary in Utah, and Sen. Tom Harkin (Iowa) led in caucuses in Idaho and Minnesota. Sen. Bob Kerrey (Neb.) dropped out of the Democratic contest, **Mar. 5**, citing a shortage of money. Clinton and Bush won the South Carolina primaries, **Mar. 7**, and Tsongas captured the Arizona caucus. Clinton won the Wyoming caucus, **Mar. 7**, and Brown the caucus in Nevada, **Mar. 8**. Harkin, who had sought to build a base among liberal and pro-labor voters, withdrew on **Mar. 9. Mar. 10** was called Super Tuesday because of the large number of delegates at stake. Most of the primaries were in the South, where Clinton won by impressive margins in Florida, Louisiana, Mississippi, Tennessee, and Texas. He also won a primary in Oklahoma and caucuses in Hawaii and Missouri. Tsongas won primaries in Massachusetts and Rhode Island and led in the Delaware caucus. Clinton drew wide support from both white and black voters in the South. Tsongas ran best among wealthy and well-educated voters. Bush easily defeated Buchanan everywhere on **Mar. 10**, but his showing was considered poor for an incumbent president. David Duke, the Louisiana legislator, ran a poor third everywhere, and got only 9 percent in his home state. On **Mar. 17**, Clinton demonstrated that he could run well outside the South, as he captured 51 percent of the primary vote in both Illinois and Michigan. Bush swept both Illinois and Michigan in the Republican primaries. On **Mar. 18**, H. Ross Perot, a Texas billionaire, criticized the Washington establishment and said he would seek the presidency as an independent if his supporters got his name on the ballots of all 50 states as a petition candidate. A U.S. Naval Academy graduate, Perot had founded Electronic Data Systems, a data-processing business, in 1962. Tsongas announced, **Mar. 19**, that he was suspending his campaign. He said he lacked the money to compete in the upcoming New York primary, and that to continue would be to play the role of the spoiler, a choice he rejected. Brown, who had limited donations to his own campaign to $100, stepped up his charges that the political system had been corrupted by money, and he tied Clinton to the system. Brown narrowly upset Clinton in the **Mar. 24** Connecticut primary. Clinton, **Mar. 29**, admitted smoking marijuana "a time or two" while studying at Oxford University in England, but said he didn't like it and "didn't inhale." Concerned that his support might be eroding, Clinton, **Mar. 30**, challenged Brown to a series of debates.

Leading Economic Indicators Rise Sharply — The Commerce Dept. reported twice in March that the leading economic indicators were rising strongly. The department said, **Mar. 3**, that the indicators had risen 0.9 in January, the biggest climb since July 1991. The Labor Dept. reported, **Mar. 6**, that the unemployment rate had risen in February to 7.3 percent, but that the nation had also added 164,000 payroll jobs. The department said, **Mar. 13**, that prices charged by producers for finished goods had risen 0.2 percent in February, and it reported, **Mar. 17**, that consumer prices had risen 0.3 percent in February. The Commerce Dept. said **Mar. 19**, that the trade deficit had narrowed to $5.77 billion in January. Revising earlier figures, the department reported, **Mar. 26**, that the gross domestic product grew at an annual rate of 0.4 percent during the 4th quarter of 1991, and that the GDP had declined 0.7 percent for all of 1991. The department said, **Mar. 31**, that the leading economic indicators had risen 0.8 percent in February.

Congress Struggles With Budget, Taxes — The House, **Mar. 4**, rejected, 370-42, the $1.52 trillion budget submitted in January by Pres. George Bush. On **Mar. 5**, the House approved a $1.5 trillion Democratic budget by a vote of 215-201. The Democratic plan projected a deficit for the 1993 fiscal year of about $325 billion. The Senate, **Mar. 11**, rejected, 60-37, a Republican-supported tax bill based on proposals put forward by Bush. The Senate, **Mar. 13**, then approved, 50-47, a bill that would cut taxes for the middle class and increase those for wealthier Americans. Senate-House conferees then resolved differences between the Senate bill and one approved in February by the House. Congress approved the conference bill, **Mar. 20**, the deadline Bush had set for Congressional action in his State of the Union address. Bush vetoed the bill, **Mar. 20**, attacking Congress for having attempted to increase taxes on upper-income taxpayers. He also rebuked Congress for approving many local pork-barrel projects. Needing a two-thirds vote to override the veto, the House Democratic leadership failed, **Mar. 25**, to get even a majority to override.

House Bank Scandal Angers Public — The U.S. House ethics committee reported, **Mar. 5**, on its investigation of the House bank. Public-opinion surveys showed that voters were angered by how the bank had been misused. The bank was a service available only to members of the House. No interest was paid nor was a fee assessed if a member overdrew an account. All checks were honored, with deposits from other accounts covering any shortfalls. The ethics committee found that 355 current and former House members had written almost 20,000 overdrafts between July 1988 and October 1991. It recommended that the names of 24 of the most serious offenders be made public. Jack Russ, sergeant at arms of the House, who had been responsible for the administration of the bank, resigned, **Mar. 12**. As a result of strong public protests, the House voted, 426-0, on **Mar. 13**, to release (at a later date) the names of all 355 members and former members. Congressional officials, **Mar. 14**, revealed the names of 21 of the 24 most serious offenders. All of them were Democrats except for former Rep. Tommy Robinson (Ark.) who had switched to the Republican Party during the period under investigation. Robinson had written the most overdrafts, 996. Among current members of the House, Rep. Robert Mrazek (N.Y.) had the highest total, 972. On **Mar. 15**, Rep. Newt Gingrich (R, Ga.), the assistant minority leader, blamed the scandal on institutional corruption, and said that the Democrats had been in power too long and must bear the blame for the scandal. Rep. Tom Foley (D, Wash.), the Speaker of the House, stressed that honoring the bad checks had not cost the taxpayers any money. On **Mar. 17**, 3 members of the Bush cabinet, including Defense Secretary Dick Cheney, admitted that they had written overdrafts while members of the House. Robert Rota, the House postmaster, resigned, **Mar. 19**. In February, 3 House post office employees had pleaded guilty to stealing cash and stamps. Attorney Gen. William Barr, **Mar. 20**, appointed Malcolm Wilkey, a retired Federal appeals court judge, as a special counsel to investigate the House bank.

Incumbents Defeated in Illinois Primary — In the Illinois Democratic primary, **Mar. 17**, challengers defeated a U.S. Senator and 2 members of the House.

Sen. Alan Dixon lost in a 3-way race to Carol Moseley Braun, the Cook County recorder of deeds. Dixon's prospects had apparently been hurt by his vote to approve Clarence Thomas as a member of the U.S. Supreme Court. Braun, a lawyer who had also served in the State Legislature for 10 years would, if elected in November, become the first black woman to serve in the Senate. Rep. Gus Savage, who had made many remarks critical of whites and Jews, lost to Melvin Reynolds, a former college professor. Rep. Charles Hayes, who had written 716 bad checks on the House bank, lost to Bobby Rush, a Chicago alderman.

Guidelines Issued on Abortion Counseling — The U.S. Health and Human Services Dept., **Mar. 20**, issued guidelines to federally funded family planning clinics on what advice could be offered on abortion. Under the new, somewhat relaxed, rules, doctors could discuss the option of abortion. However, nurses and other medical professionals would not be permitted to discuss abortion, and doctors could not refer patients to a facility whose primary business was performing abortions.

International

Middle East Talks Still Deadlocked — The 3rd round of direct talks between Arab and Israeli negotiators concluded in Washington. The Palestinians, having rejected an Israeli proposal in February, offered a plan, **Mar. 3**, for the election of a Palestinian parliament in the Israeli-occupied West Bank and Gaza Strip, and for the withdrawal of Israeli armed forces. Israel rejected this proposal, and the talks ended, **Mar. 4**, without any agreement.

British Parliamentary Election Scheduled — British Prime Minister John Major decided to call a parliamentary election. After Margaret Thatcher resigned as prime minister in November 1990, Conservative members of Parliament had chosen Major to succeed her. Major had hoped to avoid an election until the economy improved, but with the term of Parliament due to expire by summer, the prime minister, on **Mar. 11**, asked Queen Elizabeth II to dissolve Parliament. He then announced **Apr. 9** as the date of the election. Neil Kinnock, the Labour leader, said, **Mar. 11**, that 13 years of Conservative rule had left the nation in a deep recession.

Iraq Agrees to U.N. Council's Terms — A new controversy between Iraq and the U.N. Security Council flared in March, but it was apparently resolved. The Council's president for March, Diego Arria, urged, **Mar. 11**, that sanctions against Iraq remain in place until Iraq complied fully and unconditionally with the terms of the cease-fire agreement that had ended the 1991 Persian Gulf war. Rolf Ekeus, a U.N. official, said Iraq was not allowing U.N. personnel to destroy weapons-production facilities (contending that they could be converted for civilian uses) and had not accepted long-term monitoring of its military industries. The Council, **Mar. 12**, formally rejected claims by Tariq Aziz, the Iraqi envoy, that Iraq had complied with the resolutions. Unconfirmed reports circulated that the U.S. might attack strategic Iraqi targets. On **Mar. 20**, however, Ekeus said that Iraq had agreed to destroy all the components of its ballistic missile production program as well as any other equipment that the U.N. commission headed by Ekeus believed should be eliminated. Iraq also said that by April it would provide full details to the U.N. on its nuclear, chemical, and biological arms programs.

Bomb Destroys Israeli Embassy — A bomb inside a car exploded next to the Israeli embassy in Buenos Aires, Argentina, **Mar. 17**. The embassy building, a Catholic Church, and school were destroyed. At least 32 people were killed, and some 250 were injured. The Lebanese Shiite group Islamic Ji had claimed responsibility for the bombing, **Mar. 18**, stating that it was in retaliation for the assassination of Shiite leader Sheik Abbas al-Musawi by Israeli commandos in February.

S. African Vote May Mean End of Minority Rule — South African white voters gave Pres. F.W. De Klerk the authority to negotiate for an end to white minority rule. De Klerk, campaigning vigorously for a yes vote in a referendum, said he foresaw the day when a new constitution would protect all races and prevent any race from dominating the government. He warned that a no vote might bring international isolation, economic ruin, and violent black unrest. In the referendum, on **Mar. 17**, blacks could not vote, but whites turned out in large numbers and voted yes by more than a 2-1 margin. De Klerk said, "Today we have closed the book on apartheid." Nelson Mandela, president of the African National Congress, saw the vote as a step toward black rule.

U.N. Warns Libya on Bombing Suspects — The United Nations brought pressure on Libya to extradite 2 men who had been indicted in the U.S., France, and Britain in connection with the bombing of airliners over Scotland and Niger in 1988 and 1989. Libya had announced, **Mar. 23**, that it would turn over the suspects to representatives of the Arab League. Libya, however, failed to produce the 2 men. The U.N. Security Council, **Mar. 31**, voted to impose sanctions on Libya if the men were not surrendered by **Apr. 15**. Resolution 748 also asked Libya "to cease all forms of terrorist action and all assistance to terrorist groups." The resolution asked U.N. members to ban air travel to and from Libya and to cease any sales of military equipment to Libya.

General

New Evidence Offered in Earhart Mystery — An organization investigating the disappearance in 1937 of the aviator Amelia Earhart presented some new evidence, **Mar. 16**. Richard Gillespie, executive director of the International Group for Historic Aircraft Recovery, said that recent findings supported the conclusion that Earhart and her navigator, Fred Noonan, had been forced to land on Nikumaroro, a small island in the Pacific. They had been attempting to fly around the globe near the equator. Evidence they found on the island included a sheet of metal that could have come from their Lockheed Electra and part of a shoe of the size and style that Earhart wore. Two former Lockheed employees said, **Mar. 17**, that the piece of metal could not have come from Earhart's plane.

Baby Without Complete Brain Is Center of Legal Dispute — Theresa Ann Campo Pearson was born, **Mar. 21**, in Ft. Lauderdale, Fla., without a complete brain or skull. Although they knew of the condition of the fetus, the baby's parents had decided that she should be born so that her organs could be donated to help other babies. The parents sought to have the baby declared brain-dead, but Florida Circuit Court Judge Estella Moriarty ruled, **Mar. 26**, that because the baby had a functioning brain stem she could not be declared brain-dead. Two other courts rejected the parents' appeals. The baby died, **Mar. 30**, and her organs had deteriorated too much to be viable any longer for transplant.

APRIL

National

300 Named in House Check Inquiry — More than 300 members and former members of the U.S. House of Representatives were identified as having written overdraft checks at the House bank. On **Apr. 1**, the House Ethics Committee released the names of 22 described as the worst abusers. Most of the names had been leaked previously. Two of the members whose names had been revealed previously were not on the official list, because they successfully argued that the bank itself was to blame for not having credited deposits quickly. Complaints about special privileges enjoyed by other government officials grew, and on **Apr. 2**, it was reported that Sec. of State James Baker had made 11 personal trips that had cost the taxpayers $371,599. On **Apr. 3**, Senate and House leaders called a halt to free medical care and medicine for members of Congress. The House voted, **Apr. 9**, to give control of nonlegislative House matters to a professional manager, and the position of inspector general, or auditor, was also created. The manager would oversee the payroll, restaurant, and internal mail service. On **Apr. 9**, a federal grand jury charged a former House Post Office clerk with embezzlement and drug-dealing. On **Apr. 16**, the House Ethics Committee released the names of 303 more current and former members who had written at least one overdraft check. Malcolm Wilkey, who had been appointed to investigate the House bank, subpoenaed, **Apr. 21**, the financial records of all House members' accounts for a 39-month period. He said he had found evidence of a "classic check-kiting scheme."

UAW Ends Walkout at Caterpillar — A 5-month strike at Caterpillar, Inc., the manufacturer of earth-moving equipment, ended in Peoria, Ill. Salaries, health benefits, and job security were at issue, and Democratic presidential candidates had come to Peoria to support the workers. On **Apr. 1**, the company said it would start hiring replacement workers. By **Apr. 6**, 800 employees—members of the United Automobile Workers union—had returned, out of a total of 12,600. Caterpillar began testing job applicants, **Apr. 13**, and on **Apr. 14**, the UAW agreed to end the walkout and send the employees back to work without a contract.

Perot a Factor in Presidential Race — The Texas billionaire H. Ross Perot emerged as a strong contender for the presidency, though he had not yet declared his candidacy. In a *New York Times*/CBS poll reported **Apr. 1**, Pres. George Bush led nationwide, with 44 percent to 31 percent for Arkansas Gov. Bill Clinton, the likely Democratic candidate. Perot was supported by 16 percent. In a speech to the Foreign Policy Association, **Apr. 1**, Clinton criticized Bush for not condemning human-rights abuses in China and for being confrontational toward Israel. The Democratic primary campaign in New York became acrimonious, with Clinton and former California Gov. Jerry Brown exchanging accusations in debates and in speeches and television ads. Former Sen. Paul Tsongas said, **Apr. 5**, that he might re-enter the race, depending on the outcome in New York. In the primary, **Apr. 7**, Clinton received 41 percent of the vote, Tsongas 29 percent, and Brown 26 percent. On **Apr. 7**, Clinton also won primaries in Kansas, Minnesota, and Wisconsin. Despite his 2nd-place showing in New York, Tsongas said, **Apr. 9**, that he would not resume his campaign. Louisiana State Rep. David Duke announced, **Apr. 22**, that he was abandoning his campaign for the Republican presidential nomination. New national polls published **Apr. 26** and **28**, showed Perot still running behind Bush and Clinton, but his support stood at 23 percent and 30 percent, respectively. Clinton won the primary in Pennsylvania, **Apr. 28**. Bush won the Republican primary in Pennsylvania, and his campaign said he had enough delegates to win the nomination of his party.

Many in Congress Choose to Retire — By the spring of 1992, a large number of U.S. Senate and House members had chosen not to seek re-election. Some had faced an uphill battle because of redistricting of House seats after the 1990 census. Others anticipated that their opponents in the fall would make an issue out of their overdrafts at the House bank. Still others took advantage of a law permitting them to keep unspent money from previous campaigns if they retired in 1992. Some said they were fed up with the political gridlock in Washington, while others were defeated in primary elections. Sen. Kent Conrad (D, N.D.), **Apr. 2**, followed the lead of Sen. Warren Rudman (R, N.H.), who had bowed out in March. Conrad said he had promised, when elected, that he would not run again unless the U.S. budget deficit had been eliminated. Vin Weber (R, Minn.), a young and influential conservative spokesman, said he did not want to put himself and his family through what he expected would be a "vicious, negative" campaign. Weber had written 125 overdrafts. Sen. Timothy Wirth (D, Colo.) announced his retirement, **Apr. 7**, criticizing both Pres. George Bush and Congress for a lack of leadership. On **May 4**, Rep. Matthew McHugh (D, N.Y.), who had headed the House bank investigation, said he would retire—bringing the total voluntary retirements in the House to 53, a record since World War II.

'Fed' Chairman Sees Slow Growth — A forecast of slow economic growth signaled that the recovery from the recession might not be robust. The Labor Dept. reported, **Apr. 3**, that unemployment remained at 7.3 percent in March. The department said, **Apr. 9**, that prices charged by producers for finished goods had advanced 0.2 percent in March. The Federal Reserve Board, **Apr. 9**, dropped the interest rate on overnight loans between banks by one-quarter percent to 3.75 percent. The Labor Dept. reported, **Apr. 10**, that in March consumer prices had jumped 0.5 percent, the biggest one-month increase since October 1990. The Commerce Dept. reported, **Apr. 16**, that the merchandise trade deficit in February had been $3.38 billion, the smallest since 1983. On Wall Street, the Dow Jones industrial average closed, **Apr. 16**, at 3366.50, an all-time high. Alan Greenspan, chairman of the Federal Reserve Board, testified, **Apr. 17**, to the Senate Banking Committee that the economy had grown by 2 percent, at an annual rate, during the first quarter. Since World War II, the economy had grown, on average, by 6 percent in the first year of a recovery. The Commerce Dept., **Apr. 28**, confirmed the 2 percent annual growth rate during the first quarter. The department reported, **Apr. 30**, that the leading economic indicators had edged upward 0.2 percent in March.

Senate Approves a Budget for 1993 — The Senate, **Apr. 10**, approved, 54-35, a federal budget for 1993. The Senate gave its approval after narrowly rejecting an amendment that would double the cuts in the defense budget proposed by the Bush administration. A proposal to limit the growth of entitlement programs also failed. The House had passed a similar budget resolution in March.

Pentagon Assesses Persian Gulf War — The Defense Dept., **Apr. 10**, released its final assessment of the performance of U.S. forces in the Persian Gulf War in 1991. Defense Secretary Dick Cheney wrote in the report that victory was "attributable in large measure to the extraordinary effectiveness of air power." According to the report, military strategists had expected that the forces attacking Iraq might suffer 10,000 casualties. In fact, total Allied combat deaths were about 220.

Flood Disrupts Chicago Business District — On **Apr. 13**, water from the Chicago River broke through a rupture into underground tunnels and flooded basements in Chicago's central business district. It was necessary to evacuate 200,000 people. Mayor Richard Daley announced, **Apr. 14**, that he had fired his acting Transportation Commissioner, who, Daley said, had known about a crack in the tunnel system. Pres. George Bush, **Apr. 15**, declared the city a disaster area. The gap in the tunnel was not sealed until **Apr. 19**.

Opponents of Abortion Lead Protest in Buffalo — Operation Rescue, a national antiabortion organization, began a protest demonstration, **Apr. 20**, against abortion clinics in Buffalo, N.Y. The homes and offices of doctors who performed abortions were also targets of protest. Supporters of abortion rights guarded the 6 clinics in the area, and they all remained open. By the end of the protest, **May 2**, police had made 597 arrests for disorderly conduct, trespassing, and resisting arrest.

California Executes Killer of 2 Boys — The state of California carried out its first execution in 25 years. Robert Alton Harris had been convicted of shooting 2 teen-age boys to death in 1978. Sentenced to death, Harris had pursued appeals in state and federal courts. His lawyers claimed to have new evidence and also argued that execution in California's gas chamber constituted cruel and unusual punishment, forbidden by the 8th Amendment to the U.S. Constitution. A final stay of execution, issued by the U.S. 9th Circuit Court of Appeals, came after Harris had been strapped into a chair in the gas chamber, on **Apr. 21**. Harris was briefly taken from the chamber, but the U.S. Supreme Court overturned the stay and Harris was put to death.

International

France's First Woman Premier Resigns — Premier Edith Cresson of France resigned, **Apr. 2**, after less than 11 months in office. Cresson had made her mark with outspoken views, sometimes not too diplomatic. Her popularity had declined in the wake of financial scandals and a high unemployment rate. Her Socialist Party had done poorly in regional elections. Pres. Francois Mitterrand named Finance Minister Pierre Beregovoy to succeed Cresson. Beregovoy's cautious fiscal policies had protected the value of the franc and had brought the inflation rate down to 3 percent.

Sanctions Imposed on Libya — On **Apr. 2**, Libyan demonstrators in Tripoli attacked the embassies of countries that had approved U.N. sanctions against Libya in March. The sanctions, aimed at forcing Libya to hand over 2 men linked to 2 airplane bombings, took effect **Apr. 15**. Some European countries expelled employees at Libyan embassies, and Russia said it would withdraw 1,500 military advisers in Libya. Several countries turned back flights from Libya.

Peru's President Dissolves Congress — Pres. Alberto Fujimori of Peru effectively seized control of the country in April. Peru was also sagging under the weight of economic austerity measures aimed at controlling inflation and under the assault of the Maoist rebellion known as Shining Path. The rebellion had claimed 25,000 lives since 1980, and Shining Path was stepping up its attacks in and near Lima, the capital. On **Apr. 5**, Fujimori dissolved the National Congress, imposed press censorship, and ordered the arrest of some political opponents. In announcing a government of "emergency and national reconstruction," the President said Peru could not continue to be weakened by terrorism, drug trafficking, and corruption. Military troops occupied parts of the capital. In a symbolic gesture, a majority of the members of Congress voted, **Apr. 9**, to impeach Fujimori.

Earth Summit Subject of U.N. Meeting — Delegates from more than 160 countries concluded talks at U.N. headquarters in New York, **Apr. 4**, that were to lay the groundwork for an Earth Summit in Rio de Janeiro in June. The U.N. talks sought to deal with the world environment in a comprehensive way, with treaties to be signed at Rio as the ultimate objective. But delegates could not come up with preliminary agreements on global warming or protection of the forests, as divisions occurred between industrialized and developing nations. The poorer nations generally contended that they had a right to develop their resources and asked for wealthy nations to provide more financial aid if that development was to proceed in an environmentally responsible way. The Bush administration would not make specific commitments to curb emission of gases that many believed contributed to the danger of global warming.

Reshaping of Yugoslavia Continues — Amid continuing violence, the future of Yugoslavia and its breakaway republics became more distinct. Some 1,200 U.N. peacekeeping troops arrived in Croatia, **Apr. 4**. On **Apr. 7**, the nations of the European Community and the United States recognized the independence of Bosnia-Herzegovina. At the same time, the U.S. also recognized Croatia and Slovenia, several months after other nations had begun to extend diplomatic recognition. Meanwhile, the Yugoslav military, dominated by Serbs, continued to battle the secessionists. The Yugoslav parliament, **Apr. 27**, approved a constitutional amendment to create a new Yugoslavia consisting only of Serbia and Montenegro. These republics then proclaimed a new Federal Republic of Yugoslavia. Pres. Slobodan Milosevic of Serbia renounced territorial claims by the new federation on the other republics, and endorsed pursuit of a market economy in the new federation. The status of another republic, Macedonia, was in doubt. Macedonia had proclaimed independence in 1991, but its southern neighbor, Greece, opposed an independent Macedonia.

Arafat Survives Crash Landing in Desert — On **Apr. 7**, a plane carrying Yasir Arafat, chairman of the Palestine Liberation Organization, had to crash-land in the Libyan desert as a result of a sandstorm. All 3 crewmen were killed, and 5 of the 10 passengers were seriously injured, but Arafat reportedly incurred only minor injuries. The plane was spotted from the air on the morning of **Apr. 8**, and rescuers soon reached the plane. Later, Arafat developed a blood clot which doctors said was the result of head injuries incurred in the crash. He underwent surgery, **June 1**, and a cardiologist said he would suffer no lasting effects.

Rebels Seize Power in Afghanistan — Mohammad Najibullah, who had headed a communist government in Afghanistan, resigned as rebel armies closed in on the capital, Kabul. One rebel group, led by Ahmed Shah Massoud and joined by defecting military units, advanced from the north. Gulbuddin Hekmatyar, leader of a more fundamentalist Moslem faction, approached Kabul from the south. On **Apr. 9** and **10**, the government and most rebel groups agreed to a process leading to a transitional government, but Hizb-i-Islami, the Hekmatyar faction, refused to cooperate. Najibullah resigned, **Apr. 16**, and took refuge under U.N. protection in Kabul. Abdul Rahim Hatif became interim president, **April 19**, and said, **Apr. 21**, that he would turn power over to the rebels. By **Apr. 23**, forces from various rebel factions were pouring into Kabul, and by **Apr. 25**, those under the command of Massoud controlled most of the city. On **Apr. 25**, Afghan rebel leaders in Pakistan announced formation of a commission to run Afghanistan until elections could be held. But Hezb-i-Islami said it supported creation of a fundamentalist Islamic state. Sibghatullah Mojadidi, named head of the commission, arrived in Kabul, **Apr. 28**, and declared an amnesty for all members of the former government except Najibullah.

Ex-Leader of Panama Convicted — Gen. Manuel Noriega, former military ruler of Panama, was convicted, **Apr. 9**, in U.S. District Court in Miami of racketeering, drug trafficking, and money laundering. Noriega, the first foreign head of state convicted by a U.S. jury, had been seized by U.S. forces early in 1990 after the American invasion of Panama. At the trial, witnesses, many of them convicted drug traffickers themselves, tied Noriega to the Medellin drug cartel. The government sought to show that Noriega had taken millions of dollars in bribes from the cartel. Testifying for the defense, Adm. Daniel Murphy (ret.), chief of staff for Vice Pres. George Bush during the 1980s, said that Noriega had cooperated with U.S. efforts to intercept drug shipments. On **July 10**, Judge William Hoeveler sentenced Noriega to 40 years in prison.

Conservatives Win Again in Britain — The Conservative Party and Prime Minister John Major retained power in the parliamentary election held in Britain. The nation was struggling through its longest recession since the 1930s, and Labour leader Neil Kinnock made the economy his chief issue. He also warned that the Conservatives, if returned to leadership, would continue to privatize the National Health Service. Major warned that Labour's spending plans would bring back socialism and drive up taxes. In the election, **Apr. 9**, the Conservatives won, but with a sharply reduced majority. They captured 336 seats in the House of Commons to 271 for Labour. The Liberal Democrats took 20 seats and other parties, 24. Not since the early 19th century had a political party prevailed in 4 consecutive elections. It was the first triumph for Major, who had replaced Margaret Thatcher between elections in 1990. Major's new cabinet, announced **Apr. 11**, included 2 women. No women had served in his first cabinet. Kinnock, who had headed Labour since 1983, announced, **Apr. 13**, that he would step down as leader.

Nelson and Winnie Mandela Separate — Nelson Mandela, president of the African National Congress, announced, **Apr. 13**, that he and his wife, Winnie, were separating. Nelson Mandela had been in prison during most of their 33-year marriage, and his wife had carried on her husband's cause, political and economic freedom for blacks in South Africa. Winnie Mandela was appealing a prison sentence for kidnapping and as an accessory to assault.

General

Reputed Crime Boss Convicted in New York — John Gotti, who had been described by police and prosecutors as leader of the Gambino crime family, was convicted, **Apr. 2**, in U.S. District Court in Brooklyn of crimes that included murder, extortion, and obstruction of justice. A codefendant, Frank Locascio, was convicted of racketeering and murder. Gotti had been acquitted of other charges in 3 recent trials. In this instance, however, Salvatore Gravano, a former associate of Gotti, testified to Gotti's involvement in 10 murders. Gravano said he and Gotti watched the killing, on a New York City street in 1985, of Paul Castellano, reputed head of the Gambino family at that time. For cooperating, Gravano, who admitted to involvement in 19 murders himself, was assured that he would serve no more than 20 years in prison. As evidence, the government also presented tape recordings in which Gotti and others discussed criminal activities. On **June 23**, Gotti and Locascio were sentenced to life in prison without parole.

Arthur Ashe Says He Has AIDS Virus — Tennis player Arthur Ashe announced in a news conference, **Apr. 8**, that he had contracted the virus that caused acquired immune deficiency syndrome. Ashe, in 1968, had become the first black to win the U.S. Open tournament. He said he believed he had contracted the virus during a transfusion after undergoing heart surgery in 1983. He learned he had the virus while undergoing brain surgery in 1988.

Leona Helmsley Enters Prison — On **Apr. 15**, New York hotel owner Leona Helmsley entered a prison in Lexington, Ky., to begin serving a 4-year term for evading federal income taxes. Citing her own poor health and the frail condition of her elderly husband, Harry, Mrs. Helmsley had sought until the last minute to avoid being sent to prison.

52 Killed in Los Angeles as Rioting Erupts After Jury Acquits 4 Policemen in Beating of Rodney King

Rioting, looting, and arson swept South-Central Los Angeles in late April and early May after a jury that included no blacks acquitted 4 policemen on all but one count in the beating of a black man. The death toll in the violence was put at 52, and most of these deaths were homicides. More than 600 buildings were set aflame. Damage ran as high as $1 billion. Army, Marine Corps, and National Guard units helped restore order.

In March 1991, police in Los Angeles stopped a black motorist, Rodney King, and then beat him as he lay or knelt on the pavement. A man who lived nearby videotaped the attack, and the tape was shown on television newscasts across the country. The tape showed that King was struck by batons more than 50 times. He suffered serious injuries.

After a public outcry, 4 policemen, all white, were indicted for assault with a deadly weapon, excessive use of force, and other charges. Because of the concern about pretrial publicity, the trial was moved to Simi Valley, 45 miles northwest of Los Angeles. Simi Valley was a largely white commuter community. The jury that was chosen consisted of 10 whites, one Asian, and one Hispanic.

At the trial, the videotape was the principal piece of evidence presented by the prosecution. On **Apr. 29**, 1992, the jury returned its verdict. The defendants were acquitted on all charges except one, where the jury was unable to reach any verdict.

In subsequent interviews, the jurors offered explanations for their verdicts. One juror said the police were just doing what they had been taught to do, and cited the failure of the prosecution to call King to the stand as a mistake. A juror also said that King had been "in full control" during the beating.

Mayor Tom Bradley of Los Angeles said, **Apr. 29**, that the system had failed, and that the verdict "will never blind us to what we saw on that videotape." Also on **Apr. 29**, Pres. George Bush said, "The jury system has worked. What's needed now is calm, respect for the law."

Soon after the verdict, violence erupted in Los Angeles, and was concentrated in the predominantly black and Hispanic South-Central section. At the onset of the unrest, police moved in where a crowd was forming, then left. In the most publicized incident of rioting, a television crew in a helicopter recorded the beating of a white truck driver, Reginald Denny. Shown live on television, the beating prompted calls for police help, but no aid came, and Denny, seriously injured, was rescued by local black residents.

Bradley declared a state of emergency, and Gov. Pete Wilson called up National Guard units. Bush announced, **Apr. 30**, that the Justice Dept. would reopen an investigation into the beating of King.

A dusk-to-dawn curfew was imposed, **Apr. 30**, but the destruction and criminality spread that night. When Koreatown, the country's largest Korean community, became a target of the rioters, local merchants armed themselves and shot at looters and arsonists, and denounced the police for not coming to their aid.

By **Apr. 30**, violent disturbances were reported in San Francisco, Atlanta, Seattle, and Miami. Two people were killed in Las Vegas. More than 1,100 people were arrested in San Francisco. Meanwhile, Americans in many cities were demonstrating peacefully against the verdict in the King case.

On **May 1**, Bush ordered 1,500 Marines and 3,000 Army troops into Los Angeles, and Nevada Gov. Bob Miller sent 400 National Guard troops into Las Vegas. From **May 1** on, the level of violence declined.

Gov. Bill Clinton (Ark.), the front-runner for the Democratic presidential nomination, said, **May 1**, that although he understood the anger at the verdict, the violence was the work of "lawless vandals."

Bush, addressing the nation **May 1**, said he had been shocked by the verdict but that the subsequent violence reflected mob brutality rather than concern about civil rights.

On **May 3**, Mayor Bradley appointed Peter Ueberroth, organizer of the 1984 Olympic games in Los Angeles, to oversee restoration of the devastated areas. The White House announced, **May 4**, that $700 million in federal funds would be made available to help riot victims and to rebuild damaged areas and businesses.

Clinton visited Los Angeles, **May 4**, the day on which a dawn-to-dusk curfew was lifted. Presidential spokesman Marlin Fitzwater, **May 4**, blamed the riots on the antipoverty programs of Pres. Lyndon Johnson; Clinton replied, **May 5**, that social unrest was the result of "12 years of denial and neglect" under Presidents Reagan and Bush.

Los Angeles Police Chief Daryl Gates said, **May 6**, "Somewhere along the way we did not do our job . . .. There was a breakdown."

Bush toured Los Angeles, **May 7** and **8**, and announced a "weed and seed" program that would "weed" criminals from high-crime neighborhoods, which would then be "seeded" with help in health, education, job-training, and drug treatment. Within the administration, the riots had given a boost to the ideas of Housing Secretary Jack Kemp, who had long advocated free-market solutions to urban problems, including tenant ownership of public housing and incentives to businesses in inner cities.

The last federal troops left Los Angeles, **May 10**, but the National Guard remained in the impacted areas. Four men were arrested, **May 12**, in the beating of Reginald Denny.

The King jury had deadlocked on one count, a charge against policeman Laurence Powell for using excessive force. On **May 15**, Los Angeles Superior Court Judge Stanley Weisberg ruled that Powell would be tried again.

Police officials said, **May 16**, that charges had been filed in only 2 of the 50 homicides because the turmoil in the area had hampered investigations.

In a rebuff to Gates, who had campaigned against it, Los Angeles voters, **June 2**, approved a charter amendment limiting the police chief to two 5-year terms. It provided that the mayor and City Council could remove the chief, whereas under current law he could not be dismissed. Gates's critics were dismayed, **June 5**, when the chief said he might not retire, as planned, at the end of the month. On **June 8**, however, he said he would in fact retire.

On **June 18**, Congress completed action on a $1.075 billion package of aid to the cities. Bush, **June 22**, signed the bill, which was brought forth in the wake of the riots.

Gates stepped down, **June 26**, and was succeeded by Willie Williams, who had been Police Commissioner in Philadelphia. Williams was L.A.'s first black police chief.

MAY

National

FBI Gets Records of House Bank — On **May 1**, 5 Democrats in the U.S. House filed a suit seeking to prevent a special prosecutor from obtaining records of the House bank. Many House members had written checks to obtain money from the bank despite having insufficient funds on deposit. Judge John Penn of the U.S. District Court for the District of Columbia held, **May 4**, that the records belonged to the bank and that the depositors had no claim of privacy. The records were turned over to the FBI, **May 4**.

'Family Values' Debated in Presidential Race — The role of the family became an issue in the presidential campaign. Pres. George Bush and Gov. Bill Clinton (Ark.) continued to sweep toward their respective party nominations, winning primaries that no longer contained any suspense. H. Ross Perot, the Texas billionaire who was considering an independent bid for president, said, **May 5**, that he would limit his public appearances while he built an organization and developed a strategy and positions on issues. News reports on **May 7** and **8** indicated that Perot's efforts during the Vietnam war to free American prisoners of war had been part of an effort by the Nixon administration to build support for its objectives. On **May 11**, Perot's supporters filed, they said, more than 200,000 signatures supporting Perot for a place on the Texas presidential ballot. In similar rallies across the country in subsequent weeks, Perot's supporters announced that he had filed signatures for the ballot in other states. Primary victories by Bush and Clinton in Oregon and Washington, **May 19**, were overshadowed by exit polls in which large numbers of voters said they would vote for Perot in November. In a speech, **May 19**, Vice Pres. Dan Quayle discussed the violence that had occurred in Los Angeles several weeks earlier. He blamed the rioting on a "breakdown of family structure, personal responsibility and social order." Citing the story line of the television program, *Murphy Brown*, Quayle said it didn't help that the title character had had a baby out of wedlock, "mocking the importance of fathers ... and calling it just another 'life style choice.'" Bush said, **May 20**, "I believe that children should have the benefit of being born into families with a mother and a father who will give them love and care and attention all their lives." Clinton, **May 21**, said the use of the issue by Bush and Quayle had been "cynical," and that the administration had avoided taking the lead on family problems, which he linked to economic decline.

Constitution Amended on Pay Raises — A 27th Amendment became part of the U.S. Constitution in May. The amendment, proposed by James Madison, had been approved by Congress in 1789 and submitted to the states for ratification. It read, in full, "No law, varying the compensation for the services of the senators and representatives shall take effect, until an election of representatives shall have intervened." Approval of three-fourths of the states, or 38 at the present time, was required in order for an amendment to become a part of the Constitution, but after more than 200 years this amendment still lacked the requisite number. But public displeasure over Congressional pay raises had revived interest in the amendment, and on **May 7**, the Michigan legislature approved it, raising the number of states ratifying it to 38. On **May 18**, Don Wilson, the U.S. archivist, declared the amendment valid and said it had been a part of the Constitution since **May 7**. Both houses of Congress, **May 20**, voted to recognize the validity of the amendment.

Unemployment Rate Turns Downward — The Labor Dept. reported, **May 8**, that the unemployment rate had edged downward in April, to 7.2 percent, from 7.3 percent in March. The monthly decline was the first in 9 months. Also, in April, the number of Americans on company payrolls increased by 126,000, the largest monthly jump in 11 months. The department said, **May 13**, that consumer prices had edged upward 0.2 percent in April. Confidence in the economic recovery faded a bit, **May 19**, when the Commerce Dept. reported that housing starts had fallen 17 percent in April, the steepest decline in 8 years. The department said, **May 20**, that the trade deficit had expanded in March to $5.82 billion. The Dow Jones industrial average closed, **May 28**, at an all-time high of 3398.43. The Commerce Dept. said, **May 29**, that during the first quarter the gross domestic product had increased at a 2.4 percent annual rate, somewhat higher than previously reported.

Owl Habitat Opened to Logging — The Bush administration took action in the long dispute involving the northern spotted owl. Because the owl had been officially designated as an endangered species, a series of court injunctions had restricted logging in old-growth owl habitat in the Pacific Northwest. Timber interests complained about a loss of income. An amendment to the Endangered Species Act permitted an Executive Branch committee to override the authority of the act for persuasive economic reasons. On **May 14**, the committee voted, 5-2, to open 1,700 acres of federal land identified as owl habitat to logging. Although this was only a portion of the owl habitat, environmentalists protested strongly.

Publicity Effort Fails to Save Condemned Man — A publicity campaign organized by the attorneys for a condemned killer failed to save his life. Roger Coleman had been convicted of the rape and murder of his sister-in-law in 1981, and was sentenced to die in the electric chair in Virginia. Lawyers complained that it was unfair that one appeal was denied because the deadline for filing it had been missed by one day. They sought to raise doubts that Coleman could have been at the scene of the crime, and Coleman's supporters claimed that another man who had talked about the murder could have been the real culprit. Coleman was the subject of a cover story in *Time* magazine, and his case was widely debated in the media. Virginia Gov. L. Douglas Wilder allowed Coleman to take a polygraph ("lie-detector") test, **May 20**, which he failed, and he was executed that night.

International

U.N. Imposes Sanctions on Yugoslavia — The U.N. Security Council attempted to stop the bloodshed in Yugoslavia. On **May 1**, Serbian forces began shelling Sarajevo, the capital of Bosnia-Herzegovina, and also seized many towns within the secessionist republic. Hundreds of people were killed. The federal army, dominated by Serbs, signed a truce with the Bosnian government, **May 5**. A cease-fire took effect, **May 13**, but did not last long. To convey its concern, the U.S. government, **May 20**, revoked the U.S. landing rights of the Yugoslav national airline. Sec. of State James Baker announced, **May 22**, that Yugoslav consulates in New York City and San Francisco would be closed and that Yugoslav military attaches based in Washington would be expelled. On **May 22**, the U.N. General Assembly admitted as U.N. members the former republics of Croatia, Slovenia, and Bosnia-Herzegovina. On **May 27**, the European Community imposed a trade embargo on Yugoslavia. On **May 29** and **30**, Serbian forces shelled Sarajevo and the Croatian port city of Dubrovnik. The U.N. Security Council, **May 30**, approved, 13-0, broad new sanctions against Yugoslavia. The U.N. resolution demanded an end to the fighting and to all interference in Bosnia by Yugoslavia. The resolution authorized a ban on all exports to Yugoslavia except food and medical supplies, and a global ban on imports from Yugoslavia. Yugoslavia's foreign assets were frozen and commercial contacts halted. Serbian Pres. Slobodan Milosevic denied, **May 31**, that Yugoslavia had committed any aggression against Bosnia.

Afghani Rebels Reach Agreement — Rival rebel factions reached a peace settlement in Afghanistan. The rebels had seized power in April, and on **May 5**, the interim president, Sibghatullah Mojadidi, appointed a 36-member temporary cabinet. Ahmed Shah Massoud, leader of a major faction, was named defense minister. Meanwhile, a fundamentalist Moslem faction headed by Gulbuddin Hekmatyar was shelling the capital, Kabul. The assault, which killed 73 people, was halted, **May 6**, when representatives of Hekmatyar began negotiations with the ruling coalition. On **May 25**, the new government reached an agreement with Hekmatyar that provided for an immediate end to fighting in the country and that provided for national elections within 6 months.

Thai Premier Resigns After Bloodshed — Premier Suchinda Kraprayoon of Thailand resigned after his pro-military government cracked down brutally against protesters supporting democratic reform. Gen. Suchinda had led a coup in 1991 and had been appointed premier in April 1992. On **May 7**, 100,000 persons demonstrated and demanded Suchinda's resignation. Thai's major political parties agreed, **May 9**, in principle to constitutional amendments requiring that the premier be an elected member of parliament and curtailing military power. When the opposition concluded that the government might back down on its commitments, demonstrations resumed. On **May 17-19**, government troops clashed with huge crowds, sometimes shooting at the protesters. King Bhumibol Adulyadej summoned Suchinda and opposition leader Chamlong Srimuang to his palace, **May 20**. The king, who exercised great influence in the nation, insisted that the 2 discuss the controversy. Suchinda agreed to support the amendment requiring that the premier be an elected official. The government put the death toll in the clashes at 48, but nearly 600 were reported to be missing. The king, **May 22**, signed a decree protecting Suchinda and others in the military from prosecution related to the street clashes. Suchinda resigned, **May 24**, after 5 parties that had supported him withdrew their support.

Treaties on Environment Approved — Two major treaties were approved in advance of the Earth Summit scheduled for Rio de Janiero, Brazil, in June. At U.N. headquarters in New York, **May 9**, delegates from 143 countries approved a treaty asking industrialized nations to reduce emissions of so-called greenhouse gases, which were thought to cause global warming. The participating nations agreed to adopt legislation to control emissions, with the goal of returning to 1990 emission levels. The U.S. successfully resisted pressure from the European Community for treaty language freezing emissions at 1990 levels. Environmentalists criticized the Bush administration's position as too weak. In Nairobi, Kenya, **May 22**, delegates from 98 countries approved a draft treaty on biodiversity, which called on all countries to develop strategies for protecting plants and animals. The Bush administration announced, **May 29**, that the U.S. would not sign the biodiversity treaty because of concerns about how money being spent under the treaty would be dispensed and because U.S. companies developing biotechnology products would not have adequate patent protection.

Ramos Leads in Tally for Philippines Presidency — Seven men and women sought the presidency of the Philippines in an election held **May 11**. In a vote count that proceeded slowly, former Defense Secretary Fidel Ramos emerged with a slim lead. Gen. Ramos had participated in the coup that had ousted Pres. Ferdinand Marcos in 1986, and he had the support of Corazon Aquino, the outgoing president. Miriam Defensor Santiago, a former judge who was running second, had made corruption a major issue and had said, "many, if not all, of my presidential opponents are certifiable idiots." Imelda Marcos, the nation's former first lady, was among the defeated candidates, receiving about 10 percent of the vote.

General

Shuttle Crewmen Capture Wayward Satellite — Three shuttle crewmen, working outside their vehicle, captured a satellite that had gone off-course. The shuttle *Endeavour*, with a crew of 7, was launched at Cape Canaveral, Florida, **May 7**. By **May 10**, it had caught up with the *Intelsat-6* satellite owned by the International Telecommunications Satellite Organization. Designed to relay television channels and telephone calls, *Intelsat* had failed to reach a proper orbit and was not functioning. On **May 13**, in a third attempt, Navy Cmdr. Pierre Thout; Air Force Maj. Thomas Akers; and Richard Heib, an engineer, grabbed the satellite. They worked outside the shuttle for 8 hours and 29 minutes, setting U.S. records for the duration of a spacewalk and the number of astronauts outside a craft. They brought the satellite into the shuttle's cargo bay, attached a 11.5-ton solid-fuel rocket, and springs pushed it back into space. On **May 14**, the booster ignited and sent the satellite toward its proper orbit. The shuttle landed at Edwards Air Force Base, California, **May 16**. Critics of the remarkable effort in space pointed out that it may have cost nearly $1 billion to save a $270 million satellite.

Real Estate Giant Files for Bankruptcy — Olympia & York Developments Ltd., the world's largest real estate development company, filed for bankruptcy protection in Toronto, **May 14**. Olympia & York, with debts exceeding $18.5 billion, was the largest company ever to seek bankruptcy protection in Canada. It was feared that the company's problems could put banks on 3 continents in jeopardy. Olympia & York hoped to restructure its debt while retaining as many of its real estate holdings as possible. Its properties in New York included the World Financial Center. On **May 27**, Olympia & York asked a British court to appoint an administrator to take control of Canary Wharf, the largest office-development project in Europe. The court, **May 28**, appointed 3 administrators to take over the project.

Carson Retires From 'The Tonight Show' — Comedian Johnny Carson retired after 29 years as host of "The Tonight Show" on NBC. Carson had taken over the late-night program from Jack Paar in 1962. The show then originated in New York, but it was subsequently moved to California. The program was known for Carson's droll wit and for the thousands of entertainers and other celebrities who appeared on it. Some 55 million people watched Carson's final appearance on the program, **May 22**. Jay Leno succeeded Carson as the host.

JUNE

National

Clinton Assured of Democratic Nomination — Gov. Bill Clinton (Ark.) won primaries, **June 2**, in California, Ohio, New Jersey, and 3 other states, and captured enough delegates to wrap up the Democratic presidential nomination. In California, Clinton defeated former Gov. Jerry Brown of that state, 47 percent to 40 percent. Pres. George Bush, **June 2**, swept 6 primaries, although the writer and commentator Pat Buchanan continued to draw many votes—26 percent in California—as a protest candidate. Texas billionaire Ross Perot, who was mounting an independent campaign for president, was not on any ballot, **June 2**, but exit polls showed he would run well against Bush and Clinton. Perot announced, **June 3**, that his campaign staff would be headed by Hamilton Jordan and Ed Rollins. They had run successful presidential campaigns by Jimmy Carter and Ronald Reagan, respectively, and Jordan had served as Pres. Carter's chief of staff. Bush, **June 4**, held a prime-time news conference—only his second—but ABC, CBS, and NBC declined to carry it live, in the apparent belief that it was designed to boost his presidential campaign. Returning to the issue of "family values," Vice Pres. Dan Quayle, **June 9**, criticized "cultural elites" who, he said, believe "all 'life styles' are equal" and that "parents need not be married or even of opposite sexes. They are wrong." Quayle observed a spelling bee in Trenton, N.J., **June 15**, and advised a contestant, incorrectly, to add an "e" to the spelling of "potato." The Vice President quickly became the butt of many jokes. Clinton issued economic proposals, **June 21**, that included expenditure of $200 billion over 4 years on the cities, infrastructure, education, and training of workers. He proposed to raise $150 billion in new taxes over 4 years, with higher rates for wealthy Americans and fewer tax breaks for corporations. Clinton scaled down his commitment to tax breaks for the middle class. His revised plan projected a 50 percent reduction in the annual federal deficits within 4 years. Bush, **June 22**, expressed concern over a published report that Perot had investigated Bush's children. Perot, **June 23**, dismissed the report as part of a Republican attempt to destroy his credibility. The abortion controversy flared anew after the U.S. Supreme Court, **June 29**, upheld parts of a Pennsylvania law imposing some limits on a woman's ability to obtain an abortion. Bush welcomed the decision and reiterated his position: "I oppose abortion in all cases except rape or incest or where the life of the mother is at stake." Clinton, **June 29**, reaffirmed his support for the 1973 Supreme Court decision, Roe v. Wade, which established a woman's right, in many circumstances, to have an abortion, and he warned that the "constitutional right to choose is hanging by a thread."

2 California Women Win Senate Nominations — Two women, both Democrats, were nominated for the U.S. Senate in California, **June 2**. In a contest for a full 6-year term, Rep. Barbara Boxer would oppose Bruce Herschensohn, a conservative Republican television commentator, in the November election. Dianne Feinstein, a former mayor of San Francisco, would be running against Sen. John Seymour, who had been appointed to the Senate after Pete Wilson resigned in 1990 when he was elected governor. In the **June 2** primary, women won 19 major-party nominations for California's 52 U.S. House seats.

Economic Data Provide Mixed Picture — As measured by numbers, no clear trend was apparent in the U.S. economy in June. On Wall Street, **June 1**, the Dow Jones industrial average closed at an all-time high of 3413.21, but thereafter it began to decline. The Commerce Dept. reported, **June 2**, that the leading economic indicators rose 0.4 percent in April, the 4th straight increase for the index. Impacted by a large increase in the number of people looking for work, the unemployment rate jumped 0.3 percent to 7.5 percent in May, the Labor Dept. reported, **June 5**. The department reported, **June 11**, that prices charged by producers for finished goods rose 0.4 percent in May. On **June 12**, however, the department said that consumer prices had risen only 0.1 percent in May. The Commerce Dept. said, **June 18**, that the merchandise trade deficit stood at $6.97 billion in April, the biggest in more than a year. Revising its previous estimate upward, the department said, **June 25**, that the economy grew at an annual rate of 2.7 percent in the first quarter. This was the strongest advance of the Bush presidency. The department reported, **June 30**, that the leading economic indicators had jumped 0.6 percent in May, the 5th straight monthly advance.

Sex-Abuse Scandal Roils Navy — The Sec. of the Navy, H. Lawrence Garrett 3rd, resigned in June as inquiries continued in a sex-abuse scandal. In September 1991, members of the Tailhook Association, a private organization of Navy and Marine Corp fliers, attended their convention at a Las Vegas hotel. Their activities included heavy drinking and entertainment by nude dancers. After complaints from women, the Navy conducted 2 investigations and it was determined that 26 women, including 14 military officers, had been abused at the convention. An admiral had been relieved of command for ignoring a complaint. On **June 2**, Garrett ordered that disciplinary action begin against 70 officers. It was later revealed that Garrett had been nearby at the time of the misbehavior. Pres. George Bush met, **June 26**, with Navy Lt. Paula Coughlin, who said she had been assaulted by 20 or more men. Garrett resigned, **June 26**, and said he accepted "full responsibility" for the scandal.

Balanced-Budget Amendment Fails in House — A proposed amendment to the U.S. Constitution that would have required a balanced budget in the federal government was defeated in the House, **June 11**. Pres. George Bush had supported the amendment, but the House Democratic leadership had opposed it. Under the amendment, expenditures could not exceed receipts in any year unless the U.S. was at war or unless three-fifths of the entire membership of both houses of Congress voted to override the balanced-budget requirement in any year. Members of the House voted in favor of the amendment, 280-153, but this support was 9 votes short of the two-thirds majority required.

Weinberger Indicted in Iran-Contra Case — Caspar Weinberger, who had served as Sec. of Defense under Pres. Ronald Reagan, was indicted, **June 16**, in connection with the Iran-Contra case. Prosecutors investigating the arms scandal charged that Weinberger had committed perjury in Congressional testimony and that he had obstructed justice. It was alleged, for example, that he had testified untruthfully in denying knowledge of a shipment of missiles from Israel to Iran, and that he had concealed the existence of notes that he had kept on the arms shipments. Weinberger said he had refused to plead guilty to a lesser offense, and that the decision to indict him was a "moral and legal outrage."

Congress Intervenes in Railroad Dispute — The International Association of Machinists and Aerospace Workers went on strike, **June 24**, against CSX Transportation, Inc., a freight rail company. Issues at dispute included wages, work rules, and employee benefits. Other freight railroads then responded by shutting down their operations. Amtrak passenger trains were halted where their trains used the freight rails. Congress, **June 25**, completed action on legislation that sent workers back to their jobs and provided for a 38-day period for negotiations. Pres. George Bush signed the legislation, **June 26**.

International

Agreements Signed at Earth Summit — Delegates from 178 countries attended the United Nations Conference on Environment and Development in Rio de Janeiro. Some 35,000 persons participated in the conference, informally called the Earth Summit, and a number of actions to prevent further worldwide environmental degradation were approved. About 15,000 persons attended the Global Forum, which was open to nongovernmental organizations. On **June 1**, before the summit began, Pres. George Bush said the U.S. would increase its assistance to other nations' forestry programs by $150 million to $270 million in the next year. On **June 3**, as the summit opened, William Reilly, director of the U.S. Environmental Protection Agency, proposed that the White House support changes in the biodiversity convention which would permit the U.S. to reverse its position and sign the convention. The changes were rejected, and an unknown official leaked Reilly's confidential cable, reportedly angering Reilly and other U.S. delegates. Britain and Japan indicated, **June 5**, that they would sign the convention, leaving the U.S. more isolated in its opposition. By **June 12**, when Bush addressed the convention, he was one of 117 heads of state and government in Rio, possibly the greatest number ever to attend any meeting. Responding to criticism that the U.S. was not playing a leadership role, Bush said the U.S. environmental record was "second to none," and he called for an "action plan" to avert global warming. Japan said,

June 13, that it would increase its environmental aid to other countries to $1.45 billion a year. The delegates, **June 14**, approved a statement calling on all countries to develop their forest resources in a way to minimize damage to their ecosystems. The Rio Declaration and Agenda 21, approved, **June 14**, outlined cleanup strategies and means to encourage environmentally sound development. By **June 14**, as the conference closed, more than 150 countries had signed the global-warming treaty, which called for limits on the emission of greenhouse gases.

Danes Reject European Unity Treaty — The move toward European unity suffered a setback in June. The 12 nations of the European Community had adopted a treaty during a summit meeting in Maastricht, the Netherlands, in 1991. The treaty, which had to be approved by all 12 nations, sought to create a single European currency and a common foreign and defense policy. But on **June 2**, voters in Denmark, by a narrow margin of 50.7 percent to 49.3 percent, opposed ratification of the treaty. Opponents were concerned that Denmark would be dominated by the other countries, especially Germany. The EC foreign ministers, **June 4**, decided not to renegotiate the treaty to satisfy the Danes, leaving the treaty's future uncertain. Irish voters, **June 18**, voted 2-1 in favor of ratification.

'Ivan the Terrible' Case Re-Examined — A 3-judge panel for the U.S. 6th Circuit Court of Appeals announced, **June 5**, that the court would review its 1985 decision to deny John Demjanjuk an opportunity to appeal his extradition from the U.S. to Israel. Demjanjuk was later convicted in Israel of war crimes on evidence that he was the notorious "Ivan the Terrible," an especially cruel guard at the Treblinka death camp. Sentenced to death, Demjanjuk insisted he was innocent. In June, his attorney appealed Demjanjuk's conviction in Israel, offering evidence that he was a victim of mistaken identity.

Protest Halts Speech by Bush in Panama — Pres. George Bush visited Panama in June, en route to the Earth Summit in Rio de Janeiro, Brazil. Some in Panama, including supporters of the former strongman, Gen. Manuel Noriega, were hostile toward the U.S., and on **June 10**, a U.S. soldier was shot to death. Arriving **June 11**, Bush met with Pres. Guillermo Endara and then began to speak at a rally of 15,000 people in Panama City. But 150 protestors down the street began throwing rocks and bottles, and the police fired tear gas. Bush and members of the audience were affected by the gas, and the president left the area. Bush spoke later at an air base.

Debate Over Fate of American MIAs Revived — In a letter received by a Senate committee, **June 12**, Russian Pres. Boris Yeltsin disclosed that the Soviet Union had held and later released 716 American servicemen during World War II. Yeltsin said the fate of 12 U.S. airmen taken from U.S. spy planes downed in the 1950s was being investigated. During a flight to the U.S., **June 15**, Yeltsin said that some U.S. prisoners of the North Vietnamese had been held in labor camps in the Soviet Union during the Vietnam war. Pres. George Bush said, **June 16**, that Malcolm Toon, a former ambassador to the Soviet Union, would go to Russia to study the Soviet archives. During an address to Congress, **June 17**, Yeltsin gave assurance that if even one American had been held in Russia, Yeltsin would get him back to his family. The Senate Select Committee on POW-MIA Affairs opened hearings, **June 24**. Sen. John Kerry, the chairman, said that some U.S. prisoners may have been held after the supposed release of all Americans in 1973. Roger Shields, an assistant secretary of Defense in 1973, testified, **June 25**, that there had not been a complete accounting of men known to have been prisoners. Toon said, **June 26**, that he was unable to find anyone in Russia who could back up Yeltsin's statement about Vietnam-era U.S. servicemen being held there.

Bush, Yeltsin Agree to More Big Cuts in Weapons — Pres. George Bush and Russian Pres. Boris Yeltsin met and agreed in principle to major reductions in nuclear weapons that went beyond the terms of the 1991 Strategic Arms Reduction Treaty. In Washington, D.C., **June 16**, on the first day of the first official Russian-American summit, Yeltsin consented to an end to the concept of parity in the number of strategic arms. Bush and Yeltsin agreed that by 2003 the U.S. would have 3,500 warheads and the Russians 3,000. At present, both countries had about 10,000 warheads. Both countries also agreed to eliminate their land-based multiple-warhead missiles, and the U.S. agreed to reduce the number of its submarine-launched ballistic-missile warheads by half. Bush and Yeltsin signed 7 bilateral agreements, **June 17**, including one to turn their weapons agreement into a formal treaty.

Ramos Becomes President of Philippines — The slow tabulation of votes in the May presidential election in the Philippines was completed in June. Former Defense Sec. Fidel Ramos was declared the winner, **June 16**. Among the 7 candidates, Ramos received 24 percent of the vote to 20 percent for Miriam Defensor Santiago, a former judge and administrator, who placed second. Ramos, an ally of Pres. Corazon Aquino, was sworn in as her successor, **June 30**. He appealed to Communists and military rebels to end their revolts.

Shiites Free Last Western Hostages — Shiite guerrillas in Lebanon, **June 17**, freed 2 German relief workers who had been kidnapped in 1989. The workers, Heinrich Struebig and Thomas Kemptner, were the last Western hostages known to be held in Lebanon.

Czechoslovakia Moves Toward a Split — Czechoslovakia moved toward a division into separate Czech and Slovak states. Vladimir Meciar, the Slovak nationalist leader, had been pressing for a confederation in which Slovakia would control its own economy and foreign policy. The federal premier-designate, Vaclav Klaus, countered, **June 18**, with a proposal that the country split in two. Meciar welcomed the offer, and on **June 20**, he and Klaus agreed to prepare for the transition. Pres. Vaclav Havel urged, **June 21**, that the issue be decided in a national referendum.

U.N. Troops Hold Sarajevo Airport — U.N. peacekeeping troops took control of the airport outside Sarajevo, the capital of Bosnia-Herzegovina. The Bosnian government said, **June 20**, that some 40,000 people, mostly civilians, had been massacred by Serbs since Bosnia-Herzegovina voted for independence from Yugoslavia in February. U.N. Sec. General Boutros Boutros-Ghali, **June 26**, directed Serbs besieging Saravejo to put their heavy weapons under U.N. control. The assault continued, however, and on **June 28**, French Pres. Francois Mitterand ignored the danger, flying by helicopter from Croatia to Sarajevo. He toured the city and received an enthusiastic welcome from the residents. The Serbs, **June 29**, turned the Sarajevo airport over to 34 U.N. troops. This cleared the way for delivery of food and medicine to the city, and the first airplane with relief supplies arrived within hours.

Labor Party Leads in Israeli Election — In a parliamentary election, **June 23**, Israeli voters signaled their desire for a new approach to the Palestinian conflict. The ruling Likud bloc, led by Prime Minister Yitzhak Shamir, had opposed self-rule by the Palestinians and were committed to constructing more Jewish settlements in the occupied territories. The Labor Party, led by former Prime Minister Yitzhak Rabin, supported a "land-for-peace" compromise with the Palestinians. In the campaign, the Likud bloc was on the defensive because of economic problems and allegations of corruption. In the 120-seat Knesset, seats were allocated on the basis of votes cast for each party. Labor qualified for 44 seats. Meretz, a coalition of 3 parties supporting an independent Palestine, earned 12 seats. It was expected that Meretz and several small parties would join with Labor to produce a parliamentary majority for Rabin. Likud won 32 seats. Arab governments welcomed the results of the election, and it was reported that the U.S. government saw the outcome as encouraging.

Algeria's Leader Assassinated — Mohammed Boudiaf, the president of the ruling military council in Algeria, was assassinated. Boudiaf had come to power in January, when the military intervened to prevent a sweep of parliamentary elections by the fundamentalist Islamic Salvation Front. Boudiaf was giving a speech in the city of Annaba, **June 29**, when he was killed by machine-gun fire. The government announced that the assassin had been arrested.

General

Presley's Youthful Portrait Chosen for Stamp — More than 1.1 million votes were cast in an election to choose a portrait of Elvis Presley for a U.S. postage stamp. The result of the voting involving the late rock star was announced, **June 4**, by the U.S. Postal Service. By a margin of 3-1, voters preferred a portrait of Elvis as a young man over a portrait that depicted him toward the end of his career.

Biggest Quake in 40 Years Jolts California — Southern California was rocked by 2 big earthquakes in June. The quakes came 2 months after other shocks in April that had caused about 100 injuries. On **June 28**, an earthquake measuring 7.4 on the Richter scale—the highest reading in California in 40 years—shook southern California. Its epicenter was in Yucca Valley, about 90 miles east of Los Angeles. A second quake, measuring 6.5, followed 3 hours later. Its center was about 20 miles west of the first shock. Seismologists said the 2 were related. One child was killed, some 350 persons were injured, and damage was estimated at $16 million.

JULY

National

Clinton Nominated; Perot Drops Out — The Democratic Party nominated Gov. Bill Clinton (Ark.) and Sen. Albert Gore (Tenn.) as their candidates for president and vice president. The contest for the presidency took a new turn when Texas billionaire H. Ross Perot abandoned his plan to run as an independent. The economy became a more serious issue, **July 2**, when the unemployment rate was put at 7.8 percent. Pres. George Bush admitted that the increase in the jobless rate was "not good news," but he said that Congress's failure to pass his economic package was part of the problem. Clinton said, **July 2**, that Bush was "willing to do anything to keep his job, but nothing to help average hard-working Americans keep theirs." Clinton announced, **July 9**, that Gore was his choice as a running mate. Gore, who had served in the House before his election to the Senate in 1984, had run for the presidential nomination in 1988. He had served in Vietnam, though he had opposed that war, and he had supported the use of force in the Persian Gulf in 1991. Gore was a leading advocate of environmental causes. If elected, Clinton (who would be 46 in August) and Gore (44) would be the youngest team ever to win a national campaign. The ticket was also unusual in that both candidates were from neighboring southern states. Perot addressed the convention of the National Association for the Advancement of Colored People, **July 11**, and appealed for racial harmony, but his choice of words provoked complaints by some blacks that he showed insensitivity. The Democratic National Convention opened in New York City, **July 13**. As part of an effort to stress issues of interest to women, 6 women running for the U.S. Senate addressed the convention, **July 13**. The party platform, adopted **July 14**, took a strong pro-choice position on abortion, but in general was considered to be more moderate than other recent Democratic platforms. Former Pres. Jimmy Carter addressed the convention, **July 14**, as did civil rights leader Jesse Jackson, who had given a restrained endorsement of the ticket. Divisions within the Perot campaign became apparent, **July 15**, when Ed Rollins, co-manager of the effort, resigned. On **July 15**, former California Gov. Jerry Brown, still a candidate for the presidential nomination, addressed the Democratic convention and warned again of the bad influence of money in politics. He declined to endorse Clinton. In the balloting for president, Clinton received the votes of 3,372 delegates, and Brown got 596 votes. Former Massachusetts Sen. Paul Tsongas, who had endorsed Clinton, received 209 votes. Perot announced, **July 16**, that he would not seek the presidency. He said that the Democratic Party had "revitalized itself," that his candidacy would cause the election to be thrown into the House for resolution, and that this would be disruptive to the country. Perot's support in public-opinion polls had been declining. Some of Perot's supporters, who had been working to get him on the ballot in all 50 states, expressed anger and disbelief at his decision. The Bush and Clinton campaigns quickly appealed to Perot's supporters to transfer their loyalties. Gore was nominated, **July 16**, for vice president by acclamation. In his acceptance speech, **July 16**, Clinton called for a new covenant between government and the people "based not simply on what each of us can take, but what all of us must give to our nation." He recalled painful events of his childhood and stressed the importance of family. In an appeal aimed primarily at "the forgotten middle class," Clinton vowed to restore the economy. After the convention, **July 17-22**, Clinton, Gore, and their wives campaigned by bus through 8 Eastern and Midwestern states, drawing large and enthusiastic crowds. Polls showed Clinton running far ahead of Bush, with Perot backers shifting in large numbers to the Democratic ticket. In California, Clinton's lead was reported as 2-1. Bush said, **July 20**, that Clinton's economic plan was based on "smoke and mirrors." Clinton, **July 25**, urged Bush to intervene more forcefully in the Serbian-Bosnian conflict, by imposing a blockade against and possibly bombing the Serbian forces. The White House dismissed these proposals as reckless.

Unemployment at 8-Year High — The Labor Dept. reported, **July 2**, that the nation's unemployment rate stood at 7.8 percent in June, the highest level since March 1984. The jobless level had climbed 0.3 percent in each of the past 2 months. Responding to the newest data, the Federal Reserve Board, **July 2**, cut its discount rate—the interest rate it charged to banks—from 3.5 percent to 3 percent. This rate had not been so low since 1963. The Labor Dept. reported, **July 10**, that prices charged by producers for finished goods rose 0.2 percent in June. The department said, **July 14**, that consumer prices rose 0.3 percent in June. The Commerce Dept. said, **July 16**, that housing starts had declined 3.2 percent in June. The department reported,

July 17, that the U.S. merchandise trade deficit had risen to $7.38 billion in May. Federal Reserve Board Chairman Alan Greenspan predicted, **July 22**, that the economic expansion would soon gain momentum. On **July 30**, however, the Commerce Dept. reported that the gross domestic product had grown by only 1.4 percent during the 2d quarter.

Law Extends Jobless Benefits — The Senate and the House, **July 2**, approved a bill that would extend benefits to long-term unemployed persons during recessions. Pres. Bush signed the bill into law, **July 3**. An unemployed worker would now be eligible for 13 additional weeks of benefits if unemployment in his or her state had been at least 6.5 percent for 3 months and 10 percent higher than it had been in the same period during the previous 2 years. Workers could receive up to 20 additional weeks of benefits if their state's unemployment was at least 8 percent.

Exxon Valdez Captain Wins Appeal in Court — The misdemeanor conviction of the captain of the *Exxon Valdez*, which followed the worst oil spill in U.S. history, was overturned in July. The tanker struck a reef in Prince William Sound, in Alaska, in 1989 and spilled 11 million gallons of oil. The accident caused devastation of the region's marine environment. Convicted of negligence, Capt. Joseph Hazelwood had been sentenced to 1,000 hours of community service and fined $50,000. An Alaska appeals court held, **July 10**, that Hazelwood was immune from prosecution under a provision of the federal Clean Water Act of 1972, because he had reported the spill promptly to the Coast Guard.

Gingrich Barely Wins Renomination — House Minority Whip Newt Gingrich (R, Ga.), **July 21**, barely survived the tide of anti-incumbent sentiment that appeared to be sweeping the nation. Forced to run in a new district in suburban Atlanta as a result of redistricting, Gingrich received 50.7 percent of the primary vote against his Republican challenger, Herman Clark. Gingrich outspent Clark, $1.1 million to $150,000. Clark had criticized Gingrich as a "Washington insider."

International

New President Named in Algeria — Algeria's assassinated president, Mohammed Boudiaf, was buried, **July 1**. The High State Council, **July 2**, named Ali Kafi, a council-member and a leader of a veterans' organization, as the new president. Continued military control of the country seemed likely.

Rabin Becomes Israeli Prime Minister — On **July 2**, Israeli Pres. Chaim Herzog asked Yitzhak Rabin, leader of the Labor Party, to form a government. Labor had finished first in parliamentary elections in June. Rabin then put together a coalition that also included the Meretz bloc and Shas, an ultra-Orthodox religious party. The coalition parties were viewed as supportive of Rabin's conciliatory approach toward the Palestinians. The coalition controlled 62 of 120 seats in parliament. With 5 Arab members also supporting Rabin, he was approved, **July 13**, by the Knesset (parliament) as the new prime minister, by a vote of 67-53.

Iraq Allows U.N. Team to Search Building — Iraq backed down in late July to a U.N. demand that a building in Baghdad be searched for evidence of nuclear-weapons production. In early July, rumors had spread that elements of the Iraqi military had sought to overthrow Pres. Saddam Hussein. On **July 3**, Iraq's official news agency denied that a coup had been attempted, but reports persisted that Hussein had been forced to purge hundreds of his officers. On **July 6**, during a visit to a Kurdish stronghold in northern Iraq, Danielle Mitterand, wife of French Pres. Francois Mitterand, survived unharmed when a bomb exploded near her motorcade. Four people were killed. International tensions grew after members of a U.N. inspection team sought to investigate the offices of the Iraqi agriculture ministry, which they believed might contain evidence of a weapons program. The agreement that had ended the Persian Gulf war had granted U.N. authority to conduct such investigations. Iraq, **July 26**, agreed to permit an inspection after the U.N. agreed to exclude from its investigators anyone from a country that had fought against Iraq. The U.N. delegation entered the ministry, **July 28** and **29**, but reported that they had found nothing that documented the production of weapons.

Havel Resigns as Czechoslovakia's President — Vaclav Havel resigned as president of Czechoslovakia, **July 20**. At a time when the country appeared to be moving toward separate Czech and Slovak states, Havel stood for reelection, **July 3**, in the Federal Assembly (parliament). Although he was the only candidate for president, he failed to get a majority in one of the 3 houses of the Assembly, primarily because of opposition by Slovak representatives. On **July 17**, the Slovak National Council (parliament) adopted a declaration of sovereignty, 113-24. Those Slovaks opposing sovereignty were concerned about the economic impact of separating from the more prosperous Czechs. Within an hour after the vote in the Slovak parliament, Havel announced that he would resign. He said his opposition to the division of the federation made it impossible for him to remain. A playwright who had long opposed communism, Havel had become president in 1989 after the Communist regime fell. On **July 23**, the premiers of the Czech and Slovak republics agreed to a plan for the division into 2 independent states by the end of September.

Leaders of Democracies Meet in Munich — The meeting of the leaders of the world's leading industrial democracies proved to be relatively uneventful. En route to the summit, Pres. George Bush visited Poland, **July 5**. He had accompanied the remains of Ignace Paderewski, the concert pianist and Polish premier who had died in New York City in 1941. Paderewski had expressed the hope that one day he would be buried in a free Poland. In a declaration issued at the summit, **July 7**, the leaders of the 7 countries represented—Canada, France, Germany, Great Britain, Italy, Japan, and the United States—warned that they might support the use of force to get relief supplies into Bosnia, which was under assault by Serbian forces. Russian Pres. Boris Yeltsin spoke at the summit, **July 8**, and the leaders endorsed $1 billion in new aid for Russia.

Ships Enforce Yugoslav Embargo — The North Atlantic Treaty Organization and the 9-nation Western European Union agreed, **July 10**, to send warships into the Adriatic Sea to enforce the trade embargo imposed by the U.N. Security Council against Yugoslavia. Serbs in Bosnia-Herzegovina stepped up their military offensive, **July 13**. Milan Panic was approved, **July 14**, as Yugoslavia's premier, by the Yugoslav parliament. Born in Serbia, Panic was a naturalized citizen of the U.S., where he had founded a drug manufacturing company, ICN Pharmaceuticals, Inc. Panic was chosen by Serbian Pres. Slobodan Milosevic. By late July, according to the U.N., 700,000 people had been driven out of Bosnia since the war began, and there were an additional 558, 000 refugees within the country. This mass movement was the result, for the most part, of the Serbian policy of "ethnic cleansing," which aimed at driving Moslems out of areas that they shared with ethnic Serbs.

Pan Am Liable in 1988 Bombing — On **July 10**, a federal jury in New York City concluded that Pan American World Airlines was liable for damages in the terrorist bombing in 1988 that killed 270 people. A bomb had been put aboard the plane in an unaccompanied suitcase that, according to an attorney for families of the victims, airline employees had failed to inspect. The plane exploded over Lockerbie, Scotland, killing all 259 aboard and resulting in the death of 11 people on the ground. For not discovering the bomb, the jury found Pan Am to be guilty of willful misconduct. Pan Am had gone out of business since the tragedy, and it was estimated that the carrier's insurance companies might have to pay out $300 million in individual damage claims. On **July 22**, the jury made the first award on an individual claim— $9.2 million to the family of one victim.

Cocaine Kingpin Escapes From Prison — Pablo Escobar, who had become a billionaire by trafficking in cocaine, escaped from prison in Colombia. Escobar and his top aides had agreed in 1991 to accept incarceration in a luxury prison in Envigado, near his base of operations in Medellin, in return for approval of a constitutional amendment that would bar him from being extradited to the U.S. Concerned by reports that Escobar was still conducting his drug business from prison, Colombian authorities decided to transfer him, temporarily, to a military prison. On **July 21**, taking guns from guards, Escobar and his lieutenants seized officials who had come to transfer them. Soldiers attacked the prison, **July 22**, and freed the hostages, but Escobar and at least 7 other prisoners had escaped through a tunnel. At least 6 people were killed in the clashes at the prison.

Clark Clifford Indicted in Bank Scandal — Clark Clifford, a prominent figure in the Democratic Party since World War II, was indicted as the investigation of the Bank of Credit & Commerce International continued to unfold. Clifford had served as secretary of defense under Pres. Lyndon Johnson and had been an adviser to other Democratic presidents. From 1982 until 1991, Clifford and Robert Altman—who was also indicted—had been top executives with First American Bankshares Inc., the largest bank in Washington, D.C. On **July 28** in New York City, Sheik Kamal Adham, former head of the Saudi Arabian intelligence agency, pleaded guilty to conspiring with BCCI officials to purchase First American, illegally, in 1982. He agreed to cooperate with U.S. investigators. The U.S. government, **July 29**, indicted Clifford and Altman, who were also prominent lawyers, on charges that they had misled banking regulators about BCCI's control of First American. The Federal Reserve Board announced, **July 29**, that it had filed a civil suit against Clifford and Altman. Also on **July 29**, Manhattan District Attorney Robert Morgenthau announced that the 2 men had been indicted for conspiracy and bribery and on other charges. He also filed a civil suit against them. Morgenthau also announced indictments against 4 top BCCI officials, and stated that BCCI had defrauded depositors of $5 billion.

General

Pope Undergoes Operation to Remove Tumor — Pope John Paul II underwent a 4-hour operation in Rome, **July 15**. Doctors removed his gallbladder and a tumor from his colon. At first, doctors reported that the tumor was benign, but on **July 20** they said that it contained cells that were becoming malignant. They said these cells had not invaded other parts of his body and that the operation had been a success.

Mysterious Illness Resembles AIDS — The mystery surrounding acquired immune deficiency syndrome (AIDS) took a new turn in July. *Newsweek* magazine, in an issue available **July 20**, reported that immunologists had found 6 patients with AIDS symptoms whose blood showed no trace of the human immuno-deficiency virus (HIV) that caused AIDS. When the story was published, the 8th International Conference on AIDS was in progress in Amsterdam, the Netherlands. A discussion of the *Newsweek* article was organized in Amsterdam, **July 21**, and it was determined that about 30 cases fitting the description in the article had been identified. The U.S. Public Health Service reported, **July 22**, that the lifetime medical cost for an AIDS patient now averaged $102,000.

'Cop Killer' Song Dropped From Album — Time Warner Inc. became the focus of many complaints because of the lyrics in the song "Cop Killer" in the *Body Count* album recorded by the rapper Ice-T. Police associations objected to the lyrics and police officers demonstrated against Time Warner and organized boycotts. Public officials also criticized the song. Ice-T asked Time Warner to delete the song from the album, and the company announced, **July 28**, that it would do so.

AUGUST

National

Republicans Renominate Bush and Quayle — The Republican Party renominated Pres. George Bush and Vice Pres. Dan Quayle at the convention in Houston. A Gallup Poll reported, **Aug. 4**, that Pres. Bush's public-approval rating had fallen to 29 percent—a new low. On **Aug. 5**, Clinton and Al Gore, the Democratic vice presidential nominee, began a new joint campaign trip by bus, leaving St. Louis and bound for St. Paul and Minneapolis. In a press release, **Aug. 6**, Bush said Clinton supported the largest tax increase in U.S. history, $150 billion. Clinton, **Aug. 6**, said only the wealthy and corporations would bear the increase and that Pres. Ronald Reagan had signed a bigger tax-increase bill. In a letter released **Aug. 6**, former Sen. Barry Goldwater warned that the election would be a shambles for the Republicans if the party did not soften its position on abortion. Bush, who had opposed abortions in most cases, appeared to take a more restrained position, **Aug. 11**, saying in response to a question that he would seek to dissuade a granddaughter from having an abortion but would stand by any decision she ultimately made. Bush, **Aug. 11**, denied a report in a book that he had had an extramarital affair. In a speech on foreign affairs, **Aug. 13**, Clinton said Bush had failed to develop a foreign policy that reflected an understanding of domestic U.S. economic problems. The Republican platform committee, **Aug. 13**, approved a party platform with strong conservative language. As in previous years, the platform called for a constitutional amendment banning abortions. However, the final text backed off from saying that Bush's 1990 budget deal with Congress—which included a tax increase—had been a mistake. The final draft blamed the increase on Congress. Barbara Bush, the First Lady, said, **Aug. 13**, that the subject of abortion had no place in the party's platform. On **Aug. 13**, Bush appointed Sec. of State James Baker as his chief of staff. Baker, working out of the White House, would oversee the presidential campaign. Baker replaced Samuel Skinner, who was given a largely honorary post in the Republican National Committee. Lawrence Eagleburger was named acting Secretary of State. Baker had managed the successful campaigns of Ronald Reagan and Bush in 1984 and 1988, respectively. The Republican National Convention opened in Houston, **Aug. 17**. The platform was approved, as drafted, after moderates abandoned an effort to modify the language on abortion. Columnist Pat Buchanan, who had challenged Bush in the primaries, addressed the convention and endorsed the President. Former Pres. Reagan, in his speech, said he was optimistic about the nation's future. On **Aug. 19**, "family values night" at the convention, Barbara Bush and Marilyn Quayle, wife of the Vice President, addressed the delegates. Bush and Quayle were nominated for president and vice president, without any dissenting votes. Quayle, accepting his nomination, **Aug. 21**, stressed his commitment to traditional American values and called the opposing ticket too liberal. Bush then accepted renomination in a speech that reviewed momentous international events of the past 4 years, including the collapse of communism and resolution of some regional conflicts. He apologized for having raised taxes in the 1990 budget agreement with Congress, and claimed Clinton had raised taxes and fees 128 times while governor of Arkansas. For his second term, Bush endorsed "across the board" tax cuts and a cap on entitlement programs except Social Security. He endorsed giving taxpayers an option to earmark 10 percent of their taxes for a fund that would be used to help balance the budget. He renewed his support for a cut in the capital-gains tax. He blamed the country's economic problems on the failure of Congress to implement his program. Post-convention polls showed that Bush had picked up some ground on Clinton. Bush, addressing evangelical Christians, **Aug. 22**, said the Democrats had left God out of their platform. Clinton said, **Aug. 23**, that the implication that Democrats are "somehow Godless" was "deeply offensive." Independent reports in newspapers suggested that Bush's claim that Clinton had raised taxes and fees 128 times was at least a misrepresentation. On **Aug. 25**, Bush and Clinton addressed the American Legion convention. Bush defended his decision to end the Gulf war without overthrowing Pres. Saddam Hussein, saying he had decided not to "slaughter" the retreating Iraqis. Acknowledging the controversy over his failure to serve in the military during the Vietnam war, Clinton said he still believed that U.S. policy in that war was wrong.

Economic Indicators Edge Downward — Prospects for an economic recovery dimmed a bit, **Aug. 4**, when the Commerce Dept. reported that the index of leading economic indicators had edged downward in June 0.2 percent, the first decline in 6 months. The Labor Dept. reported, **Aug. 7**, that the unemployment rate had declined from its 8-year high of 7.8 percent in June to 7.7 percent in July. The number of payroll jobs was reported to be up by 198,000 in July. The department said, **Aug. 13**, that consumer prices had risen 0.1 percent in July. The Commerce Dept. reported, **Aug. 19**, that the merchandise trade deficit had narrowed to $6.59 billion in June.

Republican House Leaders Lose in Primaries — Two members of the House Republican leadership were defeated in primaries. Rep. Guy Vander Jagt, chairman of the National Republican Congressional Committee, which raised money for Republican candidates, lost a primary in Michigan, **Aug. 4**. Rep. Mickey Edwards, chairman of the House Republican Party Committee, finished third in a primary in Oklahoma, **Aug. 25**. Edwards had been declared one of the "worst abusers" of the House bank by the House Ethics Committee after he wrote 386 overdraft checks.

Trial of Ex-CIA Official Ends in Deadlock — The Iran-Contra trial of Clair George, who once ran the Central Intelligence Agency's worldwide clandestine operations, ended in a mistrial, **Aug. 26**. George had been charged with lying to Congress and to investigators about what he knew of the sale of arms to Iran and the diversion of the profits to the Nicaraguan contras. A mistrial was declared after jurors reported that they were deadlocked on all 9 counts. Some jurors who supported acquittal said George had not lied to Congress but had tried his best to answer questions about the complex and mysterious affair.

International

War in Bosnia Intensifies — On **Aug. 1**, on the outskirts of Sarajevo, Serb snipers fired on a busload of young Bosnian orphans on the first leg of a trip to asylum in Germany. A boy and a girl were killed, but 39 of the orphans arrived in Germany, **Aug. 3**. A Serb mortar barrage, **Aug. 4**, wounded the grandmother of one of the victims as she attended her grandchild's funeral. After refugees reported that the Serbs had established concentration camps in Bosnia, the U.N. Security Council demanded, **Aug. 4**, that relief agencies be allowed to inspect detention centers. Heavy fighting around Sarajevo, **Aug. 4**, forced the U.N. to suspend relief flights. On **Aug. 5**, Bill Clinton, the Democratic presidential candidate, urged that U.N. forces attack Serb artillery positions near Sarajevo. A British television crew, **Aug. 6**, visited 2 detention camps in Serbian-controlled areas of Bosnia. They filmed hundreds of prisoners who were badly malnourished and living in unhealthy conditions. Yugoslav Premier Milan Panic said, **Aug. 7**, that he would close all Serbian detention camps in Bosnia-Herzegovina. The U.N. Security Council voted, **Aug. 13**, 12-0 with 3 abstentions, to authorize military force to insure that humanitarian aid got to Bosnia-Herzegovina. U.N. members were authorized to take whatever measures they believed necessary. In a second resolution, the Security Council unanimously condemned the Serbian policy of ethnic cleansing, which involved forced evacuations. After meeting in London, the principals in the Yugoslav conflict agreed, **Aug. 27**, to an accord aimed at bringing peace. The terms included a cessation of violence in Bosnia and the release of all persons held in detention camps. It was agreed that no territory gained by force would be recognized by the international community. Pres. Slobodan Milosevic of Serbia supported the accord but claimed that Serbia had no control over camps in Bosnia.

'No-Fly Zone' Imposed on Iraq — Allied nations ordered Iraq to cease all air flights over southern Iraq. The object was to protect Shiite Moslems from attack. Earlier, on **Aug. 3** and **4**, as a show of force in the region, 2,000 U.S. Marines and other troops joined U.S.-Kuwaiti military exercises in Kuwait, which were to last 2 weeks. On **Aug. 18**, Britain and France endorsed the U.S. "no-fly zone" plan. British Prime Minister John Major said Iraq was committing "systematic murder" and "genocide" against the Shiites. Iraq, **Aug. 20**, warned it would resist Allied attempts to create a "no-fly zone," which covered about one-third of the country. Some 200 U.S. aircraft would bear the principal burden of enforcing the prohibition. Pres. George Bush, **Aug. 26**, said the Allies had acted after receiving "new evidence of harsh repression" imposed on the people in the south by the Iraqi government. The "no-fly" order went into effect, **Aug. 27**.

U.S., Israel Agree on Loan Guarantees — The impasse between Israel and the U.S. over loan guarantees was resolved. The previous Israeli government had refused to agree to the U.S. condition for granting $10 billion in guarantees, namely, that Israel would curtail construction of Jewish settlements in the occupied territories. But the new government of Prime Minister Yitzhak Rabin had halted construction of new government-financed settlements, and on **Aug. 6**, the government announced temporary suspension of the allocation of state-owned land in the territories to settlers. Rabin then met with Pres. George Bush at his vacation home in Kennebunkport, Me., and on **Aug. 11**, the 2 leaders announced that they had reached an agreement on the guarantees. It was reported that the agreement provided that any Israeli spending on the settlements would be deducted from the amount of the guarantees.

Canada, Mexico, U.S. Agree on Trade — Representatives from Canada, Mexico, and the U.S. announced, **Aug. 12**, that they had approved a draft agreement establishing free trade among the 3 countries. Over 15 years, tariffs and other restrictions on trade and investment among the countries would be eliminated. The new pact would expand on an agreement between Canada and the U.S. in effect since 1989. The legislatures in all 3 countries would need to approve the draft. Leaders of organized labor in the U.S. warned that the agreement, if approved, would prompt more U.S. companies to move to Mexico, resulting in a loss of jobs in the U.S.

General

Computer Pioneer Files for Bankruptcy — Wang Laboratories, Inc., an innovative computer company, filed for bankruptcy, **Aug. 18**. Founded by the late An Wang, acknowledged as the inventor of word processors, the company had also led the way in developing minicomputers. Analysts said the company had failed to respond effectively to the rising popularity of personal computers. In announcing that Wang would seek protection under Chapter 11 of the U.S. Bankruptcy Code, Richard Miller, chairman of the Lowell, Mass. company, said the firm would reorganize and concentrate on software.

Basketball Legend Larry Bird Retires — Larry Bird, one of basketball's greatest players, retired, **Aug. 18**, because of recurring back problems. Bird, in 1979, had led an unbeaten Indiana State team to the final game of the NCAA basketball tournament, which was won by Michigan State, led by Earvin (Magic) Johnson. Thereafter, Johnson and Bird—the latter with the Boston Celtics—dominated professional basketball and contributed to its sharp rise in popularity. Bird, a 6-foot, 9-inch forward, led Boston to 3 championships and was named the league's most valuable player 3 times. Johnson, who had already retired from pro ball, and Bird both played on the U.S. "dream team" that won the Olympic gold medal in 1992. On **Sept. 29**, Johnson announced that he would resume his career, on a limited schedule, with the Los Angeles Lakers.

Hurricane Batters Florida, Louisiana — A powerful hurricane devastated south Florida and also pounded Louisiana. The hurricane, named Andrew, was perhaps the worst natural disaster ever to strike the U.S. In Florida, the storm claimed 30 lives, destroyed or damaged 85,000 homes, and left many areas without power and water. Some 250,000 people were left homeless, and many sought refuge in 12 tent cities. Damage in Florida was estimated to be as high as $20 billion. The hurricane first struck the Bahamas, **Aug. 23**, with winds up to 120 miles an hour. Four people were reported killed there. The center of the storm struck the mainland about 10 to 15 miles south of Miami, **Aug. 24**, with winds up to 165 miles an hour. The city of Homestead and the Homestead Air Force Base were virtually leveled. With ample warning, most people had been evacuated from the hurricane's path. An 8-foot tidal surge accompanied the storm, and rain drenched south Florida. Miami survived relatively unscathed. The storm crossed the Gulf of Mexico and struck the Louisiana coast, **Aug. 25**, with the eye of the hurricane about 90 miles southwest of New Orleans. Winds were recorded at 140 miles an hour, rain was severe, and the storm spawned tornadoes. The hurricane gradually weakened as it moved north into Mississippi. After Florida officials complained, **Aug. 27**, about the slowness of the federal relief effort, Pres. George Bush ordered troops sent to the impacted area. By **Aug. 28**, 6,000 Army and Marine personnel were in south Florida, distributing food and building tent cities. On **Aug. 29**, Bush raised the commitment of Federal troops to 20,000, and private relief agencies also joined in the rescue. Sanitary conditions remained poor, and concern about disease grew.

SEPTEMBER

National

Number of Americans in Poverty Grows — The government reported that the number of Americans living in poverty was rising. The Commerce Dept. said, **Sept. 1**, that the leading economic indicators had edged upward 0.1 percent in July. The poverty report, issued by the Census Bureau, **Sept. 3**, put the number of people living in families with incomes below the poverty line at 35.7 million in 1991. That was the highest total since 1964. The poverty rate in 1991, 14.2 percent, was the highest since 1983. The bureau also said that average median family income had declined for the 2nd straight year in 1991. The Labor Dept. said, **Sept. 4**, that the unemployment rate was down 0.1 percent in August to 7.6 percent. Total unemployment in August was down by 83,000 jobs. In response to the latter figure, the Federal Reserve Board, **Sept. 4**, cut the interest rate banks charged on overnight loans to each other from 3.25 percent to 3 percent. The Labor Dept. reported, **Sept. 11**, that prices paid by producers for finished goods rose by 0.1 percent in August. The department said, **Sept. 15**, that consumer prices rose 0.3 percent in August. The Commerce Dept. said, **Sept. 17**, that the merchandise trade deficit had jumped to $7.82 billion in July. The department reported, **Sept. 22**, that housing starts had risen 10.4 percent in August. Economists saw declining mortgage rates as the major impetus for the housing market.

Race for President Heats Up — The final phase of the long presidential campaign began in September, with the candidates hitting hard at each other. On **Sept. 2**, Pres. George Bush announced a $1 billion program to subsidize U.S. wheat sales abroad, promised $755 million in aid to Texas farmers impacted by natural disasters, and approved the sale of jet fighters for the Republic of China (Taiwan). The Bush campaign, **Sept. 3**, turned down a proposal by the Commission on Presidential Debates for a series of 4 debates that would be led by a single moderator rather than a panel of questioners. Clinton was endorsed by the AFL-CIO, **Sept. 3**, and by the Sierra Club, **Sept. 4**. In a speech **Sept. 10**, Bush sought to put 13 of his economic proposals together into an integrated economic policy. New proposals included a worldwide "strategic network of free trade agreements" and a "streamlined reorganization" of the executive branch. He called for income tax cuts for individuals and small businesses. Clinton, **Sept. 11**, attacked "voices of intolerance . . . that proclaim that some families aren't real families, some Americans aren't real Americans." Bush, **Sept. 14**, said he would not sign a renewal of the Endangered Species Act unless it dealt with the impact of environmental protection on jobs. Clinton replied that the government could do more to help loggers in the Northwest while protecting the environment. Clinton, **Sept. 16**, proposed special bank accounts for less affluent Americans, with the government matching savings up to $1,800 a year that could be used for job training, education, or starting a business. Bush said, **Sept. 17**, that Clinton's economic proposals would represent "social engineering" by the government. On **Sept. 18**, the name of H. Ross Perot was placed on the ballot in Arizona, thus completing the effort by volunteers to get his name before the voters in all 50 states. Perot hinted, **Sept. 18**, that he might declare his candidacy after all. Although Clinton had said that he had never sought special treatment to avoid military service, the *New York Times* reported, **Sept. 19**, that, on request from Clinton, then-Sen. J. William Fulbright (Ark.) had tried to get a draft-exempt position for him. Adm. William Crowe, former chairman of the Joint Chiefs of Staff, endorsed Clinton, **Sept. 19**, and discounted the importance of the draft issue. Bush, **Sept. 21**, said Clinton had failed to "come clean with the American people" on the draft. Perot said, **Sept. 22**, "I think I made a mistake" in not entering the presidential race. Criticizing Bush's rejection of the proposed debate format, Clinton said, **Sept. 22**, "If I had the worst record of any president in 50 years, I wouldn't want to defend my record either." Bush, **Sept. 22**, deplored Clinton's record in Arkansas on river pollution, civil rights, health care, and early release of prisoners. Clinton said, **Sept. 24**, that he would require private employers to provide health care. Bush charged, **Sept. 26**, that Clinton would "go after the middle class" by raising their taxes. At the invitation of Perot, some principal figures in the Bush and Clinton campaigns met with the Texan and his volunteer leaders in Dallas, **Sept. 28**. Perot especially wanted to hear what plans the major parties had for balancing the federal budget. Bush, **Sept. 29**, challenged Clinton to a series of 4 debates.

Some House Members Cleared in Scandal — The U.S. Justice Dept. said, **Sept. 9**, that it was writing some current and former members of the U.S. House that they had been cleared of any wrong-doing in connection with the House bank scandal. Altogether, 329 current and former members had overdrawn their accounts. On **Sept. 10**, Joanna O'Rourke, former manager of the House Post Office, was indicted on charges related to her work at the Post Office. On **Sept. 17**, in a plea-bargain agreement, O'Rourke pleaded guilty to 2 misdemeanor charges of embezzling government property and misusing public funds.

More House Incumbents Defeated — Two more incumbent members of the U.S. House lost bids for renomination, **Sept. 15**, bringing the total for the year so far to 19, the highest in any Congressional election since World War II. Stephen Solarz (D, N.Y.), who had overdrawn his account in the House bank 743 times, lost in a district that had been redrawn to encourage Hispanics to run. The primary winner was Nydia Velazquez, a leader in the Puerto Rican community. Chester Atkins (D, Mass.), also hurt by redistricting and by 127 overdrafts, lost to Martin Meehan, a former prosecutor. On **Sept. 15**, Washington state Sen. Patty Murray (D) was nominated for the U.S. Senate, raising to 11—a record—the number of women who had captured major-party nominations for the Senate in 1992. On the same day, however, former Rep. Geraldine Ferraro (N.Y.), the 1984 Democratic nominee for vice president, narrowly lost a Senate primary to New York state Attorney Gen. Robert Abrams.

Impeachment of Judge Overturned — U.S. District Judge Stanley Sporkin, **Sept. 17**, overturned the impeachment in 1989 of former U.S. District Judge Alcee Hastings. In 1983, Hastings had been acquitted of involvement in a bribery conspiracy. Six years later, however, a panel of 12 U.S. Senators had recommended that the Florida judge be impeached and removed from the bench, and the full Senate supported the committee's recommendation. Sporkin held that the Constitution required that the full Senate must hear an impeachment trial and consider the evidence against the accused. Sporkin recommended that the case be appealed to the Supreme Court.

Kissinger Rebuts Charges on POWs — The long-simmering debate about American prisoners of war in Southeast Asia flared again. For years, assertions had been made that POWs had been left behind when the U.S. withdrew from the Vietnam war in 1973, and that U.S. officials may have known about them. Asked at a Senate committee hearing, **Sept. 21**, whether he believed any U.S. servicemen had been left behind, James Schlesinger, Sec. of Defense from 1973 to 1975, said, "As of now I can come to no other conclusion." Henry Kissinger, who had negotiated the agreement that had ended U.S. involvement in the war in 1973, testified **Sept. 22**. He denied vehemently that U.S. officials had knowingly left any prisoners after the American pull-out that year. He said, however, that the Communist government of North Vietnam had not given a satisfactory accounting for all the missing Americans.

International

France OKs European Union Treaty — France approved the European Community's Treaty on European Union that had been negotiated in Maastricht, the Netherlands, in 1991. On **Sept. 2**, the office of British Prime Minister John Major said that, in the event that French voters rejected the treaty, the British government would withdraw from Parliament the bill to ratify it. On **Sept. 3**, former Prime Minister Margaret Thatcher, an opponent of the treaty, charged that tying the value of the British pound to that of the German mark had prolonged Britain's recession. Major, **Sept. 7**, rejected calls for a referendum on the treaty in Britain. He discounted fears that a Europe united by the treaty would smother national identities. In France, the campaign for the treaty was led by Pres. François Mitterand, who denied that Germany would dominate a unified European Community and that French culture would be submerged. In the **Sept. 20** referendum, the French approved the treaty, but with only 51 percent voting in favor. France thus joined Greece, Ireland, and Luxembourg in completing ratification. Danish Premier Poul Schluter said, **Sept. 22**, that Denmark, where the treaty had been rejected, would vote again on it in 1993.

Taiwan, Saudi Arabia to Get U.S. Jets — Pres. George Bush announced, **Sept. 2**, that he had approved the sale of 150 F-16 fighter jets to the Republic of China (Taiwan). The People's Republic of China, **Sept. 3**, denounced the sale as a violation of an agreement in 1982 that curbed arms sales to Taiwan. On **Sept. 11**, Bush said his administration had approved the sale of 72 F-15 fighter jets to Saudi Arabia. Israel, **Sept. 13**, objected to the sale but indicated no attempt would be made to get Congress to disapprove it. The manufacturers benefitting from the sales were General Dynamics Corp. and McDonnell Douglas Corp., respectively. Some Democrats charged that the sales represented attempts by Bush to buy votes in an election year.

United Nations Expels Yugoslavia — The U.N. General Assembly voted to oust Yugoslavia because of its involvement in the war in Bosnia-Herzegovina. The risk involved in bringing relief supplies to the Bosnians was apparent, **Sept. 3**, when an Italian plane bringing U.N. aid crashed without explanation near Sarajevo. Four crew members were killed. On **Sept. 8**, 2 French U.N. peacekeeping officers were killed outside Sarajevo when their convoy was struck by mortar and machine-gun fire. Before the General Assembly vote, **Sept. 22**, Premier Milan Panic of Yugoslavia argued that expulsion would just strengthen the hand of "militant nationalists" in Belgrade. He condemned the "ethnic cleansing" policy practiced by the Serbs in Croatia and Bosnia. The Assembly vote was 127-6, with 26 abstentions, although the word expel was not included in the resolution. Rather, Yugoslavia's seat was declared vacant. This was the first time that a U.N. member had been removed from the organization.

Middle East Talks Remain Stalled — Arab and Israeli negotiators met again in Washington in September. The new round began **Sept. 3**, and as they continued, Israeli Prime Minister Yitzhak Rabin said that a land-for-peace agreement was likely. Pres. Hafez al-Assad, **Sept. 9**, said publicly for the first time that Syria was willing to seek a peace treaty with Israel. On **Sept. 14**, however, Syria's delegation said that Israel must withdraw from the occupied territories before a treaty could be negotiated.

Maoist Guerrilla Leader Seized in Peru — Abimael Guzman Reynoso, leader of Sendero Luminoso (Shining Path), a Maoist guerrilla organization, was seized by police in Peru, **Sept. 12**. Three other guerrilla leaders were also captured in raids on 2 houses in Lima, the capital. Shining Path's 12-year rebellion had resulted in 25,000 deaths.

General

Hurricane Losses Put at $7.3 Billion — An insurance industry group estimated, **Sept. 1**, that victims of hurricane Andrew in Florida would collect $7.3 billion in insurance claims. This figure did not include costs of damage to public property or damage in Louisiana. On a visit to south Florida, **Sept. 1**, Pres. George Bush promised that the federal government would cover almost all disaster relief costs. He also promised that Homestead Air Force Base, nearly destroyed by the hurricane, would be rebuilt. Another hurricane, named Iniki, struck Hawaii, **Sept. 11**. Described as the worst hurricane to hit the islands in the 20th century, Iniki caused 3 deaths and $1 billion in damage. On the island of Kauai, winds reached speeds of 130 miles an hour, and half of its 20,000 homes were badly damaged.

Vincent Resigns as Baseball Commissioner — Fay Vincent resigned, **Sept. 7**, as commissioner of Major League Baseball after a majority of team owners called on him to step down. In 1989, the owners had chosen Vincent to succeed A. Bartlett Giamatti, who had died, as commissioner. Vincent said he believed in exerting strong leadership, but some owners found his actions high-handed.

U.N. Acts in Famine Crisis — The United Nations stepped up its efforts to reduce the death toll from famine in Africa. The U.S. expanded its own airlift, announcing, **Sept. 4**, that it would deliver food to 2 towns in Somalia and to another in Kenya. The first 40 soldiers, all Pakistani, of a U.N. peacekeeping force arrived in Somalia, **Sept. 14**, to make sure that food reached the needy. The country was plagued by war as well as famine, and one military commander had opposed the U.N. role, arguing that his forces could distribute donated food. The population of Sudan was also suffering as the result of civil war. A U.N. official found, **Sept. 16**, that the city of Juba, which was swollen with refugees to a population of 300,000, was in desperate need of food. Altogether, some 3 million people in the country had left their homes in search of food or to escape the fighting.

50th Shuttle Trip Focuses on Science — The 50th U.S. shuttle mission began, **Sept. 12**, when the orbiter *Endeavor* was launched in Florida. The crew included the first black woman in space, the first married couple to travel in space together, and the first Japanese citizen to ride in a shuttle. Japan was the source of 34 of the 43 experiments planned for the flight. The *Endeavor* landed in Florida on **Sept. 20**.

Boy Wins Suit to Get New Parents — A 12-year-old boy won a suit in a Florida circuit court in Orlando, **Sept. 25**, that ended the parental rights of his natural mother and allowed his foster parents to adopt him. The case may have been the first in which family rights were ended as a result of a legal action brought by a child. During the trial the boy, Gregory Kingsley, testified that his mother, Rachel, had not visited him for almost 2 years while he was in foster care.

OCTOBER

National

3 Presidential Candidates Debate Issues — Pres. George Bush and Gov. Bill Clinton (Ark.), the Republican and Democratic candidates for president, participated in 3 televised debates in October. They were joined by H. Ross Perot, the Texas billionaire and an independent candidate for president. Perot declared his candidacy on **Oct. 1**, just 33 days before the election. In July, after signaling that he would run, he had removed himself from consideration. Perot made the elimination of the federal budget deficits his main issue, but he also stressed political-campaign reform. Clinton, **Oct. 1**, criticized the Bush administration's "appeasement" of the Iraqi dictator, Saddam Hussein, before the gulf war, and said Bush was too eager to befriend "potentates and dictators." On **Oct. 7**, Bush said Clinton had not told the truth about a visit to Moscow in 1969. Clinton had visited the USSR as part of a European tour related to his Oxford studies. Bush said Clinton should "level" with the voters, and he criticized Clinton's participation in anti-Vietnam war activities in England. The first debate took place in a St. Louis suburb, **Oct. 11**. In reference to his trip to Moscow, Clinton recalled that former Sen. Prescott Bush (Conn.) had spoken out against Sen. Joseph McCarthy (Wis.) in the 1950s, and he said to Bush, "Your father was right to stand up to Joe McCarthy. You were wrong to attack my patriotism." Bush announced that James Baker, his chief of staff, would oversee all domestic programs after the election. After the debate, the White House said that Bush, if re-elected, would dismiss his 3 top economic advisers. Bush, **Oct. 12**, asked for the resignations of all his Cabinet members and other top appointees, immediately after the election. He would then choose which ones to accept. In the vice presidential debate, in Atlanta, **Oct. 13**, Vice Pres. Dan Quayle declared repeatedly that Clinton lacked the character and trustworthiness to be president. Sen. Albert Gore (Tenn.) said the Bush administration was blind to the suffering caused by the recession and unwilling to abandon its "trickle down" economic policies. Vice Adm. James Stockdale (ret.), Perot's choice for vice president, deplored the acrimony displayed by the major-party nominees. In the second presidential debate, in Richmond, Va., **Oct. 15**, questions were posed by uncommitted voters from the audience. Bush said he supported term limits for members of Congress, Clinton opposed them, and Perot said he would serve only one term. The questions made it clear that the members of the audience wanted the candidates to focus on the issues and avoid mudslinging. Perot was spending lavishly from his own fortune—some $60 million, he estimated—in the campaign. Most of this went for television ads, including a series that ran for 30 minutes each. On **Oct. 16**, he laid out his plans for erasing the deficit. He called for large cuts in optional domestic programs and increases in Medicare premiums and higher taxes on some Social Security benefits. He would cut some capital-gains taxes. To reform government, he would cap political contributions at $1,000 and eliminate "all possibilities of special interests giving large sums of money to candidates." In the last presidential debate in East Lansing, Mich., **Oct. 19**, Perot charged that Bush had indicated to Pres. Saddam Hussein of Iraq that he could take the northern part of Kuwait in the summer of 1990. Bush, rushing to "defend the national honor," vigorously denied this. Bush warned that because Clinton's figures on his budget didn't add up, "he's going to sock it right to the middle class taxpayer and lower." Public-opinion surveys taken after the debates showed Clinton still ahead of Bush, with Perot third but gaining. After *The Washington Post* reported, **Oct. 22**, that the State Dept. had investigated the passport files of his mother, Clinton quipped that she was "a well-known subversive" and he deplored "a crowd . . . desperate to hold on to power." Perot revealed, **Oct. 25**, that the actual reason behind his withdrawal from the race in July was to avoid a "dirty tricks" campaign that was to be waged by the Republicans against his daughter.

Bush Veto on Abortion Counseling Upheld — In 1991 the Supreme Court had upheld an administration regulation prohibiting abortion counseling at federally financed family planning clinics. In September, Pres. Bush vetoed a bill that sought to overturn what had been called a gag rule. On **Oct. 1**, the Senate overrode the veto, 73-26. The House, **Oct. 2**, voted, 266-148, to override, falling 10 votes short of the two-thirds majority required.

Unemployment Remains High — The Labor Dept. reported, **Oct. 2**, that unemployment had edged downward 0.1 percentage point to 7.5 percent in September. In the same month, however, the U.S. had actually lost 57,000 jobs, and private-sector jobs showed a net loss of 25,000 since Pres. Bush took office. The Dow Jones industrial average closed at a low for the year, at 3,136.58, **Oct. 9**. The Commerce Dept. said, **Oct. 16**, that the U.S. trade deficit had widened sharply in August to $9 billion, as exports showed their biggest decline in 5 years.

Bush Veto Overridden for First Time — After nearly 4 years and 35 unsuccessful attempts, Congress finally overrode a veto by Pres. Bush. On **Oct. 3**, he vetoed a bill that reversed portions of a law that prohibited local governments from regulating cable-television fees. The legislation required that the Federal Communications Commission establish a "reasonable" price for basic cable services. On **Oct. 5**, the Senate, 74-25, and the House, 308-114, both voted to override by more than the two-thirds majority required.

'Iraqgate' Divides Administration — Revelations in the emerging "Iraqgate" scandal plunged members of the Bush administration into conflict in October. In 1985, Iraq asked the Atlanta branch of Banca Nazionale del Lavoro, an Italian bank, to handle its application for U.S. Dept. of Agriculture loans. Evidence emerged that some money provided by the U.S. government for the loans may have been utilized by Iraq for military weapons. In 1991, Christopher Drogoul, the branch manager, was indicted for bribery and for making unauthorized loans. On **Oct. 5**, the CIA, which had said it had no independent secret information about the case, admitted it had failed to provide all its classified intelligence reports. CIA Director Robert Gates, **Oct. 7**, ordered an internal investigation. CIA officials told the Senate Intelligence Committee, **Oct. 8**, that they had withheld information from federal prosecutors in Atlanta at the urging of the Justice Dept. The officials told the committee, **Oct. 9**, that the Justice Dept. had suppressed information provided to it by the CIA that was important to the federal investigation. After William Sessions, head of the FBI, said that the FBI would conduct an internal FBI investigation into the Justice Dept., a spokesman for the department said, **Oct. 11**, that the FBI would merely be one participant in the inquiry. Administration officials said, **Oct. 13**, that Sessions himself was the subject of an ethics investigation, and Sen. David Boren (D, Okla.), chairman of the Intelligence Committee, expressed puzzlement about the timing of the accusations. Sessions, **Oct. 15**, canceled a meeting with the ethics investigators, and his lawyer assailed the Justice Dept. for making public the details of allegations against him. On **Oct. 17**, Attorney Gen. William Barr appointed Frederick Lacey, a retired federal judge, to investigate both the leaking of allegations against Sessions as well as the administration's handling of the bank-fraud case.

International

Senate Approves Treaty on Nuclear Weapons — The Senate, **Oct. 1**, approved a treaty, signed in 1991, that would reduce the number of strategic (long-range) weapons held by the U.S. and 4 independent states that were formerly part of the Soviet Union. Under its terms, the number of U.S. warheads would drop from 12,646 (in 1990) to 8,556, and the number of Russian warheads would decline from 11,012 held by the Soviet Union (in 1990) to 6,163. Three former Soviet republics, Belarus, Kazakhstan, and Ukraine, would have no nuclear weapons. Of the 4 former Soviet republics, only Kazakhstan had approved the treaty so far.

Brazil's President Resigns, Faces Trial — The president of Brazil, Fernando Collor de Mello, surrendered his powers, **Oct. 2**. He faced trial in the Senate on accusations of complicity in a multimillion-dollar bribery scheme. Collor's wife was also under investigation, for allegedly embezzling money from a federal charity that she operated. Vice Pres. Itamar Augusto Franco became acting president, **Oct. 2**.

Peru Rebel Leader Gets Life Term — Abimael Guzman Reynoso, leader of Shining Path, the Maoist guerrilla movement in Peru who had been captured in September, was sentenced, **Oct. 7**, to life in prison after being convicted of treason. The judge, who wore a hood to protect his identity, said that Guzman had been responsible for 20,000 deaths and $20 billion in damages that had occurred during the 12-year war. Meanwhile, the rebellion continued. On **Oct. 10**, Shining Path guerrillas killed 44 people in the village of Ayacucho.

Vietnam Offers Help on Missing Combatants — Pres. George Bush said, **Oct. 23**, that Vietnam had agreed to provide to the U.S. all documents, photographs, and personal effects relating to American servicemen still missing after the Vietnam war. The U.S. listed 2,265 Americans as unaccounted for in Indochina. These included men known to be dead whose bodies had not been recovered.

(See Addenda for late Oct. 92 news.)

125 Years of *The World Almanac*

The 1993 edition of *The World Almanac* marks the 125th anniversary of the first printing of this publication in 1868. To help celebrate this anniversary, you will find a special introduction by John Chancellor (p. 33), which takes a look back at the past 125 years of U.S. history and makes an assessment of the current state of world affairs. In addition, what follows is a brief summary of past editions of this publication from 125, 100, 50, and 25 years ago.

The editors of this volume want to thank our loyal readers for their many years of devotion, interest, and concern. Throughout the years, your suggestions and criticisms have made a significant and unique contribution to our efforts to continue to make this book a compendium of universal knowledge.

This anniversary edition is dedicated to the past, present, and future readers of *The World Almanac.*

M.S.H., Editor

1868—125 Years Ago

The World Almanac was published for the first time. The 1868 edition consisted of 108 pages, with 12 additional pages of advertisements. Among the items advertised were: Land, near the "525 Miles of the Union Pacific Railroad Running West from Omaha Across the Continent" that had been completed; Steinway & Sons Pianos; The New York News Company; North American Steamship Company; P. & G. Lorillard—"Manufacturers & Dealers in Fine Tobaccos, Cigars, Genuine Maccaboy, Rappee & Extra Scotch Snuff"; The Great American Tea Company; and The Universal Clothes Wringer, "Improved with Rowell's Patent Double Gear, the Only Wringer with the Patent Stop, Without which Cog Wheels fly out of gear and are of No Use when Most Needed." This last included an illustration divided into "The Past"—a haggard-looking woman wringing out clothes over the wash-tub—and "The Present"—a young woman in elegant attire, at the crank of the Universal Clothes Wringer.

The General Index had 7 sections: Astronomical, Etc.; Political; Reconstruction; Acts of 39th Congress; Acts of 40th Congress; Statistical; and Election Returns. Astronomy, Etc. included not only the Mohammedan Calendar and the Jewish Calendar, but the Positivist's Calendar—13 months, named Moses, Homer, Aristotle, Archimedes, Cesar, St. Paul, Charlemagne, Dante, "Guttemburg;" Shakspeare, Descartes, Frederick, and Bichat; and two holidays—"The Universal Festival of the Dead," and "The General Festival of Holy Women."

The Reconstruction section included the texts of the Reconstruction Act, the Proposed 14th Constitutional Amendment, Pres. Lincoln's Plan Towards Restoration, The Policy of Pres. Johnson, Action of the Southern States, and The Policy of Congress—Reconstruction vs. Restoration. Acts of Congress included The Destitute Soldier's Act, which "furnishes every invalid soldier, who is an inmate of any regularly constituted 'Soldiers Home,' with a complete suit of clothing." The Destitute Negroes Resolution appropriated $15,000 for relief in Washington, D.C.; the Suffering South Resolution authorized "distribution, through Freedmen's Bureau, of supplies of food to prevent starvation and want to 'all classes' of destitute people in the south where the crops have failed."

Statistics included National Debts, with the aggregate debt of the States estimated at $250 million; the debt of Britain and its Colonies, more than $4.5 billion; France, nearly $2.5 billion; Austria, nearly $1.3 million, and Russia more than $1.2 billion. Still territories rather than States were Washington, Colorado, Utah, Arizona, New Mexico, Idaho, Montana, "Dacotah," and the "Indian Territory," the last consisting of almost 70,000 miles. Many statistics on cotton, and the growth of other cereals were discussed. The tobacco crop was detailed. Religious Denominations in the U.S. were led by Roman Catholics, with 4 million communicants; Methodists, 2 million; and Baptists, 1.69 million. Freemasons and Odd Fellows were also counted.

Important Events in 1867 began with Napoleon's "very pacific speech to the Diplomatic Corps. on Jan. 1. Among the last, in November, were "Jeff Davis returns to Richmond," and "The Pope orders release of all captive Garibaldians."

Distinguished Dead included the Austrian Archduke Stephen; the chemist Michael Faraday in London; Mdme. Periani, singer, at Paris; the American humorist "Artemus Ward"; Ira Aldridge, "colored tragedian"; and Hiram Woodruff, "a celebrated turfman."

U.S. Government statistics include the salaries of Pres. Andrew Johnson—$25,000; his cabinet members, $8,000; Salmon P. Chase, Chief Justice of the U.S. Supreme Court, $6,500; and associate justices, $6,000. Salaries of governors of States and Territories ranged from $1,000 in Vermont, New Hampshire, and Rhode Island, to $7,000 in California.

Among the state-by-state Election Results of 1867, Kansas voted for Negro Suffrage, 19,421 to 10,483; and against Female Suffrage, by nearly the same numbers. Southern states listed voter registration in separate "white" and "colored" columns.

1893—100 Years Ago

Highlights of the 460-page 1893 *World Almanac* included ads for Storm King Whiskey and J. Rupper's Lager "Bier"; Quickline, the "antiseptic, antipyretic, antizymotic"; the Hoffman House Bouquet Cigar; Victor Colliau's Hot Blast Colliau Cupola; the Remington Typewriter; George Theiss & Bro. Billiard Parlor & Bowling Alleys; Glenn's Sulphur Soap; Winslow's Soothing Syrup, and Syrup of Figs; Otis Elevators; and the A.P.Q Paper Co.'s "Inexhaustible Roll of Toilet Paper."

The Principal Elements of the Solar System did *not* include Pluto. Labor legislation included 8-hour-workdays. "The American Hog" was a feature of the agricultural statistics. Under Naturalization Laws in the U.S., "The naturalization of Chinamen is expressly prohibited."

Losses due to fire were divided into people, horses, and cattle; electrical statistics into Western Union Telegraph, telephones, and electric railways. There were statistics on marriage, divorce, barrenness and illegitimacy; on pauperism, murders and hangings. The education section includes American College Cheers and information about fraternities, as well as the Universities of Great Britain and Ireland. "Famous Old People of 1893" were listed, as were Living Union and Living Confederate Generals. There was information on the British Empire, immigration into the U.S., the Cleveland administration, the City of New York, and Chicago. There were facts about the Bible, Shakespeare, spelling reform, whist, chess, and scientific progress. Sports covered included canoeing, lawn tennis, cricket, curling, bicycling, lacrosse, billiards, football, "weight-throwing sports," and "Pugilism."

1943—50 Years Ago

The 1943 *World Almanac* had 960 pages, and additional pages of advertisements. Many ads concerned World War II, or anticipated the postwar period, including the back-cover ad for the Berlitz School of Languages and the inside-cover ad headed "Language Is a Weapon": "In every branch of our war services, men who speak another language are gaining advancement. And when peace comes, in every part of the globe Americans will be in charge of reconstructing a war-ravaged world." Among other ads with a war or postwar theme were: "Field Marshall's War Map"; "25,000 Doctors Now in Uniform, Now—More Than Ever—You Should Know What to Do WHEN A SCREAM OF PAIN TERRIFIES YOUR HOME"; and "Inventors—Postwar America Will Need Your Ideas." Careers were a major concern, with home study emphasized: "High School at Home, May Finish in 2 Years"; "How I Became a Hotel Hostess"; "Get Into the Baking Business"; "Law Study at Home"; "Photography for Pleasure Or Profit"; "Be a Dietician!" Cures for medical, psychological, and social problems were also prominent; "If You Can Do This Step We Can Make You a Good Dancer in 6 Hours"; "Stammering—Its Causes and Corrections"; "Which of these Mistakes in English Do YOU Make?"; "Drunkenness Is a Disease"; "Don't Worry About Rupture"; and Charles Atlas's "Will You Let Me PROVE I Can Make You Into a NEW MAN?" False teeth were available for $7.95, eyeglasses for $2.95; 6 dresses for $2.95, "Cleaned, Pressed, and Ready to Wear."

World War II was featured in more than 100 pages, including a chronology that began Dec. 7, 1941; a "Review of Fighting in the Third Year"; many maps; information on casualties, rations, appropriations and expenditures, insignia; "High Ranking Commanders," and "Conditions in Occupied Countries." Brief features were headlined "Becomes War Widow Twice in 6 Months" and "Hitler's Income $12 Million."

The Nations section began with 19 pages on the British Empire. U.S. immigration took many pages, including "Amendments to Nationality Act," "Population by Race and Nativity," "Country of Birth of Foreign-Born Whites," "U.S. German-Italian-Spanish Mother Tongue Population," "Japanese Population Under U.S. Flag," and "Bulgarians, Hungarians, and Rumanians in the U.S."

Crimes included "Lynchings in the U.S. Since 1900." Other statistics included "Telephone Conversations and Telegrams by Country." "Leading Churches in the City of New York," and "Museums and Points of Interest in Chicago" were also printed. Awards included "Air Favorites of Radio Editors"; and "American Mother of the Year."

Sports events were highlighted by the St. Louis Cardinals winning the 1942 World Series over the New York Yankees; and by "Joe Louis & His Record in 57 Ring Contests." Sports statistics were also provided on intercollegiate rowing, polo, wrestling, and log-rolling.

Noted Personalities were divided into nationalities, the inclusion of Catherine the Great allowing for the headlines "Illustrious Men of Italy," but "Illustrious Men and Women of Russia." "Chief Operas" and "Noted Violinists" were listed.

1968—25 Years Ago

The 1968 *World Almanac* had 912 pages, sold for $2.95, $3.95 in the deluxe thumb-indexed edition. This 100th-anniversary volume included a Foreword by Pres. Lyndon B. Johnson, who wrote that: "The Almanac is more than a book of facts. It provides a concise history of man's thought, of his philosophical development from the Magna Carta to the United Nations. It clarifies the complexities of government, helps us to compute our income taxes, and presents a readable synopsis of the major events of the year." An article on "The Next 100 Years" by Isaac Asimov predicted a world population of 6 billion by 2000 (the 1992 population is 5.45 billion). Among Asimov's other predictions: "the computer as it develops steadily in the next century, will make the present division of the planet obsolete"; "as the planet becomes a computer-guided community, the sense of 'foreigner' will diminish"; "ghettos and slums will disappear as copious energy makes affluence possible for all and as computerized decisions modify conditions that would otherwise be brought about by irrational feelings of bigotry"; women, also because of computerization and energy abundance, would be "equal to man economically and socially in 2068."

The War in Vietnam received a great deal of attention, including publishing the names of Medal of Honor Winners and the text of the Selective Service Act of 1967. The 6-Day Arab-Israeli War was given prominence, as were racial violence and developments in medicine and space. The JFK assassination-conspiracy probe was noted, as was a new book on that assassination.

The U.S. Population was a major topic, including tables on Immigration; Marital Status of U.S. by States; Males Per 100 Females; Urban and Rural Population, by Color; and Negro Population in 25 Largest Cities.

Among the notable events of the year: Thurgood Marshall was sworn in as the first Negro on the U.S. Supreme Court; liberalized laws, allowing for therapeutic abortions, were being enacted in many states; in crime, counterfeiting was a major problem; color TV ownership was reaching "spectacular proportions," with 19.3% of the U.S. population owning a set, compared with 7.4% two years earlier.

Sports included billiards, shuffleboard, bridge, and checkers. Baseball's Rookies of the Year were Rod Carew and Tom Seaver; Bobby Hull lead the National Hockey League with 52 goals; the World Series winners, the St. Louis Cardinals, received $8,000 per player.

The Recordings section was headlined: "Beatles Break Bing Crosby Mark"; and Americans were found to own an estimated 40 million phonographs and record players, triple the number only 20 years earlier.

PRESIDENTIAL ELECTIONS

Popular and Electoral Vote, 1988 and 1992

Source: News Election Service; 1992 totals are preliminary

	1992						1988			
	Electoral Vote			Democrat	Republican	Ind.	Electoral Vote		Democrat	Republican
States	Clinton	Bush	Perot	Clinton	Bush	Perot	Dukakis	Bush	Dukakis	Bush
Ala.. .	0	9	0	686,146	797,477	180,209	0	9	549,506	815,576
Alas..	0	3	0	57,264	73,683	50,034	0	3	72,584	119,251
Ariz. .	0	8	0	521,736	543,876	339,307	0	7	454,029	702,541
Ark. .	6	0	0	495,150	331,867	97,549	0	6	349,237	466,578
Cal. .	54	0	0	4,812,317	3,338,942	2,144,856	0	47	4,702,233	5,054,917
Col. .	8	0	0	625,402	557,408	362,506	0	8	621,453	728,177
Conn.	8	0	0	681,081	574,738	348,028	0	8	676,584	750,241
Del. .	3	0	0	125,997	102,436	59,061	0	3	108,647	139,639
D.C. .	3	0	0	186,301	19,813	9,284	3	0	159,407	27,590
Fla.. .	0	25	0	2,051,205	2,131,263	1,040,953	0	21	1,655,851	2,616,597
Ga.. .	13	0	0	1,002,433	985,682	306,489	0	12	714,792	1,081,331
Ha.. .	4	0	0	178,893	136,430	52,863	4	0	192,364	158,625
Ida.. .	0	4	0	136,249	201,787	129,897	0	4	147,272	253,881
Ill.. . .	22	0	0	2,378,873	1,717,736	832,307	0	24	2,215,940	2,310,939
Ind.. .	0	12	0	839,227	978,627	451,858	0	12	860,643	1,297,763
Ia. . .	7	0	0	583,937	503,338	251,040	8	0	670,557	545,355
Kan. .	0	6	0	386,168	443,314	312,670	0	7	422,636	554,049
Ky.. .	8	0	0	661,059	617,419	203,587	0	9	580,368	734,281
La.. .	9	0	0	815,305	729,880	210,604	0	10	717,460	883,702
Me.. .	4	0	0	261,859	207,122	205,076	0	4	243,569	307,131
Md.. .	10	0	0	941,979	671,609	271,198	0	10	826,304	876,167
Mass.	12	0	0	1,315,016	803,974	630,440	13	0	1,401,415	1,194,635
Mich..	18	0	0	1,854,603	1,585,251	819,931	0	20	1,675,783	1,965,486
Minn..	10	0	0	994,843	734,845	549,517	10	0	1,109,471	962,337
Miss..	0	7	0	391,911	478,878	83,950	0	7	363,921	557,890
Mo.. .	11	0	0	1,051,328	810,058	517,918	0	11	1,001,619	1,084,953
Mon. .	3	0	0	153,899	143,702	106,735	0	4	168,936	190,412
Neb. .	0	5	0	214,106	338,646	171,938	0	5	259,235	397,956
Nev. .	4	0	0	185,401	171,378	129,532	0	4	132,738	206,040
N.H. .	4	0	0	207,264	199,623	120,029	0	4	163,696	281,537
N.J. .	15	0	0	1,361,088	1,303,686	504,152	0	16	1,317,541	1,740,604
N.M. .	5	0	0	255,558	209,467	90,653	0	5	244,497	270,341
N.Y. .	33	0	0	3,244,562	2,240,050	1,028,607	36	0	3,347,882	3,081,871
N.C. .	0	14	0	1,103,716	1,122,608	353,845	0	13	890,167	1,237,258
N.D. .	0	3	0	97,546	133,911	69,805	0	3	127,739	166,559
Oh.. .	21	0	0	1,964,842	1,876,445	1,024,319	0	23	1,939,629	2,416,549
Okla..	0	8	0	473,066	592,929	319,978	0	8	483,423	678,367
Ore. .	7	0	0	524,161	393,273	307,244	7	0	616,206	560,126
Pa.. .	23	0	0	2,223,810	1,777,372	895,563	0	25	2,194,944	2,300,087
R.I.. .	4	0	0	198,877	121,864	94,717	4	0	225,123	177,761
S.C. .	0	8	0	475,313	572,031	137,598	0	8	370,554	606,443
S.D. .	0	3	0	124,861	136,671	73,297	0	3	145,560	165,415
Tenn..	11	0	0	933,618	840,897	199,787	0	11	679,794	947,233
Tex. .	0	32	0	2,278,912	2,460,201	1,349,644	0	29	2,352,748	3,036,829
Ut. . .	0	5	0	182,590	320,462	202,578	0	5	207,352	428,442
Vt. . .	3	0	0	125,803	85,512	61,510	0	3	115,775	124,331
Va.. .	0	13	0	1,033,825	1,146,909	344,840	0	12	859,799	1,309,162
Wash.	11	0	0	855,710	609,912	470,239	10	0	933,516	903,835
W.Va.	5	0	0	324,009	236,526	105,652	5[1]	0	341,016	310,065
Wis. .	11	0	0	1,035,942	926,245	542,610	11	0	1,126,794	1,047,499
Wyo..	0	3	0	67,863	79,558	51,209	0	3	67,113	106,867
Total.	**370**	**168**	**0**	**43,682,624**	**38,117,331**	**19,217,213**	**111[1]**	**426**	**41,805,422**	**48,881,221**

(1) Lloyd Bentsen (D.-Tex.) received 1 electoral vote from W. Va.

Presidential Election Returns by Counties

All 1992 results are preliminary. Results for New England states are for selected cities or towns due to unavailability of county results. Totals are always statewide. In Alaska, individual election districts not available.

Source: News Election Service

Alabama

	1992			1988	
County	Clinton (D)	Bush (R)	Perot (I)	Dukakis (D)	Bush (R)
Autauga	4,819	8,715	1,916	3,667	7,828
Baldwin	12,071	26,257	7,712	9,271	25,933
Barbour	4,836	4,475	1,020	3,836	4,958
Bibb	2,900	3,124	686	2,244	2,885
Blount	5,433	8,882	1,949	4,485	8,754
Bullock	3,259	1,253	266	3,122	1,421
Butler	4,021	3,493	867	3,465	3,923
Calhoun	16,453	20,723	4,717	12,451	19,806
Chambers	5,938	5,682	1,427	5,103	7,694
Cherokee	4,222	2,745	846	3,176	2,868
Chilton	5,038	8,120	1,361	3,820	8,761
Choctaw	3,941	3,069	489	3,491	3,629
Clarke	5,021	5,461	259	4,217	5,708
Clay	1,954	2,837	621	1,602	3,496
Cleburne	2,144	2,425	630	1,383	3,071
Coffee	5,776	7,591	1,861	4,319	8,890
Colbert	12,208	8,073	2,098	10,397	7,775
Conecuh	3,155	2,463	542	3,022	3,256
Coosa	2,330	1,973	476	1,860	2,405
Covington	5,004	6,840	1,880	3,845	8,130
Crenshaw	2,404	2,339	485	1,836	2,617
Cullman	10,451	14,411	4,113	8,517	14,351
Dale	4,831	7,710	2,312	3,476	9,266
Dallas	11,053	7,394	1,110	9,660	7,630
DeKalb	8,245	10,519	2,741	7,333	11,478
Elmore	6,223	11,356	2,765	4,501	10,852
Escambia	4,790	5,896	1,636	4,020	6,807
Etowah	20,558	17,467	4,277	17,762	17,828
Fayette	3,830	3,604	1,012	3,186	4,338
Franklin	5,953	4,794	1,075	4,961	5,146
Geneva	3,622	4,843	1,323	2,685	5,703
Greene	3,865	805	194	3,295	1,048
Hale	3,481	2,001	486	3,187	2,414
Henry	2,804	2,970	667	2,206	3,613
Houston	8,851	17,332	3,490	7,001	19,989
Jackson	10,628	5,711	2,462	7,418	6,090
Jefferson	125,845	149,782	22,181	107,766	148,879
Lamar	2,849	3,262	763	2,274	3,214
Lauderdale	15,936	13,728	4,009	12,862	12,942
Lawrence	6,364	3,576	1,624	4,646	3,616
Lee	13,770	16,885	4,572	9,078	17,180
Limestone	8,063	9,849	3,583	5,455	9,086
Lowndes	3,500	1,328	284	3,328	1,405
Macon	7,253	1,134	283	6,351	1,304
Madison	37,415	48,128	15,905	25,800	53,575
Marengo	5,732	4,470	810	4,402	4,241
Marion	6,167	5,692	1,389	4,505	5,955
Marshall	10,421	12,249	3,753	7,357	12,148
Mobile	53,605	70,417	14,705	45,524	72,203
Monroe	3,671	4,815	739	3,509	5,379
Montgomery	37,342	40,842	7,427	28,709	41,131
Morgan	15,091	21,076	7,608	10,594	18,679
Perry	3,712	1,829	207	3,574	2,107
Pickens	3,783	3,634	690	3,107	3,851
Pike	4,688	5,423	1,024	3,813	5,897
Randolph	3,318	3,813	919	2,462	4,625
Russell	8,647	5,587	1,360	6,589	6,333
St. Clair	6,517	12,444	2,614	4,335	10,604
Shelby	10,268	32,455	4,995	7,138	27,052
Sumter	4,810	1,807	388	4,390	2,212
Talladega	10,338	12,513	2,515	8,291	12,973
Tallapoosa	5,703	8,140	1,562	4,598	8,502
Tuscaloosa	23,495	27,454	7,011	18,166	27,396
Walker	14,831	11,301	3,344	11,338	11,011
Washington	4,046	3,270	829	3,402	3,741
Wilcox	3,439	1,671	237	3,369	1,739
Winston	3,415	5,550	1,108	2,954	6,235
Totals	**686,146**	**797,477**	**180,209**	**549,506**	**815,576**

Alabama Vote Since 1940

1940, Roosevelt, Dem., 250,726; Willkie, Rep., 42,174; Babson, Proh., 698; Browder, Com., 509; Thomas, Soc., 100.

1944, Roosevelt, Dem., 198,918; Dewey, Rep., 44,540; Watson, Proh., 1,095; Thomas, Soc., 190.

1948, Thurmond, States' Rights, 171,443; Dewey, Rep., 40,930; Wallace, Prog., 1,522; Watson, Proh., 1,085.

1952, Eisenhower, Rep., 149,231; Stevenson, Dem., 275,075; Hamblen, Proh., 1,814.

1956, Stevenson, Dem., 290,844; Eisenhower, Rep. 195,694; Independent electors, 20,323.

1960, Kennedy, Dem., 324,050; Nixon, Rep., 237,981; Faubus, States' Rights, 4,367; Decker, Proh., 2,106; King, Afro-Americans, 1,485; scattering, 236.

1964, Dem. 209,848 (electors unpledged); Goldwater, Rep., 479,085; scattering, 105.

1968, Nixon, Rep., 146,923; Humphrey, Dem., 196,579; Wallace, 3d party, 691,425; Munn, Proh., 4,022.

1972, Nixon, Rep., 728,701; McGovern, Dem., 219,108 plus 37,815 Natl. Demo. Party of Alabama; Schmitz, Conservative, 11,918; Munn., Proh., 8,551.

1976, Carter, Dem., 659,170; Ford, Rep., 504,070; Maddox, Am. Ind., 9,198; Bubar, Proh., 6,669; Hall, Com., 1,954; MacBride, Libertarian, 1,481.

1980, Reagan, Rep., 654,192; Carter, Dem., 636,730; Anderson, Independent, 16,481; Rarick, Amer. Ind., 15,010; Clark, Libertarian, 13,318; Bubar, Statesman, 1,743; Hall, Com., 1,629; DeBerry, Soc. Work., 1,303; McReynolds, Socialist, 1,006; Commoner, Citizens, 517.

1984, Reagan, Rep., 872,849; Mondale, Dem., 551,899; Bergland, Libertarian, 9,504.

1988, Bush, Rep., 815,576; Dukakis, Dem., 549,506; Paul, Lib., 8,460; Fulani, Ind., 3,311.

Alaska

	1992			1988	
Election District	Clinton (D)	Bush (R)	Perot (I)	Dukakis (D)	Bush (R)
No. 1				3,167	4,564
No. 2				1,879	2,274
No. 3				1,884	2,313
No. 4				6,057	5,963
No. 5				3,696	6,874
No. 6				1,543	2,347
No. 7				2,088	3,806
No. 8				3,815	7,629
No. 9				3,980	6,876
No. 10				3,786	6,241
No. 11				2,590	3,189
No. 12				3,733	3,511
No. 13				2,643	4,968
No. 14				3,387	6,164
No. 15				3,726	8,949
No. 16				4,174	8,851
No. 17				1,302	3,093
No. 18				1,674	5,998
No. 19				2,737	4,485
No. 20				3,389	5,225
No. 21				2,816	3,127
No. 22				1,377	1,861
No. 23				1,390	1,898
No. 24				1,381	1,818
No. 25				1,430	1,611
No. 26				1,568	2,959
No. 27				1,372	2,657
Totals	**57,264**	**73,683**	**50,034**	**72,584**	**119,251**

Alaska Vote Since 1960

1960, Kennedy, Dem., 29,809; Nixon, Rep. 30,953.

1964, Johnson, Dem., 44,329; Goldwater, Rep., 22,930.

1968, Nixon, Rep., 37,600; Humphrey, Dem., 35,411; Wallace, 3d party, 10,024.

1972, Nixon, Rep., 55,349; McGovern, Dem., 32,967; Schmitz, American, 6,903.

1976, Carter, Dem., 44,058; Ford, Rep., 71,555; MacBride, Libertarian, 6,785.

1980, Reagan, Rep., 86,112; Carter, Dem., 41,842; Clark, Libertarian, 18,479; Anderson, Ind., 11,155; Write-in, 857.

1984, Reagan, Rep., 138,377; Mondale, Dem., 62,007; Bergland, Libertarian, 6,378.

1988, Bush, Rep., 119,251; Dukakis, Dem., 72,584; Paul, Lib., 5,484; Fulani, New. Alliance, 1,024.

Arizona

	1992			1988	
County	Clinton (D)	Bush (R)	Perot (I)	Dukakis (D)	Bush (R)
Apache	11,218	4,588	1,979	8,944	5,347
Cochise	12,701	12,202	7,857	11,812	15,815
Coconino	18,558	13,520	9,207	14,660	16,649
Gila	7,571	5,781	4,694	7,147	7,861
Graham	3,389	4,160	1,859	3,407	5,120
Greenlee	1,695	1,451	794	1,733	1,526
La Paz	1,808	1,599	1,488	1,746	2,562

Maricopa	275,513	341,870	212,019	230,952	442,337
Mohave	13,216	13,659	12,674	10,197	17,651
Navajo	10,882	7,994	4,787	9,023	10,393
Pima	122,461	93,107	51,735	113,824	117,899
Pinal	14,100	10,455	8,695	13,850	14,966
Santa Cruz	3,511	3,021	1,446	3,268	3,320
Yavapai	18,041	23,089	16,188	14,514	27,842
Yuma	7,072	7,380	3,885	8,952	13,253
Totals	**521,736**	**543,876**	**339,307**	**454,029**	**702,541**

Arizona Vote Since 1940

1940, Roosevelt, Dem., 95,267; Willkie, Rep., 54,030; Babson, Proh., 742.

1944, Roosevelt, Dem., 80,926; Dewey, Rep., 56,287; Watson, Proh., 421.

1948, Truman, Dem., 95,251; Dewey, Rep., 77,597; Wallace, Prog., 3,310; Watson, Proh., 786; Teichert, Soc. Labor, 121.

1952, Eisenhower, Rep., 152,042; Stevenson, Dem., 108,528.

1956, Eisenhower, Rep., 176,990; Stevenson, Dem., 112,880; Andrews, Ind. 303.

1960, Kennedy, Dem., 176,781; Nixon, Rep., 221,241; Hass, Soc. Labor, 469.

1964, Johnson, Dem., 237,753; Goldwater, Rep., 242,535; Hass, Soc. Labor, 482.

1968, Nixon, Rep., 266,721; Humphrey, Dem., 170,514; Wallace, 3d party, 46,573; McCarthy, New Party, 2,751; Halstead, Soc. Worker, 85; Cleaver, Peace and Freedom, 217; Blomen, Soc. Labor, 75.

1972, Nixon, Rep., 402,812; McGovern, Dem., 198,540; Schmitz, Amer., 21,208; Soc. Workers, 30,945. (Due to ballot peculiarities in 3 counties (particularly Pima), thousands of voters cast ballots for the Socialist Workers Party *and* one of the major candidates. Court ordered both votes counted as official.

1976, Carter, Dem., 295,602; Ford, Rep., 418,642; McCarthy, Ind., 19,229; MacBride, Libertarian, 7,647; Camejo, Soc. Workers, 928; Anderson, Amer., 564; Maddox, Am. Ind., 85.

1980, Reagan, Rep., 529,688; Carter, Dem., 246,843; Anderson, Ind., 76,952; Clark, Libertarian, 18,784; De Berry, Soc. Workers, 1,100; Commoner, Citizens, 551; Hall, Com., 25; Griswold, Workers World, 2.

1984, Reagan, Rep., 681,416; Mondale, Dem., 333,854; Bergland, Libertarian, 10,585.

1988, Bush, Rep., 702,541; Dukakis, Dem., 454,029; Paul, Lib., 13,351; Fulani, New Alliance, 1,662.

Arkansas

County	1992 Clinton (D)	1992 Bush (R)	1992 Perot (I)	1988 Dukakis (D)	1988 Bush (R)
Arkansas	4,709	2,594	639	3,075	4,007
Ashley	5,872	2,684	929	4,466	4,111
Baxter	6,991	5,640	2,938	4,808	8,614
Benton	15,765	21,116	6,124	9,399	24,295
Boone	6,125	6,094	2,078	3,998	7,567
Bradley	2,953	1,482	381	2,167	2,089
Calhoun	1,388	1,047	256	1,024	1,316
Carroll	3,765	3,534	1,499	2,632	4,553
Chicot	3,487	1,234	346	2,426	1,901
Clark	5,761	2,403	714	4,675	3,389
Clay	4,848	1,647	568	3,442	2,766
Cleburne	5,090	3,580	1,263	3,404	4,932
Cleveland	1,893	1,127	337	1,404	1,462
Columbia	4,740	3,699	1,089	3,706	5,810
Conway	5,013	2,803	827	4,134	4,066
Craighead	13,795	9,000	2,213	9,083	11,887
Crawford	6,651	6,879	2,440	3,582	9,092
Crittenden	8,590	5,507	808	6,702	7,441
Cross	4,058	2,302	602	2,989	3,186
Dallas	2,107	1,458	342	1,990	1,947
Desha	3,815	1,279	392	2,859	2,334
Drew	3,747	1,938	596	2,578	2,995
Faulkner	12,130	8,928	2,274	7,302	10,678
Franklin	3,217	2,495	987	2,458	3,588
Fulton	2,827	1,258	631	2,018	1,918
Garland	18,803	12,821	3,474	11,406	19,281
Grant	3,190	2,272	702	2,142	2,717
Greene	7,541	3,510	1,213	5,065	5,161
Hempstead	5,474	2,387	1,022	3,841	3,938
Hot Spring	6,306	3,034	1,208	5,090	4,181
Howard	2,782	1,727	466	1,818	2,510
Independence	6,989	4,170	1,413	4,523	6,637
Izard	1,956	798	335	2,652	2,824
Jackson	4,944	1,864	673	4,199	3,049
Jefferson	21,505	7,360	2,049	16,664	12,520
Johnson	3,939	2,524	990	2,818	4,046
Lafayette	2,273	1,188	504	1,915	1,860
Lawrence	4,146	2,124	636	3,179	3,205
Lee	3,434	1,293	308	2,878	1,863
Lincoln	2,805	1,142	390	2,204	1,557
Little River	3,326	1,483	890	2,740	2,347
Logan	3,995	3,408	1,220	1,254	2,203
Lonoke	8,030	6,300	1,564	4,786	7,215
Madison	2,413	2,236	547	2,106	3,067
Marion	2,755	2,022	1,327	2,033	2,993
Miller	7,045	5,271	2,247	5,437	7,110
Mississippi	10,042	4,696	981	6,759	7,841
Monroe	2,578	1,325	355	2,052	1,862
Montgomery	1,904	1,205	576	1,362	1,752
Nevada	2,242	1,217	455	1,732	1,714
Newton	1,765	1,730	608	1,489	2,504
Ouachita	7,420	3,737	1,460	5,229	6,297
Perry	1,906	1,162	411	1,470	1,627
Phillips	6,439	2,689	628	5,580	3,892
Pike	2,167	1,577	477	1,681	2,105
Poinsett	5,338	2,425	761	3,873	3,644
Polk	3,160	2,757	1,225	2,390	4,099
Pope	7,444	7,860	1,933	4,941	10,084
Prairie	1,420	821	220	1,688	1,947
Pulaski	74,530	44,995	7,933	55,857	70,562
Randolph	3,921	1,766	578	2,781	2,560
St. Francis	6,005	2,967	712	4,656	4,298
Saline	12,670	10,102	2,751	8,436	12,353
Scott	2,228	1,695	610	1,707	2,507
Searcy	1,679	2,012	505	1,340	2,743
Sebastian	16,565	16,812	6,022	9,684	24,426
Sevier	2,558	1,592	643	2,037	2,254
Sharp	3,761	2,486	921	2,955	3,623
Stone	2,622	1,672	697	1,728	2,186
Union	8,768	7,302	1,914	5,931	10,581
Van Buren	3,795	2,608	888	2,607	3,562
Washington	22,011	20,282	5,302	12,557	23,601
White	10,493	8,535	2,365	6,957	11,094
Woodruff	2,589	674	227	1,924	1,097
Yell	4,162	2,504	940	2,763	3,535
Totals	**495,150**	**331,867**	**97,549**	**349,237**	**466,578**

Arkansas Vote Since 1940

1940, Roosevelt, Dem., 158,622; Willkie, Rep., 42,121; Babson, Proh., 793; Thomas, Soc., 305.

1944, Roosevelt, Dem., 148,965; Dewey, Rep., 63,551; Thomas, Soc. 438.

1948, Truman, Dem., 149,659; Dewey, Rep., 50,959; Thurmond, States' Rights, 40,068; Thomas, Soc., 1,037; Wallace, Prog., 751; Watson, Proh., 1.

1952, Eisenhower, Rep., 177,155; Stevenson, Dem., 226,300; Hamblen, Proh., 886; MacArthur, Christian Nationalist, 458; Hass, Soc. Labor, 1.

1956, Stevenson, Dem., 213,277; Eisenhower, Rep., 186,287; Andrews, Ind., 7,008.

1960, Kennedy, Dem., 215,049; Nixon, Rep., 184,508; Nat'l. States' Rights, 28,952.

1964, Johnson, Dem., 314,197; Goldwater, Rep., 243,264; Kasper, Nat'l. States Rights, 2,965.

1968, Nixon, Rep., 189,062; Humphrey, Dem., 184,901; Wallace, 3d party, 235,627.

1972, Nixon, Rep., 445,751; McGovern, Dem., 198,899; Schmitz, Amer. , 3,016.

1976, Carter, Dem., 498,604; Ford, Rep., 267,903; McCarthy, Ind., 639; Anderson, Amer., 389.

1980, Reagan, Rep., 403,164; Carter, Dem., 398,041; Anderson, Ind., 22,468; Clark, Libertarian, 8,970; Commoner, Citizens, 2,345; Bubar, Statesman, 1,350; Hall, Comm., 1,244.

1984, Reagan, Rep., 534,774; Mondale, Dem., 338,646; Bergland, Libertarian, 2,220.

1988, Bush, Rep., 466,578; Dukakis, Dem., 349,237; Duke, Chr. Pop., 5,146; Paul, Lib., 3,297.

California

County	1992 Clinton (D)	1992 Bush (R)	1992 Perot (I)	1988 Dukakis (D)	1988 Bush (R)
Alameda	314,761	100,574	77,105	310,283	162,815
Alpine	215	222	186	230	308
Amador	5,105	5,273	4,393	5,197	6,893
Butte	31,621	30,470	19,518	30,406	40,143
Calaveras	1,721	1,504	1,323	5,674	7,640
Colusa	1,785	2,573	1,196	2,022	3,077
Contra Costa	187,993	106,998	69,399	169,411	158,652
Del Norte	3,627	3,073	2,571	3,587	3,714
El Dorado	19,639	23,948	16,363	19,801	30,021
Fresno	85,164	80,575	33,467	92,635	94,835
Glenn	2,666	3,812	2,278	2,894	4,944
Humboldt	26,625	16,430	11,373	29,781	21,460
Imperial	10,960	9,530	4,168	10,243	12,889
Inyo	2,597	3,544	1,912	2,653	5,042
Kern	55,244	73,532	34,017	55,083	90,550

Kings	9,603	10,292	4,705	9,142	12,118
Lake	10,258	6,492	5,644	9,828	9,366
Lassen	3,330	3,741	2,927	3,446	5,157
Los Angeles	1,358,969	729,284	456,887	1,372,352	1,239,716
Madera	10,704	12,884	6,045	10,642	13,255
Marin	71,605	28,144	21,404	69,394	46,855
Mariposa	2,954	2,918	2,155	2,998	3,768
Mendocino	18,097	7,828	9,608	17,152	12,979
Merced	19,890	17,715	10,780	20,105	21,717
Modoc	1,485	1,802	1,269	1,416	2,518
Mono	1,470	1,550	1,224	1,284	2,177
Monterey	51,961	34,200	22,955	48,998	50,022
Napa	23,055	14,620	12,462	22,283	23,235
Nevada	14,213	15,843	10,232	14,980	21,383
Orange	286,003	392,450	218,108	269,013	586,230
Placer	28,002	34,048	19,720	27,516	42,096
Plumas	3,740	3,597	2,546	4,251	4,603
Riverside	156,905	146,642	95,204	133,122	199,979
Sacramento	188,663	150,755	87,180	188,557	201,832
San Benito	5,219	4,028	3,107	4,559	5,578
San Bernardino	179,159	171,038	105,929	151,118	235,167
San Diego	337,227	314,314	234,444	333,264	523,143
San Francisco	222,047	53,545	27,399	201,887	72,503
San Joaquin	57,287	50,017	27,945	61,699	75,309
San Luis Obispo	38,162	33,879	25,593	35,667	46,613
San Mateo	138,261	68,414	46,652	141,859	109,261
Santa Barbara	64,659	51,721	32,217	63,586	77,524
Santa Clara	276,391	155,984	120,128	277,810	254,442
Santa Cruz	61,084	22,596	19,680	63,133	37,728
Shasta	20,969	27,269	17,491	21,171	32,402
Sierra	653	691	519	791	860
Siskiyou	8,254	6,660	5,567	8,365	9,056
Solano	62,051	37,113	26,772	54,344	50,314
Sonoma	97,207	43,381	40,557	91,262	67,725
Stanislaus	46,065	40,447	24,413	44,685	51,648
Sutter	7,741	12,662	4,800	6,557	14,100
Tehama	7,431	7,322	5,817	7,213	9,854
Trinity	1,920	1,845	2,048	2,518	3,267
Tulare	30,170	38,982	15,788	30,711	46,891
Tuolumne	8,865	8,146	6,044	8,717	10,646
Ventura	93,920	88,550	67,672	89,065	147,604
Yolo	31,303	16,338	10,425	30,429	22,358
Yuba	5,642	7,137	3,525	5,444	8,937
Totals	**4,812,317**	**3,338,942**	**2,144,856**	**4,702,233**	**5,054,917**

California Vote Since 1940

1940, Roosevelt, Dem., 1,877,618; Willkie, Rep., 1,351,419; Thomas, Prog., 16,506; Browder, Com., 13,586; Babson, Proh., 9,400.

1944, Roosevelt, Dem., 1,988,564; Dewey, Rep., 1,512,965; Watson, Proh., 14,770; Thomas, Soc., 3,923; Teichert, Soc. Labor, 327.

1948, Truman, Dem., 1,913,134; Dewey, Rep., 1,895,269; Wallace, Prog., 190,381; Watson, Proh., 16,926; Thomas, Soc., 3,459; Thurmond, States' Rights, 1,228; Teichert, Soc. Labor, 195; Dobbs, Soc. Workers, 133.

1952, Eisenhower, Rep., 2,897,310; Stevenson, Dem., 2,197,548; Hallinan, Prog., 24,106; Hamblen, Proh., 15,653; MacArthur, (Tenny Ticket), 3,326; (Kellems Ticket) 178; Hass, Soc. Labor, 273; Hoopes, Soc., 206; scattered, 3,249.

1956, Eisenhower, Rep., 3,027,668; Stevenson, Dem., 2,420,136; Holtwick, Proh., 11,119; Andrews, Constitution, 6,087; Hass, Soc. Labor, 300; Hoopes, Soc., 123; Dobbs, Soc. Workers, 96; Smith, Christian Nat'l., 8.

1960, Kennedy, Dem., 3,224,099; Nixon, Rep., 3,259,722; Decker, Proh., 21,706; Hass, Soc. Labor, 1,051.

1964, Johnson, Dem., 4,171,877; Goldwater, Rep., 2,879,108; Hass, Soc. Labor, 489; DeBerry, Soc. Worker, 378; Munn, Proh., 305; Hensley, Universal, 19.

1968, Nixon, Rep., 3,467,664; Humphrey, Dem., 3,244,318; Wallace, 3d party, 487,270; Peace and Freedom party, 27,707; McCarthy, Alternative, 20,721; Gregory, write-in, 3,230; Mitchell, Com., 260; Munn, Proh., 59; Blomen, Soc. Labor, 341; Soeters, Defense, 17.

1972, Nixon, Rep., 4,602,096; McGovern, Dem., 3,475,847; Schmitz, Amer., 232,554; Spock, Peace and Freedom, 55,167; Hall, Com., 373; Hospers, Libertarian, 980; Munn, Proh., 53; Fisher, Soc. Labor, 197; Jenness, Soc. Workers, 574; Green, Universal, 21.

1976, Carter, Dem., 3,742,284; Ford, Rep., 3,882,244; MacBride, Libertarian, 56,388; Maddox, Am. Ind., 51,098; Wright, People's, 41,731; Camejo, Soc. Workers, 17,259; Hall, Com., 12,766; write-in, McCarthy, 58,412; other write-in, 4,935.

1980, Reagan, Rep. 4,524,858; Carter, Dem., 3,083,661; Anderson, Ind., 739,833; Clark, Libertarian, 148,434; Commoner, Ind. 61,063; Smith, Peace & Freedom, 18,116; Rarick, Amer. Ind., 9,856.

1984, Reagan, Rep. 5,305,410; Mondale, Dem., 3,815,947; Bergland, Libertarian, 48,400.

1988, Bush, Rep., 5,054,917; Dukakis, Dem., 4,702,233; Paul, Lib., 70,105; Fulani, Ind., 31,181.

Colorado

	1992			1988	
County	Clinton (D)	Bush (R)	Perot (I)	Dukakis (D)	Bush (R)
Adams	45,357	30,856	26,379	49,464	43,163
Alamosa	2,285	1,880	1,281	2,146	2,567
Arapahoe	65,995	71,354	44,001	61,113	95,926
Archuleta	815	1,239	740	795	1,440
Baca	726	1,240	647	851	1,670
Bent	985	759	506	1,088	1,032
Boulder	64,567	33,553	27,762	57,265	48,174
Chaffee	2,284	2,419	1,549	2,548	3,080
Cheyenne	301	616	292	399	760
Clear Creek	1,744	1,356	1,308	1,698	1,820
Conejos	1,705	1,160	578	1,976	1,445
Costilla	1,180	366	199	1,120	454
Crowley	570	602	276	630	862
Custer	343	651	368	310	753
Delta	3,399	4,329	2,617	3,521	5,449
Denver	121,938	55,679	36,779	127,173	77,753
Dolores	242	315	285	230	488
Douglas	7,256	14,021	9,032	6,931	17,035
Eagle	3,869	3,100	3,821	3,314	4,366
Elbert	1,237	2,205	1,567	1,566	2,805
El Paso	45,822	86,037	34,342	39,995	96,965
Fremont	5,366	5,961	3,709	5,278	7,623
Garfield	5,082	4,404	4,408	4,620	6,358
Gilpin	726	462	545	804	728
Grand	1,678	1,763	1,454	1,451	2,306
Gunnison	2,362	1,643	1,657	1,897	2,520
Hinsdale	151	188	136	111	295
Huerfano	1,224	685	385	1,876	1,079
Jackson	216	422	326	294	584
Jefferson	80,834	82,705	58,404	81,824	110,820
Kiowa	295	472	267	398	645
Kit Carson	925	1,801	919	1,196	2,262
Lake	1,426	605	863	1,516	969
La Plata	5,913	5,522	4,083	5,443	7,714
Larimer	38,232	35,995	24,879	35,703	45,967
Las Animas	3,847	1,739	953	4,075	2,162
Lincoln	645	1,084	586	874	1,356
Logan	2,718	3,420	2,184	3,382	4,485
Mesa	15,162	18,169	10,474	14,372	22,150
Mineral	171	159	117	174	217
Moffat	1,386	1,809	1,875	1,634	2,757
Montezuma	2,270	3,123	2,205	2,233	4,208
Montrose	3,668	4,792	3,062	3,748	6,012
Morgan	2,985	3,724	2,175	3,728	4,795
Otero	3,485	3,120	1,590	3,910	4,265
Ouray	461	655	466	439	814
Park	1,307	1,530	1,396	1,343	1,909
Philips	692	1,075	525	923	1,317
Pitkin	3,820	1,686	1,907	3,420	2,801
Prowers	1,770	2,370	1,184	2,207	2,978
Pueblo	30,261	16,120	9,841	32,788	20,119
Rio Blanco	778	1,231	794	803	1,821
Rio Grande	1,541	1,927	1,043	1,545	2,626
Routt	3,134	2,317	2,528	2,922	3,264
Saguache	662	539	389	1,033	945
San Juan	147	118	187	192	210
San Miguel	604	338	285	961	798
Sedgwick	397	447	295	611	921
Summit	3,344	2,256	2,715	2,595	2,893
Teller	1,873	3,050	1,927	1,656	3,760
Washington	660	1,268	671	958	1,707
Weld	19,295	20,958	13,571	20,548	26,497
Yuma	1,269	2,019	1,197	1,835	2,513
Total	**625,402**	**557,408**	**362,506**	**621,453**	**728,177**

Colorado Vote Since 1940

1940, Roosevelt, Dem., 265,554; Willkie, Rep., 279,576; Thomas, Soc., 1,899; Babson, Proh., 1,597; Browder, Com., 378.

1944, Roosevelt, Dem., 234,331; Dewey, Rep., 268,731; Thomas, Soc., 1,977.

1948, Truman, Dem., 267,288; Dewey, Rep., 239,714; Wallace, Prog., 6,115; Thomas, Soc., 1,678; Dobbs, Soc. Workers, 228; Teichert, Soc. Labor, 214.

1952, Eisenhower, Rep., 379,782; Stevenson, Dem., 245,504; MacArthur, Constitution, 2,181; Hallinan, Prog., 1,919; Hoopes, Soc., 365; Hass, Soc. Labor, 352.

1956, Eisenhower, Rep., 394,479; Stevenson, Dem., 263,997; Hass, Soc. Lab., 3,308; Andrews, Ind., 759; Hoopes, Soc., 531.

1960, Kennedy, Dem., 330,629; Nixon, Rep., 402,242; Hass, Soc. Labor, 2,803; Dobbs, Soc. Workers, 572.

1964, Johnson, Dem., 476,024; Goldwater, Rep., 296,767; Hass, Soc. Labor, 302; DeBerry, Soc. Worker, 2,537; Munn, Proh., 1,356.

1968, Nixon, Rep., 409,345; Humphrey, Dem., 335,174; Wallace, 3d party, 60,813; Blomen, Soc. Labor, 3,016; Gregory, New-party, 1,393; Munn, Proh., 275; Halstead, Soc. Worker, 235.

1972, Nixon, Rep., 597,189; McGovern, Dem., 329,980; Fisher, Soc. Labor, 4,361; Hospers, Libertarian, 1,111; Hall, Com., 432; Jenness, Soc. Workers, 555; Munn, Proh., 467; Schmitz, Amer., 17,269; Spock, Peoples, 2,403.

1976, Carter, Dem., 460,353; Ford, Rep., 584,367; McCarthy, Ind., 26,107; MacBride, Libertarian, 5,330; Bubar, Proh., 2,882.

1980, Reagan, Rep., 652,264; Carter, Dem., 367,973; Anderson, Ind., 130,633; Clark, Libertarian, 25,744; Commoner, Citizens, 5,614; Bubar, Statesman, 1,180; Pulley, Socialist, 520; Hall, Com., 487.

1984, Reagan, Rep., 821,817; Mondale, Dem., 454,975; Bergland, Libertarian, 11,257.

1988, Bush, Rep., 728,177; Dukakis, Dem., 621,453; Paul, Lib., 15,482; Dodge, Proh., 4,604.

Connecticut

	1992			1988	
County	Clinton (D)	Bush (R)	Perot (I)	Dukakis (D)	Bush (R)
Bridgeport	22,321	13,149	6,263	23,831	17,084
Hartford	26,970	6,180	3,390	27,295	8,100
New Britain	14,159	7,040	4,983	15,843	9,569
New Haven	29,774	8,931	4,130	31,951	11,616
Norwalk	16,488	14,743	6,046	14,518	18,618
Stamford	23,185	19,809	6,763	20,773	24,877
Waterbury	17,181	15,115	9,578	18,202	20,018
West Hartford	19,623	12,266	5,017	19,311	16,482
Totals	**681,081**	**574,738**	**348,028**	**676,584**	**750,241**

Connecticut Vote Since 1940

1940, Roosevelt, Dem., 417,621; Willkie, Rep., 361,021; Browder, Com., 1,091; Aiken, Soc. Labor, 971; Willkie, Union, 798.

1944, Roosevelt, Dem., 435,146; Dewey, Rep., 390,527; Thomas, Soc., 5,097; Teichert, Soc. Labor, 1,220.

1948, Truman, Dem., 423,297; Dewey, Rep., 437,754; Wallace, Prog., 13,713; Thomas, Soc., 6,964; Teichert, Soc. Labor, 1,184; Dobbs, Soc. Workers, 606.

1952, Eisenhower, Rep., 611,012; Stevenson, Dem., 481,649; Hoopes, Soc., 2,244; Hallinan, Peoples, 1,466; Hass, Soc. Labor, 535; write-in, 5.

1956, Eisenhower, Rep., 711,837; Stevenson, Dem., 405,079; scattered, 205.

1960, Kennedy, Dem., 657,055; Nixon, Rep., 565,813.

1964, Johnson, Dem., 826,269; Goldwater, Rep., 390,996; scattered, 1,313.

1968, Nixon, Rep., 556,721; Humphrey, Dem., 621,561; Wallace, 3d party, 76,650; scattered, 1,300.

1972, Nixon, Rep., 810,763; McGovern, Dem., 555,498; Schmitz, Amer., 17,239; scattered, 777.

1976, Carter, Dem., 647,895; Ford, Rep., 719,261; Maddox, George Wallace Party, 7,101; LaRouche, U.S. Labor, 1,789.

1980, Reagan, Rep., 677,210; Carter, Dem., 541,732; Anderson, Ind., 171,807; Clark, Libertarian, 8,570; Commoner, Citizens, 6,130; scattered, 836.

1984, Reagan, Rep., 890,877; Mondale, Dem., 569,597.

1988, Bush, Rep., 750,241; Dukakis, Dem., 676,584; Paul, Lib., 14,071; Fulani; New Alliance, 2,491.

Delaware

	1992			1988	
County	Clinton (D)	Bush (R)	Perot (I)	Dukakis (D)	Bush (R)
Kent	15,273	15,571	8,829	12,996	19,923
New Castle	91,551	66,423	37,518	79,147	92,587
Sussex	19,173	20,442	12,714	16,504	27,129
Totals	**125,997**	**102,436**	**59,061**	**108,647**	**139,639**

Delaware Vote Since 1940

1940, Roosevelt, Dem., 74,559; Willkie, Rep., 61,440; Babson, Proh., 220; Thomas, Soc., 115.

1944, Roosevelt, Dem., 68,166; Dewey, Rep., 56,747; Watson, Proh., 294; Thomas, Soc., 154.

1948, Truman, Dem., 67,813; Dewey, Rep., 69,688; Wallace, Prog., 1,050; Watson, Proh., 343; Thomas, Soc., 250; Teichert, Soc. Labor, 29.

1952, Eisenhower, Rep., 90,059; Stevenson, Dem., 83,315; Hass, Soc. Labor, 242; Hamblen, Proh., 234; Hallinan, Prog., 155; Hoopes, Soc., 20.

1956, Eisenhower, Rep., 98,057; Stevenson, Dem., 79,421; Oltwick, Proh., 400; Hass, Soc. Labor, 110.

1960, Kennedy, Dem., 99,590; Nixon, Rep., 96,373; Faubus, States' Rights, 354; Decker, Proh., 284; Hass, Soc. Labor, 82.

1964, Johnson, Dem., 122,704; Goldwater, Rep., 78,078; Hass, Soc. Labor, 113; Munn, Proh., 425.

1968, Nixon, Rep., 96,714; Humphrey, Dem., 89,194; Wallace, 3d party, 28,459.

1972, Nixon, Rep., 140,357; McGovern, Dem., 92,283; Schmitz, Amer., 2,638; Munn, Proh., 238.

1976, Carter, Dem., 122,596; Ford, Rep., 109,831; McCarthy, non-partisan, 2,437; Anderson, Amer., 645; LaRouche, U.S. Labor, 136; Bubar, Proh., 103; Levin, Soc. Labor, 86.

1980, Reagan, Rep., 111,252; Carter, Dem., 105,754; Anderson, Ind., 16,288; Clark, Libertarian, 1,974; Greaves, American, 400.

1984, Reagan, Rep., 152,190; Mondale, Dem., 101,656; Bergland, Libertarian, 268.

1988, Bush, Rep., 139,639; Dukakis, Dem., 108,647; Paul, Lib., 1,162; Fulani, New Alliance, 443.

District of Columbia

	1992			1988	
County	Clinton (D)	Bush (R)	Perot (I)	Dukakis (D)	Bush (R)
Totals	**186,301**	**19,813**	**9,284**	**159,407**	**27,590**

District of Columbia Vote Since 1964

1964, Johnson, Dem., 169,796; Goldwater, Rep., 28,801.

1968, Nixon, Rep., 31,012; Humphrey, Dem., 139,566.

1972, Nixon, Rep., 35,226; McGovern, Dem., 127,627; Reed, Soc. Workers, 316; Hall, Com., 252.

1976, Carter, Dem., 137,818; Ford, Rep., 27,873; Camejo, Soc. Workers, 545; MacBride, Libertarian, 274; Hall, Com., 219; LaRouche, U.S. Labor, 157.

1980, Reagan, Rep., 23,313; Carter, Dem., 130,231; Anderson, Ind., 16,131; Commoner, Citizens, 1,826; Clark, Libertarian, 1,104; Hall, Com., 369; De Berry, Soc. Work., 173; Griswold, Workers World, 52; write-ins, 690.

1984, Mondale, Dem., 180,408; Reagan, Rep., 29,009; Bergland, Libertarian, 279.

1988, Bush, Rep., 27,590; Dukakis, Dem., 159,407; Fulani, New Alliance, 2,901; Paul, Lib., 554.

Florida

	1992			1988	
County	Clinton (D)	Bush (R)	Perot (I)	Dukakis (D)	Bush (R)
Alachua	37,876	22,806	15,293	29,375	30,124
Baker	1,974	3,417	1,315	1,353	3,414
Bay	11,233	19,155	8,505	11,582	31,712
Bradford	3,040	3,671	1,572	2,386	4,218
Brevard	61,010	84,486	49,440	42,967	104,721
Broward	276,110	164,612	90,876	218,211	220,196
Calhoun	1,516	1,564	1,100	1,329	2,420
Charlotte	22,862	23,966	14,540	15,967	28,879
Citrus	15,935	16,402	12,310	12,177	21,052
Clay	10,597	26,313	8,414	7,766	25,882
Collier	18,794	38,447	14,514	12,768	38,910
Columbia	5,477	6,420	2,893	4,072	7,759
Dade	254,444	235,149	53,957	216,847	270,672
De Soto	2,646	3,070	1,687	2,181	4,237
Dixie	1,855	1,401	1,094	1,366	2,027
Duval	85,387	110,839	30,207	74,832	127,875
Escambia	28,353	43,060	16,597	29,934	64,774
Flagler	6,692	6,241	3,387	4,241	6,494
Franklin	1,534	1,660	1,143	1,283	1,911
Gadsden	7,924	3,585	1,727	6,368	5,987
Gilchrist	1,511	1,395	1,090	1,137	1,854
Glades	1,305	1,185	878	1,034	1,546
Gulf	1,938	2,650	1,245	1,687	3,040
Hamilton	1,622	1,402	695	1,314	2,062
Hardee	2,017	2,898	1,498	1,688	3,636
Hendry	2,690	3,279	2,032	2,036	3,962
Hernando	19,171	17,896	11,845	15,432	21,179
Highlands	11,234	14,497	6,702	8,087	16,713
Hillsborough	115,094	130,383	62,968	98,969	150,065
Holmes	1,683	2,927	1,339	1,639	4,221

Indian River	12,359	19,137	12,375	10,447	24,619
Jackson	5,481	6,720	2,447	5,002	8,392
Jefferson	2,270	1,506	894	2,055	2,326
Lafayette	866	1,037	612	722	1,450
Lake	23,176	30,790	15,594	16,762	37,314
Lee	53,656	73,423	38,446	40,709	87,247
Leon	42,613	27,744	15,438	33,446	36,032
Levy	4,330	3,796	2,784	3,433	5,250
Liberty	820	1,126	617	709	1,419
Madison	2,200	1,715	997	1,950	2,556
Manatee	33,826	42,708	23,282	26,618	51,160
Marion	30,823	35,438	20,524	20,679	41,488
Martin	14,772	24,368	13,433	11,486	31,270
Monroe	10,435	9,891	8,306	10,151	15,919
Nassau	3,807	5,632	2,101	4,138	8,366
Okaloosa	12,003	32,755	16,469	9,726	40,295
Okeechobee	3,418	3,298	2,645	3,007	4,733
Orange	82,024	107,940	44,487	53,991	117,141
Osceola	15,009	19,139	11,021	9,811	21,350
Palm Beach	187,754	140,193	76,167	144,143	181,408
Pasco	53,125	47,722	34,650	50,369	63,788
Pinellas	159,628	153,122	100,748	152,374	210,971
Polk	53,255	68,884	29,093	38,236	77,065
Putnam	10,707	8,909	5,975	8,569	11,621
St. Johns	12,284	20,172	7,396	7,999	19,164
St. Lucie	23,873	24,397	19,813	17,427	32,241
Santa Rosa	6,525	17,184	8,734	5,251	18,948
Sarasota	54,536	66,831	34,281	42,095	84,585
Seminole	35,649	57,085	24,477	22,627	60,328
Sumter	5,027	4,366	2,901	3,900	5,933
Suwannee	3,985	4,570	2,790	3,126	5,859
Taylor	2,568	2,693	1,929	1,762	4,054
Union	1,247	1,543	770	691	1,643
Volusia	65,213	59,155	30,813	55,437	74,116
Wakulla	2,319	2,586	1,790	1,605	3,157
Walton	3,886	5,719	3,886	3,231	7,481
Washington	2,212	3,193	1,405	2,139	4,366
Totals	**2,051,205**	**2,131,263**	**1,040,953**	**1,655,851**	**2,616,597**

Florida Vote Since 1940

1940, Roosevelt, Dem., 359,334; Willkie, Rep., 126,158.

1944, Roosevelt, Dem., 339,377; Dewey, Rep., 143,215.

1948, Truman, Dem., 281,988; Dewey, Rep., 194,280; Thurmond, States' Rights, 89,755; Wallace, Prog., 11,620.

1952, Eisenhower, Rep., 544,036; Stevenson, Dem., 444,950; scattered, 351.

1956, Eisenhower, Rep., 643,849; Stevenson, Dem., 480,371.

1960, Kennedy, Dem., 748,700; Nixon, Rep., 795,476.

1964, Johnson, Dem., 948,540; Goldwater, Rep., 905,941.

1968, Nixon, Rep., 886,804; Humphrey, Dem., 676,794; Wallace, 3d party, 624,207.

1972, Nixon, Rep., 1,857,759; McGovern, Dem., 718,117; scattered, 7,407.

1976, Carter, Dem., 1,636,000; Ford, Rep., 1,469,531; McCarthy, Ind., 23,643; Anderson, Amer., 21,325.

1980, Reagan, Rep., 2,046,951; Carter, Dem., 1,419,475; Anderson, Ind., 189,692; Clark, Libertarian, 30,524; write-ins, 285.

1984, Reagan, Rep., 2,728,775; Mondale, Dem., 1,448,344.

1988, Bush, Rep., 2,616,597; Dukakis, Dem., 1,655,851; Paul, Lib., 19,796, Fulani, New Alliance, 6,655.

Georgia

	1992			1988	
County	Clinton (D)	Bush (R)	Perot (I)	Dukakis (D)	Bush (R)
Appling	2,238	2,331	1,035	1,837	3,000
Atkinson	1,056	779	342	887	1,126
Bacon	1,423	1,301	604	780	1,407
Baker	864	421	210	707	629
Baldwin	5,813	4,262	1,679	4,008	5,852
Banks	1,530	1,551	583	984	1,590
Barrow	3,991	4,328	1,633	2,442	4,738
Bartow	6,675	7,742	2,500	4,884	8,039
Ben Hill	2,348	1,476	479	1,867	2,005
Berrien	2,103	1,637	796	1,381	2,030
Bibb	28,070	19,847	6,021	22,084	22,179
Bleckley	1,710	1,570	662	1,175	1,950
Brantley	1,883	1,541	840	1,450	1,539
Brooks	1,895	1,779	630	1,500	2,136
Bryan	1,823	2,595	1,053	1,423	2,802
Bulloch	4,903	5,690	2,020	3,417	6,354
Burke	3,647	2,390	672	2,861	2,988
Butts	2,448	1,768	619	1,730	2,184
Calhoun	1,301	464	248	901	644
Camden	2,952	3,517	1,077	2,090	2,913
Candler	1,192	1,014	541	877	1,261
Carroll	8,404	10,750	3,358	4,706	10,754
Catoosa	4,817	7,599	2,290	3,588	9,319
Charlton	1,127	1,332	427	943	1,327
Chatham	29,273	28,014	7,274	25,063	35,623
Chattahoochee	604	413	177	362	454
Chattooga	2,975	2,439	965	2,206	3,665
Cherokee	8,116	16,054	4,950	4,378	14,593
Clarke	15,403	10,459	2,986	11,154	11,150
Clay	778	264	155	595	398
Clayton	25,890	23,963	7,942	14,689	28,225
Clinch	759	790	286	594	863
Cobb	63,909	103,689	28,739	39,297	106,621
Coffee	3,275	3,778	1,256	2,777	4,019
Colquitt	3,870	4,680	1,682	2,998	5,653
Columbia	7,114	16,655	4,379	4,617	16,401
Cook	1,631	1,318	537	1,226	1,555
Coweta	7,087	9,810	3,586	4,212	9,668
Crawford	1,648	974	549	1,340	1,235
Crisp	2,610	2,253	823	1,690	2,916
Dade	1,782	2,191	823	1,120	2,539
Dawson	1,399	1,696	790	761	1,908
Decatur	3,198	3,142	1,068	2,348	3,866
DeKalb	124,559	70,282	19,741	92,521	90,179
Dodge	3,002	2,287	978	2,164	2,677
Dooly	1,993	1,034	350	1,613	1,386
Dougherty	15,236	12,455	3,178	12,579	15,520
Douglas	8,869	13,349	4,362	5,086	13,493
Early	1,970	1,454	652	1,359	1,918
Echols	312	361	238	245	422
Effingham	1,387	1,745	703	1,905	3,933
Elbert	3,021	2,369	721	2,118	2,796
Emanuel	2,596	2,297	599	2,387	3,530
Evans	1,230	1,244	480	1,023	1,707
Fannin	2,902	3,255	1,028	2,123	4,271
Fayette	8,428	17,569	5,597	4,593	16,443
Floyd	11,614	12,378	3,779	8,548	14,697
Forsyth	4,936	8,652	3,453	2,347	7,947
Franklin	2,505	2,391	1,014	1,842	2,615
Fulton	147,450	85,442	23,573	120,752	91,785
Gilmer	2,311	2,661	879	1,363	3,353
Glascock	316	516	166	210	580
Glynn	8,581	11,242	3,053	6,339	11,126
Gordon	4,103	5,265	1,818	2,369	6,051
Grady	2,520	2,473	1,128	1,883	2,989
Greene	2,259	1,307	454	1,818	1,432
Gwinnett	44,252	81,822	23,926	20,948	66,372
Habersham	3,098	4,569	1,444	2,114	4,871
Hall	11,194	16,110	5,031	7,782	17,415
Hancock	2,461	453	189	1,947	621
Haralson	3,281	3,142	1,167	2,404	4,529
Harris	2,779	3,016	954	1,905	3,414
Hart	3,614	2,607	1,376	2,476	3,044
Heard	1,456	1,190	617	874	1,551
Henry	7,817	12,614	3,769	4,348	10,882
Houston	12,254	14,099	6,252	8,664	15,748
Irwin	1,220	743	395	918	1,226
Jackson	3,792	3,976	1,381	2,607	4,407
Jasper	1,485	1,153	373	1,188	1,474
Jeff Davis	1,905	1,799	905	1,242	2,050
Jefferson	3,220	2,077	685	2,346	2,788
Jenkins	1,401	959	394	953	1,288
Johnson	1,473	1,314	502	927	1,567
Jones	3,338	2,115	1,159	2,662	3,618
Lamar	2,065	1,707	625	1,416	2,035
Lanier	811	600	298	698	725
Laurens	5,795	5,769	1,522	4,879	6,929
Lee	1,749	2,938	983	995	2,875
Liberty	3,853	2,832	1,176	2,906	3,100
Lincoln	1,327	1,149	479	893	1,417
Long	874	719	355	681	858
Lowndes	8,760	10,006	2,795	6,427	10,855
Lumpkin	2,010	1,972	1,035	1,286	2,688
McDuffie	2,640	3,055	860	1,704	3,231
McIntosh	1,925	1,027	550	1,527	1,273
Macon	2,773	1,025	385	2,268	1,412
Madison	2,393	3,351	1,129	1,639	3,724
Marion	1,145	711	198	844	804
Meriwether	4,002	2,364	942	2,934	3,101
Miller	934	826	455	515	1,105
Mitchell	3,052	1,917	818	2,260	2,590
Monroe	2,608	2,096	808	1,970	2,570
Montgomery	1,185	1,009	416	903	1,228
Morgan	2,267	2,011	666	1,508	2,108
Murray	2,764	3,256	1,186	1,679	3,996
Muscogee	25,476	21,386	4,327	18,772	23,058
Newton	5,803	5,778	1,996	3,111	5,809
Oconee	2,732	4,110	1,178	1,990	4,265
Oglethorpe	1,510	1,563	628	1,154	1,951
Paulding	5,212	7,180	2,654	2,717	7,329
Peach	3,430	2,156	906	2,972	2,782
Pickens	2,359	2,332	1,037	1,430	3,021
Pierce	1,696	1,743	737	1,558	1,947
Pike	1,651	1,822	624	1,176	2,074
Polk	4,872	4,158	1,598	2,977	5,454
Pulaski	1,756	1,075	614	1,476	1,400
Putnam	2,149	1,756	775	1,532	2,111
Quitman	523	284	113	436	296
Rabun	1,878	1,902	825	1,301	2,278
Randolph	1,756	887	315	1,369	1,319
Richmond	28,910	24,227	6,290	20,489	27,566
Rockdale	7,003	11,945	3,564	4,330	12,413
Schley	601	511	180	439	635
Screven	1,940	1,705	709	1,461	2,178
Seminole	1,193	850	468	1,171	1,469
Spalding	6,392	7,262	2,044	4,318	7,730
Stephens	2,976	4,047	1,448	2,185	4,329
Stewart	1,540	1,186	175	1,136	832

Sumter	4,489	3,616	1,046	3,332	4,289
Talbot	1,768	671	238	1,248	802
Taliaferro	755	269	80	469	306
Tattnall	2,360	2,566	996	1,694	3,172
Taylor	1,508	1,078	281	1,134	1,145
Telfair	2,238	1,324	613	1,765	1,805
Terrell	1,942	1,143	384	1,383	1,517
Thomas	4,841	5,500	1,591	3,530	6,572
Tift	3,930	4,485	1,137	2,446	4,760
Toombs	2,648	3,609	1,210	1,152	4,433
Towns	1,487	1,718	537	942	1,783
Treutlen	1,116	898	318	726	970
Troup	6,362	8,050	2,351	4,562	9,484
Turner	1,669	936	370	1,122	1,312
Twiggs	2,099	852	432	1,730	1,261
Union	2,304	2,533	804	1,258	2,396
Upson	3,740	4,052	1,182	2,666	4,614
Walker	6,147	8,398	2,719	4,753	10,487
Walton	4,821	5,619	1,923	3,091	5,974
Ware	4,573	4,579	1,263	4,292	4,819
Warren	1,239	751	180	1,091	897
Washington	3,508	2,384	820	2,615	2,752
Wayne	3,050	3,379	1,107	2,417	3,340
Webster	600	208	103	427	361
Wheeler	NA	NA	NA	658	709
White	1,756	2,477	981	1,028	2,648
Whitfield	7,335	12,003	2,866	4,618	12,761
Wilcox	1,365	916	433	1,079	1,235
Wilkes	1,955	1,535	464	1,549	1,810
Wilkinson	2,286	1,232	520	1,831	1,546
Worth	2,578	2,344	905	1,311	2,668
Totals	**1,002,433**	**985,682**	**306,489**	**714,792**	**1,081,331**

Georgia Vote Since 1940

1940, Roosevelt, Dem., 265,194; Willkie, Rep., 23,934; Ind. Dem., 22,428; total, 46,362; Babson, Proh., 983.

1944, Roosevelt, Dem., 268,187; Dewey, Rep., 56,506; Watson, Proh., 36.

1948, Truman, Dem., 254,646; Dewey, Rep., 76,691; Thurmond, States' Rights, 85,055; Wallace, Prog., 1,636; Watson, Proh., 732.

1952, Eisenhower, Rep., 198,979; Stevenson, Dem., 456,823; Liberty Party, 1.

1956, Stevenson, Dem., 444,388; Eisenhower, Rep., 222,778; Andrews, Ind., write-in, 1,754.

1960, Kennedy, Dem., 458,638; Nixon, Rep., 274,472; write-in, 239.

1964, Johnson, Dem., 522,557; Goldwater, Rep., 616,600.

1968, Nixon, Rep., 380,111; Humphrey, Dem., 334,440; Wallace, 3d party, 535,550; write-in, 162.

1972, Nixon, Rep., 881,496; McGovern, Dem., 289,529; Schmitz, Amer., 2,288; scattered.

1976, Carter, Dem., 979,409; Ford, Rep., 483,743; write-in, 4,306.

1980, Reagan, Rep., 654,168; Carter, Dem., 890,955; Anderson, Ind., 36,055; Clark, Libertarian, 15,627.

1984, Reagan, Rep., 1,068,722; Mondale, Dem., 706,628.

1988, Bush, Rep., 1,081,331; Dukakis, Dem., 714,792; Paul, Lib., 8,435; Fulani, New Alliance, 5,099.

Hawaii

County	1992 Clinton (D)	1992 Bush (R)	1992 Perot (I)	1988 Dukakis (D)	1988 Bush (R)
Hawaii	25,725	15,460	8,889	24,091	17,125
Honolulu	123,491	103,545	35,588	138,971	120,258
Kauai	10,715	6,274	1,756	11,770	8,298
Maui	18,962	11,151	6,630	17,532	12,944
Totals	**178,893**	**136,430**	**52,863**	**192,364**	**158,625**

Hawaii Vote Since 1960

1960, Kennedy, Dem., 92,410; Nixon, Rep., 92,295.

1964, Johnson, Dem., 163,249; Goldwater, Rep., 44,022.

1968, Nixon, Rep., 91,425; Humphrey, Dem., 141,324; Wallace, 3d party, 3,469.

1972, Nixon, Rep., 168,865; McGovern, Dem., 101,409.

1976, Carter, Dem., 147,375; Ford, Rep., 140,003; MacBride, Libertarian, 3,923.

1980, Reagan, Rep., 130,112; Carter, Dem., 135,879; Anderson, Ind., 32,021; Clark, Libertarian, 3,269; Commoner, Citizens, 1,548; Hall, Com., 458.

1984, Reagan, Rep., 184,934; Mondale, Dem., 147,098; Bergland, Libertarian, 2,167.

1988, Bush, Rep., 158,625; Dukakis, Dem., 192,364; Paul, Lib., 1,999; Fulani, New Alliance, 1,003.

Idaho

County	1992 Clinton (D)	1992 Bush (R)	1992 Perot (I)	1988 Dukakis (D)	1988 Bush (R)
Ada	31,357	48,231	27,745	30,525	54,951
Adams	457	754	695	643	1,107
Bannock	11,091	12,016	8,116	13,074	14,986
Bear Lake	562	1,419	684	867	2,084
Benewah	1,270	1,223	1,165	1,518	1,650
Bingham	3,565	7,333	4,144	4,346	10,131
Blaine	2,865	2,243	2,831	2,498	3,130
Boise	623	912	754	620	1,044
Bonner	4,895	3,926	4,650	5,555	5,721
Bonneville	6,998	16,528	10,235	7,032	22,613
Boundary	1,095	1,479	1,136	1,336	1,800
Butte	433	602	392	521	899
Camas	134	202	145	136	288
Canyon	9,095	19,220	8,974	10,207	21,426
Caribou	561	1,350	1,088	867	2,239
Cassias	1,351	4,052	1,785	1,833	5,345
Clark	95	195	119	133	281
Clearwater	1,433	1,152	1,098	1,861	1,659
Custer	564	829	729	616	1,253
Elmore	1,858	3,087	1,867	2,078	3,756
Franklin	524	2,115	890	806	2,992
Fremont	902	2,333	1,349	1,178	3,401
Gem	1,609	2,455	1,555	2,064	2,926
Gooding	1,501	2,132	1,572	1,872	2,908
Idaho	1,974	2,709	1,900	2,198	3,541
Jefferson	978	3,471	2,164	1,198	5,295
Jerome	1,736	2,969	1,766	1,985	3,830
Kootenai	11,553	13,065	11,261	11,621	15,093
Latah	7,233	5,353	3,602	6,544	6,367
Lemhi	996	1,540	1,146	1,157	2,378
Lewis	674	593	491	807	786
Lincoln	514	656	441	574	918
Madison	711	4,591	1,920	1,009	6,197
Minidoka	1,815	3,304	1,875	2,290	4,623
Nez Perce	7,069	5,431	4,363	7,754	7,027
Oneida	351	713	590	508	1,269
Owyhee	686	1,469	862	848	1,707
Payette	1,656	2,895	2,055	1,900	3,786
Power	837	1,352	697	1,095	1,838
Shoshone	3,182	1,441	1,878	3,379	2,134
Teton	472	762	608	531	982
Twin Falls	6,593	10,335	6,043	7,078	13,243
Valley	1,259	1,548	1,313	1,251	1,897
Washington	1,122	1,802	1,204	1,359	2,380
Totals	**136,249**	**201,787**	**129,897**	**147,272**	**253,881**

Idaho Vote Since 1940

1940, Roosevelt, Dem., 127,842; Willkie, Rep., 106,553; Thomas, Soc., 497; Browder, Com., 276.

1944, Roosevelt, Dem., 107,399; Dewey, Rep., 100,137; Watson, Proh., 503; Thomas, Soc., 282.

1948, Truman, Dem., 107,370; Dewey, Rep., 101,514; Wallace, Prog., 4,972; Watson, Proh., 628; Thomas, Soc., 332.

1952, Eisenhower, Rep., 180,707; Stevenson Dem., 95,081; Hallinan, Prog., 443; write-in, 23.

1956, Eisenhower, Rep., 166,979; Stevenson, Dem., 105,868; Andrews, Ind., 126; write-in, 16.

1960, Kennedy, Dem., 138,853; Nixon, Rep., 161,597.

1964, Johnson, Dem., 148,920; Goldwater, Rep., 143,557.

1968, Nixon, Rep., 165,369; Humphrey, Dem., 89,273; Wallace, 3d party, 36,541.

1972, Nixon, Rep., 199,384; McGovern, Dem., 80,826; Schmitz, Amer., 28,869; Spock, Peoples, 903.

1976, Carter, Dem., 126,549; Ford, Rep., 204,151; Maddox, Amer., 5,935; MacBride, Libertarian, 3,558; LaRouche, U.S. Labor, 739.

1980, Reagan, Rep., 290,699; Carter, Dem., 110,192; Anderson, Ind., 27,058; Clark, Libertarian, 8,425; Rarick, Amer., 1,057.

1984, Reagan, Rep., 297,523; Mondale, Dem., 108,510; Bergland, Libertarian, 2,823.

1988, Bush, Rep., 253,881; Dukakis, Dem., 147,272; Paul, Lib., 5,313; Fulani, Ind., 2,502.

Illinois

County	1992 Clinton (D)	1992 Bush (R)	1992 Perot (I)	1988 Dukakis (D)	1988 Bush (R)
Adams	11,748	13,529	6,157	13,768	15,831
Alexander	2,566	1,301	474	2,693	1,954
Bond	3,428	2,715	1,373	3,459	3,608
Boone	5,114	5,589	2,880	4,234	6,923
Brown	1,146	1,029	504	1,267	1,373
Bureau	7,551	6,836	3,465	7,354	8,896
Calhoun	1,519	745	532	1,544	1,238

Carroll	2,854	3,297	1,502	2,990	4,464
Cass	3,200	2,162	1,072	3,316	2,916
Champaign	35,003	27,096	13,571	29,733	33,247
Christian	9,042	5,087	3,401	8,295	7,040
Clark	3,338	3,175	1,450	3,275	4,508
Clay	2,962	2,471	1,193	2,761	3,494
Clinton	6,686	5,771	3,315	5,935	7,681
Coles	9,402	8,098	4,707	8,327	11,043
Cook	1,175,715	589,382	273,983	1,129,973	878,582
Crawford	3,964	3,606	2,062	3,555	4,951
Cumberland	2,111	1,860	1,209	1,904	2,667
DeKalb	13,744	12,655	7,680	11,811	17,182
DeWitt	3,009	3,164	1,535	2,660	3,942
Douglas	3,341	3,309	1,600	3,184	4,378
DuPage	114,533	178,197	76,825	94,285	217,907
Edgar	4,014	3,790	1,930	3,880	5,538
Edwards	1,299	1,601	634	1,218	2,212
Effingham	5,212	6,322	3,352	4,553	8,431
Fayette	4,833	3,508	1,730	4,632	5,452
Ford	2,169	3,040	1,221	2,026	4,059
Franklin	12,744	5,504	3,180	11,023	7,677
Fulton	9,725	5,062	2,874	9,046	6,999
Gallatin	2,371	990	568	2,455	1,580
Greene	3,164	2,391	1,461	3,020	3,136
Grundy	6,122	6,346	3,724	5,525	8,743
Hamilton	2,222	1,298	761	2,618	2,622
Hancock	4,213	3,714	2,091	4,740	4,568
Hardin	1,665	985	515	1,308	1,504
Henderson	2,013	1,310	715	2,085	1,726
Henry	11,077	8,989	4,231	11,594	11,358
Iroquois	4,440	6,948	3,073	4,221	9,596
Jackson	13,373	6,899	3,995	11,334	9,687
Jasper	2,284	1,995	1,160	2,135	3,024
Jefferson	8,665	5,497	3,403	7,729	7,624
Jersey	4,749	2,933	2,363	4,376	4,343
JoDaviess	4,044	4,249	2,102	4,141	4,923
Johnson	2,298	2,124	944	1,872	2,797
Kane	44,567	55,682	27,176	36,366	66,283
Kankakee	17,229	15,411	7,264	15,147	20,316
Kendall	5,423	8,521	4,394	4,347	10,653
Knox	12,524	8,331	4,357	12,752	10,842
Lake	81,693	99,000	42,384	64,327	114,115
LaSalle	23,276	16,070	10,434	22,271	22,166
Lawrence	3,270	2,681	1,498	3,140	3,655
Lee	5,530	6,652	3,191	4,608	8,903
Livingston	6,007	8,044	3,029	5,009	10,324
Logan	5,169	6,567	2,420	4,727	8,490
McDonough	5,814	5,297	2,770	5,247	7,173
McHenry	24,783	41,356	21,817	18,919	46,135
McLean	23,090	25,726	10,282	18,659	30,572
Macon	27,434	18,671	9,231	25,364	23,862
Macoupin	12,050	6,518	5,018	12,195	9,362
Madison	58,484	32,167	23,110	54,175	44,907
Marion	9,669	5,764	3,407	8,592	8,695
Marshall	2,819	2,491	1,169	2,742	3,588
Mason	3,969	2,473	1,245	3,406	3,424
Massac	3,347	2,754	891	3,227	3,507
Menard	2,264	2,834	1,179	2,103	3,560
Mercer	3,990	2,983	1,535	4,204	3,683
Monroe	4,870	4,795	2,791	4,529	6,275
Montgomery	7,424	4,407	2,956	7,293	6,388
Morgan	6,351	6,566	3,317	6,032	8,808
Moultrie	3,056	2,065	1,322	3,013	3,167
Ogle	6,512	9,008	4,455	5,641	11,644
Peoria	38,006	30,641	12,158	35,253	37,605
Perry	6,009	3,105	1,955	5,167	4,576
Piatt	3,520	3,076	1,822	3,099	4,137
Pike	4,016	3,342	1,643	4,614	3,965
Pope	1,063	951	391	996	1,202
Pulaski	1,987	1,169	379	1,793	1,666
Putnam	1,574	969	752	1,601	1,516
Randolph	8,529	4,899	3,092	7,844	7,396
Richland	3,285	3,048	1,689	2,863	4,264
Rock Island	37,412	23,212	10,416	40,174	27,412
St. Clair	57,525	31,949	17,595	55,465	41,439
Saline	7,258	3,667	2,302	6,676	5,798
Sangamon	40,034	39,629	16,860	37,729	50,175
Schuyler	1,650	1,512	815	1,866	2,178
Scott	1,057	1,132	588	1,243	1,535
Shelby	5,101	3,631	2,401	4,650	5,370
Stark	1,336	1,384	625	1,274	1,841
Stephenson	7,899	9,005	4,677	7,460	11,342
Tazewell	26,428	23,469	9,927	24,603	28,861
Union	4,681	3,003	1,373	4,197	4,244
Vermilion	18,383	11,703	8,162	17,918	16,943
Wabash	2,436	2,485	1,302	2,241	3,453
Warren	3,661	3,325	1,436	3,617	4,584
Washington	2,986	3,003	1,542	2,689	4,127
Wayne	3,332	3,809	1,702	3,135	5,481
White	4,308	3,057	1,428	4,144	4,354
Whiteside	12,329	10,146	4,589	11,328	12,978
Will	59,633	58,337	32,788	49,816	73,129
Williamson	14,361	9,462	4,779	12,712	12,274
Winnebago	48,298	42,181	21,227	45,280	55,699
Woodford	5,490	8,032	2,733	4,604	9,474
Totals	**2,378,873**	**1,717,736**	**832,307**	**2,215,940**	**2,310,939**

Illinois Vote Since 1940

1940, Roosevelt, Dem., 2,149,934; Willkie, Rep., 2,047,240; Thomas, Soc., 10,914; Babson, Proh., 9,190.

1944, Roosevelt, Dem., 2,079,479; Dewey, Rep., 1,939,314; Teichert, Soc. Labor, 9,677; Watson, Proh., 7,411; Thomas, Soc., 180.

1948, Truman, Dem., 1,994,715; Dewey, Rep., 1,961,103; Watson, Proh., 11,959; Thomas, Soc., 11,522; Teichert, Soc. Labor, 3,118.

1952, Eisenhower, Rep., 2,457,327; Stevenson, Dem., 2,013,920; Hass, Soc. Labor, 9,363; write-in, 448.

1956, Eisenhower, Rep., 2,623,327; Stevenson, Dem., 1,775,682; Hass, Soc. Labor, 8,342; write-in, 56.

1960, Kennedy, Dem., 2,377,846; Nixon, Rep., 2,368,988; Hass, Soc. Labor, 10,560; write-in, 15.

1964, Johnson, Dem., 2,796,833; Goldwater, Rep., 1,905,946; write-in, 62.

1968, Nixon, Rep., 2,174,774; Humphrey, Dem., 2,039,814; Wallace, 3d party, 390,958; Blomen, Soc. Labor, 13,878; write-in, 325.

1972, Nixon, Rep. 2,788,179; McGovern, Dem., 1,913,472; Fisher, Soc. Labor, 12,344; Schmitz, Amer., 2,471; Hall, Com., 4,541; others, 2,229.

1976, Carter, Dem., 2,271,295, Ford, Rep., 2,364,269; McCarthy, Ind., 55,939; Hall, Com., 9,250; MacBride, Libertarian, 8,057; Camejo, Soc. Workers, 3,615; Levin, Soc. Labor, 2,422; LaRouche, U.S. Labor, 2,018; write-in, 1,968.

1980, Reagan, Rep., 2,358,049; Carter, Dem., 1,981,413; Anderson, Ind., 346,754; Clark, Libertarian, 38,939; Commoner, Citizens, 10,692; Hall, Com., 9,711; Griswold, Workers World, 2,257; DeBerry, Socialist Workers, 1,302; write-ins, 604.

1984, Reagan, Rep., 2,707,103; Mondale, Dem., 2,086,499; Bergland, Libertarian, 10,086.

1988, Bush, Rep., 2,310,939; Dukakis, Dem., 2,215,940; Paul, Lib., 14,944; Fulani, Solid., 10,276.

Indiana

County	1992 Clinton (D)	1992 Bush (R)	1992 Perot (I)	1988 Dukakis (D)	1988 Bush (R)
Adams	3,708	6,078	2,865	3,811	8,137
Allen	36,524	50,453	24,522	39,238	74,638
Bartholomew	8,284	13,146	5,882	8,804	17,364
Benton	1,221	2,030	1,056	1,349	2,698
Blackford	2,088	2,347	1,319	2,253	3,336
Boone	3,982	9,485	3,826	4,168	11,608
Brown	2,029	2,633	1,635	2,115	3,348
Carroll	2,561	3,800	2,173	2,952	4,981
Cass	4,759	7,421	3,944	5,784	10,970
Clark	17,460	13,333	5,653	14,528	16,544
Clay	3,306	4,696	2,134	3,724	5,852
Clinton	3,490	6,141	2,535	4,412	8,570
Crawford	2,260	1,903	819	2,036	2,532
Daviess	3,201	5,591	1,695	3,483	6,768
Dearborn	5,116	6,974	3,384	5,066	8,195
Decatur	2,774	5,195	2,299	2,979	6,245
Dekalb	4,652	6,682	3,554	4,657	9,018
Delaware	19,556	20,473	10,453	20,548	27,348
Dubois	5,878	6,786	3,196	5,954	9,995
Elkhart	14,660	27,920	9,450	14,236	33,793
Fayette	3,969	4,376	2,299	4,118	5,949
Floyd	13,083	11,923	4,511	11,024	14,291
Fountain	2,829	3,391	2,162	3,279	5,113
Franklin	2,456	3,831	1,858	2,472	4,777
Fulton	2,552	3,982	1,963	2,788	5,234
Gibson	6,909	5,112	2,672	7,031	7,610
Grant	9,222	13,817	5,599	10,799	18,441
Greene	5,406	5,289	2,442	5,979	7,689
Hamilton	10,215	34,622	10,365	8,853	36,654
Hancock	4,752	11,072	4,752	5,355	13,374
Harrison	5,768	5,403	2,469	4,933	6,702
Hendricks	7,071	18,373	7,519	7,643	22,090
Henry	6,794	8,720	4,416	7,779	11,280
Howard	10,288	15,306	8,575	11,518	19,971
Huntington	3,922	9,171	2,970	3,873	11,675
Jackson	5,650	7,226	3,059	5,550	9,470
Jasper	3,033	4,809	2,019	3,237	6,009
Jay	3,208	3,609	1,994	3,212	5,363
Jefferson	5,510	4,937	2,565	5,221	6,949
Jennings	3,471	4,392	2,370	3,667	5,636
Johnson	8,712	20,353	8,246	9,001	24,654
Knox	6,718	6,683	3,719	7,006	9,813
Kosciusko	5,307	14,179	5,115	5,321	17,761
LaGrange	2,093	3,584	1,736	2,029	4,495
Lake	102,538	53,865	28,633	105,026	79,929
LaPorte	17,717	14,962	9,641	17,585	20,537
Lawrence	5,557	7,712	3,452	5,787	10,742
Madison	22,276	23,479	13,100	24,443	32,596
Marion	116,725	135,851	55,417	128,627	184,519
Marshall	4,912	8,048	3,522	5,488	10,490
Martin	2,118	2,523	893	2,132	3,066

Miami	3,967	6,416	3,428	4,613	8,533
Monroe	19,581	16,369	6,905	15,855	20,756
Montgomery	3,371	7,602	3,511	3,623	10,793
Morgan	4,690	10,939	5,375	5,375	14,284
Newton	1,757	2,295	1,274	1,744	3,274
Noble	4,381	5,883	3,338	4,143	7,889
Ohio	970	1,009	527	1,113	1,412
Orange	2,948	3,738	1,296	2,739	5,245
Owen	2,207	2,753	1,563	2,484	3,837
Parke	2,429	2,953	1,696	2,563	4,458
Perry	4,829	2,973	1,560	4,804	4,720
Pike	2,960	2,156	1,238	3,037	3,294
Porter	21,021	22,644	13,096	19,390	29,790
Posey	4,632	4,435	2,357	4,468	5,987
Pulaski	1,817	2,578	1,073	2,213	3,677
Putnam	3,487	5,341	3,174	3,850	7,119
Randolph	3,870	4,937	2,939	3,990	6,856
Ripley	3,469	5,008	2,402	3,605	6,414
Rush	2,168	3,873	1,948	2,451	5,112
St. Joseph	46,103	38,826	18,829	48,056	49,481
Scott	4,085	2,649	1,092	3,378	3,455
Shelby	4,560	8,075	3,521	5,382	10,176
Spencer	4,301	3,789	1,464	4,061	4,964
Starke	3,695	3,094	1,885	4,104	4,458
Steuben	3,630	4,867	2,896	3,114	6,855
Sullivan	4,211	3,052	1,857	4,320	4,246
Switzerland	1,535	1,211	636	1,479	1,572
Tippecanoe	17,343	23,050	9,684	16,256	27,897
Tipton	2,133	3,914	1,821	2,485	5,148
Union	898	1,394	664	946	1,814
Vanderburgh	33,799	30,271	12,513	31,270	38,928
Vermillion	3,652	2,360	1,794	4,044	3,674
Vigo	18,050	15,834	8,141	19,192	21,929
Wabash	4,518	7,062	3,424	4,168	9,153
Warren	1,367	1,601	1,020	1,542	2,243
Warrick	8,612	8,087	3,862	7,999	10,504
Washington	4,092	4,043	1,846	3,370	4,998
Wayne	9,960	12,221	5,095	10,209	16,388
Wells	3,282	5,799	2,890	3,437	7,712
White	2,988	4,622	2,582	3,256	6,220
Whitley	3,569	5,217	3,195	3,642	7,679
Totals	**839,227**	**978,627**	**451,858**	**860,643**	**1,297,763**

Indiana Vote Since 1940

1940, Roosevelt, Dem., 874,063; Willkie, Rep., 899,466; Babson, Proh., 6,437; Thomas, Soc., 2,075; Aiken, Soc. Labor, 706.

1944, Roosevelt, Dem., 781,403; Dewey, Rep., 875,891; Watson, Proh., 12,574; Thomas, Soc., 2,223.

1948, Truman, Dem., 807,833; Dewey, Rep., 821,079; Watson, Proh., 14,711; Wallace, Prog., 9,649; Thomas, Soc., 2,179; Teichert, Soc. Labor, 763.

1952, Eisenhower, Rep., 1,136,259; Stevenson, Dem., 801,530; Hamblen, Proh., 15,335; Hallinan, Prog., 1,222; Hass, Soc. Labor, 979.

1956, Eisenhower, Rep., 1,182,811; Stevenson, Dem., 783,908; Holtwick, Proh., 6,554; Hass, Soc. Labor, 1,334.

1960, Kennedy, Dem., 952,358; Nixon, Rep., 1,175,120; Decker, Proh., 6,746; Hass, Soc. Labor, 1,136.

1964, Johnson, Dem. 1,170,848; Goldwater, Rep., 911,118; Munn, Proh., 8,266; Hass, Soc. Labor, 1,374.

1968, Nixon, Rep., 1,067,885; Humphrey, Dem., 806,659; Wallace, 3d party, 243,108; Munn, Proh., 4,616; Halstead, Soc. Worker, 1,293; Gregory, write-in, 36.

1972, Nixon, Rep., 1,405,154; McGovern, Dem., 708,568; Reed, Soc. Workers, 5,575; Fisher, Soc. Labor, 1,688; Spock, Peace & Freedom, 4,544.

1976, Carter, Dem., 1,014,714; Ford, Rep., 1,185,958; Anderson, Amer., 14,048; Camejo, Soc. Workers, 5,695; LaRouche, U.S. Labor, 1,947.

1980 Reagan, Rep., 1,255,656; Carter, Dem., 844,197; Anderson, Ind., 111,639; Clark, Libertarian, 19,627; Commoner, Citizens, 4,852; Greaves, American, 4,750; Hall, Com., 702; DeBerry, Soc., 610.

1984 Reagan, Rep., 1,377,230; Mondale, Dem., 841,481; Bergland, Libertarian, 6,741.

1988, Bush, Rep., 1,297,763; Dukakis, Dem., 860,643; Fulani, New Alliance, 10,215.

Iowa

	1992			1988	
County	Clinton (D)	Bush (R)	Perot (I)	Dukakis (D)	Bush (R)
Adair	1,652	1,699	818	2,261	1,833
Adams	1,034	863	677	1,283	1,080
Allamakee	2,358	2,628	1,539	2,768	3,186
Appanoose	2,807	2,345	1,159	3,209	2,779
Audubon	1,583	1,369	883	1,863	1,478
Benton	4,458	3,465	2,452	5,873	4,011
Black Hawk	29,538	21,344	10,163	31,657	24,112
Boone	5,906	4,440	1,962	7,232	4,381
Bremer	4,766	4,463	2,332	4,961	5,079
Buchanan	4,116	3,253	2,085	4,778	3,495
Buena Vista	3,352	3,848	1,946	4,580	4,170
Butler	2,542	3,192	1,292	2,593	3,523
Calhoun	2,137	2,183	941	2,990	2,474
Carroll	3,795	3,437	2,188	5,437	3,701
Cass	2,226	3,173	1,608	2,934	3,962
Cedar	3,291	2,965	1,943	4,032	3,373
Cerro Gordo	11,388	8,232	4,492	12,857	9,358
Cherokee	2,590	2,750	1,500	3,574	3,218
Chickasaw	2,910	2,125	1,559	3,530	2,549
Clarke	1,916	1,417	897	2,262	1,631
Clay	3,338	3,004	1,963	4,173	3,641
Clayton	3,729	3,039	2,301	4,320	3,839
Clinton	11,665	8,739	4,404	12,549	10,243
Crawford	2,995	2,680	1,902	3,868	3,375
Dallas	6,508	5,561	2,656	7,501	4,858
Davis	1,961	1,339	715	2,246	1,563
Decatur	1,863	1,312	785	2,192	1,406
Delaware	3,092	3,191	2,092	3,947	3,425
Des Moines	11,192	6,367	3,371	11,593	7,652
Dickinson	3,100	3,188	1,972	3,342	3,678
Dubuque	20,374	13,902	8,148	23,797	14,530
Emmet	2,236	1,744	1,006	2,778	2,173
Fayette	4,300	3,728	2,397	5,304	4,921
Floyd	3,681	2,491	1,701	4,377	3,266
Franklin	2,049	2,134	1,043	2,594	2,320
Fremont	1,358	1,390	952	1,547	1,946
Greene	2,419	1,952	952	3,011	2,091
Grundy	1,992	3,149	1,066	2,211	3,433
Guthrie	2,215	1,938	1,199	2,910	2,005
Hamilton	3,249	3,015	1,339	4,156	3,277
Hancock	2,170	2,422	1,168	2,831	2,731
Hardin	3,776	3,575	1,537	5,088	3,856
Harrison	2,346	2,767	1,716	2,883	3,108
Henry	3,533	3,430	1,515	3,754	3,951
Howard	1,966	1,495	1,174	2,330	1,970
Humboldt	2,238	2,739	1,318	2,713	2,594
Ida	1,448	1,710	1,060	1,787	1,951
Iowa	2,552	2,651	1,707	3,338	3,247
Jackson	4,419	2,667	2,054	4,864	3,237
Jasper	8,104	6,857	2,969	8,940	6,703
Jefferson	2,443	2,456	1,207	3,594	3,614
Johnson	28,451	13,913	8,502	28,759	15,453
Jones	3,507	3,066	2,305	4,641	3,496
Keokuk	2,320	1,975	1,232	2,899	2,278
Kossuth	3,651	3,453	2,002	5,088	3,938
Lee	9,351	4,767	2,915	10,911	6,228
Linn	38,403	30,123	19,486	42,993	33,129
Louisa	2,086	1,689	1,044	2,268	2,060
Lucas	2,070	1,732	851	2,454	1,776
Lyon	1,317	3,267	1,064	1,706	3,517
Madison	2,521	2,439	1,161	3,421	2,410
Mahaska	3,712	4,946	1,507	4,451	4,798
Marion	5,602	6,118	1,895	6,922	5,914
Marshall	8,290	6,772	3,087	9,760	7,657
Mills	1,794	2,692	1,631	2,092	3,212
Mitchell	2,171	1,928	1,196	2,870	2,338
Monona	1,934	1,660	1,200	2,408	2,068
Monroe	1,828	1,321	612	2,338	1,313
Montgomery	1,559	2,410	1,298	1,898	3,166
Muscatine	7,078	6,076	3,576	7,059	6,904
O'Brien	2,122	3,865	1,552	2,768	4,241
Osceola	987	1,750	811	1,277	1,951
Page	1,950	3,663	1,667	2,185	4,583
Palo Alto	2,374	1,781	1,180	3,377	2,041
Plymouth	3,170	5,188	2,036	4,220	5,316
Pocahontas	1,916	1,740	942	2,722	1,871
Polk	77,363	62,758	23,559	84,476	57,854
Pottawattamie	13,342	15,731	7,910	14,958	17,193
Poweshiek	4,046	3,236	1,672	4,876	3,683
Ringgold	1,341	967	551	1,609	1,110
Sac	1,880	2,106	1,140	2,613	2,411
Scott	33,708	28,804	11,385	34,415	31,025
Shelby	2,092	2,805	1,018	2,806	3,019
Sioux	2,223	10,622	1,718	2,923	10,270
Story	17,087	12,550	6,252	19,051	13,782
Tama	3,567	2,945	1,744	4,584	3,362
Taylor	1,428	1,190	908	1,671	1,647
Union	2,553	2,217	1,271	3,236	2,751
Van Buren	1,460	1,408	807	1,612	1,692
Wapello	8,658	4,845	2,505	10,177	5,350
Warren	8,552	7,169	3,145	9,627	6,424
Washington	3,383	3,571	1,989	3,776	3,741
Wayne	1,628	1,296	640	1,988	1,467
Webster	8,556	0,984	3,266	10,267	6,926
Winnebago	2,321	2,399	1,322	2,804	2,863
Winneshiek	3,765	3,309	2,390	4,443	4,194
Woodbury	17,380	18,176	7,077	20,153	18,790
Worth	2,008	1,382	1,043	2,440	1,488
Wright	2,753	2,711	1,151	3,353	2,658
Totals	**583,934**	**503,338**	**251,040**	**670,557**	**545,355**

Iowa Vote Since 1940

1940, Roosevelt, Dem., 578,800; Willkie, Rep., 632,370; Babson, Proh., 2,284; Browder, Com., 1,524; Aiken, Soc. Labor, 452.

1944, Roosevelt, Dem., 499,876; Dewey, Rep., 547,267; Watson, Proh., 3,752; Thomas, Soc., 1,511; Teichert, Soc. Labor, 193.

1948, Truman, Dem., 522,380; Dewey, Rep., 494,018; Wallace, Prog., 12,125; Teichert, Soc. Labor, 4,274; Watson, Proh., 3,382; Thomas, Soc., 1,829; Dobbs, Soc. Workers, 26.

1952, Eisenhower, Rep., 808,906; Stevenson, Dem., 451,513; Hallinan, Prog., 5,085; Hamblen, Proh., 2,882; Hoopes, Soc., 219; Hass, Soc. Labor, 139; scattering 29.

1956, Eisenhower, Rep., 729,187; Stevenson, Dem., 501,858; Andrews (A.C.P. of Iowa), 3,202; Hoopes, Soc., 192; Hass, Soc. Labor, 125.

1960, Kennedy, Dem., 550,565; Nixon, Rep., 722,381; Hass, Soc. Labor, 230; write-in, 634.

1964, Johnson, Dem., 733,030; Goldwater, Rep., 449,148; Hass, Soc. Labor, 182; DeBerry, Soc. Worker, 159; Munn, Proh., 1,902.

1968, Nixon, Rep., 619,106; Humphrey, Dem., 476,699; Wallace, 3d party, 66,422; Munn, Proh., 362; Halstead, Soc. Worker, 3,377; Cleaver, Peace and Freedom, 1,332; Blomen, Soc. Labor, 241.

1972, Nixon, Rep., 706,207; McGovern, Dem., 496,206; Schmitz, Amer., 22,056; Jenness, Soc. Workers, 488; Fisher, Soc. Labor, 195; Hall, Com. 272; Green, Universal, 199; scattered, 321.

1976, Carter, Dem., 619,931; Ford, Rep., 632,863; McCarthy, Ind., 20,051; Anderson, Amer., 3,040; MacBride, Libertarian, 1,452.

1980, Reagan, Rep., 676,026; Carter, Dem., 508,672; Anderson, Ind., 115,633; Clark, Libertarian, 13,123; Commoner, Citizens, 2,273; McReynolds, Socialist, 534; Hall Com., 298; DeBerry, Soc. Work., 244; Greaves, American, 189; Bubar, Statesman, 150; scattering, 519.

1984, Reagan, Rep., 703,088; Mondale, Dem., 605,620; Bergland, Libertarian, 1,844.

1988, Bush, Rep., 545,355; Dukakis, Dem., 670,557; LaRouche, Ind., 3,526; Paul, Lib., 2,494.

Kansas

		1992		1988	
County	Clinton (D)	Bush (R)	Perot (I)	Dukakis (D)	Bush (R)
Allen	2,309	2,348	1,745	2,392	3,429
Anderson	1,178	1,218	1,282	1,466	1,781
Atchison	2,959	2,520	2,019	3,177	3,243
Barber	759	1,223	893	1,118	1,539
Barton	3,845	5,111	4,574	5,024	7,741
Bourbon	2,507	2,871	1,761	2,623	3,660
Brown	1,476	2,203	1,603	1,719	3,059
Butler	6,967	9,054	7,258	7,690	10,976
Chase	470	610	600	538	884
Chautauqua	598	853	607	661	1,247
Cherokee	4,083	3,586	2,066	4,069	4,281
Cheyenne	407	863	477	594	1,105
Clark	293	676	341	409	876
Clay	947	2,198	1,434	1,112	2,997
Cloud	1,720	2,130	1,573	2,022	3,043
Coffey	1,020	1,822	1,443	1,246	2,581
Comanche	325	636	324	375	738
Cowley	5,316	5,338	5,796	6,186	7,778
Crawford	7,350	5,455	3,695	7,783	6,940
Decatur	576	940	565	793	1,291
Dickinson	2,607	3,851	2,744	2,870	5,121
Doniphan	1,177	1,579	1,229	1,312	2,162
Douglas	19,407	12,926	9,617	15,752	16,149
Edwards	567	769	584	792	993
Elk	485	748	503	608	1,075
Ellis	4,544	3,984	3,886	5,289	5,194
Ellsworth	1,010	1,196	1,020	1,219	1,711
Finney	2,596	5,248	2,994	3,408	5,381
Ford	2,627	4,308	3,334	3,817	5,685
Franklin	2,957	3,650	3,171	3,592	4,777
Geary	2,559	2,928	2,057	2,721	3,782
Gove	379	792	532	663	966
Graham	554	752	603	702	1,139
Grant	619	1,561	835	907	1,654
Gray	443	1,039	686	696	1,180
Greeley	191	504	175	317	506
Greenwood	1,262	1,411	1,167	1,421	2,217
Hamilton	386	716	271	517	801
Harper	845	1,371	1,151	1,235	1,941
Harvey	5,047	6,258	3,650	5,503	6,893
Haskell	341	1,023	462	427	964
Hodgeman	258	625	343	439	732
Jackson	1,639	1,970	1,927	2,261	2,759
Jefferson	2,530	2,565	2,629	2,810	3,605
Jewell	546	1,050	698	684	1,546
Johnson	59,538	85,364	49,092	55,183	95,591
Kearny	384	943	376	524	1,073
Kingman	1,100	1,680	1,370	1,420	2,205
Kiowa	355	1,057	475	485	1,276
Labette	4,196	3,368	2,577	4,433	5,125
Lane	265	674	356	450	768
Leavenworth	8,075	7,736	7,306	8,797	9,913
Lincoln	612	893	656	796	1,229
Linn	1,352	1,410	1,355	1,497	2,163
Logan	355	905	445	503	988
Lyon	4,796	5,073	7,696	5,314	6,820
McPherson	3,633	5,717	3,544	4,354	6,563
Marion	1,627	3,142	1,553	2,024	3,685
Marshall	2,021	1,892	1,786	2,560	3,140
Meade	430	1,135	592	664	1,322
Miami	3,834	3,528	3,701	4,427	4,807
Mitchell	938	1,601	1,098	1,145	2,257
Montgomery	5,453	6,848	3,570	5,429	9,067
Morris	957	1,071	1,071	1,165	1,682
Morton	398	915	350	569	1,074
Nemaha	1,580	2,220	1,804	2,261	2,849
Neosho	2,648	2,775	2,046	3,402	3,739
Ness	565	967	678	887	1,230
Norton	779	1,468	815	855	1,923
Osage	2,295	2,549	2,526	2,840	3,496
Osborne	779	1,003	819	943	1,541
Ottawa	762	1,284	742	953	1,836
Pawnee	1,118	1,357	1,097	1,474	1,825
Phillips	843	1,579	955	960	2,316
Pottawatomie	2,065	3,045	2,730	2,544	3,897
Pratt	1,465	1,779	1,527	1,651	2,505
Rawlins	393	1,023	517	612	1,318
Reno	7,341	8,971	6,073	11,545	12,753
Republic	939	1,767	1,084	1,069	2,346
Rice	1,548	2,135	1,535	2,033	2,503
Riley	7,928	8,389	5,386	7,283	9,507
Rooks	771	1,249	1,063	1,012	1,938
Rush	689	756	665	1,020	1,045
Russell	1,178	1,434	1,371	1,448	2,403
Saline	7,907	8,572	7,101	7,998	11,371
Scott	480	1,426	621	717	1,590
Sedgwick	60,918	72,580	45,972	65,618	86,124
Seward	1,375	3,248	1,667	1,655	4,089
Shawnee	31,920	29,297	20,615	33,940	35,489
Sheridan	347	739	546	600	901
Sherman	701	1,471	771	1,082	1,929
Smith	789	1,236	816	1,004	1,951
Stafford	787	1,074	901	1,121	1,532
Stanton	224	556	214	310	592
Stevens	390	1,408	674	612	1,642
Summer	3,564	4,087	3,887	4,417	5,394
Thomas	962	1,917	1,174	1,408	2,342
Trego	608	727	574	795	979
Wabaunsee	837	1,236	1,252	1,166	1,737
Wallace	164	679	219	257	655
Washington	893	1,718	1,054	1,063	2,269
Wichita	241	706	303	399	721
Wilson	1,331	1,924	1,364	1,545	2,743
Woodson	590	662	604	761	1,062
Wyandotte	34,454	12,870	13,615	38,678	19,097
Totals	**386,168**	**443,314**	**312,670**	**422,636**	**554,049**

Kansas Vote Since 1940

1940, Roosevelt, Dem., 364,725; Willkie, Rep., 489,169; Babson, Proh., 4,056; Thomas, Soc., 2,347.

1944, Roosevelt, Dem., 287,458; Dewey, Rep., 442,096; Watson, Proh., 2,609; Thomas, Soc., 1,613.

1948, Truman, Dem., 351,902; Dewey, Rep., 423,039; Watson, Proh., 6,468; Wallace, Prog., 4,603; Thomas, Soc., 2,807.

1952, Eisenhower, Rep., 616,302; Stevenson, Dem., 273,296; Hamblen, Proh., 6,038; Hoopes, Soc., 530.

1956, Eisenhower, Rep., 566,878; Stevenson. Dem., 296,317; Holtwick, Proh., 3,048.

1960, Kennedy, Dem., 363,213; Nixon, Rep., 561,474; Decker, Proh., 4,138.

1964, Johnson, Dem., 464,028; Goldwater, Rep., 386,579; Munn, Proh., 5,393; Hass, Soc. Labor, 1,901.

1968, Nixon, Rep., 478,674; Humphrey, Dem., 302,996; Wallace, 3d, 88,921; Munn, Proh., 2,192.

1972, Nixon, Rep., 619,812; McGovern, Dem., 270,287; Schmitz, Cons., 21,808; Munn, Proh., 4,188.

1976, Carter, Dem., 430,421; Ford, Rep., 502,752; McCarthy, Ind., 13,185; Anderson, Amer., 4,724; MacBride, Libertarian, 3,242; Maddox, Cons., 2,118; Bubar, Proh., 1,403.

1980, Reagan, Rep., 566,812; Carter, Dem., 326,150; Anderson, Ind., 68,231; Clark, Libertarian, 14,470; Shelton, American, 1,555; Hall, Com., 967; Bubar, Statesman, 821; Rarick, Conservative, 789.

1984, Reagan, Rep., 674,646; Mondale, Dem., 332,471; Bergland, Libertarian, 3,585.

1988, Bush, Rep., 554,049; Dukakis, Dem., 422,636; Paul, Ind., 12,553; Fulani, Ind., 3,806.

Kentucky

County	1992 Clinton (D)	1992 Bush (R)	1992 Perot (I)	1988 Dukakis (D)	1988 Bush (R)
Adair	2,044	3,740	617	1,723	4,346
Allen	2,040	2,747	606	1,573	3,342
Anderson	2,491	2,731	1,219	2,176	3,225
Ballard	2,268	1,108	500	2,162	1,460
Barren	5,688	5,467	1,778	4,799	6,653
Bath	2,229	1,259	694	2,099	1,614
Bell	5,745	4,501	1,193	5,182	5,759
Boone	6,514	12,306	4,676	5,382	12,667
Bourbon	2,895	2,707	1,290	2,793	3,308
Boyd	10,496	7,387	3,195	9,552	9,379
Boyle	3,894	4,019	1,335	3,575	4,746
Bracken	1,259	1,162	500	1,176	1,630
Breathitt	3,496	1,303	515	3,387	2,149
Breckinridge	3,113	2,941	945	2,765	3,841
Bullitt	7,830	7,745	3,333	6,005	8,859
Butler	1,468	2,729	596	1,245	3,278
Caldwell	3,000	1,966	670	2,564	2,952
Calloway	6,181	4,654	1,853	5,287	6,225
Campbell	10,673	16,382	5,659	9,553	19,387
Carlisle	1,383	844	309	1,428	1,104
Carroll	2,119	1,046	566	1,913	1,702
Carter	4,224	3,305	989	4,570	4,325
Casey	1,409	3,317	542	1,216	3,857
Christian	6,709	7,737	1,789	5,704	9,250
Clark	4,892	4,625	1,955	4,252	5,329
Clay	2,012	4,657	656	1,709	4,156
Clinton	1,241	2,830	348	899	3,248
Crittenden	1,740	1,576	495	1,443	2,211
Cumberland	917	1,866	268	753	2,231
Daviess	16,592	14,936	5,112	14,815	17,356
Edmonson	1,653	2,486	438	1,243	2,555
Elliott	1,796	444	273	1,797	550
Estill	1,837	2,453	736	1,692	3,077
Fayette	38,306	41,908	14,215	32,554	48,065
Fleming	2,257	2,045	815	2,086	2,409
Floyd	13,351	3,540	1,723	12,327	5,296
Franklin	9,893	7,583	3,338	9,271	9,805
Fulton	1,813	1,073	306	1,531	1,474
Gallatin	1,171	699	445	1,060	881
Garrard	1,730	2,359	697	1,710	2,681
Grant	2,097	2,128	1,149	1,896	2,835
Graves	8,001	5,311	1,943	7,153	6,274
Grayson	2,808	4,391	960	2,575	5,186
Green	1,760	2,709	500	1,595	3,139
Greenup	7,214	4,975	2,188	6,956	6,559
Hancock	1,714	1,261	551	1,478	1,733
Hardin	9,456	12,357	4,018	7,262	13,240
Harlan	6,796	3,970	1,391	7,341	5,166
Harrison	2,795	2,148	1,225	2,748	2,983
Hart	2,852	2,401	579	2,519	2,927
Henderson	8,270	5,125	2,678	7,648	6,911
Henry	2,838	1,640	720	2,544	2,286
Hickman	1,296	861	294	1,158	1,142
Hopkins	8,641	5,899	2,505	7,453	7,979
Jackson	776	3,398	341	678	3,926
Jefferson	152,728	116,566	39,822	127,936	139,711
Jessamine	3,764	6,474	2,059	2,955	7,057
Johnson	2,669	4,614	1,118	3,538	4,619
Kenton	14,344	27,262	9,270	14,838	30,738
Knott	5,500	1,243	560	5,185	1,691
Knox	3,785	5,007	971	2,919	4,903
Larue	2,190	2,154	582	1,822	2,590
Laurel	4,560	8,583	1,859	3,620	9,296
Lawrence	2,400	2,084	552	2,198	2,294
Lee	1,170	1,617	356	984	1,588
Leslie	1,591	2,879	450	1,105	3,280
Letcher	5,630	2,912	1,177	4,697	3,601
Lewis	1,713	2,493	673	1,568	3,108
Lincoln	2,532	2,624	762	2,677	3,530
Livingston	2,386	1,339	578	2,052	1,834
Logan	4,064	3,710	1,043	3,379	4,295
Lyon	1,583	820	293	1,337	1,077
McCracken	13,341	10,657	3,077	12,208	12,160
McCreary	1,934	3,588	624	1,644	3,477
McLean	2,223	1,355	529	2,269	1,829
Madison	8,005	8,719	3,038	6,672	9,958
Magoffin	3,261	1,992	440	2,895	2,158
Marion	3,403	2,091	805	3,152	2,500
Marshall	6,576	4,368	1,773	5,888	5,256
Martin	1,715	1,961	393	1,581	2,587
Mason	2,657	2,432	910	2,721	3,158
Meade	3,387	2,641	1,298	3,079	3,441
Menifee	1,311	557	254	1,096	670
Mercer	3,010	3,211	1,298	2,832	3,904
Metcalfe	1,703	1,683	409	1,705	2,179
Monroe	1,515	3,776	480	1,025	4,214
Montgomery	3,686	2,590	1,308	3,082	3,435
Morgan	2,655	1,239	498	2,329	1,452
Muhlenberg	7,901	3,551	1,624	6,912	5,369
Nelson	5,437	4,495	1,638	4,788	5,283
Nicholas	1,341	894	513	1,242	1,271
Ohio	4,022	3,385	1,423	3,612	4,910
Oldham	5,457	8,263	2,855	4,025	8,716
Owen	1,830	1,108	613	1,823	1,468
Owsley	678	1,437	209	345	1,266
Pendleton	1,740	1,810	1,086	1,576	2,487
Perry	6,619	4,128	1,308	5,557	5,154
Pike	16,999	8,024	2,384	16,339	9,976
Powell	2,323	1,809	874	2,113	2,128
Pulaski	5,465	11,423	2,449	4,788	13,482
Robertson	439	329	170	515	511
Rockcastle	1,144	3,287	446	1,041	3,880
Rowan	3,366	2,335	1,169	2,968	3,093
Russell	1,950	4,641	673	1,455	4,292
Scott	3,639	3,810	1,800	3,380	4,482
Shelby	4,398	4,550	1,451	3,834	4,998
Simpson	2,834	2,280	708	2,138	2,699
Spencer	1,383	1,305	466	1,121	1,368
Taylor	3,518	4,319	1,044	2,879	5,362
Todd	1,858	1,671	612	1,632	2,282
Trigg	2,438	1,820	573	1,991	2,427
Trimble	1,413	789	413	1,342	1,083
Union	3,325	1,605	794	3,316	2,292
Warren	11,529	14,748	3,533	9,684	16,703
Washington	2,008	2,098	542	1,950	2,445
Wayne	2,516	3,412	502	2,057	3,672
Webster	3,380	1,408	854	3,019	2,159
Whitley	4,600	5,998	1,533	3,794	7,337
Wolfe	1,674	697	297	1,516	916
Woodford	3,161	3,992	1,535	2,653	4,512
Totals	**661,059**	**617,419**	**203,587**	**580,368**	**734,281**

Kentucky Vote Since 1940

1940, Roosevelt, Dem., 557,222; Willkie, Rep., 410,384; Babson, Proh., 1,443; Thomas, Soc., 1,014.

1944, Roosevelt, Dem., 472,589; Dewey, Rep., 392,448; Watson, Proh., 2,023; Thomas, Soc., 535; Teichert, Soc. Labor, 326.

1948, Truman, Dem., 466,756; Dewey, Rep., 341,210; Thurmond, States' Rights, 10,411; Wallace, Prog., 1,567; Thomas, Soc., 1,284; Watson, Proh., 1,245; Teichert, Soc. Labor, 185.

1952, Eisenhower, Rep., 495,029; Stevenson, Dem., 495,729; Hamblen, Proh., 1,161; Hass, Soc. Labor, 893; Hallinan, Proh., 336.

1956, Eisenhower, Rep., 572,192; Stevenson, Dem., 476,453; Byrd, States' Rights, 2,657; Holtwick, Proh., 2,145; Hass, Soc. Labor, 358.

1960, Kennedy, Dem., 521,855; Nixon, Rep., 602,607.

1964, Johnson, Dem., 669,659; Goldwater, Rep., 372,977; John Kasper, Nat'l. States Rights, 3,469.

1968, Nixon, Rep., 462,411; Humphrey, Dem., 397,547; Wallace, 3d p., 193,098; Halstead, Soc. Worker, 2,843.

1972, Nixon, Rep., 676,446; McGovern, Dem., 371,159; Schmitz, Amer., 17,627; Jenness, Soc. Workers, 685; Hall, Com., 464; Spock, Peoples, 1,118.

1976, Carter, Dem., 615,717; Ford, Rep., 531,852; Anderson, Amer., 8,308; McCarthy, Ind., 6,837; Maddox, Amer. Ind., 2,328; MacBride, Libertarian, 814.

1980, Reagan, Rep., 635,274; Carter, Dem., 616,417; Anderson, Ind., 31,127; Clark, Libertarian, 5,531; McCormack, Respect For Life, 4,233; Commoner, Citizens, 1,304; Pulley, Socialist, 393; Hall, Com., 348.

1984, Reagan, Rep., 815,345; Mondale, Dem., 536,756.

1988, Bush, Rep., 734,281; Dukakis, Dem., 580,368; Duke, Pop., 4,494; Paul, Lib., 2,118.

Louisiana

Parish	1992 Clinton (D)	1992 Bush (R)	1992 Perot (I)	1988 Dukakis (D)	1988 Bush (R)
Acadia	12,276	9,017	3,245	11,510	11,319
Allen	5,625	3,069	1,245	5,204	3,674
Ascension	13,036	9,794	4,080	12,147	10,726
Assumption	5,639	2,928	1,358	5,610	4,017
Avoyelles	8,696	4,851	2,139	7,353	7,659
Beauregard	5,037	5,119	2,103	4,704	6,466
Bienville	3,899	2,412	832	3,705	3,680
Bossier	11,313	15,628	4,863	9,035	20,807
Caddo	47,468	42,556	11,030	39,204	54,498
Calcasieu	33,573	24,853	10,794	33,932	29,649
Caldwell	2,061	1,752	653	1,423	2,997
Cameron	1,985	1,329	995	2,257	1,775
Catahoula	2,570	1,976	773	1,916	2,862
Claiborne	3,263	2,599	926	3,158	3,756
Concordia	4,283	3,223	1,318	3,461	5,037
DeSoto	5,671	3,634	1,334	5,366	5,022
E. Baton Rouge	68,518	81,043	16,274	59,270	86,791
East Carroll	1,835	1,142	277	1,809	1,536
East Feliciana	4,093	2,813	932	3,659	3,527
Evangeline	8,426	5,054	2,034	7,693	7,437
Franklin	4,127	3,907	1,295	3,043	5,520

Grant	3,122	3,214	1,174	2,628	4,402
Iberia	13,040	11,905	4,301	12,166	15,438
Iberville	7,908	5,114	1,522	8,678	5,855
Jackson	2,955	3,059	877	2,842	4,251
Jefferson	64,285	99,788	21,274	53,035	110,942
Jefferson Davis	7,022	4,513	2,221	6,799	5,851
Lafayette	28,583	32,406	9,124	24,133	36,648
Lafourche	16,182	12,744	5,077	15,013	16,152
LaSalle	2,382	3,068	993	1,622	4,559
Lincoln	7,205	7,020	1,751	5,427	8,853
Livingston	11,504	14,809	4,971	9,659	15,779
Madison	2,773	1,702	467	2,416	2,334
Morehouse	6,013	5,154	1,668	4,496	7,335
Natchitoches	6,974	5,694	1,592	6,151	7,224
Orleans	133,470	51,658	10,560	116,851	64,763
Ouachita	20,835	27,519	6,602	15,429	33,858
Plaquemines	4,467	5,018	1,719	3,997	6,084
Pointe Coupee	6,512	3,563	1,157	6,308	4,333
Rapides	20,873	22,783	6,581	17,928	29,977
Red River	2,360	1,649	555	2,254	2,266
Richland	3,705	3,808	1,003	2,833	5,226
Sabine	4,173	3,586	1,210	3,532	4,767
St. Bernard	12,305	16,131	4,308	11,406	19,609
St. Charles	8,987	9,337	2,722	7,973	9,685
St. Helena	3,416	1,515	570	3,013	2,006
St. James	6,682	3,400	999	6,707	3,799
St. John The Baptist	8,968	6,369	1,917	8,366	7,464
St. Landry	20,392	11,882	4,261	19,091	15,790
St. Martin	11,320	6,018	2,541	10,148	7,541
St. Mary	10,648	8,740	3,214	10,364	11,540
St. Tammany	19,797	36,740	9,008	15,638	38,334
Tangipahoa	15,194	14,148	4,560	13,527	16,669
Tensas	1,666	1,153	353	1,556	1,645
Terrebonne	13,325	14,662	5,505	12,686	18,745
Union	4,005	4,434	1,209	3,210	5,900
Vermilion	12,324	7,062	3,077	12,180	9,224
Vernon	6,000	5,912	2,294	4,998	7,453
Washington	9,095	7,227	2,303	8,369	9,374
Webster	8,380	6,640	2,629	7,434	10,204
W. Baton Rouge	5,131	3,522	1,249	4,686	3,972
West Carroll	2,068	2,082	727	1,607	3,077
West Feliciana	2,328	1,501	516	2,146	1,854
Winn	3,537	2,932	843	2,699	4,165
Totals	**815,305**	**729,880**	**210,604**	**717,460**	**883,702**

Louisiana Vote Since 1940

1940, Roosevelt, Dem., 319,751; Willkie, Rep., 52,446.

1944, Roosevelt, Dem., 281,564; Dewey, Rep., 67,750.

1948, Thurmond, States' Rights, 204,290; Truman, Dem., 136,344; Dewey, Rep., 72,657; Wallace, Prog., 3,035.

1952, Eisenhower, Rep., 306,925, Stevenson, Dem., 345,027.

1956, Eisenhower, Rep., 329,047; Stevenson, Dem., 243,977; Andrews, States' Rights, 44,520.

1960, Kennedy, Dem., 407,339; Nixon, Rep., 230,890; States' Rights (unpledged) 169,572.

1964, Johnson, Dem., 387,068; Goldwater, Rep., 509,225.

1968, Nixon, Rep., 257,535; Humphrey, Dem., 309,615; Wallace, 3d party, 530,300.

1972, Nixon, Rep., 686,852; McGovern, Dem., 298,142; Schmitz, Amer., 52,099; Jenness, Soc. Workers, 14,398.

1976, Carter, Dem., 661,365; Ford, Rep., 587,446; Maddox, Amer., 10,058; Hall, Com., 7,417; McCarthy, Ind., 6,588; MacBride, Libertarian, 3,325.

1980, Reagan, Rep., 792,853; Carter, Dem., 708,453; Anderson, Ind., 26,345; Rarick, Amer. Ind., 10,333; Clark, Libertarian, 8,240; Commoner, Citizens, 1,584; DeBerry, Soc. Work., 783.

1984, Reagan, Rep., 1,037,299; Mondale, Dem., 651,586; Bergland, Libertarian, 1,876.

1988, Bush, Rep., 883,702; Dukakis, Dem., 717,460; Duke, Pop., 18,612; Paul, Lib., 4,115.

Maine

	1992			1988	
City	Clinton (D)	Bush (R)	Perot (I)	Dukakis (D)	Bush (R)
Auburn	5,025	3,653	3,964	4,629	5,947
Augusta	4,657	3,003	3,002	4,576	5,182
Bangor	6,782	5,122	4,666	6,534	7,194
Bath	1,988	1,630	1,448	1,838	2,543
Biddeford	4,945	2,533	2,717	5,017	4,375
Brewer	1,788	1,907	1,625	1,784	2,908
Gardiner	1,391	1,054	1,115	1,395	1,609
Lewiston	9,262	4,372	6,180	9,225	7,265
Old Town	2,272	1,173	1,302	2,220	1,640
Portland	19,503	8,659	6,910	18,234	11,676
Rockland	1,120	1,181	1,059	1,198	1,850
Saco	4,000	2,769	2,303	3,169	3,852
Sanford	3,854	3,030	3,215	3,456	4,541
South Portland	5,928	3,996	2,228	5,820	5,744
Waterville	3,868	1,832	2,257	4,031	3,158
Westbrook	3,835	3,033	2,618	3,648	4,086
Totals	**261,859**	**207,122**	**205,076**	**243,569**	**307,131**

Maine Vote Since 1940

1940, Roosevelt, Dem., 156,478; Willkie, Rep., 165,951; Browder, Com., 411.

1944, Roosevelt, Dem., 140,631; Dewey, Rep., 155,434; Teichert, Soc. Labor, 335.

1948, Truman, Dem., 111,916; Dewey, Rep., 150,234; Wallace, Prog., 1,884; Thomas, Soc., 547; Teichert, Soc. Labor, 206.

1952, Eisenhower, Rep., 232,353; Stevenson, Dem., 118,806; Hallinan, Prog., 332; Hass, Soc. Labor, 156; Hoopes, Soc., 138; scattered, 1.

1956, Eisenhower, Rep., 249,238; Stevenson, Dem., 102,468.

1960, Kennedy, Dem., 181,159; Nixon, Rep., 240,608.

1964, Johnson, Dem., 262,264; Goldwater, Rep., 118,701.

1968, Nixon, Rep., 169,254; Humphrey, Dem., 217,312; Wallace, 3d party, 6,370.

1972, Nixon, Rep., 256,458; McGovern, Dem., 160,584; scattered, 229.

1976, Carter, Dem., 232,279; Ford, Rep., 236,320; McCarthy, Ind., 10,874; Bubar, Proh., 3,495.

1980, Reagan, Rep., 238,522; Carter, Dem., 220,974; Anderson, Ind., 53,327; Clark, Libertarian, 5,119; Commoner, Citizens, 4,394; Hall, Com., 591; write-ins, 84.

1984, Reagan, Rep., 336,500; Mondale, Dem., 214,515.

1988, Bush, Rep., 307,131; Dukakis, Dem., 243,569; Paul, Lib., 2,700; Fulani, New Alliance, 1,405.

Maryland

	1992			1988	
County	Clinton (D)	Bush (R)	Perot (I)	Dukakis (D)	Bush (R)
Allegany	10,884	13,085	4,838	11,844	17,462
Anne Arundel	65,183	77,203	33,922	55,440	98,540
Baltimore	137,842	121,500	50,289	121,570	163,881
Calvert	8,241	9,390	4,358	6,376	10,956
Caroline	2,690	3,696	1,668	2,440	4,661
Carroll	14,638	27,232	10,643	12,368	31,224
Cecil	9,727	10,294	5,938	7,807	13,224
Charles	13,817	16,424	6,261	11,823	20,828
Dorchester	3,735	4,678	1,946	3,709	6,343
Frederick	20,592	29,920	11,013	17,061	32,575
Garrett	2,684	5,416	1,918	2,557	6,665
Harford	25,786	34,592	16,361	19,803	38,493
Howard	41,763	36,370	15,464	34,007	44,153
Kent	2,871	2,894	1,347	2,925	3,761
Montgomery	185,377	112,396	39,946	165,187	154,191
Prince George's	163,723	60,065	22,580	133,816	86,545
Queen Anne's	4,403	6,504	2,876	3,857	7,803
St. Mary's	8,406	10,824	4,344	7,434	12,767
Somerset	2,945	3,237	1,173	2,911	4,222
Talbot	4,278	6,295	2,107	3,948	8,170
Washington	15,561	20,893	7,252	14,408	25,912
Wicomico	10,742	12,916	4,968	9,413	16,272
Worcester	5,633	6,767	3,109	4,787	8,430
Totals	**941,979**	**671,609**	**271,198**	**826,304**	**876,167**

Maryland Vote Since 1940

1940, Roosevelt, Dem., 384,546; Willkie, Rep., 269,534; Thomas, Soc., 4,093; Browder, Com., 1,274; Aiken, Soc. Labor, 657.

1944, Roosevelt, Dem., 315,490; Dewey, Rep., 292,949.

1948, Truman, Dem., 286,521; Dewey, Rep., 294,814; Wallace, Prog., 9,983; Thomas, Soc., 2,941; Thurmond, States' Rights, 2,476; Wright, write-in, 2,294.

1952, Eisenhower, Rep., 499,424; Stevenson, Dem., 395,337; Hallinan, Prog., 7,313.

1956, Eisenhower, Rep., 559,738; Stevenson, Dem., 372,613.

1960, Kennedy, Dem., 565,800; Nixon, Rep., 489,538.

1964, Johnson, Dem., 730,912; Goldwater, Rep., 385,495; write-in, 50.

1968, Nixon, Rep., 517,995; Humphrey, Dem., 538,310; Wallace, 3d party, 178,734.

1972, Nixon, Rep., 829,305; McGovern, Dem., 505,781; Schmitz, Amer., 18,726.

1976, Carter, Dem., 759,612; Ford, Rep., 672,661.

1980, Reagan, Rep., 680,606; Carter, Dem., 726,161; Anderson, Ind., 119,537; Clark, Libertarian, 14,192.

1984, Reagan, Rep., 879,918; Mondale, Dem., 787,935; Bergland, Libertarian, 5,721.

1988, Bush, Rep., 876,167; Dukakis, Dem., 826,304; Paul, Lib., 6,748; Fulani, Alliance, 5,115.

Massachusetts

City	1992 Clinton (D)	1992 Bush (R)	1992 Perot (I)	1988 Dukakis (D)	1988 Bush (R)
Boston	113,686	41,674	24,840	122,349	62,202
Brockton	13,016	8,729	7,491	14,776	16,056
Cambridge	30,360	5,809	4,074	32,027	8,770
Fall River	18,642	5,451	6,916	20,184	8,394
Framingham	15,165	8,114	6,089	15,826	12,745
Lawrence	7,686	5,074	3,241	9,255	8,265
Lowell	14,485	8,466	8,891	16,391	13,998
Lynn	15,218	7,325	7,643	18,540	12,182
New Bedford	20,873	5,253	6,964	22,609	9,901
Newton	28,991	9,621	5,681	29,039	13,892
Quincy	18,879	12,296	9,063	20,911	18,403
Somerville	19,743	5,880	4,414	21,612	8,931
Springfield	26,977	12,195	10,355	30,113	16,244
Worcester	32,270	17,195	10,477	34,369	24,355
Totals	**1,315,016**	**803,974**	**630,440**	**1,401,415**	**1,194,635**

Massachusetts Vote Since 1940

1940, Roosevelt, Dem., 1,076,522; Willkie, Rep., 939,700; Thomas, Soc., 4,091; Browder, Com., 3,806; Aiken, Soc. Labor, 1,492; Babson, Proh., 1,370.

1944, Roosevelt, Dem., 1,035,296; Dewey, Rep., 921,350; Teichert, Soc. Labor, 2,780; Watson, Proh., 973.

1948, Truman, Dem., 1,151,788; Dewey, Rep., 909,370; Wallace, Prog., 38,157; Teichert, Soc. Labor, 5,535; Watson, Proh., 1,663.

1952, Eisenhower, Rep., 1,292,325; Stevenson, Dem., 1,083,525; Hallinan, Prog., 4,636; Hass, Soc. Labor, 1,957; Hamblen, Proh., 886; scattered, 69; blanks, 41,150.

1956, Eisenhower, Rep., 1,393,197; Stevenson, Dem., 948,190; Hass, Soc. Labor, 5,573; Holtwick, Proh., 1,205; others, 341.

1960, Kennedy, Dem., 1,487,174; Nixon, Rep., 976,750; Hass, Soc. Labor, 3,892; Decker, Proh., 1,633; others, 31; blank and void, 26,024.

1964, Johnson, Dem., 1,786,422; Goldwater, Rep., 549,727; Hass, Soc. Labor, 4,755; Munn, Proh., 3,735; scattered, 159; blank, 48,104.

1968, Nixon, Rep., 766,844; Humphrey, Dem., 1,469,218; Wallace, 3d party, 87,088; Blomen, Soc. Labor, 6,180; Munn, Proh., 2,369; scattered, 53; blanks, 25,394.

1972, Nixon, Rep., 1,112,078; McGovern, Dem., 1,332,540; Jenness, Soc. Workers, 10,600; Fisher, Soc. Labor, 129; Schmitz, Amer., 2,877; Spock, Peoples, 101; Hall, Com., 46; Hospers, Libertarian, 43; scattered, 342.

1976, Carter, Dem., 1,429,475; Ford, Rep., 1,030,276; McCarthy, Ind., 65,637; Camejo, Soc. Workers, 8,138; Anderson, Amer., 7,555; La Rouche, U.S. Labor, 4,922; MacBride, Libertarian, 135.

1980, Reagan, Rep., 1,057,631; Carter, Dem., 1,053,802; Anderson, Ind., 382,539; Clark, Libertarian, 22,038; DeBerry, Soc. Workers, 3,735; Commoner, Citizens, 2,056; McReynolds, Socialist, 62; Bubar, Statesman, 34; Griswold, Workers World, 19; scattered, 2,382.

1984, Reagan, Rep., 1,310,936; Mondale, Dem., 1,239,606.

1988, Bush, Rep., 1,194,635; Dukakis, Dem., 1,401,415; Paul, Lib., 24,251; Fulani, New Alliance, 9,561.

Michigan

County	1992 Clinton (D)	1992 Bush (R)	1992 Perot (I)	1988 Dukakis (D)	1988 Bush (R)
Alcona	2,390	2,247	1,117	1,918	2,966
Alger	2,144	1,471	941	2,210	1,830
Allegan	13,005	19,255	8,838	10,785	22,163
Alpena	6,894	4,878	3,236	6,341	6,664
Antrim	3,431	3,984	2,525	3,159	5,231
Arenac	3,278	2,330	1,608	3,211	3,064
Baraga	1,695	1,160	720	1,753	1,630
Barry	8,444	9,153	6,303	7,983	12,546
Bay	26,496	16,367	11,236	28,225	20,710
Benzie	2,715	2,438	1,619	2,437	3,240
Berrien	22,180	27,399	13,133	21,948	37,799
Branch	5,849	5,954	4,668	5,231	9,225
Calhoun	25,538	19,791	13,058	22,717	26,771
Cass	8,147	7,393	4,728	7,444	10,229
Charlevoix	4,063	4,017	3,360	3,875	5,802
Cheboygan	4,459	3,867	2,495	3,943	5,395
Chippewa	5,434	5,462	2,706	5,222	6,786
Clare	5,345	3,915	2,808	4,710	5,661
Clinton	10,116	12,216	7,877	9,225	15,497
Crawford	2,252	2,193	1,441	1,825	3,097
Delta	8,387	6,027	3,485	8,891	7,114
Dickinson	5,689	4,273	3,012	6,129	6,158
Eaton	16,524	18,385	12,136	15,322	24,193
Emmet	4,245	5,312	3,575	4,170	7,105
Genesee	104,794	47,524	46,043	104,880	70,922
Gladwin	4,457	3,616	2,649	4,164	4,746
Gogebic	4,792	2,838	1,543	5,151	3,509
Grand Traverse	11,148	13,629	9,495	10,098	17,191
Gratiot	5,681	6,279	3,866	5,719	8,447
Hillsdale	5,244	7,579	4,968	4,763	10,571
Houghton	6,558	5,575	2,906	6,510	7,098
Huron	6,023	6,491	4,064	5,714	9,419
Ingham	61,596	43,926	27,683	55,984	58,363
Ionia	8,430	9,136	6,211	8,160	12,028
Iosco	5,369	4,912	3,131	4,929	7,234
Iron	3,647	1,999	1,341	3,774	2,866
Isabella	8,773	7,706	5,434	7,960	10,362
Jackson	23,693	25,421	15,214	21,865	33,885
Kalamazoo	43,568	38,035	21,666	39,457	50,205
Kalkaska	2,196	2,068	1,853	2,092	3,369
Kent	83,219	125,628	44,028	73,467	131,910
Keweenaw	582	378	212	631	536
Lake	2,351	1,194	981	1,958	1,713
Lapeer	11,982	12,326	10,541	10,736	16,670
Leelanau	3,449	3,998	2,634	3,331	5,215
Lenawee	15,400	14,288	9,515	13,690	19,115
Livingston	17,851	27,539	15,971	13,749	31,331
Luce	972	958	660	864	1,528
Mackinac	2,384	2,368	1,251	2,093	3,127
Macomb	127,788	144,199	66,358	112,856	175,632
Manistee	3,549	2,472	2,200	4,765	5,368
Marquette	16,038	9,665	5,768	15,418	11,704
Mason	4,829	5,102	3,096	4,531	6,800
Mecosta	6,096	6,047	3,607	4,736	8,181
Menominee	4,559	3,995	2,479	4,918	5,440
Midland	13,382	16,149	8,945	13,452	19,994
Missaukee	1,893	2,829	1,306	1,621	3,566
Monroe	24,957	20,450	13,551	21,847	26,189
Montcalm	8,721	8,420	5,499	7,664	10,963
Montmorency	1,903	1,794	1,077	1,563	2,514
Muskegon	32,156	23,666	15,242	28,977	33,567
Newaygo	6,455	7,332	4,056	5,389	9,896
Oakland	214,062	241,438	94,861	174,745	283,359
Oceana	3,846	3,944	2,712	3,356	5,693
Ogemaw	4,016	2,936	2,121	4,012	4,091
Ontonagon	2,449	1,464	805	2,517	2,023
Osceola	3,529	3,606	2,199	2,860	5,218
Oscoda	1,471	1,583	754	1,170	1,972
Otsego	3,129	3,393	2,635	2,835	4,620
Ottawa	22,192	56,872	16,864	18,769	61,515
Presque Isle	3,303	2,397	1,612	3,025	3,614
Roscommon	5,243	4,170	2,551	4,394	5,866
Saginaw	43,812	32,103	20,522	45,616	42,401
St. Clair	23,590	24,119	18,490	20,909	32,336
St. Joseph	7,818	9,836	6,208	7,017	13,084
Sanilac	5,876	7,891	4,837	5,445	10,653
Schoolcraft	2,139	1,253	721	2,071	1,802
Shiawassee	12,629	10,930	8,632	13,056	15,506
Tuscola	9,138	8,639	6,745	9,060	12,093
Van Buren	12,540	10,356	7,235	10,668	14,522
Washtenaw	73,201	41,303	21,747	61,799	55,029
Wayne	500,521	255,304	101,111	450,222	291,996
Wexford	4,894	4,696	2,900	4,287	6,043
Totals	**1,854,603**	**1,585,251**	**819,931**	**1,675,783**	**1,965,486**

Michigan Vote Since 1940

1940, Roosevelt, Dem., 1,032,991; Willkie, Rep., 1,039,917; Thomas, Soc., 7,593; Browder, Com., 2,834; Babson, Proh., 1,795; Aiken, Soc. Labor, 795.

1944, Roosevelt, Dem., 1,106,899; Dewey, Rep., 1,084,423; Watson, Proh., 6,503; Thomas, Soc., 4,598; Smith, America First, 1,530; Teichert, Soc. Labor, 1,264.

1948, Truman, Dem., 1,003,448; Dewey, Rep., 1,038,595; Wallace, Prog., 46,515; Watson, Proh., 13,052; Thomas, Soc. 6,063; Teichert, Soc. Labor, 1,263; Dobbs, Soc. Workers, 672.

1952, Eisenhower, Rep., 1,551,529; Stevenson, Dem., 1,230,657; Hamblen, Proh., 10,331; Hallinan, Prog., 3,922; Hass, Soc. Labor, 1,495; Dobbs, Soc. Workers, 655; scattered, 3.

1956, Eisenhower, Rep., 1,713,647; Stevenson, Dem., 1,359,898; Holtwick, Proh., 6,923.

1960, Kennedy, Dem., 1,687,269; Nixon, Rep., 1,620,428; Dobbs, Soc. Workers, 4,347; Decker, Proh., 2,029; Daly, Tax Cut, 1,767; Hass, Soc. Labor, 1,718; Ind. American, 539.

1964, Johnson, Dem., 2,136,615; Goldwater, Rep., 1,060,152; DeBerry, Soc. Workers, 3,817; Hass, Soc. Labor, 1,704; Proh. (no candidate listed), 699, scattering, 145.

1968, Nixon, Rep., 1,370,665; Humphrey, Dem., 1,593,082; Wallace, 3d party, 331,968; Halstead, Soc. Worker, 4,099; Blomen, Soc. Labor, 1,762; Cleaver, New Politics, 4,585; Munn, Proh., 60; scattering, 29.

1972, Nixon, Rep., 1,961,721; McGovern, Dem., 1,459,435; Schmitz, Amer., 63,321; Fisher, Soc. Labor, 2,437; Jenness, Soc. Workers, 1,603; Hall, Com., 1,210.

1976, Carter, Dem., 1,696,714; Ford, Rep., 1,893,742; McCarthy, Ind., 47,905; MacBride, Libertarian, 5,406; Wright, People's, 3,504, Camejo, Soc. Workers, 1,804; LaRouche, U.S. Labor, 1,366; Levin, Soc. Labor, 1,148; scattering, 2,160.

1980, Reagan, Rep., 1,915,225; Carter, Dem., 1,661,532; Anderson, Ind., 275,223; Clark, Libertarian, 41,597; Commoner, Citizens, 11,930; Hall, Com., 3,262; Griswold, Workers World, 30; Greaves, American, 21; Bubar, Statesman, 9.

1984, Reagan, Rep., 2,251,571; Mondale, Dem., 1,529,638; Bergland, Libertarian, 10,055.

1988, Bush, Rep., 1,965,486; Dukakis, Dem., 1,675,783; Paul, Lib., 18,336; Fulani, Ind., 2,513.

Minnesota

County	1992 Clinton (D)	1992 Bush (R)	1992 Perot (I)	1988 Dukakis (D)	1988 Bush (R)
Aitkin	3,400	2,151	1,951	3,863	3,011
Anoka	52,925	38,896	33,424	57,953	46,853
Becker	4,958	5,430	3,238	5,787	6,738
Beltrami	7,210	5,204	3,473	7,566	6,652
Benton	5,110	5,019	4,003	5,861	6,060
Big Stone	1,610	1,052	740	2,026	1,469
Blue Earth	11,515	8,781	7,282	12,375	11,959
Brown	4,278	5;390	3,845	5,109	6,898
Carlton	7,736	3,922	3,006	8,790	4,626
Carver	8,348	10,200	7,942	8,439	12,560
Cass	4,901	4,276	2,939	5,127	5,895
Chippewa	2,929	2,143	1,505	3,238	3,190
Chisago	7,077	4,813	5,098	7,875	6,163
Clay	9,845	9,666	3,835	11,186	10,380
Clearwater	1,587	1,315	841	1,769	1,763
Cook	1,005	878	704	1,080	1,078
Cottonwood	2,374	2,478	1,757	3,095	3,390
Crow Wing	8,812	9,051	6,333	9,674	11,017
Dakota	63,655	52,307	40,237	61,942	61,606
Dodge	2,622	3,045	2,231	2,925	3,848
Douglas	5,171	6,260	4,069	5,803	7,898
Faribault	3,339	3,439	2,322	3,879	4,846
Fillmore	3,973	3,581	3,009	4,114	5,004
Freeborn	7,644	5,013	4,803	8,836	7,226
Goodhue	7,644	6,739	5,609	9,438	9,455
Grant	1,561	1,201	885	1,950	1,693
Hennepin	278,536	179,590	123,434	292,909	240,209
Houston	3,714	3,820	2,664	3,936	4,777
Hubbard	3,362	3,227	1,949	3,306	4,365
Isanti	5,390	3,989	3,898	6,075	5,246
Itasca	9,621	5,952	5,147	10,517	8,358
Jackson	2,481	1,824	1,918	3,275	2,629
Kanabec	2,532	1,576	1,836	2,970	2,571
Kandiyohi	7,914	6,785	4,869	8,962	8,634
Kittson	1,307	1,098	558	1,650	1,381
Koochiching	3,167	1,754	1,798	3,867	2,842
LacQuiParle	2,342	1,435	1,163	2,805	2,116
Lake	3,415	1,465	1,437	3,887	1,838
Lake O'Woods	794	762	629	798	984
Le Sueur	4,664	3,858	3,363	5,410	5,415
Lincoln	1,555	1,084	967	1,891	1,479
Lyon	4,477	4,586	3,177	5,657	5,969
McLeod	4,914	5,410	4,919	5,736	7,967
Mahnomen	1,005	854	483	1,277	1,051
Marshall	2,309	2,136	1,305	3,001	2,752
Martin	4,019	4,438	3,089	4,922	5,724
Meeker	3,861	3,497	3,120	4,544	4,999
Mille Lacs	3,648	2,814	2,615	4,327	3,862
Morrison	5,588	5,038	3,710	6,469	6,598
Mower	9,935	5,147	5,001	11,893	6,969
Murray	1,993	1,609	1,588	2,840	2,316
Nicollet	6,055	5,091	3,799	6,786	6,878
Nobles	3,756	3,548	2,586	4,953	4,348
Norman	1,784	1,541	776	2,149	1,789
Olmsted	19,105	23,338	13,808	19,423	27,683
Otter Tail	8,193	10,059	5,459	10,373	14,015
Pennington	2,578	2,155	1,598	3,105	2,920
Pine	4,929	2,841	2,952	5,540	3,857
Pipestone	1,773	1,953	1,429	2,382	2,760
Polk	5,850	5,818	3,164	7,523	7,032
Pope	2,619	1,886	1,390	3,074	2,627
Ramsey	130,587	67,830	50,522	143,767	88,736
Red Lake	1,030	692	472	1,229	918
Redwood	2,740	3,408	2,710	3,178	5,076
Renville	3,414	2,852	2,598	4,454	4,356
Rice	10,908	7,014	6,056	11,570	9,460
Rock	2,005	2,064	1,244	2,435	2,737
Roseau	2,346	2,785	2,099	2,630	3,500
St. Louis	41,211	16,634	13,440	70,344	31,799
Scott	11,049	10,715	9,684	11,405	13,050
Sherburne	7,868	7,380	6,579	7,959	8,360
Sibley	2,420	2,315	2,407	3,154	3,655
Stearns	21,451	22,502	14,834	23,798	27,529
Steele	4,064	4,804	3,763	5,496	7,981
Stevens	2,466	2,229	1,086	2,721	2,679
Swift	2,980	1,603	1,359	3,579	2,156
Todd	4,059	3,990	2,976	5,023	5,633
Traverse	1,053	841	582	1,399	1,061
Wabasha	3,759	3,430	3,062	4,442	4,681
Wadena	2,340	2,492	1,535	2,484	3,733
Waseca	2,978	2,915	2,565	3,721	4,471
Washington	35,820	26,568	22,584	34,952	30,850
Watonwan	2,100	1,871	1,574	2,544	2,821
Wilkin	1,124	1,626	748	1,486	1,933
Winona	9,599	8,498	5,885	10,310	11,012
Wright	12,465	11,650	10,829	14,177	14,987
Yellow Med	2,593	1,909	1,645	3,282	2,925
Totals	**994,843**	**734,845**	**549,517**	**1,109,471**	**962,337**

Minnesota Vote Since 1940

1940, Roosevelt, Dem., 644,196; Willkie, Rep., 596,274; Thomas, Soc., 5,454; Browder, Com., 2,711; Aiken, Ind., 2,553.

1944, Roosevelt, Dem., 589,864; Dewey, Rep., 527,416; Thomas, Soc., 5,073; Teichert, Ind. Gov't., 3,176.

1948, Truman, Dem., 692,966; Dewey, Rep., 483,617; Wallace, Prog., 27,866; Thomas, Soc., 4,646; Teichert, Soc. Labor, 2,525; Dobbs, Soc. Workers, 606.

1952, Eisenhower, Rep., 763,211; Stevenson, Dem., 608,458; Hallinan, Prog., 2,666; Hass, Soc. Labor, 2,383; Hamblen, Proh., 2,147; Dobbs, Soc. Workers, 618.

1956, Eisenhower, Rep., 719,302; Stevenson, Dem., 617,525; Hass, Soc. Labor (Ind. Gov.), 2,080; Dobbs, Soc. Workers, 1,098.

1960, Kennedy, Dem., 779,933; Nixon, Rep., 757,915; Dobbs, Soc. Workers, 3,077; Industrial Gov., 962.

1964, Johnson, Dem., 991,117; Goldwater, Rep., 559,624; DeBerry, Soc. Workers, 1,177; Hass, Industrial Gov., 2,544.

1968, Nixon, Rep., 658,643; Humphrey, Dem., 857,738; Wallace, 3d party, 68,931; scattered, 2,443; Halstead, Soc. Worker, 808; Blomen, Ind. Gov't., 285; Mitchell, Com., 415; Cleaver, Peace, 935; McCarthy, write-in, 585; scattered, 170.

1972, Nixon, Rep., 898,269; McGovern, Dem., 802,346; Schmitz, Amer., 31,407; Spock, Peoples, 2,805; Fisher, Soc. Labor, 4,261; Jenness, Soc. Workers, 940; Hall, Com., 662; scattered, 962.

1976, Carter, Dem., 1,070,440; Ford, Rep., 819,395; McCarthy, Ind., 35,490; Anderson, Amer., 13,592; Camejo, Soc. Workers, 4,149; MacBride, Libertarian, 3,529; Hall, Com., 1,092.

1980, Reagan, Rep., 873, 268; Carter, Dem., 954,173; Anderson, Ind., 174,997; Clark, Libertarian, 31,593; Commoner, Citizens, 8,406; Hall, Com., 1,117; DeBerry, Soc. Workers, 711; Griswold, Workers World, 698; McReynolds, Socialist, 536; write-ins, 281.

1984, Mondale, Dem., 1,036,364; Reagan, Rep., 1,032,603; Bergland, Libertarian, 2,996.

1988, Bush., 962,337; Dukakis, Dem., 1,109,471; McCarthy, Minn. Prog., 5,403; Paul, Lib., 5,109.

Mississippi

County	1992 Clinton (D)	1992 Bush (R)	1992 Perot (I)	1988 Dukakis (D)	1988 Bush (R)
Adams	8,581	4,992	1,679	7,732	8,116
Alcorn	6,327	6,249	1,349	5,335	6,641
Amite	2,608	2,561	498	2,834	3,333
Attala	2,980	3,631	596	2,997	4,524
Benton	2,401	1,251	293	1,718	1,565
Bolivar	8,553	4,645	584	7,606	6,105
Calhoun	2,439	3,176	606	2,086	3,375
Carroll	1,182	1,695	200	1,560	2,628
Chickasaw	3,082	3,070	610	2,713	3,390
Choctaw	1,376	1,981	295	1,335	2,297
Claiborne	3,200	935	160	3,083	1,233
Clarke	2,215	4,196	450	2,576	4,522
Clay	4,572	3,283	626	3,849	3,645
Coahoma	6,323	4,061	441	6,139	4,939
Copiah	4,378	4,572	407	4,175	5,100
Covington	2,646	3,361	639	2,591	4,005
DeSoto	8,833	16,104	2,569	5,449	14,681
Forrest	7,817	12,206	1,834	6,953	14,249
Franklin	1,587	1,942	393	1,563	2,376
George	2,650	4,141	1,335	2,435	4,545
Greene	1,644	2,341	538	1,637	2,837
Grenada	4,184	4,714	609	3,683	5,352
Hancock	4,025	4,989	1,905	3,760	7,763
Harrison	14,972	24,675	6,741	14,439	32,892
Hinds	41,066	42,864	5,065	41,058	52,749

Holmes	3,997	1,663	198	5,350	2,737
Humphreys	2,573	1,719	257	2,644	2,018
Issaquena	545	297	79	511	424
Itawamba	3,597	4,097	906	3,143	4,535
Jackson	13,017	25,321	6,484	10,328	29,830
Jasper	2,966	2,716	537	3,184	3,368
Jefferson	2,761	559	152	2,693	702
Jefferson Davis	2,985	2,224	382	2,948	2,745
Jones	8,028	13,817	2,521	7,383	16,764
Kemper	2,242	1,829	278	2,069	2,128
Lafayette	4,790	4,865	786	3,967	5,841
Lamar	3,178	8,205	1,534	2,535	9,145
Lauderdale	8,274	16,671	1,600	7,967	18,302
Lawrence	2,560	2,678	763	2,517	3,682
Leake	3,333	3,943	497	2,787	4,168
Lee	7,622	12,054	1,997	6,604	13,767
Leflore	6,169	5,117	558	5,830	6,409
Lincoln	4,732	7,030	1,276	4,534	8,710
Lowndes	6,474	10,478	1,710	5,993	11,258
Madison	8,977	12,347	1,409	8,242	11,399
Marion	4,582	5,720	1,131	4,240	7,019
Marshall	7,558	3,643	670	6,982	4,668
Monroe	4,929	5,993	1,255	4,669	6,447
Montgomery	2,027	2,387	374	1,893	2,504
Neshoba	3,020	6,009	781	2,942	6,363
Newton	2,146	5,128	494	2,332	5,658
Noxubee	3,181	1,615	201	2,722	1,870
Oktibbeha	5,660	6,309	967	5,100	7,126
Panola	5,929	4,556	708	5,222	5,382
Pearl River	4,622	7,642	2,310	3,939	10,220
Perry	1,455	2,495	460	1,326	2,983
Pike	6,204	5,927	1,356	6,531	7,637
Pontotoc	2,955	4,652	776	2,772	4,939
Prentiss	3,267	4,177	727	3,429	4,348
Quitman	2,390	1,447	209	2,497	1,832
Rankin	8,155	24,537	3,454	6,201	22,937
Scott	3,349	5,268	691	2,939	5,522
Sharkey	1,529	1,005	146	1,609	1,277
Simpson	3,213	5,358	726	3,016	6,151
Smith	1,958	4,106	730	1,660	4,573
Stone	1,417	2,234	417	1,452	3,007
Sunflower	4,942	3,702	594	4,898	4,362
Tallahatchie	2,890	2,202	378	2,881	2,633
Tate	3,519	4,196	634	2,872	4,553
Tippah	3,748	4,410	791	2,958	4,593
Tishomingo	3,907	3,387	750	3,378	3,646
Tunica	1,127	681	92	1,510	896
Union	3,711	5,167	815	3,044	5,511
Walthall	2,476	2,728	711	2,354	3,103
Warren	7,946	9,933	2,081	7,437	12,507
Washington	10,361	7,480	761	10,222	10,229
Wayne	3,053	3,866	822	2,889	4,496
Webster	1,739	2,788	443	1,550	3,061
Wilkinson	3,071	1,375	344	2,678	1,528
Winston	3,902	4,298	688	3,851	5,317
Yalobusha	2,617	2,179	438	2,402	2,660
Yazoo	4,895	5,013	679	4,989	5,538
Totals	**391,911**	**478,878**	**83,950**	**363,921**	**557,890**

Mississippi Vote Since 1940

1940, Roosevelt, Dem., 168,252; Willkie, Ind. Rep., 4,550; Rep., 2,814; total, 7,364; Thomas, Soc., 103.

1944, Roosevelt, Dem., 158,515; Dewey, Rep., 3,742; Reg. Dem., 9,964; Ind. Rep., 7,859.

1948, Thurmond, States' Rights, 167,538; Truman, Dem., 19,384; Dewey, Rep., 5,043; Wallace, Prog., 225.

1952, Eisenhower, Ind. vote pledged to Rep. candidate, 112,966; Stevenson, Dem., 172,566.

1956, Stevenson, Dem., 144,498; Eisenhower, Rep., 56,372; Black and Tan Grand Old Party, 4,313; total, 60,685; Byrd, Ind., 42,966.

1960, Democratic unpledged electors, 116,248; Kennedy, Dem., 108,362; Nixon, Rep., 73,561. Mississippi's victorious slate of 8 unpledged Democratic electors cast their votes for Sen. Harry F. Byrd (D-Va.).

1964, Johnson, Dem., 52,618; Goldwater, Rep., 356,528.

1968, Nixon, Rep., 88,516; Humphrey, Dem., 150,644; Wallace, 3d party, 415,349.

1972, Nixon, Rep., 505,125; McGovern, Dem., 126,782; Schmitz, Amer., 11,598; Jenness, Soc. Workers, 2,458.

1976, Carter, Dem., 381,309; Ford, Rep., 366,846; Anderson, Amer., 6,678; McCarthy, Ind., 4,074; Maddox, Ind., 4,049; Camejo, Soc. Workers, 2,805; MacBride, Libertarian, 2,609.

1980, Reagan, Rep., 441,089; Carter, Dem., 429,281; Anderson, Ind., 12,036; Clark, Libertarian, 5,465; Griswold, Workers World, 2,402; Pulley, Soc. Worker, 2,347.

1984, Reagan, Rep., 582,377; Mondale, Dem., 352,192; Bergland, Libertarian, 2,336.

1988, Bush, Rep., 557,890; Dukakis, Dem., 363,921; Duke, Ind., 4,232; Paul, Lib., 3,329.

Missouri

	1992			1988	
County	Clinton (D)	Bush (R)	Perot (I)	Dukakis (D)	Bush (R)
Adair	4,232	4,141	2,224	3,571	5,721
Andrew	2,675	2,652	2,152	3,108	3,407
Atchison	1,208	1,140	840	1,468	1,761
Audrain	4,731	3,798	2,099	5,226	5,072
Barry	4,751	5,565	2,381	4,210	7,231
Barton	1,433	2,775	971	1,603	3,339
Bates	2,993	2,501	2,225	3,332	3,574
Benton	3,195	2,511	1,551	2,654	3,467
Bollinger	2,160	2,284	909	1,883	2,710
Boone	26,176	19,405	12,038	24,370	22,948
Buchanan	16,570	11,275	9,404	18,601	15,336
Butler	6,602	6,450	2,189	5,751	7,968
Caldwell	1,456	1,295	1,283	1,726	2,074
Callaway	5,799	4,880	3,266	5,209	6,687
Camden	5,140	5,554	3,891	3,930	7,773
Cape Girardeau	9,605	13,464	5,199	7,904	16,583
Carroll	2,104	1,774	1,495	2,330	2,811
Carter	1,169	1,101	405	1,087	1,429
Cass	10,246	10,349	9,216	10,092	12,799
Cedar	2,062	2,085	1,171	1,774	2,966
Chariton	2,141	1,378	1,067	2,347	2,193
Christian	6,242	7,422	3,422	4,724	7,670
Clark	1,815	1,039	725	1,925	1,493
Clay	30,565	23,798	20,903	29,620	30,293
Clinton	3,400	2,392	2,423	3,653	3,282
Cole	10,201	15,270	5,770	8,359	18,023
Cooper	2,709	2,867	1,735	2,510	3,737
Crawford	3,515	2,831	2,002	3,107	3,856
Dade	1,331	1,576	834	1,315	2,154
Dallas	2,533	2,116	1,392	2,293	2,898
Daviess	1,477	1,107	1,142	1,743	1,765
DeKalb	1,630	1,318	1,206	1,970	1,863
Dent	2,689	2,125	1,049	2,421	2,975
Douglas	2,126	2,569	1,081	1,735	3,225
Dunklin	6,377	4,034	1,166	5,281	5,026
Franklin	13,431	11,477	11,043	11,891	16,611
Gasconade	1,952	2,690	1,672	1,621	4,216
Gentry	1,519	1,272	921	1,872	1,554
Greene	41,137	46,457	17,770	35,475	52,211
Grundy	1,968	1,749	1,472	2,052	2,668
Harrison	1,590	1,563	1,059	1,776	2,271
Henry	4,232	2,681	2,807	4,135	4,167
Hickory	1,929	1,259	864	1,677	2,043
Holt	1,050	1,202	781	1,258	1,583
Howard	2,085	1,253	1,090	2,446	1,865
Howell	5,492	5,360	2,650	4,324	7,277
Iron	2,507	1,276	841	2,283	1,877
Jackson	145,656	78,530	66,054	147,964	107,810
Jasper	11,727	17,554	6,446	11,159	19,934
Jefferson	32,569	20,637	20,057	27,738	29,279
Johnson	5,545	5,029	4,578	5,373	7,512
Knox	1,010	724	523	1,255	1,212
Laclede	4,179	5,176	2,852	3,442	6,070
Lafayette	5,213	4,651	3,561	5,654	6,825
Lawrence	4,666	5,608	2,570	4,432	6,911
Lewis	2,196	1,461	892	2,460	1,803
Lincoln	5,168	3,719	3,572	4,605	5,305
Linn	2,916	1,967	1,524	3,150	3,061
Livingston	2,505	2,370	1,976	3,077	3,462
McDonald	2,281	3,010	1,551	2,299	3,812
Macon	3,194	2,256	1,697	3,215	3,406
Madison	2,501	1,673	899	2,167	2,528
Maries	1,732	1,356	915	1,552	1,919
Marion	5,156	4,762	1,841	5,617	5,034
Mercer	853	626	378	877	875
Miller	2,905	4,175	2,391	2,555	5,662
Missouri	3,226	1,675	776	2,814	2,218
Moniteau	2,018	2,566	1,499	1,936	3,502
Monroe	2,060	1,153	970	2,461	1,542
Montgomery	2,157	1,974	1,266	2,064	2,714
Morgan	2,906	2,819	2,028	2,604	3,958
New Madrid	4,913	2,431	977	3,812	3,387
Newton	5,987	8,921	3,229	5,798	10,617
Nodaway	3,723	3,147	2,484	4,240	4,103
Oregon	2,258	1,402	564	2,042	1,717
Osage	1,860	2,789	1,423	1,771	3,885
Ozark	1,581	1,772	906	1,329	2,404
Pemiscot	3,924	2,161	670	3,288	3,066
Perry	2,525	3,205	1,498	2,130	3,836
Pettis	6,314	6,823	4,278	5,486	9,648
Phelps	6,852	6,040	3,774	5,867	8,329
Pike	3,609	2,256	1,464	3,816	3,271
Platte	10,920	9,380	9,062	11,225	11,838
Polk	3,316	3,465	1,879	3,419	5,030
Pulaski	4,113	3,793	2,057	3,446	4,642
Putnam	838	1,143	522	803	1,365
Ralls	2,158	1,349	880	2,489	1,494
Randolph	4,951	3,025	2,212	5,291	4,384
Ray	4,457	2,563	2,567	4,879	3,763
Reynolds	2,014	776	532	1,864	1,162
Ripley	2,300	1,814	739	1,961	2,647
St. Charles	37,263	38,673	30,351	29,286	50,005
St. Clair	1,966	1,555	1,083	1,864	2,312
St. Francois	9,367	5,889	3,635	8,158	7,923
Ste. Genevieve	3,795	1,780	1,547	3,612	2,532

St. Louis	235,469	188,157	109,042	216,534	262,784
Saline	4,643	2,688	2,815	5,039	4,625
Schuyler	936	742	622	1,013	1,063
Scotland	1,070	798	617	1,117	1,248
Scott	7,452	6,265	2,763	5,914	8,013
Shannon	2,135	1,224	579	1,796	1,696
Shelby	1,435	1,169	786	1,818	1,586
Stoddard	5,772	4,637	1,871	4,701	5,822
Stone	3,256	4,035	1,884	2,889	5,080
Sullivan	1,510	1,326	596	1,562	1,897
Taney	4,682	6,081	2,395	3,888	7,043
Texas	4,597	3,470	1,900	3,887	4,584
Vernon	3,546	2,851	1,890	3,402	4,149
Warren	3,213	2,953	2,471	2,935	4,452
Washington	4,211	2,157	1,618	3,744	3,240
Wayne	1,361	1,102	404	2,456	2,648
Webster	4,149	4,361	2,108	3,890	5,123
Worth	599	483	328	732	677
Wright	2,814	3,427	1,425	2,232	4,151
Totals	**1,051,328**	**810,058**	**517,918**	**1,001,619**	**1,084,953**

Missouri Vote Since 1940

1940, Roosevelt, Dem., 958,476; Willkie, Rep., 871,009; Thomas, Soc., 2,226; Babson, Proh., 1,809; Aiken, Soc. Labor, 209.

1944, Roosevelt, Dem., 807,357; Dewey, Rep., 761,175; Thomas, Soc., 1,750; Watson, Proh., 1,175; Teichert, Soc. Labor, 221.

1948, Truman, Dem., 917,315; Dewey, Rep., 655,039; Wallace, Prog., 3,998; Thomas, Soc., 2,222.

1952, Eisenhower, Rep., 959,429; Stevenson, Dem., 929,830; Hallinan, Prog., 987; Hamblen, Proh., 885; MacArthur, Christian Nationalist, 302; America First, 233; Hoopes, Soc., 227; Hass, Soc. Labor, 169.

1956, Stevenson, Dem., 918,273; Eisenhower, Rep., 914,299.

1960, Kennedy, Dem., 972,201; Nixon, Rep., 962,221.

1964, Johnson, Dem., 1,164,344; Goldwater, Rep., 653,535.

1968, Nixon, Rep., 811,932; Humphrey, Dem., 791,444; Wallace, 3d party, 206,126.

1972, Nixon, Rep., 1,154,058; McGovern, Dem., 698,531.

1976, Carter, Dem., 999,163; Ford, Rep., 928,808; McCarthy, Ind., 24,329.

1980, Reagan, Rep., 1,074,181; Carter, Dem., 931,182; Anderson, Ind., 77,920; Clark, Libertarian, 14,422; DeBerry, Soc. Workers, 1,515; Commoner, Citizens, 573; write-ins, 31.

1984, Reagan, Rep., 1,274,188; Mondale, Dem., 848,583.

1988, Bush, Rep., 1,084,953; Dukakis, Dem., 1,001,619; Fulani, New Alliance, 6,656; Paul, write-in, 434.

Montana

		1992		1988	
County	Clinton (D)	Bush (R)	Perot (I)	Dukakis (D)	Bush (R)
Beaverhead	1,098	1,746	1,068	1,274	2,668
Big Horn	2,152	1,377	840	2,233	1,711
Blaine	1,355	971	699	1,460	1,402
Broadwater	494	830	505	592	1,054
Carbon	1,549	1,560	1,482	2,039	2,360
Carter	154	497	220	242	686
Cascade	14,717	12,490	9,149	15,718	15,946
Chouteau	959	1,380	820	1,166	1,980
Custer	1,968	2,105	1,515	2,343	3,007
Daniels	457	496	402	571	802
Dawson	1,785	1,679	1,370	2,120	2,658
Deer Lodge	3,174	832	1,206	3,185	1,168
Fallon	446	731	427	612	1,002
Fergus	1,615	2,736	1,934	2,052	3,948
Flathead	9,746	11,698	9,109	10,202	14,461
Gallatin	9,537	11,109	7,712	9,527	13,214
Garfield	125	403	281	196	631
Glacier	2,076	1,222	997	2,151	1,728
Golden Valley	142	192	157	203	335
Granite	358	556	386	511	789
Hill	3,618	2,408	2,017	4,219	3,467
Jefferson	1,415	1,541	1,172	1,746	2,007
Judith Basin	409	610	415	590	902
Lake	3,938	3,596	2,878	4,109	4,883
Lewis & Clark	11,117	9,351	5,560	11,932	10,946
Liberty	321	512	363	418	771
Lincoln	2,765	2,799	2,637	3,601	3,500
Madison	424	528	395	878	2,045
McCone	779	1,414	1,043	567	814
Meagher	260	422	310	337	656
Mineral	664	403	543	789	616
Missoula	19,757	12,471	9,440	19,178	15,965
Musselshell	648	886	691	898	1,280
Park	2,256	2,846	2,182	2,526	3,823
Petroleum	61	135	95	91	204
Phillips	634	1,026	949	905	1,462
Pondera	1,046	1,252	855	1,245	1,795
Powder River	258	547	340	395	815
Powell	989	1,058	872	1,174	1,574
Prairie	260	412	179	343	541
Ravalli	4,644	5,329	4,573	4,763	7,418
Richland	1,440	1,758	1,525	1,824	2,628
Roosevelt	1,827	1,210	1,089	2,083	1,957
Rosebud	1,669	1,130	1,099	1,869	1,822
Sanders	1,674	1,345	1,360	1,959	2,152
Sheridan	1,077	795	782	1,354	1,381
Silver Bow	9,960	3,491	4,570	11,422	5,043
Stillwater	1,178	1,390	1,055	1,407	1,920
Sweet Grass	395	880	507	462	1,242
Teton	1,042	1,367	969	1,303	1,876
Toole	854	943	903	1,070	1,505
Treasure	157	206	178	231	291
Valley	1,715	1,497	1,320	2,163	2,467
Wheatland	384	478	284	443	667
Wibaux	195	234	173	258	358
Yellowstone	20,162	22,822	13,133	21,987	28,069
Totals	**153,899**	**143,702**	**106,735**	**168,936**	**190,412**

Montana Vote Since 1940

1940, Roosevelt, Dem., 145,698; Willkie, Rep., 99,579; Thomas, Soc., 1,443; Babson, Proh., 664; Browder, Com., 489.

1944, Roosevelt, Dem., 112,556; Dewey, Rep., 93,163; Thomas, Soc., 1,296; Watson, Proh., 340.

1948, Truman, Dem., 119,071; Dewey, Rep., 96,770; Wallace, Prog., 7,313; Thomas, Soc., 695; Watson, Proh., 429.

1952, Eisenhower, Rep., 157,394; Stevenson, Dem., 106,213; Hallinan, Prog., 723; Hamblen, Proh., 548; Hoopes, Soc., 159.

1956, Eisenhower, Rep., 154,933; Stevenson, Dem., 116,238.

1960, Kennedy, Dem., 134,891; Nixon, Rep., 141,841; Decker, Proh., 456; Dobbs, Soc. Workers, 391.

1964, Johnson, Dem., 164,246; Goldwater, Rep., 113,032; Kasper, Nat'l States Rights, 519; Munn, Proh., 499; DeBerry, Soc. Worker, 332.

1968, Nixon, Rep., 138,835; Humphrey, Dem., 114,117; Wallace, 3d party, 20,015; Halstead, Soc. Worker, 457; Munn, Proh., 510; Caton, New Reform, 470.

1972, Nixon, Rep., 183,976; McGovern, Dem., 120,197; Schmitz, Amer., 13,430.

1976, Carter, Dem., 149,259; Ford, Rep., 173,703; Anderson, Amer., 5,772.

1980, Reagan, Rep., 206,814; Carter, Dem., 118,032; Anderson, Ind., 29,281; Clark, Libertarian, 9,825.

1984, Reagan, Rep., 232,450; Mondale, Dem., 146,742; Bergland, Libertarian, 5,185.

1988, Bush, Rep., 190,412; Dukakis, Dem., 168,936; Paul, Lib., 5,047; Fulani, New Alliance, 1,279.

Nebraska

		1992		1988	
County	Clinton (D)	Bush (R)	Perot (I)	Dukakis (D)	Bush (R)
Adams	3,421	6,307	3,256	4,145	8,063
Antelope	644	1,963	1,129	933	2,626
Arthur	18	147	97	58	210
Banner	68	282	125	112	361
Blaine	60	251	125	72	338
Boone	598	1,575	957	976	2,160
Box Butte	1,639	2,021	1,378	2,466	3,253
Boyd	350	726	463	480	967
Brown	306	983	521	435	1,335
Buffalo	3,727	9,670	4,067	4,700	9,980
Burt	1,217	1,657	985	1,458	2,050
Butler	1,081	1,870	1,152	1,715	2,083
Cass	2,918	4,246	2,602	3,674	4,658
Cedar	995	1,966	1,494	1,759	2,462
Chase	394	993	671	597	1,446
Cherry	557	1,697	727	642	2,240
Cheyenne	931	2,138	1,039	1,333	2,862
Clay	798	1,806	952	1,097	2,352
Colfax	1,007	1,915	1,194	1,542	2,329
Cuming	810	2,667	1,170	1,238	3,201
Custer	1,177	3,150	1,476	1,496	4,202
Dakota	2,315	2,766	1,303	2,941	2,744
Dawes	984	1,955	1,100	1,122	2,618
Dawson	1,704	4,560	2,217	2,184	5,529
Deuel	229	554	324	302	769
Dixon	832	1,471	726	1,166	1,802
Dodge	4,632	7,218	4,403	6,116	8,412
Douglas	66,368	92,447	38,332	76,444	99,806
Dundy	242	656	330	333	828
Fillmore	983	1,489	985	1,433	1,952
Franklin	474	961	522	768	1,294
Frontier	302	779	476	384	1,057
Furnas	573	1,276	761	791	1,830
Gage	3,292	3,969	2,699	4,008	5,114
Garden	212	688	383	366	986

Garfield	220	593	270	234	803
Gosper	253	489	293	331	694
Grant	74	242	123	89	301
Greeley	431	579	392	670	763
Hall	5,490	9,212	5,796	6,822	12,020
Hamilton	901	2,169	1,146	1,289	3,019
Harlan	487	987	625	725	1,403
Hayes	84	358	205	160	512
Hitchcock	354	820	538	480	1,132
Holt	775	2,940	1,640	1,327	4,081
Hooker	67	280	99	91	378
Howard	772	1,132	938	1,186	1,526
Jefferson	1,498	1,781	1,171	1,819	2,470
Johnson	819	881	640	1,162	1,182
Kearney	641	1,746	845	1,056	2,120
Keith	729	2,021	1,129	1,067	2,879
Keya Paha	103	367	157	145	446
Kimball	410	925	444	540	1,321
Knox	959	2,105	1,156	1,477	2,644
Lancaster	40,672	40,855	21,537	44,260	44,605
Lincoln	5,016	6,901	3,300	6,070	8,395
Logan	80	266	97	93	373
Loup	58	229	95	97	295
McPherson	49	217	61	60	229
Madison	2,333	7,804	3,469	2,779	9,135
Merrick	830	1,762	1,015	1,192	2,376
Morrill	575	1,181	752	753	1,554
Nance	537	813	538	794	1,185
Nemaha	1,104	1,688	1,022	1,457	2,293
Nuckolls	828	1,267	827	1,114	1,750
Otoe	2,033	2,853	1,793	2,616	3,724
Pawnee	563	665	561	767	975
Perkins	296	833	517	467	1,117
Phelps	822	2,727	1,267	1,047	3,316
Pierce	607	1,845	1,080	914	2,474
Platte	2,330	6,976	3,501	3,285	9,029
Polk	659	1,427	809	944	1,768
Red Willow	1,158	2,514	1,657	1,505	3,325
Richardson	1,497	2,029	1,343	1,926	2,702
Rock	158	586	231	198	756
Saline	2,404	1,724	1,564	3,119	2,352
Sarpy	10,648	20,362	9,218	10,936	20,179
Saunders	2,463	3,910	2,485	3,524	4,454
Scotts Bluff	4,144	7,171	3,499	4,454	8,594
Seward	2,097	3,020	1,709	2,682	3,467
Sheridan	530	1,693	745	612	2,251
Sherman	565	734	580	839	914
Sioux	145	443	205	194	568
Stanton	492	1,170	783	637	1,709
Thayer	916	1,362	1,074	1,322	1,981
Thomas	58	260	106	81	383
Thurston	864	895	485	1,225	1,105
Valley	668	1,104	646	873	1,603
Washington	2,093	4,009	2,139	2,552	4,567
Wayne	834	1,995	898	1,111	2,473
Webster	620	967	654	891	1,314
Wheeler	88	245	126	141	309
York	1,347	3,678	1,782	1,748	4,744
Totals	**214,106**	**338,646**	**171,938**	**259,235**	**397,956**

Nebraska Vote Since 1940

1940, Roosevelt, Dem., 263,677; Willkie, Rep., 352,201.

1944, Roosevelt, Dem., 233,246; Dewey, Rep., 329,880.

1948, Truman, Dem., 224,165; Dewey, Rep., 264,774.

1952, Eisenhower, Rep., 421,603; Stevenson Dem., 188,057.

1956, Eisenhower, Rep., 378,108; Stevenson, Dem., 199,029.

1960, Kennedy, Dem., 232,542; Nixon, Rep., 380,553.

1964, Johnson, Dem., 307,307; Goldwater, Rep., 276,847.

1968, Nixon, Rep., 321,163; Humphrey, Dem., 170,784; Wallace, 3d party, 44,904.

1972, Nixon, Rep., 406,298; McGovern, Dem., 169,991; scattered 817.

1976, Carter, Dem., 233,287; Ford, Rep., 359,219; McCarthy, Ind., 9,383; Maddox, Amer. Ind., 3,378; MacBride, Libertarian, 1,476.

1980, Reagan, Rep., 419,214; Carter, Dem., 166,424; Anderson, Ind., 44,854; Clark, Libertarian, 9,041.

1984, Reagan, Rep., 459,135; Mondale, Dem., 187,475; Bergland, Libertarian, 2,075.

1988, Bush, Rep., 397,956; Dukakis, Dem., 259,235; Paul, Lib., 2,534; Fulani, New Alliance, 1,740.

Nevada

County	Clinton (D)	1992 Bush (R)	Perot (I)	1988 Dukakis (D)	Bush (R)
Churchill	1,765	3,780	1,950	1,481	4,578
Clark	123,856	96,677	74,875	78,359	108,110
Douglas	3,924	6,178	4,807	3,107	7,074
Elko	2,778	5,201	3,625	2,310	5,722
Esmeralda	118	220	219	143	380
Eureka	129	330	214	151	413
Humboldt	810	1,502	1,149	1,024	2,378
Lander	423	880	652	439	1,214
Lincoln	511	888	394	466	1,035
Lyon	2,775	3,508	2,715	2,301	4,390
Mineral	909	917	746	978	1,480
Nye	2,559	2,739	2,496	1,748	3,619
Pershing	467	643	429	458	867
Storey	488	455	550	432	651
Washoe	39,443	42,556	30,927	32,902	52,654
White Pine	1,351	1,205	1,071	1,351	1,774
Totals	**185,401**	**171,378**	**129,532**	**132,738**	**206,040**

Nevada Vote Since 1940

1940, Roosevelt, Dem., 31,945; Willkie, Rep., 21,229.

1944, Roosevelt, Dem., 29,623; Dewey, Rep., 24,611.

1948, Truman, Dem., 31,291; Dewey, Rep., 29,357; Wallace, Prog., 1,469.

1952, Eisenhower, Rep., 50,502; Stevenson, Dem., 31,688.

1956, Eisenhower, Rep., 56,049; Stevenson, Dem., 40,640.

1960, Kennedy, Dem., 54,880; Nixon, Rep., 52,387.

1964, Johnson, Dem., 79,339; Goldwater, Rep., 56,094.

1968, Nixon, Rep., 73,188; Humphrey, Dem., 60,598; Wallace, 3d party, 20,432.

1972, Nixon, Rep., 115,750; McGovern, Dem. 66,016.

1976, Carter Dem., 92,479; Ford, Rep., 101,273; MacBride, Libertarian, 1,519; Maddox, Amer. Ind., 1,497; scattered 5,108.

1980, Reagan, Rep., 155,017; Carter, Dem., 66,666; Anderson, Ind., 17,651; Clark, Libertarian, 4,358.

1984, Reagan, Rep., 188,770; Mondale, Dem., 91,655; Bergland, Libertarian, 2,292.

1988, Bush, Rep., 206,040; Dukakis, Dem., 132,738; Paul, Lib., 3,520; Fulani, New Alliance, 835.

New Hampshire

City	Clinton (D)	1992 Bush (R)	Perot (I)	1988 Dukakis (D)	Bush (R)
Berlin City	2,680	1,272	1,162	2,271	2,529
Claremont	2,650	1,822	904	2,254	2,513
Concord	8,267	5,564	2,521	6,698	7,439
Dover	5,449	4,197	2,246	4,803	5,357
Keene	5,210	3,257	1,736	4,466	4,535
Laconia	2,389	3,031	1,493	2,111	3,835
Manchester	15,349	14,954	7,100	12,567	23,893
Nashua	14,777	12,514	8,406	12,833	19,369
Portsmith	6,132	3,563	2,088	5,377	4,827
Rochester	4,588	4,272	2,541	3,591	5,368
Totals	**207,264**	**199,623**	**120,029**	**163,696**	**281,537**

New Hampshire Vote Since 1940

1940, Roosevelt, Dem., 125,292; Willkie, Rep., 110,127.

1944, Roosevelt, Dem., 119,663; Dewey, Rep., 109,916; Thomas, Soc., 46.

1948, Truman, Dem., 107,995; Dewey, Rep., 121,299; Wallace, Prog., 1,970; Thomas, Soc., 86; Teichert, Soc. Labor, 83; Thurmond, States' Rights, 7.

1952, Eisenhower, Rep., 166,287; Stevenson, Dem., 106,663.

1956, Eisenhower, Rep., 176,519; Stevenson, Dem., 90,364; Andrews, Const., 111.

1960, Kennedy, Dem., 137,772; Nixon, Rep., 157,989.

1964, Johnson, Dem., 182,065; Goldwater, Rep., 104,029.

1968, Nixon, Rep., 154,903; Humphrey, Dem., 130,589; Wallace, 3d party, 11,173; New Party, 421; Halstead, Soc. Worker, 104.

1972, Nixon, Rep., 213,724; McGovern, Dem., 116,435; Schmitz, Amer., 3,386; Jenness, Soc. Workers, 368; scattered, 142.

1976, Carter, Dem., 147,645; Ford, Rep., 185,935; McCarthy, Ind., 4,095; MacBride, Libertarian, 936; Reagan, write-in, 388; La Rouche, U.S. Labor, 186; Camejo, Soc. Workers, 161, Levin, Soc. Labor, 66; scattered, 215.

1980, Reagan, Rep., 221,705; Carter, Dem., 108,864; Anderson, Ind., 49,693; Clark, Libertarian, 2,067; Commoner, Citizens, 1,325; Hall, Com., 129; Griswold, Workers World, 76; DeBerry, Soc. Workers, 72; scattered, 68.

1984, Reagan, Rep., 267,051; Mondale, Dem., 120,377; Bergland, Libertarian, 735.

1988, Bush, Rep., 281,537; Dukakis, Dem., 163,696; Paul, Lib., 4,502; Fulani, New Alliance, 790.

New Jersey

County	1992 Clinton (D)	1992 Bush (R)	1992 Perot (I)	1988 Dukakis (D)	1988 Bush (R)
Atlantic	37,833	32,564	15,389	34,047	44,748
Bergen	161,705	169,077	50,048	160,655	226,885
Burlington	68,216	58,782	33,303	61,140	87,416
Camden	99,758	63,929	35,783	90,704	100,072
Cape May	16,093	19,804	9,302	15,105	28,738
Cumberland	22,156	19,242	10,002	21,869	26,024
Essex	139,426	80,585	24,556	156,098	111,491
Gloucester	42,425	37,335	24,132	35,479	51,708
Hudson	93,553	63,545	14,155	95,696	81,807
Hunterdon	14,320	23,577	12,128	13,758	31,907
Mercer	76,017	54,880	24,284	68,712	65,384
Middlesex	123,258	104,760	43,789	117,149	143,361
Monmouth	94,512	119,490	43,288	91,844	147,320
Morris	63,069	102,524	31,039	58,721	127,420
Ocean	73,106	92,850	40,804	64,474	124,587
Passaic	69,661	70,914	21,363	66,254	88,070
Salem	10,040	10,318	7,266	9,956	15,240
Somerset	39,213	51,432	19,190	37,406	67,658
Sussex	14,775	29,510	12,537	13,676	36,086
Union	89,703	81,223	22,330	93,158	112,967
Warren	12,249	17,345	9,464	11,640	21,715
Totals	**1,361,088**	**1,303,686**	**504,152**	**1,317,541**	**1,740,604**

New Jersey Vote Since 1940

1940, Roosevelt, Dem., 1,016,404; Willkie, Rep., 944,876; Browder, Com., 8,814; Thomas, Soc., 2,823; Babson, Proh., 851; Aiken, Soc. Labor, 446.

1944, Roosevelt, Dem., 987,874; Dewey, Rep., 961,335; Teichert, Soc. Labor, 6,939; Watson, Nat'l. Proh., 4,255; Thomas, Soc., 3,385.

1948, Truman, Dem., 895,455; Dewey, Rep., 981,124; Wallace, Prog., 42,683; Watson, Proh., 10,593; Thomas, Soc., 10,521; Dobbs, Soc. Workers, 5,825; Teichert, Soc. Labor, 3,354.

1952, Eisenhower, Rep., 1,373,613; Stevenson, Dem., 1,015,902; Hoopes, Soc., 8,593; Hass, Soc. Labor, 5,815; Hallinan, Prog., 5,589; Krajewski, Poor Man's, 4,203; Dobbs, Soc. Workers, 3,850; Hamblen, Proh., 989.

1956, Eisenhower, Rep., 1,606,942; Stevenson Dem., 850,337; Holtwick, Proh., 9,147; Hass, Soc. Labor, 6,736; Andrews, Conservative, 5,317; Dobbs, Soc. Workers, 4,004; Krajewski, American Third Party, 1,829.

1960, Kennedy, Dem., 1,385,415; Nixon, Rep., 1,363,324; Dobbs, Soc. Workers, 11,402; Lee, Conservative, 8,708; Hass, Soc. Labor, 4,262.

1964, Johnson, Dem., 1,867,671; Goldwater, Rep., 963,843; DeBerry, Soc. Workers, 8,181; Hass, Soc. Labor, 7,075.

1968, Nixon, Rep., 1,325,467; Humphrey, Dem., 1,264,206; Wallace, 3d party, 262,187; Halstead, Soc. Worker, 8,667; Gregory, Peace Freedom, 8,084; Blomen, Soc. Labor, 6,784.

1972, Nixon, Rep., 1,845,502; McGovern, Dem., 1,102,211; Schmitz, Amer., 34,378; Spock, Peoples, 5,355; Fisher, Soc. Labor, 4,544; Jenness, Soc. Workers, 2,233; Mahalchik, Amer. First, 1,743; Hall, Com., 1,263.

1976, Carter, Dem., 1,444,653; Ford, Rep., 1,509,688; McCarthy, Ind., 32,717; MacBride, Libertarian, 9,449; Maddox, Amer., 7,716; Levin, Soc. Labor, 3,686; Hall, Com., 1,662; LaRouche, U.S. Labor, 1,650; Camejo, Soc. Workers, 1,184; Wright, People's, 1,044; Bubar, Proh., 554; Zeidler, Soc., 469.

1980, Reagan, Rep., 1,546,557; Carter, Dem., 1,147,364; Anderson, Ind., 234,632; Clark, Libertarian, 20,652; Commoner, Citizens, 8,203; McCormack, Right to Life, 3,927; Lynen, Middle Class, 3,694; Hall, Com., 2,555; Pulley, Soc. Workers, 2,198; McReynolds, Soc., 1,973; Gahres, Down With Lawyers, 1,718; Griswold, Workers World, 1,288; Wendelken, Ind., 923.

1984, Reagan, Rep., 1,933,630; Mondale, Dem., 1,261,323; Bergland, Libertarian, 6,416.

1988, Bush, Rep., 1,740,604; Dukakis, Dem., 1,317,541; Lewin, Peace & Freedom, 9,953; Paul, Lib., 8,421.

New Mexico

County	1992 Clinton (D)	1992 Bush (R)	1992 Perot (I)	1988 Dukakis (D)	1988 Bush (R)
Bernalillo	89,031	75,354	30,656	78,346	92,830
Catron	465	771	289	490	925
Chaves	6,359	8,872	3,590	6,730	13,367
Cibola	3,333	2,051	847	3,458	2,640
Colfax	2,606	1,730	871	2,785	2,256
Curry	3,699	7,630	2,055	3,995	8,032
De Baca	451	526	204	480	643
Dona Ana	19,894	16,299	7,681	19,608	21,582
Eddy	7,409	7,313	3,430	8,544	9,805
Grant	5,603	2,917	1,685	5,443	4,196
Guadalupe	1,224	691	173	1,243	861
Harding	268	312	98	291	377
Hidalgo	995	871	442	901	1,100
Lea	5,053	7,928	3,228	5,879	11,309
Lincoln	1,730	2,669	1,431	1,690	3,511
Los Alamos	3,835	4,249	2,299	3,275	6,622
Luna	2,633	2,165	1,442	3,066	3,415
McKinley	8,820	4,364	1,213	9,595	5,694
Mora	1,555	668	188	1,601	923
Otero	5,377	7,481	3,252	5,284	9,984
Quay	1,752	1,757	752	1,901	2,454
Rio Arriba	6,195	2,127	841	7,503	3,024
Roosevelt	2,172	3,215	1,085	2,033	3,589
Sandoval	9,874	7,532	3,613	9,332	9,411
San Juan	11,300	13,412	5,350	11,094	16,202
San Miguel	6,186	2,181	965	6,131	2,763
Santa Fe	26,373	9,454	5,647	23,581	12,891
Sierra	1,753	1,561	1,055	1,595	2,507
Socorro	2,908	2,185	917	2,960	3,114
Taos	7,050	2,260	1,300	6,271	2,897
Torrance	1,661	1,667	810	1,618	2,252
Union	519	975	355	638	1,291
Valencia	7,475	6,280	2,889	7,136	7,874
Totals	**255,558**	**209,467**	**90,653**	**244,497**	**270,341**

New Mexico Vote Since 1940

1940, Roosevelt, Dem., 103,699; Willkie, Rep., 79,315.

1944, Roosevelt, Dem., 81,389; Dewey, Rep., 70,688; Watson, Proh., 148.

1948, Truman, Dem., 105,464; Dewey, Rep., 80,303; Wallace, Prog., 1,037; Watson, Proh., 127; Thomas, Soc., 83; Teichert, Soc. Labor, 49.

1952, Eisenhower, Rep., 132,170; Stevenson, Dem., 105,661; Hamblen, Proh., 297; Hallinan, Ind. Prog., 225; MacArthur, Christian National, 220; Hass, Soc. Labor, 35.

1956, Eisenhower, Rep., 146,788; Stevenson, Dem., 106,098; Holtwick, Proh., 607; Andrews, Ind., 364; Hass, Soc. Labor, 69.

1960, Kennedy, Dem., 156,027; Nixon, Rep., 153,733; Decker, Proh., 777; Hass, Soc. Labor, 570.

1964, Johnson, Dem., 194,017; Goldwater, Rep., 131,838; Hass, Soc. Labor, 1,217; Munn, Proh., 543.

1968, Nixon, Rep., 169,692; Humphrey, Dem., 130,081; Wallace, 3d party, 25,737; Chavez, 1,519; Halstead, Soc. Worker, 252.

1972, Nixon, Rep., 235,606; McGovern, Dem., 141,084; Schmitz, Amer., 8,767; Jenness, Soc. Workers, 474.

1976, Carter, Dem., 201,148; Ford, Rep., 211,419; Camejo, Soc. Workers, 2,462; MacBride, Libertarian, 1,110; Zeidler, Soc., 240; Bubar, Proh., 211.

1980, Reagan, Rep., 250,779; Carter, Dem., 167,826; Anderson, Ind., 29,459; Clark, Libertarian, 4,365; Commoner, Citizens, 2,202; Bubar, Statesman, 1,281; Pulley, Soc. Worker, 325.

1984, Reagan, Rep., 307,101; Mondale, Dem., 201,769; Bergland, Libertarian, 4,459.

1988, Bush, Rep., 270,341; Dukakis, Dem., 244,497; Paul, Lib., 3,268; Fulani, New Alliance, 2,237.

New York

County	1992 Clinton (D)	1992 Bush (R)	1992 Perot (I)	1988 Dukakis (D)	1988 Bush (R)
Albany	66,898	43,102	18,991	86,564	59,534
Allegany	4,507	8,392	4,486	5,614	11,880
Bronx	218,218	62,156	14,535	218,245	76,043
Broome	40,370	32,275	19,491	48,130	47,610
Cattaraugus	9,489	13,148	10,156	12,447	19,691
Cayuga	12,136	11,292	9,808	15,044	16,934
Chautauqua	21,535	19,873	17,400	25,814	31,642
Chemung	14,930	15,966	7,210	15,966	20,951
Chenango	7,439	7,339	5,043	8,021	11,727
Clinton	12,628	13,349	5,135	12,670	15,702
Columbia	10,958	11,265	5,695	11,585	15,111
Cortland	7,316	7,212	4,717	7,673	10,934
Delaware	6,951	8,555	4,200	7,463	11,391
Dutchess	40,413	45,877	25,258	38,968	62,165
Erie	187,067	123,746	116,136	238,779	188,796
Essex	6,599	8,311	3,760	6,623	10,350
Franklin	7,018	6,254	3,668	7,928	9,135
Fulton	7,892	8,635	4,894	9,012	11,757
Genesee	7,703	11,342	5,982	9,945	14,182
Greene	6,851	9,337	4,278	7,265	11,874

Hamilton	945	2,021	976	2,320	
Herkimer	10,081	11,202	6,572	12,694	15,104
Jefferson	12,449	13,453	8,708	14,137	19,304
Kings	393,152	131,620	33,889	363,916	178,961
Lewis	3,421	3,787	3,211	4,252	5,787
Livingston	8,613	12,162	5,713	9,506	14,004
Madison	10,168	11,034	7,293	10,665	14,902
Monroe	139,228	133,103	61,861	153,650	155,271
Montgomery	9,274	8,686	4,953	11,371	11,128
Nassau	258,505	232,206	70,676	250,130	337,430
New York	387,537	80,889	25,816	385,675	115,927
Niagara	35,195	29,919	29,060	43,801	42,537
Oneida	35,783	38,123	19,670	47,665	55,039
Onondaga	89,444	76,844	44,156	94,751	104,080
Ontario	14,983	17,892	9,147	17,341	21,780
Orange	42,671	49,534	20,676	38,465	65,446
Orleans	5,089	7,437	4,137	5,913	9,028
Oswego	16,476	17,989	14,539	18,430	25,362
Otsego	10,737	9,571	5,566	11,069	13,021
Putnam	8,845	14,866	6,112	12,158	24,086
Queens	330,817	150,134	43,589	325,147	217,049
Rensselaer	29,209	28,658	15,629	33,066	35,412
Richmond	54,353	67,615	18,711	47,812	77,427
Rockland	52,658	47,174	14,180	47,634	63,825
St. Lawrence	17,931	13,510	9,519	18,921	20,290
Saratoga	32,835	37,160	18,572	31,684	43,498
Schenectady	31,611	25,964	14,453	36,483	33,364
Schoharie	4,678	5,325	3,131	5,389	7,008
Schuyler	2,721	3,199	2,030	2,900	4,291
Seneca	5,376	4,983	3,484	6,215	7,221
Steuben	11,949	19,521	9,164	12,824	25,359
Suffolk	209,318	221,232	103,729	199,215	311,242
Sullivan	13,393	11,171	6,214	11,635	15,713
Tioga	7,722	9,192	5,794	8,102	12,670
Tompkins	21,609	10,991	6,351	21,455	14,932
Ulster	31,759	28,489	17,297	30,744	41,173
Warren	8,721	11,061	6,334	8,580	15,860
Washington	7,795	9,389	5,792	8,201	14,103
Wayne	11,495	17,803	8,969	12,959	20,613
Westchester	160,968	136,009	34,506	169,860	197,956
Wyoming	4,792	7,362	5,544	5,228	9,451
Yates	3,338	4,344	2,240	3,507	5,488
Totals	**3,244,562**	**2,240,050**	**1,028,607**	**3,347,882**	**3,081,871**

New York Vote Since 1940

1940, Roosevelt, Dem., 2,834,500; American Lab., 417,418; total, 3,251,918; Willkie, Rep., 3,027,478; Thomas, Soc., 18,950; Babson, Proh., 3,250.

1944, Roosevelt, Dem., 2,478,598; American Lab., 496,405; Liberal, 329,325; total, 3,304,238; Dewey, Rep., 2,987,647; Teichert, Ind. Gov't., 14,352; Thomas, Soc., 10,553.

1948, Truman, Dem., 2,557,642; Liberal, 222,562; total, 2,780,204; Dewey, Rep., 2,841,163; Wallace, Amer. Lab., 509,559; Thomas, Soc., 40,879; Teichert, Ind. Gov't., 2,729; Dobbs, Soc. Workers, 2,675.

1952, Eisenhower, Rep., 3,952,815; Stevenson, Dem., 2,687,890, Liberal, 416,711; total, 3,104,601; Hallinan, American Lab., 64,211; Hoopes, Soc., 2,664; Dobbs, Soc. Workers, 2,212; Hass, Ind. Gov't., 1,560; scattering, 178; blank and void, 87,813.

1956, Eisenhower, Rep., 4,340,340; Stevenson, Dem., 2,458,212; Liberal, 292,557; total, 2,750,769; write-in votes for Andrews, 1,027; Werdel, 492; Hass, 150; Hoopes, 82; others, 476.

1960, Kennedy, Dem., 3,423,909; Liberal, 406,176; total, 3,830,085; Nixon, Rep., 3,446,419; Dobbs, Soc. Workers, 14,319; scattering, 256; blank and void, 88,896.

1964, Johnson, Dem., 4,913,156; Goldwater, Rep., 2,243,559; Hass, Soc. Labor, 6,085; DeBerry, Soc. Workers, 3,215; scattering, 188; blank and void, 151,383.

1968, Nixon, Rep., 3,007,932; Humphrey, Dem., 3,378,470; Wallace, 3d party, 358,864; Blomen, Soc. Labor, 8,432; Halstead, Soc. Worker, 11,851; Gregory, Freedom and Peace, 24,517; blank, void, and scattering, 171,624.

1972, Nixon, Rep., 3,824,642; Conservative, 368,136; McGovern, Dem., 2,767,956; Liberal, 183,128; Reed, Soc. Workers, 7,797; Fisher, Soc. Labor, 4,530; Hall, Com., 5,641; blank, void, or scattered, 161,641.

1976, Carter, Dem., 3,389,558; Ford, Rep., 3,100,791; MacBride, Libertarian, 12,197; Hall, Com., 10,270; Camejo, Soc. Workers, 6,996; LaRouche, U.S. Labor, 5,413; blank, void, or scattered, 143,037.

1980, Reagan, Rep., 2,893,831; Carter, Dem., 2,728,372; Anderson, Lib., 467,801; Clark, Libertarian, 52,648; McCormack, Right To Life, 24,159; Commoner, Citizens, 23,186; Hall, Com., 7,414; DeBerry, Soc. Workers, 2,068; Griswold, Workers World, 1,416; scattering, 1,064.

1984, Reagan, Rep., 3,664,763; Mondale, Dem., 3,119,609; Bergland, Libertarian, 11,949.

1988, Bush, Rep., 3,081,871; Dukakis, Dem., 3,347,882; Marra, Right to Life, 20,497; Fulani, New Alliance, 15,845.

North Carolina

	1992			1988	
County	Clinton (D)	Bush (R)	Perot (I)	Dukakis (D)	Bush (R)
Alamance	15,411	20,495	6,494	12,642	24,131
Alexander	4,861	6,837	2,018	4,148	7,968
Alleghany	2,271	1,851	600	2,087	2,174
Anson	5,269	2,334	921	4,831	2,782
Ashe	4,624	5,200	1,220	4,034	6,019
Avery	1,756	3,893	1,123	1,367	4,277
Beaufort	6,364	7,278	2,152	5,352	8,190
Bertie	4,382	1,755	601	3,762	2,145
Bladen	5,649	3,100	1,243	5,031	3,770
Brunswick	10,176	8,833	3,347	7,881	10,007
Buncombe	32,961	30,943	11,551	26,964	36,828
Burke	12,036	13,027	3,965	10,848	15,933
Cabarrus	13,512	21,280	6,248	10,686	22,524
Caldwell	9,033	12,543	3,965	7,862	15,176
Camden	1,153	1,039	479	1,081	1,144
Carteret	7,526	10,334	3,031	6,859	11,076
Caswell	4,724	2,793	827	4,189	3,299
Catawba	16,331	25,464	7,516	12,922	28,872
Chatham	9,520	6,506	2,409	7,600	6,999
Cherokee	3,686	4,020	1,040	2,567	4,557
Chowan	2,136	1,660	699	1,756	1,884
Clay	1,600	1,890	465	1,289	2,174
Cleveland	13,039	13,647	3,784	10,321	14,039
Columbus	11,423	5,422	1,963	9,172	6,659
Craven	9,998	11,575	3,679	7,313	12,057
Cumberland	23,842	19,998	4,862	23,789	27,057
Currituck	1,935	2,188	1,163	1,555	2,443
Dare	3,925	4,377	2,388	2,806	5,234
Davidson	16,461	24,866	8,232	13,215	28,374
Davie	4,475	6,796	1,903	3,166	7,988
Duplin	6,816	5,286	1,636	5,945	5,774
Durham	47,326	27,580	7,503	35,441	29,928
Edgecombe	11,135	6,249	2,570	9,044	6,831
Forsyth	48,895	52,493	14,222	39,726	57,688
Franklin	6,412	4,615	2,091	5,438	5,499
Gaston	19,107	34,704	7,311	14,582	34,775
Gates	2,210	1,158	466	2,024	1,451
Graham	1,544	1,914	403	1,313	2,091
Granville	6,178	4,538	1,321	5,280	4,880
Greene	2,768	2,180	780	2,729	2,498
Guilford	65,585	59,442	19,482	50,351	66,060
Halifax	9,968	5,769	2,047	8,726	7,462
Harnett	8,467	9,740	2,679	7,259	9,749
Haywood	10,379	7,290	3,290	9,010	8,957
Henderson	10,741	17,001	5,266	9,338	19,711
Hertford	4,609	2,208	836	4,943	2,977
Hoke	3,730	1,711	887	3,281	2,020
Hyde	1,206	741	348	1,316	940
Iredell	12,689	18,687	5,919	10,530	21,536
Jackson	5,751	4,375	1,367	4,933	5,166
Johnston	11,284	15,418	4,939	8,717	15,563
Jones	1,962	1,578	544	1,946	1,649
Lee	5,845	6,653	2,120	4,231	7,104
Lenoir	8,793	8,932	2,107	7,649	10,669
Lincoln	8,150	11,017	3,140	6,444	11,651
McDowell	5,309	6,090	1,881	4,449	6,526
Macon	4,545	4,713	1,800	3,773	6,026
Madison	3,980	3,121	857	3,033	3,453
Martin	4,069	2,958	981	3,598	3,149
Mecklenburg	96,966	99,355	31,083	71,907	106,236
Mitchell	1,727	4,405	877	1,377	4,620
Montgomery	4,422	3,543	1,185	3,995	4,504
Moore	9,604	12,369	4,400	7,642	14,543
Nash	10,051	12,971	4,049	8,740	15,906
New Hanover	20,282	24,332	7,400	15,401	23,807
Northampton	5,195	1,845	916	4,599	2,415
Onslow	8,042	11,829	4,270	7,162	12,253
Orange	28,594	13,009	5,534	22,326	14,503
Pamlico	2,229	1,929	809	2,188	2,297
Pasquotank	4,709	3,419	1,434	3,860	4,006
Pender	5,825	4,857	1,725	4,377	4,926
Perquimans	1,816	1,429	624	1,543	1,781
Person	4,323	4,458	1,429	3,777	4,832
Pitt	17,941	16,600	5,159	14,777	18,245
Polk	2,937	3,447	1,132	2,534	3,874
Randolph	11,274	20,704	6,808	8,641	23,881
Richmond	9,163	4,356	2,015	7,151	5,073
Robeson	19,340	7,763	3,272	16,988	9,908
Rockingham	13,880	12,678	4,671	11,551	14,591
Rowan	14,306	21,292	7,049	12,127	23,192
Rutherford	7,855	9,746	2,695	6,926	10,337
Sampson	8,698	8,007	1,852	8,009	8,524
Scotland	5,175	2,980	1,196	3,865	3,199
Stanly	7,735	11,029	2,855	6,627	11,885
Stokes	6,463	7,979	2,180	5,319	8,661
Surry	9,390	10,868	3,164	7,245	11,393
Swain	2,117	1,640	568	1,821	1,795
Transylvania	5,120	5,984	2,006	4,280	7,009

Tyrrell	928	553	189	785	637
Union	10,699	16,460	4,596	8,820	17,015
Vance	6,596	4,763	1,444	5,631	5,625
Wake	88,615	86,564	31,005	61,352	81,613
Warren	4,656	1,772	693	4,249	2,163
Washington	2,902	1,780	563	2,806	2,186
Watauga	8,262	7,888	3,005	6,048	8,662
Wayne	10,304	14,395	2,798	9,135	15,292
Wilkes	7,984	12,545	3,307	7,230	15,231
Wilson	9,862	9,656	2,507	8,214	10,997
Yadkin	3,913	7,311	1,725	3,195	7,918
Yancey	4,284	3,993	917	3,803	4,160
Totals	**1,103,716**	**1,122,608**	**353,845**	**890,167**	**1,237,258**

North Carolina Vote Since 1940

1940, Roosevelt, Dem., 609,015; Willkie, Rep., 213,633.

1944, Roosevelt, Dem., 527,399; Dewey, Rep., 263,155.

1948, Truman, Dem., 459,070; Dewey, Rep., 258,572; Thurmond, States' Rights, 69,652; Wallace, Prog., 3,915.

1952, Eisenhower, Rep., 558,107; Stevenson, Dem., 652,803.

1956, Eisenhower, Rep., 575,062; Stevenson, Dem., 590,530.

1960, Kennedy, Dem., 713,136; Nixon, Rep., 655,420.

1964, Johnson, Dem., 800,139; Goldwater Rep., 624,844.

1968, Nixon, Rep., 627,192; Humphrey, Dem., 464,113; Wallace, 3d party, 496,188.

1972, Nixon, Rep., 1,054,889; McGovern, Dem., 438,705; Schmitz, Amer., 25,018.

1976, Dem., 927,365; Ford, Rep., 741,960; Anderson, Amer., 5,607; MacBride, Libertarian, 2,219; LaRouche, U.S. Labor, 755.

1980, Reagan, Rep., 915,018; Carter, Dem., 875,635; Anderson, Ind., 52,800; Clark, Libertarian, 9,677; Commoner, Citizens, 2,287; DeBerry, Soc. Workers, 416.

1984, Reagan, Rep., 1,346,481; Mondale, Dem., 824,287; Bergland, Libertarian, 3,794.

1988, Bush, Rep., 1,237,258; Dukakis, Dem., 890,167; Fulani, New Alliance, 5,682; Paul, write-in, 1,263.

North Dakota

	1992			1988	
County	Clinton (D)	Bush (R)	Perot (I)	Dukakis (D)	Bush (R)
Adams	468	646	499	708	1,018
Barnes	2,116	2,715	1,563	2,858	3,631
Benson	899	791	550	1,691	1,316
Billings	85	157	157	211	437
Bottineau	1,258	1,785	1,032	1,684	2,530
Bowman	504	704	670	737	1,111
Burke	457	550	504	693	971
Burleigh	8,831	16,343	6,727	10,760	18,000
Cass	17,927	25,092	9,443	22,107	26,699
Cavalier	1,127	1,517	775	1,333	2,096
Dickey	916	1,513	615	1,249	2,064
Divide	633	515	456	875	869
Dunn	665	783	634	892	1,263
Eddy	577	591	432	748	891
Emmons	595	1,043	774	925	1,634
Foster	399	650	438	837	1,218
Golden Valley	254	502	350	388	781
Grand Forks	10,881	13,636	6,325	12,494	14,801
Grant	406	866	607	654	1,351
Griggs	647	771	330	846	1,020
Hettinger	465	852	497	698	1,395
Kidder	467	738	489	678	1,039
La Moure	797	1,267	677	1,223	1,642
Logan	381	703	390	540	1,111
McHenry	1,171	1,321	885	1,665	1,888
McIntosh	450	1,132	454	598	1,726
McKenzie	787	1,319	949	1,273	1,949
McLean	1,804	2,121	1,330	2,428	2,906
Mercer	1,316	2,261	1,372	1,843	3,013
Morton	3,580	5,025	2,783	4,708	5,588
Mountrail	1,389	1,014	857	1,977	1,443
Nelson	837	863	485	1,151	1,078
Oliver	326	502	405	526	696
Pembina	1,185	1,911	989	1,616	2,471
Pierce	760	1,097	551	1,008	1,422
Ramsey	1,040	1,273	787	2,665	3,103
Ransom	1,164	1,099	625	1,459	1,362
Renville	579	655	428	837	893
Richland	2,678	3,860	1,696	3,523	4,670
Rolette	2,001	894	659	2,426	1,126
Sargent	955	813	461	1,306	1,119
Sheridan	276	590	304	428	885
Sioux	460	258	244	701	325
Slope	145	226	162	202	315
Stark	2,995	4,479	3,117	3,678	6,137
Steele	598	503	267	895	690
Stutsman	3,303	4,033	2,574	4,214	5,375
Towner	728	598	401	970	946
Traill	1,636	2,018	873	1,940	2,562
Walsh	1,935	2,539	1,383	2,646	3,250
Ward	7,815	11,969	5,810	9,906	13,179
Wells	888	1,171	854	1,317	1,901
Williams	2,990	3,637	3,166	4,004	5,653
Totals	**97,546**	**133,911**	**69,805**	**127,739**	**166,559**

North Dakota Vote Since 1940

1940, Roosevelt, Dem., 124,036; Willkie, Rep., 154,590; Thomas, Soc., 1,279; Knutson, Com., 545; Babson, Proh., 325.

1944, Roosevelt, Dem., 100,144; Dewey, Rep., 118,535; Thomas, Soc., 943, Watson, Proh., 549.

1948, Truman, Dem., 95,812; Dewey, Rep., 115,139; Wallace, Prog., 8,391; Thomas, Soc., 1,000, Thurmond, States' Rights, 374.

1952, Eisenhower, Rep., 191,712; Stevenson, Dem., 76,694; MacArthur, Christian Nationalist, 1,075; Hallinan, Prog., 344; Hamblen, Proh., 302.

1956, Eisenhower, Rep., 156,766; Stevenson, Dem., 96,742; Andrews, Amer., 483.

1960, Kennedy, Dem., 123,963; Nixon, Rep., 154,310; Dobbs, Soc. Workers, 158.

1964, Johnson, Dem., 149,784; Goldwater, Rep., 108,207; DeBerry, Soc. Worker, 224; Munn, Proh., 174.

1968, Nixon, Rep., 138,669; Humphrey, Dem., 94,769; Wallace, 3d party, 14,244; Halstead, Soc. Worker, 128; Munn, Prohibition, 38; Troxell, Ind., 34.

1972, Nixon, Rep., 174,109; McGovern, Dem., 100,384; Jenness, Soc. Workers, 288; Hall, Com., 87; Schmitz, Amer., 5,646.

1976, Carter, Dem., 136,078; Ford, Rep., 153,470; Anderson, Amer., 3,698; McCarthy, Ind., 2,952; Maddox, Amer. Ind., 269; MacBride, Libertarian, 256; scattering, 371.

1980, Reagan, Rep., 193,695; Carter, Dem., 79,189; Anderson, Ind., 23,640; Clark, Libertarian, 3,743; Commoner, Libertarian, 429; McLain, Nat'l People's League, 296; Greaves, American, 235; Hall, Com., 93; DeBerry, Soc. Workers, 89; McReynolds, Soc., 82; Bubar, Statesman, 54.

1984, Reagan, Rep., 200,336; Mondale, Dem., 104,429; Bergland, Libertarian, 703.

1988, Bush, Rep., 166,559; Dukakis, Dem., 127,739; Paul, Lib., 1,315; LaRouche, Natl. Econ. Recovery, 905.

Ohio

	1992			1988	
County	Clinton (D)	Bush (R)	Perot (I)	Dukakis (D)	Bush (R)
Adams	3,958	4,679	1,972	3,740	5,916
Allen	13,501	24,864	7,951	13,727	31,021
Ashland	5,938	9,764	4,878	6,072	12,726
Ashtabula	18,696	13,149	10,670	20,536	17,654
Athens	12,968	6,922	4,916	10,795	9,314
Auglaize	4,924	10,365	4,788	4,756	13,562
Belmont	18,405	8,550	6,089	19,515	12,214
Brown	5,503	6,886	3,650	5,047	7,539
Butler	39,156	62,525	27,079	33,770	75,725
Carroll	4,665	4,357	3,410	4,667	6,179
Champaign	5,153	6,945	3,940	4,272	8,995
Clark	26,513	23,838	12,407	23,247	32,729
Clermont	17,448	31,819	14,156	15,352	37,417
Clinton	4,598	7,224	3,358	3,746	8,856
Columbiana	19,613	14,921	12,499	21,581	21,175
Coshocton	6,167	5,668	4,014	6,020	8,282
Crawford	6,306	8,545	5,681	6,018	12,472
Cuyahoga	333,700	184,996	111,217	353,401	242,439
Darke	6,967	11,000	6,142	6,851	14,914
Defiance	5,620	7,051	4,101	5,448	9,566
Delaware	9,220	18,146	9,181	7,590	20,693
Erie	14,355	12,349	8,624	15,097	16,670
Fairfield	14,173	23,954	12,127	12,504	29,208
Fayette	2,952	4,863	2,137	2,623	6,186
Franklin	174,819	184,402	78,398	147,585	226,265
Fulton	5,521	8,287	4,755	5,076	10,230
Gallia	5,300	5,734	2,514	4,834	7,399
Geauga	11,434	18,106	10,513	11,874	22,339
Greene	19,744	27,537	11,344	18,025	34,432
Guernsey	6,346	5,671	4,039	5,926	8,507
Hamilton	145,627	189,224	59,161	140,354	227,004
Hancock	7,841	16,599	6,862	7,435	19,896
Hardin	4,331	5,801	2,829	4,145	7,291
Harrison	3,808	2,278	1,664	3,881	3,298
Henry	3,905	6,146	3,127	3,764	8,618
Highland	4,828	6,933	3,260	4,278	8,776
Hocking	3,910	3,729	2,797	3,706	5,426
Holmes	1,952	5,026	1,917	2,179	5,064
Huron	7,875	9,412	6,673	7,794	12,633
Jackson	4,969	5,365	2,343	4,505	6,671
Jefferson	20,872	10,690	6,848	22,095	14,141
Knox	7,176	8,973	5,204	6,882	12,180

Lake	37,513	40,421	26,241	39,667	52,963
Lawrence	12,244	9,982	4,500	11,628	12,937
Licking	18,789	26,717	13,685	16,793	34,540
Logan	4,844	9,272	4,405	4,484	11,099
Lorain	50,418	36,411	30,025	55,600	50,410
Lucas	98,771	62,688	37,453	99,755	83,788
Madison	3,973	6,824	3,131	3,421	8,303
Mahoning	64,144	30,863	29,124	75,524	43,722
Marion	9,369	11,574	6,394	9,596	14,864
Medina	18,920	23,951	17,191	19,505	29,962
Meigs	4,186	3,893	2,074	3,699	5,486
Mercer	4,864	8,639	4,884	4,978	11,162
Miami	12,461	19,588	10,439	11,138	24,915
Monroe	4,206	1,804	1,482	4,269	2,557
Montgomery	107,174	103,998	47,489	95,737	131,596
Morgan	2,381	2,695	1,528	2,085	3,713
Morrow	3,883	5,159	3,580	3,515	7,130
Muskingum	11,554	14,030	8,588	11,691	19,736
Noble	2,175	2,212	1,405	2,079	3,155
Ottawa	8,089	6,736	4,781	8,038	9,352
Paulding	3,260	3,624	2,482	3,114	5,381
Perry	4,937	4,681	3,784	5,011	6,602
Pickaway	5,737	8,519	4,277	4,905	10,796
Pike	4,990	4,021	2,143	5,191	5,611
Portage	26,127	18,324	16,902	25,607	26,334
Preble	5,524	7,979	4,407	4,937	10,297
Putnam	3,942	9,289	3,619	4,004	11,183
Richland	19,416	23,307	13,201	19,617	30,047
Ross	10,370	10,709	5,563	9,271	14,563
Sandusky	9,819	10,689	6,613	9,709	14,203
Scioto	14,551	11,794	6,749	14,442	16,020
Seneca	9,241	9,713	6,920	9,504	13,704
Shelby	5,204	8,764	5,733	5,065	12,198
Stark	69,610	61,376	42,005	69,639	87,087
Summit	107,061	76,915	54,624	112,612	101,155
Trumbull	54,142	25,618	26,503	58,674	38,815
Tuscarawas	14,672	13,088	8,683	14,185	17,145
Union	3,432	7,716	3,382	3,130	8,846
Van Wert	3,796	7,176	3,067	3,848	9,410
Vinton	2,296	1,962	1,046	2,385	2,652
Warren	13,477	27,819	11,035	11,145	31,419
Washington	10,289	12,109	5,327	9,967	14,767
Wayne	13,836	18,193	9,352	13,571	22,320
Williams	4,814	7,574	4,840	4,666	10,782
Wood	20,587	20,362	11,520	18,579	26,013
Wyandot	2,997	4,374	2,908	2,936	6,178
Totals	**1,964,842**	**1,876,445**	**1,024,319**	**1,939,629**	**2,416,549**

Ohio Vote Since 1940

1940, Roosevelt, Dem., 1,733,139; Willkie, Rep., 1,586,773.

1944, Roosevelt, Dem., 1,570,763; Dewey, Rep., 1,582,293.

1948, Truman, Dem., 1,452,791; Dewey, Rep., 1,445,684; Wallace, Prog., 37,596.

1952, Eisenhower, Rep., 2,100,391; Stevenson, Dem., 1,600,367.

1956, Eisenhower, Rep., 2,262,610; Stevenson, Dem., 1,439,655.

1960, Kennedy, Dem., 1,944,248; Nixon, Rep., 2,217,611.

1964, Johnson, Dem., 2,498,331; Goldwater, Rep., 1,470,865.

1968, Nixon, Rep., 1,791,014; Humphrey, Dem., 1,700,586; Wallace, 3d party, 467,495; Gregory, 372; Munn, Proh., 19; Blomen, Soc. Labor, 120; Halstead, Soc. Worker, 69; Mitchell, Com., 23.

1972, Nixon, Rep., 2,441,827; McGovern, Dem., 1,558,889; Fisher, Soc. Labor, 7,107; Hall, Com., 6,437; Schmitz, Amer., 80,067; Wallace, Ind., 460.

1976, Carter, Dem., 2,011,621; Ford, Rep., 2,000,505; McCarthy, Ind., 58,258; Maddox, Amer. Ind., 15,529; MacBride, Libertarian, 8,961; Hall, Com., 7,817; Camejo, Soc. Workers, 4,717; LaRouche, U.S. Labor, 4,335; scattered, 130.

1980, Reagan, Rep., 2,206,545; Carter, Dem., 1,752,414; Anderson, Ind., 254,472; Clark, Libertarian, 49,033; Commoner, Citizens, 8,564; Hall, Com., 4,729; Congress, Ind. 4,029; Griswold, Workers World, 3,790; Bubar, Statesman, 27.

1984, Reagan, Rep., 2,678,559; Mondale, Dem., 1,825,440; Bergland, Libertarian, 5,886.

1988, Bush, Rep., 2,416,549; Dukakis, Dem., 1,939,629; Fulani, Ind., 12,017; Paul, Ind., 11,926.

Oklahoma

County	1992 Clinton (D)	1992 Bush (R)	1992 Perot (I)	1988 Dukakis (D)	1988 Bush (R)
Adair	2,645	2,994	914	2,624	3,558
Alfalfa	741	1,567	722	1,117	1,960
Atoka	2,336	1,561	1,255	2,565	1,971
Beaver	580	1,699	565	777	2,013
Beckham	2,947	2,913	1,929	3,388	3,463
Blaine	1,564	2,209	1,258	1,775	2,889
Bryan	6,259	3,452	3,713	6,849	4,615
Caddo	4,861	3,664	2,911	5,387	4,689
Canadian	7,215	16,756	8,985	7,453	17,872
Carter	7,171	5,947	5,188	7,988	8,430
Cherokee	6,794	4,977	3,297	6,483	5,838
Choctaw	3,413	1,641	1,298	3,362	2,217
Cimarron	395	965	254	470	1,153
Cleveland	24,404	35,561	20,352	22,067	36,313
Coal	1,448	714	618	1,365	891
Comanche	12,237	15,704	7,463	11,441	17,464
Cotton	1,314	910	853	1,482	1,266
Craig	2,780	2,106	1,316	2,940	2,463
Creek	9,118	10,055	5,984	9,512	11,308
Custer	3,540	5,362	2,741	3,697	6,735
Delaware	4,842	4,840	2,689	4,889	5,248
Dewey	845	1,244	684	963	1,543
Ellis	594	1,072	632	786	1,422
Garfield	6,720	13,095	5,559	8,067	15,248
Garvin	4,811	3,983	3,014	5,438	5,109
Grady	6,177	6,997	4,528	6,689	7,994
Grant	864	1,311	871	1,249	1,690
Greer	1,162	964	640	1,256	1,225
Harmon	783	496	326	890	611
Harper	486	1,038	501	593	1,281
Haskell	3,069	1,461	995	2,963	1,822
Hughes	2,850	1,522	1,158	3,259	2,037
Jackson	3,273	3,893	2,227	3,542	4,423
Jefferson	1,580	671	758	1,767	1,063
Johnston	2,096	1,191	1,040	2,042	1,518
Kay	6,643	9,115	6,984	7,751	12,646
Kingfisher	1,379	3,479	1,534	1,777	4,011
Kiowa	2,143	1,635	1,114	2,296	2,030
Latimer	2,606	1,212	1,049	2,365	1,830
Le Flore	7,843	5,850	3,021	6,594	6,964
Lincoln	3,904	5,315	3,160	4,225	6,409
Logan	4,453	6,071	3,239	4,603	6,947
Love	1,708	922	1,033	1,889	1,361
McClain	3,378	4,377	2,996	3,594	4,771
McCurtain	5,082	3,519	2,852	4,928	4,920
McIntosh	4,184	2,225	1,469	4,041	2,665
Major	731	2,154	857	982	2,638
Marshall	2,519	1,478	1,486	2,730	1,911
Mayes	6,432	5,445	3,235	6,691	6,115
Murray	2,594	1,536	1,447	2,697	2,056
Muskogee	13,619	8,782	5,454	13,760	11,147
Noble	1,333	2,474	1,449	1,661	3,015
Nowata	1,912	1,531	1,063	2,203	2,000
Okfuskee	2,141	1,580	889	2,209	1,851
Oklahoma	76,271	126,788	56,139	75,812	135,376
Okmulgee	7,767	4,586	3,013	8,262	5,674
Osage	6,894	5,891	4,477	7,778	7,162
Ottawa	6,304	4,141	2,721	6,658	5,026
Pawnee	2,612	2,675	1,656	2,781	3,324
Payne	9,886	13,032	7,852	10,568	16,027
Pittsburg	8,523	5,659	4,594	8,623	7,594
Pontotoc	6,350	5,206	3,916	6,484	6,609
Pottawatomie	8,616	10,350	6,620	8,873	12,099
Pushmataha	2,553	1,319	1,000	2,430	1,841
Roger Mills	767	890	505	866	1,132
Rogers	8,257	12,455	7,101	8,771	12,940
Seminole	4,624	3,253	2,330	4,911	4,078
Sequoyah	6,092	4,925	2,486	4,951	5,710
Stephens	7,644	7,085	5,692	7,833	9,844
Texas	1,487	4,059	1,417	1,717	4,971
Tillman	1,749	1,377	1,039	2,148	1,754
Tulsa	71,165	117,465	49,760	69,044	127,512
Wagoner	7,041	9,053	5,381	7,378	10,219
Washington	6,593	11,342	5,664	6,971	14,613
Washita	1,929	1,912	1,468	2,290	2,402
Woods	1,361	2,225	1,167	1,735	2,835
Woodward	2,063	4,006	2,411	2,408	4,996
Totals	**473,066**	**592,929**	**319,978**	**483,423**	**678,367**

Oklahoma Vote Since 1940

1940, Roosevelt, Dem., 474,313; Willkie, Rep., 348,872; Babson, Proh., 3,027.

1944, Roosevelt, Dem., 401,549; Dewey, Rep., 319,424; Watson, Proh., 1,663.

1948, Truman, Dem., 452,782; Dewey, Rep., 268,817.

1952, Eisenhower, Rep., 518,045; Stevenson, Dem., 430,939.

1956, Eisenhower, Rep., 473,769; Stevenson, Dem., 385,581.

1960, Kennedy, Dem., 370,111; Nixon, Rep., 533,039.

1964, Johnson, Dem., 519,834; Goldwater, Rep. 412,665.

1968, Nixon, Rep., 449,697; Humphrey, Dem., 301,658; Wallace, 3d party, 191,731.

1972, Nixon, Rep. 759,025; McGovern, Dem., 247,147; Schmitz, Amer., 23,728.

1976, Carter, Dem., 532,442; Ford, Rep., 545,708; McCarthy, Ind., 14,101.

1980, Reagan, Rep., 695,570; Carter, Dem., 402,026; Anderson, Ind., 38,284; Clark, Libertarian, 13,828.

1984, Reagan, Rep., 861,530; Mondale, Dem., 385,080; Bergland, Libertarian, 9,066.

1988, Bush, Rep., 678,367; Dukakis, Dem., 483,423; Paul., Lib., 6,261; Fulani, New Alliance, 2,985.

Oregon

	1992			1988	
County	Clinton (D)	Bush (R)	Perot (I)	Dukakis (D)	Bush (R)
Baker	2,377	2,842	2,166	2,896	3,696
Benton	16,502	10,336	7,385	16,930	14,004
Clackamas	51,964	43,748	35,106	59,799	61,381
Clatsop	7,678	4,679	4,295	8,074	5,956
Columbia	8,131	5,139	5,543	8,983	6,424
Coos	11,450	8,808	7,576	13,996	10,153
Crook	2,509	2,702	2,001	2,719	3,049
Curry	3,587	3,543	3,037	4,015	4,761
Deschutes	13,326	12,559	10,439	14,264	16,425
Douglas	13,982	18,678	12,184	17,255	20,120
Gilliam	374	377	283	417	470
Grant	984	1,282	1,153	1,437	2,264
Harney	973	1,580	1,024	1,379	1,833
Hood River	3,106	2,453	2,233	3,275	3,257
Jackson	26,962	25,350	17,203	28,028	32,516
Jefferson	1,827	1,568	1,509	2,346	2,509
Josephine	9,596	10,700	7,401	10,646	15,876
Klamath	7,088	10,355	6,001	8,429	13,484
Lake	991	1,764	957	1,237	2,161
Lane	66,606	35,640	31,876	69,883	47,563
Lincoln	9,265	5,343	5,865	9,598	7,364
Linn	13,801	14,158	12,171	17,007	18,312
Malheur	2,411	4,963	2,473	2,965	6,285
Marion	38,228	38,223	24,123	41,193	45,292
Morrow	1,174	1,192	1,089	1,375	1,529
Multnomah	126,887	52,734	46,356	161,361	95,561
Polk	9,211	9,498	5,579	9,626	10,553
Sherman	362	424	326	435	555
Tillamook	4,257	2,771	2,629	5,529	4,297
Umatilla	6,799	7,103	5,592	8,327	10,254
Union	3,980	4,218	3,304	4,682	5,061
Wallowa	1,187	1,596	1,189	1,425	1,993
Wasco	3,737	2,523	2,537	5,141	4,462
Washington	43,468	34,741	27,320	59,837	67,018
Wheeler	267	357	227	274	367
Yamhill	9,114	9,326	7,092	11,423	13,321
Totals	**524,161**	**393,273**	**307,244**	**616,206**	**560,126**

Oregon Vote Since 1940

1940, Roosevelt, Dem., 258,415; Willkie, Rep., 219,555; Aiken, Soc. Labor, 2,487; Thomas, Soc., 398; Browder, Com., 191; Babson, Proh., 154.

1944, Roosevelt, Dem., 248,635; Dewey, Rep., 225,365; Thomas, Soc., 3,785; Watson, Proh., 2,362.

1948, Truman, Dem., 243,147; Dewey, Rep., 260,904; Wallace, Prog., 14,978; Thomas, Soc., 5,051.

1952, Eisenhower, Rep., 420,815; Stevenson, Dem., 270,579; Hallinan, Ind., 3,665.

1956, Eisenhower, Rep., 406,393; Stevenson, Dem., 329,204.

1960, Kennedy, Dem., 367,402; Nixon, Rep., 408,060.

1964, Johnson, Dem., 501,017; Goldwater, Rep., 282,779; write-in, 2,509.

1968, Nixon, Rep., 408,433; Humphrey, Dem., 358,866; Wallace, 3d party, 49,683; write-in, McCarthy, 1,496; N. Rockefeller, 69; others, 1,075.

1972, Nixon, Rep., 486,686; McGovern, Dem., 392,760, Schmitz, Amer., 46,211; write-in, 2,289.

1976, Carter, Dem., 490,407; Ford, Rep., 492,120; McCarthy, Ind., 40,207; write-in, 7,142.

1980, Reagan, Rep., 571,044; Carter, Dem., 456,890; Anderson, Ind., 112,389; Clark, Libertarian, 25,838; Commoner, Citizens, 13,642; scattered, 1,713.

1984, Reagan, Rep., 658,700; Mondale, Dem., 536,479.

1988, Bush, Rep., 560,126; Dukakis, Dem., 616,206; Paul, Lib., 14,811; Fulani, Ind., 6,487.

Pennsylvania

	1992			1988	
County	Clinton (D)	Bush (R)	Perot (I)	Dukakis (D)	Bush (R)
Adams	9,503	13,461	6,281	8,299	15,650
Allegheny	322,645	182,901	102,460	348,814	231,137
Armstrong	12,971	9,094	6,150	13,892	11,509
Beaver	44,790	21,295	15,920	50,327	25,764
Bedford	5,835	9,204	3,725	5,754	11,123
Berks	44,382	50,590	30,876	41,040	70,153
Blair	14,822	21,376	8,262	15,588	25,623
Bradford	6,867	10,161	5,421	6,635	13,568
Bucks	96,571	93,451	53,023	82,472	127,563
Butler	22,237	23,573	14,982	22,341	27,777
Cambria	34,386	20,772	11,076	38,517	25,626
Cameron	822	1,163	672	901	1,731
Carbon	9,060	7,232	5,210	9,104	10,232
Centre	21,117	20,415	9,327	18,357	23,875
Chester	59,293	73,623	34,377	44,853	93,522
Clarion	5,565	6,437	3,599	5,616	8,026
Clearfield	12,247	11,550	6,987	12,235	14,296
Clinton	5,387	4,460	2,467	5,759	5,735
Columbia	8,238	9,705	5,671	7,767	12,114
Crawford	12,804	14,104	7,479	13,021	17,249
Cumberland	26,541	43,324	14,083	24,613	47,292
Dauphin	36,921	45,381	16,030	35,079	48,917
Delaware	111,118	107,722	43,565	96,144	147,656
Elk	5,007	4,899	3,878	5,879	6,737
Erie	56,018	39,172	21,284	53,913	48,306
Fayette	30,489	12,870	10,098	33,098	16,915
Forest	849	760	437	895	1,159
Franklin	13,314	23,101	6,857	12,368	27,086
Fulton	1,593	2,558	869	1,532	3,086
Greene	8,461	3,481	3,186	9,126	4,879
Huntingdon	5,139	7,233	3,205	4,752	8,800
Indiana	15,081	10,873	7,031	16,514	14,983
Jefferson	5,981	7,244	4,385	6,235	9,743
Juniata	2,595	3,970	1,815	2,834	4,881
Lackawanna	42,947	30,747	15,948	45,591	42,083
Lancaster	44,119	88,191	26,819	38,982	96,979
Lawrence	20,756	12,251	7,929	21,884	15,829
Lebanon	12,326	21,460	8,975	11,912	24,415
Lehigh	46,667	42,571	24,828	42,801	56,363
Luzerne	56,502	49,003	20,937	58,553	59,059
Lycoming	13,626	20,473	9,145	13,528	24,792
McKean	5,295	6,825	3,971	5,300	9,323
Mercer	23,129	15,473	10,190	24,278	21,301
Mifflin	4,934	6,275	3,377	4,790	8,170
Monroe	13,407	14,550	9,252	9,859	17,185
Montgomery	136,164	125,382	53,233	109,834	170,294
Montour	2,149	3,096	1,372	2,031	3,617
Northampton	42,132	34,346	20,310	39,264	42,748
Northumberland	12,789	15,023	7,734	14,255	20,207
Perry	4,076	7,852	3,330	3,910	8,545
Philadelphia	430,207	132,040	64,459	449,566	219,053
Pike	4,382	6,088	3,019	3,097	6,659
Potter	1,892	3,457	1,586	2,119	4,432
Schuylkill	23,672	25,707	13,384	24,797	32,666
Snyder	2,952	6,934	2,686	2,658	9,054
Somerset	12,476	13,825	6,314	13,815	16,809
Sullivan	1,030	1,337	731	1,091	1,808
Susquehanna	5,346	7,316	3,927	4,871	9,077
Tioga	4,863	7,816	3,800	4,807	9,471
Union	3,622	6,362	2,255	3,163	7,912
Venango	8,224	8,534	4,691	8,624	11,468
Warren	6,945	6,544	4,530	6,790	8,991
Washington	46,029	21,886	16,023	47,527	28,651
Wayne	4,795	8,157	3,597	3,775	9,926
Westmoreland	69,624	47,119	36,814	76,710	61,472
Wyoming	3,158	5,143	2,525	2,797	6,607
York	44,926	58,434	27,184	37,691	72,408
Totals	**2,223,810**	**1,777,372**	**895,563**	**2,194,944**	**2,300,087**

Pennsylvania Vote Since 1940

1940, Roosevelt, Dem., 2,171,035; Willkie, Rep., 1,889,848; Thomas, Soc., 10,967; Browder, Com., 4,519; Aiken, Ind. Gov., 1,518.

1944, Roosevelt, Dem., 1,940,479; Dewey, Rep., 1,835,054; Thomas, Soc., 11,721; Watson, Proh., 5,750; Teichert, Ind. Gov., 1,789.

1948, Truman, Dem., 1,752,426; Dewey, Rep., 1,902,197; Wallace, Prog., 55,161; Thomas, Soc., 11,325; Watson, Proh., 10,338; Dobbs, Militant Workers, 2,133; Teichert, Ind. Gov., 1,461.

1952, Eisenhower, Rep., 2,415,789; Stevenson, Dem., 2,146,269; Hamblen, Proh., 8,771; Hallinan, Prog., 4,200; Hoopes, Soc., 2,684; Dobbs, Militant Workers, 1,502; Hass, Ind. Gov., 1,347; scattered, 155.

1956, Eisenhower, Rep., 2,585,252; Stevenson, Dem., 1,981,769; Hass, Soc. Labor, 7,447; Dobbs, Militant Workers, 2,035.

1960, Kennedy, Dem., 2,556,282; Nixon, Rep., 2,439,956; Hass, Soc. Labor, 7,185; Dobbs, Soc. Workers, 2,678; scattering, 440.

1964, Johnson, Dem., 3,130,954; Goldwater, Rep., 1,673,657; DeBerry, Soc. Workers, 10,456; Hass, Soc. Labor, 5,092; scattering, 2,531.

1968, Nixon, Rep., 2,090,017; Humphrey, Dem., 2,259,405; Wallace, 3d party, 378,582; Blomen, Soc. Labor, 4,977; Halstead, Soc. Workers, 4,862; Gregory, 7,821; others, 2,264.

1972, Nixon, Rep., 2,714,521; McGovern, Dem., 1,796,951; Schmitz, Amer., 70,593; Jenness, Soc. Workers, 4,639; Hall, Com., 2,686; others, 2,715.

1976, Carter, Dem., 2,328,677; Ford, Rep., 2,205,604; McCarthy, Ind., 50,584; Maddox, Constitution, 25,344;

Camejo, Soc. Workers, 3,009; LaRouche, U.S. Labor, 2,744; Hall, Com., 1,891; others, 2,934.

1980, Reagan, Rep., 2,261,872; Carter, Dem., 1,937,540; Anderson, Ind., 292,921; Clark, Libertarian, 33,263; DeBerry, Soc. Workers, 20,291; Commoner, Consumer, 10,430; Hall, Com., 5,184.

1984, Reagan, Rep., 2,584,323; Mondale, Dem., 2,228,131; Bergland, Libertarian, 6,982.

1988, Bush, Rep., 2,300,087; Dukakis, Dem., 2,194,944; McCarthy, Consumer, 19,158; Paul, Lib., 12,051.

Rhode Island

City	1992 Clinton (D)	1992 Bush (R)	1992 Perot (I)	1988 Dukakis (D)	1988 Bush (R)
Cranston	17,660	11,874	7,767	19,711	17,129
East Providence	10,920	5,420	4,280	11,948	8,181
Pawtucket	13,344	5,840	5,646	15,985	9,359
Providence	30,054	10,825	7,163	34,806	15,310
Warwick	19,592	12,663	9,748	21,662	18,052
Totals	**198,877**	**121,864**	**94,717**	**225,123**	**177,761**

Rhode Island Vote Since 1940

1940, Roosevelt, Dem., 182,182; Willkie, Rep., 138,653; Browder, Com., 239; Babson, Proh., 74.

1944, Roosevelt, Dem., 175,356; Dewey, Rep., 123,487; Watson, Proh., 433.

1948, Truman, Dem., 188,736; Dewey, Rep., 135,787; Wallace, Prog., 2,619; Thomas, Soc., 429; Teichert, Soc. Labor, 131.

1952, Eisenhower, Rep., 210,935; Stevenson, Dem., 203,293; Hallinan, Prog., 187; Hass, Soc. Labor, 83.

1956, Eisenhower, Rep., 225,819; Stevenson, Dem., 161,790.

1960, Kennedy, Dem., 258,032; Nixon, Rep., 147,502.

1964, Johnson, Dem., 315,463; Goldwater, Rep., 74,615.

1968, Nixon, Rep., 122,359; Humphrey, Dem., 246,518; Wallace, 3d party, 15,678; Halstead, Soc. Worker, 383.

1972, Nixon, Rep., 220,383; McGovern, Dem., 194,645; Jenness, Soc. Workers, 729.

1976, Carter, Dem., 227,636; Ford, Rep., 181,249; MacBride, Libertarian, 715; Camejo, Soc. Workers, 462; Hall, Com., 334; Levin, Soc. Labor, 188.

1980, Reagan, Rep., 154,793; Carter, Dem., 198,342; Anderson, Ind., 59,819; Clark, Libertarian, 2,458; Hall, Com., 218; McReynolds, Socialist, 170; DeBerry, Soc. Worker, 90; Griswold, Workers World, 77.

1984, Reagan, Rep., 212,080; Mondale, Dem., 197,106; Bergland, Libertarian, 277.

1988, Bush, Rep., 177,761; Dukakis, Dem., 225,123; Paul, Lib., 825; Fulani, New Alliance, 280.

South Carolina

County	1992 Clinton (D)	1992 Bush (R)	1992 Perot (I)	1988 Dukakis (D)	1988 Bush (R)
Abbeville	3,968	3,317	1,036	3,629	3,738
Aiken	14,795	25,723	6,053	10,598	27,665
Allendale	2,153	1,048	222	1,796	1,295
Anderson	16,052	24,769	6,963	12,281	25,939
Bamberg	3,426	1,906	360	2,830	2,403
Barnwell	3,343	4,026	752	2,564	4,467
Beaufort	11,460	14,721	4,960	8,691	16,184
Berkeley	11,988	17,130	4,356	9,312	16,779
Calhoun	2,769	2,414	563	2,175	2,585
Charleston	38,184	44,931	9,925	32,977	49,149
Cherokee	5,453	6,887	2,186	4,322	7,763
Chester	5,458	3,452	1,351	3,737	3,968
Chesterfield	5,691	4,183	1,315	4,699	4,999
Clarendon	6,016	4,144	743	5,030	4,337
Colleton	5,221	4,324	1,197	4,508	4,962
Darlington	9,089	8,911	1,863	7,625	9,854
Dillon	4,953	3,575	831	3,251	3,793
Dorchester	8,766	14,291	3,493	7,371	14,756
Edgefield	3,428	3,335	596	3,020	3,814
Fairfield	4,887	2,516	651	3,827	2,714
Florence	15,562	19,792	3,495	12,531	19,490
Georgetown	7,476	6,854	1,832	5,402	7,032
Greenville	34,651	65,068	13,699	27,188	67,371
Greenwood	7,572	9,039	2,090	6,511	9,096
Hampton	4,331	2,402	563	3,435	2,826
Horry	18,896	23,489	8,472	13,316	24,843
Jasper	3,453	1,725	549	2,894	2,004
Kershaw	6,520	8,375	2,115	4,494	8,877
Lancaster	7,940	7,378	2,377	6,181	9,152
Laurens	6,632	8,336	2,154	5,930	9,731
Lee	4,408	2,815	610	3,423	2,936
Lexington	18,303	41,739	8,650	11,366	41,467
McCormick	1,843	899	295	1,722	1,172
Marion	5,634	3,404	800	5,008	4,403
Marlboro	5,109	2,531	895	3,937	2,921
Newberry	4,704	5,800	1,346	3,825	6,427
Oconee	6,597	10,327	3,396	4,299	10,184
Orangeburg	18,438	11,323	2,381	14,655	13,281
Pickens	8,265	16,995	4,126	6,103	17,448
Richland	53,625	43,722	7,916	36,420	43,841
Saluda	2,391	2,966	833	1,984	3,225
Spartanburg	25,483	37,705	8,900	22,964	40,801
Sumter	11,825	12,551	2,057	9,502	13,161
Union	4,645	4,647	1,372	4,420	6,019
Williamsburg	8,115	5,287	851	7,343	5,914
York	15,815	21,261	6,408	11,458	21,657
Totals	**475,313**	**572,031**	**137,598**	**370,554**	**606,443**

South Carolina Vote Since 1940

1940, Roosevelt, Dem., 95,470; Willkie, Rep., 1,727.

1944, Roosevelt, Dem., 90,601; Dewey, Rep., 4,547; Southern Democrats, 7,799; Watson, Proh., 365; Rep. Tolbert faction, 63.

1948, Thurmond, States' Rights, 102,607; Truman, Dem., 34,423; Dewey, Rep., 5,386; Wallace, Prog., 154; Thomas, Soc., 1.

1952, Eisenhower ran on two tickets. Under state law vote cast for two Eisenhower slates of electors could not be combined. Eisenhower, Ind., 158,289; Rep., 9,793; total, 168,082; Stevenson, Dem., 173,004; Hamblen, Proh., 1.

1956, Stevenson, Dem., 136,372; Byrd, Ind., 88,509; Eisenhower, Rep., 75,700; Andrews, Ind., 2.

1960, Kennedy, Dem., 198,129; Nixon, Rep., 188,558; write-in, 1.

1964, Johnson, Dem., 215,700; Goldwater, Rep., 309,048; write-ins: Nixon, 1, Wallace, 5; Powell, 1; Thurmond, 1.

1968, Nixon, Rep., 254,062; Humphrey, Dem., 197,486; Wallace, 3d party, 215,430.

1972, Nixon, Rep., 477,044; McGovern, Dem., 184,559, United Citizens, 2,265; Schmitz, Amer., 10,075; write-in, 17.

1976, Carter, Dem., 450,807; Ford, Rep., 346,149; Anderson, Amer., 2,996; Maddox, Amer. Ind., 1,950; write-in, 681.

1980, Reagan, Rep., 439,277; Carter, Dem., 428,220; Anderson, Ind., 13,868; Clark, Libertarian, 4,807; Rarick, Amer. Ind., 2,086.

1984, Reagan, Rep., 615,539; Mondale, Dem., 344,459; Bergland, Libertarian, 4,359.

1988, Bush, Rep., 606,443; Dukakis, Dem., 370,554; Paul, Lib., 4,935; Fulani, United Citizens, 4,077.

South Dakota

County	1992 Clinton (D)	1992 Bush (R)	1992 Perot (I)	1988 Dukakis (D)	1988 Bush (R)
Aurora	680	594	435	987	856
Beadle	3,925	3,363	1,819	4,523	4,611
Bennett	413	556	221	579	663
Bon Homme	1,294	1,212	836	1,574	1,826
Brookings	4,645	4,698	2,614	4,860	5,394
Brown	7,521	6,665	3,812	8,673	8,537
Brule	1,060	908	687	991	971
Buffalo	282	137	72	334	151
Butte	951	1,644	1,039	1,256	2,291
Campbell	222	574	252	334	909
Chas. Mix	1,639	1,570	886	2,205	1,966
Clark	799	803	761	1,164	1,247
Clay	2,826	1,869	1,303	2,859	2,307
Codington	3,701	3,943	3,262	4,570	5,050
Corson	444	483	321	722	710
Custer	1,078	1,422	845	1,180	1,806
Davison	3,284	3,110	1,706	3,705	4,024
Day	1,578	1,161	973	2,137	1,616
Deuel	880	778	761	1,246	1,251
Dewey	769	645	342	1,007	765
Douglas	481	1,175	402	695	1,438
Edmunds	894	944	415	1,259	1,327
Fall River	1,416	1,533	792	1,380	2,002
Faulk	480	658	281	714	842
Grant	1,484	1,595	1,018	1,988	2,148
Gregory	879	1,027	688	1,138	1,566
Haakon	209	860	245	379	958
Hamlin	826	1,133	774	1,258	1,380
Hand	785	1,130	624	1,101	1,461
Hanson	566	522	341	776	786
Harding	139	516	225	259	633
Hughes	2,578	4,325	1,160	2,853	4,545
Hutchinson	1,208	1,998	923	1,594	2,700
Hyde	301	440	211	436	546
Jackson	351	627	184	450	671
Jerauld	600	518	346	751	777
Jones	166	454	154	261	521

Kingsbury	1,267	1,113	744	1,472	1,592
Lake	2,388	1,890	1,299	2,663	2,439
Lawrence	3,157	3,770	2,673	3,705	5,570
Lincoln	2,943	3,365	1,593	3,190	3,537
Lyman	486	669	311	631	843
McCook	1,167	1,177	617	1,492	1,501
McPherson	478	945	322	571	1,358
Marshall	1,056	800	427	1,372	1,142
Meade	2,694	4,724	2,611	3,212	5,189
Mellette	277	417	140	385	460
Miner	698	543	332	955	795
Minnehaha	27,016	25,081	11,496	29,135	26,765
Moody	1,473	898	715	1,715	1,161
Pennington	11,106	18,052	8,358	12,068	19,510
Perkins	566	872	541	851	1,326
Potter	493	901	375	701	1,175
Roberts	1,716	1,437	954	2,267	2,012
Sanborn	632	595	376	770	815
Shannon	1,267	225	137	1,206	256
Spink	1,732	1,527	839	2,071	1,969
Stanley	427	719	240	511	698
Sully	273	565	167	393	571
Todd	915	456	246	1,117	535
Tripp	1,042	1,453	846	1,219	2,113
Turner	1,507	1,906	867	1,780	2,436
Union	2,210	1,784	1,085	2,612	1,907
Walworth	829	1,439	628	1,094	1,940
Yankton	3,404	3,430	2,511	3,777	4,186
Ziebach	280	328	117	427	362
Totals	**124,861**	**136,671**	**73,297**	**145,560**	**165,415**

South Dakota Vote Since 1940

1940, Roosevelt, Dem., 131,862; Willkie, Rep., 177,065.

1944, Roosevelt, Dem., 96,711; Dewey, Rep., 135,365.

1948, Truman, Dem., 117,653; Dewey, Rep., 129,651; Wallace, Prog., 2,801.

1952, Eisenhower, Rep., 203,857; Stevenson, Dem., 90,426.

1956, Eisenhower, Rep., 171,569; Stevenson, Dem., 122,288.

1960, Kennedy, Dem., 128,070; Nixon, Rep., 178,417.

1964, Johnson, Dem., 163,010; Goldwater, Rep., 130,108.

1968, Nixon, Rep., 149,841; Humphrey, Dem., 118,023; Wallace, 3d party, 13,400.

1972, Nixon, Rep., 166,476; McGovern, Dem., 139,945; Jenness, Soc. Workers, 994.

1976, Carter, Dem., 147,068; Ford, Rep., 151,505; MacBride, Libertarian, 1,619; Hall, Com., 318; Camejo, Soc. Workers, 168.

1980, Reagan, Rep., 198,343; Carter, Dem., 103,855; Anderson, Ind., 21,431; Clark, Libertarian, 3,824; Pulley, Soc. Workers, 250.

1984, Reagan, Rep., 200,267; Mondale, Dem., 116,113.

1988, Bush, Rep., 165,415; Dukakis, Dem., 145,560; Paul, Lib., 1,060; Fulani, New Alliance, 730.

Tennessee

	1992			1988	
County	Clinton (D)	Bush (R)	Perot (I)	Dukakis (D)	Bush (R)
Anderson	14,526	12,665	3,364	9,589	15,056
Bedford	5,978	3,836	1,541	4,046	4,856
Benton	3,896	1,625	559	2,826	2,167
Bledsoe	1,884	1,776	352	1,274	1,858
Blount	14,660	18,422	4,473	9,602	20,027
Bradley	9,889	16,528	3,212	6,122	15,829
Campbell	6,656	4,897	1,242	4,188	5,197
Cannon	2,579	1,229	495	1,726	1,604
Carroll	5,826	4,929	1,141	4,151	5,635
Carter	6,665	10,712	1,935	4,634	12,036
Cheatham	4,817	3,496	1,413	3,067	4,132
Chester	2,317	2,834	439	1,757	2,781
Claiborne	4,509	4,065	860	2,977	4,071
Clay	1,921	1,073	223	1,183	1,291
Cocke	3,493	5,293	1,124	2,115	5,430
Coffee	8,533	6,047	2,420	5,686	7,837
Crockett	2,657	2,179	507	1,742	2,214
Cumberland	6,342	7,116	2,200	3,964	7,557
Davidson	106,316	76,530	20,165	89,270	98,599
Decatur	2,633	1,667	351	1,880	2,286
De Kalb	4,373	1,714	608	2,452	2,098
Dickson	7,861	4,449	1,730	5,129	5,343
Dyer	5,845	5,667	1,240	3,690	6,508
Fayette	4,211	3,713	657	3,292	3,573
Fentress	2,730	2,391	614	1,856	3,103
Franklin	7,772	4,502	1,837	5,442	5,381
Gibson	9,477	7,073	1,513	7,542	8,415
Giles	5,601	2,827	1,309	3,918	3,518
Grainger	2,242	2,772	513	1,423	2,734
Greene	7,858	9,884	2,804	5,077	11,947
Grundy	2,993	1,001	363	2,415	1,429
Hamblen	7,204	8,898	1,764	5,061	10,418
Hamilton	46,756	53,453	14,392	40,990	68,111
Hancock	1,000	1,274	151	737	1,303
Hardeman	4,832	3,122	594	3,526	3,547
Hardin	3,922	3,875	732	2,808	4,252
Hawkins	6,623	7,758	1,847	5,212	9,356
Haywood	3,511	2,518	331	2,923	2,687
Henderson	3,502	4,719	806	2,296	5,418
Henry	6,797	3,661	1,588	5,138	4,784
Hickman	4,193	1,820	795	2,643	2,246
Houston	2,081	653	288	1,467	882
Humphreys	3,875	1,641	609	3,037	2,132
Jackson	3,208	708	332	1,962	1,168
Jefferson	4,740	6,184	1,385	3,168	6,832
Johnson	1,781	3,170	574	1,329	3,715
Knox	59,591	66,507	15,650	41,829	73,092
Lake	1,449	680	151	935	806
Lauderdale	4,452	2,928	561	3,296	3,308
Lawrence	6,716	5,608	1,405	4,903	6,273
Lewis	2,491	1,218	434	1,419	1,324
Lincoln	5,062	3,812	1,369	3,672	4,288
Loudon	5,417	6,444	1,662	3,480	7,122
McMinn	6,681	7,453	1,811	4,568	8,462
McNairy	4,691	4,097	774	3,510	4,625
Macon	2,961	2,199	443	1,538	2,962
Madison	13,520	14,836	2,626	11,001	16,952
Marion	5,589	3,262	1,186	4,175	4,407
Marshall	4,494	2,515	1,050	2,795	2,975
Maury	9,997	7,440	2,833	6,280	8,397
Meigs	1,673	1,355	453	1,048	1,507
Monroe	5,384	5,836	935	4,000	6,355
Montgomery	14,505	13,009	3,743	9,145	12,599
Moore	1,151	661	327	731	786
Morgan	3,190	2,302	698	1,941	2,576
Obion	6,017	4,406	1,312	4,785	6,037
Overton	4,488	1,656	467	2,511	1,873
Perry	1,889	706	317	1,208	854
Pickett	1,144	1,094	121	634	1,118
Polk	2,583	1,584	419	2,073	2,297
Putnam	10,858	7,998	2,471	6,606	9,547
Rhea	4,289	4,860	1,163	2,595	5,144
Roane	9,813	8,720	2,398	6,535	10,881
Robertson	8,498	5,271	1,977	5,884	5,714
Rutherford	20,726	18,549	6,865	12,245	20,397
Scott	2,738	3,011	643	1,611	2,562
Sequatchie	1,754	1,381	405	1,196	1,659
Sevier	6,719	11,714	2,760	3,643	11,920
Shelby	191,315	153,301	20,219	149,759	157,457
Smith	5,061	1,482	458	2,522	2,138
Stewart	2,779	1,046	487	1,979	1,302
Sullivan	20,981	28,817	6,730	17,396	32,996
Sumner	19,387	17,401	5,167	11,702	19,523
Tipton	5,652	6,757	1,279	3,824	6,052
Trousdale	1,846	567	243	1,193	969
Unicoi	2,375	3,344	709	1,794	3,664
Union	2,478	2,274	580	1,431	2,110
Van Buren	1,329	555	193	796	780
Warren	7,189	3,704	1,415	4,646	4,529
Washington	13,071	18,206	4,002	10,087	19,615
Wayne	1,868	2,955	418	1,516	3,405
Weakley	5,708	4,817	1,371	4,239	5,701
White	4,102	2,118	821	2,562	2,646
Williamson	13,051	22,014	5,026	7,864	20,847
Wilson	13,811	12,061	3,848	8,360	13,317
Totals	**933,618**	**840,897**	**199,787**	**679,794**	**947,233**

Tennessee Vote Since 1940

1940, Roosevelt, Dem., 351,601; Willkie, Rep., 169,153; Babson, Proh., 1,606; Thomas, Soc., 463.

1944, Roosevelt, Dem., 308,707; Dewey, Rep., 200,311; Watson, Proh., 882; Thomas, Soc., 892.

1948, Truman, Dem., 270,402; Dewey, Rep., 202,914; Thurmond, States' Rights, 73,815; Wallace, Prog., 1,864; Thomas, Soc., 1,288.

1952, Eisenhower, Rep., 446,147; Stevenson, Dem., 443,710; Hamblen, Proh., 1,432; Hallinan, Prog., 885; MacArthur, Christian Nationalist, 379.

1956, Eisenhower, Rep., 462,288; Stevenson, Dem., 456,507; Andrews, Ind., 19,820; Holtwick, Proh., 789.

1960, Kennedy, Dem., 481,453; Nixon, Rep., 556,577; Faubus, States' Rights, 11,304; Decker, Proh., 2,458.

1964, Johnson, Dem. 635,047; Goldwater, Rep., 508,965; write-in, 34.

1968, Nixon, Rep., 472,592; Humphrey, Dem., 351,233; Wallace, 3d party, 424,792.

1972, Nixon, Rep., 813,147; McGovern, Dem., 357,293; Schmitz, Amer., 30,373; write-in, 369.

1976, Carter, Dem., 825,879; Ford, Rep., 633,969; Anderson, Amer., 5,769; McCarthy, Ind., 5,004; Maddox, Am. Ind., 2,303; MacBride, Libertarian, 1,375; Hall, Com., 547; LaRouche, U.S. Labor, 512; Bubar, Proh., 442; Miller, Ind., 316; write-in, 230.

1980, Reagan, Rep., 787,761; Carter, Dem., 783,051; Anderson, Ind., 35,991; Clark, Libertarian, 7,116; Commoner, Citizens, 1,112; Bubar, Statesman, 521; McReynolds, Socialist, 519; Hall, Com., 503; DeBerry, Soc. Worker, 490; Griswold, Workers World, 400; write-ins, 152.

1984, Reagan, Rep., 990,212; Mondale, Dem., 711,714; Bergland, Libertarian, 3,072.

1988, Bush, Rep., 947,233; Dukakis, Dem., 679,794; Paul, Ind., 2,041; Duke, Ind., 1,807.

Texas

County	1992 Clinton (D)	1992 Bush (R)	1992 Perot (I)	1988 Dukakis (D)	1988 Bush (R)
Anderson	5,199	5,444	3,348	6,128	7,858
Andrews	1,081	2,266	875	1,122	3,052
Angelina	10,294	9,679	6,163	10,849	12,738
Aransas	2,246	2,826	1,676	2,305	3,858
Archer	1,284	1,560	1,106	1,627	2,010
Armstrong	278	561	187	314	720
Atascosa	3,766	3,806	2,025	4,657	4,777
Austin	2,270	3,979	1,575	2,593	4,524
Bailey	677	1,308	376	876	1,459
Bandera	1,059	2,674	1,537	1,251	3,435
Bastrop	6,252	4,980	3,240	8,004	5,991
Baylor	990	611	529	1,153	914
Bee	4,083	3,633	1,367	4,616	4,620
Bell	18,790	25,232	11,169	17,751	29,382
Bexar	172,333	168,703	72,140	174,036	193,192
Blanco	891	1,370	830	1,012	1,680
Borden	106	184	87	169	283
Bosque	2,133	2,300	1,999	2,670	3,458
Bowie	11,825	11,776	6,659	12,331	15,454
Brazoria	21,861	30,384	18,954	23,436	34,028
Brazos	14,819	23,943	10,372	14,885	29,369
Brewster	1,383	1,147	712	1,569	1,708
Briscoe	435	360	164	574	464
Brooks	2,856	585	318	2,859	608
Brown	4,260	5,301	3,027	4,763	6,810
Burleson	1,944	1,643	1,036	3,085	2,242
Burnet	3,638	4,272	2,865	4,343	5,120
Caldwell	3,748	2,723	1,776	4,649	3,553
Calhoun	2,482	2,609	1,555	3,314	3,183
Callahan	1,694	2,134	1,452	2,017	2,887
Cameron	29,828	20,507	9,258	30,972	24,263
Camp	1,938	1,219	821	2,121	1,908
Carson	825	1,647	574	1,034	2,100
Cass	5,476	3,999	2,168	5,941	5,305
Castro	1,113	1,307	485	1,436	1,604
Chambers	2,832	3,398	2,122	3,035	3,694
Cherokee	4,751	5,678	3,142	5,604	7,520
Childress	881	1,033	421	1,060	1,201
Clay	1,919	1,586	1,515	2,288	2,043
Cochran	462	761	259	681	771
Coke	580	640	393	674	863
Coleman	1,579	1,462	1,095	1,978	2,340
Collin	24,508	60,514	43,287	22,934	67,776
Collingsworth	635	697	265	809	872
Colorado	2,442	3,286	1,421	2,847	3,723
Comal	6,312	12,651	5,841	5,716	13,994
Comanche	2,297	1,626	1,382	2,622	2,120
Concho	489	414	329	643	617
Cooke	3,105	5,299	4,658	4,217	7,196
Coryell	4,158	6,144	3,974	4,026	7,461
Cottle	542	245	235	690	379
Crane	514	928	412	596	1,219
Crockett	653	624	368	881	932
Crosby	1,010	1,006	313	1,435	1,121
Culberson	424	251	171	557	417
Dallam	434	922	325	645	1,205
Dallas	232,104	255,872	170,469	243,198	347,094
Dawson	1,639	2,691	518	2,155	3,154
Deaf Smith	1,642	3,137	772	1,930	3,744
Delta	846	599	551	1,244	849
Denton	27,891	48,492	39,653	26,204	57,444
DeWitt	2,127	3,238	1,346	2,579	3,628
Dickens	536	373	250	696	435
Dimmit	3,172	844	361	2,735	900
Donley	578	893	260	661	1,043
Duval	4,006	698	326	4,177	907
Eastland	2,738	2,830	1,698	3,215	3,929
Ector	11,130	18,161	6,668	10,825	23,155
Edwards	254	460	171	368	556
Ellis	9,537	13,564	10,303	11,169	16,422
El Paso	67,715	47,224	19,738	62,622	55,573
Erath	3,531	3,834	3,046	4,113	5,427
Falls	2,669	1,774	1,185	2,877	2,344
Fannin	5,352	2,510	2,919	5,163	4,024
Fayette	2,923	3,789	2,086	3,390	4,551
Fisher	1,242	539	442	1,516	721
Floyd	947	1,676	385	1,391	1,741
Foard	435	207	152	513	306
Fort Bend	29,982	41,027	16,853	23,351	39,818
Franklin	1,338	1,058	942	1,453	1,439
Freestone	2,445	2,316	1,596	2,916	3,159
Frio	2,377	1,275	654	3,016	1,505
Gaines	1,095	2,138	696	1,310	2,265
Galveston	38,623	31,303	20,103	38,633	34,913
Garza	558	982	345	989	1,183
Gillespie	1,600	4,612	2,018	1,588	5,662
Glasscock	100	379	93	143	384
Goliad	1,069	1,233	521	1,358	1,427
Gonzales	2,006	2,502	1,018	2,897	2,983
Gray	2,426	6,105	1,810	2,460	7,259
Grayson	12,547	12,322	13,327	14,347	18,825
Gregg	12,797	20,542	8,437	12,486	26,465
Grimes	2,594	2,402	1,213	2,735	2,820
Guadalupe	6,567	10,816	5,618	7,111	13,265
Hale	2,736	6,028	1,357	3,502	6,284
Hall	819	631	263	1,029	714
Hamilton	1,100	1,232	921	1,355	1,718
Hansford	345	1,660	398	443	1,967
Hardeman	954	614	362	1,143	855
Hardin	6,780	5,902	4,147	8,245	6,897
Harris	357,446	372,679	168,776	342,919	464,217
Harrison	9,538	8,733	4,371	8,974	11,957
Hartley	406	1,081	308	505	1,229
Haskell	1,438	852	562	1,715	1,193
Hays	10,842	10,008	6,252	11,187	11,716
Hemphill	479	986	232	527	1,170
Henderson	9,105	8,368	6,746	9,819	11,005
Hidalgo	51,356	26,541	9,757	54,330	29,246
Hill	3,929	3,669	2,752	4,381	4,796
Hockley	2,301	4,261	1,291	2,850	4,368
Hood	4,359	5,313	4,457	4,255	7,400
Hopkins	4,089	3,402	3,148	4,984	5,133
Houston	3,256	3,070	1,684	3,846	3,882
Howard	3,735	5,129	1,984	4,445	6,024
Hudspeth	364	325	178	406	405
Hunt	7,452	9,737	7,383	8,820	12,331
Hutchinson	2,833	6,034	1,993	2,950	7,526
Irion	256	283	290	326	539
Jack	1,190	1,031	1,045	1,521	1,542
Jackson	1,722	2,451	976	2,141	2,954
Jasper	5,658	3,870	2,539	6,613	4,985
Jeff Davis	321	360	187	325	524
Jefferson	48,405	29,622	17,242	55,649	35,754
Jim Hogg	1,520	478	107	1,630	510
Jim Wells	7,808	3,306	1,411	8,495	4,335
Johnson	11,849	13,146	11,297	12,507	17,509
Jones	2,400	2,088	1,436	2,898	3,000
Karnes	1,899	1,990	801	2,529	2,383
Kaufman	6,498	6,578	5,913	7,358	8,466
Kendall	1,374	4,162	1,773	1,446	4,875
Kenedy	85	69	18	119	76
Kent	271	175	163	398	274
Kerr	3,707	8,787	3,790	3,587	11,207
Kimble	467	790	354	551	1,061
King	54	79	56	64	111
Kinney	598	634	299	669	771
Kleberg	5,109	3,897	1,470	5,367	4,443
Knox	854	521	438	1,013	765
Lamar	6,328	5,778	4,093	7,553	8,021
Lamb	1,737	2,998	709	2,230	3,064
Lampasas	1,458	2,233	1,432	1,954	3,000
LaSalle	1,485	585	179	1,651	693
Lavaca	2,700	3,362	1,691	3,531	4,377
Lee	1,847	2,108	1,088	2,527	2,513
Leon	2,019	2,203	1,251	2,316	2,778
Liberty	6,593	6,331	3,847	8,343	8,524
Limestone	3,188	2,358	1,505	3,476	3,257
Lipscomb	338	839	270	377	1,111
Live Oak	1,366	1,820	806	1,573	2,277
Llano	2,407	3,055	1,801	2,629	3,550
Loving	20	31	45	23	54
Lubbock	22,237	48,840	11,616	22,202	50,760
Lynn	902	1,233	291	1,086	1,279
McCulloch	1,393	1,108	986	1,665	1,618
McLennan	25,406	28,195	15,301	27,545	38,606
McMullen	78	274	89	94	302
Madison	1,553	1,544	778	1,835	1,896
Marion	2,156	1,245	882	2,255	1,857
Martin	641	986	356	632	1,017
Mason	570	776	364	671	975
Matagorda	6,200	6,969	3,758	5,675	6,787
Maverick	4,540	2,002	771	4,395	1,592
Medina	3,659	4,903	2,167	4,227	5,722
Menard	553	354	367	614	552
Midland	9,101	23,985	7,813	8,487	30,618
Milam	3,542	2,414	1,495	4,865	3,512
Mills	753	702	530	842	1,043
Mitchell	1,353	1,128	604	1,773	1,596
Montague	2,885	2,306	2,316	3,689	3,475
Montgomery	18,551	39,976	19,203	18,394	40,360
Moore	1,361	3,147	976	1,537	3,710
Morris	3,026	1,400	1,138	3,522	2,104
Motley	219	426	117	262	429
Nacogdoches	6,937	9,864	4,803	6,886	11,767
Navarro	6,006	4,897	3,800	6,749	6,445
Newton	3,073	1,105	1,032	3,640	1,659
Nolan	2,490	1,993	1,455	2,853	2,734
Nueces	46,382	36,780	17,381	49,209	46,337
Ochiltree	557	2,419	576	579	2,928
Oldham	190	560	177	303	691
Orange	15,305	9,793	7,321	17,834	11,959
Palo Pinto	3,369	2,842	3,010	3,930	4,649
Panola	3,950	3,473	1,906	4,123	4,642
Parker	7,934	10,321	9,148	8,517	14,090
Parmer	637	1,829	564	764	2,061
Pecos	1,778	1,836	895	1,960	2,483
Polk	5,942	5,390	2,884	5,943	5,831
Potter	9,527	13,510	4,655	9,563	16,400

Presidio	857	233	206	1,176	586
Rains	1,108	975	890	1,448	1,281
Randall	9,119	24,971	6,340	8,492	27,986
Reagan	337	651	259	418	935
Real	463	787	386	463	795
Red River	2,686	1,736	1,228	3,165	2,475
Reeves	2,569	1,244	734	2,812	1,724
Refugio	1,483	1,415	675	1,831	1,883
Roberts	126	391	99	135	441
Robertson	2,882	1,664	963	3,630	2,184
Rockwall	2,397	6,427	4,393	2,659	7,214
Runnels	1,399	1,652	1,279	1,720	2,417
Rusk	5,391	7,560	3,541	5,140	9,117
Sabine	2,288	1,489	1,052	2,053	1,925
San Augustine	1,737	1,243	667	2,118	1,946
San Jacinto	2,150	2,018	1,333	2,972	2,691
San Patricio	8,202	7,456	3,178	9,920	9,159
San Saba	716	723	660	1,165	1,099
Schleicher	419	452	349	494	653
Scurry	1,609	2,670	1,826	2,119	3,749
Shackelford	484	623	422	681	865
Shelby	3,986	3,217	1,487	4,261	3,999
Sherman	261	851	256	340	1,145
Smith	17,514	27,753	13,569	18,719	34,658
Somervell	782	872	903	983	1,304
Starr	7,668	1,209	345	6,958	1,218
Stephens	1,115	1,573	1,077	1,519	2,342
Sterling	127	322	182	188	464
Stonewall	561	242	322	724	421
Sutton	524	687	387	571	996
Swisher	1,413	989	541	1,893	1,271
Tarrant	156,226	183,378	129,990	151,310	242,660
Taylor	12,382	22,614	10,331	13,073	28,563
Terrell	325	176	128	390	296
Terry	1,461	2,309	619	1,941	2,645
Throckmorton	401	389	228	534	455
Titus	3,625	3,024	2,146	4,357	4,247
Tom Green	11,437	14,989	10,244	12,283	21,463
Travis	130,546	88,105	56,158	127,783	105,915
Trinity	2,784	1,988	1,133	2,657	2,448
Tyler	3,465	2,357	1,529	4,198	3,070
Upshur	4,776	4,511	2,896	5,242	5,991
Upton	489	908	313	544	1,189
Uvalde	3,416	3,542	1,338	3,684	4,266
Val Verde	4,748	4,102	2,093	5,044	5,109
Van Zandt	5,304	5,801	5,228	6,153	7,371
Victoria	7,604	13,086	5,136	8,923	15,056
Walker	5,619	6,662	3,619	5,826	8,473
Waller	4,270	3,065	1,692	3,957	3,607
Ward	1,695	1,769	948	1,858	2,709
Washington	3,283	5,817	1,738	2,960	6,041
Webb	14,509	7,789	2,517	16,227	7,528
Wharton	4,643	5,503	2,624	5,935	6,978
Wheeler	938	1,458	367	1,067	1,703
Wichita	17,021	17,956	11,478	17,956	23,324
Wilbarger	1,924	1,959	1,453	2,248	2,669
Willacy	3,357	1,480	652	3,165	1,750
Williamson	19,437	26,208	15,415	19,589	27,322
Wilson	3,711	3,766	2,105	3,953	4,436
Winkler	942	1,173	582	947	1,656
Wise	4,478	4,555	4,485	5,288	6,064
Wood	4,084	4,708	3,494	4,553	6,216
Yoakum	594	1,486	484	727	1,762
Young	2,464	2,894	2,304	3,007	4,156
Zapata	2,052	866	326	2,171	958
Zavala	3,058	571	237	3,338	628
Totals	**2,278,912**	**2,460,201**	**1,349,644**	**2,352,748**	**3,036,829**

Texas Vote Since 1940

1940, Roosevelt, Dem., 840,151; Willkie, Rep., 199,152; Babson, Proh., 925; Thomas, Soc., 728; Browder, Com., 212.

1944, Roosevelt, Dem., 821,605; Dewey, Rep., 191,425; Texas Regulars, 135,439; Watson, Proh., 1,017; Thomas, Soc., 594; America First, 250.

1948, Truman, Dem., 750,700; Dewey, Rep., 282,240; Thurmond, States' Rights, 106,909; Wallace, Prog., 3,764; Watson, Proh., 2,758; Thomas, Soc., 874.

1952, Eisenhower, Rep., 1,102,878; Stevenson, Dem., 969,228; Hamblen, Proh., 1,983; MacArthur, Christian Nationalist, 833; MacArthur, Constitution, 730; Hallinan, Prog., 294.

1956, Eisenhower, Rep., 1,080,619; Stevenson, Dem., 859,958; Andrews, Ind., 14,591.

1960, Kennedy, Dem., 1,167,932; Nixon, Rep., 1,121,699; Sullivan, Constitution, 18,169; Decker, Proh., 3,870; write-in, 15.

1964, Johnson, Dem., 1,663,185; Goldwater, Rep., 958,566; Lightburn, Constitution, 5,060.

1968, Nixon, Rep., 1,227,844; Humphrey, Dem., 1,266,804; Wallace, 3d party, 584,269; write-in, 489.

1972, Nixon, Rep., 2,298,896; McGovern, Dem., 1,154,289; Schmitz, Amer., 6,039; Jenness, Soc. Workers, 8,664; others, 3,393.

1976, Carter, Dem., 2,082,319; Ford, Rep., 1,953,300; McCarthy, Ind., 20,118; Anderson, Amer., 11,442; Camejo, Soc. Workers, 1,723; write-in, 2,982.

1980, Reagan, Rep., 2,510,705; Carter, Dem., 1,881,147; Anderson, Ind., 111,613; Clark, Libertarian, 37,643; write-in, 528.

1984, Reagan, Rep., 3,433,428; Mondale, Dem., 1,949,276.

1988, Bush, Rep., 3,036,829; Dukakis, Dem., 2,352,748; Paul, Lib., 30,355; Fulani, New Alliance, 7,208.

Utah

	1992			1988	
County	Clinton (D)	Bush (R)	Perot (I)	Dukakis (D)	Bush (R)
Beaver	666	1,037	330	816	1,286
Box Elder	2,185	7,709	4,507	2,736	12,585
Cache	4,973	15,971	8,032	5,871	21,766
Carbon	4,473	2,031	2,000	5,521	3,019
Daggett	122	171	116	132	272
Davis	14,896	38,586	23,866	16,868	50,469
Duchesne	765	1,969	1,220	1,227	3,118
Emery	1,338	1,622	1,127	1,788	2,322
Garfield	306	1,219	329	370	1,470
Grand	1,158	1,096	987	1,287	1,895
Iron	1,528	5,595	1,682	1,736	6,038
Juab	815	1,233	614	974	1,505
Kane	290	1,231	530	398	1,788
Millard	737	2,483	1,061	1,124	3,515
Morgan	519	1,341	856	647	1,889
Piute	169	427	146	206	476
Rich	151	518	185	234	621
Salt Lake	99,915	116,937	91,851	107,453	163,557
San Juan	1,367	1,884	542	1,407	2,377
Sanpete	1,302	2,989	1,736	1,822	4,579
Sevier	1,036	3,155	1,669	1,403	4,747
Summit	2,996	3,120	3,052	2,545	3,881
Tooele	3,263	3,656	3,004	4,166	5,539
Uintah	1,370	3,497	2,249	1,799	5,341
Utah	13,912	60,516	24,303	18,533	68,134
Wasatch	1,042	1,813	1,230	1,451	2,487
Washington	3,337	11,256	4,602	3,054	13,306
Wayne	235	700	250	353	784
Weber	17,724	26,700	20,502	21,431	39,676
Totals	**182,590**	**320,462**	**202,578**	**207,352**	**428,442**

Utah Vote Since 1940

1940, Roosevelt, Dem., 154,277; Willkie, Rep., 93,151; Thomas, Soc., 200; Browder, Com., 191.

1944, Roosevelt, Dem., 150,088; Dewey, Rep., 97,891; Thomas, Soc., 340.

1948, Truman, Dem., 149,151; Dewey, Rep., 124,402; Wallace, Prog., 2,679; Dobbs, Soc. Workers, 73.

1952, Eisenhower, Rep., 194,190; Stevenson, Dem., 135,364.

1956, Eisenhower, Rep., 215,631; Stevenson, Dem., 118,364.

1960, Kennedy, Dem., 169,248; Nixon, Rep., 205,361; Dobbs, Soc. Workers, 100.

1964, Johnson, Dem., 219,628; Goldwater, Rep., 181,785.

1968, Nixon, Rep., 238,728; Humphrey, Dem., 156,665; Wallace, 3d party, 26,906; Halstead, Soc. Worker, 89; Peace and Freedom, 180.

1972, Nixon, Rep., 323,643; McGovern, Dem., 126,284; Schmitz, Amer., 28,549.

1976, Carter, Dem., 182,110; Ford, Rep., 337,908; Anderson, Amer., 13,304; McCarthy, Ind., 3,907; MacBride, Libertarian, 2,438; Maddox, Am. Ind., 1,162; Camejo, Soc. Workers, 268; Hall, Com., 121.

1980, Reagan, Rep., 439,687; Carter, Dem., 124,266; Anderson, Ind., 30,284; Clark, Libertarian, 7,226; Commoner, Citizens, 1,009; Greaves, American, 965; Rarick, Amer. Ind., 522; Hall, Com., 139; DeBerry, Soc. Worker, 124.

1984, Reagan, Rep., 469,105; Mondale, Dem., 155,369; Bergland, Libertarian, 2,447.

1988, Bush, Rep., 428,442; Dukakis, Dem., 207,352; Paul, Lib., 7,473; Dennis, American, 2,158.

Vermont

	1992			1988	
City	Clinton (D)	Bush (R)	Perot (I)	Dukakis (D)	Bush (R)
Barre City	1,705	1,428	991	2,132	2,100
Bennington	3,162	2,020	1,434	3,180	2,748
Brattleboro	3,519	1,447	847	3,136	2,044
Burlington	12,510	4,462	3,241	9,748	6,382
Montpelier	2,490	1,607	657	2,351	2,013

Rutland City.	3,879	2,907	1,720	3,590	3,631
St. Albans City . . .	1,455	887	744	1,441	1,295
St. Johnsbury. . . .	1,249	1,243	836	1,188	1,974
South Burlington . .	3,714	2,119	1,254	3,373	3,136
Winooski	1,462	733	646	1,426	1,014
Totals.	**125,803**	**85,512**	**61,510**	**115,775**	**124,331**

Vermont Vote Since 1940

1940, Roosevelt, Dem., 64,269; Willkie, Rep., 78,371; Browder, Com., 411.

1944, Roosevelt, Dem., 53,820; Dewey, Rep., 71,527.

1948, Truman, Dem., 45,557; Dewey, Rep., 75,926; Wallace, Prog., 1,279; Thomas, Soc., 585.

1952, Eisenhower, Rep., 109,717; Stevenson, Dem., 43,355; Hallinan, Prog., 282; Hoopes, Soc., 185.

1956, Eisenhower, Rep., 110,390; Stevenson, Dem., 42,549; scattered, 39.

1960, Kennedy, Dem., 69,186; Nixon, Rep., 98,131.

1964, Johnson, Dem., 107,674; Goldwater, Rep., 54,868.

1968, Nixon, Rep., 85,142; Humphrey, Dem., 70,255; Wallace, 3d party, 5,104; Halstead, Soc. Worker, 295; Gregory, New Party, 579.

1972, Nixon, Rep., 117,149; McGovern, Dem., 68,174; Spock, Liberty Union, 1,010; Jenness, Soc. Workers, 296; scattered, 318.

1976, Carter, Dem., 77,798; Carter, Ind. Vermonter, 991; Ford, Rep., 100,387; McCarthy, Ind., 4,001; Camejo, Soc. Workers, 430; LaRouche, U.S. Labor, 196; scattered, 99.

1980, Reagan, Rep., 94,598; Carter, Dem., 81,891; Anderson, Ind., 31,760; Commoner, Citizens, 2,316; Clark, Libertarian, 1,900; McReynolds, Liberty Union, 136; Hall, Com. 118; DeBerry, Soc. Worker, 75; scattering, 413.

1984, Reagan, Rep., 135,865; Mondale, Dem., 95,730; Bergland, Libertarian, 1,002.

1988, Bush, Rep., 124,331; Dukakis, Dem., 115,775; Paul, Lib., 1,000; LaRouche, Ind., 275.

Virginia

	1992			1988	
County	Clinton (D)	Bush (R)	Perot (I)	Dukakis (D)	Bush (R)
Accomack.	4,950	5,666	2,277	4,443	6,926
Albemarle.	13,886	13,894	3,855	10,363	15,117
Alleghany	2,396	2,294	926	2,316	2,555
Amelia.	1,534	2,062	574	1,359	2,187
Amherst.	4,098	5,480	1,268	3,567	6,507
Appomattox.	1,919	2,830	801	1,740	3,205
Arlington.	47,739	26,371	7,987	40,314	34,191
Augusta	4,898	12,351	3,281	4,170	13,251
Bath	855	1,075	354	881	1,273
Bedford	6,770	10,479	3,247	5,406	10,702
Bland	1,001	1,360	428	937	1,556
Botetourt	4,351	5,904	1,819	3,763	5,687
Brunswick.	3,677	2,474	472	3,070	2,742
Buchanan.	7,378	3,266	807	6,935	3,912
Buckingham.	2,193	2,368	459	1,941	2,481
Campbell	5,999	10,931	2,553	4,574	12,713
Caroline.	3,770	2,950	965	3,186	3,065
Carroll.	3,790	5,664	1,387	3,190	6,377
Charles City	2,010	729	251	1,839	826
Charlotte	2,323	2,513	704	1,923	2,699
Chesterfield.	28,028	56,626	16,898	18,723	58,828
Clarke.	1,908	1,994	802	1,478	2,502
Craig.	965	1,008	304	864	1,112
Culpeper	3,444	5,217	1,640	2,555	5,896
Cumberland	1,286	1,649	373	1,132	1,978
Dickenson.	4,839	2,574	659	4,461	3,091
Dinwiddie	3,621	3,641	1,147	3,405	4,165
Essex	1,583	1,897	382	1,294	2,038
Fairfax.	159,872	170,145	52,419	125,711	200,631
Fauquier.	6,547	10,400	3,446	4,837	11,733
Floyd	2,002	2,549	666	1,727	2,921
Fluvanna	2,134	2,811	871	1,562	2,447
Franklin	6,590	6,723	2,229	5,734	7,391
Frederick	4,941	9,425	2,981	3,707	9,921
Giles.	3,346	3,123	1,147	3,042	3,400
Gloucester	4,058	6,461	2,640	3,372	7,646
Goochland	2,589	3,835	994	2,209	3,765
Grayson.	2,609	3,327	857	2,441	3,968
Greene	1,353	2,275	627	899	2,234
Greensville	2,237	1,335	360	2,083	1,610
Halifax.	4,752	5,191	1,140	4,282	5,671
Hanover.	8,021	20,337	5,680	5,985	20,570
Henrico	36,780	56,929	14,223	26,980	62,284
Henry	9,296	9,004	3,212	7,536	10,871
Highland.	494	686	212	456	807
Isle of Wight.	4,379	5,370	1,536	3,747	5,779
James City	6,536	8,781	2,675	4,642	8,945
King George	1,363	1,206	323	1,519	2,587
King and Queen . .	1,811	2,570	918	1,309	1,376
King William.	1,822	2,591	758	1,561	2,735
Lancaster	1,812	2,841	739	1,551	3,380
Lee	5,210	3,501	1,002	4,906	4,080
Loudoun.	14,654	19,581	7,528	10,101	20,448
Louisa	3,394	3,449	1,379	2,789	3,831
Lunenburg	2,082	2,227	499	1,870	2,530
Madison.	1,700	2,341	653	1,427	2,501
Mathews	1,105	2,179	884	1,235	2,752
Mecklenburg	4,273	5,401	1,128	3,275	5,887
Middlesex.	1,597	2,224	768	1,361	2,571
Montgomery	10,658	10,606	3,449	8,909	12,326
Nelson.	2,586	2,159	748	2,272	2,502
New Kent	1,738	2,707	1,016	1,427	2,917
Northampton	2,568	2,088	844	2,242	2,562
Northumberland . .	1,864	2,667	709	1,506	2,984
Nottoway	2,411	2,610	606	2,217	3,161
Orange	3,348	4,092	1,425	2,592	4,319
Page.	3,010	4,202	1,163	2,499	5,013
Patrick.	2,466	3,521	1,026	2,093	3,990
Pittsylvania	7,670	11,467	2,296	6,612	12,229
Powhatan	1,938	3,796	1,224	1,467	4,040
Prince Edward . . .	2,775	2,858	635	2,434	3,147
Prince George . . .	3,087	4,798	1,459	2,469	4,982
Prince William . . .	26,487	35,430	12,072	19,198	39,654
Pulaski.	5,633	6,148	2,066	4,686	6,844
Rappahannock . . .	1,273	1,409	487	1,003	1,657
Richmond	1,029	1,600	363	924	1,862
Roanoke	14,704	20,667	5,477	12,938	22,011
Rockbridge	2,908	3,228	1,253	2,412	3,541
Rockingham	5,406	13,014	2,961	4,716	13,241
Russell	6,480	3,896	958	6,222	4,374
Scott.	3,981	4,513	956	3,616	4,986
Shenandoah	3,944	7,719	2,063	3,276	8,612
Smyth	4,920	6,128	1,785	3,989	7,446
Southampton	3,084	2,916	750	3,000	3,439
Spotsylvania	8,133	11,829	3,918	5,486	10,978
Stafford	7,717	12,527	4,481	5,380	12,234
Surry	1,823	1,046	364	1,602	1,246
Sussex	2,189	1,518	456	1,958	1,822
Tazewell	8,584	6,374	1,872	8,098	7,165
Warren	3,554	4,319	1,650	2,769	4,700
Washington	6,913	8,763	2,280	5,819	10,722
Westmoreland . . .	2,758	2,554	818	2,311	2,974
Wise	7,646	5,119	1,825	7,017	6,189
Wythe	3,616	5,121	1,557	3,201	5,827
York	6,218	10,207	3,426	4,639	11,103
City					
Alexandria	28,551	15,390	4,638	24,358	20,913
Bedford	963	1,091	313	960	1,322
Bristol	2,947	3,613	850	2,446	4,407
Buena Vista.	1,023	849	291	828	1,121
Charlottesville . . .	8,682	4,705	1,397	7,671	5,817
Chesapeake	23,496	28,901	8,820	18,828	29,738
Clifton Forge	958	632	251	961	759
Colonial Heights . .	1,702	5,263	1,305	1,581	6,001
Covington	1,442	995	402	1,567	1,274
Danville	8,134	9,495	1,676	7,353	12,221
Emporia	1,048	1,100	157	977	1,289
Fairfax.	3,884	4,332	1,439	3,430	5,576
Falls Church	2,864	1,912	599	2,484	2,470
Franklin	1,688	1,346	272	1,630	1,557
Fredericksburg . . .	3,266	2,819	738	2,683	3,401
Galax	958	1,087	276	907	1,278
Hampton	22,028	18,162	6,542	19,106	24,034
Harrisonburg	3,414	4,935	1,162	2,799	5,376
Hopewell	2,744	3,700	1,176	2,566	4,672
Lexington	1,128	894	228	997	994
Lynchburg.	9,587	12,518	2,545	8,279	15,323
Manassas.	3,647	5,453	1,963	2,658	5,980
Manassas Park. . .	567	793	356	434	993
Martinsville	3,066	2,680	736	2,794	3,360
Newport News . . .	25,740	26,779	8,209	21,413	32,570
Norfolk	37,591	22,362	8,739	37,778	30,538
Norton.	871	472	182	795	608
Petersburg	8,671	3,125	834	8,177	4,231
Poquoson	1,086	3,354	960	877	3,840
Portsmouth	20,511	12,547	4,360	19,698	16,087
Radford	2,183	1,996	582	1,855	2,481
Richmond	47,364	24,524	6,765	42,155	31,586
Roanoke	17,539	13,245	3,708	17,185	15,389
Salem	4,028	5,143	1,430	3,760	5,694
South Boston	1,051	1,435	252	936	1,694
Staunton	2,851	4,989	1,140	2,457	5,775
Suffolk.	9,359	8,699	2,150	8,080	9,742
Virginia Beach . . .	44,578	68,933	23,385	33,780	76,481
Waynesboro	2,302	3,758	961	2,038	4,672
Williamsburg	1,858	1,349	445	1,534	1,648
Winchester	2,768	3,833	1,048	2,300	4,497
Total.	**1,033,825**	**1,146,909**	**344,840**	**859,799**	**1,309,162**

Virginia Vote Since 1940

1940, Roosevelt, Dem., 235,961; Willkie, Rep., 109,363; Babson, Proh., 882; Thomas, Soc., 282; Browder, Com., 71; Aiken, Soc. Labor, 48.

1944, Roosevelt, Dem., 242,276; Dewey, Rep., 145,243; Watson, Proh., 459; Thomas, Soc., 417; Teichert, Soc. Labor, 90.

1948, Truman, Dem., 200,786; Dewey, Rep., 172,070; Thurmond, States' Rights, 43,393; Wallace, Prog., 2,047; Thomas, Soc., 726; Teichert, Soc. Labor, 234.

1952, Eisenhower, Rep., 349,037; Stevenson, Dem., 268,677; Hass, Soc. Labor, 1,160; Hoopes, Social Dem., 504; Hallinan, Prog., 311.

1956, Eisenhower, Rep., 386,459; Stevenson, Dem., 267,760; Andrews, States' Rights, 42,964; Hoopes, Soc. Dem., 444; Hass, Soc. Labor, 351.

1960, Kennedy, Dem., 362,327; Nixon, Rep., 404,521; Coiner, Conservative, 4,204; Hass, Soc. Labor, 397.

1964, Johnson, Dem., 558,038; Goldwater, Rep., 481,334; Hass, Soc. Labor, 2,895.

1968, Nixon, Rep., 590,319; Humphrey, Dem., 442,387; Wallace, 3d party, *320,272; Blomen, Soc. Labor, 4,671; Munn, Proh., 601; Gregory, Peace and Freedom, 1,680.

*10,561 votes for Wallace were omitted in the count.

1972, Nixon, Rep., 988,493; McGovern, Dem., 438,887; Schmitz, Amer., 19,721; Fisher, Soc. Labor, 9,918.

1976, Carter, Dem., 813,896; Ford, Rep., 836,554; Camejo, Soc. Workers, 17,802; Anderson, Amer., 16,686; LaRouche, U.S. Labor, 7,508; MacBride, Libertarian, 4,648.

1980, Reagan, Rep., 989,609; Carter, Dem., 752,174; Anderson, Ind., 95,418; Commoner, Citizens, 14,024; Clark, Libertarian, 12,821; DeBerry, Soc. Worker, 1,986.

1984, Reagan, Rep., 1,337,078; Mondale, Dem., 796,250.

1988, Bush, Rep., 1,309,162; Dukakis, Dem., 859,799; Fulani, Ind., 14,312; Paul, Lib., 8,336.

Washington

County	1992 Clinton (D)	1992 Bush (R)	1992 Perot (I)	1988 Dukakis (D)	1988 Bush (R)
Adams	1,402	1,984	954	1,612	2,612
Asotin	2,889	2,119	1,683	3,422	2,874
Benton	14,175	19,897	11,543	14,817	28,688
Chelan	6,231	8,539	3,670	8,183	11,601
Clallam	9,728	8,596	6,912	11,123	11,200
Clark	39,838	34,381	24,505	40,021	37,285
Columbia	645	726	443	730	1,172
Cowlitz	13,976	9,110	8,510	16,090	12,009
Douglas	3,109	4,048	1,950	3,760	5,378
Ferry	632	525	488	972	972
Franklin	2,830	3,391	2,100	4,772	6,488
Garfield	420	573	205	593	714
Grant	6,465	8,261	4,322	7,564	10,859
Grays Harbor	10,562	5,626	6,445	14,097	8,860
Island	7,940	7,583	6,644	8,510	12,552
Jefferson	5,429	2,984	2,715	5,270	4,184
King	344,258	177,491	146,222	349,663	290,574
Kitsap	26,989	22,673	19,605	33,748	34,743
Kittitas	4,598	3,336	2,248	5,318	5,048
Klickitat	2,372	1,757	1,710	2,991	2,920
Lewis	6,164	9,845	5,677	8,629	14,184
Lincoln	1,560	1,971	1,014	1,884	2,689
Mason	7,248	5,106	5,045	7,826	7,426
Okanogan	4,489	3,691	3,094	5,630	5,856
Pacific	4,448	2,134	2,251	5,017	3,073
Pend Oreille	1,746	1,455	1,286	1,925	1,802
Pierce	75,761	54,734	46,259	96,688	94,167
San Juan	2,367	1,275	1,275	3,008	2,660
Skagit	13,420	10,961	9,452	15,159	16,550
Skamania	1,448	1,077	1,031	1,748	1,356
Snohomish	77,833	59,754	58,864	80,694	84,158
Spokane	62,420	53,007	34,882	68,520	68,787
Stevens	4,187	4,836	3,252	5,068	6,576
Thurston	32,706	21,060	16,463	33,860	31,980
Wahkiakum	582	425	497	961	629
Walla Walla	6,889	7,358	4,249	7,448	9,683
Whatcom	23,252	20,228	10,760	25,571	23,820
Whitman	7,479	6,300	3,143	7,403	7,680
Yakima	17,223	21,095	8,871	23,221	30,026
Totals	**855,710**	**609,912**	**470,239**	**933,516**	**903,835**

Washington Vote Since 1940

1940, Roosevelt, Dem., 462,145; Willkie, Rep., 322,123; Thomas, Soc., 4,586; Browder, Com., 2,626; Babson, Proh., 1,686; Aiken, Soc. Labor, 667.

1944, Roosevelt, Dem., 486,774; Dewey, Rep., 361,689; Thomas, Soc., 3,824; Watson, Proh., 2,396; Teichert, Soc. Labor, 1,645.

1948, Truman, Dem., 476,165; Dewey, Rep., 386,315; Wallace, Prog., 31,692; Watson, Proh., 6,117; Thomas, Soc., 3,534; Teichert, Soc. Labor, 1,133; Dobbs, Soc. Workers, 103.

1952, Eisenhower, Rep., 599,107; Stevenson, Dem., 492,845; MacArthur, Christian Nationalist, 7,290; Hallinan, Prog., 2,460; Hass, Soc. Labor, 633; Hoopes, Soc., 254; Dobbs, Soc. Workers, 119.

1956, Eisenhower, Rep., 620,430; Stevenson, Dem., 523,002; Hass, Soc. Labor, 7,457.

1960, Kennedy, Dem., 599,298; Nixon, Rep., 629,273; Hass, Soc. Labor, 10,895; Curtis, Constitution, 1,401; Dobbs, Soc. Workers, 705.

1964, Johnson, Dem., 779,699; Goldwater, Rep., 470,366; Hass, Soc. Labor, 7,772; DeBerry, Freedom Soc., 537.

1968, Nixon, Rep., 588,510; Humphrey, Dem., 616,037; Wallace, 3d party, 96,990; Blomen, Soc. Labor, 488; Cleaver, Peace and Freedom, 1,609; Halstead, Soc. Worker, 270; Mitchell, Free Ballot, 377.

1972, Nixon, Rep., 837,135; McGovern, Dem., 568,334; Schmitz, Amer., 58,906; Spock, Ind., 2,644; Fisher, Soc. Labor, 1,102; Jenness, Soc. Worker, 623; Hall, Com., 566; Hospers, Libertarian, 1,537.

1976, Carter, Dem., 717,323; Ford, Rep., 777,732; McCarthy, Ind., 36,986; Maddox, Amer. Ind., 8,585; Anderson, Amer., 5,046; MacBride, Libertarian, 5,042; Wright, People's, 1,124; Camejo, Soc. Workers, 905; LaRouche, U.S. Labor, 903; Hall, Com., 817; Levin, Soc. Labor, 713; Zeidler, Soc., 358.

1980, Reagan, Rep., 865,244; Carter, Dem., 650,193; Anderson, Ind., 185,073; Clark, Libertarian, 29,213; Commoner, Citizens, 9,403; DeBerry, Soc. Worker, 1,137; McReynolds, Socialist, 956; Hall, Com., 834; Griswold, Workers World, 341.

1984, Reagan, Rep., 1,051,670; Mondale, Dem., 798,352; Bergland, Libertarian, 8,844.

1988, Bush, Rep., 903,835; Dukakis, Dem., 933,516; Paul, Lib., 17,240; LaRouche, Ind., 4,412.

West Virginia

County	1992 Clinton (D)	1992 Bush (R)	1992 Perot (I)	1988 Dukakis (D)	1988 Bush (R)
Barbour	3,451	2,310	1,139	3,221	3,023
Berkeley	7,093	9,057	3,603	6,313	10,761
Boone	6,547	2,008	1,028	6,539	2,786
Braxton	3,379	1,529	815	3,377	2,024
Brooke	5,686	2,579	2,098	6,258	4,006
Cabell	13,868	12,362	4,414	15,368	17,197
Calhoun	1,617	1,083	529	1,644	1,395
Clay	1,916	1,244	458	2,263	1,536
Doddridge	968	1,499	513	955	1,880
Fayette	9,571	3,987	1,992	11,009	5,143
Gilmer	1,574	1,085	479	1,661	1,387
Grant	1,004	2,753	518	893	3,215
Greenbrier	5,766	4,424	1,893	6,091	5,395
Hampshire	2,365	2,767	1,022	2,085	3,253
Hancock	7,698	3,942	3,257	8,338	5,882
Hardy	1,915	2,142	602	1,689	2,581
Harrison	15,423	9,656	5,119	17,005	13,364
Jackson	5,094	4,182	1,901	4,573	5,696
Jefferson	5,308	4,596	2,081	4,334	5,349
Kanawha	37,905	31,063	11,567	41,144	38,140
Lewis	2,910	2,402	1,192	3,272	3,602
Lincoln	4,457	2,615	725	5,049	3,457
Logan	11,059	3,212	1,817	11,317	4,244
McDowell	6,993	1,927	698	7,204	2,463
Marion	13,979	6,364	4,691	14,441	9,229
Marshall	7,275	4,444	3,384	7,903	6,793
Mason	5,318	3,790	2,039	5,468	5,332
Mercer	9,439	7,818	2,800	10,152	10,221
Mineral	3,920	4,737	1,837	4,059	6,015
Mingo	7,277	2,554	902	7,429	2,896
Monongalia	13,952	9,660	4,502	14,178	12,091
Monroe	2,405	2,292	681	2,427	2,719
Morgan	1,832	2,561	871	1,545	3,002
Nicholas	5,022	2,947	1,492	5,173	3,731
Ohio	9,447	7,362	3,603	10,121	10,341
Pendleton	1,611	1,576	360	1,595	1,901
Pleasants	1,387	1,245	731	1,421	1,761
Pocahontas	1,741	1,398	625	1,958	1,876
Preston	3,927	4,427	2,108	4,357	5,804
Putnam	6,784	7,601	2,885	6,640	8,163
Raleigh	9,312	5,635	2,040	14,302	10,395
Randolph	5,093	3,492	1,582	5,233	4,746
Ritchie	1,473	2,182	743	1,446	2,874
Roane	2,580	2,172	906	2,447	2,861
Summers	2,639	1,644	565	3,072	2,231
Taylor	2,833	2,016	1,241	2,852	2,816
Tucker	1,799	1,254	547	1,869	1,699
Tyler	1,579	1,590	1,011	1,501	2,365
Upshur	3,134	3,481	1,542	3,065	4,813
Wayne	8,366	5,710	2,175	8,621	7,123
Webster	2,319	808	436	2,185	1,016
Wetzel	3,739	2,250	1,557	3,928	3,381
Wirt	1,042	939	393	929	1,125
Wood	13,445	15,346	6,951	12,959	19,450

Wyoming	5,773	2,807	992	6,138	3,516
Totals.	**324,009**	**236,526**	**105,652**	**341,016**	**310,065**

West Virginia Vote Since 1940

1940, Roosevelt, Dem., 495,662; Willkie, Rep., 372,414.

1944, Roosevelt, Dem., 392,777; Dewey, Rep., 322,819.

1948, Truman, Dem., 429,188; Dewey, Rep., 316,251; Wallace, Prog., 3,311.

1952, Eisenhower, Rep., 419,970; Stevenson, Dem., 453,578.

1956, Eisenhower, Rep., 449,297; Stevenson, Dem., 381,534.

1960, Kennedy, Dem., 441,786; Nixon, Rep., 395,995.

1964, Johnson, Dem., 538,087; Goldwater, Rep., 253,953.

1968, Nixon, Rep., 307,555; Humphrey, Dem., 374,091; Wallace, 3d party, 72,560.

1972, Nixon, Rep., 484,964; McGovern, Dem., 277,435.

1976, Carter, Dem., 435,864; Ford, Rep., 314,726.

1980, Reagan, Rep., 334,206; Carter, Dem., 367,462; Anderson, Ind., 31,691; Clark, Libertarian, 4,356.

1984, Reagan, Rep., 405,483; Mondale, Dem., 328,125.

1988, Bush, Rep., 310,065; Dukakis, Dem., 341,016; Fulani, New Alliance, 2,230.

Wisconsin

County	1992 Clinton (D)	1992 Bush (R)	1992 Perot (I)	1988 Dukakis (D)	1988 Bush (R)
Adams.	3,538	2,465	2,005	3,598	3,258
Ashland	4,212	2,372	1,747	4,526	2,926
Barron.	7,699	6,170	5,479	8,951	8,527
Bayfield	3,871	2,393	1,782	4,323	3,095
Brown	37,518	42,340	22,396	41,788	43,625
Buffalo.	2,996	2,029	1,889	3,481	2,783
Burnet	3,172	2,340	1,860	3,537	2,884
Calumet.	5,701	7,541	5,055	6,481	8,107
Chippewa	10,486	8,215	6,408	11,447	9,757
Clark.	5,543	4,977	4,286	6,642	6,296
Columbia	9,327	9,060	5,429	9,132	10,475
Crawford	3,440	2,390	1,797	3,608	3,238
Dane.	114,515	62,430	31,864	105,414	69,143
Dodge	11,438	14,971	9,136	12,663	17,003
Door	4,735	5,468	3,506	5,425	6,907
Douglas	12,247	5,679	4,155	13,907	6,440
Dunn.	8,045	5,283	4,809	9,205	7,273
Eau Claire.	21,051	15,778	9,673	21,150	17,664
Florence.	978	942	699	1,018	1,106
Fond duLac.	13,757	19,785	10,660	15,887	21,985
Forest	1,904	1,393	1,067	2,142	1,845
Grant	8,914	7,678	6,305	9,421	10,049
Green	5,467	4,887	3,735	5,153	6,636
Green Lake	2,771	3,895	2,827	3,033	5,205
Iowa	4,437	3,292	2,341	4,268	4,240
Iron	1,763	1,268	836	2,090	1,599
Jackson	3,681	2,644	2,040	3,924	3,555
Jefferson	11,593	13,072	7,960	11,816	14,309
Juneau	4,177	4,051	2,670	3,734	4,869
Kenosha.	27,347	19,854	14,332	30,089	21,661
Kewaunee.	4,050	3,570	2,700	4,786	4,330
La Crosse.	21,452	17,944	9,627	22,204	21,548
La Fayette	3,143	2,582	2,079	3,521	3,665
Langlade	3,630	3,890	2,444	4,254	4,884
Lincoln.	5,297	4,321	3,605	5,819	5,257
Manitowoc	15,903	14,008	11,179	19,680	16,020
Marathon	21,483	20,950	14,695	24,658	24,482
Marinette	7,626	7,984	5,462	8,030	9,637
Marquette.	2,533	2,322	1,818	2,463	3,059
Menominee	691	244	221	1,028	381
Milwaukee	232,984	148,176	74,996	268,287	168,363
Monroe	6,427	6,118	4,184	6,437	7,073
Oconto	5,903	5,820	4,405	6,549	7,084
Oneida	7,160	6,725	4,675	7,414	8,130
Outagamie	23,740	30,370	18,482	27,771	33,113
Ozaukee	11,870	22,802	7,997	12,661	22,899
Pepin	1,673	1,098	781	1,906	1,311
Pierce	7,824	4,844	4,458	8,659	6,045
Polk	7,746	5,446	4,756	8,981	6,866
Portage	15,550	10,891	7,076	16,317	12,057
Price.	3,375	2,654	2,295	3,987	3,450
Racine.	34,875	32,301	20,218	39,631	36,342
Richland.	3,559	3,244	1,889	3,643	4,026
Rock.	31,156	21,941	15,700	29,576	28,178
Rusk.	3,376	2,430	2,084	3,888	3,063
St. Croix.	10,281	8,114	7,125	11,392	9,960
Sauk.	9,128	8,886	5,280	8,324	10,225
Sawyer	2,796	2,657	1,861	3,231	3,260
Shawano	6,062	7,253	4,556	6,587	8,362
Sheboygan	20,569	22,528	11,254	23,429	23,471
Taylor	3,305	3,415	2,590	3,785	4,254
Trempealeau	6,218	3,577	3,160	6,212	4,902
Vernon	5,673	3,973	2,890	5,754	5,226
Vilas.	3,763	4,613	2,827	3,781	5,842
Walworth	11,822	15,625	9,026	12,203	18,259
Washburn.	3,080	2,586	1,982	3,393	3,074
Washington	13,336	22,735	13,042	15,907	24,328
Waukesha.	50,269	91,111	36,662	57,598	90,467
Waupaca	6,650	10,225	6,069	7,078	11,559
Waushara.	3,402	4,045	2,830	3,535	4,953
Winnebago	27,031	33,722	16,140	28,508	35,085
Wood	13,208	13,843	8,742	16,074	16,549
Totals.	**1,035,942**	**926,245**	**542,610**	**1,126,794**	**1,047,499**

Wisconsin Vote Since 1940

1940, Roosevelt, Dem., 704,821; Willkie, Rep., 679,260; Thomas, Soc., 15,071; Browder, Com., 2,394; Babson, Proh., 2,148; Aiken, Soc. Labor, 1,882.

1944, Roosevelt, Dem., 650,413; Dewey, Rep., 674,532; Thomas, Soc., 13,205; Teichert, Soc. Labor, 1,002.

1948, Truman, Dem., 647,310; Dewey, Rep., 590,959; Wallace, Prog., 25,282; Thomas, Soc., 12,547; Teichert, Soc. Labor, 399; Dobbs, Soc. Workers, 303.

1952, Eisenhower, Rep., 979,744; Stevenson, Dem., 622,175; Hallinan, Ind., 2,174; Dobbs, Ind., 1,350; Hoopes, Ind., 1,157; Hass, Ind., 770.

1956, Eisenhower, Rep., 954,844; Stevenson, Dem., 586,768; Andrews, Ind., 6,918; Hoopes, Soc., 754; Hass, Soc. Labor, 710; Dobbs, Soc. Workers, 564.

1960, Kennedy, Dem., 830,805; Nixon, Rep., 895,175; Dobbs, Soc. Workers, 1,792; Hass, Soc. Labor, 1,310.

1964, Johnson, Dem., 1,050,424; Goldwater, Rep., 638,495; DeBerry, Soc. Worker, 1,692; Hass, Soc. Labor, 1,204.

1968, Nixon, Rep., 809,997; Humphrey, Dem., 748,804; Wallace, 3d party, 127,835; Blomen, Soc. Labor, 1,338; Halstead, Soc. Worker, 1,222; scattered, 2,342.

1972 Nixon, Rep., 989,430; McGovern, Dem., 810,174; Schmitz, Amer., 47,525; Spock, Ind., 2,701; Fisher, Soc. Labor, 998; Hall, Com., 663; Reed, Ind., 506; scattered, 893.

1976, Carter, Dem., 1,040,232; Ford, Rep., 1,004,987; McCarthy, Ind., 34,943; Maddox, Amer. Ind., 8,552; Zeidler, Soc., 4,298; MacBride, Libertarian, 3,814; Camejo, Soc. Workers, 1,691; Wright, People's, 943; Hall, Com., 749; LaRouche, U.S. Lab., 738; Levin, Soc. Labor, 389; scattered, 2,839.

1980, Reagan, Rep., 1,088,845; Carter, Dem., 981,584; Anderson, Ind., 160,657; Clark, Libertarian, 29,135; Commoner, Citizens, 7,767; Rarick, Constitution, 1,519; McReynolds, Socialist, 808; Hall, Com., 772; Griswold, Workers World, 414; DeBerry, Soc. Workers, 383; scattering, 1,337.

1984, Reagan, Rep., 1,198,584; Mondale, Dem., 995,740; Bergland, Libertarian, 4,883.

1988, Bush, Rep., 1,047,499; Dukakis, Dem., 1,126,794; Paul, Lib., 5,157; Duke, Pop., 3,056.

Wyoming

County	1992 Clinton (D)	1992 Bush (R)	1992 Perot (I)	1988 Dukakis (D)	1988 Bush (R)
Albany.	5,703	4,159	2,847	5,486	5,653
Big Horn.	1,216	2,216	1,246	1,469	3,258
Campbell	2,708	5,308	3,133	2,288	6,702
Carbon	2,734	2,320	1,579	2,555	3,336
Converse	1,307	2,159	1,260	1,301	2,885
Crook	568	1,377	718	553	1,939
Fremont.	4,765	5,387	3,594	5,020	7,681
Goshen	1,754	2,395	1,144	1,875	3,075
Hot Springs.	740	978	615	800	1,490
Johnson.	656	1,614	844	707	2,081
Laramie	12,164	12,865	6,596	11,851	15,561
Lincoln.	1,430	2,591	1,495	1,592	3,237
Natrona	9,817	9,717	7,647	9,148	14,005
Niobrara.	298	635	355	354	825
Park	2,771	5,215	3,145	2,646	6,884
Platte	1,398	1,668	956	1,482	2,253
Sheridan	4,139	4,303	3,035	4,655	5,980
Sublette	536	1,168	828	576	1,636
Sweetwater.	6,414	4,476	3,878	6,720	6,780
Teton	2,854	3,120	2,340	2,217	3,616
Uinta.	2,046	2,702	2,041	1,922	3,464
Washakie	1,118	1,720	1,084	1,197	2,538
Weston	727	1,465	829	699	1,988
Totals.	**67,863**	**79,558**	**51,209**	**67,113**	**106,867**

Wyoming Vote Since 1940

1940, Roosevelt, Dem., 59,287; Willkie, Rep., 52,633; Babson, Proh., 172; Thomas, Soc., 148.

1944, Roosevelt, Dem., 49,419; Dewey, Rep., 51,921.

1948, Truman, Dem., 52,354; Dewey, Rep., 47,947; Wallace, Prog., 931; Thomas, Soc., 137; Teichert, Soc. Labor, 56.

1952, Eisenhower, Rep., 81,047; Stevenson, Dem., 47,934; Hamblen, Proh., 194; Hoopes, Soc., 40; Haas, Soc. Labor, 36.

1956, Eisenhower, Rep., 74,573; Stevenson, Dem., 49,554.

1960, Kennedy, Dem., 63,331; Nixon, Rep., 77,451.

1964, Johnson, Dem., 80,718; Goldwater, Rep., 61,998.

1968, Nixon, Rep., 70,927; Humphrey, Dem., 45,173; Wallace, 3d party, 11,105.

1972, Nixon, Rep., 100,464; McGovern, Dem., 44,358; Schmitz, Amer., 748.

1976, Carter, Dem., 62,239; Ford, Rep., 92,717; McCarthy, Ind., 624; Reagan, Ind., 307; Anderson, Amer., 290; MacBride, Libertarian, 89; Brown, Ind., 47; Maddox, Amer. Ind., 30.

1980, Reagan, Rep., 110,700; Carter, Dem., 49,427; Anderson, Ind., 12,072; Clark, Libertarian, 4,514.

1984, Reagan, Rep., 133,241; Mondale, Dem., 53,370; Bergland, Libertarian, 2,357.

1988, Bush, Rep., 106,867; Dukakis, Dem., 67,113; Paul, Lib., 2,026; Fulani, New Alliance, 545.

Electoral Votes for President

(based on 1990 Census)

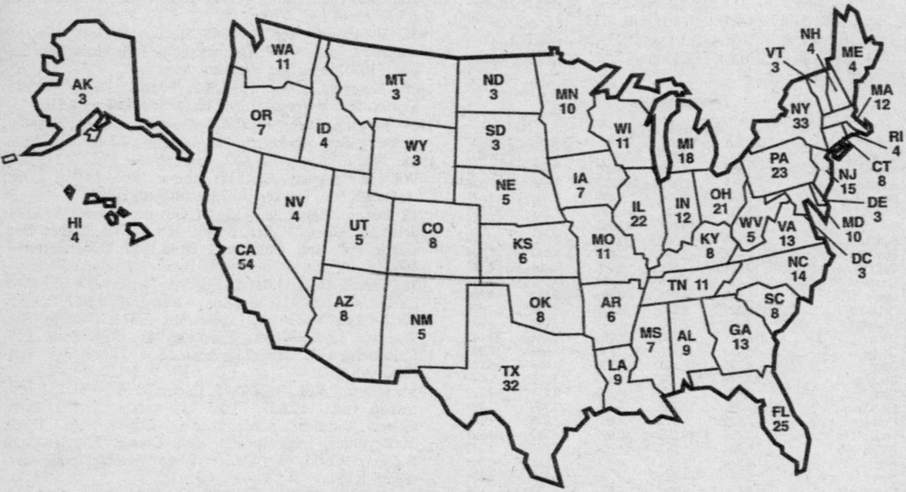

America's Third Parties

Since 1860, there have been only 4 presidential elections in which all "third parties" together polled more than 10% of the vote: the Populists (James Baird Weaver) in 1892, the National Progressives (Theodore Roosevelt) in 1912, the La Follette Progressives in 1924, and George Wallace's American Party in 1968. In 1948, the combined "third parties" (Henry Wallace's Progessives, Strom Thurmond's States' Rights party or Dixiecrats, Prohibition, Socialists, and others) received only 5.75% of the vote. In most elections since 1860, fewer than one vote in 20 has been cast for a third party. The only successful third party in American history was the Republican Party in the election of Abraham Lincoln in 1860.

Notable Third Parties

Party	Presidential nominee	Year	Issues	Strength in
Anti-Masonic	William Wirt	1832	Against secret societies and oaths	Pa., Vt.
Liberty	James G. Birney	1844	Anti-slavery	North
Free Soil	Martin Van Buren	1848	Anti-slavery	New York, Ohio
American (Know Nothing)	Millard Fillmore	1856	Anti-immigrant	Northeast, South
Greenback	Peter Cooper	1876	For "cheap money," labor rights	
Greenback	James B. Weaver	1880		National
Prohibition	John P. St. John	1884	Anti-liquor	National
Populist	James B. Weaver	1892	For "cheap money," end of national banks	South, West
Socialist	Eugene V. Debs	1900-20	For public ownership	National
Progressive (Bull Moose)	Theodore Roosevelt	1912	Against high tariffs	Midwest, West
Progressive	Robert M. LaFollette	1924	Farmer & labor rights	Midwest, West
Socialist	Norman Thomas	1928-48	Liberal reforms	National
Union	William Lemke	1936	Anti "New Deal"	National
States' Rights	Strom Thurmond	1948	For states' rights	South
Progressive	Henry Wallace	1948	Anti-cold war	New York, California
American Independent	George Wallace	1968	For states' rights	South
American	John G. Schmitz	1972	For "law and order"	Far West, Oh., La.
None (Independent)	John B. Anderson	1980	A 3d choice	National
None (Independent)	H. Ross Perot	1992	Federal budget deficit	National

Major Parties' Popular and Electoral Vote for President

(F) Federalist; (D) Democrat; (R) Republican; (DR) Democrat Republican; (NR) National Republican; (W) Whig; (P) People's; (PR) Progressive; (SR) States' Rights; (LR) Liberal Republican; Asterisk (*)—See notes.

Year	President elected	Popular	Elec.	Losing candidate	Popular	Elec.
1789	George Washington (F)	Unknown	69	No opposition	—	—
1792	George Washington (F)	Unknown	132	No opposition	—	—
1796	John Adams (F)	Unknown	71	Thomas Jefferson (DR)	Unknown	68
1800*	Thomas Jefferson (DR)	Unknown	73	Aaron Burr (DR)	Unknown	73
1804	Thomas Jefferson (DR)	Unknown	162	Charles Pinckney (F)	Unknown	14
1808	James Madison (DR)	Unknown	122	Charles Pinckney (F)	Unknown	47
1812	James Madison (DR)	Unknown	128	DeWitt Clinton (F)	Unknown	89
1816	James Monroe (DR)	Unknown	183	Rufus King (F)	Unknown	34
1820	James Monroe (DR)	Unknown	231	John Quincy Adams (DR)	Unknown	1
1824*	John Quincy Adams (DR)	105,321	84	Andrew Jackson (DR)	155,872	99
				Henry Clay (DR)	46,587	37
				William H. Crawford (DR)	44,282	41
1828	Andrew Jackson (D)	647,231	178	John Quincy Adams (NR)	509,097	83
1832	Andrew Jackson (D)	687,502	219	Henry Clay (NR)	530,189	49
1836	Martin Van Buren (D)	762,678	170	William H. Harrison (W)	548,007	73
1840	William H. Harrison (W)	1,275,017	234	Martin Van Buren (D)	1,128,702	60
1844	James K. Polk (D)	1,337,243	170	Henry Clay (W)	1,299,068	105
1848	Zachary Taylor (W)	1,360,101	163	Lewis Cass (D)	1,220,544	127
1852	Franklin Pierce (D)	1,601,474	254	Winfield Scott (W)	1,386,578	42
1856	James Buchanan (D)	1,927,995	174	John C. Fremont (R)	1,391,555	114
1860	Abraham Lincoln (R)	1,866,352	180	Stephen A. Douglas (D)	1,375,157	12
				John C. Breckinridge (D)	845,763	72
				John Bell (Const. Union)	589,581	39
1864	Abraham Lincoln (R)	2,216,067	212	George McClellan (D)	1,808,725	21
1868	Ulysses S. Grant (R)	3,015,071	214	Horatio Seymour (D)	2,709,615	80
1872*	Ulysses S. Grant (R)	3,597,070	286	Horace Greeley (D-LR)	2,834,079	—
1876*	Rutherford B. Hayes (R)	4,033,950	185	Samuel J. Tilden (D)	4,284,757	184
1880	James A. Garfield (R)	4,449,053	214	Winfield S. Hancock (D)	4,442,030	155
1884	Grover Cleveland (D)	4,911,017	219	James G. Blaine (R)	4,848,334	182
1888*	Benjamin Harrison (R)	5,444,337	233	Grover Cleveland (D)	5,540,050	168
1892	Grover Cleveland (D)	5,554,414	277	Benjamin Harrison (R)	5,190,802	145
				James Weaver (P)	1,027,329	22
1896	William McKinley (R)	7,035,638	271	William J. Bryan (D-P)	6,467,946	176
1900	William McKinley (R)	7,219,530	292	William J. Bryan (D)	6,358,071	155
1904	Theodore Roosevelt (R)	7,628,834	336	Alton B. Parker (D)	5,084,491	140
1908	William H. Taft (R)	7,679,006	321	William J. Bryan (D)	6,409,106	162
1912	Woodrow Wilson (D)	6,286,214	435	Theodore Roosevelt (PR)	4,216,020	88
				William H. Taft (R)	3,483,922	8
1916	Woodrow Wilson (D)	9,129,606	277	Charles E. Hughes (R)	8,538,221	254
1920	Warren G. Harding (R)	16,152,200	404	James M. Cox (D)	9,147,353	127
1924	Calvin Coolidge (R)	15,725,016	382	John W. Davis (D)	8,385,586	136
				Robert M. LaFollette (PR)	4,822,856	13
1928	Herbert Hoover (R)	21,392,190	444	Alfred E. Smith (D)	15,016,443	87
1932	Franklin D. Roosevelt (D)	22,821,857	472	Herbert Hoover (R)	15,761,841	59
				Norman Thomas (Socialist)	884,781	—
1936	Franklin D. Roosevelt (D)	27,751,597	523	Alfred Landon (R)	16,679,583	8
1940	Franklin D. Roosevelt (D)	27,243,466	449	Wendell Willkie (R)	22,304,755	82
1944	Franklin D. Roosevelt (D)	25,602,505	432	Thomas E. Dewey (R)	22,006,278	99
1948	Harry S. Truman (D)	24,105,812	303	Thomas E. Dewey (R)	21,970,065	189
				J. Strom Thurmond (SR)	1,169,021	39
				Henry A. Wallace (PR)	1,157,172	—
1952	Dwight D. Eisenhower (R)	33,936,252	442	Adlai E. Stevenson (D)	27,314,992	89
1956*	Dwight D. Eisenhower (R)	35,585,316	457	Adlai E. Stevenson (D)	26,031,322	73
1960*	John F. Kennedy (D)	34,227,096	303	Richard M. Nixon (R)	34,108,546	219
1964	Lyndon B. Johnson (D)	43,126,506	486	Barry M. Goldwater (R)	27,176,799	52
1968	Richard M. Nixon (R)	31,785,480	301	Hubert H. Humphrey (D)	31,275,166	191
				George C. Wallace (3d party)	9,906,473	46
1972*	Richard M. Nixon (R)	47,165,234	520	George S. McGovern (D)	29,170,774	17
1976*	Jimmy Carter (D)	40,828,929	297	Gerald R. Ford (R)	39,148,940	240
1980	Ronald Reagan (R)	43,899,248	489	Jimmy Carter (D)	35,481,435	49
				John B. Anderson (independent)	5,719,437	—
1984	Ronald Reagan (R)	54,281,858	525	Walter F. Mondale (D)	37,457,215	13
1988*	George Bush (R)	48,881,221	426	Michael S. Dukakis (D)	41,805,422	111
1992*	Bill Clinton (D)	43,682,624	370	George Bush (R)	38,117,331	168
				H. Ross Perot (independent)	19,217,213	—

1800—Elected by House of Representatives because of tied electoral vote. **1824**—Elected by House of Representatives. No candidate polled a majority. In 1824, the Democrat Republicans had become a loose coalition of competing political groups. By 1828, the supporters of Jackson were known as Democrats, and the J.Q. Adams and Henry Clay supporters as National Republicans. **1872**—Greeley died Nov. 29, 1872. His electoral votes were split among 4 individuals. **1876**—Fla., La., Ore., and S. C. election returns were disputed. Congress in joint session (Mar. 2, 1877) declared Hayes and Wheeler elected President and Vice-President. **1888**—Cleveland had more votes than Harrison but the 233 electoral votes cast for Harrison against the 168 for Cleveland elected Harrison president. **1956**—Democrats elected 74 electors but one from Alabama refused to vote for Stevenson. **1960**—Sen. Harry F. Byrd (D-Va.) received 15 electoral votes. **1972**—John Hospers of Cal. and Theodora Nathan of Ore. received one vote from an elector of Virginia. **1976**—Ronald Reagan of Cal. received one vote from an elector of Washington. **1988**—Sen. Lloyd Bentsen (D.-Tex.) received 1 electoral vote. **1992**—Preliminary totals.

CONGRESS

The One Hundred and Third Congress
With 1992 Election Results

The Senate

Terms are for 6 years and end Jan. 3 of the year preceding name. Until Jan. 1993, annual salary $129,500; President Pro Tempore, Majority Leader, and Minority Leader $143,800; cost-of-living increases scheduled for Jan. 1993. To be eligible for the U.S. Senate a person must be at least 30 years of age, a citizen of the United States for at least 9 years, and a resident of the state from which he is chosen. The Congress must meet annually on Jan. 3, unless it has, by law, appointed a different day.

The ZIP code of the Senate is 20510, the telephone number is 202-224-3121.

Senate officials: President Pro Tempore, Robert Byrd; Majority Leader, George Mitchell; Majority Whip, Wendell Ford; Minority Leader, Bob Dole; Minority Whip, Alan Simpson.

Dem., 58; Rep., 42; Total, 100. *Incumbent. Bold face denotes winner.

Preliminary Totals (Source: News Election Service)

Term ends	Senator (Party)/Service from[1]	1992 Election
	Alabama	
1999	**Richard C. Shelby*** (D)/1987	**1,011,797**
	Richard Sellers (R)	516,387
1997	Howell Heflin (D)/1979	
	Alaska	
1999	**Frank H. Murkowski*** (R)/1981	**96,656**
	Tony Smith (D)	69,862
1997	Ted Stevens (R)/12/24/68	
	Arizona	
1999	**John S. McCain*** (R)/1987	**734,769**
	Claire Sargent (D)	419,104
1995	Dennis DeConcini (D)/1977	
	Arkansas	
1999	**Dale Bumpers*** (D)/1975	**540,436**
	Mike Huckabee (R)	359,872
1997	David Pryor (D)/1979	
	California	
1999	**Barbara Boxer** (D)	**4,856,103**
	Bruce Herschensohn (R)	4,288,284
1994	**Dianne Feinstein** (D)	**5,493,418**
	John Seymour* (R) /1/10/91[2]	3,777,635
	Colorado	
1999	**Ben Nighthorse Campbell** (D)	**796,472**
	Terry Considine (R)	655,236
1997	Hank Brown (R)	
	Connecticut	
1999	**Christopher J. Dodd*** (D)/1981	**883,352**
	Brook Johnson (R)	565,601
1995	Joe Lieberman (D)/1989	
	Delaware	
1995	William V. Roth Jr. (R)/1/1/71	
1997	Joseph R. Biden Jr. (D)/1973	
	Florida	
1999	**Bob Graham*** (D)/1987	**3,197,495**
	Bill Grant (R)	1,675,314
1995	Connie Mack (R)/1989	
	Georgia	
1999	**Wyche Fowler Jr.*** (D)/1987[6]	**1,089,571**
	Paul Coverdell (R)	1,053,786
1997	Sam Nunn (D)/1972	
	Hawaii	
1999	**Daniel K. Inouye*** (D)/1963	**207,794**
	Rick Reed (R)	97,653
1995	Daniel K. Akaka (D)/5/16/90	
	Idaho	
1999	**Dirk Kempthorne** (R)	**269,209**
	Richard H. Stallings (D)	207,124
1997	Larry E. Craig (R)	
	Illinois	
1999	**Carol Moseley Braun** (D)	**2,554,794**
	Richard S. Williamson (R)	2,107,411
1997	Paul Simon (D)/1985	
	Indiana	
1999	**Daniel R. Coats*** (R)/1989	**1,253,914**
	Joseph H. Hogsett (D)	891,487
1995	Richard G. Lugar (R)/1977	
	Iowa	
1999	**Charles E. Grassley*** (R)/1981	**893,272**
	Jean Lloyd-Jones (D)	349,533
1997	Tom Harkin (D)/1985	
	Kansas	
1999	**Bob Dole*** (R)/1969	**695,708**
	Gloria O'Dell (D)	346,598
1997	Nancy L. Kassebaum (R)/12/23/78	
	Kentucky	
1999	**Wendell H. Ford*** (D)/12/28/74	**834,559**
	David L. Williams (R)	476,982
1997	Mitch McConnell (R)/1985	
	Louisiana	
1999	**John B. Breaux*** (D)/1987[3]	
1997	J. Bennett Johnston (D)/11/14/72	
	Maine	
1995	George J. Mitchell (D)/5/17/80	
1997	William S. Cohen (R)/1979	
	Maryland	
1999	**Barbara A. Mikulski*** (D)/1987	**1,247,386**
	Alan L. Keyes (R)	503,956
1995	Paul S. Sarbanes (D)/1977	
	Massachusetts	
1995	Edward M. Kennedy (D)/11/7/62	
1997	John F. Kerry (D)/1/2/85	
	Michigan	
1995	**Donald W. Riegle Jr.*** (D)/12/30/76	
1997	Carl Levin (D)/1979	
	Minnesota	
1995	David Durenberger (R)/11/8/78	
1997	Paul David Wellstone (D)	

Term ends	Senator (Party)/Service from[1]	1992 Election
	Mississippi	
1995	Trent Lott (R)/3/3/89	
1997	Thad Cochran (R)/12/27/78	
	Missouri	
1999	**Christopher "Kit" Bond*** (R)/1987	**1,208,359**
	Geri Rothman-Serot (D)	1,046,739
1995	John C. Danforth (R)/12/27/76	
	Montana	
1995	Conrad Burns (R)/1989	
1997	Max Baucus (D)/12/15/78	
	Nebraska	
1995	J. Robert Kerrey (D)/1989	
1997	J. James Exon (D)/1979	
	Nevada	
1999	**Harry M. Reid*** (D)/1987	**247,732**
	Demar Dahl (R)	194,527
1995	Richard H. Bryan (D)/1989	
	New Hampshire	
1999	**Judd Gregg** (R)	**247,215**
	John Rauh (D)	232,846
1997	Robert Smith (R)	
	New Jersey	
1995	Frank R. Lautenberg (D)/12/27/82	
1997	Bill Bradley (D)/1979	
	New Mexico	
1995	Jeff Bingaman (D)/1983	
1997	Pete V. Domenici (R)/1973	
	New York	
1999	**Alfonse M. D'Amato*** (R)/1981	**2,999,832**
	Robert Abrams (D)	2,892,112
1995	Daniel Patrick Moynihan (D)/1977	
	North Carolina	
1999	**Lauch Faircloth** (R)	**1,276,665**
	Terry Sanford* (D) 11/5/86	1,175,530
1997	Jesse Helms (R)/1973	
	North Dakota	
1999	**Byron L. Dorgan** (D)/1987	**173,836**
	Steve Sydness (R)	114,929
1995	Vacant[4]	
	Ohio	
1999	**John Glenn*** (D)/12/24/74	**2,417,802**
	Michael DeWine (R)	1,991,844
1995	Howard M. Metzenbaum (D)/12/29/76	
	Oklahoma	
1999	**Don Nickles*** (R)/1981	**757,876**
	Steve Lewis (D)	494,350
1997	David L. Boren (D)/1979	
	Oregon	
1999	**Bob Packwood*** (R)/1969	**606,688**
	Les AuCoin (D)	554,732
1997	Mark O. Hatfield (R)/1/10/67	
	Pennsylvania	
1999	**Arlen Specter*** (R)/1981	**2,342,053**
	Lynn Yeakel (D)	2,213,809
1995	Harris Wofford (D)	
	Rhode Island	
1995	John H. Chafee (R)/12/29/76	
1997	Claiborne Pell (D)/1961	
	South Carolina	
1999	**Fritz Hollings*** (D)/11/9/66	**576,975**
	Thomas Hartnett (R)	548,739
1997	Strom Thurmond (R)/11/7/56	
	South Dakota	
1999	**Thomas A. Daschle*** (D)/1987	**216,867**
	Charlene Haar (R)	108,573
1997	Larry Pressler (R)/1979	
	Tennessee	
1995	James R. Sasser (D)/1977	
1997	Albert Gore Jr. (D)/1985[5]	
	Texas	
1995	Lloyd Bentsen (D)/1971	
1997	Phil Gramm (R)/1985	
	Utah	
1999	**Robert F. Bennett** (R)	**418,187**
	Wayne Owens (D)	300,121
1995	Orrin G. Hatch (R)/1977	
	Vermont	
1999	**Patrick J. Leahy*** (D)/1975	**145,653**
	James H. Douglas (R)	116,847
1995	James M. Jeffords (R)/1989	
	Virginia	
1995	Charles S. Robb (D)/1989	
1997	John W. Warner (R)/1/2/79	
	Washington	
1999	**Patty Murray** (D)	**1,036,796**
	Rod Chandler (R)	857,547
1995	Slade Gorton (R)/1981	
	West Virginia	
1995	Robert C. Byrd (D)/1959	
1997	John D. Rockefeller IV (D)/1/15/85	
	Wisconsin	
1999	**Russell D. Feingold** (D)	**1,284,283**
	Robert W. Kasten Jr.* (R)/1981	1,123,598
1995	Herbert H. Kohl (D)/1989	
	Wyoming	
1995	Malcolm Wallop (R)/1977	
1997	Alan K. Simpson (R)/1979	

(1) Jan. 3, unless otherwise noted. (2) The short term Senate race is to fill the remainder of the term of Pete Wilson (R), who was elected in 1988 but left the Senate in 1990 to run for Governor. John Seymour (R) was appointed interim Senator in Jan. 1991. The winner of this race serves as Senator until 1994. (3) John J. Breaux (D), the incumbent, received more than 50 percent of the Louisiana vote in the Oct. 3 primary, was declared elected, and did not appear on the General Election Ballot. (4) The special Senate race to fill the vacancy created by the death of Sen. Quentin N. Burdick (D) will be held in Dec., 1992; Burdick's wife, Jocelyn, was named to fill the seat temporarily. (5) Seat to be filled to replace V.P.-elect Gore. (6) Run-off to be held.

The House of Representatives

Members' terms to Jan. 3, 1995. Annual salary $129,500; Speaker of the House, $166,200; Majority Leader and Minority Leader $143,800. To be eligible for membership, a person must be at least 25, a U.S. citizen for at least 7 years, and a resident of the state from which he or she is chosen. The ZIP code of the House is 20515, the telephone number is 202-225-3121.

House Officials: Speaker, Thomas S. Foley; Majority Leader, Richard A. Gephardt; Majority Whip, David E. Bonior; Minority Leader, Robert H. Michel; Minority Whip, Newt Gingrich.

D-Democrat; R-Republican; B-Libertarian; C-Conservative; I-Independent; L-Liberal; PF-Peace & Freedom.
Dem., 261, Rep., 173, Ind., 1. Total 435. *Incumbent. Bold face denotes winner.
Preliminary Totals. (Source: News Election Service)

Dist.	Representative (Party)	1992 Election
	Alabama	
1.	**H.L. "Sonny" Callahan*** (R)	**125,201**
	William A. Brewer (D)	77,305
2.	**Terry Everett** (R)	**112,316**
	George C. Wallace, Jr. (D)	108,999
3.	**Glen Browder*** (D)	**118,599**
	Don Sledge (R)	74,101
4.	**Tom Bevill*** (D)	**157,937**
	Martha "Mickey" Strickland (R)	66,907
5.	**Bud Cramer*** (D)	**154,679**
	Terry Smith (R)	77,592
6.	**Spencer Bachus** (R)	**146,018**
	Ben Erdreich* (D)	125,422
7.	**Earl F. Hilliard** (D)	**140,694**
	Kervin Jones (R)	35,899
	Alaska At Large	
	Don Young* (R)	**84,305**
	John C. Devens (D)	79,201
	Arizona	
1.	**Sam Coppersmith** (D)	**125,545**
	John J. Rhodes III* (R)	106,938
2.	**Ed Pastor*** (D)	**83,873**
	Don Shooter (R)	35,253
3.	**Bob Stump*** (R)	**154,242**
	Roger Hartstone (D)	86,894
4.	**John Kyl*** (R)	**149,021**
	Walter R. Mybeck II (D)	68,355
5.	**Jim Kolbe*** (R)	**166,937**
	Jim Toevs (D)	73,894
6.	**Karen English** (D)	**120,865**
	Doug Wead (R)	93,653
	Arkansas	
1.	**Blanche Lambert** (D)	**143,472**
	Terry Hayes (R)	62,704
2.	**Ray Thornton** (D)	**148,923**
	Dennis Scott (R)	51,623
3.	**Tim Hutchinson** (R)	**125,079**
	John VanWinkle (D)	117,485
4.	**Jay Dickey** (R)	**112,918**
	W. J. "Bill" McCuen (D)	101,987
	California	
1.	**Dan Hamburg** (D)	**114,151**
	Frank Riggs* (R)	106,807
2.	**Wally Herger*** (R)	**161,064**
	Elliot Roy Freedman (D)	69,504
3.	**Vic Fazio** (D)	**117,027**
	H.L. "Bill" Richardson (R)	91,865
4.	**John T. Doolittle** (R)	**125,618**
	Patricia Malberg (D)	116,190
5.	**Robert T. Matsui** (D)	**151,318**
	Robert S. Dinsmore (R)	55,381
6.	**Lynn Woolsey** (D)	**178,445**
	Bill Filante (R)	90,751
7.	**George Miller*** (D)	**147,860**
	David Scholl (R)	52,237
8.	**Nancy Polosi** (D)	**182,564**
	Marc Wolin (R)	24,064
9.	**Ronald V. Dellums** (D)	**154,122**
	G. William "Billy" Hunter (R)	48,756
10.	**Bill Baker** (R)	**137,313**
	Wendell H. Williams (D)	128,942
11.	**Richard W. Pombo** (R)	**82,911**
	Patricia Garamendi (D)	82,006
12.	**Tom Lantos** (D)	**147,658**
	Jim Tomlin (R)	49,560
13.	**Fortney "Pete" Stark** (D)	**117,701**
	Verne Teyler (R)	60,709
14.	**Anna G. Eshoo** (D)	**136,174**
	Tom Huening (R)	92,091
15.	**Norm Mineta** (D)	**157,146**
	Robert Wick (R)	76,216
16.	**Don Edwards** (D)	**89,923**
	Ted Bundesen (R)	45,450
17.	**Leon E. Panetta** (D)	**141,804**
	Bill McCambell (R)	46,827
18.	**Gary A. Condit** (D)	**125,291**
	Kim R. Almstrom (B)	23,098
19.	**Rick Lehman** (D)	**95,147**
	Tal L. Cloud (R)	94,259
20.	**Calvin Dooley** (D)	**66,291**
	Ed Hunt (R)	36,163
21.	**Bill Thomas** (R)	**119,256**
	Deborah A. Vollmer (D)	63,673
22.	**Michael Huffington** (R)	**120,356**
	Gloria Ochoa (D)	86,137
23.	**Elton Gallegly** (R)	**108,152**
	Anita Perez Ferguson (D)	83,543
24.	**Anthony C. Beilenson** (D)	**132,343**
	Tom McClintock (R)	91,463
25.	**Howard P. "Buck" McKeon** (R)	**104,552**
	James H. "Gil" Gilmartin (D)	67,687
26.	**Howard L. Berman*** (D)	**69,515**
	Gary Forsch (R)	33,595
27.	**Carlos J. Moorhead** (R)	**95,169**
	Doug Kahn (D)	78,559
28.	**David Dreier** (R)	**112,990**
	Al Wachtel (D)	72,177
29.	**Henry A. Waxman** (D)	**149,292**
	Mark A. Robbins (R)	60,995
30.	**Xavier Becerra** (D)	**45,502**
	Morry Waksberg (R)	18,150
31.	**Matthew G. Martinez** (D)	**64,430**
	Reuben D. Franco (R)	37,729
32.	**Julian C. Dixon** (D)	**142,271**
	Bob Weber (B)	11,470
33.	**Lucille Roybal-Allard** (D)	**30,235**
	Robert Guzman (R)	14,383
34.	**Esteban E. Torres*** (D)	**86,721**
	J. "Jay" Hernandez (R)	47,357
35.	**Maxine Waters** (D)	**98,338**
	Nate Truman (R)	16,122
36.	**Jane Harman** (D)	**117,202**
	Joan Milke Flores (R)	100,062
37.	**Walter R. Tucker** (D)	**92,394**
	B. Kwaku Duren (PF)	15,160
38.	**Steve Horn** (R)	**85,415**
	Evan Anderson Braude (D)	77,367
39.	**Ed Royce** (R)	**113,678**
	Molly McClanahan (D)	76,683
40.	**Jerry Lewis** (R)	**125,874**
	Donald M. "Don" Rusk (D)	62,433
41.	**Jay C. Kim** (R)	**94,867**
	Bob Baker (D)	56,339
42.	**George E. Brown, Jr.** (D)	**77,996**
	Dick Rutan (R)	67,525
43.	**Mark A. Takano** (D)	**83,291**
	Ken Calvert (R)	82,057
44.	**Al McCandless** (R)	**101,806**
	Georgia Smith (D)	76,910
45.	**Dana Rohrabacher** (R)	**116,501**
	Patricia McCabe (D)	84,267
46.	**Robert K.O. "Bob" Dornan** (R)	**49,633**
	Robert John Banuelos (D)	40,587
47.	**Christopher Cox** (R)	**151,143**
	John F. Anwiler (D)	71,657
48.	**Ron Packard** (R)	**128,213**
	Michael Farber (D)	62,318
49.	**Lynn Schenk** (D)	**118,101**
	Judy Jarvis (R)	96,135
50.	**Bob Filner** (D)	**71,251**
	Tony Valencia (R)	35,942

Dist.	Representative (Party)	1992 Election
51.	**Randy "Duke" Cunningham** (R)	**125,913**
	Bea Herbert (D)	77,023
52.	**Duncan Hunter** (R)	**101,936**
	Janet M. Gastil (D)	80,878
	Colorado	
1.	**Patricia Schroeder*** (D)	**155,037**
	Raymond Diaz Aragon (R)	70,407
2.	**David E. Skaggs*** (D)	**164,790**
	Bryan Day (R)	88,470
3.	**Scott McInnis** (R)	**141,545**
	Mike Callihan (D)	112,584
4.	**Wayne Allard*** (R)	**139,044**
	Tom Redder (D)	101,525
5.	**Joel Hefley*** (R)	**167,117**
	Charles A. Oriez (D)	60,090
6.	**Daniel Schaefer*** (R)	**140,792**
	Tom Kolbe (D)	90,525
	Connecticut	
1.	**Barbara Bailey Kennelly*** (D)	**164,381**
	Philip F. Steele (R)	74,367
2.	**Samuel Gejdenson*** (D)	**123,218**
	Edward W. Munster (R)	119,415
3.	**Rosa L. De Lauro*** (D)	**154,924**
	Thomas Scott (R)	82,717
4.	**Christopher Shays*** (R)	**145,911**
	Dave Schropfer (D)	58,543
5.	**Gary A. Franks*** (R)	**101,438**
	James J. Lawlor (D)	70,325
6.	**Nancy L. Johnson*** (R)	**165,002**
	Eugene F. Slason (D)	60,327
	Delaware At Large	
	Michael N. Castle (R)	**152,761**
	S. B. Woo (D)	117,294
	Florida	
1.	**Earl Hutto*** (D)	**110,046**
	Terry Ketchel (R)	90,089
2.	**Pete Peterson*** (D)	**155,284**
	Ray Wagner (R)	53,419
3.	**Corrine Brown** (D)	**89,625**
	Don Weidner (R)	60,586
4.	**Tillie Fowler** (R)	**124,190**
	Mattox Hair (D)	96,791
5.	**Karen L. Thurman** (D)	**129,677**
	Tom Hogan (R)	114,331
6.	**Cliff Stearns*** (R)	**142,499**
	Phil Denton (D)	75,806
7.	**John L. Mica** (R)	**125,755**
	Dan Webster (D)	96,889
8.	**Bill McCollum** (R)	**141,011**
	Chuck Kovaleski (D)	64,763
9.	**Michael Bilirakis*** (R)	**159,466**
	Cheryl Davis Knapp (D)	109,096
10.	**C.W. Bill Young** (R)	**148,378**
	Karen Moffitt (D)	114,027
11.	**Sam M. Gibbons** (D)	**100,816**
	Mark Sharpe (R)	77,451
12.	**Charles T. Canady** (R)	**103,170**
	Tom Mims (D)	94,116
13.	**Dan Miller** (R)	**158,577**
	Rand Snell (D)	115,441
14.	**Porter J. Goss** (R)	**219,383**
	James H. King (I)	47,921
15.	**Jim Bacchus** (D)	**132,386**
	Bill Tolley (R)	128,914
16.	**Tom Lewis** (R)	**157,190**
	John P. Comerford (D)	101,179
17.	**Carrie Meek** (D)	**Unopposed**
18.	**Ileana Ros-Lehtinen*** (R)	**104,715**
	Magda Montiel Davis (D)	52,095
19.	**Harry Johnston** (D)	**177,376**
	Larry Metz (R)	103,819
20.	**Peter Deutsch** (D)	**130,895**
	Beverly Kennedy (R)	91,289
21.	**Lincoln Diaz-Balart** (R)	**Unopposed**

Dist.	Representative (Party)	1992 Election
22.	**E. Clay Shaw** (R)	**128,254**
	Gwen Margolis (D)	91,540
23.	**Alcee L. Hastings** (D)	**83,944**
	Ed Fielding (R)	44,658
	Georgia	
1.	**Jack Kingston** (R)	**97,326**
	Barbara Christmas (D)	73,623
2.	**Sanford Bishop** (D)	**94,943**
	Jim Dudley (R)	54,036
3.	**Mac Collins** (R)	**112,763**
	Richard Ray* (D)	90,966
4.	**John Linder** (R)	**126,502**
	Cathey Steinberg (D)	123,819
5.	**John Lewis*** (D)	**147,443**
	Paul Stabler (R)	56,898
6.	**Newt Gingrich*** (R)	**158,670**
	Tony Center (D)	116,147
7.	**George "Buddy" Darden*** (D)	**111,259**
	Al Beverly (R)	82,820
8.	**J. Roy Rowland*** (D)	**106,957**
	Robert F. "Bob" Cunningham (R)	85,540
9.	**Nathan Deal** (D)	**113,924**
	Daniel Becker (R)	79,792
10.	**Don Johnson** (D)	**108,941**
	Ralph Hudgens (R)	92,894
11.	**Cynthia McKinney** (D)	**120,169**
	Woodrow Lovett (R)	44,243
	Hawaii	
1.	**Neil Abercrombie*** (D)	**128,942**
	Warner C. Kimo Sutton (R)	41,415
2.	**Patsy Takemoto Mink*** (D)	**131,256**
	Kamuela Price (R)	39,963
	Idaho	
1.	**Larry LaRocco*** (D)	**139,899**
	Rachel S. Gilbert (R)	90,487
2.	**Michael D. Crapo** (R)	**139,612**
	J.D. Williams (D)	81,354
	Illinois	
1.	**Bobby L. Rush** (D)	**187,926**
	Jay Walker (R)	41,363
2.	**Mel Reynolds** (D)	**172,191**
	Ron Blackstone (R)	31,118
3.	**William O. Lipinski** (D)	**156,900**
	Harry C. Lepinske (R)	91,447
4.	**Luis V. Gutierrez** (D)	**83,340**
	Hildegarde Rodriguez-Schieman (R)	24,426
5.	**Dan Rostenkowski** (D)	**128,818**
	Elias R. "Non-Incumbent" Zenkich (R)	88,360
6.	**Henry J. Hyde*** (R)	**164,668**
	Barry W. Watkins (D)	86,722
7.	**Cardiss Collins*** (D)	**166,236**
	Norman G. Boccio (R)	33,141
8.	**Philip M, Crane** (R)	**132,855**
	Sheila A. Smith (D)	96,397
9.	**Sidney R. Yates*** (D)	**156,949**
	Herbert Sohn (R)	62,327
10.	**John E. Porter*** (R)	**153,801**
	Michael J. Kennedy (D)	84,650
11.	**George F. Sangmeister** (D)	**133,400**
	Robert T. Herbolsheimer (R)	106,480
12.	**Jerry F. Costello** (D)	**168,755**
	Mike Starr (R)	68,119
13.	**Harris W. Fawell*** (R)	**179,227**
	Dennis Michael Temple (D)	82,968
14.	**J. Dennis Hastert*** (R)	**155,260**
	Jonathan Abram Reich (D)	75,282
15.	**Thomas W. Ewing*** (R)	**142,160**
	Charles D. Mattis (D)	97,184
16.	**Donald Manzullo** (R)	**142,388**
	John W. Cox Jr. (D)	113,553
17.	**Lane Evans*** (D)	**156,233**
	Ken Schloemer (R)	103,719
18.	**Robert H. Michel*** (R)	**156,414**
	Ronald C. Hawkins (D)	114,330

Dist.	Representative (Party)	1992 Election
19.	**Glenn Poshard** (D)	**186,618**
	Douglas E. Lee (R)	83,552
20.	**Richard J. Durbin*** (D)	**154,855**
	John M. Shimkus (R)	119,204
	Indiana	
1.	**Peter J. Visclosky*** (D)	**146,815**
	David J. Vucich (R)	64,767
2.	**Philip R. Sharp*** (D)	**130,881**
	William G. Frazier (R)	90,593
3.	**Timothy J. Roemer*** (D)	**121,269**
	Carl H. Baxmeyer (R)	89,709
4.	**Jill L. Long*** (D)	**129,990**
	Charles W. "Chuck" Pierson (R)	78,640
5.	**Steve Buyer** (R)	**112,370**
	James Jontz* (D)	107,870
6.	**Dan Burton*** (R)	**181,802**
	Natalie M. Bruner (D)	68,308
7.	**John T. Myers*** (R)	**129,199**
	Ellen E. Wedum (D)	87,995
8.	**Frank McCloskey*** (D)	**124,924**
	Richard E. Mourdock (R)	108,011
9.	**Lee H. Hamilton*** (D)	**161,401**
	Michael E. Bailey (R)	70,080
10.	**Andrew Jacobs Jr.*** (D)	**111,339**
	Janos Horvath (R)	61,641
	Iowa	
1.	**Jim Leach*** (R)	**177,393**
	Jan J. Zonneveld (D)	81,225
2.	**Jim Nussle*** (R)	**133,966**
	David R. Nagle (D)	130,576
3.	**Jim Ross Lightfoot** (R)	**125,779**
	Elaine Baxter (D)	120,637
4.	**Neal Smith*** (D)	**155,754**
	Paul Lunde (R)	92,627
	Kansas	
1.	**Pat Roberts*** (R)	**189,945**
	Duane E. West (D)	82,509
2.	**Jim Slattery*** (D)	**150,605**
	Jim Van Slyke (R)	109,427
3.	**Jan Meyers*** (R)	**169,668**
	Tom Love (D)	109,548
4.	**Dan Glickman*** (D)	**139,678**
	Eric R. Yost (R)	114,246
	Kentucky	
1.	**Tom Barlow** (D)	**128,233**
	Steve Hamrick (R)	82,989
2.	**William H. Natcher*** (D)	**126,808**
	Bruce R. Bartley (R)	79,619
3.	**Romano L. Mazzoli*** (D)	**148,066**
	Susan B. Stokes (R)	132,689
4.	**Jim Bunning*** (R)	**139,465**
	Dr. Floyd G. Poore (D)	86,713
5.	**Harold Rogers*** (R)	**113,681**
	John Doug Hays (D)	97,590
6.	**Scotty Baesler** (D)	**135,017**
	Charles W. Ellinger (R)	87,636
	Louisiana	
1.	**Bob Livingston*** (R)	**Declared Elected**
2.	**William J. Jefferson*** (D)	**Declared Elected**
3.	**Billy Tauzin*** (D)	**Declared Elected**
4.	**Cleo Fields** (D)	**142,822**
	Charles Jones (D)	50,796
5.	**Jim McCrery** (R)	**153,232**
	Jerry Huckaby* (D)	89,923
6.	**Richard Baker*** (R)	**123,869**
	Clyde C. Holloway (R)	120,900
7.	**James A. "Jimmy" Hayes*** (D)	**Declared Elected**

In Louisiana, all candidates of all parties run against each other in an open primary, unless they are unopposed incumbents in which case they are declared elected. All candidates who receive more than 50 percent of the primary vote are also declared elected, and do not appear on the General Election ballot.

Dist.	Representative (Party)	1992 Election
	Maine	
1.	**Thomas H. Andrews*** (D)	**230,930**
	Linda Bean (R)	125,875
2.	**Olympia J. Snowe*** (R)	**150,110**
	Patrick K. McGowan (D)	128,042
	Maryland	
1.	**Wayne T. Gilchrest*** (R)	**114,017**
	Thomas McMillen (D)	106,914
2.	**Helen Delich Bentley*** (R)	**157,194**
	Michael C. Hickey, Jr. (D)	85,931
3.	**Benjamin L. Cardin*** (D)	**156,085**
	William T.S. Bricker (R)	56,125
4.	**Albert R. Wynn*** (D)	**132,776**
	Michele Dyson (R)	42,743
5.	**Steny H. Hoyer*** (D)	**113,280**
	Lawrence J. Hogan, Jr. (R)	92,636
6.	**Roscoe G. Bartlett** (R)	**119,684**
	Thomas H. Hattery* (D)	100,753
7.	**Kweisi Mfume*** (D)	**147,133**
	Kenneth Kondner (R)	25,013
8.	**Constance A. Morella*** (R)	**189,420**
	Edward J. Heffernan (D)	72,190
	Massachusetts	
1.	**John W. Olver*** (D)	**134,954**
	Patrick Larkin (R)	113,796
2.	**Richard E. Neal*** (D)	**131,147**
	Anthony W. Ravosa, Jr. (R)	76,780
3.	**Peter I. Blute** (R)	**131,406**
	Joseph D Early* (D)	115,493
4.	**Barney Frank*** (D)	**182,207**
	Edward J. McCormick III (R)	70,628
5.	**Martin T. Meehan** (D)	**134,417**
	Paul W. Cronin (R)	96,827
6.	**Peter G. Torkildsen** (R)	**158,577**
	Nicholas Mavroules* (D)	130,597
7.	**Edward J. Markey*** (D)	**182,850**
	Stephen A. Sohn (R)	78,194
8.	**Joseph P. Kennedy II***(D)	**114,125**
	Alice Harriet Nakash (I)	23,795
9.	**John Joseph Moakley*** (D)	**175,187**
	Martin D. Conboy (R)	54,061
10.	**Gerry E. Studds*** (D)	**188,720**
	Daniel W. Daly (R)	75,686
	Michigan	
1.	**Bart Stupak** (D)	**142,379**
	Philip E. Ruppe (R)	113,818
2.	**Peter Hoekstra** (R)	**152,282**
	John H. Miltner (D)	84,179
3.	**Paul B. Henry** (R)	**164,518**
	Carol S. Kooistra (D)	96,666
4.	**Dave Camp** (R)	**155,032**
	Lisa A. Donaldson (D)	87,662
5.	**James A. Barcia** (D)	**147,657**
	Keith Muxlow (R)	92,791
6.	**Fred Upton** (R)	**141,353**
	Andy Davis (D)	85,747
7.	**Nick Smith** (R)	**133,323**
	Kenneth L. Proctor (B)	20,071
8.	**Bob Carr** (D)	**135,491**
	Dick Chrysler (R)	131,804
9.	**Dale E. Kildee** (D)	**133,980**
	Megan O'Neill (R)	112,322
10.	**David E. Bonior** (D)	**134,946**
	Douglas Carl (R)	111,776
11.	**Joseph K. Knollenberg** (R)	**166,982**
	Walter Briggs (D)	117,030
12.	**Sander Levin** (D)	**127,919**
	John Pappageorge (R)	108,582
13.	**William D. Ford** (D)	**128,237**
	R. Robert Geake (R)	94,332
14.	**John Conyers, Jr.** (D)	**165,172**
	John W. Gordon (R)	32,054

Dist.	Representative (Party)	1992 Election
15.	**Barbara-Rose Collins** (D)	**148,755**
	Charles C. Vincent (R)	31,564
16.	**John D. Dingell*** (D)	**156,964**
	Frank Beaumont (R)	75,694

Minnesota

Dist.	Representative (Party)	1992 Election
1.	**Timothy J. "Tim" Penny*** (D)	**202,944**
	Timothy R. Droogsma (R)	71,666
2.	**David Minge** (D)	**131,888**
	Cal R. Ludeman (R)	131,302
3.	**Jim Ramstad*** (R)	**199,872**
	Paul Mandell (D)	104,431
4.	**Bruce F. Vento*** (D)	**159,326**
	Ian Maitland (R)	101,313
5.	**Martin Olav Sabo*** (D)	**174,027**
	Stephen A. Moriarty (R)	77,059
6.	**Rod Grams** (R)	**132,059**
	Gerry Sikorski* (D)	99,002
7.	**Collin C. Peterson*** (D)	**133,723**
	Bernie Omann (R)	130,556
8.	**James L. Oberstar*** (D)	**144,950**
	Phil Herwig (R)	73,705

Mississippi

Dist.	Representative (Party)	1992 Election
1.	**Jamie L. Whitten*** (D)	**118,803**
	Clyde E. Whitaker (R)	81,522
2.	**Mike Espy*** (D)	**134,253**
	Dorothy Benford (R)	37,623
3.	**G. V. "Sonny" Montgomery*** (D)	**159,857**
	Michael E. Williams (R)	37,462
4.	**Mike Parker*** (D)	**131,413**
	Jack L. McMillan (R)	42,523
5.	**Gene Taylor*** (D)	**117,117**
	Paul Harvey (R)	65,447

Missouri

Dist.	Representative (Party)	1992 Election
1.	**William "Bill" Clay*** (D)	**158,418**
	Arthur S. Montgomery (R)	74,308
2.	**James M. Talent** (R)	**157,556**
	Joan Kelly Horn* (D)	148,658
3.	**Richard A. Gephardt*** (D)	**173,906**
	Malcolm L. "Mack" Holekamp (R)	89,978
4.	**Ike Skelton*** (D)	**176,252**
	John Carley (R)	75,291
5.	**Alan Wheat*** (D)	**150,693**
	Edward "Gomer" Moody (R)	93,421
6.	**Patsy Ann "Pat" Danner** (D)	**147,674**
	E. Thomas "Tom" Coleman* (R)	118,637
7.	**Melton D. "Mel" Hancock*** (R)	**157,700**
	Thomas Patrick "Pat" Deaton (D)	98,458
8.	**Bill Emerson*** (R)	**141,494**
	Thad Bullock (D)	82,904
9.	**Harold L. Volkmer*** (D)	**119,327**
	Rick Hardy (R)	115,696

Montana At Large

Dist.	Representative (Party)	1992 Election
1.	**Pat Williams*** (D)	**202,929**
	Ron Marlenee (R)	189,165

Nebraska

Dist.	Representative (Party)	1992 Election
1.	**Douglas K. Bereuter*** (R)	**140,995**
	Gerry Finnegan (D)	95,397
2.	**Peter Hoagland*** (D)	**118,486**
	Ronald L. Staskiewicz (R)	112,779
3.	**Bill Barrett*** (R)	**167,602**
	Lowell Fisher (D)	66,255

Nevada

Dist.	Representative (Party)	1992 Election
1.	**James H. Bilbray*** (D)	**127,292**
	J. Coy Pettyjohn (R)	83,527
2.	**Barbara F. Vucanovich*** (R)	**125,118**
	Pete Sferrazza (D)	113,364

New Hampshire

Dist.	Representative (Party)	1992 Election
1.	**"Bill" Zeliff*** (R)	**134,575**
	"Bob" Preston (D)	107,189
2.	**"Dick" Swett*** (D)	**157,199**
	"Bill" Hatch (R)	91,090

New Jersey

Dist.	Representative (Party)	1992 Election
1.	**Robert E. Andrews*** (D)	**150,560**
	Lee A. Solomon (R)	63,607
2.	**William J. Hughes*** (D)	**127,987**
	Frank A. LoBiondo (R)	95,231
3.	**Jim Saxton** (R)	**142,850**
	Timothy E. Ryan (D)	89,347
4.	**Christopher H. Smith*** (R)	**139,304**
	Brian M. Hughes (D)	80,550
5.	**Marge Roukema*** (R)	**186,019**
	Frank R. Lucas (D)	64,311
6.	**Frank Pallone, Jr.** (D)	**111,653**
	Joseph M. Kyrillos (R)	95,585
7.	**Bob Franks** (R)	**113,104**
	Leonard R. Sendelsky (D)	92,119
8.	**Herbert C. Klein** (D)	**91,262**
	Joseph L. Bubba (R)	80,734
9.	**Robert G. Torricelli*** (D)	**131,548**
	Patrick J. Roma (R)	83,560
10.	**Donald M. Payne*** (D)	**102,602**
	Alfred D. Palermo (R)	29,891
11.	**Dean A. Gallo*** (R)	**179,803**
	Ona Spiridellis (D)	65,024
12.	**Dick Zimmer*** (R)	**167,127**
	Frank C. Abate (D)	80,731
13.	**Robert Mendenez** (D)	**87,034**
	Fred J. Theemling, Jr. (R)	41,869

New Mexico

Dist.	Representative (Party)	1992 Election
1.	**Steven H. Schiff*** (R)	**125,056**
	Robert J. Aragon (D)	75,114
2.	**Joe Skeen*** (R)	**94,826**
	Dan Sosa, Jr. (D)	73,118
3.	**Bill Richardson*** (D)	**118,257**
	F. Gregg Bemis, Jr. (R)	52,755

New York

Dist.	Representative (Party)	1992 Election
1.	**George J. Hochbrueckner*** (D)	**111,418**
	Edward P. Romaine (R)	105,069
2.	**Rick A. Lazio** (R)	**104,264**
	Thomas J. Downey* (D)	91,465
3.	**Peter T. King** (R)	**117,692**
	Steve A. Orlins (D)	111,051
4.	**David A. Levy** (R)	**106,975**
	Philip Schiliro (D)	96,954
5.	**Gary L. Ackerman** (D)	**97,425**
	Allan E. Binder (R)	86,316
6.	**Floyd H. Flake*** (D)	**92,654**
	Dianand D. Bnaowandin (R)	21,276
7.	**Thomas J. Manton** (D)	**67,843**
	Dennis C. Shea (R)	52,734
8.	**Jerrold L. Nadler** (D)	**126,832**
	David L. Askren (R)	24,227
9.	**Charles E. Schumer** (D,L)	**111,399**
	Alice E. Gaffney (C)	14,273
10.	**Edolphus Towns** (D,L)	**93,271**
	Owen Augustin (C)	4,320
11.	**Major R. Owens** (D,L)	**75,574**
	Michael Gaffney (C)	4,122
12.	**Nydia M. Velazquez** (D)	**51,608**
	Angel Diaz (R)	13,945
13.	**Susan Molinari** (R)	**102,715**
	Sal F. Albanese (D)	70,447
14.	**Carolyn B. Maloney** (D)	**94,613**
	Bill Green* (R)	89,423
15.	**Charles B. Rangel** (D,L)	**97,398**
	Jose Suero (C)	4,817
16.	**Jose E. Serrano** (D)	**81,632**
	Michael Walters (R)	7,868
17.	**Eliot L. Engel** (D)	**92,802**
	Martin Richman (R)	15,898
18.	**Nita M. Lowey** (D)	**102,269**
	Joseph J. DioGuardi (R)	83,282
19.	**Hamilton Fish, Jr.** (R)	**125,417**
	Neil McCarthy (D)	81,941
20.	**Benjamin A. Gilman** (R)	**139,712**
	Jonathan L. Levine (D)	61,630

Dist.	Representative (Party)	1992 Election
21.	**Michael R. McNulty** (D)	**147,173**
	Nancy Norman (R)	82,668
22.	**Gerald B. H. Solomon** (R)	**154,416**
	David Roberts (D)	80,713
23.	**Sherwood L. Boehlert** (R)	**126,879**
	Paula DiPerna (D)	56,841
24.	**John M. McHugh** (R)	**116,254**
	Margaret M. Ravenscroft (D)	44,798
25.	**James T. Walsh** (R)	**132,279**
	Rhea Jezer (D)	105,364
26.	**Maurice D. Hinchey** (D)	**114,133**
	Bob Moppert (R)	105,037
27.	**Bill Paxon** (R)	**149,928**
	W. Douglas Call (D)	86,288
28.	**Louise M. Slaughter** (D)	**127,958**
	William P. Polito (R)	105,573
29.	**John J. LaFalce** (D)	**123,628**
	William E. Miller, Jr. (R)	94,804
30.	**Jack Quinn** (R)	**119,102**
	Dennis T. Gorski (D)	105,391
31.	**Amo Houghton** (R)	**143,463**
	Joseph P. Leahey (D)	49,379

North Carolina

Dist.	Representative (Party)	1992 Election
1.	**Eva Clayton** (D)	**115,291**
	Ted Tyler (R)	54,133
2.	**I.T. "Tim" Valentine Jr.*** (D)	**112,367**
	Don Davis (R)	92,164
3.	**Martin Lancaster*** (D)	**100,602**
	Tommy Pollard (R)	80,062
4.	**David E. Price*** (D)	**170,753**
	LaVinia "Vicky" Rothrock Goudie (R)	89,147
5.	**Stephen Neal*** (D)	**117,256**
	Richard M. Burr (R)	101,605
6.	**J. Howard Coble*** (R)	**161,880**
	Robin Hood (D)	66,810
7.	**Charles C. Rose III*** (D)	**89,042**
	Robert C. Anderson (R)	61,087
8.	**W. G. "Bill" Hefner*** (D)	**109,710**
	Coy C. Privette (R)	70,111
9.	**J. Alex McMillan*** (R)	**145,455**
	Rory Blake (D)	71,415
10.	**T. Cass Ballenger*** (R)	**148,900**
	Ben Neill (D)	78,979
11.	**Charles H. Taylor** (R)	**130,103**
	John S. Stevens (D)	107,894
12.	**Melvin Watt** (D)	**125,850**
	Barbara Gore Washington (R)	48,859

North Dakota At Large

Dist.	Representative (Party)	1992 Election
	Earl Pomeroy(D)	**163,865**
	John T. Korsmo (R)	114,331

Ohio

Dist.	Representative (Party)	1992 Election
1.	**David Mann** (D)	**117,689**
	Steve Grote (I)	99,741
	Jim Berns (I)	12,444
2.	**Willis D. Gradison Jr.*** (R)	**175,514**
	Thomas R. Chandler (D)	75,127
3.	**Tony P. Hall*** (D)	**144,854**
	Peter W. Davis (R)	98,049
4.	**Michael G. Oxley*** (R)	**145,484**
	Raymond M. Ball (D)	91,718
5.	**Paul E. Gillmor*** (R)	**Unopposed**
6.	**Ted Strickland** (D)	**121,223**
	Bob McEwen* (R)	117,681
7.	**David L. Hobson** (R)	**162,764**
	Clifford S. Heskett (D)	65,525
8.	**John A. Boehner*** (R)	**167,485**
	Fred Sennet (D)	68,159
9.	**Marcy Kaptur*** (D)	**176,877**
	Ken D. Brown (R)	52,431
10.	**Martin R. Hoke** (R)	**134,711**
	Mary Rose Oakar (D)	102,573
11.	**Louis Stokes** (D)	**152,328**
	Beryl E. Rothschild (R)	43,152
12.	**John R. Kasich*** (R)	**168,945**
	Bob Fitrakis (D)	68,186
13.	**Sherrod Brown** (D)	**133,489**
	Margaret R. Mueller (R)	88,202
14.	**Thomas C. Sawyer*** (D)	**163,454**
	Robert Morgan (R)	77,953
15.	**Deborah Pryce** (R)	**115,710**
	Richard Cordray (D)	97,599
16.	**Ralph Regula*** (R)	**156,963**
	Warner D. Mendenhall (D)	89,509
17.	**James A. Traficant Jr.*** (D)	**214,433**
	Salvatore Pansino (R)	40,381
18.	**Douglas Applegate*** (D)	**164,390**
	Bill Ress (R)	76,868
19.	**Eric D. Fingerhut** (D)	**137,140**
	Robert A. Gardner (R)	123,308

Oklahoma

Dist.	Representative (Party)	1992 Election
1.	**James M. Inhofe*** (R)	**119,211**
	John Selph (D)	106,619
2.	**Mike Synar*** (D)	**118,542**
	Jerry Hill (R)	87,657
3.	**Bill K. Brewster*** (D)	**155,934**
	Robert W. Stokes (R)	51,725
4.	**Dave McCurdy*** (D)	**140,841**
	Howard Bell (R)	58,235
5.	**Ernest Jim Istook** (R)	**123,237**
	Laurie Williams (D)	107,579
6.	**Glenn English*** (D)	**134,734**
	Bob Anthony (R)	64,068

Oregon

Dist.	Representative (Party)	1992 Election
1.	**Elizabeth Furse** (D)	**118,133**
	Tony Meeker (R)	100,955
2.	**Bob Smith*** (R)	**161,537**
	Denzel Ferguson (D)	80,721
3.	**Ron Wyden*** (D)	**177,745**
	Al Ritter (R)	40,752
4.	**Peter A. DeFazio*** (D)	**183,199**
	Richard L. Schulz (R)	71,366
5.	**Mike Kopetski*** (D)	**158,482**
	Jim Seagraves (R)	85,665

Pennsylvania

Dist.	Representative (Party)	1992 Election
1.	**Thomas M. Foglietta*** (D)	**150,183**
	Craig Snyder (R)	35,345
2.	**Lucien E. Blackwell*** (D)	**160,786**
	Larry Hollin (R)	47,393
3.	**Robert A. Borski*** (D)	**125,596**
	Charles F. Dougherty (R)	82,909
4.	**Ron Klink** (D)	**186,346**
	Gordon R. Johnston (R)	48,332
5.	**Bill Clinger** (D)	**Unopposed**
6.	**Tim Holden** (D)	**106,939**
	John E. Jones (R)	97,156
7.	**Curt Weldon*** (R)	**179,541**
	Frank Daly (D)	93,453
8.	**Jim Greenwood** (R)	**128,606**
	Peter H. Kostmayer* (D)	112,758
9.	**Bud Shuster*** (R, D)	**Unopposed**
10.	**Joseph M. McDade*** (R,D)	**187,318**
	Albert A. Smith (B)	19,800
11.	**Paul E. Kanjorski*** (D)	**138,557**
	Michael A. Fescina (R)	66,743
12.	**John P. Murtha*** (D)	**Unopposed**
13.	**Marjorie Margolies Mezvinsky** (D)	**127,534**
	John D. Fox (R)	126,445
14.	**William J. Coyne*** (D)	**164,827**
	Byron W. King (R)	60,932
15.	**Paul McHale** (D)	**110,865**
	Don Ritter* (R)	99,482
16.	**Robert S. Walker*** (R)	**137,818**
	Robert Peters (D)	74,648
17.	**George W. Gekas*** (R)	**150,074**
	Bill Sturges (D)	65,826
18.	**Rick Santorum** (R)	**153,154**
	Frank A. Pecora (D)	96,736
19.	**William F. Goodling*** (R)	**96,883**
	Paul V. Kilker (D)	73,849

Dist.	Representative (Party)	1992 Election
20.	**Austin J. Murphy** (D)	**114,408**
	Bill Townsend (R)	108,261
21.	**Thomas J. Ridge*** (R)	**149,857**
	John C. Harkins (D)	74,049

Rhode Island

Dist.	Representative (Party)	1992 Election
1.	**Ronald K. Machtley*** (R)	**130,173**
	David R. Carlin, Jr. (D)	45,443
2.	**John F. Reed*** (D)	**138,780**
	James W. Bell (R)	47,456

South Carolina

Dist.	Representative (Party)	1992 Election
1.	**Arthur Ravenel Jr.*** (R)	**116,136**
	Bill Oberst, Jr. (D)	59,124
2.	**Floyd D. Spence*** (R)	**147,901**
	Geb Sommer (B)	20,702
3.	**Butler Derrick*** (D)	**118,921**
	Jim Bland (R)	75,558
4.	**Bob Inglis*** (R)	**99,878**
	Liz J. Patterson (D)	94,179
5.	**John Spratt*** (D)	**112,102**
	Bill Horne (R)	71,385
6.	**James R. Clyburn** (D)	**118,862**
	John Chase (R)	64,290

South Dakota At Large

Dist.	Representative (Party)	1992 Election
	Tim Johnson* (D)	**229,646**
	John Timmer (R)	89,123

Tennessee

Dist.	Representative (Party)	1992 Election
1.	**James H. "Jimmy" Quillen*** (R)	**114,565**
	J. Carr "Jack" Christian (D)	48,237
2.	**John J. Duncan Jr.*** (R)	**148,203**
	Troy Goodale (D)	52,766
3.	**Marilyn Lloyd*** (D)	**106,899**
	Zack Wamp (R)	103,409
4.	**Jim Cooper*** (D)	**98,993**
	Dale Johnson (R)	50,047
5.	**Bob Clement*** (D)	**125,181**
	Tom Stone (R)	49,385
6.	**Bart Gordon*** (D)	**119,599**
	Marsha Blackburn (R)	85,959
7.	**Don Sundquist*** (R)	**126,766**
	David R. Davis (D)	75,008
8.	**John Tanner*** (D)	**Unopposed**
9.	**Harold E. Ford*** (D)	**123,269**
	Charles L. Black (R)	60,603

Texas

Dist.	Representative (Party)	1992 Election
1.	**Jim Chapman*** (D)	**Unopposed**
2.	**Charles Wilson*** (D)	**116,226**
	Donna Peterson (R)	90,552
3.	**Sam Johnson*** (R)	**201,670**
	Noel Kopala (B)	32,542
4.	**Ralph M. Hall*** (D)	**127,974**
	David L. Bridges (R)	83,856
5.	**John Bryant*** (D)	**98,160**
	Richard Stokley (R)	62,181
6.	**Joe Barton*** (R)	**188,762**
	John Dietrich (D)	73,787
7.	**Bill Archer*** (R)	**Unopposed**
8.	**Jack Fields*** (R)	**172,881**
	Charles Robinson (D)	53,164
9.	**Jack Brooks*** (D)	**118,607**
	Steve Stockman (R)	94,980
10.	**J. J. "Jake" Pickle*** (D)	**177,233**
	Herbert Spiro (R)	68,646
11.	**Chet Edwards*** (D)	**119,206**
	James W. Broyles (R)	57,813
12.	**Pete Geren*** (D)	**125,343**
	David Hobbs (R)	74,334
13.	**Bill Sarpalius*** (D)	**118,324**
	Beau Bolter (R)	77,746
14.	**Greg Laughlin*** (D)	**137,184**
	Humberto J. "Bert" Garza (R)	54,567
15.	**E. "Kika" de la Garza*** (D)	**86,187**
	Tom Haughey (R)	56,811
16.	**Ronald Coleman*** (D)	**66,731**
	Chip Taberski (R)	61,870
17.	**Charles W. Stenholm*** (D)	**135,953**
	Jeannie Sadowski (R)	70,007
18.	**Craig A. Washington*** (D)	**110,794**
	Edward Blum (R)	52,984
19.	**Larry Combest*** (R)	**161,896**
	Terry Lee Moser (D)	47,326
20.	**Henry B. Gonzalez*** (D)	**Unopposed**
21.	**Lamar Smith*** (R)	**190,520**
	James M. Gaddy (D)	62,705
22.	**Tom DeLay*** (R)	**146,639**
	Richard Konrad (D)	67,520
23.	**Henry Bonilla** (R)	**97,888**
	Albert G. Bustamente* (D)	63,423
24.	**Martin Frost*** (D)	**104,167**
	Steve Masterson (R)	70,036
25.	**Mike Andrews*** (D)	**97,656**
	Dolly Madison McKenna (R)	68,407
26.	**Dick Armey*** (R)	**150,209**
	John Wayne Caton (D)	55,237
27.	**Solomon P. Ortiz*** (D)	**87,517**
	Jay Kimbrough (R)	66,485
28.	**Frank Tejeda** (D)	**122,068**
	David C. Slatter (B)	18,158
29.	**Gene Green** (D)	**63,192**
	Clark Kent Ervin (R)	32,754
30.	**Eddie Bernice Johnson** (D)	**107,830**
	Lucy Cain (R)	37,853

Utah

Dist.	Representative (Party)	1992 Election
1.	**James V. Hansen*** (R)	**159,601**
	Ron Holt (D)	68,549
2.	**Karen Shepherd** (D)	**127,543**
	Enid Greene (R)	118,013
3.	**Bill Orton*** (D)	**133,919**
	Richard Harrington (R)	83,019

Vermont At Large

Dist.	Representative (Party)	1992 Election
	Bernie Sanders* (I)	**152,551**
	Tim Philbin (R)	82,443
	Lewis E. Young (D)	20,989

Virginia

Dist.	Representative (Party)	1992 Election
1.	**Herbert H. "Herb" Bateman*** (R)	**134,535**
	Andrew H. "Andy" Fox (D)	89,707
2.	**Owen B. Pickett*** (D)	**94,689**
	J. L. "Jim" Chapman (R)	75,168
3.	**Robert C. "Bobby" Scott** (D)	**131,356**
	Daniel "Dan" Jenkins (R)	35,449
4.	**Norman Sisisky*** (D)	**144,137**
	A.J. "Tony" Zevgolis (R)	66,236
5.	**L. F. Payne Jr.*** (D)	**132,867**
	W.A. "Bill" Hurlburt (R)	59,761
6.	**Robert W. "Bob" Goodlatte** (R)	**126,590**
	Stephen Alan Musselwhite (D)	83,967
7.	**Thomas J. "Tom" Bliley, Jr.** (R)	**206,385**
	Gerald E. "Jerry" Berg (I)	42,200
8.	**James P. Moran, Jr.*** (D)	**135,698**
	Kyle E. McSlarrow (R)	101,447
9.	**Frederick C. "Rick" Boucher*** (D)	**131,507**
	L. Garrett "Gary" Weddle (R)	77,718
10.	**Frank R. Wolf*** (R)	**143,777**
	Raymond E. "Ray" Vickery, Jr. (D)	75,744
11.	**Leslie L. Byrne** (D)	**113,461**
	Henry N. Butler (R)	103,091

Washington

Dist.	Representative (Party)	1992 Election
1.	**Maria Cantwell** (D)	**128,885**
	Gary Nelson (R)	96,540
2.	**Al Swift*** (D)	**116,118**
	Jack Metcalf (R)	89,923
3.	**Jolene Unsoeld*** (D)	**124,393**
	Pat Fiske (R)	96,773
4.	**Jay Inslee** (D)	**91,118**
	Richard "Doc" Hastings (R)	86,127
5.	**Thomas S. Foley*** (D)	**123,051**
	John Sonneland (R)	99,638
6.	**Norman D. Dicks*** (D)	**121,162**
	Lauri J. Phillips (R)	51,297

Dist.	Representative (Party)	1992 Election
7.	**Jim McDermott*** (D)	**198,657**
	Glenn C. Hampson (R)	45,351
8.	**Jennifer Dunn** (R)	**129,475**
	George O. Tamblyn (D)	73,654
9.	**Mike Kreidler** (D)	**91,987**
	Pete von Reichbauer (R)	71,921
	Brian Wilson (I)	5,787
	Timothy J. Brill (I)	2,886
	West Virginia	
1.	**Alan B. Mollohan*** (D)	**Unopposed**
2.	**Bob Wise** (D)	**143,923**
	Samuel A. Cravotta (R)	58,666
3.	**Nick Joe Rahall, II** (D)	**116,027**
	Ben Waldman (R)	59,291
	Wisconsin	
1.	**Les Aspin*** (D)	**147,029**
	Mark W. Neumann (R)	104,348
2.	**Scott L. Klug*** (R)	**181,845**
	Ada E. Deer (D)	107,480
3.	**Steven C. Gunderson*** (R)	**145,200**
	Paul Sacia (D)	107,458
4.	**Gerald D. Kleczka*** (D)	**172,903**
	Joseph L. Cook (R)	84,463
5.	**Thomas M. Barrett** (D)	**159,446**
	Donalda Ann Hammersmith (R)	68,676
6.	**Thomas E. Petri*** (R)	**143,843**
	Peggy A. Lautenschlager (D)	128,350
7.	**David R. Obey*** (D)	**165,975**
	Dale R. Vannes (R)	91,775
8.	**Toby Roth*** (R)	**191,037**
	Catherine L. Helms (D)	82,032
9.	**F. James Senstenbrenner Jr.*** (R)	**193,335**
	Ingrid K. Buxton (D)	77,903
	Wyoming At Large	
	Craig Thomas* (R)	**113,712**
	John Herschler (D)	77,364

Resident Commissioner (Non-Voting)

Puerto Rico

Carlos Romero Barceló (D)

Non-Voting Delegates

District of Columbia
Eleanor Holmes Norton (D)

Guam[1]
Ben G. Blaz* (R)

Virgin Islands
Ron de Lugo* (D)

American Samoa
Faleo Mavaega (D)

(1) A typhoon postponed elections on Guam.

Congressional Reapportionment for the 103rd Congress

Source: Bureau of the Census, U.S. Dept. of Commerce

As a result of population changes from 1980 to 1990, as reported in the 1990 Census, 8 states will have more representatives in the 103rd Congress, which will convene in January 1993. The states with the largest gains will be California (+7), Florida (+4), and Texas (+3), while Washington, Arizona, Georgia, North Carolina, and Virginia will each gain a seat. Thirteen states will have fewer representatives. New York will lose 3 seats, while Illinois, Michigan, Ohio, and Pennsylvania will lose 2 seats each. West Virginia, Kentucky, Louisiana, Kansas, Massachusetts, New Jersey, Iowa, and Montana will lose one seat.

The population shifts will give the West 8, and the South 7 additional seats. The Midwest will lose 8, and the Northeast 7 seats.

Political Divisions of the U.S. Senate and House of Representatives From 1955 (84th Cong.) to 1993 (103rd Cong.)

Source: Clerk of the House of Representatives; Secretary of the Senate; reflects preliminary results of 1992 elections

		Senate					House of Representatives				
Congress	Years	Number of Senators	Democrats	Republicans	Other parties	Vacant	Number of Representatives	Democrats	Republicans	Other parties	Vacant
84th	1955-57	96	48	47	1		435	232	203		
85th	1957-59	96	49	47			435	234	201		
86th	1959-61	98	64	34			[1]436	283	153		
87th	1961-63	100	64	36			[2]437	262	175		
88th	1963-65	100	67	33			435	258	176		1
89th	1965-67	100	68	32			435	295	140		
90th	1967-69	100	64	36			435	248	187		
91st	1969-71	100	58	42			435	243	192		
92d	1971-73	100	54	44	2		435	255	180		
93d	1973-75	100	56	42	2		435	242	192	1	
94th	1975-77	100	61	37	2		435	291	144		
95th	1977-79	100	61	38	1		435	292	143		
96th	1979-81	100	58	41	1		435	277	158		
97th	1981-83	100	46	53	1		435	242	190		3
98th	1983-85	100	46	54			435	269	166		
99th	1985-87	100	47	53			435	253	182		
100th	1987-89	100	54	46			435	258	177		
101st	1989-91	100	57	43			435	262	173		
102nd	1991-93	100	57	43			435	266	164	1	4
103rd	1993-95	100	58	42			435	261	173	1	

(1) Proclamation declaring Alaska a State issued Jan. 3, 1959. (2) Proclamation declaring Hawaii a State issued Aug. 21, 1959.

Congressional Bills Vetoed, 1789-1992

Source: Senate Library; Oct. 6, 1992

	Regular vetoes	Pocket vetoes	Total vetoes	Vetoes over-ridden
Washington	2	—	2	—
John Adams	—	—	—	—
Jefferson	—	—	—	—
Madison	5	2	7	—
Monroe	1	—	1	—
John Q. Adams	—	—	—	—
Jackson	5	7	12	—
Van Buren	—	1	1	—
William Harrison	—	—	—	—
Tyler	6	4	10	1
Polk	2	1	3	—
Taylor	—	—	—	—
Fillmore	—	—	—	—
Pierce	9	—	9	5
Buchanan	4	3	7	—
Lincoln	2	5	7	—
Andrew Johnson	21	8	29	15
Grant	45	48	93	4
Hayes	12	1	13	1
Garfield	—	—	—	—
Arthur	4	8	12	1
Cleveland	304	110	414	2
Benjamin Harrison	19	25	44	1
Cleveland	42	128	170	5
McKinley	6	36	42	—
Theodore Roosevelt	42	40	82	1
Taft	30	9	39	1
Wilson	33	11	44	6
Harding	5	1	6	—
Coolidge	20	30	50	4
Hoover	21	16	37	3
Franklin Roosevelt	372	263	635	9
Truman	180	70	250	12
Eisenhower	73	108	181	2
Kennedy	12	9	21	—
Lyndon Johnson	16	14	30	—
Nixon	26	17	43	7
Ford	48	18	66	12
Carter	13	18	31	2
Reagan	39	39	78	9
Bush[1]	29	5	34	1
Total[1]	**1,467**	**1,056**	**2,504**	**104**

(1) As of May 9, 1992. Excluded from the figures are 2 additional bills, which Pres. Bush claimed to be vetoes but Congress considered enacted into law because the President failed to return them to Congress; the courts will decide the status of these bills.

How a Bill Becomes a Law

1. A Senator or Representative introduces a bill by sending it to the clerk of the House, who assigns it a number and title. This procedure is termed the *first reading*. The clerk then refers the bill to the appropriate Senate or House committee.

2. If the committee opposes the bill, they immediately *table*, or kill it. Otherwise, the committee holds hearings to listen to opinions and facts offered by members and other interested people. The committee then debates the bill and possibly offers amendments. A vote is taken, and if favorable, the bill is sent back to the clerk of the House.

3. The clerk reads the bill to the House. This is termed the *second reading*. Members may then debate the bill and suggest amendments.

4. *The third reading* is simply by title, and the bill is put to a voice or roll call vote.

5. The bill then goes to the other house, where it may be defeated, or passed with or without amendments. If defeated, the bill dies. If passed with amendments, a joint Congressional committee works out the differences and arrives at a compromise.

6. After its final passage by both houses, the bill is sent to the President. If he signs it, the bill becomes a law. However, he may *veto* the bill by refusing to sign it and sending it back to the house where it originated, with his reasons for the veto.

7. The President's objections are then read and debated, and a roll-call vote taken. If the bill receives less than a two-thirds vote, it is defeated. If it receives at least two-thirds, it is sent to the other house. If that house also passes it by at least two-thirds, the President's veto is *overridden*, and the bill becomes a law.

8. If the President wishes neither to sign nor to veto the bill, he may retain it for 10 days—not including Sunday—after which it automatically becomes a law even without his signature. However, if Congress has adjourned within those 10 days, the bill is automatically killed; this indirect rejection is termed a *pocket veto*.

The Race for Governor, 1992

Source: News Election Service; results are preliminary (bold face denotes winner)

State	Democrat	Vote	Republican	Vote
Delaware	**Thomas R. Carper**	179,268	B. Gary Scott	90,747
Indiana	**Evan Bayh**	1,368,317	Linley E. Pearson	814,335
Missouri	**Mel Carnahan**	1,359,384	William L. Webster	958,256
Montana	Dorothy Bradley	197,581	**Marc Racicot**	208,488
New Hampshire	Deborah Arnie Arnesen	205,553	**Steve Merrill**	286,083
North Carolina	**James B. Hunt Jr.**	1,348,778	Jim Gardner	1,105,900
North Dakota	Nicholas Spaeth	119,975	**Edward Schafer**	171,307
Rhode Island	**Bruce Sundlun**	250,323	Elizabeth Ann Leonard	138,881
Utah	Stewart Hanson	176,412	**Mike Leavitt**	320,020
Vermont	**Howard Dean**	202,115	John McClaughry	62,805
Washington	**Mike Lowry**	1,030,084	Ken Eikenberry	913,558
W. Virginia	**Gaston Caperton**	362,111	Cleve Benedict	238,453
*Louisiana	**Edwin Edwards**	1,086,820	David Duke	701,024

* Election on Nov. 16, 1991.

Governors of States and Possessions

(reflecting Nov. 3, 1992 elections, preliminary results)

State	Capital, Zip Code	Governor	Party	Term years	Term expires	Annual salary
Alabama	Montgomery 36130	Guy Hunt	Rep.	4	Jan. 1995	$87,913
Alaska	Juneau 99811	Walter Hickel	Ind.	4	Dec. 1994	81,648
Arizona	Phoenix 85007	Fife Symington	Rep.	4	Jan. 1995	75,000
*Arkansas	Little Rock 72201	Jim Guy Tucker	Dem.	4	Jan. 1995	35,000

(continued)

State	Capital, Zip Code	Governor	Party	Term years	Term expires	Annual salary
California	Sacramento 95814	Pete Wilson	Rep.	4	Jan. 1995	$120,000
Colorado	Denver 80203	Roy Romer	Dem.	4	Jan. 1995	70,000
Connecticut	Hartford 06106	Lowell Weicker	Ind.	4	Jan. 1995	78,000
Delaware	Dover 19901	Tom Carper	Dem.	4	Jan. 1997	80,000
Florida	Tallahassee 32399.	Lawton Chiles	Dem.	4	Jan. 1995	95,000
Georgia	Atlanta 30334	Zell Miller	Dem.	4	Jan. 1995	91,092
Hawaii	Honolulu 96813	John Waihee	Dem.	4	Dec. 1994	94,780
Idaho	Boise 83720	Cecil D. Andrus	Dem.	4	Jan. 1995	75,000
Illinois	Springfield 62706	Jim Edgar	Rep.	4	Jan. 1995	97,370
Indiana	Indianapolis 46204	Evan Bayh	Dem.	4	Jan. 1997	77,200
Iowa	Des Moines 50319	Terry E. Branstad	Rep.	4	Jan. 1995	76,900
Kansas	Topeka 66612	Joan Finney	Dem.	4	Jan. 1995	74,235
Kentucky	Frankfort 40601	Brereton C. Jones	Dem.	4	Dec. 1995	79,255
Louisiana	Baton Rouge 70804	Edwin W. Edwards	Dem.	4	May 1996	73,440
Maine	Augusta 04333	John McKernan Jr.	Rep.	4	Jan. 1995	70,000
Maryland	Annapolis 21401	William Donald Schaefer	Dem.	4	Jan. 1995	120,000
Massachusetts	Boston 02113.	William Weld	Rep.	4	Jan. 1995	75,000
Michigan.	Lansing 48913	John Engler	Rep.	4	Jan. 1995	106,700
Minnesota	St. Paul 55155	Arne Carlson	Rep.	4	Jan. 1995	109,053
Mississippi.	Jackson 39205	Kirk Fordice	Rep.	4	Jan. 1996	75,600
Missouri	Jefferson City 65101	Mel Carnahan	Dem.	4	Jan. 1997	90,312
Montana.	Helena 59620	Marc Racicot	Rep.	4	Jan. 1997	55,502
Nebraska	Lincoln 68509	Ben Nelson	Dem.	4	Jan. 1995	65,000
Nevada	Carson City 89710	Robert Miller	Dem.	4	Jan. 1995	90,000
New Hampshire	Concord 03301	Steve Merrill	Rep.	2	Jan. 1995	79,541
New Jersey	Trenton 08625	James Florio	Dem.	4	Jan. 1994	85,000
New Mexico.	Santa Fe 07503	Bruce King	Dem.	4	Jan. 1995	90,000
New York	Albany 12224.	Mario M. Cuomo	Dem.	4	Jan. 1995	130,000
North Carolina	Raleigh 27603	Jim Hunt Jr.	Dem.	4	Jan. 1997	123,300
North Dakota	Bismarck 58505	Ed Schafer	Rep.	4	Jan. 1997	68,284
Ohio	Columbus 43215.	George Voinovich	Rep.	4	Jan. 1995	100,000
Oklahoma.	Oklahoma City 73105	David Walters	Dem.	4	Jan. 1995	70,000
Oregon	Salem 97310	Barbara Roberts	Dem.	4	Jan. 1995	80,000
Pennsylvania	Harrisburg 17120	Robert Casey	Dem.	4	Jan. 1995	105,000
Rhode Island	Providence 02903	Bruce Sundlun	Dem.	2	Jan. 1995	69,000
South Carolina	Columbia 29201	Carroll A. Campbell Jr.	Rep.	4	Jan. 1995	98,000
South Dakota	Pierre 57501	George S. Mickelson.	Rep.	4	Jan. 1995	63,232
Tennessee	Nashville 37219	Ned Ray McWherter	Dem.	4	Jan. 1995	85,000
Texas	Austin 78711	Ann Richards	Dem.	4	Jan. 1995	93,432
Utah	Salt Lake City 84114	Mike Leavitt	Rep.	4	Jan. 1997	70,000
Vermont	Montpelier 05602	Howard Dean	Dem.	2	Jan. 1995	80,730
Virginia	Richmond 23219	L. Douglas Wilder	Dem.	4	Jan. 1994	108,000
Washington	Olympia 98504	Mike Lowry	Dem.	4	Jan. 1997	96,700
West Virginia	Charleston 25305	Gaston Caperton	Dem.	4	Jan. 1997	72,000
Wisconsin	Madison 53703	Tommy G. Thompson	Rep.	4	Jan. 1995	92,283
Wyoming	Cheyenne 82002	Mike Sullivan	Dem.	4	Jan. 1995	70,000
Puerto Rico	San Juan 00936	Pedro Rossello	Rep.	4	Jan. 1995	—

* Tucker, the Lt. Governor, replaced Bill Clinton.

Mayors and City Managers of Selected U.S. Cities

Reflects Nov. 3, 1992 elections (preliminary results)

* Asterisk before name denotes city manager. All others are mayors. For mayors, dates are those of next election; for city managers, they are dates of appointment.

D, Democrat; R, Republican; N-P, Non-Partisan

City	Name	Term
Abilene, Tex.	Gary McCaleb, N-P	**1993, May**
Abington, Pa.	*Albert Herrmann	**1978, May**
Akron, Oh.	D.L. Plusquellic, D	**1995, Nov.**
Alameda, Cal.	E. William Withrow, R	**1994, Apr.**
Albany, Ga.	*Roy Lane	**1991, Mar.**
Albany, N.Y.	Thomas M. Whalen,3d,D	**1993, Nov.**
Albuquerque, N.M.	Louis Saavedra, N-P	**1993, Oct.**
Alexandria, La.	Edward Randolph Jr., D	**1994, Oct.**
Alexandria, Va.	*Vola Lawson	**1985, Sept.**
Alhambra, Cal.	*Julio Fuentes.	**1992, Aug.**
Allentown, Pa.	Joseph S. Daddona, D	**1993, Nov.**
Amarillo, Tex.	*John Ward	**1983, June**
Ames, Ia.	*Steven L. Schainker	**1982, Oct.**
Anaheim, Cal.	*James Roth	**1990, May**
Anchorage, Alas.	Tom Fink, R	**1994, Apr.**
Anderson, Ind.	J. Mark Lawler, D	**1995, Nov.**
Anderson, S.C.	*Richard Burnette	**1976, Sept.**
Ann Arbor, Mich.	Elizabeth Brater, D	**1993, Apr.**
Appleton, Wis.	Richard De Broux, N-P	**1996, Apr.**
Arcadia, Cal.	*George J. Watts	**1981, Feb.**
Arlington, Mass.	*Donald R. Marquis	**1966, Nov.**
Arlington, Tex.	*George Campbell	**1991, Feb.**
Arlington Hts., Ill.	William Maki, N-P	**1993, Apr.**
Arvada, Col.	*Neal G. Berlin.	**1986, Mar.**
Asheville, N.C.	*Douglas Bean	**1986, Apr.**
Athens, Ga.	Gwen O'Looney, D	**1995, Nov.**
Atlanta, Ga.	Maynard Jackson, D	**1993, Oct.**
Atlantic City, N.J.	Jim Whelan, N-P.	**1994, May**
Augusta, Ga.	Charles Devaney, N-P	**1993, Nov.**
Aurora, Col.	*John Pazour	**1990, May**
Aurora, Ill.	David L. Pierce, N-P.	**1993, Apr.**
Austin, Tex.	*Camille Barnett.	**1989, Mar.**
Bakersfield, Cal.	*J. Dale Hawley	**1988, Jan.**
Baldwin Park, Cal.	*Donald Penman	**1990, Jan.**
Baltimore, Md.	Kurt Schmoke, D	**1995, Nov.**
Baton Rouge, La.	Tom E. McHugh, D	**1996, Oct.**
Battle Creek, Mich.	*Rance L. Leaders	**1988, June**
Bayonne, N.J.	Richard Rutkowski, N-P	**1994, May**
Baytown, Tex.	*Bobby Rountree	**1989, May**
Beaumont, Tex.	*Ray A. Riley	**1989, Feb.**
Belleville, Ill.	Richard Brauer, N-P.	**1993, Apr.**
Belleville, N.J.	Marina Perna, N-P.	**1994, May**
Bellevue, Wash.	*Phillip Kushlan	**1985, Feb.**
Bellingham, Wash.	Tim Douglas, D	**1995, Dec.**

City	Name	Term
Bellflower, Cal.	*Jack Simpson	1980, July
Berkeley, Cal.	*Michael Brown	1990, Jan.
Bethlehem, Pa.	Kenneth Smith, R	1993, Nov.
Beverly Hills, Cal.	*Edward Kreins	1979, Oct.
Billings, Mont.	*Alan Tandy	1985, May
Biloxi, Miss.	Peter Halat, D	1993, June
Binghamton, N.Y.	Juanita M. Crabb, D.	1993, Nov.
Birmingham, Ala.	Richard Arrington Jr., D.	1995, Nov.
Bismarck, N.D.	Bill Sorensen, N-P	1994, Apr.
Bloomfield, N.J.	James Gasparini, D	1993, Nov.
Bloomington, Ill.	Jesse Smart, D	1993, Apr.
Bloomington, Ind.	Tomilea Allison, D	1995, Nov.
Bloomington, Minn.	*Mark Bernhardson	1991, May
Boca Raton, Fla.	Emil Danciu, N-P	1995, Mar.
Boise, Ida.	Dirk Kempthorne, R	1993, Nov.
Bossier City, La	*Lorenz Walker	1992, July
Boston, Mass.	Raymond L. Flynn, D	1995 Nov.
Boulder, Col.	*Stephen Honey	1991, Apr.
Bridgeport, Conn.	Joseph Ganim, D.	1993, Nov.
Bristol, Conn.	William Stortz, D.	1993, Nov.
Brockton, Mass.	William Farwell Jr.	1995, Nov.
Broken Arrow, Okla.	*John Vinson	1991, Aug.
Brooklyn Park, Minn.	*Craig R. Rapp	1989, Nov.
Brownsville, Tex.	*Steve Fitzgibbons	1987, Jan.
Bryan, Tex.	*Michael Conduff	1992, Aug.
Buena Park, Cal.	*Kevin O'Rourke	1985, Nov.
Buffalo, N.Y.	James D. Griffin, D	1993, Nov.
Burbank, Cal.	*Bud Ovrom	1985, June
Burlington, Vt.	Peter Clavelle, N-P	1993, Mar.
Calumet City, Ill.	Robert C. Stefaniak, D	1993, Apr.
Cambridge, Mass.	*Robert Healy	1981, July
Camden, N.J.	Aaron Thompson, D.	1993, May
Canton, Oh.	Richard Watkins, D.	1995, Nov.
Cape Coral, Fla.	*David Sallee	1992, Feb.
Carlsbad, Cal.	*Ray Patchett	1987, Sept.
Carson, Cal.	*Jack Smith	1988, Dec.
Casper, Wyo.	*Thomas Forslund	1988, June
Cedar Rapids, Ia.	Larry Serbousek, N-P.	1993, Nov.
Champaign, Ill.	*Steven C. Carter	1985, Feb.
Chandler, Ariz.	*John Pinch	1989, Jan.
Charleston, S.C.	Joseph P. Riley Jr., D	1995, Nov.
Charleston, W. Va.	Kent S. Hall, R.	1995, Apr.
Charlotte, N.C.	Richard Vinroot, R.	1993, Nov.
Charlottesville, Va.	*Cole Hendrix	1970, Jan.
Chattanooga, Tenn.	Gene Roberts, R	1993, Apr.
Chesapeake, Va.	*James W. Rein	1987, Mar.
Chester, Pa.	Barbara Bohannan-Shepperd, D	1995, Nov.
Cheyenne, Wyo.	Leo Pando, R	1996, Nov.
Chicago, Ill.	Richard M. Daley, D.	1995, Apr.
Chicopee, Mass.	Joseph Chessey, D	1993, Nov.
Chino, Cal.	*Richard Rowe	1985, Feb.
Chula Vista, Cal.	Tim Nader, N-P	1994, Nov.
Cicero, Ill.	Henry Klosak, R	1993, Apr.
Cincinnati, Oh.	*Gerald Newfarmer	1990, Sept.
Clarksville, Tenn.	Don Trotter, N-P.	1994, Nov.
Clearwater, Fla.	*Michael Wright	1991, Mar.
Cleveland, Oh.	Michael White, D	1993, Nov.
Cleveland Hgts., Oh.	*Robert Downey	1985, Jan.
Clifton, N.J.	*Roger Kemp	1987, Nov.
Col. Spgs., Col.	*Richard Zickefoose	1990, May
Columbia, Mo.	*Raymond A. Beck	1985, Aug.
Columbia, S.C.	*Miles Hadley	1989, Dec.
Columbus, Ga.	Frank Martin, D	1994, Nov.
Columbus, Oh.	Gregory Lashutka, R	1995, Nov.
Commerce, Cal.	*Robert Hinderliter	1973, Aug.
Compton, Cal.	*Howard Caldwell	1989, June
Concord, Cal.	*Rita Hardin	1990, June
Coon Rapids., Minn.	*Robert Svehla	1991, June
Coral Gables, Fla.	*H.C. Eads Jr.	1988, May
Corona, Cal.	*William Garrett	1989, Dec.
Corpus Christi, Tex.	*Juan Garza	1988, Apr.
Costa Mesa, Cal.	*Allan L. Roeder	1985, Oct.
Council Bluffs, Ia.	Tom Hanafan, N-P	1993, Nov.
Covington, Ky.	*Greg Jarvis	1989, Nov.
Cranston, R.I.	Michael Traficante, R	1994, Nov.
Crystal, Minn.	*John Irving	1963, Jan.
Culver City, Cal.	*Dale Jones	1967, Sept.
Cuyahoga Falls, Oh.	Don L. Robart, R	1993, Nov.
Dallas, Tex.	*Jan Hart	1990, Apr.
Daly City, Cal.	*David R. Rowe	1969, Sept.
Danbury, Conn.	Gene Eriquez, N-P	1993, Nov.
Danville, Va.	*A. Ray Griffin Jr.	1992, Mar.
Davenport, Ia.	*Charles Mallory	1989, Jan.
Davis, Cal.	*John Meyer	1990, Oct.
Dayton, Oh.	Richard Clay Dixon, D	1993, Nov.
Daytona Bch., Fla.	*Howard D. Tipton	1978, Oct.
Dearborn , Mich.	Michael Guido, N-P	1993, Nov.
Dearborn Hts., Mich.	Lyle Van Houton, R	1993, Nov.
Decatur, Ill.	*James Bacon Jr.	1988, Oct.
Delray Beach, Fla.	*David Handen	1990, May
Denton, Tex.	*Larry Harrell	1986, Feb.
Denver, Col.	Wellington Webb, D.	1995, Apr.
Des Moines, Ia.	John Dorrian, D	1993, Nov.
Des Plaines, Ill.	Michael Albrecht, N-P.	1993, Apr.
Detroit, Mich.	Coleman A. Young, N-P	1993, Nov.
Dotham, Ala.	*Don J. Marnon	1987, May
Downey, Cal.	*Gerald Caton	1989, Oct.
Dubuque, Ia.	*W. Kenneth Gearhart	1979, Aug.
Duluth, Minn.	John Fedo, N-P	1995, Nov.
Durham, N.C.	*Orville Powell	1983, Mar.
E. Chicago, Ind.	Robert A. Pastrick, D	1995, Nov.
E. Hartford, Conn.	Susan Kniep, R	1993, Nov.
E. Lansing, Mich.	Liz Schweitzer, N-P	1993, Nov.
E. Orange, N.J.	Cardell Cooper, D.	1993, Nov.
Eau Claire, Wis.	*Eric Anderson	1984, Jan.
Edina, Minn.	*Kenneth Rosland	1977, Nov.
Edison, N.J.	Thomas Paterniti, D	1993, Nov.
Edmond, Okla.	*C. Max Speegle	1987, Sept.
El Cajon, Cal.	Joan Shoemaker, N-P	1994, June
El Monte, Cal.	Patricia Wallach, D	1994, Apr.
El Paso, Tex.	William Tilney, D.	1993, May
Elgin, Ill.	*Larry L. Rice	1989, Oct.
Elizabeth, N.J.	J.C. Bollwage, D.	1996, Nov.
Elkhart, Ind.	James Perron, D	1995, Nov.
Elyria, Oh.	Michael Keys, D	1995, Nov.
Enfield, Conn.	*Robert J. Mulready	1983, Feb.
Enid, Okla.	*Jim Ferree	1990, May
Erie, Pa.	Joyce Savocchio, D	1993, Nov.
Escondido, Cal.	*Douglas Clark	1989, June
Euclid, Oh.	David Lynch, R	1995, Nov.
Eugene, Ore.	*Michael Gleason	1981, Jan.
Evanston, Ill.	*Eric Anderson	1991, June
Evansville, Ind.	Frank McDonald, D	1995, Nov.
Everett, Mass.	John McCarthy, D.	1993, Nov.
Everett, Wash.	Pete Kinch, N-P	1993, Nov.
Fairfield, Cal.	*Charles Long	1988, Sept.
Fall River, Mass.	John Mitchell, D	1993, Nov.
Fargo, N.D.	Jon Lindgren, D	1994, Apr.
Farmington Hills, Mich.	*William M. Costick	1981, Jan.
Fayetteville, N.C.	*John P. Smith	1981, Jan.
Fitchburg, Mass.	Jeffrey Bean, D	1993, Nov.
Flagstaff, Ariz.	*David Wilcox	1992, July
Flint, Mich.	Woodrow Stanley, N-P	1995, Nov.
Florissant, Mo.	James J. Eagan, N-P	1995, Apr.
Fontana, Cal.	Gary Boyles, N-P	1994, Nov.
Ft. Collins, Col.	*Steven Burkett	1986, Apr.
Ft. Lauderdale, Fla.	*George Hanbury 2d	1990, Apr.
Ft. Smith, Ark.	Ray Baker, N-P	1994, Dec.
Ft. Wayne, Ind.	Paul Helmke, R	1995, Nov.
Ft. Worth, Tex.	Kay Granger, N-P	1993, May
Fountain Valley, Cal.	*Judy Kelsey	1984, May
Fremont, Cal.	*Charles Kent McClain	1981, May
Fresno, Cal.	*Michael Bierman	1990, Nov.
Fullerton, Cal.	*William C. Winter	1979, Oct.
Gadsden, Ala.	David Nolen, D.	1994, July
Gainesville, Fla.	*W.D. Higginbotham Jr.	1984, Sept.
Galveston, Tex.	*Douglas W. Matthews	1985, Mar.
Gardena, Cal.	*Kenneth Landau	1985, Apr.
Garden Grove, Cal.	*George Tindall	1988, June
Garland, Tex.	*James K. Spore	1985, Mar.
Gary, Ind.	Thomas Barnes, D	1995, Nov.
Gastonia, N.C.	*Gary Hicks	1973, Dec.
Glendale, Ariz.	*Martin Vanacour	1985, Mar.
Glendale, Cal.	*David Ramsay	1988, May
Grand Forks, N.D.	Michael Polovitz, D	1996, Apr.
Gr. Rapids, Mich.	*Kurt Kimball	1987, Apr.
Greeley, Col.	William Morton, N-P.	1993, Nov.
Green Bay, Wis.	Samuel Halloin, N-P.	1995, Apr.
Greenville, S.C.	*Aubrey Watts	1992, Jan.
Greenwich, Conn.	John Margenot, D, first selectman	1993, Nov.
Groton, Conn.	Catherine Kolnaski, D.	1995, May
Gulfport, Miss.	Ken Combs, R	1993, Apr.
Hamden, Conn.	Lillian Clayman, D	1993, Nov.
Hamilton, Oh.	*Hal Shepherd	1989, Apr.
Hammond, Ind.	Thomas McDermott, R	1995, Nov.
Hampton, Va.	James Eason, N-P	1996, May
Harlingen, Tex.	*Mike Perez	1989, July
Harrisburg, Pa.	Stephen Reed, D	1993, Nov.
Hartford, Conn.	Carrie Saxon Perry, D	1993, Nov.
Haverhill, Mass.	Theodore Pelosi, R	1993, Nov.
Hawthorne, Cal.	*James Mitsch	1990, Dec.
Hayward, Cal.	Michael Sweeney, D	1994, Apr.
Henderson, Nev.	Lorna Kesterson, D	1993, June

City	Name	Term
Hesperia, Cal.	*D.J. Collins	**1992, May**
High Point, N.C.	*H. Lewis Price	**1983, July**
Hollywood, Fla.	*Robert S. Noe Jr.	**1991, Nov.**
Holyoke, Mass.	William Hamilton, R	**1993, Nov.**
Honolulu, Ha.	Frank Fasi, R	**1993, Nov.**
Houston, Tex.	Bob Lanier, N-P	**1993, Nov.**
Huntington, W. Va.	Robert Nelson, D	**1993, June**
Huntington Beach, Cal.	*Michael Ubervaga	**1990, Feb.**
Huntington Park, Cal.	Paul Perez, R	**1993, Apr.**
Huntsville, Ala.	Steve Hettinger, N-P	**1996, Sept.**
Idaho Falls, Ida.	Thomas Campbell, N-P	**1993, Nov.**
Independence, Mo.	*L.C. Kaufman	**1990, Aug.**
Indianapolis, Ind.	Steve Goldsmith, R	**1995, Nov.**
Inglewood, Cal.	*Paul Eckles	**1975, Nov.**
Iowa City, Ia.	*Stephen Atkins	**1986, July**
Irving, Tex.	*Jack Huffman	**1974, Jan.**
Irvington, N.J.	Michael Steele, D	**1994, May**
Jackson, Mich.	*William P. Buchanan	**1985, Nov.**
Jackson, Miss.	Kane Ditto, D.	**1993, May**
Jacksonville, Fla.	Ed Austin, D	**1995, May**
Janesville, Wis.	*Steven Sheiffer	**1987, May**
Jersey City, N.J.	Bret Schundler, R	**1993, May**
Johnson City, Tenn.	*John G. Campbell	**1984, June**
Joliet, Ill.	*John M. Mezera	**1987, Jan.**
Kalamazoo, Mich.	*James Holgersson	**1989, June**
Kansas City, Kan.	*David Isabell	**1985, June**
Kansas City, Mo.	Emanuel Cleaver, D.	**1995, Apr.**
Kenner, La.	Aaron Broussard, N-P	**1994, June**
Kenosha, Wis.	John Antaramian, D	**1996, Apr.**
Kettering, Oh.	Richard Hartmann, R	**1993, Nov.**
Killeen, Tex.	*Daniel Hobbs	**1990, Jan.**
Knoxville, Tenn.	Victor Ashe, R	**1995, Nov.**
Kokomo, Ind.	Robert Sargent, D.	**1995, Nov.**
LaCrosse, Wis.	Patrick Zielke, N-P	**1993, Apr.**
La Habra, Cal.	*Lee Risner	**1970, Nov.**
La Mesa, Cal.	*David Wear	**1990, Apr.**
La Mirada, Cal.	*Gary K. Sloan	**1981, Apr.**
Lafayette, Ind.	James Riehle, D.	**1995, Nov.**
Lafayette, La.	Kenneth Bowen, D	**1996, Mar.**
Lake Charles, La.	James Sudduth, D.	**1993, Apr.**
Lakeland, Fla.	*E.S. Strickland	**1986, Feb.**
Lakewood, Cal.	*Howard L. Chambers	**1976, June**
Lakewood, Col.	*Jim Zelenski, act.	**1992, June**
Lakewood, Oh.	David Harbarger, R	**1995, Nov.**
Lancaster, Pa.	Janice Stork, D	**1993, Nov.**
Lansing, Mich.	Terry John McKane, N-P	**1993, Nov.**
Laredo, Tex.	*Marvin Townsend	**1982, June**
Largo, Fla.	*Stephen Bonczek	**1988, July**
Las Cruces, N.M.	Ruben A. Smith, N-P	**1995, Nov.**
Las Vegas, Nev.	Jan Laverty Jones, N-P	**1995, June**
Lauderhill, Fla.	Ilene Lieberman, D	**1996, Mar.**
Lawrence, Kan.	*Mike Wildgen	**1990, Apr.**
Lawrence, Mass.	Kevin Sullivan, N-P	**1993, Nov.**
Lawton, Okla.	*Robert Hopkins	**1990, Jan.**
Lexington, Ky.	Scotty Baesler, N-P	**1993, Nov.**
Lima, Oh.	David Berger, N-P	**1993, Nov.**
Lincoln, Neb.	Mike Johanns, R.	**1995, May**
Little Rock, Ark.	*Thomas Dalton	**1986, June**
Livermore, Cal.	*Leland Horner	**1978, Oct.**
Livonia, Mich.	Robert Bennett, N-P	**1995, Nov.**
Long Beach, Cal.	*James Hankla	**1987, Mar.**
Longmont,Col.	*Geoff Dolan	**1987, Jan.**
Longview, Tex.	*James Baugh	**1989, Oct.**
Lorain, Oh.	Alex Olejko, D	**1995, Nov.**
Los Angeles, Cal.	Thomas Bradley, N-P	**1993, June**
Louisville, Ky.	Jerry Abramson, D	**1993, Nov.**
Lowell, Mass.	*James Campbell	**1987, Jan.**
L. Merion, Pa.	*Thomas B. Fulweiler	**1968, Jan.**
Lubbock, Tex.	*Larry Cunningham	**1976, Sept.**
Lynchburg, Va.	*Charles Church	**1991, Oct.**
Lynn, Mass.	Patrick McManus, D.	**1993, Nov.**
Lynwood, Cal.	*Faustin Gonzales	**1992, May**
Macon, Ga.	Tommy Olmstead, D	**1995, Nov.**
Madison, Wis.	Paul Soglin, R	**1995, Apr.**
Malden, Mass.	Edwin C. Lucey,	**1993, Nov.**
Manchester, Conn.	*Richard Sartor	**1989, June**
Manchester, N.H.	Ray Wieczorek, R.	**1993, Nov.**
Marietta, Ga.	Joe Mack Wilson, D.	**1993, Nov.**
McAllen, Tex.	Othal Brand, R.	**1993, Apr.**
Medford, Mass.	Michael McGlynn, D.	**1993, Nov.**
Medford, Ore.	*Harold Anderson	**1987, Sept.**
Melbourne, Fla.	*Samuel Halter	**1978, July**
Memphis, Tenn.	W.W. Herenton, N-P	**1995, Oct.**
Mentor, Oh.	*Julian Suso	**1990, Mar.**
Merced, Cal.	*James Marshall	**1992, Apr.**
Meriden, Conn.	*Michael Aldi	**1988, Mar.**
Meridian, Miss.	Jimmy Kemp, R	**1993, June**
Mesa, Ariz.	*C.K. Luster	**1979, June**
Mesquite, Tex.	*James Prugel	**1987, Dec.**
Miami, Fla.	Xavier Suarez, N-P	**1993, Nov.**
Miami Beach, Fla.	*Roger Carlton	**1992**
Middletown, Oh.	*William Klosterman	**1988, July**
Midland, Tex.	J.D. Faircloth, R.	**1994, May**
Midwest City, Okla.	*Charles Johnson	**1984, Nov.**
Milford, Conn.	Frederick Lisman, R.	**1993, Nov.**
Milwaukee, Wis.	John Norquist, D.	**1996, Apr.**
Minneapolis, Minn.	Donald Fraser, D	**1993, Nov.**
Minnetonka, Minn.	*James F. Miller	**1980, Jan.**
Mobile, Ala.	Michael Dow, N-P	**1993, Aug.**
Modesto, Cal.	*J. Edward Tewes	**1991, Mar.**
Monroe, La.	Robert Powell, D	**1996, Apr.**
Montclair, N.J.	*Bertrand Kendall	**1980, Sept.**
Montebello, Cal.	*Richard Torres	**1989, May**
Monterey Park, Cal.	*Mark Lewis	**1988, July**
Montgomery, Ala.	Emory Folmar, R	**1995, Nov.**
Mt. Prospect, Ill.	*Michael Janonis	**1992, July**
Mt. Vernon, N.Y.	Roland Blackwood, D.	**1995, Nov.**
Mountain View, Cal.	*Bruce Liedstrand	**1976, June**
Muncie, Ind.	David M. Dominick, R	**1995, Nov.**
Muskogee, Okla.	*Walter Beckham	**1984, Feb.**
Napa, Cal.	Ed Solomon, R.	**1996, June**
Naperville, Ill.	Samuel McCrane, N-P	**1995, Apr.**
Nashua, N.H.	Rob Wagner, D	**1995, Nov.**
Nashville, Tenn.	Philip Bredesen, D.	**1995, Aug.**
National City, Cal.	*Tom McCabe	**1979, Mar.**
New Britain, Conn.	Donald DeFronzo, D	**1993, Nov.**
New Haven, Conn.	John Daniels, D	**1993, Nov.**
New London, Conn.	*C.F. Driscoll	**1969, May**
New Orleans, La.	Sidney Barthelemy, D.	**1994, Mar.**
New Rochelle, N.Y.	*C. Samuel Kissinger	**1975, Apr.**
New York, N.Y.	David Dinkins, D	**1993, Nov.**
Newark, N.J.	Sharpe James, D	**1994, May**
Newport, R.I.	*Francis Edwards	**1987, Jan.**
Newport Beach, Cal.	*Kevin Murphy	**1992, Mar.**
Newport News, Va.	*Ed Maroney	**1987, Jan.**
Newton, Mass.	Theodore Mann, R	**1993, Nov.**
Niagara Falls, N.Y.	Jacob A. Palillo, R.	**1995, Nov.**
Norfolk, Va.	*James B. Oliver Jr.	**1987, Jan.**
Norman, Okla.	Bill Nations, N-P	**1995, Mar.**
North Charleston, S.C.	Bobby Kinard, R	**1995, May**
North Las Vegas	*Michael Dyal	**1982, May**
No. Little Rock, Ark.	Patrick Hayes, D	**1996, Nov.**
Norwalk, Cal.	*Richard Powers	**1988, July**
Norwalk, Conn.	Frank Esposito, R	**1993, Nov.**
Novato, Cal.	*Rod Wood	**1992, July**
Oak Park, Ill.	*J.N. Nielsen	**1986, July**
Oak Ridge, Tenn.	*Jeffrey J. Broughton	**1986, Sept.**
Oakland, Cal.	*Henry L. Gardner	**1981, June**
Oceanside, Cal.	*James Turner	**1990, Aug.**
Odessa, Tex.	*Jerry McGuire	**1992, Mar.**
Ogden, Ut.	Glenn Mecham, N-P	**1995, Nov.**
Oklahoma City, Okla.	*Paula Hearn	**1989, Oct.**
Omaha, Neb.	P.J. Morgan, R.	**1993, May**
Ontario, Cal.	*Roger Hughbanks, N-P	**1975, July**
Orange, Cal.	*Ron Thompson,	**1989, Apr.**
Orlando, Fla.	Glenda E. Hood, N-P	**1996, Sept.**
Oshkosh, Wis.	*William Frueh	**1976, Aug.**
Overland Park, Kan.	*Donald Pipes	**1977, June**
Owensboro, Ky.	*Max Rhoads	**1959, Sept.**
Oxnard, Cal.	*Vernon Hazen	**1990, Aug.**
Pacifica, Cal.	*Daniel Pincetich	**1985, Dec.**
Palm Springs, Cal.	*Dallas Flicek	**1990, Aug.**
Palo Alto, Cal.	*William Zaner	**1979, Sept.**
Parma, Oh.	Michael Ries, D	**1995, Nov.**
Pasadena, Cal.	*Philip Hawkey	**1990, June**
Pasadena, Tex.	John Ray Harrison, D.	**1993, May**
Passaic, N.J.	Joseph Lipari, D	**1993, June**
Paterson, N.J.	William Pascrell, D	**1994, May**
Pawtucket, R.I.	Robert Metivier, D.	**1993, Nov.**
Peabody, Mass.	Peter Torigian, D	**1993, Nov.**
Pembroke Pines, Fla.	*Charles Dodge	**1989, Aug.**
Pensacola, Fla.	*Rodney Kendig	**1986, June**
Peoria, Ill.	*Thomas Mikulecky	**1987, July**
Petersburg, Va.	*Richard M. Brown	**1984, Oct.**
Philadelphia, Pa.	Edward Rendell, D	**1995, Nov.**
Phoenix, Ariz.	*Frank Fairbanks	**1990, Apr.**
Pico Rivera, Cal.	*Dennis Courtemarche	**1984, Nov.**
Pine Bluff, Ark	Undecided	**1996, Nov.**
Pittsburgh, Pa.	Sophie Masloff, D	**1993, Nov.**
Pittsfield, Mass.	Edward Reilly, N-P	**1995, Nov.**
Plainfield, N.J.	*Jewel Thompson-Chin.	**1990, Sept.**
Plano, Tex.	*Thomas Muehlenbeck	**1987, Dec.**
Pocatello, Ida.	Peter Angstadt, N-P	**1993, Nov.**
Pomona, Cal.	*Lloyd Wood	**1992, Aug.**
Pompano Beach, Fla.	*Roy Stype	**1989, Oct.**

City	Name	Term
Pontiac, Mich.	Wallace Holland, R	1993, Nov.
Port Arthur, Tex.	*Mary Ellen Summerlin, D	1995, May
Portland, Me.	*Robert Ganley	1986, Sept.
Portland, Ore.	Vera Katz, D	1996, Nov.
Portsmouth, Oh.	Franklin Gerlach, N-P	1993, Nov.
Portsmouth, Va.	*V. Wayne Orton	1990, June
Poughkeepsie, N.Y.	*William J. Theysohn	1982, Mar.
Providence, R.I.	Vincent Cianci Jr., N-P	1994, Nov.
Provo, Ut.	Joseph Jenkins, R.	1993, Nov.
Pueblo, Col.	*Lewis A. Quigley	1987, Jan.
Quincy, Ill.	Verne Hagstorm, D	1993, Apr.
Quincy, Mass.	James Sheets, D	1993, Nov.
Racine, Wis.	N. Owen Davies, N-P	1995, Apr.
Raleigh, N.C.	*Dempsey Benton	1983, Dec.
Rancho Palos Verdes, Cal.	*Paul Bussey	1990, June
Rapid City, S.D.	Edward McLaughlin, R	1993, May
Reading, Pa.	Warren Haggerty Jr., D	1995, Nov.
Redding, Cal.	*Robert Christofferson	1987, Jan.
Redlands, Cal.	*James Wheaton	1991, Mar.
Redondo Beach, Cal.	*William Kirchhoff	1991, Feb.
Redwood City, Cal.	*James M. Smith	1982, Feb.
Reno, Nev.	*Clay Holstine	1991, May
Rialto, Cal.	*Gerald Johnson	1988, July
Richardson, Tex.	*Bob Hughey	1974, Jan.
Richmond, Cal.	*Larry Moore	1987, Aug.
Richmond, Va.	*Robert C. Bobb	1986, July
Riverside, Cal.	*John E. Holmes	1990, Oct.
Roanoke, Va.	David Bowers, D	1996, June
Rochester, Minn.	*Steven Kvenvold	1979, June
Rochester, N.Y.	Thomas Ryan Jr., D.	1993, Nov.
Rochester Hills, Mich.	Billie Ireland, R.	1995, Nov.
Rock Hill, S.C.	*Joe Lanford	1979, July
Rock Island, Ill.	*John Phillips	1986, Nov.
Rockford, Ill.	Charles Box, D	1993, Apr.
Rockville, Md.	*Bruce Romer	1988, Sept.
Rome, N.Y.	Joseph Griffo, R	1995, Nov.
Roseville, Mich.	Jeanne Riesterer, N-P	1993, Nov.
Roswell, N.M.	*John Capps	1992, July
Royal Oak, Mich.	*William Baldridge	1975, Sept.
Sacramento, Cal.	*Walter Slipe	1976, Mar.
Saginaw, Mich.	*J. Marvin Baldwin	1991, June
St. Clair Shores, Mich.	*Mark Wollenweber	1990, Jan.
St. Cloud, Minn.	Charles Winkleman, N-P	1993, Nov.
St. Joseph, Mo.	Glenda Kelly, N-P	1994, Apr.
St. Louis, Mo.	Vincent Schoemehl, D	1993, Apr.
St. Louis Park, Minn.	*William C. Dixon	1988, Oct.
St. Paul, Minn.	James Scheibel, N-P	1993, Nov.
St. Petersburg, Fla.	*Norman Hickey	1992, May
Salem, Ore.	*Gary Eide	1988, Jan.
Salina, Kan.	*Dennis Kissinger	1988, Jan.
Salinas, Cal.	*Roy Herte	1988, Sept.
Salt Lake City, Ut.	Deedee Corradini, N-P	1995, Nov.
San Angelo, Tex.	*Alex Briseno	1990, Apr.
San Antonio, Tex.	Nelson Wolff, N-P	1995, Apr.
San Bernardino, Cal.	Bob Holcomb, D.	1993, Mar.
San Bruno, Cal.	*Lew Pond	1990, May
San Diego, Cal.	Susan Golding, N-P	1996, Nov.
San Francisco, Cal.	Frank Jordan, N-P	1995, Nov.
San Jose, Cal.	*Leslie White	1989, May
San Leandro, Cal.	*Richard H. Randall	1986, July
San Mateo, Cal.	*Arne Croce	1990, Mar.
San Rafael, Cal.	*Pamela Nicolai	1985, Dec.
Sandy, Ut.	Larry Smith, R	1993, Nov.
Santa Ana, Cal.	*David Ream	1986, July
Santa Barbara, Cal.	*Richard Thomas	1977, Jan.
Santa Clara, Cal.	*Jennifer Sparacino	1987, Mar.
Santa Cruz, Cal.	*Richard Wilson	1981, June
Santa Fe, N.M.	Sam Pick, D	1994, Mar.
Santa Maria, Cal.	*Wayne Schwammel	1989, June
Santa Monica, Cal.	*John Jalili	1984, Dec.
Santa Rosa, Cal.	*Kenneth Blackman	1970, July
Sarasota, Fla.	*David Sollenberger	1987, July
Savannah, Ga.	*Arthur A. Mendonsa	1962, July
Schenectady, N.Y.	Frank Duci, R	1995, Nov.
Scottsdale, Ariz.	Herbert Drinkwater, N-P	1996, Apr.
Scranton, Pa.	James Connors, R	1993, Nov.
Seattle, Wash.	Norman Rice, D	1993, Nov.
Sheboygan, Wis.	Richard Schneider, N-P	1993, Apr.
Shreveport, La.	Hazel Beard, R	1994, Nov.
Simi Valley, Cal.	*M.L. Koester	1979, Sept.
Sioux City, Ia.	Robert Scott, D	1993, Nov.
Sioux Falls, S.D.	Jack White, R	1996, June
Skokie, Ill.	*Albert Rigoni	1987, Jan.
Somerville, Mass.	Michael Capuano, D	1993, Nov.

City	Name	Term
South Bend, Ind.	Joseph Kernan, D	1995, Nov.
Southfield, Mich.	*Robert Block	1985, Jan.
Sparks, Nev.	*Patricia Thompson	1983, Sept.
Spartanburg, S.C.	*Wayne Bowers	1984, Sept.
Spokane, Wash.	*Roger Crum	1992, Sept.
Springfield, Ill.	Ossie Langfelder, D.	1995, Apr.
Springfield, Mass	Robert Markel, N-P	1993, Nov.
Springfield, Mo.	*Thomas Finnie	1990, Apr.
Springfield, Oh.	*Matthew Kridler	1988, Oct.
Stamford, Conn.	Stanley Esposito, R	1993, Nov.
Sterling Hts., Mich.	*Steve Duchane	1987, Nov.
Stockton, Cal.	*Dwane Milnes	1991, Oct.
Stratford, Conn.	*Ronald Owens	1984, July
Sunnyvale, Cal.	*Thomas Lewcock	1980, Apr.
Suffolk, Va.	*Richard-Hedrick	1991, July
Sunrise, Fla.	*Patrick Salerno	1990, Dec.
Syracuse, N.Y.	Thomas G. Young, D	1993, Nov.
Tacoma, Wash.	*Ray Corpuz Jr.	1990, Jan.
Tallahassee, Fla.	*Daniel A. Kleman	1974, Aug.
Tampa, Fla.	Sandra Freedman, N-P	1995, Mar.
Taunton, Mass.	Robert Nunes, D	1993, Nov.
Taylor, Mich.	Cameron Priebe, D	1993, Nov.
Tempe, Ariz.	Harry E. Mitchell, D	1994, July
Temple, Tex.	*David Taylor	1991, Dec.
Terre Haute, Ind.	P. Pete Chalos, D	1995, Nov.
Thornton, Col.	*Jack Ethredge	1985, Jan.
Thousand Oaks, Cal.	*Grant Brimhall	1978, Jan.
Titusville, Fla.	*Norman Hickey	1974, June
Toledo, Oh.	*Thomas Hoover	1990, Sept.
Topeka, Kan.	Butch Felker, R	1993, Apr.
Torrance, Cal.	*Leroy J. Jackson	1983, Jan.
Trenton, N.J.	Douglas Palmer, N-P	1994, May
Troy, Mich.	*Frank Gerstenecker	1970, Feb
Troy, N.Y.	*Steven Dworsky	1986, July
Tucson, Ariz.	George Miller, D.	1995, Nov.
Tulsa, Okla.	Rodger Randle, D	1994, Apr.
Tuscaloosa, Ala.	Alvin DuPont, D	1993, Oct.
Tyler, Tex.	*Gary Gwyn	1982, Nov.
Union City, N.J.	Robert Menendez, D	1994, May
Univ. City, Mo.	*Frank Ollendorff	1980, Mar.
Upland, Cal.	*Ray Silver	1988, Dec.
Utica, N.Y.	Louis La Polla, R	1995, Nov.
Vallejo, Cal.	*Edward Wohlenberg	1989, Apr.
Vancouver, Wash.	*Thomas Fischbach	1990, Aug.
Ventura, Cal.	*John Baker	1986, Nov.
Vineland, N.J.	Joseph Romano, R	1996, May
Virginia Beach, Va.	*James Spore	1991, Nov.
Waco, Tex.	*John Harrison	1977, Sept.
Walnut Creek, Cal.	*Donald Blubaugh	1988, Apr.
Waltham, Mass.	William Stanley, D	1995, Nov.
Warner Robins, Ga.	Ed Martin, D	1996, Oct.
Warren, Mich.	Ronald Bonkowski, N-P	1995, Nov.
Warren, Oh.	Daniel Sferra, D	1995, Nov.
Warwick, R.I.	Kathryn O'Hare, D	1996, Nov.
Wash, D.C.	Sharon Dixon, D	1994, Nov.
Waterloo, Ia.	Albert Manning Jr., R	1993, Nov.
Waukegan, Ill.	Haig Paravonian, R	1993, Apr.
Waukesha, Wis.	Paul Vrakas, N-P	1994, Apr.
Wauwatosa, Wis.	Maricolette Walsh, N-P	1996, Apr.
W. Allis, Wis.	Joyce Ann Radtke, N-P	1996, Apr.
W. Covina, Cal.	*Herman Fast	1976, Aug.
W. Hartford, Conn.	Sandy Klebanoff, D	1993, Nov.
W. Haven, Conn.	H. Richard Borer, D	1993, Nov.
W. Palm Beach, Fla.	*Paul Steinbrenner	1986, Jan.
Westland, Mich.	Robert Thomas, D.	1993, Nov.
Westminster, Cal.	*Jerry Kenny	1989, Jan.
Westminster, Col.	*William Christopher	1978, May
Wheaton, Ill.	*Donald Rose	1980, Nov.
White Plains, N.Y.	Alfred Del Vecchio, R	1993, Nov.
Whittier, Cal.	*Thomas Mauk	1980, Oct.
Wichita, Kan.	*Chris Cherches	1985, Oct.
Wichita Falls, Tex.	*James Berzina	1983, June
Wilkes-Barre, Pa.	Lee Namey, D	1995, Nov.
Wilmington, Del.	Jim Sills, D	1996, Nov.
Wilmington, N.C.	*William B. Farris	1983, May
Winston-Salem, N.C.	*Bryce A. Stuart	1980, Jan.
Woodbridge, N.J.	James McGreevey, D.	1995, Nov.
Woonsocket, R.I.	Francis Lanctot, D.	1993, Nov.
Worcester, Mass.	*William Mulford	1985, Nov.
Wyandotte, Mich.	James R. DeSana, D	1995, Apr.
Wyoming, Mich.	*Donald Mason	1991, July
Yakima, Wash.	Pat Berndt, N-P	1995, Nov.
Yonkers, N.Y.	Terence Zaleski	1995, Nov.
York, Pa.	William Althaus, R.	1993, Nov.
Youngstown, Oh.	Patrick Ungaro, D	1993, Nov.
Yuma, Ariz.	Robert Tippert, R	1993, Nov.

AGRICULTURE

Farms—Number and Acreage by State, 1980 & 1991

Source: Natl. Agricultural Statistics Service: U.S. Dept. of Agriculture

State	Farms (1,000) 1980	Farms (1,000) 1991	Acreage (mil.) 1980	Acreage (mil.) 1991	Acreage per Farm 1980	Acreage per Farm 1991
U.S.	**2,437**	**2,105**	**1,039**	**983**	**426**	**467**
Alabama	59	46	12	10	207	215
Alaska	(z)	1	2	1	3,378	1,750
Arizona	7	8	38	36	5,080	4,500
Arkansas	58	46	17	16	280	337
California	79	83	34	30	417	365
Colorado	26	26	36	33	1,358	1,262
Connecticut	4	4	(z)	(z)	117	108
Delaware	4	3	1	1	186	197
Florida	38	40	13	11	344	263
Georgia	59	46	15	12	254	263
Hawaii	4	5	2	2	458	372
Idaho	24	21	15	14	623	631
Illinois	108	82	29	29	269	348
Indiana	88	65	17	16	193	246
Iowa	121	102	34	34	284	328
Kansas	75	69	48	48	644	694
Kentucky	103	91	15	14	143	155
Louisiana	37	30	10	9	273	293
Maine	8	7	2	1	195	200
Maryland	17	15	3	2	157	146
Massachusetts	6	7	1	1	116	99
Michigan	66	54	11	11	175	200
Minnesota	104	88	30	30	291	341
Mississippi	56	38	15	13	265	337
Missouri	121	107	31	30	261	284
Montana	24	25	62	60	2,601	2,441
Nebraska	65	56	48	47	734	841
Nevada	3	3	9	9	3,100	3,560
New Hampshire	3	3	1	(z)	160	166
New Jersey	10	8	1	1	109	106
New Mexico	13	14	47	44	3,467	3,281
New York	48	38	9	8	200	218
North Carolina	92	60	12	10	126	160
North Dakota	41	33	42	40	1,043	1,224
Ohio	96	80	16	16	171	196
Oklahoma	72	70	35	33	481	471
Oregon	34	37	18	18	517	481
Pennsylvania	61	53	9	8	145	153
Rhode Island	1	1	(z)	(z)	87	94
South Carolina	35	25	6	5	188	212
South Dakota	39	35	45	44	1,169	1,263
Tennessee	96	87	14	12	142	143
Texas	192	185	138	131	715	708
Utah	13	13	12	11	919	850
Vermont	7	7	2	2	226	219
Virginia	59	45	10	9	169	196
Washington	37	37	16	16	429	432
West Virginia	20	20	4	4	191	185
Wisconsin	94	79	19	18	200	222
Wyoming	9	9	35	35	3,846	3,867

(z) Less than 500 farms or 500,000 acres

Livestock on Farms in the U.S.

Source: Natl. Agricultural Statistics Service: U.S. Dept. of Agriculture (in thousands)

Year (On Jan. 1)	All cattle	Milk cows	All sheep	Hogs[3]
1890	60,014	15,000	44,518	48,130
1900	59,739	16,544	48,105	51,055
1910	58,993	19,450	50,239	48,072
1920	70,400	21,455	40,743	60,159
1925	63,373	22,575	38,543	55,770
1930	61,003	23,032	51,565	55,705
1935	68,846	26,082	51,808	39,066
1940	68,309	24,940	52,107	61,165
1945	85,573	27,770	46,520	59,373
1950	77,963	23,853	29,826	58,937
1955	96,592	23,462	31,582	50,474
1960	96,236	19,527	33,170	59,026
1965	109,000	16,981[2]	25,127	56,106
1970	112,369	12,091	20,423	57,046
1975	132,028	11,220	14,515	54,693
1980	111,242	10,758	12,699	67,318
1985	109,582	10,777	10,716	54,073
1990	98,162	10,153	11,363	53,821
1991	98,896	10,156	11,200	54,472
1992[1]	100,110	9,904	10,850	57,684

(1) Total estimated value on farms as of Jan. 1, 1992, was (avg. value per head in parentheses): cattle & calves $63,016,005 ($629.00) sheep & lambs $666,056 ($61.40); hogs & pigs $3,935,099 ($69.10). (2) New series, milk cows & heifers that have calved, from 1965. (3) As of Dec. 1 of preceding year.

Farm-Real Estate Debt Outstanding by Lender Groups[1]

Source: Economic Research Service, U.S. Dept. of Agriculture

Dec. 31	Total farm-real estate debt[2]	Amounts held by principal lender groups: Federal land banks[2]	Farmers Home Administration[3]	Life insurance companies[4]	All commercial banks	Other[5]
	$1,000	$1,000	$1,000	$1,000	$1,000	$1,000
1955	9,048,676	1,480,000	413,000	2,272,000	1,275,000	3,609,000
1960	12,867,524	2,539,000	723,000	2,975,000	1,592,000	5,039,000
1965	21,220,912	4,240,000	1,497,000	4,802,000	2,607,000	8,070,000
1970	30,492,357	7,145,363	2,440,043	5,610,300	3,772,377	11,524,000
1975	49,852,888	16,029,468	3,368,747	6,726,000	6,296,286	17,432,000
1980	97,486,996	36,196,103	8,163,270	12,927,800	8,563,457	31,636,000
1982	111,312,036	47,821,589	9,169,874	12,801,546	8,391,800	33,127,000
1985	105,739,201	44,583,842	10,426,971	11,830,400	11,384,920	27,507,000
1986	95,879,799	37,757,626	10,348,597	10,940,200	12,710,650	24,123,000
1987	87,717,601	32,637,687	10,083,239	9,895,800	14,455,162	20,646,000
1988	82,952,518	30,326,707	9,606,796	9,581,700	15,416,700	18,020,000
1989	80,476,478	28,501,000	8,719,822	9,597,900	16,646,179	17,011,577
1990	78,398,009	26,885,056	8,092,982	10,186,300	17,227,171	16,006,500
1991	79,133,192	26,700,747	7,462,411	10,029,300	18,436,918	16,503,786

(1) Includes operator households. (2) Includes data for joint stock land banks and real estate loans by Agricultural Credit Assn. (3) Includes loans made directly by FmHA for farm ownership, soil and water loans to individuals, Indian tribe land acquisition, grazing associations, and half of economic emergency loans. Also includes loans for rural housing on farm tracts and labor housing. (4) American Council of Life Insurance. (5) Estimated by ERS, USDA. Includes CCC storage and drying facility loans.

U.S. Farms, 1940-1991

Source: U.S. Dept. of Agriculture

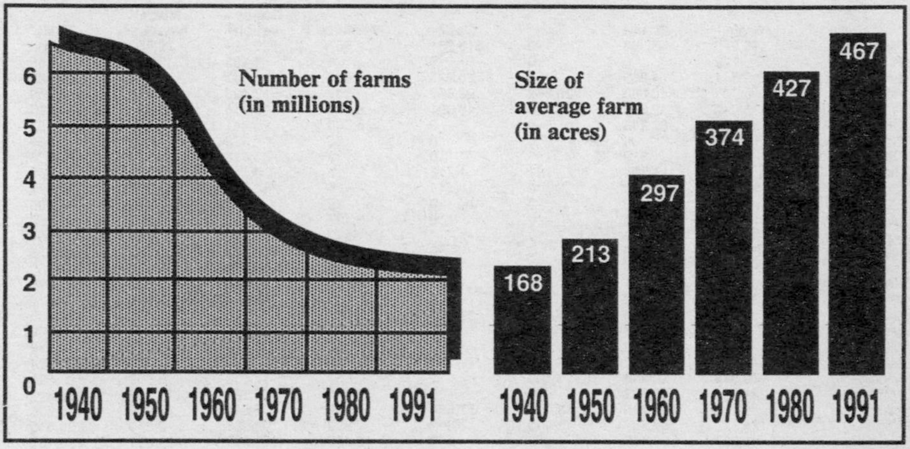

U.S. Egg Production

Source: Economic Research Service, U.S. Dept. of Agriculture

State	Eggs Produced (million) 1990	Eggs Produced (million) 1991	Price Per Dozen (cents) 1990	Price Per Dozen (cents) 1991	Value of Production (1,000 dollars) 1990	Value of Production (1,000 dollars) 1991
AL	2,206	2,186	$92.7	$91.4	$170,414	$166,500
AK	0.7	0.7	151.0	149.0	88	87
AZ	73	74	61.0	56.0	3,711	3,453
AR	3,620	3,737	86.3	91.8	260,338	285,881
CA	7,472	7,444	63.4	58.4	394,771	362,275
CO	788	873	77.8	73.0	51,089	53,108
CT	1,029	948	106.0	104.0	90,895	82,160
DE	168	164	117.0	113.0	16,380	15,443
FL	2,586	2,537	62.0	57.2	133,610	120,930
GA	4,302	4,301	80.6	80.8	288,951	289,601
HI	227.5	224.5	85.0	85.5	16,115	15,996
ID	187	203	79.1	72.9	12,326	12,332
IL	793	809	65.0	70.5	42,954	47,529
IN	5,445	5,290	62.7	60.1	284,501	264,941
IA	2,151	2,247	56.5	53.0	101,276	99,243
KS	404	389	54.5	47.8	18,348	15,495
KY	412	483	67.7	73.5	23,244	29,584
LA	273	254	115.0	115.0	26,163	24,342
ME	1,069	1,070	101.0	97.0	89,974	86,492
MD	885	898	76.3	75.4	56,271	56,424
MA	235	237	105.0	102.0	20,563	20,145
MI	1,406	1,396	58.0	53.8	67,957	62,587
MN	2,499	2,697	57.7	54.0	120,160	121,365
MS	1,434	1,468	87.8	86.7	104,921	106,063
MO	1,580	1,622	55.4	51.5	72,943	69,611
MT	172	164	68.0	66.0	9,747	9,020
NE	1,202	1,400	50.3	48.9	50,384	57,050
NV	2.2	1.8	53.9	52.7	99	79
NH	43	49	109.0	104.0	3,906	4,247
NJ	442	491	85.0	83.0	31,308	33,961
NM	283	302	74.0	70.0	17,452	17,617
NY	975	987	68.1	64.0	55,331	52,640
NC	3,033	3,045	82.8	78.7	209,277	199,701
ND	51	45	55.2	48.0	2,346	1,800
OH	4,667	4,637	59.1	54.7	229,850	211,370
OK	869	830	101.0	100.0	73,141	69,167
OR	652	686	77.0	74.6	41,837	42,646
PA	4,976	5,130	61.0	52.0	252,947	222,300
RI	53	50	102.0	99.0	4,505	4,125
SC	1,422	1,420	70.1	65.9	83,069	77,982
SD	435	602	48.0	45.8	17,400	22,976
TN	277	279	71.0	80.7	16,389	18,763
TX	3,317	3,356	76.7	72.6	212,012	203,038
UT	456	486	64.0	59.0	24,320	23,895
VT	31	30	106.0	102.0	2,738	2,550
VA	943	988	86.3	81.2	67,817	66,855
WA	1,287	1,313	74.1	71.5	79,472	78,233
WV	136	174	104.0	109.0	11,787	15,805
WI	910	873	60.1	54.0	45,576	39,285
WY	1.7	1.7	83.0	83.0	118	118
U.S.[2]	67,889	68,958	$70.9	$67.6	$4,010,791	$3,886,810

(1) Estimates cover the 12 month period Dec. 1, previous year through Nov. 30. (2) States may not add to U.S. total due to rounding.

U.S. Meat Production and Consumption

Source: Economic Research Service, U.S. Agriculture Department (million lbs.)

Year	Beef Production	Beef Consumption[1]	Veal Production	Veal Consumption[1]	Lamb and mutton Production	Lamb and mutton Consumption[1]	Pork (exclud. lard) Production	Pork (exclud. lard) Consumption[1]	All meats[3] Production	All meats[3] Consumption[1]	Lard Production	Lard Consumption[2]
1940	7,175	7,257	981	981	876	873	10,044	9,701	19,076	18,812	2,288	1,901
1950	9,534	9,529	1,230	1,206	597	596	10,714	10,390	22,075	21,721	2,631	1,891
1960	14,728	15,465	1,109	1,118	769	857	13,905	14,057	30,511	31,497	2,562	1,358
1970	21,685	23,391	588	610	551	663	14,699	14,871	37,523	39,535	1,913	939
1980	21,643	23,513	400	418	318	349	16,617	16,690	38,978	40,953	1,207	588
1990	22,743	24,031	327	325	358	419	15,354	16,030	38,787	40,806	(4)	(4)
1991	22,917	24,113	306	305	358	422	15,999	16,394	39,585	41,234	(4)	(4)

(1) Includes shipments. (2) Direct use. Excludes lard used in indirect food use such as table spreads and shortenings. (3) Meats may not add to total. (4) Discontinued series.

Government Payments by Programs and State

Source: Economic Research Service, U.S. Dept. of Agriculture (thousands)

1991[1] State	Feed Grain	Wheat	Rice	Cotton	Wool Act	Conservation[2]	Miscellaneous[3]	Total
Alabama	$6,070	$5,348	$0	$16,231	$57	$29,094	$9,550	$66,350
Alaska	78	0	0	0	1	1,155	51	1,285
Arizona	2,364	4,305	0	26,225	1,883	1,632	4,084	40,493
Arkansas	8,740	40,880	220,662	23,669	147	17,423	41,229	352,750
California	8,942	32,741	102,428	48,991	8,968	13,218	45,537	260,825
Colorado	36,302	83,243	0	0	6,360	85,241	5,956	217,102
Connecticut	437	0	0	0	26	579	309	1,351
Delaware	1,814	329	0	0	3	418	112	2,676
Florida	3,150	1,104	193	1,712	5	8,645	26,517	40,786
Georgia	19,522	18,443	0	13,611	6	31,716	14,377	97,675
Hawaii	0	0	0	0	19	815	72	906
Idaho	14,924	78,399	0	0	3,497	39,770	4,660	141,250
Illinois	346,543	36,533	0	0	547	56,030	1,754	441,407
Indiana	159,434	16,613	0	0	234	32,062	1,712	210,055
Iowa	469,701	656	0	0	2,059	168,889	3,650	644,955
Kansas	137,135	394,034	0	21	1,730	161,048	3,927	697,895
Kentucky	33,409	9,030	0	0	131	28,998	1,848	73,416
Louisiana	5,040	6,036	87,818	33,017	14	9,450	33,230	174,605
Maine	592	3	0	0	77	4,762	632	6,066
Maryland	8,297	1,680	0	0	62	2,464	2,839	15,342
Massachusetts	165	0	0	0	38	530	761	1,494
Michigan	79,344	20,238	0	0	667	17,633	5,809	123,691
Minnesota	221,988	93,583	0	0	1,391	103,525	15,332	435,819
Mississippi	5,178	12,726	43,455	57,674	10	37,046	20,209	176,298
Missouri	75,842	51,567	15,830	7,352	852	104,526	12,646	268,615
Montana	33,557	163,465	0	0	8,425	108,995	5,691	320,133
Nebraska	318,372	87,731	0	0	1,163	80,915	2,478	490,659
Nevada	191	637	0	0	965	734	3,152	5,679
New Hampshire	141	0	0	0	29	790	517	1,477
New Jersey	2,415	556	0	0	14	598	468	4,051
New Mexico	9,242	11,158	0	2,760	7,369	21,352	6,566	58,447
New York	23,847	4,638	0	0	236	8,225	4,296	41,242
North Carolina	26,548	7,385	0	3,893	55	10,774	4,182	52,837
North Dakota	83,509	299,967	0	0	1,720	116,560	32,097	533,853
Ohio	100,348	26,899	0	0	939	23,724	4,798	156,708
Oklahoma	9,269	208,695	175	10,193	2,910	54,739	4,941	290,922
Oregon	4,115	47,485	0	0	2,261	29,884	5,360	89,105
Pennsylvania	13,822	1,413	0	0	374	10,032	8,723	34,364
Rhode Island	1	0	0	0	6	91	12	110
South Carolina	13,430	9,812	0	6,474	0	14,971	4,677	49,364
South Dakota	96,842	92,281	0	0	6,831	77,302	12,981	286,237
Tennessee	14,854	10,589	91	14,561	45	26,778	3,413	70,331
Texas	125,392	136,112	79,377	140,985	73,554	178,157	44,348	777,925
Utah	2,473	7,021	0	0	5,648	10,969	7,086	33,197
Vermont	468	3	0	0	89	1,650	1,129	3,339
Virginia	11,286	3,995	0	74	609	7,369	3,283	26,616
Washington	17,317	128,79[illegible]	0	0	613	55,273	4,082	206,084
West Virginia	1,429	104	0	0	291	2,045	1,552	5,421
Wisconsin	92,658	2,639	0	0	385	47,177	7,091	149,950
Wyoming	2,116	6,797	0	0	10,204	12,410	1,714	33,241
United States	**$2,648,653**	**$2,165,672**	**$550,029**	**$406,903**	**$153,519**	**$1,858,183**	**$431,440**	**$8,214,399**

(1) Includes both cash payments and payment-in-kind (PIK). (2) Includes amount paid under agriculture and conservation programs (Conservation Reserve, Agriculture Conservation, Emergency Conservation, and Great Plains Program). (3) The programs included: Rural Clean Water, Clean Lakes, Forest Incentive, Water Bank, Milk Indemnity, Dairy Termination, Emergency Feed, Extended Warehouse Storage, Extended Farm Storage, Milk Diversion, Colorado River Salinity, Livestock Emergency Assistance, Interest Penalty Payments, Disaster, Loan Deficiency, and Market Gains.

Federal Food Assistance Programs[1]

Source: Food and Nutrition Service, U.S. Agriculture Department (millions of dollars)

	1982	1983	1984	1985	1986	1987	1988	1989	1990	1991
Food Stamp Pgm.[2]	$10,145	$11,847	$11,579	$11,703	$11,638	$11,605	$12,317	$12,908	$15,510	$18,770
P.R. Nutr. Asst.[3]	898	825	825	825	820	853	879	908	937	963
Natl. School Lunch[4]	2,942	3,203	3,335	3,380	3,537	3,685	3,730	3,770	3,834	4,224
School Breakfast	317	344	364	379	406	447	482	513	596	685
WIC[5]	949	1,126	1,388	1,489	1,583	1,680	1,798	1,913	2,122	2,301
Summer Food Svc.[4]	87	93	96	112	115	129	133	146	164	174
Child/Adult Care[4]	324	356	407	452	496	548	628	703	820	943
Special Milk	18	17	16	16	16	15	19	18	19	20
Nutrition Prg. for the Elderly[4]	102	120	127	134	137	139	146	144	142	140
Food Distrib. to Indian Reserv.	41	44	51	60	60	63	62	65	66	65
Commodity Supp. Food Pgm.[4,6]	28	42	48	48	48	56	62	73	85	93
Food Dist.—Charitable Instit.[7]	117	154	190	170	240	158	159	136	104	92
Emergency Food Assistance Pgm.	180	998	1,075	1,026	895	895	645	276	257	258
Soup Kitchens/Food Banks	0	0	0	0	0	0	0	34	77	44
Other Costs[8]	45	53	52	56	60	62	58	66	68	78
Total[9]	**$16,193**	**$19,222**	**$19,552**	**$19,851**	**$20,051**	**$20,335**	**$21,118**	**$21,673**	**$24,798**	**$28,850**

(continued)

(1) Data are for Fiscal (not Calendar) years. (2) Includes the Federal share of State Administrative Expenses and other Federal costs. (3) Puerto Rico participated in the Food Stamp Program from FY 1975 until July 1982, when it initiated a separate grant program. (4) Includes the value of commodities (entitlement, bonus and cash in lieu). (5) Includes program studies and Farmers Market demonstration projects. (6) Includes Elderly Feeding Projects. (7) Includes Summer Camps. (8) Includes Child Nutrition State Admin. Expenses, Nutrition Studies, Nutrition Education and Training, and nutrition assistance to the Northern Marianas. (9) Excludes food program administration (FPA) costs.

Farm Income—Marketings and Government Payments

Source: Economic Research Service, U.S. Dept. of Agriculture (1,000 dollars)

State	1990 Farm marketings Total	1990 Crops	1990 Livestock and products	1991 Farm marketings Total	1991 Crops	1991 Livestock and products	Government payments
AL	$2,825,642	$632,401	$2,193,241	$2,977,832	$758,659	$2,219,173	$66,350
AK	26,783	19,239	7,544	26,622	20,144	6,478	1,285
AZ	1,909,605	1,096,705	812,900	1,889,907	1,104,270	785,637	40,493
AR	4,255,795	1,554,534	2,701,261	4,310,724	1,630,656	2,680,068	352,750
CA	19,157,859	13,624,361	5,533,498	17,886,698	12,614,557	5,272,141	260,825
CO	4,216,273	1,143,550	3,072,723	3,761,320	1,097,485	2,663,835	217,102
CT	473,732	250,415	223,317	463,372	254,799	208,573	1,351
DE	636,074	176,380	459,694	619,536	181,471	438,065	2,676
FL	5,744,158	4,483,485	1,260,673	6,140,999	4,969,337	1,171,662	40,786
GA	3,865,685	1,595,816	2,269,869	3,978,361	1,824,872	2,153,489	97,675
HI	600,049	513,633	86,416	596,925	506,407	90,518	906
ID	2,885,484	1,748,066	1,137,418	2,615,946	1,543,167	1,072,779	141,250
IL	7,789,302	5,337,736	2,451,566	7,508,777	5,164,790	2,343,987	441,407
IN	4,910,528	2,870,996	2,039,532	4,474,513	2,581,688	1,892,825	210,055
IA	10,282,269	4,420,201	5,862,068	10,179,249	4,458,333	5,720,916	644,955
KS	7,019,508	2,023,972	4,995,536	6,934,986	2,132,539	4,802,447	697,895
KY	3,102,922	1,404,334	1,698,588	3,176,704	1,474,727	1,703,977	73,416
LA	1,929,030	1,296,259	632,771	1,792,907	1,172,115	620,792	174,605
ME	492,734	234,485	258,249	444,601	192,144	252,457	6,066
MD	1,364,324	541,817	822,507	1,332,494	553,596	778,898	15,342
MA	445,874	321,168	124,706	475,540	354,795	120,745	1,494
MI	3,126,461	1,719,574	1,406,887	3,081,072	1,793,369	1,287,703	123,691
MN	6,884,615	3,135,241	3,749,374	6,936,001	3,359,081	3,576,920	435,819
MS	2,432,534	1,110,744	1,321,790	2,422,070	1,147,177	1,274,893	176,298
MO	3,988,956	1,659,833	2,329,123	3,861,179	1,658,064	2,203,115	268,615
MT	1,654,141	765,972	888,169	1,531,169	740,741	790,428	320,133
NE	8,708,170	2,631,978	6,076,192	8,821,328	2,887,720	5,933,608	490,659
NV	323,953	114,813	209,140	275,836	88,746	187,090	5,679
NH	143,193	79,870	63,323	143,106	80,162	62,944	1,477
NJ	650,390	454,725	195,665	660,160	463,641	196,519	4,051
NM	1,483,015	481,616	1,001,399	1,501,152	481,764	1,019,388	58,447
NY	2,957,556	986,485	1,971,071	2,868,321	1,086,729	1,781,592	41,242
NC	4,925,996	2,268,093	2,657,903	4,924,071	2,315,591	2,608,480	52,837
ND	2,531,800	1,730,438	801,362	2,556,147	1,856,912	699,235	533,853
OH	4,146,289	2,299,495	1,846,794	3,893,074	2,211,596	1,681,478	156,708
OK	3,541,987	1,200,374	2,341,613	3,807,582	1,040,142	2,767,440	290,922
OR	2,373,519	1,620,421	753,098	2,454,389	1,630,575	823,814	89,105
PA	3,757,065	1,043,313	2,713,752	3,503,040	1,033,280	2,469,760	34,364
RI	71,346	57,614	13,732	70,917	57,642	13,275	110
SC	1,169,000	587,579	581,421	1,225,396	676,662	548,734	49,364
SD	3,259,488	965,427	2,294,061	3,264,286	1,088,201	2,176,085	286,237
TN	2,060,947	950,360	1,110,587	1,977,569	932,514	1,045,055	70,331
TX	11,831,478	4,080,572	7,750,906	12,126,182	4,212,188	7,913,994	777,925
UT	761,777	175,061	586,716	730,882	178,323	552,559	33,197
VT	456,045	59,513	396,532	433,140	65,556	367,584	3,339
VA	2,121,725	738,892	1,382,833	2,095,371	732,426	1,362,945	26,616
WA	3,798,445	2,402,296	1,396,149	3,946,524	2,656,614	1,289,910	206,084
WV	339,111	69,886	269,225	330,237	77,050	253,187	5,421
WI	5,734,009	1,160,757	4,573,252	5,449,043	1,233,998	4,215,045	149,950
WY	753,836	158,733	595,103	812,743	169,707	643,036	33,241
U.S.	$169,920,477	$79,999,228	$89,921,249	$167,292,000	$80,546,722	$86,745,278	$8,214,399

Age and Sex of the Farm and Nonfarm Population, 1990

Source: Economic Research Service, U.S. Dept. of Agriculture; Bureau of the Census, U.S. Dept. of Commerce, 1990. (Numbers in thousands)

Age	Farm Both sexes	Farm Male	Farm Female	Nonfarm Both sexes	Nonfarm Male	Nonfarm Female
Percent Distribution						
Under 15 years	20.5	20.1	20.8	22.3	23.5	21.1
15 to 19	7.8	8.0	7.5	6.9	7.2	6.7
20 to 29	10.3	10.9	9.5	15.8	15.9	15.7
30 to 39	13.0	13.1	12.9	17.1	17.3	16.8
40 to 44	7.2	6.7	7.7	7.1	7.1	7.0
45 to 49	6.3	6.5	6.0	5.6	5.6	5.6
50 to 59	13.5	13.1	14.0	8.8	8.8	8.9
60 to 69	12.3	12.3	12.3	8.4	7.9	8.7
70 to 74	4.0	4.4	3.6	3.2	2.9	3.5
75 years and over	5.3	5.0	5.7	4.7	3.6	5.8

Persons in Farm Occupations, 1820-1991

Source: Economic Research Service, U.S. Department of Agriculture; and Bureau of the Census, U.S. Department of Commerce, 1991.

(numbers in thousands)

Year	Total workers[1]	Farm occupations Number	Farm occupations % of total	Year	Total workers[1]	Farm occupations Number	Farm occupations % of total
1820	2,881	2,069	71.8	1950	59,230	6,858	11.6
1850	7,697	4,902	63.7	1960	67,990	4,132	6.1
1870	12,925	6,850	53.0	1970	79,802	2,881	3.6
1900	29,030	10,888	37.5	1980	104,058	2,818	2.7
1920	42,206	11,390	27.0	1985 (March)	106,214	2,949	2.8
1930	48,686	10,321	21.2	1990 (March)	117,491	2,864	2.4
1940	51,742	8,995	17.4	1991 (March)	116,000	2,848	2.5

(1) Total workers for 1985 to 1991 are employed workers 15 years and over; total workers for 1970 and 1980 are members of the experienced civilian labor force 16 years and over; total workers for 1900 to 1960 are members of the experienced civilian labor forced 14 years and over; and total workers for 1820 to 1890 are gainful workers 10 years and over.

Grain, Hay, Potato, Cotton, Soybean, Tobacco Production

Source: Economic Research Service, U.S. Dept. of Agriculture

1991 State	Barley (1,000 bushels)	Corn, grain (1,000 bushels)	Cotton lint (1,000 bales)	All Hay (1,000 tons)	Oats (1,000 bushels)	Potatoes (1,000 cwt.)	Soybeans (1,000 bushels)	Tobacco (1,000 pounds)	All Wheat (1,000 bushels)
Alabama	—	16,800	535	1,638	875	1,252	8,050	—	2,750
Alaska	—	—	—	—	—	—	—	—	—
Arizona	2,400	850	1,080	1,426	—	1,770	—	—	6,605
Arkansas	—	8,000	1,550	2,444	1,680	—	89,600	—	20,460
California	9,440	18,400	2,630	8,610	2,450	16,626	—	—	36,160
Colorado	10,400	128,520	—	4,062	1,800	26,168	—	—	74,000
Connecticut	—	—	—	175	—	—	—	2,831	—
Delaware	2,516	17,914	—	53	—	1,348	8,750	—	3,551
Florida	—	5,100	71	690	—	8,082	1,161	15,312	575
Georgia	—	55,000	720	1,800	3,000	—	15,930	80,600	14,025
Hawaii	—	—	—	—	—	—	—	—	—
Idaho	59,250	7,875	—	4,294	3,060	122,175	—	—	81,660
Illinois	—	1,177,000	—	3,162	6,600	1,008	341,250	—	44,800
Indiana	—	510,600	—	1,725	2,565	902	172,770	18,920	28,800
Iowa	—	1,427,400	—	6,285	21,250	208	350,325	—	1,700
Kansas	759	206,250	1	5,030	5,830	—	43,700	—	363,000
Kentucky	1,210	111,250	—	5,125	—	—	36,725	479,794	10,800
Louisiana	—	20,995	1,410	750	—	—	27,550	—	3,800
Maine	—	—	—	382	1,380	18,170	—	—	—
Maryland	4,992	42,750	—	505	420	298	17,000	12,900	9,750
Massachusetts	—	—	—	223	—	615	—	775	—
Michigan	1,419	253,000	—	5,255	5,400	11,715	52,820	—	24,080
Minnesota	43,750	720,000	—	8,090	22,800	19,314	195,275	—	67,110
Mississippi	—	11,250	2,251	1,800	—	—	46,800	—	4,500
Missouri	—	213,400	423	7,110	1,632	1,323	135,115	6,825	48,000
Montana	85,800	1,800	—	5,190	6,050	2,790	—	—	159,507
Nebraska	1,215	990,600	—	7,473	11,880	3,100	82,410	—	67,200
Nevada	360	—	—	1,158	—	2,546	—	—	660
New Hampshire	—	—	—	151	—	—	—	—	—
New Jersey	488	8,470	—	250	—	760	4,428	—	1,196
New Mexico	—	9,900	98	1,400	—	3,450	—	—	8,000
New York	—	64,680	—	4,102	5,000	6,917	—	—	5,390
North Carolina	1,645	85,500	650	1,176	2,200	3,044	38,645	634,655	19,200
North Dakota	138,670	51,300	—	4,780	32,500	30,030	19,215	—	303,670
Ohio	—	326,400	—	3,150	10,200	1,425	135,720	22,776	52,920
Oklahoma	370	9,350	250	4,520	1,292	—	5,875	—	140,000
Oregon	12,600	2,190	—	2,955	4,725	22,170	—	—	43,900
Pennsylvania	4,200	64,500	—	4,026	8,400	3,500	9,900	20,765	7,700
Rhode Island	—	—	—	16	—	241	—	—	—
South Carolina	279	21,675	340	676	2,200	—	13,860	111,180	8,525
South Dakota	17,940	240,500	—	8,045	38,500	1,775	58,320	—	96,175
Tennessee	—	43,860	700	3,263	—	—	31,500	121,524	7,680
Texas	320	165,000	4,805	9,700	7,200	3,192	5,270	—	84,000
Utah	7,885	2,940	—	2,275	616	1,620	—	—	5,807
Vermont	—	—	—	708	—	—	—	—	—
Virginia	5,695	28,140	27	2,260	—	1,485	14,500	116,849	12,250
Washington	37,050	15,840	—	2,970	2,600	75,435	—	—	98,600
West Virginia	—	2,850	—	877	225	—	—	3,420	450
Wisconsin	3,312	380,800	—	9,060	26,500	23,275	23,100	14,338	6,118
Wyoming	10,530	5,831	—	2,670	1,696	500	—	—	5,630
United States	**464,495**	**7,474,480**	**17,542**	**153,485**	**242,526**	**418,229**	**1,985,564**	**1,663,464**	**1,980,704**

Production of Chief U.S. Crops

Source: National Agricultural Statistics Service: U.S. Dept. of Agriculture

Year	Corn for grain 1,000 bushels	Oats 1,000 bushels	Barley 1,000 bushels	Sorghum for grain 1,000 bushels	All Wheat 1,000 bushels	Rye 1,000 bushels	Flax-seed 1,000 bushels	Cotton lint 1,000 bales	Cotton seed 1,000 tons
1970 . .	4,152,243	915,236	416,091	683,179	1,351,558	36,840	29,416	10,192	4,068
1975 . .	5,828,961	638,960	379,162	754,354	2,126,927	15,924	15,553	8,302	3,218
1980 . .	6,639,396	458,792	361,135	579,343	2,380,934	15,958	7,728	11,122	4,470
1982 . .	8,235,101	592,630	515,935	835,083	2,764,967	19,533	10,278	11,963	4,744
1985 . .	8,875,453	518,490	590,213	1,120,271	2,424,115	20,373	8,293	13,432	5,279
1986 . .	8,225,764	384,996	608,532	938,869	2,090,570	19,067	11,538	9,731	3,801
1987 . .	7,131,300	373,713	521,499	730,809	2,107,685	19,526	7,444	14,760	5,769
1988 . .	4,928,681	217,600	289,994	576,686	1,812,201	14,689	1,615	15,412	6,062
1989 . .	7,525,493	373,587	404,203	615,420	2,036,618	13,647	1,215	12,196	4,677
1990 . .	7,933,068	357,149	418,856	571,483	2,738,594	10,098	3,812	15,617	5,967
1991 . .	7,474,480	242,526	464,495	579,490	1,980,704	9,761	6,100	17,614	6,926

Year	Tobacco 1,000 lbs.	All Hay 1,000 tons	Beans dry edible 1,000 cwt.	Peas dry edible 1,000 cwt.	Peanuts 1,000 lbs.	Soy-beans 1,000 bushels	Pota-toes 1,000 cwt.	Sweet pota-toes 1,000 cwt.
1970	1,906,453	126,969	17,399	3,315	2,983,121	1,127,100	325,716	13,164
1975	2,182,304	132,397	17,442	2,731	3,846,722	1,548,344	321,978	12,891
1980	1,786,225	130,740	26,729	3,285	2,302,762	1,797,543	303,905	10,953
1982	1,994,494	149,241	25,563	NA	3,440,255	2,190,297	355,131	14,833
1985	1,511,638	148,719	22,298	NA	4,122,787	2,099,056	407,109	14,573
1986	1,161,940	155,385	22,960	3,196	3,697,085	1,942,558	361,511	12,368
1987	1,188,868	147,319	26,031	3,385	3,616,010	1,938,087	385,774	11,611
1988	1,369,500	126,010	19,253	3,868	3,980,917	1,548,841	356,438	10,945
1989	1,367,188	145,512	23,729	3,883	3,989,995	1,923,666	370,444	11,358
1990	1,606,851	146,985	32,429	2,372	3,602,770	1,921,787	393,867	13,020
1991	1,663,464	153,485	32,963	3,715	4,926,570	1,985,564	417,622	11,496

Year	Rice 1,000 cwt.	Sugar-cane 1,000 tons	Sugar beets 1,000 tons	Pecans 1,000 tons	Al-monds 1,000 tons	Wal-nuts 1,000 tons	Fil-berts 1,000 tons	Oranges* 1,000 boxes	Grape-fruit* 1,000 boxes
1970	NA	23,996	26,378	NA	NA	111.8	9.3	185,770	53,910
1975	NA	28,344	29,704	NA	NA	199.3	12.1	237,810	61,610
1980	146,150	26,963	23,502	91.8	264.4	197.0	15.4	273,630	73,200
1982	153,637	29,770	20,894	109.3	283.5	234.0	18.8	176,690	70,550
1985	134,913	28,213	22,529	122.2	375.6	219.0	24.6	158,350	56,150
1986	133,356	30,311	25,150	136.4	201.3	180.0	15.1	175,440	57,870
1987	129,603	29,218	28,072	131.1	519.0	247.0	21.8	181,175	63,775
1988	159,897	29,904	24,810	154.1	451.9	209.0	16.5	200,250	68,700
1989	154,487	29,426	25,131	125.3	394.7	229.0	13.0	209,050	69,500
1990	154,919	27,090	27,593	102.5	531.7	227.0	21.7	186,075	48,600
1991	154,457	30,254	28,092	149.5	385.8	259.0	25.5	178,950	55,500

NA = Not available. * Crop year ending in year cited.

Harvested Acreage of Principal U.S. Crops, 1989-1991

Source: Natl. Agricultural Statistics Service, U.S. Dept. of Agriculture (thousand acres)

State	1989	1990	1991
Alabama	2,338	2,342	2,240
Arizona	830	802	770
Arkansas	7,603	8,080	7,863
California	4,900	4,797	4,340
Colorado	5,677	5,862	5,580
Connecticut	128	129	125
Delaware	537	496	556
Florida	1,128	1,076	1,040
Georgia	4,205	3,793	3,774
Hawaii	81	79	74
Idaho	4,333	4,281	4,215
Illinois	22,977	22,759	22,906
Indiana	11,631	11,485	11,555
Iowa	24,097	23,276	23,376
Kansas	18,794	20,978	20,712
Kentucky	5,487	5,505	5,495
Louisiana	4,093	4,367	3,571
Maine	364	361	351
Maryland	1,602	1,552	1,561
Massachusetts	136	135	136
Michigan	6,360	6,510	6,713
Minnesota	18,661	18,779	18,719
Mississippi	4,614	4,723	4,481
Missouri	13,249	12,685	12,900
Montana	9,475	8,926	8,687
Nebraska	17,450	18,044	18,316
Nevada	554	520	495
New Hampshire	93	91	92
New Jersey	380	364	382
New Mexico	968	881	1,047
New York	3,560	3,538	3,443
North Carolina	4,526	4,370	4,428
North Dakota	20,660	21,229	20,925
Ohio	10,259	10,132	9,972
Oklahoma	9,396	9,688	8,614
Oregon	2,339	2,290	2,260
Pennsylvania	4,198	4,094	4,067
Rhode Island	10	10	10
South Carolina	2,283	2,049	1,827
South Dakota	15,210	15,552	15,640
Tennessee	4,570	4,477	4,379
Texas	16,697	18,550	17,608
Utah	983	992	973
Vermont	442	441	434
Virginia	2,768	2,726	2,660
Washington	4,045	4,168	4,046
West Virginia	664	668	615
Wisconsin	8,615	8,550	8,449
Wyoming	1,628	1,735	1,889
U.S.	**305,761**	**309,109**	**304,894**

Note: States may not add, due to rounding.

Average Prices Received by U.S. Farmers

Source: Natl. Agricultural Statistics Service, U.S. Dept. of Agriculture

The figures represent dollars per 100 lbs. for hogs, beef cattle, veal calves, sheep, lamb, and milk (wholesale), dollars per head for milk cows; cents per lb. for milk fat (in cream), chickens, broilers, turkeys, and wool; cents for eggs per dozen.

Weighted calendar year prices for livestock and livestock products other than wool. 1943 through 1963, wool prices are weighted on marketing year basis. The marketing year has been changed (1964) from a calendar year to a Dec.-Nov. basis for hogs, chickens, broilers and eggs.

Year	Hogs	Cattle (beef)	Calves (veal)	Sheep	Lambs	Cows (milk)	All milk	Chickens (excl. broilers)	Broilers	Turkeys	Eggs	Wool
1930	8.84	7.71	9.68	4.74	7.76	74	2.21	...	...	20.2	23.7	19.5
1940	5.39	7.56	8.83	3.95	8.10	61	1.82	13.0	17.3	15.2	18.0	28.4
1950	18.00	23.30	26.30	11.60	25.10	198	3.89	22.2	27.4	32.8	36.3	62.1
1960	15.30	20.40	22.90	5.61	17.90	223	4.21	12.2	16.9	25.4	36.1	42.0
1970	22.70	27.10	34.50	7.51	26.40	332	5.71	9.1	13.6	22.6	39.1	35.4
1975	46.10	32.20	27.20	11.30	42.10	412	8.75	9.9	26.3	34.8	54.5	44.8
1979	41.80	66.10	88.80	26.30	66.70	1,040	12.00	14.4	25.9	41.3	58.3	86.3
1980	38.00	62.40	76.80	21.30	63.60	1,190	13.05	11.0	27.7	41.3	56.3	88.1
1984	47.10	57.30	59.90	16.40	60.10	895	13.46	15.9	33.7	48.9	72.3	79.5
1985	44.00	53.70	62.10	23.90	67.70	860	12.76	14.8	30.1	49.1	57.1	63.3
1986	49.30	52.60	61.10	25.60	69.00	820	12.51	12.5	34.5	47.1	61.6	66.8
1987	51.20	61.10	78.50	29.50	77.60	920	12.54	11.0	28.7	34.8	54.9	91.7
1988	42.30	66.60	89.20	25.60	69.10	990	12.26	9.2	33.1	38.6	52.8	1.38
1989	42.50	69.50	90.80	24.40	66.10	1,030	13.56	14.9	36.6	40.9	68.9	1.24
1990	53.70	74.60	95.60	23.20	55.50	1,160	13.74	9.3	32.6	39.4	70.9	80.0
1991	49.10	72.60	98.00	19.70	52.20	1,100	12.26	7.2	30.8	38.4	67.6	55.0

The figures represent cents per lb. for cotton, apples, and peanuts; dollars per bushel for oats, wheat, corn, barley, and soybeans; dollars per 100 lbs. for rice, sorghum, and potatoes; dollars per ton for cottonseed and baled hay.

Weighted crop year prices. Crop years are as follows: apples, June-May; wheat, oats, barley, hay and potatoes, July-June; cotton, rice, peanuts and cottonseed, August-July; soybeans, September-August; and corn and sorghum grain, October-September.

Year	Corn	Wheat	Upland cotton[1]	Oats	Barley	Rice	Soybeans	Sorghum	Peanuts	Cottonseed	Hay	Potatoes	Apples
1930	.598	.663	9.46	0.311	.420	1.74	1.34	1.02	5.01	22.00	11.00	1.47	...
1940	.618	.674	9.83	0.298	.393	1.80	.892	.873	3.72	21.70	9.78	.850	...
1950	1.52	2.00	39.90	0.788	1.19	5.09	2.47	1.88	10.9	86.60	21.10	1.50	...
1960	1.00	1.74	30.08	0.599	.840	4.55	2.13	1.49	10.0	42.50	21.70	2.00	2.72
1970	1.33	1.33	21.86	0.623	.973	5.17	2.85	2.04	12.8	56.40	26.10	2.21	6.52
1975	2.54	3.55	51.10	1.45	2.42	8.35	4.92	4.21	19.6	97.00	52.10	4.48	8.80
1979	2.52	3.78	62.3	1.36	2.29	10.50	6.28	4.18	20.6	121.00	59.50	3.43	15.40
1980	3.11	3.91	74.4	1.79	2.86	12.80	7.57	5.25	25.1	129.00	71.00	6.55	12.1
1984	2.63	3.39	58.7	1.67	2.29	8.04	5.84	4.15	27.9	99.50	72.70	5.69	15.5
1985	2.23	3.08	56.8	1.23	1.98	6.53	5.05	3.45	24.4	66.00	67.60	3.92	17.3
1986	1.50	2.42	51.5	1.21	1.61	3.75	4.78	2.45	29.2	80.00	59.70	5.03	19.1
1987	1.94	2.57	63.7	1.56	1.81	7.27	5.88	3.04	28.0	82.50	65.00	4.38	12.7
1988	2.54	3.72	55.6	2.61	2.79	6.83	7.42	4.05	28.0	118.00	85.20	6.02	17.4
1989	2.36	3.72	63.6	1.49	2.42	7.35	5.69	3.75	28.0	105.00	85.40	7.36	13.9
1990	2.28	2.61	67.1	1.14	2.14	6.70	5.74	3.79	34.9	121.00	80.60	6.08	20.9
1991	2.40	3.05	57.0	1.20	2.10	7.70	5.60	4.15	28.3	71.50	71.00	5.05	25.1

(1) Beginning 1964, 480 lb. net weight bales.

Grain Storage Capacity at Principal Grain Centers in U.S.

Source: Chicago Board of Trade Market Information Department, Aug. 1992

(bushels)

Cities	Capacity
Atlantic Coast	**21,200,000**
Great Lakes	
Toledo	57,100,000
Buffalo	15,200,000
Chicago	52,400,000
Milwaukee	6,600,000
Duluth	64,500,000
River Points	
Minneapolis	105,800,000
Peoria	3,300,000
St. Louis	17,700,000
Sioux City	4,500,000
Omaha-Council Bluffs	9,200,000
Atchison	16,900,000
St. Joseph	22,300,000
Kansas City, Mo.	95,200,000
Southwest	
Fort Worth	68,000,000
Texas High Plains	72,600,000
Enid	79,700,000
Gulf Points	
South Mississippi	45,900,000
North Texas Gulf	24,700,000
South Texas Gulf	14,300,000
Plains	
Wichita	37,400,000
Topeka	55,500,000
Salina	49,500,000
Hutchinson	42,000,000
Hastings-Grand Island	25,300,000
Lincoln	33,700,000
Pacific N.W.	
Puget Sound (incl. Portland)	35,100,000
California Ports	NA

Atlantic Coast — Albany, N.Y., Philadelphia, Pa., Baltimore, Md., Norfolk, Va. **Gulf Points** — New Orleans, Baton Rouge, Ama. Belle Chase, La., Mobile, Ala. **North Texas Gulf** — Houston, Galveston, Beaumont, Port Arthur, Texas. **South Texas Gulf** — Corpus Christi, Brownsville, Texas. **Pacific N.W.** — Seattle, Tacoma, Wash., Portland, Oreg., Columbia River. **Texas High Plains** — Amarillo, Lubbock, Hereford, Plainview, Texas. NA = Not available.

World Wheat, Rice and Corn Production, 1990

Source: U.N. Food and Agriculture Organization

(thousands of metric tons)

Country	Wheat	Rice	Corn
World, total	**595,149**	**518,508**	**475,429**
Afghanistan	1,925	430	800
Argentina	10,800	467	5,049
Australia	15,712	923	202
Austria	1,370	—	1,400
Bangladesh	890	28,140	3
Belgium-Lux.	1,527	—	60
Brazil	3,140	7,425	21,298
Bulgaria	5,095	23	1,241
Burma (Myanmar)	124	13,965	186
Cambodia	—	2,400	55
Canada	31,798	—	7,033
Chile	1,718	136	823
China	96,004	188,403	87,345
Colombia	105	2,117	1,213
Cuba	—	500	95
Czechoslovakia	6,707	—	468
Denmark	4,101	—	—
Ecuador	22	760	400
Egypt	4,267	2,800	4,400
Ethiopia	870	—	2,000
Finland	627	—	—
France	33,363	109	8,996
Germany (FR)	11,053	—	1,545
Germany (NL)*	4,734	—	1
Greece	1,580	100	1,700
Hungary	6,159	35	4,500
India	49,652	112,500	9,500
Indonesia	—	44,490	6,741
Iran	7,000	1,400	7
Iraq	805	200	110
Ireland	603	—	—
Israel	160	—	22
Italy	8,109	1,282	5,864
Japan	952	13,124	1
Korea (DPR)	220	5,500	4,400
Korean Republic	1	7,786	2
Laos	—	1,491	67
Madagascar	1	2,400	170
Malaysia	—	1,650	35
Mexico	3,899	—	—
Nepal	855	3,300	950
Netherlands	1,076	—	5
New Zealand	220	—	160
Pakistan	14,315	4,713	1,279
Panama	—	—	115
Peru	95	966	621
Philippines	—	9,319	4,854
Poland	9,026	—	290
Portugal	268	153	643
Romania	7,320	67	6,810
South Africa	1,794	—	9,442
Soviet Union	108,000	2,473	16,000
Spain	4,760	569	3,051
Sri Lanka	—	2,200	36
Sweden	2,173	—	—
Switzerland	572	—	231
Syria	2,069	—	132
Thailand	—	19,000	3,675
Turkey	20,000	235	2,000
United Kingdom	13,900	—	—
United States	74,534	7,027	201,509
Uruguay	420	517	101
Venezuela	—	400	1,150
Vietnam	—	18,400	850
Yugoslavia	6,359	40	6,270

Note: Some figures are FAO estimates. Where production is small or non-existent, — is indicated. * Formerly East Germany.

Wheat, Rice and Corn—Exports and Imports of 10 Leading Countries

(thousands of metric tons)

Leading Exporters	Exports[1]		
Wheat	**1980**	**1990**	**1991p**
U.S.	41,199	29,064	34,869
Canada	16,262	21,731	24,500
France	13,423	18,600	18,000
Australia	9,577	11,760	7,600
Turkey	530	544	5,000
Argentina	3,845	5,592	4,600
United Kingdom	1,100	4,165	4,600
Germany, Fed Rep[2]	1,502	3,295	4,400
Italy	1,620	2,700	3,600
Saudi Arabia	27	1,661	2,425
Rice	**1980**	**1990**	**1991p**
Thailand	3,049	3,993	4,600
U.S.	3,028	2,317	2,123
Pakistan	1,163	1,320	1,200
Vietnam	5	1,000	1,200
China	580	689	750
Australia	468	443	600
Italy	475	580	593
India	900	500	450
Uruguay	184	270	334
Spain	45	210	210
Corn	**1980**	**1990**	**1991p**
United States	60,737	43,807	40,007
China	125	6,571	10,000
Argentina	9,098	4,000	6,400
France	2,380	5,300	5,700
Hungary	300	500	1,400
Canada	1,056	142	1,000
Thailand	2,142	1,193	800
Greece	0	400	700
Yugoslavia	300	21	600
Belgium-Luxembourg	1,742	16	200

Leading Importers	Imports[1]		
Wheat	**1980**	**1990**	**1991p**
Former Soviet Union	16,000	15,650	21,000
China	13,789	9,500	15,500
Italy	3,028	5,500	7,300
Egypt	5,423	5,668	6,000
Japan	5,840	5,622	5,750
Brazil	3,910	4,444	4,672
South Korea	2,095	4,200	4,396
Algeria	2,294	4,600	4,000
Iran	1,896	4,000	2,500
Indonesia	1,474	2,300	2,300
Rice	**1980**	**1990**	**1991p**
Iran	583	565	800
Former Soviet Union	1,283	400	800
Saudi Arabia	356	525	550
Senegal	340	430	400
Hong Kong	362	368	400
Malaysia	167	355	400
South Africa	126	346	375
Brazil	0	800	350
Turkey	32	161	350
Ivory Coast	275	310	325
Corn	**1980**	**1990**	**1991p**
Japan	13,989	16,042	16,200
Former Soviet Union	11,800	8,720	12,200
South Korea	2,355	5,571	6,800
Taiwan	2,703	5,250	5,700
South Africa	0	375	5,000
Netherlands	2,638	1,869	1,800
Zimbabwe	0	100	1,800
Malaysia	717	1,490	1,750
Spain	4,251	1,523	1,600
United Kingdom	2,349	1,250	1,575

(1) Marketing years; (2) Data for total Germany not yet available; p = preliminary

ECONOMICS

U.S. Budget Receipts and Outlays—1988-1991

Source: Financial Management Service, U.S. Dept. of the Treasury
(Fiscal year ends Sept. 30)
(millions of dollars)
(outlays incl. selected departments and agencies)

Classification	Fiscal 1988	Fiscal 1989	Fiscal 1990	Fiscal 1991
Net Receipts				
Individual income taxes	$401,181	$445,690	$466,884	$467,827
Corporation income taxes	94,195	103,291	93,507	98,086
Social insurance taxes and contributions:				
Federal old-age and survivors insurance	220,337	240,595	255,031	265,503
Federal disability insurance	21,154	23,071	26,625	28,382
Federal hospital insurance	59,859	65,396	68,556	72,842
Railroad retirement fund	3,743	3,798	3,679	3,799
Total employment taxes and contributions	**305,093**	**332,859**	**353,891**	**370,526**
Other insurance and retirement:				
Unemployment	24,584	22,011	21,635	20,922
Federal employees retirement	4,537	4,428	4,405	4,454
Non-federal employees	122	119	117	108
Total social insurance taxes and contributions	**334,335**	**359,416**	**380,047**	**396,011**
Excise taxes	35,540	34,386	35,345	42,430
Estate and gift taxes	7,594	8,745	11,500	11,138
Customs duties	15,411	16,334	16,607	15,921
Deposits of earnings-Federal Reserve Banks	17,163	19,604	24,319	19,158
All other miscellaneous receipts	2,746	3,235	2,997	3,261
Net Budget Receipts	**$908,166**	**$990,701**	**$1,031,308**	**$1,053,832**
Net Outlays				
Legislative Branch	$1,852	$2,095	$2,244	$2,295
The Judiciary	1,337	1,492	1,641	1,989
Executive Office of the President:				
The White House Office	26	27	30	32
Office of Management and Budget	41	42	44	53
Total Executive Office	**121**	**124**	**157**	**193**
Funds appropriated to the President:				
International security assistance	4,273	1,012	8,352	9,531
Multinational assistance	1,498	1,492	1,695	1,520
Agency for International Development	1,404	1,215	1,773	1,835
International Development Assistance	2,980	2,780	3,528	3,444
Total funds appropriated to the President	**7,252**	**4,257**	**10,086**	**11,724**
Agriculture Department:				
Food stamp program	13,145	13,725	15,923	19,649
Farmer's Home Admin.	7,277	7,608	6,713	6,629
Forest service	2,688	2,944	2,934	3,001
Total Agriculture Department	**44,003**	**48,316**	**46,012**	**54,119**
Commerce Department				
Total Commerce Department	**2,279**	**2,571**	**3,734**	**2,585**
Bureau of the Census	333	557	1,575	451
Defense Department:				
Military personnel	76,337	80,676	75,622	83,439
Operation and maintenance	84,475	87,001	88,340	58,151
Procurement	77,166	81,620	80,972	82,028
Research, development, test, evaluation	34,792	37,002	37,458	34,589
Military construction	5,874	5,275	5,080	3,497
Total Defense Department (military)	**281,935**	**294,881**	**289,755**	**261,925**
Defense Department (civil)	22,047	23,450	24,975	26,538
Education Department	18,246	21,608	23,109	25,339
Energy Department	11,166	11,387	12,023	12,459
Health and Human Services Department:				
Food and Drug Administration	463	510	553	648
National Institutes of Health	6,334	6,992	7,492	7,667
Public Health Service	11,408	12,250	14,007	15,348
Health Care Financing Adm.	144,654	163,028	184,893	205,776
Human Development Services	5,886	6,850	6,877	8,093
Total Health and Human Services Dept.	**158,991**	**172,301**	**193,679**	**217,541**
Social Security (Off Budget)	214,178	227,473	244,998	266,395
Housing and Urban Development Department	18,956	19,680	20,167	22,751
Interior Department	5,147	5,308	5,795	6,094
Justice Department:				
Federal Bureau of Investigation	1,384	1,528	1,473	1,695
Total Justice Department	**5,426**	**6,232**	**6,507**	**8,244**
Labor Department:				
Unemployment Trust Fund	18,598	18,730	20,250	28,434
Total Labor Department	**21,870**	**22,657**	**25,316**	**34,049**
State Department	3,421	3,722	3,979	4,252
Transportation Department.				
Federal Aviation Adm	5,192	5,740	6,391	7,241
Total Transportation Department	**26,404**	**26,607**	**28,637**	**30,503**
Treasury Department:				
Internal Revenue Service	9,363	11,049	12,053	13,689
Interest on the public debt	214,145	240,863	264,853	286,022
Total Treasury Department	**201,644**	**230,566**	**255,264**	**276,894**
Veterans Affairs Department	29,249	30,041	28,998	31,214
Environmental Protection Agency	4,872	4,906	5,108	5,770
General Services Administration	−281	−462	−123	487
National Aeronautics and Space Administration	9,092	11,036	12,429	13,878

(*continued*)

Classification	Fiscal 1988	Fiscal 1989	Fiscal 1990	Fiscal 1991
Office of Personnel Management	$29,191	$29,073	$31,949	$34,808
Small Business Administration	−54	85	692	613
Other independent agencies:				
Action	153	163	169	192
Board for International Broadcasting	194	199	208	228
Corporation for Public Broadcasting	214	228	229	299
District of Columbia	550	538	578	671
Equal Employment Opportunity Commission	176	182	181	192
Export-Import Bank of the United States	−894	47	357	−88
Federal Communications Commission	52	49	79	66
Federal Deposit Insurance Corporation	2,146	2,847	6,429	7,363
Federal Trade Commission	69	65	57	60
Interstate Commerce Comm.	43	44	43	45
Legal Services Corporation	306	309	291	344
National Archives & Record Adm.	102	71	157	172
National Foundation on the Arts and Humanities	322	309	307	325
National Labor Relations Board	132	136	141	143
National Science Foundation	1,665	1,752	1,838	2,081
Nuclear Regulatory Commission	232	189	221	−1
Railroad Retirement Board	4,147	4,315	4,477	4,358
Securities and Exchange Commission	126	140	129	143
Smithsonian Institution	260	288	302	340
Tennessee Valley Authority	1,089	348	−312	−22
U.S. Information Agency	843	888	888	1,001
Total independent agencies	**23,446**	**33,770**	**73,666**	**80,458**
Undistributed offsetting receipts	−78,474	−89,155	−99,025	−110,555
Net Budget Outlays	**1,063,318**	**1,144,020**	**1,251,776**	**1,322,561**
Less net receipts	908,166	990,701	1,031,308	1,053,832
Deficit	**$−155,151**	**$−153,319**	**$−220,469**	**$−268,729**

U.S. Net Receipts and Outlays

Source: U.S. Dept. of the Treasury; annual statements for year ending June 30
(thousands of dollars)

Yearly average	Receipts	Outlays	Yearly average	Receipts	Outlays	Yearly average	Receipts	Outlays
1789-1800[1]	$5,717	$5,776	1866-1870	$447,301	$377,642	1901-1905	$559,481	$535,559
1801-1810[2]	13,056	9,086	1871-1875	336,830	287,460	1906-1910	628,507	639,178
1811-1820[2]	21,032	23,943	1876-1880	288,124	255,598	1911-1915	710,227	720,252
1821-1830[2]	21,928	16,162	1881-1885	366,961	257,691	1916-1920	3,483,652	8,065,333
1831-1840[2]	30,461	24,495	1886-1890	375,448	279,134	1921-1925	4,306,673	3,578,989
1841-1850[2]	28,545	34,097	1891-1895	352,891	363,599	1926-1930	4,069,138	3,182,807
1851-1860	60,237	60,163	1896-1900	434,877	457,451	1931-1935	2,770,973	5,214,874
1861-1865	160,907	683,785						

(1) Average for period March 4, 1789, to Dec. 31, 1800. (2) Years ended Dec. 31, 1801 to 1842; average for 1841-1850 is for the period Jan. 1, 1841, to June 30, 1850.

Summary of Receipts, Outlays, and Surpluses or Deficits; 1934-1987

(Millions of dollars)

Source: Financial Management Service, U.S. Dept. of the Treasury

Year	Total Receipts	Total Outlays	Surplus or Deficit (−)	Year	Total Receipts	Total Outlays	Surplus or Deficit (−)
1934	2,955	6,541	−3,586	1962	99,676	106,821	−7,146
1935	3,609	6,412	−2,803	1963	106,560	111,316	−4,756
1936	3,923	8,228	−4,304	1964	112,613	118,528	−5,915
1937	5,387	7,580	−2,193	1965	116,817	118,228	−1,411
1938	6,751	6,840	−89	1966	130,835	134,532	−3,698
1939	6,295	9,141	−2,846	1967	148,822	157,464	−8,643
1940	6,548	9,468	−2,920	1968	152,973	178,134	−25,161
1941	8,712	13,653	−4,941	1969	186,882	183,640	3,242
1942	14,634	35,137	−20,503	1970	192,807	195,649	−2,842
1943	24,001	78,555	−54,554	1971	187,139	210,172	−23,033
1944	43,747	91,304	−47,557	1972	207,309	230,681	−23,373
1945	45,159	92,712	−47,553	1973	230,799	245,707	−14,908
1946	39,296	55,232	−15,936	1974	263,224	269,359	−6,135
1947	38,514	34,496	4,018	1975	279,090	332,332	−53,242
1948	41,560	29,764	11,796	1976	298,060	371,779	−73,719
1949	39,415	38,835	580	Transition quarter[1]	81,232	95,973	−14,741
1950	39,443	42,562	−3,119	1977	355,559	409,203	−53,644
1951	51,616	45,514	6,102	1978	399,561	458,729	−59,168
1952	66,167	67,686	−1,519	1979	463,302	503,464	−40,162
1953	69,608	76,101	−6,493	1980	517,112	590,920	−73,808
1954	69,701	70,855	−1,154	1981	599,272	678,209	−78,936
1955	65,451	68,444	−2,993	1982	617,766	745,706	−127,940
1956	74,587	70,640	3,947	1983	600,562	808,327	−207,764
1957	79,990	76,578	3,412	1984	666,457	851,781	−185,324
1958	79,636	82,405	−2,769	1985	734,057	946,316	−212,260
1959	79,249	92,098	−12,849	1986	769,091	990,231	−221,140
1960	92,492	92,191	301	1987	854,143	1,003,804	−149,661
1961	94,388	97,723	−3,335				

(1) Effective fiscal year 1977, fiscal year is reckoned Oct. 1-Sept. 30; Transition Quarter covers July 1, 1976-Sept. 30, 1976.

The Federal Budget Process

Source: Executive Office of the President, Office of Management and Budget.

CBO = Congressional Budget Office; GRH = Gramm-Rudman-Hollings (*Balanced Budget and Emergency Deficit Control Act of 1985*); OMB = Office of Management and Budget.

Executive budget process	Timing	Congressional budget process
Agencies subject to executive branch review submit initial budget request materials.	Sept. 1	
Fiscal year begins. President's initial GRH sequester order takes effect (amounts are withheld from obligation pending issuance of final order).	Oct. 1	Fiscal year begins.
	Oct. 10	CBO issues revised GRH report to OMB and Congress.
OMB reports on changes in initial GRH estimates and determinations resulting from legislation enacted and regulations promulgated after its initial report to Congress. President issues final GRH sequester order, which is effective immediately, and transmits message to Congress within 15 days of final order. Agencies not subject to executive branch review submit budget request materials.	Oct. 15	
	Nov. 15	Comptroller General issues GRH compliance report.
Legislative branch and the judiciary submit budget request materials.	Nov.-Dec.	
President transmits the budget to Congress.	1st Mon. after Jan. 3	Congress receives the President's budget.
OMB sends allowance letters to agencies.	Jan.-Feb.	
	Feb. 15	CBO reports to the Budget Committees on the President's budget.
	Feb. 25	Committees submit views and estimates to Budget Committee in their own house.
OMB and the President conduct reviews to establish presidential policy to guide agencies in developing the next budget.	Apr.-June	
	Apr. 1	Senate Budget Committee reports concurrent resoluion on the budget.
	Apr. 15	Congress completes action on concurrent resolution.
	May 15	House may consider appropriations bills in the absence of a concurrent resolution on the budget.
	June 10	House Appropriations Committee reports last appropriations bill.
	June 15	Congress completes action on reconciliation legislation.
	June 30	House completes action on annual appropriations bills.
President transmits the mid-session review, updating the budget estimates.	July 15	Congress receives mid-session review of the budget.
OMB provides agencies with policy guidance for the upcoming budget.	July-Aug.	
Date of "snapshot" of projected deficits for the upcoming fiscal year for initial OMB and CBO GRH reports.	Aug. 15	
	Aug. 20	CBO issues its initial GRH report to OMB and Congress.
OMB issues its initial GRH report providing estimates and determinations to the President and Congress. President issues initial GRH sequester order and sends message to Congress within 15 days.	Aug. 25	

Public Debt of the U.S.

Source: Bureau of Public Debt, U.S. Dept. of the Treasury

Fiscal year	Debt (billions)	Per. cap. (dollars)	Interest paid (billions)	Pct. of federal outlays	Fiscal year	Debt (billions)	Per. cap. (dollars)	Interest paid (billions)	Pct. of federal outlays
1870	$2.4	$61.06	—	—	1976	620.4	2,852	37.1	10.0
1880	2.0	41.60	—	—	1977	$698.8	$3,170	$41.9	10.2
1890	1.1	17.80	—	—	1978	771.5	3,463	48.7	10.6
1900	1.2	16.60	—	—	1979	826.5	3,669	59.8	11.9
1910	1.1	12.41	—	—	1980	907.7	3,985	74.9	12.7
1920	24.2	228	—	—	1981	997.9	4,338	95.6	14.1
1930	16.1	131	—	—	1982	1,142.0	4,913	117.4	15.7
1940	43.0	325	$1.0	10.5	1983	1,377.2	5,870	128.8	15.9
1945	258.7	1,849	3.8	4.1	1984	1,572.3	6,640	153.8	18.1
1950	256.1	1,688	5.7	13.4	1985	1,823.1	7,598	178.9	18.9
1955	272.8	1,651	6.4	9.4	1986	2,125.3	8,774	190.2	19.2
1960	284.1	1,572	9.2	10.0	1987	2,350.3	9,615	195.4	19.5
1965	313.8	1,613	11.3	9.6	1988	2,602.3	10,534	214.1	20.1
1970	370.1	1,814	19.3	9.9	1989	2,857.4	11,545	240.9	21.0
1975	533.2	2,475	32.7	9.8	1990	3,233.3	13,000	264.8	21.1
					1991	3,502.0	13,992	286.0	21.6

Note: Through 1976 the fiscal year ended June 30. From 1977 on, fiscal year ends Sept. 30.

U.S. Direct Investment Abroad in Selected Countries

Source: Bureau of Economic Analysis, U.S. Dept. of Commerce

(millions of dollars)

	1989	1990	1991
All countries	$370,091	424,096	450,196
Africa			
Egypt	1,744	1,465	1,515
Libya	252	240	238
Nigeria	406	161	856
S. Africa	843	956	1,015
Asia and Pacific (excl. Japan)			
Hong Kong	5,949	6,187	6,430
India	527	513	533
Indonesia	3,770	3,226	3,458
Malaysia	1,174	1,384	1,440
Philippines	1,657	1,629	1,672
Singapore	2,318	3,385	4,313
South Korea	1,855	2,178	2,392
Taiwan	1,921	2,014	2,470
Thailand	1,271	1,585	1,787
Australia	13,331	14,846	15,627
Bermuda	17,717	21,737	20,737
Canada	65,548	67,033	68,510
European Communities	149,545	177,642	188,710
Belgium	7,941	9,050	8,838
Denmark	1,234	1,597	1,835
France	14,069	18,874	20,495
Germany	24,550	27,259	32,942
Greece	265	288	291
Ireland	6,522	6,880	7,450
Italy	10,294	13,117	13,825
Luxembourg	1,127	1,390	1,455
Netherlands	18,133	22,658	24,711
Portugal	488	598	893
Spain	6,096	7,704	7,712
United Kingdom	59,827	68,224	68,261
Other Europe			
Austria	588	889	1,238
Finland	476	551	418
Norway	3,547	3,815	4,248
Sweden	1,129	1,600	1,693
Switzerland	19,209	25,199	26,443
Turkey	310	494	510
Japan	18,488	20,997	22,918
South America			
Argentina	2,684	2,956	3,412
Brazil	14,522	14,918	15,222
Chile	1,069	1,368	1,555
Colombia	1,977	1,728	1,744
Ecuador	393	387	337
Peru	939	410	352
Venezuela	1,503	1,490	2,785
Central America			
Mexico	7,280	9,398	11,570
Panama	7,889	7,409	10,980
Middle East			
Israel	756	756	718
Saudi Arabia	1,955	1,981	2,317
United Arab Emirates	652	519	544

National Income by Industry

Source: Bureau of Economic Analysis, U.S. Dept. of Commerce

(billions of dollars)

	1960	1965	1970	1975	1980	1990	1991
National income without capital consumption adjustment	$428.6	$583.6	$835.1	$1,315.0	$2,263.9	$4,497.5	$4,594.2
Domestic industries	425.1	577.8	827.8	1,297.4	2,216.3	4,486.7	4,581.1
Private industries	371.6	500.8	695.4	1,088.3	1,894.5	3,828.9	3,886.0
Agriculture, forestry, fisheries	17.8	21.0	25.9	46.5	61.4	97.1	90.2
Mining	5.6	6.1	8.4	21.2	43.8	38.1	38.2
Construction	22.5	32.3	47.4	69.9	126.6	234.4	221.4
Manufacturing	125.3	171.6	215.6	317.5	532.1	846.9	835.7
Durable goods	73.4	105.6	127.7	185.0	313.7	484.3	466.1
Nondurable goods	52.0	66.1	87.9	132.5	218.4	362.6	369.6
Transportation, public utilities	35.8	47.0	64.4	101.1	177.3	328.7	333.2
Transportation	18.5	23.7	31.5	48.0	85.8	139.4	140.4
Communication	8.2	11.5	17.6	26.8	48.1	96.4	98.5
Electric, gas, and sanitary services	9.1	11.7	86.8	90.2	43.4	92.9	94.4
Wholesale trade	25.0	32.5	47.5	83.0	143.3	263.6	269.8
Retail trade	41.3	55.1	79.9	123.1	189.4	392.1	397.8
Finance, insurance, and real estate	51.3	67.4	96.4	143.9	279.5	679.8	697.2
Services	46.9	67.9	109.8	182.1	341.0	948.3	1,002.3
Government	53.5	76.9	132.4	209.1	321.8	657.9	695.1

National Income by Type of Income

Source: Bureau of Economic Analysis, U.S. Dept. of Commerce

(billions of dollars)

	1960	1965	1970	1975	1980	1990	1991
National income[1]	$424.9	$585.2	$832.6	$1,289.1	$2,203.5	$4,459.6	$4,542.2
Compensation of employees	296.7	399.8	618.3	948.7	1,638.2	3,290.3	3,388.2
Wages and salaries	272.8	363.7	551.5	814.7	1,372.0	2,738.9	2,808.2
Government	49.2	69.9	117.1	176.1	260.1	514.0	540.5
Other	223.7	293.8	434.3	638.6	1,111.8	2,224.9	2,267.7
Supplements to wages, salary	23.8	36.1	66.8	134.0	266.3	551.4	580.0
Employer contrib. for social ins.	12.6	18.3	34.3	68.0	127.9	277.3	289.4
Other labor income	11.2	17.8	32.5	65.9	138.4	274.0	290.6
Proprietors' income	52.1	65.1	80.2	125.4	180.7	373.2	379.7
Farm	11.6	13.0	14.7	25.4	20.5	42.5	35.1
Nonfarm	40.5	52.1	65.4	100.0	160.1	330.7	344.5
Rental income of persons with capital consump. adjust.	15.3	18.1	18.2	13.5	6.6	−12.9	−12.7
Corp. profits with inventory adjustment	49.8	76.2	69.5	123.9	194.0	319.0	306.8
Corp. profits before tax	49.9	77.4	76.0	134.8	237.1	332.3	312.4
Corp. profits tax liability	22.7	30.9	34.4	50.9	84.8	135.3	124.5
Corp. profits after tax	27.2	46.5	41.7	83.9	152.3	197.0	187.9
Dividends	12.9	19.1	22.5	29.6	54.7	133.7	137.8
Undistributed profits	14.3	27.4	19.2	54.3	97.6	63.3	50.2
Inventory valuation adjustment	−.2	−1.2	−6.6	−11.0	−43.1	−14.2	3.1
Net interest	11.3	20.9	41.2	83.8	200.9	490.1	480.2

(1) *National income* is the aggregate of labor and property earnings which arises in the current production of goods and services. It is the sum of employee compensation, proprietors' income, rental income, corporate profits, and net interest. It measures the total factor costs of the goods and services produced by the economy. Income is measured before deduction of taxes on income.

Gross Domestic Product, Gross National Product, Net National Product, National Income, and Personal Income

Source: Bureau of Economic Analysis, U.S. Dept. of Commerce (billions of dollars)

	1960	1970	1975	1980	1990	1991
Gross domestic product	—	—	—	—	$5,513.8	$5,672.6
Gross national product	$515.3	$1,015.5	$1,598.4	$2,732.0	5,524.5	5,685.8
Less: Capital consumption allowances	46.4	88.8	161.8	303.8	594.8	622.9
Equals: Net national product	468.9	926.6	1,436.6	2,428.1	4,929.8	5,062.8
Less: Indirect business tax and nontax liability	45.3	94.0	140.0	213.3	439.2	471.0
Business transfer payments	2.0	4.1	7.4	12.1	27.7	31.2
Statistical discrepancy	−2.8	−1.1	2.5	4.9	8.1	19.0
Plus: Subsidies less current surplus of government enterprises	.4	2.9	2.4	5.7	4.8	0.6
Equals: National income	424.9	832.6	1,289.1	2,203.5	4,459.6	4,542.2
Less: Corporate profits with inventory valuation and capital consumption adjustment	49.5	74.7	117.6	177.2	319.0	306.8
Net interest	11.3	41.2	83.8	200.9	490.1	480.2
Contributions for social insurance	21.9	62.2	118.5	216.5	501.7	527.2
Wage accruals less disbursement	.0	.0	.1	.0	−0.1	−0.1
Plus: Government transfer payment to persons	27.5	81.8	185.7	312.6	661.7	733.2
Personal interest income	24.9	69.3	122.5	271.9	721.3	718.6
Personal dividend income	12.9	22.2	28.7	52.9	124.8	128.5
Business transfer payments	2.0	4.1	7.4	12.1	23.2	26.3
Equals: Personal income	409.4	831.8	1,313.4	2,258.5	4,679.8	4,834.4

Gross Domestic Product

Source: Bureau of Economic Analysis, U.S. Dept. of Commerce (billions of dollars)

	1990	1991	1992 (1st Quarter)
Gross domestic product	5,513.8	5,672.6	5,809.3
Personal consumption expenditures	3,742.6	3,889.1	4,023.5
Durable goods	465.9	445.2	468.3
Nondurable goods	1,217.7	1,251.9	1,270.8
Services	2,059.0	2,191.9	2,284.5
Gross private domestic investment	802.6	726.7	712.4
Fixed investment	802.7	745.2	745.0
Nonresidential	587.0	550.1	535.3
Structures	198.7	174.6	161.1
Producers' durable equipment	388.3	375.5	374.2
Residential	215.7	195.1	209.8

	1990	1991	1992 (1st Quarter)
Change in business inventories	0	−18.5	−32.7
Nonfarm	−2.0	−15.0	−29.5
Farm	2.0	−3.5	−3.2
Net exports of goods and services	−74.4	−30.7	−22.7
Exports	550.4	591.3	613.6
Imports	624.8	622.0	636.3
Government purchases	1,042.9	1,087.5	1,096.1
Federal	424.9	445.1	441.8
National defense	313.4	323.5	315.0
Nondefense	111.5	121.6	126.8
State and local	618.0	642.4	654.3

Federal Government Revenue by Major Financial Sector and Source: 1989-90

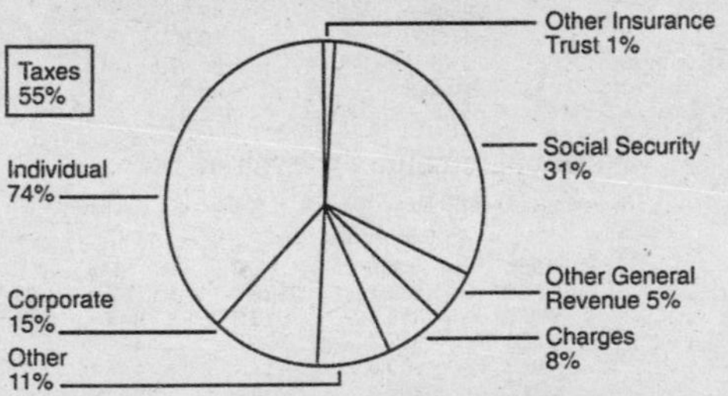

Federal Government Expenditure for Major Financial Sectors: 1989-1990

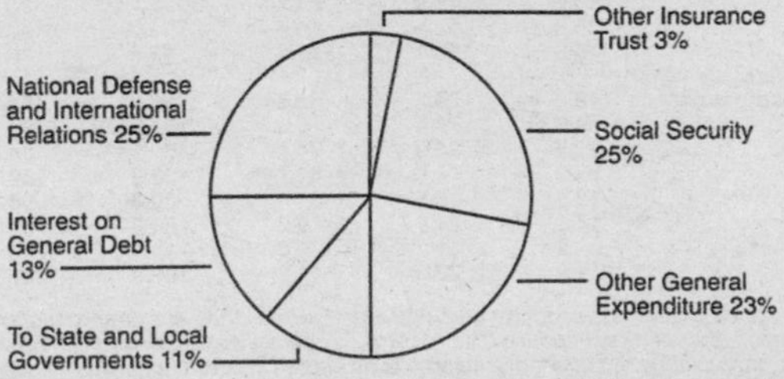

Leading U.S. Businesses in 1991

Source: FORTUNE Magazine; World Almanac Research

(millions of dollars of sales, unless otherwise noted)

Aerospace

Boeing	$29,314
United Technologies	21,262
McDonnell Douglas	18,718
Allied-Signal	11,882
Lockheed	9,809
General Dynamics	9,548
Textron	7,840
Martin Marietta	6,107
Northrop	5,706
Grumman	4,038

Apparel

Levi Strauss Assoc.	$4,903
VF	2,989
Liz Claiborne	2,029
Fruit of the Loom	1,628
Hartmarx	1,215
Leslie Fay	837
Crystal Brands	827
Kellwood	811
Phillips-Van Heusen	808
Russell	805
Gitano Group	780

Beverages

Pepsico	$19,771
Coca-Cola	11,572
Anheuser-Busch	10,996
Coca-Cola Enterprises	4,051
J.E. Seagram	3,680
Whitman	2,866
Adolph Coors	1,918
Brown-Forman	1,126
Dr Pepper/Seven-Up	601

Building Materials

PPG Industries	$5,725
Owens-Illinois	3,852
American Standard	3,595
Corning	3,287
Owens-Corning	2,783
Armstrong World Ind.	2,439
USG	1,840
Lafarge	1,569
Anchor Glass	1,167
Holnam	979

Chemicals

E.I. Du Pont De Nemours	$38,031
Dow Chemical	19,305
Monsanto	8,929
Union Carbide	7,346
W.R. Grace	6,949
Hoechst Celanese	6,856
Miles	6,197
Lyondell Petrochem.	5,757
American Cyanamid	5,040
BASF	4,962

Computers, Office Equip.

IBM	$64,792
Hewlett-Packard	14,541
Digital Equipment	14,024
Unisys	8,696
Apple Computer	6,309
Pitney Bowes	3,417
Compaq Computer	3,271
Sun Microsystems	3,260
Seagate Technology	2,691
Wang Laboratories	2,127

Electronics, Electrical Equip.

General Electric	$60,236
Westinghouse Electric	12,794
Rockwell International	12,028
Motorola	11,341
Raytheon	9,356
Emerson Electric	7,427
Texas Instruments	6,812
Whirlpool	6,770
Cooper Industries	6,163
North American Philips	6,065

Food

Philip Morris	$48,109
Conagra	19,505
Sara Lee	12,456
Archer-Daniels	8,568
Ralston Purina	7,394
Borden	7,235
General Mills	7,153
H.J. Heinz	6,682
Campbell Soup	6,230
CPC International	6,200

Forest Products

International Paper	$12,703
Georgia-Pacific	11,524
Weyerhaeuser	8,702
Kimberly-Clark	6,830
Stone Container	5,399
Scott Paper	5,000
Champion International	4,786
Mead	4,579
James River	4,562
Boise Cascade	4,044

Furniture

Johnson Controls	$4,566
Avery Dennison	2,545
Interco	1,597
LSS Holdings	1,085
Leggett & Platt	1,082
Herman Miller	884
Sealy Holdings	624
Hon Industries	612
La-Z-Boy Chair	609
Kimball International	565

Industrial and Farm Equip.

Tenneco	$14,035
Caterpillar	10,182
Deere	7,055
Dresser Industries	4,702
Black & Decker	4,637
Ingersoll-Rand	3,586
Cummins Engine	3,406
Baker Hughes	2,912
Parker Hannifin	2,441
Dover	2,196

Life Insurance[1]

Prudential of America	$148,418
Metropolitan Life	110,800
Teachers Insurance & Annuity	55,576
Aetna Life	52,355
Equitable Life Assurance	50,353
New York Life	42,750
Connecticut General Life	41,692
John Hancock Mutual Life	36,220
Northwestern Mutual Life	35,744
Travelers	35,663

Metal Products

Gillette	$4,706
Crown Cork & Seal	3,807
Masco	3,177
Tyco Laboratories	3,108
Illinois Tool Works	2,647
McDermott	2,299
Ball	2,267
Stanley Works	1,962
Harsco	1,956
Masco Industries	1,502

Metals

Aluminum Co. of Amer.	$9,981
LTV	6,117
Reynolds Metals	5,785
Bethlehem Steel	4,318
Amax	3,772
Inland Steel Ind.	3,404
Phelps Dodge	2,461
National Steel	2,330
Maxxam	2,317
Cyprus Minerals	1,659

Motor Vehicles and Parts

General Motors	$123,780
Ford Motor	88,963
Chrysler	29,370
TRW	7,913
Dana	4,591
Eaton	3,659
Navistar Intl.	3,487
Paccar	2,377
Echlin	1,695
Arvin Industries	1,680

Petroleum Refining

Exxon	$103,242
Mobil	56,910
Texaco	37,551
Chevron	36,795
Amoco	25,604
Shell Oil	22,201
Atlantic Richfield	17,683
USX	17,163
Phillips Petroleum	12,604
Sun	10,246

Pharmaceuticals

Johnson & Johnson	$12,447
Bristol-Myers Squibb	11,298
Merck	8,603
Pfizer	7,144
American Home Products	7,103
Abbott Laboratories	6,922
Eli Lilly	5,726
Warner-Lambert	5,167
Rhône-Poulenc Rorer	3,824
Schering-Plough	3,688

Publishing & Printing

R.R. Donnelly	$3,915
Times Mirror	3,624
Gannett	3,382
Berkshire Hathaway	2,914
Reader's Digest	2,394
Knight-Ridder	2,244
Tribune	2,035
McGraw-Hill	1,943
Dow Jones	1,732
New York Times	1,703

Retail[2]

Sears Roebuck	$57,242
Wal-Mart Stores	43,887
K Mart	34,969
Kroger	21,351
American Stores	20,100
J.C. Penney	17,295
Dayton Hudson	16,115
Safeway	15,119
Great Atlantic & Pacific Tea	11,391
May Department Stores	10,615

Rubber and Plastics Prods.

Goodyear Tire	$11,046
Premark Intl.	2,816
Rubbermaid	1,673
M.A. Hanna	1,150
Cooper Tire & Rubber	1,002
A. Schulman	740
Standard Products	638
Carlisle	621
Bandag	594
Constar International	548

Scientific and Photographic Equip.

Eastman Kodak	$19,649
Xerox	17,830
Minnesota Mining	13,340
Baxter International	8,921
Honeywell	6,221
EG&G	2,691
Becton Dickinson	2,172
Polaroid	2,096
Bausch & Lomb	1,536
Tektronix	1,331

Soaps, Cosmetics

Procter & Gamble	$27,406
Unilever U.S.	8,855
Colgate-Palmolive	6,094
Avon Products	3,593
Clorox	1,646
Intl. Flavors	1,017
Helene Curtis Indust.	892
Alberto-Culver	874
Stanhome	710
Safety-Kleen	697

Textiles

Wickes	$2,622

(continued)

Burlington Ind. Capital	2,081
Springs Industries	1,891
West Point-Pepperell	1,634
Shaw Industries	1,608
Amoskeag	1,244
DWG	1,222
JPS Textile Group	761
Cone Mills	700
Delta Woodside Indust.	590
Tobacco	
RJR Nabisco Holdings	$14,989
American Brands	8,379
Universal	3,274
Brooke Group	1,256
Standard Commercial	1,046
Dibrell Brothers	1,012
UST	879
Toys, Sporting Goods	
Hasbro	$2,141
Mattel	1,650
Transportation Equip.	
Brunswick	$2,088
Trinity Industries	1,263
Outboard Marine	984
Harley-Davidson	940
Avondale Industries	800
Huffy	679
Transportation[3]	
United Parcel Service	$15,048
AMR	12,993
UAL	11,748
Delta Air Lines	9,171
CSX	8,636
Federal Express	7,688
Northwest Airlines	7,534
Union Pacific	7,151
USAir Group	6,533
Continental Airlines Holdings	5,551
Utilities[1]	
GTE	$42,437
BellSouth	30,942
Bell Atlantic	27,882
US West	27,854
NYNEX	27,503
Southwestern Bell	23,179
Pacific Gas & Electric	22,901
Ameritech	22,290
Pacific Telesis Group	21,838
Southern	19,863

(1) Millions of dollars of assets as of Dec. 31, 1991; (2) Incl. revenue from nonretailing activities; (3) Incl. revenue from nontransportation activities.

U.S. Industrial Corporations with Largest Sales in 1991

Source: FORTUNE Magazine (billions of dollars)

Company, Headquarters	Sales
General Motors, Detroit, Mich.	$123.780
Exxon, Irving, Tex.	103.242
Ford Motor, Dearborn, Mich.	88.963
IBM, Armonk, N.Y.	64.792
General Electric, Fairfield, Conn.	60.236
Mobil, Fairfax, Va.	56.910
Philip Morris, New York, N.Y.	48.109
E.I. Du Pont De Nemours, Wilmington, Del.	38.031
Texaco, White Plains, N.Y.	37.551
Chevron, San Francisco, Cal.	36.795
Chrysler, Highland Park, Mich.	$29.370
Boeing, Seattle, Wash.	29.314
Procter & Gamble, Cincinnati, Oh.	27.406
Amoco, Chicago, Ill.	25.604
Shell Oil, Houston, Tex.	22.201
United Technologies, Hartford, Conn.	21.262
Pepsico, Purchase, N.Y.	19.771
Eastman Kodak, Rochester, N.Y.	19.649
Conagra, Omaha, Neb.	19.505
Dow Chemical, Midland, Mich.	19.305

Largest Corporate Mergers or Acquisitions in U.S.

(as of mid-1992)

Company	Acquirer	Dollars	Year
RJR Nabisco	Kohlberg Kravis Roberts	24.9 bln.	1988
Warner Communications	Time	13.9 bln.	1989
Gulf Oil	Chevron	13.3 bln.	1984
Kraft	Philip Morris	11.5 bln.	1988
Squibb	Bristol-Myers	11.5 bln.	1989
Getty Oil	Texaco	10.1 bln.	1984
Conoco	DuPont	8.0 bln.	1981
Standard Oil	British Petroleum	7.9 bln.*	1987
Federated Dept. Stores	Campeau	7.4 bln.	1988
NCR	AT&T	7.4 bln.	1991
MCA	Matsushita	6.5 bln.	1990
Marathon Oil	U.S. Steel	6.5 bln.	1981
Contel	GTE	6.2 bln.	1990
Beatrice	Kohlberg Kravis Roberts	6.2 bln.	1986
RCA	General Electric	6.2 bln.	1986
Superior Oil	Mobil Oil	5.7 bln.	1984
Pillsbury	Grand Metropolitan	5.7 bln.	1988
General Foods	Philip Morris	5.6 bln.	1986
Safeway Stores	Kohlberg Kravis Roberts	5.3 bln.	1986
Farmers Group	B.A.T. Industries	5.2 bln.	1988
Southern Pacific	Santa Fe Railroad	5.2 bln.	1983
Southland	J.T. Acquisition	5.1 bln.	1987
Hughes Aircraft	General Motors	5.0 bln.	1985
Nabisco	R.J. Reynolds	4.9 bln.	1985
Signal Cos.	Allied Corp.	4.9 bln.	1986
Sperry	Burroughs	4.8 bln.	1986
Connecticut General	INA	4.3 bln.	1981
Borg-Warner	AV Holdings	4.2 bln.	1987
Texasgulf	Elf Aquitaine	4.2 bln.	1981
Cities Service	Occidental Petroleum	4.0 bln.	1982
Bank America	Security Pacific	4.0 bln.	1991
Dome Petroleum	Amoco	3.8 bln.	1987
R.H. Macy	various investors	3.7 bln.	1986
American Hospital	Baxter Travenol	3.7 bln.	1986
Owens-Illinois	Kohlberg Kravis Roberts	3.6 bln.	1987
Belridge Oil	Shell Oil	3.6 bln.	1979
NWA	Checchi Group	3.6 bln.	1988
Allied Stores	Campeau	3.5 bln.	1986
Fort Howard Paper	Morgan Stanley Group	3.5 bln.	1988
ABC Broadcasting	Capital Cities Comm.	3.5 bln.	1985
Columbia Pictures	Sony	3.4 bln.	1989
Viacom	National Amusements	3.4 bln.	1987
McCaw Cellular	LIN Broadcasting	3.3 bln.	1989
Panhandle Eastern	Texas Eastern	3.2 bln.	1989
Chesebrough-Pond's	Unilever N.V.	3.1 bln.	1987
MidCon	Occidental Petroleum	3.0 bln.	1986
American Medical Intl.	IMA Holdings	3.0 bln.	1989
Texas Oil and Gas	USX Corp.	3.0 bln.	1986
Emhart	Black & Decker	2.8 bln.	1989
Carnation	Nestle	2.8 bln.	1984
Celanese	American Hoechst	2.7 bln.	1987
Esmark	Beatrice Foods	2.7 bln.	1984
G.D. Searle	Monsanto	2.7 bln.	1986
Continental Group	Kiewit-Murdock	2.7 bln.	1984
St. Joe Minerals	Fluor	2.6 bln.	1981
Electronic Data Systems	General Motors	2.6 bln.	1984
Firestone Tire	Bridgestone	2.6 bln.	1988
Macmillan	Maxwell Comm.	2.6 bln.	1988
Associated Dry Goods	May Dept. Stores	2.5 bln.	1986

* For the 45% of Standard Oil that British Petroleum did not already own.

Capital Gains Tax

Source: U.S. Chamber of Commerce

The following shows how the top effective tax rate on capital gains has changed since 1960.

Year	Effective rate (percent)	Year	Effective rate (percent)	Year	Effective rate (percent)	Year	Effective rate (percent)
1960	25.0	1970	32.2	1976	49.1	1987	28.0
1968	26.9	1971	34.4	1979	28.0	1988	33.0
1969	27.5	1972	45.5	1981	20.0	1991	28.0

Leading Franchises in 1992

Source: *Entrepreneur* magazine

Company	Business	Minimum start-up	Company	Business	Minimum start-up
McDonald's	fast food	$547,500	Jazzercise	fitness center	$2,325
Subway	fast food	44,000	Midas	auto repair	192,000
Dunkin' Donuts	donuts	160,000	Mail Boxes Etc.	shipping services	54,500
Jani-King	commercial cleaning	7,500	7-Eleven Stores	convenience stores	12,500
Baskin-Robbins USA	ice cream	134,000	H&R Block	income-tax services	5,600
ServiceMaster	home & office cleaning	16,800	Coldwell Banker Residential	real estate	28,000
Chem-Dry	cleaning services	9,950	Blockbuster Video	videotape rentals & sales	385,000
Hardee's	fast food	714,900			
Arby's	fast food	550,000	Budget Rent A Car	auto & truck rentals	165,000
Domino's Pizza	pizza	83,000	KFC	fast food	80,000
Dairy Queen	ice cream	405,000	Merle Norman Cosmetics	cosmetics	3,300
Choice Hotels	hotels	1,510,000	Re/Max International	real estate	12,800
Coverall North America	commercial cleaning	3,600	Electronic Realty Associates	real estate	18,010

Industrial Production Indexes, by Industry

Source: Federal Reserve System

Major Industry Group	1970	1975	1980	1985	1989	1990	1991
Total Index	**61**	**66**	**84**	**94**	**108**	**109**	**107**
Manufacturing	56	61	79	92	109	110	107
Durable manuf.	53	57	76	92	111	112	107
Lumber and products	67	67	77	88	103	101	94
Furniture and fixtures	56	59	78	88	105	106	99
Clay, glass, and stone prod.	71	78	92	94	108	106	95
Primary metals	115	107	111	102	109	108	100
Fabricated metal products	76	77	92	94	107	106	100
Nonelectrical machinery	33	38	61	87	122	126	124
Electrical machinery	40	45	73	93	110	111	110
Transportation equipment	55	60	72	92	107	105	99
Instruments	39	52	79	96	116	117	118
Nondurable manuf.	61	68	83	91	106	108	108
Food	64	71	85	95	105	108	109
Tobacco products	91	98	104	97	100	99	100
Textile mill products	74	78	92	90	102	101	101
Apparel products	75	71	89	93	104	99	96
Paper and products	63	66	83	92	103	105	105
Printing and publishing	53	54	70	88	109	112	112
Chemicals and products	56	69	88	91	108	110	111
Petroleum products	84	91	99	93	106	108	108
Rubber and plastic products	38	47	62	86	109	110	110
Leather and products	208	182	162	112	104	100	88
Mining	100	98	110	109	100	103	101
Utilities	73	84	96	99	107	108	109

1987 = 100.

Sales and Profits of Manufacturing Corporations by Industry Group

Source: Economic Surveys Division, Bureau of the Census, U.S. Dept. of Commerce (millions of dollars)

Industry group	Sales 1Q 1991	Sales 4Q 1991	Sales 1Q 1992	Income after taxes 1Q 1991	Income after taxes 4Q 1991	Income after taxes 1Q 1992
All manufacturing corporations	655,146	708,802	677,597	18,286	8,676	24,371
Nondurable manufacturing corporations	351,215	371,714	352,798	16,843	11,494	16,572
Food and kindred products	98,382	101,582	96,913	4,969	3,971	5,085
Tobacco manufactures	NA	NA	NA	NA	NA	NA
Textile mill products	12,958	14,864	14,556	(32)	460	294
Paper and allied products	30,067	30,866	30,735	860	(369)	796
Printing and publishing	34,870	38,627	35,706	696	1,047	878
Chemicals and allied products	70,834	76,000	75,682	5,224	4,210	6,268
Industrial chemicals and synthetics	27,002	29,297	29,216	1,836	1,143	1,675
Drugs	16,053	17,491	18,080	2,244	2,687	3,240
Petroleum and coal products	71,809	71,928	62,473	4,860	1,889	2,252
Rubber and miscellaneous plastics products	18,286	21,261	21,299	(54)	(163)	544
Other nondurable manufacturing corporations	14,208	16,586	15,434	321	449	453
Durable manufacturing corporations	303,931	337,088	324,799	1,443	(2,818)	7,769
Stone, clay, and glass products	10,903	12,782	10,978	(554)	(1,424)	(575)
Primary metal industries	28,108	28,629	28,193	289	(1,380)	260
Iron and steel	12,506	12,627	12,571	(258)	(1,148)	(140)
Nonferrous metals	15,601	16,002	15,621	547	(232)	401
Fabricated metal products	29,760	32,423	32,448	502	274	1,060
Machinery, except electrical	59,889	63,981	62,245	(1,244)	(1,266)	1,637
Electrical and electronic equipment	52,116	57,609	52,740	1,874	1,903	1,847
Transportation equipment	75,214	90,227	87,289	(1,019)	2,424	722
Motor vehicles and equipment	40,684	51,314	51,042	(1,976)	2,658	526
Aircraft, guided missiles, and parts	30,997	35,384	32,989	944	210	145
Instruments and related products	24,685	25,931	25,492	1,507	1,162	2,138
Other durable manufacturing corporations	23,257	25,507	25,415	88	337	678
All mining corporations*	**9,627**	**9,291**	**8,861**	**443**	**(266)**	**28**
All retail trade corporations*	**157,599**	**194,386**	**NA**	**736**	**2,811**	**NA**
All wholesale trade corporations*	**178,093**	**187,021**	**184,542**	**671**	**91,916**	**736**

* With assets over $50 million.

Consumer Price Index

The Consumer Price Index (CPI) is a measure of the average change in prices over time of basic consumer goods and services. From Jan. 1978, the Bureau of Labor Statistics began publishing CPI's for two population groups: (1) a CPI for All Urban Consumers (CPI-U) which covers about 80% of the total population; and (2) a CPI for Urban Wage Earners and Clerical Workers (CPI-W) which covers about 32% of the total population. The CPI-U includes, in addition to wage earners and clerical workers, groups such as professional, managerial, and technical workers, the self-employed, short-term workers, the unemployed, retirees and others not in the labor force.

The CPI is based on prices of food, clothing, shelter, fuels, transportation fares, charges for doctors' and dentists' services, drugs, and the other goods and services bought for day-to-day living. The index had been measuring price changes from a designated reference date—1967—which equaled 100.0.

Beginning with the release of data for January 1988, the standard reference base period for the Consumer Price Index is 1982-84. The rebasing is in keeping with the government's policy that index bases should be updated periodically. The 1982-84 period was chosen to coincide with the time period of the updated CPI's expenditure weights, which are based upon the Consumer Expenditure Surveys for 1982, 1983, and 1984. All of the CPI figures in the following tables have been changed to reflect the new reference base.

Consumer Price Indexes, 1992

Source: Bureau of Labor Statistics, U.S. Dept. of Labor

	CPI-U				CPI-W			
	Unadjusted indexes	Unadjusted percent change to June 1992 from-		Seasonally adjusted percent change from-	Unadjusted indexes	Unadjusted percent change to June 1992 from-		Seasonally adjusted percent change from-
(1982-84=100)	June 1992	June 1991	May 1992	May to June	June 1992	June 1991	May 1992	May to June
Food, beverages	138.3	0.4	0	0.5	137.9	0.4	0	0.1
Housing	137.7	3.2	0.7	0.4	135.1	3.1	0.7	0.4
Apparel, upkeep	131.0	3.2	−1.6	−0.2	129.8	3.3	−1.5	0.2
Transportation	126.9	2.6	0.5	0.5	126.5	2.8	0.8	0.6
Medical care	189.4	7.5	0.4	0.4	188.9	7.6	0.4	0.5
Entertainment	142.0	2.8	0	0	140.5	2.8	0	0
Other goods, services	181.5	6.8	0.1	0.2	181.8	6.6	0.1	0.1
Services	151.7	4.0	0.5	0.3	149.8	4.0	0.5	0.3
Special Indexes								
All items less food	140.7	3.7	0.4	0.4	138.2	3.6	0.4	0.4
Commodities less food	124.5	3.0	−0.1	0.4	124.1	3.0	0.2	0.5
Nondurables	132.8	1.8	0	0	132.7	1.8	0.2	0.2
Energy	105.9	2.3	3.4	2.0	105.7	2.3	3.5	1.9
All items less energy	145.0	3.2	0.1	0.2	142.8	3.0	0.1	0.1

Consumer Price Indexes for Selected Items and Groups

Source: Bureau of Labor Statistics, U.S. Dept. of Labor

(all urban consumers = CPI-U)

(1982-84 = 100. Annual averages of monthly figures)

	1970	1975	1980	1985	1988	1989	1990	1991
All Items	**38.8**	**53.8**	**82.4**	**107.6**	**118.3**	**124.0**	**130.7**	**136.2**
Food and beverages	**40.1**	**60.2**	**86.7**	**105.6**	**118.2**	**124.9**	**132.1**	**136.8**
Food	39.2	59.8	86.8	105.6	118.2	125.1	132.4	136.3
Food at home	39.9	61.8	88.4	104.3	116.6	124.2	132.3	135.8
Cereals, bakery prods.	37.1	62.9	83.9	107.9	122.1	132.4	140.0	145.8
Meats, poultry, fish, eggs	44.6	67.0	92.0	100.1	114.3	121.3	130.0	132.6
Dairy prods.	44.7	62.6	90.9	103.2	108.4	115.6	126.5	125.1
Fruits, vegetables	37.8	56.9	82.1	106.4	128.1	138.0	149.0	155.8
Sugar, sweets	30.5	65.3	90.5	105.8	114.0	119.4	124.7	129.3
Fats, oils	39.2	73.5	89.3	106.9	113.1	121.2	126.3	131.7
Nonalcoholic beverages	27.1	41.3	91.4	104.3	107.5	111.3	113.5	114.1
Other prepared foods	39.6	58.9	83.6	106.4	118.0	125.5	131.2	137.1
Food away from home	37.5	54.5	83.4	108.3	121.8	127.4	133.4	137.9
Alcoholic beverages	52.1	65.9	86.4	106.4	118.6	123.5	129.3	142.8
Housing	**36.4**	**50.7**	**81.1**	**107.7**	**118.5**	**123.0**	**128.5**	**133.6**
Shelter	35.5	48.8	81.0	109.8	127.1	132.8	140.0	146.3
Rent	46.5	58.0	80.9	111.8	127.8	132.8	146.7	155.6
Maintenance, repairs	35.8	54.1	82.4	106.5	114.7	118.0	122.2	126.3
Fuel, other utilities	29.1	45.4	75.4	106.5	104.4	107.8	111.6	115.3
Energy services	31.8	50.0	75.8	106.9	111.5	114.7	117.4	112.6
Household furnishings & operation	46.8	63.4	86.3	103.8	109.4	111.2	113.3	116.0
House furnishings	55.5	69.8	88.5	101.7	105.1	105.5	106.7	107.5
Apparel & upkeep	**59.2**	**72.5**	**90.9**	**105.0**	**115.4**	**118.6**	**124.1**	**128.7**
Apparel commodities	63.3	76.7	92.9	104.0	113.7	116.7	122.0	126.4
Men's & boys'	62.2	75.5	89.4	105.0	113.4	117.0	120.4	124.2
Women's & girls'	71.8	85.5	96.0	104.9	114.9	116.4	122.6	127.6
Footwear	56.8	69.6	91.8	102.3	109.9	114.4	117.4	120.9
Transportation	**37.5**	**50.1**	**83.1**	**106.4**	**108.7**	**114.1**	**120.5**	**123.8**
Private	37.5	50.6	84.2	106.2	107.6	112.9	118.8	121.9
New cars	53.0	62.9	88.4	106.1	116.9	119.2	121.4	126.0
Used cars	31.2	43.8	62.3	113.7	118.0	120.4	117.6	118.1
Gasoline	27.9	45.1	97.5	98.6	80.8	88.5	101.0	99.2
Public	35.2	43.5	69.0	110.5	123.3	129.5	142.6	148.9
Medical care	**34.0**	**47.5**	**74.9**	**113.5**	**138.6**	**149.3**	**162.8**	**177.0**
Entertainment	**47.5**	**62.0**	**83.6**	**107.9**	**120.3**	**126.5**	**132.4**	**138.4**

(*continued*)

	1970	1975	1980	1985	1988	1989	1990	1991
Other goods & services	**40.9**	**53.9**	**75.2**	**114.5**	**137.0**	**147.7**	**159.0**	**171.6**
Tobacco products	43.1	54.7	72.0	116.7	145.8	164.4	181.5	202.7
Personal care	43.5	57.9	81.9	106.3	119.4	125.0	130.4	134.9
Toilet goods	42.7	58.0	79.6	107.6	118.1	123.2	128.2	132.8
Personal care services	44.2	57.7	83.7	108.9	120.7	126.8	132.8	137.0
Personal, educational expenses	35.5	48.7	70.9	119.1	147.9	158.1	170.2	183.7

Consumer Price Indexes Annual Percent Change

Source: Bureau of Labor Statistics, U.S. Dept. of Labor

The Consumer Price Index (CPI-U) measures the average change in prices of goods and services purchased by all urban consumers.

	1980[1]	1981	1982	1983	1984	1985	1986	1987	1988	1989	1990	1991
All items	13.5	10.3	6.2	3.2	4.3	3.6	1.9	3.6	4.1	4.8	5.4	4.2
Food	8.6	7.8	4.1	2.1	3.8	2.3	3.2	4.1	4.1	5.8	5.8	2.9
Shelter	17.6	11.7	7.1	2.3	4.9	5.6	5.5	4.7	4.8	4.5	5.4	4.5
Rent, residential	8.9	8.7	7.6	5.8	5.2	6.2	5.8	4.1	3.8	3.9	5.6	6.1
Fuel & other utilities	16.4	14.6	9.8	5.6	4.6	1.6	−2.3	−1.1	−1.4	3.3	3.5	3.3
Apparel and upkeep	7.1	4.8	2.6	2.5	1.9	2.8	0.9	4.4	4.3	2.8	4.6	3.7
Private transportation	17.4	11.4	3.5	2.3	4.3	2.5	−4.7	−3.0	3.3	4.9	5.2	2.6
New cars	8.1	6.0	3.9	2.6	2.9	3.2	4.2	3.6	2.0	2.0	1.8	3.8
Gasoline	38.9	11.3	−5.3	−3.3	−1.6	.8	−21.9	−4.0	0.9	9.5	14.1	−1.8
Public transportation	25.7	24.1	10.9	4.8	6.2	4.5	5.9	3.5	1.8	5.0	10.1	4.4
Medical care	11.0	10.7	11.6	8.8	6.2	6.3	7.5	6.6	6.5	7.7	9.0	8.7
Entertainment	9.0	7.8	6.5	4.3	3.7	3.9	3.4	3.3	4.3	5.2	4.7	4.5
Commodities	12.3	8.4	4.1	2.9	3.4	2.1	−0.9	3.2	3.5	4.7	5.2	4.2

(1) Change from 1979.

Consumer Price Index by Region and Selected Cities

Source: Bureau of Labor Statistics, U.S. Dept. of Labor

	CPI-U Indexes			Percent change to June 1992 from—	CPI-W Indexes			Percent change to June 1992 from—
Area (1982-84 = 100)	Apr. 1992	May 1992	June 1992	June 1991	Apr. 1992	May 1992	June 1992	June 1991
U.S. city average	**139.5**	**139.7**	**140.2**	**3.1**	**137.3**	**137.6**	**138.1**	**3.0**
Northeast urban	**146.3**	**146.3**	**147.0**	**3.4**	**144.2**	**144.3**	**145.0**	**3.2**
More than 1,200,000	146.8	146.7	147.4	3.4	143.6	143.7	144.5	3.2
500,000 to 1,200,000	145.8	145.9	146.3	3.3	144.1	144.1	144.4	3.1
50,000 to 500,000	144.3	144.7	145.6	3.6	146.3	146.7	147.4	3.2
North Central urban	**135.1**	**135.5**	**136.0**	**2.6**	**132.6**	**133.1**	**133.5**	**2.4**
More than 1,200,000	136.3	136.8	137.3	2.3	132.8	133.4	134.0	2.3
360,000 to 1,200,000	133.8	133.9	133.9	1.8	131.0	131.2	131.3	1.7
50,000 to 360,000	136.4	136.9	137.5	3.8	134.5	135.0	135.6	3.5
Less than 50,000	130.3	130.4	131.0	2.4	129.7	129.9	130.6	2.4
South urban	**135.9**	**136.2**	**136.7**	**2.9**	**134.5**	**135.0**	**135.5**	**2.8**
More than 1,200,000	136.1	136.5	137.2	2.7	134.6	135.1	135.9	2.7
450,000 to 1,200,000	137.4	137.7	138.0	3.0	134.2	134.6	135.0	2.9
50,000 to 450,000	135.1	135.7	136.2	3.6	134.9	135.7	136.2	3.3
Less than 50,000	134.1	134.0	134.0	2.1	134.2	134.2	134.2	1.8
West urban	**141.3**	**141.4**	**141.6**	**3.5**	**139.0**	**139.2**	**139.5**	**3.6**
More than 1,250,000	143.2	143.5	143.7	3.6	139.3	139.7	140.1	3.7
50,000 to 330,000	138.7	137.9	138.5	4.0	137.1	136.5	137.0	3.6
Selected areas								
Chicago, Ill.–Gary-Lake County, Ill., Ind., Wis.	139.8	140.5	141.2	2.8	135.4	136.2	136.9	2.9
L.A.–Anaheim, Riverside, Cal.	145.8	146.0	146.2	3.8	141.3	141.4	141.8	4.0
New York, N.Y.–Northern N.J., Long Island, N.Y.	149.2	148.9	149.5	3.4	145.9	145.8	146.5	3.1
Philadelphia, Wilmington, Trenton, Pa., Del., N.J., M.D.	145.4	145.7	147.5	4.0	145.1	145.5	147.4	3.9
San Francisco–Oakland, San Jose, Cal.	141.6	141.9	141.9	3.1	139.6	140.1	140.3	3.2
Baltimore, Md.	—	139.5	—	—	—	138.9	—	—
Boston, Lawrence, Salem, Mass., N.H.	—	147.5	—	—	—	146.8	—	—
Cleveland, Akron, Lorain, Oh.	—	136.1	—	—	—	129.6	—	—
Miami, Ft. Lauderdale, Fla.	—	133.7	—	—	—	131.6	—	—
St. Louis, E. St. Louis, Mo., Ill.	—	134.0	—	—	—	133.6	—	—
Washington, D.C.–Md.—Va.	—	143.2	—	—	—	141.6	—	—
Dallas–Fort Worth, Tex.	132.5	—	134.2	3.2	131.5	—	133.5	3.2
Detroit, Ann Arbor, Mich.	135.3	—	135.5	1.5	131.7	—	131.8	1.3
Houston, Galveston, Brazoria, Tex.	128.7	—	129.4	3.6	128.4	—	129.2	3.2
Pittsburgh, Beaver Valley, Pa.	135.1	—	135.2	3.4	129.4	—	129.5	3.4

Percent Change in Consumer Prices in Selected Countries

Source: International Monetary Fund

Country	1970-1975, avg.	1975-1980, avg.	1980-1985, avg.	1987-1988-avg.	1988-1989, avg.	1989-1990, avg.	1990-1991, avg.
Canada	7.3	8.7	7.4	4.0	5.0	4.8	5.6
France	8.8	10.5	9.6	2.7	3.5	3.4	3.1
Germany	6.1	4.1	3.9	1.3	2.8	2.7	3.5
Italy	11.3	16.3	13.7	5.1	6.3	6.5	6.4
Japan	11.5	6.5	2.7	0.7	2.3	3.1	3.3
Spain	12.1	18.6	12.2	4.8	6.8	6.7	5.9
Sweden	8.0	10.5	9.0	5.8	6.4	10.5	9.3
Switzerland	7.7	2.3	4.3	1.9	3.2	5.4	5.8
United Kingdom	13.0	14.4	7.2	4.9	7.8	9.5	5.9
United States	6.7	8.9	5.5	4.0	4.8	5.4	4.2

Index of Leading Economic Indicators

Source: Bureau of Economic Analysis, U.S. Dept. of Commerce

The index of leading economic indicator is used to project the economy's performance six months or a year ahead. The index is made up of 11 measurements of economic activity that tend to change direction long before the overall economy does.

Components
Average work week of production workers in manufacturing
Average weekly claims for state unemployment insurance
New orders for consumer goods and materials, adjusted for inflation
Vendor performance (companies receiving slower deliveries from suppliers)
Contracts and orders for plant and equipment, adjusted for inflation

Components
New building permits issued
Change in manufacturers unfilled orders, durable goods
Change in sensitive materials prices
Index of stock prices
Money supply: M-2, adjusted for inflation
Index of consumer expectations

Distribution of Total Personal Income

Source: Bureau of Economic Analysis; U.S. Dept. of Commerce (billions of dollars)

Year	Personal income	Personal taxes	Disposable Personal income	Personal outlays	Personal Savings: Amount	Personal Savings: As pct. of disposable income
1960	$ 402.3	$ 50.4	$ 352.0	$ 332.3	$ 19.7	5.6%
1965	540.7	64.9	475.8	442.1	33.7	7.1
1970	811.1	115.8	695.3	639.5	55.8	8.0
1975	1,265.0	168.9	1,096.1	1,001.8	94.3	8.6
1980	2,165.3	336.5	1,828.9	1,718.7	110.2	6.0
1981	2.429.5	387.7	2,041.7	1,904.3	137.4	6.7
1982	2,584.6	404.1	2,180.5	2,044.5	136.0	6.2
1983	2,838.6	410.5	2,428.1	2,297.4	130.6	5.4
1984	3,108.7	440.2	2,668.6	2,504.5	164.1	6.1
1985	3,325.3	486.6	2,838.7	2,713.3	125.4	4.4
1986	3,526.2	512.9	3,013.3	2,888.5	124.9	4.1
1987	3,776.6	571.7	3,205.9	3,104.1	101.8	3.2
1988	4,070.8	591.6	3,479.2	3,333.6	145.6	4.2
1989	4,384.3	658.8	3,725.5	3,553.7	171.8	4.6
1990	4,679.8	621.0	4,058.8	3,853.1	205.8	5.1
1991	4,834.4	616.1	4,218.4	3,999.1	219.3	5.2

Notable Bankruptcy Filings

Year	Company	Year	Company	Year	Company
1970	Penn Central	1989	Southmark	1991	America West Airlines
1982	Manville	1989	Lomas Financial	1991	Orion Pictures
1983	Baldwin-United	1989	American Continental	1991	Maxwell Communications
1985	Wheeling-Pittsburgh Steel	1990	Drexel Burnham Lambert	1991	Carter Hawley Hale
1986	LTV Corp.	1990	Allied/Federal	1992	R.H. Macy
1987	Texaco	1990	Ames Department Stores	1992	Zale Corp.
1988	Financial Corp. of America	1990	Continental Airlines	1992	T.W.A.
1989	MCorp	1990	Pan Am		

Bankruptcy Petitions, 1905-1991

Source: Administrative Office of the U.S. Courts, Annual Report of the Director (thousands)

Year	Filed	Pending	Year	Filed	Pending	Year	Filed	Pending	Year	Filed	Pending
1905	17	28	1940	53	55	1975	254	202	1986	478	729
1910	18	28	1945	13	21	1980	278	346	1987	561	809
1915	28	44	1950	33	38	1981	360	362	1988	594	815
1920	14	30	1955	59	56	1982	368	461	1989	643	879
1925	46	60	1960	110	95	1983	375	537	1990	725	974
1930	63	61	1965	180	162	1984	344	578	1991	880	1,123
1935	69	65	1970	194	191	1985	365	609			

For fiscal years ending in year shown. Covers all U.S. bankruptcy courts. Bankruptcy petitions "Filed" means the commencement of a proceeding through the presentation of a petition to the clerk of the bankruptcy court; "Pending" is a proceeding in which the administration has not been completed.

Chapter 11

Chapter 11 refers to the provisions in the Federal Bankruptcy Act for court-supervised reorganization of debtor companies. A company files for Chapter 11 protection when it can no longer pay its creditors or when it expects future liabilities it cannot hope to pay, like product liability damage awards. In 1991, the U.S. Supreme Court ruled that the provision of Federal bankruptcy law that permits corporations to reorganize while continuing to operate was also available for use by individuals.

Process

1. Judge issues automatic stay

- Creditors cannot press suits for repayment.
- Debts are frozen.
- Company's day-to-day operations continue.
- Significant spending must have judge's approval.
- Secured creditors can ask court for hardship exemption from debt freeze.

2. Unsecured creditors form a committee

- Representatives are chosen to deal with the company.
- Creditors can ask the court to appoint an examiner to investigate possible fraud or mismanagement.
- Court can name a trustee to run the company.

3. The committee and company negotiate a reorganization plan.

- Parties negotiate a repayment plan for frozen debts. This step can take months or years.

4. Creditors approve the plan

- Must have assent of majority of creditors as well as creditors who are owed two-thirds of the debt.

5. Judge approves the plan

Reorganized Company Emerges

- It must meet the terms of the agreed repayment plan.
- It operates as a normal company.

State Finances

Revenues, Expenditures, Debts, Taxes, and U.S. Aid

Source: Census Bureau. U.S. Dept. of Commerce (fiscal year 1991)

State	Revenue (millions)	Expenditures (millions)	Debt (millions)	Per cap. debt	Per cap. taxes	Per cap. U.S. aid
Alabama	$9,767	$8,855	$4,214	$1,030	$964	$566
Alaska	6,355	4,941	5,291	9,282	3,168	1,239
Arizona	9,016	8,041	2,540	677	1,256	396
Arkansas	4,810	4,649	1,764	743	997	502
California	90,784	85,640	31,956	1,051	1,477	578
Colorado	7,863	6,992	2,659	787	951	466
Connecticut	9,816	11,115	13,006	3,952	1,514	646
Delaware	2,443	2,318	3,215	4,728	1,713	532
Florida	24,541	25,168	11,084	834	1,040	345
Georgia	13,866	13,286	3,652	551	1,080	510
Hawaii	4,916	4,510	4,202	3,701	2,325	644
Idaho	2,584	2,305	1,122	1,080	1,159	516
Illinois	25,092	24,619	18,238	1,580	1,151	416
Indiana	12,288	11,548	4,624	824	1,102	460
Iowa	7,137	6,820	1,620	579	1,233	518
Kansas	5,249	5,126	337	135	1,120	453
Kentucky	9,951	9,048	6,024	1,622	1,358	597
Louisiana	10,764	10,537	10,729	2,523	1,013	668
Maine	3,222	3,515	2,585	2,092	1,261	610
Maryland	12,479	12,576	7,528	1,548	1,317	457
Massachusetts	18,727	20,349	21,102	3,519	1,615	673
Michigan	24,505	24,037	10,109	1,079	1,185	555
Minnesota	13,690	12,730	3,941	889	1,588	560
Mississippi	5,792	5,171	1,413	545	948	704
Missouri	10,002	9,254	5,775	1,119	968	432
Montana	2,355	2,384	1,611	1,994	1,007	755
Nebraska	3,436	3,266	1,596	996	1,103	467
Nevada	3,555	3,436	1,708	1,330	1,312	330
New Hampshire	2,088	2,135	4,127	3,734	565	399
New Jersey	24,743	23,250	19,039	2,453	1,500	543
New Mexico	4,913	4,527	1,752	1,131	1,347	595
New York	65,715	64,321	51,804	2,868	1,567	816
North Carolina	15,266	15,036	3,490	517	1,165	454
North Dakota	1,998	1,793	964	1,517	1,189	772
Ohio	31,721	27,791	11,367	1,039	1,056	507
Oklahoma	7,819	7,267	3,730	1,174	1,216	475
Oregon	8,202	7,249	6,451	2,207	1,037	623
Pennsylvania	27,086	26,710	11,640	973	1,088	465
Rhode Island	3,305	3,465	4,393	4,375	1,251	737
South Carolina	9,289	8,970	4,189	1,176	1,104	575
South Dakota	1,629	1,417	1,754	2,494	796	713
Tennessee	9,544	9,238	2,790	563	870	551
Texas	33,773	29,526	7,687	443	923	438
Utah	4,344	4,108	1,911	1,079	1,051	551
Vermont	1,703	1,736	1,486	2,620	1,207	795
Virginia	14,523	13,352	6,500	1,034	1,090	374
Washington	16,394	15,666	6,520	1,299	1,592	551
West Virginia	5,013	4,741	2,770	1,537	1,292	596
Wisconsin	14,137	12,448	6,625	1,336	1,416	532
Wyoming	1,979	1,813	922	2,003	1,385	1,218
United States	**$660,189**	**$628,795**	**$345,554**	**$1,373**	**$1,235**	**$536**

State Revenues and Expenditures

State governments took in $517 billion in revenues and spent $507 billion in 1990.

Source	Percent	Spent on	Percent
Sales tax	28%	Education	36%
Federal government	23	Welfare	21
Individual income tax	19	Other	19
Other non-tax revenue	11	Highways	9
Fees for specific services	8	Health and hospitals	8
Other taxes	7	Interest on general debt	4
Corporation income tax	4	Corrections	3

Federal Aid to State and Local Governments

Source: U.S. Office of Management and Budget

(millions of dollars)

Type of aid, function, and major program	1980	1985	1988	1989	1990
Grant-in-aid shared revenue[1]	**$91,451**	**$105,897**	**$115,294**	**$123,563**	**$133,836**
National defense	93	157	188	253	252
Natural resources & environment	5,363	4,069	3,747	3,606	3,841
Energy	499	529	457	420	438
Agriculture	569	2,420	2,069	1,359	1,382
Transportation[1]	13,087	17,055	18,083	18,225	18,700
Community & regional development[1]	6,486	5,221	4,267	4,074	5,128
Education, employment, training, social services[1]	21,862	17,817	19,882	21,987	22,833
Health[1]	15,758	24,451	32,586	36,679	42,928
Income security[1]	18,495	27,153	31,620	32,523	35,403
Veterans benefits & services	90	91	106	127	142
Administration of justice	529	95	338	347	473
General government[2]	8,616	6,838	1,950	2,204	2,315

(1) Includes items not shown separately. (2) Includes general purpose fiscal assistance.

Federal Reserve System

(as of Aug. 1992)

The Federal Reserve System is the central bank for the United States. The system was established on December 23, 1913, originally to give the country an elastic currency, to provide facilities for discounting commercial paper, and to improve the supervision of banking. Since then, the System's responsibilities have been broadened. Over the years, stability and growth of the economy, a high level of employment, stability in the purchasing power of the dollar, and reasonable balance in transactions with foreign countries have come to be recognized as primary objectives of governmental economic policy.

The Federal Reserve System consists of the Board of Governors, the 12 District Reserve Banks and their branch offices, and the Federal Open Market Committee. Several advisory councils help the Board meet its varied responsibilities.

The hub of the System is the seven member Board of Governors in Washington. The members of the Board are appointed by the President and confirmed by the Senate, to serve 14-year terms. The President also appoints the Chairman and Vice-Chairman of the Board from among the board members for 4-year terms that may be renewed. Currently, the board members are: Alan Greenspan, Chairman; David W. Mullins Jr., Vice Chairman; Edward W. Kelley Jr.; Wayne D. Angell; John P. La Ware; Lawrence B. Lindsey; Susan M. Phillips.

The Board is the policy-making body. In addition to its policy making responsibilities, it supervises the budget and operations of the Reserve Banks, approves the appointments of their presidents and appoints 3 of each District Bank's directors, including the chairman and vice chairman of each Reserve Bank's board.

The 12 Reserve Banks and their branch offices serve as the decentralized portion of the System, carrying out day-today operations such as circulating currency and coin, providing fiscal agency functions and payments mechanism services. The District Banks are located in Boston, New York, Philadelphia, Cleveland, Richmond, Atlanta, Chicago, St. Louis, Minneapolis, Kansas City, Dallas and San Francisco.

The System's principal function is monetary policy, which it controls using three tools: reserve requirements, the discount rate and open market operations. Uniform reserve requirements, set by the Board, are applied to the transaction accounts and nonpersonal time deposits of all depository institutions. Responsibility for setting the discount rate (the interest rate at which depository institutions can borrow money from the Reserve Banks) is shared by the Board of Governors and the Reserve Banks. Changes in the discount rate are recommended by the individual Boards of Directors of the Reserve Banks and are subject to approval by the Board of Governors. The most important tool of monetary policy is open market operations (the purchase and sale of government securities). Responsibility for influencing the cost and availability of money and credit through the purchase and sale of government securities lies with the Federal Open Market Committee (FOMC). This committee is composed of the 7 members of the Board of Governors, the president of the Federal Reserve Bank of New York, and 4 other Federal Reserve Bank presidents, who serve one-year terms on a rotating basis. The committee bases its decisions on current economic and financial developments and outlook, setting yearly growth objectives for key measures of money supply and credit. The decisions of the committee are carried out by the Domestic Trading Desk of the Federal Reserve Bank of New York.

The Federal Reserve Act prescribes a Federal Advisory Council, consisting of one member from each Federal Reserve District, elected annually by the Board of Directors of each of the 12 Federal Reserve Banks. They meet with the Federal Reserve Board four times a year to discuss business and financial conditions and to make advisory recommendations.

The Consumer Advisory Council is a statutory body, including both consumer and creditor representatives, which advises the Board of Governors on its implementation of consumer regulations and other consumer-related matters.

Following the passage of the Monetary Control Act of 1980, the Board of Governors established the Thrift Institutions Advisory Council to provide information and views on the special needs and problems of thrift institutions. The group is comprised of representatives of mutual savings banks, savings and loan associations, and credit unions.

Federal Reserve Board Discount Rate

The discount rate is the rate of interest set by the Federal Reserve that member banks are charged when borrowing money through the Federal Reserve System.

	Effective Date	Rate		Effective Date	Rate		Effective Date	Rate		Effective Date	Rate
1980:	Feb. 15	13		Dec. 4	12		Nov. 21	8½	**1989:**	Feb. 24	7
	May 30	12	**1982:**	July 20	11½		Dec. 24	8	**1990:**	Dec. 18	6½
	June 13	11		Aug. 2	11	**1985:**	May 20	7½	**1991:**	Feb. 1	6
	July 28	10		Aug. 16	10½	**1986:**	March 7	7	**1991:**	Apr. 30	5½
	Sept. 26	11		Aug. 27	10		April 21	6½		Sept. 13	5
	Nov. 17	12		Oct. 12	9½		July 11	6		Nov. 6	4½
	Dec. 5	13		Nov. 22	9		Aug. 21	5½		Dec. 20	3½
1981:	May 5	14		Dec. 15	8½	**1987:**	Sept. 4	6	**1992:**	July 3	3
	Nov. 2	13	**1984:**	April 9	9	**1988:**	Aug. 9	6½			

Federal Deposit Insurance Corporation (FDIC)

The primary purpose of the Federal Deposit Insurance Corporation (FDIC) is to insure deposits in all banks approved for insurance coverage benefits under the Federal Deposit Insurance Act. The major functions of the FDIC are to pay off depositors of insured banks closed without adequate provision having been made to pay depositors' claims, to act as receiver for all national banks placed in receivership and for state banks placed in receivership when appointed receiver by state authorities, and to prevent the continuance or development of unsafe and unsound banking practices. The FDIC's income consists of assessments on insured banks and income from investments; it receives no appropriations from Congress. It may borrow from the U.S. Treasury not to exceed $30 billion outstanding, but has made no such borrowings since it was organized in 1933. The FDIC deficit (Deposit Insurance Fund) as of Jan. 1, 1992 was negative $7.0 billion.

The Savings and Loan Crisis

In Aug. 1992, the Congressional Budget Office estimated that handling losses in failed savings and loan institutions would cost $135 billion from 1989 through 1998. That is about $20 billion less than the budget office's previous estimate, and does not include $60 billion spent before 1989. Responsibility for handling savings and loan failures will shift from the Resolution Trust Corporation to the Federal Deposit Insurance Corporation on Oct. 1, 1993.

Bank Failures

Source: Federal Deposit Insurance Corp

Year	Closed or Assisted	Year	Closed or Assisted	Year	Closed or Assisted	Year	Closed or Assisted
1934	61	1961	9	1972	3	1983	48
1935	32	1963	2	1973	6	1984	72
1936	72	1964	8	1975	14	1985	120
1937	84	1965	9	1976	17	1986	145
1938	81	1966	8	1978	7	1987	184
1939	72	1967	4	1979	10	1988	221
1940	48	1969	9	1980	10	1989	207
1955	5	1970	8	1981	10	1990	169
1959	3	1971	6	1982	42	1991	127
1960	2						

Largest U.S. Commercial Banks

Source: *American Banker*, as of Dec. 31, 1991

(millions)

Bank	Assets	Bank	Assets
Citicorp, New York	$216,922.0	National City Corp., Cleveland	$24,169.7
Chemical Banking Corp., New York	138,930.0	Continental Bank Corp., Chicago	24,008.0
BankAmerica Corp., San Francisco	115,509.0	Keycorp, Albany, N.Y.	23,155.5
Nationsbank Corp., Charlotte, N.C.	110,319.0	Shawmut National Corp., Boston	22,815.5
J.P. Morgan & Co., New York	103,468.0	Corestates Financial Corp., Philadelphia	21,623.9
Chase Manhattan Corp., New York	98,197.0	National Westminster Bancorp, New York	21,459.1
Security Pacific Corp., Los Angeles	76,411.0	U.S. Bancorp, Portland, Ore.	18,875.1
Bankers Trust New York Corp., New York	63,959.0	First Bank System, Minneapolis	18,301.0
Wells Fargo & Co., San Francisco	53,547.0	Midlantic Corp., Edison, N.J.	18,170.3
First Chicago Corp., Chicago	48,963.0	Boatmen's Bancshares, St. Louis	17,634.7
First Interstate Bancorp, Los Angeles	48,922.1	Union Bank, San Francisco	17,473.7
Banc One Corp., Columbus, Ohio	46,293.1	MNC Financial, Baltimore	17,438.2
First Union Corp., Charlotte, N.C.	46,084.9	Marine Midland Banks, Buffalo	16,946.8
Fleet/Norstar Financial Group, Providence	45,444.8	First of America Bank Corp., Kalamazoo, Mich.	16,755.0
PNC Financial Corp., Pittsburgh	44,891.7	Society Corp., Cleveland	15,404.5
Bank of New York Co., New York	39,426.0	State Street Boston Corp., Boston	15,046.3
Norwest Corp., Minneapolis	38,501.6	Harris Bankcorp, Chicago	14,480.9
Suntrust Banks, Atlanta	34,553.6	Comerica, Detroit	14,450.8
Wachovia Corp., Winston-Salem	33,158.3	Manufacturers National Corp., Detroit	13,544.2
Barnett Banks, Jacksonville, Fla.	32,720.5	UJB Financial, Princeton, N.J.	13,377.7
Bank of Boston Corp., Boston	32,700.2	Northern Trust Corp., Chicago	13,192.5
Republic New York Corp., New York	31,220.8	Huntington Bancshares, Columbus, Ohio	12,332.6
First Fidelity Bancorp, Lawrenceville, N.J.	30,215.2	Firstar Corp., Milwaukee	12,309.5
NBD Bancorp, Detroit	29,513.5	Crestar Financial Corp., Richmond	11,828.3
Mellon Bank Corp., Pittsburgh	29,355.0	Bancorp Hawaii, Honolulu	11,409.3

All Banks in U.S.—Number, Deposits

Source: Federal Reserve System

Comprises all national banks in the United States and all state commercial banks, trust companies, mutual stock savings banks, private and industrial banks, and special types of institutions that are treated as banks by the federal bank supervisory agencies. Data as of June 30 prior to 1975.

Year	Number of banks						Total deposits (millions of dollars)					
		F.R.S. members			Nonmembers			F.R.S. members			Nonmembers	
	Total all banks	Total	Nat'l	State	Mutual savings	Other	Total all banks	Total	Nat'l	State	Mutual savings	Other
1925 . .	**26,479**	9,538	8,066	1,472	621	18,320	**$51,641**	$32,457	$19,912	$12,546	$7,089	$12,095
1930 . .	**23,855**	8,315	7,247	1,068	604	14,936	**59,828**	38,069	23,235	14,834	9,117	12,642
1935 . .	**16,047**	6,410	5,425	985	569	9,068	**51,149**	34,938	22,477	12,461	9,830	6,381
1940 . .	**14,955**	6,398	5,164	1,234	551	8,008	**70,770**	51,729	33,014	18,715	10,631	8,410
1945 . .	**14,542**	6,840	5,015	1,825	539	7,163	**151,033**	118,378	76,534	41,844	14,413	18,242
1950 . .	**14,674**	6,885	4,971	1,914	527	7,262	**163,770**	122,707	82,430	40,277	19,927	21,137
1955 . .	**14,309**	6,611	4,744	1,867	525	7,173	**208,850**	154,670	98,636	56,034	27,310	26,870
1960 . .	**14,006**	6,217	4,542	1,675	513	7,276	**249,163**	179,519	116,178	63,341	35,316	34,328
1965 . .	**14,295**	6,235	4,803	1,432	504	7,556	**362,611**	259,743	171,528	88,215	50,980	51,889
1970 . .	**14,167**	5,805	4,638	1,167	496	7,866	**502,542**	346,289	254,322	91,967	69,285	86,968
1975 . .	**15,108**	5,787	4,741	1,046	475	8,846	**896,879**	590,999	447,590	143,409	110,569	195,311
1980 . .	**15,145**	5,422	4,425	997	460	9,263	**1,333,399**	843,030	651,848	191,182	150,000	340,369
1985 . .	**14,713**	6,044	4,964	1,080	344	8,325	**1,973,816**	1,285,562	1,033,631	251,931	137,535	500,179
1988 . .	**13,500**	5,435	4,363	1,072	376	7,689	**2,287,274**	1,510,695	1,223,410	287,285	183,045	593,533
1989 . .	**13,102**	5,245	4,198	1,047	374	7483	**2,412,396**	1,606,884	1,307,977	298,907	188,592	616,920
1990 . .	**12,736**	5,034	4,012	1,022	361	7,341	**2,522,492**	1,679,654	1,374,004	305,650	183,522	659,316
1991 . .	**12,312**	4,812	3,827	985	355	7,145	**2,546,699**	1,694,242	1,380,499	313,743	178,167	674,290

Gold Reserves of Central Banks and Governments

Source: IMF, *International Financial Statistics*

(Million fine troy ounces)

Year end	All countries[1]	United States	Canada	Japan	Belgium	France	Germany	Italy	Nether-lands	Switzer-land	United Kingdom
1974	1,020.24	275.97	21.95	21.11	42.17	100.93	117.61	82.48	54.33	83.20	21.03
1975	1,018.71	274.71	21.95	21.11	42.17	100.93	117.61	82.48	54.33	83.20	21.03
1976	1,014.23	274.68	21.62	21.11	42.17	101.02	117.61	82.48	54.33	83.28	21.03
1977	1,029.19	277.55	22.01	21.62	42.45	101.67	118.30	82.91	54.63	83.28	22.23
1978	1,036.82	276.41	22.13	23.97	42.59	101.99	118.64	83.12	54.78	83.28	22.83
1979	944.44	264.60	22.18	24.23	34.21	81.92	95.25	66.71	43.97	83.28	18.25
1980	952.99	264.32	20.98	24.23	34.18	81.85	95.18	66.67	43.94	83.28	18.84
1981	953.72	264.11	20.46	24.23	34.18	81.85	95.18	66.67	43.94	83.28	19.03
1982	949.16	264.03	20.26	24.23	34.18	81.85	95.18	66.67	43.94	83.28	19.01
1983	947.84	263.39	20.17	24.23	34.18	81.85	95.18	66.67	43.94	83.28	19.01
1984	946.79	262.79	20.14	24.23	34.18	81.85	95.18	66.67	43.94	83.28	19.03
1985	949.39	262.65	20.11	24.33	34.18	81.85	95.18	66.67	43.94	83.28	19.03
1986	949.11	262.04	19.72	24.23	34.18	81.85	95.18	66.67	43.94	83.28	19.01
1987	944.49	262.38	18.52	24.23	33.63	81.85	95.18	66.67	43.94	83.28	19.01
1988	944.92	261.87	17.14	24.23	33.67	81.85	95.18	66.67	43.94	83.28	19.00
1989	938.95	261.93	16.10	24.23	30.23	81.85	95.18	66.67	43.94	83.28	18.99
1990	940.29	261.91	14.76	24.23	30.23	81.85	95.18	66.67	43.94	83.28	18.94
1991	939.58	261.91	12.96	24.23	30.23	81.85	95.18	66.67	43.94	83.28	18.89

(1) Covers IMF members with reported gold holdings. For countries not listed above, see *International Financial Statistics*, a monthly publication of the International Monetary Fund.

Global Stock Markets

Source: Morgan Stanley Capital International Perspective (52 weeks as of Aug. 27, 1992)

(in Local Currencies)

Index	Aug. 27, 1992	52-week Range		Index	Aug. 27, 1992	52-week Range	
The World	**374.9**	**414.6**	**363.8**	Italy	293.8	399.3	293.8
E.A.F.E.[1]	436.8	536.7	409.5	Japan	789.8	1089.8	652.0
Australia	329.2	363.5	322.9	Netherlands	325.0	360.4	313.7
Austria	317.0	457.7	309.3	New Zealand	68.6	76.5	62.3
Belgium	363.7	426.3	363.7	Norway	525.1	821.9	455.9
Canada	380.0	413.2	374.1	Singapore/Malaysia	719.8	800.1	688.3
Denmark	617.9	844.0	603.4	Spain	166.9	231.0	165.4
Finland	39.4	68.1	39.1	Sweden	966.6	1338.2	890.2
France	492.1	593.3	464.2	Switzerland	216.1	241.2	197.2
Germany	224.7	274.0	219.1	United Kingdom	682.5	821.9	675.2
Hong Kong	3924.9	4499.6	2812.0	United States	386.3	397.8	350.8

(1) Europe, Australia, Far East Index.

Dow Jones Industrial Average Since 1961

High		Year	Low		High		Year	Low	
Dec. 13	734.91	**1961**	Jan. 3	610.25	Sept. 8	907.74	**1978**	Feb. 28	742.12
Jan. 3	726.01	**1962**	June 26	535.76	Oct. 5	897.61	**1979**	Nov. 7	796.67
Dec. 18	767.21	**1963**	Jan. 2	646.79	Nov. 20	1000.17	**1980**	Apr. 21	759.13
Nov. 18	891.71	**1964**	Jan. 2	766.08	Apr. 27	1024.05	**1981**	Sept. 25	824.01
Dec. 31	969.26	**1965**	June 28	840.59	Dec. 27	1070.55	**1982**	Aug. 12	776.92
Feb. 9	995.15	**1966**	Oct. 7	744.32	Nov. 29	1287.20	**1983**	Jan. 3	1027.04
Sept. 25	943.08	**1967**	Jan. 3	786.41	Jan. 6	1286.64	**1984**	July 24	1086.57
Dec. 3	985.21	**1968**	Mar. 21	825.13	Dec. 16	1553.10	**1985**	Jan. 4	1184.96
May 14	968.85	**1969**	Dec. 17	769.93	Dec. 2	1955.57	**1986**	Jan. 22	1502.29
Dec. 29	842.00	**1970**	May 6	631.16	Aug. 25	2722.42	**1987**	Oct. 19	1738.74
Apr. 28	950.82	**1971**	Nov. 23	797.97	Oct. 21	2183.50	**1988**	Jan. 20	1879.14
Dec. 11	1036.27	**1972**	Jan. 26	889.15	Oct. 9	2791.41	**1989**	Jan. 3	2144.64
Jan. 11	1051.70	**1973**	Dec. 5	788.31	July 16	2999.75	**1990**	Oct. 11	2365.10
Mar. 13	891.66	**1974**	Dec. 6	577.60	Dec. 31	3168.83	**1991**	Jan. 9	2470.30
July 15	881.81	**1975**	Jan. 2	632.04	June 1	3413.21	**1992***	Jan. 2	3172.41
Sept. 21	1014.79	**1976**	Jan. 2	858.71				*As of	9/21/92
Jan. 3	999.75	**1977**	Nov. 2	800.85					

Stock Exchanges

N.Y. Stock Exchange Transactions

Year	Yearly volume: Stock shares	Yearly volume: Bonds par values	Year	Yearly volume: Stock shares	Yearly volume: Bonds par values
1900	138,981,000	$579,293,000	1980	11,352,294,000	5,190,304,000
1905	260,569,000	1,026,254,000	1981	11,853,740,659	5,733,071,000
1910	163,705,000	634,863,000	1982	16,458,036,768	7,155,443,000
1915	172,497,000	961,700,000	1983	21,589,576,997	7,572,315,000
1920	227,636,000	3,868,422,000	1984	23,071,031,447	6,982,291,000
1925	459,717,623	3,427,042,210	1985	27,510,706,353	9,046,453,000
1929	1,124,800,410	2,996,398,000	1986	35,680,016,341	10,475,399,000
1930	810,632,546	2,720,301,800	1987	47,801,308,660	9,726,244,000
1935	381,635,752	3,339,458,000	1988	40,438,346,358	7,594,644,000
1940	207,599,749	1,669,438,000	1989	41,698,538,270	8,836,374,000
1950	524,799,621	1,112,425,170	1990	39,836,374,000	10,893,702,000
1960	766,693,818	1,346,419,750	1991	45,424,500,000	12,693,690,000
1970	2,937,359,448	4,494,864,600			
1975	4,693,427,000	$5,178,300,000			

American Stock Exchange Transactions

Year	Yearly volume: Stock shares	Yearly volume: Bonds[1] princ. amts.	Year	Yearly volume: Stock shares	Yearly volume: Bonds[1] princ. amts.	Year	Yearly volume: Stock shares	Yearly volume: Bonds[1] princ. amts.
1929	476,140,375	$513,551,000	1970	843,116,260	$641,270,000	1986	2,978,540,000	$810,264,000
1930	222,270,065	863,541,000	1980	1,626,072,625	355,723,000	1987	3,505,950,000	684,965,000
1940	42,928,337	303,902,000	1982	1,485,831,536	325,240,000	1988	2,515,210,000	604,950,000
1945	143,309,392	167,333,000	1983	2,081,270,000	395,190,000	1989	3,125,030,000	709,010,000
1950	107,792,340	47,549,000	1984	1,545,010,000	371,990,000	1990	3,328,918,000	767,108,000
1960	286,039,982	32,670,000	1985	2,100,860,000	645,182,000	1991	3,368,380,000	952,360,000

(1) Corporate

Components of Dow Jones Industrial Average

Allied-Signal
Aluminum Co. of Amer.
American Express
AT&T
Bethlehem Steel
Boeing
Caterpillar
Chevron
Coca-Cola
Disney (Walt)
DuPont
Eastman Kodak
Exxon
General Electric
General Motors
Goodyear
IBM
International Paper
McDonald's
Merck
Minn. Mining & Manuf.
Morgan (J.P.)
Philip Morris
Procter & Gamble
Sears
Texaco
Union Carbide
United Technologies
Westinghouse
Woolworth

Components of Dow Jones Transportation Average

AMR Corp.
Airborne Freight
Alaska Air
American President
Burlington Northern
CSX
Carolina Freight
Consolidated Freightways
Consolidated Rail
Delta Air Lines
Federal Express
Norfolk Southern
Roadway Services
Ryder System
Santa Fe Pacific
Southwest Air Lines
UAL
Union Pacific
USAir Group
XTRA Corp

Components of Dow Jones Utility Average

American Electric Power
Arkla
Centerior Energy
Commonwealth Edison
Consolidated Edison
Consolidated Natural Gas
Detroit Edison
Houston Industries
Niagara Mohawk Power
Pacific Gas & Electric
Panhandle Eastern
Peoples Energy
Philadelphia Electric
Public Service Enterprises
SCE

Most Active Common Stocks in 1991

New York Exchange	Volume (millions of shares)	American Exchange	Volume (millions of shares)	NASDAQ	Volume (millions of shares)
RJR Nabisco	762.33	Fruit of the Loom	79.95	Teléfonos de México	1,540.00
Phillip Morris	497.93	Echo Bay Mines	78.69	Intel	559.92
Pepsico	489.28	Amdahl	72.72	Apple Computer	531.02
A.T.&T.	457.43	Wang Labs "B"	69.24	Sun Microsystems	403.40
I.B.M.	439.11	Hillhaven	61.79	MCI	368.03
American Express	421.37	Energy Services	59.35	Oracle	344.94
Citicorp	409.71	Bergen Brunswig	58.64	Seagate	315.69
General Motors	363.77	BAT	50.49	Telecommun. "A"	299.61
General Electric	360.50	Metro Mobile "B"	49.38	Microsoft	290.43
Wal-Mart	335.33	Hasbro	44.04	Amgen	251.27
Glaxo	333.25	Forest Labs	43.58	US Healthcare	249.32
Boeing	319.67	Nabors	32.88	Novell	248.77
Westinghouse	311.35	Ivax	32.46	Lotus	230.52
GTE	298.44	Alza	31.22	AST Research	225.90
Limited	295.54	PallCp	31.15	Champions Sports	223.08
Waste Management	291.67	Bolar Pharmaceutical	30.54	Centocor	214.20
Teléfonos de México	283.49	First Australia Prime	30.17	Quantum	191.46
Ford Motor	276.31			Dell Computer	169.98

NASDAQ in 1991

NASDAQ, The National Association of Securities Dealers Automated Quotations reported turnover volume of 41.3 billion shares in 1991. The number of companies with shares traded in this market was over 5,200 at the start of 1992, making NASDAQ the third-largest market in the world, after the New York and Tokyo exchanges.

Top Mutual Funds in 1991

Source: Lipper Analytical Services Inc.

Fund	Percent	Fund	Percent	Fund	Percent
Oppenheimer Global Bio-Tech	121.13	United New Concepts	88.26	Fidelity Sel Brokerage	82.26
CGM Cap Development	99.08	MFS Lifetime Emer Growth	87.62	Kaufmann Fund	79.18
Fidelity Sel Bio Tech	99.05	Oberweis Emerging Growth	87.06	Fidelity Sel Medical	77.83
Montgomery: Small Cap	98.75	Twentieth Cent: Ultra Inv	86.45	ABT Inv: Emerging Growth	77.23
American Heritage	96.59	J Hancock Special Equity	85.00	MIM Mutual: Stock Apprec	76.97
Financial Port: Health	91.81	Twentieth Cent: Giftrust	84.91	Financial Port: Tech	76.88
Berger One Hundred	88.81	Fidelity Sel Health	83.56		

U.S. International Transactions

Source: Bureau of Economic Analysis, U.S. Dept. of Commerce

(millions of dollars)

	1960	1965	1970	1975	1980	1985	1990	1991
Exports of goods services and income[1]	**$30,556**	**$42,722**	**$68,387**	**$157,936**	**$344,440**	**$380,051**	**$680,890**	**$704,914**
Merchandise, adjusted, excluding military[2]	19,650	26,461	42,469	107,088	224,250	215,915	388,705	415,962
Services	6,290	8,824	14,171	25,497	47,584	73,026	148,638	163,637
Income receipts on U.S. assets abroad:	4,616	7,437	11,748	25,351	71,388	82,282	143,547	125,315
Imports of goods, services and income	**-23,670**	**-32,708**	**-59,901**	**-33,745**	**-333,774**	**-473,998**	**-738,401**	**-716,624**
Merchandise, adjusted, excluding military[2]	-14,758	-21,510	-39,866	-98,185	-249,750	-338,088	-497,558	-489,398
Services	-7,674	-9,111	-14,520	-4,795	-21,996	-41,491	-116,583	-118,341
Income payments on foreign assets in the U.S.	-1,238	-2,088	-5,515	-12,564	-45,532	-67,875	-124,261	-108,886
Unilateral transfers, net	**-4,062**	**-4,583**	**-6,156**	**-7,075**	**-8,349**	**-22,950**	**-32,916**	**8,028**
U.S. assets abroad, net (increase/ capital outflow (-))	**-4,099**	**-5,716**	**-9,337**	**-39,703**	**-86,967**	**-34,069**	**-56,321**	**-62,220**
U.S. official reserve assets, net	2,145	1,225	2,481	-849	-8,155	-3,858	-2,158	5,763
U.S. Government assets, other than official reserve assets, net	-1,100	-1,605	-1,589	-3,474	-5,162	-2,821	2,304	3,397
U.S. private assets, net	-5,144	-5,336	-10,229	-35,380	-73,651	-27,391	-56,467	-71,379
Foreign assets in U.S., net (increase/ capital inflow (+))	2,294	742	6,359	15,670	58,112	130,012	99,379	66,980
Statistical discrepancy (sum of above items with sign reversed)	-1,019	-457	-219	5,917	25,386	24,825	47,370	-1,078
Memorandum:								
Balance on current account	2,824	5,431	2,331	18,116	2,317	-121,721	-90,428	-3,682

(1) Excludes transfers of goods and services under U.S. military grant programs. (2) Excludes exports of goods under U.S. military agency sales contracts identified in Census export documents, excludes imports of goods under direct defense expenditures identified in Census import documents, and reflects various other adjustments.

United States Mint

Source: United States Mint, U.S. Dept. of the Treasury

The United States Mint was created by Act of Congress April 2, 1792, which established the U.S. national coinage system. Initially, operations were conducted at Philadelphia, then the nation's capital. Supervision of the Mint was a function of the secretary of state, but in 1799, it became an independent agency reporting directly to the president. The Mint was made a statutory bureau of the Treasury Department in 1873, with a director appointed by the president to oversee its operations from headquarters offices in the Treasury Department in Washington, D.C.

The Mint manufactures all U.S. coins and distributes them through the Federal Reserve banks and branches. The Mint also maintains physical custody of the treasury's gold and silver assets, moving, storing and releasing from custody as authorized. The Mint has 4 production facilities. Mints are located in Philadelphia, Denver, San Francisco and West Point, N.Y. The Mint also includes the Bullion Depository at Fort Knox, Ky. A museum is maintained at the San Francisco Old Mint. Free tours are conducted at the Philadelphia and Denver mints.

The traditional 90% silver coinage was phased out and cupronickel clad coinage introduced when the Coinage Act of 1965 removed all silver from the dime and quarter and reduced the silver content of the half dollar to 40%. In 1970, legislative action removed the remaining silver from the half dollar and in providing for the resumption of dollar coinage, directed that both denominations produced for circulation also be cupronickel clad metal. Changes in the design, weight and size of the standard silver dollar were approved by Congress in 1978, and beginning in 1979, a smaller cupronickel dollar coin bearing the likeness of Susan B. Anthony and the Apollo II moon landing was released.

A change in the composition of the cent was effected in 1982, when the current copper-plated zinc cent was introduced to replace the traditional 95% copper cent.

The Mint manufactures and sells bronze medals of a national character, produces numismatic coins and coin sets. Congressionally authorized commemorative coinage produced by the Mint includes 90% silver half dollars produced in 1982 to mark the 250th anniversary of George Washington's birth, and 90% gold $10 coins dated 1984 and two 90% silver dollars dated 1983 and 1984, respectively, commemorating the 1984 Olympic games, and a 90% gold $5 coin, a 90% silver dollar coin and a cupronickel half dollar for the Statue of Liberty Centennial in 1986. The Mint issued a 1987 dated 90% gold $5 coin and a 1987 dated 90% silver dollar coin honoring the 200th Anniversary of the U.S. Constitution. Other Congressionally authorized commemoratives include the 1991 Eisenhower silver dollar, the 1991 Korean War Memorial silver dollar, the 1991 USO 50th Anniversary silver dollar, and the 1992 Olympic gold, silver, and clad coins. The Mint continues to produce and sell legal tender gold and silver bullion coins designated as "American Eagle Bullion Coins." Other coin programs are the 1992 White House silver dollar coins, the 1992 Christopher Columbus gold, silver and clad coins; the 1993 James Madison/Bill of Rights gold, silver and half-dollar silver coins; and the 1994 World Cup gold, silver and half-dollar silver coins. The coins have a face value of $50 (1 oz.), $25 (1/2 oz.), $10 (1/4 oz.), and $5 (1/10 oz.). The Gold Eagle comes in 4 weights, the American Eagle silver bullion coin has a face value of $1 and contains 1 troy ounce of .999 fine silver. Information concerning these and other Mint coin programs and coin availability, may be secured from the United States Mint, Customer Service Center, 10001 Aerospace Road, Lanham, MD 20706.

Domestic Coin Production

	Cents	Nickels	Dimes	Quarters	Halves	Total
1982	16,725,504,368	666,081,544	1,062,188,584	980,973,788	23,959,102	19,458,707,386
1983	14,219,554,428	1,098,341,276	1,377,154,224	1,291,341,446	66,611,244	18,053,002,618
1984	13,720,317,906	1,264,444,146	1,561,472,976	1,223,028,064	52,291,158	17,821,554,250
1985	10,935,889,813	1,106,862,408	1,293,180,932	1,295,781,850	38,520,996	14,670,235,999
1986	8,934,262,191	898,702,633	1,155,976,667	1,055,497,993	28,473,778	12,072,913,262
1987	9,561,856,445	782,090,085	1,415,912,883	1,238,094,177	99,481,000	12,998,053,071
1988	11,346,550,443	1,435,131,652	1,992,935,488	1,158,862,687	25,626,096	15,959,106,366
1989	12,837,140,268	1,497,523,652	2,240,355,488	1,417,290,422	41,196,188	18,033,506,018
1990	12,031,422,711	1,415,222,474	1,956,105,597	1,560,357,858	43,614,192	17,006,722,832
1991	9,324,386,076	1,050,600,678	1,528,461,114	1,201,934,693	29,928,678	13,135,307,239

Portraits on U.S. Treasury Bills, Bonds, Notes and Savings Bonds

Denomination	Savings bonds	Treas. bills	Treas. bonds	Treas. notes
50	Washington		Jefferson	
75	Adams			
100	Jefferson		Jackson	
200	Madison			
500	Hamilton		Washington	
1,000	Franklin	H. McCulloch	Lincoln	Lincoln
5,000	Revere	J.G. Carlisle	Monroe	Monroe
10,000	Wilson	J. Sherman	Cleveland	Cleveland
50,000		C. Glass		
100,000		A Gallatin	Grant	Grant
1,000,000		O. Wolcott	T. Roosevelt	T. Roosevelt
100,000,000				Madison
500,000,000				McKinley

Large Denominations of U.S. Currency Discontinued

The largest denomination of United States currency now being issued is the $100 bill. Issuance of currency in denominations larger than $100 was discontinued in 1969.

As large denomination bills reach the Federal Reserve Bank they are removed from circulation.

Because some of the discontinued currency is expected to be in the hands of holders for many years, the description of the various denominations below is continued:

Amt.	Portrait	Embellishment on back
$ 1	Washington	Great Seal of U.S.
2	Jefferson	Signers of Declaration
5	Lincoln	Lincoln Memorial
10	Hamilton	U.S. Treasury
20	Jackson	White House
50	Grant	U.S. Capitol
$ 100	Franklin	Independence Hall

Amt.	Portrait	Embellishment on back
500	McKinley	Ornate denominational marking
1,000	Cleveland	Ornate denominational marking
5,000	Madison	Ornate denominational marking
10,000	Chase	Ornate denominational marking
100,000*	Wilson	Ornate denominational marking

* For use only in transactions between Federal Reserve System and Treasury Department.

U.S. Currency and Coin

Source: Financial Management Service, U.S. Dept. of the Treasury (Mar. 31, 1992)

Amounts Outstanding and in Circulation

	Total currency and coin	Total	Federal Reserve notes[1]	U.S. notes	Currency no longer issued
Currency					
Amounts outstanding	$383,280,341,610	$362,732,172,712	$362,145,599,532	$322,539,016	$264,034,164
Less amounts held by:					
Treasury	703,744,663	39,898,714	4,111,591	35,578,439	208,684
Federal Reserve banks	79,362,000,205	78,762,890,910	78,762,882,355		8,555
Amounts in circulation	**$303,214,596,742**	**$283,929,383,088**	**$283,378,605,586**	**$286,960,577**	**$263,816,925**

	Total	Dollars[3]	Fractional coin
Coin[2]			
Amounts outstanding	$20,548,168,898	$2,024,703,898	$18,523,465,000
Less amounts held by:			
Treasury	663,845,949	306,530,571	357,315,378
Federal Reserve banks	599,109,295	93,618,472	505,490,823
Amounts in circulation	**$19,285,213,654**	**$1,624,554,855**	**$17,660,658,799**

Currency in Circulation by Denominations

Denomination	Total currency in circulation	Federal Reserve Notes[1]	U.S. Notes	Currency no longer issued
1 Dollar	$5,012,900,685	$4,862,382,108	$143,481	$150,375,096
2 Dollars	881,173,126	748,393,452	132,766,866	12,808
5 Dollars	6,054,762,883	5,907,970,048	111,462,110	35,330,725
10 Dollars	11,839,416,870	11,815,598,080	5,950	23,812,840
20 Dollars	66,828,099,124	66,807,965,100	3,380	20,130,644
50 Dollars	34,928,632,800	34,917,100,500	—	11,532,300
100 Dollars	158,061,214,000	157,996,554,800	42,578,700	22,080,500
500 Dollars	147,286,000	147,096,500	—	189,500
1,000 Dollars	170,672,000	170,465,000	—	207,000
5,000 Dollars	1,774,998	1,729,998	—	45,000
10,000 Dollars	3,450,000	3,350,000	—	100,000
Fractional parts	487	—	—	487
Partial notes[4]	115	—	90	25
Total currency	**$283,929,383,088**	**$283,378,605,586**	**$286,960,577**	**$263,816,925**

Comparative Totals of Money in Circulation — Selected Dates

Date	Dollars (in millions)	Per capita[5]	Date	Dollars (in millions)	Per capita[5]	Date	Dollars (in millions)	Per capita[5]
Mar. 30, 1992	303,215.0	1,219.15	June 30, 1975	81,196.4	380.08	June 30, 1940	7,847.5	59.40
Mar. 31, 1991	286,675.0	1,138.62	June 30, 1970	54,351.0	265.39	June 30, 1935	5,567.1	43.75
Mar. 31, 1990	257,664.4	1,028.71	June 30, 1965	39,719.8	204.14	June 30, 1930	4,522.0	36.74
June 30, 1989	249,182.7	1,002.54	June 30, 1960	32,064.6	177.47	June 30, 1925	4,815.2	41.56
June 30, 1988	235,415.9	956.57	June 30, 1955	30,229.3	182.90	June 30, 1920	5,467.6	51.36
June 30, 1985	185,890.7	778.58	June 30, 1950	27,156.3	179.03	June 30, 1915	3,319.6	33.01
June 30, 1980	127,097.2	558.28	June 30, 1945	26,746.4	191.14	June 30, 1910	3,148.7	34.07

(1) Issued on and after July 1, 1929. (2) Excludes coin sold to collectors at premium prices. (3) Includes $481,781,898 in standard silver dollars. (4) Represents value of certain partial denominations not presented for redemption. (5) Based on Bureau of the Census estimates of population.

The requirement for a gold reserve against U.S. notes was repealed by Public Law 90-269 approved Mar. 18, 1968. Silver certificates issued on and after July 1, 1929 became redeemable from the general fund on June 24, 1968. The amount of security after those dates has been reduced accordingly.

Consumer Credit Outstanding, 1970 to 1991

Source: Federal Reserve System

(billions of dollars)
Estimated amounts of credit outstanding as of end of year. Not seasonally adjusted.

Type of Credit	1970	1975	1980	1985	1987	1988	1989	1990	1991
Credit outstanding	**133.8**	**207.5**	**355.4**	**601.6**	**692.0**	**742.1**	**791.8**	**809.3**	**796.7**
Ratio to disposable personal income[1] (percent)	18.5	18.0	18.2	20.4	21.0	20.9	20.9	20.0	18.9
Installment	**105.5**	**168.7**	**302.1**	**526.2**	**618.5**	**673.5**	**728.9**	**748.5**	**742.1**
Automobile paper	36.3	57.2	111.9	210.4	266.4	285.4	292.1	285.1	263.1
Revolving	5.1	15.0	58.5	128.9	161.8	184.0	210.3	235.1	255.9
All other loans[4]	64.1	99.7	131.6	213.8	216.2	181.3	229.0	249.1	241.9
Commercial banks	48.7	82.9	147.0	245.1	287.2	324.8	324.8	347.1	339.6
Finance companies	27.6	32.7	62.3	111.7	189.9	144.7	138.9	133.9	121.9
Credit unions	13.0	25.7	44.0	72.7	81.0	88.3	93.1	93.1	92.3
Retailers[2]	13.9	18.2	28.7	43.0	46.0	48.4	44.2	44.8	44.0
Other[3]	2.3	9.2	20.1	53.8	64.4	67.1	61.2	51.8	44.7
Noninstallment	**28.3**	**38.8**	**53.3**	**75.3**	**73.5**	**68.7**	**62.9**	**60.7**	**54.7**

(1) Based on fourth quarter seasonally adjusted disposable personal income at annual rates as published by the U.S. Bureau of Economic Analysis. (2) Excludes 30-day charge credit held by travel and entertainment companies. (3) Comprises savings institutions and gasoline companies. (4) Comprises mobile home loans and all other installment loans not incl. in automobile or revolving credit such as loans for education, boats, trailers, or vacations.

Personal Consumption Expenditures in the U.S.

Source: Bureau of Economic Analysis, U.S. Dept. of Commerce (billions of dollars)

	1985	1986	1987	1988	1989	1990	1991
Personal consumption expenditures	**$2,629.0**	**$2,797.4**	**$3,009.4**	**$3,296.1**	**$3,523.1**	**$3,748.4**	**$3,887.7**
Food & Tobacco	**503.8**	**533.7**	**566.4**	**569.8**	**605.6**	**644.7**	**665.4**
Food purchased for off-premise consumption	322.7	339.1	353.7	351.7	373.7	398.4	407.4
Purchased meals and beverages	139.9	151.6	165.5	171.7	180.6	191.4	198.5
Tobacco products	32.2	33.6	35.6	36.2	40.5	43.4	47.8
Clothing, accessories, jewelry	**193.3**	**207.5**	**222.3**	**231.8**	**248.7**	**258.6**	**260.6**
Shoes	22.9	24.3	25.9	27.4	30.1	31.3	31.1
Clothing and accessories less shoes	133.4	142.4	152.5	158.9	170.1	175.5	177.7
Jewelry and watches	20.5	22.8	24.7	28.8	29.7	31.1	30.6
Personal care	**38.8**	**41.4**	**44.4**	**51.4**	**55.8**	**59.5**	**62.2**
Toilet articles, preparations	23.1	24.6	26.3	31.8	34.1	36.6	38.2
Barbershops, beauty parlors, baths, health clubs	15.7	16.8	18.2	19.6	21.6	22.9	24.0
Housing	**403.0**	**434.2**	**468.9**	**484.2**	**514.4**	**547.5**	**574.0**
Owner-occupied nonfarm dwellings space rent	272.7	293.7	316.9	334.1	355.8	379.8	399.1
Tenant-occupied nonfarm dwellings rent	103.8	114.3	123.6	125.3	132.6	140.8	147.3
Rental value of farm dwellings	10.9	9.7	10.3	4.9	5.0	5.2	5.3
Household operation	**334.1**	**347.5**	**363.3**	**398.9**	**422.6**	**434.7**	**441.7**
Furniture, incl. bedding	28.0	30.4	31.8	34.0	36.9	35.3	33.4
Kitchen, other household appliances	23.7	25.5	26.7	24.1	25.7	26.0	25.5
China, glassware, tableware, utensils	13.0	14.3	15.3	16.4	17.9	18.9	18.9
Other durable house furnishings	28.2	30.6	33.5	37.7	40.2	42.4	42.6
Semidurable house furnishings	14.0	15.2	16.0	19.4	20.4	21.3	21.4
Household utilities	124.2	122.4	125.8	127.3	134.1	136.4	143.2
Telephone, telegraph	40.4	42.7	44.1	50.2	51.7	53.2	54.3
Medical care	**327.5**	**357.6**	**399.0**	**487.7**	**536.4**	**595.9**	**656.0**
Drug preparations, sundries	28.1	30.2	32.3	50.8	55.0	60.3	64.6
Physicians	73.5	80.6	94.0	110.6	121.6	134.2	148.1
Dentists	21.5	22.8	25.0	27.9	30.0	32.2	34.5
Privately controlled hospitals and sanitariums	140.2	152.4	166.3	190.9	209.5	231.0	255.2
Health insurance	21.6	22.4	25.3	26.4	31.2	35.6	38.3
Personal business	**169.9**	**192.5**	**215.4**	**255.0**	**272.2**	**297.4**	**317.7**
Brokerage charges, investment counseling	14.8	19.7	20.5	19.3	21.6	22.2	24.4
Bank service charges, trust services, safe deposit box	11.7	13.0	14.6	19.8	22.0	23.7	25.2
Legal services	28.0	30.9	35.0	41.7	45.5	49.7	51.4
Funeral, burial expenses	6.3	6.6	7.0	7.8	7.9	8.3	8.9
Transportation	**359.5**	**366.3**	**379.7**	**413.2**	**437.3**	**453.7**	**438.2**
User-operated transportation	330.1	335.9	346.3	376.9	399.6	413.5	398.4
New autos	87.4	101.3	93.5	101.0	99.9	96.7	79.5
Used autos	35.1	33.6	38.5	30.5	32.5	33.7	35.8
Repair, greasing, washing, parking, storage, rental	49.1	52.0	55.9	73.5	79.1	82.5	83.7
Gasoline and oil	90.6	73.5	75.3	86.9	96.2	108.5	105.5
Tolls	1.4	1.7	1.9	1.8	2.1	2.0	2.0
Insurance premiums less claims paid	9.9	12.6	15.4	16.8	16.8	18.1	21.8
Purchased local transportation	7.2	7.8	8.2	8.3	8.1	8.9	9.1
Mass transit systems	3.6	3.8	4.0	5.4	5.3	5.7	5.7
Taxicab	3.1	3.3	3.5	2.9	2.8	3.2	3.4
Purchased intercity transportation	22.2	22.6	25.5	28.0	29.5	31.2	30.7
Railway (excl. commutation)	.6	.7	.7	.6	.7	.7	.7
Bus	1.2	1.1	1.4	2.2	1.7	1.4	1.5
Airline	18.5	18.8	20.8	23.0	24.7	26.5	25.8
Recreation	**185.7**	**201.2**	**223.2**	**246.8**	**266.0**	**280.7**	**289.7**
Books, maps	8.1	8.6	9.5	14.6	15.8	17.4	18.3
Magazines, newspapers, sheet music	13.2	13.9	15.4	20.8	22.0	24.1	24.6
Nondurable toys and sport supplies	21.1	23.1	26.2	27.5	30.0	31.4	32.3
Wheel goods, durable toys, sports equipment, boats, pleasure aircraft	26.7	29.7	33.2	30.0	31.0	30.6	30.1
Video & audio prods., computers, musical instruments	—	—	—	44.5	47.3	49.6	50.2
Flowers, seeds, potted plants	5.5	5.8	7.0	9.3	10.1	10.6	10.6
Admissions to specified spectator amusements	9.5	10.2	11.3	11.1	12.1	13.4	13.3
Motion picture theaters	3.6	3.9	4.2	3.6	3.9	3.9	3.7
Legitimate theater, opera	3.0	3.3	4.0	3.6	3.9	5.0	4.7
Spectator sports	2.9	2.9	3.0	3.9	4.3	4.5	4.8
Clubs, fraternal organizations	4.8	5.0	5.5	7.6	8.0	8.6	8.7
Commerical amusements	15.1	16.0	17.1	19.1	20.5	22.0	22.7
Education & Research	**43.3**	**46.6**	**50.9**	**71.6**	**79.4**	**86.4**	**92.8**
Higher education	15.7	16.9	17.7	36.7	40.3	44.3	48.1
Nursery, elementary and secondary schools	13.8	14.5	15.5	17.1	19.2	20.5	21.8
Religious and welfare activities	**57.1**	**62.9**	**68.1**	**86.0**	**92.7**	**102.1**	**107.7**

Foreign Direct Investment in the U.S.

Source: Bureau of Economic Analysis; U.S. Dept. of Commerce (billions of dollars)

Five countries accounted for over 75 percent of the $407 billion worth of foreign direct investment in the U.S. at the end of 1991.

	1970	1975	1980	1985	1989	1990	1991
All countries	**$13.2**	**$27.6**	**$83.0**	**$184.6**	**$401.0**	**$396,702**	**$407,577**
Canada	3.1	5.3	12.1	17.1	32.0	30.0	30.0
Germany	0.680	1.4	7.5	14.8	28.0	28.3	28.2
Japan	0.229	0.591	4.7	19.3	70.0	81.8	86.7
Netherlands	2.1	5.3	19.1	37.0	60.0	63.9	63.8
Switzerland	1.5	2.1	5.0	10.5	—	17.7	17.6
United Kingdom	4.1	6.3	14.1	43.5	119.0	102.8	106.1

North American Free Trade Agreement

The United States, Canada, and Mexico announced a comprehensive plan for free trade across North America on Aug. 12, 1992, and portrayed it as an opportunity for greater economic growth for all three nations. The agreement was greeted enthusiastically by business groups generally, but U.S. labor unions, long opposed to opening the Southern border, contended that the accord would send jobs to Mexico.

The treaty would bring together 360 million consumers in a $6.6 trillion market and would create the world's richest and largest trading bloc. The agreement must be ratified by the legislatures of the three nations. The U.S. Congress was expected to vote on the accord in the Spring of 1993.

Key Provisions

Agriculture—Tariffs on all farm products would be eliminated over 15 years. All three countries agreed to allow domestic price-support systems, provided that they did not distort trade.

Automobiles—After eight years, at least 62.5% of an automobile's value must have been produced in North America for it to qualify for duty-free status. Tariffs would be phased out over 10 years.

Banking—U.S. and Canadian banks would be allowed to acquire Mexican banks accounting for as much as 8 percent of the industry's capital. All limits on bank ownership would end Jan. 1, 2000.

Disputes—Special judges would be empaneled to resolve disagreements.

Energy—Mexico would not alter its constitution, which prohibited foreign ownership of its oil fields, but after 10 years U.S. and Canadian companies would be allowed to bid on all contracts offered by Mexican oil and electricity monopolies.

Environment—The agreement could not be used to overrule national and state environmental, health or safety laws.

Immigration—All three countries would ease restrictions on the movement of business executives and professionals.

Jobs—Visa restrictions would be reduced for business executives and professionals. Current barriers designed to limit Mexican migration to the U.S. would remain in force.

Patent and Copyright protection—Mexico would strengthen its laws providing protection to intellectual property. It would honor foreign patents for pharmaceuticals for 20 years.

Textiles—A strict "rule of origin" provision would require garments to be made from yarn and fabric also produced in North America. Tariffs would be phased out over five years.

Tariffs—Tariffs on 10,000 customs goods would be eliminated over 15 years. One-half of U.S. exports to Mexico would be considered duty-free within five years.

Trucking—Trucks would be allowed free access on cross-border routes and throughout the three countries by the end of 1999.

Highest Paid Chief Executives

Source: *Business Week*

Executive	Company	Total 1991 Pay (in millions)	Executive	Company	Total 1991 Pay (in millions)
Anthony O'Reilly	H.J. Heinz	$75.1	William LaMothe	Kellogg	$9.4
Martin Wygod	Medco Containment	33.7	Lawrence G. Rawl	Exxon	9.3
Leon Hirsch	U.S. Surgical	23.3	Charles Harper	Conagra	8.8
John Malone	Tele-Communications	18.9	Edward Hennessy Jr.	Allied-Signal	8.4
Richard Eamer	National Medical	17.5	William McGuire	United HealthCare	7.8
Sanford Weill	Primerica	15.9	Lawrence Lehmkuhl	St. Jude Medical	7.6
Hamish Maxwell	Philip Morris	15.7	Richard Fisher	Morgan Stanley	7.0
William Stiritz	Ralston Purina	13.8	Louis Gerstner Jr.	RJR Nabisco	6.8
Richard Gelb	Bristol-Myers Squibb	12.7	August Busch III	Anheuser-Busch	6.7
William Schreyer	Merrill Lynch	11.5	H.B. Atwater Jr.	General Mills	6.5

Office Vacancy Rates in U.S. Cities

Source: CB Commercial Real Estate Group

Metro Area	Vacancy rate Dec. 1991	Percent change from Dec. 1990	Metro Area	Vacancy rate Dec. 1991	Percent change from Dec. 1990
Albuquerque	19.9%	−2.5	Minn./St. Paul	19.2%	+1.2
Atlanta	18.7%	−0.3	Nashville	20.4%	−1.2
Austin, Texas	20.3%	−4.7	NYC, downtown	20.3%	+1.6
Bakersfield., Cal.	19.1%	−2.4	NYC, midtown	14.9%	+1.2
Baltimore	19.1%	+1.5	Northern N.J.	22.5%	unch.
Boston	18.2%	unch.	Oakland, Cal.	17.0%	−0.6
Charlotte, N.C.	18.4%	+3.6	Oklahoma City	24.9%	−2.2
Chicago	17.3%	−0.3	Orange Co., Cal.	21.8%	+1.1
Cincinnati	19.4%	+2.2	Orlando, Fla.	17.9%	+0.1
Cleveland	21.1%	+3.2	Palm Beach, Fla.	29.5%	+0.5
Columbus, Ohio	14.1%	−2.2	Philadelphia	16.5%	−0.3
Dallas	25.4%	−0.3	Phoenix	25.4%	−0.9
Denver	21.2%	−0.8	Portland, Ore.	14.4%	−1.2
Detroit	19.1%	+0.2	Sacramento	13.6%	+0.3
Ft. Lauderdale	26.7%	+3.7	Salt Lake City	18.7%	+0.9
Ft. Worth	20.7%	−2.3	San Diego	22.5%	+3.0
Fresno, Cal.	18.7%	+0.5	San Francisco	12.8%	−1.1
Hartford, Conn.	24.1%	−0.1	San Jose	14.4%	+2.3
Honolulu	4.7%	+1.1	Seattle	13.2%	−0.2
Houston	22.9%	−1.2	St. Louis	17.1%	unch.
Indianapolis	22.3%	+1.0	Stamford, Conn.	28.2%	−1.1
Jacksonville, Fla.	18.4%	+1.0	Tampa	20.6%	−1.4
Kansas City, Mo.	18.6%	+3.5	Tucson, Ariz.	24.2%	−0.1
Las Vegas	13.4%	+2.3	Ventura, Cal.	20.2%	−6.9
Long Island, N.Y.	18.9%	−3.6	Wash., D.C.	14.9%	−1.7
Los Angeles	19.7%	+1.8	**U.S. avg.**	**19.4%**	**−0.1**
Miami	23.5%	unch.			

Defense Contracts

Source: U.S. Dept. of Defense

(thousands of dollars)

The 50 companies (including their subsidiaries) receiving the largest dollar volume of prime contract awards from the Department of Defense during fiscal 1990.

1. McDonnell Douglas Corp.	$8,211,427
2. General Dynamics Corp.	6,306,093
3. General Electric Co.	5,588,964
4. General Motors Corp.	4,106,570
5. Raytheon Co.	4,070,955
6. Lockheed Corp.	3,552,628
7. Martin Marietta Corp.	3,491,992
8. United Technologies Corp.	2,855,766
9. Grumman Corp.	2,696,966
10. Tenneco Inc.	2,409,935
11. Boeing Co.	2,266,620
12. Westinghouse Electric Corp.	2,243,391
13. Rockwell International Corp.	2,217,299
14. Litton Industries Inc.	1,576,193
15. Honeywell Inc.	1,388,137
16. Unisys Corp.	1,375,922
17. GTE Corp.	1,294,491
18. International Business Machines Corp.	$1,285,771
19. Textron Inc.	1,190,378
20. LTV Corp.	1,182,949
21. Gencorp Inc.	1,132,819
22. TRW Inc.	1,087,295
23. American Telephone and Telegraph Co.	917,130
24. ITT Corp.	870,228
25. Ford Motor Co.	768,835
26. Northrop Corp.	746,439
27. Bath Holding Corp.	733,856
28. Allied Signal Inc.	724,513
29. Texas Instruments Inc.	704,238
30. FMC Corp.	634,030
31. Loral Corp.	618,184
32. Olin Corp.	575,720
33. McDonnell Douglas/ General Dynamics Joint Venture	555,000
34. Avondale Industries Inc.	541,482
35. Teledyne Inc.	515,255
36. Foundation Health Corp.	$515,206
37. Science Applications International Corp.	510,494
38. Hercules Inc.	491,728
39. Dyncorp	479,874
40. Massachusetts Institute of Technology	460,100
41. E Systems Inc.	460,057
42. Exxon Corp.	437,728
43. Aerospace Corp.	416,217
44. Mitre Corp.	412,354
45. Motorola Inc.	402,633
46. Royal Dutch Shell Group of Companies	395,029
47. ARCO Products Co.	390,507
48. Johns Hopkins University	374,819
49. Penn Central Corp.	373,286
50. Morrison Knudsen Corp.	370,735

Foreign Exchange Rates: 1970 to 1991

Source: International Monetary Fund

(National currency units per dollar; Data are annual averages)

Year	Australia (dollar)	Austria (schilling)	Belgium (franc)	Canada (dollar)	Denmark (krone)	France (franc)	Germany[1] (deutsche mark)	Greece (drachma)
1970	1.1136	25.880	49.680	1.0103	7.489	5.5200	3.6480	30.00
1975	1.3077	17.443	36.799	1.0175	5.748	4.2876	2.4613	32.29
1980	1.1400	12.945	29.237	1.1693	5.634	4.2250	1.8175	42.62
1982	1.0165	17.060	45.780	1.2344	8.344	6.5793	2.4280	66.87
1984	.8794	20.009	57.784	1.2951	10.357	8.7391	2.8454	112.73
1985	.7003	20.690	59.378	1.3655	10.596	8.9852	2.9440	138.12
1987	.7009	12.643	37.334	1.3260	6.840	6.0107	1.7974	135.43
1988	.7842	12.243	36.768	1.2307	6.732	5.9569	1.7562	141.89
1989	.7925	13.231	39.404	1.1840	7.310	6.3801	1.8800	162.42
1990	.7813	11.370	33.418	1.1668	6.189	5.4453	1.6157	158.51
1991	.7791	11.676	34.148	1.1457	6.396	5.6421	1.6595	182.27

Year	India (rupee)	Ireland (pound)	Italy (lira)	Japan (yen)	Malaysia (ringgit)	Netherlands (guilder)	Norway (kroner)	Portugal (escudo)
1970	7.576	2.3959	623	357.60	3.0900	3.5970	7.1400	28.75
1975	8.409	2.2216	653	296.78	2.4030	2.5293	5.2282	25.51
1980	7.887	2.0577	856	226.63	2.1767	1.9875	4.9381	50.08
1982	9.485	1.4205	1,345	249.06	2.3395	2.6719	6.4567	80.10
1984	11.363	1.0871	1,756	237.52	2.3436	3.2087	8.1615	146.39
1985	12.369	1.0656	1,909	238.54	2.4830	3.3214	8.5972	170.39
1987	12.962	1.4881	1,296	144.64	2.5196	2.0257	6.7375	140.88
1988	13.917	1.5261	1,301	128.15	2.6188	1.9766	6.5170	143.95
1989	16.226	1.4190	1,372	137.96	2.7088	2.1207	6.9045	157.46
1990	17.504	1.6585	1,198	144.79	2.7048	1.8209	6.2597	142.55
1991	22.742	1.6155	1,240	134.71	2.7501	1.8697	6.4829	144.48

Year	Singapore (dollar)	South Korea (won)	Spain (peseta)	Sweden (krona)	Switzerland (franc)	Thailand (baht)	United Kingdom (pound)
1970	3.0800	310.57	69.72	5.1700	4.3160	21.000	2.3959
1975	2.3713	484.00	57.43	4.1530	2.5839	20.379	2.2216
1980	2.1412	607.43	71.76	4.2309	1.6772	20.476	2.3243
1982	2.1406	731.93	110.09	6.2838	2.0327	23.014	1.7480
1984	2.1331	805.69	160.78	8.2718	2.3497	23.639	1.3366
1985	2.2002	870.02	170.04	8.6039	2.4571	27.159	1.2963
1987	2.1059	822.57	123.48	6.3404	1.4912	25.723	1.6389
1988	2.0124	731.57	116.49	6.1272	1.4633	25.294	1.7813
1989	1.9508	671.46	118.38	6.4469	1.6359	25.702	1.6897
1990	1.8125	707.76	101.93	5.9188	1.3892	25.585	1.7847
1991	1.7276	733.35	103.91	6.0475	1.4340	25.517	1.7694

(1) W. Germany prior to 1991.

EMPLOYMENT

U.S. Labor Force, Employment and Unemployment

Source: Bureau of Labor Statistics, U.S. Dept. of Labor; seasonally adjusted

In the second quarter of 1992, the unemployment rate reached 7.5 percent, up from 6.7 percent during that quarter in 1991, and 5.3 percent in 1990 and 1989.

Selected Unemployment Indicators

Category	1989			1990				1991				1992	
Characteristic	II	III	IV	I	II	III	IV	I	II	III	IV	I	II
Total (all civilian workers)	5.2	5.3	5.4	5.2	5.3	5.6	6.0	6.5	6.7	6.8	6.9	7.2	7.5
Men, 20 years and over	4.4	4.5	4.6	4.6	4.7	5.0	5.5	6.1	6.4	6.5	6.5	6.9	7.2
Women, 20 years and over	4.8	4.8	4.8	4.7	4.6	4.9	5.1	5.4	5.7	5.6	6.0	6.0	6.2
Both sexes, 16 to 19 years	15.1	14.7	15.2	14.7	14.9	15.9	16.6	18.0	18.7	19.0	19.0	19.6	21.0
White	4.4	4.5	4.6	4.5	4.6	4.8	5.1	5.8	6.0	6.1	6.2	6.4	6.5
Black and other	10.0	9.8	10.1	9.6	9.4	10.5	10.9	10.9	11.2	11.0	11.4	12.4	13.0
Black	11.4	11.3	11.6	10.9	10.5	11.7	12.1	12.1	12.7	12.2	12.6	13.9	14.5
Hispanic origin	8.1	8.5	8.0	7.6	7.7	8.1	8.7	9.6	9.6	10.1	10.1	11.5	11.2
Married men, spouse present	2.9	3.1	3.1	3.2	3.2	3.5	3.7	4.2	4.4	4.4	4.5	4.9	5.0
Married women, spouse present	3.9	3.8	3.8	3.7	3.6	3.8	4.1	4.3	4.5	4.5	4.7	4.8	5.1
Women who maintain families	8.0	7.9	8.0	7.9	7.7	8.5	8.7	9.1	9.3	9.0	9.2	9.5	10.1
Full-time workers	4.9	5.0	5.0	4.9	4.9	5.3	5.7	6.2	6.5	6.5	6.6	7.0	7.2
Part-time workers	7.3	7.1	7.5	7.2	7.3	7.6	7.4	8.0	8.5	8.3	8.5	9.0	9.2
Unemployed 15 weeks and over[1]	1.1	1.1	1.1	1.1	1.1	1.3	1.4	1.6	1.8	1.9	2.1	2.5	2.6
Labor force time lost[2]	6.0	6.0	6.0	5.9	6.0	6.3	6.8	7.4	7.6	7.7	7.9	8.2	8.3
Industry													
Nonagricultural private wage and salary workers	5.3	5.4	5.4	5.4	5.4	5.7	6.2	6.8	7.1	7.0	7.2	7.6	7.8
Goods-producing industries	6.0	6.4	6.4	6.5	6.5	6.9	7.9	8.7	9.1	9.0	9.2	9.5	9.9
Mining	5.1	6.7	5.4	5.3	4.2	4.3	5.2	6.5	7.7	8.7	8.6	7.6	8.2
Construction	9.8	10.4	9.5	9.5	10.6	11.2	13.5	14.6	15.1	15.8	16.2	17.3	17.1
Manufacturing	5.0	5.2	5.5	5.6	5.4	5.8	6.4	7.1	7.5	7.1	7.2	7.3	7.8
Durable goods	4.6	4.9	5.4	5.5	5.3	5.9	6.6	7.6	7.9	7.2	7.2	7.4	7.8
Nondurable goods	5.5	5.7	5.7	5.9	5.5	5.6	6.0	6.4	6.9	6.9	7.2	7.2	7.9
Service-producing industries	4.9	5.0	5.0	4.9	5.0	5.2	5.5	5.9	6.2	6.2	6.4	6.8	6.9
Transportation and public utilities	4.0	4.2	3.7	3.8	3.5	3.9	4.3	5.0	5.3	5.1	5.9	5.5	5.0
Wholesale and retail trade	5.8	6.0	6.2	6.1	6.2	6.3	6.8	7.4	7.5	7.8	7.7	8.3	8.5
Finance and service industries	4.5	4.4	4.4	4.3	4.4	4.6	4.8	5.1	5.4	5.4	5.7	6.0	6.2
Government workers	2.9	2.7	2.7	2.4	2.5	2.8	2.8	3.2	3.1	3.2	3.5	3.9	3.5
Agricultural wage and salary workers	10.0	8.6	10.7	9.4	9.6	9.7	10.2	12.0	11.2	11.5	11.9	10.7	12.4

(1) Unemployment as a percent of the civilian labor force. (2) Aggregate hours lost by the unemployed and persons on part time for economic reasons as a percent of potentially available labor force hours.

Employed Persons by Occupation, Sex, and Age

Source: Bureau of Labor Statistics, U.S. Dept. of Labor

(in thousands)

Occupation	Total 16 years and over 1990	Total 16 years and over 1991	Men 16 years and over 1990	Men 16 years and over 1991	Women 16 years and over 1990	Women 16 years and over 1991
Total	**117,914**	**116,877**	**64,435**	**63,593**	**53,479**	**53,284**
Managerial and professional specialty	30,657	31,012	16,619	16,656	14,038	14,356
Executive, administrative and managerial	14,839	14,954	8,897	8,890	5,943	6,064
Other executive, administrative, and managerial	10,362	10,412	6,592	6,611	3,770	3,801
Management-related occupations	3,893	3,951	1,950	1,943	1,943	2,008
Professional specialty	15,818	16,058	7,723	7,767	8,095	8,292
Engineers	1,862	1,846	1,714	1,694	149	152
Mathematical and computer scientists	866	923	550	583	316	339
Natural scientists	401	438	297	324	104	114
Health diagnosing occupations	871	849	716	696	155	153
Health assessment and treating occupations	2,320	2,376	320	328	2,000	2,048
Teachers, college and university	765	773	476	457	288	316
Teachers, except college and university	3,993	4,029	1,052	1,038	2,941	2,992
Lawyers and judges	756	772	599	626	157	146
Technical, sales and administrative support	36,675	36,086	12,933	12,734	23,742	23,352
Service occupations	15,759	15,986	6,288	6,429	9,470	9,557
Private household	782	787	29	32	753	755
Protective service	1,988	2,071	1,697	1,756	291	316
Service, except private household and protective	12,989	13,128	4,562	4,641	8,427	8,487
Precision production, craft, and repair	13,641	13,162	12,482	12,030	1,159	1,132
Mechanics and repairers	4,448	4,427	4,289	4,264	159	163
Construction trades	5,147	4,808	5,051	4,721	96	88
Other precision production, craft, and repair	4,046	3,927	3,142	3,045	904	881
Operators, fabricators, and laborers	17,775	17,172	13,249	12,842	4,526	4,330
Machine operators, assemblers, and inspectors	8,071	7,696	4,842	4,610	3,229	3,086
Transportation and material moving occupations	4,849	4,878	4,413	4,441	436	437
Handlers, equipment cleaners, helpers, and laborers	4,855	4,597	3,994	3,791	861	806
Farming, forestry, and fishing	3,408	3,459	2,864	2,903	544	557

Selected Unemployment Insurance Data by State

Calendar year 1991, state programs only

Source: Employment and Training Admin., U.S. Dept. of Labor

State	Insured claimants[1]	Beneficiaries[2]	Exhaustions[3]	Initial claims[4]	Benefits paid[5]	Avg. weekly benefit amt.	Employers subject to state law
AL.	197,123	171,055	37,482	414,733	$220,892,397	$119.44	77,513
AK	46,374	44,523	20,825	90,858	109,779,419	169.77	13,254
AR	147,365	103,214	28,771	250,382	176,108,254	139.54	50,302
AZ	136,916	97,919	31,022	215,948	199,168,067	143.05	79,890
CA	1,484,366	1,491,112	524,910	3,648,251	3,450,757,489	143.61	780,469
CO	115,882	82,910	31,248	164,159	175,614,793	172.68	91,401
CT	178,211	189,527	68,464	349,528	610,985,462	206.32	93,865
DC	36,775	30,994	17,724	47,460	135,225,266	220.71	20,255
DE	35,044	29,139	5,388	63,214	72,523,559	183.33	18,903
FL.	439,830	352,661	158,250	665,812	822,538,779	157.69	315,442
GA	360,857	277,517	106,192	533,261	469,312,228	148.91	144,680
HI	39,434	30,159	5,952	66,387	80,983,702	213.78	26,877
IA	121,789	92,823	21,800	181,690	187,776,654	166.85	62,884
ID	52,825	48,116	13,991	114,568	81,186,259	152.71	27,113
IL	537,107	426,600	154,704	963,980	1,317,612,196	179.86	251,257
IN	251,561	168,253	45,383	439,963	215,213,330	112.48	108,524
KS	86,461	73,820	24,533	164,445	184,497,578	176.10	58,488
KY	162,829	145,165	32,361	395,441	272,941,604	144.76	71,972
LA.	126,693	102,454	26,760	242,404	163,318,514	110.63	80,917
MA	366,541	318,141	144,970	610,814	1,312,706,433	222.49	148,474
MD	224,846	165,646	56,234	326,800	495,374,169	178.77	112,937
ME	87,546	71,441	30,056	186,113	175,678,201	164.33	33,381
MI.	684,425	513,277	171,372	1,344,235	1,547,832,094	212.42	184,203
MN	170,277	147,967	49,169	275,412	436,036,319	194.47	101,678
MO	263,050	204,688	67,714	564,778	404,254,039	142.56	127,390
MS	111,402	84,790	24,756	242,659	126,743,549	115.62	46,816
MT	31,152	26,170	8,968	54,608	46,913,180	142.89	24,192
NC	416,199	332,353	68,364	1,102,685	509,860,241	157.37	136,086
ND	18,906	16,504	6,028	34,474	28,718,996	143.98	17,776
NE	44,482	34,288	8,935	72,505	47,183,765	126.32	39,615
NH	65,729	53,567	8,556	81,397	83,619,612	130.45	32,060
NJ.	424,401	372,706	182,443	705,858	1,430,065,204	217.59	202,489
NM	40,977	33,375	11,125	71,381	70,535,566	134.53	33,931
NV	100,224	64,727	20,172	137,549	156,152,967	168.28	29,442
NY	801,617	737,436	329,288	1,426,454	2,650,319,418	190.37	436,055
OH	473,638	404,871	109,158	979,723	1,033,662,798	176.57	209,655
OK	77,739	60,384	21,268	162,473	129,788,790	152.73	65,579
OR	125,481	153,309	42,510	379,843	365,376,394	167.32	78,370
PA	659,371	559,992	169,162	1,365,413	1,725,491,156	197.10	234,321
PR	86,848	121,210	71,822	242,022	163,235,818	81.60	3,157
RI	80,813	68,584	32,197	152,679	229,166,227	204.38	31,053
SC	200,372	148,059	34,648	430,269	234,556,313	140.65	71,804
SD	10,078	8,558	822	21,701	10,839,590	121.67	19,081
TN	270,435	221,155	73,743	524,944	332,694,851	118.36	94,361
TX.	546,620	407,261	173,577	823,063	1,013,176,327	170.11	326,114
UT	50,340	39,132	10,765	70,774	73,677,820	167.96	33,887
VA	247,632	169,324	46,783	499,010	313,440,419	156.81	130,922
VI	1,175	2,128	500	3,559	3,820,223	150.90	3,157
VT.	33,776	30,682	7,658	54,615	73,361,771	153.17	18,814
WA	266,481	228,586	63,007	569,072	598,771,381	175.16	136,858
WI.	285,680	238,737	50,034	546,749	498,358,922	175.82	104,998
WV	74,500	66,274	17,589	112,796	153,346,506	159.57	35,353
WY	16,270	11,267	2,866	33,420	25,076,864	161.49	15,107
U.S..	**11,239,758**	**10,074,550**	**3,472,019**	**23,222,331**	**$25,446,271,473**	**$169.88**	**5,701,658**

(1) Claimants whose base-period earnings or whose employment, covered by the unemployment insurance program, was sufficient to make them eligible for unemployment insurance benefits as provided by state law. (2) First payments. (3) Final payments. Claimants who exhaust their benefit rights in one benefit year may be entitled to further benefits in the following benefit year. (4) Excludes intrastate transitional claims. (5) Adjusted for voided benefit checks and transfers under interstate combined wage plan.

Employment and Unemployment in the U.S.

Source: Bureau of Labor Statistics, U.S. Dept. of Labor

Civilian labor force, persons 16 years of age and over (in thousands)

Year*	Employed	Unemployed	Unemployment Rate	Year*	Employed	Unemployed	Unemployment Rate
1940[1]	47,520	8,120	14.6%	1983	100,834	10,717	9.6
1950	58,918	3,288	5.0	1984	105,005	8,539	7.5
1960	65,778	3,852	5.5	1985	107,150	8,312	7.2
1970	78,678	4,093	4.9	1986[2]	109,597	8,237	7.0
1975	85,846	7,929	8.5	1987	112,440	7,425	6.2
1978	96,048	6,202	6.1	1988	114,968	6,701	5.5
1980	99,303	7,637	7.1	1989	117,342	6,528	5.3
1981	100,397	8,273	7.6	1990	117,914	6,874	5.5
1982	99,526	10,678	9.7	1991	116,728	8,426	6.7

(1) Persons 14 years of age and over; (2) Not strictly comparable with prior years.

* **Early unemployment rates:** 1915, 9.7; 1916, 4.8; 1917, 4.8; 1918, 1.4; 1919, 2.3; 1920, 4.0; 1921, 11.9; 1922, 7.6; 1923, 3.2; 1924, 5.5; 1925, 4.0; 1926, 1.9; 1927, 4.1; 1928, 4.4; 1929, 3.2; 1930, 8.7; 1931, 15.9; 1932, 23.6; 1933, 24.9; 1934, 21.7; 1935, 20.1; 1936, 16.9; 1937, 14.3; 1938, 19.0; 1939, 17.2.

Employment and Training Services and Unemployment Insurance

Source: Employment and Training Administration, U.S. Dept. of Labor

Employment Service

The Federal-State Employment Service consists of the United States Employment Service and affiliated state employment services which make up the nation's public employment service system. During program year 1990, the public employment service listed 5.7 million job openings and placed more than 2.7 million people in jobs.

The employment service refers employable applicants to job openings that use their highest skills and helps the unemployed obtain services or training to make them employable. It also provides special attention to handicapped workers, migrants and seasonal farmworkers, workers who lose their jobs because of foreign trade competition, and other worker groups. Veterans receive priority services including referral to jobs and training. During program year 1990, 387,667 veterans were placed in jobs.

Job Training

The Job Training Partnership Act (JTPA), which became fully operational on October 1, 1983, provides job training and employment services for economically disadvantaged youth and adults, dislocated workers, and others who face significant employment barriers. The goal of the Act is to move as many jobless workers as possible into permanent, unsubsidized, self-sustaining employment.

Since its inception, JTPA has provided approximately six million Americans with training and employment services. Its placement rate is 69 percent, making it one of the most successful job and training efforts ever undertaken.

Title I of the Act's five titles basically establishes an administrative structure for the delivery of job and training services. Generally, state governors receive bloc grants from the Labor Department, and the funds are then distributed to Service Delivery Areas — areas of 200,000 population or more where local elected officials work with Private Industry Councils to plan and conduct local training projects.

Title II is in two parts, with Title II-A spelling out the Act's provision of employment and training projects for the economically disadvantaged. In program year 1990 (July 1, 1990 to Sept. 30, 1991), these projects served more than 1.7 million people.

Title II-B outlines a summer youth program offering basic and remedial education, institutional and on-the-job training, work experience, and supportive services. This program had nearly 550,000 participants in program year 1990. Beginning July 1, 1993 a new Title II-C will provide for a year-round youth training program.

Title III, Economic Dislocation and Worker Adjustment Assistance, provides for job and training help for dislocated workers — workers who lose jobs and are unlikely to return to their previous industries or occupations. This includes workers who lose their jobs because of plant closings or mass layoffs; long-term unemployed persons with limited local opportunities for jobs in their fields; farmers, ranchers, and other self-employed persons who become jobless due to general economic conditions or natural disasters; and, under certain circumstances, displaced homemakers. Such assistance benefitted over 300,000 workers in program year 1990.

Title IV authorizes programs to address the employment and training needs of specific groups facing significant barriers to productive employment, including Native Americans, migrant and seasonal farmworkers, and the disabled. In program year 1987, these programs served 33,000 Native Americans; 46,800 migrant and seasonal farmworkers; and 8,550 disabled persons.

In addition, Title IV includes the Job Corps, which each year enrolls approximately 100,000 young people between the ages of 16 and 21 in 107 residential job training centers throughout the United States; the National Commission for Employment Policy; and nationally administered programs for technical assistance, labor market information, research and evaluation, and pilots and demonstrations.

With recent amendments to JTPA, Title V is now the Jobs for Employable Dependent Individuals (JEDI) Incentive Bonus Program. Title VI provides for new State human resources investment councils, and Title VII covers transition provisions and technical conforming amendments.

Trade Adjustment Assistance for Workers

The Trade Adjustment Assistance (TAA) is available to workers who lose their jobs or whose hours of work and wages are reduced as a result of increased imports. TAA includes a variety of benefits and reemployment services to help unemployed workers prepare for and obtain suitable employment. Workers may be eligible for training, job search, relocation and other reemployment services. Additionally, weekly trade readjustment allowances (TRA) may be payable to eligible workers following their exhaustion of unemployment insurance benefits. In fiscal year 1991, about 252,000 workers received $116 million in TRA payments; about 20,100 workers entered training; about 525 workers were involved in job search visits; and about 760 workers relocated in order to obtain long term jobs.

The TAA program is administered by the Employment and Training Administration's Office of Trade Adjustment Assistance. State employment security agencies serve as agents of the U.S., under an agreement with the Secretary of Labor, for administering the TAA benefit provisions in the Trade Act of 1974, as amended.

Unemployment Insurance

Unlike old-age and survivors insurance, entirely a federal program, the unemployment insurance program is a Federal-State system that provides insured wage earners with partial replacement of wages lost during involuntary unemployment. The program protects most workers. During calendar year 1991, an estimated 104.6 million workers in commerce, industry, agriculture, and government, including the armed forces, were covered under the Federal-State system. In addition, an estimated 311,000 railroad workers were insured against unemployment by the Railroad Retirement Board.

Each state, as well as the District of Columbia, Puerto Rico, and the Virgin Islands, has its own law and operates its own program. The amount and duration of the weekly benefits are determined by state laws, based on prior wages and length of employment. States are required to extend the duration of benefits when unemployment rises to and remains above specified state levels; costs of extended benefits are shared by the state and federal governments.

Under the Federal Unemployment Tax Act, as amended in 1985, the tax rate is 6.2% on the first $7,000 paid to each employee of employers with one or more employees in 20 weeks of the year or a quarterly payroll of $1,500. A credit of up to 5.4% is allowed for taxes paid under state unemployment insurance laws that meet certain criteria, leaving the federal share at 0.8% of taxable wages.

Social Security Requirement

The Social Security Act requires, as a condition of such grants, prompt payment of due benefits. The Federal Unemployment Tax Act provides safeguards for workers' right to benefits if they refuse jobs that fail to meet certain labor standards. Through the Unemployment Insurance Service of the Employment and Training Administration, the Secretary of Labor determines whether states qualify for grants and for tax offset credit from employers.

Benefits are financed solely by employer contributions, except in Alaska, Pennsylvania and New Jersey where employees also contribute. Benefits are paid through the states' public employment offices, at which unemployed workers must register for work and to which they must report regularly for referral to a possible job during the time when they are drawing weekly benefit payments. During the fiscal year 1991, $24.42 billion in benefits was paid under state unemployment insurance programs to 10.2 million beneficiaries. They received an average weekly payment of $162.73 for total unemployment for an average of 14.8 weeks.

Women in the Labor Force, 1990-1991

Source: Bureau of Labor Statistics, U.S. Dept. of Labor (data seasonally adjusted unless otherwise indicated; numbers in thousands)

The number of unemployed women rose in 1991, reflecting continued weakness in the economy. Over the same period, the number of women with jobs did not rise for the 2nd year in a row. Prior to that, female employment had risen every year since the 1950s. The female labor force participation rate changed little during 1991, ending the year at 57.3 percent. This measure, which rose 20 percentage points from 1950 to 1990, showed little movement thereafter.

Median weekly earnings of women employed in full-time wage and salary jobs were $373 in the 4th quarter of 1991. This was 74 percent of men's earnings, an over-the-year rise of 1.8 percent. This ratio had been fluctuating around 70 percent over the 1987-89 period and had risen from 1989 to 1990. In 1979, when comparable data first became available, the ratio of women's-to-men's weekly earnings was considerably lower—63 percent.

Indicator	Annual averages[1]		Quarterly averages		
			1990	1991	
	1990	1991	IV	III	IV
Population and labor force					
Women, 16 years and over:					
Civilian noninstitutional population[1]	98,399	99,214	98,711	99,316	99,528
Civilian labor force	56,554	56,893	56,476	56,809	57,059
Civilian labor force participation rates					
Women, 16 years and over	57.5	57.3	57.2	57.2	57.3
16 to 19 years	51.8	50.2	50.4	48.4	50.3
20 years and over	57.9	57.9	57.7	57.8	57.8
20 to 24 years	71.6	70.4	71.2	69.7	70.6
25 to 54 years	74.1	74.2	73.9	74.2	74.1
55 years and over	23.0	22.8	22.8	23.0	22.6
White	57.5	57.4	57.3	57.3	57.5
Black	57.8	57.0	57.2	57.2	56.6
Employment status					
Women, 16 years and over:					
Employed	53,479	53,284	53,220	53,243	53,257
Unemployed	3,075	3,609	3,256	3,566	3,802
16 to 19 years:					
Employed	3,024	2,749	2,870	2,623	2,707
Unemployed	519	581	534	570	599
20 years and over					
Employed	50,455	50,535	50,350	50,621	50,550
Unemployed	2,555	3,028	2,722	2,996	3,203
20 to 24 years:					
Employed	5,997	5,812	5,952	5,757	5,765
Unemployed	555	628	567	625	701
25 to 54 years:					
Employed	38,068	38,383	38,058	38,497	38,522
Unemployed	1,813	2,177	1,951	2,165	2,243
55 years and over:					
Employed	6,390	6,340	6,352	6,395	6,281
Unemployed	187	222	188	221	242
Unemployment rates					
Women, 16 years and over	5.4	6.3	5.8	6.3	6.7
16 to 19 years	14.7	17.4	15.7	17.9	18.1
20 years and over	4.8	5.7	5.1	5.6	6.0
20 to 24 years	8.5	9.8	8.7	9.8	10.8
25 to 54 years	4.5	5.4	4.9	5.3	5.5
55 years and over	2.8	3.4	2.9	3.3	3.7
White, 16 years and over	4.6	5.5	4.9	5.5	5.8
White, 16 to 19 years	12.6	15.2	12.9	15.4	16.1
Black, 16 years and over	10.8	11.9	11.5	11.5	12.7
Black, 16 to 19 years	30.0	36.1	35.0	38.0	37.5
Full-time workers					
Percent of employed women working full time	74.8	74.4	74.8	74.3	74.5
Percent of unemployed women looking for full-time work	74.0	75.4	76.0	76.3	75.0
Duration of unemployment[1]					
Average (mean) number of weeks unemployed women have been looking for work	10.0	11.8	10.7	11.8	13.2
Marital status					
Married women, husband present:					
Civilian noninstitutional population[1]	53,070	53,297	53,177	53,466	53,342
Civilian labor force participation rate	58.4	58.5	58.3	58.5	58.6
Unemployment rate	3.8	4.5	4.1	4.5	4.7
Women who maintain families:					
Civilian noninstitutional population[1]	11,155	11,528	11,339	11,628	11,699
Civilian labor force participation rate	62.1	61.6	61.5	61.4	61.2
Unemployment rate	8.2	9.1	8.7	9.0	9.2

(1) Not seasonally adjusted. **Note:** Due to rounding and independent seasonal adjustment, some components may not add to totals.

Sex Discrimination and Sexual Harassment Complaints from Workers

Source: Equal Employment Opportunity Commission

	1985	1986	1987	1988	1989	1990	1991
Sex discrimination*	31,488	32,843	33,930	32,911	33,092	34,946	35,995
Sexual harassment	5,035	4,446	5,350	5,231	5,572	6,127	6,883
Lawsuits filed	NA	38	45	41	50	50	66

* Includes sexual harassment charges. NA = Not available.

Labor Force by Sex, Race, and Hispanic Origin, 1975, 1990, and Projected to 2005

Source: Women's Bureau, U.S. Labor Dept.

(labor force 16 years old and over; numbers in thousands)

	1975	1990	2005	Change 1990-2005
Total	**93,775**	**124,787**	**150,732**	**25,945**
Women	37,475	56,554	71,394	14,840
Men	56,299	68,234	79,338	11,104
White	82,831	107,177	125,785	18,608
Women	32,508	47,879	58,934	11,055
Men	50,324	59,298	66,851	7,553
Black	9,263	13,493	17,766	4,273
Women	4,247	6,785	9,062	2,277
Men	5,106	6,708	8,704	1,996
Hispanic Origin	(1)	9,576	16,790	7,214
Women	(1)	3,821	6,888	3,067
Men	(1)	5,755	9,902	4,147
Asian and other	1,643	4,116	7,181	3,065
Women	712	1,890	3,398	1,508
Men	931	2,226	3,783	1,557

(1) Comparable data on Hispanics were not available before 1980.

Fastest Growing Occupations, 1990-2005

(numbers in thousands)

Source: Bureau of Labor Statistics, U.S. Labor Dept.

Occupation	Employment 1990	Employment 2005	Change in Employment Number	Change in Employment Percent
Home health aides	287	550	263	91.7
Paralegals	90	167	77	85.2
Systems analysts and computer scientists	463	829	366	78.9
Personal and home care aides	103	183	79	76.7
Physical therapists	88	155	67	76.0
Medical assistants	165	287	122	73.9
Operations research analysts	57	100	42	73.2
Human services workers	145	249	103	71.2
Radiologic technologists and technicians	149	252	103	69.5
Medical secretaries	232	390	158	68.3

Occupations with Largest Growth, 1990-2005

(numbers in thousands)

Source: Bureau of Labor Statistics, U.S. Labor Dept.

Occupation	Employment 1990	Employment 2005	Change in Employment Number	Change in Employment Percent
Salespersons, retail	3,619	4,506	887	24.5
Registered nurses	1,727	2,494	767	44.4
Cashiers	2,633	3,318	685	26.0
General office clerks	2,737	3,407	670	24.5
Truckdrivers, light and heavy	2,362	2,979	617	26.1
General managers and top executives	3,086	3,684	598	19.4
Janitors and cleaners, including maids and housekeeping cleaners	3,007	3,562	555	18.5
Nursing aides, orderlies, and attendants	1,274	1,826	552	43.4
Food counter, fountain, and related workers	1,607	2,158	550	34.2
Waiters and waitresses	1,747	2,196	449	25.7

Occupations of Employed Persons by Work Disability Status and Sex

Source: Women's Bureau, U.S. Labor Dept. (16-64 years old; 1988)

	Persons with Work Disabilities					Persons with No Work Disabilities	
		Women					
Occupations	Men	Total	White	Black	Hispanic	Men	Women
Managerial and Professional Specialty	18.2	16.0	17.7	7.5	13.3	26.3	25.6
Technical, Sales and Administrative Support	17.5	39.5	41.2	28.3	28.5	19.9	45.3
Service	12.5	27.3	23.7	47.7	31.8	9.2	17.0
Farming, Forestry and Fishing	4.6	1.4	1.5	0.8	2.9	3.7	0.8
Precision Production, Crafts and Repair	19.6	2.2	2.4	0.5	4.6	19.8	2.2
Operators, Fabricators and Laborers	27.4	13.3	13.2	14.9	18.6	20.9	8.7

Note: Of the 6.7 million women with work disabilities in the U.S. population in 1988, 1.4 million, or 20.4%, were black and 488,000 (7.3%) were of Hispanic origin.

Work Stoppages (Strikes) in the U.S., 1955-1991

Source: Bureau of Labor Statistics, U.S. Dept. of Labor

(involving 1,000 workers or more)

Year	Number stoppages[1]	Workers involved[1] (thousands)	Work days idle[1] (thousands)	Year	Number stoppages[1]	Workers involved[1] (thousands)	Work days idle[1] (thousands)
1955	363	2,055	21,100	1977	298	1,212	21,258
1960	222	896	13,260	1978	219	1,006	23,774
1965	268	999	15,140	1979	235	1,021	20,409
1966	321	1,300	16,000	1980	187	795	20,844
1967	381	2,192	31,320	1981	145	729	16,908
1968	392	1,855	35,567	1982	96	656	9,061
1969	412	1,576	29,397	1983	81	909	17,461
1970	381	2,468	52,761	1984	62	376	8,499
1971	298	2,516	35,538	1985	54	324	7,079
1972	250	975	16,764	1986	69	533	11,861
1973	317	1,400	16,260	1987	46	174	4,481
1974	424	1,796	31,809	1988	40	118	4,364
1975	235	965	17,563	1989	51	452	16,996
1976	231	1,519	23,962	1990	44	185	5,926
				1991	40	392	4,584

(1) The number of stoppages and workers relate to stoppages that began in the year. Days of idleness include all stoppages in effect. Workers are counted more than once if they were involved in more than one stoppage during the year.

Work Stoppages Involving 5,000 Workers or More Beginning in 1991

Source: Bureau of Labor Statistics, U.S. Labor Dept.

Employer, location, and union	Began	Ended	Workers involved[1]	Estimated days idle in 1991[1]
Railroad industry Interstate Various unions	4/1	4/1	230,000	230,000
Health care industry New York, N.Y. State, County and Municipal Employees	4/17	4/17	6,000	6,000
Board of Education Intrastate-Washington National Education Association	4/19	4/30	21,000	168,000
Realty Advisory Board on Labor Relations New York, N.Y. Service Employees	4/21	5/2	30,000	186,000
Giant Eagle Markets Pittsburgh, Pa., area Food and Commercial Workers	4/22	6/2	5,500	159,500
Construction industry Philadelphia, Pa., area Carpenters	5/1	5/4	7,100	21,300
Mid-America Regional Bargaining Association Intrastate-Illinois Laborers	6/1	6/10	30,000	180,000
Caterpillar, Inc. Illinois Automobile Workers	11/4		8,000	295,200

(1) Workers and days idle are rounded to the nearest 100.

Minority Business Owners

Source: Bureau of the Census, 1982 and 1987 Economic Censuses and population estimates; latest data available as of Sept. 1992

(minority-owned firms per 1,000 population, for minority groups, and percent change 1982-87)

	1987	1982	percent change 1982-87		1987	1982	percent change 1982-87
Blacks	14.6	11.3	29.2%	Korean	102.4	68.0	50.6
Hispanics	20.9	14.3	46.2	Vietnamese	49.6	14.6	239.7
Mexican	18.8	13.7	37.2	Filipino	32.8	25.5	28.6
Puerto Rican	10.9	6.3	73.0	Hawaiian	21.5	16.6	29.5
Cuban	62.9	41.4	51.9	**American Indian**	11.8	8.8	34.1
Other Hispanic	22.9	14.2	61.3	Aleut	54.0	58.5	-7.7
Asian*	57.0	43.2	31.9	Eskimo	44.4	36.8	20.7
Asian Indian	75.7	51.3	47.6	Native American	10.3	7.4	39.2
Chinese	63.4	49.1	29.1	**Nonminority**	67.1	61.9	8.4
Japanese	66.1	59.3	11.5				

* Includes Pacific Islanders.

Sick-Days for Acute Conditions, by Age of Worker

Source: National Center for Health Statistics, 1990

(number of work-loss days per 100 currently employed people aged 18 and older per year associated with acute conditions)

	Total	18 to 24 yrs.	25 to 44 yrs.	45 to 64 yrs.
All Acute Conditions	**317.3**	**477.9**	**319.5**	**234.7**
Respiratory Conditions	112.3	142.7	107.8	97.7
Common colds	17.6	30.3	15.5	15.8
Other upper-respiratory infections	9.2	17.8	7.6	3.6
Influenza	66.4	72.2	66.2	63.1
Acute bronchitis	6.0	6.5	6.7	3.6
Pneumonia	10.6	12.2	10.3	7.3
Other	2.5	3.8	1.5	4.3
Injuries	106.3	171.6	116.2	59.7
Fractures/dislocations	23.0	28.7	29.0	8.0
Sprains/strains	33.0	43.7	39.8	17.3
Open wounds/lacerations	10.7	33.2	7.7	5.1
Contusions/superficial injuries	13.8	23.0	15.4	7.2
Other current injuries	25.8	43.0	24.4	22.2

Federal Minimum Hourly Wage Rates Since 1950

Source: U.S. Dept. of Labor.

(Employee estimates as of September 1984, except as indicated. The Fair Labor Standards Act of 1938 and subsequent amendments provide for minimum wage coverage applicable to specified nonsupervisory employment categories. Exempt from coverage are executives and administrators or professionals).

Effective date	Minimum Rates for Nonfarm Workers: Laws prior to 1966[1]	Percent, avg earnings[2]	1966 and later[3]	Minimum rates for farm workers[4]
Jan. 25, 1950	$.75	54	(X)	(X)
Mar. 1, 1956	1.00	52	(X)	(X)
Sept. 3, 1961	1.15	50	(X)	(X)
Sept. 3, 1963	1.25	51	(X)	(X)
Feb. 1, 1967	1.40	50	$1.00	$1.00
Feb. 1, 1968	1.60	54	1.15	1.15
Feb. 1, 1969	(5)	(5)	1.30	1.30
Feb. 1, 1970	(5)	(5)	1.45	(5)
Feb. 1, 1971	(5)	(5)	1.60	(5)
May 1, 1974	2.00	46	1.90	1.60
Jan. 1, 1975	2.10	45	2.00	1.80
Jan. 1, 1976	2.30	46	2.20	2.00
Jan. 1, 1977	(5)	(5)	2.30	2.20
Jan. 1, 1978	2.65	44	2.65	2.65
Jan. 1, 1979	2.90	45	2.90	2.90
Jan. 1, 1980	3.10	45	3.10	3.10
Jan. 1, 1981	3.35	43	3.35	3.35
Apr. 1, 1990	3.80[6]		3.80[6]	3.80[6]
Apr. 1, 1991	4.25[6]		4.25[6]	4.25[6]

(X) Not applicable. (1) Applies to workers covered prior to 1961 Amendments and, after Sept. 1965, to workers covered by 1961 Amendments. Rates set by 1961 Amendments were: Sept. 1961, $1.00; Sept. 1964, $1.15; and Sept. 1965, $1.25. (2) Percent of gross average hourly earnings of production workers in manufacturing. (3) Applies to workers newly covered by Amendments of 1966, 1974, and 1977, and Title IX of Education Amendments of 1972. (4) Included in coverage as of 1966, 1974, and 1977 Amendments. (5) No change in rate. (6) Training wage for workers age 16-19 in first six months of first job: 1990, $3.35; 1991, $3.62 and from Apr. 1, 1991, additional requirements re subsequent employment by a different employer for an additional 90 days. The training wage expires Mar. 31, 1993.

Year-Round, Full-Time Workers With Low Annual Earnings, by Selected Characteristics: 1964-1990

Source: Bureau of Labor Statistics, U.S. Labor Dept.

(Percent distribution)

Characteristics	1964	1969	1974	1979	1984	1989	1990
Persons 16 years old and over							
Number	11,224	7,598	6,636	7,813	10,263	13,040	14,440
Percent	100.0	100.0	100.0	100.0	100.0	100.0	100.0
Male	50.4	42.7	42.6	42.1	44.7	45.2	46.7
Female	49.6	57.3	57.4	57.9	55.3	54.8	53.3
16 to 24 years old	16.3	19.6	24.2	26.2	24.9	22.8	21.1
25 to 34 years old	15.3	15.4	17.9	21.6	25.6	29.8	30.7
35 to 54 years old	43.4	38.1	35.9	34.0	34.3	35.2	35.6
55 to 64 years old	18.1	18.6	15.6	13.7	11.6	9.3	9.6
65 years old and over	6.9	8.2	6.4	4.4	3.6	3.0	2.9
White	82.5	80.1	85.3	83.8	83.0	83.4	82.0
Black	16.5	19.1	13.0	13.9	14.1	13.3	14.3
Hispanic origin[1]	(NA)	(NA)	6.2	7.7	9.3	12.2	12.5
Persons 16 to 64 years old							
Number	10,455	6,972	6,212	7,466	9,898	12,646	14,019
Percent	100.0	100.0	100.0	100.0	100.0	100.0	100.0
Less than 12 years of school completed	(NA)	50.2	40.1	32.4	26.9	23.2	22.9
12 years of school completed	(NA)	36.6	43.5	46.2	47.5	48.8	48.5
13 or more years of school completed	(NA)	13.2	16.4	21.4	25.6	28.0	28.6
Husband in married-couple family	33.1	24.3	21.8	21.3	21.9	19.8	20.6
Wife in married-couple family	28.5	34.9	35.4	34.0	30.4	29.3	27.8
Female family householder, no spouse present	5.6	6.5	6.6	7.2	7.7	7.4	7.3
Other family member	20.7	21.1	23.0	22.5	24.4	23.8	24.3
Male unrelated individual	4.4	5.2	5.4	6.8	7.7	10.3	10.8
Female unrelated individual	7.5	8.0	7.8	8.3	7.9	9.3	9.1

(1) Persons of Hispanic Origin may be of any race. **Note:** Workers have low earnings if their annual earnings are less than the poverty level for a 4-person family; the threshold in 1964 was $3,144; in 1969, $3,676; in 1974, $4,843; in 1979, $6,905; in 1984, $9,694; in 1989, $11,570; and in 1990, $12,195.

Distribution of Wage and Salary Workers Paid Hourly Rates

Source: Bureau of Labor Statistics, U.S. Dept. of Labor; unpublished tabulations from Current Population Survey, 1991-92

(2nd quarter 1991-1st quarter 1992)

Sex and age	Total paid hourly rates	$3.80* or less	$4.25* or less	$5.00 or less	$5.01 or more
Total, 16 years and over	61,782	1,453	5,716	14,248	47,535
16 to 24 years	14,135	691	2,915	6,818	7,317
20 to 24 years	9,151	333	1,255	3,224	5,928
25 years and over	47,647	762	2,801	7,430	40,218
25 to 54 years	41,251	628	2,251	6,061	35,190
25 to 34 years	17,840	319	1,118	2,975	14,865
35 to 44 years	14,603	205	709	1,937	12,667
45 to 54 years	8,808	104	424	1,149	7,659
55 years and over	6,396	134	550	1,368	5,027
55 to 64 years	5,039	78	337	856	4,183
65 years and over	1,357	56	213	513	844
Men, 16 years and over	31,010	407	2,082	5,631	25,380
16 to 24 years	7,335	231	1,248	3,189	4,147
20 to 24 years	4,829	111	516	1,479	3,350
25 years and over	23,675	176	834	2,442	21,234
Women, 16 years and over	30,771	1,045	3,634	8,617	22,154
16 to 24 years	6,800	460	1,667	3,630	3,170
20 to 24 years	4,322	222	740	1,745	2,577
25 years and over	23,972	586	1,967	4,988	18,984
Family relationship					
Husbands	16,263	75	391	1,272	14,991
Wives	15,403	346	1,180	3,131	12,272
Women who maintain families	3,991	139	439	1,001	2,990
Men who maintain families	1,221	10	56	174	1,046
Race and hispanic origin					
White					
Total, 16 years and over	51,776	1,270	4,673	11,703	40,074
Men	26,095	329	1,646	4,540	21,556
Women	25,680	942	3,027	7,163	18,517
Black					
Total, 16 years and over	7,927	152	874	2,095	5,832
Men	3,889	69	371	898	2,991
Women	4,037	83	503	1,197	2,840
Hispanic origin					
Total, 16 years and over	5,908	102	655	1,779	4,129
Men	3,575	48	329	927	2,648
Women	2,333	54	326	851	1,481
Full- and part-time status and sex					
Full-time workers					
Total, 16 years and over	45,854	497	2,146	6,488	39,366
Men	26,030	156	891	2,905	23,126
Women	19,823	340	1,255	3,583	16,241
Part-time workers					
Total, 16 years and over	15,928	956	3,570	7,760	8,168
Men	4,908	251	1,191	2,726	2,255
Women	10,948	705	2,379	5,034	5,914

Note: Data exclude the incorporated self-employed. *$3.80 = minimum wage Apr. 1, 1990-Mar. 31, 1991; $4.25 = minimum wage from Apr. 1, 1991.

Average Hours and Earnings of Production Workers, 1964-1991

Source: Bureau of Labor Statistics, U.S. Dept. of Labor

(annual averages)

	Weekly hours	Total private[1] Hourly earnings	Weekly earnings		Weekly hours	Total private[1] Hourly earnings	Weekly earnings
1964	38.7	$2.36	$91.33	1978	35.8	5.69	203.70
1965	38.8	2.46	95.45	1979	35.7	6.16	219.91
1966	38.6	2.56	98.82	1980	35.3	6.66	235.10
1967	38.0	2.68	101.84	1981	35.2	7.25	255.20
1968	37.8	2.85	107.73	1982	34.8	7.68	267.26
1969	37.7	3.04	114.61	1983	35.0	8.02	280.70
1970	37.1	3.23	119.83	1984	35.2	8.32	292.86
1971	36.9	3.45	127.31	1985	34.9	8.57	299.09
1972	37.0	3.70	136.90	1986	34.8	8.76	304.85
1973	36.9	3.94	145.39	1987	34.8	8.98	312.50
1974	36.5	4.24	154.76	1988	34.7	9.28	322.02
1975	36.1	4.53	163.53	1989	34.6	9.66	334.24
1976	36.1	4.86	175.45	1990	34.5	10.01	345.35
1977	36.0	5.25	189.00	1991	34.3	10.33	354.32

(1) Data relate to production workers in mining and manufacturing; construction workers in construction; and nonsupervisory workers in transportation and public utilities; wholesale and retail trade; finance, insurance, and real estate; and services.

Full-Time Wage and Salary Workers with Flexible Schedules

Source: Bureau of Labor Statistics, U.S. Dept. of Labor; May 1991

(in thousands)

The number of full-time wage and salary workers with flexible work schedules was 12.1 million in May 1991, up from 9.1 million in 1985. The proportion of full-time workers with flexible schedules increased to 15.1 percent in 1991 from 12.3 percent in 1985. More than 20 percent of managers, professionals, technicians, and sales workers had flexibility, compared with only one-tenth or less of service and "blue-collar" workers. Specific occupations with the highest proportion of workers on flextime were natural scientists (45 percent), mathematical and computer scientists (44 percent), and college and university teachers (38 percent). About 18 percent of the 80.5 million full-time wage and salary employees had work schedules that differed from the regular daytime pattern—e.g., in the evening or at night, or on rotating shifts. Men were more likely than women, blacks more likely than whites, and youths more likely than older workers to work other than a normal daytime schedule.

Age, race and Hispanic origin	Both sexes Total	Both sexes With flexible schedules Number	Both sexes With flexible schedules Percent of total	Men Total	Men With flexible schedules Number	Men With flexible schedules Percent of total	Women Total	Women With flexible schedules Number	Women With flexible schedules Percent of total
Total, 16 years and over	**80,452**	**12,118**	**15.1**	**46,308**	**7,168**	**15.5**	**34,145**	**4,950**	**14.5**
16 to 19 years	1,413	150	10.6	855	82	9.6	558	67	12.0
20 years and over	79,040	11,968	15.1	45,453	7,086	15.6	33,587	4,882	14.5
20 to 24 years	8,332	999	12.0	4,694	542	11.5	3,638	456	12.5
25 to 34 years	25,523	4,008	15.7	14,917	2,358	15.8	10,606	1,650	15.6
35 to 44 years	22,749	3,744	16.5	13,001	2,213	17.0	9,749	1,531	15.7
45 to 54 years	14,306	2,184	15.3	8,003	1,299	16.2	6,302	885	14.0
55 to 64 years	7,197	880	12.2	4,286	574	13.4	2,910	306	10.5
65 years and over	933	153	16.4	552	99	17.9	382	54	14.1
16 to 24 years	9,745	1,148	11.8	5,549	625	11.3	4,196	524	12.5
25 to 54 years	62,578	9,936	15.9	35,921	5,870	16.3	26,657	4,066	15.3
55 years and over	8,130	1,033	12.7	4,838	673	13.9	3,292	360	10.9
White	68,795	10,630	15.5	40,267	6,416	15.9	28,528	4,214	14.8
Black	8,943	1,063	12.1	4,522	525	11.6	4,421	558	12.6
Hispanic origin	6,598	702	10.6	4,172	427	10.2	2,425	275	11.3

Note: Data relate to the sole or principal job of full-time wage and salary workers who were at work during the survey reference week and exclude the incorporated self-employed, who usually are classified as wage and salary workers. Detail for the above race and Hispanic-origin groups will not sum to totals because data for the "other races" group are not presented and Hispanics are included in both the white and black population groups.

Mass Layoffs, 1990-1992

Source: Bureau of Labor Statistics, U.S. Dept. of Labor

Period	Establishments	Layoff events	Separations	Initial claimants
1990				
January-March (46 states)	861	884	131,019	119,872
April-June (46 states)	839	862	150,361	108,429
July-September (45 states)	748	760	126,217	103,592
October-December (45 states)	1,069	1,095	176,280	145,362
1991				
January-March (49 states)	1,462	1,500	288,496	257,959
April-June (49 states)	1,158	1,180	204,432	157,781
July-September (48 states)	859	878	144,764	124,811
October-December (48 states)	1,149	1,163	209,864	173,584
1992				
January-March (48 states)	1,113	1,126	163,647	140,758

Note: The number of states reporting data in the 2 years varies because Maryland and Michigan began reporting in 1991 and Oregon in 1992; Indiana reported for the first half of 1990, did not report during the second half, and resumed in 1991; Ohio reported only for the first half of 1991; and Michigan did not report during the first quarter of 1992. Data were not reported for California in any quarter. Finally, for purposes of these counts, the District of Columbia is included as a state.

Reason for Separation in Mass Layoffs, Jan.-Mar. 1992

Source: Bureau of Labor Statistics, U.S. Dept. of Labor

Reason for separation	Layoff events	Separations	Unemployment Insurance Initial claimants
Total, all reasons[1]	**1,126**	**163,647**	**140,758**
Automation	9	1,422	1,230
Bankruptcy	46	8,359	4,779
Business ownership change	27	4,234	4,052
Contract cancellation	29	3,443	3,239
Contract completion	78	10,083	10,339
Domestic relocation	35	5,140	4,792
Environment related	3	362	156
Import competition	14	3,986	2,978
Material shortages	6	965	1,204
Model changeover	5	400	444
Overseas relocation	6	830	604
Plant or machine repairs	11	908	1,673
Seasonal work	331	48,784	33,925
Slack work	334	44,787	43,594
Weather-related curtailment	10	980	783
Other reasons	100	19,355	16,254
Not reported	82	9,609	10,712

(1) Data on layoffs were reported by employers in all states and the District of Columbia, except in California, Michigan, and Ohio.

Displaced Workers, January 1992

Source: Bureau of Labor Statistics, U.S. Dept. of Labor

Age, sex, race, and Hispanic origin	Total[1] (thousands)	Percent distribution by reason for job loss: Total	Plant or company closed down or moved	Slack work	Position or shift abolished
Total					
Total, 20 years and over	5,584	100.0	52.1	31.6	16.3
20 to 24 years	203	100.0	44.6	48.2	7.2
25 to 54 years	4,416	100.0	51.4	31.2	17.4
55 to 64 years	751	100.0	56.5	29.3	14.2
65 years and over	214	100.0	60.0	30.2	9.8
Men					
Total, 20 years and over	3,447	100.0	49.4	34.7	15.9
20 to 24 years	127	100.0	45.0	49.4	5.6
25 to 54 years	2,728	100.0	49.5	34.0	16.5
55 to 64 years	488	100.0	49.0	34.6	16.4
65 years and over	103	100.0	53.3	35.7	11.0
Women					
Total, 20 years and over	2,137	100.0	56.6	26.4	17.0
20 to 24 years	76	100.0	43.8	46.1	10.0
25 to 54 years	1,688	100.0	54.4	26.7	18.9
55 to 64 years	262	100.0	70.5	19.4	10.1
65 years and over	111	100.0	66.3	25.1	8.6
White					
Total, 20 years and over	4,828	100.0	52.5	30.6	16.9
Men	3,003	100.0	49.4	34.1	16.5
Women	1,825	100.0	57.6	24.8	17.6
Black					
Total, 20 years and over	626	100.0	51.3	36.3	12.4
Men	356	100.0	52.3	36.6	11.1
Women	270	100.0	50.0	35.9	14.1
Hispanic Origin					
Total, 20 years and over	511	100.0	57.0	34.5	8.5
Men	323	100.0	57.6	35.7	6.7
Women	188	100.0	56.0	32.5	11.6

(1) Data refer to persons with tenure of 3 years or more who lost or left a job between January 1987 and January 1992 because of plant closings or moves, slack work, or the abolishment of their positions or shifts.
Note: Detail for the above race and Hispanic-origin groups will not sum to totals because data for the "other races" group are not presented and Hispanics are included in both the white and black population groups

Occupational Injuries and Rates for Industries with 100,000 or More Injury Cases, 1989-90

Source: Bureau of Labor Statistics, U.S. Dept. of Labor

Industry	1989 Total cases (in thousands)	1989 Incidence rate[1]	1990 Total cases (in thousands)	1990 Incidence rate[1]
Motor vehicles and equipment manufacturing	161.4	18.9	148.5	18.9
Nursing and personal care facilities	160.0	15.2	168.2	15.4
Trucking and courier services, except air	191.0	13.3	203.8	14.1
Department stores	154.1	10.7	165.4	11.1
Grocery stores	251.8	12.5	246.4	12.1
Hotels and motels	128.1	10.8	126.0	10.4
Eating and drinking places	351.9	8.4	353.6	8.4
Hospitals	222.6	8.0	282.4	10.0

(1) Incident rates represent the number of injuries per 100 full-time workers.

Manufacturing Production Worker Statistics

Source: Bureau of Labor Statistics, U.S. Dept. of Labor (p = preliminary)

Year	All employees	Production workers	Av. weekly earnings	Avg. hourly earnings	Avg. hrs. per wk.
1955	16,882,000	13,288,000	$75.30	$1.85	40.7
1960	16,796,000	12,586,000	89.72	2.26	39.7
1965	18,062,000	13,434,000	107.53	2.61	41.2
1970	19,367,000	14,044,000	133.33	3.35	39.8
1975	18,323,000	13,043,000	190.79	4.83	39.5
1980	20,285,000	14,214,000	288.62	7.27	39.7
1985	19,260,000	13,092,000	386.37	9.54	40.5
1987	19,024,000	12,970,000	406.31	9.91	41.0
1988	19,403,000	13,254,000	418.40	10.18	41.1
1989	19,612,000	13,375,000	429.27	10.47	41.0
1990	19,111,000	12,974,000	441.86	10.83	40.8
1991	18,455,000	12,467,000	455.11	11.18	40.7
1992, June[p]	18,213,000	12,379,000	472.89	11.45	41.1

Civilian Employment of the Federal Government: May 1992

Source: Workforce Analysis and Statistics Division, U.S. Office of Personnel Management

(Payroll in thousands of dollars)

	All Areas		United States		Wash., D.C. MSA		Overseas	
Agency	Employ-ment	Payroll	Employ-ment	Payroll	Employ-ment	Payroll	Employ-ment	Payroll
Total, all agencies[1]	**3,115,056**	**$10,528,360**	**2,986,985**	**$10,185,568**	**378,845**	**$1,636,436**	**128,071**	**$342,792**
Legislative branch	**39,539**	**147,559**	**39,481**	**147,203**	**37,153**	**135,772**	**58**	**356**
Congress	20,867	65,244	20,867	65,244	20,867	65,244	—	—
U.S. Senate	7,838	24,079	7,838	24,079	7,838	24,079	—	—
House of Rep Summary	13,009	41,084	13,009	41,084	13,009	41,084	—	—
Comm. on Scty & Coop in Eur	20	81	20	81	20	81	—	—
Architect of the Capitol	2,391	8,947	2,391	8,947	2,391	8,947	—	—
Botanic Garden	55	201	55	201	55	201	—	—
Committee on Agri Workers	8	57	8	57	8	57	—	—
Congressional Budget Ofc	234	1,571	234	1,571	234	1,571	—	—
Copyright Royalty Tribunal	9	60	9	60	9	60	—	—
General Accounting Ofc	5,408	31,044	5,357	30,750	3,535	20,659	51	294
Government Printing Ofc	4,899	14,986	4,899	14,986	4,419	13,746	—	—
Library of Congress	5,062	22,451	5,055	22,389	5,043	22,343	7	62
Nat Comm on AIDS Syndrome	17	99	17	99	16	91	—	—
Nat Comm Prev Infant Mort	10	43	10	43	10	43	—	—
Ofc Technology Assessment	199	1,339	199	1,339	199	1,339	—	—
Physician Payment Rev Comm	20	78	20	78	20	78	—	—
Prosptv Paymt Assessmt Com	22	90	22	90	22	90	—	—
U.S. Tax Court	328	1,313	328	1,313	322	1,293	—	—
Judicial Branch	**27,374**	**121,926**	**27,072**	**120,588**	**2,106**	**10,545**	**302**	**1,338**
Supreme Court	364	1,028	364	1,028	364	1,028	—	—
U.S. Courts	26,932	120,495	26,630	119,157	1,664	9,114	302	1,338
U.S. Court of Vets Appeals	78	403	78	403	78	403	—	—
Executive Branch	**3,048,143**	**10,258,875**	**2,920,432**	**9,917,777**	**339,586**	**1,490,119**	**127,711**	**341,098**
Exec Ofc of the President	1,841	7,382	1,833	7,335	1,833	7,335	8	47
White House Office	386	1,435	386	1,435	386	1,435	—	—
Ofc of Vice President	21	92	21	92	21	92	—	—
Ofc of Mgt & Budget	587	2,551	587	2,551	587	2,551	—	—
Office of Administration	243	690	243	690	243	690	—	—
Council Economic Advisors	30	123	30	123	30	123	—	—
Council on Environ Qual	31	112	31	112	31	112	—	—
Ofc of Policy Development	38	105	38	105	38	105	—	—
Exec Residence at WH	92	586	92	586	92	586	—	—
National Security Council	63	222	63	222	63	222	—	—
National Space Council	8	37	8	37	8	37	—	—
Ofc of Natl Drug Control	110	487	110	487	110	487	—	—
Ofc of Sci and Tech Policy	47	145	47	145	47	145	—	—
Ofc of U.S. Trade Rep	183	790	175	743	175	743	8	47
Executive Departments	**2,063,377**	**6,282,498**	**1,955,852**	**6,010,143**	**256,174**	**1,091,483**	**107,525**	**272,355**
State	26,164	140,957	9,831	50,757	8,803	44,599	16,333	90,200
Treasury	168,970	681,808	167,838	675,689	24,504	129,348	1,132	6,119
Defense, Total	1,006,730	2,288,669	925,617	2,146,042	87,421	257,498	81,113	142,627
Dept of the Army	344,068	435,492	309,452	394,554	27,204	28,623	34,616	40,938
Army, Mil Func Total	312,984	359,033	278,458	318,376	26,043	25,132	34,526	40,657
Army, Civil Func Total	31,084	76,459	30,994	76,178	1,161	3,491	90	281
Corps of Engineers	30,948	76,170	30,858	75,889	1,025	3,202	90	281
Cemeterial Expenses	136	289	136	289	136	289	—	—
Dept of the Navy	312,303	877,800	293,372	844,356	35,614	121,663	18,931	33,444
Dept of the Air Force	212,695	584,838	203,166	567,030	6,069	35,496	9,529	17,808
Defense Log Agcy	58,104	155,955	57,648	154,210	3,195	12,670	456	1,745
Other Defense Activities	79,560	234,584	61,979	185,892	15,339	59,046	17,581	48,692
Justice	95,708	441,126	93,975	431,312	22,485	106,426	1,733	9,814
Interior	83,533	317,079	83,104	315,308	9,771	46,698	429	1,771
Agriculture	124,855	446,543	123,306	441,433	13,560	65,490	1,549	5,110
Commerce	37,485	166,039	36,601	161,886	20,254	100,466	884	4,153
Labor	17,966	90,938	17,928	90,682	6,245	33,680	38	256
Health and Human Services	132,301	555,786	131,592	552,888	31,693	154,171	709	2,898
Housing & Urban Dev	13,910	64,410	13,785	63,841	3,542	19,758	125	569
Transportation	70,400	286,103	69,858	283,784	10,571	43,676	542	2,319
Energy	20,800	116,546	20,794	116,489	7,424	46,976	6	57
Education	5,083	25,960	5,078	25,934	3,541	18,807	5	26
Veterans Affairs	259,472	660,534	256,545	654,098	6,360	23,890	2,927	6,436
Independent agencies[1]	**982,925**	**3,968,995**	**962,747**	**3,900,299**	**81,579**	**391,301**	**20,178**	**68,696**
Environmtl Protect Agcy	18,298	90,632	18,277	90,530	6,063	33,483	21	102
Equal Employ Opp Comm	2,887	13,563	2,887	13,563	748	4,000	—	—
Federal Deposit Ins Corp	22,738	119,468	22,728	119,413	3,472	21,937	10	55
Fed Emergency Mgmt Agcy	3,801	16,366	3,625	15,944	1,660	8,460	176	422
General Svcs Admin	21,105	91,013	21,009	90,611	7,019	36,456	96	402
Natl Archives & Recds, Admin.	3,157	8,693	3,157	8,693	1,220	4,641	—	—
Natl Aero Space Admin	25,638	105,249	25,631	105,177	5,876	24,178	7	72
Nuclear Regulatory Comm.	3,572	16,376	3,572	16,376	2,379	11,213	—	—
Office of Personnel Mgmt	6,872	23,609	6,848	23,557	2,891	12,569	24	52
Panama Canal Commission	8,547	27,105	18	95	6	53	8,529	27,010
Securities & Exchnge Comm	2,542	14,363	2,542	14,363	1,682	9,432	—	—
Small Business Admin	5,057	23,463	4,927	22,907	1,072	5,839	130	556
Smithsonian, Summary	5,514	21,596	5,345	21,001	4,971	19,278	169	595
Tennessee Valley Auth	19,518	70,969	19,518	70,969	10	49	—	—
U.S. Information Agency	8,289	22,457	4,256	14,191	3,992	12,932	4,033	8,266
U.S. Intnatl Dev Coop Agcy	4,586	26,781	2,424	14,249	2,421	14,228	2,162	12,532
U.S. Postal Service	798,531	3,169,978	794,676	3,153,310	21,997	99,597	3,855	16,668

(1) Included in Total are other independent agencies with fewer than 2,500 employees.

Labor Union Directory

Source: Bureau of Labor Statistics, U.S. Dept. of Labor; World Almanac questionnaire

(*) Independent union; all others affiliated with AFL-CIO.

American Federation of Labor & Congress of Industrial Organizations (AFL-CIO), 815 16th St. NW, Washington, DC 20006; 14.5 mln. members.

Actors and Artistes of America, Associated (AAAA), 165 W. 46th St., New York, NY 10036; founded 1919; Theodore Bikel, Pres.; no individual members, 7 National Performing Arts Unions are affiliates; approx. 220,000 combined membership.

Actors' Equity Association, 165 W. 46th St., New York, NY 10036; founded 1913; Colleen Dewhurst, Pres.; 39,000 active members.

Air Line Pilots Association, 1625 Massachusetts Ave. NW, Washington, DC 20036; J. Randolph Babbitt, Pres.; 43,000 members.

Aluminum Brick & Glass Workers International Union (ABGWIU), 3362 Hollenberg Drive, Bridgeton, MO 63044; founded 1953; Ernie Labaff, Pres. (since 1985); 51,800 members, 390 locals.

Automobile, Aerospace & Agricultural Implement Workers of America, International Union, United (UAW), 8000 E. Jefferson Ave., Detroit, MI 48214; founded 1935; Owen Bieber, Pres. (since 1983); 1,000,000 members, 1,194 locals.

Bakery, Confectionery & Tobacco Workers International Union (BC&T), 10401 Connecticut Ave., Kensington, MD 20895; founded 1886; John DeConcini, Pres. (since 1978); 139,000 members, 139 locals.

Boilermakers, Iron Shipbuilders, Blacksmiths, Forgers and Helpers, International Brotherhood of (IBBISB/BF&H), 570 New Brotherhood Bldg., 753 State Ave., Kansas City, KS 66101; founded 1880; Charles W. Jones, Pres. (since 1983) 95,000 members, 375 locals.

Bricklayers and Allied Craftsmen, International Union of, 815 15th St. NW, Washington, DC 20005; John T. Joyce, Pres.; 106,000 members, 525 locals.

Carpenters and Joiners of America, United Brotherhood of, 101 Constitution Ave. NW, Washington, DC 20001; founded 1881; Sigurd Lucassen, Gen. Pres.; 595,000 members, 1,500 locals.

Chemical Workers Union, International (ICWU), 1655 West Market St., Akron, OH 44313; founded 1944; Frank D. Martino, Pres. (since 1975); 50,000 members, 350 locals.

Clothing and Textile Workers Union, Amalgamated (ACTWU), 15 Union Square, New York, NY 10003; founded 1976; union founded 1914; Jack Sheinkman, Pres. (since 1987); 272,669 members, 1,400 locals.

Communications Workers of America, 501 3rd St. NW, Washington, DC 20001-2797; Morton Bahr, Pres.; 700,000 members, 1,200 locals.

Distillery, Wine & Allied Workers International Union (DWU), 66 Grand Ave., Englewood, NJ 07631; founded 1940; George J. Orlando, Pres. (since 1984); 15,500 members, 57 locals.

***Education Association, National,** 1201 16th St. NW, Washington, DC 20036; Keith Geiger, Pres. (since 1989); 2,000,000 members, 12,000 affiliates.

Electrical Workers, International Brotherhood of (IBEW), 1125 15th St., NW, Washington, DC 20005; founded 1891; J.J. Barry, Int'l Pres.; 900,000 members, 1,400 locals.

Electronic, Electrical, Salaried, Machine and Furniture Workers, International Union of (IUE), 1126 16th St. NW, Washington, DC 20036; founded 1949; William H. Bywater, Pres. (since 1982); 160,000 members, 500 locals.

Farm Workers of America, United (UFW), P.O. Box 62, Keene, CA 93531; founded 1962; Cesar E. Chavez, Pres. (since 1962); 100,000 members.

***Federal Employees, National Federation of (NFFE),** 1016 16th St. NW, Washington, DC 20036; founded 1917; Sheila K. Velazco, Pres.; 60,000+ members, 487 locals.

Fire Fighters, International Association of, 1750 New York Ave. NW, Washington, DC 20006; Alfred K. Whitehead, Pres.; 172,401 members, 1,943 locals.

Firemen and Oilers, International Brotherhood of, 1100 Circle 75 Parkway, Suite 350, Atlanta, GA 30339; Jimmy L. Walker, Pres.; 30,000 members.

Food and Commercial Workers International Union, United, (UFCW) 1775 K St., NW, Washington, DC 20006; founded 1979 following merger; William H. Wynn, Int'l Pres. (since 1977); 1.3 million members, 600 locals.

Garment Workers of America, United (UGWA), 4207 Lebanon Rd., Hermitage, TN 37076; founded 1891; Dave Johnson, Gen. Pres.; 20,000 members, 120 locals.

Glass, Molders, Pottery, Plastics & Allied Workers Intl. Union (GMP), 608 E. Baltimore Pike, P.O. Box 607, Media, PA 19063; founded 1842; James E. Hatfield, Int'l Pres. (since 1977); 90,000 members, 435 locals.

Government Employees, American Federation of (AFGE) AFL-CIO, 80 F St., NW, Washington, DC 20001; founded 1932; John N. Sturdivant, Natl. Pres. (since 1988); 172,000 members, 1,300 locals.

Grain Millers, American Federation of (AFGM), 4949 Olson Memorial Hwy., Minneapolis, MN 55422; founded 1948; Larry R. Jackson, Gen. Pres.; 30,000 members, 210 locals.

Graphic Communications International Union (GCIU), 1900 L St., NW, Washington, DC 20036; founded 1983; James J. Norton, Pres. (since 1985); 182,706 members, 520 locals.

Hotel Employees and Restaurant Employees International Union, 1219-28th St., NW, Washington, DC 20007; Edward T. Henley, Gen. Pres.; 330,000 members, 190 locals.

Industrial Workers of America, International Union, Allied (AIW), 3520 W. Oklahoma Ave., Milwaukee, WI 53215; founded 1935; Dominick D'Ambrosio, Intl. Pres. (since 1975); 61,000 members, 330 locals.

Iron Workers, International Association of Bridge Structural and Ornamental, 1750 New York Ave. NW, Washington, DC 20006; Jake West, Gen. Pres.; 145,000 members, 300 locals.

Laborers' International Union of North America (LIUNA), 905 16th St. NW, Washington, DC 20006; founded 1903; Angelo Fosco, Gen. Pres. (since 1976); 450,000 members, 696 locals.

Ladies Garment Workers Union, International (ILGWU), 1710 Broadway, New York, NY 10019; founded 1900; Jay Mazur, Pres. (since 1986); 175,000 members, 340 locals.

Leather Goods, Plastic and Novelty Workers' Union, International, 265 W. 14th St., New York, NY 10011; Domenic DiPaolo, Gen. Pres.; 20,000 members, 85 locals.

Letter Carriers, National Association of (NALC), 100 Indiana Ave. NW, Washington, DC 20001; founded 1889; Vincent R. Sombrotto, Pres. (since 1978); 311,202 members, 3,466 locals.

***Locomotive Engineers, Brotherhood of (BLE),** The Standard Bldg., Cleveland, OH 44113; founded 1863; Larry McFather, Pres. (since 1987); 56,000 members, 650 divisions.

Longshoremen's Association, International, 17 Battery Pl., New York, NY 10004; John Bowers, Pres.; 76,579 members, 331 locals.

***Longshoremen's & Warehousemen's Union, International (ILWU),** 1188 Franklin St., San Francisco, CA 94109; founded 1937; David Arian, Pres.; 55,000 members, 58 locals.

Machinists and Aerospace Workers, International Association of (IAM), 1300 Connecticut Ave. NW, Washington, DC 20036; founded 1888; George J. Kourpias, Int'l Pres.; 826,875 members, 1,700 locals.

Maintenance of Way Employees, Brotherhood of (BMWE), 12050 Woodward Ave., Detroit, MI 48203; founded 1887; Mac. A. Fleming, Pres.; 75,000 members, 827 locals.

Marine & Shipbuilding Workers of America, Industrial Union of (IUMSWA), 5101 River Rd., #110, Bethesda, MD 20816; founded 1934; (merged with Machinists and Aerospace Workers, effective Dec. 1, 1990).

Marine Engineer Beneficial Assn./National Maritime Union (MEBA/NMU), 444 N. Capitol St. NW, Suite 800, Washington, D.C. 20001; C.E. DeFries, Pres.; 50,000 members.

***Mine Workers of America, United (UMWA),** 900 15th St. NW, Washington, DC 20005; founded 1890; Richard Trumka, Int'l Pres. (since 1982); 186,000 members, 800 locals.

Musicians of the United States and Canada, American Federation of (AF of M), 1501 Broadway, Suite 600, New York, NY 10036; founded 1896; Mark Tully Massagli, Pres.; 206,000 members, 480 locals.

Newspaper Guild, The (TNG), 8611 Second Ave., Silver Spring, MD 20910; founded 1933; Charles Dale, Pres. (since 1987); 33,000 members, 80 locals.

Novelty & Production Workers, Intl. Union of Allied, 1815 Franklin Ave., Valley Stream, NY 11581; Julius Isaacson, Pres.; 30,000 members, 18 locals.

***Nurses Association, American,** 2420 Pershing Rd., Kansas City, MO 64108; Lucille A. Joel, Ed.D, R.N., F.A.A.N., Pres.; 53 constituent state assns.

(continued)

Office and Professional Employees International Union (OPEIU), 265 W. 14th St., New York, NY 10011; founded 1945 (AFL Charter); John Kelly, Int'l Pres. (since 1979); 135,000 members, 300 locals.

Oil, Chemical and Atomic Workers International Union (OCAW), PO Box 2812, Denver, CO 80201; Robert E. Wages, Pres.; 100,000 members, 400 locals.

Operating Engineers, International Union of (IUOE), 1125 17th St. NW, Washington, DC 20036; founded 1896; Frank Hanley, Gen. Pres.; 375,000 members, 200 locals.

Painters and Allied Trades, International Brotherhood of (IBPAT), 1750 New York Ave. NW, Washington, DC 20006; founded 1887; William A. Duval, Gen. Pres. (since 1984); 149,177 members, 626 locals.

Paperworkers International Union, United (UPIU), 3340 Perimeter Hill Dr., Nashville, TN 37202; founded 1884; Wayne E. Glenn, Pres. (since 1978); 230,000 members, 1,100 locals.

***Plant Guard Workers of America, International Union, United (UPGWA),** 25510 Kelly Rd., Roseville, MI 48066; founded 1948; Gene McConville, Pres.; 28,000 members, 176 locals.

Plasterers' and Cement Mason's International Association of the United States & Canada; Operative, 1125 17th St. NW, Washington, DC 20036; Vincent J. Panepinto, Gen. Pres.; 65,000 members, 365 locals.

Plumbing and Pipe Fitting Industry of the United States and Canada, United Association of Journeymen and Apprentices of the, 901 Massachusetts Ave. NW, Washington, DC 20001; Marvin J. Boede, Pres.; 325,000 members.

***Police, Fraternal Order of,** 2100 Gardiner Lane, Louisville, KY 40205; Dewey R. Stokes, Natl. Pres. and Charles R. Orms, Natl. Secy.; 225,000 members, 1,860 affiliates.

***Postal Supervisors, National Association of,** 490 L'Enfant Plaza SW, Suite 3200, Washington, DC 20024-2120; Rubin Handelman, Pres.; 44,000 members, 443 locals.

Postal Workers Union, American (APWU), 1300 L St. NW, Washington, DC 20005; founded 1971; Moe Biller, Pres. (since 1980); 330,000 members, 2,000 locals.

Railway Carmen Division of Transportation Communications Int'l. Union (BRC Division/TCU), 4929 Main St., Kansas City, MO 64112; founded 1888; W.G. Fairchild, Gen. Pres. (since 1989); 50,000 members, 310 locals.

Retail, Wholesale and Department Store Union, 30 E. 29th St., New York, NY 10016; Lenore Miller, Pres.; 200,000 members, 250 locals.

Roofers, Waterproofers & Allied Workers, United Union of, 1125 17th St. NW, Washington, DC 20036; Earl J. Kruse, Pres.; 27,000 members, 138 locals.

Rubber, Cork, Linoleum and Plastic Workers of America, United (URW), 87 South High St., Akron, OH 44308; founded 1935; Kenneth L. Coss; Int'l Pres.; 100,000 members, 400 locals.

***Rural Letter Carriers' Association, National,** 4th floor, 1630 Duke St., Alexandria, VA 22314; founded 1903; Vernon H. Meier, Pres. (since 1989); 80,000 members; 47 state organizations.

Seafarers International Union of North America (SIUNA), 5201 Auth Way, Camp Springs, MD 20746; founded 1938; Michael Sacco, Pres.; 85,000 members.

Service Employees International Union (SEIU), 1313 L St. NW, Washington, DC 20005; founded 1921; John J. Sweeney, Pres. (since 1980); 950,000 members, 300 locals.

Sheet Metal Workers' International Association (SMWIA), 1750 New York Ave. NW, Washington, DC 20006; founded 1888; Edward J. Carlough, Gen. Pres. (since 1970); 150,000 members, 245 locals.

State, County and Municipal Employees, American Federation of, 1625 L St. NW, Washington, DC 20036; Gerald McEntee, Pres.; 1,200,000 members, 2,991 locals.

Steelworkers of America, United (USWA), 5 Gateway Center, Pittsburgh, PA 15222; founded 1936; Lynn Williams, Int'l Pres. (since 1984); 750,000 members, 3,500 locals.

Teachers, American Federation of (AFT), 555 New Jersey Ave. NW, Washington, DC 20001; founded 1916; Albert Shanker, Pres. (since 1974); 750,000 members, 2,400 locals.

Teamsters, Chauffeurs, Warehousemen and Helpers of America, International Brotherhood of (IBT), 25 Louisiana Ave. NW, Washington, DC 20001; founded 1903; Ronald R. Carey, Pres.; 1,600,000 members, 700 locals.

Television and Radio Artists, American Federation of, 260 Madison Ave., New York, NY 10016; founded 1937; Reed Farrell, Pres.; 67,000 members, 38 locals.

Textile Workers of America, United (UTWA), 2 Echelon Plaza, Laurel Rd., P.O. Box 749, Voorhees, NJ 08043-0749; founded 1901; Vernon Mustard, Intl. Pres. (since 1986); 26,000 members, 180 locals.

Theatrical Stage Employes and Moving Picture Machine Operators of the United States and Canada, International Alliance of, 1515 Broadway, New York, NY 10036; Alfred W. Di Tolla, Pres.; 61,471 members, 750 locals.

Transit Union, Amalgamated (ATU), 5025 Wisconsin Ave. NW, Washington, DC 20016; founded 1892; James La Sala, Intl. Pres. (since 1986); 165,000 members, 275 locals.

Transport Workers Union of America, 80 West End Ave., New York, NY 10023; founded 1934; George Leitz, Int'l Pres. (since 1985); 100,000 members, 94 locals.

Transportation Communications International Union (TCU), 3 Research Place, Rockville, MD 20850; Richard I. Kilroy, Int'l Pres. (since 1981); 160,000 members, 750 locals.

***Transportation Union, United (UTU),** 14600 Detroit Ave., Cleveland, OH 44107; founded 1969; Fred A. Hardin, Pres. (since 1979); 100,000 members; 769 locals.

***Treasury Employees Union, National (NTEU),** 901 E. St. N.W. Suite 600, Washington, DC 20004; founded 1938; Robert M. Tobias, Natl. Pres. (since 1983); 140,000 represented, 250 chapters.

***University Professors, American Association of (AAUP),** 1012-14th St., Washington, DC 20005; founded 1915; Carol Simpson Stern, Pres.; 40,000 members, 600 chapters.

Upholstery Division - United Steelworkers of America, 25 N. 4th St., Philadelphia, PA 19106; founded 1882; Ernest F. Shock, dir.; approx. 18,000 members, 91 locals.

Utility Workers Union of America (UWUA), 815 16th St. NW, Washington, DC 20006; founded 1945; Marshall M. Hicks, Natl. Pres. (since 1980); 60,000 members, 220 locals.

International Woodworkers of America —U.S. (IWA—U.S.), 25 Cornell, Gladstone, OR 97027; founded 1987; Wilson (Bill) Hubbell, Natl. Pres.; 28,000 members, 100 locals.

U.S. Union Membership, 1930-1991

Source: Bureau of Labor Statistics, U.S. Dept. of Labor

Year	Labor[1] force (thousands)	Union[2] members (thousands)	Percent	Year	Labor[1] force (thousands)	Union[2] members (thousands)	Percent
1930	29,424	3,401	11.6	1983	88,290	17,717	20.1
1935	27,053	3,584	13.2	1984	92,194	17,340	18.8
1940	32,376	8,717	26.9	1985	94,521	16,996	18.0
1945	40,394	14,322	35.5	1986	96,903	16,975	17.5
1950	45,222	14,267	31.5	1987	99,303	16,913	17.0
1955	50,675	16,802	33.2	1988	101,407	17,002	16.8
1960	54,234	17,049	31.4	1989	103,480	16,960	16.4
1965	60,815	17,299	28.4	1990	103,905	16,740	16.1
1970	70,920	19,381	27.3	1991	102,786	16,568	16.1
1975	76,945	19,611	25.5				
1980	90,564	19,843	21.9				

(1) Does not include agricultural employment; from 1983 data do not include self-employed or unemployed persons. (2) From 1930 to 1980 data are the number of dues paying members of traditional trade unions with members counted regardless of employment status; from 1983 members include employee associations that engage in collective bargaining with employers.

TAXES

Federal Income Tax

Source: George W. Smith III, CPA, *Cut Your Own Taxes and Save,* Pharos Books.

During the past decade, the United States Congress enacted some of the most dramatic changes in our tax law. Its purpose was to create a more equitable income tax system for all taxpayers. Various provisions of these changes are still being implemented and will remain the backbone of our tax structure for decades to come.

History of the United States Income Tax

The history of taxation in the U.S. centers primarily around the income tax and is consistent with the pattern of taxation in most highly developed countries. Although the Massachusetts Bay Colony enacted an income tax in 1643, the first U.S. income tax was not created until the Civil War. However, this infant income tax had little vitality and expired soon after the war.

Congress passed another income tax act in 1894. This new law also was to be short lived. The Supreme Court held that the tax law was unconstitutional and invalidated the entire statute the following year.

By the turn of the century, income tax legislation had become a very important political issue. Congress did not give up and finally passed the Sixteenth Amendment to the United States Constitution on July 12, 1909. It was ratified by the required number of state legislatures early in 1913.

The Sixteenth Amendment laid the foundation for our modern income tax system. It states broadly and explicitly:

"The Congress shall have the power to lay and collect taxes on incomes, from whatever source derived, without apportionment among the several States, and without regard to any census or enumeration."

Congress quickly expanded on this newly sanctioned source of revenue. Corporations as well as individuals became subject to the new income tax. Since then, various revenue laws have been passed. One of the most important was the Current Tax Payment Act of 1943. This act instituted for the first time a "pay-as-you-go" tax system which required the regular withholding of tax from each employee's paycheck and the filing of estimated tax payments. This concept remains the basic method for the collection of our income taxes today.

During the past few decades, Congress enacted several major tax acts. However, the Tax Reform Act of 1986 represented the most extensive overhaul of the tax code since 1954. This Act contains approximately 1,850 separate Code amendments. Because of the scope and magnitude of all these amendments, Congress decided to redesignate the 1954 Code as the Internal Revenue Code of 1986. Many of the provisions resulting from these massive changes will affect all taxpayers not only when completing their 1992 income tax return but also for years to come.

Tax Law Changes and Recent Tax Developments

- For 1992, the highest marginal income tax rate for individuals, estates and trusts remains at 31%. There are currently three tax rates: 15%, 28% and 31%.
- The maximum income tax rate on capital gains for noncorporate taxpayers is 28%.
- An individual may not claim an exemption for a dependent child in 1992 who qualifies as a full time student and is over age 23 at the end of the year unless the child's gross income is less than $2,300.
- Effective January 1, 1992, the limitation on the exclusion of elective deferrals to 401(k) plans is increased to $8,728 from $8,475.
- Interest earned on Series EE bonds issued in 1990 or later may be exempt from federal income tax if used to pay tuition and fees for a taxpayer, spouse or dependents to attend a college, university or qualified technical school during the year the bonds are redeemed. This exclusion is subject to an income phaseout in 1992 if adjusted gross income exceeds $44,150 for a single taxpayer; $66,200 for taxpayers filing jointly. The full phaseout occurs at $59,150 for a single taxpayer and $96,200 for taxpayers filing jointly.
- Parents may elect to include on their income tax return the unearned income of a dependent child under age 14 whose income is more than $500 but less than $5,000. The income must consist solely of interest, dividends or Alaska Permanent Fund dividends. This election is not available if estimated tax payments were made in the child's name. Form 8814, Parent's Election to Report Child's Interest and Dividends, is required to report this income.
- For individuals age 55 or over, the 3 out of 5 year home use rule for the sale of a principal residence has been expanded. Certain incapacitated individuals who reside in state licensed facilities may exclude from gross income up to $125,000 of gain resulting from the sale of their home if the house was used as their principal residence for at least one year out of the last 5 years. This is a once-in-a-lifetime exclusion.
- The 25% deduction for health insurance costs of self-employed individuals has been extended through 1992.
- Face-lifts, tummy tucks, liposuction and many other elective cosmetic surgeries are no longer a deductible medical expense.
- For a taxpayer to be eligible for the child and dependent care credit, the dependent must be under age 13. The taxpayer must also report the name, address, and identification number of the child care provider on their income tax return or the taxpayer will not be entitled to the credit.
- A taxpayer must list the social security number of any dependent claimed on his income tax return who is at least 1 year old by the end of the tax year. The penalty for noncompliance can be $50 per omitted number.
- A business deduction is not allowed for the base rate charged on the first telephone line into a personal residence. This disallowance does not affect the deductibility of long distance calls or optional services such as call waiting, call forwarding, three-way calling or extra directory listings as long as they are business related.
- For 1992, the social security tax base (the maximum amount of earnings on which the social security tax can apply), increased to $55,500. The Medicare tax base increased to $130,200. For social security, the tax rate is 6.2% for employees and the same for employers. For Medicare, the rate is 1.45% for employees and the same for employers. Thus, the most an employee and an employer each will pay is 6.2% of $55,500 plus 1.45% of $130,200, or $5,328.90 each.
- IRA investments are allowed for certain gold and silver coins issued by the U.S. Government. Investments also may include certain coins issued by a state government.
- Jury duty pay surrendered by an employee to an employer in return for his normal salary is deductible as an adjustment to income, not as an itemized deduction.
- The business use of a cellular phone must be for the convenience of the employer and a condition of employment to be an allowable business deduction for employees. All phone calls must be substantiated and business related.
- Self-employed persons are entitled to an income tax deduction of one-half of their social security self-employment tax liability. The self-employment tax rate for 1992 is 15.3%. The maximum a self-employed individual will pay is $10,657.80.

- To be deductible, points paid for the purchase of a taxpayer's principal residence must meet the following requirements:
1. The purchase must be for the taxpayer's principle residence.
2. The amount paid must be clearly designated as "points," "loan origination fees," "loan discount" or "discount points."
3. Points must be computed as a percentage of the taxpayer's stated principal loan amount.
4. The payment of points must be an established business practice in the area.
5. The points must be paid from the taxpayer's own funds—the points may not be borrowed.
- Starting in 1992, the "Safe Harbor" method of calculating estimated tax payments cannot be used if: (1) a taxpayer has a $40,000 increase ($20,000 for a married taxpayer filing separately) in adjusted gross income over the year before; (2) the taxpayer's current year's adjusted gross income is at least $75,000 ($37,500 for a married taxpayer filing separately); and (3) estimated tax payments were required in any one of the three preceding years. Estimated tax payments for each quarter then must be 25% of the lesser of:

a. 90% of the tax to be shown on the return for the current year, or

b. The greater of:
1. 100% of last year's tax liability
2. 90% of this year's tax liability with some adjustments
- A sole proprietor claiming a home office deduction on Schedule C, Profit or Loss From Business, must file Form 8829, Expenses for Business Use of Your Home, with the income tax return.
- For 1992, the standard mileage rate for business use of an automobile has been increased to 28 cents per mile. This rate applies to all business miles driven. U.S. Postal Service employees who collect or deliver mail on a rural route can use a special standard mileage rate of 42 cents per mile.

1992 Individual Tax Rates

There are three tax rates for 1992: 15%, 28% and 31%. The dollar bracket amounts for 1992 have been adjusted for inflation.

Single

Tax Rates	Taxable Income
15%	$0 to $21,450
28%	$21,451 to $51,900
31%	Over $51,900

Married Filing Jointly or Qualifying Widow(er)

Tax Rates	Taxable Income
15%	$0 to $35,800
28%	$35,801 to $86,500
31%	Over $86,500

Married Filing Separately

Tax Rate	Taxable Income
15%	$0 to $17,900
28%	$17,901 to $43,250
31%	Over $43,250

Head of Household

Tax Rate	Taxable Income
15%	$0 to $28,750
28%	$28,751 to $74,150
31%	Over $74,150

The maximum tax rate on net capital gains for an individual, estate or trust is 28%.

The alternative minimum tax rate for a taxpayer other than a corporation is raised to 24%.

Standard Deduction

The standard deduction is a flat dollar amount that is subtracted from the adjusted gross income of taxpayers who do not itemize their deductions. The amount of the basic standard deduction depends upon the taxpayer's status and is adjusted annually for inflation. The standard deductions for 1992 are as follows:

1992 Basic Standard Deduction

Single	$3,600
Married filing jointly or Qualifying widow(er)	$6,000
Married filing separately	$3,000
Head of Household	$5,250

Taxpayers with itemized deductions such as medical expenses, taxes, investment and home mortgage interest, charitable contributions, moving expenses, etc., totaling more than the standard deduction amount should not use the standard deduction. Instead, they should itemize their deductions.

An individual claimed as a dependent on another person's income tax return may claim on their own tax return only the larger of $600, or the amount of earned income up to the amount of the basic standard deduction which the taxpayer would normally be allowed. Earned income includes wages, salaries, commissions, and tips. It also includes net profit from self-employment received as compensation for personal services rendered. Any part of a scholarship or fellowship grant that must be included in gross income is also earned income.

Example: A dependent parent, age 60, had unearned income (interest and dividends) of $1,700 during 1992. She had no earned income. Her basic standard deduction would be $600. She would have taxable income of $1,100. A dependent cannot claim her own personal exemption.

Example: A dependent son had $10,000 of unearned income and $100 of earned income. He is entitled to a $600 standard deduction. He is limited to this amount because he is a dependent and his earned income is less than $600. The taxpayer would, therefore, have $9,500 in taxable income.

Example: A dependent daughter with $4,000 of earned income and $600 of unearned income would claim a maximum $3,600 standard deduction because her earned income of $4,000 is greater than the standard deduction. She would have taxable income of $1,000.

Additional Standard Deduction for Age and Blindness

Elderly or blind taxpayers may claim an additional standard deduction in addition to the basic standard deduction. Taxpayers who are age 65 or over or blind at the end of 1992 qualify. Taxpayers who itemize their deductions cannot claim the additional or basic standard deductions. Individuals who claim the additional standard deduction because of blindness must attach a doctor's statement to their income tax return. The additional and basic standard deductions are adjusted each year for inflation.

1992 Additional Standard Deduction

Single or Head of Household, age 65 or over or blind	$ 900
Single or Head of Household, age 65 or over and blind	$1,800
Married filing jointly or Qualifying widow(er), age 65 or over or blind (per person)	$ 700
Married filing jointly or Qualifying widow(er), age 65 or over and blind (per person)	$1,400
Married filing separately, age 65 or over or blind	$ 700
Married filing separately, age 65 or over and blind	$1,400

Example 1: A single, sixty-five year old individual would have a standard deduction of $4,500 computed as follows:

Basic standard deduction for a single person	$3,600
Additional standard deduction for age	900
Total	$4,500

Example 2: A seventy year old husband and a fifty-eight year old blind wife filing jointly would be entitled to a standard deduction totaling $7,400 computed as follows:

(continued)

Basic standard deduction for married filing jointly	$6,000
Additional standard deduction for (husband's) age	700
Additional standard deduction for (wife's) blindness	700
Total	$7,400

Dependent and Personal Exemptions

The exemption amount for 1992 has been increased to $2,300. This amount is adjusted each year for inflation.

For tax years 1991 through 1995, the deduction for exemptions is phased out for certain higher income taxpayers. The exemption amount is reduced by 2% for each $2,500 ($1,250 for married filing separately) or a fraction thereof by which the adjusted gross income exceeds the threshold amount.

The threshold amount for 1992 at which the phaseout of the tax benefit of the personal exemption begins is as follows:

Married filing jointly	$157,900
Qualifying widow(er)	$157,900
Head of Household	$131,550
Single	$105,250
Married filing separately	$ 78,950

The exemption amount is fully phased out when adjusted gross income is more than $122,500 ($61,250 for married filing separately) over the threshold amount.

Adjustments to Income

Individual Retirement Accounts (IRAs)

Taxpayers who do not have a qualified retirement plan where they are employed may take an IRA deduction up to the lesser of $2,000, or the amount of their earned income, regardless of their total income. Income earned from IRAs will remain tax-free until the taxpayer withdraws it.

Taxpayers may still make contributions to their IRAs even if they are covered by a qualified retirement plan by their employer. However, there are limits as to the amount that can be deducted on their income tax return if they are covered by a qualified retirement plan by their employer. If either husband or wife has a qualified plan, both spouses are subject to these limitations.

For 1992, married taxpayers filing jointly with adjusted gross income of $40,000 or less may take an IRA deduction whether or not they are active participants in a qualified retirement plan. Single taxpayers in a qualified retirement plan may also deduct IRAs if their adjusted gross income is $25,000 or less. The IRA deduction phases out over the next $10,000 of adjusted gross income if taxpayers are active participants in a qualified retirement plan. Consequently, married couples filing jointly with adjusted gross income of $50,000 or more or single filers with adjusted gross income of $35,000 or more may not deduct any contributions to their IRAs.

A qualified retirement plan generally includes: (1) a qualified pension, profit-sharing or stock bonus plan; (2) a qualified annuity plan; (3) a simplified employee pension plan; or (4) a plan established for its employees by the federal, state or other political subdivision or by an agency of these entities.

Itemized Deductions

- Medical expenses are deductible but only the amount that exceeds 7.5 percent of adjusted gross income. Starting in 1991, many elective cosmetic surgeries including hair transplants and other similar procedures are no longer a deductible medical expense. Only cosmetic surgery for congenital abnormality, personal injury resulting from an accident or trauma or a disfiguring disease is allowed as a medical deduction.
- Consumer interest, such as finance charges on personal credit cards and installment interest on personal automobile loans, is no longer deductible.
- Investment interest for 1992 is only deductible to the extent of net investment income. The excess is carried over to future years.
- Mortgage interest on a taxpayer's first and second home remains fully deductible. However, there are limitations.
- Interest on home equity loans is deductible but only up to the first $100,000 in equity debt.
- Charitable contributions of tangible personal property which is related to the donee's tax-exempt purpose is not subject to the alternative minimum tax for contributions donated prior to July 1, 1992.
- State and local income taxes, real estate taxes, and personal property taxes remain fully deductible. Sales taxes are not deductible.
- Casualty and theft losses are deductible subject to the $100 limitation and the 10% of adjusted gross income rule.
- Miscellaneous deductions, such as union and professional dues, tax preparation fees, safe deposit box rental and employee business expenses are deductible but only for the amount that exceeds 2 percent of adjusted gross income.
- For 1992, certain itemized deductions otherwise allowed are reduced by the lesser of 3% of a taxpayer's adjusted gross income in excess of $105,250 ($52,625 for married taxpayers filing separately) or 80% of the amount of these itemized deductions otherwise allowable for the year. This provision does not affect medical expenses, investment interest expense, casualty losses or gambling losses to the extent of gambling gains.

Moving Expenses

Taxpayers who change jobs during the year can usually deduct part of their moving expenses. These expenses include the cost of moving household goods, travel to the new home, househunting trips, temporary living quarters and other related expenses. To qualify, the move must be job-related and it must meet several other requirements including a distance and time test. The expenses for moving household goods and traveling to a new home have some limitations. All other deductible moving expenses, such as househunting trips or temporary living quarters, are subject to a $3,000 ceiling. Meal expenses are only 80% deductible. Moving expenses are deductible only if the taxpayer itemizes deductions on Schedule A of Form 1040. Moves within the U.S. are reported on Form 3903, Moving Expenses.

Employee Business Expenses

All employee business expenses including travel, automobile, telephone, gifts and entertainment are deductible only as itemized miscellaneous deductions. Only 80% of the cost of customer meals and entertainment is deductible. These expenses are then subject to the 2% of adjusted gross income limitation for miscellaneous deductions.

Earned Income Credit, Young Child Credit, and Health Insurance Credit

Low income workers who have dependent children and maintain a household are eligible for a refundable earned income credit. The credit for 1992 is calculated on earned income such as wages and tips. For a taxpayer with one qualifying child, the maximum credit is $1,324. For a taxpayer with two or more qualifying children, it's $1,384. The credit begins to phaseout when adjusted gross income is more than $11,840. It is completely phased out when adjusted gross income is more than $22,370.

For 1992, and in addition to the basic earned income credit, a supplemental young child care credit is also available to low income workers with a qualifying child who has not attained the age of one by the close of the calendar year. The maximum credit is $376. If this supplemental credit is claimed, the dependent care credit may not be claimed.

A supplemental credit for health insurance premium costs that cover one or more qualifying children is also available. The maximum credit is $451. If medical expenses are itemized on Schedule A, or the 25% deduction for health insurance which self-employed individuals are entitled to is taken, these amounts must be reduced dollar for dollar by the amount of the allowable supplemental health insurance credit.

If an individual qualifies, the credits are refundable even if the taxpayer is not required to file an income return. However, a tax return must be filed in order to receive these credits. Taxpayers must fill out Schedule EIC and attach it to their tax return to receive these credits. To assist individuals, the IRS publishes a table showing the earned income credit at various levels of income. This chart is available free at any IRS office.

Taxing Children's Income

A child who may be claimed as a dependent by another taxpayer may not claim their own personal exemption on their tax return. Children under age 14 with at least one living parent may use up to $600 of their standard deduction against unearned income. Unearned income includes dividend and interest income. If the child's unearned income is more than $1,200, that income will be taxed at the child's tax rate, or the parent's rate, whichever is higher.

Parents have the option of including a child's unearned income on their tax return. However, if the unearned income is reported on the child's tax return, only the amount over $1,200 is subject to this treatment. Therefore, the child receives the benefit of a lower tax rate on the first $1,200 of unearned income.

Example: When a child has $3,000 of interest income, the child's taxable income would be $2,400 allowing for the deduction of the $600 standard deduction. If the parent's tax rate is 28%, the child's tax would be $596 ($92 from the tax table + 28% of $1,800).

Who Must File

Whether a U.S. citizen or resident alien living in the U.S. must file an income tax return depends on the person's gross income, filing status and age.

Generally, a U.S. citizen or resident alien will have to file an income tax return if the person's gross income for the year is at least as much as the amount shown in the following table.

Filing Status	1992 Gross Income
Single	
• Under 65	$ 5,900
• 65 or older	6,800
Married filing jointly	
• Both spouses under 65	10,600
• One spouse 65 or older	11,300
• Both spouses 65 or older	12,000
Married filing separately	2,300
Head of Household	
• Under 65	7,550
• 65 or older	8,450
Qualifying widow(er)	
• Under 65	8,300
• 65 or older	9,000

Example: John and Mary Smith intend to file a joint return for 1992. John's income is all from wages. Mary receives no income subject to tax. Neither John nor Mary is blind. John is 67 years old but Mary will not be 65 until next year. For 1992, their combined gross income subject to tax will be $11,900. They will have to file a tax return because their gross income will be at least $11,300.

If Mary was age 65, they would not have to file a 1992 tax return because their gross income would be less than $12,000 as shown in the table.

Some Exceptions to Filing Requirements. An individual must file a tax return if:

- Net earnings from self-employment for the year are $400 or more
- Advance earned income credit payments were received during the year from an employer
- Qualifications for the earned income credit, young child credit or health insurance credit are met
- There is an income tax refund
- Gross income is less than the the filing requirement amount but additional taxes are owed for:
- Social security tax on unreported tips
- Alternative minimum tax
- Recapture of investment credit
- Tax attributable to qualified retirement plans (including IRAs), annuities and modified endowment contracts

When to File

U.S. individual income tax returns for 1992 are required to be filed with the Internal Revenue Service no later than Thursday, April 15, 1993.

What if you can't file on time? File Form 4868, Application for Automatic Extension of Time to File U.S. Individual Income Tax Return. This gives you an automatic four-month extension of time until Monday, August 16, 1993 (the 15th falls on a Sunday) to file your tax return. However, this is not an extension of time to pay your taxes. You still have to pay the Internal Revenue Service any money owed by midnight April 15, 1993. Penalties and interest may be assessed for any income tax balance not paid. Form 4868 provides space for you to estimate your tax obligation, if any.

Which Form to File

Use either Form 1040EZ or Form 1040A unless filing of Form 1040 allows you to pay a lower tax. These forms are easier to complete than the longer Form 1040.

You may be able to use the short Form 1040EZ if:

- You are single and do not claim any dependents
- You are not 65 or older or blind
- You have income only from wages, salaries, tips, taxable scholarships or fellowships, and not more than $400 of interest income
- Your taxable income is less than $50,000
- You do not itemize deductions or claim any adjustments to income or have tax credits
- You did not make estimated tax payments
- You file before April 16th; you cannot file Form 1040EZ if you apply for an extension

You may be able to use Form 1040A if:

- You have income from wages, salaries, tips, taxable scholarships or fellowships, interest, and dividends
- You have income from Individual Retirement Account (IRA) distributions, pensions, annuities, unemployment compensation, and social security or railroad retirement benefits.
- Your taxable income is less than $50,000
- You do not itemize deductions
- You claim a deduction for qualified contributions to an IRA
- You claim a credit for child and dependent care expenses, credit for the elderly or the disabled, the earned income credit, the supplemental young child credit, or the health insurance credit
- You have made estimated tax payments
- You filed for an extension of time to file

Even if you do meet the above tests, you will have to file Form 1040 if any of the following situations apply:

- Your taxable income is $50,000 or more
- You itemize deductions

- You receive any nontaxable dividends or capital gain distributions
- You have foreign accounts and/or foreign trusts
- You have taxable refunds of state and local income taxes
- You have business, farm or rental income
- You have miscellaneous income not allowed on Form 1040EZ or 1040A such as alimony or lottery winnings
- You have certain adjustments to income such as alimony paid
- You can claim a foreign tax credit or certain other credits to which you are entitled
- You have other taxes such as self-employment tax or the alternative minimum tax
- You file any of these forms:

Form 2555, Foreign Earned Income

Form 3903, Moving Expense

Form 4972, Tax on Lump-Sum Distributions

Form 5329, Return for Additional Taxes Attributable to Qualified Retirement Plans

Form 8814, Parent's Election To Report Child's Interest and Dividends

Electronic Filing

Electronic filing is the process of transmitting completed personal income tax returns via computers to the Internal Revenue Service. Originating as a pilot program in 1986, over 7.5 million taxpayers filed electronically during 1992. Of these taxpayers, 75% were under the age of 45, and 62% had income under $30,000.

Electronic filing shortens the average time for processing returns. Tax refunds will usually be received within 3 weeks. Refunds may also be deposited directly into your savings or checking account. Since electronic filing automates most of the manual steps needed to process standard paper returns, processing time is faster and less expensive.

The electronic filing method is used by many tax return preparers who are equipped to send tax return information over telephone lines to an Internal Revenue Service Center. The preparer will ask you to sign a declaration form, Form 8453, U.S. Individual Income Tax Declaration for Electronic Filing. This form is not a power of attorney and it does not authorize your tax preparer to receive information from the IRS about your account.

Internal Revenue Service Audit

Although fewer than one out of every hundred individual tax returns will probably be audited this year, the IRS is good at selecting returns for audit that will yield additional income taxes.

Returns to be audited are chosen by one of the following six methods in addition to random selection:

- Discrepancies in Your Return
- Matching Information Documents
- Targeted Group Projects
- Taxpayer Compliance Measurement Program (TCMP)
- The Discriminate Function System (DIF)
- Tips from Informants

If your return is audited and you feel you are not being treated fairly, or that proper attention is not being paid to your statements, you have a right to ask for a hearing at the IRS appellate level. If you are still dissatisfied, you can take your case to the United States Tax Court. If the total amount in question is less than $10,000, your case can be handled under the Small Tax Case procedures. If you are still dissatisfied, your next move would be the United States Circuit Court of Appeals.

Your Rights As A Taxpayer

Congress responded to complaints that taxpayers were not being treated fairly by the IRS and passed a comprehensive law to force the IRS to explain, in easy to understand language, the actions it proposes to take against a taxpayer and to relax some of its audit and collection procedures. This law is called, "The Taxpayer Bill of Rights."

Some of the highlights of this bill of rights are:

- Plain English statements
- Allowing recordings of audit conferences
- Not requiring taxpayers to attend the examination
- New audit location rules
- Guidelines for installment payment of taxes
- Acting on wrong IRS advice
- Hardship relief
- Specific basis of IRS decision
- Levies on property
- Suing the IRS for damages

You can obtain a free copy of IRS Publication 1, "Your Rights As A Taxpayer," by calling 1-800-424-FORM.

State Government Individual Income Taxes

Source: Advisory Commission on Intergovernmental Relations

(As of October 1991. Only basic rates, brackets, and exemptions are shown. Local income tax rates, even those mandated by the state, are not included. Taxable income rates and brackets listed below apply to single taxpayers and married taxpayers filing "combined separate" returns in states where this is permitted.)

	Taxable Income Brackets			Personal Exemptions			Standard Deduction[a]			
State	Tax Rates (range in percent)	Lowest: Amount Under	Highest: Amount Over	Single	Married-Joint Return	Dependents	Percent	Single	Married-Joint Return	Federal Income Tax Deductible[b]
AL·*	2.0-5.0%	$500	$3,000	$1,500	$3,000	$300	20%	$2,000	$4,000	yes
AK					No state income tax					
AZ[c]	3.8-7.0	10,000	150,000	2,000	4,000	2,000	NA	3,500	7,000	no
AR	1.0-7.0	3,000	25,000	20	40	20	10	1,000	1,000	no
CA[c]*	1.0-11.0	4,394	200,000	60	120	60	NA	2,262	4,524	no
CO*					5 percent of modified federal taxable income					
CT*	1.5	Flat rate		12,000	24,000	0	NA	NA	NA	NA
DE·*	3.2-7.7	2,000	40,000	1,250	2,500	1,250	NA	1,300	1,600	no
DC	6.0-9.5	10,000	20,000	1,370	2,740	1,370	NA	2,000	2,000	no
FL					No stato income tax					
GA	1.0-6.0	750	7,000	15,000	3,000	1,500	NA	2,300	3,000	no
HI*	2.0-10.0	1,500	20,500	1,040	2,080	1,040	NA	1,500	1,900	no
ID	2.0-8.2	1,000	20,000			Same as federal				no
IL	3.0	Flat rate		1,000	2,000	1,000	NA	NA	NA	no
IN·	3.4	Flat rate		1,000	2,000	1,000	NA	NA	NA	no
IA[c]*	0.4-9.98	1,060	47,700	20	40	15	NA	1,280	3,160	yes
KS*	4.5-5.95	27,500	27,500	2,000	4,000	2,000	NA	3,000	5,000	yes
KY·*	2.0-6.0	3,000	8,000	20	40	20	NA	650	650	no
LA	2.0-6.0	10,000	50,000	4,500	9,000	1,000		Combined with exemptions		yes
ME*	2.1-9.89	4,150	37,500	2,100	4,200	2,100	NA	3,400	5,700	no
MD·*	2.0-5.0	1,000	3,000	1,200	2,400	1,200	15	2,000	4,000	no

State	Taxable Income Brackets: Tax Rates (range in percent)	Lowest: Amount Under	Highest: Amount Over	Personal Exemptions: Single	Married-Joint Return	Dependents	Standard Deduction[a]: Percent	Single	Married-Joint Return	Federal Income Tax Deductible[b]
MA*	6.25-12.0	Flat rate		2,200	4,400	1,000	NA	NA	NA	no
MI+*	4.6	Flat rate		2,100	4,200	2,100	NA	NA	NA	no
MN	6.0-8.5	13,620	44,750			Same as federal				no
MS	3.0-5.0	5,000	10,000	6,000	9,500	1,500	NA	2,300	3,400	no
MO+*	1.5-6.0	1,000	9,000	1,200	2,400	400	NA	Same as federal[e]		yes
MT[c]*	2.0-11.0	1,600	57,600	1,320	2,640	1,320	20	2,470	4,940	yes
NE*	2.37-6.92	1,800	27,000	1,290	2,580	1,290	NA	Same as federal		no
NV					No state income tax					
NH*					Limited income tax					
NJ*	2.0-3.5	20,000	75,000	1,000	2,000	1,500	NA	NA	NA	no
NM	1.8-8.5	5,200	41,600		Same as federal		NA	Same as federal		no
NY+*	4.0-7.875	5,500	13,000	0	0	1,000	NA	6,000	9,500	no
NC*	6.0-7.75	12,750	60,000	2,150	4,300	2,150	NA	3,000	5,000	no
ND*	2.67-12.0	3,000	50,000			Same as federal				yes
OH+*	0.743-6.9	5,000	100,000	650	1,300	650	NA	NA	NA	no
OK*	0.5-7.0	1,000	9,950	1,000	2,000	1,000	15	2,000	2,000	yes
OR*[c]	5.0-9.0	2,000	5,000	104	208	104	NA	1,800	3,000	yes
PA+*	2.1	Flat rate		NA	NA	NA	NA	NA	NA	no
RI					27.5 percent of federal income tax liability					no
SC[c]	2.5-7.0	2,070	10,350	2,150	4,300	2,150		Same as federal		no
SD					No state income tax					
TN*					Limited income tax					
TX					No state income tax					
UT*	2.55-7.2	750	3,750	1,613	3,226	1,613		Same as federal		yes
VT*					28.0-34.0 percent of federal income tax liability					no
VA	2.0-5.75	3,000	17,000	800	1,600	800	NA	3,000	5,000	no
WA					No state income tax					
WV	3.0-6.5	10,000	60,000	2,000	4,000	2,000	NA	NA	NA	no
WI*	4.9-6.93	7,500	15,000	0	0	50[d]	NA	5,200	8,900	no
WY					No state income tax					

Notes: (NA) = not applicable. (+) = states in which one or more local governments levy a local income tax. (a) The lesser of (1) the percentage indicated, multiplied by adjusted gross income, or (2) the dollar value listed. In some states, when a standard deduction computed using a percentage of AGI is less than the fixed amount shown above, a minimum dollar deduction is allowed. Maryland and Utah have a minimum deduction as well. (b) A state provision that allows the taxpayer to deduct fully the federal income tax reduces the effective marginal tax rate for persons in the highest state and federal tax brackets by approximately 30% of the nominal tax rate—the deduction is of a lesser benefit to other taxpayers with lower federal and state top tax brackets. (c) Indexed by an inflation factor. (d) Tax credit per dependent. Taxpayers 65 or older receive a $25 credit.

***State Notes:**

Alabama: Social Security taxes are included in itemized deductions. Taxable income brackets for married filing joint over $6,000, taxed at highest rate.

Arkansas: Tax credit per dependent. Taxpayers 65 or older receive a $20 credit.

California: Taxpayers 65 and older receive additional $60 credit.

Colorado: Modifications for federal interest income, non-Colorado state and local interest income, and Colorado pension exclusion.

Connecticut: Personal exemptions phase out incrementally for single or married filing separately from $12,000 to $24,000 Connecticut AGI to zero at $35,001; for head of household, from $19,000 to $38,000 AGI to zero at $56,001; for married filing jointly from $24,000 to $48,000 AGI to zero at $71,001. For tax years beginning in 1991, 1.5% of federal AGI with modifications; 4.5%, thereafter. A tax on dividend and interest income if federal AGI exceeds $54,000 is imposed. Rates range from 0.75% to 9.5%. Net gains from the sale or exchange of capital assets are at 4.75% but total tax payable cannot exceed 3.4% of AGI.

Delaware: Lowest personal income tax rate (3.2%) applies to income in the $2,000-5,000 bracket. Taxable income under $2,000 is not subject to tax and is refered to as the "zero bracket" amount.

District of Columbia: Exemption will increase to $1,370 by 1991.

Hawaii: A refundable food/excise tax credit of at least $55 per exemption is granted; credit of $60 per exemption is granted for 1990; a refundable medical services excise tax credit of 4% of qualified medical expenses, subject to limitation, is granted.

Idaho: Idaho allows a refundable $15/exemption credit.

Illinois: Effective 1/1/90 an additional $1,000 exemption for taxpayer or spouse 65 years of age or older. An additional $1,000 exemption for taxpayer or spouse who is blind.

Indiana: Additional $1,000 exemption if taxpayer or spouse is over 65 or blind.

Iowa: Tax may not reduce after-tax income of taxpayer below $5,000 (single) or $7,500 (married filing joint, head-of-household, surviving spouse). Only limitation for the standard deduction is that the deduction otherwise allowable of $1,260 or $3,100 may not exceed the amount of income remaining after the federal tax deduction.

Kansas: A child care credit equal to 25% of the federal child care credit is allowed to taxpayers claiming the federal credit. These rates and brackets apply to single persons not deducting federal income tax. For individuals deducting the tax, rates range from 4.75% of the first $2,000 to 8.5% on income over $30,000.

Kentucky: Tax credit per dependent. Taxpayers 65 or older receive a $60 credit.

Maine: A variable surcharge will be imposed for taxable years beginning in 1991 and 1992. A 5% surcharge will be imposed on tax liabilities arising from the first $75,000 of taxable income for married taxpayers filing a joint return ($37,500 for single filers or married filing separately and $56,250 for head of households filers). Any taxpayer with taxable income in excess of these amounts will pay a top marginal rate of 8.6% and a 15% surcharge.

Maryland: All counties have a local income tax surcharge of at least 20% of the state tax liability; most counties have a surcharge of 50%. Single taxpayers have a minimum standard deduction of $1,500, and married taxpayers a minimum standard deduction of $3,000. Blind and elderly get an additional

(*continued*)

exemption of $1,000. An additional $1,200 exemption is allowed for elderly dependents.

Massachusetts: 12% (flat rate) imposed on net capital gains, interest, and dividends of residents, and Massachusetts business income of nonresidents. All other net income taxed at 6.25%. No tax is imposed on a single person whose gross income is $8,000 or less ($12,000 married). Social Security taxes are deducted from taxable income up to $2,000 per taxpayer.

Michigan: Persons who can be claimed as a dependent on someone else's return get an exception of $1,000. If their AGI is $1,500 or less, they owe no tax.

Missouri: For taxpayers itemizing deductions, Social Security taxes are deductible.

Montana: Taxable income brackets, personal exemption level, and standard deduction levels are indexed annually for inflation.

Nebraska: Taxable income brackets will vary by filing status.

New Hampshire: There is a 5% tax on interest and dividends in excess of $1,200 ($2,400 married). There is no filing requirement for an individual whose total interest and dividend income, after deducting all interest from U.S. obligations, New Hampshire and Vermont banks or credit unions; and dividends from New Hampshire non-holding company bonds is less than $1,200 ($2,400 for joint filers) for a taxable period.

New Jersey: No taxpayer is subject to tax if gross income is $3,000 or less ($1,500 married, filing separately).

New Mexico: Several rebates are available for lower income taxpayers. An exception of $2,500 ($1,250 for married filing separate) is allowed for each "special needs" child adopted on or after 1/1/88.

New York: Rates are scheduled to be reduced further in 1992, when the top rate will be 7.6%. Beginning in 1991, a supplemental tax is imposed on taxpayers with New York adjusted gross income in excess of $100,000. Taxpayers must add back the benefit of the lower tax brackets (i.e., 4%, 5%, 6% and 7%). Taxpayers with New York AGI in excess of $150,000 are taxed at a flat rate of 7.875% in 1991.

North Carolina: Breaking points for higher marginal tax rates vary according to filing status. Taxable income brackets shown are for single taxpayers. North Carolina taxable income reflects federal reductions of personal exemptions and itemized deductions for higher income brackets.

North Dakota: Information in table applies to the long form method. As an alternative, taxpayers may use the short form method where the tax is 14% of the adjusted federal income tax liability.

Ohio: Taxpayers take a $20 tax credit per exemption.

Oklahoma: These rates and brackets apply to single persons not deducting federal income tax. For individuals deducting the tax, rates range from 0.5% of the first $1,000 to 10% on income over $16,000 (single rate).

Oregon: Federal tax deduction limited to $3,000 ($1,500 if married filing separately).

Pennsylvania: There are eight classes of income: (1) compensation; (2) net profits; (3) interest; (4) dividends; (5) sale or exchange of property; (6) rents, royalties, patents, and copyrights; (7) income derived through estates or trusts; and (8) gambling and lottery winnings in excess of $1,250 ($2,500 married). An additional 0.3% tax for second half of 1991 tax year and first half of 1992 tax year.

Tennessee: Interest and dividends taxed at 6%. Persons over 65 having total annual gross income derived from any and all sources of $9,000 or less are exempt. Blindness is a basis for total exemption.

Utah: One-half of federal tax liability is deductible. In determining Utah taxable income, 25% of federal personal exemptions are added back. Exemptions reflect this add-back.

Vermont: Refundable state earned income tax credit (28% of federal credit, maximum $566). Three percent surtax of liability between $3,400 and $13,100 and 6% liability over $13,100.

Wisconsin: The standard deduction is gradually phased out as income increases; deduction is completely phased out at $50,830 of AGI for single filers and $55,000 of AGI for joint filers.

Frequently Used Federal Tax Forms

706
U.S. Estate (and Generation-Skipping Transfer) Tax Return
Used for the estate of a deceased United States resident or citizen.

706—A
U.S. Short Form Gift Tax Return
Used by married couples to report nontaxable gifts of more than $10,000 but less than $20,000.

1040
U.S. Individual Income Tax Return
Used by citizens and residents of the United States to report income tax.

1040-ES
Estimated Tax for Individuals
Used to make estimated tax payments as a means for paying currently any income tax (including self-employment tax and the alternative minimum tax) due in excess of the tax withheld from wages, salaries, and other payments for personal services. It is not required unless the total tax exceeds withholding (if any) and applicable tax credits by $500 or more.

1040NR
U.S. Nonresident Alien Income Tax Return
Used by all nonresident alien individuals who file a U.S. tax return, whether or not engaged in a trade or business within the United States. Also used as required for filing nonresident alien fiduciary (estate and trust) returns.

1040X
Amended U.S. Individual Income Tax Return
Used to correct Form 1040, Form 1040A or 1040EZ that you have already filed.

1041
U.S. Fiduciary Income Tax Return
Used by a fiduciary for domestic estate or domestic trust.

1065
U.S. Partnership Return of Income
Used by partnerships as an information return.

1116
Computation of Foreign Tax Credit—Individual, Fiduciary, or Nonresident Alien Individual
Used to figure and support the foreign tax credit claimed for the amount of any income, war profits, and excess profits taxes paid or accrued during the tax year to any foreign country or U.S. possession.

1120
U.S. Corporation Income Tax Return
Used by a corporation to report income tax.

1120S
U.S. Income Tax Return for an S Corporation
Used by S corporations to report income and deductions under Subchapter S of the IRS code. Stockholders share of taxable income is reported on their 1040.

1139
Corporation Application for Tentative Refund
Used by corporations that have certain carrybacks and desire a quick refund of taxes.

1310
Statement of Person Claiming Refund Due a Deceased Taxpayer
Used by a claimant to secure payment of refund on behalf of a deceased taxpayer.

2106
Employee Business Expenses
For use by employee and outside salespersons to support deductions from income for travel, transportation, and expenses (except moving expenses).

2119
Sale of Your Home
For use by individuals who sold their principal residence. Also used by those individuals 55 or older who elect to exclude gain on the sale of their principal residence.

(continued)

2120
Multiple Support Declaration
Used as a statement to disclaim as an income tax exemption an individual to whose support the taxpayer and others have contributed.

2441
Child and Dependent Care Expenses
Used to figure the credit for child and dependent care expenses.

2848
Power of Attorney and Declaration of Representative
Used as an authorization for one person to act for another in any tax matter (except alcohol and tobacco taxes and firearms activities).

3903
Moving Expenses
For optional use to support deductions from income for expenses of travel, transportation (including meals and lodging), and certain expenses of selling an old residence and buying a new residence for employees or self-employed individuals moving to a new job location in the U.S. or its possessions.

4562
Depreciation and Amortization
For use by: individuals, estates and trusts, partnerships, and corporations claiming depreciation, amortization, and section 179 expense deduction. Also used to provide required information for automobiles and all other "listed property."

4684
Casualties and Thefts
For use by all taxpayers for reporting gains and losses from casualties and thefts.

4868
Application for Automatic Extension of Time To File U.S. Individual Income Tax Return
Used to apply for an automatic 4-month extension of time to file Form 1040.

5329
Return for Additional Taxes Attributable to Qualified Retirement Plans (including IRAs), Annuities, and Modified Endowment Contracts
Used to report tax on excess contributions, premature distributions, excess distributions and excess accumulations.

5500EZ
Annual Return of One-Participant (Owners and Their Spouses) Pension Benefit Plan
Used to report on a pension, profit-sharing, etc., plan covering an individual, partner or an individual and spouse or partners and spouses who wholly own a business.

6251
Alternative Minimum Tax—Individuals
Used by individuals to report tax preference items and to figure their alternative minimum tax liability.

7004
Application for Automatic Extension of Time To File Corporation Income Tax Return
Used by corporations and certain exempt organizations to request an automatic extension of 6 months to file their income tax returns.

8283
Noncash Charitable Contributions
Used by taxpayers to report contributions of property in which the total claimed fair market value of all property contributed exceeds $500.

8582
Passive Activity Loss Limitations
Used to determine limitations on passive activity losses.

8606
Nondeductible IRA Contributions, IRA Basis, and Nontaxable IRA Distributions
Used to report the nondeductible amount of IRA, contributions and distributions. It is also used to determine IRA basis.

8615
Computation of Tax for Children Under Age 14 Who Have Investment Income of More Than $1,200
Used to figure the tax on unearned income of more than $1,200 belonging to a child under age 14.

8815
Exclusion of Interest from Series EE U.S. Savings Bonds issued after 1989.
Used to figure the amount of interest on post-1989 Series EE U.S. Savings Bonds that can be excluded from income when the bonds are cashed and qualified higher education expenses are paid.

Federal Death Taxes and the State "Pick-Up" Credit

Source: Advisory Commission on Intergovernmental Relations, 1992

Federal death taxes are made up of two components—gift taxes and estate taxes. Gift taxes are levied on the donor, *while the donor is alive,* on transfers above $10,000 ($20,000 for joint gifts), *per donee,* for a single year. Estate taxes are levied on the entire taxable estate (gross estate less administrative expenses, bequests to spouse, debts, charitable contributions, and funeral expenses) *after the death of the donor.* Gift taxes paid during the donor's lifetime are credited dollar for dollar against estate taxes due at time of death.

Although estate and gift tax rates begin at the first dollar of taxable estate, there is a unified credit of $192,800 against transfer tax liability. This is equivalent to a $600,000 exemption. In addition to the unified credit, a credit for state death taxes is also allowed; see the table below for maximum state death tax credit ("Pick-Up").

Unified Transfer Tax Rates[1]			Maximum State Death Tax Credit		
Taxable Estate	Tax on Lower Amount	Rate on Excess	Adjusted Taxable Estate[2]	Federal Credit	Rate on Excess
$10,000 or less	$0	18%	$40,000-89,999	$0	0.8%
10,000-19,999	1,800	20	90,000-139,999	400	1.6
20,000-39,999	3,800	22	140,000-239,999	1,200	2.4
40,000-59,999	8,200	24	240,000-439,999	3,600	3.2
60,000-79,999	13,000	26	440,000-639,999	10,000	4.0
80,000-99,999	18,200	28	640,000-839,999	18,000	4.8
100,000-149,999	23,800	30	840,000-1,039,999	27,600	5.6
150,000-249,999	38,800	32	1,040,000-1,539,999	38,800	6.4
250,000-499,999	70,800	34	1,540,000-2,039,999	70,800	7.2
500,000-749,999	155,800	37	2,040,000-2,539,999	106,800	8.0
750,000-999,999	248,300	39	2,540,000-3,039,999	146,800	8.8
1,000,000-1,249,999	345,800	41	3,040,000-3,539,999	190,800	9.6
1,250,000-1,499,999	448,300	43	3,540,000-4,039,999	238,800	10.4
1,500,000-1,999,999	555,800	45	4,040,000-5,039,999	290,800	11.2
2,000,000-2,499,999	780,800	49	5,040,000-6,039,999	402,800	12.0
2,500,000-2,999,999	1,025,800	53	6,040,000-7,039,999	522,800	12.8
over 3,000,000[3]	1,290,800	55	7,040,000-8,039,999	650,800	13.6
			8,040,000-9,039,999	786,800	14.4
			9,040,000-10,039,999	930,800	15.2
			over 10,040,000	1,082,800	16.0

(1) For decedents dying from 1984 through 1992. (2) Taxable estate less $60,000. (3) On taxable estates between $10,000,000 and $21,040,000, an additional tax of 5% of the transfer above $10,000,000 is imposed for decedents in 1991 and 1992. For decedents in 1993 and thereafter, the additional tax rate on taxable estates between $10,000,000 and $18,340,000 is 5%.

ENERGY

Major Energy Developments

Source: Energy Information Administration, U.S. Dept. of Energy; *International Energy Annual 1990*

World Primary Energy Production Trends

Since 1981, the world's total output of primary energy—petroleum, natural gas, coal, hydroelectricity and nuclear energy—has increased steadily at an average annual rate of 2.3 percent. World production increased from 280 quadrillion Btu in 1981 to 345 quadrillion Btu in 1990. In 1990, world production of petroleum was more than 67 million barrels per day, or 136 quadrillion Btu.

Over the 10 years from 1981 to 1991, petroleum was the world's most heavily used type of energy. Between 1981 and 1990, petroleum production increased by nearly 6 million barrels per day. Africa had the largest production gain, followed by the Far East and Oceania, and Western Europe. Their combined gains over the 10-year period were 5.2 million barrels per day, nearly 87 percent of the worldwide increase. In North America, Eastern Europe, and the U.S.S.R. average daily production fell by 0.3 and 0.8 million barrels per day, respectively. OPEC production increased by 1.3 million barrels per day. Declines in oil production in the U.S. were largely offset by production increases in Canada and Mexico.

Major Energy Producers and Consumers

Only a few countries have been responsible for producing and consuming nearly half the world's energy. In 1990, three countries—the U.S., the U.S.S.R., and China—were the leading producers and consumers of world energy. These three countries produced 48 percent and consumed 49 percent of the world's total energy. The U.S.S.R. and the U.S. were the world's largest producers of energy in 1990, supplying 39 percent of the world's total. The U.S. consumed 24 percent of the world's total energy—more than any other country.

U.S. Energy Summary

Source: Energy Information Administration, U.S. Dept. of Energy; *Monthly Energy Review*, March 1992

Year-End 1991 Review: Worldwide economic recession restrained petroleum demand during 1991. That lower demand, coupled with producers' ability to replace Iraqi and Kuwaiti oil (and, to a lesser extent, oil from the troubled U.S.S.R.), kept crude oil prices below 1990 levels. In the U.S., the effects of the recession and unusually warm weather led to a decline in domestic petroleum consumption. U.S. petroleum production rose, largely due to production increases early in 1991 in support of the Persian Gulf war. However, oil exploration and development drilling was at its lowest level in decades.

The crisis in the Persian Gulf caused a sharp decline in oil production capacity in Kuwait and resulted in a United Nations embargo against Iraqi exports. As a result, U.S. imports from those countries fell almost to zero. In addition, U.S. exports of refined petroleum products increased. U.S. petroleum net imports fell to 14.1 quadrillion Btu, down 7.6 percent from the 1990 level. The decline in petroleum net imports more than offset increases in coal and natural gas net imports, and U.S. energy net imports fell 6.5 percent to 13.2 quadrillion Btu for the year.

Despite the stagnant U.S. economy, natural gas consumption rose and offset declines in the use of coal and petroleum, leading to a slight increase in total energy consumption. The higher residential consumption of electricity that resulted from increased requirements for energy for space cooling during an unusually warm summer led to a modest increase in overall use of electricity.

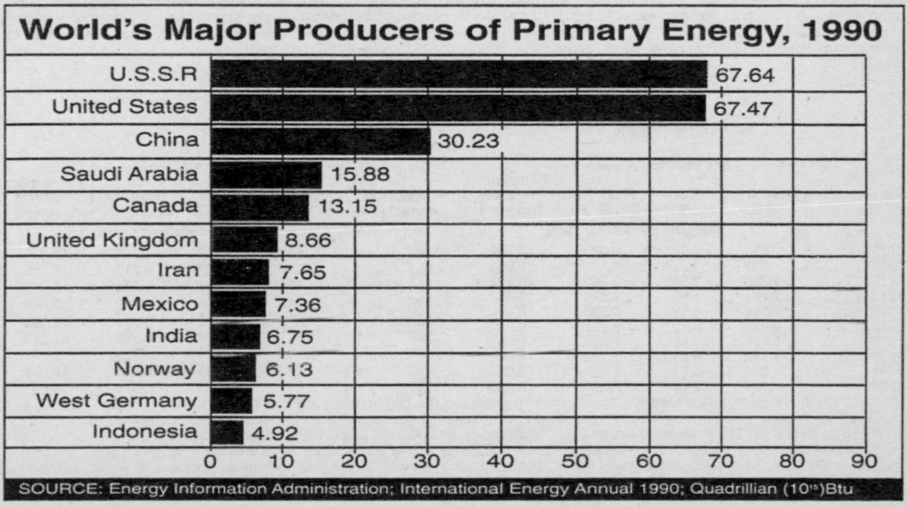

World's Major Consumers of Primary Energy, 1990

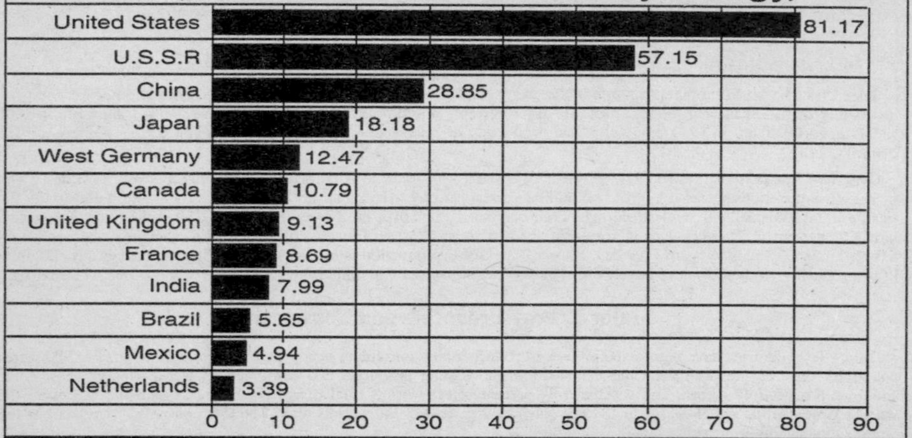

SOURCE: Energy Information Administration; International Energy Annual 1990; Quadrillian (10^{15})Btu

U.S. Production, Consumption, Net Imports, 1990 and 1991

Source: Energy Information Administration, U.S. Dept. of Energy; *Monthly Energy Review;* March 1992 (quadrillion Btu)

	1991	1991 Daily Rate	1990	1990 Daily Rate	Percent Change[1]
Production[2] . .	**67.488**	**0.185**	**67.853**	**0.186**	−0.5
Coal	21.552	.059	22.456	.062	−4.0
Natural Gas (Dry)	18.420	.050	18.362	.050	.3
Petroleum[3]	17.902	.049	17.746	.049	.9
Other[4]	9.614	.026	9.289	.025	3.5
Consumption[2] .	**81.508**	**.223**	**81.293**	**.223**	.3
Coal	18.807	.052	19.122	.052	−1.6
Natural Gas[5] .	20.156	.055	19.304	.053	4.4
Petroleum . . .	32.720	.090	33.553	.092	−2.5
Other[6]	9.825	.027	9.314	.026	5.5
Net Imports . .	**13.157**	**.036**	**14.077**	**.039**	**−6.5**
Coal[7]	−2.769	−.008	−2.705	−.007	2.4
Natural Gas . .	1.589	.004	1.463	.004	8.6
Petroleum[8] . .	14.126	.039	15.293	.042	−7.6
Other[9]	.211	.001	.025	.000	736.4

(1) Based on daily rates prior to rounding. (2) Production and consumption totals exclude wood, waste, geothermal, wind, photovoltaic, and solar thermal energy, except for small amounts used by electric utilities to generate electricity for distribution. (3) Includes crude oil, lease condensate, and natural gas plant liquids. (4) "Other" is hydroelectric and nuclear electric power, and electricity generated for distribution from wood, waste, geothermal, wind, photovoltaic, and solar thermal energy. (5) Includes supplemental gaseous fuels. (6) "Other" is hydroelectric and nuclear electric power; electricity generated for distribution from wood, waste, geothermal, wind, photovoltaic, and solar thermal energy; and net imports of electricity and coal coke. (7) Minus sign indicates exports are greater than imports. (8) Includes crude oil, lease condensate, petroleum products, pentanes plus, unfinished oils, gasoline blending components, and imports of crude oil for the Strategic Petroleum Reserve. (9) "Other" is net imports of electricity and coal coke. **Note:** Totals may not equal sum of components due to independent rounding.

U.S. Net Imports of Petroleum, 1973-1991

Source: Energy Information Administration, U.S. Dept. of Energy, *Monthly Energy Review,* March 1992

Average Annual Rate	Net Imports[1] From Arab OPEC[2]	From OPEC[3]	From All Countries	Petroleum Products Supplied
	(Thousand Barrels per Day)			
1973	914	2,991	6,025	17,308
1974	752	3,277	5,892	16,653
1975	1,382	3,599	5,846	16,322
1976	2,423	5,063	7,090	17,461
1977	3,184	6,190	8,565	18,431
1978	2,962	5,747	8,002	18,847
1979	3,054	5,633	7,985	18,513
1980	2,549	4,293	6,365	17,056
1981	1,844	3,315	5,401	16,058
1982	852	2,136	4,298	15,296
1983	630	1,843	4,312	15,231
1984	817	2,037	4,715	15,726
1985	470	1,821	4,286	15,726
1986	1,160	2,828	5,439	16,281
1987	1,272	3,053	5,914	16,665
1988	1,837	3,513	6,587	17,283
1989	2,128	4,124	7,202	17,325
1990	2,243	4,285	7,161	16,988
1991	2,048	4,033	6,575	16,641

(1) Net Imports is imports minus exports. Imports from members of the Organization of Petroleum Exporting Countries (OPEC) exclude indirect imports, which are petroleum products primarily from Caribbean and West European areas and refined from crude oil produced by OPEC. (2) The Arab members of OPEC are Algeria, Iraq, Kuwait, Libya, Qatar, Saudi Arabia, and the United Arab Emirates. Net imports from the Neutral Zone between Kuwait and Saudi Arabia are included in net imports from Arab OPEC. (3) OPEC consists of Ecuador, Gabon, Indonesia, Iran, Nigeria, and Venezuela, as well as the Arab members. **Notes:** • Beginning in October 1977, Strategic Petroleum Reserves are included; Geographic coverage is the 50 States and the District of Columbia; • Annual averages may not equal average of quarters due to independent rounding.

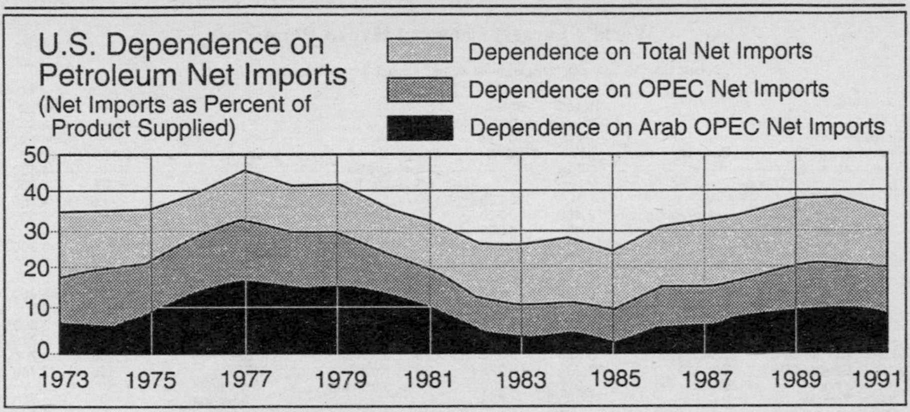

Source: Energy Information Administration; *International Energy Annual 1990*

Energy Consumption by End-Use Sector, 1973-1991

Source: Energy Information Administration, U.S. Dept. of Energy; *Monthly Energy Review*, March 1992

(quadrillion Btu)

	Residential and Commercial		Industrial		Transportation			
Total	Net	Total	Net	Total	Net	Total	Net	Total
1973	15.766	24.143	25.917	31.528	18.584	18.605	60.274	74.282
1974	15.246	23.724	24.994	30.696	18.095	18.117	58.341	72.543
1975	15.200	23.900	22.737	28.401	18.219	18.244	56.157	70.546
1976	15.997	25.020	24.038	30.234	19.076	19.101	59.119	74.362
1977	15.828	25.387	24.593	31.075	19.794	19.819	60.223	76.288
1978	16.023	26.088	24.637	31.388	20.589	20.611	61.251	78.089
1979	15.709	25.809	25.679	32.615	20.447	20.472	61.836	78.898
1980	15.075	25.653	23.854	30.609	19.669	19.695	58.597	75.955
1981	14.541	25.243	22.533	29.238	19.480	19.507	56.556	73.990
1982	14.629	25.630	20.020	26.144	19.043	19.069	53.697	70.848
1983	14.395	25.630	19.401	25.756	19.109	19.135	52.907	70.524
1984	14.964	26.452	21.183	27.846	19.773	19.801	55.923	74.101
1985	14.839	26.682	20.520	27.200	20.036	20.067	55.391	73.945
1986	14.791	26.813	20.102	26.610	20.781	20.812	55.678	74.237
1987	15.152	27.596	21.113	27.807	21.415	21.444	57.678	76.845[R]
1988	16.012	28.915	22.082	28.978	22.269	22.300	60.366	80.195
1989	16.270	29.413	22.292[R]	29.377[R]	22.524[R]	22.554[R]	61.089[R]	81.348[R]
1990	15.636	28.857[R]	22.813[R]	29.904[R]	22.497	25.528	60.950	81.293[R]
1991	16.089	29.560	22.674	29.658	22.254	22.286	61.021	81.508

R=Revised. **Notes:** Geographic coverage is the 50 States and the District of Columbia. Totals may not equal sum of components due to independent rounding and the use of sector-specific conversion factors for natural gas and coal.

Energy Consumption and Consumption per Capita by State, 1990

Source: Energy Information Administration, U.S. Dept. of Energy; *Annual Energy Review 1991*

Consumption				Consumption per Capita			
Rank State	Trillion Btu	Rank State	Trillion Btu	Rank State	Million Btu	Rank State	Million Btu
1. Texas	9,796.9	27. Mississippi	936.3	1. Alaska	1,057.5	27. Utah	315.1
2. California	7,307.0	28. Oregon	927.8	2. Wyoming	877.4	28. Illinois	309.2
3. Ohio	3,698.1	29. Arizona	916.3	3. Louisiana	827.9	29. Minnesota	301.1
4. New York	3,583.9	30. Colorado	913.2	4. Texas	576.7	30. Pennsylvania	300.5
5. Pennsylvania	3,570.5	31. Iowa	899.2	5. North Dakota	480.1	31. Virginia	296.9
6. Illinois	3,534.9	32. West Virginia	806.3	6. West Virginia	449.7	32. Maine	295.8
7. Louisiana	3,493.7	33. Arkansas	781.7	7. Indiana	440.3	33. Michigan	294.0
8. Florida	3,059.3	34. Connecticut	732.1	8. Oklahoma	429.8	34. North Carolina	293.8
9. Michigan	2,733.5	35. New Mexico	597.0	9. Montana	423.1	35. South Dakota	292.6
10. Indiana	2,441.1	36. Alaska	581.6	10. Kansas	415.7	36. New Jersey	292.3
11. New Jersey	2,260.1	37. Utah	542.9	11. Washington	401.3	37. Missouri	288.4
12. Georgia	2,073.8	38. Nebraska	507.9	12. Kentucky	394.6	38. District of Columbia	279.3
13. Washington	1,953.1	39. Wyoming	398.3	13. New Mexico	394.0	39. Wisconsin	279.1
14. North Carolina	1,948.0	40. Nevada	391.6	14. Alabama	388.9	40. Colorado	277.2
15. Virginia	1,837.2	41. Idaho	372.7	15. Idaho	370.1	41. Hawaii	269.9
16. Tennessee	1,752.9	42. Maine	363.2	16. Mississippi	363.8	42. Maryland	253.9
17. Alabama	1,571.9	43. Montana	338.1	17. Tennessee	359.4	43. Arizona	250.0
18. Missouri	1,475.8	44. North Dakota	306.8	18. Delaware	353.5	44. California	245.5
19. Kentucky	1,454.1	45. Hawaii	299.0	19. South Carolina	342.3	45. Florida	236.4
20. Wisconsin	1,365.5	46. New Hampshire	242.9	20. Ohio	340.9	46. Vermont	224.9
21. Oklahoma	1,352.3	47. Delaware	235.5	21. Arkansas	332.5	47. Massachusetts	222.9
22. Massachusetts	1,341.2	48. South Dakota	203.7	22. Oregon	326.4	48. Connecticut	222.7
23. Minnesota	1,317.6	49. Rhode Island	194.7	23. Nevada	325.7	49. New Hampshire	219.0
24. Maryland	1,214.2	50. District of Columbia	169.6	24. Iowa	323.8	50. New York	199.2
25. South Carolina	1,193.7	51. Vermont	126.6	25. Nebraska	321.8	51. Rhode Island	194.1
26. Kansas	1,030.2	**Total United States**	**81,150.8**[1]	26. Georgia	320.1	**Total United States**	**326.2**[1]

(1) The U.S. total differs from that reported elsewhere due to the use of State-level conversion factors for coal and natural gas.

World's Largest Capacity Hydro Plants

Source: U.S. Committee on Large Dams, of the Intl. Commission on Large Dams, Aug. 1992

Rank order	Name	Country	Rated capacity now (MW)	Rated capacity planned (MW)
1	Turukhansk (Lower Tungu-ska)*	USSR		20,000
2	Itaipu	Brazil/Paraguay	7,400	13,320
3	Grand Coulee	USA	6,495	10,830
4	Guri (Raûl Leoni)	Venezuela	10,300	10,300
5	Tucuruí	Brazil	2,640	7,260
6	Sayano Shu-shensk*	USSR	6,400	6,400
7=	Corpus Posadas	Argentina/Paraguay	4,700	6,000
7=	Krasnoyarsk	USSR	6,000	6,000
9	La Grande 2	Canada	5,328	5,328
10	Churchill Falls	Canada	5,225	5,225
11	Xingo	Brazil	3,012	5,020
12	Tarbela	Pakistan	1,750	4,678
13=	Bratsk	USSR	4,500	4,500
13=	Ust-Ilim	USSR	3,675	4,500
15	Cabora Bassa	Mozambique	2,425	4,150
16	Boguchany	USSR		4,000
17=	Rogun*	USSR		3,600
17=	Oak Creek	USA	3,600	3,600
19	Paulo Afonso I	Brazil	1,524	3,409
20	Pati*	Argentina		3,300
21=	Ilha Solteira	Brazil	3,200	3,200
21=	Brumley Gap*	USA	3,200	3,200
23	Chapetón*	Argentina		3,000
24	Gezhouba	China	2,715	2,715
25	John Day	USA	2,160	2,700
25	Nurek	USSR	900	2,700
25=	Yacyreta*	Argentina/Paraguay		2,700

* Planned or under construction.

Major Dams of the World

Source: U.S. Committee on Large Dams, of the Intl. Commission of Large Dams, Aug. 1992

World's Highest Dams

Rank order	Name	Country	Height above lowest formation (m)
1	Rogun*	USSR	335
2	Nurek	USSR	300
3	GrandDixence	Switzerland	285
4	Inguri	USSR	272
5	Chicoasén	Mexico	261
6	Tehri*	India	261
7	Kishau*	India	253
8=	Ertan	China	245
9=	Sayano-Shushensk*	USSR	245
10	Guavio*	Colombia	243
11	Mica	Canada	242
12	Mauvoisin	Switzerland	237
13	Chivor	Colombia	237
14	ElCajón	Honduras	234
15	Chirkei	USSR	233
16	Oroville	USA	230
17	Bhakra	India	226
18	Hoover	USA	221
19	Contra	Switzerland	220
20	Mratinje	Yugoslavia	220

* Under construction.

World's Largest Volume Embankment Dams

Rank order	Name	Country	Volume cubic meters × 1000
1	Tarbela	Pakistan	148,500
2	Fort Peck	USA	96,050
3	Tucurui	Brazil	85,200
4	Ataturk*	Turkey	85,000
5	Yacireta*	Argentina	81,000
6	Rogun*	USSR	75,500
7	Oahe	USA	70,339
8	Guri	Venezuela	70,000
9	Parambikulam	India	69,165
10	High Island West	Hong Kong	67,000
11	Gardiner	Canada	65,000
12	Afsluitdijk	Netherlands	63,400
13	Mangla	Pakistan	63,379
14	Oroville	USA	59,635
15	San Luis	USA	59,559
16	Nurek	USSR	58,000
17	Tanda	Pakistan	57,250
18	Garrison	USA	50,843
19	Chochiti	USA	50,228
20	Oosterschelde	Netherlands	50,000

* Under construction.

World's Largest Capacity Manmade Reservoirs

Rank order	Name	Country	Capacity cubic meters × 1000
1	Owen Falls	Uganda	204,800
2	Bratsk	USSR	169,000
3	Aswan (High)	Egypt	162,000
4	Kariba	Zimbabwe/Zambia	160,368
5	Akosombo	Ghana	147,960
6	Daniel Johnson	Canada	141,851
7	Guri	Venezuela	135,000
8	Krasnoyarsk	USSR	73,300
9	W A C Bennett (Portage Mt.)	Canada	70,309
10	Zeya	USSR	68,400
11	Cabora Bassa	Mozambique	63,000
12	La Grande 2	Canada	61,715
13	La Grande 3	Canada	60,020
14	Ust-Ilim	USSR	59,300
15	Boguchany*	USSR	58,200
16	Kuibyshev	USSR	58,000
17	Serra de Mesa	Brazil	54,400
18	Caniapiscau Barrage KA 3	Canada	53,790
19	Bukhtarma	USSR	49,800
20	Ataturk	Turkey	48,700

* Under construction

Major U.S. Dams and Reservoirs

Source: Committee on Register of Dams, Corps of Engineers, U.S. Army, Aug. 1991

Highest Dams

Order	Dam Name	River	State	Type	Height Feet	Height Meters	Year Complete
1	Oroville	Feather	California	E	754	230	1968
2	Hoover	Colorado	Nevada	A	725	221	1936
3	Dworshak	N Fork Clearwater	Idaho	G	718	219	1973
4	Glen Canyon	Colorado	Arizona	A	708	216	1966
5	New Bullards Bar	North Yuba	California	A	636	194	1970
6	New Melones	Stanislaus	California	R	626	191	1979
7	Swift	Lewis	Washington	E	610	186	1958
8	Mossyrock	Cowlitz	Washington	A	607	185	1968
9	Shasta	Sacramento	California	G	600	183	1945
10	Hungry Horse	S Fork Flathead	Montana	A	564	172	1953
11	Grand Coulee	Columbia	Washington	G	551	168	1942
12	Ross	Skagit	Washington	A	541	165	1949

E = Embankment, Earthfill; R = Embankment, Rockfill; G = Gravity; A = Arch.

Largest Embankment Dams

Order	Dam Name	River	State	Type	Volume Cubic yards X 1000	Volume Cubic Meters X 1000	Year Complete
1	Fort Peck	Missouri	Montana	E	125,624	96,050	1937
2	Oahe	Missouri	South Dakota	E	91,996	70,339	1958
3	Oroville	Feather	California	E	77,997	59,635	1968
4	San Luis	San Luis Creek	California	E	77,897	59,559	1967
5	Garrison	Missouri	North Dakota	E	66,498	50,843	1953
6	Cochiti	Rio Grande	New Mexico	E	65,693	50,228	1975
7	Earthquake Lake	Madison	Montana	E-G	49,998	38,228	1959
8	Fort Randall	Missouri	South Dakota	E	49,962	38,200	1952
9	Castaic	Castaic Creek	California	E	43,998	33,640	1973
10	Ludington P/S	Lake Michigan	Michigan	E	37,699	28,824	1973
11	Kingsley	N. Platte	Nebraska	E	31,999	24,466	1941
12	Warm Springs	Dry Creek	California	E	29,977	22,920	1982

E = Embankment, Earthfill; G = Gravity.

Largest Man-Made Reservoirs

Order	Dam Name	Reservoir	Location	Reservoir Capacity Acre-Feet	Reservoir Capacity Cubic Meters x 1000	Year Completed
1	Hoover	Lake Mead	Nevada	28,253,000	34,850,000	1936
2	Glen Canyon	Lake Powell	Arizona	26,997,000	33,300,000	1966
3	Garrison	Lake Sakakawea	North Dakota	22,635,000	27,920,000	1953
4	Oahe	Lake Oahe	South Dakota	22,238,000	27,430,000	1958
5	Fort Peck	Fort Peck Lake	Montana	17,933,000	22,120,000	1937
6	Grand Coulee	F D Roosevelt Lake	Washington	9,558,000	11,790,000	1942
7	Libby	Lake Koocanusa	Montana	5,813,000	7,170,000	1973
8	Fort Randall	Lake Francis Case	South Dakota	4,621,000	5,700,000	1952
9	Shasta	Lake Shasta	California	4,548,000	5,610,000	1945
10	Toledo Bend	Toledo Bend Lake	Louisiana	4,475,000	5,520,000	1968
11	Wolf Creek	Cumberland Lake	Kentucky	3,997,000	4,930,000	1951
12	Flaming Gorge	Flaming Gorge Reservoir	Utah	3,786,000	4,670,000	1964

1 acre foot = 1 acre of water, 1 foot deep

Motor Gasoline Retail Prices, U.S. City Average, 1973-1991

Source: Energy Information Administration, U.S. Dept. of Energy; *Monthly Energy Review*, March 1992

(cents per gallon, including taxes)

Average	Leaded Regular	Unleaded Regular	Unleaded Premium	All Types[1]	Average	Leaded Regular	Unleaded Regular	Unleaded Premium	All Types[1]
1973 . .	38.8	NA	NA	NA	1983 . .	115.7	124.1	138.3	122.5
1974 . .	53.2	NA	NA	NA	1984 . .	112.9	121.2	136.6	119.8
1975 . .	56.7	NA	NA	NA	1985 . .	111.5	120.2	134.0	119.6
1976 . .	59.0	61.4	NA	NA	1986 . .	85.7	92.7	108.5	93.1
1977 . .	62.2	65.6	NA	NA	1987 . .	89.7	94.8	109.3	95.7
1978 . .	62.6	67.0	NA	65.2	1988 . .	89.9	94.6	110.7	96.3
1979 . .	85.7	90.3	NA	88.2	1989 . .	99.8	102.1	119.7	106.0
1980 . .	119.1	124.5	NA	122.1	1990 . .	114.9	116.4	134.9	121.7
1981 . .	131.1	137.8	147.0[3]	135.3	1991 . .	NA	114.0	132.1	119.6
1982 . .	122.2	129.6	141.5	128.1					

(1) Also includes types of motor gasoline not shown separately. (2) In Sept. 1981, the Bureau of Labor Statistics changed the weights used in the calculation of average motor gasoline prices. From Sept. 1981 forward, gasohol is included in the average for all types, and unleaded premium is weighted more heavily. (3) Based on Sept. through Dec. data only. **Notes:** Geographic coverage for 1973-1977 is 56 urban areas; for 1978 forward, 85 urban areas. NA = Not available.

World Crude Oil and Natural Gas Reserves, January 1, 1991

Source: Energy Information Administration, U.S. Dept. of Energy; *Annual Energy Review 1991*

Region and Country	Crude Oil (billion barrels) *Oil and Gas Journal*	Crude Oil (billion barrels) *World Oil*	Natural Gas (trillion cubic feet) *Oil and Gas Journal*	Natural Gas (trillion cubic feet) *World Oil*
North America	**84.0**	**84.0**	**339.7**	**337.6**
Canada	5.8	6.4	97.6	96.7
Mexico	52.0	51.3	72.7	71.5
United States	26.3	26.3	169.3	169.3
Central and South America	**69.1**	**69.9**	**169.5**	**178.6**
Argentina	2.3	1.6	27.0	20.5
Bolivia	0.1	0.2	4.1	4.6
Brazil	2.8	2.8	4.0	4.1
Colombia	2.0	1.8	4.5	4.2
Ecuador	1.4	1.4	3.9	4.0
Trinidad and Tobago	0.5	0.6	8.9	9.2
Venezuela	59.0	60.1	105.7	121.1
Other	1.0	1.4	11.4	10.9
Western Europe	**14.7**	**23.4**	**172.4**	**225.8**
Denmark	0.8	0.8	4.5	4.1
Italy	0.7	0.7	11.6	11.4
Netherlands	0.2	0.1	60.9	69.5
Norway	7.6	16.6	60.7	108.7
United Kingdom	3.8	4.0	19.8	19.2
West Germany	0.4	0.3	6.6	6.7
Other	1.2	0.9	8.3	6.2
Eastern Europe and U.S.S.R.	**58.6**	**64.8**	**1,621.9**	**1,593.9**
U.S.S.R.	57.0	63.2	1,600.0	1,575.9
Other[2]	1.6	1.6	21.9	18.0
Middle East	**662.6**	**602.5**	**1,324.3**	**1,337.7**
Bahrain	0.1	0.1	6.3	6.1
Iran	92.8	63.0	600.3	600.5
Iraq	100.0	100.0	95.0	109.7
Kuwait[1]	97.0	98.0	53.6	52.9
Oman	4.3	4.4	7.2	10.0
Qatar	4.5	3.7	163.2	162.0
Saudi Arabia[1]	260.0	260.3	185.4	184.2
United Arab Emirates	98.1	66.5	200.4	190.7
Other	5.8	6.5	12.9	21.6
Africa	**59.9**	**62.1**	**285.1**	**289.8**
Algeria	9.2	9.5	114.7	116.5
Cameroon	0.4	0.4	3.9	3.8
Egypt	4.5	6.2	12.4	10.9
Libya	22.8	22.9	43.0	43.0
Nigeria	17.1	17.4	87.4	93.3
Tunisia	1.7	1.7	3.0	3.0
Other	4.2	4.0	20.7	19.3
Far East and Oceania	**50.2**	**54.7**	**298.6**	**363.2**
Australia	1.6	2.8	15.4	73.4
Brunei	1.3	1.1	11.2	11.9
China	24.0	30.8	35.3	33.2
India	8.0	4.2	25.0	21.1
Indonesia	11.0	10.7	91.4	101.8
Malaysia	2.9	3.6	56.9	53.6
New Zealand	0.2	0.2	4.1	3.9
Pakistan	0.2	0.3	19.4	22.7
Thailand	0.1	0.3	5.8	14.5
Other	0.9	0.7	34.1	27.1
World	**999.2**	**961.4**	**4,211.5**	**4,326.5**

(1) Includes one-half of the reserves in the Neutral Zone between Kuwait and Saudi Arabia; (2) Albania, Bulgaria, Cuba, Czechoslovakia, East Germany, Hungary, Mongolia, North Korea, Poland, Romania, Yugoslavia, and Vietnam. **Notes:** • All reserve figures except those for the U.S.S.R. and natural gas reserves in Canada are proved reserves recoverable with present technology and prices. U.S.S.R. figures are "explored reserves," which include proved, probable, and some possible. The Canadian natural gas figure includes proved and some probable. Some components may not equal total due to independent rounding.

Nuclear Electricity Gross Generation by Selected Country, Dec. 1991

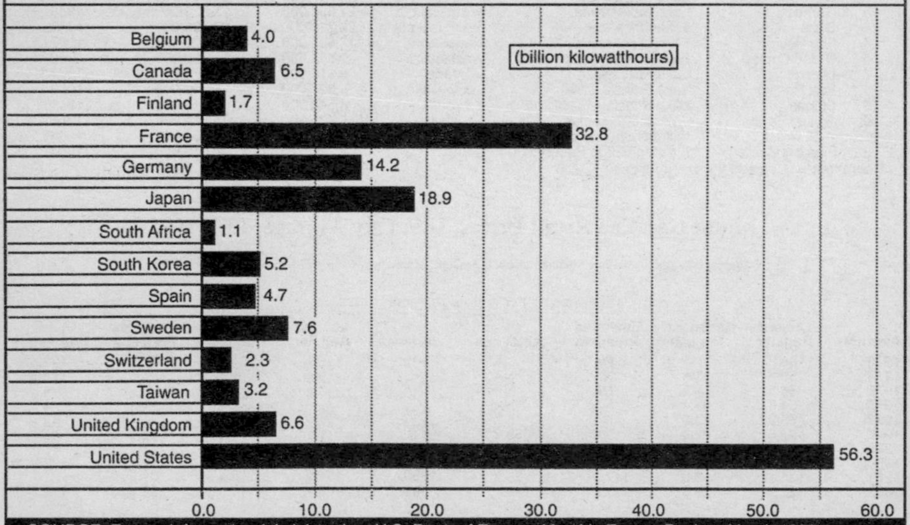

SOURCE: Energy Information Administration, U.S. Dept. of Energy; Monthly Energy Review, March 1992

World Nuclear Power

Source: International Atomic Energy Agency, Dec. 31, 1991

Country	Reactors in Operation		Reactors under Construction		Nuclear Electricity Supplied in 1991		Total Operating Experience to 31 December 1991	
	No. of Units	Total MW(e)[1]	No. of Units	Total MW(e)[1]	TW(e).h	% of Total	Years	Months
Argentina	2	935	1	692	7.2	19.1	26	7
Belgium	7	5,484	—	—	40.4	59.3	107	7
Brazil	1	626	1	1,245	1.3	0.6	9	9
Bulgaria	6	3,538	—	—	13.2	34.0	59	6
Canada	20	13,993	2	1,762	80.1	16.4	263	1
China[2]	1	288	2	1,812	—	—	0	1
Cuba	—	—	2	816	—	—	—	—
Czechoslovakia	8	3,264	6	3,336	22.2	28.6	68	1
Finland	4	2,310	—	—	18.4	33.3	51	4
France	56	56,873	5	7,005	314.9	72.7	655	3
Germany[3]	21	22,390	—	—	140.0	27.6	425	8
Hungary	4	1,645	—	—	12.9	48.4	26	2
India	7	1,374	7	1,540	4.7	1.8	93	1
Iran	—	—	2	2,392	—	—	—	—
Italy	—	—	—	—	—	—	81	0
Japan	42	32,044	10	9,192	209.5	23.8	514	3
Korea, Republic	9	7,220	3	2,550	53.5	47.5	63	1
Mexico	1	654	1	654	4.1	3.6	2	9
Netherlands	2	508	—	—	3.5	4.9	41	9
Pakistan	1	125	—	—	0.4	0.8*	20	3
Romania	—	—	5	3,125	—	—	—	—
S. Africa	2	1,842	—	—	9.1	5.9	14	3
Spain	9	7,067	—	—	53.2	35.9	110	7
Sweden	12	9,817	—	—	73.5	51.6	171	2
Switzerland	5	2,952	—	—	21.7	40.0	83	10
United Kingdom	37	11,710	1	1,188	62.0	20.6	925	10
United States[4]	111	99,757	3	3,480	612.6	21.7	1,592	3
Ex-USSR	45	34,673	25	21,255	212.1	12.6	559	3
Yugoslavia	1	632	—	—	4.7	6.3	10	3
Total	**420**	**326,611**	**76**	**62,044**	**2,009.1**	—	**6,038**	**9**

1 terawatt-hour (TW(e).h) = 10^6 megawatt-hour (MW(e).h). For an average power plant, 1 TW(e).h = 0.39 megatonnes of coal equivalent (input) and 0.23 megatonnes of oil equivalent (input). (2) Total includes data for Taiwan, China: 6 units, 4890 MW(e) in operation; 33.9 TW(e).h of nuclear electricity generation, or 37.8% of total electricity generated there; 62 yrs., 1 month of total operating experience; (3) Germany reported 5 reactors as shut down in 1990. (4) The U.S. reported 1 reactor as shut down in 1990 and 2 reactors as restarting construction suspended in 1988.

U.S. Nuclear Power Plant Operations

Source: Energy Information Administration, *Monthly Energy Review*, March 1992

	Operable Reactors Number	Nuclear-Based Electricity Generation Million Net Kilowatthours	Nuclear Portion of Domestic Electricity Generation Percent		Operable Reactors Number	Nuclear-Based Electricity Generation Million Net Kilowatthours	Nuclear Portion of Domestic Electricity Generation Percent
1976	61	191,104	9.4	1984	86	327,634	13.6
1977	65	250,883	11.8	1985	95	383,691	15.5
1978	70	276,403	12.5	1986	100	414,038	16.6
1979	68	255,155	11.4	1987	107	455,270	17.7
1980	70	251,116	11.0	1988	108	526,973	19.5
1981	74	272,674	11.9	1989	110	529,355	19.0
1982	77	282,773	12.6	1990	111	576,862[R]	20.5[R]
1983	80	293,677	12.7	1991	111	612,596	21.7

R = Revised

Status of U.S. Nuclear Reactor Units

Source: Energy Information Administration, *Monthly Energy Review*, March 1992

	Licensed for Operation		Construction Permits					
	Operable	In Startup	Granted	Pending	On Order	Announced	Total	Total Design Capacity Million Net Kilowatts
	Number of Reactor Units							
1980	70	2	82	12	3	0	169	163
1981	74	0	75	11	3	0	163	157
1982	77	2	60	3	2	0	144	135
1983	80	3	53	0	2	0	138	129
1984	86	6	38	0	2	0	132	123
1985	95	3	30	0	2	0	130	121
1986	100	7	19	0	2	0	128	119
1987	107	4	14	0	2	0	127	119
1988	108	3	12	0	0	0	123	115
1989	110	1	10	0	0	0	121	113
1990	111	0	8[R]	0	0	0	119[R]	111[R]
1991	111	0	8	0	0	0	119	111

R = Revised

SCIENCE AND TECHNOLOGY

Scientific Achievements and Discoveries: 1992

Origins of Life on Earth

- A new theory held that strong winds and the shape of the seabed could have allowed the Israelites to cross the Gulf of Suez and escape from Egypt as described in the Old Testament.
- Eight towers were discovered in Oman at a site believed to be Ubar, the fabled center of trade for frankincense; it was speculated that evidence of an ancient caravan, possibly 2,000 years old, could be tracks followed by the "Wise Men" on their way to the manger in Bethlehem.
- Israeli archeologists discovered the family tomb of Caiaphas, the Jewish High Priest who presided at the trial of Jesus; no comparable evidence existed for the remains of any other major figure in the New Testament.
- After 25 years of study, a 2.4 million-year-old skull fragment found in Kenya was identified as the earliest known fossil of the Homo line of human ancestors, extending by half a million years the age of the genus that would lead to and include modern humans.
- Possibly the largest and oldest living organism, a giant fungus spawned 1,500 to 10,000 years ago, weighing about 100 tons (about as much as a blue whale), and extending for more than 30 acres was discovered near Crystal Falls, Michigan.
- The study of 350,000-year-old human skulls excavated in 1989-90 in China challenged the widely held theory that anatomically modern human beings originated in Africa; the study provided some evidence of independent evolution in China and other parts of the world.
- A jawbone, believed to be 1.6 million years old, found in Georgia (former U.S.S.R.) was identified as the remains of Homo erectus, the species that immediately preceded Homo sapiens; if confirmed, it would be the first firm evidence that human ancestors spread out of Africa earlier than 1 million years ago.

Astronomical Findings

- Broad wrinkles discovered in the fabric of space, the first evidence of how an initially smooth cosmos evolved, were said to be the result of a "Big Bang," giving further support to this theory of the universe's creation.
- Data gathered by the Hubble Space Telescope suggested that unless large amounts of some exotic form of matter exist in space, there is not enough matter present to halt the expansion of the universe; if true, the universe would have no end and would expand forever. Observations by Hubble also led scientists to estimate that the universe was at least 15 billion years old.
- Observations appeared to confirm the theory that the Sun's primary energy source is hydrogen fusion. (The nuclear reaction that produces most of the Sun's light is the fusion of 2 hydrogen nuclei into 1 helium nucleus.) Detection of elusive neutrinos formed as a byproduct of this fusion was the first experimental proof.
- NASA called for an international effort to save Earth from asteroids, as "a significant hazard to life and property" although the chances of a major collision in the next century were "extremely small."

Medicine

- The risk of fatal colon cancer could be reduced by as much as 50 percent through regular low-dose aspirin use, according to American Cancer Society researchers.
- Sulforaphane, a poorly understood chemical, could be the main reason that people who eat broccoli, brussels sprouts, and related cruciferous vegetables have a significantly reduced risk of a wide range of cancers compared to those who avoid the foods.
- Research suggested that resistance to the drug Isoniazid, the mainstay of tuberculosis treatment, was related to a missing or defective copy of a single large gene in a strain of the tuberculosis bacterium; the discovery could lead to new medicines to treat TB and new tests to identify cases of drug-resistant TB.
- A 35-year-old man became the first human to receive a baboon liver in a transplant operation. He had received the animal organ while suffering from Hepatitis B, which was destroying his own liver. The man died 70 days after his transplant after suffering a massive stroke. At least 33 attempts at animal-to-human organ transplants have been made since 1905. The longest anyone has survived after such an operation is 9 months.
- Scientists found that sperm cells possess the same sort of odor receptors that allow the nose to smell, suggesting that swimming sperm navigate toward a fertile egg by detecting its scent.
- A new finding about dyslexia suggested that the disorder may not be a malfunction in the way people understand language, but rather a brain abnormality involving the sense of vision, and perhaps also hearing and touch.
- According to the latest research on dreams, random electrical signals generated in the brainstem elicit a mixture of images and feelings, leading the upper brain to concoct a story—the dream—to explain them. Freudian theory holds that dreaming involves disguising an unconscious wish, wherein a part of the psyche (the censor) transforms the wish into symbols whose meaning is hidden.
- A cholera outbreak aboard an Argentine airplane bound for Los Angeles was responsible for pushing the number of travel-related cholera cases to an all-time high in the U.S. The outbreak began in Peru in 1991, and has since spread to Mexico and the Caribbean, resulting in 5,000 deaths. The Centers for Disease Control said that 96 cases had been reported in the U.S. since Jan. 1992, and that 95 were travel related.
- A large study in Finland showed that high levels of iron are a strong risk factor for heart attacks. If further proof is found to substantiate the findings, it could lead to a revival of bloodletting, once a common medical practice, to remove excess iron and prevent heart disease.
- The American Academy of Pediatrics recommended that all American children over the age of 2 follow the low-fat diet now recommended for adults to prevent heart disease and obesity.

AIDS

- In Jan. 1992, the Centers for Disease Control reported that the U.S. had 206,392 people whose immune systems were severely weakened by AIDS, with 133,232 deaths.
- In Feb. 1992, the World Health Organization reported that 10-12 million adults and 1 million children worldwide had contracted H.I.V., the virus that causes AIDS, and that 2 million cases of AIDS had occurred since the disease became known in the early 1980s. About 90 percent of new adult infections resulted from heterosexual intercourse. W.H.O. estimated that by the year 2000, up to 40 million people would be infected.

Miscellany

- A new study suggested that babies learn the basic sounds of their native language by the age of 6 months; recognition of these sounds is the first step in the comprehension of spoken language. Previous studies suggested that infants' sound perception changes by about 1 year old, when children begin to understand that sounds convey word meanings.
- A study seemed to show that infants as young as 5 months know when simple calculations like one plus one or two minus one are done correctly or incorrectly; the infants indicated awareness that a wrong answer was given by staring longer at the unexpected results.
- A new light bulb, which uses a high frequency radio signal instead of a filament to produce light, was introduced, in June 1992. The new bulb is more cost effective than existing types and will last 14 years if lighted 4 hours a day (typical household usage).
- The National Institutes of Health withdrew funds from an academic conference on the search for a genetic basis for criminal behavior, forcing its indefinite postponement. The agency's objection to the conference, officials said, was that it accepted too readily the notion that violence and crime might have genetic causes. The research has faced much controversy, including charges of racism.
- According to a survey by the American Assn. for the Advancement of Science, one in four scientists suspects his or her peers of engaging in intellectual dishonesty, fakery, or fraud; only 2 percent of the respondents said they had publicly challenged suspect data.

Patents

Some of the more "interesting" patents issued in the U.S. in 1992 included:

- a device that helps people read faster by imitating the sound of the ocean—a tape player and headphones play the sound of waves washing up on the beach in a rhythm intended to help people keep their eyes moving systematically across the page
- a radio that displays written information about songs as they are being broadcast
- a wristband to fight morning sickness among pregnant women by using the principles of acupuncture, featuring a bead that presses against the Neiguan point—a point on the inside of the forearm about an inch above the wrist
- a square ball that bounces as predictably as a round one
- "aquashoes" that resemble cross-country skis and allow a person to walk on water
- a computerized beeper system to arrange on-the-spot introductions and matchmaking
- an electronic "talking stick" for blind people that can detect obstructions and warn users with words uttered through a voice synthesizer
- a kit that allows a person to erase scratches from compact disks by grinding down a portion of the outside plastic shell with sandpaper
- a mask that removes telltale odors from the breath of hunters and makes it far more difficult for deer to detect their presence
- a portable enclosure for hunters, bird watchers, and other nature lovers that allows them to hang from a branch above the ground
- a beach towel that features a kind of sundial to promote symmetrical tanning and to help sunbathers keep track of the time spent in the sun
- a protein produced by genetic engineering to duplicate an "antifreeze" produced by winter flounder to block ice crystals from forming, which will help extend the shelf life of ice creams and improve the quality of frozen fruits, vegetables, and other food
- a nail polish top coating that dries within three minutes when it is exposed to ultraviolet light
- a cotton swab on a stick that doesn't threaten to puncture a person's ear drum
- an inflatable serving tray for eating when afloat
- a ticket card holder for Lotto (a lottery game offered in many states), which enables players to compare their tickets with the winning numbers
- a variation of cocaine that can help doctors obtain medical images of the brain revealing the presence of Parkinson's disease
- the gene for a protein that could help enhance a person's sense of smell

Also of note: in Feb. 1992, scientists at the National Institutes of Health reported that an automated technique they had developed enabled them to identify and determine the basic makeup of 2,375 human brain genes, adding to 347 similar genes they reported in 1991. The U.S. government was trying to patent the genes, but faced much criticism from the private sector, who claimed that such patents could discourage work on an international project to map all human genes. The estimated 50,000 to 100,000 genes that make up the blueprint of a human being are composed of DNA (deoxyribonucleic acid), the basic material of heredity.

Inventor of the Year

Four IBM researchers, John Cocke, George Radin, Norman Kreitzer, and Francis Carruba, were named inventors of the year for 1992 by Intellectual Property Owners, a non-profit association representing people who own patents, trademarks, copyrights, and trade secrets. The invention is a broad computing concept, Reduced Instruction Set Computing (RISC), which allows for greater computer system performance through a smaller set of instructions and simpler addressing modes.

Critical Technologies

In April 1991, the White House listed 22 areas of **technological development** that should be treated as **"critical to the national prosperity and to national security."** The 22 areas of technology are: surface transportation; environment; materials processing; electronic and photomic materials; ceramics; composites; high-performance metals and alloys; flexible computer integrated manufacturing; intelligent processing equipment; micro-and nano-fabrication; systems-management; software; microelectronics and optoelectronics; high-performance computing/networking; high-definition imaging and displays; sensors and signal processing; data storage; computer simulation; applied molecular biology; medical; aeronautics; and energy.

Inventions and Discoveries

Invention	Date	Inventor	Nation.
Adding machine	1642	Pascal	French
Adding machine	1885	Burroughs	U.S.
Aerosol spray	1926	Rotheim	Norwegian
Air brake	1868	Westinghouse	U.S.
Air conditioning	1911	Carrier	U.S.
Air pump	1654	Guericke	German
Airplane, automatic pilot	1912	Sperry	U.S.
Airplane, experimental	1896	Langley	U.S.
Airplane jet engine	1939	Ohain	German
Airplane with motor	1903	Wright bros.	U.S.
Airplane, hydro	1911	Curtiss	U.S.
Airship	1852	Giffard	French
Airship, rigid dirigible	1900	Zeppelin	German
Arc welder	1919	Thomson	U.S.
Autogyro	1920	de la Cierva	Spanish
Automobile, differential gear	1885	Benz	German
Automobile, electric	1892	Morrison	U.S.
Automobile, exp'mtl	1864	Marcus	Austrian
Automobile, gasoline	1889	Daimler	German
Automobile, gasoline	1892	Duryea	U.S.
Automobile magneto	1897	Bosch	German
Automobile muffler	...	Maxim, H.P.	U.S.
Automobile self-starter	1911	Kettering	U.S.
Babbitt metal	1839	Babbitt	U.S.
Bakelite	1907	Baekeland	Belg., U.S.
Balloon	1783	Montgolfier	French
Barometer	1643	Torricelli	Italian
Bicycle, modern	1885	Starley	English
Bifocal lens	1780	Franklin	U.S.
Block signals, railway	1867	Hall	U.S.
Bomb, depth	1916	Tait	U.S.
Bottle machine	1895	Owens	U.S.
Braille printing	1829	Braille	French
Burner, gas	1855	Bunsen	German
Calculating machine	1833	Babbage	English
Camera—see also Photography			
Camera, Kodak	1888	Eastman, Walker	U.S.
Camera, Polaroid Land	1948	Land	U.S.
Car coupler	1873	Janney	U.S.
Carburetor, gasoline	1893	Maybach	German
Card time recorder	1894	Cooper	U.S.
Carding machine	1797	Whittemore	U.S.
Carpet sweeper	1876	Bissell	U.S.
Cassette, audio	1963	Philips Co.	Dutch
Cassette, videotape	1969	Sony	Japanese
Cash register	1879	Ritty	U.S.
Cathode ray oscilloscope	1897	Braun	German
Cathode ray tube	1878	Crookes	English
CAT scan (computerized tomography)	1973	Hounsfield	English
Cellophane	1908	Brandenberger	Swiss
Celluloid	1870	Hyatt	U.S.
Cement, Portland	1824	Aspdin	English
Chronometer	1761	Harrison	English
Circuit breaker	1925	Hilliard	U.S.
Circuit, integrated	1959	Kilby, Noyce, Texas Instr	U.S
Clock, pendulum	1657	Huygens	Dutch
Coaxial cable system	1929	Affel, Espensched	U.S.
Coke oven	1893	Hoffman	Austrian
Compressed air rock drill	1871	Ingersoll	U.S.
Comptometer	1887	Felt	U.S.
Computer, automatic sequence	1944	Aiken et al.	U.S.
Computer, mini	1960	Digital Corp.	U.S.
Condenser microphone (telephone)	1916	Wente	U.S.
Contraceptive, oral	1954	Pincus, Rock	U.S.
Corn, hybrid	1917	Jones	U.S.
Cotton gin	1793	Whitney	U.S.
Cream separator	1878	DeLaval	Swedish
Cultivator, disc	1878	Mallon	U.S.
Cystoscope	1878	Nitze	German
Diesel engine	1895	Diesel	German
Disk, compact	1972	RCA	U.S.
Disk, floppy	1970	IBM	U.S.
Disk player, compact	1979	Sony, Philips Co	Japan., Dutch
Disk, video	1972	Philips Co.	Dutch
Dynamite	1866	Nobel	Swedish
Dynamo, continuous current	1871	Gramme	Belgian
Dynamo, hydrogen cooled	1915	Schuler	U.S.
Electric battery	1800	Volta	Italian
Electric fan	1882	Wheeler	U.S.
Electrocardiograph	1903	Einthoven	Dutch
Electroencephalograph	1929	Berger	German
Electromagnet	1824	Sturgeon	English
Electron spectrometer	1944	Deutsch, Elliott, Evans	U.S.
Electron tube multigrid	1913	Langmuir	U.S.
Electroplating	1805	Brugnatelli	Italian
Electrostatic generator	1929	Van de Graaff	U.S.
Elevator brake	1852	Otis	U.S.
Elevator, push button	1922	Larson	U.S.
Engine, automatic transmission	1910	Fottinger	German
Engine, coal-gas 4-cycle	1876	Otto	German
Engine, compression ignition	1883	Daimler	German
Engine, electric ignition	1883	Benz	German
Engine, gas, compound	1926	Eickemeyer	U.S.
Engine, gasoline	1872	Brayton, Geo.	U.S.
Engine, gasoline	1889	Daimler	German
Engine, steam, piston	1705	Newcomen	English
Engine, steam, piston	1769	Watt	Scottish
Engraving, half-tone	1852	Talbot	U.S.
Fiberglass	1938	Owens-Corning	U.S.
Fiber optics	1955	Kapany	English
Filament, tungsten	1913	Coolidge	U.S.
Flanged rail	1831	Stevens	U.S.
Flatiron, electric	1882	Seely	U.S.
Food, frozen	1924	Birdseye	U.S.
Furnace (for steel)	1858	Siemens	German
Galvanometer	1820	Sweigger	German
Gas discharge tube	1922	Hull	U.S.
Gas lighting	1792	Murdoch	Scottish
Gas mantle	1885	Welsbach	Austrian
Gasoline (lead ethyl)	1922	Midgley	U.S.
Gasoline, cracked	1913	Burton	U.S.
Gasoline, high octane	1930	Ipatieff	Russian
Geiger counter	1913	Geiger	German
Glass, laminated safety	1909	Benedictus	French
Glider	1853	Cayley	English
Gun, breechloader	1811	Thornton	U.S.
Gun, Browning	1897	Browning	U.S.
Gun, magazine	1875	Hotchkiss	U.S.
Gun, silencer	1908	Maxim, H.P.	U.S.
Guncotton	1847	Schoenbein	German
Gyrocompass	1911	Sperry	U.S.
Gyroscope	1852	Foucault	French
Harvester-thresher	1818	Lane	U.S.
Heart, artificial	1982	Jarvik	U.S.
Helicopter	1939	Sikorsky	U.S.
Hydrometer	1768	Baume	French
Ice-making machine	1851	Gorrie	U.S.
Iron lung	1928	Drinker, Slaw	U.S.
Kaleidoscope	1817	Brewster	Scottish
Kinetoscope	1889	Edison	U.S.
Lacquer, nitrocellulose	1921	Flaherty	U.S.
Lamp, arc	1847	Staite	English

(continued)

Invention	Date	Inventor	Nation.
Lamp, flourescent	1938	General Electric, Westinghouse	U.S.
Lamp, incandescent	1879	Edison	U.S.
Lamp, incand., frosted	1924	Pipkin	U.S.
Lamp, incand., gas	1913	Langmuir	U.S.
Lamp, Klieg	1911	Kliegl, A.&J.	U.S.
Lamp, mercury vapor	1912	Hewitt	U.S.
Lamp, miner's safety	1816	Davy	English
Lamp, neon	1909	Claude	French
Lathe, turret	1845	Fitch	U.S.
Launderette	1934	Cantrell	U.S.
Lens, achromatic	1758	Dollond	English
Lens, fused bifocal	1908	Borsch	U.S.
Leydenjar (condenser)	1745	von Kleist	German
Lightning rod	1752	Franklin	U.S.
Linoleum	1860	Walton	English
Linotype	1884	Mergenthaler	U.S.
Lock, cylinder	1851	Yale	U.S.
Locomotive, electric	1851	Vail	U.S.
Locomotive, exp'mtl	1802	Trevithick	English
Locomotive, exp'mtl	1812	Fenton et al.	English
Locomotive, exp'mtl	1813	Hedley	English
Locomotive, exp'mtl	1814	Stephenson	English
Locomotive practical	1829	Stephenson	English
Locomotive, 1st U.S.	1830	Cooper, P.	U.S.
Loom, power	1785	Cartwright	English
Loudspeaker, dynamic	1924	Rice, Kellogg	U.S.
Machine gun	1861	Gatling	U.S.
Machine gun, improved	1872	Hotchkiss	U.S.
Machine gun (Maxim)	1883	Maxim, H.S.	U.S., Eng.
Magnet, electro	1828	Henry	U.S.
Mantle, gas	1885	Welsbach	Austrian
Mason jar	1858	Mason, J.	U.S.
Match, friction	1827	John Walker	English
Mercerized textiles	1843	Mercer, J.	English
Meter, induction	1888	Shallenberg	U.S.
Metronome	1816	Malezel	German
Micrometer	1636	Gascoigne	English
Microphone	1877	Berliner	U.S.
Microscope, compound	1590	Janssen	Dutch
Microscope, electronic	1931	Knoll, Ruska	German
Microscope, field ion	1951	Mueller	German
Monitor, warship	1861	Ericsson	U.S.
Monotype	1887	Lanston	U.S.
Motor, AC	1892	Tesla	U.S.
Motor, DC	1837	Davenport	U.S.
Motor, induction	1887	Tesla	U.S.
Motorcycle	1885	Daimler	German
Movie machine	1894	Jenkins	U.S.
Movie, panoramic	1952	Waller	U.S.
Movie, talking	1927	Warner Bros.	U.S.
Mower, lawn	1831	Budding, Ferrabee	English
Mowing machine	1822	Bailey	U.S.
Neoprene	1930	Carothers	U.S.
Nylon synthetic	1930	Carothers	U.S.
Nylon	1937	Du Pont lab	U.S.
Oil cracking furnace	1891	Gavrilov	Russian
Oil filled power cable	1921	Emanueli	Italian
Oleomargarine	1869	Mege-Mouries	French
Ophthalmoscope	1851	Helmholtz	German
Paper	105	Lun	Chinese
Paper machine	1809	Dickinson	U.S.
Parachute	1785	Blanchard	French
Pen, ballpoint	1838	Biro	Hungarian
Pen, fountain	1884	Waterman	U.S.
Pen, steel	1780	Harrison	English
Pendulum	1583	Galileo	Italian
Percussion cap	1807	Forsythe	Scottish
Phonograph	1877	Edison	U.S.
Photo, color	1892	Ives	U.S.
Photo film, celluloid	1893	Reichenbach	U.S.
Photo film, transparent	1884	Eastman, Goodwin	U.S.
Photoelectric cell	1895	Elster	German
Photographic paper	1835	Talbot	U.S.
Photography	1835	Talbot	English
Photography	1835	Daguerre	French
Photography	1816	Niepce	French
Photophone	1880	Bell	U.S.-Scot.
Phototelegraphy	1925	Bell Labs	U.S.
Piano	1709	Cristofori	Italian
Piano, player	1863	Fourneaux	French
Pin, safety	1849	Hunt	U.S.
Pistol (revolver)	1836	Colt	U.S.
Plow, cast iron	1785	Ransome	English
Plow, disc	1896	Hardy	U.S.
Pneumatic hammer	1890	King	U.S.
Powder, smokeless	1884	Vieille	French
Printing press, rotary	1845	Hoe	U.S.
Printing press, web	1865	Bullock	U.S.
Propeller, screw	1804	Stevens	U.S.
Propeller, screw	1837	Ericsson	Swedish

Invention	Date	Inventor	Nation.
Pulsars	1967	Bell	English
Punch card accounting	1889	Hollerith	U.S.
Quasars	1963	Schmidt	U.S.
Radar	1940	Watson-Watt	Scottish
Radio amplifier	1906	De Forest	U.S.
Radio beacon	1928	Donovan	U.S.
Radio crystal oscillator	1918	Nicolson	U.S.
Radio receiver, cascade tuning	1913	Alexanderson	U.S.
Radio receiver, heterodyne	1913	Fessenden	U.S.
Radio transmitter triode modulation	1914	Alexanderson	U.S.
Radio tube-diode	1905	Fleming	English
Radio tube oscillator	1915	De Forest	U.S.
Radio tube triode	1906	De Forest	U.S.
Radio, signals	1895	Marconi	Italian
Radio, magnetic detector	1902	Marconi	Italian
Radio FM 2-path	1933	Armstrong	U.S.
Rayon	1883	Swan	English
Razor, electric	1917	Schick	U.S.
Razor, safety	1895	Gillette	U.S.
Reaper	1834	McCormick	U.S.
Record, cylinder	1887	Bell, Tainter	U.S.
Record, disc	1887	Berliner	U.S.
Record, long playing	1947	Goldmark	U.S.
Record, wax cylinder	1888	Edison	U.S.
Refrigerants, low-boiling fluorine compound	1930	Midgely and co-workers	U.S.
Refrigerator car	1868	David	U.S.
Resin, synthetic	1931	Hill	English
Richter scale	1935	Richter	U.S.
Rifle, repeating	1860	Spencer	U.S.
Rocket engine	1926	Goddard	U.S.
Rubber, vulcanized	1839	Goodyear	U.S.
Saw, band	1808	Newberry	English
Saw, circular	1777	Miller	English
Sewing machine	1846	Howe	U.S.
Shoe-sewing machine	1860	McKay	U.S.
Shrapnel shell	1784	Shrapnel	English
Shuttle, flying	1733	Kay	English
Sleeping-car	1865	Pullman	U.S.
Slide rule	1620	Oughtred	English
Soap, hardwater	1928	Bertsch	German
Spectroscope	1859	Kirchoff, Bunsen	German
Spectroscope (mass)	1918	Dempster	U.S.
Spinning jenny	1767	Hargreaves	English
Spinning mule	1779	Crompton	English
Steamboat, exp'mtl	1778	Jouffroy	French
Steamboat, exp'mtl	1785	Fitch	U.S.
Steamboat, exp'mtl	1787	Rumsey	U.S.
Steamboat, exp'mtl	1788	Miller	Scottish
Steamboat, exp'mtl	1803	Fulton	U.S.
Steamboat, exp'mtl	1804	Stevens	U.S.
Steamboat, practical	1802	Symington	Scottish
Steamboat, practical	1807	Fulton	U.S.
Steam car	1770	Cugnot	French
Steam turbine	1884	Parsons	English
Steel (converter)	1856	Bessemer	English
Steel alloy	1891	Harvey	U.S.
Steel alloy, high-speed	1901	Taylor, White	U.S.
Steel, electric	1900	Heroult	French
Steel, manganese	1884	Hadfield	English
Steel, stainless	1916	Brearley	English
Stereoscope	1838	Wheatstone	English
Stethoscope	1819	Laennec	French
Stethoscope, binaural	1840	Cammann	U.S.
Stock ticker	1870	Edison	U.S.
Storage battery, rechargeable	1859	Plante	French
Stove, electric	1896	Hadaway	U.S.
Submarine	1891	Holland	U.S.
Submarine, even keel	1894	Lake	U.S.
Submarine, torpedo	1776	Bushnell	U.S.
Superconductivity (BCS theory)	1957	Bardeen, Cooper, Schreiffer	U.S.
Tank, military	1914	Swinton	English
Tape recorder, magnetic	1899	Poulsen	Danish
Teflon	1938	Du Pont	U.S.
Telegraph, magnetic	1837	Morse	U.S.
Telegraph, quadruplex	1864	Edison	U.S.
Telegraph, railroad	1887	Woods	U.S.
Telegraph, wireless high frequency	1895	Marconi	Italian
Telephone	1876	Bell	U.S.-Scot.
Telephone amplifier	1912	De Forest	U.S.
Telephone, automatic	1891	Stowger	U.S.
Telephone, radio	1900	Poulsen, Fessenden	Danish

Invention	Date	Inventor	Nation.
Telephone, radio	1906	De Forest	U.S.
Telephone, radio, l. d	1915	AT&T	U.S.
Telephone, recording	1898	Poulsen	Danish
Telephone, wireless	1899	Collins	U.S.
Telescope	1608	Lippershey	Neth.
Telescope	1609	Galileo	Italian
Telescope, astronomical	1611	Kepler	German
Teletype	1928	Morkrum, Kleinschmidt	U.S.
Television, iconoscope	1923	Zworykin	U.S.
Television, electronic	1927	Farnsworth	U.S.
Television, (mech. scanner)	1923	Baird	Scottish
Thermometer	1593	Galileo	Italian
Thermometer	1730	Reaumur	French
Thermometer, mercury	1714	Fahrenheit	German
Time recorder	1890	Bundy	U.S.
Time, self-regulator	1918	Bryce	U.S.
Tire, double-tube	1845	Thomson	Scottish
Tire, pneumatic	1888	Dunlop	Scottish
Toaster, automatic	1918	Strite	U.S.
Tool, pneumatic	1865	Law	English
Torpedo, marine	1804	Fulton	U.S.
Tractor, crawler	1904	Holt	U.S.
Transformer A.C.	1885	Stanley	U.S.
Transistor	1947	Shockley, Brattain, Bardeen	U.S.
Trolley car, electric	1884-87	Van DePoele, Sprague	U.S.
Tungsten, ductile	1912	Coolidge	U.S.
Tupperware	1945	Tupper	U.S.
Turbine, gas	1849	Bourdin	French
Turbine, hydraulic	1849	Francis	U.S.
Turbine, steam	1884	Parsons	English
Type, movable	1447	Gutenberg	German
Typewriter	1867	Sholes, Soule, Glidden	U.S.
Vacuum cleaner, electric	1907	Spangler	U.S.
Velcro	1948	de Mestral	Swiss
Video game ("Pong")	1972	Buschnel	U.S.
Video home system (VHS)	1975	Matsushita, JVC	Japanese
Washer, electric	1901	Fisher	U.S.
Welding, atomic hydrogen	1924	Langmuir, Palmer	U.S.
Welding, electric	1877	Thomson	U.S.
Wind tunnel	1912	Eiffel	French
Wire, barbed	1874	Glidden	U.S.
Wire, barbed	1875	Haisn	U.S.
Wrench, double-acting	1913	Owen	U.S.
X-ray tube	1913	Coolidge	U.S.
Zipper	1891	Judson	U.S.

Discoveries and Innovations: Chemistry, Physics, Biology, Medicine

	Date	Discoverer	Nation.
Acetylene gas	1862	Berthelot	French
ACTH	1927	Evans, Long	U.S.
Adrenalin	1901	Takamine	Japanese
Aluminum, electrolytic process	1886	Hall	U.S.
Aluminum, isolated	1825	Oersted	Danish
Anesthesia, ether	1842	Long	U.S.
Anesthesia, local	1885	Koller	Austrian
Anesthesia, spinal	1898	Bier	German
Aniline dye	1856	Perkin	English
Anti-rabies	1885	Pasteur	French
Antiseptic surgery	1867	Lister	English
Antitoxin, diphtheria	1891	Von Behring	German
Argyrol	1897	Bayer	German
Arsphenamine	1910	Ehrlich	German
Aspirin	1889	Dresser	German
Atabrine	...	Mietzsch, et al.	German
Atomic numbers	1913	Moseley	English
Atomic theory	1803	Dalton	English
Atomic time clock	1947	Libby	U.S.
Atom-smashing theory	1919	Rutherford	English
Bacitracin	1945	Johnson, et al.	U.S.
Bacteria (described)	1676	Leeuwenhoek	Dutch
Barbital	1903	Fischer	German
Bleaching powder	1798	Tennant	English
Blood, circulation	1628	Harvey	English
Bordeaux mixture	1885	Millardet	French
Bromine from sea	1924	Edgar Kramer	U.S.
Calcium carbide	1888	Wilson	U.S.
Calculus	1670	Newton	English
Camphor synthetic	1896	Haller	French
Canning (food)	1804	Appert	French
Carbomycin	1952	Tanner	U.S.
Carbon oxides	1925	Fisher	German
Chloamphenicol	1947	Burkholder	U.S.
Chlorine	1774	Scheele	Swedish
Chloroform	1831	Guthrie, S.	U.S.
Chlortetracycline	1948	Duggen	U.S.
Classification of plants and animals	1735	Linnaeus	Swedish
Cocaine	1860	Niermann	German
Combustion explained	1777	Lavoisier	French
Conditioned reflex	1914	Pavlov	Russian
Cortisone	1936	Kendall	U.S.
Cortisone, synthesis	1946	Sarett	U.S.
Cosmic rays	1910	Gockel	Swiss
Cyanamide	1905	Frank, Caro	German
Cyclotron	1930	Lawrence	U.S.
DDT (not applied as insecticide until 1939)	1874	Zeidler	German
Deuterium	1932	Urey, Brickwedde, Murphy	U.S.
DNA (structure)	1951	Crick Watson Wilkins	English U.S. English
Electric resistance (law)	1827	Ohm	German
Electric waves	1888	Hertz	German
Electrolysis	1852	Faraday	English
Electromagnetism	1819	Oersted	Danish
Electron	1897	Thomson, J.	English
Electron diffraction	1936	Thomson, G. Davisson	English U.S.
Electroshock treatment	1938	Cerletti, Bini	Italian
Erythromycin	1952	McGuire	U.S.
Evolution, natural selection	1858	Darwin	English
Falling bodies, law	1590	Galileo	Italian
Gases, law of combining volumes	1808	Gay-Lussac	French
Geometry, analytic	1619	Descartes	French
Gold (cyanide process for extraction)	1887	MacArthur, Forest	British
Gravitation, law	1687	Newton	English
Holograph	1948	Gabor	British
Human heart transplant	1967	Barnard	S. African
Indigo, synthesis of	1880	Baeyer	German
Induction, electric	1830	Henry	U.S.
Insulin	1922	Banting, Best, Macleod	Canadian, Scottish
Intelligence testing	1905	Binet, Simon	French
Isoniazid	1952	Hoffman-La-Roche Domagk	U.S. German
Isotopes, theory	1912	Soddy	English
Laser (light amplification by stimulated emission of radiation)	1958	Townes, Schawlow	U.S.
Light, velocity	1675	Roemer	Danish
Light, wave theory	1690	Huygens	Dutch
Lithography	1796	Senefelder	Bohemian
Lobotomy	1935	Egas Moniz	Portuguese
LSD-25	1943	Hoffman	Swiss

	Date	Discoverer	Nation.
Mendelian laws	1866	Mendel	Austrian
Mercator projection (map)	1568	Mercator (Kremer)	Flemish
Methanol	1661	Boyle	Irish
Milk condensation	1853	Borden	U.S.
Molecular hypothesis	1811	Avogadro	Italian
Motion, laws of	1687	Newton	English
Neomycin	1949	Waksman, Lechevalier	U.S.
Neutron	1932	Chadwick	English
Nitric acid	1648	Glauber	German
Nitric oxide	1772	Priestley	English
Nitroglycerin	1846	Sobrero	Italian
Oil cracking process	1891	Dewar	U.S.
Oxygen	1774	Priestley	English
Oxytetracycline	1950	Finlay, et al.	U.S.
Ozone	1840	Schonbein	German
Paper, sulfite process	1867	Tilghman	U.S.
Paper, wood pulp, sulfate process	1884	Dahl	German
Penicillin	1929	Fleming	Scottish
practical use	1941	Florey, Chain	English
Periodic law and table of elements	1869	Mendeleyev	Russian
Planetary motion, laws	1609	Kepler	German
Plutonium fission	1940	Kennedy, Wahl, Seaborg, Segre	U.S.
Polymyxin	1947	Ainsworth	English
Positron	1932	Anderson	U.S.
Proton	1919	Rutherford	N. Zealand
Psychoanalysis	1900	Freud	Austrian
Quantum theory	1900	Planck	German
Quasars	1963	Matthews, Sandage	U.S.
Quinine synthetic	1946	Woodward, Doering	U.S.
Radioactivity	1896	Becquerel	French
Radium	1898	Curie, Pierre Curie, Marie	French Pol.-Fr.
Relativity theory	1905	Einstein	German
Reserpine	1949	Jal Vaikl	Indian

	Date	Discoverer	Nation.
Schick test	1913	Schick	U.S.
Silicon	1823	Berzelius	Swedish
Streptomycin	1945	Waksman	U.S.
Sulfadiazine	1940	Roblin	U.S.
Sulfanilamide	1935	Bovet, Trefouel	French
Sulfanilamide theory	1908	Gelmo	German
Sulfapyridine	1938	Ewins, Phelps	English
Sulfathiazole	...	Fosbinder, Walter	U.S.
Sulfuric acid	1831	Phillips	English
Sulfuric acid, lead	1746	Roebuck	English
Thiacetazone	1950	Belmisch, Mietzsch, Domagk	German
Tuberculin	1890	Koch	German
Uranium fission (theory)	1939	Hahn, Meitner, Strassmann Bohr Fermi Einstein, Pegram, Wheeler	German Danish Italian U.S.
Uranium fission, atomic reactor	1942	Fermi, Szilard	U.S.
Vaccine, measles	1954	Enders, Peebles	U.S.
Vaccine, polio	1953	Salk	U.S.
Vaccine, polio, oral	1955	Sabin	U.S.
Vaccine, rabies	1885	Pasteur	French
Vaccine, smallpox	1796	Jenner	English
Vaccine, typhus	1909	Nicolle	French
Van Allen belts, radiation	1958	Van Allen	U.S.
Vitamin A	1913	McCollum, Davis	U.S.
Vitamin B	1916	McCollum	U.S.
Vitamin C	1912	Holst, Froelich	Norwegian
Vitamin D	1922	McCollum	U.S.
Wassermann test	1906	Wassermann	German
Xerography	1938	Carlson	U.S.
X-ray	1895	Roentgen	German

Chemical Elements, Atomic Weights, Discoverers

Atomic weights, based on the exact number 12 as the assigned atomic mass of the principal isotope of carbon, carbon 12, are provided through the courtesy of the International Union of Pure and Applied Chemistry and Butterworth Scientific Publications.

For the radioactive elements, with the exception of uranium and thorium, the mass number of either the isotope of longest half-life (*) or the better known isotope (**) is given.

Chemical element	Symbol	Atomic number	Atomic weight	Year discov.	Discoverer
Actinium	Ac	89	227*	1899	Debierne
Aluminum	Al	13	26.9815	1825	Oersted
Americium	Am	95	243*	1944	Seaborg, et al.
Antimony	Sb	51	121.75	1450	Valentine
Argon	Ar	18	39.948	1894	Rayleigh, Ramsay
Arsenic	As	33	74.9216	13th c.	Albertus Magnus
Astatine	At	85	210*	1940	Corson, et al.
Barium	Ba	56	137.34	1808	Davy
Berkelium	Bk	97	249**	1949	Thompson, Ghiorso, Seaborg
Beryllium	Be	4	9.0122	1798	Vauquelin
Bismuth	Bi	83	208.980	15th c.	Valentine
Boron	B	5	10.811a	1808	Gay-Lussac, Thenard
Bromine	Br	35	79.904b	1826	Balard
Cadmium	Cd	48	112.40	1817	Stromeyer
Calcium	Ca	20	40.08	1808	Davy
Californium	Cf	98	251*	1950	Thompson, et al.
Carbon	C	6	12.01115a	B.C.	Unknown
Cerium	Ce	58	140.12	1803	Klaproth
Cesium	Cs	55	132.905	1860	Bunsen, Kirchhoff
Chlorine	Cl	17	35.453b	1774	Scheele
Chromium	Cr	24	51.996b	1797	Vauquelin
Cobalt	Co	27	58.9332	1735	Brandt
Copper	Cu	29	63.546b	B.C.	
Curium	Cm	96	247*	1944	Seaborg, James, Ghiorso
Dysprosium	Dy	66	162.50	1886	Boisbaudran

Chemical element	Symbol	Atomic number	Atomic weight	Year discov.	Discoverer
Einsteinium	Es	99	254*	1952	Ghiorso, et al.
Erbium	Er	68	167.26	1843	Mosander
Europium	Eu	63	151.96	1901	Demarcay
Fermium	Fm	100	257*	1953	Ghiorso, et al.
Fluorine	F	9	18.9984	1771	Scheele
Francium	Fr	87	223*	1939	Perey
Gadolinium	Gd	64	157.25	1886	Marignac
Gallium	Ga	31	69.72	1875	Boisbaudran
Germanium	Ge	32	72.59	1886	Winkler
Gold	Au	79	196.967	B.C.	unknown
Hafnium	Hf	72	178.49	1923	Coster, Hevesy
Hahnium	Ha	105	262*	1970	Ghiorso, et al.
Helium	He	2	4.0026	1868	Janssen, Lockyer
Holmium	Ho	67	164.930	1878	Soret, Delafontaine
Hydrogen	H	1	1.00797a	1766	Cavendish
Indium	In	49	114.82	1863	Reich, Richter
Iodine	I	53	126.9044	1811	Courtois
Iridium	Ir	77	192.2	1804	Tennant
Iron	Fe	26	55.847b	B.C.	unknown
Krypton	Kr	36	83.80	1898	Ramsay, Travers
Lanthanum	La	57	138.91	1839	Mosander
Lawrencium	Lr	103	262*	1961	Ghiorso, T. Sikkeland, A.E. Larsh, and R.M. Latimer
Lead	Pb	82	207.19	B.C.	unknown
Lithium	Li	3	6.939	1817	Arfvedson
Lutetium	Lu	71	174.97	1907	Welsbach, Urbain
Magnesium	Mg	12	24.312	1829	Bussy
Manganese	Mn	25	54.9380	1774	Gahn
Mendelevium	Md	101	258*	1955	Ghiorso, et al.
Mercury	Hg	80	200.59	B.C.	unknown
Molybdenum	Mo	42	95.94	1782	Hjelm
Neodymium	Nd	60	144.24	1885	Welsbach
Neon	Ne	10	20.183	1898	Ramsay, Travers
Neptunium	Np	93	237*	1940	McMillan, Abelson
Nickel	Ni	28	58.71	1751	Cronstedt
Niobium[1]	Nb	41	92.906	1801	Hatchett
Nitrogen	N	7	14.0067	1772	Rutherford
Nobelium	No	102	259*	1958	Ghiorso, et al.
Osmium	Os	76	190.2	1804	Tennant
Oxygen	O	8	15.9994a	1774	Priestley, Scheele
Palladium	Pd	46	106.4	1803	Wollaston
Phosphorus	P	15	30.9738	1669	Brand
Platinum	Pt	78	195.09	1735	Ulloa
Plutonium	Pu	94	242**	1940	Seaborg, et al.
Polonium	Po	84	210**	1898	P. and M. Curie
Potassium	K	19	39.102	1807	Davy
Praseodymium	Pr	59	140.907	1885	Welsbach
Promethium	Pm	61	147**	1945	Glendenin, Marinsky, Coryell
Protactinium	Pa	91	231*	1917	Hahn, Meitner
Radium	Ra	88	226*	1898	P. & M. Curie, Bemont
Radon	Rn	86	222*	1900	Dorn
Rhenium	Re	75	186.2	1925	Noddack, Tacke, Berg
Rhodium	Rh	45	102.905	1803	Wollaston
Rubidium	Rb	37	85.47	1861	Bunsen, Kirchhoff
Ruthenium	Ru	44	101.07	1845	Klaus
Rutherfordium	Rf	104	261*	1969	Ghiorso, et al.
Samarium	Sm	62	150.35	1879	Boisbaudran
Scandium	Sc	21	44.956	1879	Nilson
Selenium	Se	34	78.96	1817	Berzelius
Silicon	Si	14	28.086a	1823	Berzelius
Silver	Ag	47	107.868b	B.C.	unknown
Sodium	Na	11	22.9898	1807	Davy
Strontium	Sr	38	87.62	1790	Crawford
Sulfur	S	16	32.064 a	B.C.	unknown
Tantalum	Ta	73	180.948	1802	Ekeberg
Technetium	Tc	43	99**	1937	Perrier and Segre
Tellurium	Te	52	127.60	1782	Von Reichenstein
Terbium	Tb	65	158.924	1843	Mosander
Thallium	Tl	81	204.37	1861	Crookes
Thorium	Th	90	232.038	1828	Berzelius
Thulium	Tm	69	168.934	1879	Cleve
Tin	Sn	50	118.69	B.C.	unknown
Titanium	Ti	22	47.90	1791	Gregor
Tungsten (Wolfram)	W	74	183.85	1783	d'Elhujar
Uranium	U	92	238.03	1789	Klaproth
Vanadium	V	23	50.942	1830	Sefstrom
Xenon	Xe	54	131.30	1898	Ramsay, Travers
Ytterbium	Yb	70	173.04	1878	Marignac
Yttrium	Y	39	88.905	1794	Gadolin
Zinc	Zn	30	65.37	B.C.	unknown
Zirconium	Zr	40	91.22	1789	Klaproth

(1) Formerly Columbium. (a) Atomic weights so designated are known to be variable because of natural variations in isotopic composition. The observed ranges are: hydrogen ±0.0001; boron ±0.003; carbon ±0.005; oxygen ±0.0001; silicon ±0.001; sulfur ±0.003. (b) Atomic weights so designated are believed to have the following experimental uncertainties: chlorine ±0.001; chromium ±0.001; iron ±0.003; bromine ±0.001; silver ±0.001; copper ±0.001.

METEOROLOGY

National Weather Service Watches and Warnings

Source: National Weather Service, NOAA, U.S. Dept. of Commerce; *Glossary of Meteorology*, American Meteorological Society

National Weather Service forecasters issue a Severe Thunderstorm or Tornado Watch for a specific area where threatening weather is most likely to occur during the valid time of the watch. A Severe Thunderstorm Watch is issued for a specific area where severe thunderstorms are most likely. A Tornado Watch is issued when severe thunderstorms that produce tornados are likely to occur in a specific area. A Watch alerts people to check for threatening weather, make plans for action, and listen for a Tornado Warning. A Tornado Warning means that a tornado has been sighted or indicated by radar, and that safety precautions should be taken at once. A Hurricane Watch means that an existing hurricane poses a threat to coastal and inland communities, within 24-36 hours, in the area specified by the Watch. A Hurricane Warning means hurricane force winds and/or dangerously high water and exceptionally high waves are expected in a specified coastal area within 24 hours.

Tornado—A violent rotating column of air in contact with the ground and pendant from a thundercloud, usually recognized as a funnel-shaped vortex accompanied by a loud roar. With rotating winds est. up to 300 mph., on a local scale, it is the most destructive storm. Tornado paths have varied in length from a few feet to nearly 300 miles (avg. 5 mi.); diameter from a few feet to over a mile (average 220 yards); average forward speed, 30 mph.

Cyclone—An atmospheric circulation of winds rotating counterclockwise in the northern hemisphere and clockwise in the southern hemisphere. Tornadoes, hurricanes, and the lows shown on weather maps are all examples of cyclones having various sizes and intensities. Cyclones are usually accompanied by precipitation or stormy weather.

Hurricane—A severe cyclone originating over tropical ocean waters and having winds 74 miles an hour or higher. (In the western Pacific, such storms are known as typhoons.) The area of strong winds takes the form of a circle or an oval, sometimes as much as 500 miles in diameter. In the lower latitudes hurricanes usually move toward the west or northwest at 10 to 15 mph. When the center approaches 25° to 30° North Latitude, direction of motion often changes to northeast, with increased forward speed.

Blizzard—A severe weather condition characterized by strong winds bearing a great amount of snow. The National Weather Service specifies winds of 35-miles an hour or higher, and sufficient falling and/or blowing snow to frequently reduce visibility to less than 1/4 mile for a duration of at least three hours.

Severe Thunderstorm—A thunderstorm with winds of 58 mph. or greater and/or hail three-fourths of an inch or larger in diameter.

Flood—The condition that occurs when water overflows the natural or artificial confines of a stream or other body of water, or accumulates by drainage over low-lying areas.

National Weather Service Marine Warnings and Advisories

Small Craft Advisory: A Small Craft Advisory alerts mariners to sustained (exceeding two hours) weather and/or sea conditions either present or forecast, potentially hazardous to small boats. Although there is no definition of a small craft, hazardous conditions generally include winds of 18 to 33 knots and/or dangerous wave conditions. It is the responsibility of the mariner, based on his experience, location and size or type of boat, to determine if the conditions are hazardous. When a mariner becomes aware of a Small Craft Advisory, he should immediately obtain the latest marine forecast to determine the reason for the Advisory.

Gale Warning indicates that winds within the range 34 to 47 knots, not directly associated with a tropical storm, are forecast for the area.

Tropical Storm Warning indicates that winds of 34 to 63 knots are forecast in a specified coastal area in 24 hours or less. Only issued for winds produced by tropical weather systems.

Storm Warning indicates that winds 48 knots and above, no matter how high the speed, not directly associated with a tropical storm, are forecast for the area.

Hurricane Warning indicates that winds 64 knots or greater are forecast for the area. Only issued for winds produced by tropical weather systems.

Special Marine Warning: A warning for potentially hazardous weather conditions, usually of short duration (2 hours or less) and producing wind speeds of 34 knots or more, not adequately covered by existing marine warnings.

Primary sources of dissemination are commercial radio, TV, U.S. Coast Guard radio stations, and NOAA VHF-FM broadcasts. These broadcasts on 162.40 to 162.55 MHz can usually be received 20-40 miles from the transmitting antenna site, depending on terrain and quality of the receiver used. Where transmitting antennas are on high ground, the range may be somewhat greater, reaching 60 miles or more.

Speed of Winds in the U.S.

Source: National Climatic Data Center, NESDIS, NOAA, U.S. Dept. of Commerce

Miles per hour — average through 1990. High through 1990. Wind velocities in true values.

Station	Avg.	High	Station	Avg.	High	Station	Avg.	High
Albuquerque, N.M.	9.1	(b)90	Helena, Mont.	7.8	73	Mt. Washington, N.H.	35.3	231
Anchorage, Alas.	6.9	75	Honolulu, Ha.	11.4	(b)67	New Orleans, La.	8.2	(b)98
Atlanta, Ga.	9.1	60	Houston, Tex.	7.9	51	New York, N.Y.(c)	9.4	(b)70
Baltimore, Md.	9.2	80	Indianapolis, Ind.	9.6	46	Omaha, Neb.	10.6	109
Bismarck, N.D.	10.2	(b)72	Jacksonville, Fla.	8.0	(b)82	Philadelphia, Pa.	9.5	73
Boston, Mass.	12.5	(b)61	Kansas City, Mo.	10.8	(b)70	Phoenix, Ariz.	6.3	(b)86
Buffalo, N.Y.	12.0	91	Lexington, Ky.	9.3	46	Pittsburgh, Pa.	9.1	58
Cape Hatteras, N.C.	11.1	(b)110	Little Rock, Ark.	7.8	65	Portland, Ore.	7.9	88
Casper, Wyo.	12.9	81	Los Angeles, Cal.	6.2	49	St. Louis, Mo.	9.7	(b)60
Chicago, Ill.	10.3	58	Louisville, Ky.	8.3	(b)61	Salt Lake City, Ut.	8.9	71
Cleveland, Oh.	10.6	(b)74	Memphis, Tenn.	8.9	46	San Diego, Cal.	6.9	56
Dallas, Tex.	10.8	73	Miami, Fla.	9.3	(a)74	San Francisco, Cal.	8.7	47
Denver, Col.	8.7	(b)56	Milwaukee, Wis.	11.6	54	Seattle, Wash.	9.0	66
Detroit, Mich.	10.4	48	Minneapolis, Minn.	10.6	(b)92	Spokane, Wash.	8.9	59
Galveston, Tex.	11.0	(d)100	Mobile, Ala.	9.0	63	Washington, D.C.	9.4	(b)78

(a) Highest velocity ever recorded in Miami area was 132 mph, at former station in Miami Beach in September, 1926.
(b) Previous location. (c) Data for Central Park, Battery Place data through 1960, avg. 14.5, high 113. (d) Recorded before anemometer blew away. Estimated high 120.

The Meaning of "One Inch of Rain"

An acre of ground contains 43,560 square feet. Consequently, a rainfall of 1 inch over 1 acre of ground would mean a total of 6,272,640 cubic inches of water. This is equivalent of 3,630 cubic feet.

As a cubic foot of pure water weights about 62.4 pounds, the exact amount varying with the density, it follows that the weight of a uniform coating of 1 inch of rain over 1 acre of surface would be 226,512 pounds, or about 113 short tons. The weight of 1 U.S. gallon of pure water is about 8.345 pounds. Consequently a rainfall of 1 inch over 1 acre of ground would mean 27,143 gallons of water.

1990: Warmest Year on Record

NASA's Goddard Inst. recorded the average global temperature in 1990 at **59.81 degrees**, the warmest since 1880. The British Meteorological Office reported that no year had been as warm since they began keeping records in 1850, and said that 6 of the 7 warmest years of the 20th century had occurred during the 1980s.

Tides and Their Causes

Source: U.S. Dept. of Commerce, (NOAA) Natl. Oceanic & Atmospheric Admin., (NOS) Natl. Ocean Service

The tides are a natural phenomenon involving the alternating rise and fall in the large fluid bodies of the earth caused by the combined gravitational attraction of the sun and moon. The combination of these two variable force influences produces the complex recurrent cycle of the tides. Tides may occur in both oceans and seas, to a limited extent in large lakes, the atmosphere, and, to a very minute degree, in the earth itself. The period between succeeding tides varies as the result of many factors and force influences.

The tide-generating force represents the difference between (1) the centrifugal force produced by the revolution of the earth around the common center-of-gravity of the earth-moon system and (2) the gravitational attraction of the moon acting upon the earth's overlying waters. Since, on the average, the moon is only 238,852 miles from the earth compared with the sun's much greater distance of 92,956,000 miles, this closer distance outranks the much smaller mass of the moon compared with that of the sun, and the moon's tide-raising force is, accordingly, 2¹/₅ times that of the sun.

The effect of the tide-generating forces of the moon and sun acting tangentially to the earth's surface (the so-called "tractive force") tends to cause a maximum accumulation of the waters of the oceans at two diametrically opposite positions on the surface of the earth and to withdraw compensating amounts of water from all points 90° removed from the positions of these tidal bulges. As the earth rotates beneath the maxima and minima of these tide-generating forces, a sequence of two high tides, separated by two low tides, ideally is produced each day (semidiurnal tide).

Twice in each lunar month, when the sun, moon, and earth are directly aligned, with the moon between the earth and the sun (at new moon) or on the opposite side of the earth from the sun (at full moon), the sun and the moon exert their gravitational force in a mutual or additive fashion. The highest high tides and lowest low tides are produced. These are called *spring* tides. At two positions 90° in between, the gravitational forces of the moon and sun — imposed at right angles—tend to counteract each other to the greatest extent, and the range between high and low tides is reduced. These are called *neap* tides. This semi-monthly variation between the spring and neap tides is called the *phase inequality.*

The inclination of the moon's monthly orbit to the equator and the inclination of the sun during the earth's yearly orbit to the equator produce a difference in the height of succeeding high tides and in the extent of depression of succeeding low tides which is known as the diurnal inequality. In most cases, this produces a type of tide called a mixed tide. In extreme cases, these phenomena can result in only one high tide and one low each tide (diurnal tide). There are also other monthly and yearly variations in the tide due to the elliptical shape of the orbits themselves.

The datum for Charting and Predictions is (MLLW) Mean Lower Low Water. This became effective January 1989 according to the convention of 1980 which prescribed that datums on all United States coast lines would be the same. Namely (MHHW) Mean Higher High Water, (MHW) Mean High Water, (MTL) Mean Tide Level, (MSL) Mean Sea Level, (MLW) Mean Low Water, (MLLW) Mean Lower Low Water. Diurnal range of tide is the difference in height between mean higher high water and mean lower low water. Mean range of tide is the difference in height between mean high water and mean low water.

The actual range of tide in the waters of the open oceans may amount to only one to three feet. However, as the ocean tide approaches shoal waters and its effects are augmented the tidal range may be greatly increased. In Nova Scotia along the narrow channel of the Bay of Fundy, the range of tides or difference between high and low waters, may reach 43 1/2 feet or more (under spring tide conditions) due to resonant amplification.

At New Orleans, the periodic rise and fall of the diurnal tide is affected by the seasonal stages of the Mississippi River, being about 10 inches at low stage and zero at high. The Canadian Tide Tables for 1972 gave a maximum range of nearly 50 feet at Leaf Basin, Ungava Bay, Quebec.

In every case, actual high or low tide can vary considerably from the average, due to weather conditions such as strong winds, abrupt barometric pressure changes, or prolonged periods of extreme high or low pressure.

The Average Rise and Fall of Tides[1]

Places	Ft.	In.	Places	Ft.	In.	Places	Ft.	In.
Baltimore, Md.	1	8	Mobile, Ala.	1	6	San Diego, Cal.	5	9
Boston, Mass.	10	4	New London, Conn.	3	1	Sandy Hook, N.J.	5	2
Charleston, S.C.	5	10	Newport, R.I.	3	11	San Francisco, Cal.	5	10
Cristobal, Panama	1	1	New York, N.Y.	5	1	Savannah, Ga.	8	3
Eastport, Me.	19	4	Old Pt. Comfort, Va.	3	0	Seattle, Wash.	11	4
Galveston, Tex.	1	5	Philadelphia, Pa.	6	9	Tampa, Fla.	2	10
Halifax, N.S.	4	5[2]	Portland, Me.	9	11	Vancouver, B.C.	10	6
Key West, Fla.	1	10	St. John's, Nfld.	2	7[2]	Washington, D.C.	3	2

(1) Diurnal range. (2) Mean range.

Hurricane Names in 1993

Names assigned to Atlantic hurricanes, 1993 — Arlene, Bret, Cindy, Dennis, Emily, Floyd, Gert, Harvey, Irene, Jose, Katrina, Lenny, Maria, Nate, Ophelia, Philippe, Rita, Stan, Tammy, Vince, Wilma.

Names assigned to Eastern Pacific hurricanes, 1993 — Adrian, Beatriz, Calvin, Dora, Eugene, Fernanda, Greg, Hilary, Irwin, Jova, Kenneth, Lidia, Max, Norma, Otis, Pilar, Ramon, Selma, Todd, Veronica, Wiley, Xina, York, Zelda.

Explanation of Normal Temperatures

Normal temperatures listed in the tables on pages 185 and 186 are based on records of the National Weather Service for the 30-year period from 1951-1980 inclusive. To obtain the average maximum or minimum temperature for any month, the daily temperatures are added; the total is then divided by the number of days in that month.

The normal maximum temperature for January, for example, is obtained by adding the average maximums for Jan., 1951, Jan., 1952, etc., through Jan., 1980. The total is then divided by 30. The normal minimum temperature is obtained in a similar manner by adding the average minimums for each January in the 30-year period and dividing by 30. The normal temperature for January is one half of the sum for the normal maximum and minimum temperatures for that month. The mean temperature for any one day is one-half the total of the maximum and minimum temperatures for that day.

Monthly Normal Temperature and Precipitation

Source: National Climatic Data Center, NESDIS, NOAA, U.S. Dept. of Commerce

These normals are based on records for the 30-year period 1951 to 1980 inclusive. (See explanation on page 184.) For stations that did not have continuous records from the same instrument site for the entire 30 years, the means have been adjusted to the record at the present site.

Airport station; *city office stations. T, temperature in Fahrenheit; P, precipitation in inches; L, less than .05 inch.

Station	Jan. T.	Jan. P.	Feb. T.	Feb. P.	Mar. T.	Mar. P.	Apr. T.	Apr. P.	May T.	May P.	June T.	June P.	July T.	July P.	Aug. T.	Aug. P.	Sept. T.	Sept. P.	Oct. T.	Oct. P.	Nov. T.	Nov. P.	Dec. T.	Dec. P.
Albany, N.Y.	21	2.4	23	2.3	34	3.0	47	2.9	58	3.3	67	3.3	71	3.0	69	3.3	61	3.2	51	2.9	39	3.0	26	3.0
Albuquerque, N.M.	35	0.4	39	0.4	46	0.5	55	0.4	64	0.5	75	0.5	79	1.3	76	1.5	69	0.9	57	0.9	44	0.4	36	0.5
Anchorage, Alas.	13	0.8	18	0.9	24	0.7	35	0.7	46	0.6	54	1.1	58	2.0	56	2.1	48	2.5	35	1.7	22	1.1	14	1.1
Asheville, N.C.	37	3.5	39	3.6	46	5.1	56	3.8	63	4.2	70	4.2	73	4.4	73	4.8	70	4.0	56	3.3	46	3.3	39	3.5
Atlanta, Ga.	42	4.9	45	4.4	53	5.9	62	4.4	69	4.0	76	3.4	79	4.7	78	3.4	73	3.2	62	2.5	52	3.4	45	4.2
Atlantic City, N.J.	34	3.3	35	3.2	42	3.7	51	3.1	60	2.9	68	2.9	74	3.9	74	4.5	68	2.7	58	2.8	48	3.5	38	3.5
Baltimore, Md.	33	3.0	35	3.0	43	3.7	54	3.4	63	3.4	72	3.8	77	3.9	76	4.6	69	3.5	57	3.1	46	3.1	37	3.4
Barrow, Alas.	-14	0.2	-20	0.2	-16	0.2	-2	0.2	19	0.2	33	0.4	39	0.9	38	1.0	31	0.6	14	0.6	-1	0.3	-13	0.2
Birmingham, Ala.	42	5.2	46	4.7	54	6.6	63	5.0	70	4.5	77	3.7	80	5.4	80	3.9	74	4.3	62	2.7	52	3.6	45	5.0
Bismarck, N.D.	7	0.5	15	0.5	26	0.7	43	1.5	55	2.2	64	3.0	70	2.0	69	1.7	57	1.4	46	0.8	29	0.5	15	0.5
Boise, Ida.	30	1.6	36	1.1	41	1.0	49	1.2	57	1.2	66	1.0	75	0.3	72	0.4	63	0.6	52	0.8	40	1.3	32	1.3
Boston, Mass.	30	4.0	31	3.7	38	4.1	49	3.7	59	3.5	68	2.9	74	2.7	72	3.7	65	3.4	55	3.4	45	4.2	34	4.9
Buffalo, N.Y.	24	3.0	25	2.4	33	3.0	45	3.0	56	2.9	66	2.7	71	3.0	69	4.2	62	3.4	52	2.9	40	3.6	29	3.4
Burlington, Vt.	17	1.9	18	1.7	29	2.2	43	2.8	55	3.0	65	3.6	70	3.4	67	3.9	59	3.2	48	2.8	37	2.8	23	2.4
Caribou, Me.	11	2.4	13	2.1	24	2.4	37	2.6	50	2.9	60	3.2	65	4.0	63	4.0	54	3.5	43	3.1	31	3.2	16	3.1
Charleston, S.C.	49	3.3	51	3.4	57	4.4	66	2.6	73	4.4	79	6.5	82	7.3	81	6.5	77	4.9	68	2.9	59	2.2	52	3.1
Chicago, Ill.	21	1.6	26	1.3	36	2.6	49	3.7	59	3.2	69	4.1	73	3.6	72	3.5	65	3.4	54	2.3	40	2.1	28	2.1
Cleveland, Oh.	26	2.5	27	2.2	37	3.0	48	3.3	58	3.3	68	3.5	72	3.4	70	3.4	64	2.9	53	2.5	42	2.8	31	2.8
Columbus, Oh.	27	2.8	30	2.2	40	3.2	51	3.4	61	3.8	70	4.0	74	4.0	72	3.7	66	2.8	54	1.9	42	2.6	32	2.6
Dallas-Ft. Worth, Tex.	44	1.7	49	1.9	56	2.4	66	3.6	74	4.3	82	2.6	86	2.0	86	1.8	79	3.3	68	2.5	56	1.8	48	1.7
Denver, Col.	30	0.5	34	0.7	38	1.2	47	1.8	57	2.5	67	1.6	73	1.9	71	1.5	63	1.2	52	1.0	39	0.8	33	0.6
Des Moines, Ia.	19	1.0	25	1.1	35	2.2	51	3.2	62	4.0	72	4.2	76	3.2	74	4.1	65	3.1	54	2.2	39	1.5	26	1.5
Detroit, Mich.	23	1.9	26	1.7	35	2.5	47	3.2	58	2.8	68	3.4	72	3.1	71	3.2	63	2.3	52	2.1	40	2.3	29	2.5
Dodge City, Kan.	30	0.5	35	0.5	42	1.5	54	1.8	64	3.3	75	3.0	80	3.1	78	2.5	69	1.9	58	1.3	43	0.8	34	0.5
Duluth, Minn.	6	1.2	12	0.9	23	1.8	38	2.2	50	3.2	59	4.0	65	4.0	63	4.1	54	3.3	44	2.2	28	1.7	14	1.3
Eureka, Cal.*	47	7.0	49	5.2	48	5.1	49	2.9	52	1.6	55	0.6	56	0.1	57	0.4	57	0.9	54	2.7	51	5.9	48	6.2
Fairbanks, Alas.	-13	0.5	-4	0.5	9	0.4	30	0.3	48	0.6	59	1.3	62	1.8	57	1.9	45	1.1	25	0.7	4	0.7	-10	0.7
Fresno, Cal.	46	2.0	51	1.9	54	1.6	60	1.2	68	0.3	75	0.1	81	L	79	L	74	0.2	65	0.4	53	1.2	45	1.6
Galveston, Tex.*	54	3.0	56	2.3	62	2.1	69	2.6	76	3.3	81	3.5	83	3.8	83	4.4	80	5.8	73	2.6	63	3.2	57	3.6
Grand Junction, Col.	26	0.6	34	0.5	42	0.8	52	0.7	62	0.8	72	0.4	79	0.5	76	0.9	67	0.7	55	0.9	40	0.6	28	0.6
Gr. Rapids, Mich.	22	1.9	24	1.5	33	2.5	46	3.6	58	3.0	67	3.9	71	3.0	70	3.5	62	3.1	51	2.9	39	2.9	27	2.6
Hartford, Conn.	25	3.5	28	3.2	37	4.2	49	4.0	59	3.4	69	3.4	73	3.1	71	4.0	63	3.9	52	3.5	42	4.1	29	4.2
Helena, Mon.	18	0.7	26	0.4	32	0.7	42	1.0	52	1.7	60	2.0	68	1.0	66	1.2	56	0.8	45	0.7	31	0.5	23	0.6
Honolulu, Ha.	73	3.8	73	2.7	74	3.5	76	1.5	78	1.2	79	0.5	80	0.5	81	0.6	81	0.6	80	1.9	77	3.2	74	3.4
Houston, Tex.	51	3.2	55	3.3	61	2.7	69	4.2	75	4.7	81	4.0	83	3.3	83	3.7	78	4.9	70	3.7	60	3.4	54	3.7
Huron, S.D.	11	0.4	18	0.8	29	1.2	46	2.0	57	2.7	68	3.3	74	2.3	72	2.0	61	1.4	49	1.4	32	0.7	19	0.5
Indianapolis, Ind.	26	2.7	30	2.5	40	3.6	52	3.7	63	3.7	72	4.0	75	4.3	73	3.5	67	2.7	55	2.5	42	3.0	32	3.0
Jackson, Miss.	46	5.0	49	4.9	56	5.9	65	5.9	73	4.8	79	2.9	82	4.4	81	3.7	76	3.6	65	2.6	55	4.2	49	5.4
Jacksonville, Fla.	53	3.1	55	3.5	61	3.7	68	3.3	74	4.9	79	5.4	81	6.5	81	7.2	78	7.3	70	3.4	61	1.9	55	2.6
Juneau, Alas.	22	3.7	28	3.7	31	3.3	39	2.9	46	3.4	53	3.0	56	4.1	55	5.0	49	6.4	42	7.7	33	5.2	27	4.7
Kansas City, Mo.	26	1.0	32	1.0	42	2.1	55	2.7	65	3.4	76	4.1	79	3.5	77	3.2	68	3.3	58	2.5	43	1.2	32	1.1
Knoxville, Tenn.	38	4.7	42	4.2	50	5.5	60	3.9	67	3.7	74	4.0	78	4.3	77	3.0	72	3.0	60	2.7	49	3.8	41	4.6
Lander, Wyo.	20	0.5	26	0.6	32	1.1	42	2.2	53	2.7	62	1.5	71	0.7	69	0.5	58	0.9	47	1.2	31	0.8	23	0.5
Lexington, Ky.	32	3.6	35	3.3	44	4.8	55	4.0	64	4.2	72	4.3	76	5.0	75	4.0	69	3.3	57	2.3	45	3.3	36	3.8
Little Rock, Ark.	40	3.9	44	3.8	52	4.7	62	5.4	71	5.3	79	3.7	82	3.6	81	3.1	74	4.3	63	2.8	51	4.4	43	4.2
Los Angeles, Cal.*	57	3.7	59	3.0	60	2.4	62	1.2	65	0.2	69	L	74	L	75	0.1	73	0.3	69	0.2	63	1.9	58	2.0
Louisville, Ky.	33	3.4	36	3.2	45	4.7	57	4.1	65	4.2	74	3.6	78	4.1	76	3.3	70	3.6	58	2.6	46	3.5	37	3.5
Marquette, Mich.*	12	2.0	14	1.9	23	2.8	37	3.6	50	4.0	60	3.9	65	3.2	63	3.3	54	3.9	44	3.3	30	2.9	18	2.4
Memphis, Tenn.	40	4.6	44	4.3	52	5.4	63	5.8	71	5.1	79	3.6	82	4.0	81	3.7	74	3.6	63	2.4	51	4.2	43	4.9
Miami, Fla.	67	2.1	68	2.1	72	1.9	75	3.1	79	6.5	81	9.2	83	6.0	83	7.0	82	8.1	78	7.1	73	2.7	69	1.9
Milwaukee, Wis.	19	1.6	23	1.3	32	2.6	45	3.4	55	2.6	65	3.6	71	3.5	69	3.1	62	2.9	51	2.3	37	2.0	25	2.0
Minneapolis, Minn.	11	0.8	18	0.9	29	1.7	46	2.1	59	3.2	68	4.1	73	3.5	71	3.6	61	2.5	50	1.9	33	1.3	19	0.9
Mobile, Ala.	51	4.6	54	4.9	60	6.5	68	5.4	75	5.5	81	5.1	82	7.7	82	6.8	78	6.6	69	2.6	59	3.7	53	5.4
Moline, Ill.	20	1.6	25	1.3	36	2.8	50	4.0	61	4.2	71	4.3	75	4.9	73	3.8	65	3.7	54	2.7	39	2.0	26	1.9
Nashville, Tenn.	37	4.5	40	4.0	49	5.6	60	4.8	68	4.6	76	3.7	79	3.8	78	3.4	72	3.7	60	2.6	49	3.5	41	4.6
Newark, N.J.	31	3.1	33	3.1	41	4.2	52	3.6	62	3.6	72	2.9	77	3.9	76	4.3	68	3.7	57	3.1	47	3.6	36	3.4
New Orleans, La.	52	5.0	55	5.2	61	4.7	69	4.5	75	5.1	80	4.6	82	6.7	82	6.0	79	5.9	69	2.7	60	4.1	55	5.3
New York, N.Y.*	32	3.2	33	3.1	41	4.2	53	3.8	62	3.8	71	3.2	77	3.8	75	4.0	68	3.7	58	3.4	47	4.1	36	3.8
Nome, Alas.	9	0.8	3	0.5	7	0.6	18	0.6	36	0.5	45	1.2	51	2.2	50	3.1	42	2.3	28	1.3	16	0.9	4	0.7
Norfolk, Va.	40	3.7	41	3.3	49	3.9	58	2.9	67	3.8	76	3.5	78	5.2	78	5.3	72	4.4	61	3.4	52	2.9	44	3.2
Okla. City, Okla.	36	1.0	41	1.3	49	2.1	60	2.9	68	5.5	77	3.9	82	3.0	81	2.4	73	3.4	62	2.7	49	1.5	40	1.2
Omaha, Neb.	19	0.8	25	0.9	35	1.9	50	2.9	62	4.3	71	4.1	76	3.6	74	4.1	64	2.5	54	2.1	38	1.3	26	0.8
Pago Pago, Amer. Samoa.	81	13	81	13	81	11	81	11	80	11	80	8.6	79	6.5	79	7.1	79	6.7	80	11	80	11	81	14
Philadelphia, Pa.	31	3.2	33	2.8	42	3.9	53	3.5	63	3.2	72	3.9	77	3.9	75	4.1	68	3.4	57	2.8	46	3.3	36	3.5
Phoenix, Ariz.	52	0.7	56	0.6	61	0.8	68	0.3	77	0.1	87	0.2	92	0.7	90	1.0	85	0.6	73	0.6	61	0.5	53	0.8
Pittsburgh, Pa.	27	2.9	29	2.4	39	3.6	50	3.3	60	3.5	68	3.3	72	3.8	71	3.3	64	2.8	53	2.5	42	2.3	31	2.6
Portland, Me.	22	3.8	23	3.6	32	4.0	43	3.9	53	3.3	62	3.1	68	2.8	67	2.8	59	3.3	49	3.8	38	4.7	26	4.5
Portland, Ore.	39	6.2	43	3.9	46	3.6	50	2.3	57	2.1	63	1.5	68	0.5	67	1.1	63	1.6	54	3.1	46	5.2	41	6.4
Providence, R.I.	28	4.1	29	3.7	37	4.3	48	4.0	58	3.5	67	2.8	73	3.0	71	4.0	64	3.5	53	3.8	43	4.2	32	4.5
Raleigh, N.C.	40	3.6	42	3.4	49	3.7	59	2.9	67	3.7	74	3.7	78	4.4	77	4.4	71	3.3	60	2.7	50	2.9	42	3.1
Rapid City, S.D.	21	0.4	26	0.6	33	1.0	45	2.0	56	2.6	65	3.3	73	2.1	71	1.4	61	1.0	50	0.8	35	0.5	26	0.5
Reno, Nev.	32	1.2	37	1.0	41	0.7	46	0.5	55	0.7	62	0.3	70	0.3	67	0.3	60	0.3	50	0.3	40	0.6	33	1.2
Richmond, Va.	37	3.2	39	3.1	47	3.6	58	2.9	66	3.6	74	3.6	78	5.1	77	5.0	70	3.5	59	3.7	49	3.3	40	3.4
St. Louis, Mo.	29	1.7	34	2.1	43	3.3	56	3.6	66	3.5	75	3.7	79	3.6	77	2.6	70	2.7	58	2.3	45	2.5	34	2.2
Salt Lake City, Ut.	29	1.4	34	1.3	41	1.7	49	2.2	59	1.5	68	1.0	78	0.7	75	0.9	65	0.9	53	1.1	40	1.2	30	1.4
San Antonio, Tex.	50	1.6	54	1.9	62	1.3	70	2.7	76	3.7	82	3.0	85	1.9	84	2.7	79	3.8	70	2.9	60	2.3	53	1.4
San Diego, Cal.	57	2.1	58	1.4	59	1.6	61	0.8	63	0.2	66	0.1	70	L	72	0.1	71	0.2	68	0.3	62	1.1	57	1.4
San Francisco, Cal.	49	4.7	52	3.2	53	2.6	55	1.5	58	0.3	61	0.1	62	L	63	0.1	64	0.2	61	1.1	55	2.4	49	3.6
San Juan, P.R.	77	3.0	77	2.0	78	2.3	80	3.6	79	5.6	80	4.7	82	4.9	82	5.9	82	6.0	81	5.9	80	5.6	78	4.7
Sault Ste. Marie, Mich.*	13	2.2	14	1.7	24	2.0	38	2.4	50	2.9	58	3.3	64	3.0	63	3.5	55	3.9	45	2.9	33	3.2	20	2.6
Savannah, Ga.	49	3.1	52	3.2	58	3.8	66	3.2	73	4.6	79	5.7	81	7.4	81	6.7	77	5.2	67	2.3	58	1.9	51	2.8
Seattle, Wash.	39	6.0	43	4.2	44	3.6	49	2.4	55	1.6	60	1.4	65	0.7	64	1.3	60	2.0	52	3.4	45	5.6	41	6.3
Spokane, Wash.	26	2.5	32	1.6	38	1.4	46	1.1	54	1.4	62	1.2	70	0.5	68	0.7	60	0.7	48	1.1	35	2.1	29	2.5
Springfield, Mo.	32	1.6	36	2.1	45	3.4	56	4.0	65	4.3	73	4.7	78	3.6	77	2.8	70	4.2	58	3.2	45	2.9	36	2.6
Syracuse, N.Y.	23	2.6	24	2.7	33	3.1	46	3.3	57	3.2	66	3.6	71	3.8	69	3.8	62	3.3	51	3.1	41	3.5	28	3.2
Tampa, Fla.	60	2.2	61	3.0	66	3.5	72	1.8	77	3.4	81	5.3	82	7.4	82	7.6	81	6.2	74	2.3	67	1.9	61	2.1
Washington, D.C	31	2.8	34	2.6	42	3.4	53	3.1	62	3.6	71	4.2	76	3.8	74	4.2	67	3.3	55	3.0	45	3.0	35	3.3
Wilmington, Del.	31	3.1	33	3.0	42	3.9	52	3.4	62	3.2	71	3.5	76	3.9	75	4.0	68	3.6	56	2.9	46	3.3	36	3.5

Normal Temperatures, Highs, Lows, Precipitation

Source: National Climatic Data Center, NESDIS, NOAA, U.S. Dept. of Commerce

These normals are based on records for the thirty-year period 1951-1980. (See explanation on page 184.) The extreme temperatures (through 1990) are listed for the stations shown and may not agree with the states records shown on page 188-189.

Airport stations; * designates city office stations. The minus (−) sign indicates temperatures below zero. Fahrenheit thermometer registration.

State	Station	Normal temperature — January Max.	January Min.	July Max.	July Min.	Extreme temperature — Highest	Lowest	Normal annual precipitation (inches)
Alabama	Mobile	61	41	91	73	104	3	64.64
Alabama	Montgomery	57	36	92	72	105	0	49.16
Alaska	Juneau	27	16	64	47	90	−22	53.15
Arizona	Phoenix	65	39	105	80	118	17	7.11
Arkansas	Little Rock	50	30	93	71	112	−5	49.20
California	Los Angeles*	67	48	84	64	110	28	14.85
California	San Francisco	55	42	71	53	106	20	19.71
Colorado	Denver	43	16	88	59	104	−30	15.31
Connecticut	Hartford	34	17	85	62	102	−26	44.39
Delaware	Wilmington	39	23	86	66	102	−14	41.38
Dist. of Col.	Washington	43	28	88	70	104	−5	39.00
Florida	Jacksonville	65	42	91	72	105	7	52.76
Florida	Key West	72	66	89	80	95	41	39.42
Florida	Miami	75	59	89	76	98	30	57.55
Georgia	Atlanta	51	33	88	69	105	−8	48.61
Hawaii	Honolulu	80	65	87	73	94	53	23.47
Idaho	Boise	37	23	91	59	111	−23	11.71
Illinois	Chicago	29	14	83	63	104	−27	33.34
Indiana	Indianapolis	34	18	85	65	104	−23	39.12
Iowa	Des Moines	27	10	86	66	108	−24	30.83
Iowa	Dubuque	24	7	82	62	101	−28	38.59
Kansas	Wichita	40	19	93	70	113	−21	28.61
Kentucky	Louisville	41	24	88	68	105	−20	43.56
Louisiana	New Orleans	62	43	91	74	102	11	59.74
Maine	Portland	31	12	79	57	103	−39	43.52
Maryland	Baltimore	41	24	87	67	105	−7	41.84
Massachusetts	Boston	36	23	82	65	102	−12	43.84
Michigan	Detroit	31	16	83	61	104	−21	30.97
Michigan	Sault Ste. Marie*	21	5	75	52	98	−36	33.48
Minnesota	Minn.-St. Paul	20	2	83	63	105	−34	26.36
Mississippi	Jackson	57	35	93	68	106	2	52.82
Missouri	St. Louis	38	20	89	69	107	−18	33.91
Montana	Helena	28	8	84	52	105	−42	11.37
Nebraska	Omaha	30	10	89	67	114	−23	30.34
Nevada	Las Vegas	55	33	105	76	116	8	4.19
New Hampshire	Concord	31	9	83	56	102	−37	36.53
New Jersey	Atlantic City	41	23	84	65	106	−11	41.93
New Mexico	Albuquerque	47	22	93	65	105	−17	8.12
New Mexico	Roswell	55	27	94	69	109	−9	9.70
New York	Albany	30	12	83	60	100	−28	35.74
New York	New York-La Guardia	37	26	84	69	107	−3	42.82
No. Carolina	Charlotte	50	31	88	69	104	−5	43.16
No. Carolina	Raleigh	50	29	88	67	105	−9	41.76
No. Dakota	Bismarck	18	−4	84	56	109	−44	15.36
Ohio	Cincinnati-Greater	37	20	86	65	102	−25	40.14
Ohio	Cleveland	33	19	82	61	104	−19	35.40
Oklahoma	Oklahoma City	47	25	94	71	110	−8	30.89
Oregon	Portland	44	34	80	56	107	−3	37.39
Pennsylvania	Harrisburg	37	22	86	65	107	−9	39.09
Pennsylvania	Philadelphia	39	24	86	67	104	−7	41.42
Rhode Island	Block Island	37	25	76	64	92	−4	41.91
So. Carolina	Charleston	59	37	89	72	104	6	51.59
So. Dakota	Huron	22	0	87	61	112	−39	18.66
So. Dakota	Rapid City	32	9	87	59	110	−29	16.27
Tennessee	Nashville	46	28	90	69	107	−17	48.49
Texas	Amarillo	49	22	91	66	108	−14	19.10
Texas	Galveston*	59	48	87	79	101	8	40.24
Texas	Houston	62	41	94	73	107	7	44.76
Utah	Salt Lake City	37	20	93	62	107	−30	15.31
Vermont	Burlington	25	8	81	59	101	−30	33.69
Virginia	Norfolk	48	32	90	70	104	−3	45.22
Washington	Seattle-Tacoma	44	34	75	54	99	0	38.60
Washington	Spokane	31	20	84	55	108	−25	16.71
West Virginia	Huntington	41	25	86	65	102	−16	40.74
Wisconsin	Madison	25	7	83	58	104	−37	30.84
Wisconsin	Milwaukee	26	11	80	61	103	−26	30.94
Wyoming	Cheyenne	37	15	83	55	100	−34	13.31
Puerto Rico	San Juan	83	70	88	76	98	60	53.99

Mean Annual Snowfall (inches) based on record through 1980: Boston, Mass. 42; Sault Ste. Marie, Mich., 113; Albany, N.Y. 65.2; Rochester, N.Y. 89.2; Burlington, Vt., 78.6; Cheyenne, Wyo., 53.3; Juneau, Alas. 105.8.

Wettest Spot: Mount Waialeale, Ha., on the island of Kauai, is the rainiest place in the world, according to the National Geographic Society, with an average annual rainfall of 460 inches.

Highest Temperature: A temperature of 136° F. observed at Azizia, Tripolitania in northern Africa on Sept. 13, 1922, is generally accepted as the world's highest temperature recorded under standard conditions.

The record high in the United States was 134° in Death Valley, Cal., July 10, 1913.

Lowest Temperature: A record low temperature of −128.6° F. was recorded at the Soviet Antarctica station Vostok on July 21, 1983.

The record low in the United States was −80° at Prospect Creek, Alas., Jan. 23, 1971.

The lowest official temperature on the North American continent was recorded at 81 degrees below zero in February, 1947, at a lonely airport in the Yukon called Snag.

These are the meteorological champions—the official temperature extremes—but there are plenty of other claimants to thermometer fame. However, sun readings are unofficial records, since meteorological data to qualify officially must be taken on instruments in a sheltered and ventilated location.

Annual Climatological Data

Source: National Climatic Data Center, NESDIS, NOAA, U.S. Dept. of Commerce

1991		Temperature °F				Precipitation[1]			Sleet or snow			Fastest Wind		No. of days			
Station	Elev. ft.	Highest	Date	Lowest	Date	Total (in.)	Greatest in 24 hrs.	Date	Total (in.)	Greatest in 24 hours.	Date	MPH	Date	Clear*	Cloudy*	Prec. .01 in. or more	Snow, sleet 1 in. or more
Albany, N.Y.	275	97	7/20	−4	1/22	35.72	2.26	11/22	34.0	8.2	1/11	41	12/14	60	176	125	11
Albuquerque, N.M.	5311	101	6/25	18	12/3	11.59	1.67	11/15	7.8	2.5	10/30	49	3/26	158	101	63	3
Anchorage, Alas.	114	75	6/20	−14	2/7	17.31	1.53	8/16	82.9	11.2	10/13	29	1/20	53	256	125	25
Asheville, N.C.	2140	92	9/15	4	2/16	43.66	3.73	3/28	4.5	3.1	3/8	29	3/10	73	171	139	2
Atlanta, Ga.	1010	97	9/15	13	2/16	55.85	4.22	6/18	2.1	2.1	1/24	32	5/5	88	172	125	1
Atlantic City, N.J.	11	99	7/21	2	3/9	37.31	3.01	8/18	—	—	—	35	11/10	—	—	99	0
Baltimore, Md.	148	102	7/23	12	1/23	30.16	2.36	3/23	4.6	2.1	1/11	33	12/14	95	142	100	2
Barrow, Alas.	31	66	8/13	−45	2/8	1.75	0.26	10/21	26.6	2.7	10/21	44	1/29	127	180	59	8
Birmingham, Ala.	678	98	8/6	12	2/16	53.49	2.69	9/24	T	T	11/8	—	—	—	—	130	0
Bismarck, N.D.	1647	104	7/17	−21	1/4	16.76	2.16	9/7	61.7	14.3	10/28	41	12/13	89	183	92	11
Boise, Ida.	2838	103	7/12	−12	1/5	9.47	0.64	5/17	6.6	1.2	11/24	39	5/24	114	161	76	3
Boston, Mass.	15	99	7/21	4	1/22	42.25	3.32	4/20	23.7	8.5	1/11	47	8/19	91	176	117	10
Buffalo, N.Y.	705	90	5/23	2	12/19	40.20	2.09	4/21	81.0	7.5	3/3	46	3/28	65	184	165	27
Burlington, Vt.	332	96	7/20	−9	1/25	32.52	1.79	10/5	42.1	8.7	1/11	33	7/19	53	204	149	14
Caribou, Me.	624	95	7/20	−23	1/26	35.31	2.80	8/19	89.2	6.8	12/3	35	6/28	—	—	160	29
Charleston, S.C.	40	98	7/14	19	2/16	49.67	2.78	7/6	T	T	2/15	40	6/23	74	174	131	0
Chicago, Ill.	658	101	8/2	−3	1/22	35.02	2.64	10/3	29.1	6.0	12/2	39	3/27	78	165	115	6
Cleveland, Oh.	777	97	7/20	−1	1/22	32.67	1.38	9/3	52.6	9.0	2/14	40	4/9	68	191	148	18
Columbus, Oh.	812	99	8/2	4	2/16	32.74	1.80	12/2	14.1	3.5	3/12	29	12/14	57	192	140	3
Dallas, Tex.	551	101	7/18	23	1/31	53.54	4.22	12/20	0.3	0.3	1/30	44	8/30	107	174	92	0
Denver, Co.	5283	100	6/25	−4	1/26	20.32	2.03	8/2	72.2	10.9	11/17	41	3/11	116	119	105	22
Des Moines, Ia.	938	96	7/22	−9	1/30	39.77	2.57	4/18	26.4	8.1	11/22	37	11/30	105	157	122	8
Detroit, Mich.	633	96	7/20	2	2/16	29.64	1.97	5/25	29.0	5.4	2/14	43	4/15	75	174	144	14
Dodge City, Kan.	2582	107	7/6	1	1/30	12.72	1.02	11/15	12.2	4.1	10/31	61	3/27	130	127	63	3
Duluth, Minn.	1428	92	7/17	−24	1/7	43.44	3.62	9/6	111.7	24.1	11/1	32	6/29	84	183	142	33
Fairbanks, Alas.	436	94	6/21	−45	1/15	9.40	1.17	3/24	94.8	10.2	3/24	31	1/25	67	205	113	28
Fresno, Cal.	328	112	7/5	27	1/1	10.49	1.52	3/17	T	T	3/25	30	5/16	222	74	34	0
Galveston, Tex.	7	95	8/19	36	11/9	59.08	4.51	2/4	T	T	5/4	—	—	—	—	119	0
Grand Rapids, Mich.	784	94	7/20	−1	1/24	44.93	2.63	4/8	93.5	10.4	11/3	44	11/30	76	194	145	29
Hartford, Conn.	169	101	7/21	1	1/26	47.26	4.05	8/19	28.4	8.7	1/11	35	7/21	87	167	120	8
Helena, Mont.	3828	98	8/10	−19	1/29	11.92	0.98	6/19	57.2	10.7	12/12	45	10/16	84	160	92	16
Honolulu, Ha.	7	93	9/25	55	2/26	17.94	2.60	10/15	0.0	0.0	—	28	3/16	132	73	86	0
Houston, Tex.	96	98	7/30	28	11/4	61.09	4.04	12/21	0.0	0.0	—	36	4/14	54	212	134	0
Huron, S.D.	1281	106	8/25	−22	1/3	23.40	3.21	6/1	27.4	9.6	2/17	37	4/11	95	151	70	8
Indianapolis, Ind.	792	96	9/13	0	1/22	37.53	2.96	10/25	11.1	2.2	1/26	38	3/28	82	180	124	4
Jackson, Miss.	291	99	8/2	18	2/16	63.06	4.69	3/28	T	T	11/8	35	4/11	73	184	131	0
Jacksonville, Fla.	26	98	7/22	25	2/16	79.63	4.73	9/29	T	T	3/2	39	2/15	53	179	134	0
Kansas City, Mo.	1014	103	8/2	−6	1/30	28.70	1.98	10/2	18.1	6.2	1/25	39	3/22	116	139	113	7
Knoxville, Tenn.	979	96	8/6	8	2/16	58.6	3.86	12/1	2.1	1.2	2/25	29	3/27	82	165	122	1
Lander, Wyo.	5557	98	7/14	−14	1/29	14.70	1.25	5/14	106.6	15.4	4/11	46	3/4	112	153	77	24
Lexington, Ky.	966	97	8/3	4	2/16	41.80	3.32	12/2	5.2	2.1	2/14	33	7/8	71	182	124	3
Little Rock, Ark.	257	101	7/23	18	1/1	59.65	4.27	1/5	T	T	12/19	—	—	—	—	124	0
Los Angeles, Cal.	97	107	10/10	41	3/16	15.59	3.21	2/27	—	—	—	—	—	—	—	29	0
Louisville, Ky.	477	100	8/3	7	2/16	38.15	2.19	7/9	2.6	0.6	2/25	33	3/28	86	180	128	0
Marquette, Mich.	1415	94	6/27	−20	1/30	37.07	1.76	11/23	174.1	19.1	11/23	—	—	—	—	168	45
Memphis, Tenn.	258	100	8/5	19	2/16	59.11	3.50	11/19	1.6	1.0	3/29	30	2/14	94	184	108	1
Miami, Fla.	7	95	8/20	41	2/16	71.42	8.59	10/8	0.0	0.0	—	37	8/10	51	118	160	0
Milwaukee, Wis.	672	97	7/19	−3	1/25	39.35	2.42	10/24	38.6	9.3	12/2	40	7/7	69	187	127	10
Minneapolis, Minn.	834	95	6/28	−14	1/25	36.69	2.10	11/1	88.7	21.0	11/1	35	9/25	72	194	145	21
Mobile, Ala.	211	96	7/14	22	2/16	81.67	3.96	5/25	T	T	5/6	49	7/2	79	178	141	0
Moline, Ill.	582	99	8/2	−9	1/22	34.49	2.26	10/3	25.7	5.9	1/4	43	3/23	97	164	119	8
Nashville, Tenn.	590	100	7/23	7	2/16	46.94	3.10	9/8	1.7	1.1	3/29	35	4/9	72	174	110	1
Newark, N.J.	7	102	7/21	9	1/22	43.76	2.83	3/3	14.4	5.7	1/11	35	12/14	95	137	118	3
New Orleans, La.	4	98	7/15	29	11/5	102.37	4.26	1/10	T	T	4/25	—	—	64	189	133	0
New York, N.Y.	132	99	7/21	10	1/22	38.73	3.41	8/20	15.2	6.6	2/26	39	12/14	104	135	116	2
Norfolk, Va.	24	100	7/21	19	1/22	42.92	5.90	4/20	T	T	12/21	35	3/2	98	159	105	0
Oklahoma City, Okla.	1285	100	8/8	11	11/3	43.74	4.08	9/2	3.1	1.6	11/2	40	6/13	124	151	100	1
Omaha, Neb.	997	96	7/5	−8	1/7	37.28	2.75	7/8	32.5	5.9	11/1	35	3/27	104	146	106	10
Philadelphia, Pa.	5	100	6/16	13	1/22	36.22	2.81	7/12	8.2	5.0	1/7	35	12/14	94	137	104	1
Phoenix, Ariz.	1110	113	8/8	36	12/2	8.35	1.12	10/27	T	T	3/27	35	7/28	199	73	37	0
Pittsburgh, Pa.	1137	95	8/29	4	1/22	32.02	2.18	6/30	17.8	2.4	3/13	35	12/14	59	188	137	3
Portland, Me.	43	98	6/28	−2	12/20	57.14	7.83	8/18	47.9	9.0	12/17	40	8/19	81	178	122	12
Portland, Ore.	21	100	7/23	20	1/5	33.55	1.79	6/19	0.6	0.6	1/6	38	3/3	86	212	133	0
Providence, R.I.	51	102	7/21	4	1/23	45.69	3.06	4/21	22.5	5.3	3/14	41	8/19	88	168	121	9
Raleigh, N.C.	434	96	9/14	14	12/20	35.46	2.68	7/10	T	T	11/9	29	12/3	87	152	106	0
Rapid City, S.D.	3162	103	8/27	−12	1/29	17.29	0.95	4/25	45.6	6.5	4/11	52	9/21	115	130	109	15
Reno, Nev.	4404	102	7/4	5	1/1	5.15	0.54	3/3	12.6	4.0	11/14	46	3/4	152	120	46	3
Richmond, Va.	164	100	6/16	16	1/23	35.78	2.98	6/22	2.0	1.9	2/26	30	8/20	92	164	107	1
Scottsbluff, Neb.	3957	102	7/17	−10	1/29	14.34	2.13	5/15	27.2	4.8	10/28	40	3/3	109	131	94	7
St. Louis, Mo.	535	102	8/3	8	11/8	33.48	2.47	7/10	7.9	3.9	11/6	38	3/27	96	183	109	3
Salt Lake City, Ut.	4221	101	7/5	−4	1/2	17.79	1.57	9/7	48.7	6.3	4/27	49	3/25	109	159	98	17
San Antonio, Tex.	788	103	7/31	27	11/24	42.76	6.90	12/18	T	T	5/3	28	3/2	68	171	108	0
San Diego, Cal.	13	94	8/12	42	12/2	13.51	1.99	3/1	0.0	0.0	—	—	—	125	99	37	0
San Francisco, Cal.	8	91	7/1	34	1/1	15.97	1.67	10/25	0.0	0.0	—	39	5/17	155	114	53	0
Sault Ste. Marie, Mich.	721	93	7/18	−12	2/15	33.20	1.77	9/14	107.7	7.7	4/9	35	3/28	67	204	172	35
Savannah, Ga.	46	98	8/5	21	2/16	68.42	3.66	7/30	T	T	2/15	40	3/3	90	165	118	0
Seattle, Wash.	400	99	7/23	26	12/15	35.42	3.32	4/3	2.9	2.5	3/4	—	—	68	228	128	1
Spokane, Wash.	2356	95	8/19	−2	1/4	14.45	0.76	3/2	34.8	6.1	1/6	54	10/16	99	172	109	13
Springfield, Mo.	1268	100	8/2	7	11/8	37.59	2.65	5/13	6.7	4.6	2/24	39	3/27	102	169	109	2
Syracuse, N.Y.	410	96	7/20	−4	2/12	37.05	1.96	8/9	107.8	17.3	12/4	52	5/1	80	192	168	27
Tampa, Fla.	19	96	9/7	33	2/16	43.16	3.98	7/12	0.0	0.0	—	31	1/19	90	116	115	0
Washington, D.C.	10	101	7/21	8	12/20	34.02	4.34	6/3	9.9	4.1	1/7	31	12/14	88	165	111	4
Wilmington, Del.	74	99	7/23	13	1/22	39.82	2.71	8/9	6.9	4.0	1/7	43	6/30	106	146	107	2

* To get partly cloudy days deduct the total of clear and cloudy days from 365 (1 yr.). T—trace. (1) Date shown is the starting date of the storm (in some cases it lasted more than one day).

Record Temperatures by States Through 1990

Source: National Climatic Data Center, NESDIS, NOAA, U.S. Dept. of Commerce

State	Lowest °F	Highest	Latest date	Station	Approximate elevation in feet
Alabama	−27		Jan. 30, 1966	New Market	760
		112	*Sept. 5, 1925*	*Centerville*	*345*
Alaska	−80		Jan. 23, 1971	Prospect Creek Camp	1,100
		100	*June 27, 1915*	*Fort Yukon*	*419*
Arizona	−40		Jan. 7, 1971	Hawley Lake	8,180
		127	*July 7, 1905* [1]	*Parker*	*345*
Arkansas	−29		Feb. 13, 1905	Pond	1,250
		120	*Aug. 10, 1936*	*Ozark*	*396*
California	−45		Jan. 20, 1937	Boca	5,532
		134	*July 10, 1913*	*Greenland Ranch*	*−178*
Colorado	−61		Feb. 1, 1985	Maybell	5,920
		118	*July 11, 1888*	*Bennett*	*5,484*
Connecticut	−32		Feb. 16, 1943	Falls Village	585
		105	*July 22, 1926*	*Waterbury*	*400*
Delaware	−17		Jan. 17, 1893	Millsboro	20
		110	*July 21, 1930*	*Millsboro*	*20*
Dist. of Col.	−15		Feb. 11, 1899	Washington	112
		106	*July 20, 1930*	*Washington*	*112*
Florida	−2		Feb. 13, 1899	Tallahassee	193
		109	*June 29, 1931*	*Monticello*	*207*
Georgia	−17		Jan. 27, 1940	CCC Camp F-16	1,000
		112	*Jul. 24, 1952*	*Louisville*	*132*
Hawaii	12		May 17, 1979	Mauna Kea	13,770
		100	*Apr. 27, 1931*	*Pahala*	*850*
Idaho	−60		Jan. 16, 1943	Island Park Dam	6,285
		118	*July 28, 1934*	*Orofino*	*1,027*
Illinois	−35		Jan. 22, 1930	Mount Carroll	817
		117	*July 14, 1954*	*E. St. Louis*	*410*
Indiana	−35		Feb. 2, 1951	Greensburg	954
		116	*July 14, 1936*	*Collegeville*	*672*
Iowa	−47		Jan. 12, 1912	Washta	1,157
		118	*July 20, 1934*	*Keokuk*	*614*
Kansas	−40		Feb. 13, 1905	Lebanon	1,812
		121	*July 24, 1936* [1]	*Alton (near)*	*1,651*
Kentucky	−34		Jan. 28, 1963	Cynthiana	684
		114	*July 28, 1930*	*Greensburg*	*581*
Louisiana	−16		Feb. 13, 1899	Minden	194
		114	*Aug. 10, 1936*	*Plain Dealing*	*268*
Maine	−48		Jan. 19, 1925	Van Buren	510
		105	*July 10, 1911* [1]	*North Bridgton*	*450*
Maryland	−40		Jan. 13, 1912	Oakland	2,461
		109	*July 10, 1936* [1]	*Cumberland and Frederick*	*623-325*
Massachusetts	−35		Jan. 12, 1981	Chester	640
		107	*Aug. 2, 1975*	*Chester and New Bedford*	*120-640*
Michigan	−51		Feb. 9, 1934	Vanderbilt	785
		112	*July 13, 1936*	*Mio*	*963*
Minnesota	−59		Feb. 16, 1903 [1]	Pokegama Dam	1,280
		114	*July 6, 1936* [1]	*Moorhead*	*904*
Mississippi	−19		Jan. 30, 1966	Corinth	420
		115	*July 29, 1930*	*Holly Springs*	*600*
Missouri	−40		Feb. 13, 1905	Warsaw	700
		118	*July 14, 1954* [1]	*Warsaw and Union*	*687-560*
Montana	−70		Jan. 20, 1954	Rogers Pass	5,470
		117	*July 5, 1937*	*Medicine Lake*	*1,950*
Nebraska	−47		Feb. 12, 1899	Camp Clarke	3,700
		118	*July 24, 1936* [1]	*Minden*	*2,169*
Nevada	−50		Jan. 8, 1937	San Jacinto	5,200
		122	*June 23, 1954* [1]	*Overton*	*1,240*
New Hampshire	−46		Jan. 28 1925	Pittsburgh	1,575
		106	*July 4, 1911*	*Nashua*	*125*
New Jersey	−34		Jan. 5, 1904	River Vale	70
		110	*July 10, 1936*	*Runyon*	*18*
New Mexico	−50		Feb. 1, 1951	Gavilan	7,350
		116	*July 14, 1934* [1]	*Orogrande*	*4,171*
New York	−52		Feb. 18, 1979	Old Forge	1,720
		108	*July 22, 1926*	*Troy*	*35*
North Carolina	−34		Jan. 21, 1985	Mt. Mitchell	6,525
		110	*Aug. 21, 1983*	*Fayetteville*	*213*
North Dakota	−60		Feb. 15, 1936	Parshall	1,929
		121	*July 6, 1936*	*Steele*	*1,857*
Ohio	−39		Feb. 10, 1899	Milligan	800
		113	*July 21, 1934* [1]	*Gallipolis (near)*	*673*
Oklahoma	−27		Jan. 18, 1930	Watts	958
		120	*July 26, 1943* [1]	*Tishmoningo*	*670*
Oregon	−54		Feb. 10, 1933 [1]	Seneca	4,700
		119	*Aug. 10, 1938*	*Pendleton*	*1,074*
Pennsylvania	−42		Jan. 5, 1904	Smethport	1,469
		111	*July 10, 1936* [1]	*Phoenixville*	*100*
Rhode Island	−23		Jan. 11, 1942	Kingston	100
		104	*Aug. 2, 1975*	*Providence*	*51*
South Carolina	−19		Jan. 21, 1985	Caesar's Head	3,100
		111	*June 28, 1954* [1]	*Camden*	*170*
South Dakota	−58		Feb. 17, 1936	McIntosh	2,277
		120	*July 5, 1936*	*Gannvalley*	*1,750*

State	Lowest °F	Highest	Latest date	Station	Approximate elevation in feet
Tennessee	−32		Dec. 30, 1917	Mountain City	2,471
		113	*Aug. 9, 1930* [1]	*Perryville*	*377*
Texas	−23		Feb. 8, 1933	Seminole	3,275
		120	*Aug. 12, 1936*	*Seymour.*	*1,291*
Utah	−69		Feb. 1, 1985	Peter's Sink	8,092
		117	*Jul. 5, 1985*	*Saint George*	*2,880*
Vermont	−50		Dec. 30, 1933	Bloomfield	915
		105	*July 4, 1911*	*Vernon*	*310*
Virginia	−30		Jan. 22, 1985	Mtn. Lake Bio. Stn.	3,870
		110	*July 15, 1954*	*Balcony Falls*	*725*
Washington	−48		Dec. 30, 1968	Mazama	2,120
	−48		Dec. 30, 1968	Winthrop	1,765
		118	*Aug. 5, 1961* [1]	*Ice Harbor Dam*	*475*
West Virginia	−37		Dec. 30, 1917	Lewisburg	2,200
		112	*July 10, 1936* [1]	*Martinsburg*	*435*
Wisconsin	−54		Jan. 24, 1922	Danbury	908
		114	*July 13, 1936*	*Wisconsin Dells*	*900*
Wyoming	−63		Feb. 9, 1933	Moran	6,770
		114	*July 12, 1900*	*Basin*	*3,500*

(1) Also on earlier dates at the same or other places.

International Temperature and Precipitation

Source: Environmental Data Service, U.S. Dept. of Commerce

A standard period of 30 years has been used to obtain the average daily maximum and minimum temperatures and precipitation. The length of record of extreme maximum and minimum temperatures includes all available years of data for a given location and is usually for a longer period.

		Temperature F°						
		Average Daily				Extreme		Average annual precipitation
	Elev.	January		July				
Station	Feet	Max.	Min.	Max.	Min.	Max.	Min.	(inches)
Addis Ababa, Ethiopia	8,038	75	43	69	50	94	32	48.7
Algiers, Algeria	194	59	49	83	70	107	32	30.0
Amsterdam, Netherlands	5	40	34	69	59	95	3	25.6
Athens, Greece	351	54	42	90	72	109	20	15.8
Auckland, New Zealand	23	73	60	56	46	90	33	49.1
Bangkok, Thailand	53	89	67	90	76	104	50	57.8
Beirut, Lebanon	111	62	51	87	73	107	30	35.1
Berlin, Germany	187	35	26	74	55	96	−15	23.1
Bogota, Colombia	8,355	67	48	64	50	75	30	41.8
Bombay, India	27	88	62	88	75	110	46	71.2
Bucharest, Romania	269	33	20	86	61	105	−18	22.8
Budapest, Hungary	394	35	26	82	61	103	−10	24.2
Buenos Aires, Argentina	89	85	63	57	42	104	22	37.4
Cairo, Egypt	381	65	47	96	70	117	34	1.1
Capetown, South Africa	56	78	60	63	45	103	28	20.0
Caracas, Venezuela	3,418	75	56	78	61	91	45	32.9
Casablanca, Morocco	164	63	45	79	65	110	31	15.9
Copenhagen, Denmark	43	36	29	72	55	91	−3	23.3
Damascus, Syria	2,362	53	36	96	64	113	21	8.6
Dublin, Ireland	155	47	35	67	51	86	8	29.7
Geneva, Switzerland	1,329	39	29	77	58	101	−1	33.9
Havana, Cuba	80	79	65	89	75	104	43	48.2
Hong Kong	109	64	56	87	78	97	32	85.1
Istanbul, Turkey	59	45	36	81	65	100	17	31.5
Jerusalem, Israel	2,654	55	41	87	63	107	26	19.7
Lagos, Nigeria	10	88	74	83	74	104	60	72.3
La Paz, Bolivia	12,001	63	43	62	33	80	26	22.6
Lima, Peru	394	82	66	67	57	93	49	1.6
London, England	149	44	35	73	55	99	9	22.9
Madrid, Spain	2,188	47	33	87	62	102	14	16.5
Manila, Philippines	49	86	69	88	75	101	58	82.0
Mexico City, Mexico	7,340	66	42	74	54	92	24	23.0
Montreal, Canada	187	21	6	78	61	97	−35	40.8
Moscow, Russia	505	21	9	76	55	96	−27	24.8
Nairobi, Kenya	5,971	77	54	69	51	87	41	37.7
Oslo, Norway	308	30	20	73	56	93	−21	26.9
Paris, France	164	42	32	76	55	105	1	22.3
Prague, Czechoslovakia	662	34	25	74	58	98	−16	19.3
Reykjavik, Iceland	92	36	28	58	48	74	4	33.9
Rome, Italy	377	54	39	88	64	104	20	29.5
San Salvador, El Salvador	2,238	90	60	89	65	105	45	70.0
Santiago, Chile	1,706	85	53	59	37	99	24	14.2
Sao Paolo, Brazil	2,628	77	63	66	53	100	32	57.3
Shanghai, China	16	47	32	91	75	104	10	45.0
Singapore	33	86	73	88	75	97	66	95.0
Stockholm, Sweden	146	31	23	70	55	97	−26	22.4
Sydney, Australia	62	78	65	60	46	114	35	46.5
Teheran, Iran	3,937	45	27	99	72	109	−5	9.7
Tokyo, Japan	19	47	29	83	70	101	17	61.6
Toronto, Canada	379	30	16	79	59	105	−26	32.2
Tripoli, Libya	72	61	47	85	71	114	33	15.1
Vienna, Austria	664	34	26	75	59	98	−14	25.6
Warsaw, Poland	294	30	21	75	56	98	−22	22.0

Record Maximum 24-Hour Precipitation by State

(through 1990)

Source: National Climatic Data Center, NESDIS, NOAA, U.S. Dept. of Commerce

State	Precip. (inches)	Date	Station	Elevation (feet)
Ala. . .	20.33	4/13/55	Axis	36
Alas. . .	15.20	10/12/82	Angoon	15
Ariz. . .	11.40	9/4-5/70	Workman Creek	6,970
Ark. . .	14.06	12/3/82	Big Fork	1,100
Cal. . .	26.12	1/22-23/43	Hoegees Camp	2,760
Colo. . .	11.08	6/17/65	Holly	3,390
Conn. .	12.77	8/19/55	Burlington	460
Del. . .	8.50	7/13/75	Dover	30
Fla. . .	38.70	9/5/50	Yankeetown	5
Ga. . .	18.00	8/28/11	St. George	77
Ha. . .	38.00	1/24-25/56	Kilauea Plantation	180
Id. . . .	7.17	11/23/09	Rattlesnake Creek	4,000
Ill. . . .	16.54	6/14-15/57	East St. Louis	410
Ind. . .	10.50	8/6/05	Princeton	480
Ia. . . .	16.70	8/5-6/59	Decatur Co.	1,110
Kan. . .	12.59	5/31-6/1/41	Burlington	1,010
Ky. . . .	10.40	6/28/60	Dunmor	610
La. . . .	22.00	8/28-29/62	Hackberry	10
Me. . .	8.05	9/11/54	Brunswick	70
Md. . .	14.75	7/26-27/97	Jewell	152
Mass. .	18.15	8/18-19/55	Westfield	220
Mich. .	9.78	8/31-9/1/14	Bloomingdale	750
Minn. .	10.84	7/21-22/72	Fort Ripley	1,140
Miss. .	15.68	7/9/68	Columbus	190
Mo. . .	18.18	7/20/65	Edgarton	850
Mont. .	11.50	6/20/21	Circle	2,440
Neb. . .	13.15	7/8-9/50	York	1,610
Nev. . .	7.40	3/19/07	Lewer's Ranch	5,200
N.H. . .	10.38	2/10-11/70	Mount Washington	6,260
N.J. . .	14.81	8/19/39	Tuckerton	20
N.M. . .	11.28	5/18-19/55	Lake Maloya	7,400
N.Y. . .	11.17	10/9/03	NYC Central Park	130
N.C. . .	22.22	7/15-16/16	Altapass	2,600
N.D. . .	8.10	6/29/75	Litchville	1,470
Ohio . .	10.51	7/12/66	Sandusky	610
Okla. .	15.50	9/3-4/40	Sapulpa	740
Ore. . .	10.17	12/21/15	Glenora	575
Pa. . . .	34.50*	7/17/42	Smethport	1,510
R.I. . . .	12.13	9/16-17/32	Westerly	40
S.C. . .	13.25	7/14-15/16	Effingham	110
S.D. . .	8.00	9/10/00	Elk Point	1,127
Tenn. .	11.00	3/28/02	McMinnville	900
Texas .	43.00*	7/25-26/79	Alvin	50
Utah . .	6.00*	9/5/70	Bug Point	6,600
Vt. . . .	8.77	11/3-4/27	Somerset	2,080
Va. . . .	27.00*	8/20/69	Nelson Co.	est. 500
Wash. .	12.00	1/21/35	Quinault R.S.	220
W.Va. .	19.00*	7/18/89	Rockport	700
Wis. . .	11.72	6/24/46	Mellen	1,150
Wyo. . .	6.06	8/1/85	Cheyenne	6,126

* Estimated

Wind Chill Table

Source: National Weather Service, NOAA, U.S. Dept. of Commerce

Both temperature and wind cause heat loss from body surfaces. A combination of cold and wind makes a body feel colder than the actual temperature. The table shows, for example, that a temperature of 20 degrees Fahrenheit, plus a wind of 20 miles per hour, causes a body heat loss equal to that in minus 10 degrees with no wind. In other words, the wind makes 20 degrees feel like minus 10.

Top line of figures shows actual temperatures in degrees Fahrenheit. Column at left shows wind speeds.

MPH	35	30	25	20	15	10	5	0	−5	−10	−15	−20	−25	−30	−35	−40	−45
5	33	27	21	16	12	7	0	−5	−10	−15	−21	−26	−31	−36	−42	−47	−52
10	22	16	10	3	−3	−9	−15	−22	−27	−34	−40	−46	−52	−58	−64	−71	−77
15	16	9	2	−5	−11	−18	−25	−31	−38	−45	−51	−58	−65	−72	−78	−85	−92
20	12	4	−3	−10	−17	−24	−31	−39	−46	−53	−60	−67	−74	−81	−88	−95	−103
25	8	1	−7	−15	−22	−29	−36	−44	−51	−59	−66	−74	−81	−88	−96	−103	−110
30	6	−2	−10	−18	−25	−33	−41	−49	−56	−64	−71	−79	−86	−93	−101	−109	−116
35	4	−4	−12	−20	−27	−35	−43	−52	−58	−67	−74	−82	−89	−97	−105	−113	−120
40	3	−5	−13	−21	−29	−37	−45	−53	−60	−69	−76	−84	−92	−100	−107	−115	−123
45	2	−6	−14	−22	−30	−38	−46	−54	−62	−70	−78	−85	−93	−102	−109	−117	−125

(Wind speeds greater than 45 mph have little additional chilling effect.)

Heat Index

The index is a measure of the contribution that high humidity makes with abnormally high temperatures in reducing the body's ability to cool itself. For example, the index shows that for an actual air temperature of 100 degrees Fahrenheit and a relative humidity of 50 percent, the effect on the human body would be same as 120 degrees. Sunstroke and heat exhaustion are likely when the heat index reaches 105. This index is a measure of what hot weather "feels like" to the average person for various temperatures and relative humidities.

	Air Temperature*										
	70	75	80	85	90	95	100	105	110	115	120
Relative Humidity	Apparent Temperature*										
0%	64	69	73	78	83	87	91	95	99	103	107
10%	65	70	75	80	85	90	95	100	105	111	116
20%	66	72	77	82	87	93	99	105	112	120	130
30%	67	73	78	84	90	96	104	113	123	135	148
40%	68	74	79	86	93	101	110	123	137	151	
50%	69	75	81	88	96	107	120	135	150		
60%	70	76	82	90	100	114	132	149			
70%	70	77	85	93	106	124	144				
80%	71	78	86	97	113	136					
90%	71	79	88	102	122						
100%	72	80	91	108							

*Degrees Fahrenheit.

EDUCATION

Historical Summary of Public Elementary and Secondary Schools

Source: National Center for Education Statistics, U.S. Dept. of Education

Pupils and teachers (thousands)	1899-1900	1909-10	1919-20	1929-30	1939-40	1949-50	1959-60[1]	1969-70	1979-80	1989-90
Total U.S. population	75,995	90,492	104,512	121,770	130,880	148,665	179,323	203,212	224,567	248,239
Population 5-17 years of age	21,573	24,009	27,556	31,417	30,150	30,168	43,881	52,490	48,040	45,330
Percent aged 5-17 years	28.4	26.5	26.4	25.8	23.0	20.3	24.5	25.8	21.4	18.3
Enrollment (thousands)										
Elementary and secondary	15,503	17,814	21,578	25,678	25,434	25,111	36,087	45,619	41,645	41,224
Percent pop. 5-17 enrolled	71.9	74.2	78.3	81.7	84.4	83.2	82.2	86.9	86.7	90.9
Percent in high schools	3.3	5.1	10.2	17.1	26.0	22.7	23.5	28.5	32.9	27.5
High school graduates (thousands)	62	111	231	592	1,143	1,063	1,627	2,589	2,748	2,320
Average school term (in days)	144.3	157.5	161.9	172.7	175.0	177.9	178.0	178.9	178.5	...
Total instructional staff	...	...	678	880	912	962	1,464	2,253	2,441	...
Teachers, librarians: Men	127	110	93	140	195	195	402	691	782[4]	...
Women	296	413	565	703	681	719	985	1,440	1,518[4]	...
Percent men	29.9	21.1	14.1	16.6	22.2	21.3	29.0	33.4	34.0[4]	...
Revenue & expenditures (millions)										
Total revenue	$219	$433	$970	$2,088	$2,260	$5,437	$14,746	$40,267	$96,881	$207,584
Total expenditures	214	426	1,036	2,316	2,344	5,837	15,613	40,683	95,962	211,731
Current elem. and secondary	179	356	861	1,843	1,941	4,687	12,329	34,218	86,984[1]	187,384
Capital outlay	35	69	153	370	257	1,014	2,661	4,659	6,506	...
Interest on school debt	...	...	18	92	130	100	489	1,171	1,874	...
Other	...	...	3	9	13	35	132	636	598	...
Salaries and pupil cost				(Data in unadjusted dollars)						
Average annual teacher salary[2]	$325	$485	$871	$1,420	$1,441	$3,010	$5,174	$8,840	$16,715	$32,723
Expenditure per capita total pop.	2.83	4.71	9.91	19.03	17.91	39	87	200	424	853
Current expenditure per pupil ADA[3]	16.67	27.85	53.32	86.70	88.09	209	375	816	2,272	4,960

(1) Because of a modification of the scope, "current expenditures for elementary and secondary schools" data for 1959-60 and later years are not entirely comparable with data for prior years. (2) Includes supervisors, principals, teachers and other non-supervisory instructional staff. (3) "ADA" means average daily attendance in elementary and secondary day schools. (4) Estimated.

Years of School Completed, by Race, Hispanic Origin, and Sex: 1970 and 1991

Source: Bureau of the Census, U.S. Dept. of Commerce

Persons 25 years old and over. Persons of Hispanic origin may be of any race.

		Percent of Population Completing							
		Elementary School			High School		College		
Year, Race, Hispanic Origin and Sex	Population (1,000)	1 to 4 years	5 to 7 years	8 years	1 to 3 years	4 years	1 to 3 years	4 years or more	Median years of school completed
1970, total persons[1]	**109,899**	**5.5**	**10.0**	**12.8**	**19.4**	**31.1**	**10.6**	**10.7**	**12.1**
White	98,246	4.5	9.1	13.0	18.8	32.2	11.1	11.3	12.1
Male	46,527	4.8	9.7	13.3	18.2	28.5	11.1	14.4	12.1
Female	51,718	4.1	8.6	12.8	19.4	35.5	11.1	8.4	12.1
Black	10,375	14.6	18.7	10.5	24.8	21.2	5.9	4.4	9.8
Male	4,714	17.7	19.1	10.2	22.9	20.0	6.0	4.2	9.4
Female	5,661	12.0	18.3	10.8	26.4	22.2	5.8	4.6	10.0
Hispanic	3,946	19.5	18.6	11.5	18.2	21.1	6.5	4.5	9.1
Male	1,897	19.1	18.0	11.3	18.1	19.9	7.6	5.9	9.3
Female	2,050	19.9	19.2	11.6	18.3	22.3	5.4	3.2	8.9
1991, total persons[1]	**158,694**	**2.4**	**3.8**	**4.4**	**11.0**	**38.6**	**18.4**	**21.4**	**12.7**
White	136,299	2.0	3.4	4.5	10.2	39.1	18.6	22.2	12.8
Male	65,394	2.2	3.6	4.5	9.9	36.1	18.4	25.4	12.8
Female	70,905	1.8	3.3	4.5	10.5	41.8	18.8	19.3	12.7
Black	17,096	4.7	6.4	4.1	18.0	37.7	17.5	11.5	12.4
Male	7,626	6.5	6.3	4.3	16.3	38.3	17.0	11.4	12.4
Female	9,470	3.3	6.6	3.9	19.4	37.2	17.9	11.6	12.4
Hispanic	11,208	12.5	14.8	6.3	15.1	29.3	12.3	9.7	12.0
Male	5,509	12.9	14.8	6.1	14.7	28.5	13.0	10.0	12.1
Female	5,699	12.1	14.7	6.5	15.5	30.1	11.7	9.4	12.0

(1) Includes other races, not shown separately.

Percent of Population With Less Than 12 Years of School and With 4 Years of College or More, by Race and Hispanic Origin: 1970 to 1991

Source: Bureau of the Census, U.S. Dept. of Commerce

Persons 25 years old and over. As of April 1970 and 1980, and March beginning 1985.

	Less Than 12 Years of School					4 Years of College or More				
Race and Hispanic Origin	1970	1980	1985	1990	1991	1970	1980	1985	1990	1991
All races[1]	**47.7**	**33.5**	**26.1**	**22.4**	**21.6**	**10.7**	**16.2**	**19.4**	**21.3**	**21.4**
White	45.5	31.2	24.5	20.9	20.1	11.3	17.1	20.0	22.0	22.2
Black	68.6	48.8	40.2	33.8	33.3	4.4	8.4	11.1	11.3	11.5
Hispanic origin[2]	67.9	56.0	52.1	49.2	48.7	4.5	7.6	8.5	9.2	9.7
Mexican	75.8	62.4	58.7	55.9	56.4	2.5	4.9	5.5	5.5	6.2
Puerto Rican	76.6	59.9	53.7	44.5	42.1	2.2	5.6	7.0	9.6	10.1
Cuban	56.1	44.7	48.9	36.5	39.0	11.1	16.2	16.7	20.2	18.5
Other[3]	55.1	42.6	35.8	37.9	35.6	7.0	12.4	16.4	15.5	15.6

(1) Includes races not shown separately. (2) Persons of Hispanic origin may be of any race. (3) Includes Central and South American and other Hispanic origin.

Fall Enrollment and Teachers in Full-time Day Schools

Elementary and Secondary Day Schools, Fall 1990

Source: National Center for Education Statistics, U.S. Dept. of Education; National Education Assn.

	Local school districts	Classroom teachers	Total enrollment	Pupils per teacher	Teacher's average pay (1990-1991)	Instructional aides	Expenditure per pupil
United States	**15,358**	**2,397,351**	**41,223,804**	**17.2**	**$32,977**	**395,642**	**$4,960**
Alabama	129	36,266	721,806	19.9	26,862	4,340	3,327
Alaska	56	6,710	113,874	17.0	43,435	1,512	8,374
Arizona	228	32,987	639,853	19.4	30,773	5,190	4,057
Arkansas	326	25,984	436,286	16.8	23,611	3,858	3,485
California	1,076	217,228	4,950,474	22.8	39,598	53,996	4,391
Colorado	176	32,342	574,213	17.8	31,819	4,440	4,720
Connecticut	166	34,549	469,123	13.6	43,808	6,146	7,604
Delaware	19	5,961	99,658	16.7	35,246	738	5,696
District of Columbia	1	5,950	80,694	13.6	39,497	441	8,904
Florida	67	108,088	1,861,592	17.2	30,555	21,561	4,997
Georgia	185	63,058	1,151,687	18.3	29,172	16,671	4,187
Hawaii	1	9,083	171,708	18.9	32,541	1,032	4,448
Idaho	115	11,254	220,840	19.6	25,485	1,223	3,078
Illinois	951	108,775	1,821,407	16.7	34,605	13,505	5,118
Indiana	303	54,509	954,581	17.5	32,434	11,989	4,549
Iowa	430	31,045	483,652	15.6	27,977	3,737	4,453
Kansas	304	29,140	437,034	15.0	29,767	3,182	4,752
Kentucky	176	36,777	636,401	17.3	29,115	6,522	3,675
Louisiana	66	—	784,757	—	26,240	—	3,855
Maine	283	15,513	215,149	13.9	28,531	3,290	5,373
Maryland	24	42,562	715,176	16.8	38,382	6,152	6,196
Massachusetts	352	54,003	834,314	15.4	36,090	7,914	6,237
Michigan	561	80,008	1,581,925	19.8	38,326	11,555	5,546
Minnesota	434	43,753	756,374	17.3	33,126	8,121	4,971
Mississippi	151	28,062	502,417	17.9	24,366	8,754	3,096
Missouri	543	52,304	812,234	15.5	28,290	4,670	4,507
Montana	536	9,613	152,974	15.9	26,774	1,167	4,736
Nebraska	812	18,764	274,081	14.6	26,592	3,229	4,842
Nevada	17	10,373	201,316	19.4	32,209	—	4,117
New Hampshire	170	10,637	172,785	16.2	31,273	2,140	5,304
New Jersey	606	79,886	1,089,646	13.6	38,411	9,598	7,991
New Mexico	88	16,703	301,881	18.1	25,754	3,779	3,518
New York	718	176,390	2,598,337	14.7	42,080	24,296	8,062
North Carolina	134	64,283	1,086,871	16.9	29,276	18,892	4,268
North Dakota	276	7,591	117,825	15.5	23,574	1,071	4,189
Ohio	613	102,714	1,771,516	17.2	32,615	8,926	5,136
Oklahoma	595	37,221	579,087	15.6	24,457	5,390	3,512
Oregon	299	26,163	484,652	18.5	32,300	4,543	5,521
Pennsylvania	502	100,275	1,667,834	16.6	36,057	11,332	6,061
Rhode Island	37	9,522	138,813	14.6	34,997	1,044	6,249
South Carolina	95	36,963	622,112	16.8	28,301	6,582	4,088
South Dakota	184	8,511	129,164	15.2	22,376	1,908	3,732
Tennessee	140	43,051	824,595	19.2	28,248	8,420	3,664
Texas	1,053	219,298	3,382,887	15.4	27,658	31,538	4,150
Utah	40	17,884	447,891	25.0	25,578	3,739	2,730
Vermont	336	7,257	95,762	13.2	30,986	1,915	6,227
Virginia	156	63,638	998,601	15.7	32,239	9,919	4,612
Washington	296	41,764	839,709	20.1	33,079	6,397	4,681
West Virginia	55	21,476	322,389	15.0	25,967	2,784	4,359
Wisconsin	428	49,302	797,621	16.2	33,209	7,301	5,524
Wyoming	49	6,784	98,226	14.5	28,988	1,232	5,577

Programs for the Disabled

Number of children 3 to 21 years old served annually in educational programs for the disabled.

Source: Office of Special Educ. and Rehabilitative Services, U.S. Dept. of Education

Type of Handicapped	1982-83	1983-84	1984-85	1985-86	1986-87	1987-88	1988-89	1989-90
	Number Served, in Thousands							
All disabilities	**4,255**	**4,298**	**4,315**	**4,317**	**4,374**	**4,446**	**4,544**	**4,641**
Learning disabilities	1,741	1,806	1,832	1,862	1,914	1,928	1,987	2,050
Speech impairments	1,131	1,128	1,126	1,125	1,136	953	967	973
Mental retardation	757	727	694	660	643	582	564	548
Serious emotional disturbance	352	361	372	375	383	373	376	381
Hearing impairments	73	72	69	66	65	56	56	57
Orthopedic impairments	57	56	56	57	57	47	47	48
Visual impairments	28	29	28	27	26	22	23	22
Deaf-blindness	2	2	2	2	2	12	2	2

Note: Counts are based on reports from the 50 States, District of Columbia and Puerto Rico (i.e., figures from U.S. territories are not included). Details may not add to totals because of rounding.

School and Home Computer Use, 1989

Source: Bureau of the Census, U.S. Dept. of Commerce (numbers in thousands)

Type of school and grade	All students	Use at school		Use at home		Use at home and school	
		Number	Percent	Number	Percent	Number	Percent
Public school (K-12)	39,938	18,339	45.9	6,890	17.3	4,226	10.6
Grades K-4	16,697	7,239	43.4	2,140	12.8	1,402	8.4
Grades 5-8	12,474	6,805	54.6	2,509	20.1	1,695	13.6
Grades 9-12	10,767	4,295	39.9	2,241	20.8	1,129	10.5
Private school (K-12)	4,068	2,028	49.9	1,140	28.0	717	17.6
Grades K-4	2,100	988	47.0	447	21.3	264	12.6
Grades 5-8	1,213	717	59.1	411	33.9	296	24.4
Grades 9-12	755	323	42.8	282	37.4	157	20.8

Federal Funds for Education, 1980-1992

Source: U.S. Office of Management and Budget

Federal funds obligated for programs administered by the Department of Education: Fiscal years 1980 to 1990

(In thousands of dollars)

	1980	1984	1988	1989	1990	1992[1]
Total	**$14,102,165**	**$17,072,698**	**$20,697,311**	**$24,473,634**	**$25,214,653**	**$34,122,202**
Elementary and secondary education	**4,239,022**	**4,294,269**	**5,682,997**	**5,997,160**	**7,169,693**	**8,773,507**
Grants for the disadvantaged	3,204,664	3,501,383	4,357,970	4,600,444	5,383,960	6,560,500
Special programs	788,918	549,117	1,067,213	1,129,444	1,524,001	1,910,890
Bilingual education	169,540	173,051	191,470	196,309	188,152	225,407
Indian education	75,900	70,718	66,344	70,963	73,580	76,710
School assistance in federally affected areas	**812,873**	**608,791**	**731,241**	**731,768**	**815,573**	**807,375**
Maintenance and operations	690,000	555,300	685,498	708,396	717,354	745,660
Construction	110,873	28,491	35,640	18,400	22,929	43,535
Disaster assistance	12,000	25,000	10,103	4,972	75,290	18,180
Education for the handicapped	**1,555,253**	**2,416,799**	**3,075,456**	**3,814,846**	**3,480,122**	**5,332,672**
State grant programs	815,805	1,082,180	1,115,333	1,642,647	1,258,871	2,315,464
Early childhood education[2]	38,745	53,164	210,752	319,012	280,341	697,073
Special centers, projects, and research	55,075	54,871	78,600	102,141	72,966	134,670
Captioned films and media services	17,778	14,000	13,026	13,346	15,191	17,000
Personnel training	55,375	55,540	66,153	67,023	70,838	89,800
Handicapped rehabilitation Service and research	572,475	1,157,044	1,591,592	1,670,677	1,781,915	2,078,665
Vocational education and adult programs	**1,153,743**	**954,320**	**1,000,055**	**1,052,470**	**1,138,674**	**1,893,377**
Basic programs[3]	744,653	689,324	823,299	859,239	858,716	1,297,429
Consumer and homemaking	63,169	36,792	32,752	32,816	34,517	50,142
Program improvement and supportive services	162,512	117,249	—	—	—	—
State planning and advisory councils	13,423	11,200	7,681	7,945	7,923	9,325
Adult education, grants to States	153,724	99,755	129,183	139,771	188,280	235,730
Other	16,262	—	7,140	12,699	49,238	300,751
Postsecondary student financial assistance	**5,108,534**	**7,478,401**	**8,807,929**	**11,482,608**	**11,112,068**	**15,277,415**
Educational opportunity grants[4]	2,534378	3,565,209	4,620,133	5,379,725	4,919,264	6,456,864
Work-study	596,065	561,322	604,445	620,644	615,269	617,079
Direct student loans	322,749	191,962	216,963	202,904	157,415	156,559
Guaranteed student loans	1,597,877	3,130,939	3,297,305	5,203,843	5,341,039	7,945,201
Other student assistance programs	57,465	28,969	69,083	75,492	79,081	101,712
Direct aid to postsecondary institutions	**277,068**	**311,221**	**341,063**	**398,318**	**341,634**	**542,392**
Aid to minority and developing institutions	114,680	132,081	135,222	179,062	99,812	157,143
Special programs for the disadvantaged	147,389	164,740	205,841	219,256	241,822	385,249
Cooperative education	14,999	14,400	—	—	—	—
Higher education facilities	**268,493**	**216,893**	**162,528**	**77,362**	**84,035**	**70,796**
Construction loans and insurance	35,362	54,105	89,820	37,109	30,000	8,095
Interest subsidy grants	24,626	23,925	24,466	22,524	38,471	46,695
College housing loans	208,505	138,863	48,242	17,729	15,564	16,006
Other higher education programs	**34,927**	**82,410**	**79,305**	**73,574**	**188,999**	**210,011**
International education and foreign languages	19,977	30,800	—	—	86,337	110,830
Fund for Improvement of Postsecondary Education	12,000	11,710	65,813	67,236	99,450	87,831
Other	2,950	39,900	13,492	6,338	3,212	11,350
Public Library services	**101,218**	**107,895**	**135,731**	**141,884**	**132,583**	**161,242**
Public Library services	66,451	65,000	78,922	80,944	82,505	83,898
Interlibrary cooperation	—	11,520	18,395	18,826	19,551	19,908
Public Library construction	—	21,015	23,577	27,289	14,837	30,213
Research Libraries	5,992	6,000	5,744	5,675	6,593	5,855
Other	28,775	880	9,093	9,150	9,097	21,368
Payments to special institutions	**273,860**	**249,610**	**271,658**	**284,056**	**292,736**	**340,317**
American Printing House for the Blind	4,349	5,000	5,266	5,335	5,663	5,900
National Technical Institute for the Deaf	19,799	28,000	31,594	33,326	35,594	39,530
Gallaudet College	49,409	56,288	62,195	65,998	67,643	76,540
Howard University	200,303	160,322	172,603	179,397	183,836	218,347
Departmental accounts	**$277,174**	**$352,089**	**$409,348**	**$419,588**	**$458,536**	**$713,098**
Educational research and improvement	51,415	57,165	68,147	78,263	87,074	263,564
Departmental management account	223,857	293,351	341,171	341,286	370,844	449,447
Other	1,875	1,401	—	—	—	—
Trust funds	27	172	30	39	618	87

(1) Estimated. (2) Includes preschool incentive grants. (3) Includes programs of national significance and special programs for the disadvantaged. (4) Includes Pell Grants, Supplemental Education Opportunity Grants and State Student Incentive Grants, and Income Contingent Loans. (—) Data are not available or not applicable. **NOTE:** Because of rounding, details may not add to totals.

Preprimary School Enrollment: 1970 to 1991

Source: Bureau of the Census, U.S. Dept. of Commerce

As of October. Civilian noninstitutional population. Includes public and non-public nursery school and kindergarten programs. Excludes 5 year olds enrolled in elementary school.

Item	1970	1975	1980	1985	1986	1987	1988	1989	1990	1991
Number of Children (1,000)										
Population, 3 to 5 years old	**10,949**	**10,183**	**9,284**	**10,733**	**10,866**	**10,872**	**10,894**	**11,038**	**11,207**	**11,370**
Total Enrolled[1]	**4,104**	**4,954**	**4,878**	**5,865**	**5,971**	**5,932**	**5,977**	**6,026**	**6,659**	**6,334**
Nursery	1,094	1,745	1,981	2,477	2,545	2,555	2,621	2,825	3,378	2,824
Public	332	570	628	848	829	819	852	930	1,202	996
Private	762	1,174	1,353	1,631	1,715	1,736	1,770	1,894	2,177	1,827
Kindergarten	3,010	3,211	2,897	3,388	3,426	3,377	3,356	3,201	3,281	3,510
Public	2,498	2,682	2,438	2,847	2,859	2,842	2,875	2,704	2,767	2,968
Private	511	528	459	541	567	535	481	496	513	543
White	3,443	4,105	3,994	4,757	4,851	4,748	4,891	4,911	5,389	5,104
Black	586	731	725	919	892	893	814	872	964	928
Hispanic[2]	(NA)	(NA)	370	496	593	587	544	520	642	675
3 years old	454	683	857	1,035	1,041	1,022	1,028	1,005	1,205	1,075
4 years old	1,007	1,418	1,423	1,765	1,772	1,717	1,768	1,882	2,086	1,993
5 years old	2,643	2,852	2,598	3,065	3,157	3,192	3,183	3,139	3,367	3,266
Enrollment Rate										
Total enrolled[1]	**37.5**	**48.6**	**52.5**	**54.6**	**55.0**	**54.6**	**54.4**	**54.6**	**59.4**	**59.4**
White	37.8	48.6	52.7	54.7	55.2	54.1	55.4	55.0	59.7	56.2
Black	34.9	48.1	51.8	55.8	54.1	54.2	48.2	54.2	57.8	53.1
Hispanic[2]	(NA)	(NA)	43.3	43.3	47.8	45.5	44.2	41.6	49.0	46.4
3 years old	12.9	21.5	27.3	28.8	28.9	28.6	27.6	27.1	32.6	28.2
4 years old	27.8	40.5	46.3	49.1	49.0	47.7	49.1	51.0	56.0	53.0
5 years old	69.3	81.3	84.7	86.5	86.7	86.1	86.6	86.4	88.8	86.0

(NA) Not available. (1) Includes races not shown separately. (2) Persons of Hispanic origin may be of any race. The method of identifying Hispanic children was changed in 1980 from allocation based on status of mother to status reported for each child. The number of Hispanic children using the new method is larger.

Number of Private Schools and Their Enrollment in Grades K Through 12, 1987-1988

Source: National Center for Education Statistics, U.S. Dept. of Education

Selected Characteristics	Number of Schools				Enrollment			
	Total	Catholic	Other religious	Non-sectarian	Total	Catholic	Other religious	Non-sectarian
Total	**26,836**	**9,527**	**12,132**	**5,177**	**5,226,096**	**2,822,585**	**1,590,632**	**812,879**
School Size								
Less than 150	14,065	1,971	8,689	3,406	889,794	189,893	496,799	203,102
150 to 299	7,609	4,225	2,294	1,090	1,636,110	935,288	478,285	222,537
300 to 499	3,134	2,109	649	375	1,179,644	798,886	243,511	137,247
500 to 749	1,271	767	311	193	748,262	444,801	183,324	120,137
750 or more	758	455	188	—	772,287	453,717	188,714	—
Minority status								
Less than 5%	11,856	4,052	6,559	1,245	2,164,142	1,131,135	774,261	258,746
5 to 19%	7,877	2,507	3,413	1,957	1,620,981	811,080	501,486	308,415
20 to 49%	3,392	1,221	1,115	1,056	664,382	388,519	143,014	132,850
50% or more	3,712	1,748	1,046	918	776,592	491,851	171,871	112,869
Community								
Rural/farming	5,181	1,108	3,359	715	497,868	180,483	199,011	118,375
Small city/town	6,210	2,340	2,916	954	940,971	507,869	289,409	143,693
Suburban	5,257	1,925	2,137	1,194	1,358,717	749,503	401,839	207,376
Urban	10,150	4,141	3,717	2,292	2,412,844	1,383,368	700,102	329,374

Note: Details may not add to totals due to rounding or missing values in cells with too few sample cases. (—) Too few sample cases (fewer than 30) for a reliable estimate.

National Math Test, 1990

Source: U.S. Dept. of Education

Average score of students who participated in the national eighth grade mathematics exam. The best possible score was 350. Thirteen states chose not to participate.

The National Assessment Governing Board, a federal agency that conducted the test, cautioned against using the data as a simple ranking because of the many variables involved in the calculations and the overlapping performance of many states. Some who rank in the middle in overall average, for example, have groups of students who scored among the highest in the nation.

	Average score
National	**261**
1. North Dakota	281
2. Montana	280
3. Iowa	278
4. Nebraska	276
5. Minnesota	276
6. Wisconsin	274
7. New Hampshire	273
8. Wyoming	272
9. Idaho	272
10. Oregon	271
11. Connecticut	270
12. New Jersey	269
13. Colorado	267
14. Indiana	267
15. Pennsylvania	266
16. Michigan	264
17. Virginia	264
18. Ohio	264
19. Oklahoma	263
20. New York	261
21. Delaware	261
22. Maryland	260
23. Illinois	260
24. Rhode Island	260
25. Arizona	259
26. Georgia	258
27. Texas	258
28. Kentucky	256
29. California	256
30. New Mexico	256
31. Arkansas	256
32. West Virginia	256
33. Florida	255
34. Alabama	252
35. Hawaii	251
36. North Carolina	250
37. Louisiana	246
38. Guam	231
39. D.C.	231
40. Virgin Islands	218

American College Testing (ACT) Program Mean Scores and Characteristics of College-Bound Students: 1970 to 1991

Source: The American College Testing Program

Data for academic year ending in year shown.

Type of Test and Mean Test Scores[1]	Unit	1970	1975	1980	1985	1986	1987*	1988*	1989*	1990*	1991*
Composite	Point	19.9	18.6	18.5	18.6	20.8	20.8	20.8	20.6	20.6	20.6
Male	Point	20.3	19.5	19.3	19.4	19.6	19.5	19.6	19.3	21.0	20.9
Female	Point	19.4	17.8	17.9	17.9	18.1	18.1	18.1	18.0	20.3	20.4
English	Point	18.5	17.7	17.9	18.1	18.5	18.4	18.5	18.4	20.5	20.3
Male	Point	17.6	17.1	17.3	17.6	17.9	17.9	18.0	17.8	20.1	19.8
Female	Point	19.4	18.3	18.3	18.6	18.9	18.9	19.0	18.9	20.9	20.7
Math	Point	20.0	17.6	17.4	17.2	17.3	17.2	17.2	17.1	19.9	20.0
Male	Point	21.1	19.3	18.9	18.6	18.8	18.6	18.4	18.3	20.7	20.6
Female	Point	18.8	16.2	16.2	16.0	16.0	16.1	16.1	16.1	19.3	19.4
Participants											
Total	1,000	788	714	822	739	730	777	842	855	817	796
Male	Percent	52	46	45	46	46	46	46	46	46	45
White	Percent	(NA)	77	83	82	82	81	81	80	79	79
Black	Percent	4	7	8	8	8	8	9	9	9	9
Obtaining composite scores of—											
27** or above	Percent	14	14	13	14	14	14	14	14	12**	11 **
18** or below	Pecent	21	33	33	32	31	31	31	32	35**	35 **

* Beginning with the October 1989 test (1990 scores), an entirely new ACT Assessment was introduced. The Enhanced ACT Assessment increases the emphasis on rhetorical skills in the measurement of writing proficiency, increases the number of advanced math items, and includes a new reading test which features inferential and reasoning skills and a test designed to measure science reasoning. The Enhanced ACT also provides subscores in English, Mathematics, and Reading. The "Composite" scores for 1986-89 have been converted to provide a basis of comparison; all 1990 scores are for the Enhanced ACT. It is not possible to make direct comparisons between 1990 data and data from earlier years.

** As of 1990.

(NA) Not available. (1) Minimum score, 1; maximum score, 36. (2) Test scores and characteristics of college-bound students based on a 10% sample through 1984. Beginning in 1985, these data are now based on the performance of all ACT-tested students who graduated in the spring of a given school year and who took the ACT Assessment during junior or senior year of high school.

Scholastic Aptitude Test (SAT) Mean Scores and Characteristics of College Bound Seniors: 1970 to 1992

Source: College Entrance Examination Board

(For school year ending in year shown)

Type of Test and Characteristic Test Scores[1]	Unit	1970	1975	1980	1984	1985	1987	1988	1989	1990	1991	1992
Verbal, total[1]	Point	460	434	424	426	431	430	428	427	424	422	423
Male	Point	459	437	428	433	437	435	435	434	429	426	428
Female	Point	461	431	420	420	425	425	422	421	419	418	419
Math, total[2]	Point	488	472	466	471	475	476	476	476	476	474	476
Male	Point	509	495	491	495	499	500	498	500	499	497	499
Female	Point	465	449	443	449	452	453	455	454	455	453	456
Participants (thousands)												
Total		996	992	989	977	1,080	1,134	1,088	1,025	1,033	NA	1,034
Male	Percent	NA	49.9	48.2	48.2	48.3	48.0	48.0	48.0	48.0	48.0	48.0
White	Percent	NA	86.0	82.1	80.3	80.0	78.0	77.0	75.0	73.0	72.0	71.0
Black	Percent	NA	7.9	9.1	9.1	8.9	9.0	9.0	10.0	10.0	10.0	10.0
Obtaining scores[1] of—600 or above:												
Verbal	Percent	NA	7.9	7.2	7.0	7.0	8.0	7.0	7.8	7.0	7.0	7.0
Math	Percent	NA	15.6	15.1	17.0	17.0	18.0	17.0	18.0	18.0	17.0	18.0
Below 400:												
Verbal	Percent	NA	37.8	41.8	40.0	40.0	40.0	42.0	40.5	41.0	43.0	42.0
Math	Percent	NA	28.5	30.2	29.0	28.0	29.0	27.0	28.0	28.0	29.0	27.0

(NA) Not available. (1) Minimum score, 200; maximum score, 800. (2) 1970 is an estimate based on total number of persons taking SAT.

Tuition and College Costs 1992-93

Based on the Peterson's Guides Annual Survey of Undergraduate Institutions, the average cost of tuition, mandatory fees, and college room and board at four-year private colleges is $13,422. The average cost at four-year public colleges is $5,929 for state residents and $9,528 for nonresidents. Two-year public colleges are the least expensive group of institutions; tuition and fees average $1,259 for state residents and $3,364 for nonresidents. Tuition and fees at two-year private colleges average $5,401.

The most expensive four-year institutions, including tuition, mandatory fees, and college room and board, are Sarah Lawrence College ($24,380); Brandeis University ($24,227); Barnard College ($24,162); Bard College ($24,095); Hampshire College ($23,905); Bennington College ($23,880); Tufts University ($23,787); Yale University ($23,700); Massachusetts Institute of Technology ($23,565); Tulane University ($23,516). Bennington College has the highest tuition and fees of all four-year undergraduate institutions ($19,780). The least expensive are the U.S. service academies, which are all free.

College Enrollment Rates

Source: American College Testing Program; U.S. Dept. of Labor

A record 62 percent of the high school graduates of 1991 were enrolled in a college or university last fall. Of the 2.3 million students who graduated from high school in June 1991, about 1.4 million were attending college in October. The 62 percent enrollment rate was up from the previous high of 60 percent in both 1989 and 1990. The enrollment rate for women (67 percent) continued to exceed that for men (58 percent), and the rate for whites (65 percent) remained higher than those for blacks (46 percent) and Hispanics (57 percent).

Sixty percent of the 1991 college freshmen were enrolled in 4-year colleges. About one-third of them also were in the labor force in October, while 70 percent of the students in 2-year colleges combined school with employment. The unemployment rate for the new college students averaged 11.6 percent.

About 860,000 members of the high school class of 1991 were not enrolled in college in October, and 80 percent of these were in the labor force. The unemployment rate for this group, 25.3 percent, was the highest in 8 years.

Nearly 400,000 people dropped out of high school between October 1990 and October 1991.

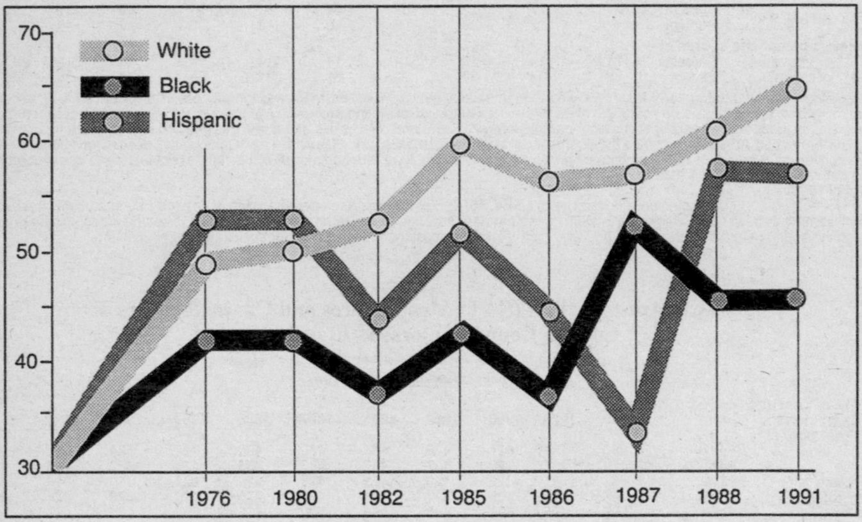

Public High School Graduation and Dropout Rates, 1990

Source: National Center for Education Statistics, U.S. Dept. of Education

	Graduation rate	rank	Dropout rate	rank
U.S.	71.2%		28.8%	
Alabama	64.7	(44)	35.3	(8)
Alaska	68.4	(38)	31.6	(14)
Arizona	72.5	(31)	27.5	(21)
Arkansas	76.7	(22)	23.3	(30)
California	67.8	(42)	32.2	(10)
Colorado	74.1	(26)	25.9	(26)
Connecticut	74.9	(25)	25.1	(27)
Delaware	68.5	(37)	31.5	(15)
D.C.	61.6	(48)	38.4	(4)
Florida	61.1	(49)	38.9	(3)
Georgia	62.7	(47)	37.3	(5)
Hawaii	86.8	(5)	13.2	(47)
Idaho	79.4	(13)	20.6	(39)
Illinois	76.6	(23)	23.4	(29)
Indiana	75.0	(24)	25.0	(28)
Iowa	87.5	(4)	12.5	(48)
Kansas	82.0	(11)	18.0	(41)
Kentucky	69.0	(36)	31.0	(16)
Louisiana	56.7	(51)	43.3	(1)
Maine	77.6	(16)	22.4	(36)
Maryland	72.8	(30)	27.2	(22)
Massachusetts	77.0	(21)	23.0	(31)
Michigan	70.1	(34)	29.9	(18)
Minnesota	89.7	(2)	10.3	(50)
Mississippi	64.2	(45)	35.8	(7)
Missouri	72.2%	(32)	27.8%	(20)
Montana	83.3	(9)	16.7	(43)
Nebraska	85.5	(7)	14.5	(45)
Nevada	77.2	(19)	22.8	(33)
New Hampshire	74.0	(27)	26.0	(25)
New Jersey	79.8	(12)	20.2	(40)
New Mexico	68.2	(39)	31.8	(13)
New York	65.1	(43)	34.9	(9)
North Carolina	68.0	(40)	32.0	(12)
North Dakota	88.1	(3)	11.9	(49)
Ohio	74.0	(27)	26.0	(25)
Oklahoma	77.5	(17)	22.5	(35)
Oregon	71.6	(33)	28.4	(19)
Pennsylvania	79.1	(14)	20.9	(38)
Rhode Island	69.6	(35)	30.4	(17)
South Carolina	58.5	(50)	41.5	(2)
South Dakota	85.7	(6)	14.3	(46)
Tennessee	67.9	(41)	32.1	(11)
Texas	64.1	(46)	35.9	(6)
Utah	83.1	(10)	16.9	(42)
Vermont[1]	91.6	(1)	8.4	(51)
Virginia	73.6	(29)	26.4	(23)
Washington	77.2	(19)	22.8	(33)
West Virginia	77.3	(18)	22.7	(34)
Wisconsin	84.2	(8)	15.8	(44)
Wyoming	78.6	(15)	21.4	(37)

(1) Based on 12th grade enrollment in fall 1989.

Public Libraries

Source: World Almanac questionnaire (1992)

City	No. bound Volumes	Circulation	Annual Acquisitions Expend.
Akron, Oh. (17)	1,498,836	3,191,088	$1,900,000
Albuquerque, N.M. (12)	810,871	2,830,979	1,150,000
Anaheim, Cal. (5)	393,231	1,550,000	450,000
Anchorage, Alas.[a] (5)	395,700	1,099,780	662,790
Arlington, Tex. (5)	246,125	1,211,662	280,533
Atlanta, Ga.[a] (33)	1,678,750	2,303,681	3,011,362
Baltimore, Md. (28)	2,217,508	1,673,310	1,904,681
Baton Rouge, La. (10)	815,467	2,276,247	1,146,850
Birmingham, Ala. (19)	889,000	2,000,000	1,200,000
Boston, Mass. (26)	6,000,000	1,600,000	2,000,000
Buffalo, N.Y. (53)	2,494,000	7,587,811	2,629,489
Charlotte, N.C.[a] (19)	1,200,000	2,700,000	1,400,000
Chicago, Ill. (Main)	1,700,000	950,000	3,600,000
Branches (82)	4,600,000	8,400,000	4,600,000
Cincinnati, Oh. (42)	4,281,202	10,413,286	5,561,019
Cleveland, Oh. (28)	2,734,894	5,624,099	6,098,471
Colorado Springs, Col. (13)	867,906	2,470,986	1,998,445
Columbus, Oh. (20)	1,928,603	8,341,885	5,178,015
Corpus Christi, Tex. (4)	362,433	1,153,718	520,756
Dallas, Tex.[a] (19)	2,409,864	4,364,027	17,201,527
Dayton, Oh. (20)	1,555,475	6,224,061	2,316,854
Denver, Col.[a] (21)	2,239,106	3,396,268	1,856,485
Des Moines, Ia. (5)	549,544	1,241,800	267,050
Detroit, Mich. (25)	2,763,442	1,494,160	1,932,650
District of Columbia[a] (25)	1,507,556	1,843,098	1,530,000
El Paso, Tex.[a] (10)	600,000	1,300,000	3,500,000
Fairfax, Va.[a] (22)	1,761,264	8,454,714	3,387,721
Ft. Worth, Tex. (10)	1,693,975	2,238,871	1,266,213
Fresno, Cal. (36)	1,192,409	2,003,511	500,000
Honolulu, Ha. (49)	2,389,153	6,290,173	3,579,085
Houston, Tex. (34)	3,982,539	6,342,340	4,038,166
Indianapolis, Ind.[a] (21)	1,500,000	5,376,388	2,170,167
Jersey City, N.J. (11)	792,423	285,549	139,412
Kansas City, Mo. (8)	1,817,937	2,032,835	1,589,306
Los Angeles, Cal.[a] (62)	5,663,240	10,382,321	4,469,364
Louisville, Ky. (14)	700,000	2,603,723	1,575,340
Memphis, Tenn.[a] (23)	1,700,000	2,700,000	3,228,007
Mesa, Ariz. (2)	556,416	2,064,658	$768,638
Miami, Fla.[a] (28)	2,386,204	4,200,000	2,200,000
Milwaukee, Wis. (12)	2,306,006	3,057,442	1,788,125
Minneapolis, Minn. (14)	1,977,573	3,065,032	2,026,182
Mobile, Ala. (6)	415,000	1,323,318	700,000
Nashville, Tenn. (16)	665,249	1,849,973	820,310
New Orleans, La. (15)	928,871	1,251,366	892,728
New York, N.Y. (research)	10,700,000	—	9,400,000
Branches (82)	4,000,000	9,908,640	6,650,000
Brooklyn[a] (58)	4,637,167	8,610,459	5,133,434
Queens[a] (61)	5,500,000	11,320,000	5,500,000
Norfolk, Va. (11)	901,775	767,110	500,626
Oklahoma City, Okla.[a] (11)	933,241	4,184,437	1,346,726
Oakland, Cal. (16)	1,300,000	1,580,000	762,000
Omaha, Neb. (9)	613,472	1,985,822	933,050
Philadelphia, Pa.[a] (53)	3,458,700	4,800,000	6,200,000
Phoenix, Az. (11)	1,783,410	5,962,000	2,200,000
Pittsburgh, Pa. (19)	1,934,390	2,925,154	1,300,000
Portland, Ore.[a] (15)	4,000,000	2,000,000	1,400,000
Richmond, Va. (8)	785,023	842,143	427,734
Rochester, N.Y. (11)	1,542,038	1,597,407	1,029,258
Sacramento, Cal.[a] (24)	1,663,893	3,977,515	2,045,262
St. Louis, Mo. (12)	1,400,000	1,830,302	1,670,000
St. Paul, Minn. (12)	599,048	2,628,951	894,113
San Diego, Cal. (32)	2,030,185	5,364,276	2,480,597
San Francisco, Cal. (27)	2,000,000	3,300,000	1,015,855
Shreveport, La. (19)	475,685	1,081,232	400,000
Syracuse, N.Y. (8)	650,080	1,911,930	1,281,088
Tampa, Fla.[a] (17)	1,100,600	3,200,000	1,800,000
Toledo, Oh. (18)	1,793,735	5,849,356	2,968,076
Tucson, Ariz. (17)	1,200,000	5,100,000	1,355,000
Tulsa, Okla. (20)	874,272	3,344,153	1,550,000
Wichita, Kan. (11)	875,558	1,718,806	464,630
Yonkers, N.Y.[a] (3)	233,532	865,901	481,286

(a) Has not provided up-to-date information. Figure in parentheses denotes number of branches.

Funding of Public Libraries

Source: National Center for Educational Statistics, U.S. Dept. of Education

States ranked by all money spent per capita for public libraries in 1990

1.	District of Columbia	$31.58
2.	New York	30.42
3.	Ohio	25.98
4.	Indiana	25.69
5.	Alaska	24.68
6.	Maryland	24.59
7.	New Jersey	23.99
8.	Connecticut	22.70
9.	Washington	21.52
10.	Wyoming	21.43
11.	Illinois	21.39
12.	Massachusetts	19.90
13.	Hawaii	19.77
14.	Minnesota	19.24
15.	Colorado	18.48
16.	Virginia	18.06
17.	Wisconsin	17.73
18.	California	$16.89
19.	Kansas	16.78
20.	Oregon	16.14
21.	Missouri	15.16
22.	New Hampshire	15.00
23.	Arizona	14.94
24.	Michigan	14.72
25.	Utah	14.28
26.	Nebraska	14.24
27.	Maine	14.16
28.	Florida	13.98
29.	Iowa	13.58
30.	Rhode Island	13.58
31.	New Mexico	13.39
32.	South Dakota	12.99
33.	Idaho	12.50
34.	Louisiana	12.43
35.	Pennsylvania	$11.76
36.	Vermont	11.61
37.	Oklahoma	11.21
38.	North Carolina	10.98
39.	Georgia	10.86
40.	Nevada	9.84
41.	North Dakota	9.42
42.	Alabama	9.02
43.	South Carolina	8.80
44.	Montana	8.79
45.	Delaware	8.68
46.	Kentucky	8.67
47.	Texas	8.27
48.	West Virginia	7.57
49.	Mississippi	7.38
50.	Tennessee	7.23
51.	Arkansas	6.44

Institutions of Higher Education—Charges: 1970 to 1991

Source: National Center for Education Statistics, U.S. Dept. of Education.

Data are for the entire academic year ending in year shown. Figures for 1970 are average charges for full-time resident degree-credit students; figures for later years are average charges per full-time equivalent student. Room and board are based on full-time students.

Academic Control and Year	Tuition and Required Fees			Board Rates			Dormitory Charges		
	All institutions	2-yr. colleges	4-yr. universities	All institutions	2-yr. colleges	4-yr. universities	All institutions	2-yr. colleges	4-yr. universities
Public:									
1970	$323	$178	$427	$511	$465	$540	$369	$308	$395
1980	583	355	840	867	894	898	715	572	749
1990	1,356	756	2,035	1,635	1,581	1,728	1,513	962	1,561
1991	1,454	824	2,159	1,691	1,594	1,767	1,612	1,050	1,658
Private:									
1970	1,533	1,034	1,809	561	546	608	436	413	503
1980	3,130	2,062	3,811	955	924	1,078	827	769	999
1990	8,147	5,196	10,348	1,948	1,811	2,339	1,923	1,663	2,411
1991	8,772	5,570	11,379	2,074	1,989	2,470	2,063	1,744	2,654

American Colleges and Universities

General Information for the 1991–92 Academic Year

Source: Peterson's Guides

These listings include all accredited undergraduate degree-granting institutions in the United States and U.S. territories that have a total institutional enrollment of 1,000 or more. Four-year colleges (those that award a bachelor's as their highest undergraduate degree) are listed first, followed by two-year colleges (those that award an associate as their highest or primary undergraduate degree).

All institutions are coeducational except those where the zip code is followed by: (1)–men only, (2)–primarily men, (3)–women only, (4)–primarily women.

Year is that of founding.

Governing official is the chief executive officer.

Institutional control: 1–independent (nonprofit), 2–independent-religious, 3–proprietary (profit making), 4–federal, 5–state, 7–commonwealth (Puerto Rico), 8–territory (U.S. territories), 9–county, 10–district, 11–city, 12–state and local, 13–state related.

Highest degree offered: B–bachelor's, M–master's, D–doctorate (includes first professional degrees).

Enrollment is the total number of matriculated undergraduate and (if applicable) graduate students.

Faculty is the total number of faculty members teaching undergraduate courses.

Any data not reported are indicated as NR.

Four-Year Colleges

Name, address	Year	Governing official, control, and highest degree offered		Enrollment	Faculty
Abilene Christian U, Abilene, TX 79699	1906	Dr. Royce Money	2-D	3,946	232
Adams State Coll, Alamosa, CO 81102	1921	Dr. William M. Fulkerson, Jr.	5-M	2,475	129
Adelphi U, Garden City, NY 11530	1896	Dr. Peter Diamandopoulos	1-D	8,535	702
Adrian Coll, Adrian, MI 49221	1859	Dr. Stanley P. Caine	2-B	1,194	134
Alabama A&M U, Normal, AL 35762	1875	Dr. David B. Henson	5-D	5,215	353
Alabama State U, Montgomery, AL 36101	1874	Dr. C.C. Baker	5-M	4,800	270
Albany State Coll, Albany, GA 31705	1903	Dr. Billy C. Black	5-M	2,746	150
Albion Coll, Albion, MI 49224	1835	Dr. Melvin L. Vulgamore	2-B	1,655	131
Albright Coll, Reading, PA 19612	1856	Dr. Ellen S. Hurwitz	2-B	1,090	129
Alcorn State U, Lorman, MS 39096	1871	Dr. Walter Washington	5-M	3,256	183
Alfred U, Alfred, NY 14802	1836	Dr. Edward G. Coll, Jr.	1-D	2,258	208
Allegheny Coll, Meadville, PA 16335	1815	Dr. Daniel F. Sullivan	2-B	1,858	198
Allentown Coll of St Francis de Sales, Center Valley, PA 18034-9568	1962	Very Rev. Daniel Gambet	2-M	2,100	96
Alma Coll, Alma, MI 48801-1599	1886	Dr. Alan J. Stone	2-B	1,224	112
Alvernia Coll, Reading, PA 19607-1799	1958	Dr. Daniel N. DeLucca	2-B	1,120	114
Alverno Coll, Milwaukee, WI 53234-3922 (3)	1887	Joel Read	1-B	2,499	196
Amber U, Garland, TX 75041	1971	Dr. Douglas W. Warner	1-M	1,610	65
American International Coll, Springfield, MA 01109	1885	Dr. Harry J. Courniotes	1-D	1,919	122
American U, Washington, DC 20016	1893	Dr. Joseph D. Duffey	2-D	10,153	1,060
Amherst Coll, Amherst, MA 01002	1821	Peter R. Pouncey	1-B	1,581	180
Anderson Coll, Anderson, SC 29621	1911	Dr. Mark L. Hopkins	2-B	1,079	73
Anderson U, Anderson, IN 46012	1917	Dr. James L. Edwards	2-M	2,162	119
Andrews U, Berrien Springs, MI 49104	1874	Dr. W. Richard Lesher	2-D	3,057	329
Angelo State U, San Angelo, TX 76909	1928	Dr. Lloyd Drexell Vincent	5-M	6,128	229
Anna Maria Coll, Paxton, MA 01612	1946	Sr. Bernadette Madore	2-M	1,554	92
Appalachian State U, Boone, NC 28608	1899	Dr. John E. Thomas	5-D	11,367	682
Aquinas Coll, Grand Rapids, MI 49506-1799	1886	Mr. R. Paul Nelson	2-M	2,574	193
Arizona State U, Tempe, AZ 85287	1885	Dr. Lattie F. Coor	5-D	42,626	1,805
Arkansas State U, State University, AR 72467	1909	Dr. John N. Mangieri	5-D	9,717	444
Arkansas Tech U, Russellville, AR 72801	1909	Dr. Kenneth G. Kersh	5-M	4,333	226
Armstrong State Coll, Savannah, GA 31419	1935	Dr. Robert A. Burnett	5-M	5,047	179
Art Ctr Coll of Design, Pasadena, CA 91103	1930	Mr. David R. Brown	1-M	1,289	306
Asbury Coll, Wilmore, KY 40390-1198	1890	Dr. Edwin G. Blue	2-B	1,086	102
Ashland U, Ashland, OH 44805	1878	Dr. Walter Waetjen	2-M	4,961	177
Assumption Coll, Worcester, MA 01615-0005	1904	Joseph H. Hagan	2-M	2,952	180
Athens State Coll, Athens, AL 35611	1822	Dr. Jerry F. Bartlett	5-B	3,500	140
Atlantic Union Coll, South Lancaster, MA 01561	1882	Dr. Lawrence T. Geraty	2-M	1,273	87
Auburn U, Auburn University, AL 36849	1856	Dr. William V. Muse	5-D	21,836	1,188
Auburn U at Montgomery, Montgomery, AL 36117-3596	1967	Dr. James O. Williams	5-D	6,485	250
Augsburg Coll, Minneapolis, MN 55454	1869	Dr. Charles S. Anderson	2-M	3,023	171
Augusta Coll, Augusta, GA 30910	1925	Dr. Martha Farmer	5-M	5,292	174
Augustana Coll, Rock Island, IL 61201	1860	Dr. Thomas Tredway	2-B	2,182	185
Augustana Coll, Sioux Falls, SD 57197	1860	Dr. Lloyd Svendsbye	2-M	1,925	142
Aurora U, Aurora, IL 60506	1893	Thomas H. Zarle	1-M	2,106	240
Austin Coll, Sherman, TX 75091	1849	Dr. Harry E. Smith	2-M	1,178	95
Austin Peay State U, Clarksville, TN 37044	1927	Dr. Oscar Page	5-M	7,670	469
Averett Coll, Danville, VA 24541	1859	Dr. Frank R. Campbell	2-M	1,603	65
Avila Coll, Kansas City, MO 64145	1916	Dr. Larry Kramer	2-M	1,330	152
Azusa Pacific U, Azusa, CA 91702	1899	Dr. Richard E. Felix	2-M	2,955	177
Babson Coll, Babson Park, MA 02157	1919	Mr. William F. Glavin	1-M	3,031	160
Baker Coll of Flint, Flint, MI 48507	1911	Mr. Edward J. Kurtz	1-B	3,861	146
Baker Coll of Muskegon, Muskegon, MI 49442	1888	Mr. Robert D. Jewell	1-B	1,860	60
Baker Coll of Owosso, Owosso, MI 48867	1984	NR	1-B	1,075	37
Baker U, Baldwin City, KS 66006	1858	Dr. Daniel M. Lambert	2-M	1,600	76
Baldwin-Wallace Coll, Berea, OH 44017	1845	Dr. Neal Malicky	2-M	4,721	335
Ball State U, Muncie, IN 47306	1918	Dr. John E. Worthen	5-D	20,488	1,168
Bard Coll, Annandale-on-Hudson, NY 12504	1860	Dr. Leon Botstein	1-M	1,160	135
Barnard Coll, New York, NY 10027-6598 (3)	1889	Ms. Ellen V. Futter	1-B	2,130	264
Barry U, Miami Shores, FL 33161	1940	Sr. Jeanne O'Laughlin	2-D	6,107	376
Barton Coll, Wilson, NC 27893	1902	Dr. James B. Hemby	2-B	1,703	106
Baruch Coll of the City U of New York, New York, NY 10010	1968	Dr. Matthew Goldstein	12-M	15,853	975
Bates Coll, Lewiston, ME 04240	1855	Dr. Donald W. Harward	1-B	1,500	165

Name, address	Year	Governing official, control, and highest degree offered	Enroll-ment	Faculty
Bayamón Central U, Bayamón, PR 00621	1970	Rev. Vincent A. M. Van Rooij, OP 2-M	2,846	108
Baylor U, Waco, TX 76798	1845	Dr. Herbert H. Reynolds 2-D	11,810	635
Beaver Coll, Glenside, PA 19038-3295	1853	Dr. Bette E. Landman 2-M	2,204	183
Bellarmine Coll, Louisville, KY 40205	1950	Dr. Joseph J. McGowan, Jr. 2-M	2,294	126
Bellevue Coll, Bellevue, NE 68005	1965	Dr. John B. Muller 1-M	2,279	83
Belmont Abbey Coll, Belmont, NC 28012	1876	Dr. Joseph Brosnan 2-B	1,016	93
Belmont U, Nashville, TN 37212	1951	Dr. William E. Troutt 2-M	2,821	262
Beloit Coll, Beloit, WI 53511	1846	Mr. Victor E. Ferrall, Jr. 1-M	1,176	127
Bemidji State U, Bemidji, MN 56601	1919	Dr. Leslie C. Duly 5-M	5,401	220
Benedict Coll, Columbia, SC 29204	1870	Dr. Marshall C. Grigsby 2-B	1,422	118
Benedictine Coll, Atchison, KS 66002	1859	Thomas O. James 2-M	1,130	88
Bentley Coll, Waltham, MA 02154-4705	1917	Dr. Joseph M. Cronin 1-M	7,277	381
Berea Coll, Berea, KY 40404	1855	Dr. John B. Stephenson 1-B	1,589	129
Berklee Coll of Music, Boston, MA 02215	1945	Dr. Lee Eliot Berk 1-B	2,360	265
Berry Coll, Rome, GA 30149-0159	1902	Dr. Gloria M. Shatto 1-M	1,740	138
Bethel Coll, St Paul, MN 55112	1871	Dr. George K. Brushaber 2-M	2,001	181
Bethune-Cookman Coll, Daytona Beach, FL 32115	1904	Dr. Oswald P. Bronson, Sr. 2-B	2,273	200
Biola U, La Mirada, CA 90639	1908	Dr. Clyde Cook 2-D	2,600	216
Birmingham-Southern Coll, Birmingham, AL 35254	1856	Dr. Neal R. Berte 2-M	1,825	141
Black Hills State U, Spearfish, SD 57799	1883	Dr. Clifford M. Trump 5-M	2,734	114
Bloomfield Coll, Bloomfield, NJ 07003	1868	Dr. John F. Noonan 2-B	1,858	230
Bloomsburg U of Pennsylvania, Bloomsburg, PA 17815	1839	Dr. Harry Ausprich 5-M	7,720	387
Bluefield State Coll, Bluefield, WV 24701	1895	Dr. Gregory D. Adkins 5-B	2,907	186
Bob Jones U, Greenville, SC 29614	1927	Dr. Bob Jones, III 2-D	3,990	346
Boise State U, Boise, ID 83725	1932	Dr. John H. Keiser 5-M	14,254	744
Boricua Coll, New York, NY 10032	1974	Dr. Victor G. Alicea 1-B	1,146	128
Boston Coll, Chestnut Hill, MA 02167	1863	Rev. J. Donald Monan, SJ 2-D	14,557	936
Boston U, Boston, MA 02215	1839	John Silber 1-D	24,348	2,141
Bowdoin Coll, Brunswick, ME 04011	1794	Mr. Robert H. Edwards 1-B	1,400	135
Bowie State U, Bowie, MD 20715	1865	Dr. James E. Lyons, Sr. 5-M	4,437	234
Bowling Green State U, Bowling Green, OH 43403	1910	Dr. Paul J. Olscamp 5-D	17,960	913
Bradley U, Peoria, IL 61625	1897	Dr. John R. Brazil 1-M	6,233	433
Brandeis U, Waltham, MA 02254-9110	1948	Dr. Samuel O. Thier 1-D	3,772	464
Brewton-Parker Coll, Mt Vernon, GA 30445	1904	Dr. Y. Lynn Holmes 2-B	1,942	81
Briar Cliff Coll, Sioux City, IA 51104	1930	Sr. Margaret Wick 2-B	1,090	85
Bridgewater State Coll, Bridgewater, MA 02325	1840	Dr. Adrian Tinsley 5-M	6,933	333
Brigham Young U, Provo, UT 84602	1875	Dr. Rex E. Lee 2-D	30,898	1,605
Brigham Young U–Hawaii Cmps, Laie, Oahu, HI 96762	1955	Dr. Alton L. Wade 2-B	2,108	149
Brooklyn Coll of the City U of New York, Brooklyn, NY 11210	1930	Dr. James W. Loughran 12-M	16,200	993
Brown U, Providence, RI 02912	1764	Vartan Gregorian 1-D	7,532	665
Bryant Coll, Smithfield, RI 02917	1863	Dr. William E. Trueheart 1-M	4,918	229
Bryn Mawr Coll, Bryn Mawr, PA 19010 (4)	1885	Mary Patterson McPherson 1-D	1,881	209
Bucknell U, Lewisburg, PA 17837	1846	Dr. Gary A. Sojka 1-M	3,578	261
Buena Vista Coll, Storm Lake, IA 50588	1891	Dr. Keith G. Briscoe 2-B	1,032	96
Butler U, Indianapolis, IN 46208	1855	Dr. Geoffrey Bannister 1-M	3,887	384
Cabrini Coll, Radnor, PA 19087-3699	1957	Dr. Antoinette Iadarola 2-M	1,559	106
Caldwell Coll, Caldwell, NJ 07006	1939	Sr. Vivien Jennings 2-B	1,306	87
California Coll for Health Sciences, National City, CA 91950	1977	NR 3-M	4,200	7
California Coll of Arts and Crafts, Oakland, CA 94618	1907	Mr. Neil J. Hoffman 1-M	1,168	167
California Inst of Tech, Pasadena, CA 91125	1891	Dr. Thomas E. Everhart 1-D	1,934	270
California Inst of the Arts, Valencia, CA 91355	1961	Dr. Steven D. Lavine 1-M	1,009	232
California Lutheran U, Thousand Oaks, CA 91360	1959	Dr. Jerry H. Miller 2-M	2,936	250
California Polytechnic State U, San Luis Obispo, San Luis Obispo, CA 93407	1901	Dr. Warren J. Baker 5-M	17,758	1,069
California State Polytechnic U, Pomona, Pomona, CA 91768	1938	Dr. Bob Suzuki 5-M	18,777	886
California State U, Bakersfield, Bakersfield, CA 93311	1970	Dr. Tomas A. Arciniega 5-M	5,425	337
California State U, Chico, Chico, CA 95929	1887	Dr. Robin Wilson 5-M	15,669	876
California State U, Dominguez Hills, Carson, CA 90747	1960	Dr. Robert Detweiler 5-M	10,357	458
California State U, Fresno, Fresno, CA 93740	1911	Dr. John D. Welty 5-M	19,824	1,220
California State U, Fullerton, Fullerton, CA 92634	1957	Dr. Milton A. Gordon 5-M	25,486	1,245
California State U, Hayward, Hayward, CA 94542	1957	Dr. Norma Rees 5-M	13,110	578
California State U, Long Beach, Long Beach, CA 90840-0119	1949	Dr. Curtis L. McCray 5-M	33,991	1,958
California State U, Los Angeles, Los Angeles, CA 90032	1947	Dr. James M. Rosser 5-D	20,801	946
California State U, Northridge, Northridge, CA 91330	1958	NR 5-M	30,441	1,547
California State U, Sacramento, Sacramento, CA 95819-6048	1947	Dr. Donald R. Gerth 5-M	25,868	1,204
California State U, San Bernardino, San Bernardino, CA 92407	1965	Dr. Anthony H. Evans 5-M	12,561	642
California State U, Stanislaus, Turlock, CA 95380	1957	Dr. John W. Moore 5-M	5,800	300
California U of Pennsylvania, California, PA 15419-1394	1852	Dr. John Pierce Watkins 5-M	6,711	385
Calumet Coll of Saint Joseph, Whiting, IN 46394	1951	Dr. Dennis C. Rittenmeyer 2-B	1,109	110
Calvin Coll, Grand Rapids, MI 49546	1876	Dr. Anthony J. Diekema 2-M	4,025	281
Campbellsville Coll, Campbellsville, KY 42718-2799	1906	Dr. Kenneth W. Winters 2-B	1,010	60
Campbell U, Buies Creek, NC 27506	1887	Dr. Norman A. Wiggins 2-D	5,777	261
Canisius Coll, Buffalo, NY 14208	1870	Rev. James M. Demske, SJ 2-M	4,629	361
Capital U, Columbus, OH 43209	1830	NR 2-D	3,453	172
Cardinal Stritch Coll, Milwaukee, WI 53217-3985	1937	Sr. Mary Lea Schneider 2-M	3,991	315
Carleton Coll, Northfield, MN 55057	1866	Dr. Stephen R. Lewis, Jr. 1-B	1,700	166
Carlow Coll, Pittsburgh, PA 15213 (4)	1929	Dr. Grace Ann Geibel, RSM 2-M	1,363	154
Carnegie Mellon U, Pittsburgh, PA 15213	1900	Dr. Robert Mehrabian 1-D	7,150	797
Carroll Coll, Helena, MT 59625	1909	Dr. Matthew Quinn 2-B	1,281	114
Carroll Coll, Waukesha, WI 53186	1846	NR 2-M	2,152	129
Carson-Newman Coll, Jefferson City, TN 37760	1851	Dr. J. Cordell Maddox 2-M	2,118	183
Carthage Coll, Kenosha, WI 53140	1847	Dr. F. Gregory Campbell 2-M	2,001	151
Case Western Reserve U, Cleveland, OH 44106	1826	Dr. Agnar Pytte 1-D	8,758	1,725
Castleton State Coll, Castleton, VT 05735	1787	Dr. Lyle A. Gray 5-M	2,079	115
Catholic U of America, Washington, DC 20064	1887	Br. F. Patrick Ellis 2-D	6,632	706
Cedar Crest Coll, Allentown, PA 18104 (4)	1867	Dr. Dorothy G. Blaney 2-B	1,005	119
Cedarville Coll, Cedarville, OH 45314	1887	Dr. Paul H. Dixon 2-B	2,046	126
Central Connecticut State U, New Britain, CT 06050	1849	Dr. John W. Shumaker 5-M	10,786	718
Central Michigan U, Mount Pleasant, MI 48859	1892	Dr. Leonard E. Plachte 5-D	16,593	813
Central Missouri State U, Warrensburg, MO 64093	1871	Dr. Ed Elliott 5-M	11,621	478

Name, address	Year	Governing official, control, and highest degree offered	Enrollment	Faculty
Central State U, Wilberforce, OH 45384	1887	Dr. Arthur E. Thomas 5-M	3,266	147
Central U of Iowa, Pella, IA 50219	1853	Dr. William M. Wiebenga 2-B	1,571	126
Central Washington U, Ellensburg, WA 98926	1891	Dr. Ivory V. Nelson 5-M	7,383	344
Central Wesleyan Coll, Central, SC 29630-1020	1906	Dr. John M. Newby 2-M	1,091	132
Chadron State Coll, Chadron, NE 69337	1911	Dr. Samuel H. Rankin 5-M	3,413	135
Chaminade U of Honolulu, Honolulu, HI 96816	1955	Mr. Kent M. Keith 2-M	2,624	195
Chapman U, Orange, CA 92666	1861	Dr. James Doti 2-M	2,323	183
Charleston Southern U, Charleston, SC 29411	1964	Dr. Jairy C. Hunter, Jr. 2-M	2,413	112
Chestnut Hill Coll, Philadelphia, PA 19118-2695 (3)	1924	Dr. Carol J. Vale, SSJ 2-M	1,228	109
Cheyney U of Pennsylvania, Cheyney, PA 19319	1837	Dr. Douglas Covington 5-M	1,607	99
Chicago State U, Chicago, IL 60628	1867	Dr. Dolores Cross 5-M	8,004	397
Christian Brothers U, Memphis, TN 38104	1871	Br. Theodore Drahmann, FSC 2-M	1,736	149
Christopher Newport U, Newport News, VA 23606	1961	Dr. Anthony Santoro 5-M	5,034	280
The Citadel, The Military Coll of South Carolina, Charleston, SC 29409 (1)	1842	Lt. Gen. Claudius E. Watts, III 5-M	3,670	152
City Coll of the City U of New York, New York, NY 10031	1847	Bernard W. Harleston 12-D	14,692	1,332
City U, Bellevue, WA 98004	1973	Dr. Michael A. Pastore 1-M	6,050	811
Clarion U of Pennsylvania, Clarion, PA 16214	1867	Dr. Diane L. Reinhard 5-M	6,209	383
Clark Atlanta U, Atlanta, GA 30314	1869	NR 1-D	3,996	246
Clarkson U, Potsdam, NY 13699	1896	Dr. Richard H. Gallagher 1-D	3,146	209
Clark U, Worcester, MA 01610-1477	1887	Dr. Richard P. Traina 1-D	2,885	NR
Clayton State Coll, Morrow, GA 30260	1969	NR 5-B	4,551	191
Cleary Coll, Ypsilanti, MI 48197	1883	Mr. Thomas Sullivan 1-B	1,100	67
Clemson U, Clemson, SC 29634	1889	Dr. Max Lennon 5-D	17,295	1,060
Cleveland State U, Cleveland, OH 44115	1964	Dr. J. Taylor Sims 5-D	18,006	690
Clinch Valley Coll of the U of Virginia, Wise, VA 24293	1954	Dr. Jimmy A. Knight 5-B	1,678	111
Coe Coll, Cedar Rapids, IA 52402	1851	Dr. John E. Brown 2-B	1,248	113
Colby Coll, Waterville, ME 04901	1813	William R. Cotter 1-B	1,716	173
Colgate U, Hamilton, NY 13346	1819	Dr. Neil R. Grabois 1-M	2,720	273
Coll for Human Services, New York, NY 10014	1964	Audrey C. Cohen 1-M	1,027	61
Coll Misericordia, Dallas, PA 18612	1924	Dr. Carol A. Smith-Jabe 2-M	1,595	120
Coll of Aeronautics, Flushing, NY 11371 (2)	1932	Dr. Richard B. Goetle, Jr. 1-B	1,300	88
Coll of Charleston, Charleston, SC 29424	1770	Dr. Alexander M. Sanders, Jr. 5-M	8,781	424
Coll of Great Falls, Great Falls, MT 59405	1932	Dr. William A. Shields 2-M	1,098	125
Coll of Insurance, New York, NY 10007	1962	Dr. Ellen Thrower 1-M	1,676	93
Coll of Mount St Joseph, Cincinnati, OH 45233-1670	1920	Francis Marie Thrailkill, OSU 2-M	2,563	205
Coll of Mount Saint Vincent, Riverdale, NY 10471	1911	Dr. Mary Clark Stuart 1-M	1,098	95
Coll of New Rochelle, New Rochelle, NY 10805 (4)	1904	Sr. Dorothy A. Kelly, OSU 1-M	2,406	105
Coll of New Rochelle, New Resources Division, New Rochelle, NY 10805	1972	NR 1-B	3,248	413
Coll of Notre Dame, Belmont, CA 94002	1851	Sr. Veronica Skillin 2-M	1,247	91
Coll of Saint Benedict, Saint Joseph, MN 56374 (3)	1887	Sr. Colman O'Connell, OSB 2-B	1,803	159
Coll of St Catherine, St Paul, MN 55105 (3)	1905	Dr. Anita Pampusch 2-M	2,539	239
Coll of Saint Elizabeth, Morristown, NJ 07960-6989 (4)	1899	Sr. Jacqueline Burns 2-B	1,202	126
Coll of St Francis, Joliet, IL 60435	1920	Dr. John C. Orr 2-M	1,970	95
Coll of Saint Mary, Omaha, NE 68124 (4)	1923	Dr. Kenneth Nielsen 2-B	1,304	136
Coll of Saint Rose, Albany, NY 12203	1920	Dr. Louis C. Vaccaro 1-M	3,715	241
Coll of St Scholastica, Duluth, MN 55811	1906	Dr. Daniel H. Pilon 2-M	1,946	139
Coll of Santa Fe, Santa Fe, NM 87501	1947	Dr. James A. Fries 1-M	1,242	81
Coll of Staten Island of the City U of New York, Staten Island, NY 10301	1955	Dr. Edmond L. Volpe 12-M	12,255	690
Coll of the Holy Cross, Worcester, MA 01610	1843	Rev. John E. Brooks, SJ 2-B	2,641	246
Coll of the Ozarks, Point Lookout, MO 65726	1906	Dr. Jerry C. Davis 2-B	1,583	111
Coll of West Virginia, Beckley, WV 25802	1933	Dr. Charles Polk 1-B	1,669	110
Coll of William and Mary, Williamsburg, VA 23185	1693	Dr. Paul R. Verkuil 5-D	7,710	596
The Coll of Wooster, Wooster, OH 44691	1866	Dr. Henry J. Copeland 2-B	1,779	155
Colorado Christian U, Lakewood, CO 80226	1914	Dr. L. David Beckman 2-M	1,000	81
The Colorado Coll, Colorado Springs, CO 80903	1874	NR 1-M	1,952	260
Colorado Sch of Mines, Golden, CO 80401	1874	Dr. George S. Ansell 5-D	2,663	215
Colorado State U, Fort Collins, CO 80523	1862	Dr. Albert C. Yates 5-D	20,967	1,019
Colorado Tech Coll, Colorado Springs, CO 80907	1965	Mr. David D. O'Donnell 3-M	1,405	76
Columbia Coll, Chicago, IL 60605	1890	Mr. John B. Duff 1-M	7,002	778
Columbia Coll, New York, NY 10027	1754	Dr. Jack Greenberg 1-B	3,325	475
Columbia Coll, Columbia, SC 29203 (3)	1854	Dr. Peter T. Mitchell 2-M	1,235	75
Columbia Union Coll, Takoma Park, MD 20912	1904	Dr. N. Clifford Sorensen 2-B	1,266	54
Columbia U, Sch of Engineering & Applied Sci, New York, NY 10027	1864	David H. Auston 1-D	1,811	112
Columbia U, Sch of General Studies, New York, NY 10027	1754	Frank Wolf 1-M	1,196	450
Columbia U, Sch of Nursing, New York, NY 10032 (4)	1935	NR 1-M	110	35
Columbus Coll, Columbus, GA 31993	1958	Dr. Frank D. Brown 5-M	4,568	228
Columbus Coll of Art and Design, Columbus, OH 43215	1879	Mr. Joseph V. Canzani 1-B	1,620	104
Concord Coll, Athens, WV 24712	1872	Dr. Jerry L. Beasley 5-B	2,937	154
Concordia Coll, Moorhead, MN 56562	1891	Dr. Paul J. Dovre 2-B	2,933	253
Concordia Coll, St Paul, MN 55104	1893	Dr. Robert Holst 2-M	1,162	109
Concordia U, River Forest, IL 60305	1864	Dr. Eugene L. Krentz 2-M	1,602	152
Concordia U Wisconsin, Mequon, WI 53092-7699	1881	Dr. R. John Buuck 2-M	2,074	136
Connecticut Coll, New London, CT 06320	1911	Claire L. Gaudiani 1-M	1,846	190
Converse Coll, Spartanburg, SC 29302 (3)	1889	Dr. Ellen Wood Hall 1-M	1,208	100
Cooper Union for the Advancement of Science & Art, New York, NY 10003	1859	Mr. John Jay Iselin 1-M	1,085	167
Coppin State Coll, Baltimore, MD 21216	1900	Dr. Calvin W. Burnett 5-M	2,816	153
Cornell Coll, Mount Vernon, IA 52314	1853	Dr. David G. Marker 2-B	1,111	127
Cornell U, Ithaca, NY 14853	1865	Dr. Frank H. T. Rhodes 1-D	18,627	1,617
Creighton U, Omaha, NE 68178	1878	Rev. Michael G. Morrison, SJ 2-D	6,140	1,252
Culver-Stockton Coll, Canton, MO 63435	1853	Dr. Edwin B. Strong, Jr. 2-B	1,169	66
Cumberland Coll, Williamsburg, KY 40769-1372	1889	Dr. James Taylor 2-M	1,812	118
Daemen Coll, Amherst, NY 14226	1947	Dr. Robert S. Marshall 1-B	1,900	131
Dakota State U, Madison, SD 57042	1881	Dr. Jerald Tunheim 5-B	1,465	59
Dallas Baptist U, Dallas, TX 75211-9288	1965	Dr. Gary R. Cook 2-M	2,635	164
Dartmouth Coll, Hanover, NH 03755	1769	James O. Freedman 1-D	5,475	468
Davenport Coll of Business, Grand Rapids, MI 49503	1866	Donald W. Maine 1-B	4,077	188
Davenport Coll of Business, Kalamazoo Cmps, Kalamazoo, MI 49007 (4)	1866	C. Dexter Rohm 1-B	1,733	105
Davenport Coll of Business, Lansing Cmps, Lansing, MI 48933	1979	Don Colizzi 1-B	1,512	86

Name, address	Year	Governing official, control, and highest degree offered		Enroll-ment	Faculty
David Lipscomb U, Nashville, TN 37204	1891	Dr. Harold Hazelip	2-M	2,257	175
Davidson Coll, Davidson, NC 28036	1837	Dr. John W. Kuykendall	2-B	1,555	127
The Defiance Coll, Defiance, OH 43512	1850	Dr. Marvin J. Ludwig	2-M	1,001	63
Delaware State Coll, Dover, DE 19901	1891	Dr. William B. DeLauder	5-M	2,882	161
Delaware Valley Coll, Doylestown, PA 18901-2697	1896	Mr. George F. West	1-B	1,204	90
Delta State U, Cleveland, MS 38733	1925	Dr. F. Kent Wyatt	5-D	4,002	236
Denison U, Granville, OH 43023	1831	Dr. Michele Tolela Myers	1-B	2,022	171
DePaul U, Chicago, IL 60604	1898	Rev. John T. Richardson, CM	2-D	16,414	1,146
DePauw U, Greencastle, IN 46135	1837	Dr. Robert Bottoms	2-B	2,171	230
Detroit Coll of Business, Dearborn, MI 48126	1962	Dr. James Mendola	1-B	4,787	134
Detroit Coll of Business, Warren Cmps, Warren, MI 48092	1975	Janet Guggenheim	1-B	1,209	95
DeVry Inst of Tech, Phoenix, AZ 85021	1967	James A. Dugan	3-B	2,719	57
DeVry Inst of Tech, City of Industry, CA 91746	1983	Paul R. McGuirk	3-B	1,884	61
DeVry Inst of Tech, Decatur, GA 30030	1969	Dr. Ronald Bush	3-B	3,133	65
DeVry Inst of Tech, Chicago, IL 60618	1931	Dr. E. Arthur Stunnard	3-B	3,331	54
DeVry Inst of Tech, Lombard, IL 60148	1982	Jerry R. Dill	3-B	2,564	54
DeVry Inst of Tech, Kansas City, MO 64131	1931	Mr. Charles R. Levalley	3-B	1,814	58
DeVry Inst of Tech, Columbus, OH 43209	1952	Mr. Richard A. Czerniak	3-B	2,745	67
DeVry Inst of Tech, Irving, TX 75038	1969	Dr. Francis V. Cannon	3-B	2,240	47
Dickinson Coll, Carlisle, PA 17013	1773	Dr. A. Lee Fritschler	1-B	2,029	186
Dickinson State U, Dickinson, ND 58601-4896	1918	Dr. Albert A. Watrel	5-B	1,491	98
Dillard U, New Orleans, LA 70122	1869	Dr. Samuel DuBois Cook	2-B	1,651	124
Dominican Coll of Blauvelt, Orangeburg, NY 10962	1952	Sr. Kathleen Sullivan	1-B	1,484	122
Dordt Coll, Sioux Center, IA 51250-1697	1955	Dr. John B. Hulst	2-B	1,046	90
Dowling Coll, Oakdale, NY 11769	1955	Dr. Victor P. Meskill	1-M	4,695	372
Drake U, Des Moines, IA 50311	1881	Dr. Michael R. Ferrari	1-D	8,096	275
Drew U, Madison, NJ 07940	1867	Mr. Thomas H. Kean	2-D	2,089	175
Drexel U, Philadelphia, PA 19104	1891	Dr. Richard D. Breslin	1-D	11,594	749
Drury Coll, Springfield, MO 65802	1873	Dr. John E. Moore, Jr.	2-M	1,579	113
Duke U, Durham, NC 27706	1838	Dr. H. Keith H. Brodie	2-D	10,736	1,530
Duquesne U, Pittsburgh, PA 15282	1878	Dr. John E. Murray, Jr.	2-D	8,015	593
D'Youville Coll, Buffalo, NY 14201	1908	Dr. Denise A. Roche, GNSH	1-M	1,581	117
Earlham Coll, Richmond, IN 47374	1847	Dr. Richard J. Wood	2-M	1,213	114
East Carolina U, Greenville, NC 27858-4353	1907	Dr. Richard Eakin	5-D	16,690	1,092
East Central U, Ada, OK 74820	1909	Dr. Bill S. Cole	5-M	4,388	200
Eastern Coll, Saint Davids, PA 19087-3696	1932	Dr. Roberta Hestenes	2-M	1,502	118
Eastern Connecticut State U, Willimantic, CT 06226	1889	David G. Carter	5-M	4,328	195
Eastern Illinois U, Charleston, IL 61920-3099	1895	Dr. Stanley G. Rives	5-M	10,450	643
Eastern Kentucky U, Richmond, KY 40475	1906	Dr. Hanly Funderburk	5-M	16,525	829
Eastern Michigan U, Ypsilanti, MI 48197	1849	Dr. William E. Shelton	5-D	25,842	1,046
Eastern Montana Coll, Billings, MT 59101	1927	Dr. Bruce H. Carpenter	5-M	3,631	191
Eastern Nazarene Coll, Quincy, MA 02170	1918	Dr. Cecil R. Paul	2-M	1,004	63
Eastern New Mexico U, Portales, NM 88130	1934	Dr. Everett L. Frost	5-M	3,879	200
Eastern Oregon State Coll, La Grande, OR 97850	1929	David E. Gilbert	5-M	1,862	164
Eastern Washington U, Cheney, WA 99004	1882	Dr. Marshall Drummond	5-M	8,348	423
East Stroudsburg U of Pennsylvania, East Stroudsburg, PA 18301	1893	Dr. James Gilbert	5-M	5,494	277
East Tennessee State U, Johnson City, TN 37614	1911	Dr. Bert C. Bach	5-D	12,135	576
East Texas Baptist U, Marshall, TX 75670-1498	1912	Dr. Harvey Lewis	2-B	1,015	75
East Texas State U, Commerce, TX 75429	1889	Dr. Jerry D. Morris	5-D	8,007	366
East Texas State U at Texarkana, Texarkana, TX 75505-0518	1971	Dr. John F. Moss	5-M	1,363	51
Eckerd Coll, St Petersburg, FL 33733	1958	Dr. Peter H. Armacost	2-B	1,368	113
Edgewood Coll, Madison, WI 53711	1927	Dr. James A. Ebben	2-M	1,591	98
Edinboro U of Pennsylvania, Edinboro, PA 16444	1857	Foster F. Diebold	5-M	8,165	439
Elizabeth City State U, Elizabeth City, NC 27909	1891	Dr. Jimmy R. Jenkins	5-B	1,762	133
Elizabethtown Coll, Elizabethtown, PA 17022	1899	Dr. Gerhard E. Spiegler	2-B	1,809	147
Elmhurst Coll, Elmhurst, IL 60126-3296	1871	Dr. Ivan E. Frick	2-B	2,848	154
Elmira Coll, Elmira, NY 14901	1855	Dr. Thomas K. Meier	1-M	1,001	75
Elms Coll, Chicopee, MA 01013 (3)	1928	Sr. Mary A. Dooley	2-M	1,250	101
Elon Coll, Elon College, NC 27244	1889	Dr. J. Fred Young	2-M	3,221	205
Embry-Riddle Aeronautical U, Daytona Beach, FL 32114-3900	1926	Kenneth Tallman	1-M	4,816	261
Embry-Riddle Aeronautical U, Coll of Continuing Ed, Daytona Beach, FL 32114	1926	NR	1-M	5,393	1,645
Embry-Riddle Aeronautical U, Western Cmps, Prescott, AZ 86301	1978	Paul S. Daly	1-B	1,607	95
Emerson Coll, Boston, MA 02116	1880	Dr. John C. Zacharis	1-D	2,626	220
Emmanuel Coll, Boston, MA 02115 (3)	1919	Sr. Janet Eisner	2-M	1,170	92
Emory U, Atlanta, GA 30322	1836	Dr. James T. Laney	2-D	9,483	621
Emporia State U, Emporia, KS 66801-5087	1863	Dr. Robert E. Glennen	5-M	6,034	244
Eugene Lang Coll, New Sch for Social Research, New York, NY 10011	1985	Donald Scott	1-B	360	60
Evangel Coll, Springfield, MO 65802	1955	Dr. Robert H. Spence	2-B	1,440	122
Evergreen State Coll, Olympia, WA 98505	1967	Dr. Jane Jervis	5-M	3,340	175
Fairfield U, Fairfield, CT 06430	1942	Rev. Aloysius P. Kelley	2-M	4,804	274
Fairleigh Dickinson U, Florham-Madison Cmps, Madison, NJ 07940	1958	Dr. Francis J. Mertz	1-M	3,428	179
Fairleigh Dickinson U, Rutherford Cmps, Rutherford, NJ 07070	1942	Dr. Francis J. Mertz	1-M	2,294	123
Fairleigh Dickinson U, Teaneck-Hackensack Cmps, Teaneck, NJ 07666	1954	Dr. Francis J. Mertz	1-D	3,271	252
Fairmont State Coll, Fairmont, WV 26554	1865	Dr. Robert J. Dillman	5-B	6,368	349
Fashion Inst of Tech, New York, NY 10001-5992	1944	Dr. Marvin J. Feldman	12-M	12,085	820
Faulkner U, Montgomery, AL 36109-3398	1942	Dr. Billy D. Hilyer	2-D	1,990	125
Fayetteville State U, Fayetteville, NC 28301	1867	Dr. Lloyd V. Hackley	5-M	3,736	216
Ferris State U, Big Rapids, MI 49307	1884	Dr. Helen Popovich	5-D	12,461	709
Ferrum Coll, Ferrum, VA 24088	1913	Dr. Jerry M. Boone	2-B	1,211	98
Fitchburg State Coll, Fitchburg, MA 01420	1894	Dr. Vincent J. Mara	5-M	5,831	243
Flagler Coll, St Augustine, FL 32085	1968	Dr. William L. Proctor	1-B	1,100	96
Florida A&M U, Tallahassee, FL 32307	1887	Dr. Frederick Humphries	5-D	9,196	670
Florida Atlantic U, Boca Raton, FL 33431	1961	Dr. Anthony James Catanese	5-D	13,558	522
Florida Inst of Tech, Melbourne, FL 32901	1958	Dr. Lynn E. Weaver	1-D	5,947	446
Florida International U, Miami, FL 33199	1965	Dr. Modesto A. Maidique	5-D	23,841	1,082
Florida Memorial Coll, Miami, FL 33054	1879	Dr. Bennie L. Reeves	2-B	2,000	NR
Florida Southern Coll, Lakeland, FL 33801	1885	Dr. Robert A. Davis	2-M	2,745	120

Name, address	Year	Governing official, control, and highest degree offered		Enrollment	Faculty
Florida State U, Tallahassee, FL 32306	1857	Dr. Dale Lick	5-D	28,607	1,577
Fontbonne Coll, St Louis, MO 63105	1917	Dr. Meneve Dunham	2-M	1,242	131
Fordham U, New York, NY 10458	1841	Rev. Joseph A. O'Hare, SJ	2-D	14,243	594
Fort Hays State U, Hays, KS 67601	1902	Dr. Edward H. Hammond	5-M	5,684	229
Fort Lauderdale Coll, Fort Lauderdale, FL 33304	1940	William P. Bedard	3-M	1,350	60
Fort Lewis Coll, Durango, CO 81301-3999	1911	Joel M. Jones	5-B	4,080	230
Fort Valley State Coll, Fort Valley, GA 31030	1895	Dr. Oscar L. Prater	5-M	2,368	154
Framingham State Coll, Framingham, MA 01701	1839	Dr. Paul F. Weller	5-M	3,878	219
Franciscan U of Steubenville, Steubenville, OH 43952	1946	Rev. Michael Scanlan, TOR	2-M	1,676	102
Francis Marion U, Florence, SC 29501-0547	1970	Dr. Thomas C. Stanton	5-M	3,903	205
Franklin and Marshall Coll, Lancaster, PA 17604-3003	1787	Dr. A. Richard Kneedler	1-B	1,793	170
Franklin Pierce Coll, Rindge, NH 03461	1962	Dr. Walter Peterson	1-B	1,298	105
Franklin U, Columbus, OH 43215	1902	Dr. Paul J. Otte	1-B	3,990	205
Freed-Hardeman U, Henderson, TN 38340	1869	Dr. Milton R. Sewell	2-M	1,247	91
Fresno Pacific Coll, Fresno, CA 93702	1944	Dr. Richard Kriegbaum	2-M	1,410	79
Friends U, Wichita, KS 67213	1898	Dr. Biff Green	2-M	1,540	100
Frostburg State U, Frostburg, MD 21532	1898	Dr. Catherine Gira	5-M	5,239	300
Furman U, Greenville, SC 29613	1826	Dr. John E. Johns	1-M	2,703	213
Gallaudet U, Washington, DC 20002-3625	1856	Dr. I. King Jordan	1-D	2,060	330
Gannon U, Erie, PA 16541	1925	Dr. M. Daniel Henry	2-M	4,440	349
Gardner-Webb Coll, Boiling Springs, NC 28017	1905	Dr. M. Christopher White	2-M	2,014	155
Geneva Coll, Beaver Falls, PA 15010	1848	Dr. John H. White	2-M	1,362	104
George Fox Coll, Newberg, OR 97132	1891	Dr. Edward F. Stevens	2-D	1,222	88
George Mason U, Fairfax, VA 22030	1957	Dr. George W. Johnson	5-D	20,693	1,041
Georgetown Coll, Georgetown, KY 40324	1829	Dr. William H. Crouch, Jr.	2-M	1,547	92
Georgetown U, Washington, DC 20057	1789	Rev. Leo J. O'Donovan, SJ	2-D	11,861	729
George Washington U, Washington, DC 20052	1821	Mr. Stephen J. Trachtenberg	1-D	16,712	1,221
Georgia Coll, Milledgeville, GA 31061	1889	Dr. Edwin G. Speir	5-M	5,350	262
Georgia Inst of Tech, Atlanta, GA 30332	1885	Dr. John P. Crecine	5-D	12,814	615
Georgian Court Coll, Lakewood, NJ 08701-2697 (4)	1908	Sr. Barbara Williams	2-M	2,032	181
Georgia Southern U, Statesboro, GA 30460	1906	Dr. Nicholas Henry	5-M	13,411	615
Georgia Southwestern Coll, Americus, GA 31709	1906	Dr. William H. Capitan	5-M	2,303	155
Georgia State U, Atlanta, GA 30303	1913	Dr. Sherman R. Day	5-D	24,024	1,172
Gettysburg Coll, Gettysburg, PA 17325	1832	Dr. Gordon A. Haaland	2-B	1,950	150
Glassboro State Coll, Glassboro, NJ 08028	1923	Dr. Herman D. James	5-M	7,983	323
Glenville State Coll, Glenville, WV 26351	1872	Dr. William K. Simmons	5-B	2,278	135
GMI Engineering & Management Inst, Flint, MI 48504-4898	1919	Dr. James E. A. John	1-M	3,104	130
Golden Gate U, San Francisco, CA 94105	1901	Dr. Thomas M. Stauffer	1-D	7,585	766
Goldey-Beacom Coll, Wilmington, DE 19808	1886	Mr. William R. Baldt	1-B	1,724	65
Gonzaga U, Spokane, WA 99258	1887	Rev. Bernard J. Coughlin, SJ	2-D	4,722	306
Gordon Coll, Wenham, MA 01984	1889	Dr. Richard F. Gross	2-B	1,200	101
Goshen Coll, Goshen, IN 46526	1894	Dr. Victor Stoltzfus	2-B	1,039	125
Governors State U, University Park, IL 60466	1969	Dr. Leo Goodman-Malamuth, II	5-M	5,615	328
Grambling State U, Grambling, LA 71245	1901	Dr. Harold Lundy	5-D	6,485	282
Grand Canyon U, Phoenix, AZ 85017	1949	Dr. Bill Williams	2-M	1,745	132
Grand Valley State U, Allendale, MI 49401	1960	Mr. Arend D. Lubbers	5-M	12,565	602
Grand View Coll, Des Moines, IA 50316-1599	1896	Dr. Arthur E. Puotinen	2-B	1,420	120
Greensboro Coll, Greensboro, NC 27401	1838	Dr. William H. Likins	2-B	1,035	81
Grinnell Coll, Grinnell, IA 50112	1846	Dr. Pamela A. Ferguson	1-B	1,291	150
Grove City Coll, Grove City, PA 16127-2104	1876	Dr. Jerry H. Combee	2-B	2,173	133
Guilford Coll, Greensboro, NC 27410	1837	Dr. William R. Rogers	2-B	1,177	111
Gustavus Adolphus Coll, St Peter, MN 56082	1862	Dr. Axel D. Steuer	2-B	2,305	206
Gwynedd-Mercy Coll, Gwynedd Valley, PA 19437	1948	Sr. Isabelle Keiss, RSM	2-M	1,975	177
Hahnemann U, Philadelphia, PA 19102	1848	Mr. Iqbal F. Paroo	1-D	1,325	430
Hamilton Coll, Clinton, NY 13323	1812	Dr. Harry C. Payne	1-B	1,698	189
Hamline U, St Paul, MN 55104	1854	Dr. Larry G. Osnes	2-D	2,443	129
Hampshire Coll, Amherst, MA 01002	1965	Dr. Gregory S. Prince, Jr.	1-B	1,235	97
Hampton U, Hampton, VA 23668	1868	Dr. William R. Harvey	1-M	5,704	390
Hanover Coll, Hanover, IN 47243	1827	Dr. Russell L. Nichols	2-B	1,070	99
Harding U, Searcy, AR 72143	1924	Dr. David B. Burks, Jr.	2-M	3,386	190
Hardin-Simmons U, Abilene, TX 79698-0001	1891	Dr. Lanny Hall	2-M	1,801	138
Harris-Stowe State Coll, St Louis, MO 63103	1857	Dr. Henry Givens, Jr.	5-B	1,850	99
Hartwick Coll, Oneonta, NY 13820	1797	Dr. Philip S. Wilder, Jr.	1-B	1,464	131
Harvard U, Cambridge, MA 02138	1636	Dr. Neil Rudenstine	1-D	18,179	800
Haverford Coll, Haverford, PA 19041	1833	Tom G. Kessinger	1-B	1,113	107
Hawaii Pacific U, Honolulu, HI 96813	1965	Mr. Chatt Wright	1-M	6,324	332
Heidelberg Coll, Tiffin, OH 44883	1850	Dr. William C. Cassell	2-M	1,429	110
Henderson State U, Arkadelphia, AR 71923	1890	Dr. Charles D. Dunn	5-M	3,646	163
Heritage Coll, Toppenish, WA 98948	1907	Dr. Kathleen Ross, SNJM	1-M	1,041	104
High Point U, High Point, NC 27261-1949	1924	Dr. Jacob C. Martinson, Jr.	2-B	2,308	94
Hillsdale Coll, Hillsdale, MI 49242	1844	Dr. George C. Roche, III	1-B	1,140	103
Hobart Coll, Geneva, NY 14456 (1)	1822	NR	2-B	1,015	180
Hofstra U, Hempstead, NY 11550	1935	Dr. James M. Shuart	1-D	11,998	979
Hollins Coll, Roanoke, VA 24020 (3)	1842	Dr. Jane Margaret O'Brien	1-M	1,102	92
Holy Family Coll, Philadelphia, PA 19114	1954	S. Francesca Onley	2-M	2,274	189
Hood Coll, Frederick, MD 21701-9988 (4)	1893	Dr. Martha E. Church	2-M	1,985	93
Hope Coll, Holland, MI 49423	1862	Dr. John Jacobson, Jr.	2-B	2,746	237
Houghton Coll, Houghton, NY 14744	1883	Dr. Daniel R. Chamberlain	2-B	1,146	100
Houston Baptist U, Houston, TX 77074	1960	Dr. E. Douglas Hodo	2-M	2,252	145
Howard Payne U, Brownwood, TX 76801	1889	Dr. Don Newbury	2-B	1,427	108
Howard U, Washington, DC 20059	1867	Franklyn G. Jenifer	1-D	10,871	2,000
Humboldt State U, Arcata, CA 95521	1913	Dr. Alistair W. McCrone	5-M	7,823	551
Hunter Coll of the City U of New York, New York, NY 10021	1870	Dr. Paul Le Clerc	12-M	18,854	696
Husson Coll, Bangor, ME 04401	1898	Dr. William H. Beardsley	1-M	1,845	64
Idaho State U, Pocatello, ID 83209	1901	Dr. Richard Bowen	5-D	11,000	464
Illinois Benedictine Coll, Lisle, IL 60532-0900	1887	Dr. Richard C. Becker	2-M	2,619	141
Illinois Inst of Tech, Chicago, IL 60616	1892	Mr. Lewis Collens	1-D	6,504	498
Illinois State U, Normal, IL 61761	1857	Dr. Thomas P. Wallace	5-D	22,361	1,003
Illinois Wesleyan U, Bloomington, IL 61702	1850	Dr. Minor Myers, Jr.	2-B	1,770	167
Immaculata Coll, Immaculata, PA 19345 (4)	1920	Sr. Marie Roseanne Bonfini	2-D	2,340	167
Incarnate Word Coll, San Antonio, TX 78209	1881	Dr. Louis J. Agnese, Jr.	2-M	2,616	159
Indiana Inst of Tech, Fort Wayne, IN 46803	1930	Donald J. Andorfer	1-B	1,047	42
Indiana State U, Terre Haute, IN 47809	1865	Dr. Richard G. Landini	5-D	11,783	814

Name, address	Year	Governing official, control, and highest degree offered		Enrollment	Faculty
Indiana U at South Bend, South Bend, IN 46634	1922	Dr. H. Daniel Cohen	5-M	7,434	469
Indiana U Bloomington, Bloomington, IN 47405	1820	Kenneth R. R. Gros Louis	5-D	35,489	1,653
Indiana U East, Richmond, IN 47374	1971	Dr. Charlie Nelms	5-B	2,197	162
Indiana U Northwest, Gary, IN 46408	1959	Dr. Peggy G. Elliott	5-M	5,565	355
Indiana U of Pennsylvania, Indiana, PA 15705	1875	Dr. Charles Fuget	5-D	14,620	805
Indiana U–Purdue U at Indianapolis, Indianapolis, IN 46202	1969	Gerald L. Bepko	5-D	27,788	2,120
Indiana U Southeast, New Albany, IN 47150	1941	Dr. Leon Rand	5-M	5,804	335
Indiana Wesleyan U, Marion, IN 46953	1920	Dr. James Barnes	2-M	2,773	105
Inter American U of PR, Arecibo U Coll, Arecibo, PR 00613	1957	Dr. Maria de los A. Ortiz	1-B	4,253	211
Iona Coll, New Rochelle, NY 10801	1940	Br. John G. Driscoll, CFC	1-M	7,602	650
Iowa State U of Science and Tech, Ames, IA 50011	1858	Dr. Martin C. Jischke	5-D	25,250	1,907
Ithaca Coll, Ithaca, NY 14850	1892	Dr. James J. Whalen	1-M	6,444	585
ITT Tech Inst, Fort Wayne, IN 46825	1967	Jack B. Cozad	3-B	1,069	34
ITT Tech Inst, Indianapolis, IN 46268	1966	Alan Crews	3-B	1,113	44
Jackson State U, Jackson, MS 39217	1877	Dr. Herman Smith	5-D	6,639	425
Jacksonville State U, Jacksonville, AL 36265	1883	Dr. Harold J. McGee	5-M	8,240	283
Jacksonville U, Jacksonville, FL 32211	1934	Dr. James J. Brady	1-M	2,517	183
James Madison U, Harrisonburg, VA 22807	1908	Dr. Ronald E. Carrier	5-M	11,264	679
Jamestown Coll, Jamestown, ND 58401	1883	Dr. James Walker	2-B	1,029	62
Jersey City State Coll, Jersey City, NJ 07305	1927	Dr. William J. Maxwell	5-M	6,807	425
John Brown U, Siloam Springs, AR 72761	1919	Dr. John E. Brown, III	2-B	1,044	79
John Carroll U, University Heights, OH 44118	1886	Rev. Michael J. Lavelle, SJ	2-M	4,666	316
John F Kennedy U, Orinda, CA 94563	1964	Charles E. Glasser	1-M	2,621	73
John Jay Coll of Criminal Justice of City U of NY, New York, NY 10019	1964	Dr. Gerald Lynch	12-D	8,500	496
Johns Hopkins U, Baltimore, MD 21218	1876	Dr. William C. Richardson	1-D	4,578	472
Johnson & Wales U, Providence, RI 02903	1914	Dr. John A. Yena	1-M	8,962	312
Johnson C Smith U, Charlotte, NC 28216	1867	Dr. Robert L. Albright	1-B	1,256	96
Johnson State Coll, Johnson, VT 05656	1828	Dr. Robert Hahn	5-M	1,730	140
Juniata Coll, Huntingdon, PA 16652-2119	1876	Dr. Robert W. Neff	1-B	1,118	104
Kalamazoo Coll, Kalamazoo, MI 49006	1833	Dr. Lawrence Bryan	1-B	1,271	109
Kansas Newman Coll, Wichita, KS 67213	1933	Sr. Tarcisia Roths	2-B	1,184	163
Kansas State U, Manhattan, KS 66506	1863	Dr. Jon Wefald	5-D	20,712	1,205
Kean Coll of New Jersey, Union, NJ 07083	1855	Dr. Elsa Gomez	5-M	11,692	783
Keene State Coll, Keene, NH 03431	1909	Dr. Judith A. Sturnick	5-M	3,926	293
Kennesaw State Coll, Marietta, GA 30061	1963	Dr. Betty L. Siegel	5-M	10,913	404
Kent State U, Kent, OH 44242-0001	1910	Dr. Carol A. Cartwright	5-D	24,524	1,351
Kentucky State U, Frankfort, KY 40601	1886	Dr. Mary L. Smith	13-M	2,518	158
Kenyon Coll, Gambier, OH 43022	1824	Dr. Philip H. Jordan, Jr.	1-B	1,507	138
King's Coll, Wilkes-Barre, PA 18711-0801	1946	Rev. James Lackenmier, CSC	2-M	2,293	153
Kutztown U of Pennsylvania, Kutztown, PA 19530	1866	Dr. David E. McFarland	5-M	8,164	406
Lafayette Coll, Easton, PA 18042	1826	Dr. Robert I. Rotberg	2-B	2,225	224
LaGrange Coll, LaGrange, GA 30240	1831	Dr. Walter Y. Murphy	2-M	1,016	65
Lake Forest Coll, Lake Forest, IL 60045	1857	Dr. Eugene Hotchkiss, III	1-M	1,059	107
Lakeland Coll, Sheboygan, WI 53082-0359	1862	Dr. David R. Black	2-M	2,318	152
Lake Superior State U, Sault Sainte Marie, MI 49783	1946	Dr. H. Erik Shaar	5-M	3,503	169
Lamar U–Beaumont, Beaumont, TX 77705	1923	NR	5-D	11,848	725
Lambuth U, Jackson, TN 38301	1843	Dr. Thomas F. Boyd	2-B	1,040	87
Lander Coll, Greenwood, SC 29649-2099	1872	Dr. William C. Moran	5-M	2,706	162
La Roche Coll, Pittsburgh, PA 15237	1963	NR	2-M	1,851	123
La Salle U, Philadelphia, PA 19141	1863	Br. Patrick Ellis	2-M	6,029	326
La Sierra U, Riverside, CA 92515	1922	Dr. Fritz Guy	2-D	1,620	112
Lawrence Tech U, Southfield, MI 48075	1932	Dr. Richard E. Marburger	1-M	5,259	307
Lawrence U, Appleton, WI 54912	1847	Dr. Richard Warch	1-B	1,225	118
Lebanon Valley Coll, Annville, PA 17003	1866	Mr. John A. Synodinos	2-M	1,410	89
Lee Coll, Cleveland, TN 37311	1918	Dr. Paul Conn	2-B	1,827	157
Lehigh U, Bethlehem, PA 18015	1865	Dr. Peter Likins	1-D	6,556	484
Lehman Coll of the City U of New York, Bronx, NY 10468	1931	Dr. Ricardo R. Fernandez	12-M	9,956	NR
Le Moyne Coll, Syracuse, NY 13214	1946	Rev. Kevin G. O'Connell, SJ	2-B	2,049	201
LeMoyne-Owen Coll, Memphis, TN 38126	1870	Dr. Doris W. Weathers	2-M	1,064	61
Lenoir-Rhyne Coll, Hickory, NC 28603	1891	Dr. John E. Trainer, Jr.	2-M	1,617	120
Lesley Coll, Cambridge, MA 02138 (3)	1909	Margaret A. McKenna	1-D	5,129	39
Lewis & Clark Coll, Portland, OR 97219	1867	Dr. Michael J. Mooney	1-D	3,112	141
Lewis-Clark State Coll, Lewiston, ID 83501	1894	Dr. Lee A. Vickers	5-B	2,816	115
Lewis U, Romeoville, IL 60441	1932	Br. James Gaffney, FSC	2-M	3,708	160
Liberty U, Lynchburg, VA 24506-8001	1971	Dr. A. Pierre Guillermin	2-D	10,549	275
Lincoln Memorial U, Harrogate, TN 37752	1897	Dr. Scott D. Miller	1-M	1,859	104
Lincoln U, Jefferson City, MO 65102	1866	Dr. Wendell G. Rayburn, Sr.	5-M	4,101	249
Lincoln U, Lincoln University, PA 19352	1854	Dr. Niara Sudarkasa	13-M	1,458	138
Lindenwood Coll, St Charles, MO 63301	1827	Dr. Dennis Spellmann	2-M	2,634	162
Lindsey Wilson Coll, Columbia, KY 42728	1903	Dr. John B. Begley	2-B	1,507	53
Linfield Coll, McMinnville, OR 97128	1849	Dr. Charles U. Walker	2-M	1,476	126
Livingston U, Livingston, AL 35470	1835	Dr. Asa N. Green	5-M	2,086	110
Lock Haven U of Pennsylvania, Lock Haven, PA 17745	1870	Dr. Craig Dean Willis	5-M	3,336	229
Long Island U, Brooklyn Cmps, Brooklyn, NY 11201	1926	Dr. David J. Steinberg	1-D	5,724	507
Long Island U, C W Post Cmps, Brookville, NY 11548	1954	NR	1-D	8,209	722
Long Island U, Southampton Cmps, Southampton, NY 11968	1963	Dr. David J. Steinberg	1-M	1,458	120
Longwood Coll, Farmville, VA 23901	1839	Dr. William F. Dorrill	5-M	3,006	210
Loras Coll, Dubuque, IA 52004	1839	Rev. Msgr. James Barta	2-M	1,682	166
Louisiana Coll, Pineville, LA 71359	1906	Dr. Robert L. Lynn	2-B	1,013	77
Louisiana State U and A&M Coll, Baton Rouge, LA 70803	1860	Dr. William E. Davis	5-D	26,138	1,348
Louisiana State U in Shreveport, Shreveport, LA 71115	1965	Dr. John R. Darling, Jr.	5-M	4,364	234
Louisiana State U Medical Ctr, New Orleans, LA 70112	1931	Dr. Perry G. Rigby	5-D	2,729	NR
Louisiana Tech U, Ruston, LA 71272	1894	Dr. Daniel D. Reneau	5-D	10,380	427
Lourdes Coll, Sylvania, OH 43560	1958	Sr. Ann Francis Klimkowski, OSF	2-B	1,242	106
Loyola Coll, Baltimore, MD 21210	1852	Rev. Joseph A. Sellinger, SJ	2-D	6,249	448
Loyola Marymount U, Los Angeles, CA 90045	1911	Rev. Thomas P. O'Malley, SJ	2-D	6,191	497
Loyola U Chicago, Chicago, IL 60611	1870	Rev. Raymond C. Baumhart, SJ	2-D	15,834	876
Loyola U, New Orleans, New Orleans, LA 70118	1912	Rev. James C. Carter, SJ	2-D	5,561	538
Lubbock Christian U, Lubbock, TX 79407	1957	Dr. Steven S. Lemley	2-M	1,055	110
Luther Coll, Decorah, IA 52101	1861	Dr. H. George Anderson	2-B	2,350	185

Name, address	Year	Governing official, control, and highest degree offered		Enroll-ment	Faculty
Lycoming Coll, Williamsport, PA 17701	1812	Dr. James E. Douthat	2-B	1,405	113
Lynchburg Coll, Lynchburg, VA 24501-3199	1903	Dr. George N. Rainsford	2-M	2,399	178
Lyndon State Coll, Lyndonville, VT 05851	1911	Dr. Margaret R. Williams	5-M	1,257	99
Lynn U, Boca Raton, FL 33431	1962	Dr. Donald E. Ross	1-M	1,140	75
Macalester Coll, St Paul, MN 55105-1899	1874	Dr. Robert M. Gavin, Jr.	2-B	1,858	185
Madonna U, Livonia, MI 48150	1947	Sr. Mary Francilene	2-M	4,436	241
Malone Coll, Canton, OH 44709	1892	Dr. E. Arthur Self	2-M	1,695	117
Manchester Coll, North Manchester, IN 46962	1889	Dr. William P. Robinson	2-M	1,122	110
Manhattan Coll, Riverdale, NY 10471	1853	Br. Thomas J. Scanlan	2-M	3,689	308
Manhattanville Coll, Purchase, NY 10577	1841	Dr. Marcia A. Savage	1-M	1,541	198
Mankato State U, Mankato, MN 56002-8400	1867	Dr. John B. Davis	5-M	14,761	552
Mannes Coll of Music, New Sch for Social Research, New York, NY 10024	1916	Dr. Charles Kaufman	1-M	237	216
Mansfield U of Pennsylvania, Mansfield, PA 16933	1857	Mr. Rod C. Kelchner	5-M	3,071	188
Marian Coll, Indianapolis, IN 46222	1851	Dr. Daniel A. Felicetti	2-B	1,263	138
Marian Coll of Fond du Lac, Fond du Lac, WI 54935	1936	Matthew G. Flanigan	2-M	1,992	84
Marietta Coll, Marietta, OH 45750	1835	Dr. Patrick D. McDonough	1-M	1,304	112
Marist Coll, Poughkeepsie, NY 12601	1929	Dr. Dennis J. Murray	1-M	4,274	345
Marquette U, Milwaukee, WI 53233	1881	Rev. Albert J. DiUlio, SJ	2-D	11,345	990
Marshall U, Huntington, WV 25755	1837	Dr. J. Wade Gilley	5-D	12,744	566
Mars Hill Coll, Mars Hill, NC 28754	1856	Dr. Fred B. Bentley	2-B	1,323	122
Marygrove Coll, Detroit, MI 48221-2599	1910	Dr. John E. Shay, Jr.	2-M	1,271	60
Marylhurst Coll, Marylhurst, OR 97036	1893	Nancy A. Wilgenbusch	2-M	1,187	223
Marymount Coll, Tarrytown, NY 10591-3796 (4)	1907	Sr. Brigid Driscoll	1-B	1,142	129
Marymount Manhattan Coll, New York, NY 10021 (4)	1936	Dr. Regina Peruggi	1-B	1,300	155
Marymount U, Arlington, VA 22207	1950	Sr. M. Majella Berg, RSHM	2-M	3,431	225
Maryville U of St Louis, St Louis, MO 63141	1872	Dr. Keith Lovin	1-M	3,546	247
Mary Washington Coll, Fredericksburg, VA 22401	1908	Dr. William M. Anderson, Jr.	5-M	3,489	227
Marywood Coll, Scranton, PA 18509	1915	Sr. Mary Reap, IHM	2-M	2,927	225
Massachusetts Coll of Art, Boston, MA 02115	1873	Dr. William F. O'Neil	5-M	1,176	89
Mass Coll of Pharmacy and Allied Health Sciences, Boston, MA 02115	1823	Dr. Louis P. Jeffrey	1-D	1,212	122
Massachusetts Inst of Tech, Cambridge, MA 02139	1861	Dr. Charles M. Vest	1-D	9,628	985
Master's Coll, Newhall, CA 91322	1927	Dr. John F. MacArthur, Jr.	2-M	1,011	87
McKendree Coll, Lebanon, IL 62254	1828	Dr. Gerrit J. TenBrink	2-B	1,303	74
McMurry U, Abilene, TX 79697	1923	Dr. Thomas K. Kim	2-B	1,499	117
McNeese State U, Lake Charles, LA 70609	1939	Dr. Robert D. Hebert	5-M	7,831	342
Medaille Coll, Buffalo, NY 14214	1875	Kevin I. Sullivan	1-B	1,127	72
Medgar Evers Coll of the City U of New York, Brooklyn, NY 11225	1969	Dr. Edison O. Jackson	12-B	4,400	272
Medical Coll of Georgia, Augusta, GA 30912	1828	Dr. Francis J. Tedesco	5-D	1,989	747
Memphis State U, Memphis, TN 38152	1912	Dr. V. Lane Rawlins	5-D	20,546	1,166
Mercer U, Macon, GA 31207	1833	Dr. R. Kirby Godsey	2-D	5,363	195
Mercy Coll, Dobbs Ferry, NY 10522	1951	Dr. Jay Sexter	1-M	5,287	494
Mercyhurst Coll, Erie, PA 16546	1926	Dr. William P. Garvey	2-M	2,201	134
Meredith Coll, Raleigh, NC 27607 (3)	1891	Dr. John E. Weems	2-M	2,141	186
Merrimack Coll, North Andover, MA 01845	1947	Rev. John E. Deegan, OSA	2-B	2,343	157
Mesa State Coll, Grand Junction, CO 81502	1925	Dr. Ray N. Kieft	5-B	4,260	246
Messiah Coll, Grantham, PA 17027	1909	Dr. D. Ray Hostetter	2-B	2,259	182
Methodist Coll, Fayetteville, NC 28311	1956	Dr. M. Elton Hendricks	2-B	1,293	85
Metropolitan State Coll of Denver, Denver, CO 80217	1963	Dr. Thomas Brewer	5-B	17,835	887
Metropolitan State U, St Paul, MN 55101	1971	Dr. Tobin G. Barrozo	5-M	5,444	576
Miami U, Oxford, OH 45056	1809	Dr. Paul G. Pearson	5-D	16,331	873
Michigan State U, East Lansing, MI 48824	1855	Dr. John DiBiaggio	5-D	42,088	4,123
Michigan Tech U, Houghton, MI 49931	1885	Dr. Curtis J. Tompkins	5-D	6,921	369
MidAmerica Nazarene Coll, Olathe, KS 66061	1966	Dr. Richard Spindle	2-M	1,370	97
Middlebury Coll, Middlebury, VT 05753	1800	Dr. John McCardell	1-D	1,960	220
Middle Tennessee State U, Murfreesboro, TN 37132	1911	Dr. James E. Walker	5-D	15,900	653
Midland Lutheran Coll, Fremont, NE 68025	1883	Dr. Carl L. Hansen	2-B	1,003	65
Midwestern State U, Wichita Falls, TX 76308	1922	Dr. Louis J. Rodriguez	5-M	5,455	220
Millersville U of Pennsylvania, Millersville, PA 17551-0302	1854	Dr. Joseph A. Caputo	5-M	6,489	406
Millikin U, Decatur, IL 62522	1901	Dr. John R. Miltner	2-B	1,841	185
Millsaps Coll, Jackson, MS 39210	1890	Dr. George M. Harmon	2-M	1,421	105
Mills Coll, Oakland, CA 94613 (3)	1852	Dr. Janet H. McKay	1-M	1,064	151
Milwaukee Sch of Engineering, Milwaukee, WI 53201	1903	Dr. Robert R. Spitzer	1-M	3,183	205
Minot State U, Minot, ND 58702	1913	Dr. Gordon B. Olson	5-M	3,721	192
Mississippi Coll, Clinton, MS 39058	1826	Dr. Lewis Nobles	2-D	3,771	234
Mississippi State U, Mississippi State, MS 39762	1878	Dr. Donald W. Zacharias	5-D	14,638	863
Mississippi U for Women, Columbus, MS 39701 (4)	1884	Dr. Clyda S. Rent	5-M	2,576	157
Missouri Baptist Coll, St Louis, MO 63141	1968	Dr. Thomas S. Field	2-B	1,209	60
Missouri Southern State Coll, Joplin, MO 64801	1937	Dr. Julio Leon	5-B	6,012	293
Missouri Valley Coll, Marshall, MO 65340	1889	Dr. Earl J. Reeves	2-B	1,032	66
Missouri Western State Coll, St Joseph, MO 64507	1915	Dr. Janet Gorman Murphy	5-B	4,981	281
Mobile Coll, Mobile, AL 36663-0220	1961	Dr. Michael A. Magnoli	2-M	1,420	101
Molloy Coll, Rockville Centre, NY 11570-1199	1955	Dr. Janet A. Fitzgerald, OP	1-M	1,516	188
Monmouth Coll, West Long Branch, NJ 07764	1933	Dr. Samuel H. Magill	1-M	4,203	322
Montana Coll of Mineral Science and Tech, Butte, MT 59701	1895	Dr. Lindsay D. Norman, Jr.	5-M	1,881	115
Montana State U, Bozeman, MT 59717	1893	Dr. Michael P. Malone	5-D	10,111	573
Montclair State Coll, Upper Montclair, NJ 07043	1908	Dr. Irvin D. Reid	5-M	13,753	719
Moody Bible Inst, Chicago, IL 60610	1886	Dr. Joseph M. Stowell, III	2-M	1,506	77
Moorhead State U, Moorhead, MN 56563	1885	Dr. Roland Dille	5-M	8,933	456
Moravian Coll, Bethlehem, PA 18018	1742	Dr. Roger Harry Martin	2-M	1,566	146
Morehead State U, Morehead, KY 40351	1922	Dr. Ronald Eaglin	5-M	8,812	414
Morehouse Coll, Atlanta, GA 30314 (1)	1867	Dr. Leroy Keith, Jr.	1-B	2,992	150
Morgan State U, Baltimore, MD 21239	1867	Dr. Earl Richardson	5-D	5,034	297
Morningside Coll, Sioux City, IA 51106	1894	Dr. Miles Tommeraasen	2-M	1,324	122
Morris Brown Coll, Atlanta, GA 30314	1881	Dr. Calvert H. Smith	2-B	2,000	128
Mount Holyoke Coll, South Hadley, MA 01075 (3)	1837	Mrs. Elizabeth T. Kennan	1-M	1,910	226
Mount Marty Coll, Yankton, SD 57078-3724	1936	Sr. Jacquelyn Ernster	2-M	1,090	81
Mount Mary Coll, Milwaukee, WI 53222 (3)	1913	Sr. Ruth Hollenbach	2-M	1,468	142
Mount Mercy Coll, Cedar Rapids, IA 52402	1928	Dr. Thomas R. Feld	2-B	1,523	109
Mount Saint Mary Coll, Newburgh, NY 12550	1960	Sr. Ann Sakac	1-M	1,662	113
Mount St Mary's Coll, Los Angeles, CA 90049 (4)	1925	Sr. Karen Kennelly	2-M	1,235	146
Mount Saint Mary's Coll, Emmitsburg, MD 21727	1808	Dr. Robert J. Wickenheiser	2-M	1,761	140
Mount Union Coll, Alliance, OH 44601	1846	Dr. Harold M. Kolenbrander	2-B	1,382	111
Mount Vernon Nazarene Coll, Mount Vernon, OH 43050	1964	Dr. E. LeBron Fairbanks	2-M	1,044	67

Name, address	Year	Governing official, control, and highest degree offered		Enroll-ment	Faculty
Muhlenberg Coll, Allentown, PA 18104	1848	Mr. Arthur R. Taylor	2-B	1,636	151
Murray State U, Murray, KY 42071	1922	Dr. Ronald J. Kurth	5-M	8,328	371
Muskingum Coll, New Concord, OH 43762	1837	Dr. Samuel W. Speck, Jr.	2-M	1,077	94
National-Louis U, Evanston, IL 60201	1886	NR	1-D	8,200	241
National U, San Diego, CA 92108	1971	Dr. Jerry C. Lee	1-D	8,847	1,109
Nazareth Coll of Rochester, Rochester, NY 14618-3790	1924	Dr. Rose Marie Beston	1-M	2,900	185
Nebraska Wesleyan U, Lincoln, NE 68504	1887	Dr. John W. White, Jr.	2-B	1,655	143
Neumann Coll, Aston, PA 19014	1965	Dr. Nan B. Hechenberger	2-M	1,268	104
New England Coll, Henniker, NH 03242-3293	1946	William R. O'Connell, Jr.	1-M	1,030	117
New Hampshire Coll, Manchester, NH 03104	1932	Dr. Richard A. Gustafson	1-M	2,724	93
New Jersey Inst of Tech, Newark, NJ 07102	1881	Dr. Saul K. Fenster	13-D	7,417	491
New Mexico Highlands U, Las Vegas, NM 87701	1893	Dr. Gilbert Sanchez	5-M	2,602	151
New Mexico Inst of Mining and Tech, Socorro, NM 87801	1889	Dr. Laurence H. Lattman	5-D	1,434	101
New Mexico State U, Las Cruces, NM 88003	1888	Dr. James E. Halligan	5-D	15,344	802
New Sch Bach of Arts, New Sch for Social Research, New York, NY 10011	1919	NR	1-B	269	545
New York Inst of Tech, Old Westbury, NY 11568-0170	1955	Dr. Matthew Schure	1-M	10,512	1,030
New York U, New York, NY 10011	1831	L. Jay Oliva	1-D	33,340	4,330
Niagara U, Niagara University, NY 14109	1856	Rev. Brian J. O'Connell, CM	1-M	3,060	220
Nicholls State U, Thibodaux, LA 70310	1948	Dr. Donald J. Ayo	5-M	7,528	265
Nichols Coll, Dudley, MA 01571	1815	Dr. Lowell C. Smith	1-M	1,892	53
Norfolk State U, Norfolk, VA 23504	1935	Dr. Harrison B. Wilson	5-M	8,298	498
North Adams State Coll, North Adams, MA 01247	1894	Dr. Thomas D. Aceto	5-M	2,202	127
North Carolina Ag and Tech State U, Greensboro, NC 27411	1891	Dr. Edward B. Fort	5-M	7,119	418
North Carolina Central U, Durham, NC 27707	1910	Dr. Donna J. Benson	5-M	5,385	396
North Carolina State U, Raleigh, NC 27695	1887	Dr. Larry K. Monteith	5-D	27,236	1,448
North Central Bible Coll, Minneapolis, MN 55404	1930	Dr. Don H. Argue	2-B	1,103	68
North Central Coll, Naperville, IL 60566-7063	1861	Dr. Harold R. Wilde	2-M	2,551	120
North Dakota State U, Fargo, ND 58105	1890	Dr. Jim Ozbun	5-D	8,842	515
Northeastern Illinois U, Chicago, IL 60625	1961	Dr. Gordon Lamb	5-M	11,274	542
Northeastern State U, Tahlequah, OK 74464-2399	1846	Dr. W. Roger Webb	5-D	9,198	329
Northeastern U, Boston, MA 02115	1898	John A. Curry	1-D	28,882	2,265
Northeast Louisiana U, Monroe, LA 71209	1931	Mr. Lawson L. Swearingen, Jr.	5-D	11,189	484
Northeast Missouri State U, Kirksville, MO 63501	1867	Dr. Russell G. Warren	5-M	5,939	464
Northern Arizona U, Flagstaff, AZ 86011	1899	Dr. Eugene M. Hughes	5-D	17,698	927
Northern Illinois U, De Kalb, IL 60115	1895	Dr. John E. LaTourette	5-D	24,895	1,307
Northern Kentucky U, Highland Heights, KY 41099	1968	Dr. Leon E. Boothe	5-D	11,540	609
Northern Michigan U, Marquette, MI 49855	1899	NR	5-M	8,542	356
Northern Montana Coll, Havre, MT 59501	1929	Dr. William Daehling	5-M	1,973	113
Northern State U, Aberdeen, SD 57401	1901	Dr. Terence Brown	5-M	2,983	131
North Georgia Coll, Dahlonega, GA 30597	1873	Dr. John H. Owen	5-M	2,699	151
North Park Coll, Chicago, IL 60625	1891	Dr. David G. Horner	2-M	1,189	158
Northwestern Coll, Orange City, IA 51041	1882	Dr. James E. Bultman	2-M	1,040	88
Northwestern Coll, St Paul, MN 55113	1902	Dr. Donald Ericksen	2-B	1,176	112
Northwestern Oklahoma State U, Alva, OK 73717	1897	Dr. Joe J. Struckle	5-M	1,999	107
Northwestern State U of Louisiana, Natchitoches, LA 71497	1884	Dr. Robert A. Alost	5-M	7,626	200
Northwestern U, Evanston, IL 60208	1851	Dr. Arnold R. Weber	1-D	14,198	915
Northwest Missouri State U, Maryville, MO 64468	1905	Dr. Dean L. Hubbard	5-M	6,021	274
Northwest Nazarene Coll, Nampa, ID 83686	1913	Dr. A. Gordon Wetmore	2-M	1,172	88
Northwood Inst, Midland, MI 48640	1959	Dr. David E. Fry	1-B	1,755	59
Norwich U, Northfield, VT 05663	1819	Dr. Richard Schneider	1-M	2,547	207
Notre Dame Coll, Manchester, NH 03104	1950	Dr. Carol J. Descoteaux, CSC	2-M	1,220	98
Nova U, Fort Lauderdale, FL 33314	1964	Dr. Stephen Feldman	1-D	10,425	251
Oakland U, Rochester, MI 48309	1957	Dr. Sandra Packard	5-D	12,530	608
Oberlin Coll, Oberlin, OH 44074	1833	S. Frederick Starr	1-M	2,912	248
Occidental Coll, Los Angeles, CA 90041	1887	Dr. John B. Slaughter	1-M	1,601	164
Oglethorpe U, Atlanta, GA 30319	1835	Dr. Donald S. Stanton	1-M	1,147	99
Ohio Dominican Coll, Columbus, OH 43219	1911	Sr. Mary Andrew Matesich	2-B	1,424	96
Ohio Northern U, Ada, OH 45810	1871	Dr. DeBow Freed	2-D	2,791	175
Ohio State U, Columbus, OH 43210	1870	Dr. E. Gordon Gee	5-D	54,313	3,900
Ohio State U-Lima Cmps, Lima, OH 45804	1960	Dr. Violet I. Meek	5-B	1,475	74
Ohio State U-Mansfield Cmps, Mansfield, OH 44906	1958	Dr. John O. Riedl, Jr.	5-B	1,428	59
Ohio State U-Marion Cmps, Marion, OH 43302	1957	Francis E. Hazard	5-B	1,026	83
Ohio State U-Newark Cmps, Newark, OH 43055	1957	Dr. Julius S. Greenstein	5-B	1,656	88
Ohio U, Athens, OH 45701	1804	Dr. Charles J. Ping	5-D	17,500	940
Ohio U-Belmont, St Clairsville, OH 43950	1957	Dr. James W. Newton	5-B	1,083	65
Ohio U-Chillicothe, Chillicothe, OH 45601	1946	Dr. Delbert Meyer	5-B	1,660	75
Ohio U-Zanesville, Zanesville, OH 43701	1946	Dr. Craig D. Laubenthal	5-M	1,767	49
Ohio Wesleyan U, Delaware, OH 43015	1842	Dr. David L. Warren	2-B	2,057	162
Oklahoma Baptist U, Shawnee, OK 74801	1910	Dr. Bob R. Agee	2-B	2,165	151
Oklahoma Christian U of Science and Arts, Oklahoma City, OK 73136	1950	Dr. J. Terry Johnson	2-M	1,689	124
Oklahoma City U, Oklahoma City, OK 73106	1904	Dr. Jerald C. Walker	2-D	4,273	233
Oklahoma Panhandle State U, Goodwell, OK 73939	1909	Dr. Theodore W. Wischropp	5-B	1,122	80
Oklahoma State U, Stillwater, OK 74078	1890	Dr. John Campbell	5-D	19,476	691
Old Dominion U, Norfolk, VA 23529	1930	Dr. James V. Koch	5-D	16,686	1,044
Olivet Nazarene U, Kankakee, IL 60901	1907	Dr. John Bowling	2-M	1,898	116
Oral Roberts U, Tulsa, OK 74171	1963	Mr. G. Oral Roberts	2-D	4,054	211
Oregon Health Sciences U, Portland, OR 97201	1974	Dr. Peter O. Kohler	5-D	1,376	76
Oregon Inst of Tech, Klamath Falls, OR 97601-8801	1947	Dr. Lawrence J. Wolf	5-B	2,661	182
Oregon State U, Corvallis, OR 97331	1868	Dr. John V. Byrne	5-D	14,915	1,714
Orlando Coll, Orlando, FL 32810	1918	Mrs. Ouida B. Kirby	3-M	2,127	106
Otterbein Coll, Westerville, OH 43081	1847	C. Brent DeVore	2-M	2,490	177
Ouachita Baptist U, Arkadelphia, AR 71923	1886	Dr. Ben M. Elrod	2-B	1,277	101
Our Lady of Holy Cross Coll, New Orleans, LA 70131	1916	Rev. Thomas E. Chambers, CSC	2-M	1,036	63
Our Lady of the Lake U of San Antonio, San Antonio, TX 78207-4666	1911	Sr. Elizabeth Anne Sueltenfuss	2-D	2,811	166
Pace U, New York, NY 10038	1906	Dr. Patricia Ewers	1-D	15,530	1,063
Pacific Lutheran U, Tacoma, WA 98447	1890	Dr. Loren J. Anderson	2-M	3,571	304
Pacific Union Coll, Angwin, CA 94508	1882	Dr. D. Malcolm Maxwell	2-M	1,577	130

Name, address	Year	Governing official, control, and highest degree offered		Enroll-ment	Faculty
Pacific U, Forest Grove, OR 97116	1849	Dr. Robert F. Duvall	1-D	1,474	98
Palm Beach Atlantic Coll, West Palm Beach, FL 33416-4708	1968	Dr. Paul R. Corts	2-M	1,500	100
Palmer Coll of Chiropractic, Davenport, IA 52803	1895	Donald P. Kern	1-D	1,700	129
Parks Coll of Saint Louis U, Cahokia, IL 62206	1927	Dr. Margaret J. Baty	2-B	1,127	67
Parsons Sch of Design, New Sch for Social Research, New York, NY 10011	1896	Charles S. Olton	1-M	1,770	332
Pembroke State U, Pembroke, NC 28372	1887	Dr. Joseph Oxendine	5-M	2,944	204
Penn State U at Erie, The Behrend Coll, Erie, PA 16563	1926	Dr. John M. Lilley	13-M	3,186	182
Penn State U at Harrisburg—The Capital Coll, Middletown, PA 17057	1966	Dr. Ruth Leventhal	13-D	3,434	178
Penn State U Univ Park Cmps, University Park, PA 16802	1855	Dr. Joab L. Thomas	13-D	38,989	2,177
Pepperdine U, Malibu, CA 90263	1937	Dr. David Davenport	2-D	6,800	294
Peru State Coll, Peru, NE 68421	1867	Dr. Robert L. Burns	5-M	1,800	60
Philadelphia Coll of Pharmacy and Science, Philadelphia, PA 19104-4495	1821	Dr. Allen Misher	1-D	1,693	198
Philadelphia Coll of Textiles and Science, Philadelphia, PA 19144	1884	Dr. James P. Gallagher	1-M	3,321	113
Pittsburg State U, Pittsburg, KS 66762	1903	Dr. Donald W. Wilson	5-M	6,166	288
Plymouth State Coll of the U System of NH, Plymouth, NH 03264	1871	Dr. Theodora J. Kalikow	5-M	4,000	200
Point Loma Nazarene Coll, San Diego, CA 92106	1902	Dr. Jim L. Bond	2-M	2,349	132
Point Park Coll, Pittsburgh, PA 15222	1960	Dr. J. Matthew Simon	1-M	2,932	212
Polytechnic U, Brooklyn Cmps, Brooklyn, NY 11201-2999	1854	Dr. George Bugliarello	1-D	2,130	393
Pomona Coll, Claremont, CA 91711	1887	Dr. Peter W. Stanley	1-B	1,375	154
Pontifical Catholic U of Puerto Rico, Ponce, PR 00732	1948	Rev. F. Tosello Giangiacomo	2-M	12,164	595
Portland State U, Portland, OR 97207-0751	1946	Dr. Judith Ramaley	5-D	14,285	628
Prairie View A&M U, Prairie View, TX 77446	1878	Mr. Julius W. Becton, Jr.	5-M	5,590	303
Pratt Inst, Brooklyn, NY 11205	1887	Dr. Warren F. Ilchman	1-M	3,218	499
Presbyterian Coll, Clinton, SC 29325	1880	Dr. Kenneth B. Orr	2-B	1,148	98
Princeton U, Princeton, NJ 08544	1746	Harold T. Shapiro	1-D	6,412	890
Providence Coll, Providence, RI 02918	1917	Rev. John F. Cunningham, OP	2-D	6,204	296
Purdue U, West Lafayette, IN 47907	1869	Dr. Steven C. Beering	5-D	36,163	2,208
Purdue U Calumet, Hammond, IN 46323-2094	1951	Dr. James Yackel	5-M	8,285	457
Purdue U North Central, Westville, IN 46391	1967	Dr. Dale W. Alspaugh	5-M	3,552	209
Queens Coll, Charlotte, NC 28274	1857	Dr. Billy O. Wireman	2-M	1,624	100
Queens Coll of the City U of New York, Flushing, NY 11367	1937	Dr. Shirley Strum Kenny	12-M	18,251	1,145
Quincy Coll, Quincy, IL 62301	1860	Rev. James Toal, OFM	2-M	1,374	99
Quinnipiac Coll, Hamden, CT 06518	1929	Dr. John L. Lahey	1-M	3,600	244
Radford U, Radford, VA 24142	1910	Dr. Donald N. Dedmon	5-M	9,204	496
Ramapo Coll of New Jersey, Mahwah, NJ 07430	1969	Dr. Robert A. Scott	5-B	4,711	286
Randolph-Macon Coll, Ashland, VA 23005	1830	Dr. Ladell Payne	2-B	1,126	141
Reed Coll, Portland, OR 97202-8199	1909	Mr. William R. Haden	1-M	1,299	132
Regis Coll, Weston, MA 02193 (3)	1927	Sr. Sheila Megley, RSM	2-B	1,147	106
Regis Coll of Regis U, Denver, CO 80221	1877	Rev. David M. Clarke, SJ	2-M	6,273	95
Rensselaer Polytechnic Inst, Troy, NY 12180	1824	Roland W. Schmitt	1-D	6,842	465
Rhode Island Coll, Providence, RI 02908	1854	Dr. John Nazarian	5-M	9,690	482
Rhode Island Sch of Design, Providence, RI 02903	1877	Dr. Thomas F. Schutte	1-M	1,960	279
Rhodes Coll, Memphis, TN 38112	1848	Dr. James H. Daughdrill, Jr.	2-B	1,429	147
Rice U, Houston, TX 77251	1912	Dr. George Rupp	1-D	4,079	542
Rider Coll, Lawrenceville, NJ 08648	1865	Dr. J. Barton Luedeke	1-M	5,651	300
Rivier Coll, Nashua, NH 03060	1933	Sr. Jeanne Perreault	2-M	2,734	186
Roanoke Coll, Salem, VA 24153	1842	Dr. David M. Gring	2-B	1,654	142
Robert Morris Coll, Coraopolis, PA 15108	1921	Dr. Edward A. Nicholson	1-M	5,492	238
Rochester Inst of Tech, Rochester, NY 14623-0887	1829	Dr. M. Richard Rose	1-D	13,018	1,076
Rockford Coll, Rockford, IL 61108	1847	Dr. Norman Fintel	1-M	1,046	123
Rockhurst Coll, Kansas City, MO 64110	1910	Rev. Thomas J. Savage, SJ	2-M	2,740	142
Roger Williams Coll, Bristol, RI 02809	1948	Dr. Natale A. Sicuro	1-B	2,111	229
Rollins Coll, Winter Park, FL 32789-4499	1885	Dr. Rita Bornstein	1-M	2,119	135
Roosevelt U, Chicago, IL 60605	1945	Dr. Theodore L. Gross	1-M	6,374	508
Rosary Coll, River Forest, IL 60305	1901	Dr. Jean Murray, OP	2-M	1,842	79
Rose-Hulman Inst of Tech, Terre Haute, IN 47803 (1)	1874	Dr. Samuel F. Hulbert	1-M	1,420	97
Rush U, Chicago, IL 60612	1969	Dr. Leo M. Henikoff	1-D	1,228	170
Russell Sage Coll, Troy, NY 12180 (3)	1916	Dr. Sara Chapman	1-M	1,191	190
Rust Coll, Holly Springs, MS 38635	1866	Dr. William A. McMillan	2-B	1,075	67
Rutgers, State U of NJ, Camden Coll of Arts & Scis, Camden, NJ 08101	1927	NR	5-B	2,780	NR
Rutgers, State U of NJ, Coll of Engineering, Piscataway, NJ 08855-0909	1864	Dr. Ellis H. Dill	5-B	2,460	NR
Rutgers, State U of NJ, Coll of Nursing, Newark, NJ 07102	1956	Dorothy J. DeMaio	5-D	437	NR
Rutgers, State U of NJ, Coll of Pharmacy, New Brunswick, NJ 08903-2101	1927	Dr. John Louis Colaizzi	5-D	847	NR
Rutgers, State U of NJ, Cook Coll, New Brunswick, NJ 08903-2101	1921	Daryl B. Lund	5-B	2,874	NR
Rutgers, State U of NJ, Douglass Coll, New Brunswick, NJ 08903-0270 (3)	1918	Dr. Mary S. Hartman	5-B	3,268	NR
Rutgers, State U of NJ, Livingston Coll, New Brunswick, NJ 08903	1969	NR	5-B	3,727	NR
Rutgers, State U of NJ, Mason Gross Sch of Arts, New Brunswick, NJ 08903-2101	1976	Marilyn F. Somville	5-M	625	NR
Rutgers, State U of NJ, Newark Coll of Arts & Scis, Newark, NJ 07102	1946	David Hosford	5-B	3,624	NR
Rutgers, State U of NJ, Rutgers Coll, New Brunswick, NJ 08903-2101	1766	James Reed	5-B	8,554	NR
Rutgers, State U of NJ, U Coll–Camden, Camden, NJ 08101	1950	Joseph Held	5-B	898	NR
Rutgers, State U of NJ, U Coll–Newark, Newark, NJ 07102-1896	1934	NR	5-B	1,967	NR
Rutgers, State U of NJ, U Coll–New Brunswick, New Brunswick, NJ 08903	1934	NR	5-B	3,221	NR
Sacred Heart U, Fairfield, CT 06432	1963	Dr. Anthony J. Cernera	2-M	4,500	276
Saginaw Valley State U, University Center, MI 48710	1963	Dr. Eric R. Gilbertson	5-M	6,474	375
St Ambrose U, Davenport, IA 52803	1882	Dr. Edward J. Rogalski	2-M	2,434	197

Name, address	Year	Governing official, control, and highest degree offered		Enroll-ment	Faculty
Saint Anselm Coll, Manchester, NH 03102	1889	Rev. Jonathan DeFelice, OSB	2-B	1,950	156
Saint Augustine's Coll, Raleigh, NC 27610-2298	1867	Dr. Prezell R. Robinson	2-B	1,907	92
St Bonaventure U, St Bonaventure, NY 14778	1858	Rev. Neil O'Connell, OFM	2-M	2,787	219
St Cloud State U, St Cloud, MN 56301-4498	1869	Dr. Brendan McDonald	5-M	17,025	797
St Edward's U, Austin, TX 78704	1885	Dr. Patricia Hayes	2-M	3,050	217
St Francis Coll, Brooklyn Heights, NY 11201	1884	Br. Donald Sullivan, OSF	1-B	1,911	119
Saint Francis Coll, Loretto, PA 15940	1847	Rev. Christian R. Oravec	2-M	1,297	80
St John Fisher Coll, Rochester, NY 14618	1948	Dr. William L. Pickett	1-M	2,194	175
Saint John's U, Collegeville, MN 56321 (1)	1857	Br. Dietrich Reinhart, O.S.B.	2-M	1,956	145
St John's U, Jamaica, NY 11439	1870	Rev. Donald J. Harrington, CM	2-D	19,037	975
Saint Joseph Coll, West Hartford, CT 06117 (3)	1932	Ms. Winifred E. Coleman	2-M	1,917	127
Saint Joseph's Coll, Rensselaer, IN 47978	1889	Fr. Charles Banet	2-M	1,021	80
St Joseph's Coll, Suffolk Cmps, Patchogue, NY 11772	1916	Sr. George Aquin O'Connor	1-B	1,826	155
Saint Joseph's U, Philadelphia, PA 19131	1851	Rev. Nicholas S. Rashford, SJ	2-M	6,643	364
St Lawrence U, Canton, NY 13617	1856	Patti McGill Peterson	1-M	2,119	177
Saint Leo Coll, Saint Leo, FL 33574	1889	Msgr. Frank Mouch	2-B	1,000	77
Saint Louis U, St Louis, MO 63103	1818	Rev. Lawrence Biondi, SJ	2-D	11,814	1,469
Saint Mary-of-the-Woods Coll, Saint Mary-of-the-Woods, IN 47876 (3)	1840	Barbara Doherty, SP	2-M	1,217	55
Saint Mary's Coll, Notre Dame, IN 46556 (3)	1844	Dr. William A. Hickey	2-B	1,675	187
Saint Mary's Coll of California, Moraga, CA 94575	1863	Br. Mel Anderson, FSC	2-M	3,650	186
St Mary's Coll of Maryland, St Mary's City, MD 20686	1840	Dr. Edward T. Lewis	5-B	1,339	142
Saint Mary's Coll of Minnesota, Winona, MN 55987-0857	1912	Br. Louis DeThomasis, FSC	2-M	3,800	128
St Mary's U of San Antonio, San Antonio, TX 78228	1852	Rev. John Moder, SM	2-D	4,055	192
Saint Michael's Coll, Colchester, VT 05439	1904	Dr. Paul J. Reiss	2-M	2,668	166
St Norbert Coll, De Pere, WI 54115	1898	Dr. Thomas A. Manion	2-M	1,877	149
St Olaf Coll, Northfield, MN 55057	1874	Dr. Melvin George	2-B	3,057	359
Saint Peter's Coll, Jersey City, NJ 07306	1872	NR	2-M	3,407	420
St Thomas Aquinas Coll, Sparkill, NY 10976	1958	Dr. Donald T. McNelis	1-M	2,075	115
St Thomas U, Miami, FL 33054	1961	Dr. Richard Greene	2-D	2,609	202
Saint Vincent Coll, Latrobe, PA 15650	1846	Rev. John F. Murtha, OSB	2-B	1,196	103
Saint Xavier U, Chicago, IL 60655	1847	Dr. Ronald Champagne	2-M	3,694	205
Salem State Coll, Salem, MA 01970	1854	Dr. Nancy D. Harrington	5-M	8,407	300
Salisbury State U, Salisbury, MD 21801-6837	1925	Dr. Thomas A. Bellavance	5-M	5,884	325
Salve Regina U, Newport, RI 02840-4192	1934	Dr. M. Lucille McKillop, RSM	2-D	2,260	231
Samford U, Birmingham, AL 35229	1841	Dr. Thomas E. Corts	2-D	4,248	323
Sam Houston State U, Huntsville, TX 77341	1879	Dr. Martin J. Anisman	5-D	12,707	437
San Diego State U, San Diego, CA 92182	1897	Dr. Thomas B. Day	5-D	32,951	2,450
San Francisco State U, San Francisco, CA 94132	1899	Dr. Robert A. Corrigan	5-D	27,991	1,556
Sangamon State U, Springfield, IL 62794-9243	1969	Dr. A. Wayne Penn	5-M	4,514	231
San Jose State U, San Jose, CA 95192	1857	Mr. J. Handel Evans	5-M	30,061	1,636
Santa Clara U, Santa Clara, CA 95053	1851	Rev. Paul L. Locatelli, SJ	2-D	7,761	551
Sarah Lawrence Coll, Bronxville, NY 10708	1926	Dr. Alice Stone Ilchman	1-M	1,150	225
Savannah Coll of Art and Design, Savannah, GA 31401	1978	Richard G. Rowan	1-M	2,209	121
Savannah State Coll, Savannah, GA 31404	1890	NR	5-M	2,656	149
Sch of the Art Inst of Chicago, Chicago, IL 60603	1866	Mr. Peter Brown	1-M	2,085	314
Sch of Visual Arts, New York, NY 10010	1947	David Rhodes	3-M	2,534	800
Seattle Pacific U, Seattle, WA 98119	1891	NR	2-M	3,394	241
Seattle U, Seattle, WA 98122	1891	Rev. William J. Sullivan, SJ	2-D	4,785	399
Seton Hall U, South Orange, NJ 07079	1856	Rev. Thomas R. Peterson, OP	2-D	10,238	640
Seton Hill Coll, Greensburg, PA 15601 (4)	1883	JoAnne W. Boyle	2-B	1,043	111
Shawnee State U, Portsmouth, OH 45662	1986	NR	5-B	3,441	266
Shaw U, Raleigh, NC 27611	1865	Dr. Talbert O. Shaw	2-B	2,149	242
Shenandoah U, Winchester, VA 22601	1875	Dr. James A. Davis	2-M	1,360	167
Shepherd Coll, Shepherdstown, WV 25443	1871	Dr. Michael P. Riccards	5-B	3,501	184
Shippensburg U of Pennsylvania, Shippensburg, PA 17257	1871	Dr. Anthony F. Ceddia	5-M	6,696	358
Siena Coll, Loudonville, NY 12211-1462	1937	Fr. William McConville, OFM	2-B	3,570	261
Siena Heights Coll, Adrian, MI 49221-1796	1919	Sr. Cathleen Real, CHM	2-M	1,186	110
Simmons Coll, Boston, MA 02115 (3)	1899	William J. Holmes	1-D	2,946	180
Simpson Coll, Indianola, IA 50125	1860	Dr. Stephen G. Jennings	2-B	1,752	137
Skidmore Coll, Saratoga Springs, NY 12866	1903	Dr. David H. Porter	1-B	2,156	208
Slippery Rock U of Pennsylvania, Slippery Rock, PA 16057	1889	Dr. Robert Aebersold	5-M	7,925	409
Smith Coll, Northampton, MA 01063 (3)	1871	Mary Maples Dunn	1-D	2,974	283
Sonoma State U, Rohnert Park, CA 94928	1961	Dr. David W. Benson	5-M	7,557	449
South Carolina State U, Orangeburg, SC 29117	1896	Dr. Carl A. Carpenter	5-D	5,145	241
South Dakota Sch of Mines and Tech, Rapid City, SD 57701-3995	1885	Dr. Richard J. Gowen	5-D	2,450	139
South Dakota State U, Brookings, SD 57007	1881	Dr. Robert T. Wagner	5-D	8,090	454
Southeastern Coll of the Assemblies of God, Lakeland, FL 33801	1935	Dr. James Hennesy	2-B	1,236	79
Southeastern Louisiana U, Hammond, LA 70402	1925	Dr. G. Warren Smith	5-M	11,392	425
Southeastern Oklahoma State U, Durant, OK 74701	1909	Dr. Larry Williams	5-M	4,182	201
Southeast Missouri State U, Cape Girardeau, MO 63701	1873	Dr. Kala M. Stroup	5-M	8,704	436
Southern Arkansas U, Magnolia, AR 71753	1909	Dr. Steven G. Gamble	5-M	2,913	130
Southern Coll of Seventh-day Adventists, Collegedale, TN 37315	1892	Dr. Donald R. Sahly	2-B	1,532	99
Southern Coll of Tech, Marietta, GA 30060-2896	1948	Dr. Stephen R. Cheshier	5-M	4,008	188
Southern Connecticut State U, New Haven, CT 06515	1893	Mr. Michael J. Adanti	5-M	12,941	761
Southern Illinois U at Carbondale, Carbondale, IL 62901	1869	Dr. John C. Guyon	5-D	24,869	1,399
Southern Illinois U at Edwardsville, Edwardsville, IL 62026	1957	Earl E. Lazerson	5-D	11,808	716
Southern Methodist U, Dallas, TX 75275	1911	Mr. A. Kenneth Pye	2-D	8,547	584
Southern Nazarene U, Bethany, OK 73008	1899	Dr. Loren P. Gresham	2-M	1,598	103
Southern Oregon State Coll, Ashland, OR 97520	1926	Dr. Joseph Cox	5-M	4,519	311
Southern U and A&M Coll, Baton Rouge, LA 70813	1880	Dr. Marvin L. Yates	5-D	10,000	603
Southern Utah U, Cedar City, UT 84720	1897	Gerald R. Sherratt	5-M	4,300	145
Southwest Baptist U, Bolivar, MO 65613	1878	Dr. James L. Sells	2-M	2,921	195
Southwestern Oklahoma State U, Weatherford, OK 73096	1903	Dr. Joe Anna Hibler	5-M	5,453	237
Southwestern U, Georgetown, TX 78626	1840	Dr. Roy B. Shilling, Jr.	2-B	1,231	127
Southwest Missouri State U, Springfield, MO 65804	1905	Dr. Russell M. Keiling	5-M	19,504	850
Southwest State U, Marshall, MN 56258	1963	Dr. Oliver Ford, III	5-B	2,856	131
Southwest Texas State U, San Marcos, TX 78666	1899	Dr. Jerome Supple	5-M	21,743	881
Spalding U, Louisville, KY 40203	1814	Dr. Eileen M. Egan	2-D	1,118	92
Spelman Coll, Atlanta, GA 30314 (3)	1881	Dr. Johnnetta B. Cole	1-B	1,850	162
Springfield Coll, Springfield, MA 01109	1885	Randolph W. Bromery	1-D	2,826	265

Name, address	Year	Governing official, control, and highest degree offered		Enrollment	Faculty
Spring Hill Coll, Mobile, AL 36608	1830	Rev. William J. Rewak, SJ	2-M	1,625	83
Stanford U, Stanford, CA 94305	1891	Mr. Gerhard Casper	1-D	13,200	1,406
State U of NY at Binghamton, Binghamton, NY 13902-6000	1946	Dr. Lois B. DeFleur	5-D	11,883	687
State U of NY at Buffalo, Buffalo, NY 14260	1846	Mr. William R. Greiner	5-D	23,573	1,091
State U of NY at Stony Brook, Stony Brook, NY 11794	1957	Dr. John H. Marburger, III	5-D	16,043	1,530
State U of NY Coll at Brockport, Brockport, NY 14420	1867	Dr. John E. Van de Wetering	5-M	8,114	536
State U of NY Coll at Buffalo, Buffalo, NY 14222	1867	Dr. F. C. Richardson	5-M	11,493	588
State U of NY Coll at Cortland, Cortland, NY 13045	1868	Dr. James M. Clark	5-M	6,361	398
State U of NY Coll at Fredonia, Fredonia, NY 14063	1826	Dr. Donald A. MacPhee	5-M	4,957	294
State U of NY Coll at Geneseo, Geneseo, NY 14454	1867	Dr. Carol C. Harter	5-M	5,630	327
State U of NY Coll at New Paltz, New Paltz, NY 12561-2449	1828	Alice Chandler	5-M	8,494	506
State U of NY Coll at Old Westbury, Old Westbury, NY 11568	1965	Dr. L. Eudora Pettigrew	5-B	4,200	259
State U of NY Coll at Oneonta, Oneonta, NY 13820	1889	Dr. Alan B. Donovan	5-M	6,000	320
State U of NY Coll at Oswego, Oswego, NY 13126	1861	Dr. Stephen Weber	5-M	8,750	393
State U of NY Coll at Plattsburgh, Plattsburgh, NY 12901	1889	Dr. Charles Warren	5-M	6,344	368
State U of NY Coll at Potsdam, Potsdam, NY 13676	1816	Dr. William Merwin	5-M	4,746	243
State U of NY Coll at Purchase, Purchase, NY 10577	1967	Dr. Sheldon Grebstein	5-M	2,540	298
State U of NY Coll of Environ Sci and Forestry, Syracuse, NY 13210-2779	1911	Dr. Ross S. Whaley	5-D	1,551	122
State U of NY Empire State Coll, Saratoga Springs, NY 12866-4391	1971	Dr. James W. Hall	5-M	10,000	360
State U of NY Health Science Ctr at Brooklyn, Brooklyn, NY 11203	1858	Dr. Donald J. Scherl	5-D	1,641	156
State U of NY Health Science Ctr at Syracuse, Syracuse, NY 13210	1950	Dr. John Bernard Henry	5-D	1,074	45
State U of NY Inst of Tech at Utica/Rome, Utica, NY 13504	1966	Dr. Peter J. Cayan	5-M	2,610	135
Stephen F Austin State U, Nacogdoches, TX 75962	1923	Dr. Daniel D. Angel	5-D	12,687	660
Stephens Coll, Columbia, MO 65215 (3)	1833	Dr. Patsy H. Sampson	1-B	1,094	94
Stetson U, DeLand, FL 32720	1883	Dr. H. Douglas Lee	2-D	2,351	188
Stevens Inst of Tech, Hoboken, NJ 07030	1870	Dr. Harold J. Raveche	1-D	3,240	250
Stockton State Coll, Pomona, NJ 08240	1971	Dr. Vera King Farris	5-B	4,965	288
Stonehill Coll, North Easton, MA 02357	1948	Rev. Bartley MacPhaidin, CSC	2-B	1,964	183
Strayer Coll, Washington, DC 20005	1892	Ron K. Bailey	3-M	3,962	90
Suffolk U, Boston, MA 02108	1906	David J. Sargent	1-D	4,203	287
Sullivan Coll, Louisville, KY 40232	1864	NR	3-B	1,713	68
Sul Ross State U, Alpine, TX 79832	1920	Dr. R. Vic Morgan	5-M	2,551	112
Susquehanna U, Selinsgrove, PA 17870	1858	Dr. Joel L. Cunningham	2-B	1,433	137
Swarthmore Coll, Swarthmore, PA 19081	1864	Dr. Alfred H. Bloom	1-B	1,320	157
Syracuse U, Syracuse, NY 13244	1870	Dr. Kenneth A. Shaw	1-D	15,960	1,489
Tampa Coll, Tampa, FL 33614	1890	Mr. David Zorn	3-M	1,527	57
Tarleton State U, Stephenville, TX 76402	1899	Dr. Dennis P. McCabe	5-M	6,420	309
Taylor U, Upland, IN 46989-1001	1846	Dr. Jay L. Kesler	1-B	1,790	128
Teikyo Marycrest U, Davenport, IA 52804-4096	1939	Dr. Wanda D. Bigham	1-M	1,312	83
Teikyo Post U, Waterbury, CT 06723-2540	1890	Dr. Phyllis C. DeLeo	1-B	1,882	165
Temple U, Philadelphia, PA 19122	1884	Mr. Peter J. Liacouras	13-D	27,892	2,374
Tennessee State U, Nashville, TN 37209-1561	1912	Dr. James A. Hefner	5-D	7,405	425
Tennessee Tech U, Cookeville, TN 38505	1915	Dr. Angelo A. Volpe	5-D	8,160	408
Texas A&I U, Kingsville, TX 78363	1925	Dr. Manuel L. Ibanez	5-D	5,937	290
Texas A&M U, College Station, TX 77843	1876	Dr. William H. Mobley	5-D	40,997	2,350
Texas A&M U at Galveston, Galveston, TX 77553	1962	Dr. David J. Schmidly	5-B	1,213	99
Texas Christian U, Fort Worth, TX 76129	1873	Dr. William Tucker	2-D	6,538	468
Texas Lutheran Coll, Seguin, TX 78155	1891	Dr. Charles H. Oestreich	2-B	1,038	81
Texas Southern U, Houston, TX 77004	1947	Dr. William H. Harris	5-D	10,269	630
Texas Tech U, Lubbock, TX 79409	1923	Robert W. Lawless	5-D	24,707	1,497
Texas Wesleyan U, Fort Worth, TX 76105	1890	Dr. W. L. Hailey	2-M	1,474	111
Texas Woman's U, Denton, TX 76204-1925 (4)	1901	Dr. Shirley Sears Chater	5-D	9,412	666
Thomas A Edison State Coll, Trenton, NJ 08608-1176	1972	Dr. George A. Pruitt	5-B	8,019	NR
Thomas Jefferson U, Philadelphia, PA 19107	1824	Paul C. Brucker, MD	1-D	1,467	83
Thomas More Coll, Crestview Hills, KY 41017	1921	Rev. William F. Cleves	2-B	1,268	110
Tiffin U, Tiffin, OH 44883	1888	Dr. George Kidd, Jr.	1-M	1,053	48
Tougaloo Coll, Tougaloo, MS 39174	1869	Dr. Adib A. Shakir	2-B	1,003	89
Touro Coll, New York, NY 10001	1971	NR	1-D	6,550	410
Towson State U, Towson, MD 21204	1866	Dr. Hoke L. Smith	5-M	15,403	925
Transylvania U, Lexington, KY 40508-1797	1780	Dr. Charles L. Shearer	2-B	1,038	102
Trenton State Coll, Trenton, NJ 08650-4700	1855	Dr. Harold Eickhoff	5-M	6,971	523
Trevecca Nazarene Coll, Nashville, TN 37210	1901	Dr. Millard Reed	2-M	1,591	131
Trinity Coll, Hartford, CT 06106	1823	Tom Gerety, Jr.	1-M	2,212	219
Trinity Coll, Washington, DC 20017-1094 (3)	1897	NR	2-M	1,093	85
Trinity Coll of Vermont, Burlington, VT 05401 (4)	1925	Sr. Janice Ryan	2-M	1,070	104
Trinity U, San Antonio, TX 78212	1869	Dr. Ronald K. Calgaard	2-M	2,518	261
Troy State U, Troy, AL 36082	1887	Dr. Jack Hawkins, Jr.	5-M	4,350	205
Troy State U at Dothan, Dothan, AL 36304	1961	Dr. Thomas Harrison	5-M	2,039	97
Troy State U in Montgomery, Montgomery, AL 36103-4419	1957	Dr. Millard E. Elrod	5-M	3,193	147
Tufts U, Medford, MA 02155	1852	Dr. Jean Mayer	1-D	7,645	619
Tulane U, New Orleans, LA 70118	1834	Dr. Eamon M. Kelly	1-D	11,487	684
Tuskegee U, Tuskegee, AL 36088	1881	Dr. Benjamin F. Payton	1-D	3,687	318
Union Coll, Schenectady, NY 12308	1795	Dr. Roger H. Hull	1-D	2,307	199
Union Inst, Cincinnati, OH 45206	1964	Robert T. Conley	1-D	1,224	739
Union U, Jackson, TN 38305	1823	Dr. Hyran E. Barefoot	2-M	1,836	111
United States Air Force Acad, Colorado Springs, CO 80840	1954	Lt. Gen. Bradley C. Hosmer	4-B	4,440	517
United States International U, San Diego, CA 92131	1952	Dr. Kenneth McLennan	1-D	3,489	84
United States Military Acad, West Point, NY 10996	1802	Lt. Gen. Howard D. Graves	4-B	4,392	535
United States Naval Acad, Annapolis, MD 21402 (2)	1845	Rear Adm. Thomas Lynch	4-B	4,265	650
Universidad del Turabo, Gurabo, PR 00798	1972	Claudio R. Prieto	1-M	7,367	312
Universidad Politécnica de Puerto Rico, Hato Rey, PR 00919	1966	Ernesto Vazquez-Barquet	1-B	4,322	186
U at Albany, State U of NY, Albany, NY 12222	1844	Dr. H. Patrick Swygert	5-D	15,333	904
U of Akron, Akron, OH 44325-0001	1870	Marion A. Ruebel	5-D	28,241	1,722
U of Alabama, Tuscaloosa, AL 35487-0132	1831	Dr. E. Roger Sayers	5-D	19,837	1,071
U of Alabama at Birmingham, Birmingham, AL 35294	1969	Dr. Charles A. McCallum	5-D	16,784	NR
U of Alabama in Huntsville, Huntsville, AL 35899	1950	Dr. Frank Franz	5-D	8,624	439
U of Alaska Anchorage, Anchorage, AK 99508	1954	Dr. Donald F. Behrend	5-M	14,861	1,162

Name, address	Year	Governing official, control, and highest degree offered		Enrollment	Faculty
U of Alaska Fairbanks, Fairbanks, AK 99775	1917	Dr. Joan K. Wadlow	5-D	4,664	711
U of Arizona, Tucson, AZ 85721	1885	Dr. Manuel T. Pacheco	5-D	35,220	1,652
U of Arkansas, Fayetteville, AR 72701	1871	Dr. Daniel E. Ferritor	5-D	14,400	799
U of Arkansas at Little Rock, Little Rock, AR 72204	1927	Dr. James H. Young	5-D	11,805	723
U of Arkansas at Monticello, Monticello, AR 71655	1909	Dr. Fred J. Taylor	5-B	2,342	126
U of Arkansas at Pine Bluff, Pine Bluff, AR 71601	1873	Dr. Lawrence A. Davis, Jr.	5-M	3,626	196
U of Arkansas for Medical Sciences, Little Rock, AR 72205	1879	Dr. Harry P. Ward	5-D	1,516	NR
U of Baltimore, Baltimore, MD 21201	1925	Dr. H. Mebane Turner	5-D	5,983	298
U of Bridgeport, Bridgeport, CT 06601	1927	Dr. Janet D. Greenwood	1-D	3,904	218
U of California at Berkeley, Berkeley, CA 94720	1868	Chang-Lin Tien	5-D	30,372	NR
U of California, Davis, Davis, CA 95616	1906	Dr. Theodore L. Hullar	5-D	23,302	1,626
U of California, Irvine, Irvine, CA 92717	1965	Jack W. Peltason	5-D	16,949	743
U of California, Los Angeles, Los Angeles, CA 90024	1919	Charles E. Young	5-D	36,366	3,250
U of California, Riverside, Riverside, CA 92521	1954	Dr. Raymond L. Orbach	5-D	8,890	718
U of California, San Diego, La Jolla, CA 92093	1959	Dr. Richard C. Atkinson	5-D	17,966	1,161
U of California, Santa Barbara, Santa Barbara, CA 93106	1891	Dr. Barbara S. Uehling	5-D	18,519	985
U of California, Santa Cruz, Santa Cruz, CA 95064	1965	Dr. Karl S. Pister	5-D	10,136	559
U of Central Arkansas, Conway, AR 72035	1907	Winfred L. Thompson	5-M	9,057	462
U of Central Florida, Orlando, FL 32816	1963	Dr. John C. Hitt	5-D	21,157	1,143
U of Central Oklahoma, Edmond, OK 73034-0172	1890	Dr. Bill J. Lillard	5-M	15,014	585
U of Charleston, Charleston, WV 25304	1888	Dr. Edwin H. Welch	1-M	1,389	230
U of Chicago, Chicago, IL 60637	1891	Hanna Holborn Gray	1-D	9,432	1,490
U of Cincinnati, Cincinnati, OH 45221	1819	Dr. Joseph A. Steger	5-D	18,398	963
U of Colorado at Boulder, Boulder, CO 80309	1876	NR	5-D	25,571	1,093
U of Colorado at Colorado Springs, Colorado Springs, CO 80933-7150	1965	Dr. Dwayne C. Nuzum	5-D	6,068	360
U of Colorado Health Sciences Ctr, Denver, CO 80262	1883	Dr. Bernard W. Nelson	5-D	1,776	NR
U of Connecticut, Storrs, CT 06269-3088	1881	Dr. Harry J. Hartley	5-D	17,127	1,250
U of Connecticut at Stamford, Stamford, CT 06903	1951	NR	5-M	1,600	93
U of Dallas, Irving, TX 75062	1956	Dr. Robert F. Sasseen	2-D	2,995	116
U of Dayton, Dayton, OH 45469-1611	1850	Br. Raymond L. Fitz, SM	2-D	9,979	765
U of Delaware, Newark, DE 19716	1743	Dr. David P. Roselle	13-D	17,323	963
U of Denver, Denver, CO 80208	1864	Mr. Daniel Ritchie	1-D	8,019	395
U of Detroit Mercy, Detroit, MI 48221	1877	Sr. Maureen A. Fay, OP	2-D	7,888	528
U of Dubuque, Dubuque, IA 52001	1852	Dr. John J. Agria	2-M	1,200	79
U of Evansville, Evansville, IN 47722	1854	Dr. James S. Vinson	2-M	2,827	159
The U of Findlay, Findlay, OH 45840	1882	Dr. Kenneth E. Zirkle	2-M	2,896	255
U of Florida, Gainesville, FL 32611	1853	Dr. John V. Lombardi	5-D	34,814	3,834
U of Georgia, Athens, GA 30602	1785	Dr. Charles B. Knapp	5-D	28,691	1,982
U of Guam, Mangilao, GU 96923	1952	Dr. Wilfred P. Leon Guerrezo	8-M	2,842	244
U of Hartford, West Hartford, CT 06117	1877	Humphrey Tonkin	1-D	7,907	740
U of Hawaii at Manoa, Honolulu, HI 96822	1907	Dr. Albert J. Simone	5-D	19,383	2,392
U of Houston–Clear Lake, Houston, TX 77058	1971	Dr. Glenn A. Goerke	5-M	7,207	321
U of Houston–Downtown, Houston, TX 77002	1974	Dr. George Magner	5-B	8,702	361
U of Houston–Victoria, Victoria, TX 77901	1973	Dr. Lesta Van Der Wert Turchen	5-M	1,159	74
U of Idaho, Moscow, ID 83843	1889	Dr. Elisabeth Zinser	5-D	9,690	570
U of Illinois at Chicago, Chicago, IL 60680	1965	Dr. James J. Stukel	5-D	24,208	2,036
U of Illinois at Urbana-Champaign, Champaign, IL 61820	1867	Dr. Morton W. Weir	5-D	36,139	2,232
U of Indianapolis, Indianapolis, IN 46227-3697	1902	Dr. G. Benjamin Lantz, Jr.	2-M	3,692	276
U of Iowa, Iowa City, IA 52242	1847	Dr. Hunter R. Rawlings, III	5-D	27,881	1,705
U of Kansas, Lawrence, KS 66045	1866	Gene A. Budig	5-D	29,150	1,265
U of Kentucky, Lexington, KY 40506-0032	1865	Dr. Charles T. Wethington, Jr.	5-D	24,556	1,993
U of La Verne, La Verne, CA 91750	1891	Dr. Stephen Morgan	1-D	5,933	572
U of Louisville, Louisville, KY 40292	1798	Dr. Donald C. Swain	5-D	21,876	1,442
U of Maine, Orono, ME 04469	1865	Dr. Frederick E. Hutchinson	5-D	12,804	769
U of Maine at Farmington, Farmington, ME 04938	1864	Dr. J. Michael Orenduff	5-B	2,386	144
U of Maine at Presque Isle, Presque Isle, ME 04769	1903	Dr. James R. Roach	5-B	1,458	105
U of Mary, Bismarck, ND 58504	1959	Sr. Thomas Welder	2-M	1,755	94
U of Mary Hardin-Baylor, Belton, TX 76513	1845	Dr. Jerry G. Bawcom	2-M	1,827	80
U of Maryland at Baltimore, Baltimore, MD 21201	1807	Dr. Errol L. Reese	5-D	4,982	190
U of Maryland Baltimore County, Baltimore, MD 21228	1966	Dr. Michael K. Hooker	5-D	10,368	616
U of Maryland Coll Park, College Park, MD 20742	1856	Dr. William E. Kirwan	5-D	34,623	2,631
U of Maryland Eastern Shore, Princess Anne, MD 21853	1886	Dr. William P. Hytche	5-D	2,397	154
U of Maryland U Coll, College Park, MD 20742	1947	Dr. T. Benjamin Massey	5-M	40,029	1,671
U of Massachusetts at Amherst, Amherst, MA 01003	1863	Richard D. O'Brien	5-D	22,070	1,223
U of Massachusetts at Boston, Boston, MA 02125-3393	1964	Dr. Sherry H. Penney	5-D	10,479	802
U of Massachusetts Dartmouth, North Dartmouth, MA 02747	1895	Dr. John R. Brazil	5-M	5,680	405
U of Massachusetts Lowell, Lowell, MA 01854	1894	Dr. William T. Hogan	5-D	13,618	623
U of Miami, Coral Gables, FL 33124	1925	Edward T. Foote, II	1-D	13,969	1,087
U of Michigan, Ann Arbor, MI 48109	1817	Dr. James J. Duderstadt	5-D	36,228	3,310
U of Michigan–Dearborn, Dearborn, MI 48128	1959	Dr. Blenda Wilson	5-M	7,044	384
U of Michigan–Flint, Flint, MI 48502	1956	Dr. Clinton B. Jones	5-M	6,603	211
U of Minnesota, Duluth, Duluth, MN 55812	1947	Dr. Lawrence A. Ianni	5-M	7,787	415
U of Minnesota, Morris, Morris, MN 56267	1959	Dr. David C. Johnson	5-B	1,915	145
U of Minnesota, Twin Cities Cmps, Minneapolis, MN 55455	1851	Nils Hasselmo	5-D	39,315	2,839
U of Mississippi, University, MS 38677	1844	Dr. R. Gerald Turner	5-D	11,033	460
U of Mississippi Medical Ctr, Jackson, MS 39216	1955	Dr. Norman Crooks Nelson	5-D	1,676	574
U of Missouri–Columbia, Columbia, MO 65211	1839	Dr. Gerald Brouder	5-D	24,660	1,804
U of Missouri–Kansas City, Kansas City, MO 64110	1929	Dr. Eleanor Brantley-Schwartz	5-D	11,159	540
U of Missouri–Rolla, Rolla, MO 65401	1870	Dr. John T. Park	5-D	5,582	358
U of Missouri–St Louis, Normandy, MO 63121-4499	1963	Dr. Blanche M. Touhill	5-D	12,941	635
U of Montana, Missoula, MT 59812	1893	Dr. George M. Dennison	5-D	10,788	520
U of Montevallo, Montevallo, AL 35115	1896	Dr. John W. Stewart	5-M	3,252	173
U of Nebraska at Kearney, Kearney, NE 68849	1903	Dr. William R. Nester	5-M	8,775	430
U of Nebraska at Omaha, Omaha, NE 68182	1908	Dr. Del D. Weber	5-M	16,835	690
U of Nebraska–Lincoln, Lincoln, NE 68588	1869	Dr. Jack Gogbel	5-D	24,620	1,514
U of Nebraska Medical Ctr, Omaha, NE 68198	1869	Dr. Charles E. Andrews	5-D	2,631	489
U of Nevada, Las Vegas, Las Vegas, NV 89154	1957	Dr. Robert Maxson	5-D	19,504	1,001
U of Nevada, Reno, Reno, NV 89557	1874	Dr. Joseph N. Crowley	5-D	10,990	480
U of New England, Biddeford, ME 04005-9526	1939	Dr. Thomas Hedley Reynolds	1-D	1,210	98
U of New Hampshire, Durham, NH 03824	1866	Dr. Dale F. Nitzschke	5-D	11,219	825
U of New Haven, West Haven, CT 06516	1920	Dr. Lawrence J. DeNardis	1-D	5,899	424
U of New Mexico, Albuquerque, NM 87131-2039	1889	Richard E. Peck	5-D	25,009	1,202
U of New Orleans, New Orleans, LA 70148	1958	Dr. Gregory M. O'Brien	5-D	16,084	666

Name, address	Year	Governing official, control, and highest degree offered		Enrollment	Faculty
U of North Alabama, Florence, AL 35632-0001	1872	Mr. Robert L. Potts	5-M	5,755	239
U of North Carolina at Asheville, Asheville, NC 28804	1927	Dr. Samuel Schuman	5-M	3,261	226
U of North Carolina at Chapel Hill, Chapel Hill, NC 27599	1795	Paul Hardin, III	5-D	23,794	2,430
U of North Carolina at Charlotte, Charlotte, NC 28223	1946	Dr. James H. Woodward, Jr.	5-M	15,058	798
U of North Carolina at Greensboro, Greensboro, NC 27412	1891	Dr. William E. Moran	5-D	11,648	715
U of North Carolina at Wilmington, Wilmington, NC 28403	1947	Dr. James R. Leutze	5-M	8,090	409
U of North Dakota, Grand Forks, ND 58202	1883	Dr. Kendall Baker	5-D	11,938	663
U of Northern Colorado, Greeley, CO 80639	1890	Dr. Herman D. Lujan	5-D	10,494	535
U of Northern Iowa, Cedar Falls, IA 50614	1876	Dr. Constantine W. Curris	5-D	13,163	782
U of North Florida, Jacksonville, FL 32216	1965	Dr. Adam W. Herbert	5-D	7,034	214
U of North Texas, Denton, TX 76203	1890	Dr. Alfred F. Hurley	5-D	27,020	1,086
U of Notre Dame, Notre Dame, IN 46556	1842	Rev. Edward A. Malloy, CSC	2-D	9,900	840
U of Oklahoma, Norman, OK 73019	1890	Dr. Richard L. Van Horn	5-D	19,650	887
U of Oklahoma Health Sciences Ctr, Oklahoma City, OK 73190	1890	Dr. Jay H. Stein	5-D	2,940	NR
U of Oregon, Eugene, OR 97403	1872	Myles Brand	5-D	16,905	1,464
U of Osteopathic Medicine and Health Sciences, Des Moines, IA 50312	1898	Dr. J. Leonard Azneer	1-D	1,090	108
U of Pennsylvania, Philadelphia, PA 19104	1740	Dr. F. Sheldon Hackney	1-D	22,220	4,152
U of Phoenix, Phoenix, AZ 85040	1976	William Gibbs	3-M	13,159	1,500
U of Pittsburgh, Pittsburgh, PA 15260	1787	Dr. J. Dennis O'Connor	13-D	27,973	3,173
U of Pittsburgh at Bradford, Bradford, PA 16701	1963	Dr. Richard E. McDowell	13-B	1,244	93
U of Pittsburgh at Greensburg, Greensburg, PA 15601	1963	Dr. George F. Chambers	13-B	1,465	91
U of Pittsburgh at Johnstown, Johnstown, PA 15904	1927	Dr. Frank H. Blackington, III	13-B	3,243	201
U of Portland, Portland, OR 97203	1901	Rev. David T. Tyson, CSC	2-M	2,646	200
U of Puerto Rico at Arecibo, Arecibo, PR 00613	1967	Prof. Salvador Salas Quintana	7-B	3,307	178
U of Puerto Rico at Bayamón, Bayamón, PR 00619	1971	Aida Canals de Bird	7-B	3,891	174
U of Puerto Rico at Ponce, Ponce, PR 00732	1970	Mr. Pedro E. Laboy	7-B	2,192	122
U of Puerto Rico, Cayey U Coll, Cayey, PR 00737	1967	Dr. Margarita Benitez	7-B	3,243	175
U of Puerto Rico, Humacao U Coll, Humacao, PR 00792	1962	Dr. Felix Castrodad	7-B	3,896	217
U of Puerto Rico, Mayagüez Cmps, Mayagüez, PR 00680	1911	Dr. Alejandro Ruiz-Acevedo	7-D	9,432	676
U of Puerto Rico Medical Sciences Cmps, San Juan, PR 00936-5067	1950	Dr. Manuel Marina	7-D	2,429	719
U of Puerto Rico, Río Piedras, Río Piedras, PR 00931	1903	Dr. Juan R. Fernandez	7-D	20,265	1,476
U of Puget Sound, Tacoma, WA 98416	1888	Dr. Philip M. Phibbs	2-M	3,210	225
U of Redlands, Redlands, CA 92373	1907	Dr. James R. Appleton	1-M	2,300	134
U of Rhode Island, Kingston, RI 02881	1892	Dr. Robert L. Carothers	5-D	12,435	748
U of Richmond, Richmond, VA 23173	1830	Dr. Richard L. Morrill	2-M	4,688	380
U of Rio Grande, Rio Grande, OH 45674	1876	Dr. Barry M. Dorsey	1-M	2,072	108
U of Rochester, Rochester, NY 14627-0001	1850	G. Dennis O'Brien	1-D	8,753	577
U of St Thomas, St Paul, MN 55105	1885	Rev. Dennis Dease	2-D	10,156	447
U of St Thomas, Houston, TX 77006	1947	Joseph M. McFadden	2-D	2,078	173
U of San Diego, San Diego, CA 92110-2492	1949	Dr. Author E. Hughes	2-D	6,041	441
U of San Francisco, San Francisco, CA 94117-1080	1855	Rev. John P. Schlegel, SJ	2-D	6,853	517
U of Science and Arts of Oklahoma, Chickasha, OK 73018-0001	1908	Dr. Roy Troutt	5-B	1,619	75
U of Scranton, Scranton, PA 18510-4501	1888	Rev. J. A. Panuska, SJ	2-M	5,113	387
U of South Alabama, Mobile, AL 36688	1963	Dr. Frederick P. Whiddon	5-D	11,990	793
U of South Carolina, Columbia, SC 29208	1801	Dr. John M. Palms	5-D	26,133	1,436
U of South Carolina–Aiken, Aiken, SC 29801	1961	Dr. Robert E. Alexander	5-B	3,642	232
U of South Carolina at Spartanburg, Spartanburg, SC 29303	1967	Dr. Olin B. Sansbury, Jr.	5-B	3,526	231
U of South Carolina–Coastal Carolina Coll, Myrtle Beach, SC 29578	1954	Dr. Ronald G. Eaglin	5-B	3,983	238
U of South Dakota, Vermillion, SD 57069-2390	1862	Dr. Betty Turner Asher	5-D	7,231	457
U of Southern California, Los Angeles, CA 90089	1880	Dr. Steven B. Sample	1-D	27,624	3,402
U of Southern Colorado, Pueblo, CO 81001	1933	Dr. Robert Shirley	5-M	4,338	264
U of Southern Indiana, Evansville, IN 47712	1965	Dr. David L. Rice	5-M	7,021	213
U of Southern Maine, Portland, ME 04103	1878	Dr. Richard L. Pattenaude	5-D	10,423	574
U of Southern Mississippi, Hattiesburg, MS 39406	1910	Dr. Aubrey K. Lucas	5-D	12,348	678
U of South Florida, Tampa, FL 33620	1956	Dr. Francis T. Borkowski	5-D	33,280	2,549
U of Southwestern Louisiana, Lafayette, LA 70504	1898	Dr. Ray P. Authement	5-D	16,185	613
U of Tampa, Tampa, FL 33606	1931	Dr. David G. Ruffer	1-M	2,527	182
U of Tennessee at Chattanooga, Chattanooga, TN 37403	1886	Dr. Frederick W. Obear	5-M	7,888	449
U of Tennessee at Martin, Martin, TN 38238	1927	Dr. Margaret N. Perry	5-M	5,494	263
U of Tennessee, Knoxville, Knoxville, TN 37996	1794	Dr. John J. Quinn	5-D	25,598	1,157
U of Tennessee, Memphis, Memphis, TN 38163	1911	NR	5-D	1,859	907
U of Texas at Arlington, Arlington, TX 76019	1895	Dr. Wendell H. Nedderman	5-D	25,135	906
U of Texas at Austin, Austin, TX 78712	1883	Dr. William H. Cunningham	5-D	49,961	2,341
U of Texas at Brownsville, Brownsville, TX 78520-4991	1973	NR	5-M	1,457	88
U of Texas at Dallas, Richardson, TX 75083-0688	1969	Dr. Robert H. Rutford	5-D	8,980	304
U of Texas at El Paso, El Paso, TX 79968	1913	Dr. Diana Natalicio	5-D	16,797	723
U of Texas at San Antonio, San Antonio, TX 78249	1969	Dr. Samuel A. Kirkpatrick	5-D	15,759	660
U of Texas at Tyler, Tyler, TX 75701	1971	Dr. George F. Hamm	5-M	3,790	213
U of Texas Health Science Ctr at Houston, Houston, TX 77225	1943	Dr. M. David Low	5-D	3,125	121
U of Texas Health Science Ctr at San Antonio, San Antonio, TX 78284	1976	Dr. John P. Howe, III	5-D	2,546	140
U of Texas Medical Branch at Galveston, Galveston, TX 77555	1891	Dr. Thomas N. James	5-D	1,960	127
U of Texas of the Permian Basin, Odessa, TX 79762-0001	1969	Dr. Edwin R. Sharpe	5-M	2,108	95
U of Texas–Pan American, Edinburg, TX 78539	1927	Dr. Miguel A. Nevarez	5-M	12,800	550
U of Texas Southwestern Medical Ctr at Dallas, Dallas, TX 75235-9096	1943	Dr. C. Kern Wildenthal	5-D	1,529	270
U of the Arts, Philadelphia, PA 19102	1870	NR	1-M	1,359	286
U of the District of Columbia, Washington, DC 20008	1976	Tilden J. LeMelle	10-M	11,422	740
U of the Pacific, Stockton, CA 95211	1851	Dr. Bill L. Atchley	1-D	5,403	356
U of the Sacred Heart, Santurce, PR 00914	1935	Jose Alberto Morales, Esq.	2-M	5,681	366
U of the South, Sewanee, TN 37375-1000	1857	Dr. Samuel R. Williamson	2-D	1,181	121
U of the State of NY, Regents Coll, Albany, NY 12203	1970	C. Wayne Williams	13-B	12,668	NR
U of the Virgin Islands, Charlotte Amalie, St Thomas, VI 00802	1962	Dr. Orville Kean	8-M	2,716	259
U of Toledo, Toledo, OH 43606	1872	Mr. Frank E. Horton	5-D	24,969	1,420
U of Tulsa, Tulsa, OK 74104	1894	Dr. Robert H. Donaldson	2-D	4,785	414
U of Utah, Salt Lake City, UT 84112	1850	Dr. Arthur K. Smith	5-D	25,581	1,290
U of Vermont, Burlington, VT 05405	1791	Thomas P. Salmon	5-D	9,492	1,017
U of Virginia, Charlottesville, VA 22906	1819	John T. Casteen, III	5-D	17,606	1,000

Name, address	Year	Governing official, control, and highest degree offered		Enrollment	Faculty
U of Washington, Seattle, WA 98195	1861	William P. Gerberding	5-D	34,269	2,834
U of West Florida, Pensacola, FL 32514-5750	1963	Dr. Morris L. Marx	5-M	7,941	255
U of Wisconsin–Eau Claire, Eau Claire, WI 54702	1916	Dr. Larry Schnack	5-M	10,495	558
U of Wisconsin–Green Bay, Green Bay, WI 54311-7001	1968	Dr. David L. Outcalt	5-M	5,423	241
U of Wisconsin–La Crosse, La Crosse, WI 54601	1909	Dr. Judith L. Kuipers	5-M	8,802	419
U of Wisconsin–Madison, Madison, WI 53706	1848	Dr. Donna E. Shalala	5-D	43,196	2,325
U of Wisconsin–Milwaukee, Milwaukee, WI 53201	1956	Dr. John H. Schroeder, Jr.	5-D	25,456	1,281
U of Wisconsin–Oshkosh, Oshkosh, WI 54901	1871	Dr. John E. Kerrigan	5-M	11,161	535
U of Wisconsin–Parkside, Kenosha, WI 53141	1968	Dr. Sheila Kaplan	5-M	5,021	295
U of Wisconsin–Platteville, Platteville, WI 53818	1866	Dr. William W. Chmurny	5-M	5,225	280
U of Wisconsin–River Falls, River Falls, WI 54022	1874	Dr. Gary A. Thibodeau	5-M	5,566	295
U of Wisconsin–Stevens Point, Stevens Point, WI 54481	1894	Dr. Keith R. Sanders	5-M	8,757	462
U of Wisconsin–Stout, Menomonie, WI 54751	1891	Dr. Charles Sorensen	5-M	7,598	406
U of Wisconsin–Superior, Superior, WI 54880	1893	Dr. Betty Youngblood	5-M	2,891	162
U of Wisconsin–Whitewater, Whitewater, WI 53190	1868	Dr. James R. Connor	5-M	10,459	476
U of Wyoming, Laramie, WY 82071	1886	Dr. Terry P. Roark	5-D	12,656	747
Upper Iowa U, Fayette, IA 52142	1857	Dr. James R. Rocheleau	1-B	2,489	230
Ursinus Coll, Collegeville, PA 19426	1869	Dr. Richard P. Richter	2-B	1,017	110
Ursuline Coll, Pepper Pike, OH 44124 (4)	1871	Sr. Anne Marie Diederich, OSU	2-M	1,583	127
Utah State U, Logan, UT 84322	1888	Dr. Stanford Cazier	5-D	16,440	970
Utica Coll of Syracuse U, Utica, NY 13502	1946	Dr. Michael K. Simpson	1-B	1,707	140
Valdosta State Coll, Valdosta, GA 31698	1906	Dr. Hugh C. Bailey	5-M	7,436	390
Valley City State U, Valley City, ND 58072	1890	Dr. Charles B. House, Jr.	5-B	1,083	68
Valparaiso U, Valparaiso, IN 46383	1859	Dr. Alan F. Harre	2-D	3,872	310
Vanderbilt U, Nashville, TN 37240	1873	Mr. Joe B. Wyatt	1-D	9,581	822
Vassar Coll, Poughkeepsie, NY 12601	1861	Frances D. Fergusson	1-M	2,345	234
Villa Julie Coll, Stevenson, MD 21153	1952	Dr. Carolyn Manuszak	1-B	1,681	129
Villanova U, Villanova, PA 19085	1842	Rev. Edmund J. Dobbin, OSA	2-D	11,858	917
Virginia Commonwealth U, Richmond, VA 23284	1838	Dr. Eugene P. Trani	5-D	21,608	2,143
Virginia Military Inst, Lexington, VA 24450 (1)	1839	Maj. Gen. John W. Knapp	5-B	1,281	98
Virginia Polytechnic Inst and State U, Blacksburg, VA 24061-0202	1872	James D. McComas	5-D	23,912	1,909
Virginia State U, Petersburg, VA 23806	1882	Dr. Wesley C. McClure	5-M	4,585	250
Virginia Union U, Richmond, VA 23220	1865	Dr. S. Dallas Simmons	2-D	1,360	115
Virginia Wesleyan Coll, Norfolk, VA 23502	1961	Dr. Lambuth M. Clarke	2-B	1,440	85
Viterbo Coll, La Crosse, WI 54601	1890	Dr. William J. Medland	2-M	1,170	109
Wagner Coll, Staten Island, NY 10301	1883	Dr. Norman R. Smith	1-M	1,521	155
Wake Forest U, Winston-Salem, NC 27109	1834	Dr. Thomas K. Hearn, Jr.	1-D	5,679	324
Walla Walla Coll, College Place, WA 99324	1892	Dr. Neils-Erik Andreasen	2-M	1,650	168
Walsh Coll, North Canton, OH 44720	1958	Rev. Richard Mucowski	2-M	1,536	113
Walsh Coll of Accountancy and Business Admin, Troy, MI 48007	1922	Mr. David A. Spencer	1-M	3,470	130
Wartburg Coll, Waverly, IA 50677	1852	Dr. Robert Vogel	2-B	1,453	122
Washburn U of Topeka, Topeka, KS 66621	1865	Dr. Hugh Thompson	11-D	6,626	377
Washington and Jefferson Coll, Washington, PA 15301	1781	Dr. Howard J. Burnett	1-B	1,126	100
Washington and Lee U, Lexington, VA 24450	1749	Dr. John D. Wilson	1-D	1,988	138
Washington State U, Pullman, WA 99164	1890	Dr. Samuel H. Smith	5-D	17,846	1,107
Washington U, St Louis, MO 63130	1853	Dr. William H. Danforth	1-D	9,599	929
Wayland Baptist U, Plainview, TX 79072	1908	Dr. Wallace E. Davis, Jr.	2-M	2,500	181
Waynesburg Coll, Waynesburg, PA 15370	1849	Mr. Timothy R. Thyreen	2-M	1,332	98
Wayne State Coll, Wayne, NE 68787	1910	Dr. Donald J. Mash	5-M	3,925	175
Wayne State U, Detroit, MI 48202	1868	Dr. David Adamany	5-D	34,004	2,426
Weber State U, Ogden, UT 84408	1889	Dr. Paul H. Thompson	5-M	14,495	454
Webster U, St Louis, MO 63119	1915	Dr. Daniel H. Perlman	1-D	4,474	410
Wellesley Coll, Wellesley, MA 02181 (3)	1870	Dr. Nannerl Keohane	1-B	2,319	325
Wentworth Inst of Tech, Boston, MA 02115	1904	Dr. John F. Van Domelen	1-B	2,779	241
Wesleyan U, Middletown, CT 06459	1831	Mr. William M. Chace	1-D	3,297	341
Wesley Coll, Dover, DE 19901	1873	Dr. Reed M. Stewart	2-B	1,294	98
West Chester U of Pennsylvania, West Chester, PA 19383	1871	Dr. Stanley Yarosewick	5-M	11,959	651
West Coast U, Los Angeles, CA 90020-1765	1909	Dr. Robert M. L. Baker, Jr.	1-M	1,600	250
Western Carolina U, Cullowhee, NC 28723	1889	Dr. Myron L. Coulter	5-M	6,372	443
Western Connecticut State U, Danbury, CT 06810	1903	Dr. Stephen Feldman	5-M	5,886	326
Western Illinois U, Macomb, IL 61455	1899	Dr. Ralph H. Wagoner	5-M	13,801	674
Western International U, Phoenix, AZ 85021	1978	Robert S. Webber	1-M	1,554	88
Western Kentucky U, Bowling Green, KY 42101	1906	Dr. Thomas C. Meredith	5-M	15,767	722
Western Maryland Coll, Westminster, MD 21157	1867	Dr. Robert H. Chambers	1-M	2,238	132
Western Michigan U, Kalamazoo, MI 49008	1903	Dr. Diether H. Haenicke	5-D	27,901	1,042
Western Montana Coll of the U of Montana, Dillon, MT 59725	1893	Dr. W. Michael Easton	5-B	1,106	42
Western New England Coll, Springfield, MA 01119	1919	Dr. Beverly W. Miller	1-D	5,189	266
Western New Mexico U, Silver City, NM 88061	1893	Dr. Jerry L. Gallentine	5-M	2,240	113
Western Oregon State Coll, Monmouth, OR 97361	1856	Dr. Richard S. Meyers	5-M	3,963	294
Western State Coll of Colorado, Gunnison, CO 81230	1911	Dr. Kaye Howe	5-B	2,450	143
Western State U Coll of Law of Orange County, Fullerton, CA 92631	1966	NR	3-D	1,723	63
Western Washington U, Bellingham, WA 98225	1893	Dr. Kenneth P. Mortimer	5-M	10,010	533
Westfield State Coll, Westfield, MA 01086	1838	Dr. Ronald L. Applbaum	5-M	5,220	213
West Georgia Coll, Carrollton, GA 30118	1933	Dr. Maurice K. Townsend	5-M	7,521	299
West Liberty State Coll, West Liberty, WV 26074	1837	Dr. Clyde D. Campbell	5-B	2,302	160
Westminster Coll, New Wilmington, PA 16172-0001	1852	Dr. Oscar E. Remick	2-M	1,554	121
Westminster Coll of Salt Lake City, Salt Lake City, UT 84105	1875	Dr. Charles H. Dick	1-M	2,112	175
Westmont Coll, Santa Barbara, CA 93108	1940	Dr. David K. Winter	2-B	1,189	103
West Texas State U, Canyon, TX 79016	1909	Dr. Barry B. Thompson	5-M	6,193	312
West Virginia Inst of Tech, Montgomery, WV 25136	1895	Dr. Robert C. Gillespie	5-M	3,051	189
West Virginia State Coll, Institute, WV 25112	1891	NR	5-B	4,986	233
West Virginia U, Morgantown, WV 26506	1867	Dr. Neil S. Bucklew	5-D	22,460	1,484
West Virginia Wesleyan Coll, Buckhannon, WV 26201	1890	Dr. Thomas B. Courtice	2-M	1,651	115
Wheaton Coll, Wheaton, IL 60187	1860	Dr. J. Richard Chase	2-M	2,520	254
Wheaton Coll, Norton, MA 02766	1834	Dale Rogers Marshall	1-B	1,302	110
Wheeling Jesuit Coll, Wheeling, WV 26003	1954	Fr. Thomas S. Acker, SJ	2-M	1,402	74
Wheelock Coll, Boston, MA 02215 (4)	1888	Dr. Gerald N. Tirozzi	1-M	1,278	175
Whitman Coll, Walla Walla, WA 99362	1859	Dr. David E. Maxwell	1-B	1,189	150
Whittier Coll, Whittier, CA 90608	1887	Dr. James L. Ash, Jr.	1-D	1,838	103
Whitworth Coll, Spokane, WA 99251	1890	Dr. Arthur J. De Jong	2-M	1,706	95

Name, address	Year	Governing official, control, and highest degree offered		Enrollment	Faculty
Wichita State U, Wichita, KS 67208	1895	Dr. Warren B. Armstrong	5-D	15,779	680
Widener U, Chester, PA 19013	1821	Mr. Robert J. Bruce	1-D	8,700	312
Wilkes U, Wilkes-Barre, PA 18766	1933	Dr. Christopher N. Breiseth	1-M	3,432	219
Willamette U, Salem, OR 97301	1842	Dr. Jerry E. Hudson	2-D	2,360	179
William Jewell Coll, Liberty, MO 64068	1849	Dr. J. Gordon Kingsley	2-B	1,366	143
William Paterson Coll of New Jersey, Wayne, NJ 07470	1855	Dr. Arnold Speert	5-M	9,706	318
Williams Coll, Williamstown, MA 01267	1793	Dr. Francis C. Oakley	1-M	2,125	271
Wilmington Coll, New Castle, DE 19720	1967	Dr. Audrey K. Doberstein	1-D	1,796	147
Wingate Coll, Wingate, NC 28174	1895	William Larry Ziglar	2-M	1,406	97
Winona State U, Winona, MN 55987	1858	Dr. Darrell Krueger	5-M	7,500	400
Winston-Salem State U, Winston-Salem, NC 27110	1892	Dr. Cleon F. Thompson, Jr.	5-B	2,604	179
Winthrop U, Rock Hill, SC 29733	1886	Dr. Anthony DiGiorgio	5-M	5,018	404
Wittenberg U, Springfield, OH 45501	1845	Dr. William A. Kinnison	2-B	2,280	182
Wofford Coll, Spartanburg, SC 29303-3663	1854	Dr. Joab M. Lesesne	2-B	1,117	88
Woodbury U, Burbank, CA 91510	1884	Dr. Paul E. Sago	1-M	1,075	123
Worcester Polytechnic Inst, Worcester, MA 01609	1865	Dr. Jon C. Strauss	1-D	3,902	342
Worcester State Coll, Worcester, MA 01602	1874	Dr. Kalyan K. Ghosh	5-M	5,746	186
Wright State U, Dayton, OH 45435	1964	Dr. Paige E. Mulhollan	5-D	17,761	950
Xavier U, Cincinnati, OH 45207	1831	Rev. James E. Hoff, SJ	2-M	6,383	399
Xavier U of Louisiana, New Orleans, LA 70125	1925	Dr. Norman C. Francis	2-D	3,099	259
Yale U, New Haven, CT 06520	1701	NR	1-D	10,778	715
Yeshiva U, New York, NY 10033-3299	1886	Dr. Norman Lamm	1-D	4,804	164
York Coll of Pennsylvania, York, PA 17403	1787	Dr. George W. Waldner	1-M	5,028	272
York Coll of the City U of New York, Jamaica, NY 11451	1967	Dr. Josephine D. Davis	12-B	6,000	200
Youngstown State U, Youngstown, OH 44555	1908	Dr. Leslie H. Cochran	5-M	15,164	933

Two-Year Colleges

The highest undergraduate degree offered for all two-year colleges is the associate degree.

Name, address	Year	Governing official	Control	Enrollment	Faculty
Abraham Baldwin Ag Coll, Tifton, GA 31794	1933	Dr. Harold J. Loyd	5	2,650	106
Adirondack Comm Coll, Queensbury, NY 12804	1960	Dr. Roger Andersen	12	3,554	195
Aiken Tech Coll, Aiken, SC 29802	1972	Dr. Paul L. Blowers	12	2,187	175
Aims Comm Coll, Greeley, CO 80632	1967	Dr. George R. Conger	10	8,832	420
Alabama Southern Comm Coll, Monroeville, AL 36460	1965	Dr. John A. Johnson	5	1,117	77
Alamance Comm Coll, Haw River, NC 27258	1959	Dr. W. Ronald McCarter	5	3,542	145
Allan Hancock Coll, Santa Maria, CA 93454	1920	Dr. Ann F. Stephenson	12	7,267	417
Allegany Comm Coll, Cumberland, MD 21502	1961	Dr. Donald L. Alexander	12	2,780	203
Allen County Comm Coll, Iola, KS 66749	1923	Dr. William A. Griffin, Jr.	12	1,318	125
Alpena Comm Coll, Alpena, MI 49707	1952	Dr. Donald L. Newport	12	2,441	128
Alvin Comm Coll, Alvin, TX 77511-4898	1949	Dr. A. Rodney Allbright	12	3,914	193
Amarillo Coll, Amarillo, TX 79178	1929	Dr. Robert L. Clinton	12	6,540	406
American Inst of Business, Des Moines, IA 50321	1921	Keith Fenton	1	1,040	55
American River Coll, Sacramento, CA 95841	1955	Dr. Queen F. Randall	10	21,330	700
Angelina Coll, Lufkin, TX 75902	1968	Dr. Larry M. Phillips	12	3,074	151
Anne Arundel Comm Coll, Arnold, MD 21012	1961	Dr. Thomas E. Florestano	12	11,398	590
Anoka-Ramsey Comm Coll, Coon Rapids, MN 55433	1965	Dr. Patrick M. Johns	5	6,830	228
Antelope Valley Coll, Lancaster, CA 93536	1929	Dr. Allan W. Kurki	12	11,000	400
Arapahoe Comm Coll, Littleton, CO 80160-9002	1965	Dr. James F. Weber	5	7,765	298
Arizona Western Coll, Yuma, AZ 85366-0929	1962	Dr. James R. Carruthers	12	5,050	243
Arkansas State U–Beebe Branch, Beebe, AR 72012	1927	Mr. William H. Owen, Jr.	5	1,694	77
Art Inst of Atlanta, Atlanta, GA 30326	1949	Hal R. Griffith	3	1,261	109
Art Inst of Dallas, Dallas, TX 75231	1978	Pat DeCoursey	3	1,000	84
Art Inst of Fort Lauderdale, Fort Lauderdale, FL 33316	1968	David P. Higley	3	2,200	150
Art Inst of Houston, Houston, TX 77056	1978	NR	3	1,083	83
Art Inst of Philadelphia, Philadelphia, PA 19103	1966	Dr. Max R. Tudor	3	1,200	90
Art Inst of Pittsburgh, Pittsburgh, PA 15222	1921	Saundra M. Van Dyke	3	2,500	102
Art Inst of Seattle, Seattle, WA 98121	1982	David J. Pauldine	3	1,314	101
Asheville-Buncombe Tech Comm Coll, Asheville, NC 28801	1959	Mr. K. Ray Bailey	5	4,090	216
Asnuntuck Comm Coll, Enfield, CT 06082	1972	Dr. Harvey S. Irlen	5	1,900	79
Athens Area Tech Inst, Athens, GA 30610-0399	1958	NR	5	1,276	77
Atlanta Metropolitan Coll, Atlanta, GA 30310	1974	Dr. Edwin A. Thompson	5	1,785	100
Atlantic Comm Coll, Mays Landing, NJ 08330	1966	Dr. William Orth	9	5,500	215
Austin Comm Coll, Austin, MN 55912	1940	Mr. Steven R. Wallace	5	1,318	73
Austin Comm Coll, Austin, TX 78714	1972	Dr. Dan Angel	10	23,563	1,388
Bakersfield Coll, Bakersfield, CA 93305	1913	Dr. Richard Wright	12	12,300	448
Barstow Coll, Barstow, CA 92311	1959	Dr. John C. Menzie	12	3,569	128
Barton County Comm Coll, Great Bend, KS 67530	1969	Dr. Jimmie L. Downing	12	4,460	205
Bay de Noc Comm Coll, Escanaba, MI 49829	1963	Dr. Dwight E. Link	9	2,255	143
Beaufort County Comm Coll, Washington, NC 27889	1968	Dr. Ron Champion	5	1,348	95
Bee County Coll, Beeville, TX 78102	1965	Dr. Norman Wallace	9	2,267	116
Belleville Area Coll, Belleville, IL 62221	1946	Dr. Joseph Cipfl	10	13,909	720
Bellevue Comm Coll, Bellevue, WA 98007-6484	1966	B. Jean Floten	5	8,690	617
Belmont Tech Coll, St Clairsville, OH 43950	1971	Dr. Wesley R. Channell	5	1,696	133
Bergen Comm Coll, Paramus, NJ 07652	1965	Dr. Jose Lopez-Isa	9	8,107	613
Berkeley Coll of Business, West Paterson, NJ 07424	1931	Kevin L. Luing	3	1,457	106
Berkshire Comm Coll, Pittsfield, MA 01201	1960	Dr. Cathryn L. Addy	5	2,641	126
Bessemer State Tech Coll, Bessemer, AL 35021	1966	Dr. W. Michael Bailey	5	1,896	102
Big Bend Comm Coll, Moses Lake, WA 98837-3299	1962	Dr. Greg Fitch	5	1,709	147
Bishop State Comm Coll, Mobile, AL 36603	1965	NR	5	2,144	91
Bismarck State Coll, Bismarck, ND 58501	1939	Dr. Kermit Lidstrom	5	2,374	117
Black Hawk Coll, Moline, IL 61265	1946	Dr. Herbert C. Lyon	12	5,614	305
Blackhawk Tech Coll, Janesville, WI 53547	1968	Dr. James C. Catania	10	2,600	137
Blinn Coll, Brenham, TX 77833	1883	Walter C. Schwartz	12	7,290	299
Blue Mountain Comm Coll, Pendleton, OR 97801	1962	Mr. Ronald L. Daniels	12	3,256	189
Blue Ridge Comm Coll, Flat Rock, NC 28731	1969	Dr. David W. Sink	12	1,586	82
Blue Ridge Comm Coll, Weyers Cave, VA 24486	1965	Dr. James R. Perkins	5	3,064	139
Borough of Manhattan Comm Coll of City U of NY, New York, NY 10007	1963	Dr. Augusta Souza Kappner	12	14,866	848
Bossier Parish Comm Coll, Bossier City, LA 71111	1967	James M. Conerly	12	4,130	165
Bowling Green State U–Firelands Coll, Huron, OH 44839	1968	Dr. Robert DeBard	5	1,405	75
Brainerd Comm Coll, Brainerd, MN 56401	1938	Sally Jane Ihne	5	1,782	88
Brazosport Coll, Lake Jackson, TX 77566	1948	Dr. John R. Grable	12	3,575	157
Brevard Comm Coll, Cocoa, FL 32922	1960	Dr. Maxwell C. King	5	15,033	925

Name, address	Year	Governing official, control		Enrollment	Faculty
Bristol Comm Coll, Fall River, MA 02720	1965	Ms. Eileen Farley	.5	3,056	183
Brookdale Comm Coll, Lincroft, NJ 07738	1967	Dr. Peter Burnham	.9	11,975	443
Brookhaven Coll, Farmers Branch, TX 75244	1978	Walter G. Bumphus	.9	8,041	385
Broome Comm Coll, Binghamton, NY 13902	1946	Dr. Donald A. Dellow	12	6,400	466
Broward Comm Coll, Fort Lauderdale, FL 33301	1960	Dr. Willis N. Holcombe	.5	28,433	775
Brunswick Coll, Brunswick, GA 31523	1961	Dr. Dorothy L. Lord	.5	1,623	75
Bryant and Stratton Business Inst, Buffalo, NY 14202	1854	Mr. William Schatt	.3	1,009	26
Bucks County Comm Coll, Newtown, PA 18940	1964	Dr. William E. Vincent	.9	11,042	375
Bunker Hill Comm Coll, Boston, MA 02129	1973	NR	.5	5,546	145
Burlington County Coll, Pemberton, NJ 08068	1966	Dr. Robert Messina	.9	7,116	150
Butler County Comm Coll, El Dorado, KS 67042	1927	Dr. Rodney V. Cox, Jr.	12	5,599	299
Butler County Comm Coll, Butler, PA 16003	1965	Dr. Thaddeus H. Penar	.9	3,071	115
Butte Coll, Oroville, CA 95965	1966	Dr. Wendell L. Reeder	10	12,838	575
Cabrillo Coll, Aptos, CA 95003	1959	Mr. John D. Hurd	10	13,500	552
Caldwell Comm Coll and Tech Inst, Hudson, NC 28638	1964	Dr. Eric B. McKeithan	.5	2,730	174
Camden County Coll, Blackwood, NJ 08012	1967	Dr. Robert W. Ramsay	12	14,352	385
Cañada Coll, Redwood City, CA 94061	1968	NR	10	7,355	263
Cape Cod Comm Coll, West Barnstable, MA 02668	1961	NR	.5	2,137	214
Cape Fear Comm Coll, Wilmington, NC 28401	1959	Dr. Richard C. Conrath	.5	3,150	153
Carl Sandburg Coll, Galesburg, IL 61401	1967	NR	12	3,600	119
Carteret Comm Coll, Morehead City, NC 28557	1963	Dr. Donald W. Bryant	.5	1,513	93
Casper Coll, Casper, WY 82601	1945	Dr. LeRoy Strausner	10	2,400	185
Catawba Valley Comm Coll, Hickory, NC 28602	1960	Dr. Cuyler A. Dunbar	12	3,427	175
Catonsville Comm Coll, Catonsville, MD 21228	1957	Dr. Frederick J. Walsh	.9	10,731	534
Cayuga County Comm Coll, Auburn, NY 13021	1953	Dr. Lawrence H. Poole	12	2,715	144
Cazenovia Coll, Cazenovia, NY 13035	1824	Dr. Stephen M. Schneeweiss	.1	1,071	145
Cecil Comm Coll, North East, MD 21901	1968	Dr. Robert L. Gell	.9	1,542	98
Cedar Valley Coll, Lancaster, TX 75134	1977	Dr. Carol J. Spencer	.5	3,281	130
Central Alabama Comm Coll, Alexander City, AL 35010	1965	Dr. James H. Cornell	.5	2,636	131
Central Arizona Coll, Coolidge, AZ 85228	1961	Dr. John J. Klein	.9	8,514	NR
Central Carolina Comm Coll, Sanford, NC 27330	1962	Dr. Marvin R. Joyner	12	2,891	177
Central Comm Coll–Grand Island Cmps, Grand Island, NE 68802	1976	Donald Nelson	12	3,684	78
Central Comm Coll–Hastings Cmps, Hastings, NE 68902	1966	Dr. Judy Dresser	12	2,841	110
Central Comm Coll–Platte Cmps, Columbus, NE 68602	1968	Dr. Peter Rush	12	3,687	84
Central Florida Comm Coll, Ocala, FL 32678	1957	NR	12	5,616	202
Central Ohio Tech Coll, Newark, OH 43055	1971	Dr. Julius S. Greenstein	.5	1,716	99
Central Oregon Comm Coll, Bend, OR 97701	1949	Dr. Robert L. Barber	10	3,118	181
Central Piedmont Comm Coll, Charlotte, NC 28235	1963	Dr. Ruth Shaw	12	15,871	1,220
Central Virginia Comm Coll, Lynchburg, VA 24502-4907	1966	Dr. Belle S. Wheelan	.5	4,077	110
Central Wyoming Coll, Riverton, WY 82501	1966	Dr. JoAnne McFarland	12	1,705	147
Cerritos Coll, Norwalk, CA 90650	1956	Dr. Ernest Martinez	12	20,676	683
Cerro Coso Comm Coll, Ridgecrest, CA 93555	1973	Dr. Raymond A. McCue	.5	4,118	241
Chabot Coll, Hayward, CA 94545	1961	Dr. Raul J. Cardoza	.5	15,103	1,045
Chaffey Coll, Rancho Cucamonga, CA 91737-3002	1883	Dr. Jerry W. Young	10	15,000	500
Champlain Coll, Burlington, VT 05401	1878	Dr. Roger H. Perry	.1	1,917	115
Charles County Comm Coll, La Plata, MD 20646	1958	Dr. John Sine	12	5,143	247
Charles Stewart Mott Comm Coll, Flint, MI 48503	1923	Dr. Charles R. Donnelly	10	10,858	404
Chattahoochee Valley State Comm Coll, Phenix City, AL 36869	1974	NR	.5	1,727	67
Chattanooga State Tech Comm Coll, Chattanooga, TN 37406	1965	Dr. James L. Catanzaro	.5	7,412	358
Chemeketa Comm Coll, Salem, OR 97309	1955	William Segura	12	10,375	881
Chesapeake Coll, Wye Mills, MD 21679	1965	Dr. John R. Kotula	12	2,042	95
Chipola Jr Coll, Marianna, FL 32446	1947	Dr. Jerry W. Kandzer	.5	2,883	137
Chippewa Valley Tech Coll, Eau Claire, WI 54701	1912	Mr. Norbert K. Wurtzel	10	3,750	400
Cincinnati Tech Coll, Cincinnati, OH 45223	1966	Dr. James P. Long	.5	5,500	274
Cisco Jr Coll, Cisco, TX 76437	1940	Dr. Roger C. Schustereit	12	2,101	98
Citrus Coll, Glendora, CA 91740	1915	NR	12	10,685	527
City Coll of San Francisco, San Francisco, CA 94112	1935	Dr. Evans S. Dobelle	12	34,000	1,117
City Colls of Chicago, Chicago City-Wide Coll, Chicago, IL 60606	1975	Mr. John Wozniak	12	2,699	116
City Colls of Chicago, Harold Washington Coll, Chicago, IL 60601	1962	Dr. Bernice Miller	12	7,709	228
City Colls of Chicago, Harry S Truman Coll, Chicago, IL 60640	1956	Dr. Wallace B. Appelson	12	6,281	170
City Colls of Chicago, Kennedy-King Coll, Chicago, IL 60621	1935	Dr. Harold Pates	12	2,932	147
City Colls of Chicago, Malcolm X Coll, Chicago, IL 60612	1911	Ms. Zerrie D. Campbell	12	2,292	142
City Colls of Chicago, Olive-Harvey Coll, Chicago, IL 60628	1970	Mr. Homer D. Franklin	12	3,952	135
City Colls of Chicago, Richard J Daley Coll, Chicago, IL 60652	1960	Mr. William P. Conway	12	5,796	161
City Colls of Chicago, Wilbur Wright Coll, Chicago, IL 60634	1934	Mr. Raymond F. LeFevour	12	6,188	161
Clackamas Comm Coll, Oregon City, OR 97045	1966	Dr. John S. Keyser	.9	7,025	527
Clark Coll, Vancouver, WA 98663	1933	Dr. Earl P. Johnson	.5	9,100	320
Clark State Comm Coll, Springfield, OH 45501	1962	Mr. Albert A. Salerno	.5	2,858	131
Clatsop Comm Coll, Astoria, OR 97103	1958	Dr. Doreen Dailey	.9	2,167	165
Cleveland Comm Coll, Shelby, NC 28150	1965	Dr. L. Steve Thornburg	.5	1,642	92
Cleveland Inst of Electronics, Cleveland, OH 44114 (2)	1934	John R. Drinko	.3	2,700	6
Cleveland State Comm Coll, Cleveland, TN 37320-3570	1967	Dr. James W. Ford	.5	3,306	161
Clinton Comm Coll, Clinton, IA 52732	1946	Desna L. Wallin	.5	1,240	75
Clinton Comm Coll, Plattsburgh, NY 12901	1969	Dr. Jay L. Fennell	12	2,080	156
Cloud County Comm Coll, Concordia, KS 66901-1002	1965	Dr. James P. Ihrig	12	3,018	224
Coahoma Comm Coll, Clarksdale, MS 38614	1949	Dr. Vivian M. Presley	12	1,478	85
Coastal Carolina Comm Coll, Jacksonville, NC 28546-6877	1964	Dr. Ronald K. Lingle, Jr.	12	3,728	170
Coastline Comm Coll, Fountain Valley, CA 92708	1976	Dr. William M. Vega	12	15,562	505
Cochise Coll, Douglas, AZ 85607	1962	Dr. Dan W. Rehurek	12	4,524	342
Coffeyville Comm Coll, Coffeyville, KS 67337	1923	Dr. Dan Kinney	12	2,300	86
Coll of Alameda, Alameda, CA 94501	1970	Marie B. Smith	12	6,100	NR
Coll of DuPage, Glen Ellyn, IL 60137	1967	Dr. Harold D. McAninch	12	30,898	1,718
Coll of Eastern Utah, Price, UT 84501	1937	Dr. Michael A. Petersen	.5	2,800	96
Coll of Lake County, Grayslake, IL 60030-1198	1967	Dr. Daniel J. La Vista	10	15,154	633
Coll of Marin, Kentfield, CA 94904	1926	Ms. Myrna R. Miller	12	10,539	464
Coll of San Mateo, San Mateo, CA 94402	1922	Richard A. Jones	12	15,200	485
Coll of Southern Idaho, Twin Falls, ID 83303	1964	Mr. Gerald R. Meyerhoeffer	12	3,144	119
Coll of The Albemarle, Elizabeth City, NC 27906-2327	1960	Dr. Parker Chesson, Jr.	.5	1,843	102

Name, address	Year	Governing official, control		Enroll-ment	Faculty
Coll of the Canyons, Santa Clarita, CA 91355	1969	Dr. Dianne G. Van Hook	12	6,250	228
Coll of the Desert, Palm Desert, CA 92260	1959	Dr. David A. George	12	12,000	315
Coll of the Mainland, Texas City, TX 77591	1967	Mr. Larry L. Stanley	12	3,742	180
Coll of the Redwoods, Eureka, CA 95501	1964	Dr. Cedric A. Sampson	12	7,638	449
Coll of the Sequoias, Visalia, CA 93277	1925	Dr. Robert A. Lombardi	12	9,289	363
Coll of the Siskiyous, Weed, CA 96094	1957	Dr. Martha Romero	12	2,446	148
Collin County Comm Coll, McKinney, TX 75070	1985	NR	12	9,729	462
Colorado Inst of Art, Denver, CO 80203	1952	W.C. Bottoms	3	1,328	77
Columbia Basin Coll, Pasco, WA 99301	1955	Dr. Marv Weiss	5	6,842	350
Columbia Coll, Columbia, CA 95310	1968	Dr. Kenneth White	12	4,188	104
Columbia-Greene Comm Coll, Hudson, NY 12534	1969	Dr. Terry A. Cline	12	1,661	110
Columbia State Comm Coll, Columbia, TN 38401	1966	Dr. Paul Sands	5	3,527	185
Columbus State Comm Coll, Columbus, OH 43216	1963	Dr. Harold M. Nestor	5	15,209	887
Comm Coll of Allegheny County Allegheny Cmps, Pittsburgh, PA 15212	1966	Dr. J. David Griffin	9	12,041	274
Comm Coll of Allegheny County Boyce Cmps, Monroeville, PA 15146	1966	Dr. Carl A. Di Sibio	9	4,483	190
Comm Coll of Allegheny County Coll Ctr–North, Pittsburgh, PA 15237	1972	Dr. Fred F. Bartok	9	4,457	1,398
Comm Coll of Allegheny County South Cmps, West Mifflin, PA 15122	1967	Dr. Thomas A. Juravich	9	5,625	760
Comm Coll of Aurora, Aurora, CO 80011-9036	1983	Larry Carter	5	4,695	197
Comm Coll of Beaver County, Monaca, PA 15061	1966	Margaret Williams-Betlyn	5	2,900	150
Comm Coll of Denver, Denver, CO 80217-3363	1970	Dr. Byron McClenney	5	6,000	271
Comm Coll of Philadelphia, Philadelphia, PA 19130	1964	Dr. Ronald J. Temple	12	17,547	989
Comm Coll of Rhode Island, Warwick, RI 02886-1807	1964	Edward Liston	5	11,344	550
Comm Coll of Southern Nevada, North Las Vegas, NV 89030	1971	Dr. Paul E. Meacham	5	19,555	730
Comm Coll of the Air Force, Maxwell Air Force Base, AL 36112-6655	1972	Col. R. A. Gregory, Jr.	4	525,337	11,000
Comm Coll of the Finger Lakes, Canandaigua, NY 14424	1965	Dr. Charles J. Meder	12	3,820	234
Comm Coll of Vermont, Waterbury, VT 05676	1970	Dr. Michael Holland	5	1,912	523
Compton Comm Coll, Compton, CA 90221-5393	1927	Dr. Warren A. Washington	12	5,700	347
Connors State Coll, Warner, OK 74469	1908	Dr. Carl O. Westbrook	5	2,224	108
Cooke County Coll, Gainesville, TX 76240	1924	Dr. Luther Bud Joyner	9	3,373	175
Copiah-Lincoln Comm Coll, Wesson, MS 39191	1928	Dr. Billy B. Thames	12	1,630	116
Corning Comm Coll, Corning, NY 14830	1956	Dr. Donald H. Hangen	12	3,540	137
Cosumnes River Coll, Sacramento, CA 95823	1970	Dr. Marc E. Hall	10	12,039	431
County Coll of Morris, Randolph, NJ 07869	1966	Dr. Edward J. Yaw	9	10,560	553
Cowley County Comm Coll and Voc-Tech Sch, Arkansas City, KS 67005	1922	Dr. Patrick J. McAtee	12	2,701	184
Crafton Hills Coll, Yucaipa, CA 92399	1972	Dr. Luis S. Gomez	12	5,738	212
Craven Comm Coll, New Bern, NC 28563	1965	Lewis S. Redd	5	2,367	157
Crowder Coll, Neosho, MO 64850	1963	Dr. Kent A. Farnsworth	12	1,748	136
Cuesta Coll, San Luis Obispo, CA 93403-8106	1964	Dr. Grace N. Mitchell	10	7,817	314
Culinary Inst of America, Hyde Park, NY 12538-1499	1946	Mr. Ferdinand E. Metz	1	1,876	101
Cumberland County Coll, Vineland, NJ 08360	1963	Dr. Roland J. Chapdelaine	12	2,700	118
Cuyahoga Comm Coll, Eastern Cmps, Highland Hills Village, OH 44122	1971	Dr. Grace Carolyn Brown	12	5,764	225
Cuyahoga Comm Coll, Metropolitan Cmps, Cleveland, OH 44115	1963	Dr. Ronald R. Zambetti	12	6,082	474
Cuyahoga Comm Coll, Western Cmps, Parma, OH 44130	1966	Mr. Ronald M. Sobel	12	12,285	577
Cuyamaca Coll, El Cajon, CA 92019	1978	Dr. Samuel M. Ciccati	5	4,862	NR
Cypress Coll, Cypress, CA 90630	1966	Dr. Kirk Avery	12	14,792	434
Dabney S Lancaster Comm Coll, Clifton Forge, VA 24422	1964	Dr. John F. Backels	5	1,653	NR
Dalton Coll, Dalton, GA 30720	1963	Dr. Derrell C. Roberts	5	2,621	99
Danville Area Comm Coll, Danville, IL 61832	1946	Dr. Harry J. Braun	12	3,450	143
Danville Comm Coll, Danville, VA 24541	1967	Dr. B. Carlyle Ramsey	5	3,593	141
Darton Coll, Albany, GA 31707	1965	Dr. Peter J. Sireno	5	2,404	127
Davidson County Comm Coll, Lexington, NC 27293	1958	Dr. J. Bryan Brooks	12	2,290	153
Daytona Beach Comm Coll, Daytona Beach, FL 32120-2811	1958	NR	5	10,190	817
Dean Jr Coll, Franklin, MA 02038	1865	Mr. Frank B. Bruno	1	1,000	90
De Anza Coll, Cupertino, CA 95014	1967	Dr. A. Robert Dehart	12	25,200	1,179
DeKalb Coll, Decatur, GA 30034	1964	Dr. Marvin M. Cole	5	15,282	486
Delaware County Comm Coll, Media, PA 19063	1967	Dr. Richard D. De Cosmo	12	9,527	532
Delaware Tech & Comm Coll, Southern Cmps, Georgetown, DE 19947	1967	Mr. Jack F. Owens	5	3,433	160
Delaware Tech & Comm Coll, Stanton/Wilmington Cmps, Newark, DE 19702	1968	Dr. Orlando J. George, Jr.	5	6,164	342
Delaware Tech & Comm Coll, Terry Cmps, Dover, DE 19901	1972	Dr. Linda C. Jolly	5	1,969	104
Delgado Comm Coll, New Orleans, LA 70119	1921	Dr. Ione Elioff	5	14,525	1,029
Del Mar Coll, Corpus Christi, TX 78404	1935	Mr. B. R. Venters	12	11,139	480
Delta Coll, University Center, MI 48710	1961	Mr. Donald J. Carlyon	10	10,985	447
Diablo Valley Coll, Pleasant Hill, CA 94523	1949	Dr. Phyllis L. Peterson	12	23,500	800
Dixie Coll, St George, UT 84770	1911	Dr. Douglas Alder	5	2,926	107
Dodge City Comm Coll, Dodge City, KS 67801	1935	Dr. Thomas E. Gamble	12	2,100	84
Doña Ana Branch Comm Coll, Las Cruces, NM 88003-0001	1973	NR	12	3,405	150
Dundalk Comm Coll, Baltimore, MD 21222	1970	Dr. Martha A. Smith	9	3,579	223
Durham Tech Comm Coll, Durham, NC 27703	1961	Dr. Phail Wynn, Jr.	5	5,304	271
Dutchess Comm Coll, Poughkeepsie, NY 12601	1957	Dr. Jerry Lee	12	7,509	391
Dyersburg State Comm Coll, Dyersburg, TN 38025-0648	1969	Dr. Karen A. Bowyer	5	2,100	132
East Arkansas Comm Coll, Forrest City, AR 72335	1974	Dr. Tom Spencer	5	1,490	89
East Central Coll, Union, MO 63084	1968	Dr. Dale Gibson	10	3,086	146
East Central Comm Coll, Decatur, MS 39327	1928	Dr. Eddie M. Smith	12	1,395	56
Eastern Arizona Coll, Thatcher, AZ 85552-0769	1888	Mr. Gherald L. Hoopes, Jr.	12	1,835	256
Eastern New Mexico U–Roswell, Roswell, NM 88202	1958	Dr. Loyd R. Hughes	5	2,074	140
Eastern Oklahoma State Coll, Wilburton, OK 74578	1907	NR	5	2,424	54
Eastern Wyoming Coll, Torrington, WY 82240	1948	Dr. Roy Mason	12	1,145	65
Eastfield Coll, Mesquite, TX 75150	1970	Dr. Rodger A. Pool	12	10,018	399
East Los Angeles Coll, Monterey Park, CA 91754	1945	Dr. Omero Suarez	12	14,587	450
Edgecombe Comm Coll, Tarboro, NC 27886	1968	Mr. Charles B. McIntyre	12	1,831	168
Edison Comm Coll, Fort Myers, FL 33906-6210	1962	Dr. Kenneth Walker	12	9,120	724
Edison State Comm Coll, Piqua, OH 45356	1973	Dr. Kenneth A. Yowell	5	3,416	160
Edmonds Comm Coll, Lynnwood, WA 98036	1967	Mr. Thomas C. Nielsen	12	8,650	257

Name, address	Year	Governing official, control	Enrollment	Faculty
El Camino Coll, Torrance, CA 90506	1947	Dr. Sam Schauerman 10	25,260	533
El Centro Coll, Dallas, TX 75202	1966	Dr. Wright L. Lassiter, Jr. 9	5,954	314
Elgin Comm Coll, Elgin, IL 60123	1949	Dr. Paul Heath 12	8,547	400
El Paso Comm Coll, El Paso, TX 79998	1969	Dr. Leonardo de la Garza 9	17,938	1,734
El Reno Jr Coll, El Reno, OK 73036	1938	Dr. Larry F. Devane 5	1,565	110
Enterprise State Jr Coll, Enterprise, AL 36331	1965	Dr. Joseph D. Talmadge 5	2,172	125
Erie Comm Coll, City Cmps, Buffalo, NY 14203-2601	1971	Dr. Louis M. Ricci 12	3,811	227
Erie Comm Coll, North Cmps, Williamsville, NY 14221-7095	1946	Dr. Louis M. Ricci 12	7,052	369
Erie Comm Coll, South Cmps, Orchard Park, NY 14127-2199	1974	Dr. Louis M. Ricci 12	3,485	247
Essex Comm Coll, Baltimore, MD 21237	1957	Dr. Donald J. Slowinski 12	11,022	532
Essex County Coll, Newark, NJ 07102	1966	Dr. Zachary Yamba 9	7,760	270
Everett Comm Coll, Everett, WA 98201	1941	Dr. Bob A. Barringer 5	7,053	231
Evergreen Valley Coll, San Jose, CA 95135	1975	NR 12	11,849	319
Fairleigh Dickinson U, Edward Williams Coll, Hackensack, NJ 07601	1964	Kenneth T. Vehrkens 1	1,414	45
Fashion Inst of Design & Merchandising, LA Cmps, Los Angeles, CA 90015	1969	Ms. Tonian Hohberg 3	3,010	180
Fayetteville Tech Comm Coll, Fayetteville, NC 28303-0236	1961	Dr. Craig Allen 5	6,819	317
Feather River Comm Coll District, Quincy, CA 95971	1968	Dr. Donald Donato 12	1,348	92
Fergus Falls Comm Coll, Fergus Falls, MN 56537	1960	Mr. Dan F. True 5	1,300	60
Fiorello H LaGuardia Comm Coll of City U of NY, Long Island City, NY 11101	1971	Raymond C. Bowen 12	9,270	633
Flathead Valley Comm Coll, Kalispell, MT 59901	1967	Dr. Howard L. Fryett 12	1,801	133
Florida Comm Coll at Jacksonville, Jacksonville, FL 32202	1963	Dr. Charles C. Spence 5	19,866	1,575
Floyd Coll, Rome, GA 30162	1970	Dr. Richard Trimble 5	2,529	66
Foothill Coll, Los Altos Hills, CA 94022	1958	Dr. Thomas H. Clements 12	19,459	613
Forsyth Tech Comm Coll, Winston-Salem, NC 27103	1964	Dr. Bob H. Greene 5	5,172	574
Fort Scott Comm Coll, Fort Scott, KS 66701	1919	Laura Meeks 12	1,918	131
Fox Valley Tech Coll, Appleton, WI 54913	1967	Dr. Stanley J. Spanbauer 12	4,810	1,241
Frederick Comm Coll, Frederick, MD 21702	1957	Dr. Lee J. Betts 12	4,255	267
Fresno City Coll, Fresno, CA 93741	1910	Dr. Brice W. Harris 10	17,941	832
Front Range Comm Coll, Westminster, CO 80030	1968	Dr. Thomas Gonzales 5	10,477	450
Fullerton Coll, Fullerton, CA 92632	1913	Dr. Philip W. Borst 12	20,736	678
Fulton-Montgomery Comm Coll, Johnstown, NY 12095	1964	Mr. John G. Boshart 12	1,745	122
Gadsden State Comm Coll, Gadsden, AL 35902-0227	1965	NR 5	5,837	290
Gainesville Coll, Gainesville, GA 30503	1964	Dr. J. Foster Watkins 5	2,680	118
Galveston Coll, Galveston, TX 77550	1967	Dr. Marc A. Nigliazzo 12	2,115	122
Garden City Comm Coll, Garden City, KS 67846	1919	Dr. James H. Tangeman 10	2,404	106
Gaston Coll, Dallas, NC 28034	1963	Dr. W. Wayne Scott 12	3,922	309
Gateway Comm Coll, Phoenix, AZ 85034	1968	Phil Randolph 12	6,869	253
Gateway Tech Coll, Kenosha, WI 53144	1911	Dr. John R. Birkholz 12	7,844	755
Genesee Comm Coll, Batavia, NY 14020	1966	Dr. Stuart Steiner 12	3,210	214
George Corley Wallace State Comm Coll, Selma, AL 36702	1966	Dr. Julius Ray Brown 5	1,801	78
George C Wallace State Comm Coll, Dothan, AL 36303	1949	Dr. Larry Beaty 5	3,781	180
Georgia Military Coll, Milledgeville, GA 31061	1879	Maj. Gen. William Acker 12	1,938	179
Germanna Comm Coll, Locust Grove, VA 22508	1970	Dr. Francis S. Turnage 5	2,500	83
Glendale Comm Coll, Glendale, AZ 85302	1965	Dr. John R. Waltrip 12	18,785	680
Glendale Comm Coll, Glendale, CA 91208	1927	Dr. John A. Davitt 12	15,126	330
Glen Oaks Comm Coll, Centreville, MI 49032	1965	Dr. Philip G. Ward 12	1,416	92
Gloucester County Coll, Sewell, NJ 08080	1967	Dr. Richard H. Jones 9	4,755	183
Gogebic Comm Coll, Ironwood, MI 49938	1932	Dr. James R. Grote 12	1,322	96
Golden West Coll, Huntington Beach, CA 92647-0592	1966	NR 5	15,302	457
Gordon Coll, Barnesville, GA 30204	1852	Dr. Jerry M. Williamson 5	1,720	89
Grand Rapids Comm Coll, Grand Rapids, MI 49503	1914	Mr. Richard Calkins 11	13,062	535
Grays Harbor Coll, Aberdeen, WA 98520	1930	Dr. Jewell Manspeaker 5	1,620	115
Grayson County Coll, Denison, TX 75020	1964	Dr. Jim M. Williams 12	3,646	176
Greater Hartford Comm Coll, Hartford, CT 06105	1967	NR 5	3,000	180
Great Lakes Jr Coll of Business, Saginaw, MI 48607	1907	NR 1	2,093	150
Greenfield Comm Coll, Greenfield, MA 01301	1962	Dr. Katherine H. Sloan 5	1,755	124
Green River Comm Coll, Auburn, WA 98002	1965	Mr. Richard A. Rutkowski 5	6,000	301
Greenville Tech Coll, Greenville, SC 29606	1962	Dr. Thomas E. Barton, Jr. 5	8,690	480
Grossmont Coll, El Cajon, CA 92020-1799	1961	Dr. Richard M. Sanchez 12	17,093	584
Guilford Tech Comm Coll, Jamestown, NC 27282	1958	Dr. Don Cameron 12	7,550	539
Gulf Coast Comm Coll, Panama City, FL 32401	1957	Dr. Robert L. McSpadden 5	7,375	312
Hagerstown Jr Coll, Hagerstown, MD 21742-6590	1946	Dr. Norman P. Shea 9	3,361	168
Harford Comm Coll, Bel Air, MD 21015	1957	Dr. Richard J. Pappas 12	5,348	216
Harrisburg Area Comm Coll, Harrisburg, PA 17110	1964	Dr. Kenneth B. Woodbury, Jr. 12	10,444	474
Hartnell Coll, Salinas, CA 93901	1920	Dr. James R. Hardt 10	7,594	356
Hawkeye Inst of Tech, Waterloo, IA 50704	1967	Dr. John E. Hawse 12	1,844	151
Haywood Comm Coll, Clyde, NC 28721	1964	Dr. Dan W. Moore 12	1,324	120
Henry Ford Comm Coll, Dearborn, MI 48128	1938	Dr. Andrew A. Mazzara 10	15,510	1,005
Herkimer County Comm Coll, Herkimer, NY 13350	1966	Dr. Ronald F. Williams 12	2,330	109
Hesser Coll, Manchester, NH 03103	1900	Linwood W. Galeucia 3	2,200	60
Hibbing Comm Coll, Hibbing, MN 55746	1916	Dr. Anthony Kuznik 5	1,115	65
Highland Comm Coll, Freeport, IL 61032	1962	Dr. Ruth Mercedes Smith 10	3,258	169
Highland Comm Coll, Highland, KS 66035	1858	Dr. Eric M. Priest 12	1,956	182
Highline Comm Coll, Des Moines, WA 98198	1961	Dr. Edward M. Command 5	10,300	432
Hill Coll of the Hill Jr Coll District, Hillsboro, TX 76645	1923	Dr. W. R. Auvenshine 10	1,700	80
Hillsborough Comm Coll, Tampa, FL 33631-3127	1968	Dr. Andreas A. Paloumpis 5	19,837	637
Hinds Comm Coll, Raymond, MS 39154	1917	NR 12	9,175	724
Hocking Tech Coll, Nelsonville, OH 45764	1968	Dr. John J. Light 5	5,481	252
Holmes Comm Coll, Goodman, MS 39079	1928	NR 12	2,233	125
Holyoke Comm Coll, Holyoke, MA 01040	1946	Dr. David M. Bartley 5	3,356	215
Horry-Georgetown Tech Coll, Conway, SC 29526	1965	Dr. D. Kent Sharples 12	2,294	113
Housatonic Comm Coll, Bridgeport, CT 06608	1966	Dr. Vincent S. Darnowski 5	2,383	90
Houston Comm Coll System, Houston, TX 77270	1971	Dr. Charles Green 12	38,005	2,587
Howard Coll, Big Spring, TX 79720	1945	Dr. Bob E. Riley 12	2,428	158
Howard Comm Coll, Columbia, MD 21044	1966	Dr. Dwight A. Burrill 12	4,883	306
Hudson County Comm Coll, Jersey City, NJ 07306	1974	NR 12	2,957	147
Hudson Valley Comm Coll, Troy, NY 12180	1953	Dr. Joseph J. Bulmer 12	9,766	507
Hutchinson Comm Coll, Hutchinson, KS 67501	1928	Dr. Edward E. Berger 12	3,888	264
ICS Ctr for Degree Studies, Scranton, PA 18515	1975	Mr. Gary Keisling 3	28,932	5

Name, address	Year	Governing official, control		Enroll-ment	Faculty
Illinois Central Coll, East Peoria, IL 61635	1967	Dr. Thomas K. Thomas	12	13,930	632
Illinois Eastern Comm Colls, Frontier Comm Coll, Fairfield, IL 62837	1976	Richard Mason	12	2,183	155
Illinois Eastern Comm Colls, Lincoln Trail Coll, Robinson, IL 62454	1969	Dr. Donald E. Donnay	12	1,040	67
Illinois Eastern Comm Colls, Olney Central Coll, Olney, IL 62450	1960	Dr. Judith M. Hansen	12	1,733	92
Illinois Eastern Comm Colls, Wabash Valley Coll, Mount Carmel, IL 62863	1960	Dr. Harry K. Benson	12	2,935	97
Illinois Valley Comm Coll, Oglesby, IL 61348	1924	Dr. Alfred E. Wisgoski	10	4,561	NR
Imperial Valley Coll, Imperial, CA 92251-2663	1922	Dr. John A. DePaoli	12	5,226	290
Independence Comm Coll, Independence, KS 67301	1925	Walter Browe	10	1,605	153
Indiana Business Coll, Indianapolis, IN 46204	1902	Kenneth J. Konesco	3	1,700	70
Indiana Vocational Tech Coll–Central Indiana, Indianapolis, IN 46206	1963	Dr. Meredith L. Carter	5	5,376	282
Indiana Vocational Tech Coll–Columbus, Columbus, IN 47203	1963	NR	5	2,614	146
Indiana Vocational Tech Coll–Eastcentral, Muncie, IN 47302	1968	Dr. Luanne G. Pruens	5	2,136	135
Indiana Vocational Tech Coll–Kokomo, Kokomo, IN 46901	1968	Dr. Ken Martin	5	1,662	105
Indiana Vocational Tech Coll–Lafayette, Lafayette, IN 47903	1968	Dr. Elizabeth J. Doversberger	5	1,620	118
Indiana Vocational Tech Coll–Northcentral, South Bend, IN 46619	1968	Dr. Carl F. Lutz	5	2,536	188
Indiana Vocational Tech Coll–Northeast, Fort Wayne, IN 46805	1969	Mr. Jon L. Rupright	5	3,740	196
Indiana Vocational Tech Coll–Northwest, Gary, IN 46409	1963	Dr. Rob Jeffs	5	2,434	172
Indiana Vocational Tech Coll–Southcentral, Sellersburg, IN 47172	1968	Jonathan W. Thomas	5	1,662	107
Indiana Vocational Tech Coll–Southwest, Evansville, IN 47710	1963	Dr. H. Victor Baldi	5	2,381	156
Indiana Vocational Tech Coll–Wabash Valley, Terre Haute, IN 47802	1966	Mr. Sam E. Borden	5	2,414	191
Indiana Vocational Tech Coll–Whitewater, Richmond, IN 47374	1963	James Steck	5	1,147	86
Indian Hills Comm Coll, Ottumwa, IA 52501	1966	Dr. Lyle A. Hellyer	12	3,176	139
Indian River Comm Coll, Fort Pierce, FL 34981-5599	1960	Dr. Edwin R. Massey	5	10,893	749
Inver Hills Comm Coll, Inver Grove Heights, MN 55076	1969	Dr. Steve Wallace	5	5,444	208
Iona Coll–Sch of Associate Degree Studies, Yonkers, NY 10701	1940	NR	1	1,403	185
Iowa Central Comm Coll, Fort Dodge, IA 50501	1966	Dr. Jack L. Bottenfield	12	2,500	155
Iowa Lakes Comm Coll, Estherville, IA 51334	1967	Mr. Richard H. Blacker	12	1,574	40
Iowa Western Comm Coll, Council Bluffs, IA 51502	1966	Dr. Carl L. Heinrich	10	3,478	166
Irvine Valley Coll, Irvine, CA 92720	1979	Dr. Anna L. McFarlin	12	10,007	223
Itasca Comm Coll, Grand Rapids, MN 55744	1922	Dr. Lawrence N. Dukes	5	1,240	75
Jackson Comm Coll, Jackson, MI 49201	1928	Dr. Clyde LeTarte	9	7,000	440
Jackson State Comm Coll, Jackson, TN 38301	1967	Dr. Walter L. Nelms	5	3,332	170
James H Faulkner State Jr Coll, Bay Minette, AL 36507	1965	Dr. Gary L. Branch	5	3,449	151
Jamestown Comm Coll, Jamestown, NY 14701	1950	Dr. Timothy G. Davies	12	4,529	306
Jefferson Coll, Hillsboro, MO 63050	1963	Dr. Gery Hochanadel	12	4,047	199
Jefferson Comm Coll, Watertown, NY 13601	1961	Dr. John W. Deans	12	2,100	180
Jefferson Davis Comm Coll, Brewton, AL 36427	1965	NR	5	1,080	44
Jefferson State Comm Coll, Birmingham, AL 35215	1965	Dr. Judy M. Merritt	5	7,494	348
Jefferson Tech Coll, Steubenville, OH 43952	1966	Dr. Edward L. Florak	12	1,719	98
John A Logan Coll, Carterville, IL 62918	1967	Dr. Ray Hancock	12	4,635	193
John C Calhoun State Comm Coll, Decatur, AL 35609	1965	Dr. Richard Carpenter	5	7,840	380
Johnson County Comm Coll, Overland Park, KS 66210	1967	Dr. Charles J. Carlsen	12	15,227	632
Johnston Comm Coll, Smithfield, NC 27577	1969	Dr. John L. Tart	5	2,574	150
John Tyler Comm Coll, Chester, VA 23831	1967	Dr. Marshall W. Smith	5	5,287	220
John Wood Comm Coll, Quincy, IL 62301	1974	Dr. Robert C. Keys	10	4,005	143
Jones County Jr Coll, Ellisville, MS 39437	1928	Dr. T. Terrell Tisdale	12	4,000	153
Jordan Coll, Cedar Springs, MI 49319	1967	Lexie K. Coxon	2	2,090	165
J Sargeant Reynolds Comm Coll, Richmond, VA 23285-5622	1972	Dr. S. A. Burnette	5	6,000	576
Kalamazoo Valley Comm Coll, Kalamazoo, MI 49009	1966	Dr. Marilyn J. Schlack	12	9,437	397
Kankakee Comm Coll, Kankakee, IL 60901	1966	Dr. Larry D. Huffman	12	4,000	213
Kansas City Kansas Comm Coll, Kansas City, KS 66112	1923	Dr. Bill Spencer	9	5,466	284
Kellogg Comm Coll, Battle Creek, MI 49017	1956	Dr. Paul R. Ohm	12	7,662	273
Kelsey Jenney Business Coll, San Diego, CA 92101	1863	NR	1	1,000	50
Kent State U, Ashtabula Cmps, Ashtabula, OH 44004	1958	Dr. John K. Mahan	5	1,020	78
Kent State U, Stark Cmps, Canton, OH 44720	1967	Dr. William G. Bittle	5	2,531	124
Kent State U, Trumbull Cmps, Warren, OH 44483	1954	David A. Allen, Jr.	5	1,771	95
Kent State U, Tuscarawas Cmps, New Philadelphia, OH 44663	1962	NR	5	1,247	79
Kilgore Coll, Kilgore, TX 75662	1935	NR	12	4,423	240
Kingsborough Comm Coll of City U of NY, Brooklyn, NY 11235	1963	Dr. Leon M. Goldstein	12	9,191	628
Kings River Comm Coll, Reedley, CA 93654	1926	Mr. Richard J. Giese	12	5,149	221
Kirkwood Comm Coll, Cedar Rapids, IA 52406	1966	Dr. Norm Nielsen	12	9,234	450
Kirtland Comm Coll, Roscommon, MI 48653	1966	Dorothy N. Franke	10	1,165	96
Kishwaukee Coll, Malta, IL 60150	1967	Dr. Norman L. Jenkins	12	4,600	NR
Labette Comm Coll, Parsons, KS 67357	1923	John A. Patterson	12	2,598	261
Lake City Comm Coll, Lake City, FL 32055	1962	Dr. Muriel Kay Heimer	5	2,551	186
Lake Land Coll, Mattoon, IL 61938	1966	Dr. Robert K. Luther	12	4,835	244
Lakeland Comm Coll, Mentor, OH 44060	1967	Dr. Ralph R. Doty	12	8,944	420
Lake Michigan Coll, Benton Harbor, MI 49022	1946	Dr. Anne E. Mulder	10	3,422	240
Lakeshore Tech Coll, Cleveland, WI 53015	1967	Dr. Dennis Ladwig	12	2,989	344
Lake-Sumter Comm Coll, Leesburg, FL 34788	1961	Dr. Carl C. Andersen	12	2,394	117
Lake Tahoe Comm Coll, South Lake Tahoe, CA 96151	1975	Dr. Guy F. Lease	12	3,000	121
Lakewood Comm Coll, White Bear Lake, MN 55110	1967	Dr. Neil Christenson	5	6,181	200
Lamar U–Port Arthur, Port Arthur, TX 77641	1909	Dr. Sam Monroe	5	2,039	109
Lane Comm Coll, Eugene, OR 97405-0640	1964	Dr. Jerry Moskus	12	9,190	487
Laney Coll, Oakland, CA 94607	1953	Mr. Odell Johnson	5	11,800	379
Lansing Comm Coll, Lansing, MI 48901	1957	Dr. Abel B. Sykes, Jr.	12	21,787	1,236
Laramie County Comm Coll, Cheyenne, WY 82007	1968	Dr. Charles Bohlen	9	4,400	213
Laredo Jr Coll, Laredo, TX 78040	1946	Dr. Roger L. Worsley	12	5,377	297
Lassen Coll, Susanville, CA 96130	1925	Dr. Larry J. Blake	12	2,808	204

Name, address	Year	Governing official, control		Enrollment	Faculty
Lawson State Comm Coll, Birmingham, AL 35221	1965	Dr. Perry W. Ward	5	1,959	79
Lee Coll, Baytown, TX 77520-4796	1934	Dr. Vivian Bowling Blevins	10	5,815	231
Lehigh County Comm Coll, Schnecksville, PA 18078	1967	NR	12	4,649	155
Lenoir Comm Coll, Kinston, NC 28501	1960	Dr. Lonnie H. Blizzard	5	2,174	163
Lewis and Clark Comm Coll, Godfrey, IL 62035	1970	NR	10	5,763	305
Lima Tech Coll, Lima, OH 45804	1971	Dr. James J. Countryman	5	2,633	167
Lincoln Land Comm Coll, Springfield, IL 62794-9256	1967	Dr. William D. Law, Jr.	10	7,877	401
Linn-Benton Comm Coll, Albany, OR 97321	1966	Mr. Jon Carnahan	12	6,767	476
Long Beach City Coll, Long Beach, CA 90808	1927	Dr. Beverly O'Neill	5	29,465	850
Longview Comm Coll, Lee's Summit, MO 64081	1969	Mr. Aldo W. Leker	12	9,844	469
Lorain County Comm Coll, Elyria, OH 44035	1963	Dr. Roy Church	12	7,746	359
Lord Fairfax Comm Coll, Middletown, VA 22645	1969	Dr. Marilyn C. Beck	5	2,857	120
Los Angeles City Coll, Los Angeles, CA 90029	1929	Jose Robledo	10	17,500	614
Los Angeles Harbor Coll, Wilmington, CA 90744	1949	Mr. James L. Heinselman	12	9,300	350
Los Angeles Mission Coll, Sylmar, CA 91342-3244	1974	Dr. Jack Fujimoto	12	7,272	115
Los Angeles Pierce Coll, Woodland Hills, CA 91371	1947	Mr. Lowell J. Erickson	12	19,201	519
Los Angeles Southwest Coll, Los Angeles, CA 90047	1967	Mrs. Patricia Wainwright	12	6,557	250
Los Angeles Trade-Tech Coll, Los Angeles, CA 90015	1925	Mr. Thomas L. Stevens	12	13,713	259
Los Angeles Valley Coll, Van Nuys, CA 91401	1949	Dr. Mary E. Lee	12	19,838	311
Los Medanos Coll, Pittsburg, CA 94565	1974	Mr. Stanley H. Chin	10	7,779	223
Louisiana State U at Alexandria, Alexandria, LA 71302	1960	Dr. Ben F. Martin	5	2,680	91
Louisiana State U at Eunice, Eunice, LA 70535	1967	Dr. Michael Smith	5	2,590	85
Lower Columbia Coll, Longview, WA 98632	1934	Dr. Vernon R. Pickett	5	4,000	199
Lurleen B Wallace State Jr Coll, Andalusia, AL 36420	1969	Mr. Seth Hammett	5	1,132	39
Luzerne County Comm Coll, Nanticoke, PA 18634-9804	1966	Donald R. Bronsard	9	6,927	382
Macon Coll, Macon, GA 31297	1968	Dr. S. Aaron Hyatt	5	4,600	100
Madison Area Tech Coll, Madison, WI 53704	1911	Dr. Beverly S. Simone	10	11,789	1,950
Manatee Comm Coll, Bradenton, FL 34206	1957	Dr. Stephen J. Korcheck	5	8,726	314
Manchester Comm Coll, Manchester, CT 06040	1963	Dr. Jonathan M. Daube	5	6,134	205
Maple Woods Comm Coll, Kansas City, MO 64156	1969	Dr. Stephen R. Brainard	12	5,007	208
Marion Tech Coll, Marion, OH 43302-5694	1971	Dr. John Richard Bryson	13	1,653	105
Marshalltown Comm Coll, Marshalltown, IA 50158	1927	Dr. William Simpson	10	1,363	92
Marymount Coll, Palos Verdes, California, Rancho Palos Verdes, CA 90274-6299	1932	Dr. Thomas D. Wood	2	1,068	91
Massachusetts Bay Comm Coll, Wellesley Hills, MA 02181	1961	Mr. Roger A. Van Winkle	5	4,674	198
Massasoit Comm Coll, Brockton, MA 02402	1968	Dr. Gerard F. Burke	5	6,421	427
Mattatuck Comm Coll, Waterbury, CT 06708	1967	Dr. Richard L. Sanders	5	4,270	114
Mayland Comm Coll, Spruce Pine, NC 28777	1971	Dr. Virginia Foxx	12	1,006	35
McHenry County Coll, Crystal Lake, IL 60012	1967	Mr. Robert C. Bartlett	12	4,368	161
McLennan Comm Coll, Waco, TX 76708	1965	Dr. Dennis F. Michaelis	9	5,704	230
Mendocino Coll, Ukiah, CA 95482	1973	Dr. Carl J. Ehmann	12	4,675	165
Merced Coll, Merced, CA 95348	1962	Dr. E. Jan Moser	12	7,835	421
Mercer County Comm Coll, Trenton, NJ 08690	1966	Mr. John P. Hanley	12	8,750	356
Merritt Coll, Oakland, CA 94619	1953	Mr. Donald Hongisto	12	6,683	NR
Mesabi Comm Coll, Virginia, MN 55792	1918	Richard Kohlhase	5	1,065	47
Mesa Comm Coll, Mesa, AZ 85202	1965	Dr. Larry K. Christiansen	12	21,451	736
Metropolitan Comm Coll, Omaha, NE 68103-0777	1974	Dr. J. Richard Gilliland	12	9,573	373
Miami-Dade Comm Coll, Miami, FL 33132	1960	Dr. Robert H. McCabe	12	55,554	2,189
Miami U–Hamilton Cmps, Hamilton, OH 45011	1968	Dr. Harriet V. Taylor	5	2,278	160
Miami U–Middletown Cmps, Middletown, OH 45042	1966	Dr. Michael P. Governanti	5	2,130	165
Middle Georgia Coll, Cochran, GA 31014	1884	Dr. Joe Ben Welch	5	1,607	82
Middlesex Comm Coll, Middletown, CT 06457	1966	Dr. Leila Gonzalez Sullivan	5	3,230	130
Middlesex Comm Coll, Bedford, MA 01730	1970	Dr. Carole A. Cowan	5	4,028	289
Middlesex County Coll, Edison, NJ 08818	1964	Dr. Flora M. Edwards	9	11,218	287
Midland Coll, Midland, TX 79705	1969	Dr. David E. Daniel	12	3,789	192
Midlands Tech Coll, Columbia, SC 29202	1974	Dr. James L. Hudgins	12	8,345	612
Mid Michigan Comm Coll, Harrison, MI 48625-9447	1965	Dr. Charles J. Corrigan	12	2,266	199
Mid-Plains Comm Coll, North Platte, NE 69101	1965	Dr. William G. Hasemeyer	10	1,947	87
Mid-State Tech Coll, Wisconsin Rapids, WI 54494	1917	Dr. M. H. Schneeberg	12	2,458	86
Milwaukee Area Tech Coll, Milwaukee, WI 53233	1912	Dr. Barbara D. Holmes	10	23,099	1,759
Mineral Area Coll, Flat River, MO 63601	1922	Dr. Dixie A. Kohn	10	2,893	75
Minneapolis Comm Coll, Minneapolis, MN 55403-1779	1965	Dr. Jacquelyn Belcher	5	4,055	175
MiraCosta Coll, Oceanside, CA 92056	1934	Dr. H. Deon Holt	5	9,137	376
Mission Coll, Santa Clara, CA 95054	1977	Dr. Floyd M. Hogue	12	11,646	313
Mississippi County Comm Coll, Blytheville, AR 72316-1109	1975	Dr. John P. Sullins	5	1,768	128
Mississippi Delta Comm Coll, Moorhead, MS 38761	1926	Mr. Harmon Boggs	10	2,958	128
Mississippi Gulf Coast Comm Coll, Perkinston, MS 39573	1911	Dr. Bobby S. Garvin	10	8,827	527
Mitchell Comm Coll, Statesville, NC 28677	1852	Dr. Douglas O. Eason	5	1,530	81
Moberly Area Comm Coll, Moberly, MO 65270	1927	Dr. Andrew Komar, Jr.	12	1,653	83
Modesto Jr Coll, Modesto, CA 95350	1921	Dr. Stanley L. Hodges	12	8,164	454
Mohave Comm Coll, Kingman, AZ 86401	1971	Dr. Charles W. Hall	5	5,622	241
Mohawk Valley Comm Coll, Utica, NY 13501	1946	Dr. Michael I. Schafer	12	6,500	340
Mohegan Comm Coll, Norwich, CT 06360	1969	Mrs. Dianne Williams	5	2,819	128
Monroe Coll, Bronx, NY 10468	1933	Stephen J. Jerome	3	2,400	100
Monroe Comm Coll, Rochester, NY 14623	1961	Dr. Peter A. Spina	12	13,548	660
Monroe County Comm Coll, Monroe, MI 48161	1964	Mr. Gerald D. Welch	9	3,668	178
Montcalm Comm Coll, Sidney, MI 48885-0300	1965	Dr. Donald C. Burns	12	2,026	112
Monterey Peninsula Coll, Monterey, CA 93940-4799	1947	Dr. David W. Hopkins, Jr.	5	8,500	235
Montgomery Coll–Germantown Cmps, Germantown, MD 20874	1975	Dr. Robert E. Parilla	12	3,989	166
Montgomery Coll–Rockville Cmps, Rockville, MD 20850	1965	Dr. Robert E. Parilla	12	14,128	690
Montgomery Coll–Takoma Park Cmps, Takoma Park, MD 20912	1946	Dr. Robert E. Parilla	12	4,944	205
Montgomery County Comm Coll, Blue Bell, PA 19422	1964	Dr. Edward M. Sweitzer	9	8,981	412
Moorpark Coll, Moorpark, CA 93021	1967	James W. Walker	9	12,412	450
Moraine Park Tech Coll, Fond du Lac, WI 54936	1967	Dr. John J. Shanahan	12	6,074	290
Moraine Valley Comm Coll, Palos Hills, IL 60465	1967	Dr. Vernon O. Crawley	12	13,938	601
Morton Coll, Cicero, IL 60650	1924	Mr. Charles P. Ferro	12	5,036	273
Motlow State Comm Coll, Tullahoma, TN 37388	1969	Dr. A. Frank Glass	5	3,033	245
Mountain Empire Comm Coll, Big Stone Gap, VA 24219	1972	Dr. Robert H. Sandel	5	3,527	133
Mountain View Coll, Dallas, TX 75211-6599	1970	Dr. William H. Jordan	9	6,600	268
Mt Hood Comm Coll, Gresham, OR 97030	1966	Dr. Paul Kreider	12	7,723	501
Mount Ida Coll, Newton Centre, MA 02159	1899	Dr. Bryan E. Carlson	1	1,750	177
Mt San Antonio Coll, Walnut, CA 91789	1946	Dr. William H. Feddersen	10	23,119	907
Mt San Jacinto Coll, San Jacinto, CA 92583	1963	Dr. Richard H. Lowe	12	6,652	181
Mount Wachusett Comm Coll, Gardner, MA 01440	1963	Daniel M. Asquino	5	2,200	112
Murray State Coll, Tishomingo, OK 73460	1908	Dr. Clyde R. Kindell	5	1,674	69

Name, address	Year	Governing official, control		Enrollment	Faculty
Muscatine Comm Coll, Muscatine, IA 52761	1929	Dr. Victor G. McAvoy	5	1,186	68
Muskegon Comm Coll, Muskegon, MI 49442	1926	Dr. James L. Stevenson	12	5,169	150
Napa Valley Coll, Napa, CA 94558	1942	Dr. Diane E. Carey	12	6,991	307
Nash Comm Coll, Rocky Mount, NC 27804	1967	Dr. J. Reid Parrott, Jr.	5	1,670	171
Nashville State Tech Inst, Nashville, TN 37209	1970	Dr. George H. Van Allen	5	6,207	294
Nassau Comm Coll, Garden City, NY 11530	1959	Dr. Sean A. Fanelli	12	17,621	1,441
National Ed Ctr–Bauder Coll Cmps, Fort Lauderdale, FL 33334	1964	NR	3	1,000	41
National Ed Ctr–Brown Inst Cmps, Minneapolis, MN 55407	1946	Ralph H. Vieau	3	1,197	79
National Ed Ctr–Spartan Sch of Aeronautics Cmps, Tulsa, OK 74158-2833 (2)	1928	Frank D. Iacobucci	3	2,495	150
National Sch of Tech, Inc, North Miami Beach, FL 33162	1977	NR	3	1,100	30
Navajo Comm Coll, Tsaile, AZ 86556	1968	Mr. Laurence Gishey	4	1,601	143
Navarro Coll, Corsicana, TX 75110	1946	Dr. Gerald Burson	12	2,938	163
Neosho County Comm Coll, Chanute, KS 66720	1936	George H. VanAllen	12	1,854	117
New Comm Coll of Baltimore, Baltimore, MD 21215	1947	Dr. James D. Tschichtelin	5	5,900	493
New England Banking Inst, Boston, MA 02111	1909	NR	1	1,197	360
New England Inst of Tech/New England Tech Coll, Warwick, RI 02886	1940	Dr. Richard I. Gouse	1	2,250	134
New Hampshire Tech Inst, Concord, NH 03302-2039	1964	Dr. David E. Larrabee, Sr.	5	1,300	114
New Mexico Jr Coll, Hobbs, NM 88240	1965	Dr. Charles D. Hays	12	2,438	96
New Mexico State U–Alamogordo, Alamogordo, NM 88310	1958	Dr. Charles R. Reidlinger	5	1,786	109
New Mexico State U–Carlsbad, Carlsbad, NM 88220	1950	Dr. Shelton W. Marlow	5	1,163	72
New Orleans Baptist Theological Sem, New Orleans, LA 70126	1917	Dr. Landrum P. Leavell, II	2	1,588	8
New River Comm Coll, Dublin, VA 24084	1969	Dr. Edwin L. Barnes	5	2,365	200
New York City Tech Coll of City U of NY, Brooklyn, NY 11201	1946	Dr. Charles W. Merideth	12	10,600	750
Niagara County Comm Coll, Sanborn, NY 14132	1962	Gerald L. Miller	12	5,480	314
Nicolet Area Tech Coll, Rhinelander, WI 54501	1968	Mr. Adrian Lorbetske	12	1,500	64
Normandale Comm Coll, Bloomington, MN 55431	1968	Dr. Thomas J. Horak	5	9,317	300
Northampton County Area Comm Coll, Bethlehem, PA 18017	1967	Dr. Robert J. Kopecek	12	6,055	465
North Arkansas Comm Coll, Harrison, AR 72601	1974	Dr. Bill Baker	12	1,333	84
North Central Michigan Coll, Petoskey, MI 49770	1958	Robert B. Graham	9	2,032	102
North Central Tech Coll, Mansfield, OH 44901	1961	Dr. Byron E. Kee	5	2,768	174
Northcentral Tech Coll, Wausau, WI 54401	1912	Dr. Donald Hagen	10	4,346	211
North Country Comm Coll, Saranac Lake, NY 12983	1967	Dr. Gordon C. Blank	12	1,604	145
North Dakota State Coll of Science, Wahpeton, ND 58076	1903	Dr. Jerry Olson	5	2,144	138
Northeast Alabama State Jr Coll, Rainsville, AL 35986	1963	Dr. Charles M. Pendley	5	1,367	47
Northeast Comm Coll, Norfolk, NE 68702	1973	Dr. Robert P. Cox	12	3,172	122
Northeastern Jr Coll, Sterling, CO 80751	1941	Dr. Henry M. Milander	12	2,040	79
Northeastern Oklahoma A&M Coll, Miami, OK 74354	1919	NR	5	2,600	133
Northeast Iowa Comm Coll, Peosta Cmps, Peosta, IA 52068	1970	Karla Berns	12	1,227	66
Northeast Mississippi Comm Coll, Booneville, MS 38829	1948	Joe M. Childers	10	3,041	NR
Northeast State Tech Comm Coll, Blountville, TN 37617	1966	Dr. R. Wade Powers	5	3,133	166
Northeast Texas Comm Coll, Mount Pleasant, TX 75456-1307	1985	NR	12	1,825	83
Northeast Wisconsin Tech Coll, Green Bay, WI 54307	1913	Dr. Gerald D. Prindiville	12	7,682	201
Northern Essex Comm Coll, Haverhill, MA 01830	1960	Dr. John R. Dimitry	5	6,416	473
Northern Nevada Comm Coll, Elko, NV 89801	1967	Dr. Ronald K. Remington	5	2,500	180
Northern New Mexico Comm Coll, Española, NM 87532	1909	Connie A. Valdez	5	1,621	148
Northern Oklahoma Coll, Tonkawa, OK 74653	1901	Dr. Joe Kinzer	5	2,082	80
Northern Virginia Comm Coll, Annandale, VA 22003	1965	Dr. Richard J. Ernst	5	38,182	1,168
North Florida Jr Coll, Madison, FL 32340	1958	Dr. William H. McCoy	5	1,048	30
North Harris Montgomery Comm Coll District, Houston, TX 77060	1972	Dr. John E. Pickelman	12	17,270	721
North Hennepin Comm Coll, Minneapolis, MN 55445	1966	Dr. Frederick W. Capshaw	5	6,300	212
North Idaho Coll, Coeur d'Alene, ID 83814	1933	Dr. Carl R. Bennett	12	3,070	186
North Iowa Area Comm Coll, Mason City, IA 50401	1918	Dr. David Buettner	12	3,000	107
North Lake Coll, Irving, TX 75038	1977	Dr. James F. Horton, Jr.	9	6,855	280
Northland Pioneer Coll, Holbrook, AZ 86025	1974	Dr. John H. Anderson	12	5,237	400
North Seattle Comm Coll, Seattle, WA 98103	1970	Peter Ku	5	9,029	246
North Shore Comm Coll, Danvers, MA 01923	1965	Dr. George Traicoff	5	3,305	NR
Northwest Alabama Comm Coll, Phil Campbell, AL 35581	1961	Dr. Charles W. Britnell	5	2,050	83
NorthWest Arkansas Comm Coll, Bentonville, AR 72712	1989	NR	12	1,807	87
Northwest Coll, Powell, WY 82435	1946	Dr. John P. Hanna	12	2,149	173
Northwestern Coll, Lima, OH 45805	1920	Mr. Loren R. Jarvis	3	1,311	64
Northwestern Connecticut Comm Coll, Winsted, CT 06098	1965	Dr. Booker T. DeVaughn	5	1,941	62
Northwestern Michigan Coll, Traverse City, MI 49684	1951	Dr. Timothy G. Quinn	12	4,428	231
Northwest Mississippi Comm Coll, Senatobia, MS 38668	1927	Dr. David M. Haraway	12	3,132	NR
Northwest Tech Coll, Archbold, OH 43502	1968	Dr. Larry G. McDougle	5	1,833	121
Norwalk Comm Coll, Norwalk, CT 06854	1961	Dr. William H. Schwab	5	3,866	135
Norwalk State Tech Coll, Norwalk, CT 06854	1961	Dr. John Karl Fisher	5	1,002	49
Oakland Comm Coll, Bloomfield Hills, MI 48304	1964	Dr. Patsy J. Fulton	12	29,084	707
Oakton Comm Coll, Des Plaines, IL 60016	1969	Dr. Thomas TenHoeve	10	11,253	495
Ocean County Coll, Toms River, NJ 08754-2001	1964	Dr. Milton Shaw	9	8,117	261
Odessa Coll, Odessa, TX 79764	1946	Dr. Philip T. Speegle	12	4,559	255
Ohio U–Ironton, Ironton, OH 45638	1956	Mr. Bill Dingus	5	2,113	105
Ohlone Coll, Fremont, CA 94539	1967	Dr. Peter Blomerley	12	9,853	434
Okaloosa-Walton Comm Coll, Niceville, FL 32578	1963	Dr. James R. Richburg	12	5,827	345
Oklahoma City Comm Coll, Oklahoma City, OK 73159	1969	Dr. Robert Gaines	5	10,126	248
Oklahoma State U, Oklahoma City, Oklahoma City, OK 73107	1961	Dr. James Hooper	5	4,236	206
Oklahoma State U, Tech Branch, Okmulgee, Okmulgee, OK 74447	1946	Dr. Robert Klabenes	5	2,120	138
Olympic Coll, Bremerton, WA 98310-1699	1946	Dr. Wallace A. Simpson	5	6,545	417
Onondaga Comm Coll, Syracuse, NY 13215	1962	Dr. Bruce H. Leslie	12	8,389	400
Orangeburg-Calhoun Tech Coll, Orangeburg, SC 29115	1968	Mr. M. Rudolph Groomes	12	1,836	120
Orange Coast Coll, Costa Mesa, CA 92628-5005	1947	Mr. David A. Grant	12	27,960	880
Orange County Comm Coll, Middletown, NY 10940	1950	Dr. William F. Messner	12	6,059	365
Owens Tech Coll, Toledo, OH 43699-1947	1966	NR	5	8,286	370
Owens Tech Coll, Findlay Cmps, Findlay, OH 45840	1983	NR	5	1,258	83
Oxnard Coll, Oxnard, CA 93033	1975	Dr. Elise D. Schneider	9	6,480	288

Name, address	Year	Governing official, control	Enroll-ment	Faculty
Palm Beach Comm Coll, Lake Worth, FL 33461	1933	Dr. Edward M. Eissey .5	14,688	650
Palo Alto Coll, San Antonio, TX 78224	1987	NR 12	5,472	317
Palomar Coll, San Marcos, CA 92069	1946	Dr. George R. Boggs 12	23,901	1,097
Palo Verde Coll, Blythe, CA 92225	1947	Dr. Wilford J. Beumel 12	1,200	60
Panola Coll, Carthage, TX 75633	1947	Dr. Gary McDaniel 12	1,457	101
Paradise Valley Comm Coll, Phoenix, AZ 85032	1985	NR 12	5,618	NR
Paris Jr Coll, Paris, TX 75460	1924	Mr. Bobby R. Walters 12	2,326	117
Parkland Coll, Champaign, IL 61821	1967	Dr. Zelema M. Harris 10	9,758	517
Pasadena City Coll, Pasadena, CA 91106	1924	Dr. Jack A. Scott 10	24,033	946
Pasco-Hernando Comm Coll, Dade City, FL 33525-7599	1972	Dr. Milton O. Jones .5	5,632	203
Passaic County Comm Coll, Paterson, NJ 07509	1968	Mr. Elliott Collins .9	3,432	204
Patrick Henry Comm Coll, Martinsville, VA 24115	1962	NR .5	2,340	88
Paul D Camp Comm Coll, Franklin, VA 23851-0737	1971	Dr. Edwin L. Barnes .5	1,557	65
Pearl River Comm Coll, Poplarville, MS 39470	1909	Dr. Ted J. Alexander 12	2,857	150
Peirce Jr Coll, Philadelphia, PA 19102	1865	Dr. Arthur J. Lendo .1	1,016	68
Pellissippi State Tech Comm Coll, Knoxville, TN 37933	1974	Mr. J. L. Goins .5	7,200	289
Peninsula Coll, Port Angeles, WA 98362	1961	Ms. Joyce M. Helens .5	1,253	141
Pennsylvania Coll of Tech, Williamsport, PA 17701	1965	Dr. Robert Breuder 13	4,741	338
Penn State U Altoona Cmps, Altoona, PA 16601	1929	Dr. Kiell Meling 13	2,043	117
Penn State U Berks Cmps, Reading, PA 19610	1924	Dr. Frederick H. Gaige 13	1,702	86
Penn State U Delaware County Cmps, Media, PA 19063	1966	Edward S. J. Tomezsko 13	1,670	99
Penn State U Hazelton Cmps, Hazelton, PA 18201	1934	Dr. James J. Staudenmeier 13	1,257	74
Penn State U McKeesport Cmps, McKeesport, PA 15132	1947	Dr. Joanne E. Burley 13	1,106	71
Penn State U New Kensington Cmps, New Kensington, PA 15068	1958	Dr. Robert D. Arbuckle 13	1,095	69
Penn State U Ogontz Cmps, Abington, PA 19001	1950	Dr. Anthony Fusaro 13	3,381	172
Penn State U Schuylkill Cmps, Schuylkill Haven, PA 17972-2208	1934	Dr. Wayne Lammie 13	1,085	60
Penn State U Shenango Cmps, Sharon, PA 16146	1965	Albert N. Skomra 13	1,086	80
Penn State U Worthington Scranton Cmps, Dunmore, PA 18512	1923	Dr. James D. Gallagher 13	1,257	85
Penn State U York Cmps, York, PA 17403	1926	Dr. John J. Romano 13	2,029	118
Penn Valley Comm Coll, Kansas City, MO 64111	1969	Dr. E. Paul Williams 12	5,842	322
Pensacola Jr Coll, Pensacola, FL 32504-8998	1948	Dr. Horace E. Hartsell .5	12,503	950
Phillips County Comm Coll, Helena, AR 72342	1965	Dr. Steven Jones 12	1,563	107
Phillips Jr Coll, Condie Cmps, Campbell, CA 95008	1968	Leslie E. Pritchard .3	1,000	45
Phoenix Coll, Phoenix, AZ 85013	1920	Ms. Myrna Harrison 12	14,319	540
Piedmont Tech Coll, Greenwood, SC 29648	1966	Dr. Lex D. Walters .5	2,287	127
Piedmont Virginia Comm Coll, Charlottesville, VA 22901	1972	Dr. Deborah M. DiCroce .5	4,249	262
Pierce Coll, Tacoma, WA 98498	1967	Dr. Frank Brouillet .5	12,500	295
Pikes Peak Comm Coll, Colorado Springs, CO 80906	1969	Dr. Marijane Axtell Paulsen .5	6,517	426
Pima Comm Coll, Tucson, AZ 85702-3010	1966	Dr. Johnas F. Hockaday .5	29,088	1,597
Pitt Comm Coll, Greenville, NC 27835-7007	1961	Dr. Charles E. Russell 12	4,397	229
Pittsburgh Inst of Aeronautics, Pittsburgh, PA 15236-0897 (2)	1929	Ivan D. Livi .1	1,012	56
Polk Comm Coll, Winter Haven, FL 33881-4299	1964	Dr. Maryly VanLeer Peck .5	6,300	260
Porterville Coll, Porterville, CA 93257	1927	Dr. Paul D. Alcantra .5	2,754	132
Portland Comm Coll, Portland, OR 97219	1961	Dr. Daniel F. Moriarty 12	27,000	1,215
Potomac State Coll of West Virginia U, Keyser, WV 26726	1901	Dr. Joseph M. Gratto .5	1,133	83
Prairie State Coll, Chicago Heights, IL 60411	1958	Dr. W. Harold Garner 12	5,657	289
Pratt Comm Coll, Pratt, KS 67124	1938	Dr. William Wojciechowski 10	2,064	48
Prince George's Comm Coll, Largo, MD 20772	1958	Dr. Robert I. Bickford .9	13,087	600
Pueblo Comm Coll, Pueblo, CO 81004	1979	Dr. Tony Zeiss .5	2,365	396
Queensborough Comm Coll of City U of NY, Bayside, NY 11364	1958	Dr. Kurt R. Schmeller 12	12,300	563
Quincy Coll, Quincy, MA 02169	1958	Dr. O. Clayton Johnson 11	1,974	69
Quinebaug Valley Comm Coll, Danielson, CT 06239	1971	Dr. Robert E. Miller .5	1,170	55
Quinsigamond Comm Coll, Worcester, MA 01606	1963	Dr. Clifford S. Peterson .5	4,558	233
Rancho Santiago Coll, Santa Ana, CA 92706	1915	NR .5	26,379	2,210
Randolph Comm Coll, Asheboro, NC 27204	1962	Dr. Larry K. Linker .5	1,480	80
Rappahannock Comm Coll, Glenns, VA 23149	1970	Dr. John H. Upton 12	2,089	129
Raritan Valley Comm Coll, Somerville, NJ 08876	1965	Dr. S. Charles Irace .9	5,638	276
Reading Area Comm Coll, Reading, PA 19603	1971	Dr. Gust Zogas 10	2,957	165
Red Rocks Comm Coll, Lakewood, CO 80401	1969	Ms. Dorothy A. Horrell .5	6,300	276
Rend Lake Coll, Ina, IL 62846	1967	Dr. Jonathan Astroth .5	4,322	201
Richard Bland Coll of the Coll of William and Mary, Petersburg, VA 23805	1961	Dr. Clarence Maze, Jr. .5	1,213	49
Richland Coll, Dallas, TX 75243-2199	1972	Dr. Stephen Mittelstet 12	13,391	665
Richland Comm Coll, Decatur, IL 62521	1971	Dr. Charles R. Novak 10	3,850	194
Richmond Comm Coll, Hamlet, NC 28345	1964	Joseph W. Grimsley .5	1,086	100
Ricks Coll, Rexburg, ID 83460	1888	Dr. Steven D. Bennion .2	7,968	322
Rio Hondo Coll, Whittier, CA 90608	1960	Dr. Alex A. Sanchez 12	17,500	710
Rio Salado Comm Coll, Phoenix, AZ 85003	1978	Dr. Linda Thor 12	10,942	596
Riverside Comm Coll, Riverside, CA 92506	1916	Dr. Charles A. Kane 12	22,000	480
Roane State Comm Coll, Harriman, TN 37748	1971	Dr. Sherry L. Hoppe .5	5,269	248
Robert Morris Coll, Chicago Cmps, Chicago, IL 60601	1913	Richard D. Pickett .1	1,733	95
Robeson Comm Coll, Lumberton, NC 28359	1965	Fred W. Williams, Jr. .5	1,450	114
Rochester Comm Coll, Rochester, MN 55904	1915	Dr. Geraldine A. Evans .5	3,987	186
Rockingham Comm Coll, Wentworth, NC 27375	1964	Dr. N. J. Owens, Jr. .5	2,020	111
Rockland Comm Coll, Suffern, NY 10901	1959	Dr. F. Thomas Clark 12	8,271	792
Rock Valley Coll, Rockford, IL 61111	1964	Dr. Karl J. Jacobs 10	7,960	214
Rogers State Coll, Claremore, OK 74017-2099	1909	Dr. Richard H. Mosier .5	3,875	270
Rogue Comm Coll, Grants Pass, OR 97527	1970	Dr. Harvey Bennett 12	2,544	334
Rose State Coll, Midwest City, OK 73110-2799	1971	Dr. Larry Nutter 12	10,018	341
Rowan-Cabarrus Comm Coll, Salisbury, NC 28145	1963	Dr. Richard L. Brownell .5	3,500	130
Roxbury Comm Coll, Roxbury Crossing, MA 02120	1973	Walter C. Howard .5	2,500	NR
Sacramento City Coll, Sacramento, CA 95822	1916	Dr. Robert M. Harris 12	16,669	420
Saddleback Coll, Mission Viejo, CA 92692	1967	NR 12	23,586	645
Saint Augustine Coll, Chicago, IL 60640	1980	Fr. Carlos A. Plazas .1	1,500	150
Saint Charles County Comm Coll, St Peters, MO 63376	1986	NR .5	3,877	186
St Clair County Comm Coll, Port Huron, MI 48061	1923	Dr. R. Ernest Dear .9	4,534	241
St Cloud Tech Coll, St Cloud, MN 56303-1240	1948	NR 12	2,388	100
St Johns River Comm Coll, Palatka, FL 32177	1958	Dr. R. L. McLendon, Jr. .5	3,344	157
St Louis Comm Coll at Florissant Valley, St Louis, MO 63135-1499	1963	Dr. Michael T. Murphy 10	10,233	416

Name, address	Year	Governing official, control		Enrollment	Faculty
St Louis Comm Coll at Forest Park, St Louis, MO 63110	1962	Dr. Henry D. Shannon	10	7,469	361
St Louis Comm Coll at Meramec, Kirkwood, MO 63122	1963	Dr. Gwendolyn W. Stephenson	10	15,566	583
St Paul Tech Coll, St Paul, MN 55102	1922	Dr. Donovan Schwichtenberg	12	3,570	565
St Petersburg Jr Coll, St Petersburg, FL 33733	1927	Dr. Carl M. Kuttler, Jr.	12	19,271	569
St Philip's Coll, San Antonio, TX 78203	1898	Dr. Stephen R. Mitchell	10	5,844	334
Salem Comm Coll, Carneys Point, NJ 08069-2799	1971	Dr. Phillip O. Barry	9	1,507	74
Salt Lake Comm Coll, Salt Lake City, UT 84130	1948	Dr. Frank W. Budd	5	15,374	702
Sampson Comm Coll, Clinton, NC 28328	1965	Dr. Clifton W. Paderick	12	1,051	97
San Antonio Coll, San Antonio, TX 78212	1925	Dr. Max Castillo	12	19,908	847
Sandhills Comm Coll, Pinehurst, NC 28374	1963	Dr. John Dempsey	12	2,509	130
San Diego City Coll, San Diego, CA 92101	1914	Dr. Jeanne L. Atherton	12	14,462	250
San Diego Mesa Coll, San Diego, CA 92111-4998	1962	Dr. Allen Brooks	10	27,000	768
San Diego Miramar Coll, San Diego, CA 92126-2999	1969	Dr. Jerome Hunter	12	8,438	209
San Jacinto Coll–Central Cmps, Pasadena, TX 77501-2007	1961	Dr. Monte Blue	12	10,064	539
San Jacinto Coll–South Cmps, Houston, TX 77089	1979	Dr. Parker Williams	12	5,619	213
San Joaquin Delta Coll, Stockton, CA 95207	1935	Dr. L. H. Horton, Jr.	10	18,981	579
San Jose City Coll, San Jose, CA 95128	1921	Dr. Byron R. Skinner	10	12,507	390
San Juan Coll, Farmington, NM 87402-4699	1958	Dr. James C. Henderson	9	3,650	165
Santa Barbara City Coll, Santa Barbara, CA 93109	1908	Dr. Peter R. MacDougall	10	11,981	471
Santa Fe Comm Coll, Gainesville, FL 32606	1966	Dr. Larry W. Tyree	12	11,728	539
Santa Fe Comm Coll, Santa Fe, NM 87502	1983	William C. Witter	12	2,964	203
Santa Monica Coll, Santa Monica, CA 90405	1929	Dr. Richard L. Moore	12	26,360	664
Santa Rosa Jr Coll, Santa Rosa, CA 95401	1918	Dr. Robert F. Agrella	12	28,844	1,479
Sauk Valley Comm Coll, Dixon, IL 61021	1965	Dr. Richard L. Behrendt	10	3,230	185
Schenectady County Comm Coll, Schenectady, NY 12305	1968	Dr. Gabriel J. Basil	12	3,514	239
Schoolcraft Coll, Livonia, MI 48152	1961	Dr. Richard W. McDowell	10	9,551	425
Scott Comm Coll, Bettendorf, IA 52722	1966	Lenny E. Stone	12	3,600	180
Scottsdale Comm Coll, Scottsdale, AZ 85250	1969	NR	12	10,322	380
Seattle Central Comm Coll, Seattle, WA 98122	1966	Dr. Charles H. Mitchell	5	9,673	388
Seminole Comm Coll, Sanford, FL 32773	1966	Dr. Earl S. Weldon	12	6,404	512
Seward County Comm Coll, Liberal, KS 67905	1969	Donald E. Guild	12	1,519	147
Shasta Coll, Redding, CA 96049	1948	George C. Kutras	12	12,820	397
Shawnee Comm Coll, Ullin, IL 62992	1967	NR	12	2,500	111
Shelby State Comm Coll, Memphis, TN 38174-0568	1970	Dr. Lawrence M. Cox	5	4,734	370
Shelton State Comm Coll, Tuscaloosa, AL 35405	1979	Dr. Tom Umphrey	5	6,665	NR
Sheridan Coll, Sheridan, WY 82801	1948	Dr. Stephen Maier	12	2,896	153
Shoals Comm Coll, Muscle Shoals, AL 35662	1989	NR	5	3,051	160
Shoreline Comm Coll, Seattle, WA 98133	1964	Dr. Ronald E. Bell	5	8,092	253
Sierra Coll, Rocklin, CA 95677	1936	Dr. Gerald C. Angove	5	14,490	492
Sinclair Comm Coll, Dayton, OH 45402	1887	Dr. David H. Ponitz	12	20,417	920
Skagit Valley Coll, Mount Vernon, WA 98273	1926	Dr. James M. Ford	5	6,236	325
Skyline Coll, San Bruno, CA 94066-1698	1969	Ms. Linda Graef Salter	9	9,028	268
Snead State Jr Coll, Boaz, AL 35957	1935	Dr. William H. Osborn	5	1,769	66
Snow Coll, Ephraim, UT 84627	1888	Dr. Gerald Day	5	2,158	97
Solano Comm Coll, Suisun City, CA 94585	1945	Dr. Virginia L. Holton	9	11,791	402
South Central Comm Coll, New Haven, CT 06511	1968	Dr. Antonio Perez	5	4,048	186
Southeast Comm Coll, Lincoln Cmps, Lincoln, NE 68520	1973	NR	10	4,115	561
Southeast Comm Coll, Milford Cmps, Milford, NE 68405	1941	Dr. Thomas Stone	10	1,010	89
Southeastern Comm Coll, North Cmps, West Burlington, IA 52655	1968	Dr. R. Gene Gardner	12	2,138	94
Southeastern Illinois Coll, Harrisburg, IL 62946	1960	Dr. Harry W. Abell	5	3,445	152
Southern Maine Tech Coll, South Portland, ME 04106	1946	Dr. Wayne H. Ross	5	1,271	148
Southern State Comm Coll, Hillsboro, OH 45133	1975	Dr. George R. McCormick	5	1,578	102
Southern Union State Jr Coll, Wadley, AL 36276	1922	Dr. Richard J. Federinko	5	2,968	151
Southern West Virginia Comm Coll, Logan, WV 25601	1971	Dr. Harry J. Boyer	5	3,242	195
South Florida Comm Coll, Avon Park, FL 33825	1965	Dr. Catherine P. Cornelius	5	1,500	266
South Georgia Coll, Douglas, GA 31533-5098	1906	Dr. Edward D. Jackson, Jr.	5	1,293	55
South Mountain Comm Coll, Phoenix, AZ 85040	1979	Raul Cardenas	12	3,349	173
South Plains Coll, Levelland, TX 79336	1958	Dr. Marvin L. Baker	12	5,528	339
South Puget Sound Comm Coll, Olympia, WA 98502	1970	Dr. Kenneth Minnaert	5	5,200	191
South Seattle Comm Coll, Seattle, WA 98106	1970	Mr. Jerry M. Brockey	5	6,500	234
Southside Virginia Comm Coll, Alberta, VA 23821	1970	Dr. John J. Cavan	5	1,565	167
South Suburban Coll, South Holland, IL 60473	1927	Dr. Richard Fonte	5	6,683	354
Southwestern Baptist Theological Sem, Fort Worth, TX 76122-0150	1908	Dr. Russell H. Dilday	2	3,359	183
Southwestern Coll, Chula Vista, CA 92010-9191	1961	Joseph M. Conte	12	17,080	678
Southwestern Comm Coll, Creston, IA 50801	1966	NR	5	1,168	65
Southwestern Comm Coll, Sylva, NC 28779	1964	Dr. Barry W. Russell	5	1,522	187
Southwestern Michigan Coll, Dowagiac, MI 49047	1964	Mr. David C. Briegel	12	3,300	182
Southwestern Oregon Comm Coll, Coos Bay, OR 97420	1961	Dr. Stephen J. Kridelbaugh	12	4,799	161
Southwest Mississippi Comm Coll, Summit, MS 39666	1918	NR	10	1,520	89
Southwest State Tech Coll, Mobile, AL 36605	1954	Dr. Thomas A. McLeod	5	1,089	84
Southwest Texas Jr Coll, Uvalde, TX 78801	1946	Mr. Billy Word	12	2,675	152
Southwest Virginia Comm Coll, Richlands, VA 24641	1968	Dr. Charles R. King	5	5,501	235
Southwest Wisconsin Tech Coll, Fennimore, WI 53809	1967	Dr. Richard A. Rogers	12	1,627	101
Spartanburg Methodist Coll, Spartanburg, SC 29301	1911	Dr. George D. Fields	2	1,100	76
Spokane Comm Coll, Spokane, WA 99207	1963	Dr. Joseph Rich	5	5,626	680
Spokane Falls Comm Coll, Spokane, WA 99204	1967	Dr. Vern Loland	5	5,813	656
Spoon River Coll, Canton, IL 61520	1959	Felix T. Haynes	5	2,300	133
Springfield Tech Comm Coll, Springfield, MA 01105	1967	Andrew M. Scibelli	5	3,525	205
Stanly Comm Coll, Albemarle, NC 28001	1971	Dr. Jan J. Crawford	5	1,301	76
Stark Tech Coll, Canton, OH 44720	1970	Dr. John J. McGrath	12	3,997	188
State Comm Coll of East St Louis, East St Louis, IL 62201	1969	NR	5	1,236	83
State Fair Comm Coll, Sedalia, MO 65301	1966	Dr. Marvin Fielding	10	2,369	98
State Tech Inst at Memphis, Memphis, TN 38134	1967	Dr. Charles Temple	5	10,010	550
State U of NY Coll of A&T at Cobleskill, Cobleskill, NY 12043	1916	Dr. Neal V. Robbins	5	2,574	164
State U of NY Coll of A&T at Morrisville, Morrisville, NY 13408	1908	Dr. Frederick W. Woodward	5	3,449	171
State U of NY Coll of Tech at Alfred, Alfred, NY 14802	1908	Dr. John O. Hunter	5	3,506	220
State U of NY Coll of Tech at Canton, Canton, NY 13617	1906	Dr. Earl W. MacArthur	5	2,297	115
State U of NY Coll of Tech at Delhi, Delhi, NY 13753	1913	Mr. Seldon M. Kruger	5	2,332	138
State U of NY Coll of Tech at Farmingdale, Farmingdale, NY 11735	1912	Dr. Frank A. Cipriani	5	9,684	514
Suffolk County Comm Coll–Ammerman Cmps, Selden, NY 11784	1962	Dr. John F. Cooper	12	12,693	471

Name, address	Year	Governing official, control		Enroll-ment	Faculty
Suffolk County Comm Coll–Eastern Cmps, Riverhead, NY 11901	1977	Steven T. Kenny	12	2,513	120
Suffolk County Comm Coll–Western Cmps, Brentwood, NY 11717	1974	Salvatore J. LaLima	12	5,657	275
Sullivan County Comm Coll, Loch Sheldrake, NY 12759-4002	1962	Dr. John F. Walter	12	2,093	167
Sumter Area Tech Coll, Sumter, SC 29150	1963	Dr. Herbert C. Robbins	5	2,345	144
Surry Comm Coll, Dobson, NC 27017	1965	Dr. Swanson Richards	5	3,036	94
Tacoma Comm Coll, Tacoma, WA 98465	1965	Dr. Raymond Needham	5	4,718	284
Tallahassee Comm Coll, Tallahassee, FL 32304	1966	Dr. James H. Hinson, Jr.	12	10,400	384
Tarrant County Jr Coll, Fort Worth, TX 76102	1967	Mr. C. A. Roberson	9	28,349	1,048
Tech Career Institutes, New York, NY 10001	1974	Dr. David M. Goodman	3	4,300	136
Tech Coll of the Lowcountry, Beaufort, SC 29902	1972	Dr. Anne S. McNutt	5	1,282	66
Temple Jr Coll, Temple, TX 76504-7435	1926	Dr. Marvin R. Felder	10	2,363	118
Terra Tech Coll, Fremont, OH 43420-9670	1968	Dr. Richard M. Simon	5	2,852	148
Texarkana Coll, Texarkana, TX 75501	1927	Dr. Carl M. Nelson	12	3,999	188
Texas State Tech Coll–Harlingen Cmps, Harlingen, TX 78550-3697	1967	Dr. J. Gilbert Leal	5	2,976	182
Texas State Tech Inst–Waco Cmps, Waco, TX 76705	1965	Mr. Don E. Goodwin	5	3,534	332
Thomas Nelson Comm Coll, Hampton, VA 23670	1968	Dr. Robert G. Templin, Jr.	5	7,900	318
Three Rivers Comm Coll, Poplar Bluff, MO 63901	1966	Dr. Stephen M. Poort	5	3,061	67
Tidewater Comm Coll, Chesapeake Cmps, Chesapeake, VA 23320	1968	Dr. Larry Whitworth	5	2,847	59
Tidewater Comm Coll, Portsmouth Cmps, Portsmouth, VA 23703	1968	Dr. Larry Whitworth	5	4,050	104
Tidewater Comm Coll, Virginia Beach Cmps, Virginia Beach, VA 23456	1968	Dr. Larry Whitworth	5	11,239	255
Tompkins Cortland Comm Coll, Dryden, NY 13053	1968	Dr. Eduardo J. Marti	12	2,904	186
Treasure Valley Comm Coll, Ontario, OR 97914	1962	Dr. Glenn Mayle	12	2,466	117
Tri-County Tech Coll, Pendleton, SC 29670	1962	Dr. Don C. Garrison	5	3,019	235
Trident Tech Coll, Charleston, SC 29411	1964	Mary H. Dellamura	12	7,588	375
Trinidad State Jr Coll, Trinidad, CO 81082	1925	Dr. Harold Deselms	5	2,392	111
Trinity Valley Comm Coll, Athens, TX 75751	1946	Mr. Ron Baugh	12	4,786	196
Triton Coll, River Grove, IL 60171	1964	Dr. Michael J. Bakalis	5	13,403	1,459
Trocaire Coll, Buffalo, NY 14220	1958	Barbara Ciarico, RSM	1	1,049	100
Truckee Meadows Comm Coll, Reno, NV 89512	1971	Dr. John Gwaltney	5	9,742	496
Tulsa Jr Coll, Tulsa, OK 74135	1968	Dr. Dean P. Van Trease	5	21,000	700
Tunxis Comm Coll, Farmington, CT 06032	1969	Ms. Marilyn Menack	5	2,443	141
Tyler Jr Coll, Tyler, TX 75711	1926	Dr. Raymond M. Hawkins	12	7,984	364
Ulster County Comm Coll, Stone Ridge, NY 12484	1961	Mr. Robert T. Brown	12	2,088	192
Umpqua Comm Coll, Roseburg, OR 97470	1964	Dr. James Kraby	12	1,846	120
Union County Coll, Cranford, NJ 07016	1933	Dr. Thomas H. Brown	12	10,227	438
U of Akron–Wayne Coll, Orrville, OH 44667	1972	Dr. William V. Muse	5	1,538	109
U of Alaska Anchorage, Kenai Peninsula Coll, Soldotna, AK 99669	1964	NR	5	1,673	85
U of Alaska Anchorage, Matanuska-Susitna Coll, Palmer, AK 99645	1958	Dr. Glenn F. Massay	5	1,689	96
U of Alaska Southeast, Sitka Cmps, Sitka, AK 99835	1962	Mr. Richard M. Griffin	5	1,200	60
U of Cincinnati Clermont Coll, Batavia, OH 45103	1972	Dr. Roger J. Barry	5	1,446	103
U of Cincinnati Raymond Walters Coll, Cincinnati, OH 45236	1967	Dr. Neal A. Raisman	5	4,300	195
U of Hawaii–Honolulu Comm Coll, Honolulu, HI 96817	1920	NR	5	4,947	238
U of Hawaii–Kapiolani Comm Coll, Honolulu, HI 96816	1957	Mr. John F. Morton	5	6,526	239
U of Hawaii–Kauai Comm Coll, Lihue, HI 96766	1965	Mr. David Iha	5	1,496	88
U of Hawaii–Leeward Comm Coll, Pearl City, HI 96782	1968	Dr. Barbara B. Polk	5	6,342	264
U of Hawaii–Maui Comm Coll, Kahului, HI 96732	1967	Dr. Clyde Sakamoto	5	2,589	147
U of Hawaii–Windward Comm Coll, Kaneohe, HI 96744	1972	Dr. Peter T. Dyer	5	1,604	80
U of Kentucky, Ashland Comm Coll, Ashland, KY 41101	1937	Dr. Anthony Newberry	5	3,084	104
U of Kentucky, Elizabethtown Comm Coll, Elizabethtown, KY 42701	1964	Dr. Charles E. Stebbins	5	3,988	136
U of Kentucky, Hazard Comm Coll, Hazard, KY 41701	1968	Dr. G. Edward Hughes	5	1,612	76
U of Kentucky, Henderson Comm Coll, Henderson, KY 42420	1963	Dr. Patrick R. Lake	5	1,479	96
U of Kentucky, Hopkinsville Comm Coll, Hopkinsville, KY 42241-2100	1965	Dr. Jim Kerley	5	3,000	113
U of Kentucky, Jefferson Comm Coll, Louisville, KY 40202	1968	Dr. Ronald J. Horvath	5	10,969	365
U of Kentucky, Lexington Comm Coll, Lexington, KY 40506	1965	Dr. Allen G. Edwards	5	4,398	302
U of Kentucky, Madisonville Comm Coll, Madisonville, KY 42431	1968	Dr. Arthur D. Stumpf	5	2,312	127
U of Kentucky, Maysville Comm Coll, Maysville, KY 41056	1967	Dr. James C. Shires	5	1,231	88
U of Kentucky, Owensboro Comm Coll, Owensboro, KY 42303	1986	NR	5	2,646	124
U of Kentucky, Paducah Comm Coll, Paducah, KY 42002	1932	Dr. Leonard O'Hara	5	3,187	102
U of Kentucky, Prestonsburg Comm Coll, Prestonsburg, KY 41653	1964	Dr. Deborah Lee Floyd	5	2,863	164
U of Kentucky, Somerset Comm Coll, Somerset, KY 42501	1965	Dr. Rollin J. Watson	5	2,600	153
U of Kentucky, Southeast Comm Coll, Cumberland, KY 40823-1099	1960	Dr. W. Bruce Ayers	5	2,250	107
U of Maine at Augusta, Augusta, ME 04330	1965	Dr. George P. Connick	5	4,687	195
U of Minnesota, Crookston, Crookston, MN 56716	1966	Dr. Donald G. Sargeant	5	1,336	75
U of New Mexico–Gallup Branch, Gallup, NM 87301	1968	Dr. John M. Phillips	5	2,359	117
U of New Mexico–Valencia Cmps, Los Lunas, NM 87031	1981	Dr. Ralph Sigala	5	1,317	88
U of Puerto Rico, Aguadilla Regional Coll, Ramey, PR 00604	1972	Miguel A. Gonzalez Valentin	7	1,310	NR
U of Puerto Rico, Carolina Regional Coll, Carolina, PR 00984-4800	1974	Dr. Andres R. Rubio	7	1,751	87
U of South Carolina at Beaufort, Beaufort, SC 29902	1959	Dr. Chris P. Plyler	5	1,050	54
U of South Carolina at Lancaster, Lancaster, SC 29721	1959	Mr. John R. Arnold	5	1,039	52
U of South Carolina at Sumter, Sumter, SC 29150	1966	Mr. J. C. Anderson, Jr.	5	1,620	95
U of Wisconsin Ctr–Fox Valley, Menasha, WI 54952	1933	Dr. Robert E. Young	5	1,447	55
U of Wisconsin Ctr–Waukesha County, Waukesha, WI 53188	1966	Dr. Mary S. Knudten	5	2,165	86
Utah Valley Comm Coll, Orem, UT 84058	1941	Dr. Kerry D. Romesburg	5	8,777	425
Valencia Comm Coll, Orlando, FL 32802	1967	Dr. Paul C. Gianini, Jr.	5	20,816	894
Vance-Granville Comm Coll, Henderson, NC 27536	1969	Dr. Ben F. Currin	5	2,534	155

Name, address	Year	Governing official, control		Enroll-ment	Faculty
Ventura Coll, Ventura, CA 93003	1925	Dr. Robert W. Long	12	12,158	541
Vernon Regional Jr Coll, Vernon, TX 76384	1972	Dr. Wade Kirk	12	1,820	112
Victoria Coll, Victoria, TX 77901	1925	Dr. Jimmy Goodson	9	3,328	120
Victor Valley Coll, Victorville, CA 92392-9699	1960	Dr. Edward O. Gould	5	8,000	353
Vincennes U, Vincennes, IN 47591	1801	Dr. Phillip M. Summers	5	7,211	400
Vincennes U–Jasper Ctr, Jasper, IN 47546	1970	NR	5	1,236	61
Virginia Highlands Comm Coll, Abingdon, VA 24210	1967	Dr. N. DeWitt Moore, Jr.	5	2,295	131
Virginia Western Comm Coll, Roanoke, VA 24038	1966	Dr. Charles L. Downs	5	7,368	202
Vista Coll, Berkeley, CA 94704	1974	Dr. Barbara Beno	12	5,100	138
Volunteer State Comm Coll, Gallatin, TN 37066	1970	Dr. Hal R. Ramer	5	4,721	263
Wake Tech Comm Coll, Raleigh, NC 27603	1958	Dr. Bruce I. Howell	12	6,560	325
Walker Coll, Jasper, AL 35501	1938	Dr. Jack L. Mott	1	1,041	50
Wallace State Comm Coll, Hanceville, AL 35077-9080	1966	Dr. James C. Bailey	5	5,291	235
Walla Walla Comm Coll, Walla Walla, WA 99362	1967	Dr. Steven L. VanAusdle	5	4,998	144
Walters State Comm Coll, Morristown, TN 37813	1970	Dr. Jack E. Campbell	5	5,042	205
Washington State Comm Coll, Marietta, OH 45750	1971	Dr. Carson K. Miller	5	2,097	79
Washtenaw Comm Coll, Ann Arbor, MI 48106	1965	Dr. Gunder A. Myran	12	10,776	688
Waterbury State Tech Coll, Waterbury, CT 06708	1964	Mr. Charles A. Ekstrom	5	1,531	45
Waubonsee Comm Coll, Sugar Grove, IL 60554	1966	Dr. John J. Swalec	10	7,402	464
Waukesha County Tech Coll, Pewaukee, WI 53072	1923	Dr. Richard T. Anderson	12	4,700	520
Wayne Comm Coll, Goldsboro, NC 27533-8002	1957	Dr. G. Herman Porter	12	2,635	137
Wayne County Comm Coll, Detroit, MI 48226	1967	Dr. Rafael Cortada	12	10,049	417
Weatherford Coll, Weatherford, TX 76086	1869	Dr. E. W. Mince	5	2,037	93
Wenatchee Valley Coll, Wenatchee, WA 98801	1939	Dr. Arnie Heuchert	12	2,790	168
Westark Comm Coll, Fort Smith, AR 72913	1928	Mr. Joel R. Stubblefield	12	5,525	230
Westchester Business Inst, White Plains, NY 10602	1915	Ernest H. Sutkowski	3	1,000	35
Westchester Comm Coll, Valhalla, NY 10595-1698	1946	Dr. Joseph N. Hankin	12	11,145	536
Western Iowa Tech Comm Coll, Sioux City, IA 51102	1966	Dr. Robert H. Kiser	5	2,075	157
Western Nebraska Comm Coll–Scottsbluff Cmps, Scottsbluff, NE 69361	1926	Dr. John N. Harms	12	1,656	56
Western Nevada Comm Coll, Carson City, NV 89703	1971	Dr. Anthony D. Calabro	5	4,847	358
Western Oklahoma State Coll, Altus, OK 73521	1926	Dr. Stephen R. Hensley	5	1,765	78
Western Piedmont Comm Coll, Morganton, NC 28655	1964	Dr. Jim A. Richardson	5	2,592	132
Western Texas Coll, Snyder, TX 79549	1969	Dr. Harry L. Krenek	12	1,070	55
Western Wisconsin Tech Coll, La Crosse, WI 54602	1911	Dr. James Lee Rasch	10	3,974	172
Western Wyoming Comm Coll, Rock Springs, WY 82902	1959	Dr. T. L. Boggs	12	2,556	112
West Hills Coll, Coalinga, CA 93210	1932	Stan R. Arterberry	5	3,500	139
West Los Angeles Coll, Culver City, CA 90230	1969	Jose L. Robledo	12	8,958	320
Westmoreland County Comm Coll, Youngwood, PA 15697	1970	Dr. Daniel C. Krezenski	9	6,400	382
West Shore Comm Coll, Scottville, MI 49454	1967	Dr. William M. Anderson	10	1,326	71
West Valley Coll, Saratoga, CA 95070	1963	Dr. Leo Chavez	12	14,224	560
West Virginia Northern Comm Coll, Wheeling, WV 26003	1972	Dr. Ron Hutkin	5	2,903	165
West Virginia U at Parkersburg, Parkersburg, WV 26101	1971	Dr. Eldon L. Miller	5	3,782	161
Wharton County Jr Coll, Wharton, TX 77488	1946	Dr. Elbert C. Hutchins	12	3,045	161
Whatcom Comm Coll, Bellingham, WA 98226	1970	Dr. Harold G. Heiner	5	2,074	104
Wilkes Comm Coll, Wilkesboro, NC 28697	1965	Dr. James R. Randolph	5	2,100	108
William Rainey Harper Coll, Palatine, IL 60067	1965	Dr. Paul N. Thompson	12	15,604	827
Willmar Comm Coll, Willmar, MN 56201	1961	Harold G. Conradi	5	1,379	77
Willmar Tech Coll, Willmar, MN 56201	1961	NR	12	1,336	91
Wilson Tech Comm Coll, Wilson, NC 27893	1958	Dr. Frank L. Eagles	5	1,383	89
Wisconsin Indianhead Tech Coll, Rice Lake Cmps, Rice Lake, WI 54868	1941	Mary Ellen Filkins	10	1,097	79
Wood Jr Coll, Mathiston, MS 39752	1886	Dr. Doyce W. Gunter	2	1,500	35
Wor-Wic Tech Comm Coll, Salisbury, MD 21801	1976	NR	12	1,692	94
Wytheville Comm Coll, Wytheville, VA 24382	1967	Dr. William F. Snyder	5	2,460	137
Yakima Valley Comm Coll, Yakima, WA 98907	1928	Dr. V. Philip Tullar	5	5,500	355
Yavapai Coll, Prescott, AZ 86301	1966	Dr. Paul Walker	12	5,499	370
York Tech Coll, Rock Hill, SC 29730	1961	Mr. Dennis F. Merrell	5	2,898	215
Yuba Coll, Marysville, CA 95901	1927	Dr. Patricia L. Wirth	12	12,979	267

College Freshman Attitudes

According to the 26th annual survey of college freshmen, conducted by the American Council on Education and the Univ. of California at Los Angeles, the number of freshmen who chose colleges because of **low tuition, financial aid** or **to live near home** reached record highs in 1991. The number of freshmen who said they went to college because they **could not find a job** was at its highest point since 1982. A record 27.7 percent of the students surveyed chose colleges based on low tuition, compared with 23.4 percent in 1990, while financial aid was the reason given by 27.8 percent compared with 25.2 percent in 1990. The results showed that 21.3 percent selected schools near their home compared with 19.8 percent in 1990. In 1991, 7.3 percent of the freshmen said they attended college because they were unable to find employment.

More than 37 percent said that there was a "very good chance" that they would have to **get a job to help pay expenses,** and the percentage of those who expect to work full time during college rose for the third straight year, reaching a record 4.8 percent.

A record 12.9 percent of the students selected a major in the **health professions** field compared to 7 percent in 1987. Those choosing **business-related majors** declined to 15.6 percent, down from 18.4 percent in 1990 and 24.6 percent in 1987.

Cigarette smoking increased to 11.3 percent after declining from 16.6 percent to 8.9 percent from 1966 to 1987.

Beer drinking reached its lowest level in the history of the survey with 57.3 percent reporting that they frequently or occasionally drink beer compared to 75.2 percent in 1981.

More than 210,000 students enrolled at 431 colleges and universities responded to the survey.

HEALTH

Ethics on Care of the Terminally Ill

A book advising terminally ill people how to commit suicide was No. 1 in the hardcover advice category on the *New York Times* Best Seller List as of Aug. 18, 1991. In Nov. 1991 an initiative in Washington State that would have legalized euthanasia was put to a vote. Although the initiative was unsuccessful, 44% of the voters supported it. As of 1992, similar initiatives were being planned in California and Oregon.

The Supreme Court heard its first ever "right-to-die" case on Dec. 6, 1989. *Cruzan v. Missouri Dept. of Health* concerned Nancy Beth Cruzan, 32, who had been unconscious since Jan. 1983, after a car accident. Her parents and a guardian appointed to represent her sought to stop the medical treatment sustaining her in a "persistent vegetative state." On June 25, 1990, the Supreme Court ruled, 5-4, that it is constitutional for the Missouri Court to require that "clear and convincing" evidence about the patient's previous wishes regarding life-sustaining treatment be presented before life-sustaining care can be withdrawn. Lacking "clear and convincing" evidence, the Cruzans' request to withdraw their daughter's feeding tube was denied. Some have interpreted the Court's decision as recognizing a constitutional right to refuse life-sustaining treatment. However, debate continued on this point.

As of January, 1988, hospitals are required by the Joint Commission on Accreditation of Health Care Organizations to have formal policies specifying when doctors and nurses can refrain from trying to resuscitate terminally ill patients. The policy must be developed in consultation with the medical staff and the nursing staff, adopted by the medical staff and then approved by the hospital's governing body. The policy must define the roles of physicians, nursing personnel, and members of the patient's family in any decision to withhold resuscitation. It must also include "provisions designed to assure that a patient's rights are respected."

In March 1986, the American Medical Association announced that it would be ethical for doctors to withhold "all means of life prolonging medical treatment," including food and water, from permanently unconscious patients even if death was not imminent. The withholding of such therapy should occur only when a patient's unconscious state "is beyond doubt irreversible and there are adequate safeguards to confirm the accuracy of the diagnosis," the association's judicial council said.

In June 1991, the AMA adopted 2 reports of their Council on Ethical and Judicial Affairs. The first, "Decisions Near the End of Life," concludes: "the principle of patient autonomy requires that physicians must respect the decision to forego life-sustaining treatment of a patient who possesses decisionmaking capacity." Life-sustaining treatment is defined as "any treatment that serves to prolong life without reversing the underlying medical condition," and includes "mechanical ventilation, renal dialysis, chemotherapy, antibiotics and artificial nutrition and hydration." The Council also reaffirmed its position that "physicians must not perform euthanasia or participate in assisted suicide." The second report, "Decisions to Forego Life-Sustaining Treatment for Incompetent Patients," encouraged the use of advance directives (living wills and the designation of durable power of attorney) by persons to ensure that their interests will be promoted in the event that they become incompetent. When there is no advance directive designating a proxy decisionmaker, the Council concludes, the patient's family should become the surrogate decisionmaker. Family is defined as "persons with whom the patient is closely associated." Surrogate decisionmakers should consider the patient's previous values and preferences and base decisions on what the patient would have likely decided had he or she been competent. When this is not possible, decisions should be based on what would objectively be in the best interests of the patient. The Council encouraged the establishment and use of ethics committees designed to facilitate sound decisionmaking, whose help should be solicited when there is no available surrogate, there is a conflict among family members, or a health care provider questions the decision of a surrogate.

A number of states have "living will" statutes that set out a procedure for a mentally competent person to declare that he or she does not wish to be subjected to a "death-prolonging" procedure. In October 1990, Congress passed the Patient Self-Determination Act, which took effect in December 1991. The Act requires that any health care facility that receives funds from Medicare or Medicaid must provide written information to all patients about advance directives and patients' rights under their state laws and document whether or not a patient has an advance directive. Information on living wills and health-care powers of attorney can be obtained from the American Bar Association's Commission on Legal Problems of the Elderly. Choice in Dying, Inc. is a patient advocacy group that will provide information by phone (212-366-5500) and send, free of charge, information appropriate to each state (200 Varick Street, New York, N.Y. 10014).

Estimated New Cancer Cases and Deaths By Sex for Selected Sites, 1992*

Source: American Cancer Society

	Estimated New Cases			Estimated Deaths		
	Total	Male	Female	Total	Male	Female
All Sites	**1,130,000**	**565,000[1]**	**565,000[1]**	**520,000**	**275,000**	**245,000**
Oral	30,300	20,600	9,700	7,950	5,175	2,775
Colon-Rectum	156,000	79,000	77,000	57,300	28,900	29,400
Lung	168,000	102,000	66,000	146,000	93,000	53,000
Skin	32,000+[2]	17,000+[2]	15,000+[2]	6,700[3]	4,100	2,600
Breast	181,000	1,000	180,000	46,300	300	46,000
Uterus	45,500[4]	—	45,500[4]	10,000	—	10,000

*Note: The estimates of new cancer cases are offered as a rough guide and should not be regarded as definitive. (1) Carcinoma in situ and non-melanoma skin cancers are not included in totals. Carcinoma in situ of the uterine cervix accounts for about 50,000 new cases annually, and carcinoma in situ of the female breast accounts for about 15,000 new cases annually. Non-melanoma skin cancer accounts for more than 600,000 new cases annually. (2) Melanoma only. (3) Melanoma 6,400; other skin 2,100. (4) Invasive cancer only.

Cancer's 7 Warning Signals*

Source: American Cancer Society

1. A change in bowel or bladder habits.
2. A sore that does not heal.
3. Unusual bleeding or discharge.
4. Thickening or lump in breast or elsewhere.
5. Indigestion or difficulty in swallowing.
6. Obvious change in wart or mole.
7. Nagging cough or hoarseness.

* If you have a warning signal, see your doctor.

Cancer Prevention

Source: American Cancer Society, 1991

PRIMARY PREVENTION: steps that might be taken to avoid those factors that might lead to the development of cancer.

Smoking Cigarette smoking is responsible for 90% of lung cancer cases among men, 79% among women—about 87% overall. Smoking accounts for about 30% of all cancer deaths. Those who smoke two or more packs of cigarettes a day have lung cancer mortality rates 15-25 times greater than nonsmokers.

Nutrition Risk for colon, breast and uterine cancers increases in obese people. High-fat diets may contribute to the development of cancers of the breast, colon and prostate. High-fiber foods may help reduce risk of colon cancer. A varied diet containing plenty of vegetables and fruits rich in vitamins A and C may reduce risk for a wide range of cancers. Salt-cured, smoked and nitrite-cured foods have been linked to esophageal and stomach cancer.

Sunlight Almost all of the more than 600,000 cases of non-melanoma skin cancer diagnosed each year in the U.S. are considered to be sun-related. Such exposure is a major factor in the development of melanoma, and the incidence increases for those living near the equator.

Alcohol Oral cancer and cancers of the larynx, throat, esophagus, and liver occur more frequently among heavy drinkers of alcohol, especially when accompanied by cigarette smoking or chewing tobacco.

Smokeless Tobacco Use of chewing tobacco or snuff increases risk of cancers of the mouth, larynx, throat, and esophagus, and is highly habit-forming.

Estrogen Estrogen treatment to control menopausal symptoms increases risk of endometrial cancer. However, including progesterone in estrogen replacement therapy helps to minimize this risk. Use of estrogen by menopausal women needs careful discussion by the woman and her physician.

Radiation Excessive exposure to ionizing radiation can increase cancer risk. Most medical and dental X rays are adjusted to deliver the lowest dose possible without sacrificing image quality. Excessive radon exposure in the home may increase lung cancer, especially in cigarette smokers. If levels are found to be too high, remedial actions should be taken.

Occupational hazards Exposure to a number of industrial agents (nickel, chromate, asbestos, vinyl chloride, etc.) increases risk of various cancers. Risk from asbestos is greatly increased when combined with smoking.

SECONDARY PREVENTION: steps to be taken to diagnose a cancer or precursor as early as possible after it has developed.

Colorectal tests The ACS recommends 3 tests for the early detection of colon and rectum cancer in people without symptoms: The digital rectal examination performed by a physician during an office visit, every year after the age of 40; the stool blood test every year after 50; and the proctosigmoidoscopy examination every 3 to 5 years, based on the advice of a physician.

Pap test For cervical cancer, women who are or have been sexually active, or have reached 18 years, should have an annual Pap test and pelvic examination. After a woman has had 3 or more consecutive satisfactory normal exams, the Pap test may be performed less frequently at the discretion of her physician.

Breast cancer detection The ACS recommends the monthly practice of breast self-examination by women 20 years and older. Physical examination of the breast should be done every 3 years from ages 20-40 and then every year. The ACS recommends a mammogram every year for asymptomatic women age 50 and over, and a baseline mammogram between ages 35-39. Women 40-49 should have mammography every 1-2 years, depending on physical and mammographic findings.

Trends in Survival By Site of Cancer, By Race

Cases Diagnosed in 1960-63, 1970-73, 1974-76, 1977-80, 1981-87

Source: American Cancer Society

	White					Black				
	Relative 5-Year Survival					Relative 5-Year Survival				
Site	1960-63	1970-73	1974-76	1977-80	1981-87	1960-63	1970-73	1974-76	1977-80	1981-87
All sites	39	43	50	51	53	27	31	39	39	38
Oral cavity & pharynx	45	43	55	54	54	—	—	35	34	31
Esophagus	4	4	5	6	9	1	4	4	4	6
Stomach	11	13	14	16	16	8	13	16	16	17
Colon	43	49	50	53	58	34	37	46	48	47
Rectum	38	45	49	51	55	27	30	41	37	44
Liver	2	3	4	3	5	—	—	1	3	5
Pancreas	1	2	3	2	3	1	2	2	5	4
Larynx	53	62	66	67	68	—	—	59	58	54
Lung & bronchus	8	10	12	13	13	5	7	11	12	11
Melanoma of skin	60	68	80	82	82	—	—	69	51	70
Breast (female)	63	68	75	75	78	46	51	63	63	63

(continued)

Site	White: Relative 5-Year Survival 1960-63	1970-73	1974-76	1977-80	1981-87	Black: Relative 5-Year Survival 1960-63	1970-73	1974-76	1977-80	1981-87
Cervix uteri	58	64	69	68	68	47	61	63	62	57
Corpus uteri	73	81	89	86	84	31	44	62	56	56
Ovary	32	36	36	38	39	32	32	41	40	36
Prostate gland	50	63	67	72	76	35	55	58	62	63
Testis	63	72	79	88	93	—	—	77	73	94
Urinary bladder	53	61	74	76	79	24	36	48	55	59
Kidney & renal pelvis	37	46	52	51	53	38	44	49	57	52
Brain & nervous system	18	20	22	24	24	19	19	27	28	33
Thyroid gland	83	86	92	92	94	—	—	87	92	94
Hodgkin's disease	40	67	71	73	77	—	—	68	73	74
Non-Hodgkin's lymphoma	31	41	47	49	51	—	—	48	49	45
Multiple myeloma	12	19	24	25	26	—	—	27	32	28
Leukemia	14	22	34	36	36	—	—	31	30	29

— Valid survival rate could not be calculated.

Cancer Death Rates by Site, U.S., 1930-1988

Source: American Cancer Society

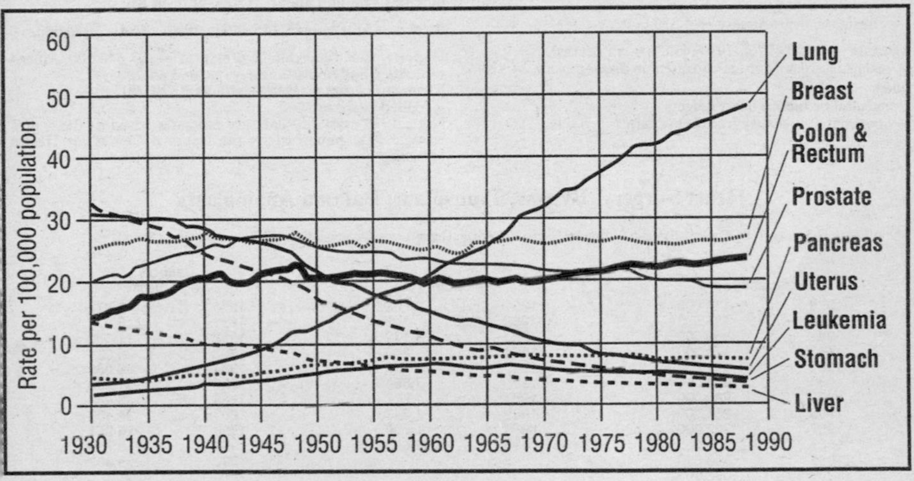

Note: Rates are for both sexes combined except breast and uterus (female only) and prostate (male only).

Heart and Blood Vessel Disease

Warning Signs

Source: American Heart Association, Dallas

Of Heart Attack

- Uncomfortable pressure, fullness, squeezing or pain in the center of the chest lasting two minutes or longer
- Pain may radiate to the shoulder, arm, neck or jaw
- Sweating may accompany pain or discomfort
- Nausea and vomiting may also occur
- Shortness of breath, dizziness, or fainting may accompany other signs

The American Heart Association advises immediate action at the onset of these symptoms. The Association points out that more than half of heart attack victims die before they reach the hospital and that the average victim waits 2 hours before seeking help.

Of Stroke

- Sudden temporary weakness or numbness of face or limbs on one side of the body
- Temporary loss of speech, or trouble speaking or understanding speech
- Temporary dimness or loss of vision, particularly in one eye
- Unexplained dizziness, unsteadiness, or sudden falls

Some Major Risk Factors

Blood pressure—High blood pressure increases the risk of stroke, heart attack, kidney failure and congestive heart failure.

Cholesterol—A cholesterol concentration over 240 mg/dl approximately doubles the risk of coronary heart disease; about 25% of the U.S. adult population falls into this category. Blood cholesterol values between 200 and 240 mg/dl are in a zone of moderate and increasing risk. An estimated 26.1 mln. (36%) of youths age 19 and under have levels of 170 mg/dl or higher, comparable to a level of 200 mg/dl in adults.

Cigarettes—Cigarette smokers have more than twice the risk of heart attack and 2-4 times the risk of sudden cardiac death than non-smokers. Young smokers have a higher risk for early death from stroke.

Obesity—47 mln. adults are 20% or more over their desirable weight. (24.4% white males, 25.7% black males, 25.1% white females, 43.8% black females.)

Cardiovascular Diseases Statistical Summary

1990

Prevalence — 70,020,000 Americans have one or more forms of heart and blood vessel disease.
- high blood pressure — 63,640,000.
- coronary heart disease — 6,230,000.
- stroke — 3,020,000.
- rheumatic heart disease — 1,320,000.

Mortality — 930,477 in 1990 (43.0% of all deaths).
- Someone dies from cardiovascular disease every 34 seconds.

Congenital or inborn heart defects —
- post-natal mortality from heart defects 5,700 in 1990.

Coronary heart disease (heart attack) — caused 489,340 deaths in 1990.
- 6,230,000 alive today have history of heart attack and/or angina pectoris.
- As many as 1,500,000 Americans will have a heart attack this year and about 500,000 of them will die.

Stroke — killed about 145,340 in 1990; afflicts 3,020,000.

Hypertension (high blood pressure) — 63,640,000 Americans age 6 and above—nearly one in 3 adults.

Rheumatic heart disease — afflicts 1,320,000.
- killed 6,000 in 1990.

Note: 1990 mortality data are estimates based on 1990 provisional data published by the National Center for Health Statistics.

Heart Surgery: Bypass, Transplant, Balloon Angioplasty

Source: Natl. Center for Health Statistics, U.S. Task Force on Organ Transplantation, United Network for Organ Sharing

Bypasses

1979	114,000
1980	137,000
1981	159,000
1982	170,000
1983	191,000
1984	202,000
1985	230,000
1986	284,000
1987	332,000
1988	353,000
1989	368,000
1990	392,000

Transplants

1981	62
1982	103
1983	172
1984	346
1985	719
1986	1,368
1987	1,512
1988	1,647
1989	1,700
1990	2,085

Balloon Angioplasty

1980	5,877
1981	5,977
1982	11,679
1983	26,021
1984	46,088
1985	81,883
1986	133,488
1987	184,453
1988	226,251
1989	258,796
1990	285,362

Immunization Schedule for Children

Source: American Academy of Pediatrics, Report of the Committee on Infectious Diseases, 1991 Red Book

Childhood immunization means protection against eight major diseases: polio, measles, mumps, rubella (German measles), whooping cough (pertussis), diphtheria, tetanus, and Haemophilus influenzae type b (Hib) infections. Check the table and ask your pediatrician if your child is up to date on vaccines. It could save a life or prevent disability. Measles, mumps, rubella, polio, pertussis, diphtheria, Haemophilus infections and tetanus are not just harmless childhood illnesses. All of them can cripple or kill.

All are preventable. In order to be completely protected against diphtheria, tetanus and pertussis, your child needs a shot of the combination diphtheria-tetanus-pertussis (DTP) vaccine at 2, 4, 6, 15 to 18 months, and a booster prior to school entry (4-6 years). At 15 months your child should have a shot for measles, mumps and rubella (MMR). A second MMR, primarily to boost measles and mumps immunity, should be given to children 11 years or older who have not had measles. In the event of measles outbreaks in the community, this MMR booster may be given on entry to kindergarten or at an earlier age. Children in high risk populations should be tested for tuberculosis in the first year. Hib conjugate vaccine is due at 2, 4, 6 and 15 months. At 14 to 16 years a tetanus-diphtheria booster shot should be given.

Individual circumstances may warrant decisions differing from the immunization guidelines given here. If you don't have a pediatrician or family physician, call your local public health department. It usually has supplies of vaccine and may give immunizations free.

***Note:** The American College of Physicians recommends that adolescents and adults consult with their physicians about further vaccinations. Those without natural infection or proper immunization against childhood diseases like measles, mumps, rubella, and polio may be at increased risk for such disease and their complications as adults; in addition, tetanus and diphtheria should be boosted periodically; and various ages, occupations, lifestyles, environmental risks, and outbreaks of disease may call for adult immunization.

(continued)

	DTP	Polio	TB Test*	Measles	Mumps	Rubella	Hib/ Conjugate	Tetanus-Diphtheria
2 months	X	X					X	
4 months	X	X					X	
6 months	X						X	
12-15 mos.			X					
15 months				X	X	X	X	
15-18 months	X	X						
4-6 years	X	X						
5-21 years				X	X	X		
14-16 years								X

*Only in high-prevalence populations.

Drug Usage: America's High School Students

Source: National Institute on Drug Abuse/Univ. of Michigan Inst. for Social Research

Reporting on their 17th national survey of American high school seniors, University of Michigan researchers noted that the proportion of high school seniors using any illicit drug in the prior year fell from 33 percent to 29 percent between 1990 and 1991, and was down considerably from the peak level of 54 percent in 1979. Similarly, among college students the use of any illicit drug in the prior year fell from 33 percent to 29 percent between 1990 and 1991, down from a peak of 56 percent in 1980.

Marijuana is still the most widely used illicit drug. Among seniors, annual use fell from 27 percent in 1990 to 24 percent in 1991, down from a peak of 51 percent in 1979. For college students, the decline in marijuana use was from 29 percent to 27 percent, down from a high of 51 percent in 1980 and 1981.

Among the seniors, the proportion using an illicit drug other than marijuana fell from 18 percent to 16 percent between 1990 and 1991, down from a peak of 34 percent in 1981. Similarly, the statistic for college students fell from 15 percent to 13 percent, down from a peak of 32 percent in 1980.

National samples of eighth and tenth grade students were included in the survey for the first time in 1991. Some 44 percent of the eighth graders, who have a modal age of 13, have already tried cigarettes. Drinking of alcoholic beverages in the past year is reported by 54 percent of eighth graders, 72 percent of tenth graders, and 79 percent of twelfth graders. Some 70 percent of the eighth graders say they have at least tried alcohol, 27 percent report having gotten drunk at least once, and 13 percent report having consumed five or more drinks in a row in just the prior two weeks.

While the study misses the 15 percent to 20 percent of a class group that drops out of school early, the investigators say there is little reason to think that trends would be different among them, although they would undoubtedly have higher rates of use overall.

In 1991, 15,500 seniors were surveyed in 136 high schools.

	Percent ever used										
	Class of 1975	Class of 1980	Class of 1984	Class of 1985	Class of 1986	Class of 1987	Class of 1988	Class of 1989	Class of 1990	Class of 1991	'90-'91 change
Marijuana/Hashish	47.3	60.3	54.9	54.2	50.9	50.2	47.2	43.7	40.7	36.7	−4.0sss
Inhalants	NA	11.9	14.4	15.4	15.9	17.0	16.7	17.6	18.0	17.6	−0.4
Inhalants Adjusted[1]	NA	17.6	19.0	18.1	20.1	18.6	17.5	18.6	18.5	18.0	−0.5
Amyl & Butyl Nitrites	NA	11.1	8.1	7.9	8.6	4.7	3.2	3.3	2.1	1.6	−0.5
Hallucinogens	16.3	13.3	10.7	10.3	9.7	10.3	8.9	9.4	9.4	9.6	+0.2
Hallucinogens Adjusted[2]	NA	15.7	13.3	12.1	11.9	10.6	9.2	9.9	9.7	10.0	+0.3
LSD	11.3	9.3	8.0	7.5	7.2	8.4	7.7	8.3	8.7	8.8	+0.1
PCP	NA	9.6	5.0	4.9	4.8	3.0	2.9	3.9	2.8	2.9	+0.1
Cocaine	9.0	15.7	16.1	17.3	16.9[5]	15.2	12.1	10.3	9.4	7.8	−1.6ss
"Crack"	NA	NA	NA	NA	NA	5.6	4.8	4.7	3.5	3.1	−0.4
Heroin	2.2	1.1	1.3	1.2	1.1	1.2	1.1	1.3	1.3	0.9	−0.4s
Other opiates[3]	9.0	9.8	9.7	10.2	9.0	9.2	8.6	8.3	8.3	6.6	−1.7sss
Stimulants Adjusted[3,4]	NA	NA	27.9	26.2	23.4	21.6	19.8	19.1	17.5	15.4	−2.1ss
Sedatives[3]	18.2	14.9	13.3	11.8	10.4	8.7	7.8	7.4	5.3	6.7	−0.8
Barbiturates[3]	16.9	11.0	9.9	9.2	8.4	7.4	6.7	6.5	6.8	6.2	−0.6
Methaqualone[3]	8.1	9.5	8.3	6.7	5.2	4.0	3.3	2.7	2.3	1.3	−1.0s
Tranquilizers[3]	17.0	15.2	12.4	11.9	10.9	10.9	9.4	7.6	7.2	7.2	0.0
Alcohol	90.4	93.2	92.6	92.2	91.3	92.2	92.0	90.7	89.5	88.0	−1.5
Cigarettes	73.6	71.0	69.7	68.8	67.6	67.2	66.4	65.7	64.4	63.1	−1.3

NA=Not available. Level of significance between the two most recent classes: s=.05, ss=.01, sss=.001. (1) Adjusted for underreporting of amyl and butyl nitrites. (2) Adjusted for underreporting of PCP. (3) Only drug use which was not under a doctor's orders. (4) Adjusted for overreporting of the non-prescription stimulants. (5) In 1986, 12.6 percent of those who used cocaine used it in powder form, while 4.1 percent used the "crack" form.

Cocaine-Related Emergencies

According to a report by the National Institute on Drug Abuse, hospital emergency-room cases resulting from cocaine abuse increased 29.3 percent in 1991.

The report also showed a 9.7 percent increase resulting from heroine abuse.

A total of 103,890 emergency-room incidents related to cocaine were reported in 1991, compared to 80,355 cases in 1990. In 1988, a total of 104,731 such cases were reported.

Effects of Commonly Abused Drugs

Source: National Institute on Drug Abuse

Tobacco

Effects and dangers: Nicotine, the active ingredient in tobacco, acts as a stimulant on the heart and nervous system. When tobacco smoke is inhaled the immediate effects on the body are a faster heart beat and elevated blood pressure. These effects, however, are quickly dissipated. Tar (in the smoke) contains many carcinogens. These compounds, many of which are in polluted air but are found in vastly greater quantities in cigarette smoke, have been identified as major causes of cancer and respiratory difficulties. Even relatively young smokers can have shortness of breath, nagging cough, or develop cardiovascular and respiratory difficulties. A third principal component of cigarette smoke, carbon monoxide, is also a cause of some of the more serious health effects of smoking. Carbon monoxide can reduce the blood's ability to carry oxygen to body tissues and can promote the development of arteriosclerosis (hardening of the arteries). Long-term effects of smoking cigarettes are emphysema, chronic bronchitis, heart disease, lung cancer, and cancer in other parts of the body.

Risks during pregnancy: Women who smoke during pregnancy are more likely to have babies that weigh less.

Alcohol

Effects: Like sedatives, it is a central nervous system depressant. In small doses, it has a tranquilizing effect on most people, although it appears to stimulate others. Alcohol first acts on those parts of the brain which affect self-control and other learned behaviors, which often leads to the aggressive behavior associated with some people who drink.

Dangers: In large doses, alcohol can dull sensation and impair muscular coordination, memory, and judgment. Taken in larger quantities over a long period time, alcohol can damage the liver and heart and can cause permanent brain damage. A large dose of alcohol can interfere with the part of the brain that controls breathing. The respiratory failure which results can bring death. Delirium tremens, the most extreme manifestation of alcohol withdrawal, can also cause death.

Risks during pregnancy: Women who drink heavily during pregnancy (more than 3 ounces of alcohol per day or about 2 mixed drinks) run a higher risk of delivering babies with physical, mental and behavioral abnormalities.

Dependence: Repeated drinking produces tolerance to the drug's effects and dependence. The drinker's body then needs alcohol to function. Once dependent, drinkers experience withdrawal symptoms when they stop drinking.

Marijuana ("grass," "pot," "weed")

What is it?: A common plant (*Cannabis sativa*), its chief psychoactive ingredient is delta-9-tetrahydrocannabinol, or THC. The amount of THC in the marijuana cigarette (joint) primarily determines its psychoactive potential.

Effects: Most users experience an increase in heart rate, reddening of the eyes, and dryness in the mouth and throat. Studies indicate the drug temporarily impairs short-term memory, alters sense of time, and reduces the ability to perform tasks requiring concentration, swift reactions, and coordination. Many feel that their hearing, vision, and skin sensitivity are enhanced by the drug, but these reports have not been objectively confirmed by research. Feelings of euphoria, relaxation, altered sense of body image, and bouts of exaggerated laughter are also commonly reported.

Dangers: Scientists believe marijuana can be particularly harmful to lungs because users typically inhale the unfiltered smoke deeply and hold it in their lungs for prolonged periods of time. Marijuana smoke has been found to have more cancer-causing agents than are found in cigarette smoke (see above). Because marijuana use increases heart rate as much as 50% and brings on chest pain in people who have a poor blood supply to the heart (and more rapidly than tobacco smoke does), doctors believe people with heart conditions or who are at high risk for heart ailments, should not use marijuana. Findings also suggest that regular use may reduce fertility in women and that men with marginal fertility or endocrine functioning should avoid marijuana use.

Risks during pregnancy: Research is limited, but scientists believe marijuana which crosses the placential barrier, may have a toxic effect on embryos and fetuses.

Dependence: Tolerance to marijuana, the need to take more and more of the drug over time to get the original effect, has been proven in humans and animals. Physical dependence has been demonstrated in research subjects who ingested an amount equal to smoking 10 to 20 joints a day. When the drug was discontinued, subjects experienced withdrawal symptoms—irritability, sleep disturbances, loss of appetite and weight, sweating, and stomach upset.

Bad reactions: Most commonly reported immediate adverse reaction to marijuana use is the "acute panic anxiety reaction," usually described as an exaggeration of normal marijuana effects in which intense fears of losing control accompany severe anxiety. The symptoms often disappear in a few hours when the acute drug effects have worn off.

Hallucinogens ("psychodelics")

What are they?: Drugs which affect perception, sensation, thinking, self-awareness, and emotion.

(1) **LSD (lysergic acid diethylamide),** a synthetic, is converted from lysergic acid which comes from fungus (ergot).

Effects: Vary greatly according to dosage, personality of the user, and conditions under which the drug is used. Basically, it causes changes in sensation. Vision alters; users describe changes in depth perception and in the meaning of the perceived object. Illusions and hallucinations often occur. Physical reactions range from minor changes such as dilated pupils, a rise in temperature and heartbeat, or a slight increase in blood pressure, to tremors. High doses can greatly alter the state of consciousness. Heavy use of the drug may produce flashbacks, recurrences of some features of a previous LSD experience days or months after the last dose.

Dangers: After taking LSD, a person loses control over normal thought processes. Although many perceptions are pleasant, others may cause panic or may make a person believe that he or she cannot be harmed. Longer-term harmful reactions include anxiety and depression, or "breaks from reality" which may last from a few days to months. Heavy users sometimes develop signs of organic brain damage, such as impaired memory and attention span, mental confusion, and difficulty with abstract thinking. It is not known yet whether such mental changes are permanent.

(2) **Mescaline:** Comes from peyote cactus and its effects are similar to those of LSD.

Phencyclidine (PCP or "angel dust")

What is it?: A drug that was developed as a surgical anesthetic for humans in the late 1950s. PCP was soon restricted to its only current legal use as a veterinary anesthetic and tranquilizer.

Effects: Vary according to dosage. Low doses may provide the usual releasing effects of many psychoactive drugs. A floaty euphoria is described, sometimes associated with a feeling of numbness (part of the drug's anesthetic effects). Increased doses produce an excited, confused intoxification, which may include muscle rigidity, loss of concentration and memory, visual disturbances, delirium, feelings of isolation, convulsions, speech impairment, violent behavior, fear of death, and changes in the user's perceptions of their bodies.

Dangers: PCP intoxication can produce violent and bizarre behavior even in people not otherwise prone to such behavior. Violent actions may be directed at themselves or others and often account for serious injuries and death. More people die from accidents caused by the erratic behavior produced by the drug than from the drug's direct effect on the body. A temporary, schizophrenic-like psychosis, which can last for days or weeks, has also occurred in users of moderate or higher doses.

Stimulants ("Uppers")

What are they?: A class of drugs which stimulate the central nervous system and produce an increase in alertness and activity.

(1) **Amphetamines** promote a feeling of alertness and increase in speech and general physical activity. Under medical supervision, the drugs are taken to control appetite.

Effects and dangers: Even small, infrequent doses can produce toxic effects in some people. Restlessness, anxiety, mood swings, panic, circulatory and cardiac disturbances, paranoid thoughts, hallucinations, convulsions, and coma

have all been reported. Heavy, frequent doses can produce brain damage which results in speed disturbances and difficulty in turning thoughts into words. Death can result from injected amphetamine overdose. Long-term users often have acne resembling a measles rash; trouble with teeth, gums and nails, and dry lifeless hair. As heavy users who inject amphetamines accumulate larger amounts of the drug in their bodies, the resulting toxicity can produce amphetamine psychosis. People in this extremely suspicious, paranoid state, frequently exhibit bizarre, sometimes violent behavior.
Dependence: People with a history of sustained low-dose use quite often become dependent and feel they need the drug to get by.
(2) **Cocaine** is a stimulant extracted from the leaves of the coca plant. It is available in many forms, the most available of which is cocaine hydrochloride. Cocaine hydrochloride is often used medically as a local anesthetic, but is also sold illegally on the street in large pieces called rocks. Street cocaine is a white, crystal-like powder that is most commonly inhaled or snorted, though some users ingest, inject, or smoke a form of the drug called freebase or crack.

Freebase and **crack** are formed by chemically converting street cocaine to a purified substance that is more suitable for smoking. Smoking freebase or crack produces a shorter, but more intense high than other ways of using the drug. It is the most direct and rapid means of getting the drug to the brain, and because larger amounts are reaching the brain more quickly, the effects of the drug are more intense and the dangers associated with its use are greater.

Ice, or crystal methamphetamine, is another stimulant that can be smoked and which has many of the same euphoric and adverse effects as crack.
Effects: The drug's usual effects are dilated pupils and increased blood pressure, heart rate, breathing rate, and body temperature. Even small doses may elicit feelings of euphoria; illusions of increased mental and physical strength and sensory awareness; and a decrease in hunger, pain, and the perceived need for sleep. Large doses significantly magnify these effects, sometimes causing irrational behavior and confusion.
Dangers: Paranoia is not an uncommon response to heavy doses. Psychosis may be triggered in users prone to mental instability. Repeated inhalation often results in nostril and nasal membrane irritation. Some regular users have reported feelings of restlessness, irritability, and anxiety. Others have experienced hallucinations of touch, sight, taste, or smell. When people stop using cocaine after taking it for a long time, they frequently become depressed. They tend to fight off this depression by taking more cocaine, just as in the up/down amphetamine cycle.
Cocaine is toxic. Although few people realize it, overdose deaths, though rare, have occurred as a result of injecting, ingesting and even snorting cocaine. The deaths are a result of seizures followed by respiratory arrest and coma, or sometimes by cardiac arrest. Other dangers associated with cocaine include the risk of infection, such as hepatitis, resulting from the use of unsterile needles and the risk of fire or explosion resulting from the use of volatile substances necessary for freebase preparation.
Dependence: Cocaine is not a narcotic; no evidence suggests that it produces a physical dependence. However, cocaine is psychologically a very dangerous, dependence-producing drug. Smoking freebase or crack increases this risk of dependence.
(3) **Caffeine** may be the world's most popular drug. It is primarily consumed in coffee and tea, but is also found in cocoa, cola and other soft drinks, as well as in many over-the-counter medicines.
Effects: Two to four cups of coffee increase heart rate, body temperature, urine production, and gastric juice secretion. Caffeine can also raise sugar levels and cause tremors, loss of coordination, decreased appetite, and postponement of fatigue. It can interfere with the depth of sleep and the amount of dream sleep by causing more rapid eye movement (REM) sleep at first, but less than average over an entire night. Extremely high doses may cause diarrhea, sleeplessness, trembling, severe headache, and nervousness.
Dependence: A form of physical dependence may result with regular consumption. In such cases, withdrawal symptoms may occur if caffeine use is stopped or interrupted. These symptoms include headache, irritability, and fatigue. Tolerance may develop with the use of six to eight cups or more a day. A regular user of caffeine who has developed a tolerance may also develop a craving for the drug's effects.
Dangers: Poisonous doses of caffeine have occurred occasionally and have resulted in convulsions, breathing failure, and even death. However, it is almost impossible to die from drinking too much coffee or tea. The deaths that have been reported have resulted from the misuse of tablets containing caffeine.

Sedatives (Tranquilizers, sleeping pills)

What are they?: Drugs which depress the central nervous system, more appropriately called sedative-hypnotics because they include drugs which calm the nerves (the sedation effect) and produce sleep (the hypnotic effect). Of drugs in this class, barbiturates ("barbs", "downers," "reds") have the highest rate of abuse and misuse. The most commonly abused barbiturates include pentobarbital (Nembutal), secobarbital (Seconal), and amobarbital (Amytal). These all have legitimate use as sedatives or sleeping aids. Among the most commonly abused nonbarbiturate drugs are glutethimide (Doriden), meprobamate (Miltown), methyprylon (Noludar), ethchlorvynol (Placidyl), and methaqualone (Sopor, Quaalude). These are prescribed to help people sleep. Benzodiazepines, especially diazepam (Valium), prescribed to relieve anxiety, are commonly abused, and their rate of abuse and misuse is increasing.
Dangers: These can kill. Barbiturate overdose is implicated in nearly one-third of all reported drug-induced deaths. Accidental deaths may occur when a user takes an unintended larger or repeated dose of sedatives because of confusion or impairment in judgment caused by initial intake of the drug. With lesser, but still large doses, users can go into coma. Moderately large doses often produce an intoxicated stupor. Users' speech is often slurred, memory vague, and judgment impaired. Taken along with alcohol, the combination can be fatal. Tranquilizers act somewhat differently from other sedatives and are considered less hazardous. But even by themselves, or in combination with other drugs (especially alcohol and other sedatives) they can be quite dangerous.
Dependence: Potential for dependence is greatest with barbiturates, but all sedatives, tranquilizers, can be addictive. Barbiturate withdrawal is often more severe than heroin withdrawal.

Narcotics

What they are?: Drugs that relieve pain and often induce sleep. The opiates, which are narcotics, include opium and drugs derived from opium, such as morphine, codeine, and heroin. Narcotics also include certain synthetic chemicals that have a morphine-like action, such as methadone.
Which are abused?: Heroin ("junk," "smack") accounts for 90% of narcotic abuse in the U.S. Sometimes medicinal narcotics are also abused, including paregoric containing codeine, and methadone, meperidine, and morphine.
Dependence: Anyone can become heroin dependent if he or she takes the drug regularly. Although environmental stress and problems of coping have often been considered as factors that lead to heroin addiction, physicians or psychologists do not agree that some people just have an "addictive personality" and are prone to dependence. All we know for certain is that continued use of heroin causes dependence.
Dangers: Physical dangers depend on the specific drug, its source, and the way it is used. Most medical problems are caused by the uncertain dosage level, use of unsterile needles and other paraphernalia, contamination of the drug, or combination of a narcotic with other drugs, rather than by the effects of the heroin (or another narcotic) itself. The life expectancy of a heroin addict who injects the drug intravenously is significantly lower than that of one who does not. An overdose can result in death. If, for example, an addict obtains pure heroin and is not tolerant of the dose, he or she may die minutes after injecting it. Infections from unsterile needles, solutions, syringes, cause many diseases. Serum hepatitis is common. Skin abscesses, inflammation of the veins and congestion of the lungs also occur.
Withdrawal: When a heroin-dependent person stops taking the drug, withdrawal begins within 4-6 hours after the last injection. Full-blown withdrawal symptoms—which include shaking, sweating, vomiting, a running nose and eyes, muscle aches, chills, abdominal pains, and diarrhea—begin some 12-16 hours after the last injection. The intensity of symptoms depends on the degree of dependence.

Basic First Aid

First aid experts stress that knowing what to do for an injured person until a doctor or trained person gets to an accident scene can save a life, especially in cases of stoppage of breath, severe bleeding, and shock.

People with special medical problems, such as diabetes, cardiovascular disease, epilepsy, or allergy, are also urged to wear some sort of emblem identifying it, as a safeguard against use of medication that might be injurious or fatal in an emergency. Emblems may be obtained from Medic Alert Foundation, Turlock, CA 95380.

Most accidents occur in homes. National Safety Council figures show that home accidents exceed those in other locations, such as in cars, at work, or in public places.

In all cases, get medical assistance as soon as possible.

Animal bite — Wound should be washed with soap under running water and animal should be caught alive for rabies test.

Asphyxiation — Start mouth-to-mouth resuscitation immediately after getting patient to fresh air.

Bleeding — Elevate the wound above the heart if possible. Press hard on wound with sterile compress until bleeding stops. Send for doctor if it is severe.

Burn — If mild, with skin unbroken and no blisters, plunge into ice water until pain subsides. Apply a dry dressing if necessary. Send for physician if burn is severe. Apply sterile compresses and keep patient quiet and comfortably warm until doctor's arrival. Do not try to clean burn, or to break blisters.

Chemical in eye — With patient lying down, pour cupsful of water immediately into corner of eye, letting it run to other side to remove chemicals thoroughly. Cover with sterile compress. Get medical attention immediately .

Choking — Do not use back slaps to dislodge obstruction. (See **Abdominal Thrust**)

Convulsions — Place person on back on bed or rug. Loosen clothing. Turn head to side. Do not place a blunt object between the victim's teeth. If convulsions do not stop, get medical attention immediately.

Cut (minor) — Apply mild antiseptic and sterile compress after washing with soap under warm running water.

Drowning — (See Mouth-to-Mouth Resuscitation) Artificial breathing must be started at once, before victim is out of the water, if possible. If the victim's stomach is bloated with water, put victim on stomach, place hands under stomach, and lift. If no pulse is felt, begin cardio-pulmonary resuscitation. This should only be done by those professionally trained. If necessary, treat for shock. (See **Shock**)

Electric shock — If possible, turn off power. Don't touch victim until contact is broken; pull him from contact with electrical source using rope, wooden pole, or loop of dry cloth. Start mouth-to-mouth resuscitation if breathing has stopped.

Foreign body in eye — Touch object with moistened corner of handkerchief if it can be seen. If it cannot be seen or does not come out after a few attempts, take patient to doctor. Do not rub eye.

Fainting — If victim feels faint, lower head to knees. Lay him down with head turned to side if he becomes unconscious. Loosen clothing and open windows. Keep patient lying quietly for at least 15 minutes after he regains consciousness. Call doctor if faint lasts for more than a few minutes.

Fall — Send for physician if patient has continued pain. Cover wound with sterile dressing and stop any severe bleeding. Do not move patient unless absolutely necessary — as in case of fire — if broken bone is suspected. Keep patient warm and comfortable.

Loss of Limb — If a limb is severed, it is important to properly protect the limb so that it can possibly be reattached to the victim. After the victim is cared for, the limb should be placed in a clean plastic bag, garbage can or other suitable container. Pack ice around the limb on the OUTSIDE of the bag to keep the limb cold. Call ahead to the hospital to alert them of the situation.

Poisoning — Call doctor. Use antidote listed on label if container is found. Call local Poison Control Center if possible. Except for lye, other caustics, and petroleum products, induce vomiting unless victim is unconscious. Give milk if poison or antidote is unknown.

Shock (injury-related) — Keep the victim lying down; if uncertain as to his injuries, keep him flat on his back. Maintain the victim's normal body temperature; if the weather is cold or damp, place blankets or extra clothing over and under the victim; if weather is hot, provide shade.

Snakebite — Immediately get victim to a hospital. If there is mild swelling or pain, apply a constricting band 2 to 4 inches above the bite.

Sting from insect — If possible, remove stinger and apply solution of ammonia and water, or paste of baking soda. Call physician immediately if body swells or patient collapses.

Unconsciousness — Send for doctor and place person on his back. Start resuscitation if he stops breathing. Never give food or liquids to an unconscious person.

Abdominal Thrust

The American Red Cross and the American Heart Association both agree that the recommended first aid for choking victims is the abdominal thrust, also known as the Heimlich maneuver, after its creator, Dr. Henry Heimlich. Slaps on the back are no longer advised and may even prove detrimental in an attempt to assist a choking victim.

- Get behind the victim and wrap your arms around him above his waist.
- Make a fist with one hand and place it, with the thumb knuckle pressing inward, just below the point of the "v" of the rib cage.
- Grasp the wrist with the other hand and give one or more upward thrusts or hugs.
- Start mouth-to-mouth resuscitation if breathing stops.

Mouth-to-Mouth Resuscitation

Stressing that your breath can save a life, the American Red Cross gives the following directions for mouth-to-mouth resuscitation if the victim is not breathing:

- Determine consciousness by tapping the victim on the shoulder and asking loudly, "Are you okay?"
- Tilt the victim's head back so that his chin is pointing upward. Do not press on the soft tissue under the chin, as this might obstruct the airway. If you suspect that an accident victim might have neck or back injuries, open the airway by placing the tips of your index and middle fingers on the corners of the victim's jaw to lift it forward without tilting the head.
- Place your cheek and ear close to the victim's mouth and nose. Look at the victim's chest to see if it rises and falls. Listen and feel for air to be exhaled for about 5 seconds.
- If there is no breathing, pinch the victim's nostrils shut with the thumb and index finger of your hand that is pressing on the victim's forehead. Another way to prevent leakage of air when the lungs are inflated is to press your cheek against the victim's nose.
- Blow air into victim's mouth by taking a deep breath and then sealing your mouth tightly around the victim's mouth. Initially, give two, quick (approx. 1.5 seconds each), full breaths without allowing the lungs to deflate completely between each breath.
- Watch the victim's chest to see if it rises.
- Stop blowing when the victim's chest is expanded. Raise your mouth; turn your head to the side and listen for exhalation.
- Watch the chest to see if it falls.
- Repeat the blowing cycle until the victim starts breathing.

Note: Infants (up to one year) and children (1 to 8 years) should be administered mouth-to-mouth resuscitation as described above, except for the following:

- Do not tilt the head as far back as an adult's head.
- Both the mouth and nose of the infant should be sealed by the mouth.
- Give breaths to a child once every four seconds.
- Blow into the infant's mouth and nose once every three seconds with less pressure and volume than for a child.

Stress: How Much Can Affect Your Health?

Source: Reprinted with permission from the *Journal of Psychosomatic Research*, Vol. 11, pp. 213-218, T.H. Holmes, M.D., R.H. Rahe, M.D.; The Social Readjustment Rating Scale © 1967, Pergamon Press, Ltd.

Change, both good and bad, can create stress and stress, if sufficiently severe, can lead to illness. Drs. Thomas Holmes and Richard Rahe, psychiatrists at the University of Washington in Seattle, developed the Social Readjustment Rating Scale. In their study, they gave a point value to stressful events. The psychiatrists discovered that in 79 percent of the persons studied, major illness followed the accumulation of stress-related changes totaling over 300 points in one year.

The Social Readjustment Rating Scale

Life Event	Value
Death of Spouse	100
Divorce	73
Marital separation from mate	65
Detention in jail or other institution	63
Death of a close family member	63
Major personal injury or illness	53
Marriage	50
Being fired at work	47
Marital reconciliation with mate	45
Retirement from work	45
Major change in the health or behavior of a family member	44
Pregnancy	40
Sexual difficulties	39
Gaining a new family member (e.g., through birth, adoption, moving in, etc.)	39
Major business readjustment (e.g., merger, reorganization, bankruptcy, etc.)	39
Major change in financial state (e.g., a lot worse off or a lot better off than usual)	38
Death of a close friend	37
Changing to a different line of work	36
Major change in the number of arguments with spouse (e.g., either a lot more or a lot less than usual regarding child-rearing, personal habits, etc.)	35
Taking out a mortgage or loan for a major purchase (e.g. for a home, business, etc.)	31
Foreclosure on a mortgage or loan	30
Major change in responsibilities at work (e.g., promotion, demotion, lateral transfer)	29
Son or daughter leaving home (e.g., marriage, attending college, etc.)	29
In-law troubles	29
Outstanding personal achievement	28
Wife beginning or ceasing work outside the home	26
Beginning or ceasing formal schooling	26
Major change in living conditions (e.g., building a new home, remodeling, deterioration of home or neighborhood)	25
Revision of personal habits (dress, manners, association, etc.)	24
Troubles with the boss	23
Major change in working hours or conditions	20
Change in residence	20
Changing to a new school	20
Major change in usual type and/or amount of recreation	19
Major change in church activities (e.g., a lot more or a lot less than usual)	19
Major change in social activities (e.g., clubs, dancing, movies, visiting, etc.)	18
Taking out a mortgage or loan for a lesser purchase (e.g., for a car, TV, freezer, etc.)	17
Major change in sleeping habits (a lot more or a lot less sleep, or change in part of day when asleep)	16
Major change in number of family get-togethers (e.g., a lot more or a lot less than usual)	15
Major change in eating habits (a lot more or a lot less food intake, or very different meal hours or surroundings)	15
Vacation	13
Christmas	12
Minor violations of the law (e.g., traffic tickets, jaywalking, disturbing the peace, etc.)	11

A Patient's Bill of Rights

Source: American Hospital Association, © copyright 1972.

Often, as a hospital patient, you feel you have little control over your circumstances. You do, however, have some important rights. They have been enumerated by the American Hospital Association.

1. The patient has the right to considerate and respectful care.
2. The patient has the right to obtain from his physician complete current information concerning his diagnosis, treatment, and prognosis in terms the patient can be expected to understand. When it is not medically advisable to give such information to the patient, the information should be made available to an appropriate person in his behalf. He has the right to know, by name, the physician responsible for coordinating his care.
3. The patient has the right to receive from his physician information necessary to give informed consent prior to the start of any procedure and/or treatment. Except in emergencies, such information for informed consent should include but not necessarily be limited to the specific procedure and/or treatment, the medically significant risks involved, and the probable duration of incapacitation. Where medically significant alternatives for care or treatment exist, or when the patient requests information concerning medical alternatives, the patient has the right to such information. The patient also has the right to know the name of the person responsible for the procedures and/or treatment.
4. The patient has the right to refuse treatment to the extent permitted by law and to be informed of the medical consequences of his action.
5. The patient has the right to every consideration of his privacy concerning his own medical care program. Case discussion, consultation, examination, and treatment are confidential and should be conducted discreetly. Those not directly involved in his care must have the permission of the patient to be present.
6. The patient has the right to expect that all communications and records pertaining to his care should be treated as confidential.
7. The patient has the right to expect that within its capacity a hospital must make reasonable response to the request of a patient for services. The hospital must provide evaluation, service, and/or referral as indicated by the urgency of the case. When medically permissable, a patient may be transferred to another facility only after he has received complete information and explanation concerning the need for and alternatives to such a transfer. The receiving institution must first have accepted the patient for transfer.
8. The patient has the right to obtain information as to any relationship of his hospital to other health care and education institutions insofar as this care is concerned. The patient has the right to obtain information as to the existence of any professional relationships among individuals, by name, who are treating him.
9. The patient has the right to be advised if the hospital proposes to engage in or perform human experimentation affecting his care or treatment. The patient has the right to refuse to participate in such research projects.
10. The patient has the right to expect reasonable continuity of care. He has the right to know in advance what appointment times and physicians are available and where. The patient has the right to expect that the hospital will provide a mechanism whereby he is informed by his physician of the patient's continuing health care requirements following discharge.
11. The patient has the right to examine and receive an explanation of his bill, regardless of the source of payment.
12. The patient has the right to know what hospital rules and regulations apply to his conduct as a patient.

Nutritive Value of Food (Calories, Proteins, etc.)

Source: Home and Garden Bulletin No. 72; available from Supt. of Documents, U. S. Government Printing Office, Washington, DC 20402

Food	Measure	Grams	Food Energy (calories)	Protein (grams)	Fat (grams)	Saturated fats (grams)	Carbohydrate (grams)	Calcium (milligrams)	Iron (milligrams)	Vitamin A (I.U.)	Thiamin (milligrams)	Riboflavin (milligrams)
Dairy products												
Cheese, cheddar	1 oz.	28	115	7	9	6.1	T	204	.2	300	.01	.11
Cheese, cottage, small curd	1 cup	210	220	26	9	6.0	6	126	.3	340	.04	.34
Cheese, cream	1 oz.	28	100	2	10	6.2	1	23	.3	400	T	.06
Cheese, Swiss	1 oz.	28	105	8	8	5.0	1	272	T	240	.01	.10
Half-and-Half	1 tbsp.	15	20	T	2	1.1	1	16	T	20	.01	.02
Cream, sour	1 tbsp.	15	25	T	3	1.6	1	14	T	90	T	.02
Milk, whole	1 cup	244	150	8	8	5.1	11	291	.1	310	.09	.40
Milk, nonfat (skim)	1 cup	244	85	8	T	.3	12	302	.1	500	.09	.37
Milkshake, chocolate	10.6 oz.	300	355	9	8	5.0	63	396	.9	260	.14	.67
Ice Cream, hardened	1 cup	133	270	5	14	8.9	32	176	.1	540	.05	.33
Sherbet	1 cup	193	270	2	4	2.4	59	103	.3	190	.03	.09
Yogurt, fruit-flavored	8 oz.	227	230	10	3	1.8	42	343	.2	120	.08	.40
Eggs												
Fried in butter	1	46	85	5	6	2.4	1	26	.9	290	.03	.13
Hard-cooked	1	50	80	6	6	1.7	1	28	1.0	260	.04	.14
Scrambled in butter (milk added)	1	64	95	6	7	2.8	1	47	.9	310	.04	.16
Fats & oils												
Butter	1 tbsp.	14	100	T	12	7.2	T	3	T	430	T	T
Margarine	1 tbsp.	14	100	T	12	2.1	T	3	T	470	T	T
Salad dressing, blue cheese	1 tbsp.	15	75	1	8	1.6	1	12	T	30	T	.02
Salad dressing, French	1 tbsp.	16	65	T	6	1.1	3	2	1	—	—	—
Salad dressing, Italian	1 tbsp.	15	85	T	9	1.6	1	2	T	T	T	T
Mayonnaise	1 tbsp.	14	100	T	11	2.0	T	3	.1	40	T	.01
Meat, poultry, fish												
Bluefish, baked with butter or margarine	3 oz.	85	135	22	4	—	0	25	0.6	40	.09	.08
Clams, raw, meat only	3 oz.	85	65	11	1	—	2	59	5.2	90	.08	.15
Crabmeat, white or king, canned	1 cup	135	135	24	3	.6	1	61	1.1	—	.11	.11
Fish sticks, breaded, cooked, frozen	1 oz.	28	50	5	3	—	2	3	.1	0	.01	.02
Salmon, pink, canned	3 oz.	85	120	17	5	.9	0	167	.7	60	.03	.16
Sardines, Atlantic, canned in oil	3 oz.	85	175	20	9	3.0	0	372	2.5	190	.02	.17
Shrimp, French fried	3 oz.	85	190	17	9	2.3	9	61	1.7	—	.03	.07
Tuna, canned in oil	3 oz.	85	170	24	7	1.7	0	7	1.6	70	.04	.10
Bacon, broiled or fried crisp	2 slices	15	85	4	8	2.5	T	2	.5	0	.08	.05
Ground beef, broiled, 10% fat	3 oz.	85	185	23	10	4.0	0	10	3.0	20	.08	.20
Roast beef, relatively lean	3 oz.	85	165	25	7	2.8	0	11	3.2	10	.06	.19
Beef steak, lean and fat	3 oz.	85	330	20	27	11.3	0	9	2.5	50	.05	.15
Beef & vegetable stew	1 cup	245	220	16	11	4.9	15	29	2.9	2,400	.15	.17
Lamb, chop, lean and fat	3.1 oz.	89	360	18	32	14.8	0	8	1.0	—	.11	.19
Liver, beef	3 oz.	85	195	22	9	2.5	5	9	7.5	45,390	.22	3.56
Ham, light cure, lean and fat	3 oz.	85	245	18	19	6.8	0	8	2.2	0	.40	.15
Pork, chop, lean and fat	2.7 oz	78	305	19	25	8.9	0	9	2.7	0	.75	.22
Bologna	1 slice	28	85	3	8	3.0	T	2	.5	—	.05	.06
Frankfurter, cooked	1	56	170	7	15	5.6	1	3	.8	—	.08	.11
Sausage, pork link, cooked	1 link	13	60	2	6	2.1	T	1	.3	0	.10	.04
Veal, cutlet, braised or boiled	3 oz.	85	185	23	9	4.0	0	9	2.7	—	.06	.21
Chicken, drumstick, fried, bones removed	1.3 oz.	38	90	12	4	1.1	T	6	.9	50	.03	.15
Chicken, half broiler, broiled, bones removed	6.2 oz.	176	240	42	7	2.2	0	16	3.0	160	.09	.34
Fruits & products												
Apple, raw, 2-3/4 in. diam.	1	138	80	T	1	—	20	10	.4	120	.04	.03
Applejuice	1 cup	248	120	T	T	—	30	15	1.5	—	.02	.05
Apricots, raw	3	107	55	1	T	—	14	18	.5	2,890	.03	.04
Banana, raw	1	119	100	1	T	—	26	10	.8	230	.06	.07
Cherries, sweet, raw	10	68	45	1	T	—	12	15	.3	70	.03	.04
Fruit cocktail, canned, in heavy syrup	1 cup	255	195	1	T	—	50	23	1.0	360	.05	.03
Grapefruit, raw, medium, white	1/2	241	45	1	T	—	12	19	.5	10	.05	.02
Grapes, Thompson seedless	10	50	35	T	T	—	9	6	.2	50	.03	.02
Lemonade, frozen, diluted	1 cup	248	105	T	T	—	28	2	.1	10	.01	.02
Cantaloupe, 5-in. diam.	1/2	477	80	2	T	—	20	38	1.1	9,240	.11	.08
Orange, 2-5/8 in. diam.	1	131	65	1	T	—	16	54	.5	260	.13	.05
Orange juice, frozen, diluted	1 cup	249	120	2	T	—	29	25	.2	540	.23	.03
Peach, raw, 2-1/2 in. diam.	1	100	40	1	T	—	10	9	.5	1,330	.02	.05
Raisins, seedless	1 cup	145	420	4	T	—	112	90	5.1	30	.16	.12
Strawberries, whole	1 cup	149	55	1	1	—	13	31	1.5	90	.04	.10
Watermelon, 4 by 8 in. wedge	1 wedge	926	110	2	1	—	27	30	2.1	2,510	.13	.13
Grain products												
Bagel, egg	1	55	165	6	2	.5	28	9	1.2	30	.14	.10
Biscuit, 2 in. diam., from home recipe	1	28	105	2	5	1.2	13	34	.4	T	.08	.08
Bread, white, enriched, soft-crumb	1 slice	25	70	2	1	.2	13	21	.6	T	.10	.06
Bread, whole wheat, soft-crumb	1 slice	28	65	3	1	.1	14	24	.8	T	.09	.03
Oatmeal or rolled oats	1 cup	240	130	5	2	.4	23	22	1.4	0	.19	.05
Bran flakes (40% bran), added sugar, salt, iron, vitamins	1 cup	35	105	4	1	—	28	19	12.4	1,650	.41	.49
Corn flakes, added sugar, salt, iron, vitamins	1 cup	25	95	2	T	—	21	*	0.6	1,180	.29	.35
Rice, puffed, added iron, thiamin, niacin	1 cup	15	60	1	T	—	13	3	.3	0	.07	.01
Wheat, shredded, plain, 1 biscuit or 1/2 cup	1 serving	25	90	2	1	—	20	11	.9	0	.06	.03
Cake, angel food, 1/12 of cake	1	53	135	3	T	—	32	50	.2	0	.03	.08
Cupcake, 2-1/2 in. diam., with chocolate icing	1	36	130	2	5	2.0	21	47	.4	60	.05	.06
Boston cream pie with custard filling, 1/12 of cake	1	69	210	3	6	1.9	34	46	.7	140	.09	.11
Fruitcake, dark, 1/30 of loaf	1	15	55	1	2	.5	9	11	.4	20	.02	.02
Cake, pound, 1/17 of loaf	1	33	160	2	10	2.5	16	6	.5	80	.05	.06
Brownies, with nuts, from commercial recipe	1	20	85	1	4	.9	13	9	.4	20	.03	.02
Cookies, chocolate chip, from home recipe	4	40	205	2	12	3.5	24	14	.8	40	.06	.06
Crackers, graham	2	14	55	1	1	.3	10	6	.5	0	.02	.08

Food	Measure	Grams	Food Energy (calories)	Protein (grams)	Fat (grams)	Saturated fats (grams)	Carbohydrate (grams)	Calcium (milligrams)	Iron (milligrams)	Vitamin A (I.U.)	Thiamin (milligrams)	Riboflavin (milligrams)
Crackers, saltines	4	11	50	1	1	.3	8	2	.5	0	.05	.05
Danish pastry, round piece	1	65	275	5	15	4.7	30	33	1.2	200	.18	.19
Doughnut, cake type	1	25	100	1	5	1.2	13	10	.4	20	.05	.05
Macaroni and cheese, from home recipe	1 cup	200	430	17	22	8.9	40	362	1.8	860	.20	.40
Muffin, corn	1	40	125	3	4	1.2	19	42	.7	120	.10	.10
Noodles, enriched, cooked	1 cup	160	200	7	2	—	37	16	1.4	110	.22	.13
Pie, apple, 1/7 of pie	1	135	345	3	15	3.9	51	11	.9	40	.15	.11
Pie, cherry, 1/7 of pie	1	135	350	4	15	4.0	52	19	.9	590	.16	.12
Pie, lemon meringue, 1/7 of pie	1	120	305	4	12	3.7	45	17	1.0	200	.09	.12
Pie, pecan, 1/7 of pie	1	118	495	6	27	4.0	61	55	3.7	190	.26	.14
Pizza, cheese, 1/8 of 12 in. diam. pie	1	60	145	6	4	1.7	22	86	1.1	230	.16	.18
Popcorn, popped, plain	1 cup	6	25	1	T	T	5	1	.2	—	—	.01
Pretzels, stick	10	3	10	T	T	—	2	1	T	0	.01	.01
Rolls, enriched, brown & serve	1	26	85	2	2	.4	14	20	.5	T	.10	.06
Rolls, frankfurter & hamburger	1	40	120	3	2	.5	21	30	.8	T	.16	.10
Spaghetti with meat balls & tomato sauce	1 cup	248	330	19	12	3.3	39	124	3.7	1,590	.25	.30
Legumes, nuts, seeds												
Beans, Great Northern, cooked	1 cup	180	210	14	1	—	38	90	4.9	0	.25	.13
Peanuts, roasted in oil, salted	1 cup	144	840	37	72	13.7	27	107	3.0	—	.46	.19
Peanut butter	1 tbsp.	16	95	4	8	1.5	3	9	.3	—	.02	.02
Sunflower seeds	1 cup	145	810	35	69	8.2	29	174	10.3	70	2.84	.33
Sugars & sweets												
Candy, caramels	1 oz.	28	115	1	3	1.6	22	42	.4	T	.01	.05
Candy, milk chocolate	1 oz.	28	145	2	9	5.5	16	65	.3	80	.02	.10
Fudge, chocolate	1 oz.	28	115	1	3	1.3	21	22	.3	T	.01	.03
Candy, hard	1 oz.	28	110	0	T	—	28	6	.5	0	0	0
Honey	1 tbsp.	21	65	T	0	0	17	1	.1	0	T	.01
Jams & Preserves	1 tbsp.	20	55	T	T	—	14	4	.2	T	T	.01
Sugar, white, granulated	1 tbsp.	12	45	0	0	0	12	0	T	0	0	0
Vegetables												
Asparagus, canned, spears	4 spears	80	15	2	T	—	3	15	1.5	640	.05	.08
Beans, green, from frozen, cuts	1 cup	135	35	2	T	—	8	54	.9	780	.09	.12
Broccoli, cooked	1 stalk	180	45	6	1	—	8	158	1.4	4,500	.16	.36
Cabbage, raw, coarsely shredded or sliced	1 cup	70	15	1	T	—	4	34	.3	90	.04	.04
Carrots, raw, 7-1/2 by 1-1/8 in.	1	72	30	1	T	—	7	27	.5	7,930	.04	.04
Celery, raw	1 stalk	40	5	T	T	—	2	16	.1	110	.01	.01
Collards, cooked	1 cup	190	65	7	1	—	10	357	1.5	14,820	.21	.38
Corn, sweet, cooked	1 ear	140	70	2	1	—	16	2	.5	310	.09	.08
Lettuce, Iceberg, chopped	1 cup	55	5	T	T	—	2	11	.3	180	.03	.03
Mushrooms, raw	1 cup	70	20	2	T	—	3	4	.6	T	.07	.32
Onions, raw, chopped	1 cup	170	65	3	T	—	15	46	.9	T	.05	.07
Peas, frozen, cooked	1 cup	160	110	8	T	—	19	30	3.0	960	.43	.14
Potatoes, baked, peeled	1	156	145	4	T	—	33	14	1.1	T	.15	.07
Potatoes, frozen, French fried	10	50	110	2	4	1.1	17	5	.9	T	.07	.01
Potatoes, mashed, milk added	1 cup	210	135	4	2	.7	27	50	.8	40	.17	.11
Potato chips	10	20	115	1	8	2.1	10	8	.4	T	.04	.01
Potato salad	1 cup	250	250	7	7	2.0	41	80	1.5	350	.20	.18
Spinach, chopped, from frozen	1 cup	205	45	6	1	—	8	232	4.3	16,200	.14	.31
Sweet potatoes, baked in skin, peeled	1	114	160	2	1	—	37	46	1.0	9,230	.10	.08
Tomatoes, raw	1	135	25	1	T	—	6	16	.6	1,110	.07	.05
Miscellaneous												
Beer	12 fl. oz.	360	150	1	0	0	14	18	T	—	.01	.11
Gin, rum, vodka, whisky, 86 proof	1-1/2 fl. oz.	42	105	—	—	0	T	—	—	—	—	—
Wine, table	3-1/2 fl. oz.	102	85	T	0	0	4	9	.4	—	T	.01
Cola-type beverage	12 fl. oz.	369	145	0	0	0	37	—	—	0	0	0
Ginger ale	12 fl. oz	366	115	0	0	0	29	—	—	0	0	0
Gelatin dessert	1 cup	240	140	4	0	0	34	—	—	—	—	—
Olives, pickled, green	4 medium	16	15	T	2	.2	T	8	.2	40	—	—
Pickles, dill, whole	1	65	5	T	T	—	1	17	.7	70	T	.01
Popsicle, 3 fl. oz.	1	95	70	0	0	0	18	0	T	0	0	0
Soup, tomato, prepared with water	1 cup	245	90	2	3	.5	16	15	.7	1,000	.05	.05

T — Indicates trace * — Varies by brand

Calories Used Per Minute According to Body Weight

Activity	Weight in Pounds 100	120	150	170	200	220
Volleyball (moderate)	2.3	2.7	3.4	3.9	4.6	5.0
Walking (3 mph)	2.7	3.2	4.0	4.6	5.4	5.9
Table tennis	2.7	3.2	4.0	4.6	5.4	5.9
Bicycling (5.5 mph)	3.1	3.8	4.7	5.3	6.3	6.9
Calisthenics	3.3	3.9	4.9	5.6	6.6	7.2
Skating (moderate)	3.6	4.3	5.4	6.1	7.2	7.9
Golf	3.6	4.3	5.4	6.1	7.2	7.9
Walking (4 mph)	3.9	4.6	5.8	6.6	7.8	8.5
Tennis	4.5	5.4	6.8	7.7	9.1	10.0
Canoeing (4 mph)	4.6	5.6	7.0	7.9	9.3	10.2
Swimming (breaststroke)	4.8	5.7	7.2	8.1	9.8	10.5
Bicycling (10 mph)	5.4	6.5	8.1	9.2	10.8	11.9
Swimming (crawl)	5.8	6.9	8.7	9.8	11.6	12.7
Jogging (11-min mile)	6.1	7.3	9.1	10.4	12.2	13.4
Handball	6.3	7.6	9.5	10.7	12.7	13.9
Racquetball	6.3	7.6	9.5	10.7	12.7	13.9
Skiing (downhill)	6.3	7.6	9.5	10.7	12.7	13.9
Mountain climbing	6.6	8.0	10.0	11.3	13.3	14.6
Squash	6.8	8.1	10.2	11.5	13.6	14.9
Skiing (cross-country)	7.2	8.7	10.8	12.3	14.5	15.9
Running (8-min. mile)	9.4	11.3	14.1	16.0	18.8	20.7

Note: Many other factors, including air temperature, clothing, and the vigor with which a person exercises, can mean an increase or decrease in the number of calories used.

Food and Nutrition

Food contains proteins, carbohydrates, fats, water, vitamins and minerals. Nutrition is the way your body takes in and uses these ingredients to maintain proper functioning.

The U.S. Dept. of Health and Human Services and the Dept. of Agriculture issued dietary guidelines Nov. 5, 1990 that were the most specific ever, and covered children from age 2 as well as adults. Recommended were: (1) no more than 30 percent of calories from fat, or about 67 grams of fat in a 2,000-calorie daily diet; and no more than 10 percent or 22 grams of that from saturated fats high in cholesterol; (2) maximum alcohol consumption of about 1 drink a day for women, 2 for men; (3) daily consumption of vegetables of 3-5 servings; fruits, 2-4; pastas, cereals or breads, 6-11; milk, 2-3; meat, poultry, fish and eggs, 2-3. (For vegetables, 1 serving=about 1 cup raw leafy greens or one-half cup other kinds; fruit, 1 medium apple, banana, or orange; grains, 1 slice of bread or 1 oz. cereal; milk, 1 cup or 1.5 oz. of cheese; meat and poultry, 2-3 oz. cooked lean beef or chicken without skin.)

Protein

Proteins, composed of amino acids, are indispensable in the diet. They build, maintain, and repair the body. Best sources: eggs, milk, fish, meat, poultry, soybeans, nuts. High quality proteins such as eggs, meat, or fish supply all 8 amino acids needed in the diet.

Fats

Fats provide energy by furnishing calories to the body, and by carrying vitamins A, D, E, and K. They are the most concentrated source of energy in the diet. Best sources: butter, margarine, salad oils, nuts, cream, egg yolks, most cheeses, lard, meat.

Carbohydrates

Carbohydrates provide energy for body function and activity by supplying immediate calories. The carbohydrate group includes sugars, starches, fiber, and starchy vegetables. Best sources: grains, legumes, nuts, potatoes, fruits.

Water

Water dissolves and transports other nutrients throughout the body, aiding the processes of digestion, absorption, circulation, and excretion. It helps regulate body temperature.

Vitamins

Vitamin A—promotes good eyesight and helps keep the skin and mucous membranes resistant to infection. Best sources: liver, carrots, sweet potatoes, kale, collard greens, turnips, fortified milk.

Vitamin B_1 (thiamine)—prevents beriberi. Essential to carbohydrate metabolism and health of nervous system.

Vitamin B_2 (riboflavin)—protects skin, mouth, eye, eyelids, and mucous membranes. Essential to protein and energy metabolism. Best sources: liver, milk, meat, poultry, broccoli, mushrooms.

Vitamin B_6 (pyridoxine)—important in the regulation of the central nervous system and in protein metabolism. Best sources: whole grains, meats, nuts, brewers' yeast.

Vitamin B_{12} (cobalamin)—needed to form red blood cells. Best sources: liver, meat, fish, eggs, soybeans.

Niacin—maintains the health of skin, tongue, and digestive system. Best sources: poultry, peanuts, fish, organ meats, enriched flour and bread.

Other B vitamins—biotin, choline, folic acid (folacin), inositol, PABA (para-aminobenzoic acid), pantothenic acid.

Vitamin C (ascorbic acid)—maintains collagen, a protein necessary for the formation of skin, ligaments, and bones. It helps heal wounds and mend fractures, and aids in resisting some types of virus and bacterial infections. Best sources: citrus fruits and juices, turnips, broccoli, Brussels sprouts, potatoes and sweet potatoes, tomatoes, cabbage.

Vitamin D—important for bone development. Best sources: sunlight, fortified milk and milk products, fish-liver oils, egg yolks, organ meats.

Vitamin E (tocopherol)—helps protect red blood cells. Best sources: vegetable oils, wheat germ, whole grains, eggs, peanuts, organ meats, margarine, green leafy vegetables.

Vitamin K—necessary for formation of prothrombin, which helps blood to clot. Also made by intestinal bacteria. Best dietary sources: green leafy vegetables, tomatoes.

Minerals

Calcium—the most abundant mineral in the body, works with phosphorus in building and maintaining bones and teeth. Best sources: milk and milk products, cheese, and blackstrap molasses.

Phosphorus—the 2d most abundant mineral, performs more functions than any other mineral, and plays a part in nearly every chemical reaction in the body. Best source: whole grains, cheese, milk.

Iron—Necessary for the formation of myoglobin, which transports oxygen to muscle tissue, and hemoglobin, which transports oxygen in the blood. Best sources: organ meats, beans, green leafy vegetables, and shellfish.

Other minerals—chromium, cobalt, copper, fluorine, iodine, magnesium, manganese, molybdenum, potassium, selenium, sodium, sulfur, and zinc.

Recommended Daily Dietary Allowances

Source: Food and Nutrition Board, Natl. Academy of Sciences—Natl. Research Council; 1989

	Age (years) and sex group	Weight (lbs.)	Protein (grams)	Fat soluble vitamins: Vitamin A[1]	Vitamin D[2]	Vitamin E[3]	Vitamin K	Vitamin C	Water soluble vitamins: Thiamin (mg.)	Riboflavin (mg.)	Niacin (mg.)[4]	Vitamin B_6 (mg.)	Folate (micrograms)	Vitamin B_{12} (micrograms)	Minerals: Calcium (mg.)	Phosphorus (mg.)	Magnesium (mg.)	Iron (mg.)	Zinc (mg.)	Iodine (micrograms)	Selenium (micrograms)
Infants. . .	to 5 mos.	13	13	375	7.5	3	5	30	0.3	0.4	5	0.3	25	0.3	400	300	40	6	5	40	10
	to 1 yr.	20	14	375	10	4	10	35	0.4	0.5	6	0.6	35	0.5	600	500	60	10	5	50	15
Children. .	1-3	29	16	400	10	6	15	40	0.7	0.8	9	1.0	50	0.7	800	800	80	10	10	70	20
	4-6	44	24	500	10	7	20	45	0.9	1.1	12	1.1	75	1.0	800	800	120	10	10	90	20
	7-10	62	28	700	10	7	30	45	1.0	1.2	13	1.4	100	1.4	800	800	170	10	10	120	30
Males . . .	11-14	99	45	1000	10	10	45	50	1.3	1.5	17	1.7	150	2.0	1200	1200	270	12	15	150	40
	15-18	145	59	1000	10	10	65	60	1.5	1.8	20	2.0	200	2.0	1200	1200	400	12	15	150	50
	19-24	160	58	1000	10	10	70	60	1.5	1.7	19	2.0	200	2.0	1200	1200	350	10	15	150	70
	25-50	174	63	1000	5	10	80	60	1.5	1.7	19	2.0	200	2.0	800	800	350	10	15	150	70
	51+	170	63	1000	5	10	80	60	1.2	1.4	15	2.0	200	2.0	800	800	350	10	15	150	70
Females .	11-14	101	46	800	10	8	45	50	1.1	1.3	15	1.4	150	2.0	1200	1200	280	15	12	150	45
	15-18	120	44	800	10	8	55	60	1.1	1.3	15	1.5	180	2.0	1200	1200	300	15	12	150	50
	19-24	128	46	800	10	8	60	60	1.1	1.3	15	1.6	180	2.0	1200	1200	280	15	12	150	55
	25-50	138	50	800	5	8	65	60	1.1	1.3	15	1.6	180	2.0	800	800	280	15	12	150	55
	51+	143	50	800	5	8	65	60	1.0	1.2	13	1.6	180	2.0	800	800	280	10	12	150	55

(1) Retinol equivalents. (2) Micrograms of cholecalciferol. (3) Milligrams alpha-tocopherol equivalents. (4) Niacin equivalents.

ASTRONOMY AND CALENDAR

Edited by Dr. Kenneth L. Franklin, Astronomer Emeritus
American Museum-Hayden Planetarium

Celestial Events Highlights, 1993

(Greenwich Mean Time, or as indicated)

This year begins with all the planets but Mercury visible in nighttime hours. At dusk, Venus is our brilliant evening star, with Saturn, for a few days, shining bravely below it after twilight ends. Before Venus leaves for the morning sky, it and the Moon play a nice pas de deux the evening of February 24, Venus being occulted for New Zealand observers on their 25th. In the east, Mars is the bright reddish object rising about sunset in the northeast. About midnight, Jupiter rises with Virgo to share the remainder of the night with Mars. Mars will fade rapidly, but linger in the evening for many months as Jupiter overtakes it in late summer; they approach each other to within a degree early in September. Then Saturn dominates the night sky until the end of the year. Early risers may enjoy watching Venus and Jupiter trade places on the mornings of November 8 and 9. During the 8th, they will be less than a moon-diameter apart.

Mercury takes a rare spotlight this year, crossing before the face of the Sun November 6. Mercury and Venus both lying in orbits closer to the Sun than the Earth, can transit the solar disk as seen from our place in space, but Mercury does it more often. There are 14 transits of Mercury during the 20th century, 4 in May, 10 in November. The last was November 13, 1986, the next, November 15, 1999. Transits of Venus are rare affairs, the last December 6, 1882, the next June 8, 2004.

Some phases of the partial solar eclipse of May 21 are visible from all of the United States except the east and southeast, but these areas do not miss much of a spectacle. The total lunar eclipse of June is partially visible from the west, but the whole north half of the western hemisphere and much of western South America will see the whole lunar eclipse November 9, weather permitting. Although totality lasts only 47 minutes, one should take advantage of it; the next one seen from about the same area will be January 21, 2000.

A few years ago, some astronomers hoped for the uncertain return of the comet responsible for the yearly Perseid meteor shower stream. But periodic comet Swift-Tuttle apparently was not observed, if it did come back. However, the Perseid meteor shower had unusual activity in 1991, possibly in 1992. Will it be even better this year? Is P/Swift-Tuttle still on its way, or should comet P/Kegler, last seen in 1737, be given responsibility for the annual "Old Faithful" of meteor showers? Keep looking up!

Of bright objects, only Venus is occulted this year, and then only twice.

January

Mercury begins the year at the edge of morning twilight, and dives deeper toward the Sun, passing superior conjunction on the 23rd, becoming an evening star.

Venus starts the year as our brilliant evening star, being 47° east of the sun on the 19th.

Mars, resembling a ruddy −1.4 magnitude star in Gemini, starts this year with a week in our morning sky before its opposition position on the 7th when it enters our evening sky, remaining there until conjunction with the Sun December 27, fading all the while.

Jupiter, brighter than Mars, begins its retrograde, western motion in our morning sky prior to its opposition at the end of March, remaining in Virgo until mid-December.

Saturn, now low in our evening twilight in Capricornus, becomes unobservable by month's end, being too close to the sun.

Moon passes Mars on the 8th, Jupiter on the 14th, and Venus on the 27th.

Jan. 3—Mars and Earth closest, 57.8 million miles apart.

Jan. 4—Earth at perihelion, 91.4 million miles from the Sun, closest this year; Quadrantid meteor shower.

Jan. 7—Mars at opposition, 58 million miles from Earth.

Jan. 8—Uranus in conjunction with the Sun, 1,910 million miles away from Earth; Moon passes 6° South of Mars; Neptune in conjunction with the Sun, nearly 2,900 million miles from us.

Jan. 14—Moon passes 7° South of Jupiter.

Jan. 19—Venus at greatest elongation, 47° east of the Sun; Sun enters Capricornus.

Jan. 23—Mercury in superior conjunction, entering the evening sky.

Jan. 25—Uranus passes 1.1° South of Neptune in Sagittarius.

Jan. 27—Moon passes 5° North of Venus.

Jan. 29—Jupiter stationary, beginning its retrograde motion.

February

Mercury briefly appears low in our western evening twilight, at greatest elongation on the 21st, 18° east of the Sun.

Venus and the crescent Moon appear in a celestial spectacle this evening, Venus at greatest brilliancy, −4.5 magnitude, passing close to the north of the crescent Moon for observers in the western United States.

Mars, in Gemini, resumes its direct, eastward motion when it becomes stationary on the 15th.

Jupiter becomes even brighter in its retrograde motion in Virgo.

Saturn is in conjunction with the Sun on the 9th passing into our morning sky, over 1,000 million miles from us.

Moon passes Mars on the 4th, Jupiter on the 10th, Neptune and Uranus on the 18th, Mercury on the 23rd, and occults Venus on the 25th.

Feb. 4—Moon passes 6° south of Mars.

Feb. 9—Saturn in conjunction with the Sun, entering our morning sky.

Feb. 10—Moon passes 6° south of Jupiter.

Feb. 15—Mars stationary, resuming direct motion.

Feb. 16—Sun enters Aquarius.

Feb. 18—Moon passes 2° north of Neptune and 3° north of Uranus in Sagittarius.

Feb. 21—Mercury at greatest elongation, 18° east of the Sun.

Feb. 23—Moon passes 3° north of Mercury.

Feb. 25—Venus at greatest brilliancy; Moon passes 0.5° south of Venus, occulting the planet.

Feb. 27—Mercury stationary, beginning retrograde motion.

March

Mercury, becoming a morning star in inferior conjunction with the Sun on the 9th, just 58 million miles away from us, may be found brighter than a 1st magnitude star in the southeast in our morning twilight by month's end.

Venus, stationary on the 9th when it begins its retrograde motion, very rapidly enters deeply into the western twilight, becoming unobservable by the 3rd week of the month.

Mars is fading rapidly in Gemini.

Jupiter is at opposition to the Sun on the 30th, being closest to the Earth on the 31st, 414 million miles away.

Saturn emerges from the dawn twilight brighter than a 1st magnitude star in Capricornus.

Moon passes Mars on the 3rd, Jupiter on the 10th, Neptune and Uranus on the 17th, Saturn on the 20th, Mercury on the 21st, Venus on the 24th, and Mars again this month on the 31st.

Mar. 1—Pluto stationary, beginning retrograde motion.

Mar. 3—Moon passes 5° south of Mars.

Mar. 9—Mercury in inferior conjunction enters our morning sky; Venus stationary, beginning retrograde motion.

Mar. 10—Moon passes 6° south of Jupiter.

Mar. 11—Sun enters Pisces.

Mar. 17—Moon passes 2° north of Neptune, and 3° north of Uranus.

Mar. 20—Moon passes 6° north of Saturn; Vernal Equinox: Spring begins in the Northern Hemisphere, Fall in the Southern.

Mar. 21—Moon passes 4° north of Mercury; Mercury stationary, resuming direct motion.

Mar. 24—Moon passes 4° south of Venus.

Mar. 30—Jupiter at opposition, 414 million miles away from Earth, entering our evening sky.

Mar. 31—Moon passes 4° south of Mars.

April

Mercury remains in the morning sky all month, at greatest elongation, 28° west of the Sun, on the 5th, passing 8° south of Venus on the 16th.

Venus at inferior conjunction with the Sun on the 1st, 26 million miles from Earth, and now a morning star, emerges from the dawn twilight by the 2nd week of the month, passing about 8° north of Mercury on the 16th.

Mars, now resembles a reddish star a bit brighter than 1st magnitude, passing Pollux in Gemini on the 14th, and moving into Cancer about a week later.

Jupiter begins the month at magnitude −2.5 in Virgo, clearly dominating the night sky, but fading almost imperceptibly.

Saturn resembles a 1st magnitude star in the morning sky, crossing the Capricornus-Aquarius border about the first of this month.

Moon passes Jupiter on the 6th, Neptune and Uranus on the 13th, Mars on the 14th, Saturn on the 16th, occults Venus on the 19th, passes Mercury on the 20th, and Mars on the 29th.

Apr. 1—Venus in inferior conjunction, to become a morning star.

Apr. 5—Mercury at greatest elongation 28° west of the Sun.

Apr. 6—Moon passes 7° south of Jupiter.

Apr. 13—Moon passes 3° north of Neptune and 4° north of Uranus.

Apr. 14—Mars passes 5° south of Pollux.

Apr. 16—Mercury passes 8° south of Venus; Moon passes 7° north of Saturn.

Apr. 18—Sun enters Aries.

Apr. 19—Moon passes 0.5° north of Venus; occultation.

Apr. 20—Venus stationary, resuming direct motion; Moon passes 8° north of Mercury.

Apr. 22—Neptune stationary, beginning retrograde motion.

Apr. 26—Uranus stationary, beginning retrograde motion.

Apr. 29—Moon passes 6° south of Mars.

May

Mercury is unobservable all month, passing superior conjunction on the 16th, to become an evening star.

Venus, in Pisces, is at its greatest brilliancy on the 7th, being magnitude −4.5.

Mars, now a little fainter than 1st magnitude, leaves Cancer for Leo at month's end.

Jupiter is the prominent evening star in our southwestern sky.

Saturn is the brightest star-like object in western Aquarius, about 1st magnitude, still in our morning sky.

Moon passes Jupiter on the 3rd, Neptune on the 10th, Uranus on the 11th, Saturn on the 14th, Venus on the 18th, partially eclipses the Sun on the 21st, passes Mars on the 27th, and passes Jupiter again on the 30th.

May 3—Moon passes 7° south of Jupiter.

May 7—Venus at greatest brilliancy.

May 10—Moon passes 3° north of Neptune.

May 11—Moon passes 4° north of Uranus.

May 13—Sun enters Taurus.

May 14—Moon passes 7° north of Saturn; Pluto at opposition near the Libra-Serpens Caput border, and at its closest distance from the Earth this year, 2,673 million miles away.

May 16—Mercury in superior conjunction, 123 million miles away.

May 18—Moon passes 6° north of Venus.

May 21—Partial Solar Eclipse.

May 27—Moon passes 7° south of Mars.

May 30—Moon passes 7° south of Jupiter.

June

Mercury May be at its most visible this year, in the west after sunset most of this month, brightest at the beginning, at greatest elongation, 25° east of the Sun, on the 17th, and stationary on the 30th, beginning its retrograde motion.

Venus is at greatest elongation, 46° west of the Sun on the 10th, close to the Pisces-Aries-Cetus corner.

Mars, in Leo all month, is slightly fainter than Regulus, which it passes just 0.8° to the north on the 22nd.

Jupiter is the brightest star-like body in Virgo, considerably north of Corvus, becoming stationary on the 1st, resuming its direct motion.

Saturn, in Aquarius, is slowly brightening as it becomes stationary on the 11th, beginning its retrograde motion.

Moon enters fully into the Earth's shadow to be totally eclipsed on the 4th, passes Neptune and Uranus on the 7th, Saturn on the 10th, Mercury on the 22nd, Mars on the 24th, and Jupiter on the 27th.

June 1—Jupiter stationary, resuming direct motion.

June 4—Total Lunar Eclipse.

June 7—Moon passes 3° north of Neptune and 4° north of Uranus.

June 10—Venus at greatest elongation, 46° west of the Sun; Saturn stationary, beginning its retrograde motion.

June 16—Moon passes 6° north of Venus.

June 17—Mercury at greatest elongation, 25° east of the Sun.

June 20—Sun enters Gemini.

June 21—Mercury passes 7° south of Pollux; Summer Solstice: Summer begins in the Northern Hemisphere, winter in the Southern Hemisphere.

June 22—Moon passes 4° south of Mercury; Mars passes 0.8° north of Regulus.

June 24—Moon passes 7° south of Mars.

June 27—Moon passes 7° south of Jupiter.

June 30—Mercury stationary, beginning its retrograde motion.

July

Mercury is effectively unobservable this month, passing inferior conjunction on the 15th.

Venus graces our morning sky, rising at a point increasingly to the left as it moves through Taurus, actually entering part of Orion by month's end.

Mars, brighter than a 2nd magnitude star, moves eastward in Leo all this month.

Jupiter is gradually accelerating its direct, eastward, motion across Virgo, fading slowly as it goes.

Saturn remains in Aquarius this month, gradually brightening as it backpedals toward Capricornus.

Moon passes Neptune and Uranus on the 4th, Saturn on the 7th, Venus on the 16th, Mars on the 23rd, Jupiter on the 24th, and Neptune and Uranus again on the 31st.

July 4—Moon passes 3° north of Neptune, and 4° north of Uranus; Earth at aphelion, 94.4 million miles from the Sun, farthest this year.

July 7—Moon passes 7° north of Saturn.

July 12—Neptune and Uranus at opposition to the Sun; Uranus is over 1,727 million miles, and Neptune 2,711 million miles from Earth.

July 15—Mercury over 53 million miles from us at inferior conjunction, passing into the morning sky; Venus passes 3° north of Aldebaran.

July 16—Moon passes 2° north of Venus.

July 20—Sun enters Cancer.

July 23—Moon passes 6° south of Mars.

July 24—Moon passes 6° south of Jupiter.

July 25—Mercury stationary, resuming direct motion.

July 31—Moon passes 3° north of Neptune, and 4° north of Uranus.

August

Mercury is at greatest elongation, 19° west of the Sun on the 4th, passes far to the south of Pollux on the 6th, and is at superior conjunction on the 29th, beyond the Sun, nearly 127 million miles away, entering the evening sky.

Venus, still prominent in our morning sky, crosses Gemini into Cancer by the end of the month.

Mars closes on Jupiter as it moves into Virgo at the beginning of the month, but it is nearly 3.5 magnitudes fainter than the king of the sky.

Jupiter continues its stately march eastward through Virgo.

Saturn possesses the night sky as it rises about sunset and sets about sunrise this month as it passes through opposition on the 19th on the Aquarius-Capricornus border.

Moon passes Saturn on the 4th, Mercury on the 6th, Venus on the 15th, Mars on the 20th, Jupiter on the 21st, Neptune and Uranus on the 28th, and Saturn again on the 31st.

Aug. 4—Mercury at greatest elongation, 19° west of the Sun; Moon passes 7° north of Saturn.

Aug. 6—Mercury passes 8° south of Pollux.

Aug. 7—Pluto stationary, resuming its direct motion in Libra.

Aug. 10—Sun enters Leo.

Aug. 12—Perseid meteor shower.

Aug. 15—Moon passes 2° south of Venus.

Aug. 19—Saturn at opposition, 818 million miles from Earth.

Aug. 20—Moon passes 5° south of Mars.

Aug. 21—Moon passes 7° south of Jupiter.

Aug. 22—Venus passes 7° south of Pollux.

Aug. 28—Moon passes 3° north of Neptune and 4° north of Uranus.

Aug. 29—Mercury at superior conjunction, entering our evening sky.

Aug. 31—Moon passes 7° north of Saturn.

September

Mercury, although in the evening sky all month, moves out of the twilight to become barely discernable in the southwest after sunset, passing Jupiter on the 24th and Spica on the 26th.

Venus has the morning sky all to itself, this month, passing 0.4° north of Regulus on the 21st.

Mars, continuing its flight across Virgo, passes 0.9° south of Jupiter on the 7th (watch this close summit meeting the evening of the 6th), and 2° north of Spica on the 16th.

Jupiter is rapidly passed by Mars the night of the 6th, going into the 7th.

Saturn, now in Capricornus until the end of the year, has the evening sky almost all to itself.

Moon passes Venus on the 14th, Mercury and Jupiter on the 17th, Mars on the 18th, Neptune and Uranus on the 24th, and Saturn on the 27th.

Sep. 7—Mars passes 0.9° south of Jupiter.

Sep. 14—Moon passes 6° south of Venus.

Sep. 16—Mars passes 2° north of Spica; Sun enters Virgo.

Sep. 17—Moon passes 5° south of Mercury, and 5° south of Jupiter.

Sep. 18—Moon passes 4° south of Mars.

Sep. 21—Venus passes 0.4° north of Regulus.

Sep. 23—Autumnal equinox; Autumn begins in the Northern Hemisphere, Spring in the Southern.

Sep. 24—Moon passes 3° north of Neptune and 4° north of Uranus; Mercury passes 2° north of Jupiter.

Sep. 26—Mercury passes 1.1° north of Spica.

Sep. 27—Moon passes 7° north of Saturn; Uranus stationary, resuming its direct motion in Sagittarius.

Sep. 30—Neptune, stationary in Sagittarius, resumes its direct motion.

October

Mercury, 2° south of Mars on the 6th, is at greatest eastern elongation on the 14th, rewarding diligent observing into the southwest, to the left of the sunset point.

Venus enters western Virgo at mid-month, still the brightest morning star.

Mars stays in Virgo for a week before entering Libra, passing Mercury twice this month, on the 6th and 28th.

Jupiter is lost to observation this month, passing through conjunction with the Sun on the 18th, to become a morning star.

Saturn is stationary on the 28th in Capricornus.

Moon passes Venus on the 14th, Mars on the 16th, Mercury on the 17th, Neptune and Uranus on the 21st, and Saturn on the 24th.

Oct. 6—Mercury passes 2° south of Mars.

Oct. 14—Moon passes 7° south of Venus; Mercury at greatest elongation, 25° east of the Sun.

Oct. 16—Moon passes 1.7° south of Mars.

Oct. 17—Moon passes 1.7° north of Mercury.

Oct. 18—Jupiter in conjunction with the Sun, 599 million miles from Earth.

Oct. 21—Moon passes 3° north of Neptune and 4° north of Uranus; Orionid meteor shower.

Oct. 24—Moon passes 7° north of Saturn.

Oct. 26—Mercury stationary, beginning its retrograde motion.

Oct. 28—Mercury passes 2° south of Mars; Saturn stationary, resuming its direct motion.

Oct. 30—Sun enters Libra.

November

Mercury enters the morning sky at its inferior conjunction on the 6th, an event visible to observers in the eastern hemisphere as Mercury crosses the face of the Sun, then to be seen in the dawn twilight by month's end.

Venus, still brilliant in the morning twilight, passes Spica on the 2nd, and Jupiter on the 8th, slowly fading from easy view by the end of the month.

Mars is lost from sight for the rest of the year, getting too close to the Sun in the evening twilight.

Jupiter emerges from the dawn twilight to replace Venus as the morning star.

Saturn has begun to slowly move toward Aquarius in eastern Capricornus.

Moon passes Jupiter and Venus on the 12th, partially eclipses the Sun on the 13th, passes Neptune and Uranus on the 18th, Saturn on the 20th, and is totally eclipsed on the 29th.

Nov. 2—Venus passes 4° north of Spica.

Nov. 6—Mercury in inferior conjunction, and in transit across the Sun, over 62 million miles away from Earth.

Nov. 8—Venus passes 0.4° north of Jupiter.

Nov. 12—Moon passes 4° south of Jupiter and 4° south of Venus.

Nov. 13—Partial Solar Eclipse.

Nov. 14—Mercury passes 0.7° north of Venus.

Nov. 15—Mercury stationary, resuming direct motion.

Nov. 17—Pluto in conjunction with the Sun, 2,855 million miles from the Earth; Leonid meteor shower.

Nov. 18—Moon passes 3° north of Neptune and 4° north of Uranus.

Nov. 20—Moon passes 7° north of Saturn.

Nov. 22—Mercury at greatest elongation, 20° west of the Sun; Sun enters Scorpius.

Nov. 29—Total Lunar Eclipse; Sun enters Ophiuchus.

December

Mercury is discernable in the dawn twilight for the first third of the month.

Venus is lost from sight until next year.

Mars is also unobservable, being in conjunction with the Sun on the 27th.

Jupiter enters Libra by mid-month, taking undisputed possession of the morning sky.

Saturn is our lone evening star, but considerably less conspicuous than Jupiter or Venus, crossing into Aquarius before the end of the year.

Moon passes Jupiter on the 10th, Neptune and Uranus on the 15th, and Saturn on the 18th.

Dec. 10—Moon passes 4° south of Jupiter.

Dec. 12—Mercury passes 5° north of Antares.

Dec. 13—Geminid meteor shower.

Dec. 15—Moon passes 3° north of Neptune and 4° north of Uranus.

Dec. 16—Sun enters Sagittarius.

Dec. 18—Moon passes 7° north of Saturn.

Dec. 21—Winter Solstice; Winter begins in the Northern Hemisphere, Summer in the Southern.

Dec. 27—Mars in conjunction with the Sun, over 225 million miles away from Earth.

Planets and the Sun

The planets of the solar system, in order of their mean distance from the sun, are Mercury, Venus, Earth, Mars, Jupiter, Saturn, Uranus, Neptune and Pluto. Both Uranus and Neptune are visible through good field glasses, but Pluto is so distant and so small that only large telescopes or long exposure photographs can make it visible.

Since Mercury and Venus are nearer to the sun than is the earth, their motions about the sun are seen from the earth as wide swings first to one side of the sun and then to the other, although they are both passing continuously around the sun in orbits that are almost circular. When their passage takes them either between the earth and the sun, or beyond the sun as seen from the earth, they are invisible to us. Because of the laws which govern the motions of planets about the sun, both Mercury and Venus require much less time to pass between the earth and the sun than around the far side of the sun, so their periods of visibility and invisibility are unequal.

The planets that lie farther from the sun than does the earth may be seen for longer periods of time and are invisible only when they are so located in our sky that they rise and set about the same time as the sun when, of course, they are overwhelmed by the sun's great brilliance. None of the planets has any light of its own but each shines only by reflecting sunlight from its surface. Mercury and Venus, because they are between the earth and the sun, show phases very much as the moon does. The planets farther from the sun are always seen as full, although Mars does occasionally present a slightly gibbous phase — like the moon when not quite full.

The planets move rapidly among the stars because they are very much nearer to us. The stars are also in motion, some of them at tremendous speeds, but they are so far away that their motion does not change their apparent positions in the heavens sufficiently for anyone to perceive that change in a single lifetime. The very nearest star is about 7,000 times as far away as the most distant planet.

Planets of the Solar System

Mercury

Mercury, nearest planet to the sun, is the second smallest of the nine planets known to be orbiting the sun. Its diameter is 3,100 miles and its mean distance from the sun is 36,000,000 miles.

Mercury moves with great speed in its journey about the sun, averaging about 30 miles a second to complete its circuit in 88 of our days. Mercury rotates upon its axis over a period of nearly 59 days, thus exposing all of its surface periodically to the sun. It is believed that the surface passing before the sun may have a temperature of about 800° F., while the temperature on the side turned temporarily away from the sun does not fall as low as might be expected. This night temperature has been described by Russian astronomers as "room temperature" — possibly about 70°. This would contradict the former belief that Mercury did not possess an atmosphere, for some sort of atmosphere would be needed to retain the fierce solar radiation that strikes Mercury. A shallow but dense layer of carbon dioxide would produce the "greenhouse" effect, in which heat accumulated during exposure to the sun would not completely escape at night. The actual presence of a carbon dioxide atmosphere is in dispute. Other research, however, has indicated a nighttime temperature approaching −300°.

This uncertainty about conditions upon Mercury and its motion arise from its shorter angular distance from the sun as seen from the earth, for Mercury is always too much in line with the sun to be observed against a dark sky, but is always seen during either morning or evening twilight.

Mariner 10 made 3 passes by Mercury in 1974 and 1975. A large fraction of the surface was photographed from varying distances, revealing a degree of cratering similar to that of the moon. An atmosphere of hydrogen and helium may be made up of gases of the solar wind temporarily concentrated by the presence of Mercury. The discovery of a weak but permanent magnetic field was a surprise. It has been held that both a fluid core and rapid rotation were necessary for the generation of a planetary magnetic field. Mercury may demonstrate these conditions to be unnecessary, or the field may reveal something about the history of Mercury.

Venus

Venus, slightly smaller than the earth, moves about the sun at a mean distance of 67,000,000 miles in 225 of our days. Its synodical revolution — its return to the same relationship with the earth and the sun, which is a result of the combination of its own motion and that of the earth — is 584 days. Every 19 months, then, Venus will be nearer to the earth than any other planet of the solar system. The planet is covered with a dense, white, cloudy atmosphere that conceals whatever is below it. This same cloud reflects sunlight efficiently so that when Venus is favorably situated, it is the third brightest object in the sky, exceeded only by the sun and the moon.

Spectral analysis of sunlight reflected from Venus' cloud tops has shown features that can best be explained by identifying the material of the clouds as sulphuric acid (oil of vitriol). Infrared spectroscopy from a balloon-borne telescope nearly 20 miles above the earth's surface gave indications of a small amount of water vapor present in the same region of the atmosphere of Venus. In 1956, radio astronomers at the Naval Research Laboratories in Washington, D. C., found a temperature for Venus of about 600° F., in marked contrast to minus 125° F., previously found at the cloud tops. Subsequent radio work confirmed a high temperature and produced evidence for this temperature to be associated with the solid body of Venus. With this peculiarity in mind, space scientists devised experiments for the U.S. space probe Mariner 2 to perform when it flew by in 1962. Mariner 2 confirmed the high temperature and the fact that it pertained to the ground rather than to some special activity of the atmosphere. In addition, Mariner 2 was unable to detect any radiation belts similar to the earth's so-called Van Allen belts. Nor was it able to detect the existence of a magnetic field even as weak as 1/100,000 of that of the earth.

In 1967, a Russian space probe, Venera 4, and the American Mariner 5 arrived at Venus within a few hours of each other. Venera 4 was designed to allow an instrument package to land gently on the planet's surface via parachute. It ceased transmission of information in about 75 minutes when the temperature it read went above 500° F. After considerable controversy, it was agreed that it still had 20 miles to go to reach the surface. The U.S. probe, Mariner 5, went around the dark side of Venus at a distance of about 6,000 miles. Again, it detected no significant magnetic field but its radio signals passed to earth through Venus' atmosphere twice — once on the night side and once on the day side. The results are startling. Venus' atmosphere is nearly all carbon dioxide and must exert a pressure at the planet's surface of up to 100 times the earth's normal sea-level pressure of one atmosphere. Since the earth and Venus are about the same size, and were presumably formed at the same time by the same general process from the same mixture of chemical elements, one is faced with the question: which is the planet with the unusual history — earth or Venus?

Radar astronomers using powerful transmitters as well as sensitive receivers and computers have succeeded in determining the rotation period of Venus. It turns out to be 243 days clockwise — in other words, contrary to the spin of most of the other planets and to its own motion around the sun. If it were exactly 243.16 days, Venus would always present the same face toward the earth at every inferior conjunction. This rate and sense of rotation allows a "day" on Venus of 117.4 earth days. Any part of Venus will receive sunlight on its clouds for over 58 days and will be in darkness for 58 days. Recent radar observations have shown surface features below the clouds. Large craters, continent-sized highlands, and extensive, dry "ocean" basins have been identified.

Mariner 10 passed Venus before traveling on to Mercury in 1974. The carbon dioxide molecule found in such abundance in the atmosphere is rather opaque to certain ultraviolet wavelengths, enabling sensitive television cameras to take pictures of the Venusian cloud cover. Photos radioed to earth show a spiral pattern in the clouds from equator to the poles.

In December, 1978, two U. S. Pioneer probes arrived at Venus. One went into orbit about Venus, the other split into 5 separate probes targeted for widely-spaced entry points to sample different conditions. The instrumentation ensemble was selected on the basis of previous missions that had shown the range of conditions to be studied. The probes confirmed expected high surface temperatures and high winds aloft. Winds of about 200 miles per hour, there, may account for the transfer of heat into the night side in spite of the low rotation speed of the planet. Surface winds were light at the time, however. Atmosphere and cloud chemistries were examined in detail, providing much data for continued analysis. The probes detected 4 layers of clouds and more light on the surface than expected solely from sunlight. This light allowed Russian scientists to obtain at least two photos showing rocks on the surface. Sulphur seems to play a large role in the chemistry of Venus, and reactions involving sulphur may be responsible for the glow. To learn more about the weather and atmospheric circulation on Venus, the orbiter takes daily photos of the daylight side cloud cover. It confirms the cloud pattern and its circulation shown by Mariner 10. The ionosphere shows large variability. The orbiter's radar operates in 2 modes: one, for ground elevation variability, and the second for ground reflectivity in 2 dimensions, thus "imaging" the surface. Radar maps of the entire planet that show the features mentioned above have been produced.

The Venus orbiter, Magellan, was launched May 5, 1989. It was equipped to observe Venus by a side-scanning radar system, together with one to gather data on variations in elevations directly beneath the craft. By mid 1991, Magellan had mapped all of the planet but a small fraction near one of the poles. The side-looking radar illuminates the surface and its features with radio waves, and records the strength and distance of returning echoes. Computer processing produces what seems to be a view of the landscape as if seen through a clear atmosphere from above, near sunset, with a resolution better than about a mile on Venus.

Craters over 20 miles wide are believed to have been caused by impacting bodies. One 150 mile-wide crater, the largest found to date, has been named for Margaret Mead. Smaller craters are probably due to volcanic action. The largest such caldera has been named Sakajawea. Many lava flows have been seen, and some old craters and plains seem to be filled with lava.

Most of the surface is believed to be younger than 1000 to 500 million years old. Modifications of previously existing surface features have been due to tectonic actions such as faulting, and to weathering. Tectonic actions in general are distinctly different from such actions on Earth. The intense heat at the surface of Venus can prevent the surface materials from cooling to the same brittle condition as on Earth. The same actions on Earth, thus, may produce somewhat different results on Venus. Although there are deep regions, somewhat similar to our ocean basins, there is no water to fill them. There seems to be no activity on Venus similar to our moving tectonic plates, but there may be local stretching and compressing that produce rift valleys and higher plains and mountains. Although there is no weathering due to water on Venus, the action of winds is in evidence. Extensive sand dunes have been seen, and wind-blown deposits indicate stable wind patterns for very long periods of time.

Magellan has been changed to a different orbit in order to see the same surface from a different direction, thus getting better third-dimension relief of the Venusian features. The orbiter's physical condition has deteriorated, thus future information may not be wholly compatible with that in hand.

Mars

Mars is the first planet beyond the earth, away from the sun. Mars' diameter is about 4,200 miles, although a determination of the radius and mass of Mars by the space-probe, Mariner 4, which flew by Mars on July 14, 1965 at a distance of less than 6,000 miles, indicated that these dimensions were slightly larger than had been previously estimated. While Mars' orbit is also nearly circular, it is somewhat more eccentric than the orbits of many of the other planets, and Mars is more than 30 million miles farther from the sun in some parts of its year than it is at others. Mars takes 687 of our days to make one circuit of the sun, traveling at about 15 miles a second. Mars rotates upon its axis in almost the same period of time that the earth does — 24 hours and 37 minutes. Mars' mean distance from the sun is 141 million miles, so that the temperature on Mars would be lower than that on the earth even if Mars' atmosphere were about the same as ours. The atmosphere is not, however, for Mariner 4 reported that atmospheric pressure on Mars is between 1% and 2% of the earth's atmospheric pressure. This thin atmosphere appears to be largely carbon dioxide. No evidence of free water was found.

There appears to be no magnetic field about Mars. This would eliminate the previous conception of a dangerous radiation belt around Mars. The same lack of a magnetic field would expose the surface of Mars to an influx of cosmic radiation about 100 times as intense as that on earth.

Deductions from years of telescopic observation indicate that 5/8ths of the surface of Mars is a desert of reddish rock, sand, and soil. The rest of Mars is covered by irregular patches that appear generally green in hues that change through the Martian year. These were formerly held to be some sort of primitive vegetation, but with the findings of Mariner 4 of a complete lack of water and oxygen, such growth does not appear possible. The nature of the green areas is now unknown. They may be regions covered with volcanic salts whose color changes with changing temperatures and atmospheric conditions, or they may be gray, rather than green. When large gray areas are placed beside large red areas, the gray areas will appear green to the eye.

Mars' axis of rotation is inclined from a vertical to the plane of its orbit about the sun by about 25° and therefore Mars has seasons as does the earth, except that the Martian seasons are longer because Mars' year is longer. White caps form about the winter pole of Mars, growing through the winter and shrinking in summer. These polar caps are now believed to be both water ice and carbon dioxide ice. It is the carbon dioxide that is seen to come and go with the seasons. The water ice is apparently in many layers with dust between them, indicating climatic cycles.

The canals of Mars have become more of a mystery than they were before the voyage of Mariner 4. Markings forming a network of fine lines crossing much of the surface of Mars have been seen there by men who have devoted much time to the study of the planet, but no canals have shown clearly enough in previous photographs to be universally accepted. A few of the 21 photographs sent back to earth by Mariner 4 covered areas crossed by canals. The pictures show faint, ill-defined, broad, dark markings, but no positive identification of the nature of the markings.

Mariners 6 & 7 in 1969 sent back many more photographs of higher quality than those of the pioneering Mariner 4. These pictures showed cratering similar to the earlier views, but in addition showed 2 other types of terrain. Some regions seemed featureless for many square miles, but others were chaotic, showing high relief without apparent organization into mountain chains or craters.

Mariner 9, the first artificial body to be placed in an orbit about Mars, has transmitted over 10,000 photographs covering 100% of the planet's surface. Preliminary study of these photos and other data shows that Mars resembles no other planet we know. Using terrestrial terms, however, scientists describe features that seem to be clearly of volcanic origin. One of these features is Nix Olympica, (now called Olympus Mons), apparently a shield volcano whose caldera is over 50 miles wide, and whose outer slopes are over 300 miles in diameter, and which stands about 90,000 feet above the surrounding plain. Some features may have been produced by cracking (faulting) of the surface and the sliding of one region over or past another. Many craters seem to have been produced by impacting bodies such as may have come from the nearby asteroid belt. Features near the south pole may have been produced by glaciers that are no longer present. Flowing water, non-existent on Mars at the present time, probably carved canyons, one 10 times longer and 3 times deeper than the Grand Canyon.

Although the Russians landed a probe on the Martian surface, it transmitted for only 20 seconds. In 1976, the U.S. landed 2 Viking spacecraft on the Martian surface. The landers had devices aboard to perform chemical analyses of the soil in search of evidence of life. The results have been inconclusive. The 2 Viking orbiters have returned the best pictures yet of Martian topographic features. Many features can be explained only if Mars once had large quantities of flowing water.

Mars' position in its orbit and its speed around that orbit in relation to the earth's position and speed bring Mars fairly close to the earth on occasions about two years apart and then move Mars and the earth too far apart for accurate observation and photography. Every 15-17 years, the close approaches are especially favorable to close observation.

Mars has 2 satellites, discovered in 1877 by Asaph Hall. The outer satellite, Deimos, revolves around Mars in about 31 hours. The inner satellite, Phobos, whips around Mars in a little more than 7 hours, making 3 trips around the planet each Martian day. Mariner and Viking photos show these bodies to be irregularly shaped and pitted with numerous craters. Phobos also shows a system of linear grooves, each about 1/3-mile across and roughly parallel. Phobos measures about 8 by 12 miles and Deimos about 5 by 7.5 miles in size.

Jupiter

Jupiter is the largest of the planets. Its equatorial diameter is 88,000 miles, 11 times the diameter of the earth. Its polar diameter is about 6,000 miles shorter. This is an equilibrium condition resulting from the liquidity of the planet and its extremely rapid rate of rotation: a Jupiter day is only 10 earth hours long. For a planet this size, this rotational speed is amazing, and it moves a point on Jupiter's equator at a speed of 22,000 miles an hour, as compared with 1,000 miles an hour for a point on the earth's equator. Jupiter is at an average distance of 480 million miles from the sun and takes almost 12 of our years to make one complete circuit of the sun.

The only directly observable chemical constituents of Jupiter's atmosphere are methane (CH_4) and ammonia (NH_3), but it is reasonable to assume the same mixture of elements available to make Jupiter as to make the sun. This would mean a large fraction of hydrogen and helium must be present also, as well as water (H_2O). The temperature at the tops of the clouds may be about minus 260° F. The clouds are probably ammonia ice crystals, becoming ammonia droplets lower down. There may be a space before water ice crystals show up as clouds: in turn, these become water droplets near the bottom of the entire cloud layer. The total atmosphere may be only a few hundred miles in depth, pulled down by the surface gravity (= 2.64 times earth's) to a relatively thin layer. Of course, the gases become denser with depth until they may turn into a slush or a slurry. Perhaps there is no surface — no real interface between the gaseous atmosphere and the body of Jupiter. Pioneers 10 and 11 provided evidence for considering Jupiter to be almost entirely liquid hydrogen. Long before a rocky core about the size of the earth is reached, hydrogen mixed with helium becomes a liquid metal at very high temperature and pressure. Jupiter's cloudy atmosphere is a fairly good reflector of sunlight and makes it appear far brighter than any of the stars.

Fourteen of Jupiter's 17 or more satellites have been found through earth-based observations. Four of the moons are large and bright, rivaling our own moon and the planet Mercury in diameter, and may be seen through a field glass. They move rapidly around Jupiter and their change of position from night to night is extremely interesting to watch. The other satellites are much smaller and in all but one instance much farther from Jupiter and cannot be seen except through powerful telescopes. The 4 outermost satellites are revolving around Jupiter clockwise as seen from the north, contrary to the motions of the great majority of the satellites in the solar system and to the direction of revolution of the planets around the sun. The reason for this retrograde motion is not known, but one theory is that Jupiter's tremendous gravitational power may have captured 4 of the minor planets or asteroids that move about the sun between Mars and Jupiter, and that these would necessarily revolve backward. At the great distance of these bodies from Jupiter — some 14 million miles — direct motion would result in decay of the orbits, while retrograde orbits would be stable. Jupiter's mass is more than twice the mass of all the other planets put together, and accounts for Jupiter's tremendous gravitational field and so, probably, for its numerous satellites and its dense atmosphere.

In December, 1973, Pioneer 10 passed about 80,000 miles from the equator of Jupiter and was whipped into a path taking it out of our solar system in about 50 years, and beyond the system of planets, on June 13, 1983. In December, 1974, Pioneer 11 passed within 30,000 miles of Jupiter, moving roughly from south to north, over the poles.

Photographs from both encounters were useful at the time but were far surpassed by those of Voyagers I and II. Thousands of high resolution multi-color pictures show rapid variations of features both large and small. The Great Red Spot exhibits internal counterclockwise rotation. Much turbulence is seen in adjacent material passing north or south of it. The satellites Amalthea, Io, Europa, Ganymede, and Callisto were photographed, some in great detail. Each is individual and unique, with no similarities to other known planets or satellites. Io has active volcanoes that probably have ejected material into a doughnut-shaped ring enveloping its orbit about Jupiter. This is not to be confused with the thin flat disk-like ring closer to Jupiter's surface. Now that such a ring has been seen by the Voyagers, older uncertain observations from Earth can be reinterpreted as early sightings of this structure.

Saturn

Saturn, last of the planets visible to the unaided eye, is almost twice as far from the sun as Jupiter, almost 900 million miles. It is second in size to Jupiter but its mass is much smaller. Saturn's specific gravity is less than that of water. Its diameter is about 71,000 miles at the equator; its rotational speed spins it completely around in a little more than 10 hours, and its atmosphere is much like that of Jupiter, except that its temperature at the top of its cloud layer is at least 100° lower. At about 300° F. below zero, the ammonia would be frozen out of Saturn's clouds. The theoretical construction of Saturn resembles that of Jupiter; it is either all gas, or it has a small dense center surrounded by a layer of liquid and a deep atmosphere.

Until Pioneer 11 passed Saturn in September 1979 only 10 satellites of Saturn were known. Since that time, the situation is quite confused. Added to data interpretations from the fly-by are earth-based observations using new techniques while the rings were edge-on and virtually invisible. It was hoped that the Voyager I and II fly-bys would help sort out the system. It is now believed that Saturn has at least 22 satellites, some sharing orbits. The Saturn satellite system is still confused.

Saturn's ring system begins about 7,000 miles above the visible disk of Saturn, lying above its equator and extending about 35,000 miles into space. The diameter of the ring system visible from Earth is about 170,000 miles; the rings are estimated to be no thicker than 10 miles. In 1973, radar observation showed the ring particles to be large chunks of material averaging a meter on a side.

Voyager I and II observations showed the rings to be considerably more complex than had been believed, so much so that interpretation will take much time. To the untrained eye, the Voyager photographs could be mistaken for pictures of a colorful phonograph record.

Uranus

Voyager II, after passing Saturn in August 1981, headed for a rendezvous with Uranus culminating in a fly-by January 24, 1986. This encounter answered many questions, and raised others.

Uranus, discovered by Sir William Herschel on Mar. 13, 1781, lies at a distance of 1.8 billion miles from the sun, taking 84 years to make its circuit around our star. Uranus has a diameter of about 32,000 miles and spins once in some 16.8 hours, according to fly-by data. One of the most fascinating features of Uranus is how far it is tipped over. Its north pole lies 98° from being directly up and down to its orbit plane. Thus, its seasons are extreme. When the sun rises at the north pole, it stays up for 42 years; then it sets and the north pole will be in darkness (and winter) for 42 years.

The satellite system of Uranus, consisting of at least 15 moons, (the 5 largest having been known before the fly-by) have orbits lying in the plane of the planet's equator. In that plane there is also a complex of rings, 9 of which were discovered in 1978. Invisible from Earth, the 9 original rings were found by observers watching Uranus pass before a star. As they waited, they saw their photoelectric equipment register several short eclipses of the star. Then the planet occulted the star as expected. After the star came out from behind Uranus, the star winked out several more times. Subsequent observations and analyses indicated the 9 narrow, nearly opaque rings circling Uranus. Evidence from the Voyager II fly-by has shown the ring particles to be predominantly a yard or so in diameter.

In addition to the 10 new, very small satellites, Voyager II returned detailed photos of the 5 large satellites. As in the case of other satellites newly observed in the Voyager program, these bodies proved to be entirely different from each other and any others. Miranda has grooved markings, reminiscent of Jupiter's Ganymede, but often arranged in a chevron pattern. Ariel shows rifts and channels. Umbriel is extremely dark, prompting some observers to regard its surface as among the oldest in the system. Titania has rifts and fractures, but not the evidence of flow found on Ariel. Oberon's main feature is its surface saturated with craters, unrelieved by other formations.

The structure of Uranus is subject to some debate. Basically, however, it may have a rocky core surrounded by a thick icy mantle on top of which is a crust of hydrogen and helium that gradually becomes an atmosphere. Perhaps continued analysis of the wealth of data returned by Voyager II will shed some light on this problem.

Neptune

Neptune, currently the most distant planet from the sun (until 1999), lies at an average distance of 2.8 billion miles. It was the last planet visited in Voyager II's epic 12 year trek from earth. While much new information was immediately perceived, much more must await further analysis of the tremendous amount of data returned from the spacecraft.

As with the other giant planets, there may be no solid surface to give real meaning to a measure of a diameter. However, a mean value of 30,600 miles may be assigned to a diameter between atmosphere levels where the pressure is about the same as sea level on earth, as determined by radio experimenters. A different radio observational technique gave evidence of a rotation period for the bulk of Neptune of 16.1 hours, a shorter value than the 18.2 hours given by the clouds seen in the blue atmosphere. Neptune orbits the sun in 164 years in nearly a circular orbit.

Voyager II, which passed 3000 miles from Neptune's north pole, found a magnetic field which is considerably asymmetric to the planet's structure, similar, but not so extreme, to that found at Uranus.

Neptune's atmosphere was seen to be quite blue, with quickly changing white clouds often suspended high above an apparent surface. In that apparent surface were found features, one of which was reminiscent of the Great Red Spot of Jupiter, even to the counterclockwise rotation expected in a high-pressure system in the southern hemisphere. Atmospheric constituents are mostly hydrocarbon compounds. Although lightning and auroras have been found on other giant planets, only the aurora phenomenon has been seen on Neptune.

Six new satellites were discerned around Neptune, one confirming a 1981 sighting that was then difficult to recover for proper identification. Five of these satellites orbit Neptune in a half day or less. Of the eight satellites of Neptune, the largest, Triton, is in a retrograde orbit suggesting that it was captured rather than being co-eval with Neptune. Triton is sufficiently large to raise significant tides on Neptune which will one day, say 100 million years from now, cause Triton to come close enough to Neptune for it to be torn apart. Nereid was found in 1949, and is in a long looping orbit suggesting it, too, was captured. Each of the satellites that has been photographed by the two Voyagers in the planetary encounters has been different from any of the other satellites, and certainly from any of the planets. Only about half of Triton has been observed, but its terrain shows cratering and a strange regional feature described as resembling the skin of a cantaloupe. Triton has a tenuous atmosphere of nitrogen with a trace of hydrocarbons, and evidence of active geysers injecting material into it. At minus 238 degrees Celsius, Triton is one of the coldest objects in the solar system observed by Voyager II.

In addition to the satellite system, Voyager II confirmed the existence of at least three rings composed of very fine particles. There may some clumpiness in their structure, but the known satellites may not contribute to the formation or maintenance of the rings, as they have in other systems.

As with the other giant planets, Neptune is emitting more energy than it receives from the sun, Voyager finding the excess to be 2.7 times the solar contribution. These excesses are thought to be cooling from internal heat sources and from the heat of formation of the planets.

Pluto

Although Pluto on the average stays about 3.6 billion miles from the sun, its orbit is so eccentric that its minimum distance of 2.7 billion miles is less than the current distance of Neptune. Thus Pluto, until 1999, is temporarily planet number 8 from the sun. At its mean distance, Pluto takes 247.7 years to circumnavigate the sun, a 3/2 resonance with Neptune. Until recently that was about all that was known of Pluto.

About a century ago, a hypothetical planet was believed to lie beyond Neptune and Uranus because neither planet followed the paths predicted by astronomers even when all known gravitational influences were considered. Little more than a guess, a mass of one Earth was assigned to the mysterious body and mathematical searches were begun. Amid some controversy about the validity of the predictive process, Pluto was found nearly where it was predicted to be. It was found by Clyde Tombaugh at the Lowell Observatory in Flagstaff, Ariz., in 1930.

At the U.S. Naval Observatory, also in Flagstaff, on July 2, 1978, James Christy obtained a photograph of Pluto that was distinctly elongated. Repeated observations of this shape and its variation were convincing evidence of the discovery of a satellite of Pluto, now named Charon. Subsequent observations show it to be 750 miles across, at a distance of over 12,000 miles from Pluto, and taking 6.4 days to move around Pluto. In this same length of time Pluto and Charon each rotate once around their individual axes. The Pluto-Charon system thus appears to rotate as virtually a ridged body. Gravitational laws allow these interactions to give us the mass of Pluto as 0.0020 of the Earth. This mass, together with a new diameter for Pluto of 1,430 miles makes the density about twice that of water. Theorists predict a rocky core for Pluto surrounded by a thick mantle of ice.

It is now clear that Pluto, the body found by Tombaugh, could not have influenced Neptune and Uranus to go astray. Theorists are again at work looking for a new planet X.

Because the rotational axis of the system is tipped from the reference plane of the solar system by about 98°.3, similar to that of Uranus, there is only a short interval every half solar period when Pluto and Charon alternately eclipse each other. Analysis of the variations in light in and out of the recent eclipses has led to the diameters quoted above, and to interesting knowledge of other aspects of the system. Each component is approximately spherical, but they are otherwise different. Pluto is red, Charon grey. Charon has a surface identified as water ice; Pluto's surface is frozen methane. There are large regions on Pluto that are dark, others, light; Pluto has spots, and, perhaps, polar caps. Although extremely cold, Pluto's methane surface produces a tenuous atmosphere that may be slowly escaping into space, perhaps going to Charon. When Pluto occulted a star, the star's light faded in such a way as to have passed through a haze layer lying above the planet's surface, indicating an inversion of temperatures, 110°K above, and 50°K below, suggesting Pluto has primitive weather.

There are tentative plans for a space-craft reconnaissance of the Pluto system, thus completing direct, close-up observation of each of the planets of the solar system.

Greenwich Sidereal Time for 0h GMT, 1993

(Add 12 hours to obtain Right Ascension of Mean Sun)

Date		h	m	Date		h	m	Date		h	m	Date		h	m
Jan.	1	06	42.6	Apr.	1	12	37.4	July	10	19	11.7	Oct.	8	01	06.5
	11	07	22.0		11	13	16.9		20	19	51.1		18	01	46.0
	21	08	01.5		21	13	56.3		30	20	30.6		28	02	25.4
	31	08	40.9	May	1	14	35.7	Aug.	9	21	10.0	Nov.	7	03	04.8
Feb.	10	09	20.3		11	15	15.1		19	21	49.4		17	03	44.2
	20	09	59.7		21	15	54.6		29	22	28.8		27	04	23.7
Mar.	2	10	39.2		31	16	34.0	Sept.	8	23	08.3	Dec.	7	05	03.1
	12	11	18.6	June	10	17	13.4		18	23	47.7		17	05	42.5
	22	11	58.0		20	17	52.9		28	00	27.1		27	06	21.9
					30	18	32.3								

Astronomical Signs and Symbols

☉	The Sun	⊕	The Earth	♅	Uranus	□	Quadrature
☾	The Moon	♂	Mars	♆	Neptune	☍	Opposition
☿	Mercury	♃	Jupiter	♇	Pluto	☊	Ascending Node
♀	Venus	♄	Saturn	☌	Conjunction	☋	Descending Node

Two heavenly bodies are in "conjunction" (☌) when they are due north and south of each other, either in Right Ascension (with respect to the north celestial pole) or in Celestial Longitude (with respect to the north ecliptic pole). If the bodies are seen near each other, they will rise and set at nearly the same time. They are in "opposition" (☍) when their Right Ascensions differ by exactly 12 hours, or their Celestial Longitudes differ by 180°. One of the two objects in opposition will rise while the other is setting. "Quadrature" (□) refers to the arrangement when the coordinates of two bodies differ by exactly 90°. These terms may refer to the relative positions of any two bodies as seen from the earth, but one of the bodies is so frequently the sun that mention of the sun is omitted; otherwise both bodies are named. The geocentric angular separation between sun and object is termed "elongation." Elongation is limited only for Mercury and Venus; the "greatest elongation" for each of these bodies is noted in the appropriate tables and is approximately the time for longest observation. When a planet is in its "ascending" (☊) or "descending" (☋) node, it is passing northward or southward, respectively, through the plane of the earth's orbit, across the celestial circle called the ecliptic. The term "perihelion" means nearest to the sun, and "aphelion," farthest from the sun. An "occultation" of a planet or star is an eclipse of it by some other body, usually the moon.

Planetary Configurations, 1993

Greenwich Mean Time (0 designates midnight; 12 designates noon; * = star; ☽ = moon)

Mo.	d. h. m.		
Jan.	3 14 -		♂ closest to ⊕
	4 03 -		⊕ closest to ☉; Perihelion
	7 23 -	☍ ♂ ☉	
	8 09 -	☌ ♅ ☉	
	8 13 -	☌ ♂ ☽	♂ 6° N
	8 22 -	☌ ♆ ☉	
	14 14 -	☌ ♃ ☽	♃ 7° N
	19 16 -		♀ Gr Elong; 47° E of ☉
	23 16 -	☌ ☿ ☉	Superior Conj.
	25 20 -	☌ ♅ ♆	♅ 1°.1 S
	27 05 -	☌ ♀ ☽	♀ 5° S
	29 13 -		♃ Stationary
Feb.	4 10 -	☌ ♂ ☽	♂ 6° N
	9 16 -	☌ ♄ ☉	
	10 22 -	☌ ♃ ☽	♃ 6° N
	15 11 -		♂ Stationary
	18 00 -	☌ ♆ ☽	♆ 2° S
	18 01 -	☌ ♅ ☽	♅ 3° S
	21 09 -		☿ Gr Elong; 18° E of ☉
	23 07 -	☌ ☿ ☽	☿ 3° S
	24 10 -		♀ Gr Brilliancy
	25 04 -	☌ ♀ ☽	♀ 0°.5 N; Occultation
	27 09 -		☿ Stationary
Mar.	1 13 -		♇ Stationary
	3 21 -	☌ ♂ ☽	♂ 5° N
	9 04 -	☌ ☿ ☉	☿ Inferior
	9 21 -		♀ Stationary
	10 04 -	☌ ♃ ☽	♃ 6° N
	17 07 -	☌ ♆ ☽	♆ 2° S
	17 09 -	☌ ♅ ☽	♅ 3° S
	20 08 -	☌ ♄ ☽	♄ 6° S
	20 14 41		Vernal Equinox; Spring begins in Northern Hemisphere
	21 13 -	☌ ☿ ☽	☿ 4° S; ☿ Stationary
	24 08 -	☌ ♀ ☽	♀ 4° N
	30 12 -	☍ ♃ ☉	
	31 19 -	☌ ♂ ☽	♂ 5° N
Apr.	1 13 -	☌ ♀ ☉	Inferior Conj.
	5 18 -		☿ Gr Elong; 28° W of ☉
	6 10 -	☌ ♃ ☽	♃ 7° N
	13 15 -	☌ ♆ ☽	♆ 3° S
	13 17 -	☌ ♅ ☽	♅ 4° S
	14 15 -	☌ ♂ *	♂ 5° S of Pollux
	16 11 -	☌ ☿ ♀	☿ 8° S
	16 20 -	☌ ♄ ☽	♄ 7° S
	19 17 -	☌ ♀ ☽	♀ 0°.5 S; Occultation
	20 02 -		♀ Stationary
	20 04 -	☌ ☿ ☽	☿ 8° S
	22 21 -		♆ Stationary
	26 12 -		♅ Stationary
	29 00 -	☌ ♂ ☽	♂ 6° N
May	3 15 -	☌ ♃ ☽	♃ 7° N
	7 04 -		♀ Gr Brilliancy
	10 23 -	☌ ♆ ☽	♆ 3° S
	11 02 -	☌ ♅ ☽	♅ 4° S
	14 07 -	☌ ♄ ☽	♄ 7° S
	14 23 -	☍ ♇ ☉	
	16 03 -	☌ ☿ ☉	Superior Conj.
	18 00 -	☌ ♀ ☽	♀ 6° S
	21 14 -		Partial Solar Eclipse
	27 07 -	☌ ♂ ☽	♂ 7° N
	30 21 -	☌ ♃ ☽	♃ 7° N
June	1 16 -		♃ Stationary
	4 13 -		Total Lunar Eclipse
	7 08 -	☌ ♆ ☽	♆ 3° S
	7 10 -	☌ ♅ ☽	♅ 4° S
	10 13 -		♀ Gr Elong; 46° W of ☉
	10 17 -	☌ ♄ ☽	♄ 7° S
	11 00 -		♄ Stationary
	16 10 -	☌ ♀ ☽	♀ 6° S
	17 17 -		☿ Gr Elong 25° E of ☉
	21 08 -	☌ ☿ *	☿ 7° S of Pollux
	21 09 00		Summer Solstice; Summer begins in Northern Hemisphere
	22 01 -	☌ ☿ ☽	☿ 4° N
	22 10 -	☌ ♂ *	♂ 0°.8 N of Regulus
	24 17 -	☌ ♂ ☽	♂ 7° N
	27 04 -	☌ ♃ ☽	♃ 7° N
	30 23 -		☿ Stationary
July	4 15 -	☌ ♆ ☽	♆ 3° S
	4 17 -	☌ ♅ ☽	♅ 4° S
	4 22 -		⊕ Farthest from ☉; Aphelion
	7 23 -	☌ ♄ ☽	♄ 7° S
	12 03 -	☍ ♆ ☉	
	12 14 -	☍ ♅ ☉	
	15 01 -	☌ ☿ ☉	Inferior Conj.
	15 07 -	☌ ♀ *	♀ 3° N of Aldebaran
	16 03 -	☌ ♀ ☽	♀ 2° S
	23 03 -	☌ ♂ ☽	♂ 6° N
	24 14 -	☌ ♃ ☽	♃ 6° N
	25 14 -		☿ Stationary
	31 21 -	☌ ♆ ☽	♆ 3° S
	31 22 -	☌ ♅ ☽	♅ 4° S
Aug.	4 02 -		☿ Gr Elong; 19° W of ☉
	4 04 -	☌ ♄ ☽	♄ 7° S
	6 02 -	☌ ☿ *	☿ 8° S
	7 01 -		♇ Stationary
	15 02 -	☌ ♀ ☽	♀ 2° N
	19 23 -	☍ ♄ ☉	
	20 16 -	☌ ♂ ☽	♂ 5° N
	21 04 -	☌ ♃ ☽	♃ 6° N
	22 23 -	☌ ♀ *	♀ 7° S of Pollux
	28 02 -	☌ ♆ ☽	♆ 3° S
	28 02 -	☌ ♅ ☽	♅ 4° S
	29 08 -	☌ ☿ ☉	Superior Conj.
	31 06 -	☌ ♄ ☽	♄ 7° S
Sept.	7 00 -	☌ ♂ ♃	♂ 0°.9 S
	14 03 -	☌ ♀ ☽	♀ 6° N
	16 10 -	☌ ♂ *	♂ 2° N of Spica
	17 08 -	☌ ☿ ☽	☿ 5° N
	17 22 -	☌ ♃ ☽	♃ 5° N
	18 06 -	☌ ♂ ☽	♂ 4° N
	21 06 -	☌ ♀ *	♀ 0°.4 N of Regulus
	23 00 22		Autumnal Equinox; Autumn begins in Northern Hemisphere
	24 07 -	☌ ♆ ☽	♆ 3° S
	24 07 -	☌ ♅ ☽	♅ 4° S
	24 12 -	☌ ☿ ♃	☿ 2° S
	26 08 -	☌ ☿ *	☿ 1°.1 N of Spica
	27 09 -	☌ ♄ ☽	♄ 7° S
	27 14 -		♅ Stationary
	30 03 -		♆ Stationary
Oct.	6 17 -	☌ ☿ ♂	☿ 2° S
	14 01 -	☌ ♀ ☽	♀ 7° N
	14 04 -		☿ Gr Elong; 25° E of ☉
	16 22 -	☌ ♂ ☽	♂ 1°.7 N
	17 05 -	☌ ☿ ☽	☿ 1°.7 S
	18 10 -	☌ ♃ ☉	
	21 14 -	☌ ♆ ☽	♆ 3° S
	21 14 -	☌ ♅ ☽	♅ 4° S
	24 13 -	☌ ♄ ☽	♄ 7° S
	26 03 -		☿ Stationary
	28 06 -	☌ ☿ ♂	☿ 2° S
	28 10 -		♄ Stationary
Nov.	2 23 -	☌ ♀ *	♀ 4° N of Spica
	6 04 -	☌ ☿ ☉	Inferior Conj. Transit over ☉
	8 13 -	☌ ♀ ♃	♀ 0°.4 N
	12 14 -	☌ ♃ ☽	♃ 4° N
	12 21 -	☌ ♀ ☽	♀ 4° N
	13 22 -		Partial Solar Eclipse
	14 13 -	☌ ☿ ♀	☿ 0°.7 N
	15 00 -		☿ Stationary
	17 18 -	☌ ♇ ☉	
	18 00 -	☌ ♆ ☽	♆ 3° S

Mo.	d. h. m.			
	18 01	-	☌ ♅ ☽	♅ 4° S
	20 22	-	☌ ♄ ☽	♄ 7° S
	22 16	-		☿ Gr Elong 20° W of ☉
	29 07	-		Total Lunar Eclipse
Dec.	10 08	-	☌ ♃ ☽	♃ 4° N
	12 22	-	☌ ☿ *	☿ 5° N of Antares

Mo.	d. h. m.			
	15 12	-	☌ ♆ ☽	♆ 3° S
	15 13	-	☌ ♅ ☽	♅ 4° S
	18 10	-	☌ ♄ ☽	♄ 7° S
	21 20 26			Winter Solstice; Winter begins in Northern Hemisphere
	27 02	-	☌ ♂ ☉	

Rising and Setting of Planets, 1993

Greenwich Mean Time (0 designates midnight)

Venus, 1993

	20° N. Latitude Rise	Set	30° N. Latitude Rise	Set	40° N. Latitude Rise	Set	50° N. Latitude Rise	Set	60° N. Latitude Rise	Set
Jan. 1	9:33	20:58	9:45	20:46	10:00	20:31	10:20	20:12	10:52	19:40
11	9:28	21:05	9:35	20:58	9:45	20:48	9:58	20:36	10:18	20:17
21	9:18	21:10	9:22	21:07	9:26	21:03	9:32	20:57	9:41	20:49
31	9:06	21:11	9:05	21:12	9:04	21:13	9:03	21:14	9:02	21:17
Feb. 10	8:49	21:08	8:44	21:13	8:39	21:18	8:31	21:26	8:19	21:39
20	8:27	20:58	8:19	21:06	8:09	21:16	7:55	21:31	7:33	21:53
Mar. 2	7:58	20:38	7:47	20:50	7:33	21:04	7:14	21:23	6:44	21:54
12	7:19	20:05	7:06	20:18	6:50	20:34	6:27	20:56	5:52	21:32
22	6:29	19:14	6:16	19:27	6:00	19:43	5:38	20:05	5:02	20:40
Apr. 1	5:33	18:10	5:22	18:20	5:09	18:34	4:51	18:51	4:22	19:20
11	4:41	17:07	4:34	17:14	4:25	17:23	4:12	17:35	3:53	17:54
21	4:01	16:18	3:56	16:23	3:50	16:29	3:42	16:36	3:30	16:48
May 1	3:32	15:46	3:28	15:49	3:24	15:54	3:18	15:59	3:09	16:08
11	3:11	15:27	3:08	15:30	3:03	15:35	2:57	15:41	2:47	15:50
21	2:56	15:16	2:51	15:21	2:45	15:27	2:37	15:35	2:25	15:48
31	2:45	15:12	2:38	15:19	2:30	15:27	2:19	15:39	2:01	15:57
June 10	2:37	15:12	2:28	15:22	2:17	15:33	2:01	15:49	1:37	16:14
20	2:32	15:16	2:20	15:28	2:05	15:43	1:45	16:03	1:13	16:36
30	2:29	15:22	2:15	15:37	1:57	15:55	1:32	16:20	0:51	17:01
July 10	2:29	15:31	2:13	15:48	1:52	16:09	1:22	16:39	0:33	17:28
20	2:33	9:07	15:41	15:59	1:51	16:23	1:17	16:57	0:20	17:54
30	2:39	9:15	15:51	16:11	1:54	16:37	1:18	17:13	0:16	18:16
Aug. 9	2:49	9:25	16:02	16:22	2:03	16:48	1:26	17:24	0:22	18:29
19	3:01	9:36	16:11	16:31	2:16	16:55	1:41	17:30	0:40	18:31
29	3:14	16:19	2:56	16:37	2:34	16:59	2:02	17:31	1:08	18:24
Sept. 8	3:28	16:25	3:13	16:40	2:54	16:59	2:27	17:25	1:42	18:09
18	3:42	16:28	3:30	16:40	3:15	16:55	2:54	17:15	2:20	17:48
28	3:56	16:29	3:48	16:38	3:37	16:48	3:22	17:02	2:59	17:24
Oct. 8	4:09	16:29	4:05	16:34	3:59	16:39	3:51	16:47	3:39	16:58
18	4:23	16:28	4:22	16:29	4:22	16:29	4:21	16:30	4:19	16:31
28	4:36	16:28	4:40	16:24	4:44	16:19	4:50	16:13	4:59	16:04
Nov. 7	4:50	16:28	4:58	16:20	5:08	16:10	5:20	15:57	5:40	15:37
17	5:05	16:30	5:17	16:18	15:32	16:03	5:51	15:43	6:22	15:12
27	5:22	16:34	5:37	16:19	5:56	16:00	6:22	15:33	7:05	14:50
Dec. 7	5:39	16:42	5:57	16:23	6:20	16:00	6:52	15:28	7:46	14:34
17	5:56	16:52	6:17	16:32	6:43	16:06	7:19	15:29	8:23	14:26
27	6:13	17:06	6:35	16:44	7:02	16:17	7:41	15:39	8:49	14:30

Mars, 1993

	20° N. Latitude Rise	Set	30° N. Latitude Rise	Set	40° N. Latitude Rise	Set	50° N. Latitude Rise	Set	60° N. Latitude Rise	Set
Jan. 1	18:01	7:30	17:36	7:54	17:05	8:25	16:19	9:11	14:48	10:42
11	17:03	6:35	16:38	7:00	16:05	7:32	15:17	8:20	13:39	9:58
21	16:07	5:40	15:41	6:06	15:08	6:39	14:19	7:28	12:36	9:11
31	15:16	4:49	14:50	5:15	14:17	5:49	13:27	6:38	11:43	8:23
Feb. 10	14:31	4:04	14:06	4:30	13:32	5:03	12:43	5:52	11:00	7:35
20	13:53	3:24	13:27	3:49	12:54	4:22	12:06	5:11	10:26	6:51
Mar. 2	13:19	2:49	12:54	3:14	12:22	3:46	11:34	4:34	9:58	6:10
12	12:50	2:18	12:25	2:43	11:54	3:14	11:08	4:00	9:36	5:32
22	12:24	1:50	12:00	2:14	11:30	2:45	10:45	3:30	9:18	4:57
Apr. 1	12:01	1:25	11:38	1:48	11:09	2:18	10:25	3:01	9:04	4:23
11	11:41	1:01	11:18	1:23	10:50	1:52	10:09	2:33	8:53	3:49
21	11:22	0:39	11:00	1:00	10:33	1:27	9:55	2:06	8:45	3:16
May 1	11:04	0:17	10:44	0:37	10:19	1:02	9:43	1:38	8:39	2:42
11	10:47	23:53	10:29	0:14	10:05	0:38	9:32	1:11	8:35	2:08
21	10:32	23:33	10:14	23:50	9:53	0:13	9:23	0:44	8:32	1:34
31	10:16	23:12	10:01	23:27	9:42	23:46	9:15	0:16	8:30	1:00
June 10	10:02	22:51	9:48	23:04	9:31	23:21	9:07	23:45	8:29	0:26
20	9:47	22:30	9:35	22:42	9:21	22:56	9:01	23:16	8:28	23:48
30	9:33	22:09	9:23	22:19	9:11	22:31	8:54	22:47	8:28	23:13
July 10	9:19	21:48	9:11	21:56	9:02	22:06	8:49	22:18	8:28	22:39
20	9:05	21:28	9:00	21:33	8:53	21:40	8:43	21:49	8:28	22:04
30	8:52	21:07	8:49	21:10	8:44	21:14	8:38	21:20	8:29	21:29
Aug. 9	8:39	20:47	8:38	20:48	8:36	20:49	8:34	20:51	8:30	20:55
19	8:27	20:26	8:28	20:25	8:29	20:24	8:30	20:22	8:32	20:20
29	8:14	20:07	8:18	20:03	8:21	19:59	8:27	19:54	8:34	19:46
Sept. 8	8:03	19:47	8:08	19:42	8:15	19:35	8:24	19:26	8:37	19:12

		20° N. Latitude		30° N. Latitude		40° N. Latitude		50° N. Latitude		60° N. Latitude	
		Rise	Set	Rise	Set	Rise	Set	Rise	Set	Rise	Set
	18	7:52	19:29	7:59	19:21	8:09	19:11	8:22	18:58	8:41	18:39
	28	7:41	19:11	7:51	19:01	8:03	18:48	8:20	18:32	8:46	18:06
Oct.	8	7:32	18:54	7:44	18:42	7:59	18:27	8:19	18:06	8:51	17:34
	18	7:23	18:38	7:37	18:24	7:55	18:06	8:19	17:42	8:58	17:03
	28	7:15	18:24	7:31	18:07	7:51	17:47	8:19	17:19	9:04	16:34
Nov.	7	7:07	18:10	7:25	17:52	7:48	17:30	8:19	16:59	9:11	16:06
	17	7:01	17:59	7:20	17:39	7:45	17:15	8:19	16:40	9:18	15:41
	27	6:54	17:48	7:15	17:28	7:41	17:01	8:18	16:24	9:23	15:20
Dec.	7	6:48	17:40	7:10	17:18	7:37	16:51	8:16	16:12	9:25	15:03
	17	6:42	17:32	7:04	17:10	7:32	16:42	8:12	16:02	9:23	14:51
	27	6:36	17:26	6:58	17:04	7:26	16:36	8:05	15:56	9:17	14:45

Jupiter, 1993

		20° N. Rise	20° N. Set	30° N. Rise	30° N. Set	40° N. Rise	40° N. Set	50° N. Rise	50° N. Set	60° N. Rise	60° N. Set
Jan.	1	0:13	12:04	0:16	12:00	0:20	11:56	0:25	11:51	0:33	11:43
	11	23:33	11:27	23:36	11:23	23:37	11:19	23:46	11:13	23:54	11:05
	21	22:55	10:49	22:58	10:45	22:59	10:41	23:09	10:35	23:17	10:26
	31	22:16	10:10	22:19	10:06	22:20	10:02	22:29	9:56	22:38	9:47
Feb.	10	21:35	9:30	21:39	9:26	21:39	9:22	21:49	9:17	21:57	9:08
	20	20:54	8:49	20:57	8:46	20:57	8:42	21:06	8:36	21:14	8:29
Mar.	2	20:11	8:07	20:14	8:04	20:13	8:01	20:22	7:56	20:29	7:49
	12	19:27	7:25	19:30	7:22	19:28	7:19	19:37	7:15	19:43	7:09
	22	18:43	6:42	18:45	6:39	18:43	6:37	18:51	6:33	18:56	6:28
Apr.	1	17:58	5:58	18:00	5:57	18:02	5:54	18:04	5:52	18:08	5:48
	11	17:13	5:15	17:15	5:14	17:16	5:12	17:18	5:10	17:21	5:07
	21	16:29	4:32	16:30	4:31	16:31	4:30	16:32	4:29	16:34	4:27
May	1	15:46	3:50	15:46	3:49	15:47	3:48	15:48	3:47	15:49	3:46
	11	15:03	3:08	15:04	3:07	15:04	3:07	15:05	3:07	15:05	3:06
	21	14:22	2:27	14:22	2:27	14:22	2:26	14:23	2:26	14:23	2:26
	31	13:42	1:47	13:42	1:47	13:42	1:47	13:43	1:46	13:43	1:46
June	10	13:03	1:08	13:03	1:08	13:04	1:07	13:04	1:07	13:05	1:06
	20	12:26	0:30	12:26	0:29	12:27	0:29	12:27	0:28	12:28	0:27
	30	11:49	23:49	11:50	23:48	11:51	23:47	11:52	23:46	11:54	23:44
July	10	11:14	23:12	11:15	23:11	11:16	23:10	11:18	23:08	11:21	23:06
	20	10:40	22:37	10:41	22:35	10:43	22:33	10:45	22:31	10:49	22:27
	30	10:06	22:01	10:08	21:59	10:11	21:57	10:14	21:54	10:19	21:49
Aug.	9	9:33	21:27	9:36	21:24	9:39	21:21	9:43	21:17	9:49	21:11
	19	9:01	20:53	9:05	20:50	9:08	20:46	9:13	20:41	9:21	20:33
	29	8:30	20:19	8:34	20:15	8:38	20:11	8:44	20:05	8:54	19:55
Sept.	8	7:59	19:46	8:03	19:41	8:09	19:36	8:16	19:29	8:27	19:18
	18	7:28	19:13	7:33	19:08	7:40	19:02	7:48	18:53	8:01	18:40
	28	6:58	18:40	7:04	18:34	7:11	18:27	7:20	18:18	7:35	18:03
Oct.	8	6:28	18:08	6:34	18:01	6:42	17:53	6:53	17:42	7:09	17:26
	18	5:58	17:35	6:05	17:28	6:14	17:19	6:26	17:07	6:44	16:49
	28	5:28	17:03	5:36	16:55	5:45	16:45	5:58	16:32	6:18	16:12
Nov.	7	4:58	16:31	5:06	16:22	5:17	16:12	5:31	15:57	5:53	15:35
	17	4:27	15:58	4:37	15:49	4:48	15:38	5:03	15:22	5:27	14:59
	27	3:57	15:26	4:07	15:16	4:19	15:04	4:35	14:47	5:01	14:22
Dec.	7	3:26	14:53	3:37	14:43	3:49	14:30	4:07	14:12	4:34	13:45
	17	2:55	14:20	3:06	14:09	3:19	13:55	3:38	13:37	4:06	13:08
	27	2:23	13:46	2:34	13:35	2:49	13:21	3:08	13:02	3:38	12:31

Saturn, 1993

		20° N. Rise	20° N. Set	30° N. Rise	30° N. Set	40° N. Rise	40° N. Set	50° N. Rise	50° N. Set	60° N. Rise	60° N. Set
Jan.	1	8:55	20:08	9:10	19:53	9:28	19:35	9:53	19:10	10:34	18:30
	11	8:20	19:34	8:34	19:19	8:52	19:01	9:17	18:37	9:56	17:58
	21	7:45	18:59	7:59	18:45	8:16	18:28	8:40	18:04	9:18	17:26
	31	7:09	18:25	7:23	18:12	7:40	17:55	8:03	17:31	8:40	16:54
Feb.	10	6:34	17:51	6:48	17:38	7:04	17:21	7:27	16:59	8:03	16:23
	20	5:59	17:17	6:12	17:04	6:28	16:48	6:50	16:26	7:25	15:51
Mar.	2	5:24	16:43	5:36	16:30	5:52	16:15	6:13	15:54	6:47	15:20
	12	4:48	16:09	5:01	15:56	5:16	15:41	5:37	15:21	6:09	14:48
	22	4:13	15:34	4:25	15:22	4:39	15:07	5:00	14:47	5:31	14:16
Apr.	1	3:37	14:59	3:49	14:48	4:03	14:33	4:23	14:14	4:53	13:43
	11	3:01	14:24	3:12	14:13	3:26	13:59	3:45	13:39	4:15	13:09
	21	2:24	13:48	2:35	13:37	2:49	13:23	3:08	13:05	3:37	12:35
May	1	1:47	13:12	1:58	13:01	2:12	12:47	2:30	12:29	2:59	12:00
	11	1:10	12:35	1:21	12:24	1:34	12:11	1:52	11:53	2:20	11:24
	21	0:32	11:57	0:43	11:47	0:56	11:33	1:14	11:15	1:42	10:47
	31	23:49	11:19	0:04	11:08	0:17	10:55	0:35	10:37	1:03	10:09
June	10	23:10	10:40	23:21	10:29	23:34	10:16	23:52	9:58	0:24	9:30
	20	22:31	10:00	22:42	9:50	22:55	9:36	23:13	9:18	23:41	8:50
	30	21:51	9:20	22:02	9:09	22:15	8:56	22:33	8:38	23:02	8:09
July	10	21:10	8:39	21:21	8:28	21:35	8:14	21:53	7:56	22:22	7:27
	20	20:29	7:57	20:41	7:46	20:54	7:32	21:13	7:14	21:43	6:44
	30	19:48	7:15	20:00	7:04	20:14	6:50	20:33	6:31	21:03	6:01
Aug.	9	19:06	6:33	19:18	6:21	19:33	6:07	19:52	5:47	20:23	5:17
	19	19:25	5:50	18:37	5:38	18:51	5:24	19:11	5:04	19:43	4:32
	29	17:43	5:08	17:55	4:56	18:10	4:41	18:31	4:20	19:03	3:48
Sept.	8	17:01	4:25	17:14	4:13	17:29	3:58	17:50	3:37	18:23	3:04
	18	16:20	3:43	16:32	3:31	16:48	3:15	17:09	2:54	17:43	2:20
	28	15:39	3:02	15:51	2:49	16:07	2:33	16:29	2:12	17:03	1:37
Oct.	8	14:58	2:20	15:11	2:08	15:27	1:52	15:49	1:30	16:23	0:55
	18	14:18	1:40	14:31	1:27	14:47	1:11	15:09	0:49	15:43	0:15

		20° N. Latitude		30° N. Latitude		40° N. Latitude		50° N. Latitude		60° N. Latitude	
		Rise	Set	Rise	Set	Rise	Set	Rise	Set	Rise	Set
	28	13:38	1:00	13:51	0:47	14:07	0:31	14:29	0:09	15:04	23:31
Nov.	7	12:59	0:21	13:12	0:08	13:28	23:49	13:50	23:27	14:24	22:52
	17	12:21	23:39	12:34	23:27	12:49	23:11	13:11	22:49	13:45	22:15
	27	11:43	23:02	11:55	22:49	12:11	22:34	12:32	22:12	13:06	21:38
Dec.	7	11:05	22:25	11:18	22:13	11:33	21:57	11:54	21:36	12:28	21:03
	17	10:28	21:49	10:41	21:37	10:56	21:22	11:16	21.01	11:49	20:29
	27	9:52	21:14	10:04	21:02	10:19	20:47	10:39	20:27	11:11	19:55

Calculation of Risetimes

The *Daily Calendar* pages contain rise and set times for the Sun and Moon for the Greenwich Meridian at north latitudes 20°, 30°, 40°, 50°, and 60°. You probably live somewhere west of the Greenwich meridian, 0° longitude, and within the range of latitudes in the table. Notice that from day to day, the values for the sun at any particular latitude do not change very much. This slow variation for the sun means that no important correction needs to be made from one day to the next, once a proper correction for your latitude has been made. Thus, whenever it rises or sets at the 0° meridian, that will also be the time of that phenomenon at your Standard Time meridian. Any correction necessary for you to be able to observe that phenomenon from your location will be to account for your distance from the Standard Time meridian, and for your latitude.

The moon, however, moves its own diameter, about a half degree, in an hour, or about 12°.5 in one complete turn of the Earth—one day. Most of this is eastward against the background stars of the sky, but some is also north or south of the equator. If there is little change on the same day of the times over the range of latitudes, the moon is near the celestial equator. All of this motion considerably affects the times of rise or set, as you can see from the adjacent entries in the table. Thus, it is necessary also to take your longitude into account in addition to your latitude. If you have no need for total accuracy, simply note that the time will be between the four values you find surrounding your location and the dates of interest.

The process of finding more accurate corrections is called interpolation. In the example, linear interpolation, involving simple differences, is used four times: twice, once each in latitude and longitude for your location on the Earth; then twice for each moon rise, once each, again, for your latitude and your longitude. In extreme cases, higher order interpolation should be used. If such cases are important to you, it is suggested that you make a plot of the times, draw smooth curves through the plots, and interpolate by eye between the relevant curves. Some people find this exercise fun.

Let's find the time the Harvest Moon rises in Duluth, Minnesota.

First, where is Duluth? Find Duluth's latitude and longitude on page 270.

I. Duluth, Minnesota 46° 46′ 56″ N
92° 06′ 24″ W

IA. Convert these values to decimals:
56″/60 = 0′.933
46′ + 0′.933 = 46′.933
46′.933/60 = 0°.782
46° + 0°.782 = 46°.782 N
24″/60 = 0′.4
6′ + 0′.4 = 6′.4
6′.4/60 = 0°.107
92° + 0°.107 = 92°.107 W

IB. Fraction Duluth lies between 40° and 50°:
46°.782 − 40 = 6.782 of the 10°, or 0.678

IC. Fraction the world must turn between Greenwich and Duluth:
92°.107/360° = 0.256

ID. The CST meridian is 90°, thus 92°.107 − 90° = 2°.107 west of 90°. In 24 hours, there are 24 × 60 = 1440 minutes; 1440/360 = 4 minutes for every degree around the Earth. So events happen for Duluth 4 × 2°.107 = 8.4 minutes later (plus) than on the CST meridian of 90°.

IE. The values in IB and IC are the interpolates for Duluth; ID is the time correction from local to standard time for Duluth. These three numbers need never be calculated for Duluth again.

IIA. We need the Greenwich times of moonrise at latitudes 40° and 50°, and for September 30 and October 1, the day of the Harvest Full Moon and the day after.

	Lat. 40°	Diff.	50°
Sep. 30	17:18	− :09	17:09
diff.	:28		:30
Oct. 1	17:46	− :07	17:39

IIB. We want IB and the Sep. 30 time difference: 0.678 × (− 9) = − 4.1 minutes. Add this to the Sep. 30 Greenwich time: 17:18 − 4 = 17:14. Do the same for Oct. 1: 0.678 × (− 7) = 4.7, or 5 minutes. Add this to the Oct. 1 Greenwich rise time: 17:46 − 5 = 17:41. These two times are for the latitude of Duluth on the two days, but for Greenwich.

IIC. To get the time for Duluth, take the difference in the times just determined, 17:41 − 17:14 = 27, and find what proportion occurred while the Earth turned from Greenwich to Duluth, 0.256: 27 × 0.256 = 6.9, or 7 minutes.

IID. The moonrise at Duluth is, thus, 17:41 + 7 = 17:48, local, or sundial, time.

IIE. Local time is 8.4 minutes later (ID) than on the CST (90°) meridian, so CST time is 17:48 − 8 = 17:40. The Daylight correction is + 1 hour, so the final Duluth time of the Harvest Moon rise is 18:40, or 6:40 PM CDT.

Star Tables

These tables include stars of visual magnitude 2.5 and brighter. Co-ordinates are for mid-1992. Where no parallax figures are given, the trigonometric parallax figure is smaller than the margin for error and the distance given is obtained by indirect methods. Stars of variable magnitude designated by v.

To find the time when the star is on meridian, subtract R.A.M.S. of the sun table on page 243 from the star's right ascension, first adding 24h to the latter, if necessary. Mark this result P.M., if less than 12h; but if greater than 12, subtract 12h and mark the remainder A.M.

Star	Magnitude	Parallax "	Light yrs.	Right ascen. h. m.	Declination ° '
α Andromedae (Alpheratz)	2.06	0.02	90	0 08.3	29 03
β Cassiopeiae	2.27v	0.07	45	0 08.8	59 05
α Phoenicis	2.39	0.04	93	0 26.0	−42 20
α Cassiopeiae (Schedir)	2.23	0.01	150	0 40.1	56 30
β Ceti	2.04	0.06	57	0 43.3	−18 01
γ Cassiopeiae	2.47v	0.03	96	0 56.3	60 41
β Andromedae	2.06	0.04	76	1 09.4	35 35
α Eridani (Achernar)	0.46	0.02	118	1 37.5	−57 16
γ Andromedae	2.26		260	2 03.5	42 18
α Arietis	2.00	0.04	76	2 06.8	23 26
o Ceti	2.00v	0.01	103	2 19.0	−3 00
α Ursae Min. (Pole Star)	2.02v		680	2 24.8	89 14
β Persei (Algol)	2.12v	0.03	105	3 07.8	40 56
α Persei	1.80	0.03	570	3 23.9	49 50
α Tauri (Aldebaran)	0.85v	0.05	68	4 35.5	16 30
β Orionis (Rigel)	0.12v		900	5 14.2	−8 13
α Aurigae (Capella)	0.08	0.07	45	5 16.2	46 00
γ Orionis (Bellatrix)	1.64	0.03	470	5 24.8	6 21
β Tauri (El Nath)	1.65	0.02	300	5 25.9	28 36
δ Orionis	2.23v		1500	5 31.7	0 18
ε Orionis	1.70		1600	5 35.9	−1 12
ζ Orionis	2.05	0.02	1600	5 40.4	−1 57
κ Orionis	2.06	0.01	2100	5 47.4	−9 40
α Orionis (Betelgeuse)	0.50v		520	5 54.8	7 24
β Aurigae	1.90	0.04	88	5 59.1	44 57
β Canis Majoris	1.98	0.01	750	6 22.4	−17 57
α Carinae (Canopus)	−0.72	0.02	98	6 23.8	−52 42
γ Geminorum	1.93	0.03	105	6 37.3	16 24
α Canis Majoris (Sirius)	−1.46	0.38	8.7	6 44.9	−16 42
ε Canis Majoris	1.50		680	6 58.4	−28 58
δ Canis Majoris	1.86		2100	7 08.1	−26 23
η Canis Majoris	2.44		2700	7 23.8	−29 17
α Geminorum (Castor)	1.99	0.07	45	7 34.2	31 54
α Canis Minoris (Procyon)	0.38	0.29	11.3	7 39.0	5 15
β Geminorum (Pollux)	1.14	0.09	35	7 44.9	28 03
ζ Puppis	2.25		2400	8 03.4	−39 59
γ Velorum	1.82		520	8 09.3	−47 19
ε Carinae	1.86		340	8 22.4	−59 29
δ Velorum	1.96	0.04	76	8 44.5	−54 41
λ Velorum	2.21	0.02	750	9 07.8	−43 24
β Carinae	1.68	0.04	86	9 13.1	−69 41
ι Carinae	2.25		750	9 16.9	−59 15
κ Velorum	2.50	0.01	470	9 21.9	−55 00
α Hydrae	1.98	0.02	94	9 27.3	−8 38
α Leonis (Regulus)	1.35	0.04	84	10 08.0	12 00
γ Leonis	1.90	0.02	90	10 19.6	19 52

Star	Magnitude	Parallax "	Light yrs.	Right ascen. h. m.	Declination ° '
β Ursae Majoris (Merak)	2.37	0.04	78	11 01.5	56 25
α Ursae Majoris (Dubhe)	1.79	0.03	105	11 03.3	61 47
β Leonis (Denebola)	2.14	0.08	43	11 48.7	14 36
γ Ursae Majoris (Phecda)	2.44	0.02	90	11 53.5	53 44
α Crucis	1.58		370	12 26.2	−63 04
γ Crucis	1.63		220	12 30.8	−57 05
γ Centauri	2.17		160	12 41.2	−48 55
β Crucis	1.25v		490	12 47.3	−59 39
ε Ursae Majoris (Alioth)	1.77v	0.01	68	12 53.7	56 00
ζ Ursae Majoris (Mizar)	2.05	0.04	88	13 23.7	54 58
α Virginis (Spica)	0.97v	0.02	220	13 24.8	−11 07
ε Centauri	2.30v		570	13 39.5	−53 26
η Ursae Majoris (Alkaid)	1.86		210	13 47.3	49 21
β Centauri	0.61v	0.02	490	14 03.4	−60 21
θ Centauri	2.06	0.06	55	14 06.3	−36 20
α Bootis (Arcturus)	−0.04	0.09	36	14 15.4	19 13
η Centauri	2.31v		390	14 35.1	−42 08
α Centauri	−0.01	0.75	4.3	14 39.2	−60 48
α Lupi	2.30v		430	14 41.5	−47 22
ε Bootis	2.40	0.01	103	14 44.7	27 06
β Ursae Minoris	2.08	0.03	105	14 50.7	74 11
α Coronae Borealis	2.23v	0.04	76	15 34.4	26 44
δ Scorpii	2.32		590	16 00.0	−22 36
α Scorpii (Antares)	0.96v	0.02	520	16 29.0	−26 25
α Trianguli Australis	1.92	0.02	82	16 48.0	−69 01
ε Scorpii	2.29	0.05	66	16 49.7	−34 17
η Ophiuchi	2.43	0.05	69	17 10.0	−15 43
λ Scorpii	1.63v		310	17 33.2	−37 06
α Ophiuchi	2.08	0.06	58	17 34.6	12 34
θ Scorpii	1.87	0.02	650	17 36.8	−43 00
κ Scorpii	2.41v		470	17 42.0	−39 02
γ Draconis	2.23	0.02	108	17 56.5	51 29
ε Sagittarii	1.85	0.02	124	18 23.7	−34 23
α Lyrae (Vega)	0.03	0.12	26.5	18 36.7	38 47
σ Sagittarii	2.02		300	18 54.9	−26 18
α Aquilae (Altair)	0.77	0.20	16.5	19 50.5	8 51
γ Cygni	2.20		750	20 22.0	40 14
α Pavonis	1.94		310	20 25.1	−56 45
α Cygni (Deneb)	1.25		1600	20 41.2	45 15
ε Cygni	2.46	0.04	74	20 45.9	33 57
α Cephei	2.44	0.06	52	21 18.4	62 33
ε Pegasi	2.39		780	21 43.9	9 51
α Gruis	1.74	0.05	64	22 07.8	−47 00
β Gruis	2.11v		280	22 42.3	−46 55
α Piscis Austrinis (Fomalhaut)	1.16	0.14	22.6	22 57.3	−29 39
β Pegasi	2.42v	0.02	210	23 03.5	28 03
α Pegasi	2.49	0.03	109	23 04.4	15 10

Constellations

Culturally, constellations are imagined patterns among the stars that, in some cases, have been recognized through millenia of tradition. In the early days of astronomy, knowledge of the constellations was necessary in order to function as an astronomer. For today's astronomers, constellations are simply areas on the entire sky in which interesting objects await observation and interpretation.

Because western culture has prevailed in establishing modern science, equally viable and interesting constellations and celestial traditions of other cultures (of Asia or Africa, for example) are not well known outside of their regions of origin. Even the patterns with which we are most familiar today have undergone considerable change over the centuries, because the western heritage embraces teachings of cultures disparate in time as well as place.

Today, students of the sky the world over recognize 88 constellations that cover the entire celestial sphere. Many of these have their origins in ancient days; many are "modern," contrived out of unformed stars by astronomers a few centuries ago. Unformed stars were those usually too faint or inconveniently placed to be included in depicting the more prominent constellations. When astronomers began to travel to South Africa in the 16th and 17th centuries, they found a sky that itself was unformed, and showing numerous brilliant stars. Thus, we find constellations in the southern hemisphere like the "air pump," the "microscope," the "furnace," and other technological marvels of the time, as well as some arguably traditional forms, such as the "fly."

Many of the commonly recognized constellations had their origins in ancient Asia Minor—Syria, Babylon, etc. These were adopted by the Greeks and Romans who translated their names and stories into their own languages, some details being modified in the process. After the declines of these cultures, most such knowledge entered oral tradition, or remained hidden in monastic libraries. Beginning in the 8th century, the Moslem explosion spread through the Mediterranean world. Wherever possible, everything was translated into Arabic to be taught in the universities the Moslems established all over their new-found world.

In the 13th century, Alphonsus XX of Spain, an avid student of astronomy, succeeded in having Claudius Ptolemy's *Almagest,* as its Arabian title was known, translated into Latin. It thus became widely available to European scholars. In the process, the constellation names were translated, but the star names were retained in their Arabic forms. Transliterating Arabic into the Roman alphabet has never been an exact art, so many of the star names we use today only "seem" Arabic to all but scholars.

Names of stars often indicated what parts of the traditional figures they represented: Deneb, the tail of the swan; Betelgeuse, the armpit of the giant. Thus, the names were an indication of the position in the sky of a particular star, provided one recognized the traditional form of the mythic figure.

In English, usage of the Latin names for the constellations couples often inconceivable creatures, represented in unimaginable configurations, with names that often seem unintelligible. Avoiding traditional names, astronomers may designate the brighter stars in a constellation with Greek letters, usually in order of brightness. Thus, the "alpha star" is often the brightest star of that constellation. The "of" implies possession, so the genetive (possessive) form of the constellation name is used, as in Alpha Orionis, the first star of Orion (Betelgeuse). Astronomers usually use a 3-letter form for the constellation name, understanding it to be read as either the nominative or genitive case of the name.

Until the 1920's, astronomers used curved boundaries for the constellation areas. As these were rather arbitrary at best, the International Astronomical Union adopted boundaries that ran due north-south and east-west, filling the sky much as the contiguous states fill up the area of the "lower 48" United States.

Within these boundaries, and occasionally crossing them, popular "asterisms" are recognized: the Big Dipper is a small part of Ursa Major, the big bear; the Sickle is the traditional head and mane of Leo, the lion; one of the horntips of Taurus, the bull, properly belongs to Auriga, the charioteer; the northeast star of the Great Square of Pegasus is Alpha Andromedae.

It is unlikely that further change will occur in the realm of the celestial constellations.

Name	Genitive	Abbreviation	Meaning
Andromeda	Andromedae	And	Chained Maiden
Antlia	Antliae	Ant	Air Pump
Apus	Apodis	Aps	Bird of Paradise
Aquarius	Aquarii	Aqr	Water Bearer
Aquila	Aquilae	Aql	Eagle
Ara	Arae	Ara	Altar
Aries	Arietis	Ari	Ram
Auriga	Aurigae	Aur	Charioteer
Bootes	Bootis	Boo	Herdsmen
Caelum	Caeli	Cae	Chisel
Camelopardalis	Camelopardalis	Cam	Giraffe
Cancer	Cancri	Cnc	Crab
Canes Venatici	Canum Venaticorum	CVn	Hunting Dogs
Canis Major	Canis Majoris	CMa	Great Dog
Canis Minor	Canis Minoris	CMi	Little Dog
Capricornus	Capricorni	Cap	Sea-goat
Carina	Carinae	Car	Keel
Cassiopeia	Cassiopeiae	Cas	Queen
Centaurus	Centauri	Cen	Centaur
Cepheus	Cephei	Cep	King
Cetus	Ceti	Cet	Whale
Chamaeleon	Chamaeleontis	Cha	Chameleon
Circinus	Circini	Cir	Compasses (art)
Columba	Columbae	Col	Dove
Coma Berenices	Comae Berenices	Com	Berenice's Hair
Corona Australis	Coronae Australis	CrA	Southern Crown
Corona Borealis	Coronae Borealis	CrB	Northern Crown
Corvus	Corvi	Crv	Crow
Crater	Crateris	Crt	Cup
Crux	Crucis	Cru	Cross (southern)
Cygnus	Cygni	Cyg	Swan
Delphinus	Delphini	Del	Dolphin
Dorado	Doradus	Dor	Goldfish
Draco	Draconis	Dra	Dragon
Equuleus	Equulei	Equ	Little Horse
Eridanus	Eridani	Eri	River
Fornax	Fornacis	For	Furnace
Gemini	Geminorum	Gem	Twins
Grus	Gruis	Gru	Crane (bird)
Hercules	Herculis	Her	Hercules
Horologium	Horologii	Hor	Clock
Hydra	Hydrae	Hya	Water Snake (female)
Hydrus	Hydri	Hyi	Water Snake (male)
Indus	Indi	Ind	Indian
Lacerta	Lacertae	Lac	Lizard
Leo	Leonis	Leo	Lion
Leo Minor	Leonis Minoris	LMi	Little Lion
Lepus	Leporis	Lep	Hare
Libra	Librae	Lib	Balance
Lupus	Lupi	Lup	Wolf
Lynx	Lyncis	Lyn	Lynx
Lyra	Lyrae	Lyr	Lyre
Mensa	Mensae	Men	Table Mountain
Microscopium	Microscopii	Mic	Microscope
Monoceros	Monocerotis	Mon	Unicorn
Musca	Muscae	Mus	Fly
Norma	Normae	Nor	Square (rule)
Octans	Octantis	Oct	Octant
Ophiuchus	Ophiuchi	Oph	Serpent Bearer
Orion	Orionis	Ori	Hunter
Pavo	Pavonis	Pav	Peacock
Pegasus	Pegasi	Peg	Flying Horse
Perseus	Persei	Per	Hero
Phoenix	Phoenicis	Phe	Phoenix
Pictor	Pictoris	Pic	Painter
Pisces	Piscium	Psc	Fishes
Piscis Austrinius	Piscis Austrini	PsA	Southern Fish
Puppis	Puppis	Pup	Stern (deck)
Pyxis	Pyxidis	Pyx	Compass (sea)
Reticulum	Reticuli	Ret	Reticle
Sagitta	Sagittae	Sge	Arrow
Sagittarius	Sagittarii	Sgr	Archer
Scorpius	Scorpii	Sco	Scorpion
Sculptor	Sculptoris	Scl	Sculptor
Scutum	Scuti	Sct	Shield
Serpens	Serpentis	Ser	Serpent
Sextans	Sextantis	Sex	Sextant
Taurus	Tauri	Tau	Bull
Telescopium	Telescopii	Tel	Telescope
Triangulum	Trianguli	Tri	Triangle
Triangulum Australe	Trianguli Australis	TrA	Southern Triangle
Tucana	Tucanae	Tuc	Toucan
Ursa Major	Ursae Majoris	UMa	Great Bear
Ursa Minor	Ursae Minoris	UMi	Little Bear
Vela	Velorum	Vel	Sail
Virgo	Virginis	Vir	Maiden
Volans	Volantis	Vol	Flying Fish
Vulpecula	Vulpeculae	Vul	Fox

Aurora Borealis and Aurora Australis

The Aurora Borealis, also called the Northern Lights, is a broad display of rather faint light in the northern skies at night. The Aurora Australis, a similar phenomenon, appears at the same time in southern skies. The aurora appears in a wide variety of forms. Sometimes it is seen as a quiet glow, almost foglike in character; sometimes as vertical streamers in which there may be considerable motion; sometimes as a series of luminous expanding arcs. There are many colors, with white, yellow, and red predominating.

The auroras are most vivid and most frequently seen at about 20 degrees from the magnetic poles, along the northern coast of the North American continent and the eastern part of the northern coast of Europe. They have been seen as far south as Key West and as far north as Australia and New Zealand, but rarely.

While the cause of the auroras is not known beyond question, there does seem to be a definite correlation between auroral displays and sun-spot activity. It is thought that atomic particles expelled from the sun by the forces that cause solar flares speed through space at velocities of 400 to 600 miles per second. These particles are entrapped by the earth's magnetic field, forming what are termed the Van Allen belts. The encounter of these clouds of the solar wind with the earth's magnetic field weakens the field so that previously trapped particles are allowed to impact the upper atmosphere. The collisions between solar and terrestrial atoms result in the glow in the upper atmosphere called the aurora. The glow may be vivid where the lines of magnetic force converge near the magnetic poles.

The auroral displays appear at heights ranging from 50 to about 600 miles and have given us a means of estimating the extent of the earth's atmosphere.

The auroras are often accompanied by magnetic storms whose forces, also guided by the lines of force of the earth's magnetic field, disrupt electrical communication.

Eclipses, 1993

There are four eclipses, two of the sun and two of the moon; there is a transit of Mercury across the Sun.

I. Partial eclipse of the Sun, May 21.

This eclipse is generally visible in the Arctic regions, Canada except most of the Maritime Provinces, most of Alaska, the continental United States south and west of the Great Lakes except most of New England to the Gulf Coast and north to the Great Lakes, Greenland, Scotland, Scandinavia, former USSR north of the Black Sea and west of the Ural Mountains.

Circumstances of the Eclipse

Event	Date		h	m
Eclipse begins	May	21	12	18.3
Greatest eclipse		21	14	19.3
Eclipse ends		21	16	19.5

Magnitude of greatest eclipse: 0.736

II. Total eclipse of the Moon, June 4.

The beginning of the umbral phase is generally visible along the east coast of Asia, and in Australia, Antarctica, the Hawaiian Islands, southern Alaska, extreme western Canada, the western United States, most of Mexico, the coastal regions of Peru and Ecuador, southwestern South America, the Pacific Ocean, and the southeastern Indian Ocean. The end is visible in most of eastern and south central Asia, Madagascar Island, Australia, Antaractica, the Hawaiian Islands, the Aleutian Islands, the Indian Ocean, and the western Pacific Ocean.

Circumstances of the Eclipse

Event	Date		h	m
Moon enters penumbra	June	4	10	10.8
Moon enters umbra		4	11	11.2
Moon enters totality		4	12	12.2
Middle of eclipse		4	13	00.5
Moon leaves totality		4	13	48.7
Moon leaves umbra		4	14	49.7
Moon leaves penumbra		4	15	50.2

Magnitude of the eclipse: 1.567.

III. Partial eclipse of the Sun, November 13.

This eclipse is generally visible in the southern tip of South America, most of Antarctica, most of New Zealand, and southeastern Australia.

Circumstances of the Eclipse

Event	Date		h	m
Eclipse begins	Nov.	13	19	46.4
Greatest eclipse		13	21	44.9
Eclipse ends		13	23	43.2

Magnitude of greatest eclipse: 0.928

IV. Total eclipse of the Moon, November 28-29.

The beginning of the umbral phase is generally visible in extreme eastern and northern Asia, the Hawaiian Islands, North America, Central America, South America, the Arctic regions, Greenland, Europe, western Africa, the extreme western former USSR, the Palmer Peninsula of Antarctica, the eastern Pacific Ocean, and the Atlantic Ocean. The end is generally visible in northeastern Asia, most of New Zealand, the Hawaiian Islands, North America, Central America, South America except the extreme east, the Arctic regions, Greenland, the northern United Kingdom, the Pacific Ocean, and most of the North Atlantic Ocean.

Circumstances of the Eclipse

Event	Date		h	m
Moon enters penumbra	Nov.	29	3	27.1
Moon enters umbra		29	4	40.4
Moon enters totality		29	6	02.2
Middle of eclipse		29	6	26.1
Moon leaves totality		29	6	50.1
Moon leaves umbra		29	8	11.9
Moon leaves penumbra		29	9	25.0

Magnitude of the eclipse: 1.092

Transit of Mercury, 1993

A transit of Mercury over the face of the Sun will occur on November 6.

The beginning of the transit will be generally visible in the Hawaiian Islands, the Aleutians Islands except the eastern end, Siberia except the northeastern tip, western Pacific Ocean, New Zealand, Australia, the Indian Ocean, Asia, Antarctica except the Palmer Peninsula, the southeastern Arabian Peninsula, and extreme eastern Africa. The end is generally visible in Asia, Siberia except the eastern end, the western Pacific Ocean, New Zealand, Australia, Antarctica except the Palmer Peninsula, the Indian Ocean, Africa east of the South Atlantic coast, Turkey, and the southern former USSR from the western Black Sea.

Geocentric Circumstances of the Transit

Event	Date		h	m
Ingress, exterior contact	Nov.	6	3	05.9
Ingress, interior contact		6	3	11.8
Least angular distance from Sun's center		6	3	56.6
Egress, interior contact		6	4	41.4
Egress, exterior contact		6	4	47.2

Least angular distance: 15′16″.7

The Planets and the Solar System

Planet	Mean daily motion ″	Orbital velocity miles per sec.	Sidereal revolution days	Synodical revolution days	Dist. from sun in millions of mi. Max.	Min.	Dist. from Earth in millions of mi. Max.	Min.	Light at[1] perihelion	aphelion
Mercury . .	14732	29.75	88.0	115.9	43.4	28.6	136	50	10.58	4.59
Venus . . .	5768	21.76	224.7	583.9	67.7	66.8	161	25	1.94	1.89
Earth. . . .	3548	18.51	365.3	—	94.6	91.4	—	—	1.03	0.97
Mars	1886	14.99	687.0	779.9	155.0	128.5	248	35	0.524	0.360
Jupiter . . .	299	8.12	4331.8	398.9	507.0	460.6	600	368	0.0408	0.0336
Saturn . . .	120	5.99	10760.0	378.1	937.5	838.4	1031	745	0.01230	0.00984
Uranus. . .	42	4.23	30684.0	369.7	1859.7	1669.3	1953	1606	0.00300	0.00250
Neptune . .	21	3.38	60188.3	367.5	2821.7	2760.4	2915	2667	0.00114	0.00109
Pluto	14	2.95	90466.8	366.7	4551.4	2756.4	4644	2663	0.00114	0.00042

1. Light at perihelion and aphelion is solar illumination in units of mean illumination at Earth.

Planet	Mean longitude of:* ascending node °	′	″	perihelion °	′	″	Inclination* of orbit to ecliptic °	′	″	Mean* distance**	Eccentricity* of orbit	Mean longitude at the epoch* °	′	″
Mercury. . . .	48	15	17	77	21	22	7	00	18	.387098	.205630	17	40	22
Venus.	76	37	19	131	28	25	3	23	41	.723330	.006775	25	41	43
Earth	—	—	—	102	49	37	0	—	—	1.000001	.016711	309	36	58
Mars	49	31	7	335	56	36	1	50	59	1.523679	.093395	206	44	55
Jupiter	100	23	56	14	13	40	1	18	13	5.202603	.048484	199	27	16
Saturn	113	36	33	92	55	51	2	29	21	.554910	.055531	331	32	30
Uranus	73	58	21	172	54	35	0	46	23	19.218446	.046298	286	27	45
Neptune . . .	131	42	48	48	1	56	1	46	14	30.110387	.008988	290	14	5
Pluto*** . . .	110	05	49	223	35	53	17	09	44	39.469800	.248646	244	33	30

* Consistent for the standard Epoch: 1993 August 1 Ephemeris Time ** Astronomical units *** Consistent for the standard Epoch: 1990 April 19 Ephemeris Time

Sun and planets	Semi-diameter at unit distance ′ ″	Semi-diameter at mean least dist. ′ ″	in miles mean s.d.	Volume ⊕=1.	Mass. ⊕=1.	Density ⊕=1.	Sidereal period of rotation d.	h.	m.	s.	Gravity at surface ⊕=1.	Reflecting power Pct.	Probable temperature °F.
Sun.	959.62	——	432449	1299370	332946	0.26	24	16	48		27.9	——	+10,000
Mercury . . .	3.37	5.5	1515	0.0559	0.0553	1.00	58	15	30		0.37	0.11	+ 620
Venus	8.34	30.1	3760	0.8541	0.8150	0.97	243	R			0.88	0.65	+ 900
Earth	——	——	3963	1.000	1.000	1.00		23	56	6.7	1.00	0.37	+ 72
Moon	2.40	932.4	1080	0.020	0.0123	0.62	27	7	43		0.17	0.12	− 10
Mars	4.69	8.95	2108.5	0.1506	0.1074	0.73		24	37	26	0.38	0.15	− 10
Jupiter	98.35	23.4	44419	1403	317.89	0.25		9	3	30	2.64	0.52	− 240
Saturn	82.83	9.7	37448	832	95.18	0.13		10	39	22	1.15	0.47	− 300
Uranus	35.4	1.9	15881	63	14.54	0.23		17	14	R	1.15	0.40	− 340
Neptune . . .	33.4	1.2	15387	55	17.15	0.30		16	6		1.12	0.35	− 370
Pluto	1.9	0.05	714	0.006	0.0020	0.37	6	9	17		0.04	0.5	? ?

(R) retrograde of Venus and Uranus.

The Sun

The sun, the controlling body of our solar system, is a star whose dimensions cause it to be classified among stars as average in size, temperature, and brightness. Its proximity to the earth makes it appear to us as tremendously large and bright. A series of thermo-nuclear reactions involving the atoms of the elements of which it is composed produces the heat and light that make life possible on earth.

The sun has a diameter of 864,000 miles and is distant, on the average, 92,900,000 miles from the earth. It is 1.41 times as dense as water. The light of the sun reaches the earth in 499.012 seconds or slightly more than 8 minutes. The average solar surface temperature has been measured by several indirect methods which agree closely on a value of 6,000° Kelvin or about 10,000° F. The interior temperature of the sun is about 35,000,000 F.°.

When sunlight is analyzed with a spectroscope, it is found to consist of a continuous spectrum composed of all the colors of the rainbow in order, crossed by many dark lines. The "absorption lines" are produced by gaseous materials in the atmosphere of the sun. More than 60 of the natural terrestrial elements have been identified in the sun, all in gaseous form because of the intense heat of the sun.

Spheres and Corona

The radiating surface of the sun is called the **photosphere,** and just above it is the **chromosphere.** The chromosphere is visible to the naked eye only at times of total solar eclipses, appearing then to be a pinkish-violet layer with occasional great prominences projecting above its general level. With proper instruments the chromosphere can be seen or photographed whenever the sun is visible without waiting for a total eclipse. Above the chromosphere is the **corona,** also visible to the naked eye only at times of total eclipse. Instruments also permit the brighter portions of the corona to be studied whenever conditions are favorable. The pearly light of the corona surges millions of miles from the sun. Iron, nickel, and calcium are believed to be principal contributors to the composition of the corona, all in a state of extreme attenuation and high ionization that indicates temperatures on the order of a million degrees Fahrenheit.

Sunspots

There is an intimate connection between sunspots and the corona. At times of low sunspot activity, the fine streamers of the corona will be much longer above the sun's equator than over the polar regions of the sun, while during high sunspot activity, the corona extends fairly evenly outward from all regions of the sun, but to a much greater distance in space. Sunspots are dark, irregularly-shaped regions whose diameters may reach tens of thousands of miles. The average life of a sunspot group is from two to three weeks, but there have been groups that have lasted for more than a year, being carried repeatedly around as the sun rotated upon its axis. The record for the duration of a sunspot is 18 months. Sunspots reach a low point every 11.3 years, with a peak of activity occurring irregularly between two successive minima.

The sun is 400,000 times as bright as the full moon and gives the earth 6 million times as much light as do all the other stars put together. Actually, most of the stars that can be easily seen on any clear night are brighter than the sun.

The Zodiac

The sun's apparent yearly path among the stars is known as the **ecliptic.** The zone 16° wide, 8° on each side of the ecliptic, is known as the **zodiac.** Inside of this zone are the apparent paths of the sun, moon, earth, and major planets. Beginning at the point on the ecliptic which marks the position of the sun at the vernal equinox, and thence proceeding eastward, the zodiac is divided into twelve signs of 30° each, as shown herewith.

These signs are named from the twelve constellations of the zodiac with which the signs coincided in the time of the astronomer Hipparchus, about 2,000 years ago. Owing to the precession of the equinoxes, that is to say, to the retrograde motion of the equinoxes along the ecliptic, each sign in the zodiac has, in the course of 2,000 years, moved backward 30° into the constellation west of it; so that the sign Aries is now in the constellation Pisces, and so on. The vernal equinox will move from Pisces into Aquarius about the middle of the 26th century. The signs of the zodiac with their Latin and English names are as follows:

Spring	1.	♈ Aries.	The Ram.
	2.	♉ Taurus.	The Bull.
	3.	♊ Gemini.	The Twins.
Summer	4.	♋ Cancer.	The Crab.
	5.	♌ Leo.	The Lion.
	6.	♍ Virgo.	The Virgin.
Autumn	7.	♎ Libra.	The Balance.
	8.	♏ Scorpius.	The Scorpion.
	9.	♐ Sagittarius.	The Archer.
Winter	10.	♑ Capricorn.	The Goat.
	11.	♒ Aquarius.	The Water Bearer.
	12.	♓ Pisces.	The Fishes.

Moon's Perigee and Apogee, 1993

Perigee

Month	Day	h	Month	Day	h
Jan.	10	12	July	22	8
Feb.	7	20	Aug.	19	7
Mar.	8	9	Sept.	16	15
Apr.	15	19	Oct.	15	2
May.	4	0	Nov.	12	12
May.	31	11	Dec.	10	14
June	25	17			

Perihelion

Month	Day	h
Jan.	4	3

Apogee

Month	Day	h	Month	Day	h
Jan.	26	10	Aug.	7	4
Feb.	22	18	Sept.	3	17
Mar.	21	19	Sept.	30	17
Apr.	18	5	Oct.	28	0
May	15	22	Nov.	24	13
June	12	16	Dec.	22	8
July	10	11			

Aphelion

Month	Day	h
July	4	22

Moon Phases, 1993

Greenwich Mean Time

New Moon				First Q				Full Moon				Last Q			
Month	Day	h	m	Month	Day	h	m	Month	Day	h	m	Month	Day	h	m
				Jan.	1	3	38	Jan.	8	12	37	Jan.	15	4	01
Jan.	22	18	27	Jan.	30	23	20	Feb.	6	23	55	Feb.	13	14	57
Feb.	21	13	05	Mar.	1	15	46	Mar.	8	9	46	Mar.	15	4	16
Mar.	23	7	14	Mar.	31	4	10	Apr.	6	18	43	Apr.	13	19	39
Apr.	21	23	49	Apr.	29	12	40	May	6	3	34	May	13	12	20
May	21	14	06	May	28	18	21	June	4	13	02	June	12	5	36
June	20	1	52	June	26	22	43	July	3	23	45	July	11	22	49
July	19	11	24	July	26	3	25	Aug.	2	12	10	Aug.	10	15	19
Aug.	17	19	28	Aug.	24	9	57	Sept.	1	2	33	Sept.	9	6	26
Sept.	16	3	10	Sept.	22	19	32	Sept.	30	18	54	Oct.	8	19	35
Oct.	15	11	36	Oct.	22	8	52	Oct.	30	12	38	Nov.	7	6	36
Nov.	13	21	34	Nov.	21	2	03	Nov.	29	6	31	Dec.	6	15	49
Dec.	13	9	27	Dec.	20	22	26	Dec.	28	23	05				

Astronomical Constants; Speed of Light

The following were adopted in 1968, in accordance with the resolutions and recommendations of the International Astronomical Union (Hamburg 1964): Speed of light, 299,792.5 kilometers per second, or about 186,282.3976 statute miles per second; solar parallax, 8".794; constant of nutation, 9".210; and constant of aberration, 20".496.

The Moon

The moon completes a circuit around the earth in a period whose mean or average duration is 27 days 7 hours 43.2 minutes. This is the moon's sidereal period. Because of the motion of the moon in common with the earth around the sun, the mean duration of the lunar month — the period from one new moon to the next new moon — is 29 days 12 hours 44.05 minutes. This is the moon's synodical period.

The mean distance of the moon from the earth according to the American Ephemeris is 238,857 miles. Because the orbit of the moon about the earth is not circular but elliptical, however, the maximum distance from the earth that the moon may reach is 252,710 miles and the least distance is 221,463 miles. All distances are from the center of one object to the center of the other.

The moon's diameter is 2,160 miles. If we deduct the radius of the moon, 1,080 miles, and the radius of the earth, 3,963 miles from the minimum distance or perigee, given above, we shall have for the nearest approach of the bodies' surfaces 216,420 miles.

The moon rotates on its axis in a period of time exactly equal to its sidereal revolution about the earth — 27.321666 days. The moon's revolution about the earth is irregular because of its elliptical orbit. The moon's rotation, however, is regular and this, together with the irregular revolution, produces what is called "libration in longitude" which permits us to see first farther around the east side and then farther around the west side of the moon. The moon's variation north or south of the ecliptic permits us to see farther over first one pole and then the other of the moon and this is "libration in latitude." These two libration effects permit us to see a total of about 60% of the moon's surface over a period of time. The hidden side of the moon was photographed in 1959 by the Soviet space vehicle Lunik III. Since then many excellent pictures of nearly all of the moon's surface have been transmitted to earth by Lunar Orbiters launched by the U.S.

The tides are caused mainly by the moon, because of its proximity to the earth. The ratio of the tide-raising power of the moon to that of the sun is 11 to 5.

Harvest Moon and Hunter's Moon

The Harvest Moon, the full moon nearest the Autumnal Equinox, ushers in a period of several successive days when the moon rises soon after sunset. This phenomenon gives farmers in temperate latitudes extra hours of light in which to harvest their crops before frost and winter come. The 1993 Harvest Moon falls on Sept. 30 GMT. Harvest moon in the south temperate latitudes falls on Apr. 6.

The next full moon after Harvest Moon is called the Hunter's Moon, accompanied by a similar phenomenon but less marked; — Oct. 30, northern hemisphere; May 6, southern hemisphere.

The Earth: Size, Computation of Time, Seasons

Size and Dimensions

The earth is the fifth largest planet and the third from the sun. Its mass is 6 sextillion, 588 quintillion short tons. Using the parameters of an ellipsoid adopted by the International Astronomical Union in 1964 and recognized by the International Union of Geodesy and Geophysics in 1967, the length of the equator is 24,901.55 miles, the length of a meridian is 24,859.82 miles, the equatorial diameter is 7,926.41 miles, and the area of this reference ellipsoid is approximately 196,938,800 square miles.

The earth is considered a solid, rigid mass with a dense core of magnetic, probably metallic material. The outer part of the core is probably liquid. Around the core is a thick shell or mantle of heavy crystalline rock which in turn is covered by a thin crust forming the solid granite and basalt base of the continents and ocean basins. Over broad areas of the earth's surface the crust has a thin cover of sedimentary rock such as sandstone, shale, and limestone formed by weathering of the earth's surface and deposition of sands, clays, and plant and animal remains.

The temperature in the earth increases about 1°F. with every 100 to 200 feet in depth, in the upper 100 kilometers of the earth, and the temperature near the core is believed to be near the melting point of the core materials under the conditions at that depth. The heat of the earth is believed to be derived from radioactivity in the rocks, pressures developed within the earth, and original heat (if the earth in fact was formed at high temperatures).

Atmosphere of the Earth

The earth's atmosphere is a blanket composed of nitrogen, oxygen, and argon, in amounts of about 78, 21, and 1% by volume. Also present in minute quantities are carbon dioxide, hydrogen, neon, helium, krypton, and xenon.

Water vapor displaces other gases and varies from nearly zero to about 4% by volume. The height of the **ozone** layer varies from approximately 12 to 21 miles above the earth. Traces exist as low as 6 miles and as high as 35 miles. Traces of methane have been found.

The atmosphere rests on the earth's surface with the weight equivalent to a layer of water 34 ft. deep. For about 300,000 ft. upward the gases remain in the proportions stated. Gravity holds the gases to the earth. The weight of the air compresses it at the bottom, so that the greatest density is at the earth's surface. Pressure, as well as density, decreases as height increases because the weight pressing upon any layer is always less than that pressing upon the layers below.

The temperature of the air drops with increased height until the **tropopause** is reached. This may vary from 25,000 to 60,000 ft. The atmosphere below the tropopause is the **troposphere;** the atmosphere for about twenty miles above the tropopause is the **stratosphere,** where the temperature generally increases with height except at high latitudes in winter. A temperature maximum near the 30-mile level is called the **stratopause.** Above this boundary is the **mesosphere** where the temperature decreases with height to a minimum, the **mesopause,** at a height of 50 miles. Extending above the mesosphere to the outer fringes of the atmosphere is the **thermosphere,** a region where temperature increases with height to a value measured in thousands of degrees Fahrenheit. The lower portion of this region, extending from 50 to about 400 miles in altitude, is characterized by a high ion density, and is thus called the **ionosphere.** The outer region is called **exosphere;** this is the region where gas molecules traveling at high speed may escape into outer space, above 600 miles.

Latitude, Longitude

Position on the globe is measured by means of meridians and parallels. Meridians, which are imaginary lines drawn around the earth through the poles, determine **longitude.** The meridian running through Greenwich, England, is the **prime meridian of longitude,** and all others are either east or west. Parallels, which are imaginary circles parallel with the equator, determine **latitude.** The length of a degree of longitude varies as the cosine of the latitude. At the equator a degree is 69.171 statute miles; this is gradually reduced toward the poles. Value of a longitude degree at the poles is zero.

Latitude is reckoned by the number of degrees north or south of the equator, an imaginary circle on the earth's surface everywhere equidistant between the two poles. According to the IAU Ellipsoid of 1964, the length of a degree of latitude is 68.708 statute miles at the equator and varies slightly north and south because of the oblate form of the globe; at the poles it is 69.403 statute miles.

Computation of Time

The earth rotates on its axis and follows an elliptical orbit around the sun. The rotation makes the sun appear to move across the sky from East to West. It determines day and night and the complete rotation, in relation to the sun, is called the **apparent** or **true solar day.** This varies but an average determines the **mean solar day** of 24 hours.

The mean solar day is in universal use for civil purposes. It may be obtained from apparent solar time by correcting observations of the sun for the equation of time, but when high precision is required, the mean solar time is calculated from its relation to sidereal time. These relations are extremely complicated, but for most practical uses, they may be considered as follows:

Sidereal time is the measure of time defined by the diurnal motion of the vernal equinox, and is determined from observation of the meridian transits of stars. One complete rotation of the earth relative to the equinox is called the **sidereal day.** The **mean sidereal day** is 23 hours, 56 minutes, 4.091 seconds of mean solar time.

The **Calendar Year** begins at 12 o'clock midnight precisely local clock time, on the night of Dec. 31-Jan. 1. The day and the calendar month also begin at midnight by the clock. The interval required for the earth to make one absolute revolution around the sun is a **sidereal year;** it consisted of 365 days, 6 hours, 9 minutes, and 9.5 seconds of mean solar time (approximately 24 hours per day) in 1900, and is increasing at the rate of 0.0001-second annually.

The **Tropical Year,** on which the return of the seasons depends, is the interval between two consecutive returns of the sun to the vernal equinox. The tropical year consists of 365 days, 5 hours, 48 minutes, and 46 seconds in 1900. It is decreasing at the rate of 0.530 seconds per century.

In 1956 the unit of time interval was defined to be identical with the second of **Ephemeris Time,** 1/31,556,925.9747 of the tropical year for 1900 January Od 12th hour E.T. A physical definition of the second based on a quantum transition of cesium (atomic second) was adopted in 1964. The atomic second is equal to 9,192,631,770 cycles of the emitted radiation. In 1967 this atomic second was adopted as the unit of time interval for the Intern'l System of Units.

The Zones and Seasons

The five zones of the earth's surface are Torrid, lying between the Tropics of Cancer and Capricorn; North Temperate, between Cancer and the Arctic Circle; South Temperate, between Capricorn and the Antarctic Circle; The Frigid Zones, between the polar Circles and the Poles.

The inclination or tilt of the earth's axis with respect to the sun determines the seasons. These are commonly marked in the North Temperate Zone, where spring begins at the vernal equinox, summer at the summer solstice, autumn at the autumnal equinox and winter at the winter solstice.

In the South Temperate Zone, the seasons are reversed. Spring begins at the autumnal equinox, summer at the winter solstice, etc.

If the earth's axis were perpendicular to the plane of the earth's orbit around the sun there would be no change of seasons. Day and night would be of nearly constant length and there would be equable conditions of temperature. But the axis is tilted 23° 27′ away from a perpendicular to the orbit and only in March and September is the axis at right angles to the sun.

The points at which the sun crosses the equator are the equinoxes, when day and night are most nearly equal. The points at which the sun is at a maximum distance from the equator are the solstices. Days and nights are then most unequal.

In June the North Pole is tilted 23° 27′ toward the sun and the days in the northern hemisphere are longer than the nights, while the days in the southern hemisphere are shorter than the nights. In December the North Pole is tilted 23° 27′ away from the sun and the situation is reversed.

The Seasons in 1993

In 1993 the 4 seasons will begin as follows: add one hour to EST for Atlantic Time; subtract one hour for Central, two hours for Mountain, 3 hours for Pacific, 4 hours for Yukon, 5 hours for Alaska-Hawaii and six hours for Bering Time. Also shown in Greenwich Mean Time.

		Date	GMT	EST
Vernal Equinox	**Spring**	Mar. 20	14:41	9:41
Summer Solstice	**Summer**	June 21	9:00	4:00
Autumnal Equinox	**Autumn**	Sept. 23	00:22	19:22*
Winter Solstice	**Winter**	Dec. 21	20:26	15:26

* Previous Day

Poles of The Earth

The geographic (rotation) poles, or points where the earth's axis of rotation cuts the surface, are not absolutely fixed in the body of the earth. The pole of rotation describes an irregular curve about its mean position.

Two periods have been detected in this motion: (1) an annual period due to seasonal changes in barometric pressure, load of ice and snow on the surface and to other phenomena of seasonal character; (2) a period of about 14 months due to the shape and constitution of the earth.

In addition there are small but as yet unpredictable irregularities. The whole motion is so small that the actual pole at any time remains within a circle of 30 or 40 feet in radius centered at the mean position of the pole.

The pole of rotation for the time being is of course the pole having a latitude of 90° and an indeterminate longitude.

Magnetic Poles

The **north magnetic pole** of the earth is that region where the magnetic force is vertically downward and the **south magnetic pole** that region where the magnetic force is vertically upward. A compass placed at the magnetic poles experiences no directive force in azimuth.

There are slow changes in the distribution of the earth's magnetic field. These changes were at one time attributed in part to a periodic movement of the magnetic poles around the geographical poles, but later evidence refutes this theory and points, rather, to a slow migration of "disturbance" foci over the earth.

There appear shifts in position of the magnetic poles due to the changes in the earth's magnetic field. The center of the area designated as the north magnetic pole was estimated to be in about latitude 70.5° N and longitude 96° W in 1905; from recent nearby measurements and studies of the secular changes, the position in 1970 is estimated as latitude 76.2° N and longitude 101° W. Improved data rather than actual motion account for at least part of the change.

The position of the south magnetic pole in 1912 was near 71° S and longitude 150° E; the position in 1970 is estimated at latitude 66° S and longitude 139.1° E.

The direction of the horizontal components of the magnetic field at any point is known as magnetic north at that point, and the angle by which it deviates east or west of true north is known as the magnetic declination, or in the mariner's terminology, the **variation of the compass.**

A compass without error points in the direction of magnetic north. (In general this is *not* the direction of the magnetic north pole.) If one follows the direction indicated by the north end of the compass, he will travel along a rather irregular curve which eventually reaches the north magnetic pole (though not usually by a great-circle route). However, the action of the compass should not be thought of as due to any influence of the distant pole, but simply as an indication of the distribution of the earth's magnetism at the place of observation.

Rotation of The Earth

The speed of rotation of the earth about its axis has been found to be slightly variable. The variations may be classified as:

(A) **Secular.** Tidal friction acts as a brake on the rotation and causes a slow secular increase in the length of the day, about 1 millisecond per century.

(B) **Irregular.** The speed of rotation may increase for a number of years, about 5 to 10, and then start decreasing. The maximum difference from the mean in the length of the day during a century is about 5 milliseconds. The accumulated difference in time has amounted to approximately 44 seconds since 1900. The cause is probably motion in the interior of the earth.

(C) **Periodic.** Seasonal variations exist with periods of one year and six months. The cumulative effect is such that each year the earth is late about 30 milliseconds near June 1 and is ahead about 30 milliseconds near Oct. 1. The maximum seasonal variation in the length of the day is about 0.5 millisecond. It is believed that the principal cause of the annual variation is the seasonal change in the wind patterns of the Northern and Southern Hemispheres. The semiannual variation is due chiefly to tidal action of the sun, which distorts the shape of the earth slightly.

The secular and irregular variations were discovered by comparing time based on the rotation of the earth with time based on the orbital motion of the moon about the earth and of the planets about the sun. The periodic variation was determined largely with the aid of quartz-crystal clocks. The introduction of the cesium-beam atomic clock in 1955 made it possible to determine in greater detail than before the nature of the irregular and periodic variations.

Morning and Evening Stars, 1993

(GMT)

	Morning	Evening
Jan.	Mercury, Jan. 1 to 23 Mars, Jan. 1 to 7 Jupiter, Jan. 1 Uranus, from Jan. 8 Neptune, from Jan. 8 Pluto	Mercury, from Jan. 23 Venus, Jan. 1 Mars, from Jan. 7 Saturn, Jan. 1 Uranus, to Jan. 8 Neptune, to Jan. 8
Feb.	Jupiter Saturn, from Feb. 9 Uranus Neptune Pluto	Mercury Venus Mars Saturn, to Feb. 9
Mar.	Mercury, from Mar. 9 Jupiter, to Mar. 30 Saturn Uranus Neptune Pluto	Mercury, to Mar. 9 Venus Mars Jupiter, from Mar. 30
Apr.	Mercury Venus, from Apr. 1 Saturn Uranus Neptune Pluto	Mars Jupiter
May	Mercury, to May 16 Venus Saturn Uranus Neptune Pluto, to May 14	Mercury, from May 16 Mars Jupiter Pluto, from May 14
June	Venus Saturn Uranus Neptune	Mercury Mars Jupiter Pluto
July	Mercury, from July 15 Venus Saturn Uranus, to July 12 Neptune, to July 12	Mercury, to July 15 Mars Jupiter Uranus, from July 12 Neptune, from July 12 Pluto
Aug.	Mercury, to Aug. 29 Venus Saturn, to Aug. 19	Mercury, from Aug. 29 Mars Jupiter Saturn, from Aug. 19 Uranus Neptune Pluto
Sept.	Venus	Mercury Mars Jupiter Saturn Uranus Neptune Pluto
Oct.	Venus Jupiter, from Oct. 18	Mercury Mars Jupiter, to Oct. 18 Saturn Uranus Neptune Pluto
Nov.	Mercury, from Nov. 6 Venus Jupiter Pluto, from Nov. 17	Mercury, to Nov. 6 Mars Saturn Uranus Neptune Pluto, to Nov. 17
Dec.	Mercury Venus Mars, from Dec. 27 Jupiter Pluto	Mars, to Dec. 27 Saturn Uranus Neptune

Chronological Eras, 1993

The year 1993 of the Christian Era comprises the latter part of the 217th and the beginning of the 218th year of the independence of the United States of America.

Era	Year	Begins in 1993	
Byzantine	7502	Sept.	14
Jewish	5754	Sept.	15 (sunset)
Roman (Ab Urbe Condita)	2746	Jan.	14
Nabonassar (Babylonian)	2742	Apr.	25
Japanese	2653	Jan.	1
Grecian (Seleucidae)	2305	Sept. or Oct.	14
Diocletian	1710	Sept.	11
Indian (Saka)	1915	Mar.	22
Mohammedan (Hegira)	1414	June	20

Chronological Cycles, 1993

Dominical Letter	C	Golden Number (Lunar Cycle)	XVIII	Roman Indiction	1
Epact	6	Solar Cycle	14	Julian Period (year of)	6706

Astronomical Twilight—Meridian of Greenwich

Date 1993		20° Begin	20° End	30° Begin	30° End	40° Begin	40° End	50° Begin	50° End	60° Begin	60° End
		h m	h m	h m	h m	h m	h m	h m	h m	h m	h m
Jan.	1	5 16	6 50	5 30	6 35	5 45	6 21	6 00	6 07	6 18	5 49
	11	5 19	6 56	5 33	6 43	5 46	6 30	6 00	6 17	6 15	6 01
	21	5 21	7 01	5 32	6 51	5 43	6 40	5 55	6 30	6 06	6 18
Feb.	1	5 21	7 07	5 29	6 58	5 38	6 51	5 45	6 44	5 51	6 38
	11	5 18	7 11	5 24	7 05	5 29	7 01	5 32	6 59	5 32	7 01

Date 1993	20° Begin	20° End	30° Begin	30° End	40° Begin	40° End	50° Begin	50° End	60° Begin	60° End
	h m	h m	h m	h m	h m	h m	h m	h m	h m	h m
21	5 13	7 15	5 17	7 12	5 17	7 12	5 16	7 14	5 09	7 23
Mar. 1	5 08	7 18	5 08	7 19	5 06	7 21	4 59	7 29	4 44	7 45
11	5 00	7 21	4 58	7 24	4 50	7 32	4 38	7 46	4 12	8 12
21	4 52	7 24	4 45	7 32	4 33	7 44	4 14	8 04	3 37	8 43
Apr. 1	4 42	7 28	4 31	7 39	4 14	7 57	3 47	8 25	2 53	9 21
11	4 32	7 32	4 18	7 47	3 56	8 09	3 20	8 47	2 03	10 10
21	4 23	7 36	4 04	7 54	3 37	8 23	2 52	9 11	0 37	11 47
May 1	4 14	7 41	3 52	8 04	3 19	8 37	2 22	9 39		
11	4 08	7 46	3 41	8 13	3 03	8 53	1 49	10 09		
21	4 02	7 52	3 32	8 22	2 48	9 07	1 13	10 46		
June 1	3 58	7 58	3 26	8 30	2 36	9 20	0 21	11 52		
11	3 56	8 03	3 22	8 36	2 29	9 30				
21	3 57	8 06	3 22	8 40	2 28	9 35				
July 1	3 59	8 07	3 25	8 41	2 30	9 35				
11	4 03	8 06	3 30	8 39	2 40	9 30				
21	4 08	8 03	3 39	8 33	2 52	9 18	1 12	11 23		
Aug. 1	4 15	7 56	3 48	8 23	3 09	9 01	1 49	10 20		
11	4 20	7 50	3 56	8 13	3 22	8 46	2 21	9 46		
21	4 24	7 41	4 05	8 01	3 34	8 27	2 47	9 15		
Sept. 1	4 29	7 31	4 14	7 46	3 51	8 08	3 13	8 43	1 40	10 02
11	4 32	7 20	4 20	7 33	4 02	7 50	3 33	8 16	2 36	9 12
21	4 35	7 11	4 26	7 19	4 14	7 31	3 52	7 52	3 11	8 31
Oct. 1	4 38	7 02	4 33	7 05	4 25	7 13	4 10	7 28	3 41	7 54
11	4 40	6 53	4 40	6 53	4 35	6 58	4 26	7 05	4 07	7 23
21	4 43	6 47	4 45	6 44	4 45	6 43	4 41	6 46	4 32	6 55
Nov. 1	4 46	6 41	4 52	6 34	4 56	6 30	4 58	6 27	4 56	6 27
11	4 50	6 38	4 59	6 28	5 06	6 21	5 13	6 14	5 17	6 08
21	4 55	6 36	5 06	6 25	5 16	6 15	5 26	6 04	5 37	5 52
Dec. 1	5 00	6 37	5 13	6 24	5 25	6 11	5 38	5 58	5 53	5 42
11	5 06	6 40	5 20	6 26	5 34	6 12	5 48	5 57	6 06	5 38
21	5 11	6 45	5 25	6 30	5 39	6 16	5 55	6 00	6 15	5 40
31	5 15	6 50	5 30	6 35	5 44	6 21	6 00	6 06	6 18	5 48

Total Eclipses, 1940-2000

Date	Duration m	s	Width miles	Path of Totality
1940 Oct. 1	5	35	135	Colombia, Brazil, Atlantic Ocean, S. Africa
1941 Sept. 21	3	21	88	Soviet Union, China, Pacific Ocean
1943 Feb. 4	2	39	142	Japan, Pacific Ocean, Alaska
1944 Jan. 25	4	08	90	Peru, Brazil, W. Africa
1945 July 9	1	15	57	US, Canada, Greenland, Scandinavia, USSR
1947 May 20	5	13	121	S. America, Atlantic Ocean, Africa
1948 Nov. 1	1	55	52	Africa, Indian Ocean
1950 Sept. 12	1	13	83	Arctic Ocean, Siberia, Pacific Ocean
1952 Feb. 25	3	09	85	Africa, Middle East, Soviet Union
1954 June 30	2	35	95	US, Canada, Iceland, Europe, Middle East
1955 June 20	7	07	157	SE Asia, Philippines, Pacific Ocean
1956 June 8	4	44	266	South Pacific Ocean
1958 Oct. 12	5	10	129	Pacific Ocean, Chile, Argentina
1959 Oct. 2	3	01	75	New England, Atlantic Ocean, Africa
1961 Feb. 15	2	45	160	Europe, Soviet Union
1962 Feb. 5	4	08	91	Borneo, New Guinea, Pacific Ocean
1963 July 20	1	39	63	Pacific Ocean, Alaska, Canada, Maine
1965 May 30	5	15	123	New Zealand, Pacific Ocean
1966 Nov. 12	1	57	52	Pacific Ocean, S. America, Atlantic Ocean
1968 Sept. 22	0	39	64	Soviet Union, China
1970 Mar. 7	3	27	95	Pacific Ocean, Mexico, Eastern US, Canada
1972 July 10	2	35	109	Siberia, Alaska, Canada
1973 June 30	7	03	159	Atlantic Ocean, Central Africa, Indian Ocean
1974 June 20	5	08	214	Indian Ocean, Australia
1976 Oct. 23	4	46	123	Africa, Indian Ocean, Australia
1977 Oct. 12	2	37	61	Pacific Ocean, Colombia, Venezuela
1979 Feb. 26	2	49	185	NW US, Canada, Greenland
1980 Feb. 16	4	08	92	Africa, Indian Ocean, India, Burma, China
1981 July 31	2	02	67	Soviet Union, Pacific Ocean
1983 June 11	5	10	123	Indian Ocean, Indonesia, New Guinea
1984 Nov. 22	1	59	53	New Guinea, Pacific Ocean
1985 Nov. 12	1	58	430	Antarctica
1986 Oct. 3h[1]	0	01	1	North Atlantic Ocean
1987 Mar. 29h	0	07	3	South Atlantic Ocean, Africa
1988 Mar. 18	3	46	104	Sumatra, Borneo, Philippines, Pacific Ocean
1990 July 22	2	32	125	Finland, Soviet Union, Aleutian Islands
1991 July 11	6	53	160	Hawaii, Mexico, C. America, Colombia, Brazil
1992 June 30	5	20	182	South Atlantic Ocean
1994 Nov. 3	4	23	117	Peru, Bolivia, Paraguay, Brazil
1995 Oct. 24	2	09	48	Iran, India, SE Asia
1997 Mar. 9	2	50	221	Mongolia, Siberia
1998 Feb. 26	4	08	94	Galapagos Islands, Panama, Colombia, Venezuela
1999 Aug. 11	2	22	69	Europe, Middle East, India

(1) "h" indicates annular-total hybrid eclipse.

1st Month — January, 1993 — 31 days

Greenwich Mean Time

NOTE: Light numbers indicate Sun. **Dark** numbers indicate **Moon.** *Degrees are North Latitude.*

FM = full moon; LQ = last quarter; NM = new moon; FQ = first quarter.

CAUTION: Must be converted to local time. For instructions see page 247.

Day of month week year	Sun on Meridian **Moon phase**	Sun's Declination	20° Rise Sun **Moon**	20° Set Sun **Moon**	30° Rise Sun **Moon**	30° Set Sun **Moon**	40° Rise Sun **Moon**	40° Set Sun **Moon**	50° Rise Sun **Moon**	50° Set Sun **Moon**	60° Rise Sun **Moon**	60° Set Sun **Moon**
	h m s	°	h m	h m	h m	h m	h m	h m	h m	h m	h m	h m
1 Fr	12 3 40	−23 1	6 35	17 32	6 56	17 11	7 22	16 46	7 59	16 09	9 02	15 05
1	**3 38 FQ**		**11 48**	**– –**	**11 39**	**0 01**	**11 28**	**0 10**	**11 13**	**0 22**	**10 50**	**0 41**
2 Sa	12 4 08	−22 56	6 36	17 33	6 56	17 12	7 22	16 46	7 58	16 10	9 02	15 07
2			**12 26**	**0 44**	**12 13**	**0 55**	**11 57**	**1 09**	**11 35**	**1 28**	**11 01**	**1 59**
3 Su	12 4 35	−22 50	6 36	17 33	6 56	17 13	7 22	16 47	7 58	16 11	9 01	15 08
3			**13 07**	**1 36**	**12 51**	**1 51**	**12 30**	**2 10**	**12 02**	**2 36**	**11 16**	**3 20**
4 Mo	12 5 03	−22 44	6 36	17 34	6 57	17 14	7 22	16 48	7 58	16 12	9 00	15 10
4			**13 54**	**2 31**	**13 34**	**2 49**	**13 09**	**3 13**	**12 35**	**3 46**	**11 37**	**4 41**
5 Tu	12 5 29	−22 38	6 36	17 35	6 57	17 14	7 22	16 49	7 58	16 13	9 00	15 12
5			**14 46**	**3 28**	**14 24**	**3 49**	**13 57**	**4 16**	**13 18**	**4 54**	**12 11**	**6 00**
6 We	12 5 56	−22 31	6 37	17 35	6 57	17 15	7 22	16 50	7 58	16 15	8 59	15 13
6			**15 43**	**4 27**	**15 21**	**4 49**	**14 53**	**5 17**	**14 13**	**5 57**	**13 02**	**7 08**
7 Th	12 6 22	−22 24	6 37	17 36	6 57	17 16	7 22	16 51	7 57	16 16	8 58	15 15
7			**16 45**	**5 25**	**16 24**	**5 47**	**15 58**	**6 14**	**15 20**	**6 52**	**14 15**	**7 59**
8 Fr	12 6 47	−22 16	6 37	17 37	6 57	17 17	7 22	16 52	7 57	16 17	8 57	15 17
8	**12 37 FM**		**17 49**	**6 21**	**17 31**	**6 41**	**17 09**	**7 05**	**16 37**	**7 38**	**15 44**	**8 34**
9 Sa	12 7 12	−22 8	6 37	17 37	6 57	17 18	7 22	16 53	7 56	16 18	8 56	15 19
9			**18 54**	**7 14**	**18 40**	**7 29**	**18 23**	**7 49**	**18 00**	**8 15**	**17 21**	**8 57**
10 Su	12 7 36	−21 59	6 37	17 38	6 57	17 18	7 22	16 54	7 56	16 20	8 55	15 21
10			**19 58**	**8 03**	**19 49**	**8 14**	**19 38**	**8 27**	**19 23**	**8 45**	**19 00**	**9 13**
11 Mo	12 7 60	−21 50	6 38	17 39	6 57	17 19	7 21	16 55	7 55	16 21	8 53	15 23
11			**21 00**	**8 48**	**20 56**	**8 54**	**20 52**	**9 01**	**20 46**	**9 11**	**20 38**	**9 25**
12 Tu	12 8 23	−21 41	6 38	17 39	6 57	17 20	7 21	16 56	7 55	16 22	8 52	15 25
12			**22 00**	**9 32**	**22 02**	**9 32**	**22 05**	**9 33**	**22 08**	**9 34**	**22 13**	**9 36**
13 We	12 8 46	−21 31	6 38	17 40	6 57	17 21	7 21	16 57	7 54	16 24	8 51	15 27
13			**23 00**	**10 14**	**23 07**	**10 10**	**23 16**	**10 04**	**23 28**	**9 57**	**23 47**	**9 46**
14 Th	12 9 08	−21 20	6 38	17 41	6 57	17 22	7 20	16 58	7 53	16 25	8 49	15 30
14			**23 59**	**10 57**	**– –**	**10 47**	**– –**	**10 36**	**– –**	**10 21**	**– –**	**9 57**
15 Fr	12 9 29	−21 10	6 38	17 41	6 57	17 23	7 20	16 59	7 53	16 27	8 48	15 32
15	**4 1 LQ**		**– –**	**11 40**	**0 11**	**11 27**	**0 26**	**11 10**	**0 46**	**10 47**	**1 19**	**10 10**
16 Sa	12 9 50	−20 58	6 38	17 42	6 57	17 23	7 20	17 00	7 52	16 28	8 46	15 34
16			**0 58**	**12 27**	**1 14**	**12 09**	**1 34**	**11 47**	**2 03**	**11 17**	**2 50**	**10 27**
17 Su	12 10 10	−20 47	6 38	17 43	6 56	17 24	7 19	17 01	7 51	16 30	8 44	15 36
17			**1 57**	**13 16**	**2 16**	**12 55**	**2 41**	**12 30**	**3 15**	**11 54**	**4 15**	**10 52**
18 Mo	12 10 29	−20 35	6 38	17 43	6 56	17 25	7 19	17 03	7 50	16 31	8 43	15 39
18			**2 54**	**14 07**	**3 16**	**13 45**	**3 43**	**13 18**	**4 22**	**12 38**	**5 31**	**11 28**
19 Tu	12 10 47	−20 23	6 38	17 44	6 56	17 26	7 18	17 04	7 49	16 33	8 41	15 41
19			**3 49**	**15 01**	**4 12**	**14 39**	**4 40**	**14 11**	**5 20**	**13 31**	**6 32**	**12 19**
20 We	12 11 05	−20 10	6 38	17 45	6 56	17 27	7 18	17 05	7 48	16 34	8 39	15 44
20			**4 41**	**15 55**	**5 03**	**15 34**	**5 30**	**15 08**	**6 08**	**14 31**	**7 15**	**13 25**
21 Th	12 11 22	−19 57	6 38	17 45	6 55	17 28	7 17	17 06	7 47	16 36	8 37	15 46
21			**5 29**	**16 49**	**5 49**	**16 31**	**6 13**	**16 08**	**6 47**	**15 35**	**7 44**	**14 40**
22 Fr	12 11 39	−19 43	6 38	17 46	6 55	17 29	7 16	17 07	7 46	16 38	8 35	15 49
22	**18 27 NM**		**6 13**	**17 42**	**6 29**	**17 27**	**6 50**	**17 08**	**7 18**	**16 42**	**8 04**	**15 59**
23 Sa	12 11 54	−19 29	6 38	17 46	6 55	17 29	7 16	17 08	7 45	16 39	8 33	15 51
23			**6 53**	**18 33**	**7 06**	**18 22**	**7 22**	**18 08**	**7 43**	**17 49**	**8 18**	**17 18**
24 Su	12 12 09	−19 15	6 37	17 47	6 54	17 30	7 15	17 10	7 44	16 41	8 31	15 54
24			**7 30**	**19 23**	**7 39**	**19 16**	**7 50**	**19 07**	**8 05**	**18 55**	**8 28**	**18 36**
25 Mo	12 12 23	−19 1	6 37	17 48	6 54	17 31	7 14	17 11	7 43	16 42	8 29	15 56
25			**8 05**	**20 11**	**8 10**	**20 08**	**8 16**	**20 05**	**8 24**	**20 00**	**8 37**	**19 52**
26 Tu	12 12 36	−18 46	6 37	17 48	6 53	17 32	7 14	17 12	7 42	16 44	8 27	15 59
26			**8 39**	**20 59**	**8 40**	**21 00**	**8 41**	**21 02**	**8 42**	**21 04**	**8 44**	**21 07**
27 We	12 12 49	−18 30	6 37	17 49	6 53	17 33	7 13	17 13	7 40	16 46	8 25	16 01
27			**9 12**	**21 47**	**9 09**	**21 53**	**9 05**	**21 59**	**9 00**	**22 08**	**8 52**	**22 23**
28 Th	12 13 00	−18 15	6 37	17 50	6 53	17 34	7 12	17 14	7 39	16 47	8 23	16 04
28			**9 47**	**22 36**	**9 39**	**22 45**	**9 30**	**22 57**	**9 18**	**23 14**	**9 00**	**23 39**
29 Fr	12 13 11	−17 59	6 36	17 50	6 52	17 35	7 11	17 15	7 38	16 49	8 21	16 06
29			**10 23**	**23 26**	**10 11**	**23 40**	**9 58**	**23 57**	**9 39**	**– –**	**9 10**	**– –**
30 Sa	12 13 21	−17 43	6 36	17 51	6 52	17 36	7 10	17 17	7 36	16 51	8 18	16 09
30	**23 20 FQ**		**11 02**	**– –**	**10 47**	**– –**	**10 28**	**– –**	**10 03**	**0 20**	**9 22**	**0 57**
31 Su	12 13 30	−17 26	6 36	17 51	6 51	17 36	7 10	17 18	7 35	16 53	8 16	16 12
31			**11 45**	**0 19**	**11 26**	**0 36**	**11 04**	**0 57**	**10 32**	**1 27**	**9 40**	**2 17**

2nd Month February, 1993 28 days

Greenwich Mean Time

NOTE: Light numbers indicate Sun. **Dark** numbers indicate **Moon.** *Degrees are North Latitude.*

FM = full moon; LQ = last quarter; NM = new moon; FQ = first quarter.

CAUTION: Must be converted to local time. For instructions see page 247.

Day of month week year	Sun on Meridian **Moon phase** h m s	Sun's Declination ° ′	20° Rise Sun **Moon** h m	20° Set Sun **Moon** h m	30° Rise Sun **Moon** h m	30° Set Sun **Moon** h m	40° Rise Sun **Moon** h m	40° Set Sun **Moon** h m	50° Rise Sun **Moon** h m	50° Set Sun **Moon** h m	60° Rise Sun **Moon** h m	60° Set Sun **Moon** h m
1 Mo	12 13 38	−17 9	6 36	17 52	6 50	17 37	7 09	17 19	7 34	16 54	8 14	16 14
32			**12 33**	**1 13**	**12 12**	**1 33**	**11 46**	**1 58**	**11 09**	**2 34**	**10 07**	**3 35**
2 Tu	12 13 45	−16 52	6 35	17 53	6 50	17 38	7 08	17 20	7 32	16 56	8 11	16 17
33			**13 26**	**2 10**	**13 04**	**2 32**	**12 36**	**2 59**	**11 57**	**3 38**	**10 47**	**4 47**
3 We	12 13 52	−16 35	6 35	17 53	6 49	17 39	7 07	17 22	7 31	16 58	8 09	16 19
34			**14 24**	**3 07**	**14 03**	**3 29**	**13 35**	**3 57**	**12 56**	**4 36**	**11 47**	**5 46**
4 Th	12 13 58	−16 17	6 35	17 54	6 48	17 40	7 06	17 23	7 29	16 59	8 07	16 22
35			**15 27**	**4 04**	**15 07**	**4 24**	**14 42**	**4 50**	**14 07**	**5 26**	**13 07**	**6 28**
5 Fr	12 14 02	−15 59	6 34	17 54	6 48	17 41	7 05	17 24	7 28	17 01	8 04	16 25
36			**16 31**	**4 58**	**16 15**	**5 15**	**15 55**	**5 37**	**15 27**	**6 08**	**14 41**	**6 57**
6 Sa	12 14 07	−15 41	6 34	17 55	6 47	17 41	7 04	17 25	7 26	17 03	8 02	16 27
37	**23 55 FM**		**17 37**	**5 49**	**17 25**	**6 03**	**17 11**	**6 19**	**16 51**	**6 42**	**16 20**	**7 17**
7 Su	12 14 10	−15 22	6 33	17 55	6 46	17 42	7 03	17 26	7 24	17 05	7 59	16 30
38			**18 41**	**6 37**	**18 35**	**6 46**	**18 27**	**6 56**	**18 17**	**7 10**	**18 01**	**7 32**
8 Mo	12 14 12	−15 3	6 33	17 56	6 46	17 43	7 01	17 28	7 23	17 06	7 57	16 33
39			**19 45**	**7 23**	**19 44**	**7 27**	**19 43**	**7 31**	**19 42**	**7 36**	**19 41**	**7 44**
9 Tu	12 14 14	−14 44	6 32	17 56	6 45	17 44	7 00	17 29	7 21	17 08	7 54	16 35
40			**20 47**	**8 08**	**20 52**	**8 06**	**20 58**	**8 03**	**21 06**	**8 00**	**21 19**	**7 55**
10 We	12 14 15	−14 25	6 32	17 57	6 44	17 45	6 59	17 30	7 19	17 10	7 51	16 38
41			**21 49**	**8 52**	**21 59**	**8 45**	**22 11**	**8 36**	**22 28**	**8 24**	**22 56**	**8 06**
11 Th	12 14 15	−14 5	6 31	17 57	6 43	17 46	6 58	17 31	7 18	17 11	7 49	16 41
42			**22 50**	**9 37**	**23 05**	**9 25**	**23 23**	**9 10**	**23 48**	**8 50**	**– –**	**8 19**
12 Fr	12 14 14	−13 45	6 31	17 58	6 43	17 46	6 57	17 32	7 16	17 13	7 46	16 43
43			**23 50**	**10 24**	**– –**	**10 08**	**– –**	**9 48**	**– –**	**9 20**	**0 30**	**8 35**
13 Sa	12 14 13	−13 25	6 30	17 58	6 42	17 47	6 56	17 33	7 14	17 15	7 44	16 46
44	**14 57 LQ**		**– –**	**11 13**	**0 09**	**10 54**	**0 32**	**10 29**	**1 04**	**9 55**	**1 59**	**8 58**
14 Su	12 14 11	−13 5	6 30	17 59	6 41	17 48	6 54	17 35	7 12	17 17	7 41	16 48
45			**0 49**	**12 04**	**1 10**	**11 43**	**1 36**	**11 16**	**2 14**	**10 38**	**3 20**	**9 31**
15 Mo	12 14 08	−12 45	6 29	17 59	6 40	17 49	6 53	17 36	7 11	17 18	7 38	16 51
46			**1 45**	**12 58**	**2 07**	**12 35**	**2 35**	**12 08**	**3 15**	**11 28**	**4 26**	**10 17**
16 Tu	12 14 05	−12 24	6 29	18 00	6 39	17 49	6 52	17 37	7 09	17 20	7 35	16 54
47			**2 38**	**13 51**	**3 00**	**13 30**	**3 27**	**13 03**	**4 06**	**12 25**	**5 14**	**11 18**
17 We	12 14 01	−12 3	6 28	18 00	6 38	17 50	6 50	17 38	7 07	17 22	7 33	16 56
48			**3 27**	**14 45**	**3 47**	**14 26**	**4 12**	**14 02**	**4 47**	**13 28**	**5 47**	**12 29**
18 Th	12 13 56	−11 42	6 27	18 01	6 37	17 51	6 49	17 39	7 05	17 24	7 30	16 59
49			**4 12**	**15 38**	**4 29**	**15 22**	**4 51**	**15 01**	**5 21**	**14 33**	**6 10**	**13 46**
19 Fr	12 13 50	−11 21	6 27	18 01	6 36	17 52	6 48	17 40	7 03	17 25	7 27	17 02
50			**4 52**	**16 29**	**5 07**	**16 16**	**5 24**	**16 01**	**5 48**	**15 39**	**6 26**	**15 04**
20 Sa	12 13 44	−10 59	6 26	18 02	6 35	17 53	6 46	17 42	7 01	17 27	7 24	17 04
51			**5 30**	**17 19**	**5 41**	**17 10**	**5 53**	**16 59**	**6 11**	**16 45**	**6 37**	**16 22**
21 Su	12 13 37	−10 38	6 26	18 02	6 34	17 53	6 45	17 43	6 59	17 29	7 22	17 07
52	**13 5 NM**		**6 06**	**18 07**	**6 12**	**18 03**	**6 20**	**17 57**	**6 31**	**17 50**	**6 47**	**17 38**
22 Mo	12 13 30	−10 16	6 25	18 02	6 33	17 54	6 44	17 44	6 57	17 30	7 19	17 09
53			**6 40**	**18 55**	**6 42**	**18 55**	**6 45**	**18 55**	**6 49**	**18 54**	**6 55**	**18 53**
23 Tu	12 13 22	−9 54	6 24	18 03	6 32	17 55	6 42	17 45	6 56	17 32	7 16	17 12
54			**7 14**	**19 43**	**7 12**	**19 47**	**7 10**	**19 52**	**7 07**	**19 58**	**7 03**	**20 09**
24 We	12 13 13	−9 32	6 24	18 03	6 31	17 55	6 41	17 46	6 54	17 34	7 13	17 15
55			**7 48**	**20 32**	**7 42**	**20 40**	**7 35**	**20 50**	**7 25**	**21 03**	**7 11**	**21 24**
25 Th	12 13 04	−9 10	6 23	18 04	6 30	17 56	6 39	17 47	6 52	17 35	7 10	17 17
56			**8 23**	**21 21**	**8 13**	**21 33**	**8 01**	**21 48**	**7 45**	**22 09**	**7 20**	**22 41**
26 Fr	12 12 54	−8 48	6 22	18 04	6 29	17 57	6 38	17 48	6 50	17 37	7 07	17 20
57			**9 01**	**22 12**	**8 47**	**22 28**	**8 31**	**22 47**	**8 08**	**23 14**	**7 32**	**23 59**
27 Sa	12 12 44	−8 25	6 21	18 04	6 28	17 58	6 37	17 50	6 48	17 39	7 04	17 22
58			**9 42**	**23 05**	**9 25**	**23 24**	**9 04**	**23 47**	**8 35**	**– –**	**7 48**	**– –**
28 Su	12 12 33	−8 2	6 21	18 05	6 27	17 58	6 35	17 51	6 46	17 40	7 02	17 25
59			**10 27**	**23 59**	**10 07**	**– –**	**9 43**	**– –**	**9 08**	**0 20**	**8 11**	**1 16**

3rd Month — March, 1993 — 31 days

Greenwich Mean Time

NOTE: Light numbers indicate Sun. **Dark** numbers indicate **Moon.** *Degrees are North Latitude.*

FM = full moon; LQ = last quarter; NM = new moon; FQ = first quarter.

CAUTION: Must be converted to local time. For instructions see page 247.

Day of month week year	Sun on Meridian **Moon phase** h m s	Sun's Declination ° ′	20° Rise Sun **Moon** h m	20° Set Sun **Moon** h m	30° Rise Sun **Moon** h m	30° Set Sun **Moon** h m	40° Rise Sun **Moon** h m	40° Set Sun **Moon** h m	50° Rise Sun **Moon** h m	50° Set Sun **Moon** h m	60° Rise Sun **Moon** h m	60° Set Sun **Moon** h m
1 Mo	12 12 21	– 7 40	6 20	18 05	6 26	17 59	6 34	17 52	6 43	17 42	6 59	17 27
60	**15 46 FQ**		**11 16**	**– –**	**10 55**	**0 20**	**10 28**	**0 46**	**9 50**	**1 24**	**8 44**	**2 29**
2 Tu	12 12 09	– 7 17	6 19	18 05	6 25	18 00	6 32	17 53	6 41	17 44	6 56	17 30
61			**12 10**	**0 54**	**11 48**	**1 16**	**11 21**	**1 44**	**10 42**	**2 23**	**9 33**	**3 31**
3 We	12 11 57	– 6 54	6 18	18 06	6 24	18 00	6 31	17 54	6 39	17 45	6 53	17 32
62			**13 09**	**1 49**	**12 48**	**2 10**	**12 22**	**2 37**	**11 45**	**3 15**	**10 42**	**4 20**
4 Th	12 11 44	– 6 31	6 18	18 06	6 23	18 01	6 29	17 55	6 37	17 47	6 50	17 35
63			**14 10**	**2 43**	**13 52**	**3 02**	**13 30**	**3 26**	**12 58**	**3 59**	**12 05**	**4 54**
5 Fr	12 11 30	– 6 8	6 17	18 06	6 22	18 02	6 27	17 56	6 35	17 49	6 47	17 37
64			**15 13**	**3 34**	**15 00**	**3 50**	**14 42**	**4 09**	**14 18**	**4 35**	**13 39**	**5 18**
6 Sa	12 11 16	– 5 45	6 16	18 07	6 21	18 02	6 26	17 57	6 33	17 50	6 44	17 40
65			**16 18**	**4 23**	**16 08**	**4 34**	**15 57**	**4 48**	**15 42**	**5 07**	**15 18**	**5 35**
7 Su	12 11 02	– 5 21	6 15	18 07	6 19	18 03	6 24	17 58	6 31	17 52	6 41	17 42
66			**17 22**	**5 10**	**17 18**	**5 16**	**17 13**	**5 24**	**17 07**	**5 34**	**16 58**	**5 49**
8 Mo	12 10 47	– 4 58	6 14	18 07	6 18	18 04	6 23	17 59	6 29	17 54	6 38	17 45
67	**9 46 FM**		**18 26**	**5 55**	**18 27**	**5 56**	**18 30**	**5 57**	**18 33**	**5 59**	**18 38**	**6 01**
9 Tu	12 10 32	– 4 35	6 14	18 08	6 17	18 04	6 21	18 00	6 27	17 55	6 35	17 47
68			**19 29**	**6 41**	**19 37**	**6 36**	**19 46**	**6 31**	**19 58**	**6 24**	**20 18**	**6 13**
10 We	12 10 16	– 4 11	6 13	18 08	6 16	18 05	6 20	18 01	6 25	17 57	6 32	17 50
69			**20 33**	**7 27**	**20 46**	**7 18**	**21 01**	**7 06**	**21 22**	**6 50**	**21 57**	**6 25**
11 Th	12 10 01	– 3 48	6 12	18 08	6 15	18 06	6 18	18 03	6 23	17 58	6 29	17 52
70			**21 36**	**8 15**	**21 53**	**8 01**	**22 14**	**7 43**	**22 43**	**7 19**	**23 32**	**6 41**
12 Fr	12 9 45	– 3 24	6 11	18 09	6 14	18 06	6 17	18 04	6 20	18 00	6 26	17 55
71			**22 38**	**9 05**	**22 58**	**8 47**	**23 23**	**8 25**	**23 58**	**7 54**	**– –**	**7 02**
13 Sa	12 9 28	– 3 0	6 10	18 09	6 12	18 07	6 15	18 05	6 18	18 02	6 23	17 57
72			**23 37**	**9 58**	**23 59**	**9 37**	**– –**	**9 11**	**– –**	**8 35**	**0 59**	**7 32**
14 Su	12 9 12	– 2 37	6 09	18 09	6 11	18 08	6 13	18 06	6 16	18 03	6 20	18 00
73			**– –**	**10 52**	**– –**	**10 30**	**0 26**	**10 03**	**1 05**	**9 24**	**2 13**	**8 15**
15 Mo	12 8 55	– 2 13	6 09	18 10	6 10	18 08	6 12	18 07	6 14	18 05	6 17	18 02
74	**4 16 LQ**		**0 33**	**11 46**	**0 55**	**11 25**	**1 22**	**10 58**	**2 01**	**10 20**	**3 09**	**9 12**
16 Tu	12 8 38	– 1 49	6 08	18 10	6 09	18 09	6 10	18 08	6 12	18 06	6 14	18 05
75			**1 24**	**12 41**	**1 44**	**12 21**	**2 10**	**11 56**	**2 46**	**11 21**	**3 48**	**10 21**
17 We	12 8 21	– 1 26	6 07	18 10	6 08	18 10	6 09	18 09	6 10	18 08	6 11	18 07
76			**2 10**	**13 14**	**2 28**	**13 17**	**2 51**	**12 56**	**3 22**	**12 26**	**4 14**	**11 36**
18 Th	12 8 03	– 1 2	6 06	18 10	6 06	18 10	6 07	18 10	6 07	18 10	6 08	18 10
77			**2 52**	**14 26**	**3 07**	**14 12**	**3 26**	**13 55**	**3 51**	**13 32**	**4 32**	**12 53**
19 Fr	12 7 46	– 0 38	6 05	18 11	6 05	18 11	6 05	18 11	6 05	18 11	6 05	18 12
78			**3 31**	**15 16**	**3 42**	**15 06**	**3 56**	**14 54**	**4 15**	**14 37**	**4 45**	**14 10**
20 Sa	12 7 28	– 0 15	6 04	18 11	6 04	18 11	6 04	18 12	6 03	18 13	6 02	18 14
79			**4 07**	**16 04**	**4 14**	**15 58**	**4 24**	**15 51**	**4 36**	**15 42**	**4 56**	**15 26**
21 Su	12 7 10	0 9	6 03	18 11	6 03	18 12	6 02	18 13	6 01	18 14	5 59	18 17
80			**4 41**	**16 52**	**4 45**	**16 51**	**4 49**	**16 49**	**4 55**	**16 46**	**5 05**	**16 41**
22 Mo	12 6 52	0 33	6 02	18 12	6 02	18 13	6 00	18 14	5 59	18 16	5 56	18 19
81			**5 15**	**17 40**	**5 15**	**17 43**	**5 14**	**17 46**	**5 14**	**17 50**	**5 13**	**17 56**
23 Tu	12 6 34	0 57	6 02	18 12	6 00	18 13	5 59	18 15	5 57	18 18	5 53	18 22
82	**7 14 NM**		**5 49**	**18 29**	**5 45**	**18 35**	**5 40**	**18 43**	**5 32**	**18 55**	**5 21**	**19 12**
24 We	12 6 16	1 20	6 01	18 12	5 59	18 14	5 57	18 16	5 54	18 19	5 50	18 24
83			**6 25**	**19 18**	**6 16**	**19 29**	**6 06**	**19 42**	**5 52**	**20 00**	**5 31**	**20 28**
25 Th	12 5 58	1 44	6 00	18 12	5 58	18 14	5 56	18 17	5 52	18 21	5 47	18 27
84			**7 02**	**20 09**	**6 50**	**20 23**	**6 34**	**20 41**	**6 14**	**21 06**	**5 42**	**21 46**
26 Fr	12 5 40	2 7	5 59	18 13	5 57	18 15	5 54	18 18	5 50	18 22	5 44	18 29
85			**7 42**	**21 01**	**7 26**	**21 18**	**7 07**	**21 40**	**6 40**	**22 11**	**5 57**	**23 03**
27 Sa	12 5 22	2 31	5 58	18 13	5 56	18 16	5 52	18 19	5 48	18 24	5 41	18 32
86			**8 25**	**21 54**	**8 07**	**22 14**	**7 43**	**22 39**	**7 11**	**23 15**	**6 17**	**– –**
28 Su	12 5 04	2 54	5 57	18 13	5 54	18 16	5 51	18 20	5 46	18 25	5 38	18 34
87			**9 13**	**22 48**	**8 52**	**23 10**	**8 26**	**23 36**	**7 50**	**– –**	**6 47**	**0 16**
29 Mo	12 4 46	3 18	5 56	18 13	5 53	18 17	5 49	18 21	5 43	18 27	5 35	18 36
88			**10 04**	**23 42**	**9 43**	**– –**	**9 16**	**– –**	**8 37**	**0 14**	**7 30**	**1 21**
30 Tu	12 4 28	3 41	5 55	18 14	5 52	18 17	5 47	18 22	5 41	18 29	5 32	18 39
89			**11 00**	**– –**	**10 39**	**0 03**	**10 12**	**0 30**	**9 35**	**1 08**	**8 30**	**2 14**
31 We	12 4 10	4 5	5 55	18 14	5 51	18 18	5 46	18 23	5 39	18 30	5 29	18 41
90	**4 10 FQ**		**11 58**	**0 34**	**11 39**	**0 54**	**11 15**	**1 19**	**10 42**	**1 53**	**9 46**	**2 52**

4th Month — April, 1993 — 30 days

Greenwich Mean Time

NOTE: Light numbers indicate Sun. **Dark** numbers indicate **Moon.** *Degrees are North Latitude.*

FM = full moon; LQ = last quarter; NM = new moon; FQ = first quarter.

CAUTION: Must be converted to local time. For instructions see page 247.

Day of month week year	Sun on Meridian **Moon** phase h m s	Sun's Declination ° '	20° Rise Sun **Moon** h m	20° Set Sun **Moon** h m	30° Rise Sun **Moon** h m	30° Set Sun **Moon** h m	40° Rise Sun **Moon** h m	40° Set Sun **Moon** h m	50° Rise Sun **Moon** h m	50° Set Sun **Moon** h m	60° Rise Sun **Moon** h m	60° Set Sun **Moon** h m
1 Th	12 3 52	4 28	5 54	18 14	5 50	18 19	5 44	18 24	5 37	18 32	5 26	18 44
91			**12 58**	**1 25**	**12 43**	**1 42**	**12 23**	**2 03**	**11 56**	**2 32**	**11 12**	**3 19**
2 Fr	12 3 34	4 51	5 53	18 15	5 48	18 19	5 43	18 25	5 35	18 33	5 22	18 46
92			**13 59**	**2 13**	**13 48**	**2 26**	**13 34**	**2 42**	**13 15**	**3 04**	**12 44**	**3 38**
3 Sa	12 3 16	5 14	5 52	18 15	5 47	18 20	5 41	18 26	5 33	18 35	5 19	18 49
93			**15 01**	**2 59**	**14 55**	**3 07**	**14 47**	**3 18**	**14 36**	**3 32**	**14 20**	**3 53**
4 Su	12 2 59	5 37	5 51	18 15	5 46	18 20	5 39	18 27	5 30	18 36	5 16	18 51
94			**16 04**	**3 44**	**16 03**	**3 47**	**16 01**	**3 51**	**16 00**	**3 57**	**15 57**	**4 06**
5 Mo	12 2 41	6 0	5 50	18 15	5 45	18 21	5 38	18 28	5 28	18 38	5 13	18 53
95			**17 07**	**4 28**	**17 11**	**4 27**	**17 16**	**4 25**	**17 24**	**4 22**	**17 36**	**4 18**
6 Tu	12 2 24	6 22	5 49	18 16	5 44	18 22	5 36	18 29	5 26	18 40	5 10	18 56
96	**18 43 FM**		**18 11**	**5 14**	**18 20**	**5 07**	**18 32**	**4 59**	**18 49**	**4 47**	**19 15**	**4 30**
7 We	12 2 07	6 45	5 49	18 16	5 42	18 22	5 35	18 30	5 24	18 41	5 07	18 58
97			**19 15**	**6 01**	**19 30**	**5 49**	**19 47**	**5 35**	**19 12**	**5 15**	**20 54**	**4 45**
8 Th	12 1 50	7 8	5 48	18 16	5 41	18 23	5 33	18 31	5 22	18 43	5 04	19 01
98			**20 19**	**6 51**	**20 38**	**6 35**	**21 00**	**6 15**	**21 33**	**5 48**	**22 28**	**5 04**
9 Fr	12 1 33	7 30	5 47	18 16	5 40	18 23	5 32	18 32	5 20	18 44	5 01	19 03
99			**21 22**	**7 44**	**21 43**	**7 25**	**22 09**	**7 01**	**22 46**	**6 27**	**23 51**	**5 30**
10 Sa	12 1 17	7 52	5 46	18 17	5 39	18 24	5 30	18 33	5 18	18 46	4 58	19 06
100			**22 21**	**8 40**	**22 43**	**8 18**	**23 10**	**7 52**	**23 48**	**7 14**	**– –**	**6 08**
11 Su	12 1 01	8 14	5 45	18 17	5 38	18 25	5 28	18 34	5 16	18 47	4 55	19 08
101			**23 16**	**9 36**	**23 36**	**9 15**	**– –**	**8 48**	**– –**	**8 09**	**0 57**	**7 01**
12 Mo	12 0 45	8 36	5 44	18 17	5 37	18 25	5 27	18 35	5 14	18 49	4 53	19 11
102			**– –**	**10 32**	**– –**	**10 12**	**0 03**	**9 47**	**0 40**	**9 10**	**1 44**	**8 08**
13 Tu	12 0 30	8 58	5 44	18 18	5 36	18 26	5 25	18 36	5 11	18 51	4 50	19 13
103	**19 39 LQ**		**0 05**	**11 27**	**0 24**	**11 09**	**0 47**	**10 47**	**1 20**	**10 16**	**2 15**	**9 22**
14 We	12 0 15	9 20	5 43	18 18	5 34	18 27	5 24	18 37	5 09	18 52	4 47	19 16
104			**0 49**	**12 20**	**1 05**	**12 06**	**1 25**	**11 47**	**1 52**	**11 22**	**2 37**	**10 40**
15 Th	12 0 00	9 41	5 42	18 18	5 33	18 27	5 22	18 38	5 07	18 54	4 44	19 18
105			**1 30**	**13 11**	**1 42**	**13 00**	**1 58**	**12 47**	**2 19**	**12 28**	**2 52**	**11 58**
16 Fr	11 59 46	10 3	5 41	18 19	5 32	18 28	5 21	18 39	5 05	18 55	4 41	19 20
106			**2 07**	**14 00**	**2 16**	**13 53**	**2 26**	**13 45**	**2 41**	**13 33**	**3 03**	**13 14**
17 SA	11 59 32	10 24	5 41	18 19	5 31	18 28	5 19	18 40	5 03	18 57	4 38	19 23
107			**2 42**	**14 48**	**2 47**	**14 46**	**2 53**	**14 42**	**3 01**	**14 37**	**3 13**	**14 29**
18 Su	11 59 19	10 45	5 40	18 19	5 30	18 29	5 18	18 41	5 01	18 58	4 35	19 25
108			**3 16**	**15 36**	**3 17**	**15 37**	**3 18**	**15 39**	**3 19**	**15 41**	**3 22**	**15 44**
19 Mo	11 59 06	11 6	5 39	18 19	5 29	18 30	5 16	18 42	4 59	19 00	4 32	19 28
109			**3 50**	**16 24**	**3 47**	**16 30**	**3 43**	**16 36**	**3 38**	**16 45**	**3 30**	**16 59**
20 Tu	11 58 53	11 27	5 38	18 20	5 28	18 30	5 15	18 43	4 57	19 02	4 29	19 30
110			**4 25**	**17 14**	**4 18**	**17 23**	**4 09**	**17 34**	**3 57**	**17 50**	**3 40**	**18 15**
21 We	11 58 41	11 47	5 38	18 20	5 27	18 31	5 14	18 44	4 55	19 03	4 26	19 33
111	**23 49 NM**		**5 02**	**18 04**	**4 51**	**18 17**	**4 37**	**18 34**	**4 19**	**18 56**	**3 51**	**19 32**
22 Th	11 58 29	12 8	5 37	18 20	5 26	18 32	5 12	18 45	4 53	19 05	4 23	19 35
112			**5 41**	**18 56**	**5 26**	**19 13**	**5 08**	**19 34**	**4 44**	**20 02**	**4 05**	**20 50**
23 Fr	11 58 18	12 28	5 36	18 21	5 25	18 32	5 11	18 46	4 51	19 06	4 20	19 38
113			**6 24**	**19 50**	**6 06**	**20 09**	**5 44**	**20 33**	**5 14**	**21 07**	**4 24**	**22 05**
24 Sa	11 58 07	12 48	5 35	18 21	5 24	18 33	5 09	18 47	4 49	19 08	4 18	19 40
114			**7 10**	**20 44**	**6 50**	**21 05**	**6 25**	**21 31**	**5 50**	**22 09**	**4 51**	**23 14**
25 Su	11 57 56	13 7	5 35	18 21	5 23	18 33	5 08	18 48	4 48	19 09	4 15	19 43
115			**8 01**	**21 38**	**7 40**	**21 59**	**7 13**	**22 26**	**6 36**	**23 04**	**5 30**	**– –**
26 Mo	11 57 46	13 27	5 34	18 22	5 22	18 34	5 07	18 49	4 46	19 11	4 12	19 45
116			**8 55**	**22 31**	**8 34**	**22 51**	**8 08**	**23 16**	**7 31**	**23 52**	**6 25**	**0 10**
27 Tu	11 57 37	13 46	5 33	18 22	5 21	18 35	5 05	18 51	4 44	19 12	4 09	19 48
117			**9 52**	**23 21**	**9 33**	**23 39**	**9 09**	**– –**	**8 34**	**– –**	**7 35**	**0 52**
28 We	11 57 28	14 5	5 33	18 22	5 20	18 35	5 04	18 52	4 42	19 14	4 06	19 50
118			**10 51**	**– –**	**10 34**	**– –**	**10 14**	**0 01**	**9 45**	**0 31**	**8 57**	**1 22**
29 Th	11 57 19	14 24	5 32	18 23	5 19	18 36	5 03	18 53	4 40	19 16	4 04	19 53
119	**12 40 FQ**		**11 50**	**0 09**	**11 37**	**0 23**	**11 22**	**0 41**	**11 00**	**1 05**	**10 25**	**1 43**
30 Fr	11 57 11	14 43	5 32	18 23	5 18	18 37	5 01	18 54	4 38	19 17	4 01	19 55
120			**12 50**	**0 54**	**12 41**	**1 04**	**12 31**	**1 16**	**12 18**	**1 33**	**11 56**	**1 59**

5th Month — May, 1993 — 31 days

Greenwich Mean Time

NOTE: Light numbers indicate Sun. **Dark** numbers indicate **Moon.** *Degrees are North Latitude.*

FM = full moon; LQ = last quarter; NM = new moon; FQ = first quarter.

CAUTION: Must be converted to local time. For instructions see page 247.

Day of month week year	Sun on Meridian Moon phase h m s	Sun's Declination ° '	20° Rise Sun Moon h m	20° Set Sun Moon h m	30° Rise Sun Moon h m	30° Set Sun Moon h m	40° Rise Sun Moon h m	40° Set Sun Moon h m	50° Rise Sun Moon h m	50° Set Sun Moon h m	60° Rise Sun Moon h m	60° Set Sun Moon h m
1 Sa	11 57 04	15 1	5 31	18 23	5 17	18 37	5 00	18 55	4 37	19 19	3 58	19 58
121			13 49	1 37	13 46	1 43	13 42	1 50	13 37	1 59	13 29	2 12
2 Su	11 56 57	15 19	5 30	18 24	5 16	18 38	4 59	18 56	4 35	19 20	3 55	20 00
122			14 50	2 20	14 52	2 21	14 54	2 22	14 58	2 23	15 03	2 24
3 Mo	11 56 51	15 37	5 30	18 24	5 16	18 39	4 58	18 57	4 33	19 22	3 53	20 03
123			15 51	3 04	15 59	3 00	16 07	2 54	16 20	2 47	16 39	2 36
4 Tu	11 56 45	15 54	5 29	18 25	5 15	18 39	4 57	18 58	4 31	19 23	3 50	20 05
124			16 54	3 49	17 06	3 40	17 21	3 28	17 42	3 13	18 16	2 49
5 We	11 56 39	16 12	5 29	18 25	5 14	18 40	4 55	18 59	4 30	19 25	3 47	20 08
125			17 58	4 37	18 15	4 23	18 35	4 06	19 04	3 43	19 52	3 05
6 Th	11 56 35	16 29	5 28	18 25	5 13	18 41	4 54	19 00	4 28	19 26	3 45	20 10
126	3 34 FM		19 02	5 29	19 22	5 11	19 46	4 49	20 21	4 18	21 21	3 28
7 Fr	11 56 30	16 45	5 28	18 26	5 12	18 41	4 53	19 01	4 26	19 28	3 42	20 13
127			20 04	6 23	20 25	6 03	20 52	5 37	21 30	5 01	22 37	4 00
8 Sa	11 56 27	17 2	5 27	18 26	5 11	18 42	4 52	19 02	4 25	19 29	3 40	20 15
128			21 02	7 20	21 23	6 59	21 50	6 32	22 28	5 54	23 34	4 46
9 Su	11 56 24	17 18	5 27	18 26	5 11	18 42	4 51	19 03	4 23	19 31	3 37	20 17
129			21 55	8 18	22 15	7 57	22 39	7 31	23 14	6 54	– –	5 48
10 Mo	11 56 21	17 34	5 26	18 27	5 10	18 43	4 50	19 03	4 20	19 32	3 35	20 20
130			22 43	9 15	23 00	8 57	23 21	8 33	23 51	7 59	0 13	7 02
11 Tu	11 56 19	17 50	5 26	18 27	5 09	18 44	4 49	19 04	4 20	19 34	3 32	20 22
131			23 25	10 11	23 39	9 55	23 56	9 35	– –	9 07	0 39	8 21
12 We	11 56 18	18 5	5 25	18 28	5 09	18 44	4 48	19 05	4 19	19 35	3 30	20 25
132			– –	11 03	– –	10 51	– –	10 36	0 20	10 14	0 57	9 40
13 Th	11 56 17	18 20	5 25	18 28	5 08	18 45	4 47	19 06	4 17	19 36	3 27	20 27
133	12 20 LQ		0 04	11 54	0 15	11 45	0 27	11 35	0 44	11 21	1 10	10 58
14 Fr	11 56 17	18 35	5 24	18 28	5 07	18 46	4 46	19 07	4 16	19 38	3 25	20 29
134			0 41	12 43	0 47	12 38	0 55	12 33	1 05	12 26	1 21	12 14
15 Sa	11 56 18	18 49	5 24	18 29	5 07	18 46	4 45	19 08	4 14	19 39	3 22	20 32
135			1 15	13 31	1 18	13 31	1 20	13 30	1 20	13 30	1 30	13 29
16 Su	11 56 19	19 3	5 24	18 29	5 06	18 47	4 44	19 09	4 13	19 41	3 20	20 34
136			1 49	14 19	1 48	14 23	1 45	14 27	1 43	14 34	1 38	14 44
17 Mo	11 56 20	19 17	5 23	18 30	5 05	18 48	4 43	19 10	4 11	19 42	3 18	20 36
137			2 24	15 07	2 18	15 15	2 11	15 25	2 02	15 38	1 48	15 59
18 Tu	11 56 23	19 30	5 23	18 30	5 05	18 48	4 42	19 11	4 10	19 43	3 16	20 39
138			3 00	15 57	2 50	16 09	2 38	16 24	2 23	16 44	1 58	17 16
19 We	11 56 25	19 43	5 23	18 30	5 04	18 49	4 41	19 12	4 09	19 45	3 13	20 41
139			3 38	16 49	3 25	17 05	3 08	17 24	2 46	17 50	2 11	18 34
20 Th	11 56 29	19 56	5 22	18 31	5 04	18 49	4 41	19 13	4 08	19 46	3 11	20 43
140			4 20	17 43	4 03	18 01	3 43	18 24	3 14	18 56	2 28	19 51
21 Fr	11 56 33	20 8	5 22	18 31	5 03	18 50	4 40	19 14	4 06	19 47	3 09	20 45
141	14 6 NM		5 06	18 38	4 46	18 58	4 22	19 24	3 49	20 00	2 53	21 03
22 Sa	11 56 37	20 21	5 22	18 32	5 03	18 51	4 39	19 15	4 05	19 49	3 07	20 48
142			5 56	19 33	5 35	19 54	5 09	20 21	4 32	20 58	3 28	22 05
23 Su	11 56 42	20 32	5 21	18 32	5 02	18 51	4 38	19 16	4 04	19 50	3 05	20 50
143			6 50	20 27	6 29	20 47	6 02	21 13	5 24	21 49	4 18	22 52
24 Mo	11 56 47	20 44	5 21	18 33	5 02	18 52	4 38	19 16	4 03	19 51	3 03	20 52
144			7 47	21 18	7 27	21 37	7 02	22 00	6 26	22 32	5 25	23 25
25 Tu	11 56 53	20 55	5 21	18 33	5 02	18 52	4 37	19 17	4 02	19 52	3 01	20 54
145			8 46	22 07	8 28	22 22	8 06	22 41	7 36	23 07	6 45	23 49
26 We	11 56 60	21 5	5 21	18 33	5 01	18 53	4 36	19 18	4 01	19 54	2 59	20 56
146			9 45	22 53	9 31	23 04	9 14	23 18	8 50	23 37	8 12	– –
27 Th	11 57 07	21 16	5 21	18 34	5 01	18 54	4 36	19 19	4 00	19 55	2 58	20 58
147			10 44	23 36	10 35	23 43	10 23	23 52	10 07	– –	9 42	0 06
28 Fr	11 57 14	21 26	5 20	18 34	5 00	18 54	4 35	19 20	3 59	19 56	2 56	21 00
148	18 21 FQ		11 43	– –	11 38	– –	11 32	– –	11 24	0 03	11 12	0 20
29 Sa	11 57 22	21 35	5 20	18 35	5 00	18 55	4 35	19 20	3 58	19 57	2 54	21 02
149			12 41	0 19	12 42	0 21	12 42	0 23	12 43	0 27	12 44	0 32
30 Su	11 57 30	21 44	5 20	18 35	5 00	18 55	4 34	19 21	3 57	19 58	2 52	21 04
150			13 41	1 01	13 46	0 58	13 53	0 55	14 02	0 50	14 16	0 43
31 Mo	11 57 38	21 53	5 20	18 35	5 00	18 56	4 34	19 22	3 57	19 59	2 51	21 06
151			14 41	1 44	14 51	1 36	15 04	1 27	15 21	1 14	15 49	0 55

6th Month **June, 1993** **30 days**

Greenwich Mean Time

NOTE: Light numbers indicate Sun. **Dark** numbers indicate **Moon.** *Degrees are North Latitude.*

FM = full moon; LQ = last quarter; NM = new moon; FQ = first quarter.

CAUTION: Must be converted to local time. For instructions see page 247.

Day of month week year	Sun on Meridian **Moon phase** h m s	Sun's Declination ° ′	20° Rise Sun **Moon** h m	20° Set Sun **Moon** h m	30° Rise Sun **Moon** h m	30° Set Sun **Moon** h m	40° Rise Sun **Moon** h m	40° Set Sun **Moon** h m	50° Rise Sun **Moon** h m	50° Set Sun **Moon** h m	60° Rise Sun **Moon** h m	60° Set Sun **Moon** h m
1 Tu	11 57 47	22 1	5 20	18 36	4 59	18 56	4 33	19 23	3 56	20 00	2 49	21 07
152			**15 43**	**2 29**	**15 57**	**2 17**	**16 16**	**2 02**	**16 41**	**1 42**	**17 23**	**0 10**
2 We	11 57 57	22 10	5 20	18 36	4 59	18 57	4 33	19 23	3 55	20 01	2 48	21 09
153			**16 45**	**3 17**	**17 03**	**3 01**	**17 26**	**2 41**	**17 59**	**2 14**	**18 54**	**1 29**
3 Th	11 58 06	22 17	5 20	18 36	4 59	18 57	4 32	19 24	3 55	20 02	2 47	21 11
154			**17 47**	**4 10**	**18 08**	**3 50**	**18 34**	**3 26**	**19 11**	**2 52**	**20 15**	**1 55**
4 Fr	11 58 16	22 24	5 20	18 37	4 59	18 58	4 32	19 25	3 54	20 03	2 45	21 12
155	**13 2 FM**		**18 47**	**5 05**	**19 08**	**4 44**	**19 35**	**4 17**	**20 13**	**3 40**	**21 21**	**2 34**
5 Sa	11 58 27	22 31	5 20	18 37	4 59	18 58	4 32	19 25	3 53	20 04	2 44	21 14
156			**19 42**	**6 03**	**20 03**	**5 41**	**20 29**	**5 15**	**21 05**	**4 36**	**22 08**	**3 29**
6 Su	11 58 37	22 38	5 20	18 38	4 59	18 59	4 32	19 26	3 53	20 05	2 43	21 15
157			**20 33**	**7 01**	**20 51**	**6 41**	**21 14**	**6 16**	**21 47**	**5 40**	**22 40**	**4 39**
7 Mo	11 58 48	22 44	5 20	18 38	4 58	18 59	4 31	19 27	3 52	20 06	2 42	21 17
158			**21 19**	**7 58**	**21 34**	**7 40**	**21 53**	**7 19**	**22 19**	**6 48**	**23 01**	**5 57**
8 Tu	11 59 00	22 50	5 20	18 38	4 58	19 00	4 31	19 27	3 52	20 06	2 41	21 18
159			**22 00**	**8 52**	**22 12**	**8 38**	**22 26**	**8 21**	**22 46**	**7 57**	**23 17**	**7 18**
9 We	11 59 11	22 55	5 20	18 39	4 58	19 00	4 31	19 28	3 52	20 07	2 40	21 19
160			**22 38**	**9 45**	**22 46**	**9 35**	**22 55**	**9 22**	**23 08**	**9 05**	**23 28**	**8 37**
10 Th	11 59 23	23 0	5 20	18 39	4 58	19 01	4 31	19 28	3 51	20 08	2 39	21 20
161			**23 13**	**10 35**	**23 17**	**10 29**	**23 22**	**10 21**	**23 28**	**10 11**	**23 38**	**9 55**
11 Fr	11 59 35	23 4	5 20	18 39	4 58	19 01	4 31	19 29	3 51	20 09	2 38	21 22
162			**23 48**	**11 24**	**23 48**	**11 22**	**23 48**	**11 19**	**23 47**	**11 16**	**23 47**	**11 11**
12 Sa	11 59 48	23 8	5 20	18 40	4 58	19 01	4 31	19 29	3 51	20 09	2 38	21 23
163	**5 36 LQ**		**– –**	**12 12**	**– –**	**12 14**	**– –**	**12 17**	**– –**	**12 20**	**23 56**	**12 26**
13 Su	12 0 00	23 12	5 20	18 40	4 58	19 02	4 31	19 30	3 50	20 10	2 37	21 23
164			**0 22**	**13 00**	**0 18**	**13 06**	**0 13**	**13 14**	**0 06**	**13 25**	**– –**	**13 41**
14 Mo	12 0 13	23 15	5 20	18 40	4 58	19 02	4 31	19 30	3 50	20 10	2 37	21 24
165			**0 57**	**13 49**	**0 49**	**13 59**	**0 39**	**14 12**	**0 26**	**14 29**	**0 06**	**14 57**
15 Tu	12 0 26	23 18	5 20	18 40	4 58	19 02	4 31	19 30	3 50	20 11	2 36	21 25
166			**1 34**	**14 40**	**1 23**	**14 54**	**1 08**	**15 11**	**0 48**	**15 35**	**0 17**	**16 14**
16 We	12 0 39	23 20	5 21	18 41	4 59	19 03	4 31	19 31	3 50	20 11	2 36	21 26
167			**2 15**	**15 33**	**1 59**	**15 50**	**1 40**	**16 11**	**1 14**	**16 41**	**0 33**	**17 32**
17 Th	12 0 52	23 22	5 21	18 41	4 59	19 03	4 31	19 31	3 50	20 12	2 36	21 26
168			**2 59**	**16 27**	**2 40**	**16 47**	**2 17**	**17 12**	**1 46**	**17 47**	**0 54**	**18 47**
18 Fr	12 1 05	23 24	5 21	18 41	4 59	19 03	4 31	19 31	3 50	20 12	2 36	21 27
169			**3 47**	**17 23**	**3 27**	**17 44**	**3 01**	**18 10**	**2 25**	**18 48**	**1 24**	**19 54**
19 Sa	12 1 18	23 25	5 21	18 42	4 59	19 04	4 31	19 32	3 50	20 12	2 36	21 27
170			**4 40**	**18 18**	**4 19**	**18 39**	**3 52**	**19 05**	**3 14**	**19 43**	**2 08**	**20 48**
20 Su	12 1 31	23 26	5 21	18 42	4 59	19 04	4 31	19 32	3 50	20 13	2 36	21 28
171	**1 52 NM**		**5 37**	**19 12**	**5 16**	**19 31**	**4 51**	**19 56**	**4 14**	**20 30**	**3 10**	**21 27**
21 Mo	12 1 44	23 26	5 21	18 42	4 59	19 04	4 31	19 32	3 51	20 13	2 36	21 28
172			**6 37**	**20 03**	**6 18**	**20 19**	**5 55**	**20 40**	**5 22**	**21 08**	**4 27**	**21 54**
22 Tu	12 1 57	23 26	5 22	18 42	5 00	19 04	4 31	19 32	3 51	20 13	2 36	21 28
173			**7 37**	**20 51**	**7 22**	**21 03**	**7 03**	**21 19**	**6 37**	**21 41**	**5 54**	**22 14**
23 We	12 2 10	23 26	5 22	18 42	5 00	19 04	4 32	19 33	3 51	20 13	2 36	21 28
174			**8 38**	**21 36**	**8 27**	**21 44**	**8 13**	**21 54**	**7 55**	**22 08**	**7 25**	**22 29**
24 Th	12 2 23	23 25	5 22	18 43	5 00	19 05	4 32	19 33	3 51	20 13	2 37	21 28
175			**9 37**	**22 19**	**9 31**	**22 22**	**9 24**	**22 27**	**9 13**	**22 33**	**8 57**	**22 41**
25 Fr	12 2 36	23 24	5 22	18 43	5 00	19 05	4 32	19 33	3 52	20 13	2 37	21 28
176			**10 37**	**23 01**	**10 35**	**23 00**	**10 34**	**22 58**	**10 32**	**22 56**	**10 29**	**22 53**
26 Sa	12 2 49	23 22	5 23	18 43	5 01	19 05	4 33	19 33	3 52	20 13	2 38	21 27
177	**22 43 FQ**		**11 35**	**23 43**	**11 39**	**23 37**	**11 44**	**23 30**	**11 50**	**23 20**	**12 00**	**23 05**
27 Su	12 3 01	23 20	5 23	18 43	5 01	19 05	4 33	19 33	3 53	20 13	2 39	21 27
178			**12 35**	**– –**	**12 43**	**– –**	**12 54**	**– –**	**13 09**	**23 45**	**13 32**	**23 18**
28 Mo	12 3 14	23 17	5 23	18 43	5 01	19 05	4 33	19 33	3 53	20 13	2 39	21 27
179			**13 35**	**0 27**	**13 48**	**0 16**	**14 04**	**0 03**	**14 27**	**– –**	**15 04**	**23 35**
29 Tu	12 3 26	23 14	5 24	18 43	5 02	19 05	4 34	19 33	3 54	20 13	2 40	21 26
180			**14 35**	**1 13**	**14 52**	**0 58**	**15 14**	**0 40**	**15 44**	**0 15**	**16 34**	**23 57**
30 We	12 3 38	23 11	5 24	18 43	5 02	19 05	4 34	19 33	3 54	20 13	2 41	21 26
181			**15 36**	**2 03**	**15 56**	**1 44**	**16 21**	**1 22**	**16 56**	**0 50**	**17 58**	**– –**

7th Month — July, 1993 — 31 days

Greenwich Mean Time

NOTE: Light numbers indicate Sun. **Dark** numbers indicate **Moon.** *Degrees are North Latitude.*

FM = full moon; LQ = last quarter; NM = new moon; FQ = first quarter.

CAUTION: Must be converted to local time. For instructions see page 247.

Day of month week year	Sun on Meridian **Moon phase** h m s	Sun's Declination ° ′	20° Rise Sun **Moon** h m	20° Set Sun **Moon** h m	30° Rise Sun **Moon** h m	30° Set Sun **Moon** h m	40° Rise Sun **Moon** h m	40° Set Sun **Moon** h m	50° Rise Sun **Moon** h m	50° Set Sun **Moon** h m	60° Rise Sun **Moon** h m	60° Set Sun **Moon** h m
1 Th	12 3 49	23 7	5 24	18 43	5 02	19 05	4 35	19 33	3 55	20 12	02 42	21 25
182			**16 35**	**2 55**	**16 57**	**2 35**	**17 23**	**2 09**	**18 02**	**1 33**	**19 09**	**0 30**
2 Fr	12 4 00	23 3	5 24	18 43	5 03	19 05	4 35	19 33	3 56	20 12	2 43	21 24
183			**17 32**	**3 51**	**17 53**	**3 30**	**18 19**	**3 03**	**18 57**	**2 24**	**20 03**	**1 17**
3 Sa	12 4 11	22 59	5 25	18 44	5 03	19 05	4 36	19 32	3 56	20 12	2 44	21 23
184	**23 45 FM**		**18 24**	**4 48**	**18 44**	**4 28**	**19 08**	**4 02**	**19 42**	**3 25**	**20 40**	**2 20**
4 Su	12 4 22	22 54	5 25	18 44	5 04	19 05	4 36	19 32	3 57	20 11	2 46	21 22
185			**19 12**	**5 45**	**19 29**	**5 27**	**19 49**	**5 03**	**20 18**	**4 30**	**21 06**	**3 34**
5 Mo	12 4 33	22 48	5 25	18 44	5 04	19 05	4 37	19 32	3 58	20 11	2 47	21 21
186			**19 55**	**6 41**	**20 08**	**6 26**	**20 25**	**6 06**	**20 48**	**5 39**	**21 23**	**4 54**
6 Tu	12 4 43	22 43	5 26	18 44	5 05	19 05	4 37	19 32	3 59	20 10	2 48	21 20
187			**20 35**	**7 35**	**20 44**	**7 23**	**20 56**	**7 08**	**21 12**	**6 48**	**21 37**	**6 15**
7 We	12 4 52	22 36	5 26	18 43	5 05	19 05	4 38	19 31	3 59	20 10	2 50	21 19
188			**21 11**	**8 26**	**21 17**	**8 18**	**21 24**	**8 09**	**21 33**	**7 55**	**21 47**	**7 34**
8 Th	12 5 02	22 30	5 26	18 43	5 05	19 04	4 39	19 31	4 00	20 09	2 51	21 18
189			**21 46**	**9 16**	**21 48**	**9 12**	**21 50**	**9 08**	**21 52**	**9 01**	**21 56**	**8 52**
9 Fr	12 5 11	22 23	5 27	18 43	5 06	19 04	4 39	19 31	4 01	20 09	2 53	21 16
190			**22 21**	**10 04**	**22 18**	**10 05**	**22 15**	**10 05**	**22 11**	**10 06**	**22 05**	**10 07**
10 Sa	12 5 19	22 16	5 27	18 43	5 06	19 04	4 40	19 30	4 02	20 08	2 54	21 15
191			**22 55**	**10 53**	**22 49**	**10 57**	**22 41**	**11 03**	**22 31**	**11 10**	**22 15**	**11 22**
11 Su	12 5 27	22 8	5 28	18 43	5 07	19 04	4 41	19 30	4 03	20 07	2 56	21 14
192	**22 49 LQ**		**23 31**	**11 41**	**23 21**	**11 50**	**23 08**	**12 00**	**22 52**	**12 15**	**22 25**	**12 37**
12 Mo	12 5 35	22 0	5 28	18 43	5 07	19 04	4 41	19 29	4 04	20 06	2 58	21 12
193			**– –**	**12 31**	**23 56**	**12 43**	**23 39**	**12 58**	**23 16**	**13 20**	**22 39**	**13 53**
13 Tu	12 5 42	21 51	5 28	18 43	5 08	19 03	4 42	19 29	4 05	20 06	3 00	21 10
194			**0 10**	**13 22**	**– –**	**13 38**	**– –**	**13 57**	**23 44**	**14 25**	**22 57**	**15 10**
14 We	12 5 49	21 43	5 29	18 43	5 08	19 03	4 43	19 28	4 06	20 05	3 02	21 09
195			**0 51**	**14 15**	**0 34**	**14 34**	**0 13**	**14 57**	**– –**	**15 30**	**23 22**	**16 26**
15 Th	12 5 55	21 33	5 29	18 43	5 09	19 03	4 44	19 28	4 07	20 04	3 03	21 07
196			**1 37**	**15 10**	**1 18**	**15 30**	**0 53**	**15 56**	**0 19**	**16 33**	**23 59**	**17 36**
16 Fr	12 6 01	21 24	5 29	18 42	5 10	19 02	4 44	19 27	4 09	20 03	3 05	21 05
197			**2 28**	**16 05**	**2 07**	**16 26**	**1 41**	**16 53**	**1 03**	**17 31**	**– –**	**18 36**
17 Sa	12 6 07	21 14	5 30	18 42	5 10	19 02	4 45	19 27	4 10	20 02	3 07	21 03
198			**3 23**	**17 00**	**3 02**	**17 20**	**2 35**	**17 46**	**1 58**	**18 21**	**0 52**	**19 23**
18 Su	12 6 11	21 4	5 30	18 42	5 11	19 01	4 46	19 26	4 11	20 01	3 09	21 02
199			**4 22**	**17 53**	**4 02**	**18 11**	**3 38**	**18 33**	**3 03**	**19 04**	**2 03**	**19 56**
19 Mo	12 6 16	20 53	5 31	18 42	5 11	19 01	4 47	19 25	4 12	20 00	3 11	21 00
200	**11 24 NM**		**5 23**	**18 43**	**5 06**	**18 58**	**4 45**	**19 16**	**4 16**	**19 40**	**3 27**	**20 19**
20 Tu	12 6 19	20 42	5 31	18 42	5 12	19 01	4 48	19 25	4 13	19 59	3 14	20 58
201			**6 25**	**19 31**	**6 12**	**19 41**	**5 56**	**19 53**	**5 34**	**20 10**	**4 59**	**20 36**
21 We	12 6 22	20 31	5 31	18 41	5 12	19 00	4 48	19 24	4 14	19 57	3 16	20 56
202			**7 27**	**20 16**	**7 19**	**20 21**	**7 09**	**20 28**	**6 55**	**20 37**	**6 33**	**20 50**
22 Th	12 6 25	20 19	5 32	18 41	5 13	19 00	4 49	19 23	4 16	19 56	3 18	20 53
203			**8 28**	**20 59**	**8 25**	**21 00**	**8 21**	**21 00**	**8 16**	**21 01**	**8 08**	**21 02**
23 Fr	12 6 27	20 7	5 32	18 41	5 14	18 59	4 50	19 22	4 17	19 55	3 20	20 51
204			**9 29**	**21 42**	**9 31**	**21 38**	**9 33**	**21 33**	**9 37**	**21 25**	**9 42**	**21 14**
24 Sa	12 6 28	19 55	5 32	18 40	5 14	18 58	4 51	19 21	4 18	19 54	3 22	20 49
205			**10 29**	**22 26**	**10 36**	**22 17**	**10 45**	**22 06**	**10 57**	**21 51**	**11 15**	**21 27**
25 Su	12 6 29	19 42	5 33	18 40	5 15	18 58	4 52	19 21	4 20	19 52	3 24	20 47
206			**11 29**	**23 12**	**11 41**	**22 59**	**11 56**	**22 42**	**12 16**	**22 19**	**12 48**	**21 43**
26 Mo	12 6 29	19 29	5 33	18 40	5 15	18 57	4 53	19 20	4 21	19 51	3 27	20 45
207	**3 25 FQ**		**12 30**	**– –**	**12 46**	**23 43**	**13 05**	**23 22**	**13 33**	**22 52**	**14 19**	**22 04**
27 Tu	12 6 29	19 15	5 34	18 39	5 16	18 57	4 54	19 19	4 22	19 50	3 29	20 42
208			**13 30**	**0 00**	**13 49**	**– –**	**14 13**	**– –**	**14 46**	**23 32**	**15 44**	**22 33**
28 We	12 6 28	19 2	5 34	18 39	5 17	18 56	4 55	19 18	4 24	19 48	3 31	20 40
209			**14 29**	**0 52**	**14 50**	**0 32**	**15 16**	**0 07**	**15 53**	**– –**	**16 59**	**23 14**
29 Th	12 6 26	18 48	5 34	18 38	5 17	18 55	4 55	19 17	4 25	19 47	3 34	20 38
210			**15 25**	**1 45**	**15 47**	**1 24**	**16 13**	**0 58**	**16 51**	**0 20**	**17 58**	**– –**
30 Fr	12 6 24	18 34	5 35	18 38	5 18	18 55	4 56	19 16	4 26	19 46	3 36	20 35
211			**16 18**	**2 41**	**16 38**	**2 20**	**17 04**	**1 54**	**17 39**	**1 16**	**18 40**	**0 10**
31 Sa	12 6 21	18 19	5 35	18 37	5 18	18 54	4 57	19 15	4 28	19 44	3 38	20 33
212			**17 07**	**3 37**	**17 25**	**3 18**	**17 47**	**2 53**	**18 18**	**2 19**	**19 09**	**1 19**

8th Month August, 1993 31 days

Greenwich Mean Time

NOTE: Light numbers indicate Sun. **Dark** numbers indicate **Moon.** *Degrees are North Latitude.*

FM = full moon; LQ = last quarter; NM = new moon; FQ = first quarter.

CAUTION: Must be converted to local time. For instructions see page 247.

Day of month week year	Sun on Meridian **Moon phase**	Sun's Declination	20° Rise Sun **Moon**	20° Set Sun **Moon**	30° Rise Sun **Moon**	30° Set Sun **Moon**	40° Rise Sun **Moon**	40° Set Sun **Moon**	50° Rise Sun **Moon**	50° Set Sun **Moon**	60° Rise Sun **Moon**	60° Set Sun **Moon**
	h m s	° ′	h m	h m	h m	h m	h m	h m	h m	h m	h m	h m
1 Su	12 6 17	18 4	5 35	18 37	5 19	18 53	4 58	19 14	4 29	19 42	3 41	20 30
213			17 51	4 33	18 06	4 16	18 24	3 55	18 50	3 26	19 30	2 36
2 Mo	12 6 13	17 49	5 36	18 36	5 20	18 53	4 59	19 13	4 31	19 41	3 43	20 28
214	12 10 FM		18 32	5 27	18 43	5 13	18 57	4 57	19 16	4 34	19 45	3 56
3 Tu	12 6 08	17 33	5 36	18 36	5 20	18 52	5 00	19 12	4 32	19 39	3 45	20 25
215			19 10	6 19	19 17	6 09	19 26	5 57	19 38	5 41	19 56	5 16
4 We	12 6 03	17 18	5 36	18 35	5 21	18 51	5 01	19 10	4 33	19 38	3 48	20 23
216			19 46	7 09	19 49	7 04	19 53	6 57	19 58	6 48	20 06	6 33
5 Th	12 5 57	17 2	5 37	18 35	5 21	18 50	5 02	19 09	4 35	19 36	3 50	20 20
217			20 20	7 58	20 19	7 57	20 18	7 55	20 17	7 53	20 15	7 50
6 Fr	12 5 50	16 45	5 37	18 34	5 22	18 49	5 03	19 08	4 36	19 34	3 52	20 18
218			20 55	8 46	20 50	8 49	20 44	8 53	20 36	8 57	20 25	9 05
7 Sa	12 5 43	16 29	5 37	18 34	5 23	18 49	5 04	19 07	4 38	19 33	3 55	20 15
219			21 30	9 35	21 21	9 41	21 11	9 50	20 57	10 01	20 35	10 19
8 Su	12 5 36	16 12	5 38	18 33	5 23	18 48	5 05	19 06	4 39	19 31	3 57	20 12
220			22 07	10 23	21 55	10 34	21 40	10 47	21 19	11 06	20 47	11 35
9 Mo	12 5 27	15 55	5 38	18 33	5 24	18 47	5 06	19 05	4 41	19 29	4 00	20 10
221			22 47	11 13	22 31	11 28	22 12	11 45	21 45	12 10	21 03	12 50
10 Tu	12 5 18	15 37	5 38	18 32	5 24	18 46	5 07	19 03	4 42	19 28	4 02	20 07
222	15 19 LQ		23 30	12 05	23 12	12 22	22 49	12 44	22 17	13 14	21 24	14 05
11 We	12 5 09	15 20	5 39	18 31	5 25	18 45	5 08	19 02	4 44	19 26	4 04	20 04
223			– –	12 58	23 57	13 17	23 32	13 42	22 56	14 17	21 55	15 17
12 Th	12 4 59	15 2	5 39	18 31	5 26	18 44	5 09	19 01	4 45	19 24	4 07	20 01
224			0 17	13 52	– –	14 13	– –	14 39	23 45	15 16	22 40	16 21
13 Fr	12 4 49	14 44	5 39	18 30	5 26	18 43	5 10	18 59	4 47	19 22	4 09	19 59
225			1 09	14 46	0 48	15 07	0 22	15 33	– –	16 09	23 41	17 13
14 Sa	12 4 38	14 26	5 40	18 29	5 27	18 42	5 10	18 58	4 48	19 20	4 12	19 56
226			2 06	15 39	1 45	15 58	1 20	16 22	0 43	16 56	– –	17 52
15 Su	12 4 26	14 7	5 40	18 29	5 27	18 41	5 11	18 57	4 49	19 18	4 14	19 53
227			3 05	16 31	2 47	16 47	2 24	17 07	1 52	17 35	0 58	18 20
16 Mo	12 4 14	13 48	5 40	18 28	5 28	18 40	5 12	18 55	4 51	19 16	4 16	19 50
228			4 07	17 20	3 52	17 32	3 34	17 47	3 08	18 08	2 26	18 40
17 Tu	12 4 01	13 29	5 41	18 27	5 28	18 39	5 13	18 54	4 52	19 15	4 19	19 48
229	19 28 NM		5 10	18 07	4 59	18 15	4 46	18 24	4 28	18 37	4 00	18 56
18 We	12 3 48	13 10	5 41	18 27	5 29	18 38	5 14	18 53	4 54	19 13	4 21	19 45
230			6 12	18 52	6 07	18 55	6 00	18 59	5 51	19 03	5 36	19 10
19 Th	12 3 35	12 50	5 41	18 26	5 30	18 37	5 15	18 51	4 55	19 11	4 24	19 42
231			7 15	19 37	7 15	19 35	7 14	19 32	7 14	19 28	7 13	19 23
20 Fr	12 3 21	12 31	5 41	18 25	5 30	18 36	5 16	18 50	4 57	19 09	4 26	19 39
232			8 17	20 22	8 22	20 15	8 28	20 06	8 37	19 54	8 50	19 36
21 Sa	12 3 06	12 11	5 42	18 24	5 31	18 35	5 17	18 48	4 58	19 07	4 28	19 36
233			9 20	21 09	9 29	20 57	9 42	20 42	9 59	20 23	10 26	19 51
22 Su	12 2 51	11 51	5 42	18 24	5 31	18 34	5 18	18 47	5 00	19 05	4 31	19 33
234			10 22	21 57	10 36	21 42	10 54	21 22	11 19	20 55	12 00	20 11
23 Mo	12 2 36	11 31	5 42	18 23	5 32	18 33	5 19	18 45	5 01	19 03	4 33	19 30
235			11 24	22 49	11 41	22 30	12 04	22 06	12 35	21 33	13 29	20 38
24 Tu	12 2 20	11 10	5 42	18 22	5 32	18 32	5 20	18 44	5 03	19 01	4 36	19 27
236	9 57 FQ		12 24	23 42	12 44	23 21	13 09	22 55	13 45	22 19	14 48	21 15
25 We	12 2 03	10 50	5 43	18 21	5 33	18 31	5 21	18 42	5 04	18 59	4 38	19 24
237			13 21	– –	13 42	– –	14 09	23 50	14 46	23 12	15 52	22 07
26 Th	12 1 47	10 29	5 43	18 20	5 34	18 29	5 22	18 41	5 06	18 57	4 40	19 21
238			14 15	0 37	14 35	0 16	15 01	– –	15 37	– –	16 39	23 11
27 Fr	12 1 29	10 8	5 43	18 20	5 34	18 28	5 23	18 39	5 07	18 55	4 43	19 19
239			15 04	1 33	15 23	1 13	15 46	0 48	16 18	0 13	17 12	– –
28 Sa	12 1 12	9 47	5 43	18 19	5 35	18 27	5 24	18 38	5 09	18 52	4 45	19 16
240			15 50	2 28	16 05	2 10	16 25	1 48	16 52	1 17	17 35	0 25
29 Su	12 0 54	9 26	5 44	18 18	5 35	18 26	5 25	18 36	5 10	18 50	4 48	19 13
241			16 31	3 22	16 43	3 07	16 59	2 49	17 19	2 24	17 52	1 43
30 Mo	12 0 35	9 4	5 44	18 17	5 36	18 25	5 26	18 35	5 12	18 48	4 50	19 10
242			17 09	4 14	17 18	4 03	17 29	3 50	17 43	3 31	18 05	3 02
31 Tu	12 0 17	8 43	5 44	18 16	5 36	18 24	5 27	18 33	5 13	18 46	4 52	19 07
243			17 46	5 04	17 50	4 57	17 56	4 49	18 04	4 37	18 16	4 19

9th Month — September, 1993 — 30 days

Greenwich Mean Time

NOTE: Light numbers indicate Sun. **Dark** numbers indicate **Moon.** *Degrees are North Latitude.*

FM = full moon; LQ = last quarter; NM = new moon; FQ = first quarter.

CAUTION: Must be converted to local time. For instructions see page 247.

Day of month week year	Sun on Meridian **Moon phase** h m s	Sun's Declination ° ′	20° Rise Sun **Moon** h m	20° Set Sun **Moon** h m	30° Rise Sun **Moon** h m	30° Set Sun **Moon** h m	40° Rise Sun **Moon** h m	40° Set Sun **Moon** h m	50° Rise Sun **Moon** h m	50° Set Sun **Moon** h m	60° Rise Sun **Moon** h m	60° Set Sun **Moon** h m
1 We	11 59 58	8 21	5 44	18 15	5 37	18 23	5 28	18 32	5 15	18 44	4 55	19 04
244	**2 33 FM**		**18 21**	**5 53**	**18 21**	**5 51**	**18 22**	**5 47**	**18 24**	**5 42**	**18 25**	**5 35**
2 Th	11 59 39	7 59	5 45	18 14	5 37	18 21	5 29	18 30	5 16	18 42	4 57	19 01
245			**18 55**	**6 42**	**18 52**	**6 43**	**18 48**	**6 45**	**18 43**	**6 47**	**18 35**	**6 50**
3 Fr	11 59 19	7 38	5 45	18 14	5 38	18 20	5 29	18 28	5 18	18 40	4 59	18 58
246			**19 30**	**7 30**	**19 23**	**7 35**	**19 14**	**7 42**	**19 03**	**7 51**	**18 45**	**8 05**
4 Sa	11 58 59	7 16	5 45	18 13	5 39	18 19	5 30	18 27	5 19	18 38	5 02	18 55
247			**20 07**	**8 19**	**19 56**	**8 28**	**19 43**	**8 39**	**19 25**	**8 55**	**18 57**	**9 19**
5 Su	11 58 39	6 53	5 45	18 12	5 39	18 18	5 31	18 25	5 21	18 36	5 04	18 52
248			**20 45**	**9 08**	**20 31**	**9 21**	**20 13**	**9 37**	**19 49**	**9 59**	**19 11**	**10 34**
6 Mo	11 58 19	6 31	5 45	18 11	5 40	18 17	5 32	18 24	5 22	18 33	5 06	18 49
249			**21 26**	**9 58**	**21 09**	**10 14**	**20 48**	**10 34**	**20 19**	**11 02**	**19 31**	**11 48**
7 Tu	11 57 59	6 9	5 46	18 10	5 40	18 15	5 33	18 22	5 24	18 31	5 09	18 46
250			**22 11**	**10 50**	**21 52**	**11 08**	**21 28**	**11 32**	**20 54**	**12 05**	**19 57**	**13 00**
8 We	11 57 38	5 46	5 46	18 09	5 41	18 14	5 34	18 20	5 25	18 29	5 11	18 43
251			**23 00**	**11 42**	**22 40**	**12 03**	**22 14**	**12 28**	**21 38**	**13 04**	**20 35**	**14 06**
9 Th	11 57 17	5 24	5 46	18 08	5 41	18 13	5 35	18 19	5 27	18 27	5 14	18 40
252	**6 26 LQ**		**23 53**	**12 35**	**23 33**	**12 56**	**23 07**	**13 22**	**22 30**	**13 58**	**21 27**	**15 02**
10 Fr	11 56 56	5 1	5 46	18 07	5 42	18 12	5 36	18 17	5 28	18 25	5 16	18 36
253			**– –**	**13 27**	**– –**	**13 47**	**– –**	**14 12**	**23 33**	**14 46**	**22 35**	**15 45**
11 Sa	11 56 36	4 38	5 47	18 06	5 42	18 10	5 37	18 15	5 30	18 22	5 18	18 33
254			**0 50**	**14 18**	**0 30**	**14 36**	**0 06**	**14 57**	**– –**	**15 28**	**23 55**	**16 18**
12 Su	11 56 14	4 15	5 47	18 05	5 43	18 09	5 38	18 14	5 31	18 20	5 21	18 30
255			**1 49**	**15 07**	**1 32**	**15 21**	**1 12**	**15 39**	**0 43**	**16 03**	**– –**	**16 41**
13 Mo	11 55 53	3 52	5 47	18 05	5 43	18 08	5 39	18 12	5 33	18 18	5 23	18 27
256			**2 50**	**15 54**	**2 37**	**16 05**	**2 21**	**16 17**	**1 59**	**16 34**	**1 25**	**17 00**
14 Tu	11 55 32	3 29	5 47	18 04	5 44	18 07	5 40	18 11	5 34	18 16	5 25	18 24
257			**3 52**	**16 40**	**3 44**	**16 46**	**3 34**	**16 53**	**3 20**	**17 01**	**2 58**	**17 15**
15 We	11 55 11	3 6	5 47	18 03	5 44	18 05	5 41	18 09	5 36	18 14	5 28	18 21
258			**4 54**	**17 26**	**4 51**	**17 26**	**4 48**	**17 27**	**4 43**	**17 27**	**4 35**	**17 28**
16 Th	11 54 50	2 43	5 48	18 02	5 45	18 04	5 42	18 07	5 37	18 12	5 30	18 18
259	**3 10 NM**		**5 58**	**18 12**	**6 00**	**18 07**	**6 03**	**18 02**	**6 07**	**17 54**	**6 13**	**17 42**
17 Fr	11 54 28	2 20	5 48	18 01	5 46	18 03	5 43	18 06	5 39	18 09	5 32	18 15
260			**7 02**	**18 59**	**7 09**	**18 50**	**7 18**	**18 38**	**7 31**	**18 22**	**7 51**	**17 57**
18 Sa	11 54 07	1 57	5 48	18 00	5 46	18 02	5 44	18 04	5 40	18 07	5 35	18 12
261			**8 06**	**19 49**	**8 18**	**19 35**	**8 34**	**19 17**	**8 55**	**18 54**	**9 29**	**18 16**
19 Su	11 53 46	1 34	5 48	17 59	5 47	18 00	5 45	18 02	5 42	18 05	5 37	18 09
262			**9 10**	**20 41**	**9 27**	**20 23**	**9 47**	**20 01**	**10 16**	**19 31**	**11 04**	**18 41**
20 Mo	11 53 25	1 10	5 48	17 58	5 47	17 59	5 46	18 01	5 43	18 03	5 39	18 06
263			**10 13**	**21 35**	**10 33**	**21 15**	**10 57**	**20 50**	**11 31**	**20 15**	**12 30**	**19 15**
21 Tu	11 53 03	0 47	5 49	17 57	5 48	17 58	5 46	17 59	5 45	18 00	5 42	18 03
264			**11 14**	**22 32**	**11 34**	**22 11**	**12 00**	**21 45**	**12 37**	**21 08**	**13 42**	**20 03**
22 We	11 52 42	0 24	5 49	17 56	5 48	17 57	5 47	17 57	5 46	17 58	5 44	18 00
265	**19 32 FQ**		**12 10**	**23 28**	**12 30**	**23 08**	**12 56**	**22 43**	**13 33**	**22 07**	**14 36**	**21 05**
23 Th	11 52 21	0 0	5 49	17 55	5 49	17 55	5 48	17 56	5 48	17 56	5 46	17 57
266			**13 01**	**– –**	**13 20**	**– –**	**13 44**	**23 43**	**14 18**	**23 11**	**15 14**	**22 16**
24 Fr	11 52 00	– 0 23	5 49	17 54	5 49	17 54	5 49	17 54	5 49	17 54	5 49	17 54
267			**13 48**	**0 24**	**14 05**	**0 06**	**14 25**	**– –**	**14 54**	**– –**	**15 40**	**23 33**
25 Sa	11 51 40	– 0 46	5 49	17 54	5 50	17 53	5 50	17 52	5 51	17 52	5 51	17 51
268			**14 31**	**1 18**	**14 44**	**1 03**	**15 00**	**0 44**	**15 23**	**0 17**	**15 58**	**– –**
26 Su	11 51 19	– 1 10	5 50	17 53	5 50	17 52	5 51	17 51	5 52	17 49	5 53	17 48
269			**15 10**	**2 10**	**15 20**	**1 59**	**15 32**	**1 44**	**15 48**	**1 24**	**16 13**	**0 51**
27 Mo	11 50 59	– 1 33	5 50	17 52	5 51	17 50	5 52	17 49	5 54	17 47	5 56	17 45
270			**15 47**	**3 01**	**15 52**	**2 53**	**16 00**	**2 43**	**16 09**	**2 29**	**16 24**	**2 08**
28 Tu	11 50 38	– 1 56	5 50	17 51	5 52	17 49	5 53	17 47	5 55	17 45	5 58	17 42
271			**16 22**	**3 50**	**16 24**	**3 46**	**16 26**	**3 41**	**16 29**	**3 34**	**16 34**	**3 24**
29 We	11 50 18	– 2 20	5 50	17 50	5 52	17 48	5 54	17 46	5 57	17 43	6 01	17 39
272			**16 56**	**4 39**	**16 54**	**4 39**	**16 52**	**4 38**	**16 49**	**4 38**	**16 44**	**4 38**
30 Th	11 49 59	– 2 43	5 51	17 49	5 53	17 47	5 55	17 44	5 58	17 41	6 03	17 36
273	**18 54 FM**		**17 31**	**5 27**	**17 26**	**5 31**	**17 18**	**5 36**	**17 09**	**5 42**	**16 55**	**5 52**

10th Month — October, 1993 — 31 days

Greenwich Mean Time

NOTE: Light numbers indicate Sun. **Dark** numbers indicate **Moon.** *Degrees are North Latitude.*

FM = full moon; LQ = last quarter; NM = new moon; FQ = first quarter.

CAUTION: Must be converted to local time. For instructions see page 247.

Day of month week year	Sun on Meridian **Moon phase**	Sun's Declination	20° Rise Sun **Moon**	20° Set Sun **Moon**	30° Rise Sun **Moon**	30° Set Sun **Moon**	40° Rise Sun **Moon**	40° Set Sun **Moon**	50° Rise Sun **Moon**	50° Set Sun **Moon**	60° Rise Sun **Moon**	60° Set Sun **Moon**
	h m s	° ′	h m	h m	h m	h m	h m	h m	h m	h m	h m	h m
1 Fr	11 49 39	− 3 6	5 51	17 48	5 53	17 46	5 56	17 43	6 00	17 39	6 05	17 33
274			**18 07**	**6 15**	**17 58**	**6 23**	**17 46**	**6 33**	**17 30**	**6 46**	**17 06**	**7 07**
2 Sa	11 49 20	− 3 30	5 51	17 47	5 54	17 44	5 57	17 41	6 01	17 36	6 08	17 30
275			**18 45**	**7 04**	**18 32**	**7 16**	**18 16**	**7 30**	**17 54**	**7 50**	**17 20**	**8 21**
3 Su	11 49 01	− 3 53	5 51	17 46	5 54	17 43	5 58	17 39	6 03	17 34	6 10	17 27
276			**19 26**	**7 54**	**19 10**	**8 09**	**18 50**	**8 28**	**18 22**	**8 53**	**17 38**	**9 36**
4 Mo	11 48 42	− 4 16	5 52	17 46	5 55	17 42	5 59	17 38	6 04	17 32	6 12	17 24
277			**20 09**	**8 45**	**19 51**	**9 03**	**19 28**	**9 25**	**18 56**	**9 56**	**18 02**	**10 48**
5 Tu	11 48 24	− 4 39	5 52	17 45	5 56	17 41	6 00	17 36	6 06	17 30	6 15	17 21
278			**20 56**	**9 37**	**20 36**	**9 57**	**20 11**	**10 21**	**19 36**	**10 56**	**18 36**	**11 55**
6 We	11 48 07	− 5 2	5 52	17 44	5 56	17 40	6 01	17 34	6 08	17 28	6 17	17 18
279			**21 47**	**10 29**	**21 26**	**10 49**	**21 01**	**11 15**	**20 25**	**11 51**	**19 22**	**12 54**
7 Th	11 47 49	− 5 25	5 52	17 43	5 57	17 38	6 02	17 33	6 09	17 26	6 20	17 15
280			**22 41**	**11 20**	**22 21**	**11 40**	**21 56**	**12 05**	**21 22**	**12 40**	**20 22**	**13 41**
8 Fr	11 47 32	− 5 48	5 53	17 42	5 57	17 37	6 03	17 31	6 11	17 24	6 22	17 12
281	**19 35 LQ**		**23 37**	**12 10**	**23 19**	**12 28**	**22 57**	**12 51**	**22 27**	**13 23**	**21 36**	**14 16**
9 Sa	11 47 16	− 6 11	5 53	17 41	5 58	17 36	6 04	17 30	6 12	17 21	6 25	17 09
282			**– –**	**12 58**	**– –**	**13 14**	**– –**	**13 33**	**23 38**	**14 00**	**22 58**	**14 42**
10 Su	11 47 00	− 6 34	5 53	17 40	5 59	17 35	6 05	17 28	6 14	17 19	6 27	17 06
283			**0 35**	**13 44**	**0 20**	**13 56**	**0 03**	**14 11**	**– –**	**14 31**	**– –**	**15 02**
11 Mo	11 46 44	− 6 57	5 54	17 40	5 59	17 34	6 06	17 27	6 15	17 17	6 29	17 03
284			**1 34**	**14 29**	**1 24**	**14 37**	**1 11**	**14 47**	**0 54**	**14 59**	**0 27**	**15 18**
12 Tu	11 46 29	− 7 19	5 54	17 39	6 00	17 33	6 07	17 25	6 17	17 15	6 32	17 00
285			**2 34**	**15 14**	**2 29**	**15 17**	**2 22**	**15 21**	**2 13**	**15 25**	**1 59**	**15 32**
13 We	11 46 15	− 7 42	5 54	17 38	6 01	17 32	6 08	17 24	6 19	17 13	6 34	16 57
286			**3 36**	**15 59**	**3 36**	**15 57**	**3 35**	**15 54**	**3 34**	**15 51**	**3 33**	**15 46**
14 Th	11 46 01	− 8 4	5 54	17 37	6 01	17 30	6 09	17 22	6 20	17 11	6 37	16 54
287			**4 39**	**16 45**	**4 44**	**16 38**	**4 50**	**16 30**	**4 58**	**16 18**	**5 10**	**16 00**
15 Fr	11 45 47	− 8 26	5 55	17 37	6 02	17 29	6 10	17 21	6 22	17 09	6 39	16 51
288	**11 36 NM**		**5 43**	**17 34**	**5 53**	**17 23**	**6 05**	**17 08**	**6 22**	**16 48**	**6 49**	**16 18**
16 Sa	11 45 34	− 8 49	5 55	17 36	6 02	17 28	6 11	17 19	6 23	17 07	6 42	16 48
289			**6 49**	**18 26**	**7 03**	**18 10**	**7 21**	**17 51**	**7 46**	**17 24**	**8 27**	**16 40**
17 Su	11 45 22	− 9 11	5 55	17 35	6 03	17 27	6 12	17 18	6 25	17 05	6 44	16 45
290			**7 55**	**19 21**	**8 12**	**19 03**	**8 35**	**18 39**	**9 06**	**18 06**	**10 00**	**17 11**
18 Mo	11 45 11	− 9 33	5 56	17 34	6 04	17 26	6 14	17 16	6 27	17 03	6 47	16 43
291			**8 58**	**20 19**	**9 18**	**19 59**	**9 44**	**19 33**	**10 19**	**18 57**	**11 21**	**17 54**
19 Tu	11 44 59	− 9 54	5 56	17 34	6 04	17 25	6 15	17 15	6 28	17 01	6 49	16 40
292			**9 59**	**21 18**	**10 19**	**20 57**	**10 45**	**20 32**	**11 22**	**19 55**	**12 25**	**18 52**
20 We	11 44 49	−10 16	5 57	17 33	6 05	17 24	6 16	17 13	6 30	16 59	6 52	16 37
293			**10 54**	**22 15**	**11 13**	**21 57**	**11 38**	**21 33**	**12 12**	**21 00**	**13 11**	**20 03**
21 Th	11 44 39	−10 37	5 57	17 32	6 06	17 23	6 17	17 12	6 31	16 57	6 54	16 34
294			**11 44**	**23 12**	**12 01**	**22 55**	**12 23**	**22 35**	**12 52**	**22 07**	**13 42**	**21 20**
22 Fr	11 44 30	−10 59	5 57	17 31	6 07	17 22	6 18	17 11	6 33	16 55	6 57	16 31
295	**8 52 FQ**		**12 29**	**– –**	**12 43**	**23 53**	**13 00**	**23 37**	**13 25**	**23 14**	**14 03**	**22 39**
23 Sa	11 44 21	−11 20	5 58	17 31	6 07	17 21	6 19	17 09	6 35	16 53	6 59	16 28
296			**13 09**	**0 05**	**13 20**	**– –**	**13 33**	**– –**	**13 51**	**– –**	**14 19**	**23 56**
24 Su	11 44 14	−11 41	5 58	17 30	6 08	17 20	6 20	17 08	6 36	16 51	7 02	16 26
297			**13 47**	**0 57**	**13 54**	**0 48**	**14 03**	**0 36**	**14 14**	**0 21**	**14 32**	**– –**
25 Mo	11 44 06	−12 2	5 58	17 30	6 09	17 19	6 21	17 07	6 38	16 49	7 04	16 23
298			**14 23**	**1 47**	**14 26**	**1 41**	**14 30**	**1 35**	**14 35**	**1 26**	**14 43**	**1 12**
26 Tu	11 44 00	−12 22	5 59	17 29	6 09	17 18	6 22	17 05	6 40	16 48	7 07	16 20
299			**14 57**	**2 35**	**14 57**	**2 34**	**14 56**	**2 32**	**14 54**	**2 30**	**14 53**	**2 27**
27 We	11 43 54	−12 43	5 59	17 28	6 10	17 17	6 23	17 04	6 41	16 46	7 09	16 17
300			**15 32**	**3 23**	**15 27**	**3 26**	**15 22**	**3 29**	**15 14**	**3 34**	**15 03**	**3 41**
28 Th	11 43 49	−13 3	6 00	17 28	6 11	17 16	6 24	17 03	6 43	16 44	7 12	16 15
301			**16 08**	**4 11**	**15 59**	**4 18**	**15 49**	**4 26**	**15 35**	**4 37**	**15 14**	**4 55**
29 Fr	11 43 45	−13 23	6 00	17 27	6 12	17 16	6 26	17 01	6 45	16 42	7 14	16 12
302			**16 45**	**5 00**	**16 33**	**5 11**	**16 18**	**5 24**	**15 59**	**5 41**	**15 28**	**6 09**
30 Sa	11 43 42	−13 43	6 01	17 27	6 12	17 15	6 27	17 00	6 46	16 40	7 17	16 09
303	**12 38 FM**		**17 25**	**5 50**	**17 10**	**6 04**	**16 51**	**6 21**	**16 25**	**6 45**	**15 44**	**7 24**
31 Su	11 43 39	−14 2	6 01	17 26	6 13	17 14	6 28	16 59	6 48	16 39	7 20	16 07
304			**18 08**	**6 41**	**17 50**	**6 58**	**17 28**	**7 19**	**16 57**	**7 48**	**16 07**	**8 37**

11th Month November, 1993 30 days

Greenwich Mean Time

NOTE: Light numbers indicate Sun. **Dark** numbers indicate **Moon.** *Degrees are North Latitude.*

FM = full moon; LQ = last quarter; NM = new moon; FQ = first quarter.

CAUTION: Must be converted to local time. For instructions see page 247.

Day of month week year	Sun on Meridian Moon phase	Sun's Declination	20° Rise Sun Moon	20° Set Sun Moon	30° Rise Sun Moon	30° Set Sun Moon	40° Rise Sun Moon	40° Set Sun Moon	50° Rise Sun Moon	50° Set Sun Moon	60° Rise Sun Moon	60° Set Sun Moon
	h m s	° ′	h m	h m	h m	h m	h m	h m	h m	h m	h m	h m
1 Mo	11 43 37	−14 22	6 01	17 26	6 14	17 13	6 29	16 58	6 50	16 37	7 22	16 04
305			18 54	7 33	18 35	7 52	18 10	8 16	17 36	8 49	16 38	9 46
2 Tu	11 43 36	−14 41	6 02	17 25	6 15	17 12	6 30	16 57	6 51	16 35	7 25	16 02
306			19 44	8 25	19 23	8 45	18 58	9 11	18 22	9 46	17 20	10 48
3 We	11 43 36	−15 0	6 02	17 25	6 15	17 11	6 31	16 55	6 53	16 34	7 27	15 59
307			20 36	9 17	20 16	9 37	19 52	10 02	19 17	10 38	18 16	11 39
4 Th	11 43 36	−15 18	6 03	17 24	6 16	17 11	6 32	16 54	6 55	16 32	7 30	15 56
308			21 31	10 07	21 13	10 25	20 50	10 49	20 19	11 22	19 25	12 17
5 Fr	11 43 37	−15 37	6 03	17 24	6 17	17 10	6 34	16 53	6 56	16 30	7 32	15 54
309			22 27	10 54	22 12	11 11	21 53	11 31	21 26	12 00	20 43	12 45
6 Sa	11 43 40	−15 55	6 04	17 23	6 18	17 09	6 35	16 52	6 58	16 29	7 35	15 51
310			23 24	11 40	23 13	11 53	22 58	12 10	22 39	12 32	22 07	13 07
7 Su	11 43 43	−16 13	6 04	17 23	6 18	17 09	6 36	16 51	7 00	16 27	7 38	15 49
311			– –	12 24	– –	12 33	– –	12 45	23 53	13 00	23 34	13 24
8 Mo	11 43 47	−16 31	6 05	17 22	6 19	17 08	6 37	16 50	7 01	16 26	7 40	15 47
312	19 35 LQ		0 22	13 07	0 15	13 12	0 06	13 18	– –	13 26	– –	13 38
9 Tu	11 43 52	−16 48	6 05	17 22	6 20	17 07	6 38	16 49	7 03	16 24	7 43	15 44
313			1 21	13 50	1 18	13 50	1 15	13 50	1 11	13 51	1 04	13 51
10 We	11 43 57	−17 5	6 06	17 22	6 21	17 07	6 39	16 48	7 05	16 23	7 45	15 42
314			2 21	14 34	2 23	14 29	2 26	14 24	2 30	14 16	2 36	14 04
11 Th	11 44 04	−17 22	6 07	17 21	6 22	17 06	6 40	16 47	7 06	16 21	7 48	15 40
315			3 22	15 20	3 30	15 11	3 39	14 59	3 51	14 44	4 10	14 20
12 Fr	11 44 11	−17 38	6 07	17 21	6 23	17 06	6 42	16 46	7 08	16 20	7 50	15 37
316			4 26	16 10	4 38	15 56	4 53	15 39	5 14	15 16	5 47	14 39
13 Sa	11 44 19	−17 54	6 08	17 21	6 23	17 05	6 43	16 45	7 09	16 19	7 53	15 35
317			5 31	17 03	5 47	16 46	6 07	16 24	6 35	15 54	7 22	15 05
14 Su	11 44 29	−18 10	6 08	17 21	6 24	17 04	6 44	16 45	7 11	16 17	7 55	15 33
318			6 36	18 00	6 55	17 41	7 19	17 16	7 53	16 41	8 51	15 42
15 Mo	11 44 39	−18 26	6 09	17 20	6 25	17 04	6 45	16 44	7 13	16 16	7 58	15 31
319	11 36 NM		7 40	19 00	8 00	18 39	8 26	18 13	9 02	17 37	10 06	16 33
16 Tu	11 44 49	−18 41	6 09	17 20	6 26	17 04	6 46	16 43	7 14	16 15	8 00	15 29
320			8 39	20 00	8 59	19 40	9 25	19 16	10 00	18 41	11 01	17 40
17 We	11 45 01	−18 56	6 10	17 20	6 27	17 03	6 47	16 42	7 16	16 14	8 03	15 26
321			9 33	20 59	9 52	20 42	10 15	20 20	10 47	19 49	11 40	18 58
18 Th	11 45 13	−19 10	6 11	17 20	6 28	17 03	6 48	16 42	7 18	16 12	8 05	15 24
322			10 22	21 55	10 37	21 41	10 57	21 23	11 23	20 59	12 06	20 18
19 Fr	11 45 27	−19 25	6 11	17 20	6 28	17 02	6 50	16 41	7 19	16 11	8 08	15 22
323			11 05	22 49	11 17	22 39	11 32	22 26	11 53	22 07	12 25	21 39
20 Sa	11 45 41	−19 39	6 12	17 19	6 29	17 02	6 51	16 40	7 21	16 10	8 10	15 20
324			11 45	23 40	11 53	23 34	12 04	23 26	12 17	23 14	12 39	22 57
21 Su	11 45 56	−19 52	6 12	17 19	6 30	17 02	6 52	16 40	7 22	16 09	8 13	15 19
325			12 22	– –	12 26	– –	12 32	– –	12 39	– –	12 51	– –
22 Mo	11 46 11	−20 5	6 13	17 19	6 31	17 01	6 53	16 39	7 24	16 08	8 15	15 17
326	8 52 FQ		12 57	0 30	12 58	0 27	12 58	0 24	12 59	0 20	13 01	0 13
23 Tu	11 46 28	−20 18	6 14	17 19	6 32	17 01	6 54	16 38	7 25	16 07	8 17	15 15
327			13 32	1 18	13 28	1 20	13 24	1 21	13 19	1 24	13 11	1 27
24 We	11 46 45	−20 30	6 14	17 19	6 33	17 01	6 55	16 38	7 27	16 06	8 20	15 13
328			14 07	2 06	14 00	2 12	13 51	2 18	13 40	2 27	13 22	2 41
25 Th	11 47 03	−20 42	6 15	17 19	6 33	17 01	6 56	16 37	7 28	16 05	8 22	15 12
329			14 44	2 55	14 33	3 04	14 20	3 15	14 02	3 31	13 35	3 55
26 Fr	11 47 21	−20 54	6 15	17 19	6 34	17 00	6 57	16 37	7 30	16 05	8 24	15 10
330			15 22	3 44	15 08	3 57	14 51	4 13	14 28	4 35	13 50	5 09
27 Sa	14 47 41	−21 5	6 16	17 19	6 35	17 00	6 58	16 37	7 31	16 04	8 26	15 08
331			16 04	4 35	15 48	4 51	15 27	5 11	14 58	5 38	14 10	6 24
28 Su	11 48 01	−21 16	6 17	17 19	6 36	17 00	6 59	16 36	7 33	16 03	8 29	15 07
332			16 50	5 27	16 31	5 46	16 07	6 09	15 34	6 41	14 38	7 35
29 Mo	11 48 22	−21 26	6 17	17 19	6 37	17 00	7 01	16 36	7 34	16 02	8 31	15 05
333			17 39	6 20	17 19	6 40	16 54	7 05	16 18	7 40	15 17	8 41
30 Tu	11 48 43	−21 37	6 18	17 19	6 37	17 00	7 02	16 36	7 35	16 02	8 33	15 04
334	12 38 FM		18 32	7 12	18 11	7 33	17 46	7 58	17 11	8 34	16 09	9 36

12th Month — December, 1993 — 31 days

Greenwich Mean Time

NOTE: Light numbers indicate Sun. **Dark** numbers indicate **Moon.** *Degrees are North Latitude.*

FM = full moon; LQ = last quarter; NM = new moon; FQ = first quarter.

CAUTION: Must be converted to local time. For instructions see page 247.

Day of month week year	Sun on Meridian **Moon phase** h m s	Sun's Declination ° ′	20° Rise Sun **Moon** h m	20° Set Sun **Moon** h m	30° Rise Sun **Moon** h m	30° Set Sun **Moon** h m	40° Rise Sun **Moon** h m	40° Set Sun **Moon** h m	50° Rise Sun **Moon** h m	50° Set Sun **Moon** h m	60° Rise Sun **Moon** h m	60° Set Sun **Moon** h m
1 We	11 49 05	−21 46	6 19	17 19	6 38	17 00	7 03	16 35	7 37	16 01	8 35	15 03
335			**19 26**	**8 04**	**19 08**	**8 23**	**18 44**	**8 47**	**18 11**	**9 21**	**17 15**	**10 19**
2 Th	11 49 28	−21 55	6 19	17 20	6 39	17 00	7 04	16 35	7 38	16 01	8 37	15 02
336			**20 23**	**8 53**	**20 07**	**9 10**	**19 46**	**9 31**	**19 18**	**10 01**	**18 31**	**10 50**
3 Fr	11 49 51	−22 4	6 20	17 20	6 40	17 00	7 05	16 35	7 39	16 00	8 39	15 00
337			**21 20**	**9 39**	**21 07**	**9 53**	**20 51**	**10 11**	**20 29**	**10 35**	**19 54**	**11 13**
4 Sa	11 50 15	−22 12	6 21	17 20	6 41	17 00	7 05	16 35	7 41	16 00	8 41	14 59
338			**22 17**	**10 23**	**22 08**	**10 34**	**21 57**	**10 47**	**21 43**	**11 04**	**21 19**	**11 31**
5 Su	11 50 40	−22 20	6 21	17 20	6 41	17 00	7 06	16 35	7 42	15 59	8 43	14 58
339			**23 14**	**11 06**	**23 10**	**11 12**	**23 04**	**11 20**	**22 57**	**11 30**	**22 47**	**11 46**
6 Mo	11 51 05	−22 28	6 22	17 20	6 42	17 00	7 07	16 35	7 43	15 59	8 44	14 57
340	**15 49 LQ**		**– –**	**11 48**	**– –**	**11 50**	**– –**	**11 52**	**– –**	**11 55**	**– –**	**11 59**
7 Tu	11 51 31	−22 35	6 22	17 21	6 43	17 00	7 08	16 35	7 44	15 59	8 46	14 57
341			**0 11**	**12 30**	**0 12**	**12 27**	**0 13**	**12 24**	**0 14**	**12 19**	**0 15**	**12 12**
8 We	11 51 57	−22 42	6 23	17 21	6 44	17 00	7 09	16 35	7 45	15 58	8 48	14 56
342			**1 10**	**13 13**	**1 16**	**13 06**	**1 22**	**12 57**	**1 31**	**12 44**	**1 45**	**12 25**
9 Th	11 52 24	−22 48	6 24	17 21	6 44	17 00	7 10	16 35	7 46	15 58	8 49	14 55
343			**2 11**	**13 59**	**2 21**	**13 48**	**2 33**	**13 33**	**2 50**	**13 13**	**3 17**	**12 42**
10 Fr	11 52 51	−22 53	6 24	17 21	6 45	17 01	7 11	16 35	7 47	15 58	8 51	14 55
344			**3 13**	**14 49**	**3 27**	**14 34**	**3 45**	**14 14**	**4 10**	**13 47**	**4 50**	**13 03**
11 Sa	11 53 19	−22 59	6 25	17 22	6 46	17 01	7 12	16 35	7 48	15 58	8 52	14 54
345			**4 16**	**15 43**	**4 34**	**15 24**	**4 56**	**15 01**	**5 28**	**14 28**	**6 20**	**13 34**
12 Su	11 53 47	−23 4	6 25	17 22	6 46	17 01	7 12	16 35	7 49	15 58	8 54	14 54
346			**5 20**	**16 41**	**5 40**	**16 21**	**6 05**	**15 55**	**6 40**	**15 19**	**7 42**	**14 17**
13 Mo	11 54 15	−23 8	6 26	17 22	6 47	17 01	7 13	16 35	7 50	15 58	8 55	14 53
347	**9 27 NM**		**6 21**	**17 41**	**6 41**	**17 21**	**7 07**	**16 55**	**7 44**	**16 19**	**8 47**	**15 16**
14 Tu	11 54 44	−23 12	6 27	17 23	6 48	17 02	7 14	16 35	7 51	15 58	8 56	14 53
348			**7 18**	**18 41**	**7 38**	**18 22**	**8 02**	**17 59**	**8 36**	**17 26**	**9 34**	**16 29**
15 We	11 55 12	−23 15	6 27	17 23	6 48	17 02	7 15	16 36	7 52	15 58	8 57	14 53
349			**8 10**	**19 40**	**8 27**	**19 24**	**8 49**	**19 04**	**9 18**	**18 36**	**10 07**	**17 50**
16 Th	11 55 42	−23 18	6 28	17 24	6 49	17 02	7 15	16 36	7 53	15 59	8 58	14 53
350			**8 57**	**20 36**	**9 11**	**20 24**	**9 28**	**20 09**	**9 52**	**19 47**	**10 29**	**19 13**
17 Fr	11 56 11	−23 21	6 28	17 24	6 50	17 03	7 16	16 36	7 53	15 59	8 59	14 53
351			**9 39**	**21 30**	**9 50**	**21 22**	**10 02**	**21 11**	**10 19**	**20 57**	**10 45**	**20 34**
18 Sa	11 56 40	−23 23	6 29	17 24	6 50	17 03	7 17	16 37	7 54	15 59	9 00	14 53
352			**10 18**	**22 21**	**10 25**	**22 17**	**10 32**	**22 12**	**10 43**	**22 04**	**10 58**	**21 53**
19 Su	11 57 10	−23 24	6 29	17 25	6 51	17 04	7 17	16 37	7 55	15 59	9 01	14 54
353			**10 55**	**23 11**	**10 57**	**23 11**	**11 00**	**23 10**	**11 04**	**23 10**	**11 09**	**23 09**
20 Mo	11 57 40	−23 26	6 30	17 25	6 51	17 04	7 18	16 38	7 55	16 00	9 01	14 54
354	**22 26 FQ**		**11 30**	**23 59**	**11 28**	**– –**	**11 26**	**– –**	**11 24**	**– –**	**11 20**	**– –**
21 Tu	11 58 10	−23 26	6 30	17 26	6 52	17 05	7 18	16 38	7 56	16 00	9 02	14 54
355			**12 05**	**– –**	**12 00**	**0 03**	**11 53**	**0 08**	**11 44**	**0 14**	**11 30**	**0 23**
22 We	11 58 40	−23 26	6 31	17 26	6 52	17 05	7 19	16 39	7 56	16 01	9 03	14 55
356			**12 41**	**0 48**	**12 32**	**0 55**	**12 21**	**1 05**	**12 05**	**1 17**	**11 42**	**1 37**
23 Th	11 59 09	−23 26	6 31	17 27	6 53	17 06	7 19	16 39	7 57	16 01	9 03	14 55
357			**13 19**	**1 37**	**13 06**	**1 48**	**12 51**	**2 02**	**12 29**	**2 21**	**11 56**	**2 51**
24 Fr	11 59 39	−23 25	6 32	17 27	6 53	17 06	7 20	16 40	7 57	16 02	9 03	14 56
358			**13 59**	**2 27**	**13 44**	**2 41**	**13 24**	**3 00**	**12 57**	**3 25**	**12 14**	**4 06**
25 Sa	12 0 09	−23 24	6 32	17 28	6 54	17 07	7 20	16 40	7 58	16 03	9 03	14 57
359			**14 43**	**3 18**	**14 25**	**3 36**	**14 02**	**3 57**	**13 31**	**4 28**	**12 38**	**5 18**
26 Su	12 0 39	−23 22	6 33	17 29	6 54	17 07	7 20	16 41	7 58	16 03	9 04	14 58
360			**15 31**	**4 11**	**15 11**	**4 30**	**14 46**	**4 54**	**14 12**	**5 29**	**13 12**	**6 27**
27 Mo	12 1 08	−23 20	6 33	17 29	6 54	17 08	7 21	16 42	7 58	16 04	9 04	14 59
361			**16 23**	**5 04**	**16 02**	**5 24**	**15 37**	**5 49**	**15 01**	**6 25**	**13 59**	**7 27**
28 Tu	12 1 37	−23 17	6 34	17 30	6 55	17 09	7 21	16 42	7 58	16 05	9 04	15 00
362	**23 5 FM**		**17 18**	**5 56**	**16 58**	**6 16**	**16 34**	**6 41**	**15 59**	**7 16**	**15 01**	**8 16**
29 We	12 2 06	−23 14	6 34	17 30	6 55	17 09	7 21	16 43	7 58	16 06	9 03	15 01
363			**18 15**	**6 47**	**17 57**	**7 05**	**17 36**	**7 28**	**17 05**	**8 00**	**16 15**	**8 52**
30 Th	12 2 35	−23 11	6 34	17 31	6 55	17 10	7 22	16 44	7 59	16 07	9 03	15 02
364			**19 13**	**7 36**	**18 59**	**7 51**	**18 41**	**8 10**	**18 17**	**8 37**	**17 37**	**9 19**
31 Fr	12 3 04	−23 7	6 35	17 31	6 56	17 11	7 22	16 44	7 59	16 08	9 03	15 04
365			**20 11**	**8 22**	**20 01**	**8 34**	**19 48**	**8 48**	**19 31**	**9 08**	**19 04**	**9 39**

Latitude, Longitude, and Altitude of North American Cities

Source: National Oceanic and Atmospheric Administration, U.S. Dept. of Commerce for geographic positions.
Source for Canadian cities: Geodetic Survey of Canada, Dept. of Energy, Mines, and Resources.
Altitudes U.S. Geological Survey and various sources. * Approx. altitude at downtown business area U.S.; in Canada at city hall except where (a) is at tower of major airport.

City	Lat. N °	'	"	Long. W °	'	"	Alt.* feet
Abilene, Tex.	32	27	05	99	43	51	1710
Akron, Oh.	41	05	00	81	30	44	874
Albany, N.Y.	42	39	01	73	45	01	20
Albuquerque, N.M.	35	05	01	106	39	05	4,945
Allentown, Pa.	40	36	11	75	28	06	255
Alert, N.W.T.	82	29	50	62	21	15	95
Altoona, Pa.	40	30	55	78	24	03	1,180
Amarillo, Tex.	35	12	27	101	50	04	3,685
Anchorage, Alas.	61	10	00	149	59	00	118
Ann Arbor, Mich.	42	16	59	83	44	52	880
Asheville, N.C.	35	35	42	82	33	26	1,985
Ashland, Ky.	38	28	36	82	38	23	536
Atlanta, Ga.	33	45	10	84	23	37	1,050
Atlantic City, N.J.	39	21	32	74	25	53	10
Augusta, Ga.	33	28	20	81	58	00	143
Augusta, Me.	44	18	53	69	46	29	45
Austin, Tex.	30	16	09	97	44	37	505
Bakersfield, Cal.	35	22	31	119	01	18	400
Baltimore, Md.	39	17	26	76	36	45	20
Bangor, Me.	44	48	13	68	46	18	20
Baton Rouge, La.	30	26	58	91	11	00	57
Battle Creek, Mich.	42	18	58	85	10	48	820
Bay City, Mich.	43	36	04	83	53	15	595
Beaumont, Tex.	30	05	20	94	06	09	20
Belleville, Ont.	44	09	42	77	23	11	257
Bellingham, Wash.	48	45	34	122	28	36	60
Berkeley, Cal.	37	52	10	122	16	17	40
Bethlehem, Pa.	40	37	16	75	22	34	235
Billings, Mon.	45	47	00	108	30	04	3,120
Biloxi, Miss.	30	23	48	88	53	00	20
Binghamton, N.Y.	42	06	03	75	54	47	865
Birmingham, Ala.	33	31	01	86	48	36	600
Bismarck, N.D.	46	48	23	100	47	17	1,674
Bloomington, Ill.	40	28	58	88	59	36	800
Boise, Ida.	43	37	07	116	11	58	2,704
Boston, Mass.	42	21	24	71	03	25	21
Bowling Green, Ky.	36	59	41	86	26	33	510
Brandon, Man.	49	51	00	99	57	00	1,265(a)
Brantford, Ont.	43	08	34	80	15	39	705(a)
Brattleboro, Vt.	42	51	06	72	33	48	300
Bridgeport, Conn.	41	10	49	73	11	22	10
Brockton, Mass.	42	05	02	71	01	25	130
Brownsville, Tex.	25	54	07	97	29	58	35
Buffalo, N.Y.	42	52	52	78	52	21	585
Burlington, Ont.	43	19	33	79	47	57	284
Burlington, Vt.	44	28	34	73	12	46	110
Butte, Mon.	46	01	06	112	32	11	5,765
Calgary, Alta.	51	02	46	114	03	24	3,427
Cambridge, Mass.	42	22	01	71	06	22	20
Camden, N.J.	39	56	41	75	07	14	30
Canton, Oh.	40	47	50	81	22	37	1,030
Carson City, Nev.	39	10	00	119	46	00	4,680
Cedar Rapids, Ia.	41	58	01	91	39	53	730
Central Islip, N.Y.	40	47	24	73	12	00	80
Champaign, Ill.	40	07	05	88	14	48	740
Charleston, S.C.	32	46	35	79	55	53	9
Charleston, W.Va.	38	21	01	81	37	52	601
Charlotte, N.C.	35	13	44	80	50	45	720
Charlottetown, P.E.I.	46	14	07	63	07	49	31
Chattanooga, Tenn.	35	02	41	85	18	32	675
Cheyenne, Wy.	41	08	09	104	49	07	6,100
Chicago, Ill.	41	52	28	87	38	22	595
Churchill, Man.	58	45	15	94	10	00	94(a)
Cincinnati, Oh.	39	06	07	84	30	35	550
Cleveland, Oh.	41	29	51	81	41	50	660
Colorado Springs	38	50	07	104	49	16	5,980
Columbia, Mo.	38	57	03	92	19	46	730
Columbia, S.C.	34	00	02	81	02	00	190
Columbus, Ga.	32	28	07	84	59	24	265
Columbus, Oh.	39	57	47	83	00	17	780
Concord, N.H.	43	12	22	71	32	25	290
Corpus Christi, Tex.	27	47	51	97	23	45	35
Dallas, Tex.	32	47	09	96	47	37	435
Dartmouth, N.S.	44	39	50	63	34	08	24
Davenport, Ia.	41	31	19	90	34	33	590
Dawson, Yukon	64	03	30	139	26	00	1,211(a)
Dayton, Oh.	39	45	32	84	11	43	574
Daytona Beach, Fla.	29	12	44	81	01	10	7
Decatur, Ill.	39	50	42	88	56	47	682
Denver, Col.	39	44	58	104	59	22	5,280
Des Moines, Ia.	41	35	14	93	37	00	803
Detroit, Mich.	42	19	48	83	02	57	585
Dodge City, Kan.	37	45	17	100	01	09	2,480
Dubuque, Ia.	42	29	55	90	40	08	620
Duluth, Minn.	46	46	56	92	06	24	610
Durham, N.C.	36	00	00	78	54	45	405
Eau Claire, Wis.	44	48	31	91	29	49	790
Edmonton, Alta.	53	32	43	113	29	21	2,186
El Paso, Tex.	31	45	36	106	29	11	3,695
Elizabeth, N.J.	40	39	43	74	12	59	21
Enid, Okla.	36	23	40	97	52	35	1,240
Erie, Pa.	42	07	15	80	04	57	685
Eugene, Ore.	44	03	16	123	05	30	422
Eureka, Cal.	40	48	08	124	09	46	45
Evansville, Ind.	37	58	20	87	34	21	385
Fairbanks, Alas.	64	48	00	147	51	00	448
Fall River, Mass.	41	42	06	71	09	18	40
Fargo, N.D.	46	52	30	96	47	18	900
Flagstaff, Ariz.	35	11	36	111	39	06	6,900
Flint, Mich.	43	00	50	83	41	33	750
Ft. Smith, Ark.	35	23	10	94	25	36	440
Fort Wayne, Ind.	41	04	21	85	08	26	790
Fort Worth, Tex.	32	44	55	97	19	44	670
Fredericton, N.B.	45	57	47	66	38	38	29
Fresno, Cal.	36	44	12	119	47	11	285
Gadsden, Ala.	34	00	57	86	00	41	555
Gainesville, Fla.	29	38	56	82	19	19	175
Gallup, N.M.	35	31	30	108	44	30	6,540
Galveston, Tex.	29	18	10	94	47	43	5
Gary, Ind.	41	36	12	87	20	19	590
Grand Junction, Col.	39	04	06	108	33	54	4,590
Grand Rapids, Mich.	42	58	03	85	40	13	610
Great Falls, Mon.	47	29	33	111	18	23	3,340
Green Bay, Wis.	44	30	48	88	00	50	590
Greensboro, N.C.	36	04	17	79	47	25	839
Greenville, S.C.	34	50	50	82	24	01	966
Guelph, Ont.	43	32	35	80	14	54	1,065
Gulfport, Miss.	30	22	04	89	05	36	20
Halifax, N.S.	44	38	54	63	34	30	60
Hamilton, Ont.	43	15	20	79	52	30	329
Hamilton, Oh.	39	23	59	84	33	47	600
Harrisburg, Pa.	40	15	43	76	52	59	365
Hartford, Conn.	41	46	12	72	40	49	40
Helena, Mon.	46	35	33	112	02	24	4,155
Hilo, Hawaii	19	43	30	155	05	24	40
Holyoke, Mass.	42	12	29	72	36	36	115
Honolulu, Ha.	21	18	22	157	51	35	21
Houston, Tex.	29	45	26	95	21	37	40
Hull, Que.	45	25	42	75	42	41	185
Huntington, W.Va.	38	25	12	82	26	33	565
Huntsville, Ala.	34	44	18	86	35	19	640
Indianapolis, Ind.	39	46	07	86	09	46	710
Iowa City, Ia.	41	39	37	91	31	53	685
Jackson, Mich.	42	14	43	84	24	22	940
Jackson, Miss.	32	17	56	90	11	06	298
Jacksonville, Fla.	30	19	44	81	39	42	20
Jersey City, N.J.	40	43	50	74	03	56	20
Johnstown, Pa.	40	19	35	78	55	03	1,185
Joplin, Mo.	37	05	26	94	30	00	990
Juneau, Alas.	58	18	12	134	24	30	50
Kalamazoo, Mich.	42	17	29	85	35	14	755
Kansas City, Kan.	39	07	04	94	38	24	750
Kansas City, Mo.	39	04	56	94	35	20	750
Kenosha, Wis.	42	35	43	87	50	11	610
Key West, Fla.	24	33	30	81	48	12	5
Kingston, Ont.	44	13	53	76	28	48	264
Kitchener, Ont.	43	26	58	80	29	12	1,100
Knoxville, Tenn.	35	57	39	83	55	07	890
Lafayette, Ind.	40	25	11	86	53	39	550
Lancaster, Pa.	40	02	25	76	18	29	355
Lansing, Mich.	42	44	01	84	33	15	830
Laredo, Tex.	27	30	22	99	30	30	440
La Salle, Que.	45	25	30	73	39	30	110
Las Vegas, Nev.	36	10	20	115	08	37	2,030
Laval, Que.	45	33	05	73	44	42	142
Lawrence, Mass.	42	42	16	71	10	08	65
Lethbridge, Alta.	49	41	38	112	49	58	2,985
Lexington, Ky.	38	02	50	84	29	46	955
Lihue, Ha.	21	58	48	159	22	30	210
Lima, Oh.	40	44	35	84	06	20	865
Lincoln, Neb.	40	48	59	96	42	15	1,150
Little Rock, Ark.	34	44	42	92	16	37	286
London, Ont.	42	59	17	81	14	03	822
Long Beach, Cal.	33	46	14	118	11	18	35
Lorain, Oh.	41	28	05	82	10	49	610
Los Angeles, Cal.	34	03	15	118	14	28	340
Louisville, Ky.	38	14	47	85	45	49	450
Lowell, Mass.	42	38	25	71	19	14	100
Lubbock, Tex.	33	35	05	101	50	33	3,195

City	Lat. N °	′	″	Long. W °	′	″	Alt.* feet
Macon, Ga.	32	50	12	83	37	36	335
Madison, Wis.	43	04	23	89	22	55	860
Manchester, N.H.	42	59	28	71	27	41	175
Marshall, Tex.	32	33	00	94	23	00	410
Memphis, Tenn.	35	08	46	90	03	13	275
Meriden, Conn.	41	32	06	72	47	30	190
Mexico City, Mexico	19	25	45	99	07	00	7,347
Miami, Fla.	25	46	37	80	11	32	10
Milwaukee, Wis.	43	02	19	87	54	15	635
Minneapolis, Minn.	44	58	57	93	15	43	815
Minot, N.D.	48	14	09	101	17	38	1,550
Mississauga, Ont.	43	33	00	79	35	00	260(a)
Mobile, Ala.	30	41	36	88	02	33	5
Moline, Ill.	41	30	31	90	30	49	585
Moncton, N.B.	46	05	18	64	46	41	38
Montgomery, Ala.	32	22	33	86	18	31	160
Montpelier, Vt.	44	15	36	72	34	41	485
Montreal, Que.	45	30	33	73	33	14	90
Moose Jaw, Sask.	50	23	34	105	32	04	1,784
Muncie, Ind.	40	11	28	85	23	16	950
Nashville, Tenn.	36	09	33	86	46	55	450
Natchez, Miss.	31	33	48	91	23	30	210
Newark, N.J.	40	44	14	74	10	19	55
New Bedford, Mass.	41	38	13	70	55	41	15
New Britain, Conn.	41	40	08	72	46	59	200
New Haven, Conn.	41	18	25	72	55	30	40
New Orleans, La.	29	56	53	90	04	10	5
New York, N.Y.	40	45	06	73	59	39	55
Niagara Falls, N.Y.	43	05	34	79	03	26	570
Niagara Falls, Ont.	43	06	22	79	03	51	590
Nome, Alas.	64	30	00	165	25	00	25
Norfolk, Va.	36	51	10	76	17	21	10
North Bay, Ont.	46	18	35	79	27	45	670
Oakland, Cal.	37	48	03	122	15	54	25
Ogden, Ut.	41	13	31	111	58	21	4,295
Oklahoma City	35	28	26	97	31	04	1,195
Omaha, Neb.	41	15	42	95	56	14	1,040
Orlando, Fla.	28	32	42	81	22	38	70
Oshawa, Ont.	43	53	46	78	51	57	350
Ottawa, Ont.	45	26	24	75	41	42	185
Paducah, Ky.	37	05	13	88	35	56	345
Pasadena, Cal.	34	08	44	118	08	41	830
Paterson, N.J.	40	55	01	74	10	21	100
Pensacola, Fla.	30	24	51	87	12	56	15
Peoria, Ill.	40	41	42	89	35	33	470
Peterborough, Ont.	44	18	32	78	19	13	673
Philadelphia, Pa.	39	56	58	75	09	21	100
Phoenix, Ariz.	33	27	12	112	04	28	1,090
Pierre, S.D.	44	22	18	100	20	54	1,480
Pittsburgh, Pa.	40	26	19	80	00	00	745
Pittsfield, Mass.	42	26	53	73	15	14	1,015
Pocatello, Ida.	42	51	38	112	27	01	4,460
Port Arthur, Tex.	29	52	30	93	56	15	10
Portland, Me.	43	39	33	70	15	19	25
Portland, Ore.	45	31	06	122	40	35	77
Portsmouth, N.H.	43	04	30	70	45	24	20
Portsmouth, Va.	36	50	07	76	18	14	10
Prince Rupert, B.C.	54	19	00	130	19	00	125(a)
Providence, R.I.	41	49	32	71	24	41	80
Provo, Ut.	40	14	06	111	39	24	4,550
Pueblo, Col.	38	16	17	104	36	33	4,690
Quebec City, Que.	46	48	51	71	12	30	163
Racine, Wis.	42	43	49	87	47	12	630
Rapid City, S.D.	44	04	52	103	13	11	3,230
Raleigh, N.C.	35	46	38	78	38	21	365
Reading, Pa.	40	20	09	75	55	40	265
Regina, Sask.	50	26	55	104	36	50	1,894(a)
Reno, Nev.	39	31	27	119	48	40	4,490
Richmond, Va.	37	32	15	77	26	09	160
Roanoke, Va.	37	16	13	79	56	44	905
Rochester, Minn.	44	01	21	92	28	03	990
Rochester, N.Y.	43	09	41	77	36	21	515
Rockford, Ill.	42	16	07	89	05	48	715
Sacramento, Cal.	38	34	57	121	29	41	30
Saginaw, Mich.	43	25	52	83	56	05	595
St. Catharines, Ont.	43	09	33	79	14	50	362(a)
St. Cloud, Minn.	45	34	00	94	10	24	1,040
Saint John, N.B.	45	16	22	66	03	48	27
St. John's, Nfld.	47	33	42	52	42	48	200(a)
St. Joseph, Mo.	39	45	57	94	51	02	850
St. Louis, Mo.	38	37	45	90	12	22	455
St. Paul, Minn.	44	57	19	93	06	07	780
St. Petersburg, Fla.	27	46	18	82	38	19	20
Salem, Ore.	44	56	24	123	01	59	155

City	Lat. N °	′	″	Long. W °	′	″	Alt.* feet
Salina, Kan.	38	50	36	97	36	46	1,229
Salt Lake City, Ut.	40	45	23	111	53	26	4,390
San Angelo, Tex.	31	27	39	100	26	03	1,845
San Antonio, Tex.	29	25	37	98	29	06	650
San Bernardino, Cal.	34	06	30	117	17	28	1,080
San Diego, Cal.	32	42	53	117	09	21	20
San Francisco, Cal.	37	46	39	122	24	40	65
San Jose, Cal.	37	20	16	121	53	24	90
San Juan, P.R.	18	27	00	66	04	15	35
Santa Barbara, Cal.	34	25	18	119	41	55	100
Santa Cruz, Cal.	36	58	18	122	01	18	20
Santa Fe, N.M.	35	41	11	105	56	10	6,950
Sarasota, Fla.	27	20	05	82	32	30	20
Saskatoon, Sask.	52	07	49	106	39	35	1,587
Sault Ste. Marie, Ont.	46	30	24	84	20	04	589
Savannah, Ga.	32	04	42	81	05	37	20
Schenectady, N.Y.	42	48	42	73	55	42	245
Scranton, Pa.	41	24	32	75	39	46	725
Seattle, Wash.	47	36	32	122	20	12	10
Sheboygan, Wis.	43	45	03	87	42	52	630
Sherbrooke, Que.	45	24	27	71	51	07	535(a)
Sheridan, Wy.	44	47	55	106	57	10	3,740
Shreveport, La.	32	30	46	93	44	58	204
Sioux City, Ia.	42	29	46	96	24	30	1,110
Sioux Falls, S.D.	43	32	35	96	43	35	1,395
Somerville, Mass.	42	23	15	71	06	07	13
South Bend, Ind.	41	40	33	86	15	01	710
Spartanburg, S.C.	34	57	03	81	56	06	875
Spokane, Wash.	47	39	32	117	25	33	1,890
Springfield, Ill.	39	47	58	89	38	51	610
Springfield, Mass.	42	06	21	72	35	32	85
Springfield, Mo.	37	13	03	93	17	32	1,300
Springfield, Oh.	39	55	38	83	48	29	980
Stamford, Conn.	41	03	09	73	32	24	35
Steubenville, Oh.	40	21	42	80	36	53	660
Stockton, Cal.	37	57	30	121	17	16	20
Sudbury, Ont.	46	29	24	80	59	24	850(a)
Superior, Wis.	46	43	14	92	06	07	630
Sydney, N.S.	46	08	15	60	11	48	15
Syracuse, N.Y.	43	03	04	76	09	14	400
Tacoma, Wash.	47	14	59	122	26	15	110
Tallahassee, Fla.	30	26	30	84	16	56	150
Tampa, Fla.	27	56	58	82	27	25	15
Terre Haute, Ind.	39	28	03	87	24	26	496
Texarkana, Tex.	33	25	48	94	02	30	324
Thunder Bay, Ont.	48	22	54	89	14	42	616
Toledo, Oh.	41	39	14	83	32	39	585
Topeka, Kan.	39	03	16	95	40	23	930
Toronto, Ont.	43	39	10	79	23	00	300
Trenton, N.J.	40	13	14	74	46	13	35
Trois-Rivieres, Que.	46	20	36	72	32	37	115(a)
Troy, N.Y.	42	43	45	73	40	58	35
Tucson, Ariz.	32	13	15	110	58	08	2,390
Tulsa, Okla.	36	09	12	95	59	34	804
Urbana, Ill.	40	06	42	88	12	06	725
Utica, N.Y.	43	06	12	75	13	33	415
Vancouver, B.C.	49	18	56	123	04	44	141
Victoria, B.C.	48	25	43	123	21	49	57
Waco, Tex.	31	33	12	97	08	00	405
Walla Walla, Wash.	46	04	08	118	20	24	936
Washington, D.C.	38	53	51	77	00	33	25
Waterbury, Conn.	41	33	13	73	02	31	260
Waterloo, Ia.	42	29	40	92	20	20	850
West Palm Beach, Fla.	26	42	36	80	03	07	15
Wheeling, W. Va.	40	04	03	80	43	20	650
Whitehorse, Yukon	60	43	17	135	03	03	2,305(a)
White Plains, N.Y.	41	02	00	73	45	48	220
Wichita, Kan.	37	41	30	97	20	16	1,290
Wichita Falls, Tex.	33	54	34	98	29	28	945
Wilkes-Barre, Pa.	41	14	32	75	53	17	640
Wilmington, Del.	39	44	46	75	32	51	135
Wilmington, N.C.	34	14	14	77	56	58	35
Windsor, Ont.	42	18	56	83	02	10	603
Winnipeg, Man.	49	53	56	97	08	23	762
Winston-Salem, N.C.	36	05	52	80	14	42	860
Worcester, Mass.	42	15	37	71	48	17	475
Yakima, Wash.	46	36	09	120	30	39	1,060
Yellowknife, N.W.T.	62	27	16	114	22	33	674(a)
Yonkers, N.Y.	40	55	55	73	53	54	10
York, Pa.	39	57	35	76	43	36	370
Youngstown, Oh.	41	05	57	80	39	02	840
Yuma, Ariz.	32	42	54	114	37	24	160
Zanesville, Oh.	39	56	18	82	00	30	720

World Cities

City	Lat. °	′	″	Long. °	′	″	Alt. feet
London, UK (Greenwich)	51	30	00N	0	0	0	245
Paris, France	48	50	14N	2	20	14E	300
Berlin, Germany	52	32	00N	13	25	00E	110
Rome, Italy	41	53	00N	12	30	00E	95
Warsaw, Poland	52	15	00N	21	00	00E	360
Moscow, Russia	55	45	00N	37	42	00E	394
Athens, Greece	37	58	00N	23	44	00E	300
Jerusalem, Israel	31	47	00N	35	13	00E	2,500
Johannesburg, So. Afr.	26	10	00S	28	02	00E	5,740
New Delhi, India	28	38	00N	77	12	00E	770
Peking, China	39	54	00N	116	28	00E	600
Rio de Janeiro, Brazil	22	53	43S	43	13	22W	30
Tokyo, Japan	35	45	00N	139	45	00E	30
Sydney, Australia	33	52	00S	151	12	00E	25

Perpetual Calendar

The number shown for each year indicates which Gregorian calendar to use. For 1583-1802, or for Julian calendar, see page 274. For years 1803-1820, use numbers for 1983-2000, respectively.

1821....2	1847....6	1873....4	1899....1	1925....5	1951....2	1977....7	2003....4	2029....2	2055....6
1822....3	1848...14	1874....5	1900....2	1926....6	1952...10	1978....1	2004...12	2030....3	2056...14
1823....4	1849....2	1875....6	1901....3	1927....7	1953....5	1979....2	2005....7	2031....4	2057....2
1824...12	1850....3	1876...14	1902....4	1928....8	1954....6	1980...10	2006....1	2032...12	2058....3
1825....7	1851....4	1877....2	1903....5	1929....3	1955....7	1981....5	2007....2	2033....7	2059....4
1826....1	1852...12	1878....3	1904...13	1930....4	1956....8	1982....6	2008...10	2034....1	2060..12
1827....2	1853....7	1879....4	1905....1	1931....5	1957....3	1983....7	2009....5	2035....2	2061..7
1828...10	1854....1	1880...12	1906....2	1932...13	1958....4	1984....8	2010....6	2036...10	2062..1
1829....5	1855....2	1881....7	1907....3	1933....1	1959....5	1985....3	2011....7	2037....5	2063..2
1830....6	1856...10	1882....1	1908...11	1934....2	1960...13	1986....4	2012....8	2038....6	2064..10
1831....7	1857....5	1883....2	1909....6	1935....3	1961....1	1987....5	2013....3	2039....7	2065..5
1832....8	1858....6	1884...10	1910....7	1936...11	1962....2	1988...13	2014....4	2040....8	2066..6
1833....3	1859....7	1885....5	1911....1	1937....6	1963....3	1989....1	2015....5	2041....3	2067..7
1834....4	1860....8	1886....6	1912....9	1938....7	1964...11	1990....2	2016...13	2042....4	2068..8
1835....5	1861....3	1887....7	1913....4	1939....1	1965....6	1991....3	2017....1	2043....5	2069..3
1836...13	1862....4	1888....8	1914....5	1940....9	1966....7	1992...11	2018....2	2044...13	2070..4
1837....1	1863....5	1889....3	1915....6	1941....4	1967....1	1993....6	2019....3	2045....1	2071..5
1838....2	1864...13	1890....4	1916...14	1942....5	1968....9	1994....7	2020...11	2046....2	2072..13
1839....3	1865....1	1891....5	1917....2	1943....6	1969....4	1995....1	2021....6	2047....3	2073..1
1840...11	1866....2	1892...13	1918....3	1944...14	1970....5	1996....9	2022....7	2048...11	2074..2
1841....6	1867....3	1893....1	1919....4	1945....2	1971....6	1997....4	2023....1	2049....6	2075..3
1842....7	1868...11	1894....2	1920...12	1946....3	1972...14	1998....5	2024....9	2050....7	2076..11
1843....1	1869....6	1895....3	1921....7	1947....4	1973....2	1999....6	2025....4	2051....1	2077..6
1844....9	1870....7	1896...11	1922....1	1948...12	1974....3	2000...14	2026....5	2052....9	2078..7
1845....4	1871....1	1897....6	1923....2	1949....7	1975....4	2001....2	2027....6	2053....4	2079..1
1846....5	1872....9	1898....7	1924...10	1950....1	1976...12	2002....3	2028...14	2054....5	2080..9

1

JANUARY

S	M	T	W	T	F	S
1	2	3	4	5	6	7
8	9	10	11	12	13	14
15	16	17	18	19	20	21
22	23	24	25	26	27	28
29	30	31				

FEBRUARY

S	M	T	W	T	F	S
			1	2	3	4
5	6	7	8	9	10	11
12	13	14	15	16	17	18
19	20	21	22	23	24	25
26	27	28				

MARCH

S	M	T	W	T	F	S
			1	2	3	4
5	6	7	8	9	10	11
12	13	14	15	16	17	18
19	20	21	22	23	24	25
26	27	28	29	30	31	

APRIL

S	M	T	W	T	F	S
						1
2	3	4	5	6	7	8
9	10	11	12	13	14	15
16	17	18	19	20	21	22
23	24	25	26	27	28	29
30						

MAY

S	M	T	W	T	F	S
	1	2	3	4	5	6
7	8	9	10	11	12	13
14	15	16	17	18	19	20
21	22	23	24	25	26	27
28	29	30	31			

JUNE

S	M	T	W	T	F	S
				1	2	3
4	5	6	7	8	9	10
11	12	13	14	15	16	17
18	19	20	21	22	23	24
25	26	27	28	29	30	

JULY

S	M	T	W	T	F	S
						1
2	3	4	5	6	7	8
9	10	11	12	13	14	15
16	17	18	19	20	21	22
23	24	25	26	27	28	29
30	31					

AUGUST

S	M	T	W	T	F	S
		1	2	3	4	5
6	7	8	9	10	11	12
13	14	15	16	17	18	19
20	21	22	23	24	25	26
27	28	29	30	31		

SEPTEMBER

S	M	T	W	T	F	S
					1	2
3	4	5	6	7	8	9
10	11	12	13	14	15	16
17	18	19	20	21	22	23
24	25	26	27	28	29	30

OCTOBER

S	M	T	W	T	F	S
1	2	3	4	5	6	7
8	9	10	11	12	13	14
15	16	17	18	19	20	21
22	23	24	25	26	27	28
29	30	31				

NOVEMBER

S	M	T	W	T	F	S
			1	2	3	4
5	6	7	8	9	10	11
12	13	14	15	16	17	18
19	20	21	22	23	24	25
26	27	28	29	30		

DECEMBER

S	M	T	W	T	F	S
					1	2
3	4	5	6	7	8	9
10	11	12	13	14	15	16
17	18	19	20	21	22	23
24	25	26	27	28	29	30
31						

2

JANUARY

S	M	T	W	T	F	S
	1	2	3	4	5	6
7	8	9	10	11	12	13
14	15	16	17	18	19	20
21	22	23	24	25	26	27
28	29	30	31			

FEBRUARY

S	M	T	W	T	F	S
				1	2	3
4	5	6	7	8	9	10
11	12	13	14	15	16	17
18	19	20	21	22	23	24
25	26	27	28			

MARCH

S	M	T	W	T	F	S
				1	2	3
4	5	6	7	8	9	10
11	12	13	14	15	16	17
18	19	20	21	22	23	24
25	26	27	28	29	30	31

APRIL

S	M	T	W	T	F	S
1	2	3	4	5	6	7
8	9	10	11	12	13	14
15	16	17	18	19	20	21
22	23	24	25	26	27	28
29	30					

MAY

S	M	T	W	T	F	S
		1	2	3	4	5
6	7	8	9	10	11	12
13	14	15	16	17	18	19
20	21	22	23	24	25	26
27	28	29	30	31		

JUNE

S	M	T	W	T	F	S
					1	2
3	4	5	6	7	8	9
10	11	12	13	14	15	16
17	18	19	20	21	22	23
24	25	26	27	28	29	30

JULY

S	M	T	W	T	F	S
1	2	3	4	5	6	7
8	9	10	11	12	13	14
15	16	17	18	19	20	21
22	23	24	25	26	27	28
29	30	31				

AUGUST

S	M	T	W	T	F	S
			1	2	3	4
5	6	7	8	9	10	11
12	13	14	15	16	17	18
19	20	21	22	23	24	25
26	27	28	29	30	31	

SEPTEMBER

S	M	T	W	T	F	S
						1
2	3	4	5	6	7	8
9	10	11	12	13	14	15
16	17	18	19	20	21	22
23	24	25	26	27	28	29
30						

OCTOBER

S	M	T	W	T	F	S
	1	2	3	4	5	6
7	8	9	10	11	12	13
14	15	16	17	18	19	20
21	22	23	24	25	26	27
28	29	30	31			

NOVEMBER

S	M	T	W	T	F	S
				1	2	3
4	5	6	7	8	9	10
11	12	13	14	15	16	17
18	19	20	21	22	23	24
25	26	27	28	29	30	

DECEMBER

S	M	T	W	T	F	S
						1
2	3	4	5	6	7	8
9	10	11	12	13	14	15
16	17	18	19	20	21	22
23	24	25	26	27	28	29
30	31					

3

JANUARY

S	M	T	W	T	F	S
		1	2	3	4	5
6	7	8	9	10	11	12
13	14	15	16	17	18	19
20	21	22	23	24	25	26
27	28	29	30	31		

FEBRUARY

S	M	T	W	T	F	S
					1	2
3	4	5	6	7	8	9
10	11	12	13	14	15	16
17	18	19	20	21	22	23
24	25	26	27	28		

MARCH

S	M	T	W	T	F	S
					1	2
3	4	5	6	7	8	9
10	11	12	13	14	15	16
17	18	19	20	21	22	23
24	25	26	27	28	29	30
31						

APRIL

S	M	T	W	T	F	S
	1	2	3	4	5	6
7	8	9	10	11	12	13
14	15	16	17	18	19	20
21	22	23	24	25	26	27
28	29	30				

MAY

S	M	T	W	T	F	S
			1	2	3	4
5	6	7	8	9	10	11
12	13	14	15	16	17	18
19	20	21	22	23	24	25
26	27	28	29	30	31	

JUNE

S	M	T	W	T	F	S
						1
2	3	4	5	6	7	8
9	10	11	12	13	14	15
16	17	18	19	20	21	22
23	24	25	26	27	28	29
30						

JULY

S	M	T	W	T	F	S
	1	2	3	4	5	6
7	8	9	10	11	12	13
14	15	16	17	18	19	20
21	22	23	24	25	26	27
28	29	30	31			

AUGUST

S	M	T	W	T	F	S
				1	2	3
4	5	6	7	8	9	10
11	12	13	14	15	16	17
18	19	20	21	22	23	24
25	26	27	28	29	30	31

SEPTEMBER

S	M	T	W	T	F	S
1	2	3	4	5	6	7
8	9	10	11	12	13	14
15	16	17	18	19	20	21
22	23	24	25	26	27	28
29	30					

OCTOBER

S	M	T	W	T	F	S
		1	2	3	4	5
6	7	8	9	10	11	12
13	14	15	16	17	18	19
20	21	22	23	24	25	26
27	28	29	30	31		

NOVEMBER

S	M	T	W	T	F	S
					1	2
3	4	5	6	7	8	9
10	11	12	13	14	15	16
17	18	19	20	21	22	23
24	25	26	27	28	29	30

DECEMBER

S	M	T	W	T	F	S
1	2	3	4	5	6	7
8	9	10	11	12	13	14
15	16	17	18	19	20	21
22	23	24	25	26	27	28
29	30	31				

4

JANUARY

S	M	T	W	T	F	S
			1	2	3	4
5	6	7	8	9	10	11
12	13	14	15	16	17	18
19	20	21	22	23	24	25
26	27	28	29	30	31	

FEBRUARY

S	M	T	W	T	F	S
						1
2	3	4	5	6	7	8
9	10	11	12	13	14	15
16	17	18	19	20	21	22
23	24	25	26	27	28	

MARCH

S	M	T	W	T	F	S
						1
2	3	4	5	6	7	8
9	10	11	12	13	14	15
16	17	18	19	20	21	22
23	24	25	26	27	28	29
30	31					

APRIL

S	M	T	W	T	F	S
		1	2	3	4	5
6	7	8	9	10	11	12
13	14	15	16	17	18	19
20	21	22	23	24	25	26
27	28	29	30			

MAY

S	M	T	W	T	F	S
				1	2	3
4	5	6	7	8	9	10
11	12	13	14	15	16	17
18	19	20	21	22	23	24
25	26	27	28	29	30	31

JUNE

S	M	T	W	T	F	S
1	2	3	4	5	6	7
8	9	10	11	12	13	14
15	16	17	18	19	20	21
22	23	24	25	26	27	28
29	30					

JULY

S	M	T	W	T	F	S
		1	2	3	4	5
6	7	8	9	10	11	12
13	14	15	16	17	18	19
20	21	22	23	24	25	26
27	28	29	30	31		

AUGUST

S	M	T	W	T	F	S
					1	2
3	4	5	6	7	8	9
10	11	12	13	14	15	16
17	18	19	20	21	22	23
24	25	26	27	28	29	30
31						

SEPTEMBER

S	M	T	W	T	F	S
	1	2	3	4	5	6
7	8	9	10	11	12	13
14	15	16	17	18	19	20
21	22	23	24	25	26	27
28	29	30				

OCTOBER

S	M	T	W	T	F	S
			1	2	3	4
5	6	7	8	9	10	11
12	13	14	15	16	17	18
19	20	21	22	23	24	25
26	27	28	29	30	31	

NOVEMBER

S	M	T	W	T	F	S
						1
2	3	4	5	6	7	8
9	10	11	12	13	14	15
16	17	18	19	20	21	22
23	24	25	26	27	28	29
30						

DECEMBER

S	M	T	W	T	F	S
	1	2	3	4	5	6
7	8	9	10	11	12	13
14	15	16	17	18	19	20
21	22	23	24	25	26	27
28	29	30	31			

5

JANUARY

S	M	T	W	T	F	S
				1	2	3
4	5	6	7	8	9	10
11	12	13	14	15	16	17
18	19	20	21	22	23	24
25	26	27	28	29	30	31

FEBRUARY

S	M	T	W	T	F	S
1	2	3	4	5	6	7
8	9	10	11	12	13	14
15	16	17	18	19	20	21
22	23	24	25	26	27	28

MARCH

S	M	T	W	T	F	S
1	2	3	4	5	6	7
8	9	10	11	12	13	14
15	16	17	18	19	20	21
22	23	24	25	26	27	28
29	30	31				

APRIL

S	M	T	W	T	F	S
			1	2	3	4
5	6	7	8	9	10	11
12	13	14	15	16	17	18
19	20	21	22	23	24	25
26	27	28	29	30		

MAY

S	M	T	W	T	F	S
					1	2
3	4	5	6	7	8	9
10	11	12	13	14	15	16
17	18	19	20	21	22	23
24	25	26	27	28	29	30
31						

JUNE

S	M	T	W	T	F	S
	1	2	3	4	5	6
7	8	9	10	11	12	13
14	15	16	17	18	19	20
21	22	23	24	25	26	27
28	29	30				

JULY

S	M	T	W	T	F	S
			1	2	3	4
5	6	7	8	9	10	11
12	13	14	15	16	17	18
19	20	21	22	23	24	25
26	27	28	29	30	31	

AUGUST

S	M	T	W	T	F	S
						1
2	3	4	5	6	7	8
9	10	11	12	13	14	15
16	17	18	19	20	21	22
23	24	25	26	27	28	29
30	31					

SEPTEMBER

S	M	T	W	T	F	S
		1	2	3	4	5
6	7	8	9	10	11	12
13	14	15	16	17	18	19
20	21	22	23	24	25	26
27	28	29	30			

OCTOBER

S	M	T	W	T	F	S
				1	2	3
4	5	6	7	8	9	10
11	12	13	14	15	16	17
18	19	20	21	22	23	24
25	26	27	28	29	30	31

NOVEMBER

S	M	T	W	T	F	S
1	2	3	4	5	6	7
8	9	10	11	12	13	14
15	16	17	18	19	20	21
22	23	24	25	26	27	28
29	30					

DECEMBER

S	M	T	W	T	F	S
		1	2	3	4	5
6	7	8	9	10	11	12
13	14	15	16	17	18	19
20	21	22	23	24	25	26
27	28	29	30	31		

6

1993

JANUARY

S	M	T	W	T	F	S
					1	2
3	4	5	6	7	8	9
10	11	12	13	14	15	16
17	18	19	20	21	22	23
24	25	26	27	28	29	30
31						

FEBRUARY

S	M	T	W	T	F	S
	1	2	3	4	5	6
7	8	9	10	11	12	13
14	15	16	17	18	19	20
21	22	23	24	25	26	27
28						

MARCH

S	M	T	W	T	F	S
	1	2	3	4	5	6
7	8	9	10	11	12	13
14	15	16	17	18	19	20
21	22	23	24	25	26	27
28	29	30	31			

APRIL

S	M	T	W	T	F	S
				1	2	3
4	5	6	7	8	9	10
11	12	13	14	15	16	17
18	19	20	21	22	23	24
25	26	27	28	29	30	

MAY

S	M	T	W	T	F	S
						1
2	3	4	5	6	7	8
9	10	11	12	13	14	15
16	17	18	19	20	21	22
23	24	25	26	27	28	29
30	31					

JUNE

S	M	T	W	T	F	S
		1	2	3	4	5
6	7	8	9	10	11	12
13	14	15	16	17	18	19
20	21	22	23	24	25	26
27	28	29	30			

JULY

S	M	T	W	T	F	S
				1	2	3
4	5	6	7	8	9	10
11	12	13	14	15	16	17
18	19	20	21	22	23	24
25	26	27	28	29	30	31

AUGUST

S	M	T	W	T	F	S
1	2	3	4	5	6	7
8	9	10	11	12	13	14
15	16	17	18	19	20	21
22	23	24	25	26	27	28
29	30	31				

SEPTEMBER

S	M	T	W	T	F	S
			1	2	3	4
5	6	7	8	9	10	11
12	13	14	15	16	17	18
19	20	21	22	23	24	25
26	27	28	29	30		

OCTOBER

S	M	T	W	T	F	S
					1	2
3	4	5	6	7	8	9
10	11	12	13	14	15	16
17	18	19	20	21	22	23
24	25	26	27	28	29	30
31						

NOVEMBER

S	M	T	W	T	F	S
	1	2	3	4	5	6
7	8	9	10	11	12	13
14	15	16	17	18	19	20
21	22	23	24	25	26	27
28	29	30				

DECEMBER

S	M	T	W	T	F	S
			1	2	3	4
5	6	7	8	9	10	11
12	13	14	15	16	17	18
19	20	21	22	23	24	25
26	27	28	29	30	31	

7 1994

JANUARY

S	M	T	W	T	F	S
						1
2	3	4	5	6	7	8
9	10	11	12	13	14	15
16	17	18	19	20	21	22
23	24	25	26	27	28	29
30	31					

FEBRUARY

S	M	T	W	T	F	S
		1	2	3	4	5
6	7	8	9	10	11	12
13	14	15	16	17	18	19
20	21	22	23	24	25	26
27	28					

MARCH

S	M	T	W	T	F	S
		1	2	3	4	5
6	7	8	9	10	11	12
13	14	15	16	17	18	19
20	21	22	23	24	25	26
27	28	29	30	31		

APRIL

S	M	T	W	T	F	S
					1	2
3	4	5	6	7	8	9
10	11	12	13	14	15	16
17	18	19	20	21	22	23
24	25	26	27	28	29	30

MAY

S	M	T	W	T	F	S
1	2	3	4	5	6	7
8	9	10	11	12	13	14
15	16	17	18	19	20	21
22	23	24	25	26	27	28
29	30	31				

JUNE

S	M	T	W	T	F	S
			1	2	3	4
5	6	7	8	9	10	11
12	13	14	15	16	17	18
19	20	21	22	23	24	25
26	27	28	29	30		

JULY

S	M	T	W	T	F	S
					1	2
3	4	5	6	7	8	9
10	11	12	13	14	15	16
17	18	19	20	21	22	23
24	25	26	27	28	29	30
31						

AUGUST

S	M	T	W	T	F	S
	1	2	3	4	5	6
7	8	9	10	11	12	13
14	15	16	17	18	19	20
21	22	23	24	25	26	27
28	29	30	31			

SEPTEMBER

S	M	T	W	T	F	S
				1	2	3
4	5	6	7	8	9	10
11	12	13	14	15	16	17
18	19	20	21	22	23	24
25	26	27	28	29	30	

OCTOBER

S	M	T	W	T	F	S
						1
2	3	4	5	6	7	8
9	10	11	12	13	14	15
16	17	18	19	20	21	22
23	24	25	26	27	28	29
30	31					

NOVEMBER

S	M	T	W	T	F	S
		1	2	3	4	5
6	7	8	9	10	11	12
13	14	15	16	17	18	19
20	21	22	23	24	25	26
27	28	29	30			

DECEMBER

S	M	T	W	T	F	S
				1	2	3
4	5	6	7	8	9	10
11	12	13	14	15	16	17
18	19	20	21	22	23	24
25	26	27	28	29	30	31

8

JANUARY

S	M	T	W	T	F	S
1	2	3	4	5	6	7
8	9	10	11	12	13	14
15	16	17	18	19	20	21
22	23	24	25	26	27	28
29	30	31				

FEBRUARY

S	M	T	W	T	F	S
			1	2	3	4
5	6	7	8	9	10	11
12	13	14	15	16	17	18
19	20	21	22	23	24	25
26	27	28	29			

MARCH

S	M	T	W	T	F	S
				1	2	3
4	5	6	7	8	9	10
11	12	13	14	15	16	17
18	19	20	21	22	23	24
25	26	27	28	29	30	31

APRIL

S	M	T	W	T	F	S
1	2	3	4	5	6	7
8	9	10	11	12	13	14
15	16	17	18	19	20	21
22	23	24	25	26	27	28
29	30					

MAY

S	M	T	W	T	F	S
		1	2	3	4	5
6	7	8	9	10	11	12
13	14	15	16	17	18	19
20	21	22	23	24	25	26
27	28	29	30	31		

JUNE

S	M	T	W	T	F	S
					1	2
3	4	5	6	7	8	9
10	11	12	13	14	15	16
17	18	19	20	21	22	23
24	25	26	27	28	29	30

JULY

S	M	T	W	T	F	S
1	2	3	4	5	6	7
8	9	10	11	12	13	14
15	16	17	18	19	20	21
22	23	24	25	26	27	28
29	30	31				

AUGUST

S	M	T	W	T	F	S
			1	2	3	4
5	6	7	8	9	10	11
12	13	14	15	16	17	18
19	20	21	22	23	24	25
26	27	28	29	30	31	

SEPTEMBER

S	M	T	W	T	F	S
						1
2	3	4	5	6	7	8
9	10	11	12	13	14	15
16	17	18	19	20	21	22
23	24	25	26	27	28	29
30						

OCTOBER

S	M	T	W	T	F	S
	1	2	3	4	5	6
7	8	9	10	11	12	13
14	15	16	17	18	19	20
21	22	23	24	25	26	27
28	29	30	31			

NOVEMBER

S	M	T	W	T	F	S
				1	2	3
4	5	6	7	8	9	10
11	12	13	14	15	16	17
18	19	20	21	22	23	24
25	26	27	28	29	30	

DECEMBER

S	M	T	W	T	F	S
						1
2	3	4	5	6	7	8
9	10	11	12	13	14	15
16	17	18	19	20	21	22
23	24	25	26	27	28	29
30	31					

9

JANUARY

S	M	T	W	T	F	S
	1	2	3	4	5	6
7	8	9	10	11	12	13
14	15	16	17	18	19	20
21	22	23	24	25	26	27
28	29	30	31			

FEBRUARY

S	M	T	W	T	F	S
				1	2	3
4	5	6	7	8	9	10
11	12	13	14	15	16	17
18	19	20	21	22	23	24
25	26	27	28	29		

MARCH

S	M	T	W	T	F	S
					1	2
3	4	5	6	7	8	9
10	11	12	13	14	15	16
17	18	19	20	21	22	23
24	25	26	27	28	29	30
31						

APRIL

S	M	T	W	T	F	S
	1	2	3	4	5	6
7	8	9	10	11	12	13
14	15	16	17	18	19	20
21	22	23	24	25	26	27
28	29	30				

MAY

S	M	T	W	T	F	S
			1	2	3	4
5	6	7	8	9	10	11
12	13	14	15	16	17	18
19	20	21	22	23	24	25
26	27	28	29	30	31	

JUNE

S	M	T	W	T	F	S
						1
2	3	4	5	6	7	8
9	10	11	12	13	14	15
16	17	18	19	20	21	22
23	24	25	26	27	28	29
30						

JULY

S	M	T	W	T	F	S
	1	2	3	4	5	6
7	8	9	10	11	12	13
14	15	16	17	18	19	20
21	22	23	24	25	26	27
28	29	30	31			

AUGUST

S	M	T	W	T	F	S
				1	2	3
4	5	6	7	8	9	10
11	12	13	14	15	16	17
18	19	20	21	22	23	24
25	26	27	28	29	30	31

SEPTEMBER

S	M	T	W	T	F	S
1	2	3	4	5	6	7
8	9	10	11	12	13	14
15	16	17	18	19	20	21
22	23	24	25	26	27	28
29	30					

OCTOBER

S	M	T	W	T	F	S
		1	2	3	4	5
6	7	8	9	10	11	12
13	14	15	16	17	18	19
20	21	22	23	24	25	26
27	28	29	30	31		

NOVEMBER

S	M	T	W	T	F	S
					1	2
3	4	5	6	7	8	9
10	11	12	13	14	15	16
17	18	19	20	21	22	23
24	25	26	27	28	29	30

DECEMBER

S	M	T	W	T	F	S
1	2	3	4	5	6	7
8	9	10	11	12	13	14
15	16	17	18	19	20	21
22	23	24	25	26	27	28
29	30	31				

10

JANUARY

S	M	T	W	T	F	S
		1	2	3	4	5
6	7	8	9	10	11	12
13	14	15	16	17	18	19
20	21	22	23	24	25	26
27	28	29	30	31		

FEBRUARY

S	M	T	W	T	F	S
					1	2
3	4	5	6	7	8	9
10	11	12	13	14	15	16
17	18	19	20	21	22	23
24	25	26	27	28	29	

MARCH

S	M	T	W	T	F	S
						1
2	3	4	5	6	7	8
9	10	11	12	13	14	15
16	17	18	19	20	21	22
23	24	25	26	27	28	29
30	31					

APRIL

S	M	T	W	T	F	S
		1	2	3	4	5
6	7	8	9	10	11	12
13	14	15	16	17	18	19
20	21	22	23	24	25	26
27	28	29	30			

MAY

S	M	T	W	T	F	S
				1	2	3
4	5	6	7	8	9	10
11	12	13	14	15	16	17
18	19	20	21	22	23	24
25	26	27	28	29	30	31

JUNE

S	M	T	W	T	F	S
1	2	3	4	5	6	7
8	9	10	11	12	13	14
15	16	17	18	19	20	21
22	23	24	25	26	27	28
29	30					

JULY

S	M	T	W	T	F	S
		1	2	3	4	5
6	7	8	9	10	11	12
13	14	15	16	17	18	19
20	21	22	23	24	25	26
27	28	29	30	31		

AUGUST

S	M	T	W	T	F	S
					1	2
3	4	5	6	7	8	9
10	11	12	13	14	15	16
17	18	19	20	21	22	23
24	25	26	27	28	29	30
31						

SEPTEMBER

S	M	T	W	T	F	S
	1	2	3	4	5	6
7	8	9	10	11	12	13
14	15	16	17	18	19	20
21	22	23	24	25	26	27
28	29	30				

OCTOBER

S	M	T	W	T	F	S
			1	2	3	4
5	6	7	8	9	10	11
12	13	14	15	16	17	18
19	20	21	22	23	24	25
26	27	28	29	30	31	

NOVEMBER

S	M	T	W	T	F	S
						1
2	3	4	5	6	7	8
9	10	11	12	13	14	15
16	17	18	19	20	21	22
23	24	25	26	27	28	29
30						

DECEMBER

S	M	T	W	T	F	S
	1	2	3	4	5	6
7	8	9	10	11	12	13
14	15	16	17	18	19	20
21	22	23	24	25	26	27
28	29	30	31			

11 1992

JANUARY

S	M	T	W	T	F	S
			1	2	3	4
5	6	7	8	9	10	11
12	13	14	15	16	17	18
19	20	21	22	23	24	25
26	27	28	29	30	31	

FEBRUARY

S	M	T	W	T	F	S
						1
2	3	4	5	6	7	8
9	10	11	12	13	14	15
16	17	18	19	20	21	22
23	24	25	26	27	28	29

MARCH

S	M	T	W	T	F	S
1	2	3	4	5	6	7
8	9	10	11	12	13	14
15	16	17	18	19	20	21
22	23	24	25	26	27	28
29	30	31				

APRIL

S	M	T	W	T	F	S
			1	2	3	4
5	6	7	8	9	10	11
12	13	14	15	16	17	18
19	20	21	22	23	24	25
26	27	28	29	30		

MAY

S	M	T	W	T	F	S
					1	2
3	4	5	6	7	8	9
10	11	12	13	14	15	16
17	18	19	20	21	22	23
24	25	26	27	28	29	30
31						

JUNE

S	M	T	W	T	F	S
	1	2	3	4	5	6
7	8	9	10	11	12	13
14	15	16	17	18	19	20
21	22	23	24	25	26	27
28	29	30				

JULY

S	M	T	W	T	F	S
			1	2	3	4
5	6	7	8	9	10	11
12	13	14	15	16	17	18
19	20	21	22	23	24	25
26	27	28	29	30	31	

AUGUST

S	M	T	W	T	F	S
						1
2	3	4	5	6	7	8
9	10	11	12	13	14	15
16	17	18	19	20	21	22
23	24	25	26	27	28	29
30	31					

SEPTEMBER

S	M	T	W	T	F	S
		1	2	3	4	5
6	7	8	9	10	11	12
13	14	15	16	17	18	19
20	21	22	23	24	25	26
27	28	29	30			

OCTOBER

S	M	T	W	T	F	S
				1	2	3
4	5	6	7	8	9	10
11	12	13	14	15	16	17
18	19	20	21	22	23	24
25	26	27	28	29	30	31

NOVEMBER

S	M	T	W	T	F	S
1	2	3	4	5	6	7
8	9	10	11	12	13	14
15	16	17	18	19	20	21
22	23	24	25	26	27	28
29	30					

DECEMBER

S	M	T	W	T	F	S
		1	2	3	4	5
6	7	8	9	10	11	12
13	14	15	16	17	18	19
20	21	22	23	24	25	26
27	28	29	30	31		

12

JANUARY

S	M	T	W	T	F	S
				1	2	3
4	5	6	7	8	9	10
11	12	13	14	15	16	17
18	19	20	21	22	23	24
25	26	27	28	29	30	31

FEBRUARY

S	M	T	W	T	F	S
1	2	3	4	5	6	7
8	9	10	11	12	13	14
15	16	17	18	19	20	21
22	23	24	25	26	27	28
29						

MARCH

S	M	T	W	T	F	S
	1	2	3	4	5	6
7	8	9	10	11	12	13
14	15	16	17	18	19	20
21	22	23	24	25	26	27
28	29	30	31			

APRIL

S	M	T	W	T	F	S
				1	2	3
4	5	6	7	8	9	10
11	12	13	14	15	16	17
18	19	20	21	22	23	24
25	26	27	28	29	30	

MAY

S	M	T	W	T	F	S
						1
2	3	4	5	6	7	8
9	10	11	12	13	14	15
16	17	18	19	20	21	22
23	24	25	26	27	28	29
30	31					

JUNE

S	M	T	W	T	F	S
		1	2	3	4	5
6	7	8	9	10	11	12
13	14	15	16	17	18	19
20	21	22	23	24	25	26
27	28	29	30			

JULY

S	M	T	W	T	F	S
				1	2	3
4	5	6	7	8	9	10
11	12	13	14	15	16	17
18	19	20	21	22	23	24
25	26	27	28	29	30	31

AUGUST

S	M	T	W	T	F	S
1	2	3	4	5	6	7
8	9	10	11	12	13	14
15	16	17	18	19	20	21
22	23	24	25	26	27	28
29	30	31				

SEPTEMBER

S	M	T	W	T	F	S
			1	2	3	4
5	6	7	8	9	10	11
12	13	14	15	16	17	18
19	20	21	22	23	24	25
26	27	28	29	30		

OCTOBER

S	M	T	W	T	F	S
					1	2
3	4	5	6	7	8	9
10	11	12	13	14	15	16
17	18	19	20	21	22	23
24	25	26	27	28	29	30
31						

NOVEMBER

S	M	T	W	T	F	S
	1	2	3	4	5	6
7	8	9	10	11	12	13
14	15	16	17	18	19	20
21	22	23	24	25	26	27
28	29	30				

DECEMBER

S	M	T	W	T	F	S
			1	2	3	4
5	6	7	8	9	10	11
12	13	14	15	16	17	18
19	20	21	22	23	24	25
26	27	28	29	30	31	

13

JANUARY

S	M	T	W	T	F	S
					1	2
3	4	5	6	7	8	9
10	11	12	13	14	15	16
17	18	19	20	21	22	23
24	25	26	27	28	29	30
31						

FEBRUARY

S	M	T	W	T	F	S
	1	2	3	4	5	6
7	8	9	10	11	12	13
14	15	16	17	18	19	20
21	22	23	24	25	26	27
28	29					

MARCH

S	M	T	W	T	F	S
		1	2	3	4	5
6	7	8	9	10	11	12
13	14	15	16	17	18	19
20	21	22	23	24	25	26
27	28	29	30	31		

APRIL

S	M	T	W	T	F	S
					1	2
3	4	5	6	7	8	9
10	11	12	13	14	15	16
17	18	19	20	21	22	23
24	25	26	27	28	29	30

MAY

S	M	T	W	T	F	S
1	2	3	4	5	6	7
8	9	10	11	12	13	14
15	16	17	18	19	20	21
22	23	24	25	26	27	28
29	30	31				

JUNE

S	M	T	W	T	F	S
			1	2	3	4
5	6	7	8	9	10	11
12	13	14	15	16	17	18
19	20	21	22	23	24	25
26	27	28	29	30		

JULY

S	M	T	W	T	F	S
					1	2
3	4	5	6	7	8	9
10	11	12	13	14	15	16
17	18	19	20	21	22	23
24	25	26	27	28	29	30
31						

AUGUST

S	M	T	W	T	F	S
	1	2	3	4	5	6
7	8	9	10	11	12	13
14	15	16	17	18	19	20
21	22	23	24	25	26	27
28	29	30	31			

SEPTEMBER

S	M	T	W	T	F	S
				1	2	3
4	5	6	7	8	9	10
11	12	13	14	15	16	17
18	19	20	21	22	23	24
25	26	27	28	29	30	

OCTOBER

S	M	T	W	T	F	S
						1
2	3	4	5	6	7	8
9	10	11	12	13	14	15
16	17	18	19	20	21	22
23	24	25	26	27	28	29
30	31					

NOVEMBER

S	M	T	W	T	F	S
		1	2	3	4	5
6	7	8	9	10	11	12
13	14	15	16	17	18	19
20	21	22	23	24	25	26
27	28	29	30			

DECEMBER

S	M	T	W	T	F	S
				1	2	3
4	5	6	7	8	9	10
11	12	13	14	15	16	17
18	19	20	21	22	23	24
25	26	27	28	29	30	31

14

JANUARY

S	M	T	W	T	F	S
						1
2	3	4	5	6	7	8
9	10	11	12	13	14	15
16	17	18	19	20	21	22
23	24	25	26	27	28	29
30	31					

FEBRUARY

S	M	T	W	T	F	S
		1	2	3	4	5
6	7	8	9	10	11	12
13	14	15	16	17	18	19
20	21	22	23	24	25	26
27	28	29				

MARCH

S	M	T	W	T	F	S
			1	2	3	4
5	6	7	8	9	10	11
12	13	14	15	16	17	18
19	20	21	22	23	24	25
26	27	28	29	30	31	

APRIL

S	M	T	W	T	F	S
						1
2	3	4	5	6	7	8
9	10	11	12	13	14	15
16	17	18	19	20	21	22
23	24	25	26	27	28	29
30						

MAY

S	M	T	W	T	F	S
	1	2	3	4	5	6
7	8	9	10	11	12	13
14	15	16	17	18	19	20
21	22	23	24	25	26	27
28	29	30	31			

JUNE

S	M	T	W	T	F	S
				1	2	3
4	5	6	7	8	9	10
11	12	13	14	15	16	17
18	19	20	21	22	23	24
25	26	27	28	29	30	

JULY

S	M	T	W	T	F	S
						1
2	3	4	5	6	7	8
9	10	11	12	13	14	15
16	17	18	19	20	21	22
23	24	25	26	27	28	29
30	31					

AUGUST

S	M	T	W	T	F	S
		1	2	3	4	5
6	7	8	9	10	11	12
13	14	15	16	17	18	19
20	21	22	23	24	25	26
27	28	29	30	31		

SEPTEMBER

S	M	T	W	T	F	S
					1	2
3	4	5	6	7	8	9
10	11	12	13	14	15	16
17	18	19	20	21	22	23
24	25	26	27	28	29	30

OCTOBER

S	M	T	W	T	F	S
1	2	3	4	5	6	7
8	9	10	11	12	13	14
15	16	17	18	19	20	21
22	23	24	25	26	27	28
29	30	31				

NOVEMBER

S	M	T	W	T	F	S
			1	2	3	4
5	6	7	8	9	10	11
12	13	14	15	16	17	18
19	20	21	22	23	24	25
26	27	28	29	30		

DECEMBER

S	M	T	W	T	F	S
					1	2
3	4	5	6	7	8	9
10	11	12	13	14	15	16
17	18	19	20	21	22	23
24	25	26	27	28	29	30
31						

Julian and Gregorian Calendars; Leap Year; Century

Calendars based on the movements of sun and moon have been used since ancient times, but none has been perfect. The Julian calendar, under which western nations measured time until 1582 A.D., was authorized by Julius Caesar in 46 B.C., the year 709 of Rome. His expert was a Greek, Sosigenes. The Julian calendar, on the assumption that the true year was 365 1/4 days long, gave every fourth year 366 days. The Venerable Bede, an Anglo-Saxon monk, announced in 730 A.D. that the 365 1/4-day Julian year was 11 min., 14 sec. too long, making a cumulative error of about a day every 128 years, but nothing was done about it for over 800 years.

By 1582 the accumulated error was estimated to have amounted to 10 days. In that year Pope Gregory XIII decreed that the day following Oct. 4, 1582, should be called Oct. 15, thus dropping 10 days.

However, with common years 365 days and a 366-day leap year every fourth year, the error in the length of the year would have recurred at the rate of a little more than 3 days every 400 years. So 3 of every 4 centesimal years (ending in 00) were made common years, not leap years. Thus 1600 was a leap year, 1700, 1800 and 1900 were not, but 2000 will be. **Leap years** are those divisible by 4 except centesimal years, which are common unless divisible by 400.

The Gregorian calendar was adopted at once by France, Italy, Spain, Portugal and Luxembourg. Within 2 years most German Catholic states, Belgium and parts of Switzerland and the Netherlands were brought under the new calendar, and Hungary followed in 1587. The rest of the Netherlands, along with Denmark and the German Protestant states made the change in 1699-1700 (German Protestants retained the old reckoning of Easter until 1776).

The British Government imposed the Gregorian calendar on all its possessions, including the American colonies, in 1752. The British decreed that the day following Sept. 2, 1752, should be called Sept. 14, a loss of 11 days. All dates preceding were marked O.S., for Old Style. In addition New Year's Day was moved to Jan. 1 from Mar. 25. (e.g., under the old reckoning, Mar. 24, 1700 had been followed by Mar. 25, 1701.) George Washington's birth date, which was Feb. 11, 1731, O.S., became Feb. 22, 1732, N.S. In 1753 Sweden too went Gregorian, retaining the old Easter rules until 1844.

In 1793 the French Revolutionary Government adopted a calendar of 12 months of 30 days each with 5 extra days in September of each common year and a 6th extra day every 4th year. Napoleon reinstated the Gregorian calendar in 1806.

The Gregorian system later spread to non-European regions, first in the European colonies, then in the independent countries, replacing traditional calendars at least for official purposes. Japan in 1873, Egypt in 1875, China in 1912 and Turkey in 1917 made the change, usually in conjunction with political upheavals. In China, the republican government began reckoning years from its 1911 founding — e.g., 1948 was designated the year 37. After 1949, the Communists adopted the Common, or Christian Era year count, even for the traditional lunar calendar.

In 1918 the revolutionary government in Russia decreed that the day after Jan. 31, 1918, Old Style, would become Feb. 14, 1918, New Style. Greece followed in 1923. (In Russia the Orthodox Church has retained the Julian calendar, as have various Middle Eastern Christian sects.) For the first time in history, all major cultures have one calendar.

To change from the Julian to the Gregorian calendar, add 10 days to dates Oct. 5, 1582, through Feb. 28, 1700; after that date add 11 days through Feb. 28, 1800; 12 days through Feb. 28, 1900; and 13 days through Feb. 28, 2100.

A **century** consists of 100 consecutive calendar years. The 1st century consisted of the years 1 through 100. The 20th century consists of the years 1901 through 2000 and will end Dec. 31, 2000. The 21st century will begin Jan. 1, 2001.

Julian Calendar

To find which of the 14 calendars printed on pages 272-273 applies to any year, starting Jan. 1, under the Julian system, find the century for the desired year in the three left-hand columns below; read across. Then find the year in the four top rows; read down. The number in the intersection is the calendar designation for that year.

Year (last two figures of desired year)

				01	02	03	04	05	06	07	08	09	10	11	12	13	14	15	16	17	18	19	20	21	22	23	24	25	26	27	28
				29	30	31	32	33	34	35	36	37	38	39	40	41	42	43	44	45	46	47	48	49	50	51	52	53	54	55	56
				57	58	59	60	61	62	63	64	65	66	67	68	69	70	71	72	73	74	75	76	77	78	79	80	81	82	83	84
Century			00	85	86	87	88	89	90	91	92	93	94	95	96	97	98	99													
0	700	1400	12	7	1	2	10	5	6	7	8	3	4	5	13	1	2	3	11	6	7	1	9	4	5	6	14	2	3	4	12
100	800	1500	11	6	7	1	9	4	5	6	14	2	3	4	12	7	1	2	10	5	6	7	8	3	4	5	13	1	2	3	11
200	900	1600	10	5	6	7	8	3	4	5	13	1	2	3	11	6	7	1	9	4	5	6	14	2	3	4	12	7	1	2	10
300	1000	1700	9	4	5	6	14	2	3	4	12	7	1	2	10	5	6	7	8	3	4	5	13	1	2	3	11	6	7	1	9
400	1100	1800	8	3	4	5	13	1	2	3	11	6	7	1	9	4	5	6	14	2	3	4	12	7	1	2	10	5	6	7	8
500	1200	1900	14	2	3	4	12	7	1	2	10	5	6	7	8	3	4	5	13	1	2	3	11	6	7	1	9	4	5	6	14
600	1300	2000	13	1	2	3	11	6	7	1	9	4	5	6	14	2	3	4	12	7	1	2	10	5	6	7	8	3	4	5	13

Gregorian Calendar

Pick desired year from table below or on page 272 (for years 1800 to 2059). The number shown with each year shows which calendar to use for that year, as shown on pages 272-273. (The Gregorian calendar was inaugurated Oct. 15, 1582. From that date to Dec. 31, 1582, use calendar 6.)

1583-1802

1583. . 7	1603. . 4	1623. . 1	1643. . 5	1663. . 2	1683. . 6	1703. . 2	1723. . 6	1743. . 3	1763. . 7	1783. . 4
1584. . 8	1604. 12	1624. . 9	1644. 13	1664. 10	1684. 14	1704. 10	1724. 14	1744. 11	1764. . 8	1784. 12
1585. . 3	1605. . 7	1625. . 4	1645. . 1	1665. . 5	1685. . 2	1705. . 5	1725. . 2	1745. . 6	1765. . 3	1785. . 7
1586. . 4	1606. . 1	1626. . 5	1646. . 2	1666. . 6	1686. . 3	1706. . 6	1726. . 3	1746. . 7	1766. . 4	1786. . 1
1587. . 5	1607. . 2	1627. . 6	1647. . 3	1667. . 7	1687. . 4	1707. . 7	1727. . 4	1747. . 1	1767. . 5	1787. . 2
1588. 13	1608. 10	1628. 14	1648. 11	1668. . 8	1688. 12	1708. . 8	1728. 12	1748. . 9	1768. 13	1788. 10
1589. . 1	1609. . 5	1629. . 2	1649. . 6	1669. . 3	1689. . 7	1709. . 3	1729. . 7	1749. . 4	1769. . 1	1789. . 5
1590. . 2	1610. . 6	1630. . 3	1650. . 7	1670. . 4	1690. . 1	1710. . 4	1730. . 1	1750. . 5	1770. . 2	1790. . 6
1591. . 3	1611. . 7	1631. . 4	1651. . 1	1671. . 5	1691. . 2	1711. . 5	1731. . 2	1751. . 6	1771. . 3	1791. . 7
1592. 11	1612. . 8	1632. 12	1652. . 9	1672. 13	1692. 10	1712. 13	1732. 10	1752. 14	1772. 11	1792. . 8
1593. . 6	1613. . 3	1633. . 7	1653. . 4	1673. . 1	1693. . 5	1713. . 1	1733. . 5	1753. . 2	1773. . 6	1793. . 3
1594. . 7	1614. . 4	1634. . 1	1654. . 5	1674. . 2	1694. . 6	1714. . 2	1734. . 6	1754. . 3	1774. . 7	1794. . 4
1595. . 1	1615. . 5	1635. . 2	1655. . 6	1675. . 3	1695. . 7	1715. . 3	1735. . 7	1755. . 4	1775. . 1	1795. . 5
1596. . 9	1616. 13	1636. 10	1656. 14	1676. 11	1696. . 8	1716. 11	1736. . 8	1756. 12	1776. . 9	1796. 13
1597. . 4	1617. . 1	1637. . 5	1657. . 2	1677. . 6	1697. . 3	1717. . 6	1737. . 3	1757. . 7	1777. . 4	1797. . 1
1598. . 5	1618. . 2	1638. . 6	1658. . 3	1678. . 7	1698. . 4	1718. . 7	1738. . 4	1758. . 1	1778. . 5	1798. . 2
1599. . 6	1619. . 3	1639. . 7	1659. . 4	1679. . 1	1699. . 5	1719. . 1	1739. . 5	1759. . 2	1779. . 6	1799. . 3
1600. 14	1620. 11	1640. . 8	1660. 12	1680. . 9	1700. . 6	1720. . 9	1740. 13	1760. 10	1780. 14	1800. . 4
1601. . 2	1621. . 6	1641. . 3	1661. . 7	1681. . 4	1701. . 7	1721. . 4	1741. . 1	1761. . 5	1781. . 2	1801. . 5
1602. . 3	1622. . 7	1642. . 4	1662. . 1	1682. . 5	1702. . 1	1722. . 5	1742. . 2	1762. . 6	1782. . 3	1802. . 6

The Julian Period

How many days have you lived? To determine this, you must multiply your age by 365, add the number of days since your last birthday until today, and account for all leap years. Chances are your answer would be wrong. Astronomers, however, find it convenient to express dates and long time intervals in days rather than in years, months and days. This is done by placing events within the Julian period.

The Julian period was devised in 1582 by Joseph Scaliger and named after his father Julius (not after the Julian calendar). Scaliger had Julian Day (JD) #1 begin at noon, Jan. 1, 4713 B. C., the most recent time that three major chronological cycles began on the same day — 1) the 28-year solar cycle, after which dates in the Julian calendar (e.g., Feb. 11) return to the same days of the week (e.g., Monday); 2) the 19-year lunar cycle, after which the phases of the moon return to the same dates of the year; and 3) the 15-year indiction cycle, used in ancient Rome to regulate taxes. It will take 7980 years to complete the period, the product of 28, 19, and 15.

Noon of Dec. 31, 1992, marks the beginning of JD 2,448,988; that many days will have passed since the start of the Julian period. The JD at noon of any date in 1992 may be found by adding to this figure the day of the year for that date, which is given in the left hand column in the chart below. Simple JD conversion tables are used by astronomers.

Days Between Two Dates

Table covers period of two ordinary years. Example—Days between Feb. 10, 1989 and Dec. 15, 1990; subtract 41 from 714; answer is 673 days. For leap year, such as 1992, one day must be added: final answer is 674.

Date	Jan.	Feb.	Mar.	April	May	June	July	Aug.	Sept.	Oct.	Nov.	Dec.
1	1	32	60	91	121	152	182	213	244	274	305	335
2	2	33	61	92	122	153	183	214	245	275	306	336
3	3	34	62	93	123	154	184	215	246	276	307	337
4	4	35	63	94	124	155	185	216	247	277	308	338
5	5	36	64	95	125	156	186	217	248	278	309	339
6	6	37	65	96	126	157	187	218	249	279	310	340
7	7	38	66	97	127	158	188	219	250	280	311	341
8	8	39	67	98	128	159	189	220	251	281	312	342
9	9	40	68	99	129	160	190	221	252	282	313	343
10	10	41	69	100	130	161	191	222	253	283	314	344
11	11	42	70	101	131	162	192	223	254	284	315	345
12	12	43	71	102	132	163	193	224	255	285	316	346
13	13	44	72	103	133	164	194	225	256	286	317	347
14	14	45	73	104	134	165	195	226	257	287	318	348
15	15	46	74	105	135	166	196	227	258	288	319	349
16	16	47	75	106	136	167	197	228	259	289	320	350
17	17	48	76	107	137	168	198	229	260	290	321	351
18	18	49	77	108	138	169	199	230	261	291	322	352
19	19	50	78	109	139	170	200	231	262	292	323	353
20	20	51	79	110	140	171	201	232	263	293	324	354
21	21	52	80	111	141	172	202	233	264	294	325	355
22	22	53	81	112	142	173	203	234	265	295	326	356
23	23	54	82	113	143	174	204	235	266	296	327	357
24	24	55	83	114	144	175	205	236	267	297	328	358
25	25	56	84	115	145	176	206	237	268	298	329	359
26	26	57	85	116	146	177	207	238	269	299	330	360
27	27	58	86	117	147	178	208	239	270	300	331	361
28	28	59	87	118	148	179	209	240	271	301	332	362
29	29	—	88	119	149	180	210	241	272	302	333	363
30	30	—	89	120	150	181	211	242	273	303	334	364
31	31	—	90	—	151	—	212	243	—	304	—	365

Date	Jan.	Feb.	Mar.	April	May	June	July	Aug.	Sept.	Oct.	Nov.	Dec.
1	366	397	425	456	486	517	547	578	609	639	670	700
2	367	398	426	457	487	518	548	579	610	640	671	701
3	368	399	427	458	488	519	549	580	611	641	672	702
4	369	400	428	459	489	520	550	581	612	642	673	703
5	370	401	429	460	490	521	551	582	613	643	674	704
6	371	402	430	461	491	522	552	583	614	644	675	705
7	372	403	431	462	492	523	553	584	615	645	676	706
8	373	404	432	463	493	524	554	585	616	646	677	707
9	374	405	433	464	494	525	555	586	617	647	678	708
10	375	406	434	465	495	526	556	587	618	648	679	709
11	376	407	435	466	496	527	557	588	619	649	680	710
12	377	408	436	467	497	528	558	589	620	650	681	711
13	378	409	437	468	498	529	559	590	621	651	682	712
14	379	410	438	469	499	530	560	591	622	652	683	713
15	380	411	439	470	500	531	561	592	623	653	684	714
16	381	412	440	471	501	532	562	593	624	654	685	715
17	382	413	441	472	502	533	503	594	625	655	686	716
18	383	414	442	473	503	534	564	595	626	656	687	717
19	384	415	443	474	504	535	565	596	627	657	688	718
20	385	416	444	475	505	536	566	597	628	658	689	719
21	386	417	445	476	506	537	567	598	629	659	690	720
22	387	418	446	477	507	538	568	599	630	660	691	721
23	388	419	447	478	508	539	569	600	631	661	692	722
24	389	420	448	479	509	540	570	601	632	662	693	723
25	390	421	449	480	510	541	571	602	633	663	694	724
26	391	422	450	481	511	542	572	603	634	664	695	725
27	392	423	451	482	512	543	573	604	635	665	696	726
28	393	424	452	483	513	544	574	605	636	666	697	727
29	394	—	453	484	514	545	575	606	637	667	698	728
30	395	—	454	485	515	546	576	607	638	668	699	729
31	396	—	455	—	516	—	577	608	—	669	—	730

Lunar Calendar, Chinese New Year, Vietnamese Tet

The ancient Chinese lunar calendar is divided into 12 months of either 29 or 30 days (compensating for the fact that the mean duration of the lunar month is 29 days, 12 hours, 44.05 minutes). The calendar is synchronized with the solar year by the addition of extra months at fixed intervals.

The Chinese calendar runs on a sexagenary cycle, i.e., 60 years. The cycles 1876-1935 and 1936-1995, with the years grouped under their twelve animal designations, are printed below. The Year 1993 (Lunar Year 4691) is found in the tenth column, under Rooster, and is known as a "Year of the Rooster." Readers can find the animal name for the year of their birth, marriage, etc., in the same chart. (Note: the first 3-7 weeks of each of the western years belong to the previous Chinese year and animal designation.)

Both the western (Gregorian) and traditional lunar calendars are used publicly in China, and two New Year's celebrations are held. On Taiwan, in overseas Chinese communities, and in Vietnam, the lunar calendar has been used only to set the dates for traditional festivals, with the Gregorian system in general use.

The four-day Chinese New Year, Hsin Nien, and the three-day Vietnamese New Year festival, Tet, begin at the first new moon after the sun enters Aquarius. The day may fall, therefore, between Jan. 21 and Feb. 19 of the Gregorian calendar. Jan. 23, 1993 marks the start of the new Chinese year. The date is fixed according to the date of the new moon in the Far East. Since this is west of the International Date Line the date may be one day later than that of the new moon in the United States.

Rat	Ox	Tiger	Hare (Rabbit)	Dragon	Snake	Horse	Sheep (Goat)	Monkey	Rooster	Dog	Pig
1876	1877	1878	1879	1880	1881	1882	1883	1884	1885	1886	1887
1888	1889	1890	1891	1892	1893	1894	1895	1896	1897	1898	1899
1900	1901	1902	1903	1904	1905	1906	1907	1908	1909	1910	1911
1912	1913	1914	1915	1916	1917	1918	1919	1920	1921	1922	1923
1924	1925	1926	1927	1928	1929	1930	1931	1932	1933	1934	1935
1936	1937	1938	1939	1940	1941	1942	1943	1944	1945	1946	1947
1948	1949	1950	1951	1952	1953	1954	1955	1956	1957	1958	1959
1960	1961	1962	1963	1964	1965	1966	1967	1968	1969	1970	1971
1972	1973	1974	1975	1976	1977	1978	1979	1980	1981	1982	1983
1984	1985	1986	1987	1988	1989	1990	1991	1992	1993	1994	1995

Standard Time, Daylight Saving Time, and Others

Source: Defense Mapping Agency Hydrographic/Topographic Center; U.S. Dept. of Transportation

Standard Time

Standard time is reckoned from Greenwich, England, recognized as the Prime Meridian of Longitude. The world is divided into 24 zones, each 15° of arc, or one hour in time apart. The Greenwich meridian (0°) extends through the center of the initial zone, and the zones to the east are numbered from 1 to 12 with the prefix "minus" indicating the number of hours to be subtracted to obtain Greenwich Time. Each zone extends 7½° on either side of its central meridian.

Westward zones are similarly numbered, but prefixed "plus" showing the number of hours that must be added to get Greenwich Time. While these zones apply generally to sea areas, it should be noted that the Standard Time maintained in many countries does not coincide with zone time. A graphical representation of the zones is shown on the Standard Time Zone Chart of the World published by the Defense Mapping Agency, Attn: PR, 8613 Lee Highway, Fairfax, VA 22031-2137.

The United States and possessions are divided into eight Standard Time zones, as set forth by the Uniform Time Act of 1966, which also provides for the use of Daylight Saving Time therein. Each zone is approximately 15° of longitude in width. All places in each zone use, instead of their own local time, the time counted from the transit of the "mean sun" across the Standard Time meridian which passes near the middle of that zone.

These time zones are designated as Atlantic, Eastern, Central, Mountain, Pacific, Yukon, Alaska-Hawaii, and Bering (Samoa), and the time in these zones is basically reckoned from the 60th, 75th, 90th, 105th, 120th, 135th, 150th and 165th meridians west of Greenwich. The line wanders to conform to local geographical regions. The time in the various zones is earlier than Greenwich Time by 4, 5, 6, 7, 8, 9, 10, and 11 hours respectively.

24-Hour Time

24-hour time is widely used in scientific work throughout the world. In the United States it is used also in operations of the Armed Forces. In Europe it is frequently used by the transportation networks in preference to the 12-hour a.m. and p.m. system. With the 24-hour system the day begins at midnight and is designated 0000 through 2359.

International Date Line

The Date Line is a zig-zag line that approximately coincides with the 180th meridian, and it is where the calendar dates are separated. The date must be advanced one day when crossing in a westerly direction and set back one day when crossing in an easterly direction.

The line is deflected eastward through the Bering Strait and westward of the Aleutians to prevent separating these areas by date. The line is again deflected eastward of the Tonga and New Zealand Islands in the South Pacific for the same reason.

Daylight Saving Time

Daylight Saving Time is achieved by advancing the clock one hour. Under the Uniform Time Act, which became effective in 1967, all states, the District of Columbia, and U.S. possessions were to observe Daylight Saving Time beginning at 2 a.m. on the first Sunday in April and ending at 2 a.m. on the last Sunday in October. Any state could, by law, exempt itself; a 1972 amendment to the act authorized states split by time zones to take that into consideration in exempting themselves. Arizona, Hawaii, Puerto Rico, the Virgin Islands, American Samoa, and part of Indiana are now exempt. Some local zone boundaries in Kansas, Texas, Florida, Michigan, and Alaska have been modified in the last several years by the Dept. of Transportation, which oversees the act. To conserve energy Congress put most of the nation on year-round Daylight Saving Time for two years effective Jan. 6, 1974 through Oct. 26, 1975; but a further bill, signed in October, 1974, restored Standard Time from the last Sunday in that month to the last Sunday in February, 1975. At the end of 1975, Congress failed to renew this temporary legislation and the nation returned to the older end-of April to end-of October DST system.

On July 8, 1986, Pres. Ronald Reagan signed legislation moving up the start of daylight saving time to the first Sunday in April. Daylight Saving Time, which used to start the last Sunday in April, will still end the last Sunday in October. The Transportation Dept. estimated that the earlier starting date will help save more than $28 million in traffic accident costs and prevent more than 1,500 injuries and 20 deaths. The new law, opposed by some farm state lawmakers, took effect in 1987.

International

Adjusting clock time to be able to use the added daylight on summer evenings is common throughout the world.

Western Europe is on daylight saving time generally from the last Sunday in March to the last Sunday in September; however, the United Kingdom continues until the last Sunday in October.

The Soviet Union lies over 11 time zones, but maintains its standard time 1 hour fast of the zone designation. Additionally, it proclaims daylight saving time as does Europe.

China lies across 5 time zones, but has decreed that the entire country be placed on zone time minus 8 hours with daylight saving time from April 12 to September 12.

Many of the countries in the Southern Hemisphere maintain daylight saving time generally from October to March; however, most countries near the equator do not deviate from standard time.

Standard Time Differences—World Cities

The time indicated in the table is fixed by law and is called the legal time, or, more generally, Standard Time. Use of Daylight Saving Time varies widely. * Indicates morning of the following day. At 12 00 noon, Eastern Standard Time, the standard time (in 24-hour time) in foreign cities is as follows:

Addis Ababa	20 00	Cape Town	19 00	Lima	12 00	St. Petersburg	20 00
Alexandria	19 00	Caracas	13 00	Lisbon	17 00	Santiago (Chile)	13 00
Amsterdam	18 00	Casablanca	17 00	Liverpool	17 00	Seoul	2 00*
Athens	19 00	Copenhagen	18 00	London	17 00	Shanghai	1 00*
Auckland	5 00*	Dacca	23 00	Madrid	18 00	Singapore	1 00*
Baghdad	20 00	Delhi	22 30	Manila	1 00*	Stockholm	18 00
Bangkok	0 00	Dublin	17 00	Mecca (Saudi Arabia)	20 00	Sydney (Australia)	3 00*
Beijing	1 00*	Gdansk	18 00	Melbourne	3 00*	Tashkent	23 00
Belfast	17 00	Geneva	18 00	Mexico City	11 00	Teheran	20 30
Berlin	18 00	Havana	12 00	Montevideo	14 00	Tel Aviv	19 00
Bogota	12 00	Helsinki	19 00	Moscow	20 00	Tokyo	2 00*
Bombay	22 30	Ho Chi Minh City	0 00	Nagasaki	2 00*	Valparaiso	13 00
Bremen	18 00	Hong Kong	1 00*	Oslo	18 00	Vladivostok	3 00*
Brussels	18 00	Istanbul	19 00	Paris	18 00	Vienna	18 00
Bucharest	19 00	Jakarta	0 00	Prague	18 00	Warsaw	18 00
Budapest	18 00	Jerusalem	19 00	Rangoon	23 30	Wellington (N.Z.)	5 00*
Buenos Aires	14 00	Johannesburg	19 00	Rio De Janeiro	14 00	Yokohama	2 00*
Cairo	19 00	Karachi	22 00	Rome	18 00	Zurich	18 00
Calcutta	22 30	Le Havre	18 00				

Standard Time Differences — North American Cities

At 12 o'clock noon, Eastern Standard Time, the standard time in N.A. cities is as follows:

Akron, Oh.	12 00	Noon	Frankfort, Ky.	12 00	Noon	*Phoenix, Ariz.	10 00	A.M.
Albuquerque, N.M.	10 00	A.M.	Galveston, Tex.	11 00	A.M.	Pierre, S.D.	11 00	A.M.
Atlanta, Ga.	12 00	Noon	Grand Rapids, Mich.	12 00	Noon	Pittsburgh, Pa.	12 00	Noon
Austin, Tex.	11 00	A.M.	Halifax, N.S.	1 00	P.M.	Portland, Me.	12 00	Noon
Baltimore, Md.	12 00	Noon	Hartford, Conn.	12 00	Noon	Portland, Ore.	9 00	A.M.
Birmingham, Ala.	11 00	A.M.	Helena, Mon.	10 00	A.M.	Providence, R.I.	12 00	Noon
Bismarck, N.D.	11 00	A.M.	*Honolulu, Ha.	7 00	A.M.	*Regina, Sask.	11 00	A.M.
Boise, Ida.	10 00	A.M.	Houston, Tex.	11 00	A.M.	Reno, Nev.	9 00	A.M.
Boston, Mass.	12 00	Noon	*Indianapolis, Ind.	12 00	Noon	Richmond, Va.	12 00	Noon
Buffalo, N.Y.	12 00	Noon	Jacksonville, Fla.	12 00	Noon	Rochester, N.Y.	12 00	Noon
Butte, Mon.	10 00	A.M.	Juneau, Alas.	8 00	A.M.	Sacramento, Cal.	9 00	A.M.
Calgary, Alta.	10 00	A.M.	Kansas City, Mo.	11 00	A.M.	St. John's, Nfld.	1 30	P.M.
Charleston, S.C.	12 00	Noon	Knoxville, Tenn.	12 00	Noon	St. Louis, Mo.	11 00	A.M.
Charleston, W.Va.	12 00	Noon	Lexington, Ky.	12 00	Noon	St. Paul, Minn.	11 00	A.M.
Charlotte, N.C.	12 00	Noon	Lincoln, Neb.	11 00	A.M.	Salt Lake City, Ut.	10 00	A.M.
Charlottetown, P.E.I.	1 00	P.M.	Little Rock, Ark.	11 00	A.M.	San Antonio, Tex.	11 00	A.M.
Chattanooga, Tenn.	12 00	Noon	Los Angeles, Cal.	9 00	A.M.	San Diego, Cal.	9 00	A.M.
Cheyenne, Wy.	10 00	A.M.	Louisville, Ky.	12 00	Noon	San Francisco, Cal.	9 00	A.M.
Chicago, Ill.	11 00	A.M.	*Mexico City	11 00	A.M.	Santa Fe, N.M.	10 00	A.M.
Cleveland, Oh.	12 00	Noon	Memphis, Tenn.	11 00	A.M.	Savannah, Ga.	12 00	Noon
Colorado Spr., Col.	10 00	A.M.	Miami, Fla.	12 00	Noon	Seattle, Wash.	9 00	A.M.
Columbus, Oh.	12 00	Noon	Milwaukee, Wis.	11 00	A.M.	Shreveport, La.	11 00	A.M.
Dallas, Tex.	11 00	A.M.	Minneapolis, Minn.	11 00	AM.	Sioux Falls, S.D.	11 00	A.M.
*Dawson, Yuk.	9 00	A.M.	Mobile, Ala.	11 00	A.M.	Spokane, Wash.	9 00	A.M.
Dayton, Oh.	12 00	Noon	Montreal, Que.	12 00	Noon	Tampa, Fla.	12 00	Noon
Denver, Col.	10 00	A.M.	Nashville, Tenn.	11 00	A.M.	Toledo, Oh.	12 00	Noon
Des Moines, Ia.	11 00	A.M.	New Haven, Conn.	12 00	Noon	Topeka, Kan.	11 00	A.M.
Detroit, Mich.	12 00	Noon	New Orleans, La.	11 00	A.M.	Toronto, Ont.	12 00	Noon
Duluth, Minn.	11 00	A.M.	New York, N.Y.	12 00	Noon	*Tucson, Ariz.	10 00	A.M.
El Paso, Tex.	10 00	A.M.	Nome, Alas.	8 00	A.M.	Tulsa, Okla.	11 00	A.M.
Erie, Pa.	12 00	Noon	Norfolk, Va.	12 00	Noon	Vancouver, B.C.	9 00	A.M.
Evansville, Ind.	11 00	A.M.	Okla. City, Okla.	11 00	A.M.	Washington, D.C.	12 00	Noon
Fairbanks, Alas.	8 00	A.M.	Omaha, Neb.	11 00	A.M.	Wichita, Kan.	11 00	A.M.
Flint, Mich.	12 00	Noon	Peoria, Ill.	11 00	A.M.	Wilmington, Del.	12 00	Noon
*Fort Wayne, Ind.	12 00	Noon	Philadelphia, Pa.	12 00	Noon	Winnipeg, Man.	11 00	A.M.
Fort Worth, Tex.	11 00	A.M.						

* Cities with an asterisk do not observe daylight saving time. During much of the year, it is necessary to add one hour to the cities which do observe daylight savings time to get the proper time relation.

Legal or Public Holidays, 1993

Technically there are no national holidays in the United States; each state has jurisdiction over its holidays, which are designated by legislative enactment or executive proclamation. In practice, however, most states observe the federal legal public holidays, even though the President and Congress can legally designate holidays only for the District of Columbia and for federal employees. Federal legal public holidays are New Year's Day, Martin Luther King Day, Washington's Birthday, Memorial Day, Independence Day, Labor Day, Columbus Day, Veterans' Day, Thanksgiving, and Christmas.

Chief Legal or Public Holidays

When a holiday falls on a Sunday or a Saturday it is usually observed on the following Monday or the preceding Friday. For some holidays, government and business closing practices vary. In most states, the office of the Secretary of State can provide details for holiday closings. The following will be legal or public holidays in most states in 1993:

Jan. 1 (Friday) — New Year's Day.

Jan. 18 (Monday) — Martin Luther King Day.

Feb. 12 (Friday) — Lincoln's Birthday.

Feb. 15 (3d Mon. in Feb.) — Washington's Birthday, or Presidents' Day, or Washington-Lincoln Day.

May 31 (last Mon. in May) — Memorial Day, or Decoration Day.

July 5 (Monday) — Independence Day, obsvd.

Sept. 6 (1st Mon. in Sept.) — Labor Day.

Oct. 11 (2d Monday in Oct.) — Columbus Day, or Discoverers' Day, or Pioneers' Day.

Nov. 11 (Thursday) — Veterans' Day.

Nov. 25 (4th Thursday in Nov.) — Thanksgiving Day.

Dec. 24 (Friday) — Christmas Day, obsvd.

In some states, the following will be legal or public holidays in 1993:

Apr. 9 (Friday) — Good Friday. In some states, observed for half or part of day.

Nov. 2 (1st Tues. after 1st Mon. in Nov.) — Election Day.

Selected Foreign Holidays

Jan. 14 — Vinegrower's Day, Bulgaria.
Jan. 20 — St. Agnes Eve, England.
Feb. 3 — Setsubun (bean-throwing festival), Japan.
Feb. 8 — Narvik Sun Pageant, Norway.
Feb. 9-12 — Carnival, Brazil.
Mar. 28 — Teacher's Day, Czechoslovakia.
Apr. 7 — World Health Day, UN nations.
Apr. 8 — Buddha's Birthday, Korea, Japan.
Apr. 22 — Independence Day, Israel
Apr. 25 — ANZAC Day, Australia, New Zealand.
May 1 — Labor Day, most socialist countries.
May 5 — Cinco de Mayo, Mexico.
May 25 — African Freedom Day, Chad, Zambia.
June 22 — Midsummer Eve, Denmark.
July 1 — Canada Day, Canada.
July 14 — Bastille Day, France.
July 24 — Simon Bolivar's Birthday, Venezuela.
Aug. 10 — Fox Hill Day, Bahamas.
Aug. 19 — Sour Herring Premiere, Sweden.
Sept. 19 — St. Gennaro, Italy.
mid Sept. — Sherry Wine Harvest, Spain.
Oct. 2 — Mahatma Gandhi's Birthday, India.
Oct. 6 — Ivy Day, Ireland.
Nov. 1 — All Saints' Day, Zaire.
Nov. 17 — Volkstrauertag (Memorial Day), Germany.
Nov. 20 — Elephant Round-up, Thailand.
Dec. 2 — Lover's Fair, Belgium.
Dec. 16-Jan. 6 — Christmas Observance, Philippines.

AEROSPACE

Memorable Manned Space Flights

Sources: National Aeronautics and Space Administration and The World Almanac

Crew, date	Mission name	Orbits[1]	Duration	Remarks
Yuri A. Gagarin (4/12/61)	Vostok 1	1	1h 48m.	1st manned orbital flight
Alan B. Shepard Jr. (5/5/61)	Mercury-Redstone 3	(2)	15m 22s	1st American in space
Virgil I. Grissom (7/21/61)	Mercury-Redstone 4	(2)	15m 37s	Spacecraft sank. Grissom rescued
Gherman S. Titov (8/6-7/61)	Vostok 2	16	25h 18m.	1st space flight of more than 24 hrs.
John H. Glenn Jr. (2/20/62)	Mercury-Atlas 6	3	4h 55m 23s	1st American in orbit
M. Scott Carpenter (5/24/62)	Mercury-Atlas 7	3	4h 56m 05s	Manual retrofire error caused 250 mi. landing overshoot
Andrian G. Nikolayev (8/11-15/62)	Vostok 3	64	94h 22m.	Vostok 3 and 4 made first group flight.
Pavel R. Popovich (8/12-15/62)	Vostok 4	48	70h 57m.	On 1st orbit it came within 3 miles of Vostok 3.
Walter M. Schirra Jr. (10/3/62)	Mercury-Atlas 8	6	9h 13m 11s	Closest splashdown to target to date (4.5 mi.).
L. Gordon Cooper (5/15-16/63)	Mercury-Atlas 9	22	34h 19m 49s	1st U.S. evaluation of effects on man of one day in space.
Valery F. Bykovsky (6/14-6/19/63)	Vostok 5	81	119h 06m.	Vostok 5 and 6 made 2d group flight
Valentina V. Tereshkova (6/16-19/63)	Vostok 6	48	70h 50m.	1st woman in space
Vladimir M. Komarov, Konstantin P. Feoktistov, Boris B. Yegorov (10/12/64)	Voskhod 1	16	24h 17m.	1st 3-man orbital flight: first without space suits
Pavel I. Belyayev, Aleksei A. Leonov (3/18/65)	Voskhod 2	17	26h 02m.	Leonov made 1st "space walk" (10 min.)
Virgil I. Grissom, John W. Young (3/23/65)	Gemini-Titan 3	3	4h 53m 00s	1st manned spacecraft to change its orbital path
James A. McDivitt, Edward H. White 2d, (6/3-7/65)	Gemini-Titan 4	62	97h 56m 11s	White was 1st American to "walk in space" (20 min.)
L. Gordon Cooper Jr., Charles Conrad Jr. (8/21-29/65)	Gemini-Titan 5	120	190h 55m 14s	1st use of fuel cells for electric power; evaluated guidance and navigation system
Frank Borman, James A. Lovell Jr. (12/4-18/65)	Gemini-Titan 7	206	330h 35m 31s	Longest duration Gemini flight
Walter M. Schirra Jr., Thomas P. Stafford (12/15-16/65)	Gemini-Titan 6-A	16	25h 51m 24s	Completed world's first space rendezvous with Gemini 7
Neil A. Armstrong, David R. Scott (3/16-17/66)	Gemini-Titan 8	6.5	10h 41m 26s	1st docking of one space vehicle with another; mission aborted, control malfunction
John W. Young, Michael Collins (7/18-21/66)	Gemini-Titan 10	43	70h 46m 39s	1st use of Agena target vehicle's propulsion systems
Charles Conrad Jr., Richard F. Gordon Jr. (9/12-15/66)	Gemini-Titan 11	44	71h 17m 08s	Docked, made 2 revolutions of earth tethered; set Gemini altitude record (739.2 mi.)
James A. Lovell Jr., Edwin E. Aldrin Jr. (11/11-15/66)	Gemini-Titan 12	59	94h 34m 31s	Final Gemini mission; record 5½ hrs. of extravehicular activity
Vladimir M. Komarov (4/23/67)	Soyuz 1	17	26h 40m.	Crashed after re-entry killing Komarov
Walter M. Schirra Jr., Donn F. Eisele, R. Walter Cunningham (10/11-22/68)	Apollo-Saturn 7	163	260h 09m 03s	1st manned flight of Apollo spacecraft command-service module only
Georgi T. Beregovoi (10/26-30/68)	Soyuz 3	64	94h 51m.	Made rendezvous with unmanned Soyuz 2
Frank Borman, James A. Lovell Jr., William A. Anders (12/21-27/68)	Apollo-Saturn 8	10[3]	147h 00m 42s	1st flight to moon (command-service module only); views of lunar surface televised to earth
Vladimir A. Shatalov (1/14-17/69)	Soyuz 4	45	71h 14m.	Docked with Soyuz 5
Boris V. Volyanov, Aleksei S. Yeliseyev, Yevgeny V. Khrunov (1/15-18/69)	Soyuz 5	46	72h 46m.	Docked with Soyuz 4; Yeliseyev and Khrunov transferred to Soyuz 4
James A. McDivitt, David R. Scott, Russell L. Schweickart (3/3-13/69)	Apollo-Saturn 9	151	241h 00m 54s	1st manned flight of lunar module

Crew, date	Mission name	Orbits[1]	Duration	Remarks
Thomas P. Stafford, Eugene A. Cernan, John W. Young (5/18-26/69)	Apollo-Saturn 10	31[4]	192h 03m 23s	1st lunar module orbit of moon.
Neil A. Armstrong, Edwin E. Aldrin Jr., Michael Collins (7/16-24/69)	Apollo-Saturn 11	30[3]	195h 18m 35s	1st lunar landing made by Armstrong and Aldrin; collected 48.5 lbs. of soil, rock samples; lunar stay time 21 h, 36m, 21 s
Georgi S. Shonin, Valery N. Kubasov (10/11-16/69)	Soyuz 6	79	118h 42m.	1st welding of metals in space.
Anatoly V. Filipchenko, Vladislav N. Volkov, Viktor V. Gorbatko (10/12-17/69)	Soyuz 7	79	118h 41m.	Space lab construction tests made; Soyuz 6, 7 and 8 — 1st time 3 spacecraft 7 crew orbited earth at once
Charles Conrad Jr., Richard F. Gordon, Alan L. Bean (11/14-24/69)	Apollo-Saturn 12	45[3]	244h 36m 25s	Conrad and Bean made 2d moon landing; collected 74.7 lbs. of samples, lunar stay time 31 h, 31 m
James A. Lovell Jr., Fred W. Haise Jr., John L. Swigart Jr. (4/11-17/70)	Apollo-Saturn 13	...	142h 54m 41s	Aborted after service module oxygen tank ruptured; crew returned safely using lunar module oxygen and power
Alan B. Shepard Jr., Stuart A. Roosa, Edgar D. Mitchell (1/31-2/9/71)	Apollo-Saturn 14	34[3]	216h 01m 57s	Shepard and Mitchell made 3d moon landing, collected 96 lbs. of lunar samples; lunar stay 33 h, 31 m
Georgi T. Dobrovolsky, Vladislav N. Volkov, Viktor I. Patsayev (6/6-30/71)	Soyuz 11	360	569h 40m.	Docked with Salyut space station; and orbited in Salyut for 23 days; crew died during re-entry from loss of pressurization
David R. Scott, Alfred M. Worden, James B. Irwin (7/26-8/7/71)	Apollo-Saturn 15	74[3]	295h 11m 53s	Scott and Irwin made 4th moon landing; first lunar rover use; first deep space walk; 170 lbs. of samples; 66 h, 55 m, stay
Charles M. Duke Jr., Thomas K. Mattingly, John W. Young (4/16-27/72)	Apollo-Saturn 16	64[3]	265h 51m 05s	Young and Duke made 5th moon landing; collected 213 lbs. of lunar samples; lunar stay line 71 h, 2 m
Eugene A. Cernan, Ronald E. Evans, Harrison H. Schmitt (12/7-19/72)	Apollo-Saturn 17	75[3]	301h 51m 59s	Cernan and Schmitt made 6th manned lunar landing; collected 243 lbs. of samples; record lunar stay of 75 h
Charles Conrad Jr., Joseph P. Kerwin, Paul J. Weitz (5/25-6/22/73)	Skylab 2	...	672h 49m 49s	1st American manned orbiting space station; made long-flights tests, crew repaired damage caused during boost
Alan L. Bean, Jack R. Lousma, Owen K. Garriott (7/28-9/25/73)	Skylab 3	...	1,427h 09m 04s	Crew systems and operational tests, exceeded pre-mission plans for scientific activities; space walk total 13h, 44 m
Gerald P. Carr, Edward G. Gibson, William Pogue (11/16/73-2/8/74)	Skylab 4	...	2,017h 16m 30s	Final Skylab mission; record space walk of 7 h, 1 m., record space walks total for a mission 22 h, 21 m
Alexi Leonov, Valeri Kubasov (7/15-7/21/75)	Soyuz 19	96	143h 31m	
Vance Brand, Thomas P. Stafford, Donald K. Slayton (7/15-7/24/75)	Apollo 18	136	217h 30m.	U.S.-USSR joint flight. Crews linked-up in space, conducted experiments, shared meals, and held a joint news conference
Leonid Kizim, Vladmir Solovyov, Oleg Atkov (2/8-10/2/84)	Salyut 7	...	237 days.	Set space endurance record (since broken)

(1) The U.S. measures orbital flights in revolutions while the Soviets use "orbits." (2) Suborbital. (3) Moon orbits in command module. (4) Moon orbits.

Fire aboard spacecraft Apollo I on the ground at Cape Kennedy, Fla. killed Virgil I. Grissom, Edward H. White and Roger B. Chaffee on Jan. 27, 1967. They were the only U.S. astronauts killed in space tests.

U.S. Space Shuttles

Name, date	Crew
Columbia (4/12-14/81)	Robert L. Crippen, John W. Young.
Columbia (11/12-14/81)	Joe Engle, Richard Truly.
Columbia (3/22-30/82)	Jack Lousma, C. Gordon Fullerton.
Columbia (6-27/7-4/82)	Thomas Mattingly 2d, Henry Hartsfield Jr.
Columbia (11/11-16/82)	Vance Brand, Robert Overmyer, William Lenoir, Joseph Allen.
Challenger (4/4-9/83)	Paul Weitz, Karol Bobko, Story Musgrave, Donald Peterson.
Challenger (6/18-24/83)	Robert L. Crippen, Norman Thagard, John Fabian, Frederick Hauck, Sally K. Ride (1st U.S. woman in space).

(continued)

Name, date	Crew
Challenger (8/30-9/5/83)	Richard Truly, Daniel Brandenstein, William Thornton, Guion Bluford (1st U.S. black in space), Dale Gardner.
Columbia (11/28-12/8/83)	John Young, Brewster Shaw Jr., Robert Parker, Owen Garriott, Byron Lichtenberg, Ulf Merbold.
Challenger (2/3-11/84)	Vance Brand, Robert Gibson, Ronald McNair, Bruce McCandless, Robert Stewart.
Challenger (4/6-13/84)	Robert L. Crippen, Francis R. Scobee, George D. Nelson, Terry J. Hart, James D. Van Hoften.
Discovery (8/30-9/5/84)	Henry W. Hartsfield Jr., Michael L. Coats, Steven A. Hawley, Judith A. Resnik, Richard M. Mullane, Charles D. Walker.
Challenger (10/5-13/84)	Robert L. Crippen, Jon A. McBride, Kathryn D. Sullivan, Sally K. Ride, Marc Garneau (first Canadian), David C. Leestma, Paul D. Scully-Power.
Discovery (11/8-16/84)	Frederick H. Hauck, David M. Walker, Dr. Anna L. Fisher, Joseph P. Allen, Dale A. Gardner.
Discovery (1/24-27/85)	Thomas K. Mattingly, Loren J. Shriver, James F. Buchli, Ellison S. Onizuka, Gary E. Payton.
Discovery (4/12-19/85)	Karol J. Bobko, Donald E. Williams, Sen. Jake Garn, Charles D. Walker, Jeffrey A. Hoffman, S. David Griggs, M. Rhea Seddon.
Challenger (4/29-5/6/85)	Robert F. Overmyer, Frederick D. Gregory, Don L. Lind, Taylor G. Wang, Lodewijk van den Berg, Norman Thagard, William Thornton.
Discovery (6/17-6/24/85)	John O. Creighton, Shannon W. Lucid, Steven R. Nagel, Daniel C. Brandenstein, John W. Fabian, Prince Sultan Salman al-Saud (first Arab), Patrick Baudry.
Challenger (7/29-8/6/85)	Roy D. Bridges Jr., Anthony W. England, Karl G. Henize, F. Story Musgrave, C. Gordon Fullerton, Loren W. Acton, John-David F. Bartoe.
Discovery (8/27-9/3/85)	John M. Lounge, James D. van Hoften, William F. Fisher, Joe H. Engle, Richard O. Covey.
Atlantis (10/4-10/7/85)	Karol J. Bobko, Ronald J. Grabe, David C. Hilmers, William A. Pailes, Robert C. Stewart.
Challenger (10/30-11/6/85)	Henry W. Hartsfield Jr., Steven R. Nagel, Bonnie J. Dunbar, James F. Buchli, Guion S. Bluford Jr., Ernst Messerschmid, Reinhard Furrer, Wubbo J. Ockels.
Atlantis (11/26-12/3/85)	Brewster H. Shaw Jr., Bryan D. O'Connor, Charles Walker, Rodolfo Neri (first Mexican), Jerry L. Ross, Sherwood C. Spring, Mary L. Cleave.
Columbia (1/12-1/18/86)	Robert L. Gibson, Charles F. Bolden Jr., George D. Nelson, Bill Nelson (first congressman), Franklin R. Chang-Diaz, Steven A. Hawley, Robert J. Cenker.
Challenger (1/28/86-exploded after takeoff)	Francis R. Scobee, Michael J. Smith, Ronald E. McNair, Ellison S. Onizuka, Judith A. Resnik, Gregory B. Jarvis, Sharon Christa McAuliffe.
Discovery (9/29-10/3/88)	Frederick H. Hauck, Richard O. Covey, David C. Hilmers, George D. Nelson, John M. Lounge.
Atlantis (12/3-12/6/88)	Robert L. Gibson, Guy S. Gardner, Richard M. Mullane, Jerry L. Ross, William M. Shepherd.
Discovery (3/13-3/18/89)	Michael L. Coats, John E. Blaha, James F. Buchli, Robert C. Springer, James P. Bagian.
Atlantis (5/4-5/8/89)	David M. Walker, Ronald J. Grabe, Mary L. Cleave, Norman E. Thagard, Mark C. Lee.
Columbia (8/8-8/13/89)	Brewster H. Shaw Jr., Richard N. Richards, David C. Leestma, James C. Adamson, Mark N. Brown.
Atlantis (10/18-10/23/89)	Donald E. Williams, Michael J. McCulley, Shannon W. Lucid, Ellen S. Baker, Franklin R. Chang-Diaz.
Discovery (11/22-11/27/89)	Frederick D. Gregory, John E. Blaha, Manley L. Carter, F. Story Musgrave, Katherine C. Thornton.
Colombia (1/9-1/20/90)	Daniel C. Brandenstein, Bonnie J. Dunbar, James D. Wetherbee, Marsha S. Ivins, G. David Low.
Atlantis (2/28-3/4/90)	John O. Creighton, John H. Casper, David C. Hilmers, Richard M. Mullane, Pierre J. Thuot.
Discovery (4/24-4/29/90)	Bruce McCandless 2d, Kathryn D. Sullivan, Loren J. Shriver, Charles F. Bolden Jr., Steven A. Hawley.
Discovery (10/6-10/10/90)	Richard N. Richards, Robert D. Cabana, Bruce E. Melnick, William M. Shepherd, Thomas D. Akers.
Atlantis (11/15-11/20/90)	Richard O. Covey, Frank L. Culbertson, Robert C. Springer, Carl J. Meade, Charles D. Gemar.
Columbia (12/2-12/10/90)	Vance D. Brand, Guy S. Gardner, Jeffrey A. Hoffman, John M. Lounge, Robert A.R. Parker, Samuel T. Durrance, Ronald A. Parise.

(*continued*)

Name, date	Crew
Atlantis (4/5-4/11/91)	Stephen R. Nagel, Kenneth D. Cameron, Linda M. Godwin, Jerry L. Ross, Jerome Apt.
Discovery (4/28-5/6/91)	Michael L. Coats, L. Blaine Hammond Jr., Guion S. Bluford Jr., Gregory J. Harbaugh, Richard J. Hieb, Donald R. McMonagle, Charles L. Veach.
Colombia (6/5-6/14/91)	Byron O. O'Connor, Sidney M. Gutierrez, James P. Bagian, Margaret Rhea Seddon, Francis A. Gaffney, Millie Hughes-Fulford, Tamara E. Jernigan.
Atlantis (8/2-8/11/91)	John E. Blaha, Michael A. Baker, Shannon W. Lucid, G. David Low, James C. Adamson.
Discovery (9/12-9/18/91)	John O. Creighton, Kenneth S. Reightler Jr., Charles D. Gemar, James F. Buchli, Mark N. Brown.
Atlantis (11/24-12/1/91)	Frederick D. Gregory, Terrence T. Hendricks, F. Story Musgrave, James S. Voss, Mario Runco Jr., Thomas J. Hennen.
Discovery (1/22-1/30/92)	Ronald J. Grabe, Stephen S. Oswald, Norman E. Thagard, William E. Readdy, David Hilmers, Roberta L. Bondar, Ulf Merbold.
Atlantis (3/24-4/2/92)	Charles F. Bolden Jr., Brian Duffy, Michael Foale, David C. Leestma, Kathryn D. Sullivan, Bryon K. Lichtenberg, Dirk D. Frimout.
Endeavour (5/7-5/16/92)	Daniel C. Brandenstein, Kevin C. Chilton, Thomas D. Akers, Richard J. Hieb, Kathryn C. Thornton, Bruce E. Melnick, Pierre J. Thout.
Columbia (6/25-7/9/92)	Richard N. Richards, Kenneth D. Bowersox, Bonnie J. Dunbar, Ellen S. Baker, Lawrence J. DeLucas, Carl J. Meade, Eugene H. Trinh. *Set Duration Record for Shuttle Flight.*
Atlantis (7/31-8/8/92)	Jeffrey A. Hoffman, Loren J. Shriver, Franco Malerda, Franklin R. Chang-Diaz, Andrew M. Allen, Marsha S. Ivins, Claude Nicollier.

Notable U.S. Unmanned and Planetary Missions

Spacecraft	Launch date (GMT)	Mission	Remarks
Mariner 2	Aug. 27, 1962	Venus	Passed within 22,000 miles from Venus 12/14/62; contact lost 1/3/63 at 54 million miles
Ranger 7	July 28, 1964	Moon	Yielded over 4,000 photos
Mariner 4	Nov. 28, 1964	Mars	Passed behind Mars 7/14/65; took 22 photos from 6,000 miles
Ranger 8	Feb. 17, 1965	Moon	Yielded over 7,000 photos
Surveyor 3	Apr. 17, 1967	Moon	Scooped and tested lunar soil
Mariner 5	June 14, 1967	Venus	In solar orbit; closest Venus fly-by 10/19/67
Mariner 6	Feb. 25, 1969	Mars	Came within 2,000 miles of Mars 7/31/69; sent back data, photos
Mariner 7	Mar. 27, 1969	Mars	Came within 2,000 miles of Mars 8/5/69
Mariner 9	May 30, 1971	Mars	First craft to orbit Mars 11/13/71; sent back over 7,000 photos
Pioneer 10	Mar. 3, 1972	Jupiter	Passed Jupiter 12/3/73; exited the solar system 6/14/83
Mariner 10	Nov. 3, 1973	Venus, Mercury	Passed Venus 2/5/74; arrived Mercury 3/29/74. First time gravity of one planet (Venus) used to whip spacecraft toward another (Mercury)
Viking 1	Aug. 20, 1975	Mars	Landed on Mars 7/20/76; did scientific research, sent photos; functioned 6 1/2 years
Viking 2	Sept. 9, 1975	Mars	Landed on Mars 9/3/76; functioned 3 1/2 years
Voyager 1	Sept. 5, 1977	Jupiter, Saturn	Encountered Jupiter 3/5/79; Saturn 11/13/80
Voyager 2	Aug. 20, 1977	Jupiter, Saturn, Uranus, Neptune	Encountered Jupiter 7/9/79; Saturn 8/26/81; Uranus 1/8 and 1/27/86; Neptune 8/24/89
Pioneer 12	May 20, 1978	Venus	Entered Venus orbit 12/4/78
Pioneer 13	Aug. 8, 1978	Venus	Encountered Venus 12/9/78
Magellan	May 4, 1989	Venus	Orbit and map Venus
Titan 4	June 14, 1989	Orbit Earth	First of 41 such rockets whose primary purpose is defense

Notable Proposed U.S. Space Missions

Source: National Aeronautics and Space Administration

Year, Month		Mission	Purpose
1993	June	Polar (a)	Study physical properties of the aurora borealis
	Sept.	Space Radar Lab (b)	Acquire radar images of Earth's surface
1995		Cassini (a)	Study Saturn
1996		X-ray Timing Explorer (a)	Study compact X-ray sources such as neutron stars and black holes
1996		Mars Environmental Survey Path Finder	Technical demonstration of Mars environmental survey program
1998		Earth Observing System (a)	Orbit and study Earth
1998		Near Earth Asteroid Rendezvous	One-year study of asteroid.
2000		Mars Rover Sample Return	Collect Martian-soil samples and return to Earth for observation

(a) Launched by expendable rocket. (b) Carried aboard shuttle.

Summary of Worldwide Payloads

(A payload is something carried into space by a rocket)

Source: National Aeronautics and Space Administration

Year	Total[1]	USSR	United States	Japan	European Space Agency	India	China
1985	164	118	33	2	1	—	1
1986	132	114	9	3	0	—	3
1987	133	116	9	3	1	—	1
1988	136	107	15	2	2	2	3
1989	129	95	22	4	2	0	0
1990	160	96	31	7	1	1	5
1991	156	101	30	2	4	1	1
Total	**4,172**	**2,761**	**1,131**	**53**	**30**	**13**	**30**

(1) Incl. launches in countries not shown.

Traffic at U.S. Airports in 1991

Source: Air Transport Association of America (Passenger arrivals and departures)

Chicago (O'Hare)	59,852,330
Dallas/Ft. Worth	48,198,208
Los Angeles	45,668,204
Atlanta	37,916,024
San Francisco	31,774,845
Denver	28,285,189
New York (JFK)	27,441,937
Miami	26,591,415
Newark	23,055,537
Phoenix	22,140,437
Boston	21,547,026
Detroit	21,309,046
Minneapolis/St. Paul	20,601,177
New York (LGA)	20,545,060
Las Vegas	20,171,557
St. Louis	19,151,278
Orlando	18,411,945
Houston	18,117,587
Charlotte	16,876,779
Pittsburgh	16,735,015

U.S. Scheduled Airline Traffic

Source: Air Transport Association of America (thousands)

	1989	1990	1991
Passenger traffic			
Revenue passengers enplaned	453,692	465,560	452,210
Revenue passenger miles	432,714,309	457,926,286	447,795,703
Available seat miles	684,375,876	733,374,893	714,974,175
Revenue passenger load factor (%)	63.2	62.4	62.6
Cargo traffic (ton miles)	12,185,968	12,549,104	12,109,348
Freight and express	10,275,002	10,546,329	10,204,874
U.S. Mail	1,878,651	2,002,775	1,904,474
Financial			
Passenger revenue	$53,802,067	$58,453,215	$56,981,690
Net profit	$127,902	– $3,921,002	– $1,869,974

Leading Passenger Airlines in 1991

Source: Air Transport Assn. of America

(In thousands)

Airline	Passengers
American	75,892
Delta	74,125
United	61,891
USAir	55,600
Northwest	41,098
Continental	36,969
Southwest	25,211
Trans World	20,523
America West	16,844
Pan American	10,559
Alaska	5,810
Aloha	4,915
Midway	4,314
Hawaiian	3,764
West Air	3,062
Air Wisconsin	2,365
Horizon Air	2,022
Trump Shuttle	1,430
Executive Airlines	944
Trans States	915

Aircraft Operating Statistics

Source: Air Transport Assn. of America

(Figures are averages for most commonly used models)

	Number of Seats	Speed Airborne	Flight Length	Fuel (Gallons Per Hour)	Aircraft Operating Cost Per Hour
B747-100	402	518	3,081	3,464	$5,946
L-1011-100/200	294	498	1,635	2,396	4,395
DC-10-10	288	485	1,386	2,170	4,222
A300-600	266	472	1,169	1,674	3,869
B767-300	227	485	1,824	1,534	3,377
B767-200	190	483	2,032	1,370	3,021
B757-200	190	453	1,054	996	2,315
A320-100/200	149	446	1,071	751	1,736
B727-200	148	428	683	1,238	2,300
MD-80	142	418	669	878	1,834
B737-300	131	411	607	711	1,818
DC-9-50	124	372	312	902	1,836
B727-100	116	421	610	1,104	2,182
B737-100/200	112	385	430	771	1,644
F-100	103	358	385	586	1,354
DC-9-30	103	381	433	768	1,638
DC-9-10	77	367	372	734	1,612

U.S. Airline Safety

Source: National Transportation Safety Board

	Departures (millions)	Fatal accidents	Fatalities	Fatal accidents per 100,000 departures		Departures (millions)	Fatal accidents	Fatalities	Fatal accidents per 100,000 departures
1977	4.9	3	78	0.061	1985	5.8	4	197	0.069
1978	5.0	5	160	0.100	1986	6.4	2	5	0.016
1979	5.4	4	351	0.074	1987	6.6	4[1]	231	0.046[1]
1980	5.4	0	0	0.000	1988	6.7	3[1]	285	0.030[1]
1981	5.2	4	4	0.077	1989	6.6	11	278	0.166
1982	5.0	4	233	0.060	1990	6.9	6	39	0.087
1983	5.0	4	15	0.079	1991	6.8	4	62	0.059
1984	5.4	1	4	0.018					

(1) Sabotage-caused accidents are incl. in the Accidents but not in the Accident rates.

National Aviation Hall of Fame

The National Aviation Hall of Fame at Dayton, Oh., is dedicated to honoring the outstanding pioneers of air and space.

Allen, William M.
Andrews, Frank M.
Armstrong, Neil A.
Arnold, Henry H. "Hap"
Atwood, John Leland
Balchen, Bernt
Baldwin, Thomas S.
Beachey, Lincoln
Beech, Olive A.
Beech, Walter H.
Bell, Alexander Graham
Bell, Lawrence D.
Bendix, Vincent T.
Boeing, William E.
Bong, Richard I.
Borman, Frank
Boyd, Albert
Bradley, Mark E.
Brown, George "Scratchley"
Byrd, Richard E.
Cessna, Clyde V.
Chamberlin, Clarence D.
Chanute, Octave
Chennault, Claire L.
Cochran (Odlum), Jacqueline
Collins, Michael
Conrad Jr., Charles
Crossfield, A. Scott
Cunningham, Alfred A.
Curtiss, Glenn H.
deSeversky, Alexander P.
Doolittle, James H.
Douglas, Donald W.
Draper, Charles S.
Eaker, Ira C.
Earhart, (Putnam), Amelia
Eielson, C. Benjamin
Ellyson, Theodore G.
Ely, Eugene B.
Everest, Frank K.
Fairchild, Sherman M.
Fleet, Reuben H.
Fokker, Anthony H.G.
Ford, Henry
Foss, Joseph
Foulois, Benjamin D.
Frye, Jack
Gabreski, Francis S.
Glenn Jr., John H.
Goddard, George W.
Goddard, Robert H.
Godfrey, Arthur
Goldwater, Barry M.
Grissom, Virgil I.
Gross, Robert E.
Grumman, Leroy R.
Guggenheim, Harry F.
Haughton, Daniel J.
Hegenberger, Albert F.
Heinemann, Edward H.
Hoover, Robert A.
Hughes, Howard R.
Ingalls, David S.
Jeppesen, Elrey B.
Johnson, Clarence L.
Jones, Thomas V.
Kenney, George C.
Kettering, Charles F.
Kindelberger, James H.
Knabenshue, A. Roy
Knight, William J.
Lahm, Frank P.
Langley, Samuel P.
Lear, William P. Sr.
LeMay, Curtis E.
LeVier, Anthony W.
Lindbergh, Anne M.
Lindbergh, Charles A.
Link, Edwin A.
Lockheed, Allan H.
Loening, Grover
Luke Jr., Frank
Macready, Carl B.
Macready, John A.
Martin, Glenn L.
McDonnell, James S.
Mitscher, Marc A.
Meyer, John C.
Mitchell, William "Billy"
Montgomery, John J.
Moorer, Thomas H.
Moss, Sanford A.
Neumann, Gerhard
Nichols, Ruth R.
Northrop, John K.
Patterson, William A.
Piper Sr., William T.
Post, Wiley H.
Read, Albert C.
Reeve, Robert C.
Rentschler, Frederick B.
Richardson, Holden C.
Rickenbacker, Edward V.
Rodgers, Calbraith P.
Rogers, Will
Rushworth, Robert A.
Ryan, T. Claude
Schirra, Walter M.
Schriever, Bernard A.
Selfridge, Thomas E.
Shepard Jr., Alan B.
Sikorsky, Igor I.
Six, Robert F.
Smith, C.R.
Spaatz, Carl A.
Sperry Sr., Elmer A.
Sperry Sr., Lawrence B.
Stanley, Robert M.
Stapp, John P.
Stearmam, Lloyd C.
Taylor, Charles E.
Thomas, Lowell
Towers, John H.
Trippe, Juan T.
Turner, Roscoe
Twining, Nathan F.
Vandenberg, Hoyt
von Braun, Wernher
von Karman, Theodore
von Ohain, Hans P.
Vought, Chance M.
Wade, Leigh
Walden, Henry W.
Wells, Edward
Wilson, Thornton A.
Wright, Orville
Wright, Wilbur
Yeager, Charles E.
Young, John W.

International Aeronautical Records

Source: The National Aeronautic Association of the USA, 1815 North Fort Myer Dr., Arlington, VA 22209, representative in the United States of the Federation Aeronautique Internationale, certifying agency for world aviation and space records. The International Aeronautical Federation was formed in 1905 by representatives from Belgium, France, Germany, Great Britain, Spain, Italy, Switzerland, and the United States, with headquarters in Paris. Regulations for the control of official records were signed Oct. 14, 1905. World records are defined as maximum performance, regardless of class or type of aircraft used. Records to Jan. 1, 1992.

World Absolute Records—Maximum Performance in Any Class

Speed over a straight course — 2,193.16 mph — Capt. Elden W. Joersz, USAF, Lockheed SR-71; Beale AFB, Cal., July 28, 1976.

Speed over a closed circuit — 2,092.294 mph — Maj. Adolphus H. Bledsoe Jr., USAF, Lockheed SR-71; Beale AFB, Cal., July 27, 1976.

Speed around the world, non-stop, nonrefueled — 115.65 mph — Richard Rutan & Jeana Yeager, U.S., Voyager, Edwards AFB, Cal., Dec. 14-23, 1986.

Altitude — (123,523.58 feet) — Alexander Fedotov, USSR, E-266M; Podmoskovnoye, USSR, Aug. 31, 1977.

Altitude in horizontal flight — 85,068.997 ft. — Capt. Robert C. Helt, USAF, Lockheed SR-71; Beale AFB, Cal., July 28, 1976.

Class K Spacecraft

Duration — 365 days, 22 hours, 39 minutes, 47 seconds — Vladimir Titov, Musa Manarov, USSR, Soyuz TM4; Dec. 21, 1987 — Dec. 21, 1988.

Altitude — 234,672.5 mi. — Frank Borman, James A. Lovell Jr., William Anders, Apollo 8; Dec. 21-27, 1968.

(continued)

Greatest mass lifted — 282,197 lbs. — Frank Borman, James A. Lovell Jr., William Anders, Apollo 8; Dec. 21-27, 1968.
Distance — 87,436,800 mi. — Anatoly Beresovoy & Valentin Lebedev, USSR, Salyut 7, Soyuz T5, Soyuz T7; May 13-Dec. 10, 1982.

World "Class" Records

All other records, international in scope, are termed World "Class" records and are divided into classes: airships, free balloons, airplanes, seaplanes, amphibians, gliders, and rotorplanes. Airplanes (Class C) are sub-divided into four groups: Group I — piston engine aircraft, Group II — turboprop aircraft, Group III — jet aircraft, Group IV — rocket powered aircraft. A partial listing of world records follows:

Airplanes (Class C-I, Group I—piston engine)

Distance, closed circuit — 24,986.727 mi. — Richard Rutan & Jeana Yeager, U.S., Voyager; Edwards AFB, Cal., Dec. 14-23, 1986.
Speed for 100 kilometers (62.137 miles) without payload — 469.549 mph — Jacqueline Cochran, U.S.; North American P-51; Coachella Valley, Cal., Dec. 10, 1947.
Speed for 1,000 kilometers (621.369 miles) without payload — 431.09 mph — Jacqueline Cochran, U.S.; North American P-51; Santa Rosasummit, Cal. — Flagstaff, Ariz. course, May 24, 1948.
Speed for 5,000 kilometers (3,106.849 miles) without payload — 338.39 mph — Capt. James Bauer, USAF, Boeing B-29; Dayton, Oh., June 28, 1946.
Speed around the world — 203.64 mph — D.N. Dalton, Australia; Beechcraft Duke; Brisbane, Aust., July 20-25, 1975. Time: 5 days, 2 hours, 19 min., 57 sec.

Light Airplanes—(Class C-1.d)

Great Circle distance without landing — 7,929.71 mi. — Peter Wilkins, Australia, Piper Malibu, Sydney, Aust. to Phoenix, Ariz., Mar. 30-Apr. 1, 1987.
Speed for 100 kilometers — (62,137 miles) in a closed circuit — 322.780 mph — Ms. R. M. Sharpe, Great Britain; Vickers Supermarine Spitfire 5-B; Wolverhampton, June 17, 1950.

Helicopters (Class E-1)

Great Circle distance without landing — 2,213.04 mi. — Robert G. Ferry, U.S.; Hughes YOH-6A helicopter; Culver City, Cal., to Ormond Beach, Fla., Apr. 6-7, 1966.
Speed around the world —35.40 mph — H. Ross Perot Jr.; Bell 206 L-11 Long Ranger N39112; Dallas, Tex.-Dallas, Tex.; Sept. 1-30, 1982; 29 days, 3 hrs., 8 min., 13 sec.

Gliders (Class D-I—single seater)

Distance, straight line — 907.7 mi. — Hans Werner Grosse, West Germany; ASK12 sailplane; Luebeck to Biarritz, Apr. 25, 1972.
Distance to a goal & return — 1,023.25 mi. — Thomas Knauff, U.S. Nimbus III; Williamsport, Pa., Apr. 25, 1983.

Airplanes (Class C-I, Group II—Turboprop)

Great Circle distance without landing — 8,732.09 mi.— Lt. Col. Edgar L. Allison Jr., USAF, Lockheed HC-130 Hercules aircraft; Taiwan to Scott AFB, Ill.; Feb. 20, 1972.
Altitude — (51,014 ft.) — Donald R. Wilson, U.S.; LTV L450F aircraft; Greenville, Tex., Mar. 27, 1972.
Speed for 1,000 kilometers (621.369 miles) without payload — 541.449 mph — Ivan Soukhomline, USSR; TU-114 aircraft; Sternberg, USSR; Mar. 24, 1960.
Speed for 5,000 kilometers (3,106.849 miles) without payload — 545.072 mph — Ivan Soukhomline, USSR; TU-114 aircraft, Sternberg, USSR; Apr. 9, 1960.
Speed around the world —304.80 mph — Joe Harnish, U.S., Gulfstream Commander 695A, Elkhart, Ind., Mar. 21-24, 1983.

Airplanes (Class C-1, Group III—Jet Engine)

Great Circle distance without landing — 12,532.28 mi. — Maj. Clyde P. Evely, USAF, Boeing B-52-H, Kadena, Okinawa to Madrid, Spain, Jan. 10-11, 1962.
Distance in a closed circuit — 12,521.78 mi. — Vladimir Tersky, USSR, AN-124, Podmoskovnoye, USSR, May 6-7, 1987.
Altitude — 123,523.58 ft. — Alexander Fedotov, USSR; E-226M airplane; Podmoskovnoye, USSR, Aug. 31, 1977.
Speed for 100 kilometers in a closed circuit — 1,618.7 mph — Alexander Fedotov, USSR; E-266 airplane, Apr. 8, 1973.
Speed for 500 kilometers in a closed circuit — 1,852.61 mph — Mikhail Komarov, USSR; E-266 airplane, Oct. 5, 1967.
Speed for 1,000 kilometers in a closed circuit — 2,092.294 mph — Maj. Adolphus H. Bledsoe Jr., USAF; Lockheed SR-71; Beale AFB, Cal., July 27, 1976.
Speed for 2,000 kilometers without payload — 1,250.42 mph — S. Agapov, USSR; Podmoscovnde, USSR; July 20, 1983.
Speed around the world — 637.71 mph — Allen E. Paulson, U.S., Gulfstream IV, Houston, Tex., Feb. 26-28, 1988.

Balloons-Class A

Altitude — (113,739.9 ft.) — Cmdr. Malcolm D. Ross, USNR; Lee Lewis Memorial Winzen Research Balloon; Gulf of Mexico, May 4, 1961.
Distance —(5,208.67 mi.) — Ben Abruzzo; Raven Experimental; Nagashima, Japan to Covello, Cal., Nov. 9-12, 1981.
Duration —137 hr., 5 min., 50 sec. — Ben Abruzzo, Larry Newman, and Maxie Anderson; Double Eagle II; Presque Isle, Maine to Miserey, France (3,107.61 mi.); Aug. 12-17, 1978.

FAI Course Records

Los Angeles to New York — 1,214.65 mph — Capt. Robert G. Sowers, USAF; Convair B-58 Hustler; elapsed time: 2 hrs. 58.71 sec., Mar. 5, 1962.
New York to Los Angeles — 1,081.80 mph — Capt. Robert G. Sowers, USAF; Convair B-58 Hustler; elapsed time: 2 hrs. 15 min. 50.08 sec., Mar. 5, 1962.
New York to Paris — 1,089.36 mph — Maj. W. R. Payne, U.S.; Convair B-58 Hustler; elapsed time: 3 hrs 19 min. 44 sec., May 26, 1961.
London to New York — 587.457 mph — Maj. Burl Davenport, USAF; Boeing KC-135; elapsed time: 5 hrs. 53 min. 12.77 sec.; June 27, 1958.
Baltimore to Moscow, USSR — 563.36 mph — Col. James B. Swindal, USAF; Boeing VC-137 (707); elapsed time: 8 hrs. 33 min. 45.4 sec., May 19, 1963.
New York to London — 1,806.964 mph — Maj. James V. Sullivan, USAF; Lockheed SR-71; elapsed time 1 hr. 54 min. 56.4 sec., Sept. 1, 1974.
London to Los Angeles — 1,435.587 mph — Capt. Harold B. Adams, USAF; Lockheed SR-71; elapsed time: 3 hrs. 47 min. 39 sec., Sept. 13, 1974.

Notable Around the World and Intercontinental Trips

	From/To	Miles	Time	Date
Nellie Bly	New York/New York		72d 06h 11m	1889
George Francis Train	New York/New York		67d 12h 03m	1890
Charles Fitzmorris	Chicago/Chicago.		60d 13h 29m	1901
J. W. Willis Sayre	Seattle/Seattle		54d 09h 42m	1903
J. Alcock-A.W. Brown (1)	Newfoundland/Ireland	1,960	16h 12m	June 14-15, 1919
Two U.S. Army airplanes	Seattle/Seattle.	26,103	35d 01h 11m	1924
Richard E. Byrd (2)	Spitsbergen/N. Pole	1,545	15h 30m	May 9, 1926
Amundsen-Ellsworth-Nobile Expedition	Spitsbergen/Teller, Alaska		80h	May 11-14,1926
E.S. Evans and L. Wells (N. Y.World) (3)	New York/New York	18,400	28d 14h 36m 05s	June 16-July 14, 1926
Charles Lindbergh (4)	New York/Paris	3,610	33h 29m 30s	May 20-21, 1927
Amelia Earhart, W. Stultz, L. Gordon	Newfoundland/Wales		20h 40m	June 17-18, 1928
Graf Zeppelin	Friedrichshafen, Ger./Lakehurst, N.J.	6,630	4d 15h 46m	Oct. 11-15, 1928
Graf Zeppelin	Friedrichshafen, Ger./Lakehurst, N.J..	21,700	20d 04h	Aug. 14-Sept. 4, 1929
Wiley Post and Harold Gatty (Monoplane Winnie Mae)	New York/New York	15,474	8d 15h 51m	July 1, 1931
C. Pangborn-H. Herndon Jr. (5)	Misawa, Japan/Wenatchee, Wash.	4,458	41h 34m	Oct. 3-5, 1931
Amelia Earhart (6)	Newfoundland/Ireland	2,026	14h 56m	May 20-21, 1932
Wiley Post (Monoplane Winnie Mae) (7)	New York/New York	15,596	115h 36m 30s	July 15-22, 1933
Hindenburg Zeppelin	Lakehurst, N.J./Frankfort, Ger.		42h 53m	Aug. 9-11, 1936
H. R. Ekins (Scripps-Howard Newspapers in race) (Zeppelin Hindenburg to Germany air planes from Frankfurt)	Lakehurst, N.J./Lakehurst, N.J..	25,654	18d 11h 14m 33s	Sept, 30-Oct. 19, 1936
Howard Hughes and 4 assistants	New York/New York	14,824	3d 19h 08m 10s	July 10-13, 1938
Douglas Corrigan	New York/Dublin		28h 13m	July 17-18, 1938
Mrs. Clara Adams (Pan American Clipper)	Port Washington, N.Y./Newark, N.J.		16d 19h 04m	June 28-July 15, 1939
Globester, U.S. Air Transport Command	Wash., D.C./Wash., D.C.	23,279	149h 44m	Oct. 4, 1945
Capt. William P. Odom (A-26 Reynolds Bombshell)	New York/New York	20,000	78h 55m 12s	Apr. 12-16, 1947
America, Pan American 4-engine Lockheed Constellation (8)	New York/New York	22,219	101h 32m	June 17-30, 1947
Col. Edward Eagan	New York/New York	20,559	147h 15m	Dec. 13, 1948
USAF B-50 Lucky Lady II (Capt. James Gallagher) (9)	Ft. Worth, Tex./Ft. Worth, Tex.	23,452	94h 01m	Feb. 26-Mar. 2, 1949
Col. D. Schilling, USAF (10)	England/Limestone, Me.	3,300	10h 01m	Sept. 22, 1950
C.F. Blair Jr.	Norway/Alaska	3,300	10h 29m	May 29, 1951
Two U.S. S-55.	Massachusetts/Scotland.	3,410	42h 30m	July 15-31, 1952
Canberra Bomber (11)	N. Ireland/Newfoundland.	2,073	04h 34m	Aug. 26, 1952
	Newfoundland/N. Ireland.	2,073	03h 25m	Aug. 26, 1952
Three USAF B-52 Stratofortresses (12).	Merced, Cal./Cal..	24,325	45h 19m	Jan. 15-18, 1957
Max Conrad.	Chicago/Rome.	5,000	34h 03m	Mar. 5-6, 1959
USSR TU-114 (13)	Moscow/New York	5,092	11h 06m	June 28, 1959
Boeing 707-320	New York/Moscow.	c.5090	08h 54m	July 23, 1959
Peter Gluckmann (solo)	San Francisco/San Francisco	22,800	29d	Aug. 22-Sept. 20, 1959
Sue Snyder	Chicago/Chicago.	21,219	62h 59m	June 22-24, 1960
Max Conrad (solo)	Miami/Miami.	25,946	8d 18h 35m 57s	Feb. 28-Mar. 8, 1961
Sam Miller & Louis Fodor	New York/New York		46h 28m	Aug. 3-4, 1963
Robert & Joan Wallick	Manila/Manila	23,129	05d 06h 17m 10s	June 2-7, 1966
Arthur Godfrey, Richard Merrill Fred Austin, Karl Keller	New York/New York	23,333	86h 9m 01s	June 4-7, 1966
Trevor K. Brougham	Darwin, Australia/Darwin.	24,800	5d 05h 57m	Aug. 5-10, 1972
Walter H. Mullikin, Albert Frink, Lyman Watt, Frank Cassaniti, Edward Shields.	New York/New York	23,137	1d 22h 50s	May 1-3,1976
David Kunst (15)	Waseca, Minn./Waseca, Minn.	14,500	4yrs 3mos 16d	June 10, 1970-Oct. 5, 1974
Arnold Palmer	Denver/Denver.	22,985	57h 25m 42s	May 17-19, 1976
Boeing 747 (14)	San Francisco/San Francisco	26,382	54h 7m 12s	Oct. 28-31, 1977
Concorde	London/Wash., D.C.	1,023 mph	03h 34m 48s	May 29, 1976
Concorde	Paris/New York	1,037.50 mph	03h 30m 11s	Aug. 22, 1978
Richard Rutan & Jeana Yeager (16).	Edwards AFB, Cal..	24,986	09d 03m 44s	Dec. 14-23, 1986

(1) Non-stop transtlantic flight. (2) Polar flight. (3) Mileage by train and auto, 4,110; by plane, 6,300; by steamship, 8,000. (4) Solo transatlantic flight in the Ryan monoplane the "Spirit of St. Louis". (5) Non-stop Pacific flight. (6) Woman's transoceanic solo flight. (7) First to fly solo around northern circumference of the world, also first to fly twice around the world. (8) Inception of regular commercial global air service. (9) First non-stop round-the-world flight, refueled 4 times in flight. (10) Non-stop jet transatlantic flight. (11) Transatlantic round trip on same day. (12) First non-stop global flight by jet planes; refueled in flight by KC-97 aerial tankers; average speed approx. 525 mph. (13) Non-stop between Moscow and New York. (14) Speed record around the world over both the earth's poles. (15) First to circle the earth on foot. (16) Circled the earth nonstop without refueling.

WEIGHTS AND MEASURES

Source: National Institute of Standards and Technology, U.S. Dept. of Commerce

The International System of Units

Two systems of weights and measures exist side by side in the United States today, with roughly equal but separate legislative sanction: the U.S. Customary System and the International (Metric) System. Throughout U.S. history, the Customary System (inherited from, but now different from, the British Imperial System) has been, as its name implies, customarily used; a plethora of federal and state legislation has given it, through implication, standing as our primary weights and measures system. However, the Metric System (incorporated in the scientists' new SI or Systeme International d'Unites) is the only system that has ever received specific legislative sanction by Congress. The "Law of 1866" reads:

> It shall be lawful throughout the United States of America to employ the weights and measures of the metric system; and no contract or dealing, or pleading in any court, shall be deemed invalid or liable to objection because the weights or measures expressed or referred to therein are weights or measures of the metric system.

Over the last 100 years, the Metric System has seen slow, steadily increasing use in the United States. In science and also in the pharmaceutical industry, the use of metrics has for many years been predominant; today, the manufacturing industry is steadily increasing its use of the metric system largely motivated by the automotive industry, which is now predominantly metric.

On Feb. 10, 1964, the National Bureau of Standards issued the following bulletin:

> Henceforth it shall be the policy of the National Bureau of Standards to use the units of the International System (SI), as adopted by the 11th General Conference on Weights and Measures (October 1960), except when the use of these units would obviously impair communication or reduce the usefulness of a report.

The Trade Act of 1988 calls for the federal government to adopt metric specifications by Dec. 31, 1992, and mandates the Commerce Dept. to oversee the program.

What had been the Metric System became the International System (SI), a more complete scientific system.

Seven units have been adopted to serve as the base for the International System as follows: **length**—meter; **mass**—kilogram; **time**—second; **electric current**—ampere; **thermodynamic temperature**—kelvin; **amount of substance**—mole; and **luminous intensity**—candela.

Prefixes

The following prefixes, in combination with the basic unit names, provide the multiples and submultiples in the International System. For example, the unit name "meter," with the prefix "kilo" added, produces "kilometer," meaning "1,000 meters."

Prefix	Symbol	Multiples	Equivalent
exa	E	10^{18}	quintillionfold
peta	P	10^{15}	quadrillionfold
tera	T	10^{12}	trillionfold
giga	G	10^{9}	billionfold
mega	M	10^{6}	millionfold
kilo	k	10^{3}	thousandfold
hecto	h	10^{2}	hundredfold
deka	da	10	tenfold

Prefix	Symbol	Submultiples	Equivalent
deci	d	10^{-1}	tenth part
centi	c	10^{-2}	hundredth part
milli	m	10^{-3}	thousandth part
micro	μ	10^{-6}	millionth part
nano	n	10^{-9}	billionth part
pico	p	10^{-12}	trillionth part
femto	f	10^{-15}	quadrillionth part
atto	a	10^{-18}	quintillionth part

Tables of Metric Weights and Measures

Linear Measure

10 millimeters (mm)	= 1 centimeter (cm)
10 centimeters	= 1 decimeter (dm) = 100 millimeters
10 decimeters	= 1 meter (m) = 1,000 millimeters
10 meters	= 1 dekameter (dam)
10 dekameters	= 1 hectometer (hm) = 100 meters
10 hectometers	= 1 kilometer (km) = 1,000 meters

Area Measure

100 square millimeters (mm^2)	= 1 square centimeter (cm^2)
10,000 square centimeters	= 1 square meter (m^2) = 1,000,000 square millimeters
100 square meters	= 1 are (a)
100 ares	= 1 hectare (ha) = 10,000 square meters
100 hectares	= 1 square kilometer (km^2) = 1,000,000 square meters

Fluid Volume Measure

10 milliliters (mL)	= 1 centiliter (cL)
10 centiliters	= 1 deciliter (dL) = 100 milliliters
10 deciliters	= 1 liter (L) = 1,000 milliliters
10 liters	= 1 dekaliter (daL)
10 dekaliters	= 1 hectoliter (hL) = 100 liters
10 hectoliters	= 1 kiloliter (kL) = 1,000 liters

Cubic Measure

1,000 cubic millimeters (mm^3)	= 1 cubic centimeter (cm^3)
1,000 cubic centimeters	= 1 cubic decimeter (dm^3) = 1,000,000 cubic millimeters
1,000 cubic decimeters	= 1 cubic meter (m^3) = 1 stere = 1,000,000 cubic centimeters = 1,000,000,000 cubic millimeters

Weight

10 milligrams (mg)	= 1 centigram (cg)
10 centigrams	= 1 decigram (dg) = 100 milligrams
10 decigrams	= 1 gram (g) = 1,000 milligrams
10 grams	= 1 dekagram (dag)
10 dekagrams	= 1 hectogram (hg) = 100 grams
10 hectograms	= 1 kilogram (kg) = 1,000 grams
1,000 kilograms	= 1 metric ton (t)

Table of U.S. Customary Weights and Measures

Linear Measure

12 inches (in)	= 1 foot (ft)
3 feet	= 1 yard (yd)
5 1/2 yards	= 1 rod (rd), pole, or perch (16 1/2 feet)
40 rods	= 1 furlong (fur) = 220 yards = 660 feet
8 furlongs	= 1 statute mile (mi) = 1,760 yards = 5,280 feet
3 miles	= 1 league = 5,280 yards = 15,840 feet
6076.11549 feet	= 1 International Nautical Mile

Liquid Measure

When necessary to distinguish the liquid pint or quart from the dry pint or quart, the word "liquid" or the abbreviation "liq" should be used in combination with the name or abbreviation of the liquid unit.

4 gills	= 1 pint (pt) = 28.875 cubic inches
2 pints	= 1 quart (qt) = 57.75 cubic inches
4 quarts	= 1 gallon (gal) = 231 cubic inches = 8 pints = 32 gills

Area Measure

Squares and cubes of units are sometimes abbreviated by using "superior" figures. For example, ft^2 means square foot, and ft^3 means cubic foot.

144 square inches	= 1 square foot (ft^2)
9 square feet	= 1 square yard (yd^2) = 1,296 square inches
30 1/4 square yards	= 1 square rod (rd^2) = 272 1/4 square feet
160 square rods	= 1 acre = 4,840 square yards = 43,560 square feet
640 acres	= 1 square mile (mi^2)
1 mile square	= 1 section (of land)
6 miles square	= 1 township = 36 sections = 36 square miles

Cubic Measure

1 cubic foot (ft^3)	= 1,728 cubic inches (in^3)
27 cubic feet	= 1 cubic yard (yd^3)

Gunter's or Surveyors' Chain Measure

7.92 inches (in)	= 1 link
100 links	= 1 chain (ch) = 4 rods = 66 feet
80 chains	= 1 survey mile (mi) = 320 rods = 5,280 feet

Troy Weight

24 grains	= 1 pennyweight (dwt)
20 pennyweights	= 1 ounce troy (oz t) = 480 grains
12 ounces troy	= 1 pound troy (lb t) = 240 pennyweights = 5,760 grains

Dry Measure

When necessary to distinguish the dry pint or quart from the liquid pint or quart, the word "dry" should be used in combination with the name or abbreviation of the dry unit.

2 pints (pt)	= 1 quart (qt) = 67.2006 cubic inches
8 quarts	= 1 peck (pk) = 537.605 cubic inches = 16 pints
4 pecks	= 1 bushel (bu) = 2,150.42 cubic inches = 32 quarts

Avoirdupois Weight

When necessary to distinguish the avoirdupois ounce or pound from the troy ounce or pound, the word "avoirdupois" or the abbreviation "avdp" should be used in combination with the name or abbreviation of the avoirdupois unit.

(The "grain" is the same in avoirdupois and troy weight.)

27 11/32 grains	= 1 dram (dr)
16 drams	= 1 ounce (oz) = 437 1/2 grains
16 ounces	= 1 pound (lb) = 256 drams = 7,000 grains
100 pounds	= 1 hundredweight (cwt)°
20 hundredweights	= 1 ton = 2,000 pounds°

In "gross" or "long" measure, the following values are recognized.

112 pounds	= 1 gross or long hundredweight°
20 gross or long hundredweights	= 1 gross or long ton = 2,240 pounds°

°When the terms "hundredweight" and "ton" are used unmodified, they are commonly understood to mean the 100-pound hundredweight and the 2,000-pound ton, respectively; these units may be designated "net" or "short" when necessary to distinguish them from the corresponding units in gross or long measure.

Tables of Equivalents

In this table it is necessary to distinguish between the "international" and the "survey" foot. The international foot, defined in 1959 as exactly equal to 0.3048 meter, is shorter than the old survey foot by exactly 2 parts in one million. The survey foot is still used in data expressed in feet in geodetic surveys within the U.S. In this table the survey foot is italicized.

When the name of a unit is enclosed in brackets thus, [1 hand], this indicates (1) that the unit is not in general current use in the United States, or (2) that the unit is believed to be based on "custom and usage" rather than on formal definition.

Equivalents involving decimals are, in most instances, rounded off to the third decimal place except where they are exact, in which cases these exact equivalents are so designated.

Lengths

1 angstrom (A)	0.1 nanometer (exactly); 0.000 1 micrometer (exactly); 0.000 000 1 millimeter (exactly); 0.000 000 004 inch
1 cable's length	120 fathoms (exactly); 720 *feet* (exactly); 219 meters
1 centimeter (cm)	0.3937 inch
1 chain (ch) (Gunter's or surveyors)	66 *feet* (exactly); 20.1168 meters
1 chain (engineers)	100 feet; 30.48 meters (exactly)
1 decimeter (dm)	3.937 inches
1 degree (geographical)	364,566.929 feet; 69.047 miles (avg.); 111.123 kilometers (avg.)
-of latitude	68.708 miles at equator; 69.403 miles at poles
-of longitude	69.171 miles at equator
1 dekameter (dam)	32.808 feet
1 fathom	6 *feet* (exactly); 1.8288 meters (exactly)
1 foot (ft)	0.3048 meters (exactly)
1 furlong (fur)	10 chains (surveyors) (exactly); 660 *feet* (exactly); 1/8 statute mile (exactly); 201.168 meters
[1 hand] (height measure for horses from ground to top of shoulders)	4 inches
1 inch (in)	2.54 centimeters (exactly)
1 kilometer (km)	0.621 mile; 3,281.5 feet
1 league (land)	3 survey miles (exactly); 4.828 kilometers
1 link (Gunter's or surveyors)	7.92 inches (exactly); 0.201 meter
1 link engineers	1 foot; 0.305 meter
1 meter (m)	39.37 inches; 1.094 yards
1 micrometer (μm) [the Greek letter mu]	0.001 millimeter (exactly); 0.000 039 37 inch
1 mil	0.001 inch (exactly); 0.025 4 millimeter (exactly)
1 mile (mi) (statute or land)	5,280 feet (exactly); 1.609 kilometers
1 international nautical mile (nmi)	1.852 kilometers (exactly); 1.150779 survey miles; 6,076.11549 feet
1 millimeter (mm)	0.039 37 inch
1 nanometer (nm)	0.001 micrometer (exactly); 0.000 000 039 37 inch
1 pica (typography)	12 points
1 point (typography)	0.013 837 inch (exactly); 0.351 millimeter
1 rod (rd), pole, or perch	16 1/2 *feet* (exactly); 5.029 meters
1 yard (yd)	0.9144 meter (exactly)

Areas or Surfaces

1 acre	43,560 square *feet* (exactly); 4,840 square yards; 0.405 hectare
1 are (a)	119.599 square yards; 0.025 acre

1 bolt (cloth measure):	
length	100 yards (on modern looms)
width	42 inches (usually, for cotton) 60 inches (usually, for wool)
1 hectare (ha)	2.471 acres
[1 square (building)]	100 square feet
1 square centimeter (cm^2)	0.155 square inch
1 square decimeter (dm^2)	15.500 square inches
1 square foot (ft^2)	929.030 square centimeters
1 square inch (in^2)	6.4516 square centimeters (exactly)
1 square kilometer (km^2)	247.104 acres 0.386 square mile
1 square meter (m^2)	1.196 square yards 10.764 square feet
1 square mile (mi^2)	258.999 hectares
1 square millimeter (mm^2)	0.002 square inch
1 square rod (rd^2) sq. pole, or sq. perch	25.293 square meters
1 square yard (yd^2)	0.836 square meter

Capacities or Volumes

1 barrel (bbl) liquid	31 to 42 gallons°

°There are a variety of "barrels," established by law or usage. For example: federal taxes on fermented liquors are based on a barrel of 31 gallons: many state laws fix the "barrel for liquids" as 31 ½ gallons; one state fixes a 36-gallon barrel for cistern measurement; federal law recognizes a 40-gallon barrel for "proof spirits"; by custom, 42 gallons comprise a barrel of crude oil or petroleum products for statistical purposes, and this equivalent is recognized "for liquids" by 4 states.

1 barrel (bbl), standard, for fruits, vegetables, and other dry commodities except dry cranberries	7,056 cubic inches 105 dry quarts 3.281 bushels, struck measure
1 barrel (bbl), standard, cranberry	5,826 cubic inches 86⁴⁵⁄₆₄ dry quarts 2.709 bushels, struck measure
1 board foot (lumber measure)	a foot-square board 1 inch thick
1 bushel (bu) (U.S.) (struck measure)	2,150.42 cubic inches (exactly) 35.239 liters
[1 bushel, heaped (U.S.)]	2,747.715 cubic inches 1.278 bushels, struck measure°

°Frequently recognized as 1¼ bushels, struck measure.

[1 bushel (bu) (British Imperial) (struck measure)]	1.032 U.S. bushels struck measure 2,219.36 cubic inches
1 cord (cd) firewood	128 cubic feet (exactly)
1 cubic centimeter (cm^3)	0.061 cubic inch
1 cubic decimeter (dm^3)	61.024 cubic inches
1 cubic inch (in^3)	0.554 fluid ounce 4.433 fluid drams 16.387 cubic centimeters
1 cubic foot (ft^3)	7.481 gallons 28.317 cubic decimeters
1 cubic meter (m^3)	1.308 cubic yards
1 cubic yard (yd^3)	0.765 cubic meter
1 cup, measuring	8 fluid ounces (exactly) ½ liquid pint (exactly)
[1 dram, fluid (fl dr) (British)]	0.961 U.S. fluid dram 0.217 cubic inch 3.552 milliliters
1 dekaliter (daL)	2.642 gallons 1.135 pecks
1 gallon (gal) (U.S.)	231 cubic inches (exactly) 3.785 liters 0.833 British gallon 128 U.S. fluid ounces (exactly)
[1 gallon (gal) British Imperial]	277.42 cubic inches 1.201 U.S. gallons 4.546 liters 160 British fluid ounces (exactly)
1 gill (gi)	7.219 cubic inches 4 fluid ounces (exactly) 0.118 liter
1 hectoliter (hL)	26.418 gallons 2.838 bushels
1 liter (L) (1 cubic decimeter exactly)	1.057 liquid quarts 0.908 dry quart 61.025 cubic inches
1 milliliter (mL) (1 cu cm exactly)	0.271 fluid dram 16.231 minims 0.061 cubic inch
1 ounce, liquid (U.S.)	1.805 cubic inches 29.573 milliliters 1.041 British fluid ounces
[1 ounce, fluid (fl oz) (British)]	0.961 U.S. fluid ounce 1.734 cubic inches 28.412 milliliters
1 peck (pk)	8.810 liters
1 pint (pt), dry	33.600 cubic inches 0.551 liter
1 pint (pt), liquid	28.875 cubic inches (exactly) 0.473 liter
1 quart (qt) dry (U.S.)	67.201 cubic inches 1.101 liters 0.969 British quart
1 quart (qt) liquid (U.S.)	57.75 cubic in (exactly) 0.946 liter 0.833 British quart
[1 quart (qt) (British)]	69.354 cubic inches 1.032 U.S. dry quarts 1.201 U.S. liquid quarts
1 tablespoon	3 teaspoons°(exactly) 4 fluid drams ½ fluid ounce (exactly)
1 teaspoon	⅓ tablespoon°(exactly) 1⅓ fluid drams°

°The equivalent "1 teaspoon—1⅓ fluid drams" has been found by the bureau to correspond more closely with the actual capacities of "measuring" and silver teaspoons than the equivalent "1 teaspoon—1 fluid dram" which is given by many dictionaries.

Weights or Masses

1 assay ton°° (AT)	29.167 grams

°°Used in assaying. The assay ton bears the same relation to the milligram that a ton of 2,000 pounds avoirdupois bears to the ounce troy; hence the weight in milligrams of precious metal obtained from one assay ton of ore gives directly the number of troy ounces to the net ton.

1 bale (cotton measure)	500 pounds in U.S. 750 pounds in Egypt
1 carat (c)	200 milligrams (exactly) 3.086 grains
1 dram avoirdupois (dr avdp)	27¹¹⁄₃₂ (=27.344) grains 1.772 grams
gamma, see microgram	
1 grain	64.799 milligrams
1 gram	15.432 grains 0.035 ounce, avoirdupois
1 hundredweight, gross or long°°° (gross cwt)	112 pounds (exactly) 50.802 kilograms
1 hundredweight, net or short (cwt. or net cwt.)	100 pounds (exactly) 45.359 kilograms
1 kilogram (kg)	2.205 pounds
1 microgram (μg [The Greek letter mu in combination with the letter g])	0.000001 gram (exactly)
1 milligram (mg)	0.015 grain
1 ounce, avoirdupois (oz avdp)	437.5 grains (exactly) 0.911 troy ounce 28.350 grams
1 ounce, troy (oz t)	480 grains (exactly) 1.097 avoirdupois ounces 31.103 grams
1 pennyweight (dwt)	1.555 grams
1 pound, avoirdupois (lb avdp)	7,000 grains (exactly) 1.215 troy pounds 453.592 37 grams (exactly)
1 pound, troy (lb t)	5,760 grains (exactly) 0.823 avoirdupois pound 373.242 grams
1 ton, gross or long°°° (gross ton)	2,240 pounds (exactly) 1.12 net tons (exactly) 1.016 metric tons

°°°The gross or long ton and hundredweight are used commercially in the United States to only a limited extent, usually in restricted industrial fields. These units are the same as British "ton" and "hundredweight."

1 ton, metric (t)	2,204.623 pounds 0.984 gross ton 1.102 net tons
1 ton, net or short (sh ton)	2,000 pounds (exactly) 0.893 gross ton 0.907 metric ton

Tables of Interrelation of Units of Measurement

Units of length and area of the international and survey measures are included in the following tables. Units unique to the survey measure are italicized. See p. 287, Tables of Equivalents; 1st para.

1 international foot = 0.999 998 survey foot (exactly)
1 survey foot = 1200/3937 meter (exactly)
1 international foot = 12 × 0.0254 meter (exactly)

Bold face type indicates exact values

Units of Length

Units	Inches	*Links*	Feet	Yards	*Rods*	*Chains*	Miles	cm	Meters
1 inch=	**1**	0.126 263	0.083 333	0.027 778	0.005 051	0.001 263	0.000 016	**2.54**	**0.025 4**
1 *link*=	**7.92**	**1**	**0.66**	**0.22**	**0.04**	**0.01**	**0.000 125**	20.117	0.201 168
1 foot=	**12**	1.515 152	**1**	0.333 333	0.060 606	0.015 152	0.000 189	**30.48**	**0.304 8**
1 yard=	**36**	4.545 45	**3**	**1**	0.181 818	0.045 455	0.000 568	**91.44**	**0.914 4**
1 *rod*=	**198**	**25**	**16.5**	**5.5**	**1**	**0.25**	**0.003 125**	502.92	5.029 2
1 *chain*=	**792**	**100**	**66**	**22**	**4**	**1**	**0.012 5**	2011.68	20.116 8
1 mile=	**63 360**	**8000**	**5280**	**1760**	**320**	**80**	**1**	**160 934.4**	**1609.344**
1 cm=	0.3937	0.049 710	0.032 808	0.010 936	0.001 988	0.000 497	0.000 006	**1**	**0.01**
1 meter=	39.37	4.970 960	3.280 840	1.093 613	0.198 838	0.049 710	0.000 621	**100**	**1**

Units of Area

Units	Sq. inches	*Sq. links*	Sq. feet	Sq. yards	*Sq. rods*	*Sq. chains*
1 sq. inch=	**1**	.015 942 3	0.006 944	0.000 771 605	0.000 025 5	0.000 001 594
1 sq. *link*=	62.726 4	**1**	**0.435 6**	**0.0484**	**0.0016**	**0.000 1**
1 sq. foot=	**144**	2.295 684	**1**	0.111 111 1	0.003 673 09	0.000 229 568
1 sq. yard=	**1296**	20.661 16	**9**	**1**	0.033 057 85	0.002 066 12
1 sq. *rod*=	**39 204**	**625**	**272.25**	**30.25**	**1**	**0.062 5**
1 sq. *chain*=	**627 264**	**10 000**	**4 356**	**484**	**16**	**1**
1 *acre*=	**6 272 640**	**100 000**	**43 560**	**4 840**	**160**	**10**
1 sq. mile=	**4 014 489 600**	**64 000 000**	**27 878 400**	**3 097 600**	**102 400**	**6400**
1 sq. cm=	0.155 000 3	0.002 471 05	0.001 076	0.000 119 599	0.000 003 954	0.000 000 247
1 sq. meter=	1550.003	24.710 44	10.763 91	1.195 990	0.039 536 70	0.002 471 044
1 *hectare*=	15 500 031	247 104	107 639.1	11 959.90	395.367 0	24.710 44

Units	*Acres*	Sq. miles	Sq. cm	Sq. meters	*Hectares*
1 sq. inch=	0.000 000 159 423	0.000 000 000 249 10	**6.451 6**	**0.000 645 16**	0.000 000 065
1 sq. *link*=	**0.000 01**	**0.000 000 015 625**	404.685 642 24	0.040 468 56	0.000 004 047
1 sq. foot=	0.000 022 956 84	0.000 000 035 870 06	929.034 1	0.092 903 41	0.000 009 290
1 sq. yard=	0.000 206 611 6	0.000 000 322 830 6	**8 361.273 6**	**0.836 127 36**	0.000 083 613
1 sq. *rod*=	**0.006 25**	**0.000 009 765 625**	252 929.5	25.292 95	0.002 529 295
1 sq. *chain*=	**0.1**	**0.000 156 25**	4 046 873	404.687 3	0.040 468 73
1 *acre*=	**1**	**0.001 562 5**	40 468 73	4 046.873	0.404 687 3
1 sq. mile=	**640**	**1**	25 899 881 103	2 589 988.11	258.998 811 034
1 sq. cm=	0.000 000 024 711	0.000 000 000 038 610	**1**	**0.000 1**	**0.000 000 01**
1 sq. meter=	0.000 247 104 4	0.000 000 386 102 2	**10 000**	**1**	**0.0001**
1 *hectare*=	2.471 044	0.003 861 006	**100 000 000**	**10 000**	**1**

Units of Mass Not Greater than Pounds and Kilograms

Units	Grains	Pennyweights	Avdp drams	Avdp ounces
1 grain=	**1**	0.041 666 67	0.036 571 43	0.002 285 71
1 pennyweight=	**24**	**1**	0.877 714 3	0.054 857 14
1 dram avdp=	**27.343 75**	1.139 323	**1**	**0.062 5**
1 ounce avdp=	**437.5**	18.229 17	**16**	**1**
1 ounce troy=	**480**	**20**	17.554 29	1.097 143
1 pound troy=	**5760**	**240**	210.651 4	13.165 71
1 pound avdp=	**7000**	291.666 7	**256**	**16**
1 milligram=	0.015 432	0.000 643 015	0.000 564 383	0.000 035 274
1 gram=	15.432 36	0.643 014 9	0.564 383 4	0.035 273 96
1 kilogram=	15 432.36	643.014 9	564.383 4	35.273 96

Units	Troy ounces	Troy pounds	Avdp pounds	Milligrams	Grams	Kilograms
1 grain=	0.002 083 33	0.000 173 611	0.000 142 857	**64.798 91**	**0.064 798 91**	0.000 064 799
1 pennyw't.=	**0.05**	0.004 166 667	0.003 428 571	**1555.173 84**	**1.555 173 84**	0.001 555 174
1 dram avdp=	0.056 966 15	0.004 747 179	0.003 906 25	1771.845 195	1.771 845 195	0.001 771 845
1 oz avdp=	0.911 458 3	0.075 954 86	**0.062 5**	**28 349.523 125**	**28.349 523 125**	0.028 349 52
1 oz troy=	**1**	0.083 333 333	0.068 571 43	**31 103.476 8**	**31.103 476 8**	0.031 103 48
1 lb troy=	**12**	**1**	0.822 857 1	**373 241.721 6**	**373.241 721 6**	0.373 241 722
1 lb avdp=	14.583 33	1.215 278	**1**	**453 592.37**	**453.592 37**	**0.453 592 37**
1 milligram=	0.000 032 151	0.000 002 679	0.000 002 205	**1**	**0.001**	**0.000 001**
1 gram=	0.032 150 75	0.002 679 229	0.002 204 623	**1000**	**1**	**0.001**
1 kilogram=	32.150 75	2.679 229	2.204 623	**1 000 000**	**1000**	**1**

Units of Mass Not Less than Avoirdupois Ounces

Units	Avdp oz	Avdp lb	Short cwt	Short tons	Long tons	Kilograms	Metric tons
1 oz av=	**1**	**0.0625**	**0.000 625**	**0.000 031 25**	0.000 027 902	0.028 349 523	0.000 028 350
1 lb av=	**16**	**1**	**0.01**	**0.000 5**	0.000 446 429	**0.453 592 37**	0.000 453 592
1 sh cwt=	**1 600**	**100**	**1**	**0.05**	0.044 642 86	**45.359 237**	**0.045 359 237**
1 sh ton=	**32 000**	**2000**	**20**	**1**	0.892 857 1	**907.184 74**	**0.907 184 74**
1 long ton=	**35 840**	**2240**	**22.4**	**1.12**	**1**	**1016.046 908 8**	1.016 046 909
1 kg=	35.273 96	2.204 623	0.022 046 23	0.001 102 311	0.000 984 207	**1**	**0.001**
1 metric ton=	35 273.96	2 204.623	22.046 23	1.102 311	0.984 206 5	**1000**	**1**

Units of Volume

Units	Cubic inches	Cubic feet	Cubic yards	Cubic cm	Cubic dm	Cubic meters
1 cubic inch=	1	0.000 578 704	0.000 021 433	16.387 064	0.016 387	0.000 016 387
1 cubic foot=	1728	1	0.037 037 04	28 316.846 592	28.316 847	0.028 316 847
1 cubic yard=	46 656	27	1	764 554.857 984	764.554 858	0.764 554 858
1 cubic cm=	0.061 023 74	0.000 035 315	0.000 001 308	1	0.001	0.000 001
1 cubic dm=	61.023 74	0.035 314 67	0.001 307 951	1 000	1	0.001
1 cubic meter	61 023.74	35.314 67	1.307 951	1 000 000	1000	1

Units of Capacity (Liquid Measure)

Units	Minims	Fluid drams	Fluid ounces	Gills	Liquid pt
1 minim=	1	0.016 666 7	0.002 083 33	0.000 520 833	0.000 130 208
1 fluid dram=	60	1	0.125	0.031 25	0.007 812 5
1 fluid ounce=	480	8	1	0.25	0.062 5
1 gill=	1920	32	4	1	0.25
1 liquid pint=	7680	128	16	4	1
1 liquid quart=	15 360	256	32	8	2
1 gallon=	61 440	1024	128	32	8
1 cubic inch=	265.974	4.432 900	0.554 112 6	0.138 528 1	0.034 632 03
1 cubic foot=	459 603.1	7 660.052	957.506 5	239.376 6	59.844 16
1 milliliter=	16.230 73	0.270 512 18	0.033 814 02	0.008 453 506	.002 113 376
1 liter=	16 230.73	270.512 18	33.814 02	8.453 506	2.113 376

Units	Liquid quarts	Gallons	Cubic inches	Cubic feet	Liters
1 minim=	0.000 065 104 17	0.000 016 276 04	0.003 759 766	0.000 002 175 790	0.000 061 611 52
1 flu. dram=	0.003 906 25	0.000 976 562 5	0.225 585 9	0.000 130 547 4	0.003 696 691
1 fluid oz=	0.031 25	0.007 812 5	1.804 687 5	0.001 044 379	0.029 573 53
1 gill=	0.125	0.031 25	7.218 75	0.004 177 517	0.118 294 118
1 liquid pt=	0.5	0.125	28.875	0.016 710 07	0.473 176 473
1 liquid qt=	1	0.25	57.75	0.033 420 14	0.946 352 946
1 gallon=	4	1	231	0.133 680 6	3.785 411 784
1 cubic in.=	0.017 316 02	0.004 329 004	1	0.000 578 703 7	0.016 387 064
1 cubic foot=	29.922 08	7.480 519	1728	1	28.316 846 592
1 liter=	1.056 688	0.264 172 05	61.023 74	0.035 314 67	1

Units of Capacity (Dry Measure)

Units	Dry pints	Dry quarts	Pecks	Bushels	Cubic in.	Liters
1 dry pint=	1	0.5	0.062 5	0.015 625	33.600 312 5	0.550 610 47
1 dry quart=	2	1	0.125	0.031 25	67.200 625	1.101 220 9
1 peck=	16	8	1	0.25	537.605	8.809 767 5
1 bushel=	64	32	4	1	2150.42	35.239 07
1 cubic inch=	0.029 761 6	0.014 880 8	0.001 860 10	0.000 465 025	1	0.016 387 06
1 liter=	1.816 166	0.908 083	0.113 510 37	0.028 377 59	61.023 74	1

Miscellaneous Measures

Caliber—the diameter of a gun bore. In the U.S., caliber is traditionally expressed in hundredths of inches, eg. .22 or .30. In Britain, caliber is often expressed in thousandths of inches, eg. .270 or .465. Now, it is commonly expressed in millimeters, eg. the 7.62 mm. M14 rifle and the 5.56 mm. M16 rifle. Heavier weapons' caliber has long been expressed in millimeters, eg. the 81 mm. mortar, the 105 mm. howitzer (light), the 155 mm. howitzer (medium or heavy).

Naval guns' caliber refers to the barrel length as a multiple of the bore diameter. A 5-inch, 50-caliber naval gun has a 5-inch bore and a barrel length of 250 inches.

Carat, karat—a measure of the amount of alloy per 24 parts in gold. Thus 24-carat gold is pure; 18-carat gold is one-fourth alloy.

Decibel (dB)—a measure of the relative loudness or intensity of sound. A 20-decibel sound is 10 times louder than a 10-decibel sound; 30 decibels is 100 times louder; 40 decibels is 1,000 times louder, etc. One decibel is the smallest difference between sounds detectable by the human ear. A 120-decibel sound is painful.

10 decibels	– a light whisper
20	– quiet conversation
30	– normal conversation
40	– light traffic
50	– typewriter, loud conversation
60	– noisy office
70	– normal traffic, quiet train
80	– rock music, subway
90	– heavy traffic, thunder
100	– jet plane at takeoff

Em—a printer's measure designating the square width of any given type size. Thus, an em of 10-point type is 10 points. An en is half an em.

Gauge—a measure of shotgun bore diameter. Gauge numbers originally referred to the number of lead balls of the gun barrel diameter in a pound. Thus, a 16 gauge shotgun's bore was smaller than a 12-gauge shotgun's. Today, an international agreement assigns millimeter measures to each gauge, eg:

Gauge	Bore diameter in mm
6	23.34
10	19.67
12	18.52
14	17.60
16	16.81
20	15.90

Horsepower—the power needed to lift 550 pounds one foot in one second, or to lift 33,000 pounds one foot in one minute. Equivalent to 746 watts or 2,546.0756 Btu/h.

Quire—25 sheets of paper

Ream—500 sheets of paper

Electrical Units

The **watt** is the unit of power (electrical, mechanical, thermal, etc.). Electrical power is given by the product of the voltage and the current.

Energy is sold by the **joule,** but in common practice the billing of electrical energy is expressed in terms of the **kilowatt-hour,** which is 3,600,000 joules or 3.6 megajoules.

The **horsepower** is a non-metric unit sometimes used in mechanics. It is equal to 746 watts.

The **ohm** is the unit of electrical resistance and represents the physical property of a conductor that offers a resistance to the flow of electricity, permitting just 1 ampere to flow at 1 volt of pressure.

Compound Interest

Compounded Annually

Principal	Period	4%	5%	6%	7%	8%	9%	10%	12%	14%	16%
$100	1 day	0.011	0.014	0.016	0.019	0.022	0.025	0.027	0.033	0.038	0.044
	1 week	0.077	0.096	0.115	0.134	0.153	0.173	0.192	0.230	0.268	0.307
	6 mos.	2.00	2.50	3.00	3.50	4.00	4.50	5.00	6.00	7.00	8.00
	1 year	4.00	5.00	6.00	7.00	8.00	9.00	10.00	12.00	14.00	16.00
	2 years	8.16	10.25	12.36	14.49	16.64	18.81	21.00	25.44	29.96	34.56
	3 years	12.49	15.76	19.10	22.50	25.97	29.50	33.10	40.49	48.15	56.09
	4 years	16.99	21.55	26.25	31.08	36.05	41.16	46.41	57.35	68.90	81.06
	5 years	21.67	27.63	33.82	40.26	46.93	53.86	61.05	76.23	92.54	110.03
	6 years	26.53	34.01	41.85	50.07	58.69	67.71	77.16	97.38	119.50	143.64
	7 years	31.59	40.71	50.36	60.58	71.38	82.80	94.87	121.07	150.23	182.62
	8 years	36.86	47.75	59.38	71.82	85.09	99.26	114.36	147.60	185.26	227.84
	9 years	42.33	55.13	68.95	83.85	99.90	117.19	135.79	177.31	225.19	280.30
	10 years	48.02	62.89	79.08	96.72	115.89	136.74	159.37	210.58	270.72	341.14
	12 years	60.10	79.59	101.22	125.22	151.82	181.27	213.84	289.60	381.79	493.60
	15 years	80.09	107.89	139.66	175.90	217.22	264.25	317.72	447.36	613.79	826.55
	20 years	119.11	165.33	220.71	286.97	366.10	460.44	572.75	864.63	1,274.35	1,846.08

Ancient Measures

Biblical

Cubit	=	21.8 inches
Omer	=	0.45 peck. 3.964 liters
Ephah	=	10 omers
Shekel	=	0.497 ounce 14.1 grams

Greek

Cubit	=	18.3 inches
Stadion	=	607.2 or 622 feet
Obolos	=	715.38 milligrams
Drachma	=	4.2923 grams
Mina	=	0.9463 pounds
Talent	=	60 mina

Roman

Cubit	=	17.5 inches
Stadium	=	202 yards
As, libra, pondus	=	325.971 grams, .71864 pounds

Weight of Water

1	cubic inch	.0360 pound	1	imperial gallon	10.0 pounds
12	cubic inches	.433 pound	11.2	imperial gallons	112.0 pounds
1	cubic foot	62.4 pounds	224	imperial gallons	2240.0 pounds
1	cubic foot	7.48052 U.S. gal	1	U.S. gallon	8.33 pounds
1.8	cubic feet	112.0 pounds	13.45	U.S. gallons	112.0 pounds
35.96	cubic feet	2240.0 pounds	269.0	U.S. gallons	2240.0 pounds

Density of Gases and Vapors

at 0°C and 760 mmHg

Source: National Institute of Standards and Technology (kilograms per cubic meter)

Gas	Wgt.	Gas	Wgt.	Gas	Wgt.
Acetylene	1.171	Ethylene	1.260	Methyl fluoride	1.545
Air	1.293	Fluorine	1.696	Mono methylamine	1.38
Ammonia	.759	Helium	.178	Neon	.900
Argon	1.784	Hydrogen	.090	Nitric oxide	1.341
Arsine	3.48	Hydrogen bromide	3.50	Nitrogen	1.250
Butane-iso	2.60	Hydrogen chloride	1.639	Nitrosyl chloride	2.99
Butane-n	2.519	Hydrogen iodide	5.724	Nitrous oxide	1.997
Carbon dioxide	1.977	Hydrogen selenide	3.66	Oxygen	1.429
Carbon monoxide	1.250	Hydrogen sulfide	1.539	Phosphine	1.48
Carbon oxysulfide	2.72	Krypton	3.745	Propane	2.020
Chlorine	3.214	Methane	.717	Silicon tetrafluoride	4.67
Chlorine monoxide	3.89	Methyl chloride	2.25	Sulfur dioxide	2.927
Ethane	1.356	Methyl ether	2.091	Xenon	5.897

Temperature Conversion Table

The numbers in **bold face type** refer to the temperature either in degrees Celsius or Fahrenheit which are to be converted. If converting from degrees Fahrenheit to Celsius, the equivalent will be found in the column on the left, while if converting from degrees Celsius to Fahrenheit the answer will be found in the column on the right.

For temperatures not shown. To convert Fahrenheit to Celsius subtract 32 degrees and multiply by 5, divide by 9; to convert Celsius to Fahrenheit, multiply by 9, divide by 5 and add 32 degrees.

Celsius		Fahrenheit	Celsius		Fahrenheit	Celsius		Fahrenheit
− 273.2	**− 459.7**	....	− 17.8	**0**	32	35.0	**95**	203
− 184	**− 300**	....	− 12.2	**10**	50	36.7	**98**	208.4
− 169	**− 273**	− 459.4	− 6.67	**20**	68	37.8	**100**	212
− 157	**− 250**	− 418	− 1.11	**30**	86	43	**110**	230
− 129	**− 200**	− 328	4.44	**40**	104	49	**120**	248
− 101	**− 150**	− 238	10.0	**50**	122	54	**130**	266
− 73.3	**− 100**	− 148	15.6	**60**	140	60	**140**	284
− 45.6	**− 50**	− 58	21.1	**70**	158	66	**150**	302
− 40.0	**− 40**	− 40	23.9	**75**	167	93	**200**	392
− 34.4	**− 30**	− 22	26.7	**80**	176	121	**250**	482
− 28.9	**− 20**	− 4	29.4	**85**	185	149	**300**	572
− 23.3	**− 10**	14	32.2	**90**	194			

Boiling and Freezing Points of Water

Water boils at 212°F at sea level. For every 550 feet above sea level, boiling point of water is lower by about 1°F. Methyl alcohol boils at 148°F. Average human oral temperature, 98.6°F. Water freezes at 32°F. Although "Centigrade" is still frequently used, the International Committee on Weights and Measures and the National Institute of Standards have recommended since 1948 that this scale be called "Celsius."

Breaking the Sound Barrier; Speed of Sound

The prefix Mach is used to describe supersonic speed. It derives from Ernst Mach, a Czech-born German physicist, who contributed to the study of sound. When a plane moves at the speed of sound it is Mach 1. When twice the speed of sound it is Mach 2. When it is near but below the speed of sound its speed can be designated at less than Mach 1, for example, Mach .90. Mach is defined as "in jet propulsion, the ratio of the velocity of a rocket or a jet to the velocity of sound in the medium being considered."

When a plane passes the sound barrier—flying faster than sound travels—listeners in the area hear thunderclaps, but pilots do not hear them.

Sound is produced by vibrations of an object and is transmitted by alternate increase and decrease in pressures that radiate outward through a material media of molecules—somewhat like waves spreading out on a pond after a rock has been tossed into it.

The frequency of sound is determined by the number of times the vibrating waves undulate per second, and is measured in cycles per second. The slower the cycle of waves, the lower the frequency. As frequencies increase, the sound is higher in pitch.

Sound is audible to human beings only if the frequency falls within a certain range. The human ear is usually not sensitive to frequencies of less than 20 vibrations per second, or more than about 20,000 vibrations per second—although this range varies among individuals. Anything at a pitch higher than the human ear can hear is termed ultrasonic.

Intensity or loudness is the strength of the pressure of these radiating waves, and is measured in decibels. The human ear responds to intensity in a range from zero to 120 decibels. Any sound with pressure over 120 decibels is painful.

The speed of sound is generally placed at 1,088 feet per second at sea level at 32°F. It varies in other temperatures and in different media. Sound travels faster in water than in air, and even faster in iron and steel. If in air it travels a mile in 5 seconds, it does a mile under water in 1 second, and through iron in 1/3 of a second. It travels through ice cold vapor at approximately 4,708 feet per second, ice-cold water, 4,938; granite, 12,960; hardwood, 12,620; brick, 11,960; glass, 16,410 to 19,690; silver, 8,658; gold, 5,717.

Colors of the Spectrum

Color, an electromagnetic wave phenomenon, is a sensation produced through the excitation of the retina of the eye by rays of light. The colors of the spectrum may be produced by viewing a light beam refracted by passage through a prism, which breaks the light into its wave lenghts.

Customarily, the primary colors of the spectrum are thought of as those 6 monochromatic colors that occupy relatively large areas of the spectrum: red, orange, yellow, green, blue, and violet. However, Sir Isaac Newton named a 7th, indigo, situated between blue and violet on the spectrum. Aubert estimated (1865) the solar spectrum to contain approximately 1,000 distinguishable hues of which according to Rood (1881) 2 million tints and shades can be distinguished; Luckiesh stated (1915) that 55 distinctly different hues have been seen in a single spectrum.

Many physicists recognize only 3 primary colors: red, yellow, and blue (Mayer, 1775); red, green, and violet (Thomas Young, 1801); red, green, and blue (Clerk Maxwell, 1860).

The color sensation of black is due to complete lack of stimulation of the retina, that of white to complete stimulation. The infra-red and ultra-violet rays, below the red (long) end of the spectrum and above the violet (short) end respectively, are invisible to the naked eye. Heat is the principal effect of the infra-red rays and chemical action that of the ultra-violet rays.

Common Fractions Reduced to Decimals

8ths	16ths	32ds	64ths	
			1	.015625
		1	2	.03125
			3	.046875
	1	2	4	.0625
			5	.078125
		3	6	.09375
			7	.109375
1	2	4	8	.125
			9	.140625
		5	10	.15625
			11	.171875
	3	6	12	.1875
			13	.203125
		7	14	.21875
			15	.234375
2	4	8	16	.25
			17	.265625
		9	18	.28125
			19	.296875
	5	10	20	.3125
			21	.328125
		11	22	.34375

8ths	16ths	32ds	64ths	
			23	.359375
3	6	12	24	.375
			25	.390625
		13	26	.40625
			27	.421875
	7	14	28	.4375
			29	.453125
		15	30	.46875
			31	.484375
4	8	16	32	.5
			33	.515625
		17	34	.53125
			35	.546875
	9	18	36	.5625
			37	.578125
		19	38	.59375
			39	.609375
5	10	20	40	.625
			41	.640625
		21	42	.65625
			43	.671875
	11	22	44	.6875

8ths	16ths	32ds	64ths	
			45	.703125
		23	46	.71875
			47	.734375
6	12	24	48	.75
			49	.765625
		25	50	.78125
			51	.796875
	13	26	52	.8125
			53	.828125
		27	54	.84375
			55	.859375
7	14	28	56	.875
			57	.890625
		29	58	.90625
			59	.921875
	15	30	60	.9375
			61	.953125
		31	62	.96875
			63	.984375
8	16	32	64	1.

Spirits Measures

Pony	0.5 jigger
Shot	0.666 jigger 1.0 ounce
Jigger	1.5 shot
Pint	16 shots 0.625 fifth
Fifth	25.6 shots 1.6 pints 0.8 quart 0.75706 liter
Quart	32 shots 1.25 fifth
Magnum	2 quarts 2.49797 bottles (wine)

For champagne and brandy only:

Jeroboam	6.4 pints 1.6 magnum 0.8 gallon

For champagne only:

Rehoboam	3 magnums
Methuselah	4 magnums
Salmanazar	6 magnums
Balthazar	8 magnums
Nebuchadnezzar	10 magnums

Wine bottle (standard):

	0.800633 quart 0.7576778 liter

Mathematical Formulas

To find the CIRCUMFERENCE of a:

Circle — Multiply the diameter by 3.14159265 (usually 3.1416).

To find the AREA of a:

Circle — Multiply the square of the diameter by .785398 (usually .7854).

Rectangle — Multiply the length of the base by the height.

Sphere (surface) — Multiply the square of the radius by 3.1416 and multiply by 4.

Square — Square the length of one side.

Trapezoid — Add the two parallel sides, multiply by the height and divide by 2.

Triangle — Multiply the base by the height and divide by 2.

To find the VOLUME of a:

Cone — Multiply the square of the radius of the base by 3.1416, multiply by the height, and divide by 3.

Cube — Cube the length of one edge.

Cylinder — Multiply the square of the radius of the base by 3.1416 and multiply by the height.

Pyramid — Multiply the area of the base by the height and divide by 3.

Rectangular Prism — Multiply the length by the width by the height.

Sphere — Multiply the cube of the radius by 3.1416, multiply by 4 and divide by 3.

Playing Cards and Dice Chances

Poker Hands

Hand	Number possible	Odds against
Royal flush	4	649,739 to 1
Other straight flush	36	72,192 to 1
Four of a kind	624	4,164 to 1
Full house	3,744	693 to 1
Flush	5,108	508 to 1
Straight	10,200	254 to 1
Three of a kind	54,912	46 to 1
Two pairs	123,552	20 to 1
One pair	1,098,240	4 to 3 (1.37 to 1)
Nothing	1,302,540	1 to 1
Total	**2,598,960**	

Dice
(probabilities on 2 dice)

Total	Odds against (Single toss)	Total	Odds against (Single toss)
2	35 to 1	8	31 to 5
3	17 to 1	9	8 to 1
4	11 to 1	10	11 to 1
5	8 to 1	11	17 to 1
6	31 to 5	12	35 to 1
7	5 to 1		

Dice
(Probabilities of consecutive winning plays)

No. consecutive wins	By 7, 11, or point	No. consecutive wins	By 7, 11 or point
1	244 in 495	6	1 in 70
2	6 in 25	7	1 in 141
3	3 in 25	8	1 in 287
4	1 in 17	9	1 in 582
5	1 in 34		

Pinochle Auction
(Odds against finding in "widow" of 3 cards)

Open places	Odds against	Open places	Odds against
1	5 to 1	4	3 to 2 for
2	2 to 1	5	2 to 1 for
3	Even		

Bridge

The odds—against suit distribution in a hand of 4-4-3-2 are about 4 to 1, against 5-4-2-2 about 8 to 1, against 6-4-2-1 about 20 to 1, against 7-4-1-1 about 254 to 1, against 8-4-1-0 about 2,211 to 1, and against 13-0-0-0 about 158,753,389,899 to 1.

Measures of Force and Pressure

Dyne = force necessary to accelerate a 1-gram mass 1 centimeter per second squared = 0.000072 poundal

Poundal = force necessary to accelerate a 1-pound mass 1 foot per second squared = 13,825.5 dynes = 0.138255 newtons

Newton = force needed to accelerate a 1-kilogram mass 1 meter per second squared

Pascal (pressure) = 1 newton per square meter = 0.020885 pound per square foot

Atmosphere (air pressure at sea level) = 2,116.102 pounds per square foot = 14.6952 pounds per square inch = 1.0332 kilograms per square centimeter = 101,323 newtons per square meter.

Large Numbers

U.S.	Number of zeros	French British, German
million	6	million
billion	9	milliard
trillion	12	billion
quadrillion	15	1,000 billion
quintillion	18	trillion
sextillion	21	1,000 trillion
septillion	24	quadrillion
octillion	27	1,000 quadrillion
nonillion	30	quintillion
decillion	33	1,000 quintillion

Roman Numerals

I	1	VI	6	XI	11	L	50	CD	400	$\overline{X}$	10,000
II	2	VII	7	XIX	19	LX	60	D	500	$\overline{L}$	50,000
III	3	VIII	8	XX	20	XC	90	CM	900	$\overline{C}$	100,000
IV	4	IX	9	XXX	30	C	100	M	1,000	$\overline{D}$	500,000
V	5	X	10	XL	40	CC	200	$\overline{V}$	5,000	$\overline{M}$	1,000,000

ARTS AND MEDIA

Notable Movies of the Year (Sept. 1991 to Aug. 1992)

Movie	Stars	Director
A League of Their Own	Tom Hanks, Geena Davis, Madonna	Penny Marshall
A Midnight Clear	Ethan Hawke, Gary Sinise, Kevin Dillon	Keith Gordon
Alien^3	Sigourney Weaver, Charles S. Dutton	David Fincher
Article 99	Ray Liotta, Kiefer Sutherland, Lea Thompson	Howard Deutch
Basic Instinct	Michael Douglas, Sharon Stone	Paul Verhoeven
Batman Returns	Michael Keaton, Michelle Pfeiffer, Danny DeVito	Tim Burton
Billy Bathgate	Dustin Hoffman, Loren Dean, Nicole Kidman, Bruce Willis	Robert Benton
Boomerang	Eddie Murphy, Robin Givens, Halle Berry	Reginald Hudlin
Bugsy	Warren Beatty, Annette Bening	Barry Levinson
Cape Fear	Robert DeNiro, Nick Nolte, Jessica Lange, Robert Mitchum	Martin Scorsese
Dead Again	Kenneth Branagh, Emma Thompson	Kenneth Branagh
Deceived	Goldie Hawn, John Heard	Damian Harris
Doc Hollywood	Michael J. Fox, Julie Warner, Woody Harrelson	Michael Caton-Jones
Far and Away	Tom Cruise, Nicole Kidman	Ron Howard
Father of the Bride	Steve Martin, Diane Keaton, Kimberley Williams	Charles Shyer
Frankie and Johnny	Al Pacino, Michelle Pfeiffer	Garry Marshall
Fried Green Tomatoes	Kathy Bates, Jessica Tandy, Mary Stuart Masterson	Jon Avnet
Grand Canyon	Danny Glover, Steve Martin, Kevin Kline, Mary McDonnell	Lawrence Kasdan
Honey, I Blew Up the Kid	Rick Moranis, Marcia Strassman	Randall Kleiser
Hook	Dustin Hoffman, Robin Williams, Julia Roberts	Steven Spielberg
Housesitter	Steve Martin, Goldie Hawn	Frank Oz
Howards End	Anthony Hopkins, Emma Thompson, Vanessa Redgrave	James Ivory
JFK	Kevin Costner, Kevin Bacon, Sissy Spacek, Tommy Lee Jones	Oliver Stone
Lethal Weapon 3	Mel Gibson, Danny Glover, Joe Pesci	Richard Donner
Little Man Tate	Jodie Foster, Dianne Wiest, Adam Hann-Byrd	Jodie Foster
Medicine Man	Sean Connery, Lorraine Bracco	John McTiernan
Mississippi Masala	Denzel Washington, Sarita Choudhury	Mira Nair
Mo' Money	Damon Wayans, Stacey Dash, Marlon Wayans	Peter Macdonald
My Cousin Vinny	Joe Pesci, Marisa Tomei	Jonathan Lynn
My Girl	Macaulay Culkin, Dan Aykroyd, Jamie Lee Curtis	Howard Zieff
Other People's Money	Danny DeVito, Gregory Peck, Penelope Ann Miller	Norman Jewison
Patriot Games	Harrison Ford, Anne Archer, James Earl Jones	Phillip Noyce
Shadows and Fog	Woody Allen, Mia Farrow, Madonna, John Cusack	Woody Allen
Sister Act	Whoopi Goldberg, Harvey Keitel, Maggie Smith	Emile Ardolino
Star Trek VI: The Undiscovered Country	William Shatner, Leonard Nimoy	Nicholas Meyer
The Addams Family	Raul Julia, Angelica Huston, Christopher Lloyd	Barry Sonnenfeld
The Fisher King	Robin Williams, Jeff Bridges, Mercedes Ruehl	Terry Gilliam
The Hand That Rocks the Cradle	Rebecca De Mornay, Annabella Sciorra	Curtis Hanson
The Mambo Kings	Armand Assante, Antonio Banderas, Cathy Moriarty	Arne Glimcher
The Player	Tim Robbins, Greta Scacchi, Fred Ward, Whoopi Goldberg	Robert Altman
The Prince of Tides	Nick Nolte, Barbra Streisand	Barbra Streisand
Unlawful Entry	Ray Liotta, Kurt Russell, Madeleine Stowe	Jonathan Kaplan
Wayne's World	Mike Myers, Dana Carvey	Penelope Spheeris
White Men Can't Jump	Wesley Snipes, Woody Harrelson, Rosie Perez	Ron Shelton

Notable New York Theater Openings, 1991-92 Season

A Life in the Theater, revival of David Mamet's play; with F. Murray Abraham, Anthony Fusco, and Larry Klein.

A Small Family Business, play by Alan Ayckbourn; with Brian Murray and Jane Carr.

A Streetcar Named Desire, revival of the 1947 Tennessee Williams classic; with Alec Baldwin, Jessica Lange, and Amy Madigan.

Babylon Gardens, play by Timothy Mason; with Timothy Hutton and Mary Louise Parker.

Catskills on Broadway, review conceived by Freddie Roman; with Freddie Roman, Marilyn Michaels, Dick Capri, and Mal Z. Lawrence.

Conversations With My Father, drama by Herb Gardner; with Judd Hirsch and Gordana Rashovich.

Crazy For You, musical featuring songs by George and Ira Gershwin; with Harry Groener, Jodi Benson, and Jane Connell.

Dancing At Lughnasa, drama by Brian Friel.

Death and the Maiden, play by Ariel Dorfman; with Glenn Close, Gene Hackman, and Richard Dreyfuss.

Falsettos, musical by William Finn and James Lapine.

Four Baboons Adoring the Sun, play by John Guare; with Stockard Channing, James Naughton, and Eugene Perry.

Guys and Dolls, revival of the Frank Loesser musical; with Peter Gallagher, Nathan Lane, Josie de Guzman, and Faith Prince.

Jake's Women, play by Neil Simon; with Alan Alda, Helen Shaver, Brenda Vaccaro, and Tracy Pollan.

Jelly's Last Jam, musical by George Wolfe inspired by the life and music of Jelly Roll Morton; with Gregory Hines.

Man of La Mancha, revival of the Mitch Leigh-Joe Darion 1965 musical; with Raul Julia, Sheena Easton, and Tony Martinez.

Marvin's Room, play by Scott McPherson; with Laura Esterman, Lisa Emery, and Mark Rosenthal.

Nick and Nora, musical by Charles Strouse and Richard Maltby Jr. based on the Dashiell Hammett "Thin Man" characters; with Barry Bostwick and Joanna Gleason.

On Borrowed Time, revival of the 1938 Paul Osborn comedy; with George C. Scott, Nathan Lane, Teresa Wright, and Conrad Bain.

Private Lives, revival of the 1930 Noel Coward comedy; with Joan Collins.

The Crucible, revival of the Arthur Miller classic; with Martin Sheen, John Fiedler, Fritz Weaver, and Michael York.

The Most Happy Fella, revival of the 1956 Frank Loesser musical; with Spiro Malas and Sophie Hayden.

The Visit, revival of the Friedrich Durrenmatt drama; with Jane Alexander.

Two Trains Running, play by August Wilson; with Roscoe Lee Browne, Larry Fishburne, and Cynthia Martells.

Record Long Run Broadway Plays[1]

Source: *Variety*

Play	Performances
Chorus Line	6,137
Oh, Calcutta (revival)	5,959
*Cats	4,069
42d Street	3,486
Grease	3,388
Fiddler on the Roof	3,242
Life With Father	3,224
Tobacco Road	3,182
Hello Dolly	2,844
My Fair Lady	2,717
Annie	2,377
Man of La Mancha	2,328
Abie's Irish Rose	2,327
Oklahoma!	2,212
*Les Miserables	2,156
Pippin	1,944
South Pacific	1,925
Magic Show	1,920
*Phantom of the Opera	1,855
Deathtrap	1,792
Gemini	1,788
Harvey	1,775
Dancin'	1,774
La Cage aux Folles	1,761
Hair	1,750
The Wiz	1,672
Born Yesterday	1,642
Ain't Misbehavin'	1,604
Best Little Whorehouse in Texas	1,584
Mary, Mary	1,572
Evita	1,567
Voice of the Turtle	1,557
Barefoot in the Park	1,530
Dreamgirls	1,521
Mame	1,508
Same Time, Next Year	1,453
Arsenic and Old Lace	1,444
The Sound of Music	1,443
How To Succeed in Business Without Really Trying	1,417
Me and My Girl	1,412
Hellzapoppin	1,404
The Music Man	1,375
Funny Girl	1,348
Mumenschanz	1,326
Oh! Calcutta! (original)	1,314
Brighton Beach Memoirs	1,299
Angel Street	1,295
Lightnin'	1,291
Promises, Promises	1,281
The King and I	1,246
Cactus Flower	1,234
Sleuth	1,222
Torch Song Trilogy	1,222
"1776"	1,217
Equus	1,209
Sugar Babies	1,208
Guys and Dolls	1,200
Amadeus	1,181
Cabaret	1,165
Mister Roberts	1,157
Annie Get Your Gun	1,147
Seven Year Itch	1,141
Butterflies Are Free	1,128

(1) Number of performances through July 5, 1992. * Still running July 5, 1992.

All-Time Top 50 American Movies

Source: *Variety*, Jan. 1992

Rental figures are in absolute dollars, reflecting actual amounts received by the distributors (estimated for movies in current release). Ticket price inflation favors recent films, but older films have the advantage of numerous reissues adding to their totals.

Rank/Title/Date	Total Rentals (millions)
1. E.T. The Extra-Terrestrial (1982)	$228.6
2. Star Wars (1977)	193.5
3. Return of the Jedi (1983)	168.0
4. Batman (1989)	150.5
5. The Empire Strikes Back (1980)	141.6
6. **Home Alone** (1990)	140.0
7. Ghostbusters* (1984)	132.7
8. Jaws (1975)	129.5
9. Raiders Of The Lost Ark (1981)	115.6
10. Indiana Jones and The Last Crusade (1989)	115.5
11. **Terminator 2** (1991)	112.0
12. Indiana Jones and The Temple Of Doom (1984)	109.0
13. Beverly Hills Cop (1984)	108.0
14. Back to the Future* (1985)	105.5
15. **Ghost** (1990)	98.2
16. Grease (1978)	96.3
17. Tootsie* (1982)	94.9
18. The Exorcist (1973)	89.0
19. Rain Man* (1989)	86.8
20. The Godfather (1972)	86.3
21. **Robin Hood: Prince of Thieves** (1991)	86.0
22. Superman (1978)	82.8
23. Close Encounters Of The Third Kind (1977/1980)	82.8
24. Pretty Woman (1990)	81.9
25. **Dances With Wolves** (1990)	81.5
26. Three Men And A Baby (1987)	81.4
27. Who Framed Roger Rabbit (1988)	81.2
28. Beverly Hills Cop II (1987)	80.9
29. The Sound Of Music* (1965)	79.8
30. Gremlins (1984)	79.5
31. Lethal Weapon 2 (1989)	79.5
32. Top Gun (1986)	79.4
33. Gone With The Wind (1939)	79.4
34. Rambo: First Blood Part II (1985)	78.9
35. The Sting (1973)	78.2
36. Rocky IV (1985)	76.0
37. Saturday Night Fever (1977)	74.1
38. Back To The Future, Part II* (1989)	72.3
39. Honey, I Shrunk The Kids (1989)	72.0
40. National Lampoon's Animal House (1978)	70.8
41. Crocodile Dundee (1986)	70.2
42. Fatal Attraction (1987)	70.0
43. Platoon* (1986)	69.9
44. **101 Dalmatians** (1961)	68.7
45. Look Who's Talking* (1989)	68.3
46. **Teenage Mutant Ninja Turtles** (1990)	67.7
47. Die Hard 2 (1990)	66.5
48. Rocky III (1982)	66.3
49. Superman II (1981)	65.1
50. Coming To America (1988)	65.0

Note: Boldface print = film new to list or significant improvement since previous year; * rentals adjusted since last report.

Top 50 Movies, 1991

Source: *Variety*, Jan. 1992

Figures represent U.S. and Canadian rentals accruing to distributors, not total ticket sales receipts taken in at theaters.

Rank/Title/Month Released	Total Rentals (millions)
1. Terminator 2; July	$112.0
2. Robin Hood: Prince of Thieves; June	86.0
3. City Slickers; June	60.8
4. Home Alone; continuing 1990	60.0
5. The Silence of the Lambs; Feb.	59.9
6. The Addams Family; Nov.	55.0
7. Dances With Wolves; continuing 1990	52.6
8. Sleeping With the Enemy; Feb.	46.3
9. The Naked Gun 2½; June	44.2
10. Teenage Mutant Ninja Turtles II; March	41.9
11. Backdraft; May	40.2
12. Hook; Dec.	40.0
13. Beauty and the Beast; Nov.	39.0
14. Hot Shots!; July	33.0
15. Cape Fear; Nov.	32.0
16. Star Trek VI: The Undiscovered Country; Dec.	32.0
17. Kindergarten Cop; continuing 1990	31.4
18. 101 Dalmatians; reissue	30.1
19. What About Bob?; May	29.2
20. Boyz n the Hood; July	26.7
21. Doc Hollywood; Aug.	24.5
22. Awakenings; Dec. 1990	23.2
23. The Rocketeer; June	23.1
24. New Jack City; March	22.0
25. My Girl; Nov.	21.6
26. The Last Boy Scout; Dec.	21.0
27. Regarding Henry; July	20.0
27. Thelma & Louise; May	20.0
29. Point Break; July	19.5
30. Dying Young; June	19.0
30. Father of the Bride; Dec.	19.0
32. Out for Justice; April	18.5
33. The Fisher King; Sept.	18.0
34. The Doctor; July	17.3
35. Bill & Ted's Bogus Journey; July	17.2

(continued)

Rank/Title/Month Released	Total Rentals (millions)
36. Freddie's Dead: The Final Nightmare; Sept.	17.0
37. Dead Again; Aug.	16.8
38. The Doors; March	16.6
39. Soapdish; May	15.7
40. Jungle Fever; June	15.7
41. White Fang; Jan.	15.2
42. King Ralph; Feb.	15.2
43. The Prince of Tides; Dec.	15.0
44. Edward Scissorhands; continuing 1990	14.5
45. Curly Sue; Oct.	14.0
45. JFK; Dec.	14.0
47. Green Card; Dec. 1990	13.7
48. Fantasia; reissue	13.6
49. The Hard Way; March	13.3
50. Class Action; March	12.8

National Film Registry

In accordance with the National Film Preservation Act passed by Congress in 1988, 25 films were placed on the National Film Registry in September 1989 as "culturally, historically, or esthetically significant," another 25 chosen in 1990, and 25 more in 1991.

Films Chosen in 1989

The Best Years of Our Lives (1946)
Casablanca (1942)
Citizen Kane (1941)
The Crowd (1928)
Dr. Strangelove (or, How I Learned to Stop Worrying and Love the Bomb) (1964)
The General (1927)
Gone With the Wind (1939)
The Grapes of Wrath (1940)
High Noon (1952)
Intolerance (1916)
The Learning Tree (1969)
The Maltese Falcon (1941)
Mr. Smith Goes to Washington (1939)
Modern Times (1936)
Nanook of the North (1921)
On the Waterfront (1954)
The Searchers (1956)
Singin' in the Rain (1952)
Snow White and the Seven Dwarfs (1937)
Some Like It Hot (1959)
Star Wars (1977)
Sunrise (1927)
Sunset Boulevard (1950)
Vertigo (1958)
The Wizard of Oz (1939)

Films Chosen in 1990

All About Eve (1950)
All Quiet on the Western Front (1930)
Bringing Up Baby (1938)
Dodsworth (1936)
Duck Soup (1933)
Fantasia (1940)
The Freshman (1925)
The Godfather (1972)
The Great Train Robbery (1903)
Harlan County, U. S. A. (1976)
How Green Was My Valley (1941)
It's A Wonderful Life (1946)
Killer of Sheep (1977)
Love Me Tonight (1932)
Meshes of the Afternoon (1943)
Ninotchka (1939)
Primary (1960)
Raging Bull (1980)
Rebel Without a Cause (1955)
Red River (1948)
The River (1937)
Sullivan's Travels (1941)
Top Hat (1935)
The Treasure of the Sierra Madre (1948)
A Woman under the Influence (1974)

Films Chosen in 1991

The Battle of San Pietro (1945)
The Blood of Jesus (1941)
Chinatown (1974)
City Lights (1931)
David Holzman's Diary (1968)
Frankenstein (1931)
Gertie the Dinosaur (1914)
Gigi (1958)
Greed (1924)
High School (1968)
I am a Fugitive from a Chain Gang (1932)
The Italian (1915)
King Kong (1933)
Lawrence of Arabia (1962)
The Magnificent Ambersons (1942)
My Darling Clementine (1946)
Out of the Past (1947)
A Place in the Sun (1951)
The Poor Little Rich Girl (1917)
The Prisoner of Zenda (1937)
Shadow of a Doubt (1943)
Sherlock, Jr. (1924)
Tevya (1939)
Trouble in Paradise (1932)
2001: A Space Odyssey (1968)

International Top 10 Movies, 1991

Source: Variety, Jan. 1992

Germany

Through first week of December '91. $1 = 1.60 marks.

Title	Gross (Millions)
1. Home Alone	$34.9
2. Dances With Wolves	32.6
3. Werner—Beinhart	25.9
4. Robin Hood: Prince of Thieves	25.1
5. Terminator 2: Judgment Day	24.2
6. The Naked Gun 2½	22.2
7. Not Without My Daughter	22.0
8. Papa Ante Portas	19.1
9. The Silence of the Lambs	17.7
10. Sleeping With the Enemy	12.8

United Kingdom

Dec. 1, 1990 to Dec. 5, 1991. £1 = $1.75.

Title	Gross (Millions)
1. Robin Hood: Prince of Thieves	$34.7
2. Terminator 2: Judgment Day	31.5
3. The Silence of the Lambs	29.9
4. Three Men and a Little Lady	22.5
5. Home Alone	20.9
6. Dances With Wolves	18.5
7. Sleeping With the Enemy	16.1
8. The Naked Gun 2½	15.2
9. Kindergarten Cop	14.4
10. The Commitments	11.5

France

Jan. 1 to Dec. 1, 1991. Ticket price calculated at an average of 34 francs (about $6).

Title	Gross (Millions)
1. Dances With Wolves	$43.8
2. Terminator 2: Judgment Day	31.2
3. Robin Hood: Prince of Thieves	29.8
4. White Fang	14.4
5. The Silence of the Lambs	11.0-11.7
6. Highlander 2	11.4
7. Kindergarten Cop	11.0
8. Une Epoque Formidable	10.0-10.1
9. Look Who's Talking Too	10.0
10. Hot Shots	9.8

Japan

December 1990 to November 1991. $1 = 130 yen.

Title	Gross (Millions)
1. Terminator 2: Judgment Day	$38.5
2. Home Alone	25.4
3. Pretty Woman	23.9
4. Total Recall	18.9
5. Omohide Poroporo	14.2
6. Doraemon	13.8
7. Dances With Wolves	11.5
7. Dragon Ball (No. 5)	11.5
9. Tora-san (No. 43)	11.0
10. Chibimaruko-chan	10.4

Italy

Dec. 17, 1990 to Dec. 15, 1991. Grosses for 98 Italian cities, representing about 40% of national box office. $1 = 1,150 lira.

Title	Gross (Millions)
1. Johnny Stecchino	$22.2
2. Dances With Wolves	19.3
3. The Little Mermaid	12.2
4. Total Recall	9.7
5. Home Alone	9.2
6. Christmas Vacation '90	8.8
6. The Sheltering Sky	8.8
8. Rocky V	8.5
8. Dying Young	8.5
10. Look Who's Talking Too	7.5

Title	Gross (Millions)
Australia	
Week ending Dec. 12, 1990 to week ending Dec. 11, 1991. Averaged at $A1 = 78 cents. Based on MPDAA weekly reports, 1991.	
1. Ghost	$16.5
2. Dances With Wolves	14.9
3. Robin Hood: Prince of Thieves	12.1
4. Home Alone	11.5
5. Terminator 2: Judgment Day	10.8
6. The Silence of the Lambs	10.6
7. Kindergarten Cop	9.3
8. Green Card	8.0
9. Three Men and a Little Lady	7.8
10. Sleeping With the Enemy	6.6
Spain	
Jan. 1 to Dec. 15, 1991. $1 = 100 pesetas. Figures supplied by the distributors.	
1. Terminator 2: Judgment Day	$12.5
2. Dances With Wolves	12.0
3. Home Alone	11.1
4. Robin Hood: Prince of Thieves	10.4
5. The Silence of the Lambs	10.0
6. High Heels	7.1
7. Regarding Henry	5.8
7. Cyrano de Bergerac	5.8
9. Kindergarten Cop	5.6
10. Look Who's Talking Too	5.0

Notable Books of 1991

Source: American Library Association

How the Garcia Girls Lost Their Accents, Julia Alvarez
The Sweet Hereafter, Russell Banks
Before Freedom Came: African-American Life in the Antebellum South, ed. Edward D.C. Campbell and Kym S. Rice
The Tomcat's Wife and Other Stories, Carol Bly
Joe, Larry Brown
A Life of Her Own: A Countrywoman in Twentieth-Century France, Emilie Carles and Robert Destanque
Black Ice, Lorene Cary
Broken Vessels, Andre Dubus
Backlash: The Undeclared War against American Women, Susan Faludi
Praying for Sheetrock, Melissa Fay Greene
The World around Midnight, Patricia Browning Griffith
The Last Fine Time, Verlyn Klinkenborg
There Are No Children Here, Alex Kotlowitz
Savage Inequalities: Children in America's Schools, Jonathan Kozol
The Promised Land: The Great Black Migration and How It Changed America, Nicholas Lemann
What Work Is, Philip Levine
The Jameses: A Family Narrative, R.W.B. Lewis
Evenings at Monginis and Other Stories, Russell Lucas
Foolscap, Michael Malone
A Dangerous Woman, Mary McGarry Morris
Music of the Swamp, Lewis Nordan
Goodness, Tim Parks
All-Bright-Court, Connie Porter
The Invisible Invaders: The Story of the Emerging Age of Viruses, Peter Radetsky
Patrimony: A True Story, Philip Roth
The Kitchen God's Wife, Amy Tan

Bestselling Books of 1991

Source: *Publishers Weekly,* Jan. 1, 1992; these books lasted longest on *Publishers Weekly's* regular weekly bestseller lists in 1991.

Hardcover Fiction

1. *The Firm,* John Grisham
2. *Loves Music, Loves to Dance,* Mary Higgins Clark
3. *Possession: A Romance,* A.S. Byatt
4. *As the Crow Flies,* Jeffrey Archer
   Star Wars: Heir to the Empire, Timothy Zahn
5. *The Kitchen God's Wife,* Amy Tan
   The Sum of All Fears, Tom Clancy
6. *Damage,* Josephine Hart
   Heartbeat, Danielle Steel

Hardcover Nonfiction

1. *Iron John: A Book About Men,* Robert Bly
2. *Wealth Without Risk,* Charles J. Givens
3. *Financial Self-Defense,* Charles J. Givens
4. *Homecoming,* John Bradshaw
5. *Parliament of Whores,* P.J. O'Rourke
6. *Chutzpah,* Alan Dershowitz
7. *Toujours Provence,* Peter Mayle
8. *Fire in the Belly: On Being a Man,* Sam Keen
   Final Exit, Derek Humphry
   DO IT! Let's Get Off Our Buts, John-Roger & Peter McWilliams
9. *Uh-Oh: Some Observations from Both Sides of the Refrigerator,* Robert Fulghum
10. *You Just Don't Understand: Women and Men in Conversation,* Deborah Tannen
    The Civil War: An Illustrated History, Geoffrey C. Ward with Ric Burns & Ken Burns
    A Life on the Road, Charles Kuralt
    The Prize: The Epic Quest for Oil, Money and Power, Daniel Yergin

Mass-Market Paperback

1. *The Silence of the Lambs,* Thomas Harris
2. *The Joy Luck Club,* Amy Tan
   Dances with Wolves, Michael Blake
3. *Red Dragon,* Thomas Harris
4. *The Burden of Proof,* Scott Turow
5. *Four Past Midnight,* Stephen King
6. *Sleeping with the Enemy,* Nancy Price
   September, Rosamunde Pilcher
7. *Memories of Midnight,* Sidney Sheldon
   The Women in His Life, Barbara Taylor Bradford
   It Was on Fire When I Lay Down on It, Robert Fulghum
8. *The Prince of Tides,* Pat Conroy
9. *"G" Is for Gumshoe,* Sue Grafton
   Not Without My Daughter, Betty Mahmoody with William Hoffer
10. *The Mummy,* Anne Rice
    Buffalo Girls, Larry McMurtry
    The Bourne Ultimatum, Robert Ludlum
    The Gold Coast, Nelson DeMille
    The Voice of the Night, Dean R. Koontz

Trade Paperback

1. *7 Habits of Highly Effective People,* Stephen Covey
2. *The T-Factor Fat Gram Counter,* Pope-Cordle & Katahn
3. *Codependent No More,* Melody Beattie
4. *All I Need to Know I Learned from My Cat,* Suzy Becker
5. *You Just Don't Understand,* Deborah Tannen
6. *From Beirut to Jerusalem,* Thomas Friedman
7. *A Year in Provence,* Peter Mayle
8. *The Revenge of the Baby-Sat,* Bill Watterson
9. *The Education of Little Tree,* Forrest Carter
10. *Life's Little Instruction Book,* H. Jackson Brown Jr.
11. *What Color is Your Parachute, 1991,* Richard N. Bolles
12. *Men at Work: The Craft of Baseball,* George F. Will
13. *Scientific Progress Goes "Boink",* Bill Watterson
    A Peace to End All Peace, David Fromkin

Notable Children's Books of 1991

Source: American Library Association

Younger Readers

Traveling to Tondo: A Tale of the Nkundo of Zaire, Verna Aardema, illus. Will Hillenbrand
Changes, Anthony Browne
Fly Away Home, Eve Bunting, illus. Ronald Himler
Bigmama's, Donald Crews
Abuela, Arthur Dorros
In the Tall, Tall Grass, Denise Fleming
Chrysanthemum, Kevin Henkes
Amazing Grace, Mary Hoffman, illus. Caroline Binch
At the Crossroads, Rachel Isadora
Jack and the Beanstalk, Steven Kellogg
The Owl and the Pussycat, Edward Lear, illus. Jan Brett
Eating Fractions, Bruce McMillan
Michael Foreman's Mother Goose
The Adventures of Isabel, Ogden Nash, illus. James Marshall
Old Mother Hubbard and Her Wonderful Dog, illus. James Marshall
Tar Beach, Faith Ringgold
Tree of Cranes, Allen Say
Albert's Alphabet, Leslie Tryon
Mouse Count, Ellen Stoll Walsh
Max's Dragon Shirt, Rosemary Wells
Piggies, Don Wood and Audrey Wood, illus. Don Wood

Middle-Grade Readers

Flight: The Journey of Charles Lindbergh, Robert Burleigh, illus. Mike Wimmer
Wanted. . .Mud Blossom, Betsy Byars, illus. Jacqueline Rogers
Nekomah Creek, Linda Crew, illus. Charles Robinson
Tiger with Wings: The Great Horned Owl, Barbara Juster Esbensen, illus. Mary Barrett Brown
Bully for You, Teddy Roosevelt!, Jean Fritz, illus. Mike Wimmer
A Wave in Her Pocket: Stories from Trinidad, Joseph Lynn, illus. Brian Pinckney
Living with Dinosaurs, Patricia Lauber, illus. Douglas Henderson
Summer of Fire: Yellowstone, 1988, Patricia Lauber
Journey, Patricia MacLachlan, illus. Barry Moser
The Discovery of the Americas, Betsy Maestro, illus. Giulio Maestro
Rats on the Roof: And Other Stories, James Marshall
Chameleons: Dragons in the Trees, James Martin, photos Art Wolfe
The Orphan Boy, M. Tolowa Mollel, illus. Paul Morin
Shiloh, Phyllis Reynolds Naylor
The Diamond Tree: Jewish Tales from around the World, Howard Schwartz and Barbara Rush, illus. Uri Shulevitz
The Frog Prince Continued, Jon Scieszka, illus. Steve Johnson
The Pennywhistle Tree, Doris Buchanan Smith
Glasses: Who Needs 'Em?, Lane Smith
The Last Princess: The Story of Princess Ka'iulani of Hawai'i, Fay Stanley, illus. Diane Stanley

Older Readers

Nothing but the Truth: A Documentary Novel, Avi
Along the Tracks, Tamar Bergman, trans. from Hebrew by Michael Swirsky
The Remarkable Voyages of Captain Cook, Rhoda Blumberg
A Separate Battle: Women and the Civil War, Ina Chang
Year of Impossible Goodbyes, Sook Nyul Choi
The Borning Room, Paul Fleischman
Monkey Island, Paula Fox
The Wright Brothers: How They Invented the Airplane, Russell Freedman
The Truth about Unicorns, James Cross Giblin, illus. Michael McDermott
The Painter's Eye: Learning to Look at Contemporary American Art, Jan Greenberg and Sandra Jordan
Stepping on the Cracks, Mary Downing Hahn
Tales of the Early World, Ted Hughes
Castle in the Air, Diana Wynne Jones
Stars Come Out Within, Jean Little
Poem-Making: Ways to Begin Writing Poetry, Myra Cohn Livingston
Thomas Jefferson: The Revolutionary Aristocrat, Milton Meltzer
Now Is Your Time! The African-American Struggle for Freedom, Walter Dean Myers
The Man from the Other Side, Uri Orlev, trans. from Hebrew by Hillel Halkin
Lyddie, Katherine Paterson
Discovering Christopher Columbus: How History Is Invented, Kathy Pelta
The Place Where Nobody Stopped, Jerry Segal, illus. Dav Pilkey
The Mozart Season, Virginia Euwer Wolff
Searching for Dragons, Patricia C. Wrede
A Young Painter: The Life and Paintings of Wang Yani . . . Zheng Zhensun and Alice Low

All Ages

Anno's Math Games III, Mitsumasa Anno
Songs of the Wild West, Alan Axelrod
Night on Neighborhood Street, Eloise Greenfield
St. Jerome and the Lion, Margaret Hodges, illus. Barry Moser
All of You Was Singing, Richard Lewis, illus. Ed Young
The Woman Who Outshone the Sun: The Legend of Lucia Zenteno, Alejandro Cruz Martinez, illus. Fernando Olivera
Animal Fables from Aesop, Barbara McClintock
The Handmade Alphabet, Laura Rankin
Appalachia: The Voice of Sleeping Birds, Cynthia Ryland, illus. Barry Moser
The Story of Christmas, illus. Jane Ray
Tuesday, David Wiesner
Pish, Posh, Said Hieronymus Bosch, Nancy Willard and Leo Dillon, illus. Diane Dillon

Young Adults (Teenagers)

The American Library Association's Young Adult Services Division has also compiled a list of best books for young adults, which consists of 35 nonfiction and 50 fiction titles; as well as a list of books especially recommended for the reluctant young adult reader, which consists of 13 nonfiction and 24 fiction titles. Single copies of these lists may be obtained, free of charge, by writing to the ALA Young Adult Library Services Assn., 50 E. Huron St., Chicago, Ill. 60611; and enclosing a stamped, self-addressed envelope; or by calling 1-800-545-2433, Extension 4390.

Top 100 U.S. Daily Newspapers

Source: *Editor & Publisher Yearbook*

In 1991, another year of recession brought the discontinuation or merging of 29 daily newspapers. The addition of 4 new dailies during the year brought the total number of daily newspapers published in the U.S. as of Feb. 1, 1992 to 1,586, a loss of 25 when compared with the 1,611 published on the same date in 1991. There was also a circulation drop of 1,748,730, when comparing the average daily circulation of 39,670,682 for the 6-month period ending Sept. 30, 1991 with the average for the same period in 1990. The trend toward morning distribution that began in the mid-1970s continued, 20 evening dailies switching to morning distribution, to bring the total number of morning papers up to 571 over 1990's count of 339, while the number of evening papers dropped from 1,084 to 1,042. Another trend continued: the number of daily newspapers publishing Sunday editions increased from 863 to 875; however, because of the loss of some relatively large circulation Sunday newspapers, total Sunday circulation was down from 62,634,512 to 62,067,820. **Note:** m = morning; e = evening.

	Newspaper		Circulation
1.	New York (NY) *Wall Street Journal*	(m)	1,795,448
2.	Arlington (VA) *USA Today*	(m)	1,418,477
3.	Los Angeles (CA) *Times*	(m)	1,177,253
4.	New York (NY) *Times*	(m)	1,110,562
5.	Washington (DC) *Post*	(m)	791,289
6.	Long Island (NY) *Newsday*	(all day)	762,639
7.	New York (NY) *Daily News*	(m)	759,068
8.	Chicago (IL) *Tribune*	(m)	723,178
9.	Detroit (MI) *Free Press*	(m)	598,418
10.	San Francisco (CA) *Chronicle*	(m)	553,433
11.	Chicago (IL) *Sun-Times*	(m)	531,462
12.	Boston (MA) *Globe*	(m)	504,675
13.	Philadelphia (PA) *Inquirer*	(m)	503,603
14.	New York (NY) *Post*	(m)	491,326
15.	Newark (NJ) *Star-Ledger*	(m)	470,672
16.	Detroit (MI) *News*	(e)	446,831
17.	Miami (FL) *Herald*	(m)	421,350
18.	Cleveland (OH) *Plain Dealer*	(m)	413,678
19.	Minneapolis (MN) *Star Tribune*	(m)	408,365
20.	Houston (TX) *Chronicle*	(all day)	404,900
21.	Dallas (TX) *Morning News*	(m)	393,511
22.	St. Petersburg (FL) *Times*	(m)	360,788
23.	Denver (CO) *Rocky Mountain News*	(m)	355,661
24.	St. Louis (MO) *Post-Dispatch*	(m)	350,350
25.	Orange County (CA) *Register*	(all day)	347,675
26.	Boston (MA) *Herald*	(m)	345,564
27.	Phoenix (AZ) *Arizona Republic*	(m)	338,562
28.	Portland (OR) *Oregonian*	(all day)	329,761
29.	Buffalo (NY) *News*	(all day)	305,437
30.	Atlanta (GA) *Constitution*	(m)	302,595
31.	Houston (TX) *Post*	(m)	300,273
32.	Tampa (FL) *Tribune*	(m)	295,941
33.	Kansas City (MO) *Star*	(m)	281,577
34.	Orlando (FL) *Sentinel*	(all day)	279,226
35.	San Diego (CA) *Union-Tribune*	(m)	273,472
36.	San Jose (CA) *Mercury News*	(all day)	270,512
37.	Sacramento (CA) *Sacramento Bee*	(m)	267,669
38.	New Orleans (LA) *Times-Picayune*	(all day)	265,080
39.	Columbus (OH) *Dispatch*	(m)	263,313
40.	Denver (CO) *Post*	(m)	252,624
41.	Fort Worth (TX) *Star-Telegram*	(all day)	244,306
42.	Milwaukee (WI) *Journal*	(e)	241,231
43.	Fort Lauderdale (FL) *Sun-Sentinel*	(m)	240,273
44.	Seattle (WA) *Times*	(e)	239,946
45.	Baltimore (MD) *Sun*	(m)	235,937
46.	Louisville (KY) *Courier-Journal*	(m)	232,034
47.	Charlotte (NC) *Observer*	(m)	229,888
48.	Indianapolis (IN) *Star*	(m)	229,777
49.	Hartford (CT) *Courant*	(m)	228,172
50.	Oklahoma City (OK) *Daily Oklahoman*	(m)	217,452
51.	Pittsburgh (PA) *Press*	(e)	211,527
52.	Seattle (WA) *Post-Intelligencer*	(m)	207,941
53.	St. Paul (MN) *Pioneer Press*	(m)	206,844
54.	Los Angeles (CA) *Daily News*	(m)	203,948
55.	Providence (RI) *Journal*	(all day)	198,734
56.	Des Moines (IA) *Register*	(m)	198,658
57.	Cincinnati (OH) *Enquirer*	(m)	198,475
58.	Philadelphia (PA) *Daily News*	(m)	197,179
59.	San Antonio (TX) *Express-News*	(all day)	187,579
60.	Jacksonville (FL) *Florida Times-Union*	(m)	181,398
61.	Dayton (OH) *Daily News*	(m)	181,022
62.	West Palm Beach (FL) *Post*	(m)	178,714
63.	Memphis (TN) *Commercial Appeal*	(m)	178,708
64.	Austin (TX) *American-Statesman*	(m)	172,269
65.	Atlanta (GA) *Journal*	(e)	171,983
66.	Asbury Park (NJ) *Press*	(e)	166,305
67.	Milwaukee (WI) *Sentinel*	(m)	166,084
68.	Birmingham (AL) *News*	(e)	162,842
69.	Hackensack (NJ) *Record*	(m)	161,797
70.	Riverside (CA) *Press-Enterprise*	(m)	158,198
71.	Pittsburgh (PA) *Post-Gazette*	(m)	156,782
72.	Norfolk (VA) *Virginian-Pilot*	(m)	156,644
73.	Akron (OH) *Beacon Journal*	(m)	156,297
74.	San Antonio (TX)*Light*	(all day)	155,326
75.	Baltimore (MD) *Evening Sun*	(e)	152,676
76.	Toledo (OH) *Blade*	(e)	150,194
77.	Grand Rapids (MI) *Press*	(e)	148,615
78.	Fresno (CA) *Bee*	(m)	148,541
79.	Raleigh (NC) *News & Observer*	(m)	141,338
80.	Richmond (VA) *Times-Dispatch*	(m)	139,351
81.	Allentown (PA) *Morning Call*	(m)	136,105
82.	Rochester (NY) *Democrat & Chronicle*	(m)	135,610
83.	Nashville (TN) *Tennessean*	(m)	135,005
84.	Columbia (SC) *State*	(m)	134,462
85.	San Francisco (CA) *Examiner*	(e)	131,253
86.	Long Beach (CA) *Press-Telegram*	(m)	129,713
87.	Tulsa (OK) *World*	(m)	128,311
88.	Las Vegas (NV) *Review-Journal*	(m)	128,032
89.	Omaha (NE) *World-Herald*	(m)	126,550
90.	Sarasota (FL) *Herald-Tribune*	(m)	122,769
91.	Tacoma (WA) *Morning News Tribune*	(m)	121,544
92.	Lexington (KY) *Herald-Leader*	(m)	121,129
93.	Wilmington (DE) *News Journal*	(all day)	120,528
94.	Albuquerque (NM) *Journal*	(m)	119,576
95.	Wichita (KS) *Eagle*	(m)	118,511
96.	Worcester (MA) *Telegram & Gazette*	(all day)	116,767
97.	Little Rock (AR) *Democrat-Gazette*	(m)	114,986
98.	Greensboro (NC) *News & Record*	(m)	114,847
99.	Salt Lake City (UT) *Tribune*	(m)	114,339
100.	Springfield (MA) *Union-News*	(all day)	112,639

Selected U.S. Daily Newspaper Circulation

Source: Audit Bureau of Circulations report of average paid circulation for 6 months to Mar. 31, 1992.

Newspaper	Daily
Albuquerque Tribune(e)	†36,016
Amarillo News(m)	43,997
Amarillo Globe-Times(e)	*21,131
Anchorage News(m)	60,873
Ann Arbor News(e)	†52,008
Athens (Ga.) News(m)	*15,097
Athens (Ga.) Banner-Herald(e)	*13,048
Augusta (Ga.) Chronicle(m)	*71,800
Augusta (Ga.) Herald(e)	*11,487
Bakersfield Californian(m)	†80,467
Bangor (Me.) News(m)	*74,167
Baton Rouge Advocate(m)	*102,010
Billings (Mont.) Gazette(m)	54,657
Binghamton (N.Y.) Press & Sun Bulletin(m)	70,739
Birmingham Post-Herald(m)	*63,720
Bismark (N.D.) Tribune(m)	31,484
Bristol (Va.) Herald-Courier Tennessean(a)	*44,222
Camden (N.J.) Courier-Post(e)	†97,540
Casper (Wyo.) Star Tribune(m)	33,659
Charleston (W.Va.) Gazette(m)	54,440
Chattanooga News-Free Press(e)	48,398
Cincinnati Post(e)	100,925
Columbus (Ga.) Ledger-Enquirer(m)	53,882
Connecticut Post(m)	67,339
Corpus Christi Caller-Times(m)	†70,265
Daytona Beach News-Journal(m)	100,588
Dubuque Telegraph-Herald(e)	34,136
El Paso Herald-Post(e)	†29,119
Erie (Pa.) News(m)	*31,782
Erie (Pa.) Times(e)	*40,566
Evansville (Ind.) Courier(m)	63,063
Evansville (Ind.) Press(e)	32,739
Everett (Wash.) Herald(m)	52,061
Fargo (N.D.) Forum(m)	55,465
Ft. Lauderdale News(e)	5,211
Ft. Myers (Fla.) News-Press(m)	103,104
Ft. Wayne Journal-Gazette(m)	†62,220
Gainesville Sun(m)	55,602
Gary Post-Tribune(m)	74,238
Greenville (S.C.) News(m)	*92,835
Greenville (S.C.) Piedmont(e)	*24,955
Honolulu Advertiser(m)	105,670
Honolulu Star-Bulletin(e)	88,460
Huntington (W.Va.) Herald-Dispatch(m)	†42,991
Hyannis: Cape Cod Times(m)	42,560
Jackson (Miss.) Clarion-Ledger(m)	108,598
Kalamazoo Gazette(e)	66,814
Knoxville News-Sentinel(m)	125,526
Lansing (Mich.) State Journal(m)	71,720
Lynchburg (Va.) News & Advance(a)	*39,715
Macon (Ga.) Telegraph & News(m)	73,460
Madison (Wis.) State Journal(m)	*83,323
Middletown (N.Y.) Times Herald Record(m)	†82,948
Mobile Press(e)	*†41,458
Mobile Register(m)	*†63,118
Modesto (Cal.) Bee(m)	†82,548
Montgomery Advertiser(m)	*51,306
Montgomery Journal(e)	*14,176
Nashville Banner(e)	61,257
Newport News (Va.) Press(m)	†103,990
Oakland Tribune(m)	107,407
Pensacola News-Journal(m)	*†60,683
Peoria Journal Star(a)	*86,361
Phoenix Gazette(e)	†93,363
Portland (Me.) Press Herald(m)	*†70,966
Reno Gazette Journal(m)	66,630
Rockford (Ill.) Register-Star(m)	75,944
Salem (Ore.) Statesman-Journal(m)	61,308
San Bernardino Sun(m)	90,239
San Juan (PR) Star(m)	†33,418
Savannah News(m)	*57,458
Savannah Press(e)	*17,214
Scranton Times(e)	*†43,914
Scranton Tribune(m)	*†30,677
Sioux City Journal(m)	*49,403
Spokane Chronicle(e)	*20,079
Springfield (Ill.) State Journal Register(m)	68,337
Syracuse Herald-Journal(e)	89,726
Syracuse Post-Standard(m)	89,699
Tallahassee Democrat(m)	58,670
Terre Haute Tribune Star(m)	36,964
Topeka Capital-Journal(m)	67,210
Tucson Star(m)	†100,331
Tulsa Tribune(e)	†66,647
Waterbury (Conn.) Republican-American(m)	60,270
Wilmington (N.C.) Star(m)	50,116
Winston-Salem Journal(m)	90,808
Yakima (Wash.) Herald-Republic(a)	†41,095
Youngstown Vindicator(e)	†89,751

(m) morning; (e) evening; (a) all day; * Mon.-Fri. average; † 3 months.

100 Bestselling U.S. Magazines

Source: Audit Bureau of Circulations, Schaumburg, Ill.

General magazines, exclusive of groups and comics; also exclusive of magazines that failed to file reports to ABC by press time. Based on total average paid circulation during the 6 months prior to Dec. 31, 1991.

Magazine	Circulation
1. Modern Maturity	22,450,000
2. NRTA/AARP Bulletin	22,174,021
3. Reader's Digest	16,306,007
4. TV Guide	15,353,982
5. National Geographic	9,921,479
6. Better Homes & Gardens	8,003,263
7. Family Circle	5,151,534
8. Good Housekeeping	5,028,151
9. McCall's	5,009,358
10. Ladies Home Journal	5,002,900
11. Woman's Day	4,751,977
12. Time	4,248,565
13. Redbook	3,841,866
14. National Enquirer	3,706,030
15. Playboy	3,498,802
16. Sports Illustrated	3,444,188
17. Newsweek	3,420,167
18. People Weekly	3,235,120
19. Star	3,207,951
20. Prevention	3,109,562
21. American Legion	2,984,389
22. Cosmopolitan	2,679,356
23. AAA World	2,630,944
24. First for Women	2,393,722
25. Southern Living	2,385,058
26. U.S. News & World Report	2,351,922
27. Smithsonian	2,204,298
28. Glamour	2,012,305
29. Field & Stream	2,003,041
30. NEA Today	1,980,823
31. Life	1,910,520
32. Home & Away	1,893,327
33. VFW	1,885,461
34. Money	1,855,426
35. Ebony	1,836,039
36. Popular Science	1,823,032
37. Seventeen	1,815,521
38. Country Living	1,758,487
39. Parents	1,737,784
40. 1,001 Home Ideas	1,675,243
41. Discovery	1,661,455
42. Popular Mechanics	1,638,015
43. Outdoor Life	1,503,691
44. Penthouse	1,501,821
45. Adventure Road	1,490,680
46. Elks	1,434,170
47. Boys' Life	1,410,305
48. Golf Digest	1,408,055
49. Sunset	1,392,691
50. Woman's World	1,363,992
51. New Woman	1,336,639
52. Bon Appetit	1,331,853
53. American Rifleman	1,329,806
54. US	1,328,442
55. Globe	1,300,379
56. Vogue	1,235,981
57. Rolling Stone	1,207,262
58. American Hunter	1,205,791
59. Sesame Street	1,200,690
60. Teen	1,152,865
61. Family Handyman	1,150,662
62. Self	1,140,928
63. Home Mechanix	1,136,419
64. Golf	1,126,738
65. Discover	1,125,357
66. Changing Times	1,115,437
67. Workbasket	1,106,910
68. Mademoiselle	1,102,547
69. Travel & Leisure	1,100,651
70. Country Home	1,050,867
71. Weight Watchers	1,006,396
72. Car and Driver	1,004,291
73. House Beautiful	1,001,732
74. Scouting	1,000,805
75. YM	995,764
76. Organic Gardening	995,265
77. Jet	971,752
78. Home	946,595
79. Elle	935,331
80. Sport	908,760
81. Yankee	903,954
82. Business Week, NA.	896,803
83. Gourmet	895,256
84. Hot Rod	890,659
85. Motor Trend	887,475
86. Consumers Digest	874,226
87. American Legion Auxiliary	863,289
88. Nation's Business	859,929
89. Popular Photography	853,338
90. Essence	853,297
91. Working Woman	849,772
92. Victoria	836,835
93. Workbench	835,486
94. National Examiner	830,174
95. Vanity Fair	813,881
96. American Health	812,672
97. Endless Vacation	811,256
98. PC Magazine	810,388
99. Health	810,064
100. Homeowner	788,232

Symphony Orchestras of the U.S.

Source: American Symphony Orchestra League, 777 14th St., N.W., Washington, DC 20005
(All orchestras listed had budgets in excess of $1.05 million in fiscal 1991.)

Symphony Orchestra[1]	Music Director[2]
Alabama (Birmingham)	Paul Polivnick
American (N.Y.C.)	Leon Botstein
Atlanta (Ga.)	Yoel Levi
Austin (Tex.)	Sung Kwak
Baltimore (Md.)	David Zinman
Boston (Mass.)	Seiji Ozawa
Brooklyn Philharmonic (N.Y.)	Dennis Russell Davies
Buffalo Philharmonic (N.Y.)	Maximiano Valdez
Charleston (S.C.)	David Stahl
Charlotte (N.C.)	Leo B. Driehuys
Chattanooga, & Opera Assn. (Tenn.)	Vacant
Chicago (Ill.)	Daniel Barenboim
Cincinnati (Oh.)	Jesus Lopez-Cobos
Cleveland (Oh.)	Christoph von Dohnanyi
Colorado (Denver)	David T. Abosch
Colorado Springs (Col.)	Christopher P. Wilkins
Columbus (Oh.)	Alessandro Siciliani
Concerto Soloists Chamber (Phila.)	Marc S. Mostovoy
Dallas (Tex.)	Eduardo Mata
Dayton Philharmonic (Oh.)	Isaiah Jackson
Delaware (Wilmington)	Stephen Gunzenhauser
Detroit (Mich.)	Neeme Jarvi
Eastern Music Festival (Greensboro, N.C.)	Sheldon Morgenstern
Florida Philharmonic (Fort Lauderdale)	James Judd
The Florida Orchestra (Tampa)	Jahja Ling
Florida (Orlando)	Kenneth Jean
Florida Symphonic Pops (Boca Raton)	Mark S. Azzolina
Fort Wayne Philharmonic (Ind.)	Ronald Ondrejka
Fort Worth (Tex.)	John Giordano
Grand Rapids (Mich.)	Catherine Comet
Grant Park (Chicago, Ill.)	Catherine M. Cahill
Handel and Haydn Society (Boston)	Christopher Hogwood
Hartford (Conn.)	Michael Lankester
Honolulu (Ha.)	Donald Johanos
Houston (Tex.)	Christoph Eschenbach
Hudson Valley Philharmonic (Poughkeepsie, N.Y.)	Vacant
Indianapolis (Ind.)	Raymond Leppard
Jacksonville (Fla.)	Roger Nierenberg
Kansas City (Mo.)	William McGlaughlin
Knoxville (Tenn.)	Kirk Trevor
Long Beach (Cal.)	JoAnn Falletta
Long Island Philharmonic (N.Y.)	Marin Alsop
Los Angeles Chamber Or. (Cal.)	Iona Brown
Los Angeles Philharmonic (Cal.)	Esa-Pekka Salonen
The Louisville Orchestra (Ky.)	Lawrence Leighton Smith
Memphis (Tenn.)	Alan Balter
Milwaukee (Wis.)	Zdenek Macal
The Minnesota Orchestra (Minneapolis)	Edo de Waart
Mississippi (Jackson)	Colman Pearce
The Nashville Symphony (Tenn.)	Kenneth S. Schermerhorn
National (Washington, D.C.)	Mstislav Rostropovich
New Haven (Conn.)	Michael Palmer
New Jersey (Newark)	Hugh Wolff
New Mexico (Albuquerque)	Neal H. Stulberg
New World Symphony (Miami Beach, Fla.)	Michael Tilson Thomas
New York Chamber Sym. of the 92nd St. Y (N.Y.C.)	Gerard Schwarz
New York Philharmonic (N.Y.C.)	Kurt Masur
North Carolina (Raleigh)	Gerhardt Zimmermann
Ohio Chamber Orchestra (Cleveland)	C. Dwight Oltman
Oklahoma City Philharmonic (Okla.)	Joel A. Levine
Omaha (Neb.)	Bruce B. Hangen
Oregon (Portland)	James DePreist
Orpheus Chamber Or. (N.Y.C., N.Y.)	None
Pacific Symphony (Irvine, Cal.)	Carl St. Clair
The Philadelphia Orchestra (Pa.)	Wolfgang Sawallisch[3]
Philharmonia Virtuosi (Dobbs Ferry, N.Y.)	Richard P. Kapp
Phoenix (Ariz.)	James L. Sedares
Pittsburgh (Pa.)	Lorin Maazel
Portland (Me.)	Toshiyuki Shimada
Puerto Rico (Santurce)	Odon Alonso
Rhode Island Philharmonic Or. (Providence)	Gustav Meier
The Richmond Symphony (Va.)	George Manahan
Rochester Philharmonic Or. (N.Y.)	Mark Elder
Sacramento (Cal.)	Alasdair P. Neale
St. Louis (Mo.)	Leonard Slatkin
St. Paul Chamber Or. (Minn.)	Hugh Wolff
San Antonio (Tex.)	Christopher P. Wilkins
San Diego (Cal.)	Yoav Talmi
San Francisco (Cal.)	Herbert Blomstedt
San Jose (Cal.)	Vacant
Savannah (Ga.)	Philip B. Greenberg
Seattle (Wash.)	Gerard Schwarz
Spokane (Wash.)	Vakhtang Jordania
Springfield (Mass.)	Raymond C. Harvey
Syracuse (N.Y.)	Kazuyoshi Akiyama
Toldeo (Oh.)	Andrew Massey
Tucson (Ariz.)	Robert E. Bernhardt
Tulsa Philharmonic Or. (Okla.)	Bernard Rubenstein
Utah (Salt Lake City)	Joseph Silverstein
The Virginia Symphony (Norfolk)	JoAnn Falletta
West Virginia (Charleston)	Thomas B. Conlin
Wichita (Kan.)	Zuohuang Chen
Winston-Salem Piedmont Triad Symphony (N.C.)	Peter J. Perret

(1) Orchestra name=place name + Symphony Orchestra, unless otherwise noted; (2) General title; listed is highest-ranking member of conducting personnel. (3) Mus. Dir. Desig.=appointment for future season.

U.S. Opera Companies with Budgets of $500,000 or More

Source: OPERA America; June, 1992

Anchorage Opera; Margaret Wood, gen. dir.
Arizona Opera Co. (Tucson); Glynn Ross, gen. dir.
Opera Theatre at Wildwood (Ariz.); Ann Chotard, art. dir.
Fullerton Civic Light Opera (Calif.); Griff Duncan, gen. mgr.
Long Beach Opera (Calif.); Michael Milenski, gen. dir.
Long Beach Civic Light Opera (Calif.); Pegge Logefeil, mng. dir.
Los Angeles Music Center Opera Assn.; Peter Hemmings, exec. dir.
Opera Pacific (Costa Mesa, Calif.); David DiChiera, gen. dir.
Sacramento Opera Assn. (Calif.); Marianne H. Oaks, gen. dir.
San Diego Civic Light Opera; C. E. Franks, exec. dir.
San Diego Opera Assn.; Ian Campbell, gen. mgr.
San Francisco Opera; Lotfi Mansouri, gen. dir.
San Francisco Opera Center (inc. Western Opera Theater); Christine Bullin, mgr.
Opera San José (Calif.); Irene Dalis, art. dir.
San José Civic Light Opera (Calif.); Dianna Shuster, dir.
Central City Opera (Denver); Daniel Rule, gen. mgr.
Opera Colorado (Denver); Nathaniel Merrill, art. dir.
Connecticut Grand Opera & Stamford State Opera, Laurence Gilgore, art. dir.
Connecticut Opera (Hartford); George Osborne, gen. dir.
Goodspeed Opera House (E. Haddam, Conn.); Michael Price, exec. dir.
Washington Opera (D.C.); Martin Feinstein, gen. dir.
Fort Lauderdale Opera; William H. Martin, gen. mgr.
Greater Miami Opera Assn.; Robert Heuer, gen. mgr.

(continued)

Orlando Opera Co. (Fla.); Robert Swedberg, gen. dir.
Palm Beach Opera; Herbert P. Benn, gen. mgr.
Sarasota Opera Assn. (Fla.); Deane Allyn, exec. dir.
The Atlanta Opera (Ga.); William Fred Scott, art. dir.; Alfred Kennedy, gen. mgr.
Augusta Opera (Ga.); Edward Bradberry, gen. dir.
Hawaii Opera Theatre; J. Mario Ramos, gen. dir.
Chicago Opera Theater; Alan Stone, art. dir.
Lyric Opera of Chicago; Ardis Krainik, gen. mgr.
Indianapolis Opera; Durand L. Pope, gen. dir.
Des Moines Metro Opera (Indianola); Robert Larsen, art. dir.
Kentucky Opera Assn. (Louisville); Thomson Smillie, gen. dir.
New Orleans Opera Assn.; Arthur Cosenza, gen. dir.
Baltimore Opera Co.; Michael Harrison, gen. dir.
Opera Company of Boston; Sarah Caldwell, art. dir.
Boston Opera Theatre; Robert Canon, exec. dir.
Michigan Opera Theatre (Detroit); David DiChiera, gen. dir.
Opera Grand Rapids (Mich.); Robert Lyall, gen. dir.
Minnesota Opera Co. (St. Paul); Kevin Smith, gen. dir.
Lyric Opera of Kansas City (Missouri); Russell Patterson, gen. dir. & art. dir.
Opera Theatre of St. Louis (Missouri); Charles MacKay, gen. dir.
Opera/Omaha (Neb.); Mary Robert, gen. dir.
Nevada Opera (Reno); Ted Puffer, gen. dir.
Opera Festival of N.J. (Princeton Junction); Deborah S. Sandler, exec. dir.
Metro Lyric Opera (Allenhurst, N.J.); Era M. Tognoli, gen. & art. dir.
New Jersey State Opera (Newark); Alfredo Silipigni, gen. dir.
Albuquerque Civic Light Opera; Linda E. McVey, exec. dir.
Santa Fe Opera (New Mexico); John Crosby, gen. dir.
Tri-Cities Opera (Binghamton, N.Y.); Edward Cordick, exec. dir.; C. Savoca, art. dir.
Chautauqua Opera (N.Y.); Linda Jackson, gen. mgr.
Glimmerglass Opera (Cooperstown, N.Y.); Paul Kellogg, gen. mgr.
Lake George Opera Festival (N.Y.); John Balme, art. dir.; Susan T. Danis, exec. dir.
Syracuse Opera; Julie Richard, mng. dir.
Light Opera of Manhattan; Raymond Allen, Jerry Gotham, art. dir.
Metropolitan Opera Assn. (New York City); Joseph Volpe, gen. mgr.
Music-Theatre Group (N.Y. & Stockbridge, Mass.); Lyn Austin, prod. dir.
New York City Opera; Christopher Keene, gen. dir.
New York City Opera Natl. Co.; Nancy Kelly, adm. dir.
Opera Orchestra of N.Y. (N.Y.C.); Eve Queler, art dir.
Opera Carolina (Charlotte, N.C.); James Wright, gen. dir.
Cincinnati Opera Assn.; James deBlasis, art. dir.
Cleveland Opera; David Bamberger, gen. dir.
Opera/Columbus (Oh.); John Gage, gen. dir.
Dayton Opera Assn. (Oh.); Jane Nelson, mng. dir.
Lyric Theatre of Oklahoma; Gayle Pearson, gen. mgr.
Tulsa Opera (Oklahoma); Myrna S. Ruffner, gen. mgr.
Portland Opera Assn. (Oregon); Robert Bailey, exec. dir.
American Music Theater Festival (Phila.); Marjorie Samoff, prod. dir.
Opera Company of Philadelphia; Robert B. Driver, gen. dir.
Pennsylvania Opera Theater (Phila.); Barbara Silverstein, art dir. & gen. mgr.
Pittsburgh Civic Light Opera; Charles Gray, exec. dir.
Pittsburgh Opera; Tito Capobianco, gen. dir.
Opera Memphis (Tenn.); Michael Ching, art. dir.; Bert Adler Wolff, gen. dir.
Austin Lyric Opera (Tex.) Walter Ducloux, art. dir.
Dallas Opera; Plato Karayanis, gen. dir.
Lyric Opera of Dallas (Tex.); John Burrows, art. dir.
Fort Worth Opera; Carl O. Johnson, art. dir.
Houston Grand Opera Assn.; R. David Gockley, gen. dir.
Texas Opera Theater (Houston); James Ireland, gen. mgr.
Utah Opera (Salt Lake City); Anne Ewers, gen. dir.
Virginia Opera (Norfolk); Peter Mark, gen. dir.
Seattle Opera Assn.; Speight Jenkins, gen. dir.
Florentine Opera of Milwaukee; Dennis Hanthorn, gen. mgr.
Skylight Opera Theatre (Milwaukee); Chas Rader-Shieber, art. dir.

Some Notable U.S. Dance Companies

Source: Dance/USA, July, 1992

African-American Dance Ensemble, Durham, NC
Alvin Ailey American Dance Theater, New York, NY
Aman Folk Ensemble, Los Angeles, CA
American Ballet Theatre, New York, NY
American Repertory Ballet Company, Princeton, NJ
Atlanta Ballet, GA
Avaz International Dance Theatre, Los Angeles, CA
Ballet Arizona, Phoenix, AZ
Ballet Austin, Austin, TX
Ballet Chicago, IL
Ballet Florida, West Palm Beach, FL
Ballet Hispanico of New York, New York, NY
BalletMet, Columbus, OH
Ballet Omaha, NE
Ballet West, Salt Lake City, UT
Tandy Beal and Company, Santa Cruz, CA
Boston Ballet, Boston, MA
Trisha Brown Company, New York, NY
Donald Byrd/The Group, New York, NY
Caribbean Dance Company, St. Croix, VI
Chen & Dancers, New York, NY
Lucinda Childs Dance Company, New York, NY
Cincinnati Ballet, Cincinnati, OH
Cleveland/San Jose Ballet, Cleveland, OH
Colorado Ballet, Denver, CO
Cunningham Dance Foundation, New York, NY
Dance Alloy, Pittsburgh, PA
Dance Exchange, Washington, DC
Dance Theatre of Harlem, New York, NY
DanceBrazil, New York, NY
Danceteller, Philadelphia, PA
Dayton Ballet Association, Dayton, OH
Dayton Contemporary Dance Company, Dayton, OH
Laura Dean Musicians and Dancers, New York, NY
Douglas Dunn & Dancers, New York, NY
Eiko & Koma, New York, NY
Eugene Ballet Company, Eugene, OR
Garth Fagan's Dance, Rochester, NY
Feld Ballet, New York, NY
Fort Worth Ballet, Fort Worth, TX
Joe Goode Performance Group, San Francisco, CA
David Gordon Pick Up Co., New York, NY
Martha Graham Dance Co., New York, NY
Hartford Ballet, Hartford, CT
Erick Hawkins Dance Co., New York, NY
Joseph Holmes Dance Theater, Chicago, IL
Houston Ballet, Houston, TX
Hubbard Street Dance Company, Chicago, IL
Jazz Tap Ensemble, Los Angeles, CA
Margaret Jenkins Dance Company, San Francisco, CA
Joffrey Ballet, New York, NY
Bill T. Jones/Arnie Zane Company, New York, NY

Rebecca Kelly Dance Company, New York, NY
KHADRA International Folk Ballet, San Francisco, CA
Ralph Lemon Company, New York, NY
Lewitzky Dance Company, Los Angeles, CA
Jose Limon Dance Company, New York, NY
LINES Contemporary Ballet, San Francisco, CA
Loretta Livingston & Dancers, Los Angeles, CA
Los Angeles Chamber Ballet, CA
Louisville Ballet, Louisville, KY
Lar Lubovitch Dance Company, New York, NY
Miami City Ballet, Miami Beach, FL
Bebe Miller and Company, New York, NY
Milwaukee Ballet, Milwaukee, WI
Elisa Monte Dance Company, New York, NY
Montgomery Ballet, Montgomery, AL
Mordine & Company, Chicago, IL
Mark Morris Dance Group, New York, NY
Jennifer Muller/The Works, New York, NY
Muntu Dance Theater, Chicago, IL
New Dance, Minneapolis, MN
New York City Ballet, New York, NY
Rosalind Newman and Dancers, New York, NY
Nikolais and Louis Dance, New York, NY
North Carolina Dance Theatre, Winston Salem, NC
Oakland Ballet, Oakland, CA
ODC/San Francisco, San Francisco, CA
Ohio Ballet, Akron, OH
Oregon Ballet Theater, Portland, OR
Pacific Northwest Ballet, Seattle, WA
Parsons Dance Company, New York, NY
Pennsylvania Ballet, Philadelphia, PA
Philadanco, Philadelphia, PA
Pilobolus Dance Theater, Washington, CT
Stuart Pimsler Dance & Theater, Columbus, OH
Pittsburgh Ballet Theatre, Pittsburgh, PA
Pittsburgh Dance Alloy, Pittsburgh, PA
Repertory Dance Theatre, Salt Lake City, UT
Richmond Ballet, Richmond, VA
Elizabeth Streb Ringside, New York, NY
Ririe-Woodbury Dance Company, Salt Lake City, UT
Cleo Parker Robinson Dance Theater, Denver, CO
Nicholas Rodriguez and Dance-Compass, Montclair, NJ
San Francisco Ballet, San Francisco, CA
Carlota Santana Spanish Dance Arts Co., New York, NY
Sarasota Ballet, FL
Solomons Company/Dance, New York, NY
Southern Ballet Theater, Winter Park, FL
State Ballet of Missouri, Kansas City, MO
Paul Taylor Dance Company, New York, NY
Joyce Trisler Danscompany, New York, NY
Tulsa Ballet Theatre, Tulsa, OK
Urban Bush Women, New York, NY
Dan Wagoner and Dancers, New York, NY
Washington Ballet, Washington, DC
June Watanabe in Company, San Rafael, CA
Nina Wiener Dance Company, New York, NY
Zenon Dance Company, Minneapolis, MN
ZeroMoving Dance Company, Philadelphia, PA
Zivili Kolo Ensemble, Granville, OH

Top 20 Cable Video Networks

Source: *Cable Television Developments*, May 1992; Natl. Cable Television Assn. Ranked by number of subscribers.

1. ESPN
Began: Sep. 1979 — Systems: 24,700*
Basic Service/Adv. — Subscribers: 59.3 million

2. CNN (Cable News Network)
Began: Jun. 1980 — Systems: 10,963
Basic Service/Adv. — Subscribers: 58.9 million

3. USA Network
Began: Apr. 1980 — Systems: 10,100*
Basic Service/Adv. — Subscribers: 58.0 million

4. TBS
Began: Dec. 1976 — Systems: 14,954*
Basic Service/Adv. — Subscribers: 57.7 million

5. The Discovery Channel
Began: Jun. 1985 — Systems: 9,232
Basic Service/Adv. — Subscribers: 56.8 million

6. TNT (Turner Network Television)
Began: Oct. 1988 — Systems: 7,833
Basic Service/Adv. — Subscribers: 56.2 million

7. Nickelodeon/Nick At Nite
Began: Apr. 1979 — Systems: 8,836
Jul. 1985 — 4,036
Basic Service/Adv. — Subscribers: 55.8 million

8. C-Span
Began: Mar. 1979 — Systems: 4,081
Basic Service/Adv. — Subscribers: 55.0 million

9. MTV: Music Television
Began: Aug. 1981 — Systems: 7,657
Basic Service/Adv. — Subscribers: 55.0 million

10. The Family Channel
Began: Apr. 1977 — Systems: 9,825
Basic Service/Adv. — Subscribers: 54.5 million

11. TNN: The Nashville Network
Began: Mar. 1983 — Systems: 12,221
Basic Service/Adv. — Subscribers: 54.5 million

12. Lifetime
Began: Feb. 1984 — Systems: 5,465
Basic Service/Adv. — Subscribers: 53.4 million

13. Arts & Entertainment Network
Began: Feb. 1984 — Systems: 7,600
Basic Service/Adv. — Subscribers: 53.0 million

14. The Weather Channel
Began: May 1982 — Systems: 4,600
Basic Service/Adv. — Subscribers: 51.0 million

15. Headline News
Began: Jan. 1982 — Systems: 6,323
Basic Service/Adv. — Subscribers: 48.3 million

16. CNBC
Began: Apr. 1989 — Systems: 3,000
Basic Service/Adv. — Subscribers: 46.0 million

17. VH-1 (Video Hits One)
Began: Jan. 1985 — Systems: 4,158
Basic Service/Adv. — Subscribers: 43.2 million

18. QVC Network
Began: Nov. 1986 — Systems: 4,071
Basic Service/Adv. — Subscribers: 42.1 million

19. AMC (American Movie Classics)
Began: Oct. 1984 — Systems: 3,200
Basic Service/Adv. — Subscribers: 38.0 million

20. WGN/UVI
Began: Nov. 1978 — Systems: 14,090*
Basic Service/Adv. — Subscribers: 34.9 million

* Includes non-cable affiliates

America's Favorite Prime-Time Television Programs, 1991

Source: Nielsen Media Research

(Nielsen People Meter Average Audience Estimates)

Regularly Scheduled Network Programs (Feb. 1992)

Percent of TV households and persons in TV households

Program	TV House-holds	Women	Men	Teens	Chil-dren
60 Minutes	23.4	18.2	17.3		
Roseanne	20.6	15.2	11.0	17.1	14.4
CBS Sunday Movie	18.9	17.5	10.0		
Home improvement	18.3	12.6	9.2	17.7	18.2
Coach	17.6	14.0	9.9	14.1	9.0
Murder, She Wrote	17.5	15.6	9.4		
Cheers	17.2	12.6	10.6		
Designing Women	17.1	14.0	9.5		
Major Dad	17.0	14.1	9.5		
NBC Sunday Movie	17.0	13.8	10.3	10.3	
Unsolved Mysteries	17.0	13.5	10.7		
Full House	16.0	11.2		16.8	19.5
Murphy Brown	16.4	13.2	8.9		
Evening Shade	16.1	13.6	9.6		
48 Hours	15.6	11.5	10.6		
Northern Exposure	14.8	11.7	9.0		
Wings	14.7				
Fresh Prince	14.7			19.0	13.0
Cosby Show	14.6			10.5	9.1
A Diff. World	14.5	11.2		12.0	9.6
CBS Tues. Movie		11.2			
Golden Girls		11.2			
In Heat of Night		11.5			
Matlock		11.5			

Program	TV House-holds	Women	Men	Teens	Chil-dren
American Detective			9.5		
Amer. Funniest Videos			8.9		10.9
FBI The Untold Stories			8.9		
ABC Sunday Movie			9.0		
ABC Monday Movie			9.0		
Beverly Hills 90210				20.5	9.0
Blossom				16.9	11.9
Doogie Howser, MD				12.8	10.2
Drexells Class				12.6	9.8
Family Matters				11.0	15.3
Herman's Head				10.8	
In Living Color				14.6	
Married With Children				12.9	
Roc				11.5	
Simpsons				16.0	16.2
Step By Step				10.5	15.0
Wonder Years				13.4	12.6
Amer. Funniest People					10.0
Baby Talk					13.5
Dinosaurs					14.9
Billy					9.5
Who's the Boss					9.0

Note: Prime time = Mon.-Sat. 8pm-11pm & Sun. 7pm-11pm, New York time.

Favorite Syndicated Programs, 1992

Source: Nielsen Media Research, Feb. 1992

(Ratings based on Designated Market Area coverage as reported by Nielsen's Cassandra Report)

Program	TV house-holds	Women	Men	Teens	Chil-dren
Wheel of Fortune	17.5	14.8	10.3	4.7	4.9
Jeopardy	14.5	11.9	8.3	3.6	3.0
Oprah Winfrey	12.9	11.0	4.0	4.7	1.7
Star Trek-Next Gen.	11.8	7.2	9.6	6.7	5.5
Wheel of Fort. (Wknd)	10.4	8.7	6.1	2.2	2.6
Entertainment Tonight	9.8	7.4	5.5	2.8	1.8
Jeopardy (Wknd)	9.1	7.5	5.5	1.8	1.9
Current Affair	8.8	6.2	5.4	2.8	1.9

Program	TV house-holds	Women	Men	Teens	Chil-dren
Inside Edition	8.0	5.9	4.4	1.9	1.0
Donahue	7.2	5.6	2.7	1.0	0.6
Golden Girls	7.2	5.6	3.3	3.9	2.5
Cheers	7.1	4.7	5.0	3.3	1.8
Full House	7.1	5.9	2.2	10.8	14.0
Hard Copy	6.8	4.9	3.9	1.7	0.9
Married With Children	6.8	4.1	4.6	6.8	4.4
Sally Jessy Raphael	6.8	5.6	2.0	1.2	0.7

Average Television Viewing Time, 1992

Source: Nielsen Media Research, Feb. 1992 (Hours:Minutes per week)

		Mon.-Fri. 10am-4:30pm	Mon.-Fri. 4:30pm-7:30pm	Mon.-Sun. 8-11pm	Sat. 7am-1pm	Mon.-Fri. 11:30pm-1am
Total Persons		4:50	4:21	9:23	:50	1:13
Total Women	18+	5:20	3:50	10:40	:43	1:28
	18-24	5:59	3:44	7:42	:41	1:19
	25-54	5:14	3:59	10:03	:40	1:25
	55+	8:47	7:11	13:07	:46	1:37
Total Men	18+	4:02	2:58	9:45	:44	1:22
	18-24	3:35	2:49	6:40	:35	1:25
	25-54	3:11	3:20	9:23	:45	1:25
	55+	6:20	6:53	12:19	:46	1:27
Female Teens		3:11	3:59	7:17	:52	:37
Male Teens		3:54	3:30	7:52	:54	:35
Children	2-5	6:07	4:22	5:42	1:31	:22
	6-11	2:14	3:53	6:32	1:20	:21

All-time Top Television Programs

Source: A.C. Nielsen estimates, Jan. 26, 1960 through Jan. 31, 1992, excluding unsponsored or joint network telecasts or programs under 30 minutes long. Ranked by percent of average audience.

Program	Date	Network	Households (000)
1. M*A*S*H Special	2/28/83	CBS	50,150
2. Dallas	11/21/80	CBS	41,470
3. Roots Pt. VIII	1/30/77	ABC	36,380
4. Super Bowl XVI	1/24/82	CBS	40,020
5. Super Bowl XVII	1/30/83	NBC	40,480
6. Super Bowl XX	1/26/86	NBC	41,490
7. Gone With The Wind-Pt. 1	11/7/76	NBC	33,960
8. Gone With The Wind-Pt. 2	11/8/76	NBC	33,750
9. Super Bowl XII	1/15/78	CBS	34,410
10. Super Bowl XIII	1/21/79	NBC	35,090
11. Bob Hope Christmas Show	1/15/70	NBC	27,260
12. Super Bowl XVIII	1/22/84	CBS	38,800
12. Super Bowl XIX	1/20/85	ABC	39,390
14. Super Bowl XIV	1/20/80	CBS	35,330
15. ABC Theater (The Day After)	11/20/83	ABC	38,550
16. Roots Pt. VI	1/28/77	ABC	32,680
16. The Fugitive	8/29/67	ABC	25,700
18. Super Bowl XXI	1/25/87	CBS	40,030
19. Roots Pt. V	1/27/77	ABC	32,540
20. Ed Sullivan	2/9/64	CBS	23,240
21. Bob Hope Christmas Special	1/14/71	NBC	27,050
22. Roots Pt. III	1/25/77	ABC	31,900
23. Super Bowl XI	1/9/77	NBC	31,610
23. Super Bowl XV	1/25/81	NBC	34,540
25. Super Bowl VI	1/16/72	CBS	27,450
26. Roots Pt. II	1/24/77	ABC	31,400
27. Beverly Hillbillies	1/8/64	CBS	22,570
28. Roots Pt. IV	1/26/77	ABC	31,190
28. Ed Sullivan	2/16/64	CBS	22,445
30. Super Bowl XXIII	1/22/89	NBC	39,320

Top-Rated TV Shows of the Past

Source: A.C. Nielsen

1950s

Program	Network	Avg. rating over decade
1. A. Godfrey's Talent Scouts	CBS	32.9
2. I Love Lucy	CBS	31.6
3. You Bet Your Life	NBC	30.1
4. Dragnet	NBC	24.6
5. The Jack Benny Show	CBS	22.3
6. A. Godfrey and Friends	CBS	19.5
7. Gunsmoke	CBS	15.6
8. The Red Skelton Show	NBC	15.2
9. December Bride	CBS	13.8
10. I've Got a Secret	CBS	12.9
11. $64,000 Question	CBS	11.2
12. Disneyland	ABC	10.8
13. The Ed Sullivan Show	CBS	10.6
14. Have Gun—Will Travel	CBS	10.3
15. The Danny Thomas Show	CBS	9.9

1960s

Program	Network	Avg. rating over decade
1. Bonanza	NBC	29.6
2. The Red Skelton Show	CBS	26.4
3. The Andy Griffith Show	CBS	22.4
4. The Beverly Hillbillies	CBS	21.9
5. The Ed Sullivan Show	CBS	21.7
6. The Lucy Show/Here's Lucy	CBS	21.3
7. The Jackie Gleason Show	CBS	16.5
8. Bewitched	ABC	14.8
9. Gomer Pyle	CBS	13.4
10. Candid Camera	CBS	11.2
11. The Dick Van Dyke Show	CBS	11.1
12. The Danny Thomas Show	CBS	10.7
13. Family Affair	CBS	9.8
14. Laugh-In	NBC	7.9
15. Rawhide	CBS	7.5

1970s

Program	Network	Avg. rating over decade
1. All in the Family	CBS	23.1
2. M*A*S*H	CBS	17.6
3. Hawaii Five-O	CBS	16.5
4. Happy Days	ABC	15.9
5. The Waltons	CBS	14.0
6. The Mary Tyler Moore Show	CBS	13.7
7. Sanford & Son	NBC	13.4
8. One Day at a Time	CBS	11.4
9. Three's Company	ABC	10.8
10. 60 Minutes	CBS	10.0
11. Maude	CBS	9.8
12. Gunsmoke	CBS	9.7
13. Charlie's Angels	ABC	9.6
14. The Jeffersons	CBS	9.4
15. Laverne & Shirley	ABC	9.3

U.S. Television Sets and Stations Received

Source: A.C. Nielsen

Set Ownership

(est. as of Jan. 1, 1992)

Total TV Households	92,100,000	
(98% of U.S. households own at least one TV set)		
Homes with:		
Color TV sets	90,800,000	98%
B&W only	1,842,000	2%
2 or more sets	59,865,000	65%
One set	32,235,000	35%
Cable (May 1992)	55,500,000	60.3%

Total TV Households:	92,100,000
Total Persons 2+:	237,680,000
Total Women 18+:	94,830,000
Total Men 18+:	86,440,000
Total Teens 12-17:	20,100,000
Total Children 2-11:	36,310,000

Stations Receivable:
(September 1990)
% of TV homes receiving:

1-6	7%
7-10	34%
11-14	34%
15-19	19%
20-29	6%
30+	*

* = Less than 1%

Recordings & Music Videos

Gold & Platinum Awards Certification Levels

(Audio and Video)

Source: Recording Industry Assn. of America, *Inside the Recording Industry: A Statistical Overview*, 1991

	Gold	Platinum	Multi-Platinum
Single	500,000 units; EP counts as two units	1 million units; EP counts as two units	2 million units; EP counts as two units
Album	500,000 units; manufacturers' $ volume at least $1 million based at 33⅓% of list price	1 million units; manufacturers' $ volume at least $2 million based at 33⅓% of list price	2 million units; manufacturers' $ volume at least $4 million based at 33⅓% of list price
Short Form	250,000 units; max. running time of 30 minutes	500,000 units; max. running time of 30 minutes	1 million units; max. running time of 30 minutes
Multi-Box	250,000 units; min. running time of 120 minutes	500,000 units; min. running time of 120 minutes	1 million units; min. running time of 120 minutes
Video Single	25,000 units; max. running time of 15 minutes; two songs per title	50,000 units; max. running time of 15 minutes; two songs per title	100,000 units; max. running time of 15 minutes; two songs per title
Video Long Form	50,000 units	100,000 units	200,000 units
Video Multi-Box	50,000 units	100,000 units	200,000 units

Listed are 1991 Multi-Platinum and Platinum Awards for music released in 1991 and for Music Videos released at any time.

Artists, Recording Titles

Albums, Multi-Platinum

(Number in parentheses—millions sold)

Paula Abdul; Spellbound (2)
Bryan Adams; (Everything I Do) I Do It for You (3)
Michael Bolton; Time, Love & Tenderness (4)
Boyz II Men; CooleyHighHarmony (2)
Garth Brooks; Ropin' the Wind (5)
Mariah Carey; Emotions (2)
Natalie Cole; Unforgettable with Love Natalie Cole (3)
Color Me Badd; I Wanna Sex You Up (2)
Amy Grant; Heart in Motion (2)
Guns 'n Roses; Use Your Illusion II (3)
Metallica; Metallica (3)
R.E.M.; Out of Time (3)
Bonnie Raitt; Luck of the Draw (2)
Van Halen; For Unlawful Carnal Knowledge (2)

Albums, Platinum

Bryan Adams; Waking up the Neighbours
Another Bad Creation; Coolin' at the Playground Ya Know
Color Me Badd; C.M.B.
Harry Connick Jr.; Blue Light, Red Light
Dire Straits; On Every Street
DJ Jazzy Jeff & Fresh Prince; Homebase
EMF; Schubert Dip
Enigma; MCMXC a.D.
Gloria Estefan & Miami Sound; Into the Light
Genesis; We Can't Dance
Ice Cube; Death Certificate
Alan Jackson; Don't Rock the Jukebox
Jesus Jones; Doubt
Reba McEntire; For My Broken Heart
N.W.A.; Efil4Zaggin
Nirvana; Nevermind
Ozzy Osbourne; No More Tears
Tom Petty & the Heartbreakers; Into the Great Wide Open
Prince & the New Power Generation; Diamonds and Pearls
Public Enemy; Apocalypse 91...The Enemy Strikes Back
Roxette; Joyride
Bob Seger; The Fire Inside
Ricky Van Shelton; Backroads
Skid Row; Slave to the Grind
Soundtrack; Beauty & the Beast
Soundtrack; New Jack City
Soundtrack; Robin Hood: Prince of Thieves
Sting; The Soul Cages
Travis Tritt; It's All About to Change
Luther Vandross; Power of Love

Singles, Multi-Platinum

(Number in parentheses—millions sold)

Bryan Adams; (Everything I Do) I Do It for You (3)
Color Me Badd; I Wanna Sex You Up (2)

Singles, Platinum

Boyz II Men: MotownPhilly
C&C Music Fact. Ft. Freedom WL; Gonna Make You Sweat
DJ Jazzy Jeff & Fresh Prince; Summertime
Naughty by Nature; O.P.P.

Music Videos, Multi-Platinum

(Number in parentheses—units sold)

Garth Brooks; Garth Brooks (200,000)
Carreras, Domingo, Pavarotti; In Concert (100,000)
Neil Diamond; Greatest Hits Live (100,000)
M.C. Hammer; Hammer Time (250,000)
M.C. Hammer; Please Hammer Don't Hurt 'Em (200,000)
Janet Jackson; Rhythm Nation Compilation (150,000)
Madonna; The Immaculate Collection (200,000)
Madonna; Four Clips (100,000)
Metallica; 2 of 1 (100,250)
George Michael; Faith (150,000)
Motley Crue; Uncensored (200,000)
New Kids on the Block; The New Kid in the Class (100,000)
New Kids on the Block; Sheik of My Dreams (100,000)
New Kids on the Block; In Step...Out of Time (100,000)
Pink Floyd; Delicate Sound of Thunder (200,000)
Vanilla Ice; Play That Funky Music White Boy (200,000)

Music Video Singles, Multi-Platinum

(Number in parentheses—units sold)

M.C. Hammer; Here Comes the Hammer (100,000)
Whitney Houston; The Star-Spangled Banner (100,000)
Madonna; Justify My Love (400,000)

100 Leading U.S. Advertisers, 1989-1990

Source: *Advertising Age*, Sept. 25, 1991 © Crain Communications Inc. 1991

(in millions)

Rank '90	Rank '89	Advertiser	Ad spending 1990
1	2	Procter & Gamble	$2,284.5
2	1	Philip Morris	2,210.2
3	3	Sears, Roebuck	1,507.1
4	4	General Motors	1,502.8
5	5	Grand Metropolitan	882.6
6	6	PepsiCo	849.1
7	17	AT&T	796.5
8	7	McDonald's	764.1
9	18	Kmart	693.2
10	16	Time Warner	676.9
11	8	Eastman Kodak	664.8
12	20	Johnson & Johnson	653.7
13	9	RJR Nabisco	636.1
14	11	Nestle SA	635.9
15	15	Warner-Lambert	630.8
16	10	Ford Motor	616.0
17	24	Toyota Motor	580.7
18	12	Kellogg	577.7
19	13	Unilever NV	568.9
20	21	General Mills	539.0
21	19	Chrysler	528.4
22	14	Anheuser-Busch	459.2
23	33	Walt Disney	435.7
24	22	Bristol-Myers Squibb	428.7
25	26	American Home Prods.	415.4
26	29	Sony	410.5
27	38	Nissan Motor	410.2
28	25	J.C. Penney	393.8
29	28	Coca-Cola	377.2
30	31	May Dept. Stores	363.6
31	23	Ralston Purina	354.5
32	42	Hershey Foods	338.7
33	37	Matsushita Electric Indus.	330.2
34	30	Quaker Oats	329.3
35	34	Dayton Hudson	$318.7
36	39	Honda Motor	318.0
37	32	H.J. Heinz	307.9
38	27	Sara Lee	306.7
39	36	U.S. Government	304.0
40	46	Pfizer Inc.	279.9
41	40	Federated Dept. Stores	273.7
42	41	Mars	272.4
43	35	R.H. Macy	272.2
44	44	Colgate-Palmolive	265.0
45	56	Mazda Motor	247.9
46	49	ConAgra	246.1
47	47	Tandy	232.7
48	45	General Electric	230.2
49	52	American Brands	227.1
50	43	American Express	217.7
51	51	Montgomery Ward	205.6
52	50	American Stores	204.7
53	53	Adolph Coors	194.6
54	48	Hasbro	191.8
55	57	SmithKline Beecham	191.4
56	73	Loews	186.2
57	58	Gillette	181.7
58	99	Nike	178.8
59	62	Goodyear Tire & Rubber	178.7
60	60	Philips NV	177.7
61	59	U.S. dairy farmers	175.9
62	55	Campbell Soup	175.3
63	61	Clorox	173.4
64	74	Paramount Commun.	162.3
65	88	Levi Strauss	158.9
66	65	S.C. Johnson	158.1
67	72	Carter Hawley Hale Stores	157.4
68	90	United Telecommun.	$155.3
69	81	Circuit City Stores	153.0
70	86	Wal-Mart Stores	151.7
71	54	IBM	148.7
72	76	Hallmark Cards	146.8
73	111	Helene Curtis	145.4
74	68	Revlon	143.6
75	82	AMR	142.5
76	63	Dow Chemical	141.9
77	67	Mobil	140.3
78	93	Mariott	139.6
79	80	Volkswagen AG	138.5
80	64	CPC International	137.0
81	77	Seagram	135.3
82	75	Hyundai	135.3
83	84	ITT	134.9
84	79	Bell Atlantic	134.2
85	125	Thompson Med./ Slim-Fast	133.4
86	92	Kroger	131.1
87	87	Wm. Wrigley Jr.	129.1
88	83	News	126.7
89	94	Delta Air Lines	126.5
90	71	Citicorp	124.9
91	70	Schering-Plough	124.9
92	95	Daimler-Benz AG	124.6
93	85	UAL	123.5
94	91	Nynex	121.5
95	105	U.S. Shoe	120.7
96	89	Wendy's Intl.	119.8
97	104	Canon	119.5
98	96	Bayer AG	115.3
99	123	Upjohn	114.9
100	101	Monsanto	114.6

Total U.S. Ad Spending by Category and Medium, 1990

Source: *Advertising Age*, Sept. 25, 1991 © Crain Communications Inc. 1991

(in millions)

Category	Total ad spending	Magazine	Sunday magazines	Newspaper	Network TV	Spot TV	Syndicated TV	Cable TV	Network radio
Retail	$6,494.2	$249.1	$119.7	$3,823.1	$356.0	$1,499.1	$20.6	$38.7	$101.5
Automotive	5,700.7	901.2	25.5	809.2	1,790.0	1,664.8	115.7	114.1	106.7
Business, consumer svcs.	3,958.5	519.1	45.0	1,320.1	698.6	861.7	56.8	100.9	114.0
Food	3,874.0	449.3	34.7	45.4	1,663.5	1,025.2	351.7	124.7	75.1
Entertainment	3,063.6	44.4	3.0	611.3	875.1	1,170.8	147.2	62.3	14.8
Toiletries & cosmetics	2,333.3	675.6	27.3	5.4	1,034.3	279.5	188.7	87.7	17.0
Travel, hotels	2,215.9	374.5	37.9	1,048.6	203.7	324.7	10.2	37.4	42.2
Drugs & remedies	1,690.7	160.4	17.5	118.1	787.2	320.0	133.9	60.5	53.4
Snacks & soft drinks	1,231.0	64.5	3.5	22.4	452.1	382.8	168.4	52.8	29.4
Direct response cos.	1,210.5	526.4	253.5	103.2	34.5	110.5	28.5	81.9	59.5
Apparel, footwear	912.1	426.5	29.4	13.1	230.5	100.7	52.9	38.9	4.0
Insurance & real estate	896.2	131.0	16.1	307.1	204.1	129.3	8.9	16.6	31.3
Beer & wine	751.5	45.5	3.5	10.3	302.1	210.4	45.2	37.0	5.0
Publishing & media	739.8	215.5	7.9	233.0	29.4	130.2	5.8	23.6	17.8
Household equip.	661.7	117.9	13.8	25.8	260.4	146.7	40.6	27.9	18.1
Sporting goods, toys	635.3	126.7	1.2	6.8	140.4	233.4	82.8	40.2	0.6
Soaps & cleansers	632.9	61.0	0.8	2.9	305.6	155.4	67.7	30.6	0.1
Computers, office equip.	604.1	285.4	5.0	71.1	152.2	28.7	7.0	19.5	20.3
Cigarettes, tobacco	585.2	311.3	52.2	30.3	0.0	4.4	0.5	0.4	3.2
Jewelry, cameras	367.4	156.3	9.9	8.0	117.8	40.7	14.9	10.8	3.5
Gasoline & lubricants	343.6	39.8	1.6	24.2	39.0	169.6	1.6	8.5	1.6
Building materials	341.4	91.1	7.4	52.3	80.6	67.8	2.4	23.0	8.0
Electronic entertainment	339.6	89.9	4.4	13.6	82.4	74.5	14.4	35.1	18.8
Liquor	290.8	232.2	10.3	8.4	0.0	1.3	0.0	0.0	0.0
Household furnishings	280.9	113.8	16.3	49.7	52.1	38.6	2.3	3.6	2.5
Pets, pet foods	213.6	28.8	3.1	7.6	104.1	38.9	15.4	10.6	2.6
Horticulture & farming	206.5	22.1	5.2	48.6	36.8	53.4	2.8	13.1	11.0
Freight	133.1	37.1	0.2	10.5	51.4	23.6	0.1	3.7	0.4
Industrial materials	129.5	64.9	1.1	9.5	44.1	2.2	0.1	4.4	1.1
Business propositions	39.1	26.4	1.4	2.5	2.3	2.8	0.0	0.4	0.4
Airplanes, aviation	23.0	19.3	0.1	2.4	0.2	0.4	0.0	0.1	0.3
Miscellaneous	238.3	130.6	18.6	57.3	1.5	1.2	0.3	1.1	2.3
Total	**$41,138.5**	**$6,737.7**	**$777.1**	**$8,901.9**	**$10,132.3**	**$9,293.3**	**$1,587.6**	**$1,110.2**	**$766.4**

AWARDS — MEDALS — PRIZES

The Alfred B. Nobel Prize Winners

Alfred B. Nobel, inventor of dynamite, bequeathed $9,000,000, the interest to be distributed yearly to those who had most benefited mankind in physics, chemistry, medicine-physiology, literature, and peace. The first Nobel Memorial Prize in Economics was awarded in 1969. No awards given for years omitted. In 1991, each prize was worth approximately $985,000 to $1 million. (For 1992, see *Addenda.)*

Physics

1991 Pierre-Giles de Gennes, French
1990 Richard E. Taylor, Can.; Jerome I. Friedman, Henry W. Kendall, both U.S.
1989 Norman F. Ramsey, U.S.; Hans G. Dehmelt, German-U.S. & Wolfgang Paul, German
1988 Leon M. Lederman, Melvin Schwartz, Jack Steinberger, all U.S.
1987 K. Alex Muller, Swiss; J. Georg Bednorz, W. German
1986 Ernest Ruska, German, Gerd Binnig, W. German, Heinrich Rohrer, Swiss
1985 Klaus von Klitzing, W. German
1984 Carlo Rubbia, Italian, Simon van der Meere, Dutch
1983 Subrahmanyan Chandrasekhar, William A. Fowler, both U.S.
1982 Kenneth G. Wilson, U.S.
1981 Nicolass Bloembergen, Arthur Schaalow, both U.S.; Kai M. Siegbahn, Swedish
1980 James W. Cronin, Val L. Fitch, U.S.
1979 Steven Weinberg, Sheldon L. Glashow, both U.S.; Abdus Salam, Pakistani
1978 Pyotr Kapitsa, USSR; Arno Penzias, Robert Wilson, both U.S.
1977 John H. Van Vleck, Philip W. Anderson, both U.S.; Nevill F. Mott, British
1976 Burton Richter, U.S.
Samuel C.C. Ting, U.S.
1975 James Rainwater, U.S.
Ben Mottelson, U.S.-Danish,
Aage Bohr, Danish
1974 Martin Ryle, British
Antony Hewish, British
1973 Ivar Giaever, U.S.
Leo Esaki, Japan
Brian D. Josephson, British
1972 John Bardeen, U.S.
Leon N. Cooper, U.S.
John R. Schrieffer, U.S.
1971 Dennis Gabor, British
1970 Louis Neel, French
Hannes Alfven, Swedish
1969 Murray Gell-Mann, U.S.
1968 Luis W. Alvarez, U.S.
1967 Hans A. Bethe, U.S.
1966 Alfred Kastler, French
1965 Richard P. Feynman, U.S.
Julian S. Schwinger, U.S.
Shinichiro Tomonaga, Japanese
1964 Nikolai G. Basov, USSR
Aleksander M. Prochorov, USSR
Charles H. Townes, U.S.
1963 Maria Goeppert-Mayer, U.S.
J. Hans D. Jensen, German
Eugene P. Wigner, U.S.
1962 Lev. D. Landau, USSR
1961 Robert Hofstadter, U.S.
Rudolf L. Mossbauer, German
1960 Donald A. Glaser, U.S.
1959 Owen Chamberlain, U.S.
Emilio G. Segre, U.S.
1958 Pavel Cherenkov, Ilya Frank, Igor Y. Tamm, all USSR
1957 Tsung-dao Lee,
Chen Ning Yang, both U.S.
1956 John Bardeen, U.S.
Walter H. Brattain, U.S.
William Shockley, U.S.
1955 Polykarp Kusch, U.S.
Willis E. Lamb, U.S.
1954 Max Born, British
Walter Bothe, German
1953 Frits Zernike, Dutch
1952 Felix Bloch, U.S.
Edward M. Purcell, U.S.
1951 Sir John D. Cockroft, British
Ernest T. S. Walton, Irish
1950 Cecil F. Powell, British
1949 Hideki Yukawa, Japanese
1948 Patrick M. S. Blackett, British
1947 Sir Edward V. Appleton, British
1946 Percy Williams Bridgman, U.S.
1945 Wolfgang Pauli, U.S.
1944 Isidor Isaac Rabi, U.S.
1943 Otto Stern, U.S.
1939 Ernest O. Lawrence, U.S.
1938 Enrico Fermi, U.S.
1937 Clinton J. Davisson, U.S.
Sir George P. Thomson, British
1936 Carl D. Anderson, U.S.
Victor F. Hess, Austrian
1935 Sir James Chadwick, British
1933 Paul A. M. Dirac, British
Erwin Schrodinger, Austrian
1932 Werner Heisenberg, German
1930 Sir Chandrasekhara V. Raman, Indian
1929 Prince Louis-Victor de Broglie, French
1928 Owen W. Richardson, British
1927 Arthur H. Compton, U.S.
Charles T. R. Wilson, British
1926 Jean B. Perrin, French
1925 James Franck,
Gustav Hertz, both German
1924 Karl M. G. Siegbahn, Swedish
1923 Robert A. Millikan, U.S.
1922 Niels Bohr, Danish
1921 Albert Einstein, Ger.-U.S.
1920 Charles E. Guillaume, French
1919 Johannes Stark, German
1918 Max K. E. L. Planck, German
1917 Charles G. Barkla, British
1915 Sir William H. Bragg, British
Sir William L. Bragg, British
1914 Max von Laue, German
1913 Heike Kamerlingh-Onnes, Dutch
1912 Nils G. Dalen, Swedish
1911 Wilhelm Wien, German
1910 Johannes D. van der Waals, Dutch
1909 Carl F. Braun, German
Guglielmo Marconi, Italian
1908 Gabriel Lippmann, French
1907 Albert A. Michelson, U.S.
1906 Sir Joseph J. Thomson, British
1905 Philipp E. A. von Lenard, Ger.
1904 John W. Strutt, Lord Rayleigh, British
1903 Antoine Henri Becquerel, French
Marie Curie, Polish-French
Pierre Curie, French
1902 Hendrik A. Lorentz,
Pieter Zeeman, both Dutch
1901 Wilhelm C. Roentgen, German

Chemistry

1991 Richard R. Ernst, Swiss
1990 Elias James Corey, U.S.
1989 Thomas R. Cech, Sidney Altman, both U.S.
1988 Johann Deisenhofer, Robert Huber, Hartmut Michel, all W. German
1987 Donald J. Cram, Charles J. Pederson, both U.S.; Jean-Marie Lehn, French
1986 Dudley Herschbach, Yuan T. Lee, both U.S.; John C. Polanyi, Canadian
1985 Herbert A. Hauptman, Jerome Karle, both U.S.
1984 Bruce Merrifield, U.S.
1983 Henry Taube, Canadian
1982 Aaron Klug, S. African
1981 Kenichi Fukui, Japan.,
Roald Hoffmann, U.S.
1980 Paul Berg., U.S.;
Walter Gilbert, U.S.,
Frederick Sanger, U.K.
1979 Herbert C. Brown, U.S.
George Wittig, German
1978 Peter Mitchell, British
1977 Ilya Prigogine, Belgian
1976 William N. Lipscomb, U.S.
1975 John Cornforth, Austral.-Brit.,
Vladimir Prelog, Yugo.-Switz.
1974 Paul J. Flory, U.S.
1973 Ernst Otto Fischer, W. German
Geoffrey Wilkinson, British
1972 Christian B. Anfinsen, U.S.
Stanford Moore, U.S.
William H. Stein, U.S.
1971 Gerhard Herzberg, Canadian
1970 Luis F. Leloir, Arg.
1969 Derek H. R. Barton, British
Odd Hassel, Norwegian
1968 Lars Onsager, U.S.
1967 Manfred Eigen, German
Ronald G. W. Norrish, British
George Porter, British
1966 Robert S. Mulliken, U.S.
1965 Robert B. Woodward, U.S.
1964 Dorothy C. Hodgkin, British
1963 Giulio Natta, Italian
Karl Ziegler, German
1962 John C. Kendrew, British
Max F. Perutz, British
1961 Melvin Calvin, U.S.
1960 Willard F. Libby, U.S.
1959 Jaroslav Heyrovsky, Czech
1958 Frederick Sanger, British
1957 Sir Alexander R. Todd, British
1956 Sir Cyril N. Hinshelwood, British
Nikolai N. Semenov, USSR
1955 Vincent du Vigneaud, U.S.
1954 Linus C. Pauling, U.S.
1953 Hermann Staudinger, German
1952 Archer J. P. Martin, British
Richard L. M. Synge, British
1951 Edwin M. McMillan, U.S.
Glenn T. Seaborg, U.S.
1950 Kurt Alder, German
Otto P. H. Diels, German
1949 William F. Giauque, U.S.
1948 Arne W. K. Tiselius, Swedish
1947 Sir Robert Robinson, British
1946 James B. Sumner, John H. Northrop, Wendell M. Stanley, U.S.
1945 Artturi I. Virtanen, Finnish
1944 Otto Hahn, German
1943 Georg de Hevesy, Hungarian
1939 Adolf F. J. Butenandt, German

Leopold Ruzicka, Swiss
1938 Richard Kuhn, German
1937 Walter N. Haworth, British
Paul Karrer, Swiss
1936 Peter J. W. Debye, Dutch
1935 Frederic Joliot-Curie, French
Irene Joliot-Curie, French
1934 Harold C. Urey, U.S.
1932 Irving Langmuir, U.S.
1931 Friedrich Bergius, German
Karl Bosch, German
1930 Hans Fischer, German
1929 Sir Arthur Harden, British
Hans von Euler-Chelpin, Swed.
1928 Adolf O. R. Windaus, German
1927 Heinrich O. Wieland, German
1926 Theodor Svedberg, Swedish
1925 Richard A. Zsigmondy, German
1923 Fritz Pregl, Austrian
1922 Francis W. Aston, British
1921 Frederick Soddy, British
1920 Walther H. Nernst, German
1918 Fritz Haber, German
1915 Richard M. Willstatter, German
1914 Theodore W. Richards, U.S.
1913 Alfred Werner, Swiss
1912 Victor Grignard, French
Paul Sabatier, French
1911 Marie Curie, Polish-French
1910 Otto Wallach, German
1909 Wilhelm Ostwald, German
1908 Ernest Rutherford, British
1907 Eduard Buchner, German
1906 Henri Moissan, French
1905 Adolf von Baeyer, German
1904 Sir William Ramsay, British
1903 Svante A. Arrhenius, Swedish
1902 Emil Fischer, German
1901 Jacobus H. van't Hoff, Dutch

Physiology or Medicine

1991 Edwin Neher, Bert Sakmann, both German
1990 Joseph E. Murray, E. Donnall Thomas, both U.S.
1989 J. Michael Bishop, Harold E. Varmus, both U.S.
1988 Gertrude B. Elion, George H. Hitchings, both U.S; Sir James Black, Brit.
1987 Susumu Tonegawa, Japanese
1986 Rita Levi-Montalcini, It.-U.S., Stanley Cohen, U.S.
1985 Michael S. Brown, Joseph L. Goldstein, both U.S.
1984 Cesar Milstein, Brit.-Argentina; Georges J. F. Koehler, German; Niels K. Jerne, Brit.-Danish
1983 Barbara McClintock, U.S.
1982 Sune Bergstrom, Bengt Samuelsson, both Swedish; John R. Vane, British.
1981 Roger W. Sperry, David H. Hubel, Tosten N. Wiesel, all U.S.
1980 Baruj Benacerraf, George Snell, both U.S.; Jean Dausset, France
1979 Allan M. Cormack, U.S.
Geoffrey N. Hounsfield, British
1978 Daniel Nathans, Hamilton O. Smith, both U.S.; Werner Arber, Swiss
1977 Rosalyn S. Yalow, Roger C.L. Guillemin, Andrew V. Schally, U.S.
1976 Baruch S. Blumberg, U.S.
Daniel Carleton Gajdusek, U.S.
1975 David Baltimore, Howard Temin, both U.S.; Renato Dulbecco, Ital.-U.S.
1974 Albert Claude, Lux.-U.S.; George Emil Palade, Rom.-U.S.; Christian Rene de Duve, Belg.
1973 Karl von Frisch, Ger.; Konrad Lorenz, Ger.-Austrian; Nikolaas Tinbergen, Brit.
1972 Gerald M. Edelman, U.S.
Rodney R. Porter, British
1971 Earl W. Sutherland Jr., U.S.
1970 Julius Axelrod, U.S.
Sir Bernard Katz, British
Ulf von Euler, Swedish
1969 Max Delbruck, Alfred D. Hershey, Salvador Luria, all U.S.
1968 Robert W. Holley, H. Gobind Khorana, Marshall W. Nirenberg, all U.S.
1967 Ragnar Granit, Swedish
Haldan Keffer Hartline, U.S.
George Wald, U.S.
1966 Charles B. Huggins, Francis Peyton Rous, both U.S.
1965 Francois Jacob, Andre Lwoff, Jacques Monod, all French
1964 Konrad E. Bloch, U.S.
Feodor Lynen, German
1963 Sir John C. Eccles, Australian
Alan L. Hodgkin, British
Andrew F. Huxley, British
1962 Francis H. C. Crick, British
James D. Watson, U.S.
Maurice H. F. Wilkins, British
1961 Georg von Bekesy, U.S.
1960 Sir F. MacFarlane Burnet, Australian
Peter B. Medawar, British
1959 Arthur Kornberg, U.S.
Severo Ochoa, U.S.
1958 George W. Beadle, U.S.
Edward L. Tatum, U.S.
Joshua Lederberg, U.S.
1957 Daniel Bovet, Italian
1956 Andre F. Cournand, U.S.
Werner Forssmann, German
Dickinson W. Richards, Jr., U.S.
1955 Alex H. T. Theorell, Swedish
1954 John F. Enders, Frederick C. Robbins, Thomas H. Weller, all U.S.
1953 Hans A. Krebs, British
Fritz A. Lipmann, U.S.
1952 Selman A. Waksman, U.S.
1951 Max Theiler, U.S.
1950 Philip S. Hench, Edward C. Kendall, both U.S.
Tadeus Reichstein, Swiss
1949 Walter R. Hess, Swiss
Antonio Moniz, Portuguese
1948 Paul H. Müller, Swiss
1947 Carl F. Cori, Gerty T. Cori, both U.S.
Bernardo A. Houssay, Arg.
1946 Hermann J. Muller, U.S.
1945 Ernst B. Chain, British
Sir Alexander Fleming, British
Sir Howard W. Florey, British
1944 Joseph Erlanger, U.S.
Herbert S. Gasser, U.S.
1943 Henrik C. P. Dam, Danish
Edward A. Doisy, U.S.
1939 Gerhard Domagk, German
1938 Corneille J. F. Heymans, Belg.
1937 Albert Szent-Gyorgyi, Hung.-U.S.
1936 Sir Henry H. Dale, British
Otto Loewi, U.S.
1935 Hans Spemann, German
1934 George R. Minot, Wm. P. Murphy, G. H. Whipple, all U.S.
1933 Thomas H. Morgan, U.S.
1932 Edgar D. Adrian, British
Sir Charles S. Sherrington, Brit.
1931 Otto H. Warburg, German
1930 Karl Landsteiner, U.S.
1929 Christiaan Eijkman, Dutch
Sir Frederick G. Hopkins, British
1928 Charles J. H. Nicolle, French
1927 Julius Wagner-Jauregg, Aus.
1926 Johannes A. G. Fibiger, Danish
1924 Willem Einthoven, Dutch
1923 Frederick G. Banting, Canadian
John J. R. Macleod, Scottish
1922 Archibald V. Hill, British
Otto F. Meyerhof, German
1920 Schack A. S. Krogh, Danish
1919 Jules Bordet, Belgian
1914 Robert Barany, Austrian
1913 Charles R. Richet, French
1912 Alexis Carrel, French
1911 Allvar Gullstrand, Swedish
1910 Albrecht Kossel, German
1909 Emil T. Kocher, Swiss
1908 Paul Ehrlich, German
Elie Metchnikoff, French
1907 Charles L. A. Laveran, French
1906 Camillo Golgi, Italian
Santiago Ramon y Cajal, Sp.
1905 Robert Koch, German
1904 Ivan P. Pavlov, Russian
1903 Niels R. Finsen, Danish
1902 Sir Ronald Ross, British
1901 Emil A. von Behring, German

Literature

1991 Nadine Gordimer, South African
1990 Octavio Paz, Mexican
1989 Camilo José Cela, Spanish
1988 Naguib Mahfouz, Egyptian
1987 Joseph Brodsky, USSR-U.S.
1986 Wole Soyinka, Nigerian
1985 Claude Simon, French
1984 Jaroslav Siefert, Czech.
1983 William Golding, British
1982 Gabriel Garcia Marquez, Colombian-Mex.
1981 Elias Canetti, Bulgarian-British
1980 Czeslaw Milosz, Polish-U.S.
1979 Odysseus Elytis, Greek
1978 Isaac Bashevis Singer, U.S. (Yiddish)
1977 Vicente Aleixandre, Spanish
1976 Saul Bellow, U.S.
1975 Eugenio Montale, Ital.
1974 Eyvind Johnson, Harry Edmund Martinson, both Swedish
1973 Patrick White, Australian
1972 Heinrich Boll, W. German
1971 Pablo Neruda, Chilean
1970 Aleksandr I. Solzhenitsyn, Russ.
1969 Samuel Beckett, Irish
1968 Yasunari Kawabata, Japanese
1967 Miguel Angel Asturias, Guate.
1966 Samuel Joseph Agnon, Israeli
Nelly Sachs, Swedish
1965 Mikhail Sholokhov, Russian
1964 Jean Paul Sartre, French (Prize declined)
1963 Giorgos Seferis, Greek
1962 John Steinbeck, U.S.
1961 Ivo Andric, Yugoslavian
1960 Saint-John Perse, French
1959 Salvatore Quasimodo, Italian
1958 Boris L. Pasternak, Russian (Prize declined)
1957 Albert Camus, French
1956 Juan Ramon Jimenez, Span.
1955 Halldor K. Laxness, Icelandic
1954 Ernest Hemingway, U.S.
1953 Sir Winston Churchill, British
1952 Francois Mauriac, French
1951 Par F. Lagerkvist, Swedish
1950 Bertrand Russell, British
1949 William Faulkner, U.S.
1948 T.S. Eliot, British
1947 Andre Gide, French
1946 Hermann Hesse, Swiss
1945 Gabriela Mistral, Chilean
1944 Johannes V. Jensen, Danish
1939 Frans E. Sillanpaa, Finnish
1938 Pearl S. Buck, U.S.
1937 Roger Martin du Gard, French
1936 Eugene O'Neill, U.S.
1934 Luigi Pirandello, Italian
1933 Ivan A. Bunin, French
1932 John Galsworthy, British
1931 Erik A. Karlfeldt, Swedish

1930 Sinclair Lewis, U.S.
1929 Thomas Mann, German
1928 Sigrid Undset, Norwegian
1927 Henri Bergson, French
1926 Grazia Deledda, Italian
1925 George Bernard Shaw, British
1924 Wladyslaw S. Reymont, Polish
1923 William Butler Yeats, Irish
1922 Jacinto Benavente, Spanish
1921 Anatole France, French
1920 Knut Hamsun, Norwegian
1919 Carl F. G. Spitteler, Swiss
1917 Karl A. Gjellerup, Danish
Henrik Pontoppidan, Danish
1916 Verner von Heidenstam, Swed.
1915 Romain Rolland, French
1913 Rabindranath Tagore, Indian
1912 Gerhart Hauptmann, German
1911 Maurice Maeterlinck, Belgian
1910 Paul J. L. Heyse, German
1909 Selma Lagerlof, Swedish
1908 Rudolf C. Eucken, German
1907 Rudyard Kipling, British
1906 Giosue Carducci, Italian
1905 Henryk Sienkiewicz, Polish
1904 Frederic Mistral, French
Jose Echegaray, Spanish
1903 Bjornsterne Bjornson, Norw.
1902 Theodor Mommsen, German
1901 Rene F. A Sully Prudhomme, French

Nobel Memorial Prize in Economics

1991 Ronald H. Coase, Br.-U.S.
1990 Harry M. Markowitz, William F. Sharpe, Merton H. Miller, all U.S.
1989 Trygve Haavelmo, Norwegian
1988 Maurice Allais, French
1987 Robert M. Solow, U.S.
1986 James M. Buchanan, U.S.
1985 Franco Modigliani, It.-U.S.
1984 Richard Stone, British
1983 Gerard Debreu, Fr.-U.S.
1982 George J. Stigler, U.S.
1981 James Tobin, U.S.
1980 Lawrence R. Klein, U.S.
1979 Theodore W. Schultz, U.S., Sir Arthur Lewis, British
1978 Herbert A. Simon, U.S.
1977 Bertil Ohlin, Swedish
James E. Meade, British
1976 Milton Friedman, U.S.
1975 Tjalling Koopmans, Dutch-U.S., Leonid Kantorovich, USSR
1974 Gunnar Myrdal, Swed., Friedrich A. von Hayek, Austrian
1973 Wassily Leontief, U.S.
1972 Kenneth J. Arrow, U.S.
John R. Hicks, British
1971 Simon Kuznets, U.S.
1970 Paul A. Samuelson, U.S.
1969 Ragnar Frisch, Norwegian
Jan Tinbergen, Dutch

Peace

1991 Daw Aung San Suu Kyi, Myanmarese
1990 Mikhail S. Gorbachev, USSR
1989 Dalai Lama, Tibet
1988 United Nations Peacekeeping Forces
1987 Oscar Arias Sanchez, Costa Rican
1986 Elie Wiesel, Romania-U.S.
1985 Intl. Physicians for the Prevention of Nuclear War, U.S.
1984 Bishop Desmond Tutu, So. African
1983 Lech Walesa, Polish
1982 Alva Myrdal, Swedish; Alfonso Garcia Robles, Mexican
1981 Office of U.N. High Commissioner for Refugees
1980 Adolfo Perez Esquivel, Argentine
1979 Mother Teresa of Calcutta, Albanian-Indian
1978 Anwar Sadat, Egyptian
Menachem Begin, Israeli
1977 Amnesty International
1976 Mairead Corrigan, Betty Williams, N. Irish
1975 Andrei Sakharov, USSR
1974 Eisaku Sato, Japanese, Sean MacBride, Irish
1973 Henry Kissinger, U.S.
Le Duc Tho, N. Vietnamese (Tho declined)
1971 Willy Brandt, W. German
1970 Norman E. Borlaug, U.S.
1969 Intl. Labor Organization
1968 Rene Cassin, French
1965 U.N. Children's Fund (UNICEF)
1964 Martin Luther King Jr., U.S.
1963 International Red Cross, League of Red Cross Societies
1962 Linus C. Pauling, U.S.
1961 Dag Hammarskjold, Swedish
1960 Albert J. Luthuli, South African
1959 Philip J. Noel-Baker, British
1958 Georges Pire, Belgian
1957 Lester B. Pearson, Canadian
1954 Office of the UN High Commissioner for Refugees
1953 George C. Marshall, U.S.
1952 Albert Schweitzer, French
1951 Leon Jouhaux, French
1950 Ralph J. Bunche, U.S.
1949 Lord John Boyd Orr of Brechin Mearns, British
1947 Friends Service Council, Brit.
Amer. Friends Service Com.
1946 Emily G. Balch, John R. Mott, both U.S.
1945 Cordell Hull, U.S.
1944 International Red Cross
1938 Nansen International Office for Refugees
1937 Viscount Cecil of Chelwood, Brit.
1936 Carlos de Saavedra Lamas, Arg.
1935 Carl von Ossietzky, German
1934 Arthur Henderson, British
1933 Sir Norman Angell, British
1931 Jane Addams, U.S.
Nicholas Murray Butler, U.S.
1930 Nathan Soderblom, Swedish
1929 Frank B. Kellogg, U.S.
1927 Ferdinand E. Buisson, French
Ludwig Quidde, German
1926 Aristide Briand, French
Gustav Stresemann, German
1925 Sir J. Austen Chamberlain, Brit.
Charles G. Dawes, U.S.
1922 Fridtjof Nansen, Norwegian
1921 Karl H. Branting, Swedish
Christian L. Lange, Norwegian
1920 Leon V.A. Bourgeois, French
1919 Woodrow Wilson, U.S.
1917 International Red Cross
1913 Henri La Fontaine, Belgian
1912 Elihu Root, U.S.
1911 Tobias M.C. Asser, Dutch
Alfred H. Fried, Austrian
1910 Permanent Intl. Peace Bureau
1909 Auguste M. F. Beernaert, Belg.
Paul H. B. B. d'Estournelles de Constant, French
1908 Klas P. Arnoldson, Swedish
Fredrik Bajer, Danish
1907 Ernesto T. Moneta, Italian
Louis Renault, French
1906 Theodore Roosevelt, U.S.
1905 Baroness Bertha von Suttner, Austrian
1904 Institute of International Law
1903 Sir William R. Cremer, British
1902 Elie Ducommun, Charles A. Gobat, both Swiss
1901 Jean H. Dunant, Swiss
Frederic Passy, French

Pulitzer Prizes in Journalism, Letters, and Music

The Pulitzer Prizes were endowed by Joseph Pulitzer (1847-1911), publisher of The World, New York, N.Y., in a bequest to Columbia University, and are awarded annually by the president of the university on recommendation of the Pulitzer Prize Board for work done during the preceding year. The administrator is Robert C. Christopher of Columbia Univ. All prizes are $3,000 (originally $500) in each category, except Meritorious Public Service for which a gold medal is given.

Journalism

Meritorious Public Service

For distinguished and meritorious public service by a United States newspaper.

1918—New York Times. Also special award to Minna Lewinson and Henry Beetle Hough.
1919—Milwaukee Journal.
1921—Boston Post.
1922—New York World.
1923—Memphis (Tenn.) Commercial Appeal.
1924—New York World.
1926—Enquirer-Sun, Columbus, Ga.
1927—Canton (Oh.) Daily News.
1928—Indianapolis Times.
1929—Evening World, New York.
1931—Atlanta (Ga.) Constitution.
1932—Indianapolis (Ind.) News.
1933—New York World-Telegram.
1934—Medford (Ore.) Mail-Tribune.
1935—Sacramento (Cal.) Bee.
1936—Cedar Rapids (Ia.) Gazette.
1937—St.Louis Post-Dispatch.
1938—Bismarck (N.D.) Tribune.
1939—Miami (Fla.) Daily News.
1940—Waterbury (Conn.) Republican and American.
1941—St.Louis Post-Dispatch.
1942—Los Angeles Times.
1943—Omaha World Herald.
1944—New York Times.
1945—Detroit Free Press.
1946—Scranton (Pa.) Times.
1947—Baltimore Sun.
1948—St. Louis Post-Dispatch.
1949—Nebraska State Journal.

1950—Chicago Daily News; St. Louis Post-Dispatch.
1951—Miami (Fla.) Herald and Brooklyn Eagle.
1952—St. Louis Post-Dispatch.
1953—Whiteville (N.C.) News Reporter; Tabor City (N.C.) Tribune.
1954—Newsday (Long Island, N.Y.)
1955—Columbus (Ga.) Ledger and Sunday Ledger-Enquirer.
1956—Watsonville (Cal.) Register-Pajaronian.
1957—Chicago Daily News.
1958—Arkansas Gazette, Little Rock.
1959—Utica (N.Y.) Observer-Dispatch and Utica Daily Press.
1960—Los Angeles Times.
1961—Amarillo (Tex.) Globe-Times.
1962—Panama City (Fla.) News-Herald.
1963—Chicago Daily News.
1964—St.Petersburg (Fla.) Times.
1965—Hutchinson (Kan.) News.
1966—Boston Globe.
1967—The Louisville Courier-Journal; The Milwaukee Journal.
1968—Riverside (Cal.) Press-Enterprise.
1969—Los Angeles Times.
1970—Newsday (Long Island, N.Y.).
1971—Winston Salem (N.C.) Journal & Sentinel.
1972—New York Times.
1973—Washington Post.
1974—Newsday (Long Island, N.Y.).
1975—Boston Globe.
1976—Anchorage Daily News.
1977—Lufkin (Tex.) News.
1978—Philadelphia Inquirer.
1979—Point Reyes (Cal.) Light.
1980—Gannett News Service.
1981—Charlotte (N.C.) Observer.
1982—Detroit News.
1983—Jackson (Miss.) Clarion-Ledger.
1984—Los Angeles Times.
1985—Ft. Worth (Tex.) Star-Telegram.
1986—Denver Post.
1987—Pittsburgh Press.
1988—Charlotte Observer.
1989—Anchorage Daily News.
1990—Philadelphia Inquirer, Gilbert M. Gaul; Washington (N.C.) Daily News.
1991—Des Moines Register, Jane Schorer.
1992—Sacramento Bee, Tom Knudson.

Reporting

This category originally embraced all fields, local, national, and international. Later separate categories were created for the different fields of reporting.

1917—Herbert Bayard Swope, New York World.
1918—Harold A. Littledale, New York Evening Post.
1920—John J. Leary, Jr., New York World.
1921—Louis Seibold, New York World.
1922—Kirke L. Simpson, Associated Press.
1923—Alva Johnston, New York Times.
1924—Magner White, San Diego Sun.
1925—James W. Mulroy and Alvin H. Goldstein, Chicago Daily News.
1926—William Burke Miller, Louisville Courier-Journal.
1927—John T. Rogers, St. Louis Post-Dispatch.
1929—Paul Y. Anderson, St. Louis Post-Dispatch.
1930—Russell D. Owens, New York Times. Also $500 to W.O. Dapping, Auburn (N.Y.) Citizen.
1931—A.B. MacDonald, Kansas City (Mo.) Star.
1932—W.C. Richards, D.D. Martin, J.S. Pooler, F.D. Webb, J.N.W. Sloan, Detroit Free Press.
1933—Francis A. Jamieson, Associated Press.
1934—Royce Brier, San Francisco Chronicle.
1935—William H.Taylor, New York Herald Tribune.
1936—Lauren D.Lyman, New York Times.
1937—John J. O'Neill, N.Y.Herald Tribune; William L. Laurence, N.Y Times; Howard W. Blakeslee, A.P.; Gobind Behari Lal, Universal Service; and David Dietz, Scripps-Howard Newspapers.
1938—Raymond Sprigle, Pittsburgh Post-Gazette.
1939—Thomas L. Stokes, Scripps-Howard Newspaper Alliance.
1940—S.Burton Heath, New York World-Telegram.
1941—Westbrook Pegler, New York World-Telegram.
1942—Stanton Delaplane, San Francisco Chronicle.
1943—George Weller, Chicago Daily News.
1944—Paul Schoenstein, New York Journal-American.
1945—Jack S. McDowell, San Francisco Call-Bulletin.
1946—William L. Laurence, New York Times.
1947—Frederick Woltman, New York World-Telegram.
1948—George E. Goodwin, Atlanta Journal.
1949—Malcolm Johnson, New York Sun.
1950—Meyer Berger, New York Times.
1951—Edward S. Montgomery, San Francisco Examiner.
1952—Geo. de Carvalho, San Francisco Chronicle.

(1) General or Spot; (2) Special or Investigative

1953—(1) Providence (R.I.) Journal and Evening Bulletin; (2) Edward J. Mowery, New York World-Telegram & Sun.
1954—(1) Vicksburg (Miss.) Sunday Post-Herald; (2) Alvin Scott McCoy, Kansas City (Mo.) Star.
1955—(1) Mrs. Caro Brown, Alice (Tex.) Daily Echo; (2) Roland K. Towery, Cuero (Tex.) Record.
1956—(1) Lee Hills, Detroit Free Press; (2) Arthur Daley, New York Times.
1957—(1) Salt Lake Tribune, Salt Lake City, Ut.; (2) Wallace Turner and William Lambert, Portland Oregonian.
1958—(1) Fargo, (N.D.) Forum; (2) George Beveridge, Evening Star, Washington, D.C.
1959—(1) Mary Lou Werner, Washington Evening Star; (2) John Harold Brislin, Scranton (Pa.) Tribune, and The Scrantonian.
1960—(1) Jack Nelson, Atlanta Constitution; (2) Miriam Ottenberg, Washington Evening Star.
1961—(1) Sanche de Gramont, New York Herald Tribune; (2) Edgar May, Buffalo Evening News.
1962—(1) Robert D.Mullins, Deseret News, Salt Lake City; (2) George Bliss, Chicago Tribune.
1963—(1) Shared by Sylvan Fox, William Longgood, and Anthony Shannon, New York World-Telegram & Sun; (2) Oscar Griffin, Jr., Pecos (Tex.) Independent and Enterprise.
1964—(1) Norman C.Miller, Wall Street Journal; (2) Shared by James V. Magee, Albert V. Gaudiosi, and Frederick A. Meyer, Philadelphia Bulletin.
1965—(1) Melvin H.Ruder, Hungry Horse News (Columbia Falls, Mon.); (2) Gene Goltz, Houston Post.
1966—(1) Los Angeles Times Staff; (2) John A. Frasca, Tampa (Fla.) Tribune.
1967—(1) Robert V.Cox, Chambersburg (Pa.) Public Opinion; (2) Gene Miller, Miami Herald.
1968—Detroit Free Press Staff; (2) J. Anthony Lukas, New York Times.
1969—(1) John Fetterman, Louisville Courier-Journal and Times; (2) Albert L.Delugach, St. Louis Globe Democrat, and Denny Walsh, Life.
1970—(1) Thomas Fitzpatrick, Chicago Sun-Times; (2) Harold Eugene Martin, Montgomery Advertiser & Alabama Journal.
1971—(1) Akron Beacon Journal Staff, (2) William Hugh Jones, Chicago Tribune.
1972—(1) Richard Cooper and John Machacek, Rochester Times-Union; (2) Timothy Leland, Gerard M. O'Neill, Stephen A. Kurkjian and Anne De Santis, Boston Globe.
1973—(1) Chicago Tribune; (2) Sun Newspapers of Omaha.
1974—(1) Hugh F. Hough, Arthur M. Petacque, Chicago Sun-Times; (2) William Sherman, New York Daily News.
1975—(1) Xenia (Oh.) Daily Gazette; (2) Indianapolis Star.
1976—(1) Gene Miller, Miami Herald; (2) Chicago Tribune.
1977—(1) Margo Huston, Milwaukee Journal; (2) Acel Moore, Wendell Rawls Jr., Philadelphia Inquirer.
1978—(1) Richard Whitt, Louisville Courier-Journal; (2) Anthony R. Dolan, Stamford (Conn.) Advocate.
1979—(1) San Diego (Cal.) Evening Tribune; (2) Gilbert M. Gaul, Elliot G.Jaspin, Pottsville (Pa.) Republican.
1980—(1) Philadelphia Inquirer; (2) Stephen A. Kurkjian, Alexander B.Hawes Jr., Nils Bruzelius, Joan Vennochi, Robert M. Porterfield, Boston Globe.
1981—(1) Longview (Wash.) Daily News staff; (2) Clark Hallas and Robert B. Lowe, Arizona Daily Star.
1982—(1) Kansas City Star, Kansas City Times; (2) Paul Henderson, Seattle Times.
1983—(1) Fort Wayne (Ind.) News-Sentinel; (2) Loretta Tofani, Washington Post.
1984—(1) Newsday (N.Y.); (2) Boston Globe.
1985—(1) Thomas Turcol, Virginian-Pilot and Ledger-Star, Norfolk, Va.; (2) William K.Marimow, Philadelphia Inquirer; Lucy Morgan & Jack Reed, St. Petersburg (Fla.) Times.
1986—(1) Edna Buchanan, Miami Herald; (2) Jeffrey A. Marx & Michael M. York, Lexington (Ky.) Herald-Leader.
1987—(1) Akron Beacon Journal; (2) Daniel R. Biddle, H.G. Bissinger, Fredric N. Tulsky, Philadelphia Inquirer; John Woestendiek, Philadelphia Inquirer.
1988—(1) Alabama Journal; Lawrence (Mass.) Eagle-Tribune; (2) Walt Bogdanich, Wall Street Journal.
1989—(1) Louisville Courier-Journal; (2) Bill Dedman, Atlanta Journal and Constitution.
1990—(1) San Jose Mercury News; (2) Lon Kilzer, Chris Ison, Star Tribune, Minneapolis-St. Paul.
1991—(1) Miami Herald; (2) Joseph T. Hallinan, Susan M. Headden, Indianapolis Star.
1992—(1) New York Newsday; (2) Lorraine Adams, Dan Malone, Dallas Morning News.

Criticism or Commentary

(1) Criticism; (2) Commentary

1970—(1) Ada Louise Huxtable, New York Times; (2) Marquis W. Childs, St.Louis Post-Dispatch.
1971—(1) Harold C.Schonberg, New York Times; (2) William A. Caldwell, The Record, Hackensack, N.J.
1972—(1) Frank Peters Jr., St. Louis Post-Dispatch; (2) Mike Royko, Chicago Daily News.
1973—(1) Ronald Powers, Chicago Sun-Times; (2) David S. Broder, Washington Post.
1974—(1) Emily Genauer, Newsday, (N.Y.); (2) Edwin A. Roberts, Jr., National Observer.
1975—(1) Roger Ebert, Chicago Sun Times; (2) Mary McGrory, Washington Star.
1976—(1) Alan M.Kriegsman, Washington Post; (2) Walter W. (Red) Smith, New York Times.
1977—(1) William McPherson, Washington Post; (2) George F. Will, Wash. Post Writers Group.
1978—(1) Walter Kerr, New York Times; (2) William Safire, New York Times.
1979—(1) Paul Gapp, Chicago Tribune; (2) Russell Baker, New York Times.
1980—(1) William A. Henry III, Boston Globe; (2) Ellen Goodman, Boston Globe.
1981—(1) Jonathan Yardley, Washington Star; (2) Dave Anderson, New York Times.
1982—(1) Martin Bernheimer, Los Angeles Times; (2) Art Buchwald, Los Angeles Times Syndicate.
1983—(1) Manuela Hoelterhoff, Wall St. Journal; (2) Claude Sitton, Raleigh (N.C.) News & Observer.
1984—Paul Goldberger, New York Times; (2) Vermont Royster, Wall St. Journal
1985—(1) Howard Rosenberg, Los Angeles Times; (2) Murray Kempton, Newsday (N.Y.).
1986—(1) Donal J. Henahan, New York Times; (2) Jimmy Breslin, New York Daily News.
1987—(1) Richard Eder, Los Angeles Times; (2) Charles Krauthammer, Washington Post.
1988—(1) Tom Shales, Washington Post; (2) Dave Barry, Miami Herald.
1989—(1) Michael Skube, News and Observer, Raleigh, N.C.; (2) Clarence Page, Chicago Tribune.
1990—(1) Allan Temko, San Francisco Chronicle; (2) Jim Murray, Los Angeles Times
1991—(1) David Shaw, Los Angeles Times; (2) Jim Hoagland, Washington Post.
1992—(1) No award; (2) Anna Quindlen, New York Times.

National Reporting

1942—Louis Stark, New York Times.
1944—Dewey L. Fleming, Baltimore Sun.
1945—James B. Reston, New York Times.
1946—Edward A. Harris, St. Louis Post-Dispatch.
1947—Edward T. Folliard, Washington Post.
1948—Bert Andrews, New York Herald Tribune; Nat S. Finney, Minneapolis Tribune.
1949—Charles P. Trussell, New York Times.
1950—Edwin O. Guthman, Seattle Times.
1952—Anthony Leviero, New York Times.
1953—Don Whitehead, Associated Press.
1954—Richard Wilson, Des Moines Register.
1955—Anthony Lewis, Washington Daily News.
1956—Charles L. Bartlett, Chattanooga Times.
1957—James Reston, New York Times.
1958—Relman Morin, AP; Clark Mollenhoff, Des Moines Register & Tribune.
1959—Howard Van Smith, Miami (Fla.) News.
1960—Vance Trimble, Scripps-Howard, Washington, D.C.
1961—Edward R. Cony, Wall Street Journal.
1962—Nathan G. Caldwell and Gene S. Graham, Nashville Tennessean.
1963—Anthony Lewis, New York Times.
1964—Merriman Smith, UPI.
1965—Louis M. Kohlmeier, Wall Street Journal.
1966—Haynes Johnson, Washington Evening Star.
1967—Monroe Karmin and Stanley Penn, Wall Street Journal.
1968—Howard James, Christian Science Monitor; Nathan K. Kotz, Des Moines Register.
1969—Robert Cahn, Christian Science Monitor.
1970—William J. Eaton, Chicago Daily News.
1971—Lucinda Franks & Thomas Powers, UPI.
1972—Jack Anderson, United Feature Syndicate.
1973—Robert Boyd and Clark Hoyt, Knight Newspapers.
1974—James R. Polk, Washington Star-News; Jack White, Providence Journal-Bulletin.
1975—Donald L. Barlett and James B. Steele, Philadelphia Inquirer.
1976—James Risser, Des Moines Register.
1977—Walter Mears, Associated Press.
1978—Gaylord D. Shaw, Los Angeles Times.
1979—James Risser, Des Moines Register.
1980—Charles Stafford, Bette Swenson Orsini, St. Petersburg (Fla.) Times.
1981—John M. Crewdson, New York Times.
1982—Rick Atkinson, Kansas City Times.
1983—Boston Globe.
1984—John Noble Wilford, New York Times.
1985—Thomas J. Knudson, Des Moines (Ia.) Register.
1986—Craig Flournoy & George Rodrigue, Dallas Morning News; Arthur Howe, Philadelphia Inquirer.
1987—Miami Herald; and New York Times.
1988—Tim Weiner, Philadelphia Inquirer.
1989—Donald L. Barlett & James B. Steele, Philadelphia Inquirer.
1990—Ross Anderson, Bill Dietrich, Mary Ann Gwinn, Eric Nalder, The Seattle Times.
1991—Marjie Lundstrom, Rochelle Sharpe, Gannett News Service.
1992—Jeff Taylor, Mike McGraw, Kansas City Star.

International Reporting

1942—Laurence Edmund Allen, Associated Press.
1943—Ira Wolfert, No. Am. Newspaper Alliance.
1944—Daniel DeLuce, Associated Press.
1945—Mark S. Watson, Baltimore Sun.
1946—Homer W. Bigart, New York Herald Tribune.
1947—Eddy Gilmore, Associated Press.
1948—Paul W. Ward, Baltimore Sun.
1949—Price Day, Baltimore Sun.
1950—Edmund Stevens, Christian Science Monitor.
1951—Keyes Beech and Fred Sparks, Chicago Daily News; Homer Bigart and Marguerite Higgins, New York Herald Tribune; Relman Morin and Don Whitehead, AP.
1952—John M. Hightower, Associated Press.
1953—Austin C. Wehrwein, Milwaukee Journal.
1954—Jim G. Lucas, Scripps-Howard Newspapers.
1955—Harrison Salisbury, New York Times.
1956—William Randolph Hearst, Jr., Frank Conniff, Hearst Newspapers; Kingsbury Smith, INS.
1957—Russell Jones, United Press.
1958—New York Times.
1959—Joseph Martin and Philip Santora, New York Daily News.
1960—A.M. Rosenthal, New York Times.
1961—Lynn Heinzerling, Associated Press.
1962—Walter Lippmann, New York Herald Tribune Synd.
1963—Hal Hendrix, Miami (Fla.) News.
1964—Malcolm W. Browne, AP; David Halberstam, New York Times.
1965—J.A. Livingston, Philadelphia Bulletin.
1966—Peter Arnett, AP.
1967—R. John Hughes, Christian Science Monitor.
1968—Alfred Friendly, Washington Post.
1969—William Tuohy, Los Angeles Times.
1970—Seymour M. Hersh, Dispatch News Service.
1971—Jimmie Lee Hoagland, Washington Post.
1972—Peter R. Kann, Wall Street Journal.
1973—Max Frankel, New York Times.
1974—Hedrick Smith, New York Times.
1975—William Mullen and Ovie Carter, Chicago Tribune.
1976—Sydney H. Schanberg, New York Times.
1978—Henry Kamm, New York Times.
1979—Richard Ben Cramer, Philadelphia Inquirer.
1980—Joel Brinkley, Jay Mather, Louisville (Ky.) Courier-Journal.
1981—Shirley Christian, Miami Herald.
1982—John Darnton, New York Times.
1983—Thomas L. Friedman, New York Times; Loren Jenkins, Washington Post.
1984—Karen Elliot House, Wall St. Journal
1985—Josh Friedman, Dennis Bell, Ozler Muhammad, Newsday (N.Y.).
1986—Lewis M. Simons, Pete Carey, Katherine Ellison, San Jose (Calif.) Mercury News.
1987—Michael Parks, Los Angeles Times.
1988—Thomas L. Friedman, New York Times.
1989—Glenn Frankel, Washington Post; Bill Keller, New York Times.
1990—Nicholas D. Kirstof, Sheryl WuDunn, New York Times.
1991—Caryle Murphy, Washington Post; Serge Schmemann, New York Times.
1992—Patrick J. Sloyan, (L.I.) Newsday.

Correspondence

For Washington or foreign correspondence. Category was merged with those in national and international reporting in 1948.
1929—Paul Scott Mowrer, Chicago Daily News.
1930—Leland Stowe, New York Herald Tribune.
1931—H.R. Knickerbocker, Philadelphia Public Ledger and New York Evening Post.
1932—Walter Duranty, New York Times, and Charles G. Ross, St. Louis Post-Dispatch.
1933—Edgar Ansel Mowrer, Chicago Daily News.
1934—Frederick T. Birchall, New York Times.
1935—Arthur Krock, New York Times.
1936—Wilfred C. Barber, Chicago Tribune.
1937—Anne O'Hare McCormick, New York Times.
1938—Arthur Krock, New York Times.
1939—Louis P. Lochner, Associated Press.
1940—Otto D. Tolischus, New York Times.
1941—Bronze plaque to commemorate work of American correspondents on war fronts.
1942—Carlos P. Romulo, Philippines Herald.
1943—Hanson W. Baldwin, New York Times.
1944—Ernest Taylor Pyle, Scripps-Howard Newspaper Alliance.
1945—Harold V. (Hal) Boyle, Associated Press.
1946—Arnaldo Cortesi, New York Times.
1947—Brooks Atkinson, New York Times.

Editorial Writing

1917—New York Tribune.
1918—Louisville (Ky.) Courier-Journal.
1920—Harvey E. Newbranch, Omaha Evening World-Herald.
1922—Frank M. O'Brien, New York Herald.
1923—William Allen White, Emporia Gazette.
1924—Frank Buxton, Boston Herald, Special Prize. Frank I. Cobb, New York World.
1925—Robert Lathan, Charleston (S.C.) News and Courier.
1926—Edward M. Kingsbury, New York Times.
1927—F. Lauriston Bullard, Boston Herald.
1928—Grover C. Hall, Montgomery Advertiser.
1929—Louis Isaac Jaffe, Norfolk Virginian-Pilot.
1931—Chas. Ryckman, Fremont (Neb.) Tribune.
1933—Kansas City (Mo.) Star.
1934—E. P. Chase, Atlantic (Ia.) News Telegraph.
1936—Felix Morley, Washington Post. George B. Parker, Scripps-Howard Newspapers.
1937—John W. Owens, Baltimore Sun.
1938—W.W. Waymack, Des Moines (Ia.) Register and Tribune.
1939—Ronald G. Callvert, Portland Oregonian.
1940—Bart Howard, St. Louis Post-Dispatch.
1941—Reuben Maury, Daily News, N.Y.
1942—Geoffrey Parsons, New York Herald Tribune.
1943—Forrest W. Seymour, Des Moines (Ia.) Register and Tribune.
1944—Henry J. Haskell, Kansas City (Mo.) Star.
1945—George W. Potter, Providence (R.I.) Journal-Bulletin.
1946—Hodding Carter, Greenville (Miss.) Delta Democrat-Times.
1947—William H. Grimes, Wall Street Journal.
1948—Virginius Dabney, Richmond (Va.) Times-Dispatch.
1949—John H. Crider, Boston (Mass.) Herald, Herbert Elliston, Washington Post.
1950—Carl M. Saunders, Jackson (Mich.) Citizen-Patriot.
1951—William H. Fitzpatrick, New Orleans States.
1952—Louis LaCoss, St. Louis Globe Democrat.
1953—Vermont C. Royster, Wall Street Journal.
1954—Don Murray, Boston Herald.
1955—Royce Howes, Detroit Free Press.
1956—Lauren K. Soth, Des Moines (Ia.) Register and Tribune.
1957—Buford Boone, Tuscaloosa (Ala.) News.
1958—Harry S. Ashmore, Arkansas Gazette.
1959—Ralph McGill, Atlanta Constitution.
1960—Lenoir Chambers, Norfolk Virginian-Pilot.
1961—William J. Dorvillier, San Juan (Puerto Rico) Star.
1962—Thomas M. Storke, Santa Barbara (Cal.) News-Press.
1963—Ira B. Harkey, Jr., Pascagoula (Miss.) Chronicle.
1964—Hazel Brannon Smith, Lexington (Miss.) Advertiser.
1965—John R. Harrison, The Gainesville (Fla.) Sun.
1966—Robert Lasch, St. Louis Post-Dispatch.
1967—Eugene C. Patterson, Atlanta Constitution.
1968—John S. Knight, Knight Newspapers.
1969—Paul Greenberg, Pine Bluff (Ark.) Commercial.
1970—Philip L. Geyelin, Washington Post.
1971—Horance G. Davis, Jr., Gainesville (Fla.) Sun.
1972—John Strohmeyer, Bethlehem (Pa.) Globe-Times.
1973—Roger B. Linscott, Berkshire Eagle, Pittsfield, Mass.
1974—F. Gilman Spencer, Trenton (N.J.) Trentonian.
1975—John D. Maurice, Charleston (W. Va.) Daily Mail.
1976—Philip Kerby, Los Angeles Times.
1977—Warren L. Lerude, Foster Church, and Norman F. Cardoza, Reno (Nev.) Evening Gazette and Nevada State Journal.
1978—Meg Greenfield, Washington Post.
1979—Edwin M. Yoder, Washington Star.
1980—Robert L. Bartley, Wall Street Journal.
1982—Jack Rosenthal, New York Times.
1983—Editorial board, Miami Herald.
1984—Albert Scardino, Georgia Gazette.
1985—Richard Aregood, Philadelphia Daily News.
1986—Jack Fuller, Chicago Tribune.
1987—Jonathan Freedman, Tribune (San Diego).
1988—Jane Healy, Orlando Sentinel.
1989—Lois Wille, Chicago Tribune.
1990—Thomas J. Hylton, Pottstown (Pa.) Mercury.
1991—Ron Casey, Harold Jackson, Joey Kennedy, Birmingham (Ala.) News.
1992—Maria Henson, Lexington (Ky.) Herald-Leader.

Editorial Cartooning

1922—Rollin Kirby, New York World.
1924—Jay N. Darling, Des Moines Register.
1925—Rollin Kirby, New York World.
1926—D. R. Fitzpatrick, St. Louis Post-Dispatch.
1927—Nelson Harding, Brooklyn Eagle.
1928—Nelson Harding, Brooklyn Eagle.
1929—Rollin Kirby, New York World.
1930—Charles Macauley, Brooklyn Eagle.
1931—Edmund Duffy, Baltimore Sun.
1932—John T. McCutcheon, Chicago Tribune.
1933—H. M. Talburt, Washington Daily News.
1934—Edmund Duffy, Baltimore Sun.
1935—Ross A. Lewis, Milwaukee Journal.
1937—C. D. Batchelor, New York Daily News.
1938—Vaughn Shoemaker, Chicago Daily News.
1939—Charles G. Werner, Daily Oklahoman.
1940—Edmund Duffy, Baltimore Sun.
1941—Jacob Burck, Chicago Times.
1942—Herbert L. Block, Newspaper Enterprise Assn.
1943—Jay N. Darling, Des Moines Register.
1944—Clifford K. Berryman, Washington Star.
1945—Bill Mauldin, United Feature Syndicate.
1946—Bruce Alexander Russell, Los Angeles Times.
1947—Vaughn Shoemaker, Chicago Daily News.
1948—Reuben L. (Rube) Goldberg, N. Y. Sun.
1949—Lute Pease, Newark (N.J.) Evening News.
1950—James T. Berryman, Washington Star.
1951—Reginald W. Manning, Arizona Republic.
1952—Fred L. Packer, New York Mirror.
1953—Edward D. Kuekes, Cleveland Plain Dealer.
1954—Herbert L. Block, Washington Post & Times-Herald.
1955—Daniel R. Fitzpatrick, St. Louis Post-Dispatch.
1956—Robert York, Louisville (Ky.) Times.
1957—Tom Little, Nashville Tennessean.
1958—Bruce M. Shanks, Buffalo Evening News.
1959—Bill Mauldin, St. Louis Post-Dispatch.
1961—Carey Orr, Chicago Tribune.
1962—Edmund S. Valtman, Hartford Times.
1963—Frank Miller, Des Moines Register.
1964—Paul Conrad, Denver Post.
1966—Don Wright, Miami News.
1967—Patrick B. Oliphant, Denver Post.
1968—Eugene Gray Payne, Charlotte Observer.
1969—John Fischetti, Chicago Daily News.
1970—Thomas F. Darcy, Newsday.
1971—Paul Conrad, L. A. Times.
1972—Jeffrey K. MacNelly, Richmond News-Leader.
1974—Paul Szep, Boston Globe.
1975—Garry Trudeau, Universal Press Syndicate.
1976—Tony Auth, Philadelphia Inquirer.
1977—Paul Szep, Boston Globe.
1978—Jeffrey K. MacNelly, Richmond News Leader.
1979—Herbert L. Block, Washington Post.
1980—Don Wright, Miami (Fla.) News.
1981—Mike Peters, Dayton (Oh.) Daily News.
1982—Ben Sargent, Austin American-Statesman.
1983—Richard Lochner, Chicago Tribune.
1984—Paul Conrad, Los Angeles Times.
1985—Jeffrey K. MacNelly, Chicago Tribune.
1986—Jules Feiffer, Village Voice (N.Y. City)
1987—Berke Breathed, Washington Post.
1988—Doug Marlette, Atlanta Constitution, Charlotte Observer.
1989—Jack Higgins, Chicago Sun-Times.
1990—Tom Toles, The Buffalo News.
1991—Jim Borgman, Cincinnati Enquirer.
1992—Signe Wilkinson, Philadelphia Daily News.

Spot News Photography

1942—Milton Brooks, Detroit News.
1943—Frank Noel, Associated Press.
1944—Frank Filan, AP; Earl L. Bunker, Omaha World-Herald.
1945—Joe Rosenthal, Associated Press, for photograph of planting American flag on Iwo Jima.
1947—Arnold Hardy, amateur, Atlanta, Ga.
1948—Frank Cushing, Boston Traveler.
1949—Nathaniel Fein, New York Herald Tribune.
1950—Bill Crouch, Oakland (Cal.) Tribune.
1951—Max Desfor, Associated Press.
1952—John Robinson and Don Ultang, Des Moines Register and Tribune.
1953—William M. Gallagher, Flint (Mich.) Journal.
1954—Mrs. Walter M. Schau, amateur.
1955—John L. Gaunt, Jr., Los Angeles Times.
1956—New York Daily News.
1957—Harry A. Trask, Boston Traveler.
1958—William C. Beall, Washington Daily News.
1959—William Seaman, Minneapolis Star.
1960—Andrew Lopez, UPI.
1961—Yasushi Nagao, Mainichi Newspapers, Tokyo.
1962—Paul Vathis, Associated Press.
1963—Hector Rondon, La Republica, Caracas, Venezuela.
1964—Robert H. Jackson, Dallas Times-Herald.
1965—Horst Faas, Associated Press.
1966—Kyoichi Sawada, UPI.
1967—Jack R. Thornell, Associated Press.
1968—Rocco Morabito, Jacksonville Journal.
1969—Edward Adams, AP.
1970—Steve Starr, AP.
1971—John Paul Filo, Valley Daily News & Daily Dispatch of Tarentum & New Kensington, Pa.
1972—Horst Faas and Michel Laurent, AP.
1973—Huynh Cong Ut, AP.
1974—Anthony K. Roberts, AP.
1975—Gerald H. Gay, Seattle Times.
1976—Stanley Forman, Boston Herald American.
1977—Neal Ulevich, Associated Press; Stanley Forman, Boston Herald American.
1978—John H. Blair, UPI.
1979—Thomas J. Kelly III, Pottstown (Pa.) Mercury.
1980—UPI.
1981—Larry C. Price, Ft. Worth (Tex.) Star-Telegram.
1982—Ron Edmonds, Associated Press.
1983—Bill Foley, AP.
1984—Stan Grossfeld, Boston Globe.
1985—The Register, Santa Ana, Calif.
1986—Carol Guzy & Michel duCille, Miami Herald.
1987—Kim Komenich, San Francisco Examiner.
1988—Scott Shaw, Odessa (Tex.) American.
1989—Ron Olshwanger, St. Louis Post-Dispatch.
1990—Oakland (Calif.) Tribune photo staff.
1991—Greg Marinovich, Associated Press.
1992—Associated Press staff.

Feature Photography

1968—Toshio Sakai, UPI.
1969—Moneta Sleet Jr., Ebony.
1970—Dallas Kinney, Palm Beach Post.
1971—Jack Dykinga, Chicago Sun-Times.
1972—Dave Kennerly, UPI.
1973—Brian Lanker, Topeka Capitol-Journal.
1974—Slava Veder, AP.
1975—Matthew Lewis, Washington Post.
1976—Louisville Courier-Journal and Louisville Times.
1977—Robin Hood, Chattanooga News-Free Press.
1978—J. Ross Baughman, AP.
1979—Staff Photographers, Boston Herald American.
1980—Erwin H. Hagler, Dallas Times-Herald.
1981—Taro M. Yamasaki, Detroit Free Press.
1982—John H. White, Chicago Sun-Times.
1983—James B. Dickman, Dallas Times-Herald.
1984—Anthony Suad, Denver Post.
1985—Stan Grossfeld, Boston Globe; Larry C. Price, Philadelphia Inquirer.
1986—Tom Gralish, Philadelphia Inquirer.
1987—David Peterson, Des Moines Register.
1988—Michel duCille, Miami Herald.
1989—Manny Crisostomo, Detroit Free Press.
1990—David C. Turnley, Detroit Free Press.
1991—William Snyder, Dallas Morning News.
1992—John Kaplan, Block Newspapers (Toledo, Oh.).

Special Citation

1938—Edmonton (Alberta) Journal, bronze plaque.
1941—New York Times.
1944—Byron Price and Mrs. William Allen White. Also to Richard Rodgers and Oscar Hammerstein 2d, for musical, Oklahoma!
1945—Press cartographers for war maps.
1947—(Pulitzer centennial year.) Columbia Univ. and the Graduate School of Journalism, and St. Louis Post-Dispatch.
1948—Dr. Frank Diehl Fackenthal.
1951—Cyrus L. Sulzberger, New York Times.
1952—Max Kase, New York Journal-American, Kansas City Star.
1953—The New York Times; Lester Markel.
1957—Kenneth Roberts, for his historical novels.
1958—Walter Lippmann, New York Herald Tribune.
1960—Garrett Mattingly, for The Armada.
1961—American Heritage Picture History of the Civil War.
1964—The Gannett Newspapers.
1973—James T. Flexner, for biography of George Washington.
1976—John Hohenberg, for services to American journalism.
1977—Alex Haley, for Roots.
1978—Richard Lee Strout, Christian Science Monitor and New Republic.
—E.B. White.
1984—Theodore Geisel ("Dr. Seuss").
1985—William Schuman, composer, educational leader.
1987—Joseph Pulitzer Jr.
1992—Art Spiegelman, Maus.

Feature Writing

1979—Jon D. Franklin, Baltimore Evening Sun.
1980—Madeleine Blais, Miami Herald Tropic Magazine.
Janet Cooke, Washington Post.
1981—Teresa Carpenter, Village Voice, New York City.
1982—Saul Pett, Associated Press.
1984—Peter M. Rinearson, Seattle Times.
1985—Alice Steinbach, Baltimore Sun.
1986—John Camp, St. Paul Pioneer Press & Dispatch
1987—Steve Twomey, Philadephia Inquirer.
1988—Jacqui Banaszynski, St. Paul Pioneer Press Dispatch.
1989—David Zucchino, Philadelphia Inquirer.
1990—Dave Curtin, Colorado Springs Gazette Telegraph.
1991—Sheryl James, St. Petersburg Times.
1992—Howell Raines, New York Times.

Explanatory Journalism

1985—Jon Franklin, Baltimore Evening Sun.
1986—New York Times Staff.
1987—Jeff Lyon & Peter Gorner, Chicago Tribune.
1988—Daniel Hertzberg, James B. Stewart, Wall Street Journal.
1989—David Hanners, William Snyder, Karen Blessen, Dallas Morning News.
1990—David A. Vise, Steve Coll, The Washington Post.
1991—Susan C. Faludi, Wall Street Journal.
1992—Robert S. Capers, Eric Lipton, Hartford (Conn.) Courant.

Specialized Reporting

1985—Randall Savage, Jackie Crosby, Macon (Ga.) Telegraph and News.
1986—Andrew Schneider & Mary Pat Flaherty, Pittsburgh Press.
1987—Alex S. Jones, New York Times.
1988—Dean Baquet, William Gaines, Ann Marie Lipinski, Chicago Tribune.
1989—Edward Humes, Orange County (Calif.) Register.
1990—Tamar Stieber, Albuquerque Journal.
1991—Natalie Angier, New York Times.
1992—Deborah Blum, Sacramento Bee.

Letters

Fiction

For fiction in book form by an American author, preferably dealing with American life.
1918—Ernest Poole, His Family.
1919—Booth Tarkington, The Magnificent Ambersons.
1921—Edith Wharton, The Age of Innocence.
1922—Booth Tarkington, Alice Adams.
1923—Willa Cather, One of Ours.
1924—Margaret Wilson, The Able McLaughlins.

1925—Edna Ferber, So Big.
1926—Sinclair Lewis, Arrowsmith. (Refused prize.)
1927—Louis Bromfield, Early Autumn.
1928—Thornton Wilder, Bridge of San Luis Rey.
1929—Julia M. Peterkin, Scarlet Sister Mary.
1930—Oliver LaFarge, Laughing Boy.
1931—Margaret Ayer Barnes, Years of Grace.
1932—Pearl S. Buck, The Good Earth.
1933—T. S. Stribling, The Store.
1934—Caroline Miller, Lamb in His Bosom.
1935—Josephine W. Johnson, Now in November.
1936—Harold L. Davis, Honey in the Horn.
1937—Margaret Mitchell, Gone with the Wind.
1938—John P. Marquand, The Late George Apley.
1939—Marjorie Kinnan Rawlings, The Yearling.
1940—John Steinbeck, The Grapes of Wrath.
1942—Ellen Glasgow, In This Our Life.
1943—Upton Sinclair, Dragon's Teeth.
1944—Martin Flavin, Journey in the Dark.
1945—John Hersey, A Bell for Adano.
1947—Robert Penn Warren, All the King's Men.
1948—James A Michener, Tales of the South Pacific.
1949—James Gould Cozzens, Guard of Honor.
1950—A. B. Guthrie Jr., The Way West.
1951—Conrad Richter, The Town.
1952—Herman Wouk, The Caine Mutiny.
1953—Ernest Hemingway, The Old Man and the Sea.
1955—William Faulkner, A Fable.
1956—MacKinlay Kantor, Andersonville.
1958—James Agee, A Death in the Family.
1959—Robert Lewis Taylor, The Travels of Jaimie McPheeters.
1960—Allen Drury, Advise and Consent.
1961—Harper Lee, To Kill a Mockingbird.
1962—Edwin O'Connor, The Edge of Sadness.
1963—William Faulkner, The Reivers.
1965—Shirley Ann Grau, The Keepers of the House.
1966—Katherine Anne Porter, Collected Stories of Katherine Anne Porter.
1967—Bernard Malamud, The Fixer.
1968—William Styron, The Confessions of Nat Turner.
1969—N. Scott Momaday, House Made of Dawn.
1970—Jean Stafford, Collected Stories.
1972—Wallace Stegner, Angle of Repose.
1973—Eudora Welty, The Optimist's Daughter.
1975—Michael Shaara, The Killer Angels.
1976—Saul Bellow, Humboldt's Gift.
1978—James Alan McPherson, Elbow Room.
1979—John Cheever, The Stories of John Cheever.
1980—Norman Mailer, The Executioner's Song.
1981—John Kennedy Toole, A Confederacy of Dunces.
1982—John Updike, Rabbit is Rich.
1983—Alice Walker, The Color Purple.
1984—William Kennedy, Ironweed.
1985—Alison Lurie, Foreign Affairs.
1986—Larry McMurtry, Lonesome Dove.
1987—Peter Taylor, A Summons to Memphis.
1988—Toni Morrison, Beloved.
1989—Anne Tyler, Breathing Lessons.
1990—Oscar Hijuelos, The Mambo Kings Play Songs of Love.
1991—John Updike, Rabbit at Rest.
1992—Jane Smiley, A Thousand Acres.

Drama

For an American play, preferably original and dealing with American life.
1918—Jesse Lynch Williams, Why Marry?
1920—Eugene O'Neill, Beyond the Horizon.
1921—Zona Gale, Miss Lulu Bett.
1922—Eugene O'Neill, Anna Christie.
1923—Owen Davis, Icebound.
1924—Hatcher Hughes, Hell-Bent for Heaven.
1925—Sidney Howard, They Knew What They Wanted.
1926—George Kelly, Craig's Wife.
1927—Paul Green, In Abraham's Bosom.
1928—Eugene O'Neill, Strange Interlude.
1929—Elmer Rice, Street Scene.
1930—Marc Connelly, The Green Pastures.
1931—Susan Glaspell, Alison's House.
1932—George S. Kaufman, Morrie Ryskind and Ira Gershwin, Of Thee I Sing.
1933—Maxwell Anderson, Both Your Houses.
1934—Sidney Kingsley, Men in White.
1935—Zoe Akins, The Old Maid.
1936—Robert E. Sherwood, Idiot's Delight.
1937—George S. Kaufman and Moss Hart, You Can't Take It With You.
1938—Thornton Wilder, Our Town.
1939—Robert E. Sherwood, Abe Lincoln in Illinois.
1940—William Saroyan, The Time of Your Life.
1941—Robert E. Sherwood, There Shall Be No Night.
1943—Thornton Wilder, The Skin of Our Teeth.
1945—Mary Chase, Harvey.
1946—Russel Crouse and Howard Lindsay, State of the Union.
1948—Tennessee Williams, A Streetcar Named Desire.
1949—Arthur Miller, Death of a Salesman.
1950—Richard Rodgers, Oscar Hammerstein 2d, and Joshua Logan, South Pacific.
1952—Joseph Kramm, The Shrike.
1953—William Inge, Picnic.
1954—John Patrick, Teahouse of the August Moon.
1955—Tennessee Williams, Cat on a Hot Tin Roof.
1956—Frances Goodrich and Albert Hackett, The Diary of Anne Frank.
1957—Eugene O'Neill, Long Day's Journey Into Night.
1958—Ketti Frings, Look Homeward, Angel.
1959—Archibald MacLeish, J. B.
1960—George Abbott, Jerome Weidman, Sheldon Harnick and Jerry Bock, Fiorello.
1961—Tad Mosel, All the Way Home.
1962—Frank Loesser and Abe Burrows, How To Succeed In Business Without Really Trying.
1965—Frank D. Gilroy, The Subject Was Roses.
1967—Edward Albee, A Delicate Balance.
1969—Howard Sackler, The Great White Hope.
1970—Charles Gordone, No Place to Be Somebody.
1971—Paul Zindel, The Effect of Gamma Rays on Man-in-the-Moon Marigolds.
1973—Jason Miller, That Championship Season.
1975—Edward Albee, Seascape.
1976—Michael Bennett, James Kirkwood, Nicholas Dante, Marvin Hamlisch, Edward Kleban, A Chorus Line.
1977—Michael Cristofer, The Shadow Box.
1978—Donald L. Coburn, The Gin Game.
1979—Sam Shepard, Buried Child.
1980—Lanford Wilson, Talley's Folly.
1981—Beth Henley, Crimes of the Heart.
1982—Charles Fuller, A Soldier's Play.
1983—Marsha Norman, 'night, Mother.
1984—David Mamet, Glengarry Glen Ross.
1985—Stephen Sondheim, James Lapine, Sunday in the Park with George.
1987—August Wilson, Fences.
1988—Alfred Uhry, Driving Miss Daisy.
1989—Wendy Wasserstein, The Heidi Chronicles.
1990—August Wilson, The Piano Lesson.
1991—Neil Simon, Lost in Yonkers.
1992—Robert Schenkkan, The Kentucky Cycle.

History

For a book on the history of the United States.
1917—J. J. Jusserand, With Americans of Past and Present Days.
1918—James Ford Rhodes, History of the Civil War.
1920—Justin H. Smith, The War with Mexico.
1921—William Sowden Sims, The Victory at Sea.
1922—James Truslow Adams, The Founding of New England.
1923—Charles Warren, The Supreme Court in United States History.
1924—Charles Howard McIlwain, The American Revolution: A Constitutional Interpretation.
1925—Frederick L. Paxton, A History of the American Frontier.
1926—Edward Channing, A History of the U.S.
1927—Samuel Flagg Bemis, Pinckney's Treaty.
1928—Vernon Louis Parrington, Main Currents in American Thought.
1929—Fred A. Shannon, The Organization and Administration of the Union Army, 1861-65.
1930—Claude H. Van Tyne, The War of Independence.
1931—Bernadotte E. Schmitt, The Coming of the War, 1914.
1932—Gen. John J. Pershing, My Experiences in the World War.
1933—Frederick J. Turner, The Significance of Sections in American History.
1934—Herbert Agar, The People's Choice.
1935—Charles McLean Andrews, The Colonial Period of American History.
1936—Andrew C. McLaughlin, The Constitutional History of the United States.
1937—Van Wyck Brooks, The Flowering of New England.
1938—Paul Herman Buck, The Road to Reunion, 1865-1900.
1939—Frank Luther Mott, A History of American Magazines.
1940—Carl Sandburg, Abraham Lincoln: The War Years.
1941—Marcus Lee Hansen, The Atlantic Migration, 1607-1860.
1942—Margaret Leech, Reveille in Washington.
1943—Esther Forbes, Paul Revere and the World He Lived In.
1944—Merle Curti, The Growth of American Thought.
1945—Stephen Bonsal, Unfinished Business.

1946—Arthur M. Schlesinger Jr., The Age of Jackson.
1947—James Phinney Baxter 3d, Scientists Against Time.
1948—Bernard De Voto, Across the Wide Missouri.
1949—Roy F. Nichols, The Disruption of American Democracy.
1950—O. W. Larkin, Art and Life in America.
1951—R. Carlyle Buley, The Old Northwest: Pioneer Period 1815-1840.
1952—Oscar Handlin, The Uprooted.
1953—George Dangerfield, The Era of Good Feelings.
1954—Bruce Catton, A Stillness at Appomattox.
1955—Paul Horgan, Great River: The Rio Grande in North American History.
1956—Richard Hofstadter, The Age of Reform.
1957—George F. Kennan, Russia Leaves the War.
1958—Bray Hammond, Banks and Politics in America—From the Revolution to the Civil War.
1959—Leonard D. White and Jean Schneider, The Republican Era; 1869-1901.
1960—Margaret Leech, In the Days of McKinley.
1961—Herbert Feis, Between War and Peace: The Potsdam Conference.
1962—Lawrence H. Gibson, The Triumphant Empire: Thunderclouds Gather in the West.
1963—Constance McLaughlin Green, Washington: Village and Capital, 1800-1878.
1964—Sumner Chilton Powell, Puritan Village: The Formation of A New England Town.
1965—Irwin Unger, The Greenback Era.
1966—Perry Miller, Life of the Mind in America.
1967—William H. Goetzmann, Exploration and Empire: the Explorer and Scientist in the Winning of the American West.
1968—Bernard Bailyn, The Ideological Origins of the American Revolution.
1969—Leonard W. Levy, Origin of the Fifth Amendment.
1970—Dean Acheson, Present at the Creation: My Years in the State Department.
1971—James McGregor Burns, Roosevelt: The Soldier of Freedom.
1972—Carl N. Degler, Neither Black Nor White.
1973—Michael Kammen, People of Paradox: An Inquiry Concerning the Origins of American Civilization.
1974—Daniel J. Boorstin, The Americans: The Democratic Experience.
1975—Dumas Malone, Jefferson and His Time.
1976—Paul Horgan, Lamy of Santa Fe.
1977—David M. Potter, The Impending Crisis.
1978—Alfred D. Chandler, Jr., The Visible Hand: The Managerial Revolution in American Business.
1979—Don E. Fehrenbacher, The Dred Scott Case: Its Significance in American Law and Politics.
1980—Leon F. Litwack, Been in the Storm So Long.
1981—Lawrence A. Cremin, American Education: The National Experience, 1783-1876.
1982—C. Vann Woodward, ed., Mary Chestnut's Civil War.
1983—Rhys L. Issac, The Transformation of Virginia, 1740-1790.
1985—Thomas K. McCraw, Prophets of Regulation.
1986—Walter A. McDougall, . . . The Heavens and the Earth.
1987—Bernard Bailyn, Voyagers to the West.
1988—Robert V. Bruce, The Launching of Modern American Science 1846-1876.
1989—Taylor Branch, Parting the Waters: America in the King Years, 1954-63; and James M. McPherson, Battle Cry of Freedom: The Civil War Era.
1990—Stanley Karnow, In Our Image: America's Empire in the Philippines.
1991—Laurel Thatcher Ulrich, A Midwife's Tale: The Life of Martha Ballard, based on her diary, 1785-1812.
1992—Mark E. Neely Jr., The Fate of Liberty: Abraham Lincoln and Civil Liberties.

Biography or Autobiography

For a distinguished biography or autobiography by an American author.
1917—Laura E. Richards and Maude Howe Elliott, assisted by Florence Howe Hall, Julia Ward Howe.
1918—William Cabell Bruce, Benjamin Franklin, Self-Revealed.
1919—Henry Adams, The Education of Henry Adams.
1920—Albert J. Beveridge, The Life of John Marshall.
1921—Edward Bok, The Americanization of Edward Bok.
1922—Hamlin Garland, A Daughter of the Middle Border.
1923—Burton J. Hendrick, The Life and Letters of Walter H. Page.
1924—Michael Pupin, From Immigrant to Inventor.
1925—M. A. DeWolfe Howe, Barrett Wendell and His Letters.
1926—Harvey Cushing, Life of Sir William Osler.
1927—Emory Holloway, Whitman: An Interpretation in Narrative.
1928—Charles Edward Russell, The American Orchestra and Theodore Thomas.
1929—Burton J. Hendrick, The Training of an American: The Earlier Life and Letters of Walter H. Page.
1930—Marquis James, The Raven (Sam Houston).
1931—Henry James, Charles W. Eliot.
1932—Henry F. Pringle, Theodore Roosevelt.
1933—Allan Nevins, Grover Cleveland.
1934—Tyler Dennett, John Hay.
1935—Douglas Southall Freeman, R. E. Lee
1936—Ralph Barton Perry, The Thought and Character of William James.
1937—Allan Nevins, Hamilton Fish: The Inner History of the Grant Administration.
1938—Divided between Odell Shepard, Pedlar's Progress; Marquis James, Andrew Jackson.
1939—Carl Van Doren, Benjamin Franklin.
1940—Ray Stannard Baker, Woodrow Wilson, Life and Letters.
1941—Ola Elizabeth Winslow, Jonathan Edwards.
1942—Forrest Wilson, Crusader in Crinoline.
1943—Samuel Eliot Morison, Admiral of the Ocean Sea (Columbus).
1944—Carleton Mabee, The American Leonardo: The Life of Samuel F. B. Morse.
1945—Russell Blaine Nye, George Bancroft; Brahmin Rebel.
1946—Linny Marsh Wolfe, Son of the Wilderness.
1947—William Allen White, The Autobiography of William Allen White.
1948—Margaret Clapp, Forgotten First Citizen: John Bigelow.
1949—Robert E. Sherwood, Roosevelt and Hopkins.
1950—Samuel Flag Bemis, John Quincy Adams and the Foundations of American Foreign Policy.
1951—Margaret Louise Colt, John C. Calhoun: American Portrait.
1952—Merlo J. Pusey, Charles Evans Hughes.
1953—David J. Mays, Edmund Pendleton, 1721-1803.
1954—Charles A. Lindbergh, The Spirit of St. Louis.
1955—William S. White, The Taft Story.
1956—Talbot F. Hamlin, Benjamin Henry Latrobe.
1957—John F. Kennedy, Profiles in Courage.
1958—Douglas Southall Freeman (decd. 1953), George Washington, Vols. I-VI: John Alexander Carroll and Mary Wells Ashworth, Vol. VII.
1959—Arthur Walworth, Woodrow Wilson: American Prophet.
1960—Samuel Eliot Morison, John Paul Jones.
1961—David Donald, Charles Sumner and The Coming of the Civil War.
1963—Leon Edel, Henry James: Vol. II. The Conquest of London, 1870-1881; Vol. III, The Middle Years, 1881-1895.
1964—Walter Jackson Bate, John Keats.
1965—Ernest Samuels, Henry Adams.
1966—Arthur M. Schlesinger Jr., A Thousand Days.
1967—Justin Kaplan, Mr. Clemens and Mark Twain.
1968—George F. Kennan, Memoirs (1925-1950).
1969—B. L. Reid, The Man from New York: John Quinn and his Friends.
1970—T. Harry Williams, Huey Long.
1971—Lawrence Thompson, Robert Frost: The Years of Triumph, 1915-1938.
1972—Joseph P. Lash, Eleanor and Franklin.
1973—W. A. Swanberg, Luce and His Empire.
1974—Louis Sheaffer, O'Neill, Son and Artist.
1975—Robert A. Caro, The Power Broker: Robert Moses and the Fall of New York.
1976—R.W.B. Lewis, Edith Wharton: A Biography.
1977—John E. Mack, A Prince of Our Disorder, The Life of T.E. Lawrence.
1978—Walter Jackson Bate, Samuel Johnson.
1979—Leonard Baker, Days of Sorrow and Pain: Leo Baeck and the Berlin Jews.
1980—Edmund Morris, The Rise of Theodore Roosevelt.
1981—Robert K. Massie, Peter the Great: His Life and World.
1982—William S. McFeely, Grant: A Biography.
1983—Russell Baker, Growing Up.
1984—Louis R. Harlan, Booker T. Washington.
1985—Kenneth Silverman, The Life and Times of Cotton Mather.
1986—Elizabeth Frank, Louise Bogan: A Portrait.
1987—David J. Garrow, Bearing the Cross: Martin Luther King Jr. and the Southern Christian Leadership Conference.
1988—David Herbert Donald, Look Homeward: A Life of Thomas Wolfe.
1989—Richard Ellmann, Oscar Wilde.
1990—Sebastian de Grazia, Machiavelli in Hell.
1991—Steven Naifeh, Gregory White Smith, Jackson Pollack: An American Saga.
1992—Lewis B. Puller Jr., Fortunate Son: The Healing of a Vietnam Vet.

American Poetry

Before this prize was established in 1922, awards were made from gifts provided by the Poetry Society: **1918**—Love Songs, by Sara Teasdale. **1919**—Old Road to Paradise, by Margaret Widemer; Corn Huskers, by Carl Sandburg.

1922—Edwin Arlington Robinson, Collected Poems.
1923—Edna St. Vincent Millay, The Ballad of the Harp-Weaver; A Few Figs from Thistles; Eight Sonnets in American Poetry, 1922; A Miscellany.
1924—Robert Frost, New Hampshire: A Poem with Notes and Grace Notes.
1925—Edwin Arlington Robinson, The Man Who Died Twice.
1926—Amy Lowell, What's O'Clock.
1927—Leonora Speyer, Fiddler's Farewell.
1928—Edwin Arlington Robinson, Tristram.
1929—Stephen Vincent Benet, John Brown's Body.
1930—Conrad Aiken, Selected Poems.
1931—Robert Frost, Collected Poems.
1932—George Dillon, The Flowering Stone.
1933—Archibald MacLeish, Conquistador.
1934—Robert Hillyer, Collected Verse.
1935—Audrey Wurdemann, Bright Ambush.
1936—Robert P. Tristram Coffin, Strange Holiness.
1937—Robert Frost, A Further Range.
1938—Marya Zaturenska, Cold Morning Sky.
1939—John Gould Fletcher, Selected Poems.
1940—Mark Van Doren, Collected Poems.
1941—Leonard Bacon, Sunderland Capture.
1942—William Rose Benet, The Dust Which Is God.
1943—Robert Frost, A Witness Tree.
1944—Stephen Vincent Benet, Western Star.
1945—Karl Shapiro, V-Letter and Other Poems.
1947—Robert Lowell, Lord Weary's Castle.
1948—W. H. Auden, The Age of Anxiety.
1949—Peter Viereck, Terror and Decorum.
1950—Gwendolyn Brooks, Annie Allen.
1951—Carl Sandburg, Complete Poems.
1952—Marianne Moore, Collected Poems.
1953—Archibald MacLeish, Collected Poems.
1954—Theodore Roethke, The Waking.
1955—Wallace Stevens, Collected Poems.
1956—Elizabeth Bishop, Poems, North and South.
1957—Richard Wilbur, Things of This World.
1958—Robert Penn Warren, Promises: Poems 1954-1956.
1959—Stanley Kunitz, Selected Poems 1928-1958.
1960—W. D. Snodgrass, Heart's Needle.
1961—Phyllis McGinley, Times Three: Selected Verse from Three Decades.
1962—Alan Dugan, Poems.
1963—William Carlos Williams, Pictures From Breughel.
1964—Louis Simpson, At the End of the Open Road.
1965—John Berryman, 77 Dream Songs.
1966—Richard Eberhart, Selected Poems.
1967—Anne Sexton, Live or Die.
1968—Anthony Hecht, The Hard Hours.
1969—George Oppen, Of Being Numerous.
1970—Richard Howard, Untitled Subjects.
1971—William S. Merwin, The Carrier of Ladders.
1972—James Wright, Collected Poems.
1973—Maxine Winokur Kumin, Up Country.
1975—Gary Snyder, Turtle Island.
1976—John Ashbery, Self-Portrait in a Convex Mirror.
1977—James Merrill, Divine Comedies.
1978—Howard Nemerov, Collected Poems.
1979—Robert Penn Warren, Now and Then: Poems 1976-1978.
1980—Donald Justice, Selected Poems.
1981—James Schuyler, The Morning of the Poem.
1982—Sylvia Plath, The Collected Poems.
1983—Galway Kinnell, Selected Poems.
1984—Mary Oliver, American Primitive.
1985—Carolyn Kizer, Yin.
1986—Henry Taylor, The Flying Change.
1987—Rita Dove, Thomas and Beulah.
1988—William Meredith, Partial Accounts: New and Selected Poems.
1989—Richard Wilbur, New and Collected Poems.
1990—Charles Simic, The World Doesn't End
1991—Mona Van Duyn, Near Changes.
1992—James Tate, Selected Poems.

General Non-Fiction

1962—Theodore H. White, The Making of the President 1960.
1963—Barbara W. Tuchman, The Guns of August.
1964—Richard Hofstadter, Anti-Intellectualism in American Life.
1965—Howard Mumford Jones, O Strange New World.
1966—Edwin Way Teale, Wandering Through Winter.
1967—David Brion Davis, The Problem of Slavery in Western Culture.
1968—Will and Ariel Durant, Rousseau and Revolution.
1969—Norman Mailer, The Armies of the Night; and Rene Jules Dubos, So Human an Animal: How We Are Shaped by Surroundings and Events.
1970—Eric H. Erikson, Gandhi's Truth.
1971—John Toland, The Rising Sun.
1972—Barbara W. Tuchman, Stilwell and the American Experience in China, 1911-1945.
1973—Frances FitzGerald, Fire in the Lake: The Vietnamese and the Americans in Vietnam; Robert Coles, Children of Crisis, Volumes II & III.
1974—Ernest Becker, The Denial of Death.
1975—Annie Dillard, Pilgrim at Tinker Creek.
1976—Robert N. Butler, Why Survive? Being Old in America.
1977—William W. Warner, Beautiful Swimmers.
1978—Carl Sagan, The Dragons of Eden.
1979—Edward O. Wilson, On Human Nature.
1980—Douglas R. Hofstadter, Gödel, Escher, Bach: An Eternal Golden Braid.
1981 —Carl E. Schorske, Fin-de-Siecle Vienna: Politics and Culture.
1982—Tracy Kidder, The Soul of a New Machine.
1983—Susan Sheehan, Is There No Place on Earth for Me?
1984—Paul Starr, Social Transformation of American Medicine.
1985—Studs Terkel, The Good War.
1986—Joseph Lelyveld, Move Your Shadow; J. Anthony Lukas, Common Ground.
1987—David K. Shipler, Arab and Jew.
1988—Richard Rhodes, The Making of the Atomic Bomb.
1989—Neil Sheehan, A Bright Shining Lie: John Paul Vann and America in Vietnam.
1990—Dale Maharidge, Michael Williamson, And Their Children After Them.
1991—Bert Holldobler, Edward O. Wilson, The Ants.
1992—Daniel Yergin, The Prize: The Epic Quest for Oil.

Music

For composition by an American (before 1977, by a composer resident in the U.S.), in the larger forms of chamber, orchestra or choral music or for an operatic work including ballet. A special posthumous award was granted in 1976 to Scott Joplin.

1943—William Schuman, Secular Cantata No. 2, A Free Song.
1944—Howard Hanson, Symphony No. 4, Op. 34.
1945—Aaron Copland, Appalachian Spring.
1946—Leo Sowerby, The Canticle of the Sun.
1947—Charles E. Ives, Symphony No. 3.
1948—Walter Piston, Symphony No. 3.
1949—Virgil Thomson, Louisiana Story.
1950—Gian-Carlo Menotti, The Consul.
1951—Douglas Moore, Giants in the Earth.
1952—Gail Kubik, Symphony Concertante.
1954—Quincy Porter, Concerto for Two Pianos and Orchestra.
1955—Gian-Carlo Menotti, The Saint of Bleecker Street.
1956—Ernest Toch, Symphony No. 3.
1957—Norman Dello Joio, Meditations on Ecclesiastes.
1958—Samuel Barber, Vanessa.
1959—John La Montaine, Concerto for Piano and Orchestra.
1960—Elliott Carter, Second String Quartet.
1961—Walter Piston, Symphony No. 7.
1962—Robert Ward, The Crucible.
1963—Samuel Barber, Piano Concerto No. 1.
1966—Leslie Bassett, Variations for Orchestra.
1967—Leon Kirchner, Quartet No. 3.
1968—George Crumb, Echoes of Time and The River.
1969—Karel Husa, String Quartet No. 3.
1970—Charles W. Wuorinen, Time's Encomium.
1971—Mario Davidovsky, Synchronisms No. 6.
1972—Jacob Druckman, Windows.
1973—Elliott Carter, String Quartet No. 3.
1974—Donald Martino, Notturno. (Special citation) Roger Sessions.
1975—Dominick Argento, From the Diary of Virginia Woolf.
1976—Ned Rorem, Air Music.
1977—Richard Wernick, Visions of Terror and Wonder.
1978—Michael Colgrass, Deja Vu for Percussion and Orchestra.
1979—Joseph Schwantner, Aftertones of Infinity.
1980—David Del Tredici, In Memory of a Summer Day.
1982—Roger Sessions, Concerto For Orchestra. (Special Citation) Milton Babbitt.
1983—Ellen T. Zwilich, Three Movements for Orchestra.
1984—Bernard Rands, Canti del Sole.
1985—Stephen Albert, Symphony, RiverRun.
1986—George Perle, Wind Quintet IV.
1987—John Harbison, The Flight Into Egypt.
1988—William Bolcom, 12 New Etudes for Piano.

1989—Roger Reynolds, Whispers Out of Time.
1990—Mel Powell, Duplicates: A Concerto For Two Pianos and Orchestra.
1991—Shulamit Ran, Symphony.
1992—Wayne Peterson, The Face of the Night, The Heart of the Dark.

Special Awards

Awarded in 1991 or 1992

Books, Allied Arts

Academy of American Poets Awards: Lamont Poetry Selection, $1,000 and purchase of 2,000 copies of book for distribution to membership: Susan Wood, *Camp Santo*; Lavan Younger Poet Awards, $1,000 each: Nicholas Christopher, J. Allyn Rosser, Peter Schmitt; Whitman Award, for first book of poems, $1,000 and purchase of 2,000 copies of book for distribution to members: Stephen Yenser, *The Fire in All Things*.

American Academy and Institute of Arts and Letters literature awards: Alice Adams, John Crowley, Richard Foreman, Vicki Hearne, Ruth Prawer Jhabvala, Tim O'Brien, Simon Schama, August Wilson; Award of Merit for Poetry: Charles Wright; Bynner Prize for Poetry: George Bradley; Forster Award in Literature: Timothy Mo; Kaufman Prize for First Fiction: Alex Ullmann; Rosenthal Foundation Award: Douglas Hobbie; Stein Award for Poetry; James Applewhite; Traveling Fellowship in Literature: Lorrie Moore; Vursell Memorial Award in Literature: Angus Fletcher; Zabel Award in Poetry: Jorie Graham.

Golden Kite Awards, by Society of Children's Book Writers: fiction: Jean Thesman, *The Raincatchers*; nonfiction: Russell Freedman, *The Wright Brothers*; picture-illustration: *Mama, Do You Love Me?*, il. Barbara Lavallee, writ. Barbara M. Joosse.

Ruth Lilly Poetry Prize, by Modern Poetry Assn. and American Council for the Arts, $25,000: John Ashberry.

Los Angeles Times Book Prizes: fiction: Allan Gurganus, *White People*; history: Nicolas Lemann, *The Promised Land*; biography: T.H. Watkins, *Righteous Pilgrim*; current interest: E.J. Dionne, *Why Americans Hate Politics*; science and technology: Grigori Medvedev, *The Truth About Chernobyl*; poetry: Philip Levine, *What Work Is*; Kirsch Award, to author with home or focus in West, for body of work: Ken Kesey; Seidenbaum Award for First Fiction: David Wong Louie, *Pangs of Love*.

National Book Awards, $10,000 each: fiction: Norman Rush, *Mating*; nonfiction: Orlando Patterson, *Freedom*; poetry: Philip Levine, *What Work Is*; National Book Foundation Medal for Distinguished Contribution to American Letters: Eudora Welty.

National Book Critics Circle Awards, for best books by American authors: fiction: Jane Smiley, *A Thousand Acres*; nonfiction: Susan Faludi: *Backlash*; poetry: Albert Goldbarth, *Heaven and Earth: A Cosmology*; criticism: Lawrence L. Langer, *Holocaust Testimonies*; Citation for Excellence in Reviewing: George Scialabba.

National Jewish Book Awards, by Jewish Book Council: autobiography/memoir: Henry Morgenthau III, *Mostly Morgenthaus*; children's literature: Uri Orlev, trans. Hillel Halkin, *The Man from the Other Side*; children's picture book: Michelle Edwards, *Chicken Man*; contemporary Jewish life: Lynn Davidman, *Tradition in a Rootless World*; fiction: Nathan Sham, trans. Dalya Bilu, *The Rosendorf Quartet*; holocaust studies: Dalia Ofer, *Escaping the Holocaust*; Israel: Itamar Rabinovich, *The Road Not Taken*; Jewish history: Yosef Hayim Yerushalmi, *Freud's Moses*; scholarship: Steven D. Fraade, *From Tradition to Commentary*; Sephardic studies: Ross Brann, *The Compunctious Poet*; visual arts: Norman L. Kleeblatt and Susan Chevlowe, eds, *Painting a Place in America*.

PEN/Faulkner Award for Fiction, $7,500: Don DeLillo, *Mao II*.

Rea Award for the Short Story, by Dungannon Foundation, to living American writer for significant contribution to the form: Eudora Welty.

Whiting Awards, $30,000 each: Stanley Couch, Rebecca Goldstein, Allegra Goodman, John Holman, Cynthia Jadohata, Scott McPherson, Thylias Moss, Rick Rofihe, Anton Shammas, Franz Wright.

Journalism Awards

Helen B. Bernstein Award, by New York Public Library, for Excellence in Journalism: Alex Kotlowitz, *There Are No Children Here*.

Maria Moors Cabot Prizes, by Columbia Univ., for advancement of press freedom and inter-American understanding, gold medal and $1,000 each: Octavio Filho, *Folha de Sao Paulo*, Brazil; Eduardo Gallardo, The Associated Press; Alejandro Junco de la Vega, *El Norte*, Monterrey, Mexico; Lucia Newman, Cable News Network.

Alfred I. duPont-Columbia Univ. Awards in Broadcast Journalism: gold baton: Bill Moyers, news documentaries; silver batons, for Persian Gulf War coverage: Peter Jennings and ABC News; Peter Arnett, Cable News Network; National Public Radio; WFAA-TV, Dallas; silver batons: Ken Burns, "The Civil War"; Pierre Sauvage, "Weapons of the Spirit"; Bill Moyers, PBS Frontline; National Geographic Society, TBS; KPIX, San Francisco; KBDI, Denver; KWWL, Waterloo, Ia.

National Journalism Awards, by Scripps Howard Foundation, $41,000 total: Stone Award for editorials: Maria Henson, *Lexington* (Ky.) *Herald-Leader*; Meeman Awards for environmental journalism: *Poughkeepsie* (N.Y.) *Journal*, and (New Orleans, La.) *Times Picayune*; Charles E. Scripps Awards for literacy: (Greenville, N.C.) *Daily Reflector*; Ernie Pyle Award for human interest writing: Chris Hedges, *New York Times*; Roy W. Howard Awards for public service: (Waterbury, Conn.) *Republican-American* and *New York Newsday*; Edward W. Scripps Award for First Amendment: (Wilkes-Barre, Pa.) *Times Leader*; Charles M. Schultz Award for college cartoonist: Steve Breen, Univ. of Calif., Riverside; broadcast journalism: small market radio: KNPR-FM, Las Vegas, Nev.; large market radio: Minnesota Public Radio, St. Paul; broadcast-cable/small market TV: WUFT-TV, Gainesville, Fla.; broadcast-cable/large market TV: KCNC-TV, Denver, Colo.; literacy: WGHP-TV, High Point, N.C.

Overseas Press Club of America, for service by foreign correspondents, editors, and photojournalists: Boyle Award, for daily or wire service reporting from abroad, $1,000: Peter Gumble, *Wall Street Journal*; Considine Award, for daily newspaper or wire service interpretation of foreign affairs, $1,000: Carol Williams, *Los Angeles Times*; Capa Gold Medal, for courageous photographic reporting from abroad: Christopher Morris, Black Star, *Time*; Rebbot Award, for photographic reporting from abroad, magazines or books, $1,000: Steve McCurry, *National Geographic*; photographic reporting from abroad, newspapers or wire services, $1,000: Associated Press photographers and David Turnley, *Detroit Free Press*; broadcast journalism: Thomas Award, for radio interpretation or documentary on foreign affairs, $1,000: Tom Gjelten and Julie McCarthy, National Public Radio; Murrow Award, for TV interpretation or documentary on foreign affairs, $1,000: Artyom Borovik and George Crile, *60 Minutes*.

Thomas Paine National Historical Assn., for journalism reflecting Paine's ideals and commitment to free expression, $1,000: Robin MacNeil.

George Polk Awards, by Long Island Univ.: career award: Claude Sitton, retired ed., (Raleigh, N.C.) *News and Observer*, former chief Southern correspondent, *New York Times*; foreign correspondents: Francis X. Clines and Barbara Crossette, *New York Times*; cultural reporting: Konstantin Akinsha and Grigory Koslov, *Art News*; national reporting: Jeff Taylor, Mike McGraw, *Kansas City Star*; regional: Dan Barry, John Sullivan, Ira Chinoy, *Providence* (R.I.) *Journal-Bulletin*; local: Holly A. Taylor, *Berkshire* (Mass.) *Eagle*; economic: Donald L. Barlett, James B. Steele, *Philadelphia Inquirer*; education: Jeff Gottlieb, *San Jose Mercury News*; war: Patrick Sloyan, *Newsday* (L.I., N.Y.); special: Andrew Schneider, Mary Pat Flaherty, *Pittsburgh Press*.

Reuben Awards, by National Cartoonists Society: cartoonist of the year: Mike Peters, "Mother Goose and Grimm," and editorial cartoons; comic strip: Lynn Johnston, "For Better or For Worse"; comic panel: Al Scaduto, "They'll Do It Every Time"; editorial cartoon: Pat Oliphant, Universal Press Syndicate; sports cartoon: Pierre Bellocq, *Daily Racing Form*; advertising illustration: W.B. Park; animation, Gil Keane, "Beauty and the Beast"; greeting card and magazine/book illustration: Patrick McDonnell; gag: Arnie Levin, *New Yorker*; comic book: Frank Miller.

Science-in-Society Awards, by National Assn. of Science Writers, $1,000 each: newspapers: Vic Cohn, *Washington Post*; magazines: Robert E. Rhoades, *National Geographic*.

Sigma Delta Awards, by Society of Professional Journalists: deadline reporting, newspaper: *Philadelphia Inquirer*; non-deadline reporting: *Kansas City Star*; investigative reporting: *St. Petersburg Times*; feature writing: Christine Evans, *Miami Herald*; editorial writing: Maria Henson, *Lexington* (Ky.) *Herald-Leader*; Washington correspondence: David Everett, *Detroit Free Press*; foreign correspondence: Carol Williams, *Los Angeles Times*; public service: Andrew Schneider and Mary Pat Flaherty, *Pittsburgh Press*; and *Modesto Bee* (Calif.); public service in magazine journalism: Steve Waldman, *Newsweek*; photography: Charles Schlosser, *Des Moines* (Ia.) *Register*; editorial cartoons: Walt Handelsman, (New Orleans, La.) *Times Picayune*.

John Peter Zenger Award, by Univ. of Arizona, for service in behalf of freedom of the press: Peter Arnett, Cable News Network.

Movie, TV, and Theater Awards

American Academy and Institute of Arts and Letters: gold medal for drama: Sam Shepard; Richard Rodgers Awards in Musical Theater: *Avenue X*, John Jiler and Ray Leslee; *The Molly Maguires*, Sid Cherry and William Strempek.

Directors Guild of America, for feature-film director: Jonathan Demme, *The Silence of the Lambs*.

New York Drama Critics Circle Awards, by New York theater critics for out-of-town publications: play: *Dancing at Lughnasa*, Brian Friel; musical: *Crazy for You*, music and lyrics by George and Ira Gershwin, book by Ken Ludwig; Gassner Award for American playwright: Scott McPherson, *Marvin's Room*; Off Broadway Play: *Marvin's Room*, Scott McPherson; Off Broadway musical: *Song of Singapore*; book, music, and lyrics: *Song of Singapore*; actor, musical: Nathan Lane, *Guys and Dolls*; actress, musical: Faith Prince, *Guys and Dolls, Nick and Nora*; acting debuts: Larry Fishburne, Cynthia Martells, *Two Trains Running*; actor: Judd Hirsch, *Conversations with My Father*; actress: Laura Esterman, *Marvin's Room*; comedy: *Catskills on Broadway*; revival: *The Visit*; musical revival: *Guys and Dolls*; choreography: Susan Stroman, *Crazy for You*; scenic design: Robin Wagner, *Crazy for You*; costumes: William Ivey Long, *Crazy for You*; lighting: Paul Gallo, *Crazy for You*.

New York Film Critics Circle Awards: film: *The Silence of the Lambs*; director: Jonathan Demme, *The Silence of the Lambs*; actor: Anthony Hopkins, *The Silence of the Lambs*; actress: Jodie Foster, *The Silence of the Lambs*; supporting actor: Samuel L. Jackson, *Jungle Fever*; supporting actress: Judy Davis, *Barton Fink* and *Naked Lunch*; screenplay: David Cronenberg, *Naked Lunch*; cinematography: Roger Deakins, *Barton Fink*; foreign film: *Europa, Europa*; documentary: *Paris Burning*; new director: John Singleton, *Boyz N the Hood*.

Emmy Awards, by Academy of Television Arts and Sciences, for primetime programs, 1991-92: Dramatic series: *Northern Exposure*, CBS; actor: Christopher Lloyd, *Avonlea*, Disney; actress: Dana Delany, *China Beach*, ABC; supporting actor: Richard Dysart, *L.A. Law*, NBC; supporting actress: Valerie Mahaffey, *Northern Exposure*, CBS; writing: Andrew Schneider and Diane Frolov, *Northern Exposure*, CBS; directing: Eric Laneuville, *I'll Fly Away*, NBC. Comedy series: *Murphy Brown*, CBS; actress: Candice Bergen, *Murphy Brown*, CBS; actor: Craig T. Nelson, *Coach*, ABC; supporting actress: Laurie Metcalf, *Roseanne*, ABC; supporting actor: Michael Jeter, *Evening Shade*, CBS; writing: Elaine Pope and Larry Charles, *Seinfeld*, NBC; directing: Barnet Kellmen, *Murphy Brown*, CBS. Variety, music, or comedy program: *The Tonight Show Starring Johnny Carson*, NBC; performance: Bette Midler, *The Tonight Show Starring Johnny Carson*, NBC: writing: *The 64th Annual Academy Awards*, ABC; directing: Patricia Birch, *Unforgettable, With Love: Natalie Cole Sings the Songs of Nat King Cole*, PBS. Made-for-TV movie: *Hallmark Hall of Fame: Miss Rose White*, NBC; Miniseries: *A Woman Named Jackie*, NBC; actor: Beau Bridges, *Without Warning: The James Brady Story*, HBO; actress: Gena Rowlands, *Face of a Stranger*, CBS; supporting actor: Hume Cronyn, *Neil Simon's 'Broadway Bound,'* ABC; actress: Amanda Plummer, *Hallmark Hall of Fame, Miss Rose White*, NBC; writing: Joshua Brand and John Falsey, *I'll Fly Away*, NBC; directing: Joseph Sargent, *Hallmark Hall of Fame, Miss Rose White*, NBC. Animation: *A Claymation Easter*, CBS. Cyd Charisse Founders Award: Robert F. Lewine. Governors Award: Ted Turner.

Tony (Antoinette Perry) **Awards:** play: *Dancing at Lughnasa*, Brian Friel; musical: *Crazy for You*; revival: *Guys and Dolls*; leading actor, play: Judd Hirsch, *Conversations with My Father*; leading actress, play: Glenn Close, *Death and the Maiden*; leading actor, musical: Gregory Hines, *Jelly's Last Jam*; leading actress, musical: Faith Prince, *Guys and Dolls*; featured actor, play: Larry Fishburne, *Two Trains Running*; featured actress, play: Brid Brennan, *Dancing at Lughnasa*; featured actor, musical: Scott Waara, *The Most Happy Fella*; featured actress, musical: Tonya Pinkins, *Jelly's Last Jam*; direction, play: Patrick Mason, *Dancing at Lughnasa*; direction, musical: Jerry Zaks, *Guys and Dolls*; book, musical: William Finn and James Lapine, *Falsettos*; original musical score: William Finn, *Falsettos*; scenic design: Tony Walton, *Guys and Dolls*; costume design: William Ivey Long, *Crazy for You*; lighting design: Jules Fisher, *Jelly's Last Jam*; choreography: Susan Stroman, *Crazy for You*.

Miscellaneous

American Academy and Institute of Arts and Letters: gold medal for graphic art: David Levine; distinguished service to the arts: W. McNeil Lowry; Brunner Memorial Prize in Architecture: Sir Norman Foster; Academy-Institute Awards: architecture: Thom Mayne and Michael Rotondi; music: Charles C. Fussell, Eugene Kurtz, Peter Lieberson, Tobias Picker; Ernst Award in Art: Hans Burkhardt; Hinrichsen Award in Music: Hi Kyung Kim; Ives Fellowship in Music: Geoffrey Stanton; Lieberson Fellowships in Music: Laura Clayton, Cindy McTee; Nevelson Award in Art: Peter Voulkos; Rosenthal Foundation Award in Art: Laura Newman.

American Assn. for the Advancement of Science: Mentor Award, $5,000: Anthony J. Andreoli, Calif. State Univ., Los Angeles, and Lafayette Frederick, Howard Univ., Washington, D.C.; Westinghouse Award for Public Understanding of Science and Technology, $5,000: Stephen H. Schneider, Natl. Center for Atmospheric Research; Hilliard Prize for Excellence in Science, Arms Control, and Intl. Security, $5,000: Robert P. Mikulak, U.S. Arms Control & Disarmament Agency; Will D. Carpenter, Monsanto Agricultural Co.; Newcomb Cleveland Prize, $5,000: Stephen P.A. Fodor, J. Leighton Read, Michael C. Pirrung, Lubert Stryer, Amy Tsai Lu, Dennis Solas.

American Institute of Architects Gold Medal, for lifetime achievement: Benjamin C. Thompson.

Charles Stark Draper Prize, Natl. Academy of Engineering, for lifetime achievement, $375,000: Sir Frank Whittle, Hans J.P. von Ohain.

Frankel Prize, by Natl. Endowment for the Humanities, for contribution to the humanities: Winton Blount, director, Alabama Shakespeare Festival; Louise Cowan, co-founder, Dallas Institute of Humanities and Culture; Karl Haas, host, "Adventures in Good Music"; John Kuo Wei Tchen, acting director, Asian-American Resource Center, Queens College, New York City; Ken Burns, producer, "The Civil War."

Friedheim Awards, by Kennedy Center, for new chamber music: first prize, $5,000: Richard Wernick, Media, Pa.

Grawemeyer Awards for Music Composition, by Univ. of Louisville, $150,000: Kryzystof Penderecki, "Adagio for Large Orchestra."

Charles Evans Hughes Gold Medal, by Natl. Conference of Christians and Jews, for courageous leadership: Thurgood Marshall.

Kennedy Center Awards, for lifetime contribution to performing arts: Roy Acuff, Betty Comden and Adolph Green, Fayard Nicholas and Harold Nicholas, Gregory Peck, Robert Shaw.

Harold W. McGraw Jr. Prize in Education, by McGraw Hill Inc., $25,000 each: Judith E. Lanier, dean of education, Michigan State Univ.; Robert H. McCable, president, Miami-Dade Community College District; Theodore R. Sizer, professor of education, Brown Univ.

Praemium Imperiale Awards, by Fujisankei Communications Group and Japan Art Assn., for lifetime achievement in the arts, $115,000 and medal each: architecture: Frank O. Gehry, U.S.; theater and film: Akira Kurosawa, Japan; painting: Pierre Soulages, France; sculpture: Anthony Caro, U.K.; music: Alfred Schnittke, Germany-Russia.

Pritzker Prize for Architecture, $100,000: Alvaro Siza, Portugal.

The Spingarn Medal

The Spingarn Medal has been awarded annually since 1914 by the National Association for the Advancement of Colored People for the highest achievement by a black American.

1946	Dr. Percy L. Julian	1960	Kenneth B. Clark	1976	Alex Haley
1947	Channing H. Tobias	1961	Robert C. Weaver	1977	Andrew Young
1948	Ralph J. Bunche	1962	Medgar Wiley Evers	1978	Mrs. Rosa L. Parks
1949	Charles Hamilton Houston	1963	Roy Wilkins	1979	Dr. Rayford W. Logan
1950	Mabel Keaton Staupers	1964	Leontyne Price	1980	Coleman Young
1951	Harry T. Moore	1965	John H. Johnson	1981	Dr. Benjamin Elijah Mays
1952	Paul R. Williams	1966	Edward W. Brooke	1982	Lena Horne
1953	Theodore K. Lawless	1967	Sammy Davis Jr.	1983	Thomas Bradley
1954	Carl Murphy	1968	Clarence M. Mitchell Jr.	1984	Bill Cosby
1955	Jack Roosevelt Robinson	1969	Jacob Lawrence	1985	Dr. Benjamin L. Hooks
1956	Martin Luther King Jr.	1970	Leon Howard Sullivan	1986	Percy E. Sutton
1957	Mrs. Daisy Bates and the Little Rock Nine	1971	Gordon Parks	1987	Frederick Douglass Patterson
1958	Edward Kennedy (Duke) Ellington	1972	Wilson C. Riles	1988	Jesse Jackson
1959	Langston Hughes	1973	Damon Keith	1989	L. Douglas Wilder
		1974	Henry (Hank) Aaron	1990	Gen. Colin L. Powell
		1975	Alvin Ailey	1991	Barbara Jordan

Miss America Winners

1921	Margaret Gorman, Washington, D.C.	1962	Maria Fletcher, Asheville, North Carolina
1922-23	Mary Campbell, Columbus, Ohio	1963	Jacquelyn Mayer, Sandusky, Ohio
1924	Ruth Malcolmson, Philadelphia, Pennsylvania	1964	Donna Axum, El Dorado, Arkansas
1925	Fay Lamphier, Oakland, California	1965	Vonda Kay Van Dyke, Phoenix, Arizona
1926	Norma Smallwood, Tulsa, Oklahoma	1966	Deborah Irene Bryant, Overland Park, Kansas
1927	Lois Delaner, Joliet, Illinois	1967	Jane Anne Jayroe, Laverne, Oklahoma
1933	Marion Bergeron, West Haven, Connecticut	1968	Debra Dene Barnes, Moran, Kansas
1935	Henrietta Leaver, Pittsburgh, Pennsylvania	1969	Judith Anne Ford, Belvidere, Illinois
1936	Rose Coyle, Philadelphia, Pennsylvania	1970	Pamela Anne Eldred, Birmingham, Michigan
1937	Bette Cooper, Bertrand Island, New Jersey	1971	Phyllis Ann George, Denton, Texas
1938	Marilyn Meseke, Marion, Ohio	1972	Laurie Lea Schaefer, Columbus, Ohio
1939	Patricia Donnelly, Detroit, Michigan	1973	Terry Anne Meeuwsen, DePere, Wisconsin
1940	Frances Marie Burke, Philadelphia, Pennsylvania	1974	Rebecca Ann King, Denver, Colorado
1941	Rosemary LaPlanche, Los Angeles, California	1975	Shirley Cothran, Fort Worth, Texas
1942	Jo-Caroll Dennison, Tyler, Texas	1976	Tawney Elaine Godin, Yonkers, N.Y.
1943	Jean Bartel, Los Angeles, California	1977	Dorothy Kathleen Benham, Edina, Minnesota
1944	Venus Ramey, Washington, D.C.	1978	Susan Perkins, Columbus, Ohio
1945	Bess Myerson, New York City, N.Y.	1979	Kylene Barker, Galax, Virginia
1946	Marilyn Buferd, Los Angeles, California	1980	Cheryl Prewitt, Ackerman, Mississippi
1947	Barbara Walker, Memphis, Tennessee	1981	Susan Powell, Elk City, Oklahoma
1948	BeBe Shopp, Hopkins, Minnesota	1982	Elizabeth Ward, Russellville, Arkansas
1949	Jacque Mercer, Litchfield, Arizona	1983	Debra Maffett, Anaheim, California
1951	Yolande Betbeze, Mobile, Alabama	1984	Vanessa Williams, Milwood, New York*
1952	Coleen Kay Hutchins, Salt Lake City, Utah		Suzette Charles, Mays Landing, New Jersey
1953	Neva Jane Langley, Macon, Georgia	1985	Sharlene Wells, Salt Lake City, Utah
1954	Evelyn Margaret Ay, Ephrata, Pennsylvania	1986	Susan Akin, Meridian, Mississippi
1955	Lee Meriwether, San Francisco, California	1987	Kellye Cash, Memphis, Tennessee
1956	Sharon Ritchie, Denver, Colorado	1988	Kaye Lani Rae Rafko, Monroe, Michigan
1957	Marian McKnight, Manning, South Carolina	1989	Gretchen Carlson, Anoka, Minnesota
1958	Marilyn Van Derbur, Denver, Colorado	1990	Debbye Turner, Columbia, Missouri
1959	Mary Ann Mobley, Brandon, Mississippi	1991	Marjorie Vincent, Illinois
1960	Lynda Lee Mead, Natchez, Mississippi	1992	Carolyn Suzanne Sapp, Hawaii
1961	Nancy Fleming, Montague, Michigan	1993	Leanza Cornett, Florida

* Resigned July 23, 1984.

Motion Picture Academy Awards (Oscars)

1927-28
Actor: Emil Jannings, *The Way of All Flesh.*
Actress: Janet Gaynor, *Seventh Heaven.*
Director: Frank Borzage, *Seventh Heaven;* Lewis Milestone, *Two Arabian Knights.*
Picture: *Wings,* Paramount.

1928-29
Actor: Warner Baxter, *In Old Arizona.*
Actress: Mary Pickford, *Coquette.*
Director: Frank Lloyd, *The Divine Lady.*
Picture: *Broadway Melody,* MGM.

1929-30
Actor: George Arliss, *Disraeli.*
Actress: Norma Shearer, *The Divorcee.*
Director: Lewis Milestone, *All Quiet on the Western Front.*
Picture: *All Quiet on the Western Front,* Univ.

1930-31
Actor: Lionel Barrymore, *Free Soul.*
Actress: Marie Dressler, *Min and Bill.*
Director: Norman Taurog, *Skippy.*
Picture: *Cimarron,* RKO.

1931-32
Actor: Fredric March, *Dr. Jekyll and Mr. Hyde;* Wallace Beery, *The Champ* (tie).
Actress: Helen Hayes, *Sin of Madelon Claudet.*
Director: Frank Borzage, *Bad Girl.*
Picture: *Grand Hotel,* MGM.
Special: Walt Disney, *Mickey Mouse.*

1932-33
Actor: Charles Laughton, *Private Life of Henry VIII.*
Actress: Katharine Hepburn, *Morning Glory.*
Director: Frank Lloyd, *Cavalcade.*
Picture: *Cavalcade,* Fox.

1934
Actor: Clark Gable, *It Happened One Night.*
Actress: Claudette Colbert, *It Happened One Night.*
Director: Frank Capra, *It Happened One Night.*
Picture: *It Happened One Night,* Columbia.

1935
Actor: Victor McLaglen, *The Informer.*
Actress: Bette Davis, *Dangerous.*
Director: John Ford, *The Informer.*
Picture: *Mutiny on the Bounty,* MGM.

1936
Actor: Paul Muni, *Story of Louis Pasteur.*
Actress: Luise Rainer, *The Great Ziegfeld.*
Sup. Actor: Walter Brennan, *Come and Get It.*
Sup. Actress: Gale Sondergaard, *Anthony Adverse.*
Director: Frank Capra, *Mr. Deeds Goes to Town.*
Picture: *The Great Ziegfeld,* MGM.

1937
Actor: Spencer Tracy, *Captains Courageous.*
Actress: Luise Rainer, *The Good Earth.*
Sup. Actor: Joseph Schildkraut, *Life of Emile Zola.*
Sup. Actress: Alice Brady, *In Old Chicago.*
Director: Leo McCarey, *The Awful Truth.*
Picture: *Life of Emile Zola,* Warner.

1938
Actor: Spencer Tracy, *Boys Town.*
Actress: Bette Davis, *Jezebel.*
Sup. Actor: Walter Brennan, *Kentucky.*
Sup. Actress: Fay Bainter, *Jezebel.*
Director: Frank Capra, *You Can't Take It With You.*
Picture: *You Can't Take It With You,* Columbia.

1939
Actor: Robert Donat, *Goodbye Mr. Chips.*
Actress: Vivien Leigh, *Gone With the Wind.*
Sup. Actor: Thomas Mitchell, *Stage Coach.*
Sup. Actress: Hattie McDaniel, *Gone With the Wind.*
Director: Victor Fleming, *Gone With the Wind.*
Picture: *Gone With the Wind,* Selznick International.

1940
Actor: James Stewart, *The Philadelphia Story.*
Actress: Ginger Rogers, *Kitty Foyle.*
Sup. Actor: Walter Brennan, *The Westerner.*
Sup. Actress: Jane Darwell, *The Grapes of Wrath.*
Director: John Ford, *The Grapes of Wrath.*
Picture: *Rebecca,* Selznick International.

1941
Actor: Gary Cooper, *Sergeant York.*
Actress: Joan Fontaine, *Suspicion.*
Sup. Actor: Donald Crisp, *How Green Was My Valley.*
Sup. Actress: Mary Astor, *The Great Lie.*
Director: John Ford, *How Green Was My Valley.*
Picture: *How Green Was My Valley,* 20th Cent.-Fox.

1942
Actor: James Cagney, *Yankee Doodle Dandy.*
Actress: Greer Garson, *Mrs. Miniver.*
Sup. Actor: Van Heflin, *Johnny Eager.*
Sup. Actress: Teresa Wright, *Mrs. Miniver.*
Director: William Wyler, *Mrs. Miniver.*
Picture: *Mrs. Miniver,* MGM.

1943
Actor: Paul Lukas, *Watch on the Rhine.*
Actress: Jennifer Jones, *The Song of Bernadette.*
Sup. Actor: Charles Coburn, *The More the Merrier.*
Sup. Actress: Katina Paxinou, *For Whom the Bell Tolls.*
Director: Michael Curtiz, *Casablanca.*
Picture: *Casablanca,* Warner.

1944
Actor: Bing Crosby, *Going My Way.*
Actress: Ingrid Bergman, *Gaslight.*
Sup. Actor: Barry Fitzgerald, *Going My Way.*
Sup. Actress: Ethel Barrymore, *None But the Lonely Heart.*
Director: Leo McCarey, *Going My Way.*
Picture: *Going My Way,* Paramount.

1945
Actor: Ray Milland, *The Lost Weekend.*
Actress: Joan Crawford, *Mildred Pierce.*
Sup. Actor: James Dunn, *A Tree Grows in Brooklyn.*
Sup. Actress: Anne Revere, *National Velvet.*
Director: Billy Wilder, *The Lost Weekend.*
Picture: *The Lost Weekend,* Paramount.

1946
Actor: Fredric March, *Best Years of Our Lives.*
Actress: Olivia de Havilland, *To Each His Own.*
Sup. Actor: Harold Russell, *The Best Years of Our Lives.*
Sup. Actress: Anne Baxter, *The Razor's Edge.*
Director: William Wyler, *The Best Years of Our Lives.*
Picture: *The Best Years of Our Lives,* Goldwyn, RKO.

1947
Actor: Ronald Colman, *A Double Life.*
Actress: Loretta Young, *The Farmer's Daughter.*
Sup. Actor: Edmund Gwenn, *Miracle on 34th Street.*
Sup. Actress: Celeste Holm, *Gentleman's Agreement.*
Director: Elia Kazan, *Gentleman's Agreement.*
Picture: *Gentleman's Agreement,* 20th Cent.-Fox.

1948
Actor: Laurence Olivier, *Hamlet.*
Actress: Jane Wyman, *Johnny Belinda.*
Sup. Actor: Walter Huston, *Treasure of Sierra Madre.*
Sup. Actress: Claire Trevor, *Key Largo.*
Director: John Huston, *Treasure of Sierra Madre.*
Picture: *Hamlet,* Two Cities Film, Universal International.

1949
Actor: Broderick Crawford, *All the King's Men.*
Actress: Olivia de Havilland, *The Heiress.*
Sup. Actor: Dean Jagger, *Twelve O'Clock High.*
Sup. Actress: Mercedes McCambridge, *All the King's Men.*
Director: Joseph L. Mankiewicz, *Letter to Three Wives.*
Picture: *All the King's Men,* Columbia.

1950
Actor: Jose Ferrer, *Cyrano de Bergerac.*
Actress: Judy Holliday, *Born Yesterday.*
Sup. Actor: George Sanders, *All About Eve.*
Sup. Actress: Josephine Hull, *Harvey.*
Director: Joseph L. Mankiewicz, *All About Eve.*
Picture: *All About Eve,* 20th Century-Fox.

1951
Actor: Humphrey Bogart, *The African Queen.*
Actress: Vivien Leigh, *A Streetcar Named Desire.*
Sup. Actor: Karl Malden, *A Streetcar Named Desire.*
Sup. Actress: Kim Hunter, *A Streetcar Named Desire.*
Director: George Stevens, *A Place in the Sun.*
Picture: *An American in Paris,* MGM.

1952
Actor: Gary Cooper, *High Noon.*
Actress: Shirley Booth, *Come Back, Little Sheba.*
Sup. Actor: Anthony Quinn, *Viva Zapata!*
Sup. Actress: Gloria Grahame, *The Bad and the Beautiful.*
Director: John Ford, *The Quiet Man.*
Picture: *Greatest Show on Earth,* C.B. DeMille, Paramount.

1953
Actor: William Holden, *Stalag 17.*
Actress: Audrey Hepburn, *Roman Holiday.*
Sup. Actor: Frank Sinatra, *From Here to Eternity.*
Sup. Actress: Donna Reed, *From Here to Eternity.*
Director: Fred Zinnemann, *From Here to Eternity.*
Picture: *From Here to Eternity,* Columbia.

1954
Actor: Marlon Brando, *On the Waterfront.*

Actress: Grace Kelly, *The Country Girl.*
Sup. Actor: Edmond O'Brien, *The Barefoot Contessa.*
Sup. Actress: Eva Marie Saint, *On the Waterfront.*
Director: Elia Kazan, *On the Waterfront.*
Picture: *On the Waterfront,* Horizon-American, Colum.

1955

Actor: Ernest Borgnine, *Marty.*
Actress: Anna Magnani, *The Rose Tattoo.*
Sup. Actor: Jack Lemmon, *Mister Roberts.*
Sup. Actress: Jo Van Fleet, *East of Eden.*
Director: Delbert Mann, *Marty.*
Picture: *Marty,* Hecht and Lancaster's Steven Prods., U.A.

1956

Actor: Yul Brynner, *The King and I.*
Actress: Ingrid Bergman, *Anastasia.*
Sup. Actor: Anthony Quinn, *Lust for Life.*
Sup. Actress: Dorothy Malone, *Written on the Wind.*
Director: George Stevens, *Giant.*
Picture: *Around the World in 80 Days,* Michael Todd, U.A.

1957

Actor: Alec Guinness, *The Bridge on the River Kwai.*
Actress: Joanne Woodward, *The Three Faces of Eve.*
Sup. Actor: Red Buttons, *Sayonara.*
Sup. Actress: Miyoshi Umeki, *Sayonara.*
Director: David Lean, *The Bridge on the River Kwai.*
Picture: *The Bridge on the River Kwai,* Columbia.

1958

Actor: David Niven, *Separate Tables.*
Actress: Susan Hayward, *I Want to Live.*
Sup. Actor: Burl Ives, *The Big Country.*
Sup. Actress: Wendy Hiller, *Separate Tables.*
Director: Vincente Minnelli, *Gigi.*
Picture: *Gigi,* Arthur Freed Production, MGM.

1959

Actor: Charlton Heston, *Ben-Hur.*
Actress: Simone Signoret, *Room at the Top.*
Sup. Actor: Hugh Griffith, *Ben-Hur.*
Sup. Actress: Shelley Winters, *Diary of Anne Frank.*
Director: William Wyler, *Ben-Hur.*
Picture: *Ben-Hur,* MGM.

1960

Actor: Burt Lancaster, *Elmer Gantry.*
Actress: Elizabeth Taylor, *Butterfield 8.*
Sup. Actor: Peter Ustinov, *Spartacus.*
Sup. Actress: Shirley Jones, *Elmer Gantry.*
Director: Billy Wilder, *The Apartment.*
Picture: *The Apartment,* Mirisch Co., U.A.

1961

Actor: Maximilian Schell, *Judgment at Nuremberg.*
Actress: Sophia Loren, *Two Women.*
Sup. Actor: George Chakiris, *West Side Story.*
Sup. Actress: Rita Moreno, *West Side Story.*
Director: Jerome Robbins, Robert Wise, *West Side Story.*
Picture: *West Side Story,* United Artists.

1962

Actor: Gregory Peck, *To Kill a Mockingbird.*
Actress: Anne Bancroft, *The Miracle Worker.*
Sup. Actor: Ed Begley, *Sweet Bird of Youth.*
Sup. Actress: Patty Duke, *The Miracle Worker.*
Director: David Lean, *Lawrence of Arabia.*
Picture: *Lawrence of Arabia,* Columbia.

1963

Actor: Sidney Poitier, *Lilies of the Field.*
Actress: Patricia Neal, *Hud.*
Sup. Actor: Melvyn Douglas, *Hud.*
Sup. Actress: Margaret Rutherford, *The V.I.P.s.*
Director: Tony Richardson, *Tom Jones.*
Picture: *Tom Jones,* Woodfall Prod., UA-Lopert Pictures.

1964

Actor: Rex Harrison, *My Fair Lady.*
Actress: Julie Andrews, *Mary Poppins.*
Sup. Actor: Peter Ustinov, *Topkapi.*
Sup. Actress: Lila Kedrova, *Zorba the Greek.*
Director: George Cukor, *My Fair Lady.*
Picture: *My Fair Lady,* Warner Bros.

1965

Actor: Lee Marvin, *Cat Ballou.*
Actress: Julie Christie, *Darling.*
Sup. Actor: Martin Balsam, *A Thousand Clowns.*
Sup. Actress: Shelley Winters, *A Patch of Blue.*
Director: Robert Wise, *The Sound of Music.*
Picture: *The Sound of Music,* 20th Century-Fox.

1966

Actor: Paul Scofield, *A Man for All Seasons.*
Actress: Elizabeth Taylor, *Who's Afraid of Virginia Woolf?*
Sup. Actor: Walter Matthau, *The Fortune Cookie.*
Sup. Actress: Sandy Dennis, *Who's Afraid of Virginia Woolf?*
Director: Fred Zinnemann, *A Man for All Seasons.*
Picture: *A Man for All Seasons,* Columbia.

1967

Actor: Rod Steiger, *In the Heat of the Night.*
Actress: Katharine Hepburn, *Guess Who's Coming to Dinner.*
Sup. Actor: George Kennedy, *Cool Hand Luke.*
Sup. Actress: Estelle Parsons, *Bonnie and Clyde.*
Director: Mike Nichols, *The Graduate.*
Picture: *In the Heat of the Night.*

1968

Actor: Cliff Robertson, *Charly.*
Actress: Katharine Hepburn, *The Lion in Winter;* Barbra Streisand, *Funny Girl* (tie).
Sup. Actor: Jack Albertson, *The Subject Was Roses.*
Sup. Actress: Ruth Gordon, *Rosemary's Baby.*
Director: Sir Carol Reed, *Oliver!*
Picture: *Oliver!*

1969

Actor: John Wayne, *True Grit.*
Actress: Maggie Smith, *The Prime of Miss Jean Brodie.*
Sup. Actor: Gig Young, *They Shoot Horses, Don't They?*
Sup. Actress: Goldie Hawn, *Cactus Flower.*
Director: John Schlesinger, *Midnight Cowboy.*
Picture: *Midnight Cowboy.*

1970

Actor: George C. Scott, *Patton* (refused).
Actress: Glenda Jackson, *Women in Love.*
Sup. Actor: John Mills, *Ryan's Daughter.*
Sup. Actress: Helen Hayes, *Airport.*
Director: Franklin Schaffner, *Patton.*
Picture: *Patton.*

1971

Actor: Gene Hackman, *The French Connection.*
Actress: Jane Fonda, *Klute.*
Sup. Actor: Ben Johnson, *The Last Picture Show.*
Sup. Actress: Cloris Leachman, *The Last Picture Show.*
Director: William Friedkin, *The French Connection.*
Picture: *The French Connection.*

1972

Actor: Marlon Brando, *The Godfather* (refused).
Actress: Liza Minnelli, *Cabaret.*
Sup. Actor: Joel Grey, *Cabaret.*
Sup. Actress: Eileen Heckart, *Butterflies are Free.*
Director: Bob Fosse, *Cabaret.*
Picture: *The Godfather.*

1973

Actor: Jack Lemmon, *Save the Tiger.*
Actress: Glenda Jackson, *A Touch of Class.*
Sup. Actor: John Houseman, *The Paper Chase.*
Sup. Actress: Tatum O'Neal, *Paper Moon.*
Director: George Roy Hill, *The Sting.*
Picture: *The Sting.*

1974

Actor: Art Carney, *Harry and Tonto.*
Actress: Ellen Burstyn, *Alice Doesn't Live Here Anymore.*
Sup. Actor: Robert DeNiro, *The Godfather, Part II.*
Sup. Actress: Ingrid Bergman, *Murder on the Orient Express.*
Director: Francis Ford Coppola, *The Godfather, Part II.*
Picture: *The Godfather, Part II.*

1975

Actor: Jack Nicholson, *One Flew Over the Cuckoo's Nest.*
Actress: Louise Fletcher, *One Flew Over the Cuckoo's Nest.*
Sup. Actor: George Burns, *The Sunshine Boys.*
Sup. Actress: Lee Grant, *Shampoo.*
Director: Milos Forman, *One Flew Over the Cuckoo's Nest.*
Picture: *One Flew Over the Cuckoo's Nest.*

1976

Actor: Peter Finch, *Network.*
Actress: Faye Dunaway, *Network.*
Sup. Actor: Jason Robards, *All the President's Men.*
Sup. Actress: Beatrice Straight, *Network.*
Director: John G. Avildsen, *Rocky.*
Picture: *Rocky.*

1977

Actor: Richard Dreyfuss, *The Goodbye Girl.*
Actress: Diane Keaton, *Annie Hall.*
Sup. Actor: Jason Robards, *Julia.*
Sup. Actress: Vanessa Redgrave, *Julia.*
Director: Woody Allen, *Annie Hall.*
Picture: *Annie Hall.*

1978

Actor: Jon Voight, *Coming Home.*
Actress: Jane Fonda, *Coming Home.*
Sup. Actor: Christopher Walken, *The Deer Hunter.*
Sup. Actress: Maggie Smith, *California Suite.*
Director: Michael Cimino, *The Deer Hunter.*
Picture: *The Deer Hunter.*

1979

Actor: Dustin Hoffman, *Kramer vs. Kramer.*
Actress: Sally Field, *Norma Rae.*
Sup. Actor: Melvyn Douglas, *Being There.*

Sup. Actress: Meryl Streep, *Kramer vs. Kramer.*
Director: Robert Benton, *Kramer vs. Kramer.*
Picture: *Kramer vs. Kramer.*

1980

Actor: Robert DeNiro, *Raging Bull.*
Actress: Sissy Spacek, *Coal Miner's Daughter.*
Sup. Actor: Timothy Hutton, *Ordinary People.*
Sup. Actress: Mary Steenburgen, *Melvin & Howard.*
Director: Robert Redford, *Ordinary People.*
Picture: *Ordinary People.*

1981

Actor: Henry Fonda, *On Golden Pond.*
Actress: Katharine Hepburn, *On Golden Pond.*
Sup. Actor: John Gielgud, *Arthur.*
Sup. Actress: Maureen Stapleton, *Reds.*
Director: Warren Beatty, *Reds.*
Picture: *Chariots of Fire.*

1982

Actor: Ben Kingsley, *Gandhi.*
Actress: Meryl Streep, *Sophie's Choice.*
Sup. Actor: Louis Gossett, Jr., *An Officer and a Gentleman.*
Sup. Actress: Jessica Lange, *Tootsie.*
Director: Richard Attenborough, *Gandhi.*
Picture: *Gandhi.*

1983

Actor: Robert Duvall, *Tender Mercies.*
Actress: Shirley MacLaine, *Terms of Endearment.*
Supporting Actor: Jack Nicholson, *Terms of Endearment.*
Supporting Actress: Linda Hunt, *The Year of Living Dangerously.*
Director: James L. Brooks, *Terms of Endearment.*
Picture: *Terms of Endearment.*

1984

Actor: F. Murray Abraham, *Amadeus.*
Actress: Sally Field, *Places in the Heart.*
Supporting Actor: Haing S. Ngor, *The Killing Fields.*
Supporting Actress: Peggy Ashcroft, *A Passage to India.*
Director: Milos Forman, *Amadeus.*
Picture: *Amadeus.*

1985

Actor: William Hurt, *Kiss of the Spider Woman.*
Actress: Geraldine Page, *The Trip to Bountiful.*
Supporting Actor: Don Ameche, *Cocoon.*
Supporting Actress: Anjelica Huston, *Prizzi's Honor.*
Director: Sydney Pollack, *Out of Africa.*
Picture: *Out of Africa.*

1986

Actor: Paul Newman, *The Color of Money.*
Actress: Marlee Matlin, *Children of a Lesser God.*
Supporting Actor: Michael Caine, *Hannah and Her Sisters.*
Supporting Actress: Dianne Wiest, *Hannah and Her Sisters.*
Director: Oliver Stone, *Platoon.*
Picture: *Platoon.*

1987

Actor: Michael Douglas, *Wall Street.*
Actress: Cher, *Moonstruck.*
Supporting Actor: Sean Connery, *The Untouchables.*
Supporting Actress: Olympia Dukakis, *Moonstruck.*
Director: Bernardo Bertolucci, *The Last Emperor.*
Picture: *The Last Emperor.*

1988

Actor: Dustin Hoffman, *Rain Man.*
Actress: Jodie Foster, *The Accused.*
Supporting Actor: Kevin Kline, *A Fish Called Wanda.*
Supporting Actress: Geena Davis, *The Accidental Tourist.*
Director: Barry Levinson, *Rain Man.*
Picture: *Rain Man.*

1989

Actor: Daniel Day-Lewis, *My Left Foot.*
Actress: Jessica Tandy, *Driving Miss Daisy.*
Supporting Actor: Denzel Washington, *Glory.*
Supporting Actress: Brenda Fricker, *My Left Foot.*
Director: Oliver Stone, *Born on the Fourth of July.*
Picture: *Driving Miss Daisy.*

1990

Actor: Jeremy Irons, *Reversal of Fortune.*
Actress: Kathy Bates, *Misery.*
Supporting Actor: Joe Pesci, *Goodfellas.*
Supporting Actress: Whoopi Goldberg, *Ghost.*
Director: Kevin Costner, *Dances With Wolves.*
Picture: *Dances With Wolves*

1991

Picture: *The Silence of the Lambs.*
Actor: Anthony Hopkins, *The Silence of the Lambs.*
Actress: Jodie Foster, *The Silence of the Lambs.*
Supporting Actor: Jack Palance, *City Slickers.*
Supporting Actress: Mercedes Ruehl, *The Fisher King.*
Director: Jonathan Demme, *The Silence of the Lambs.*
Foreign Film: *Mediterraneo*, Italy.
Art Direction: *Bugsy.*
Cinematography: *J.F.K.*
Costume Design: *Bugsy.*
Documentary Feature: *In the Shadow of the Stars.*
Documentary Short Subject: *Deadly Deception.*
Film Editing: *J.F.K.*
Makeup: *Terminator 2: Judgment Day.*
Original Score: *Beauty and the Beast.*
Original Song: "Beauty and the Beast," from *Beauty and the Beast.*
Animated Short Film: *Manipulation.*
Live Action Short Film: *Session Man.*
Sound: *Terminator 2: Judgment Day.*
Sound Effects Editing: *Terminator 2: Judgment Day.*
Visual Effects: *Terminator 2: Judgment Day.*
Lifetime Achievement Award: Satyajit Ray.
Irving G. Thalberg Award, for body of work: George Lucas.
Gordon E. Sawyer Award, for technical achievement: Ray Harryhausen.
Special Tribute: Hal Roach.

Grammy Awards

Source: National Academy of Recording Arts & Sciences

1958

Record: Domenico Modugno, *Nel Blu Dipinto Di Blu (Volare).*
Album: Henry Mancini, *The Music from Peter Gunn.*

1959

Record: Bobby Darin, *Mack the Knife.*
Album: Frank Sinatra, *Come Dance With Me.*

1960

Record: Percy Faith, *Theme From A Summer Place.*
Album: Bob Newhart, *Button Down Mind.*

1961

Record: Henry Mancini, *Moon River.*
Album: Judy Garland, *Judy At Carnegie Hall.*

1962

Record: Tony Bennett, *I Left My Heart in San Francisco.*
Album: Vaughn Meader, *The First Family.*

1963

Record: Henry Mancini, *The Days of Wine and Roses.*
Album: *The Barbra Streisand Album.*

1964

Record: Stan Getz and Astrud Gilberto, *The Girl From Ipanema.*
Album: *Getz/Gilberto.*

1965

Record: Herb Alpert, *A Taste Of Honey.*
Album: Frank Sinatra, *September of My Years.*

1966

Record: Frank Sinatra, *Strangers in the Night.*
Album: Frank Sinatra, *A Man and His Music.*

1967

Record: 5th Dimension, *Up, Up and Away.*
Album: The Beatles, *Sgt. Pepper's Lonely Hearts Club Band.*

1968

Record: Simon & Garfunkel, *Mrs. Robinson.*
Album: Glen Campbell, *By the Time I Get to Phoenix.*

1969

Record: 5th Dimension, *Aquarius/Let the Sunshine In.*
Album: *Blood, Sweat and Tears.*

1970

Record: Simon & Garfunkel, *Bridge Over Troubled Water.*
Album: *Bridge Over Troubled Water.*

1971

Record: Carole King, *It's Too Late.*
Album: Carole King, *Tapestry.*

1972

Record: Roberta Flack, *The First Time Ever I Saw Your Face.*
Album: *The Concert For Bangla Desh.*

1973

Record: Roberta Flack, *Killing Me Softly with His Song.*
Album: Stevie Wonder, *Innervisions.*

1974

Record: Olivia Newton-John, *I Honestly Love You.*
Album: Stevie Wonder, *Fulfullingness' First Finale.*

1975

Record: Captain & Tennille, *Love Will Keep Us Together.*

Album: Paul Simon, *Still Crazy After All These Years.*

1976

Record: George Benson, *This Masquerade.*
Album: Stevie Wonder, *Songs in the Key of Life.*

1977

Record: Eagles, *Hotel California.*
Album: Fleetwood Mac, *Rumours.*

1978

Record: Billy Joel, *Just the Way You Are.*
Album: Bee Gees, *Saturday Night Fever.*

1979

Record: The Doobie Brothers, *What a Fool Believes.*
Album: Billy Joel, *52nd Street.*

1980

Record: Christopher Cross, *Sailing.*
Album: Christopher Cross, *Christopher Cross.*

1981

Record: Kim Carnes, *Bette Davis Eyes.*
Album: John Lennon, Yoko Ono, *Double Fantasy.*

1982

Record: Toto, *Rosanna.*
Album: Toto, *Toto IV.*

1983

Record: Michael Jackson, *Beat It.*
Album: Michael Jackson, *Thriller.*

1984

Record: Tina Turner, *What's Love Got to Do With It.*
Album: Lionel Richie, *Can't Slow Down.*

1985

Record: USA for Africa, *We Are the World.*
Album: Phil Collins, *No Jacket Required.*

1986

Record: Steve Winwood, *Higher Love.*
Album: Paul Simon, *Graceland.*

1987

Record: Paul Simon, *Graceland.*
Album: U2, *The Joshua Tree.*

1988

Record: Bobby McFerrin, *Don't Worry, Be Happy.*
Album: George Michael, *Faith.*

1989

Record: Bette Midler, *Wind Beneath My Wings.*
Album: Bonnie Raitt, *Nick of Time.*

1990

Record: Phil Collins, *Another Day in Paradise.*
Album: Quincy Jones, *Back on the Block.*

1991

Record: Natalie Cole, with Nat "King" Cole, *Unforgettable.*
Album: Natalie Cole, with Nat "King" Cole, *Unforgettable.*
Song: Irving Gordon, *Unforgettable.*
New Artist: Marc Cohn.
Female Pop Vocal: Bonnie Raitt, *Something to Talk About.*
Male Pop Vocal: Michael Bolton, *When a Man Loves a Woman.*
Duo or Group Pop Vocal: R.E.M., *Losing My Religion.*
Traditional Pop Vocal: Natalie Cole, with Nat "King" Cole, *Unforgettable.*
Rock Song: Sting, *Soul Cages.*
Solo Rock Vocal: Bonnie Raitt, *Luck of the Draw.*
Duo or Group Rock Vocal: Bonnie Raitt, Delbert McClinton, *Good Man, Good Woman.*
Female Rhythm and Blues Vocal: (tie) Patti LaBelle, *Burnin'*; Lisa Fischer, *How Can I Ease the Pain?*
Male Rhythm and Blues Vocal: Luther Vandross, *Power of Love.*
Duo or Group Rhythm and Blues Vocal: Boyz II Men, *Cooleyhighharmony.*
Rap Solo: L.L. Cool J, *Mama Said Knock You Out.*
Duo or Group Rap Performance: D.J. Jazzy Jeff and the Fresh Prince, *Summertime.*
Hard Rock Performance: Van Halen, *For Unlawful Carnal Knowledge.*
Metal Performance: Metallica, *Metallica.*
Alternative Music Performance: R.E.M., *Out of Time.*

Newbery Medal Books

The Newbery Medal is awarded annually by the Association for Library Service to Children, a division of the American Library Association, to the author of the most distinguished contribution to American literature for children.

Year Awarded	Book, Author
1922	*The Story of Mankind,* Hendrik Willem van Loon
1923	*The Voyages of Dr. Dolittle,* Hugh Lofting
1924	*The Dark Frigate,* Charles Boardman Hawes
1925	*Tales from Silver Lands,* Charles Joseph Finger
1926	*Shen of the Sea,* Arthur Bowie Chrisman
1927	*Smoky, the Cowhorse,* Will James
1928	*Gay-Neck,* Dhan Gopal Mukerji
1929	*The Trumpeter of Krakow,* Eric P. Kelly
1930	*Hitty, Her First Hundred Years,* Rachel Field
1931	*The Cat Who Went to Heaven,* Elizabeth Coatsworth
1932	*Waterless Mountain,* Laura Adams Armer
1933	*Young Fu of the Upper Yangtze,* Elizabeth Foreman Lewis
1934	*Invincible Louisa,* Cornelia Lynde Meigs
1935	*Dobry,* Monica Shannon
1936	*Caddie Woodlawn,* Carol Ryrie Brink
1937	*Roller Skates,* Ruth Sawyer
1938	*The White Stag,* Kate Seredy
1939	*Thimble Summer,* Elizabeth Enright
1940	*Daniel Boone,* James Daugherty
1941	*Call It Courage,* Armstrong Sperry
1942	*The Matchlock Gun,* Walter D. Edmonds
1943	*Adam of the Road,* Elizabeth Janet Gray
1944	*Johnny Tremain,* Esther Forbes
1945	*Rabbit Hill,* Robert Lawson
1946	*Strawberry Girl,* Lois Lenski
1947	*Miss Hickory,* Carolyn S. Bailey
1948	*Twenty-One Balloons,* William Pène Du Bois
1949	*King of the Wind,* Marguerite Henry
1950	*The Door in the Wall,* Marguerite de Angeli
1951	*Amos Fortune, Free Man,* Elizabeth Yates
1952	*Ginger Pye,* Eleanor Estes
1953	*Secret of the Andes,* Ann Nolan Clark
1954	*. . . And Now Miguel,* Joseph Krumgold
1955	*The Wheel on the School,* Meindert DeJong
1956	*Carry On, Mr. Bowditch,* Jean Lee Latham
1957	*Miracles on Maple Hill,* Virginia Sorensen
1958	*Rifles for Watie,* Harold Keith
1959	*The Witch of Blackbird Pond,* Elizabeth George Speare
1960	*Onion John,* Joseph Krumgold
1961	*Island of the Blue Dolphins,* Scott O'Dell
1962	*The Bronze Bow,* Elizabeth George Speare
1963	*A Wrinkle in Time,* Madeleine L'Engle
1964	*It's Like This, Cat,* Emily Cheney Neville
1965	*Shadow of a Bull,* Maja Wojciechowska
1966	*I, Juan de Pareja,* Elizabeth Borton de Trevino
1967	*Up a Road Slowly,* Irene Hunt
1968	*From the Mixed-Up Files of Mrs. Basil E. Frankweiler,* E. L. Konigsburg
1969	*The High King,* Lloyd Alexander
1970	*Sounder,* William H. Armstrong
1971	*The Summer of the Swans,* Betsy Byars
1972	*Mrs. Frisby and the Rats of NIMH,* Robert C. O'Brien
1973	*Julie of the Wolves,* Jean George
1974	*The Slave Dancer,* Paula Fox
1975	*M. C. Higgins the Great,* Virginia Hamilton
1976	*Grey King,* Susan Cooper
1977	*Roll of Thunder, Hear My Cry,* Mildred D. Taylor
1978	*Bridge to Terabithia,* Katherine Paterson
1979	*The Westing Game,* Ellen Raskin
1980	*A Gathering of Days,* Joan Blos
1981	*Jacob Have I Loved,* Katherine Paterson
1982	*A Visit to William Blake's Inn: Poems for Innocent and Experienced Travelers,* Nancy Willard
1983	*Dicey's Song,* Cynthia Voigt
1984	*Dear Mr. Henshaw,* Beverly Cleary
1985	*The Hero and the Crown,* Robin McKinley
1986	*Sarah, Plain and Tall,* Patricia MacLachlan
1987	*The Whipping Boy,* Sid Fleischman
1988	*Lincoln: A Photobiography,* Russell Freedman
1989	*Joyful Noise: Poems for Two Voices,* Paul Fleischman
1990	*Number the Stars,* Lois Lowry
1991	*Maniac Magee,* Jerry Spinelli
1992	*Shiloh,* Phyllis Reynolds Naylor

NOTED PERSONALITIES

Widely Known Americans of the Present

Statesmen, journalists, authors of nonfiction, and other prominent persons not listed in other categories; as of mid-1992.

Name (Birthplace)	Birthdate
Ailes, Roger (Knoxville, Tenn.)	7/3/40
Akers, John F. (Boston, Mass.)	12/28/34
Arledge, Roone (Forest Hills, N.Y.)	7/8/31
Anderson, Jack (Long Beach, Cal.)	10/19/22
Annenberg, Walter H. (Milwaukee, Wis.)	1908
Armstrong, Neil (Wapakoneta, Oh.)	8/5/30
Ash, Mary Kay (Hot Wells, Tex.)	—
Aspin, Les (Milwaukee, Wis.)	7/21/38
Baker, James A. (Houston, Tex.)	4/28/30
Baker, Russell (Loudoun Co., Va.)	8/14/25
Barnes, Clive (London, England)	5/13/27
Barry, Dave (Armonk, N.Y.)	7/3/47
Barthelmy, Sidney K. (New Orleans, La.)	3/17/42
Bennett, William J. (Salem, Oh.)	5/4/44
Bentsen, Lloyd (Mission, Tex.)	2/11/21
Biden, Joseph R. Jr. (Scranton, Pa.)	11/20/42
Blackmun, Harry (Nashville, Ill.)	11/12/08
Blass, Bill (Ft. Wayne, Ind.)	6/22/22
Bloom, Harold (New York, N.Y.)	7/11/30
Bombeck, Erma (Dayton, Oh.)	2/21/27
Boorstin, Daniel (Atlanta, Ga.)	10/1/14
Bradlee, Ben (Boston, Mass.)	8/26/21
Bradley, Bill (Crystal City, Mo.)	7/28/43
Bradley, Ed (Philadelphia, Pa.)	6/22/41
Bradley, Thomas (Calvert, Tex.)	12/29/17
Brady, Nicholas (New York, N.Y.)	4/11/30
Braun, Carol Moseley (Chicago, Ill.)	8/16/47
Brennan, William J. (Newark, N.J.)	4/25/06
Breslin, Jimmy (Jamaica, N.Y.)	10/17/30
Brinkley, Christie (Monroe, Mich.)	2/2/53
Brinkley, David (Wilmington, N.C.)	7/10/20
Broder, David (Chicago Heights, Ill.)	9/11/29
Brody, Jane (Brooklyn, N.Y.)	5/19/41
Brokaw, Tom (Webster, S. Dak.)	2/6/40
Brothers, Joyce (New York, N.Y.)	9/20/28
Brown, Helen Gurley (Green Forest, Ark.)	2/18/22
Brown, Jerry (San Francisco, Cal.)	4/7/38
Brown, Ron (Washington, D.C.)	8/1/41
Buchanan, Pat (Washington, D.C.)	11/2/38
Buchwald, Art (Mt. Vernon, N.Y.)	10/20/25
Buckley, William F. (New York, N.Y.)	11/24/25
Buffet, Warren (Omaha, Neb.)	8/30/30
Bumpers, Dale (Charleston, Ark.)	8/12/25
Buscaglia, Leo (Los Angeles, Cal.)	3/31/24
Bush, Barbara (Rye, N.Y.)	6/8/25
Byrd, Robert (N. Wilkesboro, N.C.)	11/20/17
Canby, Vincent (Chicago, Ill.)	7/27/24
Carter, Jimmy (Plains, Ga.)	10/1/24
Carter, Rosalynn (Plains, Ga.)	8/18/27
Chancellor, John (Chicago, Ill.)	7/14/27
Chavez, Cesar (Yuma, Ariz.)	3/31/27
Cheney, Richard B. (Lincoln, Neb.)	1/30/41
Child, Julia (Pasadena, Cal.)	8/15/12
Chisholm, Shirley (Brooklyn, N.Y.)	11/30/24
Chung, Connie (Washington, D.C.)	8/20/46
Claiborne, Craig (Sunflower, Miss.)	9/4/20
Claiborne, Liz (Brussels, Belg.)	3/31/29
Clinton, Bill (Hope, Ark.)	8/19/46
Clinton, Hillary Rodham (Park Ridge, Ill.)	10/26/48
Collins, Martha (Shelby Cty, Ky.)	12/7/36
Commager, Henry Steele (Pittsburgh, Pa.)	10/25/02
Cooney, Joan Ganz (Phoenix, Ariz.)	10/30/29
Cosell, Howard (Winston-Salem, N.C.)	3/25/20
Couric, Katie (Washington, D.C.)	1/7/57
Cranston, Alan (Palo Alto, Cal.)	6/19/14
Crawford, Cindy (DeKalb, Ill.)	2/20/66
Crist, Judith (New York, N.Y.)	5/22/22
Cronkite, Walter (St. Joseph, Mo.)	11/4/16
Cuomo, Mario (Queens, N.Y.)	6/15/32
Daley, Richard M. (Chicago, Ill.)	4/24/42
Darman, Richard (Charlotte, N.C.)	5/10/43
Deford, Frank (Baltimore, Md.)	12/16/38
Dellums, Ronald (Oakland, Cal.)	11/24/35
Dershowitz, Alan (Brooklyn, N.Y.)	9/1/38
Dingell, John D. Jr. (Colorado Spngs., Col.)	7/8/26
Dinkins, David (Trenton, N.J.)	7/10/27
Dixon, Sharon Pratt (Washington, D.C.)	1/31/44
Dodd, Christopher (Willimantic, Conn.)	5/27/44
Dole, Elizabeth (Salisbury, N.C.)	7/29/36
Dole, Robert (Russell, Kan.)	7/22/23
Domenici, Pete (Albuquerque, N.M.)	5/7/32
Donaldson, Sam (El Paso, Tex.)	3/11/34
Drew, Elizabeth (Cincinnati, Oh.)	11/16/35
Dukakis, Michael S. (Boston, Mass.)	11/3/33
Eisner, Michael (New York, N.Y.)	3/7/42
Ephron, Nora (New York, N.Y.)	5/19/41
Evangelista, Linda (St. Catherine's, Canada)	5/10/65
Falwell, Jerry (Lynchburg, Va.)	8/11/33
Feinstein, Dianne (San Francisco, Cal.)	6/22/33
Ferraro, Geraldine (Newburgh, N.Y.)	8/26/35
Fitzwater, Marlin (Salina, Kan.)	11/24/42
Florio, James J. (New York, N.Y.)	8/29/37
Flynn, Raymond (Boston, Mass.)	7/22/39
Foley, Thomas S. (Spokane, Wash.)	3/6/29
Foote, Shelby (Greenville, Miss.)	11/17/16
Ford, Betty (Chicago, Ill.)	4/8/18
Ford, Gerald R. (Omaha, Neb.)	7/14/13
Frank, Barney (Bayonne, N.J.)	3/31/40
Frankel, Max (Gera, Germany)	4/3/30
Friedan, Betty (Peoria, Ill.)	2/4/21
Friedman, Milton (Brooklyn, N.Y.)	7/31/12
Galbraith, John Kenneth (Ontario, Can.)	10/15/08
Gates, Robert M. (Wichita, Kan.)	9/25/43
Gates, William (Seattle, Wash.)	10/28/55
Gephardt, Richard (St. Louis, Mo.)	1/31/41
Gibson, Charles (Evanston, Ill.)	3/9/43
Gingrich, Newt (Harrisburg, Pa.)	6/17/43
Ginsberg, Allen (Paterson, N.J.)	6/3/21
Glenn, John (Cambridge, Oh.)	7/18/21
Goldwater, Barry M. (Phoenix, Ariz.)	1/1/09
Goodman, Ellen (Newton, Mass.)	4/11/41
Gore, Albert Jr. (Washington, D.C.)	3/31/48
Gottlieb, Robert A. (New York)	4/9/31
Gould, Stephen Jay (New York, N.Y.)	9/10/41
Graham, Billy (Charlotte, N.C.)	11/7/18
Graham, Donald (Baltimore, Md.)	4/22/45
Graham, Katharine (New York, N.Y.)	6/16/17
Gramm, Phil (Ft. Bennington, Ga.)	7/8/42
Gray, William H. 3d (Baton Rouge, La.)	8/20/41
Greene, Bob (Columbus, Oh.)	5/10/47
Greenfield, Meg (Seattle, Wash.)	12/27/30
Greenspan, Alan (New York, N.Y.)	3/6/26
Gumble, Bryant (New Orleans, La.)	9/29/48
Halberstam, David (New York, N.Y.)	4/10/34
Harkin, Tom (Cumming, Ia.)	11/19/39
Harvey, Paul (Tulsa, Okla.)	9/4/18
Hatch, Orrin (Homestead, Pa.)	3/22/34
Hatfield, Mark O. (Dallas, Ore.)	7/12/22
Heflin, Howell (Poulan, Ga.)	6/19/21
Hefner, Hugh (Chicago, Ill.)	4/9/26
Helms, Jesse (Monroe, N.C.)	10/18/21
Helmsley, Leona (New York, N.Y.)	c.1920
Heloise (Waco, Tex.)	4/15/51
Hills, Carla (Los Angeles, Cal.)	1/3/34
Hollings, Ernest (Charleston, S.C.)	1/1/22
Iacocca, Lee A. (Allentown, Pa.)	10/15/24
Icahn, Carl (New York, N.Y.)	1936
Iman (Somalia, Ethiopia)	7/25/55
Inouye, Daniel K. (Honolulu, Ha.)	9/7/24
Jackson, Jesse (Greenville, S.C.)	10/8/41
Jennings, Peter (Toronto, Ont.)	8/29/38
Johnson, Lady Bird (Karnack, Tex.)	12/22/12
Jordan, Barbara (Houston, Tex.)	2/21/36
Kael, Pauline (Petaluma, Calif.)	6/19/19
Karan, Donna (Forest Hills, N.Y.)	10/2/48
Kassebaum, Nancy (Topeka, Kan.)	7/29/32
Keillor, Garrison (Anoka, Minn.)	8/7/42
Kelley, Clarence (Kansas City, Mo.)	10/24/11
Kemp, Jack (Los Angeles, Cal.)	7/13/35
Kennedy, Anthony (Sacramento, Cal.)	7/23/36
Kennedy, Edward M. (Brookline, Mass.)	2/22/32
Kennedy, Rose (Boston, Mass.)	7/22/90
Kerr, Walter (Evanston, Ill.)	7/8/13
King, Coretta Scott (Marion, Ala.)	4/27/27
King, Larry (Brooklyn, N.Y.)	11/19/34
Kinsley, Michael (Detroit, Mich.)	3/9/51
Kirkland, Lane (Camden, S.C.)	3/12/22
Kirkpatrick, Jeane (Duncan, Okla.)	11/19/26
Kissinger, Henry (Fuerth, Germany)	5/27/23
Klein, Calvin (New York, N.Y.)	11/19/42
Koch, Edward I. (New York, N.Y.)	12/12/24
Koop, C. Everett (Brooklyn, N.Y.)	10/14/16
Koppel, Ted (Lancashire, Eng.)	2/8/40
Kryzyzewski, Mike (Chicago, Ill.)	2/13/47

Name (Birthplace)	Birthdate
Kuhn, Maggie (Buffalo, N.Y.)	1905
Kunstler, William (New York, N.Y.)	7/7/19
Kuralt, Charles (Wilmington, N.C.)	9/10/34
Landers, Ann (Sioux City, Ia.)	7/4/18
Lauder, Estee (New York, N.Y.)	—
Lauren, Ralph (Bronx, N.Y.)	10/14/39
Leahy, Patrick (Montpelier, Vt.)	3/31/40
Lear, Frances (Hudson, N.Y.)	7/14/23
Lear, Norman (New Haven, Conn.)	7/27/22
Lehrer, Jim (Wichita, Kan.)	5/19/34
Lewis, Anthony (New York, N.Y.)	3/27/27
Lindbergh, Anne Morrow (Englewood, N.J.)	1906
Lorenzo, Frank (New York, N.Y.)	5/19/40
Lott, Trent (Grenada, Miss.)	10/9/41
Lugar, Richard G. (Indianapolis, Ind.)	4/4/32
Lukas, J. Anthony (New York, N.Y.)	4/25/33
Lunden, Joan (Sacramento, Calif.)	9/19/50
MacNeil, Robert (Montreal, Que.)	1/19/31
Manchester, William (Attleboro, Mass.)	4/1/22
Marshall, Thurgood (Baltimore, Md.)	7/2/08
Martin, Lynn (Evanston, Ill.)	12/26/39
Martinez, Bob (Tampa, Fla.)	12/25/34
Maslin, Janet (New York, N.Y.)	8/12/49
McClendon, Sarah (Tyler, Tex.)	7/8/10
Metzenbaum, Howard (Cleveland, Oh.)	6/4/17
Michel, Robert H. (Peoria, Ill.)	3/2/23
Mikulski, Barbara (Baltimore, Md.)	7/20/36
Mitchell, George (Waterville, Me.)	8/20/33
Mondale, Walter (Ceylon, Minn.)	1/5/28
Mosbacher, Robert (Mt. Vernon, N.Y.)	3/11/27
Moyers, Bill (Hugo, Okla.)	6/5/34
Moynihan, Daniel P. (Tulsa, Okla.)	3/16/27
Mudd, Roger (Washington, D.C.)	2/9/28
Nader, Ralph (Winsted, Conn.)	2/27/34
Nidetch, Jean (Brooklyn, N.Y.)	10/12/23
Nixon, Pat (Ely, Nev.)	3/16/12
Nixon, Richard (Yorba Linda, Cal.)	1/9/13
North, Oliver (San Antonio, Tex.)	10/7/43
Norton, Eleanor Holmes (Washington, D.C.)	6/13/37
Novak, Robert (Joliet, Ill.)	2/26/31
Novello, Antonia (Fajardo, P.R.)	8/23/44
Nunn, Sam (Perry, Ga.)	9/8/38
O'Connor, Cardinal John (Phila., Pa.)	1/15/20
O'Connor, Sandra Day (nr. Duncan, Ariz.)	3/26/30
Onassis, Jacqueline (Southampton, N.Y.)	7/28/29
O'Neill, Thomas P. (Cambridge, Mass.)	12/9/12
Packwood, Bob (Portland, Ore.)	9/11/32
Pauley, Jane (Indianapolis, Ind.)	10/31/50
Pauling, Linus (Portland, Ore.)	2/28/01
Peretz, Martin (New York, N.Y.)	7/30/39
Perot, H. Ross (Texarcana, Tex.)	6/27/30
Phillips, Kevin (New York, N.Y.)	11/30/40
Pickens, T. Boone (Holdenville, Okla.)	5/22/28
Pickering, Thomas (Orange, N.J.)	11/5/31
Plimpton, George (New York, N.Y.)	3/18/27
Podhoretz, Norman (New York, N.Y.)	1/16/30
Poussaint, Alvin F. (New York, N.Y.)	5/15/34
Powell, Colin (New York, N.Y.)	4/5/37
Quayle, Dan (Indianapolis, Ind.)	2/4/47
Quayle, Marilyn (Indianapolis, Ind.)	7/29/49
Quinn, Jane Bryant (Niagara Falls, N.Y.)	2/5/39
Rangel, Charles (New York, N.Y.)	6/11/30
Rather, Dan (Wharton, Tex.)	10/31/31
Reagan, Nancy (New York, N.Y.)	7/6/23
Reagan, Ronald (Tampico, Ill.)	2/6/11
Reasoner, Harry (Dakota City, Ia.)	4/17/23
Rehnquist, William (Milwaukee, Wis.)	10/1/24
Rich, Frank (Washington, D.C.)	6/2/49
Richards, Ann (Waco, Tex.)	9/3/33
Ride, Sally K. (Encino, Calif.)	1952
Roberts, Oral (nr. Ada, Okla.)	1/24/18
Robertson, Pat (Lexington, Va.)	3/22/30
Rockefeller, David (New York, N.Y.)	6/12/15
Rockefeller, John D. 4th "Jay" (New York, N.Y.)	6/18/37
Rockefeller, Laurance S. (New York, N.Y.)	5/26/10
Rooney, Andy (Albany, N.Y.)	1/14/19
Rostenkowski, Dan (Chicago, Ill.)	1/2/28
Rukeyser, Louis (New York, N.Y.)	1/30/33
Safer, Morley (Toronto, Ontario)	11/8/31
Safire, William (New York, N.Y.)	12/17/29
Sagan, Carl (New York, N.Y.)	11/9/34
Salk, Jonas (New York, N.Y.)	10/28/14
Sawyer, Diane (Glasgow, Ky.)	12/22/45
Scalia, Antonin (Trenton, N.J.)	3/11/36
Schlesinger, Arthur Jr. (Columbus, Oh.)	10/15/17
Schroeder, Patricia (Portland, Ore.)	7/30/40
Schuller, Robert (Alton, Ia.)	9/16/26
Schwarzkopf, H. Norman (Trenton, N.J.)	8/22/34
Scowcroft, Brent (Ogden, Ut.)	3/19/25
Seaborg, Glenn T. (Ishpeming, Mich.)	4/19/12
Shanker, Albert (New York, N.Y.)	9/14/28
Shriver, Maria (Chicago, Ill.)	11/6/55
Shultz, George P. (New York, N.Y.)	12/13/20
Silver, Joan Micklin (Omaha, Neb.)	5/25/35
Silverstein, Shel (Chicago, Ill.)	1932
Simmons, Richard (New Orleans, La.)	7/12/48
Simon, Paul (Eugene, Ore.)	11/29/28
Simpson, Alan K. (Cody, Wyo.)	9/2/31
Skinner, Samuel (Chicago, Ill.)	6/10/38
Smith, Hedrick (Kilmacolm, Scotland)	7/9/33
Smith, Liz (Ft. Worth, Tex.)	2/2/23
Solarz, Stephen J. (New York, N.Y.)	9/2/40
Souter, David H. (Melrose, Mass.)	9/17/39
Specter, J. Arlen (Wichita, Kans.)	2/12/30
Spock, Benjamin (New Haven, Conn.)	5/2/03
Stahl, Lesley (Lynn, Mass.)	12/16/41
Steinbrenner, George (Rocky River, Oh.)	7/4/30
Steinem, Gloria (Toledo, Oh.)	3/25/34
Stern, David J. (New York, N.Y.)	9/22/42
Stevens, John Paul (Chicago, Ill.)	4/20/20
Sullivan, Louis (Atlanta, Ga.)	11/3/33
Sulzberger, Arthur Ochs (New York, N.Y.)	2/5/26
Sununu, John H. (Havana, Cuba)	7/2/39
Tagliabue, Paul (Jersey City, N.J.)	11/24/40
Tarkanian, Jerry (Euclid, Oh.)	8/8/30
Tartikoff, Brandon (Long Island, N.Y.)	1949
Terkel, Studs (New York, N.Y.)	5/16/12
Thomas, Clarence (Savannah, Ga.)	6/23/48
Thurmond, J. Strom (Edgefield, S.C.)	12/5/02
Tiegs, Cheryl (Minnesota)	9/27/47
Tinker, Grant (Stamford, Conn.)	1/11/26
Tisch, Laurence (New York, N.Y.)	3/15/23
Toland, John (LaCrosse, Wis.)	6/29/12
Trillin, Calvin (Kansas City, Mo.)	12/5/35
Truman, Margaret (Independence, Mo.)	2/17/24
Trump, Donald (New York, N.Y.)	1946
Tsongas, Paul (Lowell, Mass.)	2/14/41
Turner, Ted (Cincinnati, Oh.)	1938
Udall, Morris K. (St. Johns, Ariz.)	6/15/22
Ueberroth, Peter (Chicago, Ill.)	9/2/37
Valenti, Jack (Houston, Tex.)	9/5/21
Van Buren, Abigail (Sioux City, Ia.)	7/4/18
Wallace, George (Clio, Ala.)	8/25/19
Wallace, Mike (Brookline, Mass.)	5/9/18
Walters, Barbara (Boston, Mass.)	9/25/31
Wattleton, Faye (St. Louis, Mo.)	7/8/43
Webster, William H. (St. Louis, Mo.)	3/6/24
Weicker, Lowell (Paris, France)	5/16/31
Wenner, Jann (New York, N.Y.)	1/7/46
Westheimer, Ruth (Germany)	1928
White, Bill (Lakewood, Fla.)	1/28/34
White, Byron (Ft. Collins, Col.)	6/8/17
Wicker, Tom (Hamlet, N.C.)	6/18/26
Wiesel, Elie (Sighet, Transyl.)	9/30/28
Wilder, L. Douglas (Richmond, Va.)	1/17/31
Will, George (Champaign, Ill.)	1941
Wilson, Pete (Lake Forest, Ill.)	8/23/33
Yamaguchi, Kristi (Hayward, Cal.)	7/12/71
Yard, Molly (Shanghai, China)	—
Young, Andrew (New Orleans, La.)	3/12/32
Young, Coleman (Tuscaloosa, Ala.)	5/24/18
Zahn, Paula (Omaha, Neb.)	2/24/56
Ziegler, John (Grosse Point, Mich.)	2/9/34

Noted Black Americans

Names of black athletes and entertainers are not included here as they are listed elsewhere in The World Almanac.

The Rev. Dr. Ralph David Abernathy, 1926-1990, organizer, 1957, and president, 1968, of the Southern Christian Leadership Conference.

Crispus Attucks, c. 1723-1770, agitator who led group that precipitated the "Boston Massacre," Mar. 5, 1770.

James Baldwin, 1924-1987, author, playwright; *The Fire Next Time, Blues for Mister Charlie, Just Above My Head.*

Benjamin Banneker, 1731-1806, inventor, astronomer, mathematician, and gazetteer; served on commission that surveyed and laid out Washington, D. C.

Imamu Amiri Baraka, b. LeRoi Jones, 1934, poet, playwright.

James P. Beckwourth, 1798-c. 1867, western fur-trader, scout, after whom Beckwourth Pass in northern California is named.

Dr. Mary McCleod Bethune, 1875-1955, adviser to presidents Roosevelt, Truman; division administrator, Natl. Youth Administration, 1935; founder, pres. Bethune-Cookman College.
Henry Blair, 19th century, obtained patents (believed among first issued to a black) for a corn-planter, 1834, and for a cotton-planter, 1836.
Julian Bond, b. 1940, civil rights leader first elected to the Georgia state legislature, 1965; helped found Student Nonviolent Coordinating Committee.
Edward Bouchet, 1852-1918, first black to earn a Ph.D., Yale, 1876, at a U.S. university; first black elected to Phi Beta Kappa.
Thomas Bradley, b. 1917, elected mayor of Los Angeles, 1973.
Andrew F. Brimmer, b. 1926, first black member, 1966, Federal Reserve Board.
Edward W. Brooke, b. 1919, attorney general, 1962, of Massachusetts; first black elected to U. S. Senate, 1967, since 19th century Reconstruction.
Gwendolyn Brooks, b. 1917, poet, novelist; first black to win a Pulitzer Prize, 1950, for *Annie Allen.*
Sterling A. Brown, 1901-1989, poet, literature professor; helped establish Afro-American literary criticism.
William Wells Brown, 1815-1884, novelist, dramatist; first American black to publish a novel.
Dr. Ralph Bunche, 1904-1971, first black to win the Nobel Peace Prize, 1950; undersecretary of the UN, 1950.
Sherian Grace Cadoria, b. 1940, brigadier general; highest ranking black woman in U.S. armed forces as of 1990.
Alexa Canady, b. 1950, first black woman neurosurgeon in U.S.
George E. Carruthers, b. 1940, physicist developed the Apollo 16 lunar surface ultraviolet camera/spectograph.
George Washington Carver, 1861-1943, botanist, chemurgist, and educator; his extensive experiments in soil building and plant diseases revolutionized the economy of the South.
Charles Waddell Chestnutt, 1858-1932, author known primarily for his short stories, including *The Conjure Woman.*
Shirley Chisholm, b. 1924, first black woman elected to House of Representatives, Brooklyn, N. Y., 1968.
Bishop Philip R. Cousin, b. 1933, Pres., Natl. Council of Churches of Christ in the USA, 1985-.
Countee Cullen, 1903-1946, poet, played a prominent role in the "Harlem Renaissance" of the 1920s; "Heritage," *The Black Christ.*
Lt. Gen. Benjamin O. Davis Jr. b. 1912, West Point, 1936, first black Air Force general, 1954.
Brig. Gen. Benjamin O. Davis Sr., 1877-1970, first black general, 1940, in U. S. Army.
William L. Dawson, 1886-1970, Illinois congressman, first black chairman of a major House of Representatives committee.
David Dinkins, b. 1927, first black mayor of New York City, 1990-.
Sharon Pratt Dixon, b. 1944, mayor of Washington, D.C., 1990-.
Isaiah Dorman, 19th century, U. S. Army interpreter, killed with Custer, 1876, at Battle of the Little Big Horn.
Aaron Douglas, 1900-1979, painter; called father of black American art.
Frederick Douglass, 1817-1895, author, editor, orator, diplomat; edited the abolitionist weekly, The North Star, in Rochester, N. Y.; U.S. minister and consul general to Haiti.
St. Clair Drake, 1911-1990, black studies pioneer, *Black Metropolis* (1945, with Horace R. Cayton); first permanent director, African and Afro-American Studies, Stanford Univ.
Dr. Charles Richard Drew, 1904-1950, pioneer in development of blood banks; director of American Red Cross blood donor project in World War II.
William Edward Burghardt Du Bois, 1868-1963, historian, sociologist; a founder of the National Association for the Advancement of Colored People (NAACP), 1909, and founder of its magazine The Crisis; author, *The Souls of Black Folk.*
Paul Laurence Dunbar, 1872-1906, poet, novelist; won fame with *Lyrics of Lowly Life,* 1896.
Jean Baptiste Point du Sable, c. 1750-1818, pioneer trader and first settler of Chicago, 1779.
Marian Wright Edelman, b. 1939, founder, pres. of Children's Defense Fund.
Ralph Ellison, b. 1914, novelist, essayist, *Invisible Man.*
James Farmer, b. 1920, a founder of the Congress of Racial Equality, 1942; asst. secretary, Dept. of HEW, 1969.
Henry O. Flipper, 1856-1940, first black to graduate, 1877, from West Point.
Charles Fuller, b. 1939, Pulitzer Prize-winning playwright; *A Soldier's Play.*
Mary Hatwood Futrell, b. 1940, president, Natl. Education Assn., 1983-.
Marcus Garvey, 1887-1940, founded Universal Negro Improvement Assn., 1911.
Kenneth Gibson, b. 1932, Newark, N.J., mayor, 1970-1986.
Charles Gordone, b. 1925, won 1970 Pulitzer Prize in Drama, with *No Place to Be Somebody.*
Vice Adm. Samuel L. Gravely Jr. b. 1922, first black admiral, 1971, served in World War II, Korea, and Vietnam; commander, Third Fleet.
William H. Gray 3d, b. 1941, U.S. representative from Pa., 1979—; chairman, Budget Committee, 1985-88; chairman, House Democratic Caucus, 1988-89; majority whip, 1989-.
Ewart Guinier, 1911-1990, trade unionist, first chairman of Harvard Univ.'s Department of Afro-American Studies.
Alex Haley, 1921-1992, Pulitzer Prize-winning author; *Roots, The Autobiography of Malcolm X.*
Jupiter Hammon, c. 1720-1800, poet; the first black American to have his works published, 1761.
Lorraine Hansberry, 1930-1965, playwright; won New York Drama Critics Circle Award, 1959, with *Raisin in the Sun.*
Barbara Harris, b. 1931, first woman Episcopal bishop.
Patricia Roberts Harris, 1924-1985, U. S. ambassador to Luxembourg, 1965-67; secretary, Dept. of HUD, 1977-1979, Dept. of HHS, 1979-1981.
William H. Hastie, 1904-1976 first black federal judge, appointed 1937; governor of Virgin Islands, 1946-49; judge, U.S. Circuit Court of Appeals, 1949.
Chester Himes, 1909-1984, novelist, *Cotton Comes to Harlem.*
Matthew A. Henson, 1866-1955, member of Peary's 1909 expedition to the North Pole; placed U.S. flag at the Pole.
Dr. William A. Hinton, 1883-1959, developed the Hinton and Davies-Hinton tests for detection of syphilis; first black professor, 1949, at Harvard Medical School.
Benjamin L. Hooks, b. 1925, first black member, 1972-1979, Federal Communications Comm.; exec. dir., NAACP, 1977—.
Nathan I. Huggins, 1927-1989, historian, scholar; Harvard professor from 1980, director of that university's Institute for Afro-American Research from 1981.
Langston Hughes, 1902-1967, poet; story, song lyric author, a major influence in the "Harlem Renaissance" of the 1920s; *The Weary Blues, Montage of a Dream Deferred.*
Charlayne Hunter-Gault, b. 1942, first black woman admitted to Univ. of Ga., 1961; ran *N.Y. Times* Harlem Bureau, 1968-1977; broadcast journalist, 1978—.
Rev. Jesse Jackson, b. 1941, national director, Operation Bread Basket; campaigned for Democratic presidential nomination, 1984, 1988; pres., founder, Rainbow Coalition; "shadow senator" for District of Columbia, 1991-.
Maynard Jackson, b. 1938, elected mayor of Atlanta, 1973.
Gen. Daniel James Jr. 1920-1978, first black 4-star general, 1975; Commander, North American Air Defense Command.
Pvt. Henry Johnson, 1897-1929, the first American decorated by France in World War I with the Croix de Guerre.
James Weldon Johnson, 1871-1938, poet, lyricist, novelist; first black admitted to Florida bar; U.S. consul in Venezuela and Nicaragua.
John H. Johnson, b. 1918, publisher, editor of Ebony, Jet, Ebony Jr. magazines, from 1942.
Barbara Jordan, b. 1936, former congresswoman from Texas; member, House Judiciary Committee.
Vernon E. Jordan, b. 1935, executive director, National Urban League, 1972.
Ernest Everett Just, 1883-1941, marine biologist, studied egg development; author, *Biology of Cell Surfaces,* 1941.
Leontine T.C. Kelly, b. 1920, United Methodist bishop; first black woman bishop of a major American denomination, 1989.
The Rev. Dr. Martin Luther King Jr., 1929-1968, led 382-day Montgomery, Ala., boycott that brought 1956 U.S. Supreme Court decision holding segregation on buses unconstitutional; founder, president, Southern Christian Leadership Conference, 1957; won Nobel Peace Prize, 1964.
Lewis H. Latimer, 1848-1928, associate of Edison; supervised installation of first electric street lighting in N.Y.C.
Mickey Leland, 1944-1989, U.S. representative from Texas, 1978 until death; chairman of Congressional Black Caucus, House Select Committee on Hunger.
Malcolm X, 1925-1965. Black Muslim leader and black nationalist whose ideas and oratory contributed to the black pride and black power movements in the 1960s.
Thurgood Marshall, b. 1908, first black U.S. solicitor general 1965; first black justice of the U. S. Supreme Court, 1967-1991; as a lawyer led the legal battery that won the Supreme Court decision declaring racial segregation of public schools unconstitutional, 1954.
Jan Matzeliger, 1852-1889, invented lasting machine, patented 1883, which revolutionized the shoe industry.
Benjamin Mays, 1895-1984, educator, civil rights leader; headed Morehouse College, 1940-1967.
Wade H. McCree Jr., 1920-1987, solicitor general of the U.S., 1977-1981.
Donald E. McHenry, b. 1936, U.S. ambassador to the United Nations, 1979-1981.

Ronald McNair, 1950-1986, physicist, astronaut; killed in *Challenger* explosion.
Dorie Miller, 1919-1943, Navy hero of Pearl Harbor attack; awarded the Navy Cross.
Ernest N. Morial, b. 1929, elected first black mayor of New Orleans, 1977.
Toni Morrison, b. 1931, novelist; *Song of Solomon, Sula, Tar Baby;* won 1988 Pulitzer Prize for *Beloved.*
Willard Motley, 1912-1965, novelist; *Knock on Any Door.*
Elijah Muhammad, 1897-1975, founded Black Muslims, 1931.
Pedro Alonzo Nino, navigator of the Nina, one of Columbus' 3 ships on his first voyage of discovery to the New World, 1492.
Rosa Parks, b. 1913, Montgomery Ala. citizen arrested for refusing to move to the back of the bus, Dec. 1, 1955, bringing a 382-day bus boycott led by Martin Luther King Jr.
Frederick D. Patterson, 1901-1988, founder of United Negro College Fund, 1944; Tuskegee Institute's third pres., 1935-1953.
Harold R. Perry, 1917-1991, first black American made a Roman Catholic bishop in the 20th century, 1966; first black clergyman to deliver the opening prayer in Congress, 1964.
Adam Clayton Powell, 1908-1972, early civil rights leader, congressman, 1945-1969; chairman, House Committee on Education and Labor, 1960-1967.
Colin Powell, b. 1937, first black Natl. Security Advisor, 1987-88; first black chairman of Joint Chiefs of Staff, 1989-.
Joseph H. Rainey, 1832-1887, first black elected to House of Representatives, 1869, from South Carolina.
A. Philip Randolph, 1889-1979, organized the Brotherhood of Sleeping Car Porters, 1925; organizer of 1941 and 1963 March on Washington movements; vice president, AFL-CIO.
Charles Rangel, b. 1930, congressman from N.Y.C. from 1970; member, Ways and Means Committee; chairman, Select Committee on Narcotics Abuse & Control.
Hiram R. Revels, 1822-1901, first black U.S. senator, elected in Mississippi, served 1870-1871.
Lloyd Richards, b. 1922(?), first black to direct a Broadway play, 1959; dean, Yale Univ. School of Drama & artistic director of Yale Repertory Theatre, 1979-1991.
Wilson C. Riles, b. 1917, elected, 1970, California State Superintendent of Public Instruction.
Norbert Rillieux, 1806-1894; invented a vacuum pan evaporator, 1846, revolutionizing the sugar-refining industry.
Paul Robeson, 1898-1976, actor and concert singer, graduated 1st in class at Rutgers, 1918, Phi Beta Kappa; grad. Columbia Univ. law school, 1923; associated with communist causes.
Max Robinson, 1939-1988, TV journalist, first black to anchor network news, 1978.
Carl T. Rowan, b. 1925, prize-winning journalist; director of the U.S. Information Agency, 1964, the first black to sit on the National Security Council; U. S. ambassador to Finland, 1963.
John B. Russwurm, 1799-1851, with **Samuel E. Cornish,** 1793-1858, founded, 1827, the nation's first black newspaper, Freedom's Journal, in N.Y.C.
Bayard Rustin, 1910-1987, organizer of the 1963 March on Washington; executive director, A. Philip Randolph Institute.
Peter Salem, at the Battle of Bunker Hill, June 17, 1775, shot and killed British commander Maj. John Pitcairn.
Ntozake Shange, b. 1948, writer, *For Colored Girls Who Have Considered Suicide/When the Rainbow is Enuf.*
Bishop Stephen Spottswood, 1897-1974, board chairman of NAACP, 1961-1974.
The Rev. Leon H. Sullivan, b. 1922, economic development planner, first black on General Motors Bd. of Directors.
Willard Townsend, 1895-1957, organized the United Transport Service Employees, 1935 (redcaps, etc.); vice pres. AFL-CIO.
Sojourner Truth, 1797-1883, born Isabella Baumfree; preacher, abolitonist; raised funds for Union in Civil War; worked for black educational opportunities.
Harriet Tubman, 1823-1913, Underground Railroad conductor served as nurse and spy for Union Army in the Civil War.
Nat Turner, 1800-1831, led the most significant of over 200 slave revolts in U.S., in Southampton, Va.; hanged.
Alice Walker, b. 1944, novelist, essayist, *The Color Purple.*
Booker T. Washington, 1856-1915, founder, 1881, and first president of Tuskegee Institute; author, *Up From Slavery.*
Harold Washington, 1922-1987, first black mayor of Chicago, from 1983 until death.
Dr. Robert C. Weaver, b. 1907, first black member of the U.S. Cabinet, secretary, Dept. of HUD, 1966.
Ida B. Wells (Barnett), 1862-1931, journalist who waged anti-lynching crusade.
Clifton R. Wharton Jr., b. 1926, first black pres. of major U.S. univ.; chancellor, nation's largest univ. system, 8 yrs.; chairman & CEO, country's largest pension fund, 1987—.
Phillis Wheatley, c. 1753-1784, poet; 2d American woman and first black woman to have her works published, 1770.
Bill White, b. 1934, first black baseball league president; named Natl. League head, 1989.
Walter White, 1893-1955, exec. secretary, NAACP, 1931-1955.
L. Douglas Wilder, first black governor, elected Virginia chief executive in 1989.
Roy Wilkins, 1901-1981, exec. director, NAACP, 1955-1977.
Dr. Daniel Hale Williams, 1858-1931, performed one of first 2 open-heart operations, 1893; founded Provident, Chicago's first Negro hospital; first black elected a fellow of the American College of Surgeons.
August Wilson, b. 1945, playwright, won 1987 Pulitzer Prize for *Fences,* 1990 Pulitzer for *The Piano Lesson.*
Granville T. Woods, 1856-1910, invented the third-rail system now used in subways, a complex railway telegraph device that helped reduce train accidents, and an automatic air brake.
Dr. Carter G. Woodson, 1875-1950, historian; founded Assn. for the Study of Negro Life and History, 1915, and Journal of Negro History, 1916.
Richard Wright, 1908-1960, novelist; *Native Son, Black Boy.*
Frank Yerby, 1916-1992, first best-selling American black novelist; *The Foxes of Harrow, Vixen.*
Andrew Young, b. 1932, civil rights leader, congressman from Georgia, U.S. ambassador to the United Nations, 1977-79; mayor of Atlanta, 1982-89.
Whitney M. Young Jr., 1921-1971, exec. director, 1961, National Urban League; author, lecturer, newspaper columnist.

About 5,000 blacks served in the Continental Army during the **American Revolution,** mostly in integrated units, some in all-black combat units. Some 200,000 blacks served in the Union Army during the **Civil War;** 38,000 gave their lives; 22 won the Medal of Honor, the nation's highest award. Of 367,000 blacks in the armed forces during **World War I,** 100,000 served in France. More than 1,000,000 blacks served in the armed forces during **World War II;** all-black fighter and bomber AAF units and infantry divisions gave distinguished service. In 1954 the policy of all-black units was finally abolished. Of 274,937 blacks who served in the armed forces during the **Vietnam War** (1965-1974), 5,681 were killed in combat. During the **Persian Gulf War** (1990-1991), 104,000 blacks served in the Kuwaiti theater—20 percent of U.S. soldiers, compared with 8.7% during World War II and 9.8% in Vietnam.

As of Jan., 1991, there were 314 black mayors, 2 black governors, 458 state representatives, and 26 U.S. representatives. There were then 7,480 blacks holding elected office in the U.S. and Virgin Islands, an increase of 1.5% over the previous year, according to a survey by the Joint Center for Political Studies, Washington, D.C. The number of black women in politics was increasing at a faster rate than that of any other group in American politics, according to the Center. Between 1970 and April 1991, the overall number of black women elected to local, county, state, and congressional offices rose from 131 to 1,950; in the 1990 elections, 33 of the 70 newly elected black state legislators—nearly half—were women. As of Sept. 1991, there were 2,053 black women elected officials, a 5.3% increase over the previous year.

Notable Living American Fiction Writers and Playwrights

Name (Birthplace)	Birthdate
Adams, Alice (Fredericksburg, Va.)	8/14/26
Albee, Edward (Washington, D.C.)	3/12/28
Auchincloss, Louis (Lawrence, N.Y.)	9/27/17
Barth, John (Cambridge, Md.)	5/27/30
Beattie, Ann (Washington, D.C.)	9/7/47
Bellow, Saul (Quebec, Canada)	7/10/15
Benchley, Peter (New York, N.Y.)	5/8/40
Berger, Thomas (Cincinnati, Oh.)	7/20/24
Blume, Judy (Elizabeth, N.J.)	2/12/38
Bradbury, Ray (Waukegan, Ill.)	8/22/20
Brooks, Gwendolyn (Topeka, Kan.)	6/7/17
Calisher, Hortense (New York, N.Y.)	12/20/11
Clancy, Tom (Baltimore, Md.)	1947
Clark, Mary Higgins (New York, N.Y.)	12/24/31
Clavell, James (England)	10/10/24
Cleary, Beverly (McMinnville, Ore.)	1916
Connell, Evan S. (Kansas City, Mo.)	8/17/24
Conroy, Pat (Atlanta, Ga.)	10/26/45
Crews, Harry (Alma, Ga.)	6/6/35
Crichton, Michael (Chicago, Ill.)	10/23/42
Dailey, Janet (Storm Lake, Ia.)	5/21/44
De Vries, Peter (Chicago, Ill.)	2/27/10
Didion, Joan (Sacramento, Cal.)	12/5/34

Name (Birthplace)	Birthdate
Doctorow, E. L. (New York, N.Y.)	1/6/31
Dunne, John Gregory (Hartford, Conn.)	5/25/32
Elkin, Stanley (New York, N.Y.)	5/11/30
Ellison, Ralph (Oklahoma City, Okla.)	3/1/14
Fast, Howard (New York, N.Y.)	11/11/14
Fox, Paula (New York, N.Y.)	4/22/23
French, Marilyn (New York, N.Y.)	11/21/29
Fuller, Charles (Philadelphia, Pa.)	3/5/39
Gaddis, William (New York, N.Y.)	1922
Gilroy, Frank (New York, N.Y.)	10/13/25
Godwin, Gail (Birmingham, Ala.)	6/18/37
Goldman, William (Chicago, Ill.)	8/12/31
Gordon, Mary (Long Island, N.Y.)	12/8/49
Grau, Shirley Ann (New Orleans, La.)	7/8/29
Guare, John (New York, N.Y.)	2/5/38
Hailey, Arthur (Luton, England)	4/5/20
Haley, Alex (Ithaca, N.Y.)	8/11/21
Hawkes, John (Stamford, Conn.)	8/17/25
Heller, Joseph (Brooklyn, N.Y.)	5/1/23
Helprin, Mark (New York, N.Y.)	6/28/47
Hersey, John (Tientsin, China)	6/17/14
Hinton, S.E. (Tulsa, Okla.)	1948
Irving, John (Exeter, N.H.)	3/2/42
Jong, Erica (New York, N.Y.)	3/26/42
Kennedy, William (Albany, N.Y.)	1/16/28
Kerr, Jean (Scranton, Pa.)	7/10/23
King, Stephen (Portland, Me.)	9/21/47
Kingston, Maxine Hong (Stockton, Cal.)	10/27/40
Knowles, John (Fairmont, W. Va.)	9/16/26
Krantz, Judith (New York, N.Y.)	1/9/28
LeGuin, Ursula (Berkeley, Cal.)	10/21/29
L'Engle, Madeleine (New York, N.Y.)	11/29/18
Leonard, Elmore (New Orleans, La.)	10/11/25
Levin, Ira (New York, N.Y.)	8/27/29
Ludlum, Robert (New York, N.Y.)	5/25/27
Lurie, Alison (Chicago, Ill.)	9/3/26
Mailer, Norman (Long Branch, N.J.)	1/31/23
Mamet, David (Chicago, Ill.)	11/30/47
McGuane, Thomas (Wyandotte, Mich.)	12/11/39
McMurtry, Larry (Wichita Falls, Tex.)	6/3/36
Michener, James A. (New York, N.Y.)	2/3/07
Miller, Arthur (New York, N.Y.)	10/17/15
Morris, Wright (Central City, Neb.)	1/6/10
Morrison, Toni (Lorain, Oh.)	2/18/31
Oates, Joyce Carol (Lockport, N.Y.)	6/16/38
Ozick, Cynthia (New York, N.Y.)	4/17/28
Paley, Grace (New York, N.Y.)	12/11/22
Piercy, Marge (Detroit, Mich.)	3/31/36
Potok, Chaim (New York, N.Y.)	2/17/29
Price, Reynolds (Macon, N.C.)	2/1/33
Puzo, Mario (New York, N.Y.)	10/15/20
Pynchon, Thomas (Glen Cove, N.Y.)	5/8/37
Rabe, David (Dubuque, Ia.)	3/10/40
Reed, Ishmael (Chattanooga, Tenn.)	2/22/38
Roth, Henry (Austria-Hungary)	2/8/06
Roth, Philip (Newark, N.J.)	3/19/33
Salinger, J. D. (New York, N.Y.)	1/1/19
Sanders, Lawrence (New York, N.Y.)	1920
Sendak, Maurice (New York, N.Y.)	6/10/28
Shepard, Sam (Ft. Sheridan, Ill.)	11/5/43
Simon, Neil (New York, N.Y.)	7/4/27
Spillane, Mickey (Brooklyn, N.Y.)	3/9/18
Stegner, Wallace (Lake Mills, Ia.)	2/18/09
Stern, Richard (New York, N.Y.)	2/25/28
Stone, Robert (Brooklyn, N.Y.)	8/21/37
Styron, William (Newport News, Va.)	6/11/25
Taylor, Peter (Trenton, Tenn.)	1/8/17
Theroux, Paul (Medford, Mass.)	4/10/41
Tyler, Anne (Minneapolis, Minn.)	10/25/41
Updike, John (Shillington, Pa.)	3/18/32
Uris, Leon (Baltimore, Md.)	8/3/24
Vidal, Gore (West Point, N.Y.)	10/3/25
Vonnegut, Kurt Jr. (Indianapolis, Ind.)	11/11/22
Walker, Alice (Eatonton, Ga.)	2/9/44
Wambaugh, Joseph (East Pittsburgh, Pa.)	1/22/37
Wasserstein, Wendy (New York, N.Y.)	—
Welty, Eudora (Jackson, Miss.)	4/13/09
Wideman, John Edgar (Pittsburgh, Pa.)	6/14/41
Wilson, August (Pittsburgh, Pa.)	4/27/45
Wilson, Lanford (Lebanon, Mo.)	4/13/37
Wolfe, Tom (Richmond, Va.)	3/2/31
Wolff, Tobias (Birmingham, Ala.)	6/19/45
Wouk, Herman (New York, N.Y.)	5/27/15

American Architects and Some of Their Achievements

Max Abramovitz, b. 1908, Avery Fisher Hall, Lincoln Center, N.Y.C.

Henry Bacon, 1866-1924, Lincoln Memorial.

Pietro Belluschi, b. 1899, Juilliard School of Music, Lincoln Center, N.Y.C.

Marcel Breuer, 1902-1981, Whitney Museum of American Art, N.Y.C. (with Hamilton Smith).

Charles Bulfinch, 1763-1844, State House, Boston; Capitol, Wash. D.C., (part).

Gordon Bunshaft, 1909-1990, Lever House, Park Ave, N.Y.C.; Hirshhorn Museum, Wash., D.C.

Daniel H. Burnham, 1846-1912, Union Station, Wash. D.C.; Flatiron, N.Y.C.

Irwin Chanin, 1892-1988, New York City theaters, skyscrapers.

Ralph Adams Cram, 1863-1942, Cathedral of St. John the Divine, N.Y.C.; U.S. Military Academy (part).

R. Buckminster Fuller, 1895-1983, U.S. Pavilion, Expo 67, Montreal (geodesic domes).

Cass Gilbert, 1859-1934, Custom House, Woolworth Bldg., N.Y.C.; Supreme Court bldg., Wash., D.C.

Bertram G. Goodhue, 1869-1924, Capitol, Lincoln, Neb.; St. Thomas, St. Bartholomew, N.Y.C.

Walter Gropius, 1883-1969, Pan Am Building, N.Y.C. (with Pietro Belluschi).

Peter Harrison, 1716-1775, Touro Synagogue, Redwood Library, Newport, R.I.

Wallace K. Harrison, 1895-1981, Metropolitan Opera House, Lincoln Center, N.Y.C.

Thomas Hastings, 1860-1929, Public Library, Frick Mansion, N.Y.C.

James Hoban, 1762-1831, The White House.

Raymond Hood, 1881-1934, Rockefeller Center, N.Y.C. (part); Daily News, N.Y.C.; Tribune, Chicago.

Richard M. Hunt, 1827-1895, Metropolitan Museum, N.Y.C. (part); Natl. Observatory, Wash., D.C.

William Le Baron Jenney, 1832-1907, Home Insurance, Chicago (demolished 1931).

Philip C. Johnson, b. 1906, N.Y. State Theater, Lincoln Center, N.Y.C.

Albert Kahn, 1869-1942, Athletic Club Bldg., General Motors Bldg., Detroit.

Louis Kahn, 1901-1974, Salk Laboratory, La Jolla, Cal.; Yale Art Gallery.

Christopher Grant LaFarge, 1862-1938, Roman Catholic Chapel, West Point.

Benjamin H. Latrobe, 1764-1820, U.S. Capitol (part).

William Lescaze, 1896-1969, Philadelphia Savings Fund Society; Borg-Warner Bldg., Chicago.

Bernard R. Maybeck, 1862-1957, Hearst Hall, Chick House, Univ. of Cal., First Church of Christ Scientist, Berkeley.

Charles F. McKim, 1847-1909, Public Library, Boston, Columbia Univ., N.Y.C. (part).

Charles M. McKim, b. 1920, KUHT-TV Transmitter Building, Houston; Lutheran Church of the Redeemer, Houston.

Ludwig Mies van der Rohe, 1886-1969, Seagram Building, N.Y.C. (with Philip C. Johnson); National Gallery, Berlin.

Robert Mills, 1781-1855, Washington Monument.

Richard J. Neutra, 1892-1970, Mathematics Park, Princeton; Orange Co. Courthouse, Santa Ana, Cal.

Gyo Obata, b. 1923, Natl. Air & Space Mus., Smithsonian Institution; Dallas-Ft. Worth Airport.

Frederick L. Olmsted, 1822-1903, Central Park, N.Y.C.; Fairmount Park, Philadelphia.

I(eoh) M(ing) Pei, b. 1917, National Center for Atmospheric Research, Boulder, Col.; East Wing, Natl. Gallery of Art, Wash., D.C.; Pyramid, The Louvre, Paris.

William Pereira, 1909-1985, Cape Canaveral; Transamerica Bldg., San Francisco.

John Russell Pope, 1874-1937, National Gallery.

George Browne Post, 1837-1913, New York Stock Exchange, Wisconsin state capitol.

John Portman, b. 1924, Peachtree Center, Atlanta.

James Renwick Jr., 1818-1895, Grace Church, St. Patrick's Cathedral, N.Y.C.; Smithsonian, Corcoran Galleries, Wash., D.C.

Henry H. Richardson, 1838-1886, Trinity Church, Boston.

Kevin Roche, b. 1922, Oakland Cal. Museum; Fine Arts Center, U. of Mass.

James Gamble Rogers, 1867-1947, Columbia-Presbyterian Medical Center, N.Y.C.; Northwestern Univ., Chicago.

John Wellborn Root, 1887-1963, Palmolive Building, Chicago; Hotel Statler, Washington; Hotel Tamanaco, Caracas.

Paul Rudolph, b. 1918, Jewitt Art Center, Wellesley College; Art & Architecture Bldg., Yale.

Charles M. Russell, 1866-1926, Western life.

Eero Saarinen, 1910-1961, Gateway to the West Arch, St. Louis; Trans World Flight Center, N.Y.C.

Louis Skidmore, 1897-1962, AEC town site, Oak Ridge, Tenn.; Terrace Plaza Hotel, Cincinnati.

Clarence S. Stein, 1882-1975, Temple Emanu-El, N.Y.C.

Edward Durell Stone, 1902-1978, U.S. Embassy, New Delhi, India; (H. Hartford) Gallery of Modern Art, N.Y.C.

Louis H. Sullivan, 1856-1924, Auditorium, Chicago.

Richard Upjohn, 1802-1878, Trinity Church, N.Y.C.

Ralph T. Walker, 1889-1973, N.Y. Telephone Hdqrs., N.Y.C.; IBM Research Lab., Poughkeepsie, N.Y.

Roland A. Wank, 1898-1970, Cincinnati Union Terminal; head architect TVA, 1933-44.

Stanford White, 1853-1906, Washington Arch; first Madison Square Garden, N.Y.C.

Frank Lloyd Wright, 1867 (or 1869)-1959, Imperial Hotel, Tokyo; Guggenheim Museum, N.Y.C.; Unity Church, Oak Park, Ill; Robie House, Chicago; Taliesin, Wis.

William Wurster, 1895-1973, Ghirardelli Sq., San Francisco; Cowell College, U. Cal., Berkeley.

Minoru Yamasaki, 1912-1986, World Trade Center, N.Y.C.

Noted American Cartoonists

Charles Addams, 1912-1988, macabre cartoons.

Brad Anderson, b. 1924, Marmaduke.

Peter Arno, 1904-1968, *New Yorker* urban characterizations.

Tex Avery, 1908-1980, **Friz Freleng**, b. 1905?, **Chuck Jones**, b. 1912, animators of Bugs Bunny, Porky Pig, Daffy Duck.

George Baker, 1915-1975, The Sad Sack.

C. C. Beck, 1910-1989, Captain Marvel.

Jim Berry, b. 1932, Berry's World.

Herb Block (Herblock), b. 1909, leading political cartoonist.

George Booth, b. 1926, *New Yorker* cartoonist.

Berke Breathed, b. 1957, Bloom County.

Clare Briggs, 1875-1930, Mr. & Mrs.

Dik Browne, 1917-1989, Hi & Lois, Hagar the Horrible.

Ernie Bushmiller, 1905-1982, Nancy.

Milton Caniff, 1907-1988, Terry & the Pirates; Steve Canyon.

Al Capp, 1909-1979, Li'l Abner.

Roz Chast, b. 1954, New Yorker "bonfire of the banalities" cartoons.

Paul Conrad, 1924, political cartoonist.

Roy Crane, 1901-1977, Captain Easy; Buz Sawyer.

Robert Crumb, b. 1943, "Underground" cartoonist.

Jay N. Darling (Ding), 1876-1962, political cartoonist.

Jim Davis, b. 1945, Garfield.

Billy DeBeck, 1890-1942, Barney Google.

Rudolph Dirks, 1877-1968, The Katzenjammer Kids.

Walt Disney, 1901-1966, producer of animated cartoons; created Mickey Mouse & Donald Duck.

Steve Ditko, b. 1927, Spider-Man.

Mort Drucker, b. 1929, *Mad* magazine.

Jules Feiffer, b. 1929, satirical *Village Voice* cartoonist.

Bud Fisher, 1884-1954, Mutt & Jeff.

Ham Fisher, 1900-1955, Joe Palooka.

James Montgomery Flagg, 1877-1960, illustrator; created the famous Uncle Sam recruiting poster during WWI.

Max Fleischer, 1883-1972, creator of Betty Boop, Popeye cartoons.

Hal Foster, 1892-1982, Tarzan; Prince Valiant.

Fontaine Fox, 1884-1964, Toonerville Folks.

Rube Goldberg, 1883-1970, Boob McNutt.

Chester Gould, 1900-1985, Dick Tracy.

Harold Gray, 1894-1968, Little Orphan Annie.

Matt Groening, b. 1954, Life is Hell, The Simpsons.

Cathy Guisewite, b. 1950, Cathy.

Bill Hanna, b. 1910, & **Joe Barbera**, b. 1911, animators of Tom & Jerry, Huckleberry Hound, Yogi Bear, Flintstones.

Johnny Hart, b. 1931, BC, Wizard of Id.

Jimmy Hatlo, 1898-1963, Little Iodine.

John Held Jr., 1889-1958, "Jazz Age" cartoonist.

George Herriman, 1881-1944, Krazy Kat.

Harry Hershfield, 1885-1974, Abie the Agent.

Al Hirschfeld, b. 1903, N.Y. Times theater caricaturist.

Burne Hogarth, b. 1911, Tarzan.

Helen Hokinson, 1900-1949, satirized clubwomen.

Nicole Hollander, b. 1939, Sylvia.

Lynn Johnston, b. 1947, For Better Or For Worse.

Bil Keane, b. 1922, The Family Circus.

Walt Kelly, 1913-1973, Pogo.

Hank Ketcham, b. 1920, Dennis the Menace.

Ted Key, b. 1912, Hazel.

Frank King, 1883-1969, Gasoline Alley.

Jack Kirby, b. 1917, Fantastic Four.

Rollin Kirby, 1875-1952, political cartoonist.

B(ernard) Kliban, 1935-1991, cat books.

Edward Koren, b. 1935, New Yorker woolly characters.

Walter Lantz, b. 1900, Woody Woodpecker.

Gary Larson, b. 1950, The Far Side.

Mell Lazarus, b. 1929, Momma, Miss Peach.

Stan Lee, b. 1922, Marvel Comics.

David Levine, b. 1926, New York Review of Books caricatures.

Don Martin, b. 1931, *Mad* magazine.

Bill Mauldin, b. 1921, depicted squalid life of the G.I. in WWII.

Jeff MacNelly, b. 1947, political cartoonist, and strip Shoe.

Winsor McCay, 1872-1934, Little Nemo.

John T. McCutcheon, 1870-1949, midwestern rural life.

George McManus, 1884-1954, Bringing Up Father.

Dale Messick, b. 1906, Brenda Starr.

Norman Mingo, 1896-1980, Alfred E. Neuman.

Bob Montana, 1920-1975, Archie.

Dick Moores, 1909-1986, Gasoline Alley.

Willard Mullin, 1902-1978, sports cartoonist; created Dodgers "Bum" and Mets "Kid".

Russell Myers, b. 1938, Broom Hilda.

Thomas Nast, 1840-1902, political cartoonist; created the Democratic donkey and Republican elephant.

Pat Oliphant, b. 1935, political cartoonist.

Frederick Burr Opper, 1857-1937, Happy Hooligan.

Richard Outcault, 1863-1928, Yellow Kid; Buster Brown.

Mike Peters, b. 1943, editorial cartoons; Mother Goose & Grimm.

George Price, b. 1901, New Yorker lower-class life.

Alex Raymond, 1909-1956, Flash Gordon; Jungle Jim.

Art Sansom, 1920-1991, The Born Loser.

Charles Schulz, b. 1922, Peanuts.

Elzie C. Segar, 1894-1938, Popeye.

Jerry Siegel, b. 1914, & **Joe Shuster**, b. 1914, Superman.

Sydney Smith, 1887-1935, The Gumps.

Otto Soglow, 1900-1975, Little King; Canyon Kiddies.

Art Spiegelman, b. 1948, Raw; Maus.

William Steig, b. 1907, *New Yorker* cartoonist.

James Swinnerton, 1875-1974, Little Jimmy.

Paul Terry, 1887-1971, animator of Mighty Mouse.

Bob Thaves, b. 1924, Frank and Ernest.

James Thurber, 1894-1961, *New Yorker* cartoonist.

Garry Trudeau, b. 1948, Doonesbury.

Mort Walker, b. 1923, Beetle Bailey.

Bill Watterson, b. 1958, Calvin and Hobbes.

Russ Westover, 1887-1966, Tillie the Toiler.

Frank Willard, 1893-1958, Moon Mullins.

J. R. Williams, 1888-1957, The Willets Family; Out Our Way.

Gahan Wilson, b. 1930, cartoonist of the macabre.

Tom Wilson, b. 1931, Ziggy.

Art Young, 1866-1943, political radical and satirist.

Chic Young, 1901-1973, Blondie.

Noted Political Leaders of the Past

(U.S. presidents and vice presidents, Supreme Court justices, signers of Declaration of Independence, listed elsewhere.)

Abu Bakr, 573-634, Mohammedan leader, first caliph, chosen successor to Mohammed.

Dean Acheson, 1893-1971, (U.S.) secretary of state, chief architect of cold war foreign policy.

Samuel Adams, 1722-1803, (U.S.) patriot, Boston Tea Party firebrand.

Konrad Adenauer, 1876-1967, (G.) West German chancellor.

Emilio Aguinaldo, 1869-1964, (Philip.) revolutionary, fought against Spain and the U.S.

Akbar, 1542-1605, greatest Mogul emperor of India.

Salvador Allende Gossens, 1908-1973, (Chil.) president, advocate of democratic socialism.

Herbert H. Asquith, 1852-1928, (Br.) Liberal prime minister, instituted an advanced program of social reform.

Atahualpa, ?-1533, Inca (ruling chief) of Peru.

Kemal Atatürk, 1881-1938, (Turk.) founded modern Turkey.

Clement Attlee, 1883-1967, (Br.) Labour party leader, prime minister, enacted national health, nationalized many industries.

Stephen F. Austin, 1793-1836, (U.S.) led Texas colonization.

Mikhail Bakunin, 1814-1876, (R.) revolutionary, leading exponent of anarchism.

Arthur J. Balfour, 1848-1930, (Br.) as foreign secretary under Lloyd George issued Balfour Declaration expressing official British approval of Zionism.

Bernard M. Baruch, 1870-1965, (U.S.) financier, gvt. adviser.

Fulgencio Batista y Zaldívar, 1901-1973, (Cub.) ruler overthrown by Castro.

Lord Beaverbrook, 1879-1964, (Br.) financier, statesman, newspaper owner.

Menachem Begin, 1914-1992, (Isr.) Israeli prime minister, won 1978 Nobel Peace Prize.

Eduard Benes, 1884-1948, (Czech.) president during interwar and post-WW II eras.

David Ben-Gurion, 1886-1973, (Isr.) first premier of Israel.

Thomas Hart Benton, 1782-1858, (U.S.) Missouri senator, championed agrarian interests and westward expansion.

Lavrenti Beria, 1899-1953, (USSR) Communist leader prominent in political purges under Stalin.

Aneurin Bevan, 1897-1960, (Br.) Labour party leader.

Ernest Bevin, 1881-1951, (Br.) Labour party leader, foreign minister, helped lay foundation for NATO.

Otto von Bismarck, 1815-1898, (G.) statesman known as the Iron Chancellor, uniter of Germany, 1870.

James G. Blaine, 1830-1893, (U.S.) Republican politician, diplomat, influential in launching Pan-American movement.

Léon Blum, 1872-1950, (F.) socialist leader, writer, headed first Popular Front government.

Simón Bolívar, 1783-1830, (Venez.) South American revolutionary who liberated much of the continent from Spanish rule.

William E. Borah, 1865-1940, (U.S.) isolationist senator, instrumental in blocking U.S. membership in League of Nations and the World Court.

Cesare Borgia, 1476-1507, (It.) soldier, politician, an outstanding figure of the Italian Renaissance.

Leonid Brezhnev, 1906-1982, (USSR) leader of the Soviet Union, 1964-82.

Aristide Briand, 1862-1932, (F.) foreign minister, chief architect of Locarno Pact and anti-war Kellogg-Briand Pact.

William Jennings Bryan, 1860-1925, (U.S.) Democratic, populist leader, orator, 3 times lost race for presidency.

Nikolai Bukharin, 1888-1938, (USSR) communist leader.

William C. Bullitt, 1891-1967, (U.S.) diplomat, first ambassador to USSR, ambassador to France.

Ralph Bunche, 1904-1971, (U.S.) a founder and key diplomat of United Nations for more than 20 years.

John C. Calhoun, 1782-1850, (U.S.) political leader, champion of states' rights and a symbol of the Old South.

Robert Castlereagh, 1769-1822, (Br.) foreign secy, guided Grand Alliance against Napoleon.

Camillo Benso Cavour, 1810-1861, (It.) statesman, largely responsible for uniting Italy under the House of Savoy.

Nicolae Ceausescu, 1918-1989, Rumanian Communist leader, head of state from 1967-1989.

Austen Chamberlain, 1863-1937, (Br.) Conservative party leader, largely responsible for Locarno Pact of 1925.

Neville Chamberlain, 1869-1940, (Br.) Conservative prime minister whose appeasement of Hitler led to Munich Pact.

Salmon P. Chase, 1808-1873, (U.S.) public official, abolitionist, jurist, 6th Supreme Court chief justice.

Chiang Kai-shek, 1887-1975, (Chin.) Nationalist Chinese president whose govt. was driven from mainland to Taiwan.

Chou En-lai, 1898-1976, (Chin.) diplomat, prime minister, a leading figure of the Chinese Communist party.

Winston Churchill, 1874-1965, (Br.) prime minister, soldier, author, guided Britain through WW II.

Galeazzo Ciano, 1903-1944, (It.) fascist foreign minister, helped create Rome-Berlin Axis, executed by Mussolini.

Henry Clay, 1777-1852, (U.S.) "The Great Compromiser," one of most influential pre-Civil War political leaders.

Georges Clemenceau, 1841-1929, (F.) twice premier, Wilson's chief antagonist at Paris Peace Conference after WW I.

DeWitt Clinton, 1769-1828, (U.S.) political leader, responsible for promoting idea of the Erie Canal.

Robert Clive, 1725-1774, (Br.) first administrator of Bengal, laid foundation for British Empire in India.

Jean Baptiste Colbert, 1619-1683, (F.) statesman, influential under Louis XIV, created the French navy.

Oliver Cromwell, 1599-1658, (Br.) Lord Protector of England, led parliamentary forces during Civil War.

Curzon of Kedleston, 1859-1925, (Br.) viceroy of India, foreign secretary, major force in dealing with post-WW I problems in Europe and Far East.

Édouard Daladier, 1884-1970, (F.) radical socialist politician, arrested by Vichy, interned by Germans until liberation in 1945.

Georges Danton, 1759-1794, (F.) a leading figure in the French Revolution.

Jefferson Davis, 1808-1889, (U.S.) president of the Confederate States of America.

Charles G. Dawes, 1865-1951, (U.S.) statesman, banker, advanced Dawes Plan to stabilize post-WW I German finances.

Alcide De Gasperi, 1881-1954, (It.) premier, founder of the Christian Democratic party.

Charles DeGaulle, 1890-1970, (F.) general, statesman, and first president of the Fifth Republic.

Eamon De Valera, 1882-1975, (Ir.-U.S.) statesman, led fight for Irish independence.

Thomas E. Dewey, 1902-1971, (U.S.) New York governor, twice loser in try for presidency.

Ngo Dinh Diem, 1901-1963, (Viet.) South Vietnamese president, assassinated in government take-over.

Everett M. Dirksen, 1896-1969, (U.S.) Senate Republican minority leader, orator.

Benjamin Disraeli, 1804-1881, (Br.) prime minister, considered founder of modern Conservative party.

Engelbert Dollfuss, 1892-1934, (Aus.) chancellor, assassinated by Austrian Nazis.

Andrea Doria, 1466-1560, (It.) Genoese admiral, statesman, called "Father of Peace" and "Liberator of Genoa."

Stephen A. Douglas, 1813-1861, (U.S.) Democratic leader, orator, opposed Lincoln for the presidency.

John Foster Dulles, 1888-1959, (U.S.) secretary of state under Eisenhower, cold war policy maker.

Friedrich Ebert, 1871-1925, (G.) Social Democratic movement leader, instrumental in bringing about Weimar constitution.

Sir Anthony Eden, 1897-1977, (Br.) foreign secretary, prime minister during Suez invasion of 1956.

Ludwig Erhard, 1897-1977, (G.) economist, West German chancellor, led nation's economic rise after WW II.

Hamilton Fish, 1808-1893, (U.S.) secretary of state, successfully mediated disputes with Great Britain, Latin America.

James V. Forrestal, 1892-1949, (U.S.) secretary of navy, first secretary of defense.

Francisco Franco, 1892-1975, (Sp.) leader of rebel forces during Spanish Civil War and dictator of Spain.

Benjamin Franklin, 1706-1790, (U.S.) printer, publisher, author, inventor, scientist, diplomat.

Louis de Frontenac, 1620-1698, (F.) governor of New France (Canada); encouraged explorations, fought Iroquois.

Hugh Gaitskell, 1906-1963, (Br.) Labour party leader, major force in reversing its stand for unilateral disarmament.

Albert Gallatin, 1761-1849, (U.S.) secretary of treasury who was instrumental in negotiating end of War of 1812.

Léon Gambetta, 1838-1882, (F.) statesman, politician, one of the founders of the Third Republic.

Indira Gandhi, 1917-1984, (Ind.) succeeded father, Jawaharlal Nehru, as prime minister, assassinated.

Mohandas K. Gandhi, 1869-1948, (Ind.) political leader, ascetic, led nationalist movement against British rule.

Giuseppe Garibaldi, 1807-1882, (It.) patriot, soldier, a leading figure in the Risorgimento, the Italian unification movement.

Genghis Khan, c. 1167-1227, Mongol conqueror, ruler of vast Asian empire.

William E. Gladstone, 1809-1898, (Br.) prime minister 4 times, dominant force of Liberal party from 1868 to 1894.

Paul Joseph Goebbels, 1897-1945, (G.) Nazi propagandist, master of mass psychology.

Klement Gottwald, 1896-1953, (Czech.) communist leader ushered communism into his country.

Che (Ernesto) Guevara, 1928-1967, (Arg.) guerilla leader, prominent in Cuban revolution, killed in Bolivia.

Haile Selassie, 1891-1975, (Eth.) emperor, maintained monarchy through invasion, occupation, internal resistance.

Alexander Hamilton, 1755-1804, (U.S.) first treasury secretary, champion of strong central government.

Dag Hammarskjold, 1905-1961, (Swed.) statesman, UN secretary general.

John Hancock, 1737-1793, (U.S.) revolutionary leader, first signer of Declaration of Independence.

John Hay, 1838-1905, (U.S.) secretary of state, primarily associated with Open Door Policy toward China.

Patrick Henry, 1736-1799, (U.S.) major revolutionary figure, remarkable orator.

Édouard Herriot, 1872-1957, (F.) Radical Socialist leader, twice premier, president of National Assembly.

Theodor Herzl, 1860-1904, (Aus.) founder of modern Zionism.

Heinrich Himmler, 1900-1945, (G.) chief of Nazi SS and Gestapo, primarily responsible for the Holocaust.

Paul von Hindenburg, 1847-1934, (G.) field marshal, president.

Hirohito, 1902-1989; emperor of Japan from 1926.

Adolf Hitler, 1889-1945, (G.) dictator, founder of National Socialism; wrote *Mein Kampf*, strategy for world domination.

Ho Chi Minh, 1890-1969, (Viet.) North Vietnamese president, Vietnamese Communist leader, national hero.

Harry L. Hopkins, 1890-1946, (U.S.) New Deal administrator, closest adviser to FDR during WW II.

Edward M. House, 1858-1938, (U.S.) diplomat, confidential adviser to Woodrow Wilson.

Samuel Houston, 1793-1863, (U.S.) leader of struggle to win control of Texas from Mexico.

Cordell Hull, 1871-1955, (U.S.) secretary of state, initiated reciprocal trade to lower tariffs, helped organize UN.

Hubert H. Humphrey, 1911-1978, (U.S.) Minnesota Democrat, senator, vice president, spent 32 years in public service.

Ibn Saud, c. 1888-1953, (S. Arab.) founder of Saudi Arabia and its first king.

Jacob Javits, 1904-1986 (U.S.) U.S. senator from New York for 24 years.

Jinnah, Muhammed Ali, 1876-1948, (Pak.) founder, first governor-general of Pakistan.

Benito Juarez, 1806-1872, (Mex.) rallied countrymen against foreign threats, sought to create democratic, federal republic.

Kamehameha I, c. 1758-1819, (Haw.) founder, first monarch of unified Hawaii.

Frank B. Kellogg, 1856-1937, (U.S.) secretary of state, negotiated Kellogg-Briand Pact to outlaw war.

Robert F. Kennedy, 1925-1968, (U.S.) attorney general, senator, assassinated while seeking presidential nomination.

Aleksandr Kerensky, 1881-1970, (R.) revolutionary, served as premier after Feb. 1917 revolution until Bolshevik overthrow.

Ruhollah Khomeini, 1900-1989, (Iran), religious leader with Islamic title "ayatollah," directed overthrow of shah, 1979, became source of political authority in succeeding governments.

Nikita Khrushchev, 1894-1971, (USSR) premier, first secretary of Communist party, initiated de-Stalinization.

Lajos Kossuth, 1802-1894, (Hung.) principal figure in 1848 Hungarian revolution.

Pyotr Kropotkin, 1842-1921, (R.) anarchist, championed the peasants but opposed Bolshevism.

Kublai Khan, c. 1215-1294, Mongol emperor, founder of Yüan dynasty in China.

Béla Kun, 1886-c.1939, (Hung.) communist, member of 3d International, tried to foment worldwide revolution.

Robert M. LaFollette, 1855-1925, (U.S.) Wisconsin public official, leader of progressive movement.

Pierre Laval, 1883-1945, (F.) politician, Vichy foreign minister, executed for treason.

Andrew Bonar Law, 1858-1923, (Br.) Conservative party politician, led opposition to Irish home rule.

Vladimir Ilyich Lenin (Ulyanov), 1870-1924, (USSR) revolutionary, founder of Bolshevism, Soviet leader 1917-1924.

Ferdinand de Lesseps, 1805-1894, (F.) diplomat, engineer, conceived idea of Suez Canal.

Rene Levesque, 1922-1987 (Can.) Premier of Quebec, 1976-85; led unsuccessful fight to separate from Canada.

Liu Shao-ch'i, c.1898-1974, (Chin.) communist leader, fell from grace during "cultural revolution."

Maxim Litvinov, 1876-1951, (USSR) revolutionary, commissar of foreign affairs, favored cooperation with Western powers.

David Lloyd George, 1863-1945, (Br.) Liberal party prime minister, laid foundations for modern welfare state.

Henry Cabot Lodge, 1850-1924, (U.S.) Republican senator, led opposition to participation in League of Nations.

Huey P. Long, 1893-1935, (U.S.) Louisiana political demagogue, governor, assassinated.

Rosa Luxemburg, 1871-1919, (G.) revolutionary, leader of the German Social Democratic party and Spartacus party.

J. Ramsay MacDonald, 1866-1937, (Br.) first Labour party prime minister of Great Britain.

Harold Macmillan, 1895-1987 (Br.) prime minister of Great Britain, 1957-63.

Joseph R. McCarthy, 1908-1957, (U.S.) senator notorious for his witch hunt for communists in the government.

Makarios III, 1913-1977, (Cypr.) Greek Orthodox archbishop, first president of Cyprus.

Malcolm X (Malcolm Little), 1925-1965, (U.S.) black separatist leader, assassinated.

Mao Tse-tung, 1893-1976, (Chin.) chief Chinese Marxist theorist, soldier, led Chinese revolution establishing his nation as an important communist state.

Jean Paul Marat, 1743-1793, (F.) revolutionary, politician, identified with radical Jacobins, assassinated.

José Martí, 1853-1895, (Cub.) patriot, poet, leader of Cuban struggle for independence.

Jan Masaryk, 1886-1948, (Czech.) foreign minister, died by mysterious suicide following communist coup.

Thomas G. Masaryk, 1850-1937, (Czech.) statesman, philosopher, first president of Czechoslovak Republic.

Jules Mazarin, 1602-1661, (F.) cardinal, statesman, prime minister under Louis XIII and queen regent Anne of Austria.

Giuseppe Mazzini, 1805-1872, (It.), reformer dedicated to the Risorgimento, 19th-century movement for the political and social renewal of Italy.

Tom Mboya, 1930-1969, (Kenyan) political leader, instrumental in securing independence for his country.

Cosimo I de' Medici, 1519-1574, (It.) Duke of Florence, grand duke of Tuscany.

Lorenzo de' Medici, the Magnificent, 1449-1492, (It.) merchant prince, a towering figure in Italian Renaissance.

Catherine de Medicis, 1519-1589, (F.) queen consort of Henry II, regent of France, influential in Catholic-Huguenot wars.

Golda Meir, 1898-1979, (Isr.) prime minister, 1969-74.

Klemens W.N.L. Metternich, 1773-1859, (Aus.) statesman, arbiter of post-Napoleonic Europe.

Anastas Mikoyan, 1895-1978, (USSR) prominent Soviet leader from 1917; president 1964-65.

Guy Mollet, 1905-1975, (F.) social politician, resistance leader.

Henry Morgenthau Jr., 1891-1967, (U.S.) secretary of treasury, raised funds to finance New Deal and U.S. WW II activities.

Gouverneur Morris, 1752-1816, (U.S.) statesman, diplomat, financial expert who helped plan decimal coinage system.

Wayne Morse, 1900-1974, (U.S.) senator, long-time critic of Vietnam War.

Muhammad Ali, 1769?-1849, (Egypt), pasha, founder of dynasty that encouraged emergence of modern Egyptian state.

Benito Mussolini, 1883-1945, (It.) dictator and leader of the Italian fascist state.

Imre Nagy, c. 1895-1958, (Hung.) communist premier, assassinated after Soviets crushed 1956 uprising.

Gamal Abdel Nasser, 1918-1970, (Egypt.) leader of Arab unification, second Egyptian president.

Jawaharlal Nehru, 1889-1964, (Ind.) prime minister, guided India through its early years of independence.

Kwame Nkrumah, 1909-1972, (Ghan.) dictatorial prime minister, deposed in 1966.

Frederick North, 1732-1792, (Br.) prime minister, his inept policies led to loss of American colonies.

Daniel O'Connell, 1775-1847, (Ir.) political leader, known as The Liberator.

Omar, c.581-644, Mohammedan leader, 2d caliph, led Islam to become an imperial power.

Ignace Paderewski, 1860-1941, (Pol.) statesman, pianist, composer, briefly prime minister, an ardent patriot.

Viscount Palmerston, 1784-1865, (Br.) Whig-Liberal prime minister, foreign minister, embodied British nationalism.

George Papandreou, 1888-1968, (Gk.) Republican politician, served three times as prime minister.

Franz von Papen, 1879-1969, (G.) politician, played major role in overthrow of Weimar Republic and rise of Hitler.

Charles Stewart Parnell, 1846-1891, (Ir.) nationalist leader, "uncrowned king of Ireland."

Lester Pearson, 1897-1972, (Can.) diplomat, Liberal party leader, prime minister.

Robert Peel, 1788-1850, (Br.) reformist prime minister, founder of Conservative party.

Juan Perón, 1895-1974, (Arg.) president, dictator.

Joseph Pilsudski, 1867-1935, (Pol.) statesman, instrumental in re-establishing Polish state in the 20th century.

Charles Pinckney, 1757-1824, (U.S.) founding father, his Pinckney plan was largely incorporated into constitution.

William Pitt, the Elder, 1708-1778, (Br.) statesman, called the "Great Commoner," transformed Britain into imperial power.

William Pitt, the Younger, 1759-1806, (Br.) prime minister during French Revolutionary wars.

Georgi Plekhanov, 1857-1918, (R.) revolutionary, social philosopher, called "father of Russian Marxism."

Raymond Poincaré, 1860-1934, (F.) 9th president of the Republic, advocated harsh punishment of Germany after WW I.

Georges Pompidou, 1911-1974, (F.) Gaullist political leader, president from 1969 to 1974.

Grigori Potemkin, 1739-1791, (R.) field marshal, favorite of Catherine II.

Edmund Randolph, 1753-1813, (U.S.) attorney, prominent in drafting, ratification of constitution.

John Randolph, 1773-1833, (U.S.) southern planter, strong advocate of states' rights.

Jeannette Rankin, 1880-1973, (U.S.) pacifist, first woman member of U.S. Congress.

Walter Rathenau, 1867-1922, (G.) industrialist, social theorist, statesman.

Sam Rayburn, 1882-1961, (U.S.) Democratic leader, representative for 47 years, House speaker for 17.

Paul Reynaud, 1878-1966, (F.) statesman, premier in 1940 at the time of France's defeat by Germany.

Syngman Rhee, 1875-1965, (Kor.) first president of the Republic of Korea.

Cecil Rhodes, 1853-1902, (Br.) imperialist, industrial magnate, established Rhodes scholarships in his will.

Cardinal de Richelieu, 1585-1642, (F.) statesman, known as "red eminence," chief minister to Louis XIII.
Maximilien Robespierre, 1758-1794, (F.) leading figure of French Revolution, responsible for much of Reign of Terror.
Nelson Rockefeller, 1908-1979, (U.S.) Republican gov. of N.Y., 1959-73; U.S. vice president, 1974-77.
Eleanor Roosevelt, 1884-1962, (U.S.) humanitarian, United Nations diplomat.
Elihu Root, 1845-1937, (U.S.) lawyer, statesman, diplomat, leading Republican supporter of the League of Nations.
John Russell, 1792-1878, (Br.) Liberal prime minister during the Irish potato famine.
Anwar el-Sadat, 1918-1981, (Egypt) president, 1970-1981, promoted peace with Israel; assassinated.
António de O. Salazar, 1899-1970, (Port.) statesman, long-time dictator.
José de San Martin, 1778-1850, South American revolutionary, protector of Peru.
Eisaku Sato, 1901-1975, (Jap.) prime minister, presided over Japan's post-WW II emergence as major world power.
Philipp Scheidemann, 1865-1939, (G.) Social Democratic leader, first chancellor of the German republic.
Robert Schuman, 1886-1963, (F.) statesman, founded European Coal and Steel Community.
Carl Schurz, 1829-1906, (U.S.) German-American political leader, journalist, orator, dedicated reformer.
Kurt Schuschnigg, 1897-1977, (Aus.) chancellor, unsuccessful in stopping his country's annexation by Germany.
William H. Seward, 1801-1872, (U.S.) anti-slavery activist, as Lincoln's secretary of state purchased Alaska.
Carlo Sforza, 1872-1952, (It.) foreign minister, anti-fascist.
Sitting Bull, c. 1831-1890, (Native Amer.) Sioux leader in Battle of Little Bighorn over George A. Custer, 1876; fostered Ghost Dance religion.
Alfred E. Smith, 1873-1944, (U.S.) New York Democratic governor, first Roman Catholic to run for presidency.
Jan C. Smuts, 1870-1950, (S.Af.) statesman, philosopher, soldier, prime minister.
Paul Henri Spaak, 1899-1972, (Belg.) statesman, socialist leader.
Joseph Stalin, 1879-1953, (USSR) Soviet dictator, 1924-53.
Edwin M. Stanton, 1814-1869, (U.S.) Lincoln's secretary of war during the Civil War.
Edward R. Stettinius Jr., 1900-1949, (U.S.) industrialist, secretary of state who coordinated aid to WW II allies.
Adlai E. Stevenson, 1900-1965, (U.S.) Democratic leader, diplomat, Illinois governor, presidential candidate.
Henry L. Stimson, 1867-1950, (U.S.) statesman, served in 5 administrations, influenced foreign policy in 1930s and 1940s.
Gustav Stresemann, 1878-1929, (G.) chancellor, foreign minister, dedicated to regaining friendship for post-WW I Germany.
Sukarno, 1901-1970, (Indon.) dictatorial first president of the Indonesian republic.
Sun Yat-sen, 1866-1925, (Chin.) revolutionary, leader of Kuomintang, regarded as the father of modern China.
Robert A. Taft, 1889-1953, (U.S.) conservative Senate leader, called "Mr. Republican."
Charles de Talleyrand, 1754-1838, (F.) statesman, diplomat, the major force of the Congress of Vienna of 1814-15.
U Thant, 1909-1974 (Bur.) statesman, UN secretary-general.
Norman M. Thomas, 1884-1968, (U.S.) social reformer, 6 times unsuccessful Socialist party presidential candidate.
Josip Broz Tito, 1892-1980, (Yug.) president of Yugoslavia from 1953, World War II guerrilla chief, postwar rival of Stalin, leader of 3d world movement.
Palmiro Togliatti, 1893-1964, (It.) major leader of Italian Communist party.
Hideki Tojo, 1885-1948, (Jap.) statesman, soldier, prime minister during most of WW II.
François Toussaint L'Ouverture, c. 1744-1803, (Hait.) patriot, martyr, thwarted French colonial aims.
Leon Trotsky, 1879-1940, (USSR) revolutionary, founded Red Army, expelled from party in conflict with Stalin.
Rafael L. Trujillo Molina, 1891-1961, (Dom.) absolute dictator, assassinated.
Moise K. Tshombe, 1919-1969, (Cong.) politician, president of secessionist Katanga, premier of Republic of Congo (Zaire).
William M. Tweed, 1823-1878, (U.S.) politician, absolute leader of Tammany Hall, NYC's Democratic political machine.
Walter Ulbricht, 1893-1973, (G.) communist leader of German Democratic Republic.
Arthur H. Vandenberg, 1884-1951, (U.S.) senator, proponent of anti-communist bipartisan foreign policy after WW II.
Eleutherios Venizelos, 1864-1936, (Gk.) most prominent Greek statesman in early 20th century; expanded territory.
Hendrik F. Verwoerd, 1901-1966, (S.Af.) prime minister, rigorously applied apartheid policy despite protest.
Robert Walpole, 1676-1745, (Br.) statesman, generally considered Britain's first prime minister.
Daniel Webster, 1782-1852, (U.S.) orator, politician, advocate of business interests during Jacksonian agrarianism.
Chaim Weizmann, 1874-1952, Zionist leader, scientist, first Israeli president.
Wendell L. Willkie, 1892-1944, (U.S.) Republican who tried to unseat FDR when he ran for his 3d term.
Emiliano Zapata, c. 1879-1919, (Mex.) revolutionary, major influence on modern Mexico.

Notable Military and Naval Leaders of the Past

Creighton Abrams, 1914-1974, (U.S.) commanded forces in Vietnam, 1968-72.
Harold Alexander, 1891-1969, (Br.) led Allied invasion of Italy, WW2, 1943.
Ethan Allen, 1738-1789, (U.S.) headed Green Mountain Boys; captured Ft. Ticonderoga, 1775, Amer. Revolutionary War.
Edmund Allenby, 1861-1936, (Br.) in Boer War, WW1; led Egyptian expeditionary force, 1917-18.
Benedict Arnold, 1741-1801, (U.S.) victorious at Saratoga; tried to betray West Point to British, Amer. Revolutionary War.
Henry "Hap" Arnold, 1886-1950, (U.S.) commanded Army Air Force in WW2.
John Barry, 1745-1803, (U.S.) won numerous sea battles during Amer. Revolutionary War.
Pierre Beauregard, 1818-1893, (U.S.) Confederate general ordered bombardment of Ft. Sumter that began the Civil War.
Gebhard v. Blücher, 1742-1819, (G.) helped defeat Napoleon at Waterloo.
Napoleon Bonaparte, 1769-1821, (F.) defeated Russia and Austria at Austerlitz, 1805; invaded Russia, 1812; defeated at Waterloo, 1815.
Edward Braddock, 1695-1755, (Br.) commanded forces in French and Indian War.
Omar N. Bradley, 1893-1981, (U.S.) headed U.S. ground troops in Normandy invasion, WW2, 1944.
John Burgoyne, 1722-1792, (Br.) defeated at Saratoga, Amer. Revolutionary War.
Claire Chennault, 1890-1958, (U.S.) headed Flying Tigers in WW2.
Mark Clark, 1896-1984, (U.S.) led forces in WW2 and Korean War.
Karl v. Clausewitz, 1780-1831, (G.) wrote books on military theory.
Henry Clinton, 1738-1795, (Br.) commander of forces in American Revolutionary War, 1778-81.
Lucius D. Clay, 1897-1978, (U.S.) led Berlin airlift, 1948-49.
Cochise, c. 1815-1874, (Native Amer.) Chief of Chiricahua band of Apache Indians in Arizona.
Charles Cornwallis, 1738-1805, (Br.) victorious at Brandywine, 1777; surrendered at Yorktown, Amer. Revolutionary War.
Crazy Horse, 1849-1877, (U.S.) Sioux war chief victorious at Little Big Horn.
George A. Custer, 1839-1876, (U.S.) defeated and killed at Little Big Horn.
Moshe Dayan, 1915-1981, (Isr.) directed campaigns in the 1967, 1973 Arab-Israeli wars.
Stephen Decatur, 1779-1820, (U.S.) naval hero of Barbary wars, War of 1812.
Anton Denikin, 1872-1947, (R.) led White forces in Russian civil war.
George Dewey, 1837-1917, (U.S.) destroyed Spanish fleet at Manila, 1898, Spanish-American War.
Hugh C. Dowding, 1883-1970, (Br.) headed RAF, WW2, 1936-40.
Jubal Early, 1816-1894, (U.S.) Confederate general led raid on Washington, Civil War, 1864.
Dwight D. Eisenhower, 1890-1969, (U.S.) commanded Allied forces in Europe, WW2.
David Farragut, 1801-1870, (U.S.) Union admiral captured New Orleans, Mobile Bay, Civil War.
Ferdinand Foch, 1851-1929, (F.) headed victorious Allied armies, WW1, 1918.
Nathan Bedford Forrest, 1821-1877, (U.S.) Confederate general led cavalry raids against Union supply lines, Civil War.
Frederick the Great, 1712-1786, (G.) led Prussia in The Seven Years War.
Geronimo, 1829-1909 (Native Amer.) leader of Chiricahua band of Apache Indians.
Nathanael Greene, 1742-1786, (U.S.) defeated British in Southern campaign, 1780-81.
Charles G. Gordon, 1833-1885, (Br.) led forces in China, Crimean War; killed at Khartoum.
Horatio Gates, 1728-1806, (U.S.) commanded army at Saratoga, Amer. Revolutionary War.
Ulysses S. Grant, 1822-1885, (U.S.) headed Union army, Civil War, 1864-65; forced Lee's surrender, 1865.

Heinz Guderian, 1888-1953, (G.) tank theorist, led panzer forces in Poland, France, Russia, WW2.

Douglas Haig, 1861-1928, (Br.) led British armies in France, WW2, 1915-18.

William F. Halsey, 1882-1959, (U.S.) defeated Japanese fleet at Leyte Gulf, WW2, 1944.

Sir Arthur Travers Harris, 1895-1984, (Br.) led Britain's WW2 bomber command.

Richard Howe, 1726-1799, (Br.) commanded navy in Amer. Revolutionary War, 1776-78; June 1 victory against French, 1794.

William Howe, 1729-1814, (Br.) commanded forces in American Revolutionary War, 1776-78.

Isaac Hull, 1773-1843, (U.S.) sunk British frigate *Guerriere,* War of 1812.

Thomas (Stonewall) Jackson, 1824-1863, (U.S.) Confederate general led Shenandoah Valley campaign, Civil War.

Joseph Joffre, 1852-1931, (F.) headed Allied armies, won Battle of the Marne, WW1, 1914.

John Paul Jones, 1747-1792, (U.S.) commanded *Bonhomme Richard* in victory over Serapis, Amer. Revolutionary War, 1779.

Stephen Kearny, 1794-1848, (U.S.) headed Army of the West in Mexican War.

Ernest J. King, 1878-1956, (U.S.) chief naval strategist in WW2.

Horatio H. Kitchener, 1850-1916, (Br.) led forces in Boer War; victorious at Khartoum; organized army in WW1.

Lavrenti Kornilov, 1870-1918, (R.) Commander-in-Chief, 1917; led counter-revolutionary march on Petrograd.

Thaddeus Kosciusko, 1746-1817, (P.) aided American cause in Amer. Revolutionary War.

Mikhail Kutuzov, 1745-1813, (R.) fought French at Borodino, Napoleonic Wars, 1812; abandoned Moscow; forced French retreat.

Marquis de Lafayette, 1757-1834, (F.) aided American cause in Amer. Revolutionary War.

T(homas) E. Lawrence (of Arabia), 1888-1935, (Br.) organized revolt of Arabs against Turks in WW1.

Henry (Light-Horse Harry) Lee, 1756-1818, (U.S.) cavalry officer in Amer. Revolutionary War.

Robert E. Lee, 1807-1870, (U.S.) Confederate general defeated at Gettysburg, Civil War; surrendered to Grant, 1865.

Lyman Lemnitzer, 1899-1988, (U.S.) WWII hero, later general, chairman of Joint Chiefs of Staff.

James Longstreet, 1821-1904, (U.S.) aided Lee at Gettysburg, Civil War.

Douglas MacArthur, 1880-1964, (U.S.) commanded forces in SW Pacific in WW2; headed occupation forces in Japan, 1945-51; UN commander in Korean War.

Francis Marion, 1733-1795, (U.S.) led guerrilla actions in S.C. during Amer. Revolutionary War.

Duke of Marlborough, 1650-1722, (Br.) led forces against Louis XIV in War of the Spanish Succession.

George C. Marshall, 1880-1959, (U.S.) chief of staff in WW2; authored Marshall Plan.

George B. McClellan, 1826-1885, (U.S.) Union general, commanded Army of the Potomac, Civil War, 1861-62.

George Meade, 1815-1872; (U.S.) commanded Union forces at Gettysburg, Civil War.

Billy Mitchell, 1879-1936, (U.S.) WW1 air-power advocate; court-martialed for insubordination, later vindicated.

Helmuth v. Moltke, 1800-1891; (G.) victorious in Austro-Prussian, Franco-Prussian wars.

Louis de Montcalm, 1712-1759, (F.) headed troops in Canada, French and Indian War; defeated at Quebec, 1759.

Bernard Law Montgomery, 1887-1976, (Br.) stopped German offensive at Alamein, WW2, 1942; helped plan Normandy invasion.

Daniel Morgan, 1736-1802, (U.S.) victorious at Cowpens, 1781, Amer. Revolutionary War.

Louis Mountbatten, 1900-1979, (Br.) Supreme Allied Commander of SE Asia, WW2, 1943-46.

Joachim Murat, 1767-1815, (F.) leader of cavalry at Marengo, 1800; Austerlitz, 1805; and Jena, 1806, Napoleonic Wars.

Horatio Nelson, 1758-1805, (Br.) naval commander destroyed French fleet at Trafalgar.

Michel Ney, 1769-1815, (F.) commanded forces in Switzerland, Austria, Russia, Napoleonic Wars; defeated at Waterloo.

Chester Nimitz, 1885-1966, (U.S.) commander of naval forces in Pacific in WW2.

George S. Patton, 1885-1945, (U.S.) led assault on Sicily, 1943, 3d Army invasion of German-occupied Europe, WW2.

Oliver Perry, 1785-1819, (U.S.) won Battle of Lake Erie in War of 1812.

John Pershing, 1860-1948, (U.S.) commanded Mexican border campaign, 1916; American expeditionary forces in WW1.

Henri Philippe Pétain, 1856-1951, (F.) defended Verdun, 1916; headed Vichy government in WW2.

George E. Pickett, 1825-1875, (U.S.) Confederate general famed for "charge" at Gettysburg, Civil War.

Hyman Rickover, 1900-1986 (U.S.) father of the nuclear navy.

Erwin Rommel, 1891-1944, (G.) headed Afrika Korps, WW2.

Karl v. Rundstedt, 1875-1953, (G.) supreme commander in West, WW2, 1943-45.

Aleksandr Samsonov, 1859-1914, (R.) led invasion of E. Prussia, WW1, defeated at Tannenberg, 1914.

Winfield Scott, 1786-1866, (U.S.) hero of War of 1812; headed forces in Mexican war, took Mexico City.

Philip Sheridan, 1831-1888, (U.S.) Union cavalry officer, headed Army of the Shenandoah, Civil War, 1864-65.

William T. Sherman, 1820-1891, (U.S.) Union general, sacked Atlanta during "march to the sea," Civil War, 1864.

Carl Spaatz, 1891-1974, (U.S.) directed strategic bombing against Germany, later Japan, in WW2.

Raymond Spruance, 1886-1969, (U.S.) victorious at Midway Island, WW2, 1942.

Joseph W. Stilwell, 1883-1946, (U.S.) headed forces in the China, Burma, India theater in WW2.

J.E.B. Stuart, 1833-1864, (U.S.) Confederate cavalry commander, Civil War.

George H. Thomas, 1816-1870, (U.S.) saved Union army at Chattanooga, 1863; victorious at Nashville, 1864, Civil War.

Semyon Timoshenko, 1895-1970, (USSR) defended Moscow, Stalingrad, WW2; led winter offensive, 1942-43.

Alfred v. Tirpitz, 1849-1930, (G.) responsible for submarine blockade in WW1.

Jonathan M. Wainwright, 1883-1953, (U.S.) forced to surrender on Corregidor, WW2, 1942.

George Washington, 1732-1799, (U.S.) led Continental army, Amer. Revolutionary War, 1775-83.

Archibald Wavell, 1883-1950, (Br.) commanded forces in N. and E. Africa, and SE Asia in WW2.

Anthony Wayne, 1745-1796, (U.S.) captured Stony Point, 1779, Amer. Revolutionary War; defeated Indians at Fallen Timbers, 1794.

Duke of Wellington, 1769-1852, (Br.) defeated Napoleon at Waterloo.

James Wolfe, 1727-1759, (Br.) captured Quebec from French, French and Indian War, 1759.

Georgi Zhukov, 1895-1974, (USSR) defended Moscow, 1941, led assault on Berlin, WW2.

Poets Laureate of England

There is no authentic record of the origin of the office of Poet Laureate of England. According to Warton, there was a Versificator Regis, or King's Poet, in the reign of Henry III (1216-1272), and he was paid 100 shillings a year. Geoffrey Chaucer (1340-1400) assumed the title of Poet Laureate, and in 1389 got a royal grant of a yearly allowance of wine. In the reign of Edward IV (1461-1483), John Kay held the post. Under Henry VII (1485-1509), Andrew Bernard was the Poet Laureate, and was succeeded under Henry VIII (1509-1547) by John Skelton. Next came Edmund Spenser, who died in 1599; then Samuel Daniel, appointed 1599, and then Ben Jonson, 1619. Sir William D'Avenant was appointed in 1637. He was a godson of William Shakespeare.

Others were John Dryden, 1670; Thomas Shadwell, 1688; Nahum Tate, 1692; Nicholas Rowe, 1715; the Rev. Laurence Eusden, 1718; Colley Cibber, 1730; William Whitehead, 1757, on the refusal of Gray; Rev. Thomas Warton, 1785, on the refusal of Mason; Henry J. Pye, 1790; Robert Southey, 1813, on the refusal of Sir Walter Scott; William Wordsworth, 1843; Alfred, Lord Tennyson, 1850; Alfred Austin, 1896; Robert Bridges, 1913; John Masefield, 1930; Cecil Day Lewis, 1967; Sir John Betjeman, 1972; Ted Hughes, 1984.

U.S. Poet Laureate

Robert Penn Warren, the poet, novelist, and essayist, was named the country's first official Poet Laureate on Feb. 26, 1986. The only writer to have won the Pulitzer Prize for fiction and poetry (twice), Warren was chosen by Daniel J.

Boorstin, the Librarian of Congress. The appointment began in September, 1986. Other appointments, all beginning in September, are: 1987, Richard Wilbur; 1988, Howard Nemerov; 1990, Mark Strand; 1991, Joseph Brodsky; 1992, Mona Van Duyn, the first female poet laureate.

Noted Writers of the Past

George Ade, 1866-1944, (U.S.) humorist. *Fables in Slang.*

Conrad Aiken, 1889-1973, (U.S.) poet, critic. *Ushant.*

Louisa May Alcott, 1832-1888, (U.S.) novelist. *Little Women.*

Sholom Aleichem, 1859-1916, (R.) Yiddish writer. *Tevye's Daughter, Adventures of Mottel, The Old Country.*

Vicente Aleixandre, 1898-1984, (Sp.) poet. *La destrucción o el amor, Dialogolos del conocimiento.*

Horatio Alger, 1832-1899, (U.S.) "rags-to-riches" books.

Hans Christian Andersen, 1805-1875, (Den.) author of fairy tales. *The Princess and the Pea, The Ugly Duckling.*

Maxwell Anderson, 1888-1959, (U.S.) playwright. *What Price Glory?, High Tor, Winterset, Key Largo.*

Sherwood Anderson, 1876-1941, (U.S.) short-story writer, "Death in the Woods"; *Winesburg, Ohio* (collection).

Matthew Arnold, 1822-1888, (Br.) poet, critic. "Thrysis," "Dover Beach," "The Gypsy Scholar"; "Culture and Anarchy."

Jane Austen, 1775-1817, (Br.) novelist. *Pride and Prejudice, Sense and Sensibility, Emma, Mansfield Park, Persuasion.*

Isaac Babel, 1894-1941, (R.) short-story writer, playwright. *Odessa Tales, Red Cavalry.*

James M. Barrie, 1860-1937, (Br.) playwright, novelist. *Peter Pan, Dear Brutus, What Every Woman Knows.*

Honoré de Balzac, 1799-1850, (Fr.) novelist. *Le Père Goriot, Cousine Bette, Eugénie Grandet, The Human Comedy.*

Charles Baudelaire, 1821-1867, (Fr.) symbolist poet. *Les Fleurs du Mal.*

L. Frank Baum, 1856-1919, (U.S.) writer. Wizard of Oz series of children's books.

Simone de Beauvoir, 1908-1986, (Fr.) novelist, essayist. *The Second Sex, Memoirs of a Dutiful Daughter.*

Samuel Beckett, 1906-1989, (Ir.) novelist, playwright, in French and English. *Waiting for Godot, Endgame* (plays); *Murphy, Watt, Molloy* (novels).

Brendan Behan, 1923-1964, (Ir.) playwright. *The Quare Fellow, The Hostage, Borstal Boy.*

Robert Benchley, 1889-1945, (U.S.) humorist. *From Bed to Worse, My Ten Years in a Quandary.*

Stephen Vincent Benét, 1898-1943, (U.S.) poet, novelist. *John Brown's Body.*

John Berryman, 1914-1972, (U.S.) poet. *Homage to Mistress Bradstreet.*

Ambrose Bierce, 1842-1914, (U.S.) short-story writer, journalist. *In the Midst of Life, The Devil's Dictionary.*

William Blake, 1757-1827, (Br.) poet, artist. *Songs of Innocence, Songs of Experience, The Marriage of Heaven and Hell.*

Giovanni Boccaccio, 1313-1375, (It.) poet, storyteller. *Decameron, Filostrato.*

Jorge Luis Borges, 1900-1986 (Arg.) short-story writer, poet, essayist, *Labyrinths.*

James Boswell, 1740-1795, (Sc.) biographer. *The Life of Samuel Johnson, A Journal of a Tour of the Hebrides.*

Anne Bradstreet, c. 1612-1672, (U.S.) poet. *The Tenth Muse Lately Sprung Up in America.*

Bertolt Brecht, 1898-1956, (G.) dramatist, poet. *The Threepenny Opera, Mother Courage and Her Children.*

Charlotte Brontë, 1816-1855, (Br.) novelist. *Jane Eyre.*

Emily Brontë, 1818-1848, (Br.) novelist. *Wuthering Heights.*

Elizabeth Barrett Browning, 1806-1861, (Br.) poet. *Sonnets from the Portuguese, Aurora Leigh.*

Robert Browning, 1812-1889, (Br.) poet. "My Last Duchess," "Fra Lippo Lippi," *The Ring and The Book.*

Pearl Buck, 1892-1973, (U.S.) novelist. *The Good Earth.*

Mikhail Bulgakov, 1891-1940, (R.) novelist, playwright. *The Heart of a Dog, The Master and Margarita.*

John Bunyan, 1628-1688, (Br.) writer. *Pilgrim's Progress.*

Robert Burns, 1759-1796, (Sc.) poet. "Flow Gently, Sweet Afton," "My Heart's in the Highlands," "Auld Lang Syne."

Edgar Rice Burroughs, 1875-1950, (U.S.) novelist. *Tarzan of the Apes.*

George Gordon Lord Byron, 1788-1824, (Br.) poet. *Don Juan, Childe Harold, Manfred, Cain.*

Italo Calvino, 1923-1985 (It.) novelist, short story writer. *If on a Winter's Night a Traveler ...*

Albert Camus, 1913-1960, (F.) novelist. *The Plague, The Stranger, Caligula, The Fall.*

Lewis Carroll, 1832-1898, (Br.) writer, mathematician. *Alice's Adventures in Wonderland, Through the Looking Glass.*

Karel Capek, 1890-1938, (Czech.) playwright, novelist, essayist. *R.U.R. (Rossum's Universal Robots).*

Giacomo Casanova, 1725-1798, (It.) adventurer, memoirist.

Willa Cather, 1876-1947, (U.S.) novelist, essayist. *O Pioneers!, My Ántonia, Death Comes for the Archbishop.*

Miguel de Cervantes Saavedra, 1547-1616, (Sp.) novelist, dramatist, poet. *Don Quixote de la Mancha.*

Raymond Chandler, 1888-1959, (U.S.) writer of detective fiction. Philip Marlowe series.

Geoffrey Chaucer, c. 1340-1400, (Br.) poet. *The Canterbury Tales, Troilus and Criseyde.*

John Cheever, 1912-1982, (U.S.) short story writer, novelist. *The Wapshot Scandal*, "The Country Husband."

Anton Chekhov, 1860-1904, (R.) short-story writer, dramatist. *Uncle Vanya, The Cherry Orchard, The Three Sisters.*

G.K. Chesterton, 1874-1936, (Br.) critic, novelist. Father Brown series of mysteries.

Kate Chopin, 1851-1904, (U.S.) novelist, short-story writer. *The Awakening.*

Agatha Christie, 1891-1976, (Br.) mystery writer. *And Then There Were None, Murder on the Orient Express.*

Jean Cocteau, 1889-1963, (F.) writer, visual artist, filmmaker. *The Beauty and the Beast, Enfants Terribles.*

Samuel Taylor Coleridge, 1772-1834, (Br.) poet, critic. "Kubla Khan," "The Rime of the Ancient Mariner," "Christabel."

(Sidonie) Colette, 1873-1954, (F.) novelist. *Claudine, Gigi.*

Joseph Conrad, 1857-1924, (Br.) novelist. *Lord Jim, Heart of Darkness, The Nigger of the Narcissus, Nostromo.*

James Fenimore Cooper, 1789-1851, (U.S.) novelist. *Leather-Stocking Tales.*

Pierre Corneille, 1606-1684, (F.) dramatist. *Medeé, Le Cid, Horace, Cinna, Polyeucte.*

Hart Crane, 1899-1932, (U.S.) poet. "The Bridge."

Stephen Crane, 1871-1900, (U.S.) novelist, short-story writer. *The Red Badge of Courage*, "The Open Boat."

e.e. cummings, 1894-1962, (U.S.) poet. *Tulips and Chimneys.*

Roald Dahl, (Br.) 1916-1990, (U.S.) writer. *Charlie and the Chocolate Factory.*

Gabriele D'Annunzio, 1863-1938, (It.) poet, novelist, dramatist. *The Child of Pleasure, The Intruder, The Victim.*

Dante Alighieri, 1265-1321, (It.) poet. *The Divine Comedy.*

Daniel Defoe, 1660-1731, (Br.) writer. *Robinson Crusoe, Moll Flanders, Journal of the Plague Year.*

Charles Dickens, 1812-1870, (Br.) novelist. *David Copperfield, Oliver Twist, Great Expectations, The Pickwick Papers.*

Emily Dickinson, 1830-1886, (U.S.) poet.

Isak Dinesen (Karen Blixen), 1885-1962, (Dan.) author. *Out of Africa, Seven Gothic Tales, Winter's Tales.*

John Donne, 1573-1631, (Br.) poet. *Songs and Sonnets.*

John Dos Passos, 1896-1970, (U.S.) novelist. *U.S.A.*

Fyodor Dostoyevsky, 1821-1881, (R.) novelist. *Crime and Punishment, The Brothers Karamazov, The Possessed.*

Arthur Conan Doyle, 1859-1930, (Br.) novelist, created Sherlock Holmes mystery series.

Theodore Dreiser, 1871-1945, (U.S.) novelist. *An American Tragedy, Sister Carrie.*

John Dryden, 1631-1700, (Br.) poet, dramatist, critic. *All for Love, Mac Flecknoe, Absalom and Achitopel.*

Alexandre Dumas, 1802-1870, (F.) novelist, dramatist. *The Three Musketeers, The Count of Monte Cristo.*

Alexandre Dumas (fils), 1824-1895, (F.) dramatist, novelist. *La Dame aux camélias, Le Demi-Monde.*

Ilya G. Ehrenburg, 1891-1967, (R.) writer. *The Thaw.*

George Eliot (Mary Ann Evans or Marian Evans), 1819-1880, (Br.) novelist. *Adam Bede, Silas Marner, Middlemarch, The Mill on the Floss, Daniel Deronda.*

T.S. Eliot, 1888-1965, (Br.) poet, critic. *The Waste Land*, "The Love Song of J. Alfred Prufrock," *Four Quartets.*

Ralph Waldo Emerson, 1803-1882, (U.S.) poet, essayist. "Brahma," "Nature," "The Over-Soul," "Self-Reliance."

James T. Farrell, 1904-1979, (U.S.) novelist. *Studs Lonigan.*

William Faulkner, 1897-1962, (U.S.) novelist. *Sanctuary, Light in August, The Sound and the Fury, Absalom, Absalom!*

Henry Fielding, 1707-1754, (Br.) novelist. *Tom Jones.*

F. Scott Fitzgerald, 1896-1940, (U.S.) short-story writer, novelist. *The Great Gatsby, Tender is the Night.*

Gustave Flaubert, 1821-1880, (F.) novelist. *Madame Bovary.*

C.S. Forester, 1899-1966, (Br.) novelist. Horatio Hornblower series.

E.M. Forster, 1879-1970, (Br.) novelist. *A Passage to India.*

Anatole France, 1844-1924. (F.) writer. *Penguin Island, My Friend's Book, Le Crime de Sylvestre Bonnard.*

Robert Frost, 1874-1963, (U.S.) poet. "Birches," "Fire and Ice," "Stopping by Woods on a Snowy Evening."

John Galsworthy, 1867-1933, (Br.) novelist, dramatist. *The Forsyte Saga, A Modern Comedy.*

Erle Stanley Gardner, 1889-1970, (U.S.) novelist. Perry Mason series of mysteries.

Jean Genet, 1911-1986, (Fr.) playwright, novelist. *The Blacks, The Maids, The Balcony.*
André Gide, 1869-1951, (F.) writer. *The Immoralist, The Pastoral Symphony, Strait is the Gate.*
Jean Giraudoux, 1882-1944, (F.) novelist, dramatist. *Electra, The Madwoman of Chaillot, Ondine, Tiger at the Gate.*
Johann W. von Goethe, 1749-1832, (G.) poet, dramatist, novelist. *Faust, The Sorrows of Young Werther.*
Nikolai Gogol, 1809-1852, (R.) short-story writer, dramatist, novelist. *Dead Souls, The Inspector General.*
Oliver Goldsmith, 1730?-1774, (Br.-Ir.) writer. *The Vicar of Wakefield, She Stoops to Conquer.*
Maxim Gorky, 1868-1936, (R.) writer. *The Lower Depths.*
Robert Graves, 1895-1985, (Br.) poet, classical scholar, novelist. *I, Claudius; The White Goddess.*
Thomas Gray, 1716-1771, (Br.) poet. "Elegy Written in a Country Churchyard," "The Progress of Poesy."
Graham Greene, 1904-1991, (Br.) novelist. *The Power and the Glory, The Heart of the Matter, The Ministry of Fear.*
Zane Grey, 1875-1939, (U.S.) writer of western stories.
Jakob Grimm, 1785-1863, (G.) philologist, folklorist. *German Methodology, Grimm's Fairy Tales.*
Wilhelm Grimm, 1786-1859, (G.) philologist, folklorist. *Grimm's Fairy Tales.*
Dashiell Hammett, 1894-1961, (U.S.) writer of detective fiction, created Sam Spade.
Knute Hamsun, 1859-1952 (Nor.) novelist. *Hunger.*
Thomas Hardy, 1840-1928, (Br.) novelist, poet. *The Return of the Native, Tess of the D'Urbervilles, Jude the Obscure.*
Joel Chandler Harris, 1848-1908, (U.S.) short-story writer. Uncle Remus series.
Moss Hart, 1904-1961, (U.S.) playwright. *Once in a Lifetime, You Can't Take It With You, The Man Who Came to Dinner.*
Bret Harte, 1836-1902, (U.S.) short-story writer, poet. *The Luck of Roaring Camp.*
Jaroslav Hasek, 1883-1923, (Czech.) writer. *The Good Soldier Schweik.*
Nathaniel Hawthorne, 1804-1864, (U.S.) novelist, short story writer. *The Scarlet Letter,* "The Artist of the Beautiful."
Heinrich Heine, 1797-1856, (G.) poet. *Book of Songs.*
Lillian Hellman, 1905-1984, (U.S.) playwright, author of memoirs, "The Little Foxes," *An Unfinished Woman, Pentimento.*
Ernest Hemingway, 1899-1961, (U.S.) novelist, short-story writer. *A Farewell to Arms, For Whom the Bell Tolls.*
O. Henry (W.S. Porter), 1862-1910, (U.S.) short-story writer. "The Gift of the Magi."
Hermann Hesse, 1877-1962, (G.) novelist, poet. *Death and the Lover, Steppenwolf, Siddhartha.*
Oliver Wendell Holmes, 1809-1894, (U.S.) poet, novelist. *The Autocrat of the Breakfast-Table.*
Alfred E. Housman, 1859-1936, (Br.) poet. *A Shropshire Lad.*
William Dean Howells, 1837-1920, (U.S.) novelist, critic. *The Rise of Silas Lapham.*
Langston Hughes, 1902-1967, (U.S.) poet, playwright. *The Weary Blues, One-Way Ticket, Shakespeare in Harlem.*
Victor Hugo, 1802-1885, (F.) poet, dramatist, novelist. *Notre Dame de Paris, Les Misérables.*
Aldous Huxley 1894-1963, (Br.) writer. *Brave New World.*
Henrik Ibsen, 1828-1906, (Nor.) dramatist, poet. *A Doll's House, Ghosts, The Wild Duck, Hedda Gabler.*
Washington Irving, 1783-1859, (U.S.) writer. "Rip Van Winkle," "The Legend of Sleepy Hollow."
Shirley Jackson, 1919-1965, (U.S.) writer. "The Lottery."
Henry James, 1843-1916, (U.S.) novelist, short-story writer, critic. *The Portrait of a Lady, The American, Daisy Miller.*
Robinson Jeffers, 1887-1962, (U.S.) poet, dramatist. *Tamar and Other Poems, Medea.*
Samuel Johnson, 1709-1784, (Br.) author, scholar, critic. *Dictionary of the English Language.*
Ben Jonson, 1572-1637, (Br.) dramatist, poet. *Volpone.*
James Joyce, 1882-1941, (Ir.) writer. *Ulysses, Dubliners, A Portrait of the Artist as a Young Man, Finnegans Wake.*
Franz Kafka, 1883-1924, (G.) novelist, short-story writer. *The Trial, Amerika, The Castle, The Metamorphosis.*
George S. Kaufman, 1889-1961, (U.S.) playwright. *The Man Who Came to Dinner, You Can't Take It With You, Stage Door.*
Nikos Kazantzakis, 1883?-1957, (Gk.) novelist. *Zorba the Greek, A Greek Passion.*
John Keats, 1795-1821, (Br.) poet. "Ode on a Grecian Urn," "Ode to a Nightingale," "La Belle Dame Sans Merci."
Joyce Kilmer, 1886-1918, (U.S.) poet, "Trees."
Rudyard Kipling, 1865-1936, (Br.) author, poet. "The White Man's Burden," "Gunga Din," *The Jungle Book.*
Jean de la Fontaine, 1621-1695, (F.) poet. *Fables choisies.*
Pär Lagerkvist, 1891-1974, (Swed.) poet, dramatist, novelist. *Barabbas, The Sybil.*
Selma Lagerlöf, 1858-1940, (Swed.) novelist. *Jerusalem, The Ring of the Lowenskolds.*
Alphonse de Lamartine, 1790-1869, (F.) poet, novelist, statesman. *Méditations poétiques.*
Charles Lamb, 1775-1834, (Br.) essayist. *Specimens of English Dramatic Poets, Essays of Elia.*
Giuseppe di Lampedusa, 1896-1957, (It.) novelist. *The Leopard.*
Ring Lardner, 1885-1933, (U.S.) short story writer, humorist. *You Know Me, Al.*
D. H. Lawrence, 1885-1930, (Br.) novelist. *Sons and Lovers, Women in Love, Lady Chatterley's Lover.*
Mikhail Lermontov, 1814-1841, (R.) novelist, poet. "Demon," *Hero of Our Time.*
Alain-René Lesage, 1668-1747, (F.) novelist. *Gil Blas de Santillane.*
Gotthold Lessing, 1729-1781, (G.) dramatist, philosopher, critic. *Miss Sara Sampson, Minna von Barnhelm.*
Sinclair Lewis, 1885-1951, (U.S.) novelist. *Babbitt, Arrowsmith, Dodsworth, Main Street.*
Vachel Lindsay, 1879-1931, (U.S.) poet. *General William Booth Enters into Heaven, The Congo.*
Hugh Lofting, 1886-1947, (Br.) writer. Dr. Doolittle series of children's books.
Jack London, 1876-1916, (U.S.) novelist, journalist. *Call of the Wild, The Sea-Wolf.*
Henry Wadsworth Longfellow, 1807-1882, (U.S.) poet. *Evangeline, The Song of Hiawatha.*
Amy Lowell, 1874-1925, (U.S.) poet, critic. "Lilacs."
James Russell Lowell, 1819-1891, (U.S.) poet, editor. *Poems, The Bigelow Papers.*
Robert Lowell, 1917-1977, (U.S.) poet. "Lord Weary's Castle," "For the Union Dead."
Niccolò Machiavelli, 1469-1527, (It.) writer, statesman. *The Prince, Discourses on Livy.*
Bernard Malamud, 1914-1986, (U.S.) short story writer, novelist. "The Magic Barrel," *The Assistant, The Fixer.*
Stéphane Mallarmé, 1842-1898, (F.) poet. *The Afternoon of a Faun.*
Thomas Malory, ?-1471, (Br.) writer. *Morte d'Arthur.*
Andre Malraux, 1901-1976, (F.) novelist. *Man's Fate.*
Osip Mandelstam, 1891-1938, (R.) poet. *Stone, Tristia.*
Thomas Mann, 1875-1955, (G.) novelist, essayist. *Buddenbrooks, Death in Venice, The Magic Mountain.*
Katherine Mansfield, 1888-1923, (Br.) short story writer. "Bliss," "The Garden Party."
Christopher Marlowe, 1564-1593, (Br.) dramatist, poet. *Tamburlaine the Great, Dr. Faustus, The Jew of Malta.*
John Masefield, 1878-1967, (Br.) poet. "Sea Fever," "Cargoes," *Salt Water Ballads.*
Edgar Lee Masters, 1869-1950, (U.S.) poet, biographer. *Spoon River Anthology.*
W. Somerset Maugham, 1874-1965, (Br.) author. *Of Human Bondage, The Razor's Edge, The Moon and Sixpence.*
Guy de Maupassant, 1850-1893, (F.) novelist, short-story writer. "A Life," "Bel-Ami," "The Necklace."
François Mauriac, 1885-1970, (F.) novelist, dramatist. *Viper's Tangle, The Kiss to the Leper.*
Vladimir Mayakovsky, 1893-1930, (R.) poet, dramatist. *The Cloud in Trousers.*
Mary McCarthy, 1912-1989, (U.S.) critic, novelist. *Memories of a Catholic Girlhood.*
Carson McCullers, 1917-1967, (U.S.) novelist. *The Heart is a Lonely Hunter, Member of the Wedding.*
Herman Melville, 1819-1891, (U.S.) novelist, poet. *Moby Dick, Typee, Billy Budd, Omoo.*
H.L. Mencken, 1880-1956, (U.S.) author, critic, editor. *Prejudices, The American Language.*
George Meredith, 1828-1909, (Br.) novelist, poet. *The Ordeal of Richard Feverel, The Egoist.*
Prosper Mérimée, 1803-1870, (F.) author. *Carmen.*
Edna St. Vincent Millay, 1892-1950, (U.S.) poet. *The Harp Weaver and Other Poems, A Few Figs from Thistles.*
A.A. Milne, 1882-1956, (Br.) author. *Winnie-the-Pooh.*
John Milton, 1608-1674, (Br.) poet. *Paradise Lost.*
Mishima Yukio (Hiraoka Kimitake), 1925-1970, (Jap.) writer. *Confessions of a Mask.*
Gabriela Mistral, 1889-1957, (Chil.) poet. *Sonnets of Death, Desolación, Tala, Lagar.*
Margaret Mitchell, 1900-1949, (U.S.) novelist. *Gone With the Wind.*
Jean Baptiste Molière, 1622-1673, (F.) dramatist. *Le Tartuffe, Le Misanthrope, Le Bourgeois Gentilhomme.*
Ferenc Molnár, 1878-1952, (Hung.) dramatist, novelist. *Liliom, The Guardsman, The Swan.*
Michel de Montaigne, 1533-1592, (F.) essayist. *Essais.*
Eugenio Montale, 1896-1981, (It.) poet.
Clement C. Moore, 1779-1863, (U.S.) poet, educator. "A Visit from Saint Nicholas."
Marianne Moore, 1887-1972, (U.S.) poet. *O to Be a Dragon.*
Thomas More, 1478-1535, (Br.) writer. *Utopia.*

H.H. Munro (Saki), 1870-1916, (Br.) writer. *Reginald, The Chronicles of Clovis, Beasts and Super-Beasts.*

Murasaki (Shikibu), Lady, c. 978-1031?, (Jap.) novelist. *The Tale of Genji.*

Alfred de Musset, 1810-1857, (F.) poet, dramatist. *Confession d'un enfant du siècle.*

Vladimir Nabokov, 1899-1977, (Rus.-U.S.) novelist. *Lolita.*

Ogden Nash, 1902-1971, (U.S.) poet. *Hard Lines, I'm a Stranger Here Myself, The Private Dining Room.*

Pablo Neruda, 1904-1973, (Chil.) poet. *Twenty Love Poems and One Song of Despair, Toward the Splendid City.*

Sean O'Casey, 1884-1964, (Ir.) dramatist. *Juno and the Paycock, The Plough and the Stars.*

Flannery O'Connor, 1925-1964, (U.S.) novelist, short story writer. *Wise Blood,* "A Good Man Is Hard to Find."

Clifford Odets, 1906-1963, (U.S.) playwright. *Waiting for Lefty, Awake and Sing, Golden Boy, The Country Girl.*

John O'Hara, 1905-1970, (U.S.) novelist, short-story writer. *From the Terrace, Appointment in Samarra, Pal Joey.*

Omar Khayyam, c. 1028-1122, (Per.) poet. *Rubaiyat.*

Eugene O'Neill, 1888-1953, (U.S.) playwright. *Emperor Jones, Anna Christie, Long Day's Journey into Night.*

George Orwell, 1903-1950, (Br.) novelist, essayist. *Animal Farm, Nineteen Eighty-Four.*

Thomas (Tom) Paine, 1737-1809, (U.S.) writer, political theorist. *Common Sense.*

Dorothy Parker, 1893-1967, (U.S.) poet, short-story writer. *Enough Rope, Laments for the Living.*

Boris Pasternak, 1890-1960, (R.) poet, novelist. *Doctor Zhivago, My Sister, Life.*

Samuel Pepys, 1633-1703, (Br.) public official, diarist.

S. J. Perelman, 1904-1979, (U.S.) humorist. *The Road to Miltown, Under the Spreading Atrophy.*

Francesco Petrarca, 1304-1374, (It.) poet. *Africa, Trionfi, Canzoniere, On Solitude.*

Luigi Pirandello, 1867-1936, (It.) novelist, dramatist. *Six Characters in Search of an Author.*

Edgar Allan Poe, 1809-1849, (U.S.) poet, short-story writer, critic. "Annabel Lee," "The Raven," "The Purloined Letter."

Alexander Pope, 1688-1744, (Br.) poet. *The Rape of the Lock, An Essay on Man.*

Katherine Anne Porter, 1890-1980, (U.S.) novelist, short story writer. *Ship of Fools.*

Ezra Pound, 1885-1972, (U.S.) poet. *Cantos.*

Marcel Proust, 1871-1922, (F.) novelist. *A la recherche du temps perdu (Remembrance of Things Past).*

Aleksandr Pushkin, 1799-1837, (R.) poet, prose writer. *Boris Godunov, Eugene Onegin, The Bronze Horseman.*

François Rabelais, 1495-1553, (F.) writer. *Gargantua, Pantagruel.*

Jean Racine, 1639-1699, (F.) dramatist. *Andromaque, Phèdre, Bérénice, Britannicus.*

Ayn Rand, 1905-1982 (Rus.-U.S.) novelist, philosopher. *The Fountainhead, Atlas Shrugged.*

Erich Maria Remarque, 1898-1970, (Ger.-U.S.) novelist. *All Quiet on the Western Front.*

Samuel Richardson, 1689-1761, (Br.) novelist. *Clarissa Harlowe, Pamela; or, Virtue Rewarded.*

Rainer Maria Rilke, 1875-1926, (G.) poet. *Life and Songs, Divine Elegies, Poems from the Book of Hours.*

Arthur Rimbaud, 1854-1891, (F.) poet. *A Season in Hell.*

Edwin Arlington Robinson, 1869-1935, (U.S.) poet. "Richard Cory," "Miniver Cheevy."

Theodore Roethke, 1908-1963, (U.S.) poet. *Open House, The Waking, The Far Field.*

Romain Rolland, 1866-1944, (F.) novelist, biographer. *Jean-Christophe.*

Pierre de Ronsard, 1524-1585, (F.) poet. *Sonnets pour Hélène, La Franciade.*

Edmond Rostand, 1868-1918, (F.) poet, dramatist. *Cyrano de Bergerac.*

Damon Runyon, 1880-1946, (U.S.) short-story writer, journalist. *Guys and Dolls, Blue Plate Special.*

John Ruskin, 1819-1900, (Br.) critic, social theorist. *Modern Painters, The Seven Lamps of Architecture.*

Antoine de Saint-Exupery, 1900-1944, (F.) writer. *Wind, Sand and Stars, Le Petit Prince.*

George Sand (Amandine Aurore Dupine), 1804-1876, (F.) novelist. *Consuelo, The Haunted Pool, The Master Bell-Ringer.*

Carl Sandburg, 1878-1967, (U.S.) poet. *The People, Yes; Chicago Poems, Smoke and Steel, Harvest Poems.*

George Santayana, 1863-1952, (U.S.) poet, essayist, philosopher. *The Sense of Beauty, The Realms of Being.*

William Saroyan, 1908-1981, (U.S.) playwright, novelist. *The Time of Your Life, The Human Comedy.*

Jean-Paul Sartre, 1905-1980, (Fr.) philosopher, novelist, playwright, *Nausea, No Exit, Being and Nothingness.*

Friedrich von Schiller, 1759-1805, (G.) dramatist, poet, historian. *Don Carlos, Maria Stuart, Wilhelm Tell.*

Sir Walter Scott, 1771-1832, (Sc.) novelist, poet. *Ivanhoe.*

Jaroslav Seifert, 1902-1986, (Cz.) poet.

Dr. Seuss (Theodore Seuss Geisel), 1904-1991, (U.S.) children's book author & illustrator. *The Cat in the Hat.*

William Shakespeare, 1564-1616, (Br.) dramatist, poet. *Romeo and Juliet, Hamlet, King Lear, Julius Caesar, The Merchant of Venice, Othello, Macbeth, The Tempest;* sonnets.

George Bernard Shaw, 1856-1950, (Ir.-Br.) playwright, critic. *St. Joan, Pygmalion, Major Barbara, Man and Superman.*

Mary Wollstonecraft Shelley, 1797-1851, (Br.) novelist. *Frankenstein.*

Percy Bysshe Shelley, 1792-1822, (Br.) poet. *Prometheus Unbound, Adonais,* "Ode to the West Wind," "To a Skylark."

Richard B. Sheridan, 1751-1816, (Br.) dramatist. *The Rivals, School for Scandal.*

Mikhail Sholokhov, 1906-1984 (U.S.S.R.) writer. *And Quiet Flows the Don.*

Upton Sinclair, 1878-1968, (U.S.) novelist. *The Jungle.*

Isaac Bashevis Singer, 1904-1991, (Pol.-U.S.) novelist, short-story writer, in Yiddish. *The Magician of Lubin.*

Edmund Spenser, 1552-1599, (Br.) poet. *The Faerie Queen.*

Christina Stead, 1903-1983 (Austral.) novelist, short-story writer. *The Man Who Loved Children.*

Richard Steele, 1672-1729, (Br.) essayist, playwright, began the Tatler and Spectator. *The Conscious Lovers.*

Lincoln Steffens, 1866-1936, (U.S.) editor, writer. *The Shame of the Cities.*

Gertrude Stein, 1874-1946, (U.S.) writer. *Three Lives.*

John Steinbeck, 1902-1968, (U.S.) novelist. *Grapes of Wrath, Of Mice and Men, Winter of Our Discontent.*

Stendhal (Marie Henri Beyle), 1783-1842, (F.) novelist. *The Red and the Black, The Charterhouse of Parma.*

Laurence Sterne, 1713-1768, (Br.) novelist. *Tristram Shandy.*

Wallace Stevens, 1879-1955, (U.S.) poet. *Harmonium, The Man With the Blue Guitar, Notes toward a Supreme Fiction.*

Robert Louis Stevenson, 1850-1894, (Br.) novelist, poet, essayist. *Treasure Island, A Child's Garden of Verses.*

Rex Stout, 1886-1975, (U.S.) novelist, created Nero Wolfe.

Harriet Beecher Stowe, 1811-1896, (U.S.) novelist. *Uncle Tom's Cabin.*

Lytton Strachey, 1880-1932, (Br.) biographer, critic. *Eminent Victorians, Queen Victoria, Elizabeth and Essex.*

August Strindberg, 1849-1912, (Swed.) dramatist, novelist. *The Father, Miss Julie, The Creditors.*

Jonathan Swift, 1667-1745, (Br.) writer. *Gulliver's Travels.*

Algernon C. Swinburne, 1837-1909, (Br.) poet, critic. Atalanta.

John M. Synge, 1871-1909, (Ir.) poet, dramatist. *Riders to the Sea, The Playboy of the Western World.*

Rabindranath Tagore, 1861-1941, (Ind.), author, poet. *Sadhana, The Realization of Life, Gitanjali.*

Booth Tarkington, 1869-1946, (U.S.) novelist. *Seventeen, Alice Adams, Penrod.*

Sara Teasdale, 1884-1933, (U.S.) poet. *Helen of Troy and Other Poems, Rivers to the Sea, Flame and Shadow.*

Alfred Lord Tennyson, 1809-1892, (Br.) poet. *Idylls of the King, In Memoriam,* "The Charge of the Light Brigade."

William Makepeace Thackeray, 1811-1863, (Br.) novelist. *Vanity Fair, Henry Esmond, Pendennis.*

Dylan Thomas, 1914-1953, (Welsh) poet. *Under Milk Wood, A Child's Christmas in Wales.*

Henry David Thoreau, 1817-1862, (U.S.) transcendentalist thinker, writer. *Walden.*

James Thurber, 1894-1961, (U.S.) humorist, cartoonist. "The Secret Life of Walter Mitty," *My Life and Hard Times.*

J.R.R. Tolkien, 1892-1973, (Br.) writer. *Lord of the Rings.*

Leo Tolstoy, 1828-1910, (R.) novelist, short-story writer. *War and Peace, Anna Karenina,* "The Death of Ivan Ilyich."

Anthony Trollope, 1815-1882, (Br.) novelist. *The Warden, Barchester Towers,* The Palliser novels.

Ivan Turgenev, 1818-1883, (R.) novelist, short-story writer. *Fathers and Sons, First Love, A Month in the Country.*

Mark Twain (Samuel Clemens), 1835-1910, (U.S.) novelist, humorist. *The Adventures of Huckleberry Finn, Tom Sawyer.*

Sigrid Undset, 1881-1949, (Nor.) novelist, poet. *Kristin Lavransdatter.*

Paul Valéry, 1871-1945, (F.) poet, critic. *La Jeune Parque, The Graveyard by the Sea.*

Jules Verne, 1828-1905, (F.) novelist. *Twenty Thousand Leagues Under the Sea.*

François Villon, 1431-1463?, (F.) poet. *Le petit et le Grand Testament.*

Evelyn Waugh, 1903-1966, (Br.) novelist. *The Loved One.*

H.G. Wells, 1866-1946, (Br.) novelist. *The Time Machine, The Invisible Man, The War of the Worlds.*

Rebecca West, 1893-1983 (Br.) critic. *Black Lamb and Grey Falcon.*

Edith Wharton, 1862-1937, (U.S.) novelist. *The Age of Innocence, The House of Mirth, Ethan Frome.*

E.B. White, 1899-1985 (U.S.), essayist, novelist. *Here is New York, Charlotte's Web, Stuart Little.*

T.H. White, 1906-1964, (Br.) author. *The Once and Future King, A Book of Beasts.*

Walt Whitman, 1819-1892, (U.S.) poet. *Leaves of Grass.*

John Greenleaf Whittier, 1807-1892, (U.S.) poet, journalist. *Snow-bound.*

Oscar Wilde, 1854-1900, (Ir.) playwright, story-writer. *The Picture of Dorian Gray, The Importance of Being Earnest.*

Laura Ingalls Wilder, 1867-1957, (U.S.) novelist. *Little House on the Prairie* series of children's books.

Thornton Wilder, 1897-1975, (U.S.) playwright. *Our Town, The Skin of Our Teeth, The Matchmaker.*

Tennessee Williams, 1912-1983 (U.S.) playwright. *A Streetcar Named Desire, Cat on a Hot Tin Roof, The Glass Menagerie.*

William Carlos Williams, 1883-1963, (U.S.) poet. *Tempers, Al Que Quiere!, Paterson.*

Edmund Wilson, 1895-1972, (U.S.) critic, novelist. *Axel's Castle, To the Finland Station.*

P.G. Wodehouse, 1881-1975, (U.S.) humorist. The "Jeeves" novels, *Anything Goes.*

Thomas Wolfe, 1900-1938, (U.S.) novelist. *Look Homeward, Angel, You Can't Go Home Again, Of Time and the River.*

Virginia Woolf, 1882-1941, (Br.) novelist, essayist. *Mrs. Dalloway, To the Lighthouse, The Waves, A Room of One's Own.*

William Wordsworth, 1770-1850, (Br.) poet. "Tintern Abbey," "Ode: Intimations of Immortality," *The Prelude.*

William Butler Yeats, 1865-1939, (Ir.) poet, playwright. *The Wild Swans at Coole, The Tower, Last Poems.*

Émile Zola, 1840-1902, (F.) novelist. *Nana, The Dram Shop.*

Noted Artists and Sculptors of the Past

Artists are painters unless otherwise indicated.

Washington Allston, 1779-1843, (U.S.) landscapist. Belshazzar's Feast.

Albrecht Altdorfer, 1480-1538, (Ger.) landscapist. Battle of Alexander.

Andrea del Sarto, 1486-1530, frescoes. Madonna of the Harpies.

Fra Angelico, c. 1400-1455, (It.) Renaissance muralist. Madonna of the Linen Drapers' Guild.

Alexsandr Archipenko, 1887-1964, (U.S.) sculptor. Boxing Match, Medranos.

John James Audubon, 1785-1851, (U.S.) Birds of America.

Hans Baldung Grien, 1484-1545, (Ger.) Todentanz.

Ernst Barlach, 1870-1938, (Ger.) Expressionist sculptor. Man Drawing a Sword.

Frederic-Auguste Bartholdi, 1834-1904, (Fr.) Liberty Enlightening the World, Lion of Belfort.

Fra Bartolommeo, 1472-1517, (It.) Vision of St. Bernard.

Aubrey Beardsley, 1872-1898, (Br.) illustrator. Salome, Lysistrata.

Max Beckmann, 1884-1950, (Ger.) Expressionist. The Descent from the Cross.

Gentile Bellini, 1426-1507, (It.) Renaissance. Procession in St. Mark's Square.

Giovanni Bellini, 1428-1516, (It.) St. Francis in Ecstasy.

Jacopo Bellini, 1400-1470, (It.) Crucifixion.

George Wesley Bellows, 1882-1925, (U.S.) sports artist. Stag at Sharkey's.

Thomas Hart Benton, 1889-1975, (U.S.) American regionalist. Threshing Wheat, Arts of the West.

Gianlorenzo Bernini, 1598-1680, (It.) Baroque sculpture. The Assumption.

Albert Bierstadt, 1830-1902, (U.S.) landscapist. The Rocky Mountains, Mount Corcoran.

George Caleb Bingham, 1811-1879, (U.S.) Fur Traders Descending the Missouri.

William Blake, 1752-1827, (Br.) engraver. Book of Job, Songs of Innocence, Songs of Experience.

Rosa Bonheur, 1822-1899, (Fr.) The Horse Fair.

Pierre Bonnard, 1867-1947, (Fr.) Intimist. The Breakfast Room.

Gutzon Borglum, 1871-1941, (U.S.) sculptor. Mt. Rushmore Memorial.

Hieronymus Bosch, 1450-1516, (Flem.) religious allegories. The Crowning with Thorns.

Sandro Botticelli, 1444-1510, (It.) Renaissance. Birth of Venus.

Constantin Brancusi, 1876-1957, (Rum.) Nonobjective sculptor. Flying Turtle, The Kiss.

Georges Braque, 1882-1963, (Fr.) Cubist. Violin and Palette.

Pieter Bruegel the Elder, c. 1525-1569, (Flem.) The Peasant Dance.

Pieter Bruegel the Younger, 1564-1638, (Flem.) Village Fair, The Crucifixion.

Edward Burne-Jones, 1833-1898, (Br.) Pre-Raphaelite artist-craftsman. The Mirror of Venus.

Alexander Calder, 1898-1976, (U.S.) sculptor. Lobster Trap and Fish Tail.

Michelangelo Merisi da Caravaggio, 1573-1610, (It.) Baroque. The Supper at Emmaus.

Emily Carr, 1871-1945, (Can.) landscapist. Blunden Harbour, Big Raven.

Carlo Carra, 1881-1966, (It.) Metaphysical school. Lot's Daughters.

Mary Cassatt, 1845-1926, (U.S.) Impressionist. Woman Bathing.

George Catlin, 1796-1872, (U.S.) American Indian life. Gallery of Indians.

Benvenuto Cellini, 1500-1571, (It.) Mannerist sculptor, goldsmith. Perseus.

Paul Cezanne, 1839-1906, (Fr.) Card Players, Mont-Sainte-Victoire with Large Pine Trees.

Marc Chagall, 1887-1985, (Rus.) Jewish life and folklore. I and the Village.

Jean Simeon Chardin, 1699-1779, (Fr.) still lifes. The Kiss, The Grace.

Frederic Church, 1826-1900, (U.S.) Hudson River school. Niagara, Andes of Ecuador.

Giovanni Cimabue, 1240-1302, (It.) Byzantine mosaicist. Madonna Enthroned with St. Francis.

Claude Lorrain, 1600-1682, (Fr.) ideal-landscapist. The Enchanted Castle.

Thomas Cole, 1801-1848, (U.S.) Hudson River school. The Ox-Bow.

John Constable, 1776-1837, (Br.) landscapist. Salisbury Cathedral from the Bishop's Grounds.

John Singleton Copley, 1738-1815, (U.S.) portraitist. Samuel Adams, Watson and the Shark.

Lovis Corinth, 1858-1925, (Ger.) Expressionist. Apocalypse.

Jean-Baptiste-Camille Corot, 1796-1875, (Fr.) landscapist. Souvenir de Mortefontaine, Pastorale.

Correggio, 1494-1534, (It.) Renaissance muralist. Mystic Marriages of St. Catherine.

Gustave Courbet, 1819-1877, (Fr.) Realist. The Artist's Studio.

Lucas Cranach the Elder, 1472-1553, (Ger.) Protestant Reformation portraitist. Luther.

Nathaniel Currier, 1813-1888, and **James M. Ives,** 1824-1895, (both U.S.) lithographers. A Midnight Race on the Mississippi.

John Steuart Curry, 1897-1946, (U.S.) Americana, murals. Baptism in Kansas.

Salvador Dali, 1904-1989, (Sp.) Surrealist. Persistence of Memory.

Honore Daumier, 1808-1879, (Fr.) caricaturist. The Third-Class Carriage.

Jacques-Louis David, 1748-1825, (Fr.) Neoclassicist. The Oath of the Horatii.

Arthur Davies, 1862-1928, (U.S.) Romantic landscapist. Unicorns.

Edgar Degas, 1834-1917, (Fr.) The Ballet Class.

Eugene Delacroix, 1789-1863, (Fr.) Romantic. Massacre at Chios.

Paul Delaroche, 1797-1856, (Fr.) historical themes. Children of Edward IV.

Luca Della Robbia, 1400-1482, (It.) Renaissance terracotta artist. Cantoria (singing gallery), Florence cathedral.

Donatello, 1386-1466, (It.) Renaissance sculptor. David, Gattamelata.

Jean Dubuffet, 1902-1985, (Fr.) painter, sculptor, printmaker. Group of Four Trees.

Marcel Duchamp, 1887-1968, (Fr.) Nude Descending a Staircase.

Raoul Dufy, 1877-1953, (Fr.) Fauvist. Chateau and Horses.

Asher Brown Durand, 1796-1886, (U.S.) Hudson River school. Kindred Spirits.

Albrecht Durer, 1471-1528, (Ger.) Renaissance engraver, woodcuts. St. Jerome in His Study, Melancholia I, Apocalypse.

Anthony van Dyck, 1599-1641, (Flem.) Baroque portraitist. Portrait of Charles I Hunting.

Thomas Eakins, 1844-1916, (U.S.) Realist. The Gross Clinic.

Jacob Epstein, 1880-1959, (Br.) religious and allegorical sculptor. Genesis, Ecce Homo.

Jan van Eyck, 1380-1441, (Flem.) naturalistic panels. Adoration of the Lamb.

Anselm Feuerbach, 1829-1880, (Ger.) Romantic Classicism. Judgement of Paris, Iphigenia.
John Bernard Flannagan, 1895-1942, (U.S.) animal sculptor. Triumph of the Egg.
Jean-Honore Fragonard, 1732-1806, (Fr.) Rococo. The Swing.
Daniel Chester French, 1850-1931, (U.S.) The Minute Man of Concord; seated Lincoln, Lincoln Memorial, Washington, D.C.
Caspar David Friedrich, 1774-1840, (Ger.) Romantic landscapes. Man and Woman Gazing at the Moon.
Thomas Gainsborough, 1727-1788, (Br.) portraitist. The Blue Boy.
Paul Gauguin, 1848-1903, (Fr.) Post-impressionist. The Tahitians.
Lorenzo Ghiberti, 1378-1455, (It.) Renaissance sculptor. Gates of Paradise baptistry doors, Florence.
Alberto Giacometti, 1901-1966, (It.) attenuated sculptures of solitary figures. Man Pointing.
Giorgione, c. 1477-1510, (It.) Renaissance. The Tempest.
Giotto di Bondone, 1267-1337, (It.) Renaissance. Presentation of Christ in the Temple.
Francois Girardon, 1628-1715, (Fr.) Baroque sculptor of classical themes. Apollo Tended by the Nymphs.
Vincent van Gogh, 1853-1890, (Dutch) The Starry Night, L'Arlesienne.
Arshile Gorky, 1905-1948, (U.S.) Surrealist. The Liver Is the Cock's Comb.
Francisco de Goya y Lucientes, 1746-1828, (Sp.) The Naked Maja, The Disasters of War (etchings).
El Greco, 1541-1614, View of Toledo.
Horatio Greenough, 1805-1852, (U.S.) Neo-classical sculptor. George Washington.
Matthias Grünewald, 1480-1528, (Ger.) mystical religious themes. The Resurrection.
Frans Hals, c. 1580-1666, (Dutch) portraitist. Laughing Cavalier, Gypsy Girl.
Childe Hassam, 1859-1935, (U.S.) Impressionist. Southwest Wind.
Edward Hicks, 1780-1849, (U.S.) folk painter. The Peaceable Kingdom.
Hans Hofmann, 1880-1966, (U.S.) early Abstract Expressionist. Spring. The Gate.
William Hogarth, 1697-1764, (Br.) caricaturist. The Rake's Progress.
Katsushika Hokusai, 1760-1849, (Jap.) printmaker. Crabs.
Hans Holbein the Elder, 1460-1524, (Ger.) late Gothic. Presentation of Christ in the Temple.
Hans Holbein the Younger, 1497-1543, (Ger.) portraitist. Henry VIII.
Winslow Homer, 1836-1910, (U.S.) marine themes. Marine Coast, High Cliff.
Edward Hopper, 1882-1967, (U.S.) realistic urban scenes. Sunlight in a Cafeteria.
Jean-Auguste-Dominique Ingres, 1780-1867, (Fr.) Classicist. Valpincon Bather.
George Inness, 1825-1894, (U.S.) luminous landscapist. Delaware Water Gap.
Vasily Kandinsky, 1866-1944, (Rus.) Abstractionist. Capricious Forms.
Paul Klee, 1879-1940, (Swiss) Abstractionist. Twittering Machine.
Oscar Kokoschka, 1886-1980, (Aus.) Expressionist. View of Prague.
Kathe Kollwitz, 1867-1945, (Ger.) printmaker, social justice themes. The Peasant War.
Gaston Lachaise, 1882-1935, (U.S.) figurative sculptor. Standing Woman.
John La Farge, 1835-1910, (U.S.) muralist. Red and White Peonies.
Fernand Leger, 1881-1955, (Fr.) machine art. The Cyclists.
Leonardo da Vinci, 1452-1519, (It.) Mona Lisa, Last Supper, The Annunciation.
Emanuel Leutze, 1816-1868, (U.S.) historical themes. Washington Crossing the Delaware.
Jacques Lipchitz, 1891-1973, (Fr.) Cubist sculptor. Harpist.
Filippino Lippi, 1457-1504, (It.) Renaissance. The Vision of St. Bernard.
Fra Filippo Lippi, 1406-1469, (It.) Renaissance. Coronation of the Virgin.
Morris Louis, 1912-1962, (U.S.) Abstract Expressionist. Signa, Stripes.
Aristide Maillol, 1861-1944, (Fr.) sculptor. The Mediterranean.
Edouard Manet, 1832-1883, (Fr.) forerunner of Impressionism. Luncheon on the Grass, Olympia.
Andrea Mantegna, 1431-1506, (It.) Renaissance frescoes. Triumph of Caesar.
Franz Marc, 1880-1916, (Ger.) Expressionist. Blue Horses.
John Marin, 1870-1953, (U.S.) expressionist seascapes. Maine Island.
Reginald Marsh, 1898-1954, (U.S.) satirical artist. Tattoo and Haircut.
Masaccio, 1401-1428, (It.) Renaissance. The Tribute Money.
Henri Matisse, 1869-1954, (Fr.) Fauvist. Woman with the Hat.
Michelangelo Buonarroti, 1475-1564, (It.) Pieta, David, Moses, The Last Judgment, Sistine Ceiling.
Jean-Francois Millet, 1814-1875, (Fr.) painter of peasant subjects. The Gleaners, The Man with a Hoe.
Joan Miró, 1893-1983, (Sp.) Exuberant colors, playful images. Catalan landscape, Dutch Interior.
Amedeo Modigliani, 1884-1920, (It.) Reclining Nude.
Piet Mondrian, 1872-1944, (Dutch) Abstractionist. Composition.
Claude Monet, 1840-1926, (Fr.) Impressionist. The Bridge at Argenteuil, Haystacks.
Henry Moore, 1898-1986, (Br.) sculptor of large-scale, abstract works. Reclining Figure (several).
Gustave Moreau, 1826-1898, (Fr.) Symbolist. The Apparition, Dance of Salome.
James Wilson Morrice, 1865-1924, (Can.) landscapist. The Ferry, Quebec, Venice, Looking Over the Lagoon.
Grandma Moses, 1860-1961, (U.S.) folk painter. Out for the Christmas Trees.
Edvard Munch, 1863-1944, (Nor.) Expressionist. The Cry.
Bartolome Murillo, 1618-1682, (Sp.) Baroque religious artist. Vision of St. Anthony. The Two Trinities.
Barnett Newman, 1905-1970, (U.S.) Abstract Expressionist. Stations of the Cross.
Isamu Noguchi, 1904-1988, (U.S.) trad. Japanese art, modern techniques.
Georgia O'Keeffe, 1887-1986, (U.S.) Southwest motifs. Cow's Skull.
Jose Clemente Orozco, 1883-1949, (Mex.) frescoes. House of Tears.
Charles Willson Peale, 1741-1827, (U.S.) American Revolutionary portraitist. Washington, Franklin, Jefferson, John Adams.
Rembrandt Peale, 1778-1860, (U.S.) portraitist. Thomas Jefferson.
Pietro Perugino, 1446-1523, (It.) Renaissance. Delivery of the Keys to St. Peter.
Pablo Picasso, 1881-1973, (Sp.) Guernica, Dove, Head of a Woman.
Piero della Francesca, c. 1415-1492, (It.) Renaissance. Duke of Urbino, Flagellation of Christ.
Camille Pissarro, 1830-1903, (Fr.) Impressionist. Morning Sunlight.
Jackson Pollock, 1912-1956, (U.S.) Abstract Expressionist. Autumn Rhythm.
Nicolas Poussin, 1594-1665, (Fr.) Baroque pictorial classicism. St. John on Patmos.
Maurice B. Prendergast, c. 1860-1924, (U.S.) Post-impressionist water colorist. Umbrellas in the Rain.
Pierre-Paul Prud'hon, 1758-1823, (Fr.) Romanticist. Crime pursued by Vengeance and Justice.
Pierre Cecile Puvis de Chavannes, 1824-1898, (Fr.) muralist. The Poor Fisherman.
Raphael Sanzio, 1483-1520, (It.) Renaissance. Disputa, School of Athens, Sistine Madonna.
Man Ray, 1890-1976, (U.S.) Dadaist. Observing Time, The Lovers.
Odilon Redon, 1840-1916, (Fr.) Symbolist lithographer. In the Dream.
Rembrandt van Rijn, 1606-1669, (Dutch) The Bridal Couple, The Night Watch.
Frederic Remington, 1861-1909, (U.S.) painter, sculptor, portrayer of the American West. Bronco Buster.
Pierre-Auguste Renoir, 1841-1919, (Fr.) Impressionist. The Luncheon of the Boating Party.
Joshua Reynolds, 1723-1792, (Br.) portraitist. Mrs. Siddons as the Tragic Muse.
Diego Rivera, 1886-1957, (Mex.) frescoes. The Fecund Earth.
Norman Rockwell, 1894-1978, (U.S.) illustrator. Saturday Evening Post covers.
Auguste Rodin, 1840-1917, (Fr.) sculptor. The Thinker, The Burghers of Calais.
Mark Rothko, 1903-1970, (U.S.) Abstract Expressionist. Light, Earth and Blue.
Georges Rouault, 1871-1958, (Fr.) Expressionist. The Old King.
Henri Rousseau, 1844-1910, (Fr.) primitive exotic themes. The Snake Charmer.
Theodore Rousseau, 1812-1867, (Swiss-Fr.) landscapist. Under the Birches, Evening.
Peter Paul Rubens, 1577-1640, (Flem.) Baroque. Mystic Marriage of St. Catherine.

Jacob van Ruisdael, c. 1628-1682, (Dutch) landscapist. Jewish Cemetery.

Salomon van Ruysdael, c. 1600-1670, (Dutch) landscapist. River with Ferry-Boat.

Albert Pinkham Ryder, 1847-1917, (U.S.) seascapes and allegories. Toilers of the Sea.

Augustus Saint-Gaudens, 1848-1907, (U.S.) memorial statues. Farragut, Mrs. Henry Adams (Grief).

Andrea Sansovino, 1460-1529, (It.) Renaissance sculptor. Baptism of Christ.

Jacopo Sansovino, 1486-1570, (It.) Renaissance sculptor. St. John the Baptist.

John Singer Sargent, 1856-1925, (U.S.) Edwardian society portraitist. The Wyndham Sisters, Madam X.

Georges Seurat, 1859-1891, (Fr.) Pointillist. Sunday Afternoon on the Island of Grande Jatte.

Gino Severini, 1883-1966, (It.) Futurist and Cubist. Dynamic Hieroglyph of the Bal Tabarin.

Ben Shahn, 1898-1969, (U.S.) social and political themes. Sacco and Vanzetti series, Seurat's Lunch, Handball.

Charles Sheeler, 1883-1965, (U.S.) Abstractionist. Upper Deck.

David Alfaro Siqueiros, 1896-1974, (Mex.) political muralist. March of Humanity.

John F. Sloan, 1871-1951, (U.S.) depictions of New York City. Wake of the Ferry.

David Smith, 1906-1965, (U.S.) welded metal sculpture. Hudson River Landscape, Zig, Cubi series.

Gilbert Stuart, 1755-1828, (U.S.) portraitist. George Washington.

Thomas Sully, 1783-1872, (U.S.) portraitist. Col. Thomas Handasyd Perkins, The Passage of the Delaware.

Yves Tanguy, 1900-1955, (Fr.) Surrealist. Rose of the Four Winds.

Giovanni Battista Tiepolo, 1696-1770, (It.) Rococo frescoes. The Crucifixion.

Jacopo Tintoretto, 1518-1594, (It.) Mannerist. The Last Supper.

Titian, c. 1485-1576, (It.) Renaissance. Venus and the Lute Player, The Bacchanal.

Henri de Toulouse-Lautrec, 1864-1901, (Fr.) At the Moulin Rouge.

John Trumbull, 1756-1843, (U.S.) historical themes. The Declaration of Independence.

J(oseph) M(allord) W(illiam) Turner, 1775-1851, (Br.) Romantic landscapist. Snow Storm.

Paolo Uccello, 1397-1475, (It.) Gothic-Renaissance. The Rout of San Romano.

Maurice Utrillo, 1883-1955, (Fr.) Impressionist. Sacre-Coeur de Montmartre.

John Vanderlyn, 1775-1852, (U.S.) Neo-classicist. Ariadne Asleep on the Island of Naxos.

Diego Velazquez, 1599-1660, (Sp.) Baroque. Las Meninas, Portrait of Juan de Pareja.

Jan Vermeer, 1632-1675, (Dutch) interior genre subjects. Young Woman with a Water Jug.

Paolo Veronese, 1528-1588, (It.) devotional themes, vastly peopled canvases. The Temptation of St. Anthony.

Andrea del Verrocchio, 1435-1488, (It.) Florentine sculptor. Colleoni.

Maurice de Vlaminck, 1876-1958, (Fr.) Fauvist landscapist. The Storm.

Andy Warhol, 1928-1987 (U.S.) Pop Art. Campbell's Soup Cans.

Antoine Watteau, 1684-1721, (Fr.) Rococo painter of "scenes of gallantry". The Embarkation for Cythera.

George Frederic Watts, 1817-1904, (Br.) painter and sculptor of grandiose allegorical themes. Hope, Physical Energy.

Benjamin West, 1738-1820, (U.S.) realistic historical themes. Death of General Wolfe.

James Abbott McNeill Whistler, 1834-1903, (U.S.) Arrangement in Grey and Black, No. 1: The Artist's Mother.

Archibald M. Willard, 1836-1918, (U.S.) The Spirit of '76.

Grant Wood, 1891-1942, (U.S.) Midwestern regionalist. American Gothic, Daughters of Revolution.

Ossip Zadkine, 1890-1967, (Rus.) School of Paris sculptor. The Destroyed City, Musicians, Christ.

Noted Philosophers and Religionists of the Past

Lyman Abbott, 1835-1922, (U.S.) clergyman, reformer; advocate of Christian Socialism.

Pierre Abelard, 1079-1142, (F.) philosopher, theologian, and teacher, used dialectic method to support Christian dogma.

Felix Adler, 1851-1933, (U.S.) German-born founder of the Ethical Culture Society.

St. Augustine, 354-430, Latin bishop considered the founder of formalized Christian theology.

Averroes, 1126-1198, (Sp.) Islamic philosopher.

Roger Bacon, c.1214-1294, (Br.) philosopher and scientist.

Bahaullah (Mirza Husayn Ali), 1817-1892, (Pers.) founder of Bahai faith.

Karl Barth, 1886-1968, (Sw.) theologian, a leading force in 20th-century Protestantism.

St. Benedict, c.480-547, (It.) founded the Benedictines.

Jeremy Bentham, 1748-1832, (Br.) philosopher, reformer, founder of Utilitarianism.

Henri Bergson, 1859-1941, (F.) philosopher of evolution.

George Berkeley, 1685-1753, (Ir.) philosopher, churchman.

John Biddle, 1615-1662, (Br.) founder of English Unitarianism.

Jakob Boehme, 1575-1624, (G.) theosophist and mystic.

William Brewster, 1567-1644, (Br.) headed Pilgrims, signed Mayflower Compact.

Emil Brunner, 1889-1966, (Sw.) Protestant theologian.

Giordano Bruno, 1548-1600, (It.) philosopher, first to state the cosmic theory.

Martin Buber, 1878-1965, (G.) Jewish philosopher, theologian, wrote *I and Thou.*

Buddha (Siddhartha Gautama), c.563-c.483 BC, (Ind.) philosopher, founded Buddhism.

John Calvin, 1509-1564, (F.) theologian, a key figure in the Protestant Reformation.

Rudolph Carnap, 1891-1970, (U.S.) German-born philosopher, a founder of logical positivism.

William Ellery Channing, 1780-1842, (U.S.) clergyman, early spokesman for Unitarianism.

Auguste Comte, 1798-1857, (F.) philosopher, the founder of positivism.

Confucius, 551-479 BC, (Chin.) founder of Confucianism.

John Cotton, 1584-1652, (Br.) Puritan theologian.

Thomas Cranmer, 1489-1556, (Br.) churchman, wrote much of *Book of Common Prayer;* promoter of English Reformation.

René Descartes, 1596-1650, (F.) philosopher, mathematician, "father of modern philosophy."

John Dewey, 1859-1952, (U.S.) philosopher, educator; helped inaugurate the progressive education movement.

Denis Diderot, 1713-1784, (F.) philosopher, creator of first modern encyclopedia.

Mary Baker Eddy, 1821-1910, (U.S.) founder of Christian Science, wrote *Science and Health.*

Jonathan Edwards, 1703-1758, (U.S.) preacher, theologian.

(Desiderius) Erasmus, c.1466-1536, (Du.) Renaissance humanist, wrote *On the Freedom of the Will.*

Johann Fichte, 1762-1814, (G.) philosopher, the first of the Transcendental Idealists.

George Fox, 1624-1691, (Br.) founder of Society of Friends.

St. Francis of Assisi, 1182-1226, (It.) founded Franciscans.

al Ghazali, 1058-1111, Islamic philosopher.

Georg W. Hegel, 1770-1831, (G.) Idealist philosopher.

Martin Heidegger, 1889-1976, (G.) existentialist philosopher, affected fields ranging from physics to literary criticism.

Johann G. Herder, 1744-1803, (G.) philosopher, cultural historian; a founder of German Romanticism.

David Hume, 1711-1776, (Sc.) philosopher, historian.

Jan Hus, 1369-1415, (Czech.) religious reformer.

Edmund Husserl, 1859-1938, (G.) philosopher, founded the Phenomenological movement.

Thomas Huxley, 1825-1895, (Br.) philosopher, educator.

Ignatius of Loyola, 1491-1556, (Sp.) founder of the Jesuits.

William Inge, 1860-1954, (Br.) theologian, explored the mystic aspects of Christianity.

William James, 1842-1910, (U.S.) philosopher, psychologist; advanced theory of the pragmatic nature of truth.

Karl Jaspers, 1883-1969, (G.) existentialist philosopher.

Immanuel Kant, 1724-1804, (G.) metaphysician, preeminent founder of modern critical philosophy; *Critique of Pure Reason.*

Soren Kierkegaard, 1813-1855, (Den.) philosopher, considered the father of Existentialism.

John Knox, 1505-1572, (Sc.) leader of the Protestant Reformation in Scotland.

Lao-Tzu, 604-531 BC, (Chin.) philosopher, considered the founder of the Taoist religion.

Gottfried von Leibniz, 1646-1716, (G.) philosopher, mathematician, influenced German Enlightenment.

Martin Luther, 1483-1546, (G.) leader of the Protestant Reformation, founded Lutheran church.

Maimonides, 1135-1204, (Sp.) Jewish philosopher.

Jacques Maritain, 1882-1973, (F.) Neo-Thomist philosopher.

Cotton Mather, 1663-1728, (U.S.) defender of orthodox Puritanism; founded Yale, 1701.

Philipp Melanchthon, 1497-1560, (G.) theologian, humanist; an important voice in the Reformation.

Thomas Merton, 1915-1968, (U.S.) Trappist monk, spiritual writer; *The Seven Storey Mountain.*

Mohammed, c.570-632, Arab prophet of the religion of Islam.
Dwight Moody, 1837-1899, (U.S.) evangelist.
George E. Moore, 1873-1958, (Br.) ethical theorist.
Elijah Muhammad, 1897-1975, (U.S.) leader of the Black Muslim sect.
Heinrich Muhlenberg, 1711-1787, (G.) organized the Lutheran Church in America.
John H. Newman, 1801-1890, (Br.) Roman Catholic cardinal, led Oxford Movement; *Apologia pro Vita Sua.*
Reinhold Niebuhr, 1892-1971, (U.S.) Protestant theologian, social and political critic.
Friedrich Nietzsche, 1844-1900, (G.) moral philosopher; *The Birth of Tragedy, Thus Spake Zarathustra.*
Blaise Pascal, 1623-1662, (F.) philosopher, mathematician.
St. Patrick, c.389-c.461, brought Christianity to Ireland.
St. Paul, ?-c.67, a founder of Christianity; his epistles are first Christian theological writing.
Charles S. Peirce, 1839-1914, (U.S.) philosopher, logician; originated concept of Pragmatism, 1878.
Josiah Royce 1855-1916, (U.S.) Idealist philosopher.
Charles T. Russell, 1852-1916, (U.S.) founder of Jehovah's Witnesses.
Fredrich von Schelling, 1775-1854, (G.) philosopher of romantic movement.
Friedrich Schleiermacher, 1768-1834, (G.) theologian, a founder of modern Protestant theology.
Arthur Schopenhauer, 1788-1860, (G.) philosopher.
Joseph Smith, 1805-1844, (U.S.) founded Latter Day Saints (Mormon) movement, 1830.
Herbert Spencer, 1820-1903, (Br.) philosopher of evolution.
Baruch Spinoza, 1632-1677, (Du.) rationalist philosopher.
Billy Sunday, 1862-1935, (U.S.) evangelist.
Daisetz Teitaro Suzuki, 1870-1966, (Jap.) Buddhist scholar.
Emanuel Swedenborg, 1688-1772, (Swed.) philosopher, mystic.
Thomas à Becket, 1118-1170, (Br.) archbishop of Canterbury, opposed Henry II.
Thomas à Kempis, c.1380-1471, (G.) theologian probably wrote *Imitation of Christ.*
Thomas Aquinas, 1225-1274, (It.) Roman Catholic saint, founder of system declared official Catholic philosophy; *Summa Theologica.*
Paul Tillich, 1886-1965, (U.S.) German-born philosopher and theologian; brought depth psychology to Protestantism.
John Wesley, 1703-1791, (Br.) theologian, evangelist; founded Methodism.
Alfred North Whitehead, 1861-1947, (Br.) philosopher, mathematician; *Principia Mathematica* (with Bertrand Russell).
William of Occam, c.1285-c.1349 (Br.) medieval scholastic philosopher.
Roger Williams, c.1603-1683, (U.S.) clergyman, championed religious freedom and separation of church and state.
Ludwig Wittgenstein, 1889-1951, (Aus.) philosopher, influenced language philosophy.
John Wycliffe, 1320-1384, (Br.) theologian, reformer.
Brigham Young, 1801-1877, (U.S.) Mormon leader after Smith's assassination, colonized Utah.
Huldrych Zwingli, 1484-1531, (Sw.) theologian, led Swiss Protestant Reformation.

Noted Social Reformers and Educators of the Past

Jane Addams, 1860-1935, (U.S.) co-founder of Hull House; won Nobel Peace Prize, 1931.
Susan B. Anthony, 1820-1906, (U.S.) a leader in temperance, anti-slavery, and women's suffrage movements.
Henry Barnard, 1811-1900, (U.S.) public school reformer.
Thomas Barnardo, 1845-1905, (Br.) social reformer, pioneered in the care of destitute children.
Clara Barton, 1821-1912, (U.S.) organizer of the American Red Cross.
Henry Ward Beecher, 1813-1887, (U.S.) clergyman, abolitionist.
Sarah G. Blanding, 1899-1985, (U.S.), head of Vassar College, 1946-64.
Amelia Bloomer, 1818-1894, (U.S.) social reformer, women's rights advocate.
William Booth, 1829-1912, (Br.) founded the Salvation Army.
John Brown, 1800-1859, (U.S.) abolitionist who led murder of 5 pro-slavery men, was hanged.
Nicholas Murray Butler, 1862-1947, (U.S.) educator headed Columbia Univ., 1902-45; won Nobel Peace Prize, 1931.
Frances X. (Mother) Cabrini, 1850-1917, (U.S.) Italian-born nun founded charitable institutions; first American canonized.
Carrie Chapman Catt, 1859-1947, (U.S.) suffragette, helped win passage of the 19th amendment.
Clarence Darrow, 1857-1938, (U.S.) lawyer, defender of "underdog," opponent of capital punishment.
Dorothy Day, 1897-1980, (U.S.) founder of Catholic Worker Movement.
Eugene V. Debs, 1855-1926, (U.S.) labor leader, led Pullman strike, 1894; 4-time Socialist presidential candidate.
Melvil Dewey, 1851-1931, (U.S.) devised decimal system of library-book classification.
Dorothea Dix, 1802-1887, (U.S.) crusader for humane care of mentally ill.
Frederick Douglass, 1817-1895, (U.S.) abolitionist.
W.E.B. DuBois, 1868-1963, (U.S.) Negro-rights leader, educator, and writer.
William Lloyd Garrison, 1805-1879, (U.S.) abolitionist, reformer.
Giovanni Gentile, 1875-1944, (It.) philosopher, educator; reformed Italian educational system.
Emma Goldman, 1869-1940, (Rus.-U.S.) published anarchist *Mother Earth,* birth control advocate.
Samuel Gompers, 1850-1924, (U.S.) labor leader; a founder and president of AFL.
William Green, 1873-1952, (U.S.) president of AFL, 1924-52.
Michael Harrington, 1928-1989, (U.S.) revealed poverty in affluent U.S. in *The Other America,* 1963.
Sidney Hillman, 1887-1946, (U.S.) labor leader, helped organize CIO.
John Holt, 1924-1985, (U.S.) educator and author, *How Children Fail.*
Samuel G. Howe, 1801-1876, (U.S.) social reformer, changed public attitudes toward the handicapped.
Helen Keller, 1880-1968, (U.S.) crusader for better treatment for the handicapped.
Martin Luther King Jr., 1929-1968, (U.S.) civil rights leader; won Nobel Peace Prize, 1964.
John L. Lewis, 1880-1969, (U.S.) labor leader, headed United Mine Workers, 1920-60.
Horace Mann, 1796-1859, (U.S.) pioneered modern public school system.
William H. McGuffey, 1800-1873, (U.S.) author of *Reader,* the mainstay of 19th century U.S. public education.
Alexander Meiklejohn, 1872-1964, (U.S.) British-born educator, championed academic freedom and experimental curricula.
Karl Menninger, 1893-1991, (U.S.) with brother William made Menninger Clinic, and Menninger Foundation in Topeka, Kans., the center of U.S. psychiatry.
Lucretia Mott, 1793-1880, (U.S.) reformer, pioneer feminist.
Philip Murray, 1886-1952, (U.S.) Scotch-born labor leader.
Florence Nightingale, 1820-1910, (Br.) founder of modern nursing.
Emmeline Pankhurst, 1858-1928, (Br.) woman suffragist.
Elizabeth P. Peabody, 1804-1894, (U.S.) education pioneer, founded 1st kindergarten in U.S., 1860.
Walter Reuther, 1907-1970, (U.S.) labor leader, headed UAW.
Jacob Riis, 1849-1914, (U.S.) crusader for urban reforms.
Margaret Sanger, 1883-1966, (U.S.) social reformer, pioneered the birth control movement.
Elizabeth Seton, 1774-1821, (U.S.) established parochial school education in U.S.
Earl of Shaftesbury (A.A. Cooper), 1801-1885, (Br.) social reformer.
Elizabeth Cady Stanton, 1815-1902, (U.S.) women's suffrage pioneer.
Lucy Stone, 1818-1893, (U.S.) feminist, abolitionist.
Harriet Tubman, c.1820-1913, (U.S.) abolitionist, ran Underground Railroad.
Booker T. Washington, 1856-1915, (U.S.) educator, reformer; championed vocational training for blacks.
Walter F. White, 1893-1955, (U.S.) headed NAACP, 1931-55.
William Wilberforce, 1759-1833, (Br.) social reformer, prominent in struggle to abolish the slave trade.
Emma Hart Willard, 1787-1870, (U.S.) pioneered higher education for women.
Frances E. Willard, 1839-1898, (U.S.) temperance, woman's rights leader.
Mary Wollstonecraft, 1759-1797 (Br.) wrote *Vindication of the Rights of Women.*
Whitney M. Young Jr., 1921-1971, (U.S.) civil rights leader, headed National Urban League, 1961-71.

Noted Historians, Economists, and Social Scientists of the Past

Brooks Adams, 1848-1927, (U.S.) historian, political theoretician; *The Law of Civilization and Decay.*
Henry Adams, 1838-1911, (U.S.) historian; *History of the United States of America, The Education of Henry Adams.*

Francis Bacon, 1561-1626, (Br.) philosopher, essayist, and statesman; applied scientific induction to philosophy.
George Bancroft, 1800-1891, (U.S.) historian, wrote 10-volume *History of the United States.*
Charles A. Beard, 1874-1948, (U.S.) historian; *The Economic Basis of Politics;* helped found New School for Social Research.
Bede (the Venerable), c.673-735, (Br.) scholar historian whose writings virtually comprise the learning of his time.
Ruth Benedict, 1887-1948, (U.S.) anthropologist, studied Indian tribes of the Southwest.
Bruno Bettleheim, 1903-1990, (Aust.-U.S.) psychoanalyst specializing in autistic children; *The Uses of Enchantment.*
Louis Blanc, 1811-1882, (F.) Socialist leader and historian whose ideas were a link between utopian and Marxist socialism.
Leonard Bloomfield, 1887-1949, (U.S.) linguist. *Language.*
Franz Boas, 1858-1942, (U.S.) German-born anthropologist, studied American Indians.
Van Wyck Brooks, 1886-1963, (U.S.) historian, critic of New England culture, esp. literature.
Edmund Burke, 1729-1797, (Ir.) British parliamentarian and political philosopher; influenced many Federalists.
Joseph Campbell, 1904-1987, (U.S.) wrote books on mythology, folklore.
Thomas Carlyle, 1795-1881, (Sc.) historian, critic; *Sartor Resartus, Past and Present, The French Revolution.*
Edward Channing, 1856-1931, (U.S.) historian, wrote 6-volume *A History of the United States.*
John R. Commons, 1862-1945, (U.S.) economist, labor historian; *Legal Foundations of Capitalism.*
Benedetto Croce, 1866-1952, (It.) philosopher, statesman, and historian; *Philosophy of the Spirit.*
Bernard A. De Voto, 1897-1955, (U.S.) historian; wrote trilogy on American West; edited Mark Twain manuscripts.
Ariel Durant, 1898-1981, (U.S.) historian, collaborated with husband on 11-volume *The Story of Civilization.*
Will Durant, 1885-1981, (U.S.) historian. *The Story of Civilization, The Story of Philosophy.*
Emile Durkheim, 1858-1917, (F.) a founder of modern sociology; *The Rules of Sociological Method.*
Friedrich Engels, 1820-1895, (G.) political writer, with Marx wrote the *Communist Manifesto.*
Irving Fisher, 1867-1947, (U.S.) economist, contributed to the development of modern monetary theory.
John Fiske, 1842-1901, (U.S.) historian and lecturer, popularized Darwinian theory of evolution.
Charles Fourier, 1772-1837, (F.) utopian socialist.
Henry George, 1839-1897, (U.S.) economist, reformer, led single-tax movement.
Edward Gibbon, 1737-1794, (Br.) historian, wrote *The History of the Decline and Fall of the Roman Empire.*
Francesco Guicciardini, 1483-1540, (It.) historian, wrote *Storia d'Italia,* principal historical work of the 16th-century.
Thomas Hobbes, 1588-1679, (Br.) political philosopher; *Leviathan.*
Richard Hofstadter, 1916-1970, (U.S.) historian; *The Age of Reform.*
John Maynard Keynes, 1883-1946, (Br.) economist, principal advocate of deficit spending.
Alfred L. Kroeber, 1876-1960, (U.S.) cultural anthropologist, studied Indians of North and South America.
James L. Laughlin, 1850-1933, (U.S.) economist, helped establish Federal Reserve System.
Lucien Lévy-Bruhl, 1857-1939, (F.) philosopher, studied the psychology of primitive societies; *Primitive Mentality.*
Kurt Lewin, 1890-1947, (U.S.) German-born psychologist, studied human motivation and group dynamics.
John Locke, 1632-1704, (Br.) philosopher; *Essay Concerning Human Understanding.*
Konrad Lorenz, 1904-1989, (Aus.) ethologist, pioneer in study of animal behavior.
Thomas B. Macauley, 1800-1859, (Br.) historian, statesman.
Bronislaw Malinowski, 1884-1942, (Pol.) considered the father of social anthropology.
Thomas R. Malthus, 1766-1834, (Br.) economist, famed for *Essay on the Principle of Population.*
Karl Mannheim, 1893-1947, (Hung.) sociologist, historian; *Ideology and Utopia.*
Karl Marx, 1818-1883, (G.) political philosopher, proponent of modern communism; *Communist Manifesto, Das Kapital.*
Giuseppe Mazzini, 1805-1872, (It.) political philosopher.
George H. Mead, 1863-1931, (U.S.) philosopher, social psychologist.
Margaret Mead, 1901-1978, (U.S.) cultural anthropologist, popularized field; *Coming of Age in Samoa.*
James Mill, 1773-1836, (Sc.) philosopher, historian, economist; a proponent of Utilitarianism.
John Stuart Mill, 1806-1873, (Br.) philosopher, political economist; *Essay on Liberty.*
Perry G. Miller, 1905-1963, (U.S.) historian, interpreted 17th-century New England.
Theodor Mommsen, 1817-1903, (G.) historian; *The History of Rome.*
Charles-Louis Montesquieu, 1689-1755, (F.) social philosopher; *The Spirit of Laws.*
Samuel Eliot Morison, 1887-1976, (U.S.) historian, chronicled voyages of early explorers.
Lewis Mumford, 1895-1990, (U.S.) sociologist, critic, *The Culture of Cities.*
Gunnar Myrdal, 1898-1987 (Swe.) economist, social scientist.
Allan Nevins, 1890-1971, (U.S.) historian, biographer; *The Ordeal of the Union.*
Jose Ortega y Gasset, 1883-1955, (Sp.) philosopher, advocated control by elite; *The Revolt of the Masses.*
Robert Owen, 1771-1858, (Br.) political philosopher, reformer; pioneer in cooperative movement.
Vilfredo Pareto, 1848-1923, (It.) economist, sociologist.
Francis Parkman, 1823-1893, (U.S.) historian; *France and England in North America, 1851-92.*
Marco Polo, c.1254-1324, (It.) narrated an account of his travels to China.
William Prescott, 1796-1859, (U.S.) early American historian; *The Conquest of Peru.*
Pierre Joseph Proudhon, 1809-1865, (F.) social theorist, the father of anarchism; *The Philosophy of Property.*
Francois Quesnay, 1694-1774, (F.) economic theorist, demonstrated circular flow of economic activity through society.
David Ricardo, 1772-1823, (Br.) economic theorist, advocated free international trade.
James H. Robinson, 1863-1936, (U.S.) historian, educator.
Carl Rogers, 1902-1987, (U.S.) psychotherapist, author.
Jean-Jacques Rousseau, 1712-1778, (F.) social philosopher, the father of romantic sensibility; *Confessions.*
Edward Sapir, 1884-1939 (Ger.-U.S.) anthropologist, studied ethnology and linguistics of some U.S. Indian groups.
Ferdinand de Saussure, 1857-1913, (Swiss) a founder of modern linguistics.
Hjalmar Schacht, 1877-1970, (G.) economist; Reichsbank president.
Joseph Schumpeter, 1883-1950, (U.S.) Czech.-born economist, championed big business, capitalism.
Albert Schweitzer, 1875-1965, (Alsatian) social philosopher, theologian, medical missionary.
George Simmel, 1858-1918, (G.) sociologist, philosopher; helped establish German sociology.
B.F. Skinner, 1904-1989, (U.S.) psychologist, championed behaviorism.
Adam Smith, 1723-1790, (Br.) economist, advocated laissez-faire economy and free trade.
Jared Sparks, 1789-1866, (U.S.) historian, educator, editor; *The Library of American Biography.*
Oswald Spengler, 1880-1936, (G.) philosopher and historian; *The Decline of the West.*
William G. Sumner, 1840-1910, (U.S.) social scientist, economist; championed laissez-faire economy, Social Darwinism.
Hippolyte Taine, 1828-1893, (F.) historian, basis of naturalistic school; *The Origins of Contemporary France.*
Frank W. Taussig, 1859-1940, (U.S.) economist, educator.
A(lan) J(ohn) P(ercivale) Taylor, 1906-1989, (Br.) historian, *The Origins of the Second World War.*
Nikolaas Tinbergen, 1907-1988, (Dutch-Br.) ethologist, pioneer in study of animal behavior.
Alexis de Tocqueville, 1805-1859, (F.) political scientist, historian; *Democracy in America.*
Francis E. Townsend, 1867-1960, (U.S.) led old-age pension movement, 1933.
Arnold Toynbee, 1889-1975, (Br.) historian; *A Study of History.*
Heinrich von Treitschke, 1834-1896, (G.) historian, political writer; *A History of Germany in the 19th Century.*
George Trevelyan, 1838-1928, (Br.) historian, statesman; favored "literary" over "scientific" history; *History of England.*
Barbara Tuchman, 1912-1989, (U.S.) author of popular history books, *The Guns of August, The March of Folly.*
Frederick J. Turner, 1861-1932, (U.S.) historian, educator; *The Frontier in American History.*
Thorstein B. Veblen, 1857-1929, (U.S.) economist, social philosopher; *The Theory of the Leisure Class.*
Giovanni Vico, 1668-1744, (It.) historian, philosopher; regarded by many as first modern historian. *New Science.*
Voltaire (F.M. Arouet), 1694-1778, (F.) philosopher, historian, writer of "philosophical romances; *Candide.*
Izaak Walton, 1593-1683, (Br.) wrote biographies, political-philosophical study of fishing, *The Compleat Angler.*
Sidney J., 1859-1947, and wife **Beatrice,** 1858-1943, **Webb** (Br.) leading figures in Fabian Society and British Labour Party.
Walter P. Webb, 1888-1963, (U.S.) historian of the West.

Max Weber, 1864-1920, (G.) sociologist. *The Protestant Ethic and the Spirit of Capitalism.*

Noted Scientists of the Past

Howard H. Aiken, 1900-1973, (U.S.) mathematician, credited with designing forerunner of digital computer.

Albertus Magnus, 1193-1280, (G.) theologian, philosopher, established medieval Christian study of natural science.

Andre-Marie Ampère, 1775-1836, (F.) scientist known for contributions to electrodynamics.

Amedeo Avogadro, 1776-1856, (It.) chemist, physicist, advanced important theories on properties of gases.

John Bardeen, 1908-1991, (U.S.) co-inventor of the transistor that led to modern electronics.

A.C. Becquerel, 1788-1878, (F.) physicist, pioneer in electrochemical science.

A.H. Becquerel, 1852-1908, (F.) physicist, discovered radioactivity in uranium.

Alexander Graham Bell, 1847-1922, (U.S.) inventor, first to patent and commercially exploit the telephone, 1876.

Daniel Bernoulli, 1700-1782, (Swiss) mathematician, advanced kinetic theory of gases and fluids.

Jöns Jakob Berzelius, 1779-1848, (Swed.) chemist, developed modern chemical symbols and formulas.

Henry Bessemer, 1813-1898, (Br.) engineer, invented Bessemer steel-making process.

Louis Blériot, 1872-1936, (F.) engineer, pioneer aviator, invented and constructed monoplanes.

Niels Bohr, 1885-1962, (Dan.) physicist, leading figure in the development of quantum theory.

Max Born, 1882-1970, (G.) physicist known for research in quantum mechanics.

Satyendranath Bose, 1894-1974, (In.) physicist, chemist, mathematician known for Bose statistics, forerunner of modern quantum theory.

Walter Brattain, 1902-1987, (U.S.) inventor, worked on invention of transistor.

Louis de Broglie, 1893-1987, (F.) physicist, best known for wave theory.

Robert Bunsen, 1811-1899, (G.) chemist, invented Bunsen burner.

Luther Burbank, 1849-1926, (U.S.) plant breeder whose work developed plant breeding into a modern science.

Vannevar Bush, 1890-1974, (U.S.) electrical engineer, developed differential analyzer, first electronic analogue computer.

Alexis Carrel, 1873-1944, (F.) surgeon, biologist, developed methods of suturing blood vessels and transplanting organs.

George Washington Carver, 1860?-1943, (U.S.) agricultural chemist at Tuskegee Institute, discovered hundreds of uses for peanut, sweet potato, soybean.

Henry Cavendish, 1731-1810, (Br.) chemist, physicist, discovered hydrogen.

James Chadwick, 1891-1974, (Br.) physicist, discovered the neutron.

Jean M. Charcot, 1825-1893, (F.) neurologist known for work on hysteria, hypnotism, sclerosis.

Albert Claude, 1899-1983, (Belg.) a founder of modern cell biology.

John D. Cockcroft, 1897-1967, (Br.) nuclear physicist, constructed first atomic particle accelerator with E.T.S. Walton.

Nicholas Copernicus, 1473-1543, (Pol.) astronomer who first described solar system, with earth as one of planets revolving around sun.

William Crookes, 1832-1919, (Br.) physicist, chemist, discovered thallium, invented a cathode-ray tube, radiometer.

Marie Curie, 1867-1934, (Pol.-F.) physical chemist known for work on radium and its compounds.

Pierre Curie, 1859-1906, (F.) physical chemist known for work with his wife on radioactivity.

Gottlieb Daimler, 1834-1900, (G.) engineer, inventor, pioneer automobile manufacturer.

John Dalton, 1766-1844, (Br.) chemist, physicist, formulated atomic theory, made first table of atomic weights.

Charles Darwin, 1809-1882, (Br.) naturalist, established theory of organic evolution; *Origin of Species.*

Humphry Davy, 1778-1829, (Br.) chemist, research in electrochemistry led to isolation of potassium, sodium, calcium, barium, boron, magnesium, and strontium.

Lee De Forest, 1873-1961, (U.S.) inventor, pioneer in development of wireless telegraphy, sound pictures, television.

Max Delbruck, 1907-1981, (U.S.) pioneer in modern molecular genetics.

Rudolf Diesel, 1858-1913, (G.) mechanical engineer, patented Diesel engine.

Thomas Dooley, 1927-1961, (U.S.) "jungle doctor," noted for efforts to supply medical aid to underdeveloped countries.

Christian Doppler, 1803-1853, (Aus.) physicist, demonstrated Doppler effect (change in energy wavelengths caused by motion).

Thomas A. Edison, 1847-1931, (U.S.) inventor, held over 1,000 patents, including incandescent electric lamp, phonograph.

Paul Ehrlich, 1854-1915, (G.) bacteriologist, pioneer in modern immunology and bacteriology.

Albert Einstein, 1879-1955, (Ger.-U.S.) theoretical physicist, known for formulation of relativity theory.

John F. Enders, 1897-1985, (U.S.) virologist who helped discover vaccines against polio, measles, and mumps.

Leonhard Euler, 1707-1783, (Swiss), mathematician, physicist, authored first calculus book.

Gabriel Fahrenheit, 1686-1736, (G.) physicist, introduced Fahrenheit scale for thermometers.

Michael Faraday, 1791-1867, (Br.) chemist, physicist, known for work in field of electricity.

Pierre de Fermat, 1601-1665, (F.) mathematician, discovered analytic geometry, founded modern theory of numbers and calculus of probabilities.

Enrico Fermi, 1901-1954, (It.) physicist, one of chief architects of the nuclear age.

Galileo Ferraris, 1847-1897, (It.) physicist, electrical engineer, discovered principle of rotary magnetic field.

Richard Feynman, 1918-1988, (U.S.) a leading theoretical physicist of the postwar generation.

Camille Flammarion, 1842-1925, (F.) astronomer, popularized study of astronomy.

Alexander Fleming, 1881-1955, (Br.) bacteriologist, discovered penicillin.

Jean B.J. Fourier, 1768-1830, (F.) mathematician, discovered theorem governing periodic oscillation.

James Franck, 1882-1964, (G.) physicist, proved value of quantum theory.

Sigmund Freud, 1856-1939, (Aus.) psychiatrist, founder of psychoanalysis.

Galileo Galilei, 1564-1642, (It.) astronomer, physicist, a founder of the experimental method.

Luigi Galvani, 1737-1798, (It.) physician, physicist, known as founder of galvanism.

Carl Friedrich Gauss, 1777-1855, (G.) mathematician, astronomer, physicist, made important contributions to almost every field of physical science, founded a number of new fields.

Joseph Gay-Lussac, 1778-1850, (F.) chemist, physicist, investigated behavior of gases, discovered law of combining volumes.

Josiah W. Gibbs, 1839-1903, (U.S.) theoretical physicist, chemist, founded chemical thermodynamics.

Robert H. Goddard, 1882-1945 (U.S.) physicist, father of modern rocketry.

George W. Goethals, 1858-1928, (U.S.) army engineer, built the Panama Canal.

William C. Gorgas, 1854-1920, (U.S.) sanitarian, U.S. army surgeon-general, his work to prevent yellow fever, malaria helped insure construction of Panama Canal.

Ernest Haeckel, 1834-1919, (G.) zoologist, evolutionist, a strong proponent of Darwin.

Otto Hahn, 1879-1968, (G.) chemist, worked on atomic fission.

J.B.S. Haldane, 1892-1964, (Sc.) scientist, known for work as geneticist and application of mathematics to science.

James Hall, 1761-1832, (Br.) geologist, chemist, founded experimental geology, geochemistry.

Edmund Halley, 1656-1742, (Br.) astronomer, calculated the orbits of many planets.

William Harvey, 1578-1657, (Br.) physician, anatomist, discovered circulation of the blood.

Hermann v. Helmholtz, 1821-1894, (G.) physicist, anatomist, physiologist, made fundamental contributions to physiology, optics, electrodynamics, mathematics, meteorology.

William Herschel, 1738-1822, (Br.) astronomer, discovered Uranus.

Heinrich Hertz, 1857-1894, (G.) physicist, his discoveries led to wireless telegraphy.

David Hilbert, 1862-1943, (G.) mathematician, formulated first satisfactory set of axioms for modern Euclidean geometry.

Edwin P. Hubble, 1889-1953, (U.S.) astronomer, produced first observational evidence of expanding universe.

Alexander v. Humboldt, 1769-1859, (G.) explorer, naturalist, propagator of earth sciences, originated ecology, geophysics.

Julian Huxley, 1887-1975, (Br.) biologist, a gifted exponent and philosopher of science.

Edward Jenner, 1749-1823, (Br.) physician, discovered vaccination.

William Jenner, 1815-1898, (Br.) physician, pathological anatomist.

Frederic Joliot-Curie, 1900-1958, (F.) physicist, with his wife continued work of Curies on radioactivity.

Irene Joliot-Curie, 1897-1956, (F.) physicist, continued work of Curies in radioactivity.

James P. Joule, 1818-1889, (Br.) physicist, determined relationship between heat and mechanical energy (conservation of energy).

Carl Jung, 1875-1961, (Sw.) psychiatrist, founder of analytical psychology.

Wm. Thomson Kelvin, 1824-1907, (Br.) mathematician, physicist, known for work on heat and electricity.

Sister Elizabeth Kenny, 1886-1952, (Austral.) nurse, developed method of treatment for polio.

Johannes Kepler, 1571-1630, (G.) astronomer, discovered important laws of planetary motion.

Joseph Lagrange, 1736-1813, (F.) geometer, astronomer, worked in all fields of analysis, and number theory, and analytical and celestial mechanics.

Jean B. Lamarck, 1744-1829, (F.) naturalist, forerunner of Darwin in evolutionary theory.

Edwin Land, 1910-1991, (U.S.) invented Polaroid camera.

Irving Langmuir, 1881-1957, (U.S.) physical chemist, his studies of molecular films on solid and liquid surfaces opened new fields in colloid research and biochemistry.

Pierre S. Laplace, 1749-1827, (F.) astronomer, physicist, put forth nebular hypothesis of origin of solar system.

Antoine Lavoisier, 1743-1794, (F.) chemist, founder of modern chemistry.

Ernest O. Lawrence, 1901-1958, (U.S.) physicist, invented the cyclotron.

Louis Leakey, 1903-1972, (Br.) anthropologist, discovered important fossils, remains of early hominids.

Anton van Leeuwenhoek, 1632-1723, (Du.) microscopist, father of microbiology.

Gottfried Wilhelm Leibniz, 1646-1716, (G.) mathematician, developed theories of differential and integral calculus.

Justus von Liebig, 1803-1873, (G.) chemist, established quantitative organic chemical analysis.

Joseph Lister, 1827-1912, (Br.) pioneer of antiseptic surgery.

Percival Lowell, 1855-1916, (U.S.) astronomer, predicted the existence of Pluto.

Louis (1864-1984) and **Auguste Lumière,** 1862-1954, (Fr.) invented cinematograph, first mechanism to project moving pictures on screen.

Guglielmo Marconi, 1874-1937, (It.) physicist, known for his development of wireless telegraphy.

James Clerk Maxwell, 1831-1879, (Sc.) physicist, known especially for his work in electricity and magnetism.

Maria Goeppert Mayer, 1906-1972, (G.-U.S.) physicist, independently developed theory of structure of atomic nuclei.

Lise Meitner, 1878-1968, (Aus.) physicist whose work contributed to the development of the atomic bomb.

Gregor J. Mendel, 1822-1884, (Aus.) botanist, known for his experimental work on heredity.

Franz Mesmer, 1734-1815, (G.) physician, developed theory of animal magnetism.

Albert A. Michelson, 1852-1931, (U.S.) physicist, established speed of light as a fundamental constant.

Robert A. Millikan, 1868-1953, (U.S.) physicist, noted for study of elementary electronic charge and photoelectric effect.

Thomas Hunt Morgan, 1866-1945, (U.S.) geneticist, embryologist, established chromosome theory of heredity.

Isaac Newton, 1642-1727, (Br.) natural philosopher, mathematician, discovered law of gravitation, laws of motion.

Robert N. Noyce, 1927-1989, (U.S.) inventor of the microchip, which revolutionized the electronics industry.

J. Robert Oppenheimer, 1904-1967, (U.S.) physicist, director of Los Alamos during development of the atomic bomb.

Wilhelm Ostwald, 1853-1932, (G.) physical chemist, philosopher, chief founder of physical chemistry.

Robert Morris Page, 1903-1992, (U.S.) physicist, research director of U.S. Naval Research Laboratory, a leading figure in development of radar technology.

Louis Pasteur, 1822-1895, (F.) chemist, originated process of pasteurization.

Max Planck, 1858-1947, (G.) physicist, originated and developed quantum theory.

Henri Poincaré, 1854-1912, (F.) mathematician, physicist, influenced cosmology, relativity, and topology.

Joseph Priestley, 1733-1804, (Br.) chemist, one of the discoverers of oxygen.

Rabi, Isidor Isaac, 1899-1988 (U.S.) physicist, pioneered atom exploration.

Walter S. Reed, 1851-1902, (U.S.) army pathologist, bacteriologist, proved mosquitos transmit yellow fever.

Bernhard Riemann, 1826-1866, (G.) mathematician, contributed to development of calculus, complex variable theory, and mathematical physics.

Wilhelm Roentgen, 1845-1923, (G.) physicist, discovered X-rays.

Bertrand Russell, 1872-1970, (Br.) logician, philosopher, one of the founders of modern logic, wrote *Principia Mathematica.*

Ernest Rutherford, 1871-1937, (Br.) physicist, discovered the atomic nucleus.

Giovanni Schiaparelli, 1835-1910, (It.) astronomer, hypothesized canals on the surface of Mars.

Angelo Secchi, 1818-1878, (It.) astronomer, pioneer in classifying stars by their spectra.

Harlow Shapley, 1885-1972, (U.S.) astronomer, noted for his studies of the galaxy.

Charles P. Steinmetz, 1865-1923, (G.-U.S.) electrical engineer, developed basic ideas on alternating current systems.

Leo Szilard, 1898-1964, (Hung.-U.S.) physicist, helped create first sustained nuclear reaction.

Nikola Tesla, 1856-1943, (Croatia-U.S.) electrical engineer, contributed to most developments in electronics.

Rudolf Virchow, 1821-1902, (G.) pathologist, a founder of cellular pathology.

Alessandro Volta, 1745-1827, (It.) physicist, pioneer in electricity.

Werner von Braun, 1912-1977 (G-U.S.) pioneered development of rockets for warfare and space exploration.

Alfred Russell Wallace, 1823-1913, (Br.) naturalist, proposed concept of evolution similar to Darwin.

August v. Wasserman, 1866-1925, (G.) bacteriologist, discovered reaction used as test for syphilis.

James E. Watt, 1736-1819, (Sc.) mechanical engineer, inventor, invented modern steam condensing engine.

Alfred L. Wegener, 1880-1930, (G.) meteorologist, geophysicist, postulated theory of continental drift.

Norbert Wiener, 1894-1964, (U.S.) mathematician, founder of the science of cybernetics.

Sewall Wright, 1889-1988 (U.S.) a leading evolutionary theorist.

Ferdinand v. Zeppelin, 1838-1917 (G.) soldier, aeronaut, airship designer.

Noted Business Leaders, Industrialists, and Philanthropists of the Past

Elizabeth Arden (F.N. Graham), 1884-1966, (U.S.) Canadian-born founder of cosmetics empire.

Philip D. Armour, 1832-1901, (U.S.) industrialist, streamlined meat packing.

John Jacob Astor, 1763-1848, (U.S.) German-born fur trader, banker, real estate magnate; at death, richest in U.S.

Francis W. Ayer, 1848-1923, (U.S.) ad industry pioneer.

August Belmont, 1816-1890, (U.S.) German-born financier.

James B. (Diamond Jim) Brady, 1856-1917, (U.S.) financier, philanthropist, legendary bon vivant.

Adolphus Busch, 1839-1913, (U.S.) German-born businessman, established brewery empire.

Asa Candler, 1851-1929, (U.S.) founded Coca-Cola Co.

Andrew Carnegie, 1835-1919, (U.S.) Scots-born industrialist, founded U.S. Steel; financed over 2,800 libraries.

Tom Carvel, 1908-1989, (Gr.-U.S.) founded ice cream chain.

William Colgate, 1783-1857, (U.S.) British-born businessman, philanthropist; founded soap-making empire.

Jay Cooke, 1821-1905, (U.S.) financier, sold $1 billion in Union bonds during Civil War.

Peter Cooper, 1791-1883, (U.S.) industrialist, inventor, philanthropist.

Ezra Cornell, 1807-1874, (U.S.) businessman, philanthropist; headed Western Union, established univ.

Erastus Corning, 1794-1872, (U.S.) financier, headed N.Y. Central.

Charles Crocker, 1822-1888, (U.S.) railroad builder, financier.

Samuel Cunard, 1787-1865, (Can.) pioneered trans-Atlantic steam navigation.

Marcus Daly, 1841-1900, (U.S.) Irish-born copper magnate.

George T. Delacorte, 1893-1991, (U.S.) publisher; Central Park donations included Alice in Wonderland statue.

Walt Disney, 1901-1966, (U.S.) pioneer in cinema animation, built entertainment empire.

Herbert H. Dow, 1866-1930, (U.S.) Canadian-born founder of chemical co.

James Duke, 1856-1925, (U.S.) founded American Tobacco, Duke Univ.

Eleuthere I. du Pont, 1771-1834, (U.S.) French-born gunpowder manufacturer; founded one of world's largest business empires.

Thomas C. Durant, 1820-1885, (U.S.) railroad official, financier.

William C. Durant, 1861-1947, (U.S.) industrialist, formed General Motors.

George Eastman, 1854-1932, (U.S.) inventor, manufacturer of photographic equipment.

Marshall Field, 1834-1906, (U.S.) merchant, founded Chicago's largest department store.
Harvey Firestone, 1868-1938, (U.S.) industrialist, founded tire co.
Henry M. Flagler, 1830-1913, (U.S.) financier, helped form Standard Oil; developed Florida as resort state.
Malcolm Forbes, 1919-1990, (U.S.) *Fortune* publisher.
Henry Ford, 1863-1947, (U.S.) auto maker, developed first popular low-priced car.
Henry Ford 2d, 1917-1987, (U.S.) headed auto company founded by grandfather.
Henry C. Frick, 1849-1919, (U.S.) industrialist, helped organize U.S. Steel.
Jakob Fugger (Jakob the Rich), 1459-1525, (G.) headed leading banking house, trading concern, in 16th-century Europe.
Alfred C. Fuller, 1885-1973, (U.S.) Canadian-born businessman, founded brush co.
Elbert H. Gary, 1846-1927, (U.S.) U.S. Steel head, 1903-27.
Amadeo P. Giannini, 1870-1949, (U.S.) founded Bank of America.
Stephen Girard, 1750-1831, (U.S.) French-born financier, philanthropist; richest man in U.S. at his death.
Jean Paul Getty, 1892-1976, (U.S.) founded oil empire.
Jay Gould, 1836-1892, (U.S.) railroad magnate, financier, speculator.
Hetty Green, 1834-1916, (U.S.) financier, the "witch of Wall St."; richest woman in U.S. in her day.
William Gregg, 1800-1867, (U.S.) launched textile industry in the South.
Meyer Guggenheim, 1828-1905, (U.S.) Swiss-born merchant, philanthropist; built merchandising, mining empires.
Armand Hammer, 1898-1990, (U.S.) headed Occidental Petroleum; promoted U.S.-Soviet ties.
Edward H. Harriman, 1848-1909, (U.S.) railroad financier, administrator; headed Union Pacific.
William Randolph Hearst, 1863-1951, (U.S.) a dominant figure in American journalism; built vast publishing empire.
Henry J. Heinz, 1844-1919, (U.S.) founded food empire.
James J. Hill, 1838-1916, (U.S.) Canadian-born railroad magnate, financier; founded Great Northern Railway.
Conrad N. Hilton, 1888-1979, (U.S.) intl. hotel chain founder.
Howard Hughes, 1905-1976, (U.S.) industrialist, financier, movie maker.
H.L. Hunt, 1889-1974, (U.S.) oil magnate.
Collis P. Huntington, 1821-1900, (U.S.) railroad magnate.
Henry E. Huntington, 1850-1927, (U.S.) railroad builder, philanthropist.
Walter L. Jacobs, 1898-1985, (U.S.) founder of the first rental car agency, which later became Hertz.
Howard Johnson, 1896-1972, (U.S.) founded restaurants.
Henry J. Kaiser, 1882-1967, (U.S.) industrialist, built empire in steel, aluminum.
Minor C. Keith, 1848-1929, (U.S.) railroad magnate; founded United Fruit Co.
Will K. Kellogg, 1860-1951, (U.S.) businessman, philanthropist, founded breakfast food co.
Richard King, 1825-1885, (U.S.) cattleman, founded half-million acre King Ranch in Texas.
William S. Knudsen, 1879-1948, (U.S.) Danish-born auto industry executive.
Samuel H. Kress, 1863-1955, (U.S.) businessman, art collector, philanthropist; founded "dime store" chain.
Ray A. Kroc, 1902-1984, (U.S.) builder of McDonald's fast food empire; owner, San Diego Padres baseball team.
Alfred Krupp, 1812-1887, (G.) armaments magnate.
Albert Lasker, 1880-1952, (U.S.) businessman, philanthropist.
Thomas Lipton, 1850-1931, (Scot.) merchant, built tea empire.
James McGill, 1744-1813, (Can.) Scots-born fur trader, founded univ.
Andrew W. Mellon, 1855-1937, (U.S.) financier, industrialist; benefactor of National Gallery of Art.
Charles E. Merrill, 1885-1956, (U.S.) financier, developed firm of Merrill Lynch.
John Pierpont Morgan, 1837-1913, (U.S.) most powerful figure in finance and industry at the turn-of-the-century.
Malcolm Muir, 1885-1979, (U.S.) created *Business Week* magazine; headed *Newsweek*, 1937-61.
Samuel Newhouse, 1895-1979, (U.S.) publishing and broadcasting magnate, built communications empire.
Aristotle Onassis, 1900-1975, (Gr.) shipping magnate.
William S. Paley, 1901-1989, (U.S.) built CBS communications empire.
George Peabody, 1795-1869, (U.S.) merchant, financier, philanthropist.
James C. Penney, 1875-1971, (U.S.) businessman, developed department store chain.
William C. Procter, 1862-1934, (U.S.) headed soap co.
John D. Rockefeller, 1839-1937, (U.S.) industrialist, established Standard Oil; became world's wealthiest person.
John D. Rockefeller Jr., 1874-1960, (U.S.) philanthropist, established foundation; provided land for United Nations.
Meyer A. Rothschild, 1743-1812, (G.) founded international banking house.
Thomas Fortune Ryan, 1851-1928, (U.S.) financier, dominated N.Y. City public transport; a founder of Amer. Tobacco.
Russell Sage, 1816-1906, (U.S.) financier.
David Sarnoff, 1891-1971, (U.S.) broadcasting pioneer, established first radio network, NBC.
Richard W. Sears, 1863-1914, (U.S.) founded mail-order co.
(Ernst) Werner von Siemens, 1816-1892, (G.) industrialist, inventor.
Alfred P. Sloan, 1875-1966, (U.S.) industrialist, philanthropist; headed General Motors.
A. Leland Stanford, 1824-1893, (U.S.) railroad official, philanthropist; founded univ.
Nathan Strauss, 1848-1931, (U.S.) German-born merchant, philanthropist; headed Macy's.
Levi Strauss, c.1829-1902, (U.S.) pants manufacturer.
Clement Studebaker, 1831-1901, (U.S.) wagon, carriage manufacturer.
Gustavus Swift, 1839-1903, (U.S.) pioneer meat-packer; promoted refrigerated railroad cars.
Gerard Swope, 1872-1957, (U.S.) industrialist, economist; headed General Electric.
James Walter Thompson, 1847-1928, (U.S.) ad executive.
Theodore N. Vail, 1845-1920, (U.S.) organized Bell Telephone system, headed ATT.
Cornelius Vanderbilt, 1794-1877, (U.S.) financier, established steamship, railroad empires.
Henry Villard, 1835-1900, (U.S.) German-born railroad executive, financier.
Charles R. Walgreen, 1873-1939, (U.S.) founded drugstore chain.
DeWitt Wallace, 1890-1981, (U.S.) and **Lila Wallace,** 1890-1984, (U.S.) co-founders of *Reader's Digest* magazine, philanthropists.
Sam Walton, 1918-1992, (U.S.) founder of Wal-Mart stores.
John Wanamaker, 1838-1922, (U.S.) pioneered department-store merchandising.
Aaron Montgomery Ward, 1843-1913, (U.S.) established first mail-order firm.
Thomas J. Watson, 1874-1956, (U.S.) headed IBM, 1924-49.
John Hay Whitney, 1905-1982, (U.S.) publisher, sportsman, philanthropist.
Charles E. Wilson, 1890-1961, (U.S.) auto industry executive; public official.
Frank W. Woolworth, 1852-1919, (U.S.) created 5 & 10 chain.
William Wrigley Jr., 1861-1932, (U.S.) founded chewing gum company.

Composers of the Western World

Carl Philipp Emanuel Bach, 1714-1788, (G.) Prussian and Wurtembergian Sonatas.
Johann Christian Bach, 1735-1782, (G.) Concertos; sonatas.
Johann Sebastian Bach, 1685-1750, (G.) St. Matthew Passion, The Well-Tempered Clavichord.
Samuel Barber, 1910-1981, (U.S.) Adagio for Strings, Vanessa.
Bela Bartok, 1881-1945, (Hung.) Concerto for Orchestra, The Miraculous Mandarin.
Ludwig Van Beethoven, 1770-1827, (G.) Concertos (Emperor); sonatas (Moonlight, Pastorale, Pathetique); symphonies (Eroica).
Vincenzo Bellini, 1801-1835, (It.) La Sonnambula, Norma, I Puritani.
Alban Berg, 1885-1935, (Aus.) Wozzeck, Lulu.
Hector Berlioz, 1803-1869, (F.) Damnation of Faust, Symphonie Fantastique, Requiem.
Leonard Bernstein, 1918-1990, (U.S.) Jeremiah, West Side Story.
Georges Bizet, 1838-1875, (F.) Carmen, Pearl Fishers.
Ernest Bloch, 1880-1959, (Swiss-U.S.) Schelomo, Voice in the Wilderness, Sacred Service.
Luigi Boccherini, 1743-1805, (It.) Cello Concerto in B Flat, Symphony in C.
Alexander Borodin, 1833-1887, (R.) Prince Igor, In the Steppes of Central Asia.
Johannes Brahms, 1833-1897, (G.) Liebeslieder Waltzes, Rhapsody in E Flat Major, Opus 119 for Piano, Academic Festival Overture; symphonies; quartets.
Benjamin Britten, 1913-1976, (Br.) Peter Grimes, Turn of the Screw, Ceremony of Carols, War Requiem.

Anton Bruckner, 1824-1896, (Aus.) Symphonies (Romantic), Intermezzo for String Quintet.
Ferruccio Busoni, 1866-1924, (It.) Doctor Faust, Comedy Overture.
Dietrich Buxtehude, 1637-1707, (D.) Cantatas, trio sonatas.
William Byrd, 1543-1623, (Br.) Masses, sacred songs.
(Alexis-) Emmanuel Chabrier, 1841-1894, (Fr.) Le Roi Malgre Lui, Espana.
Gustave Charpentier, 1860-1956, (F.) Louise.
Frederic Chopin, 1810-1849, (P.) Polonaises, mazurkas, waltzes, etudes, nocturnes. Polonaise No. 6 in A Flat Major (Heroic); sonatas.
Aaron Copland, 1900-1990, (U.S.) Appalachian Spring.
(Achille-) Claude Debussy, 1862-1918, (F.) Pelleas et Melisande, La Mer, Prelude to the Afternoon of a Faun.
C.P. Leo Delibes, 1836-1891, (F.) Lakme, Coppelia, Sylvia.
Norman Dello Joio, b. 1913, (U.S.), Triumph of St. Joan, Psalm of David.
Gaetano Donizetti, 1797-1848, (It.) Elixir of Love, Lucia Di Lammermoor, Daughter of the Regiment.
Paul Dukas, 1865-1935, (Fr.) Sorcerer's Apprentice.
Antonin Dvorak, 1841-1904, (C.) Symphony in E Minor (From the New World).
Edward Elgar, 1857-1934, (Br.) Pomp and Circumstance.
Manuel de Falla, 1876-1946, (Sp.) La Vide Breve, El Amor Brujo.
Gabriel Faure, 1845-1924, (Fr.) Requiem, Ballade.
Friedrich von Flotow, 1812-1883, (G.) Martha.
Cesar Franck, 1822-1890, (Belg.) D Minor Symphony.
George Gershwin, 1898-1937, (U.S.) Rhapsody in Blue, American in Paris, Porgy and Bess.
Umberto Giordano, 1867-1948, (It.) Andrea Chenier.
Alexander K. Glazunoff, 1865-1936, (R.) Symphonies, Stenka Razin.
Mikhail Glinka, 1804-1857, (R.) Ruslan and Ludmilla.
Christoph W. Gluck, 1714-1787, (G.) Alceste, Iphigenie en Tauride.
Charles Gounod, 1818-1893, (F.) Faust, Romeo and Juliet.
Edvard Grieg, 1843-1907, (Nor.) Peer Gynt Suite, Concerto in A Minor.
George Frederick Handel, 1685-1759, (G., Br.) Messiah, Xerxes, Berenice.
Howard Hanson, 1896-1981, (U.S.) Symphonies No. 1 (Nordic) and 2 (Romantic).
Roy Harris, 1898-1979, (U.S.) Symphonies, Amer. Portraits.
Joseph Haydn, 1732-1809, (Aus.) Symphonies (Clock); oratorios; chamber music.
Paul Hindemith, 1895-1963, (U.S.) Mathis Der Maler.
Gustav Holst, 1874-1934, (Br.) The Planets.
Arthur Honegger, 1892-1955, (Swiss) Judith, Le Roi David, Pacific 231.
Alan Hovhaness, b. 1911, (U.S.) Symphonies, Magnificat.
Engelbert Humperdinck, 1854-1921, (G.) Hansel and Gretel.
Charles Ives, 1874-1954, (U.S.) Third Symphony.
Aram Khachaturian, 1903-1978, (Armen.) Gayane (ballet), symphonies.
Zoltan Kodaly, 1882-1967, (Hung.) Hary Janos, Psalmus Hungaricus.
Fritz Kreisler, 1875-1962, (Aus.) Caprice Viennois, Tambourin Chinois.
Rodolphe Kreutzer, 1766-1831, (F.) 40 etudes for violin.
Edouard V.A. Lalo, 1823-1892, (F.) Symphonie Espagnole.
Ruggiero Leoncavallo, 1857-1919, (It.) Pagliacci.
Franz Liszt, 1811-1886, (Hung.) 20 Hungarian rhapsodies; symphonic poems.
Edward MacDowell, 1861-1908, (U.S.) To a Wild Rose.
Gustav Mahler, 1860-1911, (Aus.) Lied von der Erde.
Pietro Mascagni, 1863-1945, (It.) Cavalleria Rusticana.
Jules Massenet, 1842-1912, (F.) Manon, Le Cid, Thais.
Felix Mendelssohn, 1809-1847, (G.) Midsummer Night's Dream, Songs Without Words.
Gian-Carlo Menotti, b. 1911, (It.-U.S.) The Medium, The Consul, Amahl and the Night Visitors.
Giacomo Meyerbeer, 1791-1864, (G.) Robert le Diable, Les Huguenots.
Claudio Monteverdi, 1567-1643, (It.) Opera; masses; madrigals.
Wolfgang Amadeus Mozart, 1756-1791, (Aus.) Magic Flute, Marriage of Figaro; concertos; symphonies, etc.
Modest Moussorgsky, 1835-1881, (R.) Boris Godunov, Pictures at an Exhibition.
Jacques Offenbach, 1819-1880, (F.) Tales of Hoffmann.
Carl Orff, 1895-1982, (G.) Carmina Burana.
Ignace Paderewski, 1860-1941, (P.) Minuet in G.
Niccolo Paganini, 1782-1840, (It.) Violinist, many bravura variations for violin.
Giovanni P. da Palestrina, c. 1525-1594, (It.) Masses; madrigals.
Amilcare Ponchielli, 1834-1886, (It.) La Gioconda.
Francis Poulenc, 1899-1963, (F.) Dialogues des Carmelites.
Serge Prokofiev, 1891-1953, (R.) Love for Three Oranges, Lt. Kije, Peter and the Wolf.
Giacomo Puccini, 1858-1924, (It.) La Boheme, Manon Lescaut, Tosca, Madame Butterfly.
Sergei Rachmaninov, 1873-1943, (R.) 24 preludes, 4 concerti, 4 symphonies. Prelude in C Sharp Minor.
Maurice Ravel, 1875-1937, (Fr.) Bolero, Daphnis et Chloe, Rapsodie Espagnole.
Nikolai Rimsky-Korsakov, 1844-1908, (R.) Golden Cockerel, Capriccio Espagnol, Scheherazade, Russian Easter Overture.
Gioacchino Rossini, 1792-1868, (It.) Barber of Seville, Semiramide, William Tell.
Chas. Camille Saint-Saens, 1835-1921, (F.) Samson and Delilah, Danse Macabre.
Alessandro Scarlatti, 1660-1725, (It.) Cantatas; concertos.
Domenico Scarlatti, 1685-1757, (It.) Harpsichord sonatas.
Arnold Schoenberg, 1874-1951, (Aus.) Pelleas and Melisande, Transfigured Night, De Profundis.
Franz Schubert, 1797-1828, (A.) Lieder; symphonies (Unfinished); overtures (Rosamunde).
William Schuman, b. 1910, (U.S.) Credendum, New England Triptych.
Robert Schumann, 1810-1856, (G.) Symphonies, songs.
Aleksandr Scriabin, 1872-1915, (R.) Prometheus.
Dimitri Shostakovich, 1906-1975, (R.) Symphonies, Lady Macbeth of Mzensk, The Nose.
Jean Sibelius, 1865-1957, (Finn.) Finlandia, Karelia.
Bedrich Smetana, 1824-1884, (Cz.). The Bartered Bride.
Karlheinz Stockhausen, b. 1928, (G.) Kontrapunkte, Kontakte.
Richard Strauss, 1864-1949, (G.) Salome, Elektra, Der Rosenkavalier, Thus Spake Zarathustra.
Igor F. Stravinsky, 1882-1971, (R.-U.S.) Oedipus Rex, Le Sacre du Printemps, Petrushka.
Peter I. Tchaikovsky, 1840-1893, (R.) Nutcracker Suite, Swan Lake, Eugene Onegin.
Ambroise Thomas, 1811-1896, (F.) Mignon.
Virgil Thomson, 1896-1989, (U.S.) Opera, ballet; Four Saints in Three Acts.
Ralph Vaughan Williams, 1872-1958, (Br.) Job, London Symphony, Symphony No. 7 (Antartica).
Giuseppe Verdi, 1813-1901, (It.) Aida, Rigoletto, Don Carlo, Il Trovatore, La Traviata, Falstaff, Macbeth.
Heitor Villa-Lobos, 1887-1959, (Brazil) Choros.
Antonio Vivaldi, 1678-1741, (It.) Concerti, The Four Seasons.
Richard Wagner, 1813-1883, (G.) Rienzi, Tannhauser, Lohengrin, Tristan und Isolde.
Carl Maria von Weber, 1786-1826, (G.) Der Freischutz.

Composers of Operettas, Musicals, and Popular Music

Richard Adler, b. 1921, (U.S.) *Pajama Game; Damn Yankees.*
Milton Ager, 1893-1979, (U.S.) I Wonder What's Become of Sally; Hard Hearted Hannah; Ain't She Sweet?
Leroy Anderson, 1908-1975, (U.S.) Syncopated Clock.
Paul Anka, b. 1941, (Can.) My Way; She's a Lady; Tonight Show theme.
Harold Arlen, 1905-1986, (U.S.) Stormy Weather; Over the Rainbow; Blues in the Night; That Old Black Magic.
Burt Bacharach, b. 1928, (U.S.) Raindrops Keep Fallin' on My Head; Walk on By; What the World Needs Now is Love.
Ernest Ball, 1878-1927, (U.S.) Mother Machree; When Irish Eyes Are Smiling.
Irving Berlin, 1888-1989 (U.S.) *This is the Army; Annie Get Your Gun; Call Me Madam;* God Bless America; White Christmas.
Leonard Bernstein, 1918-1990, (U.S.) *On the Town; Wonderful Town; Candide; West Side Story.*
Eubie Blake, 1883-1983, (U.S.) *Shuffle Along;* I'm Just Wild about Harry.
Jerry Bock, b. 1928, (U.S.) *Mr. Wonderful; Fiorello; Fiddler on the Roof; The Rothschilds.*
Carrie Jacobs Bond, 1862-1946, (U.S.) I Love You Truly.
Nacio Herb Brown, 1896-1964, (U.S.) Singing in the Rain; You Were Meant for Me; All I Do Is Dream of You.
Hoagy Carmichael, 1899-1981, (U.S.) Stardust; Georgia on My Mind; Old Buttermilk Sky.
George M. Cohan, 1878-1942, (U.S.) Give My Regards to Broadway; You're A Grand Old Flag; Over There.
Cy Coleman, b. 1929, (U.S.) *Sweet Charity;* Witchcraft.
Noel Coward, 1899-1973 (Br.) *Bitter Sweet;* Mad Dogs and Englishmen; Mad About the Boy.
Walter Donaldson, 1893-1947, (U.S.) My Buddy; Carolina in the Morning; You're Driving Me Crazy; Makin' Whoopee.
Neil Diamond, b. 1941, (U.S.) I'm a Believer; Sweet Caroline.
Vernon Duke, 1903-1969, (U.S.) April in Paris.

Bob Dylan, b. 1941, (U.S.) Blowin' in the Wind.

Gus Edwards, 1879-1945, (U.S.) School Days; By the Light of the Silvery Moon; In My Merry Oldsmobile.

Sherman Edwards, 1919-1981, (U.S.) See You in September; Wonderful! Wonderful!

Duke Ellington, 1899-1974, (U.S.) Sophisticated Lady; Satin Doll; It Don't Mean a Thing; Solitude.

Sammy Fain, 1902-1989, (U.S.) I'll Be Seeing You; Love Is a Many-Splendored Thing.

Fred Fisher, 1875-1942, (U.S.) Peg O' My Heart; Chicago.

Stephen Collins Foster, 1826-1864, (U.S.) My Old Kentucky Home; Old Folks At Home.

Rudolf Friml, 1879-1972, (naturalized U.S.) *The Firefly; Rose Marie; Vagabond King; Bird of Paradise.*

John Gay, 1685-1732, (Br.) *The Beggar's Opera.*

George Gershwin, 1898-1937, (U.S.) Someone to Watch Over Me; I've Got a Crush on You; Embraceable You.

Ferde Grofe, 1892-1972, (U.S.) Grand Canyon Suite.

Marvin Hamlisch, b. 1944, (U.S.) The Way We Were, Nobody Does It Better, *A Chorus Line.*

W. C. Handy, 1873-1958, (U.S.) St. Louis Blues.

Ray Henderson, 1896-1970, (U.S.) *George White's Scandals;* That Old Gang of Mine; Five Foot Two, Eyes of Blue.

Victor Herbert, 1859-1924, (Ir.-U.S.) *Mlle. Modiste; Babes in Toyland; The Red Mill; Naughty Marietta; Sweethearts.*

Jerry Herman, b. 1932, (U.S.) *Hello Dolly; Mame.*

Brian Holland, b. 1941, **Lamont Dozier,** b. 1941, **Eddie Holland,** b. 1939, (all U.S.) Heat Wave; Stop! In the Name of Love; Baby, I Need Your Loving.

Scott Joplin, 1868-1917, (U.S.) *Treemonisha.*

John Kander, b. 1927, (U.S.) *Cabaret; Chicago; Funny Lady.*

Jerome Kern, 1885-1945, (U.S.) *Sally; Sunny; Show Boat.*

Carole King, b. 1942, (U.S.) Will You Love Me Tomorrow?; Natural Woman; One Fine Day; Up on the Roof.

Burton Lane, b. 1912, (U.S.) *Finian's Rainbow.*

Franz Lehar, 1870-1948, (Hung.) *Merry Widow.*

Jerry Leiber, & Mike Stoller, both b. 1933, (both U.S.) Hound Dog; Searchin'; Yakety Yak; Love Me Tender.

Mitch Leigh, b. 1928, (U.S.) *Man of La Mancha.*

John Lennon, 1940-1980, & **Paul McCartney,** b. 1942, (both Br.) I Want to Hold Your Hand; She Loves You; Hard Day's Night; Can't Buy Me Love; And I Love Her.

Frank Loesser, 1910-1969, (U.S.) *Guys and Dolls; Where's Charley?; The Most Happy Fella; How to Succeed ....*

Frederick Loewe, 1901-1988, (Aust.-U.S.) *The Day Before Spring; Brigadoon; Paint Your Wagon; My Fair Lady; Camelot.*

Henry Mancini, b. 1924, (U.S.) Moon River; Days of Wine and Roses; Pink Panther Theme.

Barry Mann, b. 1939, & **Cynthia Weil,** b. 1937, (both U.S.) You've Lost That Loving Feeling, Saturday Night at the Movies.

Jimmy McHugh, 1894-1969 (U.S.) Don't Blame Me; I'm in the Mood for Love; I Feel a Song Coming On.

Alan Menken, b. 1950, (U.S.) *Little Shop of Horrors.*

Joseph Meyer, 1894-1987, (U.S.) If You Knew Susie; California, Here I Come; Crazy Rhythm.

Chauncey Olcott, 1860-1932, (U.S.) Mother Machree.

Jerome "Doc" Pomus, 1925-1991, (U.S.) Save the Last Dance for Me, A Teenager in Love.

Cole Porter, 1893-1964, (U.S.) *Anything Goes; Kiss Me Kate; Can Can; Silk Stockings.*

Richard Rodgers, 1902-1979, (U.S.) *Connecticut Yankee; Oklahoma!; Carousel; South Pacific; The King and I; The Sound of Music.*

Smokey Robinson, b. 1940, (U.S.) Shop Around; My Guy; My Girl; Get Ready.

Sigmund Romberg, 1887-1951, (Hung.) *Maytime; The Student Prince; Desert Song; Blossom Time.*

Harold Rome, b. 1908, (U.S.) *Pins and Needles; Call Me Mister; Wish You Were Here; Fanny; Destry Rides Again.*

Vincent Rose, b. 1880-1944, (U.S.) Avalon; Whispering; Blueberry Hill.

Harry Ruby, 1895-1974, (U.S.) Three Little Words; Who's Sorry Now?

Arthur Schwartz, 1900-1984, (U.S.) *The Band Wagon;* Dancing in the Dark; By Myself; That's Entertainment.

Neil Sedaka, b. 1939, (U.S.) Breaking Up Is Hard to Do.

Paul Simon, b. 1942, (U.S.) Sounds of Silence; I Am a Rock; Mrs. Robinson; Bridge Over Troubled Waters.

Stephen Sondheim, b. 1930, (U.S.) *A Little Night Music; Company; Sweeney Todd; Sunday in the Park with George.*

John Philip Sousa. 1854-1932, (U.S.) *El Capitan;* Stars and Stripes Forever.

Oskar Straus, 1870-1954, (Aus.) *Chocolate Soldier.*

Johann Strauss, 1825-1899, (Aus.) *Gypsy Baron; Die Fledermaus;* waltzes: Blue Danube, Artist's Life.

Charles Strouse, b. 1928, (U.S.) *Bye Bye, Birdie; Annie.*

Jule Styne, b. 1905, (b. Br.-U.S.) *Gentlemen Prefer Blondes; Bells Are Ringing; Gypsy; Funny Girl.*

Arthur S. Sullivan, 1842-1900, (Br.) *H.M.S. Pinafore, Pirates of Penzance; The Mikado.*

Deems Taylor, 1885-1966, (U.S.) *Peter Ibbetson.*

Egbert van Alstyne, 1882-1951, (U.S.) In the Shade of the Old Apple Tree; Memories; Pretty Baby.

Jimmy Van Heusen, 1913-1990, (U.S.) Moonlight Becomes You; Swinging on a Star; All the Way; Love and Marriage.

Albert von Tilzer, 1878-1956, (U.S.) I'll Be With You in Apple Blossom Time; Take Me Out to the Ball Game.

Harry von Tilzer, 1872-1946, (U.S.) Only a Bird in a Gilded Cage; On a Sunday Afternoon.

Fats Waller, 1904-1943, (U.S.) Honeysuckle Rose; Ain't Misbehavin'.

Harry Warren, 1893-1981, (U.S.) You're My Everything; We're in the Money; I Only Have Eyes for You.

Jimmy Webb, b. 1946, (U.S.) Up, Up and Away; By the Time I Get to Phoenix; Didn't We?; Wichita Lineman.

Andrew Lloyd Webber, b. 1948, (Br.) *Jesus Christ Superstar, Evita, Cats, The Phantom of the Opera.*

Kurt Weill, 1900-1950, (G.-U.S.) *Threepenny Opera; Lady in the Dark; Knickerbocker Holiday; One Touch of Venus.*

Percy Wenrich, 1887-1952, (U.S.) When You Wore a Tulip; Moonlight Bay; Put On Your Old Gray Bonnet.

Richard A. Whiting, 1891-1938, (U.S.) Till We Meet Again; Sleepytime Gal; Beyond the Blue Horizon; My Ideal.

John Williams, b. 1932, (U.S.) *Jaws, E.T., Star Wars* series, *Raiders of the Lost Ark* series.

Meredith Willson, 1902-1984, (U.S.) *The Music Man.*

Stevie Wonder, b. 1950, (U.S.) You Are the Sunshine of My Life; Signed, Sealed, Delivered, I'm Yours.

Vincent Youmans, 1898-1946, (U.S.) *Two Little Girls in Blue; Wildflower; No, No, Nanette; Hit the Deck; Rainbow; Smiles.*

Lyricists

Howard Ashman, 1951-1991, (U.S.) *Little Shop of Horrors, The Little Mermaid.*

Johnny Burke, 1908-1984, (U.S.) What's New?; Misty; Imagination; Polka Dots and Moonbeams.

Sammy Cahn, b. 1913, (U.S.) High Hopes; Love and Marriage; The Second Time Around; It's Magic.

Betty Comden, b. 1919 (U.S.) and **Adolph Green,** b. 1915 (U.S.) The Party's Over; Just in Time; New York, New York.

Hal David, b. 1921 (U.S.) What the World Needs Now Is Love; Close to You.

Buddy De Sylva, 1895-1950, (U.S.) When Day is Done; Look for the Silver Lining; April Showers.

Howard Dietz, 1896-1983, (U.S.) Dancing in the Dark; You and the Night and the Music; That's Entertainment.

Al Dubin, 1891-1945, (U.S.) Tiptoe Through the Tulips; Anniversary Waltz; Lullaby of Broadway.

Fred Ebb, b. 1936 (U.S.) *Cabaret, Zorba, Woman of the Year.*

Dorothy Fields, 1905-1974, (U.S.) On the Sunny Side of the Street; Don't Blame Me; The Way You Look Tonight.

Ira Gershwin, 1896-1983, (U.S.) The Man I Love; Fascinating Rhythm; S'Wonderful; Embraceable You.

William S. Gilbert, 1836-1911, (Br.) *The Mikado; H.M.S. Pinafore, Pirates of Penzance.*

Gerry Goffin, b. 1939, (U.S.) Will You Love Me Tomorrow, Take Good Care of My Baby, Up on the Roof, One Fine Day.

Mack Gordon, 1905-1959, (Pol.-U.S.) You'll Never Know; The More I See You; Chattanooga Choo-Choo.

Oscar Hammerstein II, 1895-1960, (U.S.) Ol' Man River; *Oklahoma; Carousel.*

E. Y. (Yip) Harburg, 1898-1981, (U.S.) Brother, Can You Spare a Dime; April in Paris; Over the Rainbow.

Lorenz Hart, 1895-1943, (U.S.) Isn't It Romantic; Blue Moon; Lover; Manhattan; My Funny Valentine; Mountain Greenery.

DuBose Heyward, 1885-1940, (U.S.) Summertime; A Woman Is A Sometime Thing.

Gus Kahn, 1886-1941, (U.S.) Memories; Ain't We Got Fun.

Alan J. Lerner, 1918-1986, (U.S.) *Brigadoon; My Fair Lady; Camelot; Gigi.; On a Clear Day You Can See Forever.*

Johnny Mercer, 1909-1976, (U.S.) Blues in the Night; Come Rain or Come Shine; Laura; That Old Black Magic.

Bob Merrill, b. 1921, (U.S.) People; Don't Rain on My Parade.

Jack Norworth, 1879-1959, (U.S.) Take Me Out to the Ball Game; Shine On Harvest Moon.

Mitchell Parish, b. 1901, (U.S.) Stairway to the Stars; Stardust.

Andy Razaf, 1895-1973, (U.S.) Honeysuckle Rose, Ain't Misbehavin', S'posin'.

Leo Robin, 1900-1984, (U.S.) Thanks for the Memory; Hooray for Love; Diamonds are a Girl's Best Friend.

Paul Francis Webster, 1907-1984, (U.S.) I Got It Bad and That Ain't Good, Secret Love, The Shadow of Your Smile, Love Is a Many-Splendored Thing.

Jack Yellen, 1892-1991, (U.S.) Down by the O-Hi-O; Ain't She Sweet; Happy Days Are Here Again.

Noted Jazz Artists

Jazz has been called America's only completely unique contribution to Western culture. The following individuals have made major contributions in this field:

Julian "Cannonball" Adderley, 1928-1975: alto sax.
Louis "Satchmo" Armstrong, 1900-1971: trumpet, singer; originated the "scat" vocal.
Mildred Bailey, 1907-1951: blues singer.
Chet Baker, 1929-1988: trumpet.
Count Basie, 1904-1984: orchestra leader, piano.
Sidney Bechet, 1897-1959: early innovator, soprano sax.
Bix Beiderbecke, 1903-1931: cornet, piano, composer.
Bunny Berigan, 1909-1942: trumpet, singer.
Barney Bigard, 1906-1980: clarinet.
Art Blakey, 1919-1990: drums, leader.
Jimmy Blanton, 1921-1942: bass.
Charles "Buddy" Bolden, 1868-1931: cornet; formed the first jazz band in the 1890s.
Big Bill Broonzy, 1893-1958: blues singer, guitar.
Clifford Brown, 1930-1956: trumpet.
Ray Brown, b. 1926: bass.
Dave Brubeck, b. 1920: piano, combo leader.
Don Byas, 1912-1972: tenor sax.
Harry Carney, 1910-1974: baritone sax.
Benny Carter, b. 1907: alto sax, trumpet, clarinet.
Ron Carter, b. 1937: bass, cello.
Sidney Catlett, 1910-1951: drums.
Charlie Christian, 1919-1942: guitar.
Kenny Clarke, 1914-1985: pioneer of modern drums.
Buck Clayton, b. 1911: trumpet, arranger.
Al Cohn, 1925-1988: tenor sax, composer.
Cozy Cole, 1909-1981: drums.
Ornette Coleman, b. 1930: saxophone; unorthodox style.
John Coltrane, 1926-1967: tenor sax innovator.
Eddie Condon, 1904-1973: guitar, band leader; promoter of Dixieland.
Chick Corea, b. 1941: pianist, composer.
Tadd Dameron, 1917-1965: piano, composer.
Eddie "Lockjaw" Davis, 1921-1986: tenor sax.
Miles Davis, b. 1926: trumpet; pioneer of cool jazz.
Wild Bill Davison, 1906-1989: cornet, leader; prominent in early Chicago jazz.
Buddy De Franco, b. 1933: clarinet.
Paul Desmond, 1924-1977: alto sax.
Vic Dickenson, 1906-1984: trombone, composer.
Warren "Baby" Dodds, 1898-1959: Dixieland drummer.
Johnny Dodds, 1892-1940: clarinet.
Eric Dolphy, 1928-1964: alto sax, composer.
Jimmy Dorsey, 1904-1957: clarinet, alto sax; band leader.
Tommy Dorsey, 1905-1956: trombone; band leader.
Roy Eldridge, 1911-1989: trumpet, drums, singer.
Duke Ellington, 1899-1974: piano, band leader, composer.
Bill Evans, 1929-1980: piano.
Gil Evans, 1912-1988: composer, arranger, piano.
Ella Fitzgerald, b. 1918: singer.
"Red" Garland, 1923-1984; piano.
Erroll Garner, 1921-1977: piano, composer, "Misty."
Stan Getz, 1927-1991: tenor sax.
Dizzy Gillespie, b. 1917: trumpet, composer; bop developer.
Benny Goodman, 1909-1986: clarinet, band and combo leader.
Dexter Gordon, 1923-1990: tenor sax; bop-derived style.
Stephane Grappelli, b. 1908: violin.
Bobby Hackett, 1915-1976: trumpet, cornet.
Lionel Hampton, b. 1913: vibes, drums, piano, combo leader.
Herbie Hancock, b. 1940: piano, composer.
W. C. Handy, 1873-1958: composer, "St. Louis Blues."
Coleman Hawkins, 1904-1969: tenor sax; 1939 recording of "Body and Soul" a classic.
Roy Haynes, b. 1926: drums.
Fletcher Henderson, 1898-1952: orchestra leader, arranger; pioneered jazz and dance bands of the 30s.
Woody Herman, 1913-87: clarinet, alto sax, band leader.
Jay C. Higginbotham, 1906-1973: trombone.
Earl "Fatha" Hines, 1905-1983: piano, songwriter.
Johnny Hodges, 1906-1971: alto sax.
Billie Holiday, 1915-1959: blues singer, "Strange Fruit."
Sam "Lightnin' " Hopkins, 1912-1982: blues singer, guitar.
Mahalia Jackson, 1911-1972: gospel singer.
Milt Jackson, b. 1923: vibes, piano, guitar.
Illinois Jacquet, b. 1922: tenor sax.
Keith Jarrett, b. 1945: technically phenomenal pianist.
Blind Lemon Jefferson, 1897-1930: blues singer, guitar.
Bunk Johnson, 1879-1949: cornet, trumpet.
James P. Johnson, 1891-1955: piano, composer.
J. J. Johnson, b. 1924: trombone, composer.
Elvin Jones, b. 1927: drums.
Jo Jones, 1911-1985: drums.
Philly Joe Jones, 1923-1985: drums.
Quincy Jones, b. 1933: arranger.
Thad Jones, 1923-1986: trumpet, cornet.
Scott Joplin, 1868-1917: composer; "Maple Leaf Rag."
Stan Kenton, 1912-1979: orchestra leader, composer, piano.
Barney Kessel, b. 1923: guitar.
Lee Konitz, b. 1927: alto sax.
Gene Krupa, 1909-1973: drums, band and combo leader.
Scott LaFaro, 1936-1961: bass.
Huddie Ledbetter (Leadbelly), 1888-1949: blues singer, guitar.
John Lewis, b. 1920: composer, piano, combo leader.
Mel Lewis, 1929-1990: drummer, orchestra leader.
Jimmie Lunceford, 1902-1947: band leader, sax.
Herbie Mann, b. 1930: flute.
Wynton Marsalis, b. 1961: trumpet.
Jimmy McPartland, b. 1907: trumpet.
Marian McPartland, b. 1920: piano.
Glenn Miller, 1904-1944: trombone, dance band leader.
Charles Mingus, 1922-1979: bass, composer, combo leader.
Thelonious Monk, 1920-1982: piano, composer, combo leader; a developer of bop.
Wes Montgomery, 1925-1968: guitar.
"Jelly Roll" Morton, 1885-1941: composer, piano, singer.
Bennie Moten, 1894-1935: piano; an early organizer of large jazz orchestras.
Gerry Mulligan, b. 1927: baritone sax, arranger, leader.
Turk Murphy, 1915-1987: trombone, band leader.
Theodore "Fats" Navarro, 1923-1950: trumpet.
Red Nichols, 1905-1965: cornet, combo leader.
Red Norvo, b. 1908: vibes, band leader.
Anita O'Day, b. 1919: singer.
King Oliver, 1885-1938: cornet, band leader; teacher of Louis Armstrong.
Sy Oliver, 1910-1988: Swing Era arranger, composer, conductor.
Kid Ory, 1886-1973: trombone, "Muskrat Ramble".
Charlie "Bird" Parker, 1920-1955: alto sax, composer; rated by many as the greatest jazz improviser.
Art Pepper, 1925-1982: alto sax.
Oscar Peterson, b. 1925: piano, composer, combo leader.
Oscar Pettiford, 1922-1960: a leading bassist in the bop era.
Bud Powell, 1924-1966: piano; modern jazz pioneer.
Tito Puente, b. 1923: band leader.
Sun Ra, b. 1915?: big band leader, pianist, composer.
Gertrude "Ma" Rainey, 1886-1939: blues singer.
Don Redman, 1900-1964: composer, arranger; pioneer in the evolution of the large orchestra.
Django Reinhardt, 1910-1953: guitar; Belgian gypsy, first European to influence American jazz.
Buddy Rich, 1917-1987: drums, band leader.
Max Roach, b. 1925: drums.
Sonny Rollins, b. 1929: tenor sax.
Frank Rosollino, 1926-1978: trombone.
Jimmy Rushing, 1903-1972: blues singer.
George Russell, b. 1923: composer, piano.
Pee Wee Russell, 1906-1969: clarinet.
Artie Shaw, b. 1910: clarinet, combo leader.
George Shearing, b. 1919: piano, composer.
Horace Silver, b. 1928: piano, combo leader.
Zoot Sims, 1925-1985: tenor, alto sax; clarinet.
Zutty Singleton, 1898-1975: Dixieland drummer.
Bessie Smith, 1894-1937: blues singer.
Clarence "Pinetop" Smith, 1904-1929: piano, singer; pioneer of boogie woogie.
Willie "The Lion" Smith, 1897-1973: stride style pianist.
Muggsy Spanier, 1906-1967: cornet, band leader.
Billy Strayhorn, 1915-67: composer, piano.
Sonny Stitt, 1924-1982: alto, tenor sax.
Art Tatum, 1910-1956: piano; technical virtuoso.
Billy Taylor, b. 1921: piano, composer.
Cecil Taylor, b. 1933: piano, composer.
Jack Teagarden, 1905-1964: trombone, singer.
Dave Tough, 1908-1948: drums.
Lennie Tristano, 1919-1978: piano, composer.
Joe Turner, 1911-1985: blues singer.
McCoy Tyner, b. 1938: piano, composer.
Sarah Vaughan, 1924-1990: singer.

Joe Venuti, 1904-1978: first great jazz violinist.
Thomas "Fats" Waller, 1904-1943: piano, singer, composer. "Ain't Misbehavin' ".
Dinah Washington, 1924-1963: singer.
Chick Webb, 1902-1939: band leader, drums.
Ben Webster, 1909-1973: tenor sax.
Paul Whiteman, 1890-1967: orchestra leader; a major figure in the introduction of jazz to a large audience.
Charles "Cootie" Williams, 1908-1985: trumpet, band leader.
Mary Lou Williams, 1914-1981: piano, composer.
Teddy Wilson, 1912-1986: piano, composer.
Kai Winding, 1922-1983: trombone, composer.
Jimmy Yancey, 1894-1951: piano.
Lester "Pres" Young, 1909-1959: tenor sax, composer: a bop pioneer.

Rock & Roll Notables

For more than a quarter of a century, rock & roll has been an important force in American popular culture. The following individuals or groups have made a significant impact. Next to each is an associated single record or record album.

Paula Abdul: "Forever Your Girl"
Aerosmith: "Sweet Emotion"
The Allman Brothers Band: "Ramblin' Man"
The Animals: "House of the Rising Sun"
Paul Anka: "Lonely Boy"
The Association: "Cherish"
Frankie Avalon: "Venus"

The Band: "The Weight"
The Beach Boys: "Surfin' U.S.A."
The Beatles: *Sergeant Pepper's Lonely-Hearts Club Band*
The Bee Gees: "Stayin' Alive"
Pat Benatar: "Hit Me With Your Best Shot"
Chuck Berry: "Johnny B. Goode"
The Big Bopper: "Chantilly Lace"
Black Sabbath: "Paranoid"
Blind Faith: "Can't Find My Way Home"
Blondie: "Heart of Glass"
Blood, Sweat and Tears: "Spinning Wheel"
Bon Jovi: *Slippery When Wet*
Gary "U.S." Bonds: "Quarter to Three"
Booker T. and the MGs: "Green Onions"
Earl Bostic: "Flamingo"
David Bowie: "Let's Dance"
James Brown: "Papa's Got a Brand New Bag"
Jackson Browne: "Doctor My Eyes"
Buffalo Springfield: "For What It's Worth"
The Byrds: "Turn! Turn! Turn!"

Canned Heat: "Going Up the Country"
The Cars: "Shake It Up"
Tracy Chapman: "Fast Car"
Ray Charles: "Georgia on My Mind"
Chubby Checker: "The Twist"
Chicago: "Saturday in the Park"
Eric Clapton: "Layla"
The Coasters: "Yakety Yak"
Eddie Cochran: "Summertime Blues"
Phil Collins: "Another Day in Paradise"
Sam Cooke: "You Send Me"
Alice Cooper: "School's Out"
Elvis Costello: "Alison"
Cream: "Sunshine of Your Love"
Credence Clearwater Revival: "Proud Mary"
Crosby, Stills, Nash and Young: "Suite: Judy Blue Eyes"
The Crystals: "Da Doo Ron Ron"

DJ Jazzy Jeff & the Fresh Prince: "Summertime"
Danny and the Juniors: "At the Hop"
Bobby Darin: "Splish Splash"
Spencer Davis Group: "Gimme Some Lovin' "
Bo Diddley: "Who Do You Love?"
Dion and the Belmonts: "A Teenager in Love"
Dire Straits: *Brothers in Arms*
Fats Domino: "Blueberry Hill"
The Doobie Brothers: "What a Fool Believes"
The Doors: "Light My Fire"
The Drifters: "Save the Last Dance for Me"
Bob Dylan: "Like a Rolling Stone"

The Eagles: "Hotel California"
Earth, Wind and Fire: "Shining Star"
Emerson, Lake and Palmer: "From the Beginning"
The Eurythmics: "Sweet Dreams (Are Made of This)"
Everly Brothers: "Wake Up Little Susie"

The Five Satins: "In the Still of the Night"
Fleetwood Mac: *Rumours*
The Four Seasons: "Sherry"
The Four Tops: "I Can't Help Myself"
Aretha Franklin: "Respect"

Marvin Gaye: "I Heard It through the Grapevine"
Grand Funk Railroad: "We're an American Band"
The Grateful Dead: "Truckin' "
Guns 'N Roses: *Appetite for Destruction*

Bill Haley and the Comets: "Rock Around the Clock"
M.C. Hammer: "U Can't Touch This"
Jimi Hendrix: *Are You Experienced?*
Buddy Holly and the Crickets: "That'll Be the Day"
Whitney Houston: "The Greatest Love"

The Isley Brothers: "It's Your Thing"

The Jackson 5/The Jacksons: "ABC"
Janet Jackson: *Rhythm Nation*
Michael Jackson: *Thriller*
Tommy James & The Shondells: "Crimson and Clover"
Jay and the Americans: "This Magic Moment"
The Jefferson Airplane/Jefferson Starship: "White Rabbit"
Jethro Tull: *Aqualung*
Joan Jett: "I Love Rock' n' Roll"
Billy Joel: "Piano Man"
Elton John: "Sad Songs"
Janis Joplin: "Me and Bobby McGee"

Chaka Khan: "I Feel for You"
B.B. King: "The Thrill Is Gone"
Carole King: *Tapestry*
The Kinks: "You Really Got Me"
Kiss: "Rock' n' Roll All Night"
Gladys Knight and the Pips: "Midnight Train to Georgia"

L.L. Cool: "Mama Said Knock You Out"
Led Zeppelin: "Stairway to Heaven"
Brenda Lee: "I'm Sorry"
Jerry Lee Lewis: "Whole Lotta Shakin' Going On"
Little Anthony and the Imperials: "Tears on My Pillow"
Little Richard: "Tutti Frutti"
Lovin Spoonful: "Do You Believe in Magic?"
Frankie Lymon: "Why Do Fools Fall in Love?"
Lynyrd Skynyrd: "Freebird"

Madonna: "Material Girl"
The Mamas and the Papas: "Monday, Monday"
Bob Marley: "Jamming"
Martha and the Vandellas: "Dancin' in the Streets"
The Marvelettes: "Please Mr. Postman"
Clyde McPhatter: "Money Honey"
John Mellencamp: "Hurt So Good"
George Michael: *Faith*
Joni Mitchell: "Big Yellow Taxi"
The Monkees: "I'm a Believer"
Moody Blues: "Nights in White Satin"

Rick Nelson: "Hello Mary Lou"

Roy Orbison: "Oh Pretty Woman"

Carl Perkins: "Blue Suede Shoes"
Tom Petty and the Heartbreakers: "Refugee"
Pink Floyd: *The Wall*
Poco: *Deliverin'*
The Police: "Every Breath You Take"
Iggy Pop: "Lust for Life"
Elvis Presley: "Love Me Tender"
The Pretenders: *Learning to Crawl*
Lloyd Price: "Stagger Lee"
Prince: "Purple Rain"
Procul Harum: "A Whiter Shade of Pale"
Public Enemy: "Fight the Power"

Queen: "Bohemian Rhapsody"

The Rascals: "Good Lovin' "
Otis Redding: "The Dock of the Bay"
Lou Reed: "Walk on the Wild Side"
Righteous Brothers: "You've Lost that Lovin' Feeling"
Johnny Rivers: "Poor Side of Town"
Smokey Robinson and the Miracles: "Ooh Baby Baby"

The Rolling Stones: "Satisfaction"
The Ronettes: "Be My Baby"
Linda Ronstadt: "You're No Good"
Run D.M.C.: "Raisin' Hell"

Sam and Dave: "Soul Man"
Santana: "Black Magic Woman"
Neil Sedaka: "Breaking Up is Hard to Do"
Del Shannon: "Runaway"
The Shirelles: "Soldier Boy"
Simon and Garfunkel: "Bridge Over Troubled Water"
Carly Simon: "You're So Vain"
Sly and the Family Stone: "Everyday People"
Patti Smith: "Because the Night"
Southside Johnny and the Asbury Jukes: *This Time*
Dusty Springfield: "You Don't Have to Say You Love Me"
Bruce Springsteen: "Born in the U.S.A."
Steely Dan: "Rikki Don't Lose That Number"
Steppenwolf: "Born to Be Wild"
Rod Stewart: "Maggie Mae"
Sting: "If You Love Somebody, Set Them Free"
Donna Summer: "She Works Hard for the Money"
The Supremes: "Stop! In the Name of Love"

Talking Heads: "Once in a Lifetime"
James Taylor: "You've Got a Friend"
The Temptations: "My Girl"
Three Dog Night: "Joy to the World"
Traffic: "Feelin' Alright"
Big Joe Turner: "Shake, Rattle & Roll"
Tina Turner: "What's Love Got to Do with It?"

U2: *Joshua Tree*

Van Halen: "Jump"

Dionne Warwick: "I'll Never Fall in Love Again"
Muddy Waters: "Rollin' Stone"
Mary Wells: "My Guy"
The Who: "My Generation"
Jackie Wilson: "That's Why"
Stevie Wonder: "You Are the Sunshine of My Life"

The Yardbirds: "For Your Love"
Yes: "Yours Is No Disgrace"

Frank Zappa/Mothers of Invention: *Sheik Yerbouti*

Entertainment Personalities — Where and When Born

Actors, Actresses, Dancers, Musicians, Producers, Directors, Radio-TV Performers, Singers
(As of mid-1992)

Name	Birthplace	Born
Abbado, Claudio	Milan, Italy	6/26/33
Abbott, George	Forestville, N.Y.	6/25/87
Abdul, Paula	San Fernando, Cal.	6/19/62
Abraham, F. Murray	Pittsburgh, Pa.	10/24/39
Acuff, Roy	Maynardville, Tenn.	9/15/03
Adams, Bryan	Vancouver, B.C.	11/5/59
Adams, Don	New York, N.Y.	4/19/26
Adams, Edie	Kingston, Pa.	4/16/29
Adams, Joey	New York, N.Y.	1/6/11
Adams, Mason	New York, N.Y.	2/26/19
Adams, Maud	Lulea, Sweden	2/12/45
Adjani, Isabelle	W. Germany	6/27/55
Agutter, Jenny	London, England	12/20/52
Aiello, Danny	New York, N.Y.	6/20/33
Aimee, Anouk	Paris, France	4/27/32
Akins, Claude	Nelson, Ga.	5/25/18
Albanese, Licia	Bari, Italy	7/22/13
Alberghetti, Anna Maria	Pesaro, Italy	5/15/36
Albert, Eddie	Rock Island, Ill.	4/22/08
Alda, Alan	New York, N.Y.	1/28/36
Alexander, Jane	Boston, Mass.	10/28/39
Alexander, Jason	Newark, N.J.	9/23/59
Allen, Debbie	Houston, Tex.	1/16/50
Allen, Joan	Rochelle, Ill.	8/20/56
Allen, Karen	Carrollton, Ill.	10/5/51
Allen, Mel	Birmingham, Ala.	2/14/13
Allen, Nancy	New York, N.Y.	6/24/49
Allen, Steve	New York, N.Y.	12/26/21
Allen, Tim	Denver, Col.	6/13/-
Allen, Woody	Brooklyn, N.Y.	12/1/35
Alley, Kirstie	Wichita, Kan.	1/12/55
Allman, Gregg	Nashville, Tenn.	12/7/47
Allyson, June	New York, N.Y.	10/7/17
Alonso, Maria Conchita	Cuba	1957
Alpert, Herb	Los Angeles, Cal.	3/31/35
Altman, Robert	Kansas City, Mo.	2/20/25
Ameche, Don	Kenosha, Wis.	5/31/08
Ames, Ed	Boston, Mass.	7/9/27
Ames, Leon	Portland, Ind.	1/20/03
Amos, John	Newark, N.J.	12/27/42
Amsterdam, Morey	Chicago, Ill.	12/14/14
Anderson, Harry	Newport, R.I.	10/14/49
Anderson, Ian	Dunfermline, Scotland	8/10/47
Anderson, Loni	St. Paul, Minn.	8/5/46
Anderson, Lynn	Grand Forks, N.D.	9/26/47
Anderson, Marian	Philadelphia, Pa.	2/17/02
Anderson, Melissa Sue	Berkeley, Cal.	9/26/62
Anderson, Richard	Long Branch, N.J.	8/8/26
Anderson, Richard Dean	Minneapolis, Minn.	1/23/53
Andersson, Bibi	Stockholm, Sweden	11/11/35
Andress, Ursula	Bern, Switzerland	3/19/36
Andrews, Anthony	London, England	1/12/48
Andrews, Dana	Collins, Miss.	1/1/09
Andrews, Julie	Walton, England	10/1/35
Andrews, Maxene	Minneapolis, Minn.	1/3/18
Andrews, Patty	Minneapolis, Minn.	2/16/20
Anka, Paul	Ottawa, Ont.	7/30/41
Ann-Margret	Stockholm, Sweden	4/28/41
Anspach, Susan	New York, N.Y.	11/23/39
Anton, Susan	Oak Glen, Cal.	10/12/50
Applegate, Christina	Los Angeles, Cal.	11/25/72
Archer, Anne	Los Angeles, Cal.	8/25/50
Arkin, Alan	New York, N.Y.	3/26/34
Arnaz, Desi Jr.	Los Angeles, Cal.	1/19/53
Arnaz, Lucie	Hollywood, Cal.	7/17/51
Arness, James	Minneapolis, Minn.	5/26/23
Arnold, Eddy	Henderson, Tenn.	5/15/18
Arnold, Roseanne	Salt Lake City, Ut.	11/3/52
Arquette, Rosanna	New York, N.Y.	8/10/59
Arroyo, Martina	New York, N.Y.	2/2/37
Arthur, Beatrice	New York, N.Y.	5/13/26
Ashley, Elizabeth	Ocala, Fla.	8/30/41
Asner, Ed	Kansas City, Mo.	11/15/29
Assante, Armand	New York, N.Y.	10/4/49
Astin, John	Baltimore, Md.	3/30/30
Atherton, William	New Haven, Conn.	7/30/47
Atkins, Chet	Luttrell, Tenn.	6/20/24
Attenborough, Richard	Cambridge, England	8/29/23
Auberjonois, Rene	New York, N.Y.	6/1/40
Aumont, Jean-Pierre	Paris, France	1/5/09
Austin, Patti	New York, N.Y.	8/10/48
Autry, Alan	Shreveport, La.	7/31/52
Autry, Gene	Tioga, Tex.	9/29/07
Avalon, Frankie	Philadelphia, Pa.	9/18/39
Ax, Emmanuel	Lvov, USSR	6/8/49
Axton, Hoyt	Duncan, Okla.	3/25/38
Aykroyd, Dan	Ottawa, Ont.	7/1/52
Ayres, Lew	Minneapolis, Minn.	12/28/08
Aznavour, Charles	Paris, France	5/22/24
Bacall, Lauren	New York, N.Y.	9/16/24
Bacon, Kevin	Philadelphia, Pa.	7/8/58
Baez, Joan	Staten Island, N.Y.	1/9/41
Bain, Conrad	Lethbridge, Alta.	2/4/23
Baio, Scott	Brooklyn, N.Y.	9/22/61
Baker, Anita	Toledo, Oh.	1/26/58
Baker, Carroll	Johnstown, Pa.	5/28/31
Baker, Joe Don	Groesbeck, Tex.	2/12/36
Bakula, Scott	St. Louis, Mo.	10/9/-
Baldwin, Alec	Massapequa, N.Y.	4/3/58
Baldwin, William	Massapequa, N.Y.	1963
Ballard, Kaye	Cleveland, Oh.	11/20/26
Balsam, Martin	New York, N.Y.	11/4/19
Bancroft, Anne	New York, N.Y.	9/17/31
Banks, Jonathan	Washington, D.C.	1/31/47
Bannon, Jack	Los Angeles, Cal.	6/14/40
Barber, Red	Columbus, Miss.	2/17/08
Bardot, Brigitte	Paris, France	9/28/34
Barker, Bob	Darrington, Wash.	12/12/23
Barkin, Ellen	New York, N.Y.	4/16/55
Barrault, Jean-Louis	Vesinet, France	9/8/10

Name	Birthplace	Born
Barrie, Barbara	Chicago, Ill.	5/23/31
Barry, Gene	New York, N.Y.	6/14/19
Barty, Billy	Millsboro, Pa.	10/25/24
Baryshnikov, Mikhail	Riga, Latvia	1/28/48
Basinger, Kim	Athens, Ga.	12/8/53
Bassey, Shirley	Cardiff, Wales.	1/8/37
Bateman, Jason	Rye, N.Y.	1/14/69
Bateman, Justine	Rye, N.Y.	2/19/66
Bates, Alan	Allestree, England	2/17/34
Bates, Kathy	Memphis, Tenn.	6/28/48
Battle, Kathleen	Portsmouth, Oh.	8/13/48
Baxter, Meredith	Los Angeles, Cal.	6/21/47
Beal, John	Joplin, Mo.	8/13/09
Bean, Orson	Burlington, Vt.	7/22/28
Beasley, Allyce	New York, N.Y.	7/6/54
Beatty, Ned	Louisville, Ky.	7/6/37
Beatty, Warren	Richmond, Va.	3/30/37
Beck, John	Chicago, Ill.	1/28/43
Bedelia, Bonnie	New York, N.Y.	3/25/48
Beery, Noah Jr.	New York, N.Y.	8/10/13
Begley, Ed Jr.	Los Angeles, Cal.	9/16/49
Belafonte, Harry	New York, N.Y.	3/1/27
Bel Geddes, Barbara	New York, N.Y.	10/31/22
Belmondo, Jean-Paul	Neuilly-sur-Seine, France	4/9/33
Belushi, Jim	Chicago, Ill.	6/15/54
Benatar, Pat	Brooklyn, N.Y.	1/10/53
Benedict, Dirk	Helena, Mont.	3/1/45
Bening, Annette	Topeka, Kan.	1958
Benjamin, Richard	New York, N.Y.	5/22/38
Bennett, Tony	New York, N.Y.	8/3/26
Benson, George	Pittsburgh, Pa.	3/22/43
Benson, Robby	Dallas, Tex.	1/21/55
Beradino, John	Los Angeles, Cal.	5/1/17
Berenger, Tom	Chicago, Ill.	5/31/50
Bergen, Candice	Beverly Hills, Cal.	5/9/46
Bergen, Polly	Knoxville, Tenn.	7/14/30
Bergerac, Jacques	Biarritz, France	5/26/27
Bergman, Ingmar	Uppsala, Sweden	7/14/18
Berle, Milton	New York, N.Y.	7/12/08
Berlinger, Warren	Brooklyn, N.Y.	8/31/37
Berman, Lazar	Leningrad, USSR	2/26/30
Berman, Shelley	Chicago, Ill.	2/3/26
Bernard, Crystal	Houston, Tex.	9/30/-
Bernhard, Sandra	Flint, Mich.	1955
Bernsen, Corbin	No. Hollywood, Cal.	9/7/55
Berry, Chuck	St. Louis, Mo.	10/18/26
Berry, Ken	Moline, Ill.	11/3/33
Bertinelli, Valerie	Wilmington, Del.	4/23/60
Bikel, Theodore	Vienna, Austria	5/2/24
Birney, David	Washington, D.C.	4/23/39
Bishop, Joey	Bronx, N.Y.	2/3/18
Bisoglio, Val	New York, N.Y.	5/7/26
Bisset, Jacqueline	Weybridge, England	9/13/44
Bixby, Bill	San Francisco, Cal.	1/22/34
Black, Clint	Katy, Tex.	1962
Black, Karen	Park Ridge, Ill.	7/1/42
Blackstone Jr., Harry	Three Rivers, Mich.	6/30/34
Blades, Ruben	Panama City, Panama	7/16/48
Blaine, Vivian	Newark, N.J.	11/21/21
Blair, Linda	St. Louis, Mo.	1/22/59
Blake, Robert	Nutley, N.J.	9/18/33
Bledsoe, Tempestt	Chicago, Ill.	8/1/73
Bloom, Claire	London, England	2/15/31
Blyth, Ann	Mt. Kisco, N.Y.	8/16/28
Bochco, Steven	New York, N.Y.	12/16/43
Bogarde, Dirk	London, England	3/28/20
Bogasian, Eric	Boston, Mass.	4/24/53
Bogdanovich, Peter	Kingston, N.Y.	7/30/39
Bonet, Lisa	San Francisco, Cal.	11/16/67
Bonham-Carter, Helena	London, England	5/26/66
Bon Jovi, Jon	Sayreville, N.J.	3/2/62
Bono, Sonny	Detroit, Mich.	2/16/35
Booke, Sorrell	Buffalo, N.Y.	1/4/30
Boone, Debby	Hackensack, N.J.	9/22/56
Boone, Pat	Jacksonville, Fla.	6/1/34
Booth, Shirley	New York, N.Y.	8/30/07
Borge, Victor	Copenhagen, Denmark	1/3/09
Borgnine, Ernest	Hamden, Conn.	1/24/17
Bosco, Philip	Jersey City, N.J.	9/26/30
Bosley, Tom	Chicago, Ill.	10/1/27
Bosson, Barbara	Charleroi, Pa.	11/1/39
Bostwick, Barry	San Mateo, Cal.	2/24/46
Bottoms, Timothy	Santa Barbara, Cal.	8/30/51
Bowie, David	London, England	1/8/47
Boxleitner, Bruce	Elgin, Ill.	5/12/50
Boy George	London, England	6/14/61
Boyle, Peter	Philadelphia, Pa.	10/18/33
Bracco, Lorraine	New York, N.Y.	1955
Bracken, Eddie	New York, N.Y.	2/7/20
Branagh, Kenneth	Belfast, No. Ireland	1961
Brando, Marlon	Omaha, Neb.	4/3/24
Brazzi, Rossano	Bologna, Italy	9/18/16
Brennan, Eileen	Los Angeles, Cal.	9/3/35
Brenner, David	Philadelphia, Pa.	2/4/45
Brewer, Teresa	Toledo, Oh.	5/7/31
Bridges, Beau	Hollywood, Cal.	12/9/41
Bridges, Jeff	Los Angeles, Cal.	12/4/49
Bridges, Lloyd	San Leandro, Cal.	1/15/13
Brimley, Wilford	Salt Lake City, Ut.	9/27/34
Broderick, Matthew	New York, N.Y.	3/21/62
Brolin, James	Los Angeles, Cal.	7/18/40
Bronson, Charles	Ehrenfeld, Pa.	11/3/22
Brooks, Albert	Beverly Hills, Cal.	7/22/47
Brooks, Avery	Evansville, Ind.	10/2/-
Brooks, Garth	Tulsa, Okla.	2/7/56
Brooks, Mel	New York, N.Y.	6/28/26
Brosnan, Pierce	Co. Meath, Ireland	5/15/53
Brown, Blair	Washington, D.C.	1948
Brown, Bryan	Sydney, Australia	1947
Brown, James	Pulaski, Tenn.	6/17/28
Brown, Jim	St. Simons Island, Ga.	2/17/36
Brown, Les	Reinerton, Pa.	3/14/12
Brown, Ray	Pittsburgh, Pa.	10/13/26
Browne, Roscoe Lee	Woodbury, N.J.	5/2/25
Buckley, Betty	Ft. Worth, Tex.	7/3/47
Bujold, Genevieve	Montreal, Que.	7/1/42
Bumbry, Grace	St. Louis, Mo.	1/4/37
Burghoff, Gary	Bristol, Conn.	5/24/40
Burke, Delta	Orlando, Fla.	7/30/56
Burnett, Carol	San Antonio, Tex.	4/26/33
Burns, George	New York, N.Y.	1/20/96
Burr, Raymond	New Westminster, B.C.	5/21/17
Burrows, Darren E.	Winfield, Kan.	9/12/66
Burstyn, Ellen	Detroit, Mich.	12/7/32
Burton, LeVar	Landsthul, W. Germany	2/16/57
Busey, Gary	Goose Creek, Tex.	6/29/44
Busfield, Timothy	Lansing, Mich.	6/12/57
Butkus, Dick	Chicago, Ill.	12/9/42
Button, Dick	Englewood, N.J.	7/18/29
Buttons, Red	New York, N.Y.	2/5/19
Buzzi, Ruth	Westerly, R.I.	7/24/36
Byrne, David	Dumbarton, Scotland	5/14/52
Caan, James	New York, N.Y.	3/26/39
Caballe, Montserrat	Barcelona, Spain	4/12/33
Caesar, Sid	Yonkers, N.Y.	9/8/22
Cage, Nicolas	Long Beach, Cal.	1/7/64
Caine, Michael	London, England	3/14/33
Caldwell, Sarah	Maryville, Mo.	3/6/24
Caldwell, Zoe	Melbourne, Australia	9/14/33
Calhoun, Rory	Los Angeles, Cal.	8/8/23
Calloway, Cab	Rochester, N.Y.	12/25/07
Cameron, Kirk	Panorama City, Cal.	10/12/70
Camp, Hamilton	London, England	10/30/34
Campanella, Joseph	New York, N.Y.	11/21/27
Campbell, Glen	Billstown, Ark.	4/22/36
Candy, John	Toronto, Ont.	10/31/50
Cannell, Stephen J.	Los Angeles, Cal.	2/5/42
Cannon, Dyan	Tacoma, Wash.	1/4/37
Cantrell, Lana	Sydney, Australia	8/7/43
Cara, Irene	New York, N.Y.	3/18/59
Carey, Macdonald	Sioux City, Ia.	3/15/13
Carey, Mariah	Huntington, N.Y.	1970
Cariou, Len	Winnipeg, Canada	9/30/39
Carlin, George	New York, N.Y.	5/12/37
Carlisle, Kitty	New Orleans, La.	9/3/15
Carmen, Eric	Cleveland, Oh.	8/11/49
Carmichael, Ian	Hull, England	6/18/20
Carney, Art	Mt. Vernon, N.Y.	11/4/18
Carnovsky, Morris	St. Louis, Mo.	9/5/97
Caron, Leslie	Boulogne, France	7/1/31
Carr, Vikki	El Paso, Tex.	7/19/41
Carradine, David	Hollywood, Cal.	10/8/36
Carradine, Keith	San Mateo, Cal.	8/8/49
Carreras, Jose	Barcelona, Spain	12/5/47
Carroll, Diahann	Bronx, N.Y.	7/17/35
Carroll, Pat	Shreveport, La.	5/5/27
Carson, Johnny	Corning, Ia.	10/23/25
Carter, Dixie	McLemoresville, Tenn.	5/25/39
Carter, Jack	New York, N.Y.	6/24/23
Carter, June	Maces Spring, Va.	6/23/29
Carter, Lynda	Phoenix, Ariz.	7/24/51
Carter, Nell	Birmingham, Ala.	9/13/48
Carvey, Dana	Missoula, Mont.	6/6/55
Casadesus, Gaby	Marseilles, France	1902
Cash, Johnny	Kingsland, Ark.	2/26/32
Cash, Rosanne	Memphis, Tenn.	5/24/55

Name	Birthplace	Born
Cass, Peggy	Boston, Mass.	5/21/24
Cassidy, David	New York, N.Y.	4/12/50
Cavett, Dick	Gibbon, Neb.	11/19/36
Chamberlain, Richard	Beverly Hills, Cal.	3/31/35
Champion, Marge	Los Angeles, Cal.	9/2/23
Channing, Carol	Seattle, Wash.	1/31/23
Channing, Stockard	New York, N.Y.	2/13/44
Chaplin, Geraldine	Santa Monica, Cal.	7/31/44
Chapman, Tracy	Cleveland, Oh.	1964
Charisse, Cyd	Amarillo, Tex.	3/8/21
Charles, Ray	Albany, Ga.	9/23/30
Charo	Murcia, Spain	1/15/51
Chase, Chevy	New York, N.Y.	10/8/43
Checker, Chubby	Philadelphia, Pa.	10/3/41
Cher	El Centro, Cal.	5/20/46
Chong, Rae Dawn	California	1961
Chong, Thomas	Edmonton, Alta.	5/24/38
Christie, Julie	Assam, India	4/14/40
Christopher, William	Evanston, Ill.	10/20/32
Clapton, Eric	Surrey, England	3/30/45
Clark, Dane	New York, N.Y.	2/18/13
Clark, Dick	Mt. Vernon, N.Y.	11/30/29
Clark, Petula	Ewell, Surrey, England	11/15/32
Clark, Roy	Meherrin, Va.	4/15/33
Clark, Susan	Sarnia, Ont.	3/8/40
Clary, Robert	Paris, France	3/1/26
Clayburgh, Jill	New York, N.Y.	4/30/44
Cleese, John	England	10/27/39
Cliburn, Van	Shreveport, La.	7/12/34
Clooney, Rosemary	Maysville, Ky.	5/23/28
Close, Glenn	Greenwich, Conn.	3/19/47
Coburn, James	Laurel, Neb.	8/31/28
Coca, Imogene	Philadelphia, Pa.	11/18/08
Colbert, Claudette	Paris, France	9/13/03
Cole, Gary	Park Ridge, Ill.	9/20/57
Cole, Natalie	Los Angeles, Cal.	2/6/50
Cole, Olivia	Memphis, Tenn.	11/26/42
Coleman, Dabney	Austin, Tex.	1/3/32
Coleman, Gary	Zion, Ill.	2/8/68
Collins, Joan	London, England	5/23/33
Collins, Judy	Seattle, Wash.	5/1/39
Collins, Pauline	Exmouth, England	9/3/40
Collins, Phil	London, England	1/30/51
Comden, Betty	Brooklyn, N.Y.	5/3/19
Como, Perry	Canonsburg, Pa.	5/18/12
Conner, Nadine	Compton, Cal.	2/20/13
Connery, Sean	Edinburgh, Scotland	8/25/30
Connick Jr., Harry	New Orleans, La.	1967
Conniff, Ray	Attleboro, Mass.	11/6/16
Connors, Chuck	Brooklyn, N.Y.	4/10/21
Connors, Mike	Fresno, Cal.	8/15/25
Conrad, Robert	Chicago, Ill.	3/1/35
Conrad, William	Louisville, Ky.	9/27/20
Constantine, Michael	Reading, Pa.	5/22/27
Conti, Tom	Paisley, Scotland	11/22/41
Conway, Tim	Willoughby, Oh.	12/15/33
Cook, Barbara	Atlanta, Ga.	10/25/27
Cook, Peter	Torquay, England	11/17/37
Cooke, Alistair	Manchester, England	11/20/08
Coolidge, Rita	Nashville, Tenn.	5/1/45
Cooper, Alice	Detroit, Mich.	2/4/48
Cooper, Jackie	Los Angeles, Cal.	9/15/21
Copperfield, David	Metuchen, N.J.	9/16/56
Coppola, Francis	Detroit, Mich.	4/7/39
Corbin, Barry	Lamesa, Tex.	10/16/40
Corby, Ellen	Racine, Wis.	6/3/13
Cord, Alex	New York, N.Y.	8/3/31
Corea, Chick	Chelsea, Mass.	6/12/41
Corelli, Franco	Ancona, Italy	4/8/23
Corey, Jeff	New York, N.Y.	8/10/14
Cosby, Bill	Philadelphia, Pa.	7/12/37
Costas, Bob	New York, N.Y.	3/22/52
Costello, Elvis	London, England	8/25/54
Costner, Kevin	Compton, Cal.	1/18/55
Cotten, Joseph	Petersburg, Va.	5/15/05
Cougar, John	Seymour, Ind.	10/7/51
Courtenay, Tom	Hull, England	2/25/37
Cox, Ronny	Cloudcroft, N.M.	8/23/38
Craddock, Crash	Greensboro, N.C.	6/16/40
Crain, Jeanne	Barstow, Cal.	5/25/25
Crawford, Michael	Salisbury, England	1/19/42
Crenna, Richard	Los Angeles, Cal.	11/30/26
Crespin, Regine	Marseilles, France	2/23/26
Cronyn, Hume	London, Ont.	7/18/11
Crosby, Bob	Spokane, Wash.	8/23/13
Crosby, David	Los Angeles, Cal.	8/14/41
Cross, Ben	London, England	12/16/47
Crouse, Lindsay	New York, N.Y.	5/12/48
Crowell, Rodney	Houston, Tex.	8/17/50
Cruise, Tom	Syracuse, N.Y.	7/3/62
Crystal, Billy	Long Beach, N.Y.	3/14/47
Culkin, Macaulay	New York, N.Y.	8/26/80
Cullum, John	Knoxville, Tenn.	3/2/30
Culp, Robert	Oakland, Cal.	8/16/30
Cummings, Constance	Seattle, Wash.	5/15/10
Curtin, Jane	Cambridge, Mass.	9/6/47
Curtis, Jamie Lee	Los Angeles, Cal.	11/22/58
Curtis, Keene	Salt Lake City, Ut.	2/15/23
Curtis, Tony	New York, N.Y.	6/3/25
Cusack, Cyril	Durban, S. Africa	11/26/10
Cusack, Joan	Evanston, Ill.	10/11/62
Cusack, John	Evanston, Ill.	6/28/66
Cushing, Peter	Surrey, England	5/26/13
Dafoe, Willem	Appleton, Wis.	7/22/55
Dahl, Arlene	Minneapolis, Minn.	8/11/28
Dale, Jim	Rothwell, England	8/15/35
Dalton, Abby	Las Vegas, Nev.	8/15/32
Dalton, Timothy	Wales	3/21/44
Daltrey, Roger	London, England	3/1/44
Daly, Timothy	Suffern, N.J.	3/1/58
Daly, Tyne	Madison, Wis.	2/21/47
Damone, Vic	Brooklyn, N.Y.	6/12/28
D'Angelo, Beverly	Columbus, Oh.	1954
Dangerfield, Rodney	Babylon, N.Y.	11/22/22
Daniels, Charlie	Wilmington, N.C.	10/28/36
Daniels, Jeff	Georgia	1955
Daniels, William	Brooklyn, N.Y.	3/31/27
Danner, Blythe	Philadelphia, Pa.	2/3/44
Danson, Ted	San Diego, Cal.	12/29/47
Danza, Tony	New York, N.Y.	4/21/50
Darby, Kim	Hollywood, Cal.	7/8/48
D'Arby, Terence Trent	New York, N.Y.	3/15/62
Davidson, John	Pittsburgh, Pa.	12/13/41
Davis, Ann B.	Schenectady, N.Y.	5/5/26
Davis, Clifton	Chicago, Ill.	10/4/45
Davis, Geena	Wareham, Mass.	1/21/57
Davis, Judy	Perth, Australia	1956
Davis, Mac	Lubbock, Tex.	1/21/42
Davis, Ossie	Cogdell, Ga.	12/18/17
Dawber, Pam	Farmington Hills, Mich.	10/18/51
Dawson, Richard	Hampshire, England	11/20/32
Day, Doris	Cincinnati, Oh.	4/3/24
Day-Lewis, Daniel	London, England	4/29/57
Dean, Jimmy	Plainview, Tex.	8/10/28
De Camp, Rosemary	Prescott, Ariz.	11/14/10
DeCarlo, Yvonne	Vancouver, B.C.	9/1/22
Dee, Frances	Los Angeles, Cal.	11/26/07
Dee, Ruby	Cleveland, Oh.	10/27/23
Dee, Sandra	Bayonne, N.J.	4/23/42
Defore, Don	Cedar Rapids, Ia.	8/25/17
DeHaven, Gloria	Los Angeles, Cal.	7/23/25
De Havilland, Olivia	Tokyo, Japan	7/1/16
Delany, Dana	New York, N.Y.	3/13/57
Della Chiesa, Vivienne	Chicago, Ill.	10/9/20
Delon, Alain	Sceaux, France	11/8/35
DeLuise, Dom	Brooklyn, N.Y.	8/1/33
De Mille, Agnes	New York, N.Y.	9/18/05
Demme, Jonathan	Baldwin, N.Y.	1944
De Mornay, Rebecca	Los Angeles, Cal.	1962
Deneuve, Catherine	Paris, France	10/22/43
De Niro, Robert	New York, N.Y.	8/17/43
Dennehy, Brian	Bridgeport, Conn.	7/9/38
Dennis, Sandy	Hastings, Neb.	4/27/37
Denver, Bob	New Rochelle, N.Y.	1/9/35
Denver, John	Roswell, N.M.	12/31/43
DePalma, Brian	Newark, N.J.	9/11/40
Depardieu, Gerard	Chateauroux, France	12/27/48
Depp, Johnny	Owensboro, Ky.	6/9/63
Derek, Bo	Long Beach, Cal.	11/20/56
Derek, John	Hollywood, Cal.	8/12/26
Dern, Bruce	Chicago, Ill.	6/4/36
Dern, Laura	Santa Monica, Cal.	2/1/67
Devane, William	Albany, N.Y.	9/5/37
DeVito, Danny	Neptune, N.J.	11/17/44
DeWitt, Joyce	Wheeling, W.Va.	4/23/49
Dey, Susan	Pekin, Ill.	12/10/52
Diamond, Neil	Brooklyn, N.Y.	1/24/41
Dickinson, Angie	Kulm, N.D.	9/30/31
Diddley, Bo	McComb, Miss.	12/20/28
Diller, Phyllis	Lima, Oh.	7/17/17
Dillman, Bradford	San Francisco, Cal.	4/14/30
Dillon, Matt	New Rochelle, N.Y.	2/18/64
Dobson, Kevin	New York, N.Y.	3/18/44
Domingo, Placido	Madrid, Spain	1/21/41
Domino, Fats	New Orleans, La.	2/26/28
Donahue, Phil	Cleveland, Oh.	12/21/35

Name	Birthplace	Born
Donahue, Troy	New York, N.Y.	1/27/36
Dotrice, Roy	Guernsey, England	5/26/23
Douglas, Kirk	Amsterdam, N.Y.	12/9/18
Douglas, Michael	New Brunswick, N.J.	9/25/44
Down, Leslie-Ann	London, England	3/17/54
Downey, Robert Jr.	New York, N.Y.	4/4/65
Downs, Hugh	Akron, Oh.	2/14/21
Doyle, David	Lincoln, Neb.	12/1/29
Drake, Alfred	Bronx, N.Y.	10/7/14
Drake, Larry	Tulsa, Okla.	2/21/-
Drew, Ellen	Kansas City, Mo.	11/23/15
Dryer, Fred	Hawthorne, Cal.	7/6/46
Dreyfuss, Richard	Brooklyn, N.Y.	10/29/47
Dru, Joanne	Logan, W.Va.	1/31/23
Duffy, Julia	Minneapolis, Minn.	6/27/51
Duffy, Patrick	Townsend, Mont.	3/17/49
Dufour, Val	New Orleans, La.	2/5/27
Dukakis, Olympia	Lowell, Mass.	1931
Duke, Patty	New York, N.Y.	12/14/46
Dukes, David	San Francisco, Cal.	6/6/45
Dullea, Keir	Cleveland, Oh.	5/30/36
Dunaway, Faye	Bascom, Fla.	1/14/41
Duncan, Sandy	Henderson, Tex.	2/20/46
Dunham, Katherine	Joliet, Ill.	6/22/10
Dunne, Griffin	New York, N.Y.	6/8/55
Durbin, Deanna	Winnipeg, Man.	12/4/21
Durning, Charles	Highland Falls, N.Y.	2/28/23
Dussault, Nancy	Pensacola, Fla.	6/30/36
Duvall, Robert	San Diego, Cal.	1/5/31
Duvall, Shelley	Houston, Tex.	7/7/49
Dylan, Bob	Duluth, Minn.	5/24/41
Dysart, Richard	Augusta, Me.	3/30/29
Dzundza, George	Rosenheim, Germany	7/19/45
Easton, Sheena	Bellshill, Scotland	4/27/59
Eastwood, Clint	San Francisco, Cal.	5/31/30
Ebert, Roger	Urbana, Ill.	6/18/42
Ebsen, Buddy	Belleville, Ill.	4/2/08
Eckstine, Billy	Pittsburgh, Pa.	7/8/14
Edelman, Herb	Brooklyn, N.Y.	11/5/33
Eden, Barbara	Tucson, Ariz.	8/23/34
Edwards, Anthony	Santa Barbara, Cal.	1/19/62
Edwards, Blake	Tulsa, Okla.	7/26/22
Edwards, Ralph	Merino, Col.	6/13/13
Eichhorn, Lisa	Reading, Pa.	2/4/52
Eikenberry, Jill	New Haven, Conn.	1/21/47
Ekberg, Anita	Malmo, Sweden	9/29/31
Ekland, Britt	Stockholm, Sweden	10/6/42
Elam, Jack	Miami, Ariz.	11/13/16
Elizondo, Hector	New York, N.Y.	12/22/36
Elliott, Bob	Boston, Mass.	3/26/23
Elliott, Denholm	London, England	5/31/22
Elliott, Sam	Sacramento, Cal.	8/9/44
Englund, Robert	Hollywood, Cal.	6/6/48
Elvira (Cassandra Peterson)	Manhattan, Kan.	9/17/51
Estefan, Gloria	Havana, Cuba	9/1/58
Estevez, Emilio	New York, N.Y.	5/12/62
Estrada, Erik	New York, N.Y.	3/16/49
Evans, Dale	Uvalde, Tex.	10/31/12
Evans, Linda	Hartford, Conn.	11/18/42
Evans, Robert	New York, N.Y.	6/29/30
Everett, Chad	South Bend, Ind.	6/11/36
Everly, Don	Brownie, Ky.	2/1/37
Everly, Phil	Chicago, Ill.	1/19/38
Evigan, Greg	S. Amboy, N.J.	10/14/53
Ewell, Tom	Owensboro, Ky.	4/29/09
Fabares, Shelley	Santa Monica, Cal.	1/19/42
Fabian (Forte)	Philadelphia, Pa.	2/6/43
Fabray, Nanette	San Diego, Cal.	10/27/20
Fairbanks, Douglas Jr.	New York, N.Y.	12/9/09
Fairchild, Morgan	Dallas, Tex.	2/3/50
Falana, Lola	Philadelphia, Pa.	9/11/46
Falk, Peter	New York, N.Y.	9/16/27
Farentino, James	Brooklyn, N.Y.	2/24/38
Fargo, Donna	Mt. Airy, N.C.	11/10/45
Farr, Jamie	Toledo, Oh.	7/1/34
Farrell, Eileen	Willimantic, Conn.	2/13/20
Farrell, Mike	St. Paul, Minn.	2/6/39
Farrow, Mia	Los Angeles, Cal.	2/9/45
Faustino, David	California	3/3/74
Fawcett, Farrah	Corpus Christi, Tex.	2/2/47
Faye, Alice	New York, N.Y.	5/5/12
Feld, Fritz	Berlin, Germany	10/15/00
Feldon, Barbara	Pittsburgh, Pa.	3/12/41
Feldshuh, Tovah	New York, N.Y.	12/27/52
Feliciano, Jose	Lares, Puerto Rico	9/10/45
Fell, Norman	Philadelphia, Pa.	3/24/24
Fellini, Federico	Rimini, Italy	1/20/20

Name	Birthplace	Born
Ferrell, Conchata	Charleston, W. Va.	3/28/43
Ferrer, Mel	Elberon, N.J.	8/25/17
Fiedler, John	Platville, Wis.	2/3/25
Field, Sally	Pasadena, Cal.	11/6/46
Finney, Albert	Salford, England	5/9/36
Firkusny, Rudolf	Napajedla, Czechoslovakia	2/11/12
Firth, Peter	Yorkshire, England	10/27/53
Fischer-Dieskau, Dietrich	Berlin, Germany	5/28/25
Fishburne, Larry	Augusta, Ga.	1962
Fisher, Carrie	Beverly Hills, Cal.	10/21/56
Fisher, Eddie	Philadelphia, Pa.	8/10/28
Fitzgerald, Ella	Newport News, Va.	4/25/18
Fitzgerald, Geraldine	Dublin, Ireland	11/24/13
Flack, Roberta	Black Mountain, N.C.	2/10/39
Flanagan, Fionnula	Dublin, Ireland	12/10/41
Flanders, Ed	Minneapolis, Minn.	12/29/34
Fleming, Rhonda	Hollywood, Cal.	8/10/23
Fletcher, Louise	Birmingham, Ala.	1936
Foch, Nina	Leyden, Netherlands	4/20/24
Fogelberg, Dan	Peoria, Ill.	8/13/51
Fonda, Jane	New York, N.Y.	12/21/37
Fonda, Peter	New York, N.Y.	2/23/39
Fontaine, Joan	Tokyo, Japan	10/22/17
Ford, Faith	Alexandria, Va.	9/14/-
Ford, Glenn	Quebec, Canada	5/1/16
Ford, Harrison	Chicago, Ill.	7/13/42
Forrest, Steve	Huntsville, Tex.	9/29/24
Forsythe, John	Penns Grove, N.J.	1/29/18
Foster, Jodie	New York, N.Y.	11/19/62
Fox, James	London, England	5/19/39
Fox, Michael J.	Edmonton, Alta.	6/9/61
Foxworth, Robert	Houston, Tex.	11/1/41
Frampton, Peter	Kent, England	4/22/50
Franciosa, Anthony	New York, N.Y.	10/25/28
Francis, Anne	Ossining, N.Y.	9/16/30
Francis, Arlene	Boston, Mass.	10/20/08
Francis, Connie	Newark, N.J.	12/12/38
Frankenheimer, John	Malba, N.Y.	2/19/30
Franklin, Aretha	Memphis, Tenn.	3/25/42
Franklin, Bonnie	Santa Monica, Cal.	1/6/44
Franklin, Joe	New York, N.Y.	1929
Frann, Mary	St. Louis, Mo.	2/27/43
Franz, Dennis	Chicago, Ill.	10/28/44
Freeman Jr., Al	San Antonio, Tex.	3/21/34
Freeman, Morgan	Memphis, Tenn.	6/1/37
Friedkin, William	Chicago, Ill.	8/29/39
Frost, David	Tenterden, England	4/7/39
Funicello, Annette	Utica, N.Y.	10/22/42
Funt, Allen	New York, N.Y.	9/16/14
Gabor, Eva	Hungary	1921
Gabor, Zsa Zsa	Hungary	—
Gabriel, John	Niagara Falls, N.Y.	5/25/31
Gabriel, Peter	London, England	2/13/50
Gail, Max	Detroit, Mich.	4/5/43
Gallagher, Megan	Reading, Pa.	2/6/-
Galway, James	Belfast, Ireland	12/8/39
Garagiola, Joe	St. Louis, Mo.	2/12/26
Garcia, Andy	Havana, Cuba	1956
Gardenia, Vincent	Naples, Italy	1/7/22
Garfunkel, Art	New York, N.Y.	11/5/41
Garland, Beverly	Santa Cruz, Cal.	10/17/26
Garner, James	Norman, Okla.	4/7/28
Garr, Teri	Lakewood, Oh.	12/11/45
Garrett, Betty	St. Joseph, Mo.	5/23/19
Garson, Greer	Co. Down, N. Ireland	9/29/08
Gatlin, Larry	Seminole, Tex.	5/2/48
Gayle, Crystal	Paintsville, Ky.	1/9/51
Gaynor, Mitzi	Chicago, Ill.	9/4/30
Gazzara, Ben	New York, N.Y.	8/28/30
Gedda, Nicolai	Stockholm, Sweden	7/11/25
Gere, Richard	Philadelphia, Pa.	8/31/49
Getty, Estelle	New York, N.Y.	7/25/24
Ghostley, Alice	Eve, Mo.	8/14/26
Giannini, Giancarlo	Spezia, Italy	8/1/42
Gibbs, Marla	Chicago, Ill.	6/14/31
Gibson, Debbie	New York, N.Y.	8/31/70
Gibson, Henry	Germantown, Pa.	9/21/35
Gibson, Mel	Peekskill, N.Y.	1/3/56
Gielgud, John	London, England	4/14/04
Gifford, Frank	Santa Monica, Cal.	8/16/30
Gilbert, Melissa	Los Angeles, Cal.	5/8/64
Gilberto, Astrud	Salvador, Brazil	3/30/40
Gillette, Anita	Baltimore, Md.	8/16/38
Gilley, Mickey	Natchez, Miss.	3/9/36
Ginty, Robert	New York, N.Y.	11/14/48
Gish, Lillian	Springfield, Oh.	10/14/96
Givens, Robin	New York, N.Y.	11/27/64

Name	Birthplace	Born
Glaser, Paul Michael	Cambridge, Mass.	3/25/42
Glenn, Scott	Pittsburgh, Pa.	1/26/42
Gless, Sharon	Los Angeles, Cal.	5/31/43
Glover, Danny	San Francisco, Cal.	1947
Godard, Jean Luc	Paris, France	12/3/30
Godunov, Alexander	Sakhalin Is., USSR	11/28/49
Goldberg, Whoopi	New York, N.Y.	11/13/50
Goldblum, Jeff	Pittsburgh, Pa.	10/22/52
Goldsboro, Bobby	Marianna, Fla.	1/18/42
Goldthwait, Bob	Syracuse, N.Y.	1962
Goodman, John	St. Louis, Mo.	6/20/53
Gordon, Gale	New York, N.Y.	2/2/06
Gorme, Eydie	Bronx, N.Y.	8/16/32
Gorshin, Frank	Pittsburgh, Pa.	4/5/34
Gossett Jr., Louis	Brooklyn, N.Y.	5/27/36
Gould, Elliott	Brooklyn, N.Y.	8/29/38
Gould, Harold	Schenectady, N.Y.	12/10/23
Gould, Morton	Richmond Hill, N.Y.	12/10/13
Goulet, Robert	Lawrence, Mass.	11/26/33
Gowdy, Curt	Green River, Wyo.	7/31/19
Graham, Virginia	Chicago, Ill.	7/4/12
Grammer, Kelsey	Virgin Islands	2/20/-
Granger, Farley	San Jose, Cal.	7/1/25
Granger, Stewart	London, England	5/6/13
Grant, Amy	Augusta, Ga.	12/25/60
Grant, Lee	New York, N.Y.	10/31/29
Graves, Peter	Minneapolis, Minn.	3/18/26
Gray, Erin	Honolulu, Ha.	1/7/52
Gray, Linda	Santa Monica, Cal.	9/12/40
Grayson, Kathryn	Winston-Salem, N.C.	2/9/22
Greco, Jose	Abruzzi, Italy	12/23/18
Green, Adolph	New York, N.Y.	12/2/15
Green, Al	Forest City, Ark.	4/13/46
Greene, Michele	Las Vegas, Nev.	2/3/-
Greene, Shecky	Chicago, Ill.	4/8/26
Gregory, Cynthia	Los Angeles, Cal.	7/8/46
Gregory, Dick	St. Louis, Mo.	10/12/32
Gregory, James	Bronx, N.Y.	12/23/11
Grey, Joel	Cleveland, Oh.	4/11/32
Griffin, Merv	San Mateo, Cal.	7/6/25
Griffith, Andy	Mount Airy, N.C.	6/1/26
Griffith, Melanie	New York, N.Y.	8/9/57
Grimes, Tammy	Lynn, Mass.	1/30/34
Grizzard, George	Roanoke Rapids, N.C.	4/1/28
Grodin, Charles	Pittsburgh, Pa.	4/21/35
Groh, David	New York, N.Y.	5/21/41
Grosbard, Ulu	Antwerp, Belgium.	1/19/29
Gross, Michael	Chicago, Ill.	6/21/47
Guardino, Harry	New York, N.Y.	12/23/25
Guillaume, Robert	St. Louis, Mo.	11/30/37
Guinness, Alec	London, England	4/2/14
Gumbel, Greg	New Orleans, La.	5/3/46
Guthrie, Arlo	New York, N.Y.	7/10/47
Guttenberg, Steve	New York, N.Y.	8/24/58
Guy, Jasmine	Boston, Mass.	3/10/64
Gwynne, Fred	New York, N.Y.	7/10/26
Hackett, Buddy	Brooklyn, N.Y.	8/31/24
Hackman, Gene	San Bernardino, Cal.	1/30/30
Hagen, Uta	Gottingen, Germany	6/12/19
Haggard, Merle	Bakersfield, Cal.	4/6/37
Hagman, Larry	Weatherford, Tex.	9/21/31
Haid, Charles	San Francisco, Cal.	6/2/44
Hale, Barbara	DeKalb, Ill.	4/18/22
Hall, Arsenio	Cleveland, Oh.	2/12/55
Hall, Daryl	Pottstown, Pa.	10/11/48
Hall, Deidre	Milwaukee, Wis.	10/31/48
Hall, Huntz	New York, N.Y.	8/15/19
Hall, Monty	Winnipeg, Man.	8/25/25
Hall, Tom T.	Olive Hill, Ky.	5/25/36
Hamel, Veronica	Philadelphia, Pa.	11/20/43
Hamill, Mark	Oakland, Cal.	9/25/51
Hamilton, George	Memphis, Tenn.	8/12/39
Hamilton, Linda	Salisbury, Md.	9/26/-
Hamlin, Harry	Pasadena, Cal.	10/30/51
Hammer	Oakland, Cal.	1962
Hampton, Lionel	Birmingham, Ala.	4/12/13
Hancock, Herbie	Chicago, Ill.	4/12/40
Hanks, Tom	Oakland, Cal.	7/9/56
Hannah, Daryl	Chicago, Ill.	1961
Hardison, Kadeem	New York, N.Y.	7/24/-
Harewood, Dorian	Dayton, Oh.	8/6/51
Harmon, Mark	Burbank, Cal.	9/2/51
Harper, Jessica	Chicago, Ill.	1949
Harper, Tess	Mammoth Springs, Ark.	8/15/50
Harper, Valerie	Suffern, N.Y.	8/22/40
Harrelson, Woody	Midland, Tex.	7/23/61
Harrington, Pat Jr.	New York, N.Y.	8/13/29
Harris, Barbara	Evanston, Ill.	7/25/35
Harris, Ed	Englewood, N.J.	11/28/50
Harris, Emmylou	Birmingham, Ala.	4/2/47
Harris, Julie	Grosse Pte. Park, Mich.	12/2/25
Harris, Neil Patrick	Albuquerque, N.M.	6/15/73
Harris, Phil	Linton, Ind.	6/24/04
Harris, Richard	Co. Limerick, Ireland	10/1/33
Harris, Rosemary	Ashby, England	9/19/30
Harrison, George	Liverpool, England	2/25/43
Harrison, Gregory	Avalon, Cal.	5/31/50
Harry, Deborah	Miami, Fla.	7/1/45
Hart, Mary	Madison, S.D.	11/8/51
Hartley, Mariette	New York, N.Y.	6/21/40
Hartman, David	Pawtucket, R.I.	5/19/35
Hartman, Lisa	Houston, Tex.	6/1/56
Hartman, Phil	Ontario, Canada	9/24/48
Hasselhoff, David	Baltimore, Md.	7/17/52
Hasso, Signe	Stockholm, Sweden	8/15/10
Hauer, Rutger	Netherlands	1/23/44
Haver, June	Rock Island, Ill.	6/10/26
Havoc, June	Seattle, Wash.	11/8/16
Hawn, Goldie	Washington, D.C.	11/21/45
Hayden, Melissa	Toronto, Ont.	4/25/23
Hayes, Helen	Washington, D.C.	10/10/00
Hayes, Isaac	Covington, Tenn.	8/20/42
Hays, Robert	Bethesda, Md.	7/24/47
Heard, John	Washington, D.C.	3/7/45
Hearn, George	Memphis, Tenn.	1935
Heckart, Eileen	Columbus, Oh.	3/29/19
Helmond, Katherine	Galveston, Tex.	7/5/34
Hemingway, Margaux	Portland, Ore.	2/19/55
Hemingway, Mariel	Mill Valley, Cal.	11/21/61
Hemmings, David	Guildford, England	11/18/41
Hemsley, Sherman	Philadelphia, Pa.	2/1/38
Henderson, Florence	Dale, Ind.	2/14/34
Henderson, Skitch	Halstad, Minn.	1/27/18
Henley, Don	Gilmer, Tex.	7/22/47
Henner, Marilu	Chicago, Ill.	4/6/52
Henning, Doug	Ft. Garry, Man.	5/3/47
Hepburn, Audrey	Brussels, Belgium	5/4/29
Hepburn, Katharine	Hartford, Conn.	5/12/07
Herman, Pee-wee	Peekskill, N.Y.	8/27/52
Herrmann, Edward	Washington, D.C.	7/21/43
Hershey, Barbara	Los Angeles, Cal.	2/5/48
Hesseman, Howard	Lebanon, Ore.	2/27/40
Heston, Charlton	Evanston, Ill.	10/4/24
Hewett, Christopher	Sussex, England	4/5/-
Hildegarde	Adell, Wis.	2/1/06
Hill, Arthur	Melfort, Sask.	8/1/22
Hill, Steven	Seattle, Wash.	2/24/22
Hill, George Roy	Minneapolis, Minn.	12/20/22
Hiller, Wendy	Stockport, England	8/15/12
Hillerman, John	Denison, Tex.	12/30/32
Hines, Gregory	New York, N.Y.	2/14/46
Hines, Jerome	Hollywood, Cal.	11/8/21
Hingle, Pat	Miami, Fla.	7/19/24
Hirsch, Judd	New York, N.Y.	3/15/35
Hirt, Al	New Orleans, La.	11/7/22
Ho, Don	Kakaako, Oahu, Ha.	8/13/30
Hoffman, Dustin	Los Angeles, Cal.	8/8/37
Hogan, Paul	New South Wales, Australia	10/8/39
Holbrook, Hal	Cleveland, Oh.	2/17/25
Holder, Geoffrey	Trinidad	8/1/30
Holliday, Polly	Jasper, Ala.	7/2/37
Holliman, Earl	Delhi, La.	9/11/28
Holloway, Sterling	Cedartown, Ga.	1/4/05
Holm, Celeste	New York, N.Y.	4/29/19
Hooks, Jan	Decatur, Ga.	4/23/57
Hooks, Robert	Washington, D.C.	4/18/37
Hope, Bob	London, England	5/29/03
Hopkins, Anthony	Wales	12/31/37
Hopkins, Telma	Louisville, Ky.	10/28/48
Hopper, Dennis	Dodge City, Kan.	5/17/36
Horne, Lena	Brooklyn, N.Y.	6/30/17
Horne, Marilyn	Bradford, Pa.	1/16/34
Horsley, Lee	Muleshoe, Tex.	5/15/55
Hoskins, Bob	Suffolk, England	10/26/42
Houston, Whitney	E. Orange, N.J.	8/9/63
Howard, Ken	El Centro, Cal.	3/28/44
Howard, Ron	Duncan, Okla.	3/1/53
Howell, C. Thomas	Los Angeles, Cal.	12/7/66
Howes, Sally Ann	London, England	7/20/30
Hughes, Barnard	Bedford Hills, N.Y.	7/16/15
Hulce, Tom	Whitewater, Wis.	12/6/53
Humperdinck, Engelbert	Madras, India	5/3/36
Hunt, Linda	Morristown, N.J.	4/2/45
Hunter, Holly	Conyers, Ga.	3/20/58
Hunter, Kim	Detroit, Mich.	11/12/22

Name	Birthplace	Born
Hunter, Ross	Cleveland, Oh.	5/6/21
Hunter, Tab	New York, N.Y.	7/11/31
Hurt, John	Chesterfield, England	1/22/40
Hurt, Mary Beth	Marshalltown, Ia.	9/26/46
Hurt, William	Washington, D.C.	3/20/50
Hussey, Ruth	Providence, R.I.	10/30/14
Huston, Anjelica	Ireland	7/8/51
Hutton, Betty	Battle Creek, Mich.	2/26/21
Hutton, Timothy	Malibu, Cal.	8/16/60
Hyman, Earle	Rocky Mount, N.C.	10/11/26
Ian, Janis	New York, N.Y.	4/7/51
Idol, Billy	London, England	11/30/55
Iglesias, Julio	Madrid, Spain	9/23/43
Ingram, James	Akron, Oh.	2/16/56
Irons, Jeremy	Cowes, England	9/19/48
Irving, Amy	Palo Alto, Cal.	9/10/53
Irving, George S.	Springfield, Mass.	11/1/22
Ives, Burl	Hunt Township, Ill.	6/14/09
Ivey, Judith	El Paso, Tex.	9/4/51
Jackee	Winston-Salem, N.C.	8/14/57
Jackson, Anne	Allegheny, Pa.	9/3/25
Jackson, Glenda	Liverpool, England	5/9/36
Jackson, Janet	Gary, Ind.	5/16/66
Jackson, Jermaine	Gary, Ind.	12/11/54
Jackson, La Toya	Gary, Ind.	1/29/56
Jackson, Kate	Birmingham, Ala.	10/29/48
Jackson, Michael	Gary, Ind.	8/29/58
Jackson, Victoria	Miami, Fla.	8/2/59
Jacobi, Derek	London, England	10/22/38
Jaeckel, Richard	Long Beach, N.Y.	10/10/26
Jagger, Mick	Dartford, England	7/26/43
James, Dennis	Jersey City, N.J.	8/24/17
Janis, Conrad	New York, N.Y.	2/11/28
Jarreau, Al	Milwaukee, Wis	3/12/40
Jeffreys, Anne	Goldsboro, N.C.	1/26/23
Jennings, Waylon	Littlefield, Tex.	6/15/37
Jett, Joan	Philadelphia, Pa.	9/22/60
Jewison, Norman	Toronto, Ont.	7/21/26
Jillian, Ann	Cambridge, Mass.	1/29/50
Joel, Billy	Bronx, N.Y.	5/9/49
John, Elton	Middlesex, England	3/25/47
Johns, Glynis	Durban, S. Africa	10/5/23
Johnson, Anne-Marie	Los Angeles, Cal.	7/18/-
Johnson, Arte	Benton Harbor, Mich.	1/20/29
Johnson, Ben	Foraker, Okla.	6/13/18
Johnson, Don	Flatt Creek, Mo.	12/15/49
Johnson, Van	Newport, R.I.	8/25/16
Jones, Charlie	Ft. Smith, Ark.	11/9/30
Jones, Dean	Morgan City, Ala.	1/25/35
Jones, George	Saratoga, Tex.	9/12/31
Jones, Grace	Spanishtown, Jamaica	5/19/52
Jones, Grandpa	Niagara, Ky.	10/20/13
Jones, Henry	Philadelphia, Pa.	8/1/12
Jones, Jack	Hollywood, Cal.	1/14/38
Jones, James Earl	Tate Co., Miss.	1/17/31
Jones, Jennifer	Tulsa, Okla.	3/2/19
Jones, Shirley	Smithton, Pa.	3/31/34
Jones, Tom	Pontypridd, Wales	6/7/40
Jones, Tommy Lee	San Saba, Tex.	9/15/46
Jordan, Richard	New York, N.Y.	7/19/38
Jourdan, Louis	Marseilles, France	6/19/19
Judd, Naomi	Ashland, Ky.	1/11/46
Judd, Wynonna	Ashland, Ky.	5/3/64
Julia, Raul	San Juan, P.R.	3/9/40
Jump, Gordon	Dayton, Oh.	4/1/32
Kahn, Madeline	Boston, Mass.	9/29/42
Kanaly, Steve	Burbank, Cal.	3/14/46
Kane, Carol	Cleveland, Oh.	6/18/52
Karlen, John	New York, N.Y.	5/28/33
Karras, Alex	Gary, Ind.	7/15/35
Kasem, Casey	Detroit, Mich.	1933
Kavner, Julie	Los Angeles, Cal.	9/7/51
Kazan, Elia	Istanbul, Turkey	9/7/09
Kazan, Lainie	New York, N.Y.	5/15/42
Keach, Stacy	Savannah, Ga.	6/2/41
Keaton, Diane	Santa Ana, Cal.	1/5/46
Keaton, Michael	Pittsburgh, Pa.	9/9/51
Keel, Howard	Gillespie, Ill.	4/13/17
Keeler, Ruby	Halifax, N.S.	8/25/09
Keeshan, Bob	Lynbrook, N.Y.	6/27/27
Keitel, Harvey	Brooklyn, N.Y.	1947
Keith, Brian	Bayonne, N.J.	11/14/21
Keith, David	Knoxville, Tenn.	5/8/54
Kellerman, Sally	Long Beach, Cal.	6/2/37
Kelley, DeForest	Atlanta, Ga.	1/20/20
Kelly, Gene	Pittsburgh, Pa.	8/23/12

Name	Birthplace	Born
Kennedy, George	New York, N.Y.	2/18/25
Kennedy, Jayne	Washington, D.C.	11/27/51
Kent, Allegra	Los Angeles, Cal.	8/11/37
Kercheval, Ken	Wolcottville, Ind.	7/15/35
Kerns, Joanna	San Francisco, Cal.	2/12/53
Kerr, Deborah	Helensburgh, Scotland	9/30/21
Kerr, John	New York, N.Y.	11/15/31
Khan, Chaka	Great Lakes, Ill.	3/23/53
Kidder, Margot	Yellowknife, N.W.T.	10/17/48
Kiley, Richard	Chicago, Ill.	3/31/22
Kimbrough, Charles	St. Paul, Minn.	5/23/-
King, Alan	Brooklyn, N.Y.	12/26/27
King, B. B.	Itta Bena, Miss.	9/16/25
King, Carole	Brooklyn, N.Y.	2/9/42
King, Larry	New York, N.Y.	11/19/33
King, Perry	Alliance, Oh.	4/30/48
Kingsley, Ben	Yorkshire, England	12/31/43
Kinski, Nastassia	Berlin, W. Germany	1/24/60
Kirby, Bruno	New York, N.Y.	1949
Kirby, Durward	Covington, Ky.	8/24/12
Kirkland, Gelsey	Bethlehem, Pa.	12/29/53
Kirsten, Dorothy	Montclair, N.J.	7/6/19
Kitt, Eartha	North, S.C.	1/26/28
Klein, Robert	New York, N.Y.	2/8/42
Klemperer, Werner	Cologne, Germany	3/22/19
Kline, Kevin	St. Louis, Mo.	10/24/47
Klugman, Jack	Philadelphia, Pa.	4/27/22
Knight, Gladys	Atlanta, Ga.	5/28/44
Knotts, Don	Morgantown, W. Va.	7/21/24
Kopell, Bernie	New York, N.Y.	6/21/33
Korman, Harvey	Chicago, Ill.	2/15/27
Kotto, Yaphet	New York, N.Y.	11/15/37
Kramer, Stanley	New York, N.Y.	9/29/13
Kristofferson, Kris	Brownsville, Tex.	6/22/36
Kubelik, Rafael	Bychori, Czechoslovakia	6/29/14
Kubrick, Stanley	Bronx, N.Y.	7/26/28
Kurtz, Swoosie	Omaha, Neb.	9/6/44
LaBelle, Patti	Philadelphia, Pa.	10/4/44
Ladd, Cheryl	Huron, S.D.	7/12/51
Ladd, Diane	Meridian, Miss.	11/29/32
Lahti, Christine	Detroit, Mich.	4/5/50
Laine, Cleo	Middlesex, England	10/28/27
Laine, Frankie	Chicago, Ill.	3/30/13
Lamarr, Hedy	Vienna, Austria	11/9/13
Lamas, Lorenzo	Santa Monica, Cal.	1/20/58
Lamb, Gil	Minneapolis, Minn.	6/14/06
Lamour, Dorothy	New Orleans, La.	12/10/14
Lancaster, Burt	New York, N.Y.	11/2/13
Landau, Martin	New York, N.Y.	6/20/34
Landis, John	Chicago, Ill.	8/3/50
Lane, Cristy	E. Peoria, Ill.	1/8/40
Lane, Diane	New York, N.Y.	1/22/63
Lane, Priscilla	Indianola, Ia.	6/12/17
Lang, K.D.	Consort, Alberta	11/2/61
Lang, Stephen	New York, N.Y.	7/11/52
Lange, Hope	Redding Ridge, Conn.	11/28/31
Lange, Jessica	Cloquet, Minn.	4/20/49
Langella, Frank	Bayonne, N.J.	1/1/40
Langford, Frances	Lakeland, Fla.	4/4/13
Lansbury, Angela	London, England	10/16/25
Lansing, Robert	San Diego, Cal.	6/5/28
Laredo, Ruth	Detroit, Mich.	11/20/37
Larroquette, John	New Orleans, La.	11/25/47
Lasser, Louise	New York, N.Y.	4/11/39
Lauper, Cyndi	New York, N.Y.	6/20/53
Laurie, Piper	Detroit, Mich.	1/22/32
Lauter, Ed	Long Beach, N.Y.	10/30/40
Lavin, Linda	Portland, Me.	10/15/37
Lawrence, Carol	Melrose Park, Ill.	9/5/34
Lawrence, Steve	Brooklyn, N.Y.	7/8/35
Lawrence, Vicki	Inglewood, Cal.	3/26/49
Leach, Robin	London, England	8/29/41
Leachman, Cloris	Des Moines, Ia.	4/4/26
Lear, Norman	New Haven, Conn.	7/27/22
Learned, Michael	Washington, D.C.	4/9/39
LeBon, Simon	Bushey, England	10/27/58
Lee, Brenda	Atlanta, Ga.	12/11/44
Lee, Christopher	London, England	5/27/22
Lee, Michele	Los Angeles, Cal.	6/24/42
Lee, Peggy	Jamestown, N.D.	5/26/20
Lee, Spike	Atlanta, Ga.	3/20/57
Legrand, Michel	Paris, France	2/24/32
Leibman, Ron	New York, N.Y.	10/11/37
Leifer, Carol	E. Williston, N.Y.	1956
Leigh, Janet	Merced, Cal.	7/6/27
Leigh, Jennifer Jason	Los Angeles, Cal.	1958
Leinsdorf, Erich	Vienna, Austria	2/4/12
Leisure, David	San Diego, Cal.	11/16/-

Name	Birthplace	Born
Lemmon, Jack	Boston, Mass.	2/8/25
Leno, Jay	New Rochelle, N.Y.	4/28/50
Leonard, Sheldon	New York, N.Y.	2/22/07
Leontovich, Eugenie	Moscow, Russia	3/21/00
Leslie, Joan	Detroit, Mich.	1/26/25
Letterman, David	Indianapolis, Ind.	4/12/47
Levine, James	Cincinnati, Oh.	6/23/43
Levinson, Barry	Baltimore, Md.	6/2/32
Lewis, Emmanuel	New York, N.Y.	3/9/71
Lewis, Dawnn	New York, N.Y.	8/13/60
Lewis, Huey	New York, N.Y.	7/5/51
Lewis, Jerry	Newark, N.J.	3/16/26
Lewis, Jerry Lee	Ferriday, La.	9/29/35
Lewis, Richard	New York, N.Y.	6/29/47
Lewis, Shari	New York, N.Y.	1/17/34
Light, Judith	Trenton, N.J.	2/9/50
Lightfoot, Gordon	Orillia, Ont.	11/17/38
Linden, Hal	New York, N.Y.	3/20/31
Lindfors, Viveca	Uppsala, Sweden	12/29/20
Linkletter, Art	Saskatchewan, Canada	7/17/12
Linn-Baker, Mark	St. Louis, Mo.	6/17/53
Liotta, Ray	Newark, N.J.	12/18/-
Lithgow, John	Rochester, N.Y.	10/19/45
Little, Cleavon	Chickasha, Okla.	6/1/39
Little, Rich	Ottawa, Ont.	11/26/38
Little Richard	Macon, Ga.	12/5/32
Lloyd, Christopher	Stamford, Conn.	10/22/38
Lloyd, Emily	England	9/29/70
Locke, Sondra	Shelbyville, Tenn.	5/28/47
Lockhart, June	New York, N.Y.	6/25/25
Locklear, Heather	Los Angeles, Cal.	9/25/61
Loggia, Robert	New York, N.Y.	1/3/30
Loggins, Kenny	Everett, Wash.	1/17/47
Lollobrigida, Gina	Subiaco, Italy	7/4/27
Lom, Herbert	Prague, Czechoslovakia	1/9/17
London, Julie	Santa Rosa, Cal.	9/26/26
Long, Shelley	Ft. Wayne, Ind.	8/23/49
Lord, Jack	New York, N.Y.	12/30/22
Loren, Sophia	Rome, Italy	9/20/34
Loring, Gloria	New York, N.Y.	12/10/46
Loudon, Dorothy	Boston, Mass.	9/17/33
Louis-Dreyfus, Julia	New York, N.Y.	1/13/61
Lovitz, Jon	Tarzana, Cal.	7/21/57
Lowe, Rob	Charlottesville, Va.	3/17/64
Loy, Myrna	Helena, Mon.	8/2/05
Lucas, George	Modesto, Cal.	5/14/44
Lucci, Susan	Scarsdale, N.Y.	12/23/48
Luckinbill, Laurence	Ft. Smith, Ark.	11/21/34
Ludwig, Christa	Berlin, Germany	3/16/28
Lumet, Sidney	Philadelphia, Pa.	6/25/24
Lupino, Ida	London, England	2/4/14
LuPone, Patti	Northport, N.Y.	4/21/49
Lynch, David	Missoula, Mont.	1/20/46
Lynn, Jeffrey	Auburn, Mass.	2/16/09
Lynn, Loretta	Butcher Hollow, Ky.	4/14/-
Maazel, Lorin	Paris, France	3/6/30
MacArthur, James	Los Angeles, Cal.	12/8/37
MacCorkindale, Simon	Cambridge, England	2/12/52
MacDowell, Andie	Gaffney, S.C.	4/21/58
MacGraw, Ali	Pound Ridge, N.Y.	4/1/38
Mac Lachlan, Kyle	Yakima, Wash.	1960
MacLaine, Shirley	Richmond, Va.	4/24/34
MacLeod, Gavin	Mt. Kisco, N.Y.	2/28/30
MacNee, Patrick	London, England	2/6/22
MacNeil, Cornell	Minneapolis, Minn.	9/24/22
Macchio, Ralph	Long Island, N.Y.	11/4/62
Macy, Bill	Revere, Mass.	5/18/22
Madden, John	Austin, Minn.	4/10/36
Madigan, Amy	Chicago, Ill.	1957
Madonna (Ciccone)	Bay City, Mich.	8/16/58
Majors, Lee	Wyandotte, Mich.	4/23/40
Malbin, Elaine	New York, N.Y.	5/24/32
Malden, Karl	Chicago, Ill.	3/22/13
Malkovich, John	Christopher, Ill.	12/9/53
Malle, Louis	Thumeries, France	10/30/32
Malone, Dorothy	Chicago, Ill.	1/30/25
Manchester, Melissa	Bronx, N.Y.	2/15/51
Mancini, Henry	Cleveland, Oh.	4/16/24
Mandel, Howie	Toronto, Ont.	11/29/55
Mandrell, Barbara	Houston, Tex.	12/25/48
Mangione, Chuck	Rochester, N.Y.	11/29/40
Manilow, Barry	New York, N.Y.	6/17/46
Mann, Herbie	New York, N.Y.	4/16/30
Manoff, Dinah	New York, N.Y.	1/25/58
Mantegna, Joe	Chicago, Ill.	11/13/47
Marceau, Marcel	Strasbourg, France	3/22/23
Marchand, Nancy	Buffalo, N.Y.	6/19/28
Margolin, Janet	New York, N.Y.	7/25/43
Marin, Cheech	Los Angeles, Cal.	7/13/46
Markova, Alicia	London, England	12/1/10
Marriner, Neville	Lincoln, England	4/15/24
Marsalis, Branford	New Orleans, La.	8/26/60
Marsalis, Wynton	New Orleans, La.	10/18/61
Marsh, Jean	London, England	7/1/34
Marshall, E. G.	Owatonna, Minn.	6/18/10
Marshall, Penny	New York, N.Y.	10/15/43
Marshall, Peter	Huntington, W.Va.	3/30/27
Martin, Dean	Steubenville, Oh.	6/17/17
Martin, Dick	Detroit, Mich.	1/30/23
Martin, Steve	Waco, Tex.	4/14/45
Martin, Tony	San Francisco, Cal.	12/25/13
Martins, Peter	Copenhagen, Denmark	10/27/46
Mason, Jackie	Sheboygan, Wis.	6/9/31
Mason, Marsha	St. Louis, Mo.	4/3/42
Masterson, Mary Stuart	New York, N.Y.	1967
Mastrantonio, Mary Eliz.	Lombard, Ill.	11/17/58
Mastroianni, Marcello	Rome, Italy	9/28/23
Masur, Kurt	Brieg, Germany	7/18/27
Matheson, Tim	Glendale, Cal.	12/31/47
Mathis, Johnny	San Francisco, Cal.	9/30/35
Matlin, Marlee	Morton Grove, Ill.	1965
Matthau, Walter	New York, N.Y.	10/1/20
Mature, Victor	Louisville, Ky.	1/29/16
May, Elaine	Philadelphia, Pa.	4/21/32
Mayfield, Curtis	Chicago, Ill.	6/3/42
Mayo, Virginia	St. Louis, Mo.	11/30/20
Mazursky, Paul	Brooklyn, N.Y.	4/25/30
McArdle, Andrea	Philadelphia, Pa.	11/5/63
McBride, Patricia	Teaneck, N.J.	8/23/42
McCallum, David	Glasgow, Scotland	9/19/33
McCambridge, Mercedes	Joliet, Ill.	3/17/18
McCarthy, Andrew	New York, N.Y.	1963
McCarthy, Kevin	Seattle, Wash.	2/15/14
McCartney, Paul	Liverpool, England	6/18/42
McCarver, Tim	Memphis, Tenn.	10/16/41
McClanahan, Rue	Healdton, Okla.	2/21/36
McClure, Doug	Glendale, Cal.	5/11/35
McClurg, Edie	Kansas City, Mo.	7/23/51
McCoo, Marilyn	Jersey City, N.J.	9/30/43
McDowall, Roddy	London, England	9/28/28
McDowell, Malcolm	Leeds, England	6/13/43
McEntire, Reba	McAlester, Okla.	3/28/54
McFarland, Spanky	Dallas, Tex.	10/2/28
McFerrin, Bobby	New York, N.Y.	3/11/50
McGavin, Darren	Spokane, Wash.	5/7/22
McGillis, Kelly	Newport, Cal.	1957
McGoohan, Patrick	New York, N.Y.	3/19/28
McGovern, Elizabeth	Evanston, Ill.	7/18/61
McGovern, Maureen	Youngstown, Oh.	7/27/49
McGuire, Al	New York, N.Y.	9/7/31
McGuire, Dorothy	Omaha, Neb.	6/14/19
McKechnie, Donna	Pontiac, Mich.	11/16/42
McKee, Lonette	Detroit, Mich.	1954
McKellen, Ian	Burnley, England	5/25/39
McLerie, Allyn	Grand Mere, Que.	12/1/26
McMahon, Ed	Detroit, Mich.	3/6/23
McNichol, Kristy	Los Angeles, Cal.	9/11/62
McQueen, Butterfly	Tampa, Fla.	1/7/11
McRaney, Gerald	Collins, Miss.	8/19/48
Meadows, Audrey	Wu Chang, China	2/8/24
Meadows, Jayne	Wu Chang, China	9/27/20
Meara, Anne	New York, N.Y.	9/20/29
Mehta, Zubin	Bombay, India	4/29/36
Mendes, Sergio	Niteroi, Brazil	2/11/41
Menuhin, Yehudi	New York, N.Y.	4/22/16
Mercer, Marian	Akron, Oh.	11/26/35
Mercouri, Melina	Athens, Greece	10/18/25
Meredith, Burgess	Cleveland, Oh.	11/16/08
Merrick, David	Hong Kong	11/27/12
Merrill, Dina	New York, N.Y.	12/9/25
Merrill, Robert	Brooklyn, N.Y.	6/4/19
Messina, Jim	Maywood, Cal.	12/5/47
Metcalf, Laurie	Carbonville, Ill.	6/16/55
Meyers, Ari	San Juan, Puerto Rico	4/6/69
Michael, George	Watford, England	6/26/63
Michaels, Al	New York, N.Y.	11/12/44
Midler, Bette	Paterson, N.J.	12/1/45
Milano, Alyssa	New York, N.Y.	12/19/72
Miles, Sarah	Ingatestone, England	12/31/41
Miles, Vera	near Boise City, Okla.	8/23/29
Miller, Ann	Houston, Tex.	4/12/19
Miller, Dennis	Pittsburgh, Pa.	11/3/53
Miller, Mitch	Rochester, N.Y.	7/4/11
Miller, Roger	Ft. Worth, Tex.	1/2/36
Mills, Donna	Chicago, Ill.	12/11/42

Name	Birthplace	Born
Mills, John	Suffolk, England	2/22/08
Milner, Martin	Detroit, Mich.	12/28/27
Milnes, Sherrill	Downers Grove, Ill.	1/10/35
Milsap, Ronnie	Robinsville, N.C.	1/16/44
Milstein, Nathan	Odessa, Russia	12/31/04
Minnelli, Liza	Los Angeles, Cal.	3/12/46
Mitchell, Cameron	Dallastown, Pa.	4/11/18
Mitchell, James	Sacramento, Cal.	2/29/20
Mitchell, Joni	McLeod, Alta.	11/7/43
Mitchum, Robert	Bridgeport, Conn.	8/6/17
Modine, Matthew	Loma Linda, Cal.	3/22/59
Moffat, Donald	Plymouth, England	12/26/30
Moffo, Anna	Wayne, Pa.	6/27/27
Molinaro, Al.	Kenosha, Wis.	6/24/19
Moll, Richard	Pasadena, Cal.	1/13/43
Montalban, Ricardo	Mexico City, Mexico	11/25/20
Montgomery, Elizabeth	Hollywood, Cal.	4/15/33
Moody, Ron	London, England	1/8/24
Moore, Clayton	Chicago, Ill.	9/14/08
Moore, Demi	Roswell, N.M.	11/11/62
Moore, Dudley	London, England	4/19/35
Moore, Garry	Baltimore, Md.	1/31/15
Moore, Mary Tyler	Brooklyn, N.Y.	12/29/37
Moore, Melba	New York, N.Y.	10/29/45
Moore, Roger	London, England	10/14/27
Moore, Terry	Los Angeles, Cal.	1/1/29
Moranis, Rick	Toronto, Ont.	4/18/53
Moreno, Rita	Humacao, P.R.	12/11/31
Morgan, Dennis	Prentice, Wis.	12/10/10
Morgan, Harry	Detroit, Mich.	4/10/15
Morgan, Henry	New York, N.Y.	3/31/15
Moriarty, Michael	Detroit, Mich.	4/5/41
Morita, Pat	Isleton, Cal.	6/28/32
Morris, Greg	Cleveland, Oh.	9/27/34
Morris, Howard	New York, N.Y.	9/4/25
Morrow, Rob	New Rochelle, N.Y.	9/21/62
Morse, Robert	Newton, Mass.	5/18/31
Morton, Joe	New York, N.Y.	10/18/47
Moses, William	Los Angeles, Cal.	11/17/59
Muldaur, Diana	New York, N.Y.	8/19/38
Mulgrew, Kate	Dubuque, Ia.	4/29/55
Mulhare, Edward	Ireland	4/8/23
Mull, Martin	Chicago, Ill.	8/18/43
Mulligan, Richard	New York, N.Y.	11/13/32
Munsel, Patrice	Spokane, Wash.	5/14/25
Murphy, Ben	Jonesboro, Ark.	3/6/42
Murphy, Eddie	Brooklyn, N.Y.	4/3/61
Murphy, Michael	Los Angeles, Cal.	5/5/38
Murray, Anne	Springhill, Nova Scotia	6/20/45
Murray, Bill	Evanston, Ill.	9/21/50
Murray, Don	Hollywood, Cal.	7/31/29
Musante, Tony	Bridgeport, Conn.	6/30/36
Musburger, Brent	Portland, Ore.	5/26/39
Muti, Riccardo	Naples, Italy	7/28/41
Myers, Mike	Toronto, Ont.	1962
Nabors, Jim	Sylacauga, Ala.	6/12/33
Nash, Graham	Blackpool, England	2/2/42
Natwick, Mildred	Baltimore, Md.	6/19/08
Naughton, James	Middletown, Conn.	7/6/46
Neal, Patricia	Packard, Ky.	1/20/26
Nealon, Kevin	Bridgeport, Conn.	11/18/53
Neill, Sam	New Zealand	1948
Nelligan, Kate	London, Ontario	3/16/51
Nelson, Craig T.	Spokane, Wash.	4/4/46
Nelson, Ed	New Orleans, La.	12/21/28
Nelson, Harriet (Hilliard)	Des Moines, Ia.	7/18/14
Nelson, Judd	Portland, Me.	11/28/59
Nelson, Tracy	Santa Monica, Cal.	10/25/63
Nelson, Willie	Abbott, Tex.	4/30/33
Nero, Peter	New York, N.Y.	5/22/34
Neuwirth, Bebe	Princeton, N.J.	12/31/-
New Kids On The Block		
Knight, Jonathan	Worcester, Mass.	11/29/68
Knight, Jordan	Worcester, Mass.	5/17/70
McIntyre, Joe	Needham, Mass.	12/31/72
Wahlberg, Donnie	Boston, Mass.	8/17/69
Wood, Danny	Boston, Mass.	5/14/69
Newhart, Bob	Oak Park, Ill.	9/29/29
Newley, Anthony	Hackney, England	9/24/31
Newman, Paul	Cleveland, Oh.	1/26/25
Newman, Randy	Los Angeles, Cal.	11/28/43
Newton, Wayne	Norfolk, Va.	4/3/42
Newton-John, Olivia	Cambridge, England	9/26/47
Nicholas, Denise	Detroit, Mich.	7/12/44
Nicholas, Fayard	Philadelphia, Pa.	10/20/14
Nicholas, Harold	Philadelphia, Pa.	3/27/24
Nichols, Mike	Berlin, Germany	11/6/31
Nicholson, Jack	Neptune, N.J.	4/28/37

Name	Birthplace	Born
Nicks, Stevie	Phoenix, Ariz.	5/26/48
Nielsen, Leslie	Regina, Sask	2/11/26
Nilsson, Birgit	Karup, Sweden	5/17/18
Nimoy, Leonard	Boston, Mass.	3/26/31
Noble, James	Dallas, Tex.	3/5/22
Nolte, Nick	Omaha, Neb.	2/8/40
Norman, Jessye	Augusta, Ga.	9/15/45
Norris, Chuck	Ryan, Okla.	3/10/40
North, Sheree	Los Angeles, Cal.	1/17/33
Noth, Christopher	Madison, Wis.	11/13/-
Novak, Kim	Chicago, Ill.	2/13/33
Nureyev, Rudolf	Russia	3/17/38
Oates, John	New York, N.Y.	4/7/48
O'Brian, Hugh	Rochester, N.Y.	4/19/25
O'Brien, Margaret	San Diego, Cal.	1/15/37
Ocean, Billy	Trinidad	1/21/50
O'Connell, Helen	Lima, Oh.	5/23/21
O'Connor, Carroll	New York, N.Y.	8/2/24
O'Connor, Donald	Chicago, Ill.	8/28/25
O'Connor, Sinead	Dublin, Ireland	12/8/67
Odetta	Birmingham, Ala.	12/31/30
O'Hara, Maureen	Dublin, Ireland	8/17/20
O'Herlihy, Dan	Wexford, Ireland	5/1/19
Oldman, Gary	London, England	3/21/58
Olin, Ken	Chicago, Ill.	7/30/54
Olin, Lena	Sweden	1955
Olmos, Edward James	E. Los Angeles, Cal.	2/24/47
Olsen, Merlin	Logan, Ut.	9/15/40
O'Neal, Patrick	Ocala, Fla.	9/26/27
O'Neal, Ryan	Los Angeles, Cal.	4/20/41
O'Neal, Tatum	Los Angeles, Cal.	11/5/63
O'Neill, Ed	Youngstown, Oh.	1946
Ontkean, Michael	Vancouver, B.C.	1/24/46
Orbach, Jerry	New York, N.Y.	10/20/35
Orlando, Tony	New York, N.Y.	4/3/44
Osbourne, Ozzy	Birmingham, England	12/3/46
O'Shea, Milo	Dublin, Ireland	6/2/26
Oslin, K.T.	Crossit, Ark.	1942
Osmond, Donny	Ogden, Ut.	12/9/57
Osmond, Marie	Ogden, Ut.	10/13/59
O'Sullivan, Maureen	Boyle, Ireland	5/17/11
O'Toole, Annette	Houston, Tex.	4/1/53
O'Toole, Peter	Connemara, Ireland	8/2/32
Owens, Buck	Sherman, Tex.	8/12/29
Oz, Frank	Herford, England	5/25/44
Ozawa, Seiji	Shenyang, China	9/1/35
Paar, Jack	Canton, Oh.	5/1/18
Pacino, Al	New York, N.Y.	4/25/40
Packer, Billy	Wellsville, N.Y.	2/25/40
Page, Patti	Claremore, Okla.	11/8/27
Paige, Janis	Tacoma, Wash.	9/16/22
Palance, Jack	Lattimer, Pa.	2/18/20
Palin, Michael	England	5/5/43
Palmer, Betsy	East Chicago, Ind.	11/1/29
Papas, Irene	Greece	3/9/26
Papp, Joseph	Brooklyn, N.Y.	6/22/21
Parker, Alan	London, England	2/14/44
Parker, Eleanor	Cedarville, Oh.	6/26/22
Parker, Fess	Ft. Worth, Tex.	8/16/25
Parker, Jameson	Baltimore, Md.	11/18/47
Parker, Jean	Deer Lodge, Mon.	8/11/12
Parker, Sarah Jessica	Nelsonville, Oh.	3/25/65
Parsons, Estelle	Lynn, Mass.	11/20/27
Parton, Dolly	Sevierville, Tenn.	1/19/46
Patinkin, Mandy	Chicago, Ill.	11/30/52
Pavarotti, Luciano	Modena, Italy	10/12/35
Paycheck, Johnny	Greenfield, Oh.	5/31/41
Pearl, Minnie	Centerville, Tenn.	10/25/12
Peck, Gregory	La Jolla, Cal.	4/5/16
Pendergrass, Teddy	Philadelphia, Pa.	3/26/50
Penn, Arthur	Philadelphia, Pa.	9/27/22
Penn, Sean	Burbank, Cal.	8/17/60
Penny, Joe	London, England	9/14/56
Peppard, George	Detroit, Mich.	10/1/28
Perkins, Elizabeth	Vermont	1961
Perkins, Anthony	New York, N.Y.	4/4/32
Perlman, Itzhak	Tel Aviv, Israel	8/31/45
Perlman, Rhea	Brooklyn, N.Y.	3/31/48
Perlman, Ron	New York, N.Y.	4/13/50
Perrine, Valerie	Galveston, Tex.	9/3/43
Perry, Luke	Fredericktown, Oh.	10/11/-
Persoff, Nehemiah	Jerusalem, Palestine	8/14/20
Pesci, Joe	Newark, N.J.	2/9/43
Peters, Bernadette	New York, N.Y.	2/28/48
Peters, Brock	New York, N.Y.	7/2/27
Peters, Roberta	New York, N.Y.	5/4/30
Petty, Tom	Gainesville, Fla.	10/20/53
Pfeiffer, Michelle	Santa Ana, Cal.	4/29/57

Name	Birthplace	Born
Phillips, Lou Diamond	Philippines	2/17/62
Phillips, MacKenzie	Alexandria, Va.	11/10/59
Phillips, Michelle	Long Beach, Cal.	6/4/44
Phoenix, River	Madras, Ore.	8/23/70
Pickett, Cindy	Norman, Okla.	4/18/47
Pinchot, Bronson	New York, N.Y.	5/20/59
Piscopo, Joe	Passaic, N.J.	6/17/51
Pleasence, Donald	Worksop, England	10/5/19
Pleshette, Suzanne	New York, N.Y.	1/31/37
Plowright, Joan	Brigg, England	10/28/29
Plummer, Amanda	New York, N.Y.	3/23/57
Plummer, Christopher	Toronto, Ont.	12/13/27
Poitier, Sidney	Miami, Fla.	2/20/27
Polanski, Roman	Paris, France	8/18/33
Pollack, Sydney	Lafayette, Ind.	7/1/34
Ponti, Carlo	Milan, Italy	12/11/13
Post, Markie	Palo Alto, Cal.	11/4/50
Poston, Tom	Columbus, Oh.	10/17/27
Potts, Annie	Nashville, Tenn.	10/28/-
Powell, Jane	Portland, Ore.	4/1/28
Powers, Stefanie	Hollywood, Cal.	11/2/42
Prentiss, Paula	San Antonio, Tex.	3/4/39
Presley, Priscilla	New York, N.Y.	5/24/46
Preston, Billy	Houston, Tex.	9/9/46
Previn, Andre	Berlin, Germany	4/6/29
Price, Leontyne	Laurel, Miss.	2/10/27
Price, Ray	Perryville, Tex.	1/12/26
Price, Vincent	St. Louis, Mo.	5/27/11
Pride, Charlie	Sledge, Miss.	3/18/39
Priestley, Jason	Vancouver, B.C.	8/28/69
Prince	Minneapolis, Minn.	6/7/58
Principal, Victoria	Japan	—
Prosky, Robert	Philadelphia, Pa.	12/13/30
Pryce, Jonathan	Wales	6/1/47
Pryor, Richard	Peoria, Ill.	12/1/40
Pulliam, Keshia Knight	Newark, N.J.	4/9/79
Pyle, Denver	Bethune, Col.	5/11/20
Quaid, Dennis	Houston, Tex.	4/9/54
Quaid, Randy	Houston, Tex.	10/1/50
Quinn, Aidan	Chicago, Ill.	3/8/59
Quinn, Anthony	Chihuahua, Mexico	4/21/15
Quinn, Martha	Albany, N.Y.	5/11/59
Rabb, Ellis	Memphis, Tenn.	6/20/30
Rabbitt, Eddie	Brooklyn, N.Y.	11/27/41
Rachins, Alan	Cambridge, Mass.	10/10/47
Rae, Charlotte	Milwaukee, Wis.	4/22/26
Rainer, Luise	Vienna, Austria	1/12/09
Raitt, Bonnie	Burbank, Cal.	11/8/49
Ralston, Esther	Bar Harbor, Me.	9/17/02
Ramey, Samuel	Colby, Kan.	3/28/42
Rampal, Jean-Pierre	Marseilles, France	1/7/22
Randall, Tony	Tulsa, Okla.	2/26/20
Randolph, John	New York, N.Y.	6/1/15
Randolph, Joyce	Detroit, Mich.	10/21/25
Rashad, Phylicia	Houston, Tex.	6/17/48
Ratzenberger, John	Bridgeport, Conn.	4/6/47
Rawls, Lou	Chicago, Ill.	12/1/36
Raye, Martha	Butte, Mon.	8/27/16
Raymond, Gene	New York, N.Y.	8/13/08
Reddy, Helen	Melbourne, Australia	10/25/41
Redford, Robert	Santa Monica, Cal.	8/18/37
Redgrave, Lynn	London, England	3/8/43
Redgrave, Vanessa	London, England	1/30/37
Reed, Jerry	Atlanta, Ga.	3/20/37
Reed, Oliver	London, England	2/13/38
Reed, Rex	Ft. Worth, Tex.	10/2/38
Reed, Shanna	Kansas City, Kan.	10/30/-
Reese, Della	Detroit, Mich.	7/6/31
Reeve, Christopher	New York, N.Y.	9/25/52
Regalbuto, Joe	New York, N.Y.	8/24/-
Reid, Kate	London, England	11/4/30
Reid, Tim	Norfolk, Va.	12/19/44
Reilly, Charles Nelson	New York, N.Y.	1/13/31
Reiner, Carl	Bronx, N.Y.	3/20/22
Reiner, Rob	Bronx, N.Y.	3/6/45
Reinhold, Judge	Wilmington, Del.	5/21/56
Reinking, Ann	Seattle, Wash.	11/10/50
Resnik, Regina	New York, N.Y.	8/30/24
Reynolds, Burt	Waycross, Ga.	2/11/36
Reynolds, Debbie	El Paso, Tex.	4/1/32
Rhue, Madlyn	Washington, D.C.	10/3/34
Rich, Charlie	Forest City, Ark.	12/14/32
Richards, Keith	Kent, England	12/18/43
Richie, Lionel	Tuskegee, Ala.	6/20/50
Rickles, Don	New York, N.Y.	5/8/26
Riegert, Peter	New York, N.Y.	4/11/47
Rigg, Diana	Doncaster, England	7/20/38
Ringwald, Molly	Rosewood, Cal.	2/14/68

Name	Birthplace	Born
Ritter, John	Burbank, Cal.	9/17/48
Rivera, Chita	Washington, D.C.	1/23/33
Rivera, Geraldo	New York, N.Y.	7/4/43
Rivers, Joan	Brooklyn, N.Y.	6/8/33
Robards, Jason Jr.	Chicago, Ill.	7/26/22
Robbins, Jerome	New York, N.Y.	10/11/18
Robbins, Tim	W. Covina, Cal.	10/16/58
Roberts, Doris	St. Louis, Mo.	11/4/29
Roberts, Eric	Biloxi, Miss.	4/18/56
Roberts, Julia	Smyrna, Ga.	10/25/67
Roberts, Pernell	Waycross, Ga.	5/18/30
Roberts, Tony	New York, N.Y.	10/22/39
Robertson, Cliff	La Jolla, Cal.	9/9/25
Robertson, Dale	Harrah, Okla.	7/14/23
Robinson, Charles	Houston, Tex.	11/9/-
Robinson, Smokey	Detroit, Mich.	2/19/40
Roche, Eugene	Boston, Mass.	9/22/28
Rodgers, Jimmy	Camas, Wash.	9/18/33
Rodrigues, Percy	Montreal, Que.	6/13/24
Rodriquez, Johnny	Sabinal, Tex.	12/10/51
Rogers, Fred	Latrobe, Pa.	3/20/28
Rogers, Ginger	Independence, Mo.	7/16/11
Rogers, Kenny	Houston, Tex.	8/21/38
Rogers, Mimi	Coral Gables, Fla.	1/27/-
Rogers, Roy	Cincinnati, Oh.	11/5/12
Roland, Gilbert	Juarez, Mexico	12/11/05
Rolle, Esther	Pompano Beach, Fla.	11/8/33
Rollins, Howard	Baltimore, Md.	10/17/50
Romero, Cesar	New York, N.Y.	2/15/07
Ronstadt, Linda	Tucson, Ariz.	7/15/46
Rooney, Mickey	Brooklyn, N.Y.	9/23/20
Rose Marie	New York, N.Y.	8/15/25
Ross, Diana	Detroit, Mich.	3/26/44
Ross, Katharine	Hollywood, Cal.	1/29/42
Ross, Marion	Albert Lea, Minn.	10/25/28
Rossellini, Isabella	Rome, Italy	6/18/52
Rostropovich, Mstislav	Baku, USSR	3/12/27
Roth, David Lee	Bloomington, Ind.	10/10/55
Rourke, Mickey	Miami, Fla.	1953
Rowlands, Gena	Cambria, Wis.	6/19/34
Rubinstein, John	Los Angeles, Cal.	12/8/46
Rush, Barbara	Denver, Col.	1/4/30
Russell, Jane	Bemidji, Minn.	6/21/21
Russell, Ken	Southampton, England	7/3/27
Russell, Kurt	Springfield, Mass.	3/17/51
Russell, Mark	Buffalo, N.Y.	8/23/32
Russell, Nipsey	Atlanta, Ga.	10/13/24
Russell, Theresa	San Diego, Cal.	1957
Rutherford, Ann	Toronto, Ont.	11/2/20
Ruttan, Susan	Oregon City, Ore.	9/16/50
Ryan, Meg	Fairfield, Conn.	11/19/63
Ryan, Peggy	Long Beach, Cal.	8/28/24
Ryan, Roz	Detroit, Mich.	7/7/51
Rydell, Bobby	Philadelphia, Pa.	4/26/42
Ryder, Winona	Winona, Minn.	10/29/71
Saget, Bob	Philadelphia, Pa.	5/17/56
Sahl, Mort	Montreal, Que.	5/11/27
Saint, Eva Marie	Newark, N.J.	7/4/24
St. James, Susan	Los Angeles, Cal.	8/14/46
St. John, Jill	Los Angeles, Cal.	8/19/40
Sajak, Pat	Chicago, Ill.	10/26/47
Saks, Gene	New York, N.Y.	11/8/21
Sales, Soupy	Franklinton, N.C.	1/8/26
Samms, Emma	London, England	8/28/60
Sanderson, William	Memphis, Tenn.	1/10/48
Sandy, Gary	Dayton, Oh.	12/25/45
Sanford, Isabel	New York, N.Y.	8/29/-
Santana, Carlos	Mexico	7/20/47
Sarandon, Susan	New York, N.Y.	10/4/46
Sarnoff, Dorothy	New York, N.Y.	5/25/17
Savage, Fred	Highland Park, Ill.	7/9/76
Savalas, Telly	Garden City, N.Y.	1/21/24
Saxon, John	Brooklyn, N.Y.	8/5/35
Sayles, John	Schenectady, N.Y.	9/28/50
Scaggs, Boz	Dallas, Tex.	6/8/44
Schallert, William	Los Angeles, Cal.	7/6/22
Scheider, Roy	Orange, N.J.	11/10/32
Schell, Maria	Vienna, Austria	1/15/26
Schell, Maximilian	Vienna, Austria	12/8/30
Schenkel, Chris	Bippus, Ind.	8/21/23
Schnabel, Stefan	Berlin, Germany	2/2/12
Schneider, John	Mt. Kisco, N.Y.	4/8/54
Schreiber, Avery	Chicago, Ill.	4/9/35
Schroder, Rick	Staten Island, N.Y.	4/3/70
Schwarzenegger, Arnold	Graz, Austria	7/30/47
Schwarzkopf, Elisabeth	Jarotschin, Poland	12/9/15
Scofield, Paul	Hurst, Pierpont, England	1/21/22

Name	Birthplace	Born
Scolari, Peter	New Rochelle, Ill.	9/12/54
Scorsese, Martin	New York, N.Y.	11/17/42
Scott, George C.	Wise, Va.	10/18/27
Scott, Lizabeth	Scranton, Pa.	9/29/22
Scott, Martha	Jamesport, Mo.	9/22/14
Scotto, Renata	Savona, Italy	2/24/35
Scully, Vin	New York, N.Y.	11/29/27
Sedaka, Neil	New York, N.Y.	3/13/39
Seeger, Pete	New York, N.Y.	5/3/19
Segal, George	Great Neck, N.Y.	2/13/34
Segal, Vivienne	Philadelphia, Pa.	4/19/97
Seidelman, Susan	Philadelphia, Pa.	12/11/52
Seinfeld, Jerry	New York, N.Y.	1954
Sellecca, Connie	New York, N.Y.	5/25/55
Selleck, Tom	Detroit, Mich.	1/29/45
Severinsen, Doc	Arlington, Ore.	7/7/27
Seymour, Jane	Middlesex, England	2/15/51
Shackelford, Ted	Oklahoma City, Okla.	6/23/46
Shaffer, Paul	Thunder Bay, Ont.	11/28/49
Shandling, Garry	Tucson, Ariz.	11/29/49
Shankar, Ravi	India	4/7/20
Sharif, Omar	Alexandria, Egypt	4/10/32
Shatner, William	Montreal, Que.	3/22/31
Shea, John	N. Conway, N.H.	4/14/49
Shearer, Moira	Scotland	1/17/26
Sheedy, Ally	New York, N.Y.	6/12/62
Sheen, Charlie	New York, N.Y.	9/3/65
Sheen, Martin	Dayton, Oh.	8/3/40
Shelley, Carole	London, England	8/16/39
Shepard, Sam	Ft. Sheridan, Ill.	11/5/43
Shepherd, Cybill	Memphis, Tenn.	2/18/49
Shields, Brooke	New York, N.Y.	5/31/65
Shire, Talia	New York, N.Y.	4/25/46
Shore, Dinah	Winchester, Tenn.	3/1/17
Short, Bobby	Danville, Ill.	9/15/24
Short, Martin	Hamilton, Ont.	3/26/50
Shull, Richard B.	Evanston, Ill.	2/24/29
Sidney, Sylvia	New York, N.Y.	8/8/10
Siepi, Cesare	Milan, Italy	2/10/23
Sikking, James B.	Los Angeles, Cal.	3/5/34
Sills, Beverly	Brooklyn, N.Y.	5/25/29
Silver, Ron	New York, N.Y.	7/2/46
Simmons, Gene	Haifa, Israel	8/25/49
Simmons, Jean	London, England	1/31/29
Simmons, Richard	New Orleans, La.	7/12/48
Simon, Carly	New York, N.Y.	6/25/45
Simon, Paul	Newark, N.J.	10/13/41
Simone, Nina	Tyron, N.C.	2/21/33
Sinatra, Frank	Hoboken, N.J.	12/12/15
Sinbad	Benton Harbor, Mich.	11/10/-
Sinclair, Madge	Kingston, Jamaica	4/28/38
Siskel, Gene	Chicago, Ill.	1/26/46
Skelton, Red (Richard)	Vincennes, Ind.	7/18/13
Skerritt, Tom	Detroit, Mich.	8/25/33
Slater, Helen	Massapequa, N.Y.	12/14/63
Slezak, Erika	Hollywood, Cal.	8/5/46
Slick, Grace	Chicago, Ill.	10/30/39
Smirnoff, Yakov	Odessa, USSR	1/24/51
Smith, Allison	New York, N.Y.	12/9/69
Smith, Alexis	Penticton, B.C.	6/8/21
Smith, Buffalo Bob	Buffalo, N.Y.	11/27/17
Smith, Jaclyn	Houston, Tex.	10/26/47
Smith, Keely	Norfolk, Va.	3/9/35
Smith, Maggie	Ilford, England	12/28/34
Smith, Will	Philadelphia, Pa.	9/25/69
Smits, Jimmy	New York, N.Y.	7/9/55
Smothers, Dick	New York, N.Y.	11/20/39
Smothers, Tom	New York, N.Y.	2/2/37
Snipes, Wesley	Orlando, Fla.	1962
Snow, Hank	Nova Scotia, Canada	5/9/14
Solti, Georg	Budapest, Hungary	10/21/12
Somers, Suzanne	San Bruno, Cal.	10/16/46
Sommer, Elke	Berlin, Germany	11/5/41
Sorvino, Paul	New York, N.Y.	1939
Sothern, Ann	Valley City, N.D.	1/22/09
Soul, David	Chicago, Ill.	8/28/43
Spacek, Sissy	Quitman, Tex.	12/25/49
Spacey, Kevin	S. Orange, N.J.	1960
Spader, James	Boston, Mass.	2/7/60
Spano, Joe	San Francisco, Cal.	7/7/46
Spelling, Aaron	Dallas, Tex.	4/22/28
Spencer, John	New Jersey	1946
Spielberg, Steven	Cincinnati, Oh.	12/18/47
Springfield, Dusty	London, England	4/16/39
Springfield, Rick	Sydney, Australia	8/23/49
Springsteen, Bruce	Freehold, N.J.	9/23/49
Stack, Robert	Los Angeles, Cal.	1/13/19
Stafford, Jo	Coalinga, Cal.	11/12/18

Name	Birthplace	Born
Stahl, Richard	Detroit, Mich.	1/4/32
Stallone, Sylvester	New York, N.Y.	7/6/46
Stamos, John	Cypress, Cal.	8/19/63
Stamp, Terence	Stepney, England	7/22/39
Stander, Lionel	New York, N.Y.	1/11/08
Stang, Arnold	New York, N.Y.	9/28/25
Stanley, Kim	Tularosa, N.M.	2/11/25
Stanton, Harry Dean	Kentucky	7/14/26
Stapleton, Jean	New York, N.Y.	1/19/23
Stapleton, Maureen	Troy, N.Y.	6/21/25
Starr, Ringo	Liverpool, England	7/7/40
Steenburgen, Mary	Little Rock, Ark.	1953
Steiger, Rod	W. Hampton, N.Y.	4/14/25
Stephens, James	Mt. Kisco, N.Y.	5/18/51
Stern, Howard	New York, N.Y.	1/12/54
Stern, Isaac	Kreminiecz, Russia	7/21/20
Sternhagen, Frances	Washington, D.C.	1/13/30
Stevens, Andrew	Memphis, Tenn.	6/10/55
Stevens, Cat	London, England	7/21/48
Stevens, Connie	Brooklyn, N.Y.	8/8/38
Stevens, Rise	New York, N.Y.	6/11/13
Stevens, Stella	Yazoo City, Miss.	10/1/36
Stevenson, McLean	Normal, Ill.	11/14/29
Stevenson, Parker	Philadelphia, Pa.	6/4/52
Stewart, James	Indiana, Pa.	5/20/08
Stewart, Rod	London, England	1/10/45
Stickney, Dorothy	Dickinson, N.D.	6/21/00
Stiers, David Ogden	Peoria, Ill.	10/31/42
Stiller, Jerry	New York, N.Y.	6/8/29
Stills, Stephen	Dallas, Tex.	1/3/45
Sting (G. Sumner)	Newcastle, England	10/2/51
Stockwell, Dean	Hollywood, Cal.	3/5/36
Stoltz, Eric	American Samoa	1961
Stone, Oliver	New York, N.Y.	9/15/46
Stookey, Paul	Baltimore, Md.	12/30/37
Storch, Larry	New York, N.Y.	1/8/23
Storm, Gale	Bloomington, Tex.	4/5/22
Straight, Beatrice	Old Westbury, N.Y.	8/2/18
Strait, George	Pearsall, Tex.	5/1/52
Strasser, Robin	New York, N.Y.	5/7/45
Stratas, Teresa	Toronto, Ont.	5/26/38
Strauss, Peter	New York, N.Y.	2/20/47
Streep, Meryl	Summit, N.J.	6/22/49
Streisand, Barbra	Brooklyn, N.Y.	4/24/42
Stritch, Elaine	Detroit, Mich.	2/2/26
Struthers, Sally	Portland, Ore.	7/28/48
Stuarti, Enzo	Rome, Italy	3/3/25
Sullivan, Barry	New York, N.Y.	8/29/12
Sullivan, Susan	New York, N.Y.	11/18/44
Sumac, Yma	Ichocan, Peru	9/10/27
Summer, Donna	Boston, Mass.	12/31/48
Sutherland, Donald	St. John, New Brunswick	7/17/34
Sutherland, Joan	Sydney, Australia	11/7/26
Sutherland, Kiefer	London, England	12/20/66
Swayze, Patrick	Houston, Tex.	8/18/54
Swit, Loretta	Passaic, N.J.	11/4/37
Mr. T (Lawrence Tero)	Chicago, Ill.	5/21/52
Tallchief, Maria	Fairfax, Okla.	1/24/25
Tandy, Jessica	London, England	6/7/09
Tarkenton, Fran	Richmond, Va.	2/3/40
Taylor, Elizabeth	London, England	2/27/32
Taylor, James	Boston, Mass.	3/12/48
Taylor, Rod	Sydney, Australia	1/11/29
Te Kanawa, Kiri	Gisborne, New Zealand	3/6/44
Tebaldi, Renata	Pesaro, Italy	2/1/22
Temple, Shirley	Santa Monica, Cal.	4/23/28
Tennant, Victoria	London, England	9/30/50
Tennille, Toni	Montgomery, Ala.	5/8/43
Tharp, Twyla	Portland, Ind.	7/1/41
Thicke, Alan	Kirkland Lake, Ont.	3/1/47
Thomas, Jay	Kermit, Tex.	7/12/-
Thomas, Marlo	Detroit, Mich.	11/21/43
Thomas, Philip Michael	Columbus, Oh.	5/26/49
Thomas, Richard	New York, N.Y.	6/13/51
Thompson, Jack	Sydney, Australia	8/31/40
Thompson, Lea	Rochester, Minn.	5/31/61
Thompson, Sada	Des Moines, Ia.	9/27/29
Thulin, Ingrid	Sweden	1/27/29
Tiegs, Cheryl	Minnesota	9/27/47
Tiffany	Norwalk, Cal.	10/2/71
Tillis, Mel	Tampa, Fla.	8/8/32
Tiny Tim	New York, N.Y.	4/12/23
Todd, Richard	Dublin, Ireland	6/11/19
Tomlin, Lily	Detroit, Mich.	9/1/39
Tomlinson, David	Scotland	5/7/17
Torme, Mel	Chicago, Ill.	9/13/25
Torn, Rip	Temple, Tex.	2/6/31
Townsend, Robert	Chicago, Ill.	2/6/57

Name	Birthplace	Born
Travanti, Daniel J.	Kenosha, Wis.	3/7/40
Travers, Mary	Louisville, Ky.	11/9/36
Travis, Randy	Marshville, N.C.	5/4/59
Travolta, John	Englewood, N.J.	2/18/54
Trebek, Alex	Sudbury, Ont.	7/22/40
Trevor, Claire	New York, N.Y.	3/8/09
Troyanos, Tatiana	New York, N.Y.	9/12/38
Tucker, Michael	Baltimore, Md.	2/6/44
Tucker, Tanya	Seminole, Tex.	10/10/58
Tune, Tommy	Wichita Falls, Tex.	2/28/39
Turner, Janine	Lincoln, Neb.	12/6/62
Turner, Kathleen	Springfield, Mo.	6/19/54
Turner, Lana	Wallace, Ida.	2/8/20
Turner, Tina	Nutbush, Tenn.	11/26/38
Turturro, John	New York, N.Y.	1967
Twiggy (Leslie Hornby)	London, England	9/19/46
Twitty, Conway	Friar's Point, Miss.	9/1/33
Tyson, Cicely	New York, N.Y.	12/19/33
Uecker, Bob	Milwaukee, Wis.	1/26/35
Uggams, Leslie	New York, N.Y.	5/25/43
Ullman, Tracey	Slough, England	12/30/59
Ullmann, Liv	Tokyo, Japan	12/16/38
Underwood, Blair	Tacoma, Wash.	8/25/-
Urich, Robert	Toronto, Oh.	12/19/46
Ustinov, Peter	London, England	4/16/21
Vaccaro, Brenda	Brooklyn, N.Y.	11/18/39
Vale, Jerry	New York, N.Y.	7/8/31
Valente, Caterina	Paris, France	1/14/31
Valli, Frankie	Newark, N.J.	5/3/37
Van Ark, Joan	New York, N.Y.	6/16/43
Van Doren, Mamie	Rowena, S.D.	2/6/33
Vandross, Luther	New York, N.Y.	4/20/51
Van Dyke, Dick	West Plains, Mo.	12/13/25
Van Dyke, Jerry	Danville, Ill.	7/27/31
Van Fleet, Jo.	Oakland, Cal.	12/30/22
Van Halen, Eddie	Nijmegan, Netherlands.	1/26/57
Van Pallandt, Nina.	Copenhagen, Denmark	7/15/32
Van Patten, Dick.	New York, N.Y.	12/9/28
Van Peebles, Mario	Mexico	1/15/57
Vaughn, Robert	New York, N.Y.	11/22/32
Venuta, Benay	San Francisco, Cal.	1/27/11
Verdon, Gwen	Los Angeles, Cal.	1/13/25
Vereen, Ben	Miami, Fla.	10/10/46
Verrett, Shirley	New Orleans, La.	5/31/31
Vickers, Jon	Prince Albert, Sask.	10/26/26
Vigoda, Abe	New York, N.Y.	2/24/21
Vincent, Jan-Michael	Denver, Col.	7/15/44
Vinson, Helen	Beaumont, Tex.	9/17/07
Vinton, Bobby	Canonsburg, Pa.	4/16/35
Vitale, Dick	E. Rutherford, N.J.	6/9/40
Voight, Jon	Yonkers, N.Y.	12/29/38
Von Stade, Frederica	Somerville, N.J.	6/1/45
Von Sydow, Max	Lund, Sweden.	4/10/29
Wagner, Lindsay	Los Angeles, Cal.	6/22/49
Wagner, Robert	Detroit, Mich.	2/10/30
Wagoner, Porter	West Plains, Mo.	8/12/27
Wahl, Ken	Chicago, Ill.	2/14/56
Wain, Bea	Bronx, N.Y.	4/30/17
Waite, Ralph	White Plains, N.Y.	6/22/29
Walden, Robert	New York, N.Y.	9/25/43
Walken, Christopher	New York, N.Y.	3/31/43
Wallach, Eli.	Brooklyn, N.Y.	12/7/15
Walston, Ray	Laurel, Miss.	11/2/24
Walter, Jessica	New York, N.Y.	1/31/44
Wanamaker, Sam	Chicago, Ill.	6/14/19
Ward, Fred	San Diego, Cal.	1943
Ward, Simon	London, England	10/19/41
Warden, Jack	Newark, N.J.	9/18/20
Warfield, William	W. Helena, Ark.	1/22/20
Warner, Malcolm-Jamal	Jersey City, N.J.	8/18/70
Warren, Lesley Ann	New York, N.Y.	8/16/46
Warrick, Ruth	St. Joseph, Mo.	6/29/16
Warwick, Dionne	E. Orange, N.J.	12/12/41
Washington, Denzel	Mt. Vernon, N.Y.	12/28/54
Waterston, Sam	Cambridge, Mass.	11/15/40
Watkins, Carlene	Hartford, Conn.	6/4/52
Watts, Andre	Nuremberg, Germany	6/20/46
Wayans, Damon	New York, N.Y.	1960
Wayans, Keenan Ivory	New York, N.Y.	1958
Wayne, David	Traverse City, Mich.	1/30/14
Waxman, Al	Toronto, Ont.	3/2/35
Weaver, Dennis	Joplin, Mo.	6/4/24
Weaver, Fritz	Pittsburgh, Pa.	1/19/26
Weaver, Sigourney	New York, N.Y.	10/8/49
Weir, Peter	Sydney, Australia	8/8/44
Weitz, Bruce	Norwalk, Conn.	5/27/43
Welch, Raquel	Chicago, Ill.	9/5/40
Weld, Tuesday	New York, N.Y.	8/27/43
Wells, Kitty	Nashville, Tenn.	8/30/19
Wendt, George	Chicago, Ill.	10/17/48
Weston, Jack	Cleveland, Oh.	8/21/24
White, Barry	Galveston, Tex.	9/12/44
White, Betty	Oak Park, Ill.	1/17/22
White, Jesse	Buffalo, N.Y.	1/3/19
White, Vanna	N. Myrtle Beach, S.C.	2/18/57
Whiting, Margaret	Detroit, Mich.	7/22/24
Whitmore, James	White Plains, N.Y.	10/1/21
Widmark, Richard	Sunrise, Minn.	12/26/14
Wiest, Dianne	Kansas City, Mo.	3/28/48
Wilder, Billy	Vienna, Austria	6/22/06
Wilder, Gene	Milwaukee, Wis.	6/11/35
Williams, Andy	Wall Lake, Ia.	12/3/30
Williams, Billy Dee	New York, N.Y.	4/6/37
Williams, Cindy	Van Nuys, Cal.	8/22/47
Williams, Esther	Los Angeles, Cal.	8/8/23
Williams, Hal	Columbus, Oh.	12/14/38
Williams Jr., Hank	Shreveport, La.	5/26/49
Williams, Joe	Cordele, Ga.	12/12/18
Williams, JoBeth	Houston, Tex.	1953
Williams, Paul	Omaha, Neb.	9/19/40
Williams, Robin	Chicago, Ill.	7/21/52
Williams, Treat	Rowayton, Conn.	12/1/51
Williams, Vanessa	New York, N.Y.	3/18/63
Williamson, Nicol	Hamilton, Scotland	9/14/38
Willis, Bruce	W. Germany	3/19/55
Wilson, Demond	Valdosta, Ga.	10/13/46
Wilson, Elizabeth	Grand Rapids, Mich.	4/4/25
Wilson, Flip	Jersey City, N.J.	12/8/33
Wilson, Nancy	Chillicothe, Oh.	2/20/37
Windom, William	New York, N.Y.	9/28/23
Winfield, Paul	Los Angeles, Cal.	5/22/41
Winfrey, Oprah	Kosciusko, Miss.	1/29/54
Winger, Debra	Cleveland, Oh.	5/16/55
Winkler, Henry	New York, N.Y.	10/30/45
Winters, Jonathan	Dayton, Oh.	11/11/25
Winters, Shelley	St. Louis, Mo.	8/18/22
Winwood, Steve	Birmingham, England	5/12/48
Wiseman, Joseph	Montreal, Que.	5/15/18
Withers, Jane	Atlanta, Ga.	4/12/26
Wonder, Stevie	Saginaw, Mich.	5/13/50
Woodard, Alfre	Tulsa, Okla.	11/2/53
Woods, James	Vernal, N.J.	4/18/47
Woodward, Edward	Croyden, England	6/1/30
Woodward, Joanne	Thomasville, Ga.	2/27/30
Woolery, Chuck	Ashland, Ky.	3/16/-
Worth, Irene	Nebraska	6/23/16
Wray, Fay	Alberta, Canada	9/10/07
Wright, Martha	Seattle, Wash.	3/23/26
Wright, Max	Detroit, Mich.	8/2/-
Wright, Steven	New York, N.Y.	12/6/55
Wright, Teresa	New York, N.Y.	10/27/18
Wyatt, Jane	Campgaw, N.J.	8/10/11
Wyman, Jane	St. Joseph, Mo.	1/4/14
Wynette, Tammy	Red Bay, Ala.	5/5/42
Yarborough, Glenn	Milwaukee, Wis.	1/12/30
Yarrow, Peter	New York, N.Y.	5/31/38
York, Michael	Fulmer, England	3/27/42
York, Susannah	London, England	1/9/42
Young, Alan	Northumberland, England	11/19/19
Young, Burt	New York, N.Y.	4/30/40
Young, Loretta	Salt Lake City, Ut.	1/6/13
Young, Neil	Toronto, Ont.	11/12/45
Young, Robert	Chicago, Ill.	2/22/07
Youngman, Henny	Liverpool, England	1/12/06
Zappa, Frank	Baltimore, Md.	12/21/40
Zeffirelli, Franco	Florence, Italy	2/12/23
Zerbe, Anthony	Long Beach, Cal.	5/20/36
Zimbalist, Efrem Jr.	New York, N.Y.	11/30/23
Zukerman, Pinchas	Tel Aviv, Israel	7/16/48

Entertainment Personalities of the Past

(as of mid-1992)

Born	Died	Name
1895	1974	Abbott, Bud
1872	1953	Adams, Maude
1855	1926	Adler, Jacob P.
1903	1984	Adler, Luther
1898	1933	Adoree, Renee
1902	1986	Aherne, Brian
1931	1989	Ailey, Alvin
1909	1964	Albertson, Frank
1907	1981	Albertson, Jack
1894	1956	Allen, Fred
1906	1964	Allen, Gracie
1883	1950	Allgood, Sara
1913	1967	Andrews, Laverne
1887	1933	Arbuckle, Fatty (Roscoe)
1908	1990	Arden, Eve
1900	1976	Arlen, Richard
1868	1946	Arliss, George
1888	1945	Armetta, Henry
1900	1971	Armstrong, Louis
1917	1986	Arnaz, Desi
1890	1956	Arnold, Edward
1905	1974	Arquette, Cliff
1900	1991	Arthur, Jean
1899	1987	Astaire, Fred
1906	1987	Astor, Mary
1885	1946	Atwill, Lionel
1905	1967	Auer, Mischa
1900	1972	Austin, Gene
1913	1989	Backus, Jim
1918	1990	Bailey, Pearl
1892	1968	Bainter, Fay
1906	1975	Baker, Josephine
1904	1983	Balanchine, George
1911	1989	Ball, Lucille
1882	1956	Bancroft, George
1902	1968	Bankhead, Tallulah
1890	1952	Banks, Leslie
1890	1955	Bara, Theda
1810	1891	Barnum, Phineas T.
1879	1959	Barrymore, Ethel
1882	1942	Barrymore, John
1878	1954	Barrymore, Lionel
1848	1905	Barrymore, Maurice
1897	1963	Barthelmess, Richard
1914	1984	Basehart, Richard
1904	1984	Basie, Count
1923	1985	Baxter, Anne
1889	1951	Baxter, Warner
1904	1965	Beatty, Clyde
1902	1962	Beavers, Louise
1884	1946	Beery, Noah
1889	1949	Beery, Wallace
1901	1970	Begley, Ed
1904	1991	Bellamy, Ralph
1949	1982	Belushi, John
1906	1968	Benaderet, Bea
1906	1964	Bendix, William
1904	1965	Bennett, Constance
1910	1990	Bennett, Joan
1943	1987	Bennett, Michael
1894	1974	Benny, Jack
1924	1970	Benzell, Mimi
1899	1966	Berg, Gertrude
1903	1978	Bergen, Edgar
1915	1982	Bergman, Ingrid
1895	1976	Berkeley, Busby
1923	1986	Bernardi, Herschel
1844	1923	Bernhardt, Sarah
1893	1943	Bernie, Ben
1889	1967	Bickford, Charles
1911	1960	Bjoerling, Jussi
1895	1973	Blackmer, Sidney
1908	1989	Blanc, Mel
1928	1972	Blocker, Dan
1909	1979	Blondell, Joan
1888	1959	Blore, Eric
1901	1975	Blue, Ben
1899	1957	Bogart, Humphrey
1880	1965	Boland, Mary
1895	1969	Boles, John
1904	1987	Bolger, Ray
1903	1960	Bond, Ward
1892	1981	Bondi, Beulah
1917	1981	Boone, Richard
1833	1893	Booth, Edwin
1796	1852	Booth, Junius Brutus
1905	1965	Bow, Clara
1874	1946	Bowes, Maj. Edward
1928	1977	Boyd, Stephen
1898	1972	Boyd, William
1899	1978	Boyer, Charles
1893	1939	Brady, Alice
1894	1974	Brennan, Walter
1904	1979	Brent, George
1891	1951	Brice, Fanny
1891	1959	Broderick, Helen
1892	1973	Brown, Joe E.
1926	1966	Bruce, Lenny
1895	1953	Bruce, Nigel
1910	1982	Bruce, Virginia
1915	1985	Brynner, Yul
1903	1979	Buchanan, Edgar
1938	1982	Buono, Victor
1885	1970	Burke, Billie
1911	1967	Burnette, Smiley
1925	1984	Burton, Richard
1897	1946	Busch, Mae
1883	1966	Bushman, Francis X.
1896	1946	Butterworth, Charles
1893	1971	Byington, Spring
1904	1972	Cabot, Bruce
1918	1977	Cabot, Sebastian
1899	1986	Cagney, James
1895	1956	Calhern, Louis
1923	1977	Callas, Maria
1933	1976	Cambridge, Godfrey
1865	1940	Campbell, Mrs. Patrick
1892	1964	Cantor, Eddie
1897	1991	Capra, Frank
1878	1947	Carey, Harry
1950	1983	Carpenter, Karen
1906	1988	Carradine, John
1880	1961	Carrillo, Leo
1892	1972	Carroll, Leo G.
1905	1965	Carroll, Nancy
1910	1963	Carson, Jack
1873	1921	Caruso, Enrico
1876	1973	Casals, Pablo
1929	1989	Cassavetes, John
1893	1969	Castle, Irene
1887	1918	Castle, Vernon
1873	1938	Chaliapin, Feodor
1919	1980	Champion, Gower
1918	1961	Chandler, Jeff
1883	1930	Chaney, Lon
1905	1973	Chaney Jr., Lon
1942	1981	Chapin, Harry
1889	1977	Chaplin, Charles
1893	1961	Chatterton, Ruth
1888	1972	Chevalier, Maurice
1888	1960	Clark, Bobby
1914	1968	Clark, Fred
1920	1966	Clift, Montgomery
1932	1963	Cline, Patsy
1892	1967	Clyde, Andy
1911	1976	Cobb, Lee J.
1877	1961	Coburn, Charles
1878	1942	Cohan, George M.
1902	1986	Cohen, Myron
1919	1965	Cole, Nat (King)
1890	1965	Collins, Ray
1891	1958	Colman, Ronald
1908	1934	Columbo, Russ
1917	1982	Conried, Hans
1911	1975	Conte, Richard
1914	1984	Coogan, Jackie
1935	1964	Cooke, Sam
1901	1961	Cooper, Gary
1888	1971	Cooper, Gladys
1896	1973	Cooper, Melville
1914	1968	Corey, Wendell
1893	1974	Cornell, Katherine
1890	1972	Correll, Charles (Andy)
1905	1979	Costello, Dolores
1906	1959	Costello, Lou
1899	1973	Coward, Noel
1924	1973	Cox, Wally
1908	1983	Crabbe, Buster
1928	1978	Crane, Bob
1911	1986	Crawford, Broderick
1908	1977	Crawford, Joan
1880	1942	Crews, Laura Hope
1880	1974	Crisp, Donald
1942	1973	Croce, Jim
1903	1977	Crosby, Bing
1910	1986	Crothers, Scatman
1908	1990	Cummings, Robert
1878	1968	Currie, Finlay
1914	1978	Dailey, Dan
1923	1965	Dandridge, Dorothy
1894	1963	Daniell, Henry
1901	1971	Daniels, Bebe
1936	1973	Darin, Bobby
1921	1965	Darnell, Linda
1879	1967	Darwell, Jane
1909	1986	Da Silva, Howard
1866	1949	Davenport, Harry
1908	1989	Davis, Bette
1907	1961	Davis, Joan
1925	1990	Davis Jr., Sammy
1931	1955	Dean, James
1905	1968	Dekker, Albert
1908	1983	Del Rio, Dolores
1892	1983	Demarest, William
1881	1959	DeMille, Cecil B.
1891	1967	Denny, Reginald
1901	1974	DeSica, Vittorio
1905	1977	Devine, Andy
1942	1972	De Wilde, Brandon
1907	1974	De Wolfe, Billy
1920	1985	Diamond, Selma
1901	1992	Dietrich, Marlene
1879	1947	Digges, Dudley
1901	1966	Disney, Walt
1894	1949	Dix, Richard
1905	1958	Donat, Robert
1889	1972	Donlevy, Brian
1901	1981	Douglas, Melvyn
1907	1959	Douglas, Paul
1889	1956	Draper, Ruth
1881	1965	Dresser, Louise
1869	1934	Dressler, Marie
1820	1897	Drew, Mrs. John
1909	1951	Duchin, Eddy
1890	1974	Dumbrille, Douglass
1889	1965	Dumont, Margaret
1878	1927	Duncan, Isadora
1905	1967	Dunn, James
1898	1990	Dunne, Irene
1893	1980	Durante, Jimmy
1907	1968	Duryea, Dan
1858	1924	Duse, Eleanora
1894	1929	Eagels, Jeanne
1901	1967	Eddy, Nelson
1897	1971	Edwards, Cliff
1879	1945	Edwards, Gus
1899	1974	Ellington, Duke
1941	1974	Elliot, Cass
1891	1967	Elman, Mischa
1881	1951	Errol, Leon
1888	1976	Evans, Edith
1901	1989	Evans, Maurice
1883	1939	Fairbanks, Douglas
1914	1970	Farmer, Frances
1870	1929	Farnum, Dustin
1876	1953	Farnum, William
1882	1967	Farrar, Geraldine
1904	1971	Farrell, Glenda
1897	1961	Fay, Frank
1895	1962	Fazenda, Louise
1933	1982	Feldman, Marty
1912	1992	Ferrer, Jose
1898	1985	Fetchit, Stepin
1894	1979	Fiedler, Arthur
1918	1973	Field, Betty

Born	Died	Name
1898	1979	Fields, Gracie
1879	1946	Fields, W.C.
1931	1978	Fields, Totie
1916	1977	Finch, Peter
1902	1975	Fine, Larry
1865	1932	Fiske, Minnie Maddern
1888	1961	Fitzgerald, Barry
1895	1962	Flagstad, Kirsten
1900	1971	Flippen, Jay C.
1909	1959	Flynn, Errol
1925	1974	Flynn, Joe
1910	1968	Foley, Red
1905	1982	Fonda, Henry
1920	1978	Fontaine, Frank
1887	1983	Fontanne, Lynn
1919	1991	Fonteyn, Margot
1895	1973	Ford, John
1901	1976	Ford, Paul
1919	1991	Ford, Tennessee Ernie
1899	1966	Ford, Wallace
1927	1987	Fosse, Bob
1901	1970	Foster, Preston
1922	1991	Foxx, Redd
1857	1928	Foy, Eddie
1903	1968	Francis, Kay
1887	1966	Frawley, William
1870	1955	Friganza, Trixie
1890	1958	Frisco, Joe
1901	1960	Gable, Clark
1905	1990	Garbo, Greta
1877	1967	Garden, Mary
1922	1990	Gardner, Ava
1913	1952	Garfield, John
1922	1969	Garland, Judy
1939	1984	Gaye, Marvin
1906	1984	Gaynor, Janet
1902	1978	Geer, Will
1900	1954	George, Gladys
1892	1962	Gibson, Hoot
1894	1971	Gilbert, Billy
1895	1936	Gilbert, John
1855	1937	Gillette, William
1897	1987	Gingold, Hermione
1898	1968	Gish, Dorothy
1916	1987	Gleason, Jackie
1886	1959	Gleason, James
1884	1938	Gluck, Alma
1905	1990	Goddard, Paulette
1903	1983	Godfrey, Arthur
1882	1974	Goldwyn, Samuel
1909	1986	Goodman, Benny
1915	1969	Gorcey, Leo
1896	1985	Gordon, Ruth
1899	1982	Gosden, Freeman (Amos)
1869	1944	Gottschalk, Ferdinand
1829	1869	Gottschalk, Louis
1916	1973	Grable, Betty
1894	1991	Graham, Martha
1925	1981	Grahame, Gloria
1904	1986	Grant, Cary
1915	1987	Greene, Lorne
1879	1954	Greenstreet, Sydney
1874	1948	Griffith, David Wark
1912	1980	Griffith, Hugh
1912	1967	Guthrie, Woody
1875	1959	Gwenn, Edmund
1892	1950	Hale, Alan
1925	1981	Haley, Bill
1899	1979	Haley, Jack
1902	1985	Hamilton, Margaret
1847	1919	Hammerstein, Oscar
1893	1964	Hardwicke, Cedric
1892	1957	Hardy, Oliver
1911	1937	Harlow, Jean
1908	1990	Harrison, Rex
1870	1946	Hart, William S.
1928	1973	Harvey, Laurence
1910	1973	Hawkins, Jack
1890	1973	Hayakawa, Sessue
1885	1969	Hayes, Gabby
1902	1971	Hayward, Leland
1917	1975	Hayward, Susan
1918	1987	Hayworth, Rita
1896	1937	Healy, Ted
1910	1971	Heflin, Van
1901	1987	Heifetz, Jascha
1873	1918	Held, Anna

Born	Died	Name
1942	1970	Hendrix, Jimi
1912	1969	Henie, Sonja
1908	1992	Henreid, Paul
1936	1990	Henson, Jim
1886	1956	Hersholt, Jean
1899	1980	Hitchcock, Alfred
1914	1955	Hodiak, John
1894	1973	Holden, Fay
1918	1981	Holden, William
1922	1965	Holliday, Judy
1936	1959	Holly, Buddy
1888	1951	Holt, Jack
1918	1973	Holt, Tim
1898	1978	Homolka, Oscar
1902	1972	Hopkins, Miriam
1858	1935	Hopper, DeWolf
1915	1970	Hopper, William
1904	1989	Horowitz, Vladimir
1886	1970	Horton, Edward Everett
1874	1926	Houdini, Harry
1902	1988	Houseman, John
1906	1952	Howard, Curly
1881	1965	Howard, Eugene
1867	1961	Howard, Joe
1890	1943	Howard, Leslie
1897	1975	Howard, Moe
1891	1955	Howard, Shemp
1885	1955	Howard, Tom
1916	1988	Howard, Trevor
1885	1949	Howard, Willie
1925	1985	Hudson, Rock
1890	1977	Hull, Henry
1886	1957	Hull, Josephine
1895	1958	Humphrey, Doris
1925	1969	Hunter, Jeffrey
1901	1962	Husing, Ted
1906	1987	Huston, John
1884	1950	Huston, Walter
1892	1950	Ingram, Rex
1895	1969	Ingram, Rex
1895	1980	Iturbi, Jose
1838	1905	Irving, Henry
1875	1942	Jackson, Joe
1911	1972	Jackson, Mahalia
1891	1984	Jaffe, Sam
1903	1991	Jagger, Dean
1916	1983	James, Harry
1889	1956	Janis, Elsie
1886	1950	Jannings, Emil
1930	1980	Janssen, David
1900	1974	Jenkins, Allen
1898	1981	Jessel, George
1892	1962	Johnson, Chic
1886	1950	Jolson, Al
1889	1942	Jones, Buck
1933	1983	Jones, Carolyn
1911	1965	Jones, Spike
1943	1970	Joplin, Janis
1902	1982	Jory, Victor
1905	1981	Joslyn, Allyn
1910	1966	Kane, Helen
1887	1969	Karloff, Boris
1893	1970	Karns, Roscoe
1913	1987	Kaye, Danny
1811	1868	Kean, Charles
1806	1880	Kean, Mrs. Charles
1787	1833	Kean, Edmund
1895	1966	Keaton, Buster
1894	1973	Kellaway, Cecil
1898	1979	Kelly, Emmett
1928	1982	Kelly, Grace
1910	1981	Kelly, Patsy
1907	1968	Kelton, Pert
1926	1959	Kendall, Kay
1914	1990	Kennedy, Arthur
1890	1948	Kennedy, Edgar
1886	1956	Kibbee, Guy
1888	1964	Kilbride, Percy
1923	1986	Knight, Ted
1901	1980	Kostelanetz, Andre
1919	1962	Kovacs, Ernie
1885	1974	Kruger, Otto
1921	1991	Kulp, Nancy
1913	1964	Ladd, Alan
1895	1967	Lahr, Bert

Born	Died	Name
1919	1973	Lake, Veronica
1915	1982	Lamas, Fernando
1902	1986	Lanchester, Elsa
1919	1948	Landis, Carole
1904	1972	Landis, Jessie Royce
1936	1991	Landon, Michael
1884	1944	Langdon, Harry
1853	1929	Langtry, Lillie
1921	1959	Lanza, Mario
1870	1950	Lauder, Harry
1899	1962	Laughton, Charles
1890	1965	Laurel, Stan
1923	1984	Lawford, Peter
1898	1952	Lawrence, Gertrude
1908	1991	Lean, David
1940	1973	Lee, Bruce
1907	1952	Lee, Canada
1914	1970	Lee, Gypsy Rose
1888	1976	Lehmann, Lotte
1913	1967	Leigh, Vivien
1922	1976	Leighton, Margaret
1940	1980	Lennon, John
1898	1981	Lenya, Lotte
1870	1941	Leonard, Eddie
1900	1987	LeRoy, Mervyn
1906	1972	Levant, Oscar
1905	1980	Levene, Sam
1902	1971	Lewis, Joe E.
1892	1971	Lewis, Ted
1919	1987	Liberace
1820	1887	Lind, Jenny
1894	1989	Lillie, Beatrice
1893	1971	Lloyd, Harold
1870	1922	Lloyd, Marie
1891	1957	Lockhart, Gene
1913	1969	Logan, Ella
1909	1942	Lombard, Carole
1902	1977	Lombardo, Guy
1927	1974	Long, Richard
1895	1975	Lopez, Vincent
1888	1968	Lorne, Marion
1904	1964	Lorre, Peter
1912	1962	Lovejoy, Frank
1890	1971	Lowe, Edmund
1892	1947	Lubitsch, Ernst
1882	1956	Lugosi, Bela
1894	1971	Lukas, Paul
1892	1977	Lunt, Alfred
1926	1982	Lynde, Paul
1926	1971	Lynn, Diana
1903	1965	MacDonald, Jeanette
1902	1969	MacLane, Barton
1908	1991	MacMurray, Fred
1921	1986	MacRae, Gordon
1909	1973	Macready, George
1908	1973	Magnani, Anna
1890	1975	Main, Marjorie
1932	1967	Mansfield, Jayne
1905	1980	Mantovani, Annunzio
1897	1975	March, Fredric
1945	1981	Marley, Bob
1890	1966	Marshall, Herbert
1913	1990	Martin, Mary
1920	1981	Martin, Ross
1924	1987	Marvin, Lee
1888	1964	Marx, Arthur (Harpo)
1901	1979	Marx, Herbert (Zeppo)
1890	1977	Marx, Julius (Groucho)
1886	1961	Marx, Leonard (Chico)
1893	1977	Marx, Milton (Gummo)
1909	1984	Mason, James
1896	1983	Massey, Raymond
1885	1957	Mayer, Louis B.
1895	1973	Maynard, Ken
1884	1945	McCormack, John
1905	1990	McCrea, Joel
1895	1952	McDaniel, Hattie
1899	1981	McHugh, Frank
1907	1991	McIntire, John
1883	1959	McLaglen, Victor
1907	1971	McMahon, Horace
1930	1980	McQueen, Steve
1920	1980	Medford, Kay
1880	1946	Meek, Donald
1861	1931	Melba, Nellie
1890	1973	Melchior, Lauritz
1890	1963	Menjou, Adolphe
1902	1966	Menken, Helen

Born	Died	Name
1908	1984	Merman, Ethel
1905	1986	Milland, Ray
1904	1944	Miller, Glenn
1898	1936	Miller, Marilyn
1903	1955	Minnevitch, Borrah
1913	1955	Miranda, Carmen
1892	1962	Mitchell, Thomas
1880	1940	Mix, Tom
1926	1962	Monroe, Marilyn
1911	1973	Monroe, Vaughn
1917	1951	Montez, Maria
1904	1981	Montgomery, Robert
1901	1947	Moore, Grace
1876	1962	Moore, Victor
1906	1974	Moorehead, Agnes
1890	1949	Morgan, Frank
1900	1941	Morgan, Helen
1901	1970	Morris, Chester
1914	1959	Morris, Wayne
1943	1971	Morrison, Jim
1932	1982	Morrow, Vic
1915	1977	Mostel, Zero
1897	1969	Mowbray, Alan
1895	1967	Muni, Paul
1915	1970	Munshin, Jules
1924	1971	Murphy, Audie
1902	1992	Murphy, George
1885	1965	Murray, Mae
1896	1970	Nagel, Conrad
1900	1973	Naish, J. Carroll
1898	1961	Naldi, Nita
1906	1975	Nelson, Ozzie
1940	1985	Nelson, Rick
1885	1967	Nesbit, Evelyn
1909	1983	Niven, David
1890	1950	Nijinsky, Vaslav
1893	1974	Nilsson, Anna Q.
1902	1985	Nolan, Lloyd
1894	1930	Normand, Mabel
1899	1968	Novarro, Ramon
1903	1978	Oakie, Jack
1860	1926	Oakley, Annie
1928	1982	Oates, Warren
1911	1979	Oberon, Merle
1915	1985	O'Brien, Edmond
1899	1983	O'Brien, Pat
1908	1981	O'Connell, Arthur
1880	1959	O'Connor, Una
1908	1968	O'Keefe, Dennis
1880	1938	Oland, Warner
1860	1932	Olcott, Chauncey
1883	1942	Oliver, Edna May
1907	1989	Olivier, Laurence
1892	1963	Olsen, Ole
1849	1920	O'Neill, James
1936	1988	Orbison, Roy
1899	1985	Ormandy, Eugene
1876	1949	Ouspenskaya, Maria
1887	1972	Owen, Reginald
1860	1941	Paderewski, Ignace
1924	1987	Page, Geraldine
1889	1954	Pallette, Eugene
1914	1986	Palmer, Lilli
1894	1958	Pangborn, Franklin
1914	1992	Parks, Bert
1914	1975	Parks, Larry
1881	1940	Pasternack, Josef A.
1837	1908	Pastor, Tony
1843	1919	Patti, Adelina
1840	1889	Patti, Carlotta
1885	1931	Pavlova, Anna
1904	1984	Peerce, Jan
1899	1967	Pendleton, Nat
1905	1941	Penner, Joe
1915	1963	Piaf, Edith
1893	1979	Pickford, Mary
1897	1984	Pidgeon, Walter
1892	1957	Pinza, Ezio
1898	1963	Pitts, Zasu
1904	1976	Pons, Lily
1897	1981	Ponselle, Rosa
1904	1963	Powell, Dick
1912	1982	Powell, Eleanor
1892	1984	Powell, William
1913	1958	Power, Tyrone
1905	1986	Preminger, Otto
1935	1977	Presley, Elvis
1918	1987	Preston, Robert
1911	1978	Prima, Louis
1954	1977	Prinze, Freddie
1946	1989	Radner, Gilda
1895	1980	Raft, George
1890	1967	Rains, Claude
1892	1967	Rathbone, Basil
1897	1960	Ratoff, Gregory
1941	1967	Redding, Otis
1908	1985	Redgrave, Michael
1921	1986	Reed, Donna
1932	1992	Reed, Robert
1914	1959	Reeves, George
1873	1943	Reinhardt, Max
1935	1991	Remick, Lee
1909	1971	Rennie, Michael
1902	1983	Richardson, Ralph
1921	1985	Riddle, Nelson
1898	1977	Ritchard, Cyril
1907	1974	Ritter, Tex
1905	1969	Ritter, Thelma
1901	1965	Ritz, Al
1906	1986	Ritz, Harry
1903	1985	Ritz, Jimmy
1925	1982	Robbins, Marty
1898	1976	Robeson, Paul
1878	1949	Robinson, Bill
1893	1973	Robinson, Edward G.
1865	1942	Robson, May
1905	1977	Rochester (E. Anderson)
1897	1933	Rodgers, Jimmie
1879	1935	Rogers, Will
1880	1962	Rooney, Pat
1899	1966	Rose, Billy
1922	1987	Rowan, Dan
1887	1982	Rubinstein, Artur
1886	1970	Ruggles, Charles
1924	1961	Russell, Gail
1861	1922	Russell, Lillian
1911	1976	Russell, Rosalind
1892	1972	Rutherford, Margaret
1903	1973	Ryan, Irene
1909	1973	Ryan, Robert
1924	1963	Sabu (Dastagir)
1877	1968	St. Denis, Ruth
1884	1955	Sakall, S.Z.
1885	1936	Sale (Chic), Charles
1906	1972	Sanders, George
1895	1964	Schildkraut, Joseph
1889	1965	Schipa, Tito
1882	1951	Schnabel, Artur
1920	1981	Scott, Hazel
1898	1987	Scott, Randolph
1914	1965	Scott, Zachary
1843	1896	Scott-Siddons, Mrs.
1938	1979	Seberg, Jean
1892	1974	Seeley, Blossom
1893	1987	Segovia, Andres
1925	1980	Sellers, Peter
1902	1965	Selznick, David O.
1884	1960	Sennett, Mack
1927	1978	Shaw, Robert
1891	1972	Shawn, Ted
1868	1949	Shean, Al
1902	1983	Shearer, Norma
1915	1967	Sheridan, Ann
1875	1953	Shubert, Lee
1755	1831	Siddons, Mrs. Sarah
1921	1985	Signoret, Simone
1912	1985	Silvers, Phil
1900	1976	Sim, Alastair
1858	1942	Skinner, Otis
1863	1948	Smith, C. Aubrey
1907	1986	Smith, Kate
1854	1932	Sousa, John Philip
1884	1957	Sparks, Ned
1907	1990	Stanwyck, Barbara
1934	1970	Stevens, Inger
1882	1977	Stokowski, Leopold
1879	1953	Stone, Lewis
1904	1980	Stone, Milburn
1898	1959	Sturges, Preston
1911	1960	Sullavan, Margaret
1902	1974	Sullivan, Ed
1903	1956	Sullivan, Francis L.
1892	1946	Summerville, Slim
1899	1983	Swanson, Gloria
1904	1969	Swarthout, Gladys
1893	1957	Talmadge, Norma
1899	1972	Tamiroff, Akim
1878	1947	Tanguay, Eva
1885	1966	Taylor, Deems
1899	1958	Taylor, Estelle
1887	1946	Taylor, Laurette
1911	1969	Taylor, Robert
1847	1928	Terry, Ellen
1899	1936	Thalberg, Irving
1912	1991	Thomas, Danny
1892	1960	Thomas, John Charles
1882	1976	Thorndike, Sybil
1896	1960	Tibbett, Lawrence
1920	1991	Tierney, Gene
1909	1958	Todd, Michael
1874	1947	Toler, Sidney
1903	1968	Tone, Franchot
1867	1957	Toscanini, Arturo
1898	1968	Tracy, Lee
1900	1967	Tracy, Spencer
1903	1972	Traubel, Helen
1894	1975	Treacher, Arthur
1853	1917	Tree, Herbert Beerbohm
1890	1973	Truex, Ernest
1932	1984	Truffaut, Francois
1919	1986	Tucker, Forrest
1915	1975	Tucker, Richard
1884	1966	Tucker, Sophie
1874	1940	Turpin, Ben
1908	1959	Twelvetrees, Helen
1895	1926	Valentino, Rudolph
1901	1986	Vallee, Rudy
1911	1979	Vance, Vivian
1924	1990	Vaughan, Sarah
1893	1943	Veidt, Conrad
1926	1981	Vera-Ellen
1885	1957	Von Stroheim, Erich
1906	1981	Von Zell, Harry
1922	1992	Walker, Nancy
1914	1951	Walker, Robert
1887	1980	Walsh, Raoul
1876	1962	Walter, Bruno
1876	1958	Warner, H. B.
1924	1963	Washington, Dinah
1900	1977	Waters, Ethel
1907	1979	Wayne, John
1891	1966	Webb, Clifton
1920	1982	Webb, Jack
1903	1992	Welk, Lawrence
1915	1985	Welles, Orson
1896	1975	Wellman, William
1892	1980	West, Mae
1895	1968	Wheeler, Bert
1889	1938	White, Pearl
1891	1967	Whiteman, Paul
1865	1948	Whitty, May
1912	1979	Wilding, Michael
1877	1922	Williams, Bert
1923	1953	Williams, Hank
1905	1975	Wills, Bob
1903	1978	Wills, Chill
1917	1972	Wilson, Marie
1884	1969	Winninger, Charles
1904	1959	Withers, Grant
1907	1961	Wong, Anna May
1938	1981	Wood, Natalie
1892	1978	Wood, Peggy
1888	1963	Woolley, Monty
1902	1981	Wyler, William
1886	1966	Wynn, Ed
1916	1986	Wynn, Keenan
1890	1960	Young, Clara Kimball
1913	1978	Young, Gig
1887	1953	Young, Roland
1902	1979	Zanuck, Darryl F.
1869	1932	Ziegfeld, Florenz
1873	1976	Zukor, Adolph

Original Names of Selected Entertainers

Edie Adams: Elizabeth Edith Enke
Eddie Albert: Edward Albert Heimberger
Alan Alda: Alphonso D'Abruzzo
Jane Alexander: Jane Quigley
Fred Allen: John Sullivan
Woody Allen: Allen Konigsberg
Julie Andrews: Julia Wells
Eve Arden: Eunice Quedens
Beatrice Arthur: Bernice Frankel
Jean Arthur: Gladys Greene
Fred Astaire: Frederick Austerlitz
Alan Autry: Carlos Brown
Lauren Bacall: Betty Joan Perske
Anne Bancroft: Anna Maria Italiano
Brigitte Bardot: Camille Javal
Gene Barry: Eugene Klass
Orson Bean: Dallas Burrows
Bonnie Bedelia: Bonnie Culkin
Pat Benatar: Patricia Andrejewski
Robbie Benson: Robert Segal
Tony Bennett: Anthony Benedetto
Busby Berkeley: William Berkeley Enos
Jack Benny: Benjamin Kubelsky
Joey Bishop: Joseph Gottlieb
Robert Blake: Michael Gubitosi
Victor Borge: Borge Rosenbaum
David Bowie: David Robert Jones
Boy George: George Alan O'Dowd
Fanny Brice: Fanny Borach
Charles Bronson: Charles Buchinski
Albert Brooks: Albert Einstein
Mel Brooks: Melvin Kaminsky
George Burns: Nathan Birnbaum
Ellen Burstyn: Edna Gilhooley
Richard Burton: Richard Jenkins
Red Buttons: Aaron Chwatt
Nicolas Cage: Nicholas Coppola
Michael Caine: Maurice Micklewhite
Maria Callas: Maria Kalogeropoulos
Vikki Carr: Florencia Casillas
Diahann Carroll: Carol Diahann Johnson
Cyd Charisse: Tula Finklea
Ray Charles: Ray Charles Robinson
Cher: Cherilyn Sarkisian
Patsy Cline: Virginia Patterson Hensley
Lee J. Cobb: Leo Jacoby
Claudette Colbert: Lily Chauchoin
Michael Connors: Kreker Ohanian
Robert Conrad: Conrad Robert Falk
Alice Cooper: Vincent Furnier
David Copperfield: David Kotkin
Howard Cosell: Howard Cohen
Elvis Costello: Declan Patrick McManus
Lou Costello: Louis Cristillo
Joan Crawford: Lucille Le Sueur
Michael Crawford: Michael Dumbell-Smith
Tom Cruise: Thomas Mapother
Tony Curtis: Bernard Schwartz
Vic Damone: Vito Farinola
Rodney Dangerfield: Jacob Cohen
Bobby Darin: Walden Waldo Cassotto
Doris Day: Doris von Kappelhoff
Yvonne De Carlo: Peggy Middleton
Sandra Dee: Alexandra Zuck
John Denver: Henry John Deutschendorf Jr.
Bo Derek: Cathleen Collins
John Derek: Derek Harris
Susan Dey: Susan Smith
Angie Dickinson: Angeline Brown
Bo Diddley: Elias Bates
Phyllis Diller: Phyllis Driver
Diana Dors: Diana Fluck
Melvyn Douglas: Melvyn Hesselberg
Bob Dylan: Robert Zimmerman
Sheena Easton: Sheena Shirley Orr
Barbara Eden: Barbara Huffman
Ron Ely: Ronald Pierce
Chad Everett: Raymond Cramton
Tom Ewell: S. Yewell Tompkins
Douglas Fairbanks: Douglas Ullman
Morgan Fairchild: Patsy McClenny
Alice Faye: Ann Leppert
Stepin Fetchit: Lincoln Perry
Sally Field: Sally Mahoney
W.C. Fields: William Claude Dukenfield
Peter Finch: William Mitchell
Barry Fitzgerald: William Joseph Shields
Joan Fontaine: Joan de Havilland
John Ford: Sean O'Fearna
John Forsythe: John Freund
Redd Foxx : John Sanford
Anthony Franciosa: Anthony Papaleo
Arlene Francis: Arlene Kazanjian
Connie Francis: Concetta Franconero
Greta Garbo: Greta Gustafsson
Vincent Gardenia: Vincent Scognamiglio
John Garfield: Julius Garfinkle
Judy Garland: Frances Gumm
James Garner: James Bumgarner
Crystal Gayle: Brenda Gayle Webb
Paulette Goddard: Marion Levy
Whoopi Goldberg: Caryn Johnson
Eydie Gorme: Edith Gormezano
Stewart Granger: James Stewart
Cary Grant: Archibald Leach
Lee Grant: Lyova Rosenthal
Joel Grey: Joe Katz
Robert Guillaume: Robert Williams
Buddy Hackett: Leonard Hacker
Jean Harlow: Harlean Carpentier
Rex Harrison: Reginald Carey
Laurence Harvey: Larushka Skikne
Helen Hayes: Helen Brown
Susan Hayward: Edythe Marriner
Rita Hayworth: Margarita Cansino
Pee-Wee Herman: Paul Rubenfeld
Barbara Hershey: Barbara Herzstine
William Holden: William Beedle
Judy Holliday: Judith Tuvim
Harry Houdini: Ehrich Weiss
Leslie Howard: Leslie Stainer
Moe Howard: Moses Horowitz
Rock Hudson: Roy Scherer Jr. (later Fitzgerald)
Engelbert Humperdinck: Arnold Dorsey
Kim Hunter: Janet Cole
Mary Beth Hurt: Mary Supinger
Betty Hutton: Betty Thornberg
David Janssen: David Meyer
Elton John: Reginald Dwight
Don Johnson: Donald Wayne
Jennifer Jones: Phyllis Isley
Tom Jones: Thomas Woodward
Louis Jourdan: Louis Gendre
Boris Karloff: William Henry Pratt
Danny Kaye: David Kaminsky
Diane Keaton: Diane Hall
Michael Keaton: Michael Douglas
Howard Keel: Harold Leek
Chaka Khan: Yvette Stevens
Carole King: Carole Klein
Larry King: Larry Zeigler
Ben Kingsley: Krishna Banji
Nastassja Kinski: Nastassja Naksyznyski
Ted Knight: Tadeus Wladyslaw Konopka
Cheryl Ladd: Cheryl Stoppelmoor
Veronica Lake: Constance Ockleman
Dorothy Lamour: Mary Kaumeyer
Michael Landon: Eugene Orowitz
Mario Lanza: Alfredo Cocozza
Stan Laurel: Arthur Jefferson
Steve Lawrence: Sidney Leibowitz
Brenda Lee: Brenda Mae Tarpley
Bruce Lee: Lee Yuen Kam
Gypsy Rose Lee: Rose Louise Hovick
Michelle Lee: Michelle Dusiak
Peggy Lee: Norma Egstrom
Janet Leigh: Jeanette Morrison
Vivien Leigh: Vivien Hartley
Huey Lewis: Hugh Cregg
Jerry Lewis: Joseph Levitch
Hal Linden: Harold Lipshitz
Carole Lombard: Jane Peters
Jack Lord: John Joseph Ryan
Sophia Loren: Sophia Scicoloni
Peter Lorre: Laszio Lowenstein
Myrna Loy: Myrna Williams
Bela Lugosi: Bela Ferenc Blasko
Moms Mabley: Loretta Mary Aitken
Shirley MacLaine: Shirley Beaty
Madonna: Madonna Louise Ciccone
Lee Majors: Harvey Lee Yeary 2d
Karl Malden: Malden Sekulovich

Jayne Mansfield: Vera Jane Palmer
Fredric March: Frederick Bickel
Peter Marshall: Pierre LaCock
Dean Martin: Dino Crocetti
Ethel Merman: Ethel Zimmerman
George Michael: Georgios Panayiotou
Ray Milland: Reginald Truscott-Jones
Ann Miller: Lucille Collier
Joni Mitchell: Roberta Joan Anderson
Marilyn Monroe: Norma Jean Mortenson, (later) Baker
Yves Montand: Ivo Levi
Ron Moody: Ronald Moodnick
Demi Moore: Demi Guynes
Garry Moore: Thomas Garrison Morfit
Rita Moreno: Rosita Alverio
Harry Morgan: Harry Bratsburg
Paul Muni: Muni Weisenfreund
Mike Nichols: Michael Igor Peschowsky
Chuck Norris: Carlos Ray
Sheree North: Dawn Bethel
Hugh O'Brian: Hugh Krampke
Maureen O'Hara: Maureen Fitzsimmons
Patti Page: Clara Ann Fowler
Jack Palance: Walter Palanuik
Bert Parks: Bert Jacobson
Minnie Pearl: Sarah Ophelia Cannon
Bernadette Peters: Bernadette Lazzaro
Edith Piaf: Edith Gassion
Slim Pickens: Louis Lindley
Mary Pickford: Gladys Smith
Stephanie Powers: Stefania Federkiewicz
Paula Prentiss: Paula Ragusa
Robert Preston: Robert Preston Meservey
Prince: Prince Rogers Nelson
Tony Randall: Leonard Rosenberg
Martha Raye: Margaret O'Reed
Donna Reed: Donna Belle Mullenger
Della Reese: Delloreese Patricia Early
Joan Rivers: Joan Sandra Molinsky
Edward G. Robinson: Emmanuel Goldenberg
Ginger Rogers: Virginia McMath
Roy Rogers: Leonard Slye
Mickey Rooney: Joe Yule Jr.
Lillian Russell: Helen Leonard
Theresa Russell: Theresa Paup
Winona Ryder: Winona Horowitz
Susan St. James: Susan Miller
Soupy Sales: Milton Hines
Susan Sarandon: Susan Tomaling
Randolph Scott: George Randolph Crane
Jane Seymour: Joyce Frankenberg
Omar Sharif: Michael Shalhoub
Martin Sheen: Ramon Estevez
Beverly Sills: Belle Silverman
Talia Shire: Talia Coppola
Phil Silvers: Philip Silversmith
Suzanne Somers: Suzanne Mahoney
Ann Sothern: Harriette Lake
Robert Stack: Robert Modini
Barbara Stanwyck: Ruby Stevens
Jean Stapleton: Jeanne Murray
Ringo Starr: Richard Starkey
Connie Stevens: Concetta Ingolia
Sting: Gordon Sumner
Donna Summers: LaDonna Gaines
Robert Taylor: Spangler Arlington Brugh
Danny Thomas: Muzyad Yakhoob, later Amos Jacobs
Randy Travis: Randy Traywick
Sophie Tucker: Sophia Kalish
Tina Turner: Annie Mae Bullock
Conway Twitty: Harold Lloyd Jenkins
Rudolph Valentino: Rudolpho D'Antonguolla
Frankie Valli: Frank Castelluccio
David Wayne: Wayne McMeekan
John Wayne: Marion Morrison
Clifton Webb: Webb Parmalee Hollenbeck
Raquel Welch: Raquel Tejada
Gene Wilder: Jerome Silberman
Shelley Winters: Shirley Schrift
Stevie Wonder: Stevland Morris
Natalie Wood: Natasha Gurdin
Jane Wyman: Sarah Jane Fulks
Gig Young: Byron Barr

Selected International Figures of the Present

(Excluding heads of state, entertainers, and athletes; for heads of state, see individual nations)

Name (Birthplace)	Birthdate
Chinua Achebe (Ogidi, Nigeria)	11/16/30
Jorge Amado (Bahia, Brazil)	8/1/12
Martin Amis (Oxford, England)	8/25/49
Yasir Arafat (Jerusalem, Palestine)	1929
Moshe Arens (Kaumas, Lithuania)	12/27/25
Oscar Arias Sanchez (Heredia, Costa Rica)	9/13/41
Margaret Atwood (Ottawa, Ontario)	11/18/39
Benazir Bhutto (Karachi, Pakistan)	6/21/53
Boutros Boutros-Ghali (Cairo, Egypt)	11/14/22
British Royal Family	
Queen Elizabeth II (London, England)	4/21/26
Prince Philip (Corfu, Greece)	6/1/21
Prince Charles (London, England)	11/14/48
Princess Diana (Sandringham, England)	7/1/61
Prince William (London, England)	6/2/81
Prince Henry (London, England)	9/15/84
Princess Anne (London, England)	8/15/50
Prince Andrew (London, England)	2/19/60
Sarah Ferguson (London, England)	10/15/59
Princess Beatrice (London, England)	8/8/88
Princess Eugenie (London, England)	3/23/90
Prince Edward (London, England)	3/1/64
Princess Margaret (Glamis, Scotland)	8/21/30
Gro Harlem Bruntland (Oslo, Norway)	4/2/39
Elias Canetti (Ruschuk, Bulgaria)	7/25/05
Camilo Jose Cela (Ira Flavia, Spain)	5/11/16
Dalai Lama (Kokonor, Tibet)	6/6/35
Robertson Davies (Thamesville, Ontario)	8/28/13
Margaret Drabble (Sheffield, England)	6/5/39
Valery Giscard d'Estaing (Koblenz, Germany)	2/2/26
Carlos Fuentes (Mexico City, Mexico)	11/11/28
Athol Fugard (Kanroo, South Africa)	1932
Gabriel Garcia Marquez (Aracata, Colombia)	3/6/28
Mikhail Gorbachev (Privalnaye, Stavropol, USSR)	3/21/31
Raisa Gorbachev (Rubtsovsk, USSR)	1934
Nadine Gordimer (Springs, South Africa)	11/2/23
Germaine Greer (Melbourne, Australia)	1/29/39
Stephen Hawking (Oxford, England)	1/8/42
Michael Heseltine (Swansea, Wales)	3/21/33
Ted Hughes (Mytholmroyd, England)	8/17/30
P.D. James (Oxford, England)	8/3/20
Milan Kundera (Brno, Czechoslovakia)	4/1/29
John LeCarre (Poole, England)	10/19/31
Doris Lessing (Kermanshah, Persia)	10/22/19
Naguib Mahfouz (Cairo, Egypt)	12/11/11
Nelson Mandela (Transkei, South Africa)	1918
Winnie Mandela (Transkei, South Africa)	1934
Czeslaw Milosz (Sateinial, Lithuania)	6/3/11
Kiichi Miyazawa (Tokyo, Japan)	10/8/19
Monaco Royal Family	
Prince Ranier III (Monaco)	5/31/23
Prince Albert (Monte Carlo, Monaco)	3/14/58
Princess Caroline (Monte Carlo, Monaco)	1/23/57
Princess Stephanie (Monaco-Ville, Monaco)	2/1/65
Alice Munro (Wingham, Ontario)	7/10/31
Iris Murdoch (Dublin, Ireland)	7/15/19
Rupert Murdoch (Melbourne, Australia)	3/11/31
Yasuhiro Nakasone (Takasaki, Japan)	5/27/18
Edna O'Brien (Tuamgraney, Ireland)	12/15/31
Amoz Oz (Jerusalem, Palestine)	5/4/39
Andreas Papandreou (Chios, Greece)	2/5/19
Octavio Paz (Mexico City, Mexico)	3/31/14
Shimon Perez (Wolozyn, Poland)	8/16/23
Yitzak Rabin (Jerusalem, Palestine)	3/1/22
Mordecai Richler (Montreal, Quebec)	1/27/31
Mary Robinson (Ballina, Ireland)	5/21/44
Salman Rushdie (Bombay, India)	6/19/47
Yitzak Shamir (Kuzinoy, Poland)	11/3/14
Eduard Shevardnadze (Mamati, USSR)	1/25/28
Wole Soyinka (Abeokuta, Nigeria)	7/13/34
Muriel Spark (Edinburgh, Scotland)	2/1/18
Mother Theresa (Skopje, Yugoslavia)	8/27/10
Margaret Thatcher (Grantham, England)	10/13/25

UNITED STATES GOVERNMENT

LEGISLATIVE BRANCH

CONGRESS

Senate House

Architect of the Capitol
U.S Botanic Garden
General Accounting Office
Government Printing Office
Library of Congress
Office of Technology Assessment
Congressional Budget Office
Copyright Royalty Tribunal
U.S. Tax Court

EXECUTIVE BRANCH

PRESIDENT

Vice President Cabinet

Executive Office of the President

White House Office
Office of Management and Budget
Council of Economic Advisors
National Security Council
Office of Policy Development
Office of the U.S.Trade Representative
Council on Environmental Quality
Office of Science and Technology Policy
Office of Administration
Office of National Drug Control Policy
National Critical Materials Council
National Space Council

JUDICIAL BRANCH

Supreme Court of the United States

Courts of Appeals
District Courts
Claims Court
Court of Appeals for the Federal Circuit
Court of International Trade
Territorial Courts
Court of Military Appeals
Court of Veterans Appeals
Administrative Office of the Courts
Federal Judicial Center

The Bush Administration

As of mid-1992

Terms of office of the president and vice president, from Jan. 20, 1989 to Jan. 20, 1993. No person may be elected president of the United States for more than two 4-year terms.

President — George Bush of Texas receives salary of $200,000 a year taxable; in addition an expense allowance of $50,000 to assist in defraying expenses resulting from his official duties. Also there may be expended not exceeding $100,000, nontaxable, a year for travel expenses and $20,000 for official entertainment available for allocation within the Executive Office of the President. Congress has provided lifetime pensions of $69,630 a year, free mailing privileges, free office space, and up to $96,000 a year for office help for former Presidents except for the first 30 month period during which a former President is entitled to staff assistance for which an amount up to $150,000 a year may be paid, and $20,000 annually for their widows.

Vice President — Dan Quayle of Indiana receives salary of $166,200 a year and $10,000 for expenses, all of which is taxable.

For succession to presidency, see Succession in Index.

The Cabinet

(Salary: $143,800 per annum)

Secretary of State — Lawrence S. Eagleburger, act.
Secretary of Treasury — Nicholas F. Brady, N.J.
Secretary of Defense — Richard B. Cheney, Wyo.
Attorney General — William P. Barr, N.Y.
Secretary of Interior — Manuel Lujan, N.M.
Secretary of Agriculture — Edward Madigan, Ill.
Secretary of Commerce — Barbara H. Franklin, Pa.
Secretary of Labor — Lynn Martin, Ill.
Secretary of Health and Human Services — Louis W. Sullivan, Ga.
Secretary of Housing and Urban Development — Jack F. Kemp, N.Y.
Secretary of Transportation — Andrew S. Cord Jr., Mass.
Secretary of Energy — James D. Watkins, Cal.
Secretary of Education — Lamar Alexander, Tenn.
Secretary of Veterans Affairs — Edward J. Derwinski, Ill.

The White House Staff

1600 Pennsylvania Ave. NW 20500

Chief of Staff — James A. Baker 3d.
Asst. to the President & Deputy Chief of Staff — W. Hanson Moore.
Assistants to the President:
Counsel to the President — C. Boyden Gray.
Counsel to the President on Domestic Policy — vacant.
Presidential Personnel — Constance Warner.
Public Events & Initiatives — Sigmund A. Rogich.
Science & Technology — D. Allan Bromley.
Press Secretary — Max Marlin Fitzwater.
Legislative Affairs — Frederick D. McClure.
Communications — Stephen Prevost.
Economic & Domestic Affairs — Roger B. Porter.
Management & Admin. — Tim McBride.
Cabinet Secy. — Edith Holiday.
National Security — Brent Scowcroft.
Staff Secretary — Philip Brady.
National Service — C. Gregg Petersmeyer.
Media Affairs — J. Dorrance Smith.

Executive Agencies

Council of Economic Advisers — Michael J. Boskin.
Central Intelligence Agency — Robert M. Gates, dir.
Office of National Drug Control Policy — Robert Martinez.
Office of Management and Budget — Richard G. Darman.
U.S. Trade Representative — Carla Hills.
Council on Environmental Quality — Michael Deland, chmn.

Department of State

2201 C St. NW 20520

Secretary of State — Lawrence S. Eagleburger, act.
Deputy Secretary — vacant.
Under Sec. for Political Affairs — Arnold Kanter.
Under Sec. for Security Assistance, Science and Technology — Frank Wisner.
Under Secretary for Management — John Rogers.
Legal Advisor — Edwin Williamson.
Assistant Secretaries for:
Administration — Arthur W. Forte.
African Affairs — Herman J. Cohen.
East Asian & Pacific Affairs — Richard Clark.
Consular Affairs — Elizabeth Tamposi.
Diplomatic Security — Sheldon Krys.
Economic & Business Affairs — Eugene J. McAllister.
European & Canadian Affairs — Thomas Niles.
Intelligence & Research — Douglas P. Mulholland.
Legislative Affairs — Janet Mullins.

Inter-American Affairs — Bernard Aronson.
International Narcotics Matters — Melvin Levitsky.
International Organizations — John R. Bolton.
Near-Eastern & S. Asian Affairs — Edward Djerejian.
Public Affairs & Spokesperson — Margaret Tutwiler.
Oceans, International Environmental & Scientific Affairs — E. Curtis Bohlen.

Department of the Treasury

1500 Pennsylvania Ave. NW 20220

Secretary of the Treasury — Nicholas F. Brady.
Deputy Sec. of the Treasury — John E. Robson.
Under Sec. for Finance — Jerome Powell.
Under Sec. for International Affairs — David C. Mulford.
General Counsel — Jeanne Archibald.
Assistant Secretaries: — Desiree Tucker Sorini (Public Affairs & Public Liaison); Orin Wethington (Intl. Affairs); John Dugan (Domestic Finance); Peter Nunez (Enforcement); Gerald Murphy (Fiscal); Fred Goldberg (Tax Policy); Mary C. Sophos (Legislative Affairs); Sidney Jones (Economic Policy); Hollis S. McLoughlin (Policy Management).
Bureaus:
Alcohol, Tobacco & Firearms — Stephen E. Higgins, dir.
Comptroller of the Currency — Stephen L. Steinbrink, act.
Customs — Carol Hallett, comm.
Engraving & Printing — Peter H. Daley, dir.
Federal Law Enforcement Training Center — Charles F. Rinkevich, dir.
Financial Management Service — Russell D. Morns, comm.
Internal Revenue Service — Shirley Peterson, comm.
Mint — Eugene Essner, act. dir.
Public Debt — Richard L. Gregg, comm.
Treasurer of the U.S. — Catalina Villalpando.
U.S. Savings Bond Division — Tom Anfinson, dir.
U.S. Secret Service — John Magaw, dir.

Department of Defense

The Pentagon 20301

Secretary of Defense — Richard B. Cheney.
Deputy Secretary — Donald J. Atwood Jr.
Special Assistant — David S. Addington.
Under Secy. for Acquisition — Donald Yockey.
Under Secy. for Policy — Paul Wolfowitz.
Asst. Secretaries:
Command Control Communications & Intelligence — Duane P. Andrews.
Force Management & Personnel — Christopher Jehn.
Health Affairs — Enrique Mendez Jr.
International Security Policy — Stephen Hadley.
Legislative Affairs — David Gribbin 3d.
Products & Logistics — Colin R. McMillan.
Program Analysis & Evaluation — David S.C. Chu.
Public Affairs — Pete Williams.
Reserve Affairs — Stephen M. Duncan.
Special Operations & Low Intensity Conflict— J.R. Locher 3d.
Comptroller— vacant.
General Counsel — vacant.
Administration — Ann Reese, dir.
Operational Test & Evaluation — Robert C. Duncan, dir.
Chairman, Joint Chiefs of Staff — Gen. Colin L. Powell, USA.
Secretary of the Army — Michael P.W. Stone.
Secretary of the Navy — Sean O'Keefe, act.
Secretary of the Air Force — Donald B. Rice.

Department of Justice

Constitution Ave. & 10th St. NW 20530

Attorney General — William P. Barr.
Deputy Attorney General — George Terwilliger 3d.
Associate Attorney General — Wayne E. Budd.
Solicitor General — Kenneth W. Starr.
Intelligence Policy & Review — Mary Lawton.
Professional Responsibility —Michael E. Shaheen Jr.
Assistants:
Antitrust Division — vacant.
Civil Division — Stuart M. Gerson.
Civil Rights Division — John R. Dunne.
Criminal Division — Robert S. Mueller 3d.
Justice Management Division — Harry H. Flickinger.
Environment & Natural Resources Division — Roger B. Clegg.
Policy & Communications — Paul J. McNulty.
Legal Counsel — Timothy Flanigan, act.
Legislative Affairs — W. Lee Rawls.
Tax Division — James A. Bruton, act.
Fed. Bureau of Investigation — William S. Sessions, dir.
Exec. Off. for Immigration Review — David L. Milhollan, dir.
Bureau of Prisons — J. Michael Quinlan, dir.
Comm. Relations Service — William Lucas.
Office of Inspector General — Richard J. Hankinson.
Office of Justice Programs — Jimmy Gurulé.
Drug Enforcement Adm. — Robert C. Bonner.
Office of Special Counsel for Immigration Related Unfair Employment Practices — William Ho-Gonzalez.
Exec. Off. for U.S. Trustees — John Logan.
Exec. Off. for U.S. Attorneys — Laurence S. McWhorter.
Immigration and Naturalization Service — Gene McNary.
Pardon Attorney — Margaret Love.
U.S. Parole Commission — Carol Pavilack Getty, chmn.
U.S. Marshals Service — Henry E. Hudson, act. dir.
Foreign Claims Settlement Comm. — Stanley J. Glod, chmn.
Interpol, U.S. Natl. Central Bureau — Darrell W. Mills, chief.

Department of the Interior

C St. between 18th & 19th Sts. NW 20240

Secretary of the Interior — Manuel Lujan.
Deputy Secretary — Frank A. Bracken.
Assistant Secretaries for:
Fish, Wildlife and Parks — Mike Hayden.
Policy, Budget, and Administration — John Schrote.
Indian Affairs — Eddie Frank Brown.
Territorial & Intl. Affairs — Stella Guerra.
Land & Minerals — David C. O'Neal.
Water & Science — John M. Sayre.
Bureau of Land Management — Cy Jamison, dir.
Bureau of Mines — T.S. Ary, dir.
Bureau of Reclamation — Dennis C. Underwood, comm.
Fish & Wildlife Service — John F. Turner, dir.
Geological Survey — Dallas L. Peck, dir.
National Park Service — James M. Ridenour, dir.
Public Affairs — I. Stephen Goldstein, dir.
Office of Congressional and Legislative Affairs — James M. Hughes.
Solicitor — Thomas L. Sansonetti.

Department of Agriculture

The Mall, 12th & 14th Sts. 20250

Secretary of Agriculture — Edward Madigan.
Deputy Secretary — Ann M. Veneman.
Administration — Chuck Hilty.
Internatl. Affairs & Commodity Programs — vacant.
Food & Consumer Services — vacant.
Marketing & Inspection Services — Jo Ann Smith.
Small Community & Rural Development — Roland Vautour.
Economics — Dan Sumner.
Congressional Relations — Franklin E. Bailey.
Natural Resources & Environment — vacant.
General Counsel — Alan Raul.
Science & Education — Duane Acker.
Inspector General — Leon Snead.
Public Affairs — Roger Runningen.

Department of Commerce

14th St. between Constitution & E St. NW 20230

Secretary of Commerce — Barbara H. Franklin.
Deputy Secretary — Rockwell Schnabel.
Chief of Staff — Thomas Collamore.
General Counsel — Wendell Willkie.
Assistant Secretaries:
Chief Financial Officer & Asst. for Administration — Preston Moore.
Economic Development Adm. — L. Joyce Hampers.
Intl. Economic Policy — Thomas Duesterberg.
Import Administration — Alan Dunn.
Legislative Affairs — vacant.
Natl. Telecommunications Information Adm. — Gregory Chapados.
Patent & Trademark Office & Act. Asst. Comm. — Douglas B. Comet.
Trade Development — vacant.
Bureau of the Census — Dr. Barbara E. Bryant, dir.
Bureau of Economic Analysis — Carol Carson, dir.
Under Secy. for International Trade — vacant.
Under Secy. for Econ. Affairs — vacant.
Under Secy. for Technology — Robert M. White.
Natl. Oceanic & Atmospheric Admin. — John A. Knauss.
Natl. Technical Info. Service — Donald R. Johnson, act. dir.
Natl. Institute For Standards & Technology — John W. Lyons.
Minority Business Development Agency — Joe Lira.
Public Affairs — Carole Trimble, dir.

Department of Labor

200 Constitution Ave. NW 20210

Secretary of Labor — Lynn Martin.
Deputy Secretary — Delbert L. Spurlock Jr.
Assistant Secretaries for:
Administration and Management — Thomas C. Komarek.
Congressional & Intergovernmental Affairs — Frances McNaught.
Employment & Training — Roberts Jones.
Employment Standards — Carl Dominquez.
Labor-Management Standards — Robert M. Guttman.
Mine Safety & Health — William Tattersall.
Pension & Welfare Benefit Programs — David Ball.
Policy — Nancy Risque Rohrbach.
Veterans Employment — David Ritterpusch, act.
Solicitor of Labor — Marshall Breger.
Bureau of International Affairs — Shellyn Gae McCaffrey.
Dep. Under Secy. for Labor-Management Relations & Cooperative Programs — H. Charles Spring, act.
Office of Public Affairs — Stephen Hoffman.
Women's Bureau — Elsie Vartanian.
Inspector General — Julian De La Rosa.
Bureau of Labor Statistics — William Barron, act.

Department of Health and Human Services

200 Independence Ave. SW 20201

Secretary of HHS — Louis W. Sullivan.
Under Secretary — Kevin E. Moley.
Assistant Secretaries for:
Adm. for Children & Families — Jo Anne Barnhart.
Management & Budget — Arnold Tompkins.
Public Affairs — Alixe Glen.
Health — James Mason, M.D.
Planning & Evaluation — Martin Gerry.
Legislation — Steven Kelmar.
Personnel Administration — Thomas McFee.
General Counsel — Michael Astrue.
Inspector General — Richard P. Kusserow.
Office of Civil Rights — Edward Mercado, dir.
Surgeon General — Antonia C. Novello.
Social Security Adm. — Gwendolyn S. King.
Office of Consumer Affairs — Ann Windham Wallace, dir.
Health Care Financing Adm. — William Toby, act.

Department of Housing and Urban Development

451 7th St. SW 20410

Secretary of Housing & Urban Development — Jack Kemp.
Deputy Secretary — Alfred A. DelliBovi.
Deputies — Edwin I. Gardner, Stephen A. Glaude.
Assistant Secretaries for:
Administration — Jim E. Tarro.
Community Planning & Development — Randall H. Erben.
Fair Housing & Equal Opportunity — Gordon H. Mansfield.
Field Mgt. — Linda Marston.
Housing & Federal Housing Commissioner — Arthur J. Hill.
Labor Relations — Joseph A. Scudero.
Congressional & Intergovernmental Relations — Russell K. Paul.
Policy Development & Research — John Weicher.
Public Affairs — vacant.
Public & Indian Housing — Joseph G. Schiff.
President, Govt. Natl. Mortgage Assn. — Raoul L. Carroll.
General Counsel — Francis A. Keating 2d.
Inspector General — vacant.

Department of Transportation

400 7th St. SW 20590

Secretary of Transportation — Andrew S. Cord Jr.
Deputy Secretary — Arthur Rothkopf.
Assistant Secretaries — Jeffrey Shane (Policy and International Affairs); Kate Moore (Budget and Programs); John H. Seymour (Administration); Marion Blakey (Public Affairs); Michael J. Toohey (Governmental Affairs).
National Highway Traffic Safety Admin. — vacant.
U. S. Coast Guard Commandant — Adm. J. W. Kime.
Federal Aviation Admin. — Thomas Richards.
Federal Highway Admin. — Thomas Larson.
Federal Railroad Admin. — Gilbert Carmichael.
Maritime Admin. — Capt. Warren LeBack.
Federal Transit Admin. — Brian Clymer.
Research & Special Programs Admin. — vacant.
Saint Lawrence Seaway Development Corp. — Stan E. Parris.

Department of Energy

1000 Independence Ave. SW 20585

Secretary of Energy — James D. Watkins.
Deputy Secy. — Linda G. Stuntz, act.
Under Secretary — Tom Henderson, act.
General Counsel — Erk Fygi, act.
Inspector General — John C. Layton.
Assistant Secretaries — Gregg Ward (Congressional & Intergovernmental Affairs); Richard A Claytor (Defense Programs); John J. Easton Jr. (Domestic & International Energy Policy); William H. Young (Nuclear Energy); James G. Randolph (Fossil Energy); J. Michael Davis (Conservation & Renewable Energy); Paul L. Ziemer (Environment, Safety & Health).
Energy Information Adm. — Calvin A. Kent, adm.
Economic Regulatory Adm. — C. L. van Orman, act.
Federal Energy Regulatory Comm. — Martin L. Allday, chmn.
Hearings & Appeals — George B. Breznay, dir.
Energy Research — William Happer, dir.
Civilian Radioactive Waste Management — John W. Bartlett, dir.
Minority Economic Impact — Melva G. Wray, dir.
Board of Contract Appeals — E. Barclay van Doren, chmn.
Public Affairs — Barry M. Daniel, dir.

Department of Education

400 Maryland Ave. SW 20202

Secretary of Education — Lamar Alexander.

Deputy Secretary — David Kearns.
Chief of Staff — Stephen I. Danzansky.
Inspector General — James B. Thomas Jr.
General Counsel — Jeffrey C. Martin.
Assistant Secretaries:
- **Legislation & Congressional Affairs** — B. Robert Okum.
- **Elementary and Secondary Education** — John T. MacDonald.
- **Postsecondary Education** — Carolynn Reid-Wallace.
- **Educational Research and Improvement** — Diane S. Ravitch.
- **Adult & Vocational Education** — Betsy Brand.
- **Special Education and Rehabilitative Services** — Robert Davila.
- **Civil Rights** — Michael L. Williams.
- **Bilingual & Minority Language Affairs** — Rita Esquivel.
- **Management & Budget** — vacant.
- **Human Resources & Administration** — Donald A. Laidlaw.
- **Intergovernmental & Interagency Affairs** — Lanny Griffith.

Department of Veterans Affairs

810 Vermont Ave. NW 20420

Secretary of Veterans Affairs — Edward J. Derwinski.
Deputy — Anthony J. Principi.
Asst. Secy. For:
- **Finance & Information Resources Mgmt.** — S. Anthony McCann.
- **Human Resources Adm.** — Ronald E. Ray.
- **Acquisition & Facilities** — David Lewis.
- **Public & Intergovernmental Affairs** — Edward T. Timberlake.
- **Congressional Affairs** — Sylvia Chavez Long.
- **Policy & Planning** — Joann K. Webb.

Inspector General — Stephen Trodden.
Veterans Benefits Adm. — D'Wayne Gray, dir.
Veterans Health Adm. — James W. Holsinger Jr., dir.
National Cemetery System — Allen B. Clark, dir.
General Counsel — James A. Endicott Jr.
Board of Veterans Appeals — Charles L. Cragin, chmn.

Judiciary of the U.S.

Data as of mid-1992

Justices of the United States Supreme Court

The Supreme Court comprises the chief justice of the United States and 8 associate justices, all appointed by the president with advice and consent of the Senate. Salaries: chief justice $166,200 annually, associate justice $159,000. The Supreme Court is located at the U.S. Supreme Court Bldg., 1 First St. NE, Wash., DC 20543.

Name; apptd from *Chief Justices in italics*	Service Term	Yrs.	Born	Died
John Jay, N. Y.	1789-1795	5	1745	1829
John Rutledge, S. C.	1789-1791	1	1739	1800
William Cushing, Mass.	1789-1810	20	1732	1810
James Wilson, Pa.	1789-1798	8	1742	1798
John Blair, Va.	1789-1796	6	1732	1800
James Iredell, N. C.	1790-1799	9	1751	1799
Thomas Johnson, Md.	1791-1793	1	1732	1819
William Paterson, N. J.	1793-1806	13	1745	1806
John Rutledge, S.C.	1795(a)	—	1739	1800
Samuel Chase, Md.	1796-1811	15	1741	1811
Oliver Ellsworth, Conn.	1796-1800	4	1745	1807
Bushrod Washington, Va.	1798-1829	31	1762	1829
Alfred Moore, N. C.	1799-1804	4	1755	1810
John Marshall, Va.	1801-1835	34	1755	1835
William Johnson, S. C.	1804-1834	30	1771	1834
Henry B. Livingston, N. Y.	1806-1823	16	1757	1823
Thomas Todd, Ky.	1807-1826	18	1765	1826
Joseph Story, Mass.	1811-1845	33	1779	1845
Gabriel Duval, Md.	1811-1835	22	1752	1844
Smith Thompson, N. Y.	1823-1843	20	1768	1843
Robert Trimble, Ky.	1826-1828	2	1777	1828
John McLean, Oh.	1829-1861	32	1785	1861
Henry Baldwin, Pa.	1830-1844	14	1780	1844
James M. Wayne, Ga.	1835-1867	32	1790	1867
Roger B. Taney, Md.	1836-1864	28	1777	1864
Philip P. Barbour, Va.	1836-1841	4	1783	1841
John Catron, Tenn.	1837-1865	28	1786	1865
John McKinley, Ala.	1837-1852	15	1780	1852
Peter V. Daniel, Va.	1841-1860	19	1784	1860
Samuel Nelson, N. Y.	1845-1872	27	1792	1873
Levi Woodbury, N. H.	1845-1851	5	1789	1851
Robert C. Grier, Pa.	1846-1870	23	1794	1870
Benjamin R. Curtis, Mass.	1851-1857	6	1809	1874
John A. Campbell, Ala.	1853-1861	8	1811	1889
Nathan Clifford, Me.	1858-1881	23	1803	1881
Noah H. Swayne, Oh.	1862-1881	18	1804	1884
Samuel F. Miller, Ia.	1862-1890	28	1816	1890
David Davis, Ill.	1862-1877	14	1815	1886
Stephen J. Field, Cal.	1863-1897	34	1816	1899
Salmon P. Chase, Oh.	1864-1873	8	1808	1873
William Strong, Pa.	1870-1880	10	1808	1895
Joseph P. Bradley, N. J.	1870-1892	21	1813	1892
Ward Hunt, N. Y.	1872-1882	9	1810	1886
Morrison R. Waite, Oh.	1874-1888	14	1816	1888
John M. Harlan, Ky.	1877-1911	34	1833	1911
William B. Woods, Ga.	1880-1887	6	1824	1887
Stanley Matthews, Oh.	1881-1889	7	1824	1889
Horace Gray, Mass.	1881-1902	20	1828	1902
Samuel Blatchford, N. Y.	1882-1893	11	1820	1893
Lucius Q. C. Lamar, Miss.	1888-1893	5	1825	1893
Melville W. Fuller, Ill.	1888-1910	21	1833	1910
David J. Brewer, Kan.	1889-1910	20	1837	1910
Henry B. Brown, Mich.	1890-1906	15	1836	1913
George Shiras Jr., Pa.	1892-1903	10	1832	1924
Howell E. Jackson, Tenn.	1893-1895	2	1832	1895
Edward D. White, La.	1894-1910	16	1845	1921
Rufus W. Peckham, N. Y.	1895-1909	13	1838	1909
Joseph McKenna, Cal.	1898-1925	26	1843	1926
Oliver W. Holmes, Mass.	1902-1932	29	1841	1935
William R. Day, Oh.	1903-1922	19	1849	1923
William H. Moody, Mass.	1906-1910	3	1853	1917
Horace H. Lurton, Tenn.	1909-1914	4	1844	1914
Charles E. Hughes, N. Y.	1910-1916	5	1862	1948
Willis Van Devanter, Wy.	1910-1937	26	1859	1941
Joseph R. Lamar, Ga.	1910-1916	5	1857	1916
Edward D. White, La.	1910-1921	10	1845	1921
Mahlon Pitney, N. J.	1912-1922	10	1858	1924
James C. McReynolds, Tenn.	1914-1941	26	1862	1946
Louis D. Brandeis, Mass.	1916-1939	22	1856	1941
John H. Clarke, Oh.	1916-1922	5	1857	1945
William H. Taft, Conn.	1921-1930	8	1857	1930
George Sutherland, Ut.	1922-1938	15	1862	1942
Pierce Butler, Minn.	1922-1939	16	1866	1939
Edward T. Sanford, Tenn.	1923-1930	7	1865	1930
Harlan F. Stone, N. Y.	1925-1941	16	1872	1946
Charles E. Hughes, N. Y.	1930-1941	11	1862	1948
Owen J. Roberts, Pa.	1930-1945	15	1875	1955
Benjamin N. Cardozo, N.Y.	1932-1938	6	1870	1938
Hugo L. Black, Ala.	1937-1971	34	1886	1971
Stanley F. Reed, Ky.	1938-1957	19	1884	1980
Felix Frankfurter, Mass.	1939-1962	23	1882	1965
William O. Douglas, Conn.	1939-1975	36	1898	1980
Frank Murphy, Mich.	1940-1949	9	1890	1949
Harlan F. Stone, N. Y.	1941-1946	5	1872	1946
James F. Byrnes, S. C.	1941-1942	1	1879	1972
Robert H. Jackson, N. Y.	1941-1954	12	1892	1954
Wiley B. Rutledge, Ia.	1943-1949	6	1894	1949
Harold H. Burton, Oh.	1945-1958	13	1888	1964
Fred M. Vinson, Ky.	1946-1953	7	1890	1953
Tom C. Clark, Tex.	1949-1967	18	1899	1977
Sherman Minton, Ind.	1949-1956	7	1890	1965
Earl Warren, Cal.	1953-1969	16	1891	1974
John Marshall Harlan, N. Y.	1955-1971	16	1899	1971

Name; apptd from *Chief Justices in italics*	Service Term	Yrs.	Born	Died
William J. Brennan Jr., N. J.	1956-1990	33	1906	—
Charles E. Whittaker, Mo.	1957-1962	5	1901	1973
Potter Stewart, Oh.	1958-1981	23	1915	1985
Byron R. White, Col.	1962 —	—	1917	—
Arthur J. Goldberg, Ill.	1962-1965	3	1908	1990
Abe Fortas, Tenn.	1965-1969	4	1910	1982
Thurgood Marshall, N.Y.	1967-1991	24	1908	—
Warren E. Burger, Va.	1969-1986	17	1907	—
Harry A. Blackmun, Minn.	1970 —	—	1908	—
Lewis F. Powell Jr., Va.	1972-1987	15	1907	—
William H. Rehnquist, Ariz.	1972-1986	14	1924	—
John Paul Stevens, Ill.	1975 —	—	1920	—
Sandra Day O'Connor, Ariz.	1981 —	—	1930	—
William H. Rehnquist, Ariz.	1986 —	—	1924	—
Antonin Scalia, Va.	1986 —	—	1936	—
Anthony M. Kennedy, Cal.	1988 —	—	1936	—
David H. Souter, N.H.	1990 —	—	1939	—
Clarence Thomas, Va.	1991	—	1948	—

(a) Rejected Dec. 15, 1795.

U.S. Court of International Trade

New York, NY 10007 (Salaries, $129,500)

Chief Judge — Dominick L. DeCarlo.

Judges — Jane A. Restani, Gregory W. Carmen, Thomas J. Aquilino Jr., Nicholas Tsoucalas, R. Kenton Musgrave, Richard W. Goldberg.

U.S. Claims Court

Washington, D.C. 20005 (Salaries, $129,500)

Chief Judge — Loren A. Smith.

Judges — James F. Merow, John P. Wiese, Robert J. Yock, Reginald W. Gibson, Lawrence S. Margolis, Christine C. Nettesheim, Moody R. Tidwell 3d, Marian Blank Horn, Eric G. Bruggink, Bohdan A. Futey, Wilkes C. Robinson, Roger B. Andewelt, James T. Turner, Robert H. Hodges Jr.

U.S. Tax Court

Washington DC 20217 (Salaries, $129,500)

Chief Judge — Arthur L. Nims 3d.

Judges — Herbert L. Chabot, Edna G. Parker, Jules J. Korner 3d, Mary Ann Cohen, John O. Colvin, Perry Shields, Charles E. Clapp 2d, Lapsley W. Hamblen Jr., Joel Gerber, Julien I. Jacobs, Carolyn Miller Parr, Robert P. Ruwe, James S. Halpern.

U.S. Courts of Appeals

(Salaries, $137,300. CJ means Chief Judge)

Federal Circuit — Helen W. Nies, CJ; Giles S. Rich, Pauline Newman, Glenn L. Archer Jr., H. Robert Mayer, Paul R. Michel, S. Jay Plager; Alan D. Lourie, Raymond C. Clevenger 3d, Randall F. Rader; Clerk's Office; Washington, DC 20439.

District of Columbia — Abner J. Mikva, CJ; Patricia M. Wald, Harry T. Edwards, Ruth Bader Ginsburg, Laurence H. Silberman; James L. Buckley, Stephen F. Williams, Douglas Ginsburg, David B. Sentelle; Karen LeCraft Henderson, A. Raymond Randolph; Clerk's Office, Washington, DC 20001.

First Circuit (Me., Mass., N.H., R.I., Puerto Rico) — Stephen Breyer, CJ; Levin H. Campbell, Juan R. Torruella, Bruce M. Selya, Conrad K. Cyr; Clerk's Office, Boston, MA 02109.

Second Circuit (Conn., N.Y., Vt.) — James L. Oakes, CJ; Thomas J. Meskill, Jon O. Newman, Amalya Lyle Kearse, Richard J. Cardamone, Ralph K. Winter Jr., George C. Pratt, Roger J. Miner, Frank X. Altimari, J. Daniel Mahoney, John M. Walker; Joseph M. McLaughlin. Clerk's Office, New York, NY 10007.

Third Circuit (Del., N.J., Pa., Virgin Is.) — Dolores K. Sloviter, CJ; Edward R. Becker, Carol Los Mansmann, Walter K. Stapleton, Morton I. Greenberg, Anthony J. Scirica, William D. Hutchinson, Robert E. Cowen, Richard L. Nygaard, Samuel A. Alito Jr., Jane R. Roth; Clerk's Office, Philadelphia, PA 19106.

Fourth Circuit (Md., N.C., S.C., Va., W.Va.) — Sam J. Ervin 3d, CJ; Kenneth K. Hall, Donald Stuart Russell, H. Emory Widener Jr., James D. Phillips Jr., Francis D. Murnaghan Jr., James M. Sprouse, J. Harvie Wilkinson 3d, William W. Wilkins Jr., Paul V. Niemeyer, Clyde H. Hamilton, J. Michael Luttig; Clerk's Office, Richmond, VA 23219.

Fifth Circuit (La., Miss., Tex.) — Henry A. Politz, CJ; Carolyn D. King, Will Garwood, E. Grady Jolly, Patrick E. Higginbotham, W. Eugene Davis, Jerry E. Smith, Edith Hollan Jones, John M. Duhe Jr., Rhesa A. Barksdale, Jacques L. Wiener Jr., Emilio M. Garza, Harold R. DeMoss Jr.; Clerk's Office, New Orleans, LA 70130.

Sixth Circuit (Ky., Mich., Ohio, Tenn.) — Gilbert S. Merritt, CJ; Damon J. Keith, Boyce F. Martin Jr., Nathaniel R. Jones, Cornelia G. Kennedy, H. Ted Milburn, Ralph B. Guy Jr., David A. Nelson, James L. Ryan, Danny J. Boggs, Alan E. Norris, Richard H. Suhrheinrich, Eugene E. Siler Jr.; Clerk's Office, Cincinnati, OH 45202.

Seventh Circuit (Ill., Ind., Wis.) — William J. Bauer, CJ; Walter J. Cummings, Richard D. Cudahy, Richard A. Posner, John L. Coffey, Joel M. Flaum, Frank H. Easterbrook, Kenneth F. Ripple, Daniel A. Manion, Michael S. Kanne; Clerk's Office, Chicago, IL 60604.

Eighth Circuit (Ark., Ia., Minn., Mo., Neb., N.D., S.D.) — Richard S. Arnold, CJ; Theodore McMillian, John R. Gibson, George C. Fagg, Pasco M. Bowman 2d, Roger L. Wollman, Frank J. Magill, C. Arlen Beam, James B. Loken, David R. Hanson; Clerk's Office, St. Louis, MO 63101.

Ninth Circuit (Alaska, Ariz., Cal., Ha., Ida., Mont., Nev., Ore., Wash., Guam, N. Mariana Islands) — J. Clifford Wallace, CJ; James R. Browning, Procter Hug Jr., Thomas Tang, Jerome Farris, Betty B. Fletcher, Mary M. Schroeder, Harry Pregerson, Arthur L. Alarcon, Cecil F. Poole, Dorothy W. Nelson, William C. Canby Jr., William A. Norris, Stephen Reinhardt, Robert R. Beezer, Cynthia M. Hall, Charles E. Wiggins, Melvin Brunetti, Alex Kozinski, David R. Thompson, John T. Noonan, Diarmuid F. O'Scannlain, Edward Leavy, Stephen S. Trott, Ferdinand F. Fernandez, Pamela Ann Rymer, Thomas G. Nelson, Andrew J. Kleinfeld; Clerk's Office, San Francisco, CA 94101.

Tenth Circuit (Col., Kan., N.M., Okla., Ut., Wy.) — Monroe G. McKay, CJ; William J. Holloway Jr., James K. Logan, Stephanie K. Seymour, John P. Moore, Stephen H. Anderson, Deanell R. Tacha, Bobby R. Baldock, Wade Brorby, David M. Ebel; Clerk's Office, Denver, CO 80294.

Eleventh Circuit (Ala. Fla., Ga.)— Gerald B. Tjoflat, CJ; Peter T. Fay, Phyllis A. Kravitch, Joseph W. Hatchett, R. Lanier Anderson 3d, J.L. Edmondson, Emmett R. Cox, Stanley F. Birch Jr., Joel F. Dubina; Clerk's Office, Atlanta GA 30303.

Temporary Emergency Court of Appeals — Reynaldo G. Garza, CJ; A. Sherman Christensen, William E. Hoffman, Robert A. Grant, Charles M. Metzner, William H. Becker, John W. Peck, Frederick A. Daugherty, Wesley E. Brown, Stanley A. Weigel, Homer Thornberry, Robert E. Maxwell; Clerk's Office, Washington, DC 20001.

U.S. District Courts

(Salaries, $129,500. CJ means Chief Judge)

Alabama — Northern: Sam C. Pointer Jr., CJ; James Hughes Hancock, Robert B. Propst, U. W. Clemon, William M. Acker Jr., Edwin L. Nelson, Sharon Lovelace Blackburn; Clerk's Office, Birmingham 35203. **Middle:** Myron H. Thompson, CJ; William H. Albritton; Clerk's Office, Montgomery 36101. **Southern:** Alex T. Howard Jr., CJ; Charles R. Butler Jr., Richard W. Vollmer Jr.; Clerk's Office, Mobile 36602.

Alaska — H. Russel Holland, CJ; John Singleton; Clerk's Office, Anchorage 99513.

Arizona — William D. Browning, CJ; Richard M. Bilby, Earl H. Carroll, Paul G. Rosenblat, Robert C. Bloomfield, Roger G. Strand, Stephen M. McNamee; Clerk's Office, Phoenix 85025.

Arkansas — Eastern: Samuel M. Reasoner, CJ; Henry Woods, George Howard Jr., Susan Weber Wright; Clerk's Office, Little Rock 72203. **Western:** H. Franklin Waters, CJ; George Howard Jr., Morris S. Arnold; Clerk's Office, Fort Smith 72902.

California — Northern: Thelton E. Henderson, CJ; Robert P. Aguilar, Marilyn H. Patel, Eugene F. Lynch, John P. Vukasin Jr., Charles A. Legge, D. Lowell Jensen, Fern M. Smith, Vaughn R. Walker, James Ware, Susan B. Armstrong; Clerk's Office, San Francisco 94102. **Eastern:** Robert E. Coyle, CJ; Lawrence K. Karlton, Edward J. Garcia, William B. Shubb, David F. Levi, Oliver W. Wanger; Clerk's Office, Sacramento 95814. **Central:** Manuel L. Real, CJ; Wm. Matthew Byrne Jr., Robert M. Takasugi, Mariana R. Pfaelzer, Terry J. Hatter Jr., A. Wallace Tashima, Consuelo Bland Marshall, David V. Kenyon, Richard A. Gadbois, Edward Rafeedie, Harry L. Hupp, Alicemarie H. Stotler, James M. Ideman, William J. Rea, William D. Keller, Stephen V. Wilson, J. Spencer Letts, Dickran M. Tevrizian Jr., John G. Davies, Ronald S.W. Lew, Gary L. Taylor; Clerk's Office, Los Angeles 90012. **Southern:** Judith N. Keep, CJ; Gordon Thompson Jr., Earl B. Gilliam, Rudi M. Brewster, John S. Rhoades Sr., Marilyn L. Huff; Clerk's Office, San Diego 92189.

Colorado — Sherman G. Finesilver, CJ; Richard P. Matsch, Jim R. Carrigan, Zita L. Weinshienk, Lewis T. Babcock, Edward W. Nottingham, Daniel B. Sparr; Clerk's Office, Denver 80294.

Connecticut — Ellen B. Burns, CJ; T.F. Gilroy Daly, Warren W. Eginton, Jose A. Cabranes, Peter C. Dorsey, Alan H. Nevas; Clerk's Office, New Haven 06510.

Delaware — Joseph J. Longobardi, CJ; Joseph J. Farnan Jr.; Clerk's Office, Wilmington 19801.

District of Columbia — Aubrey E. Robinson Jr., CJ; Gerhard A. Gesell, Charles R. Richey, Louis F. Oberdorfer, Harold H. Greene, John Garrett Penn, Joyce Hens Green, Norma H. Johnson, Thomas P. Jackson, Thomas F. Hogan, Stanley S. Harris, George H. Revercomb, Stanley Sporkin, Royce C. Lamberth, Michael Boudin; Clerk's Office, Washington DC 20001.

Florida — Northern: William H. Stafford Jr. CJ; Maurice M. Paul, C. Roger Vinson, Lacey A. Collier; Clerk's Office, Tallahassee 32301. **Middle:** Susan H. Black, CJ; William Terrell Hodges, William J. Castagna; John H. Moore 2d, Elizabeth A. Kovachevich, George K. Sharp, Patricia C. Fawsett, Harvey E. Schlesinger, Ralph W. Nimmons Jr.; Clerk's Office, Jacksonville 32201. **Southern:** Norman C. Roettger Jr., CJ; James Lawrence King, Jose A. Gonzalez Jr., James C. Paine, James W. Kehoe, Edward B. Davis, Lenore C. Nesbitt, Stanley Marcus, William J. Zloch, Kenneth L. Ryskamp, Federico A. Moreno, Shelby Highsmith, Donald L. Graham; Clerk's Office, Miami 33128.

Georgia — Northern: William C. O'Kelley, CJ; Harold L. Murphy, G. Ernest Tidwell, Orinda Dale Evans, Robert L. Vining Jr., Harold T. Ward, J. Owen Forrester, Jack T. Camp; Clerk's Office, Atlanta 30335. **Middle:** Wilbur D. Owens Jr., CJ; J. Robert Elliott, Duross Fitzpatrick; Clerk's Office, Macon 31202. **Southern:** B. Avant Edenfield, CJ; Dudley H. Bowen Jr.; Clerk's Office, Savannah 31412.

Hawaii — Alan C. Kay, CJ; Harold M. Fong, David A. Ezra; Clerk's Office, Honolulu 96850.

Idaho — Harold L. Ryan, CJ; Edward J. Lodge; Clerk's Office; Boise, 83724.

Illinois — Northern: James B. Moran, CJ; John F. Grady, Marvin E. Aspen, Milton I. Shadur, Charles P. Kocoras, John A. Nordberg, William T. Hart, Paul E. Plunkett, Ilana Diamond Rovner, Charles R. Norgle Sr., James F. Holderman Jr., Ann C. Williams, Brian Barnett Duff, Harry D. Lienenweber, James B. Zagel, James H. Alesia, Suzanne B. Conlon, George M. Marovich, George W. Lindberg, Wayne R. Anderson; Clerk's Office, Chicago 60604. **Central:** Michael M. Mihm, CJ; Harold Albert Baker, Richard Mills, Joe Billy McDade; Clerk's Office, Springfield 62705. **Southern:** James L. Foreman, CJ; William L. Beatty, William D. Stiehl; Clerk's Office, E. St. Louis 62202.

Indiana — Northern: Allen Sharp, CJ; William C. Lee, James T. Moody, Robert L. Miller Jr., Rudy Lozano; Clerk's Office, South Bend 46601. **Southern:** Gene E. Brooks, CJ; S. Hugh Dillin, Sarah E. Barker, Larry J. McKinney, John D. Tinder; Clerk's Office, Indianapolis 46204.

Iowa — Northern: Donald E. O'Brien, CJ; Clerk's Office, Cedar Rapids 52401. **Southern:** Harold D. Vietor, CJ; Charles R. Wolle, R. E. Longstaff; Clerk's Office, Des Moines 50309.

Kansas — Earl E. O'Connor, CJ; Patrick F. Kelly, Sam A. Crow, C. Thomas Van Bebber, John W. Lungstrum, Monti L. Belot; Clerk's Office, Wichita 67202.

Kentucky — Eastern: William Bertelsman, CJ; Henry R. Wilhoit Jr., Karl S. Forester, Joseph M. Hood; Clerk's Office, Lexington 40586. **Western:** Thomas A. Ballantine, CJ; Ronald E. Meredith, Charles R. Simpson 3d, Edward H. Johnstone; Clerk's Office, Louisville 40202.

Louisiana — Eastern: Frederick J. R. Heebe, CJ; Morley L. Sear, Adrian A. Duplantier, Robert F. Collins, George Arceneaux Jr., Veronica D. Wicker, Peter Beer, A J. McNamara, Henry A. Mentz Jr., Martin L. C. Feldman, Marcel Livaudais Jr.; Clerk's Office, New Orleans 70130. **Middle:** John V. Parker, CJ; Frank J. Polozola; Clerk's Office, Baton Rouge 70821. **Western:** John M. Shaw, CJ; Tom Stagg, F. A. Little Jr., Donald E. Walter, Richard Haiks, James T. Trimble, Rebecca F. Doherty; Clerk's Office, Shreveport 71101.

Maine — Gene Carter, CJ; D. Brock Hornby, Martin A. Brody; Clerk's Office, Portland 04112.

Maryland — William E. Black Jr., CJ; John R. Hargrove, J. Frederick Motz, Frederic N. Smalkin, William M. Nickerson, Marvin J. Garbis, Benson Everett Legg; Clerk's Office, Baltimore 21201.

Massachusetts — Frank H. Freedman, CJ; Joseph L. Tauro, Walter Jay Skinner, A. David Mazzone, Robert E. Keeton, Rya W. Zobel, William G. Young, Mark L. Wolf, Douglas P. Woodlock, Edward F. Harrington; Clerk's Office, Boston 02109.

Michigan — Eastern: Julian A. Cook Jr., CJ; Stewart A. Newblatt, Avern Cohn, Anna Diggs Taylor, George E. Woods, George La Plata, Barbara K. Hackett, Lawrence P. Zatkoff, Patrick J. Duggan, Bernard A. Friedman, Paul V. Gadola, Gerald E. Rosen, Robert H. Cleland; Clerk's Office, Detroit 48226. **Western:** Benjamin F. Gibson, CJ; Richard A. Enslen, Robert H. Bell; Clerk's Office, Grand Rapids 49503.

Minnesota — Donald D. Alsop, CJ; Harry H. MacLaughlin, Robert G. Renner, Diana E. Murphy, Paul A. Magnuson, James M. Rosenbaum, David S. Doty; Edward J. Devitt, Earl R. Larson; Clerk's Office, St. Paul 55101.

Mississippi — Northern: L. T. Senter Jr., CJ; Neal Biggers, Glen H. Davidson; Clerk's Office, Oxford 38655. **Southern:** William H. Barbour Jr., CJ; Harry T. Wingate, Tom S. Lee, Walter J. Gex 3d, Charles W. Pickering Sr.; Clerk's Office, Jackson 39201.

Missouri — Eastern: Edward D. Filippine, CJ; Clyde S. Cahill Jr., Stephen N. Limbaugh, George F. Gunn Jr., Jean Hamilton; Clerk's Office, St. Louis 63101. **Western:** Howard F. Sachs, CJ; Joseph E. Stevens Jr., D. Brook Bartlett, Dean Whipple, Fernando J. Gaitan Jr.; Clerk's Office, Kansas City 64106.

Montana — Paul G. Hatfield, CJ; Charles C. Lovell, Jack D. Shanstrom; Clerk's Office, Billings 59101.

Nebraska — Lyle E. Strom, CJ; William G. Cambridge; Clerk's Office, Omaha 68101.

Nevada — Edward C. Reed Jr., CJ; Lloyd D. George, Howard D. McKibben, Philip M. Pro; Clerk's Office, Las Vegas 89101.

New Hampshire — Shane Devine, CJ; Norman H. Stahl; Clerk's Office, Concord 03301.

New Jersey — John F. Gerry, CJ; Anne E. Thompson, Dickinson R. Debevoise, H. Lee Sarokin, Harold A. Ackerman, John W. Bissell, Maryanne Trump Barry, Joseph H. Rodriguez, Garrett E. Brown Jr., Alfred J. Lechner Jr., Nicholas H. Politan, Alfred M. Wolin, John C. Lifland, William G. Bassler; Clerk's Office, Newark 07102.

New Mexico — Juan G. Burciaga, CJ; Santiago E. Campos, John E. Conway, James A. Parker; Clerk's Office, Albuquerque 87103.

New York — Northern: Neal P. McCurn, CJ; Thomas J. McAvoy, Con G. Cholakis; Clerk's Office, Albany 12201. **Eastern:** Thomas C. Platt Jr., CJ; Jack B. Weinstein, Charles P. Sifton, Eugene H. Nickerson, Israel Leo Glasser, Raymond J. Dearie, Leonard D. Wexler, Edward R. Korman, Reena Raggi; Arthur D. Spatt, Carol Bagley Amon, Sterling Johnson Jr.; Clerk's Office, Brooklyn 11201. **Southern:** Charles L. Brieant, CJ; David N. Edelstein, Thomas P. Griesa, Kevin Thomas Duffy, Leonard B. Sand, Gerard L. Goettel, Charles S. Haight Jr., Pierre N. Leval, John E. Sprizzo, Shirley Wohl Kram, John F. Keenan, Peter K. Leisure, Louis L. Stanton, Miriam G. Cedarbaum, Michael B. Mukasey, Kenneth Conboy, Kimba Wood, Robert P. Patterson Jr., Lawrence McKenna, John S. Martin Jr., Louis J. Freeh Jr.; Clerk's Office N. Y. City 10007. **Western:** Michael A. Telesca, CJ; Richard J. Arcara, David G. Larimer, William M. Skretny; Clerk's Office, Buffalo 14202.

North Carolina — Eastern: James C. Fox, CJ; W. Earl Britt, Terrence W. Boyle, Malcolm J. Howard; Clerk's Office, Raleigh 27611. **Middle:** Richard C. Erwin, CJ; Frank W. Bullock, N. Carlton Tilley Jr., William L. Osteen Sr.; Clerk's Office, Greensboro 27402. **Western:** Richard L. Voorhees, CJ; Robert D. Potter, Graham C. Mullen; Clerk's Office Asheville 28801.

North Dakota — Patrick A. Conmy, CJ, Rodney S. Webb; Clerk's Office, Bismarck 58502.

Ohio — Northern: Thomas D. Lambros, CJ; Frank J. Battisti, George W. White, Ann Aldrich, Alvin I. Krenzler, John W. Potter, David D. Dowd Jr., Sam H. Bell, Alice M. Batchelder; Clerk's Office, Cleveland 44114. **Southern:** John D. Holschuh, CJ; Carl B. Rubin, Walter H. Rice, S. Arthur Spiegel, Herman J. Weber, James L. Graham, George C. Smith; Clerk's Office, Columbus 43215.

Oklahoma — Northern: James O. Ellison, CJ; Thomas R. Brett, David L. Russell; Clerk's Office, Tulsa 74103. **Eastern:** Frank H. Shey, CJ; H. Dale Cook; Clerk's Office, Muskogee 74401. **Western:** Ralph G. Thompson, CJ; Wayne Alley, Lee R. West, Robin Cauthron; Clerk's Office, Oklahoma City 73102.

Oregon — James A. Redden, CJ; Owen M. Panner, Helen J. Frye, Malcolm F. Marsh, Robert E. Jones, Michael R. Hogan; Clerk's Office, Portland 97205.

Pennsylvania — Eastern: Louis Charles Bechtle, CJ; Edward N. Cahn, Norma L. Shapiro, James T. Giles, James McGirr Kelly, Thomas N. O'Neill Jr., Marvin Katz, Edmund V. Ludwig, Robert F. Kelly, Franklin S. Van Antwerpen, Robert S. Gawthrop, Lowell A. Reed Jr., Jan E. Dubois, Herbert J. Hutton, Jay C. Waldman, Ronald L. Buckwalter, Stewart Dalzell, William H. Yohn Jr., Harvey Battle 3rd; Clerk's Office, Philadelphia 19106. **Middle:** Richard P. Conaboy, CJ; Sylvia H. Rambo, William W. Caldwell, Edward M. Kosik, James F. McClure Jr.; Clerk's Office, Scranton 18501. **Western:** Maurice B. Cohill Jr., CJ; Gustave Diamond, Donald E. Ziegler, Alan N. Bloch, Glenn E. Mencer, William L. Standish, D. Brooks Smith, Donald J. Lee, Timothy K. Lewis; Clerk's Office, Pittsburgh 15230.

Rhode Island — Francis J. Boyle, CJ; Ronald R. Lagueux, Ernest C. Torres; Clerk's Office, Providence 02903.

South Carolina — Falcon B. Hawkins, CJ; C. Weston Houck, Matthew J. Perry Jr., George R. Anderson Jr., Joseph F. Anderson Jr., David C. Norton, Dennis W. Shedd, Henry M. Herlong Jr.; Clerk's Office, Columbia 29202.

South Dakota — John Baily Jones, CJ; Richard H. Battey, Donald J. Potter; Clerk's Office, Sioux Falls 57102.

Tennessee — Eastern: James H. Jarvis, CJ; Thomas G. Hill, R. Allan Edgar, Leon Jordan; Clerk's Office, Knoxville 37901. **Middle:** John T. Nixon, CJ; Thomas A. Wiseman Jr, Thomas A. Higgins; Clerk's Office, Nashville 37203. **Western:** Odell Horton, CJ; Julia S. Gibbons, James D. Todd, Jerome Turner; Clerk's Office, Memphis 38103.

Texas — Northern: Barefoot Sanders, CJ; Mary Lou Robinson, Jerry Buchmeyer, A. Joe Fish, Robert B. Maloney, Sidney A. Fitzwater, Samuel R. Cummings, John H. McBryde, Jorge A. Solis, Terry Means; Clerk's Office, Dallas 75242. **Southern:** James De Anda, CJ; Norman W. Black, George P. Kazen, Filemon B. Vela, Hayden W. Head Jr., Ricardo H. Hinojosa, Lynn N. Hughes, David Hittner, Kenneth M. Hoyt, Simeon T. Lake 3d, Melinda Harmon, John Rainey, Samuel B. Kent; Clerk's Office, Houston 77208. **Eastern:** Robert M. Parker, CJ; William Wayne Justice, Howell Cobb, Sam B. Hall Jr., Paul N. Brown, Richard A. Schell; Clerk's Office, Tyler 75702. **Western:** Lucius D. Bunton 3d, CJ; Harry Lee Hudspeth, Hipolito F. Garcia, James R. Nowlin, Edward C. Prado, Walter S. Smith Jr.; Clerk's Office, San Antonio 78206.

Utah — Bruce S. Jenkins, CJ; J. Thomas Greene, David Sam, David K. Winder, Dee V. Benson; Clerk's Office, Salt Lake City 84101.

Vermont — Fred I. Parker, CJ; Franklin S. Billings Jr.; Clerk's Office, Burlington 05402.

Virginia — Eastern: James C. Cacheris, CJ; Richard L. Williams, Robert G. Doumar, Claude M. Hilton, James R. Spencer, Thomas S. Ellis 3d, Rebecca Beach Smith; Clerk's Office, Alexandria 22320. **Western:** James C. Turk, CJ; James H. Michael Jr., Jackson L. Kiser, Samuel G. Wilson; Clerk's Office, Roanoke 24006.

Washington — Eastern: Justin L. Quackenbush, CJ; Alan A. McDonald; Fred Van Sickle, W. Fremming Nielsen; Clerk's Office, Spokane 99210. **Western:** Barbara J. Rothstein, CJ; John C. Coughenour, Carolyn R. Dimmick, Robert J. Bryan, William L. Dwyer, Thomas Zilly; Clerk's Office, Seattle 98104.

West Virginia — Northern: Robert Earl Maxwell, CJ; Frederick P. Stamp Jr.; Clerk's Office, Elkins 26241. **Southern:** Charles H. Haden 2d, CJ; Robert J. Staker, John T. Copenhaver Jr., Elizabeth V. Hallanan; Clerk's Office, Charleston 25329.

Wisconsin — Eastern: Terence T. Evans, CJ; Thomas J. Curran, J.P. Stadtmueller; Clerk's Office, Milwaukee 53202. **Western:** Barbara B. Crabb, CJ; John C. Shabaz; Clerk's Office, Madison 53701.

Wyoming — Clarence A. Brimmer, CJ; Alan B. Johnson; Clerk's Office, Cheyenne 82001.

U.S. Territorial District Courts

Guam — vacancy; Clerk's Office, Agana 96910.
Puerto Rico — Gilberto Gierbolini, CJ; Juan M. Perez-Gimenez, Carmen Consuelo Cerezo, Jaime Pieras Jr., Raymond L. Acosta, Hector M. Laffitte, Jose Antonio Fuste; Clerk's Office, San Juan 00904.
Virgin Islands — vacancy CJ; Clerk's Office, Charlotte Amalie, St. Thomas 00801.

U.S. Court of Veterans Appeals

Washington, D.C. 20004 (Salaries, $129,500)
Chief Judge — Frank Q. Nebeker.
Judges — Kenneth B. Kramer, John J. Farley 3d, Hart T. Mankin, Ronald M. Holdaway, Donald L. Ivers, Jonathan R. Steinberg.

State Officials, Salaries, Party Membership

As of mid-1992 (does **not** reflect Nov. 1992 elections); † Ind. or other party.

Alabama

Governor — Guy Hunt, R., $87,913.
Lt. Gov. — Jim Folsom Jr., D., $52 per legislative day, plus annual salary of $1,900 per month plus $1,500 per month for expenses.
Sec. of State — Billy Joe Camp, D., $57,203.
Atty. Gen. — Jimmy Evans, D., $90,474.
Treasurer — George Wallace Jr., D., $57,203.
Legislature: meets annually the 3d Tuesday in Apr. (first year of term of office, first Tuesday in Feb. (2d and 3d years), 2d Tuesday in Jan. (4th year) at Montgomery. Members receive $50 a day salary, plus $1,900 per month expenses and mileage of 10¢ per mile.
Senate — Dem., 28; Rep., 7. Total, 35.
House — Dem., 82; Rep., 23. Total, 105.

Alaska

Governor — Walter Hickel, † $81,648.
Lt. Gov. — John B. Coghill, †, $76,188.
Atty. General — Charles Cole, R., $79,860.
Legislature: meets annually in January at Juneau, for 120 days with a 10-day extension possible upon ⅔ vote. First session in odd years. Members receive $22,872 per year plus $80 a day per diem.
Senate — Dem., 10; Rep., 10. Total, 20.
House — Dem., 23; Rep., 17. Total, 40.

Arizona

Governor — Fife Symington, R., $75,000.
Sec. of State — Richard Mahoney, D., $52,000.
Atty. Gen. — Grant Woods, R., $72,800.
Treasurer — Tony West, R., $52,000.
Legislature: meets annually in January at Phoenix. Each member receives an annual salary of $15,000.
Senate — Dem., 17; Rep., 13. Total, 30.
House — Dem., 27; Rep., 33. Total, 60.

Arkansas

Governor — Bill Clinton, D., $35,000.
Lt. Gov. — Jim Guy Tucker, D., $14,000.
Sec. of State — W. J. "Bill" McCuen, D., $22,500.
Atty. Gen. — Winston Bryant, D., $26,500.
Treasurer — Jimmie Lou Fisher Lumpkin, D., $22,500.
Auditor — Julia Hughes Jones, D., $22,500.
General Assembly: meets odd years in January at Little Rock. Members receive $7,500 per year, $74 a day while in regular session, plus 21 cents a mile travel expense.
Senate — Dem., 31; Rep., 4. Total, 35.
House — Dem., 90; Rep. 9; 1 ind. Total, 100.

California

Governor — Pete Wilson, R., $120,000.
Lt. Gov. — Leo T. McCarthy, D., $90,000.
Sec. of State — March Fong Eu, D., $90,000.
Controller — Gray Davis, D., $90,000.
Atty. Gen. — Dan Lungren, R., $102,000.
Legislature: meets at Sacramento; regular sessions commence on the first Monday in Dec. of every even-numbered year; each session lasts 2 years. Members receive $52,500 per year plus mileage and $100 per diem.
Senate — Dem., 24; Rep., 13, 2 ind., 1 vac.; Total, 40.
Assembly — Dem., 47; Rep. 33; Total, 80.

Colorado

Governor — Roy Romer, D., $70,000.
Lt. Gov. — Mike Callihan, D., $48,500.

Secy. of State — Natalie Meyer, R., $48,500.
Atty. Gen. — Gale Norton, R., $60,000.
Treasurer — Gail Schoettler, D., $48,500.
General Assembly: meets annually in January at Denver. Members receive $17,500 annually.
Senate — Dem., 11; Rep., 24. Total, 35.
House — Dem., 26; Rep., 39. Total, 65.

Connecticut

Governor — Lowell Weicker, †, $78,000.
Lt. Gov. — Eunice S. Groark, †, $55,000.
Sec. of State — Pauline R. Kezer, R., $50,000.
Treasurer — Francisco Borges, D., $50,000.
Comptroller — William E. Curry Jr., D., $50,000.
Atty. Gen. — Richard Blumenthal, D., $60,000.
General Assembly: meets annually odd years in January and even years in February at Hartford. Salary $15,200 per year plus $4,500 (senator), $3,500 (representative) per year for expenses, plus travel allowance.
Senate — Dem., 20; Rep., 16. Total, 36.
House — Dem., 88; Rep., 63. Total, 151.

Delaware

Governor — Michael N. Castle, R., $80,000.
Lt. Gov. — Dale E. Wolf, R., $35,000.
Sec. of State — Jeffrey Lewis, act., R., $69,900.
Atty. Gen. — Charles Oberly 3d, D., $81,400.
Treasurer — Janet C. Rzewnicki, R., $63,000.
General Assembly: 55 day session beginning the 2d Tuesday in January until June 30. Members receive $23,000 base salary, plus $5,500 expense account.
Senate — Dem., 15; Rep., 6. Total, 21.
House — Dem., 17; Rep., 24. Total, 41.

Florida

Governor — Lawton Chiles, D., $95,000.
Lt. Gov. — Buddy McKay, D., $91,000.
Sec. of State — Jim Smith, R., $94,040.
Comptroller — Gerald Lewis, D., $94,040.
Atty. Gen. — Robert Butterworth, D., $94,040.
Treasurer — Tom Gallagher, R., $94,040.
Legislature: meets annually at Tallahassee. Members receive $22,560 per year plus expense allowance while on official business.
Senate — Dem., 22; Rep., 18. Total, 40.
House — Dem., 74; Rep., 46. Total, 120.

Georgia

Governor — Zell Miller, D., $91,092.
Lt. Gov. — Pierre Howard, D., $59,145.
Sec. of State — Max Cleland, D., $72,966.
Insurance Comm. — Tim Ryles, D., $72,954.
Atty. Gen. — Michael J. Bowers, $74,645.
General Assembly: meets annually at Atlanta. Members receive $10,509 per year, $59 per diem, and $4,800 expense reimbursement. During session $59 per day for expenses.
Senate — Dem., 45; Rep., 11. Total, 56.
House — Dem., 145; Rep., 35. Total, 180.

Hawaii

Governor — John Waihee, D., $94,780.
Lt. Gov. — Benjamin Cayetano, D., $90,041.
Atty. Gen. — Warren Price, $85,302.
Comptroller — Russel Nagata, $85,302.
Dir. of Budget & Finance — Yukio Takemoto, $85,302.
Legislature: meets annually on 3d Wednesday in January at Honolulu. Members receive $27,000 per year plus expenses.
Senate — Dem., 22. Rep., 3. Total, 25.
House — Dem., 45. Rep., 6. Total, 51.

Idaho

Governor — Cecil D. Andrus, D., $75,000.
Lt. Gov. — C. L. "Butch" Otter, R., $20,000.
Sec. of State — Pete T. Cenarrusa, R., $62,500.
Treasurer — Lydia Justice Edwards, R., $62,500.
Atty. Gen. — Larry EchoHawk, D., $67,500.
Legislature: meets annually the Monday on or nearest the 9th of January at Boise. Members receive $2,000 per year plus $70 per day during session if required to maintain a 2d residence; $40 if no 2d residence, plus $50.00 per day when engaged in legislative business when legislature is not in session.
Senate — Dem., 21; Rep., 21. Total, 42.
House — Dem., 28; Rep., 56 Total, 84.

Illinois

Governor — Jim Edgar, R., $97,370.
Lt. Gov. — Bob Kustra, R., $68,732.
Sec. of State — George H. Ryan, R., $85,915.
Comptroller — D.C. Netsch, D., $74,459.
Atty. Gen. — Roland W. Burris, D., $85,915.
Treasurer — Patrick Quinn, D., $74,459.
General Assembly: meets annually in January at Springfield. Members receive $35,661 per annum.
Senate — Dem., 31; Rep., 28. Total, 59.
House — Dem., 72; Rep., 46. Total, 118.

Indiana

Governor — Evan Bayh, D., $77,200 plus discretionary expenses.
Lt. Gov. — Frank O'Bannon, D., $64,000 plus discretionary expenses.
Sec. of State — Joseph Hogsett D., $46,000.
Atty. Gen. — Linley E. Pearson, R., $59,200.
Treasurer — Marjorie H. O'Laughlin, R., $46,000.
Auditor — Ann G. DeVore, R., $46,000.
General Assembly: meets annually in January. Members receive $11,600 per year plus $92 per day while in session, $25 per day while not in session.
Senate — Dem., 24; Rep., 26. Total, 50.
House — Dem., 52; Rep., 48. Total, 100.

Iowa

Governor — Terry E. Branstad, R., $76,900.
Lt. Gov. — Joy Corning, R., $60,000.
Sec. of State — Elaine Baxter, D., $60,000.
Atty. Gen. — Bonnie Campbell, D., $73,600.
Treasurer — Michael L. Fitzgerald, D., $60,000.
Auditor — Richard D. Johnson, R., $60,000.
Secy. of Agriculture — Dale M. Cochran, D., $60,000.
General Assembly: meets annually in January at Des Moines. Members receive $18,100 annually plus maximum expense allowance of $50 per day for first 110 days of first session, and first 100 days of 2d session (except for Polk Co. legislators); mileage expenses at 21¢ a mile.
Senate — Dem., 29; Rep., 21. Total, 50.
House — Dem., 55; Rep., 45. Total, 100.

Kansas

Governor — Joan Finney, D., $74,235.
Lt. Gov. — James Francisco, D., $20,998.
Sec. of State — Bill Graves, R., $57,668.
Atty. Gen. — Robert T. Stephan, R., $66,324.
Treasurer — Sally Thompson, D., $57,668.
Legislature: meets annually in January at Topeka. Members receive $60 a day plus $70 a day expenses while in session, plus $600 per month while not in session.
Senate — Dem., 18; Rep., 22. Total, 40.
House — Dem., 63; Rep., 62. Total, 125.

Kentucky

Governor — Brereton C. Jones, D., $79,255.
Lt. Gov. — Paul Patton, D., $67,378.
Sec. of State — Bob Babbage, D., $67,378.
Atty. Gen. — Chris Gorman, D., $67,378.
Treasurer — Francis J. Mills, D., $67,378.
Auditor — Ben Chandler, D., $67,378.
General Assembly: meets even years in January at Frankfort. Members receive $100 per day and $75 per day during session and $950 per month for expenses for interim.
Senate — Dem., 27; Rep., 11. Total, 38.
House — Dem., 68; Rep., 32. Total, 100.

Louisiana

Governor — Edwin W. Edwards, D., $73,440.
Lt. Gov. — Melinda Schwegmann, D., $63,367.
Sec. of State — Fox McKeithen, R., $60,169.
Atty. Gen. — Richard Ieyoub, D., $60,169.
Treasurer — Mary Landrieu, D., $60,169.
Legislature: meets annually for 60 legislative days commencing on the last Monday in March. Members receive $75 per day and mileage plus annual salary of $16,800.
Senate — Dem., 33; Rep., 6. Total, 39.
House — Dem., 88; Rep., 16, 1 ind. Total, 105.

Maine

Governor — John R. McKernan Jr., R., $70,000.
Sec. of State — G. William Diamond, D., $48,152.
Atty. Gen. — Michael E. Carpenter, D., $61,152.
Treasurer — Samuel Shapiro, D., $61,200.
Legislature: meets annually the first Wednesday in December at Augusta, and the Wednesday after the first Tuesday in Jan. in even numbered years. Members receive $10,500 for first regular sessions, $7,500 for second regular session plus expenses; presiding officers receive 50% more.
Senate — Dem., 22; Rep., 13. Total, 35.
House — Dem., 97; Rep., 54. Total, 151.

Maryland

Governor — William Donald Schaefer, D., $120,000.

Lt. Gov. — Melvin Steinberg, D., $100,000.
Comptroller — Louis L. Goldstein, D., $100,000.
Atty. Gen. — J. Joseph Curran Jr., D., $100,000.
Sec. of State — Winfield M. Kelly Jr., D., $70,000.
Treasurer — Lucille Maurer, D., $100,000.
General Assembly: meets 90 consecutive days annually beginning on the 2d Wednesday in January at Annapolis. Members receive $27,000 per year plus expenses.
Senate — Dem., 38; Rep., 9. Total, 47.
House — Dem., 117; Rep., 24. Total, 141.

Massachusetts

Governor — William Weld, R., $75,000.
Lt. Gov. — A. Paul Cellucci, R., $60,000.
Sec. of State — Michael Joseph Connolly, D., $60,000.
Atty. Gen. — L. Scott Harshbarger, D., $65,000.
Treasurer — Joseph Malone, R., $60,000.
Auditor — A. Joseph DeNucci, D., $60,000.
General Court (Legislature): meets each January in Boston. Salaries $30,000 per annum.
Senate — Dem., 24; Rep., 15, 1 vac. Total, 40.
House — Dem., 120; Rep., 37; ind., 1, 2 vac. Total, 160.

Michigan

Governor — John Engler, R., $106,700.
Lt. Gov. — Connie Binsfeld, R., $80,300.
Sec. of State — Richard H. Austin, D., $109,000.
Atty. Gen. — Frank J. Kelley, D., $109,000.
Treasurer — Doug Roberts, N-P, $83,100.
Legislature: meets annually in January at Lansing. Members receive $45,450 per year, plus $8,500 expense allowance.
Senate — Dem., 18; Rep., 20. Total, 38.
House — Dem., 61; Rep., 49. Total, 110.

Minnesota

Governor — Arne Carlson, R., $109,053.
Lt. Gov. — Joanell Dyrstad, IR, $59,981.
Sec. of State — Joan Anderson Growe, DFL., $59,981.
Atty. Gen. — Hubert H. Humphrey 3d, DFL., $85,194.
Treasurer — Michael McGrath, DFL., $59,981.
Auditor — Mark Dayton, IR, $65,437.
Legislature: meets for a total of 120 days within every 2 years at St. Paul. Members receive $27,979 per year, plus expense allowance during session.
Senate — DFL., 46; IR, 21. Total, 67.
House — DFL., 78; IR, 56. Total, 134.
(DFL means Democratic-Farmer-Labor. IR means Independent Republican.)

Mississippi

Governor — Kirk Fordice, R., $75,600.
Lt. Gov. — Eddie Briggs, R., $40,800.
Sec. of State — Dick Molpus, D., $54,000.
Atty. Gen. — Mike Moore, D., $61,200.
Treasurer — Marshall Bennett, D., $54,000.
Legislature: meets annually in January at Jackson. Members receive $10,100 per regular session plus travel allowance, and $500 per month while not in session.
Senate — Dem., 42; Rep., 9, 1 vac. Total, 52.
House — Dem., 98; Rep., 23, 1 ind. Total, 122.

Missouri

Governor — John D. Ashcroft, R., $90,312.
Lt. Gov. — Mel Carnahan, D., $54,343.
Sec. of State — Roy D. Blunt, R., $72,327.
Atty. Gen. — William L. Webster, R., $72,327.
Treasurer — Wendell Bailey, R., $72,327.
State Auditor — Margaret Kelly, R., $70,909.
General Assembly: meets annually in Jefferson City on the first Wednesday after first Monday in January. Members receive $22,862 annually.
Senate — Dem., 23; Rep., 11. Total, 34.
House — Dem., 99; Rep., 64. Total, 163.

Montana

Governor — Stan Stephens, R., $55,502.
Lt. Gov. — Dennis Rehberg, R., $40,466.
Sec. of State — Mike Cooney, D., $37,526.
Atty. Gen. — Marc Racicot, R., $50,841.
Legislative Assembly: meets odd years in January at Helena. Members receive $55.50 per legislative day plus $50 per day for expenses while in session.
Senate — Dem., 29; Rep., 21. Total, 50.
House — Dem., 61; Rep., 39. Total, 100.

Nebraska

Governor — Ben Nelson, D., $65,000.
Lt. Gov. — Maxine Moul, D., $47,000.
Sec. of State — Allen J. Beermann, R., $52,000.
Atty. Gen. — Don Stenberg, R., $64,500.
Treasurer — Dawn Rockey, D., $49,500.
Legislature: meets annually in January at Lincoln. Members receive salary of $12,000 annually plus expenses.
Unicameral body composed of 49 members who are elected on a nonpartisan ballot and are called senators.

Nevada

Governor — Robert Miller, D., $90,000.
Lt. Gov. — Sue Wagner, R., $20,000.
Sec. of State — Cheryl Lau, R., $62,500.
Comptroller — Darrel Daines, R., $62,500.
Atty. Gen. — Frankie Sue Del Papa, D., $85,000.
Treasurer — Bob Seale, R., $62,500.
Legislature: meets odd years in January at Carson City. Members receive $130 per day for 60 days (20 days for special sessions).
Senate — Dem., 11; Rep., 10. Total, 21.
Assembly — Dem., 22; Rep., 20. Total, 42.

New Hampshire

Governor — Judd Gregg, R., $79,541.
Sec. of State — William M. Gardner, D., $63,430.
Atty. Gen. — John Arnold, $71,007.
Treasurer — Georgie A. Thomas, R., $63,430.
General Court (Legislature): meets every year in January at Concord. Members receive $200; presiding officers $250.
Senate — Dem., 11; Rep., 13. Total, 24.
House — Rep., 267; Dem., 123., ind. 2, vac. 8; Total, 400.

New Jersey

Governor — James J. Florio, D., $85,000.
Sec. of State — Daniel Dalton, D., $95,000.
Atty. Gen. — Robert J. Del Tufo, D., $95,000.
Treasurer — Samuel Crane, act., D., $95,000.
Legislature: meets throughout the year at Trenton. Members receive $25,000 per year, except president of Senate and speaker of Assembly who receive 1/3 more.
Senate — Dem., 13; Rep., 27. Total, 40.
Assembly — Dem., 22; Rep. 58. Total, 80.

New Mexico

Governor — Bruce King, D., $90,000.
Lt. Gov. — Casey Luna, D., $65,000.
Sec. of State — Stephanie Gonzales, D., $65,000.
Atty. Gen. — Tom Udall, D., $72,500.
Treasurer — David King, D., $65,000.
Legislature: meets on the 3d Tuesday in January at Santa Fe; odd years for 60 days, even years for 30 days. Members receive $75 per day while in session.
Senate — Dem., 26; Rep., 16. Total, 42.
House — Dem., 45; Rep., 25. Total, 70.

New York

Governor — Mario M. Cuomo, D., $130,000.
Lt. Gov. — Stan Lundine, D., $110,000.
Sec. of State — Gail S. Shaffer, D., $87,338.
Comptroller — Edward V. Regan, R., $110,000.
Atty. Gen. — Robert Abrams, D., $110,000.
Legislature: meets annually in January at Albany. Members receive $57,500 per year.
Senate — Dem., 27; Rep., 34. Total, 61.
Assembly — Dem., 92; Rep., 58. Total, 150.

North Carolina

Governor — James G. Martin, R., $123,300 plus $11,500 per year expenses.
Lt. Gov. — James C. Gardner, R., $75,252 plus expenses.
Sec. of State — Rufus L. Edmisten, D., $75,252.
Atty. Gen. — Lacy Thornberg, D., $75,252.
Treasurer — Harlan E. Boyles, D., $75,252.
General Assembly: meets odd years in January at Raleigh. Members receive $12,504 annual salary and $6,624 annual expense allowance, plus $81 per diem subsistence and travel allowance while in session.
Senate — Dem., 37; Rep., 13. Total, 50.
House — Dem., 81; Rep., 39. Total, 120.

North Dakota

Governor — George A. Sinner, D., $68,284.
Lt. Gov. — Lloyd B. Omdahl, D., $56,116.
Sec. of State — Jim Kusler, D., $51,752.
Atty. Gen. — Nicholas Spaeth, D., $58,480.
Treasurer — Robert Hanson, D., $51,752.
Legislative Assembly: meets odd years in January at Bismarck. Members receive $90 per day expenses during session and $180 per month when not in session.
Senate — Dem., 27; Rep., 26. Total, 53.
House — Dem., 48; Rep., 58. Total, 106.

Ohio

Governor — George Voinovich, R., $100,000.
Lt. Gov. — Michael DeWine, R., $51,710.
Sec. of State — Bob Taft, R., $73,872.
Atty. Gen. — Lee Fisher, D., $73,872.
Treasurer — Mary Ellen Withrow, D., $73,872.
Auditor — Thomas E. Ferguson, D., $73,872.
General Assembly: meets odd years at Columbus on first Monday in January; no limit on session. Members receive $38,482 per annum.
Senate — Dem., 12; Rep., 21. Total, 33.
House — Dem., 61; Rep., 38. Total, 99.

Oklahoma

Governor — David Walters, D., $70,000.
Lt. Gov. — Jack Mildren, D., $40,000.
Sec. of State — John Kennedy, D., $42,500.
Atty. Gen. — Susan Loving, D., $55,000.
Treasurer — Claudette Henry, R., $50,000.
Auditor— Clifton Scott, D., $50,000.
Legislature: meets annually in May at Oklahoma City. Members receive $32,000 annually.
Senate — Dem., 37; Rep., 11. Total, 48.
House — Dem., 68; Rep., 33. Total, 101.

Oregon

Governor — Barbara Roberts, D., $80,000.
Sec. of State — Phil Keisling, D., $61,500.
Atty. Gen. — David B. Frohnmayer, R., $66,000.
Treasurer — Tony Meeker, R., $61,500.
Legislative Assembly: meets odd years in January at Salem. Members receive $1,029 monthly and $73 expenses per day both during & out of session.
Senate — Dem., 20; Rep., 10. Total, 30.
House — Dem., 32; Rep., 28. Total, 60.

Pennsylvania

Governor — Robert Casey, D., $105,000.
Lt. Gov. — Mark S. Singel, D., $83,000.
Sec. of the Commonwealth — Christopher Lewis, D., $72,000.
Atty. Gen. — Ernest R. Preate, R., $84,000.
Treasurer — Catherine Baker Knoll, D., $84,000.
General Assembly — convenes annually in January at Harrisburg. Members receive $47,000 per year plus expenses.
Senate — Dem., 24; Rep., 26. Total, 50.
House — Dem., 107; Rep., 96. Total, 203.

Rhode Island

Governor — Bruce Sundlun, D., $69,000.
Lt. Gov. — Roger N. Begin, D., $52,000.
Sec. of State — Kathleen S. Connell, D., $52,000.
Atty. Gen. — James E. O'Neil, D., $55,000.
Treasurer — Anthony J. Solomon, D., $52,000.
General Assembly: meets annually in January at Providence. Members receive $5 per day for 60 days, and travel allowance of 8¢ per mile.
Senate — Dem., 45; Rep., 5. Total, 50.
House — Dem., 89; Rep., 11. Total, 100.

South Carolina

Governor — Carroll A. Campbell Jr., R., $98,000.
Lt. Gov. — Nick Theodore, D., $43,000.
Sec. of State — Jim Miles, R., $85,000.
Comptroller Gen. — Earle E. Morris Jr., D., $85,000.
Atty. Gen. — T.T. Medlock, D., $85,000.
Treasurer — G.L. Patterson Jr., D., $85,000.
General Assembly: meets annually in January at Columbia. Members receive $10,400 per year and expense allowance of $79 per day, plus travel and postage allowance.
Senate — Dem., 34; Rep., 11, 1 vac. Total, 46.
House — Dem. 74; Rep., 42; 1 ind., 7 vac. Total, 124.

South Dakota

Governor — George S. Mickelson, R., $63,232.
Lt. Gov. — Walter Miller, R., $56,068.
Sec. of State — Joyce Hazeltine, R., $42,963.
Treasurer — G. Homer Harding, R., $42,963.
Atty. Gen. — Mark Bennett, R., $53,705.
Auditor — Vernon Larson, R., $42,963.
Legislature: meets annually in January at Pierre. Members receive $4,267 for 40-day session in odd-numbered years, and $3,733 for 35-day session in even-numbered years, plus $75 per legislative day.
Senate — Dem., 17; Rep., 18. Total, 35.
House — Dem., 25. Rep., 45. Total, 70.

Tennessee

Governor — Ned Ray McWherter, D., $85,000.
Lt. Gov. — John S. Wilder, D., $49,500.
Sec. of State — Bryant Millsaps, D., $73,140.
Comptroller — William Snodgrass, D., $73,140.
Atty. Gen. — Charles W. Burson, D., $85,500.
General Assembly: meets annually in January at Nashville. Members receive $16,500 yearly plus $78.00 per diem plus office expenses.
Senate — Dem., 20; Rep., 13. Total, 33.
House — Dem., 57; Rep., 42. Total, 99.

Texas

Governor — Ann Richards, D., $93,432.
Lt. Gov. — Bob Bullock, D., $7,200.
Sec. of State — John Hannah, D., $72,549.
Comptroller — John Sharp, D., $74,698.
Atty. Gen. — Dan Morales, D., $74,698.
Treasurer — Kay Bailey Hutchison, R., $74,698.
Legislature: meets odd years in January at Austin. Members receive annual salary not exceeding $7,200, per diem while in session, and travel allowance.
Senate — Dem., 23; Rep., 8. Total, 31.
House — Dem., 94; Rep., 56. Total, 150.

Utah

Governor — Norman Bangerter, R., $70,000.
Lt. Gov. — W. Val Oveson, R., $52,500.
Atty. Gen. — R. Paul Van Dam, D., $56,000.
Treasurer — Edward T. Alter, D., $53,000.
Legislature: convenes for 45 days on 2d Monday in January each year; members receive $25 per day, $15 daily expenses, and mileage.
Senate — Dem., 10; Rep., 19. Total, 29.
House — Dem., 31; Rep., 44. Total, 75.

Vermont

Governor — Howard Dean, D., $80,730.
Lt. Gov. — vacant, $33,655.
Sec. of State — James H. Douglas, R., $50,800.
Atty. Gen. — Jeffrey Amestoy, R., $61,025.
Treasurer — Paul W. Ruse Jr., D., $50,800.
Auditor of Accounts — Alexander V. Acebo, R., $50,800.
General Assembly: meets odd years in January at Montpelier. Members receive $480 per week while in session plus $95 per day for special session, plus specified expenses.
Senate — Dem., 15; Rep., 15. Total, 30.
House — Dem., 73; Rep., 75., ind. 2. Total, 150.

Virginia

Governor — L. Douglas Wilder, D., $108,000.
Lt. Gov. — Donald S. Beyer Jr., $29,550.
Atty. Gen. — Mary Sue Terry, D., $95,000.
Sec. of the Commonwealth — Pamela Womack, D., $56,603.
Treasurer — Eddie N. Moore Jr., $85,881.
General Assembly: meets annually in January at Richmond. Members receive $18,000 annually plus expense and mileage allowances.
Senate — Dem., 30; Rep., 10. Total, 40.
House — Dem., 59; Rep., 39; Ind., 2. Total, 100.

Washington

Governor — Booth Gardner, D., $96,700.
Lt. Gov. — Joel Pritchard, D., $51,100.
Sec. of State — Ralph Munro, R., $52,600.
Atty. Gen. — Ken Eikenberry, R., $75,700.
Treasurer — Daniel K. Grimm, D., $65,000.
Legislature: meets annually in January at Olympia. Members receive $17,900 annually plus per diem of $66 per diem and 24¢ per mile while in session, and $66 per diem for attending meetings during interim.
Senate — Dem., 24; Rep., 25. Total, 49.
House — Dem., 63; Rep., 35. Total, 98.

West Virginia

Governor — Gaston Caperton, D., $72,000.
Sec. of State — Ken Hechler, D., $43,200.
Atty. Gen. — Mario Palumbo, D., $50,400.
Treasurer — Larrie Bailey, D., $50,400.
Comm. of Agric. — Cleve Benedict, R., $46,800.
Auditor — Glen B. Gainer Jr., D., $46,800.
Legislature: meets annually in January at Charleston. Members receive $6,500.
Senate — Dem., 33; Rep., 1. Total, 34.
House — Dem., 74; Rep., 26. Total, 100.

Wisconsin

Governor — Tommy G. Thompson, R., $92,283.
Lt. Gov. — Scott McCallum, R., $49,673.
Sec. of State — Douglas La Follette, D., $45,088.
Treasurer — Cathy S. Zeuske, R., $45,088.
Atty. Gen. — James E. Doyle, D., $82,706.

Superintendent of Public Instruction — Herbert J. Grover, $72,337.

Legislature: meets in January at Madison. Members receive $33,622 annually plus $64 per day expenses.

Senate — Dem., 18; Rep., 15. Total, 33.

Assembly — Dem., 57; Rep., 42. Total, 99.

Wyoming

Governor — Mike Sullivan, D., $70,000.

Sec. of State — Kathy Karpan, D., $52,500.

Atty. Gen. — Joseph Meyer, $52,500.

Treasurer — Stan Smith, R., $52,500.

Auditor — Dave Ferrari, R., $52,500.

Legislature: meets odd years in January, even years in February, at Cheyenne. Members receive $75 per day while in session, plus $60 per day for expenses.

Senate — Dem., 10; Rep., 20. Total, 30.

House — Dem., 22; Rep. 42. Total, 64.

Puerto Rico

Governor — Rafael Hernández-Colón.

Legislature: composed of a Senate of 27 members and a House of Representatives of 53 members. Majority of the members of both chambers belongs to the Popular Democratic Party. They meet annually on the 2d Monday in January at San Juan.

U.S. Government Independent Agencies

Source: National Archives & Records Administration

Address: Washington, DC. Location and ZIP codes of agencies in parentheses; as of mid-1992.

ACTION — Jane A. Kenny, dir. (1100 Vermont Ave., NW, 20525).

Administrative Conference of the United States — Robert S. Ross Jr., chmn. (Suite 500, 2120 L St. NW, 20037).

African Development Foundation — Gregory Robeson Smith, pres. (1400 Eye St. NW, 20005).

Central Intelligence Agency — Robert M. Gates, dir. (Wash., DC 20505).

Commission on Civil Rights — Arthur A. Fletcher, chmn. (1121 Vermont Ave. NW, 20425).

Commodity Futures Trading Commission — Wendy L. Gramm, chmn. (2033 K St. NW, 20581).

Consumer Product Safety Commission — Jacqueline Jones-Smith, chmn. (5401 Westbard Ave., Bethesda, MD 20207).

Environmental Protection Agency — William K. Reilly, adm. (401 M St., SW, 20460).

Equal Employment Opportunity Commission — Evan J. Kemp. Jr., chmn. (1801 L St. NW., 20507).

Export-Import Bank of the United States — John D. Macomber, pres. and chmn. (811 Vermont Ave. NW 20571).

Farm Credit Administration — Harold B. Steele, chmn., Federal Farm Credit Board (1501 Farm Credit Drive, McLean, VA 22102).

Federal Communications Commission — Alfred C. Sikes, chmn. (1919 M St. NW, 20554).

Federal Deposit Insurance Corporation — William Taylor, chmn. (550 17th St. NW, 20429).

Federal Election Commission — Joan D. Aikens, chmn. (999 E. St. NW, 20463).

Federal Emergency Management Agency — Wallace E. Stickney, dir. (500 C St. SW, 20472).

Federal Housing Finance Board — Daniel F. Evans Jr., chmn. (1777 F St. NW., 20006).

Federal Labor Relations Authority — Jean McKee, chmn. (500 C St. SW, 20424).

Federal Maritime Commission — Christopher L. Koch, chmn. (1100 L St. NW 20573).

Federal Mediation and Conciliation Service — Bernard E. DeLury, dir. (2100 K St. NW, 20427).

Federal Mine Safety & Health Review Commission — Ford B. Ford, chmn. (1730 K St. NW, 20006).

Federal Reserve System — Chairman, board of governors: Alan Greenspan. (20th St. & Constitution Ave. NW, 20551).

Federal Retirement Thrift Investment Board — Roger W. Mehle, chmn. (805 15th St. NW, 20005).

Federal Trade Commission — Janet D. Steiger, chmn. (Pennsylvania Ave. at 6th St. NW, 20580).

General Accounting Office — Comptroller General of the U.S.; Charles A. Bowsher (441 G St. NW, 20548).

General Services Administration — Richard G. Austin, adm. (18th & F Sts. NW, 20405).

Government Printing Office — Public printer: Robert W. Houk. (North Capitol and H Sts. NW, 20401).

Inter-American Foundation — Frank D. Yturria, chmn. (901 N. Stuart St., Arlington, VA 22203).

Interstate Commerce Commission — Edward J. Philbin, chmn. (12th St. & Constitution Ave. NW, 20423).

Library of Congress — James H. Billington, librarian of Congress (101 Independence Ave. SE, 20540).

Merit Systems Protection Board — Daniel R. Levinson, chmn. (1120 Vermont Ave. NW, 20419).

National Aeronautics and Space Administration — Daniel S. Goldin, adm. (600 Independence Ave., SW 20546).

National Archives & Records Administration — Don W. Wilson archivist (7th St. & Pennsylvania Ave. NW, 20408).

National Credit Union Administration — Roger W. Jepsen, chmn. (1776 G St. NW, 20456).

National Foundation on the Arts and the Humanities — vacant, chmn. (arts) 1100 Pennsylvania Ave. NW, 20506; Lynne V. Cheney, chmn. (humanities) same address. Institute of Museum Services: Susannah S. Kent, dir., same address.

National Labor Relations Board — James M. Stephens, chmn. (1717 Pennsylvania Ave. NW, 20570).

National Mediation Board — Kimberly A. Madigan, chmn. (1425 K St. NW, 20572).

National Railroad Passenger Corporation (Amtrak) — W. Graham Claytor Jr., chmn. (60 Massachusetts Ave. NE, 20002).

National Science Foundation — James J. Duderstadt, chmn., National Science Board (1800 G St. NW, 20550).

National Transportation Safety Board — Susan M. Coughlin, act. chmn. (490 L'Enfant Plaza SW, 20594).

Nuclear Regulatory Commission — Ivan Selin, chmn. (1717 H St. NW, 20555).

Occupational Safety and Health Review Commission — Edwin G. Foulke Jr., chmn. (1825 K St. NW, 20006).

Office of Personnel Management — Constance B. Newman, dir., (1900 E St. NW, 20415).

Peace Corps — Elaine L. Chao, dir. (1990 K St. NW, 20526).

Postal Rate Commission — George W. Haley, chmn. (1333 H. St. NW, 20268-0001).

Railroad Retirement Board — Glen L. Bower, chmn. (Suite 558, 2000 L. St. NW, 20036), Main Office (844 Rush St., Chicago, IL 60611).

Securities and Exchange Commission — Richard C. Breeden, chmn. (450 5th St. NW, 20549).

Selective Service System — Robert W. Gambino, dir. (1023 31st St. NW, 20435).

Small Business Administration — Patricia F. Saiki, adm. (409 Third St. SW, 20416).

Smithsonian Institution — Robert McC. Adams, secy. (1000 Jefferson Dr. SW, 20560).

Tennessee Valley Authority — Chairman, board of directors: Marvin Runyon. (400 W. Summit Hill Dr., Knoxville, TN 37902 and Room 300, 412 1st St. SE, Washington, DC 20444).

United States Arms Control & Disarmament Agency — Ronald F. Lehman 2d, dir. (320 21st St. NW 20451).

United States Information Agency — Henry E. Catto, dir. (301 4th St. SW, 20547).

United States International Development Cooperation Agency — Ronald W. Roskens, act. dir. (320 21st St. NW 20523).

United States International Trade Commission — Don E. Newquist, chmn. (500 E St. SW, 20436).

United States Postal Service — vacant, postmaster general (475 L'Enfant Plaza SW, 20260).

CABINETS OF THE U. S.

Secretaries of State

The Department of Foreign Affairs was created by act of Congress July 27, 1789, and the name changed to Department of State on Sept. 15.

President	Secretary	Home	Apptd.
Washington	Thomas Jefferson	Va.	1789
"	Edmund Randolph	"	1794
"	Timothy Pickering	Pa.	1795
Adams, J.	Timothy Pickering	Pa.	1797
"	John Marshall	Va.	1800
Jefferson	James Madison	"	1801
Madison	Robert Smith	Md.	1809
"	James Monroe	Va.	1811
Monroe	John Quincy Adams	Mass.	1817
Adams, J.Q.	Henry Clay	Ky.	1825
Jackson	Martin Van Buren	N.Y.	1829
"	Edward Livingston	La.	1831
"	Louis McLane	Del.	1833
"	John Forsyth	Ga.	1834
Van Buren	John Forsyth	Ga.	1837
Harrison, W.H.	Daniel Webster	Mass.	1841
Tyler	Daniel Webster	Mass.	1841
"	Abel P. Upshur	Va.	1843
"	John C. Calhoun	S.C.	1844
Polk	John C. Calhoun	S.C.	1845
"	James Buchanan	Pa.	1845
Taylor	James Buchanan	Pa.	1849
"	John M. Clayton	Del.	1849
Fillmore	John M. Clayton	Del.	1850
"	Daniel Webster	Mass.	1850
"	Edward Everett	"	1852
Pierce	William L. Marcy	N.Y.	1853
Buchanan	William L. Marcy	N.Y.	1857
"	Lewis Cass	Mich.	1857
"	Jeremiah S. Black	Pa.	1860
Lincoln	Jeremiah S. Black	Pa.	1861
"	William H. Seward	N.Y.	1861
Johnson, A.	William H. Seward	N.Y.	1865
Grant	Elihu B. Washburne	Ill.	1869
"	Hamilton Fish	N.Y.	1869
Hayes	Hamilton Fish	N.Y.	1877
"	William M. Evarts	N.Y.	1877
Garfield	William M. Evarts	N.Y.	1881
"	James G. Blaine	Me.	1881
Arthur	James G. Blaine	Me.	1881
"	F.T. Frelinghuysen	N.J.	1881
Cleveland	F.T. Frelinghuysen	N.J.	1885
Cleveland	Thomas F. Bayard	Del.	1885
Harrison, B.	Thomas F. Bayard	Del.	1889
"	James G. Blaine	Me.	1889
"	John W. Foster	Ind.	1892
Cleveland	Walter Q. Gresham	Ind.	1893
"	Richard Olney	Mass.	1895
McKinley	Richard Olney	Mass.	1897
"	John Sherman	Oh.	1897
"	William R. Day	Oh.	1898
"	John Hay	D.C.	1898
Roosevelt, T.	John Hay	D.C.	1901
"	Elihu Root	N.Y.	1905
"	Robert Bacon	N.Y.	1909
Taft	Robert Bacon	N.Y.	1909
"	Philander C. Knox	Pa.	1909
Wilson	Philander C. Knox	Pa.	1913
"	William J. Bryan	Neb.	1913
"	Robert Lansing	N.Y.	1915
"	Bainbridge Colby	N.Y.	1920
Harding	Charles E. Hughes	N.Y.	1921
Coolidge	Charles E. Hughes	N.Y.	1923
"	Frank B. Kellogg	Minn.	1925
Hoover	Frank B. Kellogg	Minn.	1929
"	Henry L. Stimson	N.Y.	1929
Roosevelt, F.D.	Cordell Hull	Tenn.	1933
"	E.R. Stettinius Jr.	Va.	1944
Truman	E.R. Stettinius Jr.	Va.	1945
"	James F. Byrnes	S.C.	1945
"	George C. Marshall	Pa.	1947
"	Dean G. Acheson	Conn.	1949
Eisenhower	John Foster Dulles	N.Y.	1953
"	Christian A. Herter	Mass.	1959
Kennedy	Dean Rusk	N.Y.	1961
Johnson, L.B.	Dean Rusk	N.Y.	1963
Nixon	William P. Rogers	N.Y.	1969
"	Henry A. Kissinger	D.C.	1973
Ford	Henry A. Kissinger	D.C.	1974
Carter	Cyrus R. Vance	N.Y.	1977
"	Edmund S. Muskie	Me.	1980
Reagan	Alexander M. Haig Jr.	Conn.	1981
"	George P. Shultz	Cal.	1982
Bush	James A. Baker 3d	Tex.	1989

Secretaries of the Treasury

The Treasury Department was organized by act of Congress Sept. 2, 1789.

President	Secretary	Home	Apptd.
Washington	Alexander Hamilton	N.Y.	1789
"	Oliver Wolcott	Conn.	1795
Adams, J.	Oliver Wolcott	Conn.	1797
"	Samuel Dexter	Mass.	1801
Jefferson	Samuel Dexter	Mass.	1801
"	Albert Gallatin	Pa.	1801
Madison	Albert Gallatin	Pa.	1809
"	George W. Campbell	Tenn.	1814
"	Alexander J. Dallas	Pa.	1814
"	William H. Crawford	Ga.	1816
Monroe	William H. Crawford	Ga.	1817
Adams, J.Q.	Richard Rush	Pa.	1825
Jackson	Samuel D. Ingham	Pa.	1829
"	Louis McLane	Del.	1831
"	William J. Duane	Pa.	1833
"	Roger B. Taney	Md.	1833
"	Levi Woodbury	N.H.	1834
Van Buren	Levi Woodbury	N.H.	1837
Harrison, W.H.	Thomas Ewing	Oh.	1841
Tyler	Thomas Ewing	Oh.	1841
"	Walter Forward	Pa.	1841
"	John C. Spencer	N.Y.	1843
"	George M. Bibb	Ky.	1844
Polk	Robert J. Walker	Miss.	1845
Taylor	William M. Meredith	Pa.	1849
Fillmore	Thomas Corwin	Oh.	1850
Pierce	James Guthrie	Ky.	1853
Buchanan	Howell Cobb	Ga.	1857
"	Phillip F. Thomas	Md.	1860
"	John A. Dix	N.Y.	1861
Lincoln	Salmon P. Chase	Oh.	1861
"	William P. Fessenden	Me.	1864
"	Hugh McCulloch	Ind.	1865
Johnson, A.	Hugh McCulloch	Ind.	1865
Grant	George S. Boutwell	Mass.	1869
"	William A. Richardson	Mass.	1873
"	Benjamin H. Bristow	Ky.	1874
"	Lot M. Morrill	Me.	1876
Hayes	John Sherman	Oh.	1877
Garfield	William Windom	Minn.	1881
Arthur	Charles J. Folger	N.Y.	1881
"	Walter Q. Gresham	Ind.	1884
"	Hugh McCulloch	Ind.	1884
Cleveland	Daniel Manning	N.Y.	1885
"	Charles S. Fairchild	N.Y.	1887
Harrison, B.	William Windom	Minn.	1889
"	Charles Foster	Oh.	1891
Cleveland	John G. Carlisle	Ky.	1893
McKinley	Lyman J. Gage	Ill.	1897
Roosevelt, T.	Lyman J. Gage	Ill.	1901
"	Leslie M. Shaw	Ia.	1902
"	George B. Cortelyou	N.Y.	1907
Taft	Franklin MacVeagh	Ill.	1909
Wilson	William G. McAdoo	N.Y.	1913
"	Carter Glass	Va.	1918
"	David F. Houston	Mo.	1920
Harding	Andrew W. Mellon	Pa.	1921
Coolidge	Andrew W. Mellon	Pa.	1923
Hoover	Andrew W. Mellon	Pa.	1929
"	Ogden L. Mills	N.Y.	1932
Roosevelt, F.D.	William H. Woodin	N.Y.	1933
"	Henry Morgenthau, Jr.	N.Y.	1934
Truman	Fred M. Vinson	Ky.	1945
"	John W. Snyder	Mo.	1946
Eisenhower	George M. Humphrey	Oh.	1953
"	Robert B. Anderson	Conn.	1957

President	Secretary	Home	Apptd.
Kennedy	C. Douglas Dillon	N.J.	1961
Johnson, L.B.	C. Douglas Dillon	N.J.	1963
"	Henry H. Fowler	Va.	1965
"	Joseph W. Barr	Ind.	1968
Nixon	David M. Kennedy	Ill.	1969
"	John B. Connally	Tex.	1971
"	George P. Shultz	Ill.	1972
"	William E. Simon	N.J.	1974

President	Secretary	Home	Apptd.
Ford	William E. Simon	N.J.	1974
Carter	W. Michael Blumenthal	Mich.	1977
"	G. William Miller	R.I.	1979
Reagan	Donald T. Regan	N.Y.	1981
"	James A. Baker 3d	Tex.	1985
"	Nicholas F. Brady	N.J.	1988
Bush	Nicholas F. Brady	N.J.	1989

Secretaries of Defense

The Department of Defense, originally designated the National Military Establishment, was created Sept. 18, 1947. It is headed by the secretary of defense, who is a member of the president's cabinet.

The departments of the army, of the navy, and of the air force function within the Department of Defense, and their respective secretaries are no longer members of the president's cabinet.

President	Secretary	Home	Apptd.
Truman	James V. Forrestal	N.Y.	1947
"	Louis A. Johnson	W.Va.	1949
"	George C. Marshall	Pa.	1950
"	Robert A. Lovett	N.Y.	1951
Eisenhower	Charles E. Wilson	Mich.	1953
"	Neil H. McElroy	Oh.	1957
"	Thomas S. Gates Jr.	Pa.	1959
Kennedy	Robert S. McNamara	Mich.	1961
Johnson, L.B.	Robert S. McNamara	Mich.	1963
"	Clark M. Clifford	Md.	1968

President	Secretary	Home	Apptd.
Nixon	Melvin R. Laird	Wis.	1969
"	Elliot L. Richardson	Mass.	1973
"	James R. Schlesinger	Va.	1973
Ford	James R. Schlesinger	Va.	1974
"	Donald H. Rumsfeld	Ill.	1975
Carter	Harold Brown	Cal.	1977
Reagan	Caspar W. Weinberger	Cal.	1981
"	Frank C. Carlucci	Pa.	1987
Bush	Richard B. Cheney	Wyo.	1989

Secretaries of War

The War (and Navy) Department was created by act of Congress Aug. 7, 1789, and Gen. Henry Knox was commissioned secretary of war under that act Sept. 12, 1789.

President	Secretary	Home	Apptd.
Washington	Henry Knox	Mass.	1789
"	Timothy Pickering	Pa.	1795
"	James McHenry	Md.	1796
Adams, J.	James McHenry	Md.	1797
"	Samuel Dexter	Mass.	1800
Jefferson	Henry Dearborn	Mass.	1801
Madison	William Eustis	Mass.	1809
"	John Armstrong	N.Y.	1813
"	James Monroe	Va.	1814
"	William H. Crawford	Ga.	1815
Monroe	John C. Calhoun	S.C.	1817
Adams, J.Q.	James Barbour	Va.	1825
"	Peter B. Porter	N.Y.	1828
Jackson	John H. Eaton	Tenn.	1829
"	Lewis Cass	Mich.	1831
"	Benjamin F. Butler	N.Y.	1837
Van Buren	Joel R. Poinsett	S.C.	1837
Harrison, W.H.	John Bell	Tenn.	1841
Tyler	John Bell	Tenn	1841
"	John C. Spencer	N.Y.	1841
"	James M. Porter	Pa.	1843
"	William Wilkins	Pa.	1844
Polk	William L. Marcy	N.Y.	1845
Taylor	George W. Crawford	Ga.	1849
Fillmore	Charles M. Conrad	La.	1850
Pierce	Jefferson Davis	Miss.	1853
Buchanan	John B. Floyd	Va.	1857
"	Joseph Holt	Ky.	1861
Lincoln	Simon Cameron	Pa.	1861
"	Edwin M. Stanton	Pa.	1862
Johnson, A.	Edwin M. Stanton	Pa.	1865
"	John M. Schofield	Ill.	1868

President	Secretary	Home	Apptd.
Grant	John A. Rawlins	Ill.	1869
"	William T. Sherman	Oh.	1869
"	William W. Belknap	Ia.	1869
"	Alphonso Taft	Oh.	1876
"	James D. Cameron	Pa.	1876
Hayes	George W. McCrary	Ia.	1877
"	Alexander Ramsey	Minn.	1879
Garfield	Robert T. Lincoln	Ill.	1881
Arthur	Robert T. Lincoln	Ill.	1881
Cleveland	William C. Endicott	Mass.	1885
Harrison, B.	Redfield Proctor	Vt.	1889
"	Stephen B. Elkins	W.Va.	1891
Cleveland	Daniel S. Lamont	N.Y.	1893
McKinley	Russel A. Alger	Mich.	1897
"	Elihu Root	N.Y.	1899
Roosevelt, T.	Elihu Root	N.Y.	1901
"	William H. Taft	Oh.	1904
"	Luke E. Wright	Tenn.	1908
Taft	Jacob M. Dickinson	Tenn.	1909
"	Henry L. Stimson	N.Y.	1911
Wilson	Lindley M. Garrison	N.J.	1913
"	Newton D. Baker	Oh.	1916
Harding	John W. Weeks	Mass.	1921
Coolidge	John W. Weeks	Mass.	1923
"	Dwight F. Davis	Mo.	1925
Hoover	James W. Good	Ill.	1929
"	Patrick J. Hurley	Okla.	1929
Roosevelt, F.D.	George H. Dern	Ut.	1933
"	Harry H. Woodring	Kan.	1937
"	Henry L. Stimson	N.Y.	1940
Truman	Robert P. Patterson	N.Y.	1945
"	*Kenneth C. Royall	N.C.	1947

Secretaries of the Navy

The Navy Department was created by act of Congress Apr. 30, 1798.

President	Secretary	Home	Apptd.
Adams, J.	Benjamin Stoddert	Md.	1798
Jefferson	Benjamin Stoddert	Md.	1801
"	Robert Smith	Md.	1801
Madison	Paul Hamilton	S.C.	1809
"	William Jones	Pa.	1813
"	Benjamin W. Crowninshield	Mass.	1814
Monroe	Benjamin W. Crowninshield	Mass.	1817
"	Smith Thompson	N.Y.	1818
"	Samuel L. Southard	N.J.	1823
Adams, J.Q.	Samuel L. Southard	N.J.	1825
Jackson	John Branch	N.C.	1829
"	Levi Woodbury	N.H.	1831
"	Mahlon Dickerson	N.J.	1834
Van Buren	Mahlon Dickerson	N.J.	1837
"	James K. Paulding	N.Y.	1838
Harrison, W.H.	George E. Badger	N.C.	1841
Tyler	George E. Badger	N.C.	1841
"	Abel P. Upshur	Va.	1841

President	Secretary	Home	Apptd.
Tyler	David Henshaw	Mass.	1843
"	Thomas W. Gilmer	Va.	1844
"	John Y. Mason	Va.	1844
Polk	George Bancroft	Mass.	1845
"	John Y. Mason	Va.	1846
Taylor	William B. Preston	Va.	1849
Fillmore	William A. Graham	N.C.	1850
"	John P. Kennedy	Md.	1852
Pierce	James C. Dobbin	N.C.	1853
Buchanan	Isaac Toucey	Conn.	1857
Lincoln	Gideon Welles	Conn.	1861
Johnson, A.	Gideon Welles	Conn.	1865
Grant	Adolph E. Borie	Pa.	1869
"	George M. Robeson	N.J.	1869
Hayes	Richard W. Thompson	Ind.	1877
"	Nathan Goff Jr.	W.Va.	1881
Garfield	William H. Hunt	La.	1881
Arthur	William E. Chandler	N.H.	1882

President	Secretary	Home	Apptd.
Cleveland	William C. Whitney	N.Y.	1885
Harrison, B.	Benjamin F. Tracy	N.Y.	1889
Cleveland	Hilary A. Herbert	Ala.	1893
McKinley	John D. Long	Mass.	1897
Roosevelt, T.	John D. Long	Mass.	1901
"	William H. Moody	Mass.	1902
"	Paul Morton	Ill.	1904
"	Charles J. Bonaparte	Md.	1905
"	Victor H. Metcalf	Cal.	1906
"	Truman H. Newberry	Mich.	1908
Taft	George von L. Meyer	Mass.	1909
Wilson	Josephus Daniels	N.C.	1913
Harding	Edwin Denby	Mich.	1921
Coolidge	Edwin Denby	Mich.	1923
"	Curtis D. Wilbur	Cal.	1924
Hoover	Charles Francis Adams	Mass.	1929
Roosevelt, F.D.	Claude A. Swanson	Va.	1933
"	Charles Edison	N.J.	1940
"	Frank Knox	Ill.	1940
"	James V. Forrestal	N.Y.	1944
Truman	*James V. Forrestal	N.Y.	1945

* Last members of Cabinet. The War Department became the Department of the Army and it and the Navy Department became branches of the Department of Defense, created Sept. 18, 1947.

Attorneys General

The office of attorney general was organized by act of Congress Sept. 24, 1789. The Department of Justice was created June 22, 1870.

President	Attorney General	Home	Apptd.
Washington	Edmund Randolph	Va.	1789
"	William Bradford	Pa.	1794
"	Charles Lee	Va.	1795
Adams, J.	Charles Lee	Va.	1797
Jefferson	Levi Lincoln	Mass.	1801
"	John Breckenridge	Ky.	1805
"	Caesar A. Rodney	Del.	1807
Madison	Caesar A. Rodney	Del.	1797
"	William Pinkney	Md.	1811
"	Richard Rush	Pa.	1814
Monroe	Richard Rush	Pa.	1817
"	William Wirt	Va.	1817
Adams, J.Q.	William Wirt	Va.	1825
Jackson	John M. Berrien	Ga.	1829
"	Roger B. Taney	Md.	1831
"	Benjamin F. Butler	N.Y.	1833
Van Buren	Benjamin F. Butler	N.Y.	1837
"	Felix Grundy	Tenn.	1838
"	Henry D. Gilpin	Pa.	1840
Harrison, W.H.	John J. Crittenden	Ky.	1841
Tyler	John J. Crittenden	Ky.	1841
"	Hugh S. Legare	S.C.	1841
"	John Nelson	Md.	1843
Polk	John Y. Mason	Va.	1845
"	Nathan Clifford	Me.	1846
"	Isaac Toucey	Conn.	1848
Taylor	Reverdy Johnson	Md.	1849
Fillmore	John J. Crittenden	Ky.	1850
Pierce	Caleb Cushing	Mass.	1853
Buchanan	Jeremiah S. Black	Pa.	1857
"	Edwin M. Stanton	Pa.	1860
Lincoln	Edward Bates	Mo.	1861
"	James Speed	Ky.	1864
Johnson, A.	James Speed	Ky.	1865
"	Henry Stanbery	Oh.	1866
"	William M. Evarts	N.Y.	1868
Grant	Ebenezer R. Hoar	Mass.	1869
"	Amos T. Akerman	Ga.	1870
"	George H. Williams	Ore.	1871
"	Edwards Pierrepont	N.Y.	1875
"	Alphonso Taft	Oh.	1876
Hayes	Charles Devens	Mass.	1877
Garfield	Wayne MacVeagh	Pa.	1881
Arthur	Benjamin H. Brewster	"	1881
Cleveland	Augustus Garland	Ark.	1885
Harrison, B.	William H. H. Miller	Ind.	1889
Cleveland	Richard Olney	Mass.	1893
"	Judson Harmon	Oh.	1895
McKinley	Joseph McKenna	Cal.	1897
"	John W. Griggs	N.J.	1898
"	Philander C. Knox	Pa.	1901
Roosevelt, T.	Philander C. Knox	Pa.	1901
"	William H. Moody	Mass.	1904
"	Charles J. Bonaparte	Md.	1906
Taft	George W. Wickersham	N.Y.	1909
Wilson	J.C. McReynolds	Tenn.	1913
"	Thomas W. Gregory	Tex.	1914
"	A. Mitchell Palmer	Pa.	1919
Harding	Harry M. Daugherty	Oh.	1921
Coolidge	Harry M. Daugherty	Oh.	1923
"	Harlan F. Stone	N.Y.	1924
"	John G. Sargent	Vt.	1925
Hoover	William D. Mitchell	Minn.	1929
Roosevelt, F.D.	Homer S. Cummings	Conn.	1933
"	Frank Murphy	Mich.	1939
"	Robert H. Jackson	N.Y.	1940
"	Francis Biddle	Pa.	1941
Truman	Thomas C. Clark	Tex.	1945
"	J. Howard McGrath	R.I.	1949
"	J.P. McGranery	Pa.	1952
Eisenhower	Herbert Brownell Jr.	N.Y.	1953
"	William P. Rogers	Md.	1957
Kennedy	Robert F. Kennedy	Mass.	1961
Johnson, L.B.	Robert F. Kennedy	Mass.	1963
"	N. de B. Katzenbach	Ill.	1964
"	Ramsey Clark	Tex.	1967
Nixon	John N. Mitchell	N.Y.	1969
"	Richard G. Kleindienst	Ariz.	1972
"	Elliot L. Richardson	Mass.	1973
"	William B. Saxbe	Oh.	1974
Ford	William B. Saxbe	Oh.	1974
"	Edward H. Levi	Ill.	1975
Carter	Griffin B. Bell	Ga.	1977
"	Benjamin R. Civiletti	Md.	1979
Reagan	William French Smith	Cal.	1981
"	Edwin Meese 3d	Cal.	1985
"	Richard Thornburgh	Pa	1988
Bush	Richard Thornburgh	Pa.	1989
"	William P. Barr	N.Y.	1991

Secretaries of the Interior

The Department of Interior was created by act of Congress Mar. 3, 1849.

President	Secretary	Home	Apptd.
Taylor	Thomas Ewing	Oh.	1849
Fillmore	Thomas M. T. McKennan	Pa.	1850
"	Alex H. H. Stuart	Va.	1850
Pierce	Robert McClelland	Mich.	1853
Buchanan	Jacob Thompson	Miss.	1857
Lincoln	Caleb B. Smith	Ind.	1861
"	John P. Usher	Ind.	1863
Johnson, A.	John P. Usher	Ind.	1865
"	James Harlan	Ia.	1865
"	Orville H. Browning	Ill.	1866
Grant	Jacob D. Cox	Oh.	1869
Grant	Columbus Delano	Oh.	1870
"	Zachariah Chandler	Mich.	1875
Hayes	Carl Schurz	Mo.	1877
Garfield	Samuel J. Kirkwood	Ia.	1881
Arthur	Henry M. Teller	Col.	1882
Cleveland	Lucius Q.C. Lamar	Miss.	1885
"	William F. Vilas	Wis.	1888
Harrison, B.	John W. Noble	Mo.	1889
Cleveland	Hoke Smith	Ga.	1893
"	David R. Francis	Mo.	1896
McKinley	Cornelius N. Bliss	N.Y.	1897

President	Secretary	Home	Apptd.
McKinley	Ethan A. Hitchcock	Mo.	1898
Roosevelt, T.	Ethan A. Hitchcock	Mo.	1901
"	James R. Garfield	Oh.	1907
Taft	Richard A. Ballinger	Wash.	1909
"	Walter L. Fisher	Ill.	1911
Wilson	Franklin K. Lane	Cal.	1913
"	John B. Payne	Ill.	1920
Harding	Albert B. Fall	N.M.	1921
"	Hubert Work	Col.	1923
Coolidge	Hubert Work	Col.	1923
"	Roy O. West	Ill.	1929
Hoover	Ray Lyman Wilbur	Cal.	1929
Roosevelt, F.D.	Harold L. Ickes	Ill.	1933
Truman	Harold L. Ickes	Ill.	1945
"	Julius A. Krug	Wis.	1946

President	Secretary	Home	Apptd.
Truman	Oscar L. Chapman	Col.	1949
Eisenhower	Douglas McKay	Ore.	1953
"	Fred A Seaton	Neb.	1956
Kennedy	Stewart L. Udall	Ariz.	1961
Johnson, L.B.	Stewart L. Udall	Ariz.	1963
Nixon	Walter J. Hickel	Alas.	1969
"	Rogers C.B. Morton	Md.	1971
Ford	Rogers C.B. Morton	Md.	1971
"	Stanley K. Hathaway	Wyo.	1975
"	Thomas S. Kleppe	N.D.	1975
Carter	Cecil D. Andrus	Ida.	1977
Reagan	James G. Watt	Col.	1981
"	William P. Clark	Cal.	1983
"	Donald P. Hodel	Ore.	1985
Bush	Manuel Lujan	N.M.	1989

Secretaries of Agriculture

The Department of Agriculture was created by act of Congress May 15, 1862. On Feb. 8, 1889, its commissioner was renamed secretary of agriculture and became a member of the cabinet.

President	Secretary	Home	Apptd.
Cleveland	Norman J. Colman	Mo.	1889
Harrison, B.	Jeremiah M. Rusk	Wis.	1889
Cleveland	J. Sterling Morton	Neb.	1893
McKinley	James Wilson	Ia.	1897
Roosevelt, T.	James Wilson	Ia.	1901
Taft	James Wilson	Ia.	1909
Wilson	David F. Houston	Mo.	1913
"	Edwin T. Meredith	Ia.	1920
Harding	Henry C. Wallace	Ia.	1921
Coolidge	Henry C. Wallace	Ia.	1923
"	Howard M. Gore	W.Va.	1924
"	William M. Jardine	Kan.	1925
Hoover	Arthur M. Hyde	Mo.	1929
Roosevelt, F.D.	Henry A. Wallace	Ia.	1933
"	Claude R. Wickard	Ind.	1940

President	Secretary	Home	Apptd.
Truman	Clinton P. Anderson	N.M.	1945
"	Charles F. Brannan	Col.	1948
Eisenhower	Ezra Taft Benson	Ut.	1953
Kennedy	Orville L. Freeman	Minn.	1961
Johnson, L.B.	Orville L. Freeman	Minn.	1963
Nixon	Clifford M. Hardin	Ind.	1969
"	Earl L. Butz	Ind.	1971
Ford	Earl L. Butz	Ind.	1974
"	John A. Knebel	Va.	1976
Carter	Bob Bergland	Minn.	1977
Reagan	John R. Block	Ill.	1981
"	Richard E. Lyng	Cal.	1986
Bush	Clayton K. Yeutter	Neb.	1989
"	Edward Madigan	Ill.	1991

Secretaries of Commerce and Labor

The Department of Commerce and Labor, created by Congress Feb. 14, 1903, was divided by Congress Mar. 4, 1913, into separate departments of Commerce and Labor. The secretary of each was made a cabinet member.

Secretaries of Commerce and Labor

President	Secretary	Home	Apptd.
Roosevelt, T.	George B. Cortelyou	N.Y.	1903
"	Victor H. Metcalf	Cal.	1904
"	Oscar S. Straus	N.Y.	1906
Taft	Charles Nagel	Mo.	1909

Secretaries of Labor

President	Secretary	Home	Apptd.
Wilson	William B. Wilson	Pa.	1913
Harding	James J. Davis	Pa.	1921
Coolidge	James J. Davis	Pa.	1923
Hoover	James J. Davis	Pa.	1929
"	William N. Doak	Va.	1930
Roosevelt, F.D.	Frances Perkins	N.Y.	1933
Truman	L.B. Schwellenbach	Wash.	1945
"	Maurice J. Tobin	Mass.	1949
Eisenhower	Martin P. Durkin	Ill.	1953
"	James P. Mitchell	N.J.	1953
Kennedy	Arthur J. Goldberg	Ill.	1961
"	W. Willard Wirtz	Ill.	1962
Johnson, L.B.	W. Willard Wirtz	Ill.	1963
Nixon	George P. Shultz	Ill	1969
"	James D. Hodgson	Cal.	1970
"	Peter J. Brennan	N.Y.	1973
Ford	Peter J. Brennan	N.Y.	1974
"	John T. Dunlop	Cal.	1975
"	W.J. Usery Jr.	Ga.	1976
Carter	F. Ray Marshall	Tex.	1977
Reagan	Raymond J. Donovan	N.J.	1981
"	William E. Brock	Tenn.	1985
"	Ann D. McLaughlin	D.C.	1987
Bush	Elizabeth Hanford Dole	N.C.	1989
"	Lynn Martin	Ill.	1991

Secretaries of Commerce

President	Secretary	Home	Apptd.
Wilson	William C. Redfield	N.Y.	1913
"	Joshua W. Alexander	Mo.	1919
Harding	Herbert C. Hoover	Cal.	1921
Coolidge	Herbert C. Hoover	Cal.	1923
"	William F. Whiting	Mass.	1928
Hoover	Robert P. Lamont	Ill.	1929
"	Roy D. Chapin	Mich.	1932
Roosevelt, F.D.	Daniel C. Roper	S.C.	1933
"	Harry L. Hopkins	N.Y.	1939
"	Jesse Jones	Tex.	1940
"	Henry A. Wallace	Ia.	1945
Truman	Henry A. Wallace	Ia.	1945
"	W. Averell Harriman	N.Y.	1947
"	Charles Sawyer	Oh.	1948
Eisenhower	Sinclair Weeks	Mass.	1953
"	Lewis L. Strauss	N.Y.	1958
"	Frederick H. Mueller	Mich.	1959
Kennedy	Luther H. Hodges	N.C.	1961
Johnson, L.B.	Luther H. Hodges	N.C.	1963
"	John T. Connor	N.J.	1965
"	Alex B. Trowbridge	N.J.	1967
"	Cyrus R. Smith	N.Y.	1968
Nixon	Maurice H. Stans	Minn.	1969
"	Peter G. Peterson	Ill.	1972
"	Frederick B. Dent	S.C.	1973
Ford	Frederick B. Dent	S.C.	1974
"	Rogers C.B. Morton	Md.	1975
"	Elliot L. Richardson	Mass.	1975
Carter	Juanita M. Kreps	N.C.	1977
"	Philip M. Klutznick	Ill.	1979
Reagan	Malcolm Baldrige	Conn.	1981
"	C. William Verity Jr.	Oh.	1987
Bush	Robert A. Mosbacher	Tex.	1989
"	Barbara H. Franklin	Pa.	1992

Secretaries of Housing and Urban Development

The Department of Housing and Urban Development was created by act of Congress Sept. 9, 1965.

President	Secretary	Home	Apptd.	President	Secretary	Home	Apptd.
Johnson, L.B.	Robert C. Weaver	Wash.	1966	Ford	Carla Anderson Hills	Cal.	1975
"	Robert C. Wood	Mass.	1969	Carter	Patricia Roberts Harris	D.C.	1977
Nixon	George W. Romney	Mich.	1969	"	Moon Landrieu	La.	1979
"	James T. Lynn	Oh.	1973	Reagan	Samuel R. Pierce Jr.	N.Y.	1981
Ford	James T. Lynn	Oh.	1974	Bush	Jack F. Kemp	N.Y.	1989

Secretaries of Transportation

The Department of Transportation was created by act of Congress Oct. 15, 1966.

President	Secretary	Home	Apptd.	President	Secretary	Home	Apptd.
Johnson, L.B.	Alan S. Boyd	Fla.	1966	Carter	Neil E. Goldschmidt	Ore.	1979
Nixon	John A. Volpe	Mass.	1969	Reagan	Andrew L. Lewis Jr.	Pa.	1981
"	Claude S. Brinegar	Cal.	1973	"	Elizabeth Hanford Dole	N.C.	1983
Ford	Claude S. Brinegar	Cal.	1974	"	James H. Burnley	N.C.	1987
"	William T. Coleman Jr.	Pa.	1975	Bush	Samuel K. Skinner	Ill.	1989
Carter	Brock Adams	Wash.	1977	"	Andrew H. Card Jr.	Mass.	1992

Secretaries of Energy

The Department of Energy was created by federal law Aug. 4, 1977.

President	Secretary	Home	Apptd.	President	Secretary	Home	Apptd.
Carter	James R. Schlesinger	Va.	1977	Reagan	Donald P. Hodel	Ore.	1982
"	Charles Duncan Jr.	Wyo.	1979	"	John S. Herrington	Cal.	1985
Reagan	James B. Edwards	S.C.	1981	Bush	James D. Watkins	Cal.	1989

Secretaries of Health, Education, and Welfare

The Department of Health, Education and Welfare, created by Congress Apr. 11, 1953, was divided by Congress Sept. 27, 1979, into separate departments of Education, and Health and Human Services. The secretary of each is a cabinet member.

President	Secretary	Home	Apptd.	President	Secretary	Home	Apptd.
Eisenhower	Oveta Culp Hobby	Tex.	1953	Nixon	Robert H. Finch	Cal.	1969
"	Marion B. Folsom	N.Y.	1955	"	Elliot L. Richardson	Mass.	1970
"	Arthur S. Flemming	Oh.	1958	"	Caspar W. Weinberger	Cal.	1973
Kennedy	Abraham A. Ribicoff	Conn.	1961	Ford	Caspar W. Weinberger	Cal.	1974
"	Anthony J. Celebrezze	Oh.	1962	"	Forrest D. Mathews	Ala.	1975
Johnson, L.B.	Anthony J. Celebrezze	Oh.	1963	Carter	Joseph A. Califano, Jr.	D.C.	1977
"	John W. Gardner	N.Y.	1965	"	Patricia Roberts Harris	D.C.	1979
"	Wilbur J. Cohen	Mich.	1968				

Secretaries of Health and Human Services

President	Secretary	Home	Apptd.	President	Secretary	Home	Apptd.
Carter	Patricia Roberts Harris	D.C.	1979	Reagan	Otis R. Bowen	Ind.	1985
Reagan	Richard S. Schweiker	Pa.	1981	Bush	Louis W. Sullivan	Ga.	1989
"	Margaret M. Heckler	Mass.	1983				

Secretaries of Education

President	Secretary	Home	Apptd.	President	Secretary	Home	Apptd.
Carter	Shirley Hufstedler	Cal.	1979	Reagan	Lauro F. Cavazos	Tex.	1988
Reagan	Terrel Bell	Ut.	1981	Bush	Lauro F. Cavazos	Tex.	1989
"	William J. Bennett	N.Y.	1985	"	Lamar Alexander	Tenn.	1991

Secretaries of Veterans Affairs

The Department of Veterans Affairs was created Oct. 25, 1988 when Pres. Reagan signed a bill which made the Veterans Administration into a cabinet post as of Mar. 15, 1989.

President	Secretary	Home	Apptd.
Bush	Edward J. Derwinski	Ill.	1989

Librarians of Congress

Librarian	Served	Appointed by President	Librarian	Served	Appointed by President
John J. Beckley	1802-1807	Jefferson	Herbert Putnam	1899-1939	McKinley
Patrick Magruder	1807-1815	Jefferson	Archibald MacLeish	1939-1944	F. Roosevelt
George Watterston	1815-1829	Madison	Luther H. Evans	1945-1953	Truman
John Silva Meehan	1829-1861	Jackson	L. Quincy Mumford	1954-1974	Eisenhower
John G. Stephenson	1861-1864	Lincoln	Daniel J. Boorstin	1975-1987	Ford
Ainsworth Rand Spofford	1864-1897	Lincoln	James H. Billington	1987-	Reagan
John Russell Young	1897-1899	McKinley			

Speakers of the House of Representatives

Party designations: A, American; D, Democratic; DR, Democratic Republican; F, Federalist; R, Republican; W, Whig. * Served only one day.

Name	Party	State	Tenure
Frederick Muhlenberg	F	Pa.	1789-1791
Jonathan Trumbull	F	Conn.	1791-1793
Frederick Muhlenberg	F	Pa.	1793-1795
Jonathan Dayton	F	N.J.	1795-1799
Theodore Sedgwick	F	Mass.	1799-1801
Nathaniel Macon	DR	N.C.	1801-1807
Joseph B. Varnum	DR	Mass.	1807-1811
Henry Clay	DR	Ky.	1811-1814
Langdon Cheves	DR	S.C.	1814-1815
Henry Clay	DR	Ky.	1815-1820
John W. Taylor	DR	N.Y.	1820-1821
Philip P. Barbour	DR	Va.	1821-1823
Henry Clay	DR	Ky.	1823-1825
John W. Taylor	D	N.Y.	1825-1827
Andrew Stevenson	D	Va.	1827-1834
John Bell	D	Tenn.	1834-1835
James K. Polk	D	Tenn.	1835-1839
Robert M. T. Hunter	D	Va.	1839-1841
John White	W	Ky.	1841-1843
John W. Jones	D	Va.	1843-1845
John W. Davis	D	Ind.	1845-1847
Robert C. Winthrop	W	Mass.	1847-1849
Howell Cobb	D	Ga.	1849-1851
Linn Boyd	D	Ky.	1851-1855
Nathaniel P. Banks	A	Mass.	1856-1857
James L. Orr	D	S.C.	1857-1859
William Pennington	R	N.J.	1860-1861
Galusha A. Grow	R	Pa.	1861-1863
Schuyler Colfax	R	Ind.	1863-1869
*Theodore M. Pomeroy	R	N.Y.	1869-1869
James G. Blaine	R	Me.	1869-1875
Michael C. Kerr	D	Ind.	1875-1876
Samuel J. Randall	D	Pa.	1876-1881
Joseph W. Keifer	R	Oh.	1881-1883
John G. Carlisle	D	Ky.	1883-1889
Thomas B. Reed	R	Me.	1889-1891
Charles F. Crisp	D	Ga.	1891-1895
Thomas B. Reed	R	Me.	1895-1899
David B. Henderson	R	Ia.	1899-1903
Joseph G. Cannon	R	Ill.	1903-1911
Champ Clark	D	Mo.	1911-1919
Frederick H. Gillett	R	Mass.	1919-1925
Nicholas Longworth	R	Oh.	1925-1931
John N. Garner	D	Tex.	1931-1933
Henry T. Rainey	D	Ill.	1933-1935
Joseph W. Byrns	D	Tenn.	1935-1936
William B. Bankhead	D	Ala.	1936-1940
Sam Rayburn	D	Tex.	1940-1947
Joseph W. Martin Jr.	R	Mass.	1947-1949
Sam Rayburn	D	Tex.	1949-1953
Joseph W. Martin Jr.	R	Mass.	1953-1955
Sam Rayburn	D	Tex.	1955-1961
John W. McCormack	D	Mass.	1962-1971
Carl Albert	D	Okla.	1971-1977
Thomas P. O'Neill Jr.	D	Mass.	1977-1987
James Wright	D	Tex.	1987-1989
Thomas S. Foley	D	Wash.	1989-

Floor Leaders in the U.S. Senate

Majority Leaders

Name	Party	State	Tenure
Charles Curtis	R	Kan.	1925-1929
James E. Watson	R	Ind.	1929-1933
Joseph T. Robinson	D	Ark.	1933-1937
Alben W. Barkley	D	Ky.	1937-1947
Wallace H. White	R	Me.	1947-1949
Scott W. Lucas	D	Ill.	1949-1951
Ernest W. McFarland	D	Ariz.	1951-1953
Robert A. Taft	R	Oh.	1953
William F. Knowland	R	Cal.	1953-1955
Lyndon B. Johnson	D	Tex	1955-1961
Mike Mansfield	D	Mont.	1961-1977
Robert C. Byrd	D	W.Va.	1977-1981
Howard H. Baker Jr.	R	Tenn.	1981-1985
Robert J. Dole	R	Kan.	1985-1987
Robert C. Byrd	D	W.Va.	1987-1989
George J. Mitchell	D	Me.	1989-

Minority Leaders

Name	Party	State	Tenure
Oscar W. Underwood	D	Ala	1920-1923
Joseph T. Robinson	D	Ark.	1923-1933
Charles L. McNary	R	Ore.	1933-1944
Wallace H. White	R	Me.	1944-1947
Alben W. Barkley	D	Ky.	1947-1949
Kenneth S. Wherry	R	Neb.	1949-1951
Henry Styles Bridges	R	N.H.	1952-1953
Lyndon B. Johnson	D	Tex.	1953-1955
William F. Knowland	R	Cal.	1955-1959
Everett M. Dirksen	R	Ill.	1959-1969
Hugh D. Scott	R	Penn.	1969-1977
Howard H. Baker Jr.	R	Tenn.	1977-1981
Robert C. Byrd	D	W.Va.	1981-1987
Robert J. Dole	R	Kan.	1987-

Federal Bureau of Investigation

The Federal Bureau of Investigation was created July 26, 1908 and was referred to as Office of Chief Examiner. It became the Bureau of Investigation (Mar. 26, 1909), United States Bureau of Investigation (July 1, 1932), Division of Investigation (Aug. 10, 1933), and Federal Bureau of Investigation (July 1, 1935).

Director	Assumed office
Stanley W. Finch	July 26, 1908
A(lexander) Bruce Bielaski	Apr. 30, 1912
William E. Allen, act.	Feb. 10, 1919
William J. Flynn	July 1, 1919
William J. Burns	Aug. 22, 1921
J. Edgar Hoover, act.	May 10, 1924
J. Edgar Hoover	Dec. 10, 1924
L. Patrick Gray, act.	May 3, 1972
William D. Ruckelshaus, act.	Apr. 27, 1973
Clarence M. Kelley	July 9, 1973
William H. Webster	Feb. 23, 1978
John E. Otto, act.	May 27, 1987
William S. Sessions	Nov. 2, 1987

Central Intelligence Agency

On June 13, 1942 President Roosevelt established the Office of Strategic Services (OSS) and named William J. Donovan as its director. The OSS was disbanded Oct. 1, 1945 and its functions absorbed by the State and War departments. President Truman, Jan. 22, 1946, established the Central Intelligence Agency Group (CIG) to operate under the direction of the National Intelligence Authority (NIA). The National Security Act of 1947 replaced the NIA with the National Security Council and the CIG with the Central Intelligence Agency.

Director	Served	Appointed by President
Adm. Sidney W. Souers	1946	Truman
Gen. Hoyt S. Vandenberg	1946-1947	Truman
Adm. Roscoe H. Hillenkoetter	1947-1950	Truman
Gen. Walter Bedell Smith	1950-1953	Truman
Allen W. Dulles	1953-1961	Eisenhower
John A. McCone	1961-1965	Kennedy
Adm. William F. Raborn Jr.	1965-1966	Johnson
Richard Helms	1966-1973	Johnson
James R. Schlesinger	1973	Nixon
William E. Colby	1973-1976	Nixon
George Bush	1976-1977	Ford
Adm. Stansfield Turner	1977-1981	Carter
William J. Casey	1981-1987	Reagan
William H. Webster	1987-1991	Reagan
Robert M. Gates	1991-	Bush

UNITED STATES POPULATION

A Typical American as Seen Through the Eyes of the Census Bureau

by
Dr. Barbara Everitt Bryant
Director, Bureau of the Census
U.S. Department of Commerce

I am often asked to describe a typical American: What do we do? Where do we live? How much money do we make? Well, based upon the 1990 census and other survey information, I see America as a patchwork of cultures, lifestyles, and economic groups. Let's take a look at that typical and some not so typical Americans.

Who We Are

Typical America contains many racial and ethnic groups. Nearly 22 million of us (9 percent) report ourselves as being of Hispanic origin, and over 7 million of us (2.9 percent) identify ourselves as Asian-Pacific Islanders. Blacks number 30 million, or 12 percent of the population, and the American Indian/Eskimo/Aleut populations make up about 2 million (0.8 percent). That leaves over 177 million (71.3 percent) people who consider themselves to be White-non-Hispanic.

Just over 21 million of us were not born in America, but call it home. Every year, almost 25 percent of our population growth comes from immigration.

America speaks many **languages:** over 31 million of us speak a language other than English at home; over half of this number speaks Spanish.

We are also aging: since 1980, our **median age** has risen from 30.0 to 32.9 years (the median for Blacks is 28.1 and the median for Whites is 34.4). Nearly 26 percent of us are under 18 years of age, and over 12 percent are 65 and older.

Women outnumber men in America by at least 6.2 million; 51 percent of the total population is female.

There are 91.9 million **households** in our Nation; 70 percent of them contain family groups. Of all households, 55 percent are maintained by married couples, but only 26 percent of households with children under 18 include a married couple. About one-fourth of all households contains a person living alone.

What We Do

Just over 65 percent of Americans 16 years and over are in the labor force: almost 75 percent of men and nearly 57 percent of women.

Our top three **occupations** are in administrative support, including clerical; professional specialty; and executive, administrative, and managerial. Over 19 million employed persons work in the retail sales industry.

Nearly 7 million Americans suffer from a disability that prevents them from working.

Of the over 115 million employed workers, 73 percent drive to work alone and 13 percent are in carpools. Our **commuting time** averages about 22 minutes.

Working mothers are well represented in the labor force: almost 60 percent of mothers with children under 6, and 75 percent of mothers with children 6 to 17 are in the labor force.

The number of **women-owned businesses** (sole proprietorship, partnership, or subchapter 5 companies) increased by a dramatic 55 percent in the late 1980s. **Minority-owned firms** also dramatically increased in number: Asian-Pacific Islander by 89 percent, Hispanic by 81 percent, American Indian/Eskimo/Aleut by 58 percent, and Black by 38 percent.

Most **state and local government employees** are in education-related activities: two-fifths of the 8.2 million state employees and over one-half of the 10.4 million local government workers.

Personal and business services grew 13 times faster than the population in the late 1980s.

The Federal Government funds one-third of all industrial research and development.

Where We Live

Typical America, or at least half of it (55.6 percent), lives in the South and West regions of the country. Between 1980 and 1990, the West grew by 22.3 percent, and the South grew by 13.4 percent. This dramatic rate caused a shift in 19 seats in the House of Representatives. Eight states gained seats: California (+7), Florida (+4), Texas (+3), and Arizona, Georgia, North Carolina, Virginia, and Washington (+1 each); and 13 states lost seats: New York (−3), Illinois, Michigan, Ohio, and Pennsylvania (−2 each), Iowa, Kansas, Kentucky, Louisiana, Massachusetts, Montana, New Jersey, and West Virginia (−1 each).

Our five most populous states are California (29.8 million), New York (18 million), Texas (17 million), Florida (12.9 million), and Pennsylvania (11.9 million). The five states at the other end of the spectrum are Delaware (666,000), North Dakota (639,000), Vermont (563,000), Alaska (550,000), and Wyoming (454,000).

Most of us—77.5 percent—live in **metropolitan areas,** and half of us live in one of the 39 metropolitan areas with population of at least 1 million.

Our five largest metropolitan areas are scattered across the map: New York/New Jersey/Long Island/Connecticut (18.1 million), Los Angeles/Anaheim/Riverside (14.5 million), Chicago/Gary/Lake Counties (8.1 million), San Francisco/Oakland/San Jose (6.3 million), Philadelphia/Wilmington/Trenton (5.9 million). Although the New York area remains in first position, the Los Angeles area is growing at a much faster rate (26 versus 3 percent).

Within those metro areas are some big **cities.** Our five largest are New York (7.3 million), Los Angeles (3.5 million), Chicago (2.8 million), Houston (1.6 million), and Philadelphia (1.6 million).

Our five largest **counties** are Los Angeles, CA (8.9 million), Cook, IL (5.1 million), Harris, TX (2.8 million), San Diego, CA (2.5 million), and Orange, CA (2.4 million).

How We Live

The average number of people living in a household in the U.S. is 2.63.

We have a total of about 102 million **housing units** nationwide; nearly 92 million of them are occupied. The vast majority of housing units have public water and sewer, and our top two house heating fuel sources

(continued)

are utility gas (46.8 million units) and electricity (23.7 million units). About 1 million units lack complete plumbing facilities, and 1 million lack completed kitchen facilities. Nearly 5 million units do not have a telephone.

Of the 45 million **owner-occupied housing units,** nearly 30 million have mortgages. The median monthly costs for owner-occupied units is $737, and the median value of an owner-occupied, single-family home is $79,100.

If you live in one of the 32 million **renter-occupied housing units,** you pay a median rent of $447.

Quality of Life

Education: Typical America has more high school graduates than at any other time in U.S. history: over 78 percent. About 23 percent of these graduates have gone on to earn a bachelor's degree or higher.

Educational attainment has a direct impact on many aspects of life, but most directly on income. The average monthly earnings without a high school diploma are $452; with a diploma, $921; with a bachelor's degree, $1,829; with a doctorate, $3,637; and with a professional degree, $4,003.

We spend an average of $2,635 annually per student in our public schools and universities.

Assets: Homeownership accounts for over 40 percent of Americans' net worth. Interest-earning assets account for 25 percent. About 25 percent of America's households hold about 44 percent of our nation's net worth.

Pensions: Two-thirds of the work force is covered by a pension of some type. Most of us (92 percent) are covered by Social Security. Nearly all (95 percent) government employees are covered by pensions, while only 29 percent of agricultural and personal service workers are covered by employer-sponsored pensions.

Health insurance: Nearly 87 percent of us have health insurance. Those most likely to be insured are the elderly, the employed, and those with at least a high school diploma.

Child care: Working mothers spend about 7 percent of their family income on child care for their preschooler. Most of this care takes place in a home environment, such as with relatives or neighbors (66 percent). About 25 percent of child care is in organized facilities, such as nursery schools and day care centers.

Child support: Of the 5.7 million women awarded child support, 5.0 million were supposed to receive payments in 1989. Of the women due payments, about half received the full amount they were due. The average amount of child support received in 1989 was $2,995. The aggregate amount of child support received in 1989 was $11.2 billion, 69 percent of $16.3 billion due.

Assistance: About 4 percent of our adult population needs assistance with everyday activities. This need increases to 45 percent for persons 85 and over. Most caregivers are female relatives.

Voting: The 1988 Presidential election was decided by 57.4 percent of our voting-age population; 45 percent determined the outcome of the 1990 Congressional elections. Voter participation is declining; only about 62 percent of us who are old enough to vote registered to do so in the 1990 elections.

Federal Aid: In fiscal year 1990, the federal government dispensed over $1 trillion to states. California received $116 billion of these funds. On a per capita basis, Virginia received the most with spending of over $4,500 per person.

Funds were divided this way:

$498 billion in payments to individuals, such as Social Security; $147 billion in salaries to military and civilian employees; $189 billion in contracts; $134 billion in grants for Medicaid, Aid to Families With Dependent Children, and highway construction; and $36 billion in research grants and agricultural subsidies.

Lotteries: Thirty-two states operate lotteries, which produced $8.5 billion in net revenue in fiscal year 1990. During the same time, state general expenditures amounted to $506.7 billion. State expenditures for highways were up 3.7 percent in 1990 to 44.3 billion. Expenditures for hospitals rose 5.7 percent to 22.4 in 1990.

Estimated Population of American Colonies: 1630-1780

Source: Bureau of the Census U.S. Dept. of Commerce (thousands)

Colony	1780	1770	1750	1740	1720	1700	1690	1670	1650	1630
Total	**2,780.4**	**2,148.1**	**1,170.8**	**905.6**	**466.2**	**250.9**	**210.4**	**111.9**	**50.4**	**4.6**
Maine (counties)[1] ..	49.1	31.3	...	...	...	...	...	...	1.0	0.4
New Hampshire[2] ..	87.8	62.4	27.5	23.3	9.4	5.0	4.2	1.8	1.3	0.5
Vermont[3]	47.6	10.0	...	...	...	...	...	...	...	...
Plymouth and Massachusetts[1,2,4]	268.6	235.3	188.0	151.6	91.0	55.9	56.9	35.3	15.6	0.9
Rhode Island[2]	52.9	58.2	33.2	25.3	11.7	5.9	4.2	2.2	0.8	...
Connecticut[2]	206.7	183.9	111.3	89.6	58.8	26.0	21.6	12.6	4.1	...
New York[2]	210.5	162.9	76.7	63.7	36.9	19.1	13.9	5.8	4.1	0.4
New Jersey[2]	139.6	117.4	71.4	51.4	29.8	14.0	8.0	1.0	...	...
Pennsylvania[2]	327.3	240.1	119.7	85.6	31.0	18.0	11.4	...	...	...
Delaware[2]	45.4	35.5	28.7	19.9	5.4	2.5	1.5	0.7	0.2	...
Maryland[2]	245.5	202.6	141.1	116.1	66.1	29.6	24.0	13.2	4.5	...
Virginia[2]	538.0	447.0	231.0	180.4	87.8	58.6	53.0	35.3	18.7	2.5
North Carolina[2] ...	270.1	197.2	73.0	51.8	21.3	10.7	7.6	3.8	...	...
South Carolina[2] ...	180.0	124.2	64.0	45.0	17.0	5.7	3.9	0.2	...	...
Georgia[2]	56.1	23.4	5.2	2.0	...	...	...	...	...	...
Kentucky[5]	45.0	15.7	...	...	...	...	...	...	...	...
Tennessee[6]	10.0	1.0	...	...	...	...	...	...	...	...

(1) For 1660-1750, Maine counties included with Massachusetts. Maine was a part of Massachusetts until it became a separate state in 1820. (2) One of the original 13 states. (3) Admitted to statehood in 1791. (4) Plymouth became a part of the Province of Massachusetts in 1691. (5) Admitted to statehood in 1792. (6) Admitted to statehood in 1796.

U.S. Population by Age, Sex and Households, 1990

Source: Bureau of the Census, U.S. Dept. of Commerce; 1990 Census

Total population	**248,709,873**
Sex	
Male	121,239,418
Female	127,470,455
Age	
Under 5 years	18,354,443
5 to 17 years	45,249,989
18 to 20 years	11,726,868
21 to 24 years	15,010,898
25 to 44 years	80,754,835
45 to 54 years	25,223,086
55 to 59 years	10,531,756
60 to 64 years	10,616,167
65 to 74 years	18,106,558
75 to 84 years	10,055,108
85 years and over	3,080,165
Median age	32.9
Under 18 years	63,604,432
Percent of total population	25.6
65 years and over	31,241,831
Percent of total population	12.6

Households by Type	
Total households	**91,947,410**
Family households (families)	64,517,947
Married-couple families	50,708,322
Percent of total households	55.1
Other family, male householder	3,143,582
Other family, female householder	10,666,043
Nonfamily households	27,429,463
Percent of total households	29.8
Householder living alone	22,580,420
Householder 65 years and over	8,824,845
Persons living in households	242,012,129
Persons per household	2.63
Group Quarters	
Persons living in group quarters	6,697,744
Institutionalized persons	3,334,018
Other persons in group quarters	3,363,726

Projections of Total Population by Race: 1993 to 2025

Source: Bureau of the Census, U.S. Dept. of Commerce

Year	Total Population (1,000)				By Race (Preferred series)					
	Lowest series	Preferred series	Highest series	Zero migration	Number (1,000)			Percent distribution		
					White	Black	Other races	White	Black	Other races
1993	252,906	259,383	259,888	252,083	216,713	32,751	9,919	83.5	12.6	3.8
1994	254,121	261,875	262,526	253,308	218,355	33,235	10,285	83.4	12.7	3.9
1995	255,239	264,339	265,151	254,459	219,964	33,720	10,655	83.2	12.8	4.0
2000	259,576	276,382	278,228	259,304	227,634	36,177	12,571	82.4	13.1	4.5
2005	262,363	288,496	291,710	263,189	235,162	38,726	14,608	81.5	13.4	5.1
2010	264,193	301,127	305,882	266,528	242,993	41,378	16,756	80.7	13.7	5.6
2015	265,072	314,140	320,494	269,131	251,073	44,087	18,980	79.9	14.0	6.0
2020	264,536	326,987	335,022	270,493	258,959	46,781	21,247	79.2	14.3	6.5
2025	262,218	339,172	348,985	270,234	266,222	49,404	23,546	78.5	14.6	6.9

For the series shown, the following assumptions were made about fertility (ultimate lifetime births per woman), mortality (ultimate life expectancy in 2080), and immigration (ultimate yearly net immigration). Lowest series: 1.5 births per woman, 77.9 years, and 300,000 net immigration. Middle series: 1.8 births per woman, 81.2 years, and 500,000 net immigration. Highest series: 2.2 births per woman, 88.0 years, and 800,000 net immigration. Zero migration series: 1.8 births per woman and 81.2 years.

U.S. Population Abroad, by Selected Country: 1992

Source: U.S. Dept. of State

(in thousands. As of June 3. Data compiled as part of noncombatant personnel evacuation requirements report)

Area	Total[1]	Resident U.S. citizen	U.S. tourists
Total[2]	**14,285**	**6,269**	**6,674**
Argentina	38	13	25
Australia	75	65	8
Belgium	42	24	7
Brazil	46	34	11
Canada	1,561	278	1,281
Costa Rica	31	25	4
Dominican Republic	97	87	9
Egypt	21	13	2
France	224	126	91
Germany	513	107	208
Greece	70	38	30
Hong Kong	27	21	5
Ireland	71	43	28
Israel	137	124	12
Italy	155	102	28
Japan	142	38	13
Jerusalem	28	26	2
Martinique	221	(Z)	221
Mexico	802	495	300
Netherlands	35	22	5
Panama	36	8	1
Philippines	147	119	(Z)
Portugal	47	31	12
Saudi Arabia	42	31	7
South Korea	72	8	38
Spain	60	27	31
Switzerland	32	27	4
United Kingdom	414	213	162
Venezuela	50	24	26

(1) Includes Dept. of Defense noncombatant employees, other U.S. government employees, and dependents of U.S. military and civilian employees, not shown separately. (2) Includes other areas not shown separately. (Z) Less than 500.

U.S. Population by Official

(Members of the Armed Forces overseas or

State	1790[1]	1800[1]	1810[1]	1820	1830	1840	1850	1860	1870	1880	1890
Ala. . .	......	1	9	127,901	309,527	590,756	771,623	964,201	996,992	1,262,505	1,513,401
Alas. .	......	......	......	......	......	......	......	......	......	33,426	32,052
Ariz. .	......	......	......	......	......	......	......	......	9,658	40,440	88,243
Ark. . .	......	......	1	14,273	30,388	97,574	209,897	435,450	484,471	802,525	1,128,211
Cal. . .	......	......	......	......	......	......	92,597	379,994	560,247	864,694	1,213,398
Col. . .	......	......	......	......	......	......	......	34,277	39,864	194,327	413,249
Conn. .	238	251	262	275,248	297,675	309,978	370,792	460,147	537,454	622,700	746,258
Del. . .	59	64	73	72,749	76,748	78,085	91,532	112,216	125,015	146,608	168,493
D.C. . .	......	8	16	23,336	30,261	33,745	51,687	75,080	131,700	177,624	230,392
Fla. . .	......	......	......	......	34,730	54,477	87,445	140,424	187,748	269,493	391,422
Ga. . .	83	163	252	340,989	516,823	691,392	906,185	1,057,286	1,184,109	1,542,180	1,837,353
Ha. . .	......	......	......	......	......	......	......	......	......	......	......
Ida. . .	......	......	......	......	......	......	......	......	14,999	32,610	88,548
Ill. . . .	......	......	12	55,211	157,445	476,183	851,470	1,711,951	2,539,891	3,077,871	3,826,352
Ind. . .	......	6	25	147,178	343,031	685,866	988,416	1,350,428	1,680,637	1,978,301	2,192,404
Ia. . . .	......	......	......	......	......	43,112	192,214	674,913	1,194,020	1,624,615	1,912,297
Kan. . .	......	......	......	......	......	......	......	107,206	364,399	996,096	1,428,108
Ky. . .	74	221	407	564,317	687,917	779,828	982,405	1,155,684	1,321,011	1,648,690	1,858,635
La. . . .	......	......	77	153,407	215,739	352,411	517,762	708,002	726,915	939,946	1,118,588
Me. . .	97	152	229	298,335	399,455	501,793	583,169	628,279	626,915	648,936	661,086
Md. . .	320	342	381	407,350	447,040	470,019	583,034	687,049	780,894	934,943	1,042,390
Mass. .	379	423	472	523,287	610,408	737,699	994,514	1,231,066	1,457,351	1,783,085	2,238,947
Mich. .	......	......	5	8,896	31,639	212,267	397,654	749,113	1,184,059	1,636,937	2,093,890
Minn. .	......	......	......	......	......	......	6,077	172,023	439,706	780,773	1,310,283
Miss. .	......	8	31	75,448	136,621	375,651	606,526	791,305	827,922	1,131,597	1,289,600
Mo. . .	......	......	20	66,586	140,455	383,702	682,044	1,182,012	1,721,295	2,168,380	2,679,185
Mon.. .	......	......	......	......	......	......	......	......	20,595	39,159	142,924
Neb.. .	......	......	......	......	......	......	......	28,841	122,993	452,402	1,062,656
Nev.. .	......	......	......	......	......	......	......	6,857	42,491	62,266	47,355
N.H.. .	142	184	214	244,161	269,328	284,574	317,976	326,073	318,300	346,991	376,530
N.J. . .	184	211	246	277,575	320,823	373,306	489,555	672,035	906,096	1,131,116	1,444,933
N.M.. .	......	......	......	......	......	......	61,547	93,516	91,874	119,565	160,282
N.Y.. .	340	589	959	1,372,812	1,918,608	2,428,921	3,097,394	3,880,735	4,382,759	5,082,871	6,003,174
N.C.. .	394	478	556	638,829	737,987	753,419	869,039	992,622	1,071,361	1,399,750	1,617,949
N.D.. .	......	......	......	......	......	......	......	......	2,405[2]	36,909	190,983
Oh. . .	......	45	231	581,434	937,903	1,519,467	1,980,329	2,339,511	2,665,260	3,198,062	3,672,329
Okla. .	......	......	......	......	......	......	......	......	......	......	258,657
Ore.. .	......	......	......	......	......	......	12,093	52,465	90,923	174,768	317,704
Pa. . .	434	602	810	1,049,458	1,348,233	1,724,033	2,311,786	2,906,215	3,521,951	4,282,891	5,258,113
R.I. . .	69	69	77	83,059	97,199	108,830	147,545	174,620	217,353	276,531	345,506
S.C.. .	249	346	415	502,741	581,185	594,398	668,507	703,708	705,606	995,577	1,151,149
S.D.. .	......	......	......	......	......	......	......	4,837[2]	11,776[2]	98,268	348,600
Tenn. .	36	106	262	422,823	681,904	829,210	1,002,717	1,109,801	1,258,520	1,542,359	1,767,518
Tex.. .	......	......	......	......	......	......	212,592	604,215	818,579	1,591,749	2,235,527
Ut.. . .	......	......	......	......	......	......	11,380	40,273	86,786	143,963	210,779
Vt.. . .	85	154	218	235,981	280,652	291,948	314,120	315,098	330,551	332,286	332,422
Va. . .	692	808	878	938,261	1,044,054	1,025,227	1,119,348	1,219,630	1,225,163	1,512,565	1,655,980
Wash..	......	......	......	......	......	......	1,201	11,594	23,955	75,116	357,232
W. Va..	56	79	105	136,808	176,924	224,537	302,313	376,688	442,014	618,457	762,794
Wis.. .	......	......	......	......	......	30,945	305,391	775,881	1,054,670	1,315,497	1,693,330
Wy. . .	......	......	......	......	......	......	......	......	9,118	20,789	62,555
U.S. . .	**3,929**	**5,308**	**7,240**	**9,638,453**	**12,860,702**	**17,063,353[3]**	**23,191,876**	**31,443,321[3]**	**38,558,371**	**50,189,209**	**62,979,766**

Note: Where possible, population shown is that of 1990 area of state.
(1) Totals for 1790, 1800, and 1810 are in thousands. (2) 1860 figure is for Dakota Territory; 1870 figures are for parts of Dakota Territory. (3) U.S. total includes persons (5,318 in 1830 and 6,100 in 1840) on public ships in the service of the United States not credited to any region, division, or state.

Congressional Apportionment

	1990	1980		1990	1980		1990	1980		1990	1980		1990	1980
Ala.. .	7	7	Ida.. .	2	2	Minn..	8	8	N. D. .	1	1	Ut. . .	3	3
Alas. .	1	1	Ill.. . .	20	22	Miss. .	5	5	Oh.. .	19	21	Vt. . .	1	1
Ariz. .	6	5	Ind.. .	10	10	Mo.. .	9	9	Okla..	6	6	Va. . .	11	10
Ark.. .	4	4	Ia.. . .	5	6	Mon. .	1	2	Ore. .	5	5	Wash.	9	8
Cal.. .	52	45	Kan. .	4	5	Neb. .	3	3	Pa. . .	21	23	W. Va.	3	4
Col.. .	6	6	Ky. . .	6	7	Nev. .	2	2	R. I.. .	2	2	Wis. .	9	9
Conn.	6	6	La. . .	7	8	N. H. .	2	2	S. C. .	6	6	Wy.. .	1	1
Del.. .	1	1	Me.. .	2	2	N. J. .	13	14	S. D. .	1	1			
Fla.. .	23	19	Md.. .	8	8	N. M..	3	3	Tenn..	9	9	**Totals.**	**435**	**435**
Ga.. .	11	10	Mass.	10	11	N. Y..	31	34	Tex. .	30	27			
Ha.. .	2	2	Mich..	16	18	N. C..	12	11						

The primary reason the Constitution provided for a census of the population every 10 years was to give a basis for apportionment of representatives among the states. This apportionment largely determines the number of electoral votes allotted to each state.

The number of representatives of each state in Congress is determined by the state's population, but each state is entitled to one representative regardless of population. A Congressional apportionment has been made after each decennial census except that of 1920.

Under provisions of a law that became effective Nov. 15, 1941, apportionment of representatives is made by the method of equal proportions. In the application of this method, the apportionment is made so that the average population per representative has the least possible variation between one state and any other. The first House of Representatives, in 1789, had 65 members, as provided by the Constitution. As the population grew, the number of representatives was increased, but the total membership has been fixed at 435 since the apportionment based on the 1910 census.

Census from 1790 to 1990

other U.S. nationals overseas are not included.)

1900	1910	1920	1930	1940	1950	1960	1970	1980	1990
1,828,697	2,138,093	2,348,174	2,646,248	2,832,961	3,061,743	3,266,740	3,444,354	3,894,025	4,040,587
63,592	64,356	55,036	59,278	72,524	128,643	226,167	302,583	401,851	550,043
122,931	204,354	334,162	435,573	499,261	749,587	1,302,161	1,775,399	2,716,546	3,665,228
1,311,564	1,574,449	1,752,204	1,854,482	1,949,387	1,909,511	1,786,272	1,923,322	2,286,357	2,350,725
1,485,053	2,377,549	3,426,861	5,677,251	6,907,387	10,586,223	15,717,204	19,971,069	23,667,764	29,760,021
539,700	799,024	939,629	1,035,791	1,123,296	1,325,089	1,753,947	2,209,596	2,889,735	3,294,394
908,420	1,114,756	1,380,631	1,606,903	1,709,242	2,007,280	2,535,234	3,032,217	3,107,564	3,287,116
184,735	202,322	223,003	238,380	266,505	318,085	446,292	548,104	594,338	666,168
278,718	331,069	437,571	486,869	663,091	802,178	763,956	756,668	638,432	606,900
528,542	752,619	968,470	1,468,211	1,897,414	2,771,305	4,951,560	6,791,418	9,746,961	12,937,926
2,216,331	2,609,121	2,895,832	2,908,506	3,123,723	3,444,578	3,943,116	4,587,930	5,462,982	6,478,216
154,001	191,874	255,881	368,300	422,770	499,794	632,772	769,913	964,691	1,108,229
161,772	325,594	431,866	445,032	524,873	588,637	667,191	713,015	944,127	1,006,749
4,821,550	5,638,591	6,485,280	7,630,654	7,897,241	8,712,176	10,081,158	11,110,285	11,427,409	11,430,602
2,516,462	2,700,876	2,930,390	3,238,503	3,427,796	3,934,224	4,662,498	5,195,392	5,490,214	5,544,159
2,231,853	2,224,771	2,404,021	2,470,939	2,538,268	2,621,073	2,757,537	2,825,368	2,913,808	2,776,755
1,470,495	1,690,949	1,769,257	1,880,999	1,801,028	1,905,299	2,178,611	2,249,071	2,364,236	2,477,574
2,147,174	2,289,905	2,416,630	2,614,589	2,845,627	2,944,806	3,038,156	3,220,711	3,660,324	3,685,296
1,381,625	1,656,388	1,798,509	2,101,593	2,363,880	2,683,516	3,257,022	3,644,637	4,206,116	4,219,973
694,466	742,371	768,014	797,423	847,226	913,774	969,265	993,722	1,125,043	1,227,928
1,188,044	1,295,346	1,449,661	1,631,526	1,821,244	2,343,001	3,100,689	3,923,897	4,216,933	4,781,468
2,805,346	3,366,416	3,852,356	4,249,614	4,316,721	4,690,514	5,148,578	5,689,170	5,737,093	6,016,425
2,420,982	2,810,173	3,668,412	4,842,325	5,256,106	6,371,766	7,823,194	8,881,826	9,262,044	9,295,297
1,751,394	2,075,708	2,387,125	2,563,953	2,792,300	2,982,483	3,413,864	3,806,103	4,075,970	4,375,099
1,551,270	1,797,114	1,790,618	2,009,821	2,183,796	2,178,914	2,178,141	2,216,994	2,520,770	2,573,216
3,106,665	3,293,335	3,404,055	3,629,367	3,784,664	3,954,653	4,319,813	4,677,623	4,916,766	5,117,073
243,329	376,053	548,889	537,606	559,456	591,024	674,767	694,409	786,690	799,065
1,066,300	1,192,214	1,296,372	1,377,963	1,315,834	1,325,510	1,411,330	1,485,333	1,569,825	1,578,385
42,335	81,875	77,407	91,058	110,247	160,083	285,278	488,738	800,508	1,201,833
411,588	430,572	443,083	465,293	491,524	533,242	606,921	737,681	920,610	1,109,252
1,883,669	2,537,167	3,155,900	4,041,334	4,160,165	4,835,329	6,066,782	7,171,112	7,365,011	7,730,188
195,310	327,301	360,350	423,317	531,818	681,187	951,023	1,017,055	1,303,302	1,515,069
7,268,894	9,113,614	10,385,227	12,588,066	13,479,142	14,830,192	16,782,304	18,241,391	17,558,165	17,990,455
1,893,810	2,206,287	2,559,123	3,170,276	3,571,623	4,061,929	4,556,155	5,084,411	5,880,095	6,628,637
319,146	577,056	646,872	680,845	641,935	619,636	632,446	617,792	652,717	638,800
4,157,545	4,767,121	5,759,394	6,646,697	6,907,612	7,946,627	9,706,397	10,657,423	10,797,603	10,847,115
790,391	1,657,155	2,028,283	2,396,040	2,336,434	2,233,351	2,328,284	2,559,463	3,025,487	3,145,585
413,536	672,765	783,389	953,786	1,089,684	1,521,341	1,768,687	2,091,533	2,633,156	2,842,321
6,302,115	7,665,111	8,720,017	9,631,350	9,900,180	10,498,012	11,319,366	11,800,766	11,864,720	11,881,643
428,556	542,610	604,397	687,497	713,346	791,896	859,488	949,723	947,154	1,003,464
1,340,316	1,515,400	1,683,724	1,738,765	1,899,804	2,117,027	2,382,594	2,590,713	3,120,729	3,486,703
401,570	583,888	636,547	692,849	642,961	652,740	680,514	666,257	690,768	696,004
2,020,616	2,184,789	2,337,885	2,616,556	2,915,841	3,291,718	3,567,089	3,926,018	4,591,023	4,877,185
3,048,710	3,896,542	4,663,228	5,824,715	6,414,824	7,711,194	9,579,677	11,198,655	14,225,513	16,986,510
276,749	373,351	449,396	507,847	550,310	688,862	890,627	1,059,273	1,461,037	1,722,850
343,641	355,956	352,428	359,611	359,231	377,747	389,881	444,732	511,456	562,758
1,854,184	2,061,612	2,309,187	2,421,851	2,677,773	3,318,680	3,966,949	4,651,448	5,346,797	6,187,358
518,103	1,141,990	1,356,621	1,563,396	1,736,191	2,378,963	2,853,214	3,413,244	4,132,353	4,866,692
958,800	1,221,119	1,463,701	1,729,205	1,901,974	2,005,552	1,860,421	1,744,237	1,950,186	1,793,477
2,069,042	2,333,860	2,632,067	2,939,006	3,137,587	3,434,575	3,951,777	4,417,821	4,705,642	4,891,769
92,531	145,965	194,402	225,565	250,742	290,529	330,066	332,416	469,557	453,588
76,212,168	**92,228,496**	**106,021,537**	**123,202,624**	**132,164,569**	**151,325,798**	**179,323,175**	**203,302,031**	**226,542,203**	**248,709,873**

U.S. Center of Population, 1790-1990

Center of Population is that point which may be considered as center of population gravity of the U.S. or that point upon which the U.S. would balance if it were a rigid plane without weight and the population distributed thereon with each individual being assumed to have equal weight and to exert an influence on a central point proportional to his distance from that point. The 1990 center is 818.6 miles from the 1790 center of population, and 39.5 miles southwest of the 1980 center.

Year	N. Lat. °	'	"	W.Long. °	'	"	Approximate location
1790	39	16	30	76	11	12	23 miles east of Baltimore, Md.
1800	39	16	6	76	56	30	18 miles west of Baltimore, Md.
1810	39	11	30	77	37	12	40 miles northwest by west of Washington, D.C. (in Va.)
1820	39	5	42	78	33	0	16 miles east of Moorefield, W. Va.[1]
1830	38	57	54	79	16	54	19 miles west-southwest of Moorefield, W. Va.[1]
1840	39	2	0	80	18	0	16 miles south of Clarksburg, W. Va.[1]
1850	38	59	0	81	19	0	23 miles southeast of Parkersburg, W. Va.[1]
1860	39	0	24	82	48	48	20 miles south by east of Chillicothe, Oh.
1870	39	12	0	83	35	42	48 miles east by north of Cincinnati, Oh.
1880	39	4	8	84	39	40	8 miles west by south of Cincinnati, Oh. (in Ky.)
1890	39	11	56	85	32	53	20 miles east of Columbus, Ind.
1900	39	9	36	85	48	54	6 miles southeast of Columbus, Ind.
1910	39	10	12	86	32	20	In the city of Bloomington, Ind.
1920	39	10	21	86	43	15	8 miles south-southeast of Spencer, Owen County, Ind.
1930	39	3	45	87	8	6	3 miles northeast of Linton, Greene County, Ind.
1940	38	56	54	87	22	35	2 miles southeast by east of Carlisle, Haddon township, Sullivan Co., Ind.
1950 (Inc. Alaska & Hawaii)	38	48	15	88	22	8	3 miles northeast of Louisville, Clay County, Ill.
1960	38	35	58	89	12	35	6 1/2 miles northwest of Centralia, Clinton Co., Ill.
1970	38	27	47	89	42	22	5 miles east southeast of Mascoutah, St. Clair County, Ill.
1980	38	8	13	90	34	26	1/4 mile west of De Soto, Jefferson Co., Mo.
1990	37	52	20	91	12	55	9.7 miles northwest of Steelville, Mo.

(1) West Virginia was set off from Virginia Dec. 31, 1862, and admitted as a state June 20, 1863.

Race and Hispanic Origin for the United States: 1990 and 1980

Source: Bureau of the Census, U.S. Dept. of Commerce

	1990 Census		1980 Census		Percent change
	Number	Percent	Number	Percent	1980-1990
Race					
All persons	248,709,873	100.0	226,545,805	100.0	9.8
White	199,686,070	80.3	188,371,622	83.1	6.0
Black	29,986,060	12.1	26,495,025	11.7	13.2
American Indian, Eskimo, or Aleut	1,959,234	0.8	1,420,400	0.6	37.9
American Indian	1,878,285	0.8	1,364,033	0.6	37.7
Eskimo	57,152	0.0	42,162	0.0	35.6
Aleut	23,797	0.0	14,205	0.0	67.5
Asian or Pacific Islander	7,273,662	2.9	3,500,439[1]	1.5	107.8
Chinese	1,645,472	0.7	806,040	0.4	104.1
Filipino	1,406,770	0.6	774,652	0.3	81.6
Japanese	847,562	0.3	700,974	0.3	20.9
Asian Indian	815,447	0.3	361,531	0.2	125.6
Korean	798,849	0.3	354,593	0.2	125.3
Vietnamese	614,547	0.2	261,729	0.1	134.8
Hawaiian	211,014	0.1	166,814	0.1	26.5
Samoan	62,964	0.0	41,948	0.0	50.1
Guamanian	49,345	0.0	32,158	0.0	53.4
Other Asian or Pacific Islander	821,692	0.3	NA	NA	NA
Other race	9,804,847	3.9	6,758,319	3.0	45.1
Hispanic Origin					
Hispanic origin[2]	22,354,059	9.0	14,608,673	6.4	53.0
Mexican	13,495,938	5.4	8,740,439	3.9	54.4
Puerto Rican	2,727,754	1.1	2,013,945	0.9	35.4
Cuban	1,043,932	0.4	803,226	0.4	30.0
Other Hispanic	5,086,435	2.0	3,051,063	1.3	66.7
Not of Hispanic origin	226,355,814	91.0	211,937,132	93.6	6.8

(NA) Not Available from 1980 100-percent tabulations. (1) The 1980 numbers for Asians or Pacific Islanders shown in this table are not entirely comparable with 1990 counts. The 1980 count of 3,500,439 Asians or Pacific Islanders based on 100-percent tabulations includes only the nine specific Asian or Pacific Islander groups listed separately in the 1980 race item. The 1980 total Asian or Pacific Islander population of 3,726,440 from sample tabulations is comparable to the 1990 count; these figures include groups not listed separately in the race item on the 1980 census form. (2) Persons of Hispanic origin may be of any race.

Definitions of Race and Hispanic Origin Groups

Source: Bureau of the Census, U.S. Dept. of Commerce

Race

The concept of race as used by the Census Bureau reflects self-identification; it does not denote any clear-cut scientific definition of biological stock. The data for race represent self-classification by people according to the race with which they most closely identify.

Persons identified their race by classifying themselves in one of the categories listed, i.e., White, Black, American Indian, Eskimo, Aleut, Chinese, Filipino, Japanese, Asian Indian, Korean, Vietnamese, Hawaiian, Samoan, Guamanian, Other API, or Other race. In cases where persons did not identify with any of the given race categories they were directed to identify as "Other API" ("API" means Asian or Pacific Islander) or "Other race" and write in the name of their race in the space provided. Thus, data for the Asian or Pacific Islander groups not listed on the census questionnaire but contained in the tables—Cambodian, Hmong, Laotian, Thai, Bangladeshi, Burmese, Indonesian, Malayan, Okinawan, Pakistani, Sri Lankan, Tongan, Tahitian, Northern Mariana Islander, Palauan, and Fijian—were tabulated from write-in responses.

The "Other race" category includes persons not included in the race categories described above. Persons reporting in the "Other race" category and providing write-in entries such as a Spanish/Hispanic origin group (i.e., Mexican, Cuban, Puerto Rican) are included here.

Spanish/Hispanic origin

Persons of Spanish/Hispanic origin or descent are those who classify themselves in one of the specific Hispanic origin categories listed on the census questionnaire—for example, Mexican, Puerto Rican, or Cuban—as well as those who indicated that they were of other Spanish/Hispanic origin. Persons reporting "Other Spanish/Hispanic" are those whose origins are from other Spanish-speaking countries of the Caribbean, Central or South America, or from Spain, or persons identifying themselves generally as Spanish, Spanish-American, Hispano, Hispanic, Latino, etc.

Spanish origin and race are distinct; thus, persons of Spanish/Hispanic origin may be of any race.

The Census

On April 1, 1990, the Bureau of the Census began to take the 21st decennial census of the United States. The Census Bureau took the first census in 1790, when it counted 3.9 million people, and has conducted a census every 10 years over the past 200 years, as mandated by the U.S. Constitution, Article 1, Section 2. The primary purpose of the census was, and is, to provide population counts needed to apportion seats in the U.S. House of Representatives, and to subsequently determine state legislative district boundaries. In addition, the findings of the 1990 census are critical to many other national, state, and local programs, which: determine compliances with the Voting Rights Act and amendments; allocate funds from federal grant programs; identify areas needing bilingual education; assess the need for equal employment opportunity programs; allocate funds and analyze programs for American Indians and Alaska Natives; identify areas needing energy assistance; develop programs to reduce unemployment; identify areas needing programs to stimulate economic growth; establish fair lending practices; assess the need for developing or expanding low-income housing programs; and identify areas requiring child assistance programs. For state and local government programs, the census results will help: develop social services programs, including programs for the elderly and handicapped; assess transportation systems and improve commuting patterns; identify areas for low-cost housing programs; establish occupational and vocational education programs; plan school district boundaries and school construction programs; and assess the need for state housing bonds for below-market interest rates on mortgages.

Counties with 1990 Population over 1 Million

Source: Bureau of the Census, U.S. Dept. of Commerce, 1990 Census

County	April 1, 1990 census	April 1, 1980 census	Percent change, 1980-90
Los Angeles, CA	8,863,164	7,477,238	18.5
Cook, IL	5,105,067	5,253,628	−2.8
Harris, TX	2,818,199	2,409,547	17.0
San Diego, CA	2,498,016	1,861,846	34.2
Orange, CA	2,410,556	1,932,921	24.7
Kings, NY	2,300,664	2,231,028	3.1
Maricopa, AZ	2,122,101	1,509,175	40.6
Wayne, MI	2,111,687	2,337,843	-9.7
Queens, NY	1,951,598	1,891,325	3.2
Dade, FL	1,937,094	1,625,509	19.2
Dallas, TX	1,852,810	1,556,419	19.0
Philadelphia, PA	1,585,577	1,688,210	−6.1
King, WA	1,507,319	1,269,898	18.7
Santa Clara, CA	1,497,577	1,295,071	15.6
New York, NY	1,487,536	1,428,285	4.1
San Bernardino, CA	1,418,380	895,016	58.5
Cuyahoga, OH	1,412,140	1,498,400	−5.8
Middlesex, MA	1,398,468	1,367,034	2.3
Allegheny, PA	1,336,449	1,450,195	−7.8
Suffolk, NY	1,321,864	1,284,231	2.9
Nassau, NY	1,287,348	1,321,582	−2.6
Alameda, CA	1,279,182	1,105,379	15.7
Broward, FL	1,255,488	1,018,257	23.3
Bronx, NY	1,203,789	1,168,972	3.0
Bexar, TX	1,185,394	988,971	19.9
Riverside, CA	1,170,413	663,199	76.5
Tarrant, TX	1,170,103	860,880	35.9
Oakland, MI	1,083,592	1,011,793	7.1
Sacramento, CA	1,041,219	783,381	32.9
Hennepin, MN	1,032,431	941,411	9.7

Los Angeles County, the nation's largest, also had the largest numeric increase, 1.4 million, followed by San Diego and Maricopa (Phoenix) each with over 600,000, and San Bernardino and Riverside each with more than 500,000. New York City encompasses 5 counties, 4 of which exceed a million population. The largest is Kings (Brooklyn), with 2.3 million, followed by Queens, New York (Manhattan), and the Bronx. For the first time since 1950, the population of all five counties increased.

Population by State: 1990

Source: Bureau of the Census, U.S. Dept. of Commerce, 1990 Census

State	1990 population	Percent change 1980-90	Minority population 1990	Minority percent change 1980-90
U.S.	**248,709,873**	**9.8%**	**60,581,577**	**30.9%**
Cal.	29,760,021	25.7	12,730,895	61.1
N.Y.	17,990,455	2.5	5,530,266	25.9
Tex.	16,986,510	19.4	6,694,830	37.2
Fla.	12,937,926	32.7	3,462,600	52.3
Pa.	11,881,643	0.1	1,459,585	13.3
Ill.	11,430,602	0.0	2,880,394	14.5
Oh.	10,847,115	0.5	1,402,493	10.4
Mich.	9,295,297	0.4	1,645,346	11.4
N.J.	7,730,188	5.0	2,011,222	30.7
N.C.	6,628,637	12.7	1,657,510	14.1
Ga.	6,478,216	18.6	1,934,791	24.9
Va.	6,187,358	15.7	1,485,708	27.3
Mass.	6,016,425	4.9	736,133	66.2
Ind.	5,544,159	1.0	578,917	7.9
Mo.	5,117,073	4.1	668,608	10.5
Wis.	4,891,769	4.0	427,092	42.3
Tenn.	4,877,185	6.2	849,554	9.2
Wash.	4,866,692	17.8	645,070	58.8
Md.	4,781,468	13.4	1,455,359	32.2
Minn.	4,375,099	7.3	273,833	71.7
La.	4,219,973	0.3	1,443,951	5.8
Ala.	4,040,587	3.8	1,080,420	4.1
Ky.	3,685,296	0.7	307,274	1.7
Ariz.	3,665,228	34.8	1,039,043	50.2
S.C.	3,486,703	11.7	1,096,647	10.8
Colo.	3,294,394	14.0	635,449	27.2
Conn.	3,287,116	5.8	532,932	43.2
Okla.	3,145,585	4.0	597,997	31.6
Ore.	2,842,321	7.9	262,589	48.3
Ia.	2,776,755	-4.7	112,915	24.8
Miss.	2,573,216	2.1	949,018	3.5
Kan.	2,477,574	4.8	287,050	27.5
Ark.	2,350,725	2.8	417,643	2.7
W.Va.	1,793,477	-8.0	74,581	-13.3
Utah	1,722,850	17.9	151,596	37.1
Neb.	1,578,385	0.5	118,290	25.2
N.M.	1,515,069	16.3	750,905	21.7
Me.	1,227,928	9.2	24,571	30.7
Nev.	1,201,833	50.1	255,476	90.5
N.H.	1,109,252	20.5	29,768	97.1
Ha.	1,108,229	14.9	760,585	14.4
Id.	1,006,749	6.7	78,088	35.2
R.I.	1,003,464	5.9	107,355	71.8
Mont.	799,065	1.6	65,187	24.7
S.D.	696,004	0.8	61,216	14.9
Del.	666,168	12.1	138,076	24.2
N.D.	638,800	-2.1	37,208	26.1
D. of C.	606,900	-4.9	440,769	-7.0
Vt.	562,758	10.0	10,574	39.4
Alas.	550,043	36.9	143,321	47.4
Wyo.	453,588	-3.4	40,877	8.7

*Note: "Minority" includes blacks, Asians, other races, and Hispanics.

Density of Population by States

Source: Bureau of the Census; U.S. Dept. of Commerce

(Per square mile, land area only)

State	1920	1960	1980	1990
Ala.	45.8	64.2	76.6	79.6
Alas.*	0.1	0.4	0.7	1.0
Ariz.	2.9	11.5	23.9	32.3
Ark.	33.4	34.2	43.9	45.1
Cal.	22.0	100.4	151.4	190.8
Col.	9.1	16.9	27.9	31.8
Conn.	286.4	520.6	637.8	678.4
Del.	113.5	225.2	307.6	340.8
D. C.	7,292.9	12,523.9	10,132.3	9,882.8
Fla.	17.7	91.5	180.0	239.6
Ga.	49.3	67.8	94.1	111.9
Ha.*	39.9	98.5	150.1	172.5
Ida.	5.2	8.1	11.5	12.2
Ill.	115.7	180.4	205.3	205.6
Ind.	81.3	128.8	152.8	154.6
Ia.	43.2	49.2	52.1	49.7
Kan.	21.6	26.6	28.9	30.3
Ky.	60.1	76.2	92.3	92.8
La.	39.6	72.2	94.5	96.9
Me.	25.7	31.3	36.3	39.8
Md.	145.8	313.5	428.7	489.2
Mass.	479.2	657.3	733.3	767.6
Mich.	63.8	137.7	162.6	163.6
Minn.	29.5	43.1	51.2	55.0
Miss.	38.6	46.0	53.4	54.9
Mo.	49.5	62.6	71.3	74.3
Mon.	3.8	4.6	5.4	5.5
Neb.	16.9	18.4	20.5	20.5
Nev.	.7	2.6	7.3	10.9
N. H.	49.1	67.2	102.4	123.7
N. J.	420.0	805.5	986.2	1,042.0
N. M.	2.9	7.8	10.7	12.5
N. Y.	217.9	350.6	370.6	381.0
N. C.	52.5	93.2	120.4	136.1
N. D.	9.2	9.1	9.4	9.3
Oh.	141.4	236.6	263.3	264.9
Okla.	29.2	33.8	44.1	45.8
Ore.	8.2	18.4	27.4	29.6
Pa.	194.5	251.4	264.3	265.1
R. I.	566.4	819.3	897.8	960.3
S. C.	55.2	78.7	103.4	115.8
S. D.	8.3	9.0	9.1	9.2
Tenn.	56.1	86.2	111.6	118.3
Tex.	17.8	36.4	54.3	64.9
Ut.	5.5	10.8	17.8	21.0
Vt.	38.6	42.0	55.2	60.8
Va.	57.4	99.6	134.7	156.3
Wash.	20.3	42.8	62.1	73.1
W. Va.	60.9	77.2	80.8	74.5
Wis.	47.6	72.6	86.5	90.1
Wy.	2.0	3.4	4.9	4.7
U.S.	***29.9**	**50.6**	**64.0**	**70.3**

* For purposes of comparison, Alaska and Hawaii included in above tabulation for 1920, even though not states then.

The 50 Fastest-Growing Metropolitan Areas

Source: Bureau of the Census, U.S. Dept. of Commerce, 1990 Census

	1990 population	Percent-change 1980-1990
1. Naples, FL	152,099	76.9
2. Riverside-San Bernardino, CA	2,588,793	66.1
3. Fort Pierce, FL	251,071	66.1
4. Fort Myers-Cape Coral, FL	335,113	63.3
5. Las Vegas, NV	741,459	60.1
6. Ocala, FL	194,833	59.1
7. Orlando, FL	1,072,748	53.3
8. West Palm Beach-Boca Raton-Delray Beach,FL	863,518	49.7
9. Melbourne-Titusville-Palm Bay, FL	398,978	46.2
10. Austin, TX	781,572	45.6
11. Daytona Beach, FL	370,712	43.3
12. Bradenton, FL	211,707	42.6
13. Las Cruces, NM	135,510	40.7
14. Phoenix, AZ	2,122,101	40.6
15. Yuma, AZ	106,895	40.3
16. Modesto, CA	370,522	39.3
17. Stockton, CA	480,628	38.4
18. Sarasota, FL	277,776	37.3
19. Fort Worth-Arlington, TX	1,332,053	36.9
20. McAllen-Edinburg Mission, TX	383,545	35.4
21. Vallejo-Fairfield-Napa, CA	451,186	34.9
22. Bakersfield, CA	543,477	34.8
23. Sacramento, CA	1,481,102	34.7
24. Laredo, TX	133,239	34.2
25. San Diego, CA	2,498,016	34.2
26. Jacksonville, NC	149,838	32.9
27. Merced, CA	178,403	32.6
28. Atlanta, GA	2,833,511	32.5
29. Reno, NV	254,667	31.5
30. Raleigh-Durham, NC	735,480	31.2
31. Fort Walton Beach, FL	143,776	30.8
32. Dallas, TX	2,553,362	30.4
33. Bryan-College Station, TX	121,862	30.2
34. Panama City, FL	126,994	29.9
35. Anchorage, AK	226.338	29.8
36. Olympia, WA	161,238	29.8
37. Fresno, CA	667,490	29.7
38. Santo Rosa-Petaluma, CA	388,222	29.6
39. Midland, TX	106,611	29.0
40. Bremerton, WA	189,731	28.9
41. Colorado Springs, CO	397,014	28.3
42. Tampa-St. Petersburg-Clearwater, FL	2,067,959	28.2
43. Redding, CA	147,036	27.2
44. Portsmouth-Dover-Rochester, NH[1]	350,078	27.0
45. Visalia-Tulare-Porterville, CA	311,921	26.9
46. Chico, CA	182,120	26.6
47. Oxnard-Ventura, CA	669,016	26.4
48. Lakeland-Winter Haven, FL	405,382	26.0
49. Santa Fe, NM	117,043	25.7
50. Jacksonville, FL	906,727	25.5

(1) New England County Metropolitan Area (NECMA)

Metropolitan Statistical Areas: 1980–1990

Source: Bureau of the Census, U.S. Dept. of Commerce
(MSAs over 400,000 listed by 1990 population)

Metropolitan areas are defined for federal statistical use by the Office of Management and Budget, with technical assistance from the Census Bureau. Most individual metropolitan areas are designated as "metropolitan statistical areas" (MSAs). Metropolitan areas over one million may under specified circumstances be subdivided into component "primary metropolitan statistical areas" (PMSAs), in which case the area as a whole is designated a "consolidated metroplitan statistical area" (CMSA). The 1980 and 1990 data refer to the areas as defined effective June 30, 1990. After detailed results of the census become available, OMB expects to issue revised definitions of all metropolitan areas by June 30, 1992.

MSA	Population 1990 census	Population 1980 census	Percent Change 1980 to 1990
New York-Northern New Jersey-Long Island, NY-NJ-CT CMSA	18,087,251	17,539,532	3.1
Los Angeles-Anaheim-Riverside, CA CMSA	14,531,529	11,497,549	26.4
Chicago-Gary-Lake County, IL-IN-WI CMSA	8,065,633	7,937,290	1.6
San Francisco-Oakland-San Jose, CA CMSA	6,253,311	5,367,900	16.5
Philadelphia-Wilmington-Trenton, PA-NJ-DE-MD CMSA	5,899,345	5,680,509	3.9
Detroit-Ann Arbor, MI CMSA	4,665,236	4,752,764	−1.8
Boston-Lawrence-Salem, MA-NH CMSA	4,171,643	3,971,792	5.0
Washington, D.C.-MD-VA	3,923,574	3,250,921	20.7
Dallas-Fort Worth, TX CMSA	3,885,415	2,930,568	32.6
Houston-Galveston-Brazoria, TX CMSA	3,711,043	3,099,942	19.7
Miami-Fort Lauderdale, FL CMSA	3,192,582	2,643,766	20.8
Atlanta, GA	2,833,511	2,138,136	32.5
Cleveland-Akron-Lorain, OH CMSA	2,759,823	2,834,062	−2.6
Seattle-Tacoma, WA CMSA	2,559,164	2,093,285	22.3
San Diego, CA	2,498,016	1,861,846	34.2
Minneapolis-St. Paul, MN-WI	2,464,124	2,137,133	15.3
St. Louis, MO-IL	2,444,099	2,376,968	2.8
Baltimore, MD	2,382,172	2,199,497	8.3
Pittsburgh-Beaver Valley, PA CMSA	2,242,798	2,423,311	−7.4
Phoenix, AZ	2,122,101	1,509,175	40.6
Tampa-St. Petersburg-Clearwater, FL	2,067,959	1,613,600	28.2
Denver-Boulder, CO CMSA	1,848,319	1,618,461	14.2
Cincinnati-Hamilton, OH-KY-IN CMSA	1,744,124	1,660,257	5.1
Milwaukee-Racine, WI CMSA	1,607,183	1,570,152	2.4
Kansas City, MO-KS	1,566,280	1,433,464	9.3
Sacramento, CA	1,481,102	1,099,814	34.7
Portland-Vancouver, OR-WA CMSA	1,477,895	1,297,977	13.9
Norfolk-Virginia Beach-Newport News, VA	1,396,107	1,160,311	20.3
Columbus, OH	1,377,419	1,243,827	10.7
San Antonio, TX	1,302,099	1,072,125	21.5
Indianapolis, IN	1,249,822	1,166,575	7.1
New Orleans, LA	1,238,816	1,256,668	−1.4
Buffalo-Niagara Falls, NY CMSA	1,189,288	1,242,826	−4.3
Charlotte-Gastonia-Rock Hill, NC-SC	1,162,093	971,447	19.6
Providence-Pawtucket-Fall River, RI-MA CMSA	1,141,510	1,083,139	5.4
Hartford-New Britain-Middletown, CT CMSA	1,085,837	1,013,508	7.1
Orlando, FL	1,072,748	699,904	53.3
Salt Lake City-Ogden, UT	1,072,227	910,222	17.8
Rochester, NY	1,002,410	971,230	3.2
Nashville, TN	985,026	850,505	15.8
Memphis, TN-AR-MS	981,747	913,472	7.5
Oklahoma City, OK	958,839	860,969	11.4
Louisville, KY-IN	952,662	956,426	−0.4
Dayton-Springfield, OH	951,270	942,083	1.0
Greensboro-Winston-Salem-High Point, NC	942,091	851,444	10.6
Birmingham, AL	907,810	883,993	2.7
Jacksonville, FL	906,727	722,252	25.5
Albany-Schenectady-Troy, NY	874,304	835,880	4.6
Richmond-Petersburg, VA	865,640	761,311	13.7
West Palm Beach-Boca Raton-Delray Beach, FL	863,518	576,758	49.7

MSA	Population 1990 census	Population 1980 census	Percent Change 1980 to 1990
Honolulu, HI	836,231	762,565	9.7
Austin, TX	781,572	536,688	45.6
Las Vegas, NV	741,459	463,087	60.1
Raleigh-Durham, NC	735,480	560,774	31.2
Scranton-Wilkes-Barre, PA	734,175	728,796	0.7
Tulsa, OK	708,954	657,173	7.9
Grand Rapids, MI	688,399	601,680	14.4
Allentown-Bethlehem-Easton, PA-NJ	686,688	635,481	8.1
Fresno, CA	667,490	514,621	29.7
Tucson, AZ	666,880	531,443	25.5
Syracuse, NY	659,864	642,971	2.6
Greenville-Spartanburg, SC	640,861	570,210	12.4
Omaha, NE-IA	618,262	585,122	5.7
Toledo, OH	614,128	616,864	−0.4
Knoxville, TN	604,816	565,970	6.9
El Paso, TX	591,610	479,899	23.3
Harrisburg-Lebanon-Carlisle, PA	587,986	556,242	5.7
Bakersfield, CA	543,477	403,089	34.8
New Haven-Meriden, CT	530,180	500,462	5.9
Springfield, MA	529,519	515,259	2.8
Baton Rouge, LA	528,264	494,151	6.9
Little Rock-North Little Rock, AK	513,117	474,463	8.1
Charleston, SC	506,875	430,346	17.8
Youngstown-Warren, OH	492,619	531,350	−7.3
Wichita, KS	485,270	442,401	9.7
Stockton, CA	480,628	347,342	38.4
Albuquerque, NM	480,577	420,261	14.4
Mobile, AL	476,923	443,536	7.5
Columbia, SC	453,331	409,953	10.6
Worcester, MA	436,905	402,918	8.4
Johnson City-Kingsport-Bristol, TN-VA	436,047	433,638	0.6
Chattanooga, TN-GA	433,210	426,443	1.6
Lansing-East Lansing, MI	432,674	419,750	3.1
Flint, MI	430,459	450,449	−4.4
Lancaster, PA	422,822	362,346	16.7
York, PA	417,848	381,255	9.6
Lakeland-Winter Haven, FL	405,382	321,652	26.0

Final 1990 census figures show that the nation has 39 metropolitan areas of at least 1 million population, including 4 that have reached that size since 1980. **The 39 areas have 124.8 million people, or 50.2 percent of the U.S. population.** The 1950 census showed only 14 metropolitan areas of 1 million people, and their combined population of about 45 million amounted to less than 30 percent of the national total.

The census shows that the U.S. population living in all metropolitan areas totals 192,725,741, an increase of just over 20 million (11.6 percent) since 1980. The same areas grew 10.6 percent in the 1970s. The population living outside metropolitan areas totals 55,984,132, an increase of 2.1 million (3.9 percent). **The metropolitan population in 1990 constitutes 77.5 percent of the U.S. total** compared with 76.2 percent in 1980. Ninety percent of the nation's growth in the 1980s took place in metropolitan areas.

Fastest Growing Cities, 1980-1990

Source: Bureau of the Census, U.S. Dept. of Commerce, 1990 Census

Cities of more than 100,000 in 1990 that had the largest percentage increases in population from 1980.

City	Suburb of...	1990	1980	Change
1. Moreno Valley, Calif.	Riverside	118,779	28,309	319.6%
2. Mesa, Ariz.	Phoenix	288,091	152,404	89.0
3. Rancho Cucamonga, Calif.	Los Angeles	101,409	55,250	83.5
4. Plano, Tex.	Dallas	128,713	72,331	77.9
5. Irvine, Calif.	Los Angeles	110,330	62,134	77.6
6. Escondido, Calif.	San Diego	108,635	64,355	68.8
7. Oceanside, Calif.	Los Angeles	128,398	76,698	67.4
8. Santa Clarita, Calif.	Los Angeles	110,642	66,730	65.8
9. Bakersfield, Calif.	—	174,820	105,611	65.5
10. Arlington, Tex.	Dallas	261,721	160,113	63.5
11. Fresno, Calif.	—	354,202	217,491	62.9
12. Chula Vista, Calif.	San Diego	135,163	83,927	61.0
13. Las Vegas, Nev.	—	258,295	164,674	56.9
14. Modesto, Calif.	—	164,730	106,963	54.0
15. Tallahassee, Fla.	—	124,773	81,548	53.0
16. Glendale, Ariz.	Phoenix	148,134	97,172	52.4
17. Mesquite, Tex.	Dallas	101,484	67,053	51.3
18. Ontario, Calif.	Los Angeles	133,179	88,820	49.9
19. Virginia Beach, Va.	Norfolk	393,069	262,199	49.9
20. Scottsdale, Ariz.	Phoenix	130,069	88,622	46.5
21. Santa Ana, Calif.	Los Angeles	293,742	204,023	44.0
22. Stockton, Calif.	—	210,943	148,283	42.3
23. Pomona, Calif.	Los Angeles	131,723	92,742	42.0
24. Irving, Tex.	Dallas	155,037	109,943	41.0
25. Aurora, Colo.	Denver	222,103	158,588	40.1
26. Raleigh, N.C.	—	207,951	150,255	38.4
27. San Bernardino, Calif.	—	164,164	118,794	38.2
28. Santa Rosa, Calif.	San Francisco	113,313	82,658	37.1
29. Overland Park, Kan.	Kansas City	111,790	81,784	36.7
30. Vallejo, Calif.	San Francisco	109,199	80,303	36.0
31. Thousand Oaks, Calif.	Los Angeles	104,352	77,072	35.4
32. Salinas, Calif.	—	108,777	80,479	35.2
33. Durham, N.C.	—	136,611	101,149	35.1
34. Austin, Tex.	—	465,622	345,890	34.6
35. Laredo, Tex.	—	122,899	91,449	34.4
36. Sacramento, Calif.	—	369,365	275,741	34.0
37. El Monte, Calif.	Los Angeles	106,209	79,494	33.6
38. Reno, Nev.	—	133,850	100,756	32.8
39. Riverside, Calif.	—	226,505	170,591	32.8
40. Chesapeake, Va.	Norfolk	151,967	114,486	32.7
41. Tempe, Ariz.	Phoenix	141,865	106,919	32.7
42. Oxnard, Calif.	Los Angeles	142,216	108,195	31.4
43. Fremont, Calif.	San Jose/Oakland	173,339	131,945	31.4
44. Colorado Springs, Colo.	—	281,140	215,105	30.7
45. Garland, Tex.	Dallas	180,650	138,857	30.1

Population of U.S. Cities

Source: U.S. Bureau of the Census (100 most populated cities ranked by April, 1990 census)

Rank	City	1990	1980	1970	1960	1950	1900	1850
1	New York, NY	7,322,564	7,071,639	7,895,563	7,781,984	7,891,957	3,437,202	696,115
2	Los Angeles, Ca.	3,485,398	2,966,850	2,811,801	2,479,015	1,970,358	102,479	1,610
3	Chicago, Ill	2,783,726	3,005,072	3,369,357	3,550,404	3,620,962	1,698,575	29,963
4	Houston, Tx	1,630,553	1,595,138	1,233,535	938,219	596,163	44,633	2,396
5	Philadelphia, Pa	1,585,577	1,688,210	1,949,996	2,002,512	2,071,605	1,293,697	121,376
6	San Diego, Ca.	1,110,549	875,538	697,471	573,224	334,387	17,700	...
7	Detroit, Mi	1,027,974	1,203,339	1,514,063	1,670,144	1,849,568	285,704	21,019
8	Dallas, Tx	1,006,877	904,078	844,401	679,684	434,462	42,638	...
9	Phoenix, Az	983,403	789,704	584,303	439,170	106,818	5,544	...
10	San Antonio, Tx	935,933	785,880	654,153	587,718	408,442	53,321	3,488
11	San Jose, Ca	782,248	629,442	459,913	204,196	95,280	21,500	...
12	Indianapolis, In.	741,952	700,807	736,856	476,258	427,173	169,164	8,091
13	Baltimore, Md	736,014	786,775	905,787	939,024	949,708	508,957	169,054
14	San Francisco, Ca.	723,959	678,974	715,674	740,316	775,357	342,782	34,776
15	Jacksonville, Fl	672,971	540,920	504,265	201,030	204,517	28,429	1,045
16	Columbus, Oh	632,910	564,871	540,025	471,316	375,901	125,560	17,882
17	Milwaukee, Wi.	628,088	636,212	717,372	741,324	637,392	285,315	20,061
18	Memphis, Tn.	610,337	646,356	623,988	497,524	396,000	102,320	8,841
19	Washington, DC	606,900	638,333	756,668	763,956	802,178	278,718	40,001
20	Boston, Ma.	574,283	562,994	641,071	697,197	801,444	560,892	136,881
21	Seattle, Wa	516,259	493,846	530,831	557,087	467,591	80,671	...
22	El Paso, Tx.	515,342	425,259	322,261	276,687	130,485	15,906	...
23	Nashville-Davidson, Tn	510,784	455,651	426,029	170,874	174,307	80,865	10,165
24	Cleveland, Oh	505,616	573,822	750,879	876,050	914,808	381,768	17,034
25	New Orleans, La	496,938	557,515	593,471	627,525	570,445	287,104	116,375
26	Denver, Co.	467,610	492,365	514,678	493,887	415,786	133,859	...
27	Austin, Tx.	465,622	345,496	253,539	186,545	132,459	22,258	629
28	Fort Worth, Tx	447,619	385,164	393,455	356,268	278,778	26,688	...
29	Oklahoma City, Ok	444,719	403,213	368,164	324,253	243,504	10,037	...
30	Portland, Or	437,319	366,383	379,967	372,676	373,628	90,426	...
31	Kansas City, Mo.	435,146	448,159	507,330	475,539	456,622	163,752	...
32	Long Beach, Ca	429,433	361,334	358,879	344,168	250,767	2,252	...
33	Tucson, Az	405,390	330,537	262,933	212,892	45,454	7,531	...
34	St. Louis, Mo.	396,685	453,085	622,236	750,026	856,796	575,238	77,860
35	Charlotte, NC	395,934	314,447	241,420	201,564	134,042	18,091	1,065
36	Atlanta, Ga	394,017	425,022	495,039	487,455	331,314	89,872	2,572
37	Virginia Beach, Va.	393,069	262,199	172,106	8,091	5,390	...	...
38	Albuquerque, NM	384,736	331,767	244,501	201,189	96,815	6,238	...
39	Oakland, Ca	372,242	339,337	361,561	367,548	384,575	66,960	...
40	Pittsburgh, Pa	369,879	423,938	520,089	604,332	676,806	321,616	46,601
41	Sacramento, Ca.	369,365	275,741	257,105	191,667	137,572	29,282	6,820
42	Minneapolis, Mn	368,383	370,951	434,400	482,872	521,718	202,718	...
43	Tulsa, Ok.	367,302	360,919	330,350	261,685	182,740	1,390	...
44	Honolulu, CDP, Hi.	365,272	762,874	630,528	294,194	248,034	39,306	...
45	Cincinnati, Oh.	364,040	385,457	453,514	502,550	503,998	325,902	115,435
46	Miami, Fla.	358,548	346,865	334,859	291,688	249,276	1,681	...
47	Fresno, Ca	354,202	218,202	165,655	133,929	91,669	12,470	...
48	Omaha, Ne.	335,795	314,255	346,929	301,598	251,117	102,555	...
49	Toledo, Oh	332,943	354,635	383,062	318,003	303,616	131,822	3,829
50	Buffalo, NY.	328,123	357,870	462,768	532,759	580,132	352,387	42,261
51	Wichita, Ks	304,011	279,272	276,554	254,698	168,279	24,671	...
52	Santa Ana, Ca.	293,742	203,713	155,710	100,350	45,533	4,933	...
53	Mesa, Az	288,091	152,453	63,049	33,772	16,790	722	...
54	Colorado Springs, Co.	281,140	215,150	135,517	70,194	45,472	21,085	...
55	Tampa, Fl	280,015	271,523	277,714	274,970	124,681	15,839	...
56	Newark, NJ	275,221	329,248	381,930	405,220	438,776	246,070	38,894
57	St. Paul, Mn	272,235	270,230	309,866	313,411	311,349	163,065	1,112
58	Louisville, Ky	269,063	298,451	361,706	390,639	369,129	204,731	43,194
59	Anaheim, Ca	266,406	219,311	166,408	104,184	14,556	1,456	...
60	Birmingham, Al	265,968	284,413	300,910	340,887	326,037	38,415	...
61	Arlington, Tx	261,721	160,113	90,229	44,775	7,692	1,079	...
62	Norfolk, Va.	261,229	266,979	307,951	304,869	213,513	46,624	14,326
63	Las Vegas, Nv	258,295	164,674	125,787	64,405	24,624	...	...
64	Corpus Christi, Tx	257,453	231,999	204,525	167,690	108,287	4,703	...
65	St. Petersburg, Fl	238,629	238,647	216,159	181,298	96,738	1,575	...
66	Rochester, NY.	231,636	241,741	295,011	318,611	332,488	162,608	36,403
67	Jersey City, NJ	228,537	223,532	260,350	276,101	299,017	206,433	6,856
68	Riverside, Ca	226,505	170,876	140,089	84,332	46,764	7,973	...
69	Anchorage, Ak.	226,338	174,431	48,081	44,237	11,254	...	...
70	Lexington-Fayette, Ky.	225,366	204,165	108,137	62,810	55,534	26,369	8,159
71	Akron, Oh.	223,019	237,177	275,425	290,351	274,605	42,728	3,266
72	Aurora, Co	222,103	158,588	74,974	48,548	11,421	202	...
73	Baton Rouge, La	219,531	346,029	165,921	152,419	125,629	11,269	3,905
74	Stockton, Ca.	210,943	149,779	109,963	86,321	70,853	17,506	...
75	Raleigh, NC	207,951	150,255	122,830	93,931	65,679	13,643	4,518
76	Richmond, Va	203,056	219,214	249,332	219,958	230,310	85,050	27,570
77	Shreveport, La.	198,525	205,820	182,064	164,372	127,206	16,013	1,728
78	Jackson, Ms..	196,637	202,895	153,968	144,422	98,271	7,816	1,881
79	Mobile, Al.	196,278	200,452	190,026	194,856	129,009	38,469	20,515
80	Des Moines, Ia.	193,187	191,003	201,404	208,982	177,965	62,139	...
81	Lincoln, Ne	191,972	171,932	149,518	128,521	98,884	40,169	...
82	Madison, Wi	191,262	170,616	171,809	126,706	96,056	19,164	1,525
83	Grand Rapids, Mi	189,126	181,843	197,649	177,313	176,515	87,565	2,686
84	Yonkers, NY	188,082	195,351	204,297	190,634	152,798	47,931	...

Rank	City	1990	1980	1970	1960	1950	1900	1850
85	Hialeah, Fl	188,004	145,254	102,452	66,972	19,676	...	...
86	Montgomery, Al	187,106	177,857	133,386	134,393	106,525	30,346	8,728
87	Lubbock, Tx	186,206	173,979	149,101	126,691	71,747	...	...
88	Greensboro, NC	183,521	170,279	144,076	119,574	74,389	10,035	...
89	Dayton, Oh.	182,044	203,371	243,023	262,332	243,872	85,333	10,977
90	Huntington Beach, Ca.	181,519	170,505	115,960	11,492	5,237	...	...
91	Garland, Tx	180,650	138,857	81,437	38,501	10,571	819	...
92	Glendale, Ca.	180,038	139,060	133,000	119,000	96,000	...	...
93	Columbus, Ga	179,278	169,441	155,028	116,779	79,611	17,614	9,621
94	Spokane, Wa	177,196	171,300	170,516	181,608	161,721	36,848	...
95	Tacoma, Wa	176,664	158,501	154,407	147,979	143,673	37,714	...
96	Little Rock, Ar	175,795	158,461	132,483	107,813	102,213	38,307	2,167
97	Bakersfield, Cal	174,820	105,611	...	56,848	...	...	...
98	Fremont, Ca	173,339	131,945	100,869	43,790	...	...	...
99	Fort Wayne, In.	173,072	172,196	178,269	161,776	133,607	45,115	4,282
100	Newport News, Va	170,045	144,903	138,000	114,000	42,000	...	...

Cities with Largest Percentage Loss in Population, 1980-1990

Source: Bureau of the Census, U.S. Dept. of Commerce, 1990 Census

City	1990	1980	Change
1. Gary, Ind.	116,646	151,968	−23.2%
2. Newark	275,221	329,248	−16.4
3. Detroit	1,027,974	1,203,369	−14.6
4. Pittsburgh	369,879	423,960	−12.8
5. St. Louis	396,685	452,804	−12.4
6. Cleveland	505,616	573,822	−11.9
7. Flint, Mich.	140,761	159,611	−11.8
8. New Orleans	496,938	557,927	−10.9
9. Warren, Mich.	144,864	161,134	−10.1
10. Chattanooga, Tenn.	152,466	169,514	−10.1
11. Louisville, Ky.	269,063	298,694	−9.9
12. Peoria, Ill.	113,504	124,813	−9.1
13. Macon, Ga.	106,612	116,896	−8.8
14. Erie, Pa.	108,718	119,123	−8.7
15. Buffalo	328,123	357,870	−8.3
16. Birmingham, Ala.	265,968	288,297	−7.7
17. Richmond	203,056	219,214	−7.4
18. Chicago	2,783,726	3,005,072	−7.4
19. Atlanta	394,017	425,022	−7.3
20. Kansas City, Kan.	149,767	161,148	−7.1
21. Baltimore	736,014	786,741	−6.4
22. Akron, Ohio	223,019	237,590	−6.1
23. Toledo, Ohio	332,943	354,635	−6.1
24. Philadelphia	1,585,577	1,688,210	−6.1
25. Dayton, Ohio	182,044	193,549	−5.9
26. Knoxville, Tenn.	165,121	175,045	−5.7
27. Memphis	610,337	646,170	−5.5
28. Cincinnati	364,040	385,410	−5.5
29. Denver	467,610	492,694	−5.1
30. District of Columbia	606,900	638,432	−4.9

The 50 Most Racially Diverse Counties in the U.S.

Source: Bureau of the Census, U.S. Dept. of Commerce

(Rank of counties where proportions of non-Hispanic whites, non-Hispanic blacks, Hispanics, and non-Hispanic other races are nearest to being equal; 1990 Census)

Fourteen of the 50 most diverse counties have populations of 1 million or more, and 33 are in metropolitan areas. Four of New York City's five boroughs, as well as the counties that contain San Francisco, Los Angeles, Chicago, Houston, San Diego, Miami, Dallas, Philadelphia, San Jose, San Bernardino, and Oakland are on the list.

Of the 60 counties with populations more than 99.5 percent non-Hispanic white in 1990, 12 are in Nebraska, 12 are in North Dakota, 7 are in Kentucky, and 6 are in South Dakota.

Rank/County	State
1. Queens	New York
2. San Francisco	California
3. Los Angeles	California
4. Kings	New York
5. Alameda	California
6. New York	New York
7. Bronx	New York
8. Hudson	New Jersey
9. Fort Bend	Texas
10. Cibola	New Mexico
11. Harris	Texas
12. Robeson	North Carolina
13. Solano	California
14. Essex	New Jersey
15. Dade	Florida
16. Sandoval	New Mexico
17. Monterey	California
18. Fresno	California
19. San Joaquin	California
20. Santa Clara	California
21. San Mateo	California
22. Cook	Illinois
23. Merced	California
24. Hoke	North Carolina
25. Chattahoochee	Georgia
26. Kings	California
27. Dallas	Texas
28. Suffolk	Massachusetts
29. Hendry	Florida
30. Matagorda	Texas
31. Graham	Arizona
32. Denver	Colorado
33. San Juan	New Mexico
34. San Bernardino	California
35. Socorro	New Mexico
36. Aleutians West Census Area	Alaska
37. Passaic	New Jersey
38. Pinal	Arizona
39. Alexandria (city)	Virginia
40. Waller	Texas
41. Caldwell	Texas
42. San Diego	California
43. Liberty	Georgia
44. Prince George's	Maryland
45. Wharton	Texas
46. Philadelphia	Pennsylvania
47. Bell	Texas
48. Otero	New Mexico
49. Union	New Jersey
50. Coconino	Arizona

1990 Population of U.S. Counties, Under Age 18

Source: Bureau of the Census, U.S. Dept. of Commerce

(Counties with the **highest** share of residents under age 18, among counties of 10,000 or more; 1990 census)

The national average for counties' population under age 18 is 26 percent. Thirty-one percent of the nation's 64 million children are members of minorities, who, on average, have more children than do non-Hispanic whites. However, Utah, with only 8.8 percent minority population, has 11 of the 25 counties with the highest share of children. Sixty-nine percent of Utah residents belong to the Church of Jesus Christ of Latter Day Saints, and the birthrate for Mormon women was 2.5 births per woman in 1987, compared with 1.9 nationwide.

(*continued*)

Rank/County, State	Percent under 18
1. San Juan, Ut.	43.3
2. Emery, Ut.	43.0
3. Duchesne, Ut.	43.0
4. Millard, Ut.	42.9
5. Apache, Az.	41.7
6. Uintah, Ut.	41.4
7. Box Elder, Ut.	40.6
8. Jefferson, Ida.	40.4
9. Davis, Ut.	40.2
10. Uinta, Wy.	39.8
11. Wasatch, Ut.	39.5
12. Starr, Tex.	39.4
13. Sevier, Ut.	39.3
14. Bethel Census Area, Alas.	39.0
15. McKinley, N.M.	38.8
16. Bingham, Ida.	38.6
17. Navajo, Az.	38.4
18. Rolette, N.D.	38.2
19. Lincoln, Wy.	38.1
20. Sanpete, Ut.	38.0
21. Maverick, Tex.	38.0
22. Fremont, Ida.	37.9
23. Utah, Ut.	37.7
24. Glacier, Mont.	37.1
25. Webb, Tex.	36.7
26. Big Horn, Mont.	36.7
27. Hidalgo, Tex.	36.6
28. Cassia, Ida.	36.6
29. Willacy, Tex.	36.6
30. Cache, Ut.	36.5
31. Rosebud, Mont.	36.5
32. Gaines, Tex.	36.4
33. San Juan, N.M.	36.4
34. Dimmit, Tex.	36.3
35. Washington, Ut.	36.2
36. Tooele, Ut.	36.2
37. Holmes, Oh.	35.8
38. Humphreys, Miss.	35.8
39. Zavala, Tex.	35.7
40. Campbell, Wy.	35.7
41. Iron, Ut.	35.5
42. Deaf Smith, Tex.	35.3
43. Matanuska-Susitna Borough, Alas.	35.3
44. Cameron, Tex.	35.3
45. Roosevelt, Mont.	35.2
46. Bonneville, Ida.	35.2
47. Lagrange, Ind.	35.1
48. Minidoka, Ida.	35.1
49. Holmes, Miss.	35.0
50. Frio, Tex.	34.8

(Counties with the **lowest** share of residents under age 18, among counties of 10,000 or more; 1990 Census)

Of the 25 counties with the **lowest** share of children, 3 are adult resort/vacation areas: Williamsburg, Llano, and Pitkin (Aspen); 8 of the counties are popular Florida retirement places, as is Watauga; 4 (New York, San Francisco, Alexandria, and Arlington) are urban areas that contain high concentrations of affluent single residents; and the other 9 are predominantly rural counties dominated by large colleges or universities.

Rank/County, State	Percent under 18
1. Williamsburg (city), Va.	9.2
2. Radford (city), Va.	12.7
3. Arlington, Va.	15.1
4. Alexandria (city), Va.	15.4
5. Charlotte, Fl.	15.6
6. Harrisonburg (city), Va.	15.6
7. Sarasota, Fl.	15.7
8. San Francisco, Cal.	16.1
9. Llano, Tex.	16.4
10. New York, N.Y.	16.6
11. Pitkin, Col.	16.8
12. Watauga, N.C.	17.1
13. Monroe, Fl.	17.4
14. Martin, Fl.	17.6
15. Citrus, Fl.	17.6
16. Whitman, Wash.	17.8
17. Pinellas, Fl.	17.8
18. Pasco, Fl.	17.9
19. Montgomery, Va.	17.9
20. Charlottesville (city), Va.	18.0
21. Centre, Pa.	18.3
22. McDonough, Ill.	18.4
23. Monroe, Ind.	18.4
24. Hernando, Fl.	18.4
25. Fredericksburg (city), Va.	18.6
26. Highlands, Fl.	18.7
27. Amador, Cal.	18.8
28. Orange, N.C.	18.9
29. Jackson, Ill.	19.0
30. Walker, Tex.	19.0
31. Flagler, Fl.	19.1
32. Marin, Cal.	19.1
33. Fairfax (city), Va.	19.2
34. Manatee, Fl.	19.2
35. Hampshire, Mass.	19.3
36. District of Columbia, D.C.	19.3
37. Suffolk, Mass.	19.3
38. Polk, N.C.	19.4
39. Tompkins, N.Y.	19.4
40. Indian River, Fl.	19.4
41. Baxter, Ark.	19.4
42. Calloway, Ky.	19.5
43. Lee, Fl.	19.6
44. Palm Beach, Fl.	19.6
45. Salem (city), Va.	19.7
46. Volusia, Fl.	19.7
47. West Feliciana Parish, La.	19.7
48. Story, Ia.	19.8
49. Johnson, Ill.	19.8
50. Macon, N.C.	19.8

Geographical Mobility Rates, By Type of Movement: 1950-1990

(Numbers in thousands)

Source: Bureau of the Census, U.S. Dept. of Commerce

About 18 percent of Americans changed residence between March 1989 and March 1990. Rates of moving are down from the 1950s and 1960s when 20 percent or more of the population moved every year.

Metropolitan areas have shown modest net inmigration from nonmetropolitan areas during the 1980s. Suburbs gained 6.8 million persons from central cities and nonmetropolitan areas between 1989 and 1990 while losing 3.8 million outmigrants. Central cities gained 3.6 million from inmigration but lost 6.6 million movers.

Mobility period	Total, 1 year old and over	Total movers	Residing in the U.S. at beginning of the period: Total	Different house, same county	Different county: Total	Same State	Different State	Different region	Residing outside the U.S. at beginning of the period
Number									
1989-90	242,208	43,381	41,821	25,726	16,094	8,061	8,033	3,761	1,560
1985-86	232,998	43,237	42,037	26,401	15,636	8,665	6,971	3,778	1,200
1980-81	221,641	38,200	36,887	23,097	13,789	7,614	6,175	3,363	1,313
1975-76	208,069	36,793	35,645	22,399	13,246	7,106	6,140	3,279	1,148
1970-71	201,506	37,705	36,161	23,018	13,143	6,197	6,946	3,936	1,544
1965-66	190,242	37,586	36,703	24,165	12,538	6,275	6,263	3,348	883
1960-61	177,354	36,533	35,535	24,289	11,246	5,493	5,753	3,097	998
1955-56	161,497	34,040	33,098	22,186	10,912	5,859	5,053	(NA)	942
1950-51	148,400	31,464	31,158	20,694	10,464	5,276	5,188	(NA)	306
Percent									
1989-90	100.0	17.9	17.3	10.6	6.6	3.3	3.3	1.6	0.6
1985-86	100.0	18.6	18.0	11.3	6.7	3.7	3.0	1.6	0.5
1980-81	100.0	17.2	16.6	10.4	6.2	3.4	2.8	1.5	0.6
1975-76	100.0	17.7	17.1	10.8	6.4	3.4	3.0	1.6	0.6
1970-71	100.0	18.7	17.9	11.4	6.5	3.1	3.4	2.0	0.8
1965-66	100.0	19.8	19.3	12.7	6.6	3.3	3.3	1.8	0.5
1960-61	100.0	20.6	20.0	13.7	6.3	3.1	3.2	1.7	0.6
1955-56	100.0	21.1	20.5	13.7	6.8	3.6	3.1	(NA)	0.6
1950-51	100.0	21.2	21.0	13.9	7.1	3.6	3.5	(NA)	0.2

NA = Not available.

Poverty by Family Status, Sex, and Race

Source: U.S. Bureau of the Census, Current Population Reports
By thousands

	1990 No.[1]	1990 %[2]	1989 No.[1]	1989 %[2]	1986 No.[1]	1986 %[2]	1978 No.[1]	1978 %[2]
Total poor	**33,585**	**13.5**	**31,528**	**12.8**	**32,370**	**13.6**	**24,497**	**11.4**
In families	25,232	12.0	24,066	11.5	24,754	12.0	19,062	10.0
Head	7,098	10.7	6,784	10.3	7,023	10.9	5,280	9.1
Related children	12,715	19.9	12,001	19.0	12,257	19.8	9,722	15.7
Other relatives	5,419	6.7	5,281	6.6	5,475	6.9	4,509	5.7
Unrelated individuals	**7,446**	**20.7**	**6,760**	**19.2**	**6,846**	**21.6**	**5,435**	**22.1**
In families with a female householder, no husband present	12,578	37.2	11,668	35.9	11,944	38.3	9,269	35.6
Head	3,768	33.4	3,504	32.2	3,613	34.6	2,654	31.4
Related children	7,363	53.4	6,808	51.1	6,943	54.4	5,687	50.6
Other relatives	1,447	16.6	1,356	16.3	1,388	17.5	928	14.6
Unrelated female individuals	4,589	24.0	4,221	22.2	4,311	25.1	3,611	26.0
All other	12,654	7.1	12,398	7.0	12,811	7.3	9,793	5.9
Head	3,330	6.0	3,280	5.9	3,410	6.3	2,626	5.3
Related children	5,352	10.7	5,193	10.4	5,313	10.8	4,035	7.9
Other relatives	3,972	5.5	3,925	5.5	4,087	5.8	3,131	4.8
Unrelated male individuals	**2,857**	**16.9**	**2,539**	**15.7**	**2,536**	**17.5**	**1,824**	**17.1**
Total white poor	**22,326**	**10.7**	**20,785**	**10.0**	**22,183**	**11.0**	**16,259**	**8.7**
In families	15,916	9.0	15,179	8.6	16,393	9.4	12,050	7.3
Head	4,622	8.1	4,409	7.8	4,811	8.6	3,523	6.9
Female	2,010	26.8	1,858	25.4	2,041	28.2	1,391	23.5
Related children	7,696	15.1	7,164	14.1	7,714	15.3	5,674	11.0
Other relatives	3,598	5.2	3,606	5.3	3,868	5.7	2,852	4.5
Unrelated individuals	**5,739**	**18.6**	**5,063**	**16.9**	**5,198**	**19.2**	**4,209**	**19.8**
Total black poor	**9,837**	**31.9**	**9,302**	**30.7**	**8,983**	**31.1**	**7,625**	**30.6**
In families	**8,160**	**31.0**	**7,704**	**29.7**	**7,401**	**29.7**	**6,493**	**29.5**
Head	2,193	24.3	2,077	27.8	1,987	28.0	1,622	27.5
Female	1,648	48.1	1,524	46.5	1,488	50.1	1,208	50.6
Related children	4,412	44.2	4,257	43.2	4,039	42.7	3,781	41.2
Other relatives	1,556	17.6	1,370	15.9	1,375	16.5	1,094	15.7
Unrelated individuals	**1,491**	**35.1**	**1,471**	**35.2**	**1,431**	**38.5**	**1,132**	**38.6**

(1) Beginning in 1979, total includes members of unrelated subfamilies not shown separately. For earlier years, unrelated subfamily members are included in the "in family " category. (2) Percent of total population in that general category who fell below poverty level. For example, of all black female heads of households in 1978, 50.6% were poor.

Poverty Level by Family Size, 1989 and 1990

	1989	1990		1989	1990
1 persons	$ 6,310	$ 6,652	3 persons	$ 9,885	$10,419
Under 65 years	6,451	6,800	4 persons	12,674	13,359
65 years and over	5,947	6,268	5 persons	14,990	15,792
2 persons	8,076	8,509	6 persons	16,921	17,839
Householder under 65 years	8,343	8,794	7 persons	19,162	20,241
Householder 65 years and over	7,501	7,905	8 persons	21,328	22,582
			9 persons or more	25,480	26,848

Income Distribution by Population Fifths

Families, 1990	Top income of each fifth					Percent distribution of total income					
Race	Lowest	Second	Third	Fourth	Top 5%	Lowest fifth	Second fifth	Third fifth	Fourth fifth	Highest fifth	Top 5%
Total	$16,846	$29,044	$42,040	$61,490	$102,358	4.6	10.8	16.6	23.8	44.3	17.4
White	18,656	30,660	43,986	63,020	105,000	5.1	11.1	16.6	23.6	43.6	17.1
Black and other	(NA)	(NA)	(NA)	(NA)	(NA)	(NA)	(NA)	(NA)	(NA)	(NA)	(NA)
Black	8,064	16,251	27,816	43,900	73,506	3.3	8.6	15.6	25.3	47.3	17.3

Persons Below Poverty Level, 1960-1990

	Number Below Poverty Level (mil.)				Percent Below Poverty Level				
Year	All races[1]	White	Black	Hispanic origin[2]	All races[1]	White	Black	Spanish origin[2]	Average income cutoffs for non-farm family of 4[3] at poverty level
1960	39.9	28.3	NA	NA	22.2	17.8	NA	NA	$3,022
1965	33.2	22.5	NA	NA	17.3	13.3	NA	NA	3,223
1970	25.4	17.5	7.5	NA	12.6	9.9	33.5	NA	3,968
1975	25.9	17.8	7.5	3.0	12.3	9.7	31.3	26.9	5,500
1980[4]	29.3	19.7	8.6	3.5	13.0	10.2	32.5	25.7	8,414
1986[4]	32.4	22.2	9.0	5.1	13.6	11.0	31.1	27.3	11,203
1989	31.5	20.8	9.3	5.4	12.8	10.0	30.7	26.2	12,674
1990	33.6	22.3	9.8	6.0	13.5	10.7	31.9	28.1	13,359

NA = Not Available. (1) Includes other races not shown separately. (2) Persons of Spanish origin may be of any race. (3) Beginning in 1981, income cutoffs for nonfarm families are applied to both farm and nonfarm families. (4) Data based on revised poverty definition.

Poverty Rate

The poverty rate is the proportion of the population whose income falls below the government's official poverty level, which is adjusted each year to take account of inflation. The national poverty rate was higher in 1986 than in any year from 1969 through 1980. The rate reached a peak of 15.2 percent in 1983. Nationwide, children living in poverty increased 22 percent in the 1980s.

Aid to Families with Dependent Children

Source: Admin. for Children and Families, Office of Family Assistance, U.S. Dept. of Health and Human Services

FY 1991 State	Total Assistance Payments[1]	Average Monthly Caseload	Average Monthly Recipients	Average Monthly Children	Average Payment per Family	Average Payment per Person
Alabama	$67,657,691	47,465	135,440	96,251	$118.78	$41.63
Alaska	77,454,302	9,416	26,424	16,586	685.48	244.27
Arizona	178,165,986	52,645	150,435	104,848	282.03	98.69
Arkansas	59,594,434	25,998	74,567	53,281	191.02	66.60
California	5,548,946,430	729,170	2,110,168	1,449,824	634.16	219.14
Colorado	149,892,586	38,771	112,273	74,465	322.18	111.26
Connecticut	342,079,740	51,213	142,707	96,174	556.63	199.76
Delaware	32,567,344	9,373	23,639	16,050	289.56	114.81
Dist. of Columbia	97,793,691	21,043	55,739	38,978	387.28	146.21
Florida	521,734,432	166,006	452,045	319,888	261.91	96.18
Georgia	377,406,380	118,406	342,439	238,047	265.62	91.84
Guam	7,118,856	1,183	4,189	2,999	501.29	141.63
Hawaii	107,872,049	14,948	45,555	30,502	601.39	197.33
Idaho	22,183,038	6,784	18,394	12,443	272.48	100.50
Illinois	908,161,120	221,491	671,802	460,066	341.69	112.65
Indiana	193,912,239	61,127	175,844	118,658	264.36	91.90
Iowa	159,866,128	35,150	99,045	64,483	379.01	134.51
Kansas	107,812,711	26,812	79,405	53,442	335.09	113.15
Kentucky	204,357,228	78,308	214,936	139,170	217.47	79.23
Louisiana	188,152,565	92,743	278,587	198,112	169.06	56.28
Maine	112,805,198	22,717	64,249	39,930	413.81	146.31
Maryland	330,702,172	74,140	205,243	138,184	371.71	134.27
Massachusetts	666,575,185	104,914	292,187	186,508	529.46	190.11
Michigan	1,186,125,452	227,639	685,457	447,117	434.21	144.20
Minnesota	372,513,643	60,005	179,749	116,253	517.33	172.70
Mississippi	87,636,347	60,106	177,390	127,816	121.50	41.17
Missouri	255,889,307	76,922	228,134	150,196	277.22	93.47
Montana	41,850,111	10,109	30,420	19,584	345.00	114.64
Nebraska	61,397,527	15,479	45,310	30,878	330.55	112.92
Nevada	32,133,483	9,674	26,611	18,616	276.81	100.63
New Hampshire	45,375,753	8,701	23,393	14,958	434.60	161.65
New Jersey	484,687,043	118,430	336,055	230,104	341.05	120.19
New Mexico	85,959,995	24,093	73,095	47,612	297.32	98.00
New York	2,444,144,818	371,889	1,053,433	703,883	547.69	193.35
North Carolina	299,532,866	105,394	272,245	183,198	236.84	91.69
North Dakota	24,988,556	5,809	16,521	10,841	358.49	126.04
Ohio	935,661,108	238,540	678,810	443,893	326.87	114.87
Oklahoma	152,657,924	42,805	123,892	84,916	297.19	102.68
Oregon	177,278,388	37,698	105,664	69,302	391.88	139.81
Pennsylvania	871,639,962	190,439	562,830	374,996	381.42	129.06
Puerto Rico	75,988,117	60,842	193,844	132,296	104.08	32.67
Rhode Island	118,212,509	19,467	54,389	35,624	506.04	181.12
South Carolina	107,387,925	44,446	125,667	89,724	201.35	71.21
South Dakota	23,561,391	7,010	19,998	14,041	280.10	98.18
Tennessee	196,992,994	87,717	244,168	164,635	187.15	67.23
Texas	474,276,699	239,887	697,343	485,419	164.76	56.68
Utah	70,666,959	16,584	48,338	32,617	355.09	121.83
Vermont	57,006,929	9,173	26,518	16,255	517.90	179.14
Virgin Islands	3,301,413	969	3,541	2,660	283.85	77.70
Virginia	199,608,235	62,235	167,083	114,628	267.28	99.56
Washington	505,732,129	88,389	249,306	160,823	476.80	169.05
West Virginia	114,231,470	38,141	113,622	70,201	249.58	83.78
Wisconsin	447,512,859	80,326	240,326	161,386	464.27	155.18
Wyoming	24,851,687	5,968	17,072	11,390	347.03	121.31
U.S. Total	**$20,441,615,104**	**4,374,708**	**12,595,536**	**8,514,750**	**$389.39**	**$135.24**

(1) Total assistance payments include AFDC-Basic, AFDC-Unemployed Parent, Title IV-A Payments under JOBS, Home repair, and payments to Indian tribes.

1990 Census Count of the Homeless

The Bureau of the Census released results of its Shelter and Street Night (S-Night) operations conducted across the U.S. during the night of March 20-21, 1990, in an effort to include persons in the 1990 census who might not have been counted using standard procedures. Census officials said that the S-Night results and other 1990 census data that will be released in the future will *not* be considered as a count of the U.S. "homeless" population.

The operation found a total of 178,828 persons in emergency shelters for the homeless, and 49,793 persons visible at pre-identified street locations. New York City had the highest count, with 23,383 persons found in emergency shelters and 10,447 persons found in street locations. Other cities which had among the highest counts included Los Angeles, San Francisco, Washington, DC, and Chicago.

The Census Bureau's figures were disputed by almost all of the cities involved in the count. In addition to the cities' claims that the count was substantially below their own estimates, advocates for the homeless found the totals to be useless, especially when compared to previous estimates of 1 million to 3 million for the entire homeless population. In 1987, the Urban Inst., a nonprofit research organization, made an estimate of 500,000 to 600,000 homeless in America.

Immigration by Country of Last Residence 1820-1991

(thousands)

Source: U.S. Immigration and Naturalization Service

Country	Total 1820-1991	Total 1961-1970	Total 1971-1980	Total 1981-1990	1988[10]	1989[11]	1990	1991	Percent 1820-1991	Percent 1961-1970	Percent 1971-1980	Percent 1981-1990
All countries*	**58,821**	**3,321.7**	**4,493.3**	**7,338.0**	**643.0**	**1,090.9**	**1,536.5**	**1,827.2**	**100.0**	**100.0**	**100.0**	**100.0**
Europe	**37,248**	**1,123.5**	**800.4**	**761.5**	**71.8**	**94.3**	**124.0**	**146.7**	**63.3**	**33.8**	**17.8**	**10.4**
Austria[1]	1,832	20.6	9.5	18.9	2.5	2.8	3.8	3.5	3.1	.6	0.2	0.3
Hungary	1,669	5.4	6.6	5.9	0.7	0.7	1.0	0.9	2.8	.2	0.1	0.1
Belgium	211	9.2	5.3	6.6	0.7	0.7	0.8	0.7	0.4	.3	0.1	0.1
Czechoslovakia	146	3.3	6.0	5.4	0.7	0.5	0.6	0.6	0.2	.1	0.1	0.1
Denmark	371	9.2	4.4	2.8	0.6	0.6	0.7	0.6	0.6	.3	0.1	0.1
France	792	45.2	25.1	92.1	3.6	4.1	4.3	4.0	1.3	1.4	0.6	1.3
Germany[1]	7,094	190.8	74.4	159.0	9.7	10.4	12.1	10.9	12.1	5.7	1.7	2.2
Greece	707	86.0	92.4	31.9	4.7	4.6	3.9	2.9	1.2	2.6	2.1	0.4
Ireland	4,730	33.0	11.5	67.2	5.1	7.0	9.7	4.6	8.0	1.0	0.3	0.9
Italy	5,403	214.1	129.4	12.3	5.3	11.1	16.2	30.3	9.2	6.4	2.9	0.2
Netherlands	376	30.6	10.5	4.2	1.2	1.2	1.5	1.3	0.6	.9	0.2	0.1
Norway[9]	802	15.5	3.9	83.2	0.4	0.6	0.6	0.6	1.4	.5	0.1	1.1
Poland[1]	623	53.5	37.2	40.3	7.3	13.3	18.4	17.1	1.1	1.6	0.8	0.5
Portugal	506	76.1	101.7	20.5	3.3	3.9	4.0	4.6	0.9	2.3	2.3	0.3
Spain	288	44.7	39.1	11.1	2.0	2.2	2.7	2.7	0.5	1.3	0.9	0.2
Sweden[9]	1,286	17.1	6.5	8.0	1.2	1.2	1.4	1.2	2.2	.5	0.1	0.1
Switzerland	360	18.5	8.2	57.6	0.9	1.1	1.3	1.0	0.6	.6	0.2	0.8
USSR[1,3]	3,475	2.5	39.0	18.7	1.4	4.6	14.8	31.6	5.9	.1	0.9	0.3
United Kingdom[2]	5,136	213.8	137.4	159.2	14.7	17.0	19.1	16.8	8.7	6.4	3.1	2.2
Yugoslavia	139	20.4	30.5	37.3	2.0	2.5	2.8	2.8	0.2	.6	0.7	0.5
Other Europe	183	9.1	18.9	7.7	0.8	0.7	0.9	1.2	0.3	.2	0.2	0.0
Asia	**6,361**	**427.6**	**1,588.2**	**2,738.1**	**254.7**	**296.4**	**321.9**	**342.2**	**10.8**	**12.9**	**35.2**	**37.3**
China[4]	938[4]	34.8	124.3	298.9	34.3	39.3	40.6	24.0	1.6	1.0	2.8	4.1
Hong Kong	318[4]	75.0	113.5	98.2	11.8	15.2	14.4	15.9	0.5	2.3	2.5	1.3
India	498	27.2	164.1	250.7	25.3	28.6	28.8	42.7	0.8	.8	3.7	3.4
Iran	187[4]	10.3	45.1	116.0	9.8	13.0	14.9	9.9	0.3	.3	1.0	1.6
Israel	143[4]	29.6	37.7	44.2	4.4	5.5	5.9	5.1	0.2	.9	0.8	0.6
Japan	468[4]	40.0	49.8	47.0	5.1	5.4	6.4	5.6	0.8	1.2	1.1	0.6
Korea	668[4]	34.5	267.6	333.8	34.2	33.0	31.0	25.4	1.1	1.0	6.0	4.5
Philippines	1,095[5]	98.4	355.0	548.7	61.0	66.1	71.3	68.8	1.9	3.0	7.9	7.5
Turkey	416	10.1	13.4	23.4	2.2	2.5	3.2	3.5	0.7	.3	0.3	0.3
Vietnam	473[6]	4.3	172.8	281.0	12.8	13.3	14.8	14.8	0.8	1.1	3.8	3.8
Other Asia	1,157	36.5	176.1	631.4	53.7	74.5	90.6	126.4	2.0	1.1	3.8	8.6
America	**14,365**	**1,716.4**	**1,982.5**	**3,615.6**	**294.9**	**672.6**	**1,051.0**	**1,297.6**	**24.4**	**51.7**	**44.3**	**49.3**
Argentina	135[7]	49.7	29.9	27.3	2.6	3.8	6.0	4.2	0.2	1.5	0.7	0.4
Canada	4,316[7]	413.3	169.9	158.0	15.8	18.3	24.6	19.9	7.3	12.4	3.8	2.2
Colombia	315	72.0	77.3	122.9	10.2	14.9	23.8	19.3	0.5	2.2	1.7	1.7
Cuba	758[8]	208.5	264.9	144.6	16.6	9.5	9.4	9.5	1.3	6.3	5.9	2.0
Dominican Rep.	552[7]	93.3	148.1	252.0	27.2	26.7	42.1	42.4	0.9	2.8	3.3	3.4
Ecuador	166[7]	36.8	50.1	56.2	4.7	7.6	12.5	10.0	0.3	1.1	1.1	0.8
El Salvador	322[7]	15.0	34.4	213.5	12.0	57.6	79.6	46.9	0.5	.5	0.8	2.9
Haiti	282[8]	34.5	56.3	138.4	34.8	13.3	19.9	47.0	0.5	1.0	1.3	1.9
Jamaica	452[12]	74.9	137.6	208.1	20.4	23.6	23.7	23.0	0.8	2.3	3.1	2.8
Mexico	4,837[7]	453.9	640.3	1,655.7	95.2	405.6	680.2	947.9	8.2	13.7	14.3	22.6
Other America	2,231	264.4	373.8	639.3	55.3	91.6	128.8	128.4	3.8	7.9	8.3	8.7
Africa	**368**	**29.0**	**80.8**	**176.8**	**17.1**	**22.5**	**32.8**	**33.5**	**0.6**	**.9**	**1.8**	**2.4**
Oceania[13]	**212**	**25.1**	**41.2**	**45.2**	**4.3**	**5.0**	**6.8**	**7.1**	**0.4**	**.8**	**0.9**	**0.6**
Unknown or Not Reported	**268**	**0.1**	**—**	**1.0**	**0.1**	**0.1**	**0.5**	**0.2**	**0.5**	**—**	**—**	**—**

* Figures may not add to total due to rounding. (1) 1938-1945, Austria included with Germany; 1899-1919, Poland included with Austria-Hungary, Germany, and USSR. (2) Beginning 1952, includes data for United Kingdom not specified, formerly included with "Other Europe". (3) Europe and Asia. (4) Prior to 1951, included with "Other Asia". (5) Prior to 1951, Philippines included with "All other". (6) Prior to 1953, data for Vietnam not available. (7) Prior to 1951, included with "Other America". (8) Prior to 1951, included with "West Indies". (9) Norway and Sweden were combined from 1820-1868. (10) First full year with Immigration Reform and Control Act of 1986 in effect. (11) Data include 478,814 previously illegal aliens who were granted permanent resident status under section 245A of the Immigration Reform and Control Act of 1986. These aliens are not new residents of the United States. (12) Data for Jamaica not collected until 1953. (13) Includes Australia and New Zealand.

Immigrants Admitted For Top 10 Metropolitan Areas of Intended Residence: 1991

Source: Immigration and Naturalization Service, U.S. Dept. of Justice

Metropolitan statistical area of intended residence	Total Number	Total Percent
Total	1,827,167	100.00
1. Los Angeles-Long Beach, CA	257,160	14.1
2. New York, NY	163,006	8.9
3. Chicago, IL	60,590	3.3
4. San Diego, CA	59,329	3.2
5. Anaheim-Santa Ana, CA	59,015	3.2
6. Miami-Hialeah, FL	58,918	3.2
7. Houston, TX	53,690	2.9
8. Riverside-San Bernardino, CA	50,608	2.8
9. Dallas, TX	39,352	2.2
10. Washington, DC-MD-VA	36,370	2.0

U.S. Places of 5,000 or More Population—With ZIP and Area Codes

Source: Bureau of the Census; U.S. Commerce Dept., 1990 Census; updated as of April 1992

This listing presents the official 1990 Census counts. They show the official urban population of the United States. "Urban population" is defined as all persons living in (a) places of 5,000 inhabitants or more, incorporated as cities, villages, boroughs (except Alaska), and towns (except in New England, New York, New Jersey, Pennsylvania and Wisconsin), but excluding those persons living in the rural portions of extended cities; (b) unincorporated places of 5,000 inhabitants or more; and (c) other territory, incorporated or unincorporated, included in urbanized areas.

The non-urban portion of an extended city contains one or more areas, each at least 5 square miles in extent and with a population density of less than 100 persons per square mile. The area or areas constitute at least 25 percent of the legal city's land area of a total of 25 square miles or more.

In New England, New York, New Jersey, Pennsylvania, and Wisconsin, minor civil divisions called "towns" often include rural areas and one or more urban areas. Only the urban areas of these "towns" are included here, except in the case of New England where entire town populations, which may include some rural population, are shown; these towns are indicated by italics. Boroughs in Alaska may contain one or more urban areas which are included here. Population in Hawaii is counted by county subdivisions.

(u) means place is unincorporated.

The ZIP Code of each place appears before the name of that place, if it is obtainable. Telephone Area Code appears in parentheses after the name of the state or, if a state has more than one number, after the name of the place.

CAUTION—Where an asterisk (*) appears before the ZIP Code, ask your local postmaster for the correct ZIP Code for a specific address within the place listed.

Note: Due to deadline constraints, zip and area codes for places that reached 5,000 population in 1990 are not included.

Alabama (205)

ZIP code	Place	1990	1980
35007	Alabaster	14,738	7,079
35950	Albertville	14,507	12,039
35010	Alexander City	14,917	13,807
36420	Andalusia	9,269	10,415
36201	Anniston	26,634	29,135
35016	Arab	6,321	6,053
35611	Athens	16,901	14,558
36502	Atmore	8,046	8,789
35954	Attalla	6,859	7,737
36830	Auburn	33,830	28,471
36507	Bay Minette	7,168	7,455
35020	Bessemer	33,497	31,729
*35203	Birmingham	265,965	284,413
35957	Boaz	6,928	7,151
36426	Brewton	5,885	6,680
35215	Center Point(u)	22,658	23,317
36611	Chickasaw	6,649	7,402
35045	Clanton	7,669	5,832
35055	Cullman	13,367	13,084
36362	Daleville	5,117	4,250
36526	Daphne	11,290	3,406
35601	Decatur	48,776	42,002
36732	Demopolis	7,512	7,678
36301	Dothan	53,589	48,750
36330	Enterprise	20,123	18,033
36027	Eufaula	13,220	12,097
35064	Fairfield	12,200	13,242
36532	Fairhope	8,485	7,286
35630	Florence	36,426	37,029
35214	Forestdale(u)	10,395	10,814
35967	Fort Payne	11,838	11,485
36360	Fort Rucker(u)	7,593	8,932
35068	Fultondale	6,400	6,217
*35901	Gadsden	42,523	47,565
35071	Gardendale	9,251	8,005
36037	Greenville	7,492	7,807
35976	Guntersville	7,038	7,041
35570	Hamilton	5,787	5,093
35640	Hartselle	10,795	8,858
35209	Homewood	22,922	21,412
35226	Hoover	39,788	18,996
35020	Hueytown	15,280	13,452
*35804	Huntsville	159,880	142,513
35210	Irondale	9,454	6,510
36545	Jackson	5,819	6,073
36265	Jacksonville	10,283	9,735
35501	Jasper	13,553	11,894
36863	Lanett	8,985	8,922
35094	Leeds	9,946	8,638
35758	Madison	14,792	4,057
35228	Midfield	5,559	6,182
36054	Millbrook	6,046	3,101
*36601	Mobile	196,278	200,452
36460	Monroeville	6,993	5,674
*36104	Montgomery	187,543	177,857
35223	Mountain Brook	19,810	19,718
35660	Muscle Shoals	9,611	8,911
35476	Northport	17,366	14,291
36801	Opelika	22,122	21,896
36467	Opp	6,985	7,204
36203	Oxford	9,362	8,939
36360	Ozark	13,030	13,188
35124	Pelham	9,421	6,759
35125	Pell City	7,945	6,616
36867	Phenix City	25,312	26,928
36272	Piedmont	5,288	5,544
35126	Pinson-Clay-Chalkville(u)	10,987	....
35127	Pleasant Grove	8,458	7,102
36067	Prattville	19,797	18,647
36610	Prichard	34,311	39,541
35901	Rainbow City	7,673	6,299
36274	Roanoke	6,362	5,809
35653	Russellville	7,812	8,195
36201	Saks(u)	11,138	11,118
36571	Saraland	11,751	9,833
36572	Satsuma	5,194	3,822
35768	Scottsboro	13,786	14,758
36701	Selma	23,755	26,684
35660	Sheffield	10,380	11,903
35901	Southside	5,580	5,141
35150	Sylacauga	12,520	12,708
35160	Talladega	18,175	19,128
36045	Tallassee	5,112	4,763
35217	Tarrant City	8,046	8,148
36582	Theodore(u)	6,509	6,392
36619	Tillman's Corner(u)	17,988	15,941
36081	Troy	13,051	13,124
35173	Trussville	8,266	3,507
35401	Tuscaloosa	77,759	75,211
35674	Tuscumbia	8,413	9,137
36083	Tuskegee	12,257	13,327
36858	Valley	8,173	8,946
35216	Vestavia Hills	19,749	15,722

Alaska (907)

ZIP code	Place	1990	1980
*99502	Anchorage	226,338	174,431
99708	College	11,249	4,043
99702	Eielson AFB(u)	5,251	5,232
*99701	Fairbanks	30,843	22,645
99801	Juneau	26,751	19,528
99611	Kenai	6,327	4,324
99901	Ketchikan	8,263	7,198
99615	Kodiak	6,365	4,756
99835	Sitka	8,588	7,803

Arizona (602)

ZIP code	Place	1990	1980
85220	Apache Junction	18,100	9,935
85323	Avondale	16,169	8,168
85603	Bisbee	6,288	7,154
85326	Buckeye	5,038	3,434
86430	Bullhead City	21,951	10,719
86322	Camp Verde	6,243	3,824
85222	Casa Grande	19,082	14,971
*85224	Chandler	90,533	29,673
86503	Chinle(u)	5,059	2,815
85228	Coolidge	6,927	6,851
86326	Cottonwood	5,918	4,550
.....	Cottonwood-Verde Village(u)	7,037	....
85607	Douglas	12,822	13,058
85335	El Mirage	5,001	4,307
85231	Eloy	7,211	6,240

ZIP code	Place	1990	1980
*86001	Flagstaff	45,857	34,743
85232	Florence	7,510	3,391
85726	Flowing Wells	14,013	....
.....	Fortuna Foothills(u)	7,737	....
85268	Fountain Hills	10,030	2,771
85234	Gilbert	29,188	5,717
*85301	Glendale	148,134	97,172
85501	Globe	6,062	6,886
85323	Goodyear	6,258	2,747
85614	Green Valley(u)	13,231	7,999
85283	Guadalupe	5,458	4,506
86401	Kingman	12,722	9,257
86403	Lake Havasu City	24,363	15,909
*85201	Mesa	288,091	152,404
86440	Mohave Valley(u)	6,962	....
.....	New Kingman-Butler(u)	11,627	....
85621	Nogales	19,489	15,683
85737	Oro Valley	6,670	1,489
86040	Page	6,598	4,907
85253	Paradise Valley	11,671	11,085
85541	Payson	8,377	5,068
85345	Peoria	50,618	12,171
*85026	Phoenix	983,403	789,704
86301	Prescott	26,455	19,865
86314	Prescott Valley	8,858	2,284
85546	Safford	7,359	7,010
*85251	Scottsdale	130,069	88,622
86336	Sedona	7,720	5,319
85901	Show Low	5,019	4,298
85635	Sierra Vista	32,983	24,937
85635	Sierra Vista Southeast(u)	9,237	....
85350	Somerton	5,282	3,969
85713	South Tucson	5,093	6,554
*85351	Sun City(u)	38,126	40,505
85375	Sun City West(u)	15,997	3,772
85248	Sun Lakes(u)	6,578	....
85374	Surprise	7,122	3,723
*85282	Tempe	141,865	106,919
86045	Tuba City(u)	7,323	5,045
*85726	Tucson	405,390	330,537
86047	Winslow	9,095	7,921
*85364	Yuma	54,923	42,481

Arkansas (501)

ZIP code	Place	1990	1980
71923	Arkadelphia	10,014	10,005
71822	Ashdown	5,150	4,218
72501	Batesville	9,187	8,447
72714	Bella Vista(u)	9,083	2,589
72015	Benton	18,177	17,717
72712	Bentonville	11,257	8,756
72315	Blytheville	23,002	23,844
72022	Bryant	5,269	2,682
72023	Cabot	8,319	4,806
71701	Camden	14,701	15,356
72830	Clarksville	5,833	5,237
72032	Conway	26,481	20,375
71635	Crossett	6,282	6,706
71639	Dumas	5,520	6,091
71730	El Dorado	23,146	25,270
72701	Fayetteville	42,099	36,608
72335	Forrest City	13,364	13,803
72901	Fort Smith	72,798	71,626
72601	Harrison	9,936	9,567
72543	Heber Springs	5,628	4,589
72342	Helena	7,491	9,598
71801	Hope	9,768	10,290
71901	Hot Springs	32,462	35,781
71909	Hot Springs Village(u)	6,361	2,083
72076	Jacksonville	29,101	27,589
72401	Jonesboro	46,535	31,530
*72201	Little Rock	175,727	159,151
71753	Magnolia	11,151	11,909
72104	Malvern	9,236	10,163
72360	Marianna	6,033	6,220
72113	Maumelle	6,714	1,368
71953	Mena	5,475	5,154
71655	Monticello	8,116	8,259
72110	Morrilton	6,551	7,355
72653	Mountain Home	9,027	8,066
72112	Newport	7,459	8,339
*72114	North Little Rock	61,829	64,388
72370	Osceola	8,930	8,881
72450	Paragould	18,540	15,248
71601	Pine Bluff	57,140	56,636
72455	Pocahontas	6,151	5,995
72756	Rogers	24,692	17,429
72801	Russellville	21,260	14,518
72143	Searcy	15,180	13,612
72116	Sherwood	18,878	10,423
72761	Siloam Springs	8,151	7,940
72764	Springdale	29,941	23,458
72160	Stuttgart	10,420	10,941
75502	Texarkana	22,631	21,459
72472	Trumann	6,346	6,395
72956	Van Buren	14,979	12,020
71671	Warren	6,455	7,646
72390	West Helena	10,137	11,367
72301	West Memphis	28,259	28,138
72396	Wynne	8,817	7,927

California

ZIP code	Place	Area code	1990	1980
94501	Adelanto		8,517	2,164
91301	Agoura Hills	(818)	20,390	11,399
94501	Alameda	(510)	73,979	63,852
94507	Alamo(u)	(510)	12,277	8,505
94706	Albany	(510)	16,327	15,130
*91802	Alhambra	(818)	82,106	64,767
92656	Aliso Viejo(u)		7,612	....
90249	Alondra Park(u)	(310)	12,215	12,096
91901	Alpine(u)	(619)	9,695	5,368
91001	Altadena(u)	(818)	42,658	40,510
95945	Alta Sierra(u)		5,709	2,168
94590	American Canyon(u)	(707)	7,706	5,712
*92803	Anaheim	(714)	266,406	219,494
96007	Anderson	(916)	8,299	7,381
94509	Antioch	(510)	62,195	42,683
92307	Apple Valley	(619)	46,079	16,748
95003	Aptos(u)	(408)	9,061	7,039
91006	Arcadia	(818)	48,284	45,993
95521	Arcata	(707)	15,197	12,849
95825	Arden-Arcade(u)	(916)	92,040	87,570
93420	Arroyo Grande	(805)	14,378	11,290
90701	Artesia	(310)	15,464	14,301
93203	Arvin	(805)	9,286	6,863
94577	Ashland(u)	(510)	16,590	13,893
93422	Atascadero	(805)	23,138	16,232
94025	Atherton	(415)	7,163	7,797
95301	Atwater	(209)	22,282	17,530
95603	Auburn	(916)	10,592	7,540
92505	August(u)	(714)	6,376	5,445
93204	Avenal		9,770	4,137
91746	Avocado Heights(u)	(818)	14,232	11,721
91702	Azusa	(818)	41,333	29,380
*93302	Bakersfield	(805)	174,820	105,611
91706	Baldwin Park	(818)	69,330	50,554
92220	Banning	(714)	20,570	14,020
92311	Barstow	(619)	21,472	17,690
93402	Baywood-Los Osos(u)	(805)	14,377	10,933
95903	Beale AFB East(u)	(916)	6,912	6,329
92223	Beaumont	(714)	9,685	6,818
90201	Bell	(213)	34,365	25,450
90706	Bellflower	(310)	61,815	53,441
90201	Bell Gardens	(213)	42,355	34,117
94002	Belmont	(415)	24,127	24,505
94510	Benicia	(707)	24,437	15,376
95005	Ben Lomond(u)	(408)	7,884	7,238
*94704	Berkeley	(510)	102,724	103,328
*90213	Beverly Hills	(310)	31,971	32,646
92314	Big Bear Lake	(714)	5,351	4,896
94506	Black Hawk(u)		6,199	....
92316	Bloomington(u)	(714)	15,116	12,781
92225	Blythe	(619)	8,428	6,805
.....	Bonadella Ranchos-Madera Ranchos(u)		5,705	3,272
91902	Bonita(u)	(619)	12,542	6,257
92021	Bostonia(u)		13,670	....
95006	Boulder Creek(u)	(408)	6,725	5,662
95416	Boyes Hot Springs(u)		5,973	4,177
92227	Brawley	(619)	18,923	14,946
92621	Brea	(714)	32,873	27,913
94513	Brentwood	(510)	7,563	4,434
*90620	Buena Park	(714)	68,784	64,165
*91505	Burbank	(818)	93,643	84,625
94010	Burlingame	(415)	26,666	26,173
92231	Calexico	(619)	18,633	14,412
93505	California City		5,955	2,743
93010	Camarillo	(805)	52,303	37,797
93428	Cambria		5,382	3,061
95682	Cameron Park(u)	(916)	11,897	5,607
95008	Campbell	(408)	36,048	26,843
92055	Camp Pendleton North(u)	(714)	10,373	2,065
92055	Camp Pendleton South(u)	(714)	11,299	7,952
92380	Canyon Lake(u)		7,938	2,039
95010	Capitola	(408)	10,171	9,095
*92008	Carlsbad	(619)	63,126	35,490
95608	Carmichael(u)	(916)	48,702	43,108
93013	Carpinteria	(805)	13,747	10,835
90744	Carson	(310)	83,995	81,221
92077	Casa de Oro-Mt. Helix(u)	(619)	30,727	19,651
94546	Castro Valley(u)	(510)	48,619	44,011
95012	Castroville	(408)	5,272	4,396
92235	Cathedral City	(619)	30,085	11,096
95307	Ceres	(209)	26,314	13,281
90701	Cerritos	(310)	53,244	53,020
91724	Charter Oak(u)	(818)	8,858	6,840
94541	Cherryland(u)	(415)	11,088	9,425
92223	Cherry Valley(u)	(714)	5,945	5,012
95926	Chico	(916)	40,079	26,716
91710	Chino	(714)	59,682	40,165
91709	Chino Hills		27,608	....
93610	Chowchilla	(209)	5,930	5,122
*91910	Chula Vista	(619)	135,163	83,927

ZIP code	Place		1990	1980
95610	Citrus(u)	(916)	9,481	12,450
*95610	Citrus Heights(u)	(916)	107,439	85,911
91711	Claremont	(714)	32,503	31,028
94517	Clayton		7,317	4,325
95422	Clearlake		11,804	8,343
93612	Clovis	(209)	50,323	33,021
92236	Coachella	(619)	16,896	9,129
93210	Coalinga	(209)	8,212	6,593
92324	Colton	(714)	40,273	21,310
90022	Commerce	(310)	12,135	10,509
*90220	Compton	(310)	90,454	81,350
*94520	Concord	(510)	111,348	103,763
93212	Corcoran	(209)	13,364	6,454
96021	Corning	(916)	5,870	4,745
91720	Corona	(714)	76,095	37,791
92118	Coronado	(619)	26,540	18,790
94925	Corte Madera	(415)	8,272	8,074
*92626	Costa Mesa	(714)	96,357	82,562
94927	Cotati	(707)	5,714	3,346
94556	Country Club(u)	(209)	9,325	9,585
*91722	Covina	(818)	43,207	32,746
92325	Crestline(u)	(714)	8,594	6,715
90201	Cudahy	(213)	22,817	18,275
*90230	Culver City	(310)	38,793	38,139
95014	Cupertino	(408)	39,967	34,297
90630	Cypress	(714)	42,655	40,738
*94017	Daly City	(415)	92,311	78,519
92629	Dana Point	(714)	31,896	21,271
*94526	Danville	(510)	31,306	26,143
95616	Davis	(916)	46,322	36,640
90250	Del Aire(u)	(310)	8,040	8,487
93215	Delano	(805)	22,762	16,491
.....	Del Monte Forest(u)		5,069	....
92240	Desert Hot Springs	(619)	11,668	5,941
91765	Diamond Bar	(714)	53,672	30,736
93618	Dinuba	(209)	12,743	9,907
94514	Discovery Bay(u)		5,351	1,326
95620	Dixon	(916)	10,401	7,541
*90241	Downey	(310)	91,4444	82,602
91010	Duarte	(818)	20,688	16,766
94568	Dublin	(510)	23,229	13,496
93219	Earlimart(u)	(805)	5,881	4,578
90220	East Compton(u)	(310)	7,967	6,435
.....	East Foothills(u)		14,898	....
92343	East Hemet(u)	(714)	17,611	14,712
90638	East La Mirada(u)	(310)	9,367	9,688
90022	East Los Angeles(u)	(310)	126,379	110,017
94303	East Palo Alto	(415)	23,451	18,106
91117	East Pasadena(u)		5,910	....
93257	East Porterville(u)	(209)	5,790	5,218
.....	East San Gabriel(u)		12,736	....
93523	Edwards AFB(u)	(805)	7,423	8,554
*92020	El Cajon	(619)	88,693	73,892
92243	El Centro	(619)	31,405	23,996
94530	El Cerrito	(510)	22,869	22,731
95630	El Dorado Hills(u)		6,395	....
95624	Elk Grove(u)	(916)	17,483	10,959
*91734	El Monte	(818)	106,162	79,494
93446	El Paso de Robles	(310)	18,583	9,163
93030	El Rio(u)	(805)	6,419	5,674
90245	El Segundo	(310)	15,223	13,752
94803	El Sobrante(u)	(510)	9,852	10,535
92630	El Toro(u)	(714)	62,685	38,153
92709	El Toro Station(u)	(714)	6,869	7,632
94608	Emeryville	(510)	5,740	3,714
92024	Encinitas	(619)	55,386	36,550
*92025	Escondido	(619)	108,635	64,355
95501	Eureka	(707)	27,025	24,153
93221	Exeter	(209)	7,276	5,606
94930	Fairfax	(415)	6,931	7,391
94533	Fairfield	(707)	78,651	58,099
95628	Fair Oaks(u)	(916)	26,867	22,602
93238	Fairview(u)		9,045	....
92028	Fallbrook(u)	(619)	22,095	14,041
93223	Farmersville	(209)	6,235	5,544
95018	Felton	(408)	5,350	4,564
93015	Fillmore	(805)	11,992	9,602
90001	Florence-Graham(u)	(213)	57,147	48,662
95828	Florin(u)	(916)	24,330	16,523
95630	Folsom	(916)	29,802	11,003
*92335	Fontana	(714)	87,535	36,804
95841	Foothill Farms(u)	(916)	17,135	13,700
95437	Fort Bragg	(707)	6,078	5,019
95540	Fortuna	(707)	8,788	7,591
94404	Foster City	(415)	28,176	23,287
92708	Fountain Valley	(714)	53,691	55,080
95019	Freedom(u)	(408)	8,361	6,416
*94536	Fremont	(510)	173,339	131,945
*93706	Fresno	(209)	354,202	217,491
*92631	Fullerton	(714)	114,144	102,246
95632	Galt	(209)	8,889	5,514
*90247	Gardena	(310)	49,847	45,165
95205	Garden Acres(u)	(213)	8,547	7,361
*92640	Garden Grove	(714)	143,050	123,307
92392	George AFB(u)	(619)	5,085	7,061
95020	Gilroy	(408)	31,487	21,641
92509	Glen Avon(u)	(714)	12,663	8,444
*91209	Glendale	(818)	180,038	139,060
91740	Glendora	(818)	47,832	38,500

ZIP code	Place		1990	1980
93561	Golden Hills(u)		5,423	....
92324	Grand Terrace	(714)	10,946	8,498
95945	Grass Valley	(916)	9,048	6,697
93308	Greenacres(u)	(805)	7,379	5,381
93927	Greenfield	(805)	7,464	4,181
93433	Grover City	(805)	11,602	8,827
93434	Guadalupe		5,479	3,629
91745	Hacienda Heights(u)	(818)	52,354	49,422
94019	Half Moon Bay	(415)	8,886	7,282
93230	Hanford	(209)	30,897	20,958
90716	Hawaiian Gardens	(213)	13,639	10,548
90250	Hawthorne	(310)	71,349	56,437
*94544	Hayward	(510)	111,498	93,585
95448	Healdsburg	(707)	9,469	7,217
92343	Hemet	(714)	36,094	22,531
94547	Hercules	(415)	16,829	5,963
90254	Hermosa Beach	(310)	18,219	18,070
92345	Hesperia	(619)	50,418	20,612
92346	Highland	(714)	34,439	21,720
94010	Hillsborough	(415)	10,667	10,372
95023	Hollister	(408)	19,212	11,488
91720	Home Gardens(u)	(714)	7,780	5,783
*92647	Huntington Beach	(714)	181,519	170,505
90255	Huntington Park	(213)	56,065	45,932
91932	Imperial Beach	(619)	26,512	22,689
92201	Indio	(619)	36,793	21,611
*90306	Inglewood	(310)	109,602	94,162
.....	Interlaken(u)		6,404	....
95640	Ione		6,516	2,207
*92711	Irvine	(714)	110,330	62,134
93117	Isla Vista(u)	(805)	20,395	....
94904	Kentfield(u)	(415)	6,030	....
93630	Kerman	(209)	5,448	4,002
93930	King City	(408)	7,634	5,495
93631	Kingsburg	(209)	7,205	5,115
91011	La Canada-Flintridge	(818)	19,378	20,153
91214	La Crescenta-Montrose(u)	(818)	16,968	16,531
90045	Ladera Heights(u)	(310)	6,316	6,647
94549	Lafayette	(510)	23,366	20,837
.....	Laguna(u)		9,828	....
*92651	Laguna Beach	(714)	23,170	17,858
92653	Laguna Hills(u)	(714)	46,731	33,600
92677	Laguna Niguel	(714)	44,400	12,237
90631	La Habra	(310)	51,266	45,232
.....	La Habra Heights		6,226	4,786
92352	Lake Arrowhead(u)	(714)	6,539	6,272
92330	Lake Elsinore	(714)	18,285	5,982
92530	Lakeland Village(u)		5,159	2,796
93535	Lake Los Angeles(u)		7,977	....
92040	Lakeside(u)	(619)	39,412	23,921
*90714	Lakewood	(310)	73,553	74,511
91941	La Mesa	(619)	52,931	50,308
90638	La Mirada	(714)	40,452	40,986
93241	Lamont(u)	(805)	11,517	9,616
93534	Lancaster	(805)	97,291	48,027
90624	La Palma	(714)	15,392	15,399
91747	La Puente	(818)	36,955	30,882
92253	La Quinta		11,215	4,027
.....	La Riviera(u)	(916)	10,986	10,906
95403	Larkfield-Wikiup(u)		6,779	....
94939	Larkspur	(415)	11,068	11,064
95330	Lathrop		6,841	4,112
91750	La Verne	(714)	30,861	23,508
90260	Lawndale	(310)	27,331	23,460
91945	Lemon Grove	(619)	23,984	20,780
93245	Lemoore	(209)	13,622	8,832
90304	Lennox(u)	(310)	22,757	18,445
95207	Lincoln Village(u)	(916)	7,248	4,132
95901	Linda(u)	(916)	13,033	10,225
93247	Lindsay	(209)	8,338	6,936
95062	Live Oak(u)	(916)	15,212	11,482
94550	Livermore	(415)	56,741	48,349
95334	Livingston	(209)	7,317	5,326
*95240	Lodi	(209)	51,874	35,221
92354	Loma Linda	(714)	18,470	10,694
90717	Lomita	(213)	19,382	18,807
93436	Lompoc	(805)	37,649	26,267
*90801	Long Beach	(310)	429,321	361,498
95650	Loomis		5,705	3,663
90720	Los Alamitos	(310)	11,788	11,529
94022	Los Altos	(415)	26,599	25,769
94022	Los Altos Hills	(415)	7,514	7,421
*90052	Los Angeles	(213)	3,485,398	2,968,528
93635	Los Banos	(209)	14,519	10,341
95030	Los Gatos	(408)	27,357	26,906
91709	Los Serranos(u)		7,099	....
94903	Lucas Valley-Marinwood(u)	(415)	5,982	6,409
90262	Lynwood	(310)	61,945	48,289
93250	Mc Farland	(805)	7,005	5,151
95521	McKinleyville(u)	(707)	10,749	7,772
93637	Madera	(209)	29,281	21,732
.....	Madera Acres(u)		5,245	2,173
95954	Magalia(u)		8,987	....
90266	Manhattan Beach	(310)	32,063	31,542
95336	Manteca	(209)	40,773	24,925
92518	March AFB(u)	(714)	5,523	3,607
93933	Marina	(408)	26,512	20,647
90292	Marina Del Rey(u)	(310)	7,431	8,065
94553	Martinez	(510)	31,808	22,582

ZIP code	Place	Area code	1990	1980
95901	Marysville	(916)	12,324	9,898
90270	Maywood	(213)	27,850	21,810
93640	Mendota	(209)	6,821	5,038
94025	Menlo Park	(415)	28,040	26,438
92359	Mentone(u)	(714)	5,675	....
*95340	Merced	(209)	56,216	36,423
94030	Millbrae	(415)	20,414	20,058
94941	Mill Valley	(415)	13,038	12,967
95035	Milpitas	(408)	50,686	37,820
91752	Mira Loma(u)	(714)	15,786	8,707
93641	Mira Monte(u)		7,744	....
92675	Mission Viejo	(714)	72,820	48,503
*95350	Modesto	(209)	164,730	106,963
91016	Monrovia	(818)	35,761	30,531
91763	Montclair	(714)	28,434	22,628
90640	Montebello	(213)	59,564	52,929
93940	Monterey	(408)	31,954	27,558
91754	Monterey Park	(818)	60,738	54,338
93020	Moorpark	(805)	25,494	7,798
94556	Moraga	(510)	15,987	15,014
*92303	Moreno Valley	(714)	118,779	28,139
95037	Morgan Hill	(408)	23,928	17,060
93442	Morro Bay	(805)	9,664	9,064
*94042	Mountain View	(415)	67,460	58,655
92405	Muscoy(u)	(714)	7,541	6,188
94558	Napa	(707)	61,842	50,879
91950	National City	(619)	54,249	48,772
92363	Needles	(619)	5,191	4,120
94560	Newark	(510)	37,861	32,126
*92660	Newport Beach	(714)	66,643	62,556
93444	Nipomo(u)	(805)	7,109	5,247
91760	Norco	(714)	23,302	19,732
95603	North Auburn(u)	(916)	10,301	7,619
94025	North Fair Oaks(u)	(415)	13,912	10,308
95660	North Highlands(u)	(916)	42,105	37,825
90650	Norwalk	(310)	94,279	84,901
94947	Novato	(415)	47,585	43,916
95361	Oakdale	(209)	11,961	8,474
*94615	Oakland	(510)	372,242	339,337
94561	Oakley(u)		18,374	2,816
93445	Oceano(u)		6,169	4,478
*92054	Oceanside	(619)	128,398	76,698
93308	Oildale(u)	(805)	26,553	23,382
93023	Ojai	(805)	7,613	6,816
95961	Olivehurst(u)	(916)	9,738	8,929
*91761	Ontario	(714)	133,179	88,820
95060	Opal Cliffs(u)	(408)	5,940	5,041
*92667	Orange	(714)	110,658	91,450
93646	Orange Cove	(209)	5,604	4,026
95662	Orangevale(u)	(916)	26,266	20,585
94563	Orinda	(510)	16,642	17,030
95963	Orland	(916)	5,052	4,031
93647	Orosi(u)		5,486	4,076
95965	Oroville	(916)	11,960	8,683
.....	Oroville East(u)		8,462	....
*93030	Oxnard	(805)	142,216	108,195
94044	Pacifica	(415)	37,670	36,866
93950	Pacific Grove	(408)	16,117	15,755
95968	Palermo(u)		5,260	2,572
93550	Palmdale	(805)	68,842	12,277
92260	Palm Desert	(619)	23,252	11,801
.....	Palm Desert Country(u)		5,626	....
92262	Palm Springs	(619)	40,144	32,359
*94302	Palo Alto	(415)	55,900	55,225
90274	Palos Verdes Estates	(310)	13,512	14,376
95969	Paradise	(916)	25,408	22,571
90723	Paramount	(310)	47,669	36,407
95823	Parkway-So. Sacramento(u)	(916)	31,903	26,815
93648	Parlier	(209)	7,938	2,902
*91109	Pasadena	(818)	131,591	118,072
95363	Patterson	(209)	8,626	3,908
92509	Pedley(u)		8,869	....
92370	Perris	(714)	21,460	6,827
94952	Petaluma	(707)	43,184	33,834
90660	Pico Rivera	(310)	59,177	53,387
94611	Piedmont	(510)	10,602	10,498
94564	Pinole	(510)	17,460	14,253
93449	Pismo Beach	(805)	7,669	5,364
94565	Pittsburg	(510)	47,607	33,465
92670	Placentia	(714)	41,259	35,041
95667	Placerville	(916)	8,355	6,739
94523	Pleasant Hill	(510)	31,585	25,547
*94566	Pleasanton	(510)	50,570	35,160
*91766	Pomona	(714)	131,723	92,742
93257	Porterville	(209)	29,563	19707
93041	Port Hueneme	(805)	20,319	17,803
92064	Poway	(619)	43,516	33,439
93907	Prunedale(u)		7,393	....
93534	Quartz Hill(u)	(805)	9,626	7,421
92065	Ramona(u)	(619)	13,040	8,173
95670	Rancho Cordova(u)	(916)	48,731	42,881
91730	Rancho Cucamonga	(714)	101,409	55,250
92270	Rancho Mirage	(619)	9,778	6,281
90274	Rancho Palos Verdes	(310)	41,659	36,577
.....	Rancho San Diego(u)		6,977	....
92688	Rancho Santa Margarita(u)		11,390	....
96080	Red Bluff	(916)	12,363	9,490
96001	Redding	(916)	66,462	42,103
92373	Redlands	(714)	60,394	43,619
*90277	Redondo Beach	(310)	60,167	57,102
*94064	Redwood City	(415)	66,072	54,951
93654	Reedley	(209)	15,791	11,071
92376	Rialto	(714)	72,388	37,862
*94802	Richmond	(510)	87,425	74,676
93555	Ridgecrest	(619)	28,295	15,929
95003	Rio Del Mar(u)	(408)	8,919	7,067
95673	Rio Linda(u)	(916)	9,481	7,359
95366	Ripon	(209)	7,455	3,509
95367	Riverbank	(209)	8,547	5,695
*92502	Riverside	(714)	226,505	170,591
95677	Rocklin	(916)	19,033	7,344
94572	Rodeo(u)	(415)	7,589	8,286
94928	Rohnert Park	(707)	36,326	22,965
90274	Rolling Hills Estates	(310)	7,789	7,701
93560	Rosamond(u)	(805)	7,430	2,869
95401	Roseland(u)	(707)	8,779	7,915
91770	Rosemead	(818)	51,638	42,604
95826	Rosemont(u)	(916)	22,851	18,888
95678	Roseville	(916)	44,685	24,347
90720	Rossmoor(u)	(310)	9,893	10,457
91745	Rowland Heights(u)	(818)	42,647	28,252
92509	Rubidoux(u)	(714)	24,367	16,763
*95813	Sacramento	(916)	369,365	275,741
93901	Salinas	(408)	108,777	80,479
94960	San Anselmo	(415)	11,743	12,067
*92403	San Bernardino	(714)	164,164	118,794
94066	San Bruno	(415)	38,961	35,417
93001	San Buenaventura (Ventura)	(805)	92,575	73,774
94070	San Carlos	(415)	26,167	24,710
92672	San Clemente	(714)	41,100	27,325
*92109	San Diego	(619)	1,110,554	875,538
.....	San Diego Country Estates(u)		6,874	....
91773	San Dimas	(714)	32,402	24,014
*91340	San Fernando	(818)	22,580	17,731
*94101	San Francisco	(415)	723,959	678,974
91776	San Gabriel	(818)	37,120	30,072
93657	Sanger	(209)	16,839	12,542
92383	San Jacinto	(714)	16,210	7,098
*95101	San Jose	(408)	782,248	629,400
92375	San Juan Capistrano	(714)	26,183	18,959
*94577	San Leandro	(510)	68,223	63,952
94580	San Lorenzo(u)	(510)	19,987	20,545
93401	San Luis Obispo	(805)	41,958	34,252
92069	San Marcos	(619)	38,974	17,479
91108	San Marino	(818)	12,959	13,307
*94402	San Mateo	(415)	85,619	77,640
94806	San Pablo	(510)	25,158	19,750
*94901	San Rafael	(415)	48,415	44,700
94583	San Ramon	(510)	35,303	20,511
*92711	Santa Ana	(714)	293,742	204,023
*93102	Santa Barbara	(805)	85,571	74,414
*95050	Santa Clara	(408)	93,613	87,700
*91380	Santa Clarita	(805)	110,642	66,730
95060	Santa Cruz	(408)	49,711	41,483
90670	Santa Fe Springs	(310)	15,520	14,520
93454	Santa Maria	(805)	61,284	39,685
*90406	Santa Monica	(310)	86,905	88,314
93060	Santa Paula	(805)	25,062	20,658
*95402	Santa Rosa	(707)	113,313	82,658
92071	Santee	(714)	52,902	40,298
95070	Saratoga	(408)	28,061	29,261
94965	Sausalito	(415)	7,152	7,338
95066	Scotts Valley	(408)	8,667	6,891
90740	Seal Beach	(310)	25,098	25,975
93955	Seaside	(408)	38,826	36,567
95472	Sebastopol	(707)	7,004	5,595
93662	Selma	(209)	14,757	10,942
93263	Shafter	(805)	8,409	7,010
91024	Sierra Madre	(818)	10,762	10,837
90806	Signal Hill	(310)	8,371	5,734
*93065	Simi Valley	(805)	100,217	77,500
92075	Solana Beach	(619)	12,968	12,250
93960	Soledad	(408)	7,146	5,928
95476	Sonoma	(707)	8,121	6,054
95073	Soquel(u)	(408)	9,188	6,212
91733	South El Monte	(213)	20,850	16,623
90280	South Gate	(213)	86,284	66,784
95705	South Lake Tahoe	(916)	21,586	20,681
95965	South Oroville(u)	(916)	7,463	7,246
91030	South Pasadena	(818)	23,936	22,681
94080	South San Francisco	(415)	54,312	49,393
91770	South San Gabriel(u)	(213)	7,700	5,421
91744	South San Jose Hills(u)	(818)	17,814	16,049
90605	South Whittier(u)	(310)	49,514	43,815
95991	South Yuba(u)	(916)	8,816	7,530
*91979	Spring Valley(u)	(619)	55,331	40,191
94305	Stanford(u)	(415)	18,097	11,045
90680	Stanton	(714)	30,491	23,723
*95204	Stockton	(209)	210,943	148,283
94585	Suisun City	(707)	22,686	11,087
92381	Sun City(u)	(714)	14,930	8,460
*94086	Sunnyvale	(408)	117,229	106,618
96130	Susanville	(916)	7,279	6,520
93268	Taft	(805)	5,902	5,316
94941	Tamalpais-Homestead Valley(u)	(415)	9,601	8,511
93561	Tehachapi	(805)	6,182	4,126
92390	Temecula		27,099	4,289

ZIP code	Place		1990	1980
91780	Temple City	(818)	31,153	28,972
95965	Thermalito(u)		5,646	4,961
*91360	Thousand Oaks	(805)	104,352	77,072
94920	Tiburon	(415)	7,532	6,685
*90510	Torrance	(310)	133,107	129,881
95396	Tracy	(209)	33,558	18,428
93274	Tulare	(209)	33,249	22,530
95380	Turlock	(209)	42,198	26,287
92680	Tustin	(714)	50,689	32,248
92705	Tustin Foothills(u)	(714)	24,358	26,174
92277	Twentynine Palms	(619)	11,821	8,802
92278	Twentynine Palms Base(u)	(619)	10,606	7,079
.....	Twin Lakes(u)		5,379	4,502
95482	Ukiah	(707)	14,599	12,035
94587	Union City	(510)	53,762	39,406
91786	Upland	(714)	63,374	47,647
*95688	Vacaville	(707)	71,479	43,367
91744	Valinda(u)	(818)	18,735	18,700
*94590	Vallejo	(707)	109,199	80,303
92343	Valle Vista(u)	(714)	8,751	5,474
93437	Vandenberg AFB(u)	(805)	9,846	5,839
93436	Vandenberg Village(u)	(805)	5,971	5,839
92392	Victorville	(619)	40,674	14,220
90043	View Park-Windsor Hills(u)	(310)	11,769	12,101
92667	Villa Park	(714)	6,299	7,137
.....	Vincent(u)		13,713	....
93277	Visalia	(209)	75,636	49,729
92083	Vista	(619)	71,872	35,834
*91789	Walnut	(714)	29,105	12,478
*94596	Walnut Creek	(510)	60,569	54,033
90255	Walnut Park(u)	(310)	14,722	11,811
93280	Wasco	(805)	12,412	9,613
95076	Watsonville	(408)	31,099	23,662
90044	West Athens(u)	(310)	8,859	8,531
90502	West Carson(u)	(310)	20,143	17,997
90247	West Compton(u)	(310)	5,451	5,907
*91793	West Covina	(818)	96,086	80,292
90069	West Hollywood	(310)	36,118	35,754
91359	Westlake Village		7,455	6,130
92683	Westminster	(714)	78,118	71,133
90047	Westmont(u)	(213)	31,044	27,916
94565	West Pittsburg(u)	(510)	17,453	8,773
91746	West Puente Valley(u)	(818)	20,254	20,445
95691	West Sacramento	(916)	28,898	24,482
*90606	West Whittier-Los Nietos(u)	(310)	24,164	21,001
*90605	Whittier	(310)	77,671	68,558
92395	Wildomar(u)		10,411	....
95429	Willits	(707)	5,027	4,008
90222	Willowbrook(u)	(213)	32,772	30,845
95988	Willows	(916)	5,988	4,777
95492	Windsor(u)		13,371	....
95388	Winton(u)		7,559	4,995
92502	Woodcrest(u)		7,796	....
93286	Woodlake	(209)	5,678	4,343
95695	Woodland	(916)	40,230	30,235
94062	Woodside	(415)	5,034	5,291
92686	Yorba Linda	(714)	52,422	28,254
96097	Yreka City	(916)	6,948	5,916
95991	Yuba City	(916)	27,437	18,736
92399	Yucaipa(u)	(714)	32,824	27,654
92284	Yucca Valley(u)	(619)	13,701	8,294

Colorado

ZIP code	Place		1990	1980
80840	Air Force Academy	(719)	9,062	8,655
81101	Alamosa	(719)	7,579	6,830
80401	Applewood(u)	(303)	11,069	12,040
*80001	Arvada	(303)	89,235	84,576
81611	Aspen	(303)	5,049	3,678
*80010	Aurora	(303)	222,103	158,588
.....	Black Forest(u)	(719)	8,143	3,372
*80302	Boulder	(303)	83,312	76,685
80601	Brighton	(303)	14,203	12,773
80020	Broomfield	(303)	24,638	20,730
81212	Canon City	(719)	12,687	13,037
80104	Castle Rock	(303)	8,708	3,921
.....	Castlewood(u)	(303)	24,392	16,413
80110	Cherry Hills Village	(303)	5,245	5,127
81220	Cimarron Hills	(719)	11,160	6,597
81520	Clifton	(303)	12,671	5,223
*80901	Colorado Springs	(719)	281,140	215,105
80120	Columbine	(303)	23,969	23,523
80022	Commerce City	(303)	16,466	16,234
81321	Cortez	(303)	7,284	7,095
81625	Craig	(303)	8,091	8,133
*80817	Denver	(303)	467,610	492,686
80022	Derby(u)	(303)	6,043	8,578
81301	Durango	(303)	12,430	11,649
*80110	Englewood	(303)	29,387	30,021
80620	Evans	(303)	5,877	5,063
80439	Evergreen	(303)	7,582	6,376
80221	Federal Heights	(303)	9,342	7,838
80913	Fort Carson(u)	(719)	11,309	13,219
*80521	Fort Collins	(303)	87,758	65,092
80621	Fort Lupton		5,159	4,251
80701	Fort Morgan	(303)	9,068	8,768
80817	Fountain	(719)	9,984	8,324
81504	Fruitvale(u)		5,222	....
81522	Gateway(u)	(303)	7,510	....
81601	Glenwood Springs	(303)	6,561	4,637
80401	Golden	(303)	13,116	12,237
81501	Grand Junction	(303)	29,034	27,956
*80631	Greeley	(303)	60,536	53,006
80110	Greenwood Village	(303)	7,589	5,729
80501	Gunbarrel(u)	(303)	9,388	5,172
80126	Highlands Ranch(u)		10,181	....
.....	Ken Caryl	(303)	24,391	10,661
80026	Lafayette	(303)	14,548	8,985
81050	La Junta	(719)	7,697	8,338
80215	Lakewood	(303)	126,481	113,808
81052	Lamar	(719)	8,343	7,713
*80120	Littleton	(303)	33,685	28,631
80501	Longmont	(303)	51,555	42,942
80027	Louisville	(303)	12,361	5,593
*80537	Loveland	(303)	37,352	30,215
81401	Montrose	(303)	8,854	8,722
80233	Northglenn	(303)	27,195	29,847
80649	Orchard Mesa(u)		5,977	4,876
80134	Parker	(303)	5,450	290
*81003	Pueblo	(719)	98,640	101,686
.....	Redlands(u)		9,355	....
80911	Security-Widefield(u)	(719)	23,822	18,768
80221	Sherrelwood(u)	(303)	16,636	17,629
80122	Southglenn(u)	(303)	43,087	37,787
80477	Steamboat Springs	(303)	6,695	5,098
80751	Sterling	(303)	10,362	11,385
80906	Stratmoor(u)	(719)	5,854	5,519
80229	Thornton	(303)	55,031	42,054
81082	Trinidad	(719)	8,580	9,663
80229	Welby(u)	(303)	10,218	9,668
*80030	Westminster	(303)	74,625	50,211
80221	Westminster East(u)	(303)	5,197	6,002
80033	Wheat Ridge	(303)	29,419	30,293
80550	Windsor	(303)	5,062	4,277

Connecticut (203)

See Note on Page 398

ZIP code	Place	1990	1980
06401	Ansonia	18,403	19,039
06001	*Avon*	13,937	11,201
06403	*Beacon Falls*	5,083	.....
06037	*Berlin*	16,787	15,121
06801	*Bethel*	17,541	16,004
06002	*Bloomfield*	19,483	18,608
06405	*Branford*	27,603	23,363
*06602	Bridgeport	141,686	142,546
06010	Bristol	60,640	57,370
06804	*Brookfield*	14,113	12,872
06234	*Brooklyn*	6,681	5,691
06013	*Burlington*	7,026	5,660
06019	*Canton*	8,268	7,635
06040	Central Manchester(u)	30,934	21,103
06410	*Cheshire*	25,684	21,788
06413	*Clinton*	12,767	11,195
06415	*Colchester*	10,980	7,761
06340	Conning Towers-Nautilus Park(u)	10,013	9,665
06238	*Coventry*	10,063	8,895
06416	*Cromwell*	12,286	10,265
06810	Danbury	65,585	60,470
06820	*Darien*	18,130	18,892
06418	Derby	12,199	12,346
06422	*Durham*	5,732	5,143
06423	*East Haddam*	6,676	5,621
06424	*East Hampton*	10,428	8,572
06108	*East Hartford*	50,452	52,563
06512	*East Haven*	26,144	25,028
06333	*East Lyme*	13,870	11,399
06016	*East Windsor*	10,081	8,925
06425	*Easton*	6,303	5,962
06029	*Ellington*	11,197	9,711
06082	*Enfield*	45,532	42,695
06426	*Essex*	5,904	5,078
06430	*Fairfield*	53,418	54,849
06032	*Farmington*	20,608	16,407
06033	*Glastonbury Center*	27,901	24,327
06035	*Granby*	9,369	7,956
06830	*Greenwich*	58,441	59,578
06351	*Griswold*	10,384	8,967
06340	*Groton*	45,144	41,062
06340	Groton Borough	9,837	10,086
06437	*Guilford*	19,848	17,375
06438	*Haddam*	6,769	6,383
06514	*Hamden*	52,434	51,071
*06101	Hartford	139,739	136,392
06791	*Harwinton*	5,228	.....
06082	Hazardville(u)	5,179	5,436
06248	Hebron	7,079	5,453
06037	Kensington(u)	8,306	7,502
06239	*Killingly*	15,889	14,519
06249	Lebanon	6,041	.....
06339	*Ledyard*	14,913	13,735
06759	*Litchfield*	8,365	7,365
06443	*Madison*	14,031	9,768
06040	*Manchester*	49,761	51,618

ZIP code	Place	1990	1980
06250	*Mansfield*	20,634	19,994
06447	*Marlborough*	5,535	.....
06450	Meriden	59,479	57,118
06762	*Middlebury*	6,145	5,995
06457	Middletown	42,762	39,040
06460	Milford	49,938	48,168
06468	*Monroe*	16,896	14,010
06353	*Montville*	16,673	16,455
06770	Naugatuck	30,625	26,456
•06050	New Britain	75,491	73,840
06840	*New Canaan*	17,864	17,931
06810	*New Fairfield*	12,911	11,260
06057	*New Hartford*	5,769	....
•06510	New Haven	130,474	126,089
06111	*Newington*	29,208	28,841
06320	New London	28,540	28,842
06776	*New Milford*	23,629	19,420
06470	*Newtown*	20,779	19,107
06471	*North Branford*	12,996	11,554
06473	*North Haven*	22,249	22,080
06856	Norwalk	78,331	77,767
06360	Norwich	37,391	38,074
06779	Oakville(u)	8,741	8,737
06371	*Old Lyme*	6,535	6,159
06475	*Old Saybrook*	9,552	9,287
06477	*Orange*	12,830	13,237
06483	*Oxford*	8,685	.....
02891	Pawcatuck(u)	5,289	5,216
06374	*Plainfield*	14,363	17,392
06062	*Plainville*	16,401	16,733
06782	*Plymouth*	11,832	10,732
06480	*Portland*	8,418	8,383
06360	*Preston*	5,006	.....
06712	*Prospect*	7,775	6,807
06260	Putnam	6,835	6,855
.....	*Putnam*	9,031	8,580
06875	*Redding*	7,927	7,272
06877	Ridgefield Center(u)	6,363	6,066
06877	*Ridgefield*	20,919	20,120
06067	*Rocky Hill*	16,554	14,559
06483	*Seymour*	14,288	13,434
06484	Shelton	35,418	31,314
06082	Sherwood Manor(u)	6,357	6,303
06070	*Simsbury*	22,023	21,161
06071	*Somers*	9,108	.....
06488	*Southbury*	15,818	14,156
06489	*Southington*	38,518	36,879
06074	*South Windsor*	22,090	17,198
06082	Southwood Acres(u)	8,963	9,779
06075	*Stafford*	11,091	9,268
•06904	Stamford	108,056	102,466
06378	*Stonington*	16,919	6,220
06268	Storrs(u)	12,198	11,394
06497	*Stratford*	49,389	50,541
06078	*Suffield*	11,427	9,294
06786	Terryville(u)	5,426	5,234
06787	*Thomaston*	6,947	6,272
06277	*Thompson*	8,668	8,141
06082	Thompsonville(u)	8,458	....
06084	*Tolland*	11,001	9,694
06790	Torrington	33,687	30,987
06611	*Trumbull*	32,016	32,989
06066	*Vernon*	29,841	27,974
06492	*Wallingford*	40,822	37,274
•06701	Waterbury	108,961	103,266
06385	*Waterford*	17,930	17,843
06795	*Watertown*	20,456	19,489
06107	*West Hartford*	60,110	61,301
06516	West Haven	54,021	53,184
06498	*Westbrook*	5,414	5,216
06883	*Weston*	8,648	8,284
06880	*Westport*	24,410	24,407
06109	*Wethersfield*	25,651	25,651
06226	Willimantic	14,746	14,652
06279	*Willington*	5,979	.....
06897	*Wilton*	15,989	15,351
06094	*Winchester*	11,524	10,841
06280	*Windham*	22,039	21,062
06095	*Windsor*	27,817	25,204
06096	*Windsor Locks*	12,358	12,190
06098	Winsted	8,254	8,092
06716	*Wolcott*	13,700	13,008
06525	*Woodbridge*	7,924	7,761
06798	*Woodbury*	8,131	6,942
06281	*Woodstock*	6,008	5,117

Delaware (302)

ZIP code	Place	1990	1980
19713	Brookside(u)	15,307	15,255
19703	Claymont(u)	9,800	10,022
19901	Dover	27,630	23,507
19802	Edgemoor(u)	5,853	7,397
19805	Elsmere	5,935	6,493
19963	Milford	6,040	5,366
•19711	Newark	26,371	25,247
19800	Pike Creek(u)	10,163	....
19973	Seaford	5,689	5,256
19977	Smyrna	5,231	4,750
19804	Stanton(u)	5,028	5,495
19803	Talleyville(u)	6,346	6,880
•19899	Wilmington	71,529	70,195
19720	Wilmington Manor	8,568	9,233

District of Columbia (202)

ZIP code	Place	1990	1980
•20013	Washington	606,900	638,432

Florida

ZIP code	Place	Area code	1990	1980
•32701	Altamonte Springs	(407)	34,879	21,105
.....	Andover(u)		6,251	....
33572	Apollo Beach(u)		6,025	4,014
32703	Apopka	(407)	13,512	6,019
33821	Arcadia	(813)	6,488	6,002
32233	Atlantic Beach	(904)	11,636	7,847
33823	Auburndale	(813)	8,858	6,501
.....	Aventura(u)	(305)	14,914	9,698
33825	Avon Park	(813)	8,042	8,026
32807	Azalea Park(u)	(407)	8,926	8,301
33830	Bartow	(813)	14,716	14,780
.....	Bay Hill(u)		5,346	....
34667	Bayonet Point(u)	(813)	21,860	16,455
33505	Bayshore Gardens(u)	(813)	17,062	14,945
33589	Beacon Square(u)	(813)	6,265	6,513
.....	Bee Ridge		6,406	3,313
32073	Bellair-Meadowbrook Terrace(u)	(904)	15,606	12,144
33430	Belle Glade	(407)	16,177	16,535
.....	Belle Isle		5,272	2,848
32506	Belleview	(904)	19,386	15,439
32665	Beverly Hills(u)	(904)	6,163	5,024
.....	Bloomingdale(u)		13,912	....
.....	Boca Del Mar(u)		17,754	....
•33487	Boca Raton	(407)	61,492	49,447
33959	Bonita Springs(u)	(813)	13,600	5,435
•33435	Boynton Beach	(407)	46,194	35,624
•34206	Bradenton	(813)	43,779	30,228
33511	Brandon(u)	(813)	57,985	41,826
32525	Brent(u)	(904)	21,624	21,872
33317	Broadview Park(u)	(305)	6,109	6,022
33313	Broadview-Pompano Park(u)	(305)	5,230	5,256
•34601	Brooksville	(904)	7,440	5,582
33311	Browardale(u)	(305)	6,257	7,571
33142	Brownsville(u)	(813)	15,607	18,058
34743	Buena Ventura Lakes(u)		14,148	....
32401	Callaway	(904)	12,253	7,154
32920	Cape Canaveral	(407)	8,014	5,733
33904	Cape Coral	(813)	74,991	32,103
33055	Carol City(u)	(305)	53,331	47,349
33688	Carrollwood(u)	(813)	7,195	....
.....	Carrollwood Village(u)		15,051	....
32707	Casselberry	(407)	18,911	15,037
33401	Century Village(u)	(305)	8,363	10,619
•34615	Clearwater City	(813)	98,784	85,170
32711	Clermont	(904)	6,910	5,461
33440	Clewiston	(813)	6,085	5,219
32922	Cocoa	(407)	17,722	16,096
32931	Cocoa Beach	(407)	12,123	10,926
32922	Cocoa West(u)	(407)	6,160	6,432
33066	Coconut Creek	(305)	27,484	6,288
33064	Collier Manor-Cresthaven(u)	(305)	7,322	7,045
33801	Combee Settlement(u)	(813)	5,463	5,400
32809	Conway(u)	(407)	13,159	24,027
33314	Cooper City	(305)	21,269	10,140
33134	Coral Gables	(305)	40,091	43,241
33065	Coral Springs	(305)	79,443	37,349
.....	Coral Terrace(u)	(305)	23,255	22,702
32536	Crestview	(904)	9,886	7,617
33803	Crystal Lake(u)	(813)	5,300	6,827
33157	Cutler(u)	(305)	16,201	15,593
33157	Cutler Ridge(u)	(305)	21,268	20,886
33880	Cypress Gardens(u)	(813)	9,188	8,043
.....	Cypress Lake(u)	(813)	10,491	8,721
33525	Dade City	(904)	5,633	4,923
33004	Dania	(305)	13,163	11,796
33314	Davie	(305)	47,217	20,515
•32015	Daytona Beach	(904)	61,921	54,176
32713	De Bary	(407)	7,176	4,980
33441	Deerfield Beach	(305)	46,997	39,193
32433	DeFuniak Springs	(904)	5,120	5,563
32720	De Land	(904)	16,491	15,354
•33444	Delray Beach	(407)	47,181	34,329
33617	Del Rio(u)	(813)	8,248	7,409
32725	Deltona(u)	(407)	50,828	15,710
32541	Destin	(904)	8,090	3,913
.....	Doctor Phillips(u)		7,963	....
•34698	Dunedin	(813)	33,997	30,203
33610	East Lake-Orient Park (u)	(813)	6,171	5,612
33940	East Naples(u)	(813)	22,951	12,127
32032	Edgewater	(904)	15,337	6,726
32542	Eglin AFB(u)	(904)	8,347	7,574
33614	Egypt Lake(u)	(813)	14,580	11,932
34680	Elfers(u)	(813)	12,356	11,396

ZIP code	Place		1990	1980
*34223	Englewood(u)	(813)	15,025	10,229
32504	Ensley(u)	(904)	16,362	14,422
32726	Eustis	(904)	12,967	9,453
32804	Fairview Shores(u)	(305)	13,192	10,174
32034	Fernandina Beach	(904)	8,765	7,224
32730	Fern Park(u)	(407)	8,294	8,890
32504	Ferry Pass(u)	(904)	26,301	16,910
33030	Florida City	(305)	5,978	6,174
.....	Florida Ridge		12,218	4,988
32751	Forest City(u)	(407)	10,638	6,819
.....	Forest Island Park(u)		5,988	....
*33319	Fort Lauderdale	(305)	149,238	153,279
*33901	Fort Myers	(813)	45,206	36,638
33931	Fort Myers Beach(u)	(813)	9,284	5,753
.....	Fort Myers Shores(u)		5,460	4,426
*34950	Fort Pierce	(407)	36,830	33,802
33452	Fort Pierce North(u)	(407)	5,833	5,929
.....	Fort Pierce South(u)	(407)	5,320	3,324
32548	Fort Walton Beach	(904)	21,407	20,829
.....	Fruit Cove(u)		5,904	3,906
.....	Fruitville(u)	(813)	9,808	3,070
*32601	Gainesville	(904)	85,075	81,371
33801	Gibsonia(u)	(813)	5,168	5,011
33534	Gibsonton(u)	(813)	7,706	....
32960	Gifford(u)	(407)	6,278	6,240
.....	Gladeview(u)	(305)	15,637	18,919
33143	Glenvar Heights(u)	(305)	14,823	13,216
33999	Golden Gate(u)		14,148	4,327
33055	Golden Glades(u)	(305)	25,474	23,154
32733	Goldenrod(u)	(407)	12,362	13,681
32560	Gonzalez(u)	(904)	7,669	6,084
33170	Goulds(u)	(305)	7,284	7,078
.....	Greater Northdale(u)		16,318	....
33463	Greenacres City	(407)	18,683	8,870
32561	Gulf Breeze	(904)	5,530	5,478
33581	Gulf Gate Estates(u)	(813)	11,622	9,248
33707	Gulfport	(813)	11,709	11,180
33844	Haines City	(813)	11,683	10,799
33009	Hallandale	(305)	30,997	36,460
.....	Hammocks(u)		10,897	....
.....	Hamptons at Boca Raton(u)		11,686	....
*33010	Hialeah	(305)	188,008	145,254
33016	Hialeah Gardens		7,727	2,700
.....	Highpoint		13,818	....
33455	Hobe Sound(u)	(407)	11,507	6,822
34690	Holiday(u)	(813)	19,360	18,392
32017	Holly Hill	(904)	11,141	9,953
*33022	Hollywood	(305)	121,696	121,323
33030	Homestead	(305)	26,694	20,668
33030	Homestead AFB	(305)	5,153	7,594
32646	Homosassa Springs(u)		6,271	1,426
34667	Hudson(u)	(813)	7,344	5,799
33934	Immokalee(u)	(813)	14,120	11,038
32937	Indian Harbour Beach	(407)	6,933	5,967
32650	Inverness	(904)	5,797	4,095
33880	Inwood(u)	(813)	6,824	6,668
.....	Iona(u)		9,565	....
33162	Ives Estates(u)	(305)	13,531	12,623
32250	Jacksonville Beach	(904)	17,839	15,462
*32201	Jacksonville	(904)	635,230	540,920
.....	Jan Phyl Village(u)		5,308	2,785
33568	Jasmine Estates(u)	(813)	17,136	11,995
*34957	Jensen Beach(u)	(407)	9,884	6,639
33458	Jupiter	(407)	24,907	9,868
33183	Kendale Lakes(u)	(305)	48,524	32,769
33156	Kendall(u)	(305)	87,271	73,758
.....	Kendall Lakes West	(305)	6,038	....
33149	Key Biscayne(u)	(305)	8,854	6,313
33037	Key Largo(u)	(305)	11,336	7,447
33040	Key West	(305)	24,832	24,382
.....	Kings Point(u)	(305)	12,422	8,724
32741	Kissimmee	(407)	30,050	15,487
32159	Lady Lake		8,071	1,193
32055	Lake City	(904)	10,005	9,257
*33802	Lakeland	(813)	70,576	47,406
33801	Lakeland Highlands(u)	(813)	9,972	10,426
.....	Lake Lorraine(u)	(904)	6,779	5,427
33054	Lake Lucerne(u)	(305)	9,478	9,762
33612	Lake Magdalene(u)	(813)	15,973	13,331
32746	Lake Mary	(407)	5,929	2,853
33403	Lake Park	(407)	6,704	6,909
.....	Lakes by the Bay(u)		5,615	....
....	Lakeside(u)	(904)	29,137	10,534
33853	Lake Wales	(813)	9,670	8,466
.....	Lakewood Park(u)		7,211	3,411
33460	Lake Worth	(407)	28,564	27,048
34639	Land O' Lakes(u)		7,892	4,515
33460	Lantana	(407)	8,392	8,048
*34640	Largo	(813)	65,674	57,958
33313	Lauderdale Lakes	(305)	27,341	25,426
33313	Lauderhill	(305)	49,708	37,271
34272	Laurel(u)	(813)	8,245	6,368
33717	Lealman(u)	(813)	21,748	19,873
32748	Leesburg	(904)	14,903	13,191
*33936	Lehigh Acres(u)	(813)	13,611	9,604
33033	Leisure City(u)	(305)	19,379	17,905
33064	Lighthouse Point	(305)	10,378	11,488
.....	Lindgren Acres(u)	(305)	22,290	11,986
32060	Live Oak	(904)	6,332	6,732
32810	Lockhart(u)	(407)	11,636	10,569
34228	Longboat Key	(813)	5,937	4,843
*32750	Longwood	(407)	13,316	10,029
33549	Lutz(u)	(813)	10,552	5,555
32444	Lynn Haven	(904)	9,298	6,239
.....	McGregor(u)		6,504	....
32751	Maitland	(407)	8,932	8,763
33550	Mango(u)	(813)	8,700	6,493
33050	Marathon(u)	(305)	8,857	7,568
33937	Marco(u)		9,493	4,679
33063	Margate	(305)	42,985	35,900
32446	Marianna	(904)	6,292	7,006
*32901	Melbourne	(407)	59,646	46,536
33314	Melrose Park(u)	(904)	6,477	5,662
33561	Memphis(u)	(813)	6,760	5,501
32952	Merritt Island(u)	(407)	32,886	30,708
*33152	Miami	(305)	358,648	346,681
33139	Miami Beach	(305)	92,639	96,298
33023	Miami Gardens —Utopia-Carver(u)	(305)	7,448	9025
33014	Miami Lakes(u)	(305)	12,750	9,809
33153	Miami Shores	(305)	10,084	9,244
33166	Miami Springs	(305)	13,268	12,350
.....	Micco(u)		8,757	....
32068	Middleburg(u)		6,223	3,585
32570	Milton	(904)	7,216	7,206
32754	Mims(u)	(407)	9,412	7,583
33023	Miramar	(305)	40,663	32,813
32757	Mount Dora	(904)	7,196	5,883
32506	Myrtle Grove(u)	(904)	17,402	14,238
*33962	Naples	(813)	19,505	17,581
33940	Naples Park(u)	(813)	8,002	5,438
33032	Naranja(u)	(305)	5,790	10,381
32233	Neptune Beach	(904)	6,816	5,248
*34652	New Port Richey	(813)	14,044	11,196
33552	New Port Richey East(u)	(813)	9,683	6,147
32169	New Smyrna Beach	(904)	16,543	13,557
32578	Niceville	(904)	10,507	8,543
33169	Norland(u)	(305)	22,109	19,471
33308	North Andrews Gardens(u)	(305)	9,002	8,967
33141	North Bay Village		5,383	4,920
33903	North Fort Myers(u)	(813)	30,027	22,808
33068	North Lauderdale	(305)	26,506	18,479
33161	North Miami	(305)	50,001	42,566
33160	North Miami Beach	(305)	35,359	36,553
33940	North Naples(u)	(813)	13,422	7,950
33408	North Palm Beach	(407)	11,343	11,344
33596	North Port	(813)	11,973	6,205
.....	North Sarasota(u)		6,702	4,997
33860	Oak Ridge(u)	(813)	15,388	15,477
33307	Oakland Park	(305)	26,326	22,944
32670	Ocala	(904)	42,045	37,170
32548	Ocean City(u)	(904)	5,422	5,582
32761	Ocoee	(407)	12,778	7,803
33163	Ojus(u)	(305)	15,519	17,344
34677	Oldsmar		8,361	2,608
33165	Olympia Heights(u)	(305)	37,792	33,112
33054	Opa-Locka	(305)	15,283	14,460
33054	Opa-Locka North(u)	(305)	6,568	5,721
32774	Orange City		5,347	2,795
32073	Orange Park	(904)	9,488	8,766
*32820	Orlando	(407)	164,693	128,291
32811	Orlovista(u)	(407)	5,990	6,474
32176	Ormond Beach	(904)	29,721	21,438
32074	Ormond By-The-Sea(u)	(904)	8,157	7,665
32765	Oviedo	(407)	11,114	3,074
32570	Pace(u)	(904)	6,277	5,006
.....	Page Park-Pine Manor(u)		5,116	5,006
33476	Pahokee	(407)	6,822	6,346
32077	Palatka	(904)	10,201	10,175
32905	Palm Bay	(407)	62,543	18,560
33480	Palm Beach	(407)	9,814	9,729
33403	Palm Beach Gardens	(407)	22,965	14,407
32135	Palm Coast(u)		14,287	2,837
34221	Palmetto	(813)	9,268	8,637
33157	Palmetto Estates(u)	(305)	12,293	11,116
*34683	Palm Harbor(u)	(813)	50,256	5,215
33619	Palm River-Clair Mel(u)	(813)	13,691	14,447
33460	Palm Springs	(407)	9,763	8,166
33012	Palm Springs North(u)	(407)	5,300	5,838
.....	Palm Valley		9,960	....
32401	Panama City	(904)	34,378	33,346
33023	Pembroke Pines	(305)	65,452	35,776
*32502	Pensacola	(904)	58,165	57,619
33157	Perrine(u)	(305)	15,576	16,129
32347	Perry	(904)	7,151	8,254
32809	Pine Castle(u)	(407)	8,276	9,992
32808	Pine Hills(u)	(407)	35,322	35,771
.....	Pine Island Ridge		5,244	....
*34665	Pinellas Park	(813)	43,426	32,811
33168	Pinewood(u)	(305)	15,518	16,252
*33317	Plantation	(305)	66,692	48,653
33566	Plant City	(813)	22,754	17,064
*33067	Pompano Beach	(305)	72,411	52,618
33064	Pompano Beach Highlands(u)	(305)	17,915	16,154
33950	Port Charlotte(u)	(813)	41,535	25,770
32019	Port Orange	(904)	35,317	18,756
32927	Port St. John(u)		8,933	1,837
34952	Port St. Lucie	(407)	55,866	14,690

ZIP code	Place		1990	1980
34992	Port Salerno(u)		7,786	4,511
33032	Princeton(u)	(305)	7,073	....
*33950	Punta Gorda	(813)	10,747	6,797
32351	Quincy	(904)	7,452	8,591
33156	Richmond Heights(u)	(305)	8,583	8,577
33312	Riverland (u)	(305)	5,376	5,919
33569	Riverview(u)		6,478	....
33404	Riviera Beach	(407)	27,644	26,489
32955	Rockledge	(407)	16,023	11,877
.....	Royal Palm Beach	(407)	14,589	3,423
33570	Ruskin(u)	(813)	6,046	5,117
34695	Safety Harbor	(813)	15,124	6,461
32084	St. Augustine	(904)	11,692	11,985
34769	St. Cloud	(407)	12,453	7,840
*33702	St. Petersburg	(813)	240,348	238,647
33706	St. Petersburg Beach	(813)	9,200	9,354
.....	San Carlos Park(u)		11,785	3,590
33432	Sandalfoot Cove(u)	(305)	14,214	5,299
32771	Sanford	(407)	32,387	23,176
33957	Sanibel		5,468	3,363
*34236	Sarasota	(813)	50,961	48,868
33577	Sarasota Springs(u)	(813)	16,088	13,860
32937	Satellite Beach	(407)	9,889	9,163
.....	Scott Lake(u)	(305)	14,588	14,154
32958	Sebastian	(407)	10,205	2,831
*33870	Sebring	(813)	8,900	8,736
33584	Seffner(u)		5,371	....
34642	Seminole	(813)	9,251	4,856
33578	Siesta Key(u)	(813)	7,772	7,010
32688	Silver Springs Shores(u)		6,421	3,983
32809	Sky Lake(u)	(407)	6,202	6,692
32703	South Apopka(u)	(407)	6,360	5,687
33505	South Bradenton(u)	(813)	20,398	14,297
32021	South Daytona	(904)	12,488	11,252
33579	Southgate(u)	(813)	7,324	7,322
.....	South Gate Ridge(u)		5,924	4,259
33143	South Miami	(305)	10,404	10,895
33157	South Miami Heights(u)	(305)	30,030	23,559
.....	South Pasadena		5,644	4,188
32937	South Patrick Shores(u)	(407)	10,249	9,816
.....	South Sarasota(u)		5,298	4,267
33595	South Venice(u)	(813)	11,951	8,075
32401	Springfield	(904)	8,715	7,220
34606	Spring Hill(u)	(904)	31,117	6,468
32091	Starke	(904)	5,226	5,306
*34994	Stuart	(407)	11,936	9,467
33573	Sun City Center(u)	(813)	8,326	5,605
33160	Sunny Isles(u)	(305)	11,772	12,564
33304	Sunrise	(305)	64,407	39,681
33139	Sunset(u)	(305)	15,810	13,531
33144	Sweetwater	(305)	13,909	8,067
*32303	Tallahassee	(904)	124,773	81,548
33313	Tamarac	(305)	44,822	29,376
33144	Tamiami(u)	(305)	33,845	17,607
*33625	Tampa	(813)	280,015	271,577
*34689	Tarpon Springs	(813)	17,906	13,251
32778	Tavares	(904)	7,383	4,398
33617	Temple Terrace	(813)	16,444	11,097
32780	Titusville	(407)	39,394	31,910
32505	Town 'n' Country(u)	(813)	60,946	37,834
33706	Treasure Island	(813)	7,266	6,316
32807	Union Park(u)	(407)	6,890	19,175
33620	University West(u)	(904)	23,760	24,514
.....	Upper Grand Lagoon(u)		7,855	3,314
*34285	Venice	(813)	16,922	12,153
33595	Venice Gardens(u)	(813)	7,701	6,568
32960	Vero Beach	(407)	17,350	16,176
32960	Vero Beach South(u)	(407)	16,973	12,636
.....	Villages of Oriole(u)		5,698	8,724
33901	Villas(u)	(813)	9,898	8,724
32507	Warrington(u)	(904)	16,040	15,792
33314	Washington Park(u)	(305)	6,930	7,240
32703	Wekiva Springs(u)	(407)	23,026	13,386
.....	Wellington(u)		20,670	4,622
33155	Westchester(u)	(305)	29,883	29,272
.....	Westgate-Belvedere Homes(u)		6,880	....
33138	West Little River(u)	(305)	33,575	32,492
32901	West Melbourne	(407)	8,399	5,078
33144	West Miami	(305)	5,727	6,076
*33404	West Palm Beach	(407)	67,643	63,305
.....	West Park(u)		10,347	....
32505	West Pensacola(u)	(904)	22,107	24,371
33168	Westview(u)	(305)	9,668	9,102
33165	Westwood Lakes(u)	(305)	11,522	11,478
.....	Whiskey Creek(u)		5,061	....
33305	Wilton Manors	(305)	11,804	12,742
33803	Winston(u)	(813)	9,118	9,315
*32787	Winter Garden	(407)	9,745	6,789
33880	Winter Haven	(813)	24,725	21,119
*32789	Winter Park	(407)	22,623	22,339
32708	Winter Springs	(407)	22,151	10,475
32548	Wright(u)	(904)	18,945	13,011
32097	Yulee(u)		6,915	....
33599	Zephyrhills	(813)	8,220	5,742

Georgia

ZIP code	Place		1990	1980
31620	Adel	(912)	5,093	5,592
*31701	Albany	(912)	78,122	74,425
30201	Alpharetta		13,002	3,128
31709	Americus	(912)	16,512	16,120
*30601	Athens	(404)	45,734	42,549
*30304	Atlanta	(404)	394,017	425,022
*30901	Augusta	(404)	44,639	47,532
31717	Bainbridge	(912)	10,712	10,553
30032	Belvedere Park(u)	(404)	18,089	17,766
31723	Blakely	(912)	5,595	5,880
31520	Brunswick	(912)	16,433	17,605
30518	Buford	(404)	8,771	6,578
31728	Cairo	(912)	9,035	8,777
30701	Calhoun	(404)	7,135	5,563
31730	Camilla	(912)	5,008	5,414
30032	Candler-McAfee(u)	(404)	29,491	27,306
30117	Carrollton	(404)	16,029	14,078
30120	Cartersville	(404)	12,035	9,247
30125	Cedartown	(404)	7,978	8,619
30341	Chamblee	(404)	7,668	7,137
30021	Clarkston		5,385	4,539
30337	College Park	(404)	20,457	24,632
*31902	Columbus	(404)	178,681	169,441
30027	Conley(u)	(404)	5,528	6,033
30207	Conyers	(404)	7,380	6,567
31015	Cordele	(912)	10,836	11,184
.....	Country Club Estates(u)		7,500	....
30209	Covington	(404)	10,042	10,586
30720	Dalton	(404)	21,761	20,581
31742	Dawson	(912)	5,295	5,699
*30030	Decatur	(404)	17,336	18,404
31520	Dock Junction(u)	(912)	7,094	6,189
30340	Doraville	(404)	7,626	7,414
31533	Douglas	(912)	10,464	10,980
30134	Douglasville	(404)	11,635	7,641
30333	Druid Hills(u)	(404)	12,174	12,700
31021	Dublin	(912)	16,312	16,083
30136	Duluth		9,029	2,956
30338	Dunwoody(u)	(404)	26,302	17,768
31023	Eastman	(912)	5,513	5,330
30344	East Point	(404)	34,402	37,486
30635	Elberton	(404)	5,682	5,686
30809	Evans(u)	(404)	13,713	....
30060	Fair Oaks(u)	(404)	6,996	8,486
30535	Fairview(u)	(404)	6,444	6,558
30214	Fayetteville		5,827	2,715
31750	Fitzgerald	(912)	8,612	10,187
30050	Forest Park	(404)	16,925	18,782
31905	Fort Benning South(u)	(404)	14,617	15,074
30905	Fort Gordon(u)	(404)	9,140	14,069
30741	Fort Oglethorpe	(404)	5,880	5,443
31313	Fort Stewart(u)	(912)	13,774	15,031
31030	Fort Valley	(912)	8,198	9,000
.....	Gaines School(u)		11,354	....
30501	Gainesville	(404)	17,885	15,280
31408	Garden City	(912)	7,410	6,895
31754	Georgetown	(912)	5,554	2,785
30316	Gresham Park(u)	(404)	9,000	6,232
30223	Griffin	(404)	21,347	20,728
30354	Hapeville	(404)	5,483	6,166
31313	Hinesville	(912)	21,596	11,309
31545	Jesup	(912)	8,958	9,418
30144	Kennesaw	(404)	8,936	5,095
31547	Kingsland	(912)	5,474	....
30728	La Fayette	(404)	6,313	6,517
30240	La Grange	(404)	25,597	24,204
.....	Lakeview(u)		5,237	5,403
30245	Lawrenceville	(404)	17,251	8,928
30247	Lilburn		9,301	3,765
30057	Lithia Springs(u)	(404)	11,403	9,145
30059	Mableton(u)	(404)	25,725	25,111
*31201	Macon	(912)	106,612	116,896
30060	Marietta	(404)	44,129	30,821
30907	Martinez(u)	(404)	33,731	16,472
31061	Milledgeville	(912)	17,727	12,176
30655	Monroe	(404)	9,759	8,854
30260	Morrow		5,168	3,791
31768	Moultrie	(912)	14,865	15,105
30075	Mountain Park(u)	(404)	11,025	9,425
30263	Newnan	(404)	12,497	11,449
30091	Norcross	(404)	5,947	3,363
30319	North Atlanta(u)	(404)	27,812	30,521
30033	North Decatur(u)	(404)	13,936	11,830
30033	North Druid Hills(u)	(404)	14,170	12,438
30032	Panthersville(u)	(404)	9,874	11,366
30269	Peachtree City	(404)	19,027	6,429
31069	Perry	(912)	9,452	9,453
30073	Powder Springs		6,893	3,381
31643	Quitman	(912)	5,292	5,188
30074	Redan(u)		24,376	....
*30274	Riverdale	(404)	9,359	7,121
30161	Rome	(404)	30,326	28,915
30075	Roswell	(404)	47,923	23,337
31558	St. Marys		8,204	3,596
31522	St. Simons Island(u)	(912)	12,026	6,566
31082	Sandersville	(912)	6,290	6,137
30328	Sandy Springs(u)	(404)	67,842	46,877

ZIP code	Place		1990	1980
*31401	Savannah	(912)	137,560	141,654
30079	Scottdale(u)	(404)	8,636	8,770
30080	Smyrna	(404)	30,981	20,312
30278	Snellville	(404)	12,084	8,514
30901	South Augusta(u)	(404)	55,998	51,072
30458	Statesboro	(912)	15,854	14,866
30086	Stone Mountain		6,494	4,867
30747	Summerville	(404)	5,025	4,878
30401	Swainsboro	(912)	7,361	7,602
31791	Sylvester	(912)	5,702	5,860
30286	Thomaston	(404)	9,127	9,682
31792	Thomasville	(912)	17,457	18,463
30824	Thomson	(404)	6,862	7,001
31794	Tifton	(912)	14,215	13,749
30577	Toccoa	(404)	8,266	8,869
30084	Tucker(u)	(404)	25,781	25,399
30291	Union City	(404)	8,375	4,780
31601	Valdosta	(912)	39,806	37,596
30474	Vidalia	(912)	11,078	10,393
30180	Villa Rica		6,542	3,420
.....	Vinings(u)		7,417	....
31093	Warner Robins	(912)	43,726	39,893
31501	Waycross	(912)	16,410	19,371
30830	Waynesboro	(404)	5,701	5,760
30901	West Augusta(u)	(404)	27,637	24,242
31410	Wilmington Island(u)	(912)	11,230	7,546
30680	Winder	(404)	7,373	6,705

Hawaii (808)

See Note on Page 398

ZIP code	Place	1990	1980
96706	Aiea	8,906	32,879
.....	Aliamanu	8,835	....
96706	Ewa	14,315	14,369
.....	Halawa	13,408	....
.....	Heeia	5,010	5,432
.....	Hickman	6,553	4,425
96720	Hilo	37,808	35,269
*96815	Honolulu	365,272	365,048
96732	Kahului	16,889	12,978
96734	Kailua	9,126	4,751
96863	Kailua	36,818	35,812
96744	Kaneohe	35,448	29,919
.....	Kaneohe Station	11,662	....
96746	Kapaa	8,149	4,467
96753	Kihei	11,107	5,644
96761	Lahaina	9,073	6,095
96762	Laie	5,577	4,643
96766	Lihue	5,536	4,000
.....	Maili	6,059	5,026
.....	Makaha	7,990	6,582
.....	Makailo	9,828	7,691
96768	Makawao-Paia	5,405	2,900
96789	Mililani Town	29,359	21,365
96792	Nanakuli	9,575	8,185
96782	Pearl City	30,993	42,575
96788	Pukalani	5,879	3,950
.....	Schofield Barracks	19,597	....
.....	Village Park	7,407	18,851
96786	Wahiawa	17,386	16,911
96792	Waianae	8,758	7,941
96793	Wailuku	10,688	10,260
.....	Waimalu	29,967	....
96796	Waimea	5,972	1,179
96797	Waipahu	31,435	29,139
.....	Waipio	11,812	....
.....	Waipio Acre	5,304	4,091

Idaho (208)

ZIP code	Place	1990	1980
83401	Ammon	5,002	4,669
83221	Blackfoot	9,646	10,065
*83708	Boise City	125,738	102,249
83318	Burley	8,702	8,761
83605	Caldwell	18,400	17,699
83201	Chubbuck	7,794	7,052
83814	Coeur D'Alene	24,563	19,913
83714	Garden City	6,369	4,571
*83401	Idaho Falls	43,929	39,739
83338	Jerome	6,529	6,891
83501	Lewiston	28,082	27,986
83642	Meridian	9,596	6,658
83843	Moscow	18,519	16,513
83647	Mountain Home	7,913	7,540
83648	Mountain Home AFB(u)	5,936	6,403
*83651	Nampa	28,365	25,112
83661	Payette	5,667	5,448
*83201	Pocatello	46,117	46,340
83854	Post Falls	7,349	5,736
83440	Rexburg	14,302	11,559
83350	Rupert	5,455	5,476
83809	Sandpoint	5,203	4,460
83301	Twin Falls	27,591	26,209

Illinois

ZIP code	Place		1990	1980
60101	Addison	(708)	32,058	29,826
60102	Algonquin	(708)	11,663	5,834
60658	Alsip	(708)	18,227	17,134
62002	Alton	(618)	32,064	34,171
60002	Antioch	(708)	6,105	4,419
*60004	Arlington Heights	(708)	75,462	66,116
*60507	Aurora	(708)	99,581	81,293
60010	Barrington	(708)	9,504	9,029
60103	Bartlett	(708)	19,373	13,254
61607	Bartonville	(309)	5,643	6,137
60510	Batavia	(708)	17,076	12,574
.....	Beach Park	(708)	9,513	8,468
62618	Beardstown	(217)	5,270	6,338
*62220	Belleville	(618)	42,785	41,580
60104	Bellwood	(708)	20,241	19,811
61008	Belvidere	(815)	15,958	15,176
60106	Bensenville	(708)	17,767	16,106
62812	Benton	(618)	7,216	7,778
60162	Berkeley	(708)	5,137	5,467
60402	Berwyn	(708)	45,426	46,849
62010	Bethalto	(618)	9,507	8,630
60108	Bloomingdale	(708)	16,614	12,656
61701	Bloomington	(309)	51,972	44,189
60406	Blue Island	(708)	21,203	21,855
60439	Bolingbrook	(708)	40,843	37,261
60538	Boulder Hill(u)	(708)	8,894	9,333
60914	Bourbonnais	(815)	13,927	13,280
60915	Bradley	(815)	10,910	11,015
60455	Bridgeview	(708)	14,402	14,155
60153	Broadview	(708)	8,538	8,618
60513	Brookfield	(708)	18,876	19,395
60090	Buffalo Grove	(708)	36,398	22,230
60459	Burbank	(708)	27,600	28,462
60521	Burr Ridge	(708)	7,669	3,838
62206	Cahokia	(618)	17,550	18,904
60409	Calumet City	(708)	37,840	39,697
60643	Calumet Park	(708)	8,418	8,788
61520	Canton	(309)	13,951	14,626
62901	Carbondale	(618)	27,033	26,414
62626	Carlinville	(217)	5,416	5,439
62821	Carmi	(618)	5,573	6,107
60187	Carol Stream	(708)	31,716	15,472
60110	Carpentersville	(708)	23,049	23,272
60013	Cary	(708)	10,043	6,640
62801	Centralia	(618)	14,274	15,126
62206	Centreville	(618)	7,489	9,747
61820	Champaign	(217)	63,502	58,267
61920	Charleston	(217)	20,398	19,355
62629	Chatham	(217)	6,074	5,597
62233	Chester	(618)	8,204	8,401
*60607	Chicago	(312)	2,783,726	3,005,072
60411	Chicago Heights	(708)	32,966	37,026
60415	Chicago Ridge	(708)	13,643	13,473
61523	Chillicothe	(309)	5,959	6,176
60650	Cicero	(708)	67,436	61,232
60514	Clarendon Hills	(708)	6,994	6,870
61727	Clinton	(217)	7,437	8,014
62234	Collinsville	(618)	22,446	19,475
62236	Columbia	(618)	5,524	4,269
60477	Country Club Hills	(708)	15,431	14,676
60525	Countryside	(708)	5,961	6,242
60435	Crest Hill	(815)	10,994	9,252
60445	Crestwood	(708)	10,823	10,852
60417	Crete	(708)	6,773	5,417
61611	Creve Coeur	(309)	5,938	6,851
60014	Crystal Lake	(815)	24,512	18,590
61832	Danville	(217)	33,828	38,985
60559	Darien	(708)	18,193	14,956
*62521	Decatur	(217)	83,885	93,939
60015	Deerfield	(708)	17,327	17,432
60115	De Kalb	(815)	35,076	33,157
*60016	Des Plaines	(708)	53,223	53,568
61021	Dixon	(815)	15,144	15,710
60419	Dolton	(708)	23,930	24,766
60515	Downers Grove	(708)	46,858	42,259
62832	Du Quoin	(618)	6,697	6,594
62024	East Alton	(618)	7,063	7,096
61244	East Moline	(309)	20,147	20,907
61611	East Peoria	(309)	21,378	22,385
*62201	East St. Louis	(618)	40,944	55,200
62025	Edwardsville	(618)	14,579	12,480
62401	Effingham	(217)	11,851	11,270
60120	Elgin	(708)	77,010	63,668
60007	Elk Grove Village	(708)	33,429	28,679
60126	Elmhurst	(708)	42,029	44,276
60635	Elmwood Park	(708)	23,206	24,016
*60204	Evanston	(708)	73,233	73,706
60642	Evergreen Park	(708)	20,874	22,260
62837	Fairfield	(618)	5,439	5,944
62208	Fairview Heights	(618)	14,351	12,111
62839	Flora	(618)	5,054	5,379
60422	Flossmoor	(708)	8,651	8,423
60130	Forest Park	(708)	14,918	15,177
60020	Fox Lake	(708)	7,478	6,831
60423	Frankfort		7,180	4,357
.....	Frankfort Square(u)		6,227	....
60131	Franklin Park	(708)	18,485	17,507

ZIP code	Place		1990	1980
61032	Freeport	(815)	25,840	26,266
60030	Gages Lake(u)	(708)	8,349	3,814
61401	Galesburg	(309)	33,530	35,305
61254	Geneseo	(309)	5,990	6,373
60134	Geneva	(708)	12,617	9,881
62034	Glen Carbon	(618)	7,731	5,197
60022	Glencoe	(708)	8,499	9,200
60137	Glendale Heights	(708)	27,973	23,251
60137	Glen Ellyn	(708)	24,944	23,691
60025	Glenview	(708)	37,093	32,060
60425	Glenwood	(708)	9,289	10,538
62002	Godfrey(u)	(618)	5,436	....
.....	Goodings Grove(u)		14,054	....
62040	Granite City	(618)	32,769	36,815
60030	Grays Lake	(708)	7,388	5,260
62246	Greenville	(618)	5,108	....
60031	Gurnee	(708)	13,701	7,179
60103	Hanover Park	(708)	32,895	28,719
62946	Harrisburg	(618)	9,289	10,410
60033	Harvard	(815)	5,975	5,126
60426	Harvey	(708)	29,771	35,810
60656	Harwood Heights	(312)	7,680	8,228
60429	Hazel Crest	(708)	13,334	13,973
62948	Herrin	(618)	10,857	10,708
60457	Hickory Hills	(708)	13,021	13,778
62249	Highland	(618)	7,525	7,122
60035	Highland Park	(708)	30,575	30,599
60040	Highwood	(708)	5,331	5,455
60162	Hillside	(708)	7,672	8,279
60521	Hinsdale	(708)	16,029	16,726
60172	Hoffman Estates	(708)	46,561	37,272
60430	Homewood	(708)	19,278	19,724
60942	Hoopeston	(217)	5,871	6,411
60067	Inverness	(708)	6,503	4,046
60143	Itasca	(708)	6,947	7,129
62650	Jacksonville	(217)	19,324	20,284
62052	Jerseyville	(618)	7,382	7,506
*60431	Joliet	(815)	76,628	77,956
60458	Justice	(708)	11,137	10,552
60901	Kankakee	(815)	27,531	29,633
61443	Kewanee	(309)	12,969	14,508
60525	La Grange	(708)	15,362	15,693
60525	La Grange Park	(708)	12,861	13,359
60044	Lake Bluff	(708)	5,513	4,434
60045	Lake Forest	(708)	17,836	15,245
60102	Lake in the Hills	(708)	5,866	5,651
60047	Lake Zurich	(708)	14,927	8,225
60438	Lansing	(708)	28,109	29,039
61301	La Salle	(815)	9,717	10,347
60439	Lemont	(708)	7,348	5,640
60048	Libertyville	(708)	19,174	16,520
62656	Lincoln	(217)	15,418	16,327
60645	Lincolnwood	(708)	11,365	11,921
60046	Lindenhurst	(708)	8,038	6,220
60532	Lisle	(708)	19,512	13,638
62056	Litchfield	(217)	6,883	7,204
60441	Lockport	(815)	9,401	9,192
60148	Lombard	(708)	39,408	36,879
61111	Loves Park	(815)	15,462	13,192
60411	Lynwood	(708)	6,535	4,195
60534	Lyons	(708)	9,828	9,925
60050	McHenry	(815)	16,177	10,737
61111	Machesney Park	(815)	19,033	19,514
61455	Macomb	(309)	19,952	19,863
62959	Marion	(618)	14,545	14,031
60426	Markham	(708)	13,136	15,172
62258	Mascoutah	(618)	5,511	4,962
60443	Matteson	(708)	11,378	10,223
61938	Mattoon	(217)	18,441	19,293
60153	Maywood	(708)	27,139	27,998
*60160	Melrose Park	(708)	20,859	20,735
61342	Mendota	(815)	7,018	7,134
62960	Metropolis	(618)	6,734	7,171
60445	Midlothian	(708)	14,372	14,274
61264	Milan	(309)	5,753	6,371
60448	Mokena		6,128	4,578
61265	Moline	(309)	43,127	46,407
61462	Monmouth	(309)	9,489	10,706
60450	Morris	(815)	10,270	8,833
61550	Morton	(309)	13,799	14,178
60053	Morton Grove	(708)	22,373	23,747
62863	Mount Carmel	(618)	8,287	8,908
60056	Mount Prospect	(708)	53,168	52,634
62864	Mount Vernon	(618)	17,061	17,193
60060	Mundelein	(708)	21,215	17,053
62966	Murphysboro	(618)	9,176	9,866
60540	Naperville	(708)	85,351	42,601
60451	New Lenox	(815)	9,618	5,792
60648	Niles	(708)	28,384	30,363
61761	Normal	(309)	40,023	35,672
60656	Norridge	(708)	14,459	16,483
60542	North Aurora	(708)	5,940	5,205
60062	Northbrook	(708)	32,308	30,778
60064	North Chicago	(708)	34,978	38,774
60164	Northlake	(708)	12,505	12,166
60546	North Riverside	(708)	6,180	6,764
60521	Oak Brook	(708)	9,178	6,676
60452	Oak Forest	(708)	26,203	25,040
*60454	Oak Lawn	(708)	56,182	60,590
*60301	Oak Park	(708)	53,648	54,887
62269	O'Fallon	(618)	16,073	12,173
62450	Olney	(618)	8,664	9,026
60477	Orland Hills		5,510	2,784
60462	Orland Park	(708)	35,720	23,045
61350	Ottawa	(815)	17,541	18,166
60067	Palatine	(708)	39,253	32,176
60463	Palos Heights	(708)	11,478	11,096
60465	Palos Hills	(708)	17,803	16,654
62557	Pana	(217)	5,796	6,040
61944	Paris	(217)	9,016	9,885
60466	Park Forest	(708)	24,656	26,222
60068	Park Ridge	(708)	36,175	38,704
61554	Pekin	(309)	32,254	33,967
*61601	Peoria	(309)	113,504	124,160
61614	Peoria Heights	(309)	6,930	7,453
61354	Peru	(815)	9,302	10,886
60545	Plano	(708)	5,104	4,875
61764	Pontiac	(815)	11,428	11,227
61356	Princeton	(815)	7,197	7,342
60070	Prospect Heights	(708)	15,239	11,823
62301	Quincy	(217)	39,681	42,554
61866	Rantoul	(217)	17,212	20,161
60471	Richton Park	(708)	10,523	9,403
60627	Riverdale	(708)	13,671	13,233
60305	River Forest	(708)	11,669	12,392
60171	River Grove	(708)	9,961	10,368
60546	Riverside	(708)	8,774	9,236
60472	Robbins	(708)	7,498	8,853
62454	Robinson	(618)	6,740	7,285
61068	Rochelle	(815)	8,769	8,982
61071	Rock Falls	(815)	9,654	10,633
*61125	Rockford	(815)	139,943	139,712
61201	Rock Island	(309)	40,630	46,821
60008	Rolling Meadows	(708)	22,591	20,167
60441	Romeoville	(815)	14,101	15,519
60172	Roselle	(708)	20,819	17,034
60073	Round Lake Beach	(708)	16,434	12,921
60174	St. Charles	(708)	22,502	17,492
62881	Salem	(618)	7,470	7,813
60548	Sandwich	(815)	5,607	5,356
60411	Sauk Village	(708)	9,926	10,906
60172	Schaumburg	(708)	68,586	53,355
60176	Schiller Park	(708)	11,189	11,458
62225	Scott AFB(u)	(618)	7,245	8,648
60436	Shorewood	(815)	6,264	4,714
61282	Silvis	(309)	6,926	7,130
60076	Skokie	(708)	59,432	60,278
60177	South Elgin	(708)	7,474	5,970
60473	South Holland	(708)	22,105	24,977
*62703	Springfield	(217)	105,227	100,054
61362	Spring Valley	(815)	5,246	5,822
60475	Steger	(708)	8,584	9,269
61081	Sterling	(815)	15,142	16,281
60402	Stickney	(708)	5,678	5,893
60103	Streamwood	(708)	31,196	23,456
61364	Streator	(815)	14,121	14,795
60501	Summit	(708)	9,971	10,110
62221	Swansea	(618)	8,201	5,529
60178	Sycamore	(815)	9,708	9,219
62568	Taylorville	(217)	11,133	11,386
60477	Tinley Park	(708)	37,121	26,178
62294	Troy	(618)	6,046	3,772
60466	University Park	(708)	6,204	6,245
61801	Urbana	(217)	36,344	35,978
62471	Vandalia	(618)	6,114	5,338
60061	Vernon Hills	(708)	15,319	9,827
60181	Villa Park	(708)	22,253	23,155
60555	Warrenville	(708)	11,390	7,519
61571	Washington	(309)	10,099	10,364
62204	Washington Park	(618)	7,431	8,223
62298	Waterloo	(618)	5,072	4,646
60970	Watseka	(815)	5,424	5,543
60084	Wauconda	(708)	6,294	5,688
60085	Waukegan	(708)	69,392	67,653
60153	Westchester	(708)	17,301	17,730
60185	West Chicago	(708)	14,796	12,550
60558	Western Springs	(708)	11,956	12,876
62896	West Frankfort	(618)	8,526	9,437
60559	Westmont	(708)	21,228	17,353
61604	West Peoria(u)	(309)	5,314	5,219
60187	Wheaton	(708)	51,464	43,043
60090	Wheeling	(708)	29,911	23,266
60514	Willowbrook	(708)	8,701	4,953
60091	Wilmette	(708)	26,694	28,221
60190	Winfield	(708)	7,096	4,422
60093	Winnetka	(708)	12,210	12,772
60096	Winthrop Harbor	(708)	6,240	5,427
60097	Wonder Lake(u)	(815)	6,664	5,917
60191	Wood Dale	(708)	12,425	11,251
60515	Woodridge	(708)	26,256	21,763
62095	Wood River	(618)	11,490	12,446
60098	Woodstock	(815)	14,353	11,725
60482	Worth	(708)	11,208	11,592
60099	Zion	(708)	19,775	17,865

Indiana

ZIP code	Place		1990	1980
46001	Alexandria	(317)	5,709	6,028
46011	Anderson	(317)	59,459	64,695
46703	Angola	(219)	5,824	5,486
46706	Auburn	(219)	9,379	8,122
47421	Bedford	(812)	13,817	14,410
46107	Beech Grove	(317)	13,383	13,196
47401	Bloomington	(812)	60,633	52,663
46714	Bluffton	(219)	9,020	8,705
47601	Boonville	(812)	6,724	6,300
47834	Brazil	(812)	7,640	7,852
46112	Brownsburg	(317)	7,628	6,242
46032	Carmel	(317)	25,380	18,272
46303	Cedar Lake	(219)	8,885	8,754
47111	Charlestown	(812)	5,889	5,596
46304	Chesterton	(219)	9,124	8,531
47130	Clarksville	(812)	19,838	15,164
47842	Clinton	(317)	5,040	5,267
46725	Columbia City	(219)	5,706	5,091
47201	Columbus	(812)	31,802	30,614
47331	Connersville	(317)	15,550	17,023
47933	Crawfordsville	(317)	13,584	13,325
46307	Crown Point	(219)	17,728	16,455
46733	Decatur	(219)	8,642	8,649
46514	Dunlap(u)	(219)	5,705	5,397
46311	Dyer	(219)	10,923	9,555
46312	East Chicago	(219)	33,892	39,786
46514	Elkhart	(219)	43,627	41,305
46036	Elwood	(317)	9,494	10,867
*47708	Evansville	(812)	126,272	130,496
46038	Fishers		7,508	2,008
*46802	Fort Wayne	(219)	172,986	172,391
46041	Frankfort	(317)	14,754	15,168
46131	Franklin	(317)	12,907	11,563
46738	Garrett	(219)	5,349	4,751
*46401	Gary	(219)	116,646	151,968
46933	Gas City	(317)	6,296	6,370
46526	Goshen	(219)	23,797	19,665
46530	Granger(u)		20,241	....
46135	Greencastle	(317)	8,984	8,403
46140	Greenfield	(317)	11,657	11,288
47240	Greensburg	(812)	9,286	9,254
46142	Greenwood	(317)	26,265	19,327
46319	Griffith	(219)	17,914	17,026
*46320	Hammond	(219)	84,236	93,714
47348	Hartford City	(317)	6,960	7,622
46322	Highland	(219)	23,696	25,935
46342	Hobart	(219)	21,822	22,987
47542	Huntingburg	(812)	5,242	5,376
46750	Huntington	(219)	16,389	16,202
*46206	Indianapolis	(317)	731,327	700,807
47546	Jasper	(812)	10,030	9,097
47130	Jeffersonville	(812)	21,841	21,220
46755	Kendallville	(219)	7,773	7,299
46901	Kokomo	(317)	44,996	47,808
*47901	Lafayette	(317)	43,764	43,011
.....	Lakes of the Four Seasons(u)		6,556	....
46405	Lake Station	(219)	13,899	15,087
46350	La Porte	(219)	21,507	21,796
46226	Lawrence	(317)	26,779	25,591
46052	Lebanon	(317)	12,059	11,456
47441	Linton	(812)	5,814	6,315
46947	Logansport	(219)	16,865	17,731
46356	Lowell	(219)	6,430	5,827
47250	Madison	(812)	12,006	12,472
46952	Marion	(317)	32,618	35,874
46151	Martinsville	(317)	11,677	11,311
46410	Merrillville	(219)	27,257	27,677
46360	Michigan City	(219)	33,822	36,850
46544	Mishawaka	(219)	42,608	40,201
47960	Monticello	(219)	5,237	5,162
46158	Mooresville	(317)	5,541	5,349
47620	Mount Vernon	(812)	7,217	7,656
*47302	Muncie	(317)	71,035	77,216
46321	Munster	(219)	19,949	20,671
46550	Nappanee		5,574	4,694
47150	New Albany	(812)	36,322	37,103
47362	New Castle	(317)	17,753	20,056
46774	New Haven	(219)	9,320	6,714
46060	Noblesville	(317)	17,655	12,253
46962	North Manchester	(219)	6,383	5,998
47265	North Vernon	(812)	5,311	5,768
47130	Oak Park(u)	(812)	5,630	5,871
46970	Peru	(317)	12,843	13,764
46168	Plainfield	(317)	10,433	9,191
46563	Plymouth	(219)	8,303	7,693
46368	Portage	(219)	29,062	27,409
47371	Portland	(219)	6,483	7,074
47670	Princeton	(812)	8,127	8,976
47978	Rensselaer	(219)	5,045	4,944
47374	Richmond	(317)	38,705	41,349
46975	Rochester	(219)	5,969	5,050
46173	Rushville	(317)	5,533	6,113
47167	Salem	(812)	5,619	5,290
46375	Schererville	(219)	20,155	13,209
47170	Scottsburg	(812)	5,334	5,068
47172	Sellersburg	(812)	5,745	3,211
47274	Seymour	(812)	15,579	15,050
46176	Shelbyville	(317)	15,336	14,989
*46624	South Bend	(219)	105,511	109,727
46383	South Haven(u)	(219)	6,112	6,679
46224	Speedway	(317)	13,092	12,641
47586	Tell City	(812)	8,088	8,704
*47808	Terre Haute	(812)	57,483	61,125
46383	Valparaiso	(219)	24,414	22,247
47591	Vincennes	(812)	19,867	20,857
46992	Wabash	(219)	12,127	12,985
46580	Warsaw	(219)	10,968	10,647
47501	Washington	(812)	10,838	11,325
47906	West Lafayette	(317)	26,138	21,247
46391	Westville		5,255	2,887
46394	Whiting	(219)	5,155	5,630
47394	Winchester	(317)	5,095	5,659
46077	Zionsville		5,281	3,948

Iowa

ZIP code	Place		1990	1980
50511	Algona	(515)	6,015	6,289
50009	Altoona	(515)	7,191	5,764
50010	Ames	(515)	47,198	45,775
52205	Anamosa	(319)	5,100	4,958
50021	Ankeny	(515)	18,482	15,429
50022	Atlantic	(712)	7,432	7,789
52722	Bettendorf	(319)	28,139	27,381
50036	Boone	(515)	12,392	12,602
52601	Burlington	(319)	27,208	29,529
51401	Carroll	(712)	9,579	9,705
50613	Cedar Falls	(319)	34,298	36,322
*52401	Cedar Rapids	(319)	108,780	110,243
52544	Centerville	(515)	5,936	6,558
50616	Charles City	(515)	7,878	8,778
51012	Cherokee	(712)	6,026	7,004
51632	Clarinda	(712)	5,104	5,458
50428	Clear Lake City	(515)	8,183	7,458
52732	Clinton	(319)	29,201	32,828
50053	Clive	(515)	7,462	6,064
52240	Coralville	(319)	10,347	7,687
51501	Council Bluffs	(712)	54,315	56,449
50801	Creston	(515)	7,911	8,429
*52802	Davenport	(319)	95,333	103,264
52101	Decorah	(319)	8,063	7,991
51442	Denison	(712)	6,604	6,675
*50318	Des Moines	(515)	193,187	191,003
52001	Dubuque	(319)	57,546	62,374
51334	Estherville	(712)	6,720	7,518
52556	Fairfield	(515)	9,768	9,428
50501	Fort Dodge	(515)	25,894	29,423
52627	Fort Madison	(319)	11,618	13,520
50112	Grinnell	(515)	8,902	8,868
51537	Harlan	(712)	5,148	5,357
50644	Independence	(319)	5,972	6,392
50125	Indianola	(515)	11,340	10,843
52240	Iowa City	(319)	59,738	50,508
50126	Iowa Falls	(515)	5,441	6,174
52632	Keokuk	(319)	12,451	13,536
50138	Knoxville	(515)	8,232	8,143
51031	Le Mars	(712)	8,454	8,276
52057	Manchester	(319)	5,137	4,942
52060	Maquoketa	(319)	6,129	6,313
52302	Marion	(319)	20,374	19,474
50158	Marshalltown	(515)	25,178	26,938
50401	Mason City	(515)	29,040	30,144
52641	Mount Pleasant	(319)	8,027	7,322
52761	Muscatine	(319)	22,881	23,467
50201	Nevada	(515)	6,009	5,912
50208	Newton	(515)	14,789	15,292
50211	Norwalk		5,726	2,676
50662	Oelwein	(319)	6,493	7,564
52577	Oskaloosa	(515)	10,600	10,989
52501	Ottumwa	(515)	24,488	27,381
50219	Pella	(515)	9,270	8,349
50220	Perry	(515)	6,652	7,053
51566	Red Oak	(712)	6,264	6,810
51601	Shenandoah	(712)	5,572	6,274
51250	Sioux Center	(712)	5,074	4,588
*51101	Sioux City	(712)	80,505	82,003
51301	Spencer	(712)	11,066	11,726
50588	Storm Lake	(712)	8,769	8,814
50322	Urbandale	(515)	23,500	17,869
52349	Vinton	(319)	5,103	5,040
52353	Washington	(319)	7,074	6,584
*50701	Waterloo	(319)	66,467	75,985
50677	Waverly	(319)	8,539	8,444
50595	Webster City	(515)	7,894	8,572
50265	West Des Moines	(515)	31,702	21,894
50311	Windsor Heights	(515)	5,190	5,474

Kansas

ZIP code	Place		1990	1980
67410	Abilene	(913)	6,242	6,572
67005	Arkansas City	(316)	12,762	13,201
66002	Atchison	(913)	10,656	11,407
67010	Augusta	(316)	7,876	6,968

ZIP code	Place	Area code	1990	1980
66012	Bonner Springs	(913)	6,413	6,266
66720	Chanute	(316)	9,488	10,506
67337	Coffeyville	(316)	12,917	15,185
67701	Colby	(913)	5,510	5,544
66901	Concordia	(913)	6,167	6,847
67037	Derby	(316)	14,699	9,786
67801	Dodge City	(316)	21,129	18,001
67042	El Dorado	(316)	11,504	11,551
66801	Emporia	(316)	25,512	25,287
66442	Fort Riley North(u)	(913)	12,848	16,086
66701	Fort Scott	(316)	8,362	8,893
67846	Garden City	(316)	24,097	18,256
67530	Great Bend	(316)	15,427	16,608
67601	Hays	(913)	17,807	16,301
67060	Haysville	(316)	8,364	8,006
67501	Hutchinson	(316)	39,308	40,284
67301	Independence	(316)	9,942	10,598
66749	Iola	(316)	6,351	6,938
66441	Junction City	(913)	20,642	19,305
*66110	Kansas City	(913)	149,800	161,148
66043	Lansing	(913)	7,120	5,307
66044	Lawrence	(913)	65,608	52,738
66048	Leavenworth	(913)	38,495	33,656
66206	Leawood	(913)	19,693	13,360
66215	Lenexa	(913)	34,034	18,639
67901	Liberal	(316)	16,573	14,911
67460	McPherson	(316)	12,422	11,753
66502	Manhattan	(913)	37,712	32,644
66203	Merriam	(913)	11,819	10,794
66222	Mission	(913)	9,504	8,643
67114	Newton	(316)	16,700	16,332
66061	Olathe	(913)	63,352	37,258
66067	Ottawa	(913)	10,667	11,016
66204	Overland Park	(913)	111,790	81,784
.....	Park City		5,050	4,056
67357	Parsons	(316)	11,924	12,898
66762	Pittsburg	(316)	17,775	18,770
66208	Prairie Village	(913)	23,186	24,657
67124	Pratt	(316)	6,687	6,885
66203	Roeland Park	(913)	7,706	7,962
67401	Salina	(913)	42,299	41,843
*66203	Shawnee	(913)	37,962	29,653
*66603	Topeka	(913)	119,883	118,690
67880	Ulysses	(316)	5,474	4,653
67152	Wellington	(316)	8,517	8,212
*67202	Wichita	(316)	304,011	279,838
67156	Winfield	(316)	11,931	10,736

Kentucky

ZIP code	Place	Area code	1990	1980
41001	Alexandria		5,592	4,735
41101	Ashland	(606)	23,622	27,064
40004	Bardstown	(502)	6,801	6,155
41073	Bellevue	(606)	6,997	7,678
40403	Berea	(606)	9,126	8,226
42101	Bowling Green	(502)	40,641	40,450
40218	Buechel(u)	(502)	7,081	6,912
41005	Burlington(u)		6,070	....
42718	Campbellsville	(502)	9,577	8,715
40701	Corbin	(606)	7,419	8,075
*41011	Covington	(606)	43,264	49,585
41031	Cynthiana	(606)	6,497	5,881
40422	Danville	(606)	12,420	12,942
41074	Dayton	(606)	6,576	6,979
.....	Douglass Hills	(502)	5,431	4,384
41017	Edgewood	(606)	8,143	7,243
42701	Elizabethtown	(502)	18,167	15,380
41018	Elsmere	(606)	6,847	7,203
41018	Erlanger	(606)	15,979	14,466
40118	Fairdale(u)	(502)	6,563	7,315
40291	Fern Creek(u)	(502)	16,406	16,866
41139	Flatwoods	(606)	7,799	8,354
41042	Florence	(606)	18,624	15,586
42223	Fort Campbell North(u)	(502)	18,861	17,211
40121	Fort Knox(u)	(502)	21,495	31,055
41017	Fort Mitchell	(606)	7,438	7,294
41075	Fort Thomas	(606)	16,032	16,012
41011	Fort Wright		6,570	4,481
40601	Frankfort	(502)	25,968	25,973
42134	Franklin	(502)	7,607	7,738
40324	Georgetown	(502)	11,414	10,972
42141	Glasgow	(502)	12,351	12,958
40330	Harrodsburg	(606)	7,335	7,265
41701	Hazard	(606)	5,416	5,371
42420	Henderson	(502)	25,945	24,834
40228	Highview(u)	(502)	14,814	13,286
40229	Hillview	(502)	6,119	5,196
42240	Hopkinsville	(502)	29,809	27,318
41051	Independence	(606)	10,444	7,998
40299	Jeffersontown	(502)	23,221	15,795
40342	Lawrenceburg	(502)	5,911	5,167
40033	Lebanon	(502)	5,695	6,590
*40511	Lexington-Fayette	(606)	225,366	204,165
40741	London	(606)	5,757	4,002
*40201	Louisville	(502)	269,063	298,694
.....	Lyndon		8,037	1,553
42431	Madisonville	(502)	16,200	16,979
42066	Mayfield	(502)	9,935	10,705
41056	Maysville	(606)	7,169	7,983
40965	Middlesboro	(606)	11,328	12,251
40243	Middletown		5,016	4,262
42633	Monticello	(606)	5,357	5,677
40351	Morehead	(606)	8,357	7,789
40353	Mount Sterling	(606)	5,362	5,820
40047	Mount Washington	(502)	5,226	3,997
42071	Murray	(502)	14,439	14,248
40218	Newburg(u)	(502)	21,647	24,612
*41071	Newport	(606)	18,871	21,587
40356	Nicholasville	(606)	13,603	10,400
40219	Okolona(u)	(502)	18,902	20,039
42301	Owensboro	(502)	53,549	54,450
42001	Paducah	(502)	27,256	29,315
40361	Paris	(606)	8,730	7,935
41501	Pikeville	(606)	6,324	4,756
40258	Pleasure Ridge Park(u)	(502)	25,131	27,332
42445	Princeton	(502)	6,940	7,073
40160	Radcliff	(502)	19,772	14,656
40475	Richmond	(606)	21,155	21,705
42276	Russellville	(502)	7,454	7,520
.....	St. Dennis(u)		10,326	....
40207	St. Matthews	(502)	15,800	13,519
40065	Shelbyville	(502)	6,238	5,329
40216	Shively	(502)	15,535	16,645
42501	Somerset	(606)	10,733	10,649
.....	Taylor Mill		5,530	4,509
40272	Valley Station(u)	(502)	22,840	24,474
40383	Versailles	(606)	7,269	6,427
.....	Villa Hills	(606)	7,370	4,384
41101	Westwoods(u)	(606)	5,300	5,973
40769	Williamsburg	(606)	5,493	5,560
40391	Winchester	(606)	15,799	15,216

Louisiana

ZIP code	Place	Area code	1990	1980
70510	Abbeville	(318)	11,187	12,391
71301	Alexandria	(318)	49,188	51,648
70032	Arabi(u)	(504)	8,787	10,248
70094	Avondale(u)	(504)	5,813	6,699
70714	Baker	(504)	13,087	12,865
71220	Bastrop	(318)	13,916	15,527
*70821	Baton Rouge	(504)	219,531	220,394
70360	Bayou Cane(u)	(504)	15,876	15,723
70037	Belle Chasse(u)	(504)	8,512	5,412
70427	Bogalusa	(504)	14,280	16,976
71010	Bossier City	(318)	52,721	50,817
70517	Breaux Bridge	(318)	6,515	5,922
70094	Bridge(u)		8,327	....
70811	Brownfields(u)		5,229	....
71291	Brownsville-Bawcomville(u)	(318)	7,397	7,252
71322	Bunkie	(318)	5,044	5,364
70520	Carencro		5,429	3,712
70043	Chalmette(u)	(504)	31,860	33,847
71291	Claiborne(u)	(318)	8,300	6,278
70433	Covington	(504)	7,691	7,892
70526	Crowley	(318)	13,983	16,036
70345	Cut Off(u)	(504)	5,325	5,049
70726	Denham Springs	(504)	8,381	8,563
70634	De Ridder	(318)	9,868	10,337
70047	Destrehan	(504)	8,031	2,382
70346	Donaldsonville	(504)	7,949	7,901
70072	Estelle(u)	(504)	14,091	12,724
70535	Eunice	(318)	11,162	12,479
71459	Fort Polk South	(318)	10,911	12,498
70538	Franklin	(318)	9,004	9,584
70820	Gardere		7,209	....
70737	Gonzales	(504)	7,208	7,287
71245	Grambling		5,556	4,226
70053	Gretna	(504)	17,208	20,615
70401	Hammond	(504)	15,871	15,226
70123	Harahan	(504)	9,927	11,384
70058	Harvey(u)	(504)	21,222	22,709
70360	Houma	(504)	30,495	32,602
70544	Jeanerette	(318)	6,205	6,511
70121	Jefferson(u)	(504)	14,521	15,550
70546	Jennings	(318)	11,305	12,401
70062	Kenner	(504)	72,033	66,382
70445	Lacombe(u)	(504)	6,523	5,146
70501	Lafayette	(318)	94,440	80,584
70601	Lake Charles	(318)	70,580	75,226
71254	Lake Providence	(318)	5,380	6,361
70068	La Place(u)	(504)	24,194	16,112
70373	Larose(u)	(504)	5,772	5,234
71446	Leesville	(318)	7,638	9,054
70448	Mandeville	(504)	7,083	6,076
71052	Mansfield	(318)	5,389	6,485
71351	Marksville	(318)	5,526	5,113
70072	Marrero(u)	(504)	36,671	36,548
70075	Meraux(u)	(504)	8,849	....
70812	Merrydale(u)		10,395	....
*70004	Metairie(u)	(504)	149,428	164,160
71055	Minden	(318)	13,661	15,084
71201	Monroe	(318)	54,909	57,597
70380	Morgan City	(504)	14,531	16,114
70601	Moss Bluff(u)	(318)	8,039	7,004

ZIP code	Place		1990	1980
71457	Natchitoches	(318)	16,609	16,664
70560	New Iberia	(318)	31,828	32,766
*70113	New Orleans	(504)	496,938	557,927
70760	New Roads		5,303	3,924
71463	Oakdale	(318)	6,832	7,155
70810	Oak Hills Place		5,479	....
70570	Opelousas	(318)	18,151	18,903
71360	Pineville	(318)	12,251	12,034
70764	Plaquemine	(504)	7,186	7,521
70454	Ponchatoula	(504)	5,425	5,469
70767	Port Allen	(504)	6,277	6,114
70601	Prien(u)	(318)	6,448	6,224
70394	Raceland(u)	(504)	5,564	6,302
70578	Rayne	(318)	8,502	9,066
.....	Red Chute(u)		5,431	....
70084	Reserve(u)	(504)	8,847	7,288
70123	River Ridge(u)	(504)	14,800	17,146
71270	Ruston	(318)	20,071	20,585
70582	St. Martinville	(318)	7,137	7,965
70087	St. Rose(u)	(504)	6,259	....
70817	Shenandoah(u)		13,429	....
*71102	Shreveport	(318)	198,525	206,989
70458	Slidell	(504)	24,124	26,718
71075	Springhill	(318)	5,668	6,516
70663	Sulphur	(318)	20,125	19,709
71282	Tallulah	(318)	8,526	11,341
70056	Terrytown(u)	(504)	23,787	23,548
70301	Thibodaux	(504)	14,035	15,810
70053	Timberlane(u)	(504)	12,614	11,579
70809	Village St. George(u)		6,242	....
70586	Ville Platte	(318)	9,037	9,201
70092	Violet(u)	(504)	8,574	11,678
70094	Waggaman(u)	(504)	9,405	9,004
70669	Westlake	(318)	5,007	5,246
71291	West Monroe	(318)	14,096	14,993
70094	Westwego	(504)	11,218	12,663
71483	Winnfield	(318)	6,138	7,311
71295	Winnsboro	(318)	5,755	5,921
70791	Zachary	(504)	9,036	7,297

Maine (207)

See Note on Page 398

ZIP code	Place	1990	1980
04210	Auburn	24,309	23,128
04330	Augusta	21,325	21,819
04401	Bangor	33,181	31,643
04530	Bath	9,799	10,246
04915	Belfast	6,355	6,243
03901	*Berwick*	5,995	....
04005	Biddeford	20,710	19,638
04412	Brewer	9,021	9,017
04011	Brunswick Center(u)	14,683	10,990
04011	*Brunswick*	20,906	17,366
04093	*Buxton*	6,494	5,775
04843	*Camden*	5,060	....
04107	*Cape Elizabeth*	8,854	7,838
04736	Caribou	9,415	9,916
04021	*Cumberland*	5,836	5,284
03903	Eliot	5,329	....
04605	Ellsworth	5,975	5,179
04937	*Fairfield*	6,718	6,113
04105	*Falmouth*	7,610	6,853
04938	*Farmington*	7,436	6,730
04032	*Freeport*	6,905	5,863
04345	Gardiner	6,746	6,485
04038	*Gorham*	11,856	10,101
04039	Gray	5,904	....
04444	*Hampden*	5,974	5,250
.....	*Harpswell*	5,012	....
04730	Houlton Center(u)	5,627	5,730
04730	*Houlton*	6,613	6,766
04239	*Jay*	5,080	5,080
04043	*Kennebunk*	8,004	6,621
03904	Kittery Center(u)	5,151	5,465
03904	*Kittery*	9,372	9,314
04240	Lewiston	39,757	40,481
04750	*Limestone*	9,922	8,719
04457	*Lincoln*	5,587	5,066
04250	*Lisbon*	9,457	8,769
04750	Loring(u)	5,494	6,572
04462	Millinocket Center(u)	6,922	7,567
04462	*Millinocket*	7,567	7,742
04963	*Oakland*	5,595	5,162
04064	Old Orchard Beach Ctr.(u)	7,789	6,023
04064	*Old Orchard Beach*	7,789	6,291
04468	Old Town	8,317	8,422
04473	Orono Center(u)	9,789	9,891
04473	*Orono*	10,573	10,578
*04101	Portland	64,358	61,572
04769	Presque Isle	10,550	11,172
04841	Rockland	7,972	7,919
04276	Rumford Compact(u)	5,419	6,256
04276	*Rumford*	7,078	8,240
04072	Saco	15,181	12,921
04073	Sanford Center(u)	10,296	10,268
04073	*Sanford*	20,463	18,020
04074	*Scarborough*	12,518	11,347
04976	Skowhegan Center(u)	6,990	6,517
04976	*Skowhegan*	8,725	8,098
03908	*South Berwick*	5,877	....
04106	South Portland	23,163	22,712
04084	*Standish*	7,678	5,946
04086	*Topsham*	8,746	6,147
04901	Waterville	17,173	17,779
04090	*Wells*	7,778	8,211
04092	Westbrook	16,121	14,976
04082	*Windham*	13,020	11,282
04901	Winslow Center(u)	5,436	5,903
04901	*Winslow*	7,997	8,057
04364	*Winthrop*	5,986	5,889
04096	*Yarmouth*	7,862	6,585
03909	*York*	9,818	8,465

Maryland

ZIP code	Place		1990	1980
21001	Aberdeen	(410)	13,087	11,533
21005	Aberdeen Proving Ground(u)		5,267	5,722
20783	Adelphi(u)	(301)	13,524	12,530
20331	Andrews AFB(u)	(410)	10,228	10,064
*21401	Annapolis	(410)	33,187	31,740
21227	Arbutus(u)	(410)	19,750	20,163
21012	Arnold(u)	(410)	20,261	12,285
20906	Aspen Hill(u)	(301)	45,494	47,455
.....	Ballenger Creek		5,546	2,659
*21233	Baltimore	(410)	736,014	786,741
21014	Bel Air	(410)	8,860	7,814
21050	Bel Air North(u)	(410)	14,880	5,043
21014	Bel Air South(u)	(410)	26,421	8,461
20705	Beltsville(u)	(301)	14,476	12,760
*20815	Bethesda(u)	(301)	62,936	62,736
20710	Bladensburg	(301)	8,064	7,691
*20715	Bowie	(301)	37,589	33,695
.....	Bowleys Quarters(u)		5,595	....
21225	Brooklyn Park(u)	(410)	10,987	11,508
20866	Burtonsville(u)		5,853	2,046
20818	Cabin John-Brookmont(u)		5,341	5,135
20619	California(u)	(410)	7,626	5,770
.....	Calverton(u)	(301)	12,046	....
21613	Cambridge	(410)	11,514	11,703
20748	Camp Springs(u)	(301)	16,392	16,118
21401	Cape St. Clair(u)	(410)	7,878	6,022
21234	Carney(u)	(410)	25,578	21,488
21228	Catonsville(u)	(410)	35,233	33,208
.....	Chesapeake Ranch Estates(u)		5,423	....
20785	Cheverly	(301)	6,023	5,751
20815	Chevy Chase(u)	(301)	8,559	12,232
20783	Chillum(u)	(301)	31,309	32,775
20735	Clinton(u)	(301)	19,987	16,438
20904	Cloverly(u)	(301)	7,904	5,153
21030	Cockeysville(u)	(410)	18,668	17,013
20904	Colesville(u)	(301)	18,819	14,359
20740	College Park	(301)	23,714	23,614
*21044	Columbia(u)	(301)	75,883	52,518
20743	Coral Hills(u)	(410)	11,032	11,602
21114	Crofton(u)	(410)	12,781	12,009
21502	Cumberland	(301)	23,706	25,933
20872	Damascus	(301)	9,817	4,129
20747	District Heights	(301)	6,704	6,799
21222	Dundalk(u)	(410)	65,800	71,293
21601	Easton	(410)	9,372	7,536
20737	East Riverdale(u)	(301)	14,187	14,117
21219	Edgemere(u)	(410)	9,226	9,078
21040	Edgewood(u)	(410)	23,903	19,455
21784	Eldersburg(u)		9,720	4,959
.....	Elkridge(u)		12,953	....
21921	Elkton	(410)	9,073	6,468
21043	Ellicott City(u)	(410)	41,396	21,784
21221	Essex(u)	(410)	40,872	39,614
20904	Fairland(u)	(301)	19,828	5,154
21047	Fallston(u)	(410)	5,730	5,572
21061	Ferndale(u)	(410)	16,355	14,314
20747	Forestville(u)	(301)	16,731	16,401
20755	Fort Meade(u)	(301)	12,509	14,083
20744	Fort Washington(u)		24,032	....
21701	Frederick	(301)	40,148	28,086
.....	Friendly(u)	(301)	9,028	8,848
21532	Frostburg	(301)	8,075	7,715
*20877	Gaithersburg	(301)	39,542	26,424
21055	Garrison(u)		5,045	....
20874	Germantown(u)	(301)	41,145	9,721
20706	Glenarden		5,025	4,993
21061	Glen Burnie(u)	(410)	37,305	37,263
20769	Glenn Dale(u)	(301)	9,689	5,106
20772	Greater Upper Marlboro		11,528	....
20770	Greenbelt	(301)	21,096	17,332
21122	Green Haven(u)	(410)	14,416	6,577
.....	Green Valley(u)		9,424	4,504
21740	Hagerstown	(301)	35,445	34,132
21740	Halfway(u)	(301)	8,873	8,659
21078	Havre De Grace	(410)	8,952	8,763
20903	Hillandale(u)		10,318	9,686
20748	Hillcrest Heights(u)	(301)	17,136	17,021
*20780	Hyattsville	(301)	13,864	12,709
20794	Jessup(u)		6,537	4,288

ZIP code	Place	Area code	1990	1980
21085	Joppatowne(u)	(410)	11,084	11,348
20785	Kentland(u)	(301)	7,967	8,596
20772	Kettering(u)		9,901	6,972
21122	Lake Shore(u)	(410)	13,269	10,181
20785	Landover(u)	(301)	5,052	5,374
20787	Langley Park(u)	(301)	17,474	14,038
20706	Lanham-Seabrook(u)	(301)	16,792	15,814
21227	Lansdowne-Baltimore Highlands(u)		15,509	16,759
20646	La Plata	(301)	5,841	2,484
20772	Largo(u)	(301)	9,475	5,557
*20707	Laurel	(301)	19,438	12,103
20653	Lexington Pk.(u)	(410)	9,943	10,361
21090	Linthicum(u)	(410)	7,547	7,457
21207	Lochearn(u)	(410)	25,240	26,908
21037	Londontowne(u)	(410)	6,992	6,052
.....	Long Meadow(u)		5,594	1,203
21093	Lutherville-Timonium(u)		16,442	17,854
20748	Marlow Heights(u)	(301)	5,885	5,824
.....	Marlton		5,523	....
20707	Maryland City(u)		6,813	6,949
.....	Mays Chapel(u)		10,132	5,213
21220	Middle River(u)	(410)	24,616	26,756
.....	Milford Mill(u)		22,547	20,354
20717	Mitchellville		12,593	....
20879	Montgomery Village(u)	(301)	32,315	18,725
20822	Mount Rainier	(301)	7,954	7,361
21402	Naval Academy(u)	(410)	5,420	5,367
20784	New Carrollton	(301)	12,002	12,632
20815	North Bethesda(u)	(301)	29,656	22,671
20895	North Kensington(u)	(301)	8,607	9,039
20707	North Laurel(u)	(301)	15,008	6,093
.....	North Potomac(u)	(301)	18,456	....
21842	Ocean City	(410)	5,146	4,946
21113	Odenton(u)	(410)	12,833	13,270
20832	Olney(u)	(301)	23,019	13,026
21206	Overlea(u)	(410)	12,137	12,965
21117	Owings Mills(u)	(410)	9,474	9,526
20745	Oxon Hill-Glassmanor(u)	(301)	35,794	36,267
20785	Palmer Park(u)	(301)	7,019	7,986
21234	Parkville	(410)	31,617	35,159
21401	Parole		10,054	3,377
21122	Pasadena(u)	(410)	10,012	7,439
21128	Perry Hall(u)	(410)	22,723	13,455
21208	Pikesville(u)	(410)	24,815	22,555
20854	Potomac(u)	(301)	45,634	40,402
21227	Pumphrey(u)		5,483	5,666
21133	Randallstown(u)	(301)	26,277	25,927
.....	Redland(u)	(301)	16,145	10,759
21136	Reisterstown(u)	(410)	19,314	19,385
20737	Riverdale		5,185	4,761
21122	Riviera Beach(u)	(410)	11,376	8,812
*20850	Rockville	(301)	44,835	43,811
.....	Rosaryville(u)		8,976	....
21237	Rosedale(u)	(410)	18,703	19,956
.....	Rossmoor(u)		6,182	8,646
21221	Rossville(u)		9,492	8,646
20601	St. Charles(u)	(301)	28,717	13,921
21801	Salisbury	(410)	20,592	16,429
20763	Savage-Guilford(u)		9,669	2,928
20743	Seat Pleasant	(301)	5,359	5,217
21144	Severn(u)	(410)	24,499	20,147
21146	Severna Park(u)	(410)	25,879	21,253
*20907	Silver Spring(u)	(301)	76,046	72,893
21061	South Gate(u)	(410)	27,564	24,185
20895	South Kensington(u)	(301)	8,777	9,344
20707	South Laurel(u)		18,591	18,034
20746	Suitland-Silver Hills(u)	(301)	35,111	32,164
20912	Takoma Park	(301)	16,700	16,231
20748	Temple Hills(u)	(301)	6,865	6,630
21204	Towson(u)	(410)	49,445	51,083
20601	Waldorf(u)	(301)	15,058	9,782
20743	Walker Mill(u)	(301)	10,920	10,651
21157	Westminster	(410)	13,068	8,808
20902	Wheaton Glenmont(u)	(301)	53,720	48,598
21162	White Marsh(u)		8,183	....
20903	White Oak(u)	(301)	18,671	13,700
21207	Woodlawn(u)	(410)	32,907	....
21207	Woodlawn(u)		5,329	5,306

Massachusetts

See Note on Page 398

ZIP code	Place	Area code	1990	1980
02351	*Abington*	(617)	13,817	13,887
01720	*Acton*	(508)	17,872	17,544
02743	*Acushnet*	(508)	9,554	8,704
01220	Adams Center(u)	(413)	6,356	6,857
01220	*Adams*	(413)	9,445	10,381
01001	*Agawam*	(413)	27,323	26,271
01913	Amesbury Center(u)	(508)	12,109	12,236
01913	*Amesbury*	(508)	14,997	13,971
01002	Amherst Center	(413)	17,824	17,773
01002	*Amherst*	(413)	35,228	33,229
01810	Andover	(508)	8,242	8,445
01810	*Andover*	(508)	29,151	26,370
02174	*Arlington*	(617)	44,630	44,630
01430	Ashburnham	(508)	5,433	....
01721	*Ashland*	(508)	12,066	9,165
01331	Athol Center(u)	(508)	8,732	8,708
01331	*Athol*	(508)	11,451	10,634
02703	Attleboro	(508)	38,383	34,196
01501	*Auburn*	(508)	15,005	14,845
*01432	*Ayer*	(508)	6,871	6,993
02630	*Barnstable*	(508)	40,949	30,898
01730	*Bedford*	(617)	12,996	13,067
01007	*Belchertown*	(413)	10,579	8,339
02019	*Bellingham*	(508)	14,877	14,300
02178	*Belmont*	(617)	24,720	24,720
01915	Beverly	(508)	38,195	37,655
01821	*Billerica*	(508)	37,609	36,727
01504	*Blackstone*	(508)	8,023	6,570
*02109	Boston	(617)	574,283	562,994
02532	*Bourne*	(508)	16,064	13,874
01921	*Boxford*	(508)	6,266	5,374
02184	*Braintree*	(617)	33,836	36,337
02631	*Brewster*	(508)	8,440	5,226
02324	*Bridgewater*	(508)	21,249	7,242
*02403	Brockton	(508)	92,788	95,172
02146	*Brookline*	(617)	54,718	55,062
01803	*Burlington*	(617)	23,302	23,486
*02138	Cambridge	(617)	95,802	95,322
02021	*Canton*	(617)	18,530	18,182
02330	*Carver*	(508)	10,590	6,988
02632	Centerville	(508)	9,190	3,640
01507	*Charlton*	(508)	9,576	6,719
02633	*Chatham*	(508)	6,579	6,071
01824	*Chelmsford*	(508)	32,383	32,388
02150	Chelsea	(617)	28,710	25,431
*01021	Chicopee	(413)	56,632	55,112
01510	*Clinton*	(508)	13,222	7,943
01778	Cochituate(u)	(508)	6,046	6,126
02025	*Cohasset*	(617)	7,075	7,174
01742	*Concord*	(508)	17,076	16,293
01226	*Dalton*	(413)	7,155	6,797
01923	*Danvers*	(508)	24,174	24,174
02714	*Dartmouth*	(508)	27,244	23,966
02026	*Dedham*	(617)	23,782	25,298
01342	*Deerfield*	(413)	5,018	....
02638	*Dennis*	(508)	13,864	12,360
02715	*Dighton*	(508)	5,631	5,352
.....	*Douglas*	(508)	5,438	....
01826	*Dracut*	(508)	25,594	21,249
01570	*Dudley*	(508)	9,540	8,717
02332	*Duxbury*	(617)	13,895	11,807
02333	*East Bridgewater*	(508)	11,104	9,945
02536	East Falmouth(u)	(508)	5,577	5,181
01027	*Easthampton*	(413)	15,537	15,580
01028	*East Longmeadow*	(413)	13,367	12,905
02334	*Easton*	(508)	19,807	16,623
02149	Everett	(617)	35,701	37,195
02719	*Fairhaven*	(508)	16,132	15,759
*02722	Fall River	(508)	92,703	92,574
02540	*Falmouth*	(508)	27,960	41,194
01420	Fitchburg	(508)	41,194	39,580
01433	Fort Devens(u)	(508)	8,973	9,546
02035	*Foxborough*	(508)	14,637	5,706
01701	*Framingham*	(508)	64,994	65,113
02038	Franklin Center(u)	(508)	9,965	9,296
02038	*Franklin*	(508)	22,095	18,217
02702	*Freetown*	(508)	8,522	7,058
01440	Gardner	(508)	20,125	17,900
01833	*Georgetown*	(508)	6,384	5,687
01930	Gloucester	(508)	28,716	27,768
01519	*Grafton*	(508)	13,035	11,238
01033	*Granby*	(413)	5,565	5,380
01230	*Great Barrington*	(413)	7,725	7,405
01301	Greenfield Center(u)	(413)	14,016	14,198
01302	*Greenfield*	(413)	18,666	18,436
01450	*Groton*	(508)	7,511	6,154
01834	*Groveland*	(508)	5,214	5,040
02338	*Halifax*	(617)	6,526	5,513
01936	*Hamilton*	(508)	7,280	6,960
02339	*Hanover*	(617)	11,912	11,358
02341	*Hanson*	(617)	9,028	8,508
01451	*Harvard*	(508)	12,329	12,170
02645	*Harwich*	(508)	10,275	8,971
01830	Haverhill	(508)	51,418	46,865
02043	*Hingham*	(617)	19,821	5,454
02343	*Holbrook*	(617)	11,041	11,041
01520	*Holden*	(508)	14,628	13,336
01746	*Holliston*	(508)	12,926	12,622
01040	Holyoke	(413)	43,704	44,678
01747	*Hopedale*	(508)	5,666	....
01748	*Hopkinton*	(508)	9,191	7,114
01749	Hudson Center(u)	(508)	14,267	14,156
01749	*Hudson*	(508)	17,233	14,267
02045	*Hull*	(617)	10,466	10,466
02601	Hyannis(u)	(508)	14,120	9,118
01938	*Ipswich*	(508)	11,873	11,158
02364	*Kingston*	(617)	9,045	7,362
02346	*Lakeville*	(617)	7,785	5,931
01523	*Lancaster*	(508)	6,661	6,334
*01842	Lawrence	(508)	70,207	63,175
01238	*Lee*	(413)	5,849	6,247
01524	*Leicester*	(508)	10,191	9,446
01240	*Lenox*	(413)	5,069	6,523
01453	Leominster	(508)	38,145	34,508

ZIP code	Place		1990	1980
02173	*Lexington*	(617)	28,974	29,479
01773	*Lincoln*	(617)	7,666	7,098
01460	*Littleton*	(508)	7,051	6,970
01106	*Longmeadow*	(413)	15,467	15,467
*01853	Lowell	(508)	103,439	92,418
01056	*Ludlow*	(413)	18,820	18,150
01462	*Lunenburg*	(508)	9,117	8,405
*01901	Lynn	(617)	81,245	78,471
01940	*Lynnfield*	(617)	11,274	11,267
02148	Malden	(617)	53,884	53,386
01944	*Manchester*	(508)	5,286	5,424
02048	*Mansfield*	(508)	16,568	7,170
01945	*Marblehead*	(617)	19,971	19,971
01752	Marlborough	(508)	31,813	30,617
02050	*Marshfield*	(617)	21,531	20,916
02648	Marstons Mills(u)		8,017	....
02649	*Mashpee*	(508)	7,884	....
02739	*Mattapoisett*	(508)	5,850	5,597
01754	*Maynard*	(508)	10,325	10,325
02052	*Medfield*	(508)	10,531	5,985
02155	Medford	(617)	57,407	58,076
02053	*Medway*	(508)	9,931	8,447
02176	Melrose	(617)	28,150	30,055
01860	Merrimac	(508)	5,166	....
01844	*Methuen*	(508)	39,990	36,701
02346	Middleborough Center(u)	(617)	6,837	7,012
02346	*Middleborough*	(617)	17,867	16,404
01757	Milford Center(u)	(508)	23,339	21,730
01757	*Milford*	(508)	25,355	23,390
01527	*Millbury*	(508)	12,228	11,808
02054	*Millis*	(508)	7,613	6,908
02186	*Milton*	(617)	25,725	25,860
01057	*Monson*	(413)	7,776	7,315
01351	*Montague*	(413)	8,316	8,011
02554	*Nantucket*	(508)	6,012	5,087
01760	*Natick*	(508)	30,510	29,461
02192	*Needham*	(617)	27,557	27,901
*02741	New Bedford	(508)	99,922	98,478
01951	*Newbury*	(508)	5,623	....
01950	Newburyport	(508)	16,317	15,900
02158	Newton	(617)	82,585	83,622
02056	*Norfolk*	(508)	9,270	6,363
01247	North Adams	(413)	16,797	18,063
01002	North Amherst(u)	(413)	6,239	5,616
01060	Northampton	(413)	29,289	29,286
01845	*North Andover*	(508)	22,792	20,129
*02760	*North Attleborough*	(508)	25,038	16,178
01532	*Northborough*	(508)	11,929	5,761
01534	*Northbridge*	(508)	13,371	12,246
01864	*North Reading*	(508)	12,002	11,455
02766	*Norton*	(508)	14,265	12,690
02061	*Norwell*	(617)	9,279	9,182
02062	*Norwood*	(617)	28,700	29,711
01364	*Orange*	(508)	7,312	6,844
02653	*Orleans*	(508)	5,838	5,306
01540	Oxford Center(u)	(508)	5,969	6,369
01540	*Oxford*	(508)	12,588	11,680
01069	*Palmer*	(413)	12,054	11,389
01960	Peabody	(508)	47,264	45,976
02359	*Pembroke*	(617)	14,544	13,487
01463	*Pepperell*	(508)	10,098	8,061
01866	Pinehurst(u)	(508)	6,614	6,588
01201	Pittsfield	(413)	48,622	51,974
02762	*Plainville*	(508)	6,871	5,857
*02360	Plymouth Center(u)	(508)	7,258	7,232
02360	*Plymouth*	(508)	45,608	35,913
02169	Quincy	(617)	84,985	84,743
02368	*Randolph*	(617)	30,093	28,218
02767	*Raynham*	(508)	9,867	9,085
01867	*Reading*	(617)	22,539	22,678
02769	*Rehoboth*	(508)	8,656	7,570
02151	Revere	(617)	42,786	42,423
02370	*Rockland*	(617)	16,123	15,695
01966	*Rockport*	(508)	7,482	5,448
01970	Salem	(508)	38,091	38,276
01950	*Salisbury*	(508)	6,882	5,973
02563	*Sandwich*	(508)	15,489	8,727
01906	*Saugus*	(617)	25,549	25,549
02066	*Scituate*	(617)	16,786	5,180
02771	*Seekonk*	(508)	13,046	12,269
02067	*Sharon*	(617)	15,517	5,893
01464	*Shirley*	(508)	6,118	5,124
01545	*Shrewsbury*	(508)	24,146	22,674
02725	*Somerset*	(508)	17,655	18,813
02143	Somerville(u)	(617)	76,210	77,372
01002	South Amherst	(413)	5,053	4,861
01772	*Southborough*	(508)	6,628	6,193
01550	Southbridge Center(u)	(508)	12,882	14,261
01550	*Southbridge*	(508)	17,816	13,631
01075	*South Hadley*	(413)	16,685	16,399
01077	*Southwick*	(413)	7,667	7,382
02664	South Yarmouth(u)	(508)	10,358	7,525
01562	Spencer Center(u)	(508)	6,306	6,350
01562	*Spencer*	(508)	11,645	10,774
*01101	Springfield	(413)	156,983	152,319
01564	*Sterling*	(508)	6,481	5,440
02180	*Stoneham*	(617)	22,203	21,424
02072	*Stoughton*	(617)	26,777	26,710
01775	*Stow*	(508)	5,328	5,144
01566	*Sturbridge*	(508)	7,775	5,976
01776	*Sudbury*	(508)	14,358	14,027
01527	*Sutton*	(508)	6,824	5,855
01907	*Swampscott*	(617)	13,650	13,837
02777	*Swansea*	(508)	15,411	15,461
02780	Taunton	(508)	49,832	45,001
01468	*Templeton*	(508)	6,438	6,070
01876	*Tewksbury*	(508)	27,266	24,635
01983	*Topsfield*	(508)	5,754	5,709
01469	*Townsend*	(508)	8,496	7,201
01879	*Tyngsborough*	(508)	8,642	5,683
01569	*Uxbridge*	(508)	10,415	8,374
01880	*Wakefield*	(617)	24,825	24,895
02081	*Walpole*	(508)	20,212	5,495
02154	Waltham	(617)	57,878	58,200
01082	Ware Center(u)	(413)	6,533	6,806
01082	*Ware*	(413)	9,808	8,953
02571	*Wareham*	(508)	19,232	18,457
02172	*Watertown*	(617)	33,284	34,384
01778	*Wayland*	(508)	11,874	12,170
01570	Webster Center(u)	(508)	11,849	11,175
01570	*Webster*	(508)	16,196	14,480
02181	*Wellesley*	(617)	26,615	27,209
01581	*Westborough*	(508)	14,133	13,619
01583	*West Boylston*	(508)	6,611	6,204
02379	*West Bridgewater*	(508)	6,389	6,359
01742	West Concord(u)	(508)	5,761	5,331
01085	Westfield	(413)	38,372	36,465
01886	*Westford*	(508)	16,392	13,434
01473	*Westminster*	(508)	6,191	5,139
02193	*Weston*	(617)	10,200	11,169
02790	*Westport*	(508)	13,852	13,763
01089	*West Springfield*	(413)	27,537	27,042
02090	*Westwood*	(617)	12,557	13,212
02673	West Yarmouth	(508)	5,409	3,852
02188	*Weymouth*	(617)	54,063	55,601
01588	Whitinsville(u)	(508)	5,639	5,379
02382	*Whitman*	(617)	13,240	13,534
01095	*Wilbraham*	(413)	12,635	12,053
01267	*Williamstown*	(413)	8,220	8,741
01887	*Wilmington*	(508)	17,654	17,471
01475	*Winchendon*	(508)	8,805	7,019
01890	*Winchester*	(617)	20,267	20,701
02152	*Winthrop*	(617)	18,127	19,294
01801	Woburn	(617)	35,943	36,626
*01613	Worcester	(508)	169,759	161,799
02093	*Wrentham*	(508)	9,006	7,580
02675	*Yarmouth*	(508)	21,174	18,449

Michigan

ZIP code	Place		1990	1980
49221	Adrian	(517)	22,097	21,276
49224	Albion	(517)	10,066	11,059
49401	Allendale(u)		6,950	....
48101	Allen Park	(313)	31,092	34,196
48801	Alma	(517)	9,034	9,652
49707	Alpena	(517)	11,354	12,214
*48106	Ann Arbor	(313)	109,578	107,969
48057	Auburn Hills	(313)	17,076	15,388
49016	Battle Creek	(616)	53,516	35,724
48706	Bay City	(517)	38,936	41,593
48505	Beecher(u)	(313)	14,465	17,178
48809	Belding	(616)	5,969	5,634
49022	Benton Harbor	(616)	12,818	14,707
49022	Benton Heights(u)	(616)	5,465	6,787
48072	Berkley	(313)	16,960	18,637
48009	Beverly Hills	(313)	10,610	11,598
49307	Big Rapids	(616)	12,603	14,361
*48012	Birmingham	(313)	19,997	21,689
48013	Bloomfield(u)	(313)	42,137	42,876
48722	Bridgeport(u)	(517)	8,569	....
48116	Brighton	(313)	5,686	4,268
48601	Buena Vista		8,196	....
*48502	Burton	(313)	27,617	29,976
49601	Cadillac	(616)	10,104	10,199
48187	Canton(u)	(313)	57,047	....
48724	Carrollton(u)	(517)	6,521	7,482
48015	Center Line	(313)	9,026	9,293
48813	Charlotte	(517)	8,083	8,251
48017	Clawson	(313)	13,874	15,103
48043	Clinton(u)	(517)	85,866	72,400
49036	Coldwater	(517)	9,607	9,461
49321	Comstock Park(u)	(616)	6,530	5,506
49508	Cutlerville(u)	(616)	11,228	8,256
48423	Davison	(313)	5,693	6,087
*48120	Dearborn	(313)	89,286	90,660
48127	Dearborn Heights	(313)	60,838	67,706
*48233	Detroit	(313)	1,027,974	1,203,368
49047	Dowagiac	(616)	6,418	6,307
48021	East Detroit	(313)	35,283	38,280
49506	East Grand Rapids	(616)	10,807	10,914
48823	East Lansing	(517)	50,677	51,392
49001	Eastwood(u)	(616)	6,340	7,186
48229	Ecorse	(313)	12,180	14,447
49829	Escanaba	(906)	13,659	14,355
49022	Fair Plain(u)	(616)	8,051	8,289
48024	Farmington	(313)	10,170	11,022

ZIP code	Place		1990	1980
48024	Farmington Hills	(313)	74,614	58,056
48430	Fenton	(313)	8,434	8,098
48220	Ferndale	(313)	25,084	26,227
48134	Flat Rock	(313)	7,290	6,853
*48502	Flint	(313)	140,761	159,611
48433	Flushing	(313)	8,542	8,624
49506	Forest Hills		16,690	....
48026	Fraser	(313)	13,899	14,560
48135	Garden City	(313)	31,846	35,640
48439	Grand Blanc	(313)	7,760	6,848
49417	Grand Haven	(616)	11,951	11,763
48837	Grand Ledge	(517)	7,562	6,920
*49501	Grand Rapids	(616)	189,126	181,843
49418	Grandville	(616)	15,624	12,412
48838	Greenville	(616)	8,101	8,019
48138	Grosse Ile(u)	(313)	9,781	9,320
48236	Grosse Pointe	(313)	5,681	5,901
48236	Grosse Pointe Farms	(313)	10,092	10,551
48236	Grosse Pointe Park	(313)	12,857	13,562
48236	Grosse Pointe Woods	(313)	17,715	18,886
48212	Hamtramck	(313)	18,372	21,300
48225	Harper Woods	(313)	14,903	16,361
48625	Harrison(u)	(517)	24,685	23,649
48840	Haslett(u)	(517)	10,230	7,025
49058	Hastings	(616)	6,549	6,418
48030	Hazel Park	(313)	20,051	20,914
48203	Highland Park	(313)	20,121	27,909
49242	Hillsdale	(517)	8,175	7,432
49423	Holland	(616)	30,745	26,281
48442	Holly	(313)	5,595	4,874
48842	Holt(u)	(517)	11,744	10,097
49931	Houghton	(906)	7,498	7,512
48843	Howell	(517)	8,184	6,976
49426	Hudsonville		6,170	4,844
48070	Huntington Woods	(313)	6,419	6,937
48141	Inkster	(313)	30,772	35,190
48846	Ionia	(616)	5,990	5,920
49801	Iron Mountain	(906)	8,525	8,341
49938	Ironwood	(906)	6,849	7,741
49849	Ishpeming	(906)	7,200	7,538
*49201	Jackson	(517)	37,425	39,739
49428	Jenison(u)	(616)	17,882	16,330
*49001	Kalamazoo	(616)	80,277	79,722
49508	Kentwood	(616)	37,826	30,438
49801	Kingsford	(906)	5,480	5,290
49843	K.I. Sawyer(u)	(906)	6,577	7,345
48144	Lambertville(u)	(313)	7,860	6,341
*48924	Lansing	(517)	127,321	130,414
48446	Lapeer	(313)	7,759	6,198
48146	Lincoln Park	(313)	41,832	45,105
*48150	Livonia	(313)	100,850	104,814
49431	Ludington	(616)	8,507	8,937
48071	Madison Heights	(313)	32,196	35,375
49660	Manistee	(616)	6,734	7,665
49855	Marquette	(906)	21,977	23,288
49068	Marshall	(616)	6,941	7,201
48040	Marysville	(313)	8,515	7,345
48854	Mason	(517)	6,768	6,019
48122	Melvindale	(313)	11,216	12,322
49858	Menominee	(906)	9,398	10,099
48640	Midland	(517)	38,053	37,269
48042	Milford	(313)	5,500	5,041
48161	Monroe	(313)	22,902	23,531
48043	Mount Clemens	(313)	18,405	18,991
48858	Mount Pleasant	(517)	23,285	23,746
*49440	Muskegon	(616)	39,809	40,823
49444	Muskegon Heights	(616)	13,176	14,611
48047	New Baltimore	(313)	5,798	5,439
49120	Niles	(616)	12,458	13,115
.....	Northview(u)		13,712	11,662
48167	Northville	(313)	6,226	5,698
49441	Norton Shores	(616)	21,755	22,025
48050	Novi	(313)	32,998	22,525
48237	Oak Park	(313)	30,468	31,537
48864	Okemos(u)	(517)	20,216	8,882
48867	Owosso	(517)	16,322	16,455
49770	Petoskey	(616)	6,056	6,097
48170	Plymouth	(313)	9,560	9,986
48170	Plymouth Township(u)	(313)	23,646	....
*48053	Pontiac	(313)	71,136	76,715
49081	Portage	(616)	41,042	38,157
48060	Port Huron	(313)	33,694	33,981
48239	Redford(u)	(313)	54,387	58,441
48218	River Rouge	(313)	11,314	12,912
48192	Riverview	(313)	13,894	14,569
48063	Rochester	(313)	7,130	7,203
48307	Rochester Hills		61,766	40,704
48174	Romulus	(313)	22,897	24,857
48066	Roseville	(313)	51,412	54,311
*48068	Royal Oak	(313)	65,410	70,893
*48605	Saginaw	(517)	69,512	77,508
48604	Saginaw Township North	(517)	23,018	....
48603	Saginaw Township South	(517)	13,987	....
48079	St. Clair	(313)	5,116	4,780
*48083	St. Clair Shores	(313)	68,107	76,210
48879	St. Johns	(517)	7,392	7,376
49085	St. Joseph	(616)	9,214	9,622
48176	Saline	(313)	6,660	6,483
49783	Sault Ste. Marie	(906)	14,689	14,448
49455	Shelby		48,655	....
48609	Shields		6,634	....
*48075	Southfield	(313)	75,727	75,568
48198	Southgate	(313)	30,771	32,058
49090	South Haven	(616)	5,563	5,943
48178	South Lyon	(313)	6,427	5,214
48161	South Monroe(u)		5,266	4,232
49015	Springfield	(616)	5,582	5,917
*48078	Sterling Heights	(313)	117,810	108,999
49091	Sturgis	(616)	10,130	9,468
48180	Taylor	(313)	70,811	77,568
49286	Tecumseh	(517)	7,462	7,320
48182	Temperance	(313)	6,542	....
49093	Three Rivers	(616)	7,464	7,015
49684	Traverse City	(616)	15,155	15,516
48183	Trenton	(313)	20,586	22,762
48084	Troy	(313)	72,884	67,102
48087	Utica	(313)	5,081	5,282
49504	Walker	(616)	17,279	15,088
48088	Walled Lake		6,278	4,748
*48089	Warren	(313)	144,864	161,134
48095	Waterford(u)	(313)	66,692	64,250
48917	Waverly		15,614	....
48184	Wayne	(313)	19,899	21,159
48033	West Bloomfield(u)	(313)	54,843	41,962
48185	Westland	(313)	84,724	84,603
49007	Westwood(u)	(616)	8,957	8,519
48096	Wixom	(313)	8,550	6,705
48183	Woodhaven	(313)	11,631	10,902
48753	Wurtsmith AFB(u)	(517)	5,080	5,166
*48192	Wyandotte	(313)	30,938	34,006
49509	Wyoming	(616)	63,891	59,616
48197	Ypsilanti	(313)	24,846	24,031
49464	Zeeland	(616)	5,417	4,764

Minnesota

ZIP code	Place		1990	1980
56007	Albert Lea	(507)	18,310	19,200
56308	Alexandria	(612)	8,029	7,608
55303	Andover	(612)	15,216	9,387
55303	Anoka	(612)	17,192	15,634
55124	Apple Valley	(612)	34,598	21,818
55112	Arden Hills	(612)	9,199	8,012
55912	Austin	(507)	21,907	23,020
56601	Bemidji	(218)	11,165	10,949
55433	Blaine	(612)	38,975	28,558
55420	Bloomington	(612)	86,335	81,831
56401	Brainerd	(218)	12,353	11,489
55429	Brooklyn Center	(612)	28,887	31,230
55429	Brooklyn Park	(612)	56,381	43,332
55313	Buffalo	(612)	6,856	4,560
55337	Burnsville	(612)	51,288	35,674
55008	Cambridge		5,094	3,287
55316	Champlin	(612)	16,849	9,006
55317	Chanhassen	(612)	11,732	6,359
55318	Chaska	(612)	11,339	8,346
55719	Chisholm	(218)	5,290	5,930
55720	Cloquet	(218)	10,885	11,142
55421	Columbia Heights	(612)	18,910	20,029
55433	Coon Rapids	(612)	52,978	35,826
.....	Corcoran	(612)	5,199	4,252
55016	Cottage Grove	(612)	22,935	18,994
56716	Crookston	(218)	8,119	8,628
55428	Crystal	(612)	23,788	25,543
56501	Detroit Lakes	(218)	6,635	7,106
*55806	Duluth	(218)	85,493	92,811
55121	Eagan	(612)	47,409	20,700
55005	East Bethel	(612)	8,050	6,626
56721	East Grand Forks	(218)	8,658	8,537
*55343	Eden Prairie	(612)	39,311	16,263
55435	Edina	(612)	46,070	46,073
55330	Elk River	(612)	11,143	6,785
56031	Fairmont	(507)	11,265	11,506
55113	Falcon Heights	(612)	5,380	5,291
55021	Faribault	(507)	17,085	16,241
55024	Farmington	(612)	5,940	4,370
56537	Fergus Falls	(218)	12,362	12,519
55025	Forest Lake	(612)	5,833	4,596
55432	Fridley	(612)	28,335	30,228
55416	Golden Valley	(612)	20,971	22,775
55744	Grand Rapids	(218)	7,976	7,934
*55303	Ham Lake	(612)	8,924	7,832
55033	Hastings	(612)	15,478	12,827
55811	Hermantown	(218)	6,761	6,759
55746	Hibbing	(218)	18,046	21,193
55343	Hopkins	(612)	16,534	15,336
55350	Hutchinson	(612)	11,455	9,244
56649	International Falls	(218)	8,325	5,611
55075	Inver Grove Heights	(612)	22,477	17,171
55042	Lake Elmo	(612)	5,903	5,296
55044	Lakeville	(612)	24,854	14,790
.....	Lino Lakes	(612)	8,807	4,966
55355	Litchfield	(612)	6,041	5,904
55110	Little Canada	(612)	8,971	7,102
56345	Little Falls	(612)	7,374	7,250
55115	Mahtomedi		5,633	3,851
56001	Mankato	(507)	31,405	28,646

ZIP code	Place	Area code	1990	1980
55369	Maple Grove	(612)	38,736	20,525
55109	Maplewood	(612)	30,954	26,990
56258	Marshall	(507)	12,023	11,161
55118	Mendota Heights	(612)	9,381	7,288
*55401	Minneapolis	(612)	368,383	370,951
55343	Minnetonka	(612)	48,370	38,683
56265	Montevideo	(612)	5,499	5,845
55362	Monticello	(612)	5,045	....
56560	Moorhead	(218)	32,295	29,998
56267	Morris	(612)	5,613	5,367
55364	Mound	(612)	9,634	9,280
55112	Mounds View	(612)	12,541	12,593
55112	New Brighton	(612)	22,207	23,269
54428	New Hope	(612)	21,853	23,087
56073	New Ulm	(507)	13,132	13,755
55057	Northfield	(507)	14,684	12,562
56001	North Mankato	(507)	10,662	9,145
55109	North St. Paul	(612)	12,376	11,921
55119	Oakdale	(612)	18,374	12,123
55323	Orono	(612)	7,285	6,845
55060	Owatonna	(507)	19,386	18,632
55427	Plymouth	(612)	50,889	31,615
55372	Prior Lake	(612)	11,482	7,284
55303	Ramsey	(612)	12,408	10,093
55066	Red Wing	(612)	15,134	13,736
55423	Richfield	(612)	35,710	37,851
55422	Robbinsdale	(612)	14,396	14,422
55901	Rochester	(507)	70,745	57,906
55068	Rosemount	(612)	8,622	5,083
55113	Roseville	(612)	33,485	35,820
55418	St. Anthony	(612)	7,727	7,981
56301	St. Cloud	(612)	48,812	42,566
55426	St. Louis Park	(612)	43,787	42,931
*55101	St. Paul	(612)	272,235	270,230
56082	St. Peter	(507)	9,481	9,056
56377	Sartell	(612)	5,409	3,427
56379	Sauk Rapids	(612)	7,825	5,793
56337	Savage	(612)	9,906	3,954
55379	Shakopee	(612)	11,739	9,941
55126	Shoreview	(612)	24,587	17,300
55331	Shorewood		5,917	4,646
55075	South St. Paul	(612)	20,197	21,235
55432	Spring Lake Park	(612)	6,532	6,477
55082	Stillwater	(612)	13,882	12,290
56701	Thief River Falls	(218)	8,010	9,105
55110	Vadnais Heights	(612)	11,041	5,111
55792	Virginia	(218)	9,410	11,056
56387	Waite Park		5,020	3,496
56093	Waseca	(507)	8,385	8,219
55118	West St. Paul	(612)	19,248	18,527
55110	White Bear Lake	(612)	24,642	22,538
56201	Willmar	(612)	17,531	15,895
55987	Winona	(507)	25,399	25,075
55119	Woodbury	(612)	20,075	10,297
56187	Worthington	(507)	9,977	10,243

Mississippi (601)

ZIP code	Place	1990	1980
39730	Aberdeen	6,837	7,184
38821	Amory	7,093	7,307
38606	Batesville	6,403	5,162
39520	Bay St. Louis	8,063	7,850
*39530	Biloxi	46,319	49,311
38829	Booneville	7,955	6,199
39042	Brandon	11,077	9,626
39601	Brookhaven	10,243	10,800
39046	Canton	10,062	11,116
38614	Clarksdale	19,717	21,137
38732	Cleveland	15,384	14,524
39056	Clinton	21,847	14,660
39429	Columbia	6,815	7,733
39701	Columbus	23,799	27,503
38834	Corinth	11,820	13,178
39059	Crystal Springs	5,643	4,902
39532	D'Iberville	6,566	6,236
39074	Forest	5,060	5,229
39553	Gautier	10,088	10,392
38701	Greenville	45,226	40,613
38930	Greenwood	18,906	20,115
38901	Grenada	10,864	11,508
.....	Gulf Hills(u)	5,004	4,512
39501	Gulfport	40,775	39,676
39401	Hattiesburg	41,882	40,829
38635	Holly Springs	7,261	7,285
38637	Horn Lake	9,069	4,326
38751	Indianola	11,809	8,050
*39205	Jackson	196,637	202,895
39090	Kosciusko	6,986	7,415
39440	Laurel	18,827	21,897
38756	Leland	6,366	6,667
39560	Long Beach	15,804	14,199
39339	Louisville	7,165	7,323
39648	McComb	11,797	12,331
39110	Madison	7,471	2,241
39301	Meridian	41,036	46,577
39563	Moss Point	17,837	18,998
39120	Natchez	19,460	22,209
38652	New Albany	6,775	7,072
39564	Ocean Springs	14,658	14,504
39567	Orange Grove(u)	15,676	13,476
38655	Oxford	10,026	9,882
39567	Pascagoula	25,899	29,318
39571	Pass Christian	5,557	5,014
39208	Pearl	19,588	18,602
39465	Petal	7,883	8,476
39350	Philadelphia	6,758	6,434
39466	Picayune	10,633	10,361
39157	Ridgeland	11,714	5,461
38663	Ripley	5,371	4,271
.....	St. Martin(u)	6,349	....
38671	Southaven	17,949	16,441
39759	Starkville	18,458	16,139
38801	Tupelo	30,685	23,905
39180	Vicksburg	20,908	25,434
39576	Waveland	5,369	4,186
39367	Waynesboro	5,143	5,349
.....	West Hattiesburg(u)	5,450	....
39773	West Point	8,489	8,811
38967	Winona	5,705	6,177
39194	Yazoo City	12,427	12,092

Missouri

ZIP code	Place	Area code	1990	1980
63123	Affton(u)	(314)	21,106	23,181
63010	Arnold	(314)	18,828	19,141
65605	Aurora	(417)	6,459	6,437
63011	Ballwin	(314)	21,816	12,656
63137	Bellefontaine Neighbors	(314)	10,922	12,082
64012	Belton	(816)	18,150	12,708
63134	Berkeley	(314)	12,450	15,922
63031	Black Jack	(314)	6,128	5,293
64015	Blue Springs	(816)	40,096	25,936
65613	Bolivar	(417)	6,845	5,919
65233	Boonville	(816)	7,095	6,959
63114	Breckenridge Hills	(816)	5,404	5,666
63144	Brentwood	(314)	8,150	8,209
63044	Bridgeton	(314)	17,779	18,445
63701	Cape Girardeau	(314)	34,475	34,361
64836	Carthage	(417)	10,747	11,104
63830	Caruthersville	(314)	7,389	7,958
63834	Charleston	(314)	5,085	5,230
63005	Chesterfield	(314)	37,990	28,384
64601	Chillicothe	(816)	8,804	9,089
63105	Clayton	(314)	13,874	14,306
64735	Clinton	(816)	8,703	8,366
65201	Columbia	(314)	69,101	62,061
63128	Concord(u)	(314)	19,859	20,896
63126	Crestwood	(314)	11,229	12,815
63141	Creve Coeur	(314)	12,304	11,743
63136	Dellwood	(314)	5,245	6,200
63020	De Soto	(314)	5,993	5,993
63131	Des Peres	(314)	8,395	7,953
63841	Dexter	(314)	7,559	7,043
63011	Ellisville	(314)	7,545	6,233
64024	Excelsior Springs	(816)	10,354	10,424
63640	Farmington	(314)	11,598	8,270
63135	Ferguson	(314)	22,288	24,549
63028	Festus	(314)	8,105	7,574
*63033	Florissant	(314)	51,206	55,721
65473	Fort Leonard Wood(u)	(314)	15,863	21,262
65251	Fulton	(314)	10,033	11,046
64118	Gladstone	(816)	26,243	24,990
65254	Glasgow Village(u)	(314)	5,199	....
63122	Glendale	(314)	5,945	6,035
64030	Grandview	(816)	24,967	24,561
63401	Hannibal	(314)	18,004	18,811
64701	Harrisonville	(816)	7,683	6,372
*63042	Hazelwood	(314)	15,324	13,098
*64051	Independence	(816)	112,301	111,797
63755	Jackson	(314)	9,256	7,827
65101	Jefferson City	(314)	35,481	33,619
63136	Jennings	(314)	15,905	16,934
64801	Joplin	(417)	40,866	39,126
*64108	Kansas City	(816)	435,146	448,028
63857	Kennett	(314)	10,941	10,145
63501	Kirksville	(816)	17,152	17,167
63122	Kirkwood	(314)	27,291	27,739
63124	Ladue	(314)	8,847	9,369
63367	Lake St. Louis		7,400	3,843
65536	Lebanon	(417)	9,983	9,507
64063	Lee's Summit	(816)	46,418	28,741
63125	Lemay(u)	(314)	18,005	35,424
64068	Liberty	(816)	20,459	16,251
63552	Macon	(816)	5,571	5,680
63863	Malden	(314)	5,123	6,096
63011	Manchester	(314)	6,542	6,351
63143	Maplewood	(314)	9,962	10,960
65340	Marshall	(816)	12,711	12,781
63043	Maryland Heights(u)	(314)	25,407	26,413
64468	Maryville	(816)	10,663	9,558
.....	Mehlville(u)		27,557	....
65265	Mexico	(314)	11,290	12,276
65270	Moberly	(816)	12,839	13,418
65708	Monett	(417)	6,529	6,148

ZIP code	Place		1990	1980
63026	Murphy(u)	(314)	9,342	8,121
64850	Neosho	(417)	9,254	9,493
64772	Nevada	(417)	8,597	9,044
63121	Northwoods	(314)	5,106	5,831
.....	Oakville(u)		31,750	....
63366	O'Fallon	(314)	18,698	8,677
63132	Olivette	(314)	7,573	7,952
63114	Overland	(314)	17,987	19,620
63775	Perryville	(314)	6,933	7,343
63120	Pine Lawn	(314)	5,092	6,570
63901	Poplar Bluff	(314)	16,996	17,139
64083	Raymore	(816)	5,592	3,154
64133	Raytown	(816)	30,601	31,831
65738	Republic		6,292	4,485
64085	Richmond	(816)	5,738	5,499
63117	Richmond Heights	(314)	10,448	11,516
63124	Rock Hill	(314)	5,217	5,702
65401	Rolla	(314)	14,090	13,303
63074	St. Ann	(314)	14,489	15,523
63301	St. Charles	(314)	54,555	37,379
63114	St. John	(314)	7,466	7,854
*64501	St. Joseph	(816)	71,852	76,691
*63155	St. Louis	(314)	396,685	452,801
63376	St. Peters	(314)	45,779	15,700
63126	Sappington(u)	(314)	10,917	11,388
65301	Sedalia	(816)	19,800	20,927
63119	Shrewsbury	(314)	6,416	5,077
63801	Sikeston	(314)	17,641	17,431
63138	Spanish Lake(u)	(314)	20,322	20,632
*65801	Springfield	(417)	140,494	133,116
63080	Sullivan	(314)	5,661	5,461
	Town and Country		9,517	3,187
64683	Trenton	(816)	6,129	6,811
63084	Union	(314)	5,909	5,506
63130	University City	(314)	40,087	42,690
64093	Warrensburg	(816)	15,244	13,807
63090	Washington	(314)	10,704	9,251
64870	Webb City	(417)	7,449	7,309
63119	Webster Groves	(314)	22,992	23,097
63385	Wentzville	(314)	5,088	3,193
65775	West Plains	(417)	8,913	7,741

Montana (406)

ZIP code	Place	1990	1980
59711	Anaconda-Deer Lodge County	10,356	12,518
*59101	Billings	81,151	66,818
59715	Bozeman	22,660	21,645
59701	Butte-Silver Bow	33,336	37,205
*59401	Great Falls	55,097	56,884
59501	Havre	10,201	10,891
59601	Helena	24,569	23,938
.....	Helena Valley West Central(u)	6,327	....
59901	Kalispell	11,917	10,689
59044	Laurel	5,686	5,481
59457	Lewistown	6,051	7,104
59047	Livingston	6,701	6,994
59402	Malmstrom AFB(u)	5,938	6,675
59301	Miles City	8,461	9,602
*59801	Missoula	42,918	33,351
59801	Orchard Homes(u)	10,317	10,837
59270	Sidney	5,217	5,726

Nebraska

ZIP code	Place		1990	1980
69301	Alliance	(308)	9,765	9,920
68310	Beatrice	(402)	12,354	12,891
68005	Bellevue	(402)	30,982	21,813
68008	Blair	(402)	6,860	6,418
69337	Chadron	(308)	5,588	5,933
.....	Chalco(u)		7,337	....
68601	Columbus	(402)	19,480	17,328
68025	Fremont	(402)	23,680	23,979
69341	Gering	(308)	7,946	7,760
68801	Grand Island	(308)	39,457	33,180
68901	Hastings	(402)	22,837	23,045
68949	Holdrege	(308)	5,671	5,624
68847	Kearney	(308)	24,396	21,158
68128	La Vista	(402)	9,840	9,588
68850	Lexington	(308)	6,601	7,040
*68501	Lincoln	(402)	191,972	171,932
69001	McCook	(308)	8,112	8,404
68410	Nebraska City	(402)	6,547	7,127
68701	Norfolk	(402)	21,476	19,449
69101	North Platte	(308)	22,605	24,509
68113	Offutt AFB West(u)	(402)	10,883	8,787
69153	Ogallala	(308)	5,095	5,638
*68108	Omaha	(402)	335,795	313,939
68046	Papillion	(402)	10,372	6,399
68048	Plattsmouth	(402)	6,412	6,295
68127	Ralston	(402)	6,236	5,143
69361	Scottsbluff	(308)	13,711	14,156
68434	Seward	(402)	5,634	5,713
69162	Sidney	(308)	5,959	6,010
68776	South Sioux City	(402)	9,677	9,339
68787	Wayne	(402)	5,142	5,240
68467	York	(402)	7,884	7,723

Nevada (702)

ZIP code	Place	1990	1980
89005	Boulder City	12,567	9,590
*89701	Carson City	40,443	32,022
89112	East Las Vegas(u)	11,087	6,449
89801	Elko	14,736	8,758
.....	Enterprise(u)	6,412	....
89406	Fallon	6,438	4,262
89408	Fernley(u)	5,164	....
89410	Gardnerville Ranchos(u)	7,455	3,542
89015	Henderson	64,942	24,363
89450	Incline Village-Crystal Bay(u)	7,119	6,225
*89114	Las Vegas	258,204	164,674
89110	Nellis AFB(u)	8,377	7,476
*89030	North Las Vegas	47,707	42,739
89041	Pahrump(u)	7,424	84,818
89109	Paradise(u)	124,682	84,818
*89501	Reno	133,850	100,756
*89431	Sparks	53,367	40,780
.....	Spring Creek(u)	5,866	4,155
.....	Spring Valley(u)	51,726	....
89110	Sunrise Manor(u)	95,362	44,155
89431	Sun Valley(u)	11,391	8,822
89101	Winchester(u)	23,365	19,728
89445	Winnemucca	6,134	4,140

New Hampshire (603)

See Note on Page 398

ZIP code	Place	1990	1980
03031	*Amherst*	9,068	....
03811	*Atkinson*	5,188	....
03825	*Barrington*	6,164	....
03102	*Bedford*	12,563	9,481
03220	*Belmont*	5,796	....
03570	Berlin	11,824	13,084
03304	*Bow*	5,500	....
03743	Claremont	13,902	14,557
03301	Concord	36,006	30,400
03818	*Conway*	7,940	7,158
03038	Derry Compact(u)	20,446	12,248
03038	*Derry*	29,603	18,875
03820	Dover	25,042	22,377
03824	Durham Compact(u)	9,236	8,448
03824	*Durham*	11,818	10,652
03042	*Epping*	5,162	....
03833	Exeter Compact(u)	9,556	8,947
03833	*Exeter*	12,481	11,024
03835	*Farmington*	5,739	....
03235	Franklin	8,304	7,901
03246	*Gilford*	5,867	....
03045	*Goffstown*	14,621	11,315
03841	*Hampstead*	6,732	....
03842	Hampton Compact(u)	7,989	6,779
03842	*Hampton*	12,278	10,493
03755	Hanover Compact(u)	6,538	6,861
03756	*Hanover*	9,212	9,119
03049	*Hollis*	5,705	....
03106	*Hooksett*	8,767	7,303
03051	*Hudson*	19,530	7,626
03452	*Jaffrey*	5,361	....
03431	Keene	22,430	21,449
03848	*Kingston*	5,591	....
03246	Laconia	15,743	15,575
03766	Lebanon	12,183	11,134
.....	*Litchfield*	5,516	....
03561	*Littleton*	5,827	5,558
03053	*Londonderry Compact(u)*	10,114	....
03053	*Londonderry*	19,781	10,114
*03101	Manchester	99,332	90,936
03054	*Merrimack*	22,156	15,406
03055	*Milford Compact(u)*	8,015	....
03055	*Milford*	11,795	8,015
*03060	Nashua	79,662	67,865
03857	*Newmarket*	7,157	....
03773	*Newport*	6,110	6,229
03076	*Pelham*	9,408	8,090
03275	*Pembroke*	6,561	....
03458	*Peterborough*	5,239	....
03865	*Plaistow*	7,316	5,609
03264	*Plymouth*	5,811	....
03801	Portsmouth	25,925	26,254
03077	*Raymond*	8,713	5,453
03867	Rochester	26,630	21,560
03079	*Salem*	25,746	24,124
03874	*Seabrook*	6,503	5,917
03878	Somersworth	11,249	10,350
03275	Suncook(u)	5,214	4,698
.....	*Swanzey*	6,236	....
03281	*Weare*	6,193	....
03087	*Windham*	9,000	5,664

New Jersey

ZIP code	Place		1990	1980
08201	Absecon	(609)	7,298	6,859

ZIP code	Place	Area code	1990	1980
07401	Allendale	(201)	5,900	5,901
07712	Asbury Park	(908)	16,799	17,015
*08401	Atlantic City	(609)	37,986	40,199
08106	Audubon	(609)	9,205	9,533
07001	Avenel(u)	(908)	15,504	....
08007	Barrington	(609)	6,792	7,418
07002	Bayonne	(201)	61,464	65,047
08722	Beachwood	(908)	9,324	7,687
07109	Belleville(u)	(201)	34,213	35,367
08031	Bellmawr	(609)	12,603	13,721
07719	Belmar	(908)	5,877	6,771
07621	Bergenfield	(201)	24,458	25,568
07922	Berkeley Hts. Twp.(u)	(908)	11,980	12,549
08009	Berlin	(609)	5,672	5,786
07924	Bernardsville	(908)	6,597	6,715
08012	Blackwood(u)	(609)	5,120	5,219
07003	Bloomfield(u)	(201)	45,061	47,792
07403	Bloomingdale	(201)	7,530	7,867
07603	Bogota	(201)	7,824	8,344
07005	Boonton	(201)	8,343	8,620
08805	Bound Brook	(908)	9,487	9,710
08723	Brick Twp.(u)	(201)	66,473	53,629
08302	Bridgeton	(609)	18,942	18,795
08807	Bridgewater Twp.	(908)	32,509	....
08203	Brigantine	(609)	11,354	8,318
08015	Browns Mills(u)	(609)	11,429	10,568
07828	Budd Lake(u)	(201)	7,272	6,523
08016	Burlington	(609)	9,835	10,246
07405	Butler	(201)	7,392	7,616
07006	Caldwell(u)	(201)	7,549	7,624
*08101	Camden	(609)	87,492	84,910
07072	Carlstadt	(201)	5,510	6,166
08069	Carney's Point(u)	(609)	7,686	7,574
07008	Carteret	(908)	19,025	20,598
07009	Cedar Grove Twp.(u)	(201)	12,053	12,600
07928	Chatham	(201)	8,007	8,537
*08002	Cherry Hill Twp.(u)	(609)	69,319	68,785
08077	Cinnaminson Twp.(u)	(609)	14,583	16,072
07066	Clark Twp.(u)	(908)	14,629	16,699
08312	Clayton	(609)	6,155	6,013
08021	Clementon	(609)	5,601	5,764
07010	Cliffside Park	(201)	20,393	21,464
*07015	Clifton	(201)	71,984	74,388
07624	Closter	(201)	8,094	8,164
08108	Collingswood	(609)	15,289	15,838
07067	Colonia(u)	(908)	18,238	....
07016	Cranford Twp.	(908)	22,624	24,573
07626	Cresskill	(201)	7,558	7,609
.....	Crestwood Village(u)	(201)	8,030	7,965
07801	Dover	(201)	15,115	14,681
07628	Dumont	(201)	17,187	18,334
08812	Dunellen	(908)	6,528	6,593
08816	East Brunswick Twp.	(908)	43,548	37,711
07936	East Hanover	(201)	9,926	9,319
*07019	East Orange	(201)	73,552	77,878
07073	East Rutherford	(201)	7,902	7,849
07724	Eatontown	(908)	13,800	12,703
07020	Edgewater Borough	(201)	5,001	4,628
08010	Edgewater Park	(609)	8,388	9,273
08817	Edison Twp.	(201)	88,680	70,193
*07201	Elizabeth	(908)	110,002	106,201
07407	Elmwood Park	(201)	17,623	18,377
07630	Emerson	(201)	6,930	7,793
*07631	Englewood	(201)	24,850	23,701
07632	Englewood Cliffs	(201)	5,634	5,698
08618	Ewing Twp.	(609)	34,185	34,842
07006	Fairfield	(201)	7,615	7,987
07701	Fair Haven	(908)	5,270	5,679
07410	Fair Lawn	(201)	30,548	32,229
07022	Fairview	(201)	10,733	10,519
07023	Fanwood	(908)	7,115	7,767
08518	Florence-Roebling(u)	(609)	8,564	7,677
07932	Florham Park	(201)	8,521	9,359
08863	Fords(u)	(908)	14,392	....
08640	Fort Dix(u)	(609)	10,205	14,297
07024	Fort Lee	(201)	31,997	32,449
07417	Franklin Lakes	(201)	9,873	8,769
.....	Franklin Twp.	(201)	42,780	....
07728	Freehold	(908)	10,742	10,020
07026	Garfield	(201)	26,727	26,803
08753	Gilford Park(u)	(908)	8,668	6,528
08028	Glassboro	(609)	15,614	14,574
08029	Glendora(u)	(609)	5,201	5,632
07028	Glen Ridge(u)	(201)	7,076	7,855
07452	Glen Rock	(201)	10,883	11,497
08030	Gloucester City	(609)	12,649	13,121
07093	Guttenberg	(201)	8,268	7,340
*07602	Hackensack	(201)	37,049	36,039
07840	Hackettstown	(908)	8,120	8,850
08033	Haddonfield	(609)	11,628	12,337
08035	Haddon Heights	(609)	7,860	8,361
07508	Haledon	(201)	6,951	6,607
08037	Hammonton	(609)	12,208	12,298
07981	Hanover Twp.(u)	(201)	11,538	11,846
07029	Harrison	(201)	13,425	12,242
07604	Hasbrouck Heights	(201)	11,488	12,166
07506	Hawthorne	(201)	17,084	18,200
08904	Highland Park	(201)	13,279	13,396
08520	Hightstown	(609)	5,126	4,581
07642	Hillsdale	(201)	9,750	10,495
07205	Hillside Twp.(u)	(201)	21,044	21,440
07030	Hoboken	(201)	33,397	42,460
08753	Holiday City-Berkeley(u)	(908)	14,293	9,019
.....	Holiday City South(u)	(908)	5,452	....
07843	Hopatcong	(201)	15,586	15,531
07111	Irvington(u)	(201)	59,774	61,473
08830	Iselin(u)	(908)	16,141	....
08831	Jamesburg		5,294	4,114
*07303	Jersey City	(201)	228,517	223,532
07734	Keansburg	(908)	11,069	10,613
07032	Kearny	(201)	34,874	35,735
08824	Kendall Park(u)	(908)	7,127	7,419
07033	Kenilworth	(908)	7,574	8,221
07735	Keyport	(908)	7,586	7,413
07405	Kinnelon	(201)	8,470	7,770
07871	Lake Mohawk(u)	(201)	8,930	8,498
08701	Lakewood(u)	(908)	26,095	22,863
08879	Laurence Harbor(u)	(908)	6,361	6,737
08648	Lawrenceville(u)		6,446	....
.....	Leisure Village West-Pine Lake Park(u)		10,139	....
07605	Leonia	(201)	8,365	8,027
07035	Lincoln Park	(201)	10,978	8,806
07738	Lincroft(u)		6,193	....
07036	Linden	(908)	36,701	37,836
08021	Lindenwold	(609)	18,734	18,196
08221	Linwood	(609)	6,866	6,144
07424	Little Falls Twp.(u)	(201)	11,294	11,496
07643	Little Ferry	(201)	9,989	9,399
07739	Little Silver	(908)	5,721	5,548
07039	Livingston Twp.(u)	(201)	26,609	28,040
07644	Lodi	(201)	22,355	23,956
07740	Long Branch	(908)	28,658	29,819
07071	Lyndhurst Twp.(u)	(201)	18,262	20,326
08641	McGuire AFB(u)	(609)	7,580	7,853
07940	Madison	(201)	15,850	15,357
08859	Madison Park(u)	(201)	7,490	7,447
08736	Manasquan	(908)	5,369	5,354
08835	Manville	(908)	10,567	11,278
08052	Maple Shade Twp.(u)	(609)	19,211	20,525
07040	Maplewood Twp.(u)	(201)	21,756	22,950
08402	Margate City	(609)	8,431	9,179
08053	Marlton(u)	(609)	10,228	9,411
07747	Matawan	(908)	9,270	8,837
07607	Maywood	(201)	9,536	9,895
08619	Mercerville-Hamilton Sq.(u)	(609)	26,873	25,446
08840	Metuchen	(908)	12,804	13,762
08846	Middlesex	(908)	13,055	13,480
07432	Midland Park	(201)	7,047	7,381
07041	Millburn Twp.(u)	(201)	18,630	19,543
08850	Milltown	(908)	6,968	7,136
08332	Millville	(609)	25,992	24,815
*07042	Montclair(u)	(201)	37,729	38,321
07645	Montvale	(201)	6,946	7,318
08057	Moorestown-Lenola(u)	(609)	13,242	13,695
07950	Morris Plains	(201)	5,219	5,305
07960	Morristown	(201)	16,189	16,614
07092	Mountainside	(908)	6,657	7,118
08060	Mount Holly Twp.(u)	(609)	10,639	10,818
08087	Mystic Island		7,400	4,929
*07102	Newark	(201)	275,221	329,248
*08901	New Brunswick	(908)	41,711	41,442
07646	New Milford	(201)	15,990	16,876
07974	New Providence	(908)	11,439	12,426
07860	Newton	(201)	7,521	7,748
07032	North Arlington	(201)	13,790	16,587
07047	North Bergen Twp.(u)	(201)	48,414	47,019
08902	North Brunswick Twp.(u)	(908)	31,287	22,220
07006	North Caldwell(u)	(201)	6,706	5,832
08225	Northfield	(609)	7,305	7,795
07508	North Haledon	(201)	7,987	8,177
07060	North Plainfield	(908)	18,820	19,108
08260	North Wildwood		5,017	4,714
07110	Nutley	(201)	27,099	28,998
07436	Oakland	(201)	11,997	13,443
.....	Ocean Acres(u)		5,587	4,850
08226	Ocean City	(609)	15,512	13,949
07757	Oceanport	(908)	6,146	5,888
08857	Old Bridge(u)	(908)	22,151	21,815
07649	Oradell	(201)	8,024	8,658
*07050	Orange(u)	(201)	29,925	31,136
07650	Palisades Park	(201)	14,536	13,732
08065	Palmyra	(609)	7,056	7,085
07652	Paramus	(201)	25,004	26,474
07656	Park Ridge	(201)	8,102	8,515
07054	Parsippany-Troy Hills(u)	(201)	48,478	49,868
*07055	Passaic	(201)	58,041	52,463
*07510	Paterson	(201)	140,891	137,970
08066	Paulsboro	(609)	6,577	6,944
08110	Pennsauken Twp.(u)	(609)	34,733	33,775
08069	Penns Grove	(609)	5,228	5,760
08070	Pennsville Center(u)	(609)	12,218	12,467
07440	Pequannock Twp.	(201)	12,844	13,776
*08861	Perth Amboy	(908)	41,967	38,951
08865	Phillipsburg	(908)	15,757	16,647
08021	Pine Hill	(609)	9,854	8,684
08071	Pitman	(609)	9,365	9,7447
*07061	Plainfield	(908)	46,577	45,555

ZIP code	Place		1990	1980
08232	Pleasantville	(609)	16,027	13,435
08742	Point Pleasant	(908)	18,177	17,747
08742	Point Pleasant Beach	(908)	5,112	5,415
07442	Pompton Lakes	(201)	10,539	10,660
08540	Princeton	(609)	12,016	12,035
07508	Prospect Park	(201)	5,053	5,142
*07065	Rahway	(908)	25,325	26,723
08057	Ramblewood(u)	(609)	6,181	6,475
07446	Ramsey	(201)	13,228	12,899
08869	Raritan	(908)	5,798	6,128
07701	Red Bank	(908)	10,636	12,031
07657	Ridgefield	(201)	9,996	10,294
07660	Ridgefield Park	(201)	12,454	12,738
*07451	Ridgewood	(201)	24,152	25,208
07456	Ringwood	(201)	12,623	12,625
07661	River Edge	(201)	10,603	11,111
08075	Riverside Twp.(u)	(609)	7,974	7,941
07675	River Vale(u)	(201)	9,410	9,489
07726	Robertsville(u)	(908)	9,841	8,461
07662	Rochelle Park Twp.	(201)	5,587	5,603
07866	Rockaway	(201)	6,243	6,852
07203	Roselle	(908)	20,314	20,641
07204	Roselle Park	(201)	12,805	13,377
07760	Rumson	(908)	6,701	7,623
08078	Runnemede	(609)	9,042	9,461
*07070	Rutherford	(201)	17,790	19,068
07662	Saddle Brook Twp.(u)	(201)	13,296	14,084
08079	Salem	(609)	6,883	6,959
08872	Sayreville	(908)	34,998	29,969
07076	Scotch Plains Twp.(u)	(908)	21,160	20,774
07094	Secaucus	(201)	14,061	13,719
08753	Silverton	(908)	9,175	7,236
08083	Somerdale	(609)	5,440	5,900
08873	Somerset(u)	(908)	22,070	21,731
08244	Somers Point	(609)	11,216	10,330
08876	Somerville	(908)	11,632	11,973
08879	South Amboy	(908)	7,851	8,322
07079	South Orange Twp.(u)	(201)	16,390	15,864
07080	South Plainfield	(908)	20,489	20,521
08882	South River	(908)	13,692	14,361
08884	Spotswood	(908)	7,983	7,840
07081	Springfield Twp.(u)	(201)	13,420	13,955
07762	Spring Lake Heights	(908)	5,341	5,424
08084	Stratford	(609)	7,614	8,005
07747	Strathmore(u)	(201)	7,060	....
07876	Succasunna-Kenvil(u)	(201)	11,781	10,931
07901	Summit	(908)	19,757	21,071
07666	Teaneck Twp.(u)	(201)	37,825	39,007
07670	Tenafly	(201)	13,326	13,552
07724	Tinton Falls	(908)	12,361	7,740
*08753	Toms River(u)	(908)	7,524	7,465
07512	Totowa	(201)	10,177	11,448
*08608	Trenton	(609)	88,675	92,124
08520	Twin Rivers(u)	(609)	7,715	7,742
07083	Union Twp.(u)	(908)	50,024	50,184
07735	Union Beach	(908)	6,156	6,354
07087	Union City	(201)	58,012	55,593
07458	Upper Saddle River	(201)	7,198	7,958
08406	Ventnor City	(609)	11,005	11,704
07044	Verona(u)	(201)	13,597	14,166
08251	Villas(u)	(609)	8,136	5,909
08360	Vineland	(609)	54,780	53,753
07463	Waldwick	(201)	9,757	10,802
07057	Wallington	(201)	10,828	10,741
07465	Wanaque	(201)	9,711	10,025
07882	Washington	(908)	6,474	6,429
07675	Washington Twp. (Bergen)(u)	(201)	9,245	9,550
07060	Watchung	(908)	5,110	5,290
07470	Wayne Twp.(u)	(201)	47,025	46,474
07087	Weehawken Twp.(u)	(201)	12,385	13,168
07006	West Caldwell(u)	(201)	10,422	11,407
*07091	Westfield	(908)	28,870	30,447
07728	West Freehold(u)	(908)	11,166	9,929
07764	West Long Branch	(908)	7,690	7,380
07480	West Milford Twp.(u)	(201)	25,430	22,750
07093	West New York	(201)	38,125	39,194
07052	West Orange	(201)	39,103	39,510
07424	West Paterson	(201)	10,982	11,293
07675	Westwood	(201)	10,446	10,714
07885	Wharton	(201)	5,405	5,485
08610	White Horse(u)	(609)	9,397	10,098
07886	White Meadow Lake(u)	(201)	8,002	8,429
08094	Williamstown	(609)	10,891	5,768
08046	Willingboro Twp.(u)	(609)	36,291	39,912
07095	Woodbridge Twp.(u)	(908)	17,434	90,074
08096	Woodbury	(609)	10,904	10,353
07675	Woodcliff Lake	(201)	5,303	5,644
07075	Wood-Ridge	(201)	7,506	7,929
07481	Wyckoff Twp.(u)	(201)	15,372	15,500
08620	Yardville-Groveville(u)	(609)	9,248	9,414
.....	Yorketown(u)	(609)	6,313	5,330

New Mexico (505)

ZIP code	Place	1990	1980
88310	Alamogordo	27,596	24,024
*87101	Albuquerque	384,736	332,920
88021	Anthony(u)	5,160	....
88210	Artesia	10,610	10,385
87410	Aztec	5,479	5,512
87002	Belen	6,547	5,617
87001	Bernalillo	5,960	2,988
87413	Bloomfield	5,214	4,881
88220	Carlsbad	24,952	25,496
88101	Clovis	30,954	31,194
87048	Corrales	5,453	2,791
88030	Deming	10,970	9,964
87532	Espanola	8,389	6,803
87401	Farmington	33,997	31,222
87301	Gallup	19,154	18,167
87020	Grants	8,626	11,439
88240	Hobbs	29,115	29,153
88330	Holloman AFB(u)	5,891	7,245
*88001	Las Cruces	62,126	45,086
87701	Las Vegas	14,753	14,322
87544	Los Alamos(u)	11,455	11,039
87031	Los Lunas	6,013	3,525
88260	Lovington	9,322	9,727
87107	North Valley(u)	12,507	5,096
87114	Paradise Hills(u)	5,513	5,096
88130	Portales	10,690	9,940
87740	Raton	7,372	8,225
87124	Rio Rancho	32,505	9,985
88201	Roswell	44,654	39,676
87115	Sandia(u)	6,742	5,288
*87501	Santa Fe	56,551	49,160
87420	Shiprock	7,687	7,237
88061	Silver City	10,683	9,887
87801	Socorro	8,159	7,173
87105	South Valley(u)	35,701	38,916
88063	Sunland Park	8,179	4,313
87901	Truth or Consequences	6,221	5,219
88401	Tucumcari	6,831	6,765
87544	White Rock(u)	6,192	6,560
87327	Zuni Pueblo(u)	5,857	5,551

New York

ZIP code	Place		1990	1980
10901	Airmont(u)		7,835	....
*12207	Albany	(518)	101,082	101,727
11507	Albertson(u)	(516)	5,166	5,561
14411	Albion	(716)	5,863	4,897
11701	Amityville	(516)	9,286	9,076
12010	Amsterdam	(518)	20,714	21,872
12603	Arlington(u)	(914)	11,948	11,305
13021	Auburn	(315)	31,258	32,548
*11702	Babylon	(516)	12,249	12,388
11510	Baldwin(u)	(516)	22,719	31,630
11510	Baldwin Harbor(u)		7,899	....
13027	Baldwinsville	(315)	6,591	6,446
12020	Ballston Spa	(518)	5,194	....
14020	Batavia	(716)	16,310	16,703
14810	Bath	(607)	5,801	6,042
11705	Bayport(u)	(516)	7,702	9,282
11706	Bay Shore(u)	(516)	21,279	10,784
11709	Bayville	(516)	7,193	7,034
.....	Baywood(u)		7,351	....
12508	Beacon	(914)	13,243	12,937
11710	Bellmore(u)	(516)	16,438	18,106
11714	Bethpage(u)	(516)	15,761	16,840
*13902	Binghamton	(607)	53,008	55,860
11716	Bohemia(u)	(516)	9,556	9,308
11717	Brentwood(u)	(516)	45,218	44,321
10510	Briarcliff Manor	(914)	7,070	7,115
14610	Brighton (u)	(716)	34,455	35,776
14420	Brockport	(716)	8,749	9,776
10708	Bronxville	(914)	6,028	6,267
*14240	Buffalo	(716)	328,175	357,870
14424	Canandaigua	(716)	10,725	10,419
13617	Canton	(315)	6,379	7,055
11514	Carle Place(u)	(516)	5,107	5,470
11516	Cedarhurst	(516)	5,716	6,162
11720	Centereach(u)	(516)	26,720	30,136
11934	Center Moriches(u)	(516)	5,987	5,703
11721	Centerport(u)	(516)	5,333	6,576
11722	Central Islip(u)	(516)	26,028	19,734
14225	Cheektowaga(u)	(716)	84,387	92,145
10977	Chestnut Ridge		7,517	8,217
12043	Cobleskill	(518)	5,268	5,272
12047	Cohoes	(518)	16,825	18,144
12205	Colonie	(518)	8,019	8,869
11725	Commack(u)	(516)	36,124	34,719
10920	Congers(u)	(914)	8,003	7,123
11726	Copiague(u)	(516)	20,769	20,132
11727	Coram(u)	(516)	30,111	24,752
14830	Corning	(607)	11,938	12,953
13045	Cortland	(607)	19,801	20,138
10520	Croton-on-Hudson	(914)	7,018	6,889
14437	Dansville	(716)	5,002	4,979
11729	Deer Park(u)	(516)	28,840	30,394
12054	Delmar(u)	(518)	8,360	8,423
14043	Depew	(716)	17,673	19,819
13214	DeWitt(u)	(315)	8,244	9,024
11746	Dix Hills(u)	(516)	25,849	26,693
10522	Dobbs Ferry	(914)	9,940	10,053

ZIP code	Place		1990	1980
14048	Dunkirk	(716)	13,989	15,310
14052	East Aurora	(716)	6,647	6,803
10709	Eastchester(u)	(914)	18,537	20,305
12302	East Glenville(u)	(518)	6,518	6,537
11576	East Hills	(516)	6,746	7,160
11730	East Islip(u)	(516)	14,325	13,852
11758	East Massapequa(u)	(516)	19,550	13,987
11554	East Meadow(u)	(516)	36,909	39,317
11731	East Northport(u)	(516)	20,411	20,187
11772	East Patchogue(u)	(516)	20,195	18,139
14445	East Rochester	(716)	6,932	7,596
11518	East Rockaway	(516)	10,152	10,917
11786	East Shoreham		5,461	....
*14901	Elmira	(607)	33,724	35,327
11003	Elmont(u)	(516)	28,612	27,592
11731	Elmwood(u)	(516)	10,916	11,847
13760	Endicott	(607)	13,531	14,457
13760	Endwell(u)	(607)	12,602	13,745
13219	Fairmount(u)	(315)	12,266	13,415
14450	Fairport	(716)	5,943	5,970
11735	Farmingdale	(516)	8,022	7,946
11738	Farmingville(u)	(516)	14,842	13,398
*11001	Floral Park	(516)	15,947	16,805
13603	Fort Drum(u)		11,578	....
11768	Fort Salonga(u)	(516)	9,176	9,550
11010	Franklin Square(u)	(516)	28,205	29,051
14063	Fredonia	(716)	10,436	11,126
11520	Freeport	(516)	39,894	38,272
13069	Fulton	(315)	12,929	13,312
11530	Garden City	(516)	21,686	22,927
11040	Garden City Park(u)	(516)	7,437	7,712
14624	Gates-North Gates(u)	(716)	14,995	15,244
14454	Geneseo	(716)	7,187	6,746
14456	Geneva	(315)	14,143	15,133
11542	Glen Cove	(516)	24,149	24,618
12801	Glens Falls	(518)	15,023	15,897
12801	Glens Falls North(u)	(518)	7,978	6,956
12078	Gloversville	(518)	16,656	17,836
10924	Goshen	(914)	5,255	4,874
*11022	Great Neck	(516)	8,745	9,168
11020	Great Neck Plaza	(516)	5,897	5,604
14616	Greece(u)	(716)	15,632	16,177
11740	Greenlawn(u)	(516)	13,208	13,869
12083	Greenville(u)	(518)	9,528	8,706
14075	Hamburg	(716)	10,442	10,582
11946	Hampton Bays(u)	(516)	7,893	7,256
10528	Harrison	(914)	23,308	23,046
10530	Hartsdale(u)	(914)	9,587	10,216
10706	Hastings-on-Hudson	(914)	8,000	8,573
11787	Hauppauge(u)	(516)	19,750	20,960
10927	Haverstraw	(914)	9,438	8,800
*11551	Hempstead	(516)	49,453	40,404
13350	Herkimer	(315)	7,945	8,383
11557	Hewlett(u)	(516)	6,620	6,986
*11802	Hicksville(u)	(516)	40,174	43,245
10977	Hillcrest(u)	(914)	6,447	5,733
14468	Hilton		5,216	4,151
11741	Holbrook(u)	(516)	25,273	24,382
11742	Holtsville(u)	(516)	14,972	13,515
14843	Hornell	(607)	9,877	10,234
14845	Horseheads	(607)	6,802	7,348
12534	Hudson	(518)	8,034	7,986
12839	Hudson Falls	(518)	7,651	7,419
11743	Huntington(u)	(516)	18,243	21,727
11746	Huntington Station(u)	(516)	28,247	28,769
13357	Ilion	(315)	8,888	9,450
11696	Inwood(u)	(516)	7,767	8,228
14617	Irondequoit(u)	(716)	52,322	57,648
10533	Irvington	(914)	6,348	5,774
11751	Islip(u)	(516)	18,924	13,438
11752	Islip Terrace(u)	(516)	5,530	5,588
14850	Ithaca	(607)	29,541	28,732
14701	Jamestown	(716)	34,681	35,775
10535	Jefferson Valley-Yorktown(u)	(914)	14,118	13,380
11753	Jericho(u)	(516)	13,141	12,739
13790	Johnson City	(607)	16,578	17,126
12095	Johnstown	(518)	9,058	9,360
14217	Kenmore	(716)	17,180	18,474
11754	Kings Park(u)	(516)	17,773	16,131
12401	Kingston	(914)	23,095	24,481
.....	Kiryas Joel		7,437	2,088
14218	Lackawanna	(716)	20,585	22,701
10512	Lake Carmel(u)	(914)	8,489	7,295
11755	Lake Grove	(516)	9,612	9,692
11779	Lake Ronkonkoma(u)	(516)	18,997	38,336
11552	Lakeview(u)	(516)	5,476	5,276
14086	Lancaster	(716)	11,940	13,056
10538	Larchmont	(914)	6,181	6,308
12110	Latham(u)	(518)	10,131	11,182
11559	Lawrence	(516)	6,513	6,175
11756	Levittown(u)	(516)	53,286	57,045
11757	Lindenhurst	(516)	26,879	26,919
13365	Little Falls	(315)	5,829	6,156
14094	Lockport	(716)	24,426	24,844
11561	Long Beach	(516)	33,510	34,073
12211	Loudonville(u)	(518)	10,822	11,480
11563	Lynbrook	(516)	19,208	20,424
10541	Mahopac(u)	(914)	7,755	7,681
12953	Malone	(518)	6,777	7,668
11565	Malverne	(516)	9,054	9,262
10543	Mamaroneck	(914)	17,325	17,616
11030	Manhasset(u)	(516)	7,718	8,485
11050	Manorhaven	(516)	5,672	5,384
11949	Manorville(u)	(516)	6,198	....
11758	Massapequa(u)	(516)	22,018	24,454
11762	Massapequa Park	(516)	18,044	19,779
13662	Massena	(315)	11,719	12,851
11950	Mastic(u)	(516)	13,778	10,413
11951	Mastic Beach(u)	(516)	10,293	8,318
13211	Mattydale(u)	(315)	6,418	7,511
12118	Mechanicville	(518)	5,249	5,500
11763	Medford(u)	(516)	21,274	20,418
14103	Medina	(716)	6,686	6,392
11746	Melville(u)	(516)	12,586	8,139
11566	Merrick(u)	(516)	23,042	24,478
11953	Middle Island(u)	(516)	7,848	5,703
10940	Middletown	(914)	24,160	21,454
11764	Miller Place(u)	(516)	9,315	7,877
11501	Mineola	(516)	18,994	20,757
10950	Monroe	(914)	6,672	5,996
10952	Monsey(u)	(914)	13,986	12,380
12701	Monticello	(914)	6,597	6,306
10970	Mount Ivy(u)		6,013	....
10549	Mount Kisco	(914)	9,108	8,025
11766	Mount Sinai(u)	(516)	8,023	6,591
*10551	Mount Vernon	(914)	67,153	66,713
12590	Myers Corner(u)	(914)	5,599	5,180
10954	Nanuet(u)	(914)	14,065	12,578
11767	Nesconset(u)	(516)	10,712	10,706
14513	Newark	(315)	9,849	10,017
12550	Newburgh	(914)	26,454	23,438
11590	New Cassel(u)	(516)	10,257	9,635
10956	New City(u)	(914)	33,673	35,859
11040	New Hyde Park	(516)	9,728	9,801
12561	New Paltz	(914)	5,470	4,938
*10802	New Rochelle	(914)	67,265	70,794
*12550	New Windsor Center(u)	(914)	8,898	7,812
*10001	New York	(212)	7,322,564	7,071,639
*14302	Niagara Falls	(716)	61,840	71,384
11701	North Amityville(u)	(516)	13,849	13,140
11703	North Babylon(u)	(516)	18,081	19,019
11706	North Bay Shore(u)	(516)	12,799	35,020
11710	North Bellmore(u)	(516)	19,707	20,630
11713	North Bellport(u)	(516)	8,182	7,432
11757	North Lindenhurst(u)	(516)	10,563	11,511
11758	North Massapequa(u)	(516)	19,365	21,385
11566	North Merrick(u)	(516)	12,113	12,848
11040	North New Hyde Park(u)	(516)	14,359	15,114
11772	North Patchogue(u)	(516)	7,374	7,126
11768	Northport	(516)	7,572	7,651
13212	North Syracuse	(315)	7,363	7,970
10591	North Tarrytown	(914)	8,152	7,994
14120	North Tonawanda	(716)	34,989	35,760
11580	North Valley Stream(u)	(516)	14,574	14,530
11793	North Wantagh(u)	(516)	12,276	12,677
13815	Norwich	(607)	7,613	8,082
10960	Nyack	(914)	6,558	6,428
11769	Oakdale(u)	(516)	7,875	8,090
11572	Oceanside(u)	(516)	32,423	33,639
13669	Ogdensburg	(315)	13,521	12,375
11804	Old Bethpage(u)	(516)	5,610	6,215
14760	Olean	(716)	16,946	18,207
13421	Oneida	(315)	10,850	10,810
13820	Oneonta	(607)	13,954	14,933
12550	Orange Lake(u)	(914)	5,196	5,120
10562	Ossining	(914)	22,582	20,196
13126	Oswego	(315)	19,195	19,793
11771	Oyster Bay(u)	(516)	6,687	6,497
11772	Patchogue	(516)	11,060	11,291
10965	Pearl River(u)	(914)	15,314	15,893
10566	Peekskill	(914)	19,536	18,236
10803	Pelham	(914)	6,413	6,848
10803	Pelham Manor	(914)	5,443	6,130
14527	Penn Yan	(315)	5,248	5,242
11714	Plainedge(u)	(516)	8,739	9,629
11803	Plainview(u)	(516)	26,207	28,037
12901	Plattsburgh	(518)	21,255	21,057
12903	Plattsburgh AFB(u)	(518)	5,483	5,905
10570	Pleasantville	(914)	6,592	6,749
10573	Port Chester	(914)	24,728	23,565
11777	Port Jefferson	(516)	7,455	6,731
11776	Port Jefferson Station(u)	(516)	7,232	17,009
12771	Port Jervis	(914)	9,060	8,699
11050	Port Washington(u)	(516)	15,387	14,521
13676	Potsdam	(315)	10,251	10,635
*12601	Poughkeepsie	(914)	28,844	29,757
12144	Rensselaer	(518)	8,255	9,047
11961	Ridge(u)	(516)	11,734	8,977
11901	Riverhead(u)	(516)	8,814	6,339
*14603	Rochester	(716)	231,636	241,741
*11570	Rockville Centre	(516)	24,727	25,412
11778	Rocky Point(u)	(516)	8,596	7,012
12205	Roessleville(u)	(518)	10,753	11,685
13440	Rome	(315)	44,350	43,826
11779	Ronkonkoma	(516)	20,391	....
11575	Roosevelt(u)	(516)	15,030	14,109
11577	Roslyn Heights(u)	(516)	6,405	6,546
12303	Rotterdam(u)	(518)	21,228	22,933

ZIP code	Place		1990	1980
10580	Rye	(914)	14,936	15,083
10573	Rye Brook		7,765	7,996
11780	St. James(u)	(516)	12,703	12,122
14779	Salamanca	(716)	6,566	6,890
13454	Salisbury(u)		12,226	....
12983	Saranac Lake	(518)	5,377	5,578
12866	Saratoga Springs	(518)	25,001	23,906
11782	Sayville(u)	(516)	16,550	12,013
10583	Scarsdale	(914)	16,987	17,650
*12301	Schenectady	(518)	65,566	67,972
10940	Scotchtown(u)	(914)	8,765	7,352
12302	Scotia	(518)	7,359	7,280
11579	Sea Cliff	(516)	5,054	5,364
11783	Seaford(u)	(516)	15,597	16,117
11507	Searingtown(u)		5,020	....
11784	Selden(u)	(516)	20,608	17,259
13148	Seneca Falls	(315)	7,370	7,466
11733	Setauket-East Setauket(u)	(516)	13,634	10,176
11967	Shirley(u)	(516)	22,936	18,072
11787	Smithtown(u)	(516)	25,638	30,906
13209	Solvay	(315)	6,717	7,140
11789	Sound Beach(u)	(516)	9,102	8,071
11735	South Farmingdale(u)	(516)	15,377	16,439
14850	South Hill(u)	(607)	5,423	....
11746	South Huntington(u)	(516)	9,624	14,854
14094	South Lockport(u)		7,112	3,366
11971	Southold(u)		5,192	4,770
14904	Southport(u)	(607)	7,753	8,329
11581	South Valley Stream(u)	(516)	5,328	5,462
10977	Spring Valley	(914)	21,802	20,537
11790	Stony Brook(u)	(516)	13,726	16,155
10980	Stony Point(u)	(315)	10,587	8,686
10901	Suffern	(914)	11,055	10,794
11791	Syosset(u)	(516)	18,967	9,818
*13201	Syracuse	(315)	163,860	170,105
10983	Tappan(u)	(914)	6,867	8,267
10591	Tarrytown	(914)	10,739	10,648
11776	Terryville		10,275	....
10984	Thiells		5,204	....
10594	Thornwood(u)	(914)	7,025	7,197
14150	Tonawanda	(716)	17,284	18,693
14151	Tonawanda(u)	(716)	65,284	72,795
*12180	Troy	(518)	54,269	56,638
10707	Tuckahoe	(914)	6,302	6,076
11553	Uniondale(u)	(516)	20,328	20,016
*13503	Utica	(315)	68,637	75,632
10989	Valley Cottage(u)	(914)	9,007	8,214
*11580	Valley Stream	(516)	33,946	35,769
11792	Wading River		5,317	....
12586	Walden	(914)	5,836	5,659
11793	Wantagh(u)	(516)	18,567	19,817
10990	Warwick		5,984	4,320
13165	Waterloo	(315)	5,116	5,303
13601	Watertown	(315)	29,429	27,861
12189	Watervliet	(518)	11,061	11,354
14580	Webster	(716)	5,464	5,499
14895	Wellsville	(716)	5,241	5,769
11704	West Babylon(u)	(516)	42,410	41,699
11590	Westbury	(516)	13,060	13,871
14905	West Elmira(u)	(607)	5,218	5,485
12801	West Glens Falls(u)	(518)	5,964	5,331
10993	West Haverstraw	(914)	9,183	9,181
11552	West Hempstead(u)	(516)	17,689	18,536
11743	West Hills(u)	(516)	5,849	6,071
11795	West Islip(u)	(516)	28,419	29,533
12203	Westmere(u)	(518)	6,750	6,881
10996	West Point(u)	(914)	8,024	8,105
14224	West Seneca(u)	(716)	47,866	51,210
13219	Westvale(u)	(315)	5,952	6,169
11798	Wheatley Heights(u)		5,027	....
10602	White Plains	(914)	48,718	46,999
14221	Williamsville	(716)	5,583	6,017
11596	Williston Park	(516)	7,516	8,216
11797	Woodbury(u)	(516)	8,008	7,043
11598	Woodmere(u)	(516)	15,578	17,205
11798	Wyandach(u)	(516)	8,950	13,215
*10701	Yonkers	(914)	188,082	195,351
10598	Yorktown Heights(u)	(914)	7,690	7,696

North Carolina

ZIP code	Place		1990	1980
28001	Albemarle	(704)	14,939	15,110
27263	Archdale	(919)	6,975	5,326
27203	Asheboro	(919)	16,362	15,252
*28801	Asheville	(704)	61,607	54,022
28012	Belmont	(704)	8,434	4,607
28711	Black Mountain		5,418	4,083
28607	Boone	(704)	12,915	10,191
28712	Brevard	(704)	5,388	5,323
27215	Burlington	(919)	39,498	37,266
28542	Camp Le Jeune(u)	(919)	36,716	30,764
27510	Carrboro	(919)	12,134	7,336
27511	Cary	(919)	43,461	21,763
27514	Chapel Hill	(919)	38,711	32,421
*28202	Charlotte	(704)	395,934	315,474
27012	Clemmons(u)	(919)	6,020	4,842
28328	Clinton	(919)	8,385	7,552
28025	Concord	(704)	27,347	16,942
28613	Conover	(704)	5,465	4,245
28334	Dunn	(919)	8,336	8,962
*27701	Durham	(919)	136,611	101,149
27288	Eden	(919)	15,238	15,672
27932	Edenton	(919)	5,268	5,357
27909	Elizabeth City	(919)	14,292	14,004
*28302	Fayetteville	(919)	75,695	59,507
28043	Forest City	(704)	7,475	7,688
28307	Fort Bragg(u)	(919)	34,744	37,834
27529	Garner	(919)	14,967	10,073
28052	Gastonia	(704)	54,732	47,218
27530	Goldsboro	(919)	40,709	31,871
27253	Graham	(919)	10,368	8,674
*27420	Greensboro	(919)	183,894	155,642
27834	Greenville	(919)	44,972	35,740
.....	Half Moon(u)		6,306	3,592
28345	Hamlet	(919)	6,324	4,720
28532	Havelock	(919)	20,300	17,718
27536	Henderson	(919)	15,655	13,522
28739	Hendersonville	(704)	7,284	6,862
28601	Hickory	(704)	28,301	20,757
*27260	High Point	(919)	69,424	63,479
28348	Hope Mills	(919)	8,255	5,412
28540	Jacksonville	(919)	30,013	18,237
28081	Kannapolis	(704)	29,696	30,303
27284	Kernersville	(919)	10,836	5,875
28086	Kings Mountain	(704)	8,763	9,080
28501	Kinston	(919)	25,295	25,234
28352	Laurinburg	(919)	11,643	11,480
28645	Lenoir	(704)	14,192	13,748
27292	Lexington	(704)	16,581	15,711
28092	Lincolnton	(704)	6,955	4,879
28358	Lumberton	(919)	18,601	18,241
.....	Masonboro(u)		7,010	3,881
28105	Matthews	(704)	13,651	1,648
28212	Mint Hill	(704)	11,615	7,915
28110	Monroe	(704)	16,127	12,639
28115	Mooresville	(704)	9,317	8,575
28557	Morehead	(919)	6,046	4,359
28655	Morganton	(704)	15,085	13,763
27030	Mount Airy	(919)	7,156	6,862
28120	Mount Holly	(704)	7,710	4,530
28560	New Bern	(919)	17,363	14,557
27604	New Hope (Wake)(u)	(704)	5,694	6,745
28540	New River Station(u)	(919)	9,732	5,401
28658	Newton	(704)	9,304	7,624
27565	Oxford	(919)	7,965	7,709
28374	Pinehurst	(919)	5,091	1,746
28399	Piney Green-White Oak(u)	(919)	8,999	6,058
*27611	Raleigh	(919)	207,951	150,255
27320	Reidsville	(919)	12,183	12,492
27870	Roanoke Rapids	(919)	15,722	14,702
28379	Rockingham	(919)	9,399	8,300
27801	Rocky Mount	(919)	48,997	41,526
27573	Roxboro	(919)	7,332	7,532
28601	St. Stephens(u)	(704)	8,734	10,797
28144	Salisbury	(704)	23,087	22,677
27330	Sanford	(919)	14,755	14,773
.....	Seagate(u)		5,444	3,422
28150	Shelby	(704)	14,669	15,310
.....	Smith Creek(u)		7,461	....
27577	Smithfield	(919)	7,540	7,288
28387	Southern Pines	(919)	9,213	8,620
.....	South Gastonia		5,487	4,767
28390	Spring Lake	(919)	7,524	6,273
28677	Statesville	(704)	17,567	18,622
27886	Tarboro	(919)	11,037	8,741
27360	Thomasville	(919)	15,915	14,144
27370	Trinity(u)	(919)	5,469	6,887
27587	Wake Forest	(919)	5,769	3,780
27889	Washington	(919)	9,160	8,418
28786	Waynesville	(704)	6,758	6,765
28472	Whiteville	(919)	5,078	5,565
27892	Williamston	(919)	5,503	6,159
28401	Wilmington	(919)	55,530	44,000
27893	Wilson	(919)	36,930	34,424
*27102	Winston-Salem	(919)	143,485	131,885

North Dakota (701)

ZIP code	Place	1990	1980
58501	Bismarck	49,256	44,485
58301	Devils Lake	7,782	7,442
58601	Dickinson	16,097	15,924
58102	Fargo	74,084	61,383
58201	Grand Forks	49,425	43,765
58201	Grand Forks AFB(u)	9,343	9,390
58401	Jamestown	15,571	16,280
58554	Mandan	15,177	15,513
58701	Minot	34,544	32,843
58701	Minot AFB(u)	9,095	9,880
58072	Valley City	7,163	7,774
58075	Wahpeton	8,751	9,064
58078	West Fargo	12,287	10,099
58801	Williston	13,131	13,336

Ohio

ZIP code	Place	Area code	1990	1980
45810	Ada	(419)	5,428	5,669
*44309	Akron	(216)	223,019	237,177
44601	Alliance	(216)	23,376	24,315
44001	Amherst	(216)	10,332	10,638
44805	Ashland	(419)	20,079	20,326
44004	Ashtabula	(216)	21,633	23,449
45701	Athens	(614)	21,265	19,743
44202	Aurora	(216)	9,192	8,177
44515	Austintown(u)	(216)	32,371	33,636
44011	Avon	(216)	7,337	7,241
44012	Avon Lake	(216)	15,066	13,222
44203	Barberton	(216)	27,623	29,751
44140	Bay Village	(216)	17,000	17,846
44122	Beachwood	(216)	10,644	9,983
45385	Beavercreek	(513)	33,626	31,589
44146	Bedford	(216)	14,822	15,056
44146	Bedford Heights	(216)	12,131	13,214
43906	Bellaire	(614)	6,028	8,241
45305	Bellbrook	(513)	6,511	5,174
43311	Bellefontaine	(513)	12,142	11,888
44811	Bellevue	(419)	8,146	8,187
45714	Belpre	(614)	6,796	7,193
44017	Berea	(216)	19,051	19,567
43209	Bexley	(614)	13,088	13,405
43004	Blacklick Estates(u)	(614)	10,080	11,223
45242	Blue Ash	(513)	11,923	9,510
44512	Boardman(u)	(216)	38,596	39,161
43402	Bowling Green	(419)	28,176	25,728
44141	Brecksville	(216)	11,818	10,132
45211	Bridgetown North	(513)	11,748	11,460
44141	Broadview Heights	(216)	12,219	10,920
44144	Brooklyn	(216)	11,706	12,342
44142	Brook Park	(216)	22,865	26,195
44212	Brunswick	(216)	28,230	28,104
43506	Bryan	(419)	8,348	7,879
44820	Bucyrus	(419)	13,496	13,433
43725	Cambridge	(614)	11,748	13,573
44405	Campbell	(216)	10,038	11,619
44406	Canfield	(216)	5,409	5,535
*44711	Canton	(216)	84,161	93,077
45822	Celina	(419)	9,923	9,137
45459	Centerville	(513)	21,082	18,886
45211	Cheviot	(513)	9,616	9,888
45601	Chillicothe	(614)	21,923	23,420
*45234	Cincinnati	(513)	364,114	385,409
43113	Circleville	(614)	11,666	11,700
*44101	Cleveland	(216)	505,616	573,822
44118	Cleveland Heights	(216)	54,052	56,438
43410	Clyde	(419)	5,776	5,489
*43235	Columbus	(614)	632,910	565,021
44030	Conneaut	(216)	13,241	13,835
44410	Cortland	(216)	5,666	5,011
43812	Coshocton	(614)	12,193	13,405
45238	Covedale(u)	(513)	6,669	5,830
*44222	Cuyahoga Falls	(216)	48,950	50,526
*45401	Dayton	(513)	182,044	193,536
45236	Deer Park	(513)	6,181	6,745
43512	Defiance	(419)	16,768	16,810
43015	Delaware	(614)	20,030	18,780
45833	Delphos	(419)	7,093	7,314
45247	Dent(u)		6,416	....
44622	Dover	(216)	11,329	11,782
45427	Drexel(u)		5,143	....
.....	Dry Run(u)		5,389	....
43017	Dublin	(614)	16,366	3,855
44112	East Cleveland	(216)	33,096	36,957
44094	Eastlake	(216)	21,161	22,104
43920	East Liverpool	(216)	13,654	16,687
44413	East Palestine	(216)	5,168	5,306
45320	Eaton	(513)	7,396	6,839
44004	Edgewood(u)		5,189	3,099
*44035	Elyria	(216)	56,746	57,538
45322	Englewood	(513)	11,402	11,329
44117	Euclid	(216)	54,875	59,999
45324	Fairborn	(513)	31,300	29,702
45014	Fairfield	(513)	39,729	30,777
44313	Fairlawn	(216)	5,779	6,100
44126	Fairview Park	(216)	18,028	19,311
45840	Findlay	(419)	35,703	35,594
45224	Finneytown(u)		13,096	....
45405	Forest Park	(513)	18,609	18,566
45230	Forestville(u)		9,185	....
45426	Fort McKinley(u)	(513)	9,740	10,161
44830	Fostoria	(419)	14,983	15,743
45005	Franklin	(513)	11,026	10,711
43420	Fremont	(419)	17,648	17,834
43230	Gahanna	(614)	27,791	18,001
44833	Galion	(419)	11,859	12,391
44125	Garfield Heights	(216)	31,739	34,938
44041	Geneva	(216)	6,597	6,655
44420	Girard	(216)	11,304	12,517
43212	Grandview Heights	(614)	7,010	7,420
45123	Greenfield	(513)	5,172	5,150
45331	Greenville	(513)	12,863	12,999
45239	Groesbeck(u)	(513)	6,684	9,594
43123	Grove City	(614)	19,661	16,816

ZIP code	Place	Area code	1990	1980
*45012	Hamilton	(513)	61,389	63,189
45030	Harrison	(513)	7,518	5,855
43055	Heath	(614)	7,231	6,969
44124	Highland Heights	(216)	6,249	5,739
43026	Hilliard	(614)	11,796	8,131
45133	Hillsboro	(513)	6,235	6,356
44484	Howland(u)	(216)	6,732	7,441
44425	Hubbard	(216)	8,248	9,245
45424	Huber Heights	(513)	38,696	35,480
43081	Huber Ridge(u)	(614)	5,255	5,835
44236	Hudson	(216)	5,159	4,615
44839	Huron	(419)	7,067	7,123
44131	Independence	(216)	6,500	6,607
45638	Ironton	(614)	12,751	14,290
45640	Jackson	(614)	6,167	6,675
44240	Kent	(216)	28,835	26,164
43326	Kenton	(419)	8,356	8,605
45236	Kenwood(u)	(513)	7,469	9,928
45429	Kettering	(513)	60,569	61,186
44094	Kirtland	(216)	5,881	5,969
44107	Lakewood	(216)	59,718	61,963
43130	Lancaster	(614)	34,507	34,953
45039	Landen(u)		9,263	2,870
45036	Lebanon	(513)	10,453	9,636
*45802	Lima	(419)	45,549	47,827
43228	Lincoln Village(u)	(614)	9,958	10,548
43138	Logan	(614)	6,725	6,557
43140	London	(614)	7,807	6,958
*44052	Lorain	(216)	71,245	75,416
44641	Louisville	(216)	8,087	7,996
45140	Loveland	(513)	9,990	9,106
44124	Lyndhurst	(216)	15,982	18,092
44056	Macedonia	(216)	7,509	6,571
.....	Mack South(u)		5,767	....
45243	Madeira	(513)	9,141	9,341
*44901	Mansfield	(419)	50,627	53,927
44137	Maple Heights	(216)	27,089	29,735
45750	Marietta	(614)	15,026	16,467
43302	Marion	(614)	34,075	37,040
43935	Martins Ferry	(614)	7,990	9,331
43040	Marysville	(513)	9,656	7,414
45040	Mason	(513)	11,452	8,692
44646	Massillon	(216)	31,007	30,557
43537	Maumee	(419)	15,561	15,747
44124	Mayfield Heights	(216)	19,847	21,550
44256	Medina	(216)	19,231	15,268
44060	Mentor	(216)	47,491	42,065
44060	Mentor-on-the-Lake	(216)	8,271	7,919
45342	Miamisburg	(513)	17,834	15,304
44130	Middleburg Heights	(216)	14,702	16,218
45042	Middletown	(513)	46,022	43,719
45150	Milford	(513)	5,660	5,679
45242	Montgomery	(513)	9,733	10,084
45439	Moraine	(513)	5,989	5,325
45231	Mount Healthy	(513)	7,580	7,562
43050	Mount Vernon	(614)	14,550	14,323
44262	Munroe Falls	(216)	5,359	4,731
43545	Napoleon	(419)	8,884	8,614
43055	Newark	(614)	44,389	41,200
45344	New Carlisle	(513)	6,049	6,498
43764	New Lexington	(614)	5,117	5,179
44663	New Philadelphia	(216)	15,698	16,883
44446	Niles	(216)	21,128	23,088
45239	Northbrook(u)	(513)	11,471	8,357
44720	North Canton	(216)	14,748	14,228
45239	North College Hill	(513)	11,002	11,114
.....	Northgate		7,864	....
44057	North Madison(u)	(216)	8,699	8,741
44070	North Olmsted	(216)	34,204	36,486
45502	Northridge(u)	(513)	5,939	5,559
45414	Northridge(u) (Montgomery)	(513)	9,448	9,720
44039	North Ridgeville	(216)	21,564	21,522
44133	North Royalton	(216)	23,197	17,671
.....	Northview(u)	(513)	10,337	9,973
43619	Northwood	(419)	5,506	5,495
44203	Norton	(216)	11,477	12,242
44857	Norwalk	(419)	14,731	14,358
45212	Norwood	(513)	23,674	26,342
45873	Oakwood	(419)	8,957	9,372
44074	Oberlin	(216)	8,191	8,660
44138	Olmsted Falls	(216)	6,741	5,868
43616	Oregon	(419)	18,334	18,675
44667	Orrville	(216)	7,712	7,511
45431	Overlook-Page Manor(u)	(513)	13,242	14,825
45056	Oxford	(513)	18,937	17,655
44077	Painesville	(216)	15,769	16,391
44129	Parma	(216)	87,876	92,548
44130	Parma Heights	(216)	21,448	23,112
44124	Pepper Pike	(216)	6,185	6,177
44646	Perry Heights(u)	(216)	9,055	9,206
43551	Perrysburg	(419)	12,551	10,215
43147	Pickerington		5,668	3,917
45356	Piqua	(513)	20,612	20,480
44319	Portage Lakes(u)	(216)	13,373	11,310
43452	Port Clinton	(419)	7,106	7,223
45662	Portsmouth	(614)	22,676	25,943
44266	Ravenna	(216)	12,069	11,987
45215	Reading	(513)	12,038	12,843
43068	Reynoldsburg	(614)	25,748	20,661

ZIP code	Place		1990	1980
44143	Richmond Heights	(216)	9,611	10,095
44270	Rittman	(216)	6,147	6,063
44116	Rocky River	(216)	20,410	21,084
43460	Rossford	(419)	5,861	5,978
45217	St. Bernard	(513)	5,344	5,396
43950	St. Clairsville	(614)	5,162	5,452
45885	St. Marys	(419)	8,441	8,414
44460	Salem	(216)	12,233	12,869
44870	Sandusky	(419)	29,764	31,360
44870	Sandusky South(u)	(419)	6,336	6,548
44131	Seven Hills	(216)	12,339	13,650
44120	Shaker Heights	(216)	30,867	32,487
45241	Sharonville	(513)	13,153	10,108
44054	Sheffield Lake	(216)	9,825	10,484
44875	Shelby	(419)	9,564	9,703
44878	Shiloh	(419)	11,607	11,735
45365	Sidney	(513)	18,710	17,657
45236	Silverton	(513)	5,859	6,172
44139	Solon	(216)	18,548	14,341
44121	South Euclid	(216)	23,866	25,713
45066	Springboro	(513)	6,590	4,962
45246	Springdale	(216)	10,621	10,111
*45501	Springfield	(513)	70,487	72,563
43952	Steubenville	(614)	22,125	26,400
44224	Stow	(216)	27,998	25,303
44240	Streetsboro	(216)	9,932	9,055
44136	Strongsville	(216)	35,308	28,577
44471	Struthers	(216)	12,284	13,624
43560	Sylvania	(419)	17,301	15,527
44278	Tallmadge	(216)	14,870	15,269
45243	The Village of Indian Hill	(513)	5,383	5,521
44883	Tiffin	(419)	18,604	19,549
45371	Tipp City	(513)	6,027	5,595
*43601	Toledo	(419)	332,943	354,635
43964	Toronto	(614)	6,127	6,934
45067	Trenton	(513)	6,189	6,401
45426	Trotwood	(513)	8,816	7,802
45373	Troy	(513)	19,478	19,086
44087	Twinsburg	(216)	9,606	7,632
44683	Uhrichsville	(614)	5,604	6,130
45322	Union	(513)	5,531	5,219
44118	University Heights	(216)	14,787	15,401
43221	Upper Arlington	(614)	34,128	35,648
43351	Upper Sandusky	(419)	5,906	5,967
43078	Urbana	(513)	11,353	10,762
45377	Vandalia	(513)	13,882	13,161
45891	Van Wert	(419)	10,891	11,035
44089	Vermilion	(216)	11,127	11,012
44281	Wadsworth	(216)	15,718	15,166
45895	Wapakoneta	(419)	9,214	8,402
*44481	Warren	(216)	50,793	56,629
44122	Warrensville Heights	(216)	15,745	16,565
43160	Washington C.H.	(614)	13,080	12,682
43567	Wauseon	(419)	6,322	6,173
45692	Wellston	(614)	6,049	6,016
45449	West Carrollton	(513)	14,403	13,148
43081	Westerville	(614)	30,269	23,414
44145	Westlake	(216)	27,018	19,483
45694	Wheelersburg(u)		5,113	4,796
43213	Whitehall	(614)	20,572	21,299
45239	White Oak(u)	(513)	12,430	9,563
44092	Wickliffe	(216)	14,558	16,790
44890	Willard	(419)	6,210	5,720
44094	Willoughby	(216)	20,510	19,329
44094	Willoughby Hills	(216)	8,427	8,612
44094	Willowick	(216)	15,269	17,834
45177	Wilmington	(513)	11,199	10,431
45459	Woodbourne-Hyde Park(u)	(513)	7,837	8,826
44691	Wooster	(216)	22,438	19,289
43085	Worthington	(614)	14,869	14,666
45433	Wright-Patterson AFB(u)	(513)	8,579	....
45215	Wyoming	(513)	8,128	8,282
45385	Xenia	(513)	24,836	24,653
*44501	Youngstown	(216)	95,732	115,511
43701	Zanesville	(614)	26,778	28,655

Oklahoma

ZIP code	Place		1990	1980
74820	Ada	(405)	15,820	15,902
73521	Altus	(405)	21,910	23,101
73717	Alva	(405)	5,495	6,416
73005	Anadarko	(405)	6,586	6,378
73401	Ardmore	(405)	23,079	23,689
74003	Bartlesville	(918)	34,256	34,568
73008	Bethany	(405)	20,075	22,038
74008	Bixby	(918)	9,502	6,969
74631	Blackwell	(405)	7,538	8,400
74012	Broken Arrow	(918)	58,043	35,761
73018	Chickasha	(405)	14,988	15,828
73020	Choctaw	(405)	8,545	7,520
74017	Claremore	(918)	13,280	12,085
73601	Clinton	(405)	9,298	8,796
74429	Coweta		6,159	4,554
74023	Cushing	(918)	7,218	7,720
73115	Del City	(405)	23,928	28,523
73533	Duncan	(405)	21,732	22,517
74701	Durant	(405)	12,823	11,972
73034	Edmond	(405)	52,315	34,637
73644	Elk City	(405)	10,428	9,579
73036	El Reno	(405)	15,414	15,486
73701	Enid	(405)	45,309	50,363
73503	Fort Sill(u)	(405)	12,107	15,924
73542	Frederick	(405)	5,221	6,153
74033	Glenpool	(918)	6,688	2,706
73044	Guthrie	(405)	10,518	10,312
73942	Guymon	(405)	7,803	8,492
74437	Henryetta	(918)	5,872	6,432
74743	Hugo	(405)	5,978	7,172
74745	Idabel	(405)	6,957	7,622
74037	Jenks	(918)	7,493	5,876
73501	Lawton	(405)	80,561	80,054
74501	McAlester	(918)	16,370	17,255
74354	Miami	(918)	13,142	14,237
73110	Midwest City	(405)	52,267	49,559
73060	Moore	(405)	40,318	35,063
74401	Muskogee	(918)	37,708	40,011
73064	Mustang	(405)	10,434	7,496
73069	Norman	(405)	80,071	68,020
*73125	Oklahoma City	(405)	444,719	404,014
74447	Okmulgee	(918)	13,441	16,263
74055	Owasso	(918)	11,151	6,149
73075	Pauls Valley	(405)	6,150	5,664
74601	Ponca City	(405)	26,359	26,238
74953	Poteau	(918)	7,210	7,089
74361	Pryor Creek	(918)	8,327	8,483
74955	Sallisaw	(918)	7,122	6,403
74063	Sand Springs	(918)	15,346	13,121
74066	Sapulpa	(918)	18,074	15,853
74868	Seminole	(405)	7,071	8,590
74801	Shawnee	(405)	26,017	26,506
74074	Stillwater	(405)	36,676	38,268
74464	Tahlequah	(918)	10,398	9,708
74873	Tecumseh	(405)	5,570	5,123
73120	The Village	(405)	10,353	11,114
*74101	Tulsa	(918)	367,302	360,919
74301	Vinita	(918)	5,804	6,740
74467	Wagoner	(918)	6,894	6,191
73132	Warr Acres	(405)	9,288	9,940
73096	Weatherford	(405)	10,124	9,640
73801	Woodward	(405)	12,340	13,781
73099	Yukon	(405)	20,935	17,112

Oregon (503)

ZIP code	Place	1990	1980
97321	Albany	29,462	26,511
97005	Aloha(u)	34,284	28,353
97601	Altamont(u)	18,591	19,805
97520	Ashland	16,234	14,943
97103	Astoria	10,069	9,998
97814	Baker	9,140	9,471
97005	Beaverton	53,310	31,962
97701	Bend	20,469	17,263
97013	Canby	8,983	7,659
97225	Cedar Hills(u)	9,294	9,619
97291	Cedar Mill(u)	9,697	22,118
97502	Central Point	7,509	6,357
.....	City of the Dalles	11,060	10,820
97420	Coos Bay	15,076	14,424
97113	Cornelius	6,148	4,462
97330	Corvallis	44,757	40,960
97424	Cottage Grove	7,402	7,148
97338	Dallas	9,422	8,530
*97401	Eugene	112,669	105,664
97439	Florence	5,162	4,411
97116	Forest Grove	13,559	11,499
97301	Four Corners(u)	12,156	11,331
97223	Garden Home-Whitford(u)	6,652	6,926
97027	Gladstone	10,152	9,500
97526	Grants Pass	17,488	15,032
97030	Gresham	68,235	33,005
97303	Hayesville(u)	14,318	9,213
97230	Hazelwood(u)	11,480	25,541
97838	Hermiston	10,040	9,408
97123	Hillsboro	37,520	27,664
.....	Jennings Lodge(u)	6,530	....
97303	Keizer	21,884	19,785
97601	Klamath Falls	17,737	16,661
97850	La Grande	11,766	11,354
97034	Lake Oswego	30,576	22,527
97355	Lebanon	10,950	10,413
97367	Lincoln City	5,892	5,469
97128	McMinnville	17,894	14,080
97501	Medford	46,951	39,746
97862	Milton-Freewater	5,533	5,086
97222	Milwaukie	18,692	17,931
97361	Monmouth	6,288	5,594
97132	Newberg	13,086	10,394
97365	Newport	8,437	7,519
97459	North Bend	9,614	9,779
.....	North Springfield(u)	5,451	6,140
97268	Oak Grove(u)	12,576	11,640
.....	Oak Hills	6,450	....
.....	Oatfield	15,348	....
97914	Ontario	9,392	8,814

ZIP code	Place	1990	1980
97045	Oregon City	14,698	14,673
97801	Pendleton	15,126	14,521
*97208	Portland	437,319	368,148
97236	Powellhurst(u)	28,756	20,132
97754	Prineville	5,355	5,276
97225	Raleigh Hills(u)	6,066	6,517
97756	Redmond	7,163	6,452
97404	River Road(u)	9,443	10,370
.....	Rockcreek	8,282	....
97470	Roseburg	17,032	16,644
97470	Roseburg North(u)	6,831	....
97051	St. Helens	7,535	7,064
*97301	Salem	107,786	89,091
97401	Santa Clara(u)	12,834	14,288
97138	Seaside	5,359	5,193
97381	Silverton	5,635	5,168
97477	Springfield	44,683	41,621
97383	Stayton	5,011	4,396
97479	Sutherlin	5,020	4,560
97386	Sweet Home	6,850	6,921
97223	Tigard	29,344	14,799
97060	Troutdale	7,852	5,908
97062	Tualatin	15,013	7,483
.....	West Haven-Sylvan	6,009	....
97068	West Linn	16,367	11,358
97225	West Slope(u)	7,959	5,364
97501	White City(u)	5,891	5,445
97070	Wilsonville	7,106	2,920
97071	Woodburn	13,404	11,196

Pennsylvania

ZIP code	Place	Area code	1990	1980
15001	Aliquippa	(412)	13,374	17,094
*18101	Allentown	(215)	105,301	103,758
*16603	Altoona	(814)	51,881	57,078
19002	Ambler	(215)	6,609	6,628
15003	Ambridge	(412)	8,133	9,575
18403	Archbald	(717)	6,291	6,295
19003	Ardmore(u)	(215)	12,646	....
15068	Arnold	(412)	6,113	6,853
19407	Audubon(u)		6,113	6,853
15202	Avalon	(412)	5,784	6,240
15005	Baden	(412)	5,074	5,318
15234	Baldwin	(412)	21,923	24,714
18013	Bangor	(215)	5,383	5,006
15009	Beaver	(412)	5,028	5,441
15010	Beaver Falls	(412)	10,687	12,525
16823	Bellefonte	(814)	6,358	6,300
15202	Bellevue	(412)	9,126	10,128
18603	Berwick	(717)	10,976	11,850
15102	Bethel Park	(412)	33,823	34,755
*18016	Bethlehem	(215)	71,427	70,419
18447	Blakely	(717)	7,222	7,438
17815	Bloomsburg	(717)	12,439	11,717
19422	Blue Bell(u)		6,091	....
19061	Boothwyn(u)		5,069	....
16701	Bradford	(814)	9,625	11,211
15227	Brentwood	(412)	10,823	11,859
15017	Bridgeville	(412)	5,445	6,154
19007	Bristol	(215)	10,405	10,867
19015	Brookhaven	(215)	8,567	7,912
19008	Broomall(u)	(215)	10,930	....
16001	Butler	(412)	15,714	17,026
15419	California	(412)	5,748	5,703
17011	Camp Hill	(717)	7,831	8,422
15317	Canonsburg	(412)	9,200	10,459
18407	Carbondale	(717)	10,664	11,255
17013	Carlisle	(717)	18,419	18,314
15106	Carnegie	(412)	9,278	10,099
15108	Carnot-Moon(u)	(412)	10,187	11,102
15234	Castle Shannon	(412)	9,135	10,164
18032	Catasauqua	(215)	6,662	6,711
17201	Chambersburg	(717)	16,647	16,174
15022	Charleroi	(412)	5,014	5,717
*19013	Chester	(215)	41,856	45,794
19013	Chester Twp(u)	(215)	5,399	5,687
15025	Clairton	(412)	9,656	12,188
16214	Clarion	(814)	6,457	6,198
18411	Clarks Summit	(717)	5,433	5,272
16830	Clearfield	(814)	6,633	7,580
19018	Clifton Heights	(215)	7,111	7,320
19320	Coatesville	(215)	11,038	10,698
19023	Collingdale	(215)	9,175	9,539
.....	Colonial Park(u)		13,777	....
17512	Columbia	(717)	10,701	10,466
15425	Connellsville	(412)	9,229	10,319
19428	Conshohocken	(215)	8,064	8,591
15108	Coraopolis	(412)	6,747	7,308
16407	Corry	(814)	7,216	7,149
15205	Crafton	(412)	7,188	7,623
19020	Croydon(u)	(215)	9,967	....
17821	Danville	(717)	5,165	5,239
19023	Darby	(215)	11,140	11,513
19036	Darby Twp(u)	(215)	10,955	12,264
19333	Devon-Berwyn(u)	(215)	5,019	5,246
18519	Dickson City	(717)	6,276	6,699
15033	Donora	(412)	5,928	7,524

ZIP code	Place	Area code	1990	1980
15216	Dormont	(412)	9,772	11,275
19335	Downingtown	(215)	7,749	7,650
18901	Doylestown	(215)	8,575	8,717
19026	Drexel Hill(u)	(215)	29,744	....
15801	Du Bois	(814)	8,286	9,290
18512	Dunmore	(717)	15,403	16,781
15110	Duquesne	(412)	8,525	10,094
19401	East Norriton(u)	(215)	13,324	12,711
18042	Easton	(215)	26,276	26,027
18301	East Stroudsburg	(717)	8,781	8,039
17405	East York(u)		8,487	....
15005	Economy	(412)	9,305	9,538
16412	Edinboro	(814)	7,736	6,324
18704	Edwardsville	(717)	5,399	5,729
17022	Elizabethtown	(717)	9,952	8,233
16117	Ellwood City	(412)	8,894	9,998
18049	Emmaus	(215)	11,157	11,001
17025	Enola(u)		5,961	....
17522	Ephrata	(717)	12,133	11,095
*16501	Erie	(814)	108,718	119,123
18643	Exeter	(717)	5,691	5,493
19030	Fairless Hills(u)	(215)	9,026	....
16121	Farrell	(412)	6,841	8,645
19047	Feasterville-Trevose(u)	(215)	6,696	....
.....	Fernway(u)		9,072	3,843
19032	Folcroft	(215)	7,506	8,231
15221	Forest Hills	(412)	8,173	8,198
18704	Forty Fort	(717)	5,049	5,590
15238	Fox Chapel	(412)	5,319	5,049
16323	Franklin	(814)	7,329	8,146
15143	Franklin Park	(412)	10,109	6,135
18052	Fullerton(u)	(215)	13,127	8,055
17325	Gettysburg	(717)	7,025	7,194
15045	Glassport	(412)	5,582	6,242
19036	Glenolden	(215)	7,260	7,633
19038	Glenside(u)	(215)	8,704	....
15601	Greensburg	(412)	16,318	17,558
16125	Greenville	(412)	6,734	7,730
16127	Grove City	(412)	8,240	8,162
.....	Hampton Township(u)		15,568	....
17331	Hanover	(717)	14,399	14,890
19438	Harleysville(u)	(215)	7,405	3,673
*17105	Harrisburg	(717)	52,376	53,264
15636	Harrison Township(u)		11,763	....
19040	Hatboro	(215)	7,382	7,579
18201	Hazleton	(717)	24,730	27,318
18055	Hellertown	(215)	5,662	6,025
16148	Hermitage	(412)	15,260	16,365
17033	Hershey(u)	(717)	11,860	13,249
16648	Hollidaysburg	(814)	5,624	5,892
16001	Homeacre-Lyndora(u)	(412)	7,511	8,333
19044	Horsham(u)	(215)	15,051	9,900
16652	Huntingdon	(814)	6,843	7,042
15701	Indiana	(412)	15,174	16,051
15644	Jeannette	(412)	11,221	13,106
15344	Jefferson	(412)	9,533	8,643
18229	Jim Thorpe	(717)	5,048	5,263
*15901	Johnstown	(814)	28,134	35,496
15108	Kennedy Twp(u)	(412)	7,152	7,159
19348	Kennett Square	(215)	5,218	4,715
19406	King of Prussia(u)	(215)	18,406	....
18704	Kingston	(717)	14,507	15,681
16201	Kittanning	(412)	5,120	5,432
19443	Kulpsville(u)		5,183	....
*17604	Lancaster	(717)	55,551	54,725
19446	Lansdale	(215)	16,362	16,526
19050	Lansdowne	(215)	11,712	11,891
15650	Latrobe	(412)	9,265	10,799
17540	Leacock-Leola-Bareville(u)		5,685	....
17042	Lebanon	(717)	24,800	25,711
18235	Lehighton	(215)	5,914	5,826
19053	Levittown(u)	(215)	55,362	....
17837	Lewisburg	(717)	5,785	5,407
17044	Lewistown	(717)	9,341	9,830
17112	Linglestown(u)		5,862	....
19353	Lionville-Marchwood(u)	(215)	6,468	....
17543	Lititz	(717)	8,280	7,590
17745	Lock Haven	(717)	9,230	9,617
.....	Lower Allen(u)		6,329	....
15068	Lower Burrell	(412)	12,251	13,200
15237	McCandless Twp(u)	(412)	28,781	26,250
*15134	McKeesport	(412)	26,016	31,012
15136	McKees Rocks	(412)	7,691	8,742
17948	Mahanoy City	(717)	5,209	6,167
17545	Manheim	(717)	5,011	5,015
19002	Maple Glen(u)		5,881	....
16335	Meadville	(814)	14,318	15,544
17055	Mechanicsburg	(717)	9,452	9,487
*19063	Media	(215)	5,957	6,119
17057	Middletown (Dauphin)	(717)	9,254	10,122
18017	Middletown (Northampton)(u)	(215)	6,866	5,801
17551	Millersville	(717)	8,099	7,668
17847	Milton	(717)	6,746	6,730
15061	Monaca	(412)	6,739	7,661
15062	Monessen	(412)	9,901	11,928
18936	Montgomeryville(u)	(215)	9,114	....
18507	Moosic	(717)	5,397	6,068
19067	Morrisville	(215)	9,765	9,845
17851	Mount Carmel	(717)	7,196	8,190

ZIP code	Place		1990	1980
17552	Mount Joy	(717)	6,398	5,680
15228	Mount Lebanon(u)	(412)	33,362	34,414
15120	Munhall	(412)	13,158	14,535
15146	Municipality of Monroeville	(412)	29,169	30,977
15668	Municipality of Murrysville	(412)	17,240	16,036
18634	Nanticoke	(717)	12,267	13,044
18064	Nazareth	(215)	5,713	5,443
.....	Nether Providence Twp(u)	(215)	13,229	12,730
15066	New Brighton	(412)	6,854	7,364
*16101	New Castle	(412)	28,334	33,621
17070	New Cumberland	(717)	7,665	8,051
15068	New Kensington	(412)	15,894	17,660
*19401	Norristown	(215)	30,754	34,684
18067	Northampton	(215)	8,717	8,240
15104	North Braddock	(412)	7,036	8,711
15137	North Versailles(u)	(412)	12,302	13,294
16421	Northwest Harborcreek(u)	(814)	6,662	7,485
19074	Norwood	(215)	6,162	6,647
15139	Oakmont	(412)	6,961	7,039
.....	O'Hara(u)		9,096	....
16301	Oil City	(814)	11,949	13,881
18518	Old Forge	(717)	8,834	9,304
18447	Olyphant	(717)	5,222	5,204
19075	Oreland(u)		5,695	....
18071	Palmerton	(215)	5,394	5,455
17078	Palmyra	(717)	6,910	7,228
19301	Paoli(u)	(215)	5,603	5,277
.....	Park Forest Village(u)		6,703	....
17331	Parkville(u)	(717)	6,014	5,009
15235	Penn Hills(u)	(717)	51,430	57,632
.....	Penn Wynne(u)		5,807	....
18944	Perkasie	(215)	7,787	5,241
*19104	Philadelphia	(215)	1,585,577	1,688,210
19460	Phoenixville	(215)	15,066	14,165
*15219	Pittsburgh	(412)	369,879	423,959
*18640	Pittston	(717)	9,389	9,9303
15236	Pleasant Hills	(412)	8,884	9,604
15239	Plum	(412)	25,609	25,309
18651	Plymouth	(717)	7,134	7,605
19462	Plymouth Meeting(u)	(215)	6,241	....
19464	Pottstown	(215)	21,831	22,729
17901	Pottsville	(717)	16,603	18,195
.....	Progress(u)		9,654	....
19076	Prospect Park	(215)	6,764,	6,593
15767	Punxsutawney	(814)	6,782	7,479
18951	Quakertown	(215)	8,982	8,867
19087	Radnor Twp(u)	(215)	28,705	27,676
*19603	Reading	(215)	78,380	78,686
17356	Red Lion	(717)	6,130	5,824
18954	Richboro(u)	(215)	5,332	5,141
19078	Ridley Park	(215)	7,592	7,889
15949	Robinson(u)		10,830	....
15237	Ross Twp(u)	(412)	33,482	35,102
15857	St. Marys	(814)	5,511	6,417
19464	Sanatoga(u)		5,534	3,723
18840	Sayre	(717)	5,791	6,951
17972	Schuylkill Haven	(717)	5,610	5,977
15683	Scottdale	(412)	5,184	5,833
15106	Scott Twp(u)	(412)	17,118	20,413
*18503	Scranton	(717)	81,805	88,117
17870	Selinsgrove	(717)	5,384	5,227
15116	Shaler Twp(u)	(412)	30,533	33,694
17872	Shamokin	(717)	9,184	10,357
16146	Sharon	(412)	17,533	19,057
19079	Sharon Hill	(215)	5,771	6,221
17976	Shenandoah	(717)	6,221	7,589
19607	Shillington	(215)	5,062	5,601
17404	Shiloh(u)	(717)	8,245	5,315
17257	Shippensburg	(717)	5,331	5,261
15501	Somerset	(814)	6,454	6,474
18964	Souderton	(215)	5,957	6,657
.....	South Park(u)		14,292	....
17701	South Williamsport	(717)	6,496	6,581
19064	Springfield(u)	(717)	24,160	25,326
16801	State College	(814)	38,047	36,130
17113	Steelton	(717)	5,152	6,484
15136	Stowe Twp(u)	(412)	7,681	9,202
18360	Stroudsburg	(717)	5,312	5,148
16323	Sugar Creek	(717)	5,532	5,954
17801	Sunbury	(717)	11,591	12,292
19081	Swarthmore	(215)	6,157	5,950
15218	Swissvale	(412)	10,637	11,345
18704	Swoyersville	(717)	5,630	5,795
18252	Tamaqua	(717)	7,943	8,843
15084	Tarentum	(412)	5,674	6,419
18517	Taylor	(717)	6,941	7,246
16354	Titusville	(814)	6,434	6,884
19401	Trooper(u)	(215)	5,137	7,370
15145	Turtle Creek	(412)	6,556	6,959
16686	Tyrone	(814)	5,743	6,346
15401	Uniontown	(412)	12,034	14,510
19063	Upper Providence Twp(u)	(215)	9,727	9,477
15241	Upper St. Clair(u)	(412)	19,692	19,023
15690	Vandergrift	(412)	5,904	6,823
.....	Village Green-Green Ridge(u)		9,026	....
16365	Warren	(814)	11,122	12,146
15301	Washington	(412)	15,864	18,363
17268	Waynesboro	(717)	9,578	9,726
.....	Weigelstown(u)	(717)	8,665	5,213
*19380	West Chester	(215)	18,041	17,435
19380	West Goshen(u)	(215)	8,948	7,998
15122	West Mifflin	(412)	23,644	26,322
15905	Westmont	(814)	5,789	6,113
19401	West Norriton(u)	(215)	15,209	14,034
18643	West Pittston	(717)	5,590	5,980
15229	West View	(412)	7,734	7,648
18052	Whitehall	(215)	14,451	15,143
15131	White Oak	(717)	8,761	9,480
*18701	Wilkes-Barre	(717)	47,523	51,551
15221	Wilkinsburg	(412)	21,080	23,669
15145	Wilkins Twp(u)	(412)	7,487	8,472
17701	Williamsport	(717)	31,933	33,401
19090	Willow Grove(u)	(215)	16,325	....
17584	Willow Street(u)		5,817	....
15025	Wilson	(412)	7,830	7,564
19094	Woodlyn(u)	(215)	10,151	....
19118	Wyndmoor(u)	(215)	5,682	....
19610	Wyomissing	(215)	7,332	6,551
19050	Yeadon	(215)	11,980	11,727
*17405	York	(717)	42,192	44,619

Rhode Island (401)

See Note on Page 398

ZIP code	Place	1990	1980
02806	*Barrington(u)*	15,849	16,174
02809	*Bristol(u)*	21,625	20,128
02830	*Burrillville*	16,230	13,164
02863	Central Falls	17,637	16,995
02813	Charlestown	6,478	....
02816	*Coventry*	31,083	27,065
02910	Cranston	76,060	71,992
02864	*Cumberland*	29,038	27,069
02864	Cumberland Hill(u)	6,379	5,421
02818	*East Greenwich*	11,865	10,211
02914	East Providence	50,380	50,980
02822	Exeter	5,461	....
02814	*Glocester*	9,227	7,550
02828	Greenville(u)	8,303	7,576
02833	*Hopkinton*	6,873	6,406
02919	*Johnston*	26,542	24,907
02881	Kingston(u)	6,504	5,479
02865	*Lincoln*	18,045	16,949
02840	*Middletown*	19,460	17,216
02882	*Narragansett*	14,985	12,088
02840	Newport	28,227	29,259
02843	Newport East(u)	11,080	11,030
02852	*North Kingstown*	23,786	21,938
02908	*North Providence(u)*	32,090	29,188
02876	*North Smithfield*	10,497	9,972
02859	Pascoag(u)	5,011	3,807
*02860	Pawtucket	72,644	71,204
02871	*Portsmouth*	16,857	14,257
*02904	Providence	160,728	156,804
.....	Richmond	5,351	....
02857	*Scituate*	9,796	8,405
02917	*Smithfield*	19,163	16,886
02879	*South Kingstown*	24,631	20,414
02878	*Tiverton(u)*	14,312	13,526
02864	Valley Falls(u)	11,175	10,892
*02880	Wakefield-Peacedale(u)	7,134	6,474
02885	*Warren*	11,385	10,640
*02887	Warwick	85,427	87,123
02891	*Westerly*	21,605	18,580
02891	Westerly Center(u)	16,477	14,093
02893	*West Warwick(u)*	29,268	27,026
02895	Woonsocket	43,877	45,914

South Carolina (803)

ZIP code	Place	1990	1980
29620	Abbeville	5,778	5,833
29801	Aiken	20,435	14,978
29621	Anderson	26,165	27,546
29812	Barnwell	5,255	5,572
29902	Beaufort	9,576	8,634
29841	Belvedere(u)	6,133	6,859
29512	Bennettsville	9,740	8,774
29611	Berea(u)	13,535	13,164
.....	Brookdale(u)	5,339	6,123
29902	Burton(u)	0,917	3,619
29020	Camden	6,696	7,462
29033	Cayce	10,807	11,701
*29401	Charleston	80,414	69,779
29520	Cheraw	5,555	5,654
29706	Chester	7,158	6,820
29631	Clemson	11,096	8,118
29325	Clinton	9,603	8,596
*29201	Columbia	98,052	101,229
29526	Conway	9,819	10,240
29532	Darlington	7,311	7,989
29204	Dentsville(u)	11,839	13,579
29536	Dillon	6,829	7,060
29640	Easley	15,195	14,264
29501	Florence	29,956	29,842
29206	Forest Acres	7,197	6,062

ZIP code	Place	1990	1980
29340	Gaffney	13,145	13,453
29605	Gantt(u)	13,891	13,719
.....	Garden City(u)	6,305	....
29440	Georgetown	9,517	10,144
29445	Goose Creek	24,692	17,811
*29602	Greenville	58,282	58,242
29646	Greenwood	20,807	21,613
29651	Greer	10,322	10,525
29410	Hanahan	13,176	13,224
29550	Hartsville	8,372	7,631
29928	Hilton Head Island	23,694	11,239
29621	Homeland Park(u)	6,569	6,720
29063	Irmo	11,280	3,957
29456	Ladson(u)	13,540	13,246
29560	Lake City	7,153	6,731
29720	Lancaster	8,914	9,703
29360	Laurens	9,694	10,587
29571	Marion	7,658	7,700
29662	Mauldin	11,662	8,143
29430	Moncks Corner	5,607	4,179
29464	Mount Pleasant	30,108	14,464
29574	Mullins	5,910	6,068
29577	Myrtle Beach	24,848	18,446
29108	Newberry	10,542	9,866
29841	North Augusta	15,351	13,593
29406	North Charleston	70,218	62,479
29582	North Myrtle Beach	8,636	3,960
29565	Oak Grove(u)	7,173	7,092
29115	Orangeburg	13,739	14,933
.....	Parker(u)	11,072	....
29905	Parris Island(u)	7,172	7,752
.....	Red Bank(u)	5,950	....
.....	Red Hill(u)	6,112	....
29730	Rock Hill	41,643	35,327
29210	St. Andrews(u)	25,692	20,245
29609	Sans Souci(u)	7,612	8,393
29678	Seneca	7,726	7,436
.....	Seven Oaks(u)	15,722	16,604
29681	Simpsonville	11,728	9,037
29577	Socastee(u)	10,426	1,082
*29301	Spartanburg	43,467	43,826
29483	Summerville	22,519	6,492
29150	Sumter	41,943	24,921
29687	Taylors(u)	19,619	15,801
29379	Union	9,836	10,523
29607	Wade Hampton(u)	20,014	20,180
29488	Walterboro	5,595	6,209
29611	Welcome(u)	6,560	6,922
29169	West Columbia	10,944	10,409
29206	Woodfield(u)	8,862	9,588
29745	York	6,709	6,412

South Dakota (605)

ZIP code	Place	1990	1980
57401	Aberdeen	24,927	25,851
57006	Brookings	16,270	14,951
57706	Ellsworth AFB(u)	7,017	4,766
57350	Huron	12,448	13,000
57042	Madison	6,257	6,210
57301	Mitchell	13,798	13,916
57501	Pierre	12,906	11,973
57701	Rapid City	54,523	46,492
.....	Rapid Valley(u)	5,968	3,265
*57101	Sioux Falls	100,836	81,343
57783	Spearfish	6,966	5,251
57785	Sturgis	5,330	5,184
57069	Vermillion	10,034	10,136
57201	Watertown	17,592	15,649
57078	Yankton	12,703	12,011

Tennessee

ZIP code	Place	Area code	1990	1980
37701	Alcoa	(615)	6,400	6,870
37303	Athens	(615)	12,054	12,080
38134	Bartlett	(901)	26,989	17,170
37660	Bloomingdale(u)	(615)	10,953	12,088
38008	Bolivar	(901)	5,969	6,597
37027	Brentwood	(615)	16,392	9,431
37620	Bristol	(615)	23,421	23,986
38012	Brownsville	(901)	10,019	9,307
*37401	Chattanooga	(615)	152,466	169,514
37040	Clarksville	(615)	75,494	54,777
37311	Cleveland	(615)	30,354	26,415
37716	Clinton	(615)	8,972	5,245
37315	Collegedale	(615)	5,048	4,607
38017	Collierville	(901)	14,427	7,839
37663	Colonial Heights(u)	(615)	6,716	6,744
38401	Columbia	(615)	28,583	26,571
38501	Cookeville	(615)	21,744	20,535
38019	Covington	(901)	7,487	6,065
38555	Crossville	(615)	6,930	6,394
37321	Dayton	(615)	5,671	5,233
37055	Dickson	(615)	8,791	7,040
38024	Dyersburg	(901)	16,317	15,856
37801	Eagleton Village(u)	(615)	5,169	5,331
37411	East Brainerd(u)		11,594	....
37412	East Ridge	(615)	21,101	21,236
37643	Elizabethton	(615)	11,931	12,431
37650	Erwin	(615)	5,015	4,739
37922	Farragut	(615)	12,793	5,992
37334	Fayetteville	(615)	7,158	7,559
37064	Franklin	(615)	20,098	12,407
37066	Gallatin	(615)	18,794	17,191
38138	Germantown	(901)	32,893	21,467
37072	Goodlettsville	(615)	11,219	8,327
37743	Greeneville	(615)	13,532	14,097
37215	Green Hills(u)		6,763	....
37918	Halls(u)	(901)	6,450	10,363
37748	Harriman	(615)	7,119	8,303
37341	Harrison(u)	(615)	7,191	6,206
37075	Hendersonville	(615)	32,188	26,561
38343	Humboldt	(901)	9,651	10,209
38301	Jackson	(901)	49,115	49,258
37760	Jefferson City	(615)	5,494	5,612
37601	Johnson City	(615)	49,503	39,753
*37662	Kingsport	(615)	36,365	32,027
*37901	Knoxville	(615)	165,121	175,045
37766	La Follette	(615)	7,192	8,198
37086	LaVergne	(615)	7,499	5,495
38464	Lawrenceburg	(615)	10,397	10,184
37087	Lebanon	(615)	15,208	11,872
37771	Lenoir City	(615)	6,147	5,180
37091	Lewisburg	(615)	9,879	8,760
38351	Lexington	(901)	5,810	5,934
38201	McKenzie	(901)	5,168	5,405
37110	McMinnville	(615)	11,194	10,683
37355	Manchester	(615)	7,709	7,250
38237	Martin	(901)	8,600	8,898
37701	Maryville	(615)	19,208	17,480
*38101	Memphis	(901)	610,337	646,174
37343	Middle Valley(u)	(615)	12,255	11,420
38358	Milan	(901)	7,512	8,083
38053	Millington	(901)	17,866	20,236
37814	Morristown	(615)	21,385	19,570
37122	Mount Juliet		5,389	2,879
37130	Murfreesboro	(615)	44,922	32,845
*37202	Nashville-Davidson	(615)	488,374	455,651
37821	Newport	(615)	7,123	7,580
37830	Oak Ridge	(615)	27,310	27,662
38242	Paris	(901)	9,332	10,728
37148	Portland	(615)	5,165	4,030
37849	Powell(u)	(615)	7,534	7,220
38478	Pulaski	(615)	7,895	7,184
37415	Red Bank	(615)	12,316	13,129
38063	Ripley	(901)	6,188	6,366
37854	Rockwood	(615)	5,348	5,687
38372	Savannah	(901)	6,547	6,992
37862	Sevierville	(615)	7,178	4,556
37865	Seymour(u)		7,026	....
37160	Shelbyville	(615)	14,049	13,530
37377	Signal Mountain	(615)	7,034	5,818
37167	Smyrna	(615)	13,647	8,839
37379	Soddy-Daisy	(615)	8,240	8,388
.....	South Cleveland(u)		5,372	4,360
37172	Springfield	(615)	11,227	10,814
37874	Sweetwater	(615)	5,066	4,725
37388	Tullahoma	(615)	16,761	15,800
38261	Union City	(901)	10,513	10,436
37398	Winchester	(615)	6,305	5,821

Texas

ZIP code	Place	Area code	1990	1980
*79604	Abilene	(915)	106,654	98,315
75001	Addison	(214)	8,783	5,553
78516	Alamo	(512)	8,210	5,831
78209	Alamo Heights	(512)	6,502	6,252
77039	Aldine(u)	(713)	11,133	12,623
78332	Alice	(512)	19,788	20,961
75002	Allen	(214)	9,198	8,314
79830	Alpine	(915)	5,637	5,465
77511	Alvin	(713)	19,220	16,515
*79105	Amarillo	(806)	157,580	149,230
78750	Anderson Mill(u)		9,468	....
79714	Andrews	(915)	10,678	11,061
77515	Angleton	(409)	17,140	13,929
78336	Aransas Pass	(512)	7,180	7,173
*76010	Arlington	(817)	261,721	160,113
75751	Athens	(903)	10,967	10,197
75551	Atlanta	(214)	6,118	6,272
*78710	Austin	(512)	465,622	345,890
76020	Azle	(817)	8,868	5,822
75149	Balch Springs	(214)	17,406	13,746
77414	Bay City	(409)	18,170	17,837
77520	Baytown	(713)	63,850	56,923
*77704	Beaumont	(409)	114,323	118,102
76021	Bedford	(817)	43,762	20,821
78102	Beeville	(512)	13,547	14,574
77401	Bellaire	(713)	13,842	14,950
76704	Bellmead	(817)	8,336	7,569
76513	Belton	(817)	12,476	10,660
76126	Benbrook	(817)	19,564	13,579
79720	Big Spring	(915)	23,093	24,804
75418	Bonham	(903)	6,686	7,338

ZIP code	Place		1990	1980
79007	Borger	(806)	15,675	15,837
76825	Brady	(915)	5,946	5,969
76024	Breckenridge	(817)	5,665	6,921
77833	Brenham	(409)	11,952	10,966
77611	Bridge City	(409)	8,034	7,667
79316	Brownfield	(806)	9,560	10,387
78520	Brownsville	(512)	98,962	84,997
76801	Brownwood	(915)	18,387	19,396
78717	Brushy Creek(u)		5,833	....
77801	Bryan	(409)	55,002	44,337
76354	Burkburnett	(817)	10,145	10,668
76028	Burleson	(817)	16,113	11,734
76520	Cameron	(817)	5,635	5,721
79015	Canyon	(806)	11,365	10,724
78133	Canyon Lake(u)		9,975	....
78834	Carrizo Springs	(512)	5,745	6,886
75006	Carrolton	(214)	82,169	40,595
75633	Carthage	(903)	6,496	6,447
75104	Cedar Hill	(214)	19,976	6,849
78613	Cedar Park		5,161	3,474
77530	Channelview(u)	(713)	25,564	17,471
79201	Childress	(817)	5,055	5,817
76031	Cleburne	(817)	22,205	19,218
77327	Cleveland	(713)	7,124	5,977
77015	Clover Leaf(u)	(713)	18,230	17,317
77531	Clute	(409)	8,910	9,577
76834	Coleman	(915)	5,410	5,960
77840	College Station	(409)	52,456	37,272
76034	Colleyville	(817)	12,724	6,700
75428	Commerce	(903)	6,825	8,136
77301	Conroe	(409)	27,610	18,034
78109	Converse	(512)	8,887	5,150
75019	Coppell		16,881	3,826
76522	Copperas Cove	(817)	24,079	19,469
*78408	Corpus Christi	(512)	257,453	232,134
75110	Corsicana	(903)	22,911	21,712
75835	Crockett	(409)	7,024	7,405
76036	Crowley	(817)	6,974	5,852
78839	Crystal City	(512)	8,263	8,334
77954	Cuero	(512)	6,700	7,124
79022	Dalhart	(806)	6,246	6,854
*75260	Dallas	(214)	1,007,617	904,599
77535	Dayton	(409)	5,151	4,908
77536	Deer Park	(713)	27,658	22,648
78840	Del Rio	(512)	30,705	30,034
75020	Denison	(903)	21,505	23,884
76201	Denton	(817)	66,270	48,063
79323	Denver City		5,145	4,704
75115	De Soto	(214)	30,544	15,538
77539	Dickinson	(713)	9,497	7,505
78537	Donna	(512)	12,652	9,952
79029	Dumas	(806)	12,871	12,194
75116	Duncanville	(214)	35,008	27,781
76135	Eagle Mountain(u)		5,847	....
78852	Eagle Pass	(512)	20,651	21,407
78539	Edinburg	(512)	29,885	24,075
77957	Edna	(512)	5,343	5,650
77437	El Campo	(409)	10,511	10,462
*79910	El Paso	(915)	515,342	425,259
78543	Elsa	(512)	5,242	5,061
75119	Ennis	(214)	13,883	12,110
76039	Euless	(817)	38,149	24,002
76140	Everman	(817)	5,672	5,387
79838	Fabens(u)		5,599	4,285
78355	Falfurrias	(512)	5,788	6,103
75234	Farmers Branch	(214)	24,250	24,863
.....	First Colony(u)		18,327	....
78114	Floresville		5,247	4,381
75028	Flower Mound		15,527	4,402
76119	Forest Hill	(817)	11,482	11,684
79906	Fort Bliss(u)	(915)	13,915	12,687
76544	Fort Hood(u)	(817)	35,580	31,250
79735	Fort Stockton	(915)	8,524	8,688
*76101	Fort Worth	(817)	447,619	385,164
78624	Fredericksburg	(512)	6,934	6,412
77541	Freeport	(409)	11,389	13,444
77546	Friendswood	(713)	22,814	10,719
75034	Frisco		6,141	3,499
76240	Gainesville	(817)	14,256	14,081
77547	Galena Park	(713)	10,033	9,879
77550	Galveston	(409)	59,070	61,902
*75040	Garland	(214)	180,650	138,857
76528	Gatesville	(817)	11,492	6,078
78626	Georgetown	(512)	14,842	9,468
75647	Gladewater	(903)	6,027	6,548
78629	Gonzales	(512)	6,527	7,152
76046	Graham	(817)	8,986	9,170
*75050	Grand Prairie	(214)	99,616	71,462
76051	Grapevine	(817)	29,202	11,801
75401	Greenville	(903)	23,071	22,161
77619	Groves	(409)	16,745	17,090
76117	Haltom City	(817)	32,856	29,014
76541	Harker Heights	(817)	12,841	7,345
78550	Harlingen	(512)	48,735	43,543
77859	Hearne	(409)	5,132	5,418
75652	Henderson	(903)	11,139	11,473
79045	Hereford	(806)	14,745	15,853
76643	Hewitt	(817)	8,983	5,247
75205	Highland Park	(214)	8,739	8,909

ZIP code	Place		1990	1980
77562	Highlands(u)	(713)	6,632	6,467
75067	Highland Village		7,027	3,246
76645	Hillsboro	(817)	7,072	7,397
77563	Hitchcock	(409)	5,868	6,103
78861	Hondo	(512)	6,018	6,057
*77013	Houston	(713)	1,630,864	1,595,138
77338	Humble	(713)	12,060	6,729
77340	Huntsville	(409)	27,925	23,936
76053	Hurst	(817)	33,574	31,420
78362	Ingleside	(512)	5,696	5,436
76367	Iowa Park	(817)	6,072	6,184
*75061	Irving	(214)	155,037	109,943
77029	Jacinto City	(713)	9,343	8,953
75766	Jacksonville	(214)	12,765	12,264
75951	Jasper	(409)	7,160	6,959
78729	Jollyville		15,206	....
77450	Katy	(713)	8,005	5,660
75142	Kaufman	(214)	5,238	4,658
76248	Keller	(817)	13,683	4,156
79745	Kermit	(915)	6,875	8,015
78028	Kerrville	(512)	17,384	15,276
75662	Kilgore	(903)	11,066	11,331
76541	Killeen	(817)	63,535	46,296
78363	Kingsville	(512)	25,276	28,808
77325	Kingwood	(713)	37,397	16,261
78219	Kirby	(512)	8,326	6,435
78236	Lackland AFB(u)	(512)	9,352	14,459
77566	Lake Jackson	(409)	22,776	19,102
77568	La Marque	(409)	14,120	15,372
79631	Lamesa	(806)	10,809	11,790
76550	Lampasas	(512)	6,382	6,165
75146	Lancaster	(214)	22,117	14,807
77571	La Porte	(713)	27,910	14,062
78040	Laredo	(512)	122,899	91,449
77573	League City	(713)	30,159	16,578
78238	Leon Valley	(512)	9,581	9,088
79336	Levelland	(806)	13,986	13,809
75067	Lewisville	(214)	46,521	24,273
77575	Liberty	(713)	7,690	7,945
79339	Littlefield	(806)	6,489	7,409
78233	Live Oak	(512)	10,023	8,183
77351	Livingston	(409)	5,019	4,928
78644	Lockhart	(512)	9,205	7,953
75601	Longview	(903)	70,311	62,762
*79408	Lubbock	(806)	186,206	174,361
75901	Lufkin	(409)	30,206	28,562
77711	Lumberton		6,640	2,480
78501	McAllen	(512)	84,021	66,281
75069	McKinney	(214)	21,283	16,256
76063	Mansfield	(817)	15,607	8,102
76661	Marlin	(817)	6,386	7,099
75670	Marshall	(903)	23,682	24,921
78368	Mathis	(512)	5,423	5,667
78570	Mercedes	(512)	12,694	11,851
75149	Mesquite	(214)	101,484	67,053
76667	Mexia	(817)	6,933	7,094
79701	Midland	(915)	89,443	70,525
76065	Midlothian	(214)	5,141	3,219
76067	Mineral Wells	(817)	14,870	14,468
78572	Mission	(512)	28,653	22,653
.....	Mission Bend(u)		24,945	....
77459	Missouri City	(713)	36,176	24,423
79756	Monahans	(915)	8,101	8,397
75455	Mount Pleasant	(903)	12,291	11,003
75961	Nacogdoches	(409)	30,872	27,149
77868	Navasota	(409)	6,296	5,971
77627	Nederland	(409)	16,192	16,855
75570	New Boston		5,057	4,628
78130	New Braunfels	(512)	27,334	22,402
76118	North Richland Hills	(817)	45,895	30,592
*79760	Odessa	(915)	89,699	90,027
77630	Orange	(409)	19,381	23,628
75801	Palestine	(903)	18,042	15,948
79065	Pampa	(806)	19,959	21,396
75460	Paris	(903)	24,799	25,498
*77501	Pasadena	(713)	119,377	112,560
77581	Pearland	(713)	18,697	13,248
78061	Pearsall	(512)	6,924	7,383
78721	Pecan Grove(u)		9,502	....
79772	Pecos	(915)	12,069	12,855
79070	Perryton	(806)	7,607	7,991
78577	Pharr	(512)	32,921	21,381
79072	Plainview	(806)	21,700	22,187
*75075	Plano	(214)	127,885	72,331
78064	Pleasanton	(512)	7,678	6,346
77640	Port Arthur	(409)	58,551	61,251
78374	Portland	(512)	12,224	12,023
77979	Port Lavaca	(512)	10,886	10,911
77651	Port Neches	(409)	12,915	13,944
78580	Raymondville	(512)	8,880	9,493
76028	Rendon(u)		7,658	....
*75080	Richardson	(214)	74,840	72,496
76118	Richland Hills	(817)	7,978	7,977
77469	Richmond	(713)	9,801	9,692
78582	Rio Grande City(u)	(512)	9,891	8,930
77019	River Oaks	(817)	6,580	6,890
76701	Robinson	(817)	7,111	6,074
78380	Robstown	(512)	12,849	12,100
76567	Rockdale	(512)	5,235	5,611

ZIP code	Place		1990	1980
75087	Rockwall	(214)	10,486	5,939
78584	Roma		8,059	3,384
77471	Rosenberg	(713)	20,183	17,840
78664	Round Rock	(512)	30,923	12,740
75088	Rowlett	(214)	23,260	7,522
75048	Sachse		5,346	1,640
76179	Saginaw	(817)	8,551	5,736
76901	San Angelo	(915)	84,474	73,240
*78284	San Antonio	(512)	935,933	785,940
78586	San Benito	(512)	20,125	17,988
78589	San Juan	(512)	10,815	7,608
78666	San Marcos	(512)	28,743	23,420
77550	Santa Fe	(713)	8,429	6,172
78154	Schertz	(512)	10,597	7,262
77586	Seabrook	(713)	6,685	4,670
75159	Seagoville	(214)	8,969	7,304
78155	Seguin	(512)	18,853	17,854
79360	Seminole	(915)	6,342	6,080
75090	Sherman	(903)	31,601	30,413
77656	Silsbee	(409)	6,368	7,684
78387	Sinton	(512)	5,549	6,044
79364	Slaton	(806)	6,078	6,804
79549	Snyder	(915)	12,195	12,705
79910	Socorro		22,995	12,341
77587	South Houston	(713)	14,207	13,293
76051	Southlake		7,065	2,808
77373	Spring(u)	(713)	33,111	....
77477	Stafford	(713)	8,397	4,755
76401	Stephenville	(817)	13,502	11,881
77478	Sugar Land	(713)	24,528	8,826
75482	Sulphur Springs	(903)	14,062	12,804
79556	Sweetwater	(915)	11,967	12,242
76574	Taylor	(512)	11,472	10,619
76501	Temple	(817)	46,109	42,354
75160	Terrell	(214)	12,490	13,269
75501	Texarkana	(903)	31,656	31,271
77590	Texas City	(409)	40,822	41,201
75056	The Colony	(214)	22,113	11,586
77380	The Woodlands(u)	(713)	29,205	8,443
77337	Tomball	(713)	6,370	3,996
.....	Town West(u)		6,166	....
75701	Tyler	(903)	75,450	70,508
78148	Universal City	(512)	13,057	10,720
76308	University Park	(214)	22,259	22,254
78801	Uvalde	(512)	14,729	14,178
76384	Vernon	(817)	12,001	12,695
77901	Victoria	(512)	55,076	50,695
77662	Vidor	(409)	10,935	11,834
*76701	Waco	(817)	103,590	101,261
76148	Watauga	(817)	20,009	10,284
75165	Waxahachie	(214)	18,168	14,624
76086	Weatherford	(817)	14,804	12,049
78728	Wells Branch(u)		7,094	....
78596	Weslaco	(512)	21,877	19,331
79764	West Odessa(u)		16,568	....
77005	West University Place	(713)	12,920	12,010
77488	Wharton	(409)	9,011	9,033
75693	White Oak		5,136	4,415
76108	White Settlement	(817)	15,472	13,508
*76307	Wichita Falls	(817)	96,259	94,201
78239	Windcrest	(512)	5,331	5,332
76710	Woodway	(817)	8,695	7,091
75098	Wylie		8,716	3,152
77995	Yoakum	(512)	5,611	6,148
78076	Zapata(u)	(512)	7,119	3,831

Utah (801)

ZIP code	Place	1990	1980
84003	American Fork	15,696	12,564
*84010	Bountiful	36,659	32,877
84302	Brigham City	15,644	15,596
84109	Canyon Rim(u)	10,527	....
84720	Cedar City	13,443	10,972
84014	Centerville	11,500	8,069
84015	Clearfield	21,435	17,982
84015	Clinton	7,945	5,777
84121	Cottonwood Heights(u)	28,766	22,665
.....	Cottonwood West(u)	17,476	....
84020	Draper	7,257	5,521
84109	East Millcreek(u)	21,184	24,150
84025	Farmington	9,028	4,691
84004	Highland	5,002	2,435
84117	Holladay-Cottonwood(u)	14,095	22,189
84037	Kaysville	13,961	9,811
84118	Kearns(u)	28,374	21,353
*84041	Layton	41,784	22,862
84043	Lehi	8,475	6,848
.....	Little Cottonwood Creek Valley(u)	5,042	....
84321	Logan	32,771	26,844
84044	Magna(u)	17,829	13,138
84047	Midvale	11,886	10,146
84109	Millcreek(u)	32,230	....
84117	Mount Olympus(u)	7,413	6,068
84107	Murray	31,282	25,750
84404	North Ogden	11,668	9,309
84054	North Salt Lake	6,474	5,548
*84401	Ogden	63,909	64,407
.....	Oquirrh(u)	7,593	....
*84057	Orem	67,561	52,399
84651	Payson	9,510	8,246
84062	Pleasant Grove	13,476	10,833
84501	Price	8,712	9,086
*84601	Provo	86,835	74,111
84701	Richfield	5,593	5,482
84403	Riverdale	6,419	6,031
84065	Riverton	11,261	7,032
84067	Roy	24,595	19,694
84770	St. George	28,502	11,350
*84101	Salt Lake City	159,936	163,034
*84070	Sandy City	75,058	52,210
84335	Smithfield	5,566	4,993
84065	South Jordan	12,220	7,492
84403	South Ogden	12,105	11,366
84115	South Salt Lake	10,129	10,413
84660	Spanish Fork	11,272	9,825
84663	Springville	13,950	12,101
84015	Sunset	5,128	5,733
84107	Taylorsville-Bennion(u)	52,351	17,448
84074	Tooele	13,887	14,335
84047	Union(u)	13,684	9,665
84078	Vernal	6,644	6,600
84403	Washington Terrace	8,189	8,212
*84084	West Jordan	42,892	27,325
*84119	West Valley City	86,976	72,509
84070	White City(u)	6,506	7,180
84087	Woods Cross	5,384	4,263

Vermont (802)

See Note on Page 398

ZIP code	Place	1990	1980
05641	Barre	9,482	9,824
05641	*Barre*	7,411	6,509
05201	*Bennington*	16,451	15,815
05201	Bennington(u)	9,532	9,349
05301	Brattleboro Center(u)	8,612	8,596
05301	*Brattleboro*	12,241	11,886
05401	Burlington	39,127	37,712
05446	*Colchester*	14,731	12,629
05451	*Essex*	16,498	14,392
05452	Essex Junction	8,396	7,033
05047	Hartford	9,404	....
05849	Lyndon	5,371	....
05753	*Middlebury(u)*	8,034	6,007
05468	Milton	8,404	....
05602	Montpelier	8,247	8,241
05663	Northfield	5,610	....
.....	Rockingham	5,484	....
05701	Rutland	18,230	18,436
05478	St. Albans	7,339	7,308
05819	*St. Johnsbury(u)*	7,608	6,424
05482	Shelburne	5,871	....
05401	*South Burlington*	12,809	10,679
05156	*Springfield*	9,579	10,190
05488	Swanton	5,636	....
05404	Winooski	6,649	6,318

Virginia

ZIP code	Place		1990	1980
24210	Abingdon	(703)	7,003	4,318
*22313	Alexandria	(703)	111,183	103,217
22003	Annandale(u)	(703)	50,975	49,524
.....	Aquia Harbour(u)		6,308	2,870
*22210	Arlington(u)	(703)	170,936	152,599
23005	Ashland	(804)	5,864	4,640
22041	Bailey's Crossroads(u)	(703)	19,507	12,564
24523	Bedford	(703)	6,073	5,991
22307	Belle Haven(u)	(804)	6,427	6,520
23234	Bellwood(u)	(804)	6,178	6,439
23234	Bensley(u)	(804)	5,093	5,299
24060	Blacksburg	(703)	34,590	30,638
24605	Bluefield	(703)	5,363	5,946
23235	Bon Air(u)	(804)	16,413	16,224
24201	Bristol	(703)	18,426	19,042
24416	Buena Vista	(703)	6,406	6,717
.....	Bull Run(u)		5,525	....
22015	Burke(u)	(703)	57,734	33,835
24018	Cave Spring(u)	(703)	24,053	21,682
22020	Centreville(u)	(703)	26,585	7,473
22021	Chantilly(u)	(703)	29,337	12,259
*22906	Charlottesville	(804)	40,341	39,916
*23320	Chesapeake	(804)	151,982	114,486
23831	Chester(u)	(804)	14,986	11,728
24073	Christiansburg	(703)	15,004	10,345
24078	Collinsville(u)	(703)	7,280	7,517
23834	Colonial Heights	(804)	16,064	16,509
.....	Commonwealth(u)		5,538	3,505
.....	Countryside(u)		8,349	....
24426	Covington	(703)	6,991	9,063
22701	Culpeper	(703)	8,581	6,621
22191	Dale City(u)	(703)	47,170	33,127
24541	Danville	(804)	53,056	45,642
23228	Dumbarton(u)	(804)	8,526	8,149

ZIP code	Place		1990	1980
22027	Dunn Loring(u)	(703)	6,509	6,077
23222	East Highland Park(u)	(804)	11,850	11,797
23847	Emporia	(804)	5,306	4,840
23803	Ettrick(u)	...	5,290	4,890
22030	Fairfax	(703)	19,622	19,390
*22046	Falls Church	(703)	9,578	9,515
23901	Farmville	(804)	6,046	6,067
24551	Forest(u)	(804)	5,624	....
22060	Fort Belvoir(u)	(703)	8,590	7,726
22308	Fort Hunt(u)	(703)	12,989	14,294
23801	Fort Lee(u)	(804)	6,895	9,784
22310	Franconia(u)	(703)	19,882	8,476
23851	Franklin	(804)	7,864	7,308
22401	Fredericksburg	(703)	19,027	15,322
22630	Front Royal	(703)	11,880	11,126
24333	Galax	(703)	6,670	6,524
23060	Glen Allen(u)	(804)	9,010	6,202
23062	Gloucester Point(u)	(804)	8,509	5,841
22066	Great Falls(u)	...	6,945	2,419
22306	Groveton(u)	(703)	19,997	18,860
*23660	Hampton	(804)	133,811	122,617
22801	Harrisonburg	(703)	30,707	19,671
*22070	Herndon	(703)	16,139	11,449
23075	Highland Springs(u)	(804)	13,823	12,146
24019	Hollins(u)	(703)	13,305	12,295
23860	Hopewell	(804)	23,101	23,397
22303	Huntington(u)	(703)	7,489	5,813
22306	Hybla Valley(u)	(703)	15,491	15,533
22043	Idylwood(u)	(703)	14,710	11,982
22042	Jefferson(u)	(804)	25,782	24,342
22041	Lake Barcroft(u)	(703)	8,686	8,725
22191	Lake Ridge(u)	(703)	23,862	11,072
23228	Lakeside(u)	(804)	12,081	12,289
23060	Laurel(u)	(804)	13,011	10,569
22075	Leesburg	(703)	16,202	8,357
24450	Lexington	(703)	6,959	7,292
22312	Lincolnia(u)	(703)	13,041	10,350
22079	Lorton(u)	(703)	15,385	5,813
*24505	Lynchburg	(804)	66,049	66,743
22101	McLean(u)	(703)	38,168	35,664
24572	Madison Heights(u)	(804)	11,700	14,146
22110	Manassas	(703)	27,957	15,438
22110	Manassas Park	(703)	6,734	6,524
22030	Mantua(u)	(703)	6,804	6,523
24354	Marion	(703)	6,630	7,287
24112	Martinsville	(703)	16,162	18,149
23111	Mechanicsville(u)	(804)	22,027	9,269
22116	Merrifield(u)	(703)	8,399	7,525
.....	Montclair(u)	...	11,399	....
23231	Montrose(u)	(804)	6,405	5,349
22121	Mount Vernon(u)	(703)	27,485	24,058
22122	Newington(u)	(703)	17,965	8,313
*23607	Newport News	(804)	171,439	144,903
*23501	Norfolk	(804)	261,250	266,979
22151	North Springfield(u)	(703)	8,996	9,538
22124	Oakton(u)	(703)	24,610	19,150
23803	Petersburg	(804)	37,027	41,055
22043	Pimmit Hills(u)	(703)	6,019	6,658
23662	Poquoson	(804)	11,005	8,726
*23705	Portsmouth	(804)	103,910	104,577
24301	Pulaski	(703)	9,985	10,1069
22134	Quantico Station(u)	(703)	7,425	7,121
24141	Radford	(703)	15,940	13,225
22090	Reston(u)	(703)	48,556	36,407
*23232	Richmond	(804)	202,798	219,214
*24001	Roanoke	(703)	96,509	100,220
22310	Rose Hill(u)	(703)	12,675	11,926
24153	Salem	(703)	23,756	23,958
22044	Seven Corners(u)	(703)	72,80	6,058
24592	South Boston	(804)	6,997	7,093
*22150	Springfield	(703)	23,706	21,435
24401	Staunton	(703)	24,461	21,857
22170	Sterling(u)	(703)	20,512	16,080
24477	Stuarts Draft(u)	...	5,087	1,776
23162	Studley(u)	...	7,321	4,674
23434	Suffolk	(804)	52,143	47,621
22170	Sugarland Run(u)	(703)	9,357	6,258
24502	Timberlake(u)	(804)	10,314	9,697
23229	Tuckahoe(u)	(804)	42,629	39,868
22101	Tysons Corner(u)	(703)	13,124	10,065
.....	University Heights(u)	...	6,900	6,736
22180	Vienna	(703)	14,852	15,469
24179	Vinton	(703)	7,643	8,027
*23458	Virginia Beach	(804)	393,089	262,199
22980	Waynesboro	(703)	18,549	15,329
22110	West Gate(u)	(703)	6,565	7,119
22152	West Springfield(u)	(703)	28,126	25,012
23185	Williamsburg	(804)	11,530	9,870
22601	Winchester	(703)	21,947	20,217
24592	Wolf Trap(u)	(804)	13,133	9,875
22191	Woodbridge(u)	(703)	26,401	24,004
24382	Wytheville	(703)	8,036	7,135
.....	Yorkshire(u)	...	5,699	4,940

Washington

ZIP code	Place		1990	1980
98520	Aberdeen	(206)	16,565	18,739
98036	Alderwood Manor(u)	(206)	22,945	16,524
98221	Anacortes	(206)	11,451	9,013
98335	Artondale(u)	...	7,141	....
98002	Auburn	(206)	33,102	26,417
*98009	Bellevue	(206)	86,872	73,903
98225	Bellingham	(206)	52,179	45,794
98390	Bonney Lake	(206)	7,494	5,328
98011	Bothell	(206)	12,345	7,943
98310	Bremerton	(206)	38,142	36,208
98036	Brier	...	5,633	2,915
98178	Bryn Mawr-Skyway(u)	(206)	12,514	11,754
98166	Burien(u)	(206)	25,089	23,189
98607	Camas	(206)	6,442	5,681
98055	Cascade-Fairwood(u)	(206)	30,107	16,939
98684	Cascade Park East(u)	...	6,996	....
98684	Cascade Park West(u)	...	6,656	....
98531	Centralia	(206)	12,101	11,555
98532	Chehalis	(206)	6,527	6,100
99004	Cheney	(509)	7,723	7,630
99403	Clarkston	(509)	6,753	6,903
99324	College Place	(509)	6,308	5,771
.....	Country Homes(u)	...	5,126	....
98042	Covington-Sawyer-Wilderness(u)	...	24,321	....
98198	Des Moines	(206)	17,283	7,378
99213	Dishman(u)	(509)	9,671	10,169
.....	East Hill-Meridian(u)	...	42,696	....
98366	East Port Orchard(u)	...	5,409	4,631
98056	East Renton Highlands(u)	(206)	13,218	12,033
98801	East Wenatchee Bench(u)	(509)	12,539	11,410
.....	Edgewood-North Hill(u)	...	9,120	....
98020	Edmonds	(206)	30,744	27,679
98387	Elk Plain(u)	...	12,197	....
98926	Ellensburg	(509)	12,361	11,752
.....	Ellsworth North(u)	...	5,796	....
98022	Enumclaw	(206)	7,227	5,427
98823	Ephrata	(509)	5,349	5,359
99210	Esperance(u)	(509)	11,236	11,120
*98201	Everett	(206)	69,961	54,413
98411	Evergreen(u)	...	11,249	....
98055	Fairwood(u)	(206)	5,807	5,337
98003	Federal Way(u)	...	67,554	....
98248	Ferndale	(206)	5,398	3,855
98466	Fircrest	(206)	5,258	5,477
98597	Five Corners(u)	...	6,776	....
98433	Fort Lewis(u)	(206)	22,224	23,761
98930	Grandview	(509)	7,169	5,615
.....	Harbour Pointe(u)	...	9,107	....
98660	Hazel Dell North(u)	(206)	6,924	15,386
98665	Hazel Dell South(u)	(206)	5,796	....
98550	Hoquiam	(206)	8,972	9,719
98011	Inglewood-Finn Hill(u)	(206)	29,132	12,467
98027	Issaquah	(206)	7,786	5,536
98626	Kelso	(206)	11,820	11,129
98028	Kenmore(u)	(206)	8,917	7,281
99336	Kennewick	(509)	42,148	34,397
98031	Kent	(206)	37,960	22,961
98033	Kingsgate(u)	(206)	14,259	12,652
98033	Kirkland	(206)	40,059	18,785
98503	Lacey	(206)	19,279	13,940
98155	Lake Forest North(u)	(206)	8,002	7,995
.....	Lakeland North(u)	(206)	14,402	11,451
.....	Lakeland South(u)	(206)	9,027	5,225
98036	Lake Serene-North Lynnwood(u)	...	14,290	54,533
.....	Lake Shore(u)	...	6,268	....
98259	Lakewood(u)	(206)	58,412	....
98632	Longview	(206)	31,499	31,052
98264	Lynden	...	5,709	4,022
98036	Lynnwood	(206)	28,695	22,641
.....	Martha Lake(u)	(206)	10,155	7,022
98270	Marysville	(206)	10,328	5,080
98040	Mercer Island	(206)	20,816	21,522
.....	Midland(u)	...	5,587	....
98012	Mill Creek	...	7,180	1,803
.....	Minnehaha(u)	...	9,661	....
98837	Moses Lake	(509)	11,235	10,629
98043	Mountlake Terrace	(206)	19,320	16,534
98273	Mount Vernon	(206)	17,647	13,009
98275	Mukilteo	(206)	7,007	1,426
98006	Newport Hills(u)	(206)	14,736	12,245
98166	Normandy Park	...	6,709	4,268
98155	North City-Ridgecrest(u)	(206)	13,832	13,551
.....	North Creek-Canyon Park(u)	...	23,236	13,551
.....	North Hill(u)	(206)	5,706	10,170
98270	North Marysville(u)	(206)	18,711	15,159
98277	Oak Harbor	(206)	17,176	12,271
*98501	Olympia	(206)	33,840	27,447
99214	Opportunity(u)	(509)	22,326	21,241
98662	Orchards North(u)	(206)	6,479	8,828
98662	Orchards South(u)	(206)	12,956	....
99027	Otis Orchards-East Farms(u)	...	5,811	4,597
.....	Paine Field-Lake Stickney(u)	...	18,670	....
98444	Parkland(u)	(206)	20,882	23,355
98366	Parkwood(u)	...	6,853	4,599
99301	Pasco	(509)	20,337	18,428
98027	Pine Lake(u)	...	13,940	....
98362	Port Angeles	(206)	17,710	17,311
98368	Port Townsend	(206)	7,001	6,067
98390	Prairie Ridge(u)	...	8,278	....
99163	Pullman	(509)	23,478	23,579

ZIP code	Place		1990	1980
98371	Puyallup	(206)	23,878	18,251
98052	Redmond	(206)	35,800	23,318
98055	Renton	(206)	41,688	31,031
99352	Richland	(509)	32,315	33,578
98160	Richmond Beach-Innis Arden	(206)	7,242	6,700
98113	Richmond Highlands(u)	(206)	26,037	24,463
98188	Riverton-Boulevard Park(u)	(206)	15,337	14,182
.....	Sahalee(u)		13,951	....
98686	Salmon Creek(u)		11,989	....
98148	Sea-Tac(u)		22,694	....
*98109	Seattle	(206)	516,259	493,846
98284	Sedro Woolley	(206)	6,333	6,110
98942	Selah	(509)	5,113	4,500
98584	Shelton	(206)	7,241	7,629
98155	Sheridan Beach(u)	(206)	6,518	6,873
98315	Silverdale(u)	(206)	7,660	....
98201	Silver Lake-Fircrest(u)	(206)	24,474	10,299
98290	Snohomish	(206)	6,499	5,294
98373	South Hill(u)		12,963	....
98387	Spanaway(u)	(206)	15,001	8,868
*99210	Spokane	(509)	177,165	171,300
98388	Steilacoom	(206)	5,728	4,886
98371	Summit(u)		6,312	....
98390	Sumner	(206)	6,281	4,936
98944	Sunnyside	(509)	11,238	9,225
*98402	Tacoma	(206)	176,664	158,501
98501	Tanglewilde-Thompson Place(u)		6,061	5,910
98948	Toppenish	(509)	7,419	6,517
98188	Tukwila		11,874	3,578
98502	Tumwater	(206)	9,976	6,705
98406	University Place(u)	(206)	27,701	20,381
*98660	Vancouver	(206)	46,380	42,834
98662	Vancouver Mall(u)	(206)	6,938	....
99037	Veradale(u)	(509)	7,836	7,256
99362	Walla Walla	(509)	26,478	25,618
.....	Waller(u)		6,415	....
98801	Wenatchee	(509)	21,756	17,257
.....	West Lake Sammamish(u)		6,087	....
98258	West Lake Stevens(u)	(206)	12,453	....
99301	West Pasco(u)	(509)	7,312	6,210
99181	West Valley(u)		6,594	....
98166	White Center-Shorewood(u)	(206)	20,531	19,362
98072	Woodinville(u)		23,654	....
98032	Woodmont Beach(u)		7,493	....
*98901	Yakima	(509)	54,827	49,826

West Virginia (304)

ZIP code	Place	1990	1980
25801	Beckley	18,296	20,492
24701	Bluefield	12,756	16,060
26330	Bridgeport	6,739	6,604
26201	Buckhannon	5,909	6,820
*25301	Charleston	57,287	63,968
26301	Clarksburg	18,059	22,371
25301	Cross Lanes(u)	10,878	....
25064	Dunbar	8,697	9,285
26241	Elkins	7,420	8,536
26554	Fairmont	20,210	23,863
26354	Grafton	5,524	6,845
*25701	Huntington	54,844	63,684
26726	Keyser	5,870	6,569
25401	Martinsburg	14,073	13,063
26505	Morgantown	25,879	27,605
26041	Moundsville	10,753	12,419
26155	New Martinsville	6,705	7,109
25143	Nitro	6,851	8,074
25901	Oak Hill	6,812	7,120
26101	Parkersburg	33,862	39,946
.....	Pea Ridge(u)	6,535	....
24740	Princeton	7,043	7,538
25177	St. Albans	11,194	12,402
25303	South Charleston	13,645	15,968
25569	Teays Valley(u)	8,436	....
26105	Vienna	10,862	11,618
26062	Weirton	22,124	25,371
26003	Wheeling	34,882	43,070

Wisconsin

ZIP code	Place		1990	1980
54301	Allouez	(414)	14,431	14,882
54720	Altoona		5,889	4,393
54409	Antigo	(715)	8,275	8,653
59411	Appleton	(414)	65,695	58,913
54806	Ashland	(715)	8,695	9,115
54304	Ashwaubenon	(414)	16,376	14,486
53913	Baraboo	(608)	9,203	8,081
53916	Beaver Dam	(414)	14,196	14,149
.....	Bellevue Town(u)		7,541	....
53511	Beloit	(608)	35,573	35,207
54923	Berlin	(414)	5,371	5,478
53005	Brookfield	(414)	35,184	34,035
53209	Brown Deer	(414)	12,236	12,921
53105	Burlington	(414)	8,855	8,385
53012	Cedarburg	(414)	10,086	9,005
54729	Chippewa Falls	(715)	12,727	12,270
53110	Cudahy	(414)	18,659	19,547
53018	Delafield		5,347	4,083
53115	Delavan	(414)	6,073	5,684
54115	De Pere	(414)	16,569	14,892
54701	Eau Claire	(715)	56,806	51,509
53121	Elkhorn	(414)	5,337	4,605
53122	Elm Grove	(414)	6,261	6,735
53714	Fitchburg	(608)	15,648	11,965
54935	Fond Du Lac	(414)	37,757	35,863
53538	Fort Atkinson	(414)	10,213	9,785
53217	Fox Point	(414)	7,238	7,649
53132	Franklin	(414)	21,855	16,871
53022	Germantown	(414)	13,658	10,729
53209	Glendale	(414)	14,088	13,882
53024	Grafton	(414)	9,340	8,381
*54305	Green Bay	(414)	96,466	87,899
53129	Greendale	(414)	15,128	16,928
53220	Greenfield	(414)	33,403	31,353
53130	Hales Corners	(414)	7,623	7,110
53027	Hartford	(414)	8,188	7,159
53029	Hartland	(414)	6,906	5,559
54303	Howard	(414)	9,874	8,240
54016	Hudson	(715)	6,378	5,434
53545	Janesville	(608)	52,210	51,071
53549	Jefferson	(414)	6,078	5,647
54130	Kaukauna	(414)	11,982	11,310
53140	Kenosha	(414)	80,352	77,685
54136	Kimberly	(414)	5,406	5,881
54601	La Crosse	(608)	51,132	48,347
53147	Lake Geneva	(414)	5,979	5,612
54140	Little Chute	(414)	9,207	7,907
53558	McFarland	(608)	5,232	3,783
*53701	Madison	(608)	190,766	170,616
54220	Manitowoc	(414)	32,520	32,547
54143	Marinette	(715)	11,843	11,965
54449	Marshfield	(715)	19,291	18,290
54952	Menasha	(414)	14,711	14,728
53051	Menomonee Falls	(414)	26,840	27,845
54751	Menomonie	(715)	13,547	12,769
53092	Mequon	(414)	18,885	16,193
54452	Merrill	(715)	9,860	9,578
53562	Middleton	(608)	13,785	11,851
*53203	Milwaukee	(414)	628,088	636,297
53716	Monona	(608)	8,637	8,809
53566	Monroe	(608)	10,241	10,027
53150	Muskego	(414)	16,813	15,277
54956	Neenah	(414)	23,219	22,432
53151	New Berlin	(414)	33,592	30,529
54961	New London	(414)	6,658	6,210
54017	New Richmond	(715)	5,106	4,306
53154	Oak Creek	(414)	19,513	16,932
53066	Oconomowoc	(414)	10,993	9,909
54650	Onalaska	(608)	11,414	9,249
54901	Oshkosh	(414)	55,006	49,620
53072	Pewaukee		5,287	....
53818	Platteville	(608)	9,862	9,580
53158	Pleasant Prairie	(414)	11,998	12,176
54467	Plover	(715)	8,176	5,310
53073	Plymouth	(414)	6,769	6,027
53901	Portage	(608)	8,640	7,896
53074	Port Washington	(414)	9,338	8,612
53821	Prairie du Chien	(608)	5,657	5,859
*53401	Racine	(414)	84,298	85,725
53959	Reedsburg	(608)	5,834	5,038
54501	Rhinelander	(715)	7,427	7,873
54868	Rice Lake	(715)	7,998	7,691
53581	Richland Center	(608)	5,018	4,997
54971	Ripon	(414)	7,241	7,111
54022	River Falls	(715)	10,610	9,019
53207	St. Francis	(414)	9,245	10,095
54166	Shawano	(715)	7,598	7,013
53081	Sheboygan	(414)	49,587	48,085
53085	Sheboygan Falls	(414)	5,823	5,253
53211	Shorewood	(414)	14,116	14,327
53172	South Milwaukee	(414)	20,958	21,069
54656	Sparta	(608)	7,788	6,934
54481	Stevens Point	(715)	23,006	22,970
53589	Stoughton	(608)	8,786	7,589
54235	Sturgeon Bay	(414)	9,176	8,847
53590	Sun Prairie	(608)	15,333	12,931
54880	Superior	(715)	27,134	29,571
53089	Sussex		5,039	3,482
54660	Tomah	(608)	7,570	7,204
54241	Two Rivers	(414)	13,030	13,354
53593	Verona		5,374	3,336
53094	Watertown	(414)	19,142	18,113
53186	Waukesha	(414)	56,958	50,365
53597	Waunakee		5,897	3,866
53963	Waupun	(414)	8,844	8,132
54401	Wausau	(715)	37,060	32,426
53213	Wauwatosa	(414)	49,366	51,308
53214	West Allis	(414)	63,221	63,982
53095	West Bend	(414)	23,916	21,484
54476	Weston(u)	(715)	9,714	8,775
53217	Whitefish Bay	(414)	14,272	14,930
53190	Whitewater	(414)	12,636	11,520
54494	Wisconsin Rapids	(715)	18,245	17,995

Wyoming (307)

ZIP code	Place	1990	1980
*82601	Casper	46,801	51,016
*82001	Cheyenne	50,008	47,283
82414	Cody	7,897	6,599
82633	Douglas	5,076	6,030
82930	Evanston	10,903	6,265
82716	Gillette	17,635	12,134
82935	Green River	12,711	12,807
82520	Lander	7,023	7,867
82070	Laramie	26,687	24,410
82435	Powell	5,292	5,310
82301	Rawlins	9,380	11,547
82501	Riverton	9,202	9,562
82901	Rock Springs	19,050	19,458
82801	Sheridan	13,900	15,146
82240	Torrington	5,651	5,441
82401	Worland	5,742	6,391

Census and Areas of Counties and States

Source: Bureau of the Census, U.S. Dept. of Commerce
With names of county seats or court houses

Population figures listed below are final counts in the 1990 census, conducted on Apr. 1, 1990; updated as of Apr. 1992.

Alabama

(67 counties, 50,767 sq. mi. land; pop., 4,040,587)

County	Pop.	County Seat or court house	Land area sq. mi.
Autauga	34,222	Prattville	596
Baldwin	98,280	Bay Minette	1,596
Barbour	25,417	Clayton	885
Bibb	16,576	Centreville	622
Blount	39,248	Oneonta	645
Bullock	11,042	Union Springs	625
Butler	21,892	Greenville	776
Calhoun	116,034	Anniston	608
Chambers	36,876	Lafayette	597
Cherokee	19,543	Centre	553
Chilton	32,458	Clanton	694
Choctaw	16,018	Butler	913
Clarke	27,240	Grove Hill	1,238
Clay	13,252	Ashland	605
Cleburne	12,730	Heflin	560
Coffee	40,240	Elba	679
Colbert	51,666	Tuscumbia	594
Conecuh	14,054	Evergreen	850
Coosa	11,063	Rockford	652
Covington	36,478	Andalusia	1,034
Crenshaw	13,635	Luverne	609
Cullman	67,613	Cullman	738
Dale	49,633	Ozark	561
Dallas	48,130	Selma	980
De Kalb	54,651	Fort Payne	777
Elmore	49,210	Wetumpka	621
Escambia	35,518	Brewton	947
Etowah	99,840	Gadsden	534
Fayette	17,962	Fayette	627
Franklin	27,814	Russellville	635
Geneva	23,647	Geneva	576
Greene	10,153	Eutaw	645
Hale	15,498	Greensboro	643
Henry	15,374	Abbeville	561
Houston	81,331	Dothan	580
Jackson	47,796	Scottsboro	1,078
Jefferson	651,525	Birmingham	1,112
Lamar	15,715	Vernon	604
Lauderdale	79,661	Florence	669
Lawrence	31,513	Moulton	693
Lee	87,146	Opelika	608
Limestone	46,005	Athens	568
Lowndes	12,658	Hayneville	718
Macon	24,928	Tuskegee	610
Madison	238,912	Huntsville	804
Marengo	23,084	Linden	977
Marion	29,830	Hamilton	741
Marshall	70,832	Guntersville	567
Mobile	378,643	Mobile	1,233
Monroe	23,968	Monroeville	1,025
Montgomery	209,085	Montgomery	789
Morgan	100,043	Decatur	599
Perry	12,759	Marion	719
Pickens	20,699	Carrollton	881
Pike	27,595	Troy	671
Randolph	19,881	Wedowee	581
Russell	46,860	Phenix City	641
St. Clair	50,009	Ashville & Pell City	633
Shelby	99,358	Columbiana	794
Sumter	16,174	Livingston	904
Talladega	74,107	Talladega	739
Tallapoosa	38,826	Dadeville	718
Tuscaloosa	150,522	Tuscaloosa	1,325
Walker	67,670	Jasper	794
Washington	16,694	Chatom	1,080
Wilcox	13,568	Camden	888
Winston	22,053	Double Springs	614

Alaska

(25 divisions, 570,833 sq. mi. land; pop., 550,043)

Census area	Pop.	Land area sq. mi.
Aleutian Islands	2,464	10,890
Aleutians West Census Area	9,478	....
Anchorage Borough	226,338	1,732

Census division	Pop.	Land area sq. mi.
Bethel	13,656	36,104
Bristol Bay Borough	1,410	531
Dillingham	4,012	46,042
Fairbanks North Star Borough	77,720	7,404
Haines Borough	2,117	2,374
Juneau Borough	26,751	2,626
Kenai Peninsula Borough	40,802	16,056
Ketchikan Gateway Borough	13,828	1,242
Kodiak Island Borough	13,309	4,796
Lake and Peninsula Borough	1,668	....
Matanuska-Susitna Borough	39,683	24,502
Nome	8,288	23,871
North Slope Borough	5,979	90,955
Northwest Arctic Borough	6,113	....
Prince of Wales-Outer Ketchikan	6,278	7,660
Sitka Borough	8,588	2,938
Skagway-Yakutat-Angoon	4,385	13,239
Southeast Fairbanks	5,913	24,169
Valdez-Cordova	9,952	39,229
Wade Hampton	5,791	17,816
Wrangell-Petersburg	7,042	6,167
Yukon-Koyukuk	8,478	159,099

Arizona

(15 counties, 113,508 sq. mi. land; pop. 3,665,228)

County	Pop.	County Seat or court house	Land area sq. mi.
Apache	61,591	Saint Johns	11,211
Cochise	97,624	Bisbee	6,218
Coconino	96,591	Flagstaff	18,608
Gila	40,216	Globe	4,752
Graham	26,554	Safford	4,630
Greenlee	8,008	Clifton	1,837
La Paz	13,844	Parker	4,430
Maricopa	2,122,101	Phoenix	9,127
Mohave	93,497	Kingman	13,285
Navajo	77,658	Holbrook	9,955

County	Pop.	County Seat or court house	Land area sq. mi.
Pima	666,880	Tucson	9,187
Pinal	116,379	Florence	5,343
Santa Cruz	29,676	Nogales	1,238
Yavapai	107,714	Prescott	8,123
Yuma	106,895	Yuma	5,564

Arkansas

(75 counties, 52,078 sq. mi. land; pop. 2,350,725)

County	Pop.	County Seat or court house	Land area sq. mi.
Arkansas	21,653	DeWitt & Stuttgart	1,033
Ashley	24,319	Hamburg	939
Baxter	31,186	Mountain Home	586
Benton	97,499	Bentonville	876
Boone	28,297	Harrison	601
Bradley	11,793	Warren	654
Calhoun	5,826	Hampton	632
Carroll	18,654	Berryville and Eureka Sp.	642
Chicot	15,713	Lake Village	690
Clark	21,437	Arkadelphia	882
Clay	18,107	Corning; Piggott	641
Cleburne	19,411	Heber Springs	591
Cleveland	7,781	Rison	598
Columbia	25,691	Magnolia	766
Conway	19,151	Morrilton	566
Craighead	68,956	Jonesboro and Lake City	713
Crawford	42,493	Van Buren	604
Crittenden	49,939	Marion	636
Cross	19,225	Wynne	622
Dallas	9,614	Fordyce	668
Desha	16,798	Arkansas City	819
Drew	17,369	Monticello	835
Faulkner	60,006	Conway	664
Franklin	14,897	Charleston and Ozark	919
Fulton	10,037	Salem	620
Garland	73,397	Hot Spgs. Nat'l Pk.	734
Grant	13,948	Sheridan	633
Greene	31,804	Paragould	579
Hempstead	21,621	Hope	741
Hot Spring	26,115	Malvern	622
Howard	13,569	Nashville	595
Independence	31,192	Batesville	771
Izard	11,364	Melbourne	584
Jackson	18,944	Newport	641
Jefferson	85,487	Pine Bluff	913
Johnson	18,221	Clarksville	682
Lafayette	9,643	Lewisville	545
Lawrence	17,457	Walnut Ridge	592
Lee	13,053	Marianna	619
Lincoln	13,690	Star City	572
Little River	13,966	Ashdown	564
Logan	20,557	Booneville & Paris	731
Lonoke	39,268	Lonoke	802
Madison	11,618	Huntsville	837
Marion	12,001	Yellville	640
Miller	38,467	Texarkana	637
Mississippi	57,525	Blytheville and Osceola	919
Monroe	11,333	Clarendon	621
Montgomery	7,841	Mount Ida	800
Nevada	10,101	Prescott	620
Newton	7,666	Jasper	823
Ouachita	30,574	Camden	739
Perry	7,969	Perryville	560
Phillips	28,838	Helena	727
Pike	10,086	Murfreesboro	613
Poinsett	24,664	Harrisburg	763
Polk	17,347	Mena	862
Pope	45,883	Russellville	830
Prairie	9,518	Des Arc and De Valls Bluff	675
Pulaski	349,660	Little Rock	807
Randolph	16,558	Pocahontas	656
St. Francis	28,497	Forrest City	642
Saline	64,183	Benton	730
Scott	10,205	Waldron	898
Searcy	7,841	Marshall	668
Sebastian	99,590	Fort Smith; Greenwood	546
Sevier	13,637	De Queen	581
Sharp	14,109	Ash Flat	606
Stone	9,775	Mountain View	609
Union	46,719	El Dorado	1,055
Van Buren	14,008	Clinton	724
Washington	113,409	Fayetteville	956
White	54,676	Searcy	1,042
Woodruff	9,520	Augusta	594
Yell	17,759	Danville and Dardanelle	948

California

(58 counties, 156,299 sq. mi. land; pop. 29,760,021)

County	Pop.	County Seat or court house	Land area sq. mi.
Alameda	1,276,702	Oakland	736
Alpine	1,113	Markleeville	738
Amador	30,039	Jackson	589
Butte	182,120	Oroville	1,646
Calaveras	31,998	San Andreas	1,021
Colusa	16,275	Colusa	1,152
Contra Costa	803,732	Martinez	730
Del Norte	23,460	Crescent City	1,007
El Dorado	125,995	Placerville	1,715
Fresno	667,490	Fresno	5,978
Glenn	24,798	Willows	1,319
Humboldt	119,118	Eureka	3,579
Imperial	109,303	El Centro	4,173
Inyo	18,281	Independence	10,223
Kern	543,477	Bakersfield	8,130
Kings	101,469	Hanford	1,392
Lake	50,631	Lakeport	1,262
Lassen	27,598	Susanville	4,553
Los Angeles	8,863,052	Los Angeles	4,070
Madera	88,090	Madera	2,145
Marin	230,096	San Rafael	523
Mariposa	14,302	Mariposa	1,456
Mendocino	80,345	Ukiah	3,512
Merced	178,403	Merced	1,944
Modoc	9,678	Alturas	4,064
Mono	9,956	Bridgeport	3,018
Monterey	355,660	Salinas	3,303
Napa	110,765	Napa	744
Nevada	78,510	Nevada City	960
Orange	2,410,668	Santa Ana	798
Placer	172,796	Auburn	1,416
Plumas	19,739	Quincy	2,573
Riverside	1,170,413	Riverside	7,214
Sacramento	1,041,219	Sacramento	971
San Benito	36,697	Hollister	1,388
San Bernardino	1,418,380	San Bernardino	20,064
San Diego	2,498,016	San Diego	4,212
San Francisco	723,959	San Francisco	46
San Joaquin	480,628	Stockton	1,415
San Luis Obispo	217,162	San Luis Obispo	3,308
San Mateo	649,623	Redwood City	447
Santa Barbara	369,608	Santa Barbara	2,748
Santa Clara	1,497,577	San Jose	1,293
Santa Cruz	229,734	Santa Cruz	446
Shasta	147,036	Redding	3,786
Sierra	3,318	Downieville	959
Siskiyou	43,531	Yreka	6,281
Solano	340,421	Fairfield	834
Sonoma	388,222	Santa Rosa	1,604
Stanislaus	370,522	Modesto	1,506
Sutter	64,415	Yuba City	602
Tehama	49,625	Red Bluff	2,953
Trinity	13,063	Weaverville	3,190
Tulare	311,921	Visalia	4,808
Tuolumne	48,456	Sonora	2,234
Ventura	669,016	Ventura	1,862
Yolo	141,092	Woodland	1,014
Yuba	58,228	Marysville	640

Colorado

(63 counties, 103,595 sq. mi. land; pop. 3,294,394)

County	Pop.	County Seat or court house	Land area sq. mi.
Adams	265,038	Brighton	1,235
Alamosa	13,617	Alamosa	719
Arapahoe	391,511	Littleton	800
Archuleta	5,345	Pagosa Springs	1,353
Baca	4,556	Springfield	2,554
Bent	5,048	Las Animas	1,517
Boulder	225,339	Boulder	742
Chaffee	12,684	Salida	1,008
Cheyenne	2,397	Cheyenne Wells	1,783
Clear Creek	7,619	Georgetown	396
Conejos	7,453	Conejos	1,284
Costilla	3,190	San Luis	1,227
Crowley	3,946	Ordway	790
Custer	1,926	Westcliffe	740
Delta	20,980	Delta	1,141
Denver	467,610	Denver	111
Dolores	1,504	Dove Creek	1,064
Douglas	60,391	Castle Rock	841
Eagle	21,928	Eagle	1,690
Elbert	9,646	Kiowa	1,851
El Paso	397,014	Colorado Springs	2,129
Fremont	32,273	Canon City	1,538
Garfield	29,974	Glenwood Springs	2,952
Gilpin	3,070	Central City	149
Grand	7,966	Hot Sulphur Springs	1,854
Gunnison	10,273	Gunnison	3,238
Hinsdale	467	Lake City	1,115
Huerfano	6,009	Walsenburg	1,584
Jackson	1,605	Walden	1,614
Jefferson	438,430	Golden	768
Kiowa	1,688	Eads	1,758
Kit Carson	7,140	Burlington	2,160
Lake	6,007	Leadville	379
La Plata	32,284	Durango	1,692
Larimer	186,136	Fort Collins	2,604

County	Pop.	County Seat or court house	Land area sq. mi.
Las Animas	13,765	Trinidad	4,771
Lincoln	4,529	Hugo	2,586
Logan	17,567	Sterling	1,818
Mesa	93,145	Grand Junction	3,309
Mineral	558	Creede	877
Moffat	11,357	Craig	4,732
Montezuma	18,672	Cortez	2,038
Montrose	24,423	Montrose	2,240
Morgan	21,939	Fort Morgan	1,276
Otero	20,185	LaJunta	1,247
Ouray	2,295	Ouray	542
Park	7,174	Fairplay	2,192
Phillips	4,189	Holyoke	688
Pitkin	12,661	Aspen	968
Prowers	13,347	Lamar	1,629
Pueblo	123,051	Pueblo	2,377
Rio Blanco	5,972	Meeker	3,222
Rio Grande	10,770	Del Norte	913
Routt	14,088	Steamboat Springs	2,367
Saguache	4,619	Saguache	3,167
San Juan	745	Silverton	388
San Miguel	3,653	Telluride	1,287
Sedgwick	2,690	Julesburg	540
Summit	12,881	Breckenridge	607
Teller	12,468	Cripple Creek	559
Washington	4,812	Akron	2,520
Weld	131,821	Greeley	3,990
Yuma	8,954	Wray	2,365

Connecticut

(8 counties, 4,872 sq. mi. land; pop. 3,287,116)

Fairfield	827,645	Bridgeport	632
Hartford	852,783	Hartford	739
Litchfield	174,092	Litchfield	921
Middlesex	143,196	Middletown	373
New Haven	804,219	New Haven	610
New London	254,957	Norwich	669
Tolland	128,699	Rockville	412
Windham	102,525	Putnam	515

Delaware

(3 counties, 1,932 sq. mi. land; pop. 666,168)

Kent	110,993	Dover	595
New Castle	441,946	Wilmington	396
Sussex	113,229	Georgetown	942

District of Columbia

(63 sq. mi. land; pop. 606,900)

Florida

(67 counties, 54,153 sq. mi. land; pop. 12,937,926)

Alachua	181,596	Gainesville	901
Baker	18,486	Macclenny	585
Bay	126,994	Panama City	758
Bradford	22,515	Starke	293
Brevard	398,978	Titusville	995
Broward	1,255,488	Fort Lauderdale	1,211
Calhoun	11,011	Blountstown	568
Charlotte	110,975	Punta Gorda	690
Citrus	93,515	Inverness	629
Clay	105,986	Green Cove Spgs.	592
Collier	152,099	Naples	1,994
Columbia	42,613	Lake City	796
Dade	1,937,094	Miami	1,955
De Soto	23,865	Arcadia	636
Dixie	10,585	Cross City	701
Duval	672,971	Jacksonville	776
Escambia	262,798	Pensacola	660
Flagler	28,701	Bunnell	491
Franklin	8,967	Apalachicola	545
Gadsden	41,105	Quincy	518
Gilchrist	9,667	Trenton	354
Glades	7,591	Moore Haven	763
Gulf	11,504	Port St. Joe	559
Hamilton	10,930	Jasper	517
Hardee	19,499	Wauchula	637
Hendry	25,773	La Belle	1,163
Hernando	101,115	Brooksville	477
Highlands	68,432	Sebring	1,029
Hillsborough	834,054	Tampa	1,053
Holmes	15,778	Bonifay	488
Indian River	90,208	Vero Beach	497
Jackson	41,375	Marianna	942
Jefferson	11,296	Monticello	609
Lafayette	5,578	Mayo	545
Lake	152,104	Tavares	954
Lee	335,113	Fort Myers	803
Leon	192,493	Tallahassee	676
Levy	25,923	Bronson	1,100
Liberty	5,569	Bristol	837
Madison	16,569	Madison	710
Manatee	211,707	Bradenton	747
Marion	194,833	Ocala	1,610
Martin	100,900	Stuart	555
Monroe	78,024	Key West	1,034
Nassau	43,941	Fernandina Beach	649
Okaloosa	143,776	Crestview	936
Okeechobee	29,627	Okeechobee	770
Orange	677,491	Orlando	910
Osceola	107,728	Kissimmee	1,350
Palm Beach	863,518	West Palm Beach	1,993
Pasco	281,131	New Port Richey	738
Pinellas	851,659	Clearwater	280
Polk	405,382	Bartow	1,823
Putnam	65,070	Palatka	733
St. Johns	83,829	Saint Augustine	617
St. Lucie	150,171	Fort Pierce	581
Santa Rosa	81,608	Milton	1,024
Sarasota	277,776	Sarasota	573
Seminole	287,529	Sanford	298
Sumter	31,577	Bushnell	561
Suwannee	26,780	Live Oak	690
Taylor	17,111	Perry	1,058
Union	10,252	Lake Butler	246
Volusia	370,712	De Land	1,113
Wakulla	14,202	Crawfordville	601
Walton	27,760	De Funiak Springs	1,066
Washington	16,919	Chipley	590

Georgia

(159 counties, 58,056 sq. mi. land; pop. 6,478,216)

Appling	15,744	Baxley	510
Atkinson	6,213	Pearson	344
Bacon	9,566	Alma	286
Baker	3,615	Newton	347
Baldwin	39,530	Milledgeville	257
Banks	10,308	Homer	234
Barrow	29,721	Winder	163
Bartow	55,911	Cartersville	456
Ben Hill	16,245	Fitzgerald	254
Berrien	14,153	Nashville	456
Bibb	149,967	Macon	253
Bleckley	10,430	Cochran	219
Brantley	11,077	Nahunta	445
Brooks	15,398	Quitman	491
Bryan	15,438	Pembroke	441
Bulloch	43,125	Statesboro	678
Burke	20,579	Waynesboro	833
Butts	15,326	Jackson	187
Calhoun	5,013	Morgan	284
Camden	30,167	Woodbine	649
Candler	7,744	Metter	248
Carroll	71,422	Carrollton	501
Catoosa	42,464	Ringgold	162
Charlton	8,496	Folkston	780
Chatham	216,935	Savannah	443
Chattahoochee	16,934	Cusseta	250
Chattooga	22,242	Summerville	313
Cherokee	90,204	Canton	424
Clarke	87,594	Athens	122
Clay	3,364	Fort Gaines	196
Clayton	182,052	Jonesboro	148
Clinch	6,160	Homerville	821
Cobb	447,745	Marietta	343
Coffee	29,592	Douglas	602
Colquitt	36,645	Moultrie	557
Columbia	66,031	Appling	290
Cook	13,456	Adel	233
Coweta	53,853	Newnan	444
Crawford	8,991	Knoxville	328
Crisp	20,011	Cordele	275
Dade	13,147	Trenton	176
Dawson	9,429	Dawsonville	210
Decatur	25,511	Bainbridge	586
De Kalb	545,837	Decatur	270
Dodge	17,607	Eastman	504
Dooly	9,901	Vienna	397
Dougherty	96,311	Albany	330
Douglas	71,120	Douglasville	203
Early	11,854	Blakely	516
Echols	2,334	Statenville	421
Effingham	25,687	Springfield	482
Elbert	18,949	Elberton	367
Emanuel	20,546	Swainsboro	688
Evans	8,724	Claxton	186

County	Pop.	County Seat or court house	Land area sq. mi.
Fannin	15,992	Blue Ridge	384
Fayette	62,415	Fayetteville	199
Floyd	81,251	Rome	519
Forsyth	44,083	Cumming	226
Franklin	16,650	Carnesville	264
Fulton	648,951	Atlanta	534
Gilmer	13,368	Ellijay	427
Glascock	2,357	Gibson	144
Glynn	62,496	Brunswick	412
Gordon	35,072	Calhoun	355
Grady	20,279	Cairo	459
Greene	11,793	Greensboro	389
Gwinnett	352,910	Lawrenceville	435
Habersham	27,621	Clarkesville	278
Hall	95,428	Gainesville	379
Hancock	8,908	Sparta	470
Haralson	21,966	Buchanan	283
Harris	17,788	Hamilton	464
Hart	19,712	Hartwell	230
Heard	8,628	Franklin	292
Henry	58,741	McDonough	321
Houston	89,208	Perry	380
Irwin	8,649	Ocilla	362
Jackson	30,005	Jefferson	342
Jasper	8,453	Monticello	371
Jeff Davis	12,032	Hazlehurst	335
Jefferson	17,408	Louisville	529
Jenkins	8,247	Millen	353
Johnson	8,329	Wrightsville	306
Jones	20,739	Gray	394
Lamar	13,038	Barnesville	186
Lanier	5,531	Lakeland	194
Laurens	39,988	Dublin	816
Lee	16,250	Leesburg	358
Liberty	52,745	Hinesville	517
Lincoln	7,442	Lincolnton	196
Long	6,202	Ludowici	402
Lowndes	75,981	Valdosta	507
Lumpkin	14,573	Dahlonega	287
McDuffie	20,119	Thomson	256
McIntosh	8,634	Darien	425
Macon	13,114	Oglethorpe	404
Madison	21,050	Danielsville	285
Marion	5,590	Buena Vista	366
Meriwether	22,411	Greenville	506
Miller	6,280	Colquitt	284
Mitchell	20,275	Camilla	512
Monroe	17,113	Forsyth	397
Montgomery	7,163	Mount Vernon	244
Morgan	12,883	Madison	349
Murray	26,147	Chatsworth	345
Muscogee	179,278	Columbus	218
Newton	41,808	Covington	277
Oconee	17,618	Watkinsville	186
Oglethorpe	9,763	Lexington	442
Paulding	41,611	Dallas	312
Peach	21,189	Fort Valley	152
Pickens	14,432	Jasper	232
Pierce	13,328	Blackshear	344
Pike	10,224	Zebulon	219
Polk	33,815	Cedartown	311
Pulaski	8,108	Hawkinsville	249
Putnam	14,137	Eatonton	344
Quitman	2,209	Georgetown	146
Rabun	11,648	Clayton	370
Randolph	8,023	Cuthbert	431
Richmond	189,719	Augusta	326
Rockdale	54,091	Conyers	132
Schley	3,588	Ellaville	169
Screven	13,842	Sylvania	655
Seminole	9,010	Donalsonville	225
Spalding	54,457	Griffin	199
Stephens	23,257	Toccoa	177
Stewart	5,654	Lumpkin	452
Sumter	30,228	Americus	489
Talbot	6,524	Talbotton	395
Taliaferro	1,915	Crawfordville	196
Tattnall	17,722	Reidsville	484
Taylor	7,642	Butler	382
Telfair	11,000	MacRae	444
Terrell	10,653	Dawson	337
Thomas	38,986	Thomasville	551
Tift	34,998	Tifton	268
Toombs	24,072	Lyons	371
Towns	6,754	Hiawassee	165
Treutlen	5,994	Soperton	202
Troup	55,536	La Grange	414
Turner	8,703	Ashburn	289
Twiggs	9,806	Jeffersonville	362
Union	11,993	Blairsville	320
Upson	26,300	Thomaston	326
Walker	58,340	La Fayette	446
Walton	38,586	Monroe	330
Ware	35,471	Waycross	907
Warren	6,078	Warrenton	286
Washington	19,112	Sandersville	684
Wayne	22,356	Jesup	647
Webster	2,263	Preston	210
Wheeler	4,903	Alamo	299
White	13,006	Cleveland	242
Whitfield	72,462	Dalton	291
Wilcox	7,008	Abbeville	382
Wilkes	10,597	Washington	470
Wilkinson	10,228	Irwinton	451
Worth	19,745	Sylvester	575

Hawaii

(4 counties, 6,645 sq. mi. land; pop. 1,108,229)

Hawaii	120,317	Hilo	4,034
Honolulu	836,231	Honolulu	596
Kauai	51,177	Lihue	620
Maui*	100,374	Wailuku	1,175

Idaho

(44 counties, 82,412 sq. mi. land; pop. 1,006,749)

Ada	205,775	Boise	1,052
Adams	3,254	Council	1,362
Bannock	66,026	Pocatello	1,112
Bear Lake	6,084	Paris	990
Benewah	7,937	Saint Maries	784
Bingham	37,583	Blackfoot	2,096
Blaine	13,552	Hailey	2,634
Boise	3,509	Idaho City	1,901
Bonner	26,622	Sandpoint	1,726
Bonneville	72,207	Idaho Falls	1,840
Boundary	8,332	Bonners Ferry	1,268
Butte	2,918	Arco	2,236
Camas	727	Fairfield	1,071
Canyon	90,076	Caldwell	584
Caribou	6,963	Soda Springs	1,763
Cassia	19,532	Burley	2,560
Clark	762	Dubois	1,763
Clearwater	8,505	Orofino	2,460
Custer	4,133	Challis	4,927
Elmore	21,205	Mountain Home	3,071
Franklin	9,232	Preston	664
Fremont	10,937	Saint Anthony	1,852
Gem	11,844	Emmett	558
Gooding	11,633	Gooding	728
Idaho	13,783	Grangeville	8,497
Jefferson	16,543	Rigby	1,093
Jerome	15,138	Jerome	601
Kootenai	69,795	Coeur d'Alene	1,240
Latah	30,617	Moscow	1,077
Lemhi	6,899	Salmon	4,564
Lewis	3,516	Nezperce	478
Lincoln	3,308	Shoshone	1,205
Madison	23,674	Rexberg	468
Minidoka	19,361	Rupert	757
Nez Perce	33,754	Lewiston	845
Oneida	3,492	Malad City	1,200
Owyhee	8,392	Murphy	7,643
Payette	16,434	Payette	405
Power	7,086	American Falls	1,403
Shoshone	13,931	Wallace	2,641
Teton	3,439	Driggs	448
Twin Falls	53,580	Twin Falls	1,944
Valley	6,109	Cascade	3,670
Washington	8,550	Weiser	1,454

Illinois

(102 counties, 55,646 sq. mi. land; pop. 11,430,602)

Adams	66,090	Quincy	862
Alexander	10,626	Cairo	229
Bond	14,991	Greenville	378
Boone	30,806	Belvidere	283
Brown	5,836	Mount Sterling	306
Bureau	35,688	Princeton	866
Calhoun	5,322	Hardin	247
Carroll	16,805	Mount Carroll	456
Cass	13,437	Virginia	371
Champaign	173,025	Urbana	1,000
Christian	34,418	Taylorville	709
Clark	15,921	Marshall	505
Clay	14,460	Louisville	464
Clinton	33,944	Carlyle	434
Coles	51,644	Charleston	506
Cook	5,105,067	Chicago	954
Crawford	19,464	Robinson	443
Cumberland	10,670	Toledo	347
De Kalb	77,932	Sycamore	636
De Witt	16,516	Clinton	399
Douglas	19,464	Tuscola	420

County	Pop.	County Seat or court house	Land area sq. mi.
Du Page	781,666	Wheaton	337
Edgar	19,595	Paris	628
Edwards	7,440	Albion	225
Effingham	31,704	Effingham	481
Fayette	20,893	Vandalia	703
Ford	14,275	Paxton	488
Franklin	40,319	Benton	434
Fulton	38,080	Lewiston	877
Gallatin	6,909	Shawneetown	328
Greene	15,317	Carrollton	543
Grundy	32,337	Morris	432
Hamilton	8,499	McLeansboro	435
Hancock	21,373	Carthage	797
Hardin	5,189	Elizabethtown	183
Henderson	8,096	Oquawka	376
Henry	51,159	Cambridge	826
Iroquois	30,787	Watseka	1,122
Jackson	61,067	Murphysboro	605
Jasper	10,609	Newton	495
Jefferson	37,020	Mount Vernon	573
Jersey	20,539	Jerseyville	376
Jo Daviess	21,821	Galena	606
Johnson	11,347	Vienna	345
Kane	317,471	Geneva	520
Kankakee	96,255	Kankakee	678
Kendall	39,413	Yorkville	320
Knox	56,393	Galesburg	728
Lake	516,418	Waukegan	457
La Salle	106,913	Ottawa	1,150
Lawrence	15,972	Lawrenceville	374
Lee	34,392	Dixon	728
Livingston	39,301	Pontiac	1,043
Logan	30,798	Lincoln	622
McDonough	35,244	Macomb	582
McHenry	183,241	Woodstock	610
McLean	129,180	Bloomington	1,173
Macon	117,206	Decatur	578
Macoupin	47,679	Carlinville	872
Madison	249,238	Edwardsville	733
Marion	41,561	Salem	579
Marshall	12,846	Lacon	391
Mason	16,269	Havana	541
Massac	14,752	Metropolis	245
Menard	11,164	Petersburg	312
Mercer	17,290	Aledo	556
Monroe	22,422	Waterloo	382
Montgomery	30,728	Hillsboro	705
Morgan	36,397	Jacksonville	561
Moultrie	13,930	Sullivan	326
Ogle	45,957	Oregon	758
Peoria	182,827	Peoria	623
Perry	21,412	Pinckneyville	439
Piatt	15,548	Monticello	437
Pike	17,577	Pittsfield	828
Pope	4,373	Golconda	381
Pulaski	7,523	Mound City	204
Putnam	5,730	Hennepin	160
Randolph	34,583	Chester	594
Richland	16,545	Olney	364
Rock Island	148,723	Rock Island	424
St. Clair	262,852	Belleville	673
Saline	26,551	Harrisburg	383
Sangamon	178,386	Springfield	879
Schuyler	7,498	Rushville	434
Scott	5,644	Winchester	251
Shelby	22,261	Shelbyville	752
Stark	6,534	Toulon	291
Stephenson	48,052	Freeport	568
Tazewell	123,692	Pekin	652
Union	17,619	Jonesboro	416
Vermilion	88,257	Danville	899
Wabash	13,111	Mt. Carmel	222
Warren	19,181	Monmouth	541
Washington	14,965	Nashville	564
Wayne	17,241	Fairfield	715
White	16,522	Carmi	502
Whiteside	60,186	Morrison	687
Will	357,313	Joliet	847
Williamson	57,733	Marion	429
Winnebago	252,913	Rockford	519
Woodford	32,653	Eureka	528

Indiana

(92 counties, 35,870 sq. mi. land; pop. 5,544,159)

County	Pop.	County Seat or court house	Land area sq. mi.
Adams	31,095	Decatur	339
Allen	300,836	Fort Wayne	657
Bartholomew	63,657	Columbus	407
Benton	9,441	Fowler	406
Blackford	14,067	Hartford City	165
Boone	38,147	Lebanon	423
Brown	14,080	Nashville	312
Carroll	18,809	Delphi	372
Cass	38,413	Logansport	413
Clark	87,777	Jeffersonville	375
Clay	24,705	Brazil	358
Clinton	30,974	Frankfort	405
Crawford	9,914	English	306
Daviess	27,533	Washington	431
Dearborn	38,835	Lawrenceburg	305
Decatur	23,645	Greensburg	373
DeKalb	35,324	Auburn	363
Delaware	119,659	Muncie	393
Dubois	36,616	Jasper	430
Elkhart	156,198	Goshen	464
Fayette	26,015	Connersville	215
Floyd	64,404	New Albany	148
Fountain	17,808	Covington	396
Franklin	19,580	Brookville	386
Fulton	18,840	Rochester	369
Gibson	31,913	Princeton	489
Grant	74,169	Marion	414
Greene	30,410	Bloomfield	542
Hamilton	108,936	Noblesville	398
Hancock	45,527	Greenfield	306
Harrison	29,890	Corydon	485
Hendricks	75,717	Danville	408
Henry	48,139	New Castle	393
Howard	80,827	Kokomo	293
Huntington	35,427	Huntington	383
Jackson	37,730	Brownstown	509
Jasper	24,960	Rensselaer	560
Jay	21,512	Portland	384
Jefferson	29,797	Madison	361
Jennings	23,661	Vernon	377
Johnson	88,109	Franklin	320
Knox	39,884	Vincennes	516
Kosciusko	65,294	Warsaw	538
Lagrange	29,477	Lagrange	380
Lake	475,594	Crown Point	497
La Porte	107,066	La Porte	598
Lawrence	42,836	Bedford	449
Madison	130,669	Anderson	452
Marion	797,159	Indianapolis	396
Marshall	42,182	Plymouth	444
Martin	10,369	Shoals	336
Miami	36,897	Peru	376
Monroe	108,978	Bloomington	394
Montgomery	34,436	Crawfordsville	505
Morgan	55,920	Martinsville	407
Newton	13,551	Kentland	402
Noble	37,877	Albion	411
Ohio	5,315	Rising Sun	87
Orange	18,409	Paoli	400
Owen	17,281	Spencer	385
Parke	15,410	Rockville	445
Perry	19,107	Cannelton	381
Pike	12,509	Petersburg	336
Porter	128,932	Valparaiso	418
Posey	25,968	Mount Vernon	409
Pulaski	12,643	Winamac	434
Putnam	30,315	Greencastle	480
Randolph	27,148	Winchester	453
Ripley	24,616	Versailles	446
Rush	18,129	Rushville	408
St. Joseph	247,052	South Bend	457
Scott	20,991	Scottsburg	190
Shelby	40,307	Shelbyville	413
Spencer	19,490	Rockport	399
Starke	22,747	Knox	309
Steuben	27,446	Angola	309
Sullivan	18,993	Sullivan	447
Switzerland	7,738	Vevay	221
Tippecanoe	130,598	Lafayette	500
Tipton	16,119	Tipton	260
Union	6,976	Liberty	162
Vanderburgh	165,058	Evansville	235
Vermillion	16,773	Newport	257
Vigo	106,107	Terre Haute	403
Wabash	35,069	Wabash	413
Warren	8,176	Williamsport	365
Warrick	44,920	Boonville	384
Washington	23,717	Salem	515
Wayne	71,951	Richmond	404
Wells	25,948	Bluffton	370
White	23,265	Monticello	505
Whitley	27,651	Columbia City	336

Iowa

(99 counties; 55,965 sq. mi. land; pop. 2,776,755)

County	Pop.	County Seat or court house	Land area sq. mi.
Adair	8,409	Greenfield	570
Adams	4,866	Corning	426
Allamakee	13,855	Waukon	660
Appanoose	13,743	Centerville	515
Audubon	7,334	Audubon	444
Benton	22,429	Vinton	718
Black Hawk	123,798	Waterloo	573

County	Pop.	County Seat or court house	Land area sq. mi.
Boone	25,186	Boone	574
Bremer	22,813	Waverly	439
Buchanan	20,844	Independence	573
Buena Vista	19,965	Storm Lake	580
Butler	15,731	Allison	582
Calhoun	11,508	Rockwell City	573
Carroll	21,423	Carroll	570
Cass	15,128	Atlantic	565
Cedar	17,381	Tipton	582
Cerro Gordo	46,733	Mason City	575
Cherokee	14,098	Cherokee	577
Chickasaw	13,295	New Hampton	505
Clarke	8,287	Osceola	431
Clay	17,585	Spencer	573
Clayton	19,054	Elkader	795
Clinton	51,040	Clinton	710
Crawford	16,775	Denison	714
Dallas	29,755	Adel	591
Davis	8,312	Bloomfield	505
Decatur	8,338	Leon	535
Delaware	18,035	Manchester	579
Des Moines	42,614	Burlington	429
Dickinson	14,909	Spirit Lake	404
Dubuque	86,403	Dubuque	616
Emmet	11,569	Estherville	402
Fayette	21,843	West Union	731
Floyd	17,058	Charles City	501
Franklin	11,364	Hampton	583
Fremont	8,226	Sidney	517
Greene	10,045	Jefferson	572
Grundy	12,029	Grundy Center	501
Guthrie	10,935	Guthrie Center	594
Hamilton	16,071	Webster City	577
Hancock	12,638	Garner	573
Hardin	19,094	Eldora	569
Harrison	14,730	Logan	701
Henry	19,226	Mount Pleasant	436
Howard	9,809	Cresco	473
Humboldt	10,756	Dakota City	436
Ida	8,365	Ida Grove	432
Iowa	14,630	Marengo	588
Jackson	19,950	Maquoketa	650
Jasper	34,795	Newton	732
Jefferson	16,310	Fairfield	440
Johnson	96,119	Iowa City	623
Jones	19,444	Anamosa	576
Keokuk	11,624	Sigourney	580
Kossuth	18,591	Algona	976
Lee	38,687	Fort Madison and Keokuk	540
Linn	168,767	Cedar Rapids	724
Louisa	11,592	Wapello	417
Lucas	9,070	Chariton	435
Lyon	11,952	Rock Rapids	588
Madison	12,483	Winterset	563
Mahaska	21,513	Oskaloosa	572
Marion	30,001	Knoxville	575
Marshall	38,276	Marshalltown	573
Mills	13,202	Glenwood	441
Mitchell	10,928	Osage	470
Monona	10,034	Onawa	699
Monroe	8,114	Albia	434
Montgomery	12,076	Red Oak	424
Muscatine	39,907	Muscatine	449
O'Brien	15,444	Primghar	574
Osceola	7,267	Sibley	399
Page	16,870	Clarinda	535
Palo Alto	10,669	Emmetsburg	568
Plymouth	23,388	Le Mars	864
Pocahontas	9,525	Pocahontas	578
Polk	327,140	Des Moines	592
Pottawattamie	82,628	Council Bluffs	959
Poweshiek	19,033	Montezuma	586
Ringgold	5,420	Mount Ayr	536
Sac	12,324	Sac City	578
Scott	150,979	Davenport	469
Shelby	13,230	Harlan	591
Sioux	29,903	Orange City	769
Story	74,252	Nevada	574
Tama	17,419	Toledo	722
Taylor	7,114	Bedford	537
Union	12,750	Creston	427
Van Buren	7,676	Keosauqua	489
Wapello	35,696	Ottumwa	436
Warren	36,033	Indianola	573
Washington	19,612	Washington	571
Wayne	7,067	Corydon	527
Webster	40,342	Fort Dodge	718
Winnebago	12,122	Forest City	402
Winneshiek	20,847	Decorah	690
Woodbury	98,276	Sioux City	877
Worth	7,991	Northwood	402
Wright	14,269	Clarion	582

Kansas

(105 counties, 81,782 sq. mi. land; pop. 2,477,574)

County	Pop.	County Seat or court house	Land area sq. mi.
Allen	14,638	Iola	505
Anderson	7,803	Garnett	584
Atchison	16,932	Atchison	431
Barber	5,874	Medicine Lodge	1,136
Barton	29,382	Great Bend	895
Bourbon	14,966	Fort Scott	638
Brown	11,128	Hiawatha	572
Butler	50,580	El Dorado	1,443
Chase	3,021	Cottonwood Falls	777
Chautauqua	4,407	Sedan	644
Cherokee	21,374	Columbus	590
Cheyenne	3,243	Saint Francis	1,021
Clark	2,418	Ashland	975
Clay	9,158	Clay Center	632
Cloud	11,023	Concordia	718
Coffey	8,404	Burlington	615
Comanche	2,313	Coldwater	789
Cowley	36,915	Winfield	1,128
Crawford	35,568	Girard	595
Decatur	4,021	Oberlin	894
Dickinson	18,958	Abilene	852
Doniphan	8,134	Troy	388
Douglas	81,798	Lawrence	461
Edwards	3,787	Kinsley	620
Elk	3,327	Howard	650
Ellis	26,004	Hays	900
Ellsworth	6,586	Ellsworth	717
Finney	33,070	Garden City	1,302
Ford	27,463	Dodge City	1,099
Franklin	21,994	Ottawa	577
Geary	30,453	Junction City	377
Gove	3,231	Gove	1,072
Graham	3,543	Hill City	898
Grant	7,159	Ulysses	575
Gray	5,396	Cimarron	868
Greeley	1,774	Tribune	778
Greenwood	7,847	Eureka	1,135
Hamilton	2,388	Syracuse	998
Harper	7,124	Anthony	802
Harvey	31,028	Newton	540
Haskell	3,886	Sublette	578
Hodgeman	2,177	Jetmore	860
Jackson	11,525	Holton	658
Jefferson	15,905	Oskaloosa	535
Jewell	4,251	Mankato	910
Johnson	355,021	Olathe	478
Kearny	4,027	Lakin	868
Kingman	8,292	Kingman	865
Kiowa	3,660	Greensburg	723
Labette	23,693	Oswego	653
Lane	2,375	Dighton	717
Leavenworth	64,371	Leavenworth	463
Lincoln	3,653	Lincoln	720
Linn	8,254	Mound City	601
Logan	3,081	Oakley	1,073
Lyon	34,732	Emporia	844
McPherson	27,268	McPherson	900
Marion	12,888	Marion	944
Marshall	11,705	Marysville	878
Meade	4,247	Meade	979
Miami	23,466	Paola	590
Mitchell	7,203	Beloit	717
Montgomery	38,816	Independence	646
Morris	6,198	Council Grove	693
Morton	3,480	Elkhart	731
Nemaha	10,446	Seneca	719
Neosho	17,035	Erie	576
Ness	4,033	Ness City	1,074
Norton	5,947	Norton	873
Osage	15,248	Lyndon	695
Osborne	4,867	Osborne	882
Ottawa	5,634	Minneapolis	721
Pawnee	7,555	Larned	755
Phillips	6,590	Phillipsburg	887
Pottawatomie	16,128	Westmoreland	828
Pratt	9,702	Pratt	735
Rawlins	3,404	Atwood	1,069
Reno	62,389	Hutchinson	1,259
Republic	6,482	Belleville	719
Rice	10,610	Lyons	728
Riley	67,139	Manhattan	593
Rooks	6,039	Stockton	888
Rush	3,842	LaCrosse	718
Russell	7,835	Russell	869
Saline	49,301	Salina	721
Scott	5,289	Scott City	718
Sedgwick	403,662	Wichita	1,007
Seward	18,743	Liberal	640
Shawnee	160,976	Topeka	549
Sheridan	3,043	Hoxie	896
Sherman	6,926	Goodland	1,057
Smith	5,078	Smith Center	897
Stafford	5,365	Saint John	788
Stanton	2,333	Johnson	681

County	Pop.	County Seat or court house	Land area sq. mi.
Stevens	5,048	Hugoton	727
Sumner	25,841	Wellington	1,183
Thomas	8,258	Colby	1,075
Trego	3,694	WaKeeney	890
Wabaunsee	6,603	Alma	797
Wallace	1,821	Sharon Springs	914
Washington	7,073	Washington	898
Wichita	2,758	Leoti	719
Wilson	10,289	Fredonia	575
Woodson	4,116	Yates Center	498
Wyandotte	162,026	Kansas City	149

Kentucky

(120 counties, 39,732 sq. mi. land; pop. 3,685,296)

County	Pop.	County Seat or court house	Land area sq. mi.
Adair	15,360	Columbia	407
Allen	14,628	Scottsville	346
Anderson	14,571	Lawrenceburg	203
Ballard	7,902	Wickliffe	251
Barren	34,001	Glasgow	491
Bath	9,692	Owingsville	279
Bell	31,506	Pineville	361
Boone	57,589	Burlington	246
Bourbon	19,236	Paris	291
Boyd	51,150	Catlettsburg	160
Boyle	25,641	Danville	182
Bracken	7,766	Brooksville	203
Breathitt	15,703	Jackson	495
Breckinridge	16,312	Hardinsburg	572
Bullitt	47,567	Shepherdsville	299
Butler	11,245	Morgantown	428
Caldwell	13,232	Princeton	347
Calloway	30,735	Murray	386
Campbell	83,866	Newport	152
Carlisle	5,238	Bardwell	193
Carroll	9,292	Carrollton	130
Carter	24,340	Grayson	411
Casey	14,211	Liberty	446
Christian	68,941	Hopkinsville	721
Clark	29,496	Winchester	254
Clay	21,746	Manchester	471
Clinton	9,135	Albany	198
Crittenden	9,196	Marion	362
Cumberland	6,784	Burkesville	306
Daviess	87,189	Owensboro	462
Edmonson	10,357	Brownsville	303
Elliott	6,455	Sandy Hook	234
Estill	14,614	Irvine	254
Fayette	225,366	Lexington	286
Fleming	12,292	Flemingsburg	351
Floyd	43,586	Prestonsburg	394
Franklin	43,781	Frankfort	211
Fulton	8,271	Hickman	209
Gallatin	5,393	Warsaw	99
Garrard	11,579	Lancaster	231
Grant	15,737	Williamstown	260
Graves	33,550	Mayfield	556
Grayson	21,050	Leitchfield	504
Green	10,371	Greensburg	289
Greenup	36,742	Greenup	346
Hancock	7,864	Hawesville	189
Hardin	89,240	Elizabethtown	628
Harlan	36,574	Harlan	467
Harrison	16,248	Cynthiana	310
Hart	14,890	Munfordville	416
Henderson	43,044	Henderson	440
Henry	12,823	New Castle	289
Hickman	5,566	Clinton	245
Hopkins	46,126	Madisonville	551
Jackson	11,955	McKee	346
Jefferson	664,937	Louisville	385
Jessamine	30,508	Nicholasville	173
Johnson	23,248	Paintsville	262
Kenton	142,031	Covington	163
Knott	17,906	Hindman	352
Knox	29,676	Barbourville	388
Larue	11,679	Hodgenville	263
Laurel	43,438	London	436
Lawrence	13,998	Louisa	419
Lee	7,422	Beattyville	210
Leslie	13,642	Hyden	404
Letcher	27,000	Whitesburg	339
Lewis	13,029	Vanceburg	485
Lincoln	20,045	Stanford	337
Livingston	9,062	Smithland	316
Logan	24,416	Russellville	556
Lyon	6,624	Eddyville	216
McCracken	62,879	Paducah	251
McCreary	15,603	Whitley City	428
McLean	9,628	Calhoun	254
Madison	57,508	Richmond	441
Magoffin	13,077	Salyersville	310
Marion	16,499	Lebanon	347
Marshall	27,205	Benton	305
Martin	12,526	Inez	231
Mason	16,666	Maysville	241
Meade	24,170	Brandenburg	309
Menifee	5,092	Frenchburg	204
Mercer	19,148	Harrodsburg	251
Metcalfe	8,963	Edmonton	291
Monroe	11,401	Tompkinsville	331
Montgomery	19,561	Mount Sterling	199
Morgan	11,648	West Liberty	381
Muhlenberg	31,318	Greenville	475
Nelson	29,710	Bardstown	423
Nicholas	6,725	Carlisle	197
Ohio	21,105	Hartford	594
Oldham	33,263	La Grange	189
Owen	9,035	Owenton	352
Owsley	5,036	Booneville	198
Pendleton	12,036	Falmouth	280
Perry	30,283	Hazard	342
Pike	72,583	Pikeville	788
Powell	11,686	Stanton	180
Pulaski	49,489	Somerset	662
Robertson	2,124	Mount Olivet	100
Rockcastle	14,803	Mount Vernon	318
Rowan	20,353	Morehead	281
Russell	14,716	Jamestown	254
Scott	23,867	Georgetown	285
Shelby	24,824	Shelbyville	384
Simpson	15,145	Franklin	236
Spencer	6,801	Taylorsville	186
Taylor	21,146	Campbellsville	270
Todd	10,940	Elkton	376
Trigg	10,361	Cadiz	443
Trimble	6,090	Bedford	149
Union	16,557	Morganfield	345
Warren	76,673	Bowling Green	545
Washington	10,441	Springfield	301
Wayne	17,468	Monticello	459
Webster	13,955	Dixon	335
Whitley	33,326	Williamsburg	440
Wolfe	6,503	Campton	223
Woodford	19,955	Versailles	191

Louisiana

(64 parishes, 44,521 sq. mi. land; pop. 4,219,973)

County	Pop.	County Seat or court house	Land area sq. mi.
Acadia	55,882	Crowley	657
Allen	21,226	Oberlin	765
Ascension	58,214	Donaldsville	296
Assumption	22,753	Napoleonville	342
Avoyelles	39,159	Marksville	846
Beauregard	30,083	De Ridder	1,163
Bienville	15,979	Arcadia	816
Bossier	86,088	Benton	845
Caddo	248,253	Shreveport	894
Calcasieu	168,134	Lake Charles	1,082
Caldwell	9,810	Columbia	541
Cameron	9,260	Cameron	1,417
Catahoula	11,065	Harrisonburg	732
Claiborne	17,405	Homer	765
Concordia	20,828	Vidalia	717
De Soto	25,346	Mansfield	880
East Baton Rouge	380,105	Baton Rouge	458
East Carroll	9,709	Lake Providence	426
East Feliciana	19,211	Clinton	455
Evangeline	33,274	Ville Platte	667
Franklin	22,387	Winnsboro	635
Grant	17,526	Colfax	653
Iberia	68,297	New Iberia	589
Iberville	31,049	Plaquemine	638
Jackson	15,705	Jonesboro	579
Jefferson	448,306	Gretna	348
Jefferson Davis	30,722	Jennings	655
Lafayette	164,762	Lafayette	270
Lafourche	85,860	Thibodaux	1,141
La Salle	13,662	Jena	638
Lincoln	41,745	Ruston	472
Livingston	70,523	Livingston	661
Madison	12,463	Tallulah	631
Morehouse	31,938	Bastrop	807
Natchitoches	36,689	Natchitoches	1,264
Orleans	496,938	New Orleans	199
Ouachita	142,191	Monroe	627
Plaquemines	25,575	Pointe a la Hache	1,035
Pointe Coupee	22,540	New Roads	566
Rapides	131,556	Alexandria	1,341
Red River	9,387	Coushatta	394
Richland	20,629	Rayville	563
Sabine	22,646	Many	855
St. Bernard	66,631	Chalmette	486
St. Charles	42,437	Hahnville	286
St. Helena	9,874	Greensburg	409
St. James	20,879	Convent	248
St. John The Baptist	39,996	Edgard	213
St. Landry	80,331	Opelousas	936

County	Pop.	County Seat or court house	Land area sq. mi.
St. Martin	44,097	Saint Martinville	749
St. Mary	58,086	Franklin	613
St. Tammany	144,500	Covington	873
Tangipahoa	85,709	Amite	783
Tensas	7,103	Saint Joseph	623
Terrebonne	96,982	Houma	1,367
Union	20,796	Farmerville	884
Vermilion	50,055	Abbeville	1,205
Vernon	61,961	Leesville	1,332
Washington	43,185	Franklinton	676
Webster	41,989	Minden	602
West Baton Rouge	19,419	Port Allen	194
West Carroll	12,093	Oak Grove	360
West Feliciana	12,915	Saint Francisville	406
Winn	16,269	Winnfield	953

Maine

(16 counties, 30,995 sq. mi. land; pop. 1,227,928)

Androscoggin	105,259	Auburn	477
Aroostook	86,936	Houlton	6,721
Cumberland	243,135	Portland	876
Franklin	29,008	Farmington	1,699
Hancock	46,948	Ellsworth	1,537
Kennebec	115,904	Augusta	876
Knox	36,310	Rockland	370
Lincoln	30,357	Wiscasset	458
Oxford	52,602	South Paris	2,053
Penobscot	146,601	Bangor	3,430
Piscataquis	18,653	Dover-Foxcroft	3,986
Sagadahoc	33,535	Bath	257
Somerset	49,767	Skowhegan	3,930
Waldo	33,018	Belfast	730
Washington	35,308	Machias	2,586
York	164,587	Alfred	1,008

Maryland

(23 cos., 1 ind. city, 9,837 sq. mi. land; pop. 4,781,468)

Allegany	74,946	Cumberland	421
Anne Arundel	427,239	Annapolis	418
Baltimore	692,134	Towson	598
Calvert	51,372	Prince Frederick	213
Caroline	27,035	Denton	321
Carroll	123,372	Westminster	452
Cecil	71,347	Elkton	360
Charles	101,154	La Plata	452
Dorchester	30,236	Cambridge	593
Frederick	150,208	Frederick	663
Garrett	28,138	Oakland	657
Harford	182,132	Bel Air	448
Howard	187,328	Ellicott City	251
Kent	17,842	Chestertown	278
Montgomery	757,027	Rockville	495
Prince Georges	729,268	Landover	487
Queen Annes	33,953	Centreville	372
St. Mary's	75,974	Leonardtown	373
Somerset	23,440	Princess Anne	338
Talbot	30,549	Easton	259
Washington	121,393	Hagerstown	455
Wicomico	74,339	Salisbury	379
Worcester	35,028	Snow Hill	475
Independent City			
Baltimore	736,014		80

Massachusetts

(14 counties; 7,824 sq. mi. land; pop. 6,016,425)

Barnstable	186,605	Barnstable	400
Berkshire	139,352	Pittsfield	929
Bristol	506,325	Taunton	557
Dukes	11,639	Edgartown	102
Essex	670,080	Salem	495
Franklin	70,092	Greenfield	702
Hampden	456,310	Springfield	618
Hampshire	146,568	Northampton	528
Middlesex	1,398,468	East Cambridge	822
Nantucket	6,012	Nantucket	47
Norfolk	616,087	Dedham	400
Plymouth	435,276	Plymouth	655
Suffolk	663,906	Boston	57
Worcester	709,705	Worcester	1,513

Michigan

(83 counties; 56,954 sq. mi. land; pop. 9,295,297)

County	Pop.	County Seat or court house	Land area sq. mi.
Alcona	10,145	Harrisville	679
Alger	8,972	Munising	912
Allegan	90,509	Allegan	832
Alpena	30,605	Alpena	567
Antrim	18,185	Bellaire	480
Arenac	14,931	Standish	367
Baraga	7,954	L'Anse	901
Barry	50,057	Hastings	560
Bay	111,723	Bay City	447
Benzie	12,200	Beulah	322
Berrien	161,378	St. Joseph	576
Branch	41,502	Coldwater	508
Calhoun	135,982	Marshall	712
Cass	49,477	Cassopolis	496
Charlevoix	21,468	Charlevoix	421
Cheboygan	21,398	Cheboygan	720
Chippewa	34,604	Sault Ste. Marie	1,590
Clare	24,952	Harrison	570
Clinton	57,883	St. Johns	573
Crawford	12,260	Grayling	559
Delta	37,780	Escanaba	1,173
Dickinson	26,831	Iron Mountain	770
Eaton	92,879	Charlotte	579
Emmet	25,040	Petoskey	468
Genesee	430,459	Flint	642
Gladwin	21,896	Gladwin	505
Gogebic	18,052	Bessemer	1,105
Grand Traverse	64,273	Traverse City	466
Gratiot	38,982	Ithaca	570
Hillsdale	43,431	Hillsdale	603
Houghton	35,446	Houghton	1,014
Huron	34,951	Bad Axe	830
Ingham	281,912	Mason	560
Ionia	57,024	Ionia	577
Iosco	30,209	Tawas City	546
Iron	13,175	Crystal Falls	1,163
Isabella	54,624	Mount Pleasant	577
Jackson	149,756	Jackson	705
Kalamazoo	223,411	Kalamazoo	562
Kalkaska	13,497	Kalkaska	563
Kent	500,631	Grand Rapids	862
Keweenaw	1,701	Eagle River	543
Lake	8,583	Baldwin	568
Lapeer	74,768	Lapeer	658
Leelanau	16,527	Leland	341
Lenawee	91,476	Adrian	753
Livingston	115,645	Howell	574
Luce	5,763	Newberry	904
Mackinac	10,674	St. Ignace	1,025
Macomb	717,400	Mount Clemens	482
Manistee	21,265	Manistee	543
Marquette	70,887	Marquette	1,821
Mason	25,537	Ludington	494
Mecosta	37,308	Big Rapids	560
Menominee	24,920	Menominee	1,045
Midland	75,651	Midland	525
Missaukee	12,147	Lake City	565
Monroe	133,600	Monroe	557
Montcalm	53,059	Stanton	713
Montmorency	8,936	Atlanta	550
Muskegon	158,983	Muskegon	507
Newaygo	38,202	White Cloud	847
Oakland	1,083,592	Pontiac	875
Oceana	22,454	Hart	541
Ogemaw	18,681	West Branch	570
Ontonagon	8,854	Ontonagon	1,311
Osceola	20,146	Reed City	569
Oscoda	7,842	Mio	568
Otsego	17,957	Gaylord	516
Ottawa	187,768	Grand Haven	567
Presque Isle	13,743	Rogers City	656
Roscommon	19,776	Roscommon	528
Saginaw	211,946	Saginaw	815
St. Clair	145,607	Port Huron	734
St. Joseph	58,913	Centreville	503
Sanilac	39,928	Sandusky	964
Schoolcraft	8,302	Manistique	1,173
Shiawassee	69,770	Corunna	540
Tuscola	55,498	Caro	812
Van Buren	70,060	Paw Paw	611
Washtenaw	282,937	Ann Arbor	710
Wayne	2,111,687	Detroit	615
Wexford	26,360	Cadillac	566

Minnesota

(87 counties; 79,548 sq. mi. land; pop., 4,375,099)

Aitkin	12,425	Aitkin	1,834
Anoka	243,641	Anoka	430
Becker	27,881	Detroit Lakes	1,312
Beltrami	34,384	Bemidji	2,507

County	Pop.	County Seat or court house	Land area sq. mi.
Benton	30,185	Foley	408
Big Stone	6,285	Ortonville	497
Blue Earth	54,044	Mankato	749
Brown	26,984	New Ulm	610
Carlton	29,259	Carlton	864
Carver	47,915	Chaska	351
Cass	21,791	Walker	2,033
Chippewa	13,228	Montevideo	584
Chisago	30,521	Center City	417
Clay	50,422	Moorhead	1,049
Clearwater	8,309	Bagley	999
Cook	3,868	Grand Marais	1,412
Cottonwood	12,694	Windom	640
Crow Wing	44,249	Brainerd	1,008
Dakota	275,227	Hastings	574
Dodge	15,731	Mantorville	439
Douglas	28,674	Alexandria	643
Faribault	16,937	Blue Earth	714
Fillmore	20,777	Preston	862
Freeborn	33,060	Albert Lea	705
Goodhue	40,690	Red Wing	763
Grant	6,246	Elbow Lake	547
Hennepin	1,032,431	Minneapolis	541
Houston	18,497	Caledonia	564
Hubbard	14,939	Park Rapids	936
Isanti	25,921	Cambridge	440
Itasca	40,863	Grand Rapids	2,661
Jackson	11,677	Jackson	699
Kanabec	12,802	Mora	527
Kandiyohi	38,761	Willmar	784
Kittson	5,767	Hallock	1,104
Koochiching	16,299	International Falls	3,108
Lac qui Parle	8,924	Madison	772
Lake	10,415	Two Harbors	2,053
Lake of the Woods	4,076	Baudette	1,296
Le Sueur	23,239	Le Center	446
Lincoln	6,890	Ivanhoe	538
Lyon	24,789	Marshall	714
McLeod	32,030	Glencoe	489
Mahnomen	5,044	Mahnomen	559
Marshall	10,993	Warren	1,760
Martin	22,914	Fairmont	706
Meeker	20,846	Litchfield	624
Mille Lacs	18,670	Milaca	578
Morrison	29,604	Little Falls	1,124
Mower	37,385	Austin	711
Murray	9,660	Slayton	702
Nicollet	28,076	Saint Peter	440
Nobles	20,098	Worthington	714
Norman	7,975	Ada	877
Olmsted	106,470	Rochester	655
Otter Tail	50,714	Fergus Falls	1,973
Pennington	13,306	Thief River Falls	618
Pine	21,264	Pine City	1,421
Pipestone	10,491	Pipestone	466
Polk	32,498	Crookston	1,982
Pope	10,745	Glenwood	668
Ramsey	485,765	Saint Paul	154
Red Lake	4,525	Red Lake Falls	433
Redwood	17,254	Redwood Falls	882
Renville	17,673	Olivia	984
Rice	49,183	Faribault	501
Rock	9,806	Luverne	483
Roseau	15,026	Roseau	1,677
St. Louis	198,213	Duluth	6,125
Scott	57,846	Shakopee	357
Sherburne	41,945	Elk River	435
Sibley	14,366	Gaylord	593
Stearns	118,791	Saint Cloud	1,338
Steele	30,729	Owatonna	431
Stevens	10,634	Morris	560
Swift	10,724	Benson	743
Todd	23,363	Long Prairie	941
Traverse	'4,463	Wheaton	575
Wabasha	19,744	Wabasha	537
Wadena	13,154	Wadena	538
Waseca	18,079	Waseca	422
Washington	145,896	Stillwater	390
Watonwan	11,682	Saint James	435
Wilkin	7,516	Breckenridge	751
Winona	47,828	Winona	630
Wright	68,710	Buffalo	672
Yellow Medicine	11,684	Granite Falls	758

Mississippi

(82 counties, 47,233 sq. mi. land; pop. 2,573,216)

County	Pop.	County Seat or court house	Land area sq. mi.
Adams	35,356	Natchez	456
Alcorn	31,722	Corinth	401
Amite	13,328	Liberty	732
Attala	18,481	Kosciusko	737
Benton	8,046	Ashland	407
Bolivar	41,875	Cleveland & Rosedale	892
Calhoun	14,908	Pittsboro	573
Carroll	9,237	Carrollton & Vaiden	634
Chickasaw	18,085	Houston & Okolona	503
Choctaw	9,071	Ackerman	420
Claiborne	11,370	Port Gibson	494
Clarke	17,313	Quitman	692
Clay	21,120	West Point	415
Coahoma	31,665	Clarksdale	559
Copiah	27,592	Hazlehurst	779
Covington	16,527	Collins	416
De Soto	67,910	Hernando	483
Forrest	68,314	Hattiesburg	469
Franklin	8,377	Meadville	566
George	16,673	Lucedale	483
Greene	10,220	Leakesville	718
Grenada	21,555	Grenada	421
Hancock	31,760	Bay Saint Louis	478
Harrison	165,365	Gulfport	581
Hinds	254,441	Jackson & Raymond	875
Holmes	21,604	Lexington	759
Humphreys	12,134	Belzoni	430
Issaquena	1,909	Mayersville	406
Itawamba	20,017	Fulton	541
Jackson	115,243	Pascagoula	731
Jasper	17,114	Bay Springs & Paulding	678
Jefferson	8,653	Fayette	523
Jefferson Davis	14,051	Prentiss	409
Jones	62,031	Ellisville & Laurel	695
Kemper	10,356	De Kalb	766
Lafayette	31,826	Oxford	669
Lamar	30,424	Purvis	499
Lauderdale	75,555	Meridian	705
Lawrence	12,458	Monticello	435
Leake	18,436	Carthage	584
Lee	65,581	Tupelo	451
Leflore	37,341	Greenwood	605
Lincoln	30,278	Brookhaven	586
Lowndes	59,308	Columbus	517
Madison	53,794	Canton	717
Marion	25,544	Columbia	548
Marshall	30,361	Holly Springs	709
Monroe	36,582	Aberdeen	772
Montgomery	12,388	Winona	408
Neshoba	24,800	Philadelphia	571
Newton	20,291	Decatur	580
Noxubee	12,604	Macon	698
Oktibbeha	38,375	Starkville	459
Panola	29,996	Batesville & Sardis	695
Pearl River	38,714	Poplarville	819
Perry	10,865	New Augusta	651
Pike	36,882	Magnolia	410
Pontotoc	22,237	Pontotoc	499
Prentiss	23,278	Booneville	417
Quitman	10,490	Marks	406
Rankin	87,161	Brandon	782
Scott	24,137	Forest	610
Sharkey	7,066	Rolling Fork	435
Simpson	23,953	Mendenhall	591
Smith	14,798	Raleigh	635
Stone	10,750	Wiggins	446
Sunflower	35,129	Indianola	707
Tallahatchie	15,210	Charleston & Sumner	651
Tate	21,432	Senatobia	406
Tippah	19,523	Ripley	458
Tishomingo	17,683	Iuka	434
Tunica	8,164	Tunica	460
Union	22,085	New Albany	417
Walthall	14,352	Tylertown	404
Warren	47,880	Vicksburg	597
Washington	67,935	Greenville	733
Wayne	19,517	Waynesboro	813
Webster	10,222	Walthall	424
Wilkinson	9,678	Woodville	678
Winston	19,433	Louisville	610
Yalobusha	12,033	Coffeeville & Water Valley	478
Yazoo	25,506	Yazoo City	933

Missouri

(114 cos., 1 ind. city, 68,945 sq. mi. land; pop. 5,117,073)

County	Pop.	County Seat or court house	Land area sq. mi.
Adair	24,577	Kirksville	567
Andrew	14,632	Savannah	435
Atchison	7,457	Rockport	542
Audrain	23,599	Mexico	697
Barry	27,547	Cassville	773
Barton	11,312	Lamar	596
Bates	15,025	Butler	849
Benton	13,859	Warsaw	729
Bollinger	10,619	Marble Hill	621
Boone	112,379	Columbia	687
Buchanan	83,083	Saint Joseph	409
Butler	38,765	Poplar Buff	698
Caldwell	8,380	Kingston	430
Callaway	32,809	Fulton	842
Camden	27,495	Camdenton	641

County	Pop.	County Seat or court house	Land area sq. mi.
Cape Girardeau	61,633	Jackson	577
Carroll	10,748	Carrollton	695
Carter	5,515	Van Buren	509
Cass	63,808	Harrisonville	701
Cedar	12,093	Stockton	470
Chariton	9,202	Keytesville	758
Christian	32,644	Ozark	564
Clark	7,547	Kahoka	507
Clay	153,411	Liberty	403
Clinton	16,595	Plattsburg	423
Cole	63,579	Jefferson City	392
Cooper	14,835	Boonville	567
Crawford	19,173	Steelville	744
Dade	7,449	Greenfield	491
Dallas	12,646	Buffalo	543
Daviess	7,865	Gallatin	568
De Kalb	9,967	Maysville	425
Dent	13,702	Salem	755
Douglas	11,876	Ava	814
Dunklin	33,112	Kennett	547
Franklin	80,603	Union	922
Gasconade	14,006	Hermann	521
Gentry	6,848	Albany	493
Greene	207,949	Springfield	677
Grundy	10,536	Trenton	437
Harrison	8,469	Bethany	725
Henry	20,044	Clinton	729
Hickory	7,335	Hermitage	379
Holt	6,034	Oregon	457
Howard	9,631	Fayette	465
Howell	31,447	West Plains	928
Iron	10,726	Ironton	552
Jackson	633,232	Kansas City	611
Jasper	90,465	Carthage	641
Jefferson	171,380	Hillsboro	661
Johnson	42,514	Warrensburg	834
Knox	4,482	Edina	507
Laclede	27,158	Lebanon	768
Lafayette	31,107	Lexington	632
Lawrence	30,236	Mount Vernon	613
Lewis	10,233	Monticello	509
Lincoln	28,892	Troy	627
Linn	13,885	Linneus	620
Livingston	14,592	Chillicothe	537
McDonald	16,938	Pineville	540
Macon	15,345	Macon	797
Madison	11,127	Fredericktown	497
Maries	7,976	Vienna	528
Marion	27,682	Palmyra	438
Mercer	3,723	Princeton	454
Miller	20,700	Tuscumbia	593
Mississippi	14,442	Charleston	410
Moniteau	12,298	California	417
Monroe	9,104	Paris	670
Montgomery	11,355	Montgomery City	540
Morgan	15,574	Versailles	594
New Madrid	20,928	New Madrid	658
Newton	44,445	Neosho	627
Nodaway	21,709	Maryville	875
Oregon	9,470	Alton	792
Osage	12,018	Linn	606
Ozark	8,598	Gainesville	731
Pemiscot	21,921	Caruthersville	517
Perry	16,648	Perryville	473
Pettis	35,437	Sedalia	686
Phelps	35,248	Rolla	674
Pike	15,969	Bowling Green	673
Platte	57,867	Platte City	421
Polk	21,826	Bolivar	636
Pulaski	41,307	Waynesville	550
Putnam	5,079	Unionville	520
Ralls	8,476	New London	482
Randolph	24,370	Huntsville	477
Ray	21,971	Richmond	568
Reynolds	6,661	Centerville	809
Ripley	12,303	Doniphan	631
St. Charles	212,907	St. Charles	558
St. Clair	8,457	Osceola	699
St. Francis	48,904	Farmington	451
St. Louis	993,529	Clayton	506
Ste. Genevieve	16,037	Ste. Genevieve	504
Saline	23,523	Marshall	755
Schuyler	4,236	Lancaster	309
Scotland	4,822	Memphis	438
Scott	39,376	Benton	423
Shannon	7,613	Eminence	1,004
Shelby	6,942	Shelbyville	501
Stoddard	28,895	Bloomfield	815
Stone	19,078	Galena	451
Sullivan	6,326	Milan	651
Taney	25,561	Forsyth	608
Texas	21,476	Houston	1,180
Vernon	19,041	Nevada	837
Warren	19,534	Warrenton	429
Washington	20,380	Potosi	762
Wayne	11,543	Greenville	762
Webster	23,753	Marshfield	594
Worth	2,440	Grant City	266
Wright	16,758	Hartville	682
Independent City			
St. Louis	396,685		61

Montana

(56 counties, 145,556 sq. mi. land; pop., 799,065)

County	Pop.	County Seat or court house	Land area sq. mi.
Beaverhead	8,424	Dillon	5,542
Big Horn	11,337	Hardin	4,995
Blaine	6,728	Chinook	4,226
Broadwater	3,318	Townsend	1,191
Carbon	8,080	Red Lodge	2,048
Carter	1,503	Ekalaka	3,340
Cascade	77,691	Great Falls	2,698
Chouteau	5,452	Fort Benton	3,973
Custer	11,697	Miles City	3,783
Daniels	2,266	Scobey	1,426
Dawson	9,505	Glendive	2,373
Deer Lodge	10,356	Anaconda	737
Fallon	3,103	Baker	1,620
Fergus	12,083	Lewistown	4,339
Flathead	59,218	Kalispell	5,099
Gallatin	50,463	Bozeman	2,507
Garfield	1,589	Jordan	4,668
Glacier	12,121	Cut Bank	2,995
Golden Valley	912	Ryegete	1,175
Granite	2,548	Philipsburg	1,728
Hill	17,654	Havre	2,896
Jefferson	7,939	Boulder	1,657
Judith Basin	2,282	Stanford	1,870
Lake	21,041	Polson	1,494
Lewis & Clark	47,495	Helena	3,461
Liberty	2,295	Chester	1,430
Lincoln	17,481	Libby	3,613
McCone	2,276	Circle	2,643
Madison	5,989	Virginia City	3,587
Meagher	1,819	White Sulphur Springs	2,392
Mineral	3,315	Superior	1,220
Missoula	78,687	Missoula	2,598
Musselshell	4,106	Roundup	1,867
Park	14,562	Livingston	2,656
Petroleum	519	Winnett	1,654
Phillips	5,163	Malta	5,140
Pondera	6,433	Conrad	1,625
Powder River	2,090	Broadus	3,297
Powell	6,620	Deer Lodge	2,326
Prairie	1,383	Terry	1,737
Ravalli	25,010	Hamilton	2,394
Richland	10,716	Sidney	2,084
Roosevelt	10,999	Wolf Point	2,356
Rosebud	10,505	Forsyth	5,012
Sanders	8,669	Thompson Falls	2,762
Sheridan	4,732	Plentywood	1,677
Silver Bow	33,941	Butte	718
Stillwater	6,536	Columbus	1,795
Sweet Grass	3,154	Big Timber	1,855
Teton	6,271	Choteau	2,273
Toole	5,046	Shelby	1,911
Treasure	874	Hysham	979
Valley	8,239	Glasgow	4,921
Wheatland	2,246	Harlowton	1,423
Wibaux	1,191	Wibaux	889
Yellowstone	113,419	Billings	2,635

Nebraska

(93 counties, 76,644 sq. mi. land; pop., 1,578,385)

County	Pop.	County Seat or court house	Land area sq. mi.
Adams	29,625	Hastings	564
Antelope	7,965	Neligh	859
Arthur	462	Arthur	711
Banner	852	Harrisburg	747
Blaine	675	Brewster	714
Boone	6,667	Albion	687
Box Butte	13,130	Alliance	1,077
Boyd	2,835	Butte	532
Brown	3,657	Ainsworth	1,214
Buffalo	37,447	Kearney	945
Burt	7,868	Tekamah	486
Butler	8,601	David City	584
Cass	21,318	Plattsmouth	557
Cedar	10,131	Hartington	740
Chase	4,381	Imperial	894
Cherry	6,307	Valentine	5,961
Cheyenne	9,494	Sidney	1,196
Clay	7,123	Clay Center	574
Colfax	9,139	Schuyler	410
Cuming	10,117	West Point	575
Custer	12,270	Broken Bow	2,571
Dakota	16,742	Dakota City	258
Dawes	9,021	Chadron	1,397
Dawson	19,940	Lexington	982

County	Pop.	County Seat or court house	Land area sq. mi.
Deuel	2,237	Chappell	437
Dixon	6,143	Ponca	474
Dodge	34,500	Fremont	534
Douglas	416,444	Omaha	333
Dundy	2,582	Benkelman	920
Fillmore	7,103	Geneva	576
Franklin	3,938	Franklin	576
Frontier	3,101	Stockville	976
Furnas	5,553	Beaver City	721
Gage	22,794	Beatrice	858
Garden	2,460	Oshkosh	1,680
Garfield	2,141	Burwell	570
Gosper	1,928	Elwood	461
Grant	769	Hyannis	775
Greeley	3,006	Greeley	570
Hall	48,925	Grand Island	537
Hamilton	8,862	Aurora	543
Harlan	3,810	Alma	555
Hayes	1,222	Hayes Center	713
Hitchcock	3,750	Trenton	709
Holt	12,599	O'Neill	2,406
Hooker	793	Mullen	721
Howard	6,055	Saint Paul	564
Jefferson	8,759	Fairbury	575
Johnson	4,673	Tecumseh	377
Kearney	6,629	Minden	519
Keith	8,584	Ogallala	1,039
Keya Paha	1,029	Springview	769
Kimball	4,108	Kimball	952
Knox	9,534	Center	1,105
Lancaster	213,641	Lincoln	839
Lincoln	32,508	North Platte	2,525
Logan	878	Stapleton	571
Loup	683	Taylor	574
McPherson	546	Tryon	859
Madison	32,655	Madison	575
Merrick	8,042	Central City	478
Morrill	5,423	Bridgeport	1,405
Nance	4,275	Fullerton	439
Nemaha	7,980	Auburn	409
Nuckolls	5,786	Nelson	576
Otoe	14,252	Nebraska City	615
Pawnee	3,317	Pawnee City	433
Perkins	3,367	Grant	885
Phelps	9,715	Holdrege	540
Pierce	7,827	Pierce	575
Platte	29,820	Columbus	669
Polk	5,675	Osceola	437
Red Willow	11,705	McCook	718
Richardson	9,937	Falls City	553
Rock	2,019	Bassett	1,003
Saline	12,715	Wilber	575
Sarpy	102,583	Papillion	238
Saunders	18,285	Wahoo	753
Scotts Bluff	36,025	Gering	725
Seward	15,450	Seward	575
Sheridan	6,750	Rushville	2,453
Sherman	3,718	Loup City	564
Sioux	1,549	Harrison	2,070
Stanton	6,244	Stanton	431
Thayer	6,635	Hebron	575
Thomas	851	Thedford	713
Thurston	6,936	Pender	391
Valley	5,169	Ord	567
Washington	16,607	Blair	386
Wayne	9,364	Wayne	443
Webster	4,279	Red Cloud	575
Wheeler	948	Bartlett	575
York	14,428	York	576

Nevada

(16 cos., 1 ind. city, 109,894 sq. mi. land; pop., 1,201,833)

County	Pop.	County Seat or court house	Land area sq. mi.
Churchill	17,938	Fallon	4,913
Clark	741,459	Las Vegas	8,084
Douglas	27,637	Minden	751
Elko	33,530	Elko	17,181
Esmeralda	1,344	Goldfield	3,570
Eureka	1,547	Eureka	4,182
Humboldt	12,844	Winnemucca	9,704
Lander	6,266	Battle Mountain	5,621
Lincoln	3,775	Pioche	10,650
Lyon	20,001	Yerington	2,024
Mineral	6,475	Hawthorne	3,837
Nye	17,781	Tonopah	18,064
Pershing	4,336	Lovelock	6,031
Storey	2,526	Virginia City	262
Washoe	254,667	Reno	6,608
White Pine	9,264	Ely	8,905
Independent City			
Carson City	40,443	Carson City	153

New Hampshire

(10 counties, 8,993 sq. mi. land; pop., 1,109,252)

County	Pop.	County Seat or court house	Land area sq. mi.
Belknap	49,216	Laconia	404
Carroll	35,410	Ossipee	933
Cheshire	70,121	Keene	711
Coos	34,693	Lancaster	1,804
Grafton	74,929	Woodsville	1,719
Hillsborough	335,838	Nashua	876
Merrimack	120,240	Concord	936
Rockingham	245,845	Exeter	699
Strafford	104,233	Dover	370
Sullivan	38,592	Newport	540

New Jersey

(21 counties, 7,468 sq. mi. land; pop., 7,730,188)

County	Pop.	County Seat or court house	Land area sq. mi.
Atlantic	224,327	Mays Landing	568
Bergen	825,380	Hackensack	237
Burlington	395,066	Mount Holly	808
Camden	502,824	Camden	223
Cape May	95,089	Cape May Court House	263
Cumberland	138,053	Bridgeton	498
Essex	778,206	Newark	127
Gloucester	230,082	Woodbury	327
Hudson	553,099	Jersey City	46
Hunterdon	107,776	Flemington	426
Mercer	325,824	Trenton	227
Middlesex	671,780	New Brunswick	316
Monmouth	553,124	Freehold	472
Morris	421,353	Morristown	470
Ocean	433,203	Toms River	641
Passaic	453,060	Paterson	187
Salem	65,294	Salem	338
Somerset	240,279	Somerville	305
Sussex	130,943	Newton	526
Union	493,819	Elizabeth	103
Warren	91,607	Belvidere	359

New Mexico

(33 counties, 121,335 sq. mi. land; pop., 1,515,069)

County	Pop.	County Seat or court house	Land area sq. mi.
Bernalillo	480,577	Albuquerque	1,169
Catron	2,563	Reserve	6,929
Chaves	57,849	Roswell	6,066
Cibola	23,794	Grants	4,468
Colfax	12,925	Raton	3,762
Curry	42,207	Clovis	1,408
De Baca	2,252	Fort Sumner	2,323
Dona Ana	135,510	Las Cruces	3,819
Eddy	48,605	Carlsbad	4,184
Grant	27,676	Silver City	3,969
Guadalupe	4,156	Santa Rosa	3,032
Harding	987	Mosquero	2,122
Hidalgo	5,958	Lordsburg	3,445
Lea	55,765	Lovington	4,389
Lincoln	12,219	Carrizozo	4,832
Los Alamos	18,115	Los Alamos	109
Luna	18,110	Deming	2,965
McKinley	60,686	Gallup	5,442
Mora	4,264	Mora	1,930
Otero	51,928	Alamogordo	6,626
Quay	10,823	Tucumcari	2,874
Rio Arriba	34,365	Tierra Amarilla	5,856
Roosevelt	16,702	Portales	2,453
Sandoval	63,319	Bernalillo	3,707
San Juan	91,605	Aztec	5,521
San Miguel	25,743	Las Vegas	4,709
Santa Fe	98,928	Santa Fe	1,905
Sierra	9,912	Truth or Consequences	4,178
Socorro	14,764	Socorro	6,625
Taos	23,118	Taos	2,204
Torrance	10,285	Estancia	3,335
Union	4,124	Clayton	3,830
Valencia	45,235	Los Lunas	5,616

New York

(62 counties, 47,377 sq. mi. land; pop., 17,990,455)

County	Pop.	County Seat or court house	Land area sq. mi.
Albany	292,594	Albany	524
Allegany	50,470	Belmont	1,031
Bronx	1,203,789	Bronx	42
Broome	212,160	Binghamton	707
Cattaraugus	84,234	Little Valley	1,310
Cayuga	82,313	Auburn	693
Chautauqua	141,895	Mayville	1,062
Chemung	95,195	Elmira	408

County	Pop.	County Seat or court house	Land area sq. mi.
Chenango	51,768	Norwich	894
Clinton	85,969	Plattsburgh	1,039
Columbia	62,982	Hudson	636
Cortland	48,963	Cortland	500
Delaware	47,225	Delhi	1,446
Dutchess	259,462	Poughkeepsie	802
Erie	968,532	Buffalo	1,045
Essex	37,152	Elizabethtown	1,797
Franklin	46,540	Malone	1,632
Fulton	54,191	Johnstown	496
Genesee	60,060	Batavia	494
Greene	44,739	Catskill	648
Hamilton	5,279	Lake Pleasant	1,721
Herkimer	65,797	Herkimer	1,412
Jefferson	110,943	Watertown	1,272
Kings	2,300,664	Brooklyn	71
Lewis	26,796	Lowville	1,276
Livingston	62,372	Geneseo	632
Madison	69,120	Wampsville	656
Monroe	713,968	Rochester	659
Montgomery	51,981	Fonda	405
Nassau	1,287,348	Mineola	287
New York	1,487,536	New York	28
Niagara	220,756	Lockport	523
Oneida	250,836	Utica	1,213
Onondaga	468,973	Syracuse	780
Ontario	95,101	Canandaigua	644
Orange	307,647	Goshen	816
Orleans	41,846	Albion	391
Oswego	121,771	Oswego	953
Otsego	60,517	Cooperstown	1,003
Putnam	83,941	Carmel	232
Queens	1,951,598	Jamaica	109
Rensselaer	154,429	Troy	654
Richmond	378,977	Saint George	59
Rockland	265,475	New City	174
St. Lawrence	111,974	Canton	2,686
Saratoga	181,276	Ballston Spa	812
Schenectady	149,285	Schenectady	206
Schoharie	31,859	Schoharie	622
Schuyler	18,662	Watkins Glen	329
Seneca	33,683	Ovid & Waterloo	325
Steuben	99,088	Bath	1,393
Suffolk	1,321,864	Riverhead	911
Sullivan	69,277	Monticello	970
Tioga	52,337	Owego	519
Tompkins	94,097	Ithaca	476
Ulster	165,304	Kingston	1,127
Warren	59,209	Queensbury	870
Washington	59,330	Hudson Falls	836
Wayne	89,123	Lyons	604
Westchester	874,866	White Plains	433
Wyoming	42,507	Warsaw	593
Yates	22,810	Penn Yan	338

North Carolina

(100 counties, 48,843 sq. mi. land; pop., 6,628,637)

County	Pop.	County Seat or court house	Land area sq. mi.
Alamance	108,213	Graham	433
Alexander	27,544	Taylorsville	259
Alleghany	9,590	Sparta	235
Anson	23,474	Wadesboro	533
Ashe	22,209	Jefferson	426
Avery	14,867	Newland	247
Beaufort	42,283	Washington	826
Bertie	20,388	Windsor	701
Bladen	28,663	Elizabethtown	879
Brunswick	50,985	Bolivia	860
Buncombe	174,821	Asheville	659
Burke	75,744	Morganton	504
Cabarrus	98,935	Concord	364
Caldwell	70,709	Lenoir	471
Camden	5,904	Camden	240
Carteret	52,556	Beaufort	526
Caswell	20,693	Yanceyville	428
Catawba	118,412	Newton	396
Chatham	38,759	Pittsboro	708
Cherokee	20,170	Murphy	452
Chowan	13,506	Edenton	182
Clay	7,155	Hayesville	214
Cleveland	84,714	Shelby	468
Columbus	49,587	Whiteville	938
Craven	81,613	New Bern	701
Cumberland	274,566	Fayetteville	657
Currituck	13,736	Currituck	256
Dare	22,746	Manteo	391
Davidson	126,677	Lexington	548
Davie	27,859	Mocksville	267
Duplin	39,995	Kenansville	819
Durham	181,835	Durham	298
Edgecombe	56,558	Tarboro	506
Forsyth	265,878	Winston-Salem	412
Franklin	36,414	Louisburg	494
Gaston	175,093	Gastonia	357
Gates	9,305	Gatesville	338
Graham	7,196	Robbinsville	289
Granville	38,345	Oxford	534
Greene	15,384	Snow Hill	266
Guilford	347,420	Greensboro	651
Halifax	55,516	Halifax	724
Harnett	67,822	Lillington	601
Haywood	46,942	Waynesville	555
Henderson	69,285	Hendersonville	374
Hertford	22,523	Winton	356
Hoke	22,856	Raeford	391
Hyde	5,411	Swan Quarter	624
Iredell	92,931	Statesville	574
Jackson	26,846	Sylva	491
Johnston	81,306	Smithfield	795
Jones	9,414	Trenton	470
Lee	41,374	Sanford	259
Lenoir	57,274	Kinston	402
Lincoln	50,319	Lincolnton	298
McDowell	35,681	Marion	437
Macon	23,499	Franklin	517
Madison	16,953	Marshall	451
Martin	25,078	Williamston	461
Mecklenburg	511,433	Charlotte	528
Mitchell	14,433	Bakersville	222
Montgomery	23,346	Troy	490
Moore	59,013	Carthage	701
Nash	76,677	Nashville	540
New Hanover	120,284	Wilmington	185
Northampton	20,798	Jackson	538
Onslow	149,838	Jacksonville	763
Orange	93,851	Hillsborough	400
Pamlico	11,372	Bayboro	341
Pasquotank	31,298	Elizabeth City	228
Pender	28,885	Burgaw	875
Perquimans	10,447	Hertford	246
Person	30,180	Roxboro	398
Pitt	107,924	Greenville	657
Polk	14,416	Columbus	238
Randolph	106,546	Asheboro	789
Richmond	44,518	Rockingham	477
Robeson	105,179	Lumberton	949
Rockingham	86,064	Wentworth	569
Rowan	110,605	Salisbury	519
Rutherford	56,918	Rutherfordton	568
Sampson	47,297	Clinton	947
Scotland	33,754	Laurinburg	319
Stanly	51,765	Albemarle	396
Stokes	37,223	Danbury	452
Surry	61,704	Dobson	539
Swain	11,268	Bryson City	526
Transylvania	25,520	Brevard	378
Tyrrell	3,856	Columbia	407
Union	84,211	Monroe	639
Vance	38,892	Henderson	249
Wake	423,380	Raleigh	854
Warren	17,265	Warrenton	427
Washington	13,997	Plymouth	332
Watauga	36,952	Boone	314
Wayne	104,666	Goldsboro	554
Wilkes	59,393	Wilkesboro	752
Wilson	66,061	Wilson	374
Yadkin	30,488	Yadkinville	336
Yancey	15,419	Burnsville	314

North Dakota

(53 counties, 69,300 sq. mi. land; pop., 638,800)

County	Pop.	County Seat or court house	Land area sq. mi.
Adams	3,174	Hettinger	988
Barnes	12,545	Valley City	1,498
Benson	7,198	Minnewaukan	1,412
Billings	1,108	Medora	1,152
Bottineau	8,011	Bottineau	1,668
Bowman	3,596	Bowman	1,162
Burke	3,002	Bowbells	1,118
Burleigh	60,131	Bismarck	1,618
Cass	102,874	Fargo	1,767
Cavalier	6,064	Langdon	1,507
Dickey	6,107	Ellendale	1,139
Divide	2,899	Crosby	1,288
Dunn	4,005	Manning	1,993
Eddy	2,951	New Rockford	634
Emmons	4,830	Linton	1,499
Foster	3,983	Carrington	640
Golden Valley	2,108	Beach	1,003
Grand Forks	70,683	Grand Forks	1,440
Grant	3,549	Carson	1,660
Griggs	3,303	Cooperstown	708
Hettinger	3,445	Mott	1,133
Kidder	3,332	Steele	1,362
La Moure	5,383	La Moure	1,150
Logan	2,847	Napoleon	1,000
McHenry	6,528	Towner	1,887
McIntosh	4,021	Ashley	984

County	Pop.	County Seat or court house	Land area sq. mi.
McKenzie	6,383	Watford City	2,754
McLean	10,457	Washburn	2,065
Mercer	9,808	Stanton	1,044
Morton	23,700	Mandan	1,921
Mountrail	7,021	Stanley	1,837
Nelson	4,410	Lakota	991
Oliver	2,381	Center	723
Pembina	9,238	Cavalier	1,120
Pierce	5,052	Rugby	1,037
Ramsey	12,681	Devils Lake	1,241
Ransom	5,921	Lisbon	862
Renville	3,160	Mohall	874
Richland	18,148	Wahpeton	1,436
Rolette	12,772	Rolla	914
Sargent	4,549	Forman	857
Sheridan	2,148	McClusky	989
Sioux	3,761	Fort Yates	1,099
Slope	907	Amidon	1,219
Stark	22,832	Dickinson	1,338
Steele	2,420	Finley	713
Stutsman	22,241	Jamestown	2,263
Towner	3,627	Cando	1,035
Traill	8,752	Hillsboro	861
Walsh	13,840	Grafton	1,290
Ward	57,921	Minot	2,041
Wells	5,864	Fessenden	1,288
Williams	21,129	Williston	2,074

Ohio

(88 counties, 41,004 sq. mi. land; pop., 10,847,115)

County	Pop.	County Seat or court house	Land area sq. mi.
Adams	25,371	West Union	586
Allen	109,755	Lima	405
Ashland	47,507	Ashland	424
Ashtabula	99,821	Jefferson	703
Athens	59,549	Athens	508
Auglaize	44,585	Wapakoneta	398
Belmont	71,074	Saint Clairsville	537
Brown	34,966	Georgetown	493
Butler	291,479	Hamilton	470
Carroll	26,521	Carrollton	393
Champaign	36,019	Urbana	429
Clark	147,548	Springfield	398
Clermont	150,187	Batavia	456
Clinton	35,415	Wilmington	410
Columbiana	108,276	Lisbon	534
Coshocton	35,427	Coshocton	566
Crawford	47,870	Bucyrus	403
Cuyahoga	1,412,140	Cleveland	459
Darke	53,619	Greenville	600
Defiance	39,350	Defiance	414
Delaware	66,929	Delaware	443
Erie	76,779	Sandusky	264
Fairfield	103,461	Lancaster	506
Fayette	27,466	Washington C. H.	405
Franklin	961,437	Columbus	543
Fulton	38,498	Wauseon	407
Gallia	30,954	Gallipolis	471
Geauga	81,129	Chardon	408
Greene	136,731	Xenia	416
Guernsey	39,024	Cambridge	522
Hamilton	866,228	Cincinnati	412
Hancock	65,536	Findlay	532
Hardin	31,111	Kenton	471
Harrison	16,085	Cadiz	400
Henry	29,108	Napoleon	415
Highland	35,728	Hillsboro	553
Hocking	25,533	Logan	423
Holmes	32,849	Millersburg	424
Huron	56,240	Norwalk	494
Jackson	30,230	Jackson	420
Jefferson	80,298	Steubenville	410
Knox	47,473	Mount Vernon	529
Lake	215,499	Painesville	231
Lawrence	61,834	Ironton	457
Licking	128,300	Newark	686
Logan	42,310	Bellefontaine	458
Lorain	271,126	Elyria	495
Lucas	462,361	Toledo	341
Madison	37,068	London	467
Mahoning	264,806	Youngstown	417
Marion	64,274	Marion	403
Medina	122,354	Medina	422
Meigs	22,987	Pomeroy	432
Mercer	39,443	Celina	457
Miami	93,182	Troy	410
Monroe	15,497	Woodsfield	457
Montgomery	573,809	Dayton	458
Morgan	14,194	McConnelsville	420
Morrow	27,749	Mount Gilead	406
Muskingum	82,068	Zanesville	654
Noble	11,336	Caldwell	399
Ottawa	40,029	Port Clinton	253
Paulding	20,488	Paulding	419
Perry	31,557	New Lexington	412
Pickaway	48,255	Circleville	503
Pike	24,249	Waverly	443
Portage	142,585	Ravenna	493
Preble	40,113	Eaton	426
Putnam	33,819	Ottawa	484
Richland	126,137	Mansfield	497
Ross	69,330	Chillicothe	692
Sandusky	61,963	Fremont	409
Scioto	80,327	Portsmouth	613
Seneca	59,733	Tiffin	553
Shelby	44,915	Sidney	409
Stark	367,585	Canton	574
Summit	514,990	Akron	412
Trumbull	227,813	Warren	612
Tuscarawas	84,090	New Philadelphia	570
Union	31,969	Marysville	437
Van Wert	30,464	Van Wert	410
Vinton	11,098	McArthur	414
Warren	113,909	Lebanon	403
Washington	62,254	Marietta	640
Wayne	101,461	Wooster	557
Williams	36,956	Bryan	422
Wood	113,269	Bowling Green	619
Wyandot	22,254	Upper Sandusky	406

Oklahoma

(77 counties, 68,655 sq. mi. land; pop., 3,145,585)

County	Pop.	County Seat or court house	Land area sq. mi.
Adair	18,421	Stillwell	577
Alfalfa	6,416	Cherokee	864
Atoka	12,778	Atoka	980
Beaver	6,023	Beaver	1,808
Beckham	18,812	Sayre	904
Blaine	11,470	Watonga	920
Bryan	32,089	Durant	902
Caddo	29,550	Anadarko	1,286
Canadian	74,409	El Reno	901
Carter	42,919	Ardmore	828
Cherokee	34,049	Tahlequah	748
Choctaw	15,302	Hugo	762
Cimarron	3,301	Boise City	1,842
Cleveland	174,253	Norman	529
Coal	5,780	Coalgate	520
Comanche	111,486	Lawton	1,076
Cotton	6,651	Walters	656
Craig	14,104	Vinita	763
Creek	60,915	Sapulpa	930
Custer	26,897	Arapaho	981
Delaware	28,070	Jay	720
Dewey	5,551	Taloga	1,007
Ellis	4,497	Arnett	1,232
Garfield	56,735	Enid	1,060
Garvin	26,605	Pauls Valley	813
Grady	41,747	Chickasha	1,106
Grant	5,689	Medford	1,004
Greer	6,559	Mangum	638
Harmon	3,793	Hollis	537
Harper	4,063	Buffalo	1,039
Haskell	10,940	Stigler	570
Hughes	13,023	Holdenville	806
Jackson	28,764	Altus	817
Jefferson	7,010	Waurika	769
Johnston	10,032	Tishomingo	639
Kay	48,056	Newkirk	921
Kingfisher	13,212	Kingfisher	906
Kiowa	11,347	Hobart	1,019
Latimer	10,333	Wilburton	728
Le Flore	43,270	Poteau	1,585
Lincoln	29,216	Chandler	964
Logan	29,011	Guthrie	748
Love	8,157	Marietta	519
McClain	22,795	Purcell	582
McCurtain	33,433	Idabel	1,826
McIntosh	16,779	Eufaula	599
Major	8,055	Fairview	958
Marshall	10,829	Madill	372
Mayes	33,366	Pryor	644
Murray	12,042	Sulphur	420
Muskogee	68,078	Muskogee	815
Noble	11,045	Perry	736
Nowata	9,992	Nowata	540
Okfuskee	11,551	Okemah	628
Oklahoma	599,611	Oklahoma City	708
Okmulgee	36,490	Okmulgee	698
Osage	41,645	Pawhuska	2,265
Ottawa	30,561	Miami	465
Pawnee	15,575	Pawnee	551
Payne	61,507	Stillwater	691
Pittsburg	40,581	McAlester	1,251
Pontotoc	34,119	Ada	717
Pottawatomie	58,760	Shawnee	783
Pushmataha	10,997	Antlers	1,417
Roger Mills	4,147	Cheyenne	1,146

County	Pop.	County Seat or court house	Land area sq. mi.
Rogers	55,170	Claremore	683
Seminole	25,412	Wewoka	639
Sequoyah	33,828	Sallisaw	678
Stephens	42,299	Duncan	884
Texas	16,419	Guymon	2,040
Tillman	10,384	Frederick	904
Tulsa	503,341	Tulsa	572
Wagoner	47,883	Wagoner	559
Washington	48,066	Bartlesville	423
Washita	11,441	Cordell	1,006
Woods	9,103	Alva	1,291
Woodward	18,976	Woodward	1,242

Oregon

(36 counties, 96,184 sq. mi. land; pop., 2,842,321)

Baker	15,317	Baker City	3,089
Benton	70,811	Corvallis	679
Clackamas	278,850	Oregon City	1,870
Clatsop	33,301	Astoria	873
Columbia	37,557	Saint Helens	687
Coos	60,273	Coquille	1,629
Crook	14,111	Prineville	2,991
Curry	19,327	Gold Beach	1,648
Deschutes	74,958	Bend	3,055
Douglas	94,649	Roseburg	5,071
Gilliam	1,717	Condon	1,223
Grant	7,853	Canyon City	4,525
Harney	7,060	Burns	10,228
Hood River	16,903	Hood River	533
Jackson	146,389	Medford	2,801
Jefferson	13,676	Madras	1,791
Josephine	62,649	Grants Pass	1,640
Klamath	57,702	Klamath Falls	6,135
Lake	7,186	Lakeview	8,359
Lane	282,912	Eugene	4,620
Lincoln	38,889	Newport	992
Linn	91,227	Albany	2,296
Malheur	26,038	Vale	9,926
Marion	228,483	Salem	1,194
Morrow	7,625	Heppner	2,094
Multnomah	583,887	Portland	465
Polk	49,541	Dallas	741
Sherman	1,918	Moro	831
Tillamook	21,570	Tillamook	1,125
Umatilla	59,249	Pendleton	3,218
Union	23,598	La Grande	2,038
Wallowa	6,911	Enterprise	3,150
Wasco	21,683	The Dalles	2,396
Washington	311,554	Hillsboro	727
Wheeler	1,396	Fossil	1,713
Yamhill	65,551	McMinnville	718

Pennsylvania

(67 counties, 44,888 sq. mi. land; pop., 11,881,643)

Adams	78,274	Gettysburg	521
Allegheny	1,336,449	Pittsburgh	727
Armstrong	73,478	Kittanning	646
Beaver	186,093	Beaver	436
Bedford	47,919	Bedford	1,017
Berks	336,523	Reading	861
Blair	130,542	Hollidaysburg	527
Bradford	60,967	Towanda	1,152
Bucks	541,174	Doylestown	610
Butler	152,013	Butler	789
Cambria	163,029	Ebensburg	691
Cameron	5,913	Emporium	398
Carbon	56,846	Jim Thorpe	384
Centre	123,786	Bellefonte	1,106
Chester	376,396	West Chester	758
Clarion	41,699	Clarion	607
Clearfield	78,097	Clearfield	1,149
Clinton	37,182	Lock Haven	891
Columbia	63,202	Bloomsburg	486
Crawford	86,169	Meadville	1,011
Cumberland	195,257	Carlisle	547
Dauphin	237,813	Harrisburg	528
Delaware	547,651	Media	184
Elk	34,878	Ridgeway	830
Erie	275,572	Erie	804
Fayette	145,351	Uniontown	794
Forest	4,802	Tionesta	428
Franklin	121,082	Chambersburg	774
Fulton	13,837	McConnellsburg	438
Greene	39,550	Waynesburg	577
Huntingdon	44,164	Huntingdon	877
Indiana	89,994	Indiana	829
Jefferson	46,083	Brookville	657
Juniata	20,625	Mifflintown	392
Lackawanna	219,039	Scranton	461
Lancaster	422,822	Lancaster	952
Lawrence	96,246	New Castle	363
Lebanon	113,744	Lebanon	363
Lehigh	291,130	Allentown	348
Luzerne	328,149	Wilkes-Barre	891
Lycoming	118,710	Williamsport	1,237
McKean	47,131	Smethport	979
Mercer	121,003	Mercer	672
Mifflin	46,197	Lewistown	413
Monroe	95,709	Stroudsburg	609
Montgomery	678,111	Norristown	486
Montour	17,735	Danville	131
Northampton	247,105	Easton	376
Northumberland	96,771	Sunbury	461
Perry	41,172	New Bloomfield	557
Philadelphia	1,585,577	Philadelphia	136
Pike	27,966	Milford	550
Potter	16,717	Coudersport	1,081
Schuylkill	152,585	Pottsville	782
Snyder	36,680	Middleburg	329
Somerset	78,218	Somerset	1,073
Sullivan	6,104	Laporte	451
Susquehanna	40,380	Montrose	826
Tioga	41,126	Wellsboro	1,131
Union	36,176	Lewisburg	317
Venango	59,381	Franklin	679
Warren	45,050	Warren	885
Washington	204,584	Washington	958
Wayne	39,944	Honesdale	731
Westmoreland	370,321	Greensburg	1,033
Wyoming	28,076	Tunkhannock	399
York	339,574	York	906

Rhode Island

(5 counties, 1,055 sq. mi. land; pop., 1,003,464)

Bristol	48,859	Bristol	26
Kent	161,135	East Greenwich	172
Newport	87,194	Newport	107
Providence	596,270	Providence	416
Washington	110,006	West Kingston	333

South Carolina

(46 counties, 30,203 sq. mi. land; pop., 3,486,703)

Abbeville	23,862	Abbeville	508
Aiken	120,940	Aiken	1,092
Allendale	11,722	Allendale	413
Anderson	145,196	Anderson	718
Bamberg	16,902	Bamberg	395
Barnwell	20,293	Barnwell	558
Beaufort	86,425	Beaufort	579
Berkeley	128,776	Moncks Corner	1,108
Calhoun	12,753	Saint Matthews	380
Charleston	295,039	Charleston	938
Cherokee	44,506	Gaffney	396
Chester	32,170	Chester	580
Chesterfield	38,577	Chesterfield	802
Clarendon	28,450	Manning	602
Colleton	34,377	Walterboro	1,052
Darlington	61,851	Darlington	563
Dillon	29,114	Dillon	406
Dorchester	83,060	Saint George	575
Edgefield	18,375	Edgefield	490
Fairfield	22,295	Winnsboro	685
Florence	114,344	Florence	804
Georgetown	46,302	Georgetown	822
Greenville	320,167	Greenville	795
Greenwood	59,567	Greenwood	451
Hampton	18,191	Hampton	561
Horry	144,053	Conway	1,143
Jasper	15,487	Ridgeland	655
Kershaw	43,599	Camden	723
Lancaster	54,516	Lancaster	552
Laurens	58,092	Laurens	712
Lee	18,437	Bishopville	411
Lexington	167,611	Lexington	707
McCormick	8,868	McCormick	350
Marion	33,899	Marion	493
Marlboro	29,361	Bennettsville	483
Newberry	33,172	Newberry	634
Oconee	57,494	Walhalla	629
Orangeburg	84,803	Orangeburg	1,111
Pickens	93,894	Pickens	499
Richland	285,720	Columbia	762
Saluda	16,357	Saluda	456
Spartanburg	226,800	Spartanburg	814
Sumter	102,637	Sumter	665
Union	30,337	Union	515
Williamsburg	36,815	Kingstree	934
York	131,497	York	685

South Dakota

(67 counties, 75,952 sq. mi. land; pop., 696,004)

County	Pop.	County Seat or court house	Land area sq. mi.
Aurora	3,135	Plankinton	707
Beadle	18,253	Huron	1,259
Bennett	3,206	Martin	1,182
Bon Homme	7,089	Tyndall	552
Brookings	25,207	Brookings	795
Brown	35,580	Aberdeen	1,722
Brule	5,485	Chamberlain	815
Buffalo	1,759	Gannvalley	475
Butte	7,914	Belle Fourche	2,251
Campbell	1,965	Mound City	732
Charles Mix	9,131	Lake Andes	1,090
Clark	4,403	Clark	953
Clay	13,186	Vermillion	409
Codington	22,698	Watertown	694
Corson	4,195	McIntosh	2,467
Custer	6,179	Custer	1,559
Davison	17,503	Mitchell	436
Day	6,978	Webster	1,022
Deuel	4,522	Clear Lake	631
Dewey	5,523	Timber Lake	2,310
Douglas	3,746	Armour	434
Edmunds	4,356	Ipswich	1,149
Fall River	7,353	Hot Springs	4,742
Faulk	2,744	Faulkton	1,004
Grant	8,372	Milbank	681
Gregory	5,359	Burke	1,013
Haakon	2,624	Philip	1,822
Hamlin	4,974	Hayti	512
Hand	4,272	Miller	1,437
Hanson	2,994	Alexandria	433
Harding	1,669	Buffalo	2,678
Hughes	14,817	Pierre	757
Hutchinson	8,262	Olivet	816
Hyde	1,696	Highmore	860
Jackson	2,811	Kadoka	1,872
Jerauld	2,425	Wessington Spgs	530
Jones	1,324	Murdo	971
Kingsbury	5,925	De Smet	824
Lake	10,550	Madison	560
Lawrence	20,655	Deadwood	800
Lincoln	15,427	Canton	578
Lyman	3,638	Kennebec	1,679
McCook	5,688	Salem	576
McPherson	3,228	Leola	1,148
Marshall	4,844	Britton	848
Meade	21,878	Sturgis	3,481
Mellette	2,137	White River	1,311
Miner	3,272	Howard	570
Minnehaha	123,809	Sioux Falls	810
Moody	6,507	Flandreau	520
Pennington	81,343	Rapid City	2,783
Perkins	3,932	Bison	2,884
Potter	3,190	Gettysburg	869
Roberts	9,914	Sisseton	1,102
Sanborn	2,833	Woonsocket	569
Shannon	9,902	(Attached to Fall River)	2,094
Spink	7,981	Redfield	1,505
Stanley	2,453	Fort Pierre	1,431
Sully	1,589	Onida	972
Todd	8,352	(Attached to Tripp)	1,388
Tripp	6,924	Winner	1,618
Turner	8,576	Parker	617
Union	10,189	Elk Point	453
Walworth	6,087	Selby	707
Yankton	19,252	Yankton	518
Ziebach	2,220	Dupree	1,969

Tennessee

(95 counties, 41,155 sq. mi. land; pop., 4,877,185)

County	Pop.	County Seat or court house	Land area sq. mi.
Anderson	68,250	Clinton	339
Bedford	30,411	Shelbyville	475
Benton	14,524	Camden	392
Bledsoe	9,669	Pikeville	407
Blount	85,969	Maryville	558
Bradley	73,712	Cleveland	327
Campbell	35,079	Jacksboro	470
Cannon	10,467	Woodbury	266
Carroll	27,514	Huntingdon	600
Carter	51,505	Elizabethton	341
Cheatham	27,140	Ashland City	304
Chester	12,819	Henderson	289
Claiborne	26,137	Tazewell	432
Clay	7,238	Celina	227
Cocke	29,141	Newport	432
Coffee	40,339	Manchester	428
Crockett	13,378	Alamo	266
Cumberland	34,736	Crossville	682
Davidson	510,784	Nashville	501
Decatur	10,472	Decaturville	330
De Kalb	14,360	Smithville	291
Dickson	35,061	Charlotte	491
Dyer	34,854	Dyersburg	520
Fayette	25,559	Somerville	705
Fentress	14,669	Jamestown	498
Franklin	34,725	Winchester	543
Gibson	46,315	Trenton	602
Giles	25,741	Pulaski	610
Grainger	17,095	Rutledge	273
Greene	55,853	Greeneville	619
Grundy	13,362	Altamont	361
Hamblen	50,480	Morristown	156
Hamilton	285,536	Chattanooga	539
Hancock	6,739	Sneedville	223
Hardeman	23,377	Bolivar	670
Hardin	22,633	Savannah	578
Hawkins	44,565	Rogersville	486
Haywood	19,437	Brownsville	534
Henderson	21,844	Lexington	520
Henry	27,888	Paris	560
Hickman	16,754	Centerville	610
Houston	7,018	Erin	200
Humphreys	15,795	Waverly	528
Jackson	9,297	Gainesboro	308
Jefferson	33,016	Dandridge	265
Johnson	13,766	Mountain City	297
Knox	335,749	Knoxville	506
Lake	7,129	Tiptonville	169
Lauderdale	23,491	Ripley	474
Lawrence	35,303	Lawrenceburg	617
Lewis	9,247	Hohenwald	282
Lincoln	28,157	Fayetteville	571
Loudon	31,255	Loudon	235
McMinn	42,383	Athens	429
McNairy	22,422	Selmer	562
Macon	15,906	Lafayette	307
Madison	77,982	Jackson	558
Marion	24,860	Jasper	512
Marshall	21,539	Lewisburg	376
Maury	54,812	Columbia	616
Meigs	8,033	Decatur	189
Monroe	30,541	Madisonville	648
Montgomery	100,498	Clarksville	539
Moore	4,721	Lynchburg	129
Morgan	17,300	Wartburg	523
Obion	31,717	Union City	550
Overton	17,636	Livingston	433
Perry	6,612	Linden	412
Pickett	4,548	Byrdstown	159
Polk	13,643	Benton	438
Putnam	51,373	Cookeville	399
Rhea	24,344	Dayton	309
Roane	47,227	Kingston	357
Robertson	41,494	Springfield	476
Rutherford	118,570	Murfreesboro	606
Scott	18,358	Huntsville	528
Sequatchie	8,863	Dunlap	266
Sevier	51,043	Sevierville	590
Shelby	826,330	Memphis	772
Smith	14,143	Carthage	313
Stewart	9,479	Dover	454
Sullivan	143,596	Blountville	415
Sumner	103,281	Gallatin	529
Tipton	37,568	Covington	454
Trousdale	5,920	Hartsville	114
Unicoi	16,549	Erwin	186
Union	13,694	Maynardville	218
Van Buren	4,846	Spencer	273
Warren	32,992	McMinnville	431
Washington	92,315	Jonesboro	326
Wayne	13,935	Waynesboro	734
Weakley	31,972	Dresden	581
White	20,090	Sparta	373
Williamson	81,021	Franklin	584
Wilson	67,675	Lebanon	570

Texas

(254 counties, 262,017 sq. mi. land; pop., 16,986,510)

County	Pop.	County Seat or court house	Land area sq. mi.
Anderson	48,024	Palestine	1,077
Andrews	14,338	Andrews	1,501
Angelina	69,884	Lufkin	807
Aransas	17,892	Rockport	280
Archer	7,973	Archer City	907
Armstrong	2,021	Claude	909
Atascosa	30,533	Jourdanton	1,218
Austin	19,832	Bellville	656
Bailey	7,064	Muleshoe	826
Bandera	10,562	Bandera	793
Bastrop	38,263	Bastrop	895
Baylor	4,385	Seymour	862
Bee	25,135	Beeville	880

County	Pop.	County Seat or court house	Land area sq. mi.
Bell	191,088	Belton	1,055
Bexar	1,185,394	San Antonio	1,248
Blanco	5,972	Johnson City	714
Borden	799	Gail	900
Bosque	15,125	Meridian	989
Bowie	81,665	Boston	891
Brazoria	191,707	Angleton	1,407
Brazos	121,862	Bryan	589
Brewster	8,681	Alpine	6,169
Briscoe	1,971	Silverton	887
Brooks	8,204	Falfurrias	942
Brown	34,371	Brownwood	936
Burleson	13,625	Caldwell	669
Burnet	22,677	Burnet	994
Caldwell	26,392	Lockhart	546
Calhoun	19,053	Port Lavaca	540
Callahan	11,859	Baird	899
Cameron	260,120	Brownsville	906
Camp	9,904	Pittsburg	203
Carson	6,576	Panhandle	924
Cass	29,982	Linden	937
Castro	9,070	Dimmitt	899
Chambers	20,088	Anahuac	616
Cherokee	41,049	Rusk	1,052
Childress	5,953	Childress	707
Clay	10,024	Henrietta	1,086
Cochran	4,377	Morton	775
Coke	3,424	Robert Lee	908
Coleman	9,710	Coleman	1,277
Collin	264,036	McKinney	851
Collingsworth	3,573	Wellington	909
Colorado	18,383	Columbus	965
Comal	51,832	New Braunfels	555
Comanche	13,381	Comanche	930
Concho	3,044	Paint Rock	992
Cooke	30,777	Gainesville	893
Coryell	64,213	Gatesville	1,057
Cottle	2,247	Paducah	895
Crane	4,652	Crane	782
Crockett	4,078	Ozona	2,806
Crosby	7,304	Crosbyton	899
Culberson	3,407	Van Horn	3,815
Dallam	5,461	Dalhart	1,505
Dallas	1,852,810	Dallas	880
Dawson	14,349	Lamesa	903
Deaf Smith	19,153	Hereford	1,497
Delta	4,857	Cooper	278
Denton	273,525	Denton	911
Dewitt	18,840	Cuero	910
Dickens	2,571	Dickens	907
Dimmit	10,433	Carrizo Springs	1,307
Donley	3,696	Clarendon	929
Duval	12,918	San Diego	1,795
Eastland	18,488	Eastland	924
Ector	118,934	Odessa	903
Edwards	2,266	Rocksprings	2,121
Ellis	85,167	Waxahachie	939
El Paso	591,610	El Paso	1,014
Erath	27,991	Stephenville	1,080
Falls	17,712	Marlin	770
Fannin	24,804	Bonham	895
Fayette	20,095	La Grange	950
Fisher	4,842	Roby	897
Floyd	8,497	Floydada	992
Foard	1,794	Crowell	703
Fort Bend	225,421	Richmond	876
Franklin	7,802	Mount Vernon	294
Freestone	15,818	Fairfield	888
Frio	13,472	Pearsall	1,133
Gaines	14,123	Seminole	1,504
Galveston	217,399	Galveston	399
Garza	5,143	Post	895
Gillespie	17,204	Fredericksburg	1,061
Glasscock	1,447	Garden City	900
Goliad	5,980	Goliad	859
Gonzales	17,205	Gonzales	1,068
Gray	23,967	Pampa	921
Grayson	95,021	Sherman	934
Gregg	104,948	Longview	273
Grimes	18,828	Anderson	799
Guadalupe	64,873	Seguin	713
Hale	34,671	Plainview	1,005
Hall	3,905	Memphis	877
Hamilton	7,733	Hamilton	836
Hansford	5,848	Spearman	921
Hardeman	5,283	Quanah	688
Hardin	41,320	Kountze	898
Harris	2,818,199	Houston	1,734
Harrison	57,483	Marshall	908
Hartley	3,634	Channing	1,462
Haskell	6,820	Haskell	901
Hays	65,614	San Marcos	678
Hemphill	3,720	Canadian	903
Henderson	58,543	Athens	888
Hidalgo	383,545	Edinburg	1,569
Hill	27,146	Hillsboro	968
Hockley	24,199	Levelland	908
Hood	28,981	Granbury	425
Hopkins	28,833	Sulphur Springs	789
Houston	21,375	Crockett	1,234
Howard	32,343	Big Spring	901
Hudspeth	2,915	Sierra Blanca	4,567
Hunt	64,343	Greenville	840
Hutchinson	25,689	Stinnett	872
Irion	1,629	Mertzon	1,052
Jack	6,981	Jacksboro	920
Jackson	13,039	Edna	844
Jasper	31,102	Jasper	921
Jeff Davis	1,946	Fort Davis	2,257
Jefferson	239,397	Beaumont	937
Jim Hogg	5,109	Hebbronville	1,136
Jim Wells	37,679	Alice	867
Johnson	97,165	Cleburne	730
Jones	16,490	Anson	931
Karnes	12,455	Karnes City	753
Kaufman	52,220	Kaufman	788
Kendall	14,589	Boerne	663
Kenedy	460	Sarita	1,389
Kent	1,010	Jayton	878
Kerr	36,304	Kerrville	1,107
Kimble	4,122	Junction	1,250
King	354	Guthrie	914
Kinney	3,119	Brackettville	1,359
Kleberg	30,274	Kingsville	853
Knox	4,837	Benjamin	845
Lamar	43,949	Paris	919
Lamb	15,072	Littlefield	1,013
Lampasas	13,521	Lampasas	714
La Salle	5,254	Cotulla	1,517
Lavaca	18,690	Hallettsville	971
Lee	12,854	Giddings	631
Leon	12,665	Centerville	1,079
Liberty	52,726	Liberty	1,174
Limestone	20,946	Groesbeck	930
Lipscomb	3,143	Lipscomb	933
Live Oak	9,556	George West	1,057
Llano	11,631	Llano	939
Loving	107	Mentone	670
Lubbock	222,636	Lubbock	900
Lynn	6,758	Tahoka	888
McCulloch	8,778	Brady	1,071
McLennan	189,123	Waco	1,031
McMullen	817	Tilden	1,163
Madison	10,931	Madisonville	472
Marion	9,984	Jefferson	385
Martin	4,956	Staton	914
Mason	3,423	Mason	934
Matagorda	36,928	Bay City	1,127
Maverick	36,378	Eagle Pass	1,287
Medina	27,312	Hondo	1,331
Menard	2,252	Menard	902
Midland	106,611	Midland	902
Milam	22,946	Cameron	1,019
Mills	4,531	Goldthwaite	748
Mitchell	8,016	Colorado City	912
Montague	17,274	Montague	928
Montgomery	182,201	Conroe	1,047
Moore	17,865	Dumas	905
Morris	13,200	Daingerfield	256
Motley	1,532	Matador	959
Nacogdoches	54,753	Nacogdoches	939
Navarro	39,926	Corsicana	1,068
Newton	13,569	Newton	935
Nolan	16,594	Sweetwater	915
Nueces	291,145	Corpus Christi	847
Ochiltree	9,128	Perryton	919
Oldham	2,278	Vega	1,485
Orange	80,509	Orange	362
Palo Pinto	25,055	Palo Pinto	949
Panola	22,035	Carthage	812
Parker	64,785	Weatherford	902
Parmer	9,863	Farwell	885
Pecos	14,675	Fort Stockton	4,777
Polk	30,687	Livingston	1,061
Potter	97,874	Amarillo	902
Presidio	6,637	Marfa	3,857
Rains	6,715	Emory	243
Randall	89,673	Canyon	917
Reagan	4,514	Big Lake	1,173
Real	2,412	Leakey	697
Red River	14,317	Clarksville	1,054
Reeves	15,852	Pecos	2,626
Refugio	7,976	Refugio	771
Roberts	1,025	Miami	915
Robertson	15,511	Franklin	864
Rockwall	25,604	Rockwall	128
Runnels	11,294	Ballinger	1,056
Rusk	43,735	Henderson	932
Sabine	9,586	Hemphill	486
San Augustine	7,999	San Augustine	524
San Jacinto	16,372	Coldspring	572
San Patricio	58,749	Sinton	693
San Saba	5,401	San Saba	1,136
Schleicher	2,990	Eldorado	1,309
Scurry	18,634	Snyder	900
Shackelford	3,316	Albany	915

County	Pop.	County Seat or court house	Land area sq. mi.
Shelby	22,034	Center	791
Sherman	2,858	Stratford	923
Smith	151,309	Tyler	932
Somervell	5,360	Glen Rose	188
Starr	40,518	Rio Grande City	1,226
Stephens	9,010	Breckenridge	894
Sterling	1,438	Sterling City	923
Stonewall	2,013	Aspermont	925
Sutton	4,135	Sonora	1,455
Swisher	8,133	Tulia	902
Tarrant	1,170,103	Fort Worth	868
Taylor	119,655	Abilene	917
Terrell	1,410	Sanderson	2,357
Terry	13,218	Brownfield	887
Throckmorton	1,880	Throckmorton	912
Titus	24,009	Mount Pleasant	412
Tom Green	98,458	San Angelo	1,515
Travis	576,407	Austin	989
Trinity	11,445	Groveton	692
Tyler	16,646	Woodville	922
Upshur	31,370	Gilmer	587
Upton	4,447	Rankin	1,243
Uvalde	23,340	Uvalde	1,564
Val Verde	38,721	Del Rio	3,150
Van Zandt	37,944	Canton	855
Victoria	74,361	Victoria	887
Walker	50,917	Huntsville	786
Waller	23,390	Hempstead	514
Ward	13,115	Monahans	836
Washington	26,154	Brenham	610
Webb	133,239	Laredo	3,362
Wharton	39,955	Wharton	1,086
Wheeler	5,879	Wheeler	904
Wichita	122,378	Wichita Falls	606
Wilbarger	15,121	Vernon	947
Willacy	17,705	Raymondville	589
Williamson	139,551	Georgetown	1,137
Wilson	22,650	Floresville	807
Winkler	8,626	Kermit	840
Wise	34,679	Decatur	902
Wood	29,380	Quitman	689
Yoakum	8,786	Plains	800
Young	18,126	Graham	919
Zapata	9,279	Zapata	999
Zavala	12,162	Crystal City	1,298

Utah

(29 counties, 82,168 sq. mi. land; pop. 1,722,850)

Beaver	4,765	Beaver	2,590
Box Elder	36,485	Brigham City	5,724
Cache	70,183	Logan	1,165
Carbon	20,228	Price	1,479
Daggett	690	Manila	698
Davis	187,941	Farmington	305
Duchesne	12,645	Duchesne	3,238
Emery	10,332	Castle Dale	4,452
Garfield	3,980	Panguitch	5,175
Grand	6,620	Moab	3,682
Iron	20,789	Parowan	3,299
Juab	5,817	Nephi	3,392
Kane	5,169	Kanab	3,992
Millard	11,333	Fillmore	6,590
Morgan	5,528	Morgan	609
Piute	1,277	Junction	758
Rich	1,725	Randolph	1,029
Salt Lake	725,956	Salt Lake City	737
San Juan	12,621	Monticello	7,821
Sanpete	16,259	Manti	1,588
Sevier	15,431	Richfield	1,910
Summit	15,518	Coalville	1,871
Tooele	26,601	Tooele	6,946
Uintah	22,211	Vernal	4,477
Utah	263,590	Provo	1,998
Wasatch	10,089	Heber City	1,181
Washington	48,560	Saint George	2,427
Wayne	2,177	Loa	2,461
Weber	158,330	Ogden	576

Vermont

(14 counties, 9,273 sq. mi. land; pop. 562,758)

Addison	32,953	Middlebury	773
Bennington	35,845	Bennington	676
Caledonia	27,846	Saint Johnsbury	651
Chittenden	131,761	Burlington	540
Essex	6,405	Guildhall	666
Franklin	39,980	Saint Albans	649
Grand Isle	5,318	North Hero	89
Lamoille	19,735	Hyde Park	461
Orange	26,149	Chelsea	690
Orleans	24,053	Newport	697
Rutland	62,142	Rutland	932
Washington	54,928	Montpelier	690
Windham	41,588	Newfane	786
Windsor	54,055	Woodstock	972

Virginia

(95 cos., 41 ind. cities, 39,704 sq. mi. land; pop. 6,216,568)

Accomack	31,703	Accomac	476
Albemarle	68,040	Charlottesville	740
Alleghany	13,176	Covington	444
Amelia	8,787	Amelia, C.H.	366
Amherst	28,578	Amherst	470
Appomattox	12,298	Appomattox	345
Arlington	170,886	Arlington	26
Augusta	54,677	Staunton	968
Bath	4,799	Warm Springs	540
Bedford	45,656	Bedford	771
Bland	6,514	Bland	369
Botetourt	24,992	Fincastle	549
Brunswick	15,987	Lawrenceville	579
Buchanan	31,333	Grundy	508
Buckingham	12,873	Buckingham	582
Campbell	47,572	Rustburg	511
Caroline	19,217	Bowling Green	549
Carroll	26,594	Hillsville	494
Charles City	6,282	Charles City	208
Charlotte	11,688	Charlotte Courthouse	471
Chesterfield	209,564	Chesterfield	446
Clarke	12,101	Berryville	174
Craig	4,372	New Castle	336
Culpeper	27,791	Culpeper	389
Cumberland	7,825	Cumberland	292
Dickenson	17,620	Clintwood	335
Dinwiddie	22,319	Dinwiddie	502
Essex	8,689	Tappahannock	264
Fairfax	818,584	Fairfax	399
Fauquier	48,741	Warrenton	660
Floyd	12,005	Floyd	383
Fluvanna	12,429	Palmyra	282
Franklin	39,549	Rocky Mount	721
Frederick	45,723	Winchester	432
Giles	16,366	Pearisburg	369
Gloucester	30,131	Gloucester	257
Goochland	14,163	Goochland	289
Grayson	16,278	Independence	494
Greene	10,297	Stanardsville	153
Greensville	8,630	Emporia	301
Halifax	29,033	Halifax	806
Hanover	63,306	Hanover	436
Henrico	217,849	Henrico	244
Henry	56,942	Martinsville	385
Highland	2,635	Monterey	416
Isle of Wight	25,053	Isle of Wight	319
James City	34,859	Williamsburg	144
King and Queen	6,289	King and Queen	327
King George	13,527	King George	183
King William	10,913	King William	286
Lancaster	10,896	Lancaster	153
Lee	24,496	Jonesville	438
Loudoun	86,129	Leesburg	517
Louisa	20,325	Louisa	514
Lunenburg	11,419	Lunenburg	443
Madison	11,949	Madison	327
Mathews	8,348	Mathews	87
Mecklenburg	29,241	Boydton	675
Middlesex	8,653	Saluda	138
Montgomery	73,913	Christiansburg	395
Nelson	12,778	Lovingston	471
New Kent	10,445	New Kent	221
Northampton	13,061	Eastville	209
Northumberland	10,524	Heathsville	223
Nottoway	14,993	Nottoway	308
Orange	21,421	Orange	355
Page	21,690	Luray	310
Patrick	17,473	Stuart	467
Pittsylvania	55,655	Chatham	985
Powhatan	15,328	Powhatan	272
Prince Edward	17,320	Farmville	357
Prince George	27,394	Prince George	276
Prince William	215,677	Manassas	345
Pulaski	34,496	Pulaski	335
Rappahannock	6,622	Washington	267
Richmond	7,273	Warsaw	203
Roanoke	79,332	Salem	248
Rockbridge	18,350	Lexington	604
Rockingham	57,482	Harrisonburg	865
Russell	28,667	Lebanon	483
Scott	23,204	Gate City	539
Shenandoah	31,636	Woodstock	507
Smyth	32,370	Marion	435
Southampton	17,550	Courtland	599
Spotsylvania	57,403	Spotsylvania	409

County	Pop.	County Seat or court house	Land area sq. mi.
Stafford	61,236	Stafford	277
Surry	6,145	Surry	306
Sussex	10,248	Sussex	496
Tazewell	45,960	Tazewell	522
Warren	26,142	Front Royal	219
Washington	45,887	Abingdon	578
Westmoreland	15,480	Montross	250
Wise	39,573	Wise	405
Wythe	25,471	Wytheville	460
York	42,434	Yorktown	122
independent cities			
Alexandria	111,183		16
Bedford	6,073		7
Bristol	18,426		12
Buena Vista	6,406		7
Charlottesville	40,341		10
Chesapeake	151,976		353
Clifton Forge	4,679		3
Colonial Heights	16,064		8
Covington	6,991		5
Danville	53,056		44
Emporia	5,306		7
Fairfax	19,622		6
Falls Church	9,578		2
Franklin	7,864		8
Fredericksburg	19,027		10
Galax	6,670		8
Hampton	133,793		57
Harrisonburg	30,707		17
Hopewell	23,101		11
Lexington	6,959		2
Lynchburg	66,049		50
Manassas	27,957		11
Manassas Park	6,734		3
Martinsville	16,162		11
Newport News	170,045		69
Norfolk	261,229		66
Norton	4,247		7
Petersburg	38,386		23
Poquoson	11,005		10
Portsmouth	103,907		30
Radford	15,940		9
Richmond	203,056		63
Roanoke	96,397		43
Salem	23,756		14
South Boston	6,997		5
Staunton	24,461		20
Suffolk	52,141		430
Virginia Beach	393,069		310
Waynesboro	18,549		14
Williamsburg	11,530		9
Winchester	21,947		9

Washington

(39 counties, 66,511 sq. mi. land; pop., 4,866,692)

County	Pop.	County Seat or court house	Land area sq. mi.
Adams	13,603	Ritzville	1,921
Asotin	17,605	Asotin	635
Benton	112,560	Prosser	1,715
Chelan	52,250	Wenatchee	2,916
Clallam	56,210	Port Angeles	1,753
Clark	238,053	Vancouver	627
Columbia	4,024	Dayton	865
Cowlitz	82,119	Kelso	1,140
Douglas	26,205	Waterville	1,817
Ferry	6,295	Republic	2,200
Franklin	37,473	Pasco	1,243
Garfield	2,248	Pomeroy	706
Grant	54,758	Ephrata	2,660
Grays Harbor	64,175	Montesano	1,918
Island	60,195	Coupeville	212
Jefferson	20,406	Port Townsend	1,805
King	1,507,319	Seattle	2,128
Kitsap	189,731	Port Orchard	393
Kittitas	26,725	Ellensburg	2,308
Klickitat	16,616	Goldendale	1,880
Lewis	59,358	Chehalis	2,409
Lincoln	8,864	Davenport	2,310
Mason	38,341	Shelton	961
Okanogan	33,350	Okanogan	5,281
Pacific	18,882	South Bend	908
Pend Oreille	8,915	Newport	1,400
Pierce	586,203	Tacoma	1,675
San Juan	10,035	Friday Harbor	179
Skagit	79,555	Mount Vernon	1,735
Skamania	8,289	Stevenson	1,672
Snohomish	465,642	Everett	2,098
Spokane	361,364	Spokane	1,762
Stevens	30,948	Colville	2,470
Thurston	161,238	Olympia	727
Wahkiakum	3,327	Cathlamet	261
Walla Walla	48,439	Walla Walla	1,261
Whatcom	127,780	Bellingham	2,125
Whitman	38,775	Colfax	2,151
Yakima	188,823	Yakima	4,287

West Virginia

(55 counties, 24,119 sq. mi. land; pop., 1,793,477)

County	Pop.	County Seat or court house	Land area sq. mi.
Barbour	15,699	Philippi	343
Berkeley	59,253	Martinsburg	321
Boone	25,870	Madison	503
Braxton	12,998	Sutton	513
Brooke	26,992	Wellsburg	90
Cabell	96,827	Huntington	282
Calhoun	7,885	Grantsville	280
Clay	9,983	Clay	346
Doddridge	6,994	West Union	321
Fayette	47,952	Fayetteville	667
Gilmer	7,669	Glenville	340
Grant	10,428	Petersburg	480
Greenbrier	34,693	Lewisburg	1,025
Hampshire	16,498	Romney	644
Hancock	35,233	New Cumberland	84
Hardy	10,977	Moorefield	585
Harrison	69,371	Clarksburg	417
Jackson	25,938	Ripley	464
Jefferson	35,926	Charles Town	209
Kanawha	207,619	Charleston	901
Lewis	17,223	Weston	389
Lincoln	21,382	Hamlin	439
Logan	43,032	Logan	456
McDowell	35,233	Welch	535
Marion	57,249	Fairmont	312
Marshall	37,356	Moundsville	305
Mason	25,178	Point Pleasant	433
Mercer	64,980	Princeton	420
Mineral	26,697	Keyser	329
Mingo	33,739	Williamson	424
Monongalia	75,509	Morgantown	363
Monroe	12,406	Union	473
Morgan	12,128	Berkeley Springs	230
Nicholas	26,775	Summersville	650
Ohio	50,871	Wheeling	106
Pendleton	8,054	Franklin	698
Pleasants	7,546	St. Marys	131
Pocahontas	9,008	Marlinton	942
Preston	29,037	Kingwood	651
Putnam	42,835	Winfield	346
Raleigh	76,819	Beckley	608
Randolph	27,803	Elkins	1,040
Ritchie	10,233	Harrisville	454
Roane	15,120	Spencer	484
Summers	14,204	Hinton	353
Taylor	15,144	Grafton	174
Tucker	7,728	Parsons	421
Tyler	9,796	Middlebourne	258
Upshur	22,867	Buckhannon	355
Wayne	41,636	Wayne	508
Webster	10,729	Webster Springs	556
Wetzel	19,258	New Martinsville	359
Wirt	5,192	Elizabeth	235
Wood	86,915	Parkersburg	367
Wyoming	28,990	Pineville	502

Wisconsin

(72 counties, 54,426 sq. mi. land; pop., 4,891,769)

County	Pop.	County Seat or court house	Land area sq. mi.
Adams	15,682	Friendship	648
Ashland	16,307	Ashland	1,048
Barron	40,750	Barron	865
Bayfield	14,008	Washburn	1,462
Brown	194,594	Green Bay	524
Buffalo	13,584	Alma	699
Burnett	13,084	Meenon	818
Calumet	34,291	Chilton	326
Chippewa	52,360	Chippewa Falls	1,017
Clark	31,647	Neillsville	1,218
Columbia	45,088	Portage	771
Crawford	15,940	Prairie du Chien	566
Dane	367,085	Madison	1,205
Dodge	76,559	Juneau	887
Door	25,690	Sturgeon Bay	492
Douglas	41,758	Superior	1,305
Dunn	35,909	Menomonie	853
Eau Claire	85,183	Eau Claire	638
Florence	4,590	Florence	486
Fond du Lac	90,083	Fond du Lac	725
Forest	8,776	Crandon	1,011
Grant	49,266	Lancaster	1,144
Green	30,339	Monroe	583
Green Lake	18,651	Green Lake	357
Iowa	20,150	Dodgeville	760
Iron	6,153	Hurley	751
Jackson	16,588	Black River Falls	998

County	Pop.	County Seat or court house	Land area sq. mi.
Jefferson	67,783	Jefferson	562
Juneau	21,650	Mauston	774
Kenosha	128,181	Kenosha	273
Kewaunee	18,878	Kewaunee	343
La Crosse	97,904	La Crosse	457
Lafayette	16,076	Darlington	634
Langlade	19,505	Antigo	873
Lincoln	26,993	Merrill	886
Manitowoc	80,421	Manitowoc	594
Marathon	115,400	Wausau	1,559
Marinette	40,548	Marinette	1,395
Marquette	12,321	Montello	455
Menominee	3,890	Keshena	359
Milwaukee	959,275	Milwaukee	241
Monroe	36,633	Sparta	904
Oconto	30,226	Oconto	1,002
Oneida	31,679	Rhinelander	1,130
Outagamie	140,510	Appleton	642
Ozaukee	72,831	Port Washington	235
Pepin	7,107	Durand	231
Pierce	32,765	Ellsworth	576
Polk	34,773	Balsam Lake	919
Portage	61,405	Stevens Point	810
Price	15,600	Phillips	1,256
Racine	175,034	Racine	334
Richland	17,521	Richland Center	585
Rock	139,510	Janesville	724
Rusk	15,079	Ladysmith	913
St. Croix	50,251	Hudson	723
Sauk	46,975	Baraboo	838
Sawyer	14,181	Hayward	1,255
Shawano	37,157	Shawano	897
Sheboygan	103,877	Sheboygan	515
Taylor	18,901	Medford	975
Trempealeau	25,263	Whitehall	736
Vernon	25,617	Viroqua	808
Vilas	17,707	Eagle River	867
Walworth	75,000	Elkhorn	556
Washburn	13,772	Shell Lake	815
Washington	95,328	West Bend	431
Waukesha	304,715	Waukesha	554
Waupaca	46,104	Waupaca	754
Waushara	19,385	Wautoma	628
Winnebago	140,320	Oshkosh	449
Wood	73,605	Wisconsin Rapids	801

Wyoming

(23 counties, 96,989 sq. mi. land; pop., 453,588)

County	Pop.	County Seat or court house	Land area sq. mi.
Albany	30,797	Laramie	4,268
Big Horn	10,525	Basin	3,139
Campbell	29,370	Gillette	4,796
Carbon	16,659	Rawlins	7,877
Converse	11,128	Douglas	4,271
Crook	5,294	Sundance	2,855
Fremont	33,662	Lander	9,181
Goshen	12,373	Torrington	2,186
Hot Springs	4,809	Thermopolis	2,005
Johnson	6,145	Buffalo	4,166
Laramie	73,142	Cheyenne	2,684
Lincoln	12,625	Kemmerer	4,070
Natrona	61,226	Casper	5,347
Niobrara	2,499	Lusk	2,684
Park	23,178	Cody	6,936
Platte	8,145	Wheatland	2,023
Sheridan	23,562	Sheridan	2,532
Sublette	4,843	Pinedale	4,872
Sweetwater	38,823	Green River	10,352
Teton	11,172	Jackson	4,011
Uinta	18,705	Evanston	2,085
Washakie	8,388	Worland	2,243
Weston	6,518	Newcastle	2,402

Population of Outlying Areas

Source: Bureau of the Census U.S. Dept. of Commerce
Population figures are final counts from the census conducted on Apr. 1, 1990.

Puerto Rico

Zip code	Municipios	Pop.	Land area sq. mile
00601	Adjuntas	19,451	67
00602	Aguada	35,911	31
00603	Aguadilla	59,335	37
00607	Aguas Buenas	25,424	30
00609	Aibonito	24,971	31
00610	Anasco	25,234	40
00612	Arecibo	93,385	127
00615	Arroyo	18,910	15
00617	Barceloneta	20,947	24
00618	Barranquitas	25,605	34
00619	Bayamon	220,262	45
00623	Cabo Rojo	38,521	72
00625	Caguas	133,447	59
00627	Camuy	28,917	47
00629	Canovanas	36,816	33
00630	Carolina	177,806	48
00632	Catano	34,587	6
00633	Cayey	46,553	52
00635	Ceiba	17,145	27
00638	Ciales	18,084	67
00639	Cidra	35,601	36
00640	Coamo	33,837	78
00642	Comerio	20,265	29
00643	Corozal	33,095	43
00645	Culebra	1,542	13
00646	Dorado	30,759	24
00648	Fajardo	36,882	31
00650	Florida	8,689	10
00653	Guanica	19,984	37
00654	Guayama	41,588	65
00656	Guayanilla	21,581	42
00657	Guaynabo	92,886	27
00658	Gurabo	28,737	28
00659	Hatillo	32,703	42
00660	Hormigueros	15,212	11
00661	Humacao	55,203	45
00662	Isabela	39,147	56
00664	Jayuya	15,527	44
00665	Juana Diaz	45,198	61
00666	Juncos	30,612	27
00667	Lajas	23,271	60
00669	Lares	29,015	62
00670	Las Marias	9,306	46
00671	Las Piedras	27,896	34
00672	Loiza	29,307	21
00673	Luquillo	18,100	26
00701	Manati	38,692	46
00706	Maricao	6,206	37
00707	Maunabo	12,347	21
00708	Mayaguez	100,371	77
00716	Moca	32,926	50
00717	Morovis	25,288	39
00718	Naguabo	22,620	52
00719	Naranjito	27,914	28
00720	Orocovis	21,158	64
00723	Patillas	19,633	47
00724	Penuelas	22,515	45
00731	Ponce	187,749	117
00742	Quebradillas	21,425	23
00743	Rincon	12,213	14
00745	Rio Grande	45,648	62
00747	Sabana Grande	22,843	36
00751	Salinas	28,335	71
00753	San German	34,962	54
*00936	San Juan	437,745	47
00754	San Lorenzo	35,163	53
00755	San Sebastian	38,799	71
00757	Santa Isabel	19,318	35
00758	Toa Alta	44,101	28
00759	Toa Baja	89,454	24
00760	Trujillo Alto	61,120	21
00761	Utuado	34,980	115
00762	Vega Alta	34,559	28
00763	Vega Baja	55,997	48
00765	Vieques	8,602	53
00766	Villalba	23,559	37
00767	Yabucoa	36,483	55
00768	Yauco	42,058	69
Total		3,522,037	3,459

Zip code	Area	Pop.	Land area sq. mile
	American Samoa		
96799	American Samoa	46,773	77
	Guam		
96910	Agana	1,139	1
.....	Agana Hts.	3,646	1
96915	Agat	4,960	10
.....	Asan	2,070	6
96913	Barrigada	8,846	9
.....	Chalan-Pago-Ordot	4,451	6
96912	Dededo	31,728	30
96916	Inarajan	2,469	19
.....	Mangilao	10,483	10
96916	Merizo	1,742	6
.....	Mongmong-Toto-Maite	5,845	2

Zip code	Area	Pop.	Land area sq. mile
	Piti	1,827	7
96915	Santa Rita	11,857	17
.....	Sinajana	2,658	1
.....	Talofofo	2,310	17
96911	Tamuning	16,673	6
96918	Umatac	897	6
96921	Yigo	14,213	35
96914	Yona	5,338	20
Total		**133,152**	**209**

Zip code	Area	Pop.	Land area sq. mile
	Virgin Islands		
.....	St. Croix	50,139	80
.....	St. John	3,504	20
.....	St. Thomas	48,166	3
00801	Charlotte Amalie	12,331	
00820	Christiansted	2,555	
00840	Frederiksted	1,064	
Total		**101,809**	**132**
	Trust Territory of Pacific Islands		
96944	Kosrae	NA	42

Zip code	Area	Pop.	Land area sq. mile
	Marshall islands	NA	70
96940	Palau	15,122	192
96941	Ponape	NA	176
96942	Truk	NA	49
96943	Yap	NA	46
Total		**NA**	**533**
	No. Mariana Islands	**43,345**	**184**

U.S. Area and Population: 1790 to 1990

Source: Bureau of the Census

Census date	Area (square miles) Gross	Land	Water	Population Number	Per sq. mile of land	Increase over preceding census Number	%
1990 (Apr. 1)	3,787,425	3,536,342	251,083[1]	248,709,873	70.3	22,164,068	9.8
1980 (Apr. 1)	3,618,770	3,539,289	79,481	226,542,203	64.0	23,240,172	11.4
1970 (Apr. 1)	3,618,770	3,536,855	81,915	203,302,031	57.5	23,978,856	13.4
1960 (Apr. 1)	3,618,770	3,540,911	77,859	179,323,175	50.6	27,997,377	18.5
1950 (Apr. 1)	3,618,770	3,552,206	66,564	151,325,798	42.6	19,161,229	14.5
1940 (Apr. 1)	3,618,770	3,554,608	64,162	132,164,569	37.2	8,961,945	7.3
1930 (Apr. 1)	3,618,770	3,551,608	67,162	123,202,624	34.7	17,181,087	16.2
1920 (Jan. 1)	3,618,770	3,546,931	71,839	106,021,537	29.9	13,793,041	15.0
1910 (Apr. 15)	3,618,770	3,547,045	71,725	92,228,496	26.0	16,016,328	21.0
1900 (June 1)	3,618,770	3,547,314	71,456	76,212,168	21.5	13,232,402	21.0
1890 (June 1)	3,612,299	3,540,705	71,594	62,979,766	17.8	12,790,557	25.5
1880 (June 1)	3,612,299	3,540,705	71,594	50,189,209	14.2	11,630,838	30.2
1870 (June 1)	3,612,299	3,540,705	71,594	38,558,371	10.9	7,115,050	22.6
1860 (June 1)	3,021,295	2,969,640	51,655	31,443,321	10.6	8,251,445	35.6
1850 (June 1)	2,991,655	2,940,042	51,613	23,191,876	7.9	6,122,423	35.9
1840 (June 1)	1,792,552	1,749,462	43,090	17,069,453	9.8	4,203,433	32.7
1830 (June 1)	1,792,552	1,749,462	43,090	12,866,020	7.4	3,227,567	33.5
1820 (June 1)	1,792,552	1,749,462	43,090	9,638,453	5.5	2,398,572	33.1
1810 (Aug. 6)	1,722,685	1,681,828	40,857	7,239,881	4.3	1,931,398	36.4
1800 (Aug. 4)	891,364	864,746	26,618	5,308,483	6.1	1,379,269	35.1
1790 (Aug. 2)	891,364	864,746	26,618	3,929,214	4.5	—	—

(1) Comprises inland, coastal, Great Lakes, and territorial water. Data for prior years cover inland water only.

NOTE: Percent changes are computed on basis of change in population since preceding census date, and period covered therefore is not always exactly 10 years.

Population density figures given for various years represent the area within the boundaries of the United States which was under the jurisdiction on date in question, including in some cases considerable areas not organized or settled and not covered by the census. In 1870, for example, Alaska was not covered by the census.

Revised figure of 39,818,449 for the 1870 population includes adjustments for undernumeration in the Southern states. On the basis of the revised figure, the population increased by 8,375,128, or 26.6 percent between 1860 and 1870, and by 10,370,760, or 26.1 percent between 1870 and 1880.

Resident Population by Sex, Race, Residence, and Median Age: 1790 to 1990

Source: U.S. Bureau of the Census (thousands, except as indicated)

Date	Sex: Male	Sex: Female	Race: White	Race: Black Number	Race: Black Percent	Race: Other	Residence: Urban	Residence: Rural	Median Age (years): All races	Median Age: White	Median Age: Black
Conterminous U.S.[1]											
1790 (Aug. 2)	NA	NA	3,172	757	19.3	NA	202	3,728	NA	NA	NA
1810 (Aug. 6)	NA	NA	5,862	1,378	19.0	NA	525	6,714	NA	16.0	NA
1820 (Aug. 7)	4,897	4,742	7,867	1,772	18.4	NA	693	8,945	16.7	16.5	17.2
1840 (June 1)	8,689	8,381	14,196	2,874	16.8	NA	1,845	15,224	17.8	17.9	17.3
1860 (June 1)	16,085	15,358	26,923	4,442	14.1	79	6,217	25,227	19.4	19.7	17.7
1870 (June 1)	19,494	19,065	33,589	4,880	12.7	89	9,902	28,656	20.2	20.4	18.5
1880 (June 1)	25,519	24,637	43,403	6,581	13.1	172	14,130	36,026	20.9	21.4	18.0
1890 (June 1)	32,237	30,711	55,101	7,489	11.9	358	22,106	40,841	22.0	22.5	17.8
1900 (June 1)	38,816	37,178	66,809	8,834	11.6	351	30,160	45,835	22.9	23.4	19.4
1920 (Jan. 1)	53,900	51,810	94,821	10,463	9.9	427	54,158	51,553	25.3	25.6	22.3
1930 (Apr. 1)	62,137	60,638	110,287	11,891	9.7	597	68,955	53,820	26.4	26.9	23.5
1940 (Apr. 1)	66,062	65,608	118,215	12,866	9.8	589	74,424	57,246	29.0	29.5	25.3
United States											
1950 (Apr. 1)	75,187	76,139	135,150	15,045	9.9	1,131	96,847	54,479	30.2	30.7	26.2
1960 (Apr. 1)	88,331	90,992	158,832	18,872	10.5	1,620	125,269	54,054	29.5	30.3	23.5
1970 (Apr. 1)[2]	98,926	104,309	178,098	22,581	11.1	2,557	149,325	53,887	28.0	28.9	22.4
1980 (Apr. 1)[3]	110,053	116,493	194,713	26,683	11.8	5,150	167,051	59,495	30.0	30.9	24.9
1983 (July 1)	113,119	120,365	199,849	28,056	12.0	6,379	NA	NA	30.8	31.7	25.9
1984 (July 1)	115,022	121,455	201,290	28,457	12.0	6,730	NA	NA	31.1	32.0	26.3
1985 (July 1, est)	116,160	122,576	202,769	28,870	12.1	7,097	NA	NA	31.4	32.3	26.6
1990 (Apr. 1)	121,239	127,470	199,686	29,986	12.1	9,805	187,053	61,656	32.9	34.4	28.1

(NA) Not available. (1) Excludes Alaska and Hawaii. (2) The revised 1970 resident population count is 203,302,031, which incorporates changes due to errors found after tabulations were completed. The race and sex data shown here reflect the official 1970 census count while the residence data come from the tabulated count. (3) The race data shown for April 1, 1980 have been modified.

UNITED STATES FACTS

Superlative U.S. Statistics

Source: U.S. Geological Survey; U.S. Bureau of the Census

Area for 50 states and D. of C.	Total	3,618,770 sq. mi.
	Land 3,539,289 sq. mi.—Water 79,481 sq. mi.	
Largest state	Alaska	591,004 sq. mi.
Smallest state	Rhode Island	1,212 sq. mi.
Largest county (excludes Alaska)	San Bernardino County, California	20,064 sq. mi.
Smallest county	Kalawo, Hawaii	14 sq. mi.
Northernmost city	Barrow, Alaska	71°17′N.
Northernmost point	Point Barrow, Alaska	71°23′N.
Southernmost city	Hilo, Hawaii	19°43′N.
Southernmost settlement	Naalehu, Hawaii	19°03′N.
Southernmost point	Ka Lae (South Cape), Island of Hawaii	18°55′N. (155°41′W.)
Easternmost city	Eastport, Maine	66°59′02″W.
Easternmost settlement	Lubec, Maine	66°58′49″W.
Easternmost point	West Quoddy Head, Maine	66°57′W.
Westernmost city	West Unalaska, Alaska	166°32′W.
Westernmost settlement	Adak, Alaska	176°39′W.
Westernmost point	Cape Wrangell, Alaska	172°27′E.
Highest settlement	Climax, Colorado	11,560 ft.
Lowest settlement	Calipatria, California	−185 ft.
Highest point on Atlantic coast	Cadillac Mountain, Mount Desert Is., Maine	1,530 ft.
Oldest national park	Yellowstone National Park (1872), Wyoming, Montana, Idaho	3,468 sq. mi.
Largest national park	Wrangell-St. Elias, Alaska	13,018 sq. mi.
Largest national monument	Death Valley, California, Nevada	3,231 sq. mi.
Highest waterfall	Yosemite Falls—Total in three sections	2,425 ft.
	Upper Yosemite Fall	1,430 ft.
	Cascades in middle section	675 ft.
	Lower Yosemite Fall	320 ft.
Longest river	Mississippi-Missouri	3,710 mi.
Highest mountain	Mount McKinley, Alaska	20,320 ft.
Lowest point	Death Valley, California	−282 ft.
Deepest lake	Crater Lake, Oregon	1,932 ft.
Rainiest spot	Mt. Waialeale, Hawaii	Annual aver. rainfall 460 inches
Largest gorge	Grand Canyon, Colorado River, Arizona	277 miles long, 600 ft. to 18 miles wide, 1 mile deep
Deepest gorge	Hell's Canyon, Snake River, Idaho-Oregon	7,900 ft.
Strongest surface wind	Mount Washington, New Hampshire recorded 1934	231 mph
Biggest dam	New Cornelia Tailings, Ten Mile Wash, Arizona	274,026,000 cu. yds. material used
Tallest building	Sears Tower, Chicago, Illinois	1,454 ft.
Largest building	Boeing 747 Manufacturing Plant, Everett, Washington	205,600,000 cu. ft.; covers 47 acres.
Tallest structure	TV tower, Blanchard, North Dakota	2,063 ft.
Longest bridge span	Verrazano-Narrows, New York	4,260 ft.
Highest bridge	Royal Gorge, Colorado	1,053 ft. above water
Deepest well	Gas well, Washita County, Oklahoma	31,441 ft.

The 48 Contiguous States

Area for 48 states	Total	3,021,295 sq. mi.
	Land 2,962,031 sq. mi.—Water 59,264 sq. mi.	
Largest state	Texas	266,807 sq. mi
Northernmost city	International Falls, Minnesota	48°36′N.
Northernmost settlement	Angle Inlet, Minnesota	49°21′N.
Northernmost point	Northwest Angle, Minnesota	49°23′N.
Southernmost city	Key West, Florida	24°33′N.
Southernmost mainland city	Florida City, Florida	25°27′N.
Southernmost point	Key West, Florida	24°33′N.
Westernmost town	La Push, Washington	124°38′W.
Westernmost point	Cape Alava, Washington	124°44′W.
Highest mountain	Mount Whitney, California	14,494 ft.

Note to users: The distinction between cities and towns varies from state to state. In this table the U.S. Bureau of the Census usage was followed.

Geodetic Datum of North America

In July 1986, the National Oceanic and Atmospheric Administration's National Geodetic Survey (NGS) completed the readjustment and redefinition of the North American Datum. This new datum is known as the North American Datum of 1983. Rapid advances in economic growth and scientific exploration in the United States after World War II resulted in an increasing need for accurate coordinate information. To facilitate the use of satellite surveying and navigation systems, the new datum was redefined using the Geodetic Reference System 1980 as the reference ellipsoid because this model more closely approximates the true size and shape of the Earth. The readjustment of the datum resulted in position changes of as much as 330 feet in the Continental United States and as much as 1/4 mile in Hawaii, the Aleutian Islands, Puerto Rico, and the Virgin Islands.

Statistical Information about the U.S.

In the *Statistical Abstract of the United States* the Bureau of the Census, U.S. Dept. of Commerce, annually publishes a summary of social, political, and economic information. A book of almost 1,000 pages, it presents in 31 sections comprehensive data on population, housing, health, education, employment, income, prices, business, banking, energy, science, defense, trade, government finance, foreign country comparison, and other subjects. Special features include data from the 1990 Census, sections on State Rankings and Metropolitan Statistical Areas and a new section on computer technology in the office. The book is prepared under the direction of Glenn W. King, Chief, Statistical Compendia Staff, Bureau of the Census. Supplements to the *Statistical Abstract* are *County and City Data Book, 1988; Historical Statistics of the United States, Colonial Times to 1970;* and *State and Metropolitan Area Data Book, 1992.* Information concerning these and other publications may be obtained from the Supt. of Documents, Government Printing Office, Wash., D.C. 20402, or from the U.S. Bureau of the Census, Data User Services Division, Wash., D.C. 20233.

Highest and Lowest Altitudes in the U.S. and Territories

Source: U.S. Geological Survey (Minus sign means below sea level; elevations are in feet.)

	Highest Point			Lowest Point		
State	Name	County	Elev.	Name	County	Elev.
Alabama	Cheaha Mountain	Cleburne	2,405	Gulf of Mexico		Sea level
Alaska	Mount McKinley		20,320	Pacific Ocean		Sea level
Arizona	Humphreys Peak	Coconino	12,633	Colorado R.	Yuma	70
Arkansas	Magazine Mountain	Logan	2,753	Ouachita R.	Ashley-Union	55
California	Mount Whitney	Inyo-Tulare	14,494	Death Valley	Inyo	−282
Colorado	Mount Elbert	Lake	14,433	Arkansas R.	Prowers	3,350
Connecticut	Mount Frissell	Litchfield	2,380	L.I. Sound		Sea level
Delaware	On Ebright Road	New Castle	442	Atlantic Ocean		Sea level
Dist. of Col.	Tenleytown	N. W. part	410	Potomac R.		1
Florida	Sec. 30, T 6N, R 20W	Walton	345	Atlantic Ocean		Sea level
Georgia	Brasstown Bald	Towns-Union	4,784	Atlantic Ocean		Sea level
Guam	Mount Lamlam	Agat District	1,332	Pacific Ocean		Sea level
Hawaii	Mauna Kea	Hawaii	13,796	Pacific Ocean		Sea level
Idaho	Borah Peak	Custer	12,662	Snake R.	Nez Perce	710
Illinois	Charles Mound	Jo Daviess	1,235	Mississippi R.	Alexander	279
Indiana	Franklin Township	Wayne	1,257	Ohio R.	Posey	320
Iowa	Sec. 29, T 100N, R 41W	Osceola	1,670	Mississippi R.	Lee	480
Kansas	Mount Sunflower	Wallace	4,039	Verdigris R.	Montgomery	679
Kentucky	Black Mountain	Harlan	4,139	Mississippi R.	Fulton	257
Louisiana	Driskill Mountain	Bienville	535	New Orleans	Orleans	−8
Maine	Mount Katahdin	Piscataquis	5,267	Atlantic Ocean		Sea level
Maryland	Backbone Mountain	Garrett	3,360	Atlantic Ocean		Sea level
Massachusetts	Mount Greylock	Berkshire	3,487	Atlantic Ocean		Sea level
Michigan	Mount Arvon	Baraga	1,979	Lake Erie	Monroe	571
Minnesota	Eagle Mountain	Cook	2,301	Lake Superior		600
Mississippi	Woodall Mountain	Tishomingo	806	Gulf of Mexico		Sea level
Missouri	Taum Sauk Mt.	Iron	1,772	St. Francis R.	Dunklin	230
Montana	Granite Peak	Park	12,799	Kootenai R.	Lincoln	1,800
Nebraska	Johnson Township	Kimball	5,426	Missouri R.	Richardson	840
Nevada	Boundary Peak	Esmeralda	13,140	Mount Manchester	Clark	479
New Hamp.	Mt. Washington	Coos	6,288	Atlantic Ocean	Rockingham	Sea level
New Jersey	High Point	Sussex	1,803	Atlantic Ocean		Sea level
New Mexico	Wheeler Peak	Taos	13,161	Red Bluff Res.	Eddy	2,842
New York	Mount Marcy	Essex	5,344	Atlantic Ocean		Sea level
North Carolina	Mount Mitchell	Yancey	6,684	Atlantic Ocean		Sea level
North Dakota	White Butte	Slope	3,506	Red R.	Pembina	750
Ohio	Campbell Hill	Logan	1,549	Ohio R.	Hamilton	455
Oklahoma	Black Mesa	Cimarron	4,973	Little R.	McCurtain	289
Oregon	Mount Hood	Clackamas-Hood R.	11,239	Pacific Ocean		Sea level
Pennsylvania	Mt. Davis	Somerset	3,213	Delaware R.	Delaware	Sea level
Puerto Rico	Cerro de Punta	Ponce District	4,390	Atlantic Ocean		Sea level
Rhode Island	Jerimoth Hill	Providence	812	Atlantic Ocean		Sea level
Samoa	Lata Mountain	Tau Island	3,160	Pacific Ocean		Sea level
South Carolina	Sassafras Mountain	Pickens	3,560	Atlantic Ocean		Sea level
South Dakota	Harney Peak	Pennington	7,242	Big Stone Lake	Roberts	966
Tennessee	Clingmans Dome	Sevier	6,643	Mississippi R.	Shelby	178
Texas	Guadalupe Peak	Culberson	8,749	Gulf of Mexico		Sea level
Utah	Kings Peak	Duchesne	13,528	Beaverdam Wash.	Washington	2,000
Vermont	Mount Mansfield	Lamoille	4,393	Lake Champlain		95
Virginia	Mount Rogers	Grayson-Smyth	5,729	Atlantic Ocean		Sea level
Virgin Islands	Crown Mountain	St. Thomas Island	1,556	Atlantic Ocean		Sea level
Washington	Mount Rainier	Pierce	14,410	Pacific Ocean		Sea level
West Virginia	Spruce Knob	Pendleton	4,861	Potomac R.	Jefferson	240
Wisconsin	Timms Hill	Price	1,951	Lake Michigan		579
Wyoming	Gannett Peak	Fremont	13,804	B. Fourche R.	Crook	3,099

U.S. Coastline by States

Source: NOAA, U.S. Dept. of Commerce
(statute miles)

State	Coastline[1]	Shoreline[2]	State	Coastline[1]	Shoreline[2]
Atlantic coast	**2,069**	**28,673**	**Gulf coast**	**1,631**	**17,141**
Connecticut	0	618	Alabama	53	607
Delaware	28	381	Florida	770	5,095
Florida	580	3,331	Louisiana	397	7,721
Georgia	100	2,344	Mississippi	44	359
Maine	228	3,478	Texas	367	3,359
Maryland	31	3,190			
Massachusetts	192	1,519	**Pacific coast**	**7,623**	**40,298**
New Hampshire	13	131	Alaska	5,580	31,383
New Jersey	130	1,792	California	840	3,427
New York	127	1,850	Hawaii	750	1,052
North Carolina	301	3,375	Oregon	296	1,410
Pennsylvania	0	89	Washington	157	3,026
Rhode Island	40	384			
South Carolina	187	2,876	**Arctic coast, Alaska**	**1,060**	**2,521**
Virginia	112	3,315	**United States**	**12,383**	**88,633**

(1) Figures are lengths of general outline of seacoast. Measurements were made with a unit measure of 30 minutes of latitude on charts as near the scale of 1:1,200,000 as possible. Coastline of sounds and bays is included to a point where they narrow to width of unit measure, and includes the distance across at such point. (2) Figures obtained in 1939-40 with a recording instrument on the largest-scale charts and maps then available. Shoreline of outer coast, offshore islands, sounds, bays, rivers, and creeks is included to the head of tidewater or to a point where tidal waters narrow to a width of 100 feet.

States: Settled, Capitals, Entry into Union, Area, Rank

The original 13 states—The 13 colonies that seceded from Great Britain and fought the War of Independence (American Revolution) became the 13 original states. They were: Delaware, Pennsylvania, New Jersey, Georgia, Connecticut, Massachusetts, Maryland, South Carolina, New Hampshire, Virginia, New York, North Carolina, and Rhode Island. The order for the original 13 states is the order in which they ratified the Constitution.

State	Set-tled*	Capital	Entered Union Date	Entered Union Order	Extent in miles (approx. mean) Long	Extent in miles (approx. mean) Wide	Area in square miles Land	Area in square miles Inland Water	Area in square miles Total	Rank in area
Ala.	1702	Montgomery	Dec. 14, 1819	22	330	190	50,767	938	51,705	29
Alas.	1784	Juneau	Jan. 3, 1959	49	(a)1,480	810	570,833	20,171	591,004	1
Ariz.	1776	Phoenix	Feb. 14, 1912	48	400	310	113,508	492	114,000	6
Ark.	1686	Little Rock	June 15, 1836	25	260	240	52,078	1,109	53,187	27
Cal.	1769	Sacramento	Sept. 9, 1850	31	770	250	156,299	2,407	158,706	3
Col.	1858	Denver	Aug. 1, 1876	38	380	280	103,595	496	104,091	8
Conn.	1634	Hartford	Jan. 9, 1788	5	110	70	4,872	147	5,018	48
Del.	1638	Dover	Dec. 7, 1787	1	100	30	1,932	112	2,045	49
D.C.		Washington			...	...	63	6	69	51
Fla.	1565	Tallahassee	Mar. 3, 1845	27	500	160	54,153	4,511	58,664	22
Ga.	1733	Atlanta	Jan. 2, 1788	4	300	230	58,056	854	58,910	21
Ha.	1820	Honolulu	Aug. 21, 1959	50	...	...	6,425	46	6,471	47
Ida.	1842	Boise	July 3, 1890	43	570	300	82,412	1,153	83,564	13
Ill.	1720	Springfield	Dec. 3, 1818	21	390	210	55,645	700	56,345	24
Ind.	1733	Indianapolis	Dec. 11, 1816	19	270	140	35,932	253	36,185	38
Ia.	1788	Des Moines	Dec. 28, 1846	29	310	200	55,965	310	56,275	25
Kan.	1727	Topeka	Jan. 29, 1861	34	400	210	81,778	499	82,277	14
Ky.	1774	Frankfort	June 1, 1792	15	380	140	39,669	740	40,410	37
La.	1699	Baton Rouge	Apr. 30, 1812	18	380	130	44,521	3,230	47,752	31
Me.	1624	Augusta	Mar. 15, 1820	23	320	190	30,995	2,270	33,265	39
Md.	1634	Annapolis	Apr. 28, 1788	7	250	90	9,837	623	10,460	42
Mass.	1620	Boston	Feb. 6, 1788	6	190	50	7,824	460	8,284	45
Mich.	1668	Lansing	Jan. 26, 1837	26	490	240	56,954	1,573	58,527	23
Minn.	1805	St. Paul	May 11, 1858	32	400	250	79,548	4,854	84,402	12
Miss.	1699	Jackson	Dec. 10, 1817	20	340	170	47,233	457	47,689	32
Mo.	1735	Jefferson City	Aug. 10, 1821	24	300	240	68,945	752	69,697	19
Mon.	1809	Helena	Nov. 8, 1889	41	630	280	145,388	1,658	147,046	4
Neb.	1823	Lincoln	Mar. 1, 1867	37	430	210	76,644	711	77,355	15
Nev.	1849	Carson City	Oct. 31, 1864	36	490	320	109,894	667	110,561	7
N.H.	1623	Concord	June 21, 1788	9	190	70	8,993	286	9,279	44
N.J.	1660	Trenton	Dec. 18, 1787	3	150	70	7,468	319	7,787	46
N.M.	1610	Santa Fe	Jan. 6, 1912	47	370	343	121,335	258	121,593	5
N.Y.	1614	Albany	July 26, 1788	11	330	283	47,377	1,731	49,108	30
N.C.	1660	Raleigh	Nov. 21, 1789	12	500	150	48,843	3,826	52,669	28
N.D.	1812	Bismarck	Nov. 2, 1889	39	340	211	69,300	1,403	70,702	17
Oh.	1788	Columbus	Mar. 1, 1803	17	220	220	41,004	325	41,330	35
Okla.	1889	Oklahoma City	Nov. 16, 1907	46	400	220	68,655	1,301	69,956	18
Ore.	1811	Salem	Feb. 14, 1859	33	360	261	96,184	889	97,073	10
Pa.	1682	Harrisburg	Dec. 12, 1787	2	283	160	44,888	420	45,308	33
R.I.	1636	Providence	May 29, 1790	13	40	30	1,055	158	1,212	50
S.C.	1670	Columbia	May 23, 1788	8	260	200	30,203	909	31,113	40
S.D.	1859	Pierre	Nov. 2, 1889	40	380	210	75,952	1,164	77,116	16
Tenn.	1769	Nashville	June 1, 1796	16	440	120	41,155	989	42,144	34
Tex.	1682	Austin	Dec. 29, 1845	28	790	660	262,017	4,790	266,807	2
Ut.	1847	Salt Lake City	Jan. 4, 1896	45	350	270	82,073	2,826	84,899	11
Vt.	1724	Montpelier	Mar. 4, 1791	14	160	80	9,273	341	9,614	43
Va.	1607	Richmond	June 25, 1788	10	430	200	39,704	1,063	40,767	36
Wash.	1811	Olympia	Nov. 11, 1889	42	360	240	66,511	1,627	68,139	20
W.Va.	1727	Charleston	June 20, 1863	35	240	130	24,119	112	24,232	41
Wis.	1766	Madison	May 29, 1848	30	310	260	54,426	1,727	56,153	26
Wy.	1834	Cheyenne	July 10, 1890	44	360	280	96,989	820	97,809	9

* First European permanent settlement. (a) Aleutian Islands and Alexander Archipelago are not considered in these lengths.

The Continental Divide

The Continental Divide: watershed, created by mountain ranges or table-lands of the Rocky Mountains, from which the drainage is easterly or westerly; the easterly flowing waters reaching the Atlantic Ocean chiefly through the Gulf of Mexico, and the westerly flowing waters reaching the Pacific Ocean through the Columbia River, or through the Colorado River, which flows into the Gulf of California.

The location and route of the Continental Divide across the United States may briefly be described as follows:

Beginning at point of crossing the United States-Mexican boundary, near long. 108°45′W., the Divide, in a northerly direction, crosses New Mexico along the western edge of the Rio Grande drainage basin, entering Colorado near long. 106°41′W.

Thence by a very irregular route northerly across Colorado along the western summits of the Rio Grande and of the Arkansas, the South Platte, and the North Platte River basins, and across Rocky Mountain National Park, entering Wyoming near long. 106°52′W.

Thence in a northwesterly direction, forming the western rims of the North Platte, Big Horn, and Yellowstone River basins, crossing the southwestern portion of Yellowstone National Park.

Thence in a westerly and then a northerly direction forming the common boundary of Idaho and Montana, to a point on said boundary near long. 114°00′W.

Thence northeasterly and northwesterly through Montana and the Glacier National Park, entering Canada near long. 114°04′W.

Chronological List of Territories

Source: National Archives and Records Service

Name of territory	Date of Organic Act	Organic Act effective	Admission as state	Yrs. terr.
Northwest Territory(a)	July 13, 1787	No fixed date	Mar. 1, 1803(b)	16
Territory southwest of River Ohio	May 26, 1790	No fixed date	June 1, 1796(c)	6
Mississippi	Apr. 7, 1798	When president acted	Dec. 10, 1817	19
Indiana	May 7, 1800	July 4, 1800	Dec. 11, 1816	16
Orleans	Mar. 26, 1804	Oct. 1, 1804	Apr. 30, 1812(d)	7
Michigan	Jan. 11, 1805	June 30, 1805	Jan. 26, 1837	31
Louisiana-Missouri(e)	Mar. 3, 1805	July 4, 1805	Aug. 10, 1821	16
Illinois	Feb. 3, 1809	Mar. 1, 1809	Dec. 3, 1818	9
Alabama	Mar. 3, 1817	When Miss. became a state	Dec. 14, 1819	2
Arkansas	Mar. 2, 1819	July 4, 1819	June 15, 1836	17
Florida	Mar. 30, 1822	No fixed date	Mar. 3, 1845	23
Wisconsin	Apr. 20, 1836	July 3, 1836	May 29, 1848	12
Iowa	June 12, 1838	July 3, 1838	Dec. 28, 1846	7
Oregon	Aug. 14, 1848	Date of act	Feb. 14, 1859	10
Minnesota	Mar. 3, 1849	Date of act	May 11, 1858	9
New Mexico	Sept. 9, 1850	On president's proclamation	Jan. 6, 1912	61
Utah	Sept. 9, 1850	Date of act	Jan. 4, 1896	44
Washington	Mar. 2, 1853	Date of act	Nov. 11, 1889	36
Nebraska	May 30, 1854	Date of act	Mar. 1, 1867	12
Kansas	May 30, 1854	Date of act	Jan. 29, 1861	6
Colorado	Feb. 28, 1861	Date of act	Aug. 1, 1876	15
Nevada	Mar. 2, 1861	Date of act	Oct. 31, 1864	3
Dakota	Mar. 2, 1861	Date of act	Nov. 2, 1889	28
Arizona	Feb. 24, 1863	Date of act	Feb. 14, 1912	49
Idaho	Mar. 3, 1863	Date of act	July 3, 1890	27
Montana	May 26, 1864	Date of act	Nov. 8, 1889	25
Wyoming	July 25, 1868	When officers were qualified	July 10, 1890	22
Alaska(f)	May 17, 1884	No fixed date	Jan. 3, 1959	75
Oklahoma	May 2, 1890	Date of act	Nov. 16, 1907	17
Hawaii	Apr. 30, 1900	June 14, 1900	Aug. 21, 1959	59

(a) Included Ohio, Indiana, Illinois, Michigan, Wisconsin, eastern Minnesota; (b) as the state of Ohio; (c) as the state of Tennessee; (d) as the state of Louisiana; (e) organic act for Missouri Territory of June 4, 1812, became effective Dec. 7, 1812; (f) Although the May 17, 1884 act actually constituted Alaska as a district, it was often referred to as a territory, and unofficially administered as such. The Territory of Alaska was legally and formally organized by an act of Aug. 24, 1912.

Geographic Centers, U.S. and Each State

Source: U.S. Geological Survey

United States, including Alaska and Hawaii — South Dakota; Butte County, W of Castle Rock, Approx. lat. 44°58'N. long. 103°46'W.

Contiguous U. S. (48 states) — Near Lebanon, Smith Co., Kansas, lat. 39°50'N. long. 98°35'W.

North American continent — The geographic center is in Pierce County, North Dakota, 6 miles W of Balta, latitude 48°10', longitude 100°10'W.

State—county, locality

Alabama—Chilton, 12 miles SW of Clanton.
Alaska—lat. 63°50'N. long. 152°W. Approx. 60 mi. NW of Mt. McKinley.
Arizona—Yavapai, 55 miles ESE of Prescott.
Arkansas—Pulaski, 12 miles NW of Little Rock.
California—Madera, 38 miles E of Madera.
Colorado—Park, 30 miles NW of Pikes Peak.
Connecticut—Hartford, at East Berlin.
Delaware—Kent, 11 miles S of Dover.
District of Columbia—Near 4th and L Sts., NW.
Florida—Hernando, 12 miles NNW of Brooksville.
Georgia—Twiggs, 18 miles SE of Macon.
Hawaii—Hawaii, 20°15'N, 156°20'W, off Maui Island.
Idaho—Custer, at Custer, SW of Challis.
Illinois—Logan, 28 miles NE of Springfield.
Indiana—Boone, 14 miles NNW of Indianapolis.
Iowa—Story, 5 miles NE of Ames.
Kansas—Barton, 15 miles NE of Great Bend.
Kentucky—Marion, 3 miles NNW of Lebanon.
Louisiana—Avoyelles, 3 miles SE of Marksville.
Maine—Piscataquis, 18 miles north of Dover.
Maryland—Prince Georges, 4.5 miles NW of Davidsonville.
Massachusetts—Worcester, north part of city.
Michigan—Wexford, 5 miles NNW of Cadillac.
Minnesota—Crow Wing, 10 miles SW of Brainerd.
Mississippi—Leake, 9 miles WNW of Carthage.
Missouri—Miller, 20 miles SW of Jefferson City.
Montana—Fergus, 11 miles west of Lewistown.
Nebraska—Custer, 10 miles NW of Broken Bow.
Nevada—Lander, 26 miles SE of Austin.
New Hampshire—Belknap, 3 miles E of Ashland.
New Jersey—Mercer, 5 miles SE of Trenton.
New Mexico—Torrance, 12 miles SSW of Willard.
New York—Madison, 12 miles S of Oneida and 26 miles SW of Utica.
North Carolina—Chatham, 10 miles NW of Sanford.
North Dakota—Sheridan, 5 miles SW of McClusky.
Ohio—Delaware, 25 miles NNE of Columbus.
Oklahoma—Oklahoma, 8 miles N of Oklahoma City.
Oregon—Crook, 25 miles SSE of Prineville.
Pennsylvania—Centre, 2.5 miles SW of Bellefonte.
Rhode Island—Kent, 1 mile SSW of Crompton.
South Carolina—Richland, 13 miles SE of Columbia.
South Dakota—Hughes, 8 miles NE of Pierre.
Tennessee—Rutherford, 5 mi. NE of Murfreesboro.
Texas—McCulloch, 15 miles NE of Brady.
Utah—Sanpete, 3 miles N of Manti.
Vermont—Washington, 3 miles E of Roxbury.
Virginia—Buckingham, 5 miles SW of Buckingham.
Washington—Chelan, 10 mi. WSW of Wenatchee.
West Virginia—Braxton, 4 miles E of Sutton.
Wisconsin—Wood, 9 miles SE of Marshfield.
Wyoming—Fremont, 58 miles ENE of Lander.

There is no generally accepted definition of geographic center, and no satisfactory method for determining it. The geographic center of an area may be defined as the center of gravity of the surface, or that point on which the surface of the area would balance if it were a plane of uniform thickness.

No marked or monumented point has been established by any government agency as the geographic center of either the 50 states, the contiguous United States, or the North American continent. A monument was erected in Lebanon, Kan., contiguous U.S. center, by a group of citizens. A cairn in Rugby, N.D. marks the center of the North American continent.

International Boundary Lines of the U.S.

The length of the northern boundary of the contiguous U.S. — the U.S.-Canadian border, excluding Alaska — is 3,987 miles according to the U.S. Geological Survey, Dept. of the Interior. The length of the Alaskan-Canadian border is 1,538 miles. The length of the U.S.-Mexican border, from the Gulf of Mexico to the Pacific Ocean, is approximately 1,933 miles (1963 boundary agreement).

Origin of the Names of U.S. States

Source: State officials, the Smithsonian Institution, and the Topographic Division, U.S. Geological Survey.

Alabama—Indian for tribal town, later a tribe (Alabamas or Alibamons) of the Creek confederacy.

Alaska—Russian version of Aleutian (Eskimo) word, alakshak, for "peninsula," "great lands," or "land that is not an island."

Arizona—Spanish version of Pima Indian word for "little spring place," or Aztec arizuma, meaning "silver-bearing."

Arkansas—French variant of Quapaw, a Siouan people meaning "downstream people."

California—Bestowed by the Spanish conquistadors (possibly by Cortez). It was the name of an imaginary island, an earthly paradise, in "Las Serges de Esplandian," a Spanish romance written by Montalvo in 1510. Baja California (Lower California, in Mexico) was first visited by Spanish in 1533. The present U.S. state was called Alta (Upper) California.

Colorado—Spanish, red, first applied to Colorado River.

Connecticut—From Mohican and other Algonquin words meaning "long river place."

Delaware—Named for Lord De La Warr, early governor of Virginia; first applied to river, then to Indian tribe (Lenni-Lenape), and the state.

District of Columbia—For Columbus, 1791.

Florida—Named by Ponce de Leon on Pascua Florida, "Flowery Easter," on Easter Sunday, 1513.

Georgia—For King George II of England by James Oglethorpe, colonial administrator, 1732.

Hawaii—Possibly derived from native word for homeland, Hawaiki or Owhyhee.

Idaho—A coined name with an invented Indian meaning: "gem of the mountains;" originally suggested for the Pike's Peak mining territory (Colorado), then applied to the new mining territory of the Pacific Northwest. Another theory suggests Idaho may be a Kiowa Apache term for the Comanche.

Illinois—French for Illini or land of Illini, Algonquin word meaning men or warriors.

Indiana—Means "land of the Indians."

Iowa—Indian word variously translated as "one who puts to sleep" or "beautiful land."

Kansas—Sioux word for "south wind people."

Kentucky—Indian word variously translated as "dark and bloody ground," "meadow land" and "land of tomorrow."

Louisiana—Part of territory called Louisiana by Sieur de La Salle for French King Louis XIV.

Maine—From Maine, ancient French province. Also: descriptive, referring to the mainland as distinct from the many coastal islands.

Maryland—For Queen Henrietta Maria, wife of Charles I of England.

Massachusetts—From Indian tribe named after "large hill place" identified by Capt. John Smith as being near Milton, Mass.

Michigan—From Chippewa words mici gama meaning "great water," after the lake of the same name.

Minnesota—From Dakota Sioux word meaning "cloudy water" or "sky-tinted water" of the Minnesota River.

Mississippi—Probably Chippewa; mici zibi, "great river" or "gathering-in of all the waters." Also: Algonquin word, "Messipi."

Missouri—An Algonquin Indian term meaning "river of the big canoes."

Montana—Latin or Spanish for "mountainous."

Nebraska—From Omaha or Otos Indian word meaning "broad water" or "flat river," describing the Platte River.

Nevada—Spanish, meaning snow-clad.

New Hampshire—Named 1629 by Capt. John Mason of Plymouth Council for his home county in England.

New Jersey—The Duke of York, 1664, gave a patent to John Berkeley and Sir George Carteret to be called Nova Caesaria, or New Jersey, after England's Isle of Jersey.

New Mexico—Spaniards in Mexico applied term to land north and west of Rio Grande in the 16th century.

New York—For Duke of York and Albany who received patent to New Netherland from his brother Charles II and sent an expedition to capture it, 1664.

North Carolina—In 1619 Charles I gave a large patent to Sir Robert Heath to be called Province of Carolana, from Carolus, Latin name for Charles. A new patent was granted by Charles II to Earl of Clarendon and others. Divided into North and South Carolina, 1710.

North Dakota—Dakota is Sioux for friend or ally.

Ohio—Iroquois word for "fine or good river."

Oklahoma—Choctaw coined word meaning red man, proposed by Rev. Allen Wright, Choctaw-speaking Indian.

Oregon—Origin unknown. One theory holds that the name may have been derived from that of the Wisconsin River shown on a 1715 French map as "Ouaricon-sint."

Pennsylvania—William Penn, the Quaker, who was made full proprietor by King Charles II in 1681, suggested Sylvania, or woodland, for his tract. The king's government owed Penn's father, Admiral William Penn, £16,000, and the land was granted as partial settlement. Charles II added the Penn to Sylvania, against the desires of the modest proprietor, in honor of the admiral.

Puerto Rico—Spanish for Rich Port.

Rhode Island—Exact origin is unknown. One theory notes that Giovanni de Verrazano recorded an island about the size of Rhodes in the Mediterranean in 1524, but others believe the state was named Roode Eylandt by Adriaen Block, Dutch explorer, because of its red clay.

South Carolina—See North Carolina.

South Dakota—See North Dakota.

Tennessee—Tanasi was the name of Cherokee villages on the Little Tennessee River. From 1784 to 1788 this was the State of Franklin, or Frankland.

Texas—Variant of word used by Caddo and other Indians meaning friends or allies, and applied to them by the Spanish in eastern Texas. Also written texias, tejas, teysas.

Utah—From a Navajo word meaning upper, or higher up, as applied to a Shoshone tribe called Ute. Spanish form is Yutta, English Uta or Utah. Proposed name Deseret, "land of honeybees," from Book of Mormon, was rejected by Congress.

Vermont—From French words vert (green) and mont (mountain). The Green Mountains were said to have been named by Samuel de Champlain. When the state was formed, 1777, Dr. Thomas Young suggested combining vert and mont into Vermont.

Virginia—Named by Sir Walter Raleigh, who fitted out the expedition of 1584, in honor of Queen Elizabeth, the Virgin Queen of England.

Washington—Named after George Washington. When the bill creating the Territory of Columbia was introduced in the 32d Congress, the name was changed to Washington because of the existence of the District of Columbia.

West Virginia—So named when western counties of Virginia refused to secede from the United States, 1863.

Wisconsin—An Indian name, spelled Ouisconsin and Mesconsing by early chroniclers. Believed to mean "grassy place" in Chippewa. Congress made it Wisconsin.

Wyoming—The word was taken from Wyoming Valley, Pa., which was the site of an Indian massacre and became widely known by Campbell's poem, "Gertrude of Wyoming." In Algonquin it means "large prairie place."

Territorial Sea of the U.S.

According to a December 27, 1988 proclamation by Pres. Ronald Reagan: "The territorial sea of the United States henceforth extends to 12 nautical miles from the baselines of the United States determined in accordance with international law. In accordance with international law, as reflected in the applicable provisions of the 1982 United Nations Convention on the Law of the Sea, within the territorial sea of the United States, the ships of all countries enjoy the right of innocent passage and the ships and aircraft of all countries enjoy the right of transit passage through international straits."

Accession of Territory by the U.S.

Source: Bureau of the Census, U.S. Dept. of Commerce

	Acquisition date	Gross Area (Land and water) Sq. mi.
Total U.S.	**(x)**	**3,623,434**
United States	(x)	3,618,770
Territory in 1790[1]	(x)	891,364
Louisiana Purchase	1803	831,321
Purchase of Florida	1819	69,866
Texas	1845	384,958
Oregon	1846	283,439
Mexican Cession	1848	530,706
Gadsden Purchase	1853	29,640
Alaska	1867	591,004
Hawaii	1898	6,471
Other areas:		
Puerto Rico	[2]1898	3,515
Guam	[3]1898	209
American Samoa	[4]1899	77
Virgin Islands of the U.S.	1917	132
Pacific Islands, Trust Territory of the[5]	1947	533
No. Mariana Islands[5]	1947	184
All other[6]	(x)	14

(x) Not applicable. (1) Includes that part of drainage basin of Red River of the North, south of 49th parallel, sometimes considered part of Louisiana Purchase. (2) Ceded by Spain in 1898, ratified in 1899, and became Commonwealth of Puerto Rico by Act of Congress on July 25, 1952. (3) Acquired 1898; ratified 1899. (4) Acquired 1899; ratified 1900. (5) Land area only. (6) Comprises the following islands with gross areas as indicated, in sq. mi.: Midway (2), Wake (3), Palmyra (4), Navassa (2), Baker, Howland, and Jarvis (combined area, 3), Johnston Atoll (combined area, less than .5), and Kingman Reef (less than .5). Excludes Canton and Enderbury Islands (combined area 27 sq. mi.), which are considered to be under the jurisdiction of Kiribati since 1979, and Swan Islands (1 sq. mi.), which were returned to Honduras in 1972.

Public Lands of the U. S.

Source: Bureau of Land Management, U.S. Dept. of the Interior

Disposition of Public Lands 1781 to 1990

Disposition by methods not elsewhere classified[1]	Acres
Disposition by methods not elsewhere classified[1]	303,500,000
Granted or sold to homesteaders	287,500,000
Granted to railroad corporations	94,400,000
Granted to veterans as military bounties	61,000,000
Confirmed as private land claims[2]	34,000,000
Sold under timber and stone law[3]	13,900,000
Granted or sold under timber culture law[4]	10,900,000
Sold under desert land law[5]	10,700,000

Granted to states for:	Acres
Support of common schools	77,630,000
Reclamation of swampland	64,920,000
Construction of railroads	37,130,000
Support of misc. institutions[6]	21,700,000
Purposes not elsewhere classified[7]	117,600,000
Canals and rivers	6,100,000
Construction of wagon roads	3,400,000
Total granted to states	**328,480,000**

(1) Chiefly public, private, and preemption sales, but includes mineral entries, scrip locations, sales of townsites and townlots. (2) The Government has confirmed title to lands claimed under valid grants made by foreign governments prior to the acquisition of the public domain by the United States. (3) The law provided for the sale of lands valuable for timber or stone and unfit for cultivation. (4) The law provided for the granting of public lands to settlers on condition that they plant and cultivate trees on the lands granted. (5) The law provided for the sale of arid agricultural public lands to settlers who irrigate them and bring them under cultivation. (6) Universities, hospitals, asylums, etc. (7) For construction of various public improvements (individual items not specified in the granting act) reclamation of desert lands, construction of water reservoirs, etc.

Public Lands Administered by Federal Agencies

Agency (Acres, Sept. 30, 1991)	Public domain	Acquired	Total
Forest Service	161,038,854.3	28,341,223.5	189,380,077.8
Bureau of Land Management	269,710,529	2,318,889	272,029,418
Bureau of Reclamation	3,533,817.5	1,969,275.9	5,503,093.4
Fish and Wildlife Service	81,321,344	10,097,347	91,318,691
National Park Service	64,325,741.0	8,517,114.8	72,842,855.8
Bureau of Indian Affairs	2,554,358.7	193,079.6	2,747,438.3
Tennessee Valley Authority	0	1,040,231.3	1,040,231.3
Corps of Engineers	604,971.2	4,869,200.0	5,474,171.2
U.S. Army	3,187,901.0	6,495,173.0	9,683,074.0
U.S. Navy	618,005.6	1,743,750.2	2,361,755.8
U.S. Air Force	6,858,510.0	1,255,022.0	8,113,532.0
Department of Energy	1,465,862.4	700,478.8	2,166,341.2
Total, all agencies (incl. those not shown)	**660,976,655.8**	**63,089,515.1**	**724,066,170.9**

National Recreation Areas Administered by Forest Service

			Acreage
Allegheny	Pa.	1984	23,063
Arapaho	Col.	1978	34,928
Flaming Gorge	Ut.-Wyo.	1968	201,114
Grand Island	Mich.	1990	12,957
Hells Canyon	Ida.-Ore.	1975	541,336
Mount Baker	Wash.	1984	8,473
Mount Rogers	Va.	1966	154,816
Oregon Dunes	Ore.	1972	31,566
Pine Ridge	Neb.	1986	6,600
Rattlesnake	Mon.	1980	61,000
Sawtooth	Ida.	1972	756,019
Smith River	Col.	1990	331,229
Spruce Knob-Seneca Rocks	W. Va.	1965	100,000
Whiskeytown Shasta-Trinity	Cal.	1965	203,587
White Rocks	Vt.	1984	36,400
Winding Stair Mtn.	Okl.	1988	26,445

National Parks, Other Areas Administered by Nat'l. Park Service

Figures given are date area initially protected by Congress or presidential proclamation, date given current designation, and gross area in acres 12/31/90.

National Parks

Acadia, Me. (1916/1929) 41,888. Includes Mount Desert Island, half of Isle au Haut, Schoodic Point on mainland. Highest elevation on Eastern seaboard.

Arches, Ut. (1929/1971) 73,379. Contains giant red sandstone arches and other products of erosion.

Badlands, S.D. (1929/1978) 242,756; eroded prairie, bison, bighorn and antelope. Contains animal fossils of 40 million years ago.

Big Bend, Tex. (1935/1944) 801,163. Rio Grande, Chisos Mts.

Biscayne, Fla. (1968/1980) 173,467. Aquatic park encompasses chain of islands south of Miami.

Bryce Canyon, Ut. (1923/1928) 35,835. Spectacularly colorful and unusual display of erosion effects.

Canyonlands, Ut. (1964) 337,570. At junction of Colorado and Green rivers, extensive evidence of prehistoric Indians.

Capitol Reef, Ut. (1937/1971) 241,904. A 60-mile uplift of sandstone cliffs dissected by high-walled gorges.

Carlsbad Caverns, N.M. (1923/1930) 46,775. Largest known caverns; not yet fully explored.

Channel Islands, Cal. (1938/1980) 249,354. Seal lion breeding place, nesting sea birds, unique plants.

Crater Lake, Ore. (1902) 183,224. Extraordinary blue lake in crater of extinct volcano encircled by lava walls 500 to 2,000 feet high.

Denali, Alas. (1917/1980) 4,716,726. Name changed from Mt. McKinley NP. Contains highest mountain in U.S.; wildlife.

Everglades, Fla. (1934) 1,506,499. Largest remaining subtropical wilderness in continental U.S.

Gates of the Arctic, Alas. (1978/1980) 7,523,888. Vast wilderness in north central region.

Glacier, Mon. (1910) 1,013,572. Superb Rocky Mt. scenery, numerous glaciers and glacial lakes. Part of Waterton-Glacier Intl. Peace Park established by U.S. and Canada in 1932.

Glacier Bay, Alas. (1925/1980) 3,225,284. Great tidewater glaciers that move down mountain sides and break up into the sea; much wildlife.

Grand Canyon, Ariz. (1908/1919) 1,218,375. Most spectacular part of Colorado River's greatest canyon.

Grand Teton, Wy. (1929) 309,994. Most impressive part of the Teton Mountains, winter feeding ground of largest American elk herd.

Great Basin, Nev. (1922/1986) 77,100. Wide basins and high mountain ranges.

Great Smoky Mountains, N.C.-Tenn. (1926/1934) 520,269. Largest eastern mountain range, magnificent forests.

Guadalupe Mountains, Tex. (1966/1972) 86,416. Extensive Permian limestone fossil reef; tremendous earth fault.

Haleakala, Ha. (1916/1960) 28,655. Dormant volcano on Maui with large colorful craters.

Hawaii Volcanoes, Ha. (1916/1961) 229,177. Contains Kilauea and Mauna Loa, active volcanoes.

Hot Springs, Ark. (1832/1921) 5,839. Government supervised bath houses use waters of 45 of the 47 natural hot springs.

Isle Royale, Mich. (1931) 571,790. Largest island in Lake Superior, noted for its wilderness area and wildlife.

Katmai, Alas. (1918/1980) 3,716,000. Valley of Ten Thousand Smokes, scene of 1912 volcanic eruption.

Kenai Fjords, Alas. (1978/1980) 669,541. Abundant mountain goats, marine mammals, birdlife; the Harding Icefield, one of the major icecaps in U.S.

Kings Canyon, Cal. (1890/1940) 461,901. Mountain wilderness, dominated by Kings River Canyons and High Sierra; contains giant sequoias.

Kobuk Valley, Alas. (1978/1980) 1,750,421. Broad river is core of native culture.

Lake Clark, Alas. (1978/1980) 2,636,839. Across Cook Inlet from Anchorage. A scenic wilderness rich in fish and wildlife.

Lassen Volcanic, Cal. (1907/1916) 106,372. Contains Lassen Peak, recently active volcano, and other volcanic phenomena.

Mammoth Cave, Ky. (1926/1941) 52,419. 144 miles of surveyed underground passages, beautiful natural formations, river 300 feet below surface.

Mesa Verde, Col. (1906) 52,122. Most notable and best preserved prehistoric cliff dwellings in the United States.

Mount Rainier, Wash. (1899) 235,612. Greatest single-peak glacial system in the lower 48 states.

North Cascades, Wash. (1968) 504,781. Spectacular mountainous region with many glaciers, lakes.

Olympic, Wash. (1909/1938) 922,654. Mountain wilderness containing finest remnant of Pacific Northwest rain forest, active glaciers, Pacific shoreline, rare elk.

Petrified Forest, Ariz. (1906/1962) 93,533. Extensive petrified wood and Indian artifacts. Contains part of Painted Desert.

Redwood, Cal. (1968) 110,132. Forty miles of Pacific coastline, groves of ancient redwoods and world's tallest trees.

Rocky Mountain, Col. (1915) 265,198. On the continental divide, includes 107 named peaks over 11,000 feet.

Samoa, American Samoa (1988) 9,000. Features the only paleotropical rain forest.

Sequoia, Cal. (1890) 402,482. Groves of giant sequoias, highest mountain in contiguous United States — Mount Whitney (14,494 feet). World's largest tree.

Shenandoah, Va. (1926/1935) 195,039. Portion of the Blue Ridge Mountains; overlooks Shenandoah Valley; Skyline Drive.

Theodore Roosevelt, N.D. (1947/1978) 70,447. Contains part of T.R.'s ranch and scenic badlands.

Virgin Islands, V.I. (1956) 14,689. Covers 75% of St. John Island, lush growth, lovely beaches, Indian relics, evidence of colonial Danes.

Voyageurs, Minn. (1971/1975) 218,035. Abundant lakes, forests, wildlife, canoeing, boating.

Wind Cave, S.D. (1903) 28,295. Limestone caverns in Black Hills. Extensive wildlife includes a herd of bison.

Wrangell-St. Elias, Alas. (1978/1980) 8,331,604. Largest area in park system, most peaks over 16,000 feet, abundant wildlife; day's drive east of Anchorage.

Yellowstone, Ida., Mon., Wy., (1872) 2,219,791. Oldest national park. World's greatest geyser area has about 3,000 geysers and hot springs; spectacular falls and impressive canyons of the Yellowstone River; grizzly bear, moose, and bison.

Yosemite, Cal. (1890) 761,170. Yosemite Valley, the nation's highest waterfall, 3 groves of sequoias, and mountainous.

Zion, Ut. (1909/1919) 146,598. Unusual shapes and landscapes have resulted from erosion and faulting; Zion Canyon, with sheer walls ranging up to 2,500 feet, is readily accessible.

National Historical Parks

Appomattox Court House, Va. (1930/1954) 1,325. Where Lee surrendered to Grant.

Boston, Mass. (1974) 41. Includes Faneuil Hall, Old North Church, Bunker Hill, Paul Revere House.

Chaco Culture, N.M. (1907/1980) 33,974. Ruins of pueblos built by prehistoric Indians.

Chesapeake and Ohio Canal, Md.-W.Va.-D.C. (1961/1971) 20,781. 184 mile historic canal; D.C. to Cumberland, Md.

Colonial, Va. (1930/1936) 9,327. Includes most of Jamestown Island, site of first successful English colony; Yorktown, site of Cornwallis' surrender to George Washington; and the Colonial Parkway.

Cumberland Gap, Ky.-Tenn.-Va. (1940) 20,274. Mountain pass of the Wilderness Road which carried the first great migration of pioneers into America's interior.

George Rogers Clark, Vincennes, Ind. (1966) 26. Commemorates American defeat of British in west during Revolution.

Harpers Ferry, Md., W. Va. (1944/1963) 2,239. At the confluence of the Shenandoah and Potomac rivers, the site of John Brown's 1859 raid on the Army arsenal.

Independence, Pa. (1948/1956) 45. Contains several properties in Philadelphia associated with the Revolutionary War and the founding of the U.S. Includes Independence Hall.

Jean Laffite (and preserve), La. (1939/1978) 20,020. Includes Chalmette, site of 1815 Battle of New Orleans; French Quarter.

Kalaupapa, Ha. (1980) 10,779. Molokai's former leper colony site and other historic areas.

Kaloko-Honokohau, Ha. (1978) 1,161. Culture center has 234 historic features and grave of first king, Kamehameha.

Klondike Gold Rush, Alas.-Wash. (1976) 13,191. Alaskan Trails in 1898 Gold Rush. Museum in Seattle.

Lowell, Mass. (1978) 137. Seven mills, canal, 19th C. structures, park to show planned city of Industrial Revolution.

Lyndon B. Johnson, Tex. (1969/1980) 1,571. President's birthplace, boyhood home, ranch.

Minute Man, Mass. (1959) 750. Where the colonial Minute Men battled the British, April 19, 1775. Also contains Nathaniel Hawthorne's home.

Morristown, N.J. (1933) 1,671. Sites of important military encampments during the Revolutionary War; Washington's headquarters 1777, 1779-80.

Natchez, Miss. (1988) 80. Mansions, townhouses, and villas concerning history of Natchez, Miss.

Nez Perce, Ida. (1965) 2,109. Illustrates the history and culture of the Nez Perce Indian country. 20 separate sites.

Pecos, N.M. (1965/1990) 6,547. Ruins of ancient 15th century Pueblo of Pecos, archeological sites, and 2 associated Spanish colonial missions from the 17th and 18th centuries.

Pu'uhonua o Honaunau, Ha. (1955/1978) 182. Until 1819, a sanctuary for Hawaiians vanquished in battle, and those guilty of crimes or breaking taboos.

Salt River Bay, St. Croix, V.I. (1922). The only site known where, 500 years ago, members of a Columbus party landed on what is now territory of the U.S.

San Antonio Missions, Tex. (1978/1983) 493. Four of finest Spanish missions in U.S., 18th C. irrigation system.

San Francisco Maritime (1988) 50. Artifacts, photographs, and historic vessels related to the development of the Pacific Coast.

San Juan Island, Wash. (1966) 1,752. Commemorates peaceful relations of the U.S., Canada and Great Britain since the 1872 boundary disputes.

Saratoga, N.Y. (1938) 3,393. Scene of a major battle which became a turning point in the War of Independence.

Sitka, Alas. (1910/1972) 107. Scene of last major resistance of the Tlingit Indians to the Russians, 1804.

Tumacacori, Ariz. (1908/1990) 17. Historic Spanish Catholic mission building stands near the site first visited by Jesuit Father Kino in 1691.

Valley Forge, Pa. (1976) 3,468. Continental Army campsite in 1777-78 winter.

War in the Pacific, Guam (1978) 1,960. Scenic park memorial for WWII combatants in Pacific.

Women's Rights, N.Y. (1980) 6. Seneca Falls site where Susan B. Anthony, Elizabeth Cady Stanton began rights movement in 1848.

Zuni-Cibola, N. Mex. (1988) 800. Historical, archeological, and cultural site associated with the Zuni Tribe over its 1700-year cultural continuum.

National Battlefields

Antietam, Md. (1890/1978) 3,244. Battle ended first Confederate invasion of North, Sept. 17, 1862.

Big Hole, Mon. (1910/1963) 656. Site of major battle with Nez Perce Indians.

Cowpens, S.C. (1929/1972) 842. Revolutionary War battlefield.

Fort Donelson, Tenn. (1928/1985) 536. Site of first major Union victory.

Fort Necessity, Pa. (1931/1961) 903. First battle of French and Indian War.

Monocacy, Md. (1934/1976) 1,647. Civil War battle in defense of Wash., D.C., July 9, 1864.

Moores Creek, N.C. (1926/1980) 87. 1776 battle between Patriots and Loyalists commemorated here.

Petersburg, Va. (1926/1962) 2,735. Scene of 10-month Union campaign 1864-65.

Stones River, Tenn. (1927/1960) 403. Civil War battle leading to Sherman's "March to the Sea."

Tupelo, Miss. (1929/1961) 1. Crucial battle over Sherman's supply line.

Wilson's Creek, Mo. (1960/1970) 1,750. Civil War battle for control of Missouri.

National Battlefield Parks

Kennesaw Mountain, Ga. (1917/1935) 2,885. Two major battles of Atlanta campaign in Civil War.

Manassas, Va. (1940) 5,072. Two battles of Bull Run in Civil War, 1861 and 1862.

Richmond, Va. (1936) 769. Site of battles defending Confederate capital.

National Battlefield Site

Brices Cross Roads, Miss. (1929) 1. Civil War battlefield.

National Military Parks

Chickamauga and Chattanooga, Ga.-Tenn. (1890) 8,106. Four Civil War battlefields.

Fredericksburg and Spotsylvania County, Va. (1927) 7,688. Sites of several major Civil War battles and campaigns.

Gettysburg, Pa. (1895) 3,942. Site of decisive Confederate defeat in North. Gettysburg Address.

Guilford Courthouse, N.C. (1917) 220. Revolutionary War battle site.

Horseshoe Bend, Ala. (1956) 2,040. On Tallapoosa River, where Gen. Andrew Jackson broke the power of the Creek Indian Confederacy.

Kings Mountain, S.C. (1931) 3,945. Revolutionary War battle.

Pea Ridge, Ark. (1956) 4,300. Civil War battle.

Shiloh, Tenn. (1894) 3,838. Major Civil War battle; site includes some well-preserved Indian burial mounds.

Vicksburg, Miss. (1899) 1,620. Union victory gave North control of the Mississippi and split the Confederacy in two.

National Memorials

Arkansas Post, Ark. (1960) 389. First permanent French settlement in the lower Mississippi River valley.

Arlington House, the Robert E. Lee Memorial, Va. (1925/1972) 28. Lee's home overlooking the Potomac.

Chamizal, El Paso, Tex. (1966/1974) 55. Commemorates 1963 settlement of 99-year border dispute with Mexico.

Coronado, Ariz. (1941/1952) 4,750. Commemorates first European exploration of the Southwest.

DeSoto, Fla. (1948) 27. Commemorates 16th-century Spanish explorations.

Federal Hall, N.Y. (1939/1955) 0.45. First seat of U.S. government under the Constitution.

Fort Caroline, Fla. (1950) 138. On St. Johns River, overlooks site of second attempt by French Huguenots to colonize North America.

Fort Clatsop, Ore. (1958) 125. Lewis and Clark encampment 1805-06.

General Grant, N.Y. (1958) 0.76. Tombs of Pres. and wife.

Hamilton Grange, N.Y. (1962) 0.11. Home of Alexander Hamilton.

Jefferson National Expansion, St. Louis, Mo. (1935/1969) 191. Commemorates westward expansion.

John F. Kennedy Center for the Performing Arts, D.C. (1958/1964) 18.

Johnstown Flood, Pa. (1964) 164. Commemorates tragic flood of 1889.

Lincoln Boyhood, Ind. (1962) 200. Lincoln grew up here.

Lincoln Memorial, D.C. (1911) 110.

Lyndon B. Johnson Grove on the Potomac, D.C. (1973) 17.

Mount Rushmore, S.D. (1925) 1,278. World famous sculpture of 4 presidents.

Perry's Victory and International Peace Memorial, Put-in-Bay, Oh. (1936/1978) 25. The world's most massive Doric column, constructed 1912-15, to inculcate the lessons of international peace by arbitration and disarmament.

Roger Williams, R.I. (1965) 5. Memorial to founder of Rhode Island.

Thaddeus Kosciuszko, Pa. (1972) 0.02. Memorial to Polish hero of American Revolution.

Theodore Roosevelt Island, D.C. (1932) 89.

Thomas Jefferson Memorial, D.C. (1934) 18.

USS Arizona, Ha. (1980). 00. Memorializes American losses at Pearl Harbor.

Vietnam Veterans, D.C. (1980) 2. Black granite wall inscribed with names of killed in action and missing in the Vietnam War.

Washington Monument, D.C. (1848) 106.

Wright Brothers, N.C. (1927/1953) 431. Site of first powered flight.

National Historic Sites

Abraham Lincoln Birthplace, Hodgenville, Ky. (1916/1959) 117.

Adams, Quincy, Mass. (1946/1952) 10. Home of Presidents John Adams, John Quincy Adams, and celebrated descendants.

Allegheny Portage Railroad, Pa. (1964) 1,247. Part of the Pennsylvania Canal system.

Andersonville, Andersonville, Ga. (1970) 495. Noted Civil War prison.

Andrew Johnson, Greeneville, Tenn. (1935/1963) 17. Home of the President.

Bent's Old Fort, Col. (1960) 800. Old West fur-trading post.

Boston African American (1980) Pre-Civil War black history structures.

Carl Sandburg Home, N.C. (1968/1972) 264. Poet's home.

Charles Pinckney, S.C. (1988) 25.

Christiansted, St. Croix; V.I. (1952/1961) 27. Commemorates Danish colony.

Clara Barton, Md. (1974) 9. Home of founder of American Red Cross.

Edgar Allan Poe, Pa. (1978/1980) 1. Poet's home.

Edison, West Orange, N.J. (1955/1962) 21. Home and laboratory.

Eisenhower, Gettysburg, Pa. (1967/1969) 690. Home of 34th president.

Eleanor Roosevelt, Hyde Park, N.Y. (1977) 181. Personal retreat.

Eugene O'Neill, Danville, Cal. (1976) 13. Playwright's home.

Ford's Theatre, Washington, D.C. (1866/1970) 0.29. Includes theater, now restored, where Lincoln was assassinated, house where he died, and Lincoln Museum.

Fort Bowie, Ariz. (1964/1972) 1,000. Focal point of operations against Geronimo and the Apaches.

Fort Davis, Tex. (1961/1963) 460. Frontier outpost battled Comanches and Apaches.

Fort Laramie, Wy. (1938/1960) 833. Military post on Oregon Trail.

Fort Larned, Kan. (1964/1966) 718. Military post on Santa Fe Trail.

Fort Point, San Francisco, Cal. (1970) 29. Largest West Coast fortification.

Fort Raleigh, N.C. (1941) 157. First English settlement.

Fort Scott, Kan. (1965/1978) 17. Commemorates U.S. frontier of 1840-50.

Fort Smith, Ark. (1961) 75. Active post from 1817 to 1890.

Fort Union Trading Post, Mon., N.D. (1966) 442. Principal fur-trading post on upper Missouri, 1829-1867.

Fort Vancouver, Wash. (1948/1961) 209. Hdqts. for Hudson's Bay Company in 1825. Early military and political seat.

Frederick Douglass Home, D.C. (1962/1988) 9. Home of nation's leading black spokesman.

Frederick Law Olmsted, Mass. (1979) 2. Home of famous park planner (1822-1903).

Friendship Hill, Pa. (1978) 675. Home of Albert Gallatin, Jefferson's Sec'y of Treasury. Not open to public.

Golden Spike, Utah (1957) 2,735. Commemorates completion of first transcontinental railroad in 1869.

Grant-Kohrs Ranch, Mon. (1972) 1,498. Ranch house and part of 19th century ranch.

Hampton, Md. (1948) 62. 18th-century Georgian mansion.

Harry S. Truman, Mo. (1983). 0.78. Home of Pres. Truman after 1919.

Herbert Hoover, West Branch, Ia. (1965) 187. Birthplace and boyhood home of 31st president.

Home of Franklin D. Roosevelt, Hyde Park, N.Y. (1944) 290. Birthplace, home and "Summer White House".

Hopewell Furnace, Pa. (1938/1985) 848. 19th-century iron making village.

Hubbell Trading Post, Ariz. (1965) 160. Indian trading post.

James A. Garfield, Mentor, Oh. (1980) 8. President's home.

Jimmy Carter, Ga. (1987) 70. Birthplace and home of 39th president.

John Fitzgerald Kennedy, Brookline, Mass. (1967) 0.09. Birthplace and childhood home of the President.

John Muir, Martinez, Cal. (1964) 340. Home of early conservationist and writer.

Knife River Indian Villages, N.D. (1974) 1,293. Remnants of 5 Hidatsa villages.

Lincoln Home, Springfield, Ill. (1971) 12. Lincoln's residence when he was elected President, 1860.

Longfellow, Cambridge, Mass. (1972) 2. Longfellow's home, 1837-82, and Washington's hq. during Boston Siege, 1775-76.

Maggie L. Walker, Va. (1978) 1. Richmond home of black leader and 1903 founder of bank.

Manzanar, Lone Pine, Cal. (1992) 640. Commemorates Manzanar War Relocation Ctr., a Japanese-American internment camp during WWII.

Martin Luther King, Jr., Atlanta, Ga. (1980) 23. Birthplace, grave.

Martin Van Buren, N.Y. (1974) 40. Lindenwald, home of 8th president, near Kinderhook.

Mary McLeod Bethune Council House, D.C. (1991). Museum dedicated to the lives and achievements of black American women.

Ninety Six, S.C. (1976) 989. Colonial trading village.

Palo Alto Battlefield, Tex. (1978) 50. One of 2 Mexican War battles fought in U.S.

Pennsylvania Avenue, D.C. (1965) NA. Includes area between Capitol and White House, Ford's Theatre.

Puukohola Heiau, Ha. (1972) 80. Ruins of temple built by King Kamehameha.

Sagamore Hill, Oyster Bay, N.Y. (1962) 83. Home of President Theodore Roosevelt from 1885 until his death in 1919.

Saint-Gaudens, Cornish, N.H. (1964/1977) 148. Home, studio and gardens of American sculptor Augustus Saint-Gaudens.

Saint Paul's Church, N.Y. (1943/1978) 6. Eighteenth Century site of John Peter Zenger's "freedom of press" trial.

Salem Maritime, Mass. (1938) 9. Only port never seized from the patriots by the British. Major fishing and whaling port.

San Juan, P.R. (1949) 75. 16th-century Spanish fortifications.

Saugus Iron Works, Mass. (1968) 9. Reconstructed 17th-century colonial ironworks.

Springfield Armory, Mass. (1974) 55. Small arms manufacturing center for nearly 200 years.

Steamtown, Pa. (1986) 44. Railyard, roadhouse and repair shops of former Delaware, Lackawanna and Western Railroad.

Theodore Roosevelt Birthplace, N.Y., N.Y. (1962) 0.11.

Theodore Roosevelt Inaugural, Buffalo, N.Y. (1966) 1. Wilcox House where he took oath of office, 1901.

Thomas Stone, Md. (1978) 328. Home of signer of Declaration, built in 1771. Not open to public.

Tuskegee Institute, Ala. (1974) 68. College founded by Booker T. Washington in 1881 for blacks.

Ulysses S. Grant, St. Louis Co., Mo. (1989) 10. Home of Grant during pre-Civil War years.

Vanderbilt Mansion, Hyde Park, N.Y. (1940) 212. Mansion of 19th-century financier.

Weir Farm, Witon, Conn. (1990) 62. Home and studios of American Impressionist painter J. Alden Weir.

Whitman Mission, Wash. (1936/1963) 98. Site where Dr. and Mrs. Marcus Whitman ministered to the Indians until slain by them in 1847.

William Howard Taft, Cincinnati, Oh. (1969) 3. Birthplace and early home of the 27th president.

National Monuments

Name	State	Year	Acreage
Agate Fossil Beds	Neb.	1965	3,055
Alibates Flint Quarries	N.M.-Tex.	1965	1,371
Aniakchak	Alas.	1978	17
Aztec Ruins	N.M.	1923	319
Bandelier	N.M.	1916	32,737
Black Canyon of the Gunnison	Col.	1933	20,766
Booker T. Washington	Va.	1956	224
Buck Island Reef	V.I.	1961	880
Cabrillo	Cal.	1913	137
Canyon de Chelly	Ariz.	1931	83,840
Cape Krusenstern	Alas.	1978	659,807
Capulin Volcano	N.M.	1916	793
Casa Grande Ruins	Ariz.	1892	473
Castillo de San Marcos	Fla.	1924	20
Castle Clinton	N.Y.	1946	1
Cedar Breaks	Ut.	1933	6,155
Chiricahua	Ariz.	1924	11,985
Colorado	Col.	1911	20,454
Congaree Swamp	S.C.	1976	22,200
Craters of the Moon	Ida.	1924	53,545
Death Valley	Cal.-Nev.	1933	2,067,628
Devils Postpile	Cal.	1911	798
Devils Tower	Wy.	1906	1,347
Dinosaur	Col.-Ut.	1915	210,844
Effigy Mounds	Ia.	1949	1,481
El Malpais	N.M.	1987	114,335
El Morro	N.M.	1906	1,279
Florissant Fossil Beds**	Col.	1969	5,998
Fort Frederica	Ga.	1936	216
Fort Jefferson	Fla.	1935	64,700
Fort Matanzas	Fla.	1924	228
Fort McHenry National Monument and Historic Shrine	Md.	1925	43
Fort Pulaski	Ga.	1924	5,623
Fort Stanwix	N.Y.	1935	16
Fort Sumter	S.C.	1948	194
Fort Union	N.M.	1954	721
Fossil Butte	Wy.	1972	8,198
G. Washington Birthplace	Va.	1930	533
George Washington Carver	Mo.	1943	210
Gila Cliff Dwellings	N.M.	1907	533
Grand Portage	Minn.	1951	710
Great Sand Dunes	Col.	1932	38,662
Hagerman Fossil Beds	Ida.	1988	4,280
Hohokam Pima*	Ariz.	1972	1,690
Homestead Nat'l. Monument of America	Neb.	1936	195
Hovenweep	Col.-Ut.	1923	785
Jewel Cave	S.D.	1908	1,274
John Day Fossil Beds	Ore.	1974	14,014
Joshua Tree	Cal.	1936	559,955
Lava Beds	Cal.	1925	46,560
Little Big Horn Battlefield	Mon.	1879	765
Montezuma Castle	Ariz.	1906	858
Mound City Group	Oh.	1923	270
Muir Woods	Cal.	1908	554
Natural Bridges	Ut.	1908	7,636
Navajo	Ariz.	1909	360
Ocmulgee	Ga.	1934	683
Oregon Caves	Ore.	1909	488
Organ Pipe Cactus	Ariz.	1937	330,689
Petroglyph	N.M.	1990	5,207
Pinnacles	Cal.	1908	16,265
Pipe Spring	Ariz.	1923	40
Pipestone	Minn.	1937	282
Poverty Point	La.	1988	911
Rainbow Bridge	Ut.	1910	160
Russell Cave	Ala.	1961	310
Saguaro	Ariz.	1933	83,574
Salinas	N.M.	1909	1,077
Scotts Bluff	Neb.	1919	2,997
Statue of Liberty	N.J.-N.Y.	1924	58
Sunset Crater	Ariz.	1930	3,040
Timpanogos Cave	Ut.	1922	250
Tonto	Ariz.	1907	1,120

Name	State	Year	Acreage
Tuzigoot	Ariz.	1939	801
Walnut Canyon	Ariz.	1915	2,249
White Sands	N.M.	1933	143,733
Wupatki	Ariz.	1924	35,253
Yucca House*	Col.	1919	10

National Preserves

Name	State	Year	Acreage
Aniakchak	Alas.	1978	465,603
Bering Land Bridge	Alas.	1978	2,784,960
Big Cypress	Fla.	1974	716,000
Big Thicket	Tex.	1974	85,736
Denali	Alas.	1917	1,311,365
Gates of the Arctic	Alas.	1978	948,629
Glacier Bay	Alas.	1925	57,884
Katmai	Alas.	1918	374,000
Lake Clark	Alas.	1978	1,407,293
Noatak	Alas.	1978	6,574,481
Timucuan Ecological & Historic Preserve	Fla.	1988	46,000
Wrangell-St. Elias	Alas.	1978	4,856,721
Yukon-Charley Rivers	Alas.	1978	2,523,509

National Seashores

Name	State	Year	Acreage
Assateague Island	Md.-Va.	1965	39,631
Canaveral	Fla.	1975	57,662
Cape Cod	Mass.	1961	43,558
Cape Hatteras	N.C.	1937	30,319
Cape Lookout**	N.C.	1966	28,243
Cumberland Island	Ga.	1972	36,415
Fire Island	N.Y.	1964	19,579
Gulf Islands	Fla.-Miss.	1971	135,618
Padre Island	Tex.	1962	130,434
Point Reyes	Cal.	1962	71,050

National Parkways

Name	State	Year	Acreage
Blue Ridge	Va.-N.C.	1936	86,941
George Washington Memorial	Va.-Md.	1930	7,159
John D. Rockefeller Jr. Mem.	Wy.	1972	23,777
Natchez Trace	Ala.-Miss.-Tenn.	1938	51,742

National Lakeshores

Name	State	Year	Acreage
Apostle Islands	Wis.	1970	69,372
Indiana Dunes	Ind.	1966	13,845
Pictured Rocks	Mich.	1966	72,903
Sleeping Bear Dunes	Mich.	1970	71,188

National Reserve

Name	State	Year	Acreage
City of Rocks	Ida.	1988	14,407

National Rivers

Name	State	Year	Acreage
Big South Fork Natl. R. and Recreation	Tenn.-Ky.	1976	122,960
Buffalo	Ark.	1972	94,219
New River Gorge	W.Va.	1978	62,144
Ozark	Mo.	1964	80,791
Mississippi Natl. R. and Recreation	Minn.	1988	50,000
Niobrara/Missouri	Neb.-S.D.	1991	76

National Wild and Scenic Rivers

Name	State	Year	Acreage
Alagnak Wild	Alas.	1980	24,038
Bluestone	W.Va.	1988	N.A.
Delaware	N.Y.-N.J.-Pa.	1978	1,973
Lower Saint Croix	Minn.-Wis.	1972	9,475
Missouri Natl. Recreational River	Neb.	1978	0
Obed Wild	Tenn.	1976	5,075
Rio Grande	Tex.	1978	9,600
Saint Croix	Minn.-Wis.	1968	67,379
Upper Delaware	N.Y.-N.J.	1978	75,000

Parks (no other classification)

Name	State	Year	Acreage
Catoctin Mountain	Md.	1954	5,770
Constitution Gardens	D.C.	1978	52
Fort Washington	Md.	1930	341
Greenbelt	Md.	1950	1,176
Piscataway	Md.	1961	4,263
Prince William Forest	Va.	1948	18,572
Rock Creek	D.C.	1890	1,754
Wolf Trap Farm Park for the Performing Arts	Va.	1966	130

National Recreation Areas

Name	State	Year	Acreage
Amistad	Tex.	1965	57,292
Bighorn Canyon	Mon.-Wy.	1966	120,296
Chattahoochee R.	Ga.	1978	9,257
Chickasaw	Okla.	1902	9,522
Coulee Dam	Wash.	1946	100,390
Curecanti	Col.	1965	42,114
Cuyahoga Valley	Oh.	1974	32,525
Delaware Water Gap	N.J.-Pa.	1965	66,652
Gateway	N.Y.-N.J.	1972	26,311
Gauley R.	W.Va.	1988	10,300
Glen Canyon	Ariz.-Ut.	1958	1,236,880
Golden Gate	Cal.	1972	73,122
Lake Chelan	Wash.	1968	61,883
Lake Mead	Ariz.-Nev.	1936	1,495,666
Lake Meredith	Tex.	1965	44,978
Ross Lake	Wash.	1968	117,575
Santa Monica Mts.	Cal.	1978	150,050
Whiskeytown	Cal.	1965	42,503

National Mall

Name	State	Year	Acreage
National Mall	D.C.	1933	146

National Scenic Trails

Name	State	Year	Acreage
Appalachian	Me. to Ga.	1968	161,382
Natchez Trace	Ala.-Miss.-Tenn.	1983	10,995
Potomac Heritage	Md.-D.C.-Va.-Pa.	1983	***

International Historic Sites

Name	State	Year	Acreage
Saint Croix Island	Me.	1949	35

* Not open to the public. ** No federal facilities. *** Undetermined.

National Park Service Recreation Visits

Source: National Park Service

The following places had more than 2.75 million recreation visits in 1991:

Park	Recreation Visits
Blue Ridge Parkway	16,414,294
Golden Gate Natl. Recreation Area	14,650,213
Lake Mead Natl. Recreation Area	8,445,016
Great Smoky Mountains Natl. Park	8,654,459
Gateway Natl. Recreation Area	6,643,921
Natchez Trace Parkway	5,832,697
Cape Cod Natl. Seashore	5,442,379
George Washington Memorial Parkway	5,004,736
Grand Canyon Natl. Park	3,886,031
Yosemite Natl. Park	3,423,101
JFK Center for the Performing Arts	3,401,923
Independence Natl. Historical Park	3,200,377
Yellowstone Natl. Park	2,920,537
Olympic Natl. Park	2,759,673
Rocky Mountain Natl. Park	2,751,781

Attendance at all areas administered by the National Park Service in 1991 was 267,419,196 recreation visits.

Federal Indian Reservations and Trust Lands[1]

Source: Bureau of Indian Affairs, U.S. Dept. of the Interior (data as of 1990)

The total American Indian population according to the 1990 Census is 1.959 million.

State	No of Reser.	Tribally-owned acreage[2]	Individually-owned acreage[2]	No. of persons[3]	Major tribes and/or nations
Alabama	1	230	0	16,504	Poarch Creek
Alaska	1[4]	86,773	1,265,432	85,698	Aleut, Eskimo, Athapascan,[5] Haida, Tlingit, Tsimpshian
Arkansas	1	0	2.78	—	unknown
Arizona	23	19,775,959	311,579	203,527	Navajo, Apache, Papago, Hopi, Yavapai, Pima
California	96	520,049	66,769	242,164	Hoopa, Paiute, Yurok, Karok, Mission Bands
Colorado	2	764,120	2,805	27,776	Ute
Connecticut	1	1,638	0	6,654	Mashantucket Pequot
Florida	4	153,874	0	36,335	Seminole, Miccosukee
Idaho	4	609,622	327,301	13,780	Shoshone, Bannock, Nez Perce
Iowa	1	3,550	0	7,349	Sac and Fox
Kansas	4	7,219	23,763	21,965	Potawatomi, Kickapoo, Iowa
Louisiana	3	415	0	18,541	Chitimacha, Coushatta, Tunica-Biloxi
Maine	3	191,511	0	5,998	Passamaquoddy, Penobscot, Maliseet
Massachusetts	1	157	0	—	Wampanoag
Michigan	8	14,411	9,276	55,638	Chippewa, Potawatomi, Ottawa
Minnesota	14	779,138	50,338	49,909	Chippewa, Sioux
Mississippi	1	20,486	0	8,825	Choctaw
Missouri	1	0	374.37	—	unknown
Montana	7	2,663,385	2,911,450	47,679	Blackfeet, Crow, Sioux, Assiniboine, Cheyenne
Nebraska	3	23,792	43,208	12,410	Omaha, Winnebago, Santee Sioux
Nevada	19	1,147,088	78,529	19,637	Paiute, Shoshone, Washoe
New Mexico	25	7,252,326	630,293	134,355	Zuni, Apache, Navajo
New York	8	118,199	0	62,651	Seneca, Mohawk, Onondaga, Oneida
North Carolina	1	56,509	0	80,155	Cherokee
North Dakota	3	214,006	627,289	25,917	Sioux, Chippewa, Mandan, Arikara, Hidatsa
Oklahoma	1[6]	96,839	1,000,165	252,420	Cherokee, Creek, Choctaw, Chickasaw, Osage, Cheyenne, Arapahoe, Kiowa, Comanche
Oregon	7	660,367	135,053	38,496	Warm Springs, Wasco, Paiute, Umatilla, Siletz
Rhode Island	1	1,800	0	4,071	Narragansett
South Dakota	9	2,399,531	2,121,188	50,573	Sioux
Texas	3	4,726	0	65,877	Alabama-Coushatta, Tiwa, Kickapoo
Utah	4	2,286,448	32,838	24,283	Ute, Goshute, Southern Paiute
Washington	27	2,250,731	467,785	81,483	Yakima, Lummi, Quinault
Wisconsin	11	338,097	80,345	39,387	Chippewa, Oneida, Winnebago
Wyoming	1	1,958,095	101,537	9,479	Shoshone, Arapahoe

(1) As of 1988 the federal government recognized and acknowledged that it had a special relationship with, and a trust responsibility for, 307 federally recognized Indian entities in the continental U.S., plus some 200 tribal entities in Alaska. The term "Indian entities" encompasses Indian tribes, bands, villages, groups, pueblos, Eskimos, and Aleuts, eligible for federal services and classified in the following 3 categories: (a) Officially approved Indian organizations pursuant to federal statutory authority (Indian Reorganization Act; Oklahoma Indian Welfare Act and Alaska Native Act.) (b) Officially approved Indian organizations outside of specified federal statutory authority. (c) Traditional Indian organizations recognized without formal federal approval of organizational structure. Some reservation boundaries transcend state boundaries (e.g., Navajo which is in Arizona, New Mexico, and Utah). For statistical convenience under "Number of Reservations," such reservations are counted in the state where population is predominant and/or tribal headquarters is located. (2) The acreages refer only to Indian lands which are either owned by the tribes or individual Indians, and held in trust by the U.S. government. Many of these parcels are located off reservations. Not all lands within reservation boundaries are necessarily trust lands. Many parcels are privately-owned by tribes, individual Indians, and non-Indians. Also, some internal lands are the property of various governmental agencies. (3) Total Indian population in each state with reservation/trust lands, including those persons living outside of the BIA Service area. (4) Alaskan Indian Affairs are carried out under the Alaska Native Claims Settlement Act (Dec. 18, 1971). The Act provided for the establishment of regional and village corporations to conduct business for profit and non-profit purposes. There are 13 such regional corporations, each one with organized village corporations. The Annette Island Reservation remains the only federally recognized reservation in Alaska in the sense of specific reservation boundaries, trust lands, etc. (5) Aleuts and Eskimos are racially and linguistically related. Athapascans are related to the Navaho and Apache Indians. (6) Indian land status in Oklahoma is unique and there are no reservations except for Osage in the sense that the term is used elsewhere in the U.S. Likewise, many of the Oklahoma tribes are unique in their high degree of assimilation to the white culture.

American Indian Population: States Without Federal Reservations and Trust Lands

Source: Bureau of the Census, U.S. Dept. of Commerce, 1990

State	No. of Persons	State	No. of Persons	State	No. of Persons
Arkansas	12,773	Kentucky	5,769	Pennsylvania	14,733
Delaware	2,019	Maryland	12,972	South Carolina	8,246
District of Columbia	1,466	Massachusetts	12,241	Tennessee	10,039
Georgia	13,348	Missouri	19,835	Vermont	1,696
Hawaii	5,099	New Hampshire	2,134	Virginia	15,282
Illinois	21,836	New Jersey	14,970	West Virginia	2,458
Indiana	12,972	Ohio	20,358		

BIOGRAPHIES OF U.S. PRESIDENTS

George Washington (1789-1797)

George Washington, first president, was born Feb. 22, 1732 (Feb. 11, 1731, old style), the son of Augustine Washington and Mary Ball, at Wakefield on Pope's Creek, Westmoreland Co., Va. His early childhood was spent on a farm, near Fredericksburg. His father died when George was 11. He studied mathematics and surveying and when 16 went to live with his half brother Lawrence, who built and named Mount Vernon. George surveyed the lands of William Fairfax in the Shenandoah Valley, keeping a diary. He accompanied Lawrence to Barbados, West Indies, contracted small pox, and was deeply scarred. Lawrence died in 1752 and George acquired his property by inheritance. He valued land and when he died owned 70,000 acres in Virginia and 40,000 acres in what is now West Virginia.

Washington's military service began in 1753 when Gov. Dinwiddie of Virginia sent him on missions deep into Ohio country. He clashed with the French and had to surrender Fort Necessity July 3, 1754. He was an aide to Braddock and at his side when the army was ambushed and defeated on a march to Ft. Duquesne, July 9, 1755. He helped take Fort Duquesne from the French in 1758.

After his marriage to Martha Dandridge Custis, a widow, in 1759, Washington managed his family estate at Mount Vernon. Although not at first for independence, he opposed British exactions and took charge of the Virginia troops before war broke out. He was made commander-in-chief by the Continental Congress June 15, 1775.

The successful issue of a war filled with hardships was due to his leadership. He was resourceful, a stern disciplinarian, and the one strong, dependable force for unity. He favored a federal government and became chairman of the Constitutional Convention of 1787. He helped get the Constitution ratified and was unanimously elected president by the electoral college and inaugurated, Apr. 30, 1789, on the balcony of New York's Federal Hall.

He was reelected 1792, but refused to consider a 3d term and retired to Mount Vernon. He suffered acute laryngitis after a ride in snow and rain around his estate, was bled profusely, and died Dec. 14, 1799.

John Adams (1797-1801)

John Adams, 2d president, Federalist, was born in Braintree (Quincy), Mass., Oct. 30, 1735 (Oct. 19, o. s.), the son of John Adams, a farmer, and Susanna Boylston. He was a great-grandson of Henry Adams who came from England in 1636. He graduated from Harvard, 1755, taught school, studied law. In 1765 he argued against taxation without representation before the royal governor. In 1770 he defended in court the British soldiers who fired on civilians in the "Boston Massacre." He was a delegate to the first Continental Congress, and signed the Declaration of Independence. He was a commissioner to France, 1778, with Benjamin Franklin and Arthur Lee; won recognition of the U.S. by The Hague, 1782; was first American minister to England, 1785-1788, and was elected vice president, 1788 and 1792.

In 1796 Adams was chosen president by the electors. Intense antagonism to America by France caused agitation for war, led by Alexander Hamilton. Adams, breaking with Hamilton, opposed war.

To fight alien influence and muzzle criticism Adams supported the Alien and Sedition laws of 1798, which led to his defeat for reelection. He died July 4, 1826, on the same day as Jefferson (the 50th anniversary of the Declaration of Independence).

Thomas Jefferson (1801-1809)

Thomas Jefferson, 3d president, was born Apr. 13, 1743 (Apr. 2, o. s.), at Shadwell, Va., the son of Peter Jefferson, a civil engineer of Welsh descent who raised tobacco, and Jane Randolph. His father died when he was 14, leaving him 2,750 acres and his slaves. Jefferson attended the College of William and Mary, 1760-1762, read classics in Greek and Latin and played the violin. In 1769 he was elected to the House of Burgesses. In 1770 he began building Monticello, near Charlottesville. He was a member of the Virginia Committee of Correspondence and the Continental Congress. Named a member of the committee to draw up a Declaration of Independence, he wrote the basic draft. He was a member of the Virginia House of Delegates, 1776-79, elected governor to succeed Patrick Henry, 1779, reelected 1780, resigned June 1781, amid charges of ineffectual military preparation. During his term he wrote the statute on religious freedom. In the Continental Congress, 1783, he drew up an ordinance for the Northwest Territory forbidding slavery after 1800; its terms were put into the Ordinance of 1787. He was sent to Paris with Benjamin Franklin and John Adams to negotiate commercial treaties, 1784; made minister to France, 1785.

Washington appointed him secretary of state, 1789. Jefferson's strong faith in the consent of the governed, as opposed to executive control favored by Hamilton, secretary of the treasury, often led to conflict: Dec. 31, 1793, he resigned. He was the Democrat Republican candidate for president in 1796; beaten by John Adams, he became vice president. In 1800, Jefferson and Aaron Burr received equal electoral college votes for president. The House of Representatives elected Jefferson. Major events of his administration were the Louisiana Purchase, 1803, and the Lewis and Clark Expedition. He established the Univ. of Virginia and designed its buildings. He died July 4, 1826, on the same day as John Adams.

James Madison (1809-1817)

James Madison, 4th president, Democrat Republican, was born Mar. 16, 1751 (Mar. 5, 1750, o. s.) at Port Conway, King George Co., Va., eldest son of James Madison and Eleanor Rose Conway. Madison was graduated from Princeton, 1771; studied theology, 1772; sat in the Virginia Constitutional Convention, 1776. He was a member of the Continental Congress. He was chief recorder at the Constitutional Convention in 1787, and supported ratification in the Federalist Papers, written with Alexander Hamilton and John Jay. He was elected to the House of Representatives in 1789, helped frame the Bill of Rights and fought the Alien and Sedition Acts. He became Jefferson's secretary of state, 1801.

Elected president in 1808, Madison was a "strict constructionist," opposed to the free interpretation of the Constitution by the Federalists. He was reelected in 1812 by the votes of the agrarian South and recently admitted western states. Caught between British and French maritime restrictions, the U.S. drifted into war, declared June 18, 1812. The war ended in a stalemate. He retired in 1817 to his estate at Montpelier. There he edited his famous papers on the Constitutional Convention. He became rector of the Univ. of Virginia, 1826. He died June 28, 1836.

James Monroe (1817-1825)

James Monroe, 5th president, Democrat Republican, was born Apr. 28, 1758, in Westmoreland Co., Va., the son of Spence Monroe and Eliza Jones, who were of Scottish and Welsh descent, respectively. He attended the College of William and Mary, fought in the 3d Virginia Regiment at White Plains, Brandywine, Monmouth, and was wounded at Trenton. He studied law with Thomas Jefferson, 1780, was a member of the Virginia House of Delegates and of Congress, 1783-86. He opposed ratification of the Constitution because it lacked a bill of rights; was U.S. senator, 1790; minister to France, 1794-96; governor of Virginia, 1799-1802, and 1811. Jefferson sent him to France as minister, 1803. He helped Robert Livingston negotiate the Louisiana Purchase, 1803. He ran against Madison for president in 1808. He was elected to the Virginia Assembly, 1810-1811; was secretary of state under Madison, 1811-1817.

In 1816 Monroe was elected president; in 1820 reelected with all but one electoral college vote. Monroe's administration became the "Era of Good Feeling." He obtained Florida from Spain; settled boundaries with Canada, and eliminated border forts. He supported the anti-slavery position that led to the Missouri Compromise. His most significant contribution was the "Monroe Doctrine," which became a cornerstone of U.S. foreign policy. Monroe retired to Oak Hill, Va. Financial problems forced him to sell his property. He moved to New York City to live with a daughter. He died there July 4, 1831.

John Quincy Adams (1825-1829)

John Quincy Adams, 6th president, independent Federalist, later Democratic Republican, was born July 11, 1767, at Braintree (Quincy), Mass., the son of John and Abigail Adams. His father was the 2d president. He was educated in Paris, Leyden, and Harvard, graduating in 1787. He served as American minister in various European capitals, and helped draft the War of 1812 peace treaty. He was U.S. Senator, 1803-08. President Monroe made him secretary of state, 1817, and he negotiated the cession of the Floridas from Spain, supported exclusion of slavery in the Missouri Compromise, and helped formulate the Monroe Doctrine. In 1824 he was elected president by the House after he failed to win an electoral college majority. His expansion of executive powers was strongly opposed and he was beaten in 1828 by Jackson. In 1831 he entered Congress and served 17 years with distinction. He opposed slavery, the annexation of Texas, and the Mexican War. He helped establish the Smithsonian Institution. He had a stroke in the House and died in the Speaker's Room, Feb. 23, 1848.

Andrew Jackson (1829-1837)

Andrew Jackson, 7th president, was a Jeffersonian-Republican, later a Democrat. He was born in the Waxhaws district, New Lancaster Co., S.C., Mar. 15, 1767, the posthumous son of Andrew Jackson and Elizabeth Hutchinson, who were Irish immigrants. At 13, he joined the militia in the Revolution and was captured.

He read law in Salisbury, N.C., moved to Nashville, Tenn., speculated in land, married, and practiced law. In 1796 he helped draft the constitution of Tennessee and for a year occupied its one seat in Congress. He was in the Senate in 1797, and again in 1823. He defeated the Creek Indians at Horseshoe Bend, Ala., 1814. With 6,000 backwoods fighters he defeated Pakenham's 12,000 British troops at the Chalmette, outside New Orleans, Jan. 8, 1815. In 1818 he briefly invaded Spanish Florida to quell Seminoles and outlaws who harassed frontier settlements. In 1824 he ran for president against John Quincy Adams and had the most popular and electoral votes but not a majority; the election was decided by the House, which chose Adams. In 1828 he defeated Adams, carrying the West and South. He was a noisy debater and a duelist and introduced rotation in office called the "spoils system." Suspicious of privilege, he ruined the Bank of the United States by depositing federal funds with state banks. Though "Let the people rule" was his slogan, he at times supported strict constructionist policies against the expansionist West. He killed the congressional caucus for nominating presidential candidates and substituted the national convention, 1832. When South Carolina refused to collect imports under his protective tariff he ordered army and naval forces to Charleston. Jackson recognized the Republic of Texas, 1836. He died at the Hermitage, June 8, 1845.

Martin Van Buren (1837-1841)

Martin Van Buren, 8th president, Democrat, was born Dec. 5, 1782, at Kinderhook, N.Y., the son of Abraham Van Buren, a Dutch farmer, and Mary Hoes. He was surrogate of Columbia County, N.Y., state senator and attorney general. He was U.S. senator 1821, reelected, 1827, elected governor of New York, 1828. He helped swing eastern support to Jackson in 1828 and was his secretary of state 1829-31. In 1832 he was elected vice president. He was a consummate politician, known as "the little magician," and influenced Jackson's policies. In 1836 he defeated William Henry Harrison for president and took office as the Panic of 1837 initiated a 5-year nationwide depression. He inaugurated the independent treasury system. His refusal to spend land revenues led to his defeat by Harrison in 1840. He lost the Democratic nomination in 1844 to Polk. In 1848 he ran for president on the Free Soil ticket and lost. He died July 24, 1862, at Kinderhook.

William Henry Harrison (1841)

William Henry Harrison, 9th president, Whig, who served only 31 days, was born in Berkeley, Charles City Co., Va., Feb. 9, 1773, the 3d son of Benjamin Harrison, signer of the Declaration of Independence. He attended Hampden Sydney College. He was secretary of the Northwest Territory, 1798; its delegate in Congress, 1799; first governor of Indiana Territory, 1800; and superintendent of Indian affairs. With 900 men he routed Tecumseh's Indians at Tippecanoe, Nov. 7, 1811. A major general, he defeated British and Indians at Battle of the Thames, Oct. 5, 1813. He served in Congress, 1816-19; Senate, 1825-28. In 1840, he was elected president with a "log cabin and hard cider" slogan. He caught pneumonia during the inauguration and died Apr. 4, 1841.

John Tyler (1841-1845)

John Tyler, 10th president, independent Whig, was born Mar. 29, 1790, in Greenway, Charles City Co., Va., son of John Tyler and Mary Armistead. His father was governor of Virginia, 1808-11. Tyler was graduated from William and Mary, 1807; member of the House of Delegates, 1811; in congress, 1816-21; in Virginia legislature, 1823-25; governor of Virginia, 1825-26; U.S. senator, 1827-36. In 1840 he was elected vice president and, on Harrison's death, succeeded him. He favored pre-emption, allowing settlers to get government land; rejected a national bank bill and thus alienated most Whig supporters; refused to honor the spoils system. He signed the resolution annexing Texas, Mar. 1, 1845. He accepted renomination, 1844, but withdrew before election. In 1861, he chaired an unsuccessful Washington conference called to avert civil war. After its failure he supported secession, sat in the provisional Confederate Congress, became a member of the Confederate House, but died in Richmond, Jan. 18, 1862, before it met.

James Knox Polk (1845-1849)

James Knox Polk, 11th president, Democrat, was born in Mecklenburg Co., N.C., Nov. 2, 1795, the son of Samuel Polk, farmer and surveyor of Scotch-Irish descent, and Jane Knox. He graduated from the Univ. of North Carolina, 1818; member of the Tennessee state legislature, 1823-25. He served in Congress 1825-39 and as speaker 1835-39. He was governor of Tennessee 1839-41, but was defeated 1841 and 1843. In 1844, when both Clay and Van Buren announced opposition to annexing Texas, the Democrats made Polk the first dark horse nominee because he demanded control of all Oregon and annexation of Texas. Polk re-established the independent treasury system originated by Van Buren. His expansionist policy was opposed by Clay, Webster, Calhoun; he sent troops under Zachary Taylor to the Mexican border and, when Mexicans attacked, declared war existed. The Mexican war ended with the annexation of California and much of the Southwest as part of America's "manifest destiny." He compromised on the Oregon boundary ("54-40 or fight!") by accepting the 49th parallel and giving Vancouver to the British. Polk died in Nashville, June 15, 1849.

Zachary Taylor (1849-1850)

Zachary Taylor, 12th president, Whig, who served only 16 months, was born Nov. 24, 1784, in Orange Co., Va., the son of Richard Taylor, later collector of the port of Louisville, Ky., and Sarah Strother. Taylor was commissioned first lieutenant, 1808; fought in the War of 1812; the Black Hawk War, 1832; and the second Seminole War, 1837. He was called Old Rough and Ready. He settled on a plantation near Baton Rouge, La. In 1845 Polk sent him with an army to the Rio Grande. When the Mexicans attacked him, Polk declared war. Taylor was successful at Palo Alto and Resaca de la Palma, 1846; occupied Monterrey. Polk made him major general but sent many of his troops to Gen. Winfield Scott. Outnumbered 4-1, he defeated Santa Anna at Buena Vista, 1847. A national hero, he received the Whig nomination in 1848, and was elected president. He resumed the spoils system and though once a slave-holder worked to have California admitted as a free state. He died in office July 9, 1850.

Millard Fillmore (1850-1853)

Millard Fillmore, 13th president, Whig, was born Jan. 7, 1800, in Cayuga Co., N.Y., the son of Nathaniel Fillmore and Phoebe Millard. He taught school and studied law; admitted to the bar, 1823. He was a member of the state assembly, 1829-32; in Congress, 1833-35 and again 1837-43. He opposed the entrance of Texas as slave territory and voted for a protective tariff. In 1844 he was defeated for governor of New York. In 1848 he was elected vice president and succeeded as president July 10, 1850, after Taylor's death. Fillmore favored the Compromise of 1850 and signed the Fugitive Slave Law. His policies pleased neither expansionists nor slave-holders and he was not renominated in 1852. In 1856 he was nominated by the American (Know-Nothing) party and accepted by the Whigs, but defeated by Buchanan. He died in Buffalo, Mar. 8, 1874.

Franklin Pierce (1853-1857)

Franklin Pierce, 14th president, Democrat, was born in Hillsboro, N. H., Nov. 23, 1804, the son of Benjamin Pierce, veteran of the Revolution and governor of New Hampshire, 1827. He graduated from Bowdoin, 1824. A lawyer, he served in the state legislature 1829-33; in Congress, supporting Jackson, 1833-37; U.S. senator, 1837-42. He enlisted in the Mexican War, became brigadier general under Gen. Winfield Scott. In 1852 Pierce was nominated on the 49th ballot over Lewis Cass, Stephen A. Douglas, and James Buchanan, and defeated Gen. Scott, Whig. Though against slavery, Pierce was influenced by pro-slavery Southerners. He approved the Kansas-Nebraska Act, leaving slavery to popular vote ("squatter sovereignty"), 1854. He signed a reciprocity treaty with Canada and approved the Gadsden Purchase from Mexico, 1853. Denied renomination by the Democrats, he spent most of his remaining years in Concord, N.H., where he died Oct. 8, 1869.

James Buchanan (1857-1861)

James Buchanan, 15th president, Federalist, later Democrat, was born of Scottish descent near Mercersburg, Pa., Apr. 23, 1791, the son of James Buchanan, merchant, and Elizabeth Speer. He graduated from Dickinson, 1809; was a volunteer in the War of 1812; member, Pennsylvania legislature, 1814-16, Congress, 1820-31; Jackson's minister to Russia, 1831-33; U.S. senator 1834-45. As Polk's secretary of state, 1845-49, he ended the Oregon dispute with Britain, supported the Mexican War and annexation of Texas. As minister to Britain, 1853, he signed the Ostend Manifesto. Nominated by Democrats, he was elected, 1856, over John C. Fremont (Republican) and Millard Fillmore (American Know-Nothing and Whig tickets). On slavery he favored popular sovereignty and choice by state constitutions; he accepted the pro-slavery Dred Scott decision as binding. He denied the right of states to secede. A strict constructionist, he desired to keep peace and found no authority for using force. He died at Wheatland, near Lancaster, Pa., June 1, 1868.

Abraham Lincoln (1861-1865)

Abraham Lincoln, 16th president, Republican, was born Feb. 12, 1809, in a log cabin on a farm then in Hardin Co., Ky., now in Larue. He was the son of Thomas Lincoln, a carpenter, and Nancy Hanks.

The Lincolns moved to Spencer Co., Ind., near Gentryville, when Abe was 7. When his mother died his father married Mrs. Sarah Bush Johnston, 1819; she had a favorable influence on Abe. In 1830 the family moved to Macon Co., Ill. Lincoln lost election to the Illinois General Assembly, 1832, but later won 4 times, beginning in 1834. He enlisted in the militia for the Black Hawk War, 1832. In New Salem he ran a store, surveyed land, and was postmaster.

In 1837 Lincoln was admitted to the bar and became partner in a Springfield, Ill., law office. He was elected to Congress, 1847-49. He opposed the Mexican War. He supported Zachary Taylor, 1848. He opposed the Kansas-Nebraska Act and extension of slavery, 1854. He failed in his bid for the Senate, 1855. He supported John C. Fremont, 1856.

In 1858 Lincoln had Republican support in the Illinois legislature for the Senate but was defeated by Stephen A. Douglas, Dem., who had sponsored the Kansas-Nebraska Act.

Lincoln was nominated for president by the Republican party on an anti-slavery platform, 1860. He ran against Douglas, a northern Democrat; John C. Breckinridge, southern pro-slavery Democrat; John Bell,

Constitutional Union party. When he won the election, South Carolina seceded from the Union Dec. 20, 1860, followed in 1861 by 10 Southern states.

The Civil War erupted when Fort Sumter was attacked Apr. 12, 1861. On Sept. 22, 1862, 5 days after the battle of Antietam, he announced that slaves in territory then in rebellion would be free Jan. 1, 1863, date of the Emancipation Proclamation, His speeches, including his Gettysburg and Inaugural addresses, are remembered for their eloquence.

Lincoln was reelected, 1864, over Gen. George B. McClellan, Democrat. Lee surrendered Apr. 9, 1865. On Apr. 14, Lincoln was shot by actor John Wilkes Booth in Ford's Theatre, Washington. He died the next day.

Andrew Johnson (1865-1869)

Andrew Johnson, 17th president, Democrat, was born in Raleigh, N.C., Dec. 29, 1808, the son of Jacob Johnson, porter at an inn and church sexton, and Mary McDonough. He was apprenticed to a tailor but ran away and eventually settled in Greeneville, Tenn. He became an alderman, 1828; mayor, 1830; state representative and senator, 1835-43; member of Congress, 1843-53; governor of Tennessee, 1853-57; U.S. senator, 1857-62. He supported John C. Breckinridge against Lincoln in 1860. He had held slaves, but opposed secession and tried to prevent his home state, Tennessee, from seceding. In Mar. 1862, Lincoln appointed him military governor of occupied Tennessee. In 1864 he was nominated for vice president with Lincoln on the National Union ticket to win Democratic support. He succeeded Lincoln as president Apr. 15, 1865. In a controversy with Congress over the president's power over the South, he proclaimed, May 26, 1865, an amnesty to all Confederates except certain leaders if they would ratify the 13th Amendment abolishing slavery. States doing so added anti-Negro provisions that enraged Congress, which restored military control over the South. When Johnson removed Edwin M. Stanton, secretary of war, without notifying the Senate, thus repudiating the Tenure of Office Act, the House impeached him for this and other reasons. He was tried by the Senate, and acquitted by only one vote, May 26, 1868. He returned to the Senate in 1875. Johnson died July 31, 1875.

Ulysses Simpson Grant (1869-1877)

Ulysses S. Grant, 18th president, Republican, was born at Point Pleasant, Oh., Apr. 27, 1822, son of Jesse R. Grant, a tanner, and Hannah Simpson. The next year the family moved to Georgetown, Oh. Grant was named Hiram Ulysses, but on entering West Point, 1839, his name was entered as Ulysses Simpson and he adopted it. He was graduated in 1843; served under Gens. Taylor and Scott in the Mexican War; resigned, 1854; worked in St. Louis until 1860, then went to Galena, Ill. With the start of the Civil War, he was named colonel of the 21st Illinois Vols., 1861, then brigadier general; took Forts Henry and Donelson; fought at Shiloh, took Vicksburg. After his victory at Chattanooga, Lincoln placed him in command of the Union Armies. He accepted Lee's surrender at Appomattox, Apr., 1865. President Johnson appointed Grant secretary of war when he suspended Stanton, but Grant was not confirmed. He was nominated for president by the Republicans in 1868 and elected over Horatio Seymour, Democrat. The 15th Amendment, amnesty bill, and civil service reform were events of his administration. The Liberal Republicans and Democrats opposed him with Horace Greeley, 1872, but he was reelected. An attempt by the Stalwarts (Old Guard) to nominate him in 1880 failed. In 1884 the collapse of Grant & Ward, investment house, left him penniless. He wrote his personal memoirs while ill with cancer and completed them 4 days before his death at Mt. McGregor, N.Y., July 23, 1885. The book realized over $450,000.

Rutherford Birchard Hayes (1877-1881)

Rutherford B. Hayes, 19th president, Republican, was born in Delaware, Oh., Oct. 4, 1822, the posthumous son of Rutherford Hayes, a farmer, and Sophia Birchard. He was raised by his uncle Sardis Birchard. He graduated from Kenyon College, 1842, and Harvard Law School, 1845. He practiced law in Lower Sandusky, Oh., now Fremont; was city solicitor of Cincinnati, 1858-61. In the Civil War, he was major of the 23d Ohio Vols., was wounded several times, and rose to the rank of brevet major general, 1864. He served in Congress 1864-67, supporting Reconstruction and Johnson's impeachment. He was elected governor of Ohio, 1867 and 1869; beaten in the race for Congress, 1872; reelected governor, 1875. In 1876 he was nominated for president and believed he had lost the election to Samuel J. Tilden, Democrat. But a few Southern states submitted 2 different sets of electoral votes and the result was in dispute. An electoral commission, appointed by Congress, 8 Republicans and 7 Democrats, awarded all disputed votes to Hayes allowing him to become president by one electoral vote. Hayes, keeping a promise to southerners, withdrew troops from areas still occupied in the South, ending the era of Reconstruction. He proceeded to reform the civil service, alienating political spoilsmen. He advocated repeal of the Tenure of Office Act. He supported sound money and specie payments. Hayes died in Fremont, Oh., Jan. 17, 1893.

James Abram Garfield (1881)

James A. Garfield, 20th president, Republican, was born Nov. 19, 1831, in Orange, Cuyahoga Co., Oh., the son of Abram Garfield and Eliza Ballou. His father died in 1833. He worked as a canal bargeman, farmer, and carpenter; attended Western Reserve Eclectic, later Hiram College, and was graduated from Williams in 1856. He taught at Hiram, and later became principal. He was in the Ohio senate in 1859. Anti-slavery and anti-secession, he volunteered for the war, became colonel of the 42d Ohio Infantry and brigadier in 1862. He fought at Shiloh, was chief of staff for Rosecrans and was made major general for gallantry at Chickamauga. He entered Congress as a radical Republican in 1863; supported specie payment as against paper money (greenbacks). On the electoral commission in 1877 he voted for Hayes against Tilden on strict party lines. He was senator-elect in 1880 when he became the Republican nominee for president. He was chosen as a compromise over Gen. Grant, James G. Blaine, and John Sherman. This alienated the Grant following but Garfield was elected. On July 2, 1881, Garfield was shot by mentally disturbed office-seeker, Charles J. Guiteau, while entering a railroad station in Washington. He died Sept. 19, 1881, at Elberon, N.J.

Chester Alan Arthur (1881-1885)

Chester A. Arthur, 21st president, Republican, was born at Fairfield, Vt., Oct. 5, 1829, the son of the Rev. William Arthur, from County Antrim, Ireland, and Malvina Stone. He graduated from Union College, 1848, taught school at Pownall, Vt., studied law in New York. In 1853 he argued in a fugitive slave case that slaves transported through N.Y. State were thereby freed. He was made collector of the Port of New York, 1871. President Hayes, reforming the civil service, forced Arthur to resign, 1879. This made the

New York machine stalwarts enemies of Hayes. Arthur and the stalwarts tried to nominate Grant for a 3d term in 1880. When Garfield was nominated, Arthur received 2d place in the interests of harmony. When Garfield died, Arthur became president. He supported civil service reform and the tariff of 1883. He was defeated for renomination by James G. Blaine. He died in New York City Nov. 18, 1886.

Grover Cleveland (1885-1889) (1893-1897)

(According to a ruling of the State Dept., Grover Cleveland is both the 22d and the 24th president, because his 2 terms were not consecutive. By individuals, he is only the 22d.)

Grover Cleveland, 22d and 24th president, Democrat, was born in Caldwell, N.J. Mar. 18, 1837, the son of Richard F. Cleveland, a Presbyterian minister, and Ann Neale. He was named Stephen Grover, but dropped the Stephen. He clerked in Clinton and Buffalo, N.Y., taught at the N.Y. City Institution for the Blind; was admitted to the bar in Buffalo, 1859; became assistant district attorney, 1863; sheriff, 1871; mayor, 1881; governor of New York, 1882. He was an independent, honest administrator who hated corruption. He was nominated for president over Tammany Hall opposition, 1884, and defeated Republican James G. Blaine. He enlarged the civil service, vetoed many pension raids on the Treasury. In 1888 he was defeated by Benjamin Harrison, although his popular vote was larger. Reelected over Harrison in 1892, he faced a money crisis brought about by lowering of the gold reserve, circulation of paper and exorbitant silver purchases under the Sherman Act; obtained a repeal of the latter and a reduced tariff. A severe depression and labor troubles racked his administration but he refused to interfere in business matters and rejected Jacob Coxey's demand for unemployment relief. He broke the Pullman strike, 1894. In 1896, the Democrats repudiated his administration and chose silverite William Jennings Bryan as their candidate. Cleveland died in Princeton, N.J., June 24, 1908.

Benjamin Harrison (1889-1893)

Benjamin Harrison, 23d president, Republican, was born at North Bend, Oh., Aug. 20, 1833. His great-grandfather, Benjamin Harrison, was a signer of the Declaration of Independence; his grandfather, William Henry Harrison, was 9th President; his father, John Scott Harrison, was a member of Congress. His mother was Elizabeth F. Irwin. He attended school on his father's farm; graduated from Miami Univ. at Oxford, Oh., 1852; admitted to the bar, 1853, and practiced in Indianapolis. In the Civil War, he rose to the rank of brevet brigadier general, fought at Kennesaw Mountain, Peachtree Creek, Nashville, and in the Atlanta campaign. He failed to be elected governor of Indiana, 1876; but became senator, 1881. In 1888 he defeated Cleveland for president despite having fewer popular votes. He expanded the pension list, signed the McKinley high tariff bill, the Sherman Antitrust Act, and the Sherman Silver Purchase Act. During his administration, 6 states were admitted to the union. He was defeated for reelection, 1892. He represented Venezuela in a boundary arbitration with Great Britain in Paris, 1899. He died in Indianapolis, Mar. 13, 1901.

William McKinley (1897-1901)

William McKinley, 25th president, Republican, was born in Niles, Oh., Jan. 29, 1843, the son of William McKinley, an ironmaker, and Nancy Allison. McKinley attended school in Poland, Oh., and Allegheny College, Meadville, Pa., and enlisted for the Civil War at 18 in the 23d Ohio, in which Rutherford B. Hayes was a major. He rose to captain and in 1865 was made brevet major. He studied law in the Albany, N.Y., law school; opened an office in Canton, Oh., in 1867, and campaigned for Grant and Hayes. He served in the House of Representatives, 1877-83, 1885-91, and led the fight for passage of the McKinley Tariff, 1890. Defeated for reelection on the tariff issue in 1890, he was governor of Ohio, 1892-96. He had support for president in the convention that nominated Benjamin Harrison in 1892. In 1896 he was elected president on a protective tariff, sound money (gold standard) platform over William Jennings Bryan, Democratic proponent of free silver. McKinley was reluctant to intervene in Cuba but the loss of the battleship Maine at Havana crystallized opinion. He demanded Spain's withdrawal from Cuba; Spain made some concessions but Congress announced state of war as of Apr. 21. He was reelected in the 1900 campaign, defeating Bryan's anti-imperialist arguments with the promise of a "full dinner pail." McKinley was respected for his conciliatory nature, but conservative on business issues. On Sept. 6, 1901, while welcoming citizens at the Pan-American Exposition, Buffalo, N.Y., he was shot by Leon Czolgosz, an anarchist. He died Sept. 14.

Theodore Roosevelt (1901-1909)

Theodore Roosevelt, 26th president, Republican, was born in N.Y. City, Oct. 27, 1858, the son of Theodore Roosevelt, a glass importer, and Martha Bulloch. He was a 5th cousin of Franklin D. Roosevelt and an uncle of Eleanor Roosevelt. Roosevelt graduated from Harvard, 1880; attended Columbia Law School briefly; sat in the N.Y. State Assembly, 1882-84; ranched in North Dakota, 1884-86; failed election as mayor of N.Y. City, 1886; member of U.S. Civil Service Commission, 1889; president, N.Y. Police Board, 1895, supporting the merit system; assistant secretary of the Navy under McKinley, 1897-98. In the war with Spain, he organized the 1st U.S. Volunteer Cavalry (Rough Riders) as lieutenant colonel; led the charge up Kettle Hill at San Juan. Elected New York governor, 1898-1900, he fought the spoils system and achieved taxation of corporation franchises. Nominated for vice president, 1900, he became nation's youngest president when McKinley died. He was reelected in 1904. As president he fought corruption of politics by big business; dissolved Northern Securities Co. and others for violating, anti-trust laws; intervened in coal strike on behalf of the public, 1902; obtained Elkins Law forbidding rebates to favored corporations, 1903; Hepburn Law regulating railroad rates, 1906; Pure Food and Drugs Act, 1906, Reclamation Act and employers' liability laws. He organized conservation, mediated the peace between Japan and Russia, 1905; won the Nobel Peace Prize. He was the first to use the Hague Court of International Arbitration. By recognizing the new Republic of Panama he made Panama Canal possible.

In 1908 he obtained the nomination of William H. Taft, who was elected. Feeling that Taft had abandoned his policies, Roosevelt unsuccessfully sought the nomination in 1912. He bolted the party and ran on the Progressive "Bull Moose" ticket against Taft and Woodrow Wilson, splitting the Republicans and insuring Wilson's election. He was shot during the campaign but recovered. In 1916 he supported Charles E. Hughes, Republican. A strong friend of Britain, he fought American isolation in World War I. He wrote some 40 books on many topics; his *Winning of the West* is best known. He died Jan. 6, 1919, at Sagamore Hill, Oyster Bay, N.Y.

William Howard Taft (1909-1913)

William Howard Taft, 27th president, Republican, was born in Cincinnati, Oh., Sept. 15, 1857, the son of Alphonso Taft and Louisa Maria Torrey. His father was secretary of war and attorney general in Grant's cabinet; minister to Austria and Russia under Arthur. Taft was graduated from Yale, 1878; Cincinnati Law School, 1880; became law reporter for Cincinnati newspapers; was assistant prosecuting attorney, 1881-83; assistant county solicitor, 1885; judge, superior court, 1887; U.S. solicitor-general, 1890; federal circuit judge, 1892. In 1900 he became head of the U.S. Philippines Commission and was first civil governor of the Philippines, 1901-04; secretary of war, 1904; provisional governor of Cuba, 1906. He was groomed for president by Roosevelt and elected over Bryan, 1908. His administration dissolved Standard Oil and tobacco trusts; instituted Dept. of Labor; drafted direct election of senators and income tax amendments. His tariff and conservation policies angered progressives; though renominated he was opposed by Roosevelt; the result was Democrat Woodrow Wilson's election. Taft, with some reservations, supported the League of Nations. He was professor of constitutional law, Yale, 1913-21; chief justice of the U.S. Supreme Court, 1921-30; illness forced him to resign. He died in Washington, Mar. 8, 1930.

Woodrow Wilson (1913-1921)

Woodrow Wilson, 28th president, Democrat, was born at Staunton, Va., Dec. 28, 1856, as Thomas Woodrow Wilson, son of a Presbyterian minister, the Rev. Joseph Ruggles Wilson and Janet (Jessie) Woodrow. In his youth Wilson lived in Augusta, Ga., Columbia, S.C., and Wilmington, N.C. He attended Davidson College, 1873-74; was graduated from Princeton, A.B., 1879; A.M., 1882; read law at the Univ. of Virginia, 1881; practiced law, Atlanta, 1882-83; Ph.D., Johns Hopkins, 1886. He taught at Bryn Mawr, 1885-88; at Wesleyan, 1888-90; was professor of jurisprudence and political economy at Princeton, 1890-1910; president of Princeton, 1902-1910; governor of New Jersey, 1911-13. In 1912 he was nominated for president with the aid of William Jennings Bryan, who sought to block James "Champ" Clark and Tammany Hall. Wilson won the election because the Republican vote for Taft was split by the Progressives under Roosevelt.

Wilson protected American interests in revolutionary Mexico and fought for American rights on the high seas. His sharp warnings to Germany led to the resignation of his secretary of state, Bryan, a pacifist. In 1916 he was reelected by a slim margin with the slogan, "He kept us out of war." Wilson's attempts to mediate in the war failed. After 4 American ships had been sunk by the Germans, he secured a declaration of war against Germany on Apr. 6, 1917.

Wilson proposed peace Jan. 8, 1918, on the basis of his "Fourteen Points," a state paper with worldwide influence. His doctrine of self-determination continues to play a major role in territorial disputes. The Germans accepted his terms and an armistice, Nov. 11.

Wilson went to Paris to help negotiate the peace treaty, the crux of which he considered the League of Nations. The Senate demanded reservations that would not make the U.S. subordinate to the votes of other nations in case of war. Wilson refused to consider any reservations and toured the country to get support. He suffered a stroke, Oct., 1919. An invalid for months, he clung to his executive powers while his wife and doctor sought to shield him from affairs which would tire him.

He was awarded the 1919 Nobel Peace Prize, but the treaty embodying the League of Nations was rejected by the Senate, 1920. He died in Washington, Feb. 3, 1924.

Warren Gamaliel Harding (1921-1923)

Warren Gamaliel Harding, 29th president, Republican, was born near Corsica, now Blooming Grove, Oh., Nov. 2, 1865, the son of Dr. George Tyron Harding, a physician, and Phoebe Elizabeth Dickerson. He attended Ohio Central College. He was state senator, 1900-04; lieutenant governor, 1904-06; defeated for governor, 1910; chosen U.S. senator, 1915. He supported Taft, opposed federal control of food and fuel; voted for anti-strike legislation, woman's suffrage, and the Volstead prohibition enforcement act over President Wilson's veto; and opposed the League of Nations. In 1920 he was nominated for president and defeated James M. Cox in the election. The Republicans capitalized on war weariness and fear that Wilson's League of Nations would curtail U.S. sovereignty. Harding stressed a return to "normalcy"; worked for tariff revision and repeal of excess profits law and high income taxes. Two Harding appointees, Albert B. Fall (interior) and Harry Daugherty (attorney general), became involved in the Teapot Dome scandal that embittered Harding's last days. He called the International Conference on Limitation of Armaments, 1921-22. Returning from a trip to Alaska he became ill and died in San Francisco, Aug. 2, 1923.

Calvin Coolidge (1923-1929)

Calvin Coolidge, 30th president, Republican, was born in Plymouth, Vt., July 4, 1872, the son of John Calvin Coolidge, a storekeeper, and Victoria J. Moor, and named John Calvin Coolidge. Coolidge graduated from Amherst in 1895. He entered Republican state politics and served as mayor of Northampton, Mass., state senator, lieutenant governor, and, in 1919, governor. In Sept., 1919, Coolidge attained national prominence by calling out the state guard in the Boston police strike. He declared: "There is no right to strike against the public safety by anybody, anywhere, anytime." This brought his name before the Republican convention of 1920, where he was nominated for vice president. He succeeded to the presidency on Harding's death. He opposed the League of Nations; approved the World Court; vetoed the soldiers' bonus bill, which was passed over his veto. In 1924 he was elected by a huge majority. He reduced the national debt by $2 billion in 3 years. He twice vetoed the McNary-Haugen farm bill, which would have provided relief to financially hard-pressed farmers. With Republicans eager to renominate him he announced, Aug. 2, 1927: "I do not choose to run for president in 1928." He died in Northampton, Jan. 5, 1933.

Herbert Clark Hoover (1929-1933)

Herbert C. Hoover, 31st president, Republican, was born at West Branch, Ia., Aug. 10, 1874, son of Jesse Clark Hoover, a blacksmith, and Hulda Randall Minthorn. Hoover grew up in Indian Territory (now Oklahoma) and Oregon; won his A.B. in engineering at Stanford, 1891. He worked briefly with U.S. Geological Survey and western mines; then was a mining engineer in Australia, Asia, Europe, Africa, U.S. While chief engineer, imperial mines, China, he directed food relief for victims of Boxer Rebellion, 1900. He directed American Relief Committee, London, 1914-15; U.S. Comm. for Relief in Belgium, 1915-1919; was U.S. Food Administrator, 1917-1919; American Relief Administrator, 1918-1923, feeding children in defeated nations; Russian Relief, 1918-1923. He was secy. of commerce, 1921-28. He was elected president over Alfred E. Smith, 1928. In 1929 the stock market crashed and the economy collapsed. During the depression, Hoover opposed federal aid to the unemployed. He was defeated in the 1932 election by Franklin D. Roosevelt. President Truman made him coordinator of European Food Program, 1947, chairman of the Commission for Reorganization of the Executive Branch, 1947-49. He founded the Hoover Institution on War, Revolution, and Peace at Stanford Univ. He died in N.Y. City, Oct. 20, 1964.

Franklin Delano Roosevelt (1933-1945)

Franklin D. Roosevelt, 32d president, Democrat, was born near Hyde Park, N.Y., Jan. 30, 1882, the son of James Roosevelt and Sara Delano. He graduated from Harvard, 1904; attended Columbia Law School; was admitted to the bar. He went to the N.Y. Senate, 1910 and 1913. In 1913 President Wilson made him assistant secretary of the navy.

Roosevelt ran for vice president, 1920, with James Cox and was defeated. From 1920 to 1928 he was a N.Y. lawyer and vice president of Fidelity & Deposit Co. In Aug., 1921, polio paralyzed his legs. He learned to walk with leg braces and a cane.

Roosevelt was elected governor of New York, 1928 and 1930. In 1932, W. G. McAdoo, pledged to John N. Garner, threw his votes to Roosevelt, who was nominated. The depression and the promise to repeal prohibition insured his election. He asked emergency powers, proclaimed the New Deal, and put into effect a vast number of administrative changes. Foremost was the use of public funds for relief and public works, resulting in deficit financing. He greatly expanded the controls of the central government over business, and by an excess profits tax and progressive income taxes produced a redistribution of earnings on an unprecedented scale. The Wagner Act gave labor many advantages in organizing and collective bargaining. He was the last president inaugurated on Mar. 4 (1933) and the first inaugurated on Jan. 20 (1937).

Roosevelt was the first president to use radio for "fireside chats." When the Supreme Court nullified some New Deal laws, he sought power to "pack" the court with additional justices, but Congress refused to give him the authority. He was the first president to break the "no 3d term" tradition (1940) and was elected to a 4th term, 1944, despite failing health. He was openly hostile to fascist governments before World War II and launched a lend-lease program on behalf of the Allies. He wrote the principles of fair dealing into the Atlantic Charter, Aug. 14, 1941 (with Winston Churchill), and urged the Four Freedoms (freedom of speech, of worship, from want, from fear) Jan. 6, 1941. When Japan attacked Pearl Harbor, Dec. 7, 1941, the U.S. entered the war. He conferred with allied heads of state at Casablanca, Jan., 1943; Quebec, Aug., 1943; Teheran, Nov.-Dec., 1943; Cairo, Dec., 1943; Yalta, Feb., 1945. He died at Warm Springs, Ga., Apr. 12, 1945.

Harry S. Truman (1945-1953)

Harry S. Truman, 33d president, Democrat, was born at Lamar, Mo., May 8, 1884, the son of John Anderson Truman and Martha Ellen Young. A family disagreement on whether his middle name was Shippe or Solomon, after names of 2 grandfathers, resulted in his using only the middle initial S. He attended public schools in Independence, Mo., worked for the Kansas City Star, 1901, and as railroad timekeeper, and helper in Kansas City banks up to 1905. He ran his family's farm, 1906-17. He was commissioned a first lieutenant and took part in the Vosges, Meuse-Argonne, and St. Mihiel actions in World War I. After the war he ran a haberdashery, became judge of Jackson Co. Court, 1922-24; attended Kansas City School of Law, 1923-25.

Truman was elected U.S. senator in 1934; reelected 1940. In 1944 with Roosevelt's backing he was nominated for vice president and elected. On Roosevelt's death Truman became president. In 1948 he was elected president.

Truman authorized the first uses of the atomic bomb (Hiroshima and Nagasaki, Aug. 6 and 9, 1945), bringing World War II to a rapid end. He was responsible for creating NATO, the Marshall Plan, and what came to be called the Truman Doctrine (to aid nations such as Greece and Turkey, threatened by Russian or other communist takeover). He broke a Russian blockade of West Berlin with a massive airlift, 1948-49. When communist North Korea invaded South Korea, June, 1950, he won UN approval for a "police action" and sent in forces under Gen. Douglas MacArthur. When MacArthur opposed his policy of limited objectives, Truman removed him from command.

Truman was responsible for higher minimum-wage, increased social-security, and aid-for-housing laws. Truman died Dec. 26, 1972, in Kansas City, Mo.

Dwight David Eisenhower (1953-1961)

Dwight D. Eisenhower, 34th president, Republican, was born Oct. 14, 1890, at Denison, Tex., the son of David Jacob Eisenhower and Ida Elizabeth Stover. The next year, the family moved to Abilene, Kan. He graduated from West Point, 1915. He was on the American military mission to the Philippines, 1935-39 and during 4 of those years on the staff of Gen. Douglas MacArthur. He was made commander of Allied forces landing in North Africa, 1942, full general, 1943. He became supreme Allied commander in Europe, 1943, and as such led the Normandy invasion June 6, 1944. He was given the rank of general of the army Dec. 20, 1944, made permanent in 1946. On May 7, 1945, he received the surrender of the Germans at Rheims. He returned to the U.S. to serve as chief of staff, 1945-1948. In 1948, Eisenhower published *Crusade in Europe*, his war memoirs, which quickly became a best seller. From 1948 to 1953, he was president of Columbia Univ., but took leave of absence in 1950, to command NATO forces.

Eisenhower resigned from the army and was nominated for president by the Republicans, 1952. He defeated Adlai E. Stevenson in the election. He again defeated Stevenson, 1956. He called himself a moderate, favored "free market system" vs. government price and wage controls; kept goverment out of labor disputes; reorganized defense establishment; promoted missile programs. He continued foreign aid; sped end of Korean fighting; endorsed Taiwan and SE Asia defense treaties; backed UN in condemning Anglo-French raid on Egypt; advocated "open skies" policy of mutual inspection to USSR. He sent U.S. troops into Little Rock, Ark., Sept., 1957, during the segregation crisis and ordered Marines into Lebanon July-Aug., 1958.

During his retirement at his farm near Gettysburg, Pa., Eisenhower took up the role of elder statesman, counseling his 3 successors in the White House. He died Mar. 28, 1969, in Washington.

John Fitzgerald Kennedy (1961-1963)

John F. Kennedy, 35th president, Democrat, was born May 29, 1917, in Brookline, Mass., the son of Joseph P. Kennedy, financier, who later became ambassador to Great Britain, and Rose Fitzgerald. He entered Harvard, attended the London School of

Economics briefly in 1935, received a B.S., from Harvard, 1940. He served in the Navy, 1941-1945, commanded a PT boat in the Solomons and won the Navy and Marine Corps Medal. He wrote *Profiles in Courage*, which won a Pulitzer prize. He served as representative in Congress, 1947-1953; was elected to the Senate in 1952, reelected 1958. He nearly won the vice presidential nomination in 1956.

In 1960, Kennedy won the Democratic nomination for president and defeated Richard M. Nixon, Republican. He was the first Roman Catholic president.

In Apr. 1961, Kennedy's new administration suffered a severe setback when an invasion force of anti-Castro Cubans, trained and directed by the U.S. Central Intelligence Agency, failed to establish a beachhead at the Bay of Pigs in Cuba.

Kennedy's most important act was his successful demand Oct. 22, 1962, that the Soviet Union dismantle its missile bases in Cuba. He established a quarantine of arms shipments to Cuba and continued surveillance by air. He defied Soviet attempts to force the Allies out of Berlin. He made the steel industry rescind a price rise. He backed civil rights, a mental health program, arbitration of railroad disputes, and expanded medical care for the aged. Astronaut flights and satellite orbiting were greatly developed during his administration.

On Nov. 22, 1963, Kennedy was assassinated in Dallas, Tex.

Lyndon Baines Johnson (1963-1969)

Lyndon B. Johnson, 36th president, Democrat, was born near Stonewall, Tex., Aug. 27, 1908, son of Sam Ealy Johnson and Rebekah Baines. He graduated from Southwest Texas State Teachers College, 1930, attended Georgetown Univ. Law School, Washington, 1935. He taught public speaking in Houston, 1930-32; served as secretary to Rep. R. M. Kleberg, 1932-35. In 1937 Johnson won a contest to fill the vacancy caused by the death of a representative and in 1938 was elected to the full term, after which he returned for 4 terms. He was elected U.S. senator in 1948 and reelected in 1954. He became Democratic leader, 1953. Johnson had strong support for the Democratic presidential nomination in at the 1960 convention, where the nominee, John F. Kennedy, asked him to run for vice president. His campaigning helped overcome religious bias against Kennedy in the South.

Johnson became president when Kennedy was assassinated. Johnson worked hard for welfare legislation, signed civil rights, anti-proverty, and tax reduction laws. He was elected to a full term, 1964. The war in Vietnam overshadowed other developments during his administration, such as the "Great Society" social programs.

In face of increasing division in the nation and his own party over his handling of the war, Johnson announced that he would not seek another term, Mar. 31, 1968.

Retiring to his ranch near Johnson City, Tex., Johnson wrote his memoirs and oversaw the construction of the Lyndon Baines Johnson Library. He died Jan. 22, 1973.

Richard Milhous Nixon (1969-1974)

Richard M. Nixon, 37th president, Republican, was the only president to resign without completing an elected term. He was born in Yorba Linda, Cal., Jan. 9, 1913, the son of Francis Anthony Nixon and Hannah Milhous. Nixon graduated from Whittier College, 1934; Duke Univ. Law School, 1937. After practicing law in Whittier and serving briefly in the Office of Price Administration in 1942, he entered the navy, and served in the South Pacific.

Nixon was elected to the House of Representatives in 1946 and 1948. He achieved prominence as the House Un-American Activities Committee member who forced the showdown that resulted in the Alger Hiss perjury conviction. In 1950 Nixon was elected to the Senate.

He was elected vice president in the Eisenhower landslides of 1952 and 1956. With Eisenhower's endorsement, Nixon won the Republican nomination in 1960. He was defeated by Democrat John F. Kennedy, returned to Cal. and was defeated in his race for governor, 1962.

In 1968, he won the presidential nomination and went on to defeat Democrat Hubert H. Humphrey.

Nixon was the first U.S. president to visit China and Russia (1972). He and his foreign affairs advisor, Henry A. Kissinger, achieved a detente with China. Nixon appointed 4 Supreme Court justices, including the chief justice, thus altering the court's balance in favor of a more conservative view.

Reelected 1972, Nixon secured a cease-fire agreement in Vietnam and completed the withdrawal of U.S. troops.

Nixon's 2d term was cut short by a series of scandals beginning with the burglary of Democratic party national headquarters in the Watergate office complex on June 17, 1972. On July 16, 1973, a White House aide, under questioning by a Senate committee, revealed that most of Nixon's office conversations and phone calls had been recorded. Nixon claimed executive privilege to keep the tapes secret and the courts and Congress sought the tapes for criminal proceedings against former White House aides and for a House inquiry into possible impeachment.

On July 24, 1974, the Supreme Court ruled that Nixon's claim of executive privilege must fall before the special prosecutor's subpoenas of tapes relevant to criminal trial proceedings. That same day, the House Judiciary Committee opened debate on impeachment. On July 30, the committee recommended House adoption of 3 articles of impeachment charging Nixon with obstruction of justice, abuse of power, and contempt of Congress.

On Aug. 5, Nixon released transcripts of conversations held 6 days after the Watergate break-in showing that Nixon had known of, approved, and directed Watergate cover-up activities. Nixon resigned from office Aug. 9.

Gerald Rudolph Ford (1974-1977)

Gerald R. Ford, 38th president, Republican, was born July 14, 1913, in Omaha, Neb., son of Leslie King and Dorothy Gardner, and was named Leslie Jr. When he was 2, his parents were divorced and his mother moved with the boy to Grand Rapids, Mich. There she met and married Gerald R. Ford, who formally adopted the boy and gave him his own name.

He graduated from the Univ. of Michigan, 1935 and Yale Law School, 1941.

He began practicing law in Grand Rapids, but in 1942 joined the navy and served in the Pacific, leaving the service in 1946 as a lieutenant commander.

He entered congress in 1949 and spent 25 years in the House, 8 of them as Republican leader.

On Oct. 12, 1973, after Vice President Spiro T. Agnew resigned, Ford was nominated by President Nixon to replace him. It was the first use of the procedures set out in the 25th Amendment.

When Nixon resigned Aug. 9, 1974, Ford became president, the first to serve without being chosen in a national election. On Sept. 8 he pardoned Nixon for any federal crimes he might have committed as president. Ford vetoed 48 bills in his first 21 months in office, saying most would prove too costly. He visited China. In 1976, he was defeated in the election by Democrat Jimmy Carter.

Jimmy (James Earl) Carter (1977-1981)

Jimmy (James Earl) Carter, 39th president, Democrat, was the first president from the Deep South since before the Civil War. He was born Oct. 1, 1924, at Plains, Ga., where his parents, James and Lillian Gordy Carter, had a farm and several businesses.

He attended Georgia Tech, and graduated from the U.S. Naval Academy. He entered the Navy's nuclear submarine program as an aide to Adm. Hyman Rickover, and studied nuclear physics at Union College.

His father died in 1953 and Carter left the Navy to take over the family businesses — peanut-raising, warehousing, and cotton-ginning. He was elected to the Georgia state senate, was defeated for governor, 1966, but elected in 1970.

Carter won the Democratic nomination and defeated President Gerald R. Ford in the election of 1976. He played a major role in the peace negotiations between Israel and Egypt. In Nov. 1979, Iranian student militants attacked the U.S. embassy in Teheran and held members of the embassy staff hostage.

Carter was widely criticized for the poor state of the economy and high inflation. He was also viewed as weak in his handling of foreign policy. He reacted to the Soviet invasion of Afghanistan by imposing a grain embargo and boycotting the Moscow Olympic games. His failure to obtain the release of the remaining 52 hostages held in Iran plagued Carter to the end of his term. He was defeated by Ronald Reagan in the 1980 election. Carter finally succeeded in obtaining the release of the hostages on Inauguration Day, as the new president was taking the oath of office.

Ronald Wilson Reagan (1981-1989)

Ronald Wilson Reagan, 40th president, Republican, was born Feb. 6, 1911, in Tampico, Ill., the son of John Edward Reagan and Nellie Wilson. Reagan graduated from Eureka (Ill.) College in 1932. Following his graduation, he worked as a sports announcer in Des Moines, Ia.

Reagan began a successful career as a film actor in 1937, and starred in numerous movies, and later television, until the 1960s. He was a captain in the Army Air Force during World War II.

He served as president of the Screen Actors Guild from 1947 to 1952, and in 1959.

Once a liberal Democrat, Reagan became active in Republican politics during the 1964 presidential campaign of Barry Goldwater. He was elected governor of California in 1966, and reelected in 1970.

In 1980, he gained the Republican nomination and won a landslide victory over Jimmy Carter. He was easily reelected in 1984. Reagan, at 73, was the oldest man ever elected president.

Reagan successfully forged a bipartisan coalition in Congress which led to enactment of an economic program which included the largest budget and tax cuts in U.S. history, and a Social Security reform bill designed to insure the long-term solvency of the system. In 1986, he signed into law a revolutionary tax-reform bill. He was shot in an assassination attempt in 1981, and had major surgery in 1985 and 1987.

In 1983, Reagan sent a task force to lead the invasion of Grenada, and joined 3 European nations in maintaining a peacekeeping force in Beirut, Lebanon. His opposition to international terrorism led to the U.S. bombing of Libyan military installations in 1986. He strongly supported El Salvador, the Nicaraguan contras, and other anti-communist governments and forces throughout the world. Aid was sent to the rebels fighting Soviet troops in Afghanistan. When the Iran/Iraq war threatened freedom of the seas, U.S. Navy ships were sent to the Persian Gulf.

Reagan held summit meetings with Soviet leader Gorbachev in 1985 in Geneva, 1986 in Iceland, 1987 in Washington, D.C. where an historic treaty eliminating short and medium-range missiles from Europe was signed, and 1988 in Moscow where Reagan criticized the Soviet record on human rights, and met with Soviet dissidents.

Reagan faced a major crisis in 1986-1987, when it was revealed that the U.S. had sold weapons to Iran in exchange for the release of U.S. hostages being held in Lebanon; and that subsequently some of the money was diverted to the Nicaraguan contras. The scandal led to the resignation of leading White House aides; some were indicted and convicted of criminal charges.

As Reagan left office, the nation was experiencing its 6th consecutive year of economic prosperity. Along with the strong economy, the nation enjoyed low unemployment, energy costs, and inflation. Reagan, however, was unable to control the high budget deficits which plagued him throughout his administration.

George Herbert Walker Bush (1989-)

George Herbert Walker Bush, 41st president, Republican, was born June 12, 1924, in Milton, Mass., the son of Prescott Bush, U.S. senator from Connecticut, and Dorothy Walker. He served as a U.S. Navy pilot in World War II, earning the Distinguished Flying Cross and three Air Medals for service in the Pacific. After graduating from Yale Univ. (1948), he settled in Texas where, in 1953, he helped found an oil company.

After losing a bid for a U.S. Senate seat in Texas, 1964, he was elected to the House of Representatives in 1966 and 1968. He lost a 2d U.S. Senate race in 1970. He served as U.S. ambassador to the United Nations, 1971-73, headed the U.S. Liaison Office in Beijing, 1974-75, and was director of the Central Intelligence Agency, 1976-77.

Following an unsuccessful bid for the 1980 Republican presidential nomination, Bush was chosen by Ronald Reagan as his vice presidential running mate. He served as U.S. vice president, 1981-89.

In 1988, he gained the Republican presidential nomination and defeated Democrat Michael Dukakis in the election. Calling on Americans "to make kinder the face of the nation and gentler the face of the world," Bush took office faced with the ongoing U.S. budget and trade deficits as well as the rescue of insolvent U.S. savings and loan institutions.

Bush has made no major changes from Reagan's policies in his first 3 years in office. He continued to face a severe budget deficit, struggled with military cutbacks in light of reduced "cold war" tensions, and vetoed congressional actions favorable to abortion, a minimum-wage law, jobless benefits, and job discrimination that didn't reflect his own views. He later signed a job discrimination bill and a compromise bill providing for additional benefits for unemployed workers.

Bush supported Soviet reforms and eastern Europe democratization. He was criticized for his failure to support strongly enough the independence efforts of the Baltic republics and for his soft reaction to the quelling of the China democratic movement. He held 3 summit meetings with Soviet leader Gorbachev.

In Dec. 1989, Bush sent military forces to Panama which overthrew the government and captured military strongman Gen. Manuel Noriega.

Bush reacted to Iraq's Aug. 1990 invasion of Kuwait by sending U.S. forces to the Persian Gulf area and assembling a U.N. backed coalition among NATO and Arab League members. A U.S.-led international force launched air and missile attacks on Iraq, Jan. 1991, after a U.N. deadline for withdrawal from Kuwait had passed. In Feb., Allied forces retook Kuwait after a 4-day ground assault. The quick victory gave Bush one of the highest presidential approval ratings in history. His popularity plummeted by the end of 1991 as the economy struggled through a prolonged recession, and he was perceived as being indifferent to the nation's domestic problems. (*See Chronology for details of 1992.*)

Wives and Children of the Presidents

Listed in order of presidential administrations.

Name (Born–died, married)	State	Sons/daughters
Martha Dandridge Custis Washington (1732-1802, 1759)	Va.	None
Abigail Smith Adams (1744-1818, 1764)	Mass.	3/2
Martha Wayles Skelton Jefferson (1748-1782, 1772)	Va.	1/5
Dorothea "Dolley" Payne Todd Madison (1768-1849, 1794)	N.C.	None
Elizabeth Kortright Monroe (1768-1830, 1786)	N.Y.	.../2 (A)
Louisa Catherine Johnson Adams (1775-1852, 1797)	Md.(B)	3/1
Rachel Donelson Robards Jackson (1767-1828, 1791)	Va.	None
Hannah Hoes Van Buren (1783-1819, 1807)	N.Y.	4/...
Anna Symmes Harrison (1775-1864, 1795)	N.J.	6/4
Letitia Christian Tyler (1790-1842, 1813)	Va.	3/5
Julia Gardiner Tyler (1820-1889, 1844)	N.Y.	5/2
Sarah Childress Polk (1803-1891, 1824)	Tenn.	None
Margaret Smith Taylor (1788-1852, 1810)	Md.	1/5
Abigail Powers Fillmore (1798-1853, 1826)	N.Y.	1/1
Caroline Carmichael McIntosh Fillmore (1813-1881, 1858)	N.J.	None
Jane Means Appleton Pierce (1806-1863, 1834)	N.H.	3/...
Mary Todd Lincoln (1818-1882, 1842)	Ky.	4/...
Eliza McCardle Johnson (1810-1876, 1827)	Tenn.	3/2
Julia Dent Grant (1826-1902, 1848)	Mo.	3/1
Lucy Ware Webb Hayes (1831-1889, 1852)	Oh.	7/1
Lucretia Rudolph Garfield (1832-1918, 1858)	Oh.	4/1
Ellen Lewis Herndon Arthur (1837-1880, 1859)	Va.	2/1
Frances Folsom Cleveland (1864-1947, 1886)	N.Y.	2/3
Caroline Lavinia Scott Harrison (1832-1892, 1853)	Oh.	1/1
Mary Scott Lord Dimmick Harrison (1858-1948, 1896)	Pa.	.../1
Ida Saxton McKinley (1847-1907, 1871)	Oh.	.../2
Alice Hathaway Lee Roosevelt (1861-1884, 1880)	Mass.	.../1
Edith Kermit Carow Roosevelt (1861-1948, 1886)	Conn.	4/1
Helen Herron Taft (1861-1943, 1886)	Oh.	2/1
Ellen Louise Axson Wilson (1860-1914, 1885)	Ga.	.../3
Edith Bolling Galt Wilson (1872-1961, 1915)	Va.	None
Florence Kling De Wolfe Harding (1860-1924, 1891)	Oh.	None
Grace Anna Goodhue Coolidge (1879-1957, 1905)	Vt.	2/...
Lou Henry Hoover (1875-1944, 1899)	Ia.	2/...
Anna Eleanor Roosevelt Roosevelt (1884-1962, 1905)	N.Y.	4/1 (A)
Bess Wallace Truman (1885-1982, 1919)	Mo.	.../1
Mamie Geneva Doud Eisenhower (1896-1979, 1916)	Ia.	1/...(A)
Jacqueline Lee Bouvier Kennedy (b. 1929, 1953)	N.Y.	1/1 (A)
Claudia "Lady Bird" Alta Taylor Johnson (b. 1912, 1934)	Tex.	.../2
Thelma Catherine Patricia Ryan Nixon (b. 1912, 1940)	Nev.	.../2
Elizabeth Bloomer Warren Ford (b. 1918, 1948)	Ill.	3/1
Rosalynn Smith Carter (b. 1927, 1946)	Ga.	3/1
Anne Frances "Nancy" Robbins Davis Reagan (b. 1921, 1952)	N.Y.	1/1 (C)
Barbara Pierce Bush (b. 1925, 1945)	N.Y.	4/2

James Buchanan, 15th president, was unmarried. (A) plus one infant, deceased. (B) Born London, father a Md. citizen. (C) President Reagan married and divorced Jane Wyman. They had a son and a daughter.

First Lady: Barbara Bush

The first lady was born Barbara Pierce in Rye, N.Y. on June 8, 1925; the daughter of Marvin and Pauline (Robinson) Pierce. She attended Smith College, 1943-44. She married George Bush, Jan. 6, 1945. They have four sons and a daughter (another daughter died in childhood). Mrs. Bush has had a lifelong involvement in a number of causes, especially the promotion of literacy.

Burial Places of the Presidents

Washington	Mt. Vernon, Va.
J. Adams	Quincy, Mass.
Jefferson	Charlottesville, Va.
Madison	Montpelier Station, Va.
Monroe	Richmond, Va.
J.Q. Adams	Quincy, Mass.
Jackson	Nashville, Tenn.
Van Buren	Kinderhook, N.Y.
W.H. Harrison	North Bend, Oh.
Tyler	Richmond, Va.
Polk	Nashville, Tenn.
Taylor	Louisville, Ky.
Fillmore	Buffalo, N.Y.
Pierce	Concord, N.H.
Buchanan	Lancaster, Pa.
Lincoln	Springfield, Ill.
A. Johnson	Greeneville, Tenn.
Grant	New York City
Hayes	Fremont, Oh.
Garfield	Cleveland, Oh.
Arthur	Albany, N.Y.
Cleveland	Princeton, N.J.
B. Harrison	Indianapolis, Ind.
McKinley	Canton, Oh.
T. Roosevelt	Oyster Bay, N.Y.
Taft	Arlington Nat'l. Cem'y.
Wilson	Washington Cathedral
Harding	Marion, Oh.
Coolidge	Plymouth, Vt.
Hoover	West Branch, Ia.
F.D. Roosevelt	Hyde Park, N.Y.
Truman	Independence, Mo.
Eisenhower	Abilene, Kan.
Kennedy	Arlington Nat'l. Cem'y.
L.B. Johnson	Stonewall, Tex.

The Electoral College

The president and the vice president of the United States are the only elective federal officials not elected by direct vote of the people. They are elected by the members of the Electoral College, an institution that has survived since the founding of the nation despite repeated attempts in Congress to alter or abolish it. In the elections of 1824, 1876 and 1888 the presidential candidate receiving the largest popular vote failed to win a majority of the electoral votes.

On presidential election day, the first Tuesday after the first Monday in November of every 4th year, each state chooses as many electors as it has senators and representatives in Congress. In 1964, for the first time, as provided by the 23d Amendment to the Constitution, the District of Columbia voted for 3 electors. Thus, with 100 senators and 435 representatives, there are 538 members of the Electoral College, with a majority of 270 electoral votes needed to elect the president and vice president.

Political parties customarily nominate their lists of electors at their respective state conventions. An elector cannot be a member of Congress or any person holding federal office.

Some states print the names of the candidates for president and vice president at the top of the November ballot while others list only the names of the electors. In either case, the electors of the party receiving the highest vote are elected. The electors meet on the first Monday after the 2d Wednesday in December in their respective state capitals or in some other place prescribed by state legislatures. By long-established custom they vote for their party nominees, although the Constitution does not require them to do so. All of the state's electoral votes are then awarded to the winners. The only Constitutional requirement is that at least one of the persons each elector votes for shall not be an inhabitant of that elector's home state.

Certified and sealed lists of the votes of the electors in each state are mailed to the president of the U.S. Senate. He opens them in the presence of the members of the Senate and House of Representatives in a joint session held on Jan. 6 (the next day if that falls on a Sunday), and the electoral votes of all the states are then counted. If no candidate for president has a majority, the House of Representatives chooses a president from among the 3 highest candidates, with all representatives from each state combining to cast one vote for that state. If no candidate for vice president has a majority, the Senate chooses from the top 2, with the senators voting as individuals.

Voting for President

Source: Federal Election Commission; Commission for Study of American Electorate

Year	Candidates	Voter Participation (% of voting-age population)
1932	Roosevelt-Hoover	52.4
1936	Roosevelt-Landon	56.0
1940	Roosevelt-Willkie	58.9
1944	Roosevelt-Dewey	56.0
1948	Truman-Dewey	51.1
1952	Stevenson-Eisenhower	61.6
1956	Stevenson-Eisenhower	59.3
1960	Kennedy-Nixon	62.8
1964	Johnson-Goldwater	61.9
1968	Humphrey-Nixon	60.9
1972	McGovern-Nixon	55.2(a)
1976	Carter-Ford	53.5
1980	Carter-Reagan	54.0
1984	Mondale-Reagan	53.1
1988	Dukakis-Bush	50.1

(a) The sharp drop in 1972 reflects the expansion of eligibility with the enfranchisement of 18 to 21 year olds.

Party Nominees for President and Vice President

Asterisk (*) denotes winning ticket

Year	Democratic President	Democratic Vice President	Republican President	Republican Vice President
1844	James K. Polk*	George M. Dallas	Henry Clay (Whig)	Theo. Frelinghuysen
1848	Lewis Cass	William Butler	Zachary Taylor*(Whig)	Millard Fillmore
1852	Franklin Pierce*	William King	Winfield Scott (Whig)	William Graham
1856	James Buchanan*	John Breckinridge	John Fremont	William Dayton
1860	John Breckinridge	Joseph Lane	Abraham Lincoln*	Hannibal Hamlin
1864	George McClellan	G.H. Pendleton	Abraham Lincoln*	Andrew Johnson
1868	Horatio Seymour	Francis Blair	Ulysses S. Grant*	Schuyler Colfax
1872	Horace Greeley	B. Gratz Brown	Ulysses S. Grant*	Henry Wilson
1876	Samuel J. Tilden	Thomas Hendricks	Rutherford B. Hayes*	William Wheeler
1880	Winfield Hancock	William English	James A. Garfield*	Chester A. Arthur
1884	Grover Cleveland*	Thomas Hendricks	James Blaine	John Logan
1888	Grover Cleveland	A.G. Thurman	Benjamin Harrison*	Levi Morton
1892	Grover Cleveland*	Adlai Stevenson	Benjamin Harrison	Whitelaw Reid
1896	William J. Bryan	Arthur Sewall	William McKinley*	Garret Hobart
1900	William J. Bryan	Adlai Stevenson	William McKinley*	Theodore Roosevelt
1904	Alton Parker	Henry Davis	Theodore Roosevelt*	Charles Fairbanks
1908	William J. Bryan	John Kern	William H. Taft*	James Sherman
1912	Woodrow Wilson*	Thomas Marshall	William H. Taft	James Sherman[1]
1916	Woodrow Wilson*	Thomas Marshall	Charles Hughes	Charles Fairbanks
1920	James M. Cox	Franklin D. Roosevelt	Warren G. Harding*	Calvin Coolidge
1924	John W. Davis	Charles W. Bryan	Calvin Coolidge*	Charles G. Dawes
1928	Alfred E. Smith	Joseph T. Robinson	Herbert Hoover*	Charles Curtis
1932	Franklin D. Roosevelt*	John N. Garner	Herbert Hoover	Charles Curtis
1936	Franklin D. Roosevelt*	John N. Garner	Alfred M. Landon	Frank Knox
1940	Franklin D. Roosevelt*	Henry A. Wallace	Wendell L. Willkie	Charles McNary
1944	Franklin D. Roosevelt*	Harry S. Truman	Thomas E. Dewey	John W. Bricker
1948	Harry S. Truman*	Alben W. Barkley	Thomas E. Dewey	Earl Warren
1952	Adlai E. Stevenson	John J. Sparkman	Dwight D. Eisenhower*	Richard M. Nixon
1956	Adlai E. Stevenson	Estes Kefauver	Dwight D. Eisenhower*	Richard M. Nixon
1960	John F. Kennedy*	Lyndon B. Johnson	Richard M. Nixon	Henry Cabot Lodge
1964	Lyndon B. Johnson*	Hubert H. Humphrey	Barry M. Goldwater	William E. Miller
1968	Hubert H. Humphrey	Edmund S. Muskie	Richard M. Nixon*	Spiro T. Agnew
1972	George S. McGovern	R. Sargent Shriver Jr.	Richard M. Nixon*	Spiro T. Agnew
1976	Jimmy Carter*	Walter F. Mondale	Gerald R. Ford	Robert J. Dole
1980	Jimmy Carter	Walter F. Mondale	Ronald Reagan*	George Bush
1984	Walter F. Mondale	Geraldine Ferraro	Ronald Reagan*	George Bush
1988	Michael S. Dukakis	Lloyd Bentsen	George Bush*	J. Danforth "Dan" Quayle
1992	Bill Clinton	Albert Gore Jr.	George Bush	J. Danforth "Dan" Quayle

(1) Died Oct. 30; replaced on ballot by Nicholas Butler.

Presidents of the U.S.

(as of mid-1992)

No.	Name	Politics	Born	in	Inaug.	at age	Died	at age
1	George Washington	Fed.	1732, Feb. 22	Va.	1789	57	1799, Dec. 14	67
2	John Adams	Fed.	1735, Oct. 30	Mass.	1797	61	1826, July 4	90
3	Thomas Jefferson	Dem.-Rep.	1743, Apr. 13	Va.	1801	57	1826, July 4	83
4	James Madison	Dem.-Rep.	1751, Mar. 16	Va.	1809	57	1836, June 28	85
5	James Monroe	Dem.-Rep.	1758, Apr. 28	Va.	1817	58	1831, July 4	73
6	John Quincy Adams	Dem.-Rep.	1767, July 11	Mass.	1825	57	1848, Feb. 23	80
7	Andrew Jackson	Dem.	1767, Mar. 15	S.C.	1829	61	1845, June 8	78
8	Martin Van Buren	Dem.	1782, Dec. 5	N.Y.	1837	54	1862, July 24	79
9	William Henry Harrison	Whig	1773, Feb. 9	Va.	1841	68	1841, Apr. 4	68
10	John Tyler	Whig	1790, Mar. 29	Va.	1841	51	1862, Jan. 18	71
11	James Knox Polk	Dem.	1795, Nov. 2	N.C.	1845	49	1849, June 15	53
12	Zachary Taylor	Whig	1784, Nov. 24	Va.	1849	64	1850, July 9	65
13	Millard Fillmore	Whig	1800, Jan. 7	N.Y.	1850	50	1874, Mar. 8	74
14	Franklin Pierce	Dem.	1804, Nov. 23	N.H.	1853	48	1869, Oct. 8	64
15	James Buchanan	Dem.	1791, Apr. 23	Pa.	1857	65	1868, June 1	77
16	Abraham Lincoln	Rep.	1809, Feb. 12	Ky.	1861	52	1865, Apr. 15	56
17	Andrew Johnson	(1)	1808, Dec. 29	N.C.	1865	56	1875, July 31	66
18	Ulysses Simpson Grant	Rep.	1822, Apr. 27	Oh.	1869	46	1885, July 23	63
19	Rutherford Birchard Hayes	Rep.	1822, Oct. 4	Oh.	1877	54	1893, Jan. 17	70
20	James Abram Garfield	Rep.	1831, Nov. 19	Oh.	1881	49	1881, Sept. 19	49
21	Chester Alan Arthur	Rep.	1829, Oct. 5	Vt.	1881	51	1886, Nov. 18	57
22	Grover Cleveland	Dem.	1837, Mar. 18	N.J.	1885	47	1908, June 24	71
23	Benjamin Harrison	Rep.	1833, Aug. 20	Oh.	1889	55	1901, Mar. 13	67
24	Grover Cleveland	Dem.	1837, Mar. 18	N.J.	1893	55	1908, June 24	71
25	William McKinley	Rep.	1843, Jan. 29	Oh.	1897	54	1901, Sept. 14	58
26	Theodore Roosevelt	Rep.	1858, Oct. 27	N.Y.	1901	42	1919, Jan. 6	60
27	William Howard Taft	Rep.	1857, Sept. 15	Oh.	1909	51	1930, Mar. 8	72
28	Woodrow Wilson	Dem.	1856, Dec. 28	Va.	1913	56	1924, Feb. 3	67
29	Warren Gamaliel Harding	Rep.	1865, Nov. 2	Oh.	1921	55	1923, Aug. 2	57
30	Calvin Coolidge	Rep.	1872, July 4	Vt.	1923	51	1933, Jan. 5	60
31	Herbert Clark Hoover	Rep.	1874, Aug. 10	Ia.	1929	54	1964, Oct. 20	90
32	Franklin Delano Roosevelt	Dem.	1882, Jan. 30	N.Y.	1933	51	1945, Apr. 12	63
33	Harry S. Truman	Dem.	1884, May 8	Mo.	1945	60	1972, Dec. 26	88
34	Dwight David Eisenhower	Rep.	1890, Oct. 14	Tex.	1953	62	1969, Mar. 28	78
35	John Fitzgerald Kennedy	Dem.	1917, May 29	Mass.	1961	43	1963, Nov. 22	46
36	Lyndon Baines Johnson	Dem.	1908, Aug. 27	Tex.	1963	55	1973, Jan. 22	64
37	Richard Milhous Nixon (2)	Rep.	1913, Jan. 9	Cal.	1969	56		
38	Gerald Rudolph Ford	Rep.	1913, July 14	Neb.	1974	61		
39	Jimmy (James Earl) Carter	Dem.	1924, Oct. 1	Ga.	1977	52		
40	Ronald Reagan	Rep.	1911, Feb. 6	Ill.	1981	69		
41	George Bush	Rep.	1924, June 12	Mass.	1989	64		

(1) Andrew Johnson — a Democrat, nominated vice president by Republicans and elected with Lincoln on National Union ticket. (2) Resigned Aug. 9, 1974.

Presidents, Vice Presidents, Congresses

	President	Service		Vice President	Congress
1	George Washington	Apr. 30, 1789—Mar. 3, 1797	1	John Adams	1, 2, 3, 4
2	John Adams	Mar. 4, 1797—Mar. 3, 1801	2	Thomas Jefferson	5, 6
3	Thomas Jefferson	Mar. 4, 1801—Mar. 3, 1805	3	Aaron Burr	7, 8
	"	Mar. 4, 1805—Mar. 3, 1809	4	George Clinton	9, 10
4	James Madison	Mar. 4, 1809—Mar. 3, 1813		"(1)	11, 12
	"	Mar. 4, 1813—Mar. 3, 1817	5	Elbridge Gerry (2)	13, 14
5	James Monroe	Mar. 4, 1817—Mar. 3, 1825	6	Daniel D. Tompkins	15, 16, 17, 18
6	John Quincy Adams	Mar. 4, 1825—Mar. 3, 1829	7	John C. Calhoun	19, 20
7	Andrew Jackson	Mar. 4, 1829—Mar. 3, 1833		"(3)	21, 22
	"	Mar. 4, 1833—Mar. 3, 1837	8	Martin Van Buren	23, 24
8	Martin Van Buren	Mar. 4, 1837—Mar. 3, 1841	9	Richard M. Johnson	25, 26
9	William Henry Harrison (4)	Mar. 4, 1841—Apr. 4, 1841	10	John Tyler	27
10	John Tyler	Apr. 6, 1841—Mar. 3, 1845			27, 28
11	James K. Polk	Mar. 4, 1845—Mar. 3, 1849	11	George M. Dallas	29, 30
12	Zachary Taylor (4)	Mar. 5, 1849—July 9, 1850	12	Millard Fillmore	31
13	Millard Fillmore	July 10, 1850—Mar. 3, 1853			31, 32
14	Franklin Pierce	Mar. 4, 1853—Mar. 3, 1857	13	William R. King (5)	33, 34
15	James Buchanan	Mar. 4, 1857—Mar. 3, 1861	14	John C. Breckinridge	35, 36
16	Abraham Lincoln	Mar. 4, 1861—Mar. 3, 1865	15	Hannibal Hamlin	37, 38
	"(4)	Mar. 4, 1865—Apr. 15, 1865	16	Andrew Johnson	39
17	Andrew Johnson	Apr. 15, 1865—Mar. 3, 1869			39, 40
18	Ulysses S. Grant	Mar. 4, 1869—Mar. 3, 1873	17	Schuyler Colfax	41, 42
	"	Mar. 4, 1873—Mar. 3, 1877	18	Henry Wilson (6)	43, 44
19	Rutherford B. Hayes	Mar. 4, 1877—Mar. 3, 1881	19	William A. Wheeler	45, 46
20	James A. Garfield (4)	Mar. 4, 1881—Sept. 19, 1881	20	Chester A. Arthur	47
21	Chester A. Arthur	Sept. 20, 1881—Mar. 3, 1885			47, 48
22	Grover Cleveland (7)	Mar. 4, 1885—Mar. 3, 1889	21	Thomas A. Hendricks (8)	49, 50
23	Benjamin Harrison	Mar. 4, 1889—Mar. 3, 1893	22	Levi P. Morton	51, 52
24	Grover Cleveland (7)	Mar. 4, 1893—Mar. 3, 1897	23	Adlai E. Stevenson	53, 54
25	William McKinley	Mar. 4, 1897—Mar. 3, 1901	24	Garret A. Hobart (9)	55, 56
	"(4)	Mar. 4, 1901—Sept. 14, 1901	25	Theodore Roosevelt	57
26	Theodore Roosevelt	Sept. 14, 1901—Mar. 3, 1905			57, 58
	"	Mar. 4, 1905—Mar. 3, 1909	26	Charles W. Fairbanks	59, 60
27	William H. Taft	Mar. 4, 1909—Mar. 3, 1913	27	James S. Sherman (10)	61, 62
28	Woodrow Wilson	Mar. 4, 1913—Mar. 3, 1921	28	Thomas R. Marshall	63, 64, 65, 66
29	Warren G. Harding (4)	Mar. 4, 1921—Aug. 2, 1923	29	Calvin Coolidge	67

(continued)

Presidents, Vice Presidents, Congresses

(as of mid-1992)

	President	Service		Vice President	Congress
30	Calvin Coolidge	Aug. 3, 1923—Mar. 3, 1925			68
	"	Mar. 4, 1925—Mar. 3, 1929	30	Charles G. Dawes	69, 70
31	Herbert C. Hoover	Mar. 4, 1929—Mar. 3, 1933	31	Charles Curtis	71, 72
32	Franklin D. Roosevelt (16)	Mar. 4, 1933—Jan. 20, 1941	32	John N. Garner	73, 74, 75, 76
	"	Jan. 20, 1941—Jan. 20, 1945	33	Henry A. Wallace	77, 78
	"(4)	Jan. 20, 1945—Apr. 12, 1945	34	Harry S. Truman	79
33	Harry S. Truman	Apr. 12, 1945—Jan. 20, 1949			79, 80
	"	Jan. 20, 1949—Jan. 20, 1953	35	Alben W. Barkley	81, 82
34	Dwight D. Eisenhower	Jan. 20, 1953—Jan. 20, 1961	36	Richard M. Nixon	83, 84, 85, 86
35	John F. Kennedy (4)	Jan. 20, 1961—Nov. 22, 1963	37	Lyndon B. Johnson	87, 88
36	Lyndon B. Johnson	Nov. 22, 1963—Jan. 20, 1965			88
	"	Jan. 20, 1965—Jan. 20, 1969	38	Hubert H. Humphrey	89, 90
37	Richard M. Nixon	Jan. 20, 1969—Jan. 20, 1973	39	Spiro T. Agnew (11)	91, 92, 93
	"(12)	Jan. 20, 1973—Aug. 9, 1974	40	Gerald R. Ford (13)	93
38	Gerald R. Ford (14)	Aug. 9, 1974—Jan. 20, 1977	41	Nelson A. Rockefeller (15)	93, 94
39	Jimmy (James Earl)Carter	Jan. 20, 1977—Jan. 20, 1981	42	Walter F. Mondale	95, 96
40	Ronald Reagan	Jan. 20, 1981—Jan. 20, 1989	43	George Bush	97, 98, 99, 100
41	George Bush	Jan. 20, 1989—	44	Dan Quayle	101, 102

(1) Died Apr. 20, 1812. (2) Died Nov. 23, 1814. (3) Resigned Dec. 28, 1832, to become U.S. Senator. (4) Died in office. (5) Died Apr. 18, 1853. (6) Died Nov. 22, 1875. (7) Terms not consecutive. (8) Died Nov. 25, 1885. (9) Died Nov. 21, 1899. (10) Died Oct. 30, 1912. (11) Resigned Oct. 10, 1973. (12) Resigned Aug. 9, 1974. (13) First non-elected vice president, chosen under 25th Amendment procedure. (14) First non-elected president. (15) 2d non-elected vice president. (16) First president to be inaugurated under 20th Amendment, Jan. 20, 1937.

Vice Presidents of the U.S.

(as of mid-1992)

The numerals given vice presidents do not coincide with those given presidents, because some presidents had none and some had more than one.

	Name	Birthplace	Year	Home	Inaug.	Politics	Place of death	Year	Age
1	John Adams	Quincy, Mass.	1735	Mass.	1789	Fed.	Quincy, Mass.	1826	90
2	Thomas Jefferson	Shadwell, Va.	1743	Va.	1797	Dem.-Rep.	Monticello, Va.	1826	83
3	Aaron Burr	Newark, N.J.	1756	N.Y.	1801	Dem.-Rep.	Staten Island, N.Y.	1836	80
4	George Clinton	Ulster Co., N.Y.	1739	N.Y.	1805	Dem.-Rep.	Washington, D.C.	1812	73
5	Elbridge Gerry	Marblehead, Mass.	1744	Mass.	1813	Dem.-Rep.	Washington, D.C.	1814	70
6	Daniel D. Tompkins	Scarsdale, N.Y.	1774	N.Y.	1817	Dem.-Rep.	Staten Island, N.Y.	1825	51
7	John C. Calhoun (1)	Abbeville, S.C.	1782	S.C.	1825	Dem.-Rep.	Washington, D.C.	1850	68
8	Martin Van Buren	Kinderhook, N.Y.	1782	N.Y.	1833	Dem.	Kinderhook, N.Y.	1862	79
9	Richard M. Johnson	Louisville, Ky.	1780	Ky.	1837	Dem.	Frankfort, Ky.	1850	70
10	John Tyler	Greenway, Va.	1790	Va.	1841	Whig	Richmond, Va.	1862	71
11	George M. Dallas	Philadelphia, Pa.	1792	Pa.	1845	Dem.	Philadelphia, Pa.	1864	72
12	Millard Fillmore	Summerhill, N.Y.	1800	N.Y.	1849	Whig	Buffalo, N.Y.	1874	74
13	William R. King	Sampson Co., N.C.	1786	Ala.	1853	Dem.	Dallas Co., Ala.	1853	67
14	John C. Breckinridge	Lexington, Ky.	1821	Ky.	1857	Dem.	Lexington, Ky.	1875	54
15	Hannibal Hamlin	Paris, Me.	1809	Me.	1861	Rep.	Bangor, Me.	1891	81
16	Andrew Johnson	Raleigh, N.C.	1808	Tenn.	1865	(2)	Carter Co., Tenn.	1875	66
17	Schuyler Colfax	New York, N.Y.	1823	Ind.	1869	Rep.	Mankato, Minn.	1885	62
18	Henry Wilson	Farmington, N.H.	1812	Mass.	1873	Rep.	Washington, D.C.	1875	63
19	William A. Wheeler	Malone, N.Y.	1819	N.Y.	1877	Rep.	Malone, N.Y.	1887	68
20	Chester A. Arthur	Fairfield, Vt.	1829	N.Y.	1881	Rep.	New York, N.Y.	1886	57
21	Thomas A. Hendricks	Muskingum Co., Oh.	1819	Ind.	1885	Dem.	Indianapolis, Ind.	1885	66
22	Levi P. Morton	Shoreham, Vt.	1824	N.Y.	1889	Rep.	Rhinebeck, N.Y.	1920	96
23	Adlai E. Stevenson (3)	Christian Co., Ky.	1835	Ill.	1893	Dem.	Chicago, Ill.	1914	78
24	Garret A. Hobart	Long Branch, N.J.	1844	N.J.	1897	Rep.	Paterson, N.J.	1899	55
25	Theodore Roosevelt	New York, N.Y.	1858	N.Y.	1901	Rep.	Oyster Bay, N.Y.	1919	60
26	Charles W. Fairbanks	Unionville Centre, Oh.	1852	Ind.	1905	Rep.	Indianapolis, Ind.	1918	66
27	James S. Sherman	Utica, N.Y.	1855	N.Y.	1909	Rep.	Utica, N.Y.	1912	57
28	Thomas R. Marshall	N. Manchester, Ind.	1854	Ind.	1913	Dem.	Washington, D.C.	1925	71
29	Calvin Coolidge	Plymouth, Vt.	1872	Mass.	1921	Rep.	Northampton, Mass.	1933	60
30	Charles G. Dawes	Marietta, Oh.	1865	Ill.	1925	Rep.	Evanston, Ill.	1951	85
31	Charles Curtis	Topeka, Kan.	1860	Kan.	1929	Rep.	Washington, D.C.	1936	76
32	John Nance Garner	Red River Co., Tex.	1868	Tex.	1933	Dem.	Uvalde, Tex.	1967	98
33	Henry Agard Wallace	Adair County, Ia.	1888	Iowa	1941	Dem.	Danbury, Conn.	1965	77
34	Harry S. Truman	Lamar, Mo.	1884	Mo.	1945	Dem.	Kansas City, Mo.	1972	88
35	Alben W. Barkley	Graves County, Ky.	1877	Ky.	1949	Dem.	Lexington, Va.	1956	78
36	Richard M. Nixon	Yorba Linda, Cal.	1913	Cal.	1953	Rep.			
37	Lyndon B. Johnson	Johnson City, Tex.	1908	Tex.	1961	Dem.	San Antonio, Tex.	1973	64
38	Hubert H. Humphrey	Wallace, S.D.	1911	Minn.	1965	Dem.	Waverly, Minn.	1978	66
39	Spiro T. Agnew (4)	Baltimore, Md.	1918	Md.	1969	Rep.			
40	Gerald R. Ford	Omaha, Neb.	1913	Mich.	1973	Rep.			
41	Nelson A. Rockefeller	Bar Harbor, Me.	1908	N.Y.	1974	Rep.	New York, N.Y.	1979	70
42	Walter F. Mondale	Ceylon, Minn.	1928	Minn.	1977	Dem.			
43	George Bush	Milton, Mass.	1924	Tex.	1981	Rep.			
44	Dan Quayle	Indianapolis, Ind.	1947	Ind.	1989	Rep.			

(1) John C. Calhoun resigned Dec. 28, 1832, having been elected to the Senate to fill a vacancy. (2) Andrew Johnson — a Democrat nominated by Republicans and elected with Lincoln on the National Union Ticket. (3) Adlai E. Stevenson, 23d vice president, was grandfather of Democratic candidate for president, 1952 and 1956. (4) Resigned Oct. 10, 1973.

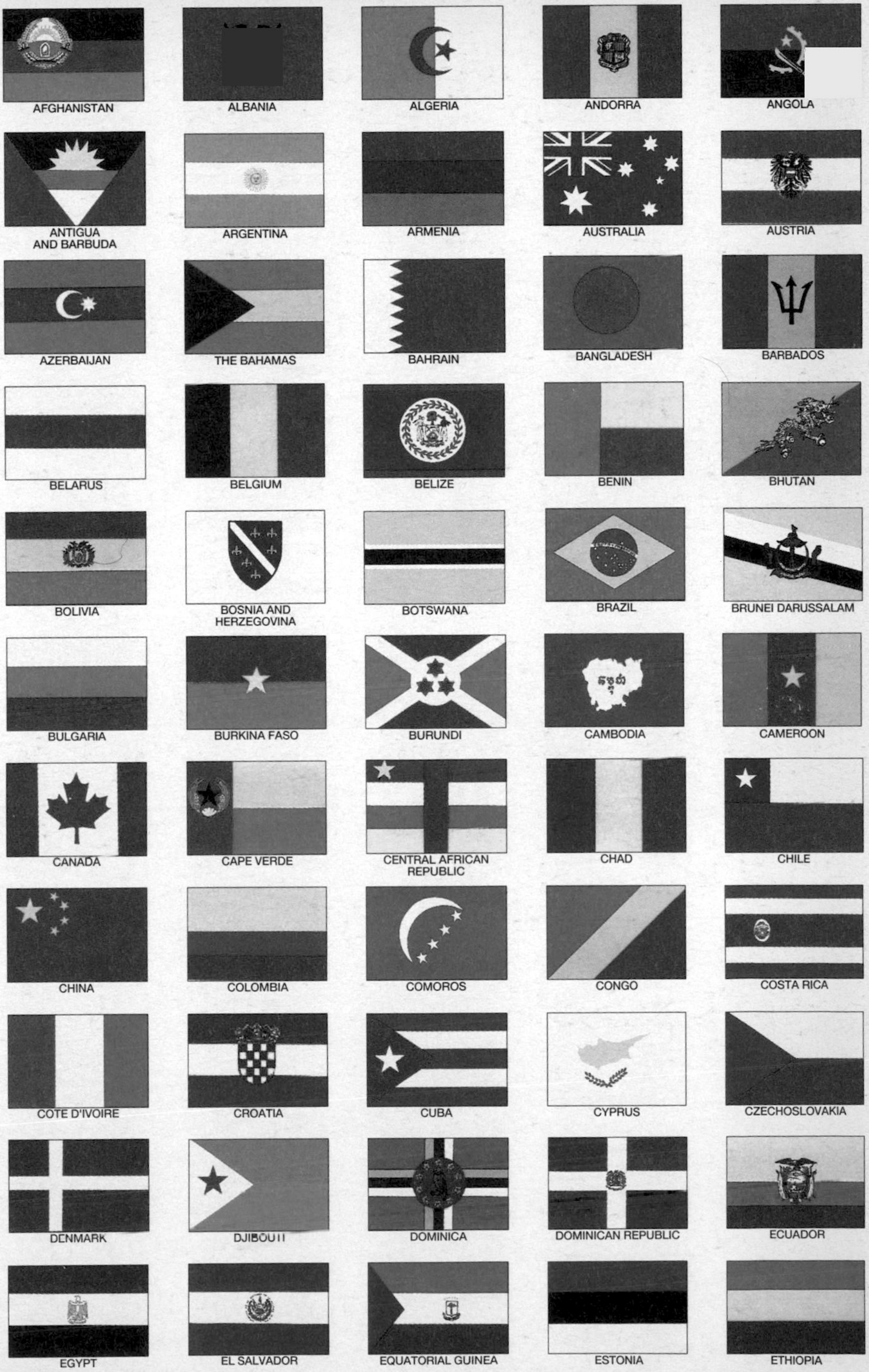
AFGHANISTAN
ALBANIA
ALGERIA
ANDORRA
ANGOLA
ANTIGUA AND BARBUDA
ARGENTINA
ARMENIA
AUSTRALIA
AUSTRIA
AZERBAIJAN
THE BAHAMAS
BAHRAIN
BANGLADESH
BARBADOS
BELARUS
BELGIUM
BELIZE
BENIN
BHUTAN
BOLIVIA
BOSNIA AND HERZEGOVINA
BOTSWANA
BRAZIL
BRUNEI DARUSSALAM
BULGARIA
BURKINA FASO
BURUNDI
CAMBODIA
CAMEROON
CANADA
CAPE VERDE
CENTRAL AFRICAN REPUBLIC
CHAD
CHILE
CHINA
COLOMBIA
COMOROS
CONGO
COSTA RICA
COTE D'IVOIRE
CROATIA
CUBA
CYPRUS
CZECHOSLOVAKIA
DENMARK
DJIBOUTI
DOMINICA
DOMINICAN REPUBLIC
ECUADOR
EGYPT
EL SALVADOR
EQUATORIAL GUINEA
ESTONIA
ETHIOPIA

F2

FIJI
FINLAND
FRANCE
GABON
THE GAMBIA
GEORGIA
GERMANY
GHANA
GREECE
GRENADA
GUATEMALA
GUINEA
GUINEA-BISSAU
GUYANA
HAITI
HONDURAS
HUNGARY
ICELAND
INDIA
INDONESIA
IRAN
IRAQ
IRELAND
ISRAEL
ITALY
JAMAICA
JAPAN
JORDAN
KAZAKHSTAN
KENYA
KIRIBATI
NORTH KOREA
SOUTH KOREA
KUWAIT
KYRGYZSTAN
LAOS
LATVIA
LEBANON
LESOTHO
LIBERIA
LIBYA
LIECHTENSTEIN
LITHUANIA
LUXEMBOURG
MADAGASCAR
MALAWI
MALAYSIA
MALDIVES
MALI
MALTA
MARSHALL ISLANDS
MAURITANIA
MAURITIUS
MEXICO
MICRONESIA, FEDERATED STATES OF

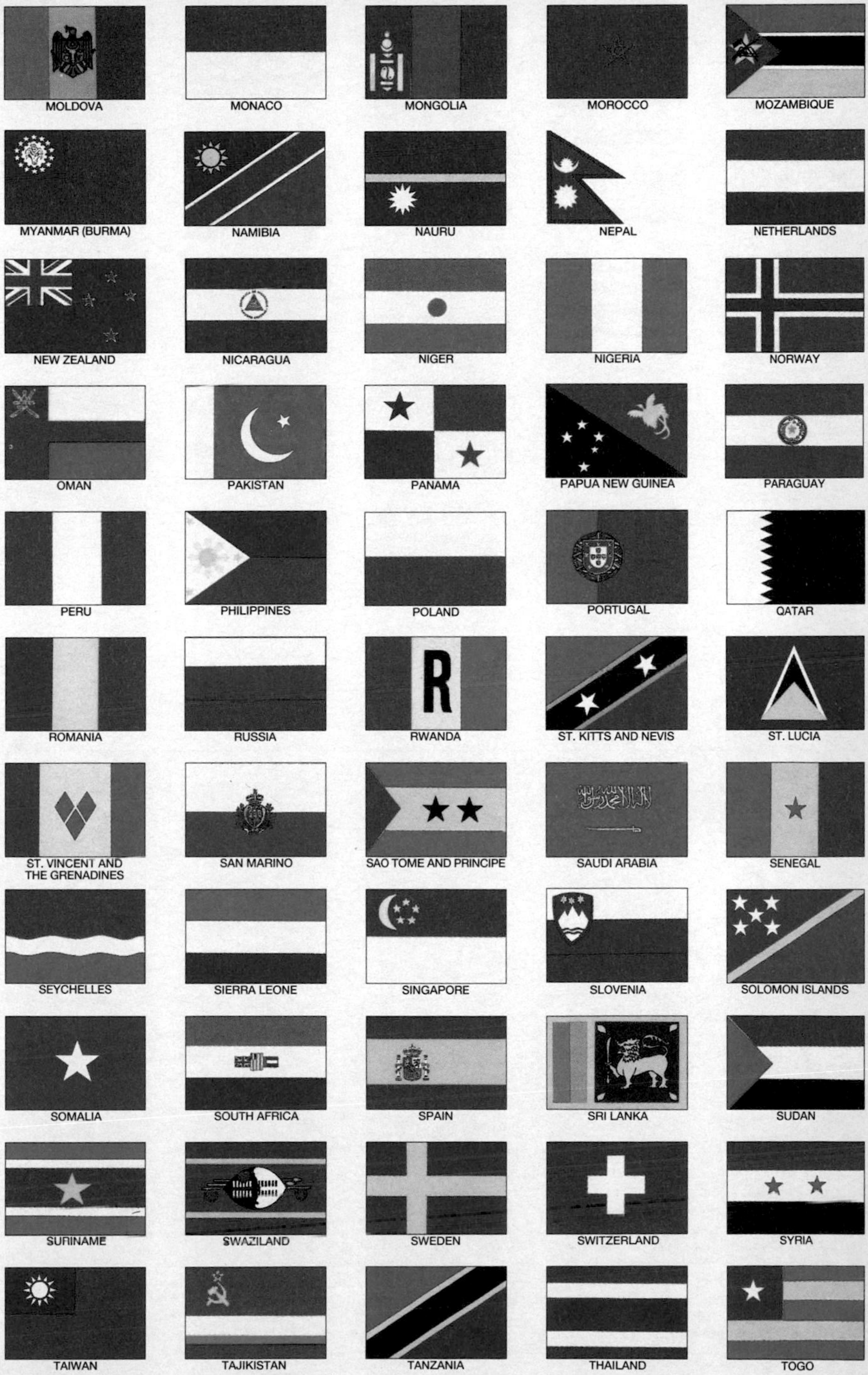
MOLDOVA
MONACO
MONGOLIA
MOROCCO
MOZAMBIQUE
MYANMAR (BURMA)
NAMIBIA
NAURU
NEPAL
NETHERLANDS
NEW ZEALAND
NICARAGUA
NIGER
NIGERIA
NORWAY
OMAN
PAKISTAN
PANAMA
PAPUA NEW GUINEA
PARAGUAY
PERU
PHILIPPINES
POLAND
PORTUGAL
QATAR
ROMANIA
RUSSIA
RWANDA
ST. KITTS AND NEVIS
ST. LUCIA
ST. VINCENT AND THE GRENADINES
SAN MARINO
SAO TOME AND PRINCIPE
SAUDI ARABIA
SENEGAL
SEYCHELLES
SIERRA LEONE
SINGAPORE
SLOVENIA
SOLOMON ISLANDS
SOMALIA
SOUTH AFRICA
SPAIN
SRI LANKA
SUDAN
SURINAME
SWAZILAND
SWEDEN
SWITZERLAND
SYRIA
TAIWAN
TAJIKISTAN
TANZANIA
THAILAND
TOGO

TONGA

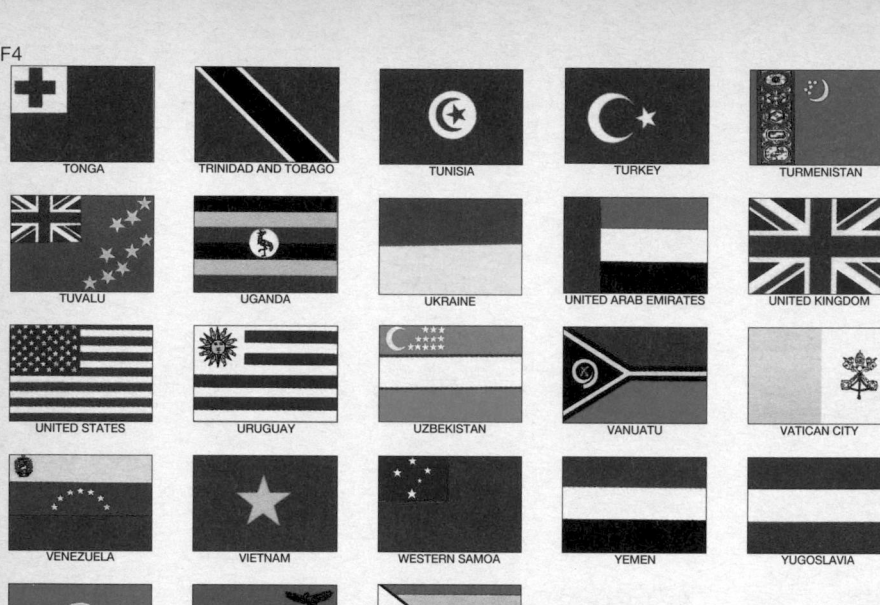

TRINIDAD AND TOBAGO

TUNISIA

TURKEY

TURMENISTAN

TUVALU

UGANDA

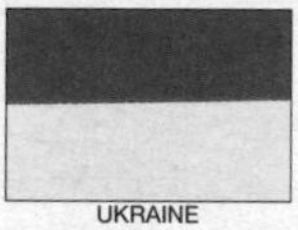
UKRAINE

UNITED ARAB EMIRATES

UNITED KINGDOM

UNITED STATES

URUGUAY

UZBEKISTAN

VANUATU

VATICAN CITY

VENEZUELA

VIETNAM

WESTERN SAMOA

YEMEN

YUGOSLAVIA

ZAIRE

ZAMBIA

ZIMBABWE

INTERNATIONAL TIME ZONES

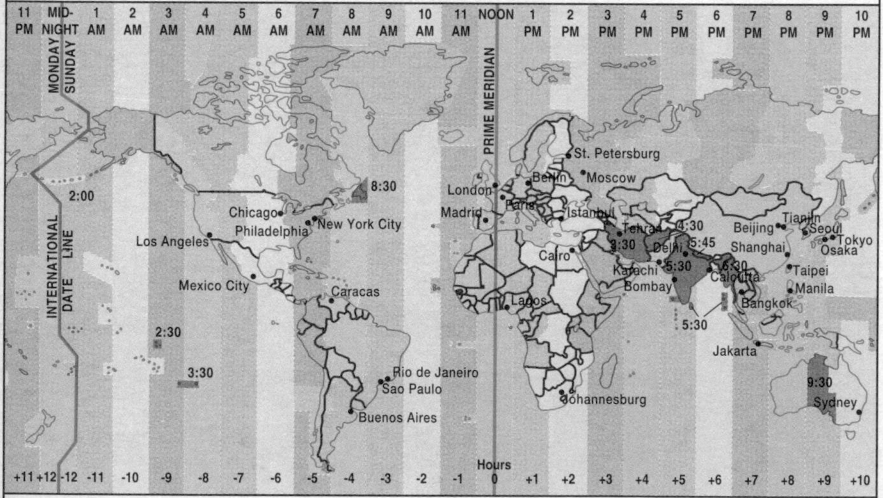

The world is divided into 24 time zones, each 15° longitude wide. The longitudinal meridian passing through Greenwich, England, is the starting point, and is called the *prime meridian.* The 12th zone is divided by the 180th meridian (International Date Line). When the line is crossed going west, the date is advanced one day; when crossed going east, the date becomes a day earlier.

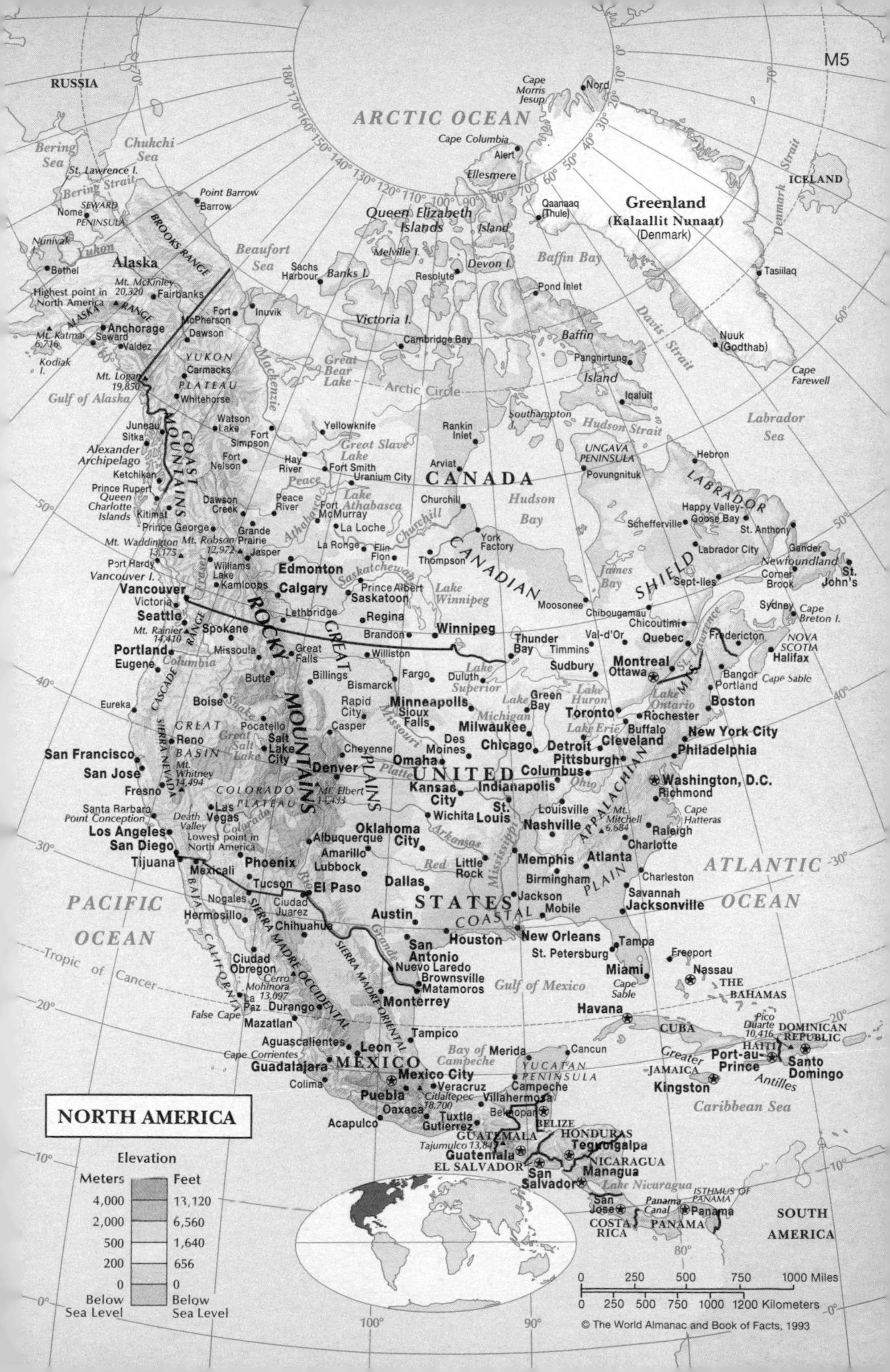
NORTH AMERICA
Elevation
Meters
Feet
4,000
13,120
2,000
6,560
500
1,640
200
656
0
0
Below Sea Level
Below Sea Level
0
250
500
750
1000 Miles
0
250
500
750
1000
1200 Kilometers
ARCTIC OCEAN
PACIFIC OCEAN
ATLANTIC OCEAN
RUSSIA
ICELAND
Greenland
(Kalaallit Nunaat)
(Denmark)
Alaska
CANADA
UNITED STATES
MEXICO
CUBA
THE BAHAMAS
HAITI
DOMINICAN REPUBLIC
JAMAICA
BELIZE
GUATEMALA
HONDURAS
EL SALVADOR
NICARAGUA
COSTA RICA
PANAMA
SOUTH AMERICA
Bering Sea
Chukchi Sea
Bering Strait
St. Lawrence I.
SEWARD PENINSULA
Nome
Nunivak I.
Yukon
Bethel
Point Barrow
Barrow
BROOKS RANGE
Beaufort Sea
Mt. McKinley 20,320
Highest point in North America
Fairbanks
ALASKA RANGE
Anchorage
Mt. Katmai 6,716
Seward
Valdez
Kodiak I.
Mt. Logan 19,850
Gulf of Alaska
Juneau
Sitka
Alexander Archipelago
Ketchikan
Prince Rupert
Queen Charlotte Islands
Kitimat
COAST MOUNTAINS
Fort McPherson
Inuvik
Dawson
YUKON PLATEAU
Carmacks
Whitehorse
Mackenzie
Watson Lake
Fort Simpson
Fort Nelson
Dawson Creek
Peace River
Hay River
Fort Smith
Uranium City
Yellowknife
Great Slave Lake
Great Bear Lake
Arctic Circle
Sachs Harbour
Banks I.
Victoria I.
Melville I.
Queen Elizabeth Islands
Cape Columbia
Alert
Ellesmere Island
Cape Morris Jesup
Nord
Resolute
Devon I.
Qaanaaq (Thule)
Baffin Bay
Pond Inlet
Cambridge Bay
Baffin Island
Pangnirtung
Iqaluit
Davis Strait
Denmark Strait
Tasiilaq
Nuuk (Godthab)
Cape Farewell
Labrador Sea
Southampton I.
Hudson Strait
Rankin Inlet
Arviat
UNGAVA PENINSULA
Povungnituk
Hebron
LABRADOR
Happy Valley-Goose Bay
Schefferville
St. Anthony
Labrador City
Gander
Newfoundland
Corner Brook
St. John's
Sept-Iles
Hudson Bay
Churchill
York Factory
CANADIAN SHIELD
James Bay
Moosonee
Chibougamau
Chicoutimi
Sydney
Cape Breton I.
NOVA SCOTIA
Halifax
Fredericton
Quebec
St. Lawrence
Val-d'Or
Timmins
Montreal
Ottawa
Sudbury
Bangor
Portland
Cape Sable
Lake Athabasca
Fort McMurray
La Loche
Athabasca
Churchill
La Ronge
Flin Flon
Thompson
Prince George
Grande Prairie
Mt. Robson 12,972
Mt. Waddington 13,175
Jasper
Williams Lake
Port Hardy
Vancouver I.
Kamloops
Edmonton
Calgary
Saskatchewan
Prince Albert
Saskatoon
Lake Winnipeg
Vancouver
Victoria
Seattle
Mt. Rainier 14,410
Spokane
Lethbridge
Regina
Brandon
Winnipeg
Thunder Bay
ROCKY MOUNTAINS
GREAT PLAINS
Portland
Columbia
Eugene
CASCADE RANGE
Missoula
Great Falls
Williston
Butte
Billings
Bismarck
Fargo
Duluth
Lake Superior
Eureka
Boise
Snake
Rapid City
Minneapolis
Sioux Falls
Lake Michigan
Green Bay
Lake Huron
Toronto
Lake Ontario
Rochester
Boston
GREAT BASIN
Great Salt Lake
Reno
Pocatello
Salt Lake City
Casper
Missouri
Milwaukee
Lake Erie
Buffalo
New York City
SIERRA NEVADA
Cheyenne
Des Moines
Chicago
Detroit
Cleveland
Philadelphia
San Francisco
San Jose
Mt. Whitney 14,494
Denver
Platte
Omaha
Pittsburgh
Columbus
APPALACHIAN
Washington, D.C.
Richmond
Fresno
COLORADO PLATEAU
Mt. Elbert 14,433
Kansas City
Indianapolis
Ohio
Santa Barbara
Point Conception
Las Vegas
Death Valley
Lowest point in North America
Colorado
Wichita
St. Louis
Louisville
Mt. Mitchell 6,684
Cape Hatteras
Los Angeles
San Diego
Tijuana
Mexicali
Phoenix
Tucson
Albuquerque
Amarillo
Lubbock
Oklahoma City
Arkansas
Nashville
Raleigh
Charlotte
Red
Little Rock
Memphis
Atlanta
Mississippi
Birmingham
Charleston
El Paso
Dallas
Savannah
Jacksonville
COASTAL PLAIN
Nogales
Ciudad Juarez
Austin
Jackson
Mobile
Hermosillo
BAJA CALIFORNIA
Chihuahua
Rio Grande
Houston
New Orleans
San Antonio
Tampa
St. Petersburg
Tropic of Cancer
Ciudad Obregon
SIERRA MADRE OCCIDENTAL
SIERRA MADRE ORIENTAL
Nuevo Laredo
Brownsville
Matamoros
Miami
Cape Sable
Freeport
Nassau
Cerro Mohinora 13,097
Monterrey
Gulf of Mexico
La Paz
False Cape
Durango
Havana
Mazatlan
Tampico
Pico Duarte 10,416
Aguascalientes
Leon
Bay of Campeche
Merida
Cancun
YUCATAN PENINSULA
Port-au-Prince
Santo Domingo
Cape Corrientes
Guadalajara
Mexico City
Greater Antilles
Kingston
Colima
Puebla
Veracruz
Citlaltepec 18,700
Campeche
Villahermosa
Oaxaca
Belmopan
Caribbean Sea
Acapulco
Tuxtla Gutierrez
Tajumulco 13,845
Guatemala
Tegucigalpa
San Salvador
Managua
Lake Nicaragua
ISTHMUS OF PANAMA
San Jose
Panama Canal
Panama
180°
170°
160°
150°
140°
130°
120°
110°
100°
90°
80°
70°
60°
50°
40°
30°
20°
10°
0°
© The World Almanac and Book of Facts, 1993

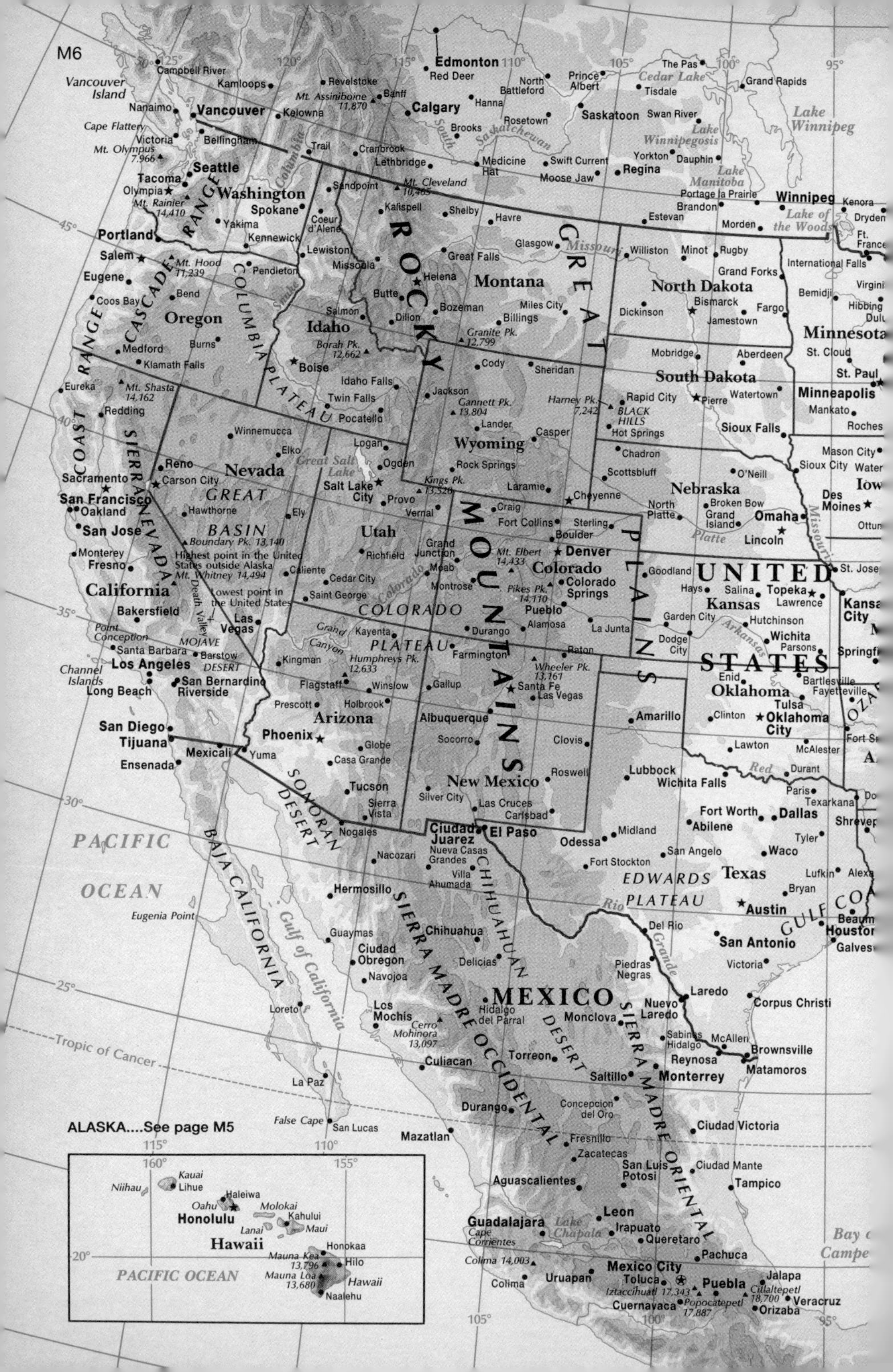
Vancouver Island
Campbell River
Kamloops
Revelstoke
Edmonton
Red Deer
The Pas
Cedar Lake
Grand Rapids
Nanaimo
Vancouver
Kelowna
Mt. Assiniboine 11,870
Banff
Calgary
Hanna
North Battleford
Prince Albert
Tisdale
Saskatoon
Swan River
Lake Winnipeg
Cape Flattery
Victoria
Mt. Olympus 7,966
Bellingham
Columbia
Trail
Cranbrook
Brooks
South Saskatchewan
Rosetown
Lake Winnipegosis
Lethbridge
Medicine Hat
Swift Current
Yorkton
Dauphin
Moose Jaw
Regina
Lake Manitoba
Tacoma
Seattle
Olympia
Washington
Sandpoint
Mt. Cleveland 10,465
Portage la Prairie
Winnipeg
Kenora
Mt. Rainier 14,410
Spokane
Kalispell
Shelby
Brandon
Estevan
Lake of the Woods
Dryden
Yakima
Havre
Morden
Portland
RANGE
Kennewick
Coeur d'Alene
Glasgow
Missouri
Williston
Minot
Rugby
Ft. Frances
Salem
Mt. Hood 11,239
Lewiston
ROCKY
Great Falls
GREAT
International Falls
Pendleton
Missoula
Helena
Montana
Grand Forks
Eugene
CASCADE
COLUMBIA
Snake
Butte
North Dakota
Virginia
Coos Bay
Bend
Bozeman
Miles City
Bismarck
Fargo
Bemidji
Hibbing
Duluth
Oregon
Salmon
Dillon
Billings
Dickinson
Jamestown
Minnesota
Idaho
Granite Pk. 12,799
Borah Pk. 12,662
Mobridge
Aberdeen
St. Cloud
Medford
Burns
Boise
Cody
Sheridan
St. Paul
Klamath Falls
PLATEAU
Idaho Falls
South Dakota
Eureka
Mt. Shasta 14,162
Jackson
Harney Pk. 7,242
Rapid City
Pierre
Watertown
Minneapolis
Twin Falls
Gannett Pk. 13,804
BLACK HILLS
Redding
Pocatello
Mankato
Lander
Hot Springs
Sioux Falls
Rochester
COAST
SIERRA
Winnemucca
Casper
Logan
Wyoming
Chadron
Elko
Mason City
Great Salt Lake
Ogden
Rock Springs
Sioux City
Waterloo
Reno
Nevada
O'Neill
Sacramento
Carson City
Salt Lake City
Scottsbluff
Iowa
Kings Pk. 13,528
Laramie
Nebraska
GREAT
Provo
Cheyenne
Des Moines
San Francisco
Oakland
Hawthorne
Vernal
Craig
North Platte
Broken Bow
Grand Island
Omaha
Ely
MOUNTAINS
Fort Collins
Sterling
BASIN
Utah
San Jose
Boulder
Missouri
Lincoln
Grand Junction
Mt. Elbert 14,433
Denver
PLAINS
Platte
Ottumwa
Boundary Pk. 13,140
Monterey
Highest point in the United States outside Alaska
Richfield
Fresno
Mt. Whitney 14,494
Colorado
UNITED
Moab
St. Joseph
NEVADA
Caliente
Goodland
Cedar City
Colorado Springs
California
Montrose
Pikes Pk. 14,110
Hays
Salina
Topeka
Death Valley
Lowest point in the United States
Saint George
Lawrence
Kansas City
Pueblo
Kansas
Bakersfield
COLORADO
Garden City
Las Vegas
Alamosa
La Junta
Hutchinson
Point Conception
MOJAVE
Kayenta
Durango
Arkansas
Grand Canyon
Dodge City
Wichita
Parsons
Santa Barbara
PLATEAU
Farmington
Raton
Springfield
Barstow
STATES
Channel Islands
Los Angeles
DESERT
Kingman
Humphreys Pk. 12,633
Wheeler Pk. 13,161
Enid
Bartlesville
Long Beach
San Bernardino
Riverside
Flagstaff
Winslow
Gallup
Santa Fe
Oklahoma
Fayetteville
Las Vegas
Tulsa
Prescott
Holbrook
Albuquerque
Amarillo
OZARK
San Diego
Arizona
Clinton
Oklahoma City
Tijuana
Phoenix
Globe
Socorro
Clovis
Fort Smith
Mexicali
Yuma
Lawton
McAlester
Ensenada
Casa Grande
Roswell
Lubbock
Red
Durant
SONORAN
Tucson
New Mexico
Wichita Falls
Paris
DESERT
Silver City
Texarkana
Sierra Vista
Las Cruces
Carlsbad
Fort Worth
Dallas
Shreveport
PACIFIC
Nogales
Ciudad Juarez
El Paso
Abilene
BAJA
Odessa
Midland
Tyler
Nacozari
Nueva Casas Grandes
San Angelo
Waco
OCEAN
Villa Ahumada
CHIHUAHUAN
Fort Stockton
EDWARDS
Texas
Lufkin
Alexandria
Hermosillo
SIERRA
PLATEAU
Bryan
CALIFORNIA
Rio
Austin
GULF COAST
Eugenia Point
Beaumont
Gulf of California
Del Rio
Houston
Guaymas
Chihuahua
San Antonio
Galveston
Ciudad Obregon
Delicias
Grande
Piedras Negras
Victoria
Navojoa
MADRE
Laredo
MEXICO
Nuevo Laredo
Corpus Christi
Loreto
Los Mochis
Hidalgo del Parral
Monclova
SIERRA
Cerro Mohinora 13,097
OCCIDENTAL
DESERT
Sabinas Hidalgo
McAllen
Brownsville
Tropic of Cancer
Culiacan
Torreon
Reynosa
Matamoros
Saltillo
Monterrey
La Paz
MADRE
Durango
Concepcion del Oro
False Cape
San Lucas
Ciudad Victoria
ALASKA....See page M5
Mazatlan
Fresnillo
ORIENTAL
Zacatecas
Kauai
Lihue
San Luis Potosi
Ciudad Mante
Niihau
Haleiwa
Oahu
Molokai
Aguascalientes
Tampico
Honolulu
Kahului
Lanai
Maui
Leon
Guadalajara
Lake Chapala
Irapuato
Hawaii
Honokaa
Cape Corrientes
Queretaro
Bay of Campeche
Mauna Kea 13,796
Hilo
Pachuca
PACIFIC OCEAN
Mauna Loa 13,680
Hawaii
Colima 14,003
Mexico City
Naalehu
Colima
Uruapan
Toluca
Puebla
Jalapa
Iztaccihuatl 17,343
Citlaltepetl 18,700
Veracruz
Cuernavaca
Popocatepetl 17,887
Orizaba
50°
45°
40°
35°
30°
25°
20°
125°
120°
115°
110°
105°
100°
95°
160°
155°

UNITED STATES,
CANADA, MEXICO
Elevation
Meters
Feet
2,000
6,560
1,000
3,280
500
1,640
200
656
0
0
Below Sea Level
Below Sea Level
0
250
500 Miles
0
250
500
750 Kilometers
90°
85°
80°
75°
70°
65°
60°
50°
45°
40°
35°
25°
20°
CANADA
CANADIAN SHIELD
James Bay
Waskaganish
Moosonee
Lake Nipigon
Geraldton
Hearst
Kapuskasing
Iroquois Falls
Timmins
Kirkland Lake
Nipigon
Marathon
Atikokan
Thunder Bay
Wawa
Chapleau
Lake Superior
Sault Ste. Marie
Sudbury
Elliot Lake
Houghton
Marquette
Iron Mountain
Cheboygan
Alpena
Georgian Bay
Lake Huron
Wisconsin
Eau Claire
Wausau
Green Bay
Appleton
La Crosse
Madison
Milwaukee
Lake Michigan
Traverse City
Michigan
Saginaw
Flint
Grand Rapids
Lansing
Detroit
Windsor
Sarnia
Kalamazoo
Rockford
Chicago
Davenport
Rock Island
Peoria
Champaign
Springfield
Illinois
Gary
South Bend
Fort Wayne
Indiana
Muncie
Indianapolis
Bloomington
Louisville
Evansville
St. Louis
Carbondale
Cape Girardeau
Poplar Bluff
Owensboro
Paducah
Bowling Green
Kentucky
Frankfort
Lexington
Toledo
Akron
Cleveland
Youngstown
Mansfield
Ohio
Wheeling
Dayton
Columbus
Parkersburg
Cincinnati
Ohio
Charleston
W.Va.
Huntington
Spruce Knob 4,861
Lake Erie
Erie
Pittsburgh
Altoona
Pa.
Harrisburg
Hagerstown
Md.
Baltimore
Annapolis
Washington, D.C.
Del.
Dover
Wilmington
Salisbury
Chesapeake Bay
Philadelphia
Trenton
N.J.
Allentown
Scranton
Newark
New York City
Long I.
Long Island Sound
Binghamton
Buffalo
Niagara Falls
Rochester
Syracuse
New York
ADIRONDACK MTS.
Albany
Lake Ontario
Toronto
Oshawa
Hamilton
London
Kitchener
Barrie
Owen Sound
Peterborough
Kingston
Bracebridge
Parry Sound
Pembroke
North Bay
Deep River
Ottawa
Hull
Cornwall
Montreal
Rouyn-Noranda
Val-d'Or
New Liskeard
Mont-Laurier
Matagami
Chibougamau
Mistassini
Alma
Chicoutimi
Shawinigan
Trois-Rivieres
Quebec
Riviere-du-Loup
Sherbrooke
St. Lawrence
St.-Georges
Burlington
Montpelier
Mt. Washington 6,288
Vt.
N.H.
Rutland
Concord
Manchester
Portsmouth
Boston
Mass.
Springfield
Cape Cod
New Bedford
Providence
R.I.
Hartford
New Haven
Conn.
Maine
Bangor
Bar Harbor
Augusta
Portland
Mt. Katahdin 5,267
Caribou
Houlton
Edmundston
Grand Falls
Fredericton
Saint John
Moncton
Calais
Sept-Iles
Port-Cartier
Baie-Comeau
Matane
Causapscal
Rimouski
Dalhousie
Bathurst
Newcastle
Gaspe
Anticosti I.
Gulf of St. Lawrence
Prince Edward I.
Charlottetown
New Glasgow
Amherst
Truro
NOVA SCOTIA
Bay of Fundy
Digby
Yarmouth
Shelburne
Cape Sable
Dartmouth
Halifax
Canso
Sydney
Cape Breton I.
Channel-Port aux Basques
APPALACHIAN MOUNTAINS
ATLANTIC COASTAL PLAIN
ATLANTIC OCEAN
Charlottesville
Richmond
Virginia
Newport News
Norfolk
Roanoke
Greensboro
Raleigh
North Carolina
Cape Hatteras
Winston-Salem
Johnson City
Knoxville
Nashville
Tennessee
Jackson
Chattanooga
Asheville
Mt. Mitchell 6,684
Charlotte
Fayetteville
New Bern
Wilmington
Greenville
Columbia
Florence
South Carolina
Charleston
Memphis
Huntsville
Tennessee
Gadsden
Athens
Atlanta
Augusta
Macon
Columbus
Georgia
Albany
Valdosta
Savannah
Brunswick
Tupelo
Birmingham
Columbus
Tuscaloosa
Montgomery
Alabama
Dothan
Greenville
Mississippi
Meridian
Jackson
Natchez
Hattiesburg
Mobile
Biloxi
Pensacola
Panama City
Tallahassee
Jacksonville
St. Augustine
Daytona Beach
Gainesville
Orlando
Cape Canaveral
Melbourne
Tampa
St. Petersburg
Florida
Lake Okeechobee
Sarasota
Fort Myers
West Palm Beach
Fort Lauderdale
Miami
Cape Sable
Florida Keys
Key West
Straits of Florida
Baton Rouge
Lafayette
New Orleans
Morgan City
PLAIN
Mississippi
Gulf of Mexico
BAHAMAS
CUBA
HAITI
DOMINICAN REPUBLIC
JAMAICA
Cancun
Merida
Cozumel I.
Campeche
YUCATAN PENINSULA

Tropic of Cancer
Equator
ATLANTIC
OCEAN
PACIFIC
OCEAN
Caribbean
Sea
MEXICO
BELIZE
Belize City
Belmopan
GUATEMALA
Guatemala
Escuintla
Volcan Tajumulco 13,845
EL SALVADOR
San Salvador
Santa Ana
HONDURAS
Gulf of Honduras
Tegucigalpa
San Pedro Sula
La Ceiba
Cerro Las Minas 9,347
NICARAGUA
Managua
Leon
Granada
Lake Nicaragua
MOSQUITO COAST
COSTA RICA
San Jose
Puntarenas
Limon
Volcan Irazu 11,260
PANAMA
Panama
Colon
David
Volcan Baru 11,401
ISTHMUS OF PANAMA
Gulf of Panama
CUBA
Havana
Isle of Youth
Santa Clara
Camaguey
Holguin
Santiago de Cuba
Guantanamo
Cayman Is. (U.K.)
THE BAHAMAS
Turks & Caicos Is. (U.K.)
JAMAICA
Kingston
Montego Bay
HAITI
Port-au-Prince
Cap-Haitien
DOMINICAN REPUBLIC
Santiago
Santo Domingo
Pico Duarte 10,417
San Juan
Ponce
Puerto Rico (U.S.)
Virgin Islands (U.S., U.K.)
Anguilla (U.K.)
ST. KITTS & NEVIS
ANTIGUA & BARBUDA
Montserrat (U.K.)
Guadeloupe (Fr.)
DOMINICA
Martinique (Fr.)
SAINT LUCIA
BARBADOS
ST. VINCENT & THE GRENADINES
GRENADA
TRINIDAD & TOBAGO
Port-of-Spain
Aruba (Neth.)
Curacao (Neth.)
Bonaire (Neth.)
Margarita Island
Pico Cristobal Colon 18,947
COLOMBIA
Barranquilla
Cartagena
Santa Marta
Valledupar
Sincelejo
Monteria
Barrancabermeja
Medellin
Manizales
Pereira
Armenia
Ibague
Bogota
Tunja
Villavicencio
Neiva
Nevada del Huila 18,865
Cali
Palmira
Buenaventura
Popayan
Pasto
Bucaramanga
Cucuta
Magdalena
VENEZUELA
Maracaibo
Lake Maracaibo
Cabimas
Valera
Merida
Pico Bolivar 16,427
San Cristobal
Coro
Barquisimeto
Valencia
Maracay
Caracas
Barcelona
Cumana
Maturin
El Tigre
San Fernando de Apure
Ciudad Bolivar
Ciudad Guayana
Puerto Ayacucho
Angel Falls
Orinoco
GUYANA
Georgetown
New Amsterdam
SURINAME
Paramaribo
French Guiana (Fr.)
Kourou
Cayenne
GUIANA HIGHLANDS
Mt. Roraima 9,094
ECUADOR
Quito
Esmeraldas
Portoviejo
Guayaquil
Ambato
Cuenca
Machala
Cotopaxi 19,347
Chimborazo 20,561
Galapagos Islands (Ecuador)
PERU
Tumbes
Talara
Sullana
Piura
Aguja Point
Chiclayo
Cajamarca
Trujillo
Chimbote
Nev. Huascaran 22,205
Nev. Yerupaja 21,709
Huanuco
Cerro de Pasco
Callao
Lima
Huancayo
Ayacucho
Ica
Cuzco
Juliaca
Puerto Maldonado
Pucallpa
Yurimaguas
Iquitos
Maranon
Ucayali
LA MONTANA
ANDES
LLANOS
Putumayo
BRAZIL
Benjamin Constant
Cruzeiro do Sul
Rio Branco
Cobija
Riberalta
Guajara-Mirim
Porto Velho
Boa Vista
Manaus
Santarem
Macapa
Marajo Island
Belem
Sao Luis
Imperatriz
Parnaiba
Teresina
Fortaleza
Natal
Joao Pessoa
Recife
Maceio
Aracaju
Salvador
Campina Grande
Juazeiro do Norte
Feira de Santana
Vitoria da Conquista
Ilheus
Gurupi
Brasilia
Cuiaba
Trinidad
BOLIVIA
Mamore
Beni
Guapore
Lake Titicaca
Amazon
Negro
Jurua
Purus
Madeira
Tapajos
Xingu
Tocantins
Araguaia
Sao Francisco
SELVAS
BRAZILIAN
MATO GROSSO PLATEAU

SOUTH AMERICA
CENTRAL AMERICA
& THE CARIBBEAN
Elevation
Meters
4,000
2,000
500
200
0
Below Sea Level
Feet
13,120
6,560
1,640
656
0
Below Sea Level
0
250
500
750 Miles
0
250
500
750
1,000 Kilometers
Tropic of Capricorn
20°
30°
40°
50°
100°
90°
80°
70°
60°
50°
40°
30°
20°
Goiania
HIGHLANDS
Montes Claros
Governador Valadares
Uberlandia
Belo Horizonte
Sao Jose do Rio Preto
Campo Grande
Grande
Pico da Bandeira 9,482
Vitoria
Ribeirao Preto
Presidente Prudente
Bauru
Juiz de Fora
Campinas
Volta Redonda
Londrina
Jundiai
Niteroi
Sorocaba
Sao Paulo
Rio de Janeiro
CAMPOS
Parana
Santos
Ponta Grossa
Curitiba
Joinvile
Florianopolis
Passo Fundo
Caxias do Sul
Santa Maria
Porto Alegre
Rivera
Pelotas
Melo
Corumba
Paraguay
CHACO
PARAGUAY
Concepcion
Coronel Oviedo
Asuncion
Iguazu Falls
Formosa
Encarnacion
Posadas
GRAN
Resistencia
Corrientes
Santo Tome
Uruguay
Curuzu Cuatia
Concordia
Salto
Paysandu
Parana
URUGUAY
Minas
Montevideo
Rio de la Plata
Nev. Sajama 21,391
Oruro
Cochabamba
Santa Cruz
Tacna
Arica
Lake Poopo
Sucre
ALTIPLANO
Potosi
Iquique
ANDES
Tarija
Pilcomayo
Calama
ATACAMA DESERT
Antofagasta
San Salvador de Jujuy
Salta
San Miguel de Tucuman
Cerro Ojos del Salado 22,572
San Felix Island (Chile)
San Ambrosio Island (Chile)
Copiapo
Cerro Bonete 22,546
Catamarca
Santiago del Estero
CHILE
La Serena
La Rioja
Cordoba
Santa Fe
Highest point in South America
Cerro Aconcagua 22,834
San Juan
PAMPAS
Vina del Mar
Mendoza
Valparaiso
Santiago
Rio Cuarto
Rosario
Cerro Tupungato 22,310
Junin
Juan Fernandez Islands (Chile)
San Bernardo
Rancagua
San Rafael
Buenos Aires
Avellaneda
La Plata
Talca
Chillan
Santa Rosa
Talcahuano
Concepcion
ARGENTINA
Bahia Blanca
Mar del Plata
Temuco
Neuquen
Punta Alta
Valdivia
Viedma
Osorno
San Carlos de Bariloche
San Matias Gulf
Puerto Montt
Valdes Peninsula
Lowest point in South America
Chiloe Island
Esquel
Trelew
Rawson
Chonos Archipelago
PATAGONIA
Comodoro Rivadavia
Gulf of San Jorge
Taitao Peninsula
Cape Tres Puntas
Bahia Grande
Stanley
Rio Gallegos
Str. of Magellan
Falkland Islands (U.K.) (Islas Malvinas)
Punta Arenas
Tierra del Fuego
Ushuaia
Cape Horn
South Georgia (U.K.)

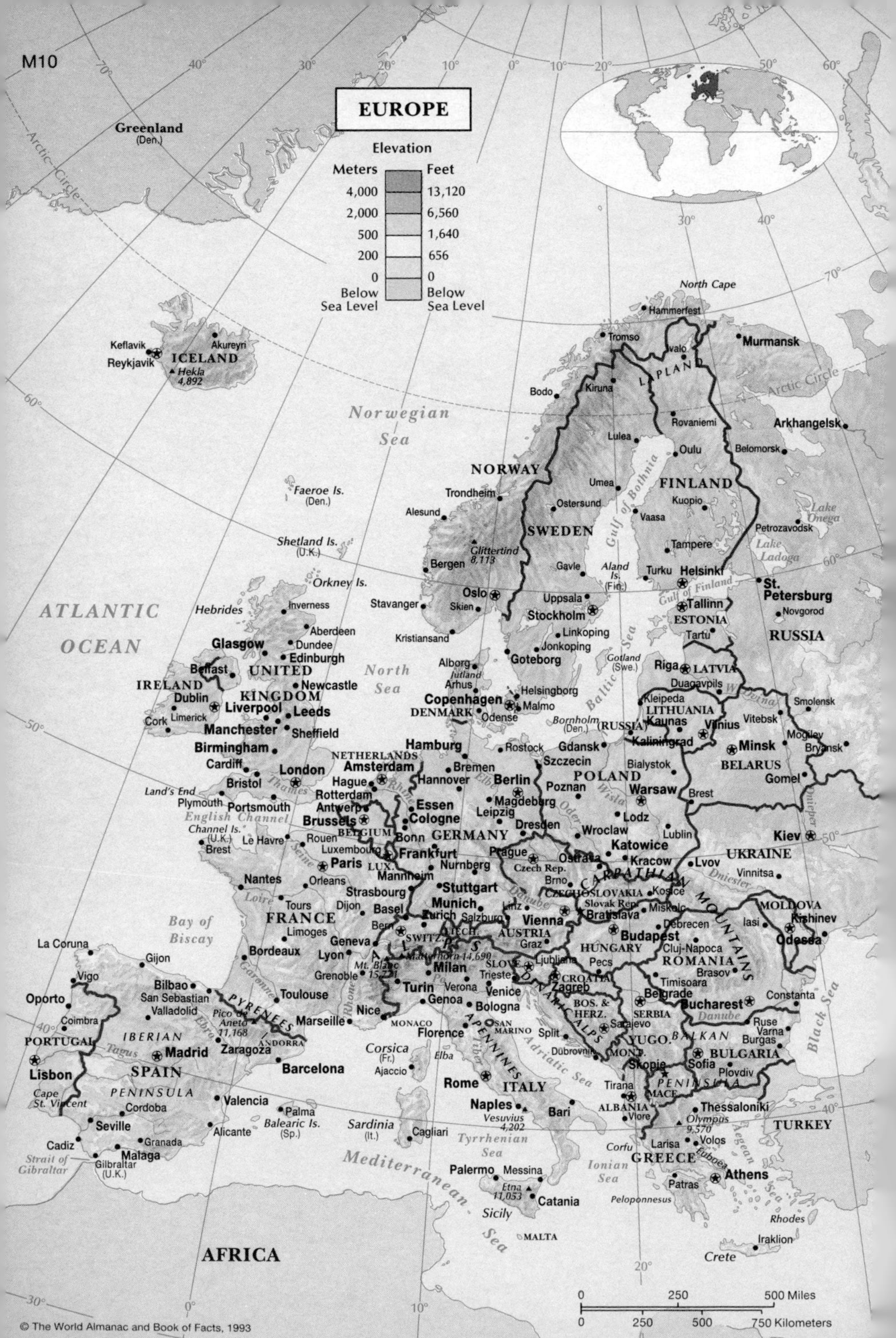
EUROPE
Elevation
Meters
Feet
4,000
13,120
2,000
6,560
500
1,640
200
656
0
0
Below Sea Level
Below Sea Level
Greenland (Den.)
Arctic Circle
ICELAND
Keflavik
Reykjavik
Akureyri
Hekla 4,892
Norwegian Sea
Faeroe Is. (Den.)
Shetland Is. (U.K.)
Orkney Is.
Hebrides
ATLANTIC OCEAN
North Cape
Hammerfest
Tromso
Murmansk
Ivalo
LAPLAND
Bodo
Kiruna
Rovaniemi
Arkhangelsk
Lulea
Oulu
Belomorsk
NORWAY
Gulf of Bothnia
FINLAND
Trondheim
Umea
Kuopio
Alesund
Ostersund
Vaasa
Lake Onega
Petrozavodsk
SWEDEN
Glittertind 8,113
Tampere
Lake Ladoga
Bergen
Gavle
Aland Is. (Fin.)
Turku
Helsinki
St. Petersburg
Gulf of Finland
Oslo
Uppsala
Tallinn
Stavanger
Skien
Stockholm
Novgorod
ESTONIA
Linkoping
Kristiansand
Jonkoping
Tartu
RUSSIA
Inverness
Aberdeen
Dundee
Glasgow
Edinburgh
Goteborg
Gotland (Swe.)
Baltic Sea
Belfast
UNITED KINGDOM
North Sea
Alborg
Jutland
Arhus
Riga
LATVIA
IRELAND
Newcastle
Helsingborg
Daugavpils
Dublin
Copenhagen
Malmo
Klaipeda
Smolensk
Liverpool
Leeds
DENMARK
Odense
LITHUANIA
Cork
Limerick
Manchester
Bornholm (Den.)
(RUSSIA)
Kaunas
Vilnius
Vitebsk
Sheffield
Kaliningrad
Minsk
Mogilev
Birmingham
Hamburg
Rostock
Gdansk
Bryansk
Cardiff
NETHERLANDS
Szczecin
Bialystok
BELARUS
Bristol
London
Amsterdam
Bremen
Berlin
POLAND
Gomel
Thames
Hague
Hannover
Elbe
Warsaw
Land's End
Rotterdam
Rhine
Poznan
Brest
Plymouth
Portsmouth
Antwerp
Essen
Magdeburg
Oder
Wisla
English Channel
Brussels
Cologne
Leipzig
Lodz
Dnieper
Channel Is. (U.K.)
BELGIUM
Bonn
Dresden
Wroclaw
Lublin
Le Havre
Rouen
GERMANY
Kiev
Brest
Seine
Luxembourg
Frankfurt
Prague
Ostrava
Katowice
UKRAINE
Paris
LUX.
Nurnberg
Czech Rep.
Kracow
Lvov
Mannheim
Brno
Vinnitsa
Nantes
Orleans
Strasbourg
Stuttgart
CARPATHIAN MOUNTAINS
Dniester
Loire
Tours
Dijon
Basel
Munich
Linz
CZECHOSLOVAKIA
Kosice
MOLDOVA
Bay of Biscay
FRANCE
Zurich
Salzburg
Danube
Vienna
Slovak Rep.
Bratislava
Miskolc
Kishinev
Bern
Debrecen
Iasi
Limoges
Geneva
SWITZ.
LIECH.
AUSTRIA
Budapest
Odesa
La Coruna
Lyon
ALPS
Matterhorn 14,690
Graz
HUNGARY
Cluj-Napoca
Bordeaux
Mt. Blanc 15,771
Milan
SLOVE.
Ljubljana
Pecs
ROMANIA
Gijon
Grenoble
Trieste
Zagreb
CROATIA
Brasov
Vigo
Bilbao
Garonne
Po
Verona
Venice
Timisoara
San Sebastian
Turin
DINARIC ALPS
Belgrade
Oporto
Valladolid
Toulouse
Genoa
Bologna
BOS. & HERZ.
Bucharest
Constanta
PYRENEES
Rhone
Nice
SERBIA
Danube
Coimbra
Pico de Aneto 11,168
Ebro
Marseille
MONACO
SAN MARINO
Sarajevo
Ruse
IBERIAN
ANDORRA
Florence
APENNINES
Split
BALKAN
Varna
PORTUGAL
Tagus
Zaragoza
Corsica (Fr.)
Tiber
Adriatic Sea
YUGO.
Burgas
Black Sea
Madrid
Elba
Dubrovnik
MONT.
Sofia
BULGARIA
Lisbon
SPAIN
Barcelona
Ajaccio
Skopje
Plovdiv
Rome
ITALY
Tirana
PENINSULA
Cape St. Vincent
PENINSULA
Valencia
MACE.
Cordoba
Palma
Naples
Bari
ALBANIA
Thessaloniki
Seville
Balearic Is. (Sp.)
Sardinia (It.)
Vesuvius 4,202
Vlore
Olympus 9,570
TURKEY
Alicante
Cagliari
Granada
Tyrrhenian Sea
Corfu
Larisa
Volos
Cadiz
Malaga
Aegean Sea
Strait of Gibraltar
Gibraltar (U.K.)
Mediterranean Sea
Euboea
GREECE
Palermo
Messina
Ionian Sea
Athens
Etna 11,053
Catania
Patras
Peloponnesus
Sicily
Rhodes
MALTA
Iraklion
AFRICA
Crete
0
250
500 Miles
0
250
500
750 Kilometers

RUSSIA, UKRAINE & CENTRAL ASIA
Elevation
Meters
Feet
4,000
13,120
2,000
6,560
500
1,640
200
656
0
0
Below Sea Level
Below Sea Level
ARCTIC OCEAN
PACIFIC OCEAN
EUROPE
SOUTH ASIA
RUSSIA
UKRAINE
KAZAKHSTAN
UZBEKISTAN
TURKMENISTAN
KYRGYZSTAN
TAJIKISTAN
GEORGIA
ARMENIA
AZERBAIJAN
Barents Sea
Kara Sea
Laptev Sea
East Siberian Sea
Chukchi Sea
Bering Strait
Bering Sea
Sea of Okhotsk
Sea of Japan
Shelikhov Gulf
Tatar Strait
Baltic Sea
Black Sea
Caspian Sea
Aral Sea
Lake Ladoga
Lake Onega
Lake Baykal
Lake Balkhash
Issyk Kul
Franz Josef Land
Novaya Zemlya
Severnaya Zemlya
New Siberian Islands
Wrangel I.
Sakhalin
Kuril Islands
KOLA PENINSULA
CRIMEA PENINSULA
KAMCHATKA PENINSULA
NORTH EUROPEAN PLAIN
URAL MOUNTAINS
WEST SIBERIAN PLAIN
CENTRAL SIBERIAN PLATEAU
VERKHOYANSK RA.
KOLYMA MOUNTAINS
STANOVOY RANGE
YABLONOVYY RANGE
SAYAN MTS.
CAUCASUS MTS.
KAZAKH UPLAND
KYZYL KUM DESERT
KARA KUM DESERT
PAMIRS
Arctic Circle
Dnieper
Don
Volga
Kama
N. Dvina
Ural
Ob
Irtysh
Yenisey
Lower Tunguska
Angara
Lena
Aldan
Indigirka
Kolyma
Amur
Syr Darya
Amu Darya
Mt. Narodnaya 6,217
Highest point in Europe Mt. El'brus 18,510
Communism Pk. 24,590
Lenina Pk. 23,405
Pobedy Pk. 24,406
Shiveluch 10,771
Klyuchevskaya 15,584
Karymsky 4,869
Alaid 7,662
Sarycheva 4,960
Tiatia 6,013
Murmansk
Belomorsk
St. Petersburg
Petrozavodsk
Arkhangelsk
Novgorod
Cherepovets
Tver
Vologda
Smolensk
Yaroslavl
Ivanovo
Kotlas
Moscow
Bryansk
Tula
Kursk
Ryazan
Nizhniy Novgorod
Kirov
Syktyvkar
Lipetsk
Voronezh
Kazan
Penza
Tolyatti
Samara
Saratov
Lvov
Vinnitsa
Kiev
Odessa
Kharkov
Krivoy Rog
Dnepropetrovsk
Zaporozhye
Donetsk
Sevastopol
Lugansk
Rostov
Volgograd
Krasnodar
Sochi
Stavropol
Astrakhan
Guryev
Grozny
Makhachkala
Batumi
Tbilisi
Yerevan
Gyandzha
Baku
Aqtau
Uralsk
Orenburg
Orsk
Ufa
Perm
Izhevsk
Berezniki
Chelyabinsk
Magnitogorsk
Yekaterinburg
Nizhniy Tagil
Serov
Tyumen
Kurgan
Tobolsk
Petropavlovsk
Vorkuta
Inta
Ukhta
Salekhard
Novyy Urengoy
Surgut
Nizhnevartovsk
Tara
Omsk
Novosibirsk
Kolpashevo
Tomsk
Achinsk
Kemerovo
Novokuznetsk
Barnaul
Pavlodar
Tselinograd
Karaganda
Semipalatinsk
Ust-Kamenogorsk
Tashtagol
Dzhezkazgan
Balkhash
Ayaguz
Kzyl-Orda
Taldy-Kurgan
Dzhambul
Alma-Ata
Bishkek
Chimkent
Tashkent
Namangan
Andizhan
Fergana
Samarkand
Bukhara
Dushanbe
Nukus
Urgench
Krasnovodsk
Ashkhabad
Dikson
Norilsk
Nordvik
Tura
Lesosibirsk
Krasnoyarsk
Kansk
Tulun
Bratsk
Ust-Kut
Irkutsk
Ulan-Ude
Chita
Lensk
Bodaybo
Vilyuysk
Yakutsk
Tiksi
Verkhoyansk
Zyryanka
Cherskiy
Susuman
Magadan
Okhotsk
Anadyr
Provideniya
Palana
Petropavlovsk-Kamchatskiy
Aldan
Berkakit
Tynda
Svobodnyy
Blagoveshchensk
Komsomolsk
Khabarovsk
Okha
Yuzhno-Sakhalinsk
Ussuriysk
Vladivostok
0 250 500 750 Miles
0 250 500 750 1,000 Kilometers
M11

SOUTH ASIA
Elevation
Meters
Feet
4,000
13,120
2,000
6,560
500
1,640
200
656
0
0
Below Sea Level
Below Sea Level
0 250 500 750 1,000 Miles
0 250 500 750 1,000 1,250 Kilometers
NORTHERN ASIA
Istanbul
Izmir
Bursa
ASIA MINOR
Black Sea
Ankara
Samsun
Konya
TURKEY
Mediterranean Sea
Mersin
Adana
Trabzon
Nicosia
CYPRUS
Erzurum
Latakia
Aleppo
Diyarbakir
Mt. Ararat 16,804
Lake Van
Beirut
LEBANON
ISRAEL
SYRIA
Tel Aviv-Yafo
Damascus
Jerusalem
Amman
JORDAN
SYRIAN DESERT
Mosul
Arbil
Karkuk
Tabriz
Lake Urmia
Caspian Sea
Dead Sea
Lowest point in Asia
Aqaba
IRAQ
Baghdad
Rasht
ELBURZ MTS.
Mt. Damavand 18,606
Tabuk
Bakhtaran
Teheran
Gorgan
Qom
Al Hillah
Euphrates
AN NAFUD
DASHT-E KAVIR
Hail
Basra
Esfahan
Mashhad
Abadan
IRAN
ZAGROS MOUNTAINS
DASHT-E LUT
Medina
Kuwait
KUWAIT
Buraydah
Yazd
Birjand
Red Sea
Shiraz
Persian Gulf
Jidda
Mecca
At Taif
SAUDI ARABIA
Riyadh
Ad Dammam
BAHRAIN
Al Hufuf
Kerman
QATAR
Doha
Zahedan
Bandar Abbas
Abu Dhabi
OMAN
UNITED ARAB EMIRATES
Dubai
Abha
Gulf of Oman
RUB AL KHALI
Muscat
Sanaa
Al Hudaydah
Sur
Ras al Hadd
YEMEN
OMAN
Aden
Al Mukalla
Salalah
Gulf of Aden
Tropic of Cancer
Arabian Sea
Socotra (Yemen)
AFRICA
Herat
Mazar-e Sharif
AFGHANISTAN
HINDU KUSH
Chitral
Kabul
Farah
Peshawar
Qandahar
Islamabad
Rawalpindi
Srinagar
Quetta
Faisalabad
Lahore
PAKISTAN
Multan
Chandigarh
Turbat
Sukkur
Indus
THAR DESERT
Delhi
New Delhi
Karachi
Hyderabad
Jaipur
Jodhpur
Agra
Kanpur
Lucknow
Ganges
Varanasi
Allahabad
Patna
Yining
Urumqi
Pobedy Peak 24,406
Kashi
Shache
TAKLIMAKAN DESERT
K2 28,250
KUNLUN MOUNTAI
PLATEAU OF TIBET
HIMALAYA
NEPAL
Pokhara
Mt. Everest 29,028
Kathmandu
Xigaze
Darjeeling
Ahmedabad
Rajkot
Indore
Bhopal
Jabalpur
Asansol
Ranchi
Khulna
Surat
DECCAN
Nagpur
Raipur
Calcutta
Bombay
PLATEAU
Poona
INDIA
Cuttack
WESTERN GHATS
EASTERN GHATS
Sholapur
Hyderabad
Vishakhapatnam
Panaji
Hubli
Vijayawada
Bay of Bengal
Bangalore
Madras
Mysore
Coimbatore
Cochin
Madurai
Trivandrum
Trincomalee
Cape Comorin
SRI LANKA
Colombo
Male
Galle
MALDIVES
Equator
INDIAN OCEAN
Chagos Archipelago (U.K.)
30°
40°
50°
60°
70°
80°
90°
20°
10°
0°

MONGOLIA
MONGOLIAN PLATEAU
ALTAY MOUNTAINS
GOBI DESERT
GREATER KHINGAN RANGE
Turpan Depression
Amur
Songhua
Moron
Darhan
Choybalsan
Dund-Us
Ulaanbaatar
Bayanhongor
Hailar
Yichun
Qiqihar
Jixi
Harbin
Changchun
Jilin
Shenyang
Fushun
Anshan
Chongjin
N. KOREA
Hamhung
Pyongyang
Inchon
Seoul
S. KOREA
Taegu
Pusan
Cheju I.
Yellow Sea
Sea of Japan
JAPAN
Hokkaido
Sapporo
Hakodate
Akita
Sendai
Niigata
Kanazawa
Honshu
Tokyo
Yokohama
Fuji-san 12,388
Kyoto
Nagoya
Kobe
Osaka
Hiroshima
Shikoku
Kitakyushu
Fukuoka
Kyushu
Nagasaki
Kagoshima
Iwo Jima (Japan)
CHINA
Hohhot
Beijing
Datong
Tianjin
Baotou
Yumen
Taiyuan
Shijiazhuang
Jinan
Qingdao
Shandong Pen.
Yinchuan
Huang
Handan
Xining
Lanzhou
Golmud
Luoyang
Xuzhou
Zhengzhou
Grand Canal
Xian
Huainan
Nanjing
Hefei
Shanghai
Hangzhou
Chang
Wuhan
Chengdu
Jingdezhen
Wenzhou
Nanchang
Lhasa
Chongqing
Zigong
Changsha
Fuzhou
Shaoyang
Hengyang
Ganzhou
Xiamen
Guiyang
Guilin
Liuzhou
Kunming
Canton (Guangzhou)
Xi
Nanning
Macau (Port.)
Hong Kong (U.K.)
Zhanjiang
Haikou
Hainan (China)
East China Sea
Ryukyu Is.
Okinawa
Naha
Taipei
TAIWAN
Kaohsiung
PACIFIC OCEAN
Tropic of Cancer
Philippine Sea
Brahmaputra
Gauhati
BANGLADESH
Dhaka
Imphal
Myitkyina
Irrawaddy
Chittagong
Mandalay
MYANMAR
Sittwe
Taunggyi
Prome
Salween
Bassein
Yangon
Moulmein
Tavoy
Mekong
Phongsali
Haiphong
Hanoi
Gulf of Tonkin
Louangphrabang
Vinh
LAOS
Vientiane
Chiang Mai
THAILAND
Hue
Da Nang
Savannakhet
Nakhon Sawan
Nakhon Ratchasima
VIETNAM
Bangkok
CAMBODIA
Batdambang
Phnom Penh
Nha Trang
Sattahip
Gulf of Thailand
Kompong Som
Ho Chi Minh City
Can Tho
Isthmus of Kra
Andaman Islands (India)
Nicobar Islands (India)
Phuket
Hat Yai
George Town
MALAYSIA
Banda Aceh
Medan
Kuala Lumpur
Kelang
Sibolga
Singapore
SINGAPORE
Pekanbaru
Padang
Jambi
Sumatra
Palembang
Bengkulu
Tanjungkarang-Telukbetung
South China Sea
Natuna Is.
Luzon
Laoag
Baguio
PHILIPPINES
Quezon City
Manila
Naga
Mindoro
Samar
Tacloban
Leyte
Iloilo
Panay
Cebu
Negros
Butuan
Puerto Princesa
Palawan
Mindanao
Davao
Zamboanga
Sandakan
Celebes Sea
Bandar Seri Begawan
BRUNEI
Tarakan
Sibu
Kuching
Samarinda
Pontianak
Borneo
Balikpapan
Sampit
Banjarmasin
Manado
Ternate
Gorontalo
Moluccas
Ambon
Celebes
Palopo
Parepare
Baubau
Ujungpandang
Banda Sea
Java Sea
INDONESIA
Jakarta
Semarang
Surabaya
Bandung
Java
Yogyakarta
Malang
Bali
Mataram
Ende
Timor
Dili
Kupang
Timor Sea
AUSTRALIA
Equator
90°
100°
110°
120°
130°
140°
150°
40°
30°
20°
10°
0°
10°

EUROPE
ASIA
Mediterranean Sea
Azores (Portugal)
Madeira Islands (Portugal)
Funchal
Canary Islands (Sp.)
Santa Cruz
Las Palmas
Strait of Gibraltar
Ceuta (Sp.)
Tangier
Tetouan
Kenitra
Rabat
Casablanca
Safi
Fes
Melilla (Sp.)
Oujda
Khouribga
Marrakech
Jebel Toubkal 13,661
Agadir
MOROCCO
ATLAS MOUNTAINS
Bechar
El Djazair (Algiers)
El Asnam
Wahran
Sidi Bel Abbes
Skikda
Bejaia
Batna
Annaba
Qacentina
Tebessa
Biskra
Djebel Chelia 7,631
Ghardaia
Touggourt
Cape Bon
Tunis
Sfax
TUNISIA
Tripoli
Misratah
Gulf of Sidra
Banghazi
Al Bayda
Tobruk
ALGERIA
I-n-Salah
I-n-Amenas
Ghadamis
LIBYA
Waha
Al Jawf
El Aaiun
Western Sahara (Occ. by Morocco)
Tropic of Cancer
AHAGGAR
Mt. Tahat 9,573
Tamanrasset
SAHARA
TIBESTI
Emi Koussi 11,204
Faya-Largeau
Mt. Greboun 6,378
AIR
NIGER
Agadez
Nouadhibou
Atar
MAURITANIA
Nouakchott
Saint-Louis
Kaedi
Ayoun el Atrous
SENEGAL
Dakar
Thies
Kaolack
THE GAMBIA
Banjul
Ziguinchor
Kayes
Senegal
GUINEA-BISSAU
Bissau
Labe
GUINEA
Conakry
Kankan
Freetown
SIERRA LEONE
Monrovia
LIBERIA
Tombouctou
Gao
MALI
Mopti
Niger
Segou
Bamako
Sikasso
BURKINA FASO
Bobo-Dioulasso
Ouagadougou
Niamey
Korhogo
CÔTE D'IVOIRE
Bouake
Yamoussoukro
GHANA
Tamale
TOGO
Lake Volta
Kumasi
Lome
BENIN
Ogbomosho
Abeokuta
Ibadan
Lagos
Ilorin
Oshogbo
Minna
Abuja
Sokoto
Maradi
Zinder
Katsina
Kano
Zaria
NIGERIA
Maiduguri
Kumo
Makurdi
Benue
Enugu
Lake Chad
N'Djamena
Maroua
Garoua
CHAD
Abeche
Sarh
Moundou
CENTRAL AFRICAN REPUBLIC
Bouar
Bambari
LIBYAN DESERT
Alexandria
Port Said
Suez Canal
Tanta
al-Jizah
Cairo
Suez
SINAI
Siwah
Al Fayyum
Asyut
EGYPT
Nile
Luxor
Al Kharijah
Aswan
Lake Nasser
Red Sea
NUBIAN DESERT
Port Sudan
Marawi
Atbarah
Kassala
Omdurman
Khartoum
Wad Madani
Blue Nile
White Nile
Al Fashir
Al Ubayyid
Nyala
SUDAN
Kusti
Malakal
Waw
Rumbek
Mitsiwa
Asmera
Al Qadarif
Ras Dashan 15,158
Mekele
Gonder
Lake Tana
Bahir Dar
Guna 13,881
Lowest point in Africa
Dese
ETHIOPIAN HIGHLANDS
Addis Ababa
Nazret
ETHIOPIA
Jima
Batu 14,131
Dire Dawa
Harer
DJIBOUTI
Lake Assal (−512)
Djibouti
Gulf of Aden
Cape Guardafui
Berbera
Hargeysa
SOMALI PENINSULA
Kelafo
Tropic of Cancer
20°
10°
0°
10°
20°
30°
40°
50°
60°
40°
30°
20°
10°

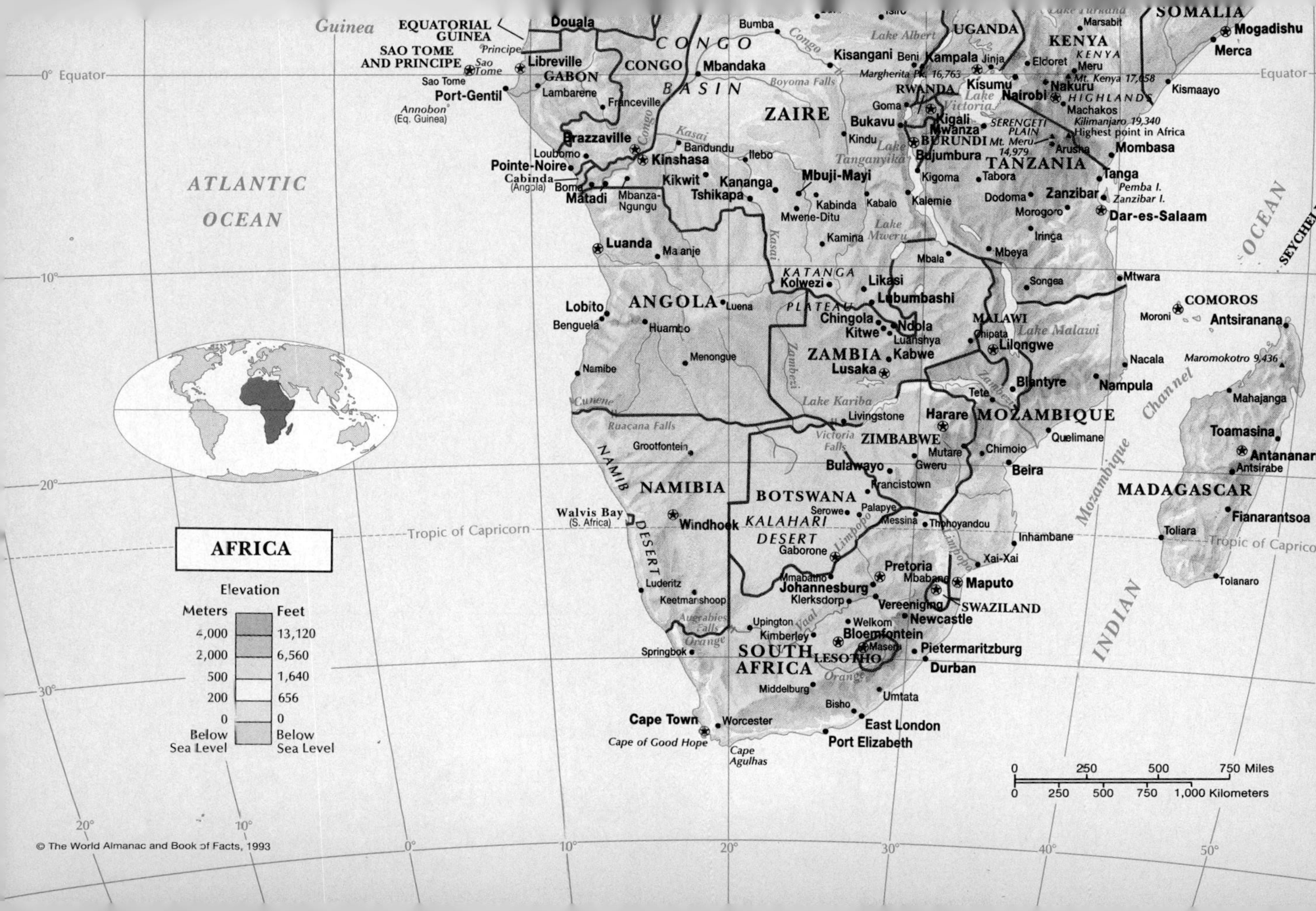
AFRICA
Elevation
Meters
4,000
2,000
500
200
0
Below Sea Level
Feet
13,120
6,560
1,640
656
0
Below Sea Level
0 250 500 750 Miles
0 250 500 750 1,000 Kilometers
ATLANTIC OCEAN
INDIAN OCEAN
Guinea
Equator
Tropic of Capricorn
0°
10°
20°
30°
40°
50°
EQUATORIAL GUINEA
SAO TOME AND PRINCIPE
Principe
Sao Tome
Annobon (Eq. Guinea)
Douala
Libreville
GABON
Lambarene
Port-Gentil
Franceville
CONGO
Brazzaville
Loubomo
Pointe-Noire
Cabinda (Angola)
Boma
Matadi
Kinshasa
Bandundu
Ilebo
Kikwit
Kananga
Tshikapa
Mbanza-Ngungu
Mbuji-Mayi
Kabinda
Mwene-Ditu
Kamina
Kabalo
Kalemie
Kindu
Bukavu
Goma
Kisangani
Beni
Mbandaka
Bumba
CONGO BASIN
ZAIRE
Boyoma Falls
Kasai
Congo
Lake Albert
Margherita Pk. 16,763
UGANDA
Kampala
Jinja
RWANDA
Kigali
BURUNDI
Bujumbura
Lake Victoria
Lake Tanganyika
Lake Mweru
Kisumu
Nairobi
Nakuru
Eldoret
Meru
Machakos
KENYA
KENYA HIGHLANDS
Mt. Kenya 17,058
Marsabit
Lake Turkana
SOMALIA
Mogadishu
Merca
Kismaayo
Mwanza
SERENGETI PLAIN
Mt. Meru 14,979
Kilimanjaro 19,340 Highest point in Africa
Arusha
Mombasa
Tanga
Pemba I.
Zanzibar I.
Zanzibar
Dar-es-Salaam
TANZANIA
Kigoma
Tabora
Dodoma
Morogoro
Iringa
Mbeya
Mbala
Songea
Mtwara
SEYCHELLES
COMOROS
Moroni
Antsiranana
Maromokotro 9,436
Mahajanga
Toamasina
Antananarivo
Antsirabe
MADAGASCAR
Fianarantsoa
Toliara
Tolanaro
Mozambique Channel
Nacala
Nampula
MALAWI
Lake Malawi
Chipata
Lilongwe
Blantyre
Zambezi
Tete
MOZAMBIQUE
Quelimane
Chimoio
Beira
Inhambane
Xai-Xai
Maputo
SWAZILAND
Mbabane
Luanda
Ma anje
ANGOLA
Luena
Lobito
Benguela
Huambo
Menongue
Namibe
Cunene
Ruacana Falls
KATANGA PLATEAU
Kolwezi
Likasi
Lubumbashi
Chingola
Kitwe
Ndola
Luanshya
ZAMBIA
Kabwe
Lusaka
Lake Kariba
Livingstone
Victoria Falls
ZIMBABWE
Harare
Mutare
Gweru
Bulawayo
Francistown
BOTSWANA
Serowe
Palapye
KALAHARI DESERT
Gaborone
Limpopo
Messina
Thohoyandou
NAMIBIA
NAMIB DESERT
Grootfontein
Walvis Bay (S. Africa)
Windhoek
Luderitz
Keetmanshoop
Augrabies Falls
Orange
Springbok
Mmabatho
Johannesburg
Pretoria
Klerksdorp
Vereeniging
Newcastle
Welkom
Upington
Kimberley
Vaal
Bloemfontein
Maseru
LESOTHO
Pietermaritzburg
Durban
SOUTH AFRICA
Middelburg
Umtata
Bisho
East London
Port Elizabeth
Worcester
Cape Town
Cape of Good Hope
Cape Agulhas

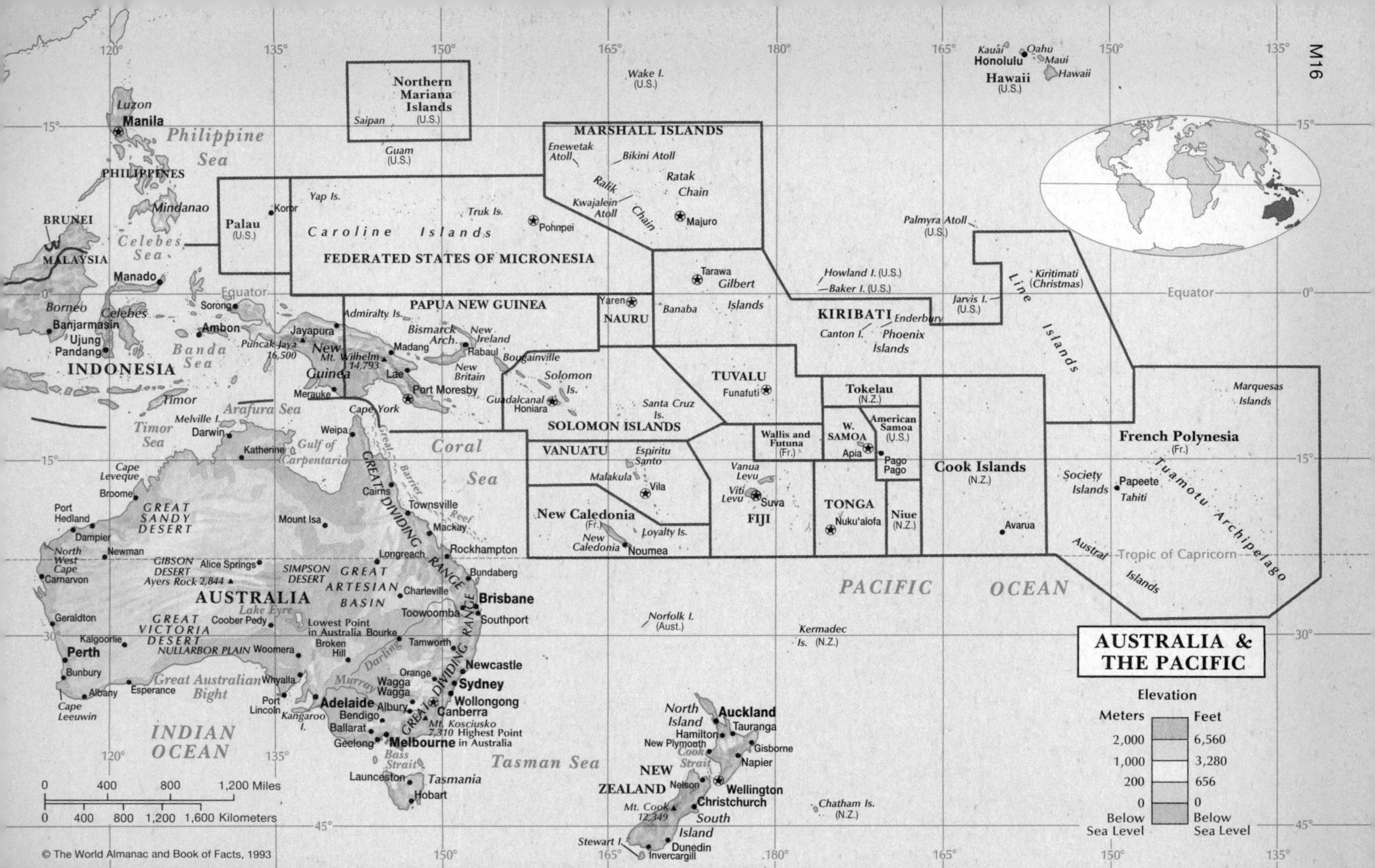
AUSTRALIA & THE PACIFIC
Elevation
Meters
2,000
1,000
200
0
Below Sea Level
Feet
6,560
3,280
656
0
Below Sea Level
0 400 800 1,200 Miles
0 400 800 1,200 1,600 Kilometers
Northern Mariana Islands (U.S.)
Saipan
Guam (U.S.)
Wake I. (U.S.)
Hawaii (U.S.)
Kauai
Oahu
Honolulu
Maui
Hawaii
MARSHALL ISLANDS
Enewetak Atoll
Bikini Atoll
Ralik Chain
Ratak Chain
Kwajalein Atoll
Majuro
Palau (U.S.)
Koror
Yap Is.
Truk Is.
Pohnpei
Caroline Islands
FEDERATED STATES OF MICRONESIA
Palmyra Atoll (U.S.)
Kiritimati (Christmas)
Line Islands
Howland I. (U.S.)
Baker I. (U.S.)
Jarvis I. (U.S.)
Tarawa
Gilbert Islands
Banaba
Yaren
NAURU
KIRIBATI
Enderbury
Canton I.
Phoenix Islands
Equator
Luzon
Manila
Philippine Sea
PHILIPPINES
Mindanao
BRUNEI
MALAYSIA
Celebes Sea
Manado
Borneo
Banjarmasin
Celebes
Ujung Pandang
Sorong
Ambon
Banda Sea
INDONESIA
Timor
Timor Sea
Arafura Sea
Jayapura
Puncak Jaya 16,500
New Guinea
Mt. Wilhelm 14,793
Merauke
PAPUA NEW GUINEA
Admiralty Is.
Bismarck Arch.
New Ireland
Madang
Rabaul
New Britain
Lae
Port Moresby
Bougainville
Solomon Is.
Guadalcanal
Honiara
Santa Cruz Is.
SOLOMON ISLANDS
TUVALU
Funafuti
Tokelau (N.Z.)
W. SAMOA
Apia
American Samoa (U.S.)
Pago Pago
Wallis and Futuna (Fr.)
VANUATU
Espiritu Santo
Malakula
Vila
Vanua Levu
Viti Levu
Suva
FIJI
TONGA
Nuku'alofa
Niue (N.Z.)
Cook Islands (N.Z.)
Avarua
New Caledonia (Fr.)
New Caledonia
Loyalty Is.
Noumea
French Polynesia (Fr.)
Marquesas Islands
Society Islands
Papeete
Tahiti
Tuamotu Archipelago
Austral Islands
Tropic of Capricorn
PACIFIC OCEAN
Norfolk I. (Aust.)
Kermadec Is. (N.Z.)
Chatham Is. (N.Z.)
Coral Sea
Cape York
Weipa
Melville I.
Darwin
Katherine
Gulf of Carpentaria
Great Barrier Reef
GREAT DIVIDING RANGE
Cairns
Townsville
Mackay
Rockhampton
Bundaberg
Brisbane
Southport
Cape Leveque
Broome
Port Hedland
Dampier
Newman
North West Cape
Carnarvon
GREAT SANDY DESERT
GIBSON DESERT
Alice Springs
Ayers Rock 2,844
Mount Isa
Longreach
SIMPSON DESERT
GREAT ARTESIAN BASIN
Charleville
Toowoomba
AUSTRALIA
Lake Eyre
Lowest Point in Australia
Bourke
Coober Pedy
GREAT VICTORIA DESERT
NULLARBOR PLAIN
Woomera
Broken Hill
Tamworth
Darling
Geraldton
Kalgoorlie
Perth
Bunbury
Albany
Cape Leeuwin
Esperance
Great Australian Bight
Whyalla
Port Lincoln
Kangaroo I.
Adelaide
Murray
Orange
Wagga Wagga
Newcastle
Sydney
Wollongong
Canberra
Albury
Bendigo
Ballarat
Geelong
Melbourne
Mt. Kosciusko 7,310 Highest Point in Australia
Bass Strait
Launceston
Tasmania
Hobart
INDIAN OCEAN
Tasman Sea
NEW ZEALAND
North Island
Auckland
Tauranga
Hamilton
New Plymouth
Gisborne
Napier
Cook Strait
Nelson
Wellington
Christchurch
South Island
Mt. Cook 12,349
Dunedin
Invercargill
Stewart I.

WORLD HISTORY

Prehistory: Our Ancestors Take Over

Homo sapiens. The precise origins of *homo sapiens,* the species to which all humans belong, are subject to broad speculation based on a small number of fossils, genetic and anatomical studies, and the geological record. But most scientists agree that we evolved from ape-like primate ancestors in a process that began millions of years ago.

Current theories trace the first hominid (human-like primate) to Africa, where 2 lines of hominids appeared some 5 or 6 million years ago. One was *Australopithecus,* a social animal, who lived from perhaps 4 to 3 million years ago, and then apparently became extinct.

The 2nd was a human line, *Homo habilis,* a large-brained specimen that walked upright and had a dextrous hand. *Homo habilis* lived in semi-permanent camps and had a food-gathering and sharing economy.

Homo erectus, our nearest ancestor, appeared in Africa perhaps 1.75 million years ago, and began spreading into Asia and Europe soon after. It had a fairly large brain and a skeletal structure similar to ours. *Homo erectus* learned to control fire, and probably had primitive language skills. The final brain development to *Homo sapiens* and then to our sub-species *Homo sapiens sapiens* occurred between 500,000 and 50,000 years ago, either in one place — probably Africa — or virtually simultaneously and independently in different places in Africa, Europe, and Asia. There is no question that all modern races are members of the same sub-species, *Homo sapiens sapiens.*

The spread of mankind into the remaining habitable continents probably took place during the last ice age up to 100,000 years ago: to the Americas across a land bridge from Asia, and to Australia across the Timor Straits.

Earliest cultures. A variety of cultural modes — in tool-making, diet, shelter, and possibly social arrangements and spiritual expression, arose as early mankind adapted to different geographic and climatic zones.

Three basic tool-making traditions are recognized by archeologists as arising and often coexisting from one million years ago to the near past: the *chopper tradition,* found largely in E. Asia, with crude chopping tools and simple flake tools; the *flake tradition,* found in Africa and W. Europe, with a variety of small cutting and flaking tools, and the *biface tradition,* found in all of Africa, W. and S. Europe, and S. Asia, producing pointed hand axes chipped on both faces. Later biface sites yield more refined axes and a variety of other tools, weapons, and ornaments using bone, antler, and wood as well as stone.

Only sketchy evidence remains for the different stages in man's increasing control over the environment. Traces of 400,000-year-old covered wood shelters have been found at Nice, France. Scraping tools at Neanderthal sites (200,000-30,000 BC in Europe, N. Africa, the Middle East and Central Asia) suggest the treatment of skins for clothing. Sites from all parts of the world show seasonal migration patterns and exploitation of a wide range of plant and animal food sources.

Painting and decoration, for which there is evidence at the Nice site, flourished along with stone and ivory sculpture after 30,000 years ago; 60 caves in France and 30 in Spain show remarkable examples of wall painting. Other examples have been found in Africa. Proto-religious rites are suggested by these works, and by evidence of ritual cannibalism by Peking Man, 500,000 BC, and of ritual burial with medicinal plants and flowers by Neanderthals at Shanidar in Iraq.

The Neolithic Revolution. Sometime after 10,000 BC, among widely separated human communities, a series of dramatic technological and social changes occurred that are summed up as the Neolithic Revolution. The cultivation of previously wild plants encouraged the growth of permanent settlements. Animals were domesticated as a work force and food source. The manufacture of pottery and cloth began. These techniques permitted a huge increase in world population and in human control over the earth.

No region can safely claim priority as the "inventor" of these techniques. Dispersed sites in Cen. and S. America, S.E. Europe, and the Middle East show roughly contemporaneous (10-8,000 BC) evidence of one or another "neolithic" trait. Dates near 6-3,000 BC have been given for E. and S. Asian, W. European, and sub-Saharan African neolithic remains. The variety of crops — field grains, rice, maize, and roots, and the varying mix of other traits suggest that the revolution occurred independently in all these regions.

History Begins: 4000 - 1000 BC

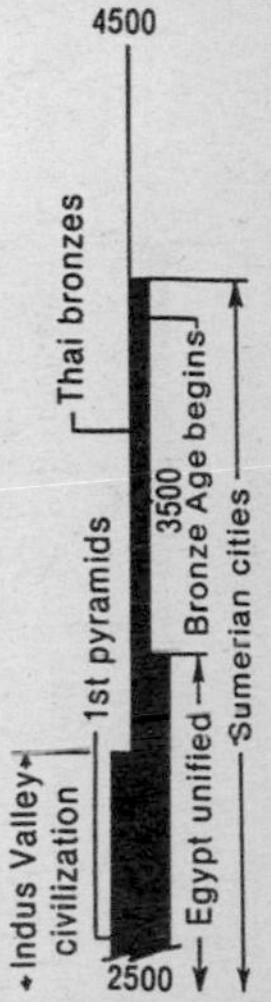

Near Eastern cradle. If history began with writing, the first chapter opened in Mesopotamia, the Tigris-Euphrates river valley. Clay tablets with pictographs were used by the Sumerians to keep records after 4000 BC. A **cuneiform** (wedge shaped) script evolved by 3000 BC as a full syllabic alphabet. Neighboring peoples adapted the script to their own language.

Sumerian life centered, from 4000 BC, on large cities (Eridu, Ur, Uruk, Nippur, Kish, Lagash) organized around temples and priestly bureaucracies, with the surrounding plains watered by vast irrigation works and worked with traction plows. Sailboats, wheeled vehicles, potters wheels, and kilns were used. Copper was smelted and tempered in Sumeria from c4000 BC and bronze was produced not long after. Ores, as well as precious stones and metals were obtained through long-distance ship and caravan trade. Iron was used from c2000 BC. Improved ironworking, developed partly by the **Hittites,** became widespread by 1200 BC.

Sumerian political primacy passed among cities and their kingly dynasties. Semitic-speaking peoples, with cultures derived from the Sumerian, founded a succession of dynasties that ruled in Mesopotamia and neighboring areas for most of 1800 years; among them the **Akkadians** (first under Sargon c2350 BC), the Amorites (whose laws, codified by **Hammurabi,** c1792-1750 BC, have Biblical parallels), and the Assyrians, with interludes of rule by the Hittites, Kassites, and Mitanni, all possibly Indo-Europeans. The political and cultural center of gravity shifted northwest with each successive empire.

Mesopotamian learning, maintained by scribes and preserved by successive rulers in vast libraries, was not abstract or theoretical. Algebraic and geometric problems could be solved on a practical basis in construction, commerce, or administration. Systematic lists of astronomical phenomena, plants, animals and stones were kept; medical texts listed ailments and their herbal cures.

The Sumerians worshipped anthropomorphic gods representing natural forces — Anu, god of heaven; Enlil (Ea), god of water. Epic poetry related these and other gods in a hierarchy. Sacrifices were made at **ziggurats** — huge stepped temples. Gods were thought to control all events, which could be foretold using oracular materials. This religious pattern persisted into the first millenium BC.

The Syria-Palestine area, site of some of the earliest urban remains (Jericho, 7000 BC), and of the recently uncovered **Ebla** civilization (fl. 2500 BC), experienced Egyptian cultural and political influence along with Mesopotamian. The **Phoenician** coast was an active commercial center. A phonetic alphabet was invented here before 1600 BC. It became the ancestor of all European, Middle Eastern, Indian, S.E.

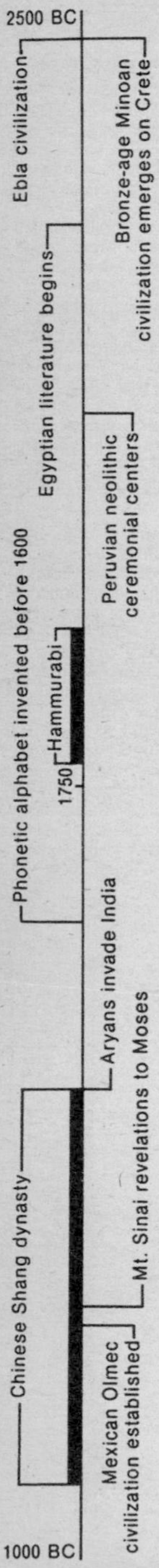

Asian, Ethiopian, and Korean alphabets.

Regional commerce and diplomacy were aided by the use of Akkadian as a *lingua franca*, later replaced by Aramaic.

Egypt. Agricultural villages along the Nile were united by 3300 BC into two kingdoms, Upper and Lower Egypt, unified under the Pharaoh Menes c3100 BC; Nubia to the south was added 2600 BC. A national bureaucracy supervised construction of canals and monuments (**pyramids** starting 2700 BC). Brilliant First Dynasty achievements in architecture, sculpture and painting, set the standards and forms for all subsequent Egyptian civilization and are still admired. **Hieroglyphic writing** appeared by 3400 BC, recording a sophisticated literature including romantic and philosophical modes after 2300 BC.

An ordered hierarchy of gods, including totemistic animal elements, was served by a powerful priesthood in Memphis. The pharaoh was identified with the falcon god Horus. Later trends were the belief in an afterlife, and the quasi-monotheistic reforms of **Akhenaton** (c1379-1362 BC).

After a period of conquest by Semitic Hyksos from Asia (c1700-1500 BC), the New Kingdom established an empire in Syria. Egypt became increasingly embroiled in Asiatic wars and diplomacy. Eventually it was conquered by Persia in 525 BC, and it faded away as an independent culture.

India. An urban civilization with a so-far-undeciphered writing system stretched across the Indus Valley and along the Arabian Sea c3000-1500 BC. Major sites are Harappa and **Mohenjo-Daro** in Pakistan, well-planned geometric cities with underground sewers and vast granaries. The entire region (600,000 sq. mi.) may have been ruled as a single state. Bronze was used, and arts and crafts were highly developed. Religious life apparently took the form of fertility cults.

Indus civilization was probably in decline when it was destroyed by **Aryan invaders** from the northwest, speaking an Indo-European language from which all the languages of Pakistan, north India and Bangladesh descend. Led by a warrior aristocracy whose legendary deeds are recorded in the **Rig Veda**, the Aryans spread east and south, bringing their pantheon of sky gods, elaborate priestly (Brahmin) ritual, and the beginnings of the caste system; local customs and beliefs were assimilated by the conquerors.

Europe. On Crete, the bronze-age **Minoan civilization** emerged c2500 BC. A prosperous economy and richly decorative art (e.g. at Knossos palace) was supported by seaborne commerce. Mycenae and other cities in Greece and Asia Minor (e.g. **Troy**) preserved elements of the culture to c1100 BC. Cretan Linear A script, c2000-1700 BC, is undeciphered; Linear B, c1300-1200 BC, records a Greek dialect.

Possible connection between Minoan-Mycenaean monumental stonework, and the great megalithic monuments and tombs of W. Europe, Iberia, and Malta (c4000-1500 BC) is unclear.

China. Proto-Chinese neolithic cultures had long covered northern and southeastern China when the first large political state was organized in the north by the **Shang dynasty** c1500 BC. Shang kings called themselves Sons of Heaven, and presided over a cult of human and animal sacrifice to ancestors and nature gods. The Chou dynasty, starting c1100 BC, expanded the area of the Son of Heaven's dominion, but feudal states exercised most temporal power.

A writing system with 2,000 different characters was already in use under the Shang, with **pictographs** later supplemented by phonetic characters. The system, with modifications, is still in use, despite changes in spoken Chinese.

Technical advances allowed urban specialists to create fine ceramic and jade products, and bronze casting after 1500 BC was the most advanced in the world.

Bronze artifacts have recently been discovered in northern Thailand dating to 3600 BC, hundreds of years before similar Middle Eastern finds.

Americas. Olmecs settled on the Gulf coast of Mexico, 1500 BC, and soon developed the first civilization in the Western Hemisphere. Temple cities and huge stone sculpture date to 1200 BC. A rudimentary calendar and writing system existed. Olmec religion, centering on a jaguar god, and art forms influenced all later Meso-American cultures.

Neolithic ceremonial centers were built on the Peruvian desert coast, c2000 BC.

Classical Era of Old World Civilizations

Greece. After a period of decline during the Dorian Greek invasions (1200-1000 BC), Greece and the Aegean area developed a unique civilization. Drawing upon Mycenaean traditions, Mesopotamian learning (weights and measures, lunisolar calendar, astronomy, musical scales), the Phoenician alphabet (modified for Greek), and Egyptian art, the revived **Greek city-states** saw a rich elaboration of intellectual life. Long-range commerce was aided by metal coinage (introduced by the Lydians in Asia Minor before 700 BC); colonies were founded around the Mediterranean and Black Sea shores (Cumae in Italy 760 BC, Massalia in France c600 BC).

Philosophy, starting with Ionian speculation on the nature of matter and the universe (Thales c634-546), and including mathematical speculation (Pythagoras c580-c500), culminated in Athens in the rationalist idealism of **Plato** (c428-347) and **Socrates** (c470-399); the latter was executed for alleged impiety. **Aristotle** (384-322) united all fields of study in his system. The arts were highly valued. Architecture culminated in the **Parthenon** in Athens (438, sculpture by Phidias); poetry and drama (Aeschylus 525-456) thrived. Male beauty and strength, a chief artistic theme, were enhanced at the gymnasium and the national games at Olympia.

Ruled by local tyrants or oligarchies, the Greeks were never politically united, but managed to resist inclusion in the Persian Empire (Darius defeated at Marathon 490 BC, Xerxes at Salamis, Plataea 479 BC). Local warfare was common; the **Peloponnesian Wars,** 431-404 BC, ended in Sparta's victory over Athens. Greek political power waned, but classical Greek cultural forms spread thoughout the ancient world from the Atlantic to India.

Hebrews. Nomadic Hebrew tribes entered Canaan before 1200 BC, settling among other Semitic peoples speaking the same language. They brought from the desert a **monotheistic faith** said to have been revealed to Abraham in Canaan c1800 BC and to Moses at Mt. Sinai c1250 BC, after the Hebrews' escape from bondage in Egypt. David (ruled 1000-961 BC) and Solomon (ruled 961-922 BC) united the Hebrews in a kingdom that briefly dominated the area. Phoenicians to the north established colonies

(*continued on p. 492*)

Paleontology: The History of Life

All dates are approximate, and are subject to change based on new fossil finds or new dating techniques, but the sequence of events is generally accepted. Dates are in years before the present.

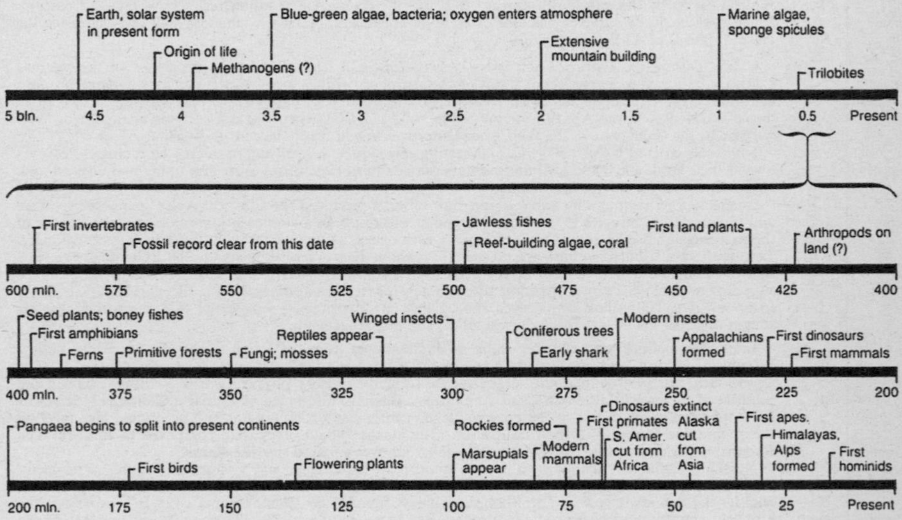

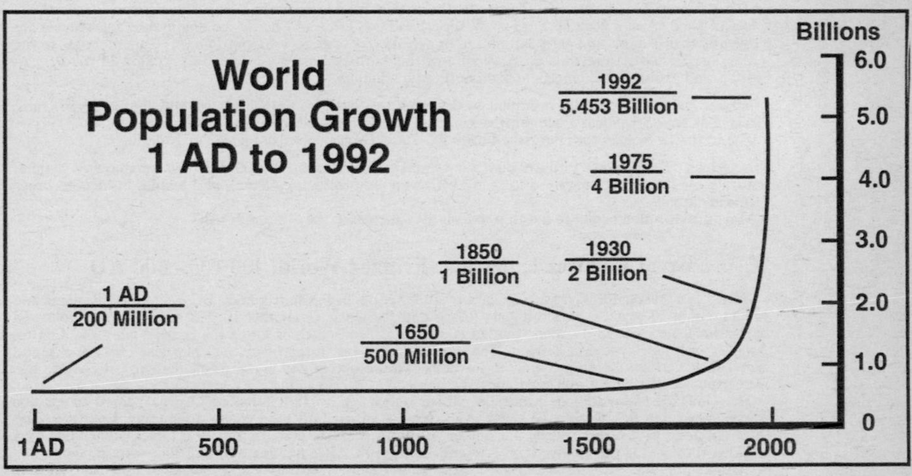

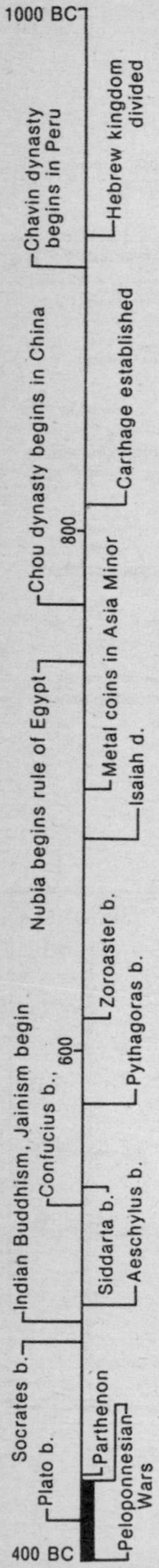

around the E. and W. Mediterranean (**Carthage** c814 BC) and sailed into the Atlantic.

A temple in Jerusalem became the national religious center, with sacrifices performed by a hereditary priesthood. Polytheistic influences, especially of the fertility cult of Baal, were opposed by **prophets** (Elijah, Amos, Isaiah).

Divided into **two kingdoms** after Solomon, the Hebrews were unable to resist the revived Assyrian empire, which conquered Israel, the northern kingdom in 722 BC. Judah, the southern kingdom, was conquered in 586 BC by the Babylonians under Nebuchadnezzar II. But with the fixing of most of the Biblical canon by the mid-fourth century BC, and the emergence of rabbis, arbiters of law and custom, Judaism successfully survived the loss of Hebrew autonomy. A Jewish kingdom was revived under the Hasmoneans (168-42 BC).

China. During the **Eastern Chou** dynasty (770-256 BC), Chinese culture spread east to the sea and south to the Yangtze. Large feudal states on the periphery of the empire contended for pre-eminence, but continued to recognize the Son of Heaven (king), who retained a purely ritual role enriched with courtly music and dance. In the Age of Warring States (403-221 BC), when the first sections of the **Great Wall** were built, the Ch'in state in the West gained supremacy, and finally united all of China.

Iron tools entered China c500 BC, and casting techniques were advanced, aiding agriculture. Peasants owned their land, and owed civil and military service to nobles. Cities grew in number and size, though barter remained the chief trade medium.

Intellectual ferment among noble scribes and officials produced the Classical Age of Chinese literature and philosophy. **Confucius** (551-479 BC) urged a restoration of a supposedly harmonious social order of the past through proper conduct in accordance with one's station and through filial and ceremonial piety. The *Analects*, attributed to him, are revered throughout East Asia. **Mencius** (d. 289 BC) added the view that the Mandate of Heaven can be removed from an unjust dynasty. The Legalists sought to curb the supposed natural wickedness of people through new institutions and harsh laws; they aided the Ch'in rise to power. The Naturalists emphasized the balance of opposites — yin, yang — in the world. **Taoists** sought mystical knowledge through meditation and disengagement.

India. The political and cultural center of India shifted from the Indus to the Ganges River Valley. Buddhism, Jainism, and mystical revisions of orthodox Vedism all developed around 500-300 BC. The *Upanishads*, last part of the *Veda*, urged escape from the illusory physical world. Vedism remained the preserve of the priestly Brahmin caste. In contrast, **Buddhism**, founded by Siddarta Gautama (c563-c483 BC), appealed to merchants in the growing urban centers, and took hold at first (and most lastingly) on the geographic fringes of Indian civilization. The classic Indian epics were composed in this era: The *Ramayana* perhaps around 300 BC, the *Mahabharata* over a period starting 400 BC.

Northern India was divided into a large number of monarchies and aristocratic republics, probably derived from tribal groupings, when the Magadha kingdom was formed in Bihar c542 BC. It soon became the dominant power. The **Maurya dynasty**, founded by Chandragupta c321 BC, expanded the kingdom, uniting most of N. India in a centralized bureaucratic empire. The third Mauryan king, **Asoka** (ruled c274-236) conquered most of the subcontinent: he converted to Buddhism, and inscribed its tenets on pillars throughout India. He downplayed the caste system and tried to end expensive sacrificial rites.

Before its final decline in India, Buddhism developed the popular worship of heavenly Bodhisatvas (enlightened beings), and produced a refined architecture (stupa—shrine—at Sanchi 100 AD) and sculpture (Gandhara reliefs 1-400 AD).

Persia. Aryan peoples (Persians, Medes) dominated the area of present Iran by the beginning of the first millenium BC. The prophet **Zoroaster** (born c628 BC) introduced a dualistic religion in which the forces of good (Ahura Mazda, Lord of Wisdom) and evil (Ahiram) battle for dominance; individuals are judged by their actions and earn damnation or salvation. Zoroaster's hymns (*Gathas*) are included in the *Avesta*, the Zoroastrian scriptures. A version of this faith became the established religion of the Persian Empire, and probably influenced later monotheistic religions.

Africa. Nubia, periodically occupied by Egypt since the third millenium, ruled Egypt c750-661, and survived as an independent Egyptianized kingdom (**Kush**; capital Meroe) for 1,000 years.

The Iron Age Nok culture flourished c500 BC-200 AD on the Benue Plateau of **Nigeria.**

Americas. The Chavin culture controlled north Peru from 900-200 BC. Its ceremonial centers, featuring the jaguar god, survived long after. Chavin architecture, ceramics, and textiles influenced other Peruvian cultures.

Mayan civilization began to develop in Central America in the 5th century BC.

Great Empires Unite the Civilized World: 400 BC - 400 AD

Persia and Alexander. Cyrus, ruler of a small kingdom in Persia from 559 BC, united the Persians and Medes within 10 years, conquered Asia Minor and Babylonia in another 10. His son Cambyses followed by **Darius** (ruled 522-486) added vast lands to the east and north as far as the Indus Valley and Central Asia, as well as Egypt and Thrace. The whole empire was ruled by an international bureaucracy and army, with Persians holding the chief positions. The resources and styles of all the subject civilizations were exploited to create a rich syncretic art.

The Hellenized kingdom of Macedon, which under Phillip II dominated Greece, passed to his son **Alexander** in 336 BC. Within 13 years, Alexander conquered all the Persian dominions. Imbued by his tutor Aristotle with Greek ideals, Alexander encouraged Greek colonization, and Greek-style cities were founded throughout the empire (e.g. Alexandria, Egypt). After his death in 323 BC, wars of succession divided the empire into three parts — **Macedon,** Egypt (ruled by the **Ptolemies**), and the **Seleucid** Empire.

In the ensuing 300 years (the **Hellenistic Era**), a cosmopolitan Greek-oriented culture permeated the ancient world from W. Europe to the borders of India, absorbing native elites everywhere.

Hellenistic philosophy stressed the private individual's search for happiness. The Cynics followed Diogenes (c372-287), who stressed satisfaction of animal needs and contempt for social convention. Zeno (c335-c263) and the Stoics exalted reason, identified it with virtue, and counseled an ascetic disregard for misfortune. The Epicureans tried to build lives of moderate pleasure without political or emotional

(*continued on p. 494*)

The Seven Wonders of the World

These ancient works of art and architecture were considered awe-inspiring in splendor and/or size by the Greek and Roman world of the Alexandrian epoch and later. Classical writers disagreed as to which works made up the list of Wonders, but the following were usually included:

The Pyramids of Egypt: The only surviving Wonder, these monumental structures of masonry located on the west bank of the Nile River above Cairo were built from 3000 to 1800 B.C. as royal tombs. Three—Khufu, Khafra, and Menkaura—were often grouped as the first Wonder of the World. The largest, **The Great Pyramid of Khufu,** or Cheops, is a solid mass of limestone blocks covering 13 acres. It is estimated to contain 2.3 million blocks of stone, the stones themselves averaging 2½ tons and some weighing 30 tons. Its construction reputedly took 100,000 laborers 20 years.

The Hanging Gardens of Babylon: These gardens were laid out on a brick terrace about 400 feet square and 75 feet above the ground. To irrigate the trees, shrubs, and flowers, screws were turned to lift water from the Euphrates River. The gardens were probably built by King Nebuchandnezzar II around 600 B.C. **The Walls of Babylon,** long, thick, and made of colorfully glazed brick, were considered by some to be among the Seven Wonders.

The Statue of Zeus (Jupiter) at Olympia: This statue of the king of the gods showed him seated on a throne. His flesh was made of ivory, his robe and ornaments of gold. Reputedly 40 feet high, the statue was made by Phidias and was placed in the great temple of Zeus in the sacred grove of Olympia around 457 B.C.

The Colossus of Rhodes: A bronze statue of the sun god Helios, the Colossus was worked on for 12 years in the early 200's B.C. by the sculptor Chares. It was probably 120 feet high. A symbol of the city of Rhodes at its height, the statue stood on a promontory overlooking the harbor.

The Temple of Artemis (Diana) at Ephesus: This largest and most complex temple of ancient times was built around 550 B.C. and was made of marble except for its tile-covered wooden roof. It was begun in honor of a non-Hellenic goddess who later became identified with the Greek goddess of the same name. Ephesus was one of the greatest of the Ionian cities.

The Mausoleum at Halicarnassus: The source of our word "mausoleum," this marble tomb was built in what is now southeastern Turkey by Artemisia for her husband Mausolus, an official of the Persian Empire who died in 353 B.C. About 135 feet high, it was adorned with the works of 4 sculptors.

The Pharos (Lighthouse) of Alexandria: This sculpture was designed around 270 B.C., during the reign of King Ptolemy II, by the Greek architect Sostratos. Estimates of its height range from 200 to 600 feet.

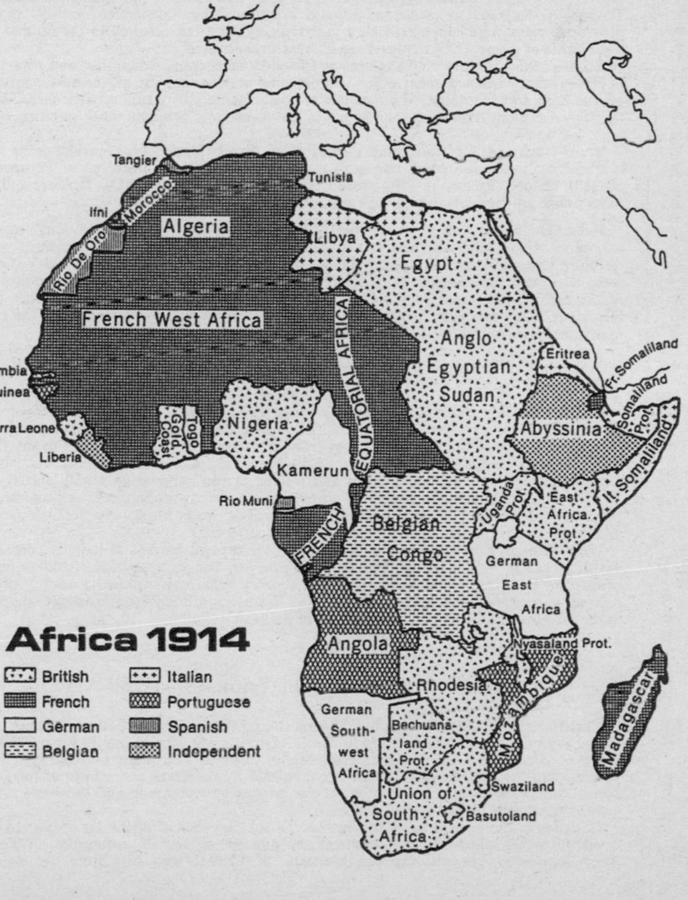

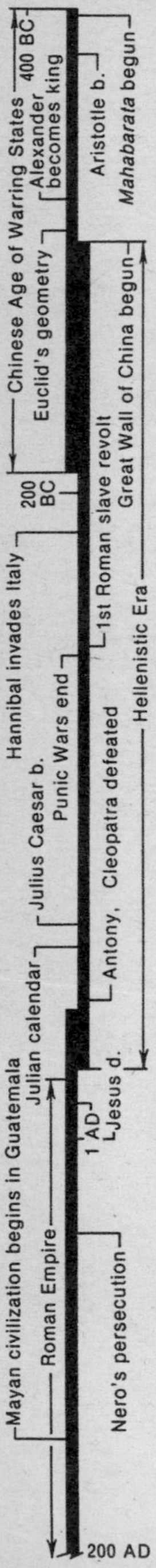

involvement. Hellenistic arts imitated life realistically, especially in sculpture and literature (comedies of Menander, 342-292).

The sciences thrived, especially at Alexandria, where the Ptolemies financed a great library and museum. Fields of study included mathematics (**Euclid's** geometry, c300 BC; Menelaus' non-Euclidean geometry, c100 AD); astronomy (heliocentric theory of Aristarchus, 310-230 BC; Julian calendar 45 BC; Ptolemy's *Almagest*, c150 AD); geography (world map of Eratosthenes, 276-194 BC); hydraulics (**Archimedes,** 287-212 BC); medicine (Galen, 130-200 AD), and chemistry. Inventors refined uses for siphons, valves, gears, springs, screws, levers, cams, and pulleys.

A restored Persian empire under the **Parthians** (N. Iranian tribesmen) controlled the eastern Hellenistic world 250 BC-229 AD. The Parthians and the succeeding Sassanian dynasty (229-651) fought with Rome periodically. The **Sassanians** revived Zoroastrianism as a state religion, and patronized a nationalistic artistic and scholarly renaissance.

Rome. The city of Rome was founded, according to legend, by Romulus in 753 BC. Through military expansion and colonization, and by granting citizenship to conquered tribes, the city annexed all of Italy south of the Po in the 100-year period before 268 BC. The Latin and other Italic tribes were annexed first, followed by the Etruscans (a civilized people north of Rome) and the Greek colonies in the south. With a large standing army and reserve forces of several hundred thousand, Rome was able to defeat Carthage in the 3 **Punic Wars,** 264-241, 218-201, 149-146 (despite the invasion of Italy by Hannibal, 218), thus gaining Sicily and territory in Spain and North Africa.

New provinces were added in the East, as Rome exploited local disputes to conquer Greece and Asia Minor in the 2d century BC, and Egypt in the first (after the defeat and suicide of **Antony and Cleopatra,** 30 BC). All the Mediterranean civilized world up to the disputed Parthian border was now Roman, and remained so for 500 years. Less civilized regions were added to the Empire: Gaul (conquered by Julius Caesar, 56-49 BC), Britain (43 AD) and Dacia NE of the Danube (117 AD).

The original aristocratic republican government, with democratic features added in the fifth and fourth centuries BC, deteriorated under the pressures of empire and class conflict (**Gracchus** brothers, social reformers, murdered 133, 121; slave revolts 135, 73). After a series of civil wars (Marius vs. Sulla 88-82, Caesar vs. Pompey 49-45, triumvirate vs. Caesar's assassins 44-43, Antony vs. Octavian 32-30), the empire came under the rule of a deified monarch (first emperor, **Augustus,** 27 BC-14 AD). Provincials (nearly all granted citizenship by Caracalla, 212 AD) came to dominate the army and civil service. Traditional Roman law, systematized and interpreted by independent jurists, and local self-rule in provincial cities were supplanted by a vast tax-collecting bureaucracy in the 3d and 4th centuries. The legal rights of women, children, and slaves were strengthened.

Roman innovations in **civil engineering** included water mills, windmills, and rotary mills, and the use of cement that hardened under water. Monumental architecture (baths, theaters, apartment houses) relied on the arch and the dome. The network of roads (some still standing) stretched 53,000 miles, passing through mountain tunnels as long as 3.5 miles. Aqueducts brought water to cities, underground sewers removed waste.

Roman art and literature were derivative of Greek models. Innovations were made in sculpture (naturalistic busts and equestrian statues), decorative wall painting (as at Pompeii), satire (Juvenal, 60-127), history (Tacitus 56-120), prose romance (Petronius, d. 66 AD). Violence and torture dominated mass public amusements, which were supported by the state.

India. The **Gupta** monarchs reunited N. India c320 AD. Their peaceful and prosperous reign saw a revival of Hindu religious thought and Brahmin power. The old Vedic traditions were combined with devotion to a plethora of indigenous deities (who were seen as manifestations of Vedic gods). **Caste lines** were reinforced, and Buddhism gradually disappeared. The art (often erotic), architecture, and literature of the period, patronized by the Gupta court, are considered to be among India's finest achievements (Kalidasa, poet and dramatist, fl. c400). Mathematical innovations included the use of zero and decimal numbers. Invasions by White Huns from the NW destroyed the empire c550.

Rich cultures also developed in S. India in this era. Emotional Tamil religious poetry aided the Hindu revival. The Pallava kingdom controlled much of S. India c350-880, and helped spread Indian civilization to S.E. Asia.

China. The Ch'in ruler Shih Huang Ti (ruled 221-210 BC), known as the First Emperor, centralized political authority in China, standardized the written language, laws, weights, measures, and coinage, and conducted a census, but tried to destroy most philosophical texts. The **Han dynasty** (206 BC-220 AD) instituted the Mandarin bureaucracy, which lasted for 2,000 years. Local officials were selected by examination in the Confucian classics and trained at the imperial university and at provincial schools. The invention of **paper** facilitated this bureaucratic system. Agriculture was promoted, but the peasants bore most of the tax burden. Irrigation was improved; water clocks and sundials were used; astronomy and mathematics thrived; landscape painting was perfected.

With the expansion south and west (to nearly the present borders of today's China), trade was opened with India, S.E. Asia, and the Middle East, over sea and caravan routes. Indian missionaries brought Mahayana Buddhism to China by the first century AD, and spawned a variety of sects. Taoism was revived, and merged with popular superstitions. Taoist and Buddhist monasteries and convents multiplied in the turbulent centuries after the collapse of the Han dynasty.

The One God Triumphs: 1-750 AD

Christianity. Religions indigenous to particular Middle Eastern nations became international in the first 3 centuries of the Roman Empire. Roman citizens worshipped **Isis** of Egypt, **Mithras** of Persia, **Demeter** of Greece, and the great mother **Cybele** of Phrygia. Their cults centered on mysteries (secret ceremonies) and the promise of an afterlife, symbolized by the death and rebirth of the god. Judaism, which had begun as the national cult of Judea, also spread by emigration and conversion. It was the only ancient religion west of India to survive.

Christians, who emerged as a distinct sect in the second half of the 1st century AD, revered **Jesus,** a Jewish preacher killed by the Romans at the request of Jewish authorities in Jerusalem c30 AD. They considered him the Savior (Messiah, or Christ) who rose from the dead and could grant eternal life to the faithful, despite their sinfulness. They believed he was an incarnation of the one god worshipped by the Jews, and that he would return soon to pass final judgment on the world. The missionary activities of such early leaders as **Paul of Tarsus** spread the faith, at first mostly among Jews or among quasi-Jews attracted by the Pauline rejection of such difficult Jewish laws as circumcision. Intermittent persecution, as in Rome under Nero in 64 AD, on grounds of suspected disloyalty, failed to disrupt the Christian communities. Each congregation, generally urban and of plebeian character, was tightly organized under a leader (bishop) elders (presbyters or priests), and assistants (deacons). Stories about Jesus (the Gospels) and the early church (Acts) were written down in the late first and early 2d centuries, and circulated along with letters of Paul. An authoritative canon of these writings was not fixed until the 4th century.

A school for priests was established at Alexandria in the second century. Its teachers (**Origen** c182-251) helped define Christian doctrine and promote the faith in Greek-style philosophical works. Pagan Neoplatonism was given Christian coloration in the works of Church Fathers such as Augustine (354-430). Christian hermits, often drawn from the lower classes, began to associate in monasteries, first in Egypt (St. Pachomius c290-345), then in other eastern lands, then in the West (**St. Benedict's rule,** 529). Popular devotion to saints, especially Mary, mother of Jesus, spread.

Under **Constantine** (ruled 306-337), Christianity became in effect the established religion of the Empire. Pagan temples were expropriated, state funds were used to build huge churches and support the hierarchy, and laws were adjusted in accordance with Christian notions. Pagan worship was banned by the end of the fourth century, and severe restrictions were placed on Judaism.

The newly established church was rocked by doctrinal disputes, often exacerbated by regional rivalries both within and outside the Empire. Chief heresies (as defined by church councils backed by imperial authority) were **Arianism,** which denied the divinity of Jesus; **Donatism,** which rejected the convergence of church and state and denied the validity of sacraments performed by sinful clergy; and the **Monophysite** position denying the dual nature of Christ.

Judaism. First century Judaism embraced several sects, including: the **Sadducees,** mostly drawn from the Temple priesthood, who were culturally Hellenized; the **Pharisees,** who upheld the full range of traditional customs and practices as of equal weight to literal scriptural law, and elaborated synagogue worship; and the **Essenes,** an ascetic, millenarian sect. Messianic fervor led to repeated, unsuccessful rebellions against Rome (66-70, 135). As a result, the Temple was destroyed, and the population decimated.

To avoid the dissolution of the faith, a program of codification of law was begun at the academy of Yavneh. The work continued for some 500 years in Palestine and Babylonia, ending in the final redaction of the **Talmud** (c600), a huge collection of legal and moral debates, rulings, liturgy, Biblical exegesis, and legendary materials.

Islam. The earliest Arab civilization emerged by the end of the 2d millenium BC in the watered highlands of Yemen. Seaborne and caravan trade in frankincense and myrrh connected the area with the Nile and Fertile Crescent. The Minaean, Sabean (Sheba), and Himyarite states successively held sway. By Mohammed's time (7th century AD), the region was a province of Sassanian Persia. In the North, the **Nabataean kingdom** at Petra and the kingdom of Palmyra were first Aramaicized and then Romanized, and finally absorbed like neighboring Judea into the Roman Empire. Nomads shared the central region with a few trading towns and oases. Wars between tribes and raids on settled communities were common, and were celebrated in a poetic tradition that by the 6th century helped establish a classic literary Arabic.

In 611 **Mohammed,** an 40-year-old Arab of Mecca, announced a revelation from the one true God, calling on him to repudiate pagan idolatry. Drawing on elements of Judaism and Christianity, and eventually incorporating some Arab pagan traditions (such as reverence for the black stone at the kaaba shrine in Mecca), Mohammed's teachings, recorded in the **Koran,** forged a new religion, Islam (submission to Allah). Opposed by the leaders of Mecca, Mohammed made a *hejira* (migration) to Medina to the north in 622, the beginning of the Moslem lunar calendar. He and his followers defeated the Meccans in 624 in the first *jihad* (holy war), and by his death (632), nearly all the Arabian peninsula accepted his religious and secular leadership.

Under the first two **caliphs** (successors) Abu Bakr (632-34) and Omar (634-44), Moslem rule was confirmed over Arabia. Raiding parties into Byzantine and Persian border areas developed into campaigns of conquest against the two empires, which had been weakened by wars and by disaffection among subject peoples (including Coptic and Syriac Christians opposed to the Byzantine orthodox church). Syria, Palestine, Egypt, Iraq, and Persia all fell to the inspired Arab armies. The Arabs at first remained a distinct minority, using non-Moslems in the new administrative system, and tolerating Christians, Jews, and Zoroastrians as self-governing "Peoples of the Book," whose taxes supported the empire.

Disputes over the succession, and puritan reaction to the wealth and refinement that empire brought to the ruling strata, led to the growth of schismatic movements. The followers of Mohammed's son-in-law Ali (assassinated 661) and his descendants became the founders of the more mystical **Shi'ite** sect, still the largest non-orthodox Moslem sect. The Karijites, puritanical, militant, and egalitarian, persist as a minor sect to the present.

Under the **Omayyad** caliphs (661-750), the boundaries of Islam were extended across N. Africa and into Spain. Arab armies in the West were stopped at Tours in 732 by the Frank **Charles Martel.** Asia Minor, the Indus Valley, and Transoxiana were conquered in the East. The vast majority of the subject population gradually converted to Islam, encouraged by tax and career privileges. The Arab language supplanted the local tongues in the central and western areas, but Arab soldiers and rulers in the East eventually became assimilated to the indigenous languages.

New Peoples Enter History: 400-900

Barbarian invasions. Germanic tribes infiltrated S and E from their Baltic homeland during the 1st millenium BC, reaching S. Germany by 100 BC and the Black Sea by 214 AD. Organized into large federated tribes under elected kings, most resisted Roman domination and raided the empire in time of civil war (Goths took Dacia 214, raided Thrace 251-269). German troops and commanders came to dominate the Roman armies by the end of the 4th century. **Huns,** invaders from Asia, entered Europe 372, driving more Germans into the western empire. Emperor Valens allowed Visigoths to cross

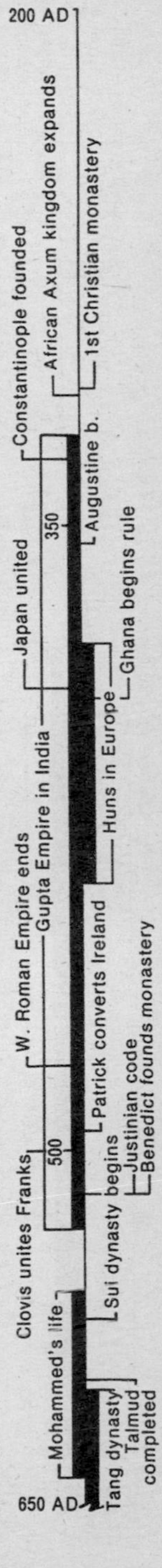

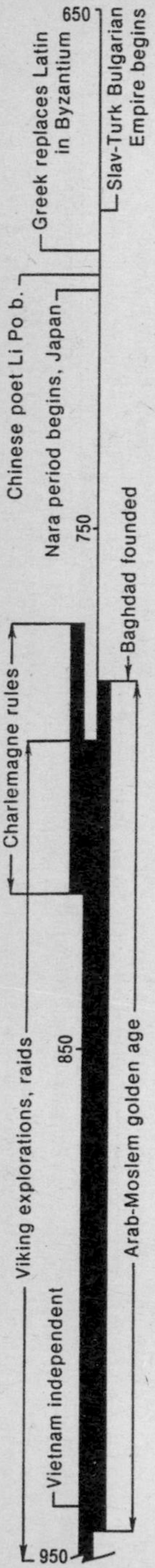

the Danube 376. Huns under Attila (d. 453) raided Gaul, Italy, Balkans. The western empire, weakened by overtaxation and social stagnation, was overrun in the 5th century. Gaul was effectively lost 406-7, Spain 409, Britain 410, Africa 429-39. Rome was sacked 410 by Visigoths under Alaric, 455 by Vandals. The last western emperor, Romulus Augustulus, was deposed 476 by the Germanic chief Odoacer.

Celts. Celtic cultures, which in pre-Roman times covered most of W. Europe, were confined almost entirely to the British Isles after the Germanic invasions. **St. Patrick** completed the conversion of Ireland (c457-92). A strong monastic tradition took hold. Irish monastic missionaries in Scotland, England, and the continent (Columba c521-597; Columban c543-615) helped restore Christianity after the Germanic invasions. The monasteries became renowned centers of classic and Christian learning, and presided over the recording of a Christianized Celtic mythology, elaborated by secular writers and bards. An intricate decorative art style developed, especially in book illumination (Lindisfarne Gospels, c700, Book of Kells, 8th century).

Successor states. The Visigoth kingdom in Spain (from 419) and much of France (to 507) saw a continuation of much Roman administration, language, and law (Breviary of Alaric 506), until its destruction by the Moslems, 711. The Vandal kingdom in Africa, from 429, was conquered by the Byzantines, 533. Italy was ruled in succession by an Ostrogothic kingdom under Byzantine suzerainty 489-554, direct Byzantine government, and the German Lombards (568-774). The latter divided the peninsula with the Byzantines and the papacy under the dynamic reformer Pope Gregory the Great (590-604) and his successors.

King Clovis (ruled 481-511) united the Franks on both sides of the Rhine, and after his conversion to orthodox Christianity, defeated the Arian Burgundians (after 500) and Visigoths (507) with the support of the native clergy and the papacy. Under the **Merovingian** kings a feudal system emerged: power was fragmented among hierarchies of military landowners. Social stratification, which in late Roman times had acquired legal, hereditary sanction, was reinforced. The Carolingians (747-987) expanded the kingdom and restored central power. **Charlemagne** (ruled 768-814) conquered nearly all the Germanic lands, including Lombard Italy, and was crowned Emperor by Pope Leo III in Rome in 800. A centuries-long decline in commerce and the arts was reversed under Charlemagne's patronage. He welcomed Jews to his kingdom, which became a center of Jewish learning (Rashi 1040-1105). He sponsored the "Carolingian Renaissance" of learning under the Anglo-Latin scholar Alcuin (c732-804), who reformed church liturgy.

Byzantine Empire. Under Diocletian (ruled 284-305) the empire had been divided into 2 parts to facilitate administration and defense. Constantine founded **Constantinople,** 330, (at old Byzantium) as a fully Christian city. Commerce and taxation financed a sumptuous, orientalized court, a class of hereditary bureaucratic families, and magnificent urban construction (Hagia Sophia, 532-37). The city's fortifications and naval innovations (Greek fire) repelled assaults by Goths, Huns, Slavs, Bulgars, Avars, Arabs, and Scandinavians. Greek replaced Latin as the official language by c700. Byzantine art, a solemn, sacral, and stylized variation of late classical styles (mosaics at S. Vitale, Ravenna, 526-48) was a starting point for medieval art in E. and W. Europe.

Justinian (ruled 527-65) reconquered parts of Spain, N. Africa, and Italy, codified Roman law (*codex Justinianus,* 529, was medieval Europe's chief legal text), closed the Platonic Academy at Athens and ordered all pagans to convert. Lombards in Italy, Arabs in Africa retook most of his conquests. The Isaurian dynasty from Anatolia (from 717) and the Macedonian dynasty (867-1054) restored military and commercial power. The Iconoclast controversy (726-843) over the permissibility of images, helped alienate the Eastern Church from the papacy.

Arab Empire. Baghdad, founded 762, became the seat of the **Abbasid** Caliphate (founded 750), while Ummayads continued to rule in Spain. A brilliant cosmopolitan civilization emerged, inaugurating an Arab-Moslem golden age. Arab lyric poetry revived; Greek, Syriac, Persian, and Sanskrit books were translated into Arabic, often by Syriac Christians and Jews, whose theology and Talmudic law, respectively, influenced Islam. The arts and music flourished at the court of **Harun al-Rashid** (786-809), celebrated in *The Arabian Nights.* The sciences, medicine, and mathematics were pursued at Baghdad, Cordova, and Cairo (founded 969). Science and Aristotelian philosophy culminated in the systems of Avicenna (980-1037), Averroes (1126-98), and Maimonides (1135-1204), a Jew; all influenced later Christian scholarship and theology. The Islamic ban on images encouraged a sinuous, geometric decorative tradition, applied to architecture and illumination. A gradual loss of Arab control in Persia (from 874) led to the capture of Baghdad by Persians, 945. By the next century, Spain and N. Africa were ruled by Berbers, while Turks prevailed in Asia Minor and the Levant. The loss of political power by the caliphs allowed for the growth of non-orthodox trends, especially the mystical **Sufi** tradition (theologian Ghazali, 1058-1111).

Africa. Immigrants from Saba in S. Arabia helped set up the **Axum** kingdom in Ethiopia in the 2d century (their language, Ge'ez, is preserved by the Ethiopian Church). In the 4th century, when the kingdom became Christianized, it defeated Kushite Meroe and expanded into Yemen. Axum was the center of a vast ivory trade; it controlled the Red Sea coast until c1100. Arab conquest in Egypt cut Axum's political and economic ties with Byzantium.

The Iron Age entered W. Africa by the end of the 1st millenium BC. **Ghana,** the first known sub-Saharan state, ruled in the upper Senegal-Niger region c400-1240, controlling the trade of gold from mines in the S to trans-Sahara caravan routes to the N. The **Bantu** peoples, probably of W. African origin, began to spread E and S perhaps 2000 years ago, displacing the Pygmies and Bushmen of central and southern Africa over a 1,500-year period.

Japan. The advanced Neolithic Yayoi period, when irrigation, rice farming, and iron and bronze casting techniques were introduced from China or Korea, persisted to c400 AD. The myriad Japanese states were then united by the **Yamato** clan, under an emperor who acted as the chief priest of the animistic **Shinto** cult. Japanese political and military intervention in Korea by the 6th century quickened a Chinese cultural invasion, bringing Buddhism, the Chinese language (which long remained a literary and governmental medium), Chinese ideographs and Buddhist styles in painting, sculpture, literature, and architecture (7th c. Horyu-ji temple at Nara). The Taika Reforms, 646, tried to centralize Japan according to Chinese bureaucratic and Buddhist philosophical values, but failed to curb traditional Japanese decentralization. A nativist reaction against the Buddhist **Nara period** (710-94) ushered in the

Heian period (794-1185) centered at the new capital, Kyoto. Japanese elegance and simplicity modified Chinese styles in architecture, scroll painting, and literature; the writing system was also simplified. The courtly novel *Tale of Genji* (1010-20) testifies to the enhanced role of women.

Southeast Asia. The historic peoples of southeast Asia began arriving some 2500 years ago from China and Tibet, displacing scattered aborigines. Their agriculture relied on rice and tubers (yams), which they may have introduced to Africa. Indian cultural influences were strongest; literacy and Hindu and Buddhist ideas followed the southern India-China trade route. From the southern tip of Indochina, the kingdom of **Funan** (1st-7th centuries) traded as far west as Persia. It was absorbed by Chenla, itself conquered by the **Khmer Empire** (600-1300). The Khmers, under Hindu god-kings (Suryavarman II, 1113-c1150), built the monumental Angkor Wat temple center for the royal phallic cult. The **Nam-Viet** kingdom in Annam, dominated by China and Chinese culture for 1,000 years, emerged in the 10th century, growing at the expense of the Khmers, who also lost ground in the NW to the new, highly-organized **Thai** kingdom. On Sumatra, the **Srivijaya** Empire at Palembang controlled vital sea lanes (7th to 10th centuries). A Buddhist dynasty, the Sailendras, ruled central **Java** (8th-9th centuries), building at Borobudur one of the largest stupas in the world.

China. The short-lived Sui dynasty (581-618) ushered in a period of commercial, artistic, and scientific achievement in China, continuing under the **T'ang** dynasty (618-906). Such inventions as the magnetic compass, gunpowder, the abacus, and printing were introduced or perfected. Medical innovations included cataract surgery. The state, from the cosmopolitan capital, Ch'ang-an, supervised foreign trade which exchanged Chinese silks, porcelains, and art works for spices, ivory, etc., over Central Asian caravan routes and sea routes reaching Africa. A golden age of poetry bequeathed tens of thousands of works to later generations (Tu Fu 712-70, Li Po 701-62). Landscape painting flourished. Commercial and industrial expansion continued under the **Northern Sung** dynasty (960-1126), facilitated by paper money and credit notes. But commerce never achieved respectability; government monopolies expropriated successful merchants. The population, long stable at 50 million, doubled in 200 years with the introduction of early-ripening rice and the double harvest. In art, native Chinese styles were revived.

Americas. An Indian empire stretched from the Valley of Mexico to Guatemala, 300-600, centering on the huge city **Teotihuacan** (founded 100 BC). To the S, in Guatemala, a high **Mayan** civilization developed, 150-900, around hundreds of rural ceremonial centers. The Mayans improved on Olmec writing and the calendar, and pursued astronomy and mathematics (using the idea of zero). In S. America, a widespread pre-Inca culture grew from **Tiahuanaco** near Lake Titicaca (Gateway of the Sun, c700).

Christian Europe Regroups and Expands: 900-1300

Scandinavians. Pagan Danish and Norse (**Viking**) adventurers, traders, and pirates raided the coasts of the British Isles (**Dublin** founded c831), France, and even the Mediterranean for over 200 years beginning in the late 8th century. Inland settlement in the W was limited to Great Britain (King Canute, 994-1035) and Normandy, settled under Rollo, 911, as a fief of France. Other Vikings reached Iceland (874), Greenland (c986), and probably N. America (Leif Eriksson c1000). Norse traders (**Varangians**) developed Russian river commerce from the 8th-11th centuries, and helped set up a state at Kiev in the late 9th century. Conversion to Christianity occurred during the 10th century, reaching Sweden 100 years later. Eleventh century Norman bands conquered S. Italy and Sicily. Duke **William of Normandy** conquered England, 1066, bringing continental feudalism and the French language, essential elements in later English civilization.

East Europe. Slavs inhabited areas of E. Central Europe in prehistoric times, and reached most of their present limits by c850. The first Slavic states were in the Balkans (Slav-Turk **Bulgarian Empire**, 680-1018) and Moravia (628). Missions of St. Cyril (whose Greek-based Cyrillic alphabet is still used by S. and E. Slavs) converted Moravia, 863. The Eastern Slavs, part-civilized under the overlordship of the Turkish-Jewish **Khazar** trading empire (7th-10th centuries), gravitated toward Constantinople by the 9th century. The **Kievan state** adopted Eastern Christianity under Prince Vladimir, 989. King Boleslav I (992-1025) began **Poland's** long history of eastern conquest. The Magyars (**Hungarians**) in present-day Hungary since 896, accepted Latin Christianity, 1001.

Germany. The German kingdom that emerged after the breakup of Charlemagne's Empire remained a confederation of largely autonomous states. The Saxon Otto I, king from 936, established the **Holy Roman Empire** of Germany and Italy in alliance with Pope John XII, who crowned him emperor, 962; he defeated the Magyars, 955. Imperial power was greatest under the **Hohenstaufens** (1138-1254), despite the growing opposition of the papacy, which ruled central Italy, and the Lombard League cities. Frederick II (1194-1250) improved administration, patronized the arts; after his death German influence was removed from Italy.

Christian Spain. From its northern mountain redoubts, Christian rule slowly migrated south through the 11th century, when Moslem unity collapsed. After the capture of **Toledo** (1085), the kingdoms of Portugal, Castile, and Aragon undertook repeated crusades of reconquest, finally completed in 1492. Elements of Islamic civilization persisted in recaptured areas, influencing all W. Europe.

Crusades. Pope Urban II called, 1095, for a crusade to restore Asia Minor to Byzantium and conquer the Holy Land from the Turks. Some 10 crusades (to 1291) succeeded only in founding 4 temporary Frankish states in the Levant. The 4th crusade sacked Constantinople, 1204. In Rhineland (1096), England (1290), France (1306), Jews were massacred or expelled, and wars were launched against Christian heretics (**Albigensian** crusade in France, 1229). Trade in eastern luxuries expanded, led by the Venetian naval empire.

Economy. The agricultural base of European life benefitted from improvements in **plow design** c1000, and by draining of lowlands and clearing of forests, leading to a rural population increase. Towns grew in N. Italy, Flanders, and N. Germany (Hanseatic League). Improvements in **loom design** permitted factory textile production. **Guilds** dominated urban trades from the 12th century. Banking (centered in Italy, 12th-15th century) facilitated long-distance trade.

The Church. The split between the Eastern and Western churches was formalized in 1054. W. and

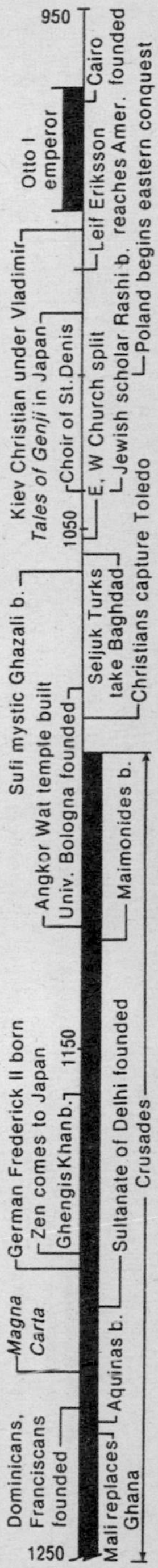

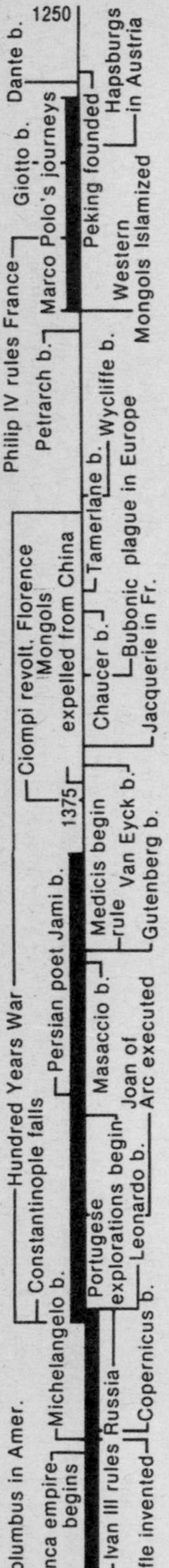

Central Europe was divided into 500 bishoprics under one united hierarchy, but conflicts between secular and church authorities were frequent (German **Investiture Controversy,** 1075-1122). Clerical power was first strengthened through the international monastic reform begun at Cluny, 910. Popular religious enthusiasm often expressed itself in heretical movements (Waldensians from 1173), but was channelled by the **Dominican** (1215) and **Franciscan** (1223) friars into the religious mainstream.

Arts. Romanesque architecture (11th-12th centuries) expanded on late Roman models, using the rounded arch and massed stone to support enlarged basilicas. Painting and sculpture followed Byzantine models. The literature of **chivalry** was exemplified by the epic (Chanson de Roland, c1100) and by courtly love poems of the troubadours of Provence and minnesingers of Germany. **Gothic architecture** emerged in France (choir of St. Denis, c1040) and spread as French cultural influence predominated in Europe. Rib vaulting and pointed arches were used to combine soaring heights with delicacy, and freed walls for display of stained glass. Exteriors were covered with painted relief sculpture and elaborate architectural detail.

Learning. Law, medicine, and philosophy were advanced at independent **universities** (Bologna, late 11th century), originally corporations of students and masters. Twelfth century translations of Greek classics, especially Aristotle, encouraged an analytic approach. Scholastic philosophy, from Anselm (1033-1109) to Aquinas (1225-74) attempted to reconcile reason and revelation.

Apogee of Central Asian Power; Islam Grows: 1250-1500

Turks. Turkic peoples, of Central Asian ancestry, were a military threat to the Byzantine and Persian Empires from the 6th century. After several waves of invasions, during which most of the Turks adopted Islam, the **Seljuk Turks** took Baghdad, 1055. They ruled Persia, Iraq, and, after 1071, Asia Minor, where massive numbers of Turks settled. The empire was divided in the 12th century into smaller states ruled by Seljuks, Kurds (**Saladin** c1137-93), and Mamelukes (a military caste of former Turk, Kurd, and Circassian slaves), which governed Egypt and the Middle East until the Ottoman era (c1290-1922).

Osman I (ruled c1290-1326) and succeeding sultans united Anatolian Turkish warriors in a militaristic state that waged holy war against Byzantium and Balkan Christians. Most of the Balkans had been subdued, and Anatolia united, when **Constantinople fell,** 1453. By the mid-16th century, Hungary, the Middle East, and North Africa had been conquered. The Turkish advance was stopped at Vienna, 1529, and at the naval battle of Lepanto, 1571, by Spain, Venice, and the papacy.

The Ottoman state was governed in accordance with orthodox Moslem law. Greek, Armenian, and Jewish communities were segregated, and ruled by religious leaders responsible for taxation; they dominated trade. State offices and most army ranks were filled by slaves through a system of child conscription among Christians.

India. Mahmud of Ghazni (971-1030) led repeated Turkish raids into N. India. Turkish power was consolidated in 1206 with the start of the **Sultanate at Delhi.** Centralization of state power under the early Delhi sultans went far beyond traditional Indian practice. Moslem rule of most of the subcontinent lasted until the British conquest some 600 years later.

Mongols. Genghis Khan (c1162-1227) first united the feuding Mongol tribes, and built their armies into an effective offensive force around a core of highly mobile cavalry. He and his immediate successors created the largest land empire in history; by 1279 it stretched from the east coast of Asia to the Danube, from the Siberian steppes to the Arabian Sea. East-West trade and contacts were facilitated (Marco Polo c1254-1324). The western Mongols were Islamized by 1295; successor states soon lost their Mongol character by assimilation. They were briefly reunited under the Turk Tamerlane (1336-1405).

Kublai Khan ruled China from his new capital Peking (founded 1264). Naval campaigns against Japan (1274, 1281) and Java (1293) were defeated, the latter by the Hindu-Buddhist maritime kingdom of Majapahit. The **Yuan** dynasty made use of Mongols and other foreigners (including Europeans) in official posts, and tolerated the return of Nestorian Christianity (suppressed 841-45) and the spread of Islam in the South and West. A native reaction expelled the Mongols, 1367-68.

Russia. The Kievan state in Russia, weakened by the decline of Byzantium and the rise of the Catholic Polish-Lithuanian state, was overrun by the Mongols, 1238-40. Only the northern trading republic of Novgorod remained independent. The grand dukes of Moscow emerged as leaders of a coalition of princes that eventually defeated the Mongols, by 1481. With the fall of Constantinople, the **Tsars** (Caesars) at Moscow (from Ivan III, ruled 1462-1505) set up an independent Russian Orthodox Church. Commerce failed to revive. The isolated Russian state remained agrarian, with the peasant class falling into serfdom.

Persia. A revival of Persian literature, using the Arab alphabet and literary forms, began in the 10th century (epic of Firdausi, 935-1020). An art revival, influenced by Chinese styles, began in the 12th. Persian cultural and political forms, and often the Persian language, were used for centuries by Turkish and Mongol elites from the Balkans to India. Persian mystics from Rumi (1207-73) to Jami (1414-92) promoted **Sufism** in their poetry.

Africa. Two Berber dynasties, imbued with Islamic militance, emerged from the Sahara to carve out empires from the Sahel to central Spain — the **Almoravids,** c1050-1140, and the fanatical **Almohads,** c1125-1269. The Ghanaian empire was replaced in the upper Niger by Mali, c1230-c1340, whose Moslem rulers imported Egyptians to help make **Timbuktu** a center of commerce (in gold, leather, slaves) and learning. The Songhay empire (to 1590) replaced Mali. To the S, forest kingdoms produced refined art works (Ife terra cotta, **Benin** bronzes). Other Moslem states in Nigeria (Hausas) and Chad originated in the 11th century, and continued in some form until the 19th century European conquest. Less developed Bantu kingdoms existed across central Africa.

Some 40 Moslem Arab-Persian trading colonies and city-states were established all along the E. African coast from the 10th century (Kilwa, Mogadishu). The interchange with Bantu peoples produced the **Swahili** language and culture. Gold, palm oil, and slaves were brought from the interior, stimulating the growth of the Monamatapa kingdom of the Zambezi (15th century). The Christian Ethiopian empire (from 13th century) continued the traditions of Axum.

Southeast Asia. Islam was introduced into Malaya and the Indonesian islands by Arab, Persian, and

Indian traders. Coastal Moslem cities and states (starting before 1300), enriched by trade, soon dominated the interior. Chief among these was the **Malacca** state, on the Malay peninsula, c1400-1511.

Arts and Statecraft Thrive in Europe: 1350-1600

Italian Renaissance & humanism. Distinctive Italian achievements in the arts in the late Middle Ages (Dante, 1265-1321, Giotto, 1276-1337) led to the vigorous new styles of the Renaissance (14th-16th centuries). Patronized by the rulers of the quarreling petty states of Italy (Medicis in Florence and the papacy, c1400-1737), the plastic arts perfected realistic techniques, including **perspective** (Masaccio, 1401-28, Leonardo 1452-1519). Classical motifs were used in architecture and increased talent and expense were put into secular buildings. The Florentine dialect was refined as a national literary language (Petrarch, 1304-74). Greek refugees from the E strengthened the respect of humanist scholars for the classic sources (Bruni 1370-1444). Soon an international movement aided by the spread of **printing** (Gutenberg c1400-1468), **humanism** was optimistic about the power of human reason (Erasmus of Rotterdam, 1466-1536, Thomas More's *Utopia*, 1516) and valued individual effort in the arts and in politics (Machiavelli, 1469-1527).

France. The French monarchy, strengthened in its repeated struggles with powerful nobles (Burgundy, Flanders, Aquitaine) by alliances with the growing commercial towns, consolidated bureaucratic control under Philip IV (ruled 1285-1314) and extended French influence into Germany and Italy (popes at Avignon, France, 1309-1417). The **Hundred Years War,** 1337-1453, ended English dynastic claims in France (battles of Crécy, 1346, Poitiers, 1356; Joan of Arc executed, 1431). A French Renaissance, dating from royal invasions of Italy, 1494, 1499, was encouraged at the court of Francis I (ruled 1515-47), who centralized taxation and law. French vernacular literature consciously asserted its independence (La Pleiade, 1549).

England. The evolution of England's unique political institutions began with the Magna Carta, 1215, by which King John guaranteed the privileges of nobles and church against the monarchy and assured jury trial. After the Wars of the Roses (1455-85), the **Tudor dynasty** reasserted royal prerogatives (Henry VIII, ruled 1509-47), but the trend toward independent departments and ministerial government also continued. English trade (wool exports from c1340) was protected by the nation's growing maritime power (**Spanish Armada** destroyed, 1588).

English replaced French and Latin in the late 14th century in law and literature (Chaucer, 1340-1400) and English translation of the Bible began (Wycliffe, 1380s). Elizabeth I (ruled 1558-1603) presided over a confident flowering of poetry (Spenser, 1552-99), drama (**Shakespeare,** 1564-1616), and music.

German Empire. From among a welter of minor feudal states, church lands, and independent cities, the **Hapsburgs** assembled a far-flung territorial domain, based in Austria from 1276. The family held the title Holy Roman Emperor from 1452 to the Empire's dissolution in 1806, but failed to centralize its domains, leaving Germany disunited for centuries. Resistance to Turkish expansion brought Hungary under Austrian control from the 16th century. The Netherlands, Luxembourg, and Burgundy were added in 1477, curbing French expansion.

The Flemish painting tradition of naturalism, technical proficiency, and bourgeois subject matter began in the 15th century (Jan Van Eyck, 1366-1440), the earliest northern manifestation of the Renaissance. **Durer** (1471-1528) typified the merging of late Gothic and Italian trends in 16th century German art. Imposing civic architecture flourished in the prosperous commercial cities.

Spain. Despite the unification of Castile and Aragon in 1479, the 2 countries retained separate governments, and the nobility, especially in Aragon and Catalonia, retained many privileges. Spanish lands in Italy (Naples, Sicily) and the Netherlands entangled the country in European wars through the mid-17th century, while explorers, traders, and conquerors built up a Spanish empire in the Americas and the Philippines.

From the late 15th century, a **golden age** of literature and art produced works of social satire (plays of Lope de Vega, 1562-1635; Cervantes, 1547-1616), as well as spiritual intensity (El Greco, 1541-1614; Velazquez, 1599-1660).

Black Death. The bubonic plague reached Europe from the E in 1348, killing as much as half the population by 1350. Labor scarcity forced a rise in wages and brought greater freedom to the peasantry, making possible **peasant uprisings** (Jacquerie in France, 1358, Wat Tyler's rebellion in England, 1381). In the *ciompi* revolt, 1378, Florentine wage earners demanded a say in economic and political power.

Explorations. Organized European maritime exploration began, seeking to evade the Venice-Ottoman monopoly of eastern trade and to promote Christianity. Expeditions from Portugal beginning 1418 explored the west coast of Africa, until **Vasco da Gama** rounded the Cape of Good Hope in 1497 and reached India. A Portuguese trading empire was consolidated by the seizure of Goa, 1510, and Malacca, 1551. Japan was reached in 1542. Spanish voyages (**Columbus,** 1492-1504) uncovered a new world, which Spain hastened to subdue. Navigation schools in Spain and Portugal, the development of large sailing ships (carracks), and the invention of the rifle, c1475, aided European penetration.

Mughals and Safavids. East of the Ottoman empire, two Moslem dynasties ruled unchallenged in the 16th and 17th centuries. The Mughal empire in India, founded by Persianized Turkish invaders from the NW under Babur, dates from their 1526 conquest of Delhi. The dynasty ruled most of India for over 200 years, surviving nominally until 1857. **Akbar** (ruled 1556-1605) consolidated administration at his glorious court, where Urdu (Persian-influenced Hindi) developed. Trade relations with Europe increased. Under Shah Jahan (1629-58), a secularized art fusing Hindu and Moslem elements flourished in miniature painting and architecture (**Taj Mahal**). Sikhism, founded c1519, combined elements of both faiths. Suppression of Hindus and Shi'ite Moslems in S India in the late 17th century weakened the empire.

Fanatical devotion to the Shi'ite sect characterized the Safavids of Persia, 1502-1736, and led to hostilities with the Sunni Ottomans for over a century. The prosperity and strength of the empire are evidenced by the mosques at its capital, **Isfahan.** The dynasty enhanced Iranian national consciousness.

China. The Ming emperors, 1368-1644, the last native dynasty in China, wielded unprecedented personal power, while the Confucian bureaucracy began to suffer from inertia. European trade (Portugese

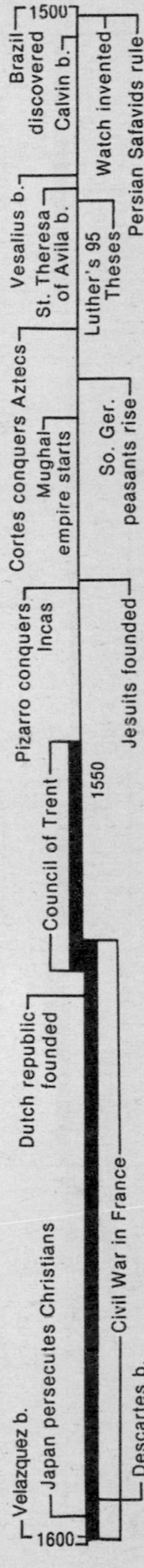

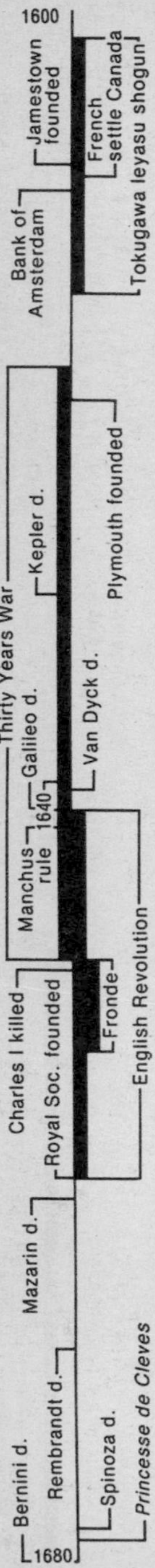

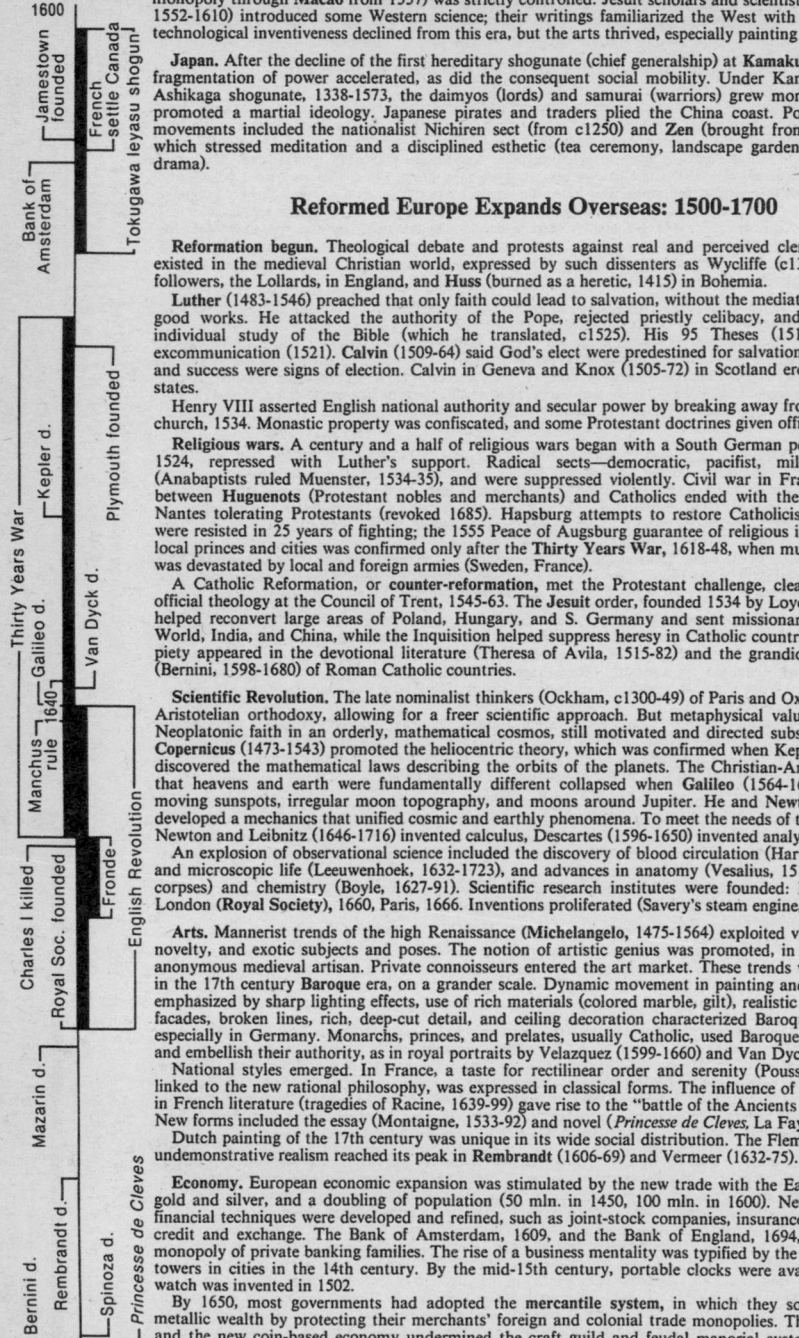

monopoly through **Macao** from 1557) was strictly controlled. Jesuit scholars and scientists (Matteo Ricci 1552-1610) introduced some Western science; their writings familiarized the West with China. Chinese technological inventiveness declined from this era, but the arts thrived, especially painting and ceramics.

Japan. After the decline of the first hereditary shogunate (chief generalship) at **Kamakura** (1185-1333), fragmentation of power accelerated, as did the consequent social mobility. Under Kamakura and the Ashikaga shogunate, 1338-1573, the daimyos (lords) and samurai (warriors) grew more powerful and promoted a martial ideology. Japanese pirates and traders plied the China coast. Popular Buddhist movements included the nationalist Nichiren sect (from c1250) and **Zen** (brought from China, 1191), which stressed meditation and a disciplined esthetic (tea ceremony, landscape gardening, judo, Noh drama).

Reformed Europe Expands Overseas: 1500-1700

Reformation begun. Theological debate and protests against real and perceived clerical corruption existed in the medieval Christian world, expressed by such dissenters as Wycliffe (c1320-84) and his followers, the Lollards, in England, and **Huss** (burned as a heretic, 1415) in Bohemia.

Luther (1483-1546) preached that only faith could lead to salvation, without the mediation of clergy or good works. He attacked the authority of the Pope, rejected priestly celibacy, and recommended individual study of the Bible (which he translated, c1525). His 95 Theses (1517) led to his excommunication (1521). **Calvin** (1509-64) said God's elect were predestined for salvation; good conduct and success were signs of election. Calvin in Geneva and Knox (1505-72) in Scotland erected theocratic states.

Henry VIII asserted English national authority and secular power by breaking away from the Catholic church, 1534. Monastic property was confiscated, and some Protestant doctrines given official sanction.

Religious wars. A century and a half of religious wars began with a South German peasant uprising, 1524, repressed with Luther's support. Radical sects—democratic, pacifist, millenarian—arose (Anabaptists ruled Muenster, 1534-35), and were suppressed violently. Civil war in France from 1562 between **Huguenots** (Protestant nobles and merchants) and Catholics ended with the 1598 Edict of Nantes tolerating Protestants (revoked 1685). Hapsburg attempts to restore Catholicism in Germany were resisted in 25 years of fighting; the 1555 Peace of Augsburg guarantee of religious independence to local princes and cities was confirmed only after the **Thirty Years War,** 1618-48, when much of Germany was devastated by local and foreign armies (Sweden, France).

A Catholic Reformation, or **counter-reformation,** met the Protestant challenge, clearly defining an official theology at the Council of Trent, 1545-63. The **Jesuit** order, founded 1534 by Loyola (1491-1556), helped reconvert large areas of Poland, Hungary, and S. Germany and sent missionaries to the New World, India, and China, while the Inquisition helped suppress heresy in Catholic countries. A revival of piety appeared in the devotional literature (Theresa of Avila, 1515-82) and the grandiose Baroque art (Bernini, 1598-1680) of Roman Catholic countries.

Scientific Revolution. The late nominalist thinkers (Ockham, c1300-49) of Paris and Oxford challenged Aristotelian orthodoxy, allowing for a freer scientific approach. But metaphysical values, such as the Neoplatonic faith in an orderly, mathematical cosmos, still motivated and directed subsequent inquiry. **Copernicus** (1473-1543) promoted the heliocentric theory, which was confirmed when Kepler (1571-1630) discovered the mathematical laws describing the orbits of the planets. The Christian-Aristotelian belief that heavens and earth were fundamentally different collapsed when **Galileo** (1564-1642) discovered moving sunspots, irregular moon topography, and moons around Jupiter. He and **Newton** (1642-1727) developed a mechanics that unified cosmic and earthly phenomena. To meet the needs of the new physics, Newton and Leibnitz (1646-1716) invented calculus, Descartes (1596-1650) invented analytic geometry.

An explosion of observational science included the discovery of blood circulation (Harvey, 1578-1657) and microscopic life (Leeuwenhoek, 1632-1723), and advances in anatomy (Vesalius, 1514-64, dissected corpses) and chemistry (Boyle, 1627-91). Scientific research institutes were founded: Florence, 1657, London (**Royal Society**), 1660, Paris, 1666. Inventions proliferated (Savery's steam engine, 1696).

Arts. Mannerist trends of the high Renaissance (**Michelangelo,** 1475-1564) exploited virtuosity, grace, novelty, and exotic subjects and poses. The notion of artistic genius was promoted, in contrast to the anonymous medieval artisan. Private connoisseurs entered the art market. These trends were elaborated in the 17th century **Baroque** era, on a grander scale. Dynamic movement in painting and sculpture was emphasized by sharp lighting effects, use of rich materials (colored marble, gilt), realistic details. Curved facades, broken lines, rich, deep-cut detail, and ceiling decoration characterized Baroque architecture, especially in Germany. Monarchs, princes, and prelates, usually Catholic, used Baroque art to enhance and embellish their authority, as in royal portraits by Velazquez (1599-1660) and Van Dyck (1599-1641).

National styles emerged. In France, a taste for rectilinear order and serenity (Poussin, 1594-1665), linked to the new rational philosophy, was expressed in classical forms. The influence of **classical values** in French literature (tragedies of Racine, 1639-99) gave rise to the "battle of the Ancients and Moderns." New forms included the essay (Montaigne, 1533-92) and novel (*Princesse de Cleves,* La Fayette, 1678).

Dutch painting of the 17th century was unique in its wide social distribution. The Flemish tradition of undemonstrative realism reached its peak in **Rembrandt** (1606-69) and Vermeer (1632-75).

Economy. European economic expansion was stimulated by the new trade with the East, New World gold and silver, and a doubling of population (50 mln. in 1450, 100 mln. in 1600). New business and financial techniques were developed and refined, such as joint-stock companies, insurance, and letters of credit and exchange. The Bank of Amsterdam, 1609, and the Bank of England, 1694, broke the old monopoly of private banking families. The rise of a business mentality was typified by the spread of clock towers in cities in the 14th century. By the mid-15th century, portable clocks were available; the first watch was invented in 1502.

By 1650, most governments had adopted the **mercantile system,** in which they sought to amass metallic wealth by protecting their merchants' foreign and colonial trade monopolies. The rise in prices and the new coin-based economy undermined the craft guild and feudal manorial systems. Expanding industries, such as clothweaving and mining, benefitted from technical advances. Coal replaced disappearing wood as the chief fuel; it was used to fuel new 16th century blast furnaces making cast iron.

New World. The **Aztecs** united much of the Mesoamerican culture area in a militarist empire by 1519, from their capital, Tenochtitlan (pop. 300,000), which was the center of a cult requiring enormous levels of ritual human sacrifice. Most of the civilized areas of S. America were ruled by the centralized **Inca Empire** (1476-1534), stretching 2,000 miles from Ecuador to N.W. Argentina. Lavish and sophisticated traditions in pottery, weaving, sculpture, and architecture were maintained in both regions.

These empires, beset by revolts, fell in 2 short campaigns to gold-seeking Spanish forces based in the Antilles and Panama. **Cortes** took Mexico, 1519-21; **Pizarro** Peru, 1531-35. From these centers, land and sea expeditions claimed most of N. and S. America for Spain. The Indian high cultures did not survive the impact of Christian missionaries and the new upper class of whites and mestizos. In turn, New World silver, and such Indian products as potatoes, tobacco, corn, peanuts, chocolate, and rubber exercised a major economic influence on Europe. While the Spanish administration intermittently concerned itself with the welfare of Indians, the population remained impoverished at most levels, despite the growth of a distinct South American civilization. European diseases reduced the native population.

Brazil, which the Portuguese discovered in 1500 and settled after 1530, and the Caribbean colonies of several European nations developed a plantation economy where sugar cane, tobacco, cotton, coffee, rice, indigo, and lumber were grown commercially by slaves. From the early 16th to the late 19th centuries, some 10 million Africans were transported to **slavery** in the New World.

Netherlands. The urban, Calvinist northern provinces of the Netherlands rebelled against Hapsburg Spain, 1568, and founded an oligarchic mercantile republic. Their strategic control of the Baltic grain market enabled them to exploit Mediterranean food shortages. Religious refugees — French and Belgian Protestants, Iberian Jews — added to the cosmopolitan commercial talent pool. After Spain absorbed Portugal in 1580, the Dutch seized Portuguese possessions and created a vast, though generally short-lived commercial empire in Brazil, the Antilles, Africa, India, Ceylon, Malacca, Indonesia, and Taiwan, and challenged or supplanted Portuguese traders in China and Japan.

England. Anglicanism became firmly established under Elizabeth I after a brief Catholic interlude under "Bloody Mary," 1553-58. But religious and political conflicts led to a rebellion by Parliament, 1642. Roundheads (Puritans) defeated Cavaliers (Royalists); Charles I was beheaded, 1649. The new **Commonwealth** was ruled as a military dictatorship by Cromwell, who also brutally crushed an Irish rebellion, 1649-51. Conflicts within the Puritan camp (democratic Levelers defeated 1649) aided the Stuart restoration, 1660, but Parliament was permanently strengthened and the peaceful **"Glorious Revolution"**, 1688, advanced political and religious liberties (writings of Locke, 1632-1704). British privateers (Drake, 1540-96) challenged Spanish control of the New World, and penetrated Asian trade routes (Madras taken, 1639). N. American colonies (Jamestown, 1607, Plymouth, 1620) provided an outlet for religious dissenters.

France. Emerging from the religious civil wars in 1628, France regained military and commercial great power status under the ministries of **Richelieu** (1624-42), Mazarin (1643-61), and Colbert (1662-83). Under Louis XIV (ruled 1643-1715) royal absolutism triumphed over nobles and local *parlements* (defeat of Fronde, 1648-53). Permanent colonies were founded in Canada (1608), the Caribbean (1626), and India (1674).

Sweden. Sweden seceded from the Scandinavian Union in 1523. The thinly-populated agrarian state (with copper, iron, and timber exports) was united by the Vasa kings, whose conquests by the mid-17th century made Sweden the dominant Baltic power. The empire collapsed in the Great Northern War (1700-21).

Poland. After the union with Lithuania in 1447, Poland ruled vast territories from the Baltic to the Black Sea, resisting German and Turkish incursions. Catholic nobles failed to gain the loyalty of the Orthodox Christian peasantry in the East; commerce and trades were practiced by German and Jewish immigrants. The bloody 1648-49 cossack uprising began the kingdom's dismemberment.

China. A new dynasty, the **Manchus,** invaded from the NE and seized power in 1644, and expanded Chinese control to its greatest extent in Central and Southeast Asia. Trade and diplomatic contact with Europe grew, carefully controlled by China. New crops (sweet potato, maize, peanut) allowed an economic and population growth (300 million pop. in 1800). Traditional arts and literature were pursued with increased sophistication (*Dream of the Red Chamber,* novel, mid-18th century).

Japan. Tokugawa Ieyasu, shogun from 1603, finally unified and pacified feudal Japan. Hereditary daimyos and samurai monopolized government office and the professions. An urban merchant class grew, literacy spread, and a cultural renaissance occurred (haiku of Basho, 1644-94). Fear of European domination led to persecution of Christian converts from 1597, and stringent isolation from outside contact from 1640.

Philosophy, Industry, and Revolution: 1700-1800

Science and Reason. Faith in human reason and science as the source of truth and a means to improve the physical and social environment, espoused since the Renaissance (Francis Bacon, 1561-1626), was bolstered by scientific discoveries in spite of theological opposition (**Galileo's forced retraction,** 1633). Descartes applied the logical method of mathematics to discover "self-evident" scientific and philosophical truths, while Newton emphasized induction from experimental observation.

The challenge of reason to traditional religious and political values and institutions began with **Spinoza** (1632-77), who interpreted the Bible historically and called for political and intellectual freedom.

French philosophes assumed leadership of the **"Enlightenment"** in the 18th century. Montesquieu (1689-1755) used British history to support his notions of limited government. Voltaire's (1694-1778) diaries and novels of exotic travel illustrated the intellectual trends toward secular ethics and relativism. Rousseau's (1712-1778) radical concepts of the **social contract** and of the inherent goodness of the common man gave impetus to anti-monarchical republicanism. The *Encyclopedia,* 1751-72, edited by Diderot and d'Alembert, designed as a monument to reason, was largely devoted to practical technology.

In England, ideals of political and religious liberty were connected with empiricist philosophy and science in the followers of Locke. But the extreme **empiricism of Hume** (1711-76) and Berkeley

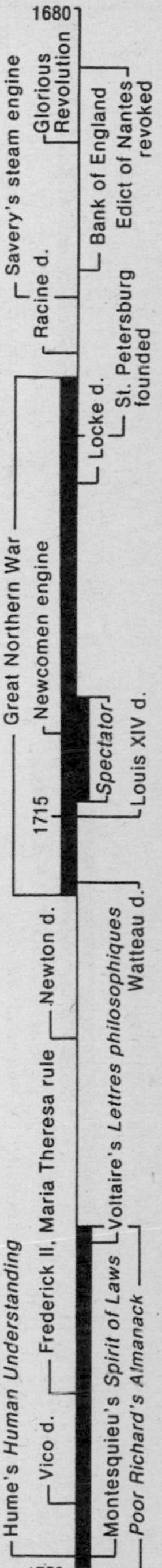

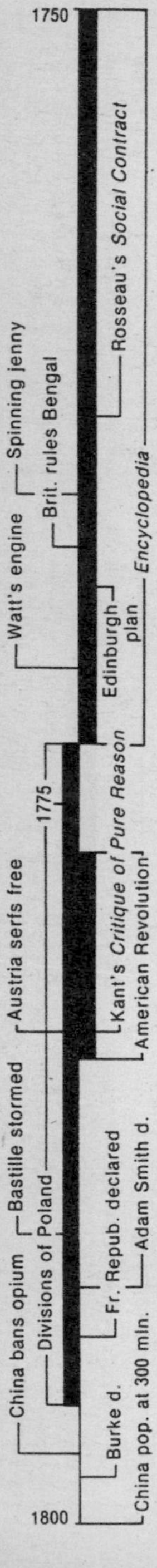

(1685-1753) posed limits to the identification of reason with absolute truth, as did the evolutionary approach to law and politics of Burke (1729-97) and the utilitarianism of Bentham (1748-1832). Adam Smith (1723-90) and other **physiocrats** called for a rationalization of economic activity by removing artificial barriers to a supposedly natural free exchange of goods.

Despite the political disunity and backwardness of most of Germany, German writers participated in the new philosophical trends popularized by Wolff (1679-1754). **Kant's** (1724-1804) **idealism,** unifying an empirical epistemology with *a priori* moral and logical concepts, directed German thought away from skepticism. Italian contributions included work on electricity by Galvani (1737-98) and Volta (1745-1827), the pioneer **historiography of Vico** (1668-1744), and writings on penal reform by Beccaria (1738-94). The American Franklin (1706-90) was celebrated in Europe for his varied achievements.

The growth of the **press** (*Spectator,* 1711-14) and the wide distribution of realistic but sentimental **novels** attested to the increase of a large bourgeois public.

Arts. Rococo art, characterized by extravagant decorative effects, asymmetries copied from organic models, and artificial pastoral subjects, was favored by the continental aristocracy for most of the century (Watteau, 1684-1721), and had musical analogies in the ornamentalized polyphony of late Baroque. The **Neoclassical** art after 1750, associated with the new scientific archeology, was more streamlined, and infused with the supposed moral and geometric rectitude of the Roman Republic (David, 1748-1825). In England, **town planning** on a grand scale began (Edinburgh, 1767).

Industrial Revolution in England. Agricultural improvements, such as the sowing drill (1701) and livestock breeding, were implemented on the large fields provided by enclosure of common lands by private owners. Profits from agriculture and from colonial and foreign trade (1800 volume, £ 54 million) were channelled through hundreds of banks and the **Stock Exchange** (founded 1773) into new industrial processes.

The Newcomen steam pump (1712) aided coal mining. Coal fueled the new efficient steam engines patented by Watt in 1769, and coke-smelting produced cheap, sturdy iron for machinery by the 1730s. The **flying shuttle** (1733) and **spinning jenny** (1764) were used in the large new cotton textile factories, where women and children were much of the work force. Goods were transported cheaply over **canals** (2,000 miles built 1760-1800).

American Revolution. The British colonies in N. America attracted a mass immigration of religious dissenters and poor people throughout the 17th and 18th centuries, coming from all parts of the British Isles, Germany, the Netherlands, and other countries. The population reached 3 million whites and blacks by the 1770s. The small native population was decimated by European diseases and wars with and between the various colonies. British attempts to control colonial trade, and to tax the colonists to pay for the costs of colonial administration and defense clashed with traditions of local self government, and eventually provoked the colonies to rebellion. (*See American Revolution in Index.*)

Central and East Europe. The monarchs of the three states that dominated eastern Europe — Austria, Prussia, and Russia — accepted the advice and legitimation of philosophes in creating more modern, centralized institutions in their kingdoms, enlarged by the division of Poland (1772-95).

Under **Frederick II** (ruled 1740-86) Prussia, with its efficient modern army, doubled in size. State monopolies and tariff protection fostered industry, and some legal reforms were introduced. Austria's heterogenecus realms were legally unified under **Maria Theresa** (ruled 1740-80) and **Joseph II** (1780-90). Reforms in education, law, and religion were enacted, and the Austrian serfs were freed (1781). With its defeat in the Seven Years' War in 1763, Austria lost Silesia and ceased its active role in Germany, but was compensated by expansion to the E and S (Hungary, Slavonia, 1699, Galicia, 1772).

Russia, whose borders continued to expand in all directions, adopted some Western bureaucratic and economic policies under **Peter I** (ruled 1682-1725) and Catherine II (ruled 1762-96). Trade and cultural contacts with the West multiplied from the new Baltic Sea capital, **St. Petersburg** (founded 1703).

French Revolution. The growing French middle class lacked political power, and resented aristocratic tax privileges, especially in light of liberal political ideals popularized by the American Revolution. Peasants lacked adequate land and were burdened with feudal obligations to nobles. Wars with Britain drained the treasury, finally forcing the king to call the **Estates-General** in 1789 (first time since 1614), in an atmosphere of food riots (poor crop in 1788).

Aristocratic resistance to absolutism was soon overshadowed by the reformist Third Estate (middle class), which proclaimed itself the **National Constituent Assembly** June 17 and took the "Tennis Court oath" on June 20 to secure a constitution. The storming of the **Bastille** July 14 by Parisian artisans was followed by looting and seizure of aristocratic property throughout France. Assembly reforms included abolition of class and regional privileges, a Declaration of Rights, suffrage by taxpayers (75% of males), and the **Civil Constitution of the Clergy** providing for election and loyalty oaths for priests. A republic was declared Sept. 22, 1792, in spite of royalist pressure from Austria and Prussia, which had declared war in April (joined by Britain the next year). Louis XVI was beheaded Jan. 21, 1793, Queen Marie Antoinette was beheaded Oct. 16, 1793.

Royalist uprisings in La Vendee and military reverses led to a **reign of terror** in which tens of thousands of opponents of the Revolution and criminals were executed. Radical reforms in the **Convention** period (Sept. 1793-Oct. 1795) included the abolition of colonial slavery, economic measures to aid the poor, support of public education, and a short-lived de-Christianization.

Division among radicals (execution of Hebert, March 1794, Danton, April, and Robespierre, July) aided the ascendance of a moderate **Directory,** which consolidated military victories. **Napoleon Bonaparte** (1769-1821), a popular young general, exploited political divisions and participated in a coup Nov. 9, 1799, making himself first consul (dictator).

India. Sikh and Hindu rebels (Rajputs, Marathas) and Afghans destroyed the power of the Mughals during the 18th century. After France's defeat in the Seven Years War, 1763, Britain was the chief European trade power in India. Its control of inland **Bengal and Bihar** was recognized by the Mughal shah in 1765, who granted the **British East India Co.** (under Clive, 1727-74) the right to collect land revenue there. Despite objections from Parliament (1784 India Act) the company's involvement in local wars and politics led to repeated acquisitions of new territory. The company exported Indian textiles, sugar, and indigo.

Change Gathers Steam: 1800-1840

French ideals and empire spread. Inspired by the ideals of the French Revolution, and supported by the expanding French armies, new republican regimes arose near France: the **Batavian** Republic in the Netherlands (1795-1806), the **Helvetic** Republic in Switzerland (1798-1803), the **Cisalpine** Republic in N. Italy (1797-1805), the **Ligurian** Republic in Genoa (1797-1805), and the **Parthenopean** Republic in S. Italy (1799). A Roman Republic existed briefly in 1798 after Pope Pius VI was arrested by French troops. In Italy and Germany, new nationalist sentiments were stimulated both in imitation of and reaction to France (anti-French and anti-Jacobin peasant uprisings in Italy, 1796-9).

From 1804, when Napoleon declared himself emperor, to 1812, a succession of military victories (Austerlitz, 1805, Jena, 1806) extended his control over most of Europe, through puppet states (**Confederation of the Rhine** united W. German states for the first time and **Grand Duchy of Warsaw** revived Polish national hopes), expansion of the empire, and alliances.

Among the lasting reforms initiated under Napoleon's absolutist reign were: establishment of the Bank of France, centralization of tax collection, codification of law along Roman models (*Code Napoleon*), and reform and extension of secondary and university education. In an 1801 concordat, the papacy recognized the effective autonomy of the French Catholic Church. Some 400,000 French soldiers were killed in the Napoleonic Wars, along with 600,000 foreign troops.

Last gasp of old regime. France's coastal blockade of Europe (**Continental System**) failed to neutralize Britain. The disastrous 1812 invasion of Russia exposed Napoleon's overextension. After an 1814 exile at Elba, Napoleon's armies were defeated at **Waterloo**, 1815, by British and Prussian troops.

At the **Congress of Vienna**, the monarchs and princes of Europe redrew their boundaries, to the advantage of Prussia (in Saxony and the Ruhr), Austria (in Illyria and Venetia), and Russia (in Poland and Finland). British conquest of Dutch and French colonies (S. Africa, Ceylon, Mauritius) was recognized, and France, under the restored Bourbons, retained its expanded 1792 borders. The settlement brought 50 years of international peace to Europe.

But the Congress was unable to check the advance of liberal ideals and of nationalism among the smaller European nations. The 1825 **Decembrist uprising** by liberal officers in Russia was easily suppressed. But an independence movement in **Greece**, stirred by commercial prosperity and a cultural revival, succeeded in expelling Ottoman rule by 1831, with the aid of Britain, France, and Russia.

A constitutional monarchy was secured in France by an **1830 revolution;** Louis Philippe became king. The revolutionary contagion spread to **Belgium,** which gained its independence from the Dutch monarchy, 1830; to **Poland,** whose rebellion was defeated by Russia, 1830-31; and to Germany.

Romanticism. A new style in intellectual and artistic life began to replace Neo-classicism and Rococo after the mid-18th century. By the early 19th, this style, Romanticism, had prevailed in the European world.

Rousseau had begun the reaction against excessive rationalism and skepticism; in education (*Emile,* 1762) he stressed subjective spontaneity over regularized instruction. In Germany, Lessing (1729-81) and Herder (1744-1803) favorably compared the German folk song to classical forms, and began a cult of Shakespeare, whose passion and "natural" wisdom was a model for the Romantic *Sturm und Drang* (storm and stress) movement. **Goethe's** *Sorrows of Young Werther* (1774) set the model for the tragic, passionate genius.

A new interest in **Gothic architecture** in England after 1760 (Walpole, 1717-97) spread through Europe, associated with an aesthetic Christian and mystic revival (Blake, 1757-1827). Celtic, Norse, and German mythology and folk tales were revived or imitated (Macpherson's Ossian translation, 1762, Grimm's *Fairy Tales,* 1812-22). The medieval revival (Scott's *Ivanhoe,* 1819) led to a new interest in history, stressing national differences and organic growth (Carlyle, 1795-1881; Michelet, 1798-1874), corresponding to theories of natural evolution (Lamarck's *Philosophie zoologique,* 1809, Lyell's *Geology,* 1830-33).

Revolution and war fed an obsession with freedom and conflict, expressed by poets (**Byron,** 1788-1824, **Hugo,** 1802-85) and philosophers (**Hegel,** 1770-1831).

Wild gardens replaced the formal French variety, and painters favored rural, stormy, and mountainous landscapes (**Turner,** 1775-1851; **Constable,** 1776-1837). Clothing became freer, with wigs, hoops, and ruffles discarded. Originality and genius were expected in the life as well as the work of inspired artists (Murger's *Scenes from Bohemian Life,* 1847-49). Exotic locales and themes (as in "Gothic" horror stories) were used in art and literature (Delacroix, 1798-1863, **Poe,** 1809-49).

Music exhibited the new dramatic style and a breakdown of classical forms (Beethoven, 1770-1827). The use of folk melodies and modes aided the growth of distinct national traditions (Glinka in Russia, 1804-57).

Latin America. Haiti, under the former slave **Toussaint L'Ouverture,** was the first Latin American independent state, 1800. All the mainland Spanish colonies won their independence 1810-24, under such leaders as **Bolivar** (1783-1830). Brazil became an independent empire under the Portuguese prince regent, 1822. A new class of military officers divided power with large landholders and the church.

United States. Heavy immigration and exploitation of ample natural resources fueled rapid economic growth. The spread of the franchise, public education, and antislavery sentiment were signs of a widespread democratic ethic.

China. Failure to keep pace with Western arms technology exposed China to greater European influence, and hampered efforts to bar imports of opium, which had damaged Chinese society and drained wealth overseas. In the **Opium War,** 1839-42, Britain forced China to expand trade opportunities and to cede Hong Kong

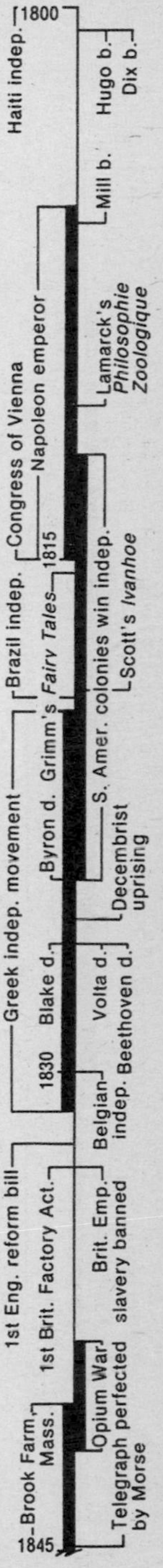

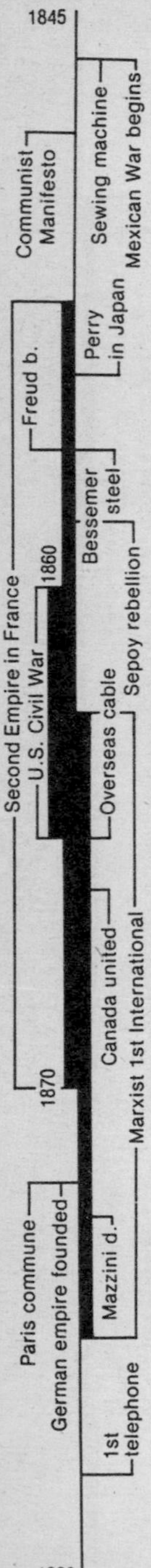

Triumph of Progress: 1840-80

Idea of Progress. As a result of the cumulative scientific, economic, and political changes of the preceding eras, the idea took hold among literate people in the West that continuing growth and improvement was the usual state of human and natural life.

Darwin's statement of the **theory of evolution** and survival of the fittest (*Origin of Species*, 1859), defended by intellectuals and scientists against theological objections, was taken as confirmation that progress was the natural direction of life. The controversy helped define popular ideas of the dedicated scientist and ever-expanding human knowledge of and control over the world (Foucault's demonstration of earth's rotation, 1851, Pasteur's germ theory, 1861).

Liberals following Ricardo (1772-1823) in their faith that unrestrained competition would bring continuous economic expansion sought to adjust political life to the new social realities, and believed that unregulated competition of ideas would yield truth (Mill, 1806-73). In England, successive reform bills (1832, 1867, 1884) gave representation to the new industrial towns, and extended the franchise to the middle and lower classes and to Catholics, Dissenters, and Jews. On both sides of the Atlantic, reformists tried to improve conditions for the mentally ill (Dix, 1802-87), women (Anthony, 1820-1906), and prisoners. Slavery was barred in the British Empire, 1833; the United States, 1865; and Brazil, 1888.

Socialist theories based on ideas of human perfectibility or historical progress were widely disseminated. Utopian socialists like Saint-Simon (1760-1825) envisaged an orderly, just society directed by a technocratic elite. A model factory town, New Lanark, Scotland, was set up by utopian Robert Owen (1771-1858), and utopian communal experiments were tried in the U.S. (Brook Farm, Mass., 1841-7). Bakunin's (1814-76) anarchism represented the opposite utopian extreme of total freedom. Marx (1818-83) posited the inevitable triumph of socialism in the industrial countries through a historical process of class conflict.

Spread of industry. The technical processes and managerial innovations of the English industrial revolution spread to Europe (especially Germany) and the U.S., causing an explosion of industrial production, demand for raw materials, and competition for markets. Inventors, both trained and self-educated, provided the means for larger-scale production (Bessemer steel, 1856, sewing machine, 1846). Many inventions were shown at the 1851 London Great Exhibition at the Crystal Palace, whose theme was universal prosperity.

Local specialization and long-distance trade were aided by a revolution in transportation and communication. Railroads were first introduced in the 1820s in England and the U.S. Over 150,000 miles of track had been laid worldwide by 1880, with another 100,000 miles laid in the next decade. Steamships were improved (*Savannah* crossed Atlantic, 1819). The telegraph, perfected by 1844 (Morse), connected the Old and New Worlds by cable in 1866, and quickened the pace of international commerce and politics. The first commercial telephone exchange went into operation in the U.S. in 1878.

The new class of industrial workers, uprooted from their rural homes, lacked job security, and suffered from dangerous overcrowded conditions at work and at home. Many responded by organizing trade unions (legalized in England, 1824; France, 1884). The U.S. Knights of Labor had 700,000 members by 1886. The First International, 1864-76, tried to unite workers internationally around a Marxist program. The quasi-Socialist Paris Commune uprising, 1871, was violently suppressed. Factory Acts to reduce child labor and regulate conditions were passed (1833-50 in England). Social security measures were introduced by the Bismarck regime in Germany, 1883-89.

Revolutions of 1848. Among the causes of the continent-wide revolutions were an international collapse of credit and resulting unemployment, bad harvests in 1845-7, and a cholera epidemic. The new urban proletariat and expanding bourgeoisie demanded a greater political role. Republics were proclaimed in France, Rome, and Venice. Nationalist feelings reached fever pitch in the Hapsburg empire, as Hungary declared independence under Kossuth, a Slav Congress demanded equality, and Piedmont tried to drive Austria from Lombardy. A national liberal assembly at Frankfurt called for German unification.

But riots fueled bourgeois fears of socialism (Marx and Engels' 1848 *Communist Manifesto*) and peasants remained conservative. The old establishment — The Papacy, the Hapsburgs (using Croats and Romanians against Hungary), the Russian army — was able to rout the revolutionaries by 1849. The French Republic succumbed to a renewed monarchy by 1852 (Emperor Napoleon III).

Great nations unified. Using the "blood and iron" tactics of Bismarck from 1862, Prussia controlled N. Germany by 1867 (war with Denmark, 1864, Austria, 1866). After defeating France in 1870 (annexation of Alsace-Lorraine), it won the allegiance of S. German states. A new **German Empire** was proclaimed, 1871. **Italy**, inspired by Mazzini (1805-72) and Garibaldi (1807-82), was unified by the reformed Piedmont kingdom through uprisings, plebiscites, and war.

The **U.S.**, its area expanded after the 1846-47 Mexican War, defeated a secession attempt by slave states, 1861-65. The Canadian provinces were united in an autonomous **Dominion of Canada**, 1867. Control in **India** was removed from the East India Co. and centralized under British administration after the 1857-58 Sepoy rebellion, laying the groundwork for the modern Indian State. Queen Victoria was named Empress of India, 1876.

Europe dominates Asia. The Ottoman Empire began to collapse in the face of Balkan nationalisms and European imperial incursions in N. Africa (Suez Canal, 1869). The Turks had lost control of most of both regions by 1882. Russia completed its expansion south by 1884 (despite the temporary setback of the Crimean War with Turkey, Britain, and France, 1853-56) taking Turkestan, all the Caucasus, and Chinese areas in the East and sponsoring Balkan Slavs against the Turks. A succession of reformist and reactionary regimes presided over a slow modernization (serfs freed, 1861). Persian independence suffered as Russia and British India competed for influence.

China was forced to sign a series of unequal treaties with European powers and Japan. Overpopulation and an inefficient dynasty brought misery and caused rebellions (Taiping, Moslems) leaving tens of millions dead. Japan was forced by the U.S. (Commodore Perry's visits, 1853-54) and Europe to end its isolation. The Meiji restoration, 1868, gave power to a Westernizing oligarchy. Intensified empire-building gave Burma to Britain, 1824-86, and Indo-China to France, 1862-95. Christian missionary activity followed imperial and trade expansion in Asia.

Respectability. The fine arts were expected to reflect and encourage the progress of morals and manners among the different classes. "Victorian" prudery, exaggerated delicacy, and familial piety were heralded by **Bowdler's** expurgated edition of Shakespeare (1818). Government-supported mass education inculcated a work ethic as a means to escape poverty (Horatio Alger, 1832-99).

The official **Beaux Arts** school in Paris set an international style of imposing public buildings (Paris Opera, 1861-74, Vienna Opera, 1861-69) and uplifting statues (Bartholdi's *Statue of Liberty,* 1885). Realist painting, influenced by photography (Daguerre, 1837), appealed to a new mass audience with social or historical narrative (Wilkie, 1785-1841, Poynter, 1836-1919) or with serious religious, moral, or social messages (pre-Raphaelites, Millet's Angelus, 1858) often drawn from ordinary life. The **Impressionists** (Pissarro, 1830-1903, Renoir, 1841-1919) rejected the central role of serious subject matter in favor of a colorful and sensual depiction of a moment, but their sunny, placid depictions of bourgeois scenes kept them within the respectable consensus.

Realistic **novelists** presented the full panorama of social classes and personalities, but retained sentimentality and moral judgment (Dickens, 1812-70, Eliot, 1819-80, Tolstoy, 1828-1910, Balzac, 1799-1850).

Veneer of Stability: 1880-1900

Imperialism triumphant. The vast **African** interior, visited by European explorers (Barth, 1821-65, Livingstone, 1813-73) was conquered by the European powers in rapid, competitive thrusts from their coastal bases after 1880, mostly for domestic political and international strategic reasons. W. African Moslem kingdoms (Fulani), Arab slave traders (Zanzibar), and Bantu military confederations (Zulu) were alike subdued. Only Christian Ethiopia (defeat of Italy, 1896) and Liberia resisted successfully. France (W. Africa) and Britain ("Cape to Cairo," Boer War, 1899-1902) were the major beneficiaries. The ideology of "the white man's burden" (Kipling, *Barrack Room Ballads,* 1892) or of a "civilizing mission" (France) justified the conquests.

West European foreign capital investments soared to nearly $40 billion by 1914, but most was in E. Europe (France, Germany) the Americas (Britain) and the white colonies. The foundation of the modern interdependent world economy was laid, with cartels dominating raw material trade.

An industrious world. Industrial and technological proficiency characterized the 2 new great powers — **Germany** and the **U.S.** Coal and iron deposits enabled Germany to reach second or third place status in iron, steel, and shipbuilding by the 1900s. German electrical and chemical industries were world leaders. The U.S. post-civil war boom (interrupted by "panics," 1884, 1893, 1896) was shaped by massive immigration from S. and E. Europe from 1880, government subsidy of railroads, and huge private monopolies (Standard Oil, 1870, U.S. Steel, 1901). The **Spanish-American War,** 1898 (Philippine rebellion, 1899-1901) and the Open Door policy in China (1899) made the U.S. a world power.

England led in **urbanization** (72% by 1890), with **London** the world capital of finance, insurance, and shipping. Electric subways (London, 1890), sewer systems (Paris, 1850s), parks, and bargain department stores helped improve living standards for most of the urban population of the industrial world.

Asians assimilate. Asian reaction to European economic, military, and religious incursions took the form of imitation of Western techniques and adoption of Western ideas of progress and freedom. The Chinese "self-strengthening" movement of the 1860s and 70s included rail, port, and arsenal improvements and metal and textile mills. Reformers like **K'ang Yu-wei** (1858-1927) won liberalizing reforms in 1898, right after the European and Japanese "scramble for concessions."

A universal education system in Japan and importation of foreign industrial, scientific, and military experts aided Japan's unprecedented rapid modernization after 1868, under the authoritarian Meiji regime. Japan's victory in the **Sino-Japanese War,** 1894-95, put Formosa and Korea in its power.

In India, the British alliance with the remaining princely states masked reform sentiment among the Westernized urban elite; higher education had been conducted largely in English for 50 years. The **Indian National Congress,** founded in 1885, demanded a larger government role for Indians.

"Fin-de-siecle" sophistication. Naturalist writers pushed realism to its extreme limits, adopting a quasi-scientific attitude and writing about formerly taboo subjects like sex, crime, extreme poverty, and corruption (Flaubert, 1821-80, Zola, 1840-1902, Hardy, 1840-1928). Unseen or repressed psychological motivations were explored in the clinical and theoretical works of **Freud** (1856-1939) and in the fiction of Dostoevsky (1821-81), James (1843-1916), Schnitzler (1862-1931) and others.

A contempt for bourgeois life or a desire to shock a complacent audience was shared by the French **symbolist** poets (Verlaine, 1844-96, Rimbaud, 1854-91), neo-pagan English writers (Swinburne, 1837-1909), continental dramatists (Ibsen, 1828-1906) and satirists (Wilde, 1854-1900). **Nietzsche** (1844-1900) was influential in his elitism and pessimism.

Post-impressionist art neglected long-cherished conventions of representation (Cezanne, 1839-1906) and showed a willingness to learn from primitive and non-European art (Gauguin, 1848-1903, Japanese prints).

Racism. Gobineau (1816-82) gave a pseudo-biological foundation to modern racist theories, which spread in the latter 19th century along with **Social Darwinism,** the belief that societies are and should be organized as a struggle for survival of the fittest. The Medieval period was interpreted as an era of natural Germanic rule (Chamberlain, 1855-1927) and notions of superiority were associated with German national aspirations (Treitschke, 1834-96). **Anti-Semitism,** with a new racist rationale, became a significant political force in Germany (Anti-Semitic Petition, 1880), Austria (Lueger, 1844-1910), and France (Dreyfus case, 1894-1906).

Last Respite: 1900-1909

Alliances. While the peace of Europe (and its dependencies) continued to hold (1907 **Hague Conference** extended the rules of war and international arbitration procedures), imperial rivalries, protectionist trade practices (in Germany and France), and the escalating arms race (British *Dreadnought* battleship launched, Germany widens Kiel canal, 1906) exacerbated minor disputes (German-French Moroccan "crises", 1905, 1911).

Security was sought through alliances: **Triple Alliance** (Germany, Austria-Hungary, Italy) renewed

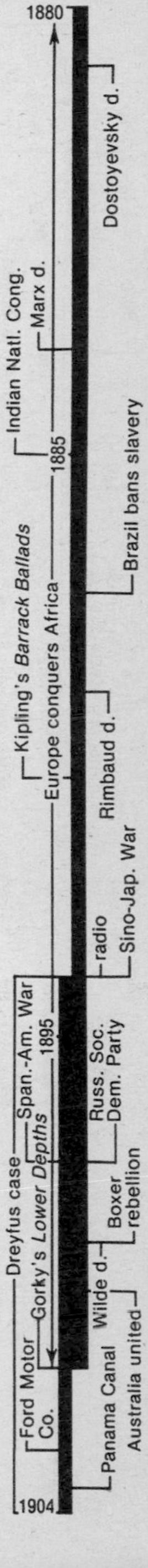

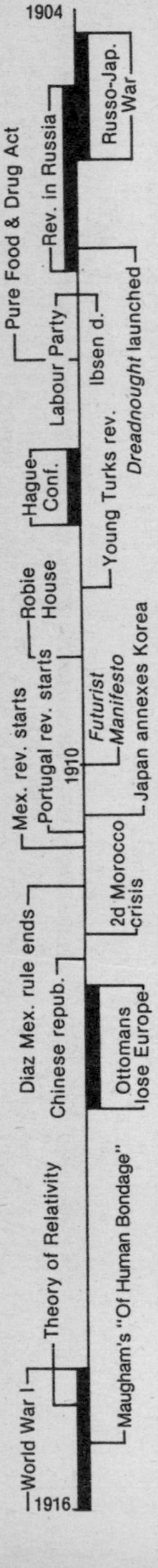

1902, 1907; Anglo-Japanese Alliance, 1902; Franco-Russian Alliance, 1899; **Entente Cordiale** (Britain, France) 1904; Anglo-Russian Treaty, 1907; German-Ottoman friendship.

Ottomans decline. The inefficient, corrupt Ottoman government was unable to resist further loss of territory. Nearly all European lands were lost in 1912 to Serbia, Greece, Montenegro, and Bulgaria. Italy took Libya and the Dodecanese islands the same year, and Britain took Kuwait, 1899, and the Sinai, 1906. The **Young Turk** revolution in 1908 forced the sultan to restore a constitution, introduced some social reform, industrialization, and secularization.

British Empire. British trade and cultural influence remained dominant in the empire, but constitutional reforms presaged its eventual dissolution: the colonies of **Australia** were united in 1901 under a self-governing commonwealth. **New Zealand** acquired dominion status in 1907. The old Boer republics joined Cape Colony and Natal in the self-governing **Union of South Africa** in 1910.

The 1909 Indian Councils Act enhanced the role of elected province legislatures in **India.** The Moslem League, founded 1906, sought separate communal representation.

East Asia. Japan exploited its growing industrial power to expand its empire. Victory in the 1904-05 war against Russia (naval battle of Tsushima, 1905) assured Japan's domination of **Korea** (annexed 1910) and Manchuria (took Port Arthur 1905).

In China, central authority began to crumble (empress died, 1908). Reforms (Confucian exam system ended 1905, modernization of the army, building of railroads) were inadequate and secret societies of reformers and nationalists, inspired by the Westernized **Sun Yat-sen** (1866-1925) fomented periodic uprisings in the south.

Siam, whose independence had been guaranteed by Britain and France in 1896, was split into spheres of influence by those countries in 1907.

Russia. The population of the Russian Empire approached 150 million in 1900. Reforms in education, law, and local institutions (*zemstvos*), and an industrial boom starting in the 1880s (oil, railroads) created the beginnings of a modern state, despite the autocratic tsarist regime. Liberals (1903 Union of Liberation), Socialists (Social Democrats founded 1898, Bolsheviks split off 1903), and populists (Social Revolutionaries founded 1901) were periodically repressed, and national minorities persecuted (anti-Jewish pogroms, 1903, 1905-6).

An industrial crisis after 1900 and harvest failures aggravated poverty in the urban proletariat, and the 1904-05 defeat by Japan (which checked Russia's Asian expansion) sparked the revolution of 1905-06. A **Duma** (parliament) was created, and an agricultural reform (under Stolypin, prime minister 1906-11) created a large class of landowning peasants (kulaks).

The world shrinks. Developments in transportation and communication and mass population movements helped create an awareness of an interdependent world. Early **automobiles** (Daimler, Benz, 1885) were experimental, or designed as luxuries. Assembly-line mass production (Ford Motor Co., 1903) made the invention practicable, and by 1910 nearly 500,000 motor vehicles were registered in the U.S. alone. **Heavier-than-air flights** began in 1903 in the U.S. (Wright brothers), preceded by glider, balloon, and model plane advances in several countries. Trade was advanced by improvements in **ship design** (gyrocompass, 1907), speed (Lusitania crossed Atlantic in 5 days, 1907), and reach (Panama Canal begun, 1904).

The first transatlantic **radio** telegraphic transmission occurred in 1901, 6 years after Marconi discovered radio. Radio transmission of human speech had been made in 1900. Telegraphic transmission of photos was achieved in 1904, lending immediacy to news reports. **Phonographs,** popularized by Caruso's recordings (starting 1902) made for quick international spread of musical styles (ragtime). **Motion pictures,** perfected in the 1890s (Dickson, Lumiere brothers), became a popular and artistic medium after 1900; newsreels appeared in 1909.

Emigration from crowded European centers soared in the decade: 9 million migrated to the U.S., and millions more went to Siberia, Canada, Argentina, Australia, South Africa, and Algeria. Some 70 million Europeans emigrated in the century before 1914. Several million Chinese, Indians, and Japanese migrated to Southeast Asia, where their urban skills often enabled them to take a predominant economic role.

Social reform. The social and economic problems of the poor were kept in the public eye by realist fiction writers (Dreiser's *Sister Carrie,* 1900; Gorky's *Lower Depths,* 1902; Sinclair's *Jungle,* 1906), journalists (U.S. **muckrakers** — Steffens, Tarbell) and artists (Ashcan school). Frequent labor strikes and occasional assassinations by anarchists or radicals (Austrian Empress, 1898; King Umberto I of Italy, 1900; U.S. Pres. McKinley, 1901; Russian Interior Minister Plehve, 1904; Portugal's King Carlos, 1908) added to social tension and fear of revolution.

But democratic reformism prevailed. In Germany, Bernstein's (1850-1932) **revisionist Marxism,** downgrading revolution, was accepted by the powerful Social Democrats and trade unions. The British Fabian Society (the Webbs, Shaw) and the Labour Party (founded 1906) worked for reforms such as social security and union rights (1906), while women's suffragists grew more militant. U.S. **progressives** fought big business (Pure Food and Drug Act, 1906). In France, the 10-hour work day (1904) and separation of church and state (1905) were reform victories, as was universal suffrage in Austria (1907).

Arts. An unprecedented period of experimentation, centered in France, produced several new **painting** styles: fauvism exploited bold color areas (Matisse, *Woman with Hat,* 1905); expressionism reflected powerful inner emotions (the Brücke group, 1905); cubism combined several views of an object on one flat surface (Picasso's *Demoiselles,* 1906-07); futurism tried to depict speed and motion (Italian Futurist Manifesto, 1910). **Architects** explored new uses of steel structures, with facades either neo-classical (Adler and Sullivan in U.S.); curvilinear Art Nouveau (Gaudi's Casa Mila, 1905-10); or functionally streamlined (Wright's Robie House, 1909).

Music and **Dance** shared the experimental spirit. Ruth St. Denis (1877-1968) and Isadora Duncan (1878-1927) pioneered modern dance, while Diaghilev in Paris revitalized classic ballet from 1909. Composers explored atonal music (Debussy, 1862-1918) and dissonance (Schönberg, 1874-1951), or revolutionized classical forms (Stravinsky, 1882-1971), often showing jazz or folk music influences.

War and Revolution: 1910-1919

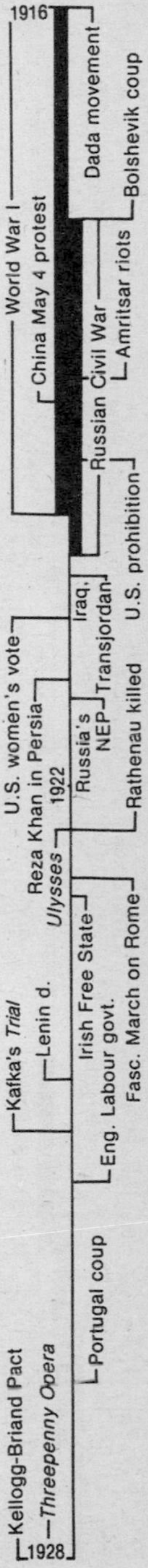

War threatens. Germany under Wilhelm II sought a political and imperial role consonant with its industrial strength, challenging Britain's world supremacy and threatening France, still resenting the loss of Alsace-Lorraine. Austria wanted to curb an expanded Serbia (after 1912) and the threat it posed to its own Slav lands. Russia feared Austrian and German political and economic aims in the Balkans and Turkey. An accelerated arms race resulted: the German standing army rose to over 2 million men by 1914. Russia and France had over a million each, Austria and the British Empire nearly a million each. Dozens of enormous battleships were built by the powers after 1906.

The **assassination of Austrian Archduke Franz Ferdinand** by a Serbian, June 28, 1914, was the pretext for war. The system of alliances made the conflict Europe-wide; Germany's invasion of Belgium to outflank France forced Britain to enter the war. Patriotic fervor was nearly unanimous among all classes in most countries.

World War I. German forces were stopped in France in one month. The rival armies dug **trench networks.** Artillery and improved machine guns prevented either side from any lasting advance despite repeated assaults (600,000 dead at **Verdun,** Feb.-July 1916). Poison gas, used by Germany in 1915, proved ineffective. Over one million U.S. troops tipped the balance after mid-1917, forcing Germany to sue for peace.

In the East, the Russian armies were thrown back (battle of **Tannenberg,** Aug. 20, 1914) and the war grew unpopular. An allied attempt to relieve Russia through Turkey failed (**Gallipoli** 1915). The new Bolshevik regime signed the capitulatory Brest-Litovsk peace in March, 1918. Italy entered the war on the allied side, May 1915, but was pushed back by Oct. 1917. A renewed offensive with Allied aid in Oct.-Nov. 1918 forced Austria to surrender.

The British Navy successfully blockaded Germany, which responded with submarine U-boat attacks; **unrestricted submarine warfare** against neutrals after Jan. 1917 helped bring the U.S. into the war. Other battlefields included Palestine and Mesopotamia, both of which Britain wrested from the Turks in 1917, and the African and Pacific colonies of Germany, most of which fell to Britain, France, Australia, Japan, and South Africa.

From 1916, the civilian population and economy of both sides were mobilized to an unprecedented degree. Over 10 million soldiers died (May 1917 French mutiny crushed).

Settlement. At the **Versailles conference** (Jan.-June 1919) and in subsequent negotiations and local wars (Russian-Polish War 1920), the map of Europe was redrawn with a nod to U.S. Pres. Wilson's principle of self-determination. Austria and Hungary were separated and much of their land was given to Yugoslavia (formerly Serbia), Romania, Italy, and the newly independent Poland and Czechoslovakia. Germany lost territory in the West, North, and East, while Finland and the Baltic states were detached from Russia. Turkey lost nearly all its Arab lands to British-sponsored Arab states or to direct French and British rule.

A huge **reparations** burden and partial demilitarization were imposed on Germany. Wilson obtained approval for a League of Nations, but the U.S. Senate refused to allow the U.S. to join.

Russian revolution. Military defeats and high casualties caused a contagious lack of confidence in Tsar Nicholas, who was forced to abdicate, Mar. 1917. A liberal provisional government failed to end the war, and massive desertions, riots, and fighting between factions followed. A moderate socialist government under Kerensky was overthrown in a violent **coup by the Bolsheviks** in Petrograd under Lenin, who disbanded the elected Constituent Assembly, Nov. 1917.

The Bolsheviks brutally suppressed all opposition and ended the war with Germany, Mar. 1918. **Civil war** broke out in the summer between the Red Army, including the Bolsheviks and their supporters, and monarchists, anarchists, nationalities (Ukrainians, Georgians, Poles) and others. Small U.S., British, French and Japanese units also opposed the Bolsheviks, 1918-19 (Japan in Vladivostok to 1922). The civil war, anarchy, and pogroms devastated the country until the 1920 Red Army victory. The wartime total monopoly of political, economic, and police power by the Communist Party leadership was retained.

Other European revolutions. An unpopular monarchy in **Portugal** was overthrown in 1910. The new republic took severe anti-clerical measures, 1911.

After a century of Home Rule agitation, during which **Ireland** was devastated by famine (one million dead, 1846-47) and emigration, republican militants staged an unsuccessful uprising in Dublin, Easter 1916. The execution of the leaders and mass arrests by the British won popular support for the rebels. The Irish Free State, comprising all but the 6 northern counties, achieved dominion status in 1922.

In the aftermath of the world war, radical revolutions were attempted in Germany (**Spartacist** uprising Jan. 1919), **Hungary** (Kun regime 1919), and elsewhere. All were suppressed or failed for lack of support.

Chinese revolution. The Manchu Dynasty was overthrown and a republic proclaimed, Oct. 1911. First president Sun Yat-sen resigned in favor of strongman Yuan Shih-k'ai. Sun organized the parliamentarian **Kuomintang** party.

Students launched protests May 4, 1919 against League of Nations concessions in China to Japan. Nationalist, liberal, and socialist ideas and political groups spread. The **Communist Party** was founded 1921. A communist regime took power in Mongolia with Soviet support in 1921.

India restive. Indian objections to British rule erupted in nationalist riots as well as in the non-violent tactics of Gandhi (1869-1948). Nearly 400 unarmed demonstrators were shot at **Amritsar,** Apr. 1919. Britain approved limited self-rule that year.

Mexican revolution. Under the long Diaz dictatorship (1876-1911) the economy advanced, but Indian and mestizo lands were confiscated, and concessions to foreigners (mostly U.S.) damaged the middle class. A **revolution in 1910** led to civil wars and U.S. intervention (1914, 1916-17). Land reform and a more democratic constitution (1917) were achieved.

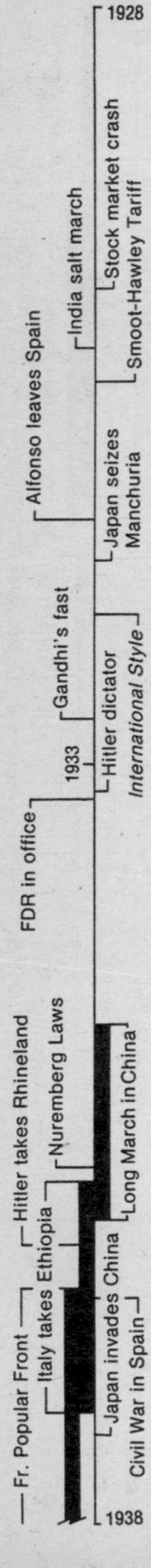

The Aftermath of War: 1920-29

U.S. Easy credit, technological ingenuity, and war-related industrial decline in Europe caused a long economic boom, in which ownership of the new products — autos, phones, radios — became democratized. Prosperity, an increase in women workers, women's suffrage (1920) and drastic change in fashion (flappers, mannish bob for women, clean-shaven men), created a wide perception of social change, despite prohibition of alcoholic beverages (1919-33). Union membership and strikes increased. Fear of radicals led to Palmer raids (1919-20) and Sacco/Vanzetti case (1921-27).

Europe sorts itself out. Germany's liberal **Weimar constitution** (1919) could not guarantee a stable government in the face of rightist violence (Rathenau assassinated 1922) and Communist refusal to cooperate with Socialists. Reparations and allied occupation of the Rhineland caused staggering inflation which destroyed middle class savings, but economic expansion resumed after mid-decade, aided by U.S. loans. A sophisticated, innovative culture developed in architecture and design (Bauhaus, 1919-28), film (Lang, *M,* 1931), painting (Grosz), music (Weill, *Threepenny Opera,* 1928), theater (Brecht, *A Man's a Man,* 1926), criticism (Benjamin), philosophy (Jung), and fashion. This culture was considered decadent and socially disruptive by rightists.

England elected its first labor governments (Jan. 1924, June 1929). A 10-day general strike in support of coal miners failed, May 1926. In **Italy,** strikes, political chaos and violence by small Fascist bands culminated in the Oct. 1922 Fascist March on Rome, which established Mussolini's dictatorship. Strikes were outlawed (1926), and Italian influence was pressed in the Balkans (Albania a protectorate 1926). A conservative dictatorship was also established in **Portugal** in a 1926 military coup.

Czechoslovakia, the only stable democracy to emerge from the war in Central or East Europe, faced opposition from Germans (in the Sudetenland), Ruthenians, and some Slovaks. As the industrial heartland of the old Hapsburg empire, it remained fairly prosperous. With French backing, it formed the Little Entente with Yugoslavia (1920) and **Romania** (1921) to block Austrian or Hungarian irredentism. **Hungary** remained dominated by the landholding classes and expansionist feeling. Croats and Slovenes in **Yugoslavia** demanded a federal state until King Alexander proclaimed a dictatorship (1929). Poland faced nationality problems as well (Germans, Ukrainians, Jews); Pilsudski ruled as dictator from 1926. The Baltic states were threatened by traditionally dominant ethnic Germans and by Soviet-supported communists.

An economic collapse and famine in **Russia,** 1921-22, claimed 5 million lives. The New Economic Policy (1921) allowed land ownership by peasants and some private commerce and industry. Stalin was absolute ruler within 4 years of Lenin's 1924 death. He inaugurated a brutal collectivization program 1929-32, and used foreign communist parties for Soviet state advantage.

Internationalism. Revulsion against World War I led to pacifist agitation, the Kellogg-Briand Pact renouncing aggressive war (1928), and **naval disarmament** pacts (Washington, 1922, London, 1930). But the League of Nations was able to arbitrate only minor disputes (Greece-Bulgaria, 1925).

Middle East. Mustafa Kemal (Ataturk) led **Turkish** nationalists in resisting Italian, French, and Greek military advances, 1919-23. The sultanate was abolished 1922, and elaborate reforms passed, including secularization of law and adoption of the Latin alphabet. Ethnic conflict led to persecution of **Armenians** (over 1 million dead in 1915, 1 million expelled), Greeks (forced Greek-Turk population exchange, 1923), and Kurds (1925 uprising).

With evacuation of the Turks from **Arab** lands, the puritanical Wahabi dynasty of eastern Arabia conquered present Saudi Arabia, 1919-25. British, French, and Arab dynastic and nationalist maneuvering resulted in the creation of two more Arab monarchies in 1921: Iraq and Transjordan (both under British control), and two French mandates: Syria and Lebanon. Jewish immigration into British-mandated **Palestine,** inspired by the Zionist movement, was resisted by Arabs, at times violently (1921, 1929 massacres).

Reza Khan ruled **Persia** after his 1921 coup (shah from 1925), centralized control, and created the trappings of a modern state.

China. The Kuomintang under **Chiang Kai-shek** (1887-1975) subdued the warlords by 1928. The Communists were brutally suppressed after their alliance with the Kuomintang was broken in 1927. Relative peace thereafter allowed for industrial and financial improvements, with some Russian, British, and U.S. cooperation.

Arts. Nearly all bounds of subject matter, style, and attitude were broken in the arts of the period. **Abstract** art first took inspiration from natural forms or narrative themes (Kandinsky from 1911), then worked free of any representational aims (Malevich's suprematism, 1915-19, Mondrian's geometric style from 1917). The **Dada** movement from 1916 mocked artistic pretension with absurd collages and constructions (Arp, Tzara, from 1916). Paradox, illusion, and psychological taboos were exploited by **surrealists** by the latter 1920s (Dali, Magritte). Architectural schools celebrated industrial values, whether vigorous abstract constructivism (Tatlin, *Monument to 3rd International,* 1919) or the machined, streamlined **Bauhaus** style, which was extended to many design fields (Helvetica type face).

Prose writers explored revolutionary narrative modes related to dreams (Kafka's *Trial,* 1925), internal monologue (Joyce's *Ulysses,* 1922), and word play (Stein's *Making of Americans,* 1925). Poets and novelists wrote of modern alienation (Eliot's *Waste Land,* 1922) and aimlessness (Lost Generation).

Sciences. Scientific specialization prevailed by the 20th century. Advances in knowledge and technological aptitude increased with the geometric increase in the number of practitioners. Physicists challenged common-sense views of causality, observation, and a mechanistic universe, putting science further beyond popular grasp (Einstein's general theory of relativity, 1915; Bohr's quantum mechanics, 1913; Heisenberg's uncertainty principle, 1927).

Rise of the Totalitarians: 1930-39

Depression. A worldwide financial panic and economic depression began with the Oct. 1929 U.S. stock market crash and the May 1931 failure of the Austrian Credit-Anstalt. A credit crunch caused international bankruptcies and **unemployment:** 12 million jobless by 1932 in the U.S., 5.6 million in Germany, 2.7 million in England. Governments responded with **tariff restrictions** (Smoot-Hawley Act 1930; Ottawa Imperial Conference, 1932) which dried up world trade. Government public works programs were vitiated by deflationary budget balancing.

Germany. Years of agitation by violent extremists was brought to a head by the Depression. Nazi leader **Hitler** was named chancellor by Pres. Hindenburg Jan. 1933, and given dictatorial power by the Reichstag in Mar. Opposition parties were disbanded, strikes banned, and all aspects of economic, cultural, and religious life brought under central government and Nazi party control and manipulated by sophisticated propaganda. Severe persecution of Jews began (**Nuremberg Laws** Sept. 1935). Many Jews, political opponents and others were sent to concentration camps (Dachau, 1933) where thousands died or were killed. Public works, renewed conscription (1935), arms production, and a 4-year plan (1936) ended unemployment.

Hitler's expansionism started with reincorporation of the Saar (1935), occupation of the **Rhineland** (Mar. 1936), and annexation of Austria (Mar. 1938). At **Munich,** Sept. 1938, an indecisive Britain and France sanctioned German dismemberment of Czechoslovakia.

Russia. Urbanization and education advanced. Rapid industrialization was achieved through successive **5-year-plans** starting 1928, using severe labor discipline and mass forced labor. Industry was financed by a decline in living standards and exploitation of agriculture, which was almost totally collectivized by the early 1930s (*kolkhoz,* collective farm; *sovkhoz,* state farm, often in newly-worked lands). Successive **purges** increased the role of professionals and management at the expense of workers. Millions perished in a series of man-made disasters: elimination of kulaks (peasant land-owners), 1929-34; severe famine, 1932-33; party purges (Great Purge, 1936-38); suppression of nationalities; and poor conditions in labor camps.

Spain. An industrial revolution during World War I created an urban proletariat, which was attracted to socialism and anarchism; Catalan nationalists challenged central authority. The 5 years after King Alfonso left Spain, Apr. 1931, were dominated by tension between intermittent leftist and anti-clerical governments and clericals, monarchists and other rightists. Anarchist and communist rebellions were crushed, but a July, 1936, extreme right rebellion led by Gen. Francisco Franco and aided by Nazi Germany and Fascist Italy succeeded, after a 3-year **civil war** (over 1 million dead in battles and atrocities). The war polarized international public opinion.

Italy. Despite propaganda for the ideal of the Corporate State, few domestic reforms were attempted. An entente with Hungary and Austria, Mar. 1934, a pact with Germany and Japan, Nov. 1937, and intervention by 50-75,000 troops in Spain, 1936-39, sealed Italy's identification with the fascist bloc (anti-Semitic laws after Mar. 1938). Ethiopia was conquered, 1935-37, and **Albania** annexed, Jan. 1939, in conscious imitation of ancient Rome.

East Europe. Repressive regimes fought for power against an active opposition (liberals, socialists, communists, peasants, Nazis). Minority groups and Jews were restricted within national boundaries that did not coincide with ethnic population patterns. In the destruction of **Czechoslovakia, Hungary** occupied southern Slovakia (Nov. 1938) and Ruthenia (Mar. 1939), and a pro-Nazi regime took power in the rest of Slovakia. Other boundary disputes (e.g. Poland-Lithuania, Yugoslavia-Bulgaria, Romania-Hungary) doomed attempts to build joint fronts against Germany or Russia. Economic depression was severe.

East Asia. After a period of liberalism in **Japan,** nativist militarists dominated the government with peasant support. Manchuria was seized, Sept. 1931-Feb. 1932, and a puppet state set up (Manchukuo). Adjacent Jehol (inner Mongolia) was occupied in 1933. China proper was invaded July 1937; large areas were conquered by Oct. 1938.

In **China** Communist forces left Kuomintang-besieged strongholds in the South in a Long March (1934-35) to the North. The Kuomintang-Communist civil war was suspended Jan. 1937 in the face of threatening Japan.

The democracies. The Roosevelt Administration, in office Mar. 1933, embarked on an extensive program of social reform and economic stimulation, including protection for labor unions (heavy industries organized), social security, public works, wages and hours laws, assistance to farmers. Isolationist sentiment (1937 Neutrality Act) prevented U.S. intervention in Europe, but military expenditures were increased in 1939.

French political instability and polarization prevented resolution of economic and international security questions. The **Popular Front** government under Blum (June 1936-Apr. 1938) passed social reforms (40-hour week) and raised arms spending. National coalition governments ruled Britain from Aug. 1931, brought some economic recovery, but failed to define a consistent foreign policy until Chamberlain's government (from May 1937), which practiced deliberate **appeasement** of Germany and Italy.

India. Twenty years of agitation for autonomy and then for independence (Gandhi's **salt march,** 1930) achieved some constitutional reform (extended provincial powers, 1935) despite Moslem-Hindu strife. Social issues assumed prominence with peasant uprisings (1921), strikes (1928), Gandhi's efforts for untouchables (1932 "fast unto death"), and social and agrarian reform by the provinces after 1937.

Arts. The streamlined, geometric design motifs of Art Deco (from 1925) prevailed through the 1930s. Abstract art flourished (Moore sculptures from 1931) alongside a new realism related to social and political concerns (**Socialist Realism** the official Soviet style from 1934; Mexican muralists Rivera, 1886-1957, and Orozco, 1883-1949), which was also expressed in fiction and poetry (Steinbeck's *Grapes of Wrath,* 1939; Sandburg's *The People, Yes,* 1936). Modern architecture (*International Style,* 1932) was unchallenged in its use of man-made materials (concrete, glass), lack of decoration, and monumentality (Rockefeller Center, 1929-40). U.S.-made films captured a world-wide audience with their larger-than-life fantasies (*Gone with the Wind,* 1939).

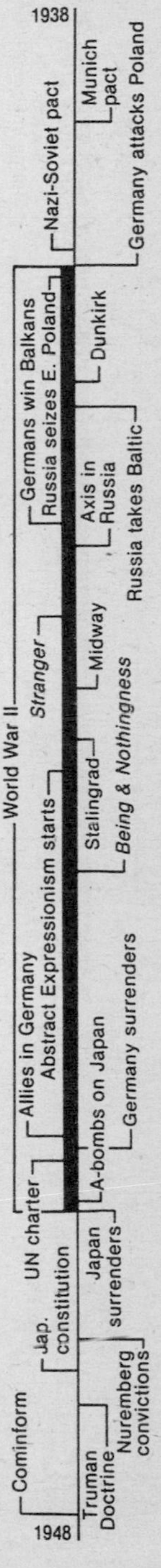

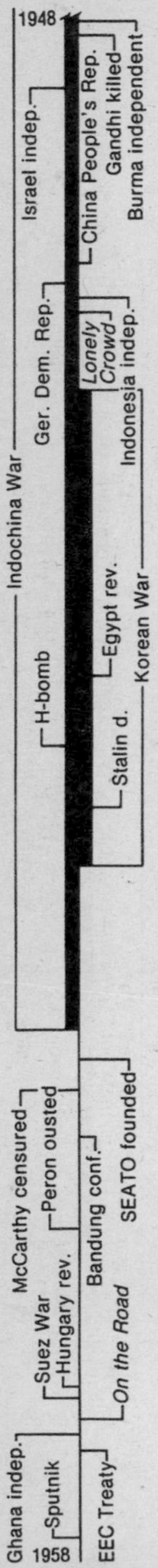

War, Hot and Cold: 1940-49

War in Europe. The Nazi-Soviet non-aggression pact (Aug. '39) freed Germany to attack Poland (Sept.). Britain and France, who had guaranteed Polish independence, declared war on Germany. Russia seized East Poland (Sept.), attacked Finland (Nov.) and took the Baltic states (July '40). Mobile German forces staged **"blitzkrieg"** attacks Apr.-June, '40, conquering neutral Denmark, Norway, and the low countries and defeating France; 350,000 British and French troops were evacuated at **Dunkirk** (May). The Battle of Britain, June-Dec. '40, denied Germany air superiority, German-Italian campaigns won the Balkans by Apr. '41. Three million Axis troops **invaded Russia** June '41, marching through the Ukraine to the Caucasus, and through White Russia and the Baltic republics to Moscow and Leningrad.

Russian winter counterthrusts, '41-'42 and '42-'43 stopped the German advance (Stalingrad Sept. '42-Feb. '43). With British and U.S. Lend-Lease aid and sustaining great casualties, the Russians drove the Axis from all E. Europe and the Balkans in the next 2 years. Invasions of N. Africa (Nov. '42), Italy (Sept. '43), and Normandy (June '44) brought U.S., British, Free French and allied troops to Germany by spring '45. Germany surrendered May 7, 1945.

War in Asia-Pacific. Japan occupied Indochina Sept. '40, dominated Thailand Dec. '41, attacked Hawaii, the Philippines, Hong Kong, Malaya Dec. 7, 1941. Indonesia was attacked Jan. '42, Burma conquered Mar. 42. Battle of **Midway** (June '42) turned back the Japanese advance. "Island-hopping" battles (Guadalcanal Aug. '42-Jan. '43, **Leyte Gulf** Oct. '44, Iwo Jima Feb.-Mar. '45, Okinawa Apr. '45) and massive bombing raids on Japan from June '44 wore out Japanese defenses. Two U.S. atom bombs, dropped Aug. 6 and 9, forced Japan to surrender Aug. 14, 1945.

Atrocities. The war brought 20th-century cruelty to its peak. Nazi murder camps (Auschwitz) systematically killed 6 million Jews. Gypsies, political opponents, sick and retarded people, and others deemed undesirable were murdered by the Nazis, as were vast numbers of Slavs, especially leaders.

Civilian deaths. German bombs killed 70,000 English civilians. Some 100,000 Chinese civilians were killed by Japanese forces in the capture of Nanking. Severe retaliation by the Soviet army, E. European partisans, Free French and others took a heavy toll. U.S. and British bombing of Germany killed hundreds of thousands, as did U.S. bombing of Japan (80-200,000 at Hiroshima alone). Some 45 million people lost their lives in the war.

Settlement. The United Nations charter was signed in San Francisco June 26, 1945 by 50 nations. The International Tribunal at Nuremberg convicted 22 German leaders for war crimes Sept. '46, 23 Japanese leaders were convicted Nov. '48. Postwar border changes included large gains in territory for the USSR, losses for Germany, a shift westward in Polish borders, and minor losses for Italy. Communist regimes, supported by Soviet troops, took power in most of E. Europe, including Soviet-occupied Germany (GDR proclaimed Oct. '49). Japan lost all overseas lands.

Recovery. Basic political and social changes were imposed on Japan and W. Germany by the western allies (Japan constitution Nov. '46, W. German basic law May '49). U.S. Marshall Plan aid ($12 billion '47-'51) spurred W. European economic recovery after a period of severe inflation and strikes in Europe and the U.S. The British Labour Party introduced a national health service and nationalized basic industries in 1946.

Cold War. Western fears of further Soviet advances (Cominform formed Oct. '47, Czechoslovakia coup, Feb. '48, Berlin blockade Apr.'48-Sept. '49) led to formation of NATO. Civil War in Greece and Soviet pressure on Turkey led to U.S. aid under the Truman Doctrine (Mar. '47). Other anti-communist security pacts were the Org. of American States (Apr. '48) and Southeast Asia Treaty Org. (Sept. '54). A new wave of Soviet purges and repression intensified in the last years of Stalin's rule, extending to E. Europe (Slansky trial in Czechoslovakia, 1951). Only Yugoslavia resisted Soviet control (expelled by Cominform, June '48; U.S. aid, June '49).

China, Korea. Communist forces emerged from World War II strengthened by the Soviet takeover of industrial Manchuria. In 4 years of fighting, the Kuomintang was driven from the mainland; the People's Republic was proclaimed Oct. 1, 1949. Korea was divided by Russian and U.S. occupation forces. Separate republics were proclaimed in the 2 zones Aug.-Sept. '48.

India. India and Pakistan became independent dominions Aug. 15, 1947. Millions of Hindu and Moslem refugees were created by the partition; riots, 1946-47, took hundreds of thousands of lives; Gandhi himself was assassinated Jan. '48. Burma became completely independent Jan. '48; Ceylon took dominion status in Feb.

Middle East. The UN approved partition of Palestine into Jewish and Arab states. Israel was proclaimed May 14, 1948. Arabs rejected partition, but failed to defeat Israel in war, May '48-July '49. Immigration from Europe and the Middle East swelled Israel's Jewish population. British and French forces left Lebanon and Syria, 1946. Transjordan occupied most of Arab Palestine.

Southeast Asia. Communists and others fought against restoration of French rule in Indochina from 1946; a non-communist government was recognized by France Mar. '49, but fighting continued. Both Indonesia and the Philippines became independent, the former in 1949 after 4 years of war with Netherlands, the latter in 1946. Philippine economic and military ties with the U.S. remained strong; a communist-led peasant rising was checked in '48.

Arts. New York became the center of the world art market; abstract expressionism was the chief mode (Pollock from '43, de Kooning from '47). Literature and philosophy explored existentialism (Camus' *Stranger*, 1942, Sartre's *Being and Nothingness*, 1943). Non-western attempts to revive or create regional styles (Senghor's Negritude, Mishima's novels) only confirmed the emergence of a universal culture. Radio and phonograph records spread American popular music (swing, bebop) around the world.

The American Decade: 1950-59

Polite decolonization. The peaceful decline of European political and military power in Asia and Africa accelerated in the 1950s. Nearly all of **N. Africa** was freed by 1956, but France fought a bitter war to retain Algeria, with its large European minority, until 1962. **Ghana,** independent 1957, led a parade of new black African nations (over 2 dozen by 1962) which altered the political character of the UN. Ethnic disputes often exploded in the new nations after decolonization (UN troops in Cyprus 1964; **Nigeria** civil war 1967-70). Leaders of the new states, mostly sharing socialist ideologies, tried to create an Afro-Asian bloc (Bandung Conf. 1955), but Western economic influence and U.S. political ties remained strong (Baghdad Pact, 1955).

Trade. World trade volume soared, in an atmosphere of monetary stability assured by international accords (**Bretton Woods** 1944). In Europe, economic integration advanced (**European Economic Community** 1957, European Free Trade Association 1960). Comecon (1949) coordinated the economies of Soviet-bloc countries.

U.S. Economic growth produced an abundance of consumer goods (9.3 million motor vehicles sold, 1955). Suburban housing tracts changed life patterns for middle and working classes (Levittown 1946-51). **Eisenhower's** landslide election victories (1952, 1956) reflected consensus politics. Censure of McCarthy (Dec. '54) curbed the political abuse of anti-communism. A system of alliances and military bases bolstered U.S. influence on all continents. Trade and payments surpluses were balanced by overseas investments and foreign aid ($50 billion, 1950-59).

USSR. In the "thaw" after Stalin's death in 1953, relations with the West improved (evacuation of Vienna, Geneva summit conf., both 1955). Repression of scientific and cultural life eased, and many prisoners were freed or rehabilitated culminating in **de-Stalinization** (1956). Khrushchev's leadership aimed at consumer sector growth, but farm production lagged, despite the virgin lands program (from 1954). The 1956 Hungarian revolution, the 1960 U-2 spy plane episode, and other incidents renewed East-West tension and domestic curbs.

East Europe. Resentment of Russian domination and Stalinist repression combined with nationalist, economic and religious factors to produce periodic violence. East Berlin workers rioted in 1953, Polish workers rioted in Poznan, June 1956, and a broad-based revolution broke out in Hungary, Oct. 1956. All were suppressed by Soviet force or threats (at least 7,000 dead in Hungary). But Poland was allowed to restore private ownership of farms, and a degree of personal and economic freedom returned to Hungary. Yugoslavia experimented with worker self-management and a market economy.

Korea. The 1945 division of Korea left industry in the North, which was organized into a militant regime and armed by Russia. The South was politically disunited. Over 60,000 North Korean troops invaded the South June 25, 1950. The U.S., backed by the UN Security Council, sent troops. UN troops reached the Chinese border in Nov. Some 200,000 Chinese troops crossed the Yalu River and drove back UN forces. Cease-fire in July 1951 found the opposing forces near the original 38th parallel border. After 2 years of sporadic fighting, an armistice was signed July 27, 1953. U.S. troops remained in the South, and U.S. economic and military aid continued. The war stimulated rapid economic recovery in Japan.

China. Starting in 1952, industry, agriculture, and social institutions were forcibly collectivized. As many as several million people were executed as Kuomintang supporters or as class and political enemies. The Great Leap Forward, 1958-60, unsuccessfully tried to force the pace of development by substituting labor for investment.

Indochina. Ho's forces, aided by Russia and the new Chinese Communist government, fought French and pro-French Vietnamese forces to a standstill, and captured the strategic Dienbienphu camp in May, 1954. The Geneva Agreements divided Vietnam in half pending elections (never held), and recognized Laos and Cambodia as independent. The U.S. aided the anti-Communist Republic of Vietnam in the South.

Middle East. Arab revolutions placed leftist, militantly nationalist regimes in power in Egypt (1952) and Iraq (1958). But Arab unity attempts failed (United Arab Republic joined Egypt, Syria, Yemen 1958-61). Arab refusal to recognize Israel (Arab League economic blockade began Sept. 1951) led to a permanent state of war, with repeated incidents (Gaza, 1955). Israel occupied Sinai, Britain and France took the Suez Canal, Oct. 1956, but were replaced by the UN Emergency Force. The Mossadegh government in Iran nationalized the British-owned oil industry May 1951, but was overthrown in a U.S.-aided coup Aug. 1953.

Latin America. Dictator Juan Peron, in office 1946, enforced land reform, some nationalization, welfare state measures, and curbs on the Roman Catholic Church, but crushed opposition. A Sept. 1955 coup deposed Peron. The 1952 revolution in Bolivia brought land reform, nationalization of tin mines, and improvement in the status of Indians, who nevertheless remained poor. The Batista regime in Cuba was overthrown, Jan. 1959, by Fidel Castro, who imposed a communist dictatorship, aligned Cuba with Russia, improved education and health care. A U.S.-backed anti-Castro invasion (Bay of Pigs, Apr. 1961) was crushed. Self-government advanced in the British Caribbean.

Technology. Large outlays on research and development in the U.S. and USSR focused on military applications (H-bomb in U.S. 1952, USSR 1953, Britain 1957, intercontinental missiles late 1950s). Soviet launching of the Sputnik satellite, Oct. 1957, spurred increases in U.S. science education funds (National Defense Education Act).

Literature and letters. Alienation from social and literary conventions reached an extreme in the theater of the absurd (Beckett's *Waiting for Godot* 1952), the "new novel" (Robbe-Grillet's *Voyeur* 1955), and avant-garde film (Antonioni's *L'Avventura* 1960). U.S. Beatniks (Kerouac's *On the Road* 1957) and others rejected the supposed conformism of Americans (Riesman's *Lonely Crowd* 1950).

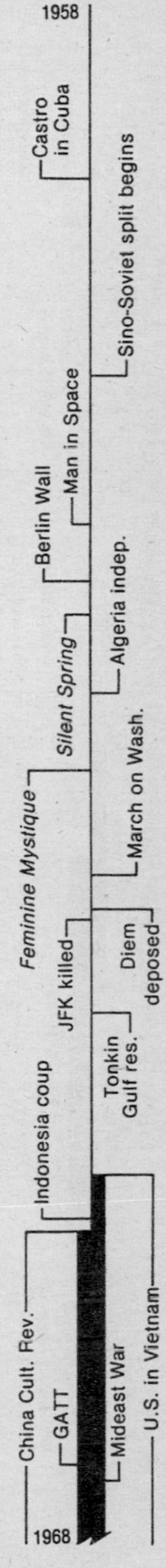

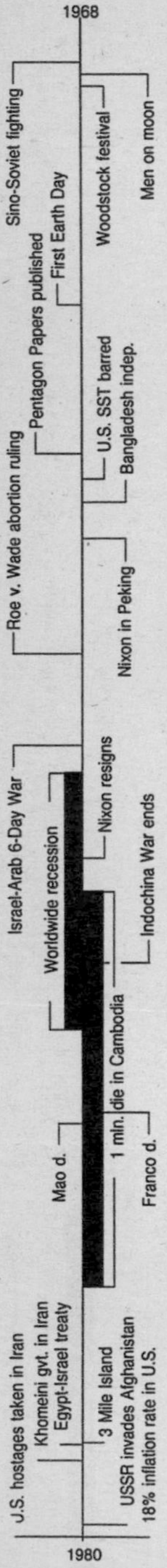

Rising Expectations: 1960-69

Economic boom. The longest sustained economic boom on record spanned almost the entire decade in the capitalist world; the closely-watched GNP figure doubled in the U.S. 1960-70, fueled by Vietnam War-related budget deficits. The **General Agreement on Tariffs and Trade,** 1967, stimulated West European prosperity, which spread to peripheral areas (Spain, Italy, E. Germany). Japan became a top economic power ($20 billion exports 1970). Foreign investment aided the industrialization of Brazil. Soviet 1965 economic reform attempts (decentralization, material incentives) were limited; but growth continued.

Reform and radicalization. Pres. John F. Kennedy, inaugurated 1961, emphasized youthful idealism, vigor; he was assassinated Nov. 22, 1963. A series of political and social reform movements took root in the U.S., later spreading to other countries with the help of ubiquitous U.S. film and television programs and heavy overseas travel (2.2 million U.S. passports issued 1970). Blacks agitated peaceably and with partial success against segregation and poverty (1963 March on Washington, 1964 **Civil Rights Act**); but some urban ghettos erupted in extensive riots (Watts, 1965; Detroit, 1967; King assassination, Apr. 4, 1968). New concern for the poor (Harrington's *Other America,* 1963) led to Pres. Johnson's **"Great Society"** programs (Medicare, Water Quality Act, Higher Education Act, all 1965). Concern with the **environment** surged (Carson's *Silent Spring,* 1962). **Feminism** revived as a cultural and political movement (Friedan's *Feminine Mystique,* 1963, National Organization for Women founded 1966) and a movement for homosexual rights emerged (Stonewall riot, in NYC, 1969). Pope John XXIII called Vatican II, 1962-65, which liberalized Roman Catholic liturgy.

Opposition to U.S. involvement in Vietnam, especially among university students (**Moratorium** protest Nov. '69) turned violent (Weatherman Chicago riots Oct. '69). New Left and Marxist theories became popular, and membership in radical groups swelled (Students for a Democratic Society, Black Panthers). Maoist groups, especially in Europe, called for total transformation of society. In France, students sparked a nationwide strike affecting 10 million workers May-June '68, but an electoral reaction barred revolutionary change.

Arts and styles. The boundary between fine and popular arts were blurred by Pop Art (Warhol) and rock musicals (Hair, 1968). Informality and exaggeration prevailed in fashion (beards, miniskirts). A non-political "counterculture" developed, rejecting traditional bourgeois life goals and personal habits, and use of marijuana and hallucinogens spread (Woodstock festival Aug. '69). Indian influence was felt in music (Beatles), religion (Ram Dass), and fashion.

Science. Achievements in space (men on moon July '69) and electronics (lasers, integrated circuits) encouraged a faith in scientific solutions to problems in agriculture ("green revolution"), medicine (heart transplants 1967) and other areas. The harmful effects of science, it was believed, could be controlled (1963 nuclear weapon test ban treaty, 1968 non-proliferation treaty).

China. Mao's revolutionary militance caused disputes with Russia under "revisionist" Khrushchev, starting 1960. The two powers exchanged fire in 1969 border disputes. China used force to capture areas disputed with India 1962. The "Great Proletarian Cultural Revolution" tried to impose a utopian egalitarian program in China and spread revolution abroad; political struggle, often violent, convulsed China 1965-68.

Indochina. Communist-led guerrillas aided by N. Vietnam fought from 1960 against the S. Vietnam government of Ngo Dinh Diem (killed 1963). The U.S. military role increased after the 1964 Tonkin Gulf incident. U.S. forces peaked at 543,400, Apr. '69. Massive numbers of N. Viet troops also fought. Laotian and Cambodian neutrality were threatened by communist insurgencies, with N. Vietnamese aid, and U.S. intrigues.

Third World. A bloc of authoritarian leftist regimes among the newly independent nations emerged in political opposition to the U.S.-led Western alliance, and came to dominate the conference of nonaligned nations (Belgrade 1961, Cairo 1964, Lusaka 1970). Soviet political ties and military bases were established in Cuba, Egypt, Algeria, Guinea, and other countries, whose leaders were regarded as revolutionary heros by opposition groups in pro-Western or colonial countries. Some leaders were ousted in coups by pro-Western groups—Zaire's Lumumba (killed 1961), Ghana's Nkrumah (exiled 1966), and Indonesia's Sukarno (effectively ousted 1965 after a Communist coup failed).

Middle East. Arab-Israeli tension erupted into a brief war June 1967. Israel emerged as a major regional power. Military shipments before and after the war brought much of the Arab world into the Soviet political sphere. Most Arab states broke U.S. diplomatic ties, while Communist countries cut their ties to Israel. Intra-Arab disputes continued: Egypt and Saudi Arabia supported rival factions in a bloody Yemen civil war 1962-70; Lebanese troops fought Palestinian commandos 1969.

East Europe. To stop the large-scale exodus of citizens, E. German authorities built a fortified wall across Berlin Aug. '61. Soviet sway in the Balkans was weakened by Albania's support of China (USSR broke ties Dec. '61) and Romania's assertion of industrial and foreign policy autonomy 1964. Liberalization in Czechoslovakia, spring 1968, was crushed by troops of 5 Warsaw Pact countries. West German treaties with Russia and Poland, 1970, facilitated the transfer of German technology and confirmed post-war boundaries.

Disillusionment: 1970-79

U.S.: Caution and neoconservatism. A relatively sluggish economy, energy and resource shortages (natural gas crunch 1975, gasoline shortage 1979) and environmental problems contributed to a **"limits of growth"** philosophy. Suspicion of science and technology killed or delayed major projects (supersonic transport dropped 1971, DNA recombination curbed 1976, Seabrook A-plant protests 1977-78) and was fed by the Three Mile Island nuclear reactor accident Mar. '79.

Mistrust of big government weakened support for government reform plans among liberals. School busing and racial quotas were opposed (**Bakke decision** June '78); the Equal Rights Amendment for women languished; civil rights for homosexuals were opposed (Dade County referendum June '77).

Completion of communist forces' takeover of **S. Vietnam** (evacuation of U.S. civilians Apr. '75), revelations of Central Intelligence Agency misdeeds (Rockefeller Commission report June '75), and **Watergate** scandals (Nixon quit Aug. '74) reduced faith in U.S. moral and material capacity to influence world affairs. Revelations of Soviet crimes (Solzhenitsyn's *Gulag Archipelago* from 1974) and Russian intervention in Africa aided a revival of anti-Communist sentiment.

Economy sluggish. The 1960s boom faltered in the 1970s; a severe recession in the U.S. and Europe 1974-75 followed a huge oil price hike Dec. '73. Monetary instability (U.S. cut ties to gold Aug. '71), the decline of the dollar, and **protectionist** moves by industrial countries (1977-78) threatened trade. Business investment and spending for research declined. Severe inflation plagued many countries (25% in Britain 1975; 18% in U.S. 1979).

China picks up pieces. After the 1976 deaths of Mao and Zhou, a power struggle for the leadership succession was won by pragmatists. A nationwide purge of orthodox Maoists was carried out and the **"Gang of Four"** led by Mao's widow Chiang Ching was arrested.

The new leaders freed over 100,000 political prisoners, and reduced public adulation of Mao. Political and trade ties were expanded with Japan, Europe, and U.S. in the late 1970's, as relations worsened with Russia, Cuba, and Vietnam (4-week invasion by China 1979). Ideological guidelines in industry, science, education, and the armed forces, which the ruling faction said had caused chaos and decline, were reversed (bonuses to workers Dec. '77; exams for college entrance Oct. '77). Severe restrictions on cultural expression were eased (Beethoven ban lifted Mar. '77).

Europe. European unity moves (EEC-EFTA trade accord 1972) faltered as economic problems appeared (Britain floated pound 1972; France floated franc 1974). Germany and Switzerland curbed guest workers from S. Europe. Greece and Turkey quarreled over Cyprus (Turks intervened 1974), Aegean oil rights.

All non-Communist Europe was under democratic rule after free elections were held in **Spain** June '76, 7 months after the death of Franco. The conservative, colonialist regime in **Portugal** was overthrown Apr. '74. In **Greece**, the 7-year-old military dictatorship yielded power in 1974. Northern Europe, though ruled mostly by Socialists (**Swedish** Socialists unseated 1976, after 44 years in power), turned conservative. The **British** Labour government imposed wage curbs 1975, and suspended nationalization schemes. Terrorism in **Germany** (1972 Munich Olympics killings) led to laws curbing some civil liberties. **French** "new philosophers" rejected leftist ideologies and the shaky Socialist-Communist coalition lost a 1978 election bid.

Religion back in politics. The improvement in Moslem countries' political fortunes by the 1950s (with the exception of Central Asia under Soviet and Chinese rule) and the growth of Arab oil wealth, was followed by a resurgence of traditional piety. **Libyan** dictator Qaddafy mixed strict Islamic laws with socialism in his militant ideology, called for an eventual Moslem return to Spain and Sicily. The illegal Moslem Brotherhood in **Egypt** was accused of violence, while extreme Moslem groups bombed theaters, 1977, to protest secular values.

In **Turkey**, the National Salvation Party was the first Islamic group to share power (1974) since secularization in the 1920s. Religious authorities, such as Ayatollah Ruhollah Khomeini, led the **Iranian** revolution and religiously motivated Moslems took part in the insurrection in Saudi Arabia that briefly seized the Grand Mosque in Mecca 1979. Moslem puritan opposition to **Pakistan** Pres. Bhutto helped lead to his overthrow July '77. However, Moslem solidarity could not prevent Pakistan's eastern province (**Bangladesh**) from declaring independence, Dec. '71, after a bloody civil war.

Moslem and Hindu resentment against coerced sterilization in **India** helped defeat the Gandhi government, which was replaced Mar. '77 by a coalition including religious Hindu parties and led by devout Hindu Desai. Moslems in the southern **Philippines,** aided by Libya, conducted a long rebellion against central rule from 1973.

Evangelical Protestant groups grew in numbers and prosperity in the U.S. A revival of interest in Orthodox Christianity occurred among **Russian** intellectuals (Solzhenitsyn). The secularist **Israeli** Labor party, after decades of rule, was ousted in 1977 by conservatives led by Begin, an observant Jew; religious militants founded settlements on the disputed West Bank, part of Biblically-promised Israel. U.S. Reform Judaism revived many previously discarded traditional practices.

The Buddhist Soka Gakkai movement launched the Komeito party in Japan 1964, which became a major opposition party in 1972 and 1976 elections.

Old-fashioned religious wars raged intermittently in **N. Ireland** (Catholic vs. Protestant 1969-) and **Lebanon** (Christian vs. Moslem 1975-) while religious militancy complicated the Israel-Arab dispute (1973 Israel-Arab war). In spite of a **1979 peace treaty between Egypt and Israel** which looked forward to a resolution of the Palestinian issue, increased religious militancy on the West Bank made a resolution unlikely.

Latin America. Repressive conservative regimes strengthened their hold on most of the continent, with the violent coup against the elected Allende government in **Chile,** Sept. '73, the 1976 military coup in **Argentina,** and coups against reformist regimes in **Bolivia,** 1971 and 1979, and **Peru,** 1976. In Central America, increasing liberal and leftist militancy led to the ouster of the Somoza regime of Nicaragua in 1979 and civil conflict in El Salvador.

Indochina. Communist victory in Vietnam, Cambodia, and Laos by May '75 did not bring peace. Attempts at radical social reorganization left over one million dead in Cambodia 1975-78 and caused hundreds of thousands of ethnic Chinese and others to flee Vietnam ("boat people" 1979). The Vietnamese invasion of Cambodia swelled the refugee population and contributed to widespread starvation in that devastated country.

Russian expansion. Soviet influence, checked in some countries (troops ousted by Egypt 1972) was projected further afield, often with the use of Cuban troops (Angola 1975-89, Ethiopia 1977-88) and aided by a growing navy, merchant fleet, and international banking ability. Detente with the West — 1972 Berlin pact, 1972 strategic arms pact (**SALT**) — gave way to a more antagonistic relationship in the late 1970s, exacerbated by the Soviet invasion of Afghanistan 1979.

Africa. The last remaining European colonies were granted independence (**Spanish Sahara** 1976, **Djibouti** 1977) and, after 10 years of civil war and many negotiation sessions, a black government took over Zimbabwe (Rhodesia) 1979; white domination remained in **S. Africa.** Great power involvement in local wars (Russia in **Angola, Ethiopia;** France in **Chad, Zaire, Mauritania**) and the use of tens of thousands of Cuban troops was denounced by some African leaders as neocolonialism. Ethnic or tribal clashes made Africa the chief world locus of sustained warfare in the late 1970s.

Arts. Traditional modes in painting, architecture, and music, pursued in relative obscurity for much of the 20th century, returned to popular and critical attention in the 1970s. The pictorial emphasis in neorealist and photorealist painting, the return of many architects to detail, decoration, and traditional natural materials, and the concern with ordered structure in musical composition were, ironically, novel experiences for artistic consumers after the exhaustion of experimental possibilities. However, these more conservative styles coexisted with modernist works in an atmosphere of variety and tolerance.

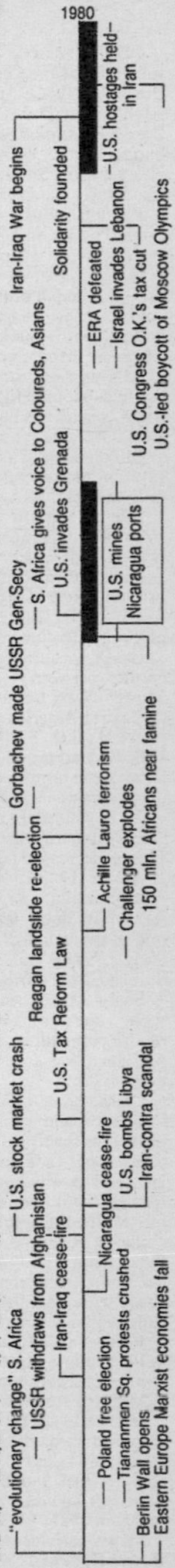

Revitalization of Capitalism, Demand for Democracy: 1980-89

USSR, Eastern Europe. A troublesome 1980-85 for the USSR was followed by 5 years of astonishing change: the **surrender of the Communist monopoly, remaking of the Soviet state, and disintegration of the Soviet empire.** After deaths of Brezhnev 1982, Andropov 1984, Chernenko 1985; harsh treatment of dissent; restriction of emigration; invasion of Afghanistan Dec.'79; Gen. Secy. **Mikhail Gorbachev** (1985-) promoted **glasnost, perestroika,** economic and social reform (Jan.'87), supported by Communist Party (July '88); signed **INF treaty** (Dec.'87). Gorbachev pledged to cut the military budget (1988); military withdrawal from Afghanistan was completed Feb.'89; democratization was not hindered in Poland, Hungary; the Soviet people chose part of the new Congress from competing candidates Mar.'89. At decade's end, Gorbachev was widely considered responsible for the **1989 ending of the Cold War.**

Poland. Solidarity, the labor union founded 1980 by **Lech Walesa,** outlawed 1982, was legalized 1988, after years of unrest. Poland's first free election since the Communist takeover brought Solidarity victory (June '89); Tadeusz Mazowiecki, a Walesa advisor, became Prime Minister in a government with the Communists (Aug.'89).

In the fall of 1989 the failure of Marxist economies in **Hungary, E. Germany, Czechoslovakia, Bulgaria, and Romania** brought the fall of the Communist monopoly, the demand for democracy. The **Berlin Wall** was opened Nov.'89.

U.S. "The Reagan Years" (1981-88) brought the **longest economic boom** in U.S. history via budget and tax cuts, deregulation, "junk bond" financing, leveraged buyouts, mergers and takeovers; a **strong anti-Communist stance,** via increased defense spending, aid to anti-communists in Central America, invasion of Cuba-threatened Grenada, championing of MX missile system and "Star Wars." Four Reagan-Gorbachev summits, 1985-88, climaxed in INF treaty 1987. Financial scandals mounted (E.F. Hutton 1985, Ivan Boesky 1986), the stock market crashed Oct.'87, the trade imbalance grew (esp. with Japan), the budget deficit soared ($3.2 trillion 1988); homelessness, drug abuse (esp. "crack") grew. The Iran-contra affair (North TV testimony July'87) was the low point, but V.P. Bush was elected pres. 1988.

Middle East. This area remained militarily unstable, with sharp divisions on economic, political, racial, and religious lines. In **Iran,** the revolution (1979-80) and violent political upheavals after, brought strong anti-U.S. stance. A dispute with **Iraq** over the Shatt al-Arab waterway became warfare Sept.'80-July'88, with millions killed.

Libya's support for international terrorism caused the U.S. to close the diplomatic mission (May'81), embargo oil (Mar.'82); U.S. accused Muammar al-Qadaffy of aiding terrorists in Dec.'85 Rome, Vienna airport attacks, retaliated by bombing Libya Apr.'86.

Israel affirmed all Jerusalem as its capital (July'80); destroyed an Iraqi atomic reactor 1981; invaded Lebanon 1982, bringing the PLO to agree to withdraw. A **Palestinian uprising,** inc. women, children hurling rocks, bottles at troops, began Dec.'87 in Israeli-occupied Gaza, spread to the West Bank; troops responded with force, killing 300 by 1988's end, with 6,000 more in detention camps.

Israeli withdrawal from **Lebanon** began Feb.'85, ended June'85, as Lebanon continued torn with military and political conflict between rival factions. Premier Karami was assassinated June'87. Artillery duels between Christian East Beirut and Moslem West Beirut, Mar.-Apr.'89, left 200 dead, 700 wounded. At 80s end, violence still dominated.

Central America. In **Nicaragua,** the leftist Sandinista National Liberation Front, in power after the 1979 civil war, faced problems due to Nicaragua's military aid to leftist guerrillas in El Salvador, U.S. backing of anti-government contras. The U.S. CIA admitted directing the mining of Nicaraguan ports 1984; U.S. sent aid, humanitarian 1985, military 1986. Profits from secret arms sales to Iran were found diverted to contras 1987. Cease-fire talks between Sandinista government and contras came in 1988, elections in Feb.'90.

In **El Salvador,** a military coup (Oct.'79) failed to halt extreme right-wing violence and left-wing activity. Archbishop Oscar Romero was assassinated Mar.'80; Jan.-June some 4,000 civilians reportedly were killed. In 1984, newly-elected Pres. Duarte decreased rights abuses. Leftist guerrillas continued their offensive 1989.

Africa. 1980-85 marked the rapid decline of the economies of virtually all Africa's 61 countries, due to accelerating desertification, the world economic recession, heavy indebtedness to overseas creditors, rapid population growth, political instability. Some 60 million Africans, almost one-fifth of the population, faced prolonged hunger 1981; much of Africa had one of the worst droughts ever 1983, and by year's end **150 million faced near-famine.** "Live Aid" marathon rock concert (July'85), U.S. and Western nations sent aid Sept.'85. Economic hardship fueled political unrest, coups. Wars in Ethiopia, Sudan, military strife in 6 other nations continued through 1989. AIDS took a heavy toll.

South Africa. Anti-apartheid sentiment gathered force, demonstrations and violent police response grew. South African white voters approved (Nov.'83) the first constitution to give "Coloureds" Asians a voice, while still excluding blacks—70% of the population. The U.S. imposed economic sanctions Aug.'85, 11 Western nations followed in Sept. **P.W. Botha,** 80s president, was succeeded by **F.W. deClerk,** Sept.'89, on a platform of "evolutionary" change via negotiation with the black population.

China. From 1980 through mid-1989 the Communist Party, under **Chairman Deng Xiaoping,** pursued **far-reaching changes** in political and economic institutions, expanding commercial and technical ties to the industrialized world, increasing the role of market forces in stimulating urban economic development. But Apr.'89, brought the demand for more changes: students camped out in Tiananmen Sq., Beijing; some 100,000 students and workers marched, at least 20 other cities saw protests. Martial law was imposed; Army troops crushed protests in Tiananmen Sq., June 3-4 with death toll estimates 500-7,000, up to 10,000 injured, up to 10,000 dissidents arrested, 31 tried and executed. The conciliatory Communist Party chief was ousted; the Politburo adopted reforms against official corruption (July).

Japan. Relations with other nations, esp. U.S., 1980-89, were dominated by **trade imbalances favoring Japan.** In 1985 the U.S. trade deficit with Japan was $49.7 billion, one-third of the total U.S. trade deficit. After Japan was found to sell semiconductors, computer memory chips below cost (Apr.'86), the U.S. was assured a "fair share" of the market, but charged Japan with failing to live up to the agreement Mar.'87. The **Omnibus Trade Bill,** Aug.'88, provided for retaliation; Pres. Bush called Japan's practices "unjustifiable," the law gave Japan 18 months to stop or face trade restrictions.

European Community. With the addition of Greece, Portugal, and Spain, the EC became a **common market of over 300 million people,** the West's largest trading entity. **Margaret Thatcher** became the first British prime minister in this century to win 3 consecutive terms 1987. France elected its first socialist president, **Francois Mitterand** 1981, re-elected 1988. Italy elected its first socialist premier, **Bettino Craxi** 1983.

International Terrorism. With the 1979 overthrow of the Shah of Iran, terrorism became a prominent political tactic that increased through the 80s, but with fewer "spectacular" attacks after 1985. Iranian militants held 52 Americans hostage in Iran for 444 days, 1979-81; a TNT-laden suicide terrorist blew up U.S. Marine headquarters in Beirut, killing 241 Americans, while a truck bomb blew up a French paratroop barracks, killing 58, 1984; the *Achille Lauro* was hijacked, an American passenger killed, and the U.S. subsequently intercepted the Egyptian plane flying the terrorists to safety 1985. Incidents rose to 700 in 1985, 1,000+ in 1988. The Pentagon reported 52 terrorist groups Jan.'89.

Assassinations included Egypt's Pres. **Anwar el-Sadat** 1981; India's Prime Minister **Indira Gandhi** 1984; Lebanese Premier **Rashid Karami** 1987; Pakistan's Pres. **Mohammed Zia-ul Haz** 1988.

UNITED STATES HISTORY

1492

Christopher Columbus and crew sighted land **Oct. 12** in the present-day Bahamas.

1497

John Cabot explored northeast coast to Delaware.

1513

Juan Ponce de Leon explored Florida coast.

1524

Giovanni da Verrazano led French expedition along coast from Carolina north to Nova Scotia; entered New York harbor.

1539

Hernando de Soto landed in Florida **May 28**; crossed Mississippi River, **1541.**

1540

Francisco Vazquez de Coronado explored Southwest north of Rio Grande. Hernando de Alarcon reached Colorado River, Don Garcia Lopez de Cardenas reached Grand Canyon. Others explored California coast.

1565

St. Augustine, Fla. founded by Pedro Menendez. Razed by Francis Drake **1586.**

1579

Francis Drake claimed California for Britain. Metal plate, found **1936,** thought to be left by Drake, termed probable hoax **1979.**

1607

Capt. John Smith and 105 cavaliers in 3 ships landed on Virginia coast, started first permanent English settlement in New World at **Jamestown** in May.

1609

Henry Hudson, English explorer of Northwest Passage, employed by Dutch, sailed into New York harbor in **Sept.,** and up Hudson to Albany. The same year, **Samuel de Champlain** explored Lake Champlain just to the north.

Spaniards settled **Santa Fe, N.M.**

1619

House of Burgesses, first representative assembly in New World, elected **July 30** at Jamestown, Va.

First black laborers — indentured servants — in English N. American colonies, landed by Dutch at Jamestown in **Aug.** Chattel slavery legally recognized, **1650.**

1620

Plymouth Pilgrims, Puritan separatists from Church of England, some living in Holland, left Plymouth, England **Sept. 16** on Mayflower. Original destination Virginia, they reached Cape Cod **Nov. 19,** explored coast; 103 passengers landed **Dec. 26** at Plymouth. Mayflower Compact was agreement to form a government and abide by its laws. Half of colony died during harsh winter.

1624

Dutch left 8 men from ship New Netherland on **Manhattan Island** in **May.** Rest sailed to Albany.

1626

Peter Minuit bought Manhattan for Dutch from Man-a-hat-a Indians **May 6** for trinkets valued at $24.

1634

Maryland founded as Catholic colony with religious tolerance.

1636

Roger Williams founded Providence, R.I., **June,** as a democratically ruled colony with separation of church and state. Charter was granted, **1644.**

Harvard College founded **Oct. 28,** now oldest in U.S.; Grammar school, compulsory education established at Boston.

1654

First Jews arrived in New Amsterdam.

1660

British Parliament passed **Navigation Act,** regulating colonial commerce to suit English needs.

1664

Three hundred **British troops Sept. 8 seized New Netherland** from Dutch, who yield peacefully. Charles II granted province of New Netherland and city of New Amsterdam to brother, Duke of York; both renamed New York. The Dutch recaptured the colony **Aug. 9, 1673,** but ceded it to Britain **Nov. 10, 1674.**

1676

Nathaniel Bacon led planters against autocratic British Gov. Berkeley, burned Jamestown, Va. Bacon died, 23 followers executed.

Bloody **Indian war** in New England ended **Aug. 12.** King Philip, Wampanoag chief, and many Narragansett Indians killed.

1682

Robert Cavelier, Sieur de La Salle, claimed lower Mississippi River country for France, called it Louisiana **Apr. 9.** Had French outposts built in Illinois and Texas, **1684.** Killed during mutiny **Mar. 19, 1687.**

1683

William Penn signed treaty with Delaware Indians and made payment for Pennsylvania lands.

1692

Witchcraft delusion at Salem (now Danvers) Mass. inspired by preaching; 19 persons executed.

1696

Capt. William Kidd, who was born in Scotland and settled in America, was hired by British to fight pirates and take booty, but himself became a pirate. Arrested and sent to England, he was hanged **1701.**

1699

French settlements made in Mississippi, Louisiana.

1704

Indians attacked Deerfield, Mass. **Feb. 28-29,** killed 40, carried off 100.

Boston News Letter, first regular newspaper, started by John Campbell, postmaster. (*Publick Occurences* was suppressed after one issue **1690.**)

1709

British-Colonial troops captured French fort, Port Royal, Nova Scotia, in **Queen Anne's War 1701-13.** France yielded Nova Scotia by treaty **1713.**

1712

Slaves revolted in New York **Apr. 6.** Six committed suicide, 21 were executed. Second rising, **1741;** 13 slaves hanged, 13 burned, 71 deported.

1716

First theater in colonies opened in Williamsburg, Va.

1728

Pennsylvania Gazette founded by Samuel Keimer in Philadelphia. Benjamin Franklin bought interest **1729.**

1732

Benjamin Franklin published first *Poor Richard's Almanac;* published annually to 1757.

1735

Freedom of the press recognized in New York by acquittal of John Peter Zenger, editor of *Weekly Journal,* on charge of libeling British Gov. Cosby by criticizing his conduct in office.

1740-41

Capt. Vitus Bering, Dane employed by Russians, reached Alaska.

1744

King George's War pitted British and colonials vs. French. Colonials captured Louisburg, Cape Breton Is. **June 17, 1745.** Returned to France **1748** by Treaty of Aix-la-Chapelle.

1752

Benjamin Franklin, flying kite in thunderstorm, proved lightning is electricity **June 15;** invented lightning rod.

1754

French and Indian War (in Europe called 7 Years War, started 1756) began when French occupied Ft. Duquesne (Pittsburgh). British moved Acadian French from Nova Scotia to Louisiana **Oct. 8, 1755.** British captured Quebec **Sept. 18, 1759** in battles in which French Gen. Montcalm and

British Gen. Wolfe were killed. Peace signed **Feb. 10 1763.** French lost Canada and American Midwest. British tightened colonial administration in North America.

1764

Sugar Act placed duties on lumber, foodstuffs, molasses and rum in colonies, to pay French and Indian War debts.

1765

Stamp Act required revenue stamps to help defray cost of royal troops. Nine colonies, led by New York and Massachusetts at Stamp Act Congress in New York **Oct. 7-25, 1765,** adopted Declaration of Rights opposing taxation without representation in Parliament and trial without jury by admiralty courts. Stamp Act **repealed Mar. 17, 1766.**

1767

Townshend Acts levied taxes on glass, painter's lead, paper, and tea. In **1770** all duties except on tea were repealed.

1770

British troops fired **Mar. 5** into Boston mob, killed 5 including **Crispus Attucks,** a black man, reportedly leader of group; later called **Boston Massacre.**

1773

East India Co. tea ships turned back at Boston, New York, Philadelphia in **May.** Cargo ship burned at Annapolis **Oct. 14,** cargo thrown overboard at **Boston Tea Party Dec. 16,** to protest the Tea Act.

1774

"Intolerable Acts" of Parliament curtailed Massachusetts self-rule; barred use of Boston harbor till tea was paid for.

First Continental Congress held in Philadelphia **Sept. 5-Oct. 26;** protested British measures, called for civil disobedience.

Rhode Island abolished slavery.

1775

Patrick Henry addressed Virginia convention, **Mar. 23** said "Give me liberty or give me death."

Paul Revere and William Dawes on night of **Apr. 18** rode to alert patriots that British were on way to Concord to destroy arms. At Lexington, Mass. **Apr. 19** Minutemen lost 8. On return from Concord British took 273 casualties.

Col. Ethan Allen (joined by Col. Benedict Arnold) captured Ft. **Ticonderoga, N.Y. May 10;** also Crown Point. Colonials headed for **Bunker Hill,** fortified Breed's Hill, Charlestown, Mass., repulsed British under Gen. William Howe twice before retreating **June 17;** British casualties 1,000; called Battle of Bunker Hill. Continental Congress **June 15** named **George Washington** commander-in-chief.

1776

France and Spain each agreed **May 2** to provide one million livres in arms to Americans.

In Continental Congress **June 7,** Richard Henry Lee (Va.) moved "that these united colonies are and of right ought to be free and independent states." Resolution adopted July 2. **Declaration of Independence** approved **July 4.**

Col. Moultrie's batteries at **Charleston, S.C.** repulsed British sea attack **June 28.**

Washington, with 10,000 men, lost **Battle of Long Island Aug. 27,** evacuated New York.

Nathan Hale executed as spy by British **Sept. 22.**

Brig. Gen. Arnold's **Lake Champlain** fleet was defeated at Valcour **Oct. 11,** but British returned to Canada. Howe failed to destroy Washington's army at **White Plains Oct. 28.** Hessians captured Ft. Washington, Manhattan, and 3,000 men **Nov. 16;** Ft. Lee, N.J. **Nov. 18.**

Washington in Pennsylvania, recrossed **Delaware River Dec. 25-26,** defeated 1,400 Hessians at Trenton, N.J. **Dec. 26.**

1777

Washington defeated Lord Cornwallis at **Princeton Jan. 3.** Continental Congress adopted Stars and Stripes. *See Flag article.*

Maj. Gen. John Burgoyne with 8,000 from Canada captured **Ft. Ticonderoga July 6.** Americans beat back Burgoyne at Bemis Heights **Oct. 7** and cut off British escape route. Burgoyne surrendered 5,000 men at **Saratoga N.Y. Oct. 17.**

Marquis de Lafayette, aged 20, made major general.

Articles of Confederation and Perpetual Union adopted by Continental Congress **Nov. 15**

France recognized independence of 13 colonies **Dec. 17.**

1778

France signed treaty of aid with U.S. **Feb. 6.** Sent fleet; British evacuated Philadelphia in consequence **June 18.**

1779

John Paul Jones on the *Bonhomme Richard* defeated *Serapis* in British North Sea waters **Sept. 23.**

1780

Charleston, S.C. fell to the British **May 12,** but a British force was defeated near **Kings Mountain, N.C. Oct. 7** by militiamen.

Benedict Arnold found to be a traitor **Sept. 23.** Arnold escaped, made brigadier general in British army.

1781

Bank of North America incorporated in Philadelphia **May 26.**

Cornwallis, sapped by patriot victories, retired to **Yorktown, Va.** Adm. De Grasse landed 3,000 French and stopped British fleet in Hampton Roads. Washington and Rochambeau joined forces, arrived near Williamsburg **Sept. 26.** When siege of Cornwallis began **Oct. 6,** British had 6,000, Americans 8,846, French 7,800. **Cornwallis surrendered Oct. 19.**

1782

New **British** cabinet agreed **in March** to **recognize U.S.** independence. Preliminary agreement signed in Paris **Nov. 30.**

1783

Massachusetts Supreme Court **outlawed slavery** in that state, noting the words in the state Bill of Rights "all men are born free and equal."

Britain, U.S. signed **peace treaty Sept. 3** (Congress ratified it **Jan. 14, 1784).**

Washington ordered army disbanded Nov. 3, bade farewell to his officers at Fraunces Tavern, N.Y. City **Dec. 4.**

Noah Webster published *American Spelling Book,* great bestseller.

1784

Jefferson's proposal to **ban slavery** in new territory after 1802 is narrowly defeated **Mar. 1.**

First successful daily newspaper, **Pennsylvania Packet & General Advertiser,** published **Sept. 21.**

1786

Delegates from 5 states at **Annapolis, Md. Sept. 11-14** asked Congress to call convention in Philadelphia to write practical constitution for the 13 states.

1787

Shays's Rebellion, of debt-ridden farmers in Massachusetts, failed **Jan. 25.**

Northwest Ordinance adopted **July 13** by Continental Congress. Determined government of Northwest Territory north of Ohio River, west of New York; 60,000 inhabitants could get statehood. Guaranteed freedom of religion, support for schools, no slavery.

Constitutional convention opened at Philadelphia **May 25** with George Washington presiding. Constitution adopted by delegates **Sept. 17;** ratification by 9th state, New Hampshire, **June 21, 1788,** meant adoption; declared in effect **Mar. 4, 1789.**

1789

George Washington chosen president by all electors voting (73 eligible, 69 voting, 4 absent); John Adams, vice president, 34 votes. **Feb. 4.** First Congress met at Federal Hall, N.Y. City; regular sessions began **Apr. 6.** Washington inaugurated there **Apr. 30.** Supreme Court created by Federal Judiciary Act **Sept. 24.** Congress submitted Bill of Rights to states **Sept. 25.**

1790

Congress passed **Census Act Mar. 1; Naturalization Act** (2-year residency) **Mar. 26.**

Congress met in Phila. **Dec. 6,** new temporary Capital.

1791

Bill of Rights went into effect **Dec. 15.**

1792

Coinage Act established **U.S. Mint** in Philadelphia **Apr. 2.**

Gen. **"Mad" Anthony Wayne** made commander in Ohio-Indiana area, trained "American Legion"; established string of forts. Routed Indians at Fallen Timbers on Maumee River **Aug. 20, 1794,** checked British at Fort Miami, Ohio.

White House cornerstone laid **Oct. 13.**

1793

Eli Whitney invented **cotton gin,** reviving southern slavery.

1794

Whiskey Rebellion, west Pennsylvania farmers protesting liquor tax of **1791,** was suppressed by 15,000 militiamen **Sept. 1794.** Alexander Hamilton used incident to establish authority of the new federal government in enforcing its laws.

1795

U.S. bought peace from **Algiers and Tunis** by paying $800,000, supplying a frigate and annual tribute of $25,000 **Nov. 28.**

Gen. Wayne signed peace with Indians at Fort Greenville.

Univ. of North Carolina became first operating state university.

1796

Washington's Farewell Address as president delivered **Sept. 19.** Gave strong warnings against permanent alliances with foreign powers, big public debt, large military establishment and devices of "small, artful, enterprising minority" to control or change government.

1797

U.S. frigate **United States** launched at Philadelphia **July 10;** Constellation at Baltimore **Sept. 7;** Constitution (Old Ironsides) at Boston **Sept. 20.**

1798

Alien & Sedition Acts passed by Federalists; intended to silence political opposition **June-July.**

War with France threatened over French raids on U.S. shipping and rejection of U.S. diplomats. Congress voided all treaties with France, ordered Navy to capture French armed ships. Navy (45 ships) and 365 privateers captured 84 French ships. USS Constellation took French warship Insurgente **1799.** Napoleon stopped French raids after becoming First Consul.

1800

Federal gvt. moves from Philadelphia to **Washington, D.C.**

1801

Tripoli declared war June 10 against U.S., which refused added tribute to commerce-raiding Arab corsairs. Land and naval campaigns forced Tripoli to conclude **peace June 4, 1805.**

1803

Supreme Court, in **Marbury v. Madison** case, for the first time overturned a U.S. law **Feb. 24.**

Napoleon, who had recovered Louisiana from Spain by secret treaty, sold all of **Louisiana,** stretching to Canadian border, to U.S., for $11,250,000 in bonds, plus $3,750,000 indemnities to American citizens with claims against France. U.S. took title **Dec. 20.** Purchases doubled U.S. area.

1804

Lewis and Clark expedition ordered by Pres. Jefferson to explore what is now northwest U.S. Started from St. Louis **May 14;** ended **Sept. 23, 1806.** Sacagawea, an Indian woman, served as guide.

Vice Pres. **Aaron Burr,** after long political rivalry, **shot Alexander Hamilton** in a duel **July 11** in Weehawken, N.J.; Hamilton died the next day.

1807

Robert Fulton made first practical steamboat trip; left N.Y. City **Aug. 17,** reached Albany, 150 mi., in 32 hrs.

Embargo Act bans all trade with foreign countries, forbids ships to set sail for foreign ports **Dec. 22.**

1808

Slave importation outlawed. Some 250,000 slaves were illegally imported **1808-1860.**

1811

William Henry Harrison, governor of Indiana, defeated Indians under the Prophet, in battle of Tippecanoe **Nov. 7.**

Cumberland Road begun at Cumberland, Md.; became important route to West.

1812

War of 1812 had 3 main causes: Britain seized U.S. ships trading with France; Britain seized 4,000 naturalized U.S. sailors by **1810;** Britain armed Indians who raided western border. U.S. stopped trade with Europe **1807** and **1809.** Trade with Britain only was stopped, **1810.**

Unaware that Britain had raised the blockade against France 2 days before, **Congress declared war June 18** by a small majority. The West favored war, New England opposed it. The British were handicapped by war with France.

U.S. naval victories in 1812 included: USS Essex captured Alert **Aug. 13;** USS Constitution destroyed Guerriere **Aug. 19;** USS Wasp took Frolic **Oct. 18;** USS United States defeated Macedonian off Azores **Oct. 25;** Constitution beat Java **Dec. 29.** British captured Detroit **Aug. 16.**

1813

Oliver H. Perry defeated British fleet at Battle of Lake Erie, **Sept. 10.** U.S. victory at Battle of the Thames, Ont., **Oct. 5,** broke Indian allies of Britain, and made Detroit frontier safe for U.S. But Americans failed in Canadian invasion attempts. York (Toronto) and Buffalo were burned.

1814

British landed in Maryland in August, defeated U.S. force **Aug. 24, burned Capitol** and White House. Maryland militia stopped British advance **Sept. 12.** Bombardment of Ft. McHenry, Baltimore, for 25 hours, **Sept. 13-14,** by British fleet failed; Francis Scott Key wrote words to **Star Spangled Banner.**

U.S. won naval Battle of **Lake Champlain Sept. 11.** Peace treaty signed at Ghent **Dec. 24.**

1815

Some 5,300 British, unaware of peace treaty, attacked U.S. entrenchments near **New Orleans, Jan. 8.** British had over 2,000 casualties, Americans lost 71.

U.S. flotilla finally ended piracy by **Algiers, Tunis, Tripoli** by **Aug. 6.**

1816

Second Bank of the U.S. chartered.

1817

Rush-Bagot treaty signed **Apr. 28-29;** limited U.S., British armaments on the Great Lakes.

1819

Spain cedes **Florida** to U.S. **Feb. 22.**

American steamship Savannah made first part steam-powered, part sail-powered crossing of Atlantic, Savannah, Ga. to Liverpool, Eng., 29 days.

1820

First organized **immigration of blacks to Africa** from U.S. began with 86 free blacks sailing **Feb.** to Sierra Leone, Brit. Colony.

Henry Clay's **Missouri Compromise** bill passed by Congress **March 3.** Slavery was allowed in Missouri, but not elsewhere west of the Mississippi River north of 36° 30′ latitude (the southern line of Missouri). Repealed **1854.**

1821

Emma Willard founded Troy Female Seminary, first U.S. women's college.

1823

Monroe Doctrine enunciated **Dec. 2,** opposing European intervention in the Americas.

1824

Pawtucket, R.I. **weavers strike** in first such action by women.

1825

Erie Canal opened; first boat left Buffalo **Oct. 26,** reached N.Y. City **Nov. 4.** Canal cost $7 million but cut travel time one-third, shipping costs nine-tenths; opened Great Lakes area, made N.Y. City chief Atlantic port.

John Stevens, of Hoboken, N.J., built and operated first experimental **steam locomotive** in U.S.

1828

South Carolina **Dec. 19** declared the right of state **nullification of federal laws,** opposing the "Tariff of Abominations."

Noah Webster published his *American Dictionary of the English Language.*

Baltimore & Ohio 1st U.S. passenger RR, was begun **July 4.**

1830

Mormon church organized by Joseph Smith in Fayette, N.Y. **Apr. 6.**

1831

William Lloyd Garrison began abolitionist newspaper *The Liberator* **Jan. 1.**

Nat Turner, black slave in Virginia, led local slave rebellion, killed 57 whites in **Aug.** Troops called in, Turner captured, tried, and hanged.

1832

Black Hawk War (Ill.-Wis.) **Apr.-Sept.** pushed Sauk and Fox Indians west across Mississippi.

South Carolina convention passed **Ordinance of Nullification in Nov.** against permanent tariff, threatening to withdraw from the Union. Congress **Feb. 1833** passed a compromise tariff act, whereupon South Carolina repealed its act.

1833

Oberlin College, first in U.S. to adopt coeducation; refused to bar students on account of race, **1835.**

1835

Seminole Indians in Florida under Osceola began attacks **Nov. 1,** protesting forced removal. The unpopular 8-year war ended **Aug. 14, 1842;** Indians were sent to Oklahoma. War cost the U.S. 1,500 soldiers.

Texas proclaimed right to secede from Mexico; Sam Houston put in command of Texas army, **Nov. 2-4.**

Gold discovered on **Cherokee land** in Georgia. Indians forced to cede lands **Dec. 20** and to cross Mississippi.

1836

Texans besieged in Alamo in San Antonio by Mexicans under Santa Anna **Feb. 23-Mar. 6;** entire garrison killed. Texas independence declared, **Mar. 2.** At San Jacinto **Apr. 21** Sam Houston and Texans defeated Mexicans.

Marcus Whitman, H.H. Spaulding and wives reached Fort Walla Walla on Columbia River, Oregon. **First white women to cross plains.**

1838

Cherokee Indians made **"Trail of Tears,"** removed from Georgia to Oklahoma starting **Oct.**

1841

First emigrant **wagon train for California,** 47 persons, left Independence, Mo. **May 1,** reached Cal. **Nov. 4.**

Brook Farm commune set up by New England Transcendentalist intellectuals. Lasts to **1846.**

1842

Webster-Ashburton Treaty signed **Aug. 9,** fixing the U.S.-Canada border in Maine and Minnesota.

First use of **anesthetic** (sulphuric ether gas).

Settlement of Oregon begins via **Oregon Trail.**

1843

More than 1,000 settlers left Independence, Mo. for Oregon **May 22,** arrived **Oct.**

1844

First message over first **telegraph line** sent **May 24** by inventor Samuel F.B. Morse from Washington to Baltimore: "What hath God wrought!"

1845

Texas Congress **voted for annexation** to U.S. **July 4.** U.S. Congress admits Texas to Union **Dec. 29.**

1846

Mexican War. Pres. James K. Polk ordered Gen. Zachary Taylor to seize disputed Texan land settled by Mexicans. After border clash, U.S. declared war **May 13;** Mexico **May 23.** Northern Whigs opposed war, southerners backed it.

Bear flag of Republic of California raised by American settlers at Sonoma **June 14.**

About 12,000 U.S. troops took Vera Cruz Mar. 27, 1847, Mexico City Sept. 14, 1847. By **treaty, Feb. 1848,** Mexico ceded claims to Texas, California, Arizona, New Mexico, Nevada, Utah, part of Colorado. U.S. assumed $3 million American claims and paid Mexico $15 million.

Treaty with Great Britain **June 15** set **boundary in Oregon** territory at 49th parallel (extension of existing line). Expansionists had used slogan "54° 40′ or fight."

Mormons, after violent clashes with settlers over polygamy, left Nauvoo, Ill. for West under Brigham Young, settled **July 1847 at Salt Lake City, Utah.**

Elias Howe invented **sewing machine.**

1847

First **adhesive U.S. postage stamps** on sale **July 1;** Benjamin Franklin 5¢, Washington 10¢.

Ralph Waldo Emerson published first book of poems; **Henry Wadsworth Longfellow** published *Evangeline.*

1848

Gold discovered Jan. 24 in California; 80,000 prospectors emigrate in **1849.**

Lucretia Mott and Elizabeth Cady Stanton lead **Seneca Falls, N.Y. Women's Rights Convention July 19-20.**

1850

Sen. Henry Clay's **Compromise of 1850** admitted California as 31st state **Sept. 9,** slavery forbidden; made Utah and New Mexico territories without decision on slavery; made Fugitive Slave Law more harsh; ended District of Columbia slave trade.

1851

Herman Melville's *Moby Dick,* **Nathaniel Hawthorne's** *House of the Seven Gables* published.

1852

Uncle Tom's Cabin, by **Harriet Beecher Stowe,** published.

1853

Commodore Matthew C. Perry, U.S.N., received by Lord of Toda, Japan **July 14; negotiated treaty to open Japan** to U.S. ships.

1854

Republican party formed at Ripon, Wis. **Feb. 28.** Opposed Kansas-Nebraska Act (became law **May 30**) which left issue of slavery to vote of settlers.

Henry David Thoreau published *Walden.*

1855

Walt Whitman published *Leaves of Grass.*

First railroad train crossed Mississippi on the river's first bridge, Rock Island, Ill.-Davenport, Ia. **Apr. 21.**

1856

Republican party's first nominee for president, **John C. Fremont,** defeated. Abraham Lincoln made 50 speeches for him.

Lawrence, Kan. sacked **May 21** by slavery party; abolitionist **John Brown** led anti-slavery men against Missourians at **Osawatomie, Kan. Aug. 30**

1857

Dred Scott decision by U.S. Supreme Court **Mar. 6** held, 6-3, that a slave did not become free when taken into a free state, Congress could not bar slavery from a territory, and blacks could not be citizens.

1858

First **Atlantic cable** completed by Cyrus W. Field **Aug. 5;** cable failed **Sept. 1.**

Lincoln-Douglas debates in Illinois **Aug. 21-Oct. 15.**

1859

First commercially productive **oil well,** drilled near Titusville, Pa., by Edwin L. Drake **Aug. 27.**

Abolitionist **John Brown** with 21 men seized U.S. Armory at **Harpers Ferry (then Va.) Oct. 16.** U.S. Marines captured raiders, killing several. Brown was hanged for treason by Virginia **Dec. 2.**

1860

New England shoe-workers, 20,000, strike **Feb. 22** win higher wages.

Abraham Lincoln, Republican, elected president in 4-way race.

First **Pony Express** between Sacramento, Cal. and St. Joseph, Mo. started **Apr. 3;** service ended **Oct. 24, 1861** when first transcontinental telegraph line was completed.

1861

Seven southern states set up **Confederate States of America Feb. 8,** with Jefferson Davis as president, captured Federal arsenals and forts. **Civil War** began as Confederates fired on **Ft. Sumter** in Charleston, S.C. **Apr. 12;** they captured it **Apr. 14.**

President **Lincoln called for 75,000 volunteers Apr. 15.** By **May,** 11 states had seceded. Lincoln blockaded southern ports **Apr. 19,** cutting off vital exports, aid.

Confederates repelled Union forces at first **Battle of Bull Run July 21.**

First **transcontinental telegraph** was put in operation.

1862

Homestead Act was approved **May 20;** it granted free family farms to settlers.

Land Grant Act approved **July 7,** providing for public land sale to benefit agricultural education; eventually led to establishment of state university systems.

Union forces were victorious in western campaigns, took **New Orleans.** Battles in East were inconclusive.

1863

Lincoln issued **Emancipation Proclamation Jan. 1,** freeing "all slaves in areas still in rebellion."

The entire **Mississippi River** was in Union hands by **July 4.** Union forces won a major victory at **Gettysburg, Pa. July 1-July 4.** Lincoln read his **Gettysburg Address Nov. 19.**

Draft riots in N.Y. City killed about 1,000, including blacks who were hanged by mobs **July 13-16.** Rioters protested provision allowing money payment in place of service. Such payments were ended 1864.

1864

Gen. Sherman marched through Georgia, taking Atlanta **Sept. 1,** Savannah **Dec. 22.**

Sand Creek massacre of Cheyenne and Arapaho Indians **Nov. 29** in a raid by 900 cavalrymen who killed 150-500 men, women, and children; 9 soldiers died. The tribes were awaiting surrender terms when attacked.

1865

Robert E. Lee surrendered 27,800 Confederate troops to Grant at Appomattox Court House, Va. **Apr. 9.** J.E. Johnston surrendered 31,200 to Sherman at Durham Station, N.C. **Apr. 18.** Last rebel troops surrendered **May 26.**

President **Lincoln was shot Apr. 14** by John Wilkes Booth in Ford's Theater, Washington; died the following morning. Booth was reported dead **Apr. 26.** Four co-conspirators were hanged **July 7.**

Thirteenth Amendment, abolishing slavery, took effect **Dec. 18.**

1866

Ku Klux Klan formed secretly in South to terrorize blacks who voted. Disbanded **1869-71.** A second Klan was organized **1915.**

Congress took control of southern Reconstruction, backed freedmen's rights.

1867

Alaska sold to U.S. by Russia for $7.2 million **Mar. 30** through efforts of Sec. of State William H. Seward.

Horatio Alger published first book, *Ragged Dick.*

The **Grange** was organized **Dec 4,** to protect farmer interests.

1868

The World Almanac, a publication of the *New York World,* appeared for the first time.

Pres. **Andrew Johnson** tried to remove Edwin M. Stanton, secretary of war; was impeached by House **Feb. 24** for violation of Tenure of Office Act; acquitted by Senate **March-May.** Stanton resigned.

1869

Financial **"Black Friday"** in New York **Sept. 24;** caused by attempt to "corner" gold.

Transcontinental railroad completed; golden spike driven at Promontory, Utah **May 10** marking the junction of Central Pacific and Union Pacific.

Knights of Labor formed in Philadelphia. By **1886,** it had 700,000 members nationally.

Woman suffrage law passed in Territory of Wyoming **Dec. 10.**

1871

Great fire destroyed Chicago Oct. 8-11; loss est. at $196 million.

1872

Amnesty Act restored civil rights to citizens of the South **May 22** except for 500 Confederate leaders.

Congress founded first national park — **Yellowstone** in Wyoming.

1873

First U.S. **postal card** issued **May 1.**

Banks failed, panic began in **Sept.** Depression lasted 5 years.

"Boss" William Tweed of N.Y. City convicted of stealing public funds. He died in jail in **1878.**

Bellevue Hospital in N.Y. City started the first **school of nursing.**

1875

Congress passed **Civil Rights Act Mar. 1** giving equal rights to blacks in public accommodations and jury duty. Act invalidated in **1883** by Supreme Court.

First **Kentucky Derby** held **May 17** at Churchill Downs, Louisville, Ky.

1876

Samuel J. Tilden, Democrat, received majority of popular votes for president over **Rutherford B. Hayes,** Republican, but 22 electoral votes were in dispute; issue left to Congress. Hayes given presidency **in Feb., 1877** after Republicans agree to end Reconstruction of South.

Col. **George A. Custer** and 264 soldiers of the 7th Cavalry killed **June 25** in "last stand," Battle of the Little Big Horn, Mont., in Sioux Indian War.

Mark Twain published *Tom Sawyer.*

1877

Molly Maguires, Irish terrorist society in Scranton, Pa. mining areas, broken up by hanging of 11 leaders for murders of mine officials and police.

Pres. Hayes sent troops in violent national **railroad strike.**

1878

First commercial **telephone** exchange opened, New Haven, Conn. **Jan. 28.**

Thomas A. Edison founded **Edison Electric Light Co. Oct. 15.**

1879

F.W. Woolworth opened his first five-and-ten store in Utica, N.Y. **Feb. 22.**

Henry George published *Progress & Poverty,* advocating single tax on land.

1881

Pres. **James A. Garfield shot** in Washington, D.C. **July 2;** died **Sept. 19.**

Booker T. Washington founded Tuskegee Institute for blacks.

Helen Hunt Jackson published *A Century of Dishonor* about mistreatment of Indians.

1883

Pendleton Act, passed **Jan. 16,** reformed federal civil service.

Brooklyn Bridge opened **May 24.**

1886

Haymarket riot and bombing, evening of **May 4,** followed bitter labor battles for 8-hour day in Chicago; 7 police and 4 workers died, 66 wounded. Eight anarchists found guilty. Gov. John P. Altgeld denounced trial as unfair.

Geronimo, Apache Indian, finally surrendered **Sept. 4.**

The **Statue of Liberty** was dedicated **Oct. 28.**

American Federation of Labor (AFL) formed **Dec. 8** by 25 craft unions.

1888

Great blizzard in eastern U.S. **Mar. 11-14;** 400 deaths.

1889

U.S. declared Oklahoma open to white settlement **Apr. 22;** within 24 hours **claims for 2 mln. acres** were staked by 50,000 settlers.

Johnstown, Pa. flood May 31; 2,200 lives lost.

1890

First execution by **electrocution:** William Kemmler **Aug. 6** at Auburn Prison, Auburn, N.Y., for murder.

Battle of **Wounded Knee, S.D. Dec. 29,** the last major conflict between Indians and U.S. troops. About 200 Indian men, women, and children, and 29 soldiers were killed.

Sherman Antitrust Act begins federal effort to curb monopolies.

Jacob Riis published *How the Other Half Lives,* about city slums.

1891

Forest Reserve Act Mar. 3 let Pres. close public forest land to settlement for establishment of national parks.

1892

Homestead, Pa., strike at Carnegie steel mills; 7 guards and 11 strikers and spectators shot to death **July 6;** setback for unions. **Ellis Island** opened as N.Y. immigration depot.

1893

Financial panic began, led to 4-year depression.

1894

Thomas A. **Edison's kinetoscope** (motion pictures) (invented **1887**) given first public showing **Apr. 14.**

Jacob S. Coxey led 500 unemployed from the Midwest into Washington, D.C. **Apr. 30.** Coxey was arrested for trespassing on Capitol grounds.

1896

William Jennings Bryan delivered "Cross of Gold" speech **July 7;** wins Democratic Party nomination.

Supreme Court, in **Plessy v. Ferguson,** approved racial segregation under the "separate but equal" doctrine.

1898

U.S. **battleship Maine** blown up **Feb. 15** at Havana, 260 killed.

U.S. blockaded Cuba Apr. 22 in aid of independence forces. U.S. declared war on Spain, **Apr. 24,** destroyed Spanish fleet in Philippines **May 1,** took Guam **June 20.**

Puerto Rico taken by U.S. **July 25-Aug. 12.** Spain agreed **Dec. 10** to cede Philippines, Puerto Rico, and Guam, and approved independence for Cuba.

U.S. annexed independent republic of **Hawaii.**

1899

Filipino insurgents, unable to get recognition of independence from U.S., started guerrilla war **Feb. 4.** Crushed with capture **May 23, 1901** of leader, Emilio Aguinaldo.

U.S. declared **Open Door Policy** to make China an open international market and to preserve its integrity as a nation.

John Dewey published *School and Society,* backing progressive education.

1900

Carry Nation, Kansas anti-saloon agitator, began raiding with hatchet.

U.S. helped suppress **"Boxers"** in Peking.

International Ladies' Garment Workers Union was founded in NYC in **Nov.**

1901

Texas had its first significant **oil strike,** near Beaumont **Jan. 10.**

Pres. William **McKinley was shot Sept. 6** by an anarchist, Leon Czolgosz; died **Sept. 14.**

1903

Treaty between U.S. and Colombia to have U.S. dig **Panama Canal** signed **Jan. 22,** rejected by Colombia. Panama declared independence with U.S. support **Nov. 3;** recognized by Pres. Theodore Roosevelt **Nov. 6.** U.S., Panama signed canal treaty **Nov. 18.**

Wisconsin set first **direct primary** voting system **May 23.**

First **automobile trip** across U.S. from San Francisco to New York **May 23-Aug. 1.**

First successful flight in heavier-than-air mechanically propelled airplane by **Orville Wright Dec. 17** near Kitty Hawk, N.C., 120 ft. in 12 seconds. Fourth flight same day by **Wilbur Wright,** 852 ft. in 59 seconds. Improved plane patented **May 22, 1906.**

Jack London published *Call of the Wild.*

Great Train Robbery, pioneering film, produced.

1904

Ida Tarbell published muckraking *History of Standard Oil.*

1905

First **Rotary Club** founded in Chicago **Dec.**

1906

San Francisco earthquake and fire **Apr. 18-19** left 503 dead, $350 million damages.

Pure Food and Drug Act and Meat Inspection Act both passed **June 30.**

1907

Financial panic and depression started **Mar. 13.**

First round-world cruise of U.S. **"Great White Fleet";** 16 battleships, 12,000 men.

1908

Henry Ford introduced **Model T** car, priced at $850 **Oct. 1.**

1909

Adm. Robert E. Peary reached **North Pole Apr. 6** on 6th attempt, accompanied by Matthew Henson, a black man, and 4 Eskimos.

National Conference on the Negro convened **May 30,** leading to founding of the National Association for the Advancement of Colored People.

1910

Boy Scouts of America founded **Feb. 8.**

1911

Supreme Court dissolved **Standard Oil Co. May 15.**

NYC's **Triangle Waist Sweatshop** caught fire, trapping and killing 146, mostly young women **Mar. 25.**

First **transcontinental airplane flight** (with numerous stops) by C.P. Rodgers, New York to Pasadena, **Sept. 17-Nov. 5;** time in air 82 hrs., 4 min.

1912

Amer. Girl Guides founded **Mar. 12;** name changed in 1913 to **Girl Scouts.**

U.S. sent marines **Aug. 14** to **Nicaragua,** which was in default of loans to U.S. and Europe.

1913

N.Y. Armory Show brought modern art to U.S. **Feb. 17.**

U.S. blockaded Mexico in support of revolutionaries.

Charles Beard published his *Economic Interpretation of the Constitution.*

Federal Reserve System was authorized **Dec. 23,** in a major reform of U.S. banking and finance.

1914

Ford Motor Co. raised basic wage rates from $2.40 for 9-hr. day to $5 for 8-hr. day **Jan. 5.**

When U.S. sailors were arrested at Tampico **Apr. 9,** Atlantic fleet was sent to **Veracruz,** occupied city.

Pres. Wilson proclaimed **U.S. neutrality** in the European war **Aug. 4.**

Panama Canal was officially opened **Aug. 15.**

The **Clayton Antitrust** Act was passed **Oct. 15,** strengthening federal anti-monopoly powers.

1915

First **telephone talk,** New York to San Francisco, **Jan. 25** by Alexander Graham Bell and Thomas A. Watson.

British ship **Lusitania** sunk **May 7** by German submarine; 128 American passengers lost (Germany had warned passengers in advance). As a result of U.S. campaign, Germany issued apology and promise of payments **Oct. 5.** Pres. Wilson asked for a military fund increase **Dec. 7.**

U.S. troops landed in **Haiti July 28.** Haiti became a virtual U.S. protectorate under **Sept. 16** treaty.

1916

Gen. John J. **Pershing entered Mexico** to pursue Francisco (Pancho) Villa, who had raided U.S. border areas. Forces withdrawn **Feb. 5, 1917.**

Rural Credits Act passed **July 17,** followed by Warehouse Act. **Aug. 11;** both provided financial aid to farmers.

Bomb exploded during **San Francisco** Preparedness Day parade **July 22,** killed 10. Thomas J. Mooney, labor organizer, and Warren K. Billings, shoe worker, were convicted; both pardoned in **1939.**

U.S. bought **Virgin Islands** from Denmark **Aug. 4.**

Jeannette Rankin, 1st U.S. Congresswoman (R-Montana) elected.

U.S. established military government in the **Dominican Republic Nov. 29.**

Trade and loans to **European Allies** soared during the year.

John Dewey published *Democracy and Education.*

Carl Sandburg published *Chicago Poems.*

1917

Germany, suffering from British blockade, declared almost unrestricted **submarine warfare Jan. 31.** U.S. cut diplomatic ties with Germany **Feb. 3,** and formally declared war **Apr. 6.**

Conscription law was passed **May 18.** First U.S. troops arrived in Europe **June 26.**

The 18th **(Prohibition)** Amendment to the Constitution was submitted to the states by Congress **Dec. 18.** On **Jan. 16, 1919,** the 36th state (Nevada) ratified it. Franklin D. Roosevelt, as 1932 presidential candidate, endorsed repeal; 21st Amendment repealed 18th; ratification completed **Dec. 5, 1933.**

1918

Pres. Wilson set out his **14 Points** as basis for peace **Jan. 8.**

Over one million **American troops** were in Europe by **July.** War ended **Nov. 11.**

Influenza epidemic killed an estimated 20 million worldwide, 548,000 in U.S.

1919

First **transatlantic flight,** by U.S. Navy seaplane, left Rockaway, N.Y. **May 8,** stopped at Newfoundland, Azores, Lisbon **May 27.**

Boston police strike Sept. 9; National Guard breaks strike.

Sherwood Anderson published *Winesburg, Ohio.*

About 250 **alien radicals** were deported **Dec. 22.**

1920

In national **Red Scare,** some 2,700 Communists, anarchists, and other radicals were arrested **Jan.-May.**

Senate refused **Mar. 19** to ratify the **League of Nations Covenant.**

Nicola Sacco, 29, shoe factory employee and radical agitator, and **Bartolomeo Vanzetti,** 32, fish peddler and anarchist, accused of killing 2 men in Mass. payroll holdup **Apr. 15.** Found guilty **1921.** A 6-year worldwide campaign for release on grounds of want of conclusive evidence and prejudice failed. Both were executed **Aug. 23, 1927.** Vindicated July 19, 1977 by proclamation of Mass. Gov. Dukakis.

First regular licensed **radio broadcasting** begun **Aug. 20.**

19th Amendment ratified **Aug. 26,** giving women right to vote.

League of Women Voters founded.

Wall St., N.Y. City, **bomb** explosion killed 30, injured 100, did $2 million damage **Sept. 16.**

Sinclair Lewis's *Main Street,* **F. Scott Fitzgerald's** *This Side of Paradise* published.

1921

Congress sharply curbed **immigration,** set national quota system **May 19.**

Joint Congressional resolution declaring **peace with Germany, Austria, and Hungary** signed **July 2** by Pres. Harding; treaties were signed in **Aug.**

Limitation of Armaments Conference met in Washington **Nov. 12 to Feb. 6, 1922.** Major powers agreed to curtail naval construction, outlaw poison gas, restrict submarine attack on merchantmen, respect integrity of China.

Ku Klux Klan began revival with violence against blacks in North, South, and Midwest.

1922

Violence during **coal-mine strike** at Herrin, Ill., **June 22-23** cost 36 lives, 21 of them non-union miners.

Reader's Digest founded.

1923

First **sound-on-film motion picture,** "Phonofilm" was shown by Lee de Forest at Rivoli Theater, N.Y. City, beginning in **April.**

1924

Law approved by Congress **June 15** making all **Indians citizens.**

Nellie Tayloe Ross elected governor of Wyoming **Nov. 9** after death of her husband **Oct. 2;** installed **Jan. 5, 1925,** first woman governor. **Miriam (Ma) Ferguson** was elected governor of Texas **Nov. 9;** installed **Jan. 20, 1925.**

George Gershwin wrote *Rhapsody in Blue.*

1925

John T. Scopes found guilty of having taught evolution in Dayton, Tenn. high school, fined $100 and costs **July 24.**

1926

Dr. Robert H. Goddard demonstrated practicality of **rockets Mar. 16** at Auburn, Mass. with first liquid fuel rocket; rocket traveled 184 ft. in 2.5 secs.

Congress established **Army Air Corps July 2.**

Air Commerce Act passed **Nov. 2,** providing federal aid for airlines and airports.

1927

About 1,000 **marines landed in China Mar. 5** to protect property in civil war.

Capt. **Charles A. Lindbergh** left Roosevelt Field, N.Y. **May 20** alone in plane Spirit of St. Louis on first New York-Paris nonstop flight. Reached Le Bourget airfield **May 21,** 3,610 miles in 33 1/2 hours.

The Jazz Singer, with **Al Jolson,** demonstrated part-talking pictures in N.Y. City **Oct. 6.**

Show Boat opened in New York **Dec. 27.**

O. E. Rolvaag published *Giants in the Earth.*

1928

Herbert Hoover elected president against **Alfred E. Smith,** the Catholic governor of New York.

Amelia Earhart became first woman to fly the Atlantic **June 17.**

1929

"St. Valentine's Day massacre" in Chicago **Feb. 14;** gangsters killed 7 rivals.

Farm price stability aided by **Agricultural Marketing Act,** passed **June 15.**

Albert B. Fall, former sec. of the interior, was convicted of accepting a bribe of $100,000 in the leasing of the **Elk Hills (Teapot Dome)** naval oil reserve; sentenced **Nov. 1** to $100,000 fine and year in prison.

Stock Market crash Oct. 29 marked end of postwar prosperity as stock prices plummeted. Stock losses for 1929-31 estimated at $50 billion; worst American depression began.

Thomas Wolfe published *Look Homeward, Angel.* **William Faulkner** published *The Sound and the Fury.*

1930

London **Naval Reduction Treaty** signed by U.S., Britain, Italy, France, and Japan **Apr. 22;** in effect **Jan. 1, 1931;** expired **Dec. 31, 1936.**

Hawley-Smoot Tariff signed; rate hikes slash world trade.

1931

Empire State Building opened in N.Y. City **May 1.**

Al Capone was convicted of tax evasion **Oct. 17.**

Pearl Buck published *The Good Earth.*

1932

Reconstruction Finance Corp. established **Jan. 22** to stimulate banking and business. Unemployment at 12 million.

Charles Lindbergh Jr. kidnaped Mar. 1, found dead **May 12.**

Bonus March on Washington **May 29** by World War I veterans demanding Congress pay their bonus in full.

1933

FDR named **Frances Perkins** U.S. Secy of Labor; 1st woman in U.S. Cabinet.

All **banks in the U.S. were ordered closed** by Pres. Roosevelt **Mar. 6.**

In the "100 days" special session, **Mar. 9—June 16,** Congress passed **New Deal** social and economic measures.

Gold standard dropped by U.S.; announced by Pres. Roosevelt **Apr. 19,** ratified by Congress **June 5.**

Prohibition ended in the U.S. as 36th state ratified 21st Amendment **Dec. 5.**

U.S. foreswore armed intervention in **Western Hemisphere** nations **Dec. 26.**

1934

U.S. troops pull out of **Haiti Aug. 6.**

1935

Comedian **Will Rogers** and aviator Wiley Post **killed Aug. 15** in Alaska plane crash.

Social Security Act passed by Congress **Aug. 14.**

Huey Long, Senator from Louisiana and national political leader, was **assassinated Sept. 8.**

Porgy and Bess, **George Gershwin** opera on American theme, opened **Oct. 10** in N.Y. City.

Committee for Industrial Organization (CIO) formed to expand industrial unionism **Nov. 9.**

1936

Boulder Dam completed.

Margaret Mitchell published *Gone With the Wind.*

1937

Joe Louis knocked out James J. Braddock, became world heavyweight champ **June 22.**

Amelia Earhart, aviator, and co-pilot Fred Noonan lost **July 2** near Howland Is. in the Pacific.

Pres. Roosevelt asked for 6 additional Supreme Court justices; **"packing" plan** defeated.

Auto, steel labor unions won first big contracts.

1938

Naval Expansion Act passed **May 17.**

National minimum wage enacted **June 25.**

Orson Welles radio dramatization of *War of the Worlds* caused nationwide scare **Oct. 30.**

1939

Pres. Roosevelt asked **defense budget hike Jan. 5, 12.**

N.Y. World's Fair opened **Apr. 30,** closed **Oct. 31;** reopened **May 11, 1940,** and finally closed **Oct. 21.**

Einstein alerts FDR to **A-bomb** opportunity in **Aug. 2** letter.

U.S. declares its neutrality in European war **Sept. 5.**

Roosevelt proclaimed a limited **national emergency Sept. 8,** an unlimited emergency **May 27, 1941.** Both ended by Pres. Truman **Apr. 28, 1952.**

John Steinbeck published *Grapes of Wrath.*

1940

U.S. okayed sale of **surplus war material** to Britain **June 3;** announced transfer of 50 overaged destroyers **Sept. 3.**

First **peacetime draft** approved **Sept. 14.**

Richard Wright published *Native Son.*

1941

The **Four Freedoms** termed essential by Pres. Roosevelt in speech to Congress **Jan. 6:** freedom of speech and religion, freedom from want and fear.

Lend-Lease Act signed **Mar. 11,** providing $7 billion in military credits for Britain. Lend-Lease for USSR approved in **Nov.**

U.S. occupied **Iceland July 7.**

The **Atlantic Charter,** 8-point declaration of principles, issued by Roosevelt and Winston Churchill **Aug. 14.**

Japan attacked **Pearl Harbor,** Hawaii, 7:55 a.m. Hawaiian time, **Dec. 7,** 19 ships sunk or damaged, 2,300 dead. U.S. declared war on Japan **Dec. 8,** on Germany and Italy **Dec. 11** after those countries declared war.

1942

Federal government forcibly moved 110,000 **Japanese-Americans** (including 75,000 U.S. citizens) from West Coast to detention camps. Exclusion lasted 3 years.

Battle of **Midway June 4-7** was Japan's first major defeat.

Marines landed on **Guadalcanal Aug. 7;** last Japanese not expelled until **Feb. 9, 1943.**

U.S., Britain invaded North Africa **Nov. 8.**

First **nuclear chain reaction** (fission of uranium isotope U-235) produced at Univ. of Chicago, under physicists Arthur Compton, Enrico Fermi, others **Dec. 2.**

1943

All war contractors barred from **racial discrimination May 27.**

Pres. Roosevelt signed **June 10** the pay-as-you-go income tax bill. Starting **July 1** wage and salary earners were subject to a **paycheck withholding** tax.

Race riot in Detroit June 21; 34 dead, 700 injured. Riot in Harlem section of N.Y. City; 6 killed.

U.S. troops invaded Italy **Sept. 9.**

Marines advanced in **Gilbert Is. in Nov.**

1944

U.S., Allied forces invaded Europe at **Normandy June 6.**

G.I. Bill of Rights signed **June 22,** providing veterans benefits.

U.S. forces landed on **Leyte,** Philippines **Oct. 20.**

1945

Yalta Conference met in the Crimea, USSR, **Feb. 3-11.** Roosevelt, Churchill, and Stalin agreed Russia would enter war against Japan.

Marines landed on **Iwo Jima Feb. 19;** U.S. forces invaded **Okinawa Apr. 1.**

Pres. Roosevelt, 63, died of cerebral hemorrhage in Warm Springs, Ga. **Apr. 12;** V.P. **Harry S. Truman** became pres.

Germany surrendered May 7.

First **atomic bomb,** produced at Los Alamos, N.M., exploded at Alamogordo, N.M. **July 16.** Bomb dropped on **Hiroshima Aug. 6,** on **Nagasaki Aug. 9.** Japan surrendered **Aug. 15.**

U.S. forces entered **Korea** south of 38th parallel to displace Japanese **Sept. 8.**

Gen. Douglas MacArthur took over supervision of Japan **Sept. 9.**

1946

Strike by 400,000 **mine workers** began **Apr. 1;** other industries followed.

Philippines given independence by U.S. **July 4.**

1947

Truman Doctrine: Pres. Truman asked Congress to aid Greece and Turkey to combat Communist terrorism **Mar. 12.** Approved **May 15.**

United Nations Security Council voted unanimously **Apr. 2** to place under **U.S. trusteeship** the Pacific islands formerly mandated to Japan.

Jackie Robinson on Brooklyn Dodgers **Apr. 11,** broke the color barrier in major league baseball.

Taft-Hartley Labor Act curbing strikes was vetoed by Truman **June 20;** Congress overrode the veto.

Proposals later known as the **Marshall Plan,** under which the U.S. would extend aid to European countries, were made by Sec. of State George C. Marshall **June 5.** Congress authorized some $12 billion in next 4 years.

1948

USSR began a land **blockade of Berlin's** Allied sectors **Apr. 1.** This blockade and Western counter-blockade were lifted **Sept. 30, 1949,** after British and U.S. planes had lifted 2,343,315 tons of food and coal into the city.

Organization of American States founded **Apr. 30.**

Alger Hiss, former State Dept. official, indicted Dec. 15 for perjury, after denying he had passed secret documents to Whittaker Chambers for transmission to a communist spy ring. His second trial ended in conviction **Jan. 21, 1950,** and a sentence of 5 years in prison.

Kinsey Report on Sexuality in the Human Male published.

1949

U.S. troops withdrawn from **Korea June 29.**

North Atlantic Treaty Organization (**NATO**) established **Aug. 24** by U.S., Canada, and 10 West European nations, agreeing that an armed attack against one or more of them would be considered an attack against all.

Mrs. I. Toguri D'Aquino (**Tokyo Rose** of Japanese wartime broadcasts) was sentenced **Oct. 7** to 10 years in prison for treason. Paroled **1956**, pardoned **1977.**

Eleven leaders of **U.S. Communist party** convicted **Oct. 14,** after 9-month trial in N.Y. City, of advocating violent overthrow of U.S. government. Ten defendants sentenced to 5 years in prison each and the 11th to 3 years. Supreme Court upheld the convictions **June 4, 1951.**

1950

U.S. **Jan 14** recalled all consular officials from **China** after the latter seized the American consulate general in Peking.

Masked bandits robbed **Brink's Inc.,** Boston express office, **Jan. 17** of $2.8 million, of which $1.2 million was in cash. Case solved **1956,** 8 sentenced to life.

Pres. Truman authorized production of **H-bomb Jan. 31.**

United Nations asked for troops to restore Korea peace **June 25.**

Truman ordered Air Force and Navy to Korea **June 27** after North Korea invaded South. Truman approved ground forces, air strikes against North **June 30.**

U.S. sent 35 military advisers to **South Vietnam June 27,** and agreed to provide military and economic aid to anti-Communist government.

Army seized all railroads Aug. 27 on Truman's order to prevent a general strike; roads returned to owners in **1952.**

U.S. forces landed at Inchon Sept. 15; UN force took Pyongyang **Oct. 20,** reached China border **Nov. 20,** China sent troops across border **Nov. 26.**

Two members of a **Puerto Rican nationalist** movement tried to kill Pres. Truman **Nov. 1.** (see Assassinations)

U.S. **Dec. 8** banned shipments to **Communist China** and to Asiatic ports trading with it.

1951

Sen. **Estes Kefauver** led Senate investigation into organized crime. Preliminary report **Feb. 28** said gambling take was over $20 billion a year.

Julius Rosenberg, his wife, Ethel, and Morton Sobell, all U.S. citizens, were found guilty **Mar. 29** of conspiracy to commit wartime espionage. Rosenbergs sentenced to death, Sobell to 30 years. Rosenbergs **executed June 19, 1953.** Sobell released **Jan. 14, 1969.**

Gen. Douglas MacArthur was removed from his Korea command **Apr. 11** for unauthorized policy statements.

Korea cease-fire talks began in July; lasted 2 years. **Fighting ended July 27, 1953.**

Tariff concessions by the U.S. to the Soviet Union, Communist China, and all communist-dominated lands were suspended **Aug. 1.**

The U.S., **Australia,** and **New Zealand** signed a mutual security pact **Sept. 1.**

Transcontinental television inaugurated **Sept. 4** with Pres. Truman's address at the Japanese Peace Treaty Conference in San Francisco.

Japanese Peace Treaty signed in San Francisco **Sept. 8** by U.S., Japan, and 47 other nations.

J.D. Salinger published *Catcher in the Rye.*

1952

U.S. seizure of nation's steel mills was ordered by Pres. Truman **Apr. 8** to avert a strike. Ruled illegal by Supreme Court **June 2.**

Peace contract between West Germany, U.S., Great Britain, and France was signed **May 26.**

The last racial and ethnic barriers to naturalization were removed, **June 26-27,** with the passage of the **Immigration and Naturalization Act of 1952.**

First **hydrogen device** explosion **Nov. 1** at Eniwetok Atoll in Pacific.

1953

Pres. Eisenhower announced **May 8** that U.S. had given France $60 million for **Indochina War.** More aid was announced in **Sept.** In **1954** it was reported that three fourths of the war's costs were met by U.S.

1954

Nautilus, first atomic-powered submarine, was launched at Groton, Conn. **Jan. 21.**

Five members of Congress were wounded in the House **Mar. 1** by 4 **Puerto Rican independence supporters** who fired at random from a spectators' gallery.

Sen. Joseph McCarthy led televised hearings **Apr. 22-June 17** into alleged Communist influence in the Army.

Racial segregation in public schools was unanimously ruled unconstitutional by the Supreme Court **May 17,** as a violation of the 14th Amendment clause guaranteeing equal protection of the laws.

Southeast Asia Treaty Organization (**SEATO**) formed by collective defense pact signed in Manila **Sept. 8** by the U.S., Britain, France, Australia, New Zealand, Philippines, Pakistan, and Thailand.

Condemnation of **Sen. Joseph R. McCarthy** (R., Wis.) voted by Senate, 67-22 **Dec. 2** for contempt of a Senate elections subcommittee, for abuse of its members, and for insults to the Senate during his Army investigation hearings.

1955

U.S. agreed **Feb. 12** to help train **South Vietnamese** army.

Supreme Court ordered **"all deliberate speed"** in integration of public schools **May 31.**

A **summit meeting** of leaders of U.S., Britain, France, and USSR took place **July 18-23** in Geneva, Switzerland.

Rosa Parks refused **Dec. 1** to give her seat to a white man on a bus in Montgomery, Ala. Bus segregation ordinance declared unconstitutional by a federal court following boycott and NAACP protest.

Merger of America's 2 largest labor organizations was effected **Dec. 5** under the name American Federation of Labor and Congress of Industrial Organizations. The merged **AFL-CIO** had a membership estimated at 15 million.

1956

Massive resistance to Supreme Court desegregation rulings was called for **Mar. 12** by 101 Southern congressmen.

Federal-Aid **Highway Act** signed **June 29,** inaugurating interstate highway system.

First transatlantic **telephone cable** went into operation **Sept. 25.**

1957

Congress approved first **civil rights bill** for blacks since Reconstruction **Apr. 29,** to protect voting rights.

National Guardsmen, called out by Arkansas Gov. Orval Faubus **Sept. 4,** barred 9 black students from entering previously all-white Central High School in **Little Rock.** Faubus complied **Sept. 21** with a federal court order to remove the National Guardsmen. The blacks entered school **Sept. 23** but were ordered to withdraw by local authorities because of fear of mob violence. Pres. Eisenhower sent federal troops **Sept. 24** to enforce the court's order.

Jack Kerouac published *On the Road.*

1958

First U.S. earth satellite to go into orbit, **Explorer I,** launched by Army **Jan. 31** at Cape Canaveral, Fla.; discovered Van Allen radiation belt.

Five thousand U.S. Marines sent to **Lebanon** to protect elected government from threatened overthrow **July-Oct.**

First domestic **jet airline** passenger service in U.S. opened by National Airlines **Dec. 10** between N.Y. and Miami.

1959

Alaska admitted as 49th state **Jan. 3; Hawaii** admitted **Aug. 21.**

St. Lawrence Seaway opened **Apr. 25.**

The George Washington, first U.S. ballistic-missile submarine, launched at Groton, Conn. **June 9.**

N.S. Savannah, world's first atomic-powered merchant ship, launched **July 21** at Camden, N.J.

Soviet Premier **Khrushchev** paid unprecedented visit to U.S. **Sept. 15-27,** made transcontinental tour.

1960

Sit-ins began **Feb. 1** when 4 black college students in Greensboro, N.C. refused to move from a Woolworth lunch counter when denied service. By **Sept. 1961** more than 70,000 students, whites and blacks, had participated in sit-ins.

U.S. launched first **weather satellite,** Tiros I, **Apr. 1.**

Congress approved a strong **voting rights act Apr. 21.**

A **U-2 reconnaisance plane** of the U.S. was shot down in the Soviet Union **May 1.** The incident led to cancellation of an imminent Paris summit conference.

Mobs attacked U.S. embassy in **Panama Sept. 17** in dispute over flying of U.S. and Panamanian flags.

U.S. announced **Dec. 15** it backed rightist group in **Laos,** which took power the next day.

1961

The U.S. severed diplomatic and consular relations with **Cuba Jan. 3,** after disputes over nationalizations of U.S. firms, U.S. military presence at Guantanamo base, etc.

Invasion of Cuba's **"Bay of Pigs" Apr. 17** by Cuban exiles trained, armed, and directed by the U.S., attempting to overthrow the regime of Premier Fidel Castro, was repulsed.

Commander Alan B. Shepard Jr. was rocketed from Cape Canaveral, Fla., 116.5 mi. above the earth in a Mercury capsule **May 5** in the first U.S. manned sub-orbital space flight.

1962

Lt. Col. John H. Glenn Jr. became the first American in orbit **Feb. 20** when he circled the earth 3 times in the Mercury capsule **Friendship 7.**

Pres. Kennedy said **Feb. 14** U.S. military advisers in Vietnam would fire if fired upon.

Supreme Court **Mar. 26** backed **one-man one-vote** apportionment of seats in state legislatures.

First U.S. **communications satellite** launched in **July.**

James Meredith became first black student at Univ. of Mississippi **Oct. 1** after 3,000 troops put down riots.

A Soviet **offensive missile buildup in Cuba** was revealed **Oct. 22** by Pres. Kennedy, who ordered a naval and air quarantine on shipment of offensive military equipment to the island. Kennedy and Soviet Premier Khrushchev reached agreement **Oct. 28** on a formula to end the crisis. Kennedy announced **Nov. 2** that Soviet missile bases in Cuba were being dismantled.

Rachel Carson's *Silent Spring* launched environmentalist movement.

1963

Supreme Court ruled **Mar. 18** that all **criminal defendants** must have counsel and that illegally acquired evidence was not admissible in state as well as federal courts.

Supreme Court ruled, 8-1, **June 17** that laws requiring **recitation of the Lord's Prayer** or Bible verses in public schools were unconstitutional.

A limited **nuclear test-ban treaty** was agreed upon **July 25** by the U.S., Soviet Union and Britain, barring all nuclear tests except underground.

Washington demonstration by 200,000 persons **Aug. 28** in support of **black demands** for equal rights. Highlight was speech in which Dr. Martin Luther King said: "I have a dream that this nation will rise up and live out the true meaning of its creed, 'We hold these truths to be self-evident: that all men are created equal.' "

South Vietnam Pres. **Ngo Dinh Diem assassinated Nov. 2;** U.S. had earlier withdrawn support.

Pres. John F. Kennedy was shot and fatally wounded by an assassin **Nov. 22** as he rode in a motorcade through downtown Dallas, Tex. Vice Pres. Lyndon B. Johnson was inaugurated president shortly after in Dallas. Lee Harvey Oswald was arrested and charged with the murder. Oswald was shot and fatally wounded **Nov. 24** by Jack Ruby, 52, a Dallas nightclub owner, who was convicted of murder **Mar. 14, 1964** and sentenced to death. Ruby died of natural causes **Jan. 3, 1967** while awaiting retrial.

U.S. troops in **Vietnam** totalled over 15,000 by year-end; aid to South Vietnam was over $500 million in **1963.**

1964

Panama suspended relations with U.S. **Jan. 9** after riots. U.S. offered **Dec. 18** to negotiate a new canal treaty.

Supreme Court ordered **Feb. 17** that **congressional districts** have equal populations.

U.S. reported **May 27** it was sending military planes to **Laos.**

Omnibus **civil rights bill** passed **June 29** banning discrimination in voting, jobs, public accommodations, etc.

Three **civil rights workers** were reported missing in Mississippi **June 22;** found buried **Aug. 4.** Twenty-one white men were arrested. On **Oct. 20, 1967,** an all-white federal jury convicted 7 of conspiracy in the slayings.

U.S. Congress **Aug. 7** passed **Tonkin Resolution,** authorizing presidential action in Vietnam, after North Vietnam boats reportedly attacked 2 U.S. destroyers **Aug. 2.**

Congress approved War on Poverty bill **Aug. 11.**

The **Warren Commission** released **Sept. 27** a report concluding that Lee Harvey Oswald was solely responsible for the Kennedy assassination.

1965

Pres. Johnson in **Feb.** ordered continuous **bombing of North Vietnam** below 20th parallel.

Some 14,000 U.S. troops sent to **Dominican Republic** during civil war **Apr. 28.** All troops withdrawn by next year.

New **Voting Rights Act** signed **Aug. 6.**

Los Angeles riot by blacks living in **Watts** area resulted in death of 34 persons and property damage est. at $200 million **Aug. 11-16.**

Water Quality Act passed **Sept. 21** to meet pollution, shortage problems.

National origins quota system of **immigration** abolished **Oct. 3.**

Electric power failure blacked out most of northeastern U.S., parts of 2 Canadian provinces the night of **Nov. 9-10.**

U.S. forces in **S. Vietnam** reached 184,300 by year-end.

1966

U.S. forces began firing into **Cambodia May 1.**

Bombing of Hanoi area of North Vietnam by U.S. planes began **June 29.** By **Dec. 31,** 385,300 U.S. troops were stationed in South Vietnam, plus 60,000 offshore and 33,000 in Thailand.

Medicare, government program to pay part of the medical expenses of citizens over 65, began **July 1.**

Edward Brooke (R, Mass.) elected **Nov. 8** as first black U.S. senator in 85 years.

1967

Black representative **Adam Clayton Powell** (D, N.Y.) was denied **Mar. 1** his seat in Congress because of charges he misused gvt. funds. Reelected in 1968, he was seated, but fined $25,000 and stripped of his 22 years' seniority.

Pres. Johnson and Soviet Premier Aleksei Kosygin met **June 23 and 25** at **Glassboro State College** in N.J.; agreed not to let any crisis push them into war.

Black riots in **Newark, N.J. July 12-17** killed 26, injured 1,500; over 1,000 arrested. In Detroit, Mich., **July 23-30** at least 40 died; 2,000 injured, 5,000 left homeless by rioting, looting, burning in city's black ghetto. Quelled by 4,700 federal paratroopers and 8,000 National Guardsmen.

Thurgood Marshall sworn in **Oct. 2** as first black U.S. Supreme Court Justice. Carl B. Stokes (D, Cleveland) and Richard G. Hatcher (D, Gary, Ind.) were elected first black mayors of major U.S. cities **Nov. 7.**

By **December** 475,000 U.S. troops were in **South Vietnam,** all North Vietnam was subject to bombing. Protests against the war mounted in U.S. during year.

1968

USS Pueblo and 83-man crew seized in Sea of Japan **Jan. 23** by North Koreans; 82 men released **Dec. 22.**

"Tet offensive": Communist troops attacked Saigon, 30 province capitals **Jan. 30,** suffer heavy casualties.

Pres. Johnson **curbed bombing** of North Vietnam **Mar. 31.** Peace talks began in Paris **May 10.** All bombing of North halted **Oct. 31.**

Martin Luther King Jr., 39, assassinated Apr. 4 in Memphis, Tenn. James Earl Ray, an escaped convict, pleaded guilty to the slaying, was sentenced to 99 years.

Sen. Robert F. Kennedy (D, N.Y.) 42, **shot June 5** in Hotel Ambassador, Los Angeles, after celebrating presidential primary victories. Died **June 6.** Sirhan Bishara Sirhan, Jordanian, convicted of murder.

Rep. Shirley Chisholm (D., N.Y.) became the first black woman elected to Congress.

1969

Expanded four-party **Vietnam peace talks** began **Jan. 18.** U.S. force peaked at 543,400 in April. Withdrawal started **July 8.** Pres. Nixon set Vietnamization policy **Nov. 3.**

U.S. astronaut **Neil A. Armstrong,** 38, commander of the Apollo 11 mission, became the first man to **set foot on the moon July 20.** Air Force Col. Edwin E. Aldrin Jr. accompanied Armstrong.

Anti-Vietnam War **demonstrations reached peak** in U.S.; some 250,000 marched in Washington, D.C. **Nov. 15.**

Massacre of hundreds of civilians at **Mylai, South Vietnam** in 1968 incident was reported **Nov. 16.**

1970

United Mine Workers official **Joseph A. Yablonski,** his wife, and their daughter were found shot **Jan. 5** in their Clarksville, Pa. home. UMW chief W. A. (Tony) Boyle was later convicted of the killing.

A federal jury **Feb. 18** found the **"Chicago 7"** innocent of conspiring to incite riots during the 1968 Democratic National Convention. However, 5 were convicted of crossing state lines with intent to incite riots.

Millions of Americans participated in anti-pollution demonstrations **Apr. 22** to mark the first **Earth Day.**

U.S. and South Vietnamese forces crossed **Cambodian** borders **Apr. 30** to get at enemy bases. Four students were killed **May 4** at **Kent St.** Univ. in Ohio by National Guardsmen during a protest against the war.

Two **women generals,** the first in U.S. history, were named by Pres. Nixon **May 15.**

A **postal reform** measure was signed **Aug. 12,** creating an independent U.S. Postal Service, thus relinquishing governmental control of the U.S. mails after almost 2 centuries.

1971

Charles Manson, 36, and 3 of his followers were found guilty **Jan. 26** of first-degree murder in the 1969 slaying of actress Sharon Tate and 6 others.

U.S. air and artillery forces aided a 44-day incursion by South Vietnam forces into **Laos** starting **Feb. 8.**

A Constitutional Amendment lowering the **voting age to 18** in all elections was approved in the Senate by a vote of 94-0 **Mar. 10.** The proposed 26th Amendment got House approval by a 400-19 vote **Mar. 23.** Thirty-eighth state ratified **June 30.**

A court-martial jury Mar. 29, convicted **Lt. William L. Calley Jr.** of premeditated murder of 22 South Vietnamese at Mylai on **Mar. 16, 1968.** He was sentenced to life imprisonment **Mar. 31.** Sentence was reduced to 20 years **Aug. 20.**

Publication of classified **Pentagon papers** on the U.S. involvement in Vietnam was begun **June 13** by the New York Times. In a 6-3 vote, the U.S. Supreme Court **June 30** upheld the right of the Times and the Washington Post to publish the documents under the protection of the First Amendment.

U.S. bombers struck massively in North Vietnam for 5 days starting **Dec. 26,** in retaliation for alleged violations of agreements reached prior to the 1968 bombing halt. U.S. forces at year-end were down to 140,000.

1972

Pres. Nixon arrived in **Peking Feb. 21** for an 8-day visit to China, which he called a "journey for peace." The unprecedented visit ended with a joint communique pledging that both powers would work for "a normalization of relations."

By a vote of 84 to 8, the Senate approved **Mar. 22** a Constitutional Amendment banning **discrimination against women** because of their sex and sent the measure to the states for ratification.

North Vietnamese forces launched the biggest attacks in 4 years across the demilitarized zone **Mar. 30.** The U.S. responded **Apr. 15** by resumption of bombing of Hanoi and Haiphong after a 4-year lull.

Nixon announced **May 8** the mining of **North Vietnam ports.** Last U.S. combat troops left **Aug. 11.**

Alabama Gov. George C. Wallace, campaigning at a Laurel, Md. shopping center **May 15, was shot** and seriously wounded as he greeted a large crowd. Arthur H. Bremer, 21, was sentenced Aug. 4 to 63 years for shooting Wallace and 3 bystanders.

In the first visit of a U.S. president to Moscow, Nixon arrived **May 22** for a week of summit talks with Kremlin leaders which culminated in a landmark **strategic arms pact.**

Five men were arrested **June 17** for breaking into the offices of the Democratic National Committee in the **Watergate** office complex in Washington, D.C.

The White House announced **July 8** that the U.S. would sell to the USSR at least $750 million of **American wheat,** corn, and other grains over a period of 3 years.

Full-scale bombing of North Vietnam resumed after Paris peace negotiations reached an impasse **Dec. 18.**

1973

Five of seven defendants in the **Watergate** break-in trial pleaded guilty **Jan. 11 and 15,** and the other 2 were convicted **Jan. 30.**

The Supreme Court ruled 7-2, **Jan. 22,** that a state may not prevent a woman from having an **abortion** during the **first 6 months of pregnancy,** invalidating abortion laws in Texas and Georgia, and, by implication, overturning restrictive abortion laws in 44 other states.

Four-party **Vietnam peace pacts** were signed in Paris **Jan. 27,** and North Vietnam released some 590 U.S. prisoners by **Apr. 1.** Last U.S. troops left **Mar. 29.**

The **end of the military draft** was announced **Jan. 27.**

China and the U.S. agreed **Feb. 22** to set up permanent liaison offices in each other's country.

Top **Nixon aides** H.R. Haldeman, John D. Ehrlichman, and John W. Dean, and Attorney General Richard Kleindienst **resigned Apr. 30** amid charges of White House efforts to obstruct justice in the Watergate case.

The Senate Armed Services Committee **July 16** began a probe into allegations that the U.S. Air Force had made 3,500 secret **B-52 raids into Cambodia** in **1969** and **1970.**

John Dean, former Nixon counsel, told Senate hearings **June 25** that Nixon, his staff and campaign aides, and the Justice Department all had conspired to cover up Watergate facts. Nixon refused July 23 to release **tapes** of relevant White House conversations. Some tapes were turned over to the court **Nov. 26.**

The U.S. officially ceased bombing in **Cambodia** at midnight **Aug. 14** in accord with a June Congressional action.

Vice Pres. Spiro T. Agnew Oct. 10 resigned and pleaded "nolo contendere" (no contest) to charges of tax evasion on payments made to him by Maryland contractors when he was governor of that state. Gerald Rudolph Ford **Oct. 12** became first appointed vice president under the 25th Amendment; sworn in **Dec. 6.**

A total ban on **oil exports** to the U.S. was imposed by Arab oil-producing nations **Oct. 19-21** after the outbreak of an Arab-Israeli war. The ban was lifted **Mar. 18, 1974.**

Atty. Gen. Elliot Richardson resigned, and his deputy William D. Ruckelshaus and Watergate Special Prosecutor Archibald Cox were fired by Pres. Nixon **Oct. 20** when Cox threatened to secure a judicial ruling that Nixon was violating a court order to turn tapes over to Watergate case Judge John Sirica.

Leon Jaworski, conservative Texas Democrat, was named **Nov. 1** by the Nixon administration to be special prosecutor to succeed Archibald Cox.

Congress overrode **Nov. 7** Nixon's veto of the **war powers** bill which curbed the president's power to commit armed forces to hostilities abroad without Congressional approval.

1974

Impeachment hearings were opened **May 9** against Nixon by the House Judiciary Committee.

John D. Ehrlichman and 3 **White House "plumbers"** were found guilty **July 12** of conspiring to violate the civil rights of Dr. Lewis Fielding, formerly psychiatrist to Pentagon Papers leaker Daniel Ellsberg, by breaking into his Beverly Hills, Cal. office.

The U.S. Supreme Court ruled, 8-0, **July 24** that Nixon had to turn over **64 tapes** of White House conversations sought by Watergate Special Prosecutor Leon Jaworski.

The House Judiciary Committee, in televised hearings **July 24-30**, recommended 3 **articles of impeachment** against Nixon. The first, voted 27-11 **July 27**, charged Nixon with taking part in a criminal conspiracy to obstruct justice in the Watergate cover-up. The second, voted 28-10 **July 29**, charged he "repeatedly" failed to carry out his constitutional oath in a series of alleged abuses of power. The third, voted 27-17 **July 30**, accused him of unconstitutional defiance of committee subpoenas. The House of Representatives voted without debate **Aug. 20**, by 412-3, to accept the committee report, which included the recommended impeachment articles.

Nixon resigned Aug. 9. His support began eroding **Aug. 5** when he released 3 tapes, admitting he originated plans to have the FBI stop its probe of the Watergate break-in for political as well as national security reasons. **Vice President Gerald R. Ford** was sworn in as the 38th U.S. president on **Aug. 9.**

An **unconditional pardon** to ex-Pres. Nixon for all federal crimes that he "committed or may have committed" while president was issued by Pres. Gerald Ford **Sept. 8.**

1975

Found guilty of **Watergate** cover-up charges **Jan. 1** were ex-Atty. Gen. John N. Mitchell, ex-presidential advisers H.R. Haldeman and John D. Ehrlichman.

U.S. civilians were evacuated from **Saigon Apr. 29** as communist forces completed takeover of South Vietnam.

U.S. merchant ship **Mayaguez** and crew of 39 seized by Cambodian forces in Gulf of Siam **May 12.** In rescue operation, U.S. Marines attacked Tang Is., planes bombed air base; Cambodia surrendered ship and crew.

Congress voted $405 million for South **Vietnam refugees May 16;** 140,000 were flown to the U.S.

Illegal **CIA operations,** including records on 300,000 persons and groups, and infiltration of agents into black, antiwar and political movements, were described by a "blue-ribbon" panel headed by Vice Pres. Rockefeller **June 10.**

FBI agents captured **Patricia (Patty) Hearst,** kidnaped **Feb. 4, 1974,** in San Francisco **Sept. 18** with others. She was indicted for bank robbery; a San Francisco jury convicted her **Mar. 20, 1976.**

1976

Payments abroad of $22 million in bribes by Lockheed Aircraft Corp. to sell its planes were revealed **Feb. 4** by a Senate subcommittee. Lockheed admitted payments in Japan, Turkey, Italy, and Holland.

The U.S. celebrated its **Bicentennial July 4,** marking the 200th anniversary of its independence with festivals, parades, and N.Y. City's Operation Sail, a gathering of tall ships from around the world viewed by 6 million persons.

A mystery ailment **"legionnaire's disease"** killed 29 persons who attended an American Legion convention **July 21-24** in Philadelphia. The cause was found to be a bacterium, it was reported **June 18, 1977.**

The Viking II set down on **Mars' Utopia Plains Sept. 3,** following the successful landing by Viking I **July 20.**

1977

Pres. Jimmy Carter **Jan. 21** pardoned most Vietnam War **draft evaders,** who numbered some 10,000.

Convicted murderer **Gary Gilmore** was executed by a Utah firing squad **Jan. 17,** in the first exercise of capital punishment anywhere in the U.S. since **1967.** Gilmore had opposed all attempts to delay the execution.

Carter signed an act **Aug. 4** creating a new Cabinet-level **Energy Department.**

1978

U.S. Senate voted **Apr. 18** to turn over the **Panama Canal** to Panama on Dec. 31, 1999; **Mar. 16** vote had given approval to a treaty guaranteeing the area's neutrality after the year 2000.

The U.S. Supreme Court **June 28** voted 5-4 not to allow a firm quota system in affirmative action plans; the Court did uphold programs that were more "flexible" in nature.

The **House Select Committee on Assassinations** opened hearings **Sept. 6** into assassinations of Pres. Kennedy and Martin Luther King Jr.; the committee recessed **Dec. 30** after concluding conspiracies likely in both cases, but with no further hard evidence for further prosecutions.

Congress passed the **Humphrey-Hawkins "full employment" Bill Oct. 15,** which set national goal of reducing unemployment to 4% by 1983, while reducing inflation to 3% in same period; Pres. Carter signed bill, **Oct. 27.**

1979

A major accident occurred, **Mar. 28,** at a nuclear reactor on **Three Mile Island** near Middletown, Pa.

The federal government announced, **Nov. 1,** a $1.5 billion loan-guarantee plan to aid the nation's 3d largest automaker, **Chrysler Corp.,** which had reported a loss of $460.6 million for the 3d quarter of 1979.

Some 90 people, including 63 Americans, were taken hostage, **Nov. 4,** at the **American embassy in Teheran,** Iran, by militant student followers of Ayatollah Khomeini who demanded the return of former Shah Mohammad Reza Pahlavi, who was undergoing medical treatment in New York City.

1980

Pres. Carter announced, **Jan. 4, punitive measures against the USSR,** inc. an embargo on the sale of grain and high technology, in retaliation for the Soviet invasion of Afghanistan. At Carter's request, the **U.S. Olympic Committee** voted, **Apr. 12,** not to attend the Moscow Summer Olympics.

Eight Americans were killed and 5 wounded, **Apr. 24,** in an ill-fated attempt to **rescue the hostages** held by Iranian **militants** at the U.S. Embassy in Teheran.

In Washington, **Mt. St. Helens erupted, May 18,** in a violent blast estimated to be 500 times as powerful as the Hiroshima atomic bomb. The blast, followed by others on **May 25** and **June 12,** left about 60 dead, and economic losses estimated at nearly $3 billion.

In a sweeping victory, **Nov. 4, Ronald Wilson Reagan** was elected 40th President of the United States, defeating incumbent Jimmy Carter. The stunning GOP victory extended to the U.S. Congress where Republicans gained control of the Senate and wrested 33 House seats from the Democrats.

Former Beatle **John Lennon** was shot and killed, **Dec. 8,** outside his apartment building in New York City.

1981

Minutes after the **inauguration of Pres. Ronald Reagan, Jan. 20,** the **52 Americans** who had been held **hostage in Iran** for 444 days were flown to freedom following an agreement in which the U.S. agreed to return to Iran $8 billion in frozen assets.

President Reagan was **shot in the chest** by a would-be assassin, **Mar. 30,** in Washington, D.C., as he walked to his limousine following an address.

The world's first reusable spacecraft, the **Space Shuttle Columbia,** was sent into space, **Apr. 12,** and completed its successful mission 2 days later.

Both houses of Congress passed, **July 29,** President Reagan's **tax-cut legislation.** The largest tax cut in the nation's history was expected to reduce taxes by $37.6 bln. in fiscal 1982, and to save taxpayers $750 bln. over the next 5 years.

Federal air traffic controllers, Aug. 3, began an **illegal nationwide strike** after their union rejected the government's final offer for a new contract. Most of the 13,000 striking controllers defied the back-to-work order, and were dismissed by President Reagan **Aug. 5.**

In a 99-0 vote, the Senate confirmed, **Sept. 21,** the appointment of **Sandra Day O'Connor** as an **associate justice of the U.S. Supreme Court.** She was the first woman appointed to that body.

President Reagan ordered **sanctions against the new Polish military government, Dec. 23,** in response to the imposition of martial law in that country.

1982

The 13-year-old lawsuit against **AT&T** by the **Justice Dept.** was settled **Jan. 8.** AT&T agreed to give up the 22 Bell System companies but in return was allowed to expand into previously prohibited areas inc. data processing, telephone and computer equipment sales, and computer communication devices.

On **Mar. 2,** the Senate voted 57-37 for a bill that virtually eliminated busing for the purposes of racial integration.

On **June 12,** in **N.Y.'s Central Park,** hundreds of thousands demonstrated against **nuclear arms.**

The Equal Rights Amendment was defeated after a 10-year struggle for ratification.

The **elections** on **Nov. 2** resulted in gains for the Democrats—the margin in the new House was 269-166. In the Senate elections, Democrats won 20 out of 33 seats, but were still the minority, 54-46.

The **highest unemployment rate since 1940,** 10.4%, was reported on **Nov. 5.** The rate for Nov. reached 10.8%, with over 11 million unemployed.

Lech Walesa, former leader of **Solidarity,** the Polish labor union, was freed **Nov. 13,** after 11 months of internment following the imposition of martial law and the outlawing of Solidarity. Pres. Reagan lifted the **U.S. embargo on sales of oil and gas equipment to the Soviet Union.**

The **Space Shuttle Columbia** completed its first operational flight **Nov. 16.**

A retired dentist, **Dr. Barney B. Clark,** 61, became the first recipient of a **permanent artificial heart** during a 7½ hour operation in Salt Lake City **Dec. 2.** The heart was designed by **Dr. Robert Jarvik,** also on the surgical team.

1983

On **Apr. 20, Pres. Reagan** signed a compromise, bipartisan bill designed to rescue the **Social Security System** from bankruptcy.

In an 8-1 decision, **the U.S. Supreme Court** held, **May 24,** that the **Internal Revenue Service** could deny **tax exemptions** to **private schools** that practiced **racial discrimination.**

Sally Ride became the first American **woman** to travel in **space, June 18,** when the **space shuttle Challenger** was launched from Cape Canaveral, Fla.

On **Oct. 23,** 241 **U.S. Marines and sailors,** members of the multinational **peacekeeping force in Lebanon,** were killed when a TNT-laden suicide **terrorist** blew up Marine headquarters at **Beirut** Intl. Airport. Almost simultaneously, a second truck bomb blew up a **French paratroop** barracks two miles away, killing more than 40.

U.S. Marines and Rangers and a small force from 6 **Caribbean** nations invaded the island of **Grenada** on **Oct. 25,** in response to a request from the **Organization of Eastern Caribbean States.** After a few days, Grenadian militia and Cuban "construction workers" were overcome, hundreds of U.S. citizens evacuated safely, and the Marxist regime deposed. The U.S. Congress applied the War Powers Resolution, requiring U.S. troops to leave Grenada by **Dec. 24.**

1984

In his **State of the Union address, Jan. 25,** Pres. Reagan called for budget cuts of $100 billion over 3 years, but opposed increased taxes.

On **Feb. 26,** as the position of Pres. Amin Gemayel of Lebanon deteriorated and his army crumbled, Pres. Reagan **removed U.S. Marines from Beirut** and placed them on U.S. ships offshore.

The space shuttle *Challenger* was launched on its 4th trip into space, **Feb. 3.** On **Feb. 7,** Navy Capt. Bruce McCandless, followed by Army Lt. Colonel Robert Stewart, **became the first humans to fly free of a spacecraft.**

During **March,** the U.S. Senate rejected 2 Constitutional amendments that would have permitted **prayer in the public schools.**

The Central Intelligence Agency **(CIA) acknowledged** in April that it had participated in the **mining of Nicaraguan harbors.** This touched off a controversy in Congress, and the Senate, **Apr. 10,** adopted a nonbinding resolution condemning U.S. participation in the mining.

From **Apr. 26 to May 1, Pres. Reagan visited China** for the first time, holding discussions with Chinese leaders.

On **May 7,** American **veterans of the Vietnam war** reached an **out-of-court settlement with 7 chemical companies** in their class-action suit the herbicide **Agent Orange.**

A federal judge in Salt Lake City held, **May 10,** that the **U.S. government had been negligent** in its above-ground testing of **nuclear weapons** in Nevada from 1951 to 1962.

On **June 6,** former vice president **Walter Mondale** won the **Democratic presidental nomination.** In a historic move, **July 12, Mondale chose a woman, Rep. Geraldine Ferraro** (N.Y.) as candidate for **vice president.**

Pres. Reagan, **Aug. 11,** signed a law prohibiting public high schools from barring students who wished to **assemble for religious or political activities outside of school hours.**

Ronald Reagan was reelected U.S. President **Nov. 6** in the greatest Republican **landslide** in history, carrying 49 states against Walter F. Mondale.

1985

The controversial MX missile survived critical votes in the Senate and House. The **Senate, Mar. 19 and 21,** voted to **authorize the missiles** and to **appropriate $1.5 million** for the construction of 21 missiles. The **House** gave its endorsement **Mar. 26 and 28.**

E.F. Hutton, one of the nation's largest brokerage companies, **pleaded guilty, May 2,** to 2,000 **federal charges** related to the manipulation of its checking accounts. The company agreed to pay $2 million in fines and to pay back up to $8 million to banks it had defrauded.

"Live Aid," a 17-hour rock concert broadcast **July 13** on radio and TV from London and Phila. to 152 countries, raised $70 million for the starving peoples of Africa.

On **Oct. 7, 5 hijackers seized an Italian cruise ship, the** *Achille Lauro,* in the open sea as it approached Port Said, Egypt. Some 400 persons were aboard, including about 340 crew. The hijackers, members of the Palestine Liberation Front, a faction broken from the PLO, demanded the release of 50 Palestinians held by Israel.

In November, for the first time in 6 years, the leaders of the U.S. and the Soviet Union met at a **summit conference.** In Geneva, Switzerland, **Pres. Reagan** and **Mikhail Gorbachev,** the general secretary of the Soviet Communist Party, talked privately for 5 hours, **Nov. 19 and 20.**

1986

On **Jan. 20,** for the 1st time, the U.S. officially observed **Martin Luther King Day.**

Moments after liftoff, **Jan. 28,** the **space shuttle** ***Challenger*** **exploded, killing 6 astronauts and Christa McAuliffe, a New Hampshire teacher.** Subsequent investigations found that NASA had abandoned "good judgment and common sense" regarding safety problems that caused the explosion.

U.S. warplanes struck targets in Tripoli and Benghazi, Libya, Apr. 14—retaliation against the Libyan bombing of a W. Berlin disco that killed 2, injured 200, Apr. 5. On **Jan. 7,** Pres. Reagan had said that the U.S. had aborted 26 "terrorist missions" in 1985. In an executive order, he banned trade with and travel to Libya, ordering Americans out. A 2nd executive order, **Jan. 8,** had frozen all Libyan government assets in the U.S. and U.S. bank branches abroad.

U.S. officials said, **June 12, that AIDS cases and deaths would increase tenfold in the next 5 years.** At that time, the government had recorded 21,517 cases, 11,713 deaths. An anti-viral drug, azidothymidine (AZT) was found to improve the health of some AIDS patient, but was not a cure.

With mounting **abuse of illegal drugs** in the U.S., specifically **cocaine as "crack,"** Congress passed anti-drug laws and the U.S. joined Bolivia in raids against cocaine processing hideouts.

The U.S., **via Congress's Sept. override of Pres. Reagan's veto,** joined other nations in imposing **economic sanctions on So. Africa,** pressuring the Botha gvt. to end apartheid.

The U.S. Senate confirmed, **Sept. 17,** Pres. Reagan's nomination of **William Rehnquist as chief justice, Antonin Scalia as associate justice of the Supreme Court.**

Congress passed, in late **Sept.,** the comprehensive **Tax Reform Law.** In effect in 1987, it simplified the system, drastically changing tax brackets, deductions, and more.

The U.S. and USSR reached tentative agreement on a **world-wide ban of medium-range missiles, Sept. 18.**

One day before the 1986 Congressional elections, it was reported that the U.S. had sent spare parts and ammunition to Iran. Over the next months it was revealed that **additional arms sales had been made to Iran, and profits diverted to a fund for Nicaraguan contras.**

In the **Congressional races, Nov. 4, Democrats won a 55-45 Senate majority,** after 6 yrs. of a Republican majority, and **enlarged their House majority by 5, to 258-177.**

The most scandalous year in Wall Street history ended with **Ivan Boesky's agreeing, Nov. 14, to plead guilty to an unspecified criminal count, pay a $100 million fine, and return profits;** he was barred for life from trading securities.

1987

Pres. Reagan produced the nation's first **trillion-dollar budget, Jan. 5.**

The stock market continued its phenomenal rise. The **Dow closed at 2002.25, Jan. 8,** its first finish above 2000. The Dow advanced for 13 consecutive trading days, another record; **Jan. 20;** the average soared 51.60 points, **Jan. 22,** a one-day record. At month's end, the cumulative advance was more than 250 points, yet another record.

The **Tower Commission Report, Feb. 27,** found **Pres. Reagan confused and uninformed;** and further faulted White House Chief of Staff Donald Regan; former Natl. Security Adviser Robert McFarlane; his successor Adm. John Poindexter; and CIA Director William Casey.

An **Iraqi warplane missile killed 37 sailors** on the frigate U.S.S. Stark in the Persian Gulf, **May 17.** Iraq called it an accident. The Stark's officers were found negligent, June 14. The U.S. escorted Kuwaiti oil tankers to the Gulf, reflagging them for the U.S.

Public hearings by the Senate and House committees investigating the **Iran-contra affair** went on from **May-Aug.** Former CIA Director Casey died, May 6, 5 months after brain surgery; Lt. Col. Oliver North, a media sensation, said he had believed all his activities authorized by his superiors; Poindexter said his own purpose had been "to provide some future deniability for the president . . ."; Shultz said Casey, McFarlane, and Poindexter had lied to him and deceived Pres. Reagan. Pres. Reagan, Aug. 12, said he had been "stubborn in pursuit of a policy that went astray," but again denied knowing of the funds' diversion to the contras.

Wall Street crashed, Oct. 19, the Dow plummeting a record 508 points—22.6 percent—after a record high of 2722.42, Aug. 25; a 200-point drop by Oct., called a correction by most; and drops of 91.55, Oct. 6; 95.46, Oct. 14; and 108.36, Oct. 16.

Pres. Reagan and **Soviet leader Gorbachev** met in Wash., **Dec. 8,** and signed **an unprecedented agreement** calling for the **dismantling of all 1,752 U.S. and 859 Soviet missiles with a 300-3,400-mile range.** The leaders agreed to meet in Moscow in 1988.

1988

Federal grand juries in Miami and Tampa returned **indictments, Feb. 4,** against **Gen. Manuel Noriega,** the effective ruler of Panama, charging that he had protected and otherwise assisted the Medellin drug cartel. Attempts by the U.S. to oust Noriega plunged Panama into political and economic turmoil.

Nearly **1.4 million illegal aliens** met the **May 4** deadline for applying for **amnesty** under a U.S. Immigration and Naturalization Service policy. An estimated 50+ percent of applications were in Calif.; nationwide, about 71 percent of the aliens had entered the U.S. from Mexico.

Much of the U.S. suffered the worst **drought** in more than 50 years. By June 23, half of the nation's agricultural counties had been designated disaster areas.

A missile, fired from the **U.S. Navy warship** *Vincennes,* in the Persian Gulf, **struck and destroyed a commercial Iranian airliner, July 3, killing all 290 persons** on the plane. Navy personnel had mistaken the airliner for an Iranian F-14 jet fighter.

Fire destroyed about 4 million acres of forest land throughout the west, including Alaska, during the late summer. Property damage was also considerable.

Failures at nuclear-power plants posed problems across the U.S., according to congressional testimony, starting **Sept. 30.** Problems cited including aging equipment, poor management and training, and lax safety standards.

George Bush, vice president under Ronald Reagan, **was elected 41st U.S. president, Nov. 8.** Bush defeated the Democratic nominee, Gov. Michael Dukakis (Mass.), by 54 to 46 percent of the popular vote, and 426 electoral votes to Dukakis's 112. **Sen. Dan Quayle** (Ind.) was the successful vice presidential nominee; Sen. Lloyd Bentsen (Tex.) was the Democratic nominee for v.p. Democrats continued to control both houses of Congress.

Drexel Burnham Lambert agreed, **Dec. 21, to plead guilty to 6 violations of federal law,** inc. insider trading, stock manipulation, and falsified records; and **to pay penalties of $650 million,** by far the largest such settlement.

1989

The Labor Dept. reported, **Jan. 6,** that **unemployment was 5.3%, a 14-year low,** at the end of **1988.** For the whole year, the economy grew 3.8%, the most in 4 years.

The **largest oil spill in U.S. history** occurred after the *Exxon Valdez* struck Bligh Reef in **Alaska's Prince William Sound, Mar. 24.** Exxon Corp. announced, Mar. 25, that it accepted full financial responsibility for the spill, initially estimated at 240,000 barrels, then announced that the spill could not be contained; as of Mar. 29, it extended 45 miles.

Former Natl. Security Council staff member **Oliver North** became the first person, **May 4, convicted in a jury trial** in connection with the **Iran-contra** scandal. The jury acquitted North on 9 charges, found him guilty of 3: aiding and abetting the obstruction of Congress; altering, destroying, removing, or concealing NSC documents; receiving as an illegal gratuity a $13,800 security system for his home. North received, July 6, a 3-year suspended prison sentence, 2 years' probation, a $150,000 fine, and an order to perform 1,200 hours of community service.

House speaker Jim Wright (D. Tex.), who faced 69 ethical charges, announced his **resignation as speaker and from the House, May 31. Rep. Tony Coehlho (D. Calif.),** also under scrutiny, announced his **resignation as majority whip and from the House.**

The **U.S. Supreme Court** announced, **July 3,** its 5-4 decision to put new **restraints on a woman's right to have an abortion,** although it did not overturn Roe v. Wade.

Jack Kemp, secy. of **Housing and Urban Development,** acknowledged, **July 11,** that an estimated **$2 billion** had been lost due to **fraud and mismanagement** during the tenure of his predecessor **Samuel Pierce.**

Legislation passed by Congress to **rescue the savings and loan industry** was signed into law, **Aug. 9,** by Pres. George Bush. The bill provided $166 billion over 10 years to close or merge insolvent S&Ls. The total cost was put at $400 billion over 30 years, most to be paid by taxpayers.

Army Gen. Colin Powell was nominated by Pres. Bush, **Aug. 10,** to serve as **chairman of the Joint Chiefs of Staff;** he became the first black to hold the post.

Minutes before the start of the 3d game of the 1989 World Series between the San Francisco Giants and the Oakland Athletics, **Oct. 17,** an **earthquake struck the San Francisco Bay area,** causing at least 59 deaths and massive property damage.

Democrats won most of the **top offices** at stake and **black candidates scored major breakthroughs,** in off-year elections, **Nov. 7.** Lt. Gov. L. Douglas Wilder, a Democrat, was elected governor of Virginia, the nation's first black governor since Reconstruction; Manhattan Borough Pres. David Dinkins, also a Democrat, became the first black elected mayor of New York City.

Pennsylvania became the first state, **Nov. 18,** to **restrict abortions,** after the U.S. Supreme Court gave states the right to do so in July.

Pres. Bush signed into law, **Nov. 19,** an **increase in the minimum wage.** Currently $3.35, the wage would rise to **$4.25** an hour by 1991, with a training wage of $3.35 for 16- to 19-year-olds in their first 3 months on a job.

U.S. troops invaded Panama, Dec. 20, overthrowing the government of Manuel Noriega, who eluded capture, took refuge in the Vatican mission, then surrendered to the U.S. Jan. 3, 1990.

1990

The **Dow Jones Industrial average** pushed to an **all-time high** on Wall Street, **July 16 and 17,** finishing at 2,999.75 and averaging above 3,000.

Pres. Bush signed a bill that would bar **discrimination** against people with **physical or mental disabilities, July 26.**

Justice William Brennan announced, **July 20,** his immediate resignation from the U.S. Supreme Court, due to illness; Pres. Bush nominated **Judge David Souter** of the U.S. Court of Appeals for the First Circuit in Boston, **July 23,** and the Senate voted to endorse him, **Sept. 27.**

Operation Desert Shield forces left for **Saudi Arabia, Aug. 7,** to defend that country following the **invasion** of its neighbor **Kuwait by Iraq.**

Pres. Bush **vetoed, Oct. 22,** a **civil rights bill** that sought in effect to reverse 6 recent Supreme Court decisions that civil rights organizations contended had weakened anti-discrimination laws on hiring and promoting.

The Democratic Party made small gains in the Senate and House in **elections, Nov. 6.** Democrats gained one seat in the Senate, for a 56-44 margin over Republicans, and gained 8 seats in the House for a 267-167 margin. One independent was elected in Vermont. About 96 percent of incumbents seeking re-election were successful; only 15 lost. In gubernatorial elections, 14 statehouses changed parties, Democrats emerging with a 28-19 margin, compared with 29-21 before the election. Independents won in Alaska and Connecticut, and a runoff would be required in Arizona.

Pres. Bush signed, **Nov. 15,** a bill designed to **reduce budget deficits** by nearly $500 billion over 5 years. The top tax rate would rise from 28 to 31 percent and exemptions for upper-income Americans would be phased out; gas, cigarette, liquor taxes would increase; a luxury tax would be imposed on some planes, cars, boats, furs, and jewelry.

Pres. Bush signed, **Nov. 15,** the **1990 Clean Air Act,** a comprehensive updating of the original Clean Air Act of 1970.

In **Dec.** unemployment reached a 3-year high of 6.1 percent. In the 2nd half of the year, more than 1 million payroll jobs were lost. Consumer prices rose 6.1 percent during the year, the highest annual rate since 1981.

1991

The **U.S. and its allies defeated Iraq** in **Jan.** and **Feb. 1991** and liberated Kuwait, which Iraq had overrun in Aug. 1990. After Iraq's invasion, for nearly 6 months, diplomats of many nations had sought to persuade Pres. Saddam Hussein to pull his occupying forces out of the oil-rich sheikhdom. Finally, In **Jan.,** the allies launched an **attack on Iraq from the air** that sharply reduced his offensive and defensive military capacity. In a **ground war in Feb.** that lasted just 100 hours, the U.S.-led attackers killed or captured many thousands of Iraqi soldiers and sent the rest into retreat before Pres. George Bush ordered a ceasefire.

The **unemployment rate in March** stood at **6.7 percent,** the highest since late 1986. However, the **Dow Jones Industrial Average** finished above 3000 for the first time, **Apr. 17,** closing at 3004.46.

Justice Thurgood Marshall, the only black ever to serve on the U.S. Supreme Court, announced, **June 27,** that he would retire when a successor was approved.

Unemployment edged up to **7.0 percent** in **June,** but the **Gross National Product,** the broadest measure of the economy, had **risen 0.4 percent** at an annual rate during the **2nd quarter of 1991,** and the chief economic advisor to the U.S. Pres. said, "The recession appears to have ended."

Pres. Bush approved, **July 10,** the recommendations of the **Defense Base Closure and Realignment Commission,** which had proposed that 34 domestic military installations be closed and 48 other realigned, due to the federal budget crunch and the end of the cold war.

Chemical Banking Corp. and **Manufacturers Hanover Corp.** announced, **July 15,** a **merger** agreement. The merger partners, both based in New York, would have combined assets of $135.46 billion.

BankAmerica and Security Pacific Corp. announced, **Aug. 12,** that they would **merge.** The agreement, if approved, would involve a $4.47 billion stock swap.

The **case against Oliver North was "terminated,"** with all charges dropped, **Sept. 16.** In 1989, North, a leading figure in the Iran/Contra affair, had been convicted of obstructing a congressional investigation, destroying documents, and accepting an illegal gratuity. In 1990, a federal appeals court had overturned one conviction and sent the others back to the federal district court.

The General Accounting Office revealed that in a recent 12-month period, **8,331 checks** had been written against **insufficient funds** in a bank that operated at the Capitol with only House members for depositors. On **Oct. 3,** House Speaker Tom Foley said the bank would be closed at the end of 1991 and that the House Ethics Committee would investigate.

The U.S. Senate approved the nomination of Clarence Thomas to serve as an **associate justice of the Supreme Court,** after investigating an allegation of sexual harassment that had been leveled against him. Thomas and his accusor, Anita Hill, a law professor at the Univ. of Oklahoma, testified before the Senate Judiciary Committee, **Oct. 11,** while a huge TV audience watched. The Senate confirmed Thomas, 52-48.

Both major parties could claim **significant victories** in the **Nov. 5 elections.** The victory of Democrat Harris Wofford over former governor and U.S. attorney general Richard Thornburgh for the U.S. Senate Seat in Pennsylvania was seen as a signal of public concern about the state of the economy. Mississippi's incumbent governor, Democrat Ray Mabus, lost to Kirk Fordice, who would become the first Republican governor of the state since Reconstruction.

A compromise bill providing for **additional benefits for unemployed workers** was signed by Pres. George Bush, **Nov. 15.** The bill would give all unemployed workers from 6 to 20 additional weeks of benefits.

Pres. George Bush signed, **Nov. 21,** a **job-discrimination bill** requiring that hiring and promotion be related to job performance. Those claiming discrimination could sue for damages, not just back pay and lost benefits.

Charles Keating was convicted of 17 counts of securities fraud, Dec. 4. The prosecution asserted that as chairman of the Lincoln Savings & Loan Assn. in Cal., Keating had induced some 17,000 investors to buy $250 million in bonds that were not insured.

Declaration of Independence

The Declaration of Independence was adopted by the Continental Congress in Philadelphia, on July 4, 1776. John Hancock was president of the Congress and Charles Thomson was secretary. A copy of the Declaration, engrossed on parchment, was signed by members of Congress on and after Aug. 2, 1776. On Jan. 18, 1777, Congress ordered that "an authenticated copy, with the names of the members of Congress subscribing the same, be sent to each of the United States, and that they be desired to have the same put upon record." Authenticated copies were printed in broadside form in Baltimore, where the Continental Congress was then in session. The following text is that of the original printed by John Dunlap at Philadelphia for the Continental Congress.

IN CONGRESS, July 4, 1776.

A DECLARATION

By the REPRESENTATIVES of the

UNITED STATES OF AMERICA,

In GENERAL CONGRESS assembled

When in the Course of human Events, it becomes necessary for one People to dissolve the Political Bands which have connected them with another, and to assume among the Powers of the Earth, the separate and equal Station to which the Laws of Nature and of Nature's God entitle them, a decent Respect to the Opinions of Mankind requires that they should declare the causes which impel them to the Separation.

We hold these Truths to be self-evident, that all Men are created equal, that they are endowed by their Creator with certain unalienable Rights, that among these are Life, Liberty, and the Pursuit of Happiness—That to secure these Rights, Governments are instituted among Men, deriving their just Powers from the Consent of the Governed, that whenever any Form of Government becomes destructive of these Ends, it is the Right of the People to alter or to abolish it, and to institute new Government, laying its Foundation on such Principles, and organizing its Powers in such Form, as to them shall seem most likely to effect their Safety and Happiness. Prudence, indeed, will dictate that Governments long established should not be changed for light and transient Causes; and accordingly all Experience hath shewn, that Mankind are more disposed to suffer, while Evils are sufferable, than to right themselves by abolishing the Forms to which they are accustomed. But when a long Train of Abuses and Usurpations, pursuing invariably the same Object, evinces a Design to reduce them under absolute Despotism, it is their Right, it is their Duty, to throw off such Government, and to provide new Guards for their future Security. Such has been the patient Sufferance of these Colonies; and such is now the Necessity which constrains them to alter their former Systems of Government. The History of the present King of Great-Britain is a History of repeated Injuries and Usurpations, all having in direct Object the Establishment of an absolute Tyranny over these States. To prove this, let Facts be submitted to a candid World.

He has refused his Assent to Laws, the most wholesome and necessary for the public Good.

He has forbidden his Governors to pass Laws of immediate and pressing Importance, unless suspended in their Operation till his Assent should be obtained; and when so suspended, he has utterly neglected to attend to them.

He has refused to pass other Laws for the Accommodation of large Districts of People, unless those People would relinquish the Right of Representation in the Legislature, a Right inestimable to them, and formidable to Tyrants only.

He has called together Legislative Bodies at Places unusual, uncomfortable, and distant from the Depository of their Public Records, for the sole Purpose of fatiguing them into Compliance with his Measures.

He has dissolved Representative Houses repeatedly, for opposing with manly Firmness his Invasions on the Rights of the People.

He has refused for a long Time, after such Dissolutions, to cause others to be elected; whereby the Legislative Powers, incapable of Annihilation, have returned to the People at large for their exercise; the State remaining in the mean time exposed to all the Dangers of Invasion from without, and Convulsions within.

He has endeavoured to prevent the Population of these States; for that Purpose obstructing the Laws for Naturalization of Foreigners; refusing to pass others to encourage their Migrations hither, and raising the Conditions of new Appropriations of Lands.

He has obstructed the Administration of Justice, by refusing his Assent to Laws for establishing Judiciary Powers.

He has made Judges dependent on his Will alone, for the Tenure of their Offices, and the Amount and payment of their Salaries.

He has erected a Multitude of new Offices, and sent hither Swarms of Officers to harrass our People, and eat out their Substance.

He has kept among us, in Times of Peace, Standing Armies, without the consent of our Legislatures.

He has affected to render the Military independent of, and superior to the Civil Power.

He has combined with others to subject us to a Jurisdiction foreign to our Constitution, and unacknowledged by our Laws; giving his Assent to their Acts of pretended Legislation:

For quartering large Bodies of Armed Troops among us:

For protecting them, by a mock Trial, from Punishment for any Murders which they should commit on the Inhabitants of these States:

For cutting off our Trade with all Parts of the World:

For imposing Taxes on us without our Consent:

For depriving us, in many Cases, of the Benefits of Trial by Jury:

For transporting us beyond Seas to be tried for pretended Offences:

For abolishing the free System of English Laws in a neighbouring Province, establishing therein an arbitrary Government, and enlarging its Boundaries, so as to render it at once an Example and fit Instrument for introducing the same absolute Rule into these Colonies:

For taking away our Charters, abolishing our most valuable Laws, and altering fundamentally the Forms of our Governments:

For suspending our own Legislatures, and declaring themselves invested with Power to legislate for us in all Cases whatsoever.

He has abdicated Government here, by declaring us out of his Protection and waging War against us.

He has plundered our Seas, ravaged our Coasts, burnt our towns, and destroyed the Lives of our People.

He is, at this Time, transporting large Armies of foreign Mercenaries to complete the works of Death, Desolation, and Tyranny, already begun with circumstances of Cruelty and Perfidy, scarcely paralleled in the most barbarous Ages, and totally unworthy the Head of a civilized Nation.

He has constrained our fellow Citizens taken Captive on the high Seas to bear Arms against their Country, to become the Executioners of their Friends and Brethren, or to fall themselves by their Hands.

He has excited domestic Insurrections amongst us, and has endeavoured to bring on the Inhabitants of our Frontiers, the merciless Indian Savages, whose known Rule of Warfare, is an undistinguished Destruction, of all Ages, Sexes and Conditions.

In every stage of these Oppressions we have Petitioned for Redress in the most humble Terms: Our repeated Petitions have been answered only by repeated Injury. A Prince, whose Character is thus marked by every act which may define a Tyrant, is unfit to be the Ruler of a free People.

Nor have we been wanting in Attentions to our British Brethren. We have warned them from Time to Time of Attempts by their Legislature to extend an unwarrantable Jurisdiction over us. We have reminded them of the Circumstances of our Emigration and Settlement here. We have appealed to their native Justice and Magnanimity, and we have conjured them by the Ties of our common Kindred to disavow these Usurpations, which, would inevitably interrupt our Connections and Correspondence. They too have been deaf to the Voice of Justice and of Consanguinity. We must, therefore, acquiesce in the Necessity, which denounces our Separation, and hold them, as we hold the rest of Mankind, Enemies in War, in Peace, Friends.

We, therefore, the Representatives of the UNITED STATES OF AMERICA, in General Congress, Assembled, appealing to the Supreme Judge of the World for the Rectitude of our Intentions, do, in the Name, and by Authority of the good People of these Colonies, solemnly Publish and Declare, That these United Colonies are, and of Right ought to be, Free and Independent States; that they are absolved from all Allegiance to the British Crown, and that all political Connection between them and the State of Great-Britain, is and ought to be totally dissolved; and that as Free and Independent States, they have full Power to levy War, conclude Peace, contract Alliances, establish Commerce, and to do all other Acts and Things which Independent States may of right do. And for the support of this declaration, with a firm Reliance on the Protection of divine Providence, we mutually pledge to each other our lives, our Fortunes, and our sacred Honor.

JOHN HANCOCK, President

Attest.
CHARLES THOMSON, Secretary.

Signers of the Declaration of Independence

Delegate and state	Vocation	Birthplace	Born	Died
Adams, John (Mass.)	Lawyer	Braintree (Quincy), Mass.	Oct. 30, 1735	July 4, 1826
Adams, Samuel (Mass.)	Political leader	Boston, Mass.	Sept. 27, 1722	Oct. 2, 1803
Bartlett, Josiah (N.H.)	Physician, judge	Amesbury, Mass.	Nov. 21, 1729	May 19, 1795
Braxton, Carter (Va.)	Farmer	Newington Plantation, Va.	Sept. 10, 1736	Oct. 10, 1797
Carroll, Chas. of Carrollton (Md.)	Lawyer	Annapolis, Md.	Sept. 19, 1737	Nov. 14, 1832
Chase, Samuel (Md.)	Judge	Princess Anne, Md.	Apr. 17, 1741	June 19, 1811
Clark, Abraham (N.J.)	Surveyor	Roselle, N.J.	Feb. 15, 1726	Sept. 15, 1794
Clymer, George (Pa.)	Merchant	Philadelphia, Pa.	Mar. 16, 1739	Jan. 23, 1813
Ellery, William (R.I.)	Lawyer	Newport, R.I.	Dec. 22, 1727	Feb. 15, 1820
Floyd, William (N.Y.)	Soldier	Brookhaven, N.Y.	Dec. 17, 1734	Aug. 4, 1821
Franklin, Benjamin (Pa.)	Printer, publisher.	Boston, Mass.	Jan. 17, 1706	Apr. 17, 1790
Gerry, Elbridge (Mass.)	Merchant	Marblehead, Mass.	July 17, 1744	Nov. 23, 1814
Gwinnett, Button (Ga.)	Merchant	Down Hatherly, England	c. 1735	May 19, 1777
Hall, Lyman (Ga.)	Physician	Wallingford, Conn.	Apr. 12, 1724	Oct. 19, 1790
Hancock, John (Mass.)	Merchant	Braintree (Quincy), Mass.	Jan. 12, 1737	Oct. 8, 1793
Harrison, Benjamin (Va.)	Farmer	Berkeley, Va.	Apr. 5, 1726	Apr. 24, 1791
Hart, John (N.J.)	Farmer	Stonington, Conn.	c. 1711	May 11, 1779
Hewes, Joseph (N.C.)	Merchant	Princeton, N.J.	Jan. 23, 1730	Nov. 10, 1779
Heyward, Thos. Jr. (S.C.)	Lawyer, farmer	St. Luke's Parish, S.C.	July 28, 1746	Mar. 6, 1809
Hooper, William (N.C.)	Lawyer	Boston, Mass.	June 28, 1742	Oct. 14, 1790
Hopkins, Stephen (R.I.)	Judge, educator	Providence, R.I.	Mar. 7, 1707	July 13, 1785
Hopkinson, Francis (N.J.)	Judge, author	Philadelphia, Pa.	Sept. 21, 1737	May 9, 1791
Huntington, Samuel (Conn.)	Judge	Windham County, Conn.	July 3, 1731	Jan. 5, 1796
Jefferson, Thomas (Va.)	Lawyer	Shadwell, Va.	Apr. 13, 1743	July 4, 1826
Lee, Francis Lightfoot (Va.)	Farmer	Westmoreland County, Va.	Oct. 14, 1734	Jan. 11, 1797
Lee, Richard Henry (Va.)	Farmer	Westmoreland County, Va.	Jan. 20, 1732	June 19, 1794
Lewis, Francis (N.Y.)	Merchant	Llandaff, Wales	Mar., 1713	Dec. 31, 1802
Livingston, Philip (N.Y.)	Merchant	Albany, N.Y.	Jan. 15, 1716	June 12, 1778
Lynch, Thomas Jr. (S.C.)	Farmer	Winyah, S.C.	Aug. 5, 1749	(at sea) 1779
McKean, Thomas (Del.)	Lawyer	New London, Pa.	Mar. 19, 1734	June 24, 1817
Middleton, Arthur (S.C.)	Farmer	Charleston, S.C.	June 26, 1742	Jan. 1, 1787
Morris, Lewis (N.Y.)	Farmer	Morrisania (Bronx County), N.Y.	Apr. 8, 1726	Jan. 22, 1798
Morris, Robert (Pa.)	Merchant	Liverpool, England	Jan. 20, 1734	May 9, 1806
Morton, John (Pa.)	Judge	Ridley, Pa.	1724	Apr., 1777
Nelson, Thos. Jr. (Va.)	Farmer	Yorktown, Va.	Dec. 26, 1738	Jan. 4, 1789
Paca, William (Md.)	Judge	Abingdon, Md.	Oct. 31, 1740	Oct. 23, 1799
Paine, Robert Treat (Mass.)	Judge	Boston, Mass.	Mar. 11, 1731	May 12, 1814
Penn, John (N.C.)	Lawyer	Near Port Royal, Va.	May 17, 1741	Sept. 14, 1788
Read, George (Del.)	Judge	Near North East, Md.	Sept. 18, 1733	Sept. 21, 1798
Rodney, Caesar (Del.)	Judge	Dover, Del.	Oct. 7, 1728	June 29, 1784
Ross, George (Pa.)	Judge	New Castle, Del.	May 10, 1730	July 14, 1779
Rush, Benjamin (Pa.)	Physician	Byberry, Pa. (Philadelphia)	Dec. 24, 1745	Apr. 19, 1813
Rutledge, Edward (S.C.)	Lawyer	Charleston, S.C.	Nov. 23, 1749	Jan. 23, 1800
Sherman, Roger (Conn.)	Lawyer	Newton, Mass.	Apr. 19, 1721	July 23, 1793
Smith, James (Pa.)	Lawyer	Dublin, Ireland	c. 1719	July 11, 1806
Stockton, Richard (N.J.)	Lawyer	Near Princeton, N.J.	Oct. 1, 1730	Feb. 28, 1781
Stone, Thomas (Md.)	Lawyer	Charles County, Md.	1743	Oct. 5, 1787
Taylor, George (Pa.)	Ironmaster	Ireland	1716	Feb. 23, 1781
Thornton, Matthew (N.H.)	Physician	Ireland	1714	June 24, 1803
Walton, George (Ga.)	Judge	Prince Edward County, Va.	1741	Feb. 2, 1804
Whipple, William (N.H.)	Merchant, judge	Kittery, Me.	Jan. 14, 1730	Nov. 28, 1785
Williams, William (Conn.)	Merchant	Lebanon, Conn.	Apr. 23, 1731	Aug. 2, 1811
Wilson, James (Pa.)	Judge	Carskerdo, Scotland	Sept. 14, 1742	Aug. 28, 1798
Witherspoon, John (N.J.)	Clergyman, educator	Gifford, Scotland	Feb. 5, 1723	Nov. 15, 1794
Wolcott, Oliver (Conn.)	Judge	Windsor, Conn.	Dec. 1, 1726	Dec. 1, 1797
Wythe, George (Va.)	Lawyer	Elizabeth City Co. (Hampton), Va.	1726	June 8, 1806

Constitution of the United States
The Original 7 Articles

PREAMBLE

We, the people of the United States, in order to form a more perfect Union, establish justice, insure domestic tranquility, provide for the common defense, promote the general welfare, and secure the blessings of liberty to ourselves and our posterity do ordain and establish this Constitution for the United States of America.

ARTICLE I.

Section 1—Legislative powers; in whom vested:

All legislative powers herein granted shall be vested in a Congress of the United States, which shall consist of a Senate and House of Representatives.

Section 2—House of Representatives, how and by whom chosen. Qualifications of a Representative. Representatives and direct taxes, how apportioned. Enumeration. Vacancies to be filled. Power of choosing officers, and of impeachment.

1. The House of Representatives shall be composed of members chosen every second year by the people of the several States, and the electors in each State shall have the qualifications requisite for electors of the most numerous branch of the State Legislature.

2. No person shall be a Representative who shall not have attained to the age of twenty-five years, and been seven years a citizen of the United States, and who shall not, when elected, be an inhabitant of that State in which he shall be chosen.

3. *(Representatives and direct taxes shall be apportioned among the several States which may be included within this Union, according to their respective numbers, which shall be determined by adding to the whole number of free persons, including those bound to service for a term of years, and excluding Indians not taxed, three-fifths of all other persons.) (The previous sentence was superseded by Amendment XIV, section 2.)* The actual enumeration shall be made within three years after the first meeting of the Congress of the United States, and within every subsequent term of ten years, in such manner as they shall by law direct. The number of Representatives shall not exceed one for every thirty thousand, but each State shall have at least one Representative; and until such enumeration shall be made, the State of New Hampshire shall be entitled to choose three, Massachusetts eight, Rhode Island and Providence Plantations one, Connecticut five, New York six, New Jersey four, Pennsylvania eight, Delaware one, Maryland six, Virginia ten, North Carolina five, South Carolina five, and Georgia three.

4. When vacancies happen in the representation from any State, the Executive Authority thereof shall issue writs of election to fill such vacancies.

5. The House of Representatives shall choose their Speaker and other officers; and shall have the sole power of impeachment.

Section 3—Senators, how and by whom chosen. How classified. Qualifications of a Senator. President of the Senate, his right to vote. President pro tem., and other officers of the Senate, how chosen. Power to try impeachments. When President is tried, Chief Justice to preside. Sentence.

1. The Senate of the United States shall be composed of two Senators from each State, *(chosen by the Legislature thereof). (The preceding five words were superseded by Amendment XVII, section 1.)* for six years; and each Senator shall have one vote.

2. Immediately after they shall be assembled in consequence of the first election, they shall be divided as equally as may be into three classes. The seats of the Senators of the first class shall be vacated at the expiration of the second year, of the second class at the expiration of the fourth year, and of the third class at the expiration of the sixth year, so that one-third may be chosen every second year; *(and if vacancies happen by resignation, or otherwise, during the recess of the Legislature of any State, the Executive thereof may make temporary appointments until the next meeting of the Legislature, which shall then fill such vacancies.) (The words in parentheses were superseded by Amendment XVII, section 2.)*

3. No person shall be a Senator who shall not have attained to the age of thirty years, and been nine years a citizen of the United States, and who shall not, when elected, be an inhabitant of that State for which he shall be chosen.

4. The Vice President of the United States shall be President of the Senate, but shall have no vote, unless they be equally divided.

5. The Senate shall choose their other officers, and also a President pro tempore, in the absence of the Vice President, or when he shall exercise the office of President of the United States.

6. The Senate shall have the sole power to try all impeachments. When sitting for that purpose, they shall be on oath or affirmation. When the President of the United States is tried, the Chief Justice shall preside: and no person shall be convicted without the concurrence of two-thirds of the members present.

7. Judgment in cases of impeachment shall not extend further than to removal from office, and disqualification to hold and enjoy any office of honor, trust or profit under the United States: but the party convicted shall nevertheless be liable and subject to indictment, trial, judgment and punishment, according to law.

Section 4—Times, etc., of holding elections, how prescribed. One session each year.

1. The times, places and manner of holding elections for Senators and Representatives, shall be prescribed in each State by the Legislature thereof; but the Congress may at any time by law make or alter such regulations, except as to the places of choosing Senators.

2. The Congress shall assemble at least once in every year, and such meeting shall *(be on the first Monday in December,) (The words in parentheses were superseded by Amendment XX, section 2).* unless they shall by law appoint a different day.

Section 5—Membership, quorum, adjournments, rules. Power to punish or expel. Journal. Time of adjournments, how limited, etc.

1. Each House shall be the judge of the elections, returns and qualifications of its own members, and a majority of each shall constitute a quorum to do business; but a smaller number may adjourn from day to day, and may be authorized to compel the attendance of absent members, in such manner, and under such penalties as each House may provide.

2. Each House may determine the rules of its proceedings, punish its members for disorderly behavior, and, with the concurrence of two-thirds, expel a member.

3. Each House shall keep a journal of its proceedings, and from time to time publish the same, excepting such parts as may in their judgment require secrecy; and the yeas and nays of the members of either House on any question shall, at the desire of one-fifth of those present, be entered on the journal.

4. Neither House, during the session of Congress, shall, without the consent of the other, adjourn for more than three days, nor to any other place than that in which the two Houses shall be sitting.

Section 6—Compensation, privileges, disqualifications in certain cases.

1. The Senators and Representatives shall receive a compensation for their services, to be ascertained by law, and paid out of the Treasury of the United States. They shall in all cases, except treason, felony and breach of the peace, be privileged from arrest during their attendance at the session of their respective Houses, and in going to and returning from the same; and for any speech or debate in either House, they shall not be questioned in any other place.

2. No Senator or Representative shall, during the time for which he was elected, be appointed to any civil office under the authority of the United States, which shall have been created, or the emoluments whereof shall have been increased during such time; and no person holding any office under the United States, shall be a member of either House

during his continuance in office.

Section 7—House to originate all revenue bills. Veto. Bill may be passed by two-thirds of each House, notwithstanding, etc. Bill, not returned in ten days, to become a law. Provisions as to orders, concurrent resolutions, etc.

1. All bills for raising revenue shall originate in the House of Representatives; but the Senate may propose or concur with amendments as on other bills.

2. Every bill which shall have passed the House of Representatives and the Senate, shall, before it becomes a law, be presented to the President of the United States; if he approves he shall sign it, but if not he shall return it, with his objections to that House in which it shall have originated, who shall enter the objections at large on their journal, and proceed to reconsider it. If after such reconsideration two-thirds of that House shall agree to pass the bill, it shall be sent, together with the objections, to the other House, by which it shall likewise be reconsidered, and if approved by two-thirds of that House, it shall become a law. But in all such cases the votes of both Houses shall be determined by yeas and nays, and the names of the persons voting for and against the bill shall be entered on the journal of each House respectively. If any bill shall not be returned by the President within ten days (Sundays excepted) after it shall have been presented to him, the same shall be a law, in like manner as if he had signed it, unless the Congress by their adjournment prevent its return, in which case it shall not be a law.

3. Every order, resolution, or vote to which the concurrence of the Senate and House of Representatives may be necessary (except on a question of adjournment) shall be presented to the President of the United States; and before the same shall take effect, shall be approved by him, or being disapproved by him, shall be repassed by two-thirds of the Senate and House of Representatives, according to the rules and limitations prescribed in the case of a bill.

Section 8—Powers of Congress.

The Congress shall have power

1. To lay and collect taxes, duties, imposts and excises, to pay the debts and provide for the common defense and general welfare of the United States; but all duties, imposts and excises shall be uniform throughout the United States;

2. To borrow money on the credit of the United States;

3. To regulate commerce with foreign nations, and among the several States, and with the Indian tribes;

4. To establish a uniform rule of naturalization, and uniform laws on the subject of bankruptcies throughout the United States;

5. To coin money, regulate the value thereof, and of foreign coin, and fix the standard of weights and measures;

6. To provide for the punishment of counterfeiting the securities and current coin of the United States;

7. To establish post-offices and post-roads;

8. To promote the progress of science and useful arts, by securing for limited times to authors and inventors the exclusive right to their respective writings and discoveries;

9. To constitute tribunals inferior to the Supreme Court;

10. To define and punish piracies and felonies committed on the high seas, and offenses against the law of nations;

11. To declare war, grant letters of marque and reprisal, and make rules concerning captures on land and water;

12. To raise and support armies, but no appropriation of money to that use shall be for a longer term than two years;

13. To provide and maintain a navy;

14. To make rules for the government and regulation of the land and naval forces;

15. To provide for calling forth the militia to execute the laws of the Union, suppress insurrections and repel invasions;

16. To provide for organizing, arming, and disciplining the militia, and for governing such part of them as may be employed in the service of the United States, reserving to the States respectively, the appointment of the officers, and the authority of training the militia according to the discipline prescribed by Congress;

17. To exercise exclusive legislation in all cases whatsoever, over such district (not exceeding ten miles square) as may, by cession of particular States, and the acceptance of Congress, become the seat of the Government of the United States, and to exercise like authority over all places purchased by the consent of the Legislature of the State in which the same shall be, for the erection of forts, magazines, arsenals, dockyards, and other needful buildings;—And

18. To make all laws which shall be necessary and proper for carrying into execution the foregoing powers, and all other powers vested by this Constitution in the Government of the United States, or in any department or officer thereof.

Section 9—Provision as to migration or importation of certain persons. Habeas corpus, bills of attainder, etc. Taxes, how apportioned. No export duty. No commercial preference. Money, how drawn from Treasury, etc. No titular nobility. Officers not to receive presents, etc.

1. The migration or importation of such persons as any of the States now existing shall think proper to admit, shall not be prohibited by the Congress prior to the year one thousand eight hundred and eight, but a tax or duty may be imposed on such importation, not exceeding ten dollars for each person.

2. The privilege of the writ of habeas corpus shall not be suspended, unless when in cases of rebellion or invasion the public safety may require it.

3. No bill of attainder or ex post facto law shall be passed.

4. No capitation, or other direct, tax shall be laid, unless in proportion to the census or enumeration herein before directed to be taken. *(Modified by Amendment XVI.)*

5. No tax or duty shall be laid on articles exported from any State.

6. No preference shall be given by any regulation of commerce or revenue to the ports of one State over those of another: nor shall vessels bound to, or from, one State, be obliged to enter, clear, or pay duties in another.

7. No money shall be drawn from the Treasury, but in consequence of appropriations made by law; and a regular statement and account of the receipts and expenditures of all public money shall be published from time to time.

8. No title of nobility shall be granted by the United States: and no person holding any office of profit or trust under them, shall, without the consent of the Congress, accept of any present, emolument, office, or title, of any kind whatever, from any king, prince, or foreign state.

Section 10—States prohibited from the exercise of certain powers.

1. No State shall enter into any treaty, alliance, or confederation; grant letters of marque and reprisal; coin money; emit bills of credit; make anything but gold and silver coin a tender in payment of debts; pass any bill of attainder, ex post facto law, or law impairing the obligation of contracts, or grant any title of nobility.

2. No State shall, without the consent of the Congress, lay any imposts or duties on imports or exports, except what may be absolutely necessary for executing its inspection laws: and the net produce of all duties and imposts, laid by any State on imports or exports, shall be for the use of the Treasury of the United States; and all such laws shall be subject to the revision and control of the Congress.

3. No State shall, without the consent of Congress, lay any duty of tonnage, keep troops, or ships of war in time of peace, enter into any agreement or compact with another State, or with a foreign power, or engage in war, unless actually invaded, or in such imminent danger as will not admit of delay.

ARTICLE II.

Section 1—President: his term of office. Electors of President; number and how appointed. Electors to vote on same day. Qualification of President. On whom his duties devolve in case of his removal, death, etc. President's compensation. His oath of office.

1. The Executive power shall be vested in a President of the United States of America. He shall hold his office during the term of four years, and together with the Vice President, chosen for the same term, be elected as follows

2. Each State shall appoint, in such manner as the Legis-

lature thereof may direct, a number of electors, equal to the whole number of Senators and Representatives to which the State may be entitled in the Congress: but no Senator or Representative, or person holding an office of trust or profit under the United States, shall be appointed an elector.

(The electors shall meet in their respective States, and vote by ballot for two persons, of whom one at least shall not be an inhabitant of the same State with themselves. And they shall make a list of all the persons voted for, and of the number of votes for each; which list they shall sign and certify, and transmit sealed to the seat of the Government of the United States, directed to the President of the Senate. The President of the Senate shall, in the presence of the Senate and House of Representatives, open all the certificates, and the votes shall then be counted. The person having the greatest number of votes shall be the President, if such number be a majority of the whole number of electors appointed; and if there be more than one who have such majority, and have an equal number of votes, then the House of Representatives shall immediately choose by ballot one of them for President; and if no person have a majority, then from the five highest on the list the said House shall in like manner choose the President. But in choosing the President, the votes shall be taken by States, the representation from each State having one vote; a quorum for this purpose shall consist of a member or members from two-thirds of the States, and a majority of all the States shall be necessary to a choice. In every case, after the choice of the President, the person having the greatest number of votes of the electors shall be the Vice President. But if there should remain two or more who have equal votes, the Senate shall choose from them by ballot the Vice President.)

(This clause was superseded by Amendment XII.)

3. The Congress may determine the time of choosing the electors, and the day on which they shall give their votes; which day shall be the same throughout the United States.

4. No person except a natural born citizen, or a citizen of the United States, at the time of the adoption of this Constitution, shall be eligible to the office of President; neither shall any person be eligible to that office who shall not have attained to the age of thirty-five years, and been fourteen years a resident within the United States.

(For qualification of the Vice President, see Amendment XII.)

5. In case of the removal of the President from office, or of his death, resignation, or inability to discharge the powers and duties of the said office, the same shall devolve on the Vice President, and the Congress may by law provide for the case of removal, death, resignation or inability, both of the President and Vice President, declaring what officer shall then act as President, and such officer shall act accordingly, until the disability be removed, or a President shall be elected.

(This clause has been modified by Amendments XX and XXV.)

6. The President shall, at stated times, receive for his services, a compensation, which shall neither be increased nor diminished during the period for which he shall have been elected, and he shall not receive within that period any other emolument from the United States, or any of them.

7. Before he enter on the execution of his office, he shall take the following oath or affirmation:

"I do solemnly swear (or affirm) that I will faithfully execute the office of President of the United States, and will to the best of my ability, preserve, protect and defend the Constitution of the United States."

Section 2—President to be Commander-in-Chief. He may require opinions of cabinet officers, etc., may pardon. Treaty-making power. Nomination of certain officers. When President may fill vacancies.

1. The President shall be Commander-in-Chief of the Army and Navy of the United States, and of the militia of the several States, when called into the actual service of the United States; he may require the opinion, in writing, of the principal officer in each of the executive departments, upon any subject relating to the duties of their respective offices, and he shall have power to grant reprieves and pardons for offenses against the United States, except in cases of impeachment.

2. He shall have power, by and with the advice and consent of the Senate, to make treaties, provided two-thirds of the Senators present concur; and he shall nominate, and by and with the advice and consent of the Senate, shall appoint ambassadors, other public ministers and consuls, judges of the Supreme Court, and all other officers of the United States, whose appointments are not herein otherwise provided for, and which shall be established by law: but the Congress may by law vest the appointment of such inferior officers, as they think proper, in the President alone, in the courts of law, or in the heads of departments.

3. The President shall have power to fill up all vacancies that may happen during the recess of the Senate, by granting commissions, which shall expire at the end of their next session.

Section 3—President shall communicate to Congress. He may convene and adjourn Congress, in case of disagreement, etc. Shall receive ambassadors, execute laws, and commission officers.

He shall from time to time give to the Congress information of the state of the Union, and recommend to their consideration such measures as he shall judge necessary and expedient; he may, on extraordinary occasions, convene both Houses, or either of them, and in case of disagreement between them, with respect to the time of adjournment, he may adjourn them to such time as he shall think proper; he shall receive ambassadors and other public ministers; he shall take care that the laws be faithfully executed, and shall commission all the officers of the United States.

Section 4—All civil offices forfeited for certain crimes.

The President, Vice President, and all civil officers of the United States, shall be removed from office on impeachment for, and conviction of, treason, bribery, or other high crimes and misdemeanors.

ARTICLE III.

Section 1—Judicial powers, Tenure. Compensation.

The judicial power of the United States, shall be vested in one Supreme Court, and in such inferior courts as the Congress may from time to time ordain and establish. The judges, both of the Supreme and inferior courts, shall hold their offices during good behavior, and shall at stated times, receive for their services, a compensation, which shall not be diminished during their continuance in office.

Section 2—Judicial power; to what cases it extends. Original jurisdiction of Supreme Court; appellate jurisdiction. Trial by jury, etc. Trial, where.

1. The judicial power shall extend to all cases, in law and equity, arising under this Constitution, the laws of the United States, and treaties made, or which shall be made, under their authority; to all cases affecting ambassadors, other public ministers and consuls; to all cases of admiralty and maritime jurisdiction; to controversies to which the United States shall be a party; to controversies between two or more States; between a State and citizens of another State; between citizens of different States, between citizens of the same State claiming lands under grants of different States, and between a State, or the citizens thereof, and foreign states, citizens or subjects.

(This section is modified by Amendment XI.)

2. In all cases affecting ambassadors, other public ministers and consuls, and those in which a State shall be party, the Supreme Court shall have original jurisdiction. In all the other cases before mentioned, the Supreme Court shall have appellate jurisdiction, both as to law and fact, with such exceptions, and under such regulations as the Congress shall make.

3. The trial of all crimes, except in cases of impeachment, shall be by jury; and such trial shall be held in the State where the said crimes shall have been committed; but when not committed within any State, the trial shall be at such place or places as the Congress may by law have directed.

Section 3—Treason Defined, Proof of, Punishment of.

1. Treason against the United States, shall consist only in levying war against them, or in adhering to their enemies,

giving them aid and comfort. No person shall be convicted of treason unless on the testimony of two witnesses to the same overt act, or on confession in open court.

2. The Congress shall have power to declare the punishment of treason, but no attainder of treason shall work corruption of blood, or forfeiture except during the life of the person attainted.

ARTICLE IV.

Section 1—Each State to give credit to the public acts, etc., of every other State.

Full faith and credit shall be given in each State to the public acts, records, and judicial proceedings of every other State. And the Congress may by general laws prescribe the manner in which such acts, records and proceedings shall be proved, and the effect thereof.

Section 2—Privileges of citizens of each State. Fugitives from justice to be delivered up. Persons held to service having escaped, to be delivered up.

1. The citizens of each State shall be entitled to all privileges and immunities of citizens in the several States.

2. A person charged in any State with treason, felony, or other crime, who shall flee from justice, and be found in another State, shall on demand of the Executive authority of the State from which he fled, be delivered up, to be removed to the State having jurisdiction of the crime.

(3. No person held to service or labor in one State, under the laws thereof, escaping into another, shall in consequence of any law or regulation therein, be discharged from such service or labor, but shall be delivered up on claim of the party to whom such service or labor may be due.) (This clause was superseded by Amendment XIII.)

Section 3—Admission of new States. Power of Congress over territory and other property.

1. New States may be admitted by the Congress into this Union; but no new State shall be formed or erected within the jurisdiction of any other State; nor any State be formed by the junction of two or more States, or parts of States, without the consent of the Legislatures of the States concerned as well as of the Congress.

2. The Congress shall have power to dispose of and make all needful rules and regulations respecting the territory or other property belonging to the United States; and nothing in this Constitution shall be so construed as to prejudice any claims of the United States, or of any particular State.

Section 4—Republican form of government guaranteed. Each state to be protected.

The United States shall guarantee to every State in this Union a Republican form of government, and shall protect each of them against invasion; and on application of the Legislature, or of the Executive (when the Legislature cannot be convened) against domestic violence.

ARTICLE V.

Constitution: how amended; proviso.

The Congress, whenever two-thirds of both Houses shall deem it necessary, shall propose amendments to this Constitution, or, on the application of the Legislatures of two-thirds of the several States, shall call a convention for proposing amendments, which, in either case, shall be valid to all intents and purposes, as part of this Constitution, when ratified by the Legislatures of three-fourths of the several States, or by conventions in three-fourths thereof, as the one or the other mode of ratification may be proposed by the Congress; provided that no amendment which may be made prior to the year one thousand eight hundred and eight shall in any manner affect the first and fourth clauses in the Ninth Section of the First Article; and that no State, without its consent, shall be deprived of its equal suffrage in the Senate.

ARTICLE VI.

Certain debts, etc., declared valid. Supremacy of Constitution, treaties, and laws of the United States. Oath to support Constitution, by whom taken. No religious test.

1. All debts contracted and engagements entered into, before the adoption of this Constitution, shall be as valid against the United States under this Constitution, as under the Confederation.

2. This Constitution, and the laws of the United States which shall be made in pursuance thereof; and all treaties made, or which shall be made, under the authority of the United States, shall be the supreme law of the land; and the judges in every State shall be bound thereby, any thing in the Constitution or laws of any State to the contrary notwithstanding.

3. The Senators and Representatives before mentioned, and the members of the several State Legislatures, and all executive and judicial officers, both of the United States and of the several States, shall be bound by oath or affirmation, to support this Constitution; but no religious test shall ever be required as a qualification to any office or public trust under the United States.

ARTICLE VII.

What ratification shall establish Constitution.

The ratification of the Conventions of nine States, shall be sufficient for the establishment of this Constitution between the States so ratifying the same.

Done in convention by the unanimous consent of the States present the Seventeenth day of September in the year of our Lord one thousand seven hundred and eighty seven, and of the independence of the United States of America the Twelfth. In witness whereof we have hereunto subscribed our names.

George Washington, President and deputy from Virginia.

New Hampshire—John Langdon, Nicholas Gilman.

Massachusetts—Nathaniel Gorham, Rufus King.

Connecticut—Wm. Saml. Johnson, Roger Sherman.

New York—Alexander Hamilton.

New Jersey—Wil: Livingston, David Brearley, Wm. Paterson, Jona: Dayton.

Pennsylvania—B. Franklin, Thomas Mifflin, Robt. Morris, Geo. Clymer, Thos. FitzSimons, Jared Ingersoll, James Wilson, Gouv. Morris.

Delaware—Geo: Read, Gunning Bedford Jun., John Dickinson, Richard Bassett, Jaco: Broom.

Maryland—James McHenry, Daniel of Saint Thomas' Jenifer, Danl. Carroll.

Virginia—John Blair, James Madison Jr.

North Carolina—Wm. Blount, Rich'd. Dobbs Spaight, Hugh Williamson.

South Carolina—J. Rutledge, Charles Cotesworth Pinckney, Charles Pinckney, Pierce Butler.

Georgia—William Few, Abr. Baldwin.

Attest: William Jackson, Secretary.

Ten Original Amendments: The Bill of Rights

In force Dec. 15, 1791

(The First Congress, at its first session in the City of New York, Sept. 25, 1789, submitted to the states 12 amendments to clarify certain individual and state rights not named in the Constitution. They are generally called the Bill of Rights.

(Influential in framing these amendments was the Declaration of Rights of Virginia, written by George Mason (1725-1792) in 1776. Mason, a Virginia delegate to the Constitutional Convention, did not sign the Constitution and opposed its ratification on the ground that it did not sufficiently oppose slavery or safeguard individual rights.

(In the preamble to the resolution offering the proposed amendments, Congress said: "The conventions of a number of the States having at the time of their adopting the Constitution, expressed a desire, in order to prevent misconstruction or abuse of its powers, that further declaratory and restrictive clauses should be added, and as extending the ground of public confidence in the government will best insure the beneficent ends of its institution, be it resolved," etc.

(Ten of these amendments now commonly known as one to 10 inclusive, but originally 3 to 12 inclusive, were ratified by the states as follows: New Jersey, Nov. 20, 1789; Maryland, Dec. 19, 1789; North Carolina, Dec. 22, 1789; South Carolina, Jan. 19, 1790; New Hampshire, Jan 25, 1790; Delaware, Jan 28, 1790; New York, Feb. 27, 1790; Pennsylvania, Mar. 10, 1790; Rhode

Island, June 7, 1790; Vermont, Nov 3, 1791; Virginia, Dec. 15, 1791; Massachusetts, Mar. 2, 1939; Georgia, Mar. 18, 1939; Connecticut, Apr. 19, 1939. These original 10 ratified amendments follow as Amendments I to X inclusive.

(Of the two original proposed amendments which were not ratified by the necessary number of states, the first related to apportionment of Representatives; the second, to compensation of members. See p. 465.)

AMENDMENT I.

Religious establishment prohibited. Freedom of speech, of the press, and right to petition.

Congress shall make no law respecting an establishment of religion, or prohibiting the free exercise thereof; or abridging the freedom of speech, or of the press; or the right of the people peaceably to assemble, and to petition the Government for a redress of grievances.

AMENDMENT II.

Right to keep and bear arms.

A well-regulated militia, being necessary to the security of a free State, the right of the people to keep and bear arms, shall not be infringed.

AMENDMENT III.

Conditions for quarters for soldiers.

No soldier shall, in time of peace be quartered in any house, without the consent of the owner, nor in time of war, but in a manner to be prescribed by law.

AMENDMENT IV.

Right of search and seizure regulated.

The right of the people to be secure in their persons, houses, papers, and effects, against unreasonable searches and seizures, shall not be violated, and no warrants shall issue, but upon probable cause, supported by oath or affirmation, and particularly describing the place to be searched, and the persons or things to be seized.

AMENDMENT V.

Provisions concerning prosecution. Trial and punishment—private property not to be taken for public use without compensation.

No person shall be held to answer for a capital, or otherwise infamous crime, unless on a presentment or indictment of a Grand Jury, except in cases arising in the land or naval forces, or in the militia, when in actual service in time of war or public danger; nor shall any person be subject for the same offense to be twice put in jeopardy of life or limb; nor shall be compelled in any criminal case to be a witness against himself, nor be deprived of life, liberty, or property, without due process of law; nor shall private property be taken for public use without just compensation.

AMENDMENT VI.

Right to speedy trial, witnesses, etc.

In all criminal prosecutions, the accused shall enjoy the right to a speedy and public trial, by an impartial jury of the State and district wherein the crime shall have been committed, which district shall have been previously ascertained by law, and to be informed of the nature and cause of the accusation; to be confronted with the witnesses against him; to have compulsory process for obtaining witnesses in his favor, and to have the assistance of counsel for his defense.

AMENDMENT VII.

Right of trial by jury.

In suits at common law, where the value in controversy shall exceed twenty dollars, the right of trial by jury shall be preserved, and no fact tried by a jury shall be otherwise reexamined in any court of the United States, than according to the rules of the common law.

AMENDMENT VIII.

Excessive bail or fines and cruel punishment prohibited.

Excessive bail shall not be required, nor excessive fines imposed, nor cruel and unusual punishments inflicted.

AMENDMENT IX.

Rule of construction of Constitution.

The enumeration in the Constitution, of certain rights, shall not be construed to deny or disparage others retained by the people.

AMENDMENT X.

Rights of States under Constitution.

The powers not delegated to the United States by the Constitution, nor prohibited by it to the States, are reserved to the States respectively, or to the people.

Amendments Since the Bill of Rights

AMENDMENT XI.

Judicial powers construed.

The judicial power of the United States shall not be construed to extend to any suit in law or equity, commenced or prosecuted against one of the United States by citizens of another State, or by citizens or subjects of any foreign state.

(This amendment was proposed to the Legislatures of the several States by the Third Congress on March 4, 1794, and was declared to have been ratified in a message from the President to Congress, dated Jan. 8, 1798.

(It was on Jan 5, 1798, that Secretary of State Pickering received from 12 of the States authenticated ratifications, and informed President John Adams of that fact.

(As a result of later research in the Department of State, it is now established that Amendment XI became part of the Constitution on Feb. 7, 1795, for on that date it had been ratified by 12 States as follows:

(1. New York, Mar. 27, 1794. 2. Rhode Island, Mar. 31, 1794. 3. Connecticut, May 8, 1794. 4. New Hampshire, June 16, 1794. 5. Massachusetts, June 26, 1794. 6. Vermont, between Oct 9, 1794, and Nov. 9, 1794. 7. Virginia, Nov. 18, 1794. 8. Georgia, Nov. 29, 1794. 9. Kentucky, Dec. 7, 1794. 10. Maryland, Dec. 26, 1794. 11. Delaware, Jan 23, 1795. 12. North Carolina, Feb. 7, 1795.

(On June 1, 1796, more than a year after Amendment XI had become a part of the Constitution (but before anyone was officially aware of this), Tennessee had been admitted as a State; but not until Oct. 16, 1797, was a certified copy of the resolution of Congress proposing the amendment sent to the Governor of Tennessee (John Sevier) by Secretary of State Pickering, whose office was then at Trenton, New Jersey, because of the epidemic of yellow fever at Philadelphia; it seems, however, that the Legislature of Tennessee took no action on Amendment XI, owing doubtless to the fact that public announcement of its adoption was made soon thereafter.

(Besides the necessary 12 States, one other, South Carolina, ratified Amendment XI, but this action was not taken until Dec. 4, 1797; the two remaining States, New Jersey and Pennsylvania, failed to ratify.)

AMENDMENT XII.

Manner of choosing President and Vice-President.

(Proposed by Congress Dec. 9, 1803; ratification completed June 15, 1804.)

The Electors shall meet in their respective States and vote by ballot for President and Vice-President, one of whom, at least, shall not be an inhabitant of the same State with themselves; they shall name in their ballots the person voted for as President, and in distinct ballots the person voted for as Vice-President, and they shall make distinct lists of all persons voted for as President, and of all persons voted for as Vice-President, and of the number of votes for each, which lists they shall sign and certify, and transmit sealed to the seat of the Government of the United States, directed to the President of the Senate; the President of the Senate shall, in the presence of the Senate and House of Representatives, open all the certificates and the votes shall then be counted;—The person having the greatest number of votes for President, shall be the President, if such number be a majority of the whole number of Electors appointed; and if no person have such majority, then from the persons having the highest numbers not exceeding three on the list of those voted for as President, the House of Representatives shall choose immediately, by ballot, the President. But in choosing the President, the votes shall be taken by States, the representation from each State having one vote; a quorum for this purpose shall consist of a member or members from two-thirds of the States, and a majority of all the States shall be necessary to a choice. *(And if the House of Representatives shall not choose a President whenever the right of choice shall devolve upon them, before the fourth day of March next following, then the Vice-President shall act as President, as in the case of the death or other constitutional disability of the President.) (The words in parentheses were superseded by Amendment XX, section 3.)* The person having the greatest number of votes as Vice-President, shall be the Vice-President, if such number be a majority of the whole number of Electors appointed, and if no person have a majority, then from the two highest numbers on the list, the Senate shall choose the Vice-President; a quorum for the purpose shall consist of two-thirds of the whole number of Senators, and a majority of the whole number shall be necessary to a choice. But no person constitutionally ineligible to the office of President shall be eligible to that of Vice-President of the United States.

THE RECONSTRUCTION AMENDMENTS

(Amendments XIII, XIV, and XV are commonly known as the Reconstruction Amendments, inasmuch as they followed the Civil War, and were drafted by Republicans who were bent on imposing their own policy of reconstruction on the South. Post-bellum legislatures there—Mississippi, South Carolina, Georgia, for example—had set up laws which, it was charged, were contrived to perpetuate Negro slavery under other names.)

AMENDMENT XIII.

Slavery abolished.

(Proposed by Congress Jan. 31, 1865; ratification completed Dec. 18, 1865. The amendment, when first proposed by a resolution in Congress, was passed by the Senate, 38 to 6, on Apr. 8, 1864, but was defeated in the House, 95 to 66 on June 15, 1864. On reconsideration by the House, on Jan. 31, 1865, the resolution passed, 119 to 56. It was approved by President Lincoln on Feb. 1, 1865, although the Supreme Court had decided in 1798 that the President has nothing to do with the proposing of amendments to the Constitution, or their adoption.)

1. Neither slavery nor involuntary servitude, except as a punishment for crime whereof the party shall have been duly convicted, shall exist within the United States or any place subject to their jurisdiction.

2. Congress shall have power to enforce this article by appropriate legislation.

AMENDMENT XIV.

Citizenship rights not to be abridged.

(The following amendment was proposed to the Legislatures of the several states by the 39th Congress, June 13, 1866, and was declared to have been ratified in a proclamation by the Secretary of State, July 28, 1868.

(The 14th amendment was adopted only by virtue of ratification subsequent to earlier rejections. Newly constituted legislatures in both North Carolina and South Carolina (respectively July 4 and 9, 1868), ratified the proposed amendment, although earlier legislatures had rejected the proposal. The Secretary of State issued a proclamation, which, though doubtful as to the effect of attempted withdrawals by Ohio and New Jersey, entertained no doubt as to the validity of the ratification by North and South Carolina. The following day (July 21, 1868), Congress passed a resolution which declared the 14th Amendment to be a part of the Constitution and directed the Secretary of State so to promulgate it. The Secretary waited, however, until the newly constituted Legislature of Georgia had ratified the amendment, subsequent to an earlier rejection, before the promulgation of the ratification of the new amendment.)

1. All persons born or naturalized in the United States, and subject to the jurisdiction thereof, are citizens of the United States and of the State wherein they reside. No State shall make or enforce any law which shall abridge the privileges or immunities of citizens of the United States; nor shall any State deprive any person of life, liberty, or property, without due process of law; nor deny to any person within its jurisdiction the equal protection of the laws.

2. Representatives shall be apportioned among the several States according to their respective numbers, counting the whole number of persons in each State, excluding Indians not taxed. But when the right to vote at any election for the choice of Electors for President and Vice-President of the United States, Representatives in Congress, the executive and judicial officers of a State, or the members of the Legislature thereof, is denied to any of the male inhabitants of such State, being twenty-one years of age, and, citizens of the United States, or in any way abridged, except for participation in rebellion, or other crime, the basis of representation therein shall be reduced in the proportion which the number of such male citizens shall bear to the whole number of male citizens twenty-one years of age in such State.

3. No person shall be a Senator or Representative in Congress, or Elector of President and Vice-President, or hold any office, civil or military, under the United States, or under any State, who, having previously taken an oath, as a member of Congress, or as an officer of the United States, or as a member of any State Legislature, or as an executive or judicial officer of any State, to support the Constitution of the United States, shall have engaged in insurrection or rebellion against the same, or given aid or comfort to the enemies thereof. But Congress may by a vote of two-thirds of each House, remove such disability.

4. The validity of the public debt of the United States, authorized by law, including debts incurred for payment of pensions and bounties for services in suppressing insurrection or rebellion, shall not be questioned. But neither the United States nor any State shall assume or pay any debt or obligation incurred in aid of insurrection or rebellion against the United States, or any claim for the loss or emancipation of any slave; but all such debts, obligations and claims, shall be held illegal and void.

5. The Congress shall have power to enforce, by appropriate legislation, the provisions of this article.

AMENDMENT XV.

Race no bar to voting rights.

(The following amendment was proposed to the legislatures of the several States by the 40th Congress, Feb. 26, 1869, and was declared to have been ratified in a proclamation by the Secretary of State, Mar. 30, 1870.)

1. The right of citizens of the United States to vote shall not be denied or abridged by the United States or by any State on account of race, color, or previous condition of servitude.

2. The Congress shall have power to enforce this article by appropriate legislation.

AMENDMENT XVI.

Income taxes authorized.

(Proposed by Congress July 12, 1909; ratification declared by the Secretary of State Feb. 25, 1913.)

The Congress shall have power to lay and collect taxes on incomes, from whatever source derived, without apportionment among the several States, and without regard to any census or enumeration.

AMENDMENT XVII.

United States Senators to be elected by direct popular vote.

(Proposed by Congress May 13, 1912; ratification declared by the Secretary of State May 31, 1913.)

1. The Senate of the United States shall be composed of two Senators from each State, elected by the people thereof, for six years; and each Senator shall have one vote. The electors in each State shall have the qualifications requisite for electors of the most numerous branch of the State Legislatures.

2. When vacancies happen in the representation of any State in the Senate, the executive authority of such State shall issue writs of election to fill such vacancies: Provided, That the Legislature of any State may empower the Executive thereof to make temporary appointments until the peo-

ple fill the vacancies by election as the Legislature may direct.

3. This amendment shall not be so construed as to affect the election or term of any Senator chosen before it becomes valid as part of the Constitution.

AMENDMENT XVIII.

Liquor prohibition amendment.

(Proposed by Congress Dec. 18, 1917; ratification completed Jan. 16, 1919. Repealed by Amendment XXI, effective Dec. 5, 1933.)

(1. After one year from the ratification of this article the manufacture, sale, or transportation of intoxicating liquors within, the importation thereof into, or the exportation thereof from the United States and all territory subject to the jurisdiction thereof for beverage purposes is hereby prohibited.

(2. The Congress and the several States shall have concurrent power to enforce this article by appropriate legislation.

(3. This article shall be inoperative unless it shall have been ratified as an amendment to the Constitution by the Legislatures of the several States, as provided in the Constitution, within seven years from the date of the submission hereof to the States by the Congress.)

(The total vote in the Senates of the various States was 1,310 for, 237 against—84.6% dry. In the lower houses of the States the vote was 3,782 for, 1,035 against—78.5% dry.

(The amendment ultimately was adopted by all the States except Connecticut and Rhode Island.)

AMENDMENT XIX.

Giving nationwide suffrage to women.

(Proposed by Congress June 4, 1919; ratification certified by Secretary of State Aug. 26, 1920.)

1. The right of citizens of the United States to vote shall not be denied or abridged by the United States or by any State on account of sex.

2. Congress shall have power to enforce this Article by appropriate legislation.

AMENDMENT XX.

Terms of President and Vice President to begin on Jan. 20; those of Senators, Representatives, Jan. 3.

(Proposed by Congress Mar. 2, 1932; ratification completed Jan. 23, 1933.)

1. The terms of the President and Vice President shall end at noon on the 20th day of January, and the terms of Senators and Representatives at noon on the 3rd day of January, of the years in which such terms would have ended if this article had not been ratified; and the terms of their successors shall then begin.

2. The Congress shall assemble at least once in every year, and such meeting shall begin at noon on the 3rd day of January, unless they shall by law appoint a different day.

3. If, at the time fixed for the beginning of the term of the President, the President elect shall have died, the Vice President elect shall become President. If a President shall not have been chosen before the time fixed for the beginning of his term, or if the President elect shall have failed to qualify, then the Vice President elect shall act as President until a President shall have qualified; and the Congress may by law provide for the case wherein neither a President elect nor a Vice President elect shall have qualified, declaring who shall then act as President, or the manner in which one who is to act shall be selected, and such person shall act accordingly until a President or Vice President shall have qualified.

4. The Congress may by law provide for the case of the death of any of the persons from whom the House of Representatives may choose a President whenever the right of choice shall have devolved upon them, and for the case of the death of any of the persons from whom the Senate may choose a Vice President whenever the right of choice shall have devolved upon them.

5. Sections 1 and 2 shall take effect on the 15th day of October following the ratification of this article (Oct., 1933).

6. This article shall be inoperative unless it shall have been ratified as an amendment to the Constitution by the Legislatures of three-fourths of the several States within seven years from the date of its submission.

AMENDMENT XXI.

Repeal of Amendment XVIII.

(Proposed by Congress Feb. 20, 1933; ratification completed Dec. 5, 1933.)

1. The eighteenth article of amendment to the Constitution of the United States is hereby repealed.

2. The transportation or importation into any State, Territory, or Possession of the United States for delivery or use therein of intoxicating liquors, in violation of the laws thereof, is hereby prohibited.

3. This article shall be inoperative unless it shall have been ratified as an amendment to the Constitution by conventions in the several States, as provided in the Constitution, within seven years from the date of the submission hereof to the States by the Congress.

AMENDMENT XXII.

Limiting Presidential terms of office.

(Proposed by Congress Mar. 24, 1947; ratification completed Feb. 27, 1951.)

1. No person shall be elected to the office of the President more than twice, and no person who has held the office of President, or acted as President, for more than two years of a term to which some other person was elected President shall be elected to the office of the President more than once. But this Article shall not apply to any person holding the office of President when this Article was proposed by the Congress, and shall not prevent any person who may be holding the office of President, or acting as President, during the term within which this Article becomes operative from holding the office of President or acting as President during the remainder of such term.

2. This article shall be inoperative unless it shall have been ratified as an amendment to the Constitution by the Legislatures of three-fourths of the several States within seven years from the date of its submission to the States by the Congress.

AMENDMENT XXIII.

Presidential vote for District of Columbia.

(Proposed by Congress June 16, 1960; ratification completed Mar. 29, 1961.)

1. The District constituting the seat of Government of the United States shall appoint in such manner as the Congress may direct:

A number of electors of President and Vice President equal to the whole number of Senators and Representatives in Congress to which the District would be entitled if it were a State, but in no event more than the least populous State; they shall be in addition to those appointed by the States, but they shall be considered, for the purposes of the election of President and Vice President, to be electors appointed by a State; and they shall meet in the District and perform such duties as provided by the twelfth article of amendment.

2. The Congress shall have power to enforce this article by appropriate legislation.

AMENDMENT XXIV.

Barring poll tax in federal elections.

(Proposed by Congress Aug. 27, 1962; ratification completed Jan. 23, 1964.)

1. The right of citizens of the United States to vote in any primary or other election for President or Vice President, for electors for President or Vice President, or for Senator or Representative in Congress, shall not be denied or abridged by the United States or any State by reason of failure to pay any poll tax or other tax.

2. The Congress shall have power to enforce this article by appropriate legislation.

AMENDMENT XXV.

Presidential disability and succession.

(Proposed by Congress July 6, 1965; ratification completed Feb. 10, 1967.)

1. In case of the removal of the President from office or of his death or resignation, the Vice President shall become President.

2. Whenever there is a vacancy in the office of the Vice President, the President shall nominate a Vice President who shall take office upon confirmation by a majority vote of both houses of Congress.

3. Whenever the President transmits to the President pro tempore of the Senate and the Speaker of the House of Representatives his written declaration that he is unable to discharge the powers and duties of his office, and until he transmits to them a written declaration to the contrary, such powers and duties shall be discharged by the Vice President as Acting President.

4. Whenever the Vice President and a majority of either the principal officers of the executive departments or of such other body as Congress may by law provide, transmit to the President pro tempore of the Senate and the Speaker of the House of Representatives their written declaration that the President is unable to discharge the powers and duties of his office, the Vice President shall immediately assume the powers and duties of the office as Acting President.

Thereafter, when the President transmits to the President pro tempore of the Senate and the Speaker of the House of Representatives his written declaration that no inability exists, he shall resume the powers and duties of his office unless the Vice President and a majority of either the principal officers of the executive department or of such other body as Congress may by law provide, transmit within four days to the President pro tempore of the Senate and the Speaker of the House of Representatives their written declaration that the President is unable to discharge the powers and duties of his office. Thereupon Congress shall decide the issue, assembling within forty-eight hours for that purpose if not in session. If the Congress, within twenty-one days after receipt of the latter written declaration, or, if Congress is not in session, within twenty-one days after Congress is required to assemble, determines by two-thirds vote of both houses that the President is unable to discharge the powers and duties of his office, the Vice President shall continue to discharge the same as Acting President; otherwise, the President shall resume the powers and duties of his office.

AMENDMENT XXVI.

Lowering voting age to 18 years.

(Proposed by Congress Mar. 23, 1971; ratification completed July 1, 1971.)

1. The right of citizens of the United States, who are 18 years of age or older, to vote shall not be denied or abridged by the United States or any state on account of age.

2. The Congress shall have the power to enforce this article by appropriate legislation.

AMENDMENT XXVII.

Congressional pay.

(Proposed by Congress Sept. 25, 1789; ratification completed May 7, 1992.)

No law, varying the compensation for the services of the Senators and Representatives, shall take effect, until an election of Representatives shall have intervened.

Origin of the Constitution

The War of Independence was conducted by delegates from the original 13 states, called the Congress of the United States of America and generally known as the Continental Congress. In 1777 the Congress submitted to the legislatures of the states the Articles of Confederation and Perpetual Union, which were ratified by New Hampshire, Massachusetts, Rhode Island, Connecticut, New York, New Jersey, Pennsylvania, Delaware, Virginia, North Carolina, South Carolina, and Georgia, and finally, in 1781, by Maryland.

The first article of the instrument read: "The stile of this confederacy shall be the United States of America." This did not signify a sovereign nation, because the states delegated only those powers they could not handle individually, such as power to wage war, establish a uniform currency, make treaties with foreign nations and contract debts for general expenses (such as paying the army). Taxes for the payment of such debts were levied by the individual states. The president under the Articles signed himself "President of the United States in Congress assembled," but here the United States were considered in the plural, a cooperating group. Canada was invited to join the union on equal terms but did not act.

When the war was won it became evident that a stronger federal union was needed to protect the mutual interests of the states. The Congress left the initiative to the legislatures. Virginia in Jan. 1786 appointed commissioners to meet with representatives of other states, with the result that delegates from Virginia, Delaware, New York, New Jersey, and Pennsylvania met at Annapolis. Alexander Hamilton prepared for their call by asking delegates from all states to meet in Philadelphia in May 1787 "to render the Constitution of the Federal government adequate to the exigencies of the union." Congress endorsed the plan Feb. 21, 1787. Delegates were appointed by all states except Rhode Island.

The convention met May 14, 1787. George Washington was chosen president (presiding officer). The states certified 65 delegates, but 10 did not attend. The work was done by 55, not all of whom were present at all sessions. Of the 55 attending delegates, 16 failed to sign, and 39 actually signed Sept. 17, 1787, some with reservations. Some historians have said 74 delegates (9 more than the 65 actually certified) were named and 19 failed to attend. These 9 additional persons refused the appointment, were never delegates and never counted as absentees. Washington sent the Constitution to Congress with a covering letter and that body, Sept. 28, 1787, ordered it sent to the legislatures, "in order to be submitted to a convention of delegates chosen in each state by the people thereof."

The Constitution was ratified by votes of state conventions as follows: Delaware, Dec. 7, 1787, unanimous; Pennsylvania, Dec. 12, 1787, 43 to 23; New Jersey, Dec. 18, 1787, unanimous; Georgia, Jan 2, 1788, unanimous; Connecticut, Jan. 9, 1788, 128 to 40; Massachusetts, Feb. 6, 1788, 187 to 168; Maryland, Apr. 28, 1788, 63 to 11; South Carolina, May 23, 1788, 149 to 73; New Hampshire, June 21, 1788, 57 to 46; Virginia, June 25, 1788, 89 to 79; New York, July 26, 1788, 30 to 27. Nine states were needed to establish the operation of the Constitution "between the states so ratifying the same" and New Hampshire was the 9th state. The government did not declare the Constitution in effect until the first Wednesday in Mar. 1789 which was Mar. 4. After that North Carolina ratified it Nov. 21, 1789, 194 to 77; and Rhode Island, May 29, 1790, 34 to 32. Vermont in convention ratified it Jan. 10, 1791, and by act of Congress approved Feb. 18, 1791, was admitted into the Union as the 14th state, Mar. 4, 1791.

On Sept. 17, 1987, the nation began a four-year celebration of the 200th anniversary of the signing of the Constitution of the United States.

As of April 1987, 32 states have voted to issue convention calls to hold a second constitutional convention. Convention bills are pending before 11 more state legislatures, while bills to rescind previous calls are under consideration in four states. When the total reaches 34, the Constitution stipulates that a convention must be held. The convention drive began in the mid 1970s to bring about the consideration of an amendment requiring a balanced federal budget.

Selected Landmark Decisions of the U.S. Supreme Court

1803: Marbury v. Madison. The Court ruled that Congress exceeded its power in the Judiciary Act of 1789; thus, the Court established its power to review acts of Congress and declare invalid those it found in conflict with the Constitution.

1819: McCulloch v. Maryland. The Court ruled that Congress had the authority to charter a national bank, under the Constitution's granting of the power to enact all laws "necessary and proper" to exact the responsibilities of government. The Court also held that the national bank was immune to state taxation.

1819: Trustees of Dartmouth College v. Woodward. The Court ruled that a state could not arbitrarily alter the terms of a college's contract. (In later years the Court widened the implications by using the same principle to limit the states' ability to interfere with business contracts.)

1857: Dred Scott v. Sanford. The Court declared unconstitutional the already-repealed Missouri Compromise of 1820 because it deprived a person of his property—a slave—without due process of law. The Court also ruled that slaves were not citizens of any state nor of the U.S. (The latter part of the decision was overturned by ratification of the 14th Amendment in 1868.)

1896: Plessy v. Ferguson. The Court ruled that a state law requiring federal railroad trains to provide separate but equal facilities for black and white passengers neither infringed upon federal authority to regulate interstate commerce nor violated the 13th and 14th Amendments. (The "separate but equal" doctrine remained effective until the 1954 Brown v. Board of Education decision.)

1904: Northern Securities Co. v. U.S. The Court ruled that a holding company formed solely to eliminate competition between two railroad lines was a combination in restraint of trade, thus a violation of the federal antitrust act.

1908: Muller v. Oregon. The Court ruled to uphold a state law limiting the maximum working hours of women. (Instead of presenting legal arguments, Louis D. Brandeis, counsel for the state, brought forth evidence from social workers, physicians, and factory inspectors that the number of hours women worked affected their health and morals.)

1911: Standard Oil. Co. of New Jersey et al. v. U.S. The Court ruled that the Standard Oil Trust must be dissolved because of its unreasonable restraint of trade, not because of its size.

1919: Schenck v. U.S. In its first decision regarding the extent of protection afforded by the First Amendment, the Court sustained the Espionage Act of 1917, maintaining that freedom of speech and press could be constrained if "the words used are in such circumstances and are of such a nature as to create a clear and present danger. . ."

1925: Gitlow v. New York. The Court ruled that the First Amendment prohibition against government abridgement of the freedom of speech applied to the states as well as to the federal government. The decision was the first of a number of rulings holding that the 14th Amendment extended the guarantees of the Bill of Rights to state action.

1935: Schechter Poultry Corp. v. U.S. The Court ruled that Congress exceeded its authority to delegate legislative powers and to regulate interstate commerce when it enacted the National Industrial Recovery Act, which afforded the U.S. president too much discretionary power.

1951: Dennis et al. v. U.S. The Court upheld convictions under the Smith Act of 1940 for speaking about communist theory that advocated the forcible overthrow of the government. (In the 1957 Yates v. U.S. decision, the Court moderated this ruling by allowing such advocacy in the abstract, if not connected to action to achieve the goal.)

1954: Brown v. Board of Education of Topeka. The Court ruled that separate public schools for black and white students were inherently unequal, thus state-sanctioned segregation in public schools violated the equal protection guarantee of the 14th Amendment. And in **Bolling v. Sharpe** the Court ruled that the congressionally-mandated segregated public school system in the District of Columbia violated the Fifth Amendment's due process guarantee of personal liberty. (The Brown ruling also led to the abolition of state-sponsored segregation in other public facilities.)

1957: Roth v. U.S., Alberts v. California. The Court ruled that obscene material was not protected by the First Amendment guarantees of freedom of speech and press, defining obscene as "utterly without redeeming social value" and appealing to "prurient interests" in the view of the average person. (This definition, the first offered by the Court, was modified in several subsequent decisions, and the "average person" standard was replaced by the "local community" standard in the **1973 Miller v. California** case.)

1961: Mapp v. Ohio. The Court ruled that evidence obtained in violation of the 4th Amendment guarantee against unreasonable search and seizure must be excluded from use at state as well as federal trials.

1962: Engel v. Vitale. The Court ruled that public school officials could not require pupils to recite a state-composed prayer at the start of each school day, even if the prayer was non-denominational and pupils who so desired could be excused from reciting it, because such official state sanction of religious utterances was an unconstitutional attempt to establish religion.

1962: Baker v. Carr. The Court held that the constitutional challenges to the unequal distribution of voters among legislative districts could be resolved by federal courts, rejecting the doctrine set out in **Colegrove v. Green** in 1946 that such apportionment challenges were "political questions."

1963: Gideon v. Wainwright. The Court ruled that the due process clause of the 14th Amendment extended to state as well as federal defendants, thus all persons charged with serious crimes must be provided with an attorney, and states were required to appoint counsel for defendants unable to pay their own attorneys' fees.

1964: New York Times Co. v. Sullivan. The Court ruled that the First Amendment guarantee of freedom of the press protected the press from libel suits for defamatory reports on public officials unless the officials proved that the reports were made from actual malice. The Court defined malice as "with knowledge that (the defamatory statement) was false or with reckless disregard of whether it was false or not."

1965: Griswold v. Conn. The Court ruled that a state unconstitutionally interfered with personal privacy in the marriage relationship when it prohibited anyone, including married couples, from using contraceptives.

1966: Miranda v. Arizona. The Court ruled that the guarantee of due process required that before any questioning of suspects in police custody, the suspects must be informed of their right to remain silent, that anything they say may be used against them, and that they have the right to counsel.

1973: Roe v. Wade, Doe v. Bolton. The Court ruled that the right to privacy inherent in the 14th Amendment's due process guarantee of personal liberty protected a woman's decision whether or not to bear a child, and was impermissibly abridged by state laws that made abortion a crime. During the first trimester of pregnancy, the Court maintained, the decision to have an abortion should be left entirely to a woman and her physician.

1974: U.S. v. Nixon. The Court ruled that neither the separation of powers nor the need to preserve the confidentiality of presidential communications could alone justify an absolute executive privilege of immunity from judicial demands for evidence to be used in a criminal trial.

1976: Gregg v. Georgia, Profitt v. Fla, Jurek v. Texas. The Court held that death, as a punishment for persons convicted of first degree murder, was not in and of itself cruel and unusual punishment in violation of the 8th Amendment.

The Court also ruled that the Amendment required the sentencing judge and jury to consider the individual character of the offender and the circumstances of the particular crime before deciding whether or not to impose the death sentence. In the associated **Woodson v. N.C., Roberts v. LA.**, the Court ruled that states could not make death the mandatory penalty for first-degree murder, since that would fail to meet the constitutional requirement for the consideration of the individual offender and offense.

1978: Regents of Univ. of Calif. v. Bakke. The Court ruled that a special admissions program for a state medical school under which a set number of places were set aside for minority group members, with white applicants denied the opportunity to compete for those seats, violated Title XIV of the 1964 Civil Rights Act, which forbids the exclusion of anyone, because of race, from participation in a federally-funded program. The Court also ruled that admissions programs that considered race as one of a complex of factors involved in the decision to admit or reject an applicant were not unconstitutional.

1979: United Steelworkers of America v. Weber, Kaiser Aluminum v. Weber, U.S. v. Weber. The Court ruled that Title VII of the 1964 Civil Rights Act, which forbids racial discrimination in employment, did not forbid employers to adopt voluntarily race-conscious affirmative action programs to encourage minority participation in areas in which they traditionally were underrepresented.

1986: Bowers v. Hardwick. The Court refused to extend the right of privacy inherent in the Constitution to homosexual activity, upholding a Georgia law that made sodomy a crime. (Although the Georgia law covered heterosexual sodomy as well as homosexual sodomy, enforcement in Georgia and most other states had been confined to homosexual activity.)

1989: Webster v. Reproductive Health Services. The Court upheld a Missouri abortion law that prohibited public employees from performing abortions unless the mother's life was in danger, barred the use of public buildings for performing abortions, and required physicians, before performing abortions of fetuses more than 20 weeks old, to perform tests to discover whether the fetus could live outside the womb.

Patrick Henry's Speech to the Virginia Convention

The following is an excerpt from Patrick Henry's speech to the Virginia Convention on Mar. 23, 1775:

Gentlemen may cry, peace, peace—but there is no peace. The war is actually begun! The next gale that sweeps from the north will bring to our ears the clash of resounding arms! Our brethren are already in the field! Why stand we here idle? What is it that gentlemen wish? What would they have? Is life so dear, or peace so sweet, as to be purchased at the price of chains and slavery? Forbid it, Almighty God! I know not what course others may take; but as for me, give me liberty, or give me death!

Common Sense

The following is an excerpt from Thomas Paine's *Common Sense.* Paine adopted the doctrine of separation from Britain after the battles of Lexington and Concord, and published his pamphlet in Jan. 1776.

The cause of America is in great measure the cause of all mankind. Many circumstances hath, and will arise, which are not local, but universal, and through which principles of all Lovers of Mankind are affected, and in the Event of which, their Affections are interested. The laying a Country desolate with Fire and Sword, declaring war against natural rights of all Mankind, and extirpating the Defenders thereof from the Face of the Earth, is the Concern of every Man to whom Nature hath given the Power of feeling; ... It is repugnant to reason, to the universal order of things, to all examples from former ages, to suppose, that this continent can longer remain subject to any external power ...

The last cord is now broken, the people of England are presenting addresses against us. There are injuries which nature cannot forgive; she would cease to be nature if she did ...

O ye that love mankind! Ye that dare oppose, not only the tyranny, but the tyrant, stand forth! Every spot of the old world is overrun with oppression. Freedom hath been hunted round the globe. Asia, and Africa, have long expelled her—Europe regards her like a stranger, and England hath given her warning to depart. O! Receive the fugitive, and prepare in time an asylum for mankind.

Law on Succession to the Presidency

If by reason of death, resignation, removal from office, inability, or failure to qualify there is neither a president nor vice president to discharge the powers and duties of the office of president, then the speaker of the House of Representatives shall upon his resignation as speaker and as representative, act as president. The same rule shall apply in the case of the death, resignation, removal from office, or inability of an individual acting as president.

If at the time when a speaker is to begin the discharge of the powers and duties of the office of president there is no speaker, or the speaker fails to qualify as acting president, then the president pro tempore of the Senate, upon his resignation as president pro tempore and as senator, shall act as president.

An individual acting as president shall continue to act until the expiration of the then current presidential term, except that (1) if his discharge of the powers and duties of the office is founded in whole or in part in the failure of both the president-elect and the vice president-elect to qualify, then he shall act only until a president or vice president qualifies, and (2) if his discharge of the powers and duties of the office is founded in whole or in part on the inability of the president or vice president, then he shall act only until the removal of the disability of one of such individuals.

If, by reason of death, resignation, removal from office, or failure to qualify, there is no president pro tempore to act as president, then the officer of the United States who is highest on the following list, and who is not under any disability to discharge the powers and duties of president shall act as president; the secretaries of state, treasury, defense, attorney general; secretaries of interior, agriculture, commerce, labor, health and human services, housing and urban development, transportation, energy, education.

(Legislation approved July 18, 1947; amended Sept. 9, 1965, Oct. 15, 1966, Aug. 4, 1977, and Sept. 27, 1979. (See also Constitutional Amendment XXV.)

Presidential Oath of Office

The Constitution (Article II) directs that the President shall take the following oath or affirmation: "I do solemnly swear (affirm) that I will faithfully execute the office of President of the United States, and will, to the best of my ability, preserve, protect, and defend the Constitution of the United States." (Custom decrees the use of the words "So help me God" at the end of the oath when taken by the President-elect, his/her left hand on the Bible for the duration of the oath, with his/her right hand slightly raised.)

How the Declaration of Independence Was Adopted

On June 7, 1776, Richard Henry Lee, who had issued the first call for a congress of the colonies, introduced in the Continental Congress at Philadelphia a resolution declaring "that these United Colonies are, and of right ought to be, free and independent states, that they are absolved from all allegiance to the British Crown, and that all political connection between them and the state of Great Britain is, and ought to be, totally dissolved."

The resolution, seconded by John Adams on behalf of the Massachusetts delegation, came up again June 10 when a committee of 5, headed by Thomas Jefferson, was appointed to express the purpose of the resolution in a declaration of independence. The others on the committee were John Adams, Benjamin Franklin, Robert R. Livingston, and Roger Sherman.

Drafting the Declaration was assigned to Jefferson, who worked on a portable desk of his own construction in a room at Market and 7th Sts. The committee reported the result June 28, 1776. The members of the Congress suggested a number of changes, which Jefferson called "deplorable." They didn't approve Jefferson's arraignment of the British people and King George III for encouraging and fostering the slave trade, which Jefferson called "an execrable commerce." They made 86 changes, eliminating 480 words and leaving 1,337. In the final form capitalization was erratic. Jefferson had written that men were endowed with "inalienable" rights; in the final copy it came out as "unalienable" and has been thus ever since.

The Lee-Adams resolution of independence was adopted by 12 yeas July 2 — the actual date of the act of independence. The Declaration, which explains the act, was adopted July 4, in the evening.

After the Declaration was adopted, July 4, 1776, it was turned over to John Dunlap, printer, to be printed on broadsides. The original copy was lost and one of his broadsides was attached to a page in the journal of the Congress. It was read aloud July 8 in Philadelphia, Easton, Pa., and Trenton, N.J. On July 9 at 6 p.m. it was read by order of Gen. George Washington to the troops assembled on the Common in New York City (City Hall Park).

The Continental Congress of July 19, 1776, adopted the following resolution:

"Resolved, That the Declaration passed on the 4th, be fairly engrossed on parchment with the title and stile of 'The Unanimous Declaration of the thirteen United States of America' and that the same, when engrossed, be signed by every member of Congress."

Not all delegates who signed the engrossed Declaration were present on July 4. Robert Morris (Pa.), William Williams (Conn.) and Samuel Chase (Md.) signed on Aug. 2, Oliver Wolcott (Conn.), George Wythe (Va.), Richard Henry Lee (Va.) and Elbridge Gerry (Mass.) signed in August and September, Matthew Thornton (N. H.) joined the Congress Nov. 4 and signed later. Thomas McKean (Del.) rejoined Washington's Army before signing and said later that he signed in 1781.

Charles Carroll of Carrollton was appointed a delegate by Maryland on July 4, 1776, presented his credentials July 18, and signed the engrossed Declaration Aug. 2. Born Sept. 19, 1737, he was 95 years old and the last surviving signer when he died Nov. 14, 1832.

Two Pennsylvania delegates who did not support the Declaration on July 4 were replaced.

The 4 New York delegates did not have authority from their state to vote on July 4. On July 9 the New York state convention authorized its delegates to approve the Declaration and the Congress was so notified on July 15, 1776. The 4 signed the Declaration on Aug. 2.

The original engrossed Declaration is preserved in the National Archives Building in Washington.

The Continental Congress: Meetings, Presidents

Meeting places	Dates of meetings	Congress presidents	Date elected
Philadelphia	Sept. 5 to Oct. 26, 1774	Peyton Randolph, Va. (1)	Sept. 5, 1774
"	"	Henry Middleton, S.C.	Oct. 22, 1774
Philadelphia	May 10, 1775 to Dec. 12, 1776	Peyton Randolph, Va.	May 10, 1775
"	"	John Hancock, Mass.	May 24, 1775
Baltimore	Dec. 20, 1776 to Mar. 4, 1777	"	
Philadelphia	Mar. 5 to Sept. 18, 1777	"	
Lancaster, Pa.	Sept. 27, 1777 (one day)	"	
York, Pa.	Sept. 30, 1777 to June 27, 1778	Henry Laurens, S.C.	Nov. 1, 1777(4)
Philadelphia	July 2, 1778 to June 21, 1783	John Jay, N.Y.	Dec. 10, 1778
"	"	Samuel Huntington, Conn.	Sept. 28, 1779
"	"	Thomas McKean, Del.	July 10, 1781
"	"	John Hanson, Md. (2)	Nov. 5, 1781
"	"	Elias Boudinot, N.J.	Nov. 4, 1782
Princeton, N.J.	June 30 to Nov. 4, 1783	Thomas Mifflin, Pa.	Nov. 3, 1783
Annapolis, Md.	Nov. 26, 1783 to June 3, 1784	"	
Trenton, N.J.	Nov. 1 to Dec. 24, 1784	Richard Henry Lee, Va.	Nov. 30, 1784
New York City	Jan. 11 to Nov. 4, 1785	"	
"	Nov. 7, 1785 to Nov. 3, 1786	John Hancock, Mass. (3)	Nov. 23, 1785
"	"	Nathaniel Gorham, Mass.	June 6, 1786
"	Nov. 6, 1786 to Oct. 30, 1787	Arthur St. Clair, Pa.	Feb. 2, 1787
"	Nov. 5, 1787 to Oct. 21, 1788	Cyrus Griffin, Va.	Jan. 22, 1788
"	Nov. 3, 1788 to Mar. 2, 1789	"	

(1) Resigned Oct. 22, 1774. (2) Titled "President of the United States in Congress Assembled," John Hanson is considered by some to be the first U.S. President as he was the first to serve under the Articles of Confederation. He was, however, little more than presiding officer of the Congress, which retained full executive power. He could be considered the head of government, but not head of state. (3) Resigned May 29, 1786, without serving, because of illness. (4) Articles of Confederation agreed upon, Nov. 15, 1777; last ratification from Maryland, Mar. 1, 1781.

Origin of the United States National Motto

In God We Trust, designated as the U. S. National Motto by Congress in 1956, originated during the Civil War as an inscription for U. S. coins, although it was used by Francis Scott Key in a slightly different form when he wrote The Star Spangled Banner in 1814. On Nov. 13, 1861, when Union morale had been shaken by battlefield defeats, the Rev. M. R. Watkinson, of Ridleyville, Pa., wrote to Secy. of the Treasury Salmon P. Chase. "From my heart I have felt our national shame in disowning God as not the least of our present national disasters," the minister wrote, suggesting "recognition of the Almighty God in some form on our coins." Secy. Chase ordered designs prepared with the inscription *In God We Trust* and backed coinage legislation which authorized use of this slogan. It first appeared on some U. S. coins in 1864, disappeared and reappeared on various coins until 1955, when Congress ordered it placed on all paper money and all coins.

The Great Seal of the U.S.

On July 4, 1776, the Continental Congress appointed a committee consisting of Benjamin Franklin, John Adams and Thomas Jefferson "to bring in a device for a seal of the United States of America." After many delays, a verbal description of a design by William Barton was finally approved by Congress on June 20, 1782. The seal shows an American bald eagle with a ribbon in its mouth bearing the device *E pluribus unum* (One out of many). In its talons are the arrows of war and an olive branch of peace. On the reverse side it shows an unfinished pyramid with an eye (the eye of Providence) above it.

The American's Creed

William Tyler Page, Clerk of the U.S. House of Representatives, wrote "The American's Creed" in 1917. It was accepted by the House on behalf of the American people on April 3, 1918.

"I believe in the United States of America as a government of the people, by the people, for the people; whose just powers are derived from the consent of the governed; a democracy in a republic; a sovereign Nation of many sovereign States; a perfect union, one and inseparable; established upon those principles of freedom, equality, justice, and humanity for which American patriots sacrificed their lives and fortunes.

"I therefore believe it is my duty to my country to love it, to support its Constitution, to obey its laws, to respect its flag, and to defend it against all enemies."

The Flag of the U.S.—The Stars and Stripes

The 50-star flag of the United States was raised for the first time officially at 12:01 a.m. on July 4, 1960, at Fort McHenry National Monument in Baltimore, Md. The 50th star had been added for Hawaii; a year earlier the 49th, for Alaska. Before that, no star had been added since 1912, when N.M. and Ariz. were admitted to the Union.

The true history of the Stars and Stripes has become so cluttered by a volume of myth and tradition that the facts are difficult, and in some cases impossible, to establish. For example, it is not certain who designed the Stars and Stripes, who made the first such flag, or even whether it ever flew in any sea fight or land battle of the American Revolution.

One thing all agree on is that the Stars and Stripes originated as the result of a resolution offered by the Marine Committee of the Second Continental Congress at Philadelphia and adopted June 14, 1777. It read:

Resolved: that the flag of the United States be thirteen stripes, alternate red and white; that the union be thirteen stars, white in a blue field, representing a new constellation.

Congress gave no hint as to the designer of the flag, no instructions as to the arrangement of the stars, and no information on its appropriate uses. Historians have been unable to find the original flag law.

The resolution establishing the flag was not even published until Sept. 2, 1777. Despite repeated requests, Washington did not get the flags until 1783, after the Revolutionary War was over. And there is no certainty that they were the Stars and Stripes.

Early Flags

Although it was never officially adopted by the Continental Congress, many historians consider the first flag of the U.S. to have been the Grand Union (sometimes called Great Union) flag. This was a modification of the British Meteor flag, which had the red cross of St. George and the white cross of St. Andrew combined in the blue canton. For the Grand Union flag, 6 horizontal stripes were imposed on the red field, dividing it into 13 alternate red and white stripes. On Jan. 1, 1776, when the Continental Army came into formal existence, this flag was unfurled on Prospect Hill, Somerville, Mass. Washington wrote that "we hoisted the Union Flag in compliment to the United Colonies."

One of several flags about which controversy has raged for years is at Easton, Pa. Containing the devices of the national flag in reversed order, this has been in the public library at Easton for over 150 years. Some contend that this flag was actually the first Stars and Stripes, first displayed on July 8, 1776. This flag has 13 red and white stripes in the canton, 13 white stars centered in a blue field.

A flag was hastily improvised from garments by the defenders of Fort Schuyler at Rome, N.Y., Aug. 3-22, 1777. Historians believe it was the Grand Union Flag.

The Sons of Liberty had a flag of 9 red and white stripes, to signify 9 colonies, when they met in New York in 1765 to oppose the Stamp Tax. By 1775, the flag had grown to 13 red and white stripes, with a rattlesnake on it.

At Concord, Apr. 19, 1775, the minute men from Bedford, Mass., are said to have carried a flag having a silver arm with sword on a red field.

At Cambridge, Mass., the Sons of Liberty used a plain red flag with a green pine tree on it.

In June 1775, Washington went from Philadelphia to Boston to take command of the army, escorted to New York by the Philadelphia Light Horse Troop. It carried a yellow flag which had an elaborate coat of arms — the shield charged with 13 knots, the motto "For These We Strive" — and a canton of 13 blue and silver stripes.

In Feb., 1776, Col. Christopher Gadsden, member of the Continental Congress, gave the S. Carolina Provincial Congress a flag "such as is to be used by the commander-in-chief of the American Navy." It had a yellow field, with a rattlesnake about to strike and the words "Don't Tread on Me."

At the battle of Bennington, Aug. 16, 1777, patriots used a flag of 7 white and 6 red stripes with a blue canton extending down 9 stripes and showing an arch of 11 white stars over the figure 76 and a star in each of the upper corners. The stars are seven-pointed. This flag is preserved in the Historical Museum at Bennington, Vt.

At the Battle of Cowpens, Jan. 17, 1781, the 3d Maryland Regt. is said to have carried a flag of 13 red and white stripes, with a blue canton containing 12 stars in a circle around one star.

Who Designed the Flag? No one knows for certain. Francis Hopkinson, designer of a naval flag, declared he also had designed the flag and in 1781 asked Congress to reimburse him for his services. Congress did not do so. Dumas Malone of Columbia Univ. wrote: "This talented man . . . designed the American flag."

Who Called the Flag Old Glory? — The flag is said to have been named Old Glory by William Driver, a sea captain of Salem, Mass. One legend has it that when he raised the flag on his brig, the Charles Doggett, in 1824, he said: "I name thee Old Glory." But his daughter, who presented the flag to the Smithsonian Institution, said he named it at his 21st birthday celebration Mar. 17, 1824, when his mother presented the homemade flag to him.

The Betsy Ross Legend — The widely publicized legend that Mrs. Betsy Ross made the first Stars and Stripes in June 1776, at the request of a committee composed of George Washington, Robert Morris, and George Ross, an uncle, was first made public in 1870, by a grandson of Mrs. Ross. Historians have been unable to find a historical record of such a meeting or committee.

Adding New Stars

The flag of 1777 was used until 1795. Then, on the admission of Vermont and Kentucky to the Union, Congress passed and Pres. Washington signed an act that after May 1, 1795, the flag should have 15 stripes, alternate red and white, and 15 white stars on a blue field in the union.

When new states were admitted it became evident that the flag would become burdened with stripes. Congress thereupon ordered that after July 4, 1818, the flag should have 13 stripes, symbolizing the 13 original states; that the union have 20 stars, and that whenever a new state was admitted a new star should be added on the July 4 following admission. No law designates the permanent arrangement of the stars. However, since 1912 when a new state has been admitted, the new design has been announced by executive order. No star is specifically identified with any state.

Code of Etiquette for Display and Use of the U.S. Flag

Although the Stars and Stripes originated in 1777, it was not until 146 years later that there was a serious attempt to establish a uniform code of etiquette for the U.S. flag. The War Department issued Feb. 15, 1923, a circular on the rules of flag usage. These were adopted almost in their entirety June 14, 1923, by a conference of 68 patriotic organizations in Washington. Finally, on June 22, 1942, a joint resolution of Congress, amended by Public Law 94-344 July 7, 1976, codified "existing rules and customs pertaining to the display and use of the flag . . ."

When to Display the Flag—The flag should be displayed on all days, especially on legal holidays and other special occasions, on official buildings when in use, in or near polling places on election days, and in or near schools when in session. A citizen may fly the flag at any time he wishes. It is customary to display the flag only from sunrise to sunset on buildings and on stationary flagstaffs in the open. However, it may be displayed at night on special occasions, preferably lighted. In Washington, the flag now flies over the White House both day and night. It flies over the Senate wing of the Capitol when the Senate is in session and over the House wing when that body is in session. It flies day and night over the east and west fronts of the Capitol, without floodlights at night but receiving light from the illuminated Capitol Dome. It flies 24 hours a day at several other places, including the Fort McHenry Nat'l Monument in Baltimore, where it inspired Francis Scott Key to write The Star Spangled Banner.

How to Fly the Flag—The flag should be hoisted briskly and lowered ceremoniously, and should never be allowed to touch the ground or the floor. When hung over a sidewalk from a rope extending from a building to a pole, the union should be away from the building. When hung over the center of a street it should have the union to the north in an east-west street and to the east in a north-south street. No other flag may be flown above or, if on the same level, to the right of the U.S. flag, except that at the United Nations Headquarters the UN flag may be placed above flags of all member nations and other national flags may be flown with equal prominence or honor with the flag of the U.S. At services by Navy chaplains at sea, the church pennant may be flown above the flag.

When two flags are placed against a wall with crossed staffs, the U.S. flag should be at right—its own right, and its staff should be in front of the staff of the other flag; when a number of flags are grouped and displayed from staffs, it should be at the center and highest point of the group.

Church and Platform Use—In an auditorium, the flag may be displayed flat, above and behind the speaker. When displayed from a staff in a church or public auditorium, the flag should hold the position of superior prominence, in advance of the audience, and in the position of honor at the clergyman's or speaker's right as he faces the audience. Any other flag so displayed should be placed on the left of the clergyman or speaker or to the right of the audience.

When the flag is displayed horizontally or vertically against a wall, the stars should be uppermost and at the observer's left.

How to Dispose of Worn Flags—The flag, when it is in such condition that it is no longer a fitting emblem for display, should be destroyed in a dignified way, preferably by burning.

When to Salute the Flag—All persons present should face the flag, stand at attention and salute on the following occasions: (1) When the flag is passing in a parade or in a review, (2) During the ceremony of hoisting or lowering, (3) When the National Anthem is played, and (4) During the Pledge of Allegiance. Those present in uniform should render the military salute. When not in uniform, men should remove the hat with the right hand holding it at the left shoulder, the hand being over the heart. Men without hats should salute in the same manner. Aliens should stand at attention. Women should salute by placing the right hand over the heart.

On Memorial Day, the flag should fly at half-staff until noon, then be raised to the peak.

As provided by Presidential proclamation the flag should fly at half-staff for 30 days from the day of death of a president or former president; for 10 days from the day of death of a vice president, chief justice or retired chief justice of the U.S., or speaker of the House of Representatives; from day of death until burial of an associate justice of the Supreme Court, cabinet member, former vice president, or Senate president pro tempore, majority or minority Senate leader, or majority or minority House leader; for a U.S. senator, representative, territorial delegate, or the resident commissioner of Puerto Rico, on day of death and the following day within the metropolitan area of the District of Columbia and from day of death until burial within the decedent's state, congressional district, territory or commonwealth; and for the death of the governor of a state, territory, or possession of the U.S., from day of death until burial within that state, territory, or possession.

When used to cover a casket, the flag should be placed so that the union is at the head and over the left shoulder. It should not be lowered into the grave nor touch the ground.

Prohibited Uses of the Flag—The flag should not be dipped to any person or thing. (An exception—customarily, ships salute by dipping their colors.) It should never be displayed with the union down save as a distress signal. It should never be carried flat or horizontally, but always aloft and free.

It should not be displayed on a float, motor car or boat except from a staff.

It should never be used as a covering for a ceiling, nor have placed upon it any word, design, or drawing. It should never be used as a receptacle for carrying anything. It should not be used to cover a statue or a monument.

The flag should never be used for advertising purposes, nor be embroidered on such articles as cushions or handkerchiefs, printed or otherwise impressed on boxes or anything that is designed for temporary use and discard; or used as a costume or athletic uniform. Advertising signs should not be fastened to its staff or halyard.

The flag should never be used as drapery of any sort, never festooned, drawn back, nor up, in folds, but always allowed to fall free. Bunting of blue, white and red always arranged with the blue above and the white in the middle, should be used for covering a speaker's desk, draping the front of a platform, and for decoration in general.

An Act of Congress approved Feb. 8, 1917, provided certain penalties for the desecration, mutilation or improper use of the flag within the District of Columbia. A 1968 federal law provided penalties of up to a year's imprisonment or a $1,000 fine or both, for publicly burning or otherwise desecrating any flag of the United States. In addition, many states have laws against flag desecration. In 1989, the Supreme Court ruled that no laws could prohibit political protesters from burning the flag. The decision had the effect of declaring unconstitutional the flag desecration laws of 48 states, as well as a similar Federal statute, in cases of peaceful political expression.

The Supreme Court, June 1990, declared that a new Federal law making it a crime to burn or deface the American flag violates the free-speech guarantee of the First Amendment. The 5-4 decision led to renewed calls in Congress for a constitutional amendment to make it possible to prosecute flag burning.

Pledge of Allegiance to the Flag

I pledge allegiance to the flag of the United States of America and to the republic for which it stands, one nation under God, indivisible, with liberty and justice for all.

This, the current official version of the Pledge of Allegiance, has developed from the original pledge, which was first published in the Sept. 8, 1892, issue of the Youth's Companion, a weekly magazine then published in Boston. The original pledge contained the phrase "my flag," which was changed more than 30 years later to "flag of the United States of America." An act of Congress in 1954 added the words "under God."

The authorship of the pledge had been in dispute for many years. The Youth's Companion stated in 1917 that the original draft was written by James B. Upham, an executive of the magazine who died in 1910. A leaflet circulated by the magazine later named Upham as the originator of the draft "afterwards condensed and perfected by him and his associates of the Companion force."

Francis Bellamy, a former member of the Youth's Companion editorial staff, publicly claimed authorship of the pledge in 1923. The United States Flag Assn., acting on the advice of a committee named to study the controversy, upheld in 1939 the claim of Bellamy, who had died 8 years earlier. The Library of Congress issued in 1957 a report attributing the authorship to Bellamy.

The National Anthem — The Star-Spangled Banner

The Star-Spangled Banner was ordered played by the military and naval services by President Woodrow Wilson in 1916. It was designated the National Anthem by Act of Congress, Mar. 3, 1931. It was written by Francis Scott Key, of Georgetown, D. C., during the bombardment of Fort McHenry, Baltimore, Md., Sept. 13-14, 1814. Key was a lawyer, a graduate of St. John's College, Annapolis, and a volunteer in a light artillery company. When a friend, Dr. Beanes, a physician of Upper Marlborough, Md., was taken aboard Admiral Cockburn's British squadron for interfering with ground troops, Key and J. S. Skinner, carrying a note from President Madison, went to the fleet under a flag of truce on a cartel ship to ask Beanes' release. Admiral Cockburn consented, but as the fleet was about to sail up the Patapsco to bombard Fort McHenry he detained them, first on H. M. S. Surprise, and then on a supply ship.

Key witnessed the bombardment from his own vessel. It began at 7 a.m., Sept. 13, 1814, and lasted, with intermissions, for 25 hours. The British fired over 1,500 shells, each weighing as much as 220 lbs. They were unable to approach closely because the Americans had sunk 22 vessels in the channel. Only four Americans were killed and 24 wounded. A British bomb-ship was disabled.

During the bombardment Key wrote a stanza on the back of an envelope. Next day at Indian Queen Inn, Baltimore, he wrote out the poem and gave it to his brother-in-law, Judge J. H. Nicholson. Nicholson suggested the tune, Anacreon in Heaven, and had the poem printed on broadsides, of which two survive. On Sept. 20 it appeared in the "Baltimore American." Later Key made 3 copies; one is in the Library of Congress and one in the Pennsylvania Historical Society.

The copy that Key wrote in his hotel Sept. 14, 1814, remained in the Nicholson family for 93 years. In 1907 it was sold to Henry Walters of Baltimore. In 1934 it was bought at auction in New York from the Walters estate by the Walters Art Gallery, Baltimore, for $26,400. The Walters Gallery in 1953 sold the manuscript to the Maryland Historical Society for the same price.

The flag that Key saw during the bombardment is preserved in the Smithsonian Institution, Washington. It is 30 by 42 ft., and has 15 alternate red and white stripes and 15 stars, for the original 13 states plus Kentucky and Vermont. It was made by Mary Young Pickersgill. The Baltimore Flag House, a museum, occupies her premises, which were restored in 1953.

The Star-Spangled Banner

I

Oh, say can you see by the dawn's early light
What so proudly we hailed at the twilight's last gleaming?
Whose broad stripes and bright stars thru the perilous fight,
O'er the ramparts we watched were so gallantly streaming?
And the rocket's red glare, the bombs bursting in air,
Gave proof through the night that our flag was still there.
Oh, say does that star-spangled banner yet wave
O'er the land of the free and the home of the brave?

II

On the shore, dimly seen through the mists of the deep,
Where the foe's haughty host in dread silence reposes,
What is that which the breeze, o'er the towering steep,
As it fitfully blows, half conceals, half discloses?
Now it catches the gleam of the morning's first beam,
In full glory reflected now shines in the stream:
'Tis the star-spangled banner! Oh long may it wave
O'er the land of the free and the home of the brave!

III

And where is that band who so vauntingly swore
That the havoc of war and the battle's confusion,
A home and a country should leave us no more!
Their blood has washed out their foul footsteps' pollution.
No refuge could save the hireling and slave
From the terror of flight, or the gloom of the grave:
And the star-spangled banner in triumph doth wave
O'er the land of the free and the home of the brave!

IV

Oh! thus be it ever, when freemen shall stand
Between their loved home and the war's desolation!
Blest with victory and peace, may the heav'n rescued land
Praise the Power that hath made and preserved us a nation.
Then conquer we must, when our cause it is just,
And this be our motto: "In God is our trust."
And the star-spangled banner in triumph shall wave
O'er the land of the free and the home of the brave!

America
(My Country 'Tis of Thee)

First sung in public on July 4, 1831, at a service in the Park Street Church, Boston, the words were written by Rev. Samuel Francis Smith, a Baptist clergyman, who set them to a melody he found in a German songbook, unaware that it was the tune for the British anthem, "God Save the King/Queen."

My country, 'tis of thee,
Sweet land of liberty, Of thee I sing.
Land where my fathers died!
Land of the Pilgrims' pride!
From ev'ry mountainside,
Let freedom ring!

My native country, thee,
Land of the noble free,
Thy name I love.
I love thy rocks and rills,
Thy woods and templed hills;
My heart with rapture thrills
Like that above.

Let music swell the breeze,
And ring from all the trees
Sweet freedom's song.
Let mortal tongues awake;
Let all that breathe partake;
Let rocks their silence break,
The sound prolong.

Our fathers' God, to Thee,
Author of liberty,
To Thee we sing.
Long may our land be bright
With freedom's holy light;
Protect us by Thy might,
Great God, our King!

America, the Beautiful

Composed by Katherine Lee Bates, a Massachusetts educator and author, in 1893. It was inspired by the view Bates experienced atop Pike's Peak. Its final form was established in 1911 and is set to the music of Samuel A. Ward's "Materna."

O beautiful for spacious skies,
For amber waves of grain,
For purple mountain majesties
Above the fruited plain.
America! America!
God shed His grace on thee,
And crown thy good with brotherhood
From sea to shining sea.

O beautiful for pilgrim feet
Whose stern impassion'd stress
A thorough-fare for freedom beat
Across the wilderness.
America! America!
God mend thine ev'ry flaw,
Confirm thy soul in self control,
Thy liberty in law.

O beautiful for heroes prov'd
In liberating strife,
Who more than self their country lov'd
And mercy more than life.
America! America!
May God thy gold refine
Till all success be nobleness,
And ev'ry gain divine.

O beautiful for patriot dream
That sees beyond the years,
Thine alabaster cities gleam,
Undimmed by human tears.
America! America!
God shed His grace on thee,
And crown thy good with brotherhood
From sea to shining sea.

The Liberty Bell: Its History and Significance

The Liberty Bell, in Independence Hall, Philadelphia, is an object of great reverence to Americans because of its association with the historic events of the War of Independence.

The original Province bell, ordered to commemorate the 50th anniversary of the Commonwealth of Pennsylvania, was cast by Thomas Lister, Whitechapel, London, and reached Philadelphia in Aug. 1752. It bore an inscription from Leviticus XXV, 10: "Proclaim liberty throughout all the land unto all the inhabitants thereof."

The bell was cracked by a stroke of its clapper in Sept. 1752 while it hung on a truss in the State House yard for testing. Pass & Stow, Philadelphia founders, recast the bell, adding 1 1/2 ounces of copper to a pound of the original metal to reduce brittleness. It was found that the bell contained too much copper, injuring its tone, so Pass & Stow recast it again, this time successfully.

In June 1753 the bell was hung in the wooden steeple of the State House, erected on top of the brick tower. In use while the Continental Congress was in session in the State House, it rang out in defiance of British tax and trade restrictions, and proclaimed the Boston Tea Party and the first public reading of the Declaration of Independence.

On Sept. 18, 1777, when the British Army was about to occupy Philadelphia, the bell was moved in a baggage train of the American Army to Allentown, Pa. where it was hidden in the Zion Reformed Church until June 27, 1778. It was moved back to Philadelphia after the British left.

In July 1781 the wooden steeple became insecure and had to be taken down. The bell was lowered into the brick section of the tower. Because of its association with the War of Independence it was not recast but remained mute in this location until 1846, the year of the Mexican War, when it was placed on exhibition in the Declaration Chamber of Independence Hall.

In 1876, when many thousands of Americans visited Philadelphia for the Centennial Exposition, it was placed in its old walnut frame in the tower hallway. In 1877 it was hung from the ceiling of the tower by a chain of 13 links. It was returned again to the Declaration Chamber and in 1896 taken back to the tower hall, where it occupied a glass case. In 1915 the case was removed so that the public might touch it. On Jan. 1, 1976, just after midnight to mark the opening of the Bicentennial Year, the bell was moved to a new glass and steel pavilion behind Independence Hall for easier viewing by the larger number of visitors expected during the year.

The measurements of the bell follow: circumference around the lip, 12 ft.; circumference around the crown, 7 ft. 6 in.; lip to the crown, 3 ft.; height over the crown, 2 ft. 3 in.; thickness at lip, 3 in.; thickness at crown, 1 1/4 in.; weight, 2080 lbs.; length of clapper, 3 ft. 2 in.; cost, £60 14s 5d.

The specific source of the crack in the bell is unknown.

Statue of Liberty National Monument

Since 1886, the Statue of Liberty Enlightening the World has stood as a symbol of freedom in New York harbor. It also commemorates French-American friendship for it was given by the people of France, designed by Frederic Auguste Bartholdi (1834-1904). A $2.5 million building housing the American Museum of Immigration was opened by Pres. Nixon Sept. 26, 1972, at the base of the statue. It houses a permanent exhibition of photos, posters, and artifacts tracing the history of American immigration. The Monument is administered by the National Park Service.

Nearby Ellis Island, gateway to America for more than 12 million immigrants between 1892 and 1954, was proclaimed part of the National Monument in 1965 by Pres. Johnson.

Edouard de Laboulaye, French historian and admirer of American political institutions, suggested that the French present a monument to the United States, the latter to provide pedestal and site. Bartholdi visualized a colossal statue at the entrance of New York harbor, welcoming the peoples of the world with the torch of liberty.

On Washington's birthday, Feb. 22, 1877, Congress approved the use of a site on Bedloe's Island suggested by Bartholdi. This island of 12 acres had been owned in the 17th century by a Walloon named Isaac Bedloe. It was called Bedloe's until Aug. 3, 1956, when Pres. Eisenhower approved a resolution of Congress changing the name to Liberty Island.

The statue was finished May 21, 1884, and formally presented to U.S. Minister Morton July 4, 1884, by Ferdinand de Lesseps, head of the Franco-American Union, promoter of the Panama Canal, and builder of the Suez Canal.

On Aug. 5, 1884, the Americans laid the cornerstone for the pedestal. This was to be built on the foundations of Fort Wood, which had been erected by the Government in 1811. The American committee had raised $125,000, but this was found to be inadequate. Joseph Pulitzer, owner of the New York World, appealed on Mar. 16, 1885, for general donations. By Aug. 11, 1885, he had raised $100,000.

The statue arrived dismantled, in 214 packing cases, from Rouen, France, in June, 1885. The last rivet of the statue was driven Oct. 28, 1886, when Pres. Grover Cleveland dedicated the monument.

The statue weighs 450,000 lbs. or 225 tons. The copper sheeting weighs 200,000 lbs. There are 167 steps from the land level to the top of the pedestal, 168 steps inside the statue to the head, and 54 rungs on the ladder leading to the arm that holds the torch.

Two years of restoration work was completed before the statue's centennial celebration on July 4, 1986. Among other repairs, the multi-million dollar project included replacing the 1,600 wrought iron bands that hold its copper skin to its frame, replacing its torch, and installing an elevator.

A four-day extravaganza of concerts, tall ships, ethnic festivals, and fireworks celebrated the 100th anniversary. The festivities included Chief Justice Warren E. Burger's swearing-in of 5,000 new citizens on Ellis Island, while 20,000 others across the country were simultaneously sworn in through a satellite telecast.

The ceremonies were followed by others on Oct. 28, 1986, the statue's 100th birthday.

Emma Lazarus' Famous Poem

A poem by Emma Lazarus is graven on a tablet within the pedestal on which the statue stands.

The New Colossus

Not like the brazen giant of Greek fame,
With conquering limbs astride from land to land;
Here at our sea-washed, sunset gates shall stand
A mighty woman with a torch, whose flame
Is the imprisoned lightning, and her name
Mother of Exiles. From her beacon-hand
Glows world-wide welcome; her mild eyes command
The air-bridged harbor that twin cities frame.
"Keep ancient lands, your storied pomp!" cries she
With silent lips. "Give me your tired, your poor,
Your huddled masses yearning to breathe free,
The wretched refuse of your teeming shore.
Send these, the homeless, tempest-tost to me,
I lift my lamp beside the golden door!"

Dimensions of the Statue	Ft.	In.
Height from base to torch (45.3 meters)	151	1
Foundation of pedestal to torch (91.5 meters)	305	1
Heel to top of head	111	1
Length of hand	16	5
Index finger	8	0
Circumference at second joint	3	6
Size of finger nail	13x10 in.	
Head from chin to cranium	17	3
Head thickness from ear to ear	10	0
Distance across the eye	2	6
Length of nose	4	6
Right arm, length	42	0
Right arm, greatest thickness	12	0
Thickness of waist	35	0
Width of mouth	3	0
Tablet, length	23	7
Tablet, width	13	7
Tablet, thickness	2	0

Lincoln's Address at Gettysburg, 1863

Fourscore and seven years ago our fathers brought forth on this continent a new nation, conceived in liberty and dedicated to the proposition that all men are created equal.

Now we are engaged in a great civil war, testing whether that nation or any nation so conceived and so dedicated can long endure. We are met on a great battle field of that war. We have come to dedicate a portion of that field, as a final resting-place for those who here gave their lives that that nation might live. It is altogether fitting and proper that we should do this.

But, in a larger sense, we can not dedicate — we can not consecrate — we can not hallow — this ground. The brave men, living and dead, who struggled here, have consecrated it, far above our poor power to add or detract. The world will little note, nor long remember, what we say here, but it can never forget what they did here. It is for us the living, rather, to be dedicated here to the unfinished work which they who fought here have thus far so nobly advanced. It is rather for us to be here dedicated to the great task remaining before us — that from these honored dead we take increased devotion to that cause for which they gave the last full measure of devotion — that we here highly resolve that these dead shall not have died in vain — that this nation, under God, shall have a new birth of freedom — and that government of the people, by the people, for the people, shall not perish from the earth.

Confederate States and Secession

The American Civil War, 1861-65, grew out of sectional disputes over the continued existence of slavery in the South and the contention of Southern legislators that the states retained many sovereign rights, including the right to secede from the Union.

The war was not fought by state against state but by one federal regime against another, the Confederate government in Richmond assuming control over the economic, political, and military life of the South, under protest from Georgia and South Carolina.

South Carolina voted an ordinance of secession from the Union, repealing its 1788 ratification of the U.S. Constitution on Dec. 20, 1860, to take effect Dec. 24. Other states seceded in 1861. Their votes in conventions were:

Mississippi, Jan. 9, 84-15; Florida, Jan. 10, 62-7; Alabama, Jan. 11, 61-39; Georgia, Jan. 19, 208-89; Louisiana, Jan. 26, 113-17; Texas, Feb. 1, 166-7, ratified by popular vote Feb. 23 (for 34,794, against 11,325); Virginia, Apr. 17, 88-55, ratified by popular vote May 23 (for 128,884; against 32,134); Arkansas, May 6, 69-1; Tennessee, May 7, ratified by popular vote June 8 (for 104,019, against 47,238); North Carolina, May 21.

Missouri Unionists stopped secession in conventions Feb. 28 and Mar. 9. The legislature condemned secession Mar. 7. Under the protection of Confederate troops, secessionist members of the legislature adopted a resolution of secession at Neosho, Oct. 31. The Confederate Congress seated the secessionists' representatives.

Kentucky did not secede and its government remained Unionist. In a part occupied by Confederate troops, Kentuckians approved secession and the Confederate Congress admitted their representatives.

The Maryland legislature voted against secession Apr. 27, 53-13. Delaware did not secede. Western Virginia held conventions at Wheeling, named a pro-Union governor June 11, 1861; admitted to Union as West Virginia June 20, 1863; its constitution provided for gradual abolition of slavery.

Confederate Government

Forty-two delegates from South Carolina, Georgia, Alabama, Mississippi, Louisiana, and Florida met in convention at Montgomery, Ala., Feb. 4, 1861. They adopted a provisional constitution of the Confederate States of America, and elected Jefferson Davis (Miss.) provisional president, and Alexander H. Stephens (Ga.) provisional vice president.

A permanent constitution was adopted Mar. 11; it abolished the African slave trade. The Congress moved to Richmond, Va. July 20. Davis was elected president in October, and was inaugurated Feb. 22, 1862.

The Congress adopted a flag, consisting of a red field with a white stripe, and a blue jack with a circle of white stars. Later the more popular flag was the red field with blue diagonal cross bars that held 13 white stars. The stars represented the 11 states actually in the Confederacy plus Kentucky and Missouri.

(See also Civil War, U.S., in Index)

The Mayflower Compact

The threat of James I to "harry them out of the land" sent a little band of religious dissenters from England to Holland in 1608. They were known as "Separatists" because they wished to cut all ties with the Established Church. In 1620, some of them, known now as the Pilgrims, joined with a larger group in England to set sail on the *Mayflower* for the New World. A joint stock company financed their venture.

In November, they sighted Cape Cod and decided to land an exploring party at Plymouth Harbor. However, a rebellious group picked up at Southampton and London troubled the Pilgrim leaders, and to control their actions forty-one of the Pilgrims drew up the "Mayflower Compact," which was signed before going ashore. The voluntary agreement to govern themselves was America's first written constitution.

In the name of God, Amen. We, whose names are underwritten, the Loyal Subjects of our dread Sovereign Lord, King *James*, by the Grace of God, of *Great Britain, France and Ireland*, King, *Defender of the Faith*, etc.

Having undertaken for the Glory of God, and Advancement of the Christian Faith, and the Honour of our King and Country, a voyage to plant the first colony in the northern Parts of Virginia; do by these Presents, solemnly and mutually in the Presence of God and one of another, convenant and combine ouselves together into a civil Body Politick, for our better Ordering and Preservation, and Furtherance of the Ends aforesaid; And by Virtue hereof to enact, constitute, and frame, such just and equal Laws, Ordinances, Acts, Constitutions and Offices, from time to time, as shall be thought most meet and convenient for the General good of the Colony; unto which we promise all due Submission and Obedience.

In Witness whereof we have hereunto subscribed our names at *Cape Cod* the eleventh of *November*, in the Reign of our Sovereign Lord, King *James* of *England, France* and *Ireland*, the eighteenth, and of *Scotland* the fifty-fourth. *Anno Domini, 1620.*

Forms of Address for Persons of Rank and Public Office

In these examples John Smith is used as a representative American name. The salutation Dear Sir or Dear Madam is always permissible when addressing a person not known to the writer. Female equivalents should be substituted where appropriate.

President of the United States

Address: The President, The White House, Washington, DC 20500. Also, The President and Mrs. ____.

Salutation: Dear Sir or Mr. President or Dear Mr. President. More intimately: My dear Mr. President. Also: Dear Mr. President and Mrs. ____

The vice president takes the same forms.

Cabinet Officers

Address: Mr. John Smith, Secretary of State, Washington, D.C. or The Hon. John Smith. Similar addresses for other members of the cabinet. Also: Secretary and Mrs. John Smith.

Salutation: Dear Sir, or Dear Mr. Secretary. Also: Dear Mr. and Mrs. Smith.

The Bench

Address: The Hon. John Smith, Chief Justice of the United States. The Hon. John Smith, Associate Justice of the Supreme Court of the United States. The Hon. John Smith, Associate Judge, U.S. District Court.

Salutation: Dear Sir, or Dear Mr. Chief Justice. Dear Mr. Justice. Dear Judge Smith.

Members of Congress

Address: The Hon. John Smith, United States Senate, Washington, DC 20510, or Sen. John Smith, etc. Also The Hon. John Smith, House of Representatives, Washington, DC 20515, or Rep. John Smith, etc.

Salutation: Dear Mr. Senator or Dear Mr. Smith; for Representative, Dear Mr. Smith.

Officers of Armed Forces

Address: Careful attention should be given to the precise rank, thus: General of the Army John Smith, Fleet Admiral John Smith. The rules for Air Force are same as Army.

Salutation: Dear Sir, or Dear General. All general officers, whatever rank, are entitled to be addressed as generals. Likewise a lieutenant colonel is addressed as colonel and first and second lieutenants are addressed as lieutenant.

Warrant officers and flight officers are addressed as Mister. Chaplains are addressed as Chaplain. A Catholic chaplain may be addressed as Father. Students of the U.S. Military Academy and Air Force Academy are addressed as Cadet, students of the U.S. Naval Academy are addressed as Midshipman/woman. Noncommissioned officers are addressed by their titles.

Ambassador, Governor, Mayor

Address: The Hon. John Smith, followed by his or her title. They can be addressed either at their embassy, or at the Department of State, Washington, D.C. An ambassador from a foreign nation may be addressed as His or Her Excellency. An American is not to be so addressed.

Salutation: Dear Mr. or Madam Ambassador. An ambassador from a foreign nation may be called Your Excellency.

Governors and mayors are often addressed as The Hon. Jane Smith, Governor of ______, or The Hon. John Smith, Mayor of ______; also Governor John Smith, State House, Albany, N.Y., or Mayor Jane Smith, City Hall, Erie, Pa.

The Clergy

Address: His Holiness, the Pope, or His Holiness Pope (name), State of Vatican City, Italy.

Salutation: Your Holiness or Most Holy Father.

Also: His Eminence, John, Cardinal Smith; salutation: Your Eminence. An archbishop or a bishop is addressed The Most Reverend, and the salutation is Your Excellency. A monsignor who is a papal chamberlain is The Very Reverend Monsignor and the salutation is Dear Sir or Very Reverend Monsignor; a monsignor who is a domestic prelate is The Right Reverend Monsignor and salutation is Right Reverend Monsignor. A priest is addressed Reverend John Smith. A brother of an order is addressed Brother —. A sister takes the same form.

A bishop of the Episcopal Church is The Right Reverend John Smith; salutation is Right Reverend Sir, or Dear Bishop Smith. If a clergyman is a doctor of divinity, he is addressed: The Reverend John Smith, D.D., and the salutation is Reverend Sir, or Dear Dr. Smith. When a clergyman does not have the degree the salutation is Dear Mr. Smith, or Dear Father Smith.

A bishop of the Methodist Church is addressed Bishop John Smith with titles following.

Royalty and Nobility

An emperor is to be addressed in a letter as Sir, or Your Imperial Majesty.

A king or queen is addressed as His Majesty (Name), King of (Name), or Her Majesty (Name), Queen of (Name), Salutation: Sir, or Madam, or May it please Your Majesty.

Princes and princesses and other persons of royal blood are addressed as His (or Her) Royal Highness, and saluted with May it please Your Royal Highness.

A duke or marquis is My Lord Duke (or Marquis), a duke is His (or Your) Grace.

HISTORICAL FIGURES

Ancient Greeks and Latins

Greeks

Aeschines, orator, 389-314BC.
Aeschylus, dramatist, 525-456BC.
Aesop, fableist, c620-c560BC.
Alcibiades, politician, 450-404BC.
Anacreon, poet, c582-c485BC.
Anaxagoras, philosopher, c500-428BC.
Anaximander, philosopher, 611-546BC.
Antiphon, speechwriter, c480-411BC.
Apollonius, mathematician, c265-170BC.
Archimedes, math. c287-212BC.
Aristophanes, dramatist, c448-380BC.
Aristotle, philosopher, 384-322BC.
Athenaeus, scholar, fl.c200.
Callicrates, architect, fl.5th cent.BC.
Callimachus, poet, c305-240BC.
Cratinus, comic dramatist, 520-421BC.
Democritus, philosopher, c460-370BC.
Demosthenes, orator, 384-322BC.
Diodorus, historian, fl.20BC.
Diogenes, philosopher, c372-c287BC.
Dionysius, historian, d.c7BC.
Empedocles, philosopher, c490-430BC.
Epicharmus, dramatist, c530-440BC.
Epictetus, philosopher, c55-c135.
Epicurus, philosopher, 341-270BC.
Eratosthenes, scientist, c276-194BC.
Euclid, mathematician, fl.c300BC.
Euripides, dramatist, c484-406BC.
Galen, physician, c129-199.
Heraclitus, philosopher, c535-c475BC.
Herodotus, historian, c484-420BC.
Hesiod, poet, 8th cent. BC.
Hippocrates, physician, c460-377BC.
Homer, poet, believed lived c850BC.
Isocrates, orator, 436-338BC.
Menander, dramatist, 342-292BC.
Phidias, sculptor, c500-435BC.
Pindar, poet, c518-c438BC.
Plato, philosopher, c428-c347BC.
Plutarch, biographer, c46-120.
Polybius, historian, c200-c118BC.
Praxiteles, sculptor, 400-330BC.
Pythagoras, phil., math., c580-c500BC.
Sappho, poet, c610-c580BC.
Simonides, poet, 556-c468BC.
Socrates, philosopher, c470-399BC.
Solon, statesman, 640-560BC.
Sophocles, dramatist, C496-406BC.
Strabo, geographer, c63BC-AD24.
Thales, philosopher, c634-c546BC.
Themistocles, politician, c524-c460BC.
Theocritus, poet, c310-250BC.
Theophrastus, phil. c372-c287BC.
Thucydides, historian, fl.5th cent.BC.
Timon, philosopher, c320-c230BC.
Xenophon, historian, c434-c355BC.
Zeno, philosopher, c495-c430BC.

Latins

Ammianus, historian, c330-395.
Apuleius, satirist, c124-c170.
Boethius, scholar, c480-524
Caesar, Julius, general, 100-44BC.
Catilina, politician, c108-62BC.
Cato(Elder), statesman, 234-149BC.
Catullus, poet, c84-54BC.
Cicero, orator, 106-43BC.
Claudian, poet, c370-c404.
Ennius, poet, 239-170BC.
Gellius, author, c130-c165.
Horace, poet, 65-8BC.
Juvenal, satirist, c60-c127.
Livy, historian, 59BC-AD17.
Lucan, poet, 39-65.
Lucilius, poet, c180-c102BC.
Lucretius, poet, c99-c55BC.
Martial, epigrammatist, c38-c103.
Nepos, historian, c100-c25BC.
Ovid,poet, 43BC-AD17.
Persius, satirist, 34-62.
Plautus, dramatist, c254-c184BC.
Pliny, scholar, 23-79.
Pliny(Younger), author, 62-113.
Quintilian, rhetorician, c35-c97.
Sallust, historian, 86-34BC.
Seneca, philosopher, 4BC-AD65.
Silius, poet, c25-101.
Statius, poet, c45-c96.
Suetonius, biographer, c69-c122.
Tacitus, historian, c56-c120.
Terence, dramatist, 185-c159BC.
Tibullus, poet, c55-c19BC.
Virgil, poet, 70-19BC.
Vitruvius, architect, fl.1st cent.BC.

Rulers of England and Great Britain

Name	England	Began	Died	Age	Rgd
	Saxons and Danes				
Egbert	King of Wessex, won allegiance of all English	829	839	—	10
Ethelwulf	Son, King of Wessex, Sussex, Kent, Essex	839	858	—	19
Ethelbald	Son of Ethelwulf, displaced father in Wessex	858	860	—	2
Ethelbert	2d son of Ethelwulf, united Kent and Wessex	860	866	—	6
Ethelred I	3d son, King of Wessex, fought Danes	866	871	—	5
Alfred	The Great, 4th son, defeated Danes, fortified London	871	899	52	28
Edward	The Elder, Alfred's son, united English, claimed Scotland	899	924	55	25
Athelstan	The Glorious, Edward's son, King of Mercia, Wessex	924	940	45	16
Edmund I	3d son of Edward, King of Wessex, Mercia	940	946	25	6
Edred	4th son of Edward	946	955	32	9
Edwy	The Fair, eldest son of Edmund, King of Wessex	955	959	18	3
Edgar	The Peaceful, 2d son of Edmund, ruled all English	959	975	32	17
Edward	The Martyr, eldest son of Edgar, murdered by stepmother	975	978	17	4
Ethelred II	The Unready, 2d son of Edgar, married Emma of Normandy	978	1016	48	37
Edmund II	Ironside, son of Ethelred II, King of London	1016	1016	27	0
Canute	The Dane, gave Wessex to Edmund, married Emma	1016	1035	40	19
Harold I	Harefoot, natural son of Canute	1035	1040	—	5
Hardecanute	Son of Canute by Emma, Danish King	1040	1042	24	2
Edward	The Confessor, son of Ethelred II (Canonized 1161)	1042	1066	62	24
Harold II	Edward's brother-in-law, last Saxon King	1066	1066	44	0
	House of Normandy				
William I	The Conqueror, defeated Harold at Hastings	1066	1087	60	21
William II	Rufus, 3d son of William I, killed by arrow	1087	1100	43	13
Henry I	Beauclerc, youngest son of William I	1100	1135	67	35
	House of Blois				
Stephen	Son of Adela, daughter of William I, and Count of Blois	1135	1154	50	19
	House of Plantagenet				
Henry II	Son of Geoffrey Plantagenet (Angevin) by Matilda, dau. of Henry I	1154	1189	56	35
Richard I	Coeur de Lion, son of Henry II, crusader	1189	1199	42	10
John	Lackland, son of Henry II, signed Magna Carta, 1215	1199	1216	50	17
Henry III	Son of John, acceded at 9, under regency until 1227	1216	1272	65	56
Edward I	Longshanks, son of Henry III	1272	1307	68	35
Edward II	Son of Edward I, deposed by Parliament, 1327	1307	1327	43	20
Edward III	Of Windsor, son of Edward II	1327	1377	65	50
Richard II	Grandson of Edw. III, minor until 1389, deposed 1399	1377	1400	33	22
	House of Lancaster				
Henry IV	Son of John of Gaunt, Duke of Lancaster, son of Edw. III	1399	1413	47	13
Henry V	Son of Henry IV, victor of Agincourt	1413	1422	34	9
Henry VI	Son of Henry V, deposed 1461, died in Tower	1422	1471	49	39

Name		Began	Died	Age	Rgd
	House of York				
Edward IV	Great-great-grandson of Edward III, son of Duke of York	1461	1483	41	22
Edward V	Son of Edward IV, murdered in Tower of London	1483	1483	13	0
Richard III	Crookback, bro. of Edward IV, fell at Bosworth Field	1483	1485	35	2
	House of Tudor				
Henry VII	Son of Edmund Tudor, Earl of Richmond, whose father had married the widow of Henry V; descended from Edward III through his mother, Margaret Beaufort via John of Gaunt. By marriage with dau. of Edward IV he united Lancaster and York	1485	1509	53	24
Henry VIII	Son of Henry VII by Elizabeth, dau. of Edward IV.	1509	1547	56	38
Edward VI	Son of Henry VIII, by Jane Seymour, his 3d queen. Ruled under regents. Was forced to name Lady Jane Grey his successor. Council of State proclaimed her queen July 10, 1553. Mary Tudor won Council, was proclaimed queen July 19, 1553. Mary had Lady Jane Grey beheaded for treason, Feb., 1554	1547	1553	16	6
Mary I	Daughter of Henry VIII, by Catherine of Aragon	1553	1558	43	5
Elizabeth I	Daughter of Henry VIII, by Anne Boleyn	1558	1603	69	44
	Great Britain				
	House of Stuart				
James I	James VI of Scotland, son of Mary, Queen of Scots. *First to call himself King of Great Britain. This became official with the Act of Union, 1707*	1603	1625	59	22
Charles I	Only surviving son of James I; beheaded Jan. 30, 1649	1625	1649	48	24
	Commonwealth, 1649-1660				
	Council of State, 1649; Protectorate, 1653				
The Cromwells	Oliver Cromwell, Lord Protector	1653	1658	59	—
	Richard Cromwell, son, Lord Protector, resigned May 25, 1659	1658	1712	86	—
	House of Stuart (Restored)				
Charles II	Eldest son of Charles I, died without issue	1660	1685	55	25
James II	2d son of Charles I. Deposed 1688. Interregnum Dec. 11, 1688, to Feb. 13, 1689	1685	1701	68	3
William III	Son of William, Prince of Orange, by Mary, dau. of Charles I	1689	1702	51	13
and Mary II	Eldest daughter of James II and wife of William III		1694	33	6
Anne	2d daughter of James II	1702	1714	49	12
	House of Hanover				
George I	Son of Elector of Hanover, by Sophia, grand-dau. of James I	1714	1727	67	13
George II	Only son of George I, married Caroline of Brandenburg	1727	1760	77	33
George III	Grandson of George II, married Charlotte of Mecklenburg	1760	1820	81	59
George IV	Eldest son of George III, Prince Regent, from Feb., 1811	1820	1830	67	10
William IV	3d son of George III, married Adelaide of Saxe-Meiningen	1830	1837	71	7
Victoria	Dau. of Edward, 4th son of George III; married (1840) Prince Albert of Saxe-Coburg and Gotha, who became Prince Consort	1837	1901	81	63
	House of Saxe-Coburg and Gotha				
Edward VII	Eldest son of Victoria, married Alexandra, Princess of Denmark	1901	1910	68	9
	House of Windsor				
	Name Adopted July 17, 1917				
George V	2d son of Edward VII, married Princess Mary of Teck	1910	1936	70	25
Edward VIII	Eldest son of George V; acceded Jan. 20, 1936, abdicated Dec. 11	1936	1972	77	1
George VI	2d son of George V; married Lady Elizabeth Bowes-Lyon	1936	1952	56	15
Elizabeth II	Elder daughter of George VI, acceded Feb. 6, 1952	1952	—	—	—

Rulers of Scotland

Kenneth I MacAlpin was the first Scot to rule both Scots and Picts, 846 AD.

Duncan I was the first general ruler, 1034. Macbeth seized the kingdom 1040, was slain by Duncan's son, Malcolm III MacDuncan (Canmore), 1057.

Malcolm married Margaret, Saxon princess who had fled from the Normans. Queen Margaret introduced English language and English monastic customs. She was canonized, 1250. Her son Edgar, 1097, moved the court to Edinburgh. His brothers Alexander I and David I succeeded. Malcolm IV, the Maiden, 1153, grandson of David I, was followed by his brother, William the Lion, 1165, whose son was Alexander II, 1214. The latter's son, Alexander III, 1249, defeated the Norse and regained the Hebrides. When he died, 1286, his granddaughter, Margaret, child of Eric of Norway and grandniece of Edward I of England, known as the Maid of Norway, was chosen ruler, but died 1290, aged 8.

John Baliol, 1292-1296. (Interregnum, 10 years).

Robert Bruce (The Bruce), 1306-1329, victor at Bannockburn, 1314.

David II, only son of Robert Bruce, ruled 1329-1371.

Robert II, 1371-1390, grandson of Robert Bruce, son of Walter, the Steward of Scotland, was called The Steward, first of the so-called Stuart line.

Robert III, son of Robert II, 1390-1406.

James I, son of Robert III, 1406-1437.

James II, son of James I, 1437-1460.

James III, eldest son of James II, 1460-1488.

James IV, eldest son of James III, 1488-1513.

James V, eldest son of James IV, 1513-1542.

Mary, daughter of James V, born 1542, became queen when one week old; was crowned 1543. Married, 1558, Francis, son of Henry II of France, who became king 1559, died 1560. Mary ruled Scots 1561 until abdication, 1567. She also married (2) Henry Stewart, Lord Darnley, and (3) James, Earl of Bothwell. Imprisoned by Elizabeth I, Mary was beheaded 1587.

James VI, 1566-1625, son of Mary and Lord Darnley, became King of England on death of Elizabeth in 1603. Although the thrones were thus united, the legislative union of Scotland and England was not effected until the Act of Union, May 1, 1707.

Prime Ministers of Great Britain

(W=Whig; T=Tory; Cl=Coalition; P=Peelite; L=Liberal; C=Conservative; La=Labour)

Sir Robert Walpole (W)	1721-1742
Earl of Wilmington (W)	1742-1743
Henry Pelham (W)	1743-1754
Duke of Newcastle (W)	1754-1756
Duke of Devonshire (W)	1756-1757
Duke of Newcastle (W)	1757-1762
Earl of Bute (T)	1762-1763
George Grenville (W)	1763-1765
Marquess of Rockingham (W)	1765-1766
William Pitt the Elder (Earl of Chatham) (W)	1766-1768
Duke of Grafton (W)	1768-1770
Frederick North (Lord North) (T)	1770-1782
Marquess of Rockingham (W)	1782
Earl of Shelburne (W)	1782-1783
Duke of Portland (Cl)	1783
William Pitt the Younger (T)	1783-1801
Henry Addington (T)	1801-1804
William Pitt the Younger (T)	1804-1806
William Wyndham Grenville, Baron Grenville (W)	1806-1807
Duke of Portland (T)	1807-1809
Spencer Perceval (T)	1809-1812
Earl of Liverpool (T)	1812-1827
George Canning (T)	1827
Viscount Goderich (T)	1827-1828
Duke of Wellington (T)	1828-1830
Earl Grey (W)	1830-1834
Viscount Melbourne (W)	1834
Sir Robert Peel (T)	1834-1835
Viscount Melbourne (W)	1835-1841
Sir Robert Peel (T)	1841-1846
Lord John Russell (later Earl) (W)	1846-1852
Earl of Derby (T)	1852
Earl of Aberdeen (P)	1852-1855
Viscount Palmerston (L)	1855-1858
Earl of Derby (C)	1858-1859
Viscount Palmerston (L)	1859-1865
Earl Russell (L)	1865-1866
Earl of Derby (C)	1866-1868
Benjamin Disraeli (C)	1868
William E. Gladstone (L)	1868-1874
Benjamin Disraeli (C)	1874-1880
William E. Gladstone (L)	1880-1885
Marquess of Salisbury (C)	1885-1886
William E. Gladstone (L)	1886
Marquess of Salisbury (C)	1886-1892
William E. Gladstone (L)	1892-1894
Earl of Rosebery (L)	1894-1895
Marquess of Salisbury (C)	1895-1902
Arthur J. Balfour (C)	1902-1905
Sir Henry Campbell-Bannerman (L)	1905-1908
Herbert H. Asquith (L)	1908-1915
Herbert H. Asquith	1915-1916
David Lloyd George (Cl)	1916-1922
Andrew Bonar Law (C)	1922-1923
Stanley Baldwin (C)	1923-1924
James Ramsay MacDonald (La)	1924
Stanley Baldwin (C)	1924-1929
James Ramsay MacDonald (La)	1929-1931
James Ramsay MacDonald (Cl)	1931-1935
Stanley Baldwin (Cl)	1935-1937
Neville Chamberlain (Cl)	1937-1940
Winston Churchill (Cl)	1940-1945
Winston Churchill (C)	1945
Clement Attlee (La)	1945-1951
Sir Winston Churchill (C)	1951-1955
Sir Anthony Eden (C)	1955-1957
Harold Macmillan (C)	1957-1963
Sir Alec Douglas-Home (C)	1963-1964
Harold Wilson (La)	1964-1970
Edward Heath (C)	1970-1974
Harold Wilson (La)	1974-1976
James Callaghan (La)	1976-1979
Margaret Thatcher (C)	1979-1990
John Major (C)	1990-

Historical Periods of Japan

Yamato	c.300-592	Conquest of Yamato plain c. 300 A.D.
Asuka	592-710	Accession of Empress Suiko, 592.
Nara	710-794	Completion of Heijo (Nara), 710; capital moves to Nagaoka, 784.
Heian	794-1192	Completion of Heian (Kyoto), 794
Fujiwara	858-1160	Fujiwara-no-Yoshifusa becomes regent, 858.
Taira	1160-1185	Taira-no-Kiyomori assumes control, 1160; Minamoto-no-Yoritomo victor over Taira, 1185.
Kamakura	1192-1333	Yoritomo becomes shogun, 1192.
Namboku	1334-1392	Restoration of Emperor Godaigo, 1334; Southern Court established by Godaigo at Yoshino, 1336.
Ashikaga	1338-1573	Ashikaga Takauji becomes shogun, 1338.
Muromachi	1392-1573	Unification of Southern and Northern Courts, 1392.
Sengoku	1467-1600	Beginning of the Onin war, 1467
Momoyama	1573-1603	Oda Nobunaga enters Kyoto, 1568; Nobunaga deposes last Ashikaga shogun, 1573; Tokugawa Ieyasu victor at Sekigahara, 1600.
Edo	1603-1867	Ieyasu becomes shogun, 1603.
Meiji	1868-1912	Enthronement of Emperor Mutsuhito (Meiji), 1867; Meiji Restoration and Charter Oath, 1868.
Taisho	1912-1926	Accession of Emperor Yoshihito, 1912.
Showa	1926-1989	Accession of Emperor Hirohito, 1926.
Heisei	1989-	Accession of Emperor Akihito, 1989

Rulers of France: Kings, Queens, Presidents

Caesar to Charlemagne

Julius Caesar subdued the Gauls, native tribes of Gaul (France) 57 to 52 BC. The Romans ruled 500 years. The Franks, a Teutonic tribe, reached the Somme from the East ca. 250 AD. By the 5th century the Merovingian Franks ousted the Romans. In 451 AD, with the help of Visigoths, Burgundians and others, they defeated Attila and the Huns at Chalons-sur-Marne.

Childeric I became leader of the Merovingians 458 AD. His son Clovis I (Chlodwig, Ludwig, Louis), crowned 481, founded the dynasty. After defeating the Alemanni (Germans) 496, he was baptized a Christian and made Paris his capital. His line ruled until Childeric III was deposed, 751.

The West Merovingians were called Neustrians, the eastern Austrasians. Pepin of Herstal (687-714) major domus, or head of the palace, of Austrasia, took over Neustria as dux (leader) of the Franks. Pepin's son, Charles, called Martel (the Hammer) defeated the Saracens at Tours-Poitiers, 732; was succeeded by his son, Pepin the Short, 741, who deposed Childeric III and ruled as king until 768.

His son, Charlemagne, or Charles the Great (742-814) became king of the Franks, 768, with his brother Carloman, who died 771. He ruled France, Germany, parts of Italy, Spain, Austria, and enforced Christianity. Crowned Emperor of the Romans by Pope Leo III in St. Peter's, Rome, Dec. 25, 800 AD. Succeeded by son, Louis I the Pious, 814. At death, 840, Louis left empire to sons, Lothair (Roman emperor); Pepin I (king of Aquitaine); Louis II (of Germany); Charles the Bald (France). They quarreled and by the peace of Verdun, 843, divided the empire.

(*continued*)

AD Name, year of accession

The Carolingians

843 Charles I (the Bald), Roman Emperor, 875
877 Louis II (the Stammerer), son
879 Louis III (died 882) and Carloman, brothers
885 Charles II (the Fat), Roman Emperor, 881
888 Eudes (Odo) elected by nobles
898 Charles III (the Simple), son of Louis II, defeated by
922 Robert, brother of Eudes, killed in war
923 Rudolph (Raoul) Duke of Burgundy
936 Louis IV, son of Charles III
954 Lothair, son, aged 13, defeated by Capet
986 Louis V (the Sluggard), left no heirs

The Capets

987 Hugh Capet, son of Hugh the Great
996 Robert II (the Wise), his son
1031 Henry I, his son
1060 Philip I (the Fair), son
1108 Louis VI (the Fat), son
1137 Louis VII (the Younger), son
1180 Philip II (Augustus), son, crowned at Reims
1223 Louis VIII (the Lion), son
1226 Louis IX, son, crusader; Louis IX (1214-1270) reigned 44 years, arbitrated disputes with English King Henry III; led crusades, 1248 (captured in Egypt 1250) and 1270, when he died of plague in Tunis. Canonized 1297 as St. Louis.
1270 Philip III (the Hardy), son
1285 Philip IV (the Fair), son, king at 17
1314 Louis X (the Headstrong), son. His posthumous son, John I, lived only 7 days
1316 Philip V (the Tall), brother of Louis X
1322 Charles IV (the Fair), brother of Louis X

House of Valois

1328 Philip VI (of Valois), grandson of Philip III
1350 John II (the Good), his son, retired to England
1364 Charles V (the Wise), son
1380 Charles VI (the Beloved), son
1422 Charles VII (the Victorious), son. In 1429 Joan of Arc (Jeanne d'Arc) promised Charles to oust the English, who occupied northern France. Joan won at Orleans and Patay and had Charles crowned at Reims July 17, 1429. Joan was captured May 24, 1430, and executed May 30, 1431, at Rouen for heresy. Charles ordered her rehabilitation, effected 1455.
1461 Louis XI (the Cruel), son, civil reformer
1483 Charles VIII (the Affable), son
1498 Louis XII, great-grandson of Charles V
1515 Francis I, of Angouleme, nephew, son-in-law. Francis I (1494-1547) reigned 32 years, fought 4 big wars, was patron of the arts, aided Cellini, del Sarto, Leonardo da Vinci, Rabelais, embellished Fontainebleau.
1547 Henry II, son, killed at a joust in a tournament. He was the husband of Catherine de Medicis (1519-1589) and the lover of Diane de Poitiers (1499-1566). Catherine was born in Florence, daughter of Lorenzo de Medicis. By her marriage to Henry II she became the mother of Francis II, Charles IX, Henry III and Queen Margaret (Reine Margot) wife of Henry IV. She persuaded Charles IX to order the massacre of Huguenots on the Feast of St. Bartholomew, Aug. 24, 1572, the day her daughter was married to Henry of Navarre.
1559 Francis II, son. In 1548, Mary, Queen of Scots since infancy, was betrothed when 6 to Francis, aged 4. They were married 1558. Francis died 1560, aged 16; Mary ruled Scotland, abdicated 1567.
1560 Charles IX, brother
1574 Henry III, brother, assassinated

House of Bourbon

1589 Henry IV, of Navarre, assassinated. Henry IV made enemies when he gave tolerance to Protestants by Edict of Nantes, 1598. He was grandson of Queen Margaret of Navarre, literary patron. He married Margaret of Valois, daughter of Henry II and Catherine de Medicis; was divorced; in 1600 married Marie de Medicis, who became Regent of France, 1610-17 for her son, Louis XIII, but was exiled by Richelieu, 1631.
1610 Louis XIII (the Just), son. Louis XIII (1601-1643) married Anne of Austria. His ministers were Cardinals Richelieu and Mazarin.
1643 Louis XIV (The Grand Monarch), son. Louis XIV was king 72 years. He exhausted a prosperous country in wars for thrones and territory. By revoking the Edict of Nantes (1685) he caused the emigration of the Huguenots. He said: "I am the state."
1715 Louis XV, great-grandson. Louis XV married a Polish princess; lost Canada to the English. His favorites, Mme. Pompadour and Mme. Du Barry, influenced policies. Noted for saying "After me, the deluge".
1774 Louis XVI, grandson; married Marie Antoinette, daughter of Empress Maria Therese of Austria. King and queen beheaded by Revolution, 1793. Their son, called Louis XVII, died in prison, never ruled.

First Republic

1792 National Convention of the French Revolution
1795 Directory, under Barras and others
1799 Consulate, Napoleon Bonaparte, first consul. Elected consul for life, 1802.

First Empire

1804 Napoleon I, emperor. Josephine (de Beauharnais) empress, 1804-09; Marie Louise, empress, 1810-1814. Her son, Francois (1811-1832), titular King of Rome, later Duke de Reichstadt and "Napoleon II," never ruled. Napoleon abdicated 1814, died 1821.

Bourbons Restored

1814 Louis XVIII king; brother of Louis XVI.
1824 Charles X, brother; reactionary; deposed by the July Revolution, 1830.

House of Orleans

1830 Louis-Philippe, the "citizen king."

Second Republic

1848 Louis Napoleon Bonaparte, president, nephew of Napoleon I. He became:

Second Empire

1852 Napoleon III, emperor; Eugenie (de Montijo) empress. Lost Franco-Prussian war, deposed 1870. Son, Prince Imperial (1856-79), died in Zulu War. Eugenie died 1920.

Third Republic—Presidents

1871 Thiers, Louis Adolphe (1797-1877)
1873 MacMahon, Marshal Patrice M. de (1808-1893)
1879 Grevy, Paul J. (1807-1891)
1887 Sadi-Carnot, M. (1837-1894), assassinated
1894 Casimir-Perier, Jean P. P. (1847-1907)
1895 Faure, Francois Felix (1841-1899)
1899 Loubet, Emile (1838-1929)
1906 Fallieres, C. Armand (1841-1931)
1913 Poincare, Raymond (1860-1934)
1920 Deschanel, Paul (1856-1922)
1920 Millerand, Alexandre (1859-1943)
1924 Doumergue, Gaston (1863-1937)
1931 Doumer, Paul (1857-1932), assassinated
1932 Lebrun, Albert (1871-1950), resigned 1940
1940 **Vichy govt.** under German armistice: Henri Philippe Petain (1856-1951) Chief of State, 1940-1944.
Provisional govt. after liberation: Charles de Gaulle (1890-1970) Oct. 1944-Jan. 21, 1946; Felix Gouin (1884-1977) Jan. 23, 1946; Georges Bidault (1899-1983) June 24, 1946.

Fourth Republic—Presidents

1947 Auriol, Vincent (1884-1966)
1954 Coty, Rene (1882-1962)

Fifth Republic—Presidents

1959 de Gaulle, Charles Andre J. M. (1890-1970)
1969 Pompidou, Georges (1911-1974)
1974 Giscard d'Estaing, Valery (1926-)
1981 Mitterrand, Francois (1916-)

Rulers of Middle Europe; Rise and Fall of Dynasties

Carolingian Dynasty

Charles the Great, or Charlemagne, ruled France, Italy, and Middle Europe; established Ostmark (later Austria); crowned Roman emperor by pope in Rome, 800 AD; died 814.

Louis I (Ludwig) the Pious, son; crowned by Charlemagne 814, d. 840.

Louis II, the German, son; succeeded to East Francia (Germany) 843-876.

Charles the Fat, son; inherited East Francia and West Francia (France) 876, reunited empire, crowned emperor by pope, 881, deposed 887.

Arnulf, nephew, 887-899. Partition of empire.

Louis the Child, 899-911, last direct descendant of Charlemagne.
Conrad I, duke of Franconia, first elected German king, 911-918, founded House of Franconia.

Saxon Dynasty; First Reich

Henry I, the Fowler, duke of Saxony, 919-936.
Otto I, the Great, 936-973, son; crowned Holy Roman Emperor by pope, 962.
Otto II, 973-983, son; failed to oust Greeks and Arabs from Sicily.
Otto III, 983-1002, son; crowned emperor at 16.
Henry II, the Saint, duke of Bavaria, 1002-1024, great-grandson of Otto the Great.

House of Franconia

Conrad II, 1024-1039, elected king of Germany.
Henry III, the Black, 1039-1056, son; deposed 3 popes; annexed Burgundy.
Henry IV, 1056-1106, son; regency by his mother, Agnes of Poitou. Banned by Pope Gregory VII, he did penance at Canossa.
Henry V, 1106-1125, son; last of Salic House.
Lothair, duke of Saxony, 1125-1137. Crowned emperor in Rome, 1134.

House of Hohenstaufen

Conrad III, duke of Swabia, 1138-1152. In 2d Crusade.
Frederick I, Barbarossa, 1152-1190; Conrad's nephew.
Henry VI, 1190-1196, took lower Italy from Normans. Son became king of Sicily.
Philip of Swabia, 1197-1208, brother.
Otto IV, of House of Welf, 1198-1215; deposed.
Frederick II, 1215-1250, son of Henry VI; king of Sicily; crowned king of Jerusalem; in 5th Crusade.
Conrad IV, 1250-1254, son; lost lower Italy to Charles of Anjou.
Conradin (1252-1268) son, king of Jerusalem and Sicily, beheaded. Last Hohenstaufen.
Interregnum, 1254-1273, Rise of the Electors.

Transition

Rudolph I of Hapsburg, 1273-1291, defeated King Ottocar II of Bohemia. Bequeathed duchy of Austria to eldest son, Albert.
Adolph of Nassau, 1292-1298, killed in war with Albert of Austria.
Albert I, king of Germany, 1298-1308, son of Rudolph.
Henry VII, of Luxemburg, 1308-1313, crowned emperor in Rome. Seized Bohemia, 1310.
Louis IV of Bavaria (Wittelsbach), 1314-1347. Also elected was Frederick of Austria, 1314-1330 (Hapsburg). Abolition of papal sanction for election of Holy Roman Emperor.
Charles IV, of Luxemburg, 1347-1378, grandson of Henry VII, German emperor and king of Bohemia, Lombardy, Burgundy; took Mark of Brandenburg.
Wenceslaus, 1378-1400, deposed.
Rupert, Duke of Palatine, 1400-1410.

Hungary

Stephen I, house of Arpad, 997-1038. Crowned king 1000; converted Magyars; canonized 1083. After several centuries of feuds Charles Robert of Anjou became Charles I, 1308-1342.
Louis I, the Great, son, 1342-1382; joint ruler of Poland with Casimir III, 1370. Defeated Turks.
Mary, daughter, 1382-1395, ruled with husband. Sigismund of Luxemburg, 1387-1437, also king of Bohemia. As bro. of Wenceslaus he succeeded Rupert as Holy Roman Emperor, 1410.
Albert, 1438-1439, son-in-law of Sigismund; also Roman emperor as Albert II. *(see under Hapsburg.)*
Ulaszlo I of Poland, 1440-1444.
Ladislaus V, posthumous son of Albert II, 1444-1457. John Hunyadi (Hunyadi Janos) governor (1446-1452), fought Turks, Czechs; died 1456.
Matthias I (Corvinus) son of Hunyadi, 1458-1490. Shared rule of Bohemia, captured Vienna, 1485, annexed Austria, Styria, Carinthia.
Ulaszlo II (king of Bohemia), 1490-1516.
Louis II, son, aged 10, 1516-1526. Wars with Suleiman, Turk. In 1527 Hungary was split between Ferdinand I, Archduke of Austria, bro.-in-law of Louis II, and John Zapolya of Transylvania. After Turkish invasion, 1547, Hungary was split between Ferdinand, Prince John Sigismund (Transylvania) and the Turks.

House of Hapsburg

Albert V of Austria, Hapsburg, crowned king of Hungary, Jan. 1438, Roman emperor, March, 1438, as Albert II; died 1439.
Frederick III, cousin, 1440-1493. Fought Turks.
Maximilian I, son, 1493-1519. Assumed title of Holy Roman Emperor (German), 1493.
Charles V, grandson, 1519-1556. King of Spain with mother co-regent; crowned Roman emperor at Aix, 1520. Confronted Luther at Worms; attempted church reform and religious conciliation; abdicated 1556.
Ferdinand I, king of Bohemia, 1526, of Hungary, 1527; disputed. German king, 1531. Crowned Roman emperor on abdication of brother Charles V, 1556.
Maximilian II, son, 1564-1576.
Rudolph II, son, 1576-1612.
Matthias, brother, 1612-1619, king of Bohemia and Hungary.
Ferdinand II of Styria, king of Bohemia, 1617, of Hungary, 1618, Roman emperor, 1619. Bohemian Protestants deposed him, elected Frederick V of Palatine, starting Thirty Years War.
Ferdinand III, son, king of Hungary, 1625, Bohemia, 1627, Roman emperor, 1637. Peace of Westphalia, 1648, ended war. Leopold I, 1658-1705; Joseph I, 1705-1711; Charles VI, 1711-1740.
Maria Theresa, daughter, 1740-1780, Archduchess of Austria, queen of Hungary; ousted pretender, Charles VII, crowned 1742; in 1745 obtained election of her husband Francis I as Roman emperor and co-regent (d. 1765). Fought Seven Years' War with Frederick II (the Great) of Prussia. Mother of Marie Antoinette, Queen of France.
Joseph II, son 1765-1790, Roman emperor, reformer; powers restricted by Empress Maria Theresa until her death, 1780. First partition of Poland. Leopold II, 1790-1792.
Francis II, son, 1792-1835. Fought Napoleon. Proclaimed first hereditary emperor of Austria, 1804. Forced to abdicate as Roman emperor, 1806; last use of title. Ferdinand I, son, 1835-1848, abdicated during revolution.

Austro-Hungarian Monarchy

Francis Joseph I, nephew, 1848-1916, emperor of Austria, king of Hungary. Dual monarchy of Austria-Hungary formed, 1867. After assassination of heir, Archduke Francis Ferdinand, June 28, 1914, Austrian diplomacy precipitated World War I.
Charles I, grand-nephew, 1916-1918, last emperor of Austria and king of Hungary. Abdicated Nov. 11-13, 1918, died 1922.

Rulers of Prussia

Nucleus of Prussia was the Mark of Brandenburg. First margrave was Albert the Bear (Albrecht), 1134-1170. First Hohenzollern margrave was Frederick, burgrave of Nuremberg, 1417-1440.
Frederick William, 1640-1688, the Great Elector. Son, Frederick III, 1688-1713, was crowned King Frederick of Prussia, 1701.
Frederick William I, son, 1713-1740.
Frederick II, the Great, son, 1740-1786, annexed Silesia part of Austria.
Frederick William II, nephew, 1786-1797.
Frederick William III, son, 1797-1840. Napoleonic wars.
Frederick William IV, son, 1840-1861. Uprising of 1848 and first parliament and constitution.

Second and Third Reich

William I, 1861-1888, brother. Annexation of Schleswig and Hanover; Franco-Prussian war, 1870-71, proclamation of German Reich, Jan. 18, 1871, at Versailles; William, German emperor (Deutscher Kaiser), Bismarck, chancellor.
Frederick III, son, 1888.
William II, son, 1888-1918. Led Germany in World War I, abdicated as German emperor and king of Prussia, Nov. 9, 1918. Died in exile in Netherlands June 4, 1941. Minor rulers of Bavaria, Saxony, Wurttemberg also abdicated.
Germany proclaimed a republic at Weimar, July 1, 1919. Presidents: Frederick Ebert, 1919-1925, Paul von Hindenburg-Beneckendorff, 1925, reelected 1932, d. Aug. 2, 1934. Adolf Hitler, chancellor, chosen successor as Leader-Chancellor (Fuehrer & Reichskanzler) of Third Reich. Annexed Austria, March, 1938. Precipitated World War II, 1939-1945. Committed suicide April 30, 1945.

Rulers of Poland

House of Piasts

Miesko I, 962?-992; Poland Christianized 966. Expansion under 3 Boleslavs: I, 992-1025, son, crowned king 1024; II, 1058-1079, great-grandson, exiled after killing bishop Stanislav who became chief patron saint of Poland: III, 1106-1138, nephew, divided Poland among 4 sons eldest suzerain.

(continued)

1138-1306, feudal division. 1226 founding in Prussia of military order Teutonic Knights. 1226 invasion by Tartars/Mongols.

Vladislav I, 1306-1333, reunited most Polish territories, crowned king 1320. Casimir III the Great, 1333-1370, son, developed economic, cultural life, foreign policy.

House of Anjou

Louis I, 1370-1382, nephew/identical with Louis I of Hungary.

Jadwiga, 1384-1399, daughter, married 1386 Jagiello, Grand Duke of Lituania.

House of Jagelloneans

Vladislav II, 1386-1434, Christianized Lituania, founded personal union between Poland & Lituania. Defeated 1410 Teutonic Knights at Grunwald.

Vladislav III, 1434-1444, son, simultaneously king of Hungary. Fought Turks, killed 1444 in battle of Varna.

Casimir IV, 1446-1492, brother, competed with Hapsburgs, put son Vladislav on throne of Bohemia, later also of Hungary.

Sigismund I, 1506-1548, brother, patronized science & arts, his & son's reign "Golden Age."

Sigismund II, 1548-1572, son, established 1569 real union of Poland and Lituania (lasted until 1795).

Elective kings

Polish nobles proclaimed 1572 Poland a Republic headed by king to be elected by whole nobility.

Stephen Batory, 1576-1586, duke of Transylvania, married Ann, sister of Sigismund II August. Fought Russians.

Sigismund III Vasa, 1587-1632, nephew of Sigismund II. 1592-1598 also king of Sweden. His generals fought Russians, Turks.

Vladislav II Vasa, 1632-1648, son. Fought Russians.

John II Casimir Vasa, 1648-1668, brother. Fought Cossacks, Swedes, Russians, Turks, Tartars (the "Deluge"). Abdicated 1668.

John III Sobieski, 1674-1696. Won Vienna from besieging Turks, 1683.

Stanislav II, 1764-1795, last king. Encouraged reforms; 1791 1st modern Constitution in Europe. 1772, 1793, 1795 Poland partitioned among Russia, Prussia, Austria. Unsuccessful insurrection against foreign invasion 1794 under Kosciuszko, Amer-Polish gen.

1795-1918 Poland under foreign rule

1807-1815 Grand Duchy of Warsaw created by Napoleon I, Frederick August of Saxony grand duke.

1815 Congress of Vienna proclaimed part of Poland "Kingdom" in personal union with Russia.

Polish uprisings: 1830 against Russia, 1846, 1848 against Austria, 1863 against Russia—all repressed.

1918-1939 Second Republic

1918-1922 Head of State Jozef Pilsudski. Presidents: Gabriel Narutowicz 1922, assassinated. Stanislav Wojciechowski 1922-1926, had to abdicate after Pilsudski's coup d'état. Ignacy Moscicki, 1926-1939, ruled with Pilsudski as (until 1935) virtual dictator.

1939-1945 Poland under foreign occupation

Nazi aggression Sept. 1939. Polish govt.-in-exile, first in France, then in England. Vladislav Raczkiewicz pres., Gen. Vladislav Sikorski, then Stanislav Mikolajczyk, prime ministers. Polish Committee of Natl. Liberation proclaimed at Lublin July 1944, transformed into govt. Jan. 1, 1945.

Rulers of Denmark, Sweden, Norway

Denmark

Earliest rulers invaded Britain; King Canute, who ruled in London 1016-1035, was most famous. The Valdemars furnished kings until the 15th century. In 1282 the Danes won the first national assembly, Danehof, from King Erik V.

Most redoubtable medieval character was Margaret, daughter of Valdemar IV, born 1353, married at 10 to King Haakon VI of Norway. In 1376 she had her first infant son Olaf made king of Denmark. After his death, 1387, she was regent of Denmark and Norway. In 1388 Sweden accepted her as sovereign. In 1389 she made her grand-nephew, Duke Erik of Pomerania, titular king of Denmark, Sweden, and Norway, with herself as regent. In 1397 she effected the Union of Kalmar of the three kingdoms and had Erik VII crowned. In 1439 the three kingdoms deposed him and elected, 1440, Christopher of Bavaria king (Christopher III). On his death, 1448, the union broke up.

Succeeding rulers were unable to enforce their claims as rulers of Sweden until 1520, when Christian II conquered Sweden. He was thrown out 1522, and in 1523 Gustavus Vasa united Sweden. Denmark continued to dominate Norway until the Napoleonic wars, when Frederick VI, 1808-1839, joined the Napoleonic cause after Britain had destroyed the Danish fleet, 1807. In 1814 he was forced to cede Norway to Sweden and Helgoland to Britain, receiving Lauenburg. Successors Christian VIII, 1839; Frederick VII, 1848; Christian IX, 1863; Frederick VIII, 1906; Christian X, 1912; Frederick IX, 1947; Margrethe II, 1972.

Sweden

Early kings ruled at Uppsala, but did not dominate the country. Sverker, c1130-c1156, united the Swedes and Goths. In 1435 Sweden obtained the Riksdag, or parliament. After the Union of Kalmar, 1397, the Danes either ruled or harried the country until Christian II of Denmark conquered it anew, 1520. This led to a rising under Gustavus Vasa, who ruled Sweden 1523-1560, and established an independent kingdom. Charles IX, 1599-1611, crowned 1604, conquered Moscow. Gustavus II Adolphus, 1611-1632, was called the Lion of the North. Later rulers: Christina, 1632; Charles X, Gustavus 1654; Charles XI, 1660; Charles XII (invader of Russia and Poland, defeated at Poltava, June 28, 1709), 1697; Ulrika Eleanora, sister, elected queen 1718; Frederick I (of Hesse), her husband, 1720; Adolphus Frederick, 1751; Gustavus III, 1771; Gustavus IV Adolphus, 1792; Charles XIII, 1809. (Union with Norway began 1814.) Charles XIV John, 1818. He was Jean Bernadotte, Napoleon's Prince of Ponte Corvo, elected 1810 to succeed Charles XIII. He founded the present dynasty: Oscar I, 1844, Charles XV, 1859; Oscar II, 1872; Gustavus V, 1907; Gustav VI Adolf, 1950; Carl XVI Gustaf, 1973.

Norway

Overcoming many rivals, Harald Haarfager, 872-930, conquered Norway, Orkneys, and Shetlands; Olaf I, great-grandson, 995-1000, brought Christianity into Norway, Iceland, and Greenland. In 1035 Magnus the Good also became king of Denmark. Haakon V, 1299-1319, had married his daughter to Erik of Sweden. Their son, Magnus, became ruler of Norway and Sweden at 6. His son, Haakon VI, married Margaret of Denmark; their son Olaf IV became king of Norway and Denmark, followed by Margaret's regency and the Union of Kalmar, 1397.

In 1450 Norway became subservient to Denmark. Christian IV, 1588-1648, founded Christiania, now Oslo. After Napoleonic wars, when Denmark ceded Norway to Sweden, a strong nationalist movement forced recognition of Norway as an independent kingdom united with Sweden under the Swedish kings, 1814-1905. In 1905 the union was dissolved and Prince Carl of Denmark became Haakon VII. He died Sept. 21, 1957, aged 85; succeeded by son, Olav V, 1957.

Rulers of the Netherlands and Belgium

The Netherlands (Holland)

William Frederick, Prince of Orange, led a revolt against French rule, 1813, and was crowned King of the Netherlands, 1815. Belgium seceded Oct. 4, 1830, after a revolt, and formed a separate government. The change was ratified by the two kingdoms by treaty Apr. 19, 1839.

Succession: William II, son, 1840; William III, son, 1849; Wilhelmina, daughter of William III and his 2d wife Princess Emma of Waldeck, 1890; Wilhelmina abdicated, Sept. 4, 1948, in favor of daughter, Juliana. Juliana abdicated Apr. 30, 1980, in favor of daughter, Beatrix.

Belgium

A national congress elected Prince Leopold of Saxe-Coburg King; he took the throne July 21, 1831, as Leopold I. Succession: Leopold II, son 1865; Albert I, nephew of Leopold II, 1909; Leopold III, son of Albert, 1934; Prince Charles, Regent 1944; Leopold returned 1950, yielded powers to son Baudouin, Prince Royal, Aug. 6, 1950, abdicated July 16, 1951. Baudouin I took throne July 17, 1951.

For political history prior to 1830 see articles on the Netherlands and Belgium.

Roman Rulers

From Romulus to the end of the Empire in the West. Rulers of the Roman Empire in the East sat in Constantinople and for a brief period in Nicaea, until the capture of Constantinople by the Turks in 1453, when Byzantium was succeeded by the Ottoman Empire.

BC	Name
	The Kingdom
753	Romulus (Quirinus)
716	Numa Pompilius
673	Tullus Hostiiius
640	Ancus Marcius
616	L. Tarquinius Priscus
578	Servius Tullius
534	L. Tarquinius Superbus
	The Republic
509	Consulate established
509	Quaestorship instituted
498	Dictatorship introduced
494	Plebeian Tribunate created
494	Plebeian Aedileship created
444	Consular Tribunate organized
435	Censorship instituted
366	Praetorship established
366	Curule Aedileship created
362	Military Tribunate elected
326	Proconsulate introduced
311	Naval Duumvirate elected
217	Dictatorship of Fabius Maximus
133	Tribunate of Tiberius Gracchus
123	Tribunate of Gaius Gracchus
82	Dictatorship of Sulla
60	First Triumvirate formed (Caesar, Pompeius, Crassus)
46	Dictatorship of Caesar
43	Second Triumvirate formed (Octavianus, Antonius, Lepidus)
	The Empire
27	Augustus (Gaius Julius Caesar Octavianus)
14	Tiberius I
37	Gaius Caesar (Caligula)
41	Claudius I
54	Nero
68	Galba
69	Galba; Otho, Vitellius
69	Vespasianus
79	Titus
81	Domitianus
96	Nerva

AD	Name
98	Trajanus
117	Hadrianus
138	Antoninus Pius
161	Marcus Aurelius and Lucius Verus
169	Marcus Aurelius (alone)
180	Commodus
193	Pertinax; Julianus I
193	Septimius Severus
211	Caracalla and Geta
212	Caracalla (alone)
217	Macrinus
218	Elagabalus (Heliogabalus)
222	Alexander Severus
235	Maximinus I (the Thracian)
238	Gordianus I and Gordianus II; Pupienus and Balbinus
238	Gordianus III
244	Philippus (the Arabian)
249	Decius
251	Gallus and Volusianus
253	Aemilianus
253	Valerianus and Gallienus
258	Gallienus (alone)
268	Claudius Gothicus
270	Quintillus
270	Aurelianus
275	Tacitus
276	Florianus
276	Probus
282	Carus
283	Carinus and Numerianus
284	Diocletianus
286	Diocletianus and Maximianus
305	Galerius and Constantius I
306	Galerius, Maximinus II, Severus I
307	Galerius, Maximinus II, Constantinus I, Licinius, Maxentius
311	Maximinus II, Constantinus I, Licinius, Maxentius
314	Maximinus II, Constantinus I, Licinius
314	Constantinus I and Licinius

AD	Name
324	Constantinus I (the Great)
337	Constantinus II, Constans I, Constantius II
340	Constantius II and Constans I
350	Constantius II
361	Julianus II (the Apostate)
363	Jovianus
	West (Rome) and East (Constantinople)
364	Valentinianus I (West) and Valens (East)
367	Valentinianus I with Gratianus (West) and Valens (East)
375	Gratianus with Valentinianus II (West) and Valens (East)
378	Gratianus with Valentinianus II (West) Theodosius I (East)
383	Valentinianus II (West) and Theodosius I (East)
394	Theodosius I (the Great)
395	Honorius (West) and Arcadius (East)
408	Honorius (West) and Theodosius II (East)
423	Valentinianus III (West) and Theodosius II (East)
450	Valentinianus III (West) and Marcianus (East)
455	Maximus (West), Avitus (West); Marcianus (East)
456	Avitus (West), Marcianus (East)
457	Majorianus (West), Leo I (East)
461	Severus II (West), Leo I (East)
467	Anthemius (West), Leo I (East)
472	Olybrius (West), Leo I (East)
473	Glycerius (West), Leo I (East)
474	Julius Nepos (West), Leo II (East)
475	Romulus Augustulus (West) and Zeno (East)
476	End of Empire in West; Odovacar, King, drops title of Emperor; murdered by King Theodoric of Ostrogoths 493 AD

Rulers of Modern Italy

After the fall of Napoleon in 1814, the Congress of Vienna, 1815, restored Italy as a political patchwork, comprising the Kingdom of Naples and Sicily, the Papal States, and smaller units. Piedmont and Genoa were awarded to Sardinia, ruled by King Victor Emmanuel I of Savoy.

United Italy emerged under the leadership of Camillo, Count di Cavour (1810-1861), Sardinian prime minister. Agitation was led by Giuseppe Mazzini (1805-1872) and Giuseppe Garibaldi (1807-1882), soldier, Victor Emmanuel I abdicated 1821. After a brief regency for a brother, Charles Albert was King 1831-1849, abdicating when defeated by the Austrians at Novara. Succeeded by Victor Emmanuel II, 1849-1861.

In 1859 France forced Austria to cede Lombardy to Sardinia, which gave rights to Savoy and Nice to France. In 1860 Garibaldi led 1,000 volunteers in a spectacular campaign, took Sicily and expelled the King of Naples. In 1860 the House of Savoy annexed Tuscany, Parma, Modena, Romagna, the Two Sicilies, the Marches, and Umbria. Victor Emmanuel assumed the title of King of Italy at Turin Mar. 17, 1861. In 1866 he allied with Prussia in the Austro-Prussian War, with Prussia's victory received Venetia. On Sept. 20, 1870, his troops under Gen. Raffaele Cadorna entered Rome and took over the Papal States, ending the temporal power of the Roman Catholic Church.

Succession: Umberto I; 1878, assassinated 1900; Victor Emmanuel III, 1900, abdicated 1946, died 1947; Umberto II, 1946, ruled a month. In 1921 Benito Mussolini (1883-1945) formed the Fascist party and became prime minister Oct. 31, 1922. He made the King Emperor of Ethiopia, 1937; entered World War II as ally of Hitler. He was deposed July 25, 1943.

At a plebiscite June 2, 1946, Italy voted for a republic; Premier Alcide de Gasperi became chief of state June 13, 1946. On June 28, 1946, the Constituent Assembly elected Enrico de Nicola, Liberal, provisional president. Successive presidents: Luigi Einaudi, elected May 11, 1948, Giovanni Gronchi, Apr. 29, 1955; Antonio Segni, May 6, 1962; Giuseppe Saragat, Dec. 28, 1964; Giovanni Leone, Dec. 29, 1971; Alessandro Pertini, July 9, 1978; Francesco Cossiga, July 9, 1985.

Rulers of Spain

From 8th to 11th centuries Spain was dominated by the Moors (Arabs and Berbers). The Christian reconquest established small kingdoms (Asturias, Aragon, Castile, Catalonia, Leon, Navarre, and Valencia). In 1474 Isabella, b. 1451, became Queen of Castile & Leon. Her husband, Ferdinand, b. 1452, inherited Aragon 1479, with Catalonia, Valencia, and the Balearic Islands, became Ferdinand V of Castile. By Isabella's request Pope Sixtus IV established the Inquisition, 1478. Last Moorish kingdom, Granada, fell 1492. Columbus opened New World of colonies, 1492. Isabella died 1504, succeeded by her daughter, Juana "the Mad," but Ferdinand ruled until his death 1516.

Charles I, b. 1500, son of Juana and grandson of Ferdinand and Isabella, and of Maximilian I of Hapsburg; succeeded later as Holy Roman Emperor, Charles V, 1520; abdicated 1556. Philip II, son, 1556-1598, inherited only Spanish throne; conquered Portugal, fought Turks, persecuted non-Catholics, sent Armada against England. Was married to Mary I of England, 1554-1558. Succession: Philip III, 1598-1621; Philip IV, 1621-1665; Charles II, 1665-1700, left Spain to Philip of Anjou, grandson of Louis XIV, who as Philip V, 1700-1746, founded Bourbon dynasty. Ferdinand VI, 1746-1759; Charles III, 1759-1788; Charles IV, 1788-1808, abdicated.

Napoleon now dominated politics and made his brother Joseph King of Spain 1808, but the Spanish ousted him in 1813. Ferdinand VII, 1808, 1814-1833, lost American colonies; succeeded by daughter Isabella II, aged 3, with wife Maria Christina of Naples regent until 1843. Isabella deposed by revolution 1868. Elected king by the Cortes, Amadeo of Savoy, 1870; abdicated 1873. First republic, 1873-74. Alphonso XII, son of Isabella, 1875-85. His posthumous son was Alphonso XIII, with his mother, Queen Maria Christina regent; Spanish-American war, Spain lost Cuba, gave up Puerto Rico, Philippines, Sulu Is., Marianas. Alphonso took throne 1902, aged 16, married British Princess Victoria Eugenia of Battenberg. The dictatorship of Primo de Rivera, 1923-30, precipitated the revolution of 1931. Alphonso agreed to leave without formal abdication. The monarchy was abolished and the second republic established, with socialist backing. Presidents were Niceto Alcala Zamora, to 1936, when Manuel Azaña was chosen.

In July, 1936, the army in Morocco revolted against the government and General Francisco Franco led the troops into Spain. The revolution succeeded by Feb., 1939, when Azaña resigned. Franco became chief of state, with provisions that if he was incapacitated the Regency Council by two-thirds vote may propose a king to the Cortes, which must have a two-thirds majority to elect him.

Alphonso XIII died in Rome Feb. 28, 1941, aged 54. His property and citizenship had been restored.

A succession law restoring the monarchy was approved in a 1947 referendum. Prince Juan Carlos, son of the pretender to the throne, was designated by Franco and the Cortes in 1969 as the future king and chief of state. Upon Franco's death, Nov. 20, 1975, Juan Carlos was proclaimed king, Nov. 22, 1975.

Leaders in the South American Wars of Liberation

Simon Bolivar (1783-1830), Jose Francisco de San Martin (1778-1850), and Francisco Antonio Gabriel Miranda (1750-1816), are among the heroes of the early 19th century struggles of South American nations to free themselves from Spain. All three, and their contemporaries, operated in periods of factional strife, during which soldiers and civilians suffered.

Miranda, a Venezuelan, who had served with the French in the American Revolution and commanded parts of the French Revolutionary armies in the Netherlands, attempted to start a revolt in Venezuela in 1806 and failed. In 1810, with British and American backing, he returned and was briefly a dictator, until the British withdrew their support. In 1812 he was overcome by the royalists in Venezuela and taken prisoner, dying in a Spanish prison in 1816.

San Martin was born in Argentina and during 1789-1811 served in campaigns of the Spanish armies in Europe and Africa. He first joined the independence movement in Argentina in 1812 and in 1817 invaded Chile with 4,000 men over the mountain passes. Here he and Gen. Bernardo O'Higgins (1778-1842) defeated the Spaniards at Chacabuco, 1817, and O'Higgins was named Liberator and became first director of Chile, 1817-23. In 1821 San Martin occupied Lima and Callao, Peru, and became protector of Peru.

Bolivar, the greatest leader of South American liberation from Spain, was born in Venezuela, the son of an aristocratic family. He first served under Miranda in 1812 and in 1813 captured Caracas, where he was named Liberator. Forced out next year by civil strife, he led a campaign that captured Bogota in 1814. In 1817 he was again in control of Venezuela and was named dictator. He organized Nueva Granada with the help of General Francisco de Paula Santander (1792-1840). By joining Nueva Granada, Venezuela, and the present terrain of Panama and Ecuador, the republic of Colombia was formed with Bolivar president. After numerous setbacks he decisively defeated the Spaniards in the second battle of Carabobo, Venezuela, June 24, 1821.

In May, 1822, Gen. Antonio Jose de Sucre, Bolivar's lieutenant, took Quito. Bolivar went to Guayaquil to confer with San Martin, who resigned as protector of Peru and withdrew from politics. With a new army of Colombians and Peruvians Bolivar defeated the Spaniards in a battle at Junín in 1824 and cleared Peru.

De Sucre organized Charcas (Upper Peru) as Republica Bolivar (now Bolivia) and acted as president in place of Bolivar, who wrote its constitution. De Sucre defeated the Spanish faction of Peru at Ayacucho, Dec. 19, 1824.

Continued civil strife finally caused the Colombian federation to break apart. Santander turned against Bolivar, but the latter defeated him and banished him. In 1828 Bolivar gave up the presidency he had held precariously for 14 years. He became ill from tuberculosis and died Dec. 17, 1830. He is buried in the national pantheon in Caracas.

Rulers of Russia; Premiers of the USSR

First ruler to consolidate Slavic tribes was Rurik, leader of the Russians who established himself at Novgorod, 862 A.D. He and his immediate successors had Scandinavian affiliations. They moved to Kiev after 972 AD and ruled as Dukes of Kiev. In 988 Vladimir was converted and adopted the Byzantine Greek Orthodox service, later modified by Slav influences. Important as organizer and lawgiver was Yaroslav, 1019-1054, whose daughters married kings of Norway, Hungary, and France. His grandson, Vladimir II (Monomakh), 1113-1125, was progenitor of several rulers, but in 1169 Andrew Bogolubski overthrew Kiev and began the line known as Grand Dukes of Vladimir.

Of the Grand Dukes of Vladimir, Alexander Nevsky, 1246-1263, had a son, Daniel, first to be called Duke of Muscovy (Moscow) who ruled 1294-1303. His successors became Grand Dukes of Muscovy. After Dmitri III Donskoi defeated the Tartars in 1380, they also became Grand Dukes of all Russia. Independence of the Tartars and considerable territorial expansion were achieved under Ivan III, 1462-1505.

Tsars of Muscovy—Ivan III was referred to in church ritual as Tsar. He married Sofia, niece of the last Byzantine emperor. His successor, Basil III, died in 1533 when Basil's son Ivan was only 3. He became Ivan IV, "the Terrible"; crowned 1547 as Tsar of all the Russias, ruled till 1584. Under the weak rule of his son, Feodor I, 1584-1598, Boris Godunov had control. The dynasty died, and after years of tribal strife and intervention by Polish and Swedish armies, the Russians united under 17-year-old Michael Romanov, distantly related to the first wife of Ivan IV. He ruled 1613-1645 and established the Romanov line. Fourth ruler after Michael was Peter I.

Tsars, or Emperors of Russia (Romanovs)—Peter I, 1682-1725, known as Peter the Great, took title of Emperor in 1721. His successors and dates of accession were: Catherine, his widow, 1725, Peter II, his grandson, 1727; Anne, Duchess of Courland, 1730, daughter of Peter the Great's brother, Tsar Ivan V; Ivan VI, 1740, great-grandson of Ivan V, child, kept in prison and murdered 1764; Elizabeth, daughter of Peter I, 1741; Peter III, grandson of Peter I, 1761, deposed 1762 for his consort, Catherine II, former princess of Anhalt Zerbst (Germany) who is known as Catherine the Great; Paul I, her son, 1796, killed 1801; Alexander I, son of Paul, 1801, defeated Napoleon; Nicholas I, his brother, 1825; Alexander II, son of Nicholas, 1855, assassinated 1881 by terrorists; Alexander III, son, 1881.

Nicholas II, son, 1894-1917, last Tsar of Russia, was forced to abdicate by the Revolution that followed losses to Germany in WWI. The Tsar, the Empress, the Tsesarevich (Crown Prince) and the Tsar's 4 daughters were murdered by the Bolsheviks in Ekaterinburg, July 16, 1918.

Provisional Government—Prince Georgi Lvov and Alexander Kerensky, premiers, 1917.

Union of Soviet Socialist Republics

Bolshevik Revolution, Nov. 7, 1917, displaced Kerensky; council of People's Commissars formed, Lenin (Vladimir Ilyich Ulyanov), premier. Lenin died Jan. 21, 1924. Aleksei Rykov (executed 1938) and V. M. Molotov held the office, but actual ruler was Joseph Stalin (Joseph Vissarionovich Djugashvili), general secretary of the Central Committee of the Communist Party. Stalin became president of the Council of Ministers (premier) May 7, 1941, died Mar. 5, 1953. Succeeded by Georgi M. Malenkov, as head of the Council and premier and Nikita S. Khrushchev, first secretary of the Central Committee. Malenkov resigned Feb. 8, 1955, became deputy premier, was dropped July 3, 1957. Marshal Nikolai A. Bulganin became premier Feb. 8, 1955; was demoted and Khrushchev became premier Mar. 27 1958. Khrushchev was ousted Oct. 14-15, 1964, replaced by Leonid I. Brezhnev as first secretary of the party and by Aleksei N. Kosygin as premier. On June 16, 1977, Brezhnev took office as president. Brezhnev died Nov. 10, 1982; 2 days later the Central Committee unanimously elected former KGB head Yuri V. Andropov president. Andropov died Feb. 9, 1984; on Feb. 13, Konstantin U. Chernenko was chosen by Central Committee as its general secretary. Chernenko died Mar. 10, 1985. On Mar. 11, he was succeeded as general secretary by Mikhail Gorbachev, who replaced Andrei Gromyko as president on Oct. 1, 1988. Gorbachev resigned Dec. 25, 1991, when the Soviet Union disbanded, replaced by the Commonwealth of Independent States, made up of 11 of 12 former Soviet constituent republics.

Governments of China

(Until 221 BC and frequently thereafter, China was not a unified state. Where dynastic dates overlap, the rulers or events referred to appeared in different areas of China.)

Hsia	c1994BC	-	c1523BC
Shang	c1523	-	c1028
Western Chou	c1027	-	770
Eastern Chou	770	-	256
Warring States	403	-	222
Ch'in (first unified empire)	221	-	206
Han	202BC	-	220AD
Western Han (expanded Chinese state beyond the Yellow and Yangtze River valleys)	202BC	-	9AD
Hsin (Wang Mang, usurper)	9AD	-	23AD
Eastern Han (expanded Chinese state into Indo-China and Turkestan)	25	-	220
Three Kingdoms (Wei, Shu, Wu)	220	-	265
Chin (western)	265	-	317
(eastern)	317	-	420
Northern Dynasties (followed several short-lived governments by Turks, Mongols, etc.)	386	-	581
Southern Dynasties (capital: Nanking)	420	-	589
Sui (reunified China)	581	-	618
Tang (a golden age of Chinese culture; capital: Sian)	618	-	906
Five Dynasties (Yellow River basin)	902	-	960
Ten Kingdoms (southern China)	907	-	979
Liao (Khitan Mongols; capital: Peking)	947	-	1125
Sung	960	-	1279
Northern Sung (reunified central and southern China)	960	-	1126
Western Hsai (non-Chinese rulers in northwest)	990	-	1227
Chin (Tartars; drove Sung out of central China)	1115	-	1234
Yuan (Mongols; Kublai Khan made Peking his capital in 1267)	1271	-	1368
Ming (China reunified under Chinese rule; capital: Nanking, then Peking in 1420)	1368	-	1644
Ch'ing (Manchus, descendents of Tartars)	1644	-	1911
Republic (disunity; provincial rulers, warlords)	1912	-	1949
People's Republic of China	1949	-	—

Leaders Since 1949

Mao Zedong	Chairman, Central People's Administrative Council, Communist Party (CPC), 1949-1976
Zhou Enlai	Premier, foreign minister, 1949-1976
Deng Xiaoping	Vice Premier, 1949-1976; 1977-1987
Liu Shaoqi	President, 1959-1969
Hua Guofeng	Premier, 1976-1980; CPC Chairman, 1976-1981
Zhao Ziyong	Premier, 1980-88; CPC Chairman, 1987-89
Hu Yaobang	CPC Chairman, 1981-1987
Li Xiannian	President, 1983-1988
Yong Shang-Kun	President, 1988-
Li Peng	Premier, 1988-

Chronological List of Popes

Source: Annuario Pontificio. Table lists year of accession of each Pope.

The Roman Catholic Church names the Apostle Peter as founder of the Church in Rome. He arrived there c. 42, was martyred there c. 67, and raised to sainthood.

The Pope's temporal title is: Sovereign of the State of Vatican City.

The Pope's spiritual titles are: Bishop of Rome, Vicar of Jesus Christ, Successor of St. Peter, Prince of the Apostles, Supreme Pontiff of the Universal Church, Patriarch of the West, Primate of Italy, Archbishop and Metropolitan of the Roman Province.

Anti-Popes are in *Italics*. Anti-Popes were illegitimate claimants of or pretenders to the papal throne.

Year	Pope
See above	St. Peter
67	St. Linus
76	St. Anacletus or Cletus
88	St. Clement I
97	St. Evaristus
105	St. Alexander I
115	St. Sixtus I
125	St. Telesphorus
136	St. Hyginus
140	St. Pius I
155	St. Anicetus
166	St. Soter
175	St. Eleutherius
189	St. Victor I
199	St. Zephyrinus
217	St. Callistus I
217	*St. Hippolytus*
222	St. Urban I
230	St. Pontian
235	St. Anterus
236	St. Fabian
251	St. Cornelius
251	*Novatian*
253	St. Lucius I
254	St. Stephen I
257	St. Sixtus II
259	St. Dionysius
269	St. Felix I
275	St. Eutychian
283	St. Caius
296	St. Marcellinus
308	St. Marcellus I
309	St. Eusebius
311	St. Melchiades
314	St. Sylvester I
336	St. Marcus
337	St. Julius I
352	Liberius
355	*Felix II*
366	St. Damasus I
366	*Ursinus*
384	St. Siricius
399	St. Anastasius I
401	St. Innocent I
417	St. Zosimus
418	St. Boniface I
418	*Eulalius*
422	St. Celestine I
432	St. Sixtus III
440	St. Leo I
461	St. Hilary
468	St. Simplicius
483	St. Felix III (II)
492	St. Gelasius I
496	Anastasius II
498	St. Symmachus
498	*Lawrence (501-505)*
514	St. Hormisdas
523	St. John I, Martyr
526	St. Felix IV (III)
530	Boniface II
530	*Dioscorus*
533	John II
535	St. Agapitus I
536	St. Silverius, Martyr
537	Vigilius
556	Pelagius I
561	John III
575	Benedict I
579	Pelagius II
590	St. Gregory I
604	Sabinian
607	Boniface III
608	St. Boniface IV
615	St. Deusdedit or Adeodatus
619	Boniface V
625	Honorius I
640	Severinus
642	Theodore I
649	St. Martin I, Martyr
654	St. Eugene I
657	St. Vitalian
672	Adeodatus II
676	Donus
678	St. Agatho
682	St. Leo II
684	St. Benedict II
685	John V
686	Conon
687	*Theodore*
687	*Paschal*
687	St. Sergius I
701	John VI
705	John VII
708	Sisinnius
708	Constantine
715	St. Gregory II
731	St. Gregory III
741	St. Zachary
752	Stephen II (III)
757	St. Paul I
767	*Constantine*
768	*Philip*
768	Stephen III (IV)
772	Adrian I
795	St. Leo III
816	Stephen IV (V)
817	St. Paschal I
824	Eugene II
827	Valentine
827	Gregory IV
844	*John*
844	Sergius II
847	St. Leo IV
855	Benedict III
855	*Anastasius*
858	St. Nicholas I
867	Adrian II
872	John VIII
882	Marinus I
884	St. Adrian III
885	Stephen V (VI)
891	Formosus
896	Boniface VI
896	Stephen VI (VII)
897	Romanus
897	Theodore II
898	John IX
900	Benedict IV
903	Leo V
903	*Christopher*
904	Sergius III
911	Anastasius III
913	Landus
914	John X
928	Leo VI
928	Stephen VII (VIII)
931	John XI
936	Leo VII
939	Stephen VIII (IX)
942	Marinus II
946	Agapitus II
955	John XII
963	Leo VIII
964	Benedict V
965	John XIII
973	Benedict VI
974	*Boniface VII*
974	Benedict VII
983	John XIV
985	John XV
996	Gregory V
997	*John XVI*
999	Sylvester II
1003	John XVII
1004	John XVIII
1009	Sergius IV
1012	Benedict VIII
1012	*Gregory*
1024	John XIX
1032	Benedict IX
1045	Sylvester III
1045	Benedict IX
1045	Gregory VI
1046	Clement II
1047	Benedict IX
1048	Damasus II
1049	St. Leo IX
1055	Victor II
1057	Stephen IX (X)
1058	*Benedict X*
1059	Nicholas II
1061	Alexander II
1061	*Honorius II*
1073	St. Gregory VII
1080	*Clement III*
1086	Bl. Victor III
1088	Bl. Urban II
1099	Paschal II
1100	*Theodoric*
1102	*Albert*
1105	*Sylvester IV*
1118	Gelasius II
1118	*Gregory VIII*
1119	Callistus II
1124	Honorius II
1124	*Celestine II*
1130	Innocent II
1130	*Anacletus II*
1138	*Victor IV*
1143	Celestine II
1144	Lucius II
1145	Bl. Eugene III
1153	Anastasius IV
1154	Adrian IV
1159	Alexander III
1159	*Victor IV*
1164	*Paschal III*
1168	*Callistus III*
1179	*Innocent III*
1181	Lucius III
1185	Urban III
1187	Clement III
1187	Gregory VIII
1191	Celestine III
1198	Innocent III
1216	Honorius III
1227	Gregory IX
1241	Celestine IV
1243	Innocent IV
1254	Alexander IV
1261	Urban IV
1265	Clement IV
1271	Bl. Gregory X
1276	Bl. Innocent V
1276	Adrian V
1276	John XXI
1277	Nicholas III
1281	Martin IV
1285	Honorius IV
1288	Nicholas IV
1294	St. Celestine V
1294	Boniface VIII
1303	Bl. Benedict XI
1305	Clement V
1316	John XXII
1328	*Nicholas V*
1334	Benedict XII
1342	Clement VI
1352	Innocent VI
1362	Bl. Urban V
1370	Gregory XI
1378	Urban VI
1378	*Clement VII*
1389	Boniface IX
1394	*Benedict XIII*
1404	Innocent VII
1406	Gregory XII
1409	*Alexander V*
1410	*John XXIII*
1417	Martin V
1431	Eugene IV
1439	*Felix V*
1447	Nicholas V
1455	Callistus III
1458	Pius II
1464	Paul II
1471	Sixtus IV
1484	Innocent VIII
1492	Alexander VI
1503	Pius III
1503	Julius II
1513	Leo X
1522	Adrian VI
1523	Clement VII
1534	Paul III
1550	Julius III
1555	Marcellus II
1555	Paul IV
1559	Pius IV
1566	St. Pius V
1572	Gregory XIII
1585	Sixtus V
1590	Urban VII
1590	Gregory XIV
1591	Innocent IX
1592	Clement VIII
1605	Leo XI
1605	Paul V
1621	Gregory XV
1623	Urban VIII
1644	Innocent X
1655	Alexander VII
1667	Clement IX
1670	Clement X
1676	Bl. Innocent XI
1689	Alexander VIII
1691	Innocent XII
1700	Clement XI
1721	Innocent XIII
1724	Benedict XIII
1730	Clement XII
1740	Benedict XIV
1758	Clement XIII
1769	Clement XIV
1775	Pius VI
1800	Pius VII
1823	Leo XII
1829	Pius VIII
1831	Gregory XVI
1846	Pius IX
1878	Leo XIII
1903	St. Pius X
1914	Benedict XV
1922	Pius XI
1939	Pius XII
1958	John XXIII
1963	Paul VI
1978	John Paul I
1978	John Paul II

WORLD EXPLORATION AND GEOGRAPHY

Early Explorers of the Western Hemisphere

The first men to discover the New World or Western Hemisphere are believed to have walked across a "land bridge" from Siberia to Alaska, an isthmus since broken by the Bering Strait. From Alaska, these ancestors of the Indians spread through North, Central, and South America. Anthropologists have placed these crossings at between 18,000 and 14,000 B.C.; but evidence found in 1967 near Puebla, Mex., indicates mankind reached there as early as 35,000-40,000 years ago.

At first, these people were hunters using flint weapons and tools. In Mexico, about 7000-6000 B.C., they founded farming cultures, developing corn, squash, etc. Eventually, they created complex civilizations — Olmec, Toltec, Aztec, and Maya and, in South America, Inca. Carbon-14 tests show men lived about 8000 B.C. near what are now Front Royal, Va., Kanawha, W. Va., and Dutchess Quarry, N.Y. The Hopewell Culture, based on farming, flourished about 1000 B.C.; remains of it are seen today in large mounds in Ohio and other states.

Norsemen (Norwegian Vikings sailing out of Iceland and Greenland) are credited by most scholars with being the first Europeans to discover America, with at least 5 voyages around 1000 A.D. to areas they called Helluland, Markland, Vinland—possibly Labrador, Nova Scotia or Newfoundland, and New England.

Christopher Columbus, the most famous explorer, was born Cristoforo Colombo in or near Genoa, Italy probably in 1451, but made his discoveries sailing for the Spanish rulers Ferdinand and Isabella. Dates of his voyages, places he discovered, and other information follow:

1492—First voyage. Left Palos, Spain, Aug. 3 with 88 men (est.). His fleet consisted of 3 vessels—the *Nina*, the *Pinta*, and the *Santa Maria*. Discovered San Salvador, (Guanahani or Watling Is., Bahamas) Oct. 12. Also Cuba, Hispaniola (Haiti-Dominican Republic); built Fort La Navidad on latter.

1493—Second voyage, first part, Sept. 25, with 17 ships, 1,500 men. Dominica (Lesser Antilles) Nov. 3; Guadeloupe, Montserrat, Antigua, San Martin, Santa Cruz, Puerto Rico, Virgin Islands. Settled Isabela on Hispaniola. **Second part** (Columbus having remained in Western Hemisphere), Jamaica, Isle of Pines, La Mona Is.

1498—Third voyage. Left Spain, May 30, 1498, 6 ships. Discovered Trinidad. Saw South American continent, Aug. 1, 1498, but called it Isla Sancta (Holy Island). Entered Gulf of Paria and landed, first time on continental soil. At mouth of Orinoco, Aug. 14, he decided this was the mainland.

1502—Fourth voyage, 4 caravels, 150 men. St. Lucia, Guanaja off Honduras; Cape Gracias a Dios, Honduras; San Juan River, Costa Rica; Almirante, Portobelo, and Laguna de Chiriqui, Panama.

Year	Explorer	Nationality and employer	Discovery or exploration
1497	John Cabot	Italian-English	Newfoundland or Nova Scotia
1498	John and Sebastian Cabot	Italian-English	Labrador to Hatteras
1499	Alonso de Ojeda	Spanish	South American coast, Venezuela
1500, Feb.	Vicente y Pinzon	Spanish	South American coast, Amazon River
1500, Apr.	Pedro Alvarez Cabral	Portuguese	Brazil (for Portugal)
1500-02	Gaspar Corte-Real	Portuguese	Labrador
1501	Rodrigo de Bastidas	Spanish	Central America
1513	Vasco Nunez de Balboa	Spanish	Pacific Ocean
1513	Juan Ponce de Leon	Spanish	Florida
1515	Juan de Solis	Spanish	Rio de la Plata
1519	Alonso de Pineda	Spanish	Mouth of Mississippi River
1519	Hernando Cortes	Spanish	Mexico
1520	Ferdinand Magellan	Portuguese-Spanish	Straits of Magellan, Tierra del Fuego
1524	Giovanni da Verrazano	Italian-French	Atlantic coast-New York harbor
1532	Francisco Pizarro	Spanish	Peru
1534	Jacques Cartier	French	Canada, Gulf of St. Lawrence
1536	Pedro de Mendoza	Spanish	Buenos Aires
1536	A.N. Cabeza de Vaca	Spanish	Texas coast and interior
1539	Francisco de Ulloa	Spanish	California coast
1539-41	Hernando de Soto	Spanish	Mississippi River near Memphis
1539	Marcos de Niza	Italian-Spanish	Southwest (now U.S.)
1540	Francisco V. de Coronado	Spanish	Southwest (now U.S.)
1540	Hernando Alarcon	Spanish	Colorado River
1540	Garcia de L. Cardenas	Spanish	Grand Canyon of the Colorado
1541	Francisco de Orellana	Spanish	Amazon River
1542	Juan Rodriguez Cabrillo	Portuguese-Spanish	San Diego harbor
1565	Pedro Menendez de Aviles	Spanish	St. Augustine
1576	Martin Frobisher	English	Frobisher's Bay, Canada
1577-80	Francis Drake	English	California coast
1582	Antonio de Espejo	Spanish	Southwest (named New Mexico)
1584	Amadas & Barlow (for Raleigh)	English	Virginia
1585-87	Sir Walter Raleigh's men	English	Roanoke Is., N.C.
1595	Sir Walter Raleigh	English	Orinoco River
1603-09	Samuel de Champlain	French	Canadian interior, Lake Champlain
1607	Capt. John Smith	English	Atlantic coast
1609-10	Henry Hudson	English-Dutch	Hudson River, Hudson Bay
1634	Jean Nicolet	French	Lake Michigan; Wisconsin
1673	Jacques Marquette, Louis Jolliet	French	Mississippi S to Arkansas
1682	Sieur de La Salle	French	Mississippi S to Gulf of Mexico
1789	Alexander Mackenzie	Canadian	Canadian Northwest

Arctic Exploration

Early Explorers

1587 — John Davis (England). Davis Strait to Sanderson's Hope, 72° 12′ N.

1596 — Willem Barents and Jacob van Heemskerck (Holland). Discovered Bear Island, touched northwest tip of Spitsbergen, 79° 49′ N, rounded Novaya Zemlya, wintered at Ice Haven.

1607 — Henry Hudson (England). North along Greenland's east coast to Cape Hold-with-Hope, 73° 30', then north of Spitsbergen to 80° 23'. Returning he discovered Hudson's Touches (Jan Mayen).

1616 — William Baffin and Robert Bylot (England). Baffin Bay to Smith Sound.

1728 — Vitus Bering (Russia). Proved Asia and America were separated by sailing through strait.

1733-40 — Great Northern Expedition (Russia). Surveyed Siberian Arctic coast.

1741 — Vitus Bering (Russia). Sighted Alaska from sea, named Mount St. Elias. His lieutenant, Chirikof, discovered coast.

1771 — Samuel Hearne (Hudson's Bay Co.). Overland from Prince of Wales Fort (Churchill) on Hudson Bay to mouth of Coppermine River.

1778 — James Cook (Britain). Through Bering Strait to Icy Cape, Alaska, and North Cape, Siberia.

1789 — Alexander Mackenzie (North West Co., Britain). Montreal to mouth of Mackenzie River.

1806 — William Scoresby (Britain). N. of Spitsbergen to 81° 30'.

1820-3 — Ferdinand von Wrangel (Russia). Completed a survey of Siberian Arctic coast. His exploration joined that of James Cook at North Cape, confirming separation of the continents.

1845 — Sir John Franklin (Britain) was one of many to seek the Northwest Passage—an ocean route connecting the Atlantic and Pacific via the Arctic. His 2 ships (the *Erebus* and *Terror*) were last seen entering Lancaster Sound July, 26.

1881 — The steamer *Jeanette* on an expedition led by Lt. Cmdr. George W. DeLong was trapped in ice and crushed, June 1881. DeLong and 11 crewmen died; 12 others survived.

1888 — Fridtjof Nansen (Norway) crossed Greenland's icecap, 1893-96 — Nansen in Fram drifted from New Siberian Is. to Spitsbergen; tried polar dash in 1895, reached Franz Josef Land.

1897 — Salomon A. Andree (Sweden) and 2 others started in balloon from Danes, Is., Spitsbergen, July 11, to drift across pole to America, and disappeared. Over 33 years later, Aug. 6, 1930, their frozen bodies were found on White Is., 82° 57' N 29° 52' E.

1903-06 — Roald Amundsen (Norway) first sailed Northwest Passage.

Discovery of North Pole

Robert E. Peary explored Greenland's coast, 1891-92, tried for North Pole, 1893. In 1900 he reached northern limit of Greenland and 83° 50' N; in 1902 he reached 84° 06' N; in 1906 he went from Ellesmere Is. to 87° 06' N. He sailed in the *Roosevelt*, July, 1908, to winter off Cape Sheridan, Grant Land. The dash for the North Pole began Mar. 1 from Cape Columbia, Ellesmere Land. Peary reached the pole, 90° N, Apr. 6, 1909.

Peary had several supporting groups carrying supplies until the last group turned back at 87° 47' N. Peary, Matthew Henson, and 4 Eskimos proceeded with dog teams and sleds. They crossed the pole several times, finally built an igloo at 90°, remained 36 hours. Started south, Apr. 7 at 4 p.m., for Cape Columbia. The Eskimos were Coqueeh, Ootah, Eginwah, and Seegloo.

1914 — Donald MacMillan (U.S.). Northwest, 200 miles, from Axel Heiberg Island to seek Peary's Crocker Land.

1915-17 — Vihjalmur Stefansson (Canada) discovered Borden, Brock, Meighen, and Lougheed Islands.

1918-20 — Roald Amundsen sailed Northeast Passage.

1925 — Amundsen and Lincoln Ellsworth (U.S.) reached 87° 44' N in attempt to fly to North Pole from Spitsbergen.

1926 — Richard E. Byrd and Floyd Bennett (U.S.) first over North Pole by air, May 9.

1926 — Amundsen, Ellsworth, and Umberto Nobile (Italy) flew from Spitsbergen over North Pole May 12, to Teller, Alaska, in dirigible *Norge*.

1928 — Nobile crossed North Pole in airship, May 24, crashed, May 25. Amundsen lost while trying to effect rescue by plane.

North Pole Exploration Records

On Aug. 3, 1958, the *Nautilus*, under Comdr. William R. Anderson, became the first ship to cross the North Pole beneath the Arctic ice.

The nuclear-powered U.S. submarine *Seadragon*, Comdr. George P. Steele 2d, made the first east-west underwater transit through the Northwest Passage during August, 1960. It sailed from Portsmouth N.H., headed between Greenland and Labrador through Baffin Bay, then west through Lancaster Sound and McClure Strait to the Beaufort Sea. Traveling submerged for the most part, the submarine made 850 miles from Baffin Bay to the Beaufort Sea in 6 days.

On Aug. 16, 1977, the Soviet nuclear icebreaker *Arktika* reached the North Pole and became the first surface ship to break through the Arctic ice pack to the top of the world.

On April 30, 1978, Naomi Uemura, a Japanese explorer, became the first man to reach the North Pole alone by dog sled. During the 54-day, 600-mile trek over the frozen Arctic, Uemura survived attacks by a marauding polar bear.

In April, 1982, Sir Ranulph Fiennes and Charles Burton, British explorers, reached the North Pole and became the first to circle the earth from pole to pole. They had reached the South Pole 16 months earlier. The 52,000-mile trek took 3 years, involved 23 people, and cost an estimated $18 million. The expedition was also the first to travel down the Scott Glacier and the first to journey up the Yukon and through the Northwest Passage in a single season.

On May 2, 1986, 6 American and Canadian explorers reached the North Pole assisted only by dogs. They became the first to reach the Pole without mechanical assistance since Robert E. Peary planted a flag there in 1909. The explorers, Americans Will Steger, Paul Schurke, Anne Bancroft, and Geoff Carroll, and Canadians Brent Boddy and Richard Weber completed the 500-mile journey in 56 days.

Antarctic Exploration

Early History

Antarctica has been approached since 1773-75, when Capt. James Cook (Britain) reached 71° 10' S. Many sea and landmarks bear names of early explorers. Bellingshausen (Russia) discovered Peter I and Alexander I Islands, 1819-21. Nathaniel Palmer (U.S.) discovered Palmer Peninsula, 60° W, 1820, without realizing that this was a continent. James Weddell (Britain) found Weddell Sea, 74° 15' S, 1823.

First to announce existence of the continent of Antarctica was Charles Wilkes (U.S.), who followed the coast for 1,500 mi., 1840. Adelie Coast, 140° E, was found by Dumont d'Urville (France), 1840. Ross Ice Shelf was found by James Clark Ross (Britain), 1841-42.

1895 — Leonard Kristensen (Norway) landed a party on the coast of Victoria Land. They were the first ashore on the main continental mass. C.E. Borchgrevink, a member of that party, returned in 1899 with a British expedition, first to winter on Antarctica.

1902-04 — Robert F. Scott (Britain) discovered Edward VII Peninsula. He reached 82° 17' S, 146° 33' E from McMurdo Sound.

1908-09 — Ernest Shackleton (Britain) introduced the use of Manchurian ponies in Antarctic sledging. He reached 88° 23' S, discovering a route on to the plateau by way of the Beardmore Glacier and pioneering the way to the pole.

Discovery of South Pole

1911 — Roald Amundsen (Norway) with 4 men and dog teams reached the pole, Dec. 14.

1912 — Capt. Scott reached the pole from Ross Island, Jan. 18, with 4 companions. They found Amundsen's tent. None of Scott's party survived. They were found, Nov. 12.

1928 — First man to use an airplane over Antarctica was Hubert Wilkins (Britain).

1929 — Richard E. Byrd (U.S.) established Little America on Bay of Whales. On 1,600-mi. airplane flight begun, Nov. 28, he crossed South Pole, Nov. 29 with 3 others.

1934-35 — Byrd led 2d expedition to Little America, explored 450,000 sq. mi., wintered alone at weather station, 80° 08′ S.

1934-37 — John Rymill led British Graham Land expedition; discovered that Palmer Peninsula is part of Antarctic mainland.

1935 — Lincoln Ellsworth (U.S.) flew south along Palmer Peninsula's east coast, then crossed continent to Little America, making 4 landings on unprepared terrain in bad weather.

1939-41 — U.S. Antarctic Service built West Base on Ross Ice Shelf under Paul Siple, and East Base on Palmer Peninsula under Richard Black. U.S. Navy plane flights discovered about 150,000 sq. miles of new land.

1940 — Byrd charted most of coast between Ross Sea and Palmer Peninsula.

1946-47 — U.S. Navy undertook Operation High-jump under Byrd. Expedition included 13 ships and 4,000 men. Airplanes photomapped coastline and penetrated beyond pole.

1946-48 — Ronne Antarctic Research Expedition, Comdr. Finn Ronne, USNR, determined the Antarctic to be only one continent with no strait between Weddell Sea and Ross Sea; discovered 250,000 sq. miles of land by flights to 79° S Lat., and made 14,000 aerial photographs over 450,000 sq. miles of land. Mrs. Ronne and Mrs. H. Darlington were the first women to winter on Antarctica.

1955-57 — U.S. Navy's Operation Deep Freeze led by Adm. Byrd. Supporting U.S. scientific efforts for the International Geophysical Year, the operation was commanded by Rear Adm. George Dufek. It established 5 coastal stations fronting the Indian, Pacific, and Atlantic oceans and also 3 interior stations; explored more than 1,000,000 sq. miles in Wilkes Land.

1957-58 — During the International Geophysical year, July 1957, through Dec. 1958, scientists from 12 countries conducted ambitious programs of Antarctic research. A network of some 60 stations on the continent and sub-Arctic islands studied oceanography, glaciology, meteorology, seismology, geomagnetism, the ionosphere, cosmic rays, aurora, and airglow.

Dr. V.E. Fuchs led a 12-man Trans-Antarctic Expedition on the first land crossing of Antarctica. Starting from the Weddell Sea, they reached Scott Station, Mar. 2, 1958, after traveling 2,158 miles in 98 days.

1958 — A group of 5 U.S. scientists led by Edward C. Thiel, seismologist, moving by tractor from Ellsworth Station on Weddell Sea, identified a huge mountain range, 5,000 ft. above the ice sheet and 9,000 ft. above sea level. The range, originally seen by a Navy plane, was named the Dufek Massif, for Rear Adm. George Dufek.

1959 — Twelve nations — Argentina, Australia, Belgium, Chile, France, Japan, New Zealand, Norway, South Africa, the Soviet Union, the United Kingdom, and the U.S. — signed a treaty suspending any territorial claims for 30 years and reserving the continent for research.

1961-62 — Scientists discovered a trough, the Bentley Trench, running from Ross Ice Shelf, Pacific, into Marie Byrd Land, around the end of the Ellsworth Mtns., toward the Weddell Sea.

1962 — First nuclear power plant began operation at McMurdo Sound.

1963 — On Feb. 22 a U.S. plane made the longest nonstop flight ever made in the S. Pole area, covering 3,600 miles in 10 hours. The flight was from McMurdo Station south past the geographical S. Pole to Shackleton Mtns., southeast to the "Area of Inaccessibility" and back to McMurdo Station.

1964 — A British survey team was landed by helicopter on Cook Island, the first recorded visit since its discovery in 1775.

1964 — New Zealanders completed one of the last and most important surveys when they mapped the mountain area from Cape Adare west some 400 miles to Pennell Glacier.

1989 — Two Americans, Victoria Murden and Shirley Metz, became the first women to reach the South Pole overland when they arrived with 9 others on Jan. 17, 1989. The 51-day trek on skis covered 740 miles.

Volcanoes

Source: Global Volcanism Network, Smithsonian Institution

More than 75 per cent of the world's 850 active volcanoes lie within the "Ring of Fire," a zone running along the west coast of the Americas from Chile to Alaska and down the east coast of Asia from Siberia to New Zealand. Twenty per cent of these volcanoes are located in Indonesia. Other prominent groupings are located in Japan, the Aleutian Islands, and Central America. Almost all active regions are found at the boundaries of the large moving plates which comprise the earth's surface. The "Ring of Fire" marks the boundary between the plates underlying the Pacific Ocean and those underlying the surrounding continents. Other active regions, such as the Mediterranean Sea and Iceland, are located on plate boundaries.

Major Historical Eruptions

Approximately 7,000 years ago, Mazama, a 9,900-feet-high volcano in southern Oregon, erupted violently, ejecting ash and lava. The ash spread over the entire northwestern United States and as far away as Saskatchewan, Canada. During the eruption, the top of the mountain collapsed, leaving a caldera 6 miles across and about a half mile deep, which filled with rain water to form what is now called Crater Lake.

In 79 A.D., Vesuvio, or Vesuvius, a 4,190 feet volcano overlooking Naples Bay became active after several centuries of quiescence. On Aug. 24 of that year, a heated mud and ash flow swept down the mountain engulfing the cities of Pompeii, Herculaneum, and Stabiae with debris over 60 feet deep. About 10 percent of the population of the 3 towns was killed.

The largest eruptions in recent centuries have been in Indonesia. In 1883, an eruption similar to the Mazama eruption occurred on the island of Krakatau. On August 27, the 2,640-feet-high peak of the volcano collapsed to 1,000 feet below sea level, leaving only a small portion of the island standing above the sea. Ash from the eruption colored sunsets around the world for 2 years. A tsunami ("tidal wave") generated by the collapse killed 36,000 people in nearby Java and Sumatra and eventually reached England. A similar, but even more powerful, eruption had taken place 68 years earlier at Tambora volcano on the Indonesian island of Sumbawa.

Notable Active Volcanoes

Name, latest activity	Location	Height (feet)
Africa		
Cameroon (1982)	Cameroon	13,354
Nyirangongo (1977)	Zaire	11,400
Nyamuragira (1991)	Zaire	10,028
Karthala (1977)	Comoro Is.	8,000
Piton de la Fournaise (1991)	Reunion Is.	5,981
Erta-Ale (1973)	Ethiopia	1,650
Antarctica		
Erebus (1991)	Ross Island	12,450
Deception Island (1970)	South Shetland Islands	1,890

(continued)

Name, latest activity	Location	Height (feet)
Asia-Oceania		
Kliuchevskol (1991)	Russia	15,584
Kerinci (1987)	Sumatra	12,467
Semeru (1991)	Java	12,060
Slamet (1988)	Java	11,247
Raung (1991)	Java	10,932
On-Take (1991)	Japan	10,049
Mayon (1988)	Philippines	9,991
Merapi (1992)	Java	9,551
Marapi (1988)	Sumatra	9,485
Ruapehu (1992)	New Zealand	9,175
Asama (1991)	Japan	8,300
Niigata Yakeyama (1989)	Japan	8,111
Canlaon (1991)	Philippines	8,070
Alaid (1972)	Kuril Is.	7,662
Ulawun (1992)	New Britain	7,532
Ngauruhoe (1975)	New Zealand	7,515
Chokai (1974)	Japan	7,300
Galunggung (1982)	Java	7,113
Azuma (1978)	Japan	6,700
Pinatubo (1992)	Philippines	5,770
Sangeang Api (1988)	Indonesia	6,351
Nasu (1977)	Japan	6,210
Tiatia (1973)	Kuril Islands	6,013
Manam (1992)	Papua New Guinea	6,000
Soputan (1989)	Indonesia	5,994
Siau (1976)	Indonesia	5,853
Kelud (1990)	Java	5,679
Kirisima (1982)	Japan	5,577
Bagana (1992)	Papua New Guinea	6,558
Akita Komaga take (1970)	Japan	5,449
Gamkonora (1981)	Indonesia	5,364
Aso (1991)	Japan	5,223
Lokon-Empung (1991)	Indonesia	5,187
Bulusan (1988)	Philippines	5,115
Sarycheva (1976)	Kuril Islands	4,960
Karkar (1981)	Papua New Guinea	4,920
Lopevi (1982)	Vanuatu	4,755
Unzen (1992)	Japan	4,462
Ambrym (1991)	Vanuatu	4,376
Awu (1992)	Indonesia	4,350
Sakurajima (1992)	Japan	3,668
Langila (1992)	New Britain	3,586
Suwanosezima (1991)	Japan	2,640
Oshima (1990)	Japan	2,550
Usu (1978)	Japan	2,400
Pagan (1990)	Mariana Is.	1,870
White Island (1992)	New Zealand	1,075
Taal (1988)	Philippines	984
Central America—Caribbean		
Acatenango (1972)	Guatemala	12,992
Fuego (1991)	Guatemala	12,582
Tacana (1988)	Guatemala	12,400
Santiaguito (Santa Maria) (1991)	Guatemala	12,362
Irazu (1992)	Costa Rica	11,260
Turrialba (1992)	Costa Rica	10,650
Poas (1992)	Costa Rica	8,930
Pacaya (1991)	Guatemala	8,346
San Miguel (1986)	El Salvador	6,994
Rincon de la Vieja (1992)	Costa Rica	6,234
El Viejo (San Cristobal) (1991)	Nicaragua	5,840
Ometepe (Concepcion) (1986)	Nicaragua	5,106
Arenal (1992)	Costa Rica	5,092
Momotombo (1982)	Nicaragua	4,199
Soufriere (1979)	St. Vincent	4,048
Telica (1987)	Nicaragua	3,409
South America		
Guallatiri (1987)	Chile	19,882
Lascar (1991)	Chile	19,652
Cotopaxi (1975)	Ecuador	19,347
Tupungatito (1986)	Chile	18,504
Ruiz (1992)	Colombia	17,716
Sangay (1988)	Ecuador	17,159
Guagua Pichincha (1988)	Ecuador	15,696
Purace (1977)	Colombia	15,601
Galeras (1992)	Colombia	13,996
Llaima (1990)	Chile	10,239
Villarrica (1991)	Chile	9,318
Hudson (1991)	Chile	8,580
Alcedo (1970)	Galapagos Is.	3,599
Mid-Pacific		
Mauna Loa (1987)	Hawaii	13,680
Kilauea (1992)	Hawaii	4,077
Mid-Atlantic Ridge		
Beerenberg (1985)	Jan Mayen Is.	7,470
Hekla (1991)	Iceland	4,892
Leirhnukur (1975)	Iceland	2,145
Krafla (1984)	Iceland	2,145
Europe		
Etna (1992)	Italy	11,053
Stromboli (1992)	Italy	3,038
North America		
Colima (1991)	Mexico	14,003
Redoubt (1991)	Alaska	10,197
Iliamna (1978)	Alaska	10,016
Shishaldin (1987)	Aleutian Is.	9,387
Mt. St. Helens (1991)	Washington	8,300+
Pavlof (1988)	Aleutian Is.	8,261
Veniaminof (1987)	Alaska	8,225
El Chichon (1983)	Mexico	7,300
Katmai (1974)	Alaska	6,715
Makushin (1987)	Aleutian Is.	6,680
Great Sitkin (1974)	Aleutian Is.	5,710
Cleveland (1987)	Aleutian Is.	5,675
Gareloi (1982)	Aleutian Is.	5,334
Korovin (1987)	Aleutian Is.	4,852
Akutan (1992)	Aleutian Is.	4,275
Kiska (1990)	Aleutian Is.	4,275
Augustine (1988)	Alaska	3,999
Okmok (1988)	Aleutian Is.	3,519
Seguam (1977)	Alaska	3,458

Notable Volcanic Eruptions

Date	Volcano	Deaths
79 A.D.	Mt. Vesuvius, Italy	16,000
1169	Mt. Etna, Sicily	15,000
1631	Mt. Vesuvius, Italy	4,000
1669	Mt. Etna, Sicily	20,000
1772	Mt. Papandayan, Java	3,000
1792	Mt. Unzen-Dake, Japan	10,400
1815	Tamboro, Java	12,000
Aug. 26-28, 1883	Krakatau, Indonesia	35,000
Apr. 8, 1902	Santa Maria, Guatemala	1,000
May 8, 1902	Mt. Pelée, Martinique	30,000
1911	Mt. Taal, Philippines	1,400
1919	Mt. Kelud, Java	5,000
Jan. 18-21, 1951	Mt. Lamington, New Guinea	3,000
Apr. 26, 1966	Mt. Kelud, Java	1,000
May 18, 1980	Mt. St. Helens, U.S.	60
Nov. 13, 1985	Nevado del Ruiz, Colombia	22,940
Aug. 24, 1986	NW Cameroon	1,700+

Mountains

Height of Mount Everest

Mt. Everest was considered to be 29,002 ft. tall when Edmund Hillary and Tenzing Norgay scaled it in 1953. This triangulation figure had been accepted since 1850. In 1954 the Surveyor General of the Republic of India set the height at 29,028 ft., plus or minus 10 ft. because of snow. The National Geographic Society accepts the new figure, but many mountaineering groups still use 29,002 ft.

In 1987, new calculations based on satellite measurements indicate that the Himalayan peak K-2 rose 29,064 feet above sea level and that Mt. Everest is 800 feet higher. The National Geographic Society has not accepted the revised figure.

United States, Canada, Mexico

Name	Place	Height (feet)
McKinley	Alaska	20,320
Logan	Yukon	19,850
Citlaltepec (Orizaba)	Mexico	18,700
St. Elias	Alas-Yukon	18,008
Popocatepetl	Mexico	17,887
Foraker	Alaska	17,400
Iztaccihuatl	Mexico	17,343
Lucania	Yukon	17,147
King	Can	16,971
Steele	Can	16,644
Bona	Alaska	16,550
Blackburn	Alaska	16,390
Kennedy	Alaska	16,286
Sanford	Alaska	16,237
South Buttress	Alaska	15,885
Wood	Yukon	15,885
Vancouver	Alas-Yukon	15,700
Churchill	Alaska	15,638
Fairweather	Alas-Yukon	15,300
Zinantecatl (Toluca)	Mexico	15,016
Hubbard	Alas-Yukon	15,015
Bear	Alaska	14,831
Walsh	Yukon	14,780
East Buttress	Alaska	14,730
Matlalcueyetl	Mexico	14,636
Hunter	Alaska	14,573
Alverstone	Alas-Yukon	14,565
Browne Tower	Alaska	14,530
Whitney	Cal	14,494
Elbert	Col	14,433
Massive	Col	14,421
Harvard	Col	14,420
Rainier	Wash	14,410
Williamson	Cal	14,375
Blanca Peak	Col	14,345
La Plata	Col	14,336
Uncompahgre	Col	14,309
Crestone	Col	14,294
Lincoln	Col	14,286
Grays Peak	Col	14,270
Antero	Col	14,269
Torreys	Col	14,267
Castle	Col	14,265
Quandary	Col	14,265
Evans	Col	14,264
Longs Peak	Col	14,256
McArthur	Yukon	14,253
Wilson	Col	14,246
White	Cal	14,246
North Palisade	Cal	14,242
Shavano	Col	14,229
Belford	Col	14,197
Princeton	Col	14,197
Crestone Needle	Col	14,197
Yale	Col	14,196
Bross	Col	14,172
Kit Carson	Col	14,165
Wrangell	Alaska	14,163
Shasta	Cal	14,162
Sill	Cal	14,162
El Diente	Col	14,159
Maroon	Col	14,156
Tabeguache	Col	14,155
Oxford	Col	14,153
Sneffels	Col	14,150
Point Success	Wash	14,150
Democrat	Col	14,148
Capitol	Col	14,130
Liberty Cap	Wash	14,112
Pikes Peak	Col	14,110
Snowmass	Col	14,092
Windom	Col	14,087
Russell	Cal	14,086
Eolus	Col	14,084
Columbia	Col	14,073
Augusta	Alas-Yukon	14,070
Missouri	Col	14,067
Humboldt	Col	14,064

South America

Peak, country	Height (feet)
Aconcagua, Argentina	22,834
Ojos del Salado, Arg.-Chile	22,572
Bonete, Argentina	22,546
Tupungato, Argentina-Chile	22,310
Pissis, Argentina	22,241
Mercedario, Argentina	22,211
Huascaran, Peru	22,205
Llullaillaco, Argentina-Chile	22,057
El Libertador, Argentina	22,047
Cachi, Argentina	22,047
Yerupaja, Peru	21,709
Galan, Argentina	21,654
El Muerto, Argentina-Chile	21,457
Sajama, Bolivia	21,391
Nacimiento, Argentina	21,302
Illimani, Bolivia	21,201
Coropuna, Peru	21,083
Laudo, Argentina	20,997
Ancohuma, Bolivia	20,958
Ausangate, Peru	20,945
Toro, Argentina-Chile	20,932
Illampu, Bolivia	20,873
Tres Cruces, Argentina-Chile	20,853
Huandoy, Peru	20,852
Parinacota, Bolivia-Chile	20,768
Tortolas, Argentina-Chile	20,745
Ampato, Peru	20,702
Condor, Argentina	20,669
Salcantay, Peru	20,574
Chimborazo, Ecuador	20,561
Huancarhuas, Peru	20,531
Famatina, Argentina	20,505
Pumasillo, Peru	20,492
Solo, Argentina	20,492
Polleras, Argentina	20,456
Pular, Chile	20,423
Chani, Argentina	20,341
Aucanquilcha, Chile	20,295
Juncal, Argentina-Chile	20,276
Negro, Argentina	20,184
Quela, Argentina	20,128
Condoriri, Bolivia	20,095
Palermo, Argentina	20,079
Solimana, Peru	20,068
San Juan, Argentina-Chile	20,049
Sierra Nevada, Arg.-Chile	20,023
Antofalla, Argentina	20,013
Marmolejo, Argentina-Chile	20,013
Chachani, Peru	19,931
Licancabur, Argentina-Chile	19,425

The highest point in the West Indies is in the Dominican Republic, Pico Duarte (10,417 ft.)

Africa, Australia, and Oceania

Peak, country	Height (feet)
Kilimanjaro, Tanzania	19,340
Kenya, Kenya	17,058
Margherita Pk., Uganda-Zaire	16,763
Jaja, New Guinea	16,500
Trikora, New Guinea	15,585
Mandala, New Guinea	15,420
Ras Dashan, Ethiopia	15,158
Meru, Tanzania	14,979
Wilhelm, Papua New Guinea	14,793
Karisimbi, Zaire-Rwanda	14,787
Elgon, Kenya-Uganda	14,178
Batu, Ethiopia	14,131
Guna, Ethiopia	13,881
Gughe, Ethiopia	13,780
Toubkal, Morocco	13,661
Kinabalu, Malaysia	13,455
Kerinci, Sumatra	12,467
Cook, New Zealand	12,349
Teide, Canary Islands	12,198
Semeru, Java	12,060
Kosciusko, Australia	7,310

Europe

Peak, country	Height (feet)
Alps	
Mont Blanc, Fr., It.	15,771
Monte Rosa (highest peak of group), Switz.	15,203
Dom, Switz.	14,911
Liskamm, It., Switz.	14,852
Weisshorn, Switz.	14,780
Taschhorn, Switz.	14,733
Matterhorn, It., Switz.	14,690
Dent Blanche, Switz.	14,293
Nadelhorn, Switz.	14,196
Grand Combin, Switz.	14,154
Lenzpitze, Switz.	14,088
Finsteraarhorn, Switz.	14,022
Castor, Switz.	13,865
Zinalrothorn, Switz.	13,849
Hohberghorn, Switz.	13,842
Alphubel, Switz.	13,799
Rimpfischhorn, Switz.	13,776
Aletschorn, Switz.	13,763
Strahlhorn, Switz.	13,747
Dent D'Herens, Switz.	13,686
Breithorn, It., Switz.	13,665
Bishorn, Switz.	13,645
Jungfrau, Switz.	13,642
Ecrins, Fr.	13,461
Monch, Switz.	13,448
Pollux, Switz.	13,422
Schreckhorn, Switz.	13,379
Ober Gabelhorn, Switz.	13,330
Gran Paradiso, It.	13,323

(continued)

Peak, country	Height (feet)
Bernina, It., Switz.	13,284
Fiescherhorn, Switz.	13,283
Grunhorn, Switz.	13,266
Lauteraarhorn, Switz.	13,261
Durrenhorn, Switz.	13,238
Allalinhorn, Switz.	13,213
Weissmies, Switz.	13,199
Lagginhorn, Switz.	13,156
Zupo, Switz.	13,120
Fletschhorn, Switz.	13,110
Adlerhorn, Switz.	13,081
Gletscherhorn, Switz.	13,068
Schalihorn, Switz.	13,040
Scerscen, Switz.	13,028
Eiger, Switz.	13,025
Jagerhorn, Switz.	13,024
Rottalhorn, Switz.	13,022

Pyrenees

Peak, country	Height (feet)
Aneto, Sp.	11,168
Posets, Sp.	11,073
Perdido, Sp.	11,007
Vignemale, Fr., Sp.	10,820
Long, Sp.	10,479
Estats, Sp.	10,304
Montcalm, Sp.	10,105

Caucasus (Europe-Asia)

Peak, country	Height (feet)
El'brus, Russia	18,510
Shkara, Russia	17,064
Dykh Tau, Russia	17,054
Kashtan Tau, Russia	16,877
Dzhangi Tau, Russia	16,565
Kazbek, Russia	16,558

Asia

Peak	Country	Height (feet)
Everest	Nepal-Tibet	29,028
K2 (Godwin Austen)	Kashmir	28,250
Kanchenjunga	India-Nepal	28,208
Lhotse I (Everest)	Nepal-Tibet	27,923
Makalu I	Nepal-Tibet	27,824
Lhotse II (Everest)	Nepal-Tibet	27,560
Dhaulagiri	Nepal	26,810
Manaslu I	Nepal	26,760
Cho Oyu	Nepal-Tibet	26,750
Nanga Parbat	Kashmir	26,660
Annapurna I	Nepal	26,504
Gasherbrum	Kashmir	26,470
Broad	Kashmir	26,400
Gosainthan	Tibet	26,287
Annapurna II	Nepal	26,041
Gyachung Kang	Nepal-Tibet	25,910
Disteghil Sar	Kashmir	25,868
Himalchuli	Nepal	25,801
Nuptse (Everest)	Nepal-Tibet	25,726
Masherbrum	Kashmir	25,660
Nanda Devi	India	25,645
Rakaposhi	Kashmir	25,550
Kamet	India-Tibet	25,447
Namcha Barwa	Tibet	25,445
Gurla Mandhata	Tibet	25,355
Ulugh Muz Tagh	Sinkiang-Tibet	25,340
Kungur	Sinkiang	25,325
Tirich Mir	Pakistan	25,230
Makalu II	Nepal-Tibet	25,120
Minya Konka	China	24,900
Kula Gangri	Bhutan-Tibet	24,784
Changtzu (Everest)	Nepal-Tibet	24,780
Muz Tagh Ata	Sinkiang	24,757
Skyang Kangri	Kashmir	24,750
Communism Peak	Russia	24,590
Jongsang Peak	India-Nepal	24,472
Pobedy Peak	Sinkiang-Kyrgyzstan	24,406
Sia Kangri	Kashmir	24,350
Haramosh Peak	Pakistan	24,270
Istoro Nal	Pakistan	24,240
Tent Peak	India-Nepal	24,165
Chomo Lhari	Bhutan-Tibet	24,040
Chamlang	Nepal	24,012
Kabru	India-Nepal	24,002
Alung Gangri	Tibet	24,000
Baltoro Kangri	Kashmir	23,990
Mussu Shan	Sinkiang	23,890
Mana	India	23,860
Baruntse	Nepal	23,688
Nepal Peak	India-Nepal	23,500
Amne Machin	China	23,490
Gauri Sankar	Nepal-Tibet	23,440
Badrinath	India	23,420
Nunkun	Kashmir	23,410
Lenin Peak	Tajikistan	23,405
Pyramid	India-Nepal	23,400
Api	Nepal	23,399
Pauhunri	India-Tibet	23,385
Trisul	India	23,360
Kangto	India-Tibet	23,260
Nyenchhen Thanglha	Tibet	23,255
Trisuli	India	23,210
Pumori	Nepal-Tibet	23,190
Dunagiri	India	23,184
Lombo Kangra	Tibet	23,165
Saipal	Nepal	23,100
Macha Pucchare	Nepal	22,958
Numbar	Nepal	22,817
Kanjiroba	Nepal	22,580
Ama Dablam	Nepal	22,350
Cho Polu	Nepal	22,093
Lingtren	Nepal-Tibet	21,972
Khumbutse	Nepal-Tibet	21,785
Hlako Gangri	Tibet	21,266
Mt. Grosvenor	China	21,190
Thagchhab Gangri	Tibet	20,970
Damavand	Iran	18,606
Ararat	Turkey	16,804

Antarctica

Peak	Height (feet)
Vinson Massif	16,864
Tyree	16,290
Shinn	15,750
Gardner	15,375
Epperly	15,100
Kirkpatrick	14,855
Elizabeth	14,698
Markham	14,290
Bell	14,117
Mackellar	14,098
Anderson	13,957
Bentley	13,934
Kaplan	13,878
Andrew Jackson	13,750
Sidley	13,720
Ostenso	13,710
Minto	13,668
Miller	13,650
Long Gables	13,620
Dickerson	13,517
Giovinetto	13,412
Wade	13,400
Fisher	13,386
Fridtjof Nansen	13,350
Wexler	13,202
Lister	13,200
Shear	13,100
Odishaw	13,008
Donaldson	12,894
Ray	12,808
Sellery	12,779
Waterman	12,730
Anne	12,703
Press	12,566
Falla	12,549
Rucker	12,520
Goldthwait	12,510
Morris	12,500
Erebus	12,450
Campbell	12,434
Don Pedro Christophersen	12,355
Lysaght	12,326
Huggins	12,247
Sabine	12,200
Astor	12,175
Mohl	12,172
Frankes	12,064
Jones	12,040
Gjelsvik	12,008
Coman	12,000

Some Notable U.S. Mountains

Name	Place	Height (feet)
Gannett Peak	Wyo.	13,804
Grand Teton	Wyo.	13,766
Kings	Utah	13,528
Cloud	Wyo.	13,175
Boundary	Nevada	13,140
Wheeler	N.M.	13,065
Granite	Montana	12,799
Borah	Idaho	12,662
Humphreys	Ariz.	12,633
Adams	Wash.	12,307
San Gorgonio	Cal.	11,502
Hood	Ore.	11,235
Lassen	Cal.	10,457
Granite	Cal.	10,321
Guadalupe	Texas	8,751
Olympus	Wash.	7,965
Harney	S.D.	7,242
Mitchell	N.C.	6,684
Clingmans Dome	N.C.-Tenn.	6,643
Washington	N.H.	6,288
Rogers	Va.	5,927
Marcy	N.Y.	5,344
Katahdin	Maine	5,268
Spruce Knob	W. Va.	4,862
Mansfield	Vt.	4,393
Black Mountain	Ky.	4,145

Ocean Areas and Average Depths

Four major bodies of water are recognized by geographers and mapmakers: the Pacific, Atlantic, Indian, and Arctic oceans. The Atlantic and Pacific oceans are considered divided at the equator into the No. and So. Atlantic; the No. and So. Pacific. The Arctic Ocean is the name for waters north of the continental land masses in the region of the Arctic Circle.

	Sq. miles	Avg. depth (feet)		Sq. miles	Avg. depth (feet)
Pacific Ocean	64,186,300	12,925	Hudson Bay	281,900	305
Atlantic Ocean	33,420,000	11,730	East China Sea	256,600	620
Indian Ocean	28,350,500	12,598	Andaman Sea	218,100	3,667
Arctic Ocean	5,105,700	3,407	Black Sea	196,100	3,906
South China Sea	1,148,500	4,802	Red Sea	174,900	1,764
Caribbean Sea	971,400	8,448	North Sea	164,900	308
Mediterranean Sea	969,100	4,926	Baltic Sea	147,500	180
Bering Sea	873,000	4,893	Yellow Sea	113,500	121
Gulf of Mexico	582,100	5,297	Persian Gulf	88,800	328
Sea of Okhotsk	537,500	3,192	Gulf of California	59,100	2,375
Sea of Japan	391,100	5,468			

Principal Ocean Depths

Source: Defense Mapping Agency Hydrographic/Topographic Center, U.S. Dept. of Defense

Name of area	Location		Depth Meters	Depth Fathoms	Feet
Pacific Ocean					
Mariana Trench	11°22'N	142°36'E	10,924	5,973	35,840
Tonga Trench	23°16'S	174°44'W	10,800	5,906	35,433
Philippine Trench	10°38'N	126°36'E	10,057	5,499	32,995
Kermadec Trench	31°53'S	177°21'W	10,047	5,494	32,963
Bonin Trench	24°30'N	143°24'E	9,994	5,464	32,788
Kuril Trench	44°15'N	150°34'E	9,750	5,331	31,988
Izu Trench	31°05'N	142°10'E	9,695	5,301	31,808
New Britain Trench	06°19'S	153°45'E	8,940	4,888	29,331
Yap Trench	08°33'N	138°02'E	8,527	4,663	27,976
Japan Trench	36°08'N	142°43'E	8,412	4,600	27,599
Peru-Chile Trench	23°18'S	71°14'W	8,064	4,409	26,457
Palau Trench	07°52'N	134°56'E	8,054	4,404	26,424
Aleutian Trench	50°51'N	177°11'E	7,679	4,199	25,194
New Hebrides Trench	20°36'S	168°37'E	7,570	4,139	24,836
North Ryukyu Trench	24°00'N	126°48'E	7,181	3,927	23,560
Mid. America Trench	14°02'N	93°39'W	6,662	3,643	21,857
Atlantic Ocean					
Puerto Rico Trench	19°55'N	65°27'W	8,605	4,705	28,232
So. Sandwich Trench	55°42'S	25°56'E	8,325	4,552	27,313
Romanche Gap	0°13'S	18°26'W	7,728	4,226	25,354
Cayman Trench	19°12'N	80°00'W	7,535	4,120	24,721
Brazil Basin	09°10'S	23°02'W	6,119	3,346	20,076
Indian Ocean					
Java Trench	10°19'S	109°58'E	7,125	3,896	23,376
Ob' Trench	09°45'S	67°18'E	6,874	3,759	22,553
Diamantina Trench	35°50'S	105°14'E	6,602	3,610	21,660
Vema Trench	09°08'S	67°15'E	6,402	3,501	21,004
Agulhas Basin	45°20'S	26°50'E	6,195	3,387	20,325
Arctic Ocean					
Eurasia Basin	82°23'N	19°31'E	5,450	2,980	17,881
Mediterranean Sea					
Ionian Basin	36°32'N	21°06'E	5,150	2,816	16,896

Note: Deeper depths have been reported in some of the above areas. However, they are not official unless confirmed by research vessels.

Principal World Rivers

Source: Geological Survey, U.S. Dept. of the Interior

River	Outflow	Length (Miles)	River	Outflow	Length (Miles)	River	Outflow	Length (Miles)
Albany	James Bay	610	Chang Jiang	E. China Sea	3,964	Dvina, North	White Sea	824
Amazon	Atlantic Ocean	4,000	Churchill, Man.	Hudson Bay	1,000	Dvina, West	Gulf of Riga	634
Amu	Aral Sea	1,578	Churchill, Que.	Atlantic Ocean	532	Ebro	Mediterranean	565
Amur	Tatar Strait	2,744	Colorado	Gulf of Calif.	1,450	Elbe	North Sea	724
Angara	Yenisey River	1,151	Columbia	Pacific Ocean	1,243	Euphrates	Shatt al-Arab	1,700
Arkansas	Mississippi	1,459	Congo	Atlantic Ocean	2,718	Fraser	Str. of Georgia	850
Back	Arctic Ocean	605	Danube	Black Sea	1,776	Gambia	Atlantic Ocean	700
Brahmaputra	Bay of Bengal	1,800	Dnieper	Black Sea	1,420	Ganges	Bay of Bengal	1,560
Bug, Southern	Dnieper River	532	Dniester	Black Sea	877	Garonne	Bay of Biscay	357
Bug, Western	Wisla River	481	Don	Sea of Azov	1,224	Huang	Yellow Sea	2,903
Canadian	Arkansas River	906	Drava	Danube River	447	Indus	Arabian Sea	1,800

River	Outflow	Length (Miles)
Irrawaddy	Bay of Bengal	1,337
Japura	Amazon River	1,750
Jordan	Dead Sea	200
Kootenay	Columbia River	485
Lena	Laptev Sea	2,734
Loire	Bay of Biscay	634
Mackenzie	Arctic Ocean	2,635
Madeira	Amazon River	2,013
Magdalena	Caribbean Sea	956
Marne	Seine River	326
Mekong	S. China Sea	2,600
Meuse	North Sea	580
Mississippi	Gulf of Mexico	2,340
Missouri	Mississippi	2,540
Murray-Darling	Indian Ocean	2,310
Negro	Amazon	1,400
Nelson	Hudson Bay	410
Niger	Gulf of Guinea	2,590
Nile	Mediterranean	4,160
Ob-Irtysh	Gulf of Ob	3,362
Oder	Baltic Sea	567
Ohio	Mississippi	1,310
Orange	Atlantic Ocean	1,300
Orinoco	Atantic Ocean	1,600
Ottawa	St. Lawrence R.	790
Paraguay	Parana River	1,584
Parana	Rio de la Plata	2,485
Peace	Slave River	1,210
Pilcomayo	Paraguay River	1,000
Po	Adriatic Sea	405
Purus	Amazon River	2,100
Red	Mississippi	1,290
Red River of N.	Lake Winnipeg	545
Rhine	North Sea	820
Rhone	Gulf of Lions	505
Rio de la Plata	Atlantic Ocean	150
Rio Grande	Gulf of Mexico	1,900
Rio Roosevelt	Aripuana	400
Saguenay	St. Lawrence R.	434
St. John	Bay of Fundy	418
St. Lawrence	Gulf of St. Law.	800
Salween	Andaman Sea	1,500
Sao Francisco	Atlantic Ocean	1,988
Saskatchewan	Lake Winnipeg	1,205
Seine	English Chan.	496
Shannon	Atlantic Ocean	230
Snake	Columbia River	1,038
Songhua	Amur River	1,150
Syr	Aral Sea	1,370
Tajo, Tagus	Atlantic Ocean	626
Tennessee	Ohio River	652
Thames	North Sea	236
Tiber	Tyrrhenian Sea	252
Tigris	Shatt al-Arab	1,180
Tisza	Danube River	600
Tocantins	Para River	1,677
Ural	Caspian Sea	1,575
Uruguay	Rio de la Plata	1,000
Volga	Caspian Sea	2,194
Weser	North Sea	454
Wisla	Bay of Danzig	675
Xi	S. China Sea	1,200
Yellow (See Huang)		
Yenisey	Kara Sea	2,543
Yukon	Bering Sea	1,979
Zambezi	Indian Ocean	1,700

Major Rivers in North America

Source: Geological Survey, U.S. Dept. of the Interior

River	Source or Upper Limit of Length	Outflow	Miles
Alabama	Gilmer County, Ga.	Mobile River	729
Albany	Lake St. Joseph, Ontario	James Bay	610
Allegheny	Potter County, Pa.	Ohio River	325
Altamaha-Ocmulgee	Junction of Yellow and South Rivers, Newton County, Ga.	Atlantic Ocean	392
Apalachicola-Chattahoochee	Towns County, Ga.	Gulf of Mexico	524
Arkansas	Lake County, Col.	Mississippi River	1,459
Assiniboine	Eastern Saskatchewan	Red River	450
Attawapiskat	Attawapiskat, Ontario	James Bay	465
Back (N.W.T.)	Contwoyto Lake	Chantrey Inlet	605
Big Black (Miss.)	Webster County, Miss.	Mississippi River	330
Brazos	Junction of Salt and Double Mountain Forks, Stonewall County, Tex.	Gulf of Mexico	923
Canadian	Las Animas County, Col.	Arkansas River	906
Cedar (Iowa)	Dodge County, Minn.	Iowa River	329
Cheyenne	Junction of Antelope Creek and Dry Fork, Converse County, Wyo.	Missouri River	290
Churchill	Methy Lake, Saskatchewan	Hudson Bay	1,000
Cimarron	Colfax County, N.M.	Arkansas River	600
Colorado (Ariz.)	Rocky Mountain National Park, Col. (90 miles in Mexico)	Gulf of Cal.	1,450
Colorado (Texas)	West Texas	Matagorda Bay	862
Columbia	Columbia Lake, British Columbia	Pacific Ocean, bet. Ore. and Wash.	1,243
Columbia, Upper	Columbia Lake, British Columbia	To mouth of Snake River	890
Connecticut	Third Connecticut Lake, N.H.	L.I. Sound, Conn.	407
Coppermine (N.W.T.)	Lac de Gras	Coronation Gulf (Arctic Ocean)	525
Cumberland	Letcher County, Ky.	Ohio River	720
Delaware	Schoharie County, N.Y.	Liston Point, Delaware Bay	390
Fraser	Near Mount Robson (on Continental Divide)	Strait of Georgia	850
Gila	Catron County, N.M.	Colorado River	649
Green (Ut.-Wyo.)	Junction of Wells and Trail Creeks, Sublette County, Wyo.	Colorado River	730
Hamilton (Lab.)	Lake Ashuanipi	Atlantic Ocean	532
Hudson	Henderson Lake, Essex County, N.Y.	Upper N.Y. Bay	306
Illinois	St. Joseph County, Ind.	Mississippi River	420
James (N.D.-S.D.)	Wells County, N.D.	Missouri River	710
James (Va.)	Junction of Jackson and Cowpasture Rivers, Botetourt County, Va.	Hampton Roads	340
Kanawha-New	Junction of North and South Forks of New River, N.C.	Ohio River	352
Kentucky	Junction of North and Middle Forks, Lee County, Ky.	Ohio River	259
Klamath	Lake Ewauna, Klamath Falls, Ore.	Pacific Ocean	250
Koyukuk	Endicott Mountains, Alaska	Yukon River	470
Kuskokwim	Alaska Range	Kuskokwim Bay	724
Liard	Southern Yukon, Alaska	Mackenzie River	693
Little Missouri	Crook County, Wyo.	Missouri River	560
Mackenzie	Great Slave Lake, N.W.T.	Arctic Ocean	2,635
Milk	Junction of North and South Forks, Alberta	Missouri River	625
Minnesota	Big Stone Lake, Minn.	Mississippi River	332
Mississippi	Lake Itasca, Minn.	Mouth of Southwest Pass	2,340
Mississippi, Upper	Lake Itasca, Minn.	To mouth of Missouri River	1,171
Mississippi-Missouri-Red Rock	Source of Red Rock, Beaverhead Co., Mon.	Mouth of Southwest Pass	3,710
Missouri	Junction of Jefferson, Madison, and Gallatin rivers, Madison County, Mon.	Mississippi River	2,315
Missouri-Red Rock	Source of Red Rock, Beaverhead Co., Mon.	Mississippi River	2,540
Mobile-Alabama-Coosa	Gilmer County, Ga.	Mobile Bay	774
Nelson (Manitoba)	Lake Winnipeg	Hudson Bay	410

River	Source or Upper Limit of Length	Outflow	Miles
Neosho	Morris County, Kan.	Arkansas River, Okla.	460
Niobrara	Niobrara County, Wyo.	Missouri River, Neb.	431
North Canadian	Union County, N.M.	Canadian River, Okla.	800
North Platte	Junction of Grizzly and Little Grizzly creeks, Jackson County, Col.	Platte River, Neb.	618
Ohio	Junction of Allegheny and Monongahela rivers, Pittsburgh, Pa.	Mississippi River	981
Ohio-Allegheny	Potter County, Pa.	Mississippi River	1,306
Osage	East-central Kansas	Missouri River	500
Ottawa	Lake Capimitchigama	St. Lawrence River	790
Ouachita	Polk County, Ark.	Red River	605
Peace	Stikine Mountains, B.C.	Slave River	1,210
Pearl	Neshoba County, Miss.	Gulf of Mexico	411
Pecos	Mora County, N.M.	Rio Grande	926
Pee Dee-Yadkin	Watauga County, N.C.	Winyah Bay	435
Pend Oreille-Clark Fork	Near Butte, Mon.	Columbia River	531
Platte	Junction of North and South Platte Rivers, Neb.	Missouri River	310
Porcupine	Ogilvie Mountains, Alaska	Yukon River, Alaska	569
Potomac	Garrett County, Md.	Chesapeake Bay	383
Powder	Junction of South and Middle Forks, Wyo.	Yellowstone River	375
Red (Okla.-Tex.-La.)	Curry County, N.M.	Mississippi River	1,290
Red River of the North	Junction of Otter Tail and Bois de Sioux Rivers, Wilkin County, Minn.	Lake Winnipeg	545
Republican	Junction of North Fork and Arikaree River, Neb.	Kansas River	445
Rio Grande	San Juan County, Col.	Gulf of Mexico	1,900
Roanoke	Junction of North and South Forks, Montgomery County, Va.	Albemarle Sound	380
Rock (Ill.-Wis.)	Dodge County, Wis.	Mississippi River	300
Sabine	Junction of South and Caddo Forks, Hunt County, Tex.	Sabine Lake	380
Sacramento	Siskiyou County, Cal.	Suisun Bay	377
St. Francis	Iron County, Mo.	Mississippi River	425
St. Lawrence	Lake Ontario	Gulf of St. Lawrence (Atlantic Ocean)	800
Salmon (Idaho)	Custer County, Ida.	Snake River	420
San Joaquin	Junction of South and Middle Forks, Madera County, Cal.	Suisun Bay	350
San Juan	Silver Lake, Archuleta County, Col.	Colorado River	360
Santee-Wateree-Catawba	McDowell County, N.C.	Atlantic Ocean	538
Saskatchewan, North	Rocky Mountains	Saskatchewan R.	800
Saskatchewan, South	Rocky Mountains	Saskatchewan R.	865
Savannah	Junction of Seneca and Tugaloo rivers, Anderson County, S.C.	Atlantic Ocean, Ga.-S.C.	314
Severn (Ontario)	Sandy Lake	Hudson Bay	610
Smoky Hill	Cheyenne County, Col.	Kansas River, Kan.	540
Snake	Teton County, Wyo.	Columbia River, Wash.	1,038
South Platte	Junction of South and Middle Forks, Park County, Col.	Platte River	424
Susitna	Alaska Range	Cook Inlet	313
Susquehanna	Otsego Lake, Otsego County, N.Y.	Chesapeake Bay	444
Tallahatchie	Tippah County, Miss.	Yazoo River	301
Tanana	Wrangell Mountains, Alaska	Yukon River	659
Tennessee	Junction of French Broad and Holston Rivers	Ohio River	652
Tennessee-French Broad	Transylvania County, N.C.	Ohio River	883
Tombigbee	Prentiss County, Miss.	Mobile River	525
Trinity	North of Dallas, Tex.	Galveston Bay	360
Wabash	Darke County, Oh.	Ohio River	512
Washita	Hemphill County, Tex.	Red River, Okla.	500
White (Ark.-Mo.)	Madison County, Ark.	Mississippi River	722
Willamette	Douglas County, Ore.	Columbia River	309
Wind-Bighorn	Junction of Wind and Little Wind Rivers, Fremont Co., Wyo. (Source of Wind R. is Togwotee Pass, Teton Co., Wyo.)	Yellowstone River	336
Wisconsin	Lac Vieux Desert, Vilas County, Wis.	Mississippi River	430
Yellowstone	Park County, Wyo.	Missouri River	692
Yukon	Coast Mountains of British Columbia	Bering Sea	1,979

Lakes of the World

Source: Geological Survey, U.S. Dept. of the Interior

A lake is a body of water surrounded by land. Although some lakes are called seas, they are lakes by definition. The Caspian Sea is bounded by the Soviet Union and Iran and is fed by eight rivers.

Name	Continent	Area (sq. mi.)	Length (miles)	Depth (feet)	Elevation (feet)
Caspian Sea	Asia-Europe	143,244	760	3,363	−92
Superior	North America	31,700	350	1,330	600
Victoria	Africa	26,828	250	270	3,720
Aral Sea	Asia	24,904(A)	280	220	174
Huron	North America	23,000	206	750	579
Michigan	North America	22,300	307	923	579
Tanganyika	Africa	12,700	420	4,823	2,534
Baykal	Asia	12,162	395	5,315	1,493
Great Bear	North America	12,096	192	1,463	512
Nyasa	Africa	11,150	360	2,280	1,550

(*continued*)

Name	Continent	Area (sq. mi.)	Length (miles)	Depth (feet)	Elevation (feet)
Great Slave	North America	11,031	298	2,015	513
Erie	North America	9,910	241	210	570
Winnipeg	North America	9,417	266	60	713
Ontario	North America	7,550	193	802	245
Balkhash	Asia	7,115	376	85	1,115
Ladoga	Europe	6,835	124	738	13
Chad	Africa	6,300	175	24	787
Maracaibo	South America	5,217	133	115	Sea level
Onega	Europe	3,710	145	328	108
Eyre	Australia	3,600	90	4	−52
Volta	Africa	3,276	250	....	....
Titicaca	South America	3,200	122	922	12,500
Nicaragua	North America	3,100	102	230	102
Athabasca	North America	3,064	208	407	700
Reindeer	North America	2,568	143	720	1,106
Rudolf	Africa	2,473	154	240	1,230
Issyk Kul	Asia	2,355	115	2,303	5,279
Torrens	Australia	2,230	130	....	92
Vanern	Europe	2,156	91	328	144
Nettilling	North America	2,140	67	....	95
Winnipegosis	North America	2,075	141	38	830
Albert	Africa	2,075	100	168	2,030
Kariba	Africa	2,050	175	390	1,590
Nipigon	North America	1,872	72	540	1,050
Gairdner	Australia	1,840	90	....	112
Urmia	Asia	1,815	90	49	4,180
Manitoba	North America	1,799	140	12	813

(A) Probably less because of the diversion of feeder rivers.

The Great Lakes

Source: National Ocean Service, U.S. Dept. of Commerce

The Great Lakes form the largest body of fresh water in the world and with their connecting waterways are the largest inland water transportation unit. Draining the great North Central basin of the U.S., they enable shipping to reach the Atlantic via their outlet, the St. Lawrence R., and also the Gulf of Mexico via the Illinois Waterway, from Lake Michigan to the Mississippi R. A third outlet connects with the Hudson R. and thence the Atlantic via the N. Y. State Barge Canal System. Traffic on the Illinois Waterway and the N.Y. State Barge Canal System is limited to recreational boating and small shipping vessels.

Only one of the lakes, Lake Michigan, is wholly in the United States; the others are shared with Canada. Ships move from the shores of Lake Superior to Whitefish Bay at the east end of the lake, thence through the Soo (Sault Ste. Marie) locks, through the St. Mary's River and into Lake Huron. To reach Gary, and Port of Indiana and South Chicago, Ill., ships move west from Lake Huron to Lake Michigan through the Straits of Mackinac.

Lake Superior is 600 feet above mean water level at Point-au-Pere, Quebec, on the International Great Lakes Datum (1955). From Duluth, Minn., to the eastern end of Lake Ontario is 1,156 mi.

	Superior	Michigan	Huron	Erie	Ontario
Length in miles	350	307	206	241	193
Breadth in miles	160	118	183	57	53
Deepest soundings in feet	1,330	923	750	210	802
Volume of water in cubic miles	2,900	1,180	850	116	393
Area (sq. miles) water surface—U.S.	20,600	22,300	9,100	4,980	3,560
Canada	11,100	.....	13,900	4,930	3,990
Area (sq. miles) entire drainage basin—U.S.	16,900	45,600	16,200	18,000	15,200
Canada	32,400	.....	35,500	4,720	12,100
Total Area (sq. miles) U.S. and Canada	**81,000**	**67,900**	**74,700**	**32,630**	**34,850**
Mean surface above mean water level at Point-au-Pere, Quebec, aver. level in feet (1900-1988)	600.61	578.34	578.34	570.53	244.74
Latitude, North	46° 25′	41° 37′	43° 00′	41° 23′	43° 11′
	49° 00′	46° 06′	46° 17′	42° 52′	44° 15′
Longitude, West	84° 22′	84° 45′	79° 43′	78° 51′	76° 03′
	92° 06′	88° 02′	84° 45′	83° 29′	79° 53′
National boundary line in miles	282.8	None	260.8	251.5	174.6
United States shore line (mainland only) miles	863	1,400	580	431	300

Highest and Lowest Continental Altitudes

Source: National Geographic Society

Continent	Highest point	Elevation (feet)	Lowest point	Elevation (feet) below sea level
Asia	Mount Everest, Nepal-Tibet	29,028	Dead Sea, Israel-Jordan	1,312
South America	Mount Aconcagua, Argentina	22,834	Valdes Peninsula, Argentina	131
North America	Mount McKinley, Alaska	20,320	Death Valley, California	282
Africa	Kilimanjaro, Tanzania	19,340	Lake Assal, Djibouti	512
Europe	Mount El'brus, Russia	18,510	Caspian Sea, Russia, Azerbaijan, Turkmenistan, Kazakhstan	92
Antarctica	Vinson Massif	16,864	Unknown	...
Australia	Mount Kosciusko, New South Wales	7,310	Lake Eyre, South Australia	52

Famous Waterfalls

Source: National Geographic Society

The earth has thousands of waterfalls, some of considerable magnitude. Their importance is determined not only by height but volume of flow, steadiness of flow, crest width, whether the water drops sheerly or over a sloping surface, and in one leap or a succession of leaps. A series of low falls flowing over a considerable distance is known as a cascade.

Estimated mean annual flow, in cubic feet per second, of major waterfalls are: Niagara, 212,200; Paulo Afonso, 100,000; Urubupunga, 97,000; Iguazu, 61,000; Patos-Maribondo, 53,000; Victoria, 35,400; and Kaieteur, 23,400.

Height = total drop in feet in one or more leaps. † = falls of more than one leap; * = falls that diminish greatly seasonally; ** = falls that reduce to a trickle or are dry for part of each year. If river names not shown, they are same as the falls. R. = river; L. = lake; (C) = cascade type.

Africa

Name and location	Elevation (Feet)
Angola	
Ruacana, Cuene R.	406
Ethiopia	
Fincha	508
Lesotho	
*Maletsunyane	630
Zimbabwe-Zambia	
*Victoria, Zambezi R.	343
South Africa	
*Augrabies, Orange R.	480
† Tugela	2,014
Tanzania-Zambia	
*Kalambo	726

Asia

Name and location	Elevation (Feet)
India—*Cauvery	330
*Jog (Gersoppa), Sharavathi R.	830
Japan	
*Kegon, Daiya R.	330

Australasia

Name and location	Elevation (Feet)
Australia	
New South Wales	
Wentworth	614
Wollomombi	1,100
Queensland	
Tully	885
† Wallaman, Stony Cr.	1,137
New Zealand	
Helena	890
† Sutherland, Arthur R.	1,904

Europe

Name and location	Elevation (Feet)
Austria—† Gastein	492
† Krimml	1,312
France—*Gavarnie	1,385
Great Britain—Scotland	
Glomach	370
Wales	
Rhaiadr	240
Italy—Frua, Toce R. (C)	470
Norway	
Mardalsfossen (Northern)	1,535
† Mardalsfossen (Southern)	2,149
† **Skjeggedal, Nybuai R.	1,378
**Skykje	984
Vetti, Morka-Koldedola R.	900
Sweden	
† Handol	427
Switzerland	
Giessbach (C)	984
† Reichenbach	656
† Simmen	459
Staubbach	984
† Trummelbach	1,312

North America

Name and location	Elevation (Feet)
Canada	
Alberta	
Panther, Nigel Cr.	600
British Columbia	
† Della	1,443
† Takakkaw, Daly Glacier	1,200
Quebec	
Montmorency	274
Canada—United States	
Niagara: American	182
Horseshoe	173
United States	
California	
*Feather, Fall R.	640
Yosemite National Park	
*Bridalveil	620
*Illilouette	370
*Nevada, Merced R.	594
**Ribbon	1,612
**Silver Strand, Meadow Br.	1,170
*Vernal, Merced R.	317
† **Yosemite	2,425
Colorado	
† Seven, South Cheyenne Cr.	300
Hawaii	
Akaka, Kolekole Str.	442
Idaho	
**Shoshone, Snake R.	212
Kentucky	
Cumberland	68
Maryland	
*Great, Potomac R. (C)	71
Minnesota	
**Minnehaha	53
New Jersey	
Passaic	70
New York	
*Taughannock	215
Oregon	
† Multnomah	620
Tennessee	
Fall Creek	256
Washington	
Mt. Rainier Natl. Park	
Sluiskin, Paradise R.	300
**Snoqualmie	268
Wisconsin	
*Big Manitou, Black R. (C)	165
Wyoming	
Yellowstone Natl. Pk. Tower	132
*Yellowstone (upper)	109
*Yellowstone (lower)	308
Mexico	
El Salto	218

South America

Name and location	Elevation (Feet)
Argentina-Brazil	
Iguazu	230
Brazil	
Glass	1,325
Patos-Maribondo, Grande R.	115
Paulo Afonso, Sao Francisco R.	275
Colombia	
Catarata de Candelas, Cusiana R.	984
*Tequendama, Bogota R.	427
Ecuador	
*Agoyan, Pastaza R.	200
Guyana	
Kaieteur, Potaro R.	741
Great, Kamarang R.	1,600
† Marina, Ipobe R.	500
Venezuela—	
† *Angel	3,212
Cuquenan	2,000

Notable Deserts of the World

Arabian (Eastern), 70,000 sq. mi. in Egypt between the Nile river and Red Sea, extending southward into Sudan.

Atacama, 600 mi. long area rich in nitrate and copper deposits in N. Chile.

Chihuahuan, 140,000 sq. mi. in Tex., N.M., Ariz., and Mexico.

Death Valley, 3,300 sq. mi. in E. Cal. and SW Nev. Contains lowest point below sea level (282 ft.) in Western Hemisphere.

Gibson, 120,000 sq. mi. in the interior of W. Australia.

Gobi, 500,000 sq. mi. in Mongolia and China.

Great Sandy, 150,000 sq. mi. in W. Australia.

Great Victoria, 150,000 sq. mi. in W. and S. Australia.

Kalahari, 225,000 sq. mi. in southern Africa.

Kara-Kum, 120,000 sq. mi. in Turkmenistan.

Kyzyl Kum, 100,000 sq. mi. in Kazakhstan & Uzbekistan.

Libyan, 450,000 sq. mi. in the Sahara extending from Lybia through SW Egypt into Sudan.

Lut (Dasht-e Lut), 20,000 sq. mi. in E. Iran.

Mojave, 15,000 sq. mi. in S. Cal.

Namib, long narrow area extending 800 miles along SW coast of Africa.

Nubian, 100,000 sq. mi. in the Sahara in NE Sudan.

Painted Desert, section of high plateau in N. Ariz. extending 150 mi.

Rub al Khali (Empty Quarter), 250,000 sq. mi. in the south Arabian Peninsula.

Sahara, 3,500,000 sq. mi. in N. Africa extending westward to the Atlantic. Largest desert in the world.

Sonoran, 70,000 sq. mi. in SW Ariz. and SE Cal. extending into Mexico.

Syrian, 100,000 sq. mi. arid wasteland extending over much of N. Saudi Arabia, E. Jordan, S. Syria, and W. Iraq.

Taklimakan, 140,000 sq. mi. in Sinkiang Province, China.

Thar (Great Indian), 100,000 sq. mi. arid area extending 400 mi. along India-Pakistan border.

Important Islands and Their Areas

Figure in parentheses shows rank among the world's 10 largest islands; some islands have not been surveyed accurately; in such cases estimated areas are shown.

Location-Ownership
Area in square miles

Arctic Ocean

Location-Ownership	Area
Canadian	
Axel Heiberg	15,779
Baffin (5)	183,810
Banks	27,038
Bathurst	7,609
Devon	20,861
Ellesmere (10)	82,119
Melville	16,369
Prince of Wales	12,830
Somerset	9,370
Southampton	15,700
Victoria (9)	81,930
Norwegian	
Svalbard	23,940
Nordaustlandet	5,410
Spitsbergen	15,060
Russian	
Franz Josef Land	8,000
Novaya Zemlya (two is.)	31,730
Wrangel	2,800

Atlantic Ocean

Location-Ownership	Area
Anticosti, Canada	3,043
Ascension, UK	34
Azores, Portugal	888
Faial	67
Sao Miguel	291
Bahamas	5,386
Bermuda Is., UK	20
Bioko Is. Equatorial Guinea	785
Block, Rhode Island	10
Canary Is., Spain	2,808
Fuerteventura	668
Gran Canaria	592
Tenerife	795
Cape Breton, Canada	3,970
Cape Verde Is.	1,557
Faeroe Is., Denmark	540
Falkland Is., UK	4,700
Fernando de Noronha Archipelago, Brazil	7
Greenland, Denmark (1)	840,000
Iceland	39,769
Long Island, N. Y.	1,396
Madeira Is., Portugal	307
Marajo, Brazil	15,444
Martha's Vineyard, Mass.	108
Mount Desert, Me.	108
Nantucket, Mass.	57
Newfoundland, Canada	42,030
Prince Edward, Canada	2,184
St. Helena, UK	47
South Georgia, UK	1,450
Tierra del Fuego, Chile and Argentina	18,800
Tristan da Cunha, UK	40
British Isles	
Great Britain, mainland (8)	84,200
Channel Islands	75
Guernsey	24
Jersey	45
Sark	2
Hebrides	2,744
Ireland	32,599
Irish Republic	27,136
Northern Ireland	5,463
Man	227
Orkney Is.	390
Scilly Is.	6
Shetland Is.	567
Skye	670
Wight	147

Baltic Sea

Location-Ownership	Area
Aland Is., Finland	581
Bornholm, Denmark	227
Gotland, Sweden	1,159

Caribbean Sea

Location-Ownership	Area
Antigua	108
Aruba, Netherlands	75
Barbados	166
Cuba	44,218
Isle of Youth	1,182
Curacao, Netherlands	171
Dominica	290
Guadeloupe, France	687
Hispaniola, Haiti and Dominican Republic	29,371
Jamaica	4,244
Martinique, France	425
Puerto Rico, U.S.	3,435
Tobago	116
Trinidad	1,864
Virgin Is., UK	59
Virgin Is., U.S.	132

Indian Ocean

Location-Ownership	Area
Andaman Is., India	2,500
Madagascar (4)	226,658
Mauritius	720
Pemba, Tanzania	380
Reunion, France	969
Seychelles	171
Sri Lanka	25,332
Zanzibar, Tanzania	640
Persian Gulf	
Bahrain	255

Mediterranean Sea

Location-Ownership	Area
Balearic Is., Spain	1,936
Corfu, Greece	229
Corsica, France	3,369
Crete, Greece	3,189
Cyprus	3,572
Elba, Italy	86
Euboea, Greece	1,411
Malta	95
Rhodes, Greece	540
Sardinia, Italy	9,262
Sicily, Italy	9,822

Pacific Ocean

Location-Ownership	Area
Aleutian Is., U.S.	6,821
Adak	289
Amchitka	121
Attu	388
Kanaga	135
Kiska	110
Tanaga	209
Umnak	675
Unalaska	1,064
Unimak	1,600
Canton, Kiribati*	4
Caroline Is.	472
Christmas, Kiribati*	94
Clipperton, France	2
Diomede, Big, Russia	11
Diomede, Little, U.S.	2
Easter, Chile	69
Fiji	7,056
Vanua Levu	2,242
Viti Levu	4,109
Funafuti, Tuvalu*	2
Galapagos Is., Ecuador	3,043
Guadalcanal	2,180
Guam	209
Hainan, China	13,000
Hawaiian Is., U.S.	6,450
Hawaii	4,037
Oahu	593
Hong Kong	29
Japan	145,809
Hokkaido	30,144
Honshu (7)	87,805
Iwo Jima	8
Kyushu	14,114
Okinawa	459
Shikoku	7,049
Kodiak, U.S.	3,670
Marquesas Is., France	492
Marshall Is.	70
Bikini*	2
Nauru	8
New Caledonia, France	6,530
New Guinea (2)	306,000
New Zealand	103,883
Chatham	372
North	44,035
South	58,305
Stewart	674
Northern Mariana Is.	184
Philippines	115,831
Leyte	2,787
Luzon	40,880
Mindanao	36,775
Mindoro	3,790
Negros	4,907
Palawan	4,554
Panay	4,446
Samar	5,050
Quemoy	56
Sakhalin, Russia	29,500
Samoa Is.	1,177
American Samoa	77
Tutuila	52
Samoa (Western)	1,133
Savaii	670
Upolu	429
Santa Catalina, U.S.	72
Tahiti, France	402
Taiwan	13,823
Tasmania, Australia	26,178
Tonga Is.	270
Vancouver, Canada	12,079
Vanuatu	5,700

East Indies

Location-Ownership	Area
Bali, Indonesia	2,171
Borneo, Indonesia-Malaysia, Brunei (3)	280,100
Celebes, Indonesia	69,000
Java, Indonesia	48,900
Madura, Indonesia	2,113
Moluccas, Indonesia	32,307
New Britain, Papua New Guinea	14,093
New Ireland, Papua New Guinea	3,707
Sumatra, Indonesia (6)	165,000
Timor	13,094

* **Atolls:** Bikini (lagoon area, 230 sq. mi., land area 2 sq. mi.); Canton (lagoon 20 sq. mi., land 4 sq. mi.), Kiribati; Christmas (lagoon 140 sq. mi., land 94 sq. mi.), Kiribati; Funafuti (lagoon 84 sq. mi., land 2 sq. mi.), Tuvalu. **Australia,** often called an island, is a continent.

Islands in minor waters; Manhattan (22 sq mi.) Staten (59 sq. mi.) and Governors (173 acres), all in New York Harbor, U.S.; Isle Royale (209 sq. mi.), Lake Superior, U.S.; Manitoulin (1,068 sq. mi.), Lake Huron, Canada; Pinang (110 sq. mi.), Strait of Malacca, Malaysia; Singapore (239 sq. mi.), Singapore Strait, Singapore.

DISASTERS

Some Notable Shipwrecks Since 1850

(Figures indicate estimated lives lost; as of mid-1991)

1854, Mar.—City of Glasgow; British steamer missing in North Atlantic; 480.

1854, Sept. 27—Arctic; U.S. (Collins Line) steamer sunk in collision with French steamer Vesta near Cape Race; 285-351.

1856, Jan. 23—Pacific; U.S. (Collins Line) steamer missing in North Atlantic; 186-286.

1858, Sept. 23—Austria; German steamer destroyed by fire in North Atlantic; 471.

1863, Apr. 27—Anglo-Saxon; British steamer wrecked at Cape Race; 238.

1865, Apr. 27—Sultana; a Mississippi River steamer blew up near Memphis, Tenn; 1,450.

1869, Oct. 27—Stonewall; steamer burned on Mississippi River below Cairo, Ill.; 200.

1870, Jan. 25—City of Boston; British (Inman Line) steamer vanished between New York and Liverpool; 177.

1870, Oct. 19—Cambria; British steamer wrecked off northern Ireland; 196.

1872, Nov. 7—Mary Celeste; U.S. half-brig sailed from New York for Genoa; found abandoned in Atlantic 4 weeks later in mystery of sea; crew never heard from; loss of life unknown.

1873, Jan. 22—Northfleet; British steamer foundered off Dungeness, England; 300.

1873, Apr. 1—Atlantic; British (White Star) steamer wrecked off Nova Scotia; 585.

1873, Nov. 23—Ville du Havre; French steamer, sunk after collision with British sailing ship Loch Earn; 226.

1875, May 7—Schiller; German steamer wrecked off Scilly Isles; 312.

1875, Nov. 4—Pacific; U.S. steamer sunk after collision off Cape Flattery; 236.

1878, Sept. 3—Princess Alice; British steamer sank after collision in Thames River; 700.

1878, Dec. 18—Byzantin; French steamer sank after Dardanelles collision; 210.

1881, May 24—Victoria; steamer capsized in Thames River, Canada; 200.

1883, Jan. 19—Cimbria; German steamer sunk in collision with British steamer Sultan in North Sea; 389.

1887, Nov. 15—Wah Yeung; British steamer burned at sea; 400.

1890, Feb. 17—Duburg; British steamer wrecked, China Sea; 400.

1890, Sept. 19—Ertogrul; Turkish frigate foundered off Japan; 540.

1891, Mar. 17—Utopia; British steamer sank in collision with British ironclad Anson off Gibraltar; 562.

1895, Jan. 30—Elbe; German steamer sank in collision with British steamer Craithie in North Sea; 332.

1895, Mar. 11—Reina Regenta; Spanish cruiser foundered near Gibraltar; 400.

1898, Feb. 15—Maine; U.S. battleship blown up in Havana Harbor; 260.

1898, July 4—La Bourgogne; French steamer sunk in collision with British sailing ship Cromartyshire off Nova Scotia; 549.

1898, Nov. 26—Portland; U.S. steamer wrecked off Cape Cod; 157.

1904, June 15—General Slocum; excursion steamer burned in East River, New York City; 1,030.

1904, June 28—Norge; Danish steamer wrecked on Rockall Island, Scotland; 620.

1906, Aug. 4—Sirio; Italian steamer wrecked off Cape Palos, Spain; 350.

1908, Mar. 23—Matsu Maru; Japanese steamer sank in collision near Hakodate, Japan; 300.

1909, Aug. 1—Waratah; British steamer, Sydney to London, vanished; 300.

1910, Feb. 9—General Chanzy; French steamer wrecked off Minorca, Spain; 200.

1911, Sept. 25—Liberté; French battleship exploded at Toulon; 285.

1912, Mar. 5—Principe de Asturias; Spanish steamer wrecked off Spain; 500.

1912, Apr. 14-15—Titanic; British (White Star) steamer hit iceberg in North Atlantic; 1,503.

1912, Sept. 28—Kichemaru; Japanese steamer sank off Japanese coast; 1,000.

1914, May 29—Empress of Ireland; British (Canadian Pacific) steamer sunk in collision with Norwegian collier in St. Lawrence River; 1,014.

1915, May 7—Lusitania; British (Cunard Line) steamer torpedoed and sunk by German submarine off Ireland; 1,198.

1915, July 24—Eastland; excursion steamer capsized in Chicago River; 812.

1916, Feb. 26—Provence; French cruiser sank in Mediterranean; 3,100.

1916, Mar. 3—Principe de Asturias; Spanish steamer wrecked near Santos, Brazil; 558.

1916, Aug. 29—Hsin Yu; Chinese steamer sank off Chinese coast; 1,000.

1917, Dec. 6—Mont Blanc, Imo; French ammunition ship and Belgian steamer collided in Halifax Harbor; 1,600.

1918, Apr. 25—Kiang-Kwan Chinese steamer sank in collision off Hankow; 500.

1918, July 12—Kawachi; Japanese battleship blew up in Tokayama Bay; 500.

1918, Oct. 25—Princess Sophia; Canadian steamer sank off Alaskan coast; 398.

1919, Jan. 17—Chaonia; French steamer lost in Straits of Messina, Italy; 460.

1919, Sept. 9—Valbanera; Spanish steamer lost off Florida coast; 500.

1921, Mar. 18—Hong Kong; steamer wrecked in South China Sea; 1,000.

1922, Aug. 26—Niitaka; Japanese cruiser sank in storm off Kamchatka, USSR; 300.

1927, Oct. 25—Principessa Mafalda; Italian steamer blew up, sank off Porto Seguro, Brazil; 314.

1928, Nov. 12—Vestris; British steamer sank in gale off Virginia; 113.

1934, Sept. 8—Morro Castle; U.S. steamer, Havana to New York, burned off Asbury Park, N.J.; 134.

1939, May 23—Squalus; U.S. submarine sank off Portsmouth, N.H.; 26.

1939, June 1—Thetis; British submarine, sank in Liverpool Bay; 99.

1942, Feb. 18—Truxtun and Pollux; U.S. destroyer and cargo ship ran aground, sank off Newfoundland; 204.

1942, Oct. 2—Curacao; British cruiser sank after collision with liner Queen Mary; 338.

1944, Dec. 17-18—3 U.S. Third Fleet destroyers sank during typhoon in Philippine Sea; 790.

1947, Jan. 19—Himera; Greek steamer hit a mine off Athens; 392.

1947, Apr. 16—Grandcamp; French freighter exploded in Texas City, Tex., Harbor, starting fires; 510.

1948, Nov.—Chinese army evacuation ship exploded and sunk off S. Manchuria; 6,000.

1948, Dec. 3—Kiangya; Chinese refugee ship wrecked in explosion S. of Shanghai; 1,100+.

1949, Sept. 17—Noronic; Canadian Great Lakes Cruiser burned at Toronto dock; 130.

1952, Apr. 26—Hobson and Wasp; U.S. destroyer and aircraft carrier collided in Atlantic; 176.

1953, Jan. 31—Princess Victoria; British ferry sank in storm off northern Irish coast; 134.

1954, Sept. 26—Toya Maru; Japanese ferry sank in Tsugaru Strait, Japan; 1,172.

1956, July 26—Andrea Doria and Stockholm; Italian liner and Swedish liner collided off Nantucket; 51.

1957, July 14—Eshghabad; Soviet ship ran aground in Caspian Sea; 270.

1961, July 8—Save; Portuguese ship ran aground off Mozambique; 259.

1962, Apr. 8—Dara; British liner exploded and sunk in Persian Gulf; 236.

1963, Apr. 10—Thresher; U.S. Navy atomic submarine sank in North Atlantic; 129.

1964, Feb. 10—Voyager, Melbourne; Australian destroyer sank after collision with Australian aircraft carrier Melbourne off New South Wales; 82.

1965, Nov. 13—Yarmouth Castle; Panamanian registered cruise ship burned and sank off Nassau; 90.

1967, July 29—Forrestal; U.S. aircraft carrier caught fire off N. Vietnam; 134.

1968, Jan. 25—Dakar; Israeli submarine vanished in Mediterranean Sea; 69.

1968, Jan. 27—Minerve; French submarine vanished in Mediterranean; 52.

1968, late May—Scorpion; U.S. nuclear submarine sank in Atlantic near Azores; 99 (located Oct. 31).

1969, June 2—Evans; U.S. destroyer cut in half by Australian carrier Melbourne, S. China Sea; 74.

1970, Mar. 4—Eurydice; French submarine sank in Mediterranean near Toulon; 57.

1970, Dec. 15—Namyong-Ho; South Korean ferry sank in Korea Strait; 308.

1974, May 1— Motor launch capsized off Bangladesh; 250.

1974, Sept. 26— Soviet destroyer burned and sank in Black Sea; 200+.

1976, Oct. 20—George Prince and Frosta; ferryboat and Norwegian tanker collided on Mississippi R. at Luling, La.; 77.

1976, Dec. 25—Patria; Egyptian liner caught fire and sank in the Red Sea; c. 100.

1977, Jan. 11—Grand Zenith; Panamanian-registered tanker sank off Cape Cod, Mass.; 38.

1979, Aug. 14—23 yachts competing in Fastnet yacht race sunk or abandoned during storm in S. Irish Sea; 18.

1981, Jan. 27—Tamponas II; Indonesian passenger ship caught fire and sank in Java Sea; 580.

1981, May 26—Nimitz; U.S. Marine combat jet crashed on deck of U.S. aircraft carrier; 14.

1983, Feb. 12—Marine Electric; coal freighter sank during storm off Chincoteague, Va.; 33.

1983, May 25—10th of Ramadan; Nile steamer caught fire and sank in L. Nassar; 357.

1986, Aug. 31—Admiral Nakhimov; Soviet passenger ship and **Pyotr Vasev,** Soviet freighter, collided in the Black Sea; 398.

1987, Mar. 6—British ferry capsized off Zeebrugge, Belgium; 188.

1987, Dec. 20—Philippine ferry *Dona Paz* and oil tanker *Victor* collided in the Tablas Strait; 3,000+.

1988, Aug. 6—Indian ferry capsized on Ganges R.; 400+.

1989, Apr. 7—Soviet submarine caught fire and sank off Norway; 42.

1989, Apr. 19—USS Iowa; U.S. battleship; explosion in gun turret; 47.

1989, Aug. 20—British barge *Bowbelle* struck British pleasure cruiser *Marchioness* on Thames R. in central London; 56.

1989, Sept. 10—Romanian pleasure boat and Bulgarian barge collided on Danube R.; 161.

1991, Apr. 10—Auto ferry and oil tanker collided outside Livorno Harbor, Italy; 140.

1991, Dec. 14—Ferry *Salem Express* rammed coral reef nr. Safaga, Egypt; 462.

Some Notable Aircraft Disasters Since 1937

Date			Aircraft	Site of accident	Deaths
1937	May	6	German zeppelin Hindenburg	Burned at mooring, Lakehurst, N.J.	36
1944	Aug.	23	U.S. Air Force B-24	Hit school, Freckelton, England	76[1]
1945	July	28	U.S. Army B-25	Hit Empire State bldg., N.Y.C.	14[1]
1947	May	30	Eastern Air Lines DC-4	Crashed near Port Deposit, Md.	53
1952	Dec.	20	U.S. Air Force C-124	Fell, burned, Moses Lake, Wash.	87
1953	Mar.	3	Canadian Pacific Comet Jet	Karachi, Pakistan	11[2]
1953	June	18	U.S. Air Force C-124	Crashed, burned near Tokyo	129
1955	Nov.	1	United Air Lines DC-6B	Exploded, crashed near Longmont, Col.	44[3]
1956	June	20	Venezuelan Super-Constellation	Crashed in Atlantic off Asbury Park, N.J.	74
1956	June	30	TWA Super-Const., United DC-7	Collided over Grand Canyon, Arizona	128
1960	Dec.	16	United DC-8 jet, TWA Super-Const.	Collided over N.Y. City	134[4]
1962	Mar.	16	Flying Tiger Super-Const.	Vanished in Western Pacific	107
1962	June	3	Air France Boeing 707 jet	Crashed on takeoff from Paris	130
1962	June	22	Air France Boeing 707 jet	Crashed in storm, Guadeloupe, W.I.	113
1963	June	3	Chartered Northw. Airlines DC-7	Crashed in Pacific off British Columbia	101
1963	Nov.	29	Trans-Canada Airlines DC-8F	Crashed after takeoff from Montreal	118
1965	May	20	Pakistani Boeing 720-B	Crashed at Cairo, Egypt, airport	121
1966	Jan.	24	Air India Boeing 707 jetliner	Crashed on Mont Blanc, France-Italy	117
1966	Feb.	4	All-Nippon Boeing 727	Plunged into Tokyo Bay	133
1966	Mar.	5	BOAC Boeing 707 jetliner	Crashed on Mount Fuji, Japan	124
1966	Dec.	24	U.S. military-chartered CL-44	Crashed into village in So. Vietnam	129[1]
1967	Apr.	20	Swiss Britannia turboprop	Crashed at Nicosia, Cyprus	126
1967	July	19	Piedmont Boeing 727, Cessna 310	Collided in air, Hendersonville, N.C.	82
1968	Apr.	20	S. African Airways Boeing 707	Crashed on takeoff, Windhoek, SW Africa	122
1968	May	3	Braniff International Electra	Crashed in storm near Dawson, Tex.	85
1969	Mar.	16	Venezuelan DC-9	Crashed after takeoff from Maracaibo, Venezuela	155[5]
1969	Dec.	8	Olympia Airways DC-6B	Crashed near Athens in storm	93
1970	Feb.	15	Dominican DC-9	Crashed into sea on takeoff from Santo Domingo	102
1970	July	3	British chartered jetliner	Crashed near Barcelona, Spain	112
1970	July	5	Air Canada DC-8	Crashed near Toronto International Airport	108
1970	Aug.	9	Peruvian turbojet	Crashed after takeoff from Cuzco, Peru	101[1]
1970	Nov.	14	Southern Airways DC-9	Crashed in mountains near Huntington, W. Va.	75[6]
1971	July	30	All-Nippon Boeing 727 and Japanese Air Force F-86	Collided over Morioka, Japan	162[7]
1971	Sept.	4	Alaska Airlines Boeing 727	Crashed into mountain near Juneau, Alaska	111
1972	Aug.	14	E. German Ilyushin-62	Crashed on take-off East Berlin	156
1972	Oct.	13	Aeroflot Ilyushin-62	E. German airline crashed near Moscow	176
1972	Dec.	3	Chartered Spanish airliner	Crashed on take-off, Canary Islands	155
1972	Dec.	29	Eastern Airlines Lockheed Tristar	Crashed on approach to Miami Int'l. Airport	101
1973	Jan.	22	Chartered Boeing 707	Burst into flames during landing, Kano Airport, Nigeria	176
1973	Feb.	21	Libyan jetliner	Shot down by Israeli fighter planes over Sinai	108
1973	Apr.	10	British Vanguard turboprop	Crashed during snowstorm at Basel, Switzerland	104
1973	June	3	Soviet Supersonic TU-144	Crashed near Goussainville, France	14[8]
1973	July	11	Brazilian Boeing 707	Crashed on approach to Orly Airport, Paris	122
1973	July	31	Delta Airlines jetliner	Crashed, landing in fog at Logan Airport, Boston	89
1973	Dec.	23	French Caravelle jet	Crashed in Morocco	106
1974	Mar.	3	Turkish DC-10 jet	Crashed at Ermenonville near Paris	346
1974	Apr.	23	Pan American 707 jet	Crashed in Bali, Indonesia	107
1974	Dec.	1	TWA-727	Crashed in storm, Upperville, Va.	92
1974	Dec.	4	Dutch-chartered DC-8	Crashed in storm near Colombo, Sri Lanka	191
1975	Apr.	4	Air Force Galaxy C-5B	Crashed near Saigon, So. Vietnam, after takeoff with load of orphans	172
1975	June	24	Eastern Airlines 727 jet	Crashed in storm, JFK Airport, N.Y. City	113
1975	Aug.	3	Chartered 707	Hit mountainside, Agadir, Morocco	188
1976	Sept.	10	British Airways Trident, Yugoslav DC-9	Collided near Zagreb, Yugoslavia	176
1976	Sept.	19	Turkish 727	Hit mountain, southern Turkey	155
1976	Oct.	13	Bolivian 707 cargo jet	Crashed in Santa Cruz, Bolivia	100[9]
1977	Jan.	13	Aeroflot TU-104	Exploded and crashed at Alma-Ata, Central Asia	90
1977	Mar.	27	KLM 747, Pan American 747	Collided on runway, Tenerife, Canary Islands	582
1977	Nov.	19	TAP Boeing 727	Crashed on Madeira	130
1977	Dec.	4	Malaysian Boeing 737	Hijacked, then exploded in mid-air over Straits of Johore	100
1977	Dec.	13	U.S. DC-3	Crashed after takeoff at Evansville, Ind.	29[10]
1978	Jan.	1	Air India 747	Exploded, crashed into sea off Bombay	213
1978	Sept.	25	Boeing 727, Cessna 172	Collided in air, San Diego, Cal.	150

Date			Aircraft	Site of accident	Deaths
1978	Nov.	15	Chartered DC-8	Crashed near Colombo, Sri Lanka	183
1979	May	25	American Airlines DC-10	Crashed after takeoff at O'Hare Intl. Airport, Chicago	275[11]
1979	Aug.	17	Two Soviet Aeroflot jetliners	Collided over Ukraine	173
1979	Oct.	31	Western Airlines DC-10	Mexico City Airport	74
1979	Nov.	26	Pakistani Boeing 707	Crashed near Jidda, Saudi Arabia	156
1979	Nov.	28	New Zealand DC-10	Crashed into mountain in Antarctica	257
1980	Mar.	14	Polish Ilyushin 62	Crashed making emergency landing, Warsaw	87[12]
1980	Aug.	19	Saudi Arabian Tristar	Burned after emergency landing, Riyadh	301
1981	Dec.	1	Yugoslavian DC-9	Crashed into mountain in Corsica	174
1982	Jan.	13	Air Florida Boeing 737	Crashed into Potomac River after takeoff	78
1982	July	9	Pan-Am Boeing 727	Crashed after takeoff in Kenner, La.	153[13]
1982	Sept.	11	U.S. Army CH-47 Chinook helicopter	Crashed during air show in Mannheim, W. Germany	46
1983	Sept.	1	S. Korean Boeing 747	Shot down after violating Soviet airspace	269
1983	Nov.	27	Colombian Boeing 747	Crashed near Barajas Airport, Madrid	183
1985	Feb.	19	Spanish Boeing 727	Crashed into Mt. Oiz, Spain	148
1985	June	23	Air-India Boeing 747	Crashed into Atlantic Ocean S. of Ireland	329
1985	Aug.	2	Delta Air Lines jumbo jet	Crashed at Dallas-Ft. Worth Intl. Airport	133
1985	Aug.	12	Japan Air Lines Boeing 747	Crashed into Mt. Ogura, Japan	520[14]
1985	Dec.	12	Arrow Air DC 8	Crashed after takeoff in Gander, Newfoundland	256[15]
1986	Mar.	31	Mexican Boeing 727	Crashed NW of Mexico City	166
1986	Aug.	31	Aeromexico DC-9	Collided with Piper PA-28 over Cerritos, Cal.	82[16]
1987	May	9	Ilyushin 62M	Crashed after takeoff in Warsaw, Poland	183
1987	Aug.	16	Northwest Airlines MD-82	Crashed after takeoff in Romulus, Mich.	156
1988	July	3	Iranian A300 Airbus	Shot down by U.S. Navy warship *Vincennes* over Persian Gulf	290
1988	Dec.	21	Pan Am Boeing 747	Exploded and crashed in Lockerbie, Scotland	270[17]
1989	Feb.	8	Boeing 707	Crashed into mountain in Azores Islands off Portugal	144
1989	June	7	Suriname DC-8	Crashed near Paramaribo Airport, Suriname	168
1989	July	19	United Airlines DC-10	Crashed while landing with a disabled hydraulic system, Sioux City, Ia.	111
1989	Sept.	19	French DC-10	Exploded in air over Niger	171
1991	May	26	Austrian Boeing 767-300	Exploded over rural Thailand	223
1991	July	11	Nigerian DC-8	Crashed while landing at Jidda, Saudi Arabia	261

(1) Including those on the ground and in buildings. (2) First fatal crash of commercial jet plane. (3) Caused by bomb planted by John G. Graham in insurance plot to kill his mother, a passenger. (4) Including all 128 aboard the planes and 6 on ground. (5) Killed 84 on plane and 71 on ground. (6) Including 43 Marshall U. football players and coaches. (7) Airliner-fighter crash, pilot of fighter parachuted to safety, was arrested for negligence. (8) First supersonic plane crash killed 6 crewmen and 8 on the ground; there were no passengers. (9) Crew of 3 killed; 97, mostly children, killed on ground. (10) Including U. of Evansville basketball team. (11) Highest death toll in U.S. aviation history. (12) Including 22 members of U.S. boxing team. (13) Including 8 on ground. (14) Worst single-plane disaster. (15) Incl. 248 members of U.S. 101st Airborne Division. (16) Incl. 15 on the ground. (17) Incl. 11 on the ground.

Notable Railroad Disasters

Date			Location	Deaths
1876	Dec.	29	Ashtabula, Oh.	92
1880	Aug.	11	Mays Landing, N. J.	40
1887	Aug.	10	Chatsworth, Ill.	81
1888	Oct.	10	Mud Run, Pa.	55
1891	June	14	Nr. Basel, Switzerland	100
1896	July	30	Atlantic City, N. J.	60
1903	Dec.	23	Laurel Run, Pa.	53
1904	Aug.	7	Eden, Col.	96
1904	Sept.	24	New Market Tenn.	56
1906	Mar.	16	Florence, Col.	35
1906	Oct.	28	Atlantic City, N. J.	40
1906	Dec.	30	Washington, D. C.	53
1907	Jan.	2	Volland, Kan.	33
1907	Jan.	19	Fowler, Ind.	29
1907	Feb.	16	New York, N.Y.	22
1907	Feb.	23	Colton, Cal.	26
1907	May	11	Lompoc, Cal.	36
1907	July	20	Salem, Mich.	33
1910	Mar.	1	Wellington, Wash.	96
1910	Mar.	21	Green Mountain, Ia.	55
1911	Aug.	25	Manchester, N. Y.	29
1912	July	4	East Corning, N. Y.	39
1912	July	5	Ligonier, Pa.	23
1914	Aug.	5	Tipton Ford, Mo.	43
1914	Sept.	15	Lebanon, Mo.	28
1915	May	22	Nr. Gretna, Scotland	227
1916	Mar.	29	Amherst, Oh.	27
1917	Sept.	28	Kellyville, Okla.	23
1917	Dec.	12	Modane, France	543[1]
1917	Dec.	20	Shepherdsville, Ky.	46
1918	June	22	Ivanhoe, Ind.	68
1918	July	9	Nashville, Tenn.	101
1918	Nov.	1	Brooklyn, N. Y.	97
1919	Jan.	12	South Byron, N. Y.	22
1919	July	1	Dunkirk, N. Y.	12
1919	Dec.	20	Onawa, Maine	23
1921	Feb.	27	Porter, Ind.	37
1921	Dec.	5	Woodmont, Pa.	27
1922	Aug.	5	Sulphur Spring, Mo.	34
1922	Dec.	13	Humble, Tex.	22
1923	Sept.	27	Lockett, Wy.	31
1925	June	16	Hackettstown, N. J.	50
1925	Oct.	27	Victoria, Miss.	21
1926	Sept.	5	Waco, Col.	30
1928	Aug.	24	I.R.T. subway, Times Sq., N. Y.	18
1937	July	16	Nr. Patna, India	107
1938	June	19	Saugus, Mont.	47
1939	Aug.	12	Harney, Nev.	24
1939	Dec.	22	Nr. Magdeburg, Germany	132
1939	Dec.	22	Nr. Friedrichshafen, Germany	99
1940	Apr.	19	Little Falls, N. Y.	31
1940	July	31	Cuyahoga Falls, Oh.	43
1943	Aug.	29	Wayland, N. Y.	27
1943	Sept.	6	Frankford Junction, Philadelphia, Pa.	79
1943	Dec.	16	Between Rennert and Buie, N. C.	72
1944	Jan.	16	Leon Province, Spain	500
1944	Mar.	2	Salerno, Italy	521
1944	July	6	High Bluff, Tenn.	35
1944	Aug.	4	Near Stockton, Ga.	47
1944	Sept.	14	Dewey, Ind.	29
1944	Dec.	31	Bagley, Utah	50
1945	Aug.	9	Michigan, N. D.	34
1946	Mar.	20	Aracaju, Mexico	185
1946	Apr.	25	Naperville, Ill.	45
1947	Feb.	18	Gallitzin, Pa.	24
1949	Oct.	22	Nr. Dwor, Poland	200+
1950	Feb.	17	Rockville Centre, N. Y.	31
1950	Sept.	11	Coshocton, Oh.	33
1950	Nov.	22	Richmond Hill, N. Y.	79
1951	Feb.	6	Woodbridge, N. J.	84
1951	Nov.	12	Wyuta, Wyo.	17
1951	Nov.	25	Woodstock, Ala.	17
1952	Mar.	4	Nr. Rio de Janeiro, Brazil	119
1952	July	9	Rzepin, Poland	160
1952	Oct.	8	Harrow, England	112
1953	Mar.	27	Conneaut, Oh.	21
1955	Apr.	3	Guadalajara, Mexico	300
1956	Jan.	22	Los Angeles, Cal.	30
1956	Feb.	28	Swampscott, Mass.	13
1956	Sept.	5	Springer, N. M.	20
1957	June	11	Vroman, Col.	12
1957	Sept.	1	Kendal, Jamaica	178
1957	Sept.	29	Montgomery, W. Pakistan	250
1957	Dec.	4	London, England	90
1958	May	8	Rio de Janeiro, Brazil	128
1958	Sept.	15	Elizabethport, N. J.	48

Date			Location	Deaths
1960	Mar.	14	Bakersfield, Cal.	14
1960	Nov.	14	Pardubice, Czech.	110
1962	Jan.	8	Woerden, Netherlands	91
1962	May	3	Tokyo, Japan	163
1962	July	28	Steelton, Pa.	19
1964	July	26	Oporto, Portugal	94
1966	Dec.	28	Everett, Mass.	13
1970	Feb.	1	Buenos Aires, Argentina	236
1971	June	10	Salem, Ill.	11
1972	June	16	Vierzy, France	107
1972	July	21	Seville, Spain	76
1972	Oct.	6	Saltillo, Mexico	208
1972	Oct.	30	Chicago, Ill.	45
1974	Aug.	30	Zagreb, Yugoslavia	153
1977	Jan.	18	Granville, Australia	82
1977	Feb.	4	Chicago, Ill., elevated train	11
1981	June	6	Bihar, India	500+
1982	Jan.	27	El Asnam, Algeria	130
1982	July	11	Tepic, Mexico	120
1983	Feb.	19	Empalme, Mexico	100
1987	Jan.	4	Essex, Md.	16
1988	Dec.	12	London, England	115
1989	Jan.	15	Maizdi Khan, Bangladesh	110+
1990	Jan.	4	Sindh Province, Pakistan	210+
1991	May	14	Shigaraki, Japan	42
1991	July	31	Camden, S.C.	7
1991	Aug.	28	N.Y. City subway	5

(1) World's worst train wreck; passenger train derailed.

Principal U.S. Mine Disasters Since 1900

Source: Bureau of Mines, U.S. Interior Department

Note: Prior to 1968, only disasters with losses of 60 or more lives are listed; since 1968, all disasters in which 5 or more people were killed are listed. Only fatalities to mining company employees are included. All bituminous-coal mines unless otherwise noted.

Date		Location	Deaths
1900	May 1	Scofield, Ut.	200
1902	May 19	Coal Creek, Tenn.	184
1902	July 10	Johnstown, Pa.	112
1903	June 30	Hanna, Wy.	169
1904	Jan. 25	Cheswick, Pa.	179
1905	Feb. 20	Virginia City, Ala.	112
1907	Jan. 29	Stuart W. Va.	84
1907	Dec. 6	Monongah, W. Va.	361
1907	Dec. 19	Jacobs Creek, Pa.	239
1908	Nov. 28	Marianna, Pa.	154
1909	Jan. 12	Switchback, W. Va.	67
1909	Nov. 13	Cherry, Ill.	259
1910	Jan. 31	Primero, Col.	75
1910	May 5	Palos, Ala.	90
1910	Nov. 8	Delagua, Col.	79
1911[1]	Apr. 7	Throop, Pa.	72
1911	Apr. 8	Littleton, Ala.	128
1911	Dec. 9	Briceville, Tenn.	84
1912	Mar. 20	McCurtain, Okla.	73
1912	Mar. 26	Jed, W. Va.	83
1913	Apr. 23	Finleyville, Pa.	96
1913	Oct. 22	Dawson, N.M.	263
1914	Apr. 28	Eccles, W. Va.	181
1915	Mar. 2	Layland, W. Va.	112
1917	Apr. 27	Hastings, Col.	121
1917[2]	June 8	Butte, Mon.	163
1917	Aug. 4	Clay, Ky.	62
1919[1]	June 5	Wilkes-Barre, Pa.	92
1922	Nov. 6	Spangler, Pa.	77
1922	Nov. 22	Dolomite, Ala.	90
1923	Feb. 8	Dawson, N.M.	120
1923	Aug. 14	Kemmerer, Wy.	99
1924	Mar. 8	Castle Gate, Ut.	171
1924	Apr. 28	Benwood, W. Va.	119
1926	Jan. 13	Wilburton, Okla.	91
1926[2]	Nov. 3	Ishpeming, Mich.	51
1927	Apr. 30	Everettville, W. Va.	97
1928	May 19	Mather, Pa.	195
1929	Dec. 17	McAlester, Okla.	61
1930	Nov. 5	Millfield, Oh.	79
1940	Jan. 10	Bartley, W. Va.	91
1940	Mar. 16	St. Clairsville, Oh.	72
1940	July 15	Portage, Pa.	63
1943	Feb. 27	Washoe, Mon.	74
1944	July 5	Belmont, Oh.	66
1947	Mar. 25	Centralia, Ill.	111
1951	Dec. 21	West Frankfort, Ill.	119
1968[3]	Mar. 6	Calumet, La.	21
1968	Nov. 20	Farmington, W. Va.	78
1970	Dec. 30	Hyden, Ky.	38
1972[2]	May 2	Kellogg, Ida.	91
1976	Mar. 9, 11	Oven Fork, Ky.	26
1977	Mar. 1	Tower City, Pa.	9
1981	Apr. 15	Redstone, Col.	15
1981	Dec. 7	Topmost, Ky.	8
1981	Dec. 8	nr. Chattanooga, Tenn.	13
1982	Jan. 20	Floyd County, Ky.	7
1983	June 21	McClure, Va	7
1984	Dec. 19	Huntington, Ut.	27
1989	Sept. 13	Wheatcroft, Ky.	10

(1) Anthracite mine. (2) Metal mine. (3) Nonmetal mine.
World's worst mine disaster killed 1,549 workers in Honkeiko Colliery in Manchuria Apr. 25, 1942.

Some Notable Tornadoes In U.S. Since 1925

Date			Location	Deaths
1925	Mar.	18	Mo., Ill. Ind.	689
1927	Apr.	12	Rock Springs, Tex.	74
1927	May	9	Arkansas, Poplar Bluff, Mo.	92
1927	Sept.	29	St. Louis, Mo.	90
1930	May	6	Hill, Navarro, Ellis Co., Tex.	41
1932	Mar.	21	Ala. (series of tornadoes)	268
1936	Apr.	5	Miss., Ga.	455
1936	Apr.	6	Gainesville, Ga.	203
1938	Sept.	29	Charleston, S.C.	32
1942	Mar.	16	Central to NE Miss.	75
1942	Apr.	27	Rogers & Mayes Co., Okla.	52
1944	June	23	Oh., Pa., W. Va., Md.	150
1945	Apr.	12	Okla.-Ark.	102
1947	Apr.	9	Tex., Okla. & Kan.	169
1948	Mar.	19	Bunker Hill & Gillespie, Ill.	33
1949	Jan.	3	La. & Ark.	58
1952	Mar.	21	Ark., Mo., Tenn. (series)	208
1953	May	11	Waco, Tex.	114
1953	June	8	Mich., Oh.	142
1953	June	9	Worcester and vicinity, Mass.	90
1953	Dec.	5	Vicksburg, Miss.	38
1955	May	25	Kan., Mo., Okla., Tex.	115
1957	May	20	Kan., Mo.	48
1958	June	4	Northwestern Wisconsin	30
1959	Feb.	10	St. Louis, Mo.	21
1960	May	5, 6	SE Oklahoma, Arkansas	30
1965	Apr.	11	Ind., Ill., Oh., Mich., Wis.	271
1966	Mar.	3	Jackson, Miss.	57
1966	Mar.	3	Mississippi, Alabama	61
1967	Apr.	21	Ill., Mich.	33
1968	May	15	Midwest	71
1969	Jan.	23	Mississippi	32
1971	Feb.	21	Mississippi delta	110
1973	May	26-27	South, Midwest (series)	47
1974	Apr.	3-4	Ala., Ga., Tenn., Ky., Oh.	350
1977	Apr.	4	Ala., Miss., Ga.	22
1979	Apr.	10	Tex., Okla.	60
1980	June	3	Grand Island, Neb. (series)	4
1982	Mar.	2-4	South, Midwest (series)	17
1982	May	29	So. Ill.	10
1983	May	18-22	Tex.	12
1984	Mar.	28	N. Carolina; S. Carolina	67
1984	Apr.	21-22	Mississippi	15
1984	Apr.	26	Series Okla to Minn.	17
1985	May	31	N.Y., Pa., Oh., Ont. (series)	90
1987	May	22	Saragosa, Tex.	29
1989	Nov.	15	Huntsville, Ala.	18
1989	Nov.	16	Newburgh, N.Y.	9
1990	June	2-3	Midwest, Great Lakes	13
1990	Aug.	28	N. Ill.	25
1991	Apr.	26	Kan., Okla.	23

Hurricanes, Typhoons, Blizzards, Other Storms

Names of hurricanes and typhoons in italics—H.—hurricane; T.—typhoon

Date	Location	Deaths
1888 Mar. 11-14	Blizzard, Eastern U.S.	400
1900 Aug.-Sept.	H., Galveston, Tex.	6,000
1906 Sept. 21	H., La., Miss.	350
1906 Sept. 18	Typhoon, Hong Kong	10,000
1926 Sept. 11-22	H., Fla., Ala.	243
1926 Oct. 20	H., Cuba	600
1928 Sept. 6-20	H., So. Fla.	1,836
1930 Sept. 3	H., Dominican Rep.	2,000
1938 Sept. 21	H., Long, Island N.Y., New England	600
1940 Nov. 11-12	Blizzard, U.S. NE, Midwest	144
1942 Oct. 15-16	H., Bengal, India	40,000
1944 Sept. 9-16	H., N.C. to New Eng.	46
1952 Oct. 22	Typhoon, Philippines	0,300
1954 Aug. 30	H. *Carol*, Northeast U.S.	68
1954 Oct. 5-18	H. *Hazel*, Eastern, U.S., Haiti.	347
1955 Aug. 12-13	H. *Connie*, Carolinas, Va., Md.	43
1955 Aug. 7-21	H. *Diane*, Eastern U.S.	400
1955 Sept. 19	H. *Hilda*, Mexico	200
1955 Sept. 22-28	H. *Janet*, Caribbean	500
1956 Feb. 1-29	Blizzard, Western Europe	1,000
1957 June 25-30	H. *Audrey*, Tex. to Ala.	390
1958 Feb. 15-16	Blizzard, NE U.S.	171
1959 Sept. 17-19	T. *Sarah*, Japan, S. Korea	2,000
1959 Sept. 26-27	T. *Vera*, Honshu, Japan	4,466
1960 Sept. 4-12	H. *Donna*, Caribbean, E. U.S.	148
1961 Sept. 11-14	H. *Carla*, Tex.	46
1961 Oct. 31	H. *Hattie*, Br. Honduras	400
1963 May 28-29	Windstorm, Bangladesh	22,000
1963 Oct. 4-8	H. *Flora*, Caribbean	6,000
1964 Oct. 4-7	H. *Hilda*, La., Miss., Ga.	38
1964 June 30	T. *Winnie*, N. Philippines	107
1964 Sept. 5	T. *Ruby*, Hong Kong and China	735
1965 May 11-12	Windstorm, Bangladesh	17,000
1965 June 1-2	Windstorm, Bangladesh	30,000
1965 Sept. 7-12	H. *Betsy*, Fla., Miss., La.	74
1965 Dec. 15	Windstorm, Bangladesh	10,000
1966 June 4-10	H. *Alma*, Honduras, SE U.S.	51
1966 Sept. 24-30	H. *Inez*, Carib., Fla., Mex.	293
1967 July 9	T. *Billie*, SW Japan	347
1967 Sept. 5-23	H. *Beulah*, Carib., Mex., Tex.	54
1967 Dec. 12-20	Blizzard, Southwest, U.S.	51
1968 Nov. 18-28	T. *Nina*, Philippines	63
1969 Aug. 17-18	H. *Camille*, Miss., La.	256
1970 July 30-Aug. 5	H. *Celia*, Cuba, Fla., Tex.	31
1970 Aug. 20-21	H. *Dorothy*, Martinique	42
1970 Sept. 15	T. *Georgia*, Philippines	300
1970 Oct. 14	T. *Sening*, Philippines	583
1970 Oct. 15	T. *Titang*, Philippinos	526
1970 Nov. 13	Cyclone, Bangladesh	300,000
1971 Aug. 1	T. *Rose*, Hong Kong	130
1972 June 19-29	H. *Agnes*, Fla. to N.Y.	118
1972 Dec. 3	T. *Theresa*, Philippines	169
1973 June-Aug.	Monsoon rains in India	1,217
1974 June 11	Storm Dinah, Luzon Is., Philip.	71
1974 July 11	T. *Gilda*, Japan, S. Korea	108
1974 Sept. 19-20	H. *Fifi*, Honduras	2,000
1974 Dec. 25	Cyclone leveled Darwin, Aus.	50
1975 Sept. 13-27	H. *Eloise*, Caribbean, NE U.S.	71
1976 May 20	T. *Olga*, floods, Philippines	215
1977 July 25, 31	T. *Thelma*, T. *Vera*, Taiwan	39
1978 Oct. 27	T. *Rita*, Philippines	c. 400
1979 Aug. 30-Sept. 7	H. *David*, Caribbean, East. U.S.	1,100
1980 Aug. 4-11	H. *Allen*, Caribbean, Texas	272
1981 Nov. 25	T. *Irma*, Luzon Is., Philippines.	176
1983 June	Monsoon rains in India	900
1983 Aug. 18	H. *Alicia*, southern Texas	17
1984 Sept. 2	T. *Ike*, southern Philippines	1,363
1985 May 25	Cyclone, Bangladesh	10,000
1985 Oct. 26-Nov. 6	H. *Juan*, SE U.S.	97
1987 Nov. 25	T. *Nina*, Philippines	650
1989 Sept. 16-22	H. *Hugo*, Caribbean, SE U.S.	504
1990 May 6-11	Cyclones, SE India	450
1991 Apr. 30	Cyclone, Bangladesh	70,000

Floods, Tidal Waves

Date		Location	Deaths
1228	....	Holland	100,000
1642	....	China	300,000
1887	....	Huang He River, China	900,000
1889	May 31	Johnstown, Pa.	2,200
1900	Sept. 8	Galveston, Tex.	5,000
1903	June 15	Heppner, Ore.	325
1911	....	Chang Jiang River, China	100,000
1913	Mar. 25-27	Ohio, Indiana	732
1915	Aug. 17	Galveston, Tex.	275
1928	Mar. 13	Collapse of St. Francis Dam, Saugus, Cal.	450
1928	Sept. 13	Lake Okeechobee, Fla.	2,000
1931	Aug.	Huang He River, China	3,700,000
1937	Jan. 22	Ohio, Miss. Valleys	250
1939	....	Northern China	200,000
1946	Apr. 1	Hawaii, Alaska	159
1947	....	Honshu Island, Japan	1,900
1951	Aug.	Manchuria	1,800
1953	Jan. 31	Western Europe	2,000
1954	Aug. 17	Farahzad, Iran	2,000
1955	Oct. 7-12	India, Pakistan	1,700
1959	Nov. 1	Western Mexico	2,000
1959	Dec. 2	Frejus, France	412
1960	Oct. 10	Bangladesh	6,000
1960	Oct. 31	Bangladesh	4,000
1962	Feb. 17	German North Sea coast	343
1962	Sept. 27	Barcelona, Spain	445
1963	Oct. 9	Dam collapse, Vaiont, Italy	1,800
1966	Nov. 3-4	Florence, Venice, Italy	113
1967	Jan. 18-24	Eastern Brazil	894
1967	Mar. 19	Rio de Janeiro, Brazil	436
1967	Nov. 26	Lisbon, Portugal	464
1968	Aug. 7-14	Gujarat State, India	1,000
1968	Oct. 7	Northeastern India	780
1969	Jan. 18-26	So. Cal.	100
1969	Mar. 17	Mundau Valley, Alagoas, Brazil	218
1969	Aug. 20-22	Western Virginia	189
1969	Sept. 15	South Korea	250
1969	Oct. 1-8	Tunisia	500
1970	May 20	Central Romania	160
1970	July 22	Himalayas, India	500
1971	Feb. 26	Rio de Janeiro, Brazil	130
1972	Feb. 26	Buffalo Creek, W. Va.	118
1972	June 9	Rapid City, S.D.	236
1972	Aug. 7	Luzon Is., Philippines	454
1973	Aug. 19-31	Pakistan	1,500
1974	Mar. 29	Tubaro, Brazil	1,000
1974	Aug. 12	Monty-Long, Bangladesh	2,500
1976	June 5	Teton Dam collapse, Ida.	11
1976	July 31	Big Thompson Canyon, Col.	139
1976	Nov. 17	East Java, Indonesia	136
1977	July 19-20	Johnstown, Pa.	68
1978	June-Sept.	Northern India	1,200
1979	Jan.-Feb.	Brazil	204
1979	July 17	Lomblem Is., Indonesia	539
1979	Aug. 11	Morvi, India	5,000-15,000
1980	Feb. 13-22	So. Cal., Ariz.	26
1981	Apr.	Northern China	550
1981	July	Sichuan, Hubei Prov., China	1,300
1982	Jan. 23	Nr. Lima, Peru	600
1982	May 12	Guangdong, China	430
1982	June 6	So. Conn.	12
1982	Sept. 17-21	El Salvador, Guatemala	1,300+
1982	Dec. 2-9	Ill., Mo., Ark.	22
1983	Feb.-Mar.	Cal. coast	13
1983	Apr. 6-12	Ala., La., Miss., Tenn.	15
1984	May 27	Tulsa, Okla.	13
1984	Aug-Sept.	S. Korea	200+
1985	July 19	Northern Italy, dam burst	361
1987	Aug.-Sept.	Northern Bangladesh	1,000+
1988	Sept.	Northern India	1,000+
1990	June 14	Shadyside, Oh.	23
1991	Dec. 18-26	Texas	18
1992	Feb. 9-15	So. Cal.	13
1992	Apr. 13	Downtown Chicago	0

Fires

Date			Location	Deaths
1835	Dec.	16	New York City, 500 bldgs. destroyed	—
1845	May		Canton, China, theater	1,670
1871	Oct.	8	Chicago, $196 million loss	250
1871	Oct.	8	Peshtigo, Wis., forest fire	1,182
1872	Nov.	9	Boston, 800 bldgs. destroyed	—
1876	Dec.	5	Brooklyn (N.Y.), theater	295
1877	June	20	St. John, N. B., Canada	100
1881	Dec.	8	Ring Theater, Vienna	850
1887	May	25	Opera Comique, Paris	200
1887	Sept.	4	Exeter, England, theater	200
1894	Sept.	1	Minn., forest fire	413
1897	May	4	Paris, charity bazaar	150
1900	June	30	Hoboken, N. J., docks	326
1902	Sept.	20	Birmingham, Ala., church	115
1903	Dec.	30	Iroquois Theater, Chicago	602
1908	Jan.	13	Rhoads Theater, Boyertown, Pa.	170
1908	Mar.	4	Collinwood, Oh., school	176
1911	Mar.	25	Triangle factory, N. Y. City	145
1913	Oct.	14	Mid Glamorgan, Wales, colliery	439
1918	Apr.	13	Norman Okla., state hospital	38
1918	Oct.	12	Cloquet, Minn., forest fire	400
1919	June	20	Mayaguez Theater, San Juan	150
1923	May	17	Camden, S. C., school	76
1924	Dec.	24	Hobart, Okla., school	35
1929	May	15	Cleveland, Oh., clinic	125
1930	Apr.	21	Columbus, Oh., penitentiary	320
1931	July	24	Pittsburgh, Pa., home for aged	48
1934	Dec.	11	Hotel Kerns, Lansing, Mich.	34
1938	May	16	Atlanta, Ga., Terminal Hotel	35
1940	Apr.	23	Natchez, Miss., dance hall	198
1942	Nov.	28	Cocoanut Grove, Boston	491
1942			St. John's, Newfoundland, hostel	100
1943	Sept.	7	Gulf Hotel, Houston	55
1944	July	6	Ringling Circus, Hartford	168
1946	June	5	LaSalle Hotel, Chicago	61
1946	Dec.	7	Winecoff Hotel, Atlanta	119
1946	Dec.	12	New York, ice plant, tenement	37
1949	Apr.	5	Effingham, Ill., hospital	77
1950	Jan.	7	Davenport, Ia., Mercy Hospital	41
1953	Mar.	29	Largo, Fla., nursing home	35
1953	Apr.	16	Chicago, metalworking plant	35
1957	Feb.	17	Warrenton, Mo., home for aged	72
1958	Mar.	19	New York City, loft building	24
1958	Dec.	1	Chicago, parochial school	95
1958	Dec.	16	Bogota, Colombia, store	83
1959	June	23	Stalheim, Norway, resort hotel	34
1960	Mar.	12	Pusan, Korea, chemical plant	68
1960	July	14	Guatemala City, mental hospital	225
1960	Nov.	13	Amude, Syria, movie theater	152
1961	Jan.	6	Thomas Hotel, San Francisco	20
1961	Dec.	8	Hartford, Conn., hospital	16
1961	Dec.	17	Niteroi, Brazil, circus	323
1963	May	4	Diourbel, Senegal, theater	64
1963	Nov.	18	Surfside Hotel, Atlantic City, N.J.	25
1963	Nov.	23	Fitchville, Oh., rest home	63
1963	Dec.	29	Roosevelt Hotel, Jacksonville, Fla.	22
1964	May	8	Manila, apartment bldg	30
1964	Dec.	18	Fountaintown, Ind., nursing home	20
1965	Mar.	1	LaSalle, Canada, apartment	28
1966	Mar.	11	Numata, Japan, 2 ski resorts	31
1966	Aug.	13	Melbourne, Australia, hotel	29
1966	Sept.	12	Anchorage, Alaska, hotel	14
1966	Oct.	17	N. Y. City bldg. (firemen)	12
1966	Dec.	7	Erzurum, Turkey, barracks	68
1967	Feb.	7	Montgomery, Ala., restaurant	25
1967	May	22	Brussels, Belgium, store	322
1967	July	16	Jay, Fla., state prison	37
1968	Feb.	26	Shrewsbury, England, hospital	22
1968	May	11	Vijayawada, India, wedding hall	58
1968	Nov.	18	Glasgow, Scotland, factory	24
1969	Jan.	26	Victoria Hotel, Dunnville, Ont.	13
1969	Dec.	2	Notre Dame, Can., nursing home	54
1970	Jan.	9	Marietta, Oh., nursing home	27
1970	Mar.	20	Seattle, Wash., hotel	19
1970	Nov.	1	Grenoble, France, dance hall	145
1970	Dec.	20	Tucson, Arizona, hotel	28
1971	Mar.	6	Burghoezli, Switzerland, psychiatric clinic	28
1971	Apr.	20	Hotel, Bangkok, Thailand	24
1971	Oct.	19	Honesdale, Pa., nursing home	15
1971	Dec.	25	Hotel, Seoul, So. Korea	162
1972	May	13	Osaka, Japan, nightclub	116
1972	July	5	Sherborne, England, hospital	30
1973	Feb.	6	Paris, France, school	21
1973	Nov.	6	Fukui, Japan, train	28
1973	Nov.	29	Kumamoto, Japan, department store	107
1973	Dec.	2	Seoul, Korea, theater	50
1974	Feb.	1	Sao Paulo, Brazil, bank building	189
1974	June	30	Port Chester, N. Y., discotheque	24
1974	Nov.	3	Seoul, So. Korea, hotel discotheque	88
1975	Dec.	12	Mina, Saudi Arabia, tent city	138
1976	Oct.	24	Bronx, N.Y., social club	25
1977	Feb.	25	Moscow, Rossiya hotel	45
1977	May	28	Southgate, Ky., nightclub	164
1977	June	9	Abidjan, Ivory Coast, nightclub	41
1977	June	26	Columbia, Tenn., jail	42
1977	Nov.	14	Manila, Pl, hotel	47
1978	Jan.	28	Kansas City, Coates House Hotel	16
1979	July	14	Saragossa, Spain, hotel	80
1979	Dec.	31	Chapais, Quebec, social club	42
1980	May	20	Kingston, Jamaica, nursing home	157
1980	Nov.	21	MGM Grand Hotel, Las Vegas	84
1980	Dec.	4	Stouffer Inn, Harrison, N.Y.	26
1981	Jan.	9	Keansburg, N.J., boarding home	30
1981	Feb.	10	Las Vegas Hilton	8
1981	Feb.	14	Dublin, Ireland, discotheque	44
1982	Sept.	4	Los Angeles, apartment house	24
1982	Nov.	8	Biloxi, Miss., county jail	29
1983	Feb.	13	Turin, Italy, movie theater	64
1983	Dec.	17	Madrid, Spain, discotheque	83
1984	May	11	Great Adventure Amusement Park, N.J.	8
1985	Apr.	21	Tabaco, Philippines, movie theater	44
1985	Apr.	26	Buenos Aires, Argentina hospital	79
1985	May	11	Bradford, England, soccer stadium	53
1986	Dec.	31	Puerto Rico, Dupont Plaza Hotel	96
1987	May 6-June 2		Northern China forest fire	193
1987	Nov.	17	London, England subway	30
1990	Mar.	25	N.Y. City social club	87
1991	Sept.	3	Hamlet, N.C. chicken-processing plant	25
1991	Oct. 20-21		Oakland, Berkeley, Cal. wildfire	24

Explosions

Date			Location	Deaths
1910	Oct.	1	Los Angeles Times Bldg.,	21
1913	Mar.	7	Dynamite, Baltimore harbor	55
1915	Sept.	27	Gasoline tank car, Ardmore, Okla.	47
1917	Apr.	10	Munitions plant, Eddystone, Pa.	133
1917	Dec.	6	Halifax Harbor, Canada	1,654
1918	May	18	Chemical plant, Oakdale, Pa.	193
1918	July	2	Explosives, Split Rock, N.Y.	50
1918	Oct.	4	Shell plant, Morgan Station, N.J.	64
1919	May	22	Food plant, Cedar Rapids, Ia.	44
1920	Sept.	16	Wall Street, New York, bomb	30
1924	Jan.	3	Food plant, Pekin, Ill.	42
1928	April	13	Dance hall, West Plains, Mo.	40
1937	Mar.	18	New London, Tex., school	413
1940	Sept.	12	Hercules Powder, Kenvil, N.J.	55
1942	June	5	Ordnance plant, Elwood, Ill.	49
1944	Apr.	14	Bombay, India, harbor	700
1944	July	17	Port Chicago, Cal., pier	322
1944	Oct.	21	Liquid gas tank, Cleveland	135
1947	Apr.	16	Texas City, Tex., pier	561
1948	July	28	Farben works, Ludwigshafen, Ger.	184
1950	May	19	Munitions barges, S. Amboy, N. J.	30
1956	Aug.	7	Dynamite trucks, Cali, Colombia	1,100
1958	Apr.	18	Sunken munitions ship, Okinawa	40
1958	May	22	Nike missiles, Leonardo, N.J.	10
1959	Apr.	10	World War II bomb, Philippines	38
1959	June	28	Rail tank cars, Meldrin, Ga.	25
1959	Aug.	7	Dynamite truck, Roseburg, Ore.	13
1959	Nov.	2	Jamuri Bazar, India, explosives	46
1959	Dec.	13	Dortmund, Ger., 2 apt. bldgs.	26
1960	Mar.	4	Belgian munitions ship, Havana	100
1960	Oct.	25	Gas, Windsor, Ont., store	11
1962	Jan.	16	Gas pipeline, Edson, Alberta, Canada	8
1962	Oct.	3	Telephone Co. office, N. Y. City	23
1963	Jan.	2	Packing plant, Terre Haute, Ind.	16

Date			Location	Deaths
1963	Mar.	9	Dynamite plant, S. Africa	45
1963	Aug.	13	Explosives dump, Gauhiti, India	32
1963	Oct.	31	State Fair Coliseum, Indianapolis	73
1964	July	23	Bone, Algeria, harbor munitions	100
1965	Mar.	4	Gas pipeline, Natchitoches, La.	17
1965	Aug.	9	Missile silo, Searcy, Ark.	53
1965	Oct.	21	Bridge, Tila Bund, Pakistan	80
1965	Oct.	30	Cartagena, Colombia	48
1965	Nov.	24	Armory, Keokuk, Ia.	20
1966	Oct.	13	Chemical plant, La Salle, Que.	11
1967	Feb.	17	Chemical plant, Hawthorne, N.J.	11
1967	Dec.	25	Apartment bldg., Moscow	20
1968	Apr.	6	Sports store, Richmond, Ind.	43
1970	Apr.	8	Subway construction, Osaka, Japan	73
1971	June	24	Tunnel, Sylmar, Cal.	17
1971	June	28	School, fireworks, Pueblo, Mex.	13
1971	Oct.	21	Shopping center, Glasgow, Scot.	20
1973	Feb.	10	Liquified gas tank, Staten Is., N.Y.	40
1975	Dec.	27	Chasnala, India, mine	431
1976	Apr.	13	Lapua, Finland, munitions works	40
1977	Nov.	11	Freight train, Iri, S. Korea	57
1977	Dec.	22	Grain elevator, Westwego, La.	35
1978	Feb.	24	Derailed tank car, Waverly, Tenn.	12
1978	July	11	Propylene tank truck, Spanish coastal campsite	150
1980	Oct.	23	School, Ortuella, Spain	64
1981	Feb.	13	Sewer system, Louisville, Ky.	0
1982	Apr.	7	Tanker truck, tunnel, Oakland, Cal.	7
1982	Apr.	25	Antiques exhibition, Todi, Italy	33
1982	Nov.	2	Salang Tunnel, Afghanistan	1,000-3,000
1984	Feb.	25	Oil pipeline, Cubatao, Brazil	508
1984	June	21	Naval supply depot, Severomorsk, USSR	200+
1984	Nov.	19	Gas storage area, NE Mexico City	334
1984	Dec.	5	Coal mine, Taipei, Taiwan	94
1985	June	25	Fireworks factory, Hallett, Okla.	21
1988	July	6	Oil rig, North Sea	167
1989	June	3	Gas pipeline, between Ufa, Asha, USSR	650+
1992	Mar.	3	Coal mine, Kozlu, Turkey	270+
1992	Apr.	22	Guadalajara, Mexico sewer	190

Notable Nuclear Accidents

Oct. 7, 1957 — A fire in the Windscale plutonium production reactor north of Liverpool, England spread radioactive material throughout the countryside. In 1983, the British government said that 39 people probably died of cancer as a result.

1957 — A chemical explosion in Kasli, USSR, in tanks containing nuclear waste, spread radioactive material and forced a major evacuation.

Jan. 3, 1961 — An experimental reactor at a federal installation near Idaho Falls, Id. killed three workers—the only deaths in U.S. reactor operations. The plant had high radiation levels but damage was contained.

Oct. 5, 1966 — A sodium cooling system malfunction caused a partial core meltdown at the Enrico Fermi demonstration breeder reactor near Detroit, Mich. Radiation was contained.

Jan. 21, 1969 — A coolant malfunction from an experimental underground reactor at Lucens Vad, Switzerland resulted in the release of a large amount of radiation into a cavern, which was then sealed.

Nov. 19, 1971 — The water-storage space at the Northern States Power Co.'s reactor in Monticello, Minn. filled to capacity and spilled over, dumping about 50,000 gallons of radioactive waste water into the Mississippi River. Some was taken into the St. Paul water system.

Mar. 22, 1975 — A technician checking for air leaks with a lighted candle caused a $100 million fire at the Brown's Ferry reactor in Decatur, Ala. The fire burned out electrical controls, lowering the cooling water to dangerous levels.

Mar. 28, 1979 — The worst commercial nuclear accident in the U.S. occured as equipment failures and human mistakes led to a loss of coolant, and partial core meltdown at the Three Mile Island reactor in Middletown, Pa.

Aug. 7, 1979 — Highly enriched uranium was released from a top-secret nuclear fuel plant near Erwin, Tenn. About 1,000 people were contaminated with up to 5 times as much radiation as would normally be received in a year.

Feb. 11, 1981 — Eight workers were contaminated when over 100,000 gallons of radioactive coolant leaked into the containment building of the TVA's Sequoyah 1 plant in Tennessee.

Apr. 25, 1981 — Some 100 workers were exposed to radioactive material during repairs of a nuclear plant at Tsuruga, Japan.

Jan. 25, 1982 — A steam-generator pipe broke at the Rochester Gas & Electric Co's Ginna plant near Rochester, N.Y. Small amounts of radioactive steam escaped into the air.

Jan. 6, 1986 — A cylinder of nuclear material burst after being improperly heated at a Kerr-McGee plant at Gore, Okla. One worker died and 100 were hospitalized.

Apr., 1986 — A serious accident at the Chernobyl nuclear plant about 60 miles from Kiev in the Soviet Union spewed clouds of radiation that spread over several European nations.

Record Oil Spills

As a rule, the number of tons can be multiplied by 7 to estimate the number of barrels spilled; the exact number of barrels in a ton varies with the type of oil. Each barrel contains 42 gallons.

Name, place	Date	Cause	Tons
Ixtoc I oil well, southern Gulf of Mexico	June 3, 1979	Blowout	600,000
Nowruz oil field, Persian Gulf	Feb., 1983	Blowout	600,000 (est.)
Atlantic Empress & Aegean Captain, off Trinidad & Tobago	July 19, 1979	Collision	300,000
Castillo de Bellver, off Cape Town, South Africa	Aug. 6, 1983	Fire	250,000
Amoco Cadiz, near Portsall, France	March 16, 1978	Grounding	223,000
Torrey Canyon, off Land's End, England	March 18, 1967	Grounding	119,000
Sea Star, Gulf of Oman	Dec. 19, 1972	Collision	115,000
Urquiola, La Coruna, Spain	May 12, 1976	Grounding	100,000
Hawaiian Patriot, northern Pacific	Feb. 25, 1977	Fire	99,000
Othello, Tralhavet Bay, Sweden	March 20, 1970	Collision	60,000-100,000

Other Notable Oil Spills

Name, place	Date	Cause	Gallons
Persian Gulf	Jan. 23, 1991 (began)	Spillage by Iraq	130,000,000*
World Glory, off South Africa	June 13, 1968	Hull failure	13,524,000
Burmah Agate, Galveston Bay, Tex.	Nov. 1, 1979	Collision	10,700,000
Exxon Valdez, Prince William Sound, Alas.	Mar. 24, 1989	Grounding	10,080,000
Keo, off Massachusetts	Nov. 5, 1969	Hull failure	8,820,000
Storage tank, Sewaren, N.J.	Nov. 4, 1969	Tank rupture	8,400,000
Ekofisk oil field, North Sea	Apr. 22, 1977	Well blowout	8,200,000
Argo Merchant, Nantucket, Mass.	Dec. 15, 1976	Grounding	7,700,000

Pipeline, West Delta, La.	Oct. 15, 1967	Dragging anchor	6,720,000
Tanker off Japan	Nov. 30, 1971	Ship broke in half	6,258,000
Storage tank, Monongahela River	Jan. 2, 1988	Tank rupture	3,800,000

* Estimated by Saudi Arabia. Some estimates are as low as 25,000,000 gallons.

Major Earthquakes

Magnitude of earthquakes (Mag.), distinct from deaths or damage caused, is measured on the Richter scale, on which each higher number represents a tenfold increase in energy measured in ground motion. Adopted in 1935, the scale has been applied in the following table to earthquakes as far back as reliable seismograms are available.

	Date	Location	Deaths	Mag.
526	May 20	Syria, Antioch	250,000	N.A.
856	....	Greece, Corinth	45,000	"
1057	....	China, Chihli	25,000	"
1268	....	Asia Minor, Cilicia	60,000	"
1290	Sept. 27	China, Chihli	100,000	"
1293	May 20	Japan, Kamakura	30,000	"
1531	Jan. 26	Portugal, Lisbon	30,000	"
1556	Jan. 24	China, Shaanxi	830,000	"
1667	Nov.	Caucasia, Shemaka	80,000	"
1693	Jan. 11	Italy, Catania	60,000	"
1730	Dec. 30	Japan, Hokkaido	137,000	"
1737	Oct. 11	India, Calcutta	300,000	"
1755	June 7	Northern Persia	40,000	"
1755	Nov. 1	Portugal, Lisbon	60,000	8.75*
1783	Feb. 4	Italy, Calabria	30,000	N.A.
1797	Feb. 4	Ecuador, Quito	41,000	"
1811-12		New Madrid, Mo. (series)	—	8.7*
1822	Sept. 5	Asia Minor, Aleppo	22,000	"
1828	Dec. 28	Japan, Echigo	30,000	"
1868	Aug. 13-15	Peru and Ecuador	40,000	"
1875	May 16	Venezuela, Colombia	16,000	"
1886	Aug. 31	Charleston, S.C.	60	6.6
1896	June 15	Japan, sea wave	27,120	N.A.
1906	Apr. 18-19	San Francisco, Cal.	503	8.3
1906	Aug. 16	Chile, Valparaiso	20,000	8.6
1908	Dec. 28	Italy, Messina	83,000	7.5
1915	Jan. 13	Italy, Avezzano	29,980	7.5
1920	Dec. 16	China, Gansu	100,000	8.6
1923	Sept. 1	Japan, Yokohama	200,000	8.3
1927	May 22	China, Nan-Shan	200,000	8.3
1932	Dec. 26	China, Gansu	70,000	7.6
1933	Mar. 2	Japan	2,990	8.9
1933	Mar. 10	Long Beach, Cal.	115	6.2
1934	Jan. 15	India, Bihar-Nepal	10,700	8.4
1935	May 31	India, Quetta	50,000	7.5
1939	Jan. 24	Chile, Chillan	28,000	8.3
1939	Dec. 26	Turkey, Erzincan	30,000	7.9
1946	Dec. 21	Japan, Honshu	2,000	8.4
1948	June 28	Japan, Fukui	5,131	7.3
1949	Aug. 5	Ecuador, Pelileo	6,000	6.8
1950	Aug. 15	India, Assam	1,530	8.7
1953	Mar. 18	NW Turkey	1,200	7.2
1956	June 10-17	N. Afghanistan	2,000	7.7
1957	July 2	Northern Iran	2,500	7.4
1957	Dec. 13	Western Iran	2,000	7.1
1960	Feb. 29	Morocco, Agadir	12,000	5.8
1960	May 21-30	Southern Chile	5,000	8.3
1962	Sept. 1	Northwestern Iran	12,230	7.1
1963	July 26	Yugoslavia, Skopje	1,100	6.0
1964	Mar. 27	Alaska	131	8.4
1966	Aug. 19	Eastern Turkey	2,520	6.9
1968	Aug. 31	Northeastern Iran	12,000	7.4
1970	Jan. 5	Yunnan Province, China	10,000	7.7
1970	Mar. 28	Western Turkey	1,086	7.4
1970	May 31	Northern Peru	66,794	7.7
1971	Feb. 9	San Fernando Valley, Cal.	65	6.6
1972	Apr. 10	Southern Iran	5,057	6.9
1972	Dec. 23	Nicaragua	5,000	6.2
1974	Dec. 28	Pakistan (9 towns)	5,200	6.3
1975	Sept. 6	Turkey (Lice, etc.)	2,312	6.8
1976	Feb. 4	Guatemala	22,778	7.5
1976	May 6	Northeast Italy	946	6.5
1976	June 26	New Guinea, Irian Jaya	443	7.1
1976	July 28	China, Tangshan	242,000	8.2
1976	Aug. 17	Philippines, Mindanao	8,000	7.8
1976	Nov. 24	E. Turkey	4,000	7.9
1977	Mar. 4	Romania	1,541	7.5
1977	Aug. 19	Indonesia	200	8.0
1977	Nov. 23	Northwestern Argentina	100	8.2
1978	June 12	Japan, Sendai	21	7.5
1978	Sept. 16	Northeast Iran	25,000	7.7
1979	Sept. 12	Indonesia	100	8.1
1979	Dec. 12	Colombia, Ecuador	800	7.9
1980	Oct. 10	Northwestern Algeria	4,500	7.3
1980	Nov. 23	Southern Italy	4,800	7.2
1982	Dec. 13	North Yemen	2,800	6.0
1983	Mar. 31	Southern Colombia	250	5.5
1983	May 26	N. Honshu, Japan	81	7.7
1983	Oct. 30	Eastern Turkey	1,300	7.1
1985	Mar. 3	Chile	146	7.8
1985	Sept. 19, 21	Mexico City	4,200+	8.1
1987	Mar. 5-6	NE Ecuador	4,000+	7.3
1988	Aug. 20	India/Nepal border	1,000+	6.5
1988	Nov. 6	China/Burma border	1,000	7.3
1988	Dec. 7	NW Armenia	55,000+	6.8
1989	Oct. 17	San Francisco Bay area	62	6.9
1990	May 30	N. Peru	115	6.3
1990	May 30	Romania	8	6.5
1990	June 21	NW Iran	40,000+	7.7
1990	July 16	Luzon, Philippines	1,621	7.7
1991	Feb. 1	Pakistan, Afghanistan border	1,200	6.8
1992	Mar. 13, 15	E. Turkey	4,000	6.2/6.0
1992	June 28	Yucca Valley, Cal.	1	7.4

(*) estimated from earthquake intensity. (N.A.) not available.

Some Recent Earthquakes

Source: Global Volcanism Network, Smithsonian Institution

Date	Location	Magnitude
June 28, 1992	Yucca Valley, Cal.	7.4
Apr. 25	N. California	7.0
Apr. 13	SE Netherlands	5.0
Mar. 13	Turkey	6.2
Feb. 27	E. New Guinea	6.7
Feb. 13	Vanuatu	6.8
Dec. 27, 1991	S. Sandwich Is.	7.1
Dec. 22	Kuril Is.	7.4
Dec. 2	Voiteg, Romania	5.6
Nov. 19	Off W. Colombia	7.0
Oct. 19	N. India	7.1
Oct. 14	Solomon Isl.	7.1
Sept. 18	Guatemala	6.0
Aug. 17	Off N. Cal.	7.1
Aug. 14	Vanuatu	6.6
July 24	N. Iraq	5.5
July 23	S. Peru	5.6
July 18	SW Romania	5.6
July 4	E. Indonesia	6.2
June 28	S. Cal.	5.9
June 20	Sulawesi, Indonesia	7.2
June 15	S. Ossetia, USSR	6.5
May 30	S. Alaska	6.8
May 24	S. Peru	6.8
May 19	Indonesia	6.9
Apr. 29	Georgia, USSR	7.2
Apr. 22	Costa Rica, Panama	7.4
Feb. 9	Solomon Islands	6.9
Jan. 5	Burma	7.1
Dec. 30, 1990	New Britain	6.7
Nov. 15	Indonesia	6.8
Nov. 6	S. Iran	6.8
Oct. 17	W. Brazil	6.7
Sept. 2	W. Equador	6.1
Aug. 3	N.W. China	6.1
July 9	Sudan	6.5
June 20	N. Iran	7.6
June 14	Kazakhstan, USSR	6.8
June 14	Panay Is., Philippines	7.1
June 7	Papua New Guinea	6.5

Historic Assassinations Since 1865

1865—Apr. 14. U. S. Pres. Abraham Lincoln, shot by John Wilkes Booth in Washington, D. C.; died Apr. 15.

1881—Mar. 13. Alexander II, of Russia—July 2. U. S. Pres. James A. Garfield, shot by Charles J. Guiteau, Washington D.C.; died Sept. 19.

1900—July 29. Umberto I, king of Italy.

1901—Sept. 6. U. S. Pres. William McKinley in Buffalo, N. Y., died Sept. 14. Leon Czolgosz executed for the crime Oct. 29.

1913—Feb. 23. Mexican Pres. Francisco I, Madero and Vice Pres. Jose Pino Suarez.—Mar. 18. George, king of Greece.

1914—June 28. Archduke Francis Ferdinand of Austria-Hungary and his wife in Sarajevo, Bosnia (later part of Yugoslavia), by Gavrilo Princip.

1916—Dec. 30. Grigori Rasputin, politically powerful Russian monk.

1918—July 12. Grand Duke Michael of Russia, at Perm.—July 16. Nicholas II, abdicated as czar of Russia; his wife, the Czarina Alexandra, their son, Czarevitch Alexis, and their daughters, Grand Duchesses Olga, Tatiana, Marie, Anastasia, and 4 members of their household were executed by Bolsheviks at Ekaterinburg.

1920—May 20. Mexican Pres. Gen. Venustiano Carranza in Tlaxcalantongo.

1922—Aug. 22. Michael Collins, Irish revolutionary.—Dec. 16. Polish President Gabriel Narutowicz in Warsaw by an anarchist.

1923—July 20. Gen. Francisco "Pancho" Villa, ex-rebel leader, in Parral, Mexico.

1928—July 17. Gen. Alvaro Obregon, president-elect of Mexico, in San Angel, Mexico.

1933—Feb. 15. In Miami, Fla. Joseph Zangara, anarchist, shot at Pres.-elect Franklin D. Roosevelt, but a woman seized his arm, and the bullet fatally wounded Mayor Anton J. Cermak, of Chicago, who died Mar. 6. Zangara was elecctrocuted on Mar. 20, 1933.

1934—July 25. In Vienna, Austrian Chancellor Engelbert Dollfuss by Nazis.

1935—Sept. 8. U. S. Sen. Huey P. Long, shot in Baton Rouge, La., by Dr. Carl Austin Weiss, who was slain by Long's bodyguards.

1940—Aug. 20. Leon Trotsky (Lev Bronstein), 63, exiled Russian war minister, near Mexico City. Killer identified as Ramon Mercador del Rio, a Spaniard, served 20 years in Mexican prison.

1948—Jan. 30. Mohandas K. Gandhi, 78, shot in New Delhi, India, by Nathuram Vinayak Godse.—Sept. 17. Count Folke Bernadotte, UN mediator for Palestine, ambushed in Jerusalem.

1951—July 20. King Abdullah ibn Hussein of Jordan. Oct. 16. Prime Min. Liaquat Ali Khan of Pakistan shot in Rawalpindi.

1956—Sept. 21. Pres. Anastasio Somoza of Nicaragua, in Leon; died Sept. 29.

1957—July 26. Pres. Carlos Castillo Armas of Guatemala, in Guatemala City by one of his own guards.

1958—July 14. King Faisal of Iraq; his uncle, Crown Prince Abdullah, and July 15, Premier Nuri as-Said, by rebels in Baghdad.

1959—Sept. 25. Prime Minister Solomon Bandaranaike of Ceylon, by Buddhist monk in Colombo.

1961—Jan. 17. Ex-Premier Patrice Lumumba of the Congo, in Katanga Province—May 30. Dominican dictator Rafael Leonidas Trujillo Molina shot to death by assassins near Ciudad Trujillo.

1963—June 12. Medgar W. Evers, NAACP's Mississippi field secretary, in Jackson, Miss.—Nov. 2. Pres. Ngo Dinh Diem of the Republic of Vietnam and his brother, Ngo Dinh Nhu, in a military coup.—Nov. 22. U. S. Pres. John F. Kennedy fatally shot in Dallas, Tex.; accused Lee Harvey Oswald murdered by Jack Ruby while awaiting trial.

1965—Jan. 21. Iranian premier Hassan Ali Mansour fatally wounded by assassin in Teheran; 4 executed.—Feb. 21. Malcolm X, black nationalist, fatally shot in N. Y. City.

1966—Sept. 6. Prime Minister Hendrik F. Verwoerd of South Africa stabbed to death in parliament at Capetown.

1968—Apr. 4. Rev. Dr. Martin Luther King Jr. fatally shot in Memphis, Tenn. by James Earl Ray.—June 5. Sen. Robert F. Kennedy (D-N. Y.) fatally shot in Los Angeles; Sirhan Sirhan, resident alien, convicted of murder.

1971—Nov. 28. Jordan Prime Minister Wasfi Tal, in Cairo, by Palestinian guerrillas.

1973—Mar. 2. U. S. Ambassador Cleo A. Noel Jr., U. S. Charge d'Affaires George C. Moore and Belgian Charge d'Affaires Guy Eid killed by Palestinian guerrillas in Khartoum, Sudan.

1974—Aug. 15. Mrs. Park Chung Hee, wife of president of So. Korea, hit by bullet meant for her husband.—Aug. 19. U. S. Ambassador to Cyprus, Rodger P. Davies, killed by sniper's bullet in Nicosia.

1975—Feb. 11. Pres. Richard Ratsimandrava, of Madagascar, shot in Tananarive.—Mar. 25. King Faisal of Saudi Arabia shot by nephew Prince Musad Abdel Aziz, in royal palace, Riyadh.—Aug. 15. Bangladesh Pres. Sheik Mujibur Rahman killed in coup.

1976—Feb. 13. Nigerian head of state, Gen. Murtala Ramat Mohammed, slain by self-styled "young revolutionaries."

1977—Mar. 16. Kamal Jumblat, Lebanese Druse chieftain, was shot near Beirut.—Mar. 18. Congo Pres. Marien Ngouabi shot in Brazzaville.

1978—July 9. Former Iraqi Premier Abdul Razak Al-Naif shot in London.

1979—Feb. 14. U.S. Ambassador Adolph Dubs shot and killed by Afghan Moslem extremists in Kabul.—Aug. 27. Lord Mountbatten, WW2 hero, and 2 others were killed when a bomb exploded on his fishing boat off the coast of Co. Sligo, Ire. The IRA claimed responsibility. —Oct. 26. So. Korean President Park Chung Hee and 6 bodyguards fatally shot by Kim Jae Kyu, head of Korean CIA, and 5 aides in Seoul.

1980—Apr. 12. Liberian President William R. Tolbert slain in military coup.—Sept. 17. Former Nicaraguan President Anastasio Somoza Debayle and 2 others shot in Paraguay.

1981—Oct. 6. Egyptian President Anwar El-Sadat fatally shot by a band of commandos while reviewing a military parade in Cairo.

1982—Sept. 14. Lebanese President-elect Bashir Gemayel killed by bomb in east Beirut.

1983—Aug. 21. Philippine opposition political leader Benigno Aquino Jr. fatally shot by a gunman at Manila International Airport.—Oct. 9. Four S. Korea cabinet ministers and 15 others killed by bomb blast in Rangoon, Burma.

1984—Oct. 31. Indian Prime Minister Indira Gandhi shot and killed by 2 of her bodyguards, who were members of the minority Sikh sect, in New Delhi.

1986—Feb. 28. Swedish Premier Olaf Palme shot and killed by a gunman in Stockholm.

1988—June 1. Lebanese Premier Rashid Karami killed when a bomb exploded aboard a helicopter in which he was traveling. —Apr. 16. PLO military chief Khalil Wazir (Abu Jihad) was gunned down by Israeli commandos in Tunisia.

1989—Aug. 18. Colombian Liberal Party presidential candidate Luis Carlos Galan was killed by Medellin cartel drug traffickers at a campaign rally in Bogota.—Nov. 22. Lebanese president Rene Moawad was killed when a bomb exploded next to his motorcade.

1990—Mar. 22. Colombian Patriotic Union presidential candidate Bernando Jamamillo Ossa was shot by a gunman at an airport in Bogota.

1991—May 21. Rajiv Gandhi, former prime minister of India, was killed when a bomb exploded during an election rally in Madras.

1992—June 29. Mohammed Boudiaf, president of Algeria, was shot by a gunman in Annaba.

Assassination Attempts

1910—Aug. 6. N. Y. City Mayor William J. Gaynor shot and seriously wounded by discharged city employee.

1912—Oct. 14. Former U. S. President Theodore Roosevelt shot and seriously wounded by demented man in Milwaukee, Wis.

1950—Nov. 1. In an attempt to assassinate President Truman, 2 members of a Puerto Rican nationalist movement—Griselio Torresola and Oscar Collazo—tried to shoot their way into Blair House. Torresola was killed, and a guard, Pvt. Leslie Coffelt was fatally shot. Collazo was convicted Mar. 7. 1951 for the murder of Coffelt.

1970—Nov. 27. Pope Paul VI unharmed by knife-wielding assailant who attempted to attack him in Manila airport.

1972—May 15. Alabama Gov. George Wallace shot in Laurel, Md. by Arthur Bremer; seriously crippled.

1972—Dec. 7. Mrs. Ferdinand E. Marcos, wife of the Philippine president, was stabbed and seriously injured in Pasay City, Philippines.

1975—Sept. 5. Pres. Gerald R. Ford was unharmed when a Secret Service agent grabbed a pistol aimed at him by Lynette (Squeaky) Fromme, a Charles Manson follower, in Sacramento.

1975—Sept. 22. Pres. Gerald R. Ford escaped unharmed when Sara Jane Moore, a political activist, fired a revolver at him.

1980—Apr. 14. Indian Prime Minister Indira Gandhi was unharmed when a man threw a knife at her in New Delhi.

1980—May 29. Civil rights leader Vernon E. Jordan Jr. shot and wounded in Ft. Wayne, Ind.

1981—Jan. 16. Irish political activist Bernadette Devlin McAliskey and her husband were shot and seriously wounded by 3 members of a protestant paramilitary group in Co. Tyrone, Ire.

1981—Mar. 30. Pres. Ronald Reagan, Press Secy. James Brady, Secret Service agent Timothy J. McCarthy, and Washington, D.C. policeman Thomas Delahanty were shot and seriously wounded by John W. Hinckley Jr. in Washington, D.C.

1981—May 13. Pope John Paul II and 2 bystanders were shot and wounded by Mehmet Ali Agca, an escaped Turkish murderer, in St. Peter's Square, Rome.

1982—May 12. Pope John Paul II was unharmed when a man with a knife was overpowered by guards, in Fatima, Portugal.

1982—June 3. Israel's ambassador to Britain Shlomo Argov was shot and seriously wounded by Arab terrorists in London.

1986—Sept. 7. Chile President Gen. Augusto Pinochet Ugarte escaped unharmed when his motorcade was attacked by rebels using rockets, bazookas, grenades, and rifles.

Notable Kidnapings in the U.S.

Edward A. Cudahy Jr., 16, in Omaha, Neb., **Dec. 18, 1900.** Returned Dec. 20 after $25,000 paid. Pat Crowe confessed.

Robert Franks, 13, in Chicago, **May 22, 1924,** by 2 youths, Richard Loeb and Nathan Leopold, who killed boy. Demand for $10,000 ignored. Loeb died in prison, Leopold paroled 1958.

Charles A. Lindbergh Jr., 20 mos. old, in Hopewell, N.J., **Mar. 1, 1932;** found dead May 12. Ransom of $50,000 was paid to man identified as Bruno Richard Hauptmann, 35, paroled German convict who entered U.S. illegally. Hauptmann was convicted after spectacular trial at Flemington, and electrocuted in Trenton, N.J. prison, Apr. 3. 1936.

William A. Hamm Jr., 39, in St. Paul, **June 15, 1933.** $100,000 paid. Alvin Karpis given life, paroled in 1969.

Charles F. Urschel, in Oklahoma City, **July 22, 1933.** Released July 31 after $200,000 paid. George (Machine Gun) Kelly and 5 others given life.

Brooke L. Hart, 22, in San Jose, Cal. Thomas Thurmond and John Holmes arrested after demanding $40,000 ransom. When Hart's body was found in San Francisco Bay, **Nov. 26, 1933,** a mob attacked the jail at San Jose and lynched the 2 kidnapers.

George Weyerhaeuser, 9, in Tacoma, Wash., **May 24, 1935.** Returned home June 1 after $200,000 paid. Kidnapers given 20 to 60 years.

Charles Mattson, 10, in Tacoma, Wash., **Dec. 27, 1936.** Found dead Jan. 11, 1937. Kidnaper asked $28,000, failed to contact.

Arthur Fried, in White Plains, N.Y., **Dec. 4, 1937.** Body not found. Two kidnapers executed.

Robert C. Greenlease, 6, taken from Kansas City, Mo. school **Sept. 28, 1953,** and held for $600,000. Body found Oct. 7. Mrs. Bonnie Brown Heady and Carl A. Hall pleaded guilty and were executed.

Peter Weinberger, 32 days old, Westbury, N.Y., **July 4, 1956,** for $2,000 ransom, not paid. Child found dead. Angelo John LaMarca, 31, convicted, executed.

Cynthia Ruotolo, 6 wks old, taken from carriage in front of Hamden, Conn. store **Sept. 1, 1956.** Body found in lake.

Lee Crary, 8 in Everett, Wash., **Sept. 22, 1957,** $10,000 ransom, not paid. He escaped after 3 days, led police to George E. Collins, who was convicted.

Frank Sinatra Jr., 19, from hotel room in Lake Tahoe, Cal., **Dec. 8, 1963.** Released **Dec. 11** after his father paid $240,000 ransom. Three men sentenced to prison; most of ransom recovered.

Barbara Jane Mackle, 20, abducted **Dec. 17, 1968,** from Atlanta, Ga., motel, was found unharmed 3 days later, buried in a coffin-like wooden box 18 inches underground, after her father had paid $500,000 ransom; Gary Steven Krist sentenced to life, Ruth Eisenmann-Schier to 7 years; most of ransom recovered.

Mrs. Roy Fuchs, 35, and 3 children held hostage 2 hours, **May 14, 1969,** in Long Island, N. Y., released after her husband, a bank manager, paid kidnapers $129,000 in bank funds; 4 men arrested, ransom recovered.

Mrs. Virginia Piper, 49, abducted **July 27, 1972,** from her home in suburban Minneapolis; found unharmed near Duluth 2 days later after her husband paid $1 million ransom to the kidnapers.

Patricia (Patty) Hearst, 19, taken from her Berkeley, Cal., apartment **Feb. 4, 1974.** Symbionese Liberation Army demanded her father, Randolph A. Hearst, publisher, give millions to poor. She was identified by FBI as taking part in a San Francisco bank holdup, **Apr. 15.** FBI, **Sept. 18, 1975,** captured Patricia and others in San Francisco; they were indicted on various charges. Patricia for bank robbery. Convicted, **Mar. 20, 1976.** She was released from prison under executive clemency, **Feb. 1, 1979.** In 1978, William and Emily Harris were sentenced to 10 years to life for the Hearst kidnaping. Both were paroled in 1983.

J. Reginald Murphy, 40, an editor of *Atlanta* (Ga.) *Constitution,* kidnaped **Feb. 20, 1974,** freed **Feb. 22** after payment of $700,000 ransom by the newspaper. Police arrested William A. H. Williams, a contractor; most of the money was recovered.

E. B. Reville, Hepzibah, Ga., banker, and wife Jean, kidnaped **Sept. 30, 1974.** Ransom of $30,000 paid. He was found alive; Mrs. Reville was found dead in car trunk **Oct. 2.**

Jack Teich, Kings Point, N.Y., steel executive, seized **Nov. 12, 1974;** released **Nov. 19** after payment of $750,000.

Sidney J. Reso, oil co. executive, seized **Apr. 29, 1992;** died May 3; Arthur D. Seale and wife, Irene J. Seale, arrested **June 19.**

ASSOCIATIONS AND SOCIETIES

Source: World Almanac questionnaire

Arranged according to key words in titles. Founding year of organization in parentheses; last figure after ZIP code indicates membership.

AFS Intercultural Programs (1917), 313 E. 43rd Street, N.Y., NY 10017; 125,000+.
ASM International (1913), 9639 Kinsman Rd., Materials Park, OH 44073-0002; 54,000.
ASTM (1898), 1916 Race St., Philadelphia, PA 19103.
Aaron Burr Assn. (1946), 4520 King Edward Ct., Annandle, VA 22003; 600.
Abortion Federation, Natl. (1977), 1436 U St. NW, Suite 103, Washington, DC 20009; 300 organizations.
Accountants, Amer. Institute of Certified Public (1887), 1211 Ave. of the Americas, N.Y., NY 10036; 305,465.
Accountants, Natl. Assn. of (1919), 10 Paragon Dr., Box 433, Montvale, NJ 07645-1760; 85,000.
Accountants, Natl. Society of Public (1945), 1010 N. Fairfax St., Alexandria, VA 22314.
Accountants for Cooperatives, Natl. Soc. of (1936), 6320 Augusta Dr., Ste. 800, Springfield, VA 22150; 2,000.
Acoustical Society of America (1929), 500 Sunnyside Blvd., Woodbury, NY 11797; 6,900.
Actors' Equity Assn. (1913), 165 W. 46 St., N.Y., NY 10036.
Actors' Fund of America (1882), 1501 Broadway, N.Y., NY 10036; 3,500.
Actuaries, American Academy of (1965), 1720 I St. NW, Wash., DC 20006; 10,500.
Actuaries, Society of (1949), 475 N. Martingale Rd., Suite 800, Schaumburg, IL 60173-2226; 13,830.
Advertisers, Assn. of Natl. (1910), 155 E. 44th St., N.Y., NY 10017.
Advertising Agencies, Amer. Assn. of (1917), 666 Third Ave., N.Y., NY 10017; 765 agencies.
Aeronautic Assn., Natl. (1905), 1815 N. Fort Myer Dr., Ste. 700, Arlington, VA 22209; 250,000.
Aeronautics and Astronautics, Amer. Institute of (1963), 1633 Broadway, N.Y., NY 10019; 38,000.
Aerospace Industries Assn. of America (1919), 1250 Eye St. NW, Wash., DC 20005; 54 cos.
Aerospace Medical Assn. (1929), 320 S. Henry St., Alexandria, VA 22314-3524; 4,350.
Afro-American Life and History, Assn. for the Study of (1915), 1401 14th St. NW, Wash., DC 20005; 1,800.
Aging Assn., Amer. (1970), 600 South 42nd St., Omaha, NE 68198-4635; 400.
Agricultural Chemicals Assn., Natl. (1933), 1155 15th St. NW, Wash., DC 20005; 80 cos.
Agricultural Economics Assn., Amer. (1910), 80 Heady Hall, Iowa State Univ., Ames, IA 50011; 4,500.
Agricultural History Society (1919), Room 932, 1301 New York Ave. NW, Wash., DC 20250; 1,400.
Agronomy, Amer. Society of (1907), 677 S. Segoe Rd., Madison, WI 53711; 12,675.
Aircraft Assn., Experimental (1953), EAA Aviation Center, Oshkosh, WI 54903-3086; 130,000.
Aircraft Owners and Pilots Assn. (1939), 421 Aviation Way, Frederick, MD 21701; 300,000.
Air Force Assn. (1946), 1501 Lee Hwy., Arlington, VA 22209.
Air Force Sergeants Assn. (1961), P.O. Box 31050, Temple Hills, MD 20748.
Air Line Employees Assn. (1948), 5600 S. Central Ave., Chicago, IL 60638; 3,679.
Air Line Pilots Assn. (1931), 1625 Massachusetts Ave. NW, Wash., DC 20036; 41,000.
Air Pollution Control Assn. (1907), P.O. Box 2861, Pittsburgh, PA 15230; 8,500.
Air Transport Assn. of America (1936), 1709 New York Ave. NW, Wash., DC 20006; 19 airlines.
Air & Waste Management Assn. (1907), P.O. Box 2861, Pittsburgh, PA 15230; 12,000.
Al-Anon Family Groups (1950), P.O. Box 862, Midtown Sta., N.Y., NY 10018; 24,918.
Alcohol Problems, Amer. Council on (1895), 3426 Bridgeland Dr., Bridgeton, MO 63044; 37 state affiliates.
Alcoholics Anonymous (1935), P.O. Box 459, Grand Central Station, N.Y., NY 10163.
Alcoholism and Drug Dependence, Natl. Council on (1944), 12 W. 21st St., N.Y., NY 10010; 200 affiliates.
Allergy and Immunology, Amer. Academy of (1943), 611 E. Wells St., Milwaukee, WI 53202; 4,200.
Alpine Club, Amer. (1902), 113 E. 90th St., N.Y., NY 10028.
Altrusa Intl. (1917), 332 S. Michigan Ave., Chicago, IL 60604.
Alzheimer's Assn. (1980), 70 E. Lake St., Chicago, IL 60601-5997; 35,000
Amer. Indian Affairs, Assn. on (1922), 245 Fifth Ave., Ste. 1801, N.Y., NY, 10016-8728; 15,000.
American Legion, The (1919), 700 N. Pennsylvania St., Indianapolis, IN 46204; 3.0 mln. **American Legion Auxiliary** (1920), 777 N. Meridian St., Indianapolis, IN 46204; 887,104.
Amer. States, Organization of (1890), 17th & Constitution Ave. NW, Wash., DC 20006; 35 countries.
Amer. Veterans (AMVETS) (1947); **AMVETS Auxiliary** (1946), 4647 Forbes Blvd., Lanham, MD 20706-9961; 200,000.
Amideast (Amer. Mideast Educational & Training Services) (1951), 1100 17th St. NW, Suite 300, Wash., DC 20036-4601.
Amnesty Intl. USA (1961), 322 Eighth Ave., N.Y., NY 10001.
Amputation Foundation, Natl. (1923), 12-45 150th St., Whitestone, NY 11357; 2,300.
Animal Protection Institute of America (1968), 2831 Fruitridge Rd., P.O. Box 95822, Sacramento, CA 95822; 135,000.
Animal Welfare Institute (1951), P.O. Box 3650, Wash., DC 20007; 12,000.
Animals, Amer. Society for Prevention of Cruelty to (ASPCA) (1866), 441 E. 92d St., N.Y., NY 10128; 400,000.
Animals, The Fund for (1967), 200 W. 57th St., N.Y., NY 10019; 200,000.
Animals, People for the Ethical Treatment of (1980), P.O. Box 42516, Wash., DC 20015; 350,000.
Antelopes, Grand United Order of (1925), 162 Fourth Ave., E. Orange, NJ 01017; 499.
Anthropological Assn., Amer. (1902), 1703 New Hampshire Ave. NW, Wash., DC 20009; 11,000.
Antiquarian Society, Amer. (1812), 185 Salisbury St., Worcester, MA 01609-1634; 552.
Anti-Vivisection Society, Amer. (1883), Suite 204, 801 Old York Rd., Jenkintown, PA 19046; 10,000+.
Appalachian Mountain Club (1876), 5 Joy St., Boston, MA 02108; 53,500.
Appalachian Trail Conference (1925), Washington & Jackson Sts., Harpers Ferry, WV 25425; 23,000.
Appraisers, Amer. Society of (1936), 535 Herndon Pwky., #150, Herndon, VA 22070; 6,000.
Arab Americans, Natl. Assn. of (1972), 2033 M St. NW, Wash., DC 20036.
Arbitration Assn., Amer. (1926), 140 W. 51st St., N.Y., NY 10020-1203; 6,523.
Arboriculture, Intl. Society of (1924), 5 Lincoln Sq., Urbana, IL 61801; 4,500.
Arc, The (1950), 500 E. Border St., Ste. 300, Arlington, TX 76010; 140,000.
Archaeological Institute of America (1879), 675 Commonwealth Ave., Boston, MA 02215; 11,500.
Archaeology, Institute of Nautical (1976), P.O. Drawer HG, College Station, TX 77841-5137; 1,100.
Archery Assn., Natl. (1879), 1750 E. Boulder St., Colorado Springs, CO 80909; 3,900.
Architects, Amer. Institute of (1857), 1735 New York Ave. NW, Wash., DC 20006; 51,000.
Architectural Historians, Society of (1940), 1232 Pine Street, Phila., PA 19107-5944; 3,500.
Armed Forces Communications and Electronics Assn. (1946), 4400 Fair Lakes Ct., Fairfax, VA 22033; 40,000.
Army, Assn. of the United States (1950), 2425 Wilson Blvd., Arlington, VA 22201; 150,000.
Arts, Amer. Council for the (1960), 1285 Avenue of the Americas, N.Y., NY 10019; 1,725.
Arts, Amer. Federation of (1909), 41 E. 65th St., N.Y., NY 10021.
Arts and Letters, Amer. Academy and Institute of (1898), 633 W. 155th St., N.Y., NY 10032; 250.
Arts and Letters, Natl. Society of (1944), 2800 Quebec St. NW, Washington, DC 20008; 1,700.
Arts & Sciences, Amer. Academy of (1780), Norton's Woods, 136 Irving St., Cambridge, MA 02138; 3,500.
Asbestos Council, Natl. (1983), 1777 NE Expressway, Ste. 150, Atlanta, GA 30329; 4,000+.
Assistance League, Natl. (1949), 5627 Fernwood Ave., Los Angeles, CA 90038; 17,000.
Association Executives, American Society of (1920), 1575 Eye St. NW, Wash., DC 20005; 18,000.
Association Publications, Society of Natl. (1963), 3299 K St. NW, Suite 700, Wash., DC 20007; 210 publications.
Astrologers, Amer. Federation of (1938), 6535 S. Rural Rd., Tempe, AZ 85283; 4,500.
Astronautical Society, Amer. (1954), 6352 Rolling Mill Pl., Suite 102, Springfield, VA 22152; 1,600.
Astronomical Society, Amer. (1899), 2000 Florida Ave., NW, Suite 300, Wash., DC 20009; 5,700.
Ataxia Foundation, Natl. (1957), 600 Twelve Oaks Cntr., 15500 Wayzata Blvd., Wayzata MN 55391; 1,400.

Atheist Assn. (1925), 910 E Street, San Diego, CA 92101.
Atheists, Amer. (1959), P.O. Box 140195, Austin, TX 78714.
Atheists, United World (1972), 7215 Cameron Rd., Austin, TX 78752; 35 org.
Athetic Assn., Natl. Jr. College (1939), P.O. Box 7305, Colorado Springs, CO 80933-7305; 550.
Athletic Assn., Natl. Scholastic (1985), 6991 Simson St., Oakland, CA 94605-2226.
Athletic Associations, Natl. Federation of State H. S. (1920), 11724 Plaza Circle, Box 20626, Kansas City, MO 64195.
Athletic Union of the U.S., Amateur (1888), 3400 W. 86th St., Indianapolis, IN 46268; 200,000+.
Athletics Congress/USA, The (1979), One Hoosier Dome, Indianapolis, IN 46225; 120,000.
Auctioneers Assn., Natl. (1949), 8880 Ballentine, Overland Park, KS 66214; 5,281.
Audubon Society, Natl. (1905), 950 Third Ave., N.Y., NY 10022; 1 mln.
Authors Guild, Inc., The (1921), 330 W. 42nd St., New York, NY 10036; 14,000.
Authors League of America (1912), 234 W. 44th St., N.Y., NY 10036; 15,000.
Autism, Society of America, (1965), 8601 Georgia Ave., Ste. 503, Silver Springs, MD 20910; 10,000.
Autograph Collectors Club, Universal (1965), P.O. Box 6181, Wash., DC 20044-6181; 2,447.
Automobile Assn., Amer. (1902), 8111 Gatehouse Rd., Falls Church, VA 22047; 28 million+.
Automobile Club, Natl. (1924), One Market Plaza, San Francisco, CA 94105; 316,000.
Automobile Club of America, Antique (1935), 501 W. Governor Rd., Hershey, PA 17033; 53,000.
Automobile Dealers Assn., Natl. (1917), 8400 Westpark Dr., McLean, VA 22102; 19,000.
Automobile License Plate Collectors' Assn. (1954), P.O. Box 77, Horner, W. VA 26372; 2,500.
Automotive Hall of Fame (1939), 3225 Cook Rd., Midland, MI 48640; 2,500.
Automotive Testers, Society of (1950), 461 Stuart Ln., Palatine, IL 60067; 326.
Avon Collectors, Inc., Natl. Assn. of (1971), P.O. Box 68, W. Newton, IN 46183; 100 clubs.

Badminton Assn., U.S. (1936), 920 O Street, Lincoln, NE 68508; 1,974.
Baker Street Irregulars (1934), 34 Pierson Ave., Norwood, NJ 07648; 275.
Bald-Headed Men of America (1973), 102 Bald Drive, Morehead City, N.C. 28557; approx. 20,000.
Ball Players of Amer., Assn. of Professional (1924), 12062 Valley View St., #211, Garden Grove, CA 92645; 15,000.
Band & Choral Directors Hall of Fame, Natl. (1985), 519 N. Halifax Ave., Daytona Beach, FL 32118.
Bankers Assn., Amer. (1875), 1120 Connecticut Ave. NW, Wash., DC 20036.
Bankers Assn. of America, Independent (1930), One Thomas Circle NW, Suite 950, Wash. DC 20005; 6,400 banks.
Bar Assn., Federal (1920), 1815 H St. NW, Wash., DC 20006; 14,300.
Barbershop Quartet Singing in Amer., Soc. for Preservation & Encouragement of (1938), 6315 Third Ave., Kenosha, WI 53140-5199; 35,000.
Baseball Congress, Amer. Amateur (1935), 118-19 Redfield Plaza, Marshall, MI 49068; 10,625 teams.
Baseball Congress, Natl. (1931), P.O. Box 1420, Wichita, KS 67201.
Baseball Research, Society for Amer. (1971), P.O. Box 93183, Cleveland, OH 44101; 6,000.
Basketball Assn., Natl. (1946), 645 Fifth Ave., N.Y., NY 10022.
Battleship Assn., Amer. (1964), P.O. Box 711247, San Diego, CA 92171; 1,300.
Beer Can Collectors of America (1970), 747 Merus Ct., Fenton, MO 63026-2092; 4,500.
Beta Gamma Sigma (1913), 605 Old Ballas Rd., Suite 200, St. Louis, MO 63141; 300,000.
Beta Sigma Phi (1931), 1800 W. 91st Place, Kansas City, MO 64114; 250,000.
Bible Society, Amer. (1816), 1865 Broadway, N.Y., NY 10023; 188,500.
Biblical Literature, Society of (1880), 1549 Clairmont Rd., Ste. 204, Decatur, GA 30033; 5,500.
Bibliographical Society of America (1904), P.O. Box 397, Grand Central Sta., N.Y., NY 10163; 1,500.
Big Brothers/Big Sisters of America (1902), 230 No. 13th St., Philadelphia, PA 19107; 494 agencies.
Biochemistry and Molecular Biology, Amer. Society for (1906), 9650 Rockville Pike, Bethesda, MD 20814-3996; 8,654.
Biological Sciences, American Institute of (1947), 730 11th St. NW, Washington, DC 20001-4521; 14,000.
Black History Honors & Awards, Contemporary & (1990), Masonic Temple Bldg., 408 17th St. N., Ste. C, Birmingham, AL 35203.
Blind, Amer. Foundation for the (1921), 15 W. 16th St., N.Y., NY 10011; 250.
Blind, Natl. Federation of the (1940), 1800 Johnson St., Baltimore, MD 21230; 50,000.
Blindness, Natl. Society to Prevent (1908), 500 E. Remington Rd., Schaumburg, IL 60173; 26 affiliates.
Blindness, Research to Prevent (1960), 598 Madison Ave., N.Y., NY 10023; 1,400.
Blue Angels Assn. (1982), 4600 Twin Oaks Dr., Apt. 702, Warrington, FL 32506; 250.
Blue Cross and Blue Shield Assn. (1946), 676 St. Clair, Chicago, IL 60611; 74 plans.
Blueberry Council, No. Amer. (1965), P.O. Box 166, Marmora, NJ 08223; 80.
Bluebird Society, No. Amer. (1978), 2 Countryside Ct., Silver Spring, MD 20906; 5,000.
B'nai B'rith Intl. (1853), 1640 Rhode Island Ave. NW, Wash., DC 20036; 500,000.
Boat Assn., Amer. Power (1903), 17640 E. Nine Mile Rd., E. Detroit, MI 48021; 5,000.
Boat Club, Chris Craft Antique (1973), 217 S. Adams St., Tallahassee, FL 32301; 2,000.
Boat Owners Assn. of the U.S. (1966), 880 S. Pickett St., Alexandria, VA 22304; 350,000.
Bodybuilders Assn., Amer. (1981), 6991 Simson St., Oakland, CA 94605-2226; 854.
Bookplate Collectors and Designers, Amer. Soc. of (1922), 605 N. Stoneman Ave. #F, Alhambra, CA 91801; 200.
Booksellers Assn., Amer. (1900), 122 E. 42d St., N.Y., NY 10168; 5,557.
Botanical Gardens & Arboreta, Amer. Assn. of (1940), 786 Church Rd, Wayne, PA 19087; 1,800.
Bottle Collectors, Federation of Historical (1969), 4098 Faxon Ave., Memphis, TN 38122; 600.
Bowling Congress, Amer. (1895), 5301 S. 76th St., Greendale, WI 53129; 2.7 mln.
Boys' Brigades of America, United (1893), 2803 Glendale Ave., Baltimore, MD 21234; 150.
Boys' Clubs of America (1906), 771 First Ave., N.Y., NY 10017; 1.2 mln.
Boy Scouts of America (1910), 1325 Walnut Hill Lane, Irving, TX 75015-2079; 3.8 mln.
Bread for the World (1975), 802 Rhode Island Ave. NE, Washington, DC 20018; 43,000.
Bridge, Tunnel and Turnpike Assn., Intl. (1932), 2120 L St. NW, Suite 305, Wash., DC 20037; 250 organizations.
Brith Sholom, Natl. (1905), 3939 Conshohocken Ave., Philadelphia, PA 19131; 4,500.
Broadcasters, Natl. Assn. of (1922), 1771 N St. NW, Wash., DC 20036.
Burroughs Bibliophiles, The (1960), 454 Elaine Dr., Pittsburgh, PA 15236; 437.
Bus Assn., Amer. (1928), 1015 15th St. NW, Suite 250, Wash., DC 20005; 3,000.
Business Bureaus, Council of Better (1970), 4200 Wilson Blvd., Arlington, VA 22203; 180 bureaus.
Business Clubs, Natl. Assn. of Amer. (1922), 3315 No. Main St., High Point, NC 27262; 6,727.
Business Communication, Assn. for (1935), Univ. of North Texas, Denton, TX 76203; 2,400.
Business Communicators, Intl. Assn. of (1970), One Hallidie Pl., Suite 600, San Francisco, CA 94102.
Business Education Assn., Natl. (1946), 1906 Association Dr., Reston, VA 22091; 18,000.
Business Real Estate & Law Assn., Amer. (1923), Dept. of Legal Studies, Univ. of Georgia, Athens, GA 30602; 1,200.
Business-Professional Advertising Assn. (1922), 100 Metroplex Dr., Edison, NJ 08817; 4,500.
Button Society, Natl. (1938), 2733 Juno Pl., Akron, OH 44313; 3,000.
Byron Society, The (1971 England, 1973 in U.S.), 259 New Jersey Ave., Collingswood, NJ 08108; 300.

CLU & CHFC, Amer. Soc. of (1928), 270 Bryn Mawr Ave., Bryn Mawr, PA 19010; 32,000.
CPCU, The Society of (1944), 720 Providence Rd., Malvern, PA 19355; 22,000.
Camp Fire Boys & Girls (1910), 4601 Madison Ave., Kansas City, MO 64112; 600,000.
Campers & Hikers Assn., Inc. (1954), 4804 Transit Rd., Depew, NY 14043; 24,000 families.
Camping Assn., Amer. (1910), 5000 SR 67 N., Martinsville, IN 46151; 5,200.

Cancer Society, Amer. (1913), 90 Park Ave., N.Y., NY 10017.
Canoe Assn., U.S. (1968), 606 Ross St., Middletown, OH 45044; 1,300.
Carillonneurs in North America, Guild of (1936), 3718 Settle Rd., Cincinnati, OH 45227; 483.
Carnegie Hero Fund Commission (1904), 2307 Oliver Bldg., Pittsburgh, PA 15222; 21 members.
Cartoonists Society, Natl. (1946), 157 W. 57th St., Suite 904, N.Y., NY 10019; 500.
Cat Fanciers' Assn. (1906), 1805 Atlantic Ave., Manasquan, NJ 08736-1005.
Catholic Bishops, Natl. Conference of/U.S. Cath. Conference (1966), 1312 Massachusetts Ave. NW, Wash., DC 20005.
Catholic Charities, USA (1910), 1731 King St., Ste 200, Alexandria, VA 22314; 3,000.
Catholic Church Extension Society of the U.S.A. (1905), 35 E. Wacker Dr., Chicago, IL 60601; 220,000.
Catholic Daughters of the Americas (1903), 10 W. 71st St., N.Y., NY 10023; 143,000.
Catholic Educational Assn., Natl. (1904), 1077-30th St. NW, Suite 100, Wash, DC 20007; 18,353.
Catholic Historical Soc., Amer. (1884), 263 S. Fourth St., P.O. Box 84, Philadelphia, PA 19106; 728.
Catholic Library Assn. (1921), 461 W. Lancaster Ave., Haverford, PA 19041; 1,518.
Catholic Press Assn. of U.S. and Canada (1911), 119 N. Park Ave., Rockville Centre, NY 11570.
Catholic Rural Life Conference, Natl. (1923), 4625 NW Beaver Ave., Des Moines, IA 50310; 2,500.
Catholic War Veterans of the U.S.A. (1935), 419 North Lee Street, Alexandria, VA 22314; 30,000.
Celiac Sprue Assn./USA (1986), 2313 Rocklyn Dr., Suite 1, Des Moines, IA 50322; 1,800.
Cemetery Assn., Amer. (1887), 5201 Leesburg Pike, Falls Church, VA 22041; 3,000.
Ceramic Society, Amer. (1898), 735 Ceramic Pl., Westerville, OH 43081; 13,000.
Cerebral Palsy Assns., United (1949), 7 Penn Plaza, N.Y., NY 10001; 180 affiliates.
Chamber of Commerce of the U.S.A. (1912), 1615 H St. NW, Wash., DC 20062; 185,000.
Chamber Music Players, Amateur (1948), 545 Eighth Ave., N.Y., NY 10018; 4,000.
Chaplain's Intl. Assn. (1960), Adjutant General Office, 5045 N. Robberson, Springfield, MO 65803; 864.
Checker Federation, Amer. (1948), 3475 Belmont Ave., Baton Rouge, LA 70808; 1,000.
Chemical Manufacturers Assn. (1872), 2501 M St. NW, Wash., DC 20037; 171 companies.
Chemical Society, Amer. (1876), 1155 16th St. NW, Wash., DC 20036; 135,000.
Chemists, Amer. Institute of (1923), 7315 Wisconsin Ave., Bethesda, Md. 20814; 5,000
Chemists, Amer. Society of Brewing (1934), 3340 Pilot Knob Rd., St. Paul MN 55121.
Chemists, Amer. Assn. of Cereal (1915), 3340 Pilot Knob Rd., St. Paul, MN 55121; 3,523.
Chess Federation, U.S. (1939), 186 Rte. 9W, New Windsor, NY 12553; 61,255.
Chess League of Amer., Correspondence (1897), P.O. Box 3481, Barrington, IL 60011-3481; 1,000.
Child Welfare League of America (1920), 440 First St. NW, Wash., DC 20001; 600 agencies.
Childbirth Without Pain Education Assn. (1959), 20134 Snowden, Detroit, MI 48235; 3,000.
Childhood Education Intl., Assn. for (1892), 11501 Georgia Ave., Suite 315, Wheaton, MD 20902; 12,000.
Children of the Amer. Revolution, Natl. Society of the (1895), 1776 D St. NW, Wash., DC 20006.
Children's Aid Society (1853), 105 E. 22d St., N.Y., NY 10010; 1,207.
Children's Book Council (1945), 568 Broadway, Suite 404, N.Y., NY 10012; 65 publishing houses.
Chiropractic Assn., Amer. (1930), 1916 Wilson Blvd., Arlington, VA 22201; 20,000.
Chiropractors Assn., Intl. (1926), 1901 L St. NW, Wash., DC 20036; 7,000.
Christian Endeavor, Intl. Society of (1881), 1221 E. Broad St., P.O. Box 1110, Columbus, OH 43216.
Christian Laity Counseling Board (1970), 5901 Plainfield Dr., Charlotte, NC 28215; 38 mln.
Christians and Jews, Natl. Conference of (1927), 71 Fifth Ave., Suite 1100 N.Y., NY 10003.
Church Business Administration, Natl. Assn. of (1956), 7001 Grapevine Hwy., Suite 324, Ft. Worth, TX 76180; 1,500.
Church Federation, Ecumenical (1982), 13014-270, N. Dalemabry, Tampa, FL 33618-2808.
Churches, U.S. Conference for the World Council of (1948), 475 Riverside Dr., N.Y., NY 10115; 317 denominations.
Church Women United (1941), The Interchurch Center, 475 Riverside Dr., Rm. 812, N.Y., NY 10115.
Cinematographers, Am. Society of (1919), 1782 N. Orange Dr., Hollywood, CA 90028; 266.
Cincinnati, Society of the (1783), 2118 Massachusetts Ave. NW, Wash., DC 20008; 3,200.
Circulation Managers Assn., Intl. (1889), 11600 Sunrise Valley Dr., Reston, VA 22091; 1,705.
Circus Fans Assn. of America (1926), P.O. Box 3187, Flint, MI 48502; 2,400.
Cities, Natl. League of (1924), 1301 Pennsylvania Ave. NW, Wash., DC 20004.
City Management Assn., Intl. (1914), 777 North Capitol St., Ste. 500, Wash., DC 20002; 6,000.
Civic League, Natl. (1894), 1601 Grant St., Suite 250, Denver, CO 80203; 1,500.
Civil Air Patrol (1941), HQ CAP-USAF, Maxwell AFB, AL 36112-5572; 63,000.
Civil Engineers, Amer. Society of (1852), 345 E. 47th St., N.Y., NY 10017; 104,000.
Civil Liberties Union, Amer. (1920), 132 W. 43rd St., N.Y. NY 10036; 250,000.
Civil War Round Table of New York (1951), P.O. Box 3485, N.Y., NY 10185; 150+.
Civic League, Natl. (1894), 55 West 44th St., N.Y., NY 10036; 3,000.
Civitan Internatl. (1920), 1401 52nd St. S., Birmingham, AL 35213-1903; 60,000.
Classical League, Amer. (1919), Hall, Miami Univ., Oxford, OH 45056; 3,604.
Clinical Pastoral Education, Assn. for (1967), 1549 Clairmont Rd., Decatur, GA 30033; 3,500.
Clinical Pathologists, Amer. Society of (1922), 2100 W. Harrison St., Chicago, IL 60612; 50,000.
Clinical Social Work, Inc., Natl. Fed. of Soc. for (1971), P.O. Box 3740, Arlington, VA 22203; 10,000+.
Coal Association, Natl. (1917), 1130 17th St. NW, Wash., DC 20036; 150 corporate members.
Co-Dependents Anonymous (1986), P.O. Box 33577, Phoenix, AZ 85067-3577.
College Athletic Conference, Eastern (1938), 1311 Craigville Beach Rd., P.O. Box 3, Centerville, MA 02632.
College Board, The (1900), 45 Columbus Ave., N.Y., NY 10023; 2,800 institutions.
College Music Society (1958), 202 W. Spruce St., Missoula, MT 59802; 4,000.
College Physical Education Assn. for Men, Natl. (1897), 108 Cooke Hall, Univ. of Minnesota, Minneapolis, MN 55455.
College Placement Council (1956), 62 Highland Ave., Bethlehem, PA 18017; 3,100.
Colleges, Amer. Assn. of Community and Jr. (1921), One Dupont Circle NW, Suite 410, Wash., DC 20036.
Colleges, Assn. of Amer. (1915), 1818 R St. NW, Wash., DC 20009; 635 institutions.
Colleges and Universities, Assn. of Intl. (1973), I301 S. Noland Rd., Independence, MO 64055; 10,860.
Collegiate Athletic Assn., Natl. (1906), 6201 College Blvd., Overland Park, KS 66211-2422; 828 inst.
Collegiate Body-Building Assn., Natl. (1983), 6991 Simson St., Oakland, CA 94605; 683.
Collegiate Schools of Business, Amer. Assembly of (1916), 605 Old Ballas Rd., St. Louis, MO 63141-7077.
Colonial Dames of Amer. (1899), 421 E. 61 St., N.Y., NY 10021; 2,049.
Colonial Dames XVII Century, Natl. Society (1915), 1300 New Hampshire Ave. NW, Wash., DC 20036; 13,000.
Colonial Wars, General Society of (1892), 840 Woodbine Ave., Glendale, OH 45246; 4,300.
Colorado Alumni Assn., U.S.S. (1984), P.O. Box 9862, McLean, VA 22102-0062; 755.
Commerce, U.S. Junior Chamber of (1920), 4 W. 21st St., Tulsa, OK 74114-1116; 225,000.
Commercial Collectors Assn., Amer. (1970), 4040 W. 70th St., Minneapolis, MN 55435; 3,225.
Commercial Law League of America (1895), 175 W. Jackson, #1541, Chicago, IL 60604; 5,300.
Commercial Travelers of America, Order of United (1888), 632 N. Park St., Columbus, OH 43215; 186,000.
Common Cause (1970), 2030 M St. NW, Wash., DC 20036.
Communication, Intl. Training In (1938), 2519 Woodland Dr., Anaheim, CA 92801; 18,000.
Communication Administration, Assn. for (1971), 5105 Backlick Rd., Annadale, VA 22003; 700.
Communities, Federation of Egalitarian (1976), E. Wind, Rt. 3WA, Box 6B2, Tecumseh, MO 65760; 140.
Community Cultural Center Assoc., Amer. (1978), 19 Foothills Dr., Pompton Plains, NJ 07444.

Composers/USA, Natl. Assn. of (1932), P.O. Box 49652, Barrington Sta., Los Angeles, CA 90049; 650.
Composers, Authors & Publishers, Amer. Society of (ASCAP) (1914), One Lincoln Plaza, N.Y., NY 10023; 24,000.
Computer Professionals, Assn. of the Inst. for Certification of (1983), 2200 E. Devon Ave., Ste. 268, Des Plaines, IL 60018; 1199.
Computing Machinery, Assn. for (1947), 11 W. 42nd St., N.Y., NY 10036; 55,000.
Concrete Institute, Amer. (1904), 22400 W. Seven Mile Rd., Detroit, MI 48219-1849.
Conscientious Objectors, Central Committee for (1948), 2208 South St., Phila., PA 19146.
Conservation Engineers, Assn. of (1961), Alabama Dept. of Conservation, 64 N. Union St., Montgomery, AL 36130; 225.
Constantian Society, The (1970), 123 Orr Rd., Pittsburgh, PA 15241; 550.
Construction Industry Manufacturers Assn. (1911), 111 E. Wisconsin Ave., Milwaukee, WI 53202; 150 companies.
Construction Specifications Institute (1948), 601 Madison St., Alexandria, VA 22314-1791; 19,200.
Consulting Organizations, Council of (1989), 521 5th Ave., N.Y., NY 10175.
Consumer Credit Assn., Intl. (1912), 243 N. Lindbergh, St. Louis, MO 63141; 20,000.
Consumer Federation of America (1968), 1424 16th St. NW, #604, Wash., DC 20036; 240 organizations.
Consumer Interests, Amer. Council on (1953), 240 Stanley Hall, Univ. of Missouri, Columbia, MO 65211; 1,700+.
Consumer Protection Institute (1970), 5901 Plainfield Dr., Charlotte, NC 28215.
Consumers League, Natl. (1899), 815 15th St. NW, Suite 928-N, Wash., DC 20009; 8,000.
Consumers Union of the U.S. (1936), 101 Truman Ave., Yonkers, NY 10703; 405,990.
Contraception, Assn. for Voluntary Surgical (1943), 79 Madison Ave., New York, NY 10016; 4,000.
Contract Bridge League, Amer. (1937), 2200 Democrat Rd., Memphis, TN 38132; 190,000.
Contract Management Assn., Natl. (1959), 6728 Old McLean Village Dr., McLean, VA 22101; 20,176.
Contractors of Amer., General (1919), 1957 E St. NW, Wash., DC 20006; 32,000.
Cooperative Business Assn., Natl. (1916), 1401 New York Ave. NW, #1100, Wash., DC 20005; 525.
Cooperative League of the U.S.A. (1916), 1401 New York Ave. NW, Suite 1100, Wash., DC 20005; 285 co-ops.
Correctional Assn., Amer. (1870), 8025 Laurel Lakes Court, Laurel, MD 20707; 24,000.
Correctional Officers, Intl. Assn. of (1977), P.O. Box 7051, Marquette, MI 49855; 10,000.
Cosmetology Assn., Natl. (1921), 3510 Olive St., St. Louis, MO 63103; 47,000.
Cosmopolitan Intl. (1914), 7341 W. 80th, Overland Park, KS 66204; 3,057.
Cotton Council of America, Natl. (1938), 1918 North Parkway, Memphis, TN 38112; 297 delegates.
Counseling and Development, Amer. Assn. for (1952), 5999 Stevenson Ave., Alexandria, VA 22304; 58,065.
Counselors and Family Therapists, Natl. Academy of (1970), 55 Morris Ave., Springfield, NJ 07081-1422; 500.
Country Music Assn. (1958), One Music Circle S., Nashville, TN 37203; 6,588.
Creative Children and Adults, Natl. Assn. for (1974), 8080 Springvalley Dr., Cincinnati, OH 45236; 1,500.
Credit Assn., International (1912), 243 N. Lindberg, St. Louis, MO 63141; 10,000.
Credit Management, Nat. Assn. of (1896), 8815 Centre Park Dr., Columbia, MD 21045.
Credit Union Natl. Assn. (1934), 5710 Mineral Point Rd., Madison, WI 53705; 52 state credit union leagues.
Crime and Delinquency, Natl. Council on (1907), 685 Market St., Suite 620, San Francisco, CA 94105; 500.
Criminal Investigators Assn., Intl. (1970), P.O. Box 15350, Chevy Chase, MD 20815; 1,000.
Criminology, Amer. Society of (1941), 1314 Kinnear Rd., Suite 212, Columbus, OH 43212; 2,800.
Crop Science Society of America (1955), 677 S. Segoe Rd., Madison, WI 53711; 5,388.
Cross-Examination Debate Assn. (1971), California State Univ.-Northridge, Northridge, CA 91330; 310.
Cryptogram Assn., Amer. (1929) 4 Hawthorne Dr., Cherry Hill, NJ 08003; 1,100.
Customs Brokers & Forwarders Assn. of Am., Natl. (1897), One World Trade Center, Ste. 1153, N.Y., NY 10048.

Dairy Council, Natl. (1915), 6300 N. River Rd., Rosemont, IL 60018.
Dairy and Food Industries Supply Assn. (1912), 6245 Executive Blvd., Rockville, MD 20852; 832.
Dairy Goat Assn., American (1904), 209 W. Main St., Spindale, NC 28160; 13,000.
Dairylea Cooperative (1907), 831 James St., Syracuse, NY13203; 3,000.
Danish Brotherhood in America (1882), 3717 Harney St., Omaha, NE 68131; 9,538.
Daughters of the American Revolution, Natl. Society, (1890), 1776 D St. NW, Wash., DC 20006-5392; 202,000.
Daughters of the Confederacy, United (1894), 328 N. Blvd., Richmond, VA 23220-4057; 25,000.
Daughters of 1812, Natl. Society, U.S. (1892), 1461 Rhode Island Ave. NW, Wash., DC 20005; 4,700.
Daughters of the Republic of Texas (1891), 510 E. Anderson Ln., Austin, TX 78752; 6,400.
Daughters of Union Veterans of the Civil War (1885), 503 S. Walnut St., Springfield, IL 62704; 5,000.
Deaf, Alexander Graham Bell Assn. for the (1890), 3417 Volta Pl. NW, Wash., DC 20007; 5,000.
Deaf, Natl. Assn. of the (1880), 814 Thayer Ave., Silver Spring, MD 20910; 22,000.
Death and Dying, Natl. Council on (1990), 250 W. 50th St., N.Y., NY 10019; 120,000.
Defense Preparedness Assn., Amer. (1919), 2101 Wilson Blvd., Ste. 400, Arlington, VA 22201-3061; 32,000.
Delta Kappa Gamma Society Intl. (1929), 416 W. 12th St., Austin, TX 78701; 165,000.
Deltiologists of America (1960), P.O. Box 8, Norwood, PA 19074; 800+.
Democratic Natl. Committee, (1792), 430 S. Capitol St. SE, Wash., DC 20003.
DeMolay, Intl. Council, Order of (1919), 10200 N. Executive Hills Blvd., Kansas City, MO 64153; 50,000.
Dental Assn., Amer. (1859), 211 E. Chicago Ave., Chicago, IL 60611; 148,542.
Descendants of the Colonial Clergy, Society of the (1933), 30 Leewood Rd., Wellesley, MA 02181; 1,400.
Descendants of the Signers of the Declaration of Independence (1907), 1300 Locust St., Phila., PA 19107; 937.
Descendants of Washington's Army at Valley Forge, Society of (1976), P.O. Box 915, Valley Forge, PA 19482-0915.
Diabetes Assn., Amer. (1940), 1660 Duke St., Alexandria, VA 22314; 259,000.
Dialect Society, Amer. (1889), c/o Allan Metcalf, English Dept., MacMurray College, Jacksonville, IL 62650; 600.
Direct Marketing Assn. (1917), 6 E. 43d St., N.Y., NY 10017.
Directors Guild of America (1936), 7920 Sunset Blvd., Los Angeles, CA 90046; 9,700.
Disabled Amer. Veterans (1920), P.O. Box 14301, Cincinnati, OH 45250; 1.1 mln.
Disc Sports, U.S. (1983), 180 Norman Rd., Rochester, NY 14623; 6,500.
Dowsers, Amer. Society of (1961), Brainerd St., Danville, VT 05828; 3,500.
Dozenal Society of America (1945), Math Dept., Nassau Community College, Garden City, NY 11530; 300.
Dracula Society, Count (1962), 334 W. 54th St., Los Angeles, CA 90037; 500.
Drug, Chemical and Allied Trades Assn. (1890), 2 Roosevelt Ave., Syosset, NY 11791; 2,018.
Ducks Unlimited (1937), One Waterfowl Way at Gilmer Rd., Long Grove, IL 60014; 640,000.
Dutch Settlers Soc. of Albany (1924), RD#2 Box 313, Altamont, NY 12009; 300.

Eagles, Fraternal Order of (1898), 12660 West Capitol Dr., Brookfield, WI 53055; 1.1 mln.
Easter Seal Society, Natl. (1919), 70 E. Lake St., Chicago, IL 60601.
Eastern Star, General Grand Chapter, Order of the (1876), 1618 New Hampshire Ave. NW, Wash., DC 20009; 1.7 mln.
Economic Assn., Amer. (1885), 2014 Broadway, Ste. 305, Nashville, TN 37203; 27,260.
Economic Development, Committee for (1942), 1700 K St., NW, Suite 700, Washington, DC 20006; 365.
Edison Electric Institute (1933), 701 Pennsylvania Ave. NW, Wash., DC 20004-2696; 180 corporations.
Edsel Club, Intl. (1969), P.O. Box 371, Sully, IA 50251; 940.
Education, Amer. Assn. for Adult and Continuing (1982), 1112 16th St. NW, Suite 420, Wash., DC 20036; 3,000.
Education, Amer. Council on (1918), One Dupont Circle NW, #800, Wash., DC 20036; 1,600 institutions.
Education, Amer. Soc. for Engineering (1893), 11 Dupont Circle NW, Suite 200, Washington, DC 20036; 10,000+.
Education, Council for Advancement & Support of (1974), 11 Dupont Circle NW, Wash., DC 20036; 2,950 schools.
Education, Council for Basic (1956), 725 15th St. NW, Wash., DC 20005; 10,000.

Education, Institute of Intl. (1919), 809 United Nations Plaza, N.Y., NY 10017; 700 U.S. colleges, univ.
Education, Natl. Assn. for Family and Community (1936), 5963 Jefferson St., Burlington, KY 41005; 353,266.
Education, Natl. Committee for Citizens in (1973), 10840 Little Patuxent Pwky., Suite 301, Columbia, MD 21044; 650.
Education, Natl. Society for the Study of (1901), 5835 Kimbark Ave., Chicago, IL 60637; 2,400.
Education Assn., Natl. (1857), 1201 16th St. NW, Wash., DC 20036; 2 mln.
Education Society, Comparative and Intl. (1956), Univ. of S. California, Univ. Park, Los Angeles, CA 90089; 2,500.
Education of Young Children, Natl. Assn. for the (1926), 1834 Connecticut Ave. NW, Wash., DC 20009; 70,000.
Educational Exchange, Council on Intl. (1947), 205 E. 42d St., N.Y., NY 10017; 200 organizations.
Educational Research Assn., Amer. (1916), 1230 17th St. NW, Wash., DC 20036; 17,000.
8th Air Force Historical Society (1975), P.O. Box 7215, St. Paul, MN 55107; 18,000.
82nd Airborne Division Assn., Inc. (1944), P.O. Box 1442, Bloomington, IN 47402; 22,000.
88th Infantry Division Assn., Inc. (1948), P.O. Box 925, Havertown, PA 19083; 5,152.
Electrical and Electronics Engineers, Institute of (1884), 345 E. 47th St., N.Y., NY 10017; 300,000.
Electrical Manufacturers Assn., Natl. (1926), 2101 L St. NW, Wash., DC 20037; 560 companies.
Electrochemical Society (1902), 10 S. Main St., Pennington, NJ 08534-2896; 6,000.
Electronic Circuits, The Institute for Interconnecting & Packaging (1957), 7380 N. Lincoln, Lincolnwood, IL 60646; 1,850 cos.
Electronic Industries Assn. (1924), 2001 Pennsylvania Ave., Wash., DC 20006-1813; 1,058 companies.
Electronics Sales & Service Dealers Assn., Natl. (1973), 2708 W. Berry, Ft. Worth, TX 76109; 900.
Electronics Technicians, Intl. Society of Certified (1970), 2708 W. Berry, Ft. Worth, TX 76109; 1,400.
Electroplaters' and Surface Finishers' Society, Amer. (1909), 12644 Research Pkwy, Orlando, FL 32826; 8,500.
Elks of the U.S.A., Benevolent and Protective Order of (1868), 2750 N. Lakeview Ave., Chicago, IL 60614; 1.5 mln.
Energy Research Institute, Clean (1974), 1251 Memorial Dr., 219 MacArthur Engineering Bldg., Coral Gables, FL, 33146.
Energy, Intl. Assn. for Hydrogen (1975), P.O. Box 242866, Miami, FL 33124-8266; 2,500.
Engine and Boat Manufacturers, Natl. Assn. of (1904), 401 N. Michigan Ave., Chicago, IL 60611.
Engineering, Natl. Academy of (1964), 2101 Constitution Ave. NW, Wash., DC 20418; 1,628.
Engineering, Soc. for the Advancement of Material & Process (1944), P.O. Box 2459, Covina, CA 91722; 10,000.
Engineering Society of N. America, Illuminating (1906), 345 E. 47th St., N.Y., NY 10017; 10,000.
Engineering Trustees, United (1904), 345 E. 47th St., N.Y., NY 10017.
Engineers, Amer. Inst. of Chemical (1908), 345 E. 47th St., N.Y., N.Y. 10017; 53,622.
Engineers, Amer. Institute of Mining, Metallurgical and Petroleum (1871), 345 E. 47th St., N.Y., NY 10017.
Engineers, Amer. Soc. of Agricultural (1907), 2950 Niles Rd., St. Joseph, MI 49085-9659; 10,000.
Engineers, Amer. Soc. of Civil (1852), 345 E. 47th St., N.Y., NY 10017; 111,112.
Engineers, American Soc. of Mechanical (1880), 345 E. 47th St., N.Y., NY 10017; 118,000.
Engineers, Amer. Soc. of Naval (1888), 1452 Duke St., Alexandria, VA 22314; 7,500.
Engineers, Amer. Soc. of Plumbing (1964), 3617 Thousand Oaks Blvd., #210, Westlake Vlge, CA 91362-3625; 4,500.
Engineers, Amer. Soc. of Safety (1911), 1800 E. Oakton St., Des Plains, IL 60018; 25,000.
Engineers, Assn. of Energy (1977), 4025 Pleasantdale Rd., Suite 420, Atlanta, GA 30340; 8,500.
Engineers, Inst. of Industrial (1948), 25 Technology Park, Atlanta, GA 30092; 43,000.
Engineers, Inst. of Transportation (1930), Suite 410, 525 School St. NW, Wash., DC 20024, 7,700.
Engineers, Natl. Society of Professional (1934), 1420 King St., Alexandria, VA 22314; 75,000.
Engineers, Soc. of Fire Protection (1950), One Liberty Sq., Boston, MA 02110.
Engineers, Soc. of Logistics (1966), 8100 Professional Pl., Ste. 211, New Carrollton, MD 20785; 8,000.
Engineers, Soc. of Manufacturing (1932), One SME Drive, P.O. Box 930, Dearborn, MI 48121; 80,000.
Engineers, Society of Mining (1871), 8307 Shaffer Pkwy., Littleton, CO 80127; 23,058.
Engineers, Society of Plastics (1942), 14 Fairfield Dr., Brookfield Ctr., CT 06805; 25,000.
Engineers, Society of Tribologists & Lubrication (1944), 838 Busse Hwy., Park Ridge, IL 60068; 4,100.
English, U.S. (1983), 818 Connecticut Ave. NW, Ste. 200, Washington, DC 20006; 250,000.
English Assn., College (1939), English Dept., Nazareth College, 4245 East Ave., Rochester, NY 14618; 1,230.
English-Speaking Union of the U.S. (1920), 16 E. 69th St., N.Y., NY 10021; 27,000.
Entomological Society of America (1889), 9301 Annapolis Rd., Lanham, MD 20706; 8,500.
Environmental Health Assn., Natl. (1937), 720 S. Colorado Blvd., Suite 970, Denver, CO 80222; 5,000.
Epigraphic Society, Inc., The (1974), 6625 Bamburgh Dr., San Diego, CA 92117; 960.
Esperanto League for North America (1952), P.O. Box 1129, El Cerrito, CA 94530; 1,100.
European Council, Ltd., Eastern (1990), 11 John St., Ste. 406, N.Y., NY 10038; 1,000.
Evangelism Crusades, Intl. (1959), 14617 Victory Blvd., Van Nuys, CA 91411; 1,500.
Exchange Club, Natl. (1911), 3050 Central Ave., Toledo, OH 43606-1700; 40,000.
Executive Management Services Corp. (1973), P.O. Box 58, Atlantic Beach, NY 11509.
Experiment in Intl. Living/School for Intl. Training (1932), P.O. Box 676, Kipling Rd., Brattleboro, VT 05302.

Fairs & Expositions, Intl. Assn. of (1919), P.O. Box 985, Springfield, MO 65801; 1,500.
Family Relations, Natl. Council on (1938), 3989 Central Ave. NE, Suite 550, Minneapolis, MN 55421; 3,800.
Family Service America (1911), 11700 W. Lake Park Dr., Park Pl, Milwaukee, WI 53224; 300 agencies.
Farm Bureau Federation, Amer. (1919), 225 Touhy Ave., Park Ridge, IL 60068; 3.8 mln. families.
Farmers of America Organization, Natl. Future (1928), 5632 Mt. Vernon Memorial Hwy., Alexandria, VA 22309-0160.
Farmers Union, Natl. (1902), Denver, CO 80251; 250,000.
Farmers' Educational and Co-Operative Union of America (1902), 10065 E. Harvard Ave., Denver, CO 80231; 250,000.
Fast Draw Assn., World (1975), 1026 Llagas Rd., Morgan Hill, CA 95037; 320.
Fat Acceptance, Natl. Assn. to Advance (NAAFA) (1969), P.O. Box 188620, Sacramento, CA 95818; 3,500.
Federal Employees, Natl. Assn. of Retired (1921), 1533 New Hampshire Ave. NW, Washington, DC 20036-1279.
Federal Employees, Natl. Fed. of (1917), 1016 16th St. NW, Wash., DC 20036.
Federal Employees Veterans Assn. (1954), Leslie Harris, 1024 E. Cliveden St., Phila., PA 19119; 4,562.
Feminists for Life of America (1972), 811 E. 47th St., Kansas City, MO 64110; 3,500.
Film Library Assn., Educational (1943), 45 John St., Suite 301, N.Y., NY 10038; 1,600.
Financial Analysts Federation (1945), #5 Boar's Head Lane, Charlottesville, VA 22901; 17,000.
Financial Executives Institute (1931), 10 Madison Ave., P.O. Box 1938, Morristown, NJ 07962-1938, 13,500.
Financiers, Intl. Soc. of (1979), P.O. Box 18508, Asheville, NC 28814; 300.
Fire Chiefs, Intl. Assn. of (1873), 1329 18th St. NW, Wash., DC 20036; 9,000.
Fire Protection Assn., Natl. (1896), Batterymarch Park, Quincy MA 02269; 38,000.
First Amendment Studies, Institute for (1984), P.O. Box 589, Great Barrington, MA 01230; 27,000.
Fish Assn., Intl. Game (1939), 1301 E. Atlantic Blvd., Pompano Beach, FL 33060; 20,000.
Fisheries Institute, Natl. (1945), 2000 M St., Washington, DC 20036; 1,250.
Fisheries Soc., American (1870), 5410 Grosvenor Lane, Ste. 110, Bethesda, MD 20814-2199; 9,000.
Fishes, Soc. for the Protection of Old (1967), School of Fisheries, WH-10 Univ. of Washington, Seattle, WA 98195; 275.
Fishing Institute, Sport (1949), 1010 Massachusetts Ave NW, Suite 320, Wash., DC 20001; 214.
Fishing Tackle Manufacturers Assn., Amer. (1950), 1250 Grove Ave., Barrington, IL 60010; 600.
Flag Research Center, The (1962), 3 Edgehill Rd., Winchester, MA 01890; 1,200.
Flight Attendants, Assn. of (1973), 1625 Massachusetts Ave. NW, Wash., DC 20036; 28,000.
Fly Fishers, Fed. of (1965), Box 1088, 200 Yellowstone Ave., W. Yellowstone, MT 59758; 10,000.
Flying Disc Fed., World (1985), Gnejsvägen 24, 85240; Sundsvall, Sweden; 15,000.

Food Brokers Assn., Natl. (1904), 1010 Massachusetts Ave. NW, Wash., DC 20001; 1,800 companies.
Food Institute, Amer. Frozen (1942), 1764 Old Meadow Ln., Suite 350, McLean, VA 22102; 531 firms.
Footwear Industries Assn., Amer. (1871), 3700 Market St., Philadelphia, PA 19104; 180.
Foreign Relations, Council on (1921), 58 E. 68th St., N.Y., NY 10021; 2,500.
Foreign Student Affairs, Natl. Assn. for (1948), 1860 19th St. NW, Wash., DC 20009; 5,500.
Foreign Study, Amer. Institute for (1964), 102 Greenwich Ave., Greenwich, CT 06830; 300,000.
Foreign Trade Council, Inc., Natl. (1914), 1625 K St. NW, Washington, DC 20006; 500 companies.
Forensic Sciences, Amer. Academy of (1948), 410 N. 21st St., Ste. 203, Colorado Springs, CO 80904; 3,435.
Forest Council (1932), 1250 Connecticut Ave. NW, Suite 320, Washington, DC 20036.
Forest History Society (1946), 701 Vickers Ave., Durham, NC 27701; 2,100.
Forest Products Assn., Natl. (1902), 1250 Connecticut Ave. NW, Wash., DC 20036; 800+ companies.
Forest Products Research Society (1947), 2801 Marshall Ct., Madison, WI 53705; 3,000.
Foresters, Society of Amer. (1900), 5400 Grosvenor La., Bethesda, MD 20814; 18,324.
Forestry Assn., Amer. (1875), 1516 P St. NW, Wash., DC 20005; 112,000.
Fortean Organization, Intl. (1965), P.O. Box 367, Arlington, VA 22210; 800.
Founders and Patriots of Amer., The Order of the (1896), 3813 Acapulco Ct., Irving, TX 75062; 1,250.
Foundrymen's Society, Amer. (1896), Golf & Wolf Rds., Des Plaines, IL 60016; 13,255.
4-H Clubs (1901-1905), Extension Service, U.S. Dept of Agriculture, Wash., DC 20250; 5.8 mln.
Franklin D. Roosevelt Philatelic Society (1963), 154 Laguna Ct., St. Augustine Shores, FL 32086; 696.
Frederick A. Cook Soc., The (1957), Sullivan County Historical Museum, P.O. Box 247, Hurleyville, NY 12747.
Freedom, Young Americans for (1960), 140 18A Sulleyfield Circle, Chantilly, VA 22021.
Freedom of Information Center (1958), 20 Walter Williams Hall, Univ. of Missouri, Columbia, MO 65211.
Freedoms Foundation at Valley Forge (1949), Valley Forge, PA 19481; 5,000.
Friedreich's Ataxia Group in America (1969), P.O. Box 11116, Oakland, CA 94611; 2,100+.
French Institute (1911), 22 E. 60th St., N.Y., NY 10022.
Friendship and Good Will, Intl. Soc. of (1978), 211 W. 4th Ave., P.O. Box 2637, Gastonia, NC 28053-2637; 4,218.
Frisbee Assn., Intl. (1967), 900 E. El Monte, San Gabriel, CA 91776; 110,000.
Frumps, Natl., of America (1965), P.O. Box 1047, Winter Park, FL 32790; 11,000.
Funeral and Memorial Societies, Continental Assn. of (1963), 2001 S. St. NW, Suite 530, Washington, DC 20009.

GASP (Group Against Smokers' Pollution) (1971), P.O. Box 632, College Park, MD 20741-0632; 10,000.
Gamblers Anonymous (1957), P.O. Box 17173, Los Angeles, CA 90017.
Garden Club of Amer. (1913), 598 Madison Ave., N.Y., NY 10022; 15,000.
Garden Clubs, Natl. Council of State (1929), 4401 Magnolia Ave., St. Louis, MO 63110; 308,623.
Garden Clubs of America, Men's (1932), 5560 Merle Hay Rd., Johnston, IA 50131; 9,500.
Gas Appliance Manufacturers Assn. (1935), 1901 N. Moore St., Arlington, VA 22209; 210 companies.
Gas Assn., Amer. (1918), 1515 Wilson Blvd., Arlington, VA 22209; 229 companies; 3,000 individuals.
Gay and Lesbian Task Force, Natl. (1973), 1734 14th St. NW, Washington, DC 20009; 20,000.
Genealogical Society, Natl. (1903), 4527 17th St. N., Arlington, VA 22207; 10,000.
Genetic Assn., Amer. (1903), P.O. Box 39, Buckeystown, MD 21717; 3,000.
Geographers, Assn. of Amer. (1904), 1710 16th St. NW, Wash., DC 20009-3198; 6,390.
Geographic Education, Natl. Council for (1915), 16A Leonard Hall, IUPA, Indiana, PA 15705; 3,700.
Geographic Society, Natl. (1888), 1145 17th St. NW, Wash., DC 20036; 10 mln.
Geographical Society, Amer. (1851), 156 Fifth Ave., Suite 600, N.Y., NY 10010-7002; 1,700.
Geolinguistics, Amer. Society of (1965), University of Rhode Island, Kingston, RI 02892; 70.
Geological Institute, Amer. (1948), 4220 King St., Alexandria, VA 22302; 19 societies.
Geological Society of America (1888), 3300 Penrose Pl., P.O. Box 9140, Boulder, CO 80301; 17,000.
Geologists, Assn. of Engineering (1960), 323 Boston Post Rd. Suite 2D, Sudbury, MA 01776; 2,800.
Geologists, Amer. Assn. of Petroleum (1917), P.O. Box 979, Tulsa, OK 74101.
Geophysicists, Society of Exploration (1930), P.O. Box 702740, Tulsa, OK 74170; 14,500.
Geriatrics Society, Amer. (1942), 770 Lexington Ave., Suite 300, N.Y., NY 10021; 6,100.
Gideons Intl. (1899), 2900 Lebanon Rd., Nashville, TN 37214; 104,000.
Gifted & Talented Club, Natl. (1987), 4049 Ross Park Dr., San Jose, CA 95118; 200.
Gifted Children, Natl. Assn. for (1957), 1155 15th St. NW, Ste. 1002, Wash., DC 20005; 6,500.
Girls Clubs of America (1945), 30 E. 33d St., N.Y., NY 10016; 250,000+.
Girl Scouts of the U.S.A. (1912), 830 Third Ave., N.Y., NY 10022; 3.2 mln.
Gladiolus Council, No. Amer. (1945), 9338 Manzanita Dr., Sun City, AZ 85373; 1,275.
Glenn Miller Birthplace Soc. (1976), P.O. Box 61, Clarinda, IA 51632-2013; 1,240.
Gold Star Mothers, Amer. (1928), 2128 Leroy Pl. NW, Wash., DC 20008; 3,000.
Golf Association, U.S. (1894), Box 708, Far Hills, NJ 07931.
Goose Island Bird & Girl Watching Society (1960), 301 Arthur Ave., Park Ridge, IL 60068; 681.
Gospel Music Assn. (1964), 7 Music Square N., Nashville, TN 37203; 2,600.
Governing Boards, Assn. of (1922), 1 Dupont Circle, Ste. 400, Washington, DC 20036; 1,107.
Government Finance Officers Assn. (1906), 180 N. Michigan Ave., Suite 800, Chicago, IL 60601; 12,500.
Graduate Schools in the U.S., Council of (1961), One Dupont Circle NW, Wash., DC 20036; 400 institutions.
Grandmothers Clubs of America, Natl. Federation of (1934), 203 N. Wabash Ave., Chicago, IL 60601; 10,000.
Grange, Natl. (1867), 1616 H St. NW, Wash., DC 20006.
Graphic Artists, Society of Amer. (1915), 32 Union Sq., East, N.Y., NY 10003; 203.
Graphic Arts, Amer. Institute of (1914), 1059 Third Ave., N.Y., NY 10021; 6,000.
Gray Panthers (1970), 1424 16th St. NW, Suite 602, Wash., DC 20036; 30,000.
Green Mountain Club, The (1910), 43 State St., Box 889, Montpelier, VT 05601; 5,500.
Grocers, Natl. Assn. of (1893), 1825 Samuel Morse Dr., Reston, VA 22090.
Grocery Manufacturers of America (1908), 1010 Wisconsin Ave., Suite 800, Wash., DC 20007; 137 companies.
Guide Dog Foundation for the Blind (1946), 371 E. Jericho Tpke., Smithtown, NY 11787-2976.
Gyro Intl. (1912), 1096 Mentor Ave., Painesville, OH 44077.

HIAS (Hebrew Immigrant Aid Society) (1880), 333 7th Ave., 17th Floor, N.Y., NY 10001-5004.
Hadassah, the Women's Zionist Organization of America (1912), 50 W. 58th St., N.Y., NY 10019; 385,000.
Hairdressers and Cosmetologists Assn., Natl. (1921), 3510 Olive St., St. Louis, MO 63103; 50,406.
Handball Assn., U.S. (1951), 930 N. Benton Ave., Tucson, AZ 85711; 9,000.
Handgun, Intl. Metallic Silhouette Assn. (1976), P.O. Box 368, Burlington, IA 52601; 1,300.
Handicapped, Federation of the (1935), 211 W. 14th St., N.Y., NY 10011; 650.
Handicapped, Natl. Assn. of the Physically (1958), Bethesda Scarlet Oaks, #117, 440 Lafayette Ave., Cincinnati, OH 45220-1000; 700.
Health Council, Natl. (1920), 1730 M St. NW, Ste. 500, Washington, DC 20036; 116.
Health Info. Management Assoc., American (1928), 919 N. Michigan Ave., #1400, Chicago, IL 60611-1683; 34,000.
Health, Physical Education, Recreation and Dance, Amer. Alliance for (1885), 1900 Association Dr., Reston, VA 22091.
Health Professions, Assn. of Schools of (1967), 1101 Connecticut Ave. NW, Ste. 700, Wash., DC 20036-4387.
Hearing Society, Intl. (1951), 20361 Middlebelt Rd., Livonia, MI 48152; 2,800.
Hearing and Speech Action, Natl. Assn. for (1910), 10801 Rockville Pike, Rockville, MD 20852; 3,500.
Heart Assn., Amer. (1924), 7320 Greenville Ave., Dallas TX 75231; 200,000.
Hearts, Mended (1951), 7320 Greenville Ave., Dallas TX 75231; 20,000.

Heating, Refrigerating & Air Conditioning Engineers, Amer. Soc. of (1894), 1791 Tullie Circle NE, Atlanta, GA 30329.
Helicopter Assn. Intl. (1948), 1619 Duke St., Alexandria, VA 22314; 1,500.
Helicopter Society, Amer. (1943), 217 N. Washington St., Alexandria VA 22314; 6,500.
Hemispheric Affairs, Council on (1975), 724 9th St. NW, Wash., DC 20001; 2,800.
Highpointers Club (1987), Box 327, Mtn. Home, AR 72653; 650.
High Points Club, World (1991), 303 Brighton Court, Oshawa, ON, Canada L1G 6H5; 35.
High School Assns., Natl. Federation of State (1920), P.O. Box 20626, Kansas City, MO 64195.
High Twelve Internatl. (1921), 11155-B2 South Towne Square, St. Louis, MO 63123; 25,000.
Hiking Society, Amer. (1977), P.O. Box 20160, Wash., DC 20041-2160; 5,000.
Historians, Organization of Amer. (1907), 112 N. Bryan St., Bloomington, IN 47408; 12,000.
Historical Assn., Amer. (1884), 400 A St. SE, Wash., DC 20003; 15,200.
Historic Preservation, Natl. Trust for (1966), 1785 Massachusetts Ave. NW, Wash., DC 20036; 240,000.
Hockey, U.S.A. (1937), 2997 Broadmoor Valley Rd., Colorado Springs, CO 80906; 250,000.
Home Builders, Natl. Assn. of (1942), 15th & M Sts. NW, Wash., DC 20005; 157,479.
Home Economics Assn., Amer. (1909), 1555 King St., Alexandria, VA 22314; 23,000.
Homemakers of America, Future (1945), 1910 Association Dr., Reston, VA 22091; 261,000+.
Honor Society, Natl. (1921), 1904 Association Dr., Reston, VA 22091; 22,000.
Hospital Marketing and Public Relations of the Amer. Hospital, Amer. Soc. for (1964), 840 N. Lake Shore Dr., 9E, Chicago, IL 60611; 3,100.
Horatio Alger Soc. (1965), 4907 Allison Dr., Lansing, MI 48910; 300.
Horse Council, American (1969), 1700 K St. NW, #300, Washington, DC 20006; 2,500.
Horse Protection Assn., Amer. (1966), 1000 29th St. NW, Suite T-100, Wash., DC 20007; 8,000.
Horse Show Assn. of America Ltd., Natl. (1883), 680 5th Ave., #1602, N.Y., NY 10019.
Horse Shows Assn., Amer. (1917), 220 E. 42 St., N.Y., NY 10017-5806; 56,500+.
Hospital Association, Amer. (1899), 840 N. Lake Shore Dr., Chicago, IL 60611; 40,000.
Hospital Marketing and Public Relations, Amer. Society for (1964), 840 N. Lake Shore Dr., Chicago, IL 60611; 3,167.
Hot Rod Assn., Natl. (1951), 2035 Financial Way, Glendora, CA 91740; 74,524.
Hotel & Motel Assn., Amer. (1910), 1201 New York Ave., NW, Washington, DC; 10,000.
Humanism, Council for Democratic and Secular (1980), Box 5, Central Park Station, Buffalo, NY 14215; 23,600.
Human Resource Management, Society for (1948), 606 N. Washington St., Alexandria, VA 22314; 45,000.
Human Rights and Social Justice, Americans for (1977), P.O. Box 6258, Ft. Worth, TX 76115.
Humane Society of the U.S. (1954), 2100 L St. NW, Wash., DC 20037; 650,000.
Humanics, American (1948), 4601 Madison Ave., Kansas City, MO 64112; 600.
Hydrogen Energy, Intl. Assn. for (1975), P.O. Box 248266, Coral Gables, FL 33124; 2,500.
Hygiene Assn., American Industrial (1939), P.O. Box 8390, 345 White Pond Dr., Akron, OH 44320.

Idaho, U.S.S. (BB-42) Assn. (1957), P.O. Box 711247, San Diego, CA 92171; 850.
Identification, Intl. Assn. for (1916), P.O. Box 2423, Alameda, CA 94501; 3,300.
Illustrators, Society of (1901), 128 E. 63 St., N.Y., NY 10021; 932.
Industrial Democracy, League for (1905), 181 Hudson St., N.Y., NY 10013; 1,500.
Industrial Designers Society of America (1965), 1142-E Walker Rd., Great Falls, VA 22066; 2,200.
Industrial Engineers, Amer. Institute of (1948), 25 Technology Park, Norcross, GA 30092; 40,000.
Industrial Health Foundation (1935), 34 Penn Circle West, Pittsburgh, PA 15206; 170 companies.
Industrial Security, Amer. Soc. for (1955), 1655 N. Ft. Myer Dr., Suite 1200, Arlington, VA 22209; 25,000.
Information, Freedom of, Center (1958), P.O. Box 858, Columbia, MO 65205.
Information and Image Management, Assn. for (1943), 1100 Wayne Ave., Ste. 1100, Silver Springs, MD 20910; 9,000.
Information Industry Assn. (1968), 555 New Jersey Ave. NW, Suite 800, Wash., DC 20001; 600 companies.
Insurance Assn., Amer. (1964), 1130 Connecticut Ave. NW, Suite 1000, Wash., DC 20036; 250+ companies.
Insurance Society, Inc., Intl. (1965), Box 870224, Rm. 328, Farrah Hall, Tuscaloosa, AL 35487; 1,000 indv., 150 corporate.
Intelligence Officers, Assn. of Former (1975), 6723 Whittier Ave., Suite 303A, McLean, VA 22101; 3,300.
Intercollegiate Athletics, Natl. Assn. of (1940), 1221 Baltimore Ave., Kansas City, MO 64105; 500 schools.
Interior Designers, Amer. Society of (1975), 608 Mass. Ave. NE, Washington, DC 20002; 33,000.
International Interculture Programs, AFS (1947), 313 E. 43rd St., N.Y., NY 10017; 100,000.
Intertel, Inc. (1966), P.O. Box 150580, Lakewood, CO 80215.
Inventors, Amer. Assn. of (1891), 2020 Pennsylvania Ave. NW, Wash., DC 20006; 5,727.
Investment Clubs, Natl. Assn. of (1951), 1515 E. Eleven Mile Rd., Royal Oak, MI 44067; 140,000.
Investment Management and Research, Assn. for (1990), 5 Boar's Head Ln., Charlottesville, VA 22901; 21,000.
Investors Corp., Natl. Assn. of (1951), 1515 E. Eleven Mile Rd., Royal Oak, MI 48067; 142,000.
Irish-American Cultural Inst. (1962), 2115 Summit Ave., Univ. of St. Thomas, St. Paul, MN 55105; 5,000.
Iron Castings Society (1897), 455 State St., Des Plaines, IL 60016; 200 firms.
Iron and Steel Engineers, Assn. of (1907), Three Gateway Center, Suite 2350, Pittsburgh, PA 15222; 9,700.
Iron and Steel Institute, Amer. (1905), 1101 17th St. NW, Ste. 1300, Wash., DC 20036; 50 companies.
Italian Historical Society of America (1949), 111 Columbia Heights, Bklyn., NY 11201.
Italy-America Chamber of Commerce (1887), 350 Fifth Ave., N.Y., NY 10118; 850.
Izaak Walton League of America, The (1922), 1401 Wilson Blvd., Level B, Arlington, VA 22209; 54,000.

(Jesse) James Farm, Friends of, (1979), Rt. 2, Box 236, Kearney, MO 64060; 300.
Jamestowne Society (1936), P.O. Box 14523, Richmond, VA 23221; 3,000.
Jane Austen Society of N. Amer. (1979), 4169 Lions Ave., N. Vancouver, B.C., Canada, V7R 352; 3,000.
Japanese Amer. Citizens League (1929), 1765 Sutter St., San Francisco, CA 94115; 26,000.
Jewish Appeal, United (1939), 99 Park Avenue, Ste. 300, N.Y., NY 10016.
Jewish Book Council (1943), 15 E. 26th St., N.Y., NY 10010.
Jewish Committee, Amer. (1906), 165 E. 56th St., N.Y., NY 10022; 50,000.
Jewish Community Centers Assn. (1917), 15 E. 26th St., N.Y., NY 10010.
Jewish Congress, Amer. (1918), 15 E. 84th St., N.Y., NY 10028; 50,000.
Jewish Federations, Council of (1932), 730 Broadway, N.Y., NY 10003; 200 agencies.
Jewish Historical Society, Amer. (1892), 2 Thornton Rd., Waltham, MA 02154; 3,800.
Jewish War Veterans of the U.S.A. (1896), 1811 R St. NW, Wash., DC 20009; 100,000.
Jewish Women, Natl. Council of (1893), 53 W. 23rd St., N.Y., NY 10010; 100,000.
Job's Daughters, Internatl. Order of (1920), 233 W. 6th St., Papillion, NE 68046; 24,000.
Jockey Club (1894), 380 Madison Ave., N.Y., NY 10017; 90.
John Birch Society (1958), P.O. Box 8040, Appleton, WI 54913.
John Pelham Historical Assn. (1982), 7 Carmel Terr., Hampton, VA 23666; 125.
Joseph Diseases Foundation, Intl. (1977), P.O. Box 2550, Livermore, CA 94550; 3,200.
Journalists, Society of Professional (1908), 16 S. Jackson, Greencastle, IN 46135; 16,000.
Journalists and Authors, Amer. Society of (1948), 1501 Broadway, Suite 1907, N.Y., NY 10036; 750+.
Judaism, Amer. Council for (1943), P.O. Box 9009, Alexandria, VA 22304.
Judicature Society, Amer. (1913), 25 E. Washington, Chicago, IL 60602; 20,000.
Juggler's Assn., Intl. (1947), P.O. Box 3707, Akron, OH 44314-3707; 3,280.
Junior Achievement (1919), 550 Summer St., Stamford, CT 06901; 300,000.
Junior Auxiliaries, Natl. Assn. of (1941), 845 S. Main, Greenville, MS 38702-1873; 10,000.

Junior Colleges, Amer. Assn. of Community and (1920), One Dupont Circle NW, Wash., DC 20036; 900.
Junior Leagues, Assn. of (1921), 660 First Ave., N.Y., NY 10016; 189,000.

Kennel Club, Amer. (1884), 51 Madison Ave., N.Y., NY 10010; 500+ clubs.
Kidney Fund, Amer. (1971), 6110 Executive Blvd., #1010, Rockville, MD 20852.
Kiwanis Intl. (1915), 3636 Woodview Trace, Indianapolis, IN 46268-3196; 329,000.
Klinefelter's Syndrome Assn. of Canada (1988), P.O. Box 5000, Penetanguishene, Ontario, Canada LOK 1PO.
Knights of Columbus (1882), One Columbus Plaza, New Haven, CT 06507; 1.4 mln.
Knights of Pythias (1864), 2785 E. Desert Inn Rd., #150, Las Vegas, NV 89121; 96,000.
Knights Templar U.S.A., Grand Encampment (1816), 14 E. Jackson Blvd., Suite 1700, Chicago, IL 60604-2293; 295,000.
Krishna Consciousness, Intl. Soc. for (ISKON) (1966) 3764 Watseka Ave., Los Angeles, CA 92109; 1 mln.

La Leche League Intl. (1956), 9616 Minneapolis Ave., P.O. Box 1209, Franklin Park, IL 60131; 40,000.
Lambs, The (1874), 3 W. 51st St., N.Y., NY 10019; 194.
Landscape Architects, Amer. Society of (1899), 4401 Connecticut Ave., NW, Wash., DC 20008-2302; 10,000.
Law, Amer. Society of International (1906), 2223 Massachusetts Ave. NW, Washington, DC 20008; 4,300.
Law Enforcement Officers Assn., Amer. (1966), 1000 Connecticut Ave. NW, Suite 9, Wash., DC 20036; 50,000.
Law Libraries, Amer. Assn. of (1906), 53 W. Jackson Blvd., Chicago, IL 60604; 4,630.
Law and Social Policy, Center for (1969), 1751 N St. NW, Wash., DC 20036.
Learned Societies, Amer. Council of (1919), 228 E. 45th St., N.Y., NY 10017; 45 societies.
Lefthanders, League of (1975), P.O. Box 89, New Milford, NJ 07646; 1,200.
Lefthanders Intl. (1975), P.O. Box 8249, Topeka, KS 66608.
Legal Administrators, Assn. of (1971), 175 E. Hawthorn Pkwy. #325, Vernon Hills, IL 60061-1428; 8,000.
Legion of Valor of the U.S.A. (1890), 92 Oak Leaf Lane, Chapel Hill, NC 27516; 750.
Leif Ericson Society (1962), Box 301, Chicago, IL 60690-0301; 1,200.
Leprosy Missions, Amer. (1906), One Alm Way, Greenville, SC 29601.
Leukemia Society of America (1949), 733 Third Ave., N.Y., NY 10017; 57 chapters.
Lewis and Clark Trail Heritage Foundation, Inc. (1969), P.O. Box 3434, Great Falls, MT 59403; 1,466.
Lewis Carroll Society of N. America (1974), 617 Rockford Rd., Silver Spring, MD 20902; 350.
Liberty Lobby (1955), 300 Independence Ave. SE, Wash., DC 20003; 20,000.
Libraries Assn., Special (1909), 1700 18th St., NW, Wash., DC 20009; 13,800.
Library Administration & Management Assn. (1957), 50 E. Huron St., Chicago, IL 60611; 5,074.
Library Assn., Amer. (1876), 50 E. Huron St., Chicago, IL 60611; 50,000.
Library Assn., Medical (1861), 6 N. Michigan Ave., Suite 300, Chicago, IL 60602; 5,000+.
Library Assn., Am. Theological (1947), 820 Church St., Ste. 300, Evanston, IL 60201; 670.
Life, Americans United for (1971), 343 S. Dearborn St., Ste. 1804, Chicago, IL 60604.
Life Insurance, Amer. Council of (1976), 1001 Pennsylvania Ave., NW, Wash., DC 20004; 616 firms.
Life Office Management Assn. (1924), 5770 Powers Ferry Rd., Atlanta, GA 30327; 870 companies.
Life Underwriters, Amer. Soc. of Certified (1929), 270 Bryn Mawr Ave., Byrn Mawr, PA 19010; 28,000.
Life Underwriters, Natl. Assn. of (1890), 1922 F St. NW, Wash., DC 20006; 135,000.
Lighter-Than-Air Society (1952), 1800 Triplett Blvd., Akron, OH 44306; 1,200.
Lions Clubs, Intl. Assn. of (1917), 300 22d St., Oak Brook, IL 60521-8842; 1,363,000.
Litchfield Institute, The (1984), 151 N. Main St., Bristol, CT 06011-0483; 44.
Literacy Intl., Laubach (1955), 1320 Jamesville Ave., Box 131, Syracuse, NY 13210.
Literacy Volunteers of America (1962), 5795 Widewaters Parkway, Syracuse, NY 13214; 100,000.
Little League Baseball (1939), Route #15, S. Williamsport, PA 17701; 17,816 charters.
Little People of America (1957), P.O. Box 9897, Washington, DC 20016; 4,000.
London Club (1975), Rt. One, Lecompton, KS 66050; 100+.
Longwave Club of America (1974), 45 Wildflower Rd., Levittown, PA 19057; 536.
Lung Assn., Amer. (1904), 1740 Broadway, N.Y., NY 10019.
Lutheran Education Assn. (1942), 7400 Augusta St., River Forest, IL 60305; 3,800.

Magazine Photographers, Am. Soc. of (1944), 419 Park Ave. South, N.Y., NY 10016; 5,000+.
Magazine Publishers of America (1919), 575 Lexington Ave., N.Y., NY 10022; 200 publishers.
Magicians, Intl. Brotherhood of (1926), 103 N. Main St., Bluffton, OH 45817; 14,000.
Magicians Assn. Worldwide, Amateur (1988), 325 Maple St., Lynne, MA 01904-0073; 18,000.
Magicians, Society of Amer. (1902), 1333 Cory St., Yellow Springs, OH 45387; 5,500.
Management Assn., Amer. (1923), 135 W. 50th St., N.Y., NY 10020; 70,000.
Management Consultants, Institute of (1968), 521 5th Ave., 35th Floor, N.Y., NY 10175-3598; 2,201.
Manufacturers, Natl. Assn. of (1897), 1331 Penna. Ave. NW, Ste. 1500N, Wash., DC 20004-1703; 12,500 companies.
Manufacturers' Agents Natl. Assn. (1947), 23016 Mill Creek Rd., P.O. Box 3467, Laguna Hills, CA 92654; 10,000.
March of Dimes Birth Defects Foundation (1938), 1275 Mamaroneck Ave., White Plains, NY 10605; 2 mln.+.
Marijuana Laws, Natl. Organization for the Reform of (NORML) (1970), 1636 R St. NW, #3, Wash., DC 20009.
Marine Corps League (1923), P.O. Box 3070, Merrifield, VA 22116-3070; 34,000.
Marine Manufacturers Assn., Natl. (1904), 401 N. Michigan Ave., Chicago, IL 60611; 1,650 companies.
Marine Technology Society (1963), 1828 L St. NW, Suite 906, Wash., DC 20036; 2,600.
Marketing Assn., Amer. (1934), 250 S. Wacker Dr., Chicago, IL 60606; 49,122.
Masonic Relief Assn. of U.S. and Canada (1885), 3827 Canal St., New Orleans, LA 70119.
Masonic Service Assn. of the U.S. (1919), 8120 Fenton St., Silver Spring, MD 20910; 43 Grand Lodges.
Masons, Ancient and Accepted Scottish Rite, Southern Jurisdiction, Supreme Council 33° (1801), 1733 16th St. NW, Wash., DC 20009; 528,837.
Masons, Supreme Council 33°, Ancient and Accepted Scottish Rite, Northern Masonic Jurisdiction (1813), 33 Marrett Rd., Lexington, MA 02173; 400,034.
Masons, Royal Arch, General Grand Chapter (1797), P.O. Box 489, 111 S. 4th St., Danville, KY 40423-0489; 265,000.
Mathematical Assn. of America (1915), 1529 Eighteenth Street, NW, Wash., DC 20036; 26,000.
Mathematical Society, Amer. (1888), 201 Charles St., Providence, RI 02904; 27,018.
Mathematical Statistics, Institute of (1935), 3401 Investment Blvd., #7, Hayward, CA 94545; 3,788.
Mathematics, Society for Industrial and Applied (1952), 3600 University City Science Ctr., Phila., PA 19104-2688; 8,100.
Mayflower Descendants, General Society of (1897), 4 Winslow St., P.O. Box 3297, Plymouth, MA 02361; 27,000.
Mayors, U.S. Conference of (1932), 1620 Eye St. NW, Wash., DC 20006; 946 cities.
Mechanics, Amer. Academy of (1969), Dept. of Civil Engineering, Northwestern Univ., Evanston, IL 60201; 1,200.
Medical Assn., Amer. (1847), 535 N. Dearborn St., Chicago, IL 60610; 290,000.
Medical Assn., Natl. (1895), 1012 Tenth St. NW, Wash., DC 20001; 14,000.
Medical Record Assn., Amer. (1928), 919 N. Michigan Ave., Chicago, IL 60611; 31,000.
Medieval Academy of America (1926), 1430 Massachusetts Ave., Cambridge, MA 02138; 3,700.
Men, Natl Coalition of Free (1977), P.O. Box 129, Manhasset, NY 11030; 2,000.
Mensa, Amer. (1960), 2626 E. 14th St., Brooklyn, NY 11235.
Mental Health Assn., Natl. (1909), 1021 Prince St., Alexandria, VA 22314; 1 mln.
Mental Health Program Directors, Natl. Assn. of State (1963), 1101 King St., Suite 160, Alexandria, VA 22314; 55.
Mentally Ill, Natl. Alliance for the (1979), 2101 Wilson Blvd., Suite 302, Arlington, VA 22201; 80,000.
Merchant Marine Library Assn., Amer. (1921), One World Trade Center, Suite 2161, N.Y., NY 10048.
Merchant Marine Veterans of WWII, U.S. (1944), P.O. Box 629, San Pedro, CA 90731; 7,182.
Merchants Assn., Natl. Retail (1911), 100 W. 31st St., N.Y., NY 10001; 45,000.

Merrill's Marauders Assn. (1946), 11244 N. 33rd St., Phoenix, AZ 85028-2723; 1,695.
Metal Finishers, Natl. Assn. of (1950), 111 E. Wacker Dr., Suite 600, Chicago, IL 60601; 900.
Metallurgy Institute, Amer. Powder (1959), 105 College Rd. East, Princeton, NJ 08540; 2,807.
Metal Powder Industries Federation, (1943), 105 College Rd. East, Princeton, NJ 08540; 250 cos.
Metals, Amer. Society for (ASM Internatl.) (1913), Metals Park, OH 44073; 53,000.
Meteorological Society, Amer. (1919), 45 Beacon St., Boston, MA 02108; 10,200.
Metric Assn., U.S. (1916), 10245 Andasol Ave., Northridge, CA 91325; 1,500.
Microbiology, Amer. Society for (1899), 1325 Massachusetts Ave. NW, Wash. DC 20005; 37,000.
Mideast Educational and Training Services, America-, (1951), 1100 17th Street, NW, Wash., DC 20036.
Military Order of the Loyal Legion of the U.S.A. (1865), 1805 Pine St., Phila., PA 19103; 800.
Military Order of the Purple Heart of the USA (1932), 5413-B Backlick Rd., Springfield, VA 22151; 30,000.
Military Order of the World Wars (1919), 435 N. Lee St., Alexandria, VA 22314; 15,000.
Military Service, Veterans of Underage (1991), 3444 Walker Dr., Ellicott City, MD 21042; 300.
Miniatures, Friends of (1988), Dollhouse Museum of the Southwest, 2208 Routh St., Dallas, TX 75201; 274.
Mining and Metallurgical Society of America (1908), 275 Madison Ave., N.Y., NY 10016; 295.
Mining, Metallurgy and Exploration, Inc., Society for (1871), 8307 Shaffer Pkwy., Littleton, CO 80127; 20,279.
Ministerial Assn., Amer. (1929), 2210 Wilshire Blvd., Suite 582, Santa Monica, CA 90403; 3,000.
Missouri Alliance for Historic Preservation (1970), P.O. Box 895, Jefferson City, MO 65102; 250.
Model Railroad Assn., Natl. (1935), 4121 Cromwell Rd., Chattanooga, TN 37421; 25,000.
Modern Language Assn. of America (1883), 10 Astor Pl., N.Y., NY 10003; 32,000.
Modern Language Teachers Assns., Natl. Federation of (1916), Gannon Univ., Erie, PA 16541; 7,200.
Moose, Loyal Order of (1888), Mooseheart, IL 60539.
Mothers, American (1935), 301 Park Ave., N.Y., NY 10022; 3,000.
Mothers-in-Law Club Intl. (1970), 420 Adelberg Ln., Cedarhurst, NY 11516; 5,000.
Mothers of Twins Clubs, Natl. Organization of (1960), P.O. Box 23188, Albuquerque, NM 87192-1188; 14,000.
Motion Picture Arts & Sciences, Academy of (1927), 8949 Wilshire Blvd., Beverly Hills, CA 90211; 5,300.
Motion Pictures, Natl. Board of Review of (1909), P.O. Box 589, Lenox Hill Sta., N.Y., NY 10021.
Motion Picture & Television Engineers, Society of (1916), 595 West Hartsdale Ave., White Plains, NY 10607; 9,500.
Motor Vehicle Administrators, Amer. Assn. of (1933), 4200 Wilson Blvd.; Suite 600, Arlington, VA 22203; 173.
Motor Vehicle Manufacturers Assn. (1903), 7430 2nd Ave., Suite 300, Detroit, MI 48202; 7 companies.
Motorcyclist Assn., American (1924), 33 Collegeview Rd., Westerville, OH 43081; 160,000.
Multiethnic Americans, Assn. of, 1060 Tennessee St., San Francisco, CA 94107.
Multiple Sclerosis Society, Natl. (1946), 733 Third Ave., N.Y., NY 10017; 400,000.
Multiracial Americans of Southern California (M.A.S.C.) (1987), 12228 Venice Blvd., #452, Los Angeles, CA 90066.
Muscular Dystrophy Assn. (1950), 3300 E. Sunrise Dr., Tucson, AZ 85718-3208.
Museums, Amer. Assn. of (1906), 1225 Eye St. NW, Ste. 200, Wash., DC 20005; 12,000.
Music Center, Amer. (1939), 30 W. 26th St., N.Y., NY 10010.
Music Council, Natl. (1940), 40 W. 37th St., N.Y., NY 10018; 50 organizations.
Music Educators Natl. Conference (1907), 1902 Association Dr., Reston, VA 22090; 60,000.
Music Scholarship Assn., Amer. (1956), 1826 Carew Tower, Cincinnati, OH 45202; 1,400.
Music Teachers Natl. Assn. (1876), 617 Vine St., Suite 1432, Cincinnati, OH 45202-2439; 22,000+.
Musicological Society, Amer. (1934), 201 S. 34th St., Phila., PA 19104-6313, 3,500.
Music Publishers' Assn., Natl. (1917), 205 E. 42nd St., N.Y., NY 10017; 300.
Muzzle Loading Rifle Assn., Natl. (1933), P.O. Box 67, Friendship, IN 47021; 26,000.
Myasthenia Gravis Foundation, The (1952), 53 W. Jackson Blvd., Ste. 1352, Chicago, IL 60604.

NAACP (Natl. Assn. for the Advancement of Colored People) (1909), 4805 Mt. Hope Drive, Baltimore, MD 21215.
NOT-SAFE (1981), Box 5743-WA, Montecito, CA 93150.
Na'amat USA (1925), 200 Madison Ave., N.Y., NY 10016.
Narcolepsy and Cataplexy Foundation of Amer. (1975), 1410 York Ave., Suite 2D, N.Y. NY 10021; 3,991.
Narcolepsy Assoc., Amer. (1977), 425 California St., Ste. 201, San Francisco, CA 94104; 3,200.
Narcotics Anonymous (1953), P.O. Box 9999, Van Nuys, CA 91409; 1 million.
National Guard Assn. of the U.S. (1878), One Massachusetts Ave. NW, Wash., DC 20001; 54,000.
Nature Conservancy (1951), 1815 N. Lynn St., Arlington, VA 22209; 575,000.
Naturist Society, The (1980), P.O. Box 132, Oshkosh, WI 54902; 15,000.
Naturopathy Institute, The (1984), P.O. Box 56, Malverne, NY 11565.
Navajo Code Talkers Assn. (1971), Box 1182, Window Rock, AZ 86515; 295.
Naval Architects & Marine Engineers, The Society of (1893), 601 Pavonia Ave., Ste. 400, Jersey City, NJ 07306.
Naval Institute, U.S. (1873), 118 Maryland Ave., Annapolis, MD 21402; 100,000.
Naval Reserve Assn. (1954), 1619 King St., Alexandria, VA 22314; 24,500.
Navigation, Institute of (1945), 1026 16th St. NW, Suite 104, Wash., DC 20036; 3,200.
Navy Club of the U.S.A. Auxiliary (1941), 418 W. Pontiac St., Ft. Wayne, IN 46807; 1,000.
Navy League of the U.S. (1902); 2300 Wilson Blvd., Arlington, VA 22201; 73,000.
Needlework Guild of America (1885), 1007-B St. Road, Southhampton, PA 18966; 100,000.
Negro College Fund, United (1944), 500 E. 62d St., N.Y., NY 10021; 42 institutions.
Neurofibromatosis Foundation, Natl. (1978), 141 Fifth Ave., Suite 7-S, N.Y., NY 10010; 7,000.
New Age Walkers (1982), 3301 Bellaire Dr., Altadena, CA 91001; 4,700.
Newspaper Editors, Amer. Society of (1922), 11600 Sunrise Valley Dr., Reston, VA 22091; 1,000.
Newspaper Marketing Assn., Intl. (1930), 11600 Sunrise Valley Dr., Reston, VA 22091; 1,300+.
Newspaper Publishers Assn., Amer. (1887), The Newspaper Center, Box 17407 Dulles Airport, Wash., DC 20041.
Newswomen's Club of N.Y. (1922), 15 Gramercy Park S., N.Y., NY 10003; 200.
Nikola Tesla Walkers (1982), 745 S. Brightview Dr., Glendora, CA 91740; 4,700.
Ninety-Nines (Intl. Organization of Women Pilots) (1929), P.O. Box 59965, Will Rogers Airport, Oklahoma City, OK 73159.
Nobel Laureate Center, Amer. (1941), 1 Morningside Dr. N., Westport, CT 06880; 480.
Non-Commissioned Officers Assn. (1960), 10635 IH 35 No., San Antonio, TX 78233; 162,000.
Northern Cross Society (1983), Route One, Big Springs, KS 66050; 50.
Notaries, Amer. Society of (1965), 918 16th St. NW, Wash., DC 20006; 23,531.
Nuclear Society, Amer. (1954), 555 N. Kensington Ave., La Grange Park, IL 60525; 15,000.
Numismatic Assn., Amer. (1891), 818 N. Cascade Ave., Colorado Springs, CO 80903-3279; 31,000.
Numismatic Society, Amer. (1858), Broadway at 155th St., N.Y., NY 10032; 2,469.
Nurses' Assn., Amer. (1896), 2420 Pershing Rd., Kansas City, MO 64108.
Nursing, Natl. League for (1952), 350 Hudson St., N.Y., NY 10014; 18,000.
Nutrition, Amer. Institute of (1928), 9650 Rockville Pike, Bethesda, MD 20814; 3,000.

ORT Federation, Amer. (Org. for Rehabilitation through Training) (1922), 817 Broadway, N.Y., NY 10003.
Odd Fellows, Independent Order of (1819), 422 N. Trade St., Winston Salem, NC 27101-2830; 475,000.
Old Crows, Assn. of (1964), 1000 N. Payne St., Alexandria, VA 22314-1696; 25,000.
Olympic Committee, U.S. (1921), 1750 E. Boulder St., Colorado Springs, CO 80909; 70 organizations.
Omnibus Soc. of Am. (1961), 3440 W. Evergreen, Chicago, IL 60651; 110.
One Shoe Crew, The, 86 Clavela Ave., Sacramento, CA 95828.
Opthalmology, Amer. Academy of (1979), 655 Beach St., San Francisco, CA 94109; 16,250.
Optical Society of America (1916), 2010 Massachusetts Ave. NW, Wash., DC 20036; 11,208.

Optimist Intl. (1919), 4494 Lindell Blvd., St. Louis, MO 63108.
Optometric Assn., Amer. (1898), 243 N. Lindbergh Blvd., St. Louis, MO 63141; 28,000.
Oral and Maxillofacial Surgeons, Amer. Assn. of (1918), 9700 W. Bryn Mawr Ave., Rosemont, IL 60018; 5,302.
Organists, Amer. Guild of (1896), 475 Riverside Dr., Suite 1260, N.Y., NY 10115; 21,000.
Oriental Society, Amer. (1842), 329 Sterling Memorial Library, Yale Sta., New Haven, CT 06520; 1,440.
Ornithologists' Union, Amer. (1883), c/o National Museum of Natural History, Smithsonian, Wash., DC 20560; 4,067.
Osteopathic Assn., Amer. (1887), 212 E. Ohio St., Chicago, IL 60611; 23,292.
Ostomy Assn., United (1970), 36 Executive Park, Suite 120, Irving, CA 92714, 42,000.
Outlaw and Lawman History, Natl. Organization for (1974), 615-C N. 8th St., Killeen, TX 76541; 559.
Overeaters Anonymous (1960), 4025 Spencer St., #203, Torrance, CA 90503; 120,000.

PTA (Natl. Congress of Parents and Teachers), Natl. (1897), 700 N. Rush St., Chicago, IL 60611; 6.6 mln.
Paleontological Research Institution (1932), 1259 Trumansburg Rd., Ithaca, NY 14850; 700+.
Paper Industry, Technical Assn. of the Pulp and (1915), 15 Technology Pkwy. S., Norcross, GA 30084; 29,950.
Paper Institute, Amer. (1964), 260 Madison Ave., N.Y., NY 10016; 166 companies.
Parasitologists, Amer. Society of (1924), 1041 New Hampshire St., Box 368, Lawrence, KS 66044; 1,491.
Parents Without Partners (1957), 8807 Colesville Rd., Silver Spring, MD 20910; 100,000.
Parkinson's Disease Foundation (1957), 650 W. 168th St., N.Y., NY 10032.
Parliamentarians, Amer. Institute of (1958), 203 W. Wayne, Ft. Wayne, IN 46802; 1,350.
Parliamentarians, Natl. Assn. of (1930), 6601 Winchester, Kansas City, MO 64133-4600; 4,400.
Parliamentary Law, Intl. Organization of Professionals in (1975), 3611 Victoria Ave., Los Angeles, CA 90016; 250.
Pasta Assn., Natl. (1904), 2101 Wilson Blvd., Suite 920, Arlington, VA 22201; 100 companies.
Pathologists, Amer. Assn. of (1976), 9650 Rockville Pike, Bethesda, MD 20814; 2,000.
Patton Historical Soc., George S. Jr. (1970), 3116 Thorn St., San Diego, CA 92104-4618.
Patriotism, Natl. Committee for Responsible (1967), P.O. Box 665, Grand Central Sta., N.Y., NY 10163; 150.
Pearl Harbor History Associates (1982), P.O. Box 205, Sperryville, VA 22740-0205; 400.
Pearl Harbor Survivors Assn. (1958), 3215 Albert St., Orlando, FL 32806.
PEN Amer. Center (1922), 568 Broadway, N.Y., NY 10012.
PEN Women, Natl. League of Amer. (1897), 1300 17th St. NW, Wash., DC 20036-1973; 5,000.
Pen Friends, Intl. (1967), Box 65, Brooklyn, NY 11229; 300,000.
Pennsylvania Society of New York (1899), 80 N. Main St., Sellersville, PA 18960; 1,800.
Pension Actuaries, Amer. Society of (1966), 4350 N. Fairfax Dr., Ste. 820, Arlington, VA 22203; 3,000.
Pension Plan, Committee for a Natl. (1979), P.O. Box 27851, Las Vegas, NV 89126; 2,000.
P.E.O. (Philanthropic Educational Organization) Sisterhood (1869), 3700 Grand Ave., Des Moines, IA 50312; 242,000.
Personnel Administration, Amer. Society for (1948), 606 N. Washington St., Alexandria, VA 22314; 40,000.
Petroleum Equipment Inst. (1951), 3739 E. 31st St., Tulsa, OK 74135; 1,200 member companies.
Petroleum Institute, Amer. (1919), 1220 L St. NW, Wash., DC 20005; 250 corporations.
Pharmaceutical Assn., Amer. (1852), 2215 Constitution Ave. NW, Wash., DC 20037; 40,000.
Phi Delta Kappa (1906), 8th & Union, Box 789, Bloomington, IN 47401-0789; 132,000.
Philatelic Pages & Panels, Amer. Soc. for (1984), 1138 Princeton Dr., Richardson, TX 75081-3615; 679.
Philatelic Society, Amer. (1886), 100 Oakwood Ave., P.O. Box 8000, State College, PA 16803; 57,000.
Philological Assn., Amer. (1869), Dept. of Classics, Fordham Univ., Bronx, NY 10458; 2,500.
Philosophical Assn., Amer. (1900), Univ. of Delaware, Newark, DE 19716; 8,000.
Philosophical Society, Amer. (1743), 104 S. 5th St., Phila., PA 19106; 700.
Photogrammetry and Remote Sensing, Amer. Society of (1934), 5410 Grosvenor Ln., Ste. 210, Bethesda, MD 20814.
Photographers of America, Professional (1880), 1090 Executive Way, Des Plaines, IL 60018; 15,000.
Photographic Society of Amer. (1934), 3000 United Founders Blvd. #103, Oklahoma City, OK 73112.
Physical Therapy Assn., Amer. (1921), 1111 N. Fairfax St., Alexandria, VA 22314; 52,000.
Physicians, Amer. Academy of Family (1947), 8880 Ward Pkwy., Kansas City, MO 64114; 70,000.
Physics, Amer. Inst. of (1931), 335 E. 45th St., N.Y., NY 10017-3483.
Physiological Society, Amer. (1887), 9650 Rockville Pike, Bethesda, MD 20814; 7,000.
Phytopathological Soc., The Amer. (1908), 3340 Pilot Knob Rd., St. Paul, MN 55121; 4,300+.
Pilgrim Society (1820), 75 Court St., Plymouth, MA 02360-3891; 600.
Pilgrims of the U.S. (1903), 80 Broadway, N.Y., NY 10005.
Pilot Intl. (1921), P.O. Box 4844, 244 College St., Macon, GA 31213-0599; 19,000.
Planetary Society (1979), 65 N. Catalina Ave., Pasadena, CA 91106; 110,000.
Planned Parenthood Federation of America (1916), 810 Seventh Ave., N.Y., NY 10019; 187 affiliates.
Planning Assn., Amer. (1909), 1776 Massachusetts Ave. NW, Wash., DC 20036; 26,000.
Plastic Modelers Society, Intl. (1965), P.O. Box 6138, Warner Robins, GA 31095-6138; 4,100.
Plastics Industry, Society of (1937), 1275 K St. NW, Suite 400, Washington, DC 20005; 2,100.
Platform Assn., Intl. (1831), Box 250, Winnetka, IL 60093.
Poetry Day Committee, Natl. (1947), 1110 N. Venetian Dr., Miami, FL 33139-1019; 17,500.
Poetry Society of America (1910), 15 Gramercy Park, N.Y., NY 10003; 1,700.
Poets, Academy of Amer. (1934), 177 E. 87th St., N.Y., NY 10128.
Police, Internatl. Assn. of Chiefs of (1893), 1110 N. Glebe Rd., Suite 200, Arlington, VA 22201; 13,500.
Police Officers Assn., Natl. Police Reserve Officers Assn., Natl. (1955/1967), 1316 Gardiner Lane, Louisville, KY 40213; 6,000.
Polish Army Veterans Assn. of America (1921), 155 Noble St., Brooklyn, NY 11222; 3,500.
Polish Cultural Society of America (1940), P.O. Box 31, Wall Street, N.Y., NY 10005; 101,261.
Polish Genealogical Society of CT (1984), 8 Lyle Rd., New Britain, CT 06053; 400.
Polish Legion of American Veterans (1921), 3024 N. Laramie Ave., Chicago, IL 60641; 15,000.
Political Items Collectors, Amer. (1945), P.O. Box 340339, San Antonio, TX 78234; 2,600.
Political Science, Academy of (1880), 475 Riverside Dr., Suite 1274, N.Y., NY 10115-0012; 9,000.
Political Science Assn., Amer. (1903), 1527 New Hampshire Ave. NW, Wash., DC 20036; 13,000.
Political & Social Science, Amer. Academy of (1891), 3937 Chestnut St., Phila., PA 19104.
Pollution Control, Internatl. Assn. for (1970), 444 N. Capital St. NW, Wash. DC 20001; 500.
Polo Assn., U.S. (1890), 4059 Iron Works Pike, Lexington, KY, 40511; 3,000.
Population Assn. of America (1931), 1722 N. St. NW, Washington, DC 20036; 2,600.
Portuguese Continental Union of the U.S.A. (1925), 899 Boylston St., Boston, MA 02115; 7,245.
Postmasters of the U.S., Natl. Assn. of (1898), 8 Herbert St., Arlington, VA 22305; 43,000.
Postmasters of the U.S., Natl. League of (1904), 1023 N. Royal St., Alexandria, VA 22314; 21,874.
Poultry Science Assn. (1921), 309 W. Clark St., Champaign, IL 61820.
Power Boat Assn., Amer. (1903), 17640 E. Nine Mile Rd., P.O. Box 377, E. Detroit, MI 48021; 9,000.
Precancel Collectors, Natl. Assn. of (1950), 5121 Park Blvd., Wildwood, NJ 08260; 7,640.
Press, Associated (1848), 50 Rockefeller Plaza, N.Y., NY 10020; 1,558 newspapers & 6,000 broadcast stations.
Press Club, Natl. (1908), 529 14th St. NW, Wash., DC 20045.
Press Intl., United (1907), 1400 I St. NW, Wash. DC 20005.
Press and Radio Club (1948), P.O. Box 70023, Montgomery, AL 36107; 739.
Printing Industries of America (1887), 100 Dangerfield Rd., Alexandria, VA 22314.
Prisoners of War, Amer. Ex- (1942), 3201 E. Pioneer Pkwy. #40, Arlington, TX 76010-5396; 34,000.
Procrastinators Club of America (1956), Box 712, Bryn Athyn, PA 19009; 6,500.
Production and Inventory Control Soc., American, 500 W. Annandale Rd., Falls Church, VA 22046-4274; 65,000.
Propeller Club of the U.S. (1927), 3927 Old Lee Highway, Ste. 101A, Fairfax, VA 22030; 13,000.

Psychiatric Assn., Amer. (1844), 1400 K St. NW, Wash., DC 20005; 37,380.
Psychical Research, Amer. Society for (1907), 5 W. 73d St., N.Y., NY 10023; 2,000.
Psychoanalytic Assn., Amer. (1911), 309 E. 49th St., N.Y., NY 10017; 3,050.
Psychological Assn., Amer. (1892), 1200 17th St. NW, Wash., DC 20036; 60,000.
Psychological Assn. for Psychoanalysis, Natl. (1948), 150 W. 13th St., N.Y., NY 10011; 347.
Psychological Minorities, Society for the Aid of (1953), 42-25 Hampton St., Elmhurst, NY 11373; 532.
Psychotherapy Assn., Amer. Group (1942), 25 E. 21st St., N.Y., NY 10010; 3,400.
Psoriasis Foundation, Natl (1968), 6443 SW Beaverton Hwy., #210, Portland, OR 97221; 14,000.
Public Administration, Amer. Soc. for (1939), 1120 G St. NW, Wash, DC 20005; 14,800.
Public Health Assn., World Fed. of (1967), 1015 15th St. NW, Wash., DC 20005; 48 natl. assn.
Public Relations Soc. of Amer. (1947), 33 Irving Pl. N.Y., NY 10003-2376; 15,462.
Publicly Traded Cos., Assn. of (1973), 1707 L St. NW, Suite 950, Wash., DC 20036; 791.
Publishers, Assn. of Amer. (1970), One Park Ave., N.Y., NY 10016; 330 publishing houses.
Puppeteers of Amer. (1937), 5 Cricklewood Path, Pasadena, CA 91107; 2,400.
Puzzle Buffs Intl. (1978), 1772 State Road, Cuyahoga Falls, OH 44223; 39,000.

Quality Control, Amer. Society for (1946), 611 E. Wisconsin Ave., Milwaukee, WI 53201-3005, 90,000.
Quota Internatl. (1919), 1420 21st St. NW, Wash., DC 20036.

Rabbinical Alliance of America (1942), 3 W. 16th St. N.Y., NY 10011; 500.
Rabbinical Assembly (1900), 3080 Broadway, N.Y., NY 10027; 1,265.
Rabbis, Central Conference of Amer. (1889), 192 Lexington Ave., N.Y., NY 10016; 1,540.
Racial Equality, Congress of (CORE) (1942), 1457 Flatbush Ave., Brooklyn, NY 11210; 100,000.
Radio, Natl. Assn. of Business and Educational (1965), 1501 Duke St., Suite 200, Alexandria, VA 22314; 4,873.
Radio Union, Intl. Amateur (1925), P.O. Box AAA, Newington, CT 06111; 126 societies.
Radio and TV Society, Intl. (1939), 420 Lexington Ave., Ste. 1714, N.Y., NY 10170; 1,800.
Radio Relay League, Amer. (1914), 225 Main St., Newington, CT 06111; 160,000.
Railroads, Assn. of Amer. (1934), 50 F St. NW, Wash., DC 20001; 113.
Railway Historical Society, Natl. (1935), P.O. Box 58153, Phila., PA 19102-8153; 19,000+.
Railway Progress Institute (1908), 700 N. Fairfax St., Suite 601, Alexandria, VA 22314-2098; 104 companies.
Rainbow Walkers (1982), 4370 Fairlawn Dr., Lake Canada, CA 91011; 1,444.
Range Management, Society for (1948), 1839 York Street, Denver, CO 80206; 5,400.
Rape, Feminist Alliance Against (1974), P.O. Box 21033, Wash., DC 20009.
Reading Assn., Intl. (1956), P.O. Box 8139, 800 Barksdale Rd., Newark, DE 19714-8139; 93,000.
Real Estate Institute, Intl. (1975), 8383 E. Evans Rd., Scottsdale, AZ 85260; 3,000.
Rebekah Assemblies, Intl. Assn. of (1916), 422 N. Trade St., Suite "R" Winston-Salem, NC 27101; 189,404.
Reconciliation, Fellowship of (1915), 523 N. Broadway, Nyack, NY 10960; 10,000.
Records Managers & Administrators, Assn. of (1975), 4200 Somerset Dr., Suite 215, Prairie Village, KS 66208; 12,000.
Recreation and Park Assn., Natl. (1965), 2775 S. Quincy St., Ste. 300, Alexandria, VA 22206; 22,182.
Recycling Coalition, Natl., 1101 30th St. NW, Ste. 305, Wash., DC 20007.
Red Cross, American (1881), 17th & D Sts. NW, Wash., DC 20006; 1.5 mln. volunteers.
Red Men, Improved Order of (1765), 4521 Speight Ave., Waco, TX, 76711; 30,000.
Redwoods League, Save-the- (1918), 114 Sansome St., Rm. 605, San Francisco, CA 94104; 45,000.
Reed Organ Society, Inc. (1982), The Musical Museum, Deansboro, NY 13328; 840.
Regional Plan Assn. (1929), 1040 Ave. of the Americas, N.Y., NY 10018; 1,000.
Rehabilitation Assn., Natl. (1925), 1910 Association Dr., Ste. 205, Reston, VA 22091.
Religion, Amer. Academy of (1909), 501 Hall of Languages, Syracuse Univ., Syracuse, NY 13244-1170; 5,600.
Religion Foundation, Freedom from (1978), P.O. Box 750, Madison, WI 53701; 3,100.
Remodeling Industry, Natl. Assn. of the (1956), 1901 N. Moore St., Suite 808, Arlington, VA 22209.
Renaissance Society of America (1954), 1161 Amsterdam Ave., N.Y., NY 10027; 3,500.
Republican National Committee (1856), 310 1st Street SE, Washington, DC 20003-1801.
Reserve Officers Assn. of the U.S. (1922), One Constitution Ave., NE, Wash., DC 20002; 123,000.
Restaurant Assn., Natl. (1919), 1200 17th St. NW, Wash., DC 20036; 20,000.
Retail Federation, Natl. (1918), 100 West 31st St., N.Y., NY 10001; 2,200.
Retired Credit Union People, Natl. Assn. for (1978), P.O. Box 391, 5910 Mineral Pt. Rd., Madison, WI 53705; 125,000.
Retired Federal Employees, Natl. Assn. of (1921), 1533 New Hampshire Ave. NW, Wash., DC 20036; 500,000.
Retired Officers Assn. (1929), 201 N. Washington St., Alexandria, VA 22314-2529; 380,000.
Retired Persons, Amer. Assn. of (1958), 1909 K St. NW, Wash., DC 20049; 32 mln.
Retired Teachers Assn., Natl. (1947), 1909 K St. NW, Wash., DC 20049; 540,000.
Revolver Assn., U.S. (1900), 96 W. Union St., Ashland, MA 01721; 1,400.
Reye's Syndrome Foundation, Natl. (1974), 426 N. Lewis, Bryan, OH 43506; 5,000+.
Richard III Society (1969), P.O. Box 13787, New Orleans, LA 70185; 700.
Rifle Assn., Natl. (1871), 1600 Rhode Island Ave. NW, Wash., DC 20036; 2.8 mln.
Road & Transportation Builders' Assn., Amer. (1902), 501 School St. SW, Wash., DC 20024-2713; 3,600.
Rodeo Cowboys Assn., Professional (1936), 101 Pro Rodeo Dr., Colorado Springs, CO 80921; 8,983.
Roller Skating, U.S. Amateur Confederation of (1937), 4730 South St., P.O. Box 6579, Lincoln, NE 68506; 20,000.
Roller Skating Rink Operators Assn. (1937), 7700 A St., P.O. Box 81846, Lincoln, NE 68501; 1,150 rinks.
Rose Society, Amer. (1899), 8877 Jefferson Paige Rd., Shreveport, LA 71119.
Rotary Intl. (1905), One Rotary Center, Evanston, IL 60201.
Running and Fitness Assn., Amer. (1968), 9310 Old Georgetown Rd., Bethesda, MD 20814; 18,000.
Ruritan Natl. (1928), Ruritan Natl. Rd., Dublin, VA 24084.

SANE/FREEZE (1987), 1819 H St. NW, Suite 640, Wash., DC 20006-3603; 170,000.
Safety and Fairness Everywhere, Natl. Assn. Taunting (1980), P.O. Box 5743WA, Montecito, CA 93150; 12,000.
Safety Council, Natl. (1913), 444 N. Michigan Ave., Chicago, IL 60611; 12,500.
Sailors, Tin Can (1976), 1231 County St., Somerset, MA 02726; 16,000.
Sailors Assn., Destroyer-Escort (1975), 352 W. Story Rd., Ocoee, FL 34761, 12,000.
St. Andrew the Apostle, The Soc. of (1983), Route 3, Sylvester, WV 25193; 450.
St. Andrew, The Brotherhood of (1883), 1109 Merchant St., P.O. Box 632, Ambridge, PA 15003; 5,000.
St. George the Martyr, Knightly Assn. of (1980), State Route #3, Sylvester, WV 25193; 10,000.
St. John of Damascus Assn. of Orthodox Iconographers, Iconologists and Architects (1979), Rt. 711 North, P.O. Box 638, Ligonier, PA 15658-0638; 400.
St. Paul, Natl. Guild of (1937), 601 Hill 'n Dale, Lexington, KY 40503; 13,652.
Salespersons, Natl. Assn. of Professional (1970), P.O. Box 76461, Atlanta, GA 30358; 35,000.
Salt Institute (1914), 700 N. Fairfax St., Ste. 600, Alexandria, VA, 22314-2040; 23 companies.
Sane Nuclear Policy, Committee for a (1957), 711 G St. SE, Wash., DC 20003; 130,000.
Savings Institutions, Natl. Council of (1983), 1101 15th St. NW, Wash., DC 20005; 550 members.
Savings & Loan League, Natl. (1943), 1101 15th St. NW, Wash., DC 20005; 300 associations.
School Administrators, Amer. Assn. of (1865), 1801 N. Moore St., Arlington, VA 22209; 18,500.
School Boards Assn., Natl. (1940), 1680 Duke St., Alexandria, VA 22314.
School Counselor Assn., Amer. (1953), 5999 Stevenson Ave., Alexandria, VA 22304; 12,500.

Schools of Art, Natl. Assn. of (also: School of Art and Design, School of Dance, Music, and Theater) (1944), 11250 Roger Bacon Dr., Reston, VA 22090; 161.
Schools & Colleges, Amer. Council on (1927), 13014 Dale Mabry Hwy., Ste. 270-B, Tampa, FL 33180-2808; 400+.
Science, Amer. Assn. for the Advancement of (1848), 1333 H St. NW, Wash., DC 20005; 135,000.
Science Fiction Society, World (1939), P.O. Box 1270, Kendall Sq. Sta., Cambridge, MA 02142; 5,000.
Science Service (1921), 1719 N St. NW, Wash., DC 20036.
Science Teachers Assn., Natl. (1985), 1742 Connecticut Ave. NW, Wash., DC 20009; 49,000.
Science Writers, Natl. Assn. of (1934), P.O. Box 294, Greenlawn, NY 11740; 1,650.
Sciences, Natl. Academy of (1863), 2101 Constitution Ave. NW, Wash., DC 20418; 1,936.
Scientists, Federation of American (1945), 307 Massachusetts Ave. NE, Wash., DC 20002; 5,000.
Scrabble Assn., Natl. (1978), Box 700, Greenport, NY 11944; 10,000.
Screen Actors Guild (1933), 7065 Hollywood Blvd. Hollywood, CA 90028; 78,000.
Screen Printing Assn. Intl. (1948), 10015 Main St., Fairfax, VA 22031.
Sculpture Soc., Natl. (1893), 15 E. 26th St., N.Y., NY 10010.
Seamen's Service, United (1942), One World Trade Ctr., Suite 1365, N.Y., NY 10048.
2d Air Division Assn. (1947), 1 Jeffrey's Neck Rd., Ipswich, MA 01938; 7,852.
Secondary School Principals, Natl. Assn. of (1916), 1904 Association Dr., Reston, VA 22091; 42,000.
Secretaries Intl., Professional (1942), 10502 NW Ambassador Dr., P.O. Box 20404, Kansas City, MO 64195-0404; 40,000.
Secretaries, Natl. Assn. of Legal (1950), 2250 E 73, Ste. 550, Tulsa, OK 74136-6805; 16,000.
Securities Industry Assn. (1972), 120 Broadway, N.Y., NY 10271; 600 firms.
Semantics, Inst. of General (1938), 163 Engle St., Englewood, NJ 07631; 300.
Separation of Church & State, Americans United for (1947), 8120 Fenton St., Silver Spring, MD 20910; 50,000.
Sertoma Internatl. (1912), 1912 E. Meyer Blvd., Kansas City, MO 64132; 30,000.
Sex Information & Education Council of the U.S. (SIECUS) (1964), 130 W. 42 St., Ste. 2500, N.Y., NY 10036; 2,000+.
Sharkhunters Intl. (1983), P.O. Box 1539, Hernanado, FL 32642; 2,500.
Shipbuilders Council of America (1921), 1110 Vermont Ave. NW, Wash., DC 20005; 50 organizations.
Ships in Bottles Assn. of Amer. (1983), P.O. Box 180550, Coronado, CA 92178; 400.
Shore & Beach Preservation Assn., Amer. (1926), P.O. Box 279, Middletown, CA 95461; 900.
Shrine, Ancient Arabic Order of the Nobles of the Mystic (1872), 2900 Rocky Pt. Dr., Tampa, FL 33607; 799,000.
Shut-Ins, Natl. Society for (1970), 237 Franklin St., Reading, PA 19602; 85.
Sierra Club (1892), 730 Polk St., San Francisco, CA 94109.
Skating Union of the U.S., Amateur (1927), 1033 Shady Lane, Glen Ellyn, IL 60137; 3,200.
Skeet Shooting Assn., Natl. (1946), P.O. Box 680007, San Antonio, TX 78268; 15,800.
Ski Assn., U.S. (1904), P.O. Box 100, Park City, UT 84060.
Small Business, Amer. Federation of (1938), 18200 Sherman St., Lansing, IL 60438-3104; 26,000.
Small Business United, Natl. (1986), 1155 15th St. NW, Suite 710, Wash., DC 20005; 50,000.
Smoking & Health, Natl. Clearinghouse for (1965), Center for Disease Control, 1600 Clifton Road NE, Atlanta, GA 30333.
Soccer Federation, U.S. (1913), Viscount Hotel, 40 JFK Intl. Airport, Jamaica, NY 11430; 700,000.
Social Biology, Society for the Study of (1926), Medical Dept., Brookhaven Natl. Laboratory, Upton, NY 11973; 415.
Social Sciences, Natl. Institute of (1865), 444 Madison Ave., Ste. 2901, N.Y., NY 10022; 300.
Social Work Education, Council on (1952), 1600 Duke Street, Alexandria, VA 22314; 2,500.
Social Workers, Natl. Assn. of (1955), 7981 Eastern Ave., Silver Spring, MD 20910; 127,000.
Socialists of America, Democratic (1981), 15 Dutch St., Suite 500, N.Y., NY 10038; 5,500.
Sociological Assn., Amer. (1905), 1722 N St. NW, Wash., DC 20036; 13,000.
Softball Association, Amateur (1933), 2801 N.E. 50th St., Oklahoma City, OK 73111; 4.5 mln.
Softball League, Cinderella (1958), P.O. Box 1411, Corning, NY 14830.
Soft Drink Assn., Natl. (1921), 1101 16th St. NW, Wash., DC 20036; 1,000.
Soil & Water Conservation Society of America (1945), 7515 N.E. Ankeny Rd., Ankeny, IA 50021; 11,000.
Soil Science Society of America (1936), 677 S. Segoe Rd., Madison, WI 53711; 6,200.
Sojourners, Natl. (1919), 8301 E. Boulevard Dr., Alexandria, VA 22308; 9,500.
Soldier's, Sailor's and Airmen's Club (1919), 283 Lexington Ave., N.Y., NY 10016.
Songwriters Guild of America, The (1931), 276 Fifth Ave., Ste. 306, N.Y., NY 10001; 3,500.
Sons of the Amer. Legion (1932), Box 1055, Indianapolis, IN 46206; 135,910.
Sons of the American Revolution, Natl. Society of (1889), 1000 S. 4th, Louisville, KY 40203; 27,000.
Sons of Confederate Veterans (1896), Southern Station, Box 5164, Hattiesburg, MS 39406-5164; 13,000.
Sons of the Desert (1965), P.O. Box 8341, Universal City, CA 91608; 10,000.
Sons of Italy in America, Order (1905), 219 E. St., NE, Wash. DC 20002; 500,000.
Sons of Norway (1895), 1455 W. Lake St., Minneapolis, MN 55408; 76,030.
Sons of Poland, Assn. of the (1903), 591 Summit Ave., Rm. 702, Jersey City, NJ 07306; 10,000.
Sons of the Republic of Texas, The (1922), 5942 Abrams Rd., #222, Dallas, TX 75231; 2,326.
Sons of the Revolution, General Society of the/Fraunces Tavern Museum (1890), 54 Pearl St., N.Y., NY 10004; 5,600.
Sons of St. Patrick, Society of the Friendly (1784), 80 Wall St., N.Y., NY 10005; 1,400.
Sons of Sherman's March to the Sea (1966), 1725 Farmers Ave., Tempe, AZ 85281; 700.
Sons of Union Veterans of the Civil War (1881), 12312 Espalier Pl., Potomac, MD 20854; 2,700.
Soroptimist Intl. of the Americas (1921), 1616 Walnut St., Phila., PA 19103; 50,000.
Southern Christian Leadership Conference (1957), 334 Auburn Ave. NE, Atlanta, GA 30303; 1 mln.
Space Education Assoc., U.S. (1973), 746 Turnpike Rd., Elizabethtown, PA 17022-1161; 1,500.
Speech Communication Assn. (1914), 5105 Backlick Rd., Annandale, VA 22003; 7,000.
Speech-Language-Hearing Assn., Amer. (1925), 10801 Rockville Pike, Rockville, MD 20852; 64,000.
Speleological Society, Natl. (1941), 2813 Cave Ave., Huntsville, AL 35810; 10,300.
Spiritual Awareness, Assn. for (1984), P.O. Box 224, Clifton Hill, MO 65244; 2,050.
Sports Car Club of America (1944), P.O. Box 3278, Englewood, CO 80155-3278; 51,081.
Sports Club, Indoor (1930), 1145 Highland St., Napoleon, OH 43545; 950.
Sportscasters Assn., Amer. (1979), 5 Beekman St., N.Y., NY 10038; 550.
Standards Institute, Amer. Natl. (1918), 1430 Broadway, N.Y., NY 10018; 1,000.
State Communities Aid Assn. (1872), 151 Chestnut St., Albany, NY 12210; 95.
State Governments, Council of (1933), P.O. Box 11910, Iron Works Pike, Lexington, KY 40578; 50 states, 4 territories.
State & Local History, Amer. Assn. for (1940), 172 Second Ave. N., Nashville, TN 37201; 5,800.
Statistical Assn., Amer. (1839), 1429 Duke St., Alexandria, VA 22314-3402; 15,000.
Steamship Historical Society of America (1935), 300 Ray Dr., Ste. 4, Providence, RI 02906; 3,300.
Steel Construction, Amer. Institute of (1921), 400 N. Michigan Ave., Chicago, IL 60611-4185; 2,600+.
Stock Car Auto Racing, Natl. Assn. for (NASCAR) (1948), P.O. Box 2875, Daytona Beach, FL 32120; 40,000.
Stock Exchange, Amer. (1911), 86 Trinity Pl., N.Y., NY 10006; 871.
Stock Exchange, N.Y. (1792), 11 Wall St., N.Y., NY 10005.
Stock Exchange, Phila. (1790), 1900 Market St., Phila., PA 19103; 505.
Structural Stability Research Council (1944), Fritz Engineering Laboratory No. 13, Lehigh Univ., Bethlehem, PA 18015.
Student Assn., U.S. (1947), 1012 14th St. NW, Suite 403, Wash., DC 20005.
Student Councils, Natl. Assn. of (1931), 1904 Association Dr., Reston, VA 22091; 9,000 schools.
Stuttering Project, Natl. (1977), 2151 Irving St., Ste. 208, San Francisco, CA 94122-1609; 3,750.
Sudden Infant Death Syndrome Alliance, Natl. (1987), 10500 Little Patuxent Pkwy., Ste. 420, Columbia, MD 21044.
Sugar Brokers Assn., Natl. (1903), 1 World Trade Center, N.Y., NY 10047; 100.
Sunbathing Assn., Amer. (1931), 1703 N. Main St., Kissimmee, FL 34744; 40,000.

Sunday League (1933), 279 Highland Ave., Newark, NJ 07104; 25,000.
Surfing Committee, U.S. (1960), Box 3029, Palm Beach, FL 33480; 1,375,000.
Surgeons, Amer. College of (1913), 55 E. Erie St., Chicago IL 60611-2797; 52,127.
Surgeons, Intl. College of (1935), 1516 N. Lake Shore Dr., Chicago IL 60610; 6,800.
Surgeons of the U.S., Assn. of Military (1891), 9320 Old Georgetown Rd., Bethesda, MD 20814; 14,500.
Surveying & Mapping, Amer. Congress on (1941), 5410 Grosvenor Ln., Bethesda, MD 20814-2122; 7,000.
Symphony Orchestra League, Amer. (1942), 777 14th St. NW, Wash., DC 20005; 899 orchestras.
Systems Management, Assn. for (1947), 1433 West Bagley Rd., Berea, OH 44017; 8,000.

Table Tennis Assn., U.S. (1933), Olympic Complex, 1750 E. Boulder St., Colorado Springs, CO 80909; 7,000.
Tailhook Assn., The (1957), P.O. Box 40, Bonita, CA 91908.
Tall Buildings and Urban Habitat, Council on (1969), Lehigh Univ., Bethlehem, PA 18015; 2,500.
Tax Accountants, Natl. Assn. of Enrolled Federal (1960), 6108 N. Harding Ave., Chicago, IL 60659-3108; 450.
Tax Administrators, Federation of (1937), 444 N. Capitol St. NW, Wash., DC 20001.
Tax Assn., Natl.–Tax Institute of America (1907), 5310 E. Main St., Suite 104, Columbus, OH 43213; 1,800.
Tax Foundation, Inc. (1937), 470 L'Enfant Plaza SW, Suite 7112, Wash., DC 20024; 10,000.
Tax Free America (1986), 11015 Cumpston St., N. Hollywood, CA 91601; 400,000.
Taxpayers Union, Natl. (1969), 325 Pennsylvania Ave. SE, Wash., DC 20003; 200,000.
Tea Assn. of the U.S.A. (1899), 230 Park Ave., N.Y., NY 10169; 140.
Teachers Assn., Amer. String (1946), UGA Sta. Box 2066, Athens, GA 30612-0066; 6,800.
Teachers of English, Natl. Council of (1911), 1111 Kenyon Rd., Urbana, IL 61801; 125,000.
Teachers of English to Speakers of Other Languages (1966), 1600 Cameron St., Suite 300, Alexandria, VA 22314.
Teachers of French, Amer. Assn. of (1927), 57 E. Armory Ave., Champaign, IL 61820; 11,000.
Teachers of Mathematics, Natl. Council of (1920), 1906 Association Dr., Reston, VA 22091; 91,740.
Teachers of Singing, Natl. Assn. of (1944), 2800 Univ. Blvd. N, J.U. Sta., Jacksonville, FL 32211; 4,600.
Teachers of Spanish & Portuguese, Amer. Assn. of (1917), P.O. Box 6349, 218 Lee Hall, MSU., MS 39762-6349.
Technicians Assn., Market (1973), 71 Broadway, 2nd Fl., N.Y., NY 10006; 500.
Telephone Pioneers of Amer. (1911), 930 15th St., 12th Fl., Denver, CO 80202; 810,000.
Television Arts & Sciences, Natl. Academy of (1947), 111 W. 57th St., Suite 1020, N.Y., NY 10019; 12,000.
Television Bureau of Advertising (1954), 477 Madison Ave., N.Y., NY 10022.
Television & Radio Artists, Amer. Federation of (1937), 1350 Ave. of the Americas, N.Y., NY 10019; 66,000.
Telluride Assn. (1911), 217 West Ave., Ithaca, NY 14850.
Tennis Assn., U.S. (1881), 1212 Ave. of Americas, N.Y., NY 10036.
Terraplane Club, Hudson-Essex (1959), 100 E. Cross St., Ypsilanti, MI 48197; 3,200.
Tesla Memorial Soc., Inc. (1979), 453 Martin Rd., Buffalo, NY 14218; 1,400+.
Testing & Materials, Amer. Society for (1898), 1916 Race St., Phila., PA 19103; 32,000.
Texas State Genealogical Society (1960), 2507 Tannehill, Houston, TX 77008-3052; 1,000.
Textile Assn. of Los Angeles (1944), 110 E. 9th St., Suite C765, Los Angeles, CA 90079; 914.
Textile Assn., Northern (1854), 230 Congress St., Boston, MA 02110; 150.
Textile Manufacturers Institute, Amer. (1949), 1801 K St. NW, Suite 900, Wash., DC 20006.
Theatre Organ Society, Amer. (1955), P.O. Box 3043, Olivenhain, CA 92024; 6,000.
Theodore Roosevelt Assn. (1919), P.O. Box 720, Oyster Bay, NY 11771; 2,000.
Theological Schools in the U.S. and Canada, Assn. of (1918), 10 Summit Park Dr., Pittsburgh, PA 15275-1103.
Theosophical Society in America, The (1875), 1926 N. Main St., Wheaton, IL 60187; 4,905.
Thoreau Society (1941), 156 Belknap St., Concord, MA 01742; 1,500.
Thoroughbred Racing Assns. (1942), 420 Fair Hill Dr., Ste. 1, Elkton, MD 21921; 57 racing associations.
Titanic Historical Society (1963), P.O. Box 51053, Indian Orchard, MA 01151-0053; 5,000.
Toastmasters Intl. (1924), 23182 Arroyo Vista, Rancho Santa Margarita, CA 92688; 175,000.
Topical Assn., Amer. (1949), P.O. Box 630, Johnstown, PA 15907; 7,000.
Torch Clubs, Internatl. Assn. of (1924), 435 N. Michigan Ave., #1717, Chicago, IL 60611; 3,250.
Toy Manufacturers of America (1916), 200 Fifth Ave., N.Y., NY 10010; 240.
Traffic and Transportation, Amer. Society of (1946), 1816 Norris Pl. #4, Louisville, KY 40205; 2,400.
Trail Association, North Country (1980), 2780 Mundy Ave., White Cloud, MI 49349; 200.
Transit Assn., Amer. Public (1974), 1201 New York Ave. NW, Wash., DC 20005; 11,000 organizations.
Translators Assn., Amer. (1960), 109 Croton Ave., Ossining, NY 10562; 3,000.
Transportation and Logistics, Inc., Amer. Society of (1946), P.O. Box 33095, Louisville, KY 40232; 1,700.
Trapshooting Assn., Amateur (1923), 601 W. National Rd. Vandalia, OH 45377; 100,000+.
Traumatic Stress Studies, Inc., The Intl. Soc. for (1985), 435 N. Michigan Ave., Ste. 1717, Chicago, IL 60611; 1,675.
Travel Agents, Amer. Society of (1931), 1101 King St., Alexandria, VA 22314; 20,000.
Travel Industry Assn. of America (1941), 1133 21st St. NW, Wash., DC 20036; 1,900.
Travelers Protective Assn. of America (1890), 3755 Lindell Blvd., St. Louis, MO 63108; 175,000.
Trilateral Commission, The (1973), 345 E. 46th St., N.Y., NY 10017; 325.
Triple Nine Society (1979), 2119 College St., Cedar Falls, IA 50613; 700.
Trucking Assn., Amer. (1933), 2200 Mill Rd., Alexandria, VA 22314-4677; 4,100.
True Sisters, United Order (1846), 212 Fifth Ave., N.Y., NY 10010; 8,500.
Truth Seeker Co., Inc. (1873), 910 E Street, San Diego, CA 92101; 3,000.
Tuberous Sclerosis Assn. of Amer. (1970), P.O. Box 44, Rockland, MA 02370; 2,500.

UFOs, Natl. Investigation Committee on (1967), 14617 Victory Blvd., Suite 4, Van Nuys, CA 91411.
UNICEF, U.S. Committee for (1947), 333 E. 38th St., N.Y., NY 10016.
USO (United Service Organizations) (1941), 601 Indiana Ave., NW, Wash., DC 20004.
Underwriters, Amer. Soc. of Chartered Life (1927), 270 Bryn Mawr Ave., Bryn Mawr, PA 19010; 30,000.
Underwriters, Soc. of Chartered Property and Casualty (1944), Kahler Hall, 720 Providence Rd., Malvern, PA 19355.
Uniformed Services Society of Military Widows, Natl. Assn. for (1968), 5535 Hempstead Way, Springfield, VA 22151.
United Nations Assn. of the U.S.A. (1923, as League of Nations Assn.) 485 Fifth Ave., N.Y., NY 10017; 31,000.
U.S., Amer. Assn. for Study of the, in World Affairs (1948), 3813 Annandale Rd., Annandale, VA 22003; 1,500.
United Way of America (1918), 801 N. Fairfax St., Alexandria, VA 22309; 1,200.
Universities, Assn. of Amer. (1914), One Dupont Circle, Suite 730, Wash., DC 20036; 59 institutions.
Universities & Colleges, Assn. of Governing Bds. of (1921), One Dupont Circle NW, Suite 400, Wash., DC 20036.
University Continuing Education Assn., Natl. (1915), One Dupont Circle, Ste. 615, Wash., DC 20036; 2,000.
University Extension Assn., Natl. (1915), One Dupont Circle, Suite 400, NW, Wash., DC 20036; 1,100.
University Foundation, Intl. (1973), 1301 S. Noland Rd., Independence, MO 64055; 67,525.
University Professors, Amer. Assn. of (1915), 1012 14th St. NW, Suite 500, Wash., DC 20005; 41,000.
University Women, Amer. Assn. of (1881), 1111 16th St. NW, Wash., DC 20036.
Urban Coalition, Natl. (1967), 1120 G St. NW, Suite 900, Wash., DC 20005; 42 affiliates.
Urban League, Natl. (1910), 500 E. 62d St., N.Y., NY 10020.
Useless Skills, Institute of Totally (1987), 20 Richmond St., Dover, NH 03820; 250.
Utility Commissioners, Natl. Assn. of Regulatory (1889), 1102 Interstate Commerce Commission Bldg., 12th & Constitution Ave. NW, Wash., DC 20423; 370.

Vampire Research Center (1972), P.O. Box 252, Elmhurst, NY 11373; 500.
Variety Clubs Intl. (1928), 1560 Bdway., N.Y., NY 10036.

VASA Order of America (1896), 65 Bryant Rd., Cranston, R.I. 02910; 30,000.

Ventriloquists, No. American Assn. of (1944), 800 W. Littleton Blvd., Box 420, Littleton, CO 80120; 1,450.

Veterans Assn., Blinded (1945), 477 H St. NW, Wash., DC 20001; 7,284.

Veterans Assn., China-Burma-India (1948), 750 N. Lincoln Memorial Dr., Milwaukee, WI 53202; 7,000.

Veterans Committee, Amer. (1944), 6309 Bannockurn Dr., Bethesda, MD 20817; 15,000.

Veterans of Foreign Wars of the U.S. (1899) **& Ladies Auxiliary** (1914), 406 W. 34th St., Kansas City, MO 64111.

Veterans of the Vietnam War (1980), 760 Jumper Rd., Wilkes-Barre, PA 18702-8033; 30,000.

Veterans of World War I (1958), 941 N. Capitol St. NE, Room 1201-C, Wash., DC 20002-4234; 62,000.

Veterans of WWII, Submarine (1955), 6523 San Joaquin St., Sacramento, CA 95820; 8,000.

Veterinary Medical Assn., Amer. (1863), 1931 N. Meacham Rd., Schaumburg, IL 60173; 52,000.

Victorian Society in America (1966), 219 S. Sixth St., Phila., PA 19106; 4,000.

Virgil Fox Society, The (1977), 88 Chestnut St., Brooklyn, NY 11208; 350.

Volleyball Assn., U.S. (1928), 3595 E. Fountain Blvd., Ste. I-2, Colorado Springs, CO 80910; 70,000.

Walking Assn. (1976), 655 E. Rancho Catalina Pl., Tucson, AZ 85704.

Walking Society, American (1980), Viana House, Box 1315, Beverly Hills, CA 90213; 2.8 mln.

War Mothers, Amer. (1917), 2615 Woodley Pl. NW, Wash., DC 20008; 3,000.

Warrant and Warrant Officers' Assn., Chief, U.S. Coast Guard (1929), c/o Fort McNair Yacht Basin, 200 V Street, SW, Wash., DC 20024; 3,346.

Washington, DC Area Trucking Assn. (1933), 2200 Mill Rd., Alexandria, VA 22314; 130 companies.

Watch & Clock Collectors, Natl. Assn. of (1940), 514 Poplar St., Columbia, PA 17512; 34,000.

Watercolor Soc., American (1867), 47 Fifth Ave., N.Y., NY 10003; 502.

Water Environment Federation (1928), 601 Wythe St., Alexandria, VA 22314; 38,000.

Water Pollution Control Admin., Assn. of State and Interstate (1961), 444 N. Capital St. NW, Suite 330, Wash., DC 20001.

Water Pollution Control Federation (1928), 601 Wythe St., Alexandria, VA 22314-1994; 32,000.

Water Resources Assn., Amer. (1964), 5410 Grosvenor Ln., Suite 220, Bethesda, MD 20814-2192; 4,000.

Water Ski Assn., Amer. (1939), 799 Overlook Dr. SE, Winter Haven, FL 33884; 29,000.

Water Assn., Natl. Ground (1948), 6375 Riverside Drive, Dublin, OH 43017; 24,000.

Water Works Assn., Amer. (1881), 6666 W. Quincy Ave., Denver, CO 80235; 52,000.

Welding Society, Amer. (1919), 550 NW LeJeune Rd., Miami, FL 33126; 39,500.

Wheelchair Athletic Assn., Natl. (1957), 3595 E. Fountain Blvd., Suite L-1, Colorado Springs, CO 80916; 1,500.

Widows, Society of Military (1968), 5535 Hemstead Way, Springfield, VA 22151; 2,000.

Wilderness Society (1935), 900 17th St. NW, Wash., DC 20006; 350,000.

Wild Horse Organized Assistance (WHOA!) (1971), 140 Greenstone Dr., Reno, NV 89512; 10,000.

Wildlife, Defenders of (1947), 1244 19th St. NW, Wash., DC 20036; 80,000.

Wildlife Federation, Natl. (1936), 1400 16th St. NW, Wash., DC 20036; 5.1 mln.

Wildlife Foundation, No. Amer. (1929), 102 Wilmot Rd., #410, Deerfield, IL 60015; 6,000.

Wildlife Fund, World (1961), 1250 24th St. NW, Wash., DC 20037; 1 mln.

Wildlife Management Institute (1911), 1101-14th St., Suite 725, NW, Wash., DC 20005.

William Penn Assn. (1886), 709 Brighton Rd., Pittsburgh, PA 15233; 90,000.

Wireless Pioneers, Society of (1968), 146 Coleen St., Livermore, CA 94550; 5,340.

Wizard of Oz Club, Intl. (1957), Box 95, Kinderhook, IL 62345; 3,000.

Women, Natl. Assn. of Bank (1920), 500 No. Michigan Ave., Suite 1400, Chicago, IL 60611; 30,000.

Women, Natl. Council of (1888), 777 United Nations Plaza, N.Y., NY 10017; approx. 800.

Women, Natl. Organization for (NOW) (1966), 1000 16th St., NW, Ste. 700 Wash., DC 20036; 250,000.

Women Artists, Natl. Assn. of (1889), 41 Union Sq., N.Y., NY 10003; 725.

Women Engineers, Society of (1950), 345 E. 47th St., N.Y., NY 10017; 16,000.

Women for America, Concerned (1979), 370 L'Enfant Promenade SW, #800, Washington, DC 20024; 600,000.

Women in Communications (1909), 2101 Wilson Blvd., Ste. 417, Arlington, VA 22201; 12,000.

Women in Radio and TV, Inc. (1951), 1101 Connecticut Ave. NW, #700, Washington, DC 20036; 2,500.

Women Geographers, Society of (1925), 1619 New Hampshire Ave. NW, Wash., DC 20009; 500.

Women Intl., Financial (1921), 500 N. Michigan Ave., Ste. 1400, Chicago, IL 60611; 35,000.

Women Strike for Peace (1961), 110 Maryland Ave. NE, Ste. 302, Washington, DC 20002; 3,000.

Women of the U.S., Natl. Council of (1888), 777 U.N. Plaza, N.Y., NY 10017; 28 organizations.

Women Voters of the U.S., League of (1920), 1730 M St. NW, Wash., DC 20036; 120,000.

Women World War Veterans (1919), 237 Madison Ave., N.Y., NY 10016; 35,000.

Women's Army Corps Veterans Assn. (1947), Hwy. 21, Anniston, AL 36206; 3,500.

Women's Association, American Business (1949), 9100 Ward Parkway, P.O. Box 8728, Kansas City, MO 64114.

Women's Christian Temperance Union, Natl. (1874), 1730 Chicago Ave., Evanston, IL 60201; 40,000.

Women's Clubs, General Federation of (1890), 1734 N St. NW., Wash. DC, 20036.

Women's Clubs, Natl. Federation of Business & Professional (1919), 2012 Massachusetts Ave. NW, Wash., DC 20036.

Women's Educational & Industrial Union (1877), 356 Boylston St., Boston, MA 02116; 1,131.

Women's Intl. League for Peace & Freedom (1915), 1213 Race St., Phila., PA 19107; 50,000.

Women's Legal Defense Fund (1971), 1875 Connecticut Ave. NW, Suite 710, Washington, DC 20009; 1,700.

Women's Overseas Service League (1921), P.O. Box 39058, Friendship Station, Washington, DC 20016; 1,150.

Woodmen of America, Modern (1883), 1701 1st Ave., Rock Island, IL 61201; 648,711.

Woodmen of the World Life Insurance Soc. (1890), 1700 Farnam St., Omaha, NE 68102; 965,000.

Workmen's Circle (1900), 45 E. 33d St., N.Y., NY 10016.

World Federalist Assn. (1975), 418 7th St. SE, Washington, DC 20003; 9,000.

World Future Society (1966), 7910 Woodmont Ave., Ste. 450, Bethesda, MD 20814; 30,000.

World Health, Amer. Assn. for (1953), 1129 20th St., NW, Suite 400, Washington, DC 20036; 1,000.

World Peace, Intl Assn. of Educators for (1969), P.O. Box 3282, Mastin Lake Sta., Huntsville, AL 35810-0282; 20,500.

World's Fair Collectors Soc. (1968), P.O. Box 20806, Sarasota, FL 34276; 500.

Writers Guild of America, West (1933), 8955 Beverly Blvd., W. Hollywood, CA 90048; 7,500+.

Yeoman F. Natl. (1936), 223 El Camino Real, Vallejo, CA 94590; 800.

Young America's Foundation (1971), 110 Elden St., Herndon, VA 22070.

Young Men's Christian Assns. of the U.S.A., (1851), 101 N. Wacker Dr., Chicago, IL 60606; 13 mln.

YM-YMHAs of Greater New York, Associated (1957), 130 E. 59th St., N.Y., NY 10020; 55,100.

Young Women's Christian Assn. of the U.S.A. (1906), 726 Broadway, N.Y., NY 10003; 1.6 mln.

Youth Hostels, American (1934), P.O. Box 37613, Wash., DC 20013; 124,000+.

Zero Population Growth (1968), 1400 16th St. NW, Suite 320, Wash., DC 20036; 45,000.

Ziegfeld Club (1936), 593 Park Ave., N.Y., NY 10021; 303.

Zionist Organization of America (1897), 4 E. 34th St., N.Y., NY 10016; 140,000.

Zoological Parks & Aquariums, Amer. Assn. of (1924), Oglebay Park, Wheeling, WV 26003; 6,000.

Zoologists, Amer. Society of (1890), 104 Sirius Circle, Thousand Oaks, CA 91360; 3,709.

POSTAL INFORMATION

U.S. Postal Service

The Postal Reorganization Act, creating a government-owned postal service under the executive branch and replacing the old Post Office Department, was signed into law by President Nixon on Aug. 12, 1970. The service officially came into being on July 1, 1971.

The U.S. Postal Service is governed by an 11-person Board of Governors. Nine members are appointed to 9-year terms by the president with Senate approval. These 9, in turn, choose a postmaster general, who is no longer a member of the president's cabinet. The board and the new postmaster general choose the 11th member, who serves as deputy postmaster general. An independent Postal Rate Commission of 5 members, appointed by the president, recommends postal rates to the governors for their approval.

As of Sept. 30, 1991, there were 28,912 post offices throughout the U.S. and possessions.

U.S. Domestic Rates

Postal rates and fees shown below were implemented on Feb. 3, 1991. Domestic rates apply to the U.S., its territories and possessions and APOs and FPOs.

First Class

Letters written, and matter sealed against inspection, 29¢ for 1st oz. or fraction, 23¢ for each additional oz. or fraction.

U.S. Postal cards; single 19¢; double 38¢; private postcards, same.

First class includes written matter, namely letters, postal cards, postcards (private mailing cards) and all other matter wholly or partly in writing, whether sealed or unsealed, except manuscripts for books, periodical articles and music, manuscript copy accompanying proofsheets or corrected proofsheets of the same and the writing authorized by law on matter of other classes. Also matter sealed or closed against inspection, bills and statements of accounts.

Express Mail

Express Mail Service is available for any mailable article up to 70 pounds, and guarantees delivery between major U.S. cities or your money back. Articles received by the acceptance time authorized by the postmaster at a postal facility offering Express Mail will be delivered by 3 p.m. the next day to some locations or will be delivered by noon the next day to other destinations. Or, if you prefer, your shipment can be picked up as early as 10 a.m. the next business day. Second day service is available to locations not on the Next Day Delivery Network. Rates include insurance, Shipment Receipt, and Record of Delivery at the destination post office.

Consult Postmaster for other Express Mail Services and rates. (The Postal Service will refund, upon application to originating office, the postage for any Express Mail shipments not meeting the service standard except for those delayed by strike or work stoppage, delay or cancellation of flights, or governmental action beyond the control of the Postal Service.)

Third Class

Third class (limit up to but not including 16 ounces): Mailable matter not in 1st and 2d classes.

Single mailing: Publications, small parcels, printed matter, booklets and catalogs, 29¢ the first ounce, 52¢ for over 1 to 2 ozs., 75¢ for over 2 to 3 ozs., 98¢ for over 3 to 4 ozs., $1.21 for over 4 to 6 ozs., $1.33 for over 6 to 8 ozs., $1.44 for over 8 to 10 ozs., $1.56 for over 10 to 12 ozs., $1.67 for over 12 to 14 ozs., $1.79 for over 14 but less than 16 ozs.

Bulk mailing: At least 200 pieces or 50 pounds of such items as solicitations, newsletters, advertising materials, books and cassettes, each item of which individually weighs less than one pound. Minimum rate per piece: Basic presort, $0.198 for pieces weighing 3.3067 ounces or less; for pieces weighing more than 3.3067 ounces, the rate is $0.109 per piece + $0.600 per pound. Contact your post office for the discounts offered for presorted, destination entry and automation compatible mail.

Separate rates for some nonprofit organizations. Bulk mailing fee, $75 per calendar year. Apply to postmaster for permit. One-time fee for permit imprint, $75.

Parcel Post—Fourth Class

Fourth class or parcel post (16 ounces and over): merchandise, printed matter, etc., may be sealed, subject to inspection.

Priority Mail

First class mail of more than 11 ounces can be sent "Priority Mail" service. The most expeditious handling and transportation available will be used for fastest delivery.

A new pickup service has been initiated for Priority Mail. It costs $4.50 for each stop by the Postal Service. There is also a new flat rate Priority Mail envelope, applicable at the 2-pound rate for matter sent in the Special Postal Service-provided envelope.

Forwarding Addresses

The mailer, in order to obtain a forwarding address, must endorse the envelope or cover "Address Correction Requested." The destination post office then will determine whether a forwarding address has been left on file and provide it for a fee of 35¢ per manual correction and 20¢ per automated correction.

Priority Mail

Packages weighing up to 70 pounds and not exceeding 108 inches in length and girth combined, including written and other material of the first class, whether sealed or unsealed, fractions of a pound being charged as a full pound.

Rates according to zone apply between the U.S. and Puerto Rico and Virgin Islands.

Parcels weighing less than 15 pounds, measuring over 84 inches but not exceeding 108 inches in length and girth combined are chargeable with a minimum rate equal to that for a 15 pound parcel for the zone to which addressed.

Zones	To 2 lbs	3 lbs	4 lbs	5 lbs	Zones	To 2 lbs	3 lbs	4 lbs	5 lbs
1, 2, 3, ...	$2.90	$4.10	$4.65	$5.45	6.	$2.90	$4.10	$4.65	$5.45
4.	2.90	4.10	4.65	5.45	7.	2.90	4.10	4.65	5.45
5.	2.90	4.10	4.65	5.45	8.	2.90	4.10	4.65	5.45

*Consult postmaster for parcels over 5 lbs.

Special Handling

Third and fourth class parcels will be handled and delivered as expeditiously as practicable (but not special delivery) upon payment, in addition to the regular postage: up to 10 lbs., $1.80; over 10 lbs., $2.50. Such parcels must be endorsed, Special Handling.

Special Delivery

First class mail up to 2 lbs. $7.65, over 2 lbs. and up to 10 lbs., $7.95; over 10 lbs. $8.55. All other classes up to 2 lbs. $8.05, over 2 and up to 10 lbs., $8.65, over 10 lbs. $9.30.

Bound Printed Matter Rates
(Single Piece Zone Rate)

Fourth-Class Mail: Single-Piece Bound Printed Matter

Weight lbs.	Local	Rate Zones 1&2	3	4	5	6	7	8
1.5	$0.93	$1.27	$1.30	$1.36	$1.45	$1.54	$1.65	$1.75
2	0.94	1.30	1.34	1.42	1.53	1.66	1.81	1.93
2.5	0.96	1.33	1.38	1.48	1.62	1.78	1.97	2.12
3	0.98	1.35	1.42	1.54	1.71	1.90	2.12	2.31
3.5	0.99	1.38	1.46	1.60	1.80	2.02	2.28	2.50
4	1.01	1.41	1.50	1.66	1.89	2.14	2.44	2.69
4.5	1.02	1.44	1.54	1.72	1.98	2.26	2.59	2.88
5	1.04	1.47	1.58	1.78	2.07	2.38	2.75	3.07
6	1.07	1.53	1.66	1.89	2.24	2.61	3.06	3.44
7	1.10	1.59	1.74	2.01	2.42	2.85	3.38	3.82
8	1.14	1.64	1.82	2.13	2.60	3.09	3.69	4.20
9	1.17	1.70	1.90	2.25	2.77	3.33	4.01	4.57
10	1.20	1.76	1.98	2.37	2.95	3.57	4.32	4.95

(Includes both catalogs and similar bound printed matter.)

(Bound printed matter must weigh at least 1 pound and not more than 10 pounds. Bound printed matter includes catalogs, directories and books not eligible for special fourth-class rates.)

Domestic Mail Special Services

Registry — Only matter prepaid with postage at First-class postage rates may be registered. Stamps or meter stamps must be attached. The face of the article must be at least 5" long, 3½" high. The mailer is required to declare the value of mail presented for registration.

Registered Mail

Value	Insured	Uninsured
$0.00 to $100	$4.50	$4.40
$100.01 to $500 . . .	4.85	4.70
$500.01 to $1,000 . .	5.25	5.05
$1,000.01 to $2,000 .	5.70	5.40
$2,000.01 to $3,000 .	6.15	5.75
$3,000.01 to $4,000 .	6.60	6.10
$4,000.01 to $5,000 .	7.05	6.45
$5,000.01 to $6,000 .	7.50	6.80
$6,000.01 to $7,000 .	7.95	7.15
$7,000.01 to $8,000 .	8.40	7.50
$8,000.01 to $9,000 .	8.85	7.85
$9,000.01 to $10,000	9.30	8.20

Consult postmaster for registry rates above $10,000.

C.O.D.: Unregistered — is applicable to first-, third-, fourth-class, and express mail matter. Such mail must be based on bona fide orders or be in conformity with agreements between senders and addressees. **Registered** — for details consult postmaster.

Insurance — is applicable to third and fourth class matter. Matter for sale addressed to prospective purchasers who have not ordered it or authorized its sending will not be insured.

Insured Mail

$0.01 to $50	$0.75
50.01 to $100.	1.60
100.01 to $150.	2.40
150.01 to $200.	2.40
200.01 to $300.	3.50
300.01 to $400.	4.60
400.01 to $500.	5.40
500.01 to $600.	6.20

Liability for insured mail is limited to $600.

Certified mail — service is available for any matter having no intrinsic value on which 1st class or air mail postage is paid. Receipt is furnished at time of mailing and evidence of delivery obtained. The fee is $1.00 in addition to postage. Return receipt, restricted delivery, and special delivery are available upon payment of additional fees. No indemnity.

Special Fourth Class Rate
(limit 70 lbs.)

First pound or fraction, $1.05 (59¢ if 500 pieces or more of special rate matter are presorted to 5 digit ZIP code or 88¢ if 500 pieces or more are presorted to Bulk Mail Cntrs.); each additional pound or fraction through 7 pounds, 43¢; each additional pound, 25¢. Only the following specific articles: Books of at least 8 printed pages consisting wholly of reading matter or scholarly bibliography, or reading matter with incidental blank spaces for notations and containing no advertising matter other than incidental announcements of books; 16-millimeter or narrower width films in final form and catalogs of such films of 24 pages or more (at least 22 of which are printed) except films and film catalogs sent to or from commercial theaters; printed music in bound or sheet form; printed objective test materials; sound recordings, playscripts and manuscripts for books, periodicals, and music; printed educational reference charts; loose-leaf pages and binders thereof consisting of medical information for distribution to doctors, hospitals, medical schools, and medical students; computer-readable media containing prerecorded information and guides for use with such media. Package must be marked "Special 4th Class Rate" stating item contained.

Library Rate (limit 70 lbs.)

First pound 65¢, each additional pound through 7 pounds, 24¢; each additional pound, 12¢. Books when loaned or exchanged between and sent to or from schools, colleges, public libraries, and certain non-profit organizations; books, printed music, bound academic theses, periodicals, sound recordings, other library materials, museum materials (specimens, collections), scientific or mathematical kits, instruments or other devices; also catalogs, guides or scripts for some of these materials. Must be marked "Library Rate".

Also qualifying for library rate are: Books mailed from publishers or distributors to schools, libraries, colleges or universities or to bookstores owned, operated and controlled by schools, colleges or universities.

Parcel Post Rate Schedule
(Inter BMC/ASF Zip Codes Only, Machinable Parcels, No Discount, No Surcharge)

Weight up to but not exceeding—(pounds)	Zones 1 and 2	3	4	5	6	7	8
2.	$2.19	$2.32	$2.46	$2.74	$2.85	$2.85	$2.85
3.	2.29	2.49	2.70	3.12	3.54	4.00	4.05
4.	2.39	2.65	2.94	3.50	4.06	4.35	4.60
5.	2.49	2.81	3.17	3.88	4.58	5.20	5.40
6.	2.59	2.98	3.41	4.26	5.10	6.33	8.55
7.	2.68	3.14	3.65	4.64	5.62	7.06	9.60
8.	2.78	3.31	3.89	5.02	6.14	7.78	10.65
9.	2.88	3.47	4.12	5.40	6.67	8.51	11.70
10.	2.98	3.63	4.36	5.78	7.19	9.24	12.75
11.	3.08	3.80	4.60	6.16	7.71	9.97	13.75

Weight up to but not exceeding—(pounds)	Zones 1 and 2	3	4	5	6	7	8
12.	3.18	3.96	4.83	6.54	8.23	10.69	14.80
13.	3.25	4.08	4.99	6.79	8.57	11.17	15.85
14.	3.32	4.19	5.16	7.04	8.92	11.65	16.90
15.	3.38	4.28	5.27	7.23	9.17	11.99	17.95
16.	3.43	4.36	5.39	7.40	9.40	12.31	19.00
17.	3.48	4.44	5.49	7.56	9.62	12.61	19.91
18.	3.53	4.51	5.60	7.72	9.83	12.90	20.38
19.	3.58	4.59	5.69	7.87	10.03	13.17	20.83
20.	3.63	4.65	5.79	8.01	10.22	13.43	21.26
21.	3.68	4.72	5.88	8.15	10.40	13.68	21.66
22.	3.72	4.79	5.97	8.28	10.57	13.91	22.05
23.	3.77	4.85	6.05	8.40	10.74	14.14	22.43
24.	3.81	4.91	6.13	8.52	10.90	14.36	22.78
25.	3.85	4.97	6.21	8.64	11.05	14.57	23.13

Postal Union Mail Special Services

Registration — available to practically all countries. Fee $4.40. The maximum indemnity payable — generally only in case of complete loss (of both contents and wrapper) — is $24.60. To Canada only the fee is $4.50 providing indemnity for loss up to $100, $4.85 for loss up to $500, and $5.25 for loss up to $1,000.

Return receipt — showing to whom and date delivr'd, 90¢.

Special delivery — Available to most countries. Consult post office. Fees for International Special Delivery same for air or surface: for letters, letter packages and post cards not over 2 pounds, $5.60. If over 2 pounds, $6.00, for printed matter, matter for the blind, or small packets, $5.90 if not over 2 pounds; if over 2 pounds, $6.75.

Marking — an article intended for special delivery service must have affixed to the cover near the name of the country of destination "EXPRES" (special delivery) label, obtainable at the post office, or it may be marked on the cover boldly in red "EXPRES" (special delivery).

Special handling — entitles AO surface packages to priority handling between mailing point and U.S. point of dispatch. Fees: $1.80 for packages to 10 pounds, and $2.50 for packages over 10 pounds.

Airmail — there is daily air service to practically all countries.

Prepayment of replies from other countries — a mailer who wishes to prepay a reply by letter from another country may do so by sending his correspondent one or more international reply coupons, which may be purchased at United States post offices. One coupon should be accepted in any country in exchange for stamps to prepay a surface letter of the first unit of weight to the U.S.

Additional international special services: Insurance: Available to many countries for loss of or damage to items paid at parcel post rate. Consult postmaster for indemnity limits for individual countries.

Limit of Indemnity Not Over	Fees Canada	All other Countries
$50	$0.75	$1.60
100	1.60	2.40
200	2.40	3.50
300	3.50	4.60
400	4.60	5.40
500	5.40	6.20
600	6.20	6.60
700		6.90
800		7.20
900		7.50
1,000		7.80
1,100		8.10
1,200		8.40

Restricted Delivery: Available to many countries for registered mail, limits who may receive an item. Fee: $2.50.

Post Office-Authorized 2-Letter State Abbreviations

The abbreviations below are approved by the U.S. Postal Service for use in addresses only. They do not replace the traditional abbreviations in other contexts. The official list follows, including the District of Columbia, Guam, Puerto Rico, the Canal Zone, and the Virgin Islands (all capital letters are used):

Alabama . . . AL
Alaska . . . AK
American Samoa . . . AS
Arizona . . . AZ
Arkansas . . . AR
California . . . CA
Colorado . . . CO
Connecticut . . . CT
Delaware . . . DE
Dist. of Col. . . . DC
Federated States of Micronesia . . . FM
Florida . . . FL
Georgia . . . GA
Guam . . . GU
Hawaii . . . HI
Idaho . . . ID
Illinois . . . IL
Indiana . . . IN
Iowa . . . IA
Kansas . . . KS
Kentucky . . . KY
Louisiana . . . LA
Maine . . . ME
Marshall Islands . . . MH
Maryland . . . MD
Massachusetts . . . MA
Michigan . . . MI
Minnesota . . . MN
Mississippi . . . MS
Missouri . . . MO
Montana . . . MT
Nebraska . . . NE
Nevada . . . NV
New Hampshire . . . NH
New Jersey . . . NJ
New Mexico . . . NM
New York . . . NY
North Carolina . . . NC
North Dakota . . . ND
Northern Mariana Is. . . . MP
Ohio . . . OH
Oklahoma . . . OK
Oregon . . . OR
Pennsylvania . . . PA
Puerto Rico . . . PR
Rhode Island . . . RI
South Carolina . . . SC
South Dakota . . . SD
Tennessee . . . TN
Texas . . . TX
Utah . . . UT
Vermont . . . VT
Virginia . . . VA
Virgin Islands . . . VI
Washington . . . WA
West Virginia . . . WV
Wisconsin . . . WI
Wyoming . . . WY

Also approved for use in addressing mail are the following abbreviations:

Alley . . . Aly
Arcade . . . Arc
Avenue . . . Ave
Boulevard . . . Blvd
Branch . . . Br
Bypass . . . Byp
Causeway . . . Cswy
Center . . . Ctr
Circle . . . Cir
Court . . . Ct
Courts . . . Cts
Crescent . . . Cres
Drive . . . Dr
Expressway . . . Expy
Extended . . . Ext
Extension . . . Ext
Freeway . . . Fwy
Gardens . . . Gdns
Grove . . . Grv
Heights . . . Hts
Highway . . . Hwy
Lane . . . Ln
Manor . . . Mnr
Place . . . Pl
Plaza . . . Plz
Point . . . Pt
Road . . . Rd
Rural . . . R
Square . . . Sq
Street . . . St
Terrace . . . Ter
Trail . . . Trl
Turnpike . . . Tpke
Viaduct . . . Via
Vista . . . Vis

Size Standards for Domestic Mail

Minimum Size

Pieces which do not meet the following requirements are prohibited from the mails:

a. All pieces must be at least .007 of an inch thick, and
b. All pieces (except keys and identification devices) which are 1/4 inch or less thick must be:
   (1) Rectangular in shape,
   (2) At least 3 1/2 inches high, and
   (3) At least 5 inches long.

Note: Pieces greater than 1/4 inch thick can be mailed even if they measure less than 3 1/2 by 5 inches.

Nonstandard Mail

All First-Class Mail, except presort and carrier route First-Class mail, weighing one ounce or less and all single-piece rate Third-Class mail weighing one ounce or less is nonstandard (and subject to a 10¢ surcharge in addition to the applicable postage and fees) if:

1. Any of the following dimensions are exceeded:
   Length—11 1/2 inches,
   Height—6 1/8 inches,
   Thickness—1/4 inch, or
2. The length divided by the height is not between 1.3 and 2.5, inclusive. The nonstandard surcharge for presort and carrier route First-Class mail is 5¢.

Air Mail, Parcel Post International Rates

Aerogrammes — 45¢ each to all countries.
Air mail postcards (single) - 40¢ to all countries except Canada and Mexico (30¢ each)
International letters and letter packages: airmail to Canada and Mexico (there are no surface rates to these countries)—weight not over 0.5 ozs., 40¢ to Canada, 35¢ to Mexico; not over 1.0 ozs., 40¢ to Canada, 45¢ to Mexico; not over 2 ozs., 63¢ to Canada, 65¢ to Mexico; not over 3 ozs., 86¢ to Canada, 90¢ to Mexico; airmail to countries other than Canada and Mexico—not over 0.5 ozs., 50¢; not over 1.0 oz., 95¢; not over 1.5 ozs., $1.34; not over 2.0 ozs., $1.73; not over 2.5 ozs., $2.12; not over 3 ozs., $2.51; surface rates to countries other than Canada and Mexico—not over 1 oz., 70¢; not over 2 ozs., 95¢; not over 3 ozs., $1.20; not over 4 ozs., $1.45; not over 5 ozs., $1.70; not over 6 ozs., $1.95; not over 7 ozs., $2.20; not over 8 ozs., $2.45.

Weight steps	Air Parcel post rate groups A	B	C	D	E
First 1 pound	$6.00	$7.75	$9.25	$10.70	$12.30
Each additional pound or fraction up to 5 pounds	3.00	4.25	5.00	6.00	7.00
Each additional pound or fraction over 5 pounds	2.00	3.00	4.00	5.00	6.00

Air Parcel Post Rate Groups

Country	Rate group	Maximum weight limits
Afghanistan	D.	44
Albania	C.	44
Algeria	D.	44
Andorra	B.	44
Angola	E.	22
Anguilla	A.	22
Antigua & Barbuda	A.	22
Argentina	D.	44
Aruba	A.	44
Ascension	No Air Service	
Australia	D.	44
Austria	B.	44
Azores	C.	44
Bahamas	A.	22
Bahrain	D.	22
Bangladesh	E.	22
Barbados	B.	44
Belgium	D.	44
Belize	A.	44
Benin	C.	44
Bermuda	A.	44
Bhutan	E.	44
Bolivia	B.	44
Botswana	E.	22
Brazil	E.	44
British Virgin Islands	A.	44
Brunei	D.	22
Bulgaria	D.	44
Burkina Faso	D.	44
Burma	D.	22
Burundi	E.	44
Cameroon	D.	44
Canada	Separate Rate Group.	66
Cape Verde	D.	22
Cayman Islands	A.	44
Central African Rep.	E.	44
Chad	D.	44
Chile	D.	44
China (Peoples Republic of)	D.	44
Colombia	B.	44
Comoros	E.	44
Congo	D.	44
Corsica	E.	44
Costa Rica	A.	44
Cote d'Ivoire (Ivory Coast)	D.	44
Cuba	No Parcel Post Service.	
Cyprus	C.	44
Czecholovakia	C.	33
Denmark	C.	66
Djibouti	D.	44
Dominica	A.	22
Dominican Rep.	A.	44
Eat Timor	No Parcel Post Service.	
Ecuador	C.	44
Egypt	D.	44
El Salvador	B.	44
Equatorial Guinea	D.	44
Estonia	E.	22
Ethiopia	D.	44
Falkland Islands	D.	44
Faroe Islands	C.	44
Fiji	B.	44
Finland	D.	44
France	E.	44
French Guiana	C.	44
French Polynesia	D.	44
Gabon	D.	44
Gambia	B.	22
Germany	C.	44
Ghana	D.	22
Gibraltar	C.	44
Great Britain and Northern Ireland	C.	50
Greece	C.	44
Greenland	D.	44
Grenada	A.	44
Guadeloupe	A.	44
Guatemala	A.	44
Guinea	B.	44
Guinea-Bissau	B.	22
Guyana	B.	44
Haiti	A.	44
Honduras	B.	44
Hong Kong	C.	44

Country	Rate group	Maximum weight limits
Hungary	C.	44
Iceland	C.	44
India	D.	44
Indonesia	E.	44
Iran	D.	44
Iraq	D.	44
Ireland (Eire)	C.	50
Israel	C.	33
Italy (incl. San Marino).	C.	44
Jamaica	A.	22
Japan	E.	44
Jordan	C.	44
Kampuchea (Cambodia)	No Parcel Post Service.	
Kenya	D.	44
Kirabati	B.	44
Korea, Democratic People's Republic	No Parcel Post Service.	
Korea, Republic of (South).	C.	44
Kuwait	C.	44
Lao	E.	44
Latvia	E.	44
Lebanon	C.	11
Lesotho	E.	44
Liberia	C.	22
Libya	D.	44
Liechtenstein	B.	44
Lithuania	E.	22
Luxembourg	B.	44
Macao	C.	44
Madagascar	E.	44
Madeira Islands	B.	44
Malawi	D.	22
Malaysia	D.	22
Maldives	D.	22
Mali	C.	44
Malta	C.	22
Martinique	A.	44
Mauritania	D.	44
Mauritius	E.	22
Mexico	A.	44
Monaco	E.	44
Mongolia	No Parcel Post Service.	
Montserrat	A.	44
Morocco	C.	44
Mozambique	E.	22
Nauru	C.	44
Nepal	D.	44
Netherlands	C.	44
Netherlands Antilles	A.	44
New Caledonia	D.	44
New Zealand	D.	44
Nicaragua	B.	44
Niger	D.	44
Nigeria	C.	22
Norway	D.	44
Oman	D.	22
Pakistan	D.	22
Panama	A.	44
Papua New Guinea	D.	44
Paraguay	D.	44
Peru	B.	44
Philippines	D.	44
Pitcairn Islands	B.	22
Poland	B.	33
Portugal	C.	22
Qatar	C.	44
Reunion	E.	44
Romania	C.	44
Rwanda	D.	44
Saint Christopher & Nevis	A.	44
Saint Helena	C.	44
Saint Lucia	A.	44
Saint Pierre & Miguelon	A.	44
Saint Vincent & the Grenadines	A.	22
San Marino	C.	44
Sao Tome & Principe	D.	44
Saudia Arabia	D.	22
Senegal	D.	44
Seychelles	D.	22
Sierre Leone	D.	44
Singapore	D.	44
Solomon Islands	C.	44
Somalia	D.	44
South Africa (including South West Africa & Namibia)	D.	44
Spain	C.	44
Sri Lanka	D.	44
Sudan	D.	44
Suriname	B.	44
Swaziland	D.	44
Sweden	D.	44
Switzerland	B.	44
Syria	C.	44
Taiwan	C.	44
Tanzania	E.	22
Thailand	D.	44
Togo	D.	44
Tonga	B.	22
Trinidad & Tobago	B.	22
Tristan da Cunha	E.	22
Tunisia	C.	44
Turkey	C.	44
Turks and Caicos Islands	A.	22
Tuvalu	B.	44
Uganda	D.	22
Union of Soviet Socialist Republics	E.	22
United Arab Emirates	D.	44
Uruguay	B.	44
Vanuatu	B.	44
Vatican City State	C.	44
Venezuela	B.	44
Vietnam	No Parcel Post Service.	
Wallis & Futuna Islands	D.	44
Western Samoa	B.	22
Yemen, Republic of	E.	44
Yugoslavia	C.	33
Zaire	E.	33
Zambia	E.	44
Zimbabwe	E.	44

Postcards

Surface rates to Canada and Mexico, 30¢; to all other countries, 35¢. By air, Canada and Mexico, 30¢; to all other countries, 40¢. Maximum size permitted, 6 x 4¼ in.; minimum, 5½ x 3½.

Gross Postal Revenues at Large Cities

Fiscal year	Boston	Chicago	L.A.	New York	Phila.	St. Louis	Wash., D.C.
1975	$136,453,079	$365,378,795	$193,229,077	$453,905,277	$134,571,376	$85,591,774	$115,489,343
1980	224,428,760	528,233,991	271,136,828	666,377,778	221,161,624	127,427,555	187,334,312
1981	256,524,082	551,088,016	301,159,594	741,286,845	235,118,018	142,548,957	201,191,995
1982	292,971,572	597,246,568	338,798,409	848,507,590	265,242,959	160,590,946	215,772,861
1983	294,932,399	589,476,264	330,734,928	856,569,717	273,210,529	165,000,437	212,117,368
1984	314,230,399	598,141,605	338,760,060	907,426,500	295,917,848	177,041,331	225,378,646
1985	339,550,469	563,693,370	358,859,412	938,829,064	300,811,081	194,786,119	236,131,464
1986	378,861,842	579,432,633	381,254,469	960,987,314	330,671,509	211,134,497	253,607,563
1987	405,124,317	612,014,066	389,819,485	962,000,684	367,123,549	221,972,462	290,840,099
1988	428,049,178	618,237,375	415,847,750	999,747,864	384,189,378	245,040,401	341,131,117
1989	421,170,296	610,124,516	439,708,491	1,052,810,676	374,566,877	264,109,672	307,918,572
1990	426,200,044	593,027,761	434,305,082	1,224,750,953	325,928,242	267,125,823	307,899,289
1991	444,507,711	611,177,108	459,350,229	1,011,569,765	318,670,932	268,635,552	321,003,265

Other cities for fiscal year 1991: Dallas, $490,854,925; Atlanta, $430,470,095; Houston, $388,100,645; Minneapolis, $317,553,446; San Francisco, $295,253,161; Baltimore, $273,518,266; Hartford, CT, $283,357,489; Columbus, OH, $349,575,092.

LANGUAGE

Sources for this section: *The World Almanac Guide to Good Word Usage; The Columbia Encyclopedia; Webster's Third New International Dictionary; The Oxford English Dictionary, 2nd ed.; The Associated Press Stylebook and Libel Manual; The Encyclopedia Americana.*

Neologisms

("New" words; from the Second Edition of the *Oxford English Dictionary*, Oxford Univ. Press, 1989.)

antiquark: the antiparticle of a quark.

arcade game: a (mechanical or electronic) game of a type orig. popularized in amusement arcades.

assertiveness training: a technique by which diffident persons are trained to behave (more) assuredly.

astroturfed: carpeted with astroturf.

birth parent: a natural (as opposed to an adoptive) parent.

build-down: a systematic reduction of nuclear armaments, by destroying two or more for each new one deployed.

bulimarexic: suffering from or characteristic of bulimia nervosa; one who suffers from bulimia nervosa.

camp-on: a facility of some telephone systems by which the caller of an engaged number can arrange for the system to ring it automatically as soon as it becomes free (in some cases ringing the caller also if he has replaced his receiver).

car-phone: a radio-telephone designed for use in a motor vehicle.

designer drug: a drug synthesized to mimic a legally restricted or prohibited drug without itself being subject to restriction.

fast tracker: a high-flyer; an ambitious or thrusting person.

foodie: also foody. One who is particular about food, a gourmet.

gender gap: the difference in (esp. political) attitudes between men and women.

hate mail: letters (often anonymous) in which the senders express their hostility towards the recipient.

Jazzercise: a proprietary name for a program of physical exercises arranged to be carried out in a class to the accompaniment of jazz music; also, exercise of this kind.

microwavable: of food and food containers: suitable for cooking or heating in a microwave oven.

NIMBY, nimby: "not in my backyard," a slogan expressing objection to the siting of something considered unpleasant, such as nuclear waste, in one's own locality.

passive smoking: the inhalation of smoke involuntarily from the tobacco being smoked by others, considered as a health risk.

rainbow coalition: a political grouping of minority peoples and other disadvantaged elements, esp. for the purpose of electing a candidate.

right to die: the alleged right of a brain-damaged or otherwise incurably ill person to the termination of life-sustaining treatment.

skanking: a style of West Indian dancing to reggae music, in which the body bends forward at the waist, and the knees are raised and the hands claw the air in time to the beat; dancing in this style.

street credibility: popularity with, or accessibility to, ordinary people, esp. those involved in urban street culture; the appearance or fact of being "street-wise"; hence (apparent) familiarity with contemporary trends, fashions, social issues.

yuppiedom: the condition or fact of being a yuppie; the domain of yuppies; yuppies as a class.

Eponyms (words named for people)

Bloody Mary—a vodka and tomato juice drink; after the nickname of Mary I, Queen of England, 1553-58, notorious for her persecution of Protestants.

Bloomers—full, loose trousers gathered at the knee; after Mrs. Amelia Bloomer, an American social reformer who advocated such clothing, 1851.

Bobbies—in Great Britain, police officers; after Sir Robert Peel, the statesman who organized the London police force, 1850.

Bowdlerize—to delete written matter considered indelicate; after Thomas Bowdler, British editor of an expurgated Shakespeare, 1825.

Boycott—to combine against in a policy of nonintercourse for economic or political reasons; after Charles C. Boycott, an English land agent in County Mayo, Ireland, ostracized in 1880 for refusing to reduce rents.

Braille—a system of writing for the blind; after Louis Braille, the French teacher of the blind who invented it, 1852.

Caesarean section—surgical removal of a child from the uterus through an abdominal incision; after Julius Caesar, born c. 102 B.C., in this manner, according to legend.

Casanova—a man who is a promiscuous and unscrupulous lover; after Giovanni Casanova, an Italian adventurer, 1725-98.

Chauvinist—excessively patriotic; after Nicolas Chauvin, a legendary French soldier devoted to Napoleon.

Derby—a stiff felt hat with a dome-shaped crown and rather narrow rolled brim; after Edward Stanley, 12th Earl of Derby, who in 1780 founded the Derby horse race at Epsom Downs, England, to which these hats are worn.

Gerrymander—to divide an election district in an unnatural way, to favor one political party; after Elbridge Gerry, and the salamander, for the salamander-like shape of a Mass. election district created, 1812, during Gerry's governorship.

Guillotine—a machine for beheading; after Joseph Guillotine, a French physician who proposed its use in 1789 as more humane than hanging.

Leotard—a close-fitting garment for the torso, worn by dancers, acrobats, and the like; after Julius Leotard, a 19th-century French aerial gymnast.

Silhouette—an outline image; from Etienne de Silhouette, the French finance minister, 1757, who advocated economies that included buying such paper portraits instead of painted miniatures.

Foreign Words and Phrases

(L=Latin; F=French; Y=Yiddish; R=Russian; G=Greek; I=Italian; S=Spanish)

ad hoc (L; ad HOK): for the particular end or purpose at hand

ad infinitum (L; ad in-FI-NITE-UM): endless

ad nauseam (L; ad NAWZ-ee-um): to a sickening degree

apropos (L; ap-ruh-POH): to the point; appropriate

bête noire (F; BET NWAHR): a thing or person viewed with particular dislike.

bon appetit (F; BOH nap-uh-teet): good appetite

bona fide (L; BOH nuh-feyed): genuine

carte blanche (F; kahrt BLANNSH): full discretionary power

cause celebre (F; kawz suh-LEB-ruh): a notorious incident

C'est la vie (F; se lah VEE): That's life

chutzpah (Y; KHOOT-spuh): amazing nerve bordering on arrogance

coup de grace (F; kooh duh GRAHS): the final blow

coup d'etat (F; kooh duh tah): forceful overthrow of a government

creme de la creme (F; KREM duh luh KREM): the best of the best

cum laude/magna cum laude/summa cum laude (L; KUHM loud-ay; MAHN-ya . . .; SOO-ma . . .): with praise or honor; with great praise or honor; with the highest praise or honor

de facto (L; di FAK-toh): in fact; generally agreed to without a formal decision

deja vu (F; DAY-zhah VOOH): the sensation that something happening has happened before

de jure (L; dee JOOR-ee, day YOOR-ay): determined by law, as opposed to de facto

de rigueur (F; duh ree-GUR): necessary according to convention

detente (F; day-TAHNT): an easing or relaxation of strained relations

éminence grise (F; ay-meh-NAHNN-suh GREEZ): one who wields power behind the scenes

enfant terrible (F; ahnn-FAHNN te-REE-bluh): one whose unconventional behavior causes embarrassment

en masse (F; ahn MAHS): in a large body

ergo (L; ER-goh): therefore

esprit de corps (F; es-PREE duh KAWR): group spirit; feeling of camaraderie

Eureka (G; YOOR-EE-kuh): I have found it

ex post facto (L; eks pohst FAK-toh): an explanation or regulation concocted after the event

fait accompli (F; fayt uh-kom-PLEE): an accomplished fact

faux pas (F; fowe PAH): a social blunder

glasnost (R; glahs-nust): openness, candor

hoi polloi (G; hoy puh-LOY): the masses

in loco parentis (L; in LOH-Koh puh-REN-tis): in place of a parent

in memoriam (L; in muh-MAWR-ee-uhm): in memory of

in situ (L; in SEYE-tyooh): in the original arrangement

in toto (L; in TOH-toh): totally

je ne sais quoi (F; zhuh nuh say KWAH): I don't know what; the little something that eludes description

joie de vivre (F; zhwah duh VEEV-ruh): joy of living, love of life

mea culpa (L; MAY-uh CUL-puh): my fault

meshugga (Y; meh-SHOOG-uh): crazy

modus operandi (L; MOH-duhs op-uh-RAN-dee): method of operation

noblesse oblige (F; noh-BLES uh-BLEEZH); the obligation of nobility to help the less fortunate

non compos mentis (L; non KOM-puhs MEN-tis): out of control of the mind; insane

nouveau riche (L; nooh-voh REESH); pejorative for recent rich who spend money conspicuously

perestroika (R; PAIR-es TROY-kuh): restructuring

persona non grata (L; per-SOH-nah non GRAH-tah): unacceptable person

post-mortem (L; pohst-MORE-tuhm): after death; autopsy; analysis after event

prima donna (I; pree-muh DAH-nuh): temperamental person

pro tempore (L; proh TEM-puh-ree): for the time being

que sera sera (S; keh sair-ah sair-AH): what will be, will be

quid pro quo (L; kwid proh KWOH): something given or received for something else

raison d'etre (F; RAY-zohnn DET-ruh): reason for being

shlemiel (Y; shleh-MEEL): an unlucky bungling person

savoir-faire (F; sav-wahr-FAIR): dexterity in social and practical affairs

semper fidelis (L; SEM-puhr fee-DAY-lis): always faithful

status quo (L; STAY-tus QWOH): existing order of things

tour de force (L; TOOR duh FAWRS): feat accomplished through great skill

terra firma (L; TER-uh FUR-muh): solid ground

verbatim (L; ver-BAY-tuhm): word for word

vis-a-vis (F; vee-ZUH-VEE): compared with

Esperanto

In 1887, Dr. L. L. Zamenhof, a linguist and physician, published a slim textbook on his "Internacia Lingvo" (International Language) under the pseudonym "Doktoro Esperanto." The term "Esperanto" became attached to the language itself as it gained adherents rapidly until the outbreak of World War I. Hardly recovered from the effects of the war, Esperanto was savaged by Nazism, Stalinism, Fascism, the Japanese militarists of the 1930's, and chauvinistic groups in many other countries. Not until the late 1950's did the number of speakers begin to show the steady increase which continues as Esperanto begins its second century.

Controlled experiments show that because of its logical structure, phonemic spelling, and regular grammar Esperanto can be learned to a given criterion of performance in from one-twentieth to one-fifth the time needed for the learning of a typical national language.

Inteligenta persono lernas la lingvon Esperanto rapide kaj facile. Esperanto estas la moderna, kultura lingvo por la tuta mondo.

Common Abbreviations

Usage of periods after abbreviations varies, but recently the tendency has been toward omission. Definitions preceding those in parentheses are in Latin.

A.A. = Alcoholics Anonymous
A.A.A. = American Automobile Association
AC = alternating current
A.D. = anno Domini (in the year of the Lord)
A.M. = ante meridiem (before noon)
A.F.L. = American Federation of Labor
A.M.A. = American Medical Association
anon. = anonymous
ASAP = as soon as possible
ASCAP = American Society of Composers, Authors, and Publishers
B.A. = Bachelor of Arts
bbl. = barrel(s)
B.C. = before Christ
B.C.E. = before the Christian era
B.S. = Bachelor of Science
B.T.U. = British thermal unit
bu. = bushel
C. = centigrade, Celsius
c. = copyright
c. (or ca.) = circa (about)
C.I.A. = Central Intelligence Agency
C.E.O. = chief executive officer
C.I.O. = Congress of Industrial Organizations
cm = centimeter
C.O.D. = cash (or collect) on delivery
C.P. = Communist Party
C.P.A. = Certified Public Accountant
C.P.R. = cardio-pulmonary resuscitation
D.A. = District Attorney
D.A.R. = Daughters of the American Revolution
DC = direct current
D.D. = Doctor of Divinity
D.D.S. = Doctor of Dental Surgery
DNA = deoxyribonucleic acid
DOA = dead on arrival
ed. = edited, edition, editor
e.g. = exempli gratia (for example)
esp. = especially
et. al. = et alii (and others)
etc. = et cetera (and so forth)
F. = Fahrenheit
F.B.I. = Federal Bureau of Investigation
f.o.b. = freight on board
FYI = for your information
g.n.p. = gross national product
G.O.P. = Grand Old party (Republican)
Hon. = the Honorable
H.R.H. = His (Her) Royal Highness
i.e. = id est (that is)
I.Q. = Intelligence Quotient
I.R.A. = Irish Republican Army
I.R.S. = Internal Revenue Service
J.D. = Juris Doctor (Doctor of Laws)
J.P. = Justice of the Peace
K = 1,000
k. = karat
kg. = kilogram
km. = kilometer
l = liter
lb. = libra (pound)
M.A. = Master of Arts
M.D. = Medicinae Doctor (Doctor of Medicine)
mfg. = manufacturing
ml = milliliter
mm = millimeter
M.S. = Master of Science
mph = miles per hour
MS = manuscript
MSG = monosodium glutamate
Msgr. = Monsignor
NCO = Noncommissioned Officer
No. = numero (number)
op. = opus (work)
oz. = ounce
p. = page
P.M. = post meridiem (afternoon)
POW = prisoner of war
P.S. = post scriptum (postscript)
pt. = pint(s), part, point
qt. = quart(s)
REM = rapid eye movement
R.F.D. = rural free delivery
R.I.P. = Requiescat in pace (May he rest in peace)
R.N. = Registered Nurse
ROTC = Reserve Officers' Training Corps
rpm = revolutions per minute
RR = railroad
R.S.V.P. = Répondez, s'il vous plait (Please answer)
S.A.S.E. = self-addressed stamped envelope
S.P.C.A. = Society for the Prevention of Cruelty to Animals
St. = saint, street
T. = ton
T.N.T. = trinitrotoluene
UFO = unidentified flying object
UHF = ultra high frequency
U.S.S. = United States Ship
v. (or vs.) = versus (against)
VHF = very high frequency
w = watt

Latin and Greek Prefixes and Suffixes

Latin prefix/English meaning
a, abs/from
alti, alto/high
ambi/both
ante/before
aqui/water
arbori/tree
audio/hearing
avi/bird
brevi/short
centi/hundred
cerebro/brain
circum/around
ferri, ferro/iron
fissi/split
igni/fire
inter/between
juxta/close
lacto/milk
luni/moon
magni/great
mal/bad
multi/many
naso/nose
nati/birth
oculo/eye
oleo/oil
omni/all
ovi, ovo/egg
plano/flat
post/after
pre/before
pro/for
pulmo/lung
re/again
recti/straight
retro/backward
somni/sleep
stelli/star
sub/under
super/above
terri/land
trans/through
ultra/beyond
uni/one

Latin suffix/English meaning
cide, cidal/kill
fid/split
fuge, fugal/flee from
grade/walking
pennale/wing
vorous/eating

Greek prefix/English meaning
a/not
anti/against
astro/star
auto/self
biblio/book
bio/life
cardio/heart
chloro/green
chrono/time
cosmo/universe
ex/outside
geo/earth
geronto/old age
gluc/sweet
grapho/writing
helio/sun
hemi/half
hetero/different
homeo/similar
homo/same
hydro/water
hyper/above
kinesi/movement
litho/stone
logo/word
macro/large
mega/great
meso/middle
meta/beyond
micro/small
mono/one
necro/dead body
neo/new
ornitho/bird
osteo/bone
pan/all
para/close
phono/sound
photo/light
poly/many
proto/first
pseudo/false
psycho/mind, spirit
pyro/fire
rhino/nose
theo/god
thermo/heat
toxico/poison
zoo/living

Greek suffix/English meaning
algia/pain
archy/government
gamy/marriage
gnomy/knowledge
iasis/disease
itis/inflammation
lepsy/seizure
logy/science of
machy/battle
meter/measure
oid/like
oma/tumor
phobe/fear
scope/observation
sect/cutting
soma/body
sophy/wisdom

Commonly Confused English Words

adverse: unfavorable
averse: opposed

affect: to influence
effect: to cause

aggravate: to make worse
annoy: to irritate

allusion: an indirect reference
illusion: an unreal impression

anxious: apprehensive
eager: avid

complement: to make complete; something that completes
compliment: to praise; praise

capital: the seat of government
capitol: the building in which a legislative body meets

discreet: prudent
discrete: separate

disinterested: impartial
uninterested: without interest

emigrate: to leave for another place of residence
immigrate: to come to another place of residence

elicit: to draw or bring out
illicit: illegal

denote: to mean
connote: to suggest beyond the explicit meaning

farther: more distant in space
further: an extension of time or degree

historic: an important occurrence
historical: any occurrence in the past

imply: to relay information but not explicitly
infer: to understand information that is not relayed explicitly

imminent: ready to take place
eminent: standing out

incredible: unbelievable
incredulous: skeptical

include: used when the items following are part of a whole
comprise: used when the items following are all of a whole

ingenious: clever
ingenuous: innocent

insidious: intended to trick
invidious: detrimental to reputation

literally: actually
figuratively: metaphorically

oral: spoken, as opposed to written
verbal: referring to skill with language, as opposed to other skills

prevaricate: to lie
procrastinate: to put off

pestilence: a contagious or infectious epidemic disease
petulance: rudeness

prostrate: stretched out flat, face down
prostate: of or relating to the prostate gland

qualitative: relating to quality
quantitative: relating to number

National Spelling Bee Champions

The Scripps Howard National Spelling Bee, conducted by Scripps Howard Newspapers and other leading newspapers since 1939, was instituted by the Louisville (Ky.) Courier-Journal in 1925. Children under 16 years of age and not beyond the eighth grade are eligible to compete for cash prizes at the finals, which are held annually in Washington, D.C. The 1992 winners are: first prize, **Amanda Good,** *The Richmond Times Leader* (Richmond, Va.); second prize, **Todd Erik Wallace,** *The Morning News* (Blackfoot, Ida.); third prize, **Srinivas Ayyagari,** *The Commercial Appeal* (Memphis, Tenn.).

Winning Words

These were the last words given in each of the years 1965-1991 at the Scripps Howard National Spelling Bee. They were all correctly spelled, thereby determining the national champion.

1965 — eczema
1966 — ratoon
1967 — chihuahua
1968 — abalone
1969 — interlocutory
1970 — croissant
1971 — shalloon
1972 — macerate
1973 — vouchsafe
1974 — hydrophyte
1975 — incisor
1976 — narcolepsy
1977 — cambist
1978 — deification
1979 — maculature
1980 — elucubrate
1981 — sarcophagus
1982 — psoriasis
1983 — purim
1984 — luge
1985 — milieu
1986 — odontalgia
1987 — staphylococci
1988 — elegiacal
1989 — spoliator
1990 — fibranne
1991 — antipyretic
1992 — lyceum

Commonly Misspelled English Words

accidentally
accommodate
acquainted
all right
already
amateur
appearance
appropriate
bureau
character
commitment
conscious
conscientious
convenience
deceive
describe
description
desirable
despair
desperate
eliminate
embarrass
fascinating
finally
foreign
forty
government
grammar
humorous
hurrying
incidentally
independent
inoculate
irresistible
laboratory
lightning
maintenance
marriage
miniature
mysterious
necessary
opportunity
optimistic
performance
permanent
rhythm
ridiculous
similar
sincerely
transferred

Foreign Idioms

English	Italian
Naked as a jaybird	Naked as a worm (Nudo come un verme)
A bird in the hand is worth two in the bush.	Better a finch in hand than a thrush on a branch. (Meglio fringuello in man che tordo in frasca.)
To kill two birds with one stone	To catch two pigeons with one bean (Pigliare due piccioni con una fava)
To eat crow	To swallow the toad (Inghiottire il rospo)
To eat like a pig	To eat like a buffalo (Mangiare come un bufalo)
Don't bite off more than you can chew.	Don't take a step longer than your leg. (Non fare il passo piu lungo della gamba.)
Pride goes before a fall.	Pride rode out on horseback and came back on foot. (La superbia andò a cavallo e tornò a piedi.)
To go by fits and starts	To go by hiccups (Andare a singhiozzo)
There is honor among thieves.	A dog doesn't eat a dog. (Cane non mangia cane.)
Once in a blue moon	Every death of a pope (Ad oogni morte di papa)

English	French
Don't waste your breath!	Save your saliva! (Espargne ta salive!)
To turn up like a bad penny	To arrive like a hair in the soup. (Arriver comme un cheveu sur la soupe.)
To talk to yourself	To talk to angels (Parler aux anges)
Let's get back to the subject.	Let's get back to our sheep. (Revenons à nos moutons.)
To pull a long face	To make a funny nose (Faire un drole de nez)
He laughs in your face.	He laughs in your nose. (Il vous rit au nez.)
By rule of thumb	From the view of the nose (A vue de nez)
To be knock-kneed	To have your legs in an X (Avoir les jambes en X)
Put that in your pipe and smoke it!	Put this in your pocket with your handkerchief on top! (Mets-le dans ta poche avec ton mouchoir dessus!)
It's Greek to me!	It's Chinese! (C'est de chinois!)

English	Spanish
To hit the ceiling	To scream at the sky (Poner el grito en el cielo)
Go fly a kite!	Go fry asparagus! (Véte a freír esparragos!)
There's always room for one more.	Where six can eat, seven can eat. (Donde comen seis, comen siete.)
To have the tables turned	To go out for wool and come home shorn (Ir por lana y volver esquilado)
To cut off your nose to spite your face	To throw stones at your own roof (Tirar piedras contra su propio tejado)
To slam the door in your face	To slam the door on your nostrils (Cerrarle la puerta en las narices)
Give him an inch, he'll take a mile.	Give him a hand and he takes a foot. (Le da la mano y se toma el pie.)
To be alive and kicking	To be alive and wagging your tail (Estar vivo y coleando)
You can't make a silk purse out of a sow's ear.	A monkey dressed in silk is still a monkey. (Aunque la mona se vista de seda, mona se queda.)
To swear a blue streak	To toss out toads and snakes (Echar sapos y culebras)

English	Yiddish
Go jump in the lake!	Go whistle in the ocean! (Gai feifen ahfenyam!)
You can only do one thing at a time.	You can't dance at two weddings at the same time. (Me ken nit tantzen auf tsvai chassenes mit ain mol.)
He's as slow as molasses.	He creeps like a bedbug. (Er kricht vi a vantz.)
He repeats himself..	He grinds ground flour. (Er molt gemolen mel.)
Where there's smoke, there's fire.	When bells ring, it's usually a holiday. (Az es klingt, iz misstomeh chogeh.)
Are you in a hurry?	Are you standing on one leg? (Bist ahf ain fus?)
Drop dead!	You should lie in the earth! (Zolst ligen in drerd!)
He makes a lot of trouble for me.	He makes my wedding black. (Er macht mir a shvartzeh chasseneh.)
Go fight City Hall.	Go fight with God. (Shlog zich mit Got arum.)
Thanks for nothing.	Many thanks in your belly button. (A shainem dank dir ir pupik.)

Names of the Days

English	French	Italian	Spanish	German
Sunday	Dimanche	domenica	domingo	Sonntag
Monday	Lundi	lunedi	lunes	Montag
Tuesday	Mardi	martedi	martes	Dienstag
Wednesday	Mercredi	mercoledi	miércoles	Mittwoch
Thursday	Jeudi	giovedi	jueves	Donnerstag
Friday	Vendredi	venerdi	viernes	Freitag
Saturday	Samedi	sabato	sábado	Samstag

Idioms: Their Meaning and Derivation

dyed in the wool: to have traits deeply ingrained; from the fact that if wool is dyed before being made into yarn, or while still raw wool, the color is more firmly fixed.

feet of clay: a blemish in the character of one previously held above reproach; from Daniel's interpretation of Nebuchadnezzar's dream in the Old Testament. The king dreamed of an image made of precious metals, except for feet made of clay and iron. Daniel said that the feet symbolized human vulnerability to weakness and destruction.

hands down: effortlessly; incontestably; from the way a jockey, sure of victory, drops his hands, loosening his grip on the reins.

in seventh heaven: in a state of bliss; especially in Islamic beliefs, the heaven of heavens, the home of God and the highest angels.

kiss of death: something that seems good but is in reality the instrument of one's downfall; from the earlier phrase "Judas kiss," betraying Jesus to the authorities.

mad as a hatter: crazy; from mercury's use in the making of felt hats, thus hatters often were afflicted with a violent twitching of the muscles as a result of its effects.

red herring: a false lead; a herring cured by smoke; from the persistent odor, hence the use, trailed over the ground, for training a dog to follow this scent over any other.

red-letter day: a memorable day; from the custom of using red or purple colors to mark holy days on the calendar.

to bark up the wrong tree: to pursue a false lead; an Americanism that comes from hunting, some say specifically nocturnal racoon hunting, in which dogs often lost track of their quarry.

to buckle down: to adopt an attitude of effort and determination; probably from the act of buckling on armor to prepare for battle.

to go at it with hammer and tongs: no holds barred; from the blacksmith who, with his tongs (long-handled pincers) took a piece of red-hot metal from the forge, laid it on the anvil, and beat it into shape with his hammer.

to hold water: to pass a test for soundness; from testing a pitcher by filling it with water.

to knuckle under: to submit to another; from the time when one knelt before a conquerer, putting the "knuckles" of one's knees (the rounded part of the bone where the joint is bent) on the ground.

to make hay while the sun shines: to seize the opportunity; from hay's composition of mown grass dried for fodder, with the sun as the cheapest and most available drying agent.

to strike while the iron is hot: to seize the opportunity; from the blacksmith's need to swing the hammer while the metal on the anvil is glowing, or he must start up the forge again and reheat the iron.

Pen Names

Currer, Ellis, and Acton Bell (Charlotte, Emily, and Anne Bronte)
Isak Dinesen (Karen Blixen)
George Eliot (Mary Ann or Marian Evans)
O. Henry (W.S. Porter)
George Sand (Amandine Aurore Dupine)
Stendahl (Marie Henri Beyle)
Dr. Seuss (Theodore Geisel)
Mark Twain (Samuel Clemens)

Designations of Some King Louis of France

Louis I (778-840): the Debonair or the Pious
Louis II (846-879): the Stammerer
Louis V (966-987): the Lazy
Louis VI (1081-1137): the Fat
Louis VII (1121-1180): the Young
Louis VIII (1187-1226): the Lion
Louis X (1289-1316): the Quarrelsome
Louis XII (1462-1515): Father of the People
Louis XIV (1638-1715): the Great or the Sun King
Louis XV (1710-1774): the Well-Beloved
Louis XVII (1785-1795?): the Lost Dauphin

Young of Animals Have Special Names

The young of many animals, birds and fish have come to be called by special names. A young eel, for example, is an elver. Many young animals, of course, are often referred to simply as infants, babies, younglets, or younglings.

bunny: rabbit.
calf: cattle, elephant, antelope, rhino, hippo, whale, etc.
cheeper: grouse, partridge, quail.
chick, chicken: fowl.
cockerel: rooster.
codling, sprag: codfish.
colt: horse (male).
cub: lion, bear, shark, fox, etc.
cygnet: swan.
duckling: duck.
eaglet: eagle.
elver: eel.
eyas: hawk, others.
fawn: deer.
filly: horse (female).
fingerling: fish generally.
flapper: wild fowl.
fledgling: birds generally.
foal: horse, zebra, others.
fry: fish generally.
gosling: goose.
heifer: cow.
joey: kangaroo, others.
kid: goat.
kit: fox, beaver, rabbit, cat.
kitten, kitty, catling: cats, other fur-bearers.
lamb, lambkin, cosset, hog: sheep.
leveret: hare.
nestling: birds generally.
owlet: owl.
parr, smolt, grilse: salmon.
piglet, shoat, farrow, suckling: pig.
polliwog, tadpole: frog.
poult: turkey.
pullet: hen.
pup: dog, seal, sea lion, fox.
puss, pussy: cat.
spike, blinker, tinker: mackerel.
squab: pigeon.
squeaker: pigeon, others.
whelp: dog, tiger, beasts of prey.
yearling: cattle, sheep, horse, etc.

A Collection of Animal Collectives

The English language boasts an abundance of names to describe groups of things, particularly pairs or aggregations of animals. Some of these words have fallen into comparative disuse, but many of them are still in service, helping to enrich the vocabularies of those who like their language to be precise, who tire of hearing a group referred to as "a bunch of," or who enjoy the sound of words that aren't overworked.

bale of turtles
band of gorillas
bed of clams, oysters
bevy of quail, swans
brace of ducks
brood of chicks
cast of hawks
cete of badgers
charm of goldfinches
cloud of gnats
clowder of cats
clutch of chicks
clutter of cats
colony of ants
congregation of plovers
covey of quail, partridge
crash of rhinoceri
cry of hounds
down of hares
drift of swine
drove of cattle, sheep
exaltation of larks
flight of birds
flock of sheep, geese
gaggle of geese
gam of whales
gang of elks
grist of bees
herd of elephants
horde of gnats
husk of hares
kindle or **kendle** of kittens
knot of toads
leap of leopards
leash of greyhounds, foxes
litter of pigs
mob of kangaroos
murder of crows
muster of peacocks
mute of hounds
nest of vipers
nest, nide of pheasants
pack of hounds, wolves
pair of horses
pod of whales, seals
pride of lions
school of fish
sedge or **siege** of cranes
shoal of fish, pilchards
skein of geese
skulk of foxes
sleuth of bears
sounder of boars, swine
span of mules
spring of teals
swarm of bees
team of ducks, horses
tribe or **trip** of goats
troop of kangaroos, monkeys
volery of birds
watch of nightingales
wing of plovers
yoke of oxen

The Principal Languages of the World

Source: S. Culbert, NI-25, University of Washington, Seattle, WA 98195

Languages with over 100,000,000 Speakers

(mid-1992)

	Speakers (millions) Native	Total
Mandarin	817	907
Hindi	321	383
Spanish	320	362
English	316	456
Bengali	180	189
Arabic	178	208
Russian	173	293
Portuguese	165	177
Japanese	125	126
German	98	119
French	71	123
Malay-Indonesian	48	148

Total number of speakers (native plus non-native) of languages spoken by at least one million speakers

Achinese (N Sumatra, Indonesia)	3
Afrikaans (So. Africa)	10
Akan (or Twi-Fanti) (Ghana)	3
Albanian (Albania; Kosovo)	5
Amharic (Ethiopia)	18
Arabic (see above)	208
Armenian (Armenia)	5
Assamese[1] (India, Bangladesh)	23
Aymara (Bolivia; Peru)	2
Azerbaijani (Azerbaijan)	15
Balinese (Bali, Indonesia)	3
Baluchi (Baluchistan, Pakistan)	4
Bashkir (Bashkortostan, in Russia)	1
Batak Toda (Indonesia)	4
Baule (Côte d'Ivoire)	2
Beja (Kassala, Sudan; Ethiopia)	1
Bemba (Zambia)	2
Bengali[1] (see above)	189
Berber[2]	
Beti (Cameroon; Gabon; Eq. Guinea)	2
Bhili (India)	3
Bikol (SE Luzon, Philippines)	4
Brahui (Pakistan; Afghan.; Iran)	1
Bugis (Indonesia; Malaysia)	4
Bulgarian (Bulgaria)	9
Burmese (Myanmar)	31
Buji (S Guizhou, S China)	2
Byelorussian (Belarus)	10
Cantonese (China; Hong-kong)	65
Catalan (NE Spain; S France; Andorra)	9
Cebuano (Bohol Sea, Philippines)	13
Chagga (Kilimanjaro area, Tanzania)	1
Chiga (Ankole, Uganda)	1
Chinese[3]	
Chuvash (Chuvash, in Russia)	2
Czech (Czechoslovakia)	12
Danish (Denmark)	5
Dimli (EC Turkey)	1
Dogri (Jammu-Kashmir, CE India)	1
Dong (SC China)	2
Dutch-Flemish (Netherlands; Belg.)	21
Dyerma (SW Niger)	2
Edo (Bendel, S Nigeria)	1
Efik (incl. Ibibio) (SE Nigeria)	6
English (see above)	456
Esperanto	2
Estonian (Estonia)	1
Ewe (SE Ghana; S Togo)	3
Fang-Bulu (Dialects of Beti, q. v.)	
Farsi (Iranian form of Persian, q. v.)	
Finnish (Finland; Sweden)	6
Fon (SC Benin; S Togo)	1
French (see above)	123
Fula (or Peulh) (Cameroon; Nigeria)	13
Fulakunda (Senegambia; Guinea B.)	2
Futa Jalon (Guinea; Sierra Leone)	3
Galician (Galicia, NW Spain)	3
Galla (see Oromo)	
Ganda (or Luganda) (S Uganda)	3
Georgian (Georgia)	4
German (see above)	119
Gilaki (Gilan, NW Iran)	2
Gogo (Riff Valley, Tanzania)	1
Gondi (Central India)	2
Greek (Greece)	11
Guarani (Paraguay)	4
Gujarati[1] (WC India; S Pakistan)	39
Gusii (Kisii District, Nyanza, Kenya)	2
Hadiyya (Arusi, Ethiopia)	2
Hakka (or Kejia) (SE China)	33
Hani (S China)	1
Hausa (N Nigeria; Niger; Cameroon)	36
Haya (Kagera, NW Tanzania)	1
Hebrew (Israel)	4
Hindi[1,4] (see above)	383
Ho (Bihar and Orissa States, India)	1
Hungarian (or Magyar) (Hungary)	14
Iban (Indonesia; Malaysia)	1
Ibibio (see Efik)	
Igbo (or Ibo) (lower Niger, Nigeria)	17
Ijaw (Niger River delta, Nigeria)	2
Ilocano (NW Luzon, Philippines)	7
Indonesian (see Malay-Indonesian)	
Italian (Italy)	63
Japanese (see above)	126
Javanese (Java, Indonesia)	61
Kabyle (W Kabylia, N Algeria)	3
Kamba (E Kenya)	3
Kannada[1] (S India)	43
Kanuri (Nigeria; Niger; Chad; Cam.)	4
Karen (see Pho and Sgaw)	

(continued)

Karo-Dairi (N Sumatra, Indonesia)	2
Kashmiri[1] (N India; NE Pakistan)	4
Kazakh (Kazakhstan)	8
Kanuzi-Dongola (S Egypt; Sudan)	1
Khalka (see Mongolian)	
Khmer (Kampuchea; Vietnam; Thai.)	7
Khmer, Northern (Thailand)	1
Kikuyu (or Gekoyo) (WC Kenya)	5
Kituba (Bas-Zaire, Bandundu, Zaire)	4
Kongo (W Zaire; S Congo; NW Ang.)	3
Konkani (Maharashtra and SW India)	4
Korean (Korea; China; Japan)	73
Kurdish (south-west of Caspian Sea)	10
Kyrgyz (Kyrgyzstan)	2
Lao[5] (Laos)	4
Lampung (Sumatra, Indonesia)	1
Latvian (Latvia)	2
Lingala (incl. Bangala) (Zaire)	6
Lithuanian (Lithuania)	3
Luba-Lulua (or Chiluba) (Zaire)	6
Luba-Shaba (Shaba, Zaire)	1
Lubu (E Sumatra, Indonesia)	1
Luhya (W Kenya)	1
Luo (Kenya; Nyanza, Tanzania)	3
Luri (SW Iran; Iraq)	3
Lwena (E Angola; W Zambia)	3
Macedonian (Macedonia)	2
Madurese (Madura, Indonesia)	10
Magindanaon (S Philippines)	1
Makassar (S Sulawesi, Indonesia)	2
Makua (S Tanzania; N Mozambique)	3
Malagasy (Madagascar)	12
Malay-Indonesian (see above)	148
Malay, Pattani (SE Thailand)	1
Malayalam[1] (Kerala, S India)	35
Malinke-Bambara-Dyula (W Africa)	9
Mandarin (see above)	907
Marathi[1] (Maharashtra, India)	67
Mazandarani (S Mazandaran, N Iran)	2
Mbundu (Benguela, Angola)	4
Mbundu (Luanda, Angola)	3
Meithei (NE India; Bangladesh)	1
Mende (Sierra Leone)	2
Meru (Eastern Province, C Tanzania)	1
Miao (or Hmong) (S China; SE Asia)	5
Mien (China; Viet.; Laos; Thailand)	2
Min (SE China; Taiwan; Malaysia)	50
Minangkabau (W Sumatra, Indon.)	6
Moldavian (included with Romanian)	
Mongolian (Mongolia; NE China)	5
Mordvin (Mordova, in Russia)	1
Moré (central part of Burkina Faso)	4
Nepali (Nepal; NE India; Bhutan)	14
Ngulu (Mozambique; Malawi)	2
Nkole (Western Prov., Uganda)	1
Norwegian (Norway)	5
Nung (NE of Hanoi, Vietnam; China)	1
Nupe (Kwara, Niger States, Nigeria)	1
Nyamwezi-Sukuma (NW Tanzania)	4
Nyanja (Malawi; Zambia; Zimbabwe)	4
Oriya[1] (Central and E India)	31
Oromo (West Ethiopia; N Kenya)	10
Pampangan (NW of Manila, Philip.)	2
Panay-Hiligaynon (Philippines)	6
Pangasinan (Lingayen G., Philip.)	1
Pashtu (Pakistan; Afghanistan; Iran)	21
Pedi (see Sotho, Northern)	
Persian (Iran; Afghanistan)	34
Polish (Poland)	44
Portuguese (see above)	177
Provençal (S France)	4
Punjabi[1] (Punjab, Pakistan; India)	89
Pushto (see Pashtu) (many spellings)	
Quechua A (Peru; Boliv.; Ec.; Arg.)	8
Rejang (SW Sumatra, Indonesia)	1
Riff (N Morocco; Algerian coast)	1
Romanian (Romania; Moldova)	26
Romany (Vlach only) (Eur.; Amer.)	2
Ruanda (Rwanda; Uganda; Zaire)	8
Rundi (Burundi)	6
Russian (see above)	293
Samar-Leyte (Central E Philippines)	3
Sango (Central African Republic)	3
Santali (E India; Nepal)	5
Sasak (Lombok, Alas Strait, Indon.)	1
Serbo-Croatian (NW Balkan area)	20
Sgaw (SW Myanmar)	1
Shan (Shan, E Myanmar)	3
Shilha (W Algeria; S Morocco)	3
Shona (Zimbabwe)	8
Sidamo (Sidamo, S Ethiopia)	1
Sindhi[1] (SE Pakistan; W India)	17
Sinhalese (Sri Lanka)	13
Slovak (Czechoslovakia)	5
Slovene (Slovenia)	2
Soga (Busoga, Uganda)	1
Somali (Som.; Eth.; Ken.; Djibouti)	7
Songye (Kasai Or., NW Shala, Zaire)	1
Soninke (Mali; countries to W S E)	1
Sotho, Northern (So. Africa)	3
Sotho, Southern (So. Afr.; Lesotho)	4
Spanish (see above)	362
Sundanese (Sunda Strait, Indonesia)	25
Swahili (Kenya; Tanz.; Zaire; Ug.)	46
Swedish (Sweden; Finland)	9
Sylhetti (Bangladesh)	5
Tagalog (Philippines)	43
Tajiki (Tajikistan; Uzbek.; Kyrgyz.)	4
Tamazight (N Morocco; W Algeria)	3
Tamil[1] (Tamil Nadu, India; Sri Lanka)	67
Tatar (Tatarstan, in Russia)	8
Tausug (Philippines; Malaysia)	1
Telugu[1] (Andhra Pradesh, SE India)	71
Temne (central Sierra Leone)	1
Thai[5] (Thailand)	49
Tho (N Vietnam; S China)	1
Thonga (Mozambique; So. Africa)	3
Tibetan (SW China; N India; Nepal)	5
Tigrinya (S Eritrea, Tigre, Ethiopia)	4
Tiv (SE Nigeria; Cameroon)	2
Tong (see Dong)	
Tonga (SW Zambia; NW Zimbabwe)	2
Tswana (Botswana; So. Africa)	4
Tudza (N Vietnam; S China)	1
Tulu (S India)	2
Tumbuka (N Malawi; NE Zambia)	2
Turkish (Turkey)	57
Turkmen (Turkmenistan; Afghanistan)	3
Twi-Fante (see Akan)	
Uighur (Xinjiang, NW China)	7
Ukrainian (Ukraine, Russia, Poland)	46
Urdu[1,4] (Pakistan; India)	96
Uzbek (Uzbekistan)	13
Vietnamese (Vietnam)	61
Wolaytta (SE Ethiopia)	2
Wolof (Senegal)	6
Wu (Shanghai region, China)	64
Xhosa (SW Cape Prov., So. Africa)	7
Yao (see Mien)	
Yao (Malawi; Tanzania; Mozambique)	1
Yi (S and SW China)	6
Yiddish[6]	
Yoruba (SW Nigeria; Zou, Benin)	19
Zande (NE Zaire; SW Sudan)	1
Zhuang (S China)	15
Zulu (N. Natal, So. Africa; Lesotho)	7

(1) One of the fifteen languages of the Constitution of India. (2) See Kabyle, Riff, Shilha, and Tamazight. (3) See Mandarin, Cantonese, Wu, Min, and Hakka. The "common speech" (Putonghua) of the "national language" (Guoyu) is a standardized form of Mandarin as spoken in the area of Beijing. (4) Hindi and Urdu are essentially the same language, Hindustani. As the official language of Pakistan it is written in a modified Arabic script and called Urdu. As the official language of India it is written in the Devanagari script and called Hindi. (5) The distinctions between some Thai dialects and Lao is political rather than linguistic. (6) Yiddish is usually considered a variant of German, though it has its own standard grammar, dictionaries, a highly developed literature; and is written in Hebrew characters.

Computer Language

Source: *Electronic Computer Glossary* by Alan Freedman, The Computer Language Co. Inc., 1992

access: (used as a verb) to store data on and retrieve data from a disk or other device connected to the computer.

acoustic coupler: a device that connects a terminal or computer to the handset of a telephone. It may also include the **modem.**

address: a number of a particular memory or disk location. Like a post office box.

analog: a representation of an object that resembles the original. For example, the telephone system converts sound waves into analogous electrical waves.

artificial intelligence: a broad range of computer applications that resemble human intelligence and behavior, such as expert systems and robots.

ASCII: acronym for American Standard Code for Information Interchange. A widely-used code for storing data.

assembly language: a machine oriented language using mnemonics to represent each machine-language instruction. Each CPU has its own assembly language.

authorization code: an identification number or password used to gain access to a computer system.

backup file: a copy of a current file used if the current file is destroyed.

BASIC: Beginner's All-purpose Symbolic Instruction Code; a computer language used by many small and personal computer systems.

baud rate: the switching speed of a line. One baud equals one bit per second or more.

(*continued*)

binary: refers to the base-2 number system in which the only allowable digits are 0 and 1.
bit: short for binary digit, the smallest unit of information stored in a computer. It always has the binary value of "O" or "1."
bubble memory: a memory that circulates tiny bubble-like magnetic bits in a solid state structure. Not widely used.
buffer: a temporary place to put information for processing.
bug: a mistake that occurs in a program within a computer or in the unit's electrical system. When a mistake is found and corrected, it's called debugging.
byte: an 8-bit sequence of binary digits. Each byte corresponds to 1 character of data, representing a single letter, number, or symbol. Bytes are the most common unit for measuring computer and disk storage capacity.
C: a high-level programming language often used to write commercial products due to its transportability to many different computer systems.
CAD/CAM: abbreviation for computer-aided design/computer-aided manufacturing.
cathode ray tube terminal: a device used as a computer terminal which contains a television-like screen for displaying data. Most CRT terminals also have a typewriter-like keyboard.
CD-ROM: Information is retrieved by a laser beam that scans tracks of microscopic holes in a rotating compact disk. They can store 550 million characters, but cannot store new information.
COBOL: Common Business Oriented Language; one of the most widely used business programming languages.
chip: a common term for an integrated circuit, a collection of interconnected microminiature electronic components.
code: lines of programming statements written by a programmer.
command: an action statement or order to the computer.
compiler: a program that translates a high-level language, such as BASIC, into machine language.
connect time: the time a user at a terminal (a work station away from the main computer) is logged-on to a computer system.
CPU: the Central Processing Unit within the computer that executes the instructions the user gives the system.
cursor: the symbol on the computer monitor that marks the place where the operator is working.
database: a large amount of data stored in a well organized format. A database management system is a program that allows access to the information.
dedicated: designed for a single use.
density: the number of bits that can be stored in a linear inch.
desktop publishing: using a personal computer to produce high-quality printed output camera ready for the printer.
diagnostics: software programs that test the operational capability of hardware components.
directory: an index to the location of files on a disk.
disk: a revolving plate on which information and programs are stored. See also **Floppy disk.**
disk drive: a peripheral machine that stores information on disks.
documentation: user or operator instructions that come with some hardware and software that tells how to use the material.
DOS: a single-user operating system commonly used on PCs.
download: to transmit data from a central to a remote computer or from a file server to a personal computer.
dump: a printout of the contents of memory or a file.
fax: facsimile, the communication of a printed page between remote locations.
field: the physical unit of data in a record.
file: any collection of data treated as a single unit.
file server: a computer that stores data and programs that are shared by many users in a network.
floppy disk: a small inexpensive disk used to record and store information. It must be used in conjunction with a disk drive.
font: a set of characters of a particular design and size.
foreground/background: an operating system prioritizing method in multitasking computer systems. Programs running in the foreground have highest priority.
format: the arrangement by which information is stored.
function: in programming, a routine, or set of instructions, that performs a particular task.
gigabyte: one billion bytes.
hacker: a very technical person in the computer field; the term is sometimes used in a derogatory manner to refer to people who gain unauthorized access into computer systems and data banks.
hardware: the physical apparatus that makes up a computer, silicon chips, transformers, boards and wires. Also used to describe various pieces of equipment including the CPU, printer, modem, CRT (cathode ray tube).
hexadecimal: refers to the base-16 number system, which is used as a shorthand for referencing machine codes.
intelligent terminal: a terminal with built-in processing capability. It has memory, but no disk or tape storage.
interface: the hardware or software necessary to connect one device or system to another.
K: abbreviation for Kilo-byte used to denote 1,024 units of stored matter.
language: any set of compiled, unified, or related commands or instructions that are acceptable to a computer.
laptop computer: a portable computer that usually weighs less than 12 pounds and has a self-contained power supply.
light pen: an input device that uses a light-sensitive stylus connected by a wire to a video terminal.
load: the actual operation of putting information and data into the computer or memory.
loop: in programming, the repetition of some function within the program.
machine readable: any paper form or storage medium that can be automatically read by the computer.
master file: a collection of records pertaining to one of the main subjects of an information system.
megabyte: one million bytes.
memory: the computer's internal work space.
menu: programs, functions or other choices displayed on the monitor for user selection.
microcomputer: a computer that uses a microprocessor for its CPU. All personal computers are microcomputers.
microprocessor: a complete CPU on a single chip.
minicomputer: an intermediate computer system sized between the very small microcomputer and the large computer.
modem: stands for Modulator-Demodulator. A device that adapts a terminal or computer to an analog telephone line.
mouse: a puck-like object that is used as a pointing and drawing device.
multitasking: the ability to run more than one program at the same time.
network: in communications, the path between terminals and computers. In database management, a database design.
noise: random disturbances that degrade or disrupt data communications.
operating system: a master control program that runs the computer and acts as a scheduler and traffic cop.
OS/2: a single-user, multitasking operating system that was designed to be the successor to DOS.
password: a word or code used to identify an authorized user.
PC: microcomputer that serves one user.
peripheral: any hardware device connected to a computer, such as printers or joy sticks.
pixel: picture element, the smallest display element on a video display screen.
program: coded instructions telling a computer how to perform a specific function.
RAM: stands for Random Access Memory. Same as **memory.**
random access: the ability to retrieve records in a file without reading any previous records.
record: a group of related fields that are used to store data about a subject. A collection of records is a *file*, and a collection of files is a *database.*
ROM: stands for Read Only Memory. A permanent memory.

semiconductor: a solid state substance that can be electrically altered, such as a transistor.
software: the programs, or sets of instructions, that tell the computer what to do.
spreadsheet: a software program that simulates a paper spreadsheet, or worksheet, in which columns of numbers are totaled.
superconductor: a material that has almost no resistance to the flow of electricity.
telecommuting: working at home and communicating via computer with the office.
user friendly: hardware or software that is easy to use.
user interface: hardware and software that provide the interface between the user and the computer.
virtual reality: artificial reality that projects the user into a 3-dimensional space.
virus: a program that infects a computer system. It is secretly attached to a program and does its dirty work after the program has been run once.
voice recognition: the understanding of spoken words by a machine.
window: a separate viewing area on a display screen.
word processor: a text–editing program or system that allows electronic writing and correcting of articles, etc.

Economic and Financial Glossary

Acquisition: The purchase of one company by another.

Balanced Budget: The federal government budget is balanced when receipts are equal to current expenditure.

Balance of payments: The difference between all payments made to and from foreign countries over a set period of time. A *favorable* balance exists when more payments are coming in than going out; an *unfavorable* balance, when the reverse is true. Payments include gold, the cost of merchandise and services, interest and dividend payments, money spent by travelers, and repayment of principal on loans.

Balance of trade (trade gap): The difference between exports and imports, both in actual funds and credit. A nation's balance of trade is *favorable* when exports exceed imports and *unfavorable* when the reverse is true.

Bear Market: A market in which prices are falling.

Bearer Bond: A bond issued in bearer form rather than being registered in the owner's name. Ownership is determined by possession.

Bond: A written promise or IOU by the issuer to repay a fixed amount of borrowed money on a specified date and to pay a set annual rate of interest in the meantime, usually at semi-annual intervals. Bonds are generally considered safe because the borrower (whether a company or the government) usually must make interest payments before the money is spent on anything else.

Bull Market: A market in which prices are on the rise.

Commercial Paper: An extremely short-term corporate IOU, generally due in 270 days or less. Available in face amounts of $100,000, $250,000, $500,000, $1,000,000 and combinations thereof.

Convertible Bond: A corporate bond (see below) which may be converted into a stated number of shares of common stock. Its price tends to fluctuate along with fluctuations in the price of the stock and with changes in interest rates.

Corporate Bond: Evidence of debt by a corporation. The bond normally has a stated life and pays a fixed rate of interest. Considered safer than the common or preferred stock of the same company.

Cost of living: The cost of maintaining a standard of living measured in terms of purchased goods and services. A rise in the cost of living mirrors the rate of inflation.

Cost-of-living benefits: Benefits that go to those persons whose money receipts increase automatically as prices rise.

Credit crunch (liquidity crisis): The period when cash for lending to business and consumers is in short supply.

Debenture: An unsecured long-term debt obligation backed only by the general credit of the issuing corporation.

Deficit spending: The practice whereby a government goes into debt to finance some of its expenditures.

Depression: A long period of economic decline when prices are low, unemployment is high, and there are many business failures.

Devaluation: The official lowering of a nation's currency, decreasing its value in relation to foreign currencies.

Discount Rate: The rate of interest set by the Federal Reserve that member banks are charged when borrowing money through the Federal Reserve System.

Disposable income: Income after taxes which is available to persons for spending and saving.

Dividend: Payment by a corporation to its shareholders, usually in the form of cash, stock shares, or other property.

Dow-Jones Industrial Average: A measure of stock market prices, based on 30 leading companies on the New York Stock Exchange.

Econometrics: The application of mathematical and statistical methods to the study of economic and financial data.

Economic Growth: The steady process of increasing productive capacity of the economy, and hence of increasing national income.

Federal Deposit Insurance Corporation (FDIC): A government-sponsored corporation that insures accounts in national banks and other qualified institutions.

Federal Reserve System: The entire banking system of the U.S., incorporating 12 Federal Reserve banks (one in each of 12 Federal Reserve districts), and 24 Federal Reserve branch banks, all national banks and state-chartered commercial banks and trust companies that have been admitted to its membership. The system greatly influences the nation's monetary and credit policies.

Full employment: The economy is said to be at full employment when only fractional unemployment exists. That is, everyone who wishes to work at the going wage-rate for his type of labor is employed. Since it takes time to switch from one job to another, there will be at any given time a small amount of unemployment.

Golden Parachute: Provisions in the employment contracts of executives guaranteeing substantial severance benefits if they lose their position in a corporate takeover.

Government Bond: An IOU of the U.S. Treasury, considered the safest security in the investment world. They are divided into two categories, those that are not marketable and those that are. *Savings Bonds* cannot be bought and sold once the original purchase is made. These include the familiar Series EE bonds. You buy them at 50 percent of their face value and when they mature, 12 years later, they will pay you back 100 percent of face value if you cash them in. Another type, Series H, are not discounted, but issued in amounts of $500, $1,000, $5,000, and $10,000 and pay their interest in semiannual checks. Marketable bonds fall into 12 categories. *Treasury Bills* are short-term U.S. obligations, maturing in 3, 6, or 12 months. They are sold at a discount of the face value, and the minimum denomination is $10,000. *Treasury Notes* mature in up to 10 years. Denominations range from $500, $1,000 to $5,000, $10,000 and up. *Treasury Bonds* mature in 10 to 30 years. The minimum investment is $1,000.

Greenmail: A company buys back its own shares from a suitor for more than the going market price to avoid a hostile takeover.

Gross Domestic Product (GDP): The market value of all goods and services that have been bought for final use during a year. It became the official measure of the U.S. economy in 1991, and replaced the *Gross National Product (GNP)* which had been in use since 1941. The GDP covers workers and capital employed within the nation's borders. The GNP covers production by American residents, regardless of location. The switch aligned the U.S. with most other industrialized countries, making comparisons easier.

Individual Retirement Account (IRA): A self-funded retirement plan that allows employed individuals to contribute a maximum yearly sum toward their retirement. Interest earned in the account is tax deferred.

Inflation: An increase in the average level of prices.

Insider Information: Important facts about the condition or plans of a corporation that have not been released to the general public.

Interest: Money paid for the use of money. There are two kinds of interest. Simple interest is interest that is earned and paid. Compound interest is the accumulated interest that is added to the principal amount.

Junk Bonds: Debt securities that sell at relatively low prices, because of the low credit rating of their issuers. They pay significantly higher yields than top-grade bonds to reflect their added risk. In the 1980s, they have been used to finance hostile takeovers.

Key leading indicators: A series of eleven indicators from different segments of the economy used by the Commerce Department to foretell what will happen in the economy in the near future.

Leveraged Buy-Out: An acquisition of a public company by a small group, often including the company's management, which takes the company private. Much of the purchase price is borrowed with the debt repaid from company profits or by selling company assets.

Liquid Assets: Assets that include cash or those items that are easily converted into cash.

Margin Account: A brokerage account that allows a person to trade securities on credit.

Money supply: The currency held by the public plus checking accounts in commercial banks and savings institutions.

Mortgage-Backed Securities: Created when a bank, builder or government agency gathers together a group of mortgages and then sells bonds to other institutions and the public. The investors receive their proportionate share of the interest payments on the loans as well as the principal payments. Usually, these mortgages are guaranteed by the government, making them a fairly safe investment despite the fact that their market value does fluctuate.

Municipal Bond: Issued by governmental units such as states, cities, local taxing authorities and other agencies. Interest is exempt from U.S. — and sometimes state and local — income tax. *Municipal Bond Unit Investment Trusts* allow you to invest in a portfolio of many different municipal bonds chosen by professionals. The income is exempt from federal income taxes.

Mutual Fund: A portfolio, or selection, of professionally bought and managed stocks in which you pool your money along with thousands of other people. A share price is based on net asset value, or the value of all the investments owned by the funds, less any debt, and divided by the total number of shares. The major advantage is less risk — it is spread out over many stocks and, if one or two do badly, the remainder may shield you from the losses. *Bond Funds* are mutual funds that deal in the bond market exclusively. *Money Market Mutual Funds* buy in the so-called "Money Market" — institutions that need to borrow large sums of money for short terms. Usually the individual investor cannot afford the denominations required in the "Money Market" (i.e. treasury bills, commercial paper, certificates of deposit), but through a money market mutual fund he can take advantage of these instruments when interest rates are high. These funds offer special checking account advantages.

National debt: The debt of the national government as distinguished from the debts of the political subdivisions of the nation and private business and individuals.

National debt ceiling: Limit set by Congress beyond which the national debt cannot rise. This limit is periodically raised by congressional vote.

Option: A contractual agreement between a buyer and a seller to buy or sell shares of a security. A **Call** option contract gives the right to purchase shares of a specific stock at a stated price within a given period of time. A **Put** option contract gives the buyer the right to sell shares of a specific stock at a stated price within a given period of time.

Per capita income: The nation's total income divided by the number of people in the nation.

Prime interest rate: The rate charged by banks on short-term loans to large commercial customers with the highest credit rating.

Producer price index: A statistical measure of the change in the price of wholesale goods. It is reported for 3 different stages of the production chain: crude, intermediate, and finished goods.

Program Trading: A term used for trading techniques involving large numbers and large blocks of stocks, usually used in conjunction with computer programs. Techniques include *Index Arbitrage* in which traders profit from price differences between stocks and futures contracts on stock indexes, and *Portfolio Insurance* which is the use of stock-index futures to protect stock investors from large losses when the market drops.

Public debt: The total of the nation's debts owed by state, local, and national government. This is considered a good measure of how much of the nation's spending is financed by borrowing rather than taxation.

Recession: A mild decrease in economic activity marked by a decline in real GNP, employment, and trade, usually lasting 6 months to a year, and marked by widespread decline in many sectors of the economy.

Savings Association Insurance Fund (SAIF): Created in 1989 to insure accounts in savings and loan associations up to $100,000.

Seasonal adjustment: Statistical changes made to compensate for regular fluctuations in data that are so great they tend to distort the statistics and make comparisons meaningless. For instance, seasonal adjustments are made in midwinter for a slowdown in housing construction and for the rise in farm income in the fall after the summer crops are harvested.

Stagnation: A period of economic slowdown in which there is little growth in GDP, capital investment, and real income.

Stock: *Common Stocks* are shares of ownership in a corporation; they are the most direct way to participate in the fortunes of a company. There can be wide swings in the prices of this kind of stock. *Preferred Stock* is a type of stock on which a fixed dividend must be paid before holders of common stock are issued their share of the issuing corporation's earnings. Prices are higher and yields lower than comparable bonds. However, they are attractive to corporate investors because 85 percent of preferred dividends are tax exempt to corporations. *Convertible Preferred Stock* can be converted into the common stock of the company that issued the preferred. This stock has the advantage of producing a higher yield than common stock and it also has appreciation potential. *Over-the-Counter Stock* is not traded on the major or regional exchanges, but rather through dealers from whom you buy directly. These stocks tend to belong to smaller companies. *Blue Chip* stocks are so called because they have been leading stocks for a long time. *Growth* stocks are stocks whose earnings have grown over several years.

Stock-index Futures: A futures contract is an agreement to buy or sell a specific amount of a commodity or financial instrument at a particular price at a set date. Futures on a stock index (such as the Standard & Poor's 500) are bets on the future price of that group of stocks.

Supply-side economics: The school of economic thinking which stresses the importance of the costs of production as a means of revitalizing the economy. Advocates policies that raise capital and labor output by increasing the incentives to produce.

Takeover: The passing of control of one company by another company or group by sale or merger. A friendly takeover occurs when the acquired company's management is agreeable to the merger; when management is opposed to the merger it is an unfriendly takeover. Takeover **arbitrage** is the purchase and/or selling of the securities of companies involved in takeover situations in order to realize a profit.

Tender Offer: A public offer to buy a company's stock; usually priced at a premium above the market.

Unit Investment Trust: A portfolio of many different corporate bonds, preferred stocks, government-backed securities or utility common stocks in which you can invest with as little as $1,000. Professional managers choose the securities, arrange for safe-keeping and collect the income. You receive your pro rata share of income every month.

Zero Coupon Bond: A corporate or government bond that is issued at a deep discount from the maturity value and pays no interest during the life of the bond. It is redeemable at face value.

CITIES OF THE U.S.[1]

Sources: Bureau of the Census: population (1990 Census); population growth (1980-1990). Geography Division, Bureau of the Census: population density (1990); area (1990). Bureau of Labor Statistics: employment (Metropolitan Statistical Area, Jan. 1992). Bureau of Economic Analysis: per capita personal income (MSA, 1990).

Akron, Ohio

Population: 223,019; **Pop. density:** 4,055 per sq. mi.; **Pop. growth:** –6.0%. **Area:** 55 sq. mi. **Employment:** 306,948 employed, 8.0% unemployed; **Per capita income:** $18,029; % change 1980-90: 83.3.

History: settled 1825; inc. as city 1865; located on Ohio-Erie Canal and is a port of entry; since 1870 the rubber capital of the U.S.

Transportation: 1 airport; major trucking industry; Conrail; metro transit system. **Communications:** 4 TV, 7 radio stations; CATV. **Medical facilities:** 11 hospitals; specialized children's treatment center. **Educational facilities:** 13 univ. and colleges; 68 public schools. **Further information:** Akron Regional Development Board or Akron-Summit Convention and Visitors Bureau, Cascade Plaza, Akron, OH 44308.

Albuquerque, New Mexico

Population: 384,736; **Pop. density:** 4,050 per sq. mi.; **Pop. growth:** 15.6%. **Area:** 95 sq. mi. **Employment:** 252,438 employed, 5.1% unemployed; **Per capita income:** $17,518; % change 1980-90: 89.6.

History: founded 1706 by the Spanish; inc. 1890.

Transportation: 1 international airport; 2 railroads; 2 bus lines. **Communications:** 5 TV, 31 radio stations; CATV. **Medical facilities:** 10 major hospitals. **Educational facilities:** 1 university. **Further information:** Convention & Visitors Bureau, 625 Silver S.W., Albuquerque, NM 87125.

Anaheim, California

Population: 266,406; **Pop. density:** 6,498 per sq. mi.; **Pop. growth:** 21.4%. **Area:** 41 sq. mi. **Employment:** 1,279,875 employed, 5.3% unemployed; **Per capita income:** $24,400; % change 1980-90: 86.9.

History: founded 1858; inc. 1876; now known as home of Disneyland (since 1955).

Transportation: 3 municipal airports; 4 railroads; Greyhound buses. **Communications:** 12 TV, 4 radio stations; CATV. **Medical facilities:** 6 general hospitals. **Educational facilities:** 3 colleges, 5 junior colleges; 62 elementary, 8 junior high, 8 high schools. **Further information:** Chamber of Commerce, 100 South Anaheim Blvd., Suite 300, Anaheim, CA 92805.

Anchorage, Alaska

Population: 226,338; **Pop. density:** 131 per sq. mi.; **Pop. growth:** 29.8%. **Area:** 1,732 sq. mi. **Employment** (1990): 111,068 employed, 5.2% unemployed; **Per capita income:** $25,035; % change 1980-90: 66.7.

History: founded 1914 as a construction camp for railroad; HQ of Alaska Defense Command, WWII; severely damaged in earthquake 1964.

Transportation: 1 international airport, 3 other airports. **Communications:** 6 TV, 16 radio stations. **Medical facilities:** 3 hospitals. **Educational facilities:** 2 univ., 1 comm. college. **Further information:** Chamber of Commerce, 437 E St., Anchorage, AK 99501.

Arlington, Texas

Population: 261,721; **Pop. density:** 3,313 per sq. mi.; **Pop. growth:** 63.5%. **Area:** 79 sq. mi. **Employment:** 677,742 employed, 7.8% unemployed; **Per capita income:** $18,478; % change 1980-90: 72.7.

History: settled in 1840s between Dallas & Ft. Worth; inc. 1884.

Transportation: Dallas/Ft. Worth airport is 20 minutes away; 11 railway lines; intercity transport system in planning stage. **Communications:** 13 TV, 53 radio stations; CATV. **Medical facilities:** 4 hospitals. **Educational facilities:** 51 public schools; 1 univ. **Further information:** Chamber of Commerce, 316 W. Main St., Arlington, TX 76010.

Atlanta, Georgia

Population: 394,017; **Pop. density:** 3,008 per sq. mi.; **Pop. growth:** –7.3%. **Area:** 131 sq. mi. **Employment:** 1,444,109 employed, 4.9% unemployed; **Per capita income:** $20,263; % change 1980-90: 98.6.

History: founded as "Terminus" 1837; renamed Atlanta 1845 after Atlantis; inc. 1847; played major role in Civil War and burned during Gen. Sherman's "March to the Sea."

Transportation: 1 international airport; 7 railroad lines, 2 systems; 2 bus terminals; rapid rail. **Communications:** 9 TV, 41 radio stations; 21 cable TV companies. **Medical facilities:** 60 hospitals; VA hospital; Natl. Centers for Disease Control; Natl. Cancer Center. **Educational facilities:** 37 colleges, universities, seminaries, junior colleges. **Further information:** Chamber of Commerce, 235 International Blvd., Atlanta, GA 30303.

Aurora, Colorado

Population: 222,103; **Pop. density:** 3,702 per sq. mi.; **Pop. growth:** 40.1%. **Area:** 60 sq. mi. **Employment:** 844,801 employed, 5.7% unemployed; **Per capita income:** $20,885 (1988); % change 1980-90: 76.9.

History: residential suburb 5 mi. east of Denver; fast-growing trade center for large livestock and farm area.

Transportation: 1 international airport; 4 railroads; 2 bus lines; city bus system. **Further information:** ECO Aurora, Inc., 1470 S. Havana, Ste. 708, Aurora, CO 80012.

Austin, Texas

Population: 465,622; **Pop. density:** 4,014 per sq. mi.; **Pop. growth:** 34.6%. **Area:** 116 sq. mi. **Employment:** 429,271 employed, 5.7% unemployed; **Per capita income:** $17,345; % change 1980-90: 85.0.

History: first permanent settlement 1835; capital of Rep. of Texas 1838; named after Stephen Austin; inc. 1840.

Transportation: 1 international airport; 4 railroads. **Communications:** 5 TV, 18 radio stations. **Medical facilities:** 15 hospitals. **Educational facilities:** 7 universities and colleges. **Further information:** Chamber of Commerce, P.O. Box 1967, Austin, TX 78767.

Bakersfield, California

Population: 174,820; **Pop. density:** 2,033 per sq. mi.; **Pop. growth:** 65.5%. **Area:** 86 sq. mi. **Employment** (1990): 212,539 employed, 10.5% unemployed; **Per capita income:** $15,881; % change 1980-90: 49.4.

History: incorporated in 1898.

Transportation: 1 airport; 3 railroads; Greyhound buses; local bus system. **Medical facilities:** 4 major hospitals; 9 convalescent; 2 psychiatric; 3 physical rehab.

(1) Based on 1990 census, the 100 most populated cities (inc.=incorporated; est.=established; NA=not available).

centers; 3 clinics; 2 urgent care centers. **Educational facilities:** 58 public schools; 1 community college; 1 university; 9 vocational schools; 1 adult school; 1 college of law. **Further information:** Greater Bakersfield Chamber of Commerce, 1033 Truxtun Avenue, Bakersfield, CA 93301.

Baltimore, Maryland

Population: 736,014; **Pop. density:** 9,200 per sq. mi.; **Pop. growth:** −6.4%. **Area:** 80 sq. mi. **Employment:** 1,105,609 employed, 8.0% unemployed; **Per capita income:** $21,461; % change 1980-90: 101.3.

History: founded by Maryland legislature 1729; inc. 1797; bombing of its Ft. McHenry 1814 inspired Francis Scott Key to write "Star-Spangled Banner;" rebuilt after fire 1904.

Transportation: 1 major airport; 3 railroads, bus system; subway system, 2 underwater tunnels. **Communications:** 6 TV, 33 radio stations. **Medical facilities:** 29 hospitals; 2 major medical centers. **Educational facilities:** 189 public schools; over 30 universities and colleges. **Further information:** Greater Baltimore Committee, Suite 900, Two Hopkins Plaza, Baltimore, MD 21202.

Baton Rouge, Louisiana

Population: 219,531; **Pop. density:** 3,599 per sq. mi.; **Pop. growth:** −0.4%. **Area:** 61 sq. mi. **Employment:** 256,347 employed; 6.1% unemployed; **Per capita income:** $16,345; % change 1980-90: 68.5.

History: claimed by Spain at time of La. Purchase 1803; est. independence by rebellion 1810; inc. as town 1817; held by Union during most of Civil War.

Transportation: 1 airport, 7 airlines; 1 bus line; 3 railroad trunk lines. **Communications:** 5 TV, 19 radio stations; CATV. **Medical facilities:** 7 hospitals. **Educational facilities:** 96 public, 46 private schools; 2 univ. **Further information:** Chamber of Commerce, P.O. Box 3217, Baton Rouge, LA 70821.

Birmingham, Alabama

Population: 265,968; **Pop. density:** 2,687 per sq. mi.; **Pop. growth:** −6.5%. **Area:** 99 sq. mi. **Employment:** 413,164 employed, 5.7% unemployed; **Per capita income:** $17,479; % change 1980-90: 94.1.

History: settled due to discovery of elements needed for steel production; inc. 1871; named after Great Britain's steel making center.

Transportation: 1 airport; 4 major rail freight lines, Amtrak; 1 bus line; 75 truck line terminals; 4 interstate highways. **Communications:** 5 TV, 22 radio stations; 1 educational TV, 1 educational radio station. **Medical facilities:** Univ. of Alabama in Birmingham Medical Center; VA hospital with organ transplant program; 15 other hospitals. **Educational facilities:** 1 university, 2 colleges, 2 junior colleges. **Further information:** Chamber of Commerce, 2027 First Ave. N., Birmingham, AL 35202.

Boston, Massachusetts

Population: 574,283; **Pop. density:** 12,484 per sq. mi.; **Pop. growth:** 2.0%. **Area:** 46 sq. mi. **Employment:** 1,415,342 employed, 7.1% unemployed; **Per capita income:** $24,315; % change 1980-90: 118.4.

History: settled 1630 by John Winthrop; capital of Mass. Bay Colony; figured strongly in Am. Revolution, earning distinction as the "Cradle of Liberty;" inc. 1822.

Transportation: 1 major airport; 2 railroads; city rail and subway system; 2 underwater tunnels. **Communications:** 8 TV, 17 radio stations; CATV. **Medical facilities:** 16 hospitals; 8 major medical research centers. **Educational facilities:** 11 universities and colleges. **Further information:** Chamber of Commerce, Federal Reserve Bank, 600 Atlantic Ave., 13th Fl., Boston, MA 02106.

Buffalo, New York

Population: 328,123; **Pop. density:** 7,812 per sq. mi.; **Pop. growth:** −8.3%. **Area:** 42 sq. mi. **Employment:** 415,251 employed, 8.7% unemployed; **Per capita income:** $18,305; % change 1980-90: 85.6.

History: founded 1790 by the Dutch; raided twice by British during War of 1812; as western terminus for Erie Canal became a center for trade and manufacturing; inc. 1832.

Transportation: 1 international airport; 6 major railroads; metro rail system; water service to Great Lakes-St. Lawrence seaways system, and Atlantic seaboard. **Communications:** 5 TV, 23 radio stations, 2 cable systems. **Medical facilities:** 21 hospitals. **Educational facilities:** 2 universities, 9 colleges; 78 public schools. **Further information:** Greater Buffalo Chamber of Commerce, 107 Delaware Ave., Buffalo, NY 14202.

Charlotte, North Carolina

Population: 395,934; **Pop. density:** 2,869 per sq. mi.; **Pop. growth:** 25.5%. **Area:** 138 sq. mi. **Employment:** 603,194 employed, 6.1% unemployed; **Per capita income:** $18,455; % change 1980-90: 105.2.

History: settled by Scotch-Irish immigrants 1740s; inc. 1767 and named after Queen Charlotte, George III's wife; scene of first major U.S. gold discovery 1799.

Transportation: 1 airport; 2 major railway lines; 2 bus lines; 200 trucking firms. **Communications:** 6 TV, 20 radio stations. **Medical facilities:** 12 hospitals, 1 medical center. **Educational facilities:** 2 universities, 5 colleges. **Further information:** Chamber of Commerce, P.O. Box 32785, Charlotte, NC 28232.

Chicago, Illinois

Population: 2,783,726; **Pop. density:** 12,209 per sq. mi.; **Pop. growth:** −7.4%. **Area:** 228 sq. mi. **Employment:** 2,992,903 employed, 8.5% unemployed; **Per capita income:** $22,385; % change 1980-90: 90.9.

History: site acquired from Indians 1795; area began settlement with opening of Erie Canal 1825; chartered as city 1837; boomed with arrival of railroads from east and canal to Mississippi R.; much of city destroyed by fire 1871; major grain & livestock market.

Transportation: 3 airports; major railroad system; major trucking industry. **Communications:** 9 TV, 31 radio stations. **Medical facilities:** over 123 hospitals. **Educational facilities:** 95 institutions of higher learning. **Further information:** Association of Commerce and Industry, 200 N. LaSalle St., Chicago, IL 60601.

Cincinnati, Ohio

Population: 364,040; **Pop. density:** 4,667 per sq. mi.; **Pop. growth:** −5.5%. **Area:** 78 sq. mi. **Employment:** 775,228 employed, 6.0% unemployed; **Per capita income:** $19,010; % change 1980-90: 89.9.

History: founded 1788 and named after the Society of Cincinnati, an organization of Revolutionary War officers; chartered as village 1802; inc. as city 1819.

Transportation: 1 international airport; 3 railroads; 1 bus system. **Communications:** 6 TV, 3 CATV systems; 27 radio stations. **Medical facilities:** 32 hospitals; Children's Hospital Medical Center; VA hospital. **Educational facilities:** 4 universities; 5 colleges, 8 technical & 2-year colleges. **Further information:** Chamber of Commerce, 300 Carew Tower, 441 Vine St., Cincinnati, OH 45202.

Cleveland, Ohio

Population: 505,616; **Pop. density:** 6,400 per sq. mi.; **Pop. growth:** −11.9%. **Area:** 79 sq. mi. **Employment:**

869,106 employed, 6.9% unemployed; **Per capita income:** $20,758; % change 1980-90: 84.5.

History: surveyed in 1796; inc. as village 1814, as city 1836; annexed Ohio City 1854.

Transportation: 1 intl. airport; rail service; major port; rapid transit system. **Communications:** 7 TV, 20 radio stations. **Medical facilities:** numerous hospitals; major medical research center. **Educational facilities:** 124 public schools; 8 universities and colleges. **Further information:** Convention & Visitor's Bureau, 3100 Terminal Tower, Cleveland, OH 44115.

Colorado Springs, Colorado

Population: 281,140; **Pop. density:** 2,730 per sq. mi.; **Pop. growth:** 30.7%. **Area:** 103 sq. mi. **Employment** (1990): 178,193 employed, 6.3% unemployed; **Per capita income:** $16,807; % change 1980-90: 83.2.

History: founded 1859 at the foot of Pikes Peak; inc. 1886.

Transportation: 1 municipal airport; 2 railroads; Greyhound-Trailways bus line. **Communications:** 5 TV, 22 radio stations. **Medical facilities:** 9 hospitals. **Educational facilities:** 3 universities, 7 colleges. **Further information:** Chamber of Commerce, P.O. Drawer B, Colorado Springs, CO 80901.

Columbus, Georgia

Population: 179,278; **Pop. density:** 822 per sq. mi.; **Pop. growth:** 5.4%. **Area:** 218 sq. mi. **Employment** (1990): 93,912 employed, 6.1% unemployed; **Per capita income:** $14,722; % change 1980-90: 100.5.

History: settled and inc. 1828; a port city on Chattahouchee R.

Transportation: 1 airport; metro bus system; 2 bus lines; 2 railroads. **Communications:** 5 TV, 11 radio stations. **Medical facilities:** 5 hospitals. **Educational facilities:** 53 public schools; 1 college. **Further information:** Chamber of Commerce, P.O. Box 1200, Columbus, GA 31902.

Columbus, Ohio

Population: 632,910; **Pop. density:** 3,497 per sq. mi.; **Pop. growth:** 12.0%. **Area:** 181 sq. mi. **Employment:** 699,231 employed, 5.6% unemployed; **Per capita income:** $18,319; % change 1980-90: 90.6.

History: first settlement 1797; laid out as new capital 1812 with current name; became city 1834.

Transportation: 2 airports; 3 railroads; 4 intercity bus lines. **Communications:** 5 TV, 19 radio stations. **Medical facilities:** 22 hospitals. **Educational facilities:** 12 universities and colleges. **Further information:** Chamber of Commerce, P.O. Box 1527, Columbus, OH 43216.

Corpus Christi, Texas

Population: 257,453; **Pop. density:** 2,476 per sq. mi.; **Pop. growth:** 10.9%. **Area:** 104 sq. mi. **Employment** (1990): 151,158 employed, 6.9% unemployed; **Per capita income:** $14,813; % change 1980-90: 65.5.

History: settled 1839 and inc. 1852.

Transportation: 1 international airport; 2 bus lines, metro bus system; 3 freight railroads. **Communications:** 6 TV, 17 radio stations. **Medical facilities:** 14 hospitals including a children's center. **Educational facilities:** 54 public schools; 1 univ., 1 college. **Further information:** Chamber of Commerce, PO Box 640, Corpus Christi, TX 78403.

Dallas, Texas

Population: 1,006,877; **Pop. density:** 3,024 per sq. mi.; **Pop. growth:** 11.3%. **Area:** 333 sq. mi. **Employment:** 1,339,254 employed, 7.8% unemployed; **Per capita income:** $20,522; % change 1980-90: 75.4.

History: first settled 1841; platted 1846; inc. 1871; developed as the financial and commercial center of Southwest; known for its oil industry and cotton market.

Transportation: 1 international airport; Amtrak; major transit system. **Communications:** 10 TV, 49 radio stations. **Medical facilities:** 70 hospitals; major medical center. **Educational facilities:** 7 univ., 2 colleges. **Further information:** Chamber of Commerce, 1201 Elm, Dallas, TX 75270.

Dayton, Ohio

Population: 182,044; **Pop. density:** 3,793 per sq, mi.; **Pop, growth:** −5.9%. **Area:** 48 sq. mi. **Employment:** 442,795 employed, 6.9% unemployed; **Per capita income:** $17,965; % change 1980-90: 84.4.

History: settled 1796; inc. 1805; disastrous flood 1913; site where Wright Bros. invented first airplane to sustain flight 1903.

Transportation: 1 international airport, 12 airlines, 2 railroads; 4 bus lines; countywide Dayton Regional Transit Authority. **Communications:** 5 TV, 8 radio stations. **Medical facilities:** 15 hospitals including VA facility. **Educational facilities:** 26 institutions of higher learning. **Further information:** Dayton Area Chamber of Commerce, Fifth and Main, Chamber Plaza, Dayton, OH 45402.

Denver, Colorado

Population: 467,610; **Pop. density:** 4,213 per sq. mi.; **Pop. growth:** −5.1%. **Area:** 111 sq. mi. **Employment:** 844,801 employed, 5.7% unemployed; **Per capita income:** $20,885; % change 1980-90: 76.9.

History: settled 1858 by gold prospectors and miners; inc. 1861; growth spurred by gold and silver boom; the financial and industrial center of Rocky Mt. region.

Transportation: 1 international airport; 5 major rail freight lines, Amtrak; 2 bus lines. **Communications:** 7 TV, 35 radio stations. **Medical facilities:** 34 hospitals. **Educational facilities:** 2 universities; 3 colleges. **Further information:** Chamber of Commerce, 1301 Welton St., Denver, CO 80204.

Des Moines, Iowa

Population: 193,187 **Pop. density:** 2,927 per sq. mi.; **Pop. growth:** 1.1%. **Area:** 66 sq. mi. **Employment** (1990): 227,940 employed, 3.2% unemployed; **Per capita income:** $19,662; % change 1980-90: 78.5.

History: Fort Des Moines built 1843; settled and inc. 1851; chartered as city 1857.

Transportation: 1 international airport; 3 bus lines; 4 railroads; metro bus system. **Communications:** 5 TV, 18 radio stations; CATV. **Medical facilities:** 8 hospitals. **Educational facilities:** 1 univ., 2 colleges. **Further information:** Chamber of Commerce, 8th & High Sts., Des Moines, IA 50309.

Detroit, Michigan

Population: 1,027,974; **Pop. density:** 7,559 per sq. mi.; **Pop. growth:** −14.6%. **Area:** 136 sq. mi. **Employment:** 1,900,789 employed, 10.0% unemployed; **Per capita income:** $20,453; % change 1980-90: 83.1.

History: founded by French 1701; controlled by British 1760; acquired by U.S. 1796; destroyed by fire 1805; capital of state 1837-47; inc. as city 1824; auto manufacturing began 1899.

Transportation: 1 international airport; 10 railroads; major international port; public transit system. **Communications:** 9 TV, 37 radio stations. **Medical facilities:** 28 hospitals, major medical center. **Educational facilities:** 13 universities and colleges. **Further information:** Chamber of Commerce, 150 Michigan Avenue, Detroit, MI 48226.

El Paso, Texas

Population: 515,342; **Pop. density:** 2,156 per sq. mi. **Pop. growth:** 21.2%. **Area:** 239 sq. mi. **Employment:** 224,377 employed, 12.4% unemployed; **Per capita income:** $11,545; % change 1980-90: 71.8.

History: first settled 1827; inc. 1873; arrival of railroad 1881 boosted city's population and industries.

Transportation: International airport; 5 major rail lines; 8 bus lines; 9 major highways; gateway to Mexico. **Communications:** 6 TV, 23 radio stations. **Medical facilities:** 16 hospitals; cancer treatment center. **Educational facilities:** 2 colleges and universities. **Further information:** Convention and Visitors Bureau, 5 Civic Center Plaza, El Paso, TX 79901.

Fort Wayne, Indiana

Population: 173,072; **Pop. density:** 3,328 per sq. mi.; **Pop. growth:** 0.4%. **Area:** 52 sq. mi. **Employment** (1990): 189,481 employed, 5.3% unemployed; **Per capita income:** $18,570; % change 1980-90: 89.8.

History: French fort 1680; U.S. fort 1794; settled by 1832; inc. 1840 prior to Wabash-Erie canal completion 1843.

Transportation: 1 airport, 9 airlines; 3 railroads; 5 bus lines. **Communications:** 5 TV stations; 13 radio stations. **Medical facilities:** 3 major hospitals; VA hospital. **Educational facilities:** 82 public schools; 5 colleges. **Further information:** Chamber of Commerce, 826 Ewing Street, Fort Wayne, IN 46802.

Fort Worth, Texas

Population: 447,619; **Pop. density:** 1,865 per sq. mi.; **Pop. growth:** 16.2%. **Area:** 240 sq. mi. **Employment:** 677,742 employed, 7.8% unemployed; **Per capita income:** $18,478; % change 1980-90: 72.7.

History: est. as military post 1849; inc. 1873; oil discovered 1917; Fort Worth is a sister city to Dallas.

Transportation: 1 intl. airport; 8 major railroads, Amtrak; local bus service; 2 transcontinental, 2 intrastate bus lines. **Communications:** 9 TV, 37 radio stations. **Medical facilities:** 35 hospitals; 2 children's hospitals; 4 government hospitals. **Educational facilities:** 8 colleges & universities. **Further information:** Chamber of Commerce, 700 Throckmorton, Fort Worth, TX 76102.

Fremont, California

Population: 173,339; **Pop. density:** 2,211 per sq. mi.; **Pop. growth:** 31.4%. **Area:** 78.4 sq. mi. **Employment** (1990): 1,052,453 employed, 4.1% unemployed; **Per capita income:** $23,452.

History: area first settled by Spanish 1769; during 1800s a collection of towns formed the area; inc. 1956.

Transportation: intracity bus line; Bay Area Rapid Transit System (southern terminal). **Communications:** NA. **Medical facilities:** 1 hospital. **Educational facilities:** 43 public schools; 1 jr. college. **Further information:** Chamber of Commerce, One Fremont Pl., 39650 Liberty St., Ste. 130, Fremont, CA 94538.

Fresno, California

Population: 354,202; **Pop. density:** 5,449 per sq. mi.; **Pop. growth:** 62.9%. **Area:** 65 sq. mi. **Employment:** 272,468 employed, 15.0% unemployed; **Per capita income:** $16,365; % change 1980-90: 55.2.

History: founded 1872; inc. as city 1885.

Transportation: 2 municipal airports; Amtrak; 1 bus line; intracity bus system. **Communications:** 11 TV stations, 5 CATV services; 58 radio stations. **Medical facilities:** 6 general hospitals including a VA facility. **Educational facilities:** 8 colleges and univ.; 85 public schools. **Further information:** Chamber of Commerce, P.O. Box 1469, Fresno, CA 93721.

Garland, Texas

Population: 180,650; **Pop. density:** 3,226 per sq. mi.; **Pop. growth:** 30.1%. **Area:** 56 sq. mi. **Employment** (1990): 1,364,875 employed, 5.1% unemployed; **Per capita income:** $20,522; % change 1980-90: 75.4.

History: city in Dallas co., 14 mi. NE of Dallas.

Transportation: 45 miles from Dallas/Ft. Worth airport; 2 railroads. **Communications:** 3 TV stations (from Dallas). **Medical facilities:** total of 306 hospital beds. **Educational facilities:** 53 public schools; 1 univ., 2 community colleges. **Further information:** Chamber of Commerce, P.O. Box 460939, Garland, TX 75046.

Glendale, California

Population: 180,038; **Pop. density:** 5,886 per sq. mi.; **Pop. growth:** 29%. **Area:** 30.59 sq. mi. **Employment** (1990): 4,173,000 employed, 5.8% unemployed; **Per capita income:** $20,786; % change 1980-90: 77.1.

History: Township in 1887, incorporated in 1906. Adjacent to Los Angeles.

Transportation: 1 airport; 1 railroad; in triangle surrounded by 3 freeways; Southern California Rapid Transit system; Glendale Beeline bus. **Communications:** 2 radio stations, 1 cable company. **Medical facilities:** 1,100 beds in three hospitals. **Educational facilities:** 1 community college. **Further information:** Chamber of Commerce, 200 S. Louise, Glendale, CA 91205.

Grand Rapids, Michigan

Population: 189,126; **Pop. density:** 4,358 per sq. mi.; **Pop. growth:** 4.0%. **Area:** 43.4 sq. mi. **Employment:** 360,039 employed, 7.5% unemployed; **Per capita income:** $18,588; % change 1980-90: 90.2.

History: originally site of Ottowa Indian village; trading post 1826; became lumbering center and chartered as town 1850.

Transportation: 1 international airport; 4 railroads; 5 bus lines; transit bus system. **Communications:** 6 TV, 25 radio stations. **Medical facilities:** 10 hospitals. **Educational facilities:** 64 public schools; 8 colleges. **Further information:** Chamber of Commerce, 17 Fountain St., NW, Grand Rapids, MI 49503.

Greensboro, North Carolina

Population: 183,521; **Pop. density:** 3,059 per sq. mi.; **Pop. growth:** 17.9%. **Area:** 60 sq. mi. **Employment:** 488,023 employed, 5.7% unemployed; **Per capita income:** $18,621; % change 1980-90: 99.9.

History: settled 1749; site of Revolutionary War conflict 1781 between Nathanael Greene and Cornwallis; inc. 1807.

Transportation: 1 regional airport; 2 railroads; Trailways/Greyhound bus service. **Communications:** all cable TV stations; 11 radio stations. **Medical facilities:** 4 hospitals. **Educational facilities:** 38 public schools; 2

univ., 1 college. **Further information:** Chamber of Commerce, P.O. Box 3246, Greensboro, NC 27402.

Hialeah, Florida

Population: 188,004; **Pop. density:** 9,691 per sq. mi.; **Pop. growth:** 29.4%. **Area:** 19.4 sq. mi. **Employment:** NA. **Per capita income:** $17,823; % change 1980-90: 74.1.

History: inc. 1925; built over drained swamplands NW of Miami.

Transportation: Miami Int'l. airport is 5 miles away; Amtrak; 2 rail freight lines. **Communications:** NA. **Medical facilities:** 3 hospitals. **Educational facilities:** 2 universities. **Further information:** Hialeah Dept. of Eco. Development, Office of the Mayor, 501 Palm Ave., Hialeah, FL 33010.

Honolulu, Hawaii

Population: 365,272; **Pop. density:** 613 per sq. mi.; **Pop. growth:** 0.1%. **Area:** 596 sq. mi. **Employment:** 393,099 employed, 2.9% unemployed (MSA); **Per capita income:** $21,307; % change 1980-90: 96.3.

History: harbor first discovered 1794; city began 1816; became capital 1816.

Transportation: 1 major airport; large, active port for passengers and cargo. **Communications:** 10 TV, 28 radio stations. **Medical facilities:** 33 hospitals. **Educational facilities:** 163 public schools (state); 102 private schools (state); 4 univ., 1 college. **Further information:** Visitors Bureau, 2270 Kalakaua Avenue, Honolulu, HI 96815.

Houston, Texas

Population: 1,630,553; **Pop. density:** 2,933 per sq. mi.; **Pop. growth:** 2.2%. **Area:** 556 sq. mi. **Employment:** 1,639,236 employed; 7.5% unemployed; **Per capita income:** $19,175; % change 1980-90: 56.4.

History: founded 1836; inc. 1837; capital of Rep. of Texas 1837-39, 1842-45; developed rapidly after completion of canal to Gulf of Mexico 1914; important oil center.

Transportation: 2 commercial airports; 5 railroads; major bus transit system; major international port. **Communications:** 9 TV, 45 radio stations. **Medical facilities:** 59 hospitals; major medical center. **Educational facilities:** 27 universities and colleges. **Further information:** Chamber of Commerce, 1100 Milam, Houston, TX 77002.

Huntington Beach, California

Population: 181,519; **Pop. density:** 6,723 per sq. mi.; **Pop. growth:** 6.5%. **Area:** 27 sq. mi. **Employment** (1990): 1,326,417 employed, 3.3% unemployed; **Per capita income:** $24,400; % change 1980-90: 73.4.

History: settled in early 1880s; inc. 1909; oil discovered 1920, led to city's development.

Transportation: 1 airport; 1 railroad; 2 bus lines. **Communications:** 1 TV station; CATV. **Medical facilities:** 2 hospitals. **Educational facilities:** 45 public schools; 1 junior college. **Further information:** Chamber of Commerce, Seacliff Village, 2213 Main #32, Huntington Beach, CA 92648.

Indianapolis, Indiana

Population: 741,952; **Pop. density:** 2,108 per sq. mi.; **Pop. growth:** 4.3%. **Area:** 352 sq. mi. **Employment:** 642,571 employed, 4.7% unemployed; **Per capita income:** $19,522; % change 1980-90: 89.9.

History: settled in 1820, made into capital 1825.

Transportation: 1 international airport; 5 railroads; 3 interstate bus lines. **Communications:** 7 TV, 25 radio stations. **Medical facilities:** 17 hospitals; 1 major medical and research center. **Educational facilities:** 6 universities and colleges; major public library system. **Further information:** Chamber of Commerce, 320 N. Meridian Street, Indianapolis, IN 46204.

Jackson, Mississippi

Population: 196,637; **Pop. density:** 1,852 per sq. mi.; **Pop. growth:** −3.1%. **Area:** 106.2 sq. mi. **Employment** (1990): 190,476 employed, 5.3% unemployed; **Per capita income:** $15,644; % change 1980-90: 79.9.

History: originally known as Le Fleur's Bluff, selected as capital 1821 and named for Andrew Jackson; inc. 1833; scene of secession convention 1861; captured by Sherman 1863.

Transportation: 5 airlines; 2 bus lines; Ill. Central railroad. **Communications:** 5 TV, 25 radio stations. **Medical facilities:** 12 hospitals including a VA facility. **Educational facilities:** 1 univ., 5 colleges. **Further information:** Chamber of Commerce, P.O. Box 22548, Jackson, MS 39225.

Jacksonville, Florida

Population: 672,971; **Pop. density:** 885 per sq. mi.; **Pop. growth:** 17.9%. **Area:** 760 sq. mi. **Employment:** 425,169 employed, 7.7% unemployed; **Per capita income:** $17,675; % change 1980-90: 94.7.

History: settled 1816 as Cowford; renamed after Andrew Jackson 1822; inc. 1832; rechartered 1851; scene of conflicts in Seminole and Civil Wars.

Transportation: 1 international airport; 3 railroads; 2 interstate bus lines. **Communications:** 6 TV, 21 radio stations. **Medical facilities:** 14 hospitals. **Educational facilities:** 5 universities and colleges. **Further information:** Chamber of Commerce, 3 Independent Drive, P.O. Box 329, Jacksonville, FL 32201.

Jersey City, New Jersey

Population: 228,537; **Pop. density:** 17,313 per sq. mi.; **Pop. growth:** 2.2%. **Area:** 13.2 sq. mi. **Employment:** 245,237 employed, 10.3% unemployed; **Per capita income:** $18,463; % change 1980-90: 98.4.

History: bought from Indians 1830; chartered as town by British 1668; scene of Revolutionary War conflict 1779; chartered under present name 1838; important station on Underground Railroad.

Transportation: bus and subway system. **Medical facilities:** 10 hospitals. **Educational facilities:** 3 colleges. **Further information:** Chamber of Commerce & Industry of Hudson County, 911 Bergen Ave., Jersey City, NJ 07303.

Kansas City, Missouri

Population: 435,146; **Pop. density:** 1,377 per sq. mi.; **Pop. growth:** −2.9%. **Area:** 316 sq. mi. **Employment:** 820,893 employed, 5.5% unemployed; **Per capita income:** $19,482; % change 1980-90: 82.0.

History: settled by 1838 at confluence of the Missouri and Kansas rivers; inc. 1851.

Transportation: 1 international airport; a major rail center; 191 trunk lines; several barge companies. **Communications:** 7 TV, 29 radio stations. **Medical facilities:** 14 hospitals; VA facility. **Educational facilities:** 9 colleges & universities. **Further information:** Chamber of Commerce, 600 Boatmen's Center, 920 Main St., Kansas City, MO 64105.

Las Vegas, Nevada

Population: 258,295; **Pop. density:** 4,696 per sq. mi.; **Pop. growth:** 56.9%. **Area:** 55 sq. mi. **Employment:** 385,434 employed, 7.0% unemployed; **Per capita income:** $18,625; % change 1980-90: 70.5.

History: occupied by Mormons 1855-57; bought by railroad 1903; city of Las Vegas inc. 1911; gambling legalized 1931.

Transportation: 1 international airport; 2 railroads; bus system. **Communcations:** 7 TV and 28 radio stations. **Medical facilities:** 8 hospitals. **Educational facilities:** 130 public schools; 1 college; 1 univ. **Further information:** Chamber of Commerce, 2301 E. Sahara Ave., Las Vegas, NV, 89104.

Lexington–Fayette, Kentucky

Population: 225,366; **Pop. density:** 794 per sq. mi.; **Pop. growth:** 10.4%. **Area:** 284 sq. mi. **Employment** (1990): 192,241 employed, 3.6% unemployed; **Per capita income:** $18,488; % change 1980-90: 96.2.

History: site was founded and named 1775 by hunters who heard of the Revolutionary War battle at Lexington, Mass.; settled 1779; inc. 1832.

Transportation: 8 airlines, 2 railroads; city buses. **Communications:** 5 TV stations, CATV; 9 radio stations. **Medical facilities:** 5 general, 5 specialized hospitals. **Educational facilities:** 2 univ., 2 colleges. **Further information:** Chamber of Commerce, 330 East Main, Lexington, KY 40507.

Lincoln, Nebraska

Population: 191,972; **Pop. density:** 3,200 per sq. mi.; **Pop. growth:** 11.7%. **Area:** 60 sq. mi. **Employment** (1990): 128,118 employed, 1.7% unemployed; **Per capita income:** $17,816; % change 1980-90: 81.6.

History: originally called Lancaster, chosen state capital 1867 and renamed after Abraham Lincoln; inc. 1869.

Transportation: 1 airport; Greyhound, Amtrak, 2 railroads. **Communications:** 1 TV, 13 radio stations. **Medical facilities:** 4 hospitals including a VA facility. **Educational facilities:** 2 univ., 1 college, 46 public, 15 private schools. **Further information:** Chamber of Commerce, 1221 N St., Lincoln, NE 68508.

Little Rock, Arkansas

Population: 175,795; **Pop. density:** 2,225 per sq. mi.; **Pop. growth:** 10.5%. **Area:** 79 sq. mi. **Employment:** 254,628 employed, 6.8% unemployed; **Per capita income:** $16,949; % change 1980-90: 86.0.

History: founded 1821; inc. as city 1835.

Transportation: 1 airport, 7 airlines; 3 railroads; 1 bus line. **Communications:** 7 TV stations; 34 radio stations. **Medical facilities:** 16 hospitals; veterans' medical center. **Educational facilities:** 49 public schools; 8 colleges and universities; Univ. of Arkansas. **Further information:** Chamber of Commerce, One Spring St., Little Rock, AR 72201.

Long Beach, California

Population: 429,433; **Pop. density:** 8,589 per sq. mi.; **Pop. growth:** 18.8%. **Area:** 50 sq. mi. **Employment:** 4,111,000 employed, 8.6% unemployed; **Per capita income:** $20,786; % change 1980-90: 77.1.

History: settled as early as 1769 by Spanish; by 1884 present site developed due to its harbor; inc. 1888; oil discovered 1921.

Transportation: 1 airport; 3 railroads; major international port; 6 bus lines, "lite" rail service. **Communications:** CATV; 4 radio stations. **Medical facilities:** 10 hospitals. **Educational facilities:** 78 public schools; 1 university, 1 college. **Further information:** Chamber of Commerce, One World Trade Center, Long Beach, CA 90831.

Los Angeles, California

Population: 3,485,398; **Pop. density:** 7,495 per sq. mi.; **Pop. growth:** 17.4%. **Area:** 465 sq. mi. **Employment:** 4,111,000 employed, 8.6% unemployed; **Per capita income:** $20,786; % change 1980-90: 77.1.

History: founded by Spanish 1781; captured by U.S. 1846; inc. 1850; Hollywood a district of L.A.

Transportation: 1 intl. airport; 4 railroads; major freeway system; intracity transit system. **Communications:** 19 TV, 71 radio stations. **Medical facilities:** 822 hospitals and clinics. **Educational facilities:** 11 universities and colleges; 1,642 public schools; 800 private schools. **Further information:** Chamber of Commerce, 404 S. Bixel St., P.O. Box 3696, Los Angeles, CA 90051.

Louisville, Kentucky

Population: 269,063; **Pop. density:** 4,484 per sq. mi.; **Pop. growth:** −9.9%. **Area:** 60 sq. mi. **Employment:** 474,814 employed, 6.1% unemployed. **Per capita income:** $18,263; % change 1980-90: 91.5.

History: settled 1778; named for Louis XVI of France; inc. 1828; base for Union forces in Civil War.

Transportation: 2 municipal airports; 1 terminal, 6 trunk-line railroads; 3 bus lines; 5 barge lines. **Communications:** 4 TV, 20 radio stations, 2 educational, CATV. **Medical facilities:** 21 hospitals. **Educational facilities:** 10 colleges & universities, 9 business colleges & technical schools. **Further information:** Chamber of Commerce, One Riverfront Plaza, Louisville, KY 40202.

Lubbock, Texas

Population: 186,206; **Pop. density:** 2,069 per sq. mi.; **Pop. growth:** 6.8%. **Area:** 90 sq. mi. **Employment** (1990): 109,078 employed, 4.8% unemployed; **Per capita income:** $15,443; % change 1980-90: 71.6.

History: settled 1879; inc. in 1909 through merger of two towns.

Transportation: 1 international airport; 2 railroads, bus line. **Communications:** 5 TV, 18 radio stations. **Medical facilities:** 7 hospitals. **Educational facilities:** 51 public schools; 2 univ., 1 college. **Further information:** Chamber of Commerce, P.O. Box 561, Lubbock, TX 79408.

Madison, Wisconsin

Population: 191,262; **Pop. density:** 3,188 per sq. mi.; **Pop. growth:** 12.1%. **Area:** 60 sq. mi. **Employment** (1990): 221,228 employed, 2.5% unemployed; **Per capita income:** $20,087; % change 1980-90: 83.9.

History: first white settlement 1832; named after James Madison who died in 1836; chartered 1856.

Transportation: 1 airport, 8 airlines; 2 railroads; intracity bus system. **Communications:** 6 TV, 18 radio stations. **Medical facilities:** 6 hospitals. **Educational facilities:** 39 public schools; 3 colleges and universities; Univ. of Wisconsin. **Further information:** Chamber of Commerce, P.O. Box 71, Madison, WI 53701.

Memphis, Tennessee

Population: 610,337; **Pop. density:** 2,312 per sq. mi.; **Pop. growth:** −5.5%. **Area:** 264 sq. mi. **Employment:** 430,872 employed, 6.7% unemployed; **Per capita income:** $17,797; % change 1980-90: 95.7.

History: French, Spanish and U.S. forts by 1797; settled by 1819; inc. as town 1826, as city 1840; surrendered charter to state 1879 after yellow fever epidemics; rechartered as city 1893.

Transportation: 1 international airport; 6 railroads; bus system. **Communications:** 6 TV, 29 radio stations. **Medical facilities:** 21 hospitals. **Educational facilities:** 12 universities and colleges; 205 public, 76 private schools. **Further information:** Memphis Area Chamber of Commerce, 22 N. Front St., Box 224, Memphis TN 38101.

Mesa, Arizona

Population: 288,091; **Pop. density:** 4,237 per sq. mi.; **Pop. growth:** 89.0%. **Area:** 68 sq. mi. **Employment** (1990): 1,033,954 employed, 4.3% unemployed; **Per capita income:** $18,042; % change 1980-90: 76.7.

History: founded by Mormons 1878; inc. 1883; 15 mi. from Phoenix; population boomed fivefold from 1960-80.

Transportation: 1 intl. airports; 2 railroads; trolley and bus lines. **Medical facilities:** 4 major hospitals. **Educational facilities:** 49 public schools; 1 college, 1 univ. **Further information:** Convention and Visitor's Bureau, 120 N. Center, Mesa, AZ 85201.

Miami, Florida

Population: 358,548; **Pop. density:** 10,546 per sq. mi.; **Pop. growth:** 3.4%. **Area:** 34 sq. mi. **Employment:** 841,349 employed; 10.8% unemployed; **Per capita income:** $17,823; % change 1980-90: 74.1.

History: site of fort 1836; settlement began 1870; inc. 1896 and modern city developed into resort and recreation center; land speculation 1920s added to city's growth, as did Cuban immigration in 1970s and 1980s.

Transportation: 1 international airport; 2 passenger railroads, 1 all-freight; 2 bus lines; 65 truck lines. **Communications:** 6 commercial, 5 educational TV stations; 31 radio stations. **Medical facilities:** 41 hospitals, VA Hospital. **Educational facilities:** 6 colleges & universities. **Further information:** Metro-Dade Department of Tourism, 234 W. Flagler St., Miami, FL 33130.

Milwaukee, Wisconsin

Population: 628,088; **Pop. density:** 6,543 per sq. mi.; **Pop. growth:** −1.3%. **Area:** 96 sq. mi. **Employment:** 708,897 employed, 5.0% unemployed; **Per capita income:** $19,817; % change 1980-90: 78.3.

History: Indian trading post by 1674; settlement began 1835; inc. as city 1848; beer industry is famous.

Transportation: 1 international airport; 2 railroads; major port; 4 bus lines. **Communications:** 12 TV, 33 radio stations. **Medical facilities:** 25 hospitals; major medical center. **Educational facilities:** 12 universities and colleges. **Further information:** Association of Commerce, 756 N. Milwaukee Street, Milwaukee, WI 53202.

Minneapolis, Minnesota

Population: 368,383; **Pop. density:** 6,698 per sq. mi.; **Pop. growth:** −0.7%. **Area:** 55 sq. mi. **Employment:** 1,317,095 employed; 4.9% unemployed; **Per capita income:** $21,330; % change 1980-90: 85.3.

History: site visited by Hennepin 1680; included in area of military reservations 1819; inc. 1867.

Transportation: 1 international airport; 6 railroads; mass transit systems; 5 major barge lines. **Communications:** 6 TV, 39 radio stations. **Medical facilities:** 36 hospitals, including leading heart hospital at Univ. of Minnesota. **Educational facilities:** 48 public school districts; 13 colleges and universities. **Further information:** Greater Minneapolis Chamber of Commerce, 81 S. 9th St., Ste. 200, Minneapolis, MN 55402.

Mobile, Alabama

Population: 196,278; **Pop. density:** 1,596 per sq. mi.; **Pop. growth:** −2.1%. **Area:** 123 sq. mi. **Employment:** 205,323 employed, 7.0% unemployed; **Per capita income:** $14,434; % change 1980-90: 80.5.

History: settled by French 1711; later occupied by U.S. 1813; inc. as town 1814, as city 1819; only seaport of Alabama.

Transportation: 4 rail freight lines, Amtrak, 4 major airlines, 65 truck lines; leading river system. **Communications:** 7 TV, 19 radio stations; CATV. **Medical facilities:** 7 hospitals. **Educational facilities:** 1 univ., 2 colleges. **Further information:** Chamber of Commerce, P.O. Box 2187, Mobile, AL 36652.

Montgomery, Alabama

Population: 187,106; **Pop. density:** 1,462 per sq. mi.; **Pop. growth:** 5.2%. **Area:** 128 sq. mi. **Employment** (1990): 129,185 employed, 6.2% unemployed; **Per capita income:** $16,751; % change 1980-90: 99.0.

History: inc. as town 1819, as city 1837; first capital of Confederacy 1861.

Transportation: 12 airlines; 2 railroads; 1 bus line; Alabama River is navigable to Gulf of Mexico. **Communications:** 5 TV, 6 radio stations; CATV. **Medical facilities:** 16 hospitals; VA and 32 clinics. **Educational facilities:** 48 public, 28 private schools, 5 universities. **Further information:** Chamber of Commerce, P.O. Box 79, Montgomery, AL 36101.

Nashville-Davidson, Tennessee

Population: 510,784; **Pop. density:** 1,064 per sq. mi.; **Pop. growth:** 6.9%. **Area:** 480 sq. mi. **Employment:** 489,366 employed, 6.0% unemployed; **Per capita income:** $18,339; % change 1980-90: 101.9.

History: settled 1779; first chartered 1806; important Union base during Civil War; home of the Grand Ole Opry.

Transportation: 1 airport, 2 railroads; 3 bus lines; transit system. **Communications:** 7 TV, 30 radio stations. **Medical facilities:** 14 hospitals; VA Hospital, speech-hearing center. **Educational facilities:** 16 colleges & universities. **Further information:** Chamber of Commerce, 161 4th Ave., Nashville, TN 37219.

Newark, New Jersey

Population: 275,221; **Pop. density:** 11,468 per sq. mi.; **Pop. growth:** −16.4%. **Area:** 24 sq. mi. **Employment:** 865,210 employed, 7.6% unemployed; **Per capita income:** $26,600; % change 1980-90: 121.5.

History: settled by Puritans 1666; used as supply base by Washington 1776; inc. as town 1833, as city 1836.

Transportation: 1 international airport; 2 railroads; bus system; 2 subways. **Communications:** 3 TV, 5 radio stations. **Medical facilities:** 6 hospitals. **Educational facilities:** 5 universities and colleges; 71 public schools. **Further information:** Metro Newark Chamber of Commerce, 40 Clinton St., Newark, NJ 07102.

Newport News, Virginia

Population: 170,045; **Pop. density:** 2,464 per sq. mi.; **Pop. growth:** 17.4%. **Area:** 69 sq. mi. **Employment:** 599,524 employed, 7.3% unemployed; **Per capita income:** $16,613; % change 1980-90: 83.5.

History: the cities of Warwick and Newport News consolidated in 1958 into the larger city of Newport News; one of the world's major shipbuilding centers.

Transportation: 1 international airport; 2 railroads; Greyhound buses; local bus system. **Communications:** 7 TV, 20 radio stations received in area. **Medical facilities:**

3 hospitals; adolescent psychiatry hospital. **Educational facilities:** 33 public schools. **Further information:** Peninsula Chamber of Commerce, A-12, Coliseum Mall, 1800 West Mercury Blvd., Hampton, VA 23666.

New Orleans, Louisiana

Population: 496,938; **Pop. density:** 2,497 per sq. mi.; **Pop. growth:** −10.9%. **Area:** 199 sq. mi. **Employment:** 532,823 employed, 6.2% unemployed; **Per capita income:** $16,560; % change 1980-90: 69.7.

History: founded by French 1718, became major seaport on Mississippi R.; acquired by U.S. as part of La. Purchase 1803; inc. as city 1805; 29-day Battle of New Orleans fought during War of 1812.

Transportation: 2 airports; major railroad center; major international port. **Communications:** 7 TV, 18 radio stations. **Medical facilities:** numerous hospitals; major medical research center. **Educational facilities:** 13 universities and colleges. **Further information:** Chamber of Commerce, 301 Camp Street, New Orleans, LA 70130.

New York City, New York

Population: 7,322,564; **Pop. density:** 24,327 per sq. mi.; **Pop. growth:** 3.5%. **Area:** 301 sq. mi. **Employment:** 3,518,675 employed, 9.9% unemployed; **Per capita income:** $23,744; % change 1980-90: 108.6.

History: trading post established by H. Hudson 1609; British took control from Dutch 1664 and named New York; briefly capital of U.S.; Washington inaugurated as president 1789; comprised of 5 boroughs: The Bronx, Brooklyn, Manhattan, Queens, Staten Island.

Transportation: 2 airports; 2 rail terminals; major subway network; ferry system; 4 underwater tunnels. **Communications:** 13 TV stations, 117 radio stations. **Medical facilities:** 100 hospitals; 5 medical research centers. **Educational facilities:** 94 universities and colleges; 976 public schools, 914 private schools. **Further information:** Convention and Visitors Bureau, 2 Columbus Circle, New York, NY 10019.

Norfolk, Virginia

Population: 261,229; **Pop. density:** 4,929 per sq. mi.; **Pop. growth:** −2.2%. **Area:** 53 sq. mi. **Employment:** 599,524 employed, 7.3% unemployed; **Per capita income:** $16,613; % change 1980-90: 83.5.

History: founded 1682; burned by patriots to prevent capture by British during Revolutionary War; rebuilt and inc. as town 1805, as city 1845; location of world's largest naval base.

Transportation: 1 international airport; 4 major railroad systems in area. **Communications:** 7 TV, 38 radio stations. **Medical facilities:** 11 hospitals. **Educational facilities:** 53 public schools; 2 universities, 1 college. **Further information:** Hampton Roads Chamber of Commerce, 480 Bank St., Norfolk, VA 23510.

Oakland, California

Population: 372,242; **Pop. density:** 6,893 per sq. mi.; **Pop. growth:** 9.7%. **Area:** 54 sq. mi. **Employment:** 1,039,427 employed, 5.9% unemployed; **Per capita income:** $23,452; % change 1980-90: 89.6.

History: area settled by Spanish 1820; inc. as city under present name 1854.

Transportation: 1 international airport; western terminus for 3 railroads; underground, underwater 75-mile subway. **Communications:** 1 TV, 3 radio stations. **Medical facilities:** 7 hospitals, including Children's Hospital Medical Center, VA hospital. **Educational facilities:** 94 public schools; 8 "eastbay" colleges and universities. **Further information:** Chamber of Commerce, 475 14th St., Oakland, CA 94612-1903.

Oklahoma City, Oklahoma

Population: 444,719; **Pop. density:** 736 per sq. mi.; **Pop. growth:** 10.1%. **Area.** 604 sq. mi. **Employment:** 457,034 employed, 6.1% unemployed; **Per capita income:** $16,501; % change 1980-90: 55.7.

History: settled during landrush in Midwest 1889; inc. 1890; oil discovered 1928.

Transportation: 1 international airport; 3 railroads; public transit system; 5 major bus lines. **Communications:** 8 TV, 24 radio stations; cable TV. **Medical facilities:** 12 hospitals, VA hospital. **Educational facilities:** 87 public schools; 17 colleges and universities. **Further information:** Chamber of Commerce, One Santa Fe Plaza, Oklahoma City, OK 73102.

Omaha, Nebraska

Population: 335,795; **Pop. density:** 3,690 per sq. mi.; **Pop. growth:** 7.0%. **Area:** 91 sq. mi. **Employment:** 327,218 employed, 3.7% unemployed; **Per capita income:** $18,583; % change 1980-90: 83.7.

History: founded 1854; inc. 1857; large livestock market; home for U.S. Strategic Air Command.

Transportation: 8 major airlines; 4 major railroads; intercity bus line. **Communications:** 8 TV, 22 radio stations. **Medical facilities:** 17 hospitals; institute for cancer research. **Educational facilities:** 229 public, 138 private schools; 3 universities, 6 colleges. **Further information:** Chamber of Commerce, 1301 Harney St., Omaha, NE 68102.

Philadelphia, Pennsylvania

Population: 1,585,577; **Pop. density:** 11,659 per sq. mi.; **Pop. growth:** −6.1%. **Area:** 136 sq. mi. **Employment:** 2,258,027 employed, 6.9% unemployed; **Per capita income:** $21,347; % change 1980-90: 101.0.

History: first settled by Swedes 1636; by English 1681; named Philadelphia 1682; chartered 1701; Continental Congress met 1774, 1775; Dec. of Independence signed 1776; national capital 1790-1800; cap. of Penn. 1683-1799.

Transportation: 1 major airport; 3 railroads; major freshwater port; subway, el, rail commuter, bus, and streetcar system. **Communications:** 6 TV stations; 53 radio stations. **Medical facilities:** 124 hospitals. **Educational facilities:** 88 degree-granting institutions. **Further information:** Office of City Representative, 1660 Municipal Services Bldg., Philadelphia, PA 19107.

Phoenix, Arizona

Population: 983,403; **Pop. density:** 3,035 per sq. mi.; **Pop. growth:** 24.5%. **Area:** 324 sq. mi. **Employment:** 975,054 employed, 7.8% unemployed; **Per capita income:** $18,042; % change 1980-90: 76.7.

History: settled in 1870; inc. as city 1881.

Transportation: 1 intl. airport; 2 railroads; 2 transcontinental bus lines; public transit system. **Communications:** 8 TV, 35 radio stations; CATV. **Medical facilities:** 42 hospitals, 1 medical research center. **Educational facilities:** 411 public schools; 11 institutions of higher learning. **Further information:** Chamber of Commerce, 34 W. Monroe, Suite 900, Phoenix, AZ 85003.

Pittsburgh, Pennsylvania

Population: 369,879; **Pop. density:** 6,725 per sq. mi.; **Pop. growth:** −12.8%. **Area:** 55 sq. mi. **Employment:** 940,557 employed, 7.2% unemployed; **Per capita income:** $19,159; % change 1980-90: 82.7.

History: settled around Ft. Pitt 1758; inc. as city 1816; has one of largest inland ports; by Civil War, already a center for iron production.

Transportation: 1 international airport; 20 railroads; 2 bus lines; trolley/subway system. **Communications:** 6 TV, 25 radio stations. **Medical facilities:** 32 hospitals; VA installation. **Educational facilities:** 86 public schools; 3 universities, 6 colleges. **Further information:** Chamber of Commerce, 3 Gateway Ctr., Pittsburgh, PA 15222.

Portland, Oregon

Population: 437,319; **Pop. density:** 4,246 per sq. mi.; **Pop. growth:** 18.8%. **Area:** 103 sq. mi. **Employment:** 652,212 employed, 6.5% unemployed; **Per capita income:** $19,352; % change 1980-90: 74.0.

History: settled by pioneers 1845, developed as trading center, aided by California Gold Rush 1849; chartered as city 1851.

Transportation: 1 international airport; 3 major rail freight lines, Amtrak; 2 intercity bus lines; 27-mi. frontage freshwater port; mass transit bus and rail system. **Communications:** 5 TV, 23 radio stations. **Medical facilities:** 32 hospitals; VA hospital. **Educational facilities:** 11 colleges and universities, 3 community colleges. **Further information:** Chamber of Commerce, 221 N.W. 2nd Ave., Portland, OR 97209.

Raleigh, North Carolina

Population: 207,951; **Pop. density:** 3,851 per sq. mi.; **Pop. growth:** 38.4%. **Area:** 54 sq. mi. **Employment:** 405,432 employed, 4.2% unemployed; **Per capita income:** $19,814; % change 1980-90: 110.5.

History: named after Sir Walter Raleigh, site chosen for capital 1788; laid out 1792; inc. 1795; occupied by Gen. Sherman 1865.

Transportation: 1 airport, 7 airlines; 3 railroads; 1 bus line. **Communications:** 6 TV stations; 20 radio stations. **Medical facilities:** 11 hospitals. **Educational facilities:** 4 colleges and universities, 4 junior colleges; 82 public schools. **Further information:** Chamber of Commerce, 800 S. Salisbury St., P.O. Box 2978, Raleigh, NC 27602.

Richmond, Virginia

Population: 203,056; **Pop. density:** 3,384 per sq. mi.; **Pop. growth:** −7.4%. **Area:** 60 sq. mi. **Employment:** 441,886 employed, 6.3% unemployed; **Per capita income:** $21,114; % change 1980-90: 100.1.

History: first settled 1607; attacked by British under Benedict Arnold 1781; inc. as city 1782; capital of Confederate States of America, 1861.

Transportation: 1 international airport; 4 railroads, 3 intracity bus lines; deepwater terminal accessible to ocean-going ships. **Communications:** 6 TV, 26 radio stations; CATV. **Medical facilities:** Medical Coll. of Virginia renowned for heart and kidney transplants; 19 other hospitals including VA facility. **Educational facilities:** 173 public, 45 private schools; 9 colleges and universities. **Further information:** Chamber of Commerce, P.O. Box 12324, Richmond, VA 23241.

Riverside, California

Population: 226,505; **Pop. density:** 3,190 per sq. mi.; **Pop. growth:** 32.8%. **Area:** 71 sq. mi. **Employment:** 996,742 employed, 9.8% unemployed; **Per capita income:** $16,755; % change 1980-90: 66.1.

History: founded 1870; inc. 1886; known for its citrus industry.

Communications: 11 TV, 13 radio stations. **Educational facilities:** 1 univ., 1 college. **Further information:** Chamber of Commerce, 4261 Main St., Riverside, CA 92501.

Rochester, New York

Population: 231,636; **Pop. density:** 6,813 per sq. mi.; **Pop. growth:** −4.2%. **Area:** 34 sq. mi. **Employment:** 475,377 employed, 6.5% unemployed; **Per capita income:** $20,338; % change 1980-90: 91.7.

History: first permanent white settlement 1812; inc. as village 1817, as city 1834; developed as Erie Canal town.

Transportation: 1 airport; Amtrak; 3 bus lines; intracity transit service; Port of Rochester. **Communications:** 5 TV, 18 radio stations. **Medical facilities:** 8 general hospitals. **Educational facilities:** 10 colleges, 3 community colleges. **Further information:** Chamber of Commerce, 55 St. Paul St., Rochester, NY 14604.

Sacramento, California

Population: 369,365; **Pop. density:** 3,848 per sq. mi.; **Pop. growth:** 34.0%. **Area:** 96 sq. mi. **Employment:** 715,641 employed, 7.8% unemployed; **Per capita income:** $19,180; % change 1980-90: 80.8.

History: settled 1839; important trading center during California Gold Rush 1840s.

Transportation: metropolitan airport; 2 mainline transcontinental rail carriers; bus and light rail system. **Communications:** 7 TV, 25 radio stations. **Medical facilities:** 8 hospitals. **Educational facilities:** 2 universities, 4 community colleges. **Further information:** Chamber of Commerce, 917 7th St., P.O. Box 1017, Sacramento, CA 95805.

St. Louis, Missouri

Population: 396,685; **Pop. density:** 6,503 per sq. mi.; **Pop. growth:** −12.4%. **Area:** 61 sq. mi. **Employment:** 1,195,276 employed, 7.6% unemployed; **Per capita income:** $20,200; % change 1980-90: 92.3.

History: founded 1764 as a fur trading post by French; acquired by U.S. 1803; chartered as city 1822; gateway to Missouri R.

Transportation: 1 international airport; major rail center, 17 trunk line railroads; major inland port; 14 bus lines; 14 barge lines. **Communications:** 6 TV, 35 radio stations. **Medical facilities:** 65 hospitals. **Educational facilities:** 5 universities, 26 colleges and seminaries. **Further information:** Regional Commerce and Growth Assoc., Ten Broadway, St. Louis, MO 63102.

St. Paul, Minnesota

Population: 272,235; **Pop. density:** 5,235 per sq. mi.; **Pop. growth:** 0.7%. **Area:** 52 sq. mi. **Employment:** 1,317,095 employed, 4.9% unemployed; **Per capita income:** $21,330; % change 1980-90: 85.3.

History: founded in early 1840s as "Pig's Eye Landing;" became capital of the Minnesota territory 1849 and chartered as St. Paul.

Transportation: 1 international airport; 6 major rail lines; 3 interstate bus lines; public transit system. **Communications:** 6 TV, 35 radio stations; CATV. **Medical facilities:** 7 hospitals. **Educational facilities:** 2 univ., 5 colleges. **Further information:** Chamber of Commerce, 600 N. Central Tower, 445 Minnesota St., St. Paul, MN 55101.

St. Petersburg, Florida

Population: 238,629; **Pop. density:** 4,186 per sq. mi.; **Pop. growth:** 0.0%. **Area:** 57 sq. mi. **Employment:** 930,789 employed, 7.5% unemployed; **Per capita income:** $18,274; % change 1980-90: 95.4.

History: settled in 1888; inc. 1892.

Transportation: 1 international airport; bus system; 1 full-service port. **Communications:** 9 TV, 49 radio stations. **Medical facilities:** 9 hospitals. **Educational facilities:** 128 public schools; 6 colleges. **Further information:**

Chamber of Commerce, P.O. Box 1371, St. Petersburg, FL 33731.

San Antonio, Texas

Population: 935,933; **Pop. density:** 3,559 per sq. mi.; **Pop. growth:** 19.1%. **Area:** 263 sq. mi. **Employment:** 564,509 employed, 7.5% unemployed; **Per capita income:** $15,517; % change 1980-90: 80.5.

History: first Spanish garrison 1718; Battle at the Alamo fought here 1835; city subsequently captured by Texans; inc. 1837.

Transportation: 1 intl. airport; 4 railroads; 6 bus lines; public transit system. **Communications:** 7 TV, 31 radio stations. **Medical facilities:** 26 hospitals; major medical center. **Educational facilities:** 14 universities and colleges. **Further information:** Chamber of Commerce, 602 E. Commerce, P.O. Box 1628, San Antonio, TX 78296.

San Diego, California

Population: 1,110,549; **Pop. density:** 3,470 per sq. mi.; **Pop. growth:** 26.8%. **Area:** 320 sq. mi. **Employment:** 1,100,006 employed, 6.6% unemployed; **Per capita income:** $19,588; % change 1980-90: 84.5.

History: claimed by the Spanish 1542, first mission est. 1769; scene of conflict during Mexican-American War 1846; inc. 1850.

Transportation: 1 major airport; 1 railroad; major freeway system; bus system; trolley system. **Communications:** 8 TV, 22 radio stations. **Medical facilities:** 31 hospitals. **Educational facilities:** 5 universities, 7 colleges. **Further information:** Greater SD Chamber of Commerce, 402 W. Broadway, Suite 1000, San Diego, CA 92101-3585.

San Francisco, California

Population: 723,959; **Pop. density:** 15,934 per sq. mi.; **Pop. growth:** 6.6%. **Area:** 46 sq. mi. **Employment:** 834,471 employed, 5.4% unemployed; **Per capita income:** $29,942; % change 1980-90: 101.2.

History: sited by Spanish 1542, settled by 1776; claimed by U.S. 1846; became a major city during California Gold Rush 1849; inc. as city 1850; earthquake devasted city 1906.

Transportation: 1 major airport; intracity railway system; 2 railway transit systems; bus and railroad service; ferry system; 1 underwater tunnel. **Communications:** 14 TV and cable stations; 69 radio stations. **Medical facilities:** 23 hospitals; 1 major medical center. **Educational facilities:** 4 universities and colleges. **Further information:** Chamber of Commerce, 465 California Street, San Francisco, CA 94104.

San Jose, California

Population: 782,248; **Pop. density:** 4,951 per sq. mi.; **Pop. growth:** 24.3%. **Area:** 158 sq. mi. **Employment:** 771,483 employed, 6.3% unemployed; **Per capita income:** $25,193; % change 1980-90: 93.7.

History: founded by the Spanish 1777 between San Francisco and Monterey; briefly capital of Calif. 1849-51; inc. 1850.

Transportation: 1 international airport; 2 railroads; bus system. **Communications:** 4 TV, 14 radio stations. **Medical facilities:** 6 hospitals. **Educational facilities:** 3 universities and colleges. **Further information:** Chamber of Commerce, 180 S. Market St., San Jose, CA 95113.

Santa Ana, California

Population: 293,742; **Pop. density:** 10,879 per sq. mi.; **Pop. growth:** 44.0%. **Area:** 27 sq. mi. **Employment:** 1,279,875 employed, 5.3% unemployed (county); **Per capita income:** $24,400; % change 1980-90: 86.9.

History: founded 1869; inc. as city 1886.

Transportation: 1 airport; 5 major freeways including main Los Angeles-San Diego artery; Amtrak. **Communications:** CATV system. **Medical facilities:** 4 hospitals. **Educational facilities:** 1 university, 1 community college. **Further information:** Chamber of Commerce, 600 W. Santa Ana Blvd., P.O. Box 205, Santa Ana, CA 92702.

Seattle, Washington

Population: 516,259; **Pop. density:** 6,146 per sq. mi.; **Pop. growth:** 4.5%. **Area:** 84 sq. mi. **Employment:** 1,054,941 employed, 6.1% unemployed; **Per capita income:** $22,540; % change 1980-90: 81.2.

History: settled 1851; inc. 1869; suffered severe fire 1889; played prominent role during Alaska Gold Rush 1897; growth followed opening of Panama Canal 1914; center of aircraft industry WWII.

Transportation: 1 international airport; 2 railroads; ferries serve Puget Sound, Alaska, Canada. **Communications:** 7 TV, 42 radio stations. **Medical facilities:** 27 hospitals. **Educational facilities:** 4 colleges; 11 community colleges. **Further information:** Greater Seattle Chamber of Commerce, 600 University St., Ste. 1200, Seattle, WA 98101-3186.

Shreveport, Louisiana

Population: 198,525; **Pop. density:** 2,482 per sq. mi.; **Pop. growth:** −4.1%. **Area:** 80 sq. mi. **Employment** (1990): 143,749 employed, 6.7% unemployed; **Per capita income:** $15,741; % change 1980-90: 74.0.

History: founded 1833 near site of a 160-mile log jam cleared by Capt. Henry Shreve; inc. 1839; oil discovered 1906.

Transportation: 1 airport; 2 bus lines. **Communications:** 5 TV, 16 radio stations; CATV. **Medical facilities:** 11 hospitals. **Educational facilities:** 3 univ., 3 colleges. **Further information:** Chamber of Commerce, P.O. Box 20074, Shreveport, LA 71120.

Spokane, Washington

Population: 177,196; **Pop. density:** 3,408 per sq. mi.; **Pop. growth:** 3.4%. **Area:** 52 sq. mi. **Employment** (1990): 161,428 employed, 5.4% unemployed; **Per capita income:** $16,365; % change 1980-90: 73.9.

History: settled 1872; inc. as village of Spokane Falls 1881 but destroyed in fire 1889; reinc. as city of Spokane 1891.

Transportation: 1 international airport; 2 railroads; bus system. **Communications:** 5 TV and 25 radio stations. **Medical facilities:** 6 major hospitals. **Educational facilities:** 8 colleges and universities; 14 public school districts, 11 high schools. **Further information:** Chamber of Commerce, W. 1020 Riverside Ave., P.O. Box 2147, Spokane, WA 99210.

Stockton, California

Population: 210,943; **Pop. density:** 5,274 per sq. mi.; **Pop. growth:** 42.3%. **Area:** 40 sq. mi. **Employment** (1990): 178,724 employed, 9.8% unemployed; **Per capita income:** $15,453; % change 1980-90: 48.9.

History: site purchased 1842; settled 1847; inc. 1850; chief distributing point for agricultural products of San Joaquin Valley.

Transportation: 1 airport, 7 railroads; 2 bus lines, city bus system. **Communications:** 5 TV stations. **Medical**

facilities: 4 hospitals; regional burn center. **Educational facilities:** 45 public schools; 4 colleges and universities. **Further information:** Chamber of Commerce, 445 W. Weber Ave., Suite 220, Stockton, CA 95203.

Tacoma, Washington

Population: 176,664; **Pop. density:** 3,696 per sq. mi.; **Pop. growth:** 11.5%. **Area:** 47.8 sq. mi. **Employment:** 239,410 employed, 7.9% unemployed; **Per capita income:** $16,194; % change 1980-90: 67.1.

History: discovered 1792 by the British; first permanent settlement 1864; terminus for the Northern Pacific Railroad; inc. 1884.

Transportation: 1 airport; 1 railroad; transit system; Port of Tacoma. **Communications:** NA. **Medical facilities:** 6 hospitals, VA facility. **Educational facilities:** 2 univ., 2 colleges. **Further information:** Chamber of Commerce, P.O. Box 1933, Tacoma, WA 98401-1933.

Tampa, Florida

Population: 280,015; **Pop. density:** 3,334 per sq. mi.; **Pop. growth:** 3.1%. **Area:** 84 sq. mi. **Employment:** 930,789 employed, 7.5% unemployed; **Per capita income:** $18,274; % change 1980-90: 95.4.

History: U.S. army fort on site 1824; inc. 1855.

Transportation: 1 international airport; Port of Tampa, 140 steamship lines; 2 bus lines. **Communications:** 7 TV, 27 radio stations. **Medical facilities:** 19 hospitals. **Educational facilities:** 131 public schools; 4 colleges and universities. **Further information:** Chamber of Commerce, 801 E. Kennedy Blvd., P.O. Box 420, Tampa, FL 33601.

Toledo, Ohio

Population: 332,943; **Pop. density:** 3,964 per sq. mi.; **Pop. growth:** −6.1%. **Area:** 84 sq. mi. **Employment:** 275,738 employed, 9.0% unemployed; **Per capita income:** $17,697; % change 1980-90: 75.0.

History: site of Ft. Industry, 1794; settled 1817; figured in "Toledo War" 1835-36 between Ohio and Michigan over their borders; inc. 1837.

Transportation: 10 major airlines; 9 railroads; 100 motor freight lines; 2 interstate bus lines. **Communications:** 5 TV, 17 radio stations; 4 cablevision cos. **Medical facilities:** 9 major hospital complexes. **Educational facilities:** 7 colleges and universities. **Further information:** Office of Tourism and Conventions, 218 Huron, Toledo, OH 43604.

Tucson, Arizona

Population: 405,390; **Pop. density:** 4,095 per sq. mi.; **Pop. growth:** 22.6%. **Area:** 99 sq. mi. **Employment:** 300,100 employed, 6.1% unemployed; **Per capita income:** $15,191; % change 1980-90: 72.8.

History: settled 1775 by Spanish as a presidio; acquired by U.S. in Gadsen Purchase 1853; inc. 1877.

Transportation: 1 international airport; 3 railroads; bus system. **Communications:** 6 TV, 27 radio stations; CATV. **Medical facilities:** 15 hospitals. **Educational facilities:** 2 univ., 1 college; 165 public schools. **Further information:** Chamber of Commerce, P.O. Box 991, Tucson, AZ 85702.

Tulsa, Oklahoma

Population: 367,302; **Pop. density:** 1,979 per sq. mi.; **Pop. growth:** 1.8%. **Area:** 185.6 sq. mi. **Employment:** 319,209 employed, 7.2% unemployed; **Per capita income:** $17,782; % change 1980-90: 61.5.

History: settled in 1830s by Creek Indians; modern town founded 1882 and inc. 1898; oil discovered early 20th century.

Transportation: 1 international airport; 5 rail lines; 2 bus lines; transit bus system. **Communications:** 7 TV, 23 radio stations. **Medical facilities:** 6 hospitals. **Educational facilities:** 57 public and 23 private schools; 6 colleges and universities. **Further information:** Chamber of Commerce, 616 S. Boston Ave., Tulsa, OK 74119.

Virginia Beach, Virginia

Population: 393,069; **Pop. density:** 1,541 per sq. mi.; **Pop. growth:** 49.9%. **Area:** 255 sq. mi. **Employment:** 599,524 employed, 7.3% unemployed; **Per capita income:** $16,613; % change 1980-90: 83.5.

History: area founded by Capt. John Smith 1607; formed by merger with Princess Anne co. 1963.

Transportation: 1 airport; 2 railroads; 2 bus lines; public transit system. **Communications:** 6 TV, 40 radio stations. **Medical facilities:** 2 hospitals. **Educational facilities:** 62 public schools; 1 university, 2 colleges. **Further information:** Chamber of Commerce, 4512 Virginia Beach Blvd., Virginia Beach, VA 23462.

Washington, District of Columbia

Population: 606,900; **Pop. density:** 9,633 per sq. mi.; **Pop. growth:** −4.9%. **Area:** 63 sq. mi. **Employment:** 2,088,874 employed, 5.3% unemployed; **Per capita income:** $25,363; % change 1980-90: 100.1.

History: capital of the U.S.; 10-mile-square diamond at Potomac R. chosen by George Washington 1790 on land ceded from Va. and Md.; Congress first met 1800; inc. 1802; sacked by British, War of 1812.

Transportation: 2 airports; rail transit system; extensive local bus service; 1 bus, 2 rail lines. **Communications:** 5 TV, 61 radio stations. **Medical facilities:** 43 hospitals; major medical research center. **Educational facilities:** 6 universities and colleges. **Further information:** Convention and Visitors Association, 1411 K St. NW, Suite 500, Washington, DC 20005.

Wichita, Kansas

Population: 304,011; **Pop. density:** 3,010 per sq. mi.; **Pop. growth:** 8.6%. **Area:** 101 sq. mi. **Employment:** 250,824 employed, 4.3% unemployed; **Per capita income:** $18,825; % change 1980-90: 69.4.

History: founded 1864; inc. 1871.

Transportation: 1 airport; 3 major rail freight lines; 2 bus lines. **Communications:** 5 TV, 23 radio stations. **Medical facilities:** 7 hospitals. **Educational facilities:** 95 public schools; 2 univ., 2 colleges. **Further information:** Chamber of Commerce, 350 W. Douglas, Wichita, KS 67202.

Yonkers, New York

Population: 188,082; **Pop. density:** 10,449 per sq. mi.; **Pop. growth:** −3.7%. **Area:** 18 sq. mi. **Employment** (city): 96,287 employed, 7.1% unemployed; **Per capita income:** $23,744.

History: founded 1641 by the Dutch; inc. as town 1855; chartered as city 1872; borders NYC to the North.

Transportation: intracity bus system; rail service. **Communications:** see New York City. **Medical facilities:** 3 hospitals. **Educational facilities:** 30 public schools; 3 colleges. **Further information:** Chamber of Commerce, 480 N. Broadway, Yonkers, NY 10701.

STATES AND OTHER AREAS OF THE U.S.

Sources: Population: Commerce Dept., Bureau of the Census (1991 est., inc. armed forces personnel in each state but excluding such personnel stationed overseas); area: Bureau of the Census, Geography Division; forested land: Agriculture Dept., Forest Service; lumber production: Bureau of the Census, Industry Division; mineral production: Interior Dept., Bureau of Mines; commercial fishing: Commerce Dept., Natl. Marine Fisheries Service; value of construction: McGraw-Hill Information Systems Co., F.W. Dodge Division; per capita income: Commerce Dept., Bureau of Economic Analysis; unemployment: Labor Dept., Bureau of Labor Statistics; finance: Federal Deposit Insurance Corp., U.S. League of Savings Institutions; federal employees: Labor Dept., Office of Personnel Management; energy: Energy Dept., Energy Information Administration; education: Education Dept., National Education Assn. Other information from sources in individual states, usually Commerce Dept.

Alabama

Heart of Dixie, Camellia State

People. Population (1991): 4,089,232; **rank:** 22. **Pop. density:** 80.6 per sq. mi. **Racial distrib.** (1990): 73.6% White; 25.3% Black; 0.6% Hispanic. **Net change** (1990-91): 1.2%.

Geography. Total area: 51,705 sq. mi.; **rank:** 29. **Land area:** 50,750 sq. mi. **Acres forested land:** 21,725,000. **Location:** in the east south central U.S., extending N-S from Tenn. to the Gulf of Mexico; east of the Mississippi River. **Climate:** long, hot summers; mild winters; generally abundant rainfall. **Topography:** coastal plains inc. Prairie Black Belt give way to hills, broken terrain; highest elevation, 2,407 ft. **Capital:** Montgomery.

Economy. Principal industries: pulp and paper, chemicals, electronics, apparel, textiles, primary metals, lumber and wood prods., food processing, fabricated metals, automotive tires, oil and gas exploration. **Principal manufactured goods** (1991-1992): electronics, cast iron and plastic pipe, fabricated steel prods., ships, paper products, chemicals, steel, mobile homes, fabrics, poultry processing, soft drinks, furniture, tires. **Agriculture: Chief crops** (1991-92): peanuts, cotton, soybeans, cottonseed, catfish, hay, corn, wheat, potatoes, pecans, peaches, sweet potatoes. **Livestock** (1990): 1.8 mln. cattle; 400,000 hogs/pigs; 14.8 mln. poultry, 2.7 mln. foodsize catfish. **Timber/lumber** (1990): pine, hardwoods; 2.2 bln. bd. ft. **Nonfuel Minerals** (1991): $531 mln., mostly stone, cement, clays, lime, sand & gravel. **Commercial fishing** (1991): $36.7 mln. **Chief ports:** Mobile. **Value of construction** (1991): $2.7 bln. **Employment distribution** (1991): 20% mfg.; 35% trade; 16% serv. **Per capita income** (1991): $15,567. **Unemployment** (1991): 7.2%. **Tourism** (1991): tourists spent $3.4 bln. **Sales Tax** (1991): 4%.

Finance. FDIC-insured commercial banks & trust companies (1990): 221. **Deposits:** $29.7 bln. **Savings institutions** (1991): 27. **Assets:** $4.9 bln.

Federal government. No. federal civilian employees (Mar. 1991): 45,831. **Avg. salary:** $32,678. **Notable federal facilities:** George C. Marshall NASA Space Center, Huntsville; Gunter & Maxwell AFB, Montgomery; Ft. Rucker, Ozark; Ft. McClellan, Anniston; Natl. Fertilizer Development Center, Muscle Shoals; Navy Station & U.S. Corps of Engineers, Mobile; Redstone Arsenal, Huntsville.

Energy. Electricity production (1991, MWh, by source): Hydroelectric: 11.9 mln. Mineral: 45.5 mln. Nuclear: 19.4 mln.

Education. Student-teacher ratio (1990): 19.9. **Avg. salary, public school teachers** (1991-92): $26,954.

State data. Motto: We dare defend our rights. **Flower:** Camellia. **Bird:** Yellowhammer. **Tree:** Southern Pine. **Song:** Alabama. **Entered union** Dec. 14, 1819; rank, 22d. **State fair** at: Birmingham; early Oct.

History. First Europeans were Spanish explorers in the early 1500s. The French made the first permanent settlement, on Mobile Bay, 1701-02; later, English settled in the northern areas. France ceded the entire region to England at the end of the French and Indian War, 1763, but Spanish Florida claimed the Mobile Bay area until U. S. troops took it, 1813. Gen. Andrew Jackson broke the power of the Creek Indians, 1814, and they were removed to Oklahoma. The Confederate States were organized Feb. 4, 1861, at Montgomery, the first capital.

Tourist attractions. Jefferson Davis' "first White House" of the Confederacy; Montgomery's Civil Rights Memorial; Ivy Green, Helen Keller's birthplace, Tuscumbia; statue of Vulcan, Birmingham; George Washington Carver Museum, Tuskegee Univ.; W.C. Handy Home & Museum, Florence; Alabama Space and Rocket Center, Huntsville; Alabama Shakespeare Festival, Montgomery; Moundville State Monument, Moundville; Pike Pioneer Museum, Troy, USS Alabama Memorial Park, Mobile; 28 hunting areas, 24 public lakes, 82 campgrounds, 21 state parks.

At Russell Cave National Monument, near Bridgeport: a detailed record of occupancy by humans from about 10,000 BC to 1650 AD.

Famous Alabamians include Hank Aaron, Tallulah Bankhead, Hugo L. Black, Paul "Bear" Bryant, George Washington Carver, Nat King Cole, William C. Handy, Bo Jackson, Helen Keller, Harper Lee, Joe Louis, Willie Mays, John Hunt Morgan, Jesse Owens, George Wallace, Booker T. Washington, Hank Williams.

Alabama Business Council (State Chamber of Commerce). 468 S. Perry St., P.O. Box 76, Montgomery, AL 36195.

Toll-free travel information. 1-800-392-8096; 1-800-ALABAMA out of state.

Alaska

The Last Frontier (unofficial)

People. Population (1991): 570,345; **rank:** 48. **Racial distrib.** (1990): 75.5% White; 4.1% Black; 3.2% Hispanic; 15.6% Amer. Ind., Eskimo or Aleut; 3.6% Asian or Pacific Is. **Pop. density:** 0.99 per sq. mi. **Net change** (1990-91): 3.7%.

Geography. Total area: 591,000 sq. mi.; **rank:** 1. **Land area:** 570,373 sq. mi. **Acres forested land:** 129,045,000. **Location:** NW corner of North America, bordered on east by Canada. **Climate:** SE, SW, and central regions, moist and mild; far north extremely dry. Extended summer days, winter nights, throughout. **Topography:** includes Pacific and Arctic mountain systems, central plateau, and Arctic slope. Mt. McKinley, 20,320 ft., is the highest point in North America. **Capital:** Juneau.

Economy. Principal industries: oil, gas, tourism, commercial fishing, mining, forestry. **Principal manufactured goods:** fish products, lumber and pulp, furs. **Agriculture** (1991): Chief crops: barley, hay, greenhouse nursery prods., potatoes, lettuce, milk. **Livestock** (1990): 7,500 cattle; 2,500 sheep; 5,000 poultry; 37,000 reindeer. **Timber/lumber:** spruce, yellow cedar, hemlock. **Nonfuel minerals** (1991): $539.4 mln.; crushed and broken stone, gold, sand & gravel. **Commercial fishing** (1991): $1.2 bln. **Chief ports:** Anchorage, Dutch Harbor, Kodiak, Seward, Skagway, Juneau, Sitka, Valdez, Wrangell. **International airports at:** Anchorage, Fairbanks, Ketchikan, Juneau. **Value of construction** (1991): $735 mln. **Employment distribution** (1991): 29.7% gvt.; 21.3% serv.; 19.6% trade. **Per capita income** (1991): $21,932. **Unemployment** (1991): 8.5%. **Tourism** (1987-88): $500 mln.

Finance. FDIC-insured commercial banks & trust companies (1990): 7. Deposits: $3.3 bln. **Commercial bank deposits, per capita** (1990): $7,475. **Savings institutions** (1991): 1. **Assets:** $111 mln.

Federal government. No. federal civilian employees (Mar. 1991): 11,636. **Avg. salary:** $36,468.

Energy. Electricity production (1991, MWh, by source): Hydroelectric: 0.8 mln. Mineral: 25.8 mln.

Education. Student-teacher ratio (1990): 17.0. **Avg. salary, public school teachers** (1991-92): $44,725.

State data. Motto: North to the future. **Flower:** Forget-Me-Not. **Bird:** Willow Ptarmigan. **Tree:** Sitka Spruce. **Song:** Alaska's Flag. **Entered union:** Jan. 3, 1959; rank, 49th. **State fair at:** Palmer; late Aug.—early Sept.

History. Vitus Bering, a Danish explorer working for Russia, was the first European to land in Alaska, 1741. Alexander Baranov, first governor of Russian America, set up headquarters at Archangel, near present Sitka, in 1799. Secretary of State William H. Seward in 1867 bought Alaska from Russia for $7.2 million, a bargain some called "Seward's Folly." In 1896 gold was discovered and the famed Gold Rush was on.

Tourist attractions: Portage Glacier, Mendenhall Glacier, Glacier Bay National Park, Katmai National Park & Preserve, Denali National Park, one of North America's great wildlife sanctuaries, surrounding Mt. McKinley, No. America's highest peak. Pribilof Islands fur seal rookeries, restored St. Michael's Russian Orthodox Cathedral, Sitka.

Famous Alaskans include Tom Bodett, Susan Butcher, Ernest Gruening, Sydney Laurence, Libby Riddles, Jefferson "Soapy" Smith.

Tourist information. Alaska Division of Tourism, P.O. Box 110801, Juneau, AK 99811-0801.

Arizona

Grand Canyon State

People. Population (1991): 3,749,693; **rank:** 23. **Pop. density:** 33.0 per sq. mi. **Racial distrib.** (1990): 80.8% White; 3.0% Black; 5.6% American Indian; 18.8% Hispanic. **Net change** (1990-91): 2.3%.

Geography. Total area: 114,000 sq. mi.; **rank:** 6. **Land area:** 113,642 sq. mi. **Acres forested land:** 19,384,000. **Location:** in the southwestern U.S. **Climate:** clear and dry in the southern regions and northern plateau; high central areas have heavy winter snows. **Topography:** Colorado plateau in the N, containing the Grand Canyon; Mexican Highlands running diagonally NW to SE; Sonoran Desert in the SW. **Capital:** Phoenix.

Economy: Principal industries: manufacturing, tourism, mining, agriculture. **Principal manufactured goods:** electronics, printing and publishing, foods, primary and fabricated metals, aircraft and missiles, apparel. **Agriculture: Chief crops:** cotton, sorghum, barley, corn, wheat, sugar beets, citrus fruits. **Livestock** (1992): 900,000 cattle; 100,000 hogs/pigs; 225,000 sheep; 325,000 poultry. **Timber/lumber** (1990): pine, fir, spruce; 433 mln. bd. ft. **Nonfuel Minerals** (1991): $2.8 bln.; copper, gold, molybdenum, silver. **International airports at:** Phoenix, Tucson, Yuma. **Value of construction** (1991): $4.6 bln. **Employment distribution** (1991): 25.6% services; 24.6% trade; 19.1% gvt.; 11.3% mfg. **Per capita income** (1991): $16,401. **Unemployment** (1991): 5.7%. **Tourism** (1989): tourists spent $5.6 bln. **Sales tax:** 5.0% (Maricopa, Pinal Countries, 5.5%).

Finance. FDIC-insured commercial bank & trust companies (1990): 39. **Deposits:** $25.9 bln. **Savings institutions** (1991): 1. **Assets:** $73 mln.

Federal government: No. federal civilian employees (Mar. 1991): 28,663. **Avg. salary:** $30,466. **Notable federal facilities:** Williams, Luke, Davis-Monthan AF bases; Ft. Huachuca Army Base; Yuma Proving Grounds.

Energy. Electricity production (1991, MWh, by source): Hydroelectric: 4.8 mln.; Mineral: 31.7; Nuclear: 18.7.

Education. Student-teacher ratio (1990): 19.4. **Avg. salary, public school teachers** (1991-92): $31,892.

State data. Motto: Ditat Deus (God enriches). **Flower:** Blossom of the Saguaro cactus. **Bird:** Cactus wren. **Tree:** Paloverde. **Song:** Arizona. **Entered union** Feb. 14, 1912; rank, 48th. **State fair** at: Phoenix; late Oct.–early Nov.

History. Marcos de Niza, a Franciscan, and Estevan, a black slave, explored the area, 1539. Eusebio Francisco Kino, Jesuit missionary, taught Indians Christianity and farming, 1690-1711, left a chain of missions. Spain ceded Arizona to Mexico, 1821. The U. S. took over at the end of the Mexican War, 1848. The area below the Gila River was obtained from Mexico in the Gadsden Purchase, 1854. Long Apache wars did not end until 1886, with Geronimo's surrender.

Tourist attractions. The Grand Canyon of the Colorado, an immense, vari-colored fissure 217 mi. long, 4 to 13 mi. wide at the brim, 4,000 to 5,500 ft. deep; the Painted Desert, extending for 30 mi. along U.S. 66; the Petrified Forest; Canyon Diablo, 225 ft. deep and 500 ft. wide; Meteor Crater, 4,150 ft. across, 570 ft. deep, made by a prehistoric meteor. Also, London Bridge at Lake Havasu City.

Famous Arizonans include Cochise, Geronimo, Barry Goldwater, Zane Grey, Carl Hayden, George W. P. Hunt, Helen Jacobs, Percival Lowell, Sandra Day O'Connor, William H. Pickering, John J. Rhodes, Morris Udall, Stewart Udall, Frank Lloyd Wright.

Tourist information. Phoenix & Valley of the Sun Visitor and Convention Bureau, 1-602-254-6500.

Arkansas

Land of Opportunity

People. Population (1991): 2,371,950; **rank:** 33. **Pop. density:** 45.5 per sq. mi. **Racial distrib.** (1990): 82.7% White; 15.9% Black; 0.8% Hispanic. **Net change** (1990-91): 0.9%.

Geography. Total area: 53,187 sq. mi.; **rank:** 27. **Land area:** 52,075 sq. mi. **Acres forested land:** 16,987,000. **Location:** in the west south-central U.S. **Climate:** long, hot summers, mild winters; generally abundant rainfall. **Topography:** eastern delta and prairie, southern lowland forests, and the northwestern highlands, which include the Ozark Plateaus. **Capital:** Little Rock.

Economy. Principal industries: manufacturing, agriculture, tourism, forestry. **Principal manufactured goods:** food prods., chemicals, lumber, paper, electric motors, furniture, home appliances, auto components, airplane parts, apparel, machinery, petroleum prods., steel. **Agriculture: Chief crops:** soybeans, rice, cotton, tomatoes, grapes, apples, commercial vegetables, peaches, wheat. **Livestock** (1990): 1.69 mln. cattle; 760,000 hogs/pigs; $1.84 bln. poultry. **Timber/lumber** (1990): oak, hickory, gum, cypress, pine; 1.8 bln. bd. ft. **Nonfuel Minerals** (1991): 242.5 mln.; bromine, abrasives, bauxite, sand and gravel. **Chief ports:** Little Rock, Pine Bluff, Osceola, Helena, Fort Smith, Van Buren, Camden, Dardanelle, North Little Rock, West Memphis, Crossett, McGehee. **Value of construction** (1991): $1.6 bln. **Employment distribution** (1991): 23.9% mfg.; 21.1% trade; 20.3% serv.; 16.7% gvt. **Per capita income** (1991): $14,753. **Unemployment** (1991): 7.3%. **Tourism** (1991): travelers spent $2.5 bln.

Finance. FDIC-insured commercial banks & trust companies (1990): 257. **Deposits:** $17.7 bln. **Savings institutions** (1991): 19. **Assets:** $2.5 bln.

Federal government. No. federal civilian employees (Mar. 1991): 12,249. **Avg. salary:** $29,044. **Notable federal facilities:** Nat'l. Center for Toxicological Research, Jefferson; Pine Bluff Arsenal, Little Rock AFB.

Energy. Electricity production (1991, MWh, by source): Hydroelectric: 5.8 mln.; Mineral: 14.8 mln.; Nuclear: 12.9 mln.

Education. Student-teacher ratio (1990): 16.8. **Avg. salary, public school teachers** (1991-92): $26,569.

State data. Motto: Regnat Populus (The people rule). **Flower:** Apple Blossom. **Bird:** Mockingbird. **Tree:** Pine. **Song:** Arkansas. **Entered union:** June 15, 1836; rank, 25th. **State fair at:** Little Rock; late Sept.- early Oct.

History. First European explorers were de Soto, 1541, Jolliet, 1673; La Salle, 1682. First settlement was by the French under Henri de Tonty, 1686, at Arkansas Post. In 1762 the area was ceded by France to Spain, then back again in 1800, and was part of the Louisiana Purchase by the U.S. in 1803. Arkansas seceded from the Union in 1861, only after the Civil War began, and more than 10,000 Arkansans fought on the Union side.

Tourist attractions. 5 natl. parks & 48 state parks, inc. Hot Springs National Park, water ranging from 95° to

147°F. Eureka Springs, resort since 1879; Blanchard Caverns, near Mountain View, are among the nation's largest; Crater of Diamonds, near Murfreesboro, only U.S. diamond mine; Buffalo Natl. River; Mid-America Museum, Ozark Folk Center.

Famous Arkansans include Daisy Bates, Dee Brown, Glen Campbell, Johnny Cash, Hattie Caraway, "Dizzy" Dean, Orval Faubus, James W. Fulbright, Douglas MacArthur, John L. McClellan, James S. McDonnel, Dick Powell, Winthrop Rockefeller, Mary Steenburgen, Edward Durell Stone, Archibald Yell.

Chamber of Commerce. One Spring Bldg., Little Rock, AR 72201-2486.

Toll-free travel information. 1-800-NATURAL.

California

Golden State

People. Population (1991): 30,379,872; **rank:** 1. **Pop. density:** 194.8 per sq. mi. **Racial distrib.** (1990): 69.0% White; 7.4% Black; 9.6% Asian; 25.8% Hispanic. **Net change** (1990-91): 2.1%.

Geography. Total area 158,706 sq. mi.; **rank:** 3. **Land area:** 155,973 sq. mi. **Acres forested land:** 39,381,000. **Location:** on western coast of the U.S. **Climate:** moderate temperatures and rainfall along the coast; extremes in the interior. **Topography:** long mountainous coastline; central valley; Sierra Nevada on the east; desert basins of the southern interior; rugged mountains of the north. **Capital:** Sacramento.

Economy. Principal industries: agriculture, manufacturing, services, trade. **Principal manufactured goods:** foods, printed material, primary and fabricated metals, machinery, electric and electronic equipment, transportation equipment, instruments. **Agriculture: Chief crops:** grapes, cotton, flowers, oranges, nursery products, hay, tomatoes, lettuce, strawberries, almonds, broccoli, walnuts, sugar beets, peaches, potatoes. **Livestock** (1991): 8 mln. cattle & calves; 80,000 hogs/pigs; 735,000 sheep; 34.5 mln. chickens exc. broilers. **Timber/lumber** (1990): fir, pine, redwood, oak; 5.2 bln. bd. ft. **Nonfuel Minerals:** (1991): $3.02 bln.; mostly asbestos, boron minerals, cement, diatomite, calcined gypsum, construction sand & gravel. **Commercial fishing** (1991): $139.6 mln. **Chief ports:** Long Beach, Los Angeles, San Diego, Oakland, San Francisco, Sacramento, Stockton. **International airports at:** Los Angeles, San Francisco, San Jose, San Diego. **Value of construction** (1991): $29.4 bln. **Employment distribution** (1991): 27.6% serv.; 23.3% trade; 16.2% mfg.; 16.6% gvt. **Per capita income** (1991): $20,952. **Unemployment** (1991): 7.5%. **Tourism** (1991): $48.5 bln. **Sales tax:** 7¼-8¾%.

Finance. FDIC-insured commercial banks & trust companies (1990): 479. **Deposits:** $238.6 bln. **Savings institutions** (1991): 117. **Assets:** $295.2 bln.

Federal government. No. federal civilian employees (Mar. 1991): 204,902. **Avg. salary:** $33,611. **Notable federal facilities:** Vandenberg, Beale, Travis, McClellan AF bases, San Francisco Mint.

Energy. Electricity production (1991, MWh, by source): Hydroelectric: 13.2 mln.; Mineral: 36.9 mln.; Nuclear: 34.7 mln.

Education. Student-teacher ratio (1990): 22.8. **Avg. salary, public school teachers** (1991-92): $41,811.

State Data. Motto: Eureka (I have found it). **Flower:** Golden poppy. **Bird:** California valley quail. **Tree:** California redwood. **Song:** I Love You, California. **Entered Union** Sept. 9, 1850; rank, 31st. **State fair** at: Sacramento; late Aug.—early Sept.

History. First European explorers were Cabrillo, 1542, and Drake, 1579. First settlement was the Spanish Alta California mission at San Diego, 1769, first in a string founded by Franciscan Father Junipero Serra. U. S. traders and settlers arrived in the 19th century and staged the abortive Bear Flag Revolt, 1846; the Mexican War began later in 1846 and U.S. forces occupied California; Mexico ceded the province to the U.S., 1848, the same year the Gold Rush began.

Tourist attractions. Scenic regions are Yosemite Valley; Lassen and Sequoia-Kings Canyon national parks; Lake Tahoe; the Mojave and Colorado deserts; San Francisco Bay; Napa Valley; and Monterey Peninsula. Oldest living things on earth are believed to be a stand of Bristlecone pines in the Inyo National Forest, est. to be 4,600 years old. The world's tallest tree, the Howard Libbey redwood, 362 ft. with a girth of 44 ft., stands on Redwood Creek, Humboldt County.

Also, RMS Queen Mary, Spruce Goose, both Long Beach; Palomar Observatory; Disneyland; J. Paul Getty Museum, Malibu; Tournament of Roses and Rose Bowl; Universal Studios, Hollywood; Los Angeles County Art Museum; San Diego Zoo.

Famous Californians include Luther Burbank, John C. Fremont, Bret Harte, Wm. R. Hearst, Jack London, Aimee Semple McPherson, John Muir, Richard M. Nixon, William Saroyan, Junipero Serra, Leland Stanford, John Steinbeck, Earl Warren.

Chamber of Commerce: 1201 K St., Sacramento, CA 95814.

Toll-free travel information. 1-800-862-2543, x T100.

Colorado

Centennial State

People. Population (1991): 3,376,669; **rank:** 26. **Pop. density:** 32.6 per sq. mi. **Racial distrib.** (1990): 88.2% White; 4.0% Black; 12.9% Hispanic. **Net change** (1990-91): 2.5%.

Geography. Total area: 104,091 sq. mi.; **rank:** 8. **Land area:** 103,730 sq. mi. **Acres forested land:** 21,338,000. **Location:** in west central U.S. **Climate:** low relative humidity, abundant sunshine, wide daily, seasonal temperatures ranges; alpine conditions in the high mountains. **Topography:** eastern dry high plains; hilly to mountainous central plateau; western Rocky Mountains of high ranges alternating with broad valleys and deep, narrow canyons. **Capital:** Denver.

Economy. Principal industries: manufacturing, government, tourism, agriculture, aerospace, electronics equipment. **Principal manufactured goods:** computer equipment, instruments, foods, machinery, aerospace products. **Agriculture: Chief crops:** corn, wheat, hay, sugar beets, barley, potatoes, apples, peaches, pears, dry edible beans, sorghum, onions, oats. **Livestock** (1989): 2.8 mln. cattle; 220,000 hogs/pigs; 825,000 sheep; 4.0 mln. poultry. **Timber/lumber** (1990): oak, ponderosa pine, Douglas fir; 130 mln. bd. ft. **Nonfuel Minerals** (1991): $386 mln.; gold, construction sand & gravel, crushed stone. **International airports at:** Denver. **Value of construction** (1991): $4.5 bln. **Employment distribution** (1987 est.): 26.7% serv.; 20.8% trade; 17.0% gvt.; 10.0% mfg. **Per capita income** (1991): $19,440. **Unemployment** (1991): 5.0%. **Tourism** (1989): $5.6 bln. **Sales Tax:** 3%.

Finance. FDIC-insured commercial banks & trust companies (1990): 450. **Deposits:** $21.9 bln. **Savings Institutions** (1991): 18. **Assets:** $8.4 bln.

Federal government. No. federal civilian employees (Mar. 1991): 37,783. **Avg. salary:** $33,383. **Notable federal facilities:** U.S. Air Force Academy; U.S. Mint; Ft. Carson, Lowry AFB; Solar Energy Research Institute; U.S. Rail Transport. Test Center; N. Amer. Aerospace Defense Command; Consolidated Space Operations Center; U.S. Documents Center, Fitzsimons Army Medical Center, Federal Center.

Energy. Electricity production (1991, MWh, by source): Hydroelectric: 1.5 mln.; Mineral: 27.5 mln.

Education. Student-teacher ratio (1990): 17.8. **Avg. salary, public school teachers** (1991-92): $32,926.

State data. Motto: Nil Sine Numine (Nothing without Providence). **Flower:** Rocky Mountain columbine. **Bird:** Lark bunting. **Tree:** Colorado blue spruce. **Song:** Where the Columbines Grow. Entered union Aug. 1, 1876; rank 38th. **State fair** at: Pueblo; last week in Aug.

History. Early civilization centered around Mesa Verde 2,000 years ago. The U.S. acquired eastern Colorado in the Louisiana Purchase, 1803; Lt. Zebulon M. Pike explored the area, 1806, discovering the peak that bears his name. After the Mexican War, 1846-48, U.S. immigrants settled in the east, former Mexicans in the south.

Tourist attractions. 310 or more sunshine days per year; more than 1,000 peaks of 2 or more miles; Rocky Mountain National Park; Garden of the Gods; Great Sand Dunes, Dinosaur, Black Canyon of the Gunnison, and Colorado national monuments; Pikes Peak and Mt. Evans highways; Mesa Verde National Park (Ancient Anasazi Indian cliff dwellings); 35 major ski areas; the Grand Mesa tableland comprises Grand Mesa Forest, 659,584 acres, with 200 lakes stocked with trout. Mining towns of Central City, Silverton, Cripple Creek; Burlington's Old Town; Bent's Fort, outside La Junta; Georgetown Loop Historic Mining Railroad Park, Cumbres & Toltec Scenic Railroad.

Famous Coloradans include Frederick Bonfils, Molly Brown, William N. Byers, M. Scott Carpenter, Jack Dempsey, Mamie Eisenhower, Douglas Fairbanks, Scott Hamilton, "Baby Doe" Tabor, Lowell Thomas, Byron R. White, Paul Whiteman.

Toll-free travel information. 1-800-433-2656.

Connecticut

Constitution State, Nutmeg State

People. Population (1991): 3,291,094; **rank:** 27. **Pop. density:** 679.3 per sq. mi. **Racial distrib.** (1990): 87.0% White; 8.3% Black; 6.5% Hispanic. **Net change** (1990-91): 0.1%.

Geography. Total area: 5,018 sq. mi.; **rank:** 48. **Land area:** 4,845 sq. mi. **Acres forested land:** 1,815,800. **Location:** New England state in the northeastern corner of the U.S. **Climate:** moderate; winters avg. slightly below freezing, warm, humid summers. **Topography:** western upland, the Berkshires, in the NW, highest elevations; narrow central lowland N-S; hilly eastern upland drained by rivers. **Capital:** Hartford.

Economy. Principal industries: manufacturing, retail trade, government, services, finances, insurance, real estate. **Principal manufactured goods:** aircraft engines and parts, submarines, helicopters, instruments, machinery & computer equipment, electronics & electrical equipment. **Agriculture: Chief crops:** nursery stock, vegetables, sweet corn, tobacco, apples. **Livestock** (1989): 73,000 cattle; 6,800 hogs/pigs; 8,400 sheep; 5.6 mln. poultry. **Timber/lumber** (1990): oak, birch, beech, maple; 46 mln. bd ft. **Nonfuel Minerals** (1991): $83.7 mln.; crushed stone; construction sand & gravel. **Commercial fishing** (1991): $44.8 mln. **Chief ports:** New Haven, Bridgeport, New London. **International airports at:** Windsor Locks. **Value of construction** (1991): $2.8 bln. **Employment distribution** (1989): 21.4% mfg.; 25.3% serv. **Per capita income** (1991): $25,881. **Unemployment** (1991): 6.7%. **Tourism** (1989): out-of-state visitors spent $3.2 bln. **Sales tax:** 8.0%.

Finance. FDIC-insured commercial banks & trust companies (1990): 70. **Deposits:** $30.7 bln. **Savings institutions** (1991): 18. **Assets:** $7.2 bln.

Federal Government. No. federal civilian employees (Mar. 1991): 9,458. **Avg. salary:** $34,708. **Notable federal facilities:** U.S. Coast Guard Academy; U.S. Navy Submarine Base.

Energy. Electricity production (1991, MWh, by source): Hydroelectric: 0.5 mln.; Mineral: 0.3 mln.; Nuclear: 12.4 mln.

Education. Student-teacher ratio (1990): 13.6. **Avg. salary, public school teachers** (1991-92): $47,300.

State data. Motto: Qui Transtulit Sustinet (He who transplanted still sustains). **Flower:** Mountain laurel. **Bird:** American robin. **Tree:** White oak. **Song:** Yankee Doodle. **Fifth** of the 13 original states to ratify the Constitution, Jan. 9, 1788.

History. Adriaen Block, Dutch explorer, was the first European visitor, 1614. By 1634, settlers from Plymouth Bay started colonies along the Connecticut River and in 1637 defeated the Pequot Indians. In the Revolution, Connecticut men fought in most major campaigns and turned back British raids on Danbury and other towns, while Connecticut privateers captured British merchant ships.

Tourist attractions. Mark Twain House, Hartford; Yale University's Art Gallery, Peabody Museum, all in New Haven; Mystic Seaport; Mystic Marine Life Aquarium; P.T. Barnum Museum, Bridgeport; Gillette Castle, Hadlyme; U.S.S. Nautilus Memorial, Groton (1st nuclear-powered submarine).

Famous "Nutmeggers" include Ethan Allen, Phineas T. Barnum, Samuel Colt, Jonathan Edwards, Nathan Hale, Katharine Hepburn, Isaac Hull, J. Pierpont Morgan, Israel Putnam, Harriet Beecher Stowe, Mark Twain, Noah Webster, Eli Whitney.

Tourist information. State Dept. of Economic Development, 865 Brook St., Rocky Hill, CT 06067.

Toll-free travel information. 1-800-CT-BOUND (282-6863).

Delaware

First State, Diamond State

People. Population (1991): 679,942; **rank:** 46. **Pop. density:** 347.8 per sq. mi. **Racial distrib.** (1990): 80.3% White; 16.9% Black; 2.4% Hispanic. **Net change** (1990-91): 2.1%.

Geography. Total area: 2,045 sq. mi.; **rank:** 49. **Land area:** 1,955 sq. mi. **Acres forested land:** 398,000. **Location:** occupies the Delmarva Peninsula on the Atlantic coastal plain. **Climate:** moderate. **Topography:** Piedmont plateau to the N, sloping to a near sea-level plain. **Capital:** Dover.

Economy. Principal industries: chemistry, agriculture, finance, poultry, shellfish, tourism, auto assembly, food processing, transportation equipment. **Principal manufactured goods:** nylon, apparel, luggage, foods, autos, processed meats and vegetables, railroad and aircraft equipment. **Agriculture: Chief crops:** soybeans, potatoes, corn, mushrooms, lima beans, green peas, barley, cucumbers, snap beans, watermelons, apples. **Livestock** (1992): 31,000 cattle; 236.5 mln. broilers. **Nonfuel Minerals** (1991): $6 mln; construction sand & gravel, magnesium compounds. **Commercial fishing** (1991): $4.5 mln. **Chief ports:** Wilmington. **International airports at:** Philadelphia/Wilmington. **Value of construction** (1991): $793 mln. **Employment distribution** (1991): 79.4% non-manufacturing; 20.6% mfg. **Per capita income** (1991): $20,349. **Unemployment** (1991): 6.2%. **Tourism** (1989); travelers spent $785 mln.

Finance. FDIC-insured commercial banks & trust companies (1990): 47. **Deposits:** $27.0 bln. **Savings institutions** (1991): 4. **Assets:** $668.5 mln.

Federal government. No. federal civilian employees (Mar. 1991): 2,772. **Avg. salary:** $29,620. **Notable federal facilities:** Dover Air Force Base, Federal Wildlife Refuge, Bombay Hook.

Energy. Electricity production (1991, MWh, by source): Mineral: 5.8 mln.

Education. Student-teacher ratio (1990): 16.7. **Avg. salary, public school teachers** (1991-92): $34,548.

State data. Motto: Liberty and independence. **Flower:** Peach blossom. **Bird:** Blue hen chicken. **Tree:** American holly. **Song:** Our Delaware. **First** of original 13 states to ratify the Constitution, Dec. 7, 1787. **State fair** at: Harrington; end of July.

History. The Dutch first settled in Delaware near present Lewes, 1631, but were wiped out by Indians. Swedes settled at present Wilmington, 1638; Dutch settled anew, 1651, near New Castle and seized the Swedish settlement, 1655, only to lose all Delaware and New Netherland to the British, 1664.

Tourist attractions. Ft. Christina Monument, the site of founding of New Sweden; John Dickinson "Penman of the Revolution" home, Dover; Henry Francis du Pont Winterthur Museum; Hagley Museum, Wilmington; Rehoboth Beach, "nation's summer capitol," Rehoboth; Dover Downs Intl. Speedway, Dover; Old Swedes (Trinity Parish) Church, erected 1698, is the oldest Protestant church in the U.S. still in use.

Famous Delawareans include Thomas F. Bayard, Henry Seidel Canby, E. I. du Pont, John P. Marquand, Howard Pyle, Caesar Rodney.

Chamber of Commerce. One Commerce Center, Wilmington, DE 19801.

Toll-free travel information. 1-800-441-8846.

Florida

Sunshine State

People. Population (1991): 13,276,771; **rank:** 4. **Pop. density:** 245.9 per sq. mi. **Racial distrib.** (1990): 83.1% White; 13.6% Black; 12.2% Hispanic. **Net change** (1990-91): 2.5%.

Geography: Total area: 58,664 sq. mi.; **rank:** 22. **Land area:** 53,997 sq. mi. **Acres forested land:** 16,721,000. **Location:** peninsula jutting southward 500 mi. bet. the Atlantic and the Gulf of Mexico. **Climate:** subtropical N of Bradenton-Lake Okeechobee-Vero Beach line; tropical S of line. **Topography:** land is flat or rolling; highest point is 345 ft. in the NW. **Capital:** Tallahassee.

Economy. Principal industries: services, trade, gvt., manufacturing, tourism. **Principal manufactured goods:** electric & electronic equip., transp. equipment; food; printing & publishing; machinery. **Agriculture: Chief crops:** citrus fruits, vegetables, potatoes, melons, strawberries, sugar cane. **Livestock** (1987): 1.97 mln. cattle; 150,000 hogs/pigs; 7,360 sheep; 13.5 mln. poultry. **Timber/lumber** (1990): pine, cypress, cedar; 582 mln. bd. ft. **Nonfuel Minerals** (1991): $1.4 bln.; mostly cement, phosphate rock, crushed stone. **Commercial fishing** (1991): $162.1 mln. **Chief ports:** Pensacola, Tampa, Miami, Port Everglades, Jacksonville, St. Petersburg, Canaveral. **International airports at:** Miami, Tampa, Jacksonville, Orlando, Ft. Lauderdale, W. Palm Beach. **Value of construction** (1991): $15.5 bln. **Per capita income** (1991): $18,880. **Unemployment** (1991): 7.3% **Tourism** (1990): out-of-state visitors spent $26.6 bln. **Sales tax:** 6%.

Finance. FDIC-insured commercial banks & trust companies (1990): 427. **Deposits:** $112.1 bln. **Savings institutions** (1991): 89. **Assets:** $39.3 bln.

Federal government. No. federal civilian employees (Mar. 1991): 63,798. **Avg. salary:** $32,271. **Notable federal facilities:** John F. Kennedy Space Center, NASA-Kennedy Space Center's Spaceport USA; Eglin Air Force Base.

Energy. Electricity production (1991, MWh, by source): Hydroelectric: 0.2 mln.; Mineral: 76.7 mln.; Nuclear: 18.5 mln.

Education. Student-teacher ratio (1990): 17.2. **Avg. salary, public school teachers** (1991-92): $31,119.

State data. Motto: In God we trust. **Flower:** Orange blossom. **Bird:** Mockingbird. **Tree:** Sabal palmetto palm. **Song:** Old Folks at Home. **Entered union** Mar. 3, 1845; rank, 27th. **State fair** at: Tampa; early to mid-Feb.

History. First European to see Florida was Ponce de Leon, 1513. France established a colony, Fort Caroline, on the St. Johns River, 1564; Spain settled St. Augustine, 1565, and Spanish troops massacred most of the French. Britain's Francis Drake burned St. Augustine, 1586. Britain held the area briefly, 1763-83, returning it to Spain. After Andrew Jackson led a U.S. invasion, 1818, Spain ceded Florida to the U.S., 1819. The Seminole War, 1835-42, resulted in removal of most Indians to Oklahoma. Florida seceded from the Union, 1861, was readmitted, 1868.

Tourist attractions. Miami, with a variety of luxury hotels at Miami Beach; St. Augustine, oldest city in U.S.; Walt Disney World's Magic Kingdom and EPCOT; Spaceport U.S.A.

Everglades National Park preserves the beauty of the vast Everglades swamp. Castillo de San Marcos, St. Augustine, is a national monument. Also, the Ringling Museum of Art, and the Ringling Museum of the Circus, both in Sarasota; Sea World, Orlando; Cypress Gardens, Winter Haven; Busch Gardens, Tampa; Universal Studios.

Famous Floridians include Henry M. Flagler, James Weldon Johnson, MacKinlay Kantor, Henry B. Plant, Marjorie Kinnan Rawlings, Joseph W. Stilwell, Charles P. Summerall.

Tourist information. Florida Division of Tourism, 126 Van Buren St., Tallahassee, FL 32399-2000, 1-904-487-1462.

Georgia

Empire State of the South, Peach State

People. Population (1991): 6,622,713; **rank:** 11. **Pop. density:** 114.3 per sq. mi. **Racial distrib.** (1990): 71.0% White; 27.0% Black; 1.7% Hispanic. **Net change** (1990-91): 2.2%.

Geography. Total area: 58,910 sq. mi.; **rank:** 21. **Land area:** 57,919 sq. mi. **Acres forested land:** 23,907,000. **Location:** South Atlantic state. **Climate:** maritime tropical air masses dominate in summer; continental polar air masses in winter; east central area drier. **Topography:** most southerly of the Blue Ridge Mtns. cover NE and N central; central Piedmont extends to the fall line of rivers; coastal plain levels to the coast flatlands. **Capital:** Atlanta.

Economy. Principal industries: services, manufacturing, gvt., retail trade. **Principal manufactured goods** (1991): textiles, food, and kindred prods. **Agriculture: Chief crops:** (1991): peanuts, cotton, corn, tobacco, hay soybeans. **Livestock** (1991): 8.8 mln. poultry; 1.4 mln. cattle; 1.1 hogs/pigs. **Timber/lumber** (1990): pine, hardwood; 2.8 bln. bd. ft. **Nonfuel Minerals** (1991): $1.4 bln.; mostly crushed stone. **Commercial fishing** (1991): $23.7 mln. **Chief ports:** Savannah, Brunswick. **International airports at:** Atlanta. **Value of construction** (1991): $6.8 bln. **Employment distribution** (1991): 20% services; 19% mfg.; 18% retail trade; 18% gvt. **Per capita income** (1991): $17,364. **Unemployment** (1991): 5.0%. **Tourism** (1991): tourists spent $10.4 bln. **Sales tax:** 4%.

Finance. FDIC-insured commercial banks & trust companies (1990): 400. **Deposits:** $49.9 bln. **Savings institutions** (1991): 50. **Assets:** $15.0 bln.

Federal government. No. federal civilian employees (Mar. 1991): 68,924. **Avg. salary:** $30,777. **Notable federal facilities:** Dobbins AFB; Fts. Benning, Gordon, McPherson; Fed. Law Enforcement Training Ctr., Glynco, Warner Robins AFB; Centers for Disease Control, Atlanta.

Energy. Electricity production (1991, MWh, by source): Hydroelectric: 3.5 mln.; Mineral: 39.8 mln.; Nuclear: 27.6 mln.

Education. Student-teacher ratio (1990): 18.3. **Avg. salary, public school teachers** (1991-92): $29,680.

State data. Motto: Wisdom, justice and moderation. **Flower:** Cherokee rose. **Bird:** Brown thrasher. **Tree:** Live oak. **Song:** Georgia On My Mind. **Fourth** of the 13 original states to ratify the Constitution, Jan. 2, 1788.

History. Gen. James Oglethorpe established the first settlements, 1733, for poor and religiously-persecuted Englishmen. Oglethorpe defeated a Spanish army from Florida at Bloody Marsh, 1742. In the Revolution, Georgians seized the Savannah armory, 1775, and sent the munitions to the Continental Army; they fought seesaw campaigns with Cornwallis' British troops, twice liberating Augusta and forcing final evacuation by the British from Savannah, 1782.

Tourist attractions. Atlanta area: State Capitol, Stone Mt. Park, Six Flags over Georgia, Kennesaw Mt. Natl. Battlefield Park, Martin Luther King Center, Underground Atlanta, Jimmy Carter Lib. & Museum. NW: Chickamauga Battlefield Park, Chattahoochee Natl. Forest. NE: alpine village of Helen; Dahlonega, site of America's first gold rush; Brasstown Bald Mt., Lake Lanier. SW: Roosevelt's Little White House, Callaway Gardens, Andersonville Natl. Historic Site. SE: Okefenokee Swamp. Coastal: Jekyll Island, St. Simons Island, Cumberland Island Natl. Seashore, historic riverfront district in Savannah, Ft. Pulaski.

Famous Georgians include Hank Aaron, Griffin Bell, James Bowie, Erskine Caldwell, Jimmy Carter, Ray Charles, Lucius D. Clay, Ty Cobb, John C. Fremont, Joel Chandler Harris, Gladys Knight, Juliette Gordon Low, Martin Luther King Jr., Sidney Lanier, Margaret Mitchell, Flannery O'Connor, Jackie Robinson, Joseph Wheeler.

Chamber of Commerce. 235 International Blvd., Atlanta, GA 30303.

Toll-free travel information. 1-800-VISIT GA.

Hawai'i

The Aloha State

People. Population (1991): 1,134,750; **rank:** 40. **Pop. density:** 176.7 per sq. mi. **Racial distrib.** (1990): 33.4% White; 2.5% Black; 61.8% Asian or Pacific Is.; 7.3% Hispanic. **Net change** (1990-91): 2.4%.

Geography. Total area: 6,471 sq. mi.; **rank:** 47. **Land area:** 6,423 sq. mi. **Acres forested land:** 1,748,000. **Location:** Hawaiian Islands lie in the North Pacific, 2,397 mi. SW from San Francisco. **Climate:** subtropical, with wide variations in rainfall; Waialeale, on Kaua'i, wettest spot in U.S. (annual rainfall 444 in.) **Topography:** islands are tops of a chain of submerged volcanic mountains; active volcanoes: Mauna Loa, Kilauea. **Capital:** Honolulu.

Economy. Principal industries: tourism, defense and other government, sugar refining, pineapple and diversified agriculture, aquaculture, fishing, motion pictures. **Principal manufactured goods:** sugar, canned pineapple, clothing, foods, printing and publishing. **Agriculture: Chief crops:** sugar, pineapples, macadamia nuts, fruits, coffee, vegetables, melons, and floriculture. **Livestock** (1990): 214,000 cattle and calves; 36,000 hogs/pigs; 1.18 mln. chickens. **Nonfuel Minerals** (1991): $100.3 mln.; mostly crushed stone, sand, gravel & cement. **Commercial fishing** (1991): $57.7 mln. **Chief ports:** Honolulu, Nāwiliwili, Barbers Point, Kahului, Hilo. **International airports at:** Honolulu. **Value of construction** (1991): $2.7 bln. **Employment distribution** (1991): 25.3% trade; 29.4% serv.; 20.2% gvt. **Per capita income** (1991): $21,306. **Unemployment** (1991): 2.8%. **Tourism** (1990): visitors spent $9.4 bln. **General excise tax:** 4%. **Sales tax:** 4%.

Finance. FDIC-insured commercial banks & trust companies: (1990): 21. **Deposits:** $13.8 bln. **Savings institutions** (1991): 6. **Assets:** $7.3 bln.

Federal government. No. federal civilian employees (Mar. 1991): 21,651. **Avg. salary:** $32,872. **Notable federal facilities:** Pearl Harbor Naval Shipyard; Hickam AFB; Schofield Barracks.

Energy. Electricity production (1991, MWh, by source): Hydroelectric: .02 mln.; Mineral: 5.8 mln.

Education. Student-teacher ratio (1990): 18.9. **Avg. Salary, public school teachers** (1991-92): $34,528.

State data. Motto: The life of the land is perpetuated in righteousness. **Flower:** Yellow Hibiscus. **Bird:** Hawaiian goose. **Tree:** Kukui (Candlenut). **Song:** Hawai'i Pono'i. **Entered union** Aug. 21, 1959; rank, 50th. **State fair** at: Honolulu; late May–mid-June.

History. Polynesians from islands 2,000 mi. to the south settled the Hawaiian Islands, probably between 300 A.D. and 600 A.D. First European visitor was British Capt. James Cook, 1778. Missionaries arrived, 1820, taught religion, reading and writing. King Kamehameha III and his chiefs created the first Constitution and a Legislature which set up a public school system. Sugar production began in 1835 and it became the dominant industry. In 1893, Queen Lili'uokalani was deposed, followed, 1894, by a republic headed by Sanford B. Dole. Annexation by the U.S. came in 1898.

Tourist attractions. Hawaii Volcanoes, Haleakala National Parks; Polynesian Cultural Center, Waikiki Beach, Nu'uanu Pali, Bishop Museum, Waimea Canyon, Wailua River State Park, Honolulu Academy of Arts.

Famous Islanders include Bernice Pauahi Bishop, John A. Burns, Father Damien de Veuster, Daniel K. Inouye, Duke Kahanamoku, King Kamehameha the Great, Queen Ka'ahumanu, Queen Liliuokalani, Ellison Onizuka.

Chamber of Commerce. Dillingham Bldg., 735 Bishop St., Honolulu, HI 96813.

Idaho

Gem State

People. Population (1991): 1,039,295; **rank:** 42. **Pop. density:** 12.6 per sq. mi. **Racial distrib.** (1990): 94.4% White; 0.3% Black; 5.3% Hispanic. **Net change** (1990-91): 3.2%.

Geography. Total area: 83,564 sq. mi.; **rank:** 13. **Land area:** 82,751 sq. mi. **Acres forested land:** 21,818,000. **Location:** Pacific Northwest-Mountain state bordering on British Columbia. **Climate:** tempered by Pacific westerly winds; drier, colder, continental clime in SE; altitude an important factor. **Topography:** Snake R. plains in the S; central region of mountains, canyons, gorges (Hells Canyon, 7,900 ft., deepest in N.A.); subalpine northern region. **Capital:** Boise.

Economy. Principal industries: agriculture, manufacturing, tourism, lumber, mining, electronics. **Principal manufactured goods:** processed foods, lumber and wood products, chemical products, primary metals, fabricated metal products, machinery, electronic components. **Agriculture: Chief crops:** potatoes, peas, sugar beets, alfalfa seed, wheat, hops, barley, plums and prunes, mint, onions, corn, cherries, apples, hay. **Livestock** (1989): 1.66 mln. cattle; 296,000 sheep; 72,000 hogs; 1.1 mln. poultry. **Timber/lumber** (1990): yellow, white pine; Douglas fir; white spruce; 2.1 bln. bd. ft. **Nonfuel Minerals** (1991): $283 mln.; phosphate rock, silver, gold, sand & gravel. **Chief ports:** Lewiston. **Value of construction** (1991) $1.05 bln. **Employment distribution** (1990): 21% trade; 17% serv., 13% mfg.; 7% agric. **Per capita income** (1991): $15,401. **Unemployment** (1991): 6.1%. **Tourism** (1989): travellers spent $1.4 bln. **Sales tax:** 5%.

Finance. FDIC-insured commercial banks & trust companies (1990): 22. **Deposits:** $6.6 bln. **Savings institutions** (1991): 3. **Assets:** $459.2 mln.

Federal government. No. federal civilian employees (Mar. 1991): 7,393. **Avg. salary:** $31,575. **Notable federal facilities:** Ida. Nat'l. Engineering Lab, Idaho Falls; Mt. Home Air Force Base, Mt. Home.

Energy. Electricity production (1991, MWh, by source): Hydroelectric: 5.8 mln.

Education: Student-teacher ratio (1990): 19.6. **Avg. salary, public school teachers** (1991-92): $26,759.

State data. Motto: Esto Perpetua (It is perpetual). **Flower:** Syringa. **Bird:** Mountain bluebird. **Tree:** White pine. **Song:** Here We Have Idaho. **Entered union** July 3, 1890; rank, 43d. **State fair** at: Boise, late Aug.; and Blackfoot, early Sept.

History. Exploration of the Idaho area began with Lewis and Clark, 1805-06. Next came fur traders, setting up posts, 1809-34, and missionaries, establishing missions, 1830s-1850s. Mormons made their first permanent settlement at Franklin, 1860. Idaho's Gold Rush began that same year, and brought thousands of permanent settlers. Strangest of the Indian Wars was the 1,300-mi. trek in 1877 of Chief Joseph and the Nez Perce tribe, pursued by troops that caught them a few miles short of the Canadian border. In 1890, Idaho adopted a progressive Constitution and became a state.

Tourist attractions. Hells Canyon, deepest gorge in N.A.; World Center for Birds of Prey; Craters of the Moon; Sun Valley, year-round resort in the Sawtooth Mtns.; Crystal Falls Cave; Shoshone Falls; Lava Hot Springs; Lake Pend Oreille; Lake Coeur d'Alene; Sawtooth Natl. Recreation Area; River of No Return Wilderness Area.

Famous Idahoans include William E. Borah, Frank Church, Fred T. Dubois, Chief Joseph, Sacagawea.

Tourist information. Department of Commerce, 700 W. State St., Boise, ID 83720.

Toll-free travel information. 1-800-635-7820.

Illinois

The Prairie State

People. Population (1991): 11,542,841; **rank:** 6. **Pop. density:** 207.6 per sq. mi. **Racial distrib.** (1990): 78.3% White; 14.8% Black; 7.9% Hispanic. **Net change** (1990-91): 1.0%.

Geography. Total area: 56,345 sq. mi.; **rank:** 24. **Land area:** 55,593 sq. mi. **Acres forested land:** 4,265,000. **Location:** east-north central state; western, southern, and eastern boundaries formed by Mississippi, Ohio, and Wabash Rivers, respectively. **Climate:** temperate; typically cold, snowy winters, hot summers. **Topography:** prairie and fertile plains throughout; open hills in the southern region. **Capital:** Springfield.

Economy. Principal industries: services, manufacturing, travel, wholesale and retail trade, finance, insurance, real estate, construction, gvt., health care, agriculture. **Principal manufactured goods:** machinery, electric and electronic equipment, primary and fabricated metals, chemical products, printing and publishing, food and kindred prods. **Agriculture: Chief crops:** corn, soybeans, wheat, oats, hay. **Livestock** (1991): 1.98 mln. cattle; 5.9 mln. hogs/pigs; 129,000 sheep; 3.31 mln. poultry. **Timber/lumber** (1990): oak, hickory, maple, cottonwood; 87 mln. bd. ft. **Nonfuel Minerals** (1991): $609.5 mln.; mostly crushed stone, cement, construction & industrial sand & gravel, lime. **Commercial fishing** (1991): $377,000. **Chief ports:** Chicago. **International airports at:** Chicago. **Value of construction** (1991): $9.15 bln. **Employment distribution** (1991): 26.0% serv.; 24.0% trade; 18.1% mfg. **Per capita income** (1991): $20,824. **Unemployment** (1991): 7.1%. **Tourism** (1991): out-of-state visitors spent $15 bln. **Sales tax:** 6.25%.

Finance. FDIC-insured commercial banks & trust companies (1990): 1,102. **Deposits:** $128.9 bln. **Savings institutions** (1991): 176. **Assets:** $45.3 bln.

Federal government. No. federal civilian employees (Mar. 1991): 53,215. **Avg. salary:** $33,155. **Notable federal facilities:** Fermi Nat'l. Accelerator Lab; Argonne Nat'l. Lab; Ft. Sheridan; Rock Island; Great Lakes, Naval Training Station, Scott AFB.

Energy. Electricity production (1991, MWh, by source): Hydroelectric: 0.04 mln.; Mineral: 42.5 mln.; Nuclear: 67.5 mln.

Education. Student-teacher ratio (1990): 16.7. **Avg. salary, public school teachers** (1991-92): $36,623.

State data. Motto: State sovereignty—national union. **Flower:** Native violet. **Bird:** Cardinal. **Tree:** White oak. **Song:** Illinois. **Entered union** Dec. 3, 1818; rank, 21st. **State fair** at: Springfield; mid-Aug.; DuQuoin, late Aug.

History. Fur traders were the first Europeans in Illinois, followed shortly, 1673, by Jolliet and Marquette, and, 1680, La Salle, who built a fort near present Peoria. First settlements were French, at Fort St. Louis on the Illinois River, 1692, and Kaskaskia, 1700. France ceded the area to Britain, 1763; Amer. Gen. George Rogers Clark, 1778, took Kaskaskia from the British without a shot. Defeat of Indian tribes in Black Hawk War, 1832, and railroads in 1850s, inspired change.

Tourist attractions: Chicago museums, parks; Lincoln shrines at Springfield, New Salem, Sangamon; Cahokia Mounds, E. St. Louis; Starved Rock State Park; Crab Orchard Wildlife Refuge; Mormon settlement at Nauvoo; Fts. Kaskaskia, Chartres, Massac (parks); Shawnee Natl. Forest, Southern Illinois; Illinois State Museum, Springfield; Dickson Mounds Museum, btwn. Havana & Lewistown.

Famous Illinoisans include Jane Addams, Saul Bellow, Jack Benny, Ray Bradbury, Gwendolyn Brooks, William Jennings Bryan, St. Francis Xavier Cabrini, Clarence Darrow, John Deere, Stephen A. Douglas, James T. Farrell, George W. Ferris, Marshall Field, Betty Friedan, Benny Goodman, Ulysses S. Grant, Ernest Hemingway, Wild Bill Hickock, Abraham Lincoln, Vachel Lindsay, Edgar Lee Masters, Oscar Mayer, Cyrus McCormick, Ronald Reagan, Carl Sandburg, Adlai Stevenson, Frank Lloyd Wright, Philip Wrigley.

Tourist information. Illinois Dept. of Commerce and Community Affairs, 620 E. Adams St., Springfield, IL 62701. **Toll-free literature:** 1-800-223-0121.

Indiana

Hoosier State

People. Population (1991): 5,609,616; **rank:** 14. **Pop. density:** 152.1 per sq. mi. **Racial distrib.** (1990): 90.6 White; 7.8% Black; 1.8% Hispanic. **Net change** (1990-91): 1.2%.

Geography. Total area: 36,185 sq. mi.; **rank:** 38. **Land area:** 35,870 sq. mi. **Acres forested land:** 4,439,900. **Location:** east north-central state; Lake Michigan on northern border. **Climate:** 4 distinct seasons with a temperate climate. **Topography:** hilly southern region; fertile rolling plains of central region; flat, heavily glaciated north; dunes along Lake Michigan shore. **Capital:** Indianapolis.

Economy: Principal industries: manufacturing, wholesale and retail trade, agriculture, government, services. **Principal manufactured goods:** primary and fabricated metals, transportation equipment, electrical and electronic equipment, non-electrical machinery, plastics, chemical products, foods. **Agriculture: Chief crops** (1987): corn, sorghum, oats, wheat, rye, soybeans, hay. **Livestock** (1987): 1.2 mln. cattle; 4.4 mln. hogs/pigs; 82,757 sheep; 28 mln. chickens. **Timber/lumber** (1990): oak, tulip, beech, sycamore; 245 mln. bd. ft. **Nonfuel Minerals** (1991): $385.7 mln.; mostly crushed stone, abrasives, cement, construction sand & gravel. **Commercial fishing** (1991): $1.02 mln. **Chief ports:** Burns Harbor, Portage; Southwind Maritime, Mt. Vernon; Clark Maritime, Jeffersonville. **International airports at:** Indianapolis. **Value of construction** (1991): $5.2 bln. **Employment distribution** (1989): 27.9% mfg.; 24.8% trade; 19.8% serv; 12.3 gvt. **Per capita income** (1991): $17,217. **Unemployment** (1991): 5.9%. **Tourism** (1985): tourists spent $3 bln. **Sales tax**: 5%, with exemptions.

Finance. FDIC-insured commercial banks & trust companies (1990): 307. **Deposits:** $46.3 bln. **Savings institutions** (1991): 89. **Assets:** $13.4 bln.

Federal government. No. federal civilian employees (Mar. 1991): 25,726. **Avg. salary:** $30,744. **Notable federal facilities:** Naval Avionics Ctr.; Ft. Benjamin Harrison; Grissom AFB; Navy Weapons Support Ctr., Crane.

Energy. Electricity production (1991 MWh, by source): Hydroelectric: 0.5 mln.; Mineral: 83.9 mln.

Education. Student-teacher ratio (1990): 17.5. **Avg. salary, public school teachers** (1991-92): $33,755.

State data. Motto: Crossroads of America. **Flower:** Peony. **Bird:** Cardinal. **Tree:** Tulip poplar. **Song:** On the Banks of the Wabash, Far Away. **Entered union** Dec. 11, 1816; rank, 19th. **State fair** at: Indianapolis; mid-Aug.

History: Pre-historic Indian Mound Builders of 1,000 years ago were the earliest known inhabitants. A French trading post was built, 1731-32, at Vincennes and La Salle visited the present South Bend area, 1679 and 1681. France ceded the area to Britain, 1763. During the Revolution, American Gen. George Rogers Clark captured Vincennes, 1778, and defeated British forces 1779; at war's end Britain ceded the area to the U.S. Miami Indians defeated U.S. troops twice, 1790, but were beaten, 1794, at Fallen Timbers by Gen. Anthony Wayne. At Tippecanoe, 1811, Gen. William H. Harrison defeated Tecumseh's Indian confederation.

Tourist attractions. Lincoln Boyhood, George Rogers Clark memorials; Wyandotte Cave; Vincennes, Tippecanoe sites; Indiana Dunes; Hoosier Nat'l. Forest; Benjamin Harrison Home.

Famous "Hoosiers" include Larry Bird, Ambrose Burnside, Hoagy Carmichael, Jim Davis, James Dean, Eugene V. Debs, Theodore Dreiser, Paul Dresser, Gil Hodges, David Letterman, Jane Pauley, Cole Porter, Gene Stratton Porter, Ernie Pyle, James Whitcomb Riley, Oscar Robertson, Red Skelton, Booth Tarkington, Lew Wallace, Wendell L. Willkie, Wilbur Wright.

Chamber of Commerce. One North Capital, Suite 200, Indianapolis, IN 46204.

Toll-free travel information. 1-800-289-6646.

Iowa

Hawkeye State

People. Population (1991): 2,795,220; **rank:** 30. **Pop. density:** 50.0 per sq. mi. **Racial distrib.** (1990): 96.6% White; 1.7% Black; 1.2% Hispanic. **Net change** (1990-91): 0.7%.

Geography. Total area: 56,275 sq. mi.; **rank:** 25. **Land area:** 55,875 sq. mi. **Acres forested land:** 1,562,000. **Location:** Midwest state bordered by Mississippi R. on the E and Missouri R. on the W. **Climate:** humid, continental. **Topography:** Watershed from NW to SE; soil especially rich and land level in the N central counties. **Capital:** Des Moines.

Economy. Principal industries: agriculture, communications, construction, finance, insurance, trade, service, mfg. **Principal manufactured goods:** tires, farm machinery, electronic products, appliances, office furniture, chemicals, fertilizers, auto accessories. **Agriculture: Chief crops:** silage and grain corn, soybeans, oats, hay. **Livestock** (1991): 4.0 mln. cattle; 14.0 mln. swine; 465,000 sheep & lambs; 8.8 mln. turkeys. **Timber/lumber** (1990): red cedar; 38 mln. bd. ft. **Nonfuel Minerals** (1991): $328.8 mln.; mostly crushed stone, portland cement, construction sand & gravel. **Value of construction** (1991): 2.3 bln. **Employment distribution** (1992): 25.2% trade; 24.4% serv; 18.3% mfg.; 18.2% gvt. **Per capita income** (1991): $17,505. **Unemployment** (1991): 4.6%. **Tourism** (1989): tourists spent $2.3 bln. **Sales tax:** 4%.

Finance. FDIC-insured commercial banks & trust companies (1990): 567. **Deposits:** $27.6 bln. **Savings institutions** (1991): 31. **Assets:** $4.5 bln.

Federal government. No. federal civilian employees (Mar. 1991): 7,772. **Avg. salary:** $30,723.

Energy. Electricity production (1991, MWh, by source): Hydroelectric: 0.81 mln.; Mineral: 23.4 mln.; Nuclear: 3.8 mln.

Education. Student-teacher ratio (1990): 15.6. **Avg. salary, public school teachers** (1991-92): $29,196.

State data. Motto: Our liberties we prize and our rights we will maintain. **Flower:** Wild rose. **Bird:** Eastern goldfinch. **Tree:** Oak. **Rock:** Geode. **Entered union** Dec. 28, 1846; rank, 29th. **State fair** at: Des Moines; mid-Aug.

History. A thousand years ago several groups of prehistoric Indian Mound Builders dwelt on Iowa's fertile plains. Marquette and Jolliet gave France its claim to the area, 1673. It became U.S. territory through the 1803 Louisiana Purchase. Indian tribes were moved into the area from states further east, but by mid-19th century were forced to move on to Kansas. Before and during the Civil War, Iowans strongly supported Abraham Lincoln and became traditional Republicans.

Tourist attractions. Herbert Hoover birthplace and library, West Branch; Effigy Mounds Nat'l. Monument, Marquette, a pre-historic Indian burial site; Amana Colonies; Davenport Municipal Art Gallery's collection of Grant Wood's paintings and memorabilia; Living History Farms, Des Moines; Adventureland, Altoona; Boone & Scenic Valley Railroad, Boone; Greyhound Parks in Dubuque, Council Bluffs & Waterloo; Prairie Meadows horse racing, Altoona; riverboat cruises and casino gambling, Mississippi River; Iowa Great Lakes, Okoboji.

Famous Iowans include James A. Van Allen, Marquis Childs, Buffalo Bill Cody, Mamie Dowd Eisenhower, George Gallup, Susan Glaspell, James Norman Hall, Harry Hansen, Herbert Hoover, Glenn Miller, Billy Sunday, Carl Van Vechten, Henry Wallace, John Wayne, Meredith Willson, Grant Wood.

Tourist information. Division of Tourism, Iowa Dept. of Economic Development, 200 E. Grand Ave. Des Moines, IA 50309.

Toll-free travel information. 1-800-345-IOWA.

Kansas

Sunflower State

People. Population (1991): 2,494,560; **rank:** 32. **Pop. density:** 30.5 per sq. mi. **Racial distrib.** (1990): 90.1% White; 5.8% Black; 3.8% Hispanic. **Net change** (1990-91): 0.7%.

Geography. Total area: 82,277 sq. mi.; **rank:** 14. **Land area:** 81,823 sq. mi. **Acres forested land:** 1,358,000. **Location:** West North Central state, with Missouri R. on E. **Climate:** temperate but continental, with great extremes bet. summer and winter. **Topography:** hilly Osage Plains in the E; central region level prairie and hills; high plains in the W. **Capital:** Topeka.

Economy. Principal industries: manufacturing, finance, insurance, real estate, services. **Principal manufactured goods:** transportation equip., machinery and computer equipment, food and kindred products, printing and publishing. **Agriculture: Chief crops:** wheat, sorghum, corn, hay, soybeans. **Livestock** (1991): 5.7 mln. cattle; 1.4 mln. hogs/pigs; 190,000 sheep & lambs; 1.8 mln. poultry. **Timber/lumber:** oak, walnut. **Nonfuel Minerals** (1991): $332 mln.; cement, salt, crushed stone. **Chief ports:** Kansas City. **International airports at:** Wichita. **Value of construction** (1991): $2.2 bln. **Employment distribution** (1990): 24.6% trade; 22.3% serv.; 19.8% gvt.; 17.1% mfg. **Per capita income** (1991): $18,511. **Unemployment** (1991): 4.4%. **Tourism** (1991): out-of-state visitors spent $2.1 bln. **Sales tax:** 6.9% maximum.

Finance. FDIC-insured commercial banks & trust companies (1990): 561. **Deposits:** $25.1 bln. **Savings institutions** (1991): 33. **Assets** : $8.7 bln.

Federal government. No. federal civilian employees (Mar. 1991): 16,223. **Avg. salary:** $30,539. **Notable federal facilities:** McConnell AFB; Fts. Riley, Leavenworth.

Energy. Electricity production (1991, MWh, by source): Mineral: 23.2 mln; Nuclear: 3.8 mln.

Education. Student-teacher ratio (1990): 15.0. **Avg. salary, public school teachers** (1991-92): $30,808.

State data. Motto: Ad Astra per Aspera (To the stars through difficulties). **Flower:** Native sunflower. **Bird:** Western meadowlark. **Tree:** Cottonwood. **Song:** Home on the Range. **Entered union** Jan. 29, 1861; rank, 34th. **State fair** at: Hutchinson; begins Friday after Labor Day.

History. Coronado marched through the Kansas area, 1541; French explorers came next. The U.S. took over in the Louisiana Purchase, 1803. In the pre-war North-South struggle over slavery, so much violence swept the area it was called Bleeding Kansas. Railroad construction after the war made Abilene and Dodge City terminals of large cattle drives from Texas.

Tourist attractions. Eisenhower Center and "Place of Meditation," Abilene; Agricultural Hall of Fame and National Ctr., Bonner Springs, displays farm equipment; Dodge City-Boot Hill & Frontier Town; Cowtown-historic frontier town, Wichita; Ft. Scott & Ft. Larned-restored 1800s cavalry forts. Kansas Cosmosphere and Space Discovery Center, Hutchinson.

Famous Kansans include Thomas Hart Benton, John Brown, Walter P. Chrysler, John Steuart Curry, Amelia Earhart, Dwight D. Eisenhower, Ron Evans, Wild Bill Hickok, Cyrus Holliday, William Inge, Walter Johnson, Alf Landon, Carry Nation, Gordon Parks, Jim Ryun, William Allen White.

Tourist information. Kansas Dept. of Commerce, Travel and Tourism Div., 400 SW 8th St., 5th Fl., Topeka, KS 66603; 1-913-296-2009.

Toll-free travel information. 1-800-2KANSAS.

Kentucky

Bluegrass State

People. Population (1991): 3,713,475 **rank:** 24. **Pop. density:** 93.5 per sq. mi. **Racial Distrib.** (1990): 92.0% White; 7.1% Black; Hispanic 0.6%. **Net change** (1990-91): 0.8%.

Geography. Total area: 40,410 sq. mi.; **rank:** 37. **Land area:** 39,732 sq. mi. **Acres forested land:** 12,256,000. Location: east south central state, bordered on N by Illinois, Indiana, Ohio; on E by West Virginia and Virginia; in S by Tennessee; on W by Missouri. **Climate:** moderate, with plentiful rainfall. **Topography:** mountainous in E; rounded hills of the Knobs in the N; Bluegrass, heart of state; wooded rocky hillsides of the Pennyroyal; Western Coal Field; the fertile Purchase the SW. **Capital:** Frankfort.

Economy. Principal industries: manufacturing, coal mining, construction, agriculture. **Principal manufactured goods:** industrial machinery, electrical & electronic prods., apparel and textile prods., transportation equip., printing and publishing. **Agriculture: Chief crops** (1990): tobacco, soybeans, corn. **Livestock** (1991): 2.5 mln. cattle; 920,000 hogs/pigs; 35,000 sheep; 2.2 mln. chickens; 1990 receipts for horse & mule sales, $490 mln. **Timber/lumber** (1990): hardwoods, pines; 526 mln. bd. ft. **Nonfuel Minerals** (1991): $352 mln.; mostly crushed stone. **Chief ports:** Paducah, Louisville, Covington, Owensboro, Ashland, Henderson County, Lyon County, Hickman-Fulton County. **International airports at:** Covington. **Value of construction** (1991): $3.7 bln. **Employment distribution** (1991): 25.6% trade; 21% mfg.; 21.2% serv.; 14.1% gvt. **Per capita income** (1991): $15,539. **Unemployment** (1991): 7.4%. **Tourism** (1991): tourists spent $5.3 bln. **Sales tax:** 6%.

Finance. FDIC-insured commercial banks & trust companies (1990): 335. **Deposits:** $30.9 bln. **Savings institutions** (1991): 58. **Assets:** $7.5 bln.

Federal government. No. federal civilian employees (Mar. 1991): 28,135. **Avg. salary:** $27,436. **Notable federal facilities:** U.S. Gold Bullion Depository, Fort Knox; Federal Correctional Institution, Lexington.

Energy. Electricity production (1991, MWh, by source): Hydroelectric: 3.4 mln.; Mineral: 60.8 mln.

Education. Student-teacher ratio (1990): 17.3. **Avg. salary, public school teachers** (1991-92): $30,880.

State data. Motto: United we stand, divided we fall. **Flower:** Goldenrod. **Bird:** Cardinal. **Tree:** Kentucky coffee tree. **Song:** My Old Kentucky Home. **Entered union** June 1, 1792; rank, 15th. **State fair** at: Louisville.

History. Kentucky was the first area west of the Alleghenies settled by American pioneers; first permanent settlement, Harrodsburg, 1774. Daniel Boone blazed the Wilderness Trail through the Cumberland Gap and founded Fort Boonesborough, 1775. Indian attacks, spurred by the British, were unceasing until, during the Revolution, Gen. George Rogers Clark captured British forts in Indiana and Illinois, 1778. In 1792, after Virginia dropped its claims to the region, Kentucky became the 15th state.

Tourist attractions. Kentucky Derby and accompanying festivities, Louisville; Land Between the Lakes Nat'l. Recreation Area encompassing Kentucky Lake and Lake Barkley; Mammoth Cave National Park with 330 mi. of explored passageways, 200-ft. high rooms, blind fish, and Echo River, 360 ft. below ground; Shaker Village of Pleasant Hill, Harrodsburg; Lincoln birthplace, Hodgenville; My Old Kentucky Home, Bardstown; Cumberland Gap Natl. Historical Park, Middlesboro; Kentucky Horse Park, Lexington.

Famous Kentuckians include Muhammad Ali, John James Audubon, Alben Barkley, Daniel Boone, Louis D. Brandeis, John C. Breckinridge, Kit Carson, Albert B. "Happy" Chandler, Cassius Marcellus Clay, Henry Clay, Jefferson Davis, "Casey" Jones, Abraham Lincoln, Mary Todd Lincoln, Thomas Hunt Morgan, Carry Nation, Col. Harland Sanders, Diane Sawyer, Jesse Stuart, Adlai Stevenson, Zachary Taylor, Robert Penn Warren, Whitney Young, Jr.

Chamber of Commerce. 452 Versailles Rd., P.O. Box 817, Frankfort, KY 40602.

Toll-free travel information. 1-800-225-TRIP, extension 67 in U.S., Ontario & Quebec, Canada.

Louisiana

Pelican State

People. Population (1991): 4,251,569; **rank:** 21. **Pop. density:** 97.6 per sq. mi. **Racial distrib.** (1990): 67.3% White; 30.8% Black; 2.2% Hispanic. **Net change** (1990-91): 0.7%.

Geography. Total area: 47,752 sq. mi.; **rank:** 31. **Land area:** 43,566 sq. mi. **Acres forested land:** 13,883,000. **Location:** south central Gulf Coast state. **Climate:** subtropical, affected by continental weather patterns. **Topography:** lowlands of marshes and Mississippi R. flood plain; Red R. Valley lowlands; upland hills in the Florida Parishes; average elevation, 100 ft. **Capital:** Baton Rouge.

Economy. Principal industries: wholesale and retail trade, government, manufacturing, construction, transportation, mining. **Principal manufactured goods** (1991): chemical products, foods, transportation equipment, electronic equipment, petroleum products, lumber, wood, and paper. **Agriculture: Chief crops** (1991): soybean, sugarcane, rice, corn, cotton, sweet potatoes, pecans, sorghum. **Livestock** (1991): 1.02 mln. cattle; 60,000 hogs/pigs; 16,000 sheep; 1.85 mln. poultry. **Timber lumber** (1990): pines, hardwoods, oak; 939 mln. bd. ft. **Nonfuel Minerals** (1991): $233.9 mln., mostly salt, sand & gravel, sulfur. **Commercial fishing** (1991): $243.6 mln. **Chief ports:** New Orleans, Baton Rouge, Lake Charles, S. Louisiana Port Commission at La Place, Shreveport. **International airports at:** New Orleans. **Value of construction** (1991): $2.9 bln. **Employment distribution** (1991): 22.8% trade; 23.8% serv.; 21.2% gvt.; 11.4% mfg. **Per capita income** (1991): $15,143. **Unemployment** (1991): 7.1%. **Tourism** (1990): out-of-state visitors spent $4.7 bln. **Sales tax:** 4%.

Finance. FDIC-insured commercial banks & trust companies (1990): 232. **Deposits:** $31.5 bln. **Savings institutions** (1991): 42. **Assets:** $4.4 bln.

Federal government. No. federal civilian employees (Mar. 1991): 21,637. **Avg. salary:** $30,311. **Notable federal facilities:** Barksdale, England, Ft. Polk military bases; Strategic Petroleum Reserve, New Orleans; Michoud Assembly Plant, New Orleans; U.S. Public Service Hospital, Carville.

Energy. Electricity production (1991, MWh, by source): Mineral: 29.9 mln; Nuclear: 9.5 mln.

Education. Student-teacher ratio (1990): 17.5. **Avg. salary, public school teachers** (1991-92): $27,087.

State data. Motto: Union, justice and confidence. **Flower:** Magnolia. **Bird:** Eastern brown pelican. **Tree:** Cypress. **Song:** Give Me Louisiana. **Entered union** Apr. 30, 1812; rank, 18th. **State fair** at: Shreveport; Oct.

History. The area was first visited, 1530, by Cabeza de Vaca and Panfilo de Narvaez. The region was claimed for France by LaSalle, 1682. First permanent settlement was by French at Biloxi, now in Mississippi, 1699. France ceded the region to Spain, 1762, took it back, 1800, and sold it to the U.S., 1803, in the Louisiana Purchase. During the Revolution, Spanish Louisiana aided the Americans. Admitted to statehood, 1812, Louisiana was the scene of the Battle of New Orleans, 1815.

Louisiana Creoles are descendants of early French and/or Spanish settlers. About 4,000 Acadians, French settlers in Nova Scotia, Canada, were forcibly transported by the British to Louisiana in 1755 (an event commemorated in Longfellow's *Evangeline*) and settled near Bayou Teche; their descendants became known as Cajuns. Another group, the Islenos, were descendants of Canary Islanders brought to Louisiana by a Spanish governor in 1770. Traces of Spanish and French survive in local dialects.

Tourist attractions. Mardi Gras, French Quarter, Superdome, Dixieland jazz, Aquarium of the Americas, all New Orleans; Battle of New Orleans site; Longfellow-Evangeline Memorial Park; Kent House Museum, Alexandria; Hodges Gardens, Natchilotches.

Famous Louisianans include Louis Armstrong, Pierre Beauregard, Judah P. Benjamin, Braxton Bragg, Grace King, Huey Long, Leonidas K. Polk, Henry Miller Shreve, Edward D. White Jr.

Tourist Information. State Dept. of Culture, Recreation & Tourism, P.O. Box 94291, Baton Rouge, LA 70804-9291.

Toll-free travel information. 1-800-33-GUMBO.

Maine

Pine Tree State

People. Population (1991): 1,234,602; **rank:** 39. **Pop. density:** 40.0 per sq. mi. **Racial distrib.** (1990): 98.4% White; 0.4% Black; 0.6% Hispanic. **Net change** (1990-91): 0.5%.

Geography. Total area: 33,265 sq. mi.; **rank:** 39. **Land area:** 30,865 sq. mi. **Acres forested land:** 17,713,000. **Location:** New England state at northeastern tip of U.S. **Climate:** Southern interior and coastal, influenced by air masses from the S and W; northern clime harsher, avg. +100 in. snow in winter. **Topography:** Appalachian Mtns. extend through state; western borders have rugged terrain; long sand beaches on southern coast; northern coast mainly rocky promontories, peninsulas, fjords. **Capital:** Augusta.

Economy. Principal industries: manufacturing, services, trade, government, finance, insurance, real estate, construction. **Principal manufactured goods:** paper and wood products, leather goods. **Agriculture: Chief crops:** potatoes, apples, hay, blueberries. **Livestock** (1986): 135,000 cattle; 79,000 hogs/pigs; 17,000 sheep; 4.9 mln. poultry. **Timber/lumber** (1990): pine, spruce, fir; 814 mln. bd ft. **Nonfuel Minerals** (1991): $53 mln.; construction sand & gravel, cement, crushed stone, dimension stone. **Commercial fishing** (1991): $155.3 mln. **Chief ports:** Searsport, Portland, Eastport. **International airports at:** Portland, Bangor. **Value of construction** (1991): $768.7 mln. **Employment distribution** (1987): 24.3% trade; 21.4% serv.; 20.1% mfg.; 18.9% gvt. **Per capita income** (1991): $17,306. **Unemployment** (1991): 7.5%. **Tourism** (1989): $2 bln. **Sales tax**: 6%.

Finance. FDIC-insured commercial banks & trust companies (1990): 21. **Deposits**: $6.7 bln. **Savings institutions** (1991): 13. **Assets**: $685.7 mln.

Federal government. No. federal civilian employees (Mar. 1991): 12,279. **Avg. salary:** $30,165. **Notable federal facilities:** Kittery Naval Shipyard; Brunswick Naval Air Station; Loring Air Force Base.

Energy. Electricity production (1991, MWh, by source): Hydroelectric: 1.7 mln.; Mineral: 1.5 mln.; Nuclear: 5.9 mln.

Education. Student-teacher ratio (1990): 13.9. **Avg. salary, public school teachers** (1991-92): $29,672.

State data. Motto: Dirigo (I direct). **Flower:** White pine cone and tassel. **Bird:** Chickadee. **Tree:** Eastern white pine. **Song:** State of Maine Song. **Entered union:** Mar. 15, 1820; rank, 23d.

History. Maine's rocky coast was explored by the Cabots, 1498-99. French settlers arrived, 1604, at the St. Croix River; English, 1607, on the Kennebec. In 1691, Maine was made part of Massachusetts. In the Revolution, a Maine regiment fought at Bunker Hill; a British fleet destroyed Falmouth (now Portland), 1775, but the British ship Margaretta was captured near Machiasport. In 1820, Maine broke off from Massachusetts, became a separate state.

Tourist attractions. Acadia Nat'l. Park, Bar Harbor, on Mt. Desert Is.; Funtown, Saco; Bath Iron Works and Marine Museum; Boothbay (Harbor) Railway Museum; Portland Art Museum; Sugarloaf/USA Ski Area; Ogunquit, Portland, York.

Famous "Down Easters" include James G. Blaine, Cyrus H.K. Curtis, Hannibal Hamlin, Longfellow, Sir Hiram and Hudson Maxim, Edna St. Vincent Millay, Kate Douglas Wiggin, Ben Ames Williams.

Chamber of Commerce and Industry. 126 Sewall St., Augusta, ME 04330.

Toll-free travel information. 1-800-533-9595, winter only, out of state only; 1-207-289-2423 year round.

Maryland

Old Line State, Free State

People. Population (1991): 4,859,790; **rank:** 19 **Pop. density:** 497.2 per sq. mi. **Racial distrib.** (1990): 71.0% White; 24.9% Black; 2.9 Asian; 2.6% Hispanic. **Net change** (1990-91): 1.6%.

Geography. Total area: 10,460 sq. mi.; **rank:** 42. **Land area:** 9,775 sq. mi. **Acres forested land:** 2,632,000. **Location:** Middle Atlantic state stretching from the Ocean to the Allegheny Mtns. **Climate:** continental in the west; humid subtropical in the east. **Topography:** Eastern Shore of coastal plain and Maryland Main of coastal plain, piedmont plateau, and the Blue Ridge, separated by the Chesapeake Bay. **Capital:** Annapolis.

Economy. Principal industries: manufacturing, services, tourism. **Principal manufactured goods:** electric and electronic equipment; food and kindred products; chemicals and allied products. **Agriculture: Chief crops** (1990): corn, soybeans, greenhouse & nursery prods. **Livestock** (1990): 328,000 cattle; 180,000 hogs/pigs; 32,000 sheep; 257.8 mln. poultry. **Timber/lumber:** hardwoods. **Nonfuel Minerals** (1991): $290 mln.; crushed stone, sand & gravel, portland cement. **Commercial fishing** (1991): $47.1 mln. **Chief ports:** Baltimore. **International airports at:** Baltimore-Washington Intl. **Value of construction** (1991): $5.1 bln. **Employment distribution** (1991): 29.5% serv.; 24.2% trade; 19.8% gvt. **Per capita income** (1991): $22,080. **Unemployment** (1991): 5.9%. **Tourism** (1991): tourists spent $4.3 bln. **Sales tax:** 5.9%.

Finance. FDIC-insured commercial banks & trust companies (1990): 108. **Deposits:** $41.7 bln. **Savings institutions** (1991): 87. **Assets:** $19.7 bln.

Federal government. No. federal civilian employees (Mar. 1991): 105,862. **Avg. salary:** $37,558. **Notable federal facilities:** U.S. Naval Academy, Annapolis; Natl. Agric. Research Cen.; Ft. George G. Meade, Aberdeen Proving Ground; Goddard Space Flight Center; Natl. Institutes of Health; Natl. Institute of Standards & Technology; Food & Drug Administration; Bureau of the Census.

Energy. Electricity production (1991, MWh, by source): Hydroelectric: 1.2 mln.; Mineral: 22.5 mln.; Nuclear: 1.1 mln.

Education. Student-teacher ratio (1990): 16.8. **Avg. salary, public school teachers** (1991-92): $38,843.

State data. Motto. Fatti Maschii, Parole Femine (Manly deeds, womanly words). **Flower:** Black-eyed susan. **Bird:** Baltimore oriole. **Tree:** White oak. **Song:** Maryland, My Maryland. **Seventh** of the original 13 states to ratify Constitution, Apr. 28, 1788. **State fair** at: Timonium; late Aug.-early Sept.

History. Capt. John Smith first explored Maryland, 1608. William Claiborne set up a trading post on Kent Is. in Chesapeake Bay, 1631. Britain granted land to Cecilius Calvert, Lord Baltimore, 1632; his brother led 200 settlers to St. Marys River, 1634. The bravery of Maryland troops in the Revolution, as at the Battle of Long Island, won the state its nickname, The Old Line State. In the War of 1812, when a British fleet tried to take Fort McHenry, Marylander Francis Scott Key, 1814, wrote *The Star-Spangled Banner.*

Tourist Attractions. Racing events include the Preakness and Maryland Million, both at Pimlico track, Baltimore, and the International at Laurel Race Course; Balitmore Orioles pro baseball at Oriole Park, Camden Yards. Also Annapolis yacht races; Ocean City beach resort; restored Ft. McHenry, Baltimore, near which Francis Scott Key wrote *The Star-Spangled Banner;* Antietam Battlefield, 1862, near Hagerstown; South Mountain Battlefield, 1862; Edgar Allan Poe house, Baltimore; National Aquarium, Baltimore Harborplace; The State House, Annapolis, 1772, the oldest still in use in the U.S.; Montgomery & Prince George's County, gateway to Washington, D.C.

Famous Marylanders include Benjamin Banneker, Francis Scott Key, H.L. Mencken, William Pinkney, Upton Sinclair, Roger B. Taney, Charles Willson Peale.

Maryland Chamber and Economic Growth Associates, Inc. 111 S. Calvert St., Suite 2220, Baltimore, MD 21202.

Toll-free travel information. 1-800-543-1036.

Massachusetts

Bay State, Old Colony

People. Population (1991): 5,995,959; **rank:** 13. **Pop. density:** 765.0 per sq. mi. **Racial distrib.** (1990): 89.8% White; 5.0% Black; 2.4% Asian; 4.8% Hispanic. **Net change** (1990-91): −0.3%.

Geography. Total area: 8,284 sq. mi.; **rank:** 45. **Land area:** 7,838 sq. mi. **Acres forested land:** 3,097,000. **Location:** New England state along Atlantic seaboard. **Climate:** temperate, with colder and drier clime in western region. **Topography:** jagged indented coast from Rhode Island around Cape Cod; flat land yields to stony upland pastures near central region and gentle hilly country in west; except in west, land is rocky, sandy, and not fertile. **Capital:** Boston.

Economy. Principal industries (1990): services, trade, manufacturing. **Principal manufactured goods** (1990): electric and electronic equipment, machinery, industrial machinery and equipment, printing and publishing, fabricated metal products. **Agriculture: Chief crops:** cranberries, greenhouse, nursery, vegetables. **Livestock** (1983): 120,000 cattle; 50,000 hogs/pigs; 8,000 sheep; 125,000 horses, ponies; 3.6 mln. poultry. **Timber/lumber** (1990): white pine, oak, other hard woods; 45 mln. bd. ft. **Nonfuel Minerals** (1991): $101 mln.; mostly construction sand & gravel, crushed stone. **Commercial fishing** (1991): $295.8 mln. **Chief ports:** Boston, Fall River, New Bedford, Salem, Gloucester, Plymouth. **International airport at:** Boston. **Value of construction** (1991): $4.9 bln. **Employment distribution** (1990): 30.8% trade; 23.5% serv.; 17.5% mfg. **Per capita income** (1991): $22,897. **Unemployment** (1991): 9.0%. **Tourism** (1987): out-of-state visitors spent $12.9 bln. **Sales tax:** 5%.

Finance. FDIC-insured commercial banks & trust companies (1990): 94. **Deposits:** $66.7 bln. **Savings institutions** (1991): 23. **Assets:** $3.4 bln.

Federal government. No. federal civilian employees (Mar. 1991): 31,030. **Avg. salary:** $33,165. **Notable federal facilities:** Ft. Devens; Thomas P. O'Neill Jr. Federal Bldg., J.W. McCormack Bldg., John Fitzgerald Kennedy Federal Bldg., Boston; Q.M. Laboratory, Natick.

Energy. Electricity production (1991, MWh, by source): Hydroelectric: 0.5 mln.; Mineral: 27.6 mln.; Nuclear: 4.9 mln.

Education. Student-teacher ratio (1990): 15.4. **Avg. salary, public school teachers** (1991-92): $38,066.

State data. Motto: Ense Petit Placidam Sub Libertate Quietem (By the sword we seek peace, but peace only under liberty). **Flower:** Mayflower. **Bird:** Chickadee. **Tree:** American elm. **Song:** All Hail to Massachusetts. **Sixth** of the original 13 states to ratify Constitution, Feb. 6, 1788.

History. Pilgrims settled in Plymouth, 1620; the following year they gave thanks for their survival with the first Thanksgiving Day. Indian opposition reached a high point in King Philip's War, 1675-76, won by the colonists. Demonstrations against British restrictions set off the "Boston Massacre," 1770, and Boston "tea party," 1773. First bloodshed of the Revolution was at Lexington, 1775.

Tourist attractions. Cape Cod—Plymouth Rock, Plymouth Plantation, Mayflower II, Provincetown artists colony; Boston—Freedom Trail, Museum of Fine Arts, Children's Museum, Museum of Science, New England Aquarium, JFK Library, Boston Ballet, Boston Pops, Boston Symphony Orchestra; Berkshires—Tanglewood, Jacob's Pillow Dance Festival, Hancock Shaker Village, Berkshire Scenic Railroad; Old Sturbridge Village; Walden Pond; Naismith Memorial Basketball Hall of Fame, Springfield.

Famous "Bay Staters" include John Adams, John Quincy Adams, Samuel Adams, Louisa May Alcott, Horatio Alger, Susan B. Anthony, Crispus Attucks, Clara Barton, Alexander Graham Bell, Emily Dickinson, Ralph Waldo Emerson, John Hancock, Nathaniel Hawthorne, Oliver W. Holmes, Winslow Homer, Elias Howe, John Fitzgerald Kennedy, Samuel F.B. Morse, Edgar Allan Poe, Paul Revere, Henry David Thoreau, James McNeil Whistler, John Greenleaf Whittier.

Tourist information. Massachusetts Office of Travel & Tourism, 100 Cambridge St., 13th Floor, Boston, MA 02202.

Toll-free travel information. 1-800-624-MASS.

Michigan

Great Lakes State, Wolverine State

People. Population (1991): 9,367,627; **rank:** 8. **Pop. density:** 164.9 per sq. mi. **Racial distrib.** (1990): 83.4% White; 13.9% Black; 2.2% Hispanic. **Net change** (1990-91): 0.8%.

Geography. Total area: 58,527 sq. mi.; **rank:** 23. **Land area:** 56,809 sq. mi. **Acres forested land:** 18,220,000. **Location:** east north central state bordering on 4 of the 5 Great Lakes, divided into an Upper and Lower Peninsula by the Straits of Mackinac, which link lakes Michigan and Huron. **Climate:** well-defined seasons tempered by the Great Lakes. **Topography:** low rolling hills give way to northern tableland of hilly belts in Lower Peninsula; Upper Peninsula is level in the east, with swampy areas; western region is higher and more rugged. **Capital:** Lansing.

Economy. Principal industries: manufacturing, services, tourism, agriculture, mining. **Principal manufactured goods:** transportation equipment, machinery, fabricated metals, primary metals, food prods., rubber & plastics. **Agriculture: Chief crops:** corn, winter wheat, soybeans, dry beans, oats, hay, sugar beets, honey, asparagus, sweet corn, apples, cherries, grapes, peaches, blueberries, flowers. **Livestock** (1986): 1.4 mln. cattle; 1.2 mln. hogs/pigs; 108,000 sheep; 8.9 mln. poultry. **Timber/lumber** (1990): maple, oak, aspen; 341 mln. bd. ft. **Nonfuel Minerals** (1991): $1.4 bln.; iron ore, Portland cement, crushed stone, sand & gravel. **Commercial fishing** (1991): $10.5 mln. **Chief ports:** Detroit, Saginaw River, Escanaba, Muskegon, Saulte Ste. Marie, Port Huron, Marine City. **International airports at:** Detroit, Sault St. Marie. **Value of construction** (1991): $7.2 bln. **Employment distribution** (1990): 24% mfg.; 24% serv.; **Per capita income** (1991): $18,679. **Unemployment** (1991): 9.2%. **Tourism** (1990): travellers spent $16.5 bln. **Sales tax:** 4%.

Finance. FDIC-insured commercial banks & trust companies (1990): 255. **Deposits:** $73.2 bln. **Savings institutions** (1991): 36. **Assets:** $29.7 bln.

Federal government. No. federal civilian employees (Mar. 1991): 26,725. **Avg. salary:** $32,370. **Notable federal facilities:** Isle Royal, Sleeping Bear Dunes national parks.

Energy. Electricity production (1991, MWh, by source): Hydroelectric: 1.0 mln.; Mineral: 54.6 mln.; Nuclear: 25.2 mln.

Education. Student-teacher ratio (1990): 19.8. **Avg. salary, public school teachers** (1991-92): $40,251.

State data. Motto: Si Quaeris Peninsulam Amoenam Circumspice (If you seek a pleasant peninsula, look about you). **Flower:** Apple blossom. **Bird:** Robin. **Tree:** White pine. **Song:** Michigan, My Michigan. **Entered union** Jan. 26, 1837; rank, 26th. **State fair** at: Detroit, late Aug.-early Sept.; Upper Peninsula (Escanaba) mid-Aug; Michigan Festival, mid.-Aug.

History. French fur traders and missionaries visited the region, 1616, set up a mission at Sault Ste. Marie, 1641, and a settlement there, 1668. The whole region went to Britain, 1763. Anthony Wayne defeated their Indian allies at Fallen Timbers, Ohio, 1794. The British returned, 1812, seized Ft. Mackinac and Detroit. Oliver H. Perry's Lake Erie victory and William H. Harrison's troops, who carried the war to the Thames River in Canada, 1813, freed Michigan once more.

Tourist attractions. Henry Ford Museum, Greenfield Village, reconstruction of a typical 19th cent. American village, both in Dearborn; Michigan Space Ctr., Jackson; Tahquamenon *(Hiawatha)* Falls; DeZwaan windmill and Tulip Festival, Holland; "Soo Locks," St. Marys Falls Ship Canal, Sault Ste. Marie.

Famous Michiganians include Ralph Bunche, Thomas A. Edison, Gerald R. Ford, Paul de Kruif, Edna Ferber, Henry Ford, Aretha Franklin, Edgar Guest, Lee Iacocca, Robert Ingersoll, Magic Johnson, Will Kellogg, Ring Lardner, Elmore Leonard, Charles Lindbergh, Joe Louis, Madonna, Pontiac, Diana Ross, Tom Selleck, Lily Tomlin, Stewart Edward White, Malcolm X.

Chamber of Commerce: 200 N. Washington Sq., Suite 400, Lansing, MI 48933.

Toll-free travel information. 1-800-543-2937.

Minnesota

North Star State, Gopher State

People. Population (1991): 4,432,361; **rank:** 20. **Pop. density:** 55.7 per sq. mi. **Racial distrib.** (1990): 94.4% White; 2.2% Black; 1.8% Asian; 1.2% Hispanic. **Net change** (1990-91): 1.3%.

Geography. Total area: 84,402 sq. mi.; **rank:** 12. **Land area:** 79,617 sq. mi. **Acres forested land:** 16,583,000. **Location:** north central state bounded on the E by Wisconsin and Lake Superior, on the N by Canada, on the W by the Dakotas, and on the S by Iowa. **Climate:** northern part of state lies in the moist Great Lakes storm belt; the western border lies at the edge of the semi-arid Great Plains. **Topography:** central hill and lake region covering approx. half the state; to the NE, rocky ridges and deep lakes; to the NW, flat plain; to the S, rolling plains and deep river valleys. **Capital:** St. Paul.

Economy. Principal industries: agri business, forest products, mining, manufacturing, tourism. **Principal manufactured goods:** food processing, non-electrical machinery, chemicals, paper, electric and electronic equipment, printing and publishing, instruments, fabricated metal products. **Agriculture: Chief crops:** corn, soybeans, wheat, sugar beets, sunflowers, barley. **Livestock** (1990): 2.95 mln. cattle; 4.25 mln. hogs/pigs; 285,000 sheep; 12.7 mln. poultry. **Timber/lumber** (1990): needleleaves and hardwoods; 109 mln. bd. ft. **Nonfuel Minerals** (1991): 1.4 bln.; mostly iron ore, construction sand & gravel, industrial sand and gravel, crushed stone. **Commercial fishing** (1991): $111,000. **Chief ports:** Duluth, St. Paul, Minneapolis. **International airports at:** Minneapolis-St. Paul. **Value of construction** (1991): $4.4 bln. **Employment distribution** (1990): 24.4% trade; 26.0% serv.; 18.3% mfg.; 15.8% gvt. **Per capita income** (1991): $19,107. **Unemployment** (1991): 5.1%. **Tourism** (1987): out-of-state visitors spent $3.6 bln. **Sales tax:** 6½%.

Finance. FDIC-insured commercial banks & trust companies (1990): 628. **Deposits:** $39.6 bln. **Savings institutions** (1991): 26. **Assets:** $6.9 bln.

Federal government. No. federal civilian employees (Mar. 1991): 14,718. **Avg. salary:** $32,809.

Energy. Electricity production (1991, MWh, by source): Hydroelectric: 0.7 mln.; Mineral: 21.1 mln.; Nuclear: 8.7 mln.

Education. Student-teacher ratio (1990): 17.3. **Avg. salary, public school teachers** (1991-92): $34,782.

State data. Motto: L'Etoile du Nord (The star of the north). **Flower:** Pink and white lady's-slipper. **Bird:** Common loon. **Tree:** Red pine. **Song:** Hail! Minnesota. **Entered union** May 11, 1858; rank, 32d. **State fair** at: Saint Paul; late Aug. to early Sept.

History. Fur traders and missionaries from French Canada opened the region in the 17th century. Britain took the area east of the Mississippi, 1763. The U.S. took over that portion after the Revolution and in 1803 bought the western area as part of the Louisiana Purchase. The U.S. built present Ft. Snelling, 1820, bought lands from the Indians, 1837. Sioux Indians staged a bloody uprising, 1862, and were driven from the state.

Tourist attractions. Minnehaha Falls, Minneapolis, inspiration for Longfellow's *Hiawatha;* over 15,000 lakes; 66 state parks; 25 historical sites; Minneapolis Aquatennial; Ordway Theater, St. Paul; Guthrie Theater, Minneapolis; professional baseball, football, hockey. Voyageurs Nat'l. Park, a water wilderness along the Canadian border; Mayo Clinic, Rochester; St. Paul Winter Carnival; North Shore (of Lake Superior).

Famous Minnesotans include F. Scott Fitzgerald, Cass Gilbert, Hubert Humphrey, Sister Elizabeth Kenny, Sinclair Lewis, Paul Manship, E. G. Marshall, William and Charles Mayo, Walter F. Mondale, Charles Schulz, Harold Stassen, Thorstein Veblen.

Tourist Information. Minnesota Office of Tourism, 375 Jackson St., 250 Skyway Level, St. Paul, MN 55101.

Toll-free travel information. 1-800-328-1461.

Mississippi

Magnolia State

People. Population (1991): 2,592,003; **rank:** 31. **Pop. density:** 55.3 per sq. mi. **Racial distrib.** (1990): 63.5% White; 35.6% Black; 0.6% Hispanic. **Net change** (1990-91): 0.7%.

Geography. Total area: 47,689 sq. mi.; **rank:** 32. **Land area:** 46,914 sq. mi. **Acres forested land:** 16,693,000. **Location:** south central state bordered on the W by the Mississippi R. and on the S by the Gulf of Mexico. **Climate:** semi-tropical, with abundant rainfall, long growing season, and extreme temperatures unusual. **Topography:** low, fertile delta bet. the Yazoo and Mississippi rivers; loess bluffs stretching around delta border; sandy Gulf coastal terraces followed by piney woods and prairie; rugged, high sandy hills in extreme NE followed by black prairie belt. Pontotoc Ridge, and flatwoods into the north central highlands. **Capital:** Jackson.

Economy. Principal industries: manufacturing, government, wholesale and retail trade. **Principal manufactured goods:** apparel, food & kindred prods., furniture, lumber and wood products, electrical machinery, transportation equip. **Agriculture: Chief crops** (1990): cotton, catfish, rice, soybeans. **Livestock** (1990): 1.3 mln. cattle; 149,000 hogs/pigs; 413 mln. broilers. **Timber/lumber** (1990): pine, oak, hardwoods; 1.3 bln. bd. ft. **Nonfuel Minerals** (1991): $93.6 mln., mostly construction sand & gravel. **Commercial fishing** (1991): $34.3 mln. **Chief ports:** Pascagoula, Vicksburg, Gulfport, Natchez, Greenville. **Value of construction** (1991): $1.9 bln. **Employment distribution** (1991): 26.2% mfg.; 21.8% gvt.; 21.2% trade; 17.2% serv. **Per capita income** (1991): $13,343. **Unemployment** (1991): 8.6%. **Tourism** (1990): out-of-state visitors spent $1.68 bln. **Sales tax:** 7%.

Finance. FDIC-insured commercial banks & trust companies (1990): 122. **Deposits:** $18.2 bln. **Savings institutions** (1991): 23. **Assets:** $2.9 bln.

Federal government. No. federal civilian employees (Mar. 1991): 18,067. **Avg. salary:** $30,662. **Notable federal facilities:** Columbus, Keesler AF bases; Meridian Naval Air Station, John C. Stennis Space Center; U.S. Army Corps of Engineers Waterway Experiment Station.

Energy. Electricity production (1991, MWh, by source): Mineral: 9.6 mln.; Nuclear: 8.0 mln.

Education. Student-teacher ratio (1990): 17.9. **Avg. salary, public school teachers** (1991-92): $24,428.

State data. Motto: Virtute et Armis (By valor and arms). **Flower:** Magnolia. **Bird:** Mockingbird. **Tree:** Magnolia. **Song:** Go, Mississippi! **Entered union** Dec. 10, 1817; rank, 20th. **State fair** at: Jackson; Fall.

History. De Soto explored the area, 1540, discovered the Mississippi River, 1541. La Salle traced the river from Illinois to its mouth and claimed the entire valley for France, 1682. First settlement was the French Ft. Maurepas, near Ocean Springs, 1699. The area was ceded to Britain, 1763; American settlers followed. During the Revolution, Spain seized part of the area and refused to leave even after the U.S. acquired title at the end of the Revolution, finally moving out, 1798. Mississippi seceded 1861. Union forces captured Corinth and Vicksburg and destroyed Jackson and much of Meridian.

Tourist attractions. Vicksburg National Military Park and Cemetery, other Civil War sites; Natchez Trace; Indian mounds; Antebellum Home; pilgrimages in Natchez and some 25 other cities; Mardi Gras and blessing of the shrimp fleet, June, both in Biloxi.

Famous Mississippians include Dana Andrews, Jimmy Buffet, Hodding Carter III, William Faulkner, Shelby Foote, Fannie Lou Hamer, Jim Henson, Robert Johnson, James Earl Jones, B.B. King, L.Q.C. Lamar, Willie Morris, Elvis Presley, Leontyne Price, Charlie Pride, Eudora Welty, Tennessee Williams, Oprah Winfrey, Richard Wright, Tammy Wynette.

Dept. of Economic & Community Development. P.O. Box 1849, Jackson, MS 39205.

Toll-free travel information. 1-800-359-3297; 1-800-647-2290 out of state.

Missouri

Show Me State

People. Population (1991): 5,157,751; **rank:** 15. **Pop. density:** 74.9 per sq. mi. **Racial distrib.** (1990): 87.7% White; 10.7% Black; 1.2% Hispanic. **Net change** (1990-91): 0.8%.

Geography. Total area: 69,697 sq. mi.; **rank:** 19. **Land area:** 68,898 sq. mi. **Acres forested land:** 12,523,000. **Location:** West North central state near the geographic center of the conterminous U.S.; bordered on the E by the Mississippi R., on the NW by the Missouri R. **Climate:** continental, susceptible to cold Canadian air, moist, warm Gulf air, and drier SW air. **Topography:** Rolling hills, open, fertile plains, and well-watered prairie N of the Missouri R.; south of the river land is rough and hilly with deep, narrow valleys; alluvial plain in the SE; low elevation in the west. **Capital:** Jefferson City.

Economy. Principal industries: agriculture, manufacturing, aerospace, tourism. **Principal manufactured goods:** transportation equipment, food and related products, electrical and electronic equipment, chemicals. **Agriculture: Chief crops:** soybeans, corn, wheat, hay. **Livestock** (1990): 4.5 mln. cattle; 2.8 mln. hogs/pigs; 134,000 sheep; 8.0 mln. chickens, 18.0 mln. turkeys. **Timber/lumber** (1990): oak, hickory; 256 mln. bd. ft. **Nonfuel Minerals** (1991): $880 mln., mostly lead, crushed stone, Portland cement. **Chief ports:** St. Louis, Kansas City. **International airports at:** St. Louis, Kansas City. **Value of construction** (1991): $3.9 bln. **Employment distribution** (1990): 24.7% services; 24.0% trade; 18.7% mfg.; 15.7% gvt. **Per capita income** (1991): $17,842. **Unemployment** (1991): 6.6%. **Tourism** (1990): total travelers spent $5 bln. **Sales tax**: 4.225%.

Finance. FDIC-insured commercial banks & trust companies (1990): 549. **Deposits**: $49.7 bln. **Savings institutions** (1991): 65. **Assets**: $15.0 bln.

Federal government: No. federal civilian employees (Mar. 1991): 45,573. **Avg. salary:** $30,508. **Notable federal facilities:** Federal Reserve banks, St. Louis, Kansas City; Ft. Leonard Wood, Rolla; Jefferson Barracks, St. Louis; Whiteman AFB, Knob Noster.

Energy. Electricity production (1991 MWh, by source): Hydroelectric: 1.3 mln.; Mineral: 36.9 mln.; Nuclear: 8.7 mln.

Education. Student-teacher ratio (1990): 15.5. **Avg. salary, public school teachers** (1991-92); $28,880.

State data. Motto: Salus Populi Suprema Lex Esto (The welfare of the people shall be the supreme law). **Flower:** Hawthorn. **Bird:** Bluebird. **Tree:** Dogwood. **Song:** Missouri Waltz. **Entered union** Aug. 10, 1821; rank, 24th. **State fair** at: Sedalia; 3d week in Aug.

History. DeSoto visited the area, 1541. French hunters and lead miners made the first settlement, c. 1735, at Ste. Genevieve. The U.S. acquired Missouri as part of the Louisiana Purchase, 1803. The fur trade and the Santa Fe Trail provided prosperity; St. Louis became the "jump-off" point for pioneers on their way West. Pro- and anti-slavery forces battled each other there during the Civil War.

Tourist attractions. Mark Twain Area, Hannibal; Pony Express Museum, St. Joseph; Harry S. Truman Library, Independence; Gateway Arch, St. Louis; Silver Dollar City, Branson Worlds of Fun, Kansas City; Lake of the Ozarks, Churchill Memorial, Fulton; State Capitol, Jefferson City.

Famous Missourians include Josephine Baker, Thomas Hart Benton, George Caleb Bingham, Gen. Omar Bradley, George Washington Carver, Walter Cronkite, Dale Carnegie, Walt Disney, T.S. Eliot, Betty Grable, Jesse James, J. C. Penney, John J. Pershing, Joseph Pulitzer, Ginger Rogers, Bess Truman, Harry S. Truman, Mark Twain, Tennessee Williams.

Chamber of Commerce: 400 E. High St., P.O. Box 149, Jefferson City, MO 65101.

Toll-free travel information. 1-800-877-1234.

Montana

Treasure State

People. Population (1991): 808,487; **rank:** 44. **Pop. density:** 5.55 per sq. mi. **Racial distrib.** (1990): 92.7% White; 0.3% Black; 6.0% Amer. Indian; 1.5% Hispanic. **Net change** (1990-91): 1.2%.

Geography. Total area: 147,046 sq. mi.; **rank:** 4. **Land area:** 145,556 sq. mi. **Acres forested land:** 21,910,000. **Location:** Mountain state bounded on the E by the Dakotas, on the S by Wyoming, on the S/SW by Idaho, and on the N by Canada. **Climate:** colder, continental climate with low humidity. **Topography:** Rocky Mtns. in western third of the state; eastern two-thirds gently rolling northern Great Plains. **Capital:** Helena.

Economy. Principal industries: agriculture, timber, mining, tourism, oil & gas. **Principal manufactured goods:** food prods., wood & paper prods., primary metals, printing & publishing, petroleum & coal prods. **Agriculture: Chief crops:** wheat, barley, sugar beets, hay, oats. **Livestock** (1991): 2.4 mln. cattle; 185,000 hogs/pigs; 683,000 sheep; 760,000 poultry. **Timber/lumber** (1990): Douglas fir, pines, larch; 1.5 bln. bd. ft. **Nonfuel Minerals** (1991): $532 mln. mostly metallics. **International airports at:** Great Falls, Billings, Kalispell, Missoula. **Value of construction** (1991): $450.7 mln. **Employment distribution** (1990): 26.8% serv.; 22.2% trade; 18.5% govt.; 7.3% agric; 5.9% mfg. **Per capita income** (1991): $16,043. **Unemployment** (1991): 6.9%. **Tourism** (1990): non-resident visitors spent $751 mln.

Finance. FDIC-insured commercial banks & trust companies (1990): 158. **Deposits**: $6.0 bln. **Savings institutions** (1991): 9. **Assets**: $1.3 bln.

Federal government. No. federal civilian employees (Mar. 1991): 8,478. **Avg. salary:** $31,247. **Notable federal facilities:** Malmstrom AFB; Ft. Peck, Hungry Horse, Libby, Yellowtail dams, numerous missile silos.

Energy. Electricity production (1991, MWh, by source): Hydroelectric: 9.8 mln; Mineral: 15.5 mln.

Education. Student-teacher ratio (1990): 15.9. **Avg. salary, public school teachers** (1991-92): $27,513.

State data. Motto: Oro y Plata (Gold and silver). **Flower:** Bitterroot. **Bird:** Western meadowlark. **Tree:** Ponderosa pine. **Song:** Montana. **Entered union** Nov. 8, 1889; rank, 41st. **State fair** at: Great Falls; late July to early Aug.

History. French explorers visited the region, 1742. The U.S. acquired the area partly through the Louisiana Purchase, 1803, and partly through the explorations of Lewis and Clark, 1805-06. Fur traders and missionaries established posts in the early 19th century. Indian uprisings reached their peak with the Battle of the Little Bighorn, 1876. Mining activity and the coming of the Northern Pacific Railway, 1883, brought population growth.

Tourist attractions. Glacier Natl. Park, on the Continental Divide, is a scenic and recreational wonderland, with 60 glaciers, 200 lakes, and many trout streams. Yellowstone Natl. Park has 3 of the 5 entrances in Montana, with 2,221,000 acres of scenic beauty, inc. geysers, mountains, canyons, streams, lakes, forests, waterfalls.

Also, Museum of the Plains Indian, Blackfeet Reservation near Browning; Little Bighorn Battlefield Natl. Monument & Custer Natl. Cemetery; Flathead Lake, in the NW, Lewis and Clark Caverns State Park, near Whitehall; 7 Indian reservations, covering over 5 million acres; state capitol and historical society, Helena.

Famous Montanans include Gary Cooper, Marcus Daly, Chet Huntley, Will James, Myrna Loy, Mike Mansfield, Brent Musberger, Jeannette Rankin, Charles M. Russell, Lester Thurow.

Chamber of Commerce. 2030 11th Ave., P.O. Box 1730, Helena, MT 59624.

Toll-free travel information. 1-800-541-1447.

Nebraska

Cornhusker State

People. Population (1991): 1,592,717; **rank:** 36. **Pop. density:** 20.7 per sq. mi. **Racial distrib.** (1990): 93.8% White; 3.6% Black; 2.3% Hispanic. **Net change** (1990-91): 0.9%.

Geography. Total area: 77,355 sq. mi.; **rank:** 15. **Land area:** 76,878 sq. mi. **Acres forested land:** 722,000. **Location:** West North Central state with the Missouri R. for a NE/E border. **Climate:** continental semi-arid. **Topography:** till plains of the central lowland in the eastern third rising to the Great Plains and hill country of the north central and NW. **Capital:** Lincoln.

Economy. Principal industries: agriculture, food processing, manufacturing. **Principal manufactured goods:** foods, machinery, electric and electronic equipment, primary and fabricated metal products, transportation equipment, instruments & related prod. **Agriculture: Chief crops:** corn, sorghum, soybeans, hay, wheat, beans, oats, potatoes, sugar beets. **Livestock** (1990): 6 mln. cattle; 4.2 mln. hogs/pigs; 160,000 sheep; 6.2 mln. chickens, 2.1 mln. turkeys. **Nonfuel Minerals** (1991): $85.4 mln.; mostly Portland cement, crushed stone, construction sand & gravel. **Chief ports:** Omaha, Sioux City, Brownville, Blair, Plattsmouth, Nebraska City. **Value of construction** (1991): $1.2 bln. **Employment distribution** (1990): 25.5% trade; 24.4% serv.; 19.7% gvt.; 13.8% mfg.; 8.8% agric. **Per capita income** (1991): $17,852. **Unemployment** (1991): 2.7%. **Tourism** (1991): traveler expenditures $1.7 bln. **Sales tax:** 5%, + some local sales taxes of .5-1.5%.

Finance. FDIC-insured commercial banks & trust companies (1990): 392. **Deposits:** $16.3 bln. **Savings institutions** (1991): 17. **Assets:** $8.1 bln.

Federal government. No. federal civilian employees (Mar. 1991): 9,113. **Avg. salary:** $31,277. **Notable federal facilities:** Strategic Air Command Base, Omaha.

Energy. Electricity production (1991, MWh, by source): Hydroelectric: 0.5 mln.; Mineral: 12.0 mln.; Nuclear: 5.6 mln.

Education. Student-teacher ratio (1990): 14.6. **Avg. salary, public school teachers** (1991-92): $27,231.

State data. Motto: Equality before the law. **Flower:** Goldenrod. **Bird:** Western meadowlark. **Tree:** Cottonwood. **Song:** Beautiful Nebraska. **Entered union** Mar. 1, 1867; rank, 37th. **State fair** at: Lincoln; late Aug. to mid-Sept.

History. Spanish and French explorers and fur traders visited the area prior to the Louisiana Purchase, 1803. Lewis and Clark passed through, 1804-06. First permanent settlement was Bellevue, near Omaha, 1823. Many Civil War veterans settled under free land terms of the 1862 Homestead Act; struggles followed between homesteaders and ranchers.

Tourist attractions. Architecturally unique, 400′ tall state capitol, Lincoln; Stuhr Museum of the Prairie Pioneer, Grand Island; Museum of the Fur Trade, Chadron; State Museum (Elephant Hall), Lincoln; Joslyn Art Museum, Omaha; Strategic Air Command Museum, Bellevue; Boys Town, founded by Fr. Flanagan, west of Omaha; Arbor Lodge State Park, Nebraska City; Buffalo Bill Ranch State Historical Park, North Platte; Pioneer Village, Minden; Oregon Trail landmarks, Scotts Bluff National Monument, Chimney Rock Historic Site, Ft. Robinson; Hastings Museum, McDonald Planetarium, Hastings.

Famous Nebraskans include Fred Astaire, Charles W. and William Jennings Bryan, Johnny Carson, Willa Cather, William F. "Buffalo Bill" Cody, Loren Eiseley, Rev. Edward J. Flanagan, Henry Fonda, Gerald R. Ford, Rollin Kirby, Harold Lloyd, Wright Morris, J. Sterling Morton, John Neidhardt, George Norris, Gen. John J. Pershing, Chief Red Cloud, Mari Sandoz, Malcolm X, Roscoe Pound.

Chamber of Commerce. 1320 Lincoln Mall, Box 95128, Lincoln, NE 68501.

Toll-free travel information. 1-800-742-7595; 1-800-228-4307 out of state.

Nevada

Sagebrush State, Battle Born State, Silver State

People. Population (1991): 1,283,832; **rank:** 38. **Pop. density:** 11.7 per sq. mi. **Racial distrib.** (1990): 84.3% White; 6.6% Black; 3.2% Asian; 10.4% Hispanic. **Net change** (1990-91): 6.8%.

Geography. Total area: 110,561 sq. mi.; **rank:** 7. **Land area:** 109,806 sq. mi. **Acres forested land:** 8,928,000. **Location:** Mountain state bordered on N by Oregon and Idaho, on E by Utah and Arizona, on SE by Arizona, and on SW/W by California. **Climate:** semi-arid and arid. **Topography:** rugged N-S mountain ranges; highest elevation, Boundary Peak, 13,140 ft.; southern area is within the Mojave Desert; lowest elevation, Colorado River at southern tip of state, 479 ft. **Capital:** Carson City.

Economy. Principal industries: gaming, tourism, mining, manufacturing, government, agriculture, warehousing, trucking. **Principal manufactured goods:** gaming devices, chemicals, aerospace prods.; lawn & garden irrigation equip.; seismic & machinery-monitoring devices. **Agriculture: Chief crops:** hay, alfalfa seed, potatoes, onions, garlic, barley, wheat. **Livestock** (1991): 520,000 cattle; 14,000 hogs/pigs; 98,500 sheep; 14,000 poultry. **Timber/lumber:** piñon, juniper, other pines. **Nonfuel Minerals** (1991): $2.5 bln.; mostly gold, construction sand & gravel. **International airports at** Las Vegas, Reno. **Value of construction** (1991): $2.4 bln. **Employment distribution** (1991): 44.3% serv.; 20.3% trade; 12.8% gvt. **Per capita income** (1991): $19,175. **Unemployment** (1991): 5.5%. **Tourism** (1991): out-of-state travelers spent over $10 bln. **Sales tax:** 6.5-7%.

Finance. FDIC-insured commercial banks & trust companies (1990): 19. **Deposits:** $8.3 bln. **Savings institutions** (1991): 5. **Assets:** $3.9 bln.

Federal government. No. federal civilian employees (Mar. 1991): 6,875. **Avg. salary:** $32,916. **Notable federal facilities:** Nevada Test Site; Hawthorne Army Ammunition Plant, Nellis Air Force Base & Gunnery Range; Fallon Naval Air Station; Palomino Valley Wild Horse & Burro Placement Center.

Energy. Electricity production (1991, MWh, by source): Hydroelectric: 1.0 mln.; Mineral: 16.6 mln.

Education. Student-teacher ratio (1990): 19.4. **Avg. salary, public school teachers** (1991-92): $33,175.

State data. Motto: All for our country. **Flower:** Sagebrush. **Bird:** Mountain bluebird. **Trees:** Single-leaf pinon and bristlecone pine. **Song:** Home Means Nevada. **Entered union** Oct. 31, 1864; rank, 36th. **State fair** at Reno; early Sept.

History. Nevada was first explored by Spaniards in 1776. Hudson's Bay Co. trappers explored the north and central region, 1825; trader Jedediah Smith crossed the state, 1826 and 1827. The area was acquired by the U.S., in 1848, at the end of the Mexican War. First settlement, Mormon Station, now Genoa, was est. 1849. In the early 20th century, Nevada adopted progressive measures such as the initiative, referendum, recall, and woman suffrage.

Tourist attractions. Legalized casino gambling provided the impetus for the development of resort facilities at Lake Tahoe, Reno, Las Vegas, and elsewhere. Ghost towns, rodeos, mountain climbing, skiing, golfing, trout fishing, water sports and hunting important. Notable are Hoover Dam, Lake Mead Natl. Recreation Area, Lake Tahoe, Great Basin Natl. Park, Valley of Fire State Park & Virginia City. Annual events inc. Helldorado Days & Rodeo, Las Vegas; Reno Rodeo; Basque Festival, Elko; Nevada Day, Carson City; Cowboy Poetry Gathering, Elko.

Famous Nevadans include Walter Van Tilburg Clark, Sarah Winnemucca Hopkins, Paul Laxalt, John William

Mackay, Pat McCarran, Dat So La Lee, Key Pittman, William Morris Stewart.

Tourist Information. Commission on Tourism, Capitol Complex, Carson City, NV 89710.

Toll-free travel information. 1-800-638-2328.

New Hampshire

Granite State

People. Population (1991): 1,104,695; **rank:** 41. **Pop. density:** 123.2 per sq. mi. **Racial distrib.** (1990): 98.0% White; 0.6% Black; 1.0% Hispanic. **Net change** (1990-91): −0.4%.

Geography. Total area: 9,279 sq. mi.; **rank:** 44. **Land area:** 8,969 sq. mi. **Acres forested land:** 5,021,000. **Location:** New England state bounded on S by Massachusetts, on W by Vermont, on N/NW by Canada, on E by Maine and the Atlantic O. **Climate:** highly varied, due to its nearness to high mountains and ocean. **Topography:** low, rolling coast followed by countless hills and mountains rising out of a central plateau. **Capital:** Concord.

Economy. Principal industries: tourism, manufacturing, agriculture, trade, mining. **Principal manufactured goods:** machinery, electrical & electronic products, plastics, fabricated metal products. **Agriculture: Chief crops:** dairy products, nursery and greenhouse products, hay, vegetables, fruit, maple syrup & sugar prods. **Livestock** (1991): 55,000 cattle; 9,500 hogs/pigs; 9,000 sheep; 310,000 poultry. **Timber/lumber** (1990): white pine, hemlock, oak, birch; 201 mln. bd. ft. **Nonfuel Minerals** (1991): $26 mln.; mostly construction sand & gravel, crushed & dimension stone. **Commercial fishing** (1991): $13.3 mln. **Chief ports:** Portsmouth, Hampton, Rye. **Value of construction** (1991): $815 mln. **Employment distribution** (1991): 20.8% mfg.; 23.7% trade; 26.6% serv; 15.7% gvt. **Per capita income** (1991): $20,951. **Unemployment** (1991): 7.2%. **Tourism** (1991): out-of-state visitors spent $3.5 bln.

Finance. FDIC-insured commercial banks & trust companies (1990): 43. **Deposits:** $8.1 bln. **Savings institutions** (1991): 9. **Assets**: $1.5 bln.

Federal government. No. federal civilian employees (Mar. 1991): 3,596. **Avg. salary:** $35,103.

Energy. Electricity production (1991, MWh, by source): Hydroelectric: 1.1 mln.; Mineral: 4.7 mln.; Nuclear: 8.1 mln.

Education: Student-teacher ratio (1990): 16.2. **Avg. salary, public school teachers** (1991-92): $33,175.

State data. Motto: Live free or die. **Flower:** Purple lilac. **Bird:** Purple finch. **Tree:** White birch. **Song:** Old New Hampshire. **Ninth** of the original 13 states to ratify the Constitution, June 21, 1788.

History. First explorers to visit the New Hampshire area were England's Martin Pring, 1603, and Champlain, 1605. First settlement was Odiorne's Point (now port of Rye), 1623. Indian raids were halted, 1759, by Robert Rogers' Rangers. Before the Revolution, New Hampshire men seized a British fort at Portsmouth, 1774, and drove the royal governor out, 1775. Three regiments served in the Continental Army and scores of privateers raided British shipping.

Tourist attractions. Mt. Washington, highest peak in Northeast, hub of network of trails; Lake Winnipesaukee; White Mt. Natl. Forest; Crawford, Franconia, Pinkham notches in White Mt. region—Franconia famous for the Old Man of the Mountain, described by Hawthorne as the Great Stone Face; the Flume, a spectacular gorge; the aerial tramway on Cannon Mt; Strawbery Banke, Portsmouth; Shaker Village, Canterbury; St. Gaudens, natl. historic site, Cornish; Mt. Monadnock.

Famous New Hampshirites include Salmon P. Chase, Ralph Adams Cram, Mary Baker Eddy, Daniel Chester French, Robert Frost, Horace Greeley, Sarah Buell Hale, Franklin Pierce, Augustus Saint-Gaudens, Daniel Webster.

Tourist Information. Department of Resources and Economic Development, Division of Travel & Tourism Development, P.O. Box 856, Concord, NH 03302-0856; 603-271-2666.

New Jersey

Garden State

People. Population (1991): 7,760,487; **rank:** 9. **Pop. density:** 1,046.0 per sq. mi. **Racial distrib.** (1990): 79.3% White; 13.4% Black; 3.5% Asian; 9.6% Hispanic. **Net change** (1990-91): 0.4%.

Geography. Total area: 7,787 sq. mi.; **rank:** 46. **Land area:** 7,419 sq. mi. **Acres forested land:** 1,985,000. **Location:** Middle Atlantic state bounded on the N and E by New York and the Atlantic O., on the S and W by Delaware and Pennsylvania. **Climate:** moderate, with marked difference bet. NW and SE extremities. **Topography:** Appalachian Valley in the NW also has highest elevation, High Pt., 1,801 ft.; Appalachian Highlands, flat-topped NE-SW mountain ranges; Piedmont Plateau, low plains broken by high ridges (Palisades) rising 400-500 ft.; Coastal Plain, covering three-fifths of state in SE, gradually rises from sea level to gentle slopes. **Capital:** Trenton.

Economy. Principal industries: services, trade, manufacturing. **Principal manufactured goods:** chemicals, electronic and electrical equipment, non-electrical machinery, fabricated metals. **Agriculture: Chief crops:** hay, corn, soybeans, tomatoes, blueberries, peaches, cranberries. **Livestock** (1992): 77,000 cattle; 24,000 hogs/pigs; 13,000 sheep; 2.1 mln. poultry. **Timber/lumber** (1989): pine, cedar, mixed hardwoods; 4 mln. bd. ft. **Nonfuel Minerals** (1991): $203 mln.; mostly crushed stone, construction sand & gravel. **Commercial fishing** (1991): $96.9 mln. **Chief ports:** Newark, Elizabeth, Hoboken, Camden. **International airports at:** Newark. **Value of construction** (1991): $6.2 bln. **Employment distribution** (1991): 27.5% serv.; 23.5% trade; 16.0% mfg.; 16.2% gvt. **Per capita income** (1991): $25,372. **Unemployment** (1991): 6.6%. **Tourism** (1988): tourists spent $13.6 bln. **Sales tax**: 7%.

Finance. FDIC-insured commercial banks & trust companies (1990): 127. **Deposits**: $73.3. **Savings institutions** (1991): 96. **Assets**: $34.4 bln.

Federal government. No. federal civilian employees (Mar. 1991): 38,347. **Avg. salary:** $35,343. **Notable federal facilities:** McGuire AFB Fort Dix; Fort Monmouth; Picatinny Arsenal; Lakewood Naval Air Station, Lakehurst Naval Air Engineering Center.

Energy. Electricity production (1991, MWh, by source): Mineral: 9.2 mln.; Nuclear: 19.9 mln.

Education. Student-teacher ratio (1990): 13.6. **Avg. salary, public school teachers** (1991-92): $41,381.

State Data. Motto: Liberty and prosperity. **Flower:** Purple violet. **Bird:** Eastern goldfinch. **Tree:** Red oak. **Third** of the original 13 states to ratify the Constitution, Dec. 18, 1787. **State fair:** usually Aug.

History. The Lenni Lenape (Delaware) Indians had mostly peaceful relations with European colonists who arrived after the explorers Verrazano, 1524, and Hudson, 1609. The Dutch were first; when the British took New Netherland, 1664, the area between the Delaware and Hudson Rivers was given to Lord John Berkeley and Sir George Carteret. New Jersey was the scene of nearly 100 battles, large and small, during the Revolution, including Trenton, 1776, Princeton, 1777, Monmouth, 1778.

Tourist attractions. 127 miles of beaches; Miss America Pageant and hotel-casinos, Atlantic City; Grover Cleveland birthplace, Caldwell. Cape May Historic District; Edison Labs, W. Orange; Great Adventure amusement park; Liberty State Park; Meadowlands Sports Complex; Pine Barrens wilderness area; Princeton University; numerous Revolutionary War historical sites.

Famous New Jerseyans include Count Basie, Judy Blume, Aaron Burr, Grover Cleveland, James Fenimore Cooper, Stephen Crane, Thomas Edison, Albert Einstein, Alexander Hamilton, Joyce Kilmer, Gen. George McClellan, Thomas Paine, Molly Pitcher, Paul Robeson, Philip Roth, Walter Schirra, Frank Sinatra, Bruce Springsteen, Walt Whitman, William Carlos Williams, Woodrow Wilson.

Chamber of Commerce. 51 Commerce St., Newark, NJ 07102.
Toll-free travel information. 1-800-JERSEY-7.

New Mexico

Land of Enchantment

People. Population (1991): 1,547,721; **rank:** 37. **Pop. density:** 12.8 per sq. mi. **Racial distrib.** (1990): 75.6% White; 2.0% Black; 8.9% Amer. Indian; 38.2% Hispanic. **Net change** (1990-91): 2.2%.

Geography. Total area: 121,593 sq. mi.; **rank:** 5. **Land area:** 121,364 sq. mi. **Acres forested land:** 18,526,000. **Location:** southwestern state bounded by Colorado on the N, Oklahoma, Texas, and Mexico on the E and S, and Arizona on the W. **Climate:** dry, with temperatures rising or falling 5°F with every 1,000 ft. elevation. **Topography:** eastern third, Great Plains; central third Rocky Mtns. (85% of the state is over 4,000 ft. elevation); western third high plateau. **Capital:** Santa Fe.

Economy. Principal industries: government, services, trade. **Principal manufactured goods:** foods, machinery, apparel, lumber, printing, transportation equipment. **Agriculture: Chief crops:** hay, onions, wheat, pecans, corn, cotton, sorghum. **Livestock** (1990): 1.34 mln. cattle; 27,000 hogs; 462,000 sheep; 1.43 mln. poultry. **Timber/lumber** (1990): Ponderosa pine, Douglas fir; 185 mln. bd. ft. **Nonfuel Minerals** (1991): $1 bln.; copper, potash, construction sand & gravel. **International airports at:** Albuquerque. **Value of construction** (1991): $1.5 bln. **Employment distribution** (1990): 26% serv.; 2% agric.; 10% mfg.; 26.2% gvt. **Per capita income** (1991): $14,844. **Unemployment** (1991): 6.9%. **Tourism** (1990): out-of-state visitors spent $2.2 bln. **Sales tax:** 5-6.75%.

Finance. FDIC-insured commercial banks & trust companies (1990): 91. **Deposits:** $9.5 bln. **Savings institutions** (1991): 13. **Assets:** $1.2 bln.

Federal government. No. federal civilian employees (Mar. 1991): 23,173. **Avg. salary:** $31,353. **Notable federal facilities:** Kirtland, Cannon, Holloman AF bases; Los Alamos Scientific Laboratory; White Sands Missile Range, National Solar Observatory, National Radio Astronomy Observatory.

Energy. Electricity production (1991, MWh, by source): Hydroelectric: 0.1 mln.; Mineral: 22.3 mln.

Education. Student-teacher ratio (1990): 18.1. **Avg. salary, public school teachers** (1991-92): $26,653.

State data. Motto: Crescit Eundo (It grows as it goes). **Flower:** Yucca. **Bird:** Roadrunner. **Tree:** Pinon. **Song:** O, Fair New Mexico, Asi Es Nuevo Mexico. **Entered union** Jan. 6, 1912; rank, 47th. **State fair** at: Albuquerque; mid-Sept.

History. Franciscan Marcos de Niza and a black slave Estevan explored the area, 1539, seeking gold. First settlements were at San Juan Pueblo, 1598, and Santa Fe, 1610. Settlers alternately traded and fought with the Apaches, Comanches, and Navajos. Trade on the Santa Fe Trail to Missouri started 1821. The Mexican War was declared May, 1846, Gen. Stephen Kearny took Santa Fe, August. In the 1870s, cattlemen staged the famed Lincoln County War in which Billy (the Kid) Bonney played a leading role. Pancho Villa raided Columbus, 1916.

Tourist Attractions. Carlsbad Caverns, a national park, has caverns on 3 levels and the largest natural cave "room" in the world, 1,500 by 300 ft., 300 ft. high; White Sands Natl. Monument, the largest gypsum deposit in the world.

Pueblo ruins from 100 AD, Chaco Canyon; Acoma, the "sky city," built atop a 357-ft. mesa; 19 Pueblo, 4 Navajo, and 2 Apache reservations. Also, ghost towns, dude ranches, skiing, hunting, and fishing.

Famous New Mexicans include Billy (the Kid) Bonney, Kit Carson, Peter Hurd, Archbishop Jean Baptiste Lamy, Nancy Lopez, Bill Mauldin, Georgia O'Keeffe, Kim Stanley, Al Unser, Bobby Unser, Lew Wallace.

Tourist information. New Mexico Dept. of Tourism, P.O. Box 20003, Santa Fe, N.M. 87503.
Toll-free travel information. 1-800-545-2040.

New York

Empire State

People. Population (1991): 18,057,602 **rank:** 2. **Pop. density:** 382.4 per sq. mi. **Racial distrib.** (1990): 74.4% White; 15.9% Black; 3.9% Asian; 12.3% Hispanic. **Net change** (1990-91): 0.4%.

Geography. Total area: 49,108 sq. mi.; **rank:** 30. **Land area:** 47,224 sq. mi. **Acres forested land:** 18,775,000. **Location:** Middle Atlantic state, bordered by the New England states, Atlantic Ocean, New Jersey and Pennsylvania, Lakes Ontario and Erie, and Canada. **Climate:** variable; the SE region moderated by the ocean. **Topography:** highest and most rugged mountains in the NE Adirondack upland; St. Lawrence-Champlain lowlands extend from Lake Ontario NE along the Canadian border; Hudson-Mohawk lowland follows the flows of the rivers N and W, 10-30 mi. wide; Atlantic coastal plain in the SE; Appalachian Highlands, covering half the state westward from the Hudson Valley, include the Catskill Mtns., Finger Lakes; plateau of Erie-Ontario lowlands. **Capital:** Albany.

Economy. Principal industries: manufacturing, finance, communications, tourism, transportation, services. **Principal manufactured goods:** books and periodicals, clothing and apparel, pharmaceuticals, machinery, instruments, toys and sporting goods, electronic equipment, automotive and aircraft components. **Agriculture: Chief crops:** apples, cabbage, cauliflower, celery, cherries, grapes, corn, peas, snap beans, sweet corn. **Products:** milk, cheese, maple syrup, wine. **Livestock** (1990): 1.6 mln. cattle; 103,000 hogs/pigs; 92,000 sheep; 9.8 mln. poultry. **Timber/lumber** (1990): saw log production; 368 mln. bd. ft. **Nonfuel Minerals** (1991): $676.8 mln.; mostly crushed stone, salt, cement, construction sand & gravel, zinc. **Commercial fishing** (1991): $53.2 mln. **Chief ports:** New York, Buffalo, Albany. **International airports at:** New York, Buffalo, Syracuse, Massena, Ogdensburg, Watertown, Niagara Falls, Newburgh, Sullivan county. **Value of construction** (1991): $12.3 bln. **Employment distribution** (1991): 29% serv.; 20% trade; 18% gvt.; 13% mfg. **Per capita income** (1991): $22,456. **Unemployment** (1991): 7.2%. **Tourism** (1990): tourists spent $20.0 bln. **Sales tax:** 4-8¼%.

Finance. FDIC-insured commercial banks & trust companies (1990): 191. **Deposits:** $263.2 bln. **Savings institutions** (1991): 70. **Assets:** $42.7 bln.

Federal government. No. federal civilian employees (Mar. 1991): 68,980. **Avg. salary:** $32,881. **Notable federal facilities:** West Point Military Academy; Merchant Marine Academy; Ft. Drum; Griffiss, Plattsburgh AF bases; Watervliet Arsenal.

Energy. Electricity production (1991, MWh, by source): Hydroelectric: 21.2 mln.; Mineral: 56.4 mln.; Nuclear: 27.7 mln.

Education: Student-teacher ratio (1990): 14.7. **Avg. salary, public school teachers** (1991-92): $44,200.

State data. Motto: Excelsior (Ever upward). **Flower:** Rose. **Bird:** Bluebird. **Tree:** Sugar maple. **Song:** I Love New York. **Eleventh** of the original 13 states to ratify the Constitution, July 26, 1788. **State fair** at: Syracuse, late Aug.-early Sept.

History. In 1609 Henry Hudson discovered the river that bears his name and Champlain explored the lake, far upstate, which was named for him. Dutch built posts near Albany 1614 and 1624; in 1626 they settled Manhattan. A British fleet seized New Netherland, 1664. Ninety-two of the 300 or more engagements of the Revolution were fought in New York, including the Battle of Bemis Heights-Saratoga, a turning point of the war.

Tourist attractions. New York City; Adirondack and Catskill mtns.; Finger Lakes, Great Lakes; Long Island beaches; Thousand Islands; Niagara Falls; Saratoga Springs racing and spas; Philipsburg Manor, Sunnyside, the restored home of Washington Irving, The Dutch Church of Sleepy Hollow, all in North Tarrytown; Corning Glass Center and Steuben factory, Corning; Fenimore House, National Baseball Hall of Fame and Museum, both in Cooperstown; Ft. Ticonderoga overlooking lakes George and Champlain; Albany's Empire State Plaza, Lake Placid Olympic Village.

The Franklin D. Roosevelt National Historic Site, Hyde Park, includes the graves of Pres. and Mrs. Roosevelt, the family home since 1867, the Roosevelt Library. Sagamore Hill, Oyster Bay, the Theodore Roosevelt estate, includes his home.

Famous New Yorkers include Susan B. Anthony, Peter Cooper, George Eastman, Millard Fillmore, George and Ira Gershwin, Julia Ward Howe, Charles Evans Hughes, Henry and William James, Herman Melville, Franklin Delano Roosevelt, Theodore Roosevelt, Alfred E. Smith, Elizabeth Cady Stanton, Martin Van Buren, Walt Whitman.

Tourist information: N.Y. State Dept. of Economic Development, 1 Commerce Plaza, Albany, NY 12245.

Toll-free travel information. 1-800-CALLNYS, from 50 states & U.S. territories; 1-518-474-4116 from other areas and Canada.

North Carolina

Tar Heel State, Old North State

People. Population (1991): 6,736,827; **rank:** 10. **Pop. density:** 138.3 per sq. mi. **Racial distrib.** (1990): 75.6% White; 22.0% Black; 1.2% Amer. Indian; 1.2% Hispanic. **Net change** (1990-91): 1.8%.

Geography. Total area: 52,669 sq. mi.; **rank:** 28. **Land area:** 48,718 sq. mi. **Acres forested land:** 18,891,000. **Location:** South Atlantic state bounded by Virginia, South Carolina, Georgia, Tennessee, and the Atlantic O. **Climate:** sub-tropical in SE, medium-continental in mountain region; tempered by the Gulf Stream and the mountains in W. **Topography:** coastal plain and tidewater, two-fifths of state, extending to the fall line of the rivers; piedmont plateau, another two-fifths, 200 mi. wide of gentle to rugged hills; southern Appalachian Mtns. contains the Blue Ridge and Great Smoky mtns. **Capital:** Raleigh.

Economy. Principal industries: manufacturing, agriculture, tobacco, tourism. **Principal manufactured goods:** textiles, tobacco products, electrical/electronic equip., chemicals, furniture, food products, non-electrical machinery. **Agriculture: Chief crops:** tobacco, soybeans, corn, peanuts, small sweet potatoes, feed grains, vegetables, fruits. **Livestock** (1991): 950,000 cattle; 2.8 mln. hogs/pigs; 19.3 mln. chickens. **Timber/lumber** (1990): yellow pine, oak, hickory, poplar, maple. 1.5 bln. bd. ft. **Nonfuel Minerals** (1991): Total $517.2 mln., mostly clay, sand & gravel, crushed stone. **Commercial fishing** (1991): $66.7 mln. **Chief ports:** Morehead City, Wilmington. **Value of construction** (1991): $6.9 bln. **Employment distribution** (1991): 26.9% mfg.; 22.9% trade; 17.6% serv.; 19.5% gvt. **Per capita income** (1991): $16,642. **Unemployment** (1991): 5.8%. **Tourism** (1990): out-of-state visitors spent $6.4 bln. **Sales tax:** 5.0%.

Finance. FDIC-insured commercial banks & trust companies (1990): 79. **Deposits:** $49.6 bln. **Savings institutions** (1991): 113. **Assets:** $17.3 bln.

Federal government. No. federal civilian employees (Mar. 1991): 29,136. **Avg. salary:** $29,621. **Notable federal facilities:** Ft. Bragg; Camp LeJeune Marine Base; U.S. EPA Research and Development Labs, Cherry Point Marine Corps Air Station; Natl. Humanities Center; Natl. Inst. of Environmental Health Science; Natl. Center for Health Statistics Lab, Research Triangle Park.

Energy. Electricity production (1991, MWh, by source): Hydroelectric: 5.2 mln.; Mineral: 41.4 mln.; Nuclear: 25.8 mln.

Education. Student-teacher ratio (1990): 16.9. **Avg. salary, public school teachers** (1991-92): $29,334.

State data. Motto: Esse Quam Videri (To be rather than to seem). **Flower:** Dogwood. **Bird:** Cardinal. **Tree:** Pine. **Song:** The Old North State. **Twelfth** of the original 13 states to ratify the Constitution, Nov. 21, 1789. **State fair** at: Raleigh; mid-Oct.

History. The first English colony in America was the first of 2 established by Sir Walter Raleigh on Roanoke Is., 1585 and 1587. The first group returned to England; the second, the "Lost Colony," disappeared without trace. Permanent settlers came from Virginia, c. 1660. Roused by British repressions, the colonists drove out the royal governor, 1775; the province's congress was the first to vote for independence; ten regiments were furnished to the Continental Army. Cornwallis' forces were defeated at Kings Mountain, 1780, and forced out after Guilford Courthouse, 1781.

Tourist attractions. Cape Hatteras and Cape Lookout national seashores; Great Smoky Mtns. (half in Tennessee); Guilford Courthouse and Moore's Creek parks, 66 Revolutionary battle sites; Bennett Place, NW of Durham, where Gen. Joseph Johnston surrendered the last Confederate army to Gen. Wm. Sherman; Ft. Raleigh, Roanoke Is., where Virginia Dare, first child of English parents in the New World, was born Aug. 18, 1587; Wright Brothers National Memorial, Kitty Hawk; N.C. Zoo, Asheboro; N.C. Symphony, & N.C. Museum, Raleigh.

Famous North Carolinians include Richard J. Gatling, Billy Graham, Andrew Jackson, Andrew Johnson, Michael Jordan, Wm. Rufus King, Dolley Madison, Edward R. Murrow, James K. Polk, Enos Slaughter, Thomas Wolfe.

Tourist information. Travel & Tourism Division, 430 No. Salisbury St., Raleigh, NC 27603.

Toll-free travel information. 1-800-VISITNC.

North Dakota

Peace Garden State

People. Population (1991): 634,604; **rank:** 47. **Pop. density:** 9.2 per sq. mi. **Racial distrib.** (1990): 94.6% White; 0.6% Black; 4.1% Amer. Indian; 0.7% Hispanic. **Net change** (1990-1991): −0.7%.

Geography. Total area: 70,702 sq. mi.; **rank:** 17. **Land area:** 68,994 sq. mi. **Acres forested land:** 460,000. **Location:** West North Central state, situated exactly in the middle of North America, bounded on the N by Canada, on the E by Minnesota, on the S by South Dakota, on the W by Montana. **Climate:** continental, with a wide range of temperature and moderate rainfall. **Topography:** Central Lowland in the E comprises the flat Red River Valley and the Rolling Drift Prairie; Missouri Plateau of the Great Plains on the W. **Capital:** Bismarck.

Economy. Principal industries: agriculture, mining, tourism, manufacturing, telecommunications, energy. **Principal manufactured goods:** farm equipment, processed foods, fabricated metal, high-tech. electronics. **Agriculture: Chief crops:** spring wheat, durum, barley, rye, flaxseed, oats, potatoes, dried edible beans, honey, soybeans, sugarbeets, sunflowers, hay. **Livestock** (1987): 2.0 mln. cattle; 285,000 hogs/pigs; 180,000 sheep; 1.4 mln. poultry. **Nonfuel Minerals** (1991): $18 mln. mostly construction sand & gravel, lime. **International airports at:** Fargo, Grand Forks, Bismarck, Minot. **Value of construction** (1991): $490.4 mln. **Employment distribution:** 21.9% trade; 20.4% gvt.; 18.6% serv.; 17.2% agric. **Per capita income** (1991): $16,088. **Unemployment** (1991): 4.1%. **Tourism** (1988): $565 mln. **Sales tax:** 5%-6%.

Finance. FDIC-insured commercial banks & trust companies (1990): 152. **Deposits:** $6.2 bln. **Savings institutions** (1991): 4. **Assets:** $5.3 bln.

Federal government. No. federal civilian employees (Mar. 1991): 5,459. **Avg. salary:** $29,147. **Notable federal facilities:** Strategic Air Command bases at Minot, Grand Forks; Northern Prairie Wildlife Research Center; Garrison Dam; Theodore Roosevelt Natl. Park; Grand Forks Energy Research Center; Ft. Union Natl. Historic Site.

Energy. Electricity production (1991, MWh, by source): Hydroelectric: 1.7 mln.; Mineral: 24.2 mln.

Education. Student-teacher ratio (1990): 15.5. **Avg. salary, public school teachers** (1991-92): $24,145.

State data. Motto: Liberty and union, now and forever, one and inseparable. **Flower:** Wild prairie rose. **Bird:** Western Meadowlark. **Tree:** American elm. **Song:** North Dakota Hymn. **Entered union** Nov. 2, 1889; rank, 39th. **State fair** at: Minot; 3d week in July.

History. Pierre La Verendrye was the first French fur trader in the area, 1738, followed later by the English. The U.S. acquired half the territory in the Louisiana Purchase, 1803. Lewis and Clark built Ft. Mandan, spent the winter of 1804-05 there. In 1818, American ownership of the other half was confirmed by agreement with Britain. First permanent settlement was at Pembina, 1812. Missouri River steamboats reached the area, 1832; the first railroad, 1873, bringing many homesteaders. The state was first to hold a presidential primary, 1912.

Tourist attractions. North Dakota Heritage Center, state capitol grounds; Bonanzaville, Fargo, restored pioneer town; Ft. Union Trading Post Natl. Historic Site, built 1829; Lake Sakakawea, 180 miles of fishing, boating, 1,600 miles of shoreline. Interntl. Peace Garden, 2,200-acre tract extending across the border into Manitoba; 65,000-acre Theodore Roosevelt National Park, Badlands, contains the president's Elkhorn Ranch; Ft. Abraham Lincoln State Park and Museum, S of Mandan.

Famous North Dakotans include Maxwell Anderson, Angie Dickinson, John Bernard Flannagan; Louis L'Amour, Peggy Lee, Eric Sevareid, Vilhjalmur Stefansson, Lawrence Welk.

Chamber of Commerce. P.O. Box 2467, Fargo, ND 58108.

Toll-free travel information. 1-800-437-2077.

Ohio

Buckeye State

People. Population (1991): 10,938,800; **rank:** 7. **Pop. density:** 267.1 per sq. mi. **Racial distrib.** (1990): 87.8% White; 10.6% Black; 1.3% Hispanic. **Net change** (1990-91): 0.8%.

Geography. Total area: 41,330 sq. mi.; **rank:** 35. **Land area:** 40,953 sq. mi. **Acres forested land:** 7,309,000. **Location:** East North Central state bounded on the N by Michigan and Lake Erie; on the E and S by Pennsylvania, West Virginia; and Kentucky; on the W by Indiana. **Climate:** temperate but variable; weather subject to much precipitation. **Topography:** generally rolling plain; Allegheny plateau in E; Lake [Erie] plains extend southward; central plains in the W. **Capital:** Columbus.

Economy. Principal industries: manufacturing, trade, services. **Principal manufactured goods:** transportation equipment, machinery, primary and fabricated metal products. **Agriculture: Chief crops:** corn, hay, winter wheat, oats, soybeans. **Livestock** (1990): 1.8 mln. cattle; 2.0 mln. hogs/pigs; 270,000 sheep; 24.0 mln. poultry. **Timber/lumber** (1990): oak, ash, maple, walnut, beech; 311 mln. bd. ft. **Nonfuel Minerals** (1991): $668 mln.; mostly crushed stone, construction sand & gravel, lime, Portland cement. **Commercial fishing** (1991): $3.6 mln. **Chief ports:** Toledo, Conneaut, Cleveland, Ashtabula. **International airports at:** Cleveland, Cincinnati, Columbus, Dayton. **Value of construction** (1991): $9.5 bln. **Employment distribution** (1991): 22.2% mfg.; 24.0% trade; 25.0% serv.; 15.1% gvt. **Per capita income** (1991): $17,916. **Unemployment** (1991): 6.4%. **Tourism** (1989): travelers spent $7.8 bln.

Finance. FDIC-insured commercial banks & trust companies (1990): 287. **Deposits:** $85.0 bln. **Savings institutions** (1991): 192. **Assets:** $40.6.

Federal government. No. federal civilian employees (Mar. 1991): 54,417. **Avg. salary:** $33,852. **Notable federal facilities:** Wright Patterson AF base; Defense Construction Supply Center; Lewis Research Ctr.; Portsmouth Gaseous Diffusion Plant; Mound Laboratory.

Energy. Electricity production (1991, MWh, by source): Hydroelectric: 0.2 mln.; Mineral: 105.1 mln.; Nuclear: 11.3.

Education. Student-teacher ratio (1990): 17.2. **Avg. salary, public school teachers** (1991-92): $34,359.

State data. Motto: With God, all things are possible. **Flower:** Scarlet carnation. **Bird:** Cardinal. **Tree:** Buckeye. **Song:** Beautiful Ohio. **Entered union** Mar. 1, 1803; rank, 17th. **State fair** at: Columbus; August.

History. LaSalle visited the Ohio area, 1669. American fur-traders arrived, beginning 1685; the French and Indians sought to drive them out. During the Revolution, Virginians defeated the Indians, 1774, but hostilities were renewed, 1777. The region became U.S. territory after the Revolution. First organized settlement was at Marietta, 1788. Indian warfare ended with Anthony Wayne's victory at Fallen Timbers, 1794. In the War of 1812, Oliver H. Perry's victory on Lake Erie and William H. Harrison's invasion of Canada, 1813, ended British incursions.

Tourist attractions. Mound City Group National Monuments, a group of 24 prehistoric Indian burial mounds; Neil Armstrong Air and Space Museum, Wapakoneta; Air Force Museum, Dayton; Pro Football Hall of Fame, Canton; King's Island amusement park, King's Island; Cedar Point amusement park, Sandusky. birthplaces, homes, and memorials to Ohio's 8 U.S. presidents: Wm. Henry Harrison, Grant, Garfield, Hayes, McKinley, Harding, Taft, Benjamin Harrison; Lake Erie Islands, Sandusky; Amish Region, Tuscarawas/Holmes counties; German Village, Columbus; Sea World, Aurora; Jack Nicklaus Sports Center, Mason; Bob Evans Farm, Rio Grande.

Famous Ohioans include Sherwood Anderson, Neil Armstrong, George Bellows, Ambrose Bierce, Clarence Darrow, Paul Laurence Dunbar, Thomas Edison, Clark Gable, John Glenn, Bob Hope, Jack Nicklaus, Jesse Owens, Eddie Rickenbacker, John D. Rockefeller Sr. and Jr., Pete Rose, Gen. Wm. Sherman, Harriet Beecher Stowe, Charles Taft, Robert A. Taft, William H. Taft, James Thurber, Orville Wright.

Chamber of Commerce. 35 E. Gay St., Columbus, OH 43215.

Toll-free travel information. 1-800-BUCKEYE.

Oklahoma

Sooner State

People. Population (1991): 3,174,775; **rank:** 28. **Pop. density:** 46.2 per sq. mi. **Racial distrib.** (1990): 82.1% White; 7.4% Black; 8.0% Amer. Indian; 2.7% Hispanic. **Net change** (1990-91): 0.9%.

Geography. Total area: 69,919 sq. mi.; **rank:** 18. **Land area:** 68,679 sq. mi. **Acres forested land:** 7,283,000. **Location:** West South Central state bounded on the N by Colorado and Kansas; on the E by Missouri and Arkansas; on the S and W by Texas and New Mexico. **Climate:** temperate; southern humid belt merging with colder northern continental; humid eastern and dry western zones. **Topography:** high plains predominate the W, hills and small mountains in the E; the east central region is dominated by the Arkansas R. Basin, and the Red R. Plains, in the S. **Capital:** Oklahoma City.

Economy. Principal industries: manufacturing, mineral and energy exploration and production, agriculture, services, printing & publishing. **Principal manufactured goods:** non-electrical machinery, fabricated metal products, petroleum. **Agriculture: Chief crops:** wheat, hay, peanuts, grain sorghum, soybeans, corn, pecans, oats, barley, rye. **Livestock** (1990): 5.2 mln. cattle; 215,000 hogs/pigs; 135,000 sheep; 4.75 mln. poultry. **Timber/lumber** (1990): pine, oaks, hickory; 244 mln. bd. ft. **Nonfuel Minerals** (1991): $261 mln.; mostly crushed stone, portland cement, iodine. **Chief ports:** Catoosa, Muskogee. **International airports at:** Oklahoma City, Tulsa. **Value of construction** (1991): $2.0 bln. **Employment distribution** (1990): 23.3% trade; 22.2% gvt.; 23.0% serv.; 14.0% mfg. **Per capita income** (1991): $15,827. **Unemployment** (1991): 6.7%. **Tourism** (1989): tourists spent $2.37 bln.

Finance. FDIC-insured commercial banks & trust companies (1990): 423. **Deposits:** $22.8 bln. **Savings institutions** (1991): 20. **Assets:** $5.4 bln.

Federal government. No. federal civilian employees (Mar. 1991): 35,038. **Avg. salary:** $30,446. **Notable federal facilities:** Federal Aviation Agency and Tinker AFB, both Oklahoma City; Ft. Sill, Lawton; Altus AFB, Altus; Vance AFB, Enid.

Energy. Electricity production (1991, MWh, by source): Hydroelectric: 3.3 mln.; Mineral: 31.4 mln.

Education. Student-teacher ratio (1990): 15.6. **Avg. salary, public school teachers** (1991-92): $25,721.

State data. Motto: Labor Omnia Vincit (Labor conquers all things). **Flower:** Mistletoe. **Bird:** Scissortailed flycatcher. **Tree:** Redbud. **Song:** Oklahoma! **Entered union** Nov. 16, 1907; rank, 46th. **State fair** at: Oklahoma City; last week of Sept.

History. Part of the Louisiana Purchase, 1803, Oklahoma was known as Indian Territory (but was not given territorial government) after it became the home of the "Five Civilized Tribes"—Cherokee, Choctaw, Chickasaw, Creek, and Seminole—1828-1846. The land was also used by Comanche, Osage, and other Plains Indians. As white settlers pressed west, land was opened for homesteading by runs and lottery, the first run taking place Apr. 22, 1889. The most famous run was to the Cherokee Outlet, 1893.

Tourist attractions. State park system—camping, hiking, water sports; Cherokee Heritage Center, Tahlequah; Cherokee strip centennial celebration; Will Rogers Memorial, Claremore; National Cowboy Hall of Fame, and Remington Park Race Track, both Oklahoma City; restored Ft. Gibson Stockade, near Muskogee, the Army's largest outpost in Indian lands; Indian pow-wows; rodeos; fishing; hunting; Ouachita National Forest; Enterprise Square, museum devoted to American economic system; Woolaroc Museum & Wildlife Preserve, Bartlesville.

Famous Oklahomans include Carl Albert, Johnny Bench, L. Gordon Cooper, Woody Guthrie, Gen. Patrick J. Hurley, Karl Jansky, Mickey Mantle, Carry Nation, Wiley Post, Oral Roberts, Will Rogers, Maria Tallchief, Jim Thorpe.

Chamber of Commerce. 4020 N. Lincoln Blvd., Oklahoma City, OK 73105.

Tourism Dept. P.O. Box 60789, Oklahoma City, OK 73146-0789.

Toll-free travel information. 1-800-652-6552.

Oregon

Beaver State

People. Population (1991): 2,921,921; **rank:** 29. **Pop. density:** 30.4 per sq. mi. **Racial distrib.** (1990): 92.8% White; 1.6% Black; 4.0% Hispanic. **Net change** (1990-91): 2.8%.

Geography. Total area: 97,073 sq. mi.; **rank:** 10. **Land area:** 96,003 sq. mi. **Acres forested land:** 28,057,000. **Location:** Pacific state, bounded on N by Washington; on E by Idaho; on S by Nevada and California; on W by the Pacific. **Climate:** coastal mild and humid climate; continental dryness and extreme temperatures in the interior. **Topography:** Coast Range of rugged mountains; fertile Willamette R. Valley to E and S; Cascade Mtn. Range of volcanic peaks E of the valley; plateau E of Cascades, remaining two-thirds of state. **Capital:** Salem.

Economy. Principal industries: forestry, agriculture, tourism, high technology, manufacturing. **Principal manufactured goods:** lumber & wood products, foods, machinery, fabricated metals, paper, printing & publishing, primary metals. **Agriculture: Chief crops:** hay, grass seed, farm forest prods., wheat, potatoes, onions, pears. **Livestock** (1989): 1.4 mln. cattle; 90,000 hogs/pigs; 455,000 sheep; 3.1 mln. poultry. **Timber/lumber** (1990): Douglas fir, hemlock, ponderosa pine; 7.3 bln. bd. ft. **Nonfuel Minerals** (1991): $270 mln.; mostly portland cement, crushed stone, construction sand & gravel. **Commercial fishing** (1991): $62.9 mln. **Chief ports:** Portland, Astoria, Newport, Coos Bay. **International airports at:** Portland. **Value of construction** (1991): $2.5 bln. **Employment distribution** (1989): 25.7% trade; 23.2% serv.; 18.0% mfg.; 17.8% gvt. **Per capita income** (1991): $17,592. **Unemployment** (1991): 6.0%. **Tourism** (1989): travel expenditures, $2.1 bln.

Finance: FDIC-insured commercial banks & trust companies (1990): 49. **Deposits:** $17.9 bln. **Savings institutions** (1991): 8. **Assets:** $1.3 bln.

Federal government. No. federal civilian employees (Mar. 1991): 20,334. **Avg. salary:** $31,941. **Notable federal facilities:** Bonneville Power Administration.

Energy: Electricity production (1991, MWh, by source): Hydroelectric: 30.6 mln.; Mineral: 5.8 mln.

Education. Student-teacher ratio (1990): 18.5. **Avg. salary, public school teachers** (1991-92): $33,656.

State data. Motto: She flies with her own wings. **Flower:** Oregon grape. **Bird:** Western meadowlark. **Tree:** Douglas fir. **Song:** Oregon, My Oregon. **Entered union** Feb. 14, 1859; rank, 33d. **State fair** at: Salem; late Aug. to early Sept.

History. American Capt. Robert Gray discovered and sailed into the Columbia River, 1792; Lewis and Clark, traveling overland, wintered at its mouth 1805-06; fur traders followed. Settlers arrived in the Willamette Valley, 1834. In 1843 the first large wave of settlers arrived via the Oregon Trail. Early in the 20th century, the "Oregon System," reforms which included the initiative, referendum, recall, direct primary, and woman suffrage, was adopted.

Tourist attractions. John Day Fossil Beds National Monument; Columbia River Gorge; Mt. Hood & Timberline Lodge; Crater Lake National Park; Oregon Dunes National Recreation Area; Ft. Clatsop National Memorial; Oregon Caves National Monument; Shakespearean Festival, Ashland; High Desert Museum, Bend. Also, skiing, fishing; Annual Albany Timber Carnival, Pendelton Round-Up, Portland Rose Festival.

Famous Oregonians include Ernest Bloch, Ernest Haycox, Chief Joseph, Edwin Markham, Tom McCall, Dr. John McLoughlin, Joaquin Miller, Linus Pauling, John Reed, Alberto Salazar, Mary Decker Slaney, William Simon U'Ren.

Tourist Information: Economic Development Department, 775 Summer St. NE, Salem, OR 97310.

Toll-free travel information. 1-800-543-8838; 1-800-547-7842 out of state.

Pennsylvania

Keystone State

People. Population (1991): 11,961,074; **rank:** 5. **Pop. density:** 266.9 per sq. mi. **Racial distrib.** (1990): 88.5% White; 9.2% Black; 2.0% Hispanic. **Net change** (1980-90): 0.1%.

Geography. Total area: 45,308 sq. mi.; **rank:** 33. **Land area:** 44,820 sq. mi. **Acres forested land:** 16,997,000. **Location:** Middle Atlantic state, bordered on the E by the Delaware R., on the S by the Mason-Dixon Line; on the W by West Virginia and Ohio; on the N/NE by Lake Erie and New York. **Climate:** continental with wide fluctuations in seasonal temperatures. **Topography:** Allegheny Mtns. run SW to NE, with Piedmont and Coast Plain in the SE triangle; Allegheny Front a diagonal spine across the state's center; N and W rugged plateau falls to Lake Erie Lowland. **Capital:** Harrisburg.

Economy. Principal industries: steel, travel, health, apparel, machinery, food & agriculture. **Principal manufactured goods:** primary metals, foods, fabricated metal products, non-electrical machinery, electrical machinery. **Agriculture: Chief crops:** corn, hay, mushrooms, apples, potatoes, winter wheat, oats, vegetables, tobacco, grapes. **Livestock** (1985): 1.96 mln. cattle; 800,000 hogs/pigs; 88,000 sheep; 22.5 mln. poultry. **Timber/lumber** (1990): pine, oak, maple; 681 mln. bd. ft. **Nonfuel Minerals** (1991): $881 mln.; mostly crushed stone, cement, lime, construction sand & gravel. **Commercial fishing** (1991): $323,000. **Chief ports:** Philadelphia, Pittsburgh, Erie. **International airports at:** Philadelphia, Pittsburgh, Erie, Harrisburg. **Value of construction** (1991): $9.7 bln. **Employment distribution** (1986): 24.4% serv.; 23.9% trade; 23.3% mfg.; 14.9% gvt. **Per capita income** (1991): $19,128 **Unemployment** (1991): 6.9%. **Tourism** (1985): out-of-state visitors spent $8.9 bln.

Finance. FDIC-insured commercial banks & trust companies (1990): 297. **Deposits:** $130.1 bln. **Savings institutions** (1991): 124. **Assets:** $28.4 bln.

Federal government. No. federal civilian employees (Mar. 1991): 81,612. **Avg. salary:** $30,269. **Notable federal facilities:** Army War College, Carlisle; Ships Control Ctr., Mechanicsburg; New Cumberland Army Depot; Philadelphia Navy Yard, Philadelphia.

Energy. Electricity production (1991, MWh, by source): Hydroelectric: 0.71 mln.; Mineral: 31.4 mln.; Nuclear: 57.5 mln.

Education. Student-teacher ratio (1990): 16.6. **Avg. salary, public school teachers** (1991-92): $38,540.

State data. Motto: Virtue, liberty and independence. **Flower:** Mountain laurel. **Bird:** Ruffed grouse. **Tree:** Hemlock. **Second** of the original 13 states to ratify the Constitution, Dec. 12, 1787. **State fair** at: Harrisburg; 2d week in Jan.

History. First settlers were Swedish, 1643, on Tinicum Is. In 1655 the Dutch seized the settlement but lost it to the British, 1664. The region was given by Charles II to William Penn, 1681, Philadelphia (brotherly love) was the capital of the colonies during most of the Revolution, and of the U.S., 1790-1800. Philadelphia was taken by the British, 1777; Washington's troops encamped at Valley Forge in the bitter winter of 1777-78. The Declaration of Independence, 1776, and the Constitution, 1787, were signed in Philadelphia.

Tourist attractions. Independence Hall & Natl. Historic Park, Franklin Institute Science Museum, Philadelphia Museum of Art, all in Philadelphia; Valley Forge Natl. Historic Park, Gettysburg Natl. Military Park; Pennsylvania Dutch Country; Hershey; Dusquesne Incline, Carnegie Institute, Heinz Hall, all in Pittsburgh; year 'round outdoor sports in Pocono Mtns., Pine Creek River Gorge, Alleghenies, Laurel Highlands & Presque Isle State Park.

Famous Pennsylvanians include Marian Anderson, Maxwell Anderson, James Buchanan, Andrew Carnegie, Stephen Foster, Benjamin Franklin, George C. Marshall, Andrew W. Mellon, Robert E. Peary, Mary Roberts Rinehart, Betsy Ross.

Chamber of Commerce. 222 N. 3d St., Harrisburg, PA 17101.

Toll-free travel information. 1-800-VISITPA.

Rhode Island

Little Rhody, Ocean State

People. Population (1991): 1,004,328; **rank:** 43. **Pop. density:** 961.1 per sq. mi. **Racial distrib.** (1990): 91.4% White; 3.9% Black; 4.6% Hispanic. **Net change** (1990-91): 0.1%.

Geography. Total area: 1,212 sq. mi.; **rank:** 50. **Land area:** 1,045 sq. mi. **Acres forested land:** 399,000. **Location:** New England state. **Climate:** invigorating and changeable. **Topography:** eastern lowlands of Narragansett Basin; western uplands of flat and rolling hills. **Capital:** Providence.

Economy. Principal industries: manufacturing, services. **Principal manufactured goods:** costume jewelry, toys, machinery, textiles, electronics. **Agriculture: Chief crops:** nursery prods., turf, potatoes, apples. **Timber/lumber:** oak. **Nonfuel Minerals** (1991): $12.6 mln.; construction sand & gravel, crushed stone. **Commercial fishing** (1991): $85.1 mln. **Chief ports:** Providence, Quonset Point, Newport. **Value of construction** (1991): $675 mln. **Employment distribution** (1991): 30% services; 21.7% mfg.; 21.0% trade. **Per capita income** (1991): $18,840. **Unemployment** (1991): 8.5%. **Tourism** (1987): visitors spent $1.1 bln. **Sales tax:** 7%.

Finance. FDIC-insured commercial banks & trust companies (1990): 13. **Deposits:** $11.2 bln. **Savings institutions** (1991): 3. **Assets:** $2.3 bln.

Federal government. No. federal civilian employees (Mar. 1991): 5,765. **Avg. salary:** $33,597. **Notable federal facilities:** Naval War College; Naval Underwater Systems Center.

Energy. Electricity production (1991, MWh, by source): Mineral: 0.2 mln.

Education. Student-teacher ratio (1990): 14.6. **Avg. salary, public school teachers** (1991-92): $36,047.

State data. Motto: Hope. **Flower:** Violet. **Bird:** Rhode Island red. **Tree:** Red maple. **Song:** Rhode Island. **Thirteenth** of original 13 states to ratify the Constitution, May 29, 1790.

History. Rhode Island is distinguished for its battle for freedom of conscience and action, begun by Roger Williams, founder of Providence, who was exiled from Massachusetts Bay Colony in 1636, and Anne Hutchinson, exiled in 1638. Rhode Island gave protection to Quakers in 1657 and to Jews from Holland in 1658.

The colonists broke the power of the Narragansett Indians in the Great Swamp Fight, 1675, the decisive battle in King Philip's War. British trade restrictions angered the colonists and they burned the British revenue cutter Gaspee, 1772. The colony declared its independence May 4, 1776. Gen. John Sullivan and Lafayette won a partial victory, 1778, but failed to oust the British.

Tourist attractions. Newport mansions; summer resorts and water sports; various yachting races inc. Newport to Bermuda. Touro Synagogue, Newport, 1763; first Baptist Church in America, Providence, 1638; Gilbert Stuart birthplace, Saunderstown; Narragansett Indian Fall Festival.

Famous Rhode Islanders include Ambrose Burnside, George M. Cohan, Nelson Eddy, Jabez Gorham, Nathanael Greene, Christopher and Oliver La Farge, Matthew C. and Oliver Perry, Gilbert Stuart.

Chamber of Commerce. 30 Exchange Terr., Providence, RI 02908.

Toll-free travel information. 1-800-556-2484.

South Carolina

Palmetto State

People. Population (1991): 3,559,618. **rank:** 25. **Pop. density:** 118.2 per sq. mi. **Racial distrib.** (1990): 69.0% White; 29.8% Black; 0.9% Hispanic. **Net change** (1990-91): 2.1%.

Geography. Total area: 31,113 sq. mi.; **rank:** 40. **Land area:** 30,111 sq. mi. **Acres forested land:** 12,257,000. **Location:** south Atlantic coast state, bordered by North Carolina on the N; Georgia on the SW and W; the Atlantic O. on the E, SE and S. **Climate:** humid sub-tropical. **Topo- graphy:** Blue Ridge province in NW has highest peaks; piedmont lies between the mountains and the fall line; coastal plain covers two-thirds of the state. **Capital:** Columbia.

Economy: Principal industries: tourism, agriculture, manufacturing. **Principal manufactured goods:** textiles, chemicals and allied products, machinery & fabricated metal products, apparel and related products. **Agriculture: Chief crops:** tobacco, soybeans, corn, cotton, peaches, hay. **Livestock** (1991): 575,000 cattle; 410,000 hogs/pigs; 7.13 mln. chickens, excl. broilers. **Timber/lumber** (1990): pine, oak; 1.6 bln. **Nonfuel Minerals** (1991): $380.5 mln.; mostly crushed stone, cement, clay. **Commercial fishing** (1991): $28.5 mln. **Chief ports:** Charleston, Georgetown, Port Royal. **International airports at:** Charleston. **Value of construction** (1991): $3.5 bln. **Employment distribution** (1990): 25.7% mfg.; 28.2% serv.; 20.2% trade; 6.6% gvt. **Per capita income** (1991): $15,420. **Unemployment** (1991): 6.2%. **Tourism** (1988): $4.6 bln. **Sales tax:** 5%.

Finance. FDIC-insured commercial banks & trust companies (1990): 84. **Deposits:** $18.0 bln. **Savings institutions** (1991): 45. **Assets:** $10.7 bln.

Federal government: No. federal civilian employees (Mar. 1991): 24,710. **Avg. Salary:** $29,680. **Notable federal facilities:** Polaris Submarine Base; Barnwell Nuclear Power Plant; Ft. Jackson; Parris Island; Savannah River Plant.

Energy. Electricity production (1991, MWh, by source): Hydroelectric: 1.2 mln.; Mineral: 19.0 mln.; Nuclear: 34.1 mln.

Education. Student-teacher ratio (1990): 16.8. **Avg. salary, public school teachers** (1991-92): $28,209.

State data. Motto: Dum Spiro Spero (While I breathe, I hope). **Flower:** Yellow jessamine. **Bird:** Carolina wren. **Tree:** Palmetto. **Song:** Carolina. **Eighth** of the original 13 states to ratify the Constitution, May 23, 1788. **State fair** at: Columbia; mid-Oct.

History. The first English colonists settled, 1670, on the Ashley River, moved to the site of Charleston, 1680. The colonists seized the government, 1775, and the royal governor fled. The British took Charleston, 1780, but were defeated at Kings Mountain that year, and at Cowpens and Eutaw Springs, 1781. In the 1830s, South Carolinians, angered by federal protective tariffs, adopted the Nullification Doctrine, holding a state can void an act of Congress. The state was the first to secede and, in 1861, Confederate troops fired on and forced the surrender of U. S. troops at Ft. Sumter, in Charleston Harbor, launching the Civil War.

Tourist attractions. Restored historic Charleston harbor area and Charleston gardens: Middleton Place, Magnolia, Cypress; other gardens at Brookgreen, Edisto, Glencairn; state parks; coastal islands; shore resorts such as Myrtle Beach and Hilton Head Island; fishing and quail hunting; Revolutionary War battle sites; Andrew Jackson State Park & Museum; Carl Sandburg Home, Hendersonville; Ft. Sumter National Monument, in Charleston Harbor; Charleston Museum, est. 1773, is the oldest museum in the U.S.; South Carolina State Museum, one of largest museums in South, Columbia; Riverbanks Zoo, Columbia.

Famous South Carolinians include Charles Bolden, James F. Byrnes, John C. Calhoun, DuBose Heyward, Ernest F. Hollings, Andrew Jackson, Jesse Jackson, James Longstreet, Francis Marion, Ronald McNair, Charles Pinckney, John Rutledge, Thomas Sumter, Strom Thurmond; John B. Watson.

Tourist information: Chamber of Commerce, 930 Richland St., P.O. Box 1360, Columbia, SC 29201; and So. Carolina Dept. of Parks, Recreation, & Tourism, (803) 734-0122; Greater Columbia Convention & Visitors' Bureau, 301 Gervais St., Columbia, SC 29201, (803) 254-0479.

South Dakota

Coyote State, Rushmore State

People. Population (1991): 703,301; **rank:** 45. **Pop. density:** 9.17 per sq. mi. **Racial distrib.** (1990): 91.6% White; 0.5% Black; 7.3% Amer. Indian; 0.8% Hispanic. **Net change** (1990-91): 1.0%.

Geography. Total area: 77,116 sq. mi.; **rank:** 16. **Land area:** 75,898 sq. mi. **Acres forested land:** 1,690,000. **Location:** West North Central state bounded on the N by North Dakota; on the E by Minnesota and Iowa; on the S by Nebraska; on the W by Wyoming and Montana. **Climate:** characterized by extremes of temperature, persistent winds, low precipitation and humidity. **Topography:** Prairie Plains in the E; rolling hills of the Great Plains in the W; the Black Hills, rising 3,500 ft. in the SW corner. **Capital:** Pierre.

Economy: Principal industries: agriculture, services, manufacturing. **Principal manufactured goods** (1989): food & kindred prods., machinery, electric & electronic equipment. **Agriculture: Chief crops** (1991): corn, oats, wheat, sunflowers, soybeans, sorghum. **Livestock** (1991): 3.6 mln. cattle; 2.0 mln. hogs/pigs; 602,000 sheep. **Timber/lumber** (1990): ponderosa pine; 223 mln. bd. ft. **Nonfuel Minerals** (1991): $287 mln.; mostly gold, portland cement. **Value of construction** (1991): $372.9 mln. **Employment distribution** (1991): 21.4% serv.; 10.1% mfg. **Per capita income** (1991): $16,392. **Unemployment** (1991): 3.4%. **Tourism** (1991): travellers' impact $951 mln. **Sales tax:** 4%.

Finance. FDIC-insured commercial banks & trust companies (1990): 125. **Deposits:** $9.6 bln. **Savings institutions** (1991): 10. **Assets:** $1.2 bln.

Federal government. No. federal civilian employees (Mar. 1991): 7,048. **Avg. salary:** $28,742. **Notable federal facilities:** Bureau of Indian Affairs, Ellsworth AFB, Corp of Engineers, Nat'l Park Service.

Energy. Electricity production (1991, MWh, by source): Hydroelectric: 2.4 mln.; Mineral: 2.1 mln.

Education: Student-teacher ratio (1990): 15.2. **Avg. salary, public school teachers** (1991-92): $23,300.

State data. Motto: Under God, the people rule. **Flower:** Pasque flower. **Bird:** Ringnecked pheasant. **Tree:** Black Hills spruce. **Song:** Hail, South Dakota. **Entered union** Nov. 2, 1889; rank, 40th. **State fair** at: Huron; late Aug.-early Sept.

History. Les Verendryes explored the region, 1742-43. Lewis and Clark passed through the area, 1804 and 1806. First white American settlement was at Fort Pierre, 1817. Gold was discovered, 1874, on the Sioux Reservation; miners rushed in. The U.S. first tried to stop them, then relaxed its opposition. The "great Dakota Boom" began 1879. A new Indian uprising came in 1890, climaxed by the massacre of Indian families at Wounded Knee.

Tourist attractions. Black Hills; Mt. Rushmore, with colossal likeness of the faces of U.S. Presidents Washington, Jefferson, Lincoln & T. Roosevelt carved by sculptor Gutzon Borglum; Needles Highway; Harney Peak, at 7,242 ft. the tallest peak between the Rockies and the Alps; Deadwood, an 1876 Gold Rush town; Custer State Park's buffalo and burro herds; Jewel Cave, the 4th largest cave in the world; Badlands Natl. Park's "moonscape"; "Great Lakes of So. Dakota"; Ft. Sisseton, restored 1864 army frontier post; Great Plains Zoo & Museum; Corn Palace in Mitchell; Wind Cave; Mammoth Site, ongoing excavation of prehistoric mammoths; Crazy Horse, mountain carving in progress.

Famous South Dakotans include Sparky Anderson, Catherine Bach, Tom Brokaw, "Calamity Jane", Mary Hart, Crazy Horse, Myron Floren, Alvin H. Hansen, Cheryl Ladd, Dr. Ernest O. Lawrence, George McGovern, Billy Mills, Allen Neuharth, Pat O'Brien, Sitting Bull.

Tourist information. South Dakota Tourism, 711 E. Wells Ave., Pierre, SD 57501-3369.

Toll-free travel information. 1-800-843-1930.

Tennessee

Volunteer State

People. Population (1991): 4,952,726 **rank:** 18. **Pop. density:** 120.2 per sq. mi. **Racial distrib.** (1990): 83.0% White; 16.0% Black; 0.7% Hispanic. **Net change** (1990-91): 1.5%.

Geography. Total area: 42,144 sq. mi.; **rank:** 34. **Land area:** 41,220 sq. mi. **Acres forested land:** 13,258,000. **Location:** East South Central state bounded on the N by Kentucky and Virginia; on the E by North Carolina; on the S by Georgia, Alabama, and Mississippi; on the W by Arkansas and Missouri. **Climate:** humid continental to the N; humid sub-tropical to the S. **Topography:** rugged country in the E; the Great Smoky Mtns. of the Unakas; low ridges of the Appalachian Valley; the flat Cumberland Plateau; slightly rolling terrain and knobs of the Interior Low Plateau, the largest region; Eastern Gulf Coastal Plain to the W, is laced with meandering streams; Mississippi Alluvial Plain, a narrow strip of swamp and flood plain in the extreme W. **Capital:** Nashville.

Economy. Principal industries: trade, services, construction; transp., commun., public utilities; finance, ins., real estate. **Principal manufactured goods:** chemicals, food, transportation equip., industrial machinery & equip., fabr. metal prods., rubber/plastic prods., paper & allied prods., printing and publishing. **Agriculture: Chief crops** (1991): soybeans, greenhouse/nursery, cotton/lint. **Livestock** (1991): 2.25 mln. cattle; 0.6 mln. hogs/pigs; 1.6 mln. poultry. **Timber/lumber** (1990): red oak, white oak, yellow poplar, hickory; 516 mln. bd. ft. **Nonfuel Minerals** (1991): $550.9 mln.; mostly clay, sand and gravel, crushed stone. **Chief ports:** Memphis, Nashville, Chattanooga, Knoxville. **International airports at:** Memphis, Nashville. **Value of construction** (1991): $4.3 bln. **Employment distribution** (1991): 23.0% mfg.; 23.4% trade; 23% serv.; 16.2% gvt. **Per capita income** (1991): $16,325. **Unemployment** (1991): 6.6%. **Tourism** (1989): out-of-state visitors spent $3.3 bln. **Sales tax:** 6.0% state, up to 2.75% local.

Finance. FDIC-insured commercial banks & trust companies (1990): 260. **Deposit:** $38.4 bln. **Savings institutions** (1991): 44. **Assets:** $9.6 bln.

Federal government. No. federal civilian employees (Mar. 1991): 41,684. **Avg. salary:** $31,658. **Notable federal facilities:** Tennessee Valley Authority; Oak Ridge Nat'l. Laboratories.

Energy: Electricity production (1991, mWh, by source): Hydroelectric: 1.2 mln.; Mineral: 37.3 mln.; Nuclear: 10.0 mln.

Education. Student-teacher ratio (1990): 19.2. **Avg. salary, public school teachers** (1991-92): $28,726.

State data. Motto: Agriculture and commerce. **Flower:** Iris. **Bird:** Mockingbird. **Tree:** Tulip poplar. **Song:** The Tennessee Waltz. **Entered union** June 1, 1796; rank, 16th. **State fair** at: Nashville; mid-Sept.

History. Spanish explorers first visited the area, 1541. English traders crossed the Great Smokies from the east while France's Marquette and Jolliet sailed down the Mississippi on the west, 1673. First permanent settlement was by Virginians on the Watauga River, 1769. During the Revolution, the colonists helped win the Battle of Kings Mountain, N.C., 1780, and joined other eastern campaigns. The state seceded from the Union 1861, and saw many engagements of the Civil War, but 30,000 soldiers fought for the Union.

Tourist attractions. Natural wonders include Reelfoot Lake, the reservoir basin of the Mississippi R. formed by the 1811 earthquake; Lookout Mountain, Chattanooga; Fall Creek Falls, 256 ft. high; Great Smoky Mountains National Park; Lost Sea, Sweetwater; Cherokee Natl. Forest.

Also, the Hermitage, 13 mi. E of Nashville, home of Andrew Jackson; the homes of presidents Polk and Andrew Johnson; American Museum of Science, Oak Ridge; the Parthenon, Nashville, a replica of the Parthenon of Athens; the Grand Old Opry, Nashville, Opryland, USA, theme park, Nashville; Graceland, home of Elvis Presley, Memphis; Alex Haley Home & Museum, Henning; Casey Jones Home & Museum, Jackson.

Famous Tennesseans include Roy Acuff, Davy Crockett, David Farragut, William C. Handy, Sam Houston, Cordell Hull, Grace Moore, Minnie Pearl, Dinah Shore, Alvin York.

Tourist information. Dept. of Tourist Development, 5th Floor, Rachel Jackson Bldg., Nashville, TN 37219.

Texas

Lone Star State

People. Population (1991): 17,348,206; **rank:** 3. **Pop. density:** 66.2 per sq. mi. **Racial distrib.** (1990): 75.2% White; 11.9% Black; 25.5% Hispanic. **Net change** (1990-91): 2.1%.

Geography: Total area: 266,807 sq. mi.; **rank:** 2. **Land area:** 261,914 sq. mi.; **Acres forested land:** 13,656,000. **Location:** Southwestern state, bounded on the SE by the Gulf of Mexico; on the SW by Mexico, separated by the Rio Grande; surrounding states are Louisiana, Arkansas, Oklahoma, New Mexico. **Climate:** extremely varied; driest region is the Trans-Pecos; wettest is the NE. **Topography:** Gulf Coast Plain in the S and SE; North Central Plains slope upward with some hills; the Great Plains extend over the Panhandle, are broken by low mountains; the Trans-Pecos is the southern extension of the Rockies. **Capital:** Austin.

Economy. Principal industries: trade, services, manufacturing. **Principal manufactured goods:** machinery, transportation equipment, foods, electrical and electronic equip., chemicals and allied prods., apparel. **Agriculture: Chief crops:** cotton, grain sorghum, grains, vegetables, citrus and other fruits, pecans, peanuts. **Livestock** (1989): 13.7 mln. cattle; 510,000 hogs/pigs; 1.73 mln. sheep; 18.2 mln. poultry. **Timber/lumber** (1990): pine, cypress; 1.1 bln. bd. ft. **Nonfuel Minerals** (1991): $1.4 bln.; mostly cement, stone, sand & gravel. **Commercial fishing** (1991): $214.4 mln. **Chief ports:** Houston, Galveston, Brownsville, Beaumont, Port Arthur, Corpus Christi. **Major international airports at:** Houston, Dallas/Ft. Worth, San Antonio. **Value of construction** (1991) $14.3 bln. **Employment distribution** (1991): 24.2% trade; 24.8% serv.; 17.8% gvt.; 13.8% mfg. **Per capita income** (1991): $17,305. **Unemployment** (1991): 6.6%. **Tourism** (1987): out-of-state visitors spent $17.6 bln. **Sales tax:** 6%, + optional 1% local, 1% transit.

Finance. FDIC-insured commercial banks & trust companies (1990): 1,236. **Deposits:** $138.8 bln. **Savings institutions** (1991): 68 **Assets:** $48.9 bln.

Federal government. No. federal civilian employees (Mar. 1991): $121,747. **Avg. salary:** $30,441. **Notable federal facilities:** Fort Hood (Killeen); Kelly AFB, and Ft. Sam Houston, both San Antonio.

Energy. Electricity production (1991, MWh, by source): Hydroelectric: 2.1 mln.; Mineral: 162 mln.; Nuclear: 13.6 mln.

Education. Student-teacher ratio (1990): 15.4. **Avg. salary, public school teachers** (1991-92): $29,041.

State data. Motto: Friendship. **Flower:** Bluebonnet. **Bird:** Mockingbird. **Tree:** Pecan. **Song:** Texas, Our Texas. **Entered union** Dec. 29, 1845; rank, 28th. **State fair** at: Dallas; mid-Oct.

History. Pineda sailed along the Texas coast, 1519; Cabeza de Vaca and Coronado visited the interior, 1541. Spaniards made the first settlement at Ysleta, near El Paso, 1682. Americans moved into the land early in the 19th century. Mexico, of which Texas was a part, won independence from Spain, 1821; Santa Anna became dictator, 1835. Texans rebelled; Santa Anna wiped out defenders of the Alamo, 1836. Sam Houston's Texans defeated Santa Anna at San Jacinto and independence was proclaimed the same year. In 1845, Texas was admitted to the Union.

Tourist attractions. Padre Island National Seashore; Big Bend, Guadalupe Mtns. national parks; The Alamo; Ft. Davis; Six Flags Amusement Park. Named for Pres. Lyndon B. Johnson are a state park, a natl. historic site marking his birthplace, boyhood home, and ranch, all near Johnson City, and a library in Austin.

Famous Texans include Stephen F. Austin, James Bowie, Carol Burnett, J. Frank Dobie, Dwight D. Eisenhower, Sam Houston, Howard Hughes, Lyndon B. Johnson, Mary Martin, Chester Nimitz, Katharine Ann Porter, Sam Rayburn.

Chamber of Commerce. 900 Congress, Suite 501, Austin, TX 78701.

Utah

Beehive State

People. Population (1991): 1,770,212; **rank:** 35. **Pop. density:** 21.5 per sq. mi. **Racial distrib.** (1990): 93.8% White; 0.7% Black; 4.9% Hispanic. **Net change** (1990-91): 2.7%.

Geography. Total area: 84,899 sq. mi.; **rank:** 11. **Land area:** 82,168 sq. mi. **Acres forested land:** 16,234,000. **Location:** Middle Rocky Mountain state; its southeastern corner touches Colorado, New Mexico, and Arizona, and is the only spot in the U.S. where 4 states join. **Climate:** arid; ranging from warm desert in SW to alpine in NE. **Topography:** high Colorado plateau is cut by brilliantly-colored canyons of the SE; broad, flat, desert-like Great Basin of the W; the Great Salt Lake and Bonneville Salt Flats to the NW; Middle Rockies in the NE run E-W; valleys and plateaus of the Wasatch Front. **Capital:** Salt Lake City.

Economy. Principal industries: services, trade, manufacturing, government, construction. **Principal manufactured goods:** guided missiles and parts, electronic components, food products, fabricated metals, steel, electrical equipment. **Agriculture: Chief crops:** hay, wheat, apples, barley, alfalfa seed, corn, potatoes, cherries, onions. **Livestock:** 855,000 cattle; 34,000 hogs/pigs; 600,000 sheep; 3.8 mln. poultry. **Timber/lumber:** aspen, spruce, pine. **Nonfuel Minerals** (1991): $1.2 bln.; mostly copper, gold, magnesium. **International airports at:** Salt Lake City. **Value of construction** (1991): $1.7 bln. **Employment distribution** (1991): 25.3% serv.; 24.0% trade; 20.7% govt; 14.2% mfg. **Per capita income** (1991): $14,529. **Unemployment** (1991): 4.9%. **Tourism** (1986): travellers spent $2.0 bln. **Sales tax:** 6.25%.

Finance. FDIC-insured commercial banks & trust companies (1990): 57. **Deposits:** $9.8 bln. **Savings institutions** (1991): 6. **Assets:** $3.0 bln.

Federal government. No. federal civilian employees (Mar. 1991): 31,982. **Avg. salary:** $29,108. **Notable federal facilities:** Hill AFB; Tooele Army Depot, IRS Western Service Center.

Energy. Electricity production (1991, MWh, by source): Hydroelectric: 0.6 mln.; Mineral: 27.0 mln.

Education. Student-teacher ratio (1990): 25.0. **Avg. salary, public school teachers** (1991-92): $26,524.

State data. Motto: Industry. **Flower:** Sego lily. **Bird:** Seagull. **Tree:** Blue spruce. **Song:** Utah, We Love Thee. **Entered union** Jan. 4, 1896; rank, 45th. **State fair** at: Salt Lake City; Sept.

History. Spanish Franciscans visited the area, 1776, the first white men to do so. American fur traders followed. Permanent settlement began with the arrival of the Mormons, 1847. They made the arid land bloom and created a prosperous economy, organized the State of Deseret, 1849, and asked admission to the Union. This was not achieved until 1896, after a long period of controversy over the Mormon Church's doctrine of polygamy, which it discontinued in 1890.

Tourist attractions. Temple Square, Mormon Church hdqtrs., Salt Lake City; Great Salt Lake; fishing streams, lakes and reservoirs, numerous winter sports; campgrounds. Natural wonders may be seen at Zion, Canyonlands, Bryce Canyon, Arches, and Capitol Reef national parks; Dinosaur, Rainbow Bridge, Timpanogos Cave, and Natural Bridges national monuments. Also Lake Powell and Flaming Gorge reservoirs.

Famous Utahans include Maude Adams, Ezra Taft Benson, John Moses Browning, Mariner Eccles, Philo Farnsworth, James Fletcher, David M. Kennedy, J. Willard Marriott, Osmond Family, Merlin Olsen, Ivy Baker Priest, George Romney, Brigham Young, Loretta Young.

Tourist information. Utah Travel Council, Council Hall, Salt Lake City, UT 84114.

Vermont

Green Mountain State

People. Population (1991): 566,619; **rank:** 49. **Pop. density:** 61.3 per sq. mi. **Racial distrib.** (1990): 98.6% White; 0.3% Black; 0.6% Asian; 0.7% Hispanic. **Net change** (1990-91): 0.7%.

Geography. Total area: 9,614 sq. mi.; **rank:** 43. **Land area:** 9,249 sq. mi. **Acres forested land:** 4,479,000. **Location:** northern New England state. **Climate:** temperate, with considerable temperature extremes; heavy snowfall in mountains. **Topography:** Green Mtns. N-S backbone 20-36 mi. wide; avg. altitude 1,000 ft. **Capital:** Montpelier.

Economy. Principal industries: manufacturing, tourism, agriculture, trade; finance, insurance, real estate, government. **Principal manufactured goods:** machine tools, furniture, scales, books, computer components, fishing rods. **Agriculture: Chief crops:** dairy products, apples, maple syrup, silage corn, hay. **Livestock** (1989): 320,000 cattle; 5,100 hogs/ pigs; 20,456 sheep; 406,000 poultry. **Timber/lumber** (1990): pine, spruce, fir, hemlock; 186 mln. bd. ft. **Nonfuel Minerals** (1991): $83.7 mln.; mostly dimension stone, crushed stone, construction sand & gravel. **International airports at:** Burlington. **Value of construction** (1991): $543.8 mln. **Employment distribution** (1990): 27% serv.; 23% trade; 18% mfg. **Per capita income** (1991): $17,747. **Unemployment** (1991): 6.4%. **Tourism** (1990): visitors spent $1.25 bln. **Sales tax.** 5%.

Finance. FDIC-insured commercial banks & trust companies (1990): 27. **Deposits:** $5.1 bln. **Savings institutions** (1991): 4. **Assets:** $564.1 mln.

Federal government. No. federal civilian employees (Mar. 1991): 2,576. **Avg. salary:** $30,575.

Energy. Electricity production (1991, MWh, by source): Hydroelectric: 1.0 mln.; Mineral: 0.2 mln.; Nuclear: 3.8 mln.

Education. Student-teacher ratio (1990): 13.2. **Avg. salary, public school teachers** (1991-92): $33,420.

State data. Motto: Freedom and unity. **Flower:** Red clover. **Bird:** Hermit thrush. **Tree:** Sugar maple. **Song:** Hail, Vermont. **Entered union** Mar. 4, 1791; rank, 14th. **State fair** at: Rutland; early Sept.

History. Champlain explored the lake that bears his name, 1609. First American settlement was Ft. Dummer, 1724, near Brattleboro. Ethan Allen and the Green Mountain Boys captured Ft. Ticonderoga, 1775; John Stark defeated part of Burgoyne's forces near Bennington, 1777. In the War of 1812, Thomas MacDonough defeated a British fleet on Champlain off Plattsburgh, 1814.

Tourist attractions. Year-round outdoor sports, esp. hiking, camping and skiing; there are 24 alpine ski areas & 47 cross country areas in the state. Popular are the Shelburne Museum; Rock of Ages Tourist Center, Graniteville; Vermont Marble Exhibit, Proctor; Bennington Battle Monument; Pres. Coolidge homestead, Plymouth; Maple Grove Maple Museum, St. Johnsbury.

Famous Vermonters include Ethan Allen, Chester A. Arthur, Calvin Coolidge, Adm. George Dewey, John Dewey, Stephen A. Douglas, Dorothy Canfield Fisher, James Fisk.

Tourist Information. Vermont Dept. of Travel and Tourism, 134 State St., Montpelier, VT 05602.

Virginia

Old Dominion

People. Population (1991): 6,285,931; **rank:** 12. **Pop. density:** 158.7 per sq. mi. **Racial distrib.** (1990): 77.4% White; 18.8% Black; 2.6% Asian; 2.6% Hispanic. **Net change** (1990-91): 1.6%.

Geography. Total area: 40,767 sq. mi.; **rank:** 36. **Land area:** 39,598 sq. mi. **Acres forested land:** 15,968,000. **Location:** South Atlantic state bounded by the Atlantic O. on the E and surrounded by North Carolina, Tennessee, Kentucky, West Virginia, and Maryland. **Climate:** mild and equable. **Topography:** mountain and valley region in the W, including the Blue Ridge Mtns.; rolling piedmont plateau; tidewater, or coastal plain, including the eastern shore. **Capital:** Richmond.

Economy. Principal industries: services, trade, government, manufacturing, tourism, agriculture. **Principal manufactured goods:** textiles, transportation equipment, electric & electronic equipment, food processing, chemicals, printing. **Agriculture: Chief crops** (1990): tobacco, soybeans, peanuts, winterwheat, corn, far grain, tomatoes, apples, summer & sweet potatoes. **Livestock** (1990): 1.73 mln. cattle; 430,000 hogs/pigs; 157,000 sheep; 1.96 mln. broilers, 1.7 mln. turkeys. **Timber/lumber** (1990): pine and hardwoods; 1.2 bln. bd. ft. **Nonfuel Minerals** (1991): $415 mln.; mostly crushed stone. **Commercial fishing** (1991): $95.0 mln. **Chief ports:** Hampton Roads, Richmond, Alexandria. **International airports at:** Norfolk, Dulles, Richmond, Newport News. **Value of construction** (1990): $7.1 bln. **Employment distribution** (1990): 25.4% serv.; 22.6% trade; 20.0% gvt.; 14.7% mfg. **Per capita income** (1991): $19,976. **Unemployment** (1991): 5.8%. **Tourism** (1989): domestic travellers spent $8 bln. **Sales tax:** 4.5%.

Finance. FDIC-insured commercial banks & trust companies (1990): 180. **Deposits:** $52.4 bln. **Savings institutions** (1991): 49. **Assets:** $16.1 bln.

Federal government. No. federal civilian employees (Mar. 1991): 137,269. **Avg. salary:** $35,806. **Notable federal facilities:** Pentagon; Naval Sta., Norfolk; Naval Air Sta., Norfolk, Virginia Beach; Naval Shipyard, Portsmouth; Marine Corps Base, Quantico; Langley AFB; NASA at Langley.

Energy. Electricity production (1991, MWh, by source): Mineral: 20.7 mln.; Nuclear: 21.7 mln.

Education. Student-teacher ratio (1990): 15.7. **Avg. salary, public school teachers** (1991-92): $31,921.

State data. Motto: Sic Semper Tyrannis (Thus always to tyrants). **Flower:** Dogwood. **Bird:** Cardinal. **Tree:** Dogwood. **Song:** Carry Me Back to Old Virginia. **Tenth** of the original 13 states to ratify the Constitution, June 25, 1788. **State fair** at: Richmond; late Sept.-early Oct.

History. English settlers founded Jamestown, 1607. Virginians took over much of the government from royal Gov. Dunmore in 1775, forcing him to flee. Virginians under George Rogers Clark freed the Ohio-Indiana-Illinois area of British forces. Benedict Arnold burned Richmond and Petersburg for the British, 1781. That same year, Britain's Cornwallis was trapped at Yorktown and surrendered.

Tourist attractions. Colonial Williamsburg; Busch Gardens; Wolf Trap Farm, near Falls Church; Arlington National Cemetery; Mt. Vernon, home of George Washington; Jamestown Festival Park; Yorktown; Jefferson's Monticello, Charlottesville; Robert E. Lee's birthplace, Stratford Hall, and grave, at Lexington; Appomattox; Shenandoah National Park; Blue Ridge Parkway; Virginia Beach; King's Dominion, near Richmond.

Famous Virginians include Richard E. Byrd, James B. Cabell, William Henry Harrison, Patrick Henry, Thomas Jefferson, Joseph E. Johnston, Robert E. Lee, Meriwether Lewis and William Clark, James Madison, George Mason, James Monroe, John Marshall, Edgar Allan Poe, Walter Reed, Zachary Taylor, John Tyler, Maggie Walker, Booker T. Washington, George Washington, Woodrow Wilson.

Chamber of Commerce: 9th South Fifth St., Richmond, VA 23219.

Toll-free travel information. 1-800-VISITVA.

Washington

Evergreen State

People. Population (1991): 5,017,724; **rank:** 16. **Pop. density:** 75.4 per sq. mi. **Racial distrib.** (1990): 88.5% White; 3.1% Black; 4.3% Asian; 4.4% Hispanic. **Net change** (1990-91): 3.1%.

Geography. Total area: 68,139 sq. mi.; **rank:** 20. **Land area:** 66,582 sq. mi. **Acres forested land:** 21,856,000. **Location:** northwestern coastal state bordered by Canada on the N; Idaho on the E; Oregon on the S; and the Pacific O. on the W. **Climate:** mild, dominated by the Pacific O. and protected by the Rockies. **Topography:** Olympic Mtns. on NW peninsula; open land along coast to Columbia R.; flat terrain of Puget Sound Lowland; Cascade Mtns. region's high peaks to the E; Columbia Basin in central portion; highlands to the NE; mountains to the SE. **Capital:** Olympia.

Economy. Principal industries: aerospace, forest products, food products, primary metals, agriculture. **Principal manufactured goods:** aircraft, pulp and paper, lumber and plywood, aluminum, processed fruits and vegetables. **Agriculture: Chief crops:** hops, spearmint oil, raspberries, apples, asparagus, pears, cherries, peppermint oil, potatoes. **Livestock** (1986): 1.3 mln. cattle; 50,000 hogs/pigs; 59,000 sheep; 5.7 mln. poultry. **Timber/lumber** (1990): Douglas fir, hemlock, cedar, pine; 4.4 bln. bd. ft. **Nonfuel Minerals** (1991): $443 mln.; mostly construction sand & gravel, crushed stone, Portland cement. **Commercial fishing** (1991): $109.5 mln. **Chief ports:** Seattle, Tacoma, Vancouver, Kelso-Longview. **International airports at:** Seattle/Tacoma, Spokane, Boeing Field. **Value of construction** (1991): $6.1 bln. **Employment distribution** (1989): 24.4% trade; 20.7% serv.; 18.3% gvt.; 17.3% mfg. **Per capita income** (1991): $19,442. **Unemployment** (1991): 6.3%. **Tourism** (1988): $4.6 bln. **Sales tax:** 6.5%.

Finance. FDIC-insured commercial banks & trust companies (1990): 1,062. **Deposits:** $31.9 bln. **Savings institutions** (1991): 20. **Assets:** $15.8 bln.

Federal government. No. federal civilian employees (Mar. 1991): 49,153. **Avg. salary:** $32,875. **Notable federal facilities:** Bonneville Power Admin.; Ft. Lewis; McChord AFB; Hanford Nuclear Reservation; Bremerton Naval Shipyards.

Energy. Electricity production (1991, MWh, by source): Hydroelectric: 62.0 mln.; Mineral: 9.6 mln.; Nuclear: 6.4 mln.

Education. Student-teacher ratio (1990): 20.1. **Avg. salary, public school teachers** (1991-92): $34,880.

State data. Motto. Alki (By and by). **Flower:** Western rhododendron. **Bird:** Willow goldfinch. **Tree:** Western hemlock. **Song:** Washington, My Home. **Entered union** Nov. 11, 1889; rank, 42d. **State fairs at:** S.E. Washington, W. Washington, N. Cent. Washington District, Cent. Washington.

History. Spain's Bruno Hezeta sailed the coast, 1775. American Capt. Robert Gray sailed up the Columbia River, 1792. Canadian fur traders set up Spokane House, 1810; Americans under John Jacob Astor established a post at Fort Okanogan, 1811. Missionary Marcus Whitman settled near Walla Walla, 1836. Final agreement on the border of Washington and Canada was made with Britain, 1846, and gold was discovered in the state's northeast, 1855, bringing new settlers.

Tourist attractions. Mt. Rainier, Olympic and North Cascades National Parks; Mt. St. Helens; Pacific beaches; Puget Sound; wineries; Indian cultures; year-round outdoor recreation: Seattle Waterfront, Seattle Center, Space Needle, San Juan Islands, Grand Coulee Dam, Spokane's Riverfront Park.

Famous Washingtonians include Bing Crosby, William O. Douglas, Henry M. Jackson, Gary Larson, Mary McCarthy, Edward R. Murrow, Theodore Roethke, Marcus Whitman, Minoru Yamasaki.

Local Chambers of Commerce. P.O. Box 658, Olympia, WA 98507.

Toll-free travel information. 1-800-544-1800.

West Virginia

Mountain State

People. Population (1991): 1,800,936. **rank:** 34. **Pop. density:** 74.8 per sq. mi. **Racial distrib.** (1990): 96.2% White; 3.1% Black; 0.5% Hispanic. **Net change** (1990-91): 0.4%.

Geography. Total area: 24,232 sq. mi.; **rank:** 41. **Land area:** 24,087 sq. mi. **Acres forested land:** 11,942,000. **Location:** South Atlantic state bounded on the N by Ohio, Pennsylvania, Maryland; on the S and W by Virginia, Kentucky, Ohio; on the E by Maryland and Virginia. **Climate:** humid continental climate except for marine modification in the lower panhandle. **Topography:** ranging from hilly to mountainous; Allegheny Plateau in the W, covers two-thirds of the state; mountains here are the highest in the state, over 4,000 ft. **Capital:** Charleston.

Economy. Principal industries: manufacturing, services, mining, tourism. **Principal manufactured goods:** machinery, plastic and hardwood prods., fabricated metals, basic organic and inorganic chemicals, aluminum, steel. **Agriculture: Chief crops:** apples, peaches, hay, tobacco, corn, wheat, oats. **Chief products:** dairy prods., eggs. **Livestock** (1989): 500,000 cattle; 37,000 hogs/pigs; 82,000 sheep; 810,000 chickens. **Timber/ lumber** (1990): oak, yellow poplar, hickory, walnut, cherry; 397 mln. bd. ft. **Nonfuel Minerals** (1991): $114 mln.; mostly crushed stone. **Chief port:** Huntington. **Value of construction** (1991): $885.2 mln. **Employment distribution** (1989): 23% trade; 21% gvt.; 22% serv.; 14% mfg. **Per capita income** (1991): $14,174. **Unemployment** (1991): 10.5%. **Tourism** (1989): travel-related expenditures were $2.3 bln. **Sales tax:** 6%.

Finance. FDIC-insured commercial banks & trust companies (1990): 185. **Deposits:** $14.5 bln. **Savings institutions** (1991): 12. **Assets:** $1.2 bln.

Federal government. No. federal civilian employees (Mar. 1991): 10,432. **Avg. salary:** $30,143. **Notable federal facilities:** National Radio Astronomy Observatory, Green Bank; Bureau of Public Debt. Bldg., Parkersburg; Natl. Park, Harper's Ferry; Correctional Institution for Women, Alderson.

Energy. Electricity production (1991, MWh, by source): Hydroelectric: 0.5 mln.; Mineral: 58.9 mln.

Education. Student-teacher ratio (1990): 15.0. **Avg. salary, public school teachers** (1991-92): $27,298.

State Data. Motto: Montani Semper Liberi (Mountaineers are always free) **Flower:** Big rhododendron. **Bird:** Cardinal. **Tree:** Sugar maple. **Songs:** The West Virginia

Hills; This Is My West Virginia; West Virginia, My Home, Sweet Home. **Entered union** June 20, 1863; rank, 35th. **State fair** at: Lewisburg (Fairlea), late Aug.

History. Early explorers included George Washington, 1753, and Daniel Boone. The area became part of Virginia and often objected to rule by the eastern part of the state. When Virginia seceded, 1861, the Wheeling Conventions repudiated the act and created a new state, Kanawha, subsequently changed to West Virginia. It was admitted to the Union as such, 1863.

Tourist attractions. Harpers Ferry National Historic Park has been restored to its condition in 1859, when John Brown seized the U.S. Armory.

Also Science and Cultural Center, Charleston; White Sulphur and Berkeley Springs mineral water spas; Monongahela Natl. Forest; state parks and forests; trout fishing; turkey, deer, and bear hunting; white water rafting, paddleboat tours, skiing; glass tours at Fenton Glass in Williamstown, Viking Glass in New Martinsville, Blenko Glass in Milton; Sternwheel Regatta, Charleston; Mountain State Forest Festival; Mountain State Arts & Crafts Fair, Ripley.

Famous West Virginians include Newton D. Baker, Pearl Buck, John W. Davis, Thomas "Stonewall" Jackson, Don Knotts, Dwight Whitney Morrow, Nick Nolte, Michael Owens, Cyrus Vance, Col. Charles "Chuck" Yeager.

Tourist information. Dept. of Commerce, State Capitol, Charleston WV 25305.

Toll-free travel information. 1-800-CALLW.VA.

Wisconsin

Badger State

People. Population (1991): 4,955,127; **rank:** 17. **Pop. density:** 91.2 per sq. mi. **Racial distrib.** (1990): 92.2% White; 5.0% Black; 1.9% Hispanic. **Net change** (1990-91): 1.3%.

Geography. Total area: 56,153 sq. mi.; **rank:** 26. **Land area:** 54,314 sq. mi. **Acres forested land:** 15,319,000. **Location:** North central state, bounded on the N by Lake Superior and Upper Michigan; on the E by Lake Michigan; on the S by Illinois; on the W by the St. Croix and Mississippi rivers. **Climate:** long, cold winters and short, warm summers tempered by the Great Lakes. **Topography:** narrow Lake Superior Lowland plain met by Northern Highland which slopes gently to the sandy crescent Central Plain; Western Upland in the SW; 3 broad parallel limestone ridges running N-S are separated by wide and shallow lowlands in the SE. **Capital:** Madison.

Economy. Principal industries: manufacturing, trade, services, government, transportation, communications, agriculture, tourism. **Principal manufactured goods:** machinery, foods, fabricated metals, transportation equipment, paper and wood products. **Agriculture: Chief crops:** corn, beans, beets, peas, hay, oats, cabbage, cranberries. **Chief products:** milk, butter, cheese. **Livestock** (1990): 4.2 mln. cattle, 1.3 mln. hogs/pigs; 84,000 sheep; 4.2 mln. poultry. **Timber/lumber** (1990): maple, birch, oak, evergreens; 522 mln. bd. ft. **Nonfuel Minerals** (1991): $212 mln.; mostly crushed stone, construction & industrial sand & gravel, lime. **Commercial fishing** (1991): $5.1 mln. **Chief ports:** Superior, Ashland, Milwaukee, Green Bay, Kewaunee, Pt. Washington, Manitowoc, Sheboygan, Marinette, Kenosha. **International airports at:** Milwaukee. **Value of construction** (1991): $4.2 bln. **Employment distribution** (1990): 24.1% trade; 25.0% mfg.; 23.1% serv.; 13.9% gvt. **Per capita income** (1991): $18,046. **Unemployment** (1991): 5.4%. **Tourism** (1989): out-of-state visitors spent $5.4 bln. **Sales tax:** 5%.

Finance. FDIC-insured commercial banks & trust companies (1990): 504. **Deposits:** $37.6 bln. **Savings institutions** (1991): 61. **Assets:** $17.8 bln.

Federal government. No. federal civilian employees (Mar. 1991): 12,052. **Avg. salary:** $29,988. **Notable federal facilities:** Ft. McCoy.

Energy. Electricity production (1991, MWh, by source): Hydroelectric: 2.4 mln.; Mineral: 27.7 mln.; Nuclear: 10.9 mln.

Education. Student-teacher ratio (1990): 16.2. **Avg. salary, public school teachers** (1991-92): $33,873.

State data. Motto: Forward. **Flower:** Wood violet. **Bird:** Robin. **Tree:** Sugar maple. **Song:** On, Wisconsin! **Entered union** May 29, 1848; rank, 30th. **State fair** at: West Allis; mid-Aug.

History. Jean Nicolet was the first European to see the Wisconsin area, arriving in Green Bay, 1634; French missionaries and fur traders followed. The British took over, 1763. The U.S. won the land after the Revolution but the British were not ousted until after the War of 1812. Lead miners came next, then farmers. Railroads were started in 1851, serving growing wheat harvests and iron mines.

Tourist attractions. Old Wade House and Carriage Museum, Greenbush; Villa Louis, Prairie du Chien; Circus World Museum, Baraboo; Wisconsin Dells; Old World Wisconsin, Eagle; Door County peninsula; Chequamegon and Nicolet national forests; Lake Winnebago; numerous lakes for water sports, ice boating and fishing; skiing and hunting.

Famous Wisconsinites include Edna Ferber, King Camp Gillette, Harry Houdini, Robert LaFollette, Alfred Lunt, Georgia O'Keeffe, Spencer Tracy, Thorstein Veblen, Orson Welles, Thornton Wilder, Frank Lloyd Wright.

Tourist information. Wisconsin Dept. of Development, Division of Tourism, 123 W. Washington Ave., Madison, WI 53702.

Toll-free travel information. 1-800-372-2737.

Wyoming

Equality State

People. Population (1991): 459,511; **rank:** 50. **Pop. density:** 4.7 per sq. mi. **Racial distrib.** (1990): 94.2% White; 0.8% Black; 2.1% Amer. Indian; 5.7% Hispanic. **Net change** (1990-91): 1.3%.

Geography. Total area: 97,809 sq. mi.; **rank:** 9. **Land area:** 97,105 sq. mi. **Acres forested land:** 9,966,000. **Location:** Mountain state lying in the high western plateaus of the Great Plains. **Climate:** semi-desert conditions throughout; true desert in the Big Horn and Great Divide basins. **Topography:** the eastern Great Plains rise to the foothills of the Rocky Mtns.; the Continental Divide crosses the state from the NW to the SE. **Capital:** Cheyenne.

Economy. Principal industries: mineral extraction, tourism and recreation, agriculture. **Principal manufactured goods:** refined petroleum products, foods, wood products, stone, clay and glass products. **Agriculture: Chief crops:** wheat, beans, barley, oats, sugar beets, hay. **Livestock** (1992): 1.3 mln. cattle; 24,000 hogs/pigs; 850,000 sheep. **Timber/lumber** (1990): Ponderosa & lodgepole pine, Douglas fir, Engelmann spruce; 309 mln. bd. ft. **Nonfuel Minerals** (1991): $941 mln.; mostly portland cement, crushed stone. **International airports at:** Casper. **Value of construction** (1991): $512.5 mln. **Employment distribution** (1991): 23% trade; 18% services; 9.6% mining. **Per capita income** (1991): $17,118. **Unemployment** (1991): 5.1%. **Tourism** (1989): out-of-state visitors spent $1.5 bln. **State sales tax.** 3%.

Finance. FDIC-insured commercial banks & trust companies (1990): 71. **Deposits:** $3.9 bln. **Savings institutions** (1991): 6. **Assets:** $812.2 mln.

Federal government. No. federal civilian employees (Mar. 1991): 4,749. **Avg. salary:** $30,627. **Notable federal facilities:** Warren AFB.

Energy. Electricity production (1991, MWh, by source): Hydroelectric: 0.4 mln.; Mineral: 36.7 mln.

Education. Student-teacher ratio (1990): 36.7. **Avg. salary, public school teachers** (1991-92): $29,000.

State data. Motto: Equal Rights. **Flower:** Indian paintbrush. **Bird:** Meadowlark. **Tree:** Cottonwood. **Song:** Wyoming. **Entered union** July 10, 1890; rank, 44th. **State fair** at: Douglas; late Aug.

History. Francés Francois and Louis Verendrye were the first Europeans, 1743. John Colter, American, was first to traverse Yellowstone Park, 1807-08. Trappers and fur traders followed in the 1820s. Forts Laramie and

Bridger became important stops on the pioneer trail to the West Coast. Indian wars followed massacres of army detachments in 1854 and 1866. Population grew after the Union Pacific crossed the state, 1869. Women won the vote, for the first time in the U.S., from the Territorial Legislature, 1869.

Tourist attractions. Yellowstone National Park, 3,472 sq. mi. in the NW corner of Wyoming and the adjoining edges of Montana and Idaho, the oldest U.S. national park, est. 1872, has some 10,000 geysers, hot springs, mud volcanoes, fossil forests, a volcanic glass (obsidian) mountain, the 1,000-ft.-deep canyon and 308-ft.-high waterfall of the Yellowstone River, and a wide variety of animals living free in their natural habitat.

Also, Grand Teton National Park, with mountains 13,000 ft. high; National Elk Refuge, covering 25,000 acres; Devils Tower, a columnar rock of igneous origin 1,280 ft. high; Fort Laramie and surrounding areas of pioneer trails; Buffalo Bill Museum, Cody; Cheyenne Frontier Days Celebration, last full week in July, the state's largest rodeo, and world's largest purse.

Famous Wyomingites include James Bridger, Buffalo Bill Cody, Nellie Tayloe Ross.

Tourist information. Travel Commission, Etchepare Circle, Cheyenne, WY 82002.

Toll-free travel information. 1-800-CALLWYO.

District of Columbia

Area: 69 sq. mi. **Population** (1991): 598,790. **Motto:** Justitia omnibus, Justice for all. **Flower:** American beauty rose. **Tree:** Scarlet oak. **Bird:** Wood thrush. The city of Washington is coextensive with the District of Columbia.

The District of Columbia is the seat of the federal government of the United States. It lies on the west central edge of Maryland on the Potomac River, opposite Virginia. Its area was originally 100 sq. mi. taken from the sovereignty of Maryland and Virginia. Virginia's portion south of the Potomac was given back to that state in 1846.

The 23d Amendment, ratified in 1961, granted residents the right to vote for president and vice president for the first time and gave them 3 members in the Electoral College. The first such votes were cast in Nov. 1964.

Congress, which has legislative authority over the District under the Constitution, established in 1878 a government of 3 commissioners appointed by the president. The Reorganization Plan of 1967 substituted a single commissioner (also called mayor), assistant, and 9-member City Council. Funds were still appropriated by Congress; residents had no vote in local government, except to elect school board members.

In Sept. 1970, Congress approved legislation giving the District one delegate to the House of Representatives. The delegate could vote in committee but not on the House floor. The first was elected 1971.

In May 1974 voters approved a charter giving them the right to elect their own mayor and a 13-member city council; the first took office Jan. 2, 1975. The district won the right to levy its own taxes but Congress retained power to veto council actions, and approve the city's annual budget.

Proposals for a "federal town" for the deliberations of the Continental Congress were made in 1783, 4 years before the adoption of the Constitution that gave the Confederation a national government. Rivalry between northern and southern delegates over the site appeared in the First Congress, 1789. John Adams, presiding officer of the Senate, cast the deciding vote of that body for Germantown, Pa. In 1790 Congress compromised by making Philadelphia the temporary capital for 10 years. The Virginia members of the House wanted a capital on the eastern bank of the Potomac; they were defeated by the Northerners, while the Southerners defeated the Northern attempt to have the nation assume the war debts of the 13 original states, the Assumption Bill fathered by Alexander Hamilton. Hamilton and Jefferson arranged a compromise: the Virginia men voted for the Assumption Bill, and the Northerners conceded the capital to the Potomac. President Washington chose the site in Oct. 1790 and persuaded landowners to sell their holdings to the government at £25, then about $66, an acre. The capital was named Washington.

Washington appointed Pierre Charles L'Enfant, a French engineer who had come over with Lafayette, to plan the capital on an area not over 10 mi. square. The L'Enfant plan, for streets 100 to 110 feet wide and one avenue 400 feet wide and a mile long, seemed grandiose and foolhardy. But Washington endorsed it. When L'Enfant ordered a wealthy landowner to remove his new manor house because it obstructed a vista, and demolished it when the owner refused, Washington stepped in and dismissed the architect. The official map and design of the city was completed by Benjamin Banneker, a distinguished black architect and astronomer, and Andrew Ellicott.

On Sept. 18, 1793, Pres. Washington laid the cornerstone of the north wing of the Capitol. On June 3, 1800, Pres. John Adams moved to Washington and on June 10, Philadelphia ceased to be the temporary capital. The City of Washington was incorporated in 1802; the District of Columbia was created as a municipal corporation in 1871, embracing Washington, Georgetown, and Washington County.

Outlying U.S. Areas

Commonwealth of Puerto Rico

(Estado Libre Asociado de Puerto Rico)

People. Population (1991): 3,566,000. **Pop. density:** 1,042.4 per sq. mi. **Urban** (1990): 66.8%. **Racial distribution** (1990): 99.9% Hispanic. **Net migration rate** (1991): 10 migrants/1,000 pop.

Geography. Total area: 3,435 sq. mi. **Land area:** 3,421 sq. mi. **Location:** island lying between the Atlantic to the N and the Caribbean to the S; it is easternmost of the West Indies group called the Greater Antilles, of which Cuba, Hispaniola, and Jamaica are the larger islands. **Climate:** mild, with a mean temperature of 77°. **Topography:** mountainous throughout three-fourths of its rectangular area, surrounded by a broken coastal plain; highest peak is Cerro Puntita, 4,389 ft. **Capital:** San Juan.

Economy. Principal industries: manufacturing. **Principal manufactured goods:** pharmaceuticals; chemicals, machinery and metals, electric machinery and equipment, petroleum refining, food products, apparel. **Agriculture: Chief crops:** sugarcane, coffee, pineapples, plantains; bananas; yams; taniers; pineapples; pidgeon peas; peppers; pumpkins; coriander; lettuce; tobacco. **Livestock** (1990): 600,000 cattle; 206,000 pigs; 7.4 mln. poultry. **Nonfuel Minerals** (1991): $119.2 mln., mostly cement. **Commercial fishing** (1984): $7.9 mln. **Chief ports/river shipping:** San Juan, Ponce, Mayaguez, Guayanillá, Guánica, Yabucoa, Aguirre. **Major airports at:** San Juan, Ponce, Mayaguez, Aguadilla. **Value of construction** (1987): $2.5 bln. **Employment distribution** (1990): 28% gvt.; 15% mfg.; 14% trade; 3% agric. **Per capita income** (1985): $4,301. **Unemployment** (1991): 16%. **Tourism** (1990): Visitors spent $1.37 bln.

Finance. No. FDIC-insured commercial banks & trust companies (1987): 14. **Deposits:** $9.7 bln. **No. savings institutions** (1991): 10. **Assets:** $5.4 bln.

Federal government. No. federal civilian employees (1985): 9,989. **Notable federal facilities:** U.S. Naval Station at Roosevelt Roads; U.S. Army Salinas Training Area and Ft. Allen; Sabana SECA Communications Center (U.S. Navy); Ft. Buchanan.

Energy Production (1985): Steam and gas: 11,938 mln. kwh; Other: 209 mln. kwh.

Education. Student-teacher ratio (1990): 18.8. **Avg. salary, public school teachers** (1985): $12,000.

Misc. Data. Motto. Joannes Est Nomen Eius (John is his name). **Flower:** Maga. **Bird:** Reinita. **Tree:** Ceiba. **National anthem:** La Borinqueña.

History: Puerto Rico (or Borinquen, after the original Arawak Indian name Boriquen), was discovered by Columbus, Nov. 19, 1493. Ponce de Leon conquered it for Spain, 1509, and established the first settlement at Caparra, across the bay from San Juan.

Sugar cane was introduced, 1515, and slaves were imported 3 years later. Gold mining petered out, 1570. Spaniards fought off a series of British and Dutch attacks; slavery was abolished, 1873. Under the treaty of Paris, Puerto Rico was ceded to the U.S. after the Spanish-American War, 1898. In 1952 the people voted in favor of Commonwealth status.

The Commonwealth of Puerto Rico is a self-governing part of the U.S. with a primary Hispanic culture. Puerto Ricans are U.S. citizens and about 2.0 million now live on the mainland, although since 1974 there has also been a reverse migration flow.

The current commonwealth political status of Puerto Rico gives the island's citizens virtually the same control over their internal affairs as the fifty states of the U.S. However, they do not vote in national elections, although they do vote in national primary elections.

Puerto Rico is represented in Congress solely by a resident commissioner who has a voice but no vote, except in committees.

No federal income tax is collected from residents on income earned from local sources in Puerto Rico.

Puerto Rico's famous "Operation Bootstrap," begun in the late 1940s, succeeded in changing the island from "The Poorhouse of the Caribbean" to an area with the highest per capita income in Latin America. This pioneering program encouraged manufacturing and the development of the tourist trade by selective tax exemption, low-interest loans, and other incentives. Despite the marked success of Puerto Rico's development efforts over an extended period of time, per capita income in Puerto Rico is low in comparison to that of the U.S. Economic growth slowed in fiscal 1991 from the 2.2% of fiscal 1990. In Mar., 1991 Gov. Rafael Hernández Colón signed a law making Spanish the island's only official language, ending 89 yrs. of Spanish and English as joint official languages.

General tourist attractions: Ponce Museum of Art; forts El Morro and San Cristobal; Old Walled City of San Juan; Arecibo Observatory; Cordillera Central and state parks; El Yunque Rain Forest; San Juan Cathedral; Porta Coeli Chapel and Museum of Religious Art, Interamerican Univ., San Germán; Condado Convention Center; Casa Blanca, Ponce de León family home, Puerto Rican Family Museum of 16th and 17 centuries and the Fine Arts Center in San Juan.

Cultural facilities, festivals, etc.: Festival Casals classical music concerts, mid-June; Puerto Rico Symphony Orchestra at Music Conservatory; Botanical Garden and Museum of Anthropology, Art, and History at the University of Puerto Rico; Institute of Puerto Rican Culture, at the Dominican Convent, and many popular festivals throughout the island.

Famous Puerto Ricans include: José Celso Barbosa, Julia de Burgos, Pablo Casals, Orlando Cepeda, Roberto Clemente, José de Diego, José Feliciano, Luis A. Ferré, José Ferrer, Doña Felisa Rincón de Gautier, Commodore Diégo E. Hernández, Rafael Hernández (El Jibarito), Raúl Julia, Luis Muñoz Marín, René Marqués, Luis Palés Matos, Concha Meléndez, Rita Moreno, Adm. Horacio Rivero, Rafael Hernández Colón, Marta Casals Istomin, Miguel Hernández Agosto.

Chamber of Commerce: 100 Tetuán P.O.Box. S-3789, San Juan, PR 00904; Ponce & South: El Señorial Bldg., Ponce, PR 00731.

Guam

Where America's Day Begins

People. Population (1990): 133,152, a 26% increase over the 1980 figure of 105,979. **Pop. density:** 631.6 per sq. mi. **Urban** (1980): 39.5%. **Major ethnic groups** (1987): Chamorro 47%, Filipino 28.6%, stateside immigrants 18%, remainder Micronesians. Native Guamanians, ethnically called Chamorros, are basically of Indonesian stock, with a mixture of Spanish and Filipino. In addition to the offical language, they speak the native Chamorro. **Migration** (1990): About 52% of population were born elsewhere; of these, 48% in Asia, 40% in U.S.

Geography. Total area: 209 sq. mi. land, 30 mi. long and 4 to 8.5 mi. wide. **Location:** largest and southernmost of the Mariana Islands in the West Pacific, 3,700 mi. W of Hawaii. **Climate:** tropical, with temperatures from 70° to 90°F; avg. annual rainfall, about 70 in. **Topography:** coralline limestone plateau in the N; southern chain of low volcanic mountains sloping gently to the W, more steeply to coastal cliffs on the E; general elevation, 500 ft.; highest pt., Mt. Lamlam, 1,334 ft. **Capital:** Agana.

Economy. Principal industries: construction, light manufacturing, tourism, banking, defense. **Principal manufactured goods:** textiles, foods. **Agriculture: Chief crops:** cabbages, eggplants, cucumber, long beans, tomatoes, bananas, coconuts, watermelon, yams, canteloupe, papayas, maize, sweet potatoes. **Livestock** (1984): 2,000 cattle; 14,000 hogs/pigs. **Chief ports:** Apra Harbor. **International airports at:** Tamuning. **Value of construction** (1980): $80.60 mln. **Employment distribution** (1987): 61.3% private sector; 38.7% gvt. **Per capita income** (1986): $7,116. **Median household income** (1989): $30,755; persons per household 3.97; persons per family 4.26. **Unemployment** (1990): 3.8%. **Tourism** (1980): visitors' receipts $117.9 mln.

Finance. Notable industries: insurance, real estate, finance. **No. banks:** 13; **No. savings and loan assns.:** 2.

Federal government. No. federal employees (1980): 6,600. **Notable federal facilities:** Anderson AFB; naval, air and port bases.

Education. Public elem. and second. school enrollment (1987): 25,676; **Percent of enrollment:** 91.2; **Expenditures per pupil:** $3,344.

Misc. Data. Flower: Puti Tai Nobio (Bougainvillea). **Bird:** Toto (Fruit dove). **Tree:** Ifit (Intsiabijuga). **Song:** Stand Ye Guamians.

History. Magellan arrived in the Marianas Mar. 6, 1521. They were colonized in 1668 by Spanish missionaries who named them the Mariana Islands in honor of Maria Anna, queen of Spain. When Spain ceded Guam to the U.S., it sold the other Marianas to Germany. Japan obtained a League of Nations mandate over the German islands in 1919; in Dec. 1941 it seized Guam; the island was retaken by the U.S. in July 1944.

Guam is a self-governing organized unincorporated U.S. territory. The Organic Act of 1950 provides for a governor and a 21-member unicameral legislature, elected biennially by the residents who are American citizens.

In 1972 a U.S. law gave Guam one delegate to the U.S. House of Representatives; the delegate may vote in committee but not on the House floor.

Guam's quest to change its status to a U.S. Commonwealth began in the late 1970's. A Commission on Self-Determination, created in 1984, developed a Draft Commonwealth Act, which was in Congress for review as of mid-1992.

General tourist attractions. annual mid-Aug. Merizo Water Festival; Tarzan Falls; beaches; water sports, duty-free port shopping.

Virgin Islands

St. John, St. Croix, St. Thomas

People. Population (1990): 101,809 (50,139, St. Croix; 48,166, St. Thomas; 3,504, St. John). **Pop. density:** 748.60 per sq. mi. **Urban** (1980): 39%. **Racial distribution:** (1980) 15% White; 85% Black. **Major ethnic groups:** West Indian, French, Hispanic.

Geography. Total area: 133 sq. mi.; **Land area:** 136 sq. mi. **Location:** 3 larger and 50 smaller islands and cays in the S and W of the V.I. group (British V.I. colony to the N and E) which is situated 70 mi. E of Puerto Rico, located W of the Anegada Passage, a major channel connecting the Atlantic O. and the Caribbean Sea. **Climate:** subtropical; the sun tempered by gentle trade winds; humidity is low; average temperature, 78° F. **Topography:** St. Thomas is mainly a ridge of hills running E and W, and has little tillable land; St. Croix rises abruptly in the N but slopes to the S to flatlands and lagoons; St. John has steep, lofty hills and valleys with little level tillable land. **Capital:** Charlotte Amalie, St. Thomas.

Economy. Principal industries: tourism, rum, alumina prod., petroleum refining, watch industry, textiles, electronics. **Principal manufactured goods:** rum, textiles, pharmaceuticals, perfumes. **Gross Domestic Product** (1987): $1.246 bln. **Agriculture: Chief crops:** truck garden produce. **Minerals:** sand, gravel. **Chief ports:** Cruz Bay, St. John; Frederiksted and Christiansted, St. Croix; Charlotte Amalie, St. Thomas. **International airports on:** St. Thomas, St. Croix. **Value of construction** (1987): $167.0 mln. **Per capita income** (1989): $11,052. **Unemployment** (1991): 2.9%. **Tourism** (1988): $662.8. **No. banks** (1990): 8.

Education (1987): **No. public schools:** 34 elem. and second.; 1 college. **Avg. starting salary, public school teachers:** $18,001.

Misc. data. Flower: Yellow elder or yellow trumpet, local designation Ginger Thomas. **Bird:** Yellow breast. **Song:** Virgin Islands March.

History. The islands were discovered by Columbus in 1493. Spanish forces, 1555, defeated the Caribes and claimed the territory; by 1596 the native population was annihilated. First permanent settlement in the U.S. territory, 1672, by the Danes; U.S. purchased the islands, 1917, for defense purposes.

The Virgin Islands has a republican form of government, headed by a governor and lieut. governor elected, since 1970, by popular vote for 4-year terms. There is a 15-member unicameral legislature, elected by popular vote. Residents of the V.I. have been U.S. citizens since 1927. Since 1973 they have elected a delegate to the U.S. House of Representatives, who may vote in committee but not in the House.

General tourist attractions. Magens Bay, St. Thomas; duty-free shopping; Virgin Islands National Park, 14,488 acres on St. John of lush growth, beaches, Indian relics, and evidence of colonial Danes.

Tourist information. Dept. of Economic Development & Agriculture, St. Thomas, P.O. Box 6400, St. Thomas, VI 00801; St. Croix, P.O. Box 4535, Christiansted, St. Croix 00820.

American Samoa

Capital: Pago Pago, Island of Tutuila. **Area:** 77 sq. mi. **Population:** (1990) 46,773. **Motto:** Samoa Muamua le Atua (In Samoa, God is First). **Song:** Amerika Samoa. **Flower:** Paogo (Ula-fala). **Plant:** Ava.

Blessed with spectacular scenery and delightful South Seas climate, American Samoa is the most southerly of all lands under U. S. sovereignty. It is an unincorporated territory consisting of 6 small islands of the Samoan group: **Tutuila, Aunu'u, Manu'a Group (Ta'u, Olosega and Ofu),** and **Rose.** Also administered as part of American Samoa is **Swain's Island,** 210 mi. to the NW, acquired by the U.S. in 1925. The islands are 2,300 mi. SW of Honolulu.

American Samoa became U. S. territory in Feb., 1900 by a treaty with the United Kingdom and Germany in 1899. The islands were ceded by local chiefs in April, 1900 and July, 1904, and became U.S territories. The U.S. acquired commercial rights pursuant to the convention 1899, a tripartite agreement among Great Britain, Germany, and the U.S.

Samoa (Western), comprising the larger islands of the Samoan group, was a New Zealand mandate and UN Trusteeship until it became an independent nation Jan. 1, 1962 *(see Index.)*

Tutuila and Annu'u have an area of 53 sq. mi. Ta'u has an area of 17 sq. mi., and the islets of Ofu and Olosega, 5 sq. mi. with a population of a few thousand. Swain's Island has nearly 2 sq. mi. and a population of about 100.

About 70% of the land is bush. Chief products and exports are fish products. Taro, bread-fruit, yams, coconuts, pineapples, oranges, and bananas are also produced.

From 1900-1951, American Samoa was under the jurisdiction of the U.S. Navy. Since 1951, it has been under the Interior Dept. On Jan. 3, 1978, the first popularly elected Samoan governor and lieutenant governor were inaugurated. Previously, the governor was appointed by the Secretary of the Interior. American Samoa has a bicameral legislature and elects its own member of Congress, who can introduce legislation and vote in committee, but not in the House.

The American Samoans are of Polynesian origin. They are nationals of the U.S.; approximately 20,000 live in Hawaii, 65,000 in California and Washington.

Minor Caribbean Island

Navassa lies between Jamaica and Haiti, 100 miles south of Guantanamo Bay, Cuba; it covers about 3 sq. mi., is reserved by the U.S. for a lighthouse and is uninhabited. It is administered by the U.S. Coast Guard.

Wake, Midway, Other Islands

Wake Island, and its sister islands, **Wilkes** and **Peale,** lie in the Pacific Ocean on the direct route from Hawaii to Hong Kong, about 2,300 mi. W of Hawaii and 1,290 mi. E of Guam. The group is 4.5 mi. long, 1.5 mi. wide, and totals less than 3 sq. mi.

The U.S. flag was hoisted over Wake Island, July 4, 1898, formal possession taken Jan. 17, 1899; Wake has been administered by the U.S. Air Force since 1972. The population consists of about 200 persons.

The **Midway Islands,** acquired in 1867, consist of 2, **Sand** and **Eastern,** in the North Pacific 1,150 mi. NW of Hawaii, with area of about 3 sq. mi., administered by the U.S. Navy. There is no indigenous population; its population is about 450.

Johnston Atoll, 717 miles SW of Hawaii, area 1 sq. mi. is operated by The Defense Nuclear Agency, and the Fish and Wildlife Service, U.S. Dept. of the Interior, and **Kingman Reef,** 920 miles S of Hawaii, is under Navy control.

Howland, Jarvis, and **Baker Islands,** 1,500-1,650 miles southwest of the Hawaiian group, uninhabited since World War II, are under the Interior Dept.

Palmyra is an atoll about 1,000 miles south of Hawaii, 2 sq. mi. Privately owned, it is under the Interior Dept.

Islands Under Trusteeship

The Trust Territory of the Pacific Islands was established in 1947, as the only strategic trusteeship of the 11 trusteeships established by the U.N. For nearly 4 decades, the territory had a heterogeneous population of about 140,000 people scattered among more than 2,100 islands and atolls in 3 major archipelagos: the Carolines, the Marshalls, and the Marianas. The entire geographic area is sometimes referred to as "Micronesia," meaning "little islands." The area of the Trust Territory covered some 3 million sq. miles of the Pacific Ocean, slightly larger than the continental U.S. However, its islands constituted a land area of only 715.8 sq. miles—half the size of Rhode Island. It formerly contained 4 political jurisdictions: The Commonwealth of the Northern Mariana Islands (CNMI), the Federated States of Micronesia (FSM), the Republic of the Marshall Islands (RMI), and Palau. As of Oct. 21, 1986, the RMI entered into free association with the U.S., as did the FSM effective Nov. 3, 1986. The CNMI became a commonwealth of the U.S., also effective Nov. 3. Only Palau remains under trusteeship.

Commonwealth of the Northern Mariana Islands

Located in the perpetually warm climes between Guam and the Tropic of Cancer, the 16 islands of the Northern

Marianas form a 300-mile-long archipelago, comprising a total land area of 183.5 sq. miles. The native population, 1990, is 43,345, and is concentrated on the 3 largest of the 6 inhabited islands: **Saipan,** the seat of government and commerce (38,896), **Rota** (2,295), and **Tinian** (2,118).

The people of the Northern Marianas are predominantly of Chamorro cultural extraction, although numbers of Carolinians and immigrants from other areas of E. Asia and Micronesia have also settled in the islands. Pursuant to the Covenant of 1976, which established the Northern Marianas as a commonwealth in political union with the U.S., most natives and many domiciliaries of these islands achieved U.S. citizenship on Nov. 13, 1986, when the U.S. terminated its administration of the U.N. trusteeship as it affected the Northern Marianas. From July 18, 1947, the U.S. had administered the Northern Marianas under a trusteeship agreement with the U.N. Security Council. English is among the several languages commonly spoken.

The Northern Mariana Islands has been self-governing since 1978, when both a constitution drafted and adopted by the people became effective, and a bicameral legislature with offices of governor and lieutenant governor was inaugurated. Commercial activity has increased steadily in the last few years, with 3,537 business licenses issued in the CNM, mostly in tourism, construction, and light industry. In 1990, more than 417,146 tourists visited. An agreement with the U.S. for 1986-1992 entitles the Northern Marianna Islands to $228 million for capital development, government operations and special programs.

Palau

Palau consists of more than 200 islands in 16 states in the Caroline chain, of which 8 are permanently inhabited. The capital of Palau, Koror, lies 3,997 miles SW of Honolulu and 813 miles S of Guam. Population of Palau is 15,122 (1990), 10,501 (1990) in Koror. Average year-round temperature is 80 degrees, average annual rainfall 150 inches.

Until 1979, a High Commissioner appointed by the U.S. president, himself appointed a district administrator for Palau to oversee programs and administration there. In support of the evolving political status, the U.S. recognized the Constitution of Palau and the establishment of the Government of Palau, consistent with U.S. responsibilities in Palau as the administered authority of the Trust Territory of the Pacific Islands (TTPI).

The Assistant Secretary of the Interior for Territorial and International Affairs has been delegated U.S. authority with respect to Palau and may suspend any newly enacted national law in Palau and every newly enacted state law in Palau that involves finance or the expenditure of funds if the law is inconsistent with the trusteeship agreement or U.S. laws or regulations applicable to the TTPI. The Government of the TTPI maintains an office and staff in Palau. The Constitution became effective in 1980. The President and Vice President are elected by popular vote. A Council of Chiefs advises the President on matters concerning traditional law and custom. Palau has a bicameral national legislature composed of a House of Delegates and a Senate.

Washington, Capital of the U.S.

Arlington National Cemetery

Arlington National Cemetery, on the former Custis estate in Virginia, is the site of the **Tomb of the Unknown Soldier** and the final resting place of John Fitzgerald Kennedy, president of the United States, who was buried there Nov. 25, 1963. A torch burns day and night over his grave. The remains of his brother Sen. Robert F. Kennedy (N.Y.) were interred on June 8, 1968, in an area adjacent. Many other famous Americans are also buried at Arlington, as well as 175,000 American soldiers from every major war.

U.S. Marine Corps War Memorial (Iwo Jima)

North of the National Cemetery, approximately 350 yards, stands the bronze statue of the raising of the United States flag on Mt. Suribachi during WWII, executed by Felix de Weldon from the photograph by Joe Rosenthal, and presented to the nation by members and friends of the U.S. Marine Corps.

Vietnam War Memorial

Dedicated on November 13, 1982, it is a symbol of the U.S.' honor and recognition of the men and women who served in the armed forces in the Vietnam War. It is inscribed with the names of the more than 58,000 who gave their lives or remain missing.

The Capitol

The United States Capitol was originally designed by Dr. William Thornton, an amateur architect, who submitted a plan in the spring of 1793 that won him $500 and a city lot.

The south, or House wing, was completed in 1807 under the direction of Benjamin H. Latrobe.

The present Senate and House wings and the iron dome were designed and constructed by Thomas U. Walter, the 4th architect of the Capitol, between 1851-1863.

The present cast iron dome at its greatest exterior measures 135 ft. 5 in., and it is topped by the bronze Statue of Freedom that stands 19½ ft. and weighs 14,985 pounds. On its base are the words "E Pluribus Unum" (Out of Many One).

The Capitol is normally open from 9 a.m. to 4:30 p.m. Tours through the Capitol, including the House and Senate galleries, are conducted from 9 a.m. to 4 p.m. without charge.

Folger Shakespeare Library

The Folger Shakespeare Library on Capitol Hill, Washington, D. C., is a research institution devoted to the advancement of learning in the background of Anglo-American civilization in the 16th and 17th centuries, and in most aspects of the continental Renaissance. It has the largest collection of Shakespeareana in the world, with 79 copies of the First Folio.

Library of Congress

Established by and for Congress in 1800, the Library of Congress has extended its services over the years to other government agencies and other libraries, to scholars, and to the general public, and it now serves as the national library. It contains over 80 million items in 470 languages.

The library's exhibit halls are open to the public. Guided tours are given every hour from 9 a.m. through 4 p.m. Monday through Friday.

Thomas Jefferson Memorial

Dedicated in 1943, **The Thomas Jefferson Memorial** stands on the south shore of the Tidal Basin in West Potomac park. It is a circular stone structure, with Vermont marble on the exterior and Georgia white marble inside and combines architectural elements of the dome of the Pantheon in Rome and the rotunda designed by Jefferson for the University of Virginia.

The memorial is open daily from 8 a.m. to midnight. An elevator and curb ramps for the handicapped are in service.

Lincoln Memorial

The Lincoln Memorial in West Potomac Park, on the axis of the Capitol and the Washington Monument, consists of a large marble hall enclosing a heroic statue of Abraham Lincoln in meditation sitting on a large armchair. It was dedicated on Memorial Day, May 30, 1922. The Memorial was designed by Henry Bacon. The statue was made by Daniel Chester French and sculpted by the Piccirilli family. Murals and ornamentation on the bronze ceiling beams are by Jules Guerin.

The memorial is open daily from 8 a.m. to midnight. An elevator for the handicapped is in service.

John F. Kennedy Center

John F. Kennedy Center for the Performing Arts, designated by Congress as the National Cultural Center and the official memorial in Washington to President Kennedy, opened September 8, 1971. Tours are available daily between 10:00 a.m. and 1:00 p.m.

Mount Vernon

Mount Vernon on the south bank of the Potomac R., 16 miles below Washington, D. C., is part of a large tract of land in northern Virginia.

The present house is an enlargement of one apparently built on the site of an earlier one by Augustine Washington, who lived there 1735-1738. His son Lawrence came there in 1743, when he renamed the plantation Mount Vernon in honor of Admiral Vernon under whom he had served in the West Indies. Lawrence Washington died in 1752 and was succeeded as proprietor of Mount Vernon by his half-brother, George Washington.

National Archives

The Declaration of Independence, the Constitution of the United States, and the Bill of Rights are on permanent display in the National Archives Exhibition Hall. They are sealed in glass-and-bronze cases. The National Archives also holds the permanently valuable federal records of the United States government.

National Gallery of Art

The National Gallery of Art, situated in an area bounded by Constitution Avenue and the Mall, between Third and Seventh Streets, was established by Joint Resolution of Congress Mar. 24, 1937, and opened Mar. 17, 1941.

Normally open daily from 10 a.m. to 5 p.m.; noon to 9 p.m. Sunday. Summer, 10 a.m. to 9 p.m., noon to 9 p.m. on Sunday.

The Pentagon

The Pentagon, headquarters of the Department of Defense, is one of the world's largest office buildings. Situated in Arlington, Va., it houses more than 23,000 employees in offices that occupy 3,707,745 square feet.

Tours are available Monday through Friday (excluding federal holidays), from 9 a.m. to 3:30 p.m.

Smithsonian Institution

The Smithsonian Institution, established in 1846, the world's largest museum complex, is comprised of 14 museums and the National Zoo. It holds some 100 million artifacts and specimens in its trust "for the increase and diffusion of knowledge among men." Nine museums are located on the National Mall between the Washington Monument and the Capitol; 4 other museums and the zoo are elsewhere in Washington, and the Cooper-Hewitt Museum in New York City. The National Air and Space Museum, National Museum of Natural History, and the National Portrait Gallery are some of the more popular museums. They are open daily, except Dec. 25, from 10 a.m. to 5:30 p.m. unless otherwise noted.

Washington Monument

The Washington Monument, dedicated in 1885, is a tapering shaft or obelisk of white marble, 555 ft., 5-1/8 inches in height and 55 ft., 1-1/2 inches square at base. Eight small windows, 2 on each side, are located at the 500-ft. level, where points of interest are indicated.

Open daily except Dec. 25, 9 a.m. to 5 p.m., 8 a.m. to 12 p.m. in summer.

The White House

The White House, the president's residence, stands on 18 acres on the south side of Pennsylvania Avenue, between the Treasury and the Executive Office Building.

The walls are of sandstone, quarried at Aquia Creek, Va. The exterior walls were painted, causing the building to be termed the "White House." On Aug. 24, 1814, during Madison's administration, the house was burned by the British. James Hoban rebuilt it by Oct. 1817.

The White House is normally open from 10 a.m. to 12 noon, Tuesday through Saturday. Only the public rooms on the ground floor and state floor may be visited.

Naturalization: How to Become an American Citizen

Source: The Federal Statutes

A person who desires to be naturalized as a citizen of the United States may obtain the necessary application form as well as detailed information from the nearest office of the Immigration and Naturalization Service or from the clerk of a court handling naturalization cases.

An applicant must be at least 18 years old. He must have been a lawful resident of the United States continuously for 5 years. For husbands and wives of U.S. citizens the period is 3 years in most instances. Special provisions apply to certain veterans of the Armed Forces.

An applicant must have been physically present in this country for at least half of the required 5 years' residence.

Every applicant for naturalization must:

(1) demonstrate an understanding of the English language, including an ability to read, write, and speak words in ordinary usage in the English language (persons physically unable to do so, and persons who, on the date of their examinations, are over 50 years of age and have been lawful permanent residents of the United States for 20 years or more are exempt).

(2) have been a person of good moral character, attached to the principles of the Constitution, and well disposed to the good order and happiness of the United States for five years just before filing the petition or for whatever other period of residence is required in his case and continue to be such a person until admitted to citizenship; and

(3) demonstrate a knowledge and understanding of the fundamentals of the history, and the principles and form of government, of the U.S.

At the preliminary hearing the applicant may be represented by a lawyer or social service agency. There is a 30-day wait. If action is favorable, there is a final hearing before a judge, who administers the following oath of allegiance:

I hereby declare, on oath, that I absolutely and entirely renounce and abjure all allegiance and fidelity to any foreign prince, potentate, state or sovereignty, to whom or which I have heretofore been a subject or citizen; that I will support and defend the Constitution and laws of the United States of America against all enemies, foreign and domestic; that I will bear true faith and allegiance to the same; that I will bear arms on behalf of the United States when required by the law; that I will perform noncombatant service in the armed forces of the United States when required by the law; that I will perform work of national importance under civilian direction when required by the law; and that I take this obligation freely without any mental reservation or purpose of evasion; so help me God.

Notable Tall Buildings in North American Cities

Height from sidewalk to roof, including penthouse and tower if enclosed as integral part of structure; actual number of stories beginning at street level. Asterisks (*) denote buildings still under construction Jan. 1993. Year is date of completion

City	Hgt. ft.	Stories
Albany, N.Y.		
Erastus Corning II Tower	589	44
State Office Building	388	34
Agency (4 bldgs.), So. Mall	310	23
Atlanta, Ga.		
C & S Plaza (1992)	1,050	57
One Peachtree Center (1992)	880	63
Atlantic Center/IBM (1988)	828	52
191 Peachtree (1990)	770	54
Westin Peachtree Plaza (1973)	723	71
Georgia Pacific Tower (1981)	697	51
Promenade II/AT&T (1989)	691	40
Southern Bell Telephone (1980)	677	47
GLG Grand/Occidental Hotel (1992)	609	53
Concourse Tower #5 (1988)	570	32
2 Peachtree Tower (1968)	556	44
Marriott Marquis (1985)	554	52
Concourse Tower #6 (1991)	553	32
Equitable Building, 100 Peachtree (1967)	453	34
101 Marietta Tower, 101 Marietta (1975)	446	36
Ravinia #3 (1991)	444	34
AT&T Long Line Bldg (1975)	433	...
Bell South Enterprises (1990)	428	28
Atlanta Plaza I (1986)	425	32
Park Place, 2660 Peachtree (1986)	420	40
Club Towers Apts. (1989)	410	38
South Trust Bank (1961)	409	32
Peachtree Summit (1975)	406	31
North Avenue Tower (1979)	403	26
Tower Place, 3361 Piedmont Rd. (1974)	401	29
First Union Bank (1987)	396	30
Richard B. Russell, Federal Bldg. (1978)	383	26
Atlanta Hilton Hotel (1974)	383	32
Peachtree Center, Harris Bldg. (1975)	382	31
Marquis One (1985)	378	30
Marquis Two (1987)	378	30
Trust Company Bank (1968)	377	28
Coastal States Insurance (1971)	377	27
Peachtree Center Cain Building (1972)	376	30
Peachtree Center Building (1966)	374	31
One Georgia Center (1966)	371	29
Mayfair Apts. Tower (1990)	370	34
The Campanile, 1145 Peachtree (1987)	367	25
Riverwood Tower/Barnett Bank (1989)	362	26
Austin, Tex.		
One American Center (1982)	395	32
One Congress Plaza (1987)	391	30
NCNB Tower (1975)	328	26
Baltimore, Md.		
U.S. Fidelity & Guaranty Co.	529	40
Maryland National Bank Bldg.	509	34
6 St. Paul Place	493	37
World Trade Center Bldg.	395	32
Tremont Plaza Hotel	395	37
250 W. Pratt St.	360	26
Harbor Court	356	28
Blaustein Bldg.	342	30
Union Trust Tower	335	24
Central Savings Bank Bldg.	330	28
Charles Center South	330	26
Baton Rouge, La.		
State Capitol (1932)	460	34
Hancock Bank Bldg. (1974)	315	24
Birmingham, Ala.		
Southtrust Tower	454	34
First Natl. Southern Natural Bldg.	390	30
Am South/Sonat Tower	390	30
South Central Bell Hdqts. Bldg.	390	30
City Federal Bldg.	325	27
Boston, Mass.		
John Hancock Tower	790	60
Prudential Center	750	52
Boston Co. Bldg., Court St.	605	41
Federal Reserve Bldg.	604	32
International Place, 100 Oliver St.	600	46
First National Bank of Boston	591	37
One Financial Center	590	46
Shawmut Bank Bldg.	520	38
Exchange Place, 53 State St.	510	39
Sixty State St.	509	38
One Post Office Sq.	507	40
One Beacon St.	507	40
New England Merch. Bank Bldg.	500	40
U.S. Custom House	496	32
John Hancock Bldg.	495	26
State St. Bank Bldg.	477	34
125 High St. (1990)	455	30
One Hundred Summer St.	450	33
McCormack Bldg.	401	22
Keystone Custodian Funds	400	32
Saltonstall Office Bldg.	396	22
Devonshire, 250 Wash. St.	396	40
Harbor Towers (2 bldgs.)	396	40
Westin Hotel, Copley Place	395	36
Federal Center (1988)	393	28
75 State St. (1988)	390	31
John F. Kennedy Bldg.	387	24
Marriott Hotel, Copley Place	383	39
101 Federal St. (1988)	382	31
Longfellow Towers (2 bldgs.)	380	38
Buffalo, N.Y.		
Marine Midland Center (1971)	529	40
City Hall (1926)	378	32
Rand Bldg., not incl. 40-ft. beacon (1929)	351	29
Main Place Tower (1969)	350	26
Calgary, Alta.		
Petro-Canada Tower #2	689	52
Benkers Hall (1989)	645	50
Calgary Tower	626	...
Canterra Tower (1988)	580	46
First Canadian Centre	547	44
Scotia Centre	504	38
Nova Bldg., 801 7th Ave. SW	500	37
Petro-Canada Tower #1	469	33
Two Bow Valley Square	468	39
Fifth & Fifth Bldg.	460	35
Home Oil Tower	463	34
Canada Trust Tower (1991)	462	40
Shell Tower	460	34
Dome Oil Tower	449	33
Four Bow Valley Square	441	37
Esso Plaza (twin towers)	435	34
Oxford Square	421	33
Family Life Bldg.	410	33
Pan Canadian Bldg., 150 9th Ave. SW	410	28
Norcen Tower	408	33
Alberta Stock Exchange Bldg.	407	33
Amoco Centre (1988)	396	30
Western Centre	385	40
Calgary Place	385	30
Three Bow Valley Square	382	33
Charlotte, N.C.		
NationsBank Corp. Center (1992)	871	60
One First Union Center (1988)	580	42
NationsBank Plaza (1974)	503	40
Interstate Tower (1990)	462	32
Two First Union Center (1971)	433	32
Wachovia Center (1974)	420	32
Carillon (1991)	394	24
Charlotte Plaza (1982)	388	27
First Citizens Plaza (1987)	320	23
Chicago, Ill.		
Sears Tower (world's tallest) (1974)	1,454	110
Amoco (1974)	1,136	80
John Hancock Center (1969)	1,127	100
311 S. Wacker (1990)	970	65
Two Prudential Plaza (1990)	901	64
AT&T Corporate Center (1989)	891	60
900 N. Michigan (1989)	871	66
Water Tower Place (1976)	859	74
First Natl. Bank (1969)	852	60
Three First National Plaza (1981)	775	57
Olympia Centre (1984)	727	63

City	Hgt. ft.	Stories
Leo Burnett Bldg. (1989)	**700**	46
600 N. Lakeshore Dr.	**697**	75
IBM Plaza (1991)	**695**	52
One Magnificent Mile (1983)	**673**	58
Daley Center (1965)	**662**	31
1,000 Lake Shore Plaza (1964)	**648**	55
Lake Point Tower (1968)	**645**	70
Board of Trade, incl. 81 ft. statue (1930)	**605**	44
Prudential Bldg., 130 E. Randolph (1955).	**601**	41
Antenna tower, 311 ft., makes total	**912**	...
CNA Plaza (1972)	**600**	44
Huron Apts.	**599**	56
Marina City Apts., 2 buildings	**588**	61
Mid Continental Plaza (1972)	**580**	50
Associates Center (1983)	**575**	41
Pittsfield, 55 E. Washington St. (1927)	**572**	38
Onterie Center (1985)	**570**	58
Civic Opera Bldg. (1929)	**555**	45
Newberry Plaza, State & Oak (1974)	**553**	56
One South Wacker Dr. (1983)	**550**	40
Harbor Point (1975)	**550**	54
Madison Plaza (1982)	**551**	45
190 S. LaSalle (1986)	**550**	40
LaSalle Natl. Bank (1934)	**535**	44
One N. LaSalle Street (1930)	**530**	49
111 E. Chestnut St. (1972)	**529**	56
Chicago Mercantile Exchange (2 bldgs)	**525**	40
River Plaza, Rush & Hubbard (1988)	**524**	56
35 E. Wacker Drive (1926)	**523**	40
United Ins. Bldg., 1 E. Wacker Dr. (1962)	**522**	41
Lincoln Tower, 75 E. Wacker Dr. (1928)	**519**	42
Quaker Tower (1987)	**518**	35
Carbide & Carbon, 230 N. Mich. (1929)	**503**	37
Walton Colonnade (1972)	**500**	44
Xerox Center (1980)	**500**	40
One Financial Place (1985)	**498**	40
LaSalle-Wacker, 221 N. LaSalle St.	**491**	41
Amer. Nat'l. Bank, 33 N. LaSalle St.	**479**	40
Bankers, 105 W. Adams St. (1927)	**476**	41
Brunswick Bldg. (1965)	**475**	37
310 Center (1924)	**475**	37
American Furniture Mart (1926)	**474**	24
333 Wacker Dr. (1983)	**472**	36

Cincinnati, Oh.

City	Hgt. ft.	Stories
Carew Tower (1931)	**568**	49
Central Trust Tower (1979)	**504**	33
Dubois Tower, 5th & Walnut (1969)	**423**	32
Omni-Netherland Plaza	**372**	31
Central Trust Center	**355**	27
Atrium Two (1984)	**350**	30
Star Bank Center (1981)	**351**	26
Clarion North Tower	**350**	33
Cinn. Commerce Center (1984)	**346**	29

Cleveland, Oh.

City	Hgt. ft.	Stories
Society Center (1991)	**948**	57
Terminal Tower (1930)	**708**	52
BP America (1985)	**658**	46
Plaza Tower at Erieview (1964)	**529**	40
One Cleveland Center (1983)	**450**	31
Bank One Center (1991)	**446**	28
Justice Center, 1250 Ontario (1976)	**420**	26
Federal Bldg. (1967)	**419**	32
National City Center (1980)	**410**	35
Cleveland St. J. F. Rhodes Tower (1971)	**373**	20
Eaton Center (1983)	**360**	28
Ohio-Bell. (1927)	**360**	22

Columbus, Oh.

City	Hgt. ft.	Stories
James A. Rhodes (State Office Tower)	**629**	41
LeVeque Tower, 50 W. Broad	**555**	47
Ohio Bureau of Worker's Compensation & Ind. Comm. (1990)	**530**	33
Huntington Center, 41 S. High St.	**512**	37
Verne-Riffe State Office Tower	**503**	33
One Nationwide Plaza	**482**	40
One Riverside Plaza	**456**	31
Borden Bldg., 180 E. Broad	**438**	34
Three Nationwide Plaza (1989)	**408**	27
One Columbus	**366**	26
Columbus Center, 100 E. Broad	**357**	24

Dallas, Tex.

City	Hgt. ft.	Stories
National Bank Plaza (1985)	**939**	72
Bank One Center (1987)	**787**	60
Texas Commerce Tower (1987)	**738**	55
First Interstate Bank Tower (1986)	**721**	60
Renaissance Tower (1987)	**710**	56
Trammell Crow Center (1984)	**686**	50
First City Center (1984)	**655**	50
Thanksgiving Tower (1982)	**645**	50
First National Bank	**625**	52
Republic Bank Tower	**598**	50
SW Bell Admin. Tower	**580**	37
Lincoln Plaza (1984)	**579**	45
Olympia York Tower (1982)	**562**	36
Cityplace Center East (1988)	**560**	50
Southland Center Tower (1959)	**550**	42
Maxus Energy (1980)	**550**	34
2001 Bryan St. (1973)	**512**	40
San Jacinto Tower (1982)	**456**	33
NationsBank Center Tower 1 (1954)	**452**	36
Stouffer Hotel	**451**	29
Skyway Tower (1981)	**448**	31
One Main Place (1968)	**445**	34
1600 Pacific Bldg. (1964)	**434**	32
Magnolia Bldg. (1923)	**430**	27
Mart Hotel	**400**	29
Complex Union Tower	**400**	33

Dayton, Oh.

City	Hgt. ft.	Stories
Kettering Tower, 2d & Main (1970)	**405**	30
Mead World Hqtrs, 10 W. 2d St. (1976)	**385**	28

Denver, Col.

City	Hgt. ft.	Stories
Republic Plaza	**714**	56
Mountain Bell Center	**709**	54
United Bank of Denver	**698**	52
1999 Broadway	**544**	43
Arco Tower	**527**	41
Anaconda Tower	**507**	40
Amoco Bldg., 17th Ave. & Broadway	**448**	36
17th Street Plaza	**438**	35
Stollar Plaza	**437**	31
First Interstate Tower North	**434**	32
One Denver Place	**428**	34
Brooks Towers, 1020 15th St.	**420**	42
Tabor Center, #1	**408**	32
Manville Plaza	**404**	29
Colorado Nat'l. Bank, 17th & Curtis	**389**	26
First Interstate Tower South	**385**	28
Security Life Bldg.	**384**	33
Mellon Financial Center	**374**	31
Dominion Plaza	**368**	30
Lincoln Center	**366**	30
Denver Natl. Bank Plaza	**363**	29
Bank Western	**357**	27
Colorado State Bank	**352**	26

Des Moines, Ia.

City	Hgt. ft.	Stories
Principal Financial Group Bldg. (1990)	**630**	44
Ruan Center (1974)	**457**	35
Financial Center, 7th & Walnut (1973)	**345**	25
Marriott Hotel, 700 Grand Ave. (1981)	**340**	33
Plaza, 3d & Walnut (1984)	**340**	25

Detroit, Mich.

City	Hgt. ft.	Stories
Westin Hotel	**720**	71
Penobscot Bldg.	**557**	47
1 Detroit Center	**491**	40
Guardian	**485**	40
Renaissance Center (4 bldgs.)	**479**	39
Book Tower	**472**	35
150 W. Jefferson Bldg.	**470**	29
Prudential 3000 Town Center	**448**	32
Cadillac Tower	**437**	40
David Stott	**436**	38
ANR Bldg.	**430**	32
Fisher	**420**	28
J. L. Hudson Bldg.	**397**	28
McNamara Federal Office Bldg.	**393**	27
2000 Prudential Town Ctr.	**392**	28
American Center	**374**	27
Top of Troy Bldg.	**374**	27
Comerica Bldg., 211 N. Fort	**370**	28
Edison Plaza	**366**	25
David Broderick Tower	**358**	34
1st National Bldg.	**350**	25
Buhl, 535 Griswold	**350**	26

Edmonton, Alta.

City	Hgt. ft.	Stories
Manulife Place (1983)	**479**	39
Royal Trust Tower (1973)	**476**	30
AGT Tower (1971)	**441**	34
Canada Trust Tower (1982)	**440**	34
Metropolitan Place (1980)	**370**	30
Scotia Place (1983)	**366**	30

City	Hgt. ft.	Stories
CN Tower (1966)	365	26
Phipps McKinnon (1977)	359	21
Fort Wayne, Ind.		
One Summit Square (1981)	442	26
Ft. Wayne Natl. Bank (1970)	339	26
Fort Worth, Tex.		
City Center Tower II (1984)	546	38
Burnett Plaza (1983)	538	40
Continental Plaza (1982)	520	40
1st City Bank Tower (1982)	475	33
Team Bank-Ft. Worth (1974)	457	37
Texas Bldg. (1955)	420	31
Hartford, Conn.		
City Place	535	38
Travelers Ins. Co. Bldg.	527	34
Goodwin Square	522	30
Hartford Plaza	420	22
Connecticut Natl. Bank & Trust	360	26
One Commercial Plaza	349	27
Bushnell Tower	349	27
Honolulu, Hi.		
Waterfront Towers (1990)	400	46
Nauru Tower (1991)	400	45
Ala Moana Hotel	396	38
Pacific Tower	350	30
Franklin Towers	350	41
Honolulu Tower	350	40
Discovery Bay	350	42
Hyatt Regency Waikiki	350	39
Maile Court Hotel	350	43
Regency Tower, 2525 Date St.	350	42
Pearlridge Square	350	43
Yacht Harbor Towers	350	40
Canterbury Place	350	40
Royal Iolani	350	38
Island Colony	350	44
Century Center	350	41
Pacific Beach Hotel	350	43
Hawaiian Monarch Hotel	350	43
Waikiki Hobron	350	43
Honolulu Tower 2	350	40
Tapa Tower, 2005 Kalia Rd.	350	36
Executive Center, 1088 Bishop St.	350	41
1001 Bishop	350	28
Houston, Tex.		
Texas Commerce Tower	1,002	75
Allied Bank Plaza, 1000 Louisiana	992	71
Transco Tower	901	64
RepublicBank Center	780	56
Heritage Plaza, 1111 Bagby	762	53
InterFirst Plaza	744	55
1600 Smith St.	729	54
Chevron Tower, 1301 McKinney	725	52
One Shell Plaza (not incl. 285 ft. TV tower)	714	50
Four Allen Center	692	50
Capital Natl. Bank Plaza	685	50
One Houston Center	678	47
First City Tower	662	47
1100 Milam Bldg.	651	47
San Felipe Plaza	620	45
Exxon Bldg.	606	44
The America Tower	577	42
Marathon Oil Tower	572	41
Two Houston Center	570	40
Dresser Tower	550	40
1415 Louisiana Tower	550	44
Pennzoil, 700 Milam (2 bldgs.)	523	36
Two Allen Center	521	36
Entex Bldg.	518	35
Huntington	506	34
Tenneco Bldg.	502	33
Conoco Tower	465	32
One Allen Center	452	34
Summit Tower West	441	31
Coastal Tower	441	31
Four Leafs Towers (2 bldgs.)	439	40
Phoenix Tower	434	34
Gulf Bldg.	428	37
The Spires	426	41
Central Tower (4 Oaks Place)	420	30
First City Natl. Bank	410	32
Houston Lighting & Power	410	27

City	Hgt. ft.	Stories
Niels Esperson Bldg.	409	31
Hyatt Regency Houston	401	34
Indianapolis, Ind.		
Bank One Tower (1989)	728	51
AUL Tower (1981)	533	38
Market Tower (1988)	515	32
Indiana Natl. Bank Tower (1969)	504	35
Riley Towers (2 bldgs.) (1963)	427	30
300 N. Meridian Bldg. (1988)	408	28
First Indiana Plaza (1988)	396	31
City-County Bldg. (1962)	375	28
Jacksonville, Fla.		
Barnett Tower (1990)	631	43
Independent Square (1975)	535	37
Southern Bell (1983)	447	30
Gulf Life Tower (1967)	435	27
American Heritage Life (1989)	375	23
Blue Cross-Blue Shield (1973)	350	22
Kansas City, Mo.		
One Kansas City Place	626	42
AT&T Town Pavilion	590	38
Hyatt Regency	504	40
Kansas City Power and Light Bldg.	476	32
City Hall	443	29
Federal Office Bldg.	413	35
Commerce Tower	402	32
City Center Sq.	402	30
Southwest Bell Telephone Bldg.	394	27
Pershing Road Associates	352	28
Las Vegas, Nev.		
Fitzgerald Casino-Hotel	400	34
Landmark Hotel	356	31
Las Vegas Hilton	345	30
Lexington, Ky.		
Lexington Financial Center (1986)	410	30
Kincaid Tower (1980)	333	22
Little Rock, Ark.		
TCBY Towers (1986)	546	40
First Commercial Bank (1975)	454	30
Worthen Bank & Trust (1969)	375	24
Stephens Bldg. (1985)	365	25
Tower Bldg. (1960)	350	18
Union National Bank (1968)	331	21
Los Angeles, Cal.		
First Interstate World Center (1989)	1,017	73
First Interstate Bank	858	62
Cal. Plaza 11A	750	57
Wells Fargo Tower	750	54
Security Pacific Plaza	735	55
So. Cal. Gas Center (1990)	733	55
777 Tower	725	52
Mitsui Fudoson (1990)	716	52
Atlantic Richfield Tower	699	52
Bank of America Tower	699	52
444 S. Flower St.	625	48
AT&T Bldg.	620	42
One California Plaza	578	42
Century Plaza Towers (2 bldgs.)	571	44
IBM Tower	560	45
Citicorp Plaza	534	42
1999 Ave. of the Stars (1989)	533	39
Manulife Tower (1990)	517	37
Union Bank Square	516	41
MCA-Getty	506	36
WTC Bldg.	496	36
Fox Plaza	492	34
ARCO Center	462	33
City Hall	454	28
Equitable Life Bldg.	454	34
Transamerica Center	452	32
Mutual Benefit Life Ins. Bldg.	435	31
Warner Center Plaza III	415	25
Broadway Plaza	414	33
1900 Ave. of Stars	398	27
1 Wilshire Bldg.	395	28
The Evian	390	31
400 S. Hope St.	375	26
Westin Bonaventure Hotel	367	35
Beaudry Center	365	29
Cal. Fed. Savings & Loan Bldg.	363	28
Century City North	363	26
Home Savings Tower	356	25

Louisville, Ky.

City	Hgt. ft.	Stories
First Natl. Bank (1972)	512	40
Citizen's Plaza (1971)	420	30
Humana Bldg.	350	27
Meindinger Tower (1982)	338	26
Brown & Williamson Tower (1982)	338	26

Memphis, Tenn.

City	Hgt. ft.	Stories
100 N. Main Bldg.	430	37
Commerce Square	396	31
Sterick Bldg.	365	31
Clark, 5100 Poplar	365	32
Morgan Keegan Tower, 50 Front St.	341	23
First Natl. Bank Bldg.	332	25

Miami, Fla.

City	Hgt. ft.	Stories
Southeast Financial Center (1983)	764	55
Centrust Tower (1987)	562	35
Metro-Dade Administration Bldg.	510	30
Florida National Tower (1986)	484	35
One Biscayne Corp.	456	40
Amerifirst Bldg. (1973)	375	32
Hotel Inter-Continental Miami	366	35
Venitia, 1635 Bayshore Dr.	365	42
Dade County Court House	357	28

Milwaukee, Wis.

City	Hgt. ft.	Stories
First Wis. Center	625	42
100 E. Wisconsin	549	37
Milwaukee Center	425	29
Faison Bldg. (1989)	417	34
411 E. Wisconsin	385	30
Northwestern Mutual Tower (1989)	350	19
City Hall	350	9

Minneapolis, Minn.

City	Hgt. ft.	Stories
IDS Center (1973)	787	51
Norwest (1988)	777	57
*First Bank Place	774	53
Multifoods Tower (1983)	651	52
Piper Jaffray Tower (1984)	627	42
*Dain Bosworth Plaza	550	40
Pillsbury Center, 200 S. 6th St. (1981)	545	40
Lincoln Centre, 333 S. 7th (1987)	496	31
Foshay Tower, not including 163-ft. antenna tower (1929)	496	32
Plaza VII, 45 S. 7th (1987)	494	36
100 South Fifth (1987)	490	36
Telephone Bldg. (1931)	423	27
Hennepin Co. Govt. Center (1974)	413	24
First Bank Place West (1960)	386	26
Marriott Hotel (1983)	379	31

Montreal, Que.

City	Hgt. ft.	Stories
Place Victoria	624	47
Place Ville Marie	616	42
Canadian Imperial Bank of Commerce	604	43
Le Complexe Desjardins		
La Tour du Sud	498	40
La Tour du L'Est	428	32
La Tour du Nord	355	27
Trust Royal Bldg.	429	32
Chateau Champlain Hotel	420	38
Port Royal Apts.	400	33
Royal Bank Tower	397	22
Sun Life Bldg.	390	26
500 Place d'Armes	390	32

Nashville, Tenn.

City	Hgt. ft.	Stories
Third National Financial Center	490	30
American General Center	452	31
Landmark Center	409	30
Nashville City Center (1987)	402	27
James K. Polk State Office Bldg.	392	32
Stouffer Hotel (1987)	385	35
First American Center	354	28
One Nashville Plaza	346	23

Newark, N.J.

City	Hgt. ft.	Stories
Natl. Newark & Essex Bldg.	465	36
Raymond-Commerce	448	37
Park Plaza Bldg.	400	26
Prudential Plaza	370	24
Public Service Elec. & Gas	360	26
Prudential Ins. Co., 753 Broad St.	360	26
AT&T Bldg.	359	31
Gateway 1	355	28

New Orleans, La.

City	Hgt. ft.	Stories
One Shell Square (1972)	697	51
Place St. Charles (1985)	645	53
Plaza Tower (1969)	531	45
Energy Centre (1984)	530	39
LL&E Tower (1987)	481	36
Sheraton Hotel (1985)	478	47
Marriott Hotel (1972)	450	42
Texaco Bldg. (1983)	442	33
Canal Place One (1979)	439	32
1010 Common (1971)	438	31
Int'l. Trade Mart Bldg.	407	33
225 Baronne St. (1965)	362	28
One Poydras Plaza (1983)	360	28
Hyatt-Regency Hotel (1976)	360	25
Hibernia Bank Bldg. (1920)	355	23

New York, N.Y.

City	Hgt. ft.	Stories
World Trade Center (2 towers) (1973)	1,368/ 1,362	110/110
Empire State, 34th St. & 5th Ave.	1,250	102
TV tower, 164 ft., makes total (1931)	1,414	...
Chrysler, Lexington & 43d (1930)	1,046	77
Amer. International, 70 Pine (1932)	950	67
40 Wall Tower (1929)	927	71
Citicorp Center (1977)	914	46
G.E. Bldg., Rockefeller Center (1933)	850	70
Chase Manhattan Plaza (1960)	813	60
200 Park Ave. (1963)	808	59
Cityspire (1989)	802	72
Woolworth, 233 Broadway (1913)	792	60
1 Worldwide Plaza	778	47
1 Penn Plaza (1972)	764	57
Carnegie Tower	756	59
Exxon, 1251 Ave. of Americas (1971)	750	54
Equitable Center Tower West (1985)	750	58
60 Wall St. (1989)	745	50
1 Liberty Plaza (1972)	743	50
Citibank (1907)	741	57
World Financial Center, Tower C (1988)	739	54
One Astor Plaza (1969)	730	54
Solow Bldg. (1979)	725	50
Marine Midland	724	52
Metropolitan Tower (1988)	716	66
Union Carbide Bldg. (1960)	707	52
General Motors Bldg. (1968)	705	50
Metropolitan Life (1909)	700	50
500 5th Ave. (1928)	697	58
Chem. Bank, N.Y. Trust Bldg. (1963)	687	50
55 Water St.	687	53
1585 Broadway	685	42
Chanin, Lexington & 42d (1929)	680	56
15 Columbus Circle (1970)	679	44
McGraw Hill, 1221 Ave. of Am. (1972)	674	51
Citicorp (Queens) (1990)	673	50
Lincoln, 60 E. 42d Street (1939)	673	53
1633 Broadway	670	48
Trump Tower, 725 5th Ave. (1983)	664	68
599 Lexington Ave. (1988)	653	47
Museum Tower Apts. (1985)	650	58
712 5th Ave. (1990)	650	56
American Brands, 245 Park Ave.	648	47
A. T. & T. Tower (1983)	648	37
World Financial Center Tower B (1986)	645	50
General Electric, 570 Lexington (1931)	640	50
Irving Trust, 1 Wall St. (1932)	640	50
345 Park Ave.	634	44
Grace Plaza, 1114 Ave. of Am.	630	50
1 New York Plaza (1969)	630	50
Home Insurance Co. Bldg.	630	44
N.Y. Telephone, 1095 Ave. of Am.	630	40
Central Park Place (1988)	628	56
888 7th Ave.	628	42
1 Hammarskjold Plaza	628	50
Waldorf-Astoria, 301 Park Ave. (1931)	625	47
Burlington House (1970)	625	50
Olympic Tower, 645 5th Ave. (1976)	620	51
10 E. 40th St.	620	48
101 Park Ave.	618	50
750 7th Ave.	615	35
New York Life, 51 Madison Ave. (1928)	615	40
Rihga Royal Hotel	610	54
17 State St.	610	41
Penney Bldg., 1301 Ave. of Am.	609	46
IBM, 590 Madison Ave. (1983)	603	41
780 3rd Ave.	600	50
Celanese Bldg. (1973)	592	45

City	Hgt. ft.	Stories
U.S. Court House, 505 Pearl St. (1976)	590	37
*Kalikow Hotel	588	58
Federal Bldg., Foley Square	587	41
Time & Life, 1271 Ave. of Am. (1959)	587	47
Cooper Bregstein Bldg., 1250 Bway.	580	40
Stevens Tower, 1185 Ave. of Am.	580	42
Municipal, Bldg. (1919)	580	34
520 Madison Ave. (1983)	577	42
1 Madison Square Plaza (1968)	576	42
World Financial Center Tower A (1986)	575	42
One Financial Sq. (1987)	575	37
Park Ave. Plaza (1981)	575	44
Westvaco Bldg. 299 Park Ave.	574	42
Marriott Marquis Hotel (1985)	574	42
Socony Mobil Bldg., East 42d St.	572	45
Sperry Rand Bldg., 1290 Ave. of Am.	570	43
600 3d Ave.	570	42
Helmsley Bldg., 230 Park (1929)	565	35
1 Bankers Trust Plaza	565	40
Hemsley Palace Hotel (1980)	563	51
30 Broad St.	562	48
Park Ave Tower (1986)	561	36
Sherry-Netherland, 5th Ave. & 59th St.	560	40
Continental Can, 633 3d Ave. (1983)	557	39
Sperry & Hutchinson, 330 Madison	555	39
Continental Corp., 180 Maiden Lane	555	41
Galleria, 117 E. 57th St. (1975)	552	57
Interchem Bldg., 1133 Ave. of Am.	552	45
151 E. 44th St.	550	44
N.Y. Telephone, 323 Bway. (1979)	550	45
919 3d Ave.	550	47
Burroughs Bldg., 605 3d Ave.	550	44
Bankers Trust, 33 E. 48 St. (1963)	547	41
Transportation Bldg., 225 Bway.	546	45
Equitable, 120 Broadway (1915)	545	42
1 Brooklyn Bridge Plaza (1976)	540	42
Paine Webber Bldg. (1961)	540	42
Ritz Tower, Park Ave. & 57th St.	540	41
Bankers Trust, 6 Wall St.	540	39
1166 Ave. of Americas	540	44
1700 Broadway	533	41
Downtown Athletic Club, 19 West St.	530	45
Nelson Towers, 7th Ave. & 34th St.	525	45
767 3d Ave.	525	39
Hotel Pierre, 5th Ave. & 61st St. (1928)	525	44
House of Seagram (1958)	525	38
7 World Trade Center (1985)	525	44
Random House, 825 3d Ave.	522	40
3 Park Ave.	522	42
North American Plywood, 800 3d Ave.	520	41
Du Mont Bldg., 515 Madison Ave.	520	42
26 Broadway	520	31
Newsweek Bldg., 444 Madison Ave.	518	43
Sterling Drug Bldg., 90 Park Ave.	515	41
First National City Bank	515	41
Bank of New York, 48 Wall St.	513	32
Navarre, 512 7th Ave.	513	43
Manhattan Savings Bank, Bklyn.	512	42
ITT—American, 437 Madison Ave.	512	40
International, Rockefeller Ctr.	512	41
1407 Broadway Realty Corp.	512	44
United Nations, 405 E. 42 St. (1953)	505	39
Oakland, Cal.		
Ordway Bldg., 2150 Valdez St.	404	28
Kaiser Bldg.	390	28
Lake Merritt Plaza	371	27
*Federal Bldg. (2 Bldgs.)	368	19
American President Lines (1990)	360	29
Raymond Kaiser Engineer Bldg.	336	25
Clorox Bldg.	330	24
Oklahoma City, Okla.		
Liberty Tower (1971)	500	36
First National Center (1974)	493	33
City Place (1985)	440	32
First Oklahoma Tower (1982)	425	31
Kerr-McGee Center (1973)	393	30
Mid America Tower (1981)	362	19
Omaha, Neb.		
Woodmen Tower	469	30
Northwestern Bell Telephone Hdqrs.	334	16
Masonic Manor	320	22
First Natl. Center	320	22
Orlando, Fla.		
Sun Bank Center Tower (1988)	441	31
DuPont Center Bldg. (1988)	409	28

Ottawa, Ont.

City	Hgt. ft.	Stories
Place de Ville, Tower C	368	29
R.H. Coats Bldg.	326	27
Philadelphia, Pa.		
One Liberty Place (1987)	960	61
Two Liberty Place (1989)	845	52
Mellon Bank Center (1989)	795	54
Bell Atlantic Tower (1991)	739	53
Blue Cross Tower (1990)	700	50
Commerce Sq., #1 (1990)	572	40
Commerce Sq., #2 (1992)	572	40
City Hall Tower, incl. 37-ft. statue of Wm. Penn. (1901)	548	7
1818 Market St. (1974)	500	40
Provident Mutual Life (1983)	491	40
Meridan Bank (1972)	492	38
Phila. Saving Fund Society (1932)	492	39
Central Penn Natl. Bank (1970)	490	36
Centre Square (2 towers) (1973)	490/416	38/32
Industrial Valley Bank (1968)	482	32
Philadelphia National Bank (1930)	475	25
Two Mellon Plaza (1930)	450	30
2000 Market St. (1973)	435	29
Two Logan Square (1987)	435	34
2 Girard Plaza (1930)	412	30
Fidelity Bank Bldg. (1927)	405	30
Lewis Tower, 15th & Locust (1929)	400	33
One Logan Square (1982)	400	32
1500 Locust St. (1973)	390	44
Philadelphia Electric Co. (1970)	384	29
Academy House, 1420 Locust St.	377	37
Penn Mutual Life (1931)	375	20
The Drake, 15th & Spruce (1928)	375	33
INA Annex	369	27
Medical Tower, 255 So. 17th (1931)	364	33
United Engineers, 17th & Ludlow (1976)	344	22
Inquirer Building (1924)	340	18
Phoenix, Ariz.		
Valley National Bank (1972)	483	40
Arizona Bank Downtown(1976)	407	31
Phoenix Plaza (1990)	397	25
First Interstate Bank Plaza (1971)	372	27
Phoenix Center (1979)	361	28
Citibank Plaza (1980)	356	27
One Renaissance Sq. (1987)	347	26
Two Renaissance Sq. (1989)	347	26
Merabank Tower	341	26
Pittsburgh, Pa.		
USX Towers	841	64
One Mellon Bank Center	725	54
One PPG Place	635	40
Fifth Avenue Place (1987)	616	32
One Oxford Centre	615	46
Gulf, 7th Ave. and Grant St.	582	44
University of Pittsburgh	535	42
Mellon Bank Bldg.	520	41
1 Oliver Plaza	511	39
Grant, Grant St. at 3rd Ave.	485	40
Koppers, 7th Ave. and Grant	475	34
Equibank Bldg.	445	34
CNG Tower (1987)	430	32
Pittsburgh National Bldg.	424	30
Alcoa Bldg., 425 Sixth Ave.	410	30
Liberty Tower	358	29
Westinghouse Bldg.	355	23
Oliver, 535 Smithfield St.	347	25
Gateway Bldg. No. 3	344	24
Centre City Tower	341	26
Federal Bldg., 1000 Liberty Ave.	340	23
Bell Telephone, 416 7th Ave.	339	21
Hilton Hotel	333	22
Frick, 437 Grant St.	330	20
Portland, Ore.		
First Interstate Tower	546	41
U.S. Bancorp Tower	536	39
Koin Tower Plaza	509	35
Standard Insurance Center	367	27
Pacwest Center	356	31
Providence, R.I.		
Fleet National Bank	420	26
Rhode Island Hospital Trust Tower	410	30
40 Westminster Bldg.	301	24

Raleigh, N.C.

City	Hgt. ft.	Stories
BB & T/2 Hanover Sq. (1991)	431	29
First Union Capitol Center (1991)	390	29

Richmond, Va.

City	Hgt. ft.	Stories
James Monroe Bldg.	450	29
City Hall (incl. penthouse)	425	17
Crestar Bank Hdqt. Bldg.	400	24
Federal Reserve Bank	393	26
Sovran Center	333	25

Rochester, N.Y.

City	Hgt. ft.	Stories
Xerox Tower (1967)	443	30
Lincoln First Tower (1973)	392	27
Eastman Kodak Bldg. (1914)	340	19

Sacramento, Cal.

City	Hgt. ft.	Stories
Wells Fargo Center	405	30
Park Plaza Tower	373	26
Renaissance Tower	372	28

St. Louis, Mo.

City	Hgt. ft.	Stories
Gateway Arch	630	...
Metropolitan Square Tower	591	42
S.W. Bell Telephone Bldg.	587	44
Mercantile Center Tower	550	37
Centerre Plaza	433	31
Laclede Gas. Bldg., 8th & Olive	400	31
S.W. Bell Telephone Bldg.	398	31
Civil Courts	387	13
Queeny Tower	321	24
Counsel Tower	320	30

St. Paul, Minn.

City	Hgt. ft.	Stories
First Natl. Bank Bldg., incl. 100-ft. sign	517	32
Minn. World Trade Center	471	36
Galtier Plaza's Jackson Tower	440	46
Osborn Bldg., 320 Wabasha	368	20
Kellogg Square Apts.	366	32
Northwestern Bell Telephone (2 bldgs.)	340	16
Pointe of St. Paul	340	34
American National Bank Bldg.	335	25
North Central Tower, 445 Minn.	328	27
Amhoist/Park Tower	324	26

Salt Lake City, Ut.

City	Hgt. ft.	Stories
L.D.S. Church Office Bldg.	420	30
Beneficial Life Tower	351	21
Utah One Center (1992)	350	24

San Antonio, Tex.

City	Hgt. ft.	Stories
Tower of the Americas (1968)	622	...
Marriott Rivercenter (1988)	546	38
NBC Plaza (1988)	444	32
Tower Life (1929)	404	30
NCNB Plaza (1983)	387	28
Nix Professional Bldg. (1931)	375	23

San Diego, Cal.

City	Hgt. ft.	Stories
Symphony Tower (1989)	499	34
First Interstate Bank (1985)	398	23
Union Bank (1969)	388	27
First National Bank (1982)	379	27
The Meridan	375	27
Imperial Bank	355	24
Executive Complex (1963)	350	25
Wells Fargo Bldg. (1982)	348	20
Great American Bldg. (1974)	339	24

San Francisco, Cal.

City	Hgt. ft.	Stories
Transamerica Pyramid (1972)	853	48
Bank of America (1969)	778	52
101 California St. (1986)	600	48
5 Fremont Center (1983)	600	43
Embarcadero Center, No. 4 (1982)	570	45
Security Pacific Bank	569	45
One Market Plaza, Spear St. (1976)	565	43
Wells Fargo Bldg.	561	43
Standard Oil, 575 Market St. (1975)	551	39
One Sansome-Citicorp	550	39
Shaklee Bldg., 444 Market	537	38
Aetna Life	529	38
First & Market Bldg. (1973)	529	38
Metropolitan Life (1973)	524	38
Crocker National Bank	500	38
Hilton Hotel	493	46
Pacific Gas & Electric (1970)	492	34
Union Bank (1972)	487	37
Pacific Insurance (1972)	476	34
Bechtel Bldg., Fremont St. (1977)	475	33
333 Market Bldg. (1979)	474	33
Hartford Bldg. (1965)	465	33
Mutual Benefit Life (1969)	438	32
Russ Bldg. (1928)	435	31
Pacific Telephone Bldg. (1925)	435	26
Pacific Gateway (1983)	416	30
Embarcadero Center, No. 3 (1976)	412	31
Embarcadero Center, No. 2 (1974)	412	31
595 Market Bldg. (1979)	410	31
101 Montgomery St.	405	28
Cal. State Automobile Assn. (1974)	399	29
Alcoa Bldg.	398	27
St. Francis Hotel (1970)	395	32
Shell Bldg. (1928)	386	29
Del Monte	378	28
Meridien Hotel (1984)	374	34

Seattle, Wash.

City	Hgt. ft.	Stories
Columbia Seafirst Center (1985)	954	76
Two Union Square (1989)	740	56
Washington Mutual Tower (1988)	730	55
AT&T Gateway Tower (1990)	722	62
1001 4th Pl. (1969)	609	50
Space Needle (1962)	605	...
Pacific First Center (1989)	580	44
First Interstate Center (1983)	574	48
Seafirst 5th Ave. Plaza (1981)	543	42
Security Pacific Bank Tower (1977)	514	42
Smith Tower (1914)	500	42
520 Pike Tower (1984)	498	29
Key Tower (1986)	493	40
Federal Office Bldg.	487	37
US West Communications	466	33
One Union Square (1981)	456	38
1111 3d Ave. Bldg. (1980)	454	35
Westin Bldg., 2001 6th Ave. (1981)	409	34
Westin Hotel	397	40
Unigard Financial Center (1973)	389	27
Century Square (1986)	379	30
Sheraton Seattle Hotel	371	34
Fourth & Blanchard Bldg. (1979)	360	24
Crown Plaza Hotel	352	33

Tampa, Fla.

City	Hgt. ft.	Stories
Barnett Plaza (1986)	577	42
Tampa City Center (1981)	537	39
First Financial Tower (1973)	458	36
NCNB Plaza (1988)	454	33

Toledo, Oh.

City	Hgt. ft.	Stories
Owens-Illinois Corp. Headquarters	411	32
Owens-Corning Fiberglas Tower	400	30
Ohio Citizens Bank Bldg.	368	27
Toledo Govt. Center	327	22

Toronto, Ont.

City	Hgt. ft.	Stories
CN Tower, World's tallest self-supporting structure (1976)	1,821	...
First Canadian Place (1979)	970	72
Bay/Adelaide Project (1991)	951	57
Scotia Plaza (1988)	902	68
Canada Trust Tower (1990)	869	52
Bay-Wellington Tower (1990)	705	47
Commerce Court West (1972)	784	57
Toronto-Dominion Tower (TD Centre) (1967)	758	56
Royal Trust Tower (TD Centre) (1969)	600	46
Royal Bank Plaza—South Tower (1977)	589	41
Manulife Centre (1975)	545	53
IBM Tower (TD Centre) (1986)	520	36
Two Bloor West (1974)	488	34
Exchange Tower (1981)	480	36
Commerce Court North (1930)	476	34
Simpson Tower (1968)	473	33
Eaton Tower (1990)	471	34
Cadillac-Fairview Tower (1982)	466	36
Palace Point (1991)	455	46
Palace Pier (1978)	453	46
Continental Bank Bldg. (1980)	450	35
Sheraton Centre (1972)	443	43
Hudson's Bay Centre (1974)	442	35
Royal York Hotel (1929)	439	26
Ernst & Yonge Tower (1990)	438	31
Old Toronto Exchange Bldg. (1990)	436	31
Leaside Towers (2 bldgs.) (1970)	423	44
Metro Hall (1991)	420	27
Commercial Union Tower (1974)	420	32

City	Hgt. ft.	Stories
Maple Leaf Mills Tower	419	30
Plaza 2 Hotel	415	41
Sun Life Bldg. (1981)	410	28
Tulsa, Okla.		
Bank of Oklahoma Tower	667	52
City of Faith Clinic Tower	640	60
1st National Tower	516	41
Mid-Continent Tower	513	36
4th Natl. Bank of Tulsa	412	33
320 South Boston Bldg.	400	24
Occidential Place	388	28
Univ. Club Tower	377	32
City of Faith Hospital	348	30
Philtower	343	24
Vancouver, B.C.		
Royal Centre Tower (1973)	460	36
Canada Trust Tower, 1055 Melville	454	35
Scotiabank Tower	451	36
Bentall IV (1981)	450	35
Vancouver Center (1977)	450	36
Park Place (1984)	450	35
T-D Bank Tower (1978)	440	30
200 Granville Square (1973)	438	28
Harbour Centre (1977)	428	21
Bentall III (1974)	399	31
Winston-Salem, N.C.		
Wachovia Bldg. (1965)	410	30
One Triad Park (1987)	340	20
Reynolds Bldg. (1929)	315	21

Other Notable Tall Buildings in U.S.

Cape Canaveral, Fla., Vehicle Assembly Bldg., 40 (552); Akron, OH., First National Tower, 28 (330); Amarillo, Tex., American Natl. Bank, 33 (374); Atlantic City, N.J., Taj Mahal, 51 (429); Charleston, W. Va., Kanawha Valley Bldg., 20 (384); Galveston, Tex., American National Ins., 20 (358); Hamilton, Ont., Century Twenty One, 43 (418); Harrisburg, PA., State Office Tower #2, 21 (334); Knoxville, Tenn., United American Bank, 30 (400); Lincoln, Neb., State Capitol (432); Mobile, Ala., First Natl. Bank, 33 (420); Niagara Falls, Ont., Skylon, (520); Shreveport La., Commercial National Tower, 24 (365); Springfield, Mass., Valley Bank Tower, 29 (370); Tallahassee, Fla., State Capitol Tower, 22 (345).

Some Notable Foreign Structures

Structure	Hgt. ft.	Stories
Bank of China, Hong Kong	1,209	72
Central Plaza, Hong Kong	1,028	78
Bank of China, Hong Kong	1,001	70
Moscow State Univ (incl. spire)	994	32
Eiffel Tower, Paris	984	-
MesseTurm. Bldg, Frankfurt	841	70
One Canada Sq, London	800	56
Tokyo City Hall	797	-
Palace of Science & Culture, Warsaw	790	42
Rialto Tower, Melbourne	786	60
M.L.C. Centre, Sydney	765	60
Ikebukuro Office Tower, Tokyo	742	60
Central Park, Perth	739	51
Chifley Tower, Sydney	727	42
Bourke Place, Melbourne	724	48
Carlton Centre, Johannesburg	722	50
Shinjuku Center, Tokyo	709	55
Shinjuku Mitsui, Tokyo	696	55
Tour Maine Montparnasse, Paris	688	56
Shinjuku Nomura, Tokyo	666	53
Overseas-Chinese Banking Corp., Singapore	660	52
Shinjuku Sumitomo, Tokyo	656	52
Parque Central Torre Oficinas, Caracas	656	56
Ukraine Hotel, Moscow	650	60
Natwest Tower, London	600	50
Tour Elf Aquitaine, Paris	578	48
Ulm Cathedral, Germany	530	-
Cologne Cathedral, Germany	515	-
Tour du Cite Administrative, Brussels	492	36

Notable Bridges in North America

Source: Survey of State Highway Engineers (1991)

Asterisk (*) designates railroad bridge. Span of a bridge is distance (in feet) between its supports.

Year	Bridge	Location	Longest span
	Suspension		
1964	Verrazano-Narrows	New York, N.Y.	4,260
1937	Golden Gate	San Fran. Bay, Cal.	4,200
1957	Mackinac	Sts. of Mackinac	3,800
1931	Geo. Washington	Hudson River, N.Y.-N.J.	3,500
1950	Tacoma Narrows	Washington	2,800
1936	[1]Transbay	San Fran. Bay, Cal.	2,310
1939	Bronx-Whitestone	East R., N.Y.C.	2,300
1970	Pierre Laporte	Quebec	2,190
1951	Del. Memorial	Wilmington, Del.	2,150
1968	Del. Mem. (new)	Wilmington, Del.	2,150
1957	Walt Whitman	Phila., Pa.	2,000
1929	Ambassador	Detroit-Canada	1,850
1961	Throgs Neck	Long Is. Sound	1,800
1926	Benjamin Franklin	Philadelphia	1,750
1924	Bear Mt., N.Y.	Hudson River	1,632
1952	[2]Wm. Preston Lane Mem.	Sandy Point, Md.	1,600
1903	Williamsburg	East R., N.Y.C.	1,600
1969	Newport	Narragansett Bay, R.I.	1,600
1883	Brooklyn	East R., N.Y.C.	1,595
1939	Lion's Gate	Burrard Inlet, B.C.	1,550
1930	Mid-Hudson, N.Y.	Poughkeepsie	1,500
1964	Vincent Thomas	Los Angeles Harbor	1,500
1909	Manhattan	East R., N.Y.C.	1,470
1936	Triboro	East R., N.Y.C.	1,380
1931	St. Johns	Portland, Ore.	1,207
1929	Mount Hope	Rhode Island	1,200
1960	Ogdensburg, N.Y.	St. Lawrence R.	1,150
1939	Deer Isle	Maine	1,080
1931	Maysville (Ky.)	Ohio River	1,060
1867	Cincinnati	Ohio River	1,057
1971	Dent	Clearwater Co., Ida.	1,050
1900	Miampimi	Mexico	1,030
1849	Wheeling, W. Va.	Ohio River	1,010
	Cantilever		
1917	Quebec	Quebec	1,800
1981	Ravenswood	W. Va.	1,723
1974	Commodore Barry	Chester, Pa.	1,622
1958	Mississippi R.	New Orleans, La.	1,575
1988	Mississippi R.	New Orleans, La	1,575
1936	Transbay	San Fran. Bay	1,400
1968	W. 17th St.	Huntington, W. Va.	1,312
1968	Mississippi R.	Baton Rouge, La.	1,235
1955	Tappan Zee	Hudson River	1,212
1930	Lewis and Clark	Longview, Wash.	1,200
1909	Queensboro	East R., N.Y.C.	1,182
1927	Carquinez Strait	California	1,100
1958	Parallel Span	"	1,100
1930	Jacques Cartier	Montreal, P.Q.	1,097
1968	Isaiah D. Hart	Jacksonville, Fla.	1,088
1957	[3]Richmond	San Fran. Bay, Cal.	1,070
1929	Grace Memorial	Charleston, S.C.	1,050
1980	Newburgh-Beacon	Hudson R., N.Y.	1,000
1963	Newburgh-Beacon	Hudson R., N.Y.	1,000
1949	Martin Luther King	St. Louis, Mo.	962
1982	Yeager	Charleston, W. Va.	947
1975	Caruthersville, Mo.	Mississippi R.	920
1977	Saint Marys	Saint Marys, W. Va.	900

Year	Bridge	Location	Longest span
1969	Silver Memorial	Pt. Pleasant, W. Va.	900
1987	Carl Perkins	Ohio River/So. Portsmouth, Ky.	900
1986	Mississippi River	Natchez, Miss.	875
1940	Mississippi River	Natchez, Miss.	875
1938	Blue Water	Pt. Huron, Mich.	871
1972	Mississippi River	Vicksburg, Miss	870
1972	N. Fork American R.	Auburn, Cal.	862
1940	*Baton Rouge	Mississippi R.	848
1899	*Cornwall	St. Lawrence R.	843
1940	Mississippi River	Greenville, Miss.	840
1961	Helena, Ark.	Mississippi R.	840
1963	Brent Spence	Covington, Ky.	831
1963	Cincinnati, Oh.	Ohio River	830
1963	Mississippi, R.	Donaldsonville, La.	825
1940	Mississippi River	Vicksburg, Miss.	825
1929	Louisville	Ohio River	820
1961	Campbellton-Cross Point	New Brunswick-Quebec.	815
1950	Maurice J. Tobin	Boston, Mass.	800
1935	Rip Van Winkle	Catskill, N.Y.	800
1938	Cairo	Ohio River, Ill.-Ky.	800
1932	Washington Mem.	Seattle, Wash.	800
1936	McCullough	Coos Bay, Ore.	793
1935	[4]Huey P Long	New Orleans	790
1916	*Memphis (Harahan)	Mississippi R.	790
1892	*Memphis	Mississippi R.	790
1949	Memphis-Arkansas	Mississippi R.	790
1904	*Mingo Jct., W. Va.	Ohio River	769
1910	*Beaver, Pa.	Ohio River	767

Simple Truss

Year	Bridge	Location	Longest span
1976	Chester	Chester, W. Va.	745
1917	*Metropolis	Ohio River	720
1929	Irvin S. Cobb	Ohio River-Ill.-Ky.	716
1922	*Tanana River.	Nenana, Alaska	700
1933	*Henderson	Ohio River-Ind.-Ky.	665
1967	I-77, Ohio River	Williamstown, W. Va.	650
1917	4 MacArthur, Ill.-Mo.	St. Louis	647
1919	Louisville	Ohio River	644
1933	Atchafalaya	Morgan City, La.	608
1924	*Castleton	Hudson River	598
1937	Delaware R.	Easton, Pa.	550
1930	Swindell Bridge	Pittsburgh, Pa.	545
1889	*Cincinnati	Ohio River	542
1952	Allegheny R., Tpk.	Pittsburgh, Pa.	534
1930	*Martinez	California	528
1951	Rankin	Pittsburgh, Pa.	525
1914	Old Brownsville	Brownsville, Pa.	520
1906	Donora-Webster	Donora-Webster, Pa.	515
1909	Hulton	Pittsburgh, Pa.	505
1967	Tanana River	Alaska	500

Steel Truss

Year	Bridge	Location	Longest span
1988	Glade Creek	Raleigh Co., W.Va.	784
1973	Atchafalaya R.	Krotz Springs, La.	780
1972	Atchafalaya R.	Simmesport, La.	720
1957	SR-3, Rappahannock R.	Middlesex Co., Va.	648
1940	Jamestown	Jamestown, R.I.	640
1949	Memphis	Mississippi R., Ark.	621
1978	Atchafalaya R.	Morgan City, La.	607
1938	US-22	Delaware River, N.J.	540
1955	Interstate (I-5)	Columbia River, Ore.-Wash.	531
1910	[4]McKinley, St. Louis	Mississippi River.	517
1972	Mississippi River	Muscatine, Ia.	512
1896	Newport	Ohio River, Ky.	511
1970	Lake Koocanusa	Lincoln Co., Mon.	500
1931	US-60	Cumberland R., Ky.	500
1958	Lake Oahe.	Mobridge, S.D.	500
1958	Lake Oahe.	Gettysburg, S.D.	500

Continuous Truss

Year	Bridge	Location	Longest span
1966	Columbia R. (Astoria)	Ore.-Wash.	1,232
1977	Francis Scott Key	Baltimore, Md.	1,200
1943	Dubuque, Ia.	Mississippi R.	845
1956	[7]Earl C. Clements	Ohio R., Ill-Ky.	825
1953	John E. Mathews	Jacksonville, Fla.	810
1940	Gov. Nice Mem.	Potomac River, Md.	800
1957	Kingston-Rhinecliff	Hudson R., N.Y.	800
1986	Rochester-Monaca	Rochester-Monaca, Pa.	780
1918	*Sciotoville	Ohio River	775
1976	I-275, Lawrenceburg Bridge	Ohio River	750
1981	Sewickley	Sewickley, Pa.	750
1984	13th St. Bridge, Ohio R.	Ashland, Ky.	740
1959	Monaca-E. Rochester	Monaca-East Rochester, Pa.	730
1976	Betsy Ross	Philadelphia, Pa.	729
1929	Madison-Milton	Ohio River	727
1977	I-275, Brent Bridge	Ohio River	720
1970	Vanport	Vanport, Pa.	715
1966	[5]Matthew E. Welsh	Mauckport	707
1962	Champlain	Montreal, P.Q.	707
1973	Girard Point	Philadelphia, Pa.	700
1954	Pa. Tpk., Delaware R.	Philadelphia, Pa.	682
1949	George Platt.	Philadelphia, Pa.	680
1938	Port Arthur-Orange	Texas.	680
1929	*Cincinnati	Ohio River	675
1928	Cape Girardeau, Mo.	Mississippi R.	672
1946	Chester, Ill.	Mississippi R.	670
1970	Gulfgate	Port Arthur, Tex.	664
1953	Jefferson City	Missouri River	640
1930	Quincy, Ill.	Mississippi R.	628
1961	Shippingport	Shippingport, Pa.	620
1959	US 181, over harbor	Corpus Christi, Tex.	620
1934	Bourne	Cape Cod Canal	616
1935	Sagamore	Cape Cod Canal	616
1965	Clarion R. (I-80)	Clarion, Pa.	612
1975	Donora-Monesson	Donora-Monesson, Pa.	608
1957	Blatnik	Duluth, Minn.	600
1965	Rio Grande Gorge	Taos, N.M.	600
1941	Columbia River	Kettle Falls, Wash.	600
1954	Columbia River	Umatilla, Ore.	600
1954	Columbia River	The Dalles, Ore.	576
1962	W. Br. Feather River	Oroville, Cal.	576
1967	Glenwood	Pittsburgh, Pa.	567
1936	Meredosia	Illinois River	567
1936	Mark Twain Mem.	Hannibal, Mo.	562
1957	Mackinac	Mackinac Straits, Mich.	560

Continuous Box and Plate Girder

Year	Bridge	Location	Longest span
1988	Piney Creek-US19	Beckley, W. Va.	1,760
1973	Danville-US119	Danville, W. Va.	1,545
1983	Mississippi R.	Luling, La.	1,222
1974	Dunbar-S. Charleston	South Charleston, W. Va.	842
1988	Beaver Creek-I-64	Beckley, W. Va.	764
1982	Houston Ship Chan.	Houston, Tex.	750
1967	San Mateo-Hayward No. 2	San Fran. Bay, Cal.	750
1977	Intracoastal Canal	Gibbstown, La.	750
1976	Intracoastal Canal	Forked Is., La.	750
1969	[6]San Diego-Coronado	San Diego Bay, Cal.	660
1987	Columbia R.	Umatilla Ore.	629
1981	Douglas	Juneau, Alaska	620
1976	Wax L. Outlet	Calumet, La.	618
1975	S. Charleston-I-64	South Charleston, W. Va.	612
1981	Glenn Jackson (I-205)	Columbia R., Ore.-Wash.	600
1967	Poplar St.	St. Louis, Mo.	600
1982	Illinois R.	Pekin, Ill.	550
1982	I-440	Arkansas R.	540
1977	US-64, Tennessee R.	Savannah, Tenn.	525
1988	Mon City	Monongahela, Pa.	520
1965	McDonald-Cartier	Ottawa, Ont.	520
1986	Veterans	Pittsburgh, Pa.	440
1986	SR 76, Cumberland R.	Dover, Tenn.	440
1985	SR 20, Tennessee R.	Perryville, Tenn.	440
1970	Willamette R., I-205.	West Linn, Ore.	430
1974	I-430	Arkansas R.	430
1985	I-435	Missouri R., Ks.-Mo.	425
1984	US-36	Missouri R., Ks.-Mo.	425
1972	I-635, Kansas City	Missouri R., Kan.-Mo.	425
1985	FAU 3456, Tennessee R.	Chattanooga, Tenn.	420
1967	I-24, Tennessee R.	Marion Co., Tenn.	420
1978	Snake River	Clarkston, Wash.	420
1975	36th St.	Charleston, W.Va.	420
1976	35th St. Bridge, Kanawha.	Charleston, W. Va.	415
1986	SR 1, Tennessee R.	New Johnsonville, Tenn.	411
1979	Arkansas R.	Clarksville, Ark.	410
1975	Yukon River	Alaska	410

Continuous Plate

Year	Bridge	Location	Longest span
1973	Ship Channel (I-610)	Houston, Tex.	630
1971	W. Atchafalaya	Henderson, La.	573
1981	Illinois 23.	Illinois R., Ill.	510
1968	Trinity R.	Dallas, Tex.	480
1978	San Joaquin R.	Antioch, Cal.	460

Year	Bridge	Location	Longest span
1977	Thomas Johnson Mem.	Solomons, Md.	451
1975	Lewis Bridge	St. Louis, Mo.	450
1975	I-129	Missouri R., Ia.	450
1967	Mississippi River	LaCrescent, Minn.	450
1972	Whiskey Bay Pilot Channel	Ramah, La.	425
1966	I-480	Missouri R., Ia.-Neb.	425
1970	I-435	Missouri R., Mo.	425
1972	I-80	Missouri R., Ia.-Neb.	425
1978	I-24	Cumberland R., Ky.	420

Cable-Stayed

Year	Bridge	Location	Longest span
1991	Talmadge Mem'l	Savannah, Ga.	1,100
1979	Intercity	Pasco-Kennewick, Wash.	970
1985	E. Huntington	Huntington, W. Va.	900
1985	Mississippi R.	Quincy, Ill.	900
1980	Veterans Mem'l	Weirton, W. Va.-Steubenville, Oh.	820
1991	Neches R.	Port Arthur - Orange, Tex.	640
1990	James River	Henrico Co., Va.	630
1972	Sitka Harbor	Sitka, Alaska	450
1976	Capt. William Moore	Skagway, Alaska	250

I-Beam Girder

Year	Bridge	Location	Longest span
1980	Shreveport Int.	Louisiana	438
1948	US-27	Licking River, Ky.	316
1947	US-31E	Green River, Ky.	316
1941	US-62	Rolling Fork, Ky.	240
1942	Licking River	Owingsville, Ky.	240
1954	Fuller Warren	Jacksonville, Fla.	224

Steel Arch

Year	Bridge	Location	Longest span
1977	New River Gorge	Fayetteville, W. Va.	1,700
1931	Bayonne, N.J.	Kill Van Kull	1,652
1973	Fremont	Portland, Ore.	1,255
1964	Port Mann	British Columbia	1,200
1916	*Hell Gate	East R., N.Y.C.	1,038
1959	Glen Canyon	Colorado River	1,028
1967	Trois-Rivieres	St. Lawrence R., P.Q.	1,100
1962	Lewiston-Queenston	Niagara River, Ont.	1,000
1976	Perrine	Twin Falls, Ida.	993
1941	Rainbow	Niagara Falls	984
1986	Moundsville Bridge, Ohio R.	Moundsville, W. Va.	912
1984	I-255	Mississippi R., Mo.	909
1972	[9]I-40, Mississippi R.	Memphis, Tenn.	900
1970	Lake Quinsigamond	Worcester, Mass.	849
1966	Charles Braga	Somerset, Mass.	840
1936	Henry Hudson	Harlem River, N.Y.C.	840
1967	Lincoln Trail	Ohio R., Ind.-Ky.	825
1978	I-57, Cairo, Ill.	Mississippi R.	821
1980	I-65 Mobile River	Mobile, Ala.	800
1961	Sherman Minton	Louisville, Ky.	800
1936	French King	Conn. R. (Rt. 2, Mass.)	782
1978	I-470 Bridge, Ohio R.	Wheeling, W. Va.	780
1930	West End	Pittsburgh	780

Concrete Arch

Year	Bridge	Location	Longest span
1971	Selah Creek (twin)	Selah, Wash.	549
1968	Cowlitz River	Mossyrock, Wash.	520
1931	Westinghouse	Pittsburgh	460
1923	Cappelen	Minneapolis	400

Twin Concrete Trestle

Year	Bridge	Location	Longest span
1979	I-55/I-10	Manchae, La.	181,157
1969	L. Pontchartrain Cswy.	Mandeville, La.	126,720
1972	Atchafalaya Flwy.	Baton Rouge, La.	93,984
1963	[8]L. Pontchartrain	Slidell, La.	28,547

Concrete Slab Dam

Year	Bridge	Location	Longest span
1927	Conowingo Dam	Maryland	4,611
1952	SR-4, Roanoke R.	Mecklenburg Co., Va.	2,785
1936	Hoover Dam	Boulder City, Nev.	1,324

Drawbridges

Vertical Lift

Year	Bridge	Location	Longest span
1959	*Arthur Kill	N.Y.-N.J.	558
1965	Pennsylvania Railroad	Kirkwood-Mt. Pleasant, Del.	548
1935	*Cape Cod Canal	Massachusetts	544
1960	*Delair, N.J.	Delaware River	542
1937	Marine Parkway	Jamaica Bay, N.Y.C.	540
1931	Burlington, N.J.	Delaware R.	534
1908	*Willamette R.	Portland, Ore.	521
1968	Second Narrows	Vancouver, B.C.	493
1912	*A-S-B Fratt	Kansas City	428
1945	*Harry S. Truman	Kansas City	427
1955	Roosevelt Island	East River, N.Y.C.	418
1980	US-17, James R.	Isle of Wight, Co., Va.	415
1932	*M-K-T R.R.	Missouri R.	414
1969	Wilm'gtn Mem.	Wilmington, N.C.	408
1930	Aerial	Duluth, Minn.	386
1941	Main St.	Jacksonville, Fla.	386
1962	Burlington	Ontario	370
1941	Acosta	St. Johns R., Fla.	365
1922	*Cincinnati	Ohio River	365
1967	SR-156, James R.	Prince George Co., Va.	364
1964	Red R.	Alexandria, La.	360
1957	Industrial Canal	New Orleans, La.	360
1950	Red R.	Moncla, La.	360
1936	Tribo	Harlem River, N.Y.C.	344
1961	[4]Corpus Christi Harbor	Corpus Christi, Tex.	344
1939	U.S. 1&9, Passaic R.	Newark, N.J.	333
1929	Carlton	Bath-Woolwich, Me.	328
1930	*Martinez	California	328
1960	St. Andrews Bay	Panama City, Fla.	327
1929	*Penn-Lehigh	Newark Bay	322
1987	Industrial Canal Bridge	New Orleans, La.	320
1920	*Chattanooga	Tennessee R.	310

Bascule

Year	Bridge	Location	Longest span
1969	E. Pearl River	Slidell, La.	482
1955	Chehalis R.	Aberdeen, Wash.	340
1917	SR-8, Tennessee River	Chattanooga, Tenn.	306
1940	Lorain, Ohio	Black River	300
1968	Elizabeth River	Chesapeake, Va.	280
1913	Broadway	Portland, Ore.	278
1982	Columbus Drive	Chicago R.	269
1954	Fuller Warren	St. Johns R., Fla.	267
1958	Morrison	Portland, Ore.	262
1926	Burnside	Portland, Ore.	252

Swing Bridges

Year	Bridge	Location	Longest span
1926	[4]Fort Madison	Mississippi R.	525
1930	Rigolets Pass	New Orleans, La.	400
1950	Douglass Memorial	Wash. D.C.	386
1945	Lord Delaware	Mattaponi River, Va.	252
1957	Eltham	Pamunkey River, Va.	237

Swing Span

Year	Bridge	Location	Longest span
1903	*East Omaha	Missouri R.	519
1952	US-17	York River, Va.	500
1897	*Duluth, Minn.	St. Louis Bay	486
1899	*C.M.&N.R.R.	Chicago	474
1913	Rt. 82, Conn-R.	E. Haddam, Ct.	465
1914	*Coos Bay	Oregon	458

Floating Pontoon

Year	Bridge	Location	Longest span
1963	Evergreen Pt.	Seattle, Wash.	7,518
1961	Hood Canal	Pt. Gamble, Wash.	6,471
1989	3rd Lake Washington Bridge	Seattle, Wash.	6,130

(1) The Transbay Bridge has 2 spans of 2,310 ft. each. (2) A second bridge in parallel was completed in 1973. (3) The Richmond Bridge has twin spans 1,070 ft. each. (4) Railroad and vehicular bridge. (5) Two spans each 707 ft. (6) Two spans each 660 ft. (7) Two spans each 825 ft. (8) Total length of bridge. (9) Two spans each 900 ft.

Notable International Bridges

Angostura, suspension type, span 2,336 feet, 1967 at Ciudad Bolivar, Venezuela. Total length, 5,507. (continued)

Bendorf Bridge on the Rhine River, 5 mi. n. of Coblenz, completed 1965, is a 3-span cement girder bridge, 3,378 ft. overall length, 101 ft. wide, with the main span 682 ft.

Bosporus Bridge linking Europe and Asia opened at Istanbul in 1973, at 3,524 ft. is the fifth longest suspension bridge in the world.

Gladesville Bridge at Sydney, Australia, has the longest concrete arch in the world (1,000 ft. span).

Humber Bridge, with a suspension span of 4,626 ft., the longest in the world, crosses the Humber estuary 5 miles west of the city of Kingston upon Hull, England. Unique in a large suspension bridge are the towers of reinforced concrete instead of steel.

Second Narrow's Bridge, Canada's longest railway lift span connecting Vancouver and North Vancouver over Burrard Inlet.

Oland Island Bridge in Sweden was completed in 1972. It is 19,882 feet long, Europe's longest.

Oosterscheldebrug, opened Dec. 15, 1965, is a 3.125-mile causeway for automobiles over a sea arm in Zeeland, the Netherlands. It completes a direct connection between Flushing and Rotterdam.

Rio-Niteroi, Guanabara Bay, Brazil, completed in 1972, is world's longest continuous box and plate girder bridge, 8 miles, 3,363 feet long, with a center span of 984 feet and a span on each side of 656 feet.

Tagus River Bridge near Lisbon, Portugal, has a 3,323-ft. main span. Opened Aug. 6, 1966, it was named Salazar Bridge for the former premier.

Zoo Bridge across the Rhine at Cologne, with steel box girders, has a main span of 850 ft.

Oldest Bridge in Continuous Use

Completed in 1841, the 178 ft. long, wood truss (with orthotropic steel deck) covered bridge spans the Housatonic River on Rt. 128 in West Cornwall, Connecticut.

Underwater Vehicular Tunnels in North America

(3,000 feet in length or more)

Name	Location	Waterway	Lgth. Ft.
Bart Trans-Bay Tubes (Rapid Transit)	San Francisco, Cal.	S.F. Bay	3.6 miles
Brooklyn-Battery	New York, N.Y.	East River	9,117
Holland Tunnel	New York, N.Y.	Hudson River	8,557
Lincoln Tunnel	New York, N.Y.	Hudson River	8,216
Thimble Shoal Channel	Northampton Co., Va.	Chesapeake Bay	8,187
Chesapeake Channel	Northampton Co., Va.	Chesapeake Bay	7,941
Baltimore Harbor Tunnel	Baltimore, Md.	Patapsco River	7,650
Hampton Roads (twin)	Hampton, Va.	Hampton Roads	7,479
Fort McHenry Tunnel (2)	Baltimore, Md.	Baltimore Harbor	7,200
Queens Midtown	New York, N.Y.	East River	6,414
Sumner Tunnel	Boston, Mass.	Boston Harbor	5,650
Louis-Hippolyte Lafontaine Tunnel	Montreal, Que.	St. Lawrence River	5,280
Detroit-Windsor	Detroit, Mich.	Detroit River	5,135
Callahan Tunnel	Boston, Mass.	Boston Harbor	5,046

Land Vehicular Tunnels in U.S.

(over 2,000 feet in length.)

Name	Location	Lgth. Ft.	Name	Location	Lgth. Ft.
E. Johnson Memorial	I-70, Col.	8,959	Lehigh	Penna. Turnpike	4,379
Eisenhower Memorial	I-70, Col.	8,941	Wawona	Yosemite Natl. Park	4,233
Allegheny (twin)	Penna. Turnpike	6,072	Big Walker Mt.	Bland Co., Va.	4,229
Liberty Tubes	Pittsburgh, Pa.	5,920	Fort Pitt	Pittsburgh, Pa.	3,560
Zion Natl. Park	Rte. 9, Utah.	5,766	Dingess Tunnel	Mingo Co., W.Va.	3,400
East River Mt. (twin)	Bland Co., Va.	5,412	Mall Tunnel	Dist. of Columbia.	3,400
Tuscarora (twin)	Penna. Turnpike	5,400	Caldecott	Oakland, Cal.	3,371
Kittatinny (twin)	Penna. Turnpike	4,660	Cody No. 1	U.S. 14, 16, 20, Wyo.	3,202
Blue Mountain (twin)	Penna. Turnpike	4,435			

World's Longest Railway Tunnels

Source: Railway Directory & Year Book. Tunnels over 5 miles in length.

Tunnel	Date	Miles	Operating railway	Country
Seikan	1985	33.5	Japanese Railway	Japan
Dai-shimizu	1979	14	Japanese Railway	Japan
Simplon No. 1 and 2	1906, 1922	12	Swiss Fed. & Italian St.	Switz.-Italy
Kanmon	1975	12	Japanese Railway	Japan
Apennine	1934	11	Italian State	Italy
Rokko	1972	10	Japanese Railway	Japan
Mt. MacDonald	1989	9.1	Canadian Pacific	Canada
Gotthard	1882	9	Swiss Federal	Switzerland
Lotschberg	1913	9	Bern-Lotschberg-Simplon	Switzerland
Hokuriku	1962	9	Japanese Railway	Japan
Mont Cenis (Frejus)	1871	8	Italian State	France-Italy
Shin-Shimizu	1961	8	Japanese Railway	Japan
Aki	1975	8	Japanese Railway	Japan
Cascade	1929	8	Burlington Northern	U.S.
Flathead	1970	8	Burlington Northern	U.S.

TRADE AND TRANSPORTATION

U.S. Foreign Trade with Leading Countries, 1991

Source: Office of Industry and Trade Information, U.S. Dept. of Commerce
(millions of dollars, not seasonally adjusted)

Country	Trade Balance	Rank	Exports	Rank	Imports	Rank
Total	$–65,399.0	(X)	$421,730.0	(X)	$487,129.0	(X)
Japan	–43,385.2	1	48,125.3	2	91,510.6	1
China	–12,690.7	2	6,278.3	16	18,969.0	6
Taiwan	–9,840.6	3	13,182.4	9	23,023.0	5
Canada	–5,914.4	4	85,149.7	1	91,064.1	2
Germany	–4,834.1	5	21,302.4	5	26,136.5	4
Saudi Arabia	–4,342.9	6	6,557.3	15	10,900.1	11
Nigeria	–4,336.7	7	831.4	52	5,168.2	19
Venezuela	–3,522.2	8	4,656.3	20	8,178.5	14
Italy	–3,194.4	9	8,569.8	12	11,764.2	10
Thailand	–2,369.3	10	3,752.7	23	6,122.0	16
Malaysia	–2,201.6	11	3,899.9	22	6,101.5	17
Angola	–1,589.2	12	186.1	79	1,775.3	33
Republic of Korea	–1,513.5	13	15,594.8	6	17,018.5	8
Algeria	–1,376.0	14	726.7	54	2,102.6	30
Indonesia	–1,349.0	15	1,891.5	34	3,240.5	26
Sweden	–1,237.7	16	3,286.8	25	4,524.5	21
Philippines	–1,206.4	17	2,264.9	29	3,471.2	25
India	–1,193.1	18	1,999.3	32	3,192.5	27
Singapore	–1,152.9	19	8,803.8	11	9,956.7	12
Hong Kong	–1,141.4	20	8,137.1	14	9,278.5	13
Colombia	–784.3	21	1,952.0	33	2,736.2	29
Gabon	–626.6	22	85.0	104	711.6	50
Macao	–570.2	23	10.4	151	580.6	56
Brazil	–568.9	24	6,147.9	17	6,716.8	15
Sri Lanka	–483.4	25	120.8	93	604.2	55
Developed Countries	–28,281.4	(X)	263,480.2	(X)	291,761.6	(X)
Developing Countries	–27,852.5	(X)	146,744.8	(X)	174,597.3	(X)
Eastern Europe	2,987.0	(X)	4,786.9	(X)	1,800.0	(X)
Selected Asia	–12,675.6	(X)	6,294.6	(X)	18,970.1	(X)
Unidentified (1)	423.6	(X)	423.6	(X)	(X)	(X)
Asia—Near East	–497.3	(X)	15,315.4	(X)	15,812.7	(X)
Asia—(NICS)	–13,648.4	(X)	45,628.2	(X)	59,276.6	(X)
Asia—South	–1,784.7	(X)	3,258.2	(X)	5,042.9	(X)
Assn. of South East Asia Nations (ASEAN)	–8,143.4	(X)	20,774.9	(X)	28,918.3	(X)
Western Europe	16,419.9	(X)	118,681.8	(X)	102,262.0	(X)
European Community (EC)	16,965.3	(X)	103,122.1	(X)	86,156.8	(X)
European Free Trade Association	–1,795.1	(X)	12,506.9	(X)	14,302.0	(X)
Twenty Latin American Republics	–584.1	(X)	58,891.2	(X)	59,475.2	(X)
Central American Common Market	314.5	(X)	3,286.6	(X)	2,972.1	(X)
Latin American Free Trade Association	–1,454.5	(X)	52,487.6	(X)	53,942.1	(X)
N. Atlantic Treaty Organization (NATO) Allies	11,592.1	(X)	189,703.6	(X)	178,111.5	(X)
Organization for Economic Cooperation & Development (OECD) in Europe	16,627.7	(X)	118,106.3	(X)	101,478.6	(X)
Organization of Petroleum Exporting Countries (OPEC)	–13,590.1	(X)	19,054.3	(X)	32,644.4	(X)
Pacific Rim Countries	–70,641.0	(X)	117,767.1	(X)	188,408.1	(X)

(1) The export totals reflect shipments of certain grains, oilseeds and satellites that are not in the country/area totals.
(2) Developed countries include Australia, Canada, Japan, New Zealand, South Africa, and Western Europe.
Developing countries include the rest of the world except Eastern Europe and Selected Asia countries.
Eastern Europe - Albania, Bulgaria, Czechoslovakia, Hungary, Poland, Romania, USSR.
Selected Asia - China, Mongolia, North Korea, Vietnam.
Asia Near East - Bahrain, Iran, Iraq, Israel, Jordan, Kuwait, Lebanon, Oman, Qatar, Saudi Arabia, Syrian Arab Republic, United Arab Emirates, Yemen.
Asia - NICS - Hong Kong, Singapore, South Korea, Taiwan.
Asia - South - Afghanistan, Bangladesh, India, Nepal, Pakistan, Sri Lanka.
ASEAN - Brunei, Indonesia, Malaysia, Philippines, Singapore, Thailand.
Western Europe - Andorra, Austria, Belgium, Cyprus, Denmark, Faroe Islands, Finland, France, Germany, Gibraltar, Greece, Iceland, Ireland, Italy, Liechtenstein, Luxembourg, Malta and Gozo, Monaco, Netherlands, Norway, Portugal, San Marino, Spain, Svalbard - Jan Mayen Island, Sweden, Switzerland, Turkey, United Kingdom, Vatican City, Yugoslavia.
European Community - Belgium, Denmark, France, Germany, Greece, Ireland, Italy, Luxembourg, Netherlands, Portugal, Spain, United Kingdom.
European Free Trade Association - Austria, Finland, Iceland, Liechtenstein, Norway, Sweden, Switzerland.
20 Latin American Republics - Argentina, Bolivia, Brazil, Chile, Colombia, Costa Rica, Cuba, Dominican Republic, Ecuador, El Salvador, Guatemala, Haiti, Honduras, Mexico, Nicaragua, Panama, Paraguay, Peru, Uruguay, Venezuela.
Central American Common Market - Costa Rica, El Salvador, Guatemala, Honduras, Nicaragua.
LAFTA - Argentina, Bolivia, Brazil, Chile, Colombia, Ecuador, Mexico, Paraguay, Peru, Uruguay, Venezuela.
NATO Allies - Belgium, Canada, Denmark, France, Germany, Greece, Iceland, Italy, Luxembourg, Netherlands, Norway, Portugal, Spain, Turkey, and United Kingdom.
OECD - Austria, Belgium, Denmark, Finland, France, Germany, Greece, Iceland, Ireland, Italy, Liechtenstein, Luxembourg, Monaco, Netherlands, Norway, Portugal, San Marino, Spain, Svalbard - Jan Mayen Island, Sweden, Switzerland, Turkey, United Kingdom.
OPEC - Algeria, Ecuador, Gabon, Indonesia, Iran, Iraq, Kuwait, Libya, Nigeria, Qatar, Saudi Arabia, United Arab Emirates, Venezuela.
Pacific Rim countries - Australia, Brunei, China, Hong Kong, Indonesia, Japan, Macao, Malaysia, New Zealand, Papua New Guinea, Philippines, Republic of Korea, Singapore, Taiwan.
(X) Not applicable. **Note:** Details may not equal totals due to rounding.

U.S. Exports and General Imports by Principal Commodity Groupings, 1991

Source: Office of Industry and Trade Information. U.S. Dept. of Commerce

(millions of dollars, not seasonally adjusted, current dollar basis)

Item	Exports	Imports
Total	$421,730.0	$487,129.0
Agricultural commodities	**38,510.0**	**22,140.4**
Animal feeds	3,192.3	312.1
Bulbs	113.0	177.9
Cereal flour	812.7	640.7
Cocoa	22.7	823.4
Coffee	9.8	1,738.1
Corn	5,145.7	39.2
Cotton, raw and linters	2,514.3	16.3
Dairy products; eggs	454.5	452.4
Furskins, raw	106.5	56.7
Grains, unmilled	701.2	112.0
Hides and skins	1,276.1	109.7
Live animals	687.6	1,172.4
Meat and preparations	3,629.6	2,908.3
Oils/fats, animal	446.8	28.5
Oils/fats, vegetable	596.2	735.1
Plants	99.2	104.8
Rice	753.5	80.1
Seeds	273.6	132.2
Soybeans	3,994.9	27.4
Sugar	12.1	713.2
Tobacco, unmanufactured	1,429.6	989.3
Vegetables and fruit	5,341.7	5,391.4
Wheat	3,350.2	66.0
Other agricultural	3,546.4	5,313.1
Manufactured goods	**325,978.0**	**392,432.6**
ADP equipment; office mach.	25,978.8	30,019.1
Airplanes	24,335.1	3,347.3
Airplane parts	10,283.6	4,046.0
Aluminum	3,127.8	2,408.8
Artwork/antiques	1,239.4	1,978.7
Basketware, etc.	1,289.9	1,910.8
Chemicals-cosmetics	2,360.8	1,415.2
Chemicals-dyeing	1,649.2	1,416.4
Chemicals-fertilizers	2,977.3	917.6
Chemicals-inorganic	4,082.7	3,296.5
Chemicals-medicinal	4,608.5	3,046.9
Chemicals-organic	10,898.2	8,132.8
Chemicals-plastics	10,315.5	3,783.6
Chemicals-other	6,019.4	2,121.9
Clothing	3,214.8	26,202.2
Copper	1,328.0	1,572.8
Electrical machinery	30,050.1	35,067.0
Footwear	542.9	9,554.0
Furniture and parts	2,119.6	4,936.1
Gem diamonds	209.3	4,002.0
General industrial mach.	17,152.8	14,396.1
Glass	1,144.6	769.5
Glassware	448.5	936.5
Gold, nonmonetary	3,279.2	1,922.1
Iron and steel mill prod.	4,210.8	8,301.1
Lighting, plumbing	876.5	1,246.0
Metal manufactures	$5,188.8	$6,372.2
Metalworking machinery	2,709.3	3,605.0
Motorcycles, bicycles	1,307.6	1,636.3
Nickel	218.5	1,061.0
Optical goods	713.4	1,483.5
Paper and paperboard	5,965.4	8,020.6
Photographic equipment	2,926.1	3,640.9
Plastic articles	2,240.1	3,114.0
Platinum	310.9	1,658.9
Pottery	87.1	1,242.3
Power generating mach.	16,960.3	14,194.8
Printed materials	3,588.9	1,701.6
Records/magnetic media	4,266.9	2,788.1
Rubber articles	579.1	704.8
Rubber tires and tubes	1,274.0	2,308.8
Scientific instruments	13,499.0	6,732.6
Ships, boats	1,155.0	248.9
Silver and bullion	237.2	363.2
Spacecraft	257.3	(—)
Specialized ind. mach.	16,686.3	10,863.9
Telecommunications equip.	9,998.7	23,445.7
Textile yarn, fabric	5,481.9	6,981.1
Toys/games/sporting goods	2,087.0	8,820.9
Travel goods	159.3	2,346.1
Vehicles/new cars-Canada	6,194.9	13,517.8
Vehicles/new cars-Japan	495.8	20,422.4
Vehicles/new cars-Other	3,069.7	10,812.5
Vehicles/trucks	3,878.7	8,292.8
Vehicles/chassis/bodies	241.3	351.9
Vehicles/parts	14,370.9	14,066.5
Watches/clocks/parts	225.0	2,285.0
Wood manufactures	1,250.5	1,907.4
Zinc	39.5	651.5
Other manufactured goods	24,569.8	30,042.4
Mineral fuel	**12,081.3**	**54,055.6**
Coal	4,775.6	310.0
Crude oil	33.4	36,901.9
Petroleum preparations	4,399.4	12,312.0
Liquified propane/butane	253.0	858.6
Natural gas	308.2	2,482.4
Electricity	43.8	486.7
Other mineral fuels	2,267.9	704.0
Selected commodities:		
Fish and preparations	3,062.7	5,637.6
Cork, wood, lumber	5,113.8	3,056.8
Pulp and waste paper	3,600.4	2,163.4
Metal ores; scrap	4,038.7	3,560.6
Crude fertilizers	1,385.4	982.3
Cigarettes	4,238.1	129.9
Alcoholic bev., distilled	279.0	1,594.9
All other	**2,821.6**	**1,374.7**

Note: Details may not equal totals due to rounding.

Value of U.S. Exports, Imports, and Merchandise Balance

Source: Office of Trade and Investment Analysis. U.S. Dept. of Commerce

(millions of dollars)

	Principal Census trade totals					Other Census totals		
Year	U.S. exports and reexports excluding military grant-aid	U.S. general imports f.a.s. transaction values[1]	U.S. merchandise balance f.a.s.[1]	U.S. general imports c.i.f.	U.S. balance exports f.a.s. imports c.i.f.	Military grant-aid shipments	Exports of domestic merchandise	Re-exports
1950	$9,997	$8,954	$1,043	$ —	$ —	$282	$10,146	$133
1955	14,298	11,566	2,732	—	—	1,256	15,426	128
1960	19,659	15,073	4,586	—	—	949	20,408	201
1965	26,742	21,520	5,222	—	—	779	27,178	343
1970	42,681	40,356	2,325	42,833	−152	565	42,612	634
1975	107,652	98,503	9,149	105,935	1,716	461	106,622	1,490
1980	220,626	244,871	−24,245	256,984	−36,358	156	216,668	4,115
1985	213,133	345,276[2]	−132,143	361,626	−148,493	13	206,925	6,221
1990	394,030	495,042	−101,012	516,987	−122,957	15	375,606	18,439
1991	421,730	487,129	−65,399	508,363	−86,633	NA	401,109	20,621

Note: Export values include both commercially-financed shipments and shipments under government-financed programs such as AID and PL-480. (1) Prior to 1974, imports are customs values, i.e. generally at prices in principal foreign markets. (2) In 1981 import value changes back to customs value. NA=Not available.

Notable Ocean Passages by Ships

Compiled by N.R.P. Bonsor

Date	Ship		From	To	Nautical miles	Time D. H. M	Speed (knots)
Sailing Vessels							
1846	Yorkshire		Liverpool	New York	3150	16. 0. 0	8.46†
1853	Northern Light		San Francisco	Boston	—	76. 6. 0	—
1854	James Baines		Boston Light	Light Rock	—	12. 6. 0	—
1854	Flying Cloud		New York	San Francisco	15091	89. 0. 0	7.07†
1868-9	Thermopylae		Liverpool	Melbourne	—	63.18.15	—
—	Red Jacket		New York	Liverpool	3150	13. 1.25	10.05†
—	Starr King		50 S. Lat	Golden Gate	—	36. 0. 0	—
—	Golden Fleece		Equator	San Francisco	—	12.12. 0	—
1905	Atlantic		Sandy Hook	England	3013	12. 4. 0	10.32
Atlantic Crossing by Passenger Steamships							
1819 (5/22 - 6/20)	Savannah (a)	US	Savannah	Liverpool	—	29. 4. 0	—
1838 (5/7 - 5/22)	Great Western	Br	New York	Avonmouth	3218	14.15.59	9.14
1840 (8/4 - 8/14)	Britannia (b)	Br	Halifax	Liverpool	2610	9.21.44	10.98†
1854 (6/28 - 7/7)	Baltic	US	Liverpool	New York	3037	9.16.52	13.04
1856 (8/6 - 8/15)	Persia	Br	Sandy Hook	Liverpool	3046	8.23.19	14.15†
1876 (12/16-12/24)	Britannic	Br	Sandy Hook	Queenstown	2882	7.12.41	15.94
1895 (5/18 - 5/24)	Lucania	Br	Sandy Hook	Queenstown	2897	5.11.40	22.00
1898 (3/30 - 4/5)	Kaiser Wilhelm der Grosse	Ger	Needles	Sandy Hook	3120	5.20. 0	22.29
1901 (7/10 - 7/17)	Deutschland	Ger	Sandy Hook	Eddystone	3082	5.11. 5	23.51
1907 (10/6 - 10/10)	Lusitania	Br	Queenstown	Sandy Hook	2780	4.19.52	23.99
1924 (8/20 - 8/25)	Mauretania	Br	Ambrose	Cherbourg	3198	5. 1.49	26.25
1929 (7/17 - 7/22)	Bremen*	Ger	Cherbourg	Ambrose	3164	4.17.42	27.83
1933 (6/27 - 7/2)	Europa	Ger	Cherbourg	Ambrose	3149	4.16.48	27.92
1933 (8/11 - 8/16)	Rex	It	Gibraltar	Ambrose	3181	4.13.58	28.92
1935 (5/30 - 6/3)	Normandie*	Fr	Bishop Rock	Ambrose	2971	4. 3. 2	29.98
1938 (8/10 - 8/14)	Queen Mary	Br	Ambrose	Bishop Rock	2938	3.20.42	31.69
1952 (7/11 - 7/15)	United States	US	Bishop Rock	Ambrose	2906	3.12.12	34.51
1952 (7/3 - 7/7)	United States*(e)	US	Ambrose	Bishop Rock	2942	3.10.40	35.59
Other Ocean Passages							
1928 (June)	USS Lexington		San Pedro	Honolulu	2226	3. 0.36	30.66
1944 (Jul-Sep)	St. Roch (c) (Can)		Halifax	Vancouver	7295	86. 0. 0	—
1945 (7/16-7/19)	USS Indianapolis (d)		San Francisco	Oahu, Hawaii	2091	3. 2.20	28.07
1945 (11/26)	USS Lake Champlain		Gibraltar	Newport News	3360	4. 8.51	32.04
1950 (Jul-Aug)	USS Boxer		Japan	San Francisco	5000	7.18.36	26.80†
1951 (6/1-6/9)	USS Philippine Sea		Yokohama	Alameda	5000	7.13. 0	27.62†
1958 (2/25-3/4)	USS Skate (f)		Nantucket	Portland, Eng	3161	8.11. 0	15.57
1958 (3/23-3/29)	USS Skate (f)		Lizard, Eng	Nantucket	—	7. 5. 0	—
1958 (7/23-8/7)	USS Nautilus (g)		Pearl Harbor	Iceland (via N. Pole)	—	15. 0. 0	—
1960 (2/16-5/10)	USS Triton (h)		New London	Rehoboth, Del	41500	84. 0. 0	20.59†
1960 (8/15-8/20)	USS Seadragon (i)		Baffin Bay	NW Passage, Pac	850	6. 0. 0	—
1962 (10/30-11/11)	African Comet* (U.S.)		New York	Cape Town	6786	12.16.22	22.03
1973 (8/20)	Sea-Land Exchange (k) (U.S.)		Bishop Rock	Ambrose	2912	3.11.24	34.92
1973 (8/24)	Sea-Land Trade (U.S.)		Kobe	Race Rock, BC	4126	5. 6. 0	32.75

† The time taken and/or distance covered is approximate and so, therefore, is the average speed.

* Maiden voyage. (a) The Savannah, a fully rigged sailing vessel with steam auxiliary (over 300 tons, 98.5 ft. long, beam 25.8 ft., depth 12.9 ft.) was launched in the East River in 1818. It was the first ship to use steam in crossing any ocean. It was supplied with engines and detachable iron paddle wheels. On its famous voyage it used steam 105 hours. (b) First Cunard liner. (c) First ship to complete NW Passage in one season. (d) Carried Hiroshima atomic bomb in World War II. (e) Set world speed record; average speed eastbound on maiden voyage 35.59 knots (about 41 m.p.h.). (f) First atomic submarine to cross Atlantic both ways submerged. (g) World's first atomic submarine also first to make undersea voyage under polar ice cap, 1,830 mi. from Point Barrow, Alaska, to Atlantic Ocean, Aug. 1-4, 1958, reaching North Pole Aug. 3. Second undersea transit of the North Pole made by submarine USS Skate Aug. 11, 1958, during trip from New London, Conn., and return. (h) World's largest submarine. Nuclear-powered Triton was submerged during nearly all its voyage around the globe. It duplicated the route of Ferdinand Magellan's circuit (1519-1522) 30,708 mi., starting from St. Paul Rocks off the NE coast of Brazil, Feb. 24-Apr. 25, 1960, then sailed to Cadiz, Spain, before returning home. (i) First underwater transit of Northwest Passage. (k) Fastest freighter crossing of Atlantic.

Commerce at Principal U.S. Ports

Source: Corps of Engineers, Dept. of the Army (by tonnage, 1992)

Rank	Port	Total	Foreign
1.	Port of South Louisiana, LA	193,042,300	90,880,628
2.	New York, NY	140,027,575	49,263,710
3.	Houston, TX	126,177,644	62,942,126
4.	Valdez Harbor, AK	95,953,448	16,804
5.	Baton Rouge, LA	78,112,575	34,711,325
6.	Corpus Christi, TX	62,023,736	35,828,603
7.	New Orleans, LA	61,249,051	29,374,508
8.	Port of Plaquemine, LA	56,527,861	17,280,970
9.	Norfolk Harbor, VA	53,722,133	44,735,594
10.	Long Beach, CA	52,425,196	22,817,148
11.	Tampa Harbor, FL	51,579,204	21,201,181
12.	Texas City, TX	48,071,122	28,654,514
13.	Los Angeles, CA	46,352,315	24,878,485
14.	Philadelphia, PA	41,836,960	26,934,370
15.	Mobile, AL	41,136,445	19,339,687
16.	Lake Charles, LA	40,882,809	24,319,311
17.	Duluth-Supr., MN	40,766,373	5,734,197
18.	Baltimore Hrbr., MD	39,551,292	24,210,416
19.	Pittsburgh, PA	35,492,000	0
20.	Port Arthur, TX	30,679,583	20,146,433
21.	Portland, OR	27,475,429	16,234,007
22.	St. Louis, Metro., MO	27,108,441	0
23.	Beaumont, TX	26,728,664	7,923,165
24.	Pascagoula, MS	26,479,086	16,253,470
25.	Marcus Hook, PA	25,864,205	10,259,286
26.	Newport News, VA	24,935,372	21,725,456
27.	Paulsboro, NJ	23,331,201	11,838,939
28.	Chicago, IL	22,533,880	2,683,349
29.	Boston, MA, Port of	21,888,634	13,434,735
30.	Seattle, WA	21,569,739	13,097,094
31.	Tacoma Hrbr., WA	21,433,431	16,439,133
32.	Richmond, CA	21,155,885	6,930,842
33.	Detroit, MI	17,734,779	3,834,568
34.	Huntington, WV	17,310,165	0
35.	Anacortes, WA	15,437,562	2,259,074
36.	Indiana Harbor, IN	14,672,845	259,858
37.	Toledo Harbor, OH	14,667,771	7,124,201
38.	Jacksonville, FL	14,597,933	6,800,723
39.	San Juan, PR	14,536,669	6,126,030
40.	Freeport, TX	14,494,397	7,145,703

Commerce on U.S. Inland Waterways

Source: Corps of Engineers, Depart. of the Army, 1991

Mississippi River System and Gulf Intracoastal Waterway

Waterway	Tons
Mississippi River, Minneapolis to the Gulf	462,735,996
Mississippi River, Minneapolis to St. Louis	79,356,272
Mississippi River, St. Louis to Cairo	101,799,998
Mississippi River, Cairo to Baton Rouge	181,802,058
Mississippi River, Baton Rouge to New Orleans	331,655,147
Mississippi River, New Orleans to Gulf	281,225,303
Gulf Intracoastal Waterway	112,739,177
Mississippi River System	626,384,122

Ton-Mileage of Freight Carried on Inland Waterways

System	Ton-miles
Atlantic Coast Waterways	28,204,948
Gulf Coast Waterways	42,545,820
Pacific Coast Waterways	23,999,523
Mississippi River System, including Ohio River and Tributaries	268,089,639
Great Lakes System, U.S. Commerce only	85,847,239
Total:	**448,687,169**

Note: Tons are for calendar year 1989; all tons are in U.S. short tons (2,000 lbs per ton); ton-miles(000) have been omitted.

Important Waterways and Canals

The St. Lawrence & Great Lakes Waterway, the largest inland navigation system on the continent, extends from the Atlantic Ocean to Duluth at the western end of Lake Superior, a distance of 2,342 miles. With the deepening of channels and locks to 27 ft., ocean carriers are able to penetrate to ports in the Canadian interior and the American midwest.

The major canals are those of the St. Lawrence Great Lakes waterway — the 3 new canals of the St. Lawrence Seaway, with their 7 locks, providing navigation for vessels of 26-foot draught from Montreal to Lake Ontario; the Welland Ship Canal by-passing the Niagara River between Lake Ontario and Lake Erie with its 8 locks, and the Sault Ste. Marie Canal and lock between Lake Huron and Lake Superior. These 16 locks overcome a drop of 580 ft. from the head of the lakes to Montreal. From Montreal to Lake Ontario the former bottleneck of narrow, shallow canals and of slow passage through 22 locks has been overcome, giving faster and safer movement for larger vessels. The new locks and linking channels now accommodate all but the largest ocean-going vessels and the upper St. Lawrence and Great Lakes are open to 80% of the world's saltwater fleet.

Subsidiary Canadian canals or branches include the St. Peters Canal between Bras d'Or Lakes and the Atlantic Ocean in Nova Scotia; the St. Ours and Chambly Canals on the Richelieu River, Quebec; the Ste. Anne and Carillon Canals on the Ottawa River; the Rideau Canal between the Ottawa River and Lake Ontario, the Trent and Murrary Canals between Lake Ontario and Georgian Bay in Ontario and the St. Andrew's Canal on the Red River. The commercial value of these canals is not great but they are maintained to control water levels and permit the passage of small vessels and pleasure craft. The Canso Canal, completed 1957, permits shipping to pass through the causeway connecting Cape Breton Island with the Nova Scotia mainland.

The Welland Canal overcomes the 326-ft. drop of Niagara Falls and the rapids of the Niagara River. It has 8 locks, each 859 ft. long, 80 ft. wide and 30 ft. deep. Regulations permit ships of 730-ft. length and 75-ft. beam to transit.

Shortest Navigable Distances Between Ports

Source: Distances Between Ports. (Pub. 151 6th Edition 1991) Defense Mapping Agency Hydrographic/Topographic Center
Distances shown are in nautical miles (1,852 meters or about 6,076.115 feet). To get statute miles, multiply by 1.15.

TO — FROM	New York	Montreal	Colon[1]
Algiers, Algeria	3,617	3,592	4,745
Amsterdam, Netherlands	3,418	3,162	4,825
Baltimore, Md.	410	1,820	1,901
Barcelona, Spain	3,710	3,695	4,842
Boston, Mass.	378	1,309	2,157
Buenos Aires, Argentina	5,871	6,455	5,346
Cape Town, S. Africa[2]	6,766	7,115	6,429
Cherbourg, France	3,127	2,878	4,541
Cobh, Ireland	2,879	2,603	4,308
Copenhagen, Denmark	3,720	3,241	5,129
Dakar, Senegal	3,335	3,562	3,694
Galveston, Tex.	1,895	3,165	1,492
Gibraltar[3]	3,204	3,184	4,329
Glasgow, Scotland	3,065	2,691	4,746
Halifax, N.S.	600	958	2,295
Hamburg, Germany	3,636	3,398	5,054
Hamilton, Bermuda	697	1,621	1,659
Havana, Cuba	1,199	2,473	998
Helsinki, Finland	4,208	3,778	5,902
Istanbul, Turkey	5,001	4,981	6,129
Kingston, Jamaica	1,474	2,690	551
Lagos, Nigeria	4,883	5,130	5,033
Lisbon, Portugal	2,980	2,941	4,155
Marseille, France	3,891	3,870	5,019
Montreal, Quebec	1,516		3,126
Naples, Italy	4,181	4,159	5,309
Nassau, Bahamas	962	2,274	1,166
New Orleans, La.	1,761	2,991	1,389
New York, N.Y.		1,516	1,974
Norfolk, Va.	287	1,697	1,779
Oslo, Norway	3,701	3,222	5,306
Piraeus, Greece	4,687	4,661	5,806
Port Said, Egypt	5,123	5,093	6,238
Rio de Janeiro, Brazil	4,770	5,342	4,367
St. John's, Nfld.	1,093	1,038	2,345
San Juan, Puerto Rico	1,399	2,445	993
Southampton, England	3,156	3,063	4,514

TO — FROM	San. Fran.	Vancouver	Panama[1]
Acapulco, Mexico	1,833	2,645	1,426
Anchorage, Alas.	1,872	1,347	5,117
Bombay, India	9,791	9,519	9,248
Calcutta, India	9,006	8,728	10,929
Colon, Panama[1]	3,289	4,076	44
Jakarta, Indonesia	7,642	7,413	10,570
Haiphong, Vietnam	6,657	6,358	9,806
Hong Kong	6,044	5,756	9,195
Honolulu, Hawaii	2,091	2,423	4,685
Los Angeles, Cal.	369	1,162	2,913
Manila, Philippines	6,221	5,756	9,347
Melbourne, Australia	6,970	7,342	7,928
Pusan, S. Korea	4,914	4,623	8,074
Ho Chi Min City, Vietnam	6,878	6,606	10,017
San Francisco, Cal.		812	3,245
Seattle, Wash.	796	126	4,020
Shanghai, China	5,398	5,110	8,566
Singapore	7,353	7,078	10,505
Suva, Fiji	4,749	5,199	6,325
Valparaiso, Chile	5,140	5,915	2,616
Vancouver, B.C.	812		4,032
Vladivostok, Russia	4,563	4,262	7,739
Yokohama, Japan	4,536	4,262	7,682

TO — FROM	Port Said	Cape Town[2]	Singapore
Bombay, India	3,046	4,616	2,441
Calcutta, India	4,691	5,638	1,649
Dar es Salaam, Tanzania	3,238	2,365	4,042
Jakarta, Indonesia	5,293	5,212	526
Hong Kong	6,472	7,006	1,454
Kuwait City, Kuwait	3,306	5,169	3,845
Manila, Philippines	6,348	6,777	1,330
Melbourne, Australia	7,837	6,104	3,844
Ho Chi Min City, Vietnam	5,667	6,263	649
Singapore	5,018	5,611	
Yokohama, Japan	7,907	8,503	2,889

(1) Colon on the Atlantic is 44 nautical miles from Panama (port) on the Pacific. (2) Cape Town is 35 nautical miles northwest of the Cape of Good Hope. (3) Gibraltar (port) is 24 nautical miles east of the Strait of Gibraltar.

Major Merchant Fleets of the World

Source: Maritime Administration, U.S. Commerce Department (tonnage in thousands)

Fleets of oceangoing steam and motor ships totalling 1 million gross tons and over as of Jan. 1, 1992. Excludes ships operating exclusively on the Great Lakes and inland waterways and special types such as channel ships, icebreakers, cable ships, etc., and merchant ships owned by any military force. Gross tonnage is a volume measurement; each cargo gross ton represents 100 cubic ft. of enclosed space. Deadweight tonnage is the carrying capacity of a ship in long tons (2,240 lbs.). Tonnage figures may not add, due to rounding.

	Total			Type of Vessel: Freighters			Bulk Carriers			Tankers		
	Number	Gross Tons	Dwt. Tons	Number	Gross Tons	Dwt. Tons	Number	Gross Tons	Dwt. Tons	Number	Gross Tons	Dwt. Tons
All Countries[1]	23,943	397,225	652,025	12,581	99,931	122,349	5,473	139,295	247,679	5,542	153,309	280,572
United States[2]	619	15,466	23,254	359	6,538	7,155	24	584	1,014	226	8,189	14,993
Privately owned	394	12,729	19,716	167	4,341	4,487	23	569	989	201	7,740	14,210
Government owned	225	2,737	3,538	192	2,197	2,668	1	15	25	25	449	783
Argentina	108	1,336	2,132	56	468	689	12	366	636	40	502	807
Australia	76	2,209	3,307	25	270	300	30	1,015	1,702	21	924	1,305
Bahamas	756	18,264	30,585	302	2,468	3,093	175	4,971	8,493	233	9,878	18,771
Brazil	259	5,645	9,634	83	632	828	89	2,870	5,027	85	2,141	3,777
British Dep Terr	712	14,132	23,634	393	3,069	3,996	192	5,910	10,587	121	5,109	9,032
Bulgaria	117	1,268	1,911	59	371	462	37	605	971	19	290	476
China (Communist)	1,359	13,407	20,549	880	6,196	8,647	278	5,317	9,035	183	1,749	2,790
Cyprus	1,210	20,036	35,746	599	3,936	5,762	469	10,446	18,950	136	5,615	11,017
Denmark (Dis)	269	5,005	7,658	171	2,198	2,406	15	552	1,022	83	2,255	4,230
France	102	2,941	4,641	48	984	1,040	7	178	292	42	1,753	3,295
Germany, Federal	491	5,078	6,395	396	3,799	4,623	29	662	1,050	57	421	662
Greece	914	23,004	43,184	216	1,622	2,390	449	11,458	21,347	223	9,737	19,357
India	293	5,957	9,948	99	972	1,436	121	3,064	5,256	70	1,907	3,249
Indonesia	389	1,615	2,558	267	872	1,365	18	167	246	96	559	933
Iran	126	4,449	8,271	40	411	572	49	1,054	1,751	37	2,984	5,948
Isle of Man	84	1,527	2,644	31	258	287	13	318	555	40	951	1,802
Italy	493	6,826	10,310	189	1,452	1,480	61	2,388	4,318	226	2,652	4,444
Japan	944	21,674	33,376	382	4,099	3,364	266	9,209	16,948	281	8,166	13,006
Korea (South)	445	7,023	11,436	233	1,898	2,191	150	4,495	8,122	62	630	1,123
Kuwait	28	1,326	2,268	5	111	148	—	—	—	23	1,215	2,120
Liberia	1,550	52,622	93,522	380	5,908	6,344	553	16,713	30,885	597	29,426	56,170
Luxemborg	47	1,593	2,639	13	216	242	17	881	1,630	17	496	767
Malaysia	169	1,676	2,496	103	600	852	19	364	661	47	712	983
Malta	640	8,705	14,962	303	1,860	2,769	196	3,951	6,957	136	2,848	5,218
Marshall Islands	18	1,436	2,855	2	60	59	9	387	699	7	989	2,097
Netherlands	362	3,051	4,125	281	1,757	2,261	15	393	632	61	770	1,214
Norway (Nis)	770	21,298	38,015	198	1,782	1,975	236	6,775	12,439	323	12,425	23,540
Panama	3,040	46,183	74,905	1,662	13,129	15,961	711	16,233	28,003	637	16,529	30,808
Philippines	536	7,934	13,438	236	1,320	1,785	250	6,207	10,924	40	363	706
Poland	230	2,950	4,173	134	1,182	1,306	88	1,639	2,672	5	109	185
Romania	282	3,524	5,554	202	1,193	1,605	63	1,665	2,784	17	666	1,165
Singapore	478	8,684	14,045	238	2,646	3,208	78	2,240	4,022	161	3,786	6,813
Spain	267	2,713	5,108	154	384	607	43	764	1,386	68	1,547	3,109
Sweden	172	2,570	3,471	85	988	947	19	415	692	64	1,033	1,812
Taiwan	211	5,826	9,152	127	2,188	2,542	65	2,876	5,287	19	762	1,323
Turkey	347	4,081	7,236	200	722	1,083	94	2,547	4,674	50	798	1,473
U.S.S.R.	2,233	17,233	22,879	1,601	9,470	11,100	231	3,927	6,223	372	3,589	5,497
United Kingdom	166	2,879	3,266	68	1,229	1,199	20	177	274	63	1,153	1,706
Vanuatu	109	1,897	2,844	53	633	605	46	1,019	1,759	9	239	478
Yugoslavia	65	1,113	1,869	31	327	471	31	775	1,382	3	11	16

(1) Includes Combination Passenger & Cargo Ships; (2) Excludes non-merchant type and/or Navy-owned vessels that are currently in the Nat. Reserve Fleet.

Fastest Scheduled Passenger Train Runs in the U.S. and Canada

Source: Darrell J. Smith, Natl. Railroad Passenger Corp.; 1992 timetables

Railroad	Train	From	To	Mi.	Min.	MPH
Amtrak	Eight Metroliner Service trains	Wilmington	Baltimore	68.4	42	97.7
Amtrak	16 Metroliner Service trains	Baltimore	Wilmington	68.4	43	95.0
Amtrak	Express Metroliner Service train 203	Metropark	Baltimore	160.0	103	93.0
Amtrak	Express Metroliner Service train 202	New Carrollton	New York	216.0	141	91.9
Amtrak	Express Metroliner Service train 220	Washington	Philadelphia	135.0	88	91.8
Amtrak	Express Metroliner Service train 223	New York	Baltimore	185.0	123	90.2
Amtrak	Two Metroliner Service trains	Newark	Philadelphia	80.7	55	87.7
Amtrak	Nine Metroliner Service trains	Newark	Philadelphia	80.7	56	86.8
VIA	Renaissance	Dorval	Kingston	165.0	117	84.6
VIA	York	Kingston	Cornwall	108.0	77	84.4
Amtrak	Three Metroliner Service trains	Philadelphia	Newark	80.7	58	83.2
VIA	York	Cornwall	Kingston	108.0	78	83.1
VIA	Renaissance	Kingston	Dorval	165.0	120	82.5

Note: The fastest scheduled passenger train runs in the world are those of France's TGV Atlantique, between Paris and various cities in western France, at 186.4 mph.

Top 50 U.S. Industrial Exporters

Source: FORTUNE magazine; June 29, 1992

Rank 1991	Rank 1990	Company	1991 $ millions	% change from 1990	As % of total sales %
1	1	Boeing	17,856	11.0	60.9
2	2	General Motors	11,284	9.4	9.1
3	3	General Electric	8,614	20.8	14.3
4	5	Intl. Business Machines	7,668	23.8	11.8
5	4	Ford Motor	7,340[1]	3.4	8.3
6	6	Chrysler	6,168	23.3	21.0
7	9	McDonnell Douglas	6,160	74.1	32.9
8	7	E.I. Du Pont De Nemours	3,812	(12.4)	10.0
9	10	Caterpillar	3,710	8.0	36.4
10	8	United Technologies	3,587	(0.5)	16.9
11	13	Hewlett-Packard	3,223	14.5	22.2
12	12	Philip Morris	3,061	4.5	6.4
13	11	Eastman Kodak	3,020	2.1	15.4
14	14	Motorola	2,928	4.5	25.8
15	27	Archer-Daniels-Midland	2,600[2]	123.6	30.3
16	17	Digital Equipment	2,200	14.6	15.7
17	24	Intel	1,929	60.4	40.4
18	18	Allied-Signal	1,729	(5.9)	14.6
19	30	Sun Microsystems	1,606	43.7	49.3
20	15	Unisys	1,598	(27.5)	18.4
21	21	Raytheon	1,556	8.4	16.6
22	20	Weyerhaeuser	1,550	(0.6)	17.8
23	22	Dow Chemical	1,376	2.4	7.1
24	19	General Dynamics	1,370	(15.6)	14.3
25	28	Merck	1,342	16.1	15.6
26	25	Minnesota Mining & Mfg.	1,275	6.3	9.6
27	33	International Paper	1,200	9.1	9.4
28	23	Union Carbide	1,200	(6.3)	16.3
29	31	Textron	1,171	6.2	14.9
30	34	Hoechst Celanese	1,158	6.7	16.9
31	26	Westinghouse Electric	1,141	(4.5)	8.9
32	35	Monsanto	1,128	4.5	12.6
33	37	Xerox	1,040	15.6	5.8
34	36	Aluminum Co. of America	967	4.4	9.7
35	41	Abbott Laboratories	957	17.5	13.8
36	16	Occidental Petroleum	951	(54.2)	9.2
37	29	Compaq Computer	950[3]	(15.3)	29.0
38	39	FMC	913	7.7	23.2
39	38	Miles	877[4]	1.4	14.2
40	47	Cooper Industries	835	26.0	13.5
41	40	Rockwell Intl.	828	(0.8)	6.9
42	43	Honeywell	808	7.7	13.0
43	45	Bristol-Myers Squibb	807[5]	8.9	7.1
44	50	Lockheed	794	35.0	8.1
45	32	Exxon	744	(32.4)	0.7
46	42	Deere	713	(5.9)	10.1
47	44	Amoco	712	(4.2)	2.8
48	46	Tenneco	692	(2.7)	4.9
49	49	Ethyl	655	10.5	25.4
50	48	Reynolds Metals	603	(5.6)	10.4
		Total	$130,407		

(1) Excludes some U.S. export figures. (2) Includes sales value of grain merchandise; 1990 figure did not. (3) Includes Canadian exports. (4) A wholly owned subsidiary of Bayer AG, Germany. (5) FORTUNE est.

Passenger Car Production, U.S. Plants

Source: Motor Vehicle Manufacturers Assn.

	1990	1991
Chrysler Corp.		
Horizon	4,327	0
Sundance	87,587	61,605
Acclaim	120,440	82,358
Total Plymouth	**212,354**	**143,963**
LeBaron A	8,071	0
LeBaron J	52,026	29,388
Fifth Avenue (Y)	41,366	36,706
Imperial	16,280	9,335
New Yorker (C)	34,876	15,142
Total Chrysler-Plymouth	**364,973**	**234,534**
Omni	4,078	0
Daytona	33,376	11,492
Shadow	95,681	69,463
Spirit	105,587	80,216
Dynasty	123,047	114,439
Viper	0	3
Total Dodge	**361,769**	**275,613**
Total Chrysler Corp.	**726,742**	**510,147**
Ford Motor Co.		
Thunderbird	107,366	71,395
Taurus	329,852	317,810
Tempo	125,151	112,105
Escort	242,031	188,450
Mustang	129,066	81,594
Total Ford	**933,466**	**771,354**
Cougar	73,373	52,157
Sable	101,334	110,619
Topaz	46,729	49,493
Town Car	145,806	126,354
Mark	18,023	9,297
Continental	58,620	52,406
Total Lincoln-Mercury	**443,885**	**400,326**
Total Ford Motor Co.	**1,377,351**	**1,171,680**
General Motors Corp.		
Geo Prizm	102,296	94,927
Cavalier	360,798	252,857
Camaro	70,982	52,177
Beretta-Corsica	269,143	240,745
Caprice	200,006	0
Corvette	22,154	21,082
Total Chevrolet	**1,025,379**	**786,012**
Sunbird	167,405	118,615
Firebird	40,375	20,322
Grand Am	204,812	147,467
6000	51,529	19,603
Grand Prix	112,936	114,718
Bonneville H.	72,198	86,355
Total Pontiac	**649,255**	**509,080**
Calais	99,981	34,616
Ciera	65,339	111,628
Cutlass Supreme	93,786	105,151
Delta 88 B	3,430	0
Delta 88 H.	99,088	100,862
Oldsmobile 98.	42,346	75,362
Toronado	14,772	5,934
Achieva	0	6,199
Total Oldsmobile	**418,742**	**439,752**
Skylark	94,118	61,537
Century	63,780	98,670
LeSabre B	4,022	0
LeSabre Roadmaster	154,066	171,491
Electra-Park Avenue	62,243	93,700
Reatta	5,587	1,210
Riviera	21,307	10,314
Total Buick	**405,123**	**436,922**
Cadillac DeVille/Fleetwood/Brougham	191,657	182,457
Eldorado	22,048	16,276
Seville	35,328	26,786
Allante	3,507	2,900
Total Cadillac	**252,540**	**228,419**
Total Saturn	**4,245**	**95,821**
Total General Motors Corp.	**2,755,284**	**2,496,006**
Diamond Star	**148,379**	**153,936**
Honda	**435,437**	**451,199**
Mazda	**184,428**	**165,314**
Nissan	**95,844**	**133,505**
Subaru	**32,461**	**57,945**
Toyota	**321,523**	**298,847**
Total Passenger Cars 1991	**—**	**5,438,579**
Total Passenger Cars 1990	**6,077,449**	**—**
1991/1990 Percent Change	**−10.93**	**−11.17**

Selected Motor Vehicle Statistics

Source: Federal Highway Adm.; National Transportation Safety Board; Insurance Institute for Highway Safety

State	Driver's age Jan. 1, 1992 (1) Regular	Driver's age Jan. 1, 1992 (2) Juvenile	State gas tax gal. cents (April 1, 1992)	Safety belt use law[4] (Aug. 1, 1991)	Licensed drivers per 1,000 resident population	Registered motor vehicles per 1,000 resident population	Licensed drivers per registered motor vehicle	Gallons of fuel per vehicle	Miles per gallon	Annual miles per vehicle	Vehicle miles per licensed driver
Alabama. . . .	16	—	13	S	681	927	0.74	701	16.14	11,309	15,384
Alaska	16	—	8	S	571	868	0.66	670	12.45	8,336	12,660
Arizona	16	—	18	S	653	771	0.85	697	18.01	12,550	14,819
Arkansas . . .	16	—	18.7	S	732	616	1.19	1,098	13.22	14,514	12,201
California . . .	16/18	14	16	S*	667	737	0.91	669	17.66	11,809	13,047
Colorado . . .	18	16	22	S	620	958	0.65	538	16.02	8,613	13,303
Connecticut . .	16/18	—	26	P	674	798	0.84	567	17.68	10,028	11,880
Delaware . . .	16/18	—	19	S	728	790	0.92	733	16.97	12,447	13,507
Dist. of Col. . .	18	16	18	S	680	432	1.57	719	18.09	13,007	8,263
Florida	16	—	11.6	S	714	846	0.84	610	16.48	10,046	11,916
Georgia	16	—	7.5	S	691	847	0.82	788	16.83	13,253	16,244
Hawaii	15	—	16	P	612	696	0.88	501	20.86	10,455	11,903
Idaho	17	15	21	S	699	1,046	0.67	563	16.61	9,349	13,986
Illinois	16/18	—	19	S	638	689	0.93	786	13.47	10,585	11,424
Indiana	16/18	—	15	S	650	787	0.82	760	16.19	12,300	14,910
Iowa	16/18	—	20	P	674	948	0.71	635	13.75	8,736	12,279
Kansas	16	14	17	S	692	812	0.85	743	15.29	11,354	13,327
Kentucky . . .	16	—	15.4	No	652	790	0.83	780	14.82	11,562	14,007
Louisiana . . .	15/17	15	20	S	610	710	0.86	723	17.39	12,578	14,625
Maine	16/17	16	19	No	722	795	0.91	706	17.22	12,155	13,383
Maryland . . .	16/18	16	18.5	S	703	754	0.93	643	17.47	11,240	12,057
Massachusetts	17/18	16½	21	No	703	619	1.14	697	17.77	12,381	10,907
Michigan . . .	16/18	14	15	S	693	776	0.89	649	17.33	11,248	12,591
Minnesota . .	16/18	15	20	S	578	802	0.72	629	17.65	11,102	15,400
Mississippi . .	15	—	18.2	P	732	729	1.00	813	16.00	13,009	12,946
Missouri	16	—	11.03	S	721	763	0.94	840	15.52	13,031	13,797
Montana . . .	15/16	13	20	S	755	979	0.77	684	15.54	10,639	13,804
Nebraska . . .	16	14	24.1	No**	690	877	0.79	694	14.54	10,086	12,821
Nevada	16	14	21.5	S	704	710	0.99	890	13.46	11,969	12,069
New Hampshire .	16/18	16	18.6	No	761	853	0.89	577	18.05	10,409	11,671
New Jersey .	17	16	10.5	S	722	731	0.99	654	15.94	10,424	10,551
New Mexico .	15/16	—	17	P	709	859	0.83	768	16.15	12,410	15,038
New York . . .	17/18	16	22.89	P	570	567	1.01	655	16.01	10,485	10,425
North Carolina	16/18	—	22.3	P	686	779	0.88	744	16.34	12,148	13,780
North Dakota .	16	14	17	No	665	986	0.67	640	14.66	9,383	13,909
Ohio	16/18	14	21	S	685	775	0.88	665	15.56	10,341	11,710
Oklahoma . .	16	—	17	S	724	842	0.86	767	16.28	12,488	14,525
Oregon	16	14	22	P	778	860	0.90	677	16.16	10,934	12,090
Pennsylvania .	17/18	16	22.4	S	665	671	0.99	682	15.76	10,752	10,850
Rhode Island .	16/18	—	26	S	669	670	1.00	598	17.49	10,455	10,473
South Carolina	16	15	16	S	680	723	0.94	869	15.70	13,643	14,487
South Dakota	16	14	18	No	707	1,011	0.70	652	15.22	9,931	14,194
Tennessee . .	16	14	20	S	684	911	0.75	681	15.43	10,511	14,008
Texas	16/18	15	20	P	656	754	0.87	772	16.42	12,675	14,567
Utah	16/18	—	19	S	607	700	0.87	730	16.64	12,149	14,000
Vermont . . .	18	16	16	No	732	820	0.89	695	18.18	12,642	14,173
Virginia	16/19	—	17.7	S	709	798	0.89	705	17.28	12,187	13,712
Washington . .	16/18	—	23	S	694	875	0.79	609	17.23	10,500	13,236
West Virginia .	16/18	16	20.35	No	716	683	1.05	822	15.32	12,587	12,011
Wisconsin . . .	16/18	14	22.2	S	680	751	0.91	668	18.05	12,058	13,305
Wyoming . . .	16	14	9	S	735	1,164	0.63	869	12.71	11,039	17,488
Average . . .					**672**	**759**	**0.89**	**697**	**16.32**	**11,383**	**12,858**

(1) Unrestricted operation of private passenger car. When 2 ages are shown, license is issued at lower age upon completion of approved driver education course. (2) Juvenile license issued with consent of parent or guardian. (3) Estimated. (4) P = an officer may stop a vehicle for a violation (primary); S = an officer may only issue a seat belt citation when the vehicle is stopped for another moving violation (secondary); *California will enforce its law primarily beginning Jan. 1, 1993. **Nebraska's seat belt law will be enforced secondarily from Jan. 1, 1993.

Best-Selling Cars in the U.S.

Source: *Ward's Automotive Yearbooks*

1965-1969: Full-size Chevrolet Impala, Caprice, Biscayne, Bel Air
1970: Full-size Ford Custom LTD, Galaxie 500
1971-1972: Full-size Chevrolet Impala, Caprice, Biscayne, Bel Air
1973-1974: Full-size Chevrolet Impala, Caprice, Bel Air
1975: Full-size Chevrolet Impala, Caprice
1976: Oldsmobile Cutlass
1977-1979: Full-size Chevrolet Impala, Caprice
1980: Chevrolet Citation
1981: Chevrolet Chevette
1982-1983: Ford Escort
1984-1985: Chevrolet Cavalier
1986: Chevrolet Celebrity
1987-1988: Ford Escort/EXP
1989-1990: Honda Accord
1990-1991: Honda Accord

World Motor Vehicle Production, 1950-1991

Source: Motor Vehicle Manufacturers Association

(in thousands)

Year	United States	Canada	Europe	Japan	Other	World Total	U.S. Percent of World Total
1950	8,006	388	1,991	32	160	10,577	75.7%
1960	7,905	398	6,830	482	873	16,488	47.9
1970	8,284	1,160	13,243	5,289	1,427	29,403	28.2
1980	8,010	1,374	15,446	11,043	2,641	38,514	20.8
1981	7,943	1,323	14,440	11,180	2,344	37,230	21.3
1982	6,986	1,276	14,808	10,732	2,311	36,113	19.3
1983	9,205	1,524	15,708	11,112	2,206	39,755	23.2
1984	10,939	1,829	15,293	11,465	2,532	42,058	26.0
1985	11,653	1,933	15,959	12,271	2,995	44,811	26.0
1986	11,335	1,854	16,701	12,260	3,147	45,297	25.0
1987	10,925	1,635	17,548	12,249	3,546	45,903	23.8
1988	11,214	1,949	18,234	12,700	4,113	48,210	23.3
1989	10,874	2,002	18,979	13,026	4,220	49,101	22.1
1990	9,783	1,925	18,566	13,487	4,414	48,275	20.3
1991	8,811	1,905	17,598	13,245	4,878	46,437	18.0

Note: As far as can be determined, production refers to vehicles locally manufactured.

World Motor Vehicle Production, 1991

Source: Motor Vehicle Manufacturers Association

Country	Passenger Cars	Commercial Vehicles	Total
Argentina	114,113	24,845	138,958
Australia	278,421	14,904	293,325
Austria	13,682	5,506	19,188
Belgium	253,491	84,170	337,661
Brazil	705,363	254,763	960,126
Canada	1,072,352	833,103	1,905,455
China	40,300	604,196	644,496
Czechoslovakia	172,726	28,587	201,313
France	3,187,634	423,139	3,610,773
Germany, East	150,000	35,000	185,000
Germany, West	4,659,480	355,523	5,015,003
Hungary	0	5,001	5,001
India	176,995	176,589	353,584
Italy	1,631,941	245,385	1,877,326
Japan	9,753,069	3,492,363	13,245,432
Korea, South	1,158,245	339,573	1,497,818
Mexico	720,384	268,989	989,373
The Netherlands	84,709	26,103	110,812
Poland	154,578	30,000	184,578
Spain	1,773,752	307,959	2,081,711
Sweden	269,431	75,259	344,690
United Kingdom	1,236,900	217,141	1,454,041
United States	5,438,579	3,371,942	8,810,521
U.S.S.R.	1,170,000	759,000	1,929,000
Yugoslavia	215,789	26,126	241,915
Total	**34,431,934**	**12,005,146**	**46,437,080**

Note: As far as can be determined, production in this table refers to vehicles locally manufactured.

Domestic and Imported Retail Car Sales in the U.S., 1980-1991

Source: Motor Vehicle Manufacturers Assn.

Calendar Year	Domestic	Imports: From Japan	From Germany	Other Countries	Total	U.S. Total	Import Percent: Total	Japan	U.S. Sponsored Imports
1980	6,581,307	1,905,968	305,219	186,700	2,397,887	8,979,194	26.7	21.2	223,310
1981	6,208,760	1,858,896	282,881	185,502	2,327,279	8,536,039	27.3	21.8	174,665
1982	5,758,586	1,801,969	247,080	174,508	2,223,557	7,982,143	27.9	22.6	139,767
1983	6,795,295	1,915,621	279,748	191,403	2,386,772	9,182,067	26.0	20.9	136,798
1984	7,951,523	1,906,206	344,416	188,220	2,438,842	10,390,365	23.5	18.3	116,965
1985	8,204,542	2,217,837	423,983	195,925	2,837,745	11,042,287	25.7	20.1	206,252
1986	8,214,897	2,382,614	443,721	418,286	3,244,621	11,459,518	28.3	20.8	314,358
1987	7,080,858	2,190,405	347,881	657,415	3,195,701	10,276,559	31.1	21.3	348,154
1988	7,526,038	2,022,602	280,099	700,991	3,003,692	10,529,730	28.5	19.2	393,412
1989	7,072,902	1,897,143	248,561	553,660	2,699,364	9,772,266	27.6	19.4	340,425
1990	6,896,888	1,719,839	266,775	417,802	2,404,416	9,301,304	25.8	18.5	296,778
1991	6,136,787	1,500,309	192,778	344,814	2,037,899	8,174,686	24.9	18.4	254,572

Top 10 Selling Passenger Cars in the U.S. By Calendar Year, 1989-1991 (Domestic and Import)

Source: Motor Vehicle Manufacturers Assn.

1991

1.	Honda Accord	399,297
2.	Ford Taurus	299,659
3.	Toyota Camry	263,818
4.	Chevrolet Cavalier	259,385
5.	Ford Escort	247,864
6.	Chevrolet Corsica/Beretta	231,227
7.	Chevrolet Lumina	217,555
8.	Honda Civic	205,715
9.	Toyota Corolla	199,083
10.	Ford Tempo	189,457

1990

1.	Honda Accord	417,179
2.	Ford Taurus	313,274
3.	Chevrolet Cavalier	295,123
4.	Ford Escort	288,727
5.	Toyota Camry	284,595
6.	Chevrolet Corsica/Beretta	277,176
7.	Toyota Corolla	228,211
8.	Honda Civic	220,852
9.	Chevrolet Lumina	218,288
10.	Ford Tempo	215,290

1989

1.	Honda Accord	362,707
2.	Ford Taurus	348,081
3.	Ford Escort	333,535
4.	Chevrolet Corsica/Beretta	328,006
5.	Chevrolet Cavalier	295,715
6.	Toyota Camry	257,466
7.	Ford Tempo	228,426
8.	Nissan Sentra	221,292
9.	Pontiac Grand Am	202,185
10.	Toyota Corolla	199,975

Licensed Drivers, by Age

Source: Federal Highway Administration, U.S. Dept. of Transportation

Age	1990 Male	1990 Female	1990 Total	1990 Percent male	Estimated 1991 Male (1,000)	Estimated 1991 Female (1,000)	Estimated 1991 Total (1,000)	Percent change total drivers 1980-1990
Under 16	23,351	19,853	43,204	54.05	24	20	44	−53.54
16	768,602	673,955	1,442,557	53.28	778	684	1,462	−20.87
17	1,135,673	996,499	2,132,171	53.26	1,149	1,011	2,160	−23.58
18	1,377,523	1,217,402	2,594,926	53.09	1,394	1,235	2,629	−20.08
19	1,607,564	1,428,625	3,036,188	52.95	1,626	1,449	3,075	−14.28
(19 and under)	4,912,712	4,336,334	9,249,046	53.12	4,971	4,399	9,370	−19.55
20	1,690,511	1,538,307	3,228,818	52.36	1,710	1,560	3,270	−11.20
21	1,694,002	1,555,250	3,249,253	52.14	1,714	1,578	3,292	−12.96
22	1,701,410	1,561,245	3,262,654	52.15	1,721	1,584	3,305	−14.39
23	1,766,508	1,631,178	3,397,686	51.99	1,787	1,655	3,442	−13.72
24	1,951,212	1,807,015	3,758,227	51.92	1,974	1,833	3,807	−4.00
(20-24)	8,803,643	8,092,995	16,896,638	52.10	8,906	8,210	17,116	−11.22
25-29	10,238,989	9,656,202	19,895,190	51.46	10,357	9,794	20,151	5.13
30-34	10,506,510	10,071,064	20,577,574	51.06	10,629	10,216	20,845	18.47
35-39	9,683,644	9,371,273	19,054,916	50.82	9,796	9,506	19,302	39.13
40-44	8,609,620	8,294,564	16,904,185	50.93	8,710	8,414	17,124	51.82
45-49	6,642,056	6,378,114	13,020,170	51.01	6,719	6,470	13,189	29.22
50-54	5,376,194	5,107,829	10,484,023	51.28	5,439	5,181	10,620	3.91
55-59	4,855,447	4,582,612	9,438,059	51.45	4,912	4,649	9,561	−3.40
60-64	4,738,465	4,497,035	9,235,500	51.31	4,794	4,562	9,356	12.19
65-69	4,266,307	4,108,841	8,375,148	50.94	4,316	4,168	8,484	27.28
70 and over	7,158,862	6,725,937	13,884,800	51.56	7,242	6,823	14,065	56.11
Total	85,792,450	81,222,800	167,015,250	51.37	86,791	82,392	169,183	14.95

Countries with Safety Belt Use Laws

Source: Motor Vehicle Manufacturers Assn.

Country	Effective Date
Australia	1/72
Austria	7/76
Belgium	6/75
Brazil	6/72
Bulgaria	1976
Canadian Provinces	
Alberta	7/87
British Columbia	10/77
Manitoba	4/84
Newfoundland	7/82
New Brunswick	11/83
Nova Scotia	1/85
Ontario	1/76
Prince Edward Island	1/88
Quebec	7/76
Saskatchewan	7/77
Czechoslovakia	1/69
Denmark	1/76
Finland	7/75
France	10/79
Greece	12/79
Hong Kong	10/83
Hungary	7/77
Iceland	10/81
Ireland	2/79
Israel	7/75
Ivory Coast	1970
Japan	12/71
Jordan	12/83
Luxembourg	6/75
Malaysia	4/79
Netherlands	6/75
New Zealand	6/72
Norway	9/75
Poland	1/84
Portugal	1/78
Singapore	7/81
South Africa	12/77
Spain	10/74
Sweden	1/75
Switzerland	1/76
Turkey	10/84

Tips for Fuel-Efficient Driving

Source: U.S. Environmental Protection Agency

When Buying a New Vehicle

- **Buy the type of vehicle that best suits your needs.** Check the federal *Gas Mileage Guide*, available free at all auto dealerships, to compare the fuel economy of similar models. In general, *larger displacement engines and higher horsepower ratings will result in lower fuel economy.* The additional power and torque may be useful for mountain driving or trailer towing situations, but your fuel economy will suffer during almost all types of driving. *Avoid unnecessary optional equipment* (especially heavy options such as four-wheel drive and options such as air conditioning that tax the engine). Extra equipment adds weight and decreases the fuel economy of the vehicle. Beware of "sport" packages, which often include fuel-guzzling features such as energy robbing tires that are not reflected by *Guide* mileage values.

Conserving Fuel with your Current Vehicle:

- **Drive your vehicle wisely.** *Avoid idles* of more than one minute (turn off your engine in traffic jams, limit vehicle warm-ups in winter, park and go in instead of using drive-up lanes at restaurants and banks). *Go easy on the brakes and gas pedal* (anticipate stops and avoid "jack-rabbit" starts). Pay attention to speed. *You can improve your fuel economy about 15 percent by driving 55 mph rather than 65 mph.* Put your vehicle's transmission into overdrive or a "fuel economy" position when cruising on the highway. If you have manual transmission, follow recommended shift guidelines or heed your shift indicator light. *Do not carry unneeded items* that add weight. Reduce drag by placing items inside the vehicle or trunk rather than on roof racks. *Use air conditioning only when necessary.*
- **Maintain your vehicle regularly.** *Periodic tune-ups improve vehicle fuel economy and performance.* Dragging brakes, low transmission fluid levels, out of tune engines, and old plugged fuel or air filters all hurt fuel economy.

(*continued*)

Inflate tires to maximum recommended pressure and perform periodic *wheel alignments. Use energy conserving oils* which increase fuel economy by reducing internal engine friction (the best are labeled "Energy Conserving II").

- **Keep track of your vehicle's fuel economy.** A marked increase in the amount of fuel you use could indicate the need for a tune-up, or serve as an early signal for necessary repairs.
- **Use your vehicle effectively.** *Use your vehicle only when necessary.* Combine errands into one trip. If you have access to more than one vehicle, drive the one that's most fuel efficient whenever possible. Consider carpooling, bicycling, walking, or public transportation.

Transportation Energy Consumption

Source: *Monthly Energy Review*, March 1992; Energy Information Administration, U.S. Dept. of Energy

(quadrillion Btu)

	Coal	Natural Gas[1]	Petroleum	Primary Consumption	Electricity	Net Consumption	Electrical System Energy Losses	Total Consumption[2]
Total								
1973	0.003	0.743	17.831	18.576	0.008	18.584	0.020	18.605
1974	.002	.685	17.399	18.086	.009	18.095	.022	18.117
1975	.001	.595	17.614	18.209	.010	18.219	.025	18.244
1976	—	.559	18.506	19.065	.010	19.076	.025	19.101
1977	—	.543	19.241	19.784	.010	19.794	.025	19.819
1978	(3)	.539	20.041	20.580	.009	20.589	.022	20.611
1979	(3)	.612	19.825	20.436	.010	20.447	.025	20.472
1980	(3)	.650	19.008	19.658	.011	19.669	.026	19.695
1981	(3)	.658	18.811	19.469	.011	19.480	.026	19.507
1982	(3)	.612	18.420	19.032	.011	19.043	.026	19.069
1983	(3)	.505	18.593	19.098	.011	19.109	.026	19.135
1984	(3)	.545	19.216	19.761	.012	19.773	.028	19.801
1985	(3)	.519	19.504	20.024	.013	20.036	.030	20.067
1986	(3)	.499	20.269	20.768	.013	20.781	.030	20.812
1987	(3)	.535	20.867	21.402	.013	21.415	.029	21.444
1988	(3)	.632	21.624	22.255	.014	22.269	.031	22.300
1989	(3)	.648	21.861	22.510	.014	22.524	.031	22.554
1990	(3)	.680	21.804	22.483	.014	22.497	.031	22.528
1991	(3)	.826	21.414	22.240	.015	22.254	.032	22.286

(1) Pipeline fuel only, including supplemental gaseous fuels. (2) Excludes wood, waste, geothermal, wind, photovoltaic, and solar thermal energy, except for small amounts used by electric utilities to generate electricity for distribution. (3) Since 1978, the small amounts of coal consumed for transportation are reported as industrial sector consumption. R=Revised data. (—) Less than 0.5 trillion Btu. **Notes.** • Geographic coverage is the 50 States and the District of Columbia. • Totals may not equal sum of components due to independent rounding.

Personal Consumption Expenditures for Transportation

Source: Motor Vehicle Manufacturers Association; Bureau of Economic Analysis, U.S. Dept. of Commerce

(in millions of dollars)

	1980	1982	1984	1986	1988	1989	1990	1991
User-Operated Transportation								
New Autos	$46,395	$53,336	$77,560	$100,328	$101,041	$99,984	$96,601	$79,161
Net Purchases of Used Autos	10,848	13,551	21,152	25,356	30,532	32,491	35,816	36,120
Other Motor Vehicles[1]	11,489	15,605	28,589	40,818	45,577	51,703	48,876	45,668
Tires, Tubes and Accessories and Parts	14,889	15,230	17,302	18,353	20,685	21,417	22,383	23,081
Repair, Greasing, Washing, Parking, Storage and Rental	33,662	37,903	49,723	60,695	73,531	81,412	88,630	93,624
Gasoline and Oil	86,689	94,125	94,532	79,699	86,899	95,487	106,803	102,859
Bridge, Tunnel, Ferry and Road Tolls	1,104	1,306	1,387	1,794	1,774	2,059	2,178	2,248
Insurance Premiums, Less Claims Paid	9,443	9,150	10,099	12,724	16,842	16,823	18,045	21,802
Total User-Operated Transportation	**$214,879**	**$240,205**	**$300,344**	**$339,767**	**$376,881**	**$401,376**	**$419,332**	**$404,563**
Purchased Local Transportation								
Transit Systems	$2,927	$3,839	$4,244	$4,913	$5,377	$5,343	$5,723	$5,641
Taxicabs	1,866	1,513	2,498	2.998	2,935	2,841	3,017	3,338
Total Purchased Local Transportation	**$4,793**	**$5,352**	**$6,742**	**$7,911**	**$8,312**	**$8,184**	**$8,740**	**$8,979**
Purchased Intercity Transportation								
Railway Excluding Commutation	$300	$317	$415	$472	$500	$671	$708	$722
Bus	1,403	1,665	1,632	1,469	2,181	1,759	1,467	1,729
Airline	13,454	14,708	17,721	18,993	22,993	24,708	25,222	23,954
Other	910	1,173	1,380	1,737	2,229	2,387	2,644	2,793
Total Purchased Intercity Transportation	**$15,057**	**$17,861**	**$21,128**	**$22,671**	**$27,991**	**$29,525**	**$30,041**	**$29,198**
Total Transportation	**$235,739**	**$263,416**	**$326,214**	**$370,349**	**$413,184**	**$439,005**	**$458,113**	**$442,740**
Total Personal Consumption Expenditures	**$1,748,077**	**$2,059,179**	**$2,460,288**	**$2,850,553**	**$3,296,126**	**$3,617,802**	**$3,742,801**	**$3,683,763**

(1) New and used trucks, recreation vehicles, etc.

Road Mileage Between Selected U.S. Cities

	Atlanta	Boston	Chicago	Cincinnati	Cleveland	Dallas	Denver	Des Moines	Detroit	Houston
Atlanta, Ga.	...	1,037	674	440	672	795	1,398	870	699	789
Boston, Mass.	1,037	...	963	840	628	1,748	1,949	1,280	695	1,804
Chicago, Ill.	674	963	...	287	335	917	996	327	266	1,067
Cincinnati, Oh.	440	840	287	...	244	920	1,164	571	259	1,029
Cleveland, Oh.	672	628	335	244	...	1,159	1,321	652	170	1,273
Dallas Tex.	795	1,748	917	920	1,159	...	781	684	1,143	243
Denver, Col.	1,398	1,949	996	1,164	1,321	781	...	669	1,253	1,019
Detroit, Mich.	699	695	266	259	170	1,143	1,253	584	...	1,265
Houston, Tex.	789	1,804	1,067	1,029	1,273	243	1,019	905	1,265	...
Indianapolis, Ind.	493	906	181	106	294	865	1,058	465	278	987
Kansas City, Mo.	798	1,391	499	591	779	489	600	195	743	710
Los Angeles, Cal.	2,182	2,979	2,054	2,179	2,367	1,387	1,059	1,727	2,311	1,538
Memphis, Tenn.	371	1,296	530	468	712	452	1,040	599	713	561
Milwaukee, Wis.	761	1,050	87	374	422	991	1,029	361	353	1,142
Minneapolis, Minn.	1,068	1,368	405	692	740	936	841	252	671	1,157
New Orleans, La.	479	1,507	912	786	1,030	496	1,273	978	1,045	356
New York, N.Y.	841	206	802	647	473	1,552	1,771	1,119	637	1,608
Omaha, Neb.	986	1,412	459	693	784	644	537	132	716	865
Philadelphia, Pa.	741	296	738	567	413	1,452	1,691	1,051	573	1,508
Pittsburgh, Pa.	687	561	452	287	129	1,204	1,411	763	287	1,313
Portland Ore.	2,601	3,046	2,083	2,333	2,418	2,009	1,238	1,786	2,349	2,205
St. Louis, Mo.	541	1,141	289	340	529	630	857	333	513	779
San Francisco	2,496	3,095	2,142	2,362	2,467	1,753	1,235	1,815	2,399	1,912
Seattle, Wash.	2,618	2,976	2,013	2,300	2,348	2,078	1,307	1,749	2,279	2,274
Tulsa, Okla.	772	1,537	683	736	925	257	681	443	909	478
Washington, D.C.	608	429	671	481	346	1,319	1,616	984	506	1,375

	Indianapolis	Kansas City	Los Angeles	Louisville	Memphis	Milwaukee	Minneapolis	New Orleans	New York	Omaha
Atlanta, Ga.	493	798	2,182	382	371	761	1,068	479	841	986
Boston, Mass.	906	1,391	2,979	941	1,296	1,050	1,368	1,507	206	1,412
Chicago, Ill.	181	499	2,054	292	530	87	405	912	802	459
Cincinnati, Oh.	106	591	2,179	101	468	374	692	786	647	693
Cleveland Oh.	294	779	2,367	345	712	422	740	1,030	473	784
Dallas, Tex.	865	489	1,387	819	452	991	936	496	1,552	644
Denver, Col.	1,058	600	1,059	1,120	1,040	1,029	841	1,273	1,771	537
Detroit, Mich.	278	743	2,311	360	713	353	671	1,045	637	716
Houston, Tex.	987	710	1,538	928	561	1,142	1,157	356	1,608	865
Indianapolis, Ind.	...	485	2,073	111	435	268	586	796	713	587
Kansas City, Mo.	485	...	1,589	520	451	537	447	806	1,198	201
Los Angeles, Cal.	2,073	1,589	...	2,108	1,817	2,087	1,889	1,883	2,786	1,595
Memphis, Tenn.	435	451	1,817	367	...	612	826	390	1,100	652
Milwaukee, Wis.	268	537	2,087	379	612	...	332	994	889	493
Minneapolis, Minn.	586	447	1,889	697	826	332	...	1,214	1,207	357
New Orleans, La.	796	806	1,883	685	390	994	1,214	...	1,311	1,007
New York, N.Y.	713	1,198	2,786	748	1,100	889	1,207	1,311	...	1,251
Omaha, Neb.	587	201	1,595	687	652	493	357	1,007	1,251	...
Philadelphia, Pa.	633	1,118	2,706	668	1,000	825	1,143	1,211	100	1,183
Pittsburgh, Pa.	353	838	2,426	388	752	539	857	1,070	368	895
Portland, Ore.	1,227	1,809	959	2,320	2,259	2,010	1,678	2,505	2,885	1,654
St. Louis, Mo.	235	257	1,845	263	285	363	552	673	948	449
San Francisco	2,256	1,835	379	2,349	2,125	2,175	1,940	2,249	2,934	1,683
Seattle, Wash.	2,194	1,839	1,131	2,305	2,290	1,940	1,608	2,574	2,815	1,638
Tulsa, Okla.	631	248	1,452	659	401	757	695	647	1,344	387
Washington, D.C.	558	1,043	2,631	582	867	758	1,076	1,078	233	1,116

	Philadelphia	Pittsburgh	Portland	St. Louis	Salt Lake City	San Francisco	Seattle	Toledo	Tulsa	Washington
Atlanta, Ga.	741	687	2,601	541	1,878	2,496	2,618	640	772	608
Boston, Mass.	296	561	3,046	1,141	2,343	3,095	2,976	739	1,537	429
Chicago, Ill.	738	452	2,083	289	1,390	2,142	2,013	232	683	671
Cincinnati, Oh.	567	287	2,333	340	1,610	2,362	2,300	200	736	481
Cleveland Oh.	413	129	2,418	529	1,715	2,467	2,348	111	925	346
Dallas, Tex.	1,452	1,204	2,009	630	1,242	1,753	2,078	1,084	257	1,319
Denver, Col.	1,691	1,411	1,238	857	504	1,235	1,307	1,218	681	1,616
Detroit, Mich.	576	287	2,349	513	1,647	2,399	2,279	59	909	506
Houston, Tex.	1,508	1,313	2,205	779	1,438	1,912	2,274	1,206	478	1,375
Indianapolis, Ind.	633	353	2,227	235	1,504	2,256	2,194	219	631	558
Kansas City, Mo.	1,118	838	1,809	257	1,086	1,839	687	248	1,043	
Los Angeles, Cal.	2,706	2,426	959	1,845	715	379	1,131	2,276	1,452	2,631
Memphis, Tenn.	1,000	752	2,259	285	1,535	2,125	2,290	654	401	867
Milwaukee, Wis.	825	539	2,010	363	1,423	2,175	1,940	319	757	758
Minneapolis, Minn.	1,143	857	1,678	552	1,186	1,940	1,608	637	695	1,076
New Orleans, La.	1,211	1,070	2,505	673	1,738	2,249	2,574	986	647	1,078
New York, N.Y.	100	368	2,885	948	2,182	2,934	2,815	578	1,344	233
Omaha, Neb.	1,183	895	1,654	449	931	1,683	1,638	681	387	1,116
Philadelphia, Pa.	...	288	2,821	868	2,114	2,866	2,751	514	1,264	133
Pittsburgh, Pa.	288	...	2,535	588	1,826	2,578	2,465	228	984	221
Portland, Ore.	2,821	2,535	...	2,060	767	636	172	2,315	1,913	2,754
St. Louis, Mo.	868	588	2,060	...	1,337	2,089	2,081	454	396	793
San Francisco	2,866	2,578	636	2,089	752	...	808	2,364	1,760	2,799
Seattle, Wash.	2,751	2,465	172	2,081	836	808	...	2,245	1,982	2,684
Tulsa, Okla.	1,264	984	1,913	396	1,172	1,760	1,982	850	...	1,189
Washington, D.C.	133	221	2,754	793	2,047	2,799	2,684	447	1,189	...

Air Distances Between Selected World Cities in Statute Miles

Point-to-point measurements are usually from City Hall.

	Bangkok	Beijing	Berlin	Cairo	Cape Town	Caracas	Chicago	Hong Kong	Hono-lulu	Lima
Bangkok	...	2,046	5,352	4,523	6,300	10,555	8,570	1,077	6,609	12,244
Bejing	2,046	...	4,584	4,698	8,044	8,950	6,604	1,217	5,077	10,349
Berlin	5,352	4,584	...	1,797	5,961	5,238	4,414	5,443	7,320	6,896
Cairo	4,523	4,698	1,797	...	4,480	6,342	6,141	5,066	8,848	7,726
Cape Town	6,300	8,044	5,961	4,480	...	6,366	8,491	7,376	11,535	6,072
Caracas	10,555	8,950	5,238	6,342	6,366	...	2,495	10,165	6,021	1,707
Chicago	8,570	6,604	4,414	6,141	8,491	2,495	...	7,797	4,256	3,775
Hong Kong	1,077	1,217	5,443	5,066	7,376	10,165	7,797	...	5,556	11,418
Honolulu	6,609	5,077	7,320	8,848	11,535	6,021	4,256	5,556	...	5,947
London	5,944	5,074	583	2,185	5,989	4,655	3,958	5,990	7,240	6,316
Los Angeles	7,637	6,250	5,782	7,520	9,969	3,632	1,745	7,240	2,557	4,171
Madrid	6,337	5,745	1,165	2,087	5,308	4,346	4,189	6,558	7,872	5,907
Melbourne	4,568	5,643	9,918	8,675	6,425	9,717	9,673	4,595	5,505	8,059
Mexico City	9,793	7,753	6,056	7,700	8,519	2,234	1,690	8,788	3,789	2,639
Montreal	8,338	6,519	3,740	5,427	7,922	2,438	745	7,736	4,918	3,970
Moscow	4,389	3,607	1,006	1,803	6,279	6,177	4,987	4,437	7,047	7,862
New York	8,669	6,844	3,979	5,619	7,803	2,120	714	8,060	4,969	3,639
Paris	5,877	5,120	548	1,998	5,786	4,732	4,143	5,990	7,449	6,370
Rio de Janeiro	9,994	10,768	6,209	6,143	3,781	2,804	5,282	11,009	8,288	2,342
Rome	5,494	5,063	737	1,326	5,231	5,195	4,824	5,774	8,040	6,750
San Francisco	7,931	5,918	5,672	7,466	10,248	3,902	1,859	6,905	2,398	4,518
Singapore	883	2,771	6,164	5,137	6,008	11,402	9,372	1,605	6,726	11,689
Stockholm	5,089	4,133	528	2,096	6,423	5,471	4,331	5,063	6,875	7,166
Tokyo	2,865	1,307	5,557	5,958	9,154	8,808	6,314	1,791	3,859	9,631
Warsaw	5,033	4,325	322	1,619	5,935	5,559	4,679	5,147	7,366	7,215
Washington, D.C.	8,807	6,942	4,181	5,822	7,895	2,047	596	8,155	4,838	3,509

	London	Los Angeles	Madrid	Mel-bourne	Mexico City	Mon-treal	Mos-cow	New Delhi	New York	Paris
Bangkok	5,944	7,637	6,337	4,568	9,793	8,338	4,389	1,813	8,669	5,877
Bejing	5,074	6,250	5,745	5,643	7,753	6,519	3,607	2,353	6,844	5,120
Berlin	583	5,782	1,165	9,918	6,056	3,740	1,006	3,598	3,979	548
Cairo	2,185	7,520	2,087	8,675	7,700	5,427	1,803	2,758	5,619	1,998
Cape Town	5,989	9,969	5,308	6,425	8,519	7,922	6,279	5,769	7,803	5,786
Caracas	4,655	3,632	4,346	9,717	2,234	2,438	6,177	8,833	2,120	4,732
Chicago	3,958	1,745	4,189	9,673	1,690	745	4,987	7,486	714	4,143
Hong Kong	5,990	7,240	6,558	4,595	8,788	7,736	4,437	2,339	8,060	5,990
Honolulu	7,240	2,557	7,872	5,505	3,789	4,918	7,047	7,412	4,969	7,449
London	...	5,439	785	10,500	5,558	3,254	1,564	4,181	3,469	214
Los Angeles	5,439	...	5,848	7,931	1,542	2,427	6,068	7,011	2,451	5,601
Madrid	785	5,848	...	10,758	5,643	3,448	2,147	4,530	3,593	655
Melbourne	10,500	7,931	10,758	...	8,426	10,395	8,950	6,329	10,359	10,430
Mexico City	5,558	1,542	5,643	8,426	...	2,317	6,676	9,120	2,090	5,725
Montreal	3,254	2,427	3,448	10,395	2,317	...	4,401	7,012	331	3,432
Moscow	1,564	6,068	2,147	8,950	6,676	4,401	...	2,698	4,683	1,554
New York	3,469	2,451	3,593	10,359	2,090	331	4,683	7,318	...	3,636
Paris	214	5,601	655	10,430	5,725	3,432	1,554	4,102	3,636	...
Rio de Janeiro	5,750	6,330	5,045	8,226	4,764	5,078	7,170	8,753	4,801	5,684
Rome	895	6,326	851	9,929	6,377	4,104	1,483	3,684	4,293	690
San Francisco	5,367	347	5,803	7,856	1,887	2,543	5,885	7,691	2,572	5,577
Singapore	6,747	8,767	7,080	3,759	10,327	9,203	5,228	2,571	9,534	6,673
Stockholm	942	5,454	1,653	9,630	6,012	3,714	716	3,414	3,986	1,003
Tokyo	5,959	5,470	6,706	5,062	7,035	6,471	4,660	3,638	6,757	6,053
Warsaw	905	5,922	1,427	9,598	6,337	4,022	721	3,277	4,270	852
Washington, D.C.	3,674	2,300	3,792	10,180	1,885	489	4,876	7,500	205	3,840

	Rio de Janiero	Rome	San Fran-cisco	Singa-pore	Stock-holm	Teheran	Tokyo	Vienna	Warsaw	Wash., D.C.
Bangkok	9,994	5,494	7,931	883	5,089	3,391	2,865	5,252	5,033	8,807
Bejing	10,768	5,063	5,918	2,771	4,133	3,490	1,307	4,648	4,325	6,942
Berlin	6,209	737	5,672	6,164	528	2,185	5,557	326	322	4,181
Cairo	6,143	1,326	7,466	5,137	2,096	1,234	5,958	1,481	1,619	5,822
Cape Town	3,781	5,231	10,248	6,008	6,423	5,241	9,154	5,656	5,935	7,895
Caracas	2,804	5,195	3,902	11,402	5,471	7,320	8,808	5,372	5,559	2,047
Chicago	5,282	4,824	1,859	9,372	4,331	6,502	6,314	4,698	4,679	596
Hong Kong	11,009	5,774	6,905	1,605	5,063	3,843	1,791	5,431	5,147	8,155
Honolulu	8,288	8,040	2,398	6,726	6,875	8,070	3,859	7,632	7,366	4,838
London	5,750	895	5,367	6,747	942	2,743	5,959	771	905	3,674
Los Angeles	6,330	6,326	347	8,767	5,454	7,682	5,470	6,108	5,922	2,300
Madrid	5,045	851	5,803	7,080	1,653	2,978	6,706	1,128	1,427	3,792
Melbourne	8,226	9,929	7,856	3,759	9,630	7,826	5,062	9,790	9,598	10,180
Mexico City	4,764	6,377	1,887	10,327	6,012	8,184	7,035	6,320	6,337	1,885
Montreal	5,078	4,104	2,543	9,203	3,714	5,880	6,471	4,009	4,022	489
Moscow	7,170	1,483	5,885	5,228	716	1,532	4,660	1,043	721	4,876
New York	4,801	4,293	2,572	9,534	3,986	6,141	6,757	4,234	4,270	205
Paris	5,684	690	5,577	6,673	1,003	2,625	6,053	645	852	3,840
Rio de Janeiro	...	5,707	6,613	9,785	6,683	7,374	11,532	6,127	6,455	4,779
Rome	5,707	...	6,259	6,229	1,245	2,127	6,142	477	820	4,497
San Francisco	6,613	6,259	...	8,448	5,399	7,362	5,150	5,994	5,854	2,441
Singapore	9,785	6,229	8,448	...	5,936	4,103	3,300	6,035	5,843	9,662
Stockholm	6,683	1,245	5,399	5,936	...	2,173	5,053	780	494	4,183
Tokyo	11,532	6,142	5,150	3,300	5,053	4,775	...	5,689	5,347	6,791
Warsaw	6,455	820	5,854	5,843	494	1,879	5,689	347	...	4,472
Washington, D.C.	4,779	4,497	2,441	9,662	4,183	6,341	6,791	4,438	4,472	...

ENVIRONMENT

Environmental Quality Index

Source: Feb.-Mar. 1992 issue of *National Wildlife* magazine

In 1992, *National Wildlife* magazine published the twenty-fourth in its series of annual reports on the environment. According to the report, 1991 was a year of **heightened conflict** over the allocation of America's natural resources, as a recession underlined the industrial and job-related uses of these resources, while news of pollution suggested a need for further conservation.

Wildlife: The northern spotted owl along with its habitat, old-growth forests of the Pacific NW, remained at the center of controversy in 1991. At issue were the conflicting interests of the endangered owl and the timber industry. Federal courts forced the U.S. Fish & Wildlife Service to identify prime owl habitat, in compliance with the Endangered Species Act. Conflict also occurred over possible protection of the delta smelt in California, and of the Snake River salmon, which would jeopardize long-standing water subsidies for agriculture. Such conflicts between conservation and commerce raised the larger issue of the Endangered Species Act itself, and the possibility that its goals or authority might be redefined. Meanwhile, captive-breeding programs improved the prospects for two imperiled species as two California condors and 50 black-footed ferrets were released into the wild.

Air: There was also some compromise between industry and environmentalists in 1991. After decades in court, the owners of a coal-burning power plant in northern Arizona agreed in August to control air pollution in the Grand Canyon by decade's end. That same month, the oil industry agreed to supply cleaner-burning gas to the smoggiest U.S. cities beginning in 1995. Other good news: the amount of toxic chemicals released into the air in the U.S. decreased for the third straight year. On the darker side, however, a study released in April by the Natl. Academy of Sciences concluded that "Despite great uncertainties, greenhouse warming is a potential threat sufficient to justify action now." Other developments included satellite reports indicating that the thinning of the ozone layer was worse, and longer-lasting, than expected, and two studies linking air pollution to health risks.

Water: There was mixed news in 1991 about U.S. coastal waters and bays. The Natl. Oceanic & Atmospheric Admin. (NOAA) reported levels of toxic compounds and trace minerals to be generally stable or decreasing. Scientists found less DDT, chlordane and PCBs, all of which are now banned. The persistence of toxics already in place remained problematic, especially in the Great Lakes. There was also troubling news concerning declines in the nation's freshwater and coastal fish, due to habitat pollution and overfishing. Studies showed a decline in the total U.S. catch from 400 mln. pounds in 1983 to 282 mln. in 1990. Meanwhile, Congress began consideration of rewriting laws on wetlands protection and on runoff pollution from farms and city streets. In Florida, the state agreed to accept responsibility for cleaning up polluted runoff water before it flows into Everglades Natl. Park. Another concern was the quantity of available water, with the NOAA predicting shortages in the 1990s.

Energy: Despite a continued drop in U.S. oil production, gas prices remained low in 1991, largely due to increased production by Saudi Arabia. A World Resources Institute analysis of 1988 data showed per capita energy use in the U.S. to be double that of Europe, and triple that of Japan, where gas is significantly more expensive. The national energy strategy, unveiled by the Administration in Feb., did not directly address this apparent U.S. dependence on cheap fuel, instead placing emphasis on domestic oil and natural gas production. The strategy also proposed easing the regulation of pipeline building and nuclear power plant construction, as well as setting efficiency standards for lighting. In Nov., the Senate rejected an Administration energy bill that included provisions for oil and gas development in the Arctic refuge.

Forests: The U.S. Forest Service celebrated its 100th anniversary in 1991, amid continuing debate concerning the health of U.S. forests. The debate centered on two issues: the number of trees constituting the maximum **sustainable** harvest on public lands, and the quality, or biodiversity, of those lands. In addition to the possibility of overcutting, questions were also raised concerning the commercial viability of public land timber sales. Meanwhile, the northern spotted owl remained the best known example of the argument over biodiversity, but a botanical indicator, the Pacific yew tree, also came into prominence. Once burned as a "weed," the yew is now known to be the chief source of **taxol**, possibly a potent new cancer-treating compound. At mid-year, the Forest Service reached an agreement with Bristol-Myers Squibb to provide enough yews for test programs, while learning at the company's expense how to cultivate and harvest yews.

Soil: A survey released in 1991 by the Soil and Water Conservation Society raised some doubts concerning the apparent early progress of the 1985 federal Farm Bill. The bill links federal farm subsidies with progress in erosion control, grasslands conservation, and wetlands protection, but the survey reported significant compliance problems. Active opposition by many U.S. farmers and developers magnified these problems with regard to the wetlands protection provisions. Under a new definition, announced by the Administration in August, a wetland is "ground on which standing water can be found for 15 consecutive days in any year, or which was saturated to the surface for at least 21 days a year." Meanwhile, on dry land, questions of overgrazing on the nearly 300 mln. acres of publicly owned rangeland heightened tensions between ranchers against environmentalists.

The Earth Summit, 1992

The U.N. Conference on Environment & Development, more widely known as the Earth Summit, was held June 3-14, 1992, in Rio de Janeiro, Brazil. In the largest such gathering ever, 117 heads of state attended the closing round of summit talks, while, in all, delegates from 178 nations reached accords at the conference. The focus was on **sustainable development,** reconciling economic needs with environmental responsibility. The environmental implications of industrialization in developing nations were of central concern. This created a formidable conflict of interests, with developing nations contending that the industrialized nations should help them pay for the costs of environmental regulations. The Earth Summit covered a range of other issues, though, notably, not overpopulation. Delegates reached consensus agreements, in principle, on non-binding accords on sustainable development and forest preservation. Amid criticism, the U.S. did not sign the Biodiversity Convention, claiming economic inequities, but did sign a weakened Global Warming Convention. Largely, the need to find common ground between many nations resulted in the elimination of specific environmental target levels and aid figures.

Hazardous Waste Sites

Source: Environmental Protection Agency, *Natl. Priorities List Fact Book, Feb. 1992*

State/Territory	Final General	Federal	Total*
California	67	20	95
Pennsylvania	90	4	100
Florida	47	4	55
Arkansas	10	0	12
Virginia	19	1	22
Colorado	13	3	17
Indiana	32	0	33
Kansas	9	1	11
Louisiana	10	1	12
Massachusetts	22	3	26
Missouri	19	3	23
North Carolina	21	1	23
Oregon	7	1	9
South Carolina	22	1	24
Utah	7	4	13
Virgin Islands	0	0	1
Wisconsin	39	0	40
Guam	1	0	2
Tennessee	12	2	15
Alabama	10	2	12
Alaska	2	4	6
American Samoa	0	0	0
Arizona	7	3	10
Commonwealth of Marianas	0	0	0
Connecticut	14	1	15
Delaware	19	1	20
District of Columbia	0	0	0
Georgia	11	2	13
Hawaii	0	1	2
Idaho	7	2	9
Illinois	32	4	37
Iowa	19	1	20
Kentucky	17	0	19
Maine	7	2	9
Maryland	8	2	10
Michigan	77	0	77
Minnesota	39	2	41
Mississippi	2	0	2
Montana	8	0	8
Nebraska	5	1	8
Nevada	1	0	1
New Hampshire	15	1	17
New Jersey	102	6	108
New Mexico	8	2	10
New York	79	4	84
North Dakota	2	0	2
Ohio	30	3	33
Oklahoma	9	1	10
Puerto Rico	8	1	9
Rhode Island	9	2	12
South Dakota	2	1	4
Texas	25	3	29
Trust Territories	0	0	0
Vermont	8	0	8
Washington	31	14	49
West Virginia	5	0	5
Wyoming	2	1	3
Total	**1067**	**116**	**1235***

* Includes previously proposed sites

Total Toxic Chemical Releases, 1990

Source: Environmental Protection Agency; Citizen Action and Citizens Fund

In 1990, the nation's manufacturing companies reported releasing a grand total of 4.8 billion pounds of toxic chemicals. The 10 companies that released the most toxic chemicals accounted for 1.1 billion pounds, or 23 percent of all reported toxic chemical releases. These chemicals were released to air, water and land, injected underground, discharged to public sewage treatment plants and sent off-site to treatment, storage and disposal operations.

Total Releases of Toxic Chemicals: Top 10 Manufacturing Companies, 1990

Source: Environmental Protection Agency, Citizens Fund calculations.
(pounds)

Company	Air Releases	Water Releases	Land Releases	Under-ground	Public Sewage	Off-Site Transfers	Total Releases	% of Grand Total Releases
1. E. I. Du Pont De Nemours	44,685,429	1,386,397	653,476	151,074,953	538,181	21,136,642	219,475,078	4.54
2. American Cyanamid Co.	3,985,306	1,134,329	24,962	161,349,715	3,295,927	1,966,361	171,756,600	3.56
3. Monsanto Co.	7,758,881	1,777,576	86,984	86,878,372	34,270,406	6,801,034	137,573,253	2.85
4. Freeport McMoran Inc.	15,415,482	78,013,500	6,794,555	0	0	0	100,223,537	2.07
5. Kennecott Corp.	559,315	5,200	9,126,620	0	0	86,862,050	96,553,185	2.00
6. Renco Group Inc.	95,049,161	0	220	0	0	260	95,049,641	1.97
7. Asarco Inc.	1,915,615	11,321	72,398,274	6,000,060	14,988	2,646,359	82,986,617	1.72
8. 3M Co.	62,054,298	3,976,617	29,233	20	815,060	5,885,726	72,760,954	1.51
9. General Motors	41,989,117	113,572	10,827,522	10	3,484,067	14,661,255	71,075,543	1.47
10. BP	5,805,443	376,842	14,198	53,070,902	44,014	414,362	59,725,761	1.24

Total Releases of Toxic Chemicals: Top 10 Manufacturing Facilities, 1990

Source: Environmental Protection Agency, Citizens Fund calculations.
(pounds)

Facility	City	State	Total Releases
1. American Cyanamid Co. Fortier Plant	Westwego	LA	162,040,814
2. Kennecott Utah Copper	Bingham Canyon	UT	96,553,185
3. Magnesium Corp. Of America	Tooele	UT	95,049,611
4. Monsanto Co.	Alvin	TX	64,823,729
5. Vulcan Chemicals	Wichita	KS	59,195,030
6. Freeport McMoran/Agrico Chemical Co. Div.	Saint James	LA	56,538,815
7. Inland Steel Co.	East Chicago	IN	52,982,076
8. Du Pont Johnsonville Plant	New Johnsonville	TN	50,003,965
9. Courtaulds North America Inc.	Lemoyne	AL	45,971,234
10. Asarco Inc. E. Helena Plant	East Helena	MT	40,304,583

Total Releases of Toxic Chemicals By Manufacturing Industry, 1990

Source: Environmental Protection Agency, Citizens Fund calculations. (pounds)

Industry	Air Releases	Water Releases	Land Releases	Under-ground	Public Sewage	Off-Site Transfers	Total Releases
Food	25,181,182	3,836,018	8,249,810	35,308	41,653,992	4,681,783	83,638,093
Tobacco	2,445,939	22,892	1,500	0	8,841	36,881	2,516,053
Textiles	26,116,480	538,526	35,857	35	8,493,765	2,644,962	37,829,625
Apparel	1,107,185	47,992	770	0	147,989	146,409	1,450,345
Lumber	33,926,967	94,265	125,561	75	102,679	6,761,567	41,011,114
Furniture	58,307,140	1,890	76,226	40	303,805	4,092,757	62,781,858
Paper	186,080,400	35,769,305	7,199,262	60	51,662,928	15,489,726	296,201,681
Printing	49,691,542	993	4,674	35	290,663	4,166,955	54,154,862
Chemicals	668,599,119	132,097,533	82,944,632	658,422,678	264,887,189	240,244,461	2,047,194,572
Petroleum	51,309,937	3,222,867	2,331,757	16,309,280	6,938,724	7,085,540	87,198,105
Plastics	171,231,387	446,448	197,024	14,274	4,545,702	19,004,409	195,439,244
Leather	11,376,028	388,353	20,603	0	8,407,074	2,440,868	22,632,926
Stone/Clay	19,433,483	169,309	1,467,201	7,555,070	972,955	9,764,217	39,362,235
Primary Metals	206,678,273	9,243,900	269,560,231	16,494,058	7,810,400	280,193,593	789,980,455
Fabricated Metals	117,886,413	344,798	958,329	770	5,786,173	60,520,209	185,496,692
Machinery	47,252,538	201,431	124,606	518	2,504,602	12,483,336	62,567,031
Electrical	75,681,780	413,429	2,735,053	18,673	11,674,909	33,097,093	123,620,937
Transportation	172,157,405	221,501	1,874,109	320	8,856,716	34,517,122	217,627,173
Instruments	27,406,914	58,190	5,321	20	1,738,917	9,070,543	38,279,905
Misc. Manufacturing	22,994,654	17,038	3,424	90	635,478	6,256,794	29,907,478
Mixed Industry	217,620,289	10,043,050	62,846,302	26,355,817	19,819,292	60,781,879	397,466,629

Gestation, Longevity, and Incubation of Animals

Longevity figures were supplied by Ronald T. Reuther. They refer to animals in captivity; the potential life span of animals is rarely attained in nature. Maximum longevity figures are from the Biology Data Book, 1972. Figures on gestation and incubation are averages based on estimates by leading authorities.

Animal	Gestation (day)	Average longevity (years)	Maximum longevity (yrs., mos.)
Ass	365	12	35-10
Baboon	187	20	35-7
Bear: Black	219	18	36-10
Grizzly	225	25	—
Polar	240	20	34-8
Beaver	122	5	20-6
Buffalo (American)	278	15	—
Bactrian camel	406	12	29-5
Cat (domestic)	63	12	28
Chimpanzee	231	20	44-6
Chipmunk	31	6	8
Cow	284	15	30
Deer (white-tailed)	201	8	17-6
Dog (domestic)	61	12	20
Elephant (African)	—	35	60
Elephant (Asian)	645	40	70
Elk	250	15	26-6
Fox (red)	52	7	14
Giraffe	425	10	33-7
Goat (domestic)	151	8	18
Gorilla	257	20	39-4
Guinea pig	68	4	7-6
Hippopotamus	238	25	—
Horse	330	20	46
Kangaroo	42	7	—

Animal	Gestation (day)	Average longevity (years)	Maximum longevity (yrs., mos.)
Leopard	98	12	19-4
Lion	100	15	25-1
Monkey (rhesus)	164	15	—
Moose	240	12	—
Mouse (meadow)	21	3	—
Mouse (dom. white)	19	3	3-6
Opossum (American)	14-17	1	—
Pig (domestic)	112	10	27
Puma	90	12	19
Rabbit (domestic)	31	5	13
Rhinoceros (black)	450	15	—
Rhinoceros (white)	—	20	—
Sea lion (California)	350	12	28
Sheep (domestic)	154	12	20
Squirrel (gray)	44	10	—
Tiger	105	16	26-3
Wolf (maned)	63	5	—
Zebra (Grant's)	365	15	—

Incubation time (days)

Chicken	21
Duck	30
Goose	30
Pigeon	18
Turkey	26

Speeds of Animals

Source: Natural History magazine, March 1974. Copyright © The American Museum of Natural History, 1974.

Animal	Mph	Animal	Mph	Animal	Mph
Cheetah	70	Mongolian wild ass	40	Human	27.89
Pronghorn antelope	61	Greyhound	39.35	Elephant	25
Wildebeest	50	Whippet	35.50	Black mamba snake	20
Lion	50	Rabbit (domestic)	35	Six-lined race runner	18
Thomson's gazelle	50	Mule deer	35	Wild turkey	15
Quarterhorse	47.5	Jackal	35	Squirrel	12
Elk	45	Reindeer	32	Pig (domestic)	11
Cape hunting dog	45	Giraffe	32	Chicken	9
Coyote	43	White-tailed deer	30	Spider (Tegenaria atrica)	1.17
Gray fox	42	Wart hog	30	Giant tortoise	0.17
Hyena	40	Grizzly bear	30	Three-toed sloth	0.15
Zebra	40	Cat (domestic)	30	Garden snail	0.03

Most of these measurements are for maximum speeds over approximate quarter-mile distances. Exceptions are the lion and elephant, whose speeds were clocked in the act of charging; the whippet, which was timed over a 200-yard course; the cheetah over a 100-yard distance; man for a 15-yard segment of a 100-yard run (of 13.6 seconds); and the black mamba, six-lined race runner, spider, giant tortoise, three-toed sloth, and garden snail, which were measured over various small distances.

Some Endangered Species

Source: Fish and Wildlife Service, U.S. Dept. of Interior; as of July 30, 1992

Common name	Scientific name	Range
Mammals		
Asian wild ass	Equus hemianus	Southwestern & Central Asia
Point Arena mountain beaver	Aplodontia rufa nigra	U.S. (Cal.)
Bobcat	Felis rufus escuinapae	Central Mexico
Ozark big-eared bat	Plecotus townsendii ingens	U.S. (Mo., Okla., Ariz.)
Brown or grizzly bear	Ursus arctos horribilis	U.S. (48 conterminous states)
Cheetah	Acinonyx jubatus	Africa to India
Eastern cougar	Felis concolor cougar	Eastern N.A.
Columbian white-tailed deer	Odocoilcus virginianus leucurus	U.S. (Wash., Ore.)
Chinese river dolphin	Lipotes vexillifer	China
Asian elephant	Elephas maximus	Southcentral, Southeast Asia
San Joaquin kit fox	Vulpes macrotis mutica	U.S. (Cal.)
Gorilla	Gorilla gorilla	Central & W. Africa
Leopard	Panthera pardus	Africa, Asia
Asiatic lion	Panthera leo persica	Turkey to India
Howler monkey	Alouatta pigra	Mexico to S. America
Southeastern beach mouse	Peromyscus polionotus phasma	U.S. (Fla.)
Ocelot	Felis pardalis	U.S. (Tex., Ariz.)
Southern sea otter	Enhydra lutris hereis	U.S. (Wash., Ore., Cal.)
Giant panda	Ailuropoda melanoleuca	China
Florida panther	Felis concolor coryi	U.S. (La., Ark. east to S.C., Fla.)
Utah prairie dog	Cynomys parvidens	U.S. (Ut.)
Morro Bay kangaroo rat	Dipodomys heermanni morroensis	U.S. (Cal.)
Black rhinoceros	Diceros bicornis	Sub-Saharan Africa
Carolina northern flying squirrel	Glaucomys sabrinus coloratus	U.S. (N.C., Tenn.)
Tiger	Panthera tigris	Asia
Hualapai Mexican vole	Microtus mexicanus hualpaiensis	U.S. (Ariz.)
Gray whale	Eschrichtius robustus	N. Pacific Ocean
Wild yak	Bos grunniens	China (Tibet), India
Mountain zebra	Equus zebra zebra	South Africa
Red wolf	Canis rufus	U.S. (Southeast to central Tex.)
Birds		
Masked bobwhite (quail)	Colinus virginianus ridgwayi	U.S. (Ariz.)
California condor	Gymnogyps californianus	U.S. (Ore., Cal.)
Hooded crane	Grus monacha	Japan, USSR
White-necked crow	Corvus leucognaphalus	U.S. (P.R.), Dominican Rep., Haiti
Eskimo curlew	Numenius borealis	Alaska and N. Canada
Bald eagle	Haliaeetus leucocephalus	U.S. (most states), Canada
American peregrine falcon	Falco peregrinus anatum	Canada to Mexico
Hawaiian hawk	Buteo solitarius	U.S. (Hi.)
Indigo macaw	Anodorhynchus leari	Brazil
West African ostrich	Struthio camelus spatzi	Spanish Sahara
Golden parakeet	Aratinga guarouba	Brazil
Australian parrot	Geopsittacus occidentalis	Australia
Attwater's greater prairie-chicken	Tympanuchus cupido attwateri	U.S. (Tex.)
Bachman's warbler (wood)	Vermivora bachmanii	U.S. (Southeast), Cuba
Kirtland's warbler (wood)	Dendroica kirtlandii	U.S., Canada, Bahama Is.
Ivory-billed woodpecker	Campephilus principalis	U.S. (Southcentral and Southeast), Cuba
Reptiles		
American alligator	Alligator mississippiensis	U.S (Southeastern)
American crocodile	Crocodylus acutus	U.S. (Fla.)
Atlantic salt marsh snake	Nerodia fasciatia taeniata	U.S. (Fla.)
Plymouth red-bellied turtle	Pseudemys rubiventris bangsi	U.S. (Mass.)
Fishes		
Yaqui catfish	Ictalupus pricei	U.S. (Ariz.)
Bonytail chub	Gila elegans	U.S. (Ariz., Cal., Col., Nev., Ut., Wyo.)
Gila trout	Salmo gilae	U.S. (Ariz., N.M.)
Plants		
Florida golden aster	Chrysopsis floridana	U.S. (Fla.)
Maguire daisy	Erigeron maguireivar masguirei	U.S. (Ut.)
Short's Goldenrod	Solidago shortii	U.S. (Ky.)
Bakersfield cactus	Opuntia treleasei	U.S. (Cal.)
Mountain golden heather	Hudsonia montana	U.S. (N.C.)
Santa Cruz cypress	Cypressus abramsiana	U.S. (Cal.)
Chapman rhododendron	Rhododendron chapmanii	U.S. (Fla.)
Wheeler's peperomia	Peperomia wheeleri	U.S. (P.R.)
Texas wild-rice	Zizania texana	U.S. (Tex.)
Autumn buttercup	Ranunculus acriformis	U.S. (Ut.)
Cooley's meadowrue	Thalictrum cooleyi	U.S. (N.C., Fla.)
Tennessee yellow-eyed grass	Xyris tennesseensis	U.S. (Ala., Ga., Tenn.)

Major Venomous Animals

Snakes

Coral snake - 2 to 4 ft. long, in Americas south of Canada; bite is nearly painless; very slow onset of paralysis, difficulty breathing; mortality high without antivenin.

Rattlesnake - 2 to 8 ft. long, throughout W. Hemisphere. Rapid onset of symptoms of severe pain, swelling; mortality low, but amputation of affected limb is sometimes necessary; antivenin. Probably higher mortality rate for Mojave rattler.

Cottonmouth water moccasin - up to 5 ft. long, wetlands of southern U.S. from Virginia to Texas. Rapid onset of symptoms of severe pain, swelling; mortality low, but tissue destruction can be extensive; antivenin.

Copperhead - less than 4 ft. long, from New England to Texas; pain and swelling; very seldom fatal; antivenin seldom needed.

Bushmaster - up to 12 ft. long, wet tropical forests of C. and S. America; few bites occur, but mortality rate is high.

Barba Amarilla or **Fer-de-lance** - up to 7 ft. long, from tropical Mexico to Brazil; severe tissue damage common; moderate mortality; antivenin.

Asian pit vipers - from 2 to 5 ft. long throughout Asia; reactions and mortality vary but most bites cause tissue damage and mortality is generally low.

Sharp-nosed pit viper or **One Hundred Pace Snake** - up to 5 ft. long, in southern Vietnam and Taiwan, China; the most toxic of Asian pit vipers; very rapid onset of swelling and tissue damage, internal bleeding; moderate mortality; antivenin.

Boomslang - under 6 ft. long, in African savannahs; rapid onset of nausea and dizziness, often followed by slight recovery and then sudden death from internal hemorrhaging; bites rare, mortality high; antivenin.

European vipers - from 1 to 3 ft. long; bleeding and tissue damage; mortality low; antivenins.

Puff adder - up to 5 ft. long, fat; south of the Sahara and throughout the Middle East; rapid large swelling, great pain, dizziness; moderate mortality often from internal bleeding; antivenin.

Gaboon viper - over 6 ft. long, fat; 2-inch fangs; south of the Sahara; massive tissue damage, internal bleeding; few recorded bites.

Saw-scaled or carpet viper - up to 2 ft. long, in dry areas from India to Africa; severe bleeding, fever; high mortality, causes more human fatalities than any other snake; antivenin.

Desert horned viper - in dry areas of Africa and western Asia; swelling and tissue damage; low mortality; antivenin.

Russell's viper or tic-palonga - over 5 ft. long, throughout Asia; internal bleeding; moderate mortality rate; bite reports common; antivenin.

Black mamba - up to 14 ft. long, fast-moving; S. and C. Africa; rapid onset of dizziness, difficulty breathing, erratic heart-beat; mortality high, nears 100% without antivenin.

Kraits - in S. Asia; rapid onset of sleepiness; numbness; up to 50% mortality even with antivenin treatment.

Common or Asian cobra - 4 to 8 ft. long, throughout S. Asia; considerable tissue damage, sometimes paralysis; mortality probably not more than 10%; antivenin.

King cobra - up to 16 ft. long, throughout S. Asia; rapid swelling, dizziness, loss of consciousness, difficulty breathing, erratic heart-beat; mortality varies sharply with amount of venom involved, most bites involve non-fatal amounts; antivenin.

Yellow or Cape cobra - 7 ft. long, in southern Africa; most toxic venom of any cobra; rapid onset of swelling, breathing and cardiac difficulties; mortality high without treatment; antivenin.

Ringhals, or spitting, cobra - 5 ft. and 7 ft. long; southern Africa; squirt venom through holes in front of fangs as a defense; venom is severely irritating and can cause blindness.

Australian brown snakes - very slow onset of symptoms of cardiac or respiratory distress; moderate mortality; antivenin.

Tiger snake - 2 to 6 ft. long, S. Australia; pain, numbness, mental disturbances with rapid onset of paralysis; may be the most deadly of all land snakes though antivenin is quite effective.

Death adder - less than 3 ft. long, Australia; rapid onset of faintness, cardiac and respiratory distress; at least 50% mortality without antivenin.

Taipan - up to 11 ft. long, in Australia and New Guinea; rapid paralysis with severe breathing difficulty; mortality nears 100% without antivenin.

Sea snakes - throughout Pacific, Indian oceans except NE Pacific; almost painless bite, variety of muscle pain, paralysis; mortality rate low, many bites are not envenomed; some antivenins.

Notes: Not all snake bites by venomous snakes are actually envenomed. Any animal bite, however, carries the danger of tetanus and anyone suffering a venomous snake bite should seek medical attention. Antivenins are not certain cures; they are only an aid in the treatment of bites. Mortality rates above are for envenomed bites; low mortality, up to 2% result in death; moderate, 2–5%; high, 5–15%. Even when the victim recovers fully, prolonged hospitalization and extensive medical procedures are usually required.

Lizards

Gila monster - up to 24 inches long with heavy body and tail, in high desert in southwest U.S. and N. Mexico; immediate severe pain followed by vomiting, thirst, difficulty swallowing, weakness approaching paralysis; no recent mortality.

Mexican beaded lizard - similar to Gila monster, Mexican westcoast; reaction and mortality rate similar to Gila monster.

Insects

Ants, bees, wasps, hornets, etc. Global distribution. Usual reaction is piercing pain in area of sting. Not directly fatal, except in cases of massive multiple stings. Many people suffer allergic reactions - swelling, rashes, partial paralysis –and a few may die within minutes from severe sensitivity to the venom (anaphylactic shock).

Spiders, scorpions

Black widow - small, round-bodied with hour-glass marking; the widow and its relatives are found around the world in tropical and temperate zones; sharp pain, weakness, clammy skin, muscular rigidity, breathing difficulty and, in small children, convulsions; low mortality; antivenin.

Recluse or fiddleback and brown spiders - small, oblong body; throughout U.S.; pain with later ulceration at place of bite; in severe cases fever, nausea, and stomach cramps; ulceration may last months; very low mortality.

Atrax spiders - several varieties, often large, in Australia; slow onset of breathing, circulation difficulties; low mortality.

Tarantulas - large, hairy spiders found around the world; American tarantulas, and probably all others, are **harmless,** though their bite may cause some pain and swelling.

Scorpions - crab-like body with stinger in tail, various sizes, many varieties throughout tropical and subtropical areas; various symptoms may include severe pain spreading from the wound, numbness, severe emotional agitation, cramps; severe reactions include vomiting, diarrhea, respiratory failure; low mortality, usually in children; antivenins.

Sea Life

Sea wasps - jellyfish, with tentacles up to 30 ft. long, in the S. Pacific; very rapid onset of circulatory problems; high mortality largely because of speed of toxic reaction; antivenin.

Portuguese man-of-war - jellyfish-like, with tentacles up to 70 ft. long, in most warm water areas; immediate severe pain; not fatal, though shock may cause death in a rare case.

Octopi - global distribution, usually in warm waters; all varieties produce venom but only a few can cause death; rapid onset of paralysis with breathing difficulty.

Stingrays - several varieties of differing sizes, found in tropical and temperate seas and some fresh water; severe pain, rapid onset of nausea, vomiting, breathing difficulties; wound area may ulcerate, gangrene may appear; seldom fatal.

Stonefish - brownish fish which lies motionless as a rock on bottom in shallow water; throughout S. Pacific and Indian oceans; extraordinary pain, rapid paralysis; low mortality.

Cone-shells - molluscs in small, beautiful shells in the S. Pacific and Indian oceans; shoot barbs into victims; paralysis; low mortality.

How Much Water Is Used . . .?

Source: American Water Works Assn.

1. In the average residence during a year? **107,000 gallons**
2. By an average person daily? **168 gallons**
3. To flush a toilet? **5-7 gallons**
4. To take a shower? **25-50 gallons**
5. To brush your teeth (water running)? **2 gallons**
6. To shave (water running)? **10-15 gallons**
7. To wash dishes by hand? **20 gallons**
8. To run a dishwasher? **10 gallons**

Mammals: Orders and Major Families

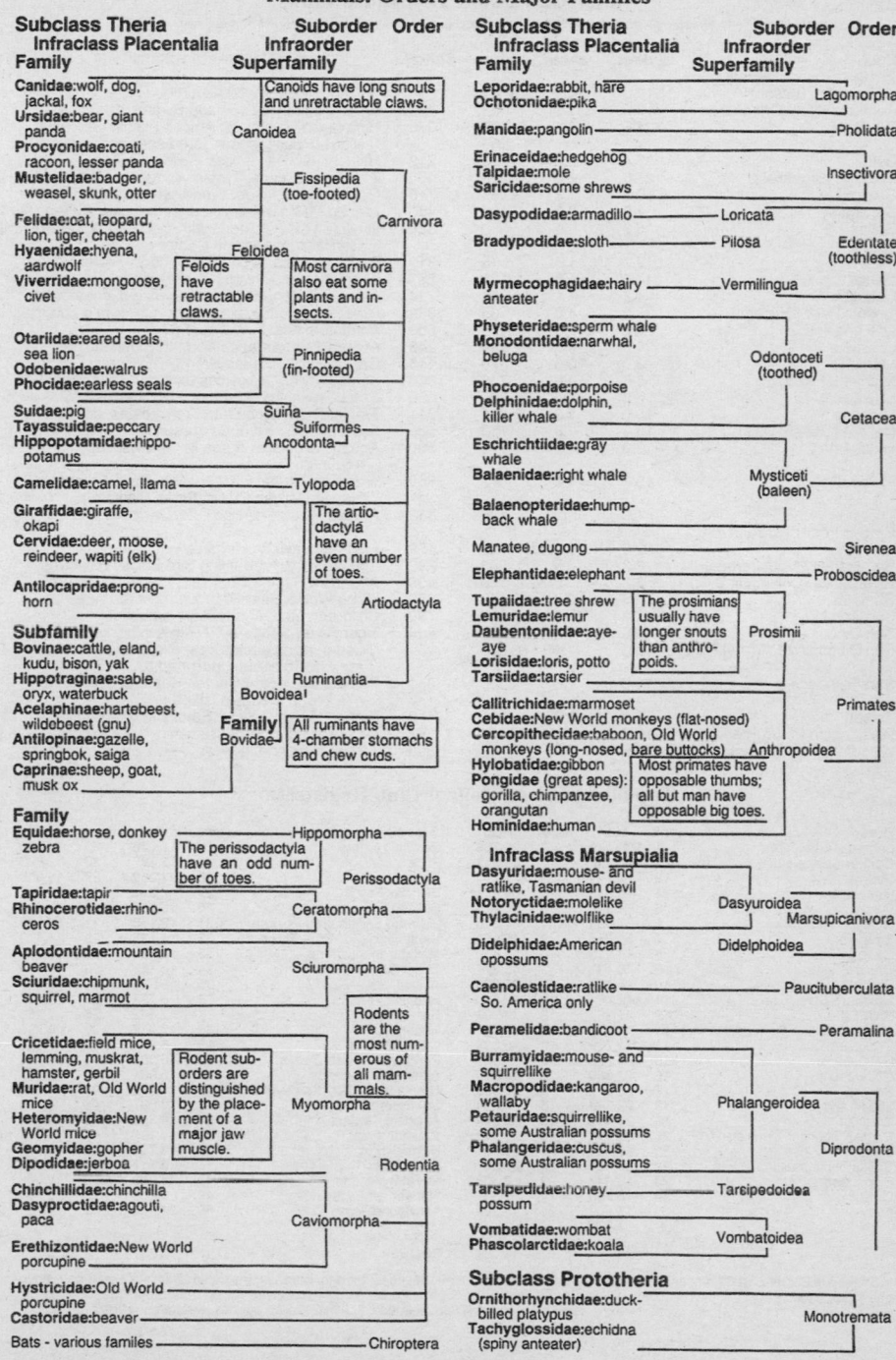

Subclass Theria
Infraclass Placentalia

Family — Suborder / Infraorder / Superfamily — Order

- **Carnivora**
  - Fissipedia (toe-footed)
    - Canoidea
      - **Canidae:** wolf, dog, jackal, fox
      - **Ursidae:** bear, giant panda
      - **Procyonidae:** coati, racoon, lesser panda
      - **Mustelidae:** badger, weasel, skunk, otter
      - Canoids have long snouts and unretractable claws.
    - Feloidea
      - **Felidae:** cat, leopard, lion, tiger, cheetah
      - **Hyaenidae:** hyena, aardwolf
      - **Viverridae:** mongoose, civet
      - Feloids have retractable claws.
    - Most carnivora also eat some plants and insects.
  - Pinnipedia (fin-footed)
    - **Otariidae:** eared seals, sea lion
    - **Odobenidae:** walrus
    - **Phocidae:** earless seals
- **Artiodactyla**
  - The artiodactyla have an even number of toes.
  - Suiformes
    - Suina
      - **Suidae:** pig
      - **Tayassuidae:** peccary
    - Ancodonta
      - **Hippopotamidae:** hippopotamus
  - Tylopoda
    - **Camelidae:** camel, llama
  - Ruminantia
    - **Giraffidae:** giraffe, okapi
    - **Cervidae:** deer, moose, reindeer, wapiti (elk)
    - **Antilocapridae:** pronghorn
    - Bovoidea
      - **Family** Bovidae
        - **Subfamily**
          - **Bovinae:** cattle, eland, kudu, bison, yak
          - **Hippotraginae:** sable, oryx, waterbuck
          - **Acelaphinae:** hartebeest, wildebeest (gnu)
          - **Antilopinae:** gazelle, springbok, saiga
          - **Caprinae:** sheep, goat, musk ox
    - All ruminants have 4-chamber stomachs and chew cuds.
- **Perissodactyla**
  - The perissodactyla have an odd number of toes.
  - Hippomorpha
    - **Family**
    - **Equidae:** horse, donkey zebra
  - Ceratomorpha
    - **Tapiridae:** tapir
    - **Rhinocerotidae:** rhinoceros
- **Rodentia**
  - Rodents are the most numerous of all mammals.
  - Rodent suborders are distinguished by the placement of a major jaw muscle.
  - Sciuromorpha
    - **Aplodontidae:** mountain beaver
    - **Sciuridae:** chipmunk, squirrel, marmot
  - Myomorpha
    - **Cricetidae:** field mice, lemming, muskrat, hamster, gerbil
    - **Muridae:** rat, Old World mice
    - **Heteromyidae:** New World mice
    - **Geomyidae:** gopher
    - **Dipodidae:** jerboa
  - Caviomorpha
    - **Chinchillidae:** chinchilla
    - **Dasyproctidae:** agouti, paca
    - **Erethizontidae:** New World porcupine
  - **Hystricidae:** Old World porcupine
  - **Castoridae:** beaver
- **Chiroptera**
  - Bats - various familes
- **Lagomorpha**
  - **Leporidae:** rabbit, hare
  - **Ochotonidae:** pika
- **Pholidata**
  - **Manidae:** pangolin
- **Insectivora**
  - **Erinaceidae:** hedgehog
  - **Talpidae:** mole
  - **Saricidae:** some shrews
- **Edentate (toothless)**
  - Loricata
    - **Dasypodidae:** armadillo
  - Pilosa
    - **Bradypodidae:** sloth
  - Vermilingua
    - **Myrmecophagidae:** hairy anteater
- **Cetacea**
  - Odontoceti (toothed)
    - **Physeteridae:** sperm whale
    - **Monodontidae:** narwhal, beluga
    - **Phocoenidae:** porpoise
    - **Delphinidae:** dolphin, killer whale
  - Mysticeti (baleen)
    - **Eschrichtiidae:** gray whale
    - **Balaenidae:** right whale
    - **Balaenopteridae:** humpback whale
- **Sirenea**
  - Manatee, dugong
- **Proboscidea**
  - **Elephantidae:** elephant
- **Primates**
  - Prosimii
    - **Tupaiidae:** tree shrew
    - **Lemuridae:** lemur
    - **Daubentoniidae:** aye-aye
    - **Lorisidae:** loris, potto
    - **Tarsiidae:** tarsier
    - The prosimians usually have longer snouts than anthropoids.
  - Anthropoidea
    - **Callitrichidae:** marmoset
    - **Cebidae:** New World monkeys (flat-nosed)
    - **Cercopithecidae:** baboon, Old World monkeys (long-nosed, bare buttocks)
    - **Hylobatidae:** gibbon
    - **Pongidae** (great apes): gorilla, chimpanzee, orangutan
    - **Hominidae:** human
    - Most primates have opposable thumbs; all but man have opposable big toes.

Infraclass Marsupialia

- **Marsupicanivora**
  - Dasyuroidea
    - **Dasyuridae:** mouse- and ratlike, Tasmanian devil
    - **Notoryctidae:** molelike
    - **Thylacinidae:** wolflike
  - Didelphoidea
    - **Didelphidae:** American opossums
- **Paucituberculata**
  - **Caenolestidae:** ratlike So. America only
- **Peramalina**
  - **Peramelidae:** bandicoot
- **Diprodonta**
  - Phalangeroidea
    - **Burramyidae:** mouse- and squirrellike
    - **Macropodidae:** kangaroo, wallaby
    - **Petauridae:** squirrellike, some Australian possums
    - **Phalangeridae:** cuscus, some Australian possums
  - Tarsipedoidea
    - **Tarsipedidae:** honey possum
  - Vombatoidea
    - **Vombatidae:** wombat
    - **Phascolarctidae:** koala

Subclass Prototheria

- **Monotremata**
  - **Ornithorhynchidae:** duck-billed platypus
  - **Tachyglossidae:** echidna (spiny anteater)

Major U.S. Public Zoological Parks

Source: World Almanac questionnaire, 1992; budget and attendance in millions. (*) park has not provided up-to-date data.

Zoo	Budget	Attendance	Acres	Species	Major attractions
Arizona-Sonora Desert Museum (Tucson)*	$12.0	0.6	186	600	"Living" museum, 90% outdoors
Audubon (New Orleans)	10.0	1.0	58	419	White alligators, Louisiana Swamp
Bronx (N.Y.C.)	24.6	2.1	265	670	Himalayan Highlands, African Plains, Wild Asia, MouseHouse, endangered species
Buffalo	3.4	0.5+	23	212	Habicat, Gorilla Habitat, Children's Zoo
Chicago (Brookfield)	27.0	2.0	215	400+	7 Seas Seascape, Tropic World
Cincinnati	10.0	1.3	67	715	Gorilla World, Insect World, white bengal tigers
Cleveland	2.9	0.9	165	460	African Plains, rhino/cheetah, Animals of China
Dallas	6.2	0.6	70	330	25-acre Wilds of Africa with monorail, nature trail, Gorilla Conservation Center
Denver	9.7	1.3	75	310	Bear Mountain, Wolf Pack Woods, Feline House
Detroit	7.0	1.0	125	253	Penguinarium, Chimps of Harambee
Houston	4.8	1.1	43	724	Children's Zoo, white tigers, white rhinoceros
Lincoln Park (Chicago)	18.0	4.0	35	339	Great Ape House, bird house, Children's Zoo
Los Angeles	7.2	1.8	113	500+	Adventure Island, World of Birds
Louisville	4.0	0.5	132	245	African Panorama, polar bear, Siberian tiger
Memphis	3.0	0.6	70	416	Cat Country, Primate World, The Forest
Miami Metrozoo	6.5	0.6	740	300	Koalas, Aviary, cageless exhibits, Asian River Life
Milwaukee	12.0	1.4	200	350	Sea Lion Exhibit, Predator Prey, new Aviary
Minnesota	10.0	1.2	485	311	Tropics Trail, Minnesota Trail, koalas, dolphins
National (Wash. D.C.)	13.0	3.0	163	509	Giant pandas, Komodo dragon lizards, gorillas
Oklahoma City	9.0	0.5	110	500+	Aquaticus dolphin & sea lion shows, 300 aquariums
Philadelphia	15.7	1.3	42	560	World of Primates, Treehouse, Rare Animal House, African Plains, Small Mammals
Phoenix	7.0	1.0	125	335	African Veldt, Children's Zoo, Arizona Trail
Gladys Porter (Brownsville, Tex.)	2.0	0.3	31	459	Free-flight aviary, Herpetarium, Aquatic wing.
Rio Grande (Albuquerque)	3.2	0.5	60	292	Ape Country, Free-flying Bird Show, Rainforest
Riverbanks (Columbia, S.C.)	3.2	1.0	170	439	Aquarium Reptile Complex, Riverbanks Farm
St. Louis	14.7	2.7	83	657	Living World, Bear Pits, Jungle of the Apes
San Antonio	7.0	1.0	35	730	Children's Zoo, Australian Walkabout
San Diego*	40.0	3.5	100	800	Tiger River, Southeast Asian exhibit, koalas
San Diego (Wild Animal Park)	15.0	1.4	2,200	450	Mixed-species enclosures; exotic species, monorail with 50-minute, narrated tour
San Francisco	11.0	1.0	65	351	Primate Discovery Center, Koala Crossing, Gorilla World, Penguin Island
Toledo	7.8	0.8	30	400	Hippoquarium, African Savanna, Children's Zoo
Washington Pk (Portland)	11.9	1.1	64	192	Alaska Tundra, Penguinarium, Africa exhibit
Woodland Pk (Seattle)	7.5	0.9	92	300	African Savanna, gorillas, Asian Elephant Forest

Top 50 American Kennel Club Registrations

Breed	Rank	1991	Rank	1990	Breed	Rank	1991	Rank	1990
Labrador Retrievers	1	105,876	2	95,768	Boston Terriers	26	17,075	25	15,401
Cocker Spaniels	2	96,937	1	105,642	Pugs	27	15,387	28	12,833
Poodles	3	77,709	3	71,757	Brittanys	28	14,282	27	14,049
Rottweilers	4	76,889	5	60,471	Bichons Frises	29	12,245	30	10,847
German Shepherd Dogs	5	68,844	6	59,556	Bulldogs	30	12,186	32	10,281
Golden Retrievers	6	67,284	4	64,848	German Shorthaired Pointers	31	12,158	31	10,478
Beagles	7	56,956	9	42,499	West Highland White Terriers	32	11,128	29	11,419
Dachshunds	8	48,713	8	44,470	Miniature Pinschers	33	10,772	37	8,176
Chow Chows	9	45,131	7	45,271	Great Danes	34	10,159	33	9,118
Shetland Sheepdogs	10	44,106	11	39,870	Akitas	35	9,949	34	8,643
Miniature Schnauzers	11	42,404	10	39,910	Scottish Terriers	36	8,724	35	8,397
Shih Tzu	12	41,367	12	39,503	Samoyeds	37	7,649	36	8,389
Pomeranians	13	41,034	14	34,475	Keeshonden	38	7,017	39	6,799
Yorkshire Terriers	14	39,772	13	36,033	Cairn Terriers	39	6,911	38	7,025
Dalmatians	15	30,225	19	21,603	Pembroke Welsh Corgis	40	6,039	41	5,041
Chihuahuas	16	29,860	15	24,593	Alaskan Malamutes	41	5,631	40	5,647
Boxers	17	26,722	17	23,659	Chesapeake Bay Retrievers	42	4,738	43	4,272
Lhasa Apsos	18	23,543	16	24,024	Saint Bernards	43	4,637	44	4,120
Siberian Huskies	19	23,436	18	21,944	Airedale Terriers	44	4,328	42	4,300
English Springer Spaniels	20	22,448	20	21,342	Weimaraners	45	4,136	45	3,731
Doberman Pinschers	21	20,734	22	20,255	Schipperkes	46	3,705	46	3,372
Basset Hounds	22	20,497	21	20,945	Old English Sheepdogs	47	3,417	47	3,352
Pekingese	23	18,843	23	18,505	Great Pyrenees	48	3,269	50	2,982
Collies	24	18,129	24	17,337	Norwegian Elkhounds	49	3,205	48	3,186
Maltese	25	17,502	26	15,364	Newfoundlands	50	3,180	51	2,791

Cat Breeds

There are 27 cat breeds recognized: abyssinian, american shorthair, balinese, birman, bombay, burmese, colorpoint shorthair, egyptian mau, exotic shorthair, havana brown, himalayan, japanese bobtail, korat, leopard cat, lilac foreign shorthair, maine coon cat, manx, ocicat, oriental shorthair, persian, rex, russian blue, scottish fold, siamese, sphynx, turkish angora, wirehair shorthair.

Minerals

Source: Bureau of Mines, U.S. Dept. of the Interior, as of mid-1992

Aluminum: the second most abundant metal element in the Earth's crust. Bauxite is the main source of aluminum; convert to aluminum equivalent by multiplying by 0.211. Guinea and Australia have 42 percent of the world's reserves. Aluminum is used in the U.S. in packaging 35%, transportation 20% and building 17%.

Chromium: some 95% of the world's chromite is found in South Africa and Zimbabwe. The chemical and metallurgical industries use about 90% of the chromite consumed in the U.S.

Cobalt: used in superalloys for jet engines; chemicals (paint driers, catalysts, magnetic coatings); permanent magnets; and cemented carbides for cutting tools. Principal cobalt producing countries include Zaire, Zambia, and the former USSR. The U.S. uses about one-third of total world consumption. Although its resources are relatively large, the U.S. has produced no cobalt since 1971; most cobalt resources are low grade and production from these deposits is not economically feasible.

Columbium: used mostly as an additive in steelmaking and in superalloys. Brazil and Canada are the world's leading producers. There is no U.S. columbium mining industry.

Copper: main uses of copper in the U.S. are in building construction 40%, electrical and electronic products 26%, industrial machinery and equipment 14%, transportation 11%, consumer & general products 9%. The leading producer is Chile, followed by the U.S., USSR, Canada, Zambia, Peru, and Poland. Principal mining states are Arizona, New Mexico, and Utah.

Gold: used in the U.S. in jewelry and arts 53%, industrial (mainly electronic) 25%, dental 9%. South Africa has about half of the world's resources; significant quantities are also present in the U.S., Canada, the former USSR, and Brazil. Gold mining in the U.S. takes place in nearly all of the western states and Alaska.

Iron ore: the source of primary iron for the world's iron and steel industries. Major iron ore producers include the former USSR, Brazil, Australia, and China.

Lead: the U.S., Australia, China and the former USSR are the world's largest producers of lead. Transportation accounted for the major end use in the U.S. with 75% used in batteries, gasoline additives, and other applications. Other uses include emergency power supply batteries, construction sheeting, sporting ammunition and TV tubes. The U.S. produces and consumes more than 20% of the world's lead metal.

Manganese: essential to iron and steel production. The U.S., Japan, and Western Europe are all nearly deficient in economically minable manganese. South Africa and the USSR have over 80% of the world's reserves.

Nickel: vital to stainless steel industry and played a key role in the development of the chemical and aerospace industries. Leading producers include the former USSR, Canada, Australia, and New Caledonia.

Platinum-Group Metals: the platinum group comprises 6 closely related metals: platinum, palladium, rhodium, ruthenium, iridium, and osmium. They commonly occur together in nature and are among the scarcest of the metallic elements. They are consumed in the U.S. by the following industries: automotive 38%, electrical and electronic 30%, and dental 9%. The USSR and South Africa have nearly all the world's reserves.

Silver: used in the following U.S. industries: photography; electrical and electronic products; sterlingware, electroplated ware, and jewelry. Silver is mined in more than 54 countries. Nevada produces over 28% of the U.S. silver, Idaho 18%.

Tantalum: a refractory metal with unique electrical, chemical, and physical properties used mostly in the U.S to produce electronic components, mainly tantalum capacitors. Australia, Brazil, Canada and Thailand are the leading producers. There is no U.S. tantalum mining industry.

Titanium: a metal which is mostly used in jet engines, airframes, and space and missile applications. It is produced in the USSR, Japan, and the western and central U.S., the United Kingdom, and China.

Vanadium: used as an alloying element in steel, as an alloying agent in aerospace titanium alloys, and as a catalyst in the production of sulfuric acid and maleic anhydride. The USSR and South Africa are the world's largest producers.

Zinc: used as protective coating on steel, as diecastings, as an alloying metal with copper to make brass, and as chemical compounds in rubber and paints. It is mined in over 50 countries with Canada the leading producer, followed by Australia, the former USSR, Peru, China and the U.S. In the U.S., mine production comes mostly from Tennessee, Missouri, New York and Alaska.

World Mineral Reserve Base

Source: Bureau of Mines, U.S. Dept. of the Interior, as of 1991

Mineral	Reserve Base[1]	Mineral	Reserve Base[1]
Aluminum	25,000 mln. metric tons[2]	Nickel	121,000 thousand metric tons
Chromium	6,800 mln. metric tons	Platinum—Group Metals	66 mln. kilograms
Cobalt	8,340 thou. metric tons	Silver	420,000 metric tons
Columbium	3,549 kilograms	Tantalum	34.5 mln. kilograms
Copper	550 mln. metric tons	Titanium	330 mln. metric tons
Gold	49,400 metric tons	Vanadium	18,300 thousand short tons
Iron	229,000 mln. metric tons[3]	Zinc	325 mln. metric tons
Lead	125 mln. metric tons		
Manganese	5,300,000 thousand short tons		

(1) Includes demonstrated resources that are currently economic (reserves), marginally economic (marginal reserves), and some of those that are currently subeconomic. (2) Bauxite. (3) Crude ore.

U.S. Nonfuel Mineral Production—10 Leading States in 1991

Source: Bureau of Mines, U.S. Dept. of the Interior

Rank/State	Value (millions)	Percent of U.S. total	Principal minerals
1. California	$3,017	9.80	Cement, boron minerals, sand & gravel (construction), stone (crushed)
2. Arizona	3,791	9.06	Copper, gold, sand and gravel
3. Nevada	2,510	8.15	Gold, sand & gravel (construction), silver
4. Florida	1,422	4.62	Stone (crushed), cement, phosphate rock
5. Michigan	1,398	4.54	Cement, sand & gravel, stone
6. Georgia	1,392	4.52	Clays, stone (crushed)
7. Minnesota	1,389	4.51	Iron ore, sand & gravel (construction), stone (crushed)
8. Texas	1,379	4.48	Cement, stone (crushed), sand & gravel (construction), salt
9. Utah	1,182	3.84	Cement, lime, sand & gravel (construction), salt
10. New Mexico	976	3.17	Potassium salts, copper

U.S. Nonfuel Mineral Production

Source: Bureau of Mines, U.S. Dept. of the Interior

Production as measured by mine shipments, sales, or marketable production (including consumption by producers)

		1987	1988	1989	1990	1991[E]
Antimony (ore and concentrate)		W	W	W	W	NA
Bauxite	thousand metric tons, dried equivalent	576	588	W	W	NA
Beryllium	metric tons	220	212	184	200	NA
Copper (recoverable content of ores, etc.)	metric tons	1,244	1,417	1,498	1,550	NA
Gold (recoverable content of ores, etc.)	metric tons	153.9	200.9	265.5	300.0	NA
Iron ore, usable (includes byproduct material)	million metric tons	47.6	57.5	59.0	53.9	NA
Lead (recoverable content of ores, etc.)	thousand metric tons	311	385	411	484	466
Magnesium metal (primary)	thousand tons	124	142	152	150	NA
Molybdenum (content of ore and concentrate)	thousand kilograms	34,067	43,044	65,095	60,300	NA
Nickel (content of ore and concentrate)	metric tons	NA	NA	330	5,523	NA
Silver (recoverable content of ores, etc.)	metric tons	1,241	1,661	2,007	2,125	1,848
Tungsten ore and concentrate		W	W	W	W	W
Zinc (recoverable content of ores, etc.)	thousand metric tons	216	244	276	515	518
Asbestos	thousand metric tons	51	18	17	20	W
Barite	thousand metric tons	406	404	290	430	448
Boron minerals	thousand metric tons	625	578	562	608	568
Bromine	million kilograms	152	163	175	177	170
Cement: (Portland, Masonry, etc.)	thousand short tons	78,198	76,867	77,189	77,111	72,300
Clays	thousand metric tons	43,234	44,515	42,254	42,904	43,000
Diatomite	thousand metric tons	596	629	617	631	610
Feldspar	thousand metric tons	655	650	655	630	580
Fluorspar	thousand metric tons	64	64	66	64	58
Garnet (industrial)	metric tons	38,353	42,409	42,605	47,009	50,930
Gem stones		NA	NA	NA	NA	NA
Gypsum	thousand short tons	15,612	16,390	17,624	16,406	15,456
Helium (extracted from natural gas)	million cubic feet	1,968	2,281	2,390	2,800	NA
Helium (Grade A)	million cubic feet	2,230	2,574	2,879	3,200	NA
Iodine	thousand kilograms	W	1,015	1,508	1,973	1,999
Lime	thousand short tons	15,733	17,052	17,152	17,452	17,270
Mica (scrap & flake)	thousand metric tons	146	130	119	109	103
Peat	thousand short tons	955	844	761	763	697
Perlite	thousand short tons	533	576	601	635	567
Phosphate rock	thousand metric tons	40,954	45,389	49,817	46,343	48,100
Pumice & Pumicite	thousand metric tons	356	353	424	443	401
Salt	thousand short tons	36,943	39,170	39,278	40,558	40,700
Sand and gravel (construction)	thousand short tons	895,200	923,400	897,300	910,600	780,300
Sand and gravel (industrial)	thousand short tons	28,010	28,480	29,205	28,406	25,600
Sodium sulfate (natural)	thousand short tons	382	398	375	390	400
Stone (crushed)	million short tons	1,200	1,250	1,213	1,222	1,062
Stone (dimension)	thousand short tons	1,179	1,160	1,207	1,190	1,330
Sulfur	thousand metric tons	10,539	10,746	11,592	11,560	10,816
Talc and pyrophyllite	thousand metric tons	1,163	1,234	1,253	1,267	1,037
Vermiculite	thousand short tons	303	304	275	230	185

(E) Estimated. (W) Withheld to avoid disclosing company proprietary data. * Talc only. (NA) Not available.

U.S. Reliance on Foreign Supplies of Minerals

Source: Bureau of Mines, U.S. Dept. of the Interior

Mineral	Percent imported in 1991	Major sources (1987-90)	Major uses
Columbium	100%	Brazil, Canada, Germany	Steelmaking and aerospace alloys
Graphite	100	Mexico, China, Brazil, Madagascar	Metallurgical processes
Manganese	100	S. Africa, France, Gabon, Australia	Steelmaking
Mica (sheet)	100	India, Belgium, France, Brazil	Electronic and electrical equipment
Strontium (Celestite)	100	Mexico, Spain, Germany	Television picture tubes, pyrotechnics
Bauxite and alumina	100	Australia, Guinea, Jamaica, Brazil	Aluminum production
Diamonds (industrial)	92	South Africa, Britain, Ireland, Zaire	Machinery for grinding and cutting
Fluorspar	87	Mexico, South Africa	Raw material for metallurgical and chemical industries
Platinum group	88	South Africa, Britain, USSR	Catalytic converters for autos, electrical and electronic equipment
Cobalt	84	Zaire, Zambia, Canada, Norway	Aerospace alloys, magnets, cutting tools, chemicals
Tantalum	85	Germany, Thailand, Brazil, Australia	Electronic components
Nickel	72	Canada, Australia, Norway	Stainless steel and other alloys
Chromium	80	South Africa, Turkey, Zimbabwe, Yugoslavia	Stainless steel
Tin	76	Bolivia, Brazil, Indonesia	Cans, electrical construction
Tungsten	73	China, Bolivia, Germany, Peru	Lamp filaments
Barite	70	China, Morocco, India	Oil drilling fluids
Potash	67	Canada, Israel, USSR	Fertilizer
Cadmium	94	Canada, Australia, Mexico, Germany	Batteries, plating and coating of metals
Silver	NA	Canada, Mexico, Britain, Peru	Photography, electrical and electronic prods.

U.S. Copper, Lead, and Zinc Production

Source: Bureau of Mines, U.S. Dept. of the Interior

Year	Copper Quantity (metric tons)	Copper Value ($1,000)	Lead Quantity (metric tons)	Lead Value ($1,000)	Zinc Quantity (metric tons)	Zinc Value ($1,000)
1950	827	379,122	390,839	113,078	565,516	167,000
1960	1,037	733,706	223,774	57,722	395,013	112,365
1965	1,226	957,028	273,196	93,959	554,429	178,284
1970	1,560	1,984,484	518,698	178,609	484,560	163,650
1975	1,282	1,814,763	563,783	267,230	425,792	366,097
1980	1,181	2,666,931	550,366	515,189	317,103	261,671
1985	1,105	1,631,000	413,955	174,008	226,545	201,607
1987	1,244	2,262,000	311,381	246,720	216,281	200,529
1988	1,417	3,764,000	384,983	315,222	244,314	324,249
1989	1,497	4,323,000	410,915	356,476	275,883	499,103
1990	587	4,310,000	483,704	490,750	515,355	847,485
1991	635	3,942,000	465,931	343,907	517,814	602,462

U.S. Pig Iron and Raw Steel Output

Source: American Iron and Steel Institute (net tons)

Year	Total pig iron	Raw steel
1940	46,071,666	66,982,686
1945	53,223,169	79,701,648
1950	64,586,907	96,836,075
1955	76,857,417	117,036,085
1960	66,480,648	99,281,601
1965	88,184,901	131,461,601
1970	91,435,000	131,514,000
1975	101,208,000	116,642,000
1980	68,721,000	111,835,000
1985	50,446,000	88,259,000
1986	43,952,000	81,606,000
1987	48,410,000	89,151,000
1988	55,745,000	99,924,000
1989	55,873,000	97,943,000
1990	54,750,000	98,906,000
1991	48,637,000	87,896,000

Steel figures include only that portion of the capacity and production of steel for castings used by foundries which were operated by companies producing steel ingots.

World Gold Production

Source: Bureau of Mines, U.S. Dept. of the Interior

(Troy Ounces)

		Africa			North and South America						Other	
Year	World prod.	South Africa	Ghana	Zaire	United States	Canada	Mexico	Colombia	Australia	China	Philippines	USSR
1972	44,843,374	29,245,273	724,051	140,724	1,449,943	2,078,567	146,061	188,137	754,866	—	606,730	—
1975	38,476,371	22,937,820	523,889	103,217	1,052,252	1,653,611	144,710	308,864	526,821	—	502,577	—
1977	38,906,145	22,501,886	480,884	80,418	1,100,347	1,733,609	212,709	257,070	624,270	—	558,554	—
1978	38,983,019	22,648,558	402,034	76,077	998,832	1,735,077	202,003	246,446	647,579	—	586,531	—
1979	38,768,978	22,617,179	362,000	69,992	964,390	1,644,265	190,364	269,369	596,910	—	535,166	—
1980	39,197,315	21,669,468	353,000	39,963	969,782	1,627,477	195,991	510,439	547,591	—	753,452	8,425,000
1982	43,082,814	21,355,111	331,000	62,233	1,465,686	2,081,230	214,349	472,674	866,815	1,800,000	834,439	8,550,000
1984	46,929,444	21,860,933	287,000	117,115	2,084,615	2,682,786	270,998	730,670	1,295,963	1,900,000	827,149	8,650,000
1985	49,283,691	21,565,230	299,363	63,022	2,427,232	2,815,118	265,693	1,142,385	1,881,491	1,950,000	1,062,997	8,700,000
1986	51,534,056	20,513,665	287,127	167,827	3,739,015	3,364,700	250,615	1,285,878	2,413,842	2,100,000	1,296,400	8,850,000
1987	53,033,614	19,176,500	327,598	140,561	4,947,040	3,724,000	256,822	853,600	3,558,954	2,300,000	1,048,081	8,850,000
1988	58,453,814	19,881,126	372,979	140,000	6,459,539	4,110,000	296,689	933,000	4,887,000	2,500,000	1,134,920	9,000,000
1989	63,497,633	19,531,550	429,469	112,528	8,536,010	5,092,670	266,850	870,962	6,523,377	2,572,056	1,125,275	9,162,949
1990	67,977,286	19,380,009	541,406	136,187	9,329,994	5,381,159	268,073	943,687	7,849,175	3,215,070	790,618	9,709,511
1991	67,259,264	19,322,568	845,867	144,695	9,320,006	5,552,683	270,066	964,521	7,530,273	3,858,084	801,774	7,716,168

(e) estimated.

U.S. and World Silver Production

Source: Bureau of Mines, U.S. Dept. of the Interior

(metric tons)

Largest production of silver in the United States in 1915—2,332 metric tons.

Year	United States	World
1930	1,578	7,736
1935	1,428	6,865
1940	2,164	8,565
1945	904	5,039
1950	1,347	6,323
1955	1,134	6,967
1960	1,120	7,505
1965	1,238	8,007
1970	1,400	9,670
1975	1,087	9,428
1980	1,006	10,556
1985	1,227	13,051
1986	1,074	12,970
1987	1,241	14,019
1988	1,661	14,514
1989	2,007	15,059
1990	2,125	15,167
1991	1,848	15,122

Aluminum Summary, 1980 to 1991

Source: Bureau of Mines, U.S. Dept. of the Interior

Item	Unit	1980	1985	1987	1988	1989	1990	1991
U.S. production	1,000 metric ton	5,914	5,262	5,329	6,066	6,084	6,441	6,622
Primary aluminum	1,000 metric ton	4,654	3,500	3,343	3,944	4,030	4,048	4,121
Secondary aluminum[1]	1,000 metric ton	1,260	1,762	1,986	2,122	2,054	2,393	2,501
Primary aluminum value	Bil. dol	7.3	6.3	5.3	9.5	7.8	6.6	5.4
Price (Primary alum.)[2]	Cents/lb	71.6	81.0	72.3	110.1	87.8	74.0	59.5
Imports for consumption[3]	1,000 metric ton	647	1,420	1,850	1,620	1,470	1,514	1,490
Exports[3]	1,000 metric ton	1,346	908	917	1,247	1,613	1,659	1,762
World production	1,000 metric ton	15,383	15,398	16,514	17,548	18,199	18,025	18,243

(1) Recoverable metal content from purchased scrap, old and new; (2) Average prices for primary aluminum, quoted by *Metals Week;* (3) Crude and semicrude (including metal and alloys, plates, bars, etc., and scrap).

Giant Trees of the U.S.

Source: The American Forestry Assn., Washington, D.C.

Approximately 850 native and naturalized species of trees are grown in the U.S. The oldest thing on earth is a bristlecone pine tree in California named Methusalah, believed to be 4700 years old. The world's largest living thing, the General Sherman giant sequoia in California, weighs more than 1,400 tons—as much as 9 blue whales or 360 elephants.

Recognition as the National Champion of each species is determined by total mass of each tree, based on this formula: the circumference in inches as measured at a point 4½ feet above the ground plus the total height of the tree in feet plus ¼ of the average crown spread in feet. Trees within 5 points of each other are declared co-champions. Of all the trees nominated at the beginning of AFA's Big Tree program in 1940, only 4 trees have never lost their title—the giant sequoia (Sequoia Natl. Park, Cal.), white oak (Wye Mills State Park, Md.), western juniper (Stanislaus Natl. Forest, Cal.), and Rocky Mountain juniper (Cache Natl. Forest, Ut.). The coast redwood Dyerville Giant (Dyerville, Cal.) was also one of the original champs until it fell in March 1991. Florida has more national champs (113) than any other state. No champions have been identified for nearly 200 species, including white fir, papaya, eucalyptus, California Sycamore, and Saguaro.

Anyone can nominate candidates for the National Register of Big Trees. For information, write to American Forestry Assn., P.O. Box 2000, Washington, DC 20013. The following is a small selection of the trees registered.

(Figure in parentheses is year of most recent measurement; * = co-champion)

Species	Height (ft.)	Location
Ailanthus (1952)	64	Head of Harbor, L.I.
Alder, Hazel (1989)	35	Norfolk, Va.
Allthorn (1989)*	13	Midland, Tex.
Anacahuite (1992)	25	Mercedes, Tex.
Apple, Common (1986)	70	East End, Va.
Apple, Oregon Crab (1989)	79	Nisqually Natl. Wildlife Refuge, Wash.
Ash, Carolina (1988)	48	Chesapeake, Va.
Ash, Texas (1989)	66	Lost Maples State Natl. Area, Tex.
Ash, Velvet (1992)	81	Modesto, Cal.
Aspen, Bigtooth (1989)*	66	Caroline Co., Md.
Avocado (1982)	40	Hallandale, Fla.
Basswood, White (1986)	75	Henderson Co., N.C.
Beech, American (1984)	130	Ashtabula Co., Oh.
Birch, Gray (1989)	77	Somers, Ct.
Birch, River (1988)*	90	Appleton Comm., Tenn.
Birch, Water (1973)	53	Wallowa Co., Ore.
Blackbead, Ebony (1986)	40	Hidalgo Co., Tex.
Bladdernut, Sierra (1986)	28	Fresno, Co., Cal.
Bluewood (1989)	30	San Juan, Tex.
Boxwood, Florida (1986)	27	Monroe Co., Fla.
Buckeye, Bottlebrush (1989)	20	Cashiers, N.C.
Buffaloberry, Silver (1975)	22	Malheur Co., Ore.
Bumelia, Tough (1987)	41	Amelia Is., Fla.
Butternut (1989)*	88	Eugene, Ore.
California Laurel (1978)	88	Siskiyou Natl. For., Ore.
Camphor-Tree (1977)	72	Hardee Co., Fla.
Catalpa, Southern (1981)	80	Henderson Co., Ill.
Catclaw, Wright (1986)	36	Uvalde Co., Tex.
Cedar, Atlantic white (1985)	88	Escambia Co., Ala.
Cherry, Bitter (1985)	104	Vashon Is., Wash.
Chestnut, American (1992)	110	Grand Traverse, Mich.
Coconut, Palm (1979)	92	Hilo, Hi.
Crab Apple, Southern (1992)	36	Swannanoa, N.C.
Cranberrybush, American (1989)*	25	Trenton, Mich.
Cypress, McNab (1981)	55	Amador Co., Cal.
Dahoon, Myrtle (1972)	46	Lawtey, Fla.
Devilwood (1989)	36	Perry, Fla.
Dogwood, Blackfruit (1986)	18	Shasta Co., Cal.
Dogwood, Swamp (1989)*	23	Chesapeake, Va.
Douglas-Fir, Coast (1992)	329	Coos Co., Ore.
Elder, American (1987)	16	Jefferson Natl. For., Va.
Elder, Pacific Red (1989)	30	Lincoln Co., Ore.
Elm, American (1991)	100	Louisville, Kan.
Fiddlewood, Florida (1988)	39	Dade Co., Fla.
Fig, Shortleaf (1986)	41	Monroe Co., Fla.
Fir, Grand (1987)	251	Olympic Natl. Park, Wash.
Franklinia (1968)	36	Wyndmoor, Pa.
Fringetree (1989)*	32	Fairfax Co., Va.
Gallberry, Large (1989)	27	Great Dismal Swamp Natl. Wildlife Refuge, Va.
Geiger Tree (1988)	25	Lee Co., Fla.
Guajillo (1989)	15	Starr Co., Tex.
Guiana Plum (1976)	31	Coral Gables, Fla.
Hackberry, Common (1989)	111	Rock Co., Wis.
Haw, May (1989)	12	Williamsburg, Va.
Hawthorne, Fleshy (1988)	8	Kirkwood, Mo.
Hazel, California (1984)	47	Seattle, Wash.
Hemlock, Western (1991)*	227	Olympic Natl. Park, Wash.
Hickory, Mockernut (1985)*	125	Monroe Co., Ala.
Hickory, Shellbark (1986)	105	Rixeyville, Va.
Holly, Carolina (1986)	25	Jacksonville, Fla.
Honeylocust (1972)	115	Wayne Co., Mich.
Huisache (1989)	33	Big Bend Natl. Park, Tex.
Jerusalem-thorn (1969)	36	Florence, Ariz.
Jujube, Common (1989)	43	Fort Worth, Tex.
Juniper, Western (1945)	86	Stanislaus Natl. Forest., Cal.
Larch, European (1989)	83	Greenwich, Ct.
Laurel, English (1985)	32	Seattle, Wash.
Loblolly Bay (1963)	94	Ocala Natl. Forest, Fla.
Locust, Black (1974)	96	Dansville, N.Y.
Magnolia, Umbrella (1969)	50	Bucks Co., Pa.
Mahogany, W. Indies (1988)	70	Lee Co., Fla.
Mango (1991)	40	Pompano Beach, Fla.
Manzanita, Common (1989)	22	Guerneville, Cal.
Maple, Black (1976)	118	Allegan Co., Mich.
Maple, Douglas (1985)*	65	Ahsahka, Ida.
Mesquite, Honey (1984)	52	Real County, Tex.
Mountain-Laurel (1989)	25	Asheville, N.C.
Mulberry, Black (1971)	68	Westminster, Md.
Nannyberry (1989)	40	Oakland Co., Mich.
Oak, Bluejack (1985)	64	Cherokee Co., Tex.
Oak, Chestnut (1972)	75	Northport, N.Y.
Oak, Harvard (1986)	30	Yoakum Co., Tex.
Oysterwood (1986)	24	Monroe Co., Fla.
Palm, Texas Sabal (1989)	45	Hidalgo Cty., Tex.
Paloverde, Blue (1976)	53	Riverside Co., Cal.
Paper-Mulberry (1989)	34	Yorktown, Va.
Pawpaw, Common (1986)	60	Newton Co., Miss.
Peach (1986)	18	Morrisville, Va.
Pear, Common (1991)	59	Waitsburg, Wash.
Pecan (1980)	143	Cocke Co., Tenn.
Persimmon, Texas (1965)	26	Uvalde Co., Tex.
Pine, Bishop (1986)	112	Mendocino Co., Cal.
Pine, Intermountain (1951)	47	Inyo Natl. Forest, Cal.
Pine, Virginia (1989)	120	Chambers Co., Ala.
Pistache, Texas (1976)	39	Val Verde Co., Tex.
Plum, Chicasaw (1988)	32	Henderson Co., N.C.
Plum, Wildgoose (1989)	26	New Salem Village, Ill.
Poison-Sumac (1972)	16	Robins Is., N.Y.
Poplar, Balsam (1984)	138	Marquette, Mich.
Portiatree (1968)	42	Kekaha, Ha.
Privet, California (1989)*	28	Yorktown, Va.
Redbud, Eastern (1989)	36	Nashville, Tenn.
Redwood, Coast (1972)	362	Humboldt Redwoods State Park, Cal.
Ribbonbush (1977)	23	No. Warner Springs, Cal.
Russian-Olive (1982)	58	Cortez, Col.
Saffron-Plum (1987)	31	Santa Ana, Tex.
Sassafras (1954)	76	Owensboro, Ky.
Sequoia, Giant (1975)	275	Sequoia Natl. Park, Cal.
Serviceberry, Downy (1986)	60	Burkes Garden, Va.
Silktree, Mimosa (1986)*	54	Webster Parish, La.
Sophora, Mescalbean (1983)	27	Comal Co., Tex.
Spruce, Norway (1989)	94	Susquehanna City, Pa.
Stewartia, Virginia (1987)	15	Chesapeake, Va.
Sugarberry (1976)	78	Society Hills, S.C.
Sweetgum, American (1986)	136	Craven Co., N.C.
Sycamore, Arizona (1981)	114	Sierra Co., N.M.
Tamarisk (1981)	34	Columbus, N.M.
Thatchpalm, Florida (1986)	23	Monroe Co., Fla.
Walnut, Arizona (1987)	85	Mimbres Valley, N.M.
Walnut, Black (1991)	105	Southhampton Co., Va.
Willow, Sitka (1988)	34	Coupeville, Wash.
Willow, Weeping (1982)*	114	Asheville, N.C.
Yew, Florida (1986)	20	Torreya State Park, Fla.
Yucca, Mojave (1987)	24	Needles Res. Area, Cal.
Yucca, Torrey (1987)	23	Lincoln Natl. Forest, N.M.

SOCIAL SECURITY

Social Security Programs

Source: Social Security Administration, U.S. Dept. of Health and Human Services

Old-Age, Survivors, and Disability Insurance; Medicare; Supplemental Security Income

Social Security Benefits

Social Security benefits are based on a worker's primary insurance amount (PIA), which is related by law to the average indexed monthly earnings (AIME) on which social security contributions have been paid. The full PIA is payable to a retired worker who becomes entitled to benefits at age 65 and to an entitled disabled worker at any age. Spouses and children of retired or disabled workers and survivors of deceased workers receive set proportions of the PIA subject to a family maximum amount. The PIA is calculated by applying varying percentages to succeeding parts of the AIME. The formula is adjusted annually to reflect changes in average annual wages.

Automatic increases in Social Security benefits are initiated for December of a year whenever the Consumer Price Index (CPI) of the Bureau of Labor Statistics for the third calendar quarter of a year increases relative to the CPI for the base quarter, which is either the third calendar quarter of the preceding year or the quarter in which an increase legislated by Congress becomes effective. The size of the benefit increase is determined by the actual percentage rise of the CPI between the quarters measured.

Average monthly benefits payable to all retired workers was $629.00 in December 1992. The average amount for disabled workers in that month was $609.00.

Minimum and maximum monthly retired-worker benefits payable to individuals who retired at age 65[1]

Year of attainment of age 65[2]	Minimum benefit: Payable at the time of retirement	Minimum benefit: Payable effective December 1990	Maximum benefit: Payable at the time of retirement, Men[3]	Maximum benefit: Payable at the time of retirement, Women	Maximum benefit: Payable effective December 1990, Men[3]	Maximum benefit: Payable effective December 1990, Women
1965 . . .	$44.00	$253.40	$131.70	$135.90	$677.40	$699.10
1970 . . .	64.00	253.40	189.80	196.40	750.70	777.40
1980 . . .	133.90	253.40	572.00	...	1083.00	...
1985 . . .	(4)	(4)	717.20	...	928.60	...
1990 . . .	(4)	(4)	975.00	...	1060.70	...

(1) Assumes retirement at beginning of year. (2) The final benefit amount payable after SMI premium or any other deductions is rounded to next lower $1 (if not already a multiple of $1). (3) Benefit for both men and women are shown in men's columns except where women's benefit appears separately. (4) Minimum eliminated for workers who reach age 62 after 1981.

Amount of Work Required

To qualify for benefits, the worker must have worked in covered employment long enough to become insured. Just how long depends on when the worker reaches age 62 or, if earlier, when he or she dies or becomes disabled.

A person is fully insured if he or she has one quarter of coverage for every year after 1950 (or year age 21 is reached, if later) up to but not including the year in which the worker reaches age 62, dies, or becomes disabled. In 1992, a person earns one quarter of coverage for each $570 of annual earnings in covered employment, up to a maximum of 4 quarters per year.

The law permits special monthly payments under the Social Security program to certain very old persons who are not eligible for regular social security benefits since they had little or no opportunity to earn social security work credits during their working lifetime.

To get disability benefits, in addition to being fully insured, the worker must also have credit for 20 quarters of coverage out of the 40 calendar quarters before he or she becomes disabled. A disabled blind worker need meet only the fully insured requirement. Persons disabled before age 31 can qualify with a briefer period of coverage. Certain survivor benefits are payable if the deceased worker had 6 quarters of coverage in the 13 quarters preceding death.

Work credit for fully insured status for benefits

Born after 1929; die, become disabled, or reach age 62 in	Years needed
1983	8
1984	8¼
1985	8½
1986	8¾
1987	9
1988	9¼
1989	9½
1990	9¾
1991	10

Contribution and benefit base

Calendar year	OASDI Base	HI Base
1983	$35,700	—
1984	37,800	—
1985	39,600	—
1986	42,000	—
1987	43,800	—
1988	45,000	—
1989	48,000	—
1990	51,300	$125,000[1]
1991	53,400	130,200
1992	55,500	

(1) While the OASDI and HI bases were the same amount prior to 1991, they have differed since that time.

Tax-rate schedule
[Percent of covered earnings]

Year	Total	OASDI	HI
	Employees and employers, each		
1979-80	6.13	5.08	1.05
1981	6.65	5.35	1.30
1982-83	6.70	5.40	1.30
1984	7.00	5.70	1.30
1985	7.05	5.70	1.35
1986-87	7.15	5.70	1.45
1988-89	7.51	6.06	1.45
1990 and after	7.65	6.20	1.45
	Self-employed		
1979-80	8.10	7.05	1.05
1981	9.30	8.00	1.30
1982-83	9.35	8.05	1.30
1984	14.00	11.40	2.60
1985	14.10	11.40	2.70
1986-87	14.30	11.40	2.90
1988-89	15.02	12.12	2.90
1990 and after	15.30	12.40	2.90

What Aged Workers Get

When a person has enough work in covered employment and reaches retirement age (currently 65 for full benefit, 62 for reduced benefit), he or she may retire and get monthly old-age benefits. The age at which unreduced benefits are payable will be increased gradually from 65 to 67 over a 21-year period beginning with workers age 62 in the year 2000; (reduced benefits will still be available as early as age 62 but with a larger reduction at age 62.) If a person aged 65 or older continues to work and has earnings of more than $10,200 in 1992, $1 in benefits will be withheld for every $3 above $10,200. The annual exempt amount for people under age 65 is $7,440 in 1992 and $1 in benefits is withheld for every $2 in earnings above the exempt amount for them. The annual exempt amount is raised automatically as the general earnings level rises. The eligible worker who is 70 receives the full benefit regardless of earnings.

For workers who reach age 65 from 1982 through 1989, the worker's benefit is raised by 3% for each year for which the worker between 65 and 70 (72 before 1984) did not receive benefits because of earnings from work or because the worker had not applied for benefits. The delayed retirement credit is 1 percent a year for workers reaching age 65 before 1982. The delayed retirement credit will gradually rise to 8% per year from 1990 through 2008. The rate for workers reaching age 65 in 1992-93 is 4%.

Effective December 1991, the special benefit for persons aged 72 or over who do not meet the regular coverage requirements is $173.60 a month. Like the monthly benefits, these payments are subject to cost-of-living increases. The special payment is not made to persons on the public assistance or supplemental security income rolls.

Workers retiring before age 65 have their benefits permanently reduced by 5/9 of 1% for each month they receive benefits before age 65. Thus, workers entitled to benefits in the month they reach age 62 receive 80% of the PIA, while a worker retiring at age 65 receives a benefit equal to 100% of the PIA. The nearer to age 65 the worker is when he or she begins collecting a benefit, the larger the benefit will be.

Benefits for Worker's Spouse

The spouse of a worker who is getting Social Security retirement or disability payments may become entitled to a spouse's insurance benefit when he or she reaches 65 of one-half of the worker's PIA. Reduced spouse's benefits are available at age 62 (25/36 of 1% reduction for each month of entitlement before age 65). Benefits are also payable to the aged-divorced spouse of an insured worker if he or she was married to the worker for at least 10 years.

Benefits for Children of Retired or Disabled Workers

If a retired or disabled worker has a child under 18 the child will get a benefit that is half of the worker's unreduced benefit, and so will the worker's spouse, even if he or she is under 62 if he or she is caring for an entitled child of the worker who is under 16 or who became disabled before age 22. Total benefits paid on a worker's earnings record are subject to a maximum and if the total that would be paid to a family exceeds that maximum, the individual dependents' benefits are adjusted downward. (Total benefits paid to the family of a worker who retired in January 1992 at age 65 and who always had the maximum amount of earnings creditable under Social Security can be no higher than $1,906.50.)

When entitled children reach 18, their benefits will generally stop, except that a child disabled before 22 may get a benefit as long as his or her disability meets the definition in the law. Additionally, benefits will be paid to a child until age 19 if the child is in full-time attendance at an elementary or secondary school.

Benefits may also be paid to a grandchild or step-grandchild of a worker or of his or her spouse, in special circumstances.

OASDI	May 1991	May 1990	May 1989
Monthly beneficiaries, total (in thousands)	**40,119**	**39,440**	**38,835**
Aged 65 and over, total	29,516	28,979	28,393
Retired workers	22,432	21,960	21,455
Survivors and dependents	7,078	7,010	6,926
Special age-72 beneficiaries	6	9	12
Under age 65, total	10,603	10,462	10,442
Retired workers	2,539	2,545	2,560
Disabled workers	3,076	2,934	2,850
Survivors and dependents	4,988	4,982	5,032
Total monthly benefits (in millions)	**$21,880**	**$20,244**	**$18,870**

What Disabled Workers Get

If a worker becomes so severely disabled that he or she is unable to work, he or she may be eligible to receive a monthly disability benefit. Benefits continue until it is determined that the individual is no longer disabled. Each beneficiary's eligibility is reviewed periodically. When a disabled worker beneficiary reaches 65, the disability benefit becomes a retired-worker benefit.

Benefits generally like those provided for dependents of retired-worker beneficiaries may be paid to dependents of disabled beneficiaries. However, the maximum family benefit in disability cases is generally lower than in retirement cases.

Survivor Benefits

If an insured worker should die, one or more types of benefits may be payable to survivors, again subject to a maximum family benefit as described above.

1. If claiming benefits at 65, the surviving spouse will receive a benefit that is 100% of the deceased worker's PIA. The surviving spouse may choose to get the benefit as early as age 60, but the benefit is then reduced by 19/40 of 1% for each month it is paid before age 65. However, for those whose spouses claimed their benefits before 65, the benefit is limited to the reduced amount the worker would be getting if alive but not less than 82 1/2% of the worker's PIA. Marriage after the worker's death ends the surviving spouses benefit rights. However, if he or she marries and the marriage is ended, he or she regains benefit rights (A marriage after age 60, 50 if disabled, is deemed not to have occurred for benefit purposes.). This benefit may also be paid to the divorced spouse, if the marriage lasted for at least 10 years.

Disabled widows and widowers may under certain circumstances qualify for benefits after attaining age 50 at the rate of 71.5% of the deceased worker's PIA. The widow or widower must have become totally disabled before or within 7 years after the spouse's death, the last month in which he or she received mother's or father's insurance benefits, or the last month he or she previously received surviving spouse's benefits.

2. A benefit for each child until the child reaches 18. The monthly benefit of each child of a worker who has died is three-quarters of the amount the worker would have received if he or she had lived and drawn full retirement benefits. A child with a disability that began before age 22 may receive benefits. Also, a child may receive benefits until age 19 if he or she is in full-time attendance at an elementary or secondary school.

3. A mother's or father's benefit for the widow(er), if children of the worker under 16 are in his or her care. The benefit is 75% of the PIA and he or she draws it until the youngest child reaches 16, at which time payments stop even if the child's benefit continues. They may start again when he or she is 60 (50 if disabled) unless he or she is married. If he or she has a disabled child beneficiary aged 16 or over in care, benefits also continue.

4. Dependent parents may be eligible for benefits, if they have been receiving at least half their support from the worker before his or her death, have reached age 62, and (except in certain circumstances) have not remarried since the worker's death. Each parent gets 75% of the worker's PIA; if only one parent survives the benefit is 82 1/2%.

5. A lump sum cash payment of $255. Payment is made only when there is a spouse who was living with the worker or a spouse or child eligible for immediate monthly survivor benefits.

Self-Employed

A self-employed person who has net earnings of $400 or more in a year must report such earnings for social security tax and credit purposes. The person reports net returns from the business. Income from real estate, savings, dividends, loans, pensions or insurance policies may not be included unless they are part of the business.

A self-employed person gets a quarter of coverage for each $570 (for 1992), up to a maximum of 4 quarters of coverage.

The nonfarm self-employed have the option of reporting their earnings as ²/₃ of their gross income from self-employment but not more than $1,600 a year and not less than their actual net earnings. This option can be used only if actual net earnings from self-employment income is less than $1,600 and may be used only 5 times. Also, the self-employed person must have actual net earnings of $400 or more in 2 of the 3 taxable years immediately preceding the year in which he or she uses the option.

When a person has both taxable wages and earnings from self-employment, the wages are credited for Social Security purposes first; only as much of the self-employment income as will bring total earnings up to the current taxable maximum is subject to the self-employment tax.

Farm Owners and Workers

Self-employed farmers whose gross annual earnings from farming are $2,400 or less may report 2/3 of their gross earnings instead of net earnings for social security purposes. Farmers whose gross income is over $2,400 and whose net earnings are less than $1,600 can report $1,600. Cash or crop shares received from a tenant or share farmer count if the owner participated materially in production or management. The self-employed farmer pays contributions at the same rate as other self-employed persons.

Agricultural employees. A worker's earnings from farm work count toward benefits (1) if the employer pays him $150 or more in cash during the year; or (2) if the employer spends $2,500 or more in the year for agricultural labor. Under these rules a person gets credit for one calendar quarter for each $570 in cash pay in 1992 up to four quarters.

Foreign farm workers admitted to the United States on a temporary basis are not covered.

Household Workers

Anyone working as maid, cook, laundress, nursemaid, baby-sitter, chauffeur, gardener and at other household tasks in the house of another is covered by Social Security if he or she is paid $50 or more in cash in a calendar quarter by any one employer. Room and board do not count, but carfare counts if paid in cash. The job does not have to be regular or fulltime. The employee should get a Social Security card at the social security office and show it to the employer.

The employer deducts the amount of the employee's social security tax from the worker's pay, adds an identical amount as the employer's social security tax and sends the total amount to the federal government, with the employee's social security number.

Medicare

The Medicare health insurance program provides acute-care coverage for Social Security and Railroad Retirement beneficiaries aged 65 and over and, for persons entitled for 24 months to receive a social security disability benefit, and certain persons with end-stage kidney disease. The Medicare program cost almost $114 billion in 1991 and served about 35 million people.

Persons eligible for Medicare may choose to have their covered services provided through a Health Maintenance Organization.

Hospital insurance.—

The hospital insurance program pays the cost of covered services for hospital and posthospital care as follows:

- Medicare pays for all necessary inpatient hospital care for the first 60 days of each benefit period, except for a deductible ($652 in 1992). For days 61-90, Medicare pays for covered services except for a coinsurance amount ($163 per day in 1992). After 90 days, the beneficiary has 60 reserve days for which Medicare helps pay. The coinsurance amount for reserve days was $326 in 1992.
- Up to 100 days' care in a skilled-nursing facility (skilled-nursing home) in each benefit period. Hospital insurance pays for all covered services for the first 20 days, for the 21-100th day, the beneficiary pays coinsurance ($81.50 in 1992).
- Visits by nurses or other health workers (not doctors) from a home health agency.
- Hospice care for terminally ill individuals.

Medical insurance. Aged persons can receive benefits under this supplementary program only if they sign up for them and agree to a monthly premium ($31.80 in 1992). The Federal Government pays the rest of the cost.

The medical insurance program pays 80% of the approval amount (after the first $100 in each calendar year) for the following services:

Medicare helps pay for covered services you receive from your doctor in his or her office, in a hospital, in a skilled nursing facility, in your home, or any other location.

Doctors' services covered by Medicare include:

- Medical and surgical services, including anesthesia.
- Diagnostic tests and procedures that are part of your treatment.
- Radiology and pathology services by doctors while you are a hospital inpatient or outpatient.
- Treatment of mental illness. Medicare payments for non-hospital treatment are limited—you may get the services from doctors, comprehensive outpatient rehabilitation facilities (CORFs), physician assistants, psychologists and clinical social workers.

These services for nonhospital treatment of a mental illness are subject to a special payment rule. In effect, once the annual deductible is met, Medicare pays only 50% (not 80%) of approved charges for these services. On assigned claims, beneficiaries are responsible for paying the remaining 50%. For unassigned claims, beneficiaries may have to pay more.

Partial hospitalization services for treatment of mental illness are not subject to this special payment rule. Also, brief office visits for the sole purpose of monitoring or changing drug prescriptions used in the treatment of mental illness are not subject to this special payment rule.

- Other services such as:

— X-rays.
— Services of your doctor's office nurse.
— Drugs and biologicals that cannot be self-administered.
— Transfusions of blood and blood components.
— Medical supplies.
— Physical/occupational therapy and speech pathology services.

To get medical insurance protection, persons approaching age 65 may enroll in the 7-month period that includes 3 months before the 65th birthday, the month of the birthday, and 3 months after the birthday, but if they wish coverage to begin in the month they reach 65 they must enroll in the 3 months **before** their birthday. Persons not enrolling within their first enrollment period may enroll later, during the first 3 months of each year but their premium is 10% higher for each 12-month period elapsed since they first could have enrolled.

The monthly premium is deducted from the cash benefit for persons receiving Social Security, Railroad Retirement, or Civil Service retirement benefits. Income from the medical premiums and the federal matching payments are put in a Supplementary Medical Insurance Trust Fund, from which benefits and administrative expenses are paid.

Medicare card. Persons qualifying for hospital insurance under Social Security receive a health insurance card similar to cards now used by Blue Cross and other health agencies. The card indicates whether the individual has taken out medical insurance protection. It is to be shown to the hospital, skilled-nursing facility, home health agency, doctor, or whoever provides the covered services.

Payments are made only in the 50 states, Puerto Rico, the Virgin Islands, Guam, and American Samoa, except that hospital services may be provided in border areas immediately outside the U.S. if comparable services are not accessible in the U.S. for a beneficiary who becomes ill or is injured in the U.S.

Social Security Financing

Social Security is paid for by a tax on earnings (for 1992, up to $55,500 for Old Age, Survivors, and Disability Insurance and up to $130,200 for Hospital Insurance with the Medicare Program; the taxable earnings base is now subject to automatic adjustment to reflect increases in average wages). The employed worker and his or her employer share the tax equally.

Employers remit amounts withheld from employee wages for Social Security and income taxes to the Internal Revenue Service; employer Social Security taxes are also payable at the same time. (Self-employed workers pay their Social Security taxes along with their regular income tax forms). The Social Security taxes (along with revenues arising from partial taxation of the Social Security benefits of certain high-income people) are transferred to the Social Security Trust Funds (Federal Old-Age and Survivors Insurance Trust Fund, the Federal Disability Insurance Trust Fund, and the Federal Hospital Insurance Trust Fund); they can be used only to pay benefits, the cost of rehabilitation services, and administrative expenses. Money not immediately needed for these purposes is by law invested in obligations of the Federal Government, which must pay interest on the money borrowed and must repay the principal when the obligations are redeemed or mature.

Supplemental Security Income

On Jan. 1, 1974, the Supplemental Security Income (SSI) program established by the 1972 Social Security Act amendments replaced the former federal grants to states for aid to the needy aged, blind, and disabled in the 50 states and the District of Columbia. The program provides both for federal payments based on uniform national standards and eligibility requirements and for state supplementary payments varying from state to state. The Social Security Administration administers the federal payments financed from general funds of the Treasury—and the state supplements as well, if the state elects to have its supplementary program federally administered. The states may supplement the federal payment for all recipients and must supplement it for persons otherwise adversely affected by the transition from the former public assistance programs. In May 1992, the number of persons receiving federal payments and federally administered state payments was 5,322,877 and the amount of these payments was $1.90 billion.

The maximum monthly federal SSI payment for an individual with no other countable income, living in his own household, was $422.00 in 1992. For a couple it was $633.00.

Examples of monthly cash benefit awards for selected beneficiary families with first entitlement in 1992, effective January 1992

Beneficiary Family	Low Earnings ($10,243 in 1992) (45% of average)	Career Earnings Level Average Earnings ($22,762 in 1992)[1]	Maximum Earnings ($55,500 in 1992)
Primary Insurance amount (worker retiring at 65)	$481.10	$749.90	$1,088.70
Maximum family benefit (worker retiring at 65)	721.80	1,449.40	1,906.50
Disability maximum family benefit (worker disabled at 55; in 1991)*	669.80	1,177.60	1,654.00
Disabled worker: (worker disabled at 55)			
Worker alone	478.00	785.00	1,103.00
Worker, spouse, and 1 child	668.00	1,177.00	1,653.00
Retired worker claiming benefits at age 62:			
Worker alone[2]	384.00	635.00	870.00
Worker with spouse claiming benefits at—			
Age 65 or over	624.00	1,032.00	1,414.00
Age 62[2]	556.00	933.00	1,278.00
Widow or widower claiming benefits at—			
Age 65 or over[3]	481.00	794.00	1,088.00
Age 60	343.00	568.00	778.00
Disabled widow or widower claiming benefits at age 50-59[4]	343.00	568.00	778.00
1 surviving child	360.00	596.00	816.00
Widow or widower age 65 or over and 1 child[5]	841.00	1,390.00	1,904.00
Widowed mother or father and 1 child[5]	720.00	1,192.00	1,632.00
Widowed mother or father and 2 children[5]	720.00	1,449.00	1,905.00

* Assumes work beginning at age 22. (1) Estimate. (2) Assumes maximum reduction. (3) A widow(er)'s benefit amount is limited to the amount the spouse would have been receiving if still living but not less than 82.5 percent of the PIA. (4) Effective January 1984, disabled widow(er)s claiming benefit at ages 50-59 will receive benefit equal to 71.5 percent of the PIA (based on 1983 Social Security Amendment provision). (5) Based on worker dying at age 65.

Social Security Trust Funds

Old-Age and Survivors Insurance Trust Fund, 1940-1991

(in millions)

	Income					Disbursements						
Fiscal year[1]	Total	Net contributions[2]	Income from taxation of benefits	Payments from the general fund of the Treasury[3]	Net interest[4]	Total	Benefit payments[5]	Administrative expenses	Transfers to Railroad Retirement program	Interfund borrowing transfers[6]	Net increase in fund	Fund at end of period
1940	$592	$550	—	—	$42	$28	$16	$12	—	—	$564	$1,745
1950	2,367	2,106	—	$4	257	784	727	57	—	—	1,583	12,893
1960	10,360	9,843	—	—	517	11,073	10,270	202	$600	—	−713	20,829
1970	31,746	29,955	—	442	1,350	27,321	26,268	474	579	—	4,425	32,616
1980	100,051	97,608	—	557	1,886	103,228	100,626	1,160	1,442	—	−3,177	24,566
1985	179,881	175,305	$3,151	105	1,321	169,210	165,310	1,589	2,310	$−4,364	6,308	33,877
1990	278,607	261,506	2,924	34	14,143	223,481	218,948	1,564	2,969	—	55,126	203,445
1991	293,288	270,841	5,790	−2,089	18,746	241,316	236,195	1,746	3,375	—	51,972	255,417

(1) Under the Congressional Budget Act of 1974 (Public Law 93-344), fiscal years 1977 and later consist of the 12 months ending on September 30 of each year. Fiscal years prior to 1977 consisted of the 12 months ending on June 30 of each year.

(2) Beginning in 1983, includes transfers from general fund of Treasury representing contributions that would have been paid on deemed wage credits for military service in 1957 and later, if such credits were considered to be covered wages.

(3) Includes payments (1) in 1947-52 and in 1967 and later, for costs of noncontributory wage credits for military service performed before 1957; (2) in 1972-83, for costs of deemed wage credits for military service performed after 1956; and (3) in 1969 and later, for costs of benefits to certain uninsured persons who attained age 72 before 1968.

(4) Net interest includes net profits or losses on marketable investments. Beginning in 1967, administrative expenses are charged currently to the trust fund on an estimated basis, with a final adjustment, including interest, made in the following fiscal year. The amounts of these interest adjustments are included in net interest. For years prior to 1967, a description of the method of accounting for administrative expenses is contained in the 1970 Annual Report. Beginning in October 1973, the figures shown include relatively small amounts of gifts to the fund. Figures for 1983-86 reflect payments from a borrowing trust fund to a lending trust fund for interest on amounts owed under the interfund borrowing provisions. During 1983-91, interest paid from the trust fund to the general fund on advance tax transfers is reflected. The amounts shown for 1985 and 1986 include interest adjustments of $76.5 million and $11.5 million, respectively, on unnegotiated checks issued before April 1985.

(5) Beginning in 1967, includes payments for vocational rehabilitation services furnished to disabled persons receiving benefits because of their disabilities. Beginning in 1983, amounts are reduced by amount of reimbursement for unnegotiated benefit checks.

(6) Negative figures represent amounts repaid from the OASI Trust Fund to the DI and HI Trust Funds.

Disability Insurance Trust Fund, 1960-1991

(In millions)

	Income					Disbursements						
Fiscal year[1]	Total	Net contributions[2]	Income from taxation of benefits	Payments from the general fund of the Treasury[3]	Net interest[4]	Total	Benefit payments[5]	Administrative expenses	Transfers to Railroad Retirement program	Interfund borrowing transfers[6]	Net increase in fund	Fund at end of period
1960	$1,034	$987	—	—	$47	$533	$528	$32	−$27	—	$501	$2,167
1970	4,380	4,141	—	$16	223	2,954	2,795	149	10	—	1,426	5,104
1980	17,376	16,805	—	118	453	15,320	14,998	334	−12	—	2,056	7,680
1985	17,984	16,876	$217	—	891	19,294	18,648	603	43	$2,540	1,230	5,873
1990	28,215	27,291	158	—	766	25,124	24,327	717	80	—	3,091	11,455
1991	29,322	28,953	131	−775	1,014	27,780	26,909	789	82	—	1,543	12,997

(1) Under the Congressional Budget Act of 1974 (Public Law 93-344), fiscal years 1977 and later consist of the 12 months ending on September 30 of each year. The act further provides that the calendar quarter July-September 1976 is a period of transition from fiscal year 1976, which ended on June 30, 1976, to fiscal year 1977, which began on October 1, 1976.

(2) Beginning in 1983, includes government contributions on deemed wage credits for military service in 1957 and later.

(3) Includes payments (1) in 1967 and later, for costs of noncontributory wage credits for military service performed before 1957; and (2) in 1972-83, for costs of deemed wage credits for military service performed after 1956.

(4) Net interest includes net profits or losses on marketable investments. Beginning in 1967, administrative expenses are charged currently to the trust fund on an estimated basis, with a final adjustment, including interest, made in the following fiscal year. The amounts of these interest adjustments are included in net interest. For years prior to 1967, a description of the method of accounting for administrative expenses is contained in the 1970 Annual Report of the Board of Trustees of the Federal Old-Age and Survivors Insurance and Disability Insurance Trust Funds. Beginning in 1983, these figures reflect payments from a borrowing trust fund to a lending trust fund for interest on amounts owed under the interfund borrowing provisions. Also, beginning in 1983, interest paid from the trust fund to the general fund on advance tax transfers is reflected. The amount shown for 1985 includes an interest adjustment of $14.8 million on unnegotiated checks issued before April 1985.

(5) Beginning in 1967, includes payments for vocational rehabilitation services furnished to disabled persons receiving benefits because of their disabilities. Beginning in 1983, amounts are reduced by amount of reimbursement for unnegotiated benefit checks. The amount shown for 1983 is reduced by $48 million for all unnegotiated checks issued before 1983; reductions in subsequent years are relatively small.

(6) Negative figure represents amounts lent by the DI Trust Fund to the OASI Trust Fund. Positive figures represent repayment of these amounts.

Supplementary Medical Insurance Trust Fund, 1970-1991

(In millions)

	Income				Disbursements			
Fiscal year[1]	Premium from participants	Government contributions[2]	Interest and other income[3]	Total income	Benefit payments	Administrative expenses	Total disbursements	Balance in fund at end of year[4]
1970	$936	$928	$12	$1,876	$1,979	$217	$2,196	$57
1975	1,887	2,330	105	4,322	3,765	405	4,170	1,424
1980	2,928	6,932	415	10,275	10,144	593	10,737	4,532
1985	5,524	17,898	1,155	24,577	21,808	922	22,730	10,646
1990	11,494[5]	33,210	1,434[5]	46,138[5]	41,498	1,524[5]	43,022[5]	14,527[5]
1991	11,807	34,730	1,629	48,166	45,514	1,505	47,019	15,675

(1) For 1967 through 1976, fiscal years cover the interval from July 1 through June 30; fiscal years 1977 and later cover the interval from October 1 through September 30. (2) The payments shown as being from the general fund of the Treasury include certain interest-adjustment items. (3) Other income includes recoveries of amounts reimbursed from the trust fund which are not obligations of the trust fund and other miscellaneous income. (4) The financial status of the program depends on both the total net assets and the liabilities of the program. (5) Includes the impact of the Medicare Catastrophic Coverage Act of 1988 (Public Law 100-360).

Hospital Insurance Trust Fund, 1970-1991

(In millions)

	Income							Disbursements			Trust Fund	
Fiscal Year[1]	Payroll taxes	Transfers from railroad retirement account	Reimbursement for uninsured persons	Premiums from voluntary enrollees	Payments for military wage credits	Interest on investments and other income[2]	Total income	Benefits payments[3]	Administrative expense[4]	Total disbursements	Net increase fund	Fund at end of year
1970	$4,785	$64	617	—	$11	$137	$5,614	$4,804	$149	$4,953	$661	$2,677
1975	11,291	132	481	6	48	609	12,568	10,353	259	10,612	1,956	9,870
1980	23,244	244	697	17	141	1,072	25,415	23,790	497	24,288	1,127	14,490
1985	46,490	371	766	38	86	3,182	50,933	47,841	813	48,654	4,103[5]	21,277[5]
1990	70,655	367	413	113	107	7,908	79,563	65,912	774	66,687	12,876	95,631
1991	74,655	352	605	367	−1,011[6]	8,969	83,938	68,705	934	69,638	14,299	109,930

(1) Fiscal years 1976 and earlier consist of the 12 months ending on June 30 of each year; fiscal years 1977 and later consist of the 12 months ending on September 30 of each year. (2) Other income includes recoveries of amounts reimbursed from the trust fund which are not obligations of the trust fund and a small amount of miscellaneous income. (3) Includes costs of Peer Review Organizations (beginning with the implementation of the Prospective Payment System on October 1, 1983). (4) Includes costs of experiments and demonstration projects. (5) In fiscal year 1983, $12,437 million was loaned to the Old-Age and Survivors Insurance Trust Fund under the interfund borrowing provisions of the Social Security Act. Repayments of $1,824 million and $10,613 million were made in fiscal years 1985 and 1986, respectively. (6) Includes the lump sum general revenue adjustment of $-1,100 million, as provided for by section 151 of P.L. 98-21.

NOTE: Totals do not necessarily equal the sum of rounded components.

NATIONAL DEFENSE

Data as of July, 1992

Chairman, Joint Chiefs of Staff
Gen. Colin L. Powell

The Joint Chiefs of Staff consists of the Chairman and Vice Chairman of the Joint Chiefs of Staff; the Chief of Staff, U.S. Army; the Chief of Naval Operations; the Chief of Staff, U.S. Air Force; and the Commandant of the Marine Corps.

Army

Chief of Staff—Gordon R. Sullivan

Generals

	Date of Rank
Burba, Edwin H. Jr.	Sept. 27, 1989
Franks, Frederick M. Jr.	Aug. 23, 1991
Galvin, John R.	Feb. 25, 1985
Joulwan, George A.	Nov. 21, 1990
Powell, Colin L.	Apr. 4, 1989
Reimer, Dennis J.	June 21, 1991
RisCassi, Robert W.	Jan. 17, 1989
Ross, Jimmy D.	Feb. 1, 1992
Saint, Crosbie E.	June 24, 1988
Stiner, Carl W.	July 1, 1990

Air Force

Chief of Staff—Merrill A. McPeak.

Generals

Adams, Jimmie V.	Feb. 13, 1991
Butler, George L.	Jan. 25, 1991
Carns, Michael P.C.	May 16, 1991
Davis, James B.	June 1992
Horner, Charles A.	June 1992
Johnson, Hansford T.	Oct. 1, 1989
Loh, John M.	June 1, 1990
McCarthy, James P.	Oct. 1, 1989
Oaks, Robert C.	July 1, 1990
Yates, Ronald W.	Apr. 1, 1990

Navy

Chief of Naval Operations
Admiral Frank B. Kelso II (submariner)

Admirals

	Date of Rank
Arthur, Stanley R. (aviator)	———
Boorda, Jeremy M. (surface warfare)	Mar. 2, 1992
DeMars, Bruce (submariner)	Nov. 1, 1988
Jeremiah, David E. (surface warfare)	Oct. 1, 1987
Kelly, Robert J. (aviator)	Mar. 1, 1991
Kelso, Frank B. (submariner)	June 30, 1986
Larson, Charles R. (submariner)	Mar. 1, 1990
Mauz, Henry N. Jr. (surface warfare)	———
Miller, Paul D. (surface warfare)	Feb. 1, 1991
Smith, William D. (submariner)	Feb. 22, 1991

Marine Corps

Corps Commandant, with rank of General

Carl E. Mundy Jr.	July 1, 1991

ACMC/Chief of Staff, with rank of Gen.

John R. Dailey	Aug. 1, 1990
Joseph P. Hoar	Sept. 1, 1991

Coast Guard

Commandant, with rank of Admiral

J. William Kime	May 31, 1990

Vice Commandant, with rank of Vice Admiral

Robert T. Nelson	June 5, 1992

Unified Defense Commands Commanders-in-Chief

Atlantic Command (LANTCOM) — Adm. Paul D. Miller.

U.S. European Command, Brussels — Maj. Gen. John Shalikashvili (USA) (concurrently NATO Supreme Allied Commander).

U.S. Southern Command, Quarry Heights, Panama Canal Zone — Gen. George A. Joulwan (USA).

U.S. Atlantic Command, Norfolk, Virginia — Adm. Paul D. Miller, (USN) (concurrently NATO Supreme Allied Commander, Atlantic).

U.S. Pacific Command, Hawaii — Adm. Charles R. Larson (USN)

U.S. Space Command, Gen. Charles A. Horner (USAF)

***Strategic U.S. Command,** Omaha — Gen. George L. Butler (USAF)

***US Forces Command** — Gen. Edwin H. Burba (USA)

***U.S. Transportation Command,** Gen. Hansford T. Johnson (USAF)

U.S. Special Operations Command, MacDill AFB, Fla. — Gen. Carl W. Stiner (USA)

U.S. Central Command, Gen. Joseph P. Hoar (USMC)

North Atlantic Treaty Organization International Commands

Supreme Allied Commander, Europe (SACEUR) — Gen. John R. Galvin (USA)

Deputy Supreme Allied Commander Europe (DSACEUR) — Gen. Sir Brian Kenny, UK, Army (UKA)

Deputy Supreme Allied Commander Europe (DSACEUR) — Gen. Dieter Clauss (GEA)

Commander-in-Chief Allied Forces Northern Europe — Gen. Sir Patrick Palmer, UK, Army, KBE, MC (UKA)

Commander-in-Chief Allied Forces Central Europe — Gen. Hans-Henning von Sandrart (GEA)

Commander-in-Chief Allied Forces Southern Europe — Adm. Jeremy M. Boorda

Commander-in-Chief United Kingdom Air Forces — Gen. Michael Graydon (UKAF)

Chairman, NATO Military Committee — Gen. Viglik Eide (Norway)

Principal U.S. Military Training Centers

Army

Name, P.O. address	Zip	Nearest city
Aberdeen Proving Ground, MD	21005	Aberdeen
Carlisle Barracks, PA	17013	Carlisle
Fort Benning, GA	31905	Columbus
Fort Bliss, TX	79916	El Paso
Fort Bragg, NC	28307	Fayetteville
Fort Devens, MA	01433	Ayer
Fort Dix, NJ	08640	Trenton
Fort Eustis, VA	23604	Newport News
Fort Gordon, GA	30905	Augusta
Fort Benjamin Harrison, IN	46216	Indianapolis
Fort Sam Houston, TX	78234	San Antonio
Fort Huachuca, AZ	85613	Sierra Vista
Fort Jackson, SC	29207	Columbia
Fort Knox, KY	40121	Louisville
Fort Leavenworth, KS	66027	Leavenworth
Fort Lee, VA	23801	Petersburg
Fort McClellan, AL	36205	Anniston
Fort Monmouth, NJ	07703	Red Bank
Fort Rucker, AL	36362	Dothan
Fort Sill, OK	73503	Lawton
Fort Leonard Wood, MO	65473	Rolla
Joint Readiness, Ft. Chaffee, AR	72905	Fort Smith
National Training Center	92311	Barstow, CA
Redstone Arsenal, AL	35809	Huntsville
The Judge Advocate General School, VA	22901	Charlottesville
U.S. Military Acad., NY	10996	West Point

Navy

Name, P.O. address	Zip	Nearest city
Great Lakes, IL	60088	North Chicago
San Diego, CA	92133	San Diego
Orlando, FL	32813	Orlando
Annapolis, MD	21402	Annapolis

Marine Corps

Name, P.O. address	Zip	Nearest city
MCB Camp Lejeune, NC	28542	Jacksonville
MCB Camp Pendleton, CA	92055	Oceanside
MCB Camp Butler, Okinawa	FPO Seattle 98773	Futenma, Okinawa
MCAGCC Twentynine Palms, CA.	92278	Palm Springs
MCCDC Quantico, VA	22134	Quantico
MCRD Parris Island, SC	29905	Beaufort
MCRD San Diego, CA	92140	San Diego
MCAS Cherry Point, NC	28533	Havelock
MCAS El Toro (Santa Ana), CA.	92709	Santa Ana
MCAS Tustin, CA	92780	Santa Ana
MCAS New River, NC	28545	Jacksonville
MCAS Iwakuni, Japan	FPO Seattle 98764	Iwakuni
MCAS Kaneohe Bay, Oahu, HI	San Francisco 96863	Kailua
MCAS Futenma, Okinawa FPO Seattle	98772	Futenma
MCAS Beaufort, SC	29904	Beaufort
MCAS Yuma, AZ	85369	Yuma
MCMWTC Bridgeport, CA	93517	Bridgeport
MCLB Albany, GA	31704	Albany
MCLB Barstow, CA	92311	Barstow

MCB = Marine Corps Base. MCCDC = Marine Corps Combat Development Command. MCAS = Marine Corps Air Station. MCRD = Marine Corps Recruit Depot. MCAGCC = Marine Corps Air-Ground Combat Center. MCMWTC = Marine Corps Mountain Warfare Training Center. MCLB = Marine Corps Logistics Base.

Air Force

Name, P.O. address	Zip	Nearest city
Chanute AFB, IL	61868	Rantoul
Goodfellow AFB, TX	76908	San Angelo
Gunter AFB, AL*	36114	Montgomery
Keesler AFB, MS	39534	Biloxi
Lackland AFB, TX	78236	San Antonio
Lowry AFB, CO	80230	Denver
Maxwell AFB, AL*	36112	Montgomery
Sheppard AFB, TX	76311	Wichita Falls

* Air University Bases. All others are Air Training Command Bases.

Personal Salutes and Honors

The United States national salute, 21 guns, is also the salute to a national flag. The independence of the United States is commemorated by the salute to the union — one gun for each state — fired at noon on July 4 at all military posts provided with suitable artillery.

A-21-gun salute on arrival and departure, with 4 ruffles and flourishes, is rendered to the President of the United States, to an ex-President and to a President-elect. The national anthem or *Hail to the Chief*, as appropriate, is played for the President, and the national anthem for the others. A 21-gun salute on arrival and departure with 4 ruffles and flourishes, also is rendered to the sovereign or chief of state of a foreign country or a member of a reigning royal family; the national anthem of his or her country is played. The music is considered an inseparable part of the salute and will immediately follow the ruffles and flourishes without pause.

Rank	Salute—guns Arrive	—Leave	Ruffles, flourishes	Music
Vice President of United States	19		4	Hail Columbia
Speaker of the House	19		4	March
American or foreign ambassador	19		4	Nat. anthem of official
Premier or prime minister	19		4	Nat. anthem of official
Secretary of Defense, Army, Navy or Air Force	19	19	4	Honors March
Other Cabinet members, Senate President pro tempore, Governor, or Chief Justice of U.S.	19		4	Honors March
Chairman, Joint Chiefs of Staff	19	19	4	
Army Chief of Staff, Chief of Naval Operations, Air Force Chief of Staff, Marine Commandant	19	19	4	General's or Admiral's March
General of the Army, General of the Air Force, Fleet Admiral	19	19	4	
Generals, Admirals	17	17	4	
Assistant secretaries of Defense, Army, Navy or Air Force	17	17	4	Honors March
Chairman of a committee of Congress	17		4	Honors March

Other salutes (on arrival only) include 15 guns for U.S. envoys or ministers and foreign envoys or ministers accredited to the U.S.; 15 guns for a lieutenant general or vice admiral; 13 guns for a major general or rear admiral (upper half); 13 guns for U.S. ministers resident and ministers resident accredited to the U.S.; 11 guns for a brigadier general or rear admiral (lower half); 11 guns for U.S. charges d'affaires and like officials accredited to U.S.; and 11 guns for consuls general accredited to U.S.

Military Units, U.S. Army and Air Force

Army units. Squad. In infantry usually ten men under a staff sergeant. **Platoon.** In infantry 4 squads under a lieutenant. **Company.** Headquarters section and 4 platoons under a captain. (Company in the artillery is a battery; in the cavalry, a troop.) **Battalion.** Hdqts. and 4 or more companies under a lieutenant colonel. (Battalion size unit in the cavalry is a squadron.) **Brigade.** Hdqts. and 3 or more battalions under a colonel. **Division.** Hdqts. and 3 brigades with artillery, combat support, and combat service support units under a major general. **Army Corps.** Two or more divisions with corps troops under a lieutenant general. **Field Army.** Hdqts. and two or more corps with field Army troops under a general.

Air Force Units. Flight. Numerically designated flights are the lowest level unit in the Air Force. They are used primarily where there is a need for small mission elements to be incorporated into an organized unit. **Squadron.** A squadron is the basic unit in the Air Force. It is used to designate the mission units in operational commands. **Group.** The group is a flexible unit composed of two or more squadrons whose functions may be either tactical, support or administrative in nature. **Wing.** An operational wing normally has two or more assigned mission squadrons in an area such as combat, flying training or airlift. **Air Division.** The organization of the air division may be similar to that of the numbered air force, though on a much smaller scale. Functions are usually limited to operations and logistics. **Numbered Air Forces.** Normally an operationally oriented agency, the numbered air force is designed for the control of two or more air divisions or units of comparable strength. It is a flexible organization and may be of any size. Its wings may be assigned to air divisions or directly under the numbered air force. **Major Command.** A major subdivision of the Air Force that is assigned a major segment of the USAF mission.

U.S. Army Insignia and Chevrons

Source: Department of the Army

Grade **Insignia**

General of the Armies

General John J. Pershing, the only person to have held this rank, was authorized to prescribe his own insignia, but never wore in excess of four stars. The rank originally was established by Congress for George Washington in 1799, and he was promoted to the rank by joint resolution of Congress, approved by Pres. Ford Oct. 19, 1976.

General of Army . . . Five silver stars fastened together in a circle and the coat of arms of the United States in gold color metal with shield and crest enameled.

General . . . . Four silver stars
Lieutenant General . . . . . Three silver stars
Major General . . . . Two silver stars
Brigadier General . . . . . . One silver star
Colonel . . . . Silver eagle
Lieutenant Colonel . . . . . Silver oak leaf
Major . . . . Gold oak leaf
Captain . . . . Two silver bars
First Lieutenant . . . . One silver bar
Second Lieutenant . . . . . . One gold bar

Warrant officers

Grade Four—Silver bar with 4 enamel black squares.
Grade Three—Silver bar with 3 enamel black squares.
Grade Two—Silver bar with 2 enamel black squares.
Grade One—Silver bar with 1 enamel black squares.

Non-commissioned Officers

Sergeant Major of the Army (E-9). Same as Command Sergeant Major (below) but with 2 stars. Also wears distinctive red and white shield on lapel.

Command Sergeant Major (E-9). Three chevrons above three arcs with a 5-pointed star with a wreath around the star between the chevrons and arcs.

Sergeant Major (E-9). Three chevrons above three arcs with a five-pointed star between the chevrons and arcs.

First Sergeant (E-8). Three chevrons above three arcs with a lozenge between the chevrons and arcs.

Master Sergeant (E-8). Three chevrons above three arcs.

Sergeant First Class (E-7). Three chevrons above two arcs.

Staff Sergeant (E-6). Three chevrons above one arc.

Sergeant (E-5). Three chevrons.

Corporal (E-4). Two chevrons.

Specialists

Specialist (E-4). Eagle device only.

Other enlisted

Private First Class (E-3). One chevron above one arc.

Private (E-2). One chevron.

Private (E-1). None.

U.S. Army

Source: Department of the Army

Army Military Personnel on Active Duty[1]

June 30[2]	Total strength	Commissioned officers			Warrant officers		Enlisted personnel		
		Total	Male	Female[3]	Male[4]	Female	Total	Male	Female
1940	267,767	17,563	16,624	939	763	—	249,441	249,441	—
1942	3,074,184	203,137	190,662	12,475	3,285	—	2,867,762	2,867,762	—
1943	6,993,102	557,657	521,435	36,222	21,919	0	6,413,526	6,358,200	55,325
1944	7,992,868	740,077	692,351	47,726	36,893	10	7,215,888	7,144,601	71,287
1945	8,266,373	835,403	772,511	62,892	56,216	44	7,374,710	7,283,930	90,780
1946	1,889,690	257,300	240,643	16,657	9,826	18	1,622,546	1,605,847	16,699
1950	591,487	67,784	63,375	4,409	4,760	22	518,921	512,370	6,551
1955	1,107,606	111,347	106,173	5,174	10,552	48	985,659	977,943	7,716
1960	871,348	91,056	86,832	4,224	10,141	39	770,112	761,833	8,279
1965	967,049	101,812	98,029	3,783	10,285	23	854,929	846,409	8,520
1970	1,319,735	143,704	138,469	5,235	23,005	13	1,153,013	1,141,537	11,476
1975	781,316	89,756	85,184	4,572	13,214	22	678,324	640,621	37,703
1980 (Sept 30)	772,661	85,339	77,843	7,496	13,265	113	673,944	612,593	61,351
1984 (Sept. 30)	775,594	92,484	82,497	9,987	15,156	243	667,711	601,695	66,616
1985 (Sept. 30)	776,244	94,103	83,563	10,540	15,296	288	666,557	598,639	67,918
1988 (Mar. 30)	764,247	93,173	81,904	11,269	14,664	363	656,047	584,305	71,742
1989 (Mar. 30)	760,237	91,550	80,113	11,437	14,517	417	653,753	581,106	72,647
1990 (Mar. 30)	746,220	91,330	79,520	11,810	15,177	470	639,713	567,015	72,698
1991 (Mar. 30)	740,023	89,448	77,489	11,959	14,771	505	635,299	564,180	71,119
1992 (Mar. 30)	661,391	85,953	74,326	11,627	13,840	494	561,104	496,335	64,769

(1) Represents strength of the active Army, including Philippine Scouts, retired Regular Army personnel on extended active duty, and National Guard and Reserve personnel on extended active duty; excludes U.S. Military Academy cadets, contract surgeons, and National Guard and Reserve personnel not on extended active duty.

(2) Data for 1940 to 1947 include personnel in the Army Air Forces and its predecessors (Air Service and Air Corps).

(3) Includes: women doctors, dentists, and Medical Service Corps officers for 1946 and subsequent years, women in the Army Nurse Corps for all years, and the Women's Army Corps and Women's Medical Specialists Corps (dieticians, physical therapists, and occupational specialists) for 1943 and subsequent years.

(4) Act of Congress approved April 27, 1926, directed the appointment as warrant officers of field clerks still in active service. Includes flight officers as follows: 1943, 5,700; 1944, 13,615; 1945, 31,117; 1946, 2,580.

The Federal Service Academies

U.S. Military Academy, West Point, N.Y. Founded 1802. Awards B.S. degree and Army commission for a 5-year service obligation. For admissions information, write Admissions Office, USMA, West Point, NY 10996.

U.S. Naval Academy, Annapolis, Md. Founded 1845. Awards B.S. degree and Navy or Marine Corps commission for a 5-year service obligation. For admissions information, write Dean of Admissions, Naval Academy, Annapolis, MD 21402.

U.S. Air Force Academy, Colorado Springs, Col. Founded 1954. Awards B.S. degree and Air Force commission for a 5-year service obligation. For admissions information, write Registrar, U.S. Air Force Academy, CO 80840.

U.S. Coast Guard Academy, New London, Conn. Founded 1876. Awards B.S. degree and Coast Guard commission for a 5-year service obligation. For admissions information, write Director of Admissions, Coast Guard Academy, New London, CT 06320.

U.S. Merchant Marine Academy, Kings Point, N.Y. Founded 1943. Awards B.S. degree, a license as a deck, engineer, or dual officer, and a U.S. Naval Reserve commission. Service obligations vary according to options taken by the graduate. For admissions information, write Admission Office, U.S. Merchant Marine Academy, Kings Point, NY 11024.

U.S. Navy Insignia

Source: Department of the Navy

Navy

Stripes and corps device are of gold embroidery.

Stripes

Fleet Admiral . . . . . 1 two inch with 4 one-half inch.
Admiral . . . . 1 two inch with 3 one-half inch.
Vice Admiral. . . . . . 1 two inch with 2 one-half inch.
Rear Admiral (upper half) . . . . 1 two inch with 1 one-half inch.
Rear Admiral (lower half) . . . . 1 two inch.
Captain. . . . . 4 one-half inch.
Commander . . . . . . 3 one-half inch.
Lieut. Commander . . 2 one-half inch, with 1 one-quarter inch between.
Lieutenant . . . . 2 one-half inch.
Lieutenant (j.g.) . . . . 1 one-half inch with one-quarter inch above.
Ensign . . . . 1 one-half inch.

Warrant Officers—One 1/2" broken with 1/2" intervals of blue as follows:

Warrant Officer W-4—1 break
Warrant Officer W-3—2 breaks, 2" apart
Warrant Officer W-2—3 breaks, 2" apart

The breaks are symmetrically centered on outer face of the sleeve.

Enlisted personnel (non-Commissioned petty officers)...A rating badge worn on the upper left arm, consisting of a spread eagle, appropriate number of chevrons, and centered specialty mark.

Marine Corps

Marine Corps and Army officer insignia are similar. Marine Corps and Army enlisted insignia, although basically similar, differ in color, design, and fewer Marine Corps subdivisions. The Marine Corps' distinctive cap and collar ornament is a combination of the American eagle, globe, and anchor.

Coast Guard

Coast Guard insignia follow Navy custom, with certain minor changes such as the officer cap insignia. The Coast Guard shield is worn on both sleeves of officers and on the right sleeve of all enlisted personnel.

U.S. Navy Personnel on Active Duty

June 30	Officers	Nurses	Enlisted	Off. Cand.	Total
1940	13,162	442	144,824	2,569	160,997
1945	320,293	11,086	2,988,207	61,231	3,380,817
1950	42,687	1,964	331,860	5,037	381,538
1960	67,456	2,103	544,040	4,385	617,984
1970	78,488	2,273	605,899	6,000	692,660
1980	63,100[1]	—	464,100[2]	—	527,200
1990 (Sept.)	74,429[1]	—	530,133[2]	—	604,562
1992 (Mar.)	71,826	—	500,459	—	572,285

(1) Nurses are included. (2) Officer candidates are included.

Marine Corps Personnel On Active Duty

Year	Officers	Enlisted	Total	Year	Officers	Enlisted	Total	Year	Officers	Enlisted	Total
1955	18,417	186,753	205,170	1970	24,941	234,796	259,737	1988	20,079	177,271	197,350
1960	16,203	154,418	170,621	1980	18,198	170,271	188,469	1989	20,099	176,857	196,956
1965	17,258	172,955	190,213	1985	20,175	177,850	198,025	1990	19,958	176,694	196,652

Veteran Population

Source: Dept. of Veterans Affairs; U.S. Census, 1990

Total Veterans in civil life[a,b,c]	**27,183,662**
Total Wartime Veterans	**20,985,702**
Total Vietnam Era	8,232,414
Vietnam Era with Service in Korean Conflict	585,506
Vietnam Era with no Prior Wartime Service	7,646,908
Total Korean Conflict	4,931,165
Korean Conflict with Service in WWII	883,307
Korean Conflict with no Prior Wartime Service	4,047,858
World War II	9,228,738
World War I	62,198
Total Peacetime Veterans	**6,197,960**
Total Post Vietnam Era	3,054,763
Service Between Korean Conflict and Vietnam Era Only	2,944,497
Other Peacetime	198,700

NOTE: Detail may not add to total shown due to rounding. (a) The category "War veterans" equals the sum of Vietnam era (no service in Korean conflict), Korean conflict (no service in World War II), World War II and World War I. The data refer only to veterans living in the U.S. and Puerto Rico since data on veterans living elsewhere are not available. (b) There is 1 living Spanish-American War veteran. There are also an indeterminate number of Mexican Border period veterans, 59 of whom were receiving benefits in March 1991. (c) Estimates for Persian Gulf war not shown separately; data indicate that, as of Mar. 31, 1991, there were approx. 130,000 Persian Gulf war veterans. About 80 percent are included with the Post-Vietnam era peacetime veteran totals; approx. 20 percent are listed as Vietnam era veterans.

Compensation and Pension Case Payments

Fiscal year	Living veteran cases no.	Deceased veteran cases no.	Total cases no.	Total disbursement dollars	Fiscal year	Living veteran cases no.	Deceased veteran cases no.	Total cases no.	Total disbursement dollars
1900	752,510	241,019	993,529	138,462,130	1960	3,008,935	950,802	3,959,737	3,314,761,383
1910	602,622	318,461	921,083	159,974,056	1970	3,127,338	1,487,176	4,614,514	5,113,649,490
1920	419,627	349,916	769,543	316,418,029	1980	3,195,395	1,450,785	4,646,180	11,045,412,000
1930	542,610	298,223	840,833	418,432,808	1990	2,746,329	837,596	3,583,925	15,535,069,000
1940	610,122	239,176	849,298	429,138,465	1991	2,709,500	799,677	3,509,177	15,975,440,000
1950	2,368,238	658,123	3,026,361	2,009,462,298					

USAF and Air Reserve Forces Personnel by Categories

Category	FY '87	FY '88	FY '89	FY '90	FY '91[1]	FY '92[1]
Air Force Military						
Officers	107,300	105,100	103,700	100,000	96,700	92,000
Airmen	495,200	466,900	462,800	430,800	407,500	390,500
Cadets	4,500	4,500	4,400	4,400	4,300	4,300
Total, Air Force Military	**607,000**	**576,500**	**570,900**	**535,200**	**508,500**	**486,800**
Career Reenlistments	41,400	51,500	39,400	44,600	36,300	38,800
Rate	87%	86%	87%	82%	85%	85%
First-Term Reenlistments	25,600	26,500	18,100	23,600	20,700	17,900
Rate	62%	50%	59%	51%	55%	55%
Civilian Personnel						
Direct Hire (including Technicians)	251,771	241,120	248,666	237,844	227,732	214,505
Indirect Hire—Foreign Nationals	12,559	12,041	11,909	11,031	11,397	9,653
Total, Civilian Personnel	**264,330**	**253,161**	**260,575**	**248,875**	**239,129**	**224,158**
Total, Military and Civilian[1]	**871,230**	**829,607**	**831,455**	**784,075**	**747,629**	**710,958**
Technicians (included above as Direct Hire Civilians)						
AFRES Technicians	8,772	9,111	10,061	9,596	10,316	10,343
ANG Technicians	23,221	23,409	23,644	24,119	23,521	24,639
Air Reserve Forces						
Air National Guard, Selected Reserve	114,600	115,221	114,975	117,786	116,610	118,100
Air Force Reserve, Paid	80,415	82,116	83,214	83,814	85,591	81,200
Air Force Reserve, Nonpaid[3]	43,783	51,658	49,553	68,714	65,296	65,746
Total, Ready Reserve[3]	**238,798**	**248,995**	**247,742**	**270,314**	**267,497**	**265,046**
Standby	24,479	21,772	17,299	15,369	17,075	17,075
Total, Air Reserve Forces[4]	**263,277**	**270,767**	**265,041**	**285,683**	**284,572**	**282,121**

Note: Totals may not add due to rounding. (1) President's budget request. (2) FY '87-90 are actual figures; FY '91-92 are estimates; excludes nonchargeable personnel. (3) Excludes training/pay categories J, K, and L. (4) Excludes Retired Air Force Reserve.

U.S. Air Force Personnel Strength: 1907–1992

Year[1]	Strength	Year[1]	Strength	Year[1]	Strength	Year[1]	Strength
1907	3	1941	152,125	1950	411,277	1988	575,603
1918	195,023	1942	764,415	1960	814,213	1989	570,965
1920	9,050	1943	2,197,114	1970	791,078	1990	535,200
1930	13,531	1944	2,372,292	1980	557,969	1991	508,500
1940	51,165	1945	2,282,259	1986	608,200	1992	494,000

(1) Prior to 1947, data are for U.S. Army Air Corps and Air Service of the Signal Corps.

Coast Guard Personnel on Active Duty: 1970-1992

Source: U.S. Dept. of Transportation, *Annual Report of the Secretary of Transportation.*

Year	Total	Officers	Cadets	Enlisted	Year	Total	Officers	Cadets	Enlisted
1970	37,689	5,512	653	31,524	1985	38,595	6,775	733	31,087
1975	36,788	5,630	1,177	29,981	1986	37,284	6,577	754	29,953
1980	39,381	6,463	877	32,041	1987	38,576	6,644	859	31,073
1981	39,760	6,519	981	32,260	1988	37,723	6,530	887	30,306
1982	38,248	6,431	902	30,915	1990	37,308	6,475	820	29,860
1983	39,708	6,535	811	32,362	1991	37,390	6,783	897	29,710
1984	38,705	6,790	759	31,156	1992	39,314	7,171	858	31,285

Women in the Armed Forces

Women in the Army, Navy, Air Force, Marines, and Coast Guard are all fully integrated with male personnel. Expansion of military women's programs began in the Department of Defense in fiscal year 1973.

As of mid-1990, women made up 10.8 percent of the armed forces. Almost 25% of all medical and dental specialists are women; only 0.8 percent serve in the infantry, gun crews, or seamanship.

Although women are prohibited by law and directives based on law from serving in combat positions, policy changes in the Department of Defense have made possible the assignment of women to almost all other career fields. Career progression for women is now comparable to that for male personnel. Women are routinely assigned to overseas locations formerly closed to female personnel. Women are in command of activities and units that have missions other than administration of women.

Admission of women to the service academies began in the fall of 1976.

Army — Information: Chief, Office of Public Affairs, Dept. of Army, Wash., DC 20310; (as of Mar. 30, 1992): 76,890 women, 64,769 enlisted women, 11,627 women commissioned officers, 494 women warrant officers.

Army Nurse Corps — Brig. Gen. Nancy R. Adams, Chief Army Nurse Corps, Office of the Surgeon General, Dept. of Army, 5109 Leesburg Pike, Falls Church, VA 22041.

Navy — Information: Chief of Information, Dept. of Navy, Wash., DC 20350-1200; 8,232 women officers; 51,729 enlisted women; 674 cadets and midshipwomen, as of 6/30/91.

Navy Nurse Corps — Rear Adm. Mary Stratton, Dir., Navy Nurse Corps, Dept. of Navy, Wash., DC 20372-2000; 2,308 women officers; 809 men. (As of 6/30/91).

Air Force — Information: Office of Public Affairs, Dept. of the Air Force, Wash., DC 20330; 13,323 women officers; 58,540 enlisted women.

Air Force Nurse Corps — Brig. Gen. Sue Turner, Chief, Air Force Nurse Corps, Office of the Surgeon Gen., USAF, Bolling AFB, Wash., DC 20332.

Marine Corps — Information: Commandant of the Marine Corps (Code PA), Headquarters, Marine Corps, Wash., DC 20380-0001; 677 women officers; 8,679 enlisted women.

Coast Guard — Information: Commander Judith Hammond c/o Commandant (G-PDP), U.S. Coast Guard, 2100 Second St., SW, Wash., DC 20593-0001; 366 women commissioned officers; 16 woman warrant officer; 2,066 enlisted women.

Active Duty U.S. Military Personnel Strengths—Worldwide

(As of Dec. 31, 1991)

Source: U.S. Department of Defense

U.S. Territories & Special Locations	
Continental U.S.	1,198,992
Alaska	22,823
Hawaii	45,175
Guam	5,823
Marshall Islands	38
Puerto Rico	3,560
Transients	66,780
Afloat	186,486
Total[1]	**1,529,981**
Western & Southern Europe	
Belgium	2,277
Germany	183,507
Greece	1,331
Greenland	157
Iceland	3,186
Italy	14,421
Netherlands	2,629
Norway	221
Portugal	1,648
Spain	5,414
Turkey	5,436
United Kingdom	23,348
Afloat	18,114
Total[1]	**262,128**
European NATO	**243,744**
East Asia & Pacific	
Australia	691
Japan	45,067
Philippines	5,787
Rep. of Korea	39,513
Thailand	127
Afloat	17,726
Total[1]	**109,186**
Africa, Near East & South Asia	
Bahrain	289
Diego Garcia	972
Egypt	1,145
Saudi Arabia	3,217
Afloat	14,613
Total[1]	**20,634**
Other Western Hemisphere	
Bermuda	1,155
Canada	521
Cuba (Guantanamo)	2,996
Honduras	836
Panama	10,987
Afloat	2,226
Total[1]	**19,403**
Total Worldwide	**1,944,243**
Ashore	1,705,078
Afloat	239,165

(1) Area totals include countries with less than 100 assigned U.S. military members.

Estimates of Total Dollar Costs of American Wars

(In millions of dollars, except percent)

Source: *The Military Budget and National Economic Priorities*, revised and updated by James L. Clayton, Univ. of Utah.

Item	World War II	Vietnam Conflict	Korean Conflict	World War I	Civil War: Union	Civil War: Confederacy	Spanish American War	American Revolution	War of 1812	Mexican War
Original increment, direct costs:[1]										
Current dollars	360,000	140,600	50,000	32,700	2,300	1,000	270	100-140	89	82
Constant (1967) dollars	816,300	148,800	69,300	100,000	8,500	3,700	1,100	400-680	170	300
Percent 1 year's GNP	188	14	15	43	74	123	2	104	14	4
Service-connected veterans' benefits[2]	87,629	26,175	17,024	19,273	3,290	—	2,111	28	20	26
Interest, pmts. on war loans[3]	(5)	(5)	(5)	11,000	1,200	(5)	60	20	14	10
Current cost to 1986[4]	447,629	166,775	67,024	62,973	6,790	(5)	2,441	170	120	120

(1) Figures are rounded and taken from Claudia D. Goldin, *Encyclopedia of American Economic History*. (2) Total cost to Oct. 1, 1986. For World War I and later wars, benefits are actual service-connected figures from 1986 *Annual Report* of Veterans Administration. For earlier wars, service-connected veterans' benefits are estimated at 40 percent of total, the approximate ratio of service-connected to total benefits since World War I. (3) Total cost to 1986. Interest payments are a very rough approximation based on the percentage of the original costs of each war financed by money creation and debt, the difference between the level of public debt at the beginning of the war and at its end, and the approximate time required to pay off the war debts. (4) Figures are rounded estimates. (5) Unknown.

The Medal of Honor

The Medal of Honor is the highest military award for bravery that can be given to any individual in the United States. The first Army Medals were awarded on March 25, 1863, and the first Navy Medals went to sailors and Marines on April 3, 1863.

The Medal of Honor, established by Joint Resolution of Congress, 12 July 1862 (amended by Act of 9 July 1918 and Act of 25 July 1963) is awarded in the name of Congress to a person who, while a member of the Armed Forces, distinguishes himself conspicuously by gallantry and intrepidity at the risk of his life above and beyond the call of duty while engaged in an action against any enemy of the United States; while engaged in military operations involving conflict with an opposing foreign force; or while serving with friendly foreign forces engaged in an armed conflict against an opposing armed force in which the United States is not a belligerent party. The deed performed must have been one of personal bravery or self-sacrifice so conspicuous as to clearly distinguish the individual above his comrades and must have involved risk of life. Incontestable proof of the performance of service is exacted and each recommendation for award of this decoration is considered on the standard of extraordinary merit.

Prior to World War I, the 2,625 Army Medal of Honor awards up to that time were reviewed to determine which past awards met new stringent criteria. The Army removed 911 names from the list, most of them former members of a volunteer infantry group during the Civil War who had been induced to extend their enlistments when they were promised the Medal.

Since that review Medals of Honor have been awarded in the following numbers:

World War I	96	Korean War	131
World War II	432	Vietnam	238

Armed Services Senior Enlisted Adviser

The U.S. Army, Navy and Air Force in 1966-67 each created a new position of senior enlisted adviser whose primary job is to represent the point of view of his services' enlisted men and women on matters of welfare, morale, and any problems concerning enlisted personnel. The senior adviser will have direct access to the military chief of his branch of service and policy-making bodies.

The senior enlisted adviser for each Dept. is:

Army—Sgt. Major of the Army Richard A. Kidd.

Navy—Master Chief Petty Officer of the Navy John Hagan.

Air Force—Chief Master Sgt. of the AF Gary R. Pfingston.

Marines—Sgt. Major of the Marine Corps Harold G. Overstreet.

Nuclear Arms Treaties and Negotiations: An Historical Overview

Aug. 4, 1963—Nuclear Test Ban Treaty, signed in Moscow by the U.S., USSR, and Great Britain, prohibited testing of nuclear weapons in space, above ground, and under water.

Jan. 1967—Outer Space Treaty banned the introduction of nuclear weapons into space.

1968—Non-proliferation of Nuclear Weapons Treaty, with U.S., USSR, and Great Britain as major signers, limited the spread of military nuclear technology by agreement not to assist nonnuclear nations in getting or making nuclear weapons.

May 26, 1972—SALT I (Strategic Arms Limitations Talks) agreement, in negotiation since Nov. 17, 1969, signed in Moscow by U.S. and USSR. In the area of defensive nuclear weapons, the treaty limited antiballistic missiles to 2 sites of 100 antiballistic missile launchers in each country (amended in 1974 to one site in each country). The treaty also imposed a 5-year freeze on testing and deployment of intercontinental ballistic missiles and submarine-launched ballistic missiles. An interim short-term agreement putting a ceiling on numbers of offensive nuclear weapons was also signed. SALT I was in effect until Oct. 3, 1977.

July 3, 1974—Protocol on antiballistic missile systems and a treaty and protocol on limiting underground testing of nuclear weapons was signed by U.S. and USSR in Moscow.

Nov. 24, 1974—Vladivostok Agreement announced establishing the framework for a more comprehensive agreement on offensive nuclear arms, setting the guidelines of a second SALT treaty.

Sept. 1977—U.S. and USSR agreed to continue to abide by SALT I, despite its expiration date.

June 18, 1979—SALT II, signed in Vienna by the U.S. and USSR, constrained offensive nuclear weapons, limiting each side to 2,400 missile launchers and heavy bombers with that ceiling to apply until Jan. 1, 1985. The treaty also set a combined total of 1,320 ICBMs and SLBMs with multiple warheads on each side. Although approved by the U.S. Senate Foreign Relations Committee, the treaty never reached the Senate floor because Pres. Jimmy Carter withdrew his support for the treaty following the December 1979 invasion of Afghanistan by Soviet troops.

Nov. 18, 1981—U.S. Pres. Ronald Reagan proposed his controversial "zero option" to cancel deployment of new U.S. intermediate-range missiles in Western Europe in return for Soviet dismantling of comparable forces (600 SS-20, SS-4, and SS-5 missiles already stationed in the European part of its territory).

Nov. 30, 1981—Geneva talks on limiting intermediate nuclear forces based in and around Europe began.

May 9, 1982—U.S. Pres. Ronald Reagan proposed 2-step plan for strategic arms reductions and announced that he had proposed to the USSR that START (Strategic Arms Reduction Talks) begin in June.

May 18, 1982—Soviet Pres. Leonid Brezhnev rejected Reagan's plan as one-sided, but responded positively to the call for arms reduction talks.

June 29, 1982—START (Strategic Arms Reduction Talks) began in Geneva.

1985-1987—Disarmament talks between the U.S. and the USSR began in Geneva, Switzerland on March 12, 1985.

Dec. 8, 1987—I.N.F. (Intermediate-Range Nuclear Forces) Treaty signed in Washington, D.C. by USSR leader Mikhail Gorbachev and U.S. Pres. Ronald Reagan eliminating all medium- and shorter-range nuclear missiles; ratified with conditions by U.S Senate on May 27, 1988.

July 31, 1991—Strategic Arms Reduction Treaty (START) signed, in Moscow, by Soviet Pres. Mikhail Gorbachev and U.S. Pres. George Bush to reduce strategic offensive arms by approximately 30 percent in three phases over seven years. START is the first treaty to mandate reductions by the superpowers. (The treaty will need approval by the U.S. Senate and Soviet legislature.)

(For details and 1991-1992 developments see Index and Chronology.)

Leading Arms Exporters, 1989

Source: U.S. Arms Control and Disarmament Agency

(value of exports in millions of dollars)

1. Soviet Union	$19,600	6. W. Germany	$1,200	11. N. Korea	$400
2. United States	11,200	7. Czechoslovakia	875	12. Poland	400
3. United Kingdom	3,000	8. Israel	625	13. Egypt	370
4. France	2,700	9. Sweden	575	14. E. Germany	330
5. China	2,000	10. Canada	410	15. Bulgaria	160

Based on a report delivered to Congress, July 1992, based on data supplied by the Defense Dept. and U.S. intelligence agencies, arms sales to the "third world" fell sharply in 1991. Total sales fell 40 percent, to $24.7 billion, the lowest level in 7 years. The U.S., which surpassed the Soviet Union as the biggest supplier in 1990, accounted for 57 percent of all sales in 1991. Saudi Arabia spent $5.6 billion, nearly 40 percent of total U.S. sales to the third world.

Leading Arms Importers, 1989

Source: U.S. Arms Control and Disarmament Agency

	Principal supplier[1]	Imports (millions of dollars)		Principal supplier[1]	Imports (millions of dollars)
1. Saudi Arabia	United Kingdom	$4,200	11. Turkey	United States	$1,100
2. Afghanistan	Soviet Union	3,800	12. Syria	Soviet Union	1,000
3. India	Soviet Union	3,500	13. Libya	Soviet Union	975
4. Greece	United States	2,000	14. Ethiopia	Soviet Union	925
5. Iraq	Soviet Union	1,900	15. Soviet Union	Czechoslovakia	900
6. United States	—	1,600	16. W. Germany	United States	875
7. Japan	United States	1,400	17. United Arab Emirates	France	850
8. Iran	—	1,300	18. E. Germany	Soviet Union	825
9. Vietnam	Soviet Union	1,300	19. Angola	Soviet Union	750
10. Cuba	Soviet Union	1,200	20. Spain	United States	750

(1) Supplies more than 50 percent of total value of imports.

Percentage of Central Government Expenditures Spent on Defense, 1989

Source: U.S. Arms Control and Disarmament Agency

1. Afghanistan	NA
2. Syria	69.8
3. Iraq	NA
4. Yugoslavia	53.4
5. Cambodia	NA
6. Qatar	NA
7. Soviet Union	45.7
8. Vietnam	NA
9. Mozambique	42.1
10. Oman	41.4
11. United Arab Emirates	40.7
12. Chad	NA
13. Korea, North	39.5
14. Saudi Arabia	38.6
15. El Salvador	37.3
16. Nicaragua	NA
17. Jordan	32.7
18. Burma	30.8
19. Ethiopia	30.5
20. Taiwan	30.4
21. Yemen (Sanaa)	29.8
22. Bulgaria	29.7
23. Libya	29.2
24. Madagascar	28.9
25. Angola	NA
26. United States	25.5
27. Bolivia	25.4
28. Israel	25.2
29. Yemen (Aden)	NA
30. Pakistan	24.6

NA = not available.

Armed Forces Per 1,000 Persons, 1989

Source: U.S. Arms Control and Disarmament Agency

1. Jordan	60.5
2. Iraq	55.3
3. Korea, North	49.5
4. Israel	44.0
5. Yemen (Aden)	34.9
6. Syria	33.3
7. Cuba	28.3
8. Libya	21.0
9. Singapore	20.7
10. Nicaragua	20.4
11. United Arab Emirates	20.3
12. Oman	20.3
13. Greece	20.1
14. Cyprus	19.9
15. Taiwan	18.6
16. Bulgaria	16.7
17. Germany, East	15.9
18. Mongolia	15.5
19. Vietnam	15.4
20. Korea, South	15.1
21. Qatar	15.1
22. Cambodia	14.5
23. Laos	14.1
24. Turkey	13.9
25. Albania	13.5
26. Angola	12.9
27. Soviet Union	12.8
28. Iran	11.2
29. Czechoslovakia	11.2
30. Belgium	11.1

Monthly Military Pay Scale

Source: U.S. Dept. of Defense

(effective Jan. 1, 1992)

	Years of Service						
Rank/Grade	2	4	8	12	16	20	26
General—0-10	$6643.50	$6643.50	$6898.20	$7280.40	$7801.20	$8323.50	$8842.20[1]
Lt. General—0-9	5836.50	5961.00	6112.50	6366.90	6898.20	7280.40	7801.20
Major General—0-8	5306.10	5431.80	5836.50	6112.50	6366.90	6898.20	7068.30
Brig. General—0-7	4571.40	4571.40	4776.60	5053.50	5836.50	6238.20	6238.20
Colonel—0-6	3485.70	3714.30	3714.30	3714.30	4447.50	4776.60	5480.70
Lt. Colonel—0-5	2979.30	3185.40	3185.40	3458.40	3966.60	4320.90	4471.80
Major—0-4	2604.60	2778.30	2954.70	3333.60	3638.70	3739.20	3739.20
Captain—0-3	2222.40	2628.60	2853.00	3156.30	3233.70	3233.70	3233.70
1st Lt.—0-2	1892.70	2350.50	2399.40	2399.40	2399.40	2399.40	2399.40
2d Lt.—0-1	1566.30	1892.70	1892.70	1892.70	1892.70	1892.70	1892.70
Chief Warrant—W-4	2172.60	2222.40	2425.80	2704.20	2929.20	3104.70	3458.40
Warrant Officer—W-1	1539.90	1668.30	1818.90	1971.00	2121.90	2274.30	2274.30
Sgt. Major—E-9	0.00	0.00	0.00	2408.70	2519.70	2626.20	3032.70
Master Sgt.—E-8	0.00	0.00	1975.50	2085.60	2196.30	2301.90	2708.40
Sgt. 1st class—E-7	1488.90	1598.10	1705.20	1814.70	1950.60	2031.00	2436.90
Staff Sgt.—E-6	1293.30	1404.60	1509.60	1645.80	1752.30	1779.00	1779.00
Sergeant—E-5	1133.40	1240.20	1375.50	1482.60	1509.60	1509.60	1509.60
Corporal—E-4	1025.70	1170.00	1216.20	1216.20	1216.20	1216.20	1216.20
Pvt. 1st class—E-3	965.40	1043.40	1043.40	1043.40	1043.40	1043.40	1043.40
Private—E-2	880.50	880.50	880.50	880.50	880.50	880.50	880.50
Recruit—E-1	785.70	785.70	785.70	785.70	785.70	785.70	785.70

(1) Basic pay is limited to $8,733.30.

Chairmen of the Joint Chiefs of Staff

Gen. of the Army Omar N. Bradley, USA	Aug. 16, 1949 – Aug. 14, 1953
Adm. Arthur W. Radford, USN	Aug. 15, 1953 – Aug. 14, 1957
Gen. Nathan F. Twining, USAF	Aug. 15, 1957 – Sept. 30, 1960
Gen. Lyman L. Lemnitzer, USA	Oct. 1, 1960 – Sept. 30, 1962
Gen. Maxwell D. Taylor, USA	Oct. 1, 1962 – July 3, 1964
Gen. Earle G. Wheeler, USA	July 3, 1964 – July 2, 1970
Adm. Thomas H. Moorer, USN	July 3, 1970 – June 30, 1974
Gen. George S. Brown, USAF	July 1, 1974 – June 20, 1978
Gen. David C. Jones, USAF	June 21, 1978 – June 18, 1982
Gen. John W. Vessey Jr., USA	June 18, 1982 – Sept. 30, 1985
Adm. William J. Crowe, Jr., USN	Oct. 1, 1985 – Sept. 30, 1989
Gen. Colin L. Powell, USA	Oct. 1, 1989 –

Casualties in Principal Wars of the U.S.

Data on Revolutionary War casualties is from *The Toll of Independence*, Howard H. Peckham, ed., U. of Chicago Press, 1974.

Data prior to World War I are based on incomplete records in many cases. Casualty data are confined to dead and wounded personnel and therefore exclude personnel captured or missing in action who were subsequently returned to military control. Dash (—) indicates information is not available.

Wars	Branch of service	Number serving	Casualties: Battle deaths	Other deaths	Wounds not mortal[8]	Total
Revolutionary War	**Total**	**—**	**6,824**	**18,500**	**8,445**	**33,769**
1775-1783	Army	184,000	5,992	—	7,988	13,980
	Navy &	to	—	—	—	—
	Marines	250,000	832	—	457	1,289
War of 1812	**Total**	**286,730[9]**	**2,260**	—	**4,505**	**6,765**
1812-1815	Army	—	1,950	—	4,000	5,950
	Navy	—	265	—	439	704
	Marines	—	45	—	66	111
Mexican War	**Total**	**78,718[9]**	**1,733**	**11,550**	**4,152**	**17,435**
1846-1848	Army	—	1,721	11,500	4,102	17,373
	Navy	—	1	—	3	4
	Marines	—	11	—	47	58
Civil War	**Total**	**2,213,363[9]**	**140,414**	**224,097**	**281,881**	**646,392**
(Union forces only)	Army	2,128,948	138,154	221,374	280,040	639,568
1861-1865	Navy	—	2,112	2,411	1,710	6,233
	Marines	84,415	148	312	131	591
Confederate forces	**Total**	**—**	**74,524**	**59,297**	**—**	**133,821**
(estimate)[1]	Army	600,000	—	—	—	—
1863-1866	Navy	to	—	—	—	—
	Marines	1,500,000	—	—	—	—
Spanish-American War	**Total**	**306,760**	**385**	**2,061**	**1,662**	**4,108**
	Army[4]	280,564	369	2,061	1,594	4,024
1898	Navy	22,875	10	0	47	57
	Marines	3,321	6	0	21	27
World War I	**Total**	**4,743,826**	**53,513**	**63,195**	**204,002**	**320,710**
April 6, 1917-	Army[5]	4,057,101	50,510	55,868	193,663	300,041
Nov. 11, 1918	Navy	599,051	431	6,856	819	8,106
	Marines	78,839	2,461	390	9,520	12,371
	Coast Guard	8,835	111	81	—	192
World War II	**Total**	**16,353,659**	**292,131**	**115,185**	**670,846**	**1,078,162**
Dec. 7, 1941-	Army[6]	11,260,000	234,874	83,400	565,861	884,135
Dec. 31, 1946[2]	Navy[7]	4,183,466	36,950	25,664	37,778	100,392
	Marines	669,100	19,733	4,778	67,207	91,718
	Coast Guard	241,093	574	1,343	—	1,917
Korean War	**Total**	**5,764,143**	**33,629**	**20,617**	**103,284**	**157,530**
June 25, 1950-	Army	2,834,000	27,704	9,429	77,596	114,729
July 27, 1953[3]	Navy	1,177,000	458	4,043	1,576	6,077
	Marines	424,000	4,267	1,261	23,744	29,272
	Air Force	1,285,000	1,200	5,884	368	7,452
	Coast Guard	44,143	—	—	—	—
Vietnam (preliminary)[10]	**Total**	**8,744,000**	**47,356**	**10,795**	**153,303**	**211,324**
Aug. 4, 1964-	Army	4,368,000	30,904	7,274	96,802	134,972
Jan. 27, 1973	Navy	1,842,000	1,626	923	4,178	6,697
	Marines	794,000	13,082	1,754	51,392	66,213
	Air Force	1,740,000	1,739	842	931	3,435
	Coast Guard	—	5	2	—	7

(1) Authoritative statistics for the Confederate Forces are not available. An estimated 26,000-31,000 Confederate personnel died in Union prisons.

(2) Data are for the period Dec. 1, 1941 through Dec. 31, 1946 when hostilities were officially terminated by Presidential Proclamation, but few battle deaths or wounds not mortal were incurred after the Japanese acceptance of Allied peace terms on Aug. 14, 1945. Numbers serving from Dec. 1, 1941-Aug. 31, 1945 were: Total—14,903,213; Army—10,420,000; Navy—3,883,520; and Marine Corps—599,693.

(3) Tentative final data based upon information available as of Sept. 30, 1954, at which time 24 persons were still carried as missing in action.

(4) Number serving covers the period April 21-Aug. 13, 1898, while dead and wounded data are for the period May 1-Aug. 31, 1898. Active hostilities ceased on Aug. 13, 1898, but ratifications of the treaty of peace were not exchanged between the United States and Spain until April 11, 1899.

(5) Includes Air Service Battle deaths and wounds not mortal include casualties suffered by American forces in Northern Russia to Aug. 25, 1919 and in Siberia to April 1, 1920. Other deaths covered the period April 1, 1917-Dec. 31, 1918.

(6) Includes Army Air Forces.

(7) Battle deaths and wounds not mortal include casualties incurred in Oct. 1941 due to hostile action.

(8) Marine Corps data for World War II, the Spanish-American War and prior wars represent the number of individuals wounded, whereas all other data in this column represent the total number (incidence) of wounds.

(9) As reported by the Commissioner of Pensions in his Annual Report for Fiscal Year 1903.

(10) Number serving covers the period Aug. 4 1964-Jan. 27, 1973 (date of ceasefire). Number of casualties incurred in connection with the conflict in Vietnam from Jan. 1, 1961-Sept. 30, 1977. Includes casualties incurred in Mayaguez Incident. Wounds not mortal exclude 150,375 persons not requiring hospital care.

CONSUMER INFORMATION

Consumer Information Catalog

Source: Consumer Information Center, U.S. General Services Administration

The *Consumer Information Catalog* is a free listing of about 200 of the best federal consumer publications. They range from booklets on financial planning to planning a diet, from learning about federal benefits to getting an education, from fixing a car to dealing effectively with consumer problems, to getting a passport or a birth certificate. Many of these booklets are free.

The *Consumer Information Catalog* is published quarterly by the Consumer Information Center of the U.S. General Services Administration, so you will be able to send for the most current booklets. For your free copy of the *Consumer Information Catalog*, send your name and address to: Consumer Information Catalog, Pueblo, CO 81009. Educators, libraries, and other non-profit groups who are able to distribute 25 or more copies of the *Consumer Information Catalog* on a quarterly basis should write to the same address for an application to be placed on the mailing list. Costs prevent the Consumer Information Center from maintaining a mailing list for individuals.

The booklets listed below are available *free* from the *Consumer Information Catalog* as of Fall, 1992. Quantities of some may be limited. There is a $1 fee for handling. To order, please send your name and address, the item numbers of the booklets you want, and the $1 fee to: S. James, Consumer Information Center, Pueblo, CO 81009.

Some Free Publications

Parenting

Handbook on Child Support Enforcement. The basic steps to follow if you need child support enforcement services; tips on solving enforcement problems. 40 pp. (1989) **509Y.**

Growing Up Drug Free. Shows what children should understand about drugs, including alcohol and tobacco, identifies classes and types of drugs, and resource contacts. 55 pp. (1989) **508Y.**

Education

Schools Without Drugs. Guide for parents, schools, students, and communities on how to fight drug use by children. Describes extent of the problem, effects of various drugs, and signs of use. Includes legal considerations and an extensive list of resources. 94 pp. (1989) **512Y.**

The Student Guide: Financial Aid. Describes federal grants, loans, and work/study programs for college, vocational and technical school students after high school. 50 pp. (1992-3) **522Y.**

AIDS and the Education of Our Children. Facts about AIDS, its transmission, and how teens are at risk. Methods of protection, guidelines for selecting educational materials, and sources for more information. 34 pp. (1988) **506Y.**

Federal Benefits

Request for Earnings and Benefit Estimate Statement. A form to complete and return to Social Security to get your earnings history and an estimate of future benefits. 3 pp. (1989) **521Y.**

Understanding Social Security. An easy to understand overview of the Social Security system. Explains retirement, disability, and survivor's benefits; Medicare coverage; and Supplemental Security Income. 41 pp. (1991) **523Y.**

Food & Nutrition

Food Additives ... give consistency; maintain nutritional value, and enhance the flavor of foods. Find out what food additives are, how they are approved and regulated, and when they are most often used. 14 pp. (1992) **605Y.**

Food Irradiation—Toxic to Bacteria, Safe for Humans. Irradiation kills harmful organisms so they cannot survive or multiply in your food. Learn how this safe and effective process works and why it is especially useful in certain foods. 4 pp. (1991) **529Y.**

Preventing Food-Borne Illness. Discusses symptoms, prevention tips, and safe storage. Also charts common disease-causing organisms and where they come from. 7 pp. (1991) **534Y.**

Quick Consumer Guide to Safe Food Handling. Reduce the risk of food poisoning when shopping for, preparing, serving and reheating food by learning how long some foods can be safely frozen or refrigerated. 8 pp. (1990) **535Y.**

Diet, Nutrition, and Cancer Prevention: The Good News. This booklet will help you select, prepare and serve healthier food. Includes lists of high-fiber and low-fat foods. 15 pp. (1986) **526Y.**

Health

Contact Lenses: The Better the Care the Safer the Wear. Discusses the risks of infection, and has a step-by-step chart for proper care of hard, gas-permeable and extended-wear soft lenses. 3 pp. (1991) **539Y.**

Getting the Lead Out. Learn the serious health risks of lead poisoning from paint, soil, glassware, water pipes, etc., and why infants and children are most at risk. Includes information on symptoms, treatments, how to reduce exposure to lead and more. 6 pp. (1991) **614Y.**

Guide to Choosing a Nursing Home. Suggestions to help plan, visit and evaluate your need. Includes information on food services, payment, Medicare/Medicaid coverage, insurance, contracts, and more. 19 pp. (1992) **606Y.**

Who Donates Better Blood for You Than You? Discusses the advantages of donating blood to yourself before undergoing surgery. 3 pp. (1991) **544Y.**

Smart Advice for Women 40 and Over: Have a Mammogram. A mammogram is an X-ray of the breast designed to find cancer in its earliest stages. Learn how often, and why, you should have one. 4 pp. (1990) **543Y.**

Facing Forward: A Guide for Cancer Survivors. Advice on coping with the psychological, physical, and financial effects of this illness. Provides practical information on health care (both emotional and physical), insurance coverage, job concerns, and more. 45 pp. (1990) **541Y.**

Good News for Blacks About Cancer. Blacks have a higher than average risk of getting certain cancers. Learn preventative actions to minimize your risk. 9 pp. (1987) **542Y.**

AIDS. How AIDS is spread, how to prevent it, and what to do if you think you've been infected. 2 pp. (1988) **552Y.**

Breast Lumps: Questions and Answers. Straightforward discussion of benign and cancerous growths. Questions to ask your doctor, where to go for more information, and a self-examination guide. 23 pp. (1988) **554Y.**

Getting a Second Opinion. Answers questions of the prospective patient. Includes toll-free number for locating specialists. 5 pp. (1989) **557Y.**

Mental Health

A Consumer's Guide to Mental Health Services. Answers commonly asked questions about mental health and the different methods of treating mental illness. Lists resources for further help and information. 28 pp. (1987) **562Y.**

Plain Talk About Depression. Nine million Americans suffer from depressive illness during any six month period. Learn about the symptoms and causes; how it's diagnosed and treated; and how to help. 4 pp. (1989) **563Y.**

Plain Talk About Mutual Help Groups. Gain strength through sharing with others who have similiar problems: An overview of the many support groups available. 6 pp. (1989) **564Y.**

What to Do When a Friend Is Depressed. Identifies common myths, warning signals, and suggests ways to help. 6 pp. (1989) **569Y.**

Plain Talk about Stress. What stress is and how to deal with it. 2 pp. (1987) **566Y.**

Plain Talk About Wife Abuse. The causes, emotional and physical consequences, and where an abused wife can get help. 3 pp. (1983) **567Y.**

Schizophrenia: Questions and Answers. Describes this chronic, debilitating illness affecting millions of Americans: its nature, causes, treatments, how others can help, and the outlook for recovery. 25 pp. (1986) **568Y.**

Money Management

Information About Marketable Treasury Securities. Learn about bills, notes, and bonds sold at original issue through your local Federal Reserve Bank or Bureau of the Public Debt. 16 pp. (1991) **575Y.**

Investment Swindles: How They Work and How to Avoid Them. How to protect yourself against illegal telemarketing and direct mail offers. 20 pp. (1987) **576Y.**

Investors' Bill of Rights. Tips to help you make an informed decision on investment risks and costs. 7 pp. (1987) **577Y.**

How to Get the Most for Your Money

Source: *Consumer's Resource Handbook*

Before Making a Purchase:

(1) Analyze what you need and what features are important to you.

(2) Compare brands. Use word-of-mouth recommendations and formal product comparison reports. Check with your local library for magazines and other publicatons containing consumer information.

(3) Compare stores. Look for a store with a good reputation and take advantage of sales.

(4) Check for any additional charges, such as delivery and service costs.

(5) Compare warranties.

(6) Read terms of contracts carefully.

(7) Check the return or exchange policy.

After Your Purchase:

(1) Follow proper use and care instructions for products.

(2) Read and understand the warranty provisions. Keep in mind that you may have additional warranty rights in your state. Check with your state or local consumer office to find out.

(3) If trouble develops, report the problem as soon as possible. Do not try to fix the product yourself as this may void the warranty.

(4) Keep a record of efforts to have your problem remedied. This record should include names of people you speak to, times, dates, and other relevant information.

(5) Send for the *Consumer's Resource Handbook* (see *Source*, above) to find out where and how to get your problem resolved.

(6) Clearly state your problem and the solution you want.

(7) Include all relevant details, along with copies of documents (proof of purchase).

(8) Briefly describe what you have done to resolve the problem.

(9) Allow each person you contact a reasonable period of time to resolve your problem before contacting another source for assistance.

Handling Your Own Complaint:

(1) Identify your problem and what you believe would be a fair settlement. Do you want your money back? Would you like the product repaired? Will an exchange do?

(2) Gather documentation regarding your complaint. Sales receipts, repair orders, warranties, cancelled checks, or contracts will back up your complaint and help the company solve your problem.

(3) Go back to where you made the purchase. Contact the person who sold you the item or performed the service. Calmly and accurately explain the problem and what action you would like taken. If that person is not helpful, ask for the supervisor or manager and repeat your complaint. A large percentage of consumer problems are resolved at this level. Chances are yours will be too.

(4) Don't give up if you are not satisfied with the response. If the company operates nationally or the product is a national brand, write a letter to the person responsible for consumer complaints at the company's headquarters. A listing of many of these companies can be found in the World Almanac's Business Directory on pages 781–787. If the company doesn't have a consumer office, direct your letter to the president of the company.

How to Write a Complaint Letter:

(1) If you have already contacted the person who sold you the product or service or the company is out of town, you will need to write a letter to pursue your complaint.

(2) If you need the president's name and the address of the company, first check in your phone directory to see if the company has a local office. If it does, call and ask for the name and address of the company's president. If there is no local listing, check *Standard & Poor's Register of Corporations, Directors and Executives.* It lists over 37,000 American business firms and can be found in most libraries.

(3) If you don't have the name of the manufacturer of the product, check your local library for the *Thomas Register.* It lists the manufacturers of thousands of products.

Basic Tips on Letter Writing:

(1) Include your name, address, and home and work phone numbers.

(2) Type your letter if possible. If it is handwritten, make sure it is neat and easy to read.

(3) Make your letter brief and to the point. Include all important facts about your purchase, including the date and place where you made the purchase, and any information you can give about the product or service such as serial or model numbers or specific type of service.

(4) State exactly what you want done about the problem and how long you are willing to wait to get it resolved. Be reasonable.

(5) Include all documents regarding your problems. Be sure to send COPIES, not originals.

(6) Avoid writing an angry, sarcastic, or threatening letter. The person reading your letter probably was not responsible for your problem, but may be very helpful in resolving it.

(7) Keep a copy of the letter for your records.

Business Directory

Listed below are major U.S. corporations, and major foreign corporations, whose operations—products and services—directly concern the American consumer. At the end of each listing is a representative sample of some of the company's products.

Company . . . Address . . . Phone Number . . . Chief executive officer . . . Business.

A & W Brands Inc. . . . 709 Westchester Ave., White Plains, NY 10604 . . . (914) 397-1700 . . . M.L. Lowenkron . . . soft drinks.

AMR Corp. . . . PO Box 619616, Dallas/Ft. Worth Airport, TX 75261 . . . (817) 963-1234 . . . Robert Crandall . . . Air transportation (American Airlines).

Abbott Laboratories . . . One Abbott Park Rd., Abbot Park, IL 60064 (708) 937-6100 . . . D.L. Burnham . . . health care prods.

Aetna Life & Casualty Co. . . . 151 Farmington Ave., Hartford, CT 06156 . . . (203) 273-0123 . . . Ronald E. Compton . . . insurance, financial services.

H.F. Ahmanson & Co. . . . 660 S. Figueroa St., Los Angeles, CA 90017 . . . (213) 955-4200 . . . R.H. Deihi . . . operates largest S&L assn. in U.S. (Home Savings of America).

Alberto-Culver Co. . . . 2525 Armitage Ave., Melrose Park, IL 60160 . . . (708) 450-3000 . . . Leonard H. Lavin . . . hair care preparations, feminine hygiene products, household and grocery items.

Albertson's Inc. . . . 250 Parkcenter Blvd., Boise, ID 83726 . . . (208) 385-6200 . . . Gary Michael . . . supermarkets.

Alcan Aluminium Ltd. . . . 1188 Sherbrooke St. W., Montreal, Que., Canada H3A 3G2 . . . (514) 848-8050 . . . David Morton . . . aluminum producer.

Alexander & Alexander Services Inc. . . . 1211 Ave. of the Amer., New York, NY 10036 . . . (212) 840-8500 . . . T.H. Irvin . . . insurance & financial services.

Allied-Signal Inc. . . . Box 2245R, Morristown, NJ 07960 . . . (201) 455-2000 . . . Lawrence Bossidy . . . aerospace, engineered materials, automotive prods.

Alltel Corp. . . . One Allied Dr., Little Rock, AR 72202 . . . (501) 661-8000 . . . J.T. Ford . . . telephone service in Midwest, South, and Eastern U.S.

Aluminum Co. of America . . . 1501 Alcoa Bldg., Pittsburgh, PA 15219 . . . (412) 553-4545 . . . Paul O'Neill . . . mining, refining, & processing of aluminum.

Amerada Hess Corp. . . . 1185 Ave. of the Americas, N.Y., NY 10036 . . . (212) 997-8500 . . . L. Hess . . . integrated petroleum co.

American Brands, Inc. . . . 1700 E. Putnam Ave., Old Greenwich, CT 06870 (203) 698-5000 . . . W.J. Alley . . . tobacco (Pall Mall, Carlton, Half and Half, Paleden pipe tobacco), whiskey (Jim Beam), snack foods, life insurance, office prods., food, financial services, toiletries.

American Cyanamid Co. . . . One Cyanamid Plaza, Wayne, NJ 07470 . . . (201) 831-2000 . . . G.J. Sella Jr. . . . medical, agricultural, chemical, and consumer prods.

American Express Co. . . . 200 Vesey St., N.Y., N.Y. 10285 (212) 640-2000 . . . J.D. Robinson 3d . . . travelers checks, credit card services, insurance, investment services (Shearson Lehman).

American Greetings Corp. . . . 10500 American Rd., Cleveland, OH 44144 . . . (216) 252-7300 . . . M. Weiss . . . greeting cards, stationery, gift items.

American Home Products Corp. . . . 685 3d Ave., N.Y., NY 10017 . . . (212) 878-5000 . . . J.R. Stafford . . . prescription and ethical drugs (Advil, Anacin, Robitussin), household prods. (Woolite, Easy-Off oven cleaner; Black Flag, Wizard air fresheners), food (Chef Boy-ar-dee).

American Stores Co. . . . 709 E. South Temple., Salt Lake City, Utah 84102 . . . (801) 539-0112 . . . J.L. Scott & Victor Lund . . . retail food markets, dept. & drug stores.

American Telephone & Telegraph Co. . . . 550 Madison Ave. N.Y., NY 10022 . . . (212) 605-5500 . . . Robert Allen . . . communications, financial services.

Amoco Corp. . . . 200 E. Randolph Dr., Chicago, IL 60601 . . . (312) 856-6111 . . . H.L. Fuller . . . oil and gas exploration, production, and marketing.

Anheuser-Busch, Inc. . . . One Busch Place, St. Louis, MO 63118 . . . (314) 577-2000 . . . August A. Busch 3d . . . brewing (Budweiser, Michelob, Bud Light, Natural Light, King Cobra, Busch), theme parks, snack foods (Eagle).

Apple Computer, Inc. . . . 10260 Bandley Dr., Cupertino, CA 95014 . . . (408) 996-1010 . . . John Sculley . . . Manuf. personal computers.

Armstrong World Industries . . . P.O. Box 3001, 313 W. Liberty St., Lancaster, PA 17604 . . . (717) 397-0611 . . . W.W. Adams . . . interior furnishings.

Arvin Industries, Inc. . . . 1531 13th St., Columbus, IN 47201 . . . (812) 379-3000 . . . J.K. Baker . . . auto emission & noise control systems.

Ashland Oil, Inc. . . . P.O. Box 391, Ashland, KY 41114 . . . (212) 421-1250 . . . J.R. Hall . . . petroleum refiner, chemicals.

Atlantic Richfield Co. . . . 515 S. Flower St., Los Angeles, CA 90071-2256 . . . (213) 486-3511 . . . L.M. Cook . . . petroleum, chemicals, other natural resources.

Avery Denison Corp. . . . 150 N. Orange Grove Blvd., Pasadena, CA 91103 . . . (818) 304-2000 . . . Charles D. Miller . . . self-adhesive labels, office prods., specialty chemicals.

Avon Products, Inc. . . . 9 West 57th St., N.Y., NY 10019 . . . (212) 546-6015 . . . J. E. Preston . . . cosmetics, fragrances, toiletries, health care.

Bally Manufacturing Corp. . . . 8700 W. Bryn Mawr Ave., Chicago, IL 60631 . . . (312) 399-1300 . . . A.M. Goldberg . . . lottery and gaming equip., hotel-casino operator, health & fitness centers.

Bausch & Lomb . . . One Lincoln First Square, Rochester, NY 14601 . . . (716) 338-6000 . . . D.E. Gill . . . manuf. of vision care products, accessories.

Baxter International Inc. . . . One Baxter Pky., Deerfield, IL 60015 . . . (708) 948-2000 . . . Vernon R. Loucks Jr. . . . medical care prods & services.

Bell Atlantic Corp. . . . 1600 Market St., Philadelphia, PA 19103 . . . (215) 963-6000 . . . R.W. Smith . . . telephone service in mid-Atlantic region.

BellSouth Corp. . . . 1155 Peachtree St. NE, Atlanta, GA 30367 . . . (404) 249-2000 . . . J.L. Clendenin . . . telephone service in the South.

Bethlehem Steel Corp. . . . 8th & Eaton Ave., Bethlehem, PA 18016 . . . (215) 694-2424 . . . W.F. Williams . . . steel & steel prods.

Bic Corporation . . . Wiley Street, Milford, CT 06401 . . . (203) 783-2070 . . . Bruno Bich . . . writing instruments, disposable lighters, and shavers.

Black & Decker Corp. . . . 701 E. Joppa Rd., Towson, MD 21204 . . . (410) 583-3900 . . . N.D. Archibald . . . manuf. power tools, household prods., small appliances.

H & R Block, Inc. . . . 4410 Main St., Kansas City, MO 64111 . . . (816) 753-6900 . . . Henry W. Bloch . . . tax preparation.

Blockbuster Entertainment Corp. . . . 901 E. Las Olas Blvd., Ft. Lauderdale, FL 33301 . . . (305) 524-8200 . . . H. Wayne Huizenga . . . video rental superstores.

Boeing Company . . . 7755 E. Marginal Way So., Seattle, WA 98108 . . . (206) 655-2121 . . . F.A. Shrontz . . . aircraft manuf.

Boise Cascade Corp. . . . One Jefferson Square, Boise, ID 83728 . . . (208) 384-6161 . . . J.B. Fery . . . timber, paper, wood prod.

Borden, Inc. . . . 277 Park Ave., N.Y., NY 10172 . . . (212) 573-4000 . . . A.S. D'Amato . . . food, cheese and cheese products, snacks (Cracker Jack), beverages, adhesives (Elmer's, Krazy Glue), pasta (Prince, Creamette), pasta sauce (Aunt Millie's, Classico).

Bristol-Myers Squibb Co. . . . 345 Park Ave., N.Y., NY 10022 . . . (212) 546-4000 . . . Richard L. Gelb . . . toiletries (Ban anti-perspirant), hair items (Clairol), drugs (Bufferin, Nuprin, Comtrex, Excedrin), household prods. (Drano, Windex), infant formula (Enfamil).

Brown-Forman Inc. . . . 850 Dixie Highway, Louisville, KY 40210 . . . (502) 585-1100 . . . W.L.L. Brown Jr. . . . distilled spirits (Jack Daniel's, Early Times), wines (Bolla, Fontana Candita), champagne (Korbel), liquor (Southern Comfort), Lenox china and crystal.

Brown Group, Inc. . . . 8400 Maryland Ave., St. Louis, MO 63105 . . . (314) 854-4000 . . . B.A. Brightwater Jr. . . . manuf. and wholesaler of women's and children's shoes (Buster Brown, Naturalizer); specialty retailing.

Brunswick Corp. . . . One Brunswick Plaza, Skokie, IL 60077 . . . (708) 470-4700 . . . J.F. Reichert . . . marine, recreation prods., bowling centers & equip., fishing equip.

Burlington Coat Factory Warehouse Corp. . . . 1830 Route 130 North, Burlington, NJ 08016 . . . (609) 387-7800 . . . M.G. Milstein . . . discount apparel stores.

Burlington Northern Inc. . . . 777 Maun St., Ft. Worth, TX 76102 . . . (817) 878-2000 . . . G. Grinstein . . . rail transportation.

CBS Inc. . . . 51 W. 52d St., N.Y., NY 10019 . . . (212) 975-4321 . . . L.A. Tisch . . . broadcasting.

CPC International, Inc. . . . International Plaza, Englewood Cliffs, NJ 07632 . . . (201) 894-4000 . . . Charles Shoemate . . . branded food items (Hellman's, Best Foods, Mazola oil,

Skippy peanut butter, Knorr Soups, Thomas English muffins), corn wet milling prods.

Caesar's World, Inc....1801 Century Park East, Los Angeles, CA 90067...(213) 552-2711...H. Gluck...hotels & casinos, resort hotels.

Campbell Soup Co....Campbell Pl., Camden, NJ 08103...(609) 342-3823...D.W. Johnson...canned soups, spaghetti (Franco-American), vegetable juice (V-8), pork and beans, pet foods, restaurants, confections, Le Menu frozen dinners, Prego spaghetti sauce, Mrs. Paul's frozen fish, Pepperidge Farm breads.

Capital Cities/ABC, Inc....77 W. 66th Street, New York, NY 10023...(212) 456-7777...D.B. Burke...operates television and radio stations, newspapers, cable TV (ESPN); newspapers, specialized business and consumer periodicals.

Carnival Cruise Lines Inc....3655 NW 87 Ave., Miami, FL 33178-2428...(305) 599-2600...M. Arison...Cruise Line.

Carter-Wallace, Inc....1345 Ave. of the Amer., New York, NY 10105...(212) 339-5000...H.H. Hoyt Jr....personal care items, anti-perspirant (Arrid), shave lathers (Rise), condoms (Trojan), laxative (Carter's Pills), pet products.

Caterpillar Inc....100 N.E. Adams St., Peoria, IL 61629...(309) 675-1000...Donald Fites...heavy duty earthmoving equip.

Chase Manhattan Corp....1 Chase Manhattan Plaza, New York, NY 10081...(212) 552-2222...Thomas Labrecque ...Bank holding co.

Chevron Corp....225 Bush St., San Francisco, CA 94104...(415) 894-7700...K.T. Derr...integrated oil co.

Chrysler Corp....12000 Chrysler Dr., Highland Pk., MI 48288...(313) 956-5252...Lee Iacocca...cars, trucks.

Circuit City Stores, Inc....9950 Maryland Dr., Richmond, VA 23233...(804) 527-4000...R.L. Sharp...retailer of electronic equip., consumer appliances.

Circus Circus Enterprises, Inc. ...2880 Las Vegas Blvd. S., Las Vegas, NV 89109...(702) 734-0410...W.G. Bennett ...casino operator.

Citicorp...399 Park Ave., N.Y., NY 10043...(212) 559-1000...J.S. Reed...largest U.S. commercial bank.

Clayton Homes...P.O. Box 15169, Knoxville, TN 37901...(615) 970-7200...J.L. Clayton...produces & sells manufactured homes.

Clorox Co....1221 Broadway, Oakland, CA 94612...(415) 271-7000...C.R. Weaver...retail consumer prods (Formula 409, Pine-Sol, Kingsford charcoal briquets, Hidden Valley Ranch salad dressing, Soft Scrub cleanser).

Coachman Industries Inc....601 E. Beardsley Ave., Elkhart, IN 46514...(219) 262-0123...T.H. Corson...manuf. recreational vehicles.

Coca-Cola Co....One Coca-Cola Plaza N.W., Atlanta, GA 30313...(404) 676-2121...R.C. Goizueta...soft drinks (Coca-Cola, Sprite, Ramblin root beer), syrups, citrus and fruit juices (Minute Maid, Hi-C).

Colgate-Palmolive Co....300 Park Ave., N.Y., NY 10022...(212) 310-2000...R. Mark...soaps (Palmolive, Irish Spring), detergents (Fab, Ajax, Fresh Start), tooth paste (Colgate, Ultra Brite), household prods. (Handy Wipes, Curad bandages).

Commodore International Ltd....1200 Wilson Dr., West Chester, PA 19380...(215) 431-9100...I. Gould...microcomputer systems, semiconductors component, consumer electronics, office equipment.

Compaq Computer Corp....20555 SH 149, Houston, TX 77070...(713) 370-0670...E. Pfeiffer...portable, desktop computers.

Control Data Corp....8100 34th Ave. South, Minneapolis, MN 55440...(612) 853-8100...L. Perlman...computer systems & services.

Adolph Coors Co....Golden, CO 80401...(303) 279-6565...W. K. Coors...brewery.

Corning Inc....Houghton Park, Corning, NY 14831...(607) 974-9000...J.R. Houghton ...glass mfg.

Crane Co....757 3d Ave., N.Y., NY 10017...(212) 415-7300...R.S. Evans...fluid & pollution controls, aircraft and aerospace, building prods.

A.T. Cross Co....One Albion Rd., Lincoln, RI 02865...(401) 333-1200...B.R. Boss...writing instruments.

Crystal Brands, Inc....Crystal Brands Rd., Southport, CT 06490...(203) 254-6200...R.F. Kral...apparel, accessories (Evan Picone, Izod).

Culbro Corp....387 Park Avenue South, New York, NY 10016...(212) 561-8700...E. M. Cullman...cigars (Corina, Robert Burns, White Owl, Tiparillo's), snack foods.

Dana Corp....4500 Dorr St., Toledo, OH 43615...(419) 535-4500...S.J. Morcott...truck and auto parts supplies.

Data General Corp....4400 Computer Dr., Westboro, MA 01580...(508) 366-8911...R.L. Skates...computer & communications sytems manuf.

Dayton Hudson Corp....777 Nicollet Mall, Minneapolis, MN 55402...(612) 370-6948...K.A. Macke...department, specialty, stores, Mervyn's, Target.

Deere & Co....John Deere Rd., Moline, IL 61265...(309) 765-8000...H.W. Becherer...farm, industrial, and outdoor power equip.

Delta Air Lines, Inc....Hartsfield Atlanta Intl. Airport, Atlanta, GA 30320...(404) 715-2600...Ronald W. Allen...air transportation.

Dial Corp....Dial Tower, Phoenix, AZ 85077-2346...(602) 207-4000...J.W. Teets...consumer prods. (Dial, Purex), contract and fast food services, manuf. buses.

Diebold, Inc....P.O. Box 8230, Canton, OH 44711...(216) 489-4000...R.P. Barone...manuf. equip. for financial insts.

Digital Equipment Corp....146 Main St., Maynard, MA 01754-2571...(508) 493-5111...Kenneth H. Olsen...computer systems manuf.

Walt Disney Co....500 S. Buena Vista St., Burbank, CA 91521...(818) 560-1000...M.D. Eisner...motion pictures, CATV, amusement parks, Disneyland, Walt Disney World, Epcot Center.

Dole Food Co....31355 Oak Crest Drive, Westlake Village, CA 91361...(818) 879-6600...David Murdock...food products, fresh fruits and vegetables, real estate.

Dollar General Corp....104 Woodmont Blvd., Ste. 5000, Nashville, TN 37205...(615) 386-4000...Cal Turner...self-service discount stores.

R.R. Donnelley & Sons Co....2223 Martin Luther King Drive, Chicago, IL 60616...(312) 326-8000...J.R. Walter...largest commercial printer.

Dow Chemical Co....2030 Dow Center, Midland, MI 48674...(517) 636-1000...F.P. Popoff...chemicals, plastics, metals, consumer prods. (Ziploc, Saran Wrap, Fantastik).

Dow Jones & Co....200 Liberty St., New York, NY 10281...(212) 416-2000...P. R. Kann...financial news service, publishing (Wall Street Journal, Barron's, Ottaway Newspapers).

Dun & Bradstreet Corp....299 Park Ave., New York, NY 10171...(212) 593-6800...C.W. Moritz...business information and computer services, publishing, broadcasting.

E.I. du Pont de Nemours & Co....1007 Market St., Wilmington, DE 19898...(302) 774-1000...Edgar Woolard Jr....chemicals, petroleum, consumer prods., coal.

Eastman Kodak Co....343 State St., Rochester, NY 14650...(716) 724-4685...K.R. Whitmore...photographic prods, chemicals, health care (Sterling Drug).

Eaton Corp....1111 Superior Ave., Cleveland, OH 44114...(216) 523-5000...W.E. Butler...manuf. of electronic, electrical prods., vehicle components.

Emerson Electric Co....8000 W. Florissant Ave., St. Louis, MO 63136...(314) 553-2000...C.F. Knight...electrical/ electronics products & systems

Ethyl Corp....330 S. 4th St., Richmond, VA 23217...(804) 788-5000...B.C. Gottwald...petroleum and industrial chemicals.

Exxon Corp....225 E. John W. Carpenter Freeway, Irving, TX 75062-2298...(214) 444-1000...L.G. Rawl...world's largest oil co.

Family Dollar Stores, Inc....P.O. Box 1017, Charlotte, NC 28201...(704) 847-6961...L. Levine...discount variety stores.

Fabri-Centers of America, Inc...5555 Darrow Rd., Hudson, OH. 44236...(216) 656-2600...Alan Rosskamm...specialty fabric stores.

Fedders Corp....158 Highway 206, P.O. Box 265, Peapack, NJ 07977...(908) 234-2100...S. Giordano...manuf. of room air conditioners.

Federal Express Corp....P.O. Box 727, Memphis, TN 38194...(901) 922-6443...F.W. Smith...small package delivery service.

Fieldcrest Cannon, Inc....326 East Stadium Dr., Eden, NC 27288...(919) 627-3000...J.M. Fitzgibbons...household textile prods., rugs (Karastan, Laurelcrest).

Fleetwood Enterprises, Inc....P.O. Box 7638, Riverside, CA 92523...(714) 351-3500...John C. Crean...manufactured homes, recreational vehicles.

Fluor Corp....3333 Michelson Dr., Irvine, CA 92730...(714) 975-6961...L.G. McGraw...engineering and construction, natural resources.

Ford Motor Co....The American Rd., Dearborn, MI 48121...(313) 845-8540...H.A. Poling...motor vehicles, Ford Tractor, Lincoln-Mercury.

Fruit of The Loom, Inc....233 S. Wacker, 6300 Sears Tower, Chicago, IL 60606...(312) 876-1724...W. Farley...manuf. of men's and boy's underwear.

GTE Corp.... One Stamford Forum, Stamford, CT 06904...(203) 965-2789...J.L. Johnson...telecommunications system prods.
Gannett Co., Inc....1100 Wilson Blvd, Arlington, VA 22234...(703) 284-6000...J.J. Curley...newspaper publishing (USA Today), TV stations, outdoor advertising.
The GAP, Inc...1 Harrison, San Francisco, CA 94105...(415) 952-4400...D.G. Fisher...casual and activewear retailer.
Gencorp...175 Ghent Rd., Fairlawn, OH 44313-3300...(216) 869-4200...A.W. Reynolds...aerospace, auto prods., polymer prods.
Genentech, Inc....460 Point San Bruno Blvd., S. San Francisco, CA 94080...(415) 266-1000...G.K. Raab...world's largest biotechnology corp.
General Cinema Corp....27 Boylston St., Chestnut Hill, MA 02167...(617) 232-8200...R.J. Tarr Jr....movie exhibitor, retailing, publishing.
General Dynamics Corp....3190 Fairview Park Dr., Falls Church, VA 22042...(703) 876-3000...William Anders ... military and commercial aircraft, tactical missiles.
General Electric Co....3135 Easton Ave., Fairfield, CT 06431...(203) 373-2211...J. F. Welch Jr....electrical, electronic equip, finance (Kidder, Peabody & Co.), radio, television (NBC), polymer plastic prods.
General Mills, Inc....P.O. Box 1113, Minneapolis, MN 55440...(612) 540-2444...H.B. Atwater Jr....foods, restaurants, Total, Bisquick, Wheaties, Cheerios, Hamburger Helper, Gorton's, Betty Crocker, Red Lobster Inns.
General Motors Corp....3044 W. Grand Rapids, Detroit, MI 48202-3091...(313) 556-5000...R. C. Stempel...world's largest auto manuf.
Genesco Inc.... Genesco Park, Nashville, TN 37202...(615) 367-7000...W.S. Wire 2d...footwear and men's clothing, Jarman, Johnston & Murphy.
Genuine Parts Co....2999 Circle 75 Pkwy, Atlanta, GA 30339...(404) 953-1700...L. L. Prince...distributes auto replacement parts (NAPA).
Georgia-Pacific Corp....133 Peachtree St., NE, Atlanta, GA 30303...(404) 521-5210...T.M. Hahn Jr....building prods., pulp, paper, chemicals.
Gerber Products Co....445 State St., Fremont, MI 49412...(616) 928-2718...A.A. Piergallini...baby foods, clothing, nursery accessories.
Giant Food Inc....6300 Sheriff Rd., Landover, MD 20785...(301) 341-4100...I. Cohen...supermarkets.
Gillette Co.... Prudential Tower Bldg., Boston, MA 02199...(617) 421-7000...Alfred Zeier...razors, pens (Paper Mate), toiletries (Right Guard deodorants, Foamy shaving cream, Earth Born shampoo), hair products (Toni, Adorn).
Goodyear Tire & Rubber Co....1144 E. Market St., Akron, OH 44316...(216) 796-8576...Stanley Gault...tires, rubber prods.
W.R. Grace & Co.... One Town Center Rd., Boca Raton, FL 33486-1010...(407) 362-2000...J.P. Bolduc...chemicals, natural resources, health care.
Great Atlantic & Pacific Tea Co....2 Paragon Dr., Montvale, NJ 07645...(201) 573-9700...James Wood...supermarket chain.
Grumman Corp....1111 Stewart Ave., Bethpage, NY 11714...(516) 575-3344...Renso Caporali...aerospace, truck bodies, electronics.

Hannaford Bros. Co....145 Pleasant Hill Rd., Scarborough, ME 04074...(207) 883-2911...Hugh G. Farrington...operates supermarkets, drug stores.
Harley-Davidson, Inc....3700 W. Juneau Ave., Milwaukee, WI 53208...(414) 342-4680...R.F. Terrlink...manuf. of motorcycles, parts & accessories.
Hartmarx...101 N. Wacker Dr., Chicago, IL 60606...(312) 372-6300...H.A. Weinberg...apparel manufacturer and retailer (Hickey-Freeman, Hart Schaffner & Marx).
Hasbro Inc....1027 Newport Ave., Pawtucket, R.I. 02862...(401) 431-8697...A.G. Hassenfeld...toy manuf. & marketer (Milton Bradley, Playskool, G.I. Joe, Cabbage Patch Kids, Scrabble).
H.J. Heinz Co....P.O. Box 57, Pittsburgh, PA 15230...(412) 456-6014...Anthony J.F. O'Reilly...foods (Star-Kist, Ore-Ida, '57 Varieties), 9-Lives cat food, Weight Watchers.
Helene Curtis...325 N. Wells St., Chicago, IL 60610...(312) 661-0222...R.J. Gidwitz...hair care prods. (Finesse, Sauve, Salon Selectives).
Hershey Foods Corp....100 Crystal A Dr., Hershey, PA 17033...(717) 534-7552...R.A. Zimmerman...chocolate & confectionery prods., (Reese's peanut butter cups, Kit Kat, Peter Paul Mounds, Almond Joy), pasta (San Giorgio, Ronzoni).
Hewlett-Packard Co....P.O. Box 10301, Palo Alto, CA 94303...(415) 857-1501...John A. Young...manuf. electronic instruments.
Hillenbrand Industries, Inc.... Highway 46, Batesville, IN 47006...(812) 934-7000...D.A. Hillenbrand...manuf. burial caskets, electronically operated hospital beds, luggage.
Home Depot, Inc....2727 Paces Ferry Rd., Atlanta, GA 30339...(404) 433-8211...Bernard Marcus...retailer of building materials & home improvement prods.
Honda Motor Co., LTD...1290 Ave. of the Americas, N.Y., NY 10020...(212) 765-3804...N. Kawamoto...manuf. autos, motorcycles.
Honeywell, Inc.... Honeywell Plaza, Minneapolis, MN 55408...(612) 870-5200...J.J. Renier...industrial systems & controls, aerospace guidance systems, information systems.
Geo. A. Hormel & Co....501 16th Ave. N.E., Austin, MN 55912...(507) 437-5611...R.L. Knowlton...meat packaging, pork and beef prods (Spam, Dinty Moore, Mary Kitchen).
Houghton Mifflin Co.... One Beacon St., Boston, MA 02108...(617) 725-5000...Nader F. Darehshori...book publishing.
Household International Inc....2700 Sanders Rd., Prospect Heights, IL 60070...(708) 564-5000...D.C. Clark...financial and insurance services.
Huffy Corp....7701 Byers Rd., Miamisburg, OH 45342...(513) 866-6251...H.A. Shaw 3d...bicycle manuf.
Humana, Inc....500 W. Main St., Louisville, KY 40201-1438...(502) 580-1000...D. A. Jones...operates hospitals, provides health care plans.

ITT Corp....1330 Ave. of the Amer., N.Y., NY 10022...(212) 258-1000...R.V. Araskog...manuf., installs communciation and electronic equip., auto equip., insurance, financial services, hotels, educational services.
Imperial Oil Ltd....111 St. Clair Ave. W., Toronto, Ont., Canada M5W 1K3...(416) 968-4111...A.R. Haynes...Canada's largest oil co.
International Business Machines Corp.... Old Orchard Rd., Armonk, NY 10504...(914) 765-1900...J.F. Akers...information-handling systems, equip., and services.
International Paper Co....2 Manhattanville Rd., Purchase , NY 10577...(914) 397-1500...J.A. Georges...paper, wood prods.
Johnson & Johnson...501 George St., New Brunswick, NJ 08903...(201) 524-0400...R.S. Larsen...surgical dressings, pharmaceuticals (Tylenol), consumer prods.
Jostens, Inc....5501 Norman Center Dr., Minneapolis, MN 55437...(612) 830-3300...H. W. Lurton...school rings, yearbooks.

K mart Corp....3100 W. Big Beaver Rd., Troy, MI 48084...(313) 643-1000...J. E. Antonini...largest U.S. chain of discount stores, book stores (Walden Book), cafeterias, drug stores (Pay Less Drug Stores), home improvement retail stores.
Kellogg Co.... One Kellogg Sq., Battle Creek, MI 49016...(616) 961-6122...Arnold G. Laugbo...ready to eat cereals & other food prods., Mrs. Smith's Pie Co., Eggo.
Kimberly-Clark Corp....P.O. Box 619100, Dallas, TX 75261-9100...(214) 830-1200...Wayne R. Sanders...paper and lumber prods., consumer prods. (Kleenex, Huggies).
King World Productions, Inc....830 Morris Turnpike, Short Hills, NJ 07078...(201) 376-1313...M. King...syndicator of first-run TV programs.
Knight-Ridder, Inc.... One Herold Plaza, Miami, FL 33101...(305) 376-3838...J.K. Batten...newspaper publishing, TV broadcasting, book publishing, information services.
Kroger Co....1014 Vine St., Cincinnati, OH 45201...(513) 762-4000...Joseph Pichler...grocery chain.

L.A. Gear, Inc....4221 Redwood Ave., Los Angeles, CA 90006...(213) 822-1995...Stanley P. Gold...athletic & leisure footwear, casual apparel.
La-Z-Boy Chair Co....1284 N. Telegraph Rd., Monroe, MI 48161...(313) 242-1444...C. T. Knabusch...reclining chair mfg.
Land's End, Inc.... Land's End Lane, Dodgeville, WI 53595...(608) 935-9341...R.C. Anderson...direct-mail catalog co.
Eli Lilly & Company... Lilly Corp. Center, Indianapolis, IN 46285...(317) 276-2000...Vaughn D. Bryson...mfg. human health and agricultural products.
The Limited, Inc.... Two Limited Pkwy., Columbus, OH 43216...(614) 479-7000...L.H. Wexner...women's apparel stores (Lane Bryant, Lerner, Victoria's Secret), Abercrombie & Fitch.
Litton Industries, Inc....360 N. Crescent Dr., Beverly Hills, CA 90210...(310) 859-5000...O.L. Hoch...industrial systems & services, advanced electronic systems, electronic & electrical prods., marine engineering.

Lockheed Corp....4500 Park Granada Blvd., Calabasas, CA 91399...(818) 712-2000...D.M. Tellep...commercial and military aircraft, missiles.

Loews Corp....667 Madison Ave., N.Y., NY 10021...(212) 545-2000...Laurence A. Tisch...tobacco prods. (Kent, Newport, True), watches, hotels, real estate, insurance.

Long's Drug Stores Corp....141 North Civic Dr., Walnut Creek, CA 94596...(510) 937-1170...R.M. Long...drug store chain.

Lowe's Cos., Inc....P.O. Box 1111, N. Wilkesboro, NC 28656...(919) 651-4000...L.G. Herring...retailer of building materials & related prods.

Luby's Cafeterias, Inc....211 Northeast Loop 410, San Antonio, TX 78265...(512) 654-9000...R. Erben...operates cafeterias in SW U.S.

MCI Communications Corp...1801 Pennsylvania, NW, Washington, DC 20006...(202) 872-1600...Bert Roberts...long-distance telephone carrier.

Manor Care, Inc....10750 Columbia Pike, Silver Spring, MD 20901...(301) 681-9400...S. Bainum Jr...operates nursing centers.

Marriott Corp.... Marriott Dr., Wash., DC 20058...(301) 380-9000...J. Willard Marriott Jr....hotels, food service.

Martin Marietta Corp....6801 Rockledge Dr., Bethesda, MD 20817...(301) 897-6000...N.R. Augustine...electronics, aerospace.

Mattel, Inc....333 Continental Blvd., El Segundo, CA 90245...(213) 524-2000...J.W. Amerman...toy & hobby prods (Barbie doll, Hot Wheels).

May Department Stores Co....611 Olive Street, St. Louis, MO 63101...(314) 342-6300...D.C. Farrell...department stores (Hecht's, Famous Barr, G. Fox, Lord & Taylor, Foley's).

Maytag Corp....403 W. 4th St. North, Newton, IA 50208...(515) 792-7000...Daniel J. Krumm...manuf. home laundry equip, appliances (Magic Chef, Admiral, Norge).

McCormick & Co., Inc....18 Loveton Circle, P.O. Box 600, Sparks, MD 21152-6000...(301) 771-7301...Bailey Thomas...leading manuf. of seasoning & flavoring prods.

McDonald's Corp.... McDonald's Plaza, Oak Brook, IL 60521...(708) 575-7428...M.R. Quinlan...fast service restaurants.

McDonnell Douglas Corp....P.O. Box 516, St. Louis, MO 63166-0516...(314) 232-0232...J. F. McDonnell...commercial & military aircraft, space systems & missiles.

McGraw-Hill, Inc....1221 Ave. of the Americas, New York, NY 10020...(212) 512-2000...J.L. Dionne...book, magazine publishing (Business Week), information & financial services (Standard and Poor's), TV stations.

Mead Corporation... Courthouse Plaza Northeast, Dayton, OH 45463...(513) 495-6323...B.R. Roberts...printing and writing paper, paperboard, packaging, shipping containers, pulp and lumber.

Media General, Inc....333 E. Grace St., Richmond, VA 23219...(804) 649-6000...J.S. Bryan 3d...broadcasting, newspaper publishing.

Medtronic, Inc....7000 Central Ave. N.E., Minneapolis, MN 55432...(612) 574-4000...W.W. George...manuf. prosthetic and therapeutic devices.

Melville Corp....1 Theall Rd., Rye, NY 10580...(914) 925-4000...S.P. Goldstein...shoe stores (Thom McAn), apparel (Marshalls, Chess King), drug stores.

Merck & Co., Inc....P.O. Box 2000, Rahway, NJ 07065...(201) 594-4000...P. Roy Vagelos...human & animal health care prods.

Meredith Corp....1716 Locust St., Des Moines, IA 50336...(515) 284-3000...J.D. Rehm...magazine publishing (Better Homes and Gardens, Ladies Home Journal), book publishing, broadcasting.

Merrill Lynch & Co., Inc.... World Financial Center, N. Tower, N.Y., NY 10281-1220...(212) 449-1000...Daniel P. Tully...securities broker, financial services.

Minnesota Mining & Manuf. Co....3M Center, St. Paul, MN 55144-1000...(612) 733-1110...L.D. DeSimone...abrasives, adhesives, building services & chemicals, electrical, health care, photographic, printing, recording materials, consumer prods. (Scotch Tape, Post-It).

Mobil Corp....3225 Gallows Rd., Fairfax, VA 22037...(703) 846-3000...A.E. Murray...international oil co., chemicals.

Monsanto Company...800 N. Lindbergh Blvd., St. Louis, MO 63167...(314) 694-1000...R. J. Mahoney...chemicals, agricultural prods., pharmaceuticals, consumer prods. (Nutra-Sweet).

Motorola, Inc....1303 E. Algonquin Rd., Schaumburg, IL 60196...(708) 576-5000...G. Fisher...electronic equipment and components.

National Medical Enterprises, Inc....P.O. Box 4070, Santa Monica, CA 90404...(310) 998-8000...R.K. Eamer ...operates hospitals.

National Semiconductor Corp....2900 Semiconductor Dr., Santa Clara, CA 95052-8090...(408) 721-5000...P. Sprague ...manuf. of semiconductors.

Navistar Intl. Corp....455 N. Cityfront Plaza Dr., Chicago, IL 60611...(312) 836-2000...J.C. Cotting...manuf. heavy duty trucks, parts.

New York Times Co....229 W. 43rd St., N.Y., NY 10036...(212) 556-3660...A. O. Sulzberger...newspapers, radio, CATV stations, magazines (Family Circle, Golf Digest).

Nike, Inc....9000 SW Nimbus, Beaverton, OR 97005...(503) 644-9000...Philip Knight...athletic & leisure footware.

Norfolk Southern Corp....3 Commercial Place, Norfolk, VA 23510...(804) 629-2640...A.B. McKinnon...operates Norfolk & Southern railways, freight carrier (North American Van Lines).

Northrop Corp....1840 Century Park E., Los Angeles, CA 90067...(213) 553-6262...K. Kresa...aircraft, electronics, communications.

Nynex Corp....335 Madison Ave., N.Y., NY 10017...(212) 370-7400...W.C. Ferguson...telephone co. in northeast U.S.

Occidental Petroleum Corp....10889 Wilshire Blvd., Los Angeles, CA 90024...(213) 879-1700...Ray Irani...oil, gas, chemicals, coal, agriculture.

Ogden Corp....2 Pennsylvania Plaza, New York NY 10121...(212) 868-6100...R. Ablon...transportation, foods, metals, financial services.

Olin Corp....120 Long Ridge Rd., Stamford, CT 06904...(203) 356-2000...J.W. Johnstone Jr....chemicals, water treatment prods., aerospace.

Olsten Corp.... One Merrick Ave., Westbury, NY 11590...(516) 832-8200...F. N. Liguori...provides temporary workers.

Oshkosh B' Gosh, Inc....112 Otter Ave, Oshkosh, WI 54901...(414) 231-8800...Douglas Hyde...manuf. of children's wear.

Outboard Marine Corp....100 Sea Horse Dr., Waukegan, IL 60085...(708) 689-6200...J.C. Chapman...outboard motors (Evinrude, Johnson), boats.

Owens-Corning Fiberglas Corp.... Fiberglas Tower, Toledo, OH 43659...(419) 248-8000...Glen Hiner...glass fiber and related prods.

Oxford Industries, Inc....222 Piedmont Ave., N.E., Atlanta, GA 30308...(404) 659-2424...J.H. Lanier...manuf. men's and women's apparel.

Pacific Telesis Group...130 Kearny St., San Francisco, CA 94108...(415) 394-3000...S. L. Ginn...telephone service.

Paramount Communications Inc.,...15 Columbus Circle, N.Y., NY 10023...(212) 373-8000...M.S. Davis...entertainment (Paramount Pictures, Madison Square Garden), publishing (Simon & Schuster, Prentice Hall).

J.C. Penney Co....14841 N. Dallas Pkwy., P.O. Box 659000, Dallas, TX 75265-9000...(214) 591-1000...W. R. Howell ...dept. stores, catalog sales, drug stores, insurance.

Pennzoil Co....P.O. Box 2967, Houston, TX 77252-8000...(713) 546-4000...J.L. Pate...Integrated oil and gas co.

Pep Boys—Manny, Moe & Jack...3111 W. Allegheny Ave., Philadelphia, Pa. 19132...(215) 229-9000...M. G. Leibovitz... automotive parts and accessories, retail stores.

PepsiCo, Inc.... PepsiCo. World HQ, Purchase, NY 10577...(914) 253-2000...D.W. Calloway...soft drinks, (Pepsi-Cola, Slice), snack foods (Ruffles, Lays, Doritos), restaurants (Pizza Hut, KFC, Taco Bell).

Perry Drug Stores, Inc....5400 Perry Dr., P.O. Box 436021, Pontiac, MI 48056-6021...(313) 334-1300...J.A. Robinson...drug stores, health care.

Petrie Stores Corp....70 Enterprise Ave., Secaucus, NJ 07094...(201) 866-3600...M.J. Petrie...operates chain of women's specialty stores.

Pfizer Inc....235 E. 42d St., N.Y., NY 10017...(212) 573-2323...W.C. Steere Jr....pharmaceutical, hospital, agricultural, chemical prods., consumer prods (Visine eye drops, Ben-Gay pain relief).

Philip Morris Cos., Inc....120 Park Ave., N.Y., NY 10017...(212) 880-5000...Michael A. Miles...cigarettes (Marlboro, Virginia Slims), beer (Miller High Life, Lite, Lowenbrau brands), packaged foods (Jell-o, Ronzoni pasta, Entenmann baked goods, Maxwell House coffee, Kool Aid, Oscar Mayer meats, Tang, Cheez Whiz & Velveeta cheese prods.).

Phillips-Van Heusen Corp....1290 Ave. of the Americas, New York, NY 10019...(212) 541-5200...L. S. Phillips...manuf. apparel for men & women; operates retail stores.

Pitney Bowes, Inc.... Walter H. Wheeler Jr. Dr., Stamford, CT 06926...(203) 356-5000...G. B. Harvey...postage meters, mail handling equip., office equipment.

Playboy Enterprises, Inc....680 N. Lake Shore Dr., Chicago, IL 60611...(312) 751-8000...C. Hefner...magazine publishing, CATV, merchandising.

Polaroid Corp....549 Technology Sq., Cambridge, MA 02139...(617) 577-2000...I.M. Booth...photographic equip., supplies and optical goods.

Premark Intl., Inc....1717 Deerfield Rd. Deerfield, IL 60015...(708) 405-6000...W.L. Batts...consumer prods. (Tupperware, Hobart, West Bend).

The Price Co....2657 Ariane Dr., San Diego, CA 92117...(619) 581-4600...Robert Price...Operates "Price Club" wholesale retail warehouses.

Primerica, Corp....65 E. 55 St., N.Y., NY 10022...(212) 891-8900...S. I. Weill...insurance financial services (Smith Barney).

Procter & Gamble Co....391 E. 6th St., Cincinnati, OH 45202...(513) 562-1100...E. L. Artzt...soap & detergent (Ivory, Cheer, Tide, Zest), shortenings (Crisco), toiletries (Crest toothpaste, Prell, and Head and Shoulders shampoos, Noxzema, Old Spice) pharmaceuticals (Pepto-Bismol), Pampers disposable diapers, Folgers coffee, Hawaiian Punch, Charmin toilet tissues, Bounty towels, Vicks cough medicines.

Promus Cos. Inc....1023 Cherrry Rd., Memphis, TN 38117...(901) 762-8852...M.D. Rose...casinos (Harrah), lodging (Hampton Inn, Embassy Suites).

Quaker Oats Co.... Quaker Tower, P.O. Box 9001, Chicago, IL 60604...(312) 222-7818...William D. Smithburg...foods, cereal (Quaker Oat Bran, Life, Cap'n Crunch, Puffed Wheat, Puffed Rice), foods (Aunt Jemima, Celeste pizza, Van Camp's pork and beans, Gatorade), pet foods (Ken-L-Ration, Gaines).

Quaker State Corp....255 Elm St., Oil City, PA 16301...(814) 676-7676...J.W. Corn...refining, marketing petroleum prods., filters, mining & marketing coal.

Ralston Purina Co.... Checkerboard Sq., St. Louis, MO 63164...(314) 982-2161...W. P. Stiritz...pet and livestock food (Purina), consumer prods. (Chex cereal, Beech-Nut baby food, Wonder bread, Hostess baked goods, Eveready batteries).

Raytheon Company...141 Spring St., Lexington, MA 02173...(617) 862-6600...Dennis J. Picard...electronics, aviation, appliances...Amana Refrigeration, Beech Aircraft.

Reader's Digest Assn.... Pleasantville, NY 10570...(914) 238-1000...George V. Grune...magazines, books.

Reebok Intl. Ltd....100 Technology Ctr. Dr., Stoughton, MA 02072...(617) 341-5000...P.B. Fireman...athletic & casual footwear, sportswear.

Reynolds Metals Co....6601 W. Broad St., Richmond, VA 23261...(804) 281-2000...Richard G. Holder...aluminum prods.

Rite Aid Corp....P.O. Box 3165, Harrisburg, PA 17105...(717) 761-2633...A. Grass...discount drug stores, beauty aid stores, auto parts stores.

Rockwell Intl. Corp....625 Liberty Ave, Pittsburgh, PA 15222...(412) 565-2000...D. R. Beall...aerospace, electronic, automotive prods.

Rubbermaid Inc....1147 Akron Rd., Wooster, OH 44691...(216) 264-6464...Walter Williams...rubber and plastic consumer prods.

Russell Corp....P.O. Box 272, Alexander City, AL 35010...(205) 329-4000...Eugene C. Gwaltney, chmn....manuf. leisure apparel, athletic uniforms.

Ryder System, Inc....3600 NW 82d Ave., Miami, FL 33166...(305) 593-3726...M. A. Burns...truck leasing service.

Santa Fe Pacific Corp....1700 E. Golf Rd., Schaumberg, IL 60173...(708) 995-6000...Robert D. Krebs...railroad, real estate, construction, natural resources.

Sara Lee Corp....3 First National Plaza, Chicago, IL 60602...(312) 726-2600...J.H. Bryan Jr....baked goods, fresh and processed meats, fresh and frozen fruits and vegetables and other packaged foods, beverages, tobacco products, hosiery, intimate apparel and knitwear, Hanes, Kiwi, Shasta, Hillshire Farm, L'eggs, Isotoner.

Schering-Plough Corp.... One Giralda Farms, Madison, NJ 07940...(201) 822-7000...R. P. Luciano...pharmaceuticals, consumer prods.

Schlumberger Ltd....277 Park Ave., New York, NY 10172...(212) 350-9400...D.E. Baird...oilfield services, electronics, measurement and control devices.

Scott Paper Co.... Scott Plaza, Phila., PA 19113...(215) 522-5000...P. E. Lippincott...toilet tissue, paper towels, napkins.

E.W. Scripps Co....1105 N. Market St., Wilmington, DE 19801...(302) 478-4141...C.E. Scripps, chmn....newspapers, TV & radio stations.

Seagram Co. Ltd....1430 Peel St., Montreal, Que., Canada H3A 1S9...(514) 849-5271...E.M. Bronfman...distilled spirits & wine (Crown Royal, Chivas Regal, Calvert, Wolfschmidt Vodka, Paul Masson, Christian Brothers, Martell, Myer's Jamaica Rum); juice (Tropicana).

Sears, Roebuck & Co.... Sears Tower, Chicago, IL 60684...(312) 875-2500...E.A. Brennan...merchandising, insurance (Allstate), financial services (Dean Witter), real estate (Coldwell Banker).

Service Merchandise, Inc....P.O. Box 24600, Nashville, TN 37202-4600...(615) 660-6000...R. Zimmerman...operates catalog showrooms.

Shaw Industries, Inc....616 E. Walnut Ave., Dalton, GA 30722...(404) 278-3812...R.E. Shaw...manuf. tufted carpeting (Magee, Philadelphia).

Sherwin-Williams Co....101 Prospect Ave. N.W., Cleveland, OH 44115...(216) 566-2000...John G. Breen...world's largest paint producer (Dutch Boy, Kem-Tone).

Skyline Corp....2520 By-Pass Rd., Elkhart, IN 46515...(219) 294-6521...Arthur J. Decio...mfg. housing and recreational vehicles.

Smucker (J.M.) Co.... Strawberry Lane, Orrville, OH 44667 ... (216) 682-3000 ... Timothy Smucker, chmn. ... preserves, jams, jellies, toppings.

Snap-on Tools Corp....2801 80th St., Kenosha, WI 53140...(414) 656-5449...R. A. Cornog...manuf. mechanic's tools, equip.

Sony Corp....9 W. 57th St., New York, NY 10019...(212) 371-5800...N. Ohga...manuf. televisions, radios, tape recorders, audio equip., video tape recorders (Walkman, Betamax); entertainment (Sony Pictures).

Southwest Airlines Co....P.O. Box 36611, Dallas, TX 75235-1611...(214) 904-4000...H.D. Kelleher...air transportation.

Southwestern Bell Corp.... One Bell Center, St. Louis, MO 63101...(314) 235-9800...E.E. Whitacre Jr....telephone communications.

Stanley Works...1000 Stanley Drive, P.O. Box 7000, New Britain CT 06050...(203) 225-5111...R.H. Ayers...hand tools, hardware, door opening equipment.

Stride Rite Corp....5 Cambridge Center, Cambridge, MA 02142...(617) 491-8800...Erwin Shames...manuf. & retailer children's footwear.

Sun Company, Inc....1801 Market St., Philadelphia, PA 19103-1699 ...(215) 977-3000...R.H. Campbell...energy resources co.

Syms Corp.... Syms Way, Secaucus, NJ 07094...(201) 902-9600...S. Syms...operates off-price apparel stores.

Tambrands Inc....777 Westchester Ave., White Plains, NY 10604...(914) 696-6688...C. Chapman...feminine hygiene products (Tampax, Maxithins).

Tandem Computers...19333 Vallco Pkwy., Cupertino, CA 95014-2599...(408) 285-6000...T. Perkins...supplier of computer systems and networks.

Tandy Corp....1800 One Tandy Center, Fort Worth, TX 76102...(817) 390-3700...J.F. Roach...consumer electronics retailing & mfg., Radio Shack.

Teledyne, Inc....1901 Ave. of the Stars, Los Angeles, CA 90067-6046...(213) 277-3311...William Rutledge...electronics, aerospace prods., industrial prods., insurance, finance.

Tenneco, Inc....P.O. Box 2511, Houston, TX 77001...(713) 757-2131...M. H. Walsh...oil, natural gas pipelines, shipbuilding, farm equip.

Texaco Inc....2000 Westchester Ave., White Plains, NY 10650...(914) 253-4000...J.W. Kinnear...petroleum and petroleum prods.

Texas Instruments Inc....13500 N. Central Expressway, Dallas, TX 75265...(214) 995-2551...Jerry Junkins...electrical & electronics prods.

Textron Inc....40 Westminster St., Providence, RI 02903...(401) 421-2800...J.F. Handymon...aerospace, consumer, industrial, metal prods, consumer finance, insurance, management services.

Tiffany & Co....727 5th Ave, New York, NY 10022...(212) 755-8000...W.R. Chaney...designs, manuf., and distributes jewelry & gift items.

Time Warner Inc.... Time & Life Bldg., Rockefeller Center, New York, NY 10020...(212) 522-1212...Steve Ross ... magazine publisher (Time, Sports Illustrated, Fortune, Money, People), CATV (HBO, Cinemax), publishing (Little, Brown, Warner Books).

Tootsie Roll Industries, Inc....7401 S. Cicero Ave., Chicago, IL 60629...(312) 838-3400...M.J. Gordon...candy (Tootsie Roll, Mason Dots, Charms).

Toro Co....8111 Lyndale Ave. South, Bloomington, MN 55420...(612) 887-8801...K. B. Melrose...lawn and turf maintenance (Lawn Boy); snow removal equipment.

Toys "R" Us...461 From Rd., Paramus, NJ 07652...(201) 262-7800...Charles Lazarus...toy retailer, clothing stores (Kids "R" Us).

Transamerica Corp....600 Montgomery St., San Francisco, CA 94111...(415) 983-4000...Frank C. Herringer...insurance, financial, business services.

Travelers Corp.... One Tower Sq., Hartford, CT 06183...(203) 277-0111...E. H. Budd...insurance.
Tribune Co....435 N. Michigan Ave., Chicago, IL 60611...(312) 222-3883...C.T. Brumback...newpaper publishing, broadcasting, entertainment (Chicago Cubs baseball team).
Trinity Industries, Inc....2525 Stemmons Freeway, P.O. Box 10587, Dallas, TX 75207...(214) 631-4420...W.R. Wallace...manufactures variety of metal products.
TRW Inc....1900 Richmond Rd., Cleveland, OH 44124...(216) 291-7000...J.T. Gorman...car and truck operations, electronics, and space systems.
Turner Broadcasting System, Inc....1 CNN Center, Atlanta, GA 30303...(404) 827-1700...R.E. Turner...operates cable TV networks: CNN, TBS, TNT; owns MGM film library; owns Atlanta Braves, Hawks.
Tyson Foods...2210 W. Oaklawn, Springdale, AR 72764...(501) 756-4000...Don Tyson...produces & markets fresh & processed poultry.

USAIR Group, Inc....1911 Jefferson Davis Hwy., Arlington, VA 22202...(703) 418-7000...Seth E. Schofield...air carrier of passengers, property, and mail.
UST Inc....100 W. Putnam Ave., Greenwich, CT 06830...(203) 661-1100...L.F. Bantle...smokeless tobacco (Copenhagen, Skoal, Happy Days), pipes, pipe tobacco.
USX-U.S. Steel Group...600 Grant St., Pittsburgh, PA 15230...(412) 433-1121...C.A. Corry...steel manuf.
Unilever, PLC...390 Park Ave., New York, NY 10022...(212) 906-3398...Michael Perry, chmn....soap, detergent, margarine, frozen food, toothpaste, tea, dried soups, ice cream, cosmetics, fragrances (Lever Brothers, Lipton, Pond's Vaseline Intensive Care, Obsession, Q-Tips, Cutex).
Union Carbide Corp....39 Old Ridgebury Rd., Danbury, CT 06817...(203) 794-2000...R.D. Kennedy...chemicals, industrial gases.
Union Pacific Corp.... Martin Tower, Bethlehem, PA 18018...(215) 861-3200...D. Lewis...railroad, natural resources.
Unisys Corp....P.O. Box 500, Blue Bell, PA 19424-0001...(215) 986-6999...James Unruh...business equip., data processing prods.
U.S. Shoe Corp.... One Eastwood Dr., Cincinnati, OH 45227...(513) 527-7000...B.B. Hudson...apparel, retailer (Casual Corner), shoes (Red Cross, Joyce), eye-care stores (LensCrafters).
United Technologies Corp.... United Technologies Bldg., Hartford, CT 06101...(203) 728-7000...R.F. Daniell ... aerospace, industrial prods. & services, Carrier Corp., Otis Elevator; Pratt & Whitney, Sikorsky Aircraft.
Univar Corp....6100 Carillon Pt., Kirkland, WA 98033...(206) 899-3400...J.W. Bernard...industrial and agricultural chemicals, laboratory and graphic arts products distributor, home furnishing supplies and fabrics distributors.
Universal Foods Corp....433 East Michigan St., Milwaukee, WI 53202...(414) 271-6755...G.A. Osborn...yeast products, cheese products, dehydrated seasonings, food colors and flavors, imported gourmet foods.
Upjohn Co....700 Portage Rd., Kalamazoo, MI 49001...(616) 323-4000...T. Cooper...pharmaceuticals (Lopid, Dilantin, Accupril), chemicals, agricultural and health care prods.

VF Corp....1047 No. Park Rd., Wyomissing, PA 19610...(215) 378-1151...L.R. Pugh...apparel, Vanity Fair, Lee, Wrangler jeans, Bassett-Walker, Jantzen.

Wal-Mart Stores Inc.... Box 116, Bentonville, AR 72716...(501) 273-4000...S. Robson Walton, chmn....retail dept. stores.
Walgreen Co....200 Wilmot Rd., Deerfield, IL 60015...(312) 940-2500...Charles R. Walgreen 3d...retail drug chain, restaurants.
Wang Laboratories, Inc.... One Industrial Ave., Lowell, MA 01851...(508) 459-5000...R.W. Miller...word processors.
Warner-Lambert Co....201 Tabor Rd., Morris Plains, NJ 07950...(201) 540-2000...M.R. Goodes, chmn....health care prods. (Benadryl), consumer prods. (Efferdent dental cleanser, Hall cough tablets, Schick razors, Rolaids antacid, Listerine mouthwash).
Washington Post Co....1150 15th St., N.W., Washington, DC 20071...(202) 334-6000...D.E. Graham...newspapers, magazines (Newsweek), TV stations.
Weis Markets, Inc....1000 South Second Street, Sunbury, PA 17801...(717) 286-4571...S. Weis...operates supermarkets, distributes frozen foods and grocery items.
Wells Fargo & Co....420 Montgomery St., San Francisco, CA 94163...(415) 396-3606...C.E. Reichardt...banking.
Wendy's Intl., Inc....4288 W. Dublin-Granville Rd., Dublin, OH 43017...(614) 764-3100...J.W. Near...quick service restaurants.
Westinghouse Electric Corp.... Westinghouse Bldg., Gateway Center, Pittsburgh, PA 15222 ... (412) 244-2000 ... P.E. Lego...manuf. electrical, mechanical equip.; radio and television stations.
Westvaco Corp....299 Park Avenue, New York, NY 10171...(212) 688-5000...J.A. Luke...manufactures paper for graphic reproduction, communications, and packaging (largest producer of envelopes in the world).
Weyerhaeuser Co.... Tacoma, WA 98477...(206) 924-2345...George H. Weyerhaeuser...manuf., distribution of forest prods.
Whirlpool Corp.... Benton Harbor, MI 49022...(616) 926-5000...D.R. Whitwam...major home appliances.
Whitman Corp....111 Crossroads of Commerce, 3501 Algonquin Rd., Rolling Meadows, IL 60008...(708) 818-5000...Bruce S. Chelberg... diversified prods. and services, consumer prods., food, auto prods. (Midas).
Willamette Industries, Inc....3800 1st Interstate Tower, 1300 SW 5th Ave., Portland, OR 97201...(503) 227-5581...William Swindells... building materials and paper prods.
Winn-Dixie Stores, Inc....5050 Edgewood Ct., Jacksonville, FL 32205...(904) 783-5000...A.D. Davis, chmn....supermarket chain.
Winnebago Industries, Inc....P.O. Box 152, Forest City, IA 50436...(515) 582-3535...J.K. Hanson, chmn....manuf. of motor homes, recreation vehicles.
Wolverine World Wide Corp....9341 Courtland Dr., Rockford, MI 49351...(616) 866-5500...T.D. Gleason...manuf. footwear (Hush Puppies).
Woolworth Corp....233 Broadway, N.Y., NY 10279...(212) 553-2000...H.E. Sells...variety stores, shoe stores (Kinney), men's clothing (Richman Brothers), children's apparel (Kid's Mart), athletic footwear (Foot Locker).
Wm. Wrigley Jr. Co....410 N. Michigan Ave., Chicago, IL 60611...(312) 644-2121...William Wrigley...chewing gum.

Xerox Corp....P.O. Box 1600, Stamford, CT 06904...(203) 968-3000...Paul Allaire...equip. for reproduction, reduction, and transmission of printed information.

Zenith Electronics Corp....1000 Milwaukee Ave., Glenview, IL 60025...(708) 391-8181...Jerry K. Pearlman...consumer electronic prods.

Who Owns What: Familiar Consumer Products

The following is a list of familiar consumer products and their parent companies. The address of the parent company can be found on pages 701-706.

Admiral appliances: Maytag
Advil: American Home Products
Ajax cleanser: Colgate-Palmolive
Allstate Insurance Co.: Sears, Roebuck
Almond Joy candy: Hershey
Anacin: American Home Products
Arrid anti-perspirant: Carter-Wallace
Aunt Millie's pasta sauce: Borden

Ban anti-perspirant: Bristol-Myers
Beech Aircraft: Raytheon
Beech Nut babyfood: Ralston Purina
Ben-Gay: Pfizer
Betty Crocker products: General Mills
Budweiser beer: Anheuser-Busch
Bufferin: Bristol-Myers Squibb
Business Week magazine: McGraw-Hill
Buster Brown shoes: Brown Group

Cap'n Crunch cereal: Quaker Oats
Carrier air conditioners: United Technologies
Celeste Pizza: Quaker Oats
Charmin toilet tissues: Procter & Gamble
Chef Boy-ar-dee products: American Home Products
Cheer detergent: Procter & Gamble
Cheerios cereal: General Mills
Clairol hair products: Bristol-Myers Squibb
Clorets mints: Warner-Lambert
Copenhagen snuff: UST
Cracker Jack: Borden
Crest toothpaste: Procter & Gamble
Crisco shortening: Procter & Gamble

Dean Witter financial services: Sears, Roebuck
Doritos chips: PepsiCo
Drano: Bristol-Meyers Squibb

Dristan: American Home Products
Duncan Hines cookies: Procter & Gamble
Easy-Off oven cleaner: American Home Products
Efferdent dental cleanser: Warner-Lambert
ESPN: Capital Cities/ABC
Eveready batteries: Ralston Purina
Excedrin: Bristol-Myers
Fab detergent: Colgate-Palmolive
Family Circle magazine: New York Times
Foamy shaving cream: Gillette
Folger coffee: Procter & Gamble
Formula 409 spray cleaner: Clorox
Franco-American foods: Campbell Soup
Frito-Lay snacks: PepsiCo
Gatorade: Quaker Oats
Gleem toothpaste: Procter & Gamble
Hampton Inns: Promus
Handy Wipes: Colgate-Palmolive
Hanes hosiery: Sara Lee
Hawaiian Punch: Procter & Gamble
Head and Shoulders shampoo: Procter & Gamble
Hellman's mayonnaise: CPC International
Hi-C fruit drinks: Coca Cola
Hillshire Farm meats: Sara Lee
Home Box Office: Time
Hostess baked goods: Ralston Purina
Hush Puppies shoes: Wolverine World Wide
Ivory soap products: Procter & Gamble
Jack Daniel bourbon: Brown-Forman
Jell-o: Philip Morris
Jim Beam whiskey: American Brands
Ken-L-Ration pet foods: Quaker Oats
Kent cigarettes: Loews
Kinney shoe stores: Woolworth
Knorr soups: CPC International
Kool Aid: Philip Morris
La Menu frozen dinners: Campbell Soup
Ladies Home Journal magazine: Meredith
Lee jeans: VF Corp.
Lenox china: Brown-Forman
Lens Crafters: U.S. Shoe
Lerner stores: The Limited
Lipton tea: Unilever
Listerine mouthwash: Warner-Lambert
Log Cabin syrup: Philip Morris
Lord & Taylor dept. stores: May Dept. Stores
Lunch Bucket meals: Greyhound Dial
Marlboro cigarettes: Philip Morris
Mazola oil: CPC International
Maxwell House coffee: Philip Morris
Michelob beer: Anheuser-Busch
Midas automotive centers: Whitman
Miller beer: Philip Morris
Milton Bradley games: Hasbro
Minute Rice: Philip Morris
Mrs. Paul's frozen fish: Campbell Soup
NBC Broadcasting: General Electric
Newsweek magazine: Washington Post
9-Lives cat food: H.J. Heinz
North American Van Lines: Norfolk Southern
Nuprin: Bristol-Myers Squibb
Obsession fragrance: Unilever
Old Spice: Procter & Gamble
Ore-Ida frozen foods: H.J. Heinz
Pampers: Procter & Gamble
Paper Mate pens: Gillette
People magazine: Time
Pepto-Bismol: Procter & Gamble
Pepperidge Farm products: Campbell Soup
Pizza Hut restaurants: PepsiCo
Playskool toys: Hasbro
Prego spaghetti sauce: Campbell Soup
Prell shampoo: Procter & Gamble
Prentice-Hall publishing: Paramount
Post-It stickers: Minn. Min. & Manuf.
Purex detergent: Dial
Q-Tips: Unilever
Radio Shack retail outlets: Tandy
Ramblin root beer: Coca Cola
Red Lobster Inns: General Mills
Reese's peanut butter cups: Hershey
Right Guard deodorant: Gillette
Rise shave lathers: Carter-Wallace
Robitussin: American Home Products
Rolaids antacid: Warner-Lambert
Ronzoni pasta: Hershey
Ruffles chips: PepsiCo
San Giorgio pasta: Hershey
Saran Wrap: Dow Chemical
Scotch tape: Minn. Min. & Manuf.
Scrabble: Hasbro
Skippy peanut butter: CPC International
Simon & Schuster publishing: Paramount
Southern Comfort liquor: Brown-Forman
Sports Illustrated magazine: Time
Sprite soda: Coca-Cola
Sugartwin: Alberto Culver
Taco Bell restaurants: PepsiCo
Thom McAn shoe stores: Melville
Thomas English muffins: CPC International
Tide detergent: Procter & Gamble
Trojan condoms: Carter-Wallace
Tropicana juices: Seagram
Tupperware: Premark
Tylenol: Johnson & Johnson
Ultra Brite toothpaste: Colgate-Palmolive
V-8 vegetable juice: Campbell Soup
Vanity Fair apparel: VF Corp.
Velveeta cheese prods.: Philip Morris
Vicks cough medicines: Procter & Gamble
Virginia Slims cigarettes: Philip Morris
Walden Book stores: K mart
Walkman: Sony
Wall Street Journal: Dow Jones
Weight Watchers: H.J. Heinz
Wheaties cereal: General Mills
White Owl cigars: Culbro
Wizard air freshener: American Home Products
Wyler's drink mixes: Borden

Tips for Shopping by Mail, Telephone, and Television

Source: *Consumer's Resource Handbook*

1. Be suspicious of exaggerated product claims or very low prices, and read product descriptions very carefully—sometimes pictures of products are misleading.

2. If you have any doubts about the company, check with the U.S. Postal Service, your state or local consumer protection agency or Better Business Bureau before ordering.

3. Ask about the firm's return policy. If it is not stated, ask before you order. For example, does the company pay charges for shipping and return? Is a warranty or guarantee available? Does the company sometimes substitute comparable goods for the product you want to order?

4. Keep a complete record of your order; including the company's name, address and telephone number, the price of the items ordered, any handling or other charges, the date you mailed (or telephoned) in the order, and your method of payment. Keep copies of canceled checks and/or statements.

5. If you order by mail, your order should be shipped within 30 days after the company receives your complete order, unless another period is agreed upon when placing the order or is stated in an advertisement. If your order is delayed, a notice of delay should be sent to you within the promised shipping period along with an option to cancel the order.

6. If you buy a product through a television shopping program, check the cost of the same item sold by other sources, including local stores, catalogs, etc.

7. If your want to buy a product based on a telephone call from the company, ask for the name, address, and phone number where you can reach the caller after considering the offer.

8. Never give your credit card or social security number over the telephone as proof of your identity.

9. Postal regulations allow you to write a check payable to the sender, rather than the delivery company, for cash on delivery (C.O.D.) orders. If, after examining the merchandise, you feel there has been misrepresentation or fraud, you can stop payment on the check and file a complaint with the U.S. Postal Inspector's Office.

10. You can have a charge removed from your bill if you did not receive the goods or services or if your order was obtained through misrepresentation or fraud. You must notify the credit card company in writing, at the billing inquiries/disputes address, within 60 days after the charge first appeared on your bill.

Interest Laws and Consumer Finance Loan Rates

Source: Revised by Christian T. Jones. Editor, Consumer Finance Law Bulletin, San Diego, Ca.

All states have laws regulating interest rates. These laws fix a legal or conventional rate which applies when there is no contract for interest. They also fix a general maximum contract rate, but there are so many exceptions that the general contract maximum actually applies only to exceptional cases. Also, federal law has preempted state limits on first home mortgages, subject to each state's right to reinstate its own law, and given depository institutions parity with other state lenders.

Legal rate of interest. The legal or conventional rate of interest applies to money obligations when no interest rate is contracted for and also to judgments. The rate is usually somewhat below the general interest rate.

General maximum contract rates. General interest laws in most states set the maximum rate between 8% and 16% per year. The general maximum is fixed by the state constitution at 5% over the Federal Reserve Discount rate in Arkansas. Loans to corporations are frequently exempted or subject to a higher maximum. In recent years, it has also been common to provide special rates for home mortgage loans and variable usury rates that are indexed to market rates.

Specific enabling acts. In many states special statutes permit industrial loan companies, second mortgage lenders, and banks to charge 1.5% a month or more. Laws regulating revolving loans, charge accounts and credit cards generally limit charges between 1.5% and 2% per month plus annual fees for credit cards. Rates for installment sales contracts in most states are somewhat higher. Credit unions may generally charge 1% to 1.5% a month. Pawnbrokers' rates vary widely. Savings and loan associations, and loans insured by federal agencies, are also specially regulated. A number of states allow regulated lenders to charge any rate agreed to with the customer either for all credit or over a certain dollar amount.

Consumer finance loan statutes. Most consumer finance loan statutes are based on early models drafted by the Russell Sage Foundation (1916-42) to provide small loans to wage earners under license and other protective regulations. Since 1969 the model has frequently been the Uniform Consumer Credit Code which applies to credit sales and loans for consumer purposes. In general, licensed lenders may charge 3% a month and reduced rates for additional amounts. An add-on of 17% ($17 per $100) per year yields about 2.5% per month if paid in equal monthly installments. Discount rates produce higher yields than add-on rates of the same amount. In the table below, unless otherwise stated, monthly and annual rates are based on reducing principal balances, annual add-on rates are based on the original principal for the full term, and two or more rates apply to different portions of balance or original principal.

States with consumer finance loan laws and the rates of charge as of August 1, 1992

Maximum monthly rates computed on unpaid balances, unless otherwise stated.

Ala. . . Annual add-on: 15% to $750, 10% to $2,000 (min. 1.5% on unpaid balances). Higher rates for loans up to $749. Over $2,000, any agreed rate. Fee: 4% (max. $25); 5% real estate.
Alas. . . 3% to $850, 2% to $10,000. Over $10,000, any agreed rate.
Ariz. . . To $1,000: 3%. Over $1,000: 3% to $500, 2% to $10,000. Over $10,000, any agreed rate.
Cal. . . 2.5% to $225, 2% to $900, 1.5% to $1,650, 1% to $2,500 (1.6% min.). Over $2,500, any agreed rate. 5% fee (max. $50) to $2,500
Colo. . . 36% per year to $630, 21% to $2,100, 15% to $25,000 (21% min.).
Conn. . Annual Add-on: 17% to $600, 11% to $5,000; 11% over $1,800 to $5,000 for certain secured loans. Any agreed rate for second mortgages.
Del. . . Any agreed rate.
D.C. . . 24% per year.
Fla. . . 30% per year to $1,000, 24% to $2,000, 18% to $25,000.
Ga. . . 10% per year discount to 18 months, add-on to 36½months; 8% fee to $600, 4% on excess plus $2 per month. Over $3,000, any agreed rate.
Ha. . . 3.5% to $100, 2.5% to $300; 2% on entire balance over $300 or discount rates.
Ida. . . Any agreed rate.
Ill. . . . Any agreed rate.
Ind. . . 36% per year to $810, 21% to $2,700, 15% to $25,000 (21% min.).
Ia. . . . 3% to $1,000, 2% to $2,800, 1.5% to $10,000; or equivalent flat rate. Over $10,000: 21% per year.
Kan. . . 36% per year to $780, 21% to $2,600, 14.45% to $25,000 (18% min.). Fee: 2% (max. $100); 3% real estate.
Ky. . . . 3% to $1,000, 2% to $3,000. Over $3,000, 2%.
La. . . . 36% per year to $1,400, 27% to $4,000, 24% to $7,000, 21% over $7,000, plus $25 fee.
Me. . . 30% per year to $700, 21% to $2,000, 15% to $25,000 (18% min.).
Md. . . 2.75% to $1,000, 2% to $2,000. Over $2,000, 2%.
Mass. . 23% per year plus $20 annual fee to $6,000; any agreed rate over $6,000.
Mich. . . 22% per year to $8,000; 18% for second mortgages, plus 2% fee (max. $200).
Minn. . . 33% per year to $750, 19% over $750 (21.75% min.).
Miss. . . 36% per year to $1,000, 33% to $1,800, 24% to $5,000, 14% over $5,000. Over $25,000, 18%. 2% fee (max. $50).
Mo. . . 2.218% to $1,200, 1.67% over $1,200, plus 5% fee (max. $15); 1.67% plus 2% for second mortgages.
Mont. . Any agreed rate.
Neb. . . 24% per year to $1,000. 21% over, plus fee of 7% to $2,000 and 5% over (max. $500).
Nev. . . Any agreed rate.
N.H. . . 2% to $600, 1.5% to $1,500; Any agreed rate over $1,500 or for real estate mortgages.
N.J. . . 30% per year to $5,000 or for second mortgages.
N.M. . . Any agreed rate.
N.Y. . . 25% per year to 6/30/93.
N.C. . . 3% to $1,000, 1.5% to $7,500; 1.5% on entire amount to $10,000. 1.5% or variable plus 2% fee for second mortgages.
N.D. . . 2.5% to $250, 2% to $500, 1.75% to $750, 1.5% to $1,000; any agreed rate over $1,000.
Ohio . . 28% per year to $1,000, 22% to $5,000; 25% on entire amount over $5,000; plus fee.
Okla. . . 30% per annum to $870, 21% to $2,900, 15% to $45,000. (21% min.). Special rates to $500.
Ore. . . Any agreed rate.
Pa. . . . 9.5% per year discount to 48 months, 6% for remaining time plus 2% fee (max. $100); or 2% on unpaid balances; 1.85% for second mortgages over $5,000, plus 2% fee.
P.R. . . Variable: 25% max., 19% min.
R.I. . . . 3% to $300, 2.5% for loans between $300 and $800; 2% for larger loans to $5,000. 1.75% over $5,000.
S.C. . . Any agreed and posted rate.
S.D. . . Any agreed rate.
Tenn. . Over $100, 24% per year or discount rates plus fees.
Texas . Annual add-on: 18% to $1,170, 8% to $9,750 or formula rate (18% to 24% per year on unpaid balances.)
Utah . . Any agreed rate.
Vt. . . . 2% to $1,000, 1% to $3,000 (min. 1.5%); 1.5% for second mortgages.
Va. . . . 2¾% to $800, 2% to $2,000, 1.5% to $3,500; or annual add-on of 19% to $800, 15% to $2,000, 12% to $2,800; 2% fee. Any agreed rate over $3,500 for second mortgages, plus 2% fee.
Wash. . 25% per year plus fees.
W.Va. . 36% per year to $500, 24% to $1,500, 18% to $2,000. Over $2,000, 27% per year to $2,000, 25% to $10,000, 18% on remainder, 2% fee.
Wis. . . Any agreed rate.
Wyo. . . 36% per year to $1,000, 21% to $25,000. No limit over $25,000.

How to Check Your Credit File

Any individual can investigate the contents of his or her credit file by directly contacting one or more of the approximately 2,000 credit bureaus, or consumer credit clearinghouses, in the United States. The nearest ones can be found by calling a local Better Business Bureau or by looking in the telephone Yellow Pages under "Credit Rating or Reporting Agencies."

Although the Fair Credit Reporting Act requires that a bureau give a person no more than an oral or written credit history review, many bureaus will go beyond the technical requirements of the law and furnish the same computer-generated compilation of facts that they give the banks, retailers and other companies that subscribe to their service. An individual who has been denied credit on the basis of negative information from a credit bureau can obtain this review without charge within 30 days of the denial. Sometimes there is a small fee for such a credit check.

After inspecting this record of past credit behavior, a consumer can question any item believed to be inaccurate, misleading or vague. The credit bureau must then investigate and remove any item that cannot be substantiated.

When a bureau affirms, rather than removes, a questionable item, an individual can present a 100-word explanation that must be placed in his or her file. And whenever an adverse item is deleted from the file or an explantory statement is added to one, a consumer may request that the credit bureau inform every credit grantor who received a report within the last six months.

Credit Card Rates

(As of Aug. 1, 1992)

(Prepared by Christian T. Jones, San Diego, CA)

Nearly all states have special laws dealing with rates charged for credit cards issued by state banks and other financial institutions. Although some state laws apply only to banks, under Federal parity law, the same charges can be made by other financial institutions. A national bank can charge the highest rates allowed for revolving credit extended by any other creditor in the state where the bank is located for similar types of credit, and such rates may also be charged to residents of any other state. Maximum rates and fees shown below; rates are yearly.

Ala.	No limit.
Alas.	17% plus fee.
Ariz.	No limit.
Ark.	5% over FRB discount rate (max. 17%).
Cal.	No limit.
Colo.	21%.
Conn.	18%.
D.C.	24%.
Del.	No limit.
Fla.	No limit.
Ga.	No limit on rate or fee.
Ha.	24%.
Ida.	No limit.
Ill.	No limit; plus fees.
Ind.	36-21-15%, @ $810, $2,700; or 21%.
Ia.	No limit.
Kan.	18-14.45% @ $1,000.
Ky.	21%; $20 annual fee.
La.	18%; 4% cash advance and $12 annual fees.
Me.	18%; $12 annual fee.
Md.	24%; 2% fee.
Mass.	18% or formula rate.
Mich.	18%; no limit on annual fee.
Minn.	18%; $50 annual fee.
Miss.	21%; or 18% plus $12 annual fee.
Mo.	22-10% @ $1,000.
Mont.	No limit.
Neb.	18% plus fees.
Nev.	No limit.
N.H.	No limit.
N.J.	30%; $15 annual fee or $50 over $5,000.
N.M.	No limit.
N.Y.	25% plus annual fee to 6/30/93.
N.C.	18%; $24 annual fee.
N.D.	No limit.
Oh.	25% to 1/1/96.
Okla.	30-21-15% @ $870, $2,900; or 21%.
Ore.	No limit.
Pa.	12% loans; 15% purchases; $15 annual fee.
P.R.	17% loans; 26% purchases.
R.I.	18%.
S.C.	No limit.
S.D.	No limit.
Tenn.	24%.
Tex.	Set by rule (max. 24%, min. 18%.)
Utah	No limit.
Vt.	18%; no limit on annual fee.
Va.	No limit.
Wash.	12% or 4% over U.S. T-bill rate.
W.Va.	18%.
Wis.	No limit.
Wyo.	36-21% @ $1,000; no limit over $25,000.

The Cost of Raising a Child

Source: Family Economics Research Group, U.S. Dept. of Agriculture

Projected annual expenditures in current dollars on a child born in 1990, by income group for married-couple families.

		Income group[1]		
Year	Age of child	Low	Medium	High
1990	under 1	$4,330	$6,140	$8,770
1991	1	4,590	6,510	9,300
1992	2	4,870	6,900	9,850
1993	3	5,510	7,790	11,030
1994	4	5,850	8,260	11,690
1995	5	6,200	8,750	12,390
1996	6	6,550	9,220	12,950
1997	7	6,950	9,770	13,730
1998	8	7,360	10,360	14,550
1999	9	7,570	10,690	15,120
2000	10	8,020	11,340	16,030
2001	11	8,500	12,020	16,990
2002	12	10,360	14,190	19,680
2003	13	10,980	15,040	20,860
2004	14	11,640	15,940	22,110
2005	15	13,160	17,950	24,610
2006	16	13,950	19,030	26,090
2007	17	14,780	20,170	27,650
Total		$151,170	$210,070	$293,400

(1) Low income is under $29,900 in 1990; middle is $29,900 to $48,299; high is $48,300 or more. Projection assumes 6 percent annual inflation.

Tourism: Foreign Visitors to the U.S., 1990

Source: U.S. Travel & Tourism Admin.; Bureau of Economic Analysis

Country of origin	Visitors (millions)	Expenditures (millions)	Expenditures per visitor
Japan	3.2	$7,694	$2,381
Canada	17.3	5,690	330
Mexico	6.8	4,004	592
United Kingdom	2.2	3,581	1,596
Germany	1.2	2,139	1,778
France	0.7	$1,219	$1,703
Australia	0.5	1,061	2,279
Italy	0.4	781	1,973
Netherlands	0.3	404	1,422
New Zealand	0.2	379	2,181
All countries	39.1	$40,579	$1,038

Note: Excludes international passenger fare payments and cruise travel. Numbers may not add up due to rounding.

U.S. Passport, Visa, and Health Requirements

Source: Bureau of Consular Affairs, U.S. Dept. of State as of mid-1992

Passports are issued by the U.S. Department of State to citizens and nationals of the United States for the purpose of documenting them for foreign travel and identifying them as Americans.

How to Obtain a Passport

Applicants who have never been issued a passport in their own name must execute an application in person before (1) a passport agent; (2) a clerk of any federal court or state court of record or a judge or clerk of any probate court accepting applications; (3) a postal employee designated by the postmaster at a post office which has been selected to accept passport applications; or (4) a U.S. diplomatic or consular officer abroad. A DSP-11 is the correct form to use for applicants who must apply in person. All persons are required to obtain individual passports in their own name. An applicant who is 13 years of age or older is required to appear in person before the clerk or agent executing the application. A parent or legal guardian may execute the application for children under 13.

A full validity passport previously issued to the applicant, or one in which he was included, will be accepted as proof of U.S. citizenship. If the applicant has no prior passport and was born in the U.S. a certified copy of their birth certificate shall be presented to the agent accepting the passport application. To be acceptable, the certificate must show the given name and surname, the date and place of birth, and that the birth record was filed shortly after birth. A delayed birth certificate (a record filed more than one year after the date of birth) is acceptable provided that it shows acceptable secondary evidence was used for creating this record.

If such primary evidence is not obtainable, a notice from state registrar shall be submitted stating that no birth record exists. The notice shall be accompanied by the best obtainable secondary evidence such as a baptismal certificate, or a hospital birth record.

A naturalized citizen with no previous passport must present a Certificate of Naturalization. A person born abroad claiming U.S. citizenship through either a native-born or naturalized citizen parent must submit a Certificate of Citizenship issued by the Immigration and Naturalization Service; or a Consular Report of Birth or Certification of Birth Abroad issued by the Dept. of State. If one of the above documents has not been obtained, evidence of citizenship of the parent(s) through whom citizenship is claimed and evidence which would establish the parent/child relationship must be submitted. Additionally, if citizenship is derived through birth to citizen parent(s), the following documents will be required: parents' marriage certificate plus an affidavit from parent(s) showing periods and places of residence or physical presence in the U.S. and abroad, specifying periods spent abroad in the employment of the U.S. government, including the armed forces, or with certain international organizations. If citizenship is derived through naturalization of parents, evidence of admission to the U.S. for permanent residence also will be required.

Persons who possess the most recent passport in their current name issued within the last 12 years and after their 16th birthday may be eligible to apply for a new passport by mail. A form DSP-82, Application for Passport by Mail must be filled out and mailed to the nearest passport agency, together with their previous passport, 2 recent identical photographs and $55.00. The DSP-82 may not be used if the most recent passport has been altered or mutilated.

Contract Employees — Persons traveling because of a contract with the U.S. Government must submit with their application: letters from their employer stating position, destination and purpose of travel, armed forces contract number, and expiration date of contract when pertinent.

Photographs, Fees and Identity

Photographs — Submit 2 identical photographs which are sufficiently recent (normally not more than 6 months old) to be a good likeness of and satisfactorily identify the applicant. Photographs should be 2 × 2 inches in size. The image size measured from the bottom of the chin to the top of the head (including hair) should be not less than one inch nor more than 1 3/8 inches. Photographs should be portrait-type prints. They must be clear, front view, full face, with a plain, white or off-white background. Photographs which depict the applicant as relaxed and smiling are encouraged.

Fees — The passport fee is $30.00 for passports issued to persons under 18 years of age. These passports are valid for 5 years from the date of issue. The passport fee is $55.00 for passports issued to persons 18 and older. These passports are valid for 10 years from the date of issuance. An additional fee of $10.00 is charged for the execution of the application. There is no acceptance fee when using DSP-82, "Application For Passport By Mail." Applicants eligible to use this form pay only the $55.00 passport fee.

Identity—Applicants must also establish their identity to the satisfaction of the person accepting the application and to Passport Services. To establish identity, applicants may use a previous U.S. passport, a Certificate of Naturalization, a Certificate of Citizenship, a valid driver's license, or a government identification card. Applicants may not use a Social Security card, learner's or temporary driver's license, credit card, or expired identity card. Extremely old documents cannot be used by themselves. Applicants unable to establish their identity must take the identification cards they have in their own name (i.e. Social Security card) and in addition, they must be accompanied by a person who has known them for at least 2 years and who is a U.S. citizen or legal U.S. permanent resident alien. That person must sign an affidavit before the individual who executes the passport application. The witness will be required to establish his or her own identity.

The loss or theft of a valid passport is a serious matter and should be reported immediately to Passport Services, 1425 K Street, N.W., Dept. of State, Wash., D.C. 20524, tel: (202) 647-0518 or to the nearest passport agency, or the nearest U.S. embassy or consulate when abroad.

Foreign Regulations

A visa, usually rubber stamped in a passport by a representative of the country to be visited, indicates that the bearer of the passport is permitted to enter that country for a certain purpose and length of time. In most instances, you must obtain necessary visas before you leave the U.S. Apply directly to the embassy or nearest consulate of each country you plan to visit, or consult a travel agent.

The State Dept's. "Foreign Entry Requirements," contains entry requirements and application instructions for most foreign countries and is available for 50¢ from the Consumer Information Center, Dept. 438T, Pueblo, CO 81009.

The process may take several weeks, so it is important to apply well in advance and verify requirements with the embassy or nearest consulate of each country before applying.

Aliens — An alien leaving the U.S. must request a passport from the embassy of the country of their nationality, must have a permit from his local Collector of Internal Revenue, and if they wish to return, should request a re-entry permit from the Immigration and Naturalization Service if it is required.

How to Obtain Birth, Marriage, Death Records

The pamphlets, "How You May Save Time Proving Your Age and Other Birth Facts," and "Where to Write for Vital Records: Births, Deaths, Marriages, and Divorces," are available from the U.S. Dept. of Health and Human Services, National Center for Health Statistics, Rockville, MD 20852; "Guide to Geneological Research in the National Archives" is sold by the National Archives Trust Fund Board, P.O. Box 100793, Atlanta, GA 30384. "Where to Write for Birth and Death Records of U.S. Citizens Who Were Born or Died Outside the U.S. and Birth Certifications for Alien Children Adopted by U.S. Citizens" is available from Passport Services, Correspondence Branch, U.S. Dept. of State, Washington, DC 20524.

Copyright Law of The United States

Source: Copyright Office, Library of Congress

What Copyright Is

Copyright is a form of protection provided by the laws of the United States (title 17, U.S. Code) to the authors of "original works of authorship" including literary, dramatic, musical, artistic, and certain other intellectual works. This protection is available to both published and unpublished works. Section 106 of the Copyright Act generally gives the owner of copyright the exclusive right to do and to authorize others to do the following:

- *To reproduce* the copyrighted work in copies or phonorecords;
- To prepare *derivative works* based upon the copyrighted work;
- *To distribute copies or phonorecords* of the copyrighted work to the public by sale or other transfer of ownership, or by rental, lease, or lending;
- *To perform the copyrighted work publicly,* in the case of literary, musical, dramatic, and choreographic works, pantomimes, and motion pictures and other audiovisual works; and
- *To display the copyrighted work publicly,* in the case of literary, musical, dramatic, and choreographic works, pantomimes, and pictorial, graphic, or sculptural works, including the individual images of a motion picture or other audiovisual work.

It is illegal for anyone to violate any of the rights provided by the Act to the owner of copyright. These rights, however, are not unlimited in scope. Sections 107 through 119 of the Copyright Act establish limitations on these rights. In some cases, these limitations are specified exemptions from copyright liability. One major limitation is the doctrine of "fair use," which is given a statutory basis by section 107 of the Act. In other instances, the limitation takes the form of a "compulsory license" under which certain limited uses of copyrighted works are permitted upon payment of specified royalties and compliance with statutory conditions.

Copyright protection subsists from the time the work is created in fixed form; that is, it is an incident of the process of authorship. The copyright in the work of authorship *immediately* becomes the property of the author who created it. Only the author or those deriving their rights from the author can rightfully claim copyright.

In the case of works made for hire, the employer and not the employee is presumptively considered the author. Section 101 of the copyright statute defines a "work made for hire" as:

(1) a work prepared by an employee within the scope of his or her employment; or

(2) a work specially ordered or commissioned for use as a contribution to a collective work, as a part of a motion picture or other audiovisual work, as a translation, as a supplementary work, as a compilation, as an instructional text, as a test, as answer material for a test, or as an atlas, if the parties expressly agree in a written instrument signed by them that the work shall be considered a work made for hire.

The authors of a joint work are co-owners of the copyright in the work, unless there is an agreement to the contrary.

Copyright in each separate contribution to a periodical or other collective work is distinct from copyright in the collective work as a whole and vests initially with the author of the contribution.

Works published on or after January 1, 1978, are subject to protection under the copyright statute if, on the date of first publication, one or more of the authors is a national or domiciliary of the U.S., or is a national, domiciliary, or sovereign authority of a foreign nation that is a party to a copyright treaty to which the U.S. is also a party, or is a stateless person, regardless of domicile, or if the work is first published either in the U.S. or in a foreign nation that on the date of first publication is a party to the Universal Copyright Convention or the Berne Union.

What Works Are Protected

Copyright protects "original works of authorship" that are fixed in a tangible form of expression. The fixation need not be directly perceptible, so long as it may be communicated with the aid of a machine or device. Copyrightable works include the following categories:

(1) literary works;

(2) musical works, including any accompanying words;

(3) dramatic works, including any accompanying music;

(4) pantomimes and choreographic works;

(5) pictorial, graphic, and sculptural works;

(6) motion pictures and other audiovisual works;

(7) sound recordings; and

(8) architectural works.

These categories should be viewed quite broadly: for example, computer programs and most "compilations" are registrable as "literary works"; maps and architectural plans are registrable as "pictorial, graphic, and sculptural works."

What Is Not Protected By Copyright

Several categories of material are generally not eligible for statutory copyright protection. These include among others:

- Works that have *not* been fixed in a tangible form of expression. For example: choreographic works that have not been notated or recorded, or improvisational speeches or performances that have not been written or recorded.
- Titles, names, short phrases, and slogans; familiar symbols or designs; mere variations of typographic ornamentation, lettering, or coloring; mere listings of ingredients or contents.
- Ideas, procedures, methods, systems, processes, concepts, principles, discoveries, or devices, as distinguished from a description, explanation, or illustration.
- Works consisting *entirely* of information that is common property and containing no original authorship. For example: standard calendars, height and weight charts, tape measures and rulers, and lists or tables taken from public documents or other common sources.

Notice of Copyright

For works first published on and after March 1, 1989, use of the copyright notice is optional, though highly recommended. Before March 1, 1989, the use of the notice was mandatory on all published works, and any work first published before that date *must* bear a notice or risk loss of copyright protection.

Use of the notice is recommended because it informs the public that the work is protected by copyright, identifies the copyright owner, and shows the year of first publication. Furthermore, in the event that a work is infringed, if the work carries a proper notice, the court will not allow a defendant to claim "innocent infringement"—that is, that he or she did not realize that the work is protected. (A successful innocent infringement claim may result in a reduction in damages that the copyright owner would otherwise receive.)

The use of the copyright notice is the responsibility of the copyright owner and does not require advance permission from, or registration with, the Copyright Office.

For visually perceptible copies, the form of the notice consists of the following: © (the letter C in a circle), the word "Copyright," or "Copr.," and the year of first publication, and the name of the owner of copyright in the work. Example: © 1992 Judy Smith. The notice must be affixed in such manner and location as to give reasonable notice of the claim of copyright.

The notice of copyright prescribed for all published phonorecords of sound recordings consists of the symbol ℗ (the letter P in a circle), the year of first publication of the sound recording, and the name of the owner of copyright in the sound recording. Example ℗ 1992 XYZ Records, Inc. The notice on phonorecords may appear on the surface of the phonorecord or on the phonorecord label or container, provided the manner of placement and location give reasonable notice of the claim.

How Long Copyright Protection Endures

Works Originally Copyrighted on or After January 1, 1978

A work that is created (fixed in tangible form for the first time) on or after January 1, 1978, is automatically protected from the moment of its creation, and is ordinarily given a term enduring for the author's life, plus an additional 50 years after the author's death. In the case of "a joint work prepared by two or more authors who did not work for hire," the term lasts for 50 years after the last surviving author's death. For works made for hire, and for anonymous and pseudonymous works (unless the author's identity is revealed in Copyright Office records), the duration of copyright will be 75 years from publication or 100 years from creation, whichever is shorter.

Works that were created but not published or registered for copyright before January 1, 1978, have been automatically brought under the statute and are now given Federal copyright protection. The duration of copyright in these works will generally be computed in the same way as for works created on or after January 1, 1978: the life-plus-50 or 75/100-year terms will apply to them as well. The law provides that in no case will the term of copyright for works in this category expire before December 31, 2002, and for works published on or before December 31, 2002, the term of copyright will not expire before December 31, 2027.

Works Copyrighted Before January 1, 1978

Under the law in effect before 1978, copyright was secured either on the date a work was published or on the date of registration if the work was registered in unpublished form. In either case, the copyright endured for a first term of 28 years from the date it was secured. During the last (28th) year of the first term, the copyright was eligible for renewal. The current copyright law has extended the renewal term from 28 to 47 years for copyrights that were subsisting on January 1, 1978, making these works eligible for a total term of protection of 75 years. On June 26, 1992, President Bush signed Public Law 102-307, which amends the Copyright Law to extend automatically the term of copyrights secured between January 1, 1964 and December 31, 1977 to a further term of 47 years and increases the filing fee from $12.00 to $20.00. This fee increase applies to all renewal applications filed on or after June 29, 1992.

P.L. 102-307 makes renewal registration optional. There is no need to make the renewal filing in order to extend the original 28-year copyright term to the full 75 years.

International Copyright Protection

There is no such thing as an "international copyright" that will automatically protect an author's writings throughout the entire world. Protection against unauthorized use in a particular country depends, basically, on the national laws of that country. However, most countries do offer protection to foreign works under certain conditions, and these conditions have been greatly simplified by international copyright treaties and conventions. The U.S. belongs to both global, multilateral copyright treaties—the Universal Copyright Convention (UCC) and the Berne Convention for the Protection of Literary and Artistic Works.

A U.S. author may obtain copyright protection in all countries that are members of the Berne Union and the Universal Copyright Convention. A work first published in the U.S. or another Berne Union country (or first published in a non-Berne Union country, followed by publication within 30 days in a Berne Union country) is eligible for protection in all Berne member countries. There are no special requirements. In UCC member countries, where no formalities are required, the works of U.S. authors are also automatically protected. Member countries whose laws impose formalities protect U.S. works if all published copies bear a Convention notice, which consists of the symbol ©, together with the name of the copyright owner and the year of publication. Example: © JOHN DOE 1992.

For a list of countries that maintain copyright relations with the U.S., write or call the Copyright Office and ask for Circular 38a.

Copyright Registration

Copyright registration is a legal formality intended to make a public record of the basic facts of a particular copyright. Except in specific situations, registration is not a condition for protection, but the copyright law provides several inducements or advantages to encourage copyright owners to register. Among these advantages are the following:

- Registration establishes a public record of the copyright claim;
- Before an infringement suit may be filed in court, registration is necessary for works of U.S. origin and for foreign works not originating in a Berne Union country. (For more information on when a work is of U.S. origin, request Circular 93 from the Copyright Office);
- If made before or within 5 years of publication, registration will establish prima facie evidence in court of the validity of the copyright and of the facts stated in the certificate; and
- If registration is made within 3 months after publication of the work or prior to an infringement of the work, statutory damages and attorney's fees will be available to the copyright owner in court actions. Otherwise, only an award of actual damages and profits is available to the copyright owner.

Copyright registration allows the owner of the copyright to record the registration with the U.S. Customs Service for protection against the importation of infringing copies. For additional information, request Publication No. 563 from:

Commissioner of Customs
ATTN: IPR Branch,
Room 2104
U.S. Customs Service
1301 Constitution Avenue, N.W.
Washington, D.C. 20229

Registration may be made at any time within the life of the copyright. When a work has been registered in unpublished form, it is not necessary to make another registration when the work becomes published (although the copyright owner may register the published edition, if desired).

The process of registration is quite simple. An appropriate form is requested from the Copyright Office and completed. It is returned to the Copyright Office along with a $20 nonrefundable filing fee and the appropriate deposit(s) of the work for which registration is sought. In a common example—a published book—the deposit is two copies of the best edition of the book. A certificate of registration is sent once the paperwork is completed, a process that usually takes 12 to 16 weeks due to the large volume of registrations the Office must handle.

Although a copyright registration is not required, the Copyright Act establishes a mandatory deposit requirement for works published in the U.S. In general, the owner of copyright, or the owner of the exclusive right of publication in the work, has a legal obligation to deposit in the Copyright Office, within three months of publication in the U.S., two copies (or, in the case of sound recordings, two phonorecords) for the use of the Library of Congress. Failure to make the deposit can result in fines and other penalties, but does not affect copyright protection. Certain categories of works are *exempt entirely* from the mandatory deposit requirements, and the obligation is reduced for certain other categories.

Information on registration and application forms may be obtained free of charge by writing the Copyright Office, Information Section, LM-401, Library of Congress, Washington, DC 20559. Registration application forms and circulars may be ordered on a 24-hour basis by calling (202) 707-9100. Request Circular 1 for additional general information on copyright, including a list of which application forms to use when registering specific types of works.

Birthstones

Source: Jewelry Industry Council

Month	Ancient	Modern
January	Garnet	Garnet
February	Amethyst	Amethyst
March	Jasper	Bloodstone or Aquamarine
April	Sapphire	Diamond
May	Agate	Emerald
June	Emerald	Pearl, Moonstone, or Alexandrite
July	Onyx	Ruby
August	Carnelian	Sardonyx or Peridot
September	Chrysolite	Sapphire
October	Aquamarine	Opal or Tourmaline
November	Topaz	Topaz
December	Ruby	Turquoise or Zircon

Mortgage Payment Tables

Source: *The Mortgage Money Guide*, Federal Trade Commission

8% Annual Percent Rate

Monthly Payments (Principal and Interest)*

Amount Financed	10 Years	15 Years	20 Years	25 Years	30 Years
$ 25,000	303.32	238.91	209.11	192.95	183.44
35,000	424.65	334.48	292.75	270.14	256.82
45,000	545.97	430.04	376.40	347.32	330.19
50,000	606.64	477.83	418.22	385.91	366.88
60,000	727.97	573.39	501.86	463.09	440.26
70,000	849.29	668.96	585.51	540.27	513.64
80,000	970.62	764.52	669.15	617.45	587.01
90,000	1091.95	860.09	752.80	694.63	660.39
100,000	1213.28	955.65	836.44	771.82	733.76
120,000	1455.94	1146.78	1003.72	926.18	880.52
140,000	1698.58	1337.92	1171.02	1080.54	1027.28
160,000	1941.24	1529.04	1338.30	1234.90	1174.02
180,000	2183.90	1720.18	1505.60	1389.26	1320.78
200,000	2426.56	1911.30	1672.88	1543.64	1467.52

10% Annual Percentage Rate

Monthly Payments (Principal and Interest)*

Amount Financed	10 Years	15 Years	20 Years	25 Years	30 Years
$ 25,000	330.38	268.65	241.26	227.18	219.39
35,000	462.53	376.11	337.76	318.05	307.15
45,000	594.68	483.57	434.26	408.92	394.91
50,000	660.75	537.30	482.51	454.35	438.79
60,000	792.90	644.76	579.01	545.22	526.54
70,000	925.06	752.22	675.52	636.09	614.30
80,000	1057.20	859.68	772.02	726.96	702.06
90,000	1189.36	967.14	868.52	817.83	789.81
100,000	1321.51	1074.61	965.02	908.70	877.57
120,000	1585.80	1289.52	1158.02	1090.44	1053.08
140,000	1850.12	1504.44	1351.04	1272.18	1228.60
160,000	2114.40	1719.36	1544.04	1453.92	1404.12
180,000	2378.72	1934.28	1737.04	1635.66	1579.62
200,000	2643.02	2149.22	1930.04	1817.40	1755.14

12% Annual Percentage Rate

Monthly Payments (Principal and Interest)*

Amount Financed	10 Years	15 Years	20 Years	25 Years	30 Years
$ 25,000	358.68	300.05	275.28	263.31	257.16
35,000	502.15	420.06	385.39	368.63	360.02
45,000	645.62	540.08	495.49	473.96	462.88
50,000	717.36	600.09	550.55	526.62	514.31
60,000	860.83	720.11	660.66	631.93	617.17
70,000	1004.30	840.12	770.77	737.26	720.03
80,000	1147.77	960.14	880.87	842.58	822.90
90,000	1291.24	1080.15	990.98	947.90	925.75
100,000	1434.71	1200.17	1101.09	1053.23	1028.62
120,000	1721.66	1440.22	1321.32	1263.86	1234.34
140,000	2008.60	1680.24	1541.54	1474.52	1440.06
160,000	2295.54	1920.28	1761.74	1685.16	1645.80
180,000	2582.48	2160.30	1981.96	1895.80	1851.50
200,000	2869.42	2400.34	2202.18	2106.46	2057.24

14% Annual Percentage Rate

Monthly Payments (Principal and Interest)*

Amount Financed	10 Years	15 Years	20 Years	25 Years	30 Years
$ 25,000	388.17	332.94	310.89	300.95	296.22
35,000	543.44	466.11	435.24	421.32	414.71
45,000	698.70	599.29	559.59	541.70	533.20
50,000	776.34	665.88	621.77	601.89	592.44
60,000	931.60	799.05	746.12	722.26	710.93
70,000	1086.87	932.22	870.47	842.64	829.42
80,000	1242.14	1065.40	994.82	963.01	947.90
90,000	1397.40	1198.57	1119.17	1083.38	1066.38
100,000	1552.67	1331.75	1243.53	1203.77	1184.88
120,000	1863.20	1598.10	1492.24	1444.52	1421.86
140,000	2173.74	1864.44	1740.94	1685.28	1658.84
160,000	2484.28	2130.80	1989.64	1926.02	1895.80
180,000	2794.80	2397.14	2238.34	2166.76	2132.76
200,000	3105.34	2663.50	2487.06	2407.54	2369.76

Median Price of Existing Single-Family Homes

Source: National Association of Realtors

City[1]	1988	1990	Apr. 1992
Akron, Oh.	$59,900	$67,700	$75,500
Albuquerque, N.M.	80,400	84,500	86,700
Anaheim/Santa Ana, Cal.	203,900	242,400	235,100
Atlanta, Ga.	NA	86,400	85,800
Baltimore, Md.	88,700	105,900	111,500
Baton Rouge, La.	64,700	64,900	71,800
Birmingham, Ala.	75,700	80,800	89,500
Boston, Mass.	181,200	174,200	168,200
Bradenton, Fla.	66,100	69,600	80,400
Buffalo, N.Y.	65,500	77,200	79,700
Charleston, S.C.	73,100	76,200	82,000
Chicago, Ill.	89,000	116,800	131,100
Cincinnati, Oh.	69,700	79,800	87,500
Cleveland, Oh.	69,200	80,600	88,100
Columbia, S.C.	69,700	77,100	85,100
Columbus, Oh.	72,600	81,600	90,300
Corpus Christi, Tex.	64,900	63,200	62,500
Dallas, Tex.	90,800	89,500	90,500
Daytona Beach, Fla.	62,600	64,100	63,600
Denver, Col.	81,800	86,400	91,300
Des Moines, Ia.	55,800	60,500	71,200
Detroit, Mich.	73,100	76,700	77,500
El Paso, Tex.	59,600	63,600	65,900
Grand Rapids, Mich.	57,900	68,300	73,000
Hartford, Conn.	167,600	157,300	141,500
Honolulu, Hi.	210,000	352,000	342,000
Houston, Tex.	61,800	70,700	78,200
Indianapolis, Ind.	66,100	74,800	80,100
Jacksonville, Fla.	67,700	72,400	75,100
Kansas City, Mo.	70,500	74,100	76,100
Knoxville, Tenn.	67,000	75,400	78,300
Las Vegas, Nev.	78,800	93,000	101,400
Los Angeles, Cal.	178,900	212,800	218,000
Louisville, Ky.	$54,500	$60,800	$69,700
Madison, Wis.	72,000	82,300	89,400
Memphis, Tenn.	76,300	78,100	83,600
Miami, Fla.	82,900	89,300	97,300
Milwaukee, Wis.	74,500	84,400	96,100
Minneapolis, Minn.	85,200	88,700	94,800
Mobile, Ala.	53,000	59,100	63,300
Nashville, Tenn.	77,600	81,800	89,000
New Haven, Conn.	169,400	153,300	142,400
New Orleans, La.	73,100	67,800	68,400
New York, N.Y.	183,800	174,900	169,300
Oklahoma City, Okla.	56,200	53,200	59,800
Omaha, Neb.	59,500	63,000	67,400
Orlando, Fla.	79,100	62,800	86,200
Philadelphia, Pa.	102,400	108,700	119,800
Phoenix, Ariz.	80,000	84,000	84,700
Pittsburgh, Pa.	63,200	70,100	74,800
Portland, Ore.	64,400	79,500	92,300
Providence, R.I.	130,600	127,900	120,300
Sacramento, Cal.	94,600	137,100	135,600
St. Louis, Mo.	78,100	75,700	81,600
Salt Lake City, Ut.	67,700	69,400	73,000
San Antonio, Tex.	65,000	63,600	68,000
San Diego, Cal.	153,400	183,600	182,700
San Francisco, Cal.	212,900	259,300	243,900
Seattle, Wash.	94,000	142,000	141,300
Spokane, Wash.	51,100	55,500	71,300
Syracuse, N.Y.	74,600	80,700	77,400
Tampa, Fla.	65,600	71,400	70,100
Toledo, Oh.	58,400	62,800	74,000
Tulsa, Okla.	65,000	63,900	68,500
Washington, D.C.	132,500	150,200	152,500

(1) All areas are metropolitan statistical areas as defined by the U.S. Office of Management and Budget. They include the named central city and surrounding suburban areas. NA=not available.

Housing Affordability

Source: National Association of Realtors

	Median-priced existing home	Average mortgage rate	Monthly principal and interest payment	Payment as percentage of median income
1981	$66,400	15.12%	$677	36.3%
1982	67,800	15.38	702	35.9
1983	70,300	12.85	616	30.1
1984	72,400	12.49	618	28.2
1985	75,500	11.74	609	26.2
1986	80,300	10.25	563	23.0
1987	$85,600	9.28%	$565	21.9%
1988	90,600	9.31	591	22.0
1989	93,100	10.11	660	23.1
1990	97,500	10.04	673	22.7
1991	99,700	9.51	671	22.3
1992	100,900	8.48	620	20.0

Note: The average mortgage rate is based on the effective rate of loans closed on existing homes monitored by the Federal Home Loan Bank Board.

The 1992 numbers are for May.

Income Needed to Get a Mortgage

Source: National Association of Realtors

The following shows the minimum annual gross income needed for various size home loans at different rates. The figures are based on a 30-year loan and assume that the borrower's monthly payments can't exceed 28% of gross income, the ceiling most lenders use. The figures do not include property taxes and insurance as part of the monthly payment.

Interest rate (Percent)	$50,000	$75,000	Loan amount $100,000 income needed	$150,000	$200,000
8	$15,724	$23,586	$31,447	$47,171	$62,895
8½	16,477	24,715	32,954	49,430	65,907
9	17,242	25,863	34,484	51,726	68,968
9½	18,018	27,028	36,037	54,055	72,074
10	18,085	28,208	37,611	56,415	75,221
10½	19,602	29,403	39,203	58,805	78,406
11	20,407	30,611	40,814	61,221	81,628
11½	21,221	31,831	42,441	63,662	84,883
12	22,042	33,063	44,084	66,125	88,167
12½	22,870	34,305	45,740	68,610	91,479
13	23,704	35,556	47,409	71,113	94,817

Marriage Laws

Source: Gary N. Skoloff, Skoloff & Wolfe, Livingston, N.J.; as of May 1, 1992

State	Age with parental consent		Age without consent		Physical exam & blood test for male and female			
	Male	Female	Male	Female	Maximum period between exam and license	Scope of medical exam	Waiting period Before license	Waiting period After license
Alabama*	14a	14a	18	18	—	b	—	s
Alaska	16z	16z	18	18	—	b	3 da., w	—
Arizona	16z	16z	18	18	—	—	—	—
Arkansas	17c	16c	18	18	—	—	v	—
California	aa	aa	18	18	30 da., w	zzz	—	h
Colorado*	16z	16z	18	18	—	bb	—	s
Connecticut	16z	16z	18	18	—	bb	4 da., w	ttt
Delaware	18c	16c	18	18	—	—	—	e, s
Florida	16a, c	16a, c	18	18	—	b	3 da.	s
Georgia*	aa	aa	16	16	—	b	3 da., g	s*
Hawaii	16d	16d	18	18	—	b	—	—
Idaho*	16z	16z	18	18	—	bb	—	—
Illinois	16	16	18	18	30 da.	b, n	—	ee
Indiana	17c	17c	18	18	—	bb	72 hrs.	t
Iowa*	18z	18z	18	18	—	—	3 da., v	tt
Kansas*[y]	18z	18z	18	18	—	—	3 da., w	—
Kentucky	18c, z	18c, z	18	18	—	—	—	—
Louisiana	18z	18z	18	18	10 da.	b	72 hrs., w	—
Maine	16z	16z	18	18	—	—	3 da., v, w	h
Maryland	16c, f	16c, f	18	18	—	—	48 hrs., w	ff
Massachusetts	14j	12j	18	18	60 da.	bb	3 da., v	—
Michigan	16c, d	16c	18	18	30 da.	b	3 da., w	—
Minnesota	16z	16z	18	18	—	—	5 da., w	—
Mississippi	aa	aa	17gg	15gg	30 da.	b	3 da., w	—
Missouri	15d, 18z	15d, 18z	18	18	—	—	—	—
Montana*[yy]	16	16	18	18	—	b	—	ff
Nebraska[yy]	17	17	18	18	—	bb	—	—
Nevada	16z	16z	18	18	—	—	—	—
New Hampshire	14j	13j	18	18	—	l,zzz	3 da., v	h
New Jersey	16z, c	16z, c	18	18	30 da.	b	72 hrs., w	s
New Mexico[y]	16d	16d	18	18	30 da.	b	—	—
New York	14j	14j	18	18	—	nn	—	24 hrs., w, t
North Carolina	16c, g	16c, g	18	18	—	m	—	—
North Dakota	16	16	18	18	—	—	—	t
Ohio*	18c, z	16c, z	18	18	30 da.	b	5 da.,w	t
Oklahoma*	16c	16c	18	18	30 da., w	b	—	s
Oregon	17	17	18	18	—	—	3 da., w	—
Pennsylvania*	16d	16d	18	18	30 da.	b	3 da., w	t
Puerto Rico[y]	18c, d, z	16c, d, z	21	21	—	b	—	—
Rhode Island*	18d	16d	18	18	—	bb	—	—
South Carolina*	16c	14c	18	18	—	—	1 da.	—
South Dakota	16c	16c	18	18	—	—	—	tt
Tennesee	16d	16d	18	18	—	—	3 da., cc	s
Texas*[y]	14j, k	14j, k	18	18	—	—	—	s
Utah*	14	14	18x	18x	30 da.	b	—	s
Vermont	16z	16z	18	18	30 da.	b	1 da., w	—
Virginia	16a, c	16a, c	18	18	—	b	—	t
Washington	17d	17d	18	18	—	bbb	3 da.	t
West Virginia	18c	18c	18	18	—	b	3 da., w	—
Wisconsin	16d	16d	18	18	—	b	5 da., w	s
Wyoming	16d	16d	18	18	—	bb	—	—
Dist. of Columbia*	16a	16a	18	18	30 da.	b	3 da. w	—

* Indicates 1987 common-law marriage recognized; in many states, such marriages are only recognized if entered into many years before. (a) Parental consent not required if minor was previously married. (aa) No age limits. (b) Venereal diseases. (bb) Venereal diseases and Rubella (for female). In Colorado and Wyoming, Rubella for female under 45 and Rh type. (bbb) No medical exam required; however, applicants must file affidavit showing non-affliction of contagious venereal disease. (c) Younger parties may obtain license in case of pregnancy or birth of child. (cc) Unless parties are over 18 years of age. (d) Younger parties may obtain license in special circumstances. (e) Residents before expiration of 24-hour waiting period; non-residents formerly residents, before expiration of 96-hour waiting period; others 96 hours. (ee) License effective 1 day after issuance, unless court orders otherwise, valid for 60 days only. (f) If parties are at least 16 years of age, proof of age and the consent of parents in person is required. If a parent is ill, an affidavit by the incapacitated parent and a physician's affidavit to that effect required. (ff) License valid for 180 days only. (g) Unless parties are 18 years of age or more, or female is pregnant, or applicants are the parents of a living child born out of wedlock. (gg) Notice to parents necessary if parties are under 21. (h) License valid for 90 days only. (j) Parental consent and/or permission of judge required. (k) Below age of consent parties need parental consent and permission of judge. (l) With each certificate issued to couples, a list of family planning agencies and services available to them is provided. (m) Mental incompetence, infectious tuberculosis, venereal diseases and Rubella (certain counties only). (n) Venereal diseases; test for sickle cell anemia given at request of examining physician. (nn) Tests for sickle cell anemia may be required for certain applicants. Marriage prohibited unless it is established that procreation is not possible. (p) If one or both parties are below the age for marriage without parental consent (3 day waiting period). (s) License valid for 30 days only. (t) License valid for 60 days only. (tt) License valid for 20 days only. (ttt) License valid for 65 days. (v) Parties must file notice of intention to marry with local clerk. (w) Waiting period may be avoided. (x) Authorizes counties to provide for premarital counseling as a requisite to issuance of license to persons under 19 and persons previously divorced. (y) Marriages by proxy are valid. (yy) Proxy marriages are valid under certain conditions. (z) Younger parties may marry with parental consent and/or permission of judge. In Connecticut, judicial approval. (zz) With consent of court. (zzz) Required offer of HIV test, and/or must be provided with information on AIDS.

Divorce Laws

Adapted from a revision by Gary N. Skoloff of the N.J. Bar, as of May 1, 1992. Important: almost all states also have other laws, as well as qualifications of the laws shown below and proposed divorce-reform laws pending. It would be wise to consult a lawyer in conjunction with the use of this chart.

Some grounds for absolute divorce

	Residence	Adultery	Cruelty	Desertion	Alcoholism	Impotency	Non-support	Insanity	Pregnancy at marriage	Bigamy	Separation	Felony conviction or imprisonment	Drug addiction	Fraud force, duress
PR	1 yr.	Yes	Yes	1 yr.	Yes	Yes	No	Yes	No	A	2 yrs.	Yes*	Yes	No
AL	6 mos.*	Yes	Phys. only	1 yr.	Yes	Yes*	2 yrs.	5 yrs.	Yes	A	2 yrs.*	2 yrs*	Yes	A
AK	*	Yes	Yes	1 yr.	1 yr.	Yes	No	18 mos.	No	A	No	Yes	Yes	A
AZ	90 da.	No	No	No	No	No	No	No	No	No	No	No	No	No
AR	60 da.	Yes	Yes	No	1 yr.	Yes	Yes	3 yrs.	No	No	18 mos.	Yes	No	A
CA	6 mos.	No	No	No	No	A	No	Yes, A	No	A	No	No	No	A
CO	90 da.	No	No	No	No	No	No	No	No	A	No	No	No	A
CT	1 yr.*	Yes	Yes	1 yr.	Yes	No	No	5 yrs.	No	A	18 mos.*	life*	No	Yes
DE	6 mos.	Yes	Yes	Yes	Yes	A	No	A	No	Yes	6 mos.	Yes	Yes	A
FL	6 mos.	No	No	No	No	No	No	3 yrs.	No	No	No	No	No	No
GA	6 mos.	Yes	Yes	1 yr.	Yes	Yes	No	2 yrs.	Yes	A	No	Yes*	Yes	Yes
HI	6 mos.*	No	No	No	No	No	No	A	No	A	2 yrs.*	No	No	A
ID	6 wks.	Yes	Yes	Yes	Yes	A	Yes	3 yrs.	Yes	A	5 yrs.	Yes	No	A
IL	90 da.	Yes	Yes	1 yr.	2 yrs.	Yes	No	No	No	Yes	2 yrs.*	Yes	2 yrs.	No
IN	6 mos.*	No	No	No	No	Yes	No	2 yrs.	No	A	No	Yes	No	A
IA	1 yr.*	No	No	No	No	A	No	A	No	A	No	No	No	No
KS	60 da.	No	No	No	No	No	Yes	2 yrs.	A	A	No	No	No	A
KY	180 da.	No	No	No	No	A	No	No	No	A	No	No	No	A
LA	1 yr.*	Yes	No	No	No	No	No	No	No	A	6 mos.	Yes*	No	A
ME	6 mos.*	Yes	Yes	3 yrs.	Yes	Yes	Yes	A	No	A	No	No	Yes	No
MD	1 yr.*	Yes	No	1 yr.*	No	No	No	3 yrs.	No	A	1 yr.*	1 yr.*	No	No
MA	1 yr.*	Yes	Yes	1 yr.	Yes	Yes	Yes	No	No	A	No	5 yrs.	Yes	No
MI	180 da.	No	No	No	No	No	No	No	No	No	No	No	No	A
MN	180 da.	No	No	No	No	No	No	No	No	No	No	No	No	A
MS	6 mos.	Yes	Yes	1 yr.	Yes	Yes	No	3 yrs.	Yes	Yes	No	Yes*	Yes	A
MO	90 da.	No	No	No	No	No	No	No	No	No	No	No	No	A
MT	90 da.	No	No	No	No	A	No	No	No	No	180 da.*	No	No	A
NE	1 yr.*	No	No	No	No	A	No	No	No	A	No	No	No	A
NV	6 wks.	No	No	No	No	No	No	2 yrs.	No	A	1 yr.	No	No	A
NH	1 yr.*	Yes	Yes	2 yrs.	2 yrs.	Yes	2 yrs.	No	No	A	Yes	1 yr.*	No	No
NJ	1 yr.*	Yes	Yes	1 yr.	1 yr.	A	No	2 yrs.	No	A	18 mos.	18 mos.	1 yr.	A
NM	6 mos.	Yes	Yes	Yes*	No	No	No	No	No	No	No	No	No	No
NY	1 yr.*	Yes	Yes	1 yr.	No	No	No	No	No	A	1 yr.	3 yrs.	No	A
NC	6 mos.	No	No	No	No	A	No	3 yrs.	No	A	1 yr.	No	No	No
ND	6 mos.	Yes	Yes	1 yr.	1 yr.	A	1 yr.	5 yrs.*	No	A	No	Yes	1 yr.	A
OH	6 mos.	Yes	Yes	1 yr.	Yes	Yes	Yes	No	No	Yes, A	1 yr.	Yes	No	Yes, A
OK	6 mos.	Yes	Yes	1 yr.	Yes	Yes	Yes	5 yrs.	Yes	Yes	No	Yes	No	Yes
OR	6 mos.*	No	No	No	No	No	No	No	No	No	No	No	No	A
PA	6 mos.	Yes	Yes	1 yr.	No	No	No	18 mos.*	No	Yes	2 yrs.*	Yes	No	No
RI	1yr.	Yes	Yes	5 yrs.*	Yes	Yes	1 yr.	No	No	Yes	3 yrs.	Yes	Yes	No
SC	1 yr.*	Yes	Phys. only	1 yr.	Yes	No	No	No	No	No	1 yr.	No	Yes	No
SD	none*	Yes	Yes	1 yr.	1 yr.	A	1 yr.	5 yrs.	No	A	No	Yes	No	A*
TN	6 mos.*	Yes	Yes	1 yr.	Yes	Yes	Yes	No	Yes	Yes	2 yrs.	Yes	Yes	A
TX	6 mos.*	Yes	Yes	1 yr.	*	A	No	3 yrs.	No	No	3 yrs.	1 yr.	No	No
UT	3 mos.*	Yes	Yes	1 yr.	Yes	Yes	Yes	Yes	No	A	3 yrs.*	Yes	No	No
VT	6 mos.*	Yes	Yes	7 yrs.*	No	No	Yes	5 yrs.	No	A	6 mos.	3 yrs.	No	A
VA	6 mos.*	Yes	Yes*	1 yr.	No	A	No	No	A	A	1 yr.*	1 yr.*	No	A
WA	bona fide res.	No	No	No	No	No	No	No	No	No	No	No	No	No
WV	1 yr.*	Yes	Yes	6 mos.	Yes	A	No	3 yrs.	A	A	1 yr.	Yes	Yes	No
WI	6 mos.	No	No	No	No	A	No	No	No	A	1 yr.	No	No	A
WY	60 da.*	No	No	No	No	No	No	2 yrs.	No	A	No	No	No	No
DC	6 mos.	No	No	No	No	A	No	A*	No	A	6 mos.-1 yr.	No	No	A

(*) indicates qualification-check local statutes; (A) indicates grounds for annulment.

Wedding Anniversaries

The traditional names for wedding anniversaries go back many years in social usage. As such names as wooden, crystal, silver, and golden were applied it was considered proper to present the married pair with gifts made of these products or of something related. The list of traditional gifts, with a few allowable revisions in parentheses, is presented below, followed by modern gifts in **bold face.**

1st-Paper, **clocks**
2d-Cotton, **china**
3d-Leather, **crystal & glass**
4th-Linen (silk), **electrical appliances**
5th-Wood, **silverware**
6th-Iron, **wood**
7th-Wool (copper), **desk sets**
8th-Bronze, **linens & lace**
9th-Pottery (china), **leather**
10th-Tin (aluminum), **diamond jewelry**
11th-Steel, **fashion jewelry, accessories**
12th-Silk, **pearls or colored gems**
13th-Lace, **textiles & furs**
14th-Ivory, **gold jewelry**
15th-Crystal, **watches**
20th-China, **platinum**
25th-Silver, **sterling silver jubilee**
30th-Pearl, **diamond**
35th-Coral (jade), **jade**
40th-Ruby, **ruby**
45th-Sapphire, **sapphire**
50th-Gold, **gold**
55th-Emerald, **emerald**
60th-Diamond, **diamond**

RELIGIOUS INFORMATION

Census of Religious Groups in the U.S.

Source: *1992 Yearbook of American and Canadian Churches;* World Almanac Questionnaire

According to the National Council of Churches of Christ in the U.S.A. (unpublished data) there were a total of 156,336,384 members of religious groups in the U.S. in 1991.

Comparisons of membership statistics from group to group are not necessarily meaningful. Membership definitions vary—e.g., Roman Catholics count members from infancy, but some Protestant groups count only "adult" members, usually 13 years or older; some groups compile data carefully, but others estimate; not all groups report annually.

The number of churches appear in parentheses. Asterisk (*) indicates church declines to publish membership figures; (**) indicates figures date from 1981 or earlier.

Group	Members
Adventist churches:	
Advent Christian Ch. (334)	27,590
Primitive Advent Christian Ch. (10)	339
Seventh-day Adventists (4,217)	717,446
American Rescue Workers (20)	**2,700**
Anglican Orthodox Church (40)	**6,000**
Baha'i Faith (1,700)	**110,000**
Baptist churches:	
Amer. Baptist Assn. (1,705)	250,000
Amer. Baptist Chs. in U.S.A. (5,808)	1,535,971
Baptist General Conference (799)	134,717
Baptist Missionary Assn. of America (1,372)	229,166
Conservative Baptist Assn. of America (1,126)	210,000
Duck River (and Kindred) Assn. of Baptists (85)	**8,632
Free Will Baptists (2,506)	197,206
Gen. Assn. of Regular Baptist Chs. (1,574)	168,068
Natl. Baptist Convention of America (11,398)	**2,668,799
Natl. Baptist Convention, U.S.A. (30,000)	7,800,000
Natl. Primitive Baptist Convention (616)	**250,000
No. Amer. Baptist Conference (279)	44,493
Progressive National Baptist Convention (1,400)	2,500,000
Seventh Day Baptist General Conference (86)	5,200
Southern Baptist Convention (37,922)	15,038,409
Brethren (German Baptists):	
Brethren Ch. (Ashland, Ohio) (124)	13,060
Church of the Brethren (1,095)	148,253
Fellowship of Grace Brethren (319)	39,481
Brethren, River:	
Brethren in Christ Ch. (189)	17,277
Buddhist Churches of America (67)	**19,441**
Christadelphians (850)	**15,800**
The Christian and Missionary Alliance (1,856)	**279,207**
Christian Catholic Church (6)	**2,500**
Christian Church (Disciples of Christ) (4,069)	**1,039,692**
Christian Churches and Churches of Christ (5,579)	**1,070,616**
Christian Congregation (1,453)	**109,919**
Christian Methodist Episcopal Church (2,340)	**718,922**
Christian Nation Church U.S.A. (5)	**200**
Christian Union (114)	**6,000**
Churches of Christ (13,134)	**1,683,346**
Churches of Christ in Christian Union (214)	**9,221**
Churches of God:	
Chs. of God, General Conference (349)	33,371
Ch. of God (Anderson, Ind.) (2,339)	205,884
Ch. of God (Seventh Day), Denver, Col. (153)	5,749
Church of God in Christ (15,300)	5,499,875
Church of Christ, Scientist (3,000)	*
Church of God by Faith (145)	**8,235**
Church of the Nazarene (5,172)	**573,834**
Conservative Congregational Christian Conference (178)	**28,355**
Eastern Orthodox churches:	
Albanian Orth. Diocese of America (2)	1,870
American Carpatho-Russian Orth. Greek Catholic Ch. (72)	14,058
Antiochian Orth. Christian Archdiocese of No. Amer. (160)	350,000
Diocese of the Armenian Ch. of America (66)	**450,000
Bulgarian Eastern Orth. Ch. (9)	10,000
Coptic Orthodox Ch. (42)	165,000
Greek Orth. Archdiocese of N. and S. America (535)	**1,950,000
Orthodox Ch. in America (440)	**1,000,000
Patriarchal Parishes of the Russian Orth. Ch. in the U.S.A. (38)	9,780
Romanian Orth. Episcopate of America (37)	65,000
Serbian Eastern Orth. Ch. (68)	67,000
Syrian Orth. Ch. of Antioch (Archdiocese of the U.S.A. and Canada) (28)	30,000
Ukrainian Orth. Ch. of America (Ecumenical Patriarchate) (27)	5,000
Ukrainian Orthodox Church in the U.S.A. (107)	**87,745
The Episcopal Church in the U.S.A. (7,354)	**2,446,050**
Reformed Episcopal Church in America (83)	6,565
American Ethical Union (Ethical Culture Movement) (21)	**3,212**
Evangelical Church (185)	**16,398**
Evangelical Congregational Church (155)	**34,700**
The Evangelical Covenant Church (590)	**89,735**
Evangelical Free Church of America (1,087)	**192,352**
Evangelical associations:	
Apostolic Christian Chs. of America (80)	11,450
Apostolic Christian Ch. (Nazarene) (48)	2,799
Friends:	
Evangelical Friends International (246)	26,322
Friends General Conference (505)	31,690
Friends United Meeting (526)	54,945
Grace Gospel Fellowship (50)	**4,500**
Independent Fundamental Churches of America (700)	**78,174**
Jehovah's Witnesses (9,347)	**858,367**
Jewish organizations	
Union of Amer. Hebrew Congregations (Reform) (848)	1,300,000
Union of Orthodox Jewish Congregations of America (1,200)	1,000,000
United Synagogue of America (Conservative) (800)	2,000,000
Latter-day Saints:	
Ch. of Jesus Christ (Bickertonites) (63)	2,707
Ch. of Jesus Christ of Latter-day Saints (Mormon) (9,213)	4,267,000
Reorganized Ch. of Jesus Christ of Latter Day Saints (1,025)	189,524
Lutheran churches:	
Ch. of the Lutheran Brethren of America (111)	12,220
Ch. of the Lutheran Confession (69)	8,753
Evangelical Lutheran Ch. in America (11,087)	5,240,739
Evangelical Lutheran Synod (128)	21,630
Assn. of Free Lutheran Congregations (210)	27,650
Latvian Evangelical Lutheran Church of America (56)	12,553
Lutheran Ch.-Missouri Synod (5,296)	2,602,849
Protestant Conference (Lutheran) (7)	1,086
Wisconsin Evangelical Lutheran Synod (1,211)	420,039
Mennonite churches:	
Beachy Amish Mennonite Chs. (99)	6,872
Evangelical Mennonite Ch. (26)	3,958
The U.S. Conference of Mennonite Brethren Chs. (130)	16,794
General Conference Mennonite Church (1,023)	92,682
The General Conference Mennonite Ch. (218)	33,535
Hutterian Brethren (375)	38,000
Mennonite Ch. (1,034)	92,517
Old Order Amish Ch. (785)	70,650
Old Order (Wisler) Mennonite Ch. (36)	**9,731
Methodist churches:	
African Methodist Episcopal Ch. (6,200)	**2,210,000
African Methodist Episcopal Zion Ch. (3,000)	1,200,000
Evangelical Methodist Ch. (130)	8,282
Free Methodist Ch. of North America (1,096)	74,313
Fundamental Methodist Ch. (12)	1,075
Primitive Methodist Ch., U.S.A. (85)	8,244
Reformed Methodist Union Episcopal Ch. (18)	3,800
Southern Methodist Ch. (130)	7,572
United Methodist Ch. (37,407)	8,904,824
Missionary Church (302)	**26,910**
Moravian churches:	
Moravian Ch. Northern Province (98)	31,032
Moravian Ch. in America Southern Province (55)	21,269

(continued)

Group	Members
Unity of the Brethren (25)	3,196
Moslems	**8,000,000**
New Apostolic Church of North America (506)	**38,612**
North American Old Roman Catholic Church (133)	**62,611**
Old Catholic churches:	
Christ Catholic Ch. (12)	1,444
Pentecostal churches:	
Apostolic Faith (Portland, Ore.) (50)	4,100
Assemblies of God (11,353)	2,181,502
Bible Church of Christ (6)	6,812
Bible Way Church of Our Lord Jesus Christ World Wide (350)	**30,000
Church of God (Cleveland, Tenn.) (5,841)	620,393
Church of God of Prophecy (2,096)	72,904
Congregational Holiness Ch. (174)	**8,347
Gen. Council, Christian Ch. of No. Amer. (104)	13,500
Intl. Ch. of the Foursquare Gospel (1,451)	199,385
National Gay Pentecostal Alliance (2)	*
Open Bible Standard Chs. (335)	41,000
Pentecostal Assemblies of the World (550)	**4,500
Pentecostal Church of God (1,174)	91,300
Pentecostal Free-Will Baptist Ch. (141)	11,757
United Pentecostal Ch. Intl. (3,626)	500,000
Polish Natl. Catholic Church of America (162)	****282,411**
Presbyterian churches:	
Associated Reformed Presbyterian Ch. (Gen. Synod) (189)	37,988
Cumberland Presbyterian Ch. (796)	98,891

Group	Members
Evangelical Presbyterian Ch. (155)	52,645
Orthodox Presbyterian Ch. (188)	19,094
Presbyterian Ch. in America (1,167)	223,935
Presbyterian Ch. (U.S.A.) (11,501)	3,788,009
Reformed Presbyterian Ch. in No. Amer. (68)	5,174
Reformed churches:	
Christian Reformed Ch. in N. America (715)	226,163
Hungarian Reformed Ch. in America (27)	9,780
Protestant Reformed Chs. in America (21)	**4,544
Reformed Ch. in America (924)	326,850
Reformed Ch. in the U.S. (34)	3,778
The Roman Catholic Church (23,685)	**58,568,015**
The Salvation Army (1,133)	**445,566**
The Schwenkfelder Church (5)	**2,488**
Social Brethren (40)	****1,784**
Natl. Spiritualist Assn. of Churches (120)	**3,406**
Gen. Convention, The Swedenborgian Church (50)	**2,423**
Unitarian Universalist Assn. (1,020)	**141,315**
United Brethren:	
Ch. of the United Brethren in Christ (260)	25,775
United Christian Ch. (12)	420
United Church of Christ (6,260)	**1,599,212**
Universal Fellowship of Metropolitan Community Chs. (195)	**25,076**
Vedanta Society (13)	**2,500**
Volunteers of America (607)	****36,634**
The Wesleyan Church (1,628)	**110,561**

Number of U.S. Churches and Members, by Religious Groups

Comparisons of statistics of the various religious groups tabulated below are not meaningful because definitions of membership vary greatly from one religious body to another. For example, Roman Catholics count all baptized individuals, including infant members, as do many Protestant bodies. Some Protestant bodies, however, count as members those who have been received into the church at baptism, which can take place as early as age 9, thereby leaving out of official counts of membership many millions of children. Jewish statistics are estimates of the number of individuals in households in which one or more Jews reside and, therefore, include non-Jews living in such households as the result of intermarriage. The total number of persons in Jewish households is estimated to be 7 percent larger than the number of Jewish persons residing in these households.

	Number of Bodies Reporting	Number of Churches	Number of Members
Buddhists	1	67	19,441
Eastern Churches	18	1,702	3,976,153
Jews*	1	3,416	5,981,000
Old Catholic, Polish National Catholic, Armenian Churches	7	441	949,916
Protestants**	186	327,717	86,684,476
Roman Catholics	1	23,685	58,568,015
Miscellaneous***	5	1,166	157,383
Totals	219	358,194	156,336,384

* Including Orthodox, Conservative, and Reformed branches.
** Some bodies included here, such as various Latter-Day Saints groups and Jehovah's Witnesses, are strictly speaking, not Protestant in the usual sense.
*** This is a grouping of bodies officially non-Christian, Including those such as Spiritualists, Ethical Culture Movement, and Unitarian-Universalists.

Adherents of All Religions by Continental Areas, Mid-1991

Source: 1992 Encyclopedia Britannica Book of the Year

	Africa	Asia	Europe	Latin America	Northern America	Oceania	(former) U.S.S.R.	World
Christians	317,453,000	257,926,000	412,790,000	427,416,000	237,261,000	22,316,000	108,498,000	1,783,660,000
Roman Catholics	119,244,000	121,311,000	262,026,000	397,810,000	96,315,000	8,095,000	5,551,000	1,010,352,000
Protestants	84,729,000	79,969,000	73,766,000	16,930,000	95,610,000	7,415,000	9,790,000	368,209,000
Orthodox	27,698,000	3,587,000	36,080,000	1,730,000	5,964,000	568,000	93,056,000	168,683,000
Anglicans	26,063,000	694,000	32,879,000	1,275,000	7,284,000	5,640,000	400	73,835,400
Other Christians	59,719,000	52,365,000	8,039,000	9,671,000	32,088,000	598,000	100,600	162,580,600
Moslems	269,959,000	625,194,000	12,545,000	1,326,000	2,642,000	101,000	38,959,000	950,726,000
Nonreligious	1,840,000	700,523,000	52,289,000	16,828,000	25,265,000	3,246,000	84,477,000	884,468,000
Hindus	1,431,000	714,652,000	703,000	867,000	1,259,000	355,000	2,000	719,269,000
Buddhists	20,000	307,323,000	271,000	530,000	554,000	25,000	404,000	309,127,000
Atheists	307,000	158,429,000	17,563,000	3,162,000	1,310,000	527,000	55,511,000	236,809,000
Chinese folk religionists	12,000	183,361,000	60,000	71,000	121,000	20,000	1,000	183,646,000
New Religionists	20,000	138,767,000	50,000	520,000	1,410,000	10,000	1,000	140,778,000
Tribal religionists	68,484,000	24,487,000	1,000	918,000	40,000	66,000	0	93,996,000
Sikhs	26,000	17,934,000	231,000	8,000	252,000	9,000	500	18,460,500
Jews	327,000	5,484,000	1,465,000	1,071,000	6,952,000	96,000	2,220,000	17,615,000
Shamanists	1,000	10,044,000	2,000	1,000	1,000	1,000	252,000	10,302,000
Confucians	1,000	5,883,000	2,000	2,000	26,000	1,000	2,000	5,917,000
Baha'is	1,451,000	2,630,000	90,000	785,000	363,000	76,000	7,000	5,402,000
Jains	51,000	3,649,000	15,000	4,000	4,000	1,000	0	3,724,000
Shintoists	200	3,160,000	500	500	1,000	500	100	3,162,800
Other religionists	420,000	12,065,000	1,466,000	3,501,000	482,000	4,000	330,000	18,268,000
Total Population	**661,803,200**	**3,171,511,000**	**499,543,500**	**457,010,500**	**277,943,000**	**26,854,500**	**290,664,600**	**5,385,330,300**

(continued)

Percentage of adherents as part of world population: Christians, 33.1; Roman Catholics, 18.8; Protestants, 6.8; Moslems, 17.7; Nonreligious, 16.4; Hindus, 13.4; Buddhists, 5.7; Atheists, 4.4; Jews, 0.3.

Adherents: As defined and enumerated for each of the world's countries in *World Christian Encyclopedia* (1982), projected to mid-1991, adjusted for recent data.

Christians: Followers of Jesus Christ affiliated to churches (church members, including children: 1,658,149,700) plus persons professing in censuses or polls though not so affiliated.

Other Christians: Catholics (non-Roman), marginal Protestants, crypto-Christians, and adherents of African, Asian, black, and Latin-American indigenous churches.

Muslims: 83% Sunnites, 16% Shiites, 1% other schools. The definition excludes former ethnic Muslims who have now abandoned Islam, also followers of syncretistic religions combining Islam with other belief systems. In the U.S., a recent detailed survey showed that most Asian immigrants previously thought to be Muslims were now in fact Christians.

Hindus: 70% Vaishnavites, 25% Shaivites, 2% neo-Hindus and reform Hindus.

Buddhists: 56% Mahayana, 38% Theravada, 6% Tantrayana.

Atheists: Persons professing atheism, skepticism, disbelief, or irreligion, including antireligious (opposed to all religion).

Chinese folk religionists: Followers of traditional Chinese religion (local deities, ancestor veneration, Confucian ethics, Taoism, universism, divination, some Buddhist elements).

New-Religionists: Followers of Asian 20th-century New Religions, New Religious movements, radical new crisis religions, and non-Christian syncretistic mass religions, all founded since 1800 and mostly since 1945.

Jews: 84% Ashkenazis, 10% Orientals, 4% Sephardis. The definition includes nonpracticing Jews, underground Jews, and crypto-Jews in Muslim countries.

Confucians: Non-Chinese followers of Confucius and Confucianism, mostly Koreans in Korea.

Other religionists: Including 50 minor world religions and a large number of spiritist religions, New Age religions, quasi religions, pseudoreligions, parareligions, religious or mystic systems, religious and semireligious brotherhoods of numerous varieties.

Total Population: UN medium variant figures for mid-1991, as given in *World Population Prospects 1990* (New York: UN, 1991).

Headquarters, Leaders of U.S. Religious Groups

Year organized in parentheses. See *Associations and Societies* section for religious organizations.

Adventist churches:

Advent Christian Church (1860) — Pres., Rev. Glennon Balser; sec., Rev. John Gallagher; P.O. Box 23152, Charlotte, NC 28212.

Primitive Advent Christian Church — Pres., Roger Hammons; sec.-treas., Hugh W. Good; 395 Frame Rd., Elkview, WV 25071.

Seventh-day Adventists (1863) — Pres., Robert S. Folkenberg; sec., G. Ralph Thompson; 12501 Old Columbia Pike, Silver Spring, MD 20904-6600.

Baptist churches:

American Baptist Assn. (1905) — Pres., James A. Kirkland sec.-treas., D.S. Madden; 4605 N. State Line, Texarkana, TX 75503.

American Baptist Churches in the U.S.A. (1907) — Pres., James A. Scott; gen. sec., Daniel E. Weiss, P.O. Box 851, Valley Forge, PA 19482.

Baptist General Conference (1879) — Pres., Dr. Robert S. Ricker, 2002 S. Arlington Heights Rd., Arlington Heights, IL 60005.

Baptist Missionary Assn. of America (formerly **North American Baptist Assn.**) (1950) — Pres., Rev. Vernon R. Lee, rec. sec., Rev. Ralph Cottrell, P.O. Box 1203, Van, TX 75790.

Conservative Baptist Assn. of America (1947) — Gen. Dir., Dr. Tim Blanchard, Box 66, Wheaton, IL 60189.

Free Will Baptists (1727) — Mod., Rev. Ralph Hampton; exec. sec., Dr. Melvin Worthington; P.O. Box 5002, Antioch, TN 37011-5002.

General Assn. of General Baptists (1823) — Mod., Rev. Ray Phelps; clerk, Rev. Franklin Dumond; 100 Stinson Dr., Poplar Bluff, MO 63901.

General Assn. of Regular Baptist Churches (1932) — Chpsn., Dr. David Nettleton; sec., Dr. John Greening, 1300 N. Meacham Rd., Schaumburg, IL 60173.

Natl. Baptist Convention, U.S.A. (1880) — Pres., Dr. T.J. Jemison; gen. sec., Dr. W. Franklyn Richardson; 1620 Whites Creek Pike, Nashville, TN 37207.

North American Baptist Conference (1865) — Mod., Rev. Richard Russell; exec. dir., Dr. John Binder, 1 S. 210 Summit Ave., Oakbrook Terrace, IL 60181.

Progressive National Baptist Convention (1967) — Pres., Dr. Charles G. Adams; gen. sec., Rev. Tyrone S. Pitts, 601 50th St. N.E., Washington DC 20019.

Southern Baptist Convention (1845) — Pres., Morris M. Chapman; rec. sec., David W. Atchison; 901 Commerce St., Ste. 750, Nashville, TN 37203.

Brethren in Christ Church (1798) — Mod., Rev. Harvey R. Sider, gen. sec., Dr. R. Donald Shafer; P.O. Box 290, Grantham, PA 17027.

Brethren (German Baptists):

Brethren Church (Ashland, Oh.) (1882) — Dir., Pastoral Min., Rev. Dale Cooksey; 524 College Ave., Ashland, OH 44805.

Church of the Brethren (1708) — Mod., Charles L. Boyer; sec., Anne Myers; 1451 Dundee Ave., Elgin, IL 60120.

Buddhist Churches of America (1899) — Bishop, Seigen H. Yamaoka; exec. asst., Rev. Seikan Fukuma; 1710 Octavia St., San Francisco, CA 94109.

The Christian and Missionary Alliance (1887) — Pres., David L. Rambo; sec., R.H. Maugham; P.O. Box 35000, Colorado Springs, CO 80935.

Christian Church (Disciples of Christ) (1809) — Gen. minister and pres., C. William Nichols; v.p. for communication, Claudia E. Grant; 222 S. Downey Ave., Box 1986, Indianapolis, IN 46206.

Christian Methodist Episcopal Church (1870) — Exec. sec., Dr. W. Clyde Williams; sec., Rev. Edgar L. Wade; First Memphis Plaza, 4466 Elvis Presley Blvd., Memphis, TN 38116.

Churches of Christ in Christian Union (1909) — Gen. supt., Dr. Daniel Tipton; gen. sec., Rev. Robert Barth; 1426 Lancaster Pike, Box 30, Circleville, OH 43113.

Grace Brethren Church, Fellowship of (1882) — Mod., David Plaster; sec., John Snow, P.O. Box 6, Portis, KS 67474.

Churches of God:

Churches of God, General Conference (1825) — Pres., Pastor George Reser; journalizing sec., Pastor David L. Meador, 5665 New Design Rd., Frederick, MD 21701.

Church of God (Anderson, Ind.) (1880) — Exec. sec., Edward L. Foggs; Box 2420, Anderson, IN 46018.

Church of God in Christ (1906) — Pres. Bishop, Rt. Rev., Louis Henry Ford; 272 S. Main St., Memphis, TN 38101.

Church of Christ, Scientist (1879) — Chpsn., Virginia S. Harris; clk., Olga M. Chaffee, The First Church of Christ, Scientist, 175 Huntington Ave., Boston, MA 02115.

Church of the Nazarene (1908) — Gen. sec., Jack Stone; 6401 The Paseo, Kansas City, MO 64131.

National Association of Congregational Christian Churches (1955) — Mod., Steven S. Hoth; exec. sec., Michael S. Robertson, 8473 S. Howell Ave., Oak Creek, WI 53154.

Eastern Orthodox churches:

American Carpatho - Russian Onthodox Greek Catholic (Ecumenical Patriarchate) (1938) — Bishop, Rt. Bishop Nicholas (Smisko); Chancellor, Very Rev. Msgr. Frank P. Milloro, 312 Garfield St., Johnstown, PA 15906.

(continued)

Antiochian Orthodox Christian Archdiocese of North America (formerly **Syrian Antiochian Orthodox Archdiocese**) (1894) — Primate, Metropolitan Archbishop Saliba; aux., Archbishop Michael Shaheen, Bishop Antoun Khouri; 358 Mountain Rd., Englewood, NJ 07631.

Diocese of the Armenian Church of America (1889) — Primate, Eastern Diocese, His Eminence Bishop Khajag Barsamian; sec., Edward Onanian; 630 Second Ave., New York, NY 10016; Western Diocese, Primate, His Eminence Archbishop Vatche Hovsepian, 1201 N. Vine St., Hollywood, CA 90038.

Coptic Orthodox Ch. — Archpriest Fr. Gabriel Abdelsayed, 427 West Side Ave., Jersey City, NJ 07304.

Greek Orthodox Archdiocese of North and South America (1864) — Pres., Archbishop Iakovos; sec., Basil C. Foussianes; 8-10 E. 79th St., N.Y., NY 10021.

Orthodox Church in America (formerly **Russian Orthodox Greek Catholic Church of North America**) (1792) — Primate, Metropolitan Theodosius; chancellor, V. Rev. Robert S. Kondratick, P.O. Box 675, Syosset, NY 11791.

Romanian Orthodox Episcopate of America (1929) — Ruling Bishop, His Grace Bishop Nathaniel (Popp); sec., Rev. Fr. Laurence Lazar; 2522 Grey Tower Rd., Jackson, MI 49201.

Serbian Orthodox Church for the U.S.A. and Canada — Most Rev. Metropolitan Christopher, Rt. Rev. Georgije, Rt. Rev. Chrysostom, Rt. Rev. Bishop Mitrophan; St. Sava Monastery, Box 519, Libertyville, IL 60048.

Syrian Orthodox Church of Antioch (Archdiocese of the U.S.A. and Canada) (1957) — Primate, Archbishop Mar Athanasius Y. Samuel; gen. sec., Very Rev. Chorepiscopus John Meno, 45 Fairmount Ave., Hackensack, NJ 07601.

Ukrainian Orthodox Church in America (Ecumenical Patriarchate) (1928) — Primate, Rev. Bishop Vsevolod; 90-34 139th St., Jamaica, NY 11435.

Ukrainian Orthodox Church of the U.S.A. (1919) — Patriarch, His Holiness Patriarch Mstyslav I; Box 495, South Bound Brook, NJ 08880.

The Episcopal Church (1789) — Presiding bishop and primate, Most Rev. Edmond L. Browning; sec., Rev. Donald A. Nickerson Jr.; 815 Second Ave., New York, NY 10017.

Reformed Episcopal Church in America (1873) — Presiding Bishop, Franklin Sellers; sec., Rev. Willie J. Hill, 271 W. Tulpehocken St., Philadelphia, PA 19144.

The Evangelical Covenant Church (1885) — Pres., Dr. Paul E. Larsen; sec., John R. Hunt; 5101 N. Francisco Ave., Chicago, IL 60625.

Evangelical Friends (1965) — Mid-America YM, Roscoe Townsend, 2018 Maple, Wichita, KS 67213.

International — North Amer. Region (1990) (formerly **Evangelical Friends Alliance**) — 393 S. Vaughn Way, Aurora, CO 80012.

Friends:

Friends General Conference (1900) — Gen. sec., Meredith Walton; 1216 Arch St., 2B, Phila., PA 19107.

Friends United Meeting (formerly **Five Years Meeting of Friends**) (1902) — Presiding clerk, Sarah Wilson; 101 Quaker Hill Dr., Richmond, IN 47374.

Independent Fundamental Churches of America (1930) — Natl. Exec. Dir., Dr. Richard Gregory; P.O. Box 810, Grandville, MI 49418.

Jehovah's Witnesses (1879) — Pres., Frederick W. Franz, 25 Columbia Heights, Brooklyn, NY 11201.

Jewish congregations:

Union of American Hebrew Congregations (Reform) — Pres., Rabbi Alexander M. Schindler; 838 5th Ave., N.Y., NY 10021.

Union of Orthodox Jewish Congregations of America — Pres., Sheldon Rudoff; 333 7th Ave., N.Y., NY 10001.

United Synagogue of America (Conservative) — Pres., Alan Tichnor; 155 5th Ave., N.Y., NY 10010.

Latter-day Saints:

The Church of Jesus Christ (Bickertonites) (1830) — Pres., Dominic R. Thomas; exec. sec., Paul Palmieri; Sixth & Lincoln Sts., Monongahela, PA 15063.

The Church of Jesus Christ of Latter-day Saints (Mormon) (1830) — Pres., Ezra Taft Benson; 50 E. North Temple St., Salt Lake City, UT 84150.

Reorganized Church of Jesus Christ of Latter Day Saints (1830) — Pres., Wallace B. Smith; sec., A. Bruce Lindgren; The Auditorium, P.O. Box 1059, Independence, MO 64051.

Lutheran churches:

Church of the Lutheran Brethren of America (1900) — Pres., Rev. Robert M. Overgard Sr.; sec., Rev. Richard Vettrus; 1007 Westside Dr., Box 655, Fergus Falls, MN 56538.

Church of the Lutheran Confession (1961) — Pres., Rev. Daniel Fleischer; sec., Rev. Paul Nolting; 460 75th Ave., NE, Minneapolis, MN 55432.

Evangelical Lutheran Church in America (1987) — Bishop, Rev. Dr. Herbert W. Chilstrom; sec., Rev. Dr. Lowell G. Almen; 8765 W. Higgins Rd., Chicago, IL 60631.

Evangelical Lutheran Synod (1853) — Pres., Rev. George Orvick; sec., Rev. Alf Merseth; 447 N. Division St., Mankato, MN 56001.

Assn. of Free Lutheran Congregations (1962) — Pres. Rev. Robert L. Lee; sec., Rev. Richard Anderson; 3110 E. Medicine Lake Blvd., Minneapolis, MN 55441.

Lutheran Church — Missouri Synod (1847) — Pres., Dr. Ralph A. Bohlmann; sec., Dr. Walter L. Rosin; 1333 S. Kirkwood, St. Louis, MO 63122.

Wisconsin Evangelical Lutheran Synod (1850) — Pres., Rev. Carl H. Mischke; sec., Prof. David Worgull; 2929 N. Mayfair Rd., Milwaukee, WI 53222.

Mennonite churches:

The General Conference of Mennonite Brethren Churches (1860) — Mod. Edmund Janzen; sec., Roland Reimer, 1631 N. Callahan, Wichita, KS 67212.

General Conference Mennonite Church (1860) — Mod. Florence Driedger; 722 Main St., Newton, KS 67114

Mennonite Church (1690) — Mod., David W. Mann; 421 S. Second St. Ste. 600, Elkhart, IN 46516.

Methodist churches:

African Methodist Episcopal Church (1787) — Sr. Bishop, John H. Adams; gen. sec., Dr. O. Urcille Infill Sr., Box 19039, E. Germantown Sta., Philadelphia, PA 19138.

African Methodist Episcopal Zion Church (1796) — Sr. Bishop, William Milton Smith; sec., John Henry Miller Sr., 8605 Caswell Ct., Raleigh, NC 27612.

Free Methodist Church of North America (1860) — Bishops G.E. Bates, D.M. Foster, B. Akulu Ilangyi, D. Ward, N. Nzeyimana, R.D. Snyder; gen. conf. sec., Melvin J. Spencer; P.O. Box 535002, Indianapolis, IN 46253.

The United Methodist Church (1968) — Sec., Gen. Conference, Carolyn M. Marshall; 204 N. Newlin St., Veedersburg, IN 47987.

Universal Fellowship of Metropolitan Community Churches (1968) — Mod., Rev. Elder Troy D. Perry; clerk, Elder Larry Rodriguez; 5300 Santa Monica Blvd., Los Angeles, CA 90029.

Moravian Church (Unitas Fratrum) (1740) **Northern Province** — Pres., Dr. Gordon L. Sommers, 1021 Center St., P.O. Box 1245, Bethlehem, PA 18016. **Southern Province** — Pres., Rev. Graham H. Rights, 459 S. Church St., Winston-Salem, NC 27108.

Missionary Church (1883) — Pres. Dr. John Moran; sec., Rev. Dave Engbrecht; 3901 S. Wayne Ave., Ft. Wayne, IN 46516.

Pentecostal churches:

Assemblies of God (1914) — Gen. supt., G. Raymond Carlson; gen. sec., Joseph R. Flower; 1445 Boonville Ave., Springfield, MO 65802.

Bible Way Church of Our Lord Jesus Christ World Wide (1957) — Pres. Bishop, Lawrence G. Campbell; gen. sec., Bishop Edward Williams; 1100 New Jersey Ave., NW, Washington, DC 20001.

Gen. Council, Christian Church of No. America (1948) — Gen. overseer; David Farina; gen. sec.-treas., Rev. R. Allen Noyd; Rt. 18 & Rutledge Rd., Box 141-A, RD #1, Transfer, PA 16154.

The Church of God (1903) — Gen. overseer, Bishop Voy M. Bullen; gen. sec.-treas., Marie Powell; Box 13036, 1207 Willow Brook, Huntsville, AL 35802.

Church of God (Cleveland, Tenn.) (1886) — Gen. overseer, R. Lamar Vest; gen. sec.-treas., Gene D. Rice; P.O. Box 2430, Cleveland, TN 37320.

International Church of the Foursquare Gospel (1927) — Pres., Dr. John R. Holland; sec., Dr. John W. Bowers; 1910 W. Sunset Blvd., Ste. 200, Los Angeles, CA 90026.

National Gay Pentecostal Alliance (1980) — Presbyter, Rev. Wm. H. Carey, P.O. Box 1391, Schenectady, NY 12301.

Open Bible Standard Churches (1919) — Pres., Ray E. Smith; sec.-treas., Patrick L. Bowlin; 2020 Bell Ave., Des Moines, IA 50315.

Pentecostal Church of God (1919) — Gen. supt., Dr. James D. Gee; gen. sec., Dr. Ronald R. Minor; 4901 Pennsylvania, P.O. Box 850, Joplin, MO 64802.

Pentecostal Free Will Baptist Church (1959) — Gen. supt., Rev. Don Sauls; gen. sec., Rev. J.T. Hammond; Box 1568, Dunn, NC 28335.

United Pentecostal Church International (1945) — Gen. supt., Rev. Nathaniel A. Urshan; gen. sec.-treas., Rev. C. M. Becton; 8855 Dunn Rd., Hazelwood, MO 63042.

Presbyterian churches:

Cumberland Presbyterian Church (1810) — Mod., Floyd T.

Hensley; stated clerk, Robert Prosser, 1978 Union Ave., Memphis, TN 38104.

Evangelical Presbyterian Church (1981) — Mod., Dr. William M. Flannagan; stated clerk, Dr. L. Edward Davis; 26049 Five Mile Rd., Detroit, MI 48239.

The Orthodox Presbyterian Church (1936) — Mod., Rev. William E. Warren; stated clerk, Rev. Donald J. Duff; 303 Horsham Rd., Ste. G, Horsham, PA 19044.

Presbyterian Church in America (1973) — Mod., Mark Belz; stated clerk, Dr. Paul R. Gilchrist; 1852 Century Pl., Atlanta, GA 30345.

Presbyterian Church (U.S.A.) (1983) — Mod., Herbert D. Valentine; stated clerk, James E. Andrews; 100 Witherspoon St., Louisville, KY 40202.

Reformed Presbyterian Church of No. America (1871) — Mod., Dr. Roy Blackwood Jr.; clerk, J. Bruce Martin, 1328 Goodlin, Clay Center, KS 67432.

Reformed churches:

Christian Reformed Church in North America (1857) — Gen. sec., Rev. Leonard J. Hofman; 2850 Kalamazoo Ave., SE, Grand Rapids, MI 49560.

Reformed Church in America (1628) — Pres., Louis E. Lotz; gen. sec., Edwin G. Mulder; 475 Riverside Dr., N.Y., NY 10115.

Roman Catholic Church — National Conference of Catholic Bishops. Pres., Archbishop Daniel Pilarczyk; sec., Bishop Raymond W. Lessard; 3211 Fourth St., Washington, DC 20017.

The Salvation Army (1880) — Natl. Cmdr., Commissioner James Osborne; natl. chief sec., Com. Kenneth Hood; 615 Slaters La., Alexandria, VA 22313.

Sikh (1972) — The Sikh Foundation, Mr. Kawad Kohli, 1 Younge St., Ste. 1801, Toronto, ON M5E 5E1.

Unitarian Universalist Assn. (1961) — Pres., Rev. William Schulz; sec., Ralph Robins; 25 Beacon St., Boston, MA 02108.

United Brethren in Christ (1789) — Chpsn., Bishop C. Ray Miller; 302 Lake St., Huntington, IN 46750.

United Church of Christ (1957) — Pres., Rev. Paul H. Sherry sec., Edith Guffey; 700 Prospect Ave. E., Cleveland, OH 44115.

Volunteers of America (1896) — Chpsn., Walter Faster; 3813 N. Causeway Blvd., Metairie, LA 70002.

The Wesleyan Church (1968) — Gen. supt., Drs. O.D. Emery, Earle L. Wilson, Lee M. Haines, H.C. Wilson; gen. sec., Dr. Ronald R. Brannon, P.O. Box 50434; Indianapolis, IN 46250.

Jewish Holy Days, Festivals, and Fasts

	1992 (5752-53)	1993 (5753-54)	1994 (5754-55)	1995 (5755-56)	1996 (5756-57)
Tu B'Shvat	Jan. 20 Mon.	Feb. 6 Sat.	Jan. 27 Thu.	Jan. 16 Mon.	Feb. 5 Mon.
Ta'anis Esther (Fast of Esther)	Mar. 18 Wed.	Mar. 4 Thu.*	Feb. 24 Thu.	Mar. 15 Wed.	Mar. 4 Mon.
Purim	Mar. 19 Thu.	Mar. 7 Sun.	Feb. 25 Fri.	Mar. 16 Thu.	Mar. 5 Tue.
Passover	Apr. 18 Sat.	Apr. 6 Tue.	Mar. 27 Sun.	Apr. 15 Sat.	Apr. 4 Thu.
	Apr. 25 Sat.	Apr. 13 Tue.	Apr. 3 Sun.	Apr. 22 Sat.	Apr. 11 Thu.
Lag B'Omer	May 21 Thu.	May 9 Sun.	Apr. 29 Fri.	May 18 Thu.	May 7 Tue.
Shavuot	June 7 Sun.	May 26 Wed.	May 16 Mon.	June 4 Sun	May 24 Fri.
	June 8 Mon.	May 27 Thu.	May 17 Tue.	June 5 Mon.	May 25 Sat.
Fast of the 17th Day of Tammuz	July 19 Sun.*	July 6 Tue.	June 26 Sun.	July 16 Sun.*	July 4 Thu.
Fast of the 9th Day of Ac	Aug. 9 Sun.*	July 27 Tue.	July 17 Sun.	Aug. 6 Sun.	July 25 Thu.
Rosh Hashanah	Sept. 28 Mon.	Sept. 16 Thu.	Sept. 6 Tue.	Sept. 25 Mon.	Sept. 14 Sat.
	Sept. 29 Tue.	Sept. 17 Fri.	Sept. 7 Wed.	Sept. 26 Tue.	Sept. 15 Sun.
Fast of Gedalya	Sept. 30 Wed.	Sept. 19 Sun.*	Sept. 8 Thu.	Sept. 27 Wed.	Sept. 16 Mon.
Yom Kippur	Oct. 7 Wed.	Sept. 25 Sat.	Sept. 15 Thu.	Oct. 4 Wed.	Sept 23 Mon.
Sukkot	Oct. 12 Mon.	Sept. 30 Thu.	Sept. 20 Tue.	Oct. 9 Mon.	Sept. 28 Sat.
	Oct. 18 Sun.	Oct. 6 Wed.	Sept. 26 Mon.	Oct. 15 Sun.	Oct. 4 Fri.
Shmini Atzeret	Oct. 19 Mon.	Oct. 7 Thu.	Sept. 27 Tue.	Oct. 16 Mon.	Oct. 5 Sat.
	Oct. 20 Tue.	Oct. 8 Fri.	Sept. 28 Wed.	Oct. 17 Tue.	Oct. 6 Sun.
Chanukah	Dec. 20 Sun.	Dec. 9 Thu.	Nov. 28 Mon.	Oct. 18 Mon.	Dec. 6 Fri.
	Dec. 27 Sun.	Dec. 16 Thu.	Dec. 5 Mon.	Oct. 25 Mon.	Dec. 13 Fri.
Fast of the 10th of Tevet	Jan. 3, Sun.	Dec. 24 Fri.	Dec. 13 Tue.	Jan. 2 Tue.	Dec. 20 Fri.

The months of the Jewish year are: 1) Tishri; 2) Cheshvan (also Marcheshvan); 3) Kislev; 4) Tebet (also Tebeth); 5) Shebat (also Shebhat); 6) Adar; 6a) Adar Sheni (II) added in leap years; 7) Nisan; 8) Iyar; 9) Sivan; 10) Tammuz; 11) Av (also Abh); 12) Elul. All Jewish holy days, etc., begin at sunset on the day previous. *Date changed to avoid Sabbath.

Greek Orthodox Movable Ecclesiastical Dates

	1992	1993	1994	1995	1996
Triódion begins	February 16	February 7	February 20	February 12	February 4
Sat. of Souls	February 29	February 20	March 5	February 25	February 17
Meat Fare	March 1	February 21	March 6	February 26	February 18
2nd Sat. of Souls	March 7	February 27	March 12	March 4	February 24
Lent Begins	March 9	March 1	March 14	March 6	February 26
St. Theodore 3rd Sat. of Souls	March 14	March 6	March 19	March 11	March 2
Sunday of Orthodoxy	March 15	March 7	March 20	March 12	March 3
Sat. of Lazarus	April 18	April 10	April 23	April 15	April 6
Palm Sunday	April 19	April 11	April 24	April 16	April 7
Holy (Good) Friday	April 24	April 16	April 29	April 21	April 12
Western Easter	April 19	April 11	April 3	April 16	April 7
Orthodox Easter	April 26	April 18	May 1	April 23	April 14
Ascension	June 4	May 27	June 9	June 1	May 23
Sat. of Souls	June 13	June 5	June 18	June 10	June 1
Pentecost	June 14	June 6	June 19	June 11	June 2
All Saints	June 21	June 13	June 26	June 18	June 9

Islamic (Moslem) Calendar 1992-1993 (1413-1414)

The Islamic Calendar is a lunar reckoning from the year of the *hegira*, 622 A.D., when Muhammed moved from Mecca to Medina. It runs in cycles of 30 years, of which the 2nd, 5th, 7th, 10th, 13th, 16th, 18th, 21st, 24th, 26th, and 29th are leap years; 1413 is the 3rd year, 1414 the 4th year of the cycle. Common years have 354 days, leap years 355, the extra day being added to the last month, Zu'lhijjah. Except for this case, the 12 months beginning with Muharram have alternately 30 and 29 days.

Year	Name of month	Month begins
1413	Muharram (New Year)	July 2, 1992
1413	Safar	Aug. 1, 1992
1413	Rabia I	Aug. 30, 1992
1413	Rabia II	Sept. 29, 1992
1413	Jumada I	Oct. 28, 1992
1413	Jumada II	Nov. 27, 1992
1413	Rajab	Dec. 26, 1992
1413	Shaban	Jan. 25, 1993
1413	Ramadan	Feb. 22, 1993
1413	Shawwal	Mar. 25, 1993
1413	Zu'lkadah	Apr. 23, 1993
1413	Zu'lhijjah	May 23, 1993
1414	Muharram (New Year)	June 21, 1993
1414	Safar	July 21, 1993
1414	Rabia I	Aug. 19, 1993
1414	Rabia II	Sept. 18, 1993
1414	Jamada I	Oct. 17, 1993

Episcopal Church Calendar and Liturgical Colors

Source: The Episcopal Church Center, New York City

White—from Christmas Day through the First Sunday after Epiphany; Maundy Thursday (as an alternative to crimson at the Eucharist); from the Vigil of Easter to the Day of Pentecost (Whitsunday); Trinity Sunday; Feasts of the Lord (except Holy Cross Day); the Confession of St. Peter; the Conversion of St. Paul; St. Joseph; St. Mary Magdalene; St. Mary the Virgin; St. Michael and All Angels; All Saints' Day; St. John the Evangelist; memorials of other saints who were not martyred; Independence Day and Thanksgiving Day; weddings and funerals. **Red**—the Day of Pentecost; Holy Cross Day; feasts of apostles and evangelists (except those listed above); feasts and memorials of martyrs (including Holy Innocents' Day). **Violet**—Advent and Lent. **Crimson** (dark red)—Holy Week. **Green**—the seasons after Epiphany and after Pentecost. **Black**—optional alternative for funerals. Alternative colors used in some churches: **Blue**—Advent; **Lenten White**—Ash Wednesday to Palm Sunday.

In the Episcopal Church the days of fasting are Ash Wednesday and Good Friday. Other days of special devotion (abstinence) are the 40 days of Lent and all Fridays of the year, except those in Christmas and Easter seasons and any Feasts of the Lord which occur on a Friday or during Lent. Ember Days (optional) are days of prayer for the Church's ministry. They fall on the Wednesday, Friday, and Saturday after the first Sunday in Lent, the Day of Pentecost, Holy Cross Day, and the Third Sunday of Advent. Rogation Days (also optional) are the three days before Ascension Day, and are days of prayer for God's blessing on the crops, on commerce and industry, and for the conservation of the earth's resources.

Days, etc.	1992	1993	1994	1995	1996
Golden Number	17	18	19	1	2
Sunday Letter	ED	C	B	A	GF
Sundays after Epiphany	8	7	6	8	7
Ash Wednesday	Mar. 4	Feb. 24	Feb. 16	Mar. 1	Feb. 21
First Sunday in Lent	Mar. 8	Feb. 28	Feb. 20	Mar. 5	Feb. 25
Passion/Palm Sunday	Apr. 12	Apr. 4	Mar. 27	Apr. 9	Mar. 31
Good Friday	Apr. 17	Apr. 9	Apr. 1	Apr. 14	Apr. 5
Easter Day	Apr. 19	Apr. 11	Apr. 3	Apr. 16	Apr. 7
Ascension Day	May 28	May 20	May 12	May 25	May 16
The Day of Pentecost	June 7	May 30	May 22	June 4	May 26
Trinity Sunday	June 14	June 6	May 29	June 11	June 2
Numbered Proper of 2 Pentecost	#7	#6	#5	#6	#5
First Sunday of Advent	Nov. 29	Nov. 28	Nov. 27	Dec. 3	Dec. 1

Ash Wednesday and Easter Sunday

Year	Ash Wed.	Easter Sunday	Year	Ash Wed.	Easter Sunday	Year	Ash Wed.	Easter Sunday	Year	Ash Wed.	Easter Sunday
1901	Feb. 20	Apr. 7	1951	Feb. 7	Mar. 25	2001	Feb. 28	Apr. 15	2051	Feb. 15	Apr. 2
1902	Feb. 12	Mar. 30	1952	Feb. 27	Apr. 13	2002	Feb. 13	Mar. 31	2052	Mar. 6	Apr. 21
1903	Feb. 25	Apr. 12	1953	Feb. 18	Apr. 5	2003	Mar. 5	Apr. 20	2053	Feb. 19	Apr. 6
1904	Feb. 17	Apr. 3	1954	Mar. 3	Apr. 18	2004	Feb. 25	Apr. 11	2054	Feb. 11	Mar. 29
1905	Mar. 8	Apr. 23	1955	Feb. 23	Apr. 10	2005	Feb. 9	Mar. 27	2055	Mar. 3	Apr. 18
1906	Feb. 28	Apr. 15	1956	Feb. 15	Apr. 1	2006	Mar. 1	Apr. 16	2056	Feb. 16	Apr. 2
1907	Feb. 13	Mar. 31	1957	Mar. 6	Apr. 21	2007	Feb. 21	Apr. 8	2057	Mar. 7	Apr. 22
1908	Mar. 4	Apr. 19	1958	Feb. 19	Apr. 6	2008	Feb. 6	Mar. 23	2058	Feb. 27	Apr. 14
1909	Feb. 24	Apr. 11	1959	Feb. 11	Mar. 29	2009	Feb. 25	Apr. 12	2059	Feb. 12	Mar. 30
1910	Feb. 9	Mar. 27	1960	Mar. 2	Apr. 17	2010	Feb. 17	Apr. 4	2060	Mar. 3	Apr. 18
1911	Mar. 1	Apr. 16	1961	Feb. 15	Apr. 2	2011	Mar. 9	Apr. 24	2061	Feb. 23	Apr. 10
1912	Feb. 21	Apr. 7	1962	Mar. 7	Apr. 22	2012	Feb. 22	Apr. 8	2062	Feb. 8	Mar. 26
1913	Feb. 5	Mar. 23	1963	Feb. 27	Apr. 14	2013	Feb. 13	Mar. 31	2063	Feb. 28	Apr. 15
1914	Feb. 25	Apr. 12	1964	Feb. 12	Mar. 29	2014	Mar. 5	Apr. 20	2064	Feb. 20	Apr. 6
1915	Feb. 17	Apr. 4	1965	Mar. 3	Apr. 18	2015	Feb. 18	Apr. 5	2065	Feb. 11	Mar. 29
1916	Mar. 8	Apr. 23	1966	Feb. 23	Apr. 10	2016	Feb. 10	Mar. 27	2066	Feb. 24	Apr. 11
1917	Feb. 21	Apr. 8	1967	Feb. 8	Mar. 26	2017	Mar. 1	Apr. 16	2067	Feb. 16	Apr. 3
1918	Feb. 13	Mar. 31	1968	Feb. 28	Apr. 14	2018	Feb. 14	Apr. 1	2068	Mar. 7	Apr. 22
1919	Mar. 5	Apr. 20	1969	Feb. 19	Apr. 6	2019	Mar. 6	Apr. 21	2069	Feb. 27	Apr. 14
1920	Feb. 18	Apr. 4	1970	Feb. 11	Mar. 29	2020	Feb. 26	Apr. 12	2070	Feb. 12	Mar. 30
1921	Feb. 9	Mar. 27	1971	Feb. 24	Apr. 11	2021	Feb. 17	Apr. 4	2071	Mar. 4	Apr. 19
1922	Mar. 1	Apr. 16	1972	Feb. 16	Apr. 2	2022	Mar. 2	Apr. 17	2072	Feb. 24	Apr. 10
1923	Feb. 14	Apr. 1	1973	Mar. 7	Apr. 22	2023	Feb. 22	Apr. 9	2073	Feb. 8	Mar. 26
1924	Mar. 5	Apr. 20	1974	Feb. 27	Apr. 14	2024	Feb. 14	Mar. 31	2074	Feb. 28	Apr. 15
1925	Feb. 25	Apr. 12	1975	Feb. 12	Mar. 30	2025	Mar. 5	Apr. 20	2075	Feb. 20	Apr. 7
1926	Feb. 17	Apr. 4	1976	Mar. 3	Apr. 18	2026	Feb. 18	Apr. 5	2076	Mar. 4	Apr. 19
1927	Mar. 2	Apr. 17	1977	Feb. 23	Apr. 10	2027	Feb. 10	Mar. 28	2077	Feb. 24	Apr. 11
1928	Feb. 22	Apr. 8	1978	Feb. 8	Mar. 26	2028	Mar. 1	Apr. 16	2078	Feb. 16	Apr. 3
1929	Feb. 13	Mar. 31	1979	Feb. 28	Apr. 15	2029	Feb. 14	Apr. 1	2079	Mar. 8	Apr. 23
1930	Mar. 5	Apr. 20	1980	Feb. 20	Apr. 6	2030	Mar. 6	Apr. 21	2080	Feb. 21	Apr. 7
1931	Feb. 18	Apr. 5	1981	Mar. 4	Apr. 19	2031	Feb. 26	Apr. 13	2081	Feb. 12	Mar. 30
1932	Feb. 10	Mar. 27	1982	Feb. 24	Apr. 11	2032	Feb. 11	Mar. 28	2082	Mar. 4	Apr. 19
1933	Mar. 1	Apr. 16	1983	Feb. 16	Apr. 3	2033	Mar. 2	Apr. 17	2083	Feb. 17	Apr. 4
1934	Feb. 14	Apr. 1	1984	Mar. 7	Apr. 22	2034	Feb. 22	Apr. 9	2084	Feb. 9	Mar. 26
1935	Mar. 6	Apr. 21	1985	Feb. 20	Apr. 7	2035	Feb. 7	Mar. 25	2085	Feb. 28	Apr. 15
1936	Feb. 26	Apr. 12	1986	Feb. 12	Mar. 30	2036	Feb. 27	Apr. 13	2086	Feb. 13	Mar. 31
1937	Feb. 10	Mar. 28	1987	Mar. 4	Apr. 19	2037	Feb. 18	Apr. 5	2087	Mar. 5	Apr. 20
1938	Mar. 2	Apr. 17	1988	Feb. 17	Apr. 3	2038	Mar. 10	Apr. 25	2088	Feb. 25	Apr. 11
1939	Feb. 22	Apr. 9	1989	Feb. 8	Mar. 26	2039	Feb. 23	Apr. 10	2089	Feb. 16	Apr. 3
1940	Feb. 7	Mar. 24	1990	Feb. 28	Apr. 15	2040	Feb. 15	Apr. 1	2090	Mar. 1	Apr. 16
1941	Feb. 26	Apr. 13	1991	Feb. 13	Mar. 31	2041	Mar. 6	Apr. 21	2091	Feb. 21	Apr. 8
1942	Feb. 18	Apr. 5	1992	Mar. 4	Apr. 19	2042	Feb. 19	Apr. 6	2092	Feb. 13	Mar. 30
1943	Mar. 10	Apr. 25	1993	Feb. 24	Apr. 11	2043	Feb. 11	Mar. 29	2093	Feb. 25	Apr. 12
1944	Feb. 23	Apr. 9	1994	Feb. 16	Apr. 3	2044	Mar. 2	Apr. 17	2094	Feb. 17	Apr. 4
1945	Feb. 14	Apr. 1	1995	Mar. 1	Apr. 16	2045	Feb. 22	Apr. 9	2095	Mar. 9	Apr. 24
1946	Mar. 6	Apr. 21	1996	Feb. 21	Apr. 7	2046	Feb. 7	Mar. 25	2096	Feb. 29	Apr. 15
1947	Feb. 19	Apr. 6	1997	Feb. 12	Mar. 30	2047	Feb. 27	Apr. 14	2097	Feb. 13	Mar. 31
1948	Feb. 11	Mar. 28	1998	Feb. 25	Apr. 12	2048	Feb. 19	Apr. 5	2098	Mar. 5	Apr. 20
1949	Mar. 2	Apr. 17	1999	Feb. 17	Apr. 4	2049	Mar. 3	Apr. 18	2099	Feb. 25	Apr. 12
1950	Feb. 22	Apr. 9	2000	Mar. 8	Apr. 23	2050	Feb. 23	Apr. 10	2100	Feb. 10	Mar. 28

The Ten Commandments

According to Judeo-Christian tradition, as related in the Bible, the Ten Commandments were revealed by God to Moses, and form the basic moral component of God's covenant with Israel. The Ten Commandments appear in two different places in the Old Testament—Exodus 20:1-17 and Deuterotomy 5:6-21—the phrasing similar but not identical. Most Protestant, Anglican, and Orthodox Christians enumerate the commandments differently from Roman Catholics and Lutherans. Jewish tradition considers the introduction, "I am the Lord . . ." to be the first commandment and makes the prohibition against "other gods" and idolatry the second.

Abridged Text of the Ten Commandments in Exodus 20:1-17

I. I am the Lord your God, who brought you out of the land of Egypt, out of the house of bondage. You shall have no other gods before me.
II. You shall not make for yourself a graven image. You shall not bow down to them or serve them.
III. You shall not take the name of the Lord your God in vain.
IV. Remember the sabbath day, to keep it holy.
V. Honor your father and your mother.
VI. You shall not kill.
VII. You shall not commit adultery.
VIII. You shall not steal.
IX. You shall not bear false witness against your neighbor.
X. You shall not covet.

Books of the Bible

Old Testament—Standard Protestant English Versions

Genesis	II Chronicles	Daniel
Exodus	Ezra	Hosea
Leviticus	Nehemiah	Joel
Numbers	Esther	Amos
Deuteronomy	Job	Obadiah
Joshua	Psalms	Jonah
Judges	Proverbs	Micah
Ruth	Ecclesiastes	Nahum
I Samuel	Song of Solomon	Habakkuk
II Samuel	Isaiah	Zephaniah
I Kings	Jeremiah	Haggai
II Kings	Lamentations	Zechariah
I Chronicles	Ezekiel	Malachi

New Testament—Standard Protestant English Versions

Matthew	Ephesians	Hebrews
Mark	Phillippians	James
Luke	Colossians	I Peter
John	I Thessalonians	II Peter
Acts	II Thessalonians	I John
Romans	I Timothy	II John
I Corinthians	II Timothy	III John
II Corinthians	Titus	Jude
Galatians	Philemon	Revelation

Catholic Versions

All the Catholic books of the Bible (Old Testament and New Testament) have the same names as Protestant Versions. A Catholic Version (and Pre-Reformation Bibles) simply has the books **Tobit, Judith, Wisdom, Sirach (Ecclesiasticus), Baruch, I Maccabees,** and **II Maccabees** as part of the Old Testament. The Old Testament books that a Catholic Bible includes and a Protestant Bible does not are called "Deuterocanonical Books."

Roman Catholic Hierarchy

Source: U.S. Catholic Conference; Mid-year, 1992

Supreme Pontiff

At the head of the Roman Catholic Church is the Supreme Pontiff, Pope John Paul II, Karol Wojtyla, born at Wadowice (Krakow), Poland, May 18, 1920; ordained priest Nov. 1, 1946; appointed bishop July 4, 1958; promoted to archbishop of Krakow Jan. 13, 1964; proclaimed cardinal June 26, 1967; elected pope as successor of Pope John Paul I Oct. 16, 1978; installed as pope Oct. 22, 1978.

College of Cardinals

Members of the Sacred College of Cardinals are chosen by the Pope to be his chief assistants and advisors in the administration of the church. Among their duties is the election of the Pope when the Holy See becomes vacant. The title of cardinal is a high honor, but it does not represent any increase in the powers of holy orders.

In its present form, the College of Cardinals dates from the 12th century. The first cardinals, from about the 6th century, were deacons and priests of the leading churches of Rome, and bishops of neighboring diocese. The title of cardinal was limited to members of the college in 1567. The number of cardinals was set at 70 in 1586 by Pope Sixtus V. From 1959 Pope John XXIII began to increase the number. However, the number of cardinals eligible to participate in papal elections was limited to 120. There were lay cardinals until 1918, when the Code of Canon Law specified that all cardinals must be priests. Pope John XXIII in 1962 established that all cardinals must be bishops. The first age limits were set in 1971 by Pope Paul VI, who decreed that at age 80 cardinals must retire from curial departments and offices and from participation in papal elections. They continue as members of the college, with all rights and privileges.

U.S. Cardinals

Name	Office	Born	Named Cardinal
Baum, William W.	Major Penitentiary of Apostolic Penitentiary, the Vatican	1926	1976
Bevilacqua, Anthony J.	Archbishop of Philadelphia	1923	1991
Bernardin, Joseph L.	Archbishop of Chicago	1928	1983
Carberry, John J.*	Archbishop emeritus of St. Louis	1904	1969
Hickey, James A.	Archbishop of Washington	1920	1988
Krol, John J.*	Archbishop emeritus of Philadelphia	1910	1967
Law, Bernard F.	Archbishop of Boston	1931	1985
Mahony, Roger	Archbishop of Los Angeles	1936	1991
O'Connor, John J.	Archbishop of New York	1920	1985
Szoka, Edmund C.	Pres. of Prefecture of Economic Affairs of Holy See, the Vatican	1927	1988

*Asterisk indicates cardinals ineligible to take part in papal elections.

Major Christian Denominations:

Italics indicate that area which, generally speaking, most

Denomination	Origins	Organization	Authority	Special rites
Baptists	In radical Reformation objections to infant baptism, demands for church-state separation; John Smyth, English Separatist in 1609; Roger Williams, 1638, Providence, R.I.	Congregational, *i.e.*, each local church is autonomous.	Scripture; some Baptists, particularly in the South, interpret the Bible literally.	Baptism, after about age 12, by total immersion; Lord's Supper.
Church of Christ (Disciples)	Among evangelical Presbyterians in Ky. (1804) and Penn. (1809), in distress over Protestant factionalism and decline of fervor. Organized 1832.	Congregational.	"*Where the Scriptures speak, we speak; where the Scriptures are silent, we are silent.*"	Adult baptism, Lord's Supper (weekly).
Episcopalians	Henry VIII separated English Catholic Church from Rome, 1534, for political reasons. Protestant Episcopal Church in U.S. founded 1789.	*Bishops, in apostolic succession, are elected by diocesan representatives; part of Anglican Communion, symbolically headed by Archbishop of Canterbury.*	Scripture as interpreted by tradition, esp. *39 Articles* (1563); not dogmatic. Tri-annual convention of bishops, priests, and laymen.	Infant baptism, Holy Communion, others. Sacrament is symbolic, but has real spiritual effect.
Lutherans	Martin Luther in Wittenberg, Germany, 1517, objected to Catholic doctrine of salvation by merit and sale of indulgences; break complete by 1519.	Varies from congregational to episcopal; in U.S. a combination of regional synods and congregational polities is most common.	*Scripture, and tradition as spelled out in Augsburg Confession (1530) and other creeds. These confessions of faith are binding although interpretations vary.*	Infant baptism, Lord's Supper. Christ's true body and blood present "in, with, and under the bread and wine."
Methodists	Rev. John Wesley began movement, 1738, within Church of England. First U.S. denomination Baltimore, 1784.	Conference and superintendent system. *In United Methodist Church, general superintendents are bishops—not a priestly order, only an office—who are elected for life.*	Scripture as interpreted by tradition, reason, and experience.	Baptism of infants or adults, Lord's Supper commanded. Other rites, inc. marriage, ordination, solemnize personal commitments.
Mormons	In visions of the Angel Moroni by Joseph Smith, 1827, in New York, in which he received a new revelation on golden tablets: *The Book of Mormon.*	Theocratic; all male adults are in priesthood which culminates in Council of 12 Apostles and 1st Presidency (1st President, 2 counselors).	*The Bible, Book of Mormon and other revelations to Smith, and certain pronouncements of the 1st Presidency.*	Baptism, at age 8, laying on of hands (which confers the gift of the Holy Spirit), Lord's Supper. Temple rites: baptism for the dead, marriage for eternity, others.
Orthodox	Original Christian proselytizing in 1st century; broke with Rome, 1054, after centuries of doctrinal disputes and diverging traditions.	Synods of bishops in autonomous, usually national, churches elect a patriarch, archbishop or metropolitan. These men, as a group, are the heads of the church.	Scripture, tradition, and the first 7 church councils up to Nicaea II in 787. Bishops in council have authority in doctrine and policy.	Seven sacraments: infant baptism and anointing, Eucharist (both bread and wine), ordination, penance, anointing of the sick, marriage.
Pentecostal	In Topeka, Kansas (1901), and Los Angeles (1906) in reaction to loss of evangelical fervor among Methodists and other denominations.	Originally a movement, not a formal organization, Pentecostalism now has a variety of organized forms and continues also as a movement.	Scripture, individual charismatic leaders, the teachings of the Holy Spirit.	*Spirit baptism, esp. as shown in "speaking in tongues"; healing and sometimes exorcism; adult baptism, Lord's Supper.*
Presbyterians	In Calvinist Reformation in 1500s; differed with Lutherans over sacraments, church government. John Knox founded Scotch Presbyterian church about 1560.	*Highly structured representational system of ministers and laypersons (presbyters) in local, regional and national bodies. (synods).*	Scripture.	Infant baptism, Lord's Supper; bread and wine symbolize Christ's spiritual presence.
Roman Catholics	Traditionally, by Jesus who named St. Peter the 1st Vicar; historically, in early Christian proselytizing and the conversion of imperial Rome in the 4th century.	Hierarchy with supreme power vested in Pope elected by cardinals. Councils of Bishops advise on matters of doctrine and policy.	*The Pope, when speaking for the whole church in matters of faith and morals, and tradition, which is partly recorded in scripture and expressed in church councils.*	Seven sacraments: baptism, contrition and penance, confirmation, Eucharist, marriage, ordination, and anointing of the sick (unction).
United Church of Christ	*By ecumenical union, 1957, of Congregationalists and Evangelical & Reformed, representing both Calvinist and Lutheran traditions.*	Congregational; a General Synod, representative of all congregations, sets general policy.	Scripture.	Infant baptism, Lord's Supper.

How Do They Differ?

distinguishes that denomination from any other.

Practice	Ethics	Doctrine	Other	Denomination
Worship style varies from staid to evangelistic. Extensive missionary activity.	Usually opposed to alcohol and tobacco; sometimes tends toward a perfectionist ethical standard.	*No creed; true church is of believers only, who are all equal.*	Since no authority can stand between the believer and God, the Baptists are strong supporters of church-state separation.	**Baptists**
Tries to avoid any rite or doctrine not explicitly part of the 1st century church. Some congregations may reject instrumental music.	Some tendency toward perfectionism; increasing interest in social action programs.	Simple New Testament faith; avoids any elaboration not firmly based on Scripture.	Highly tolerant in doctrinal and religious matters; strongly supportive of scholarly education.	**Church of Christ (Disciples)**
Formal, based on *Book of Common Prayer* (1549); services range from austerely simple to highly elaborate.	Tolerant; sometimes permissive; some social action programs.	*Apostles' Creed* is basic; otherwise, considerable variation ranges from rationalist and liberal to acceptance of most Roman Catholic dogma.	Strongly ecumenical, holding talks with all other branches of Christendom.	**Episcopalians**
Relatively simple formal liturgy with emphasis on the sermon.	Generally, conservative in personal and social ethics; doctrine of "2 kingdoms" (worldly and holy) supports conservatism in secular affairs.	Salvation by faith alone through grace. Lutheranism has made major contributions to Protestant theology.	Though still somewhat divided along ethnic lines (German, Swede, etc.), main divisions are between fundamentalists and liberals.	**Lutherans**
Worship style varies widely by denomination, local church, geography.	Originally pietist and perfectionist; always strong social activist elements.	No distinctive theological development; 25 Articles abridged from Church of England's 39 not binding.	In 1968, United Methodist Church joined pioneer English- and German-speaking groups. UMs leaders in ecumenical movement.	**Methodists**
Staid service with hymns, sermon. Secret temple ceremonies may be more elaborate. Strong missionary activity.	Temperance; strict tithing. Combine a strong work ethic with communal self-reliance.	God is a material being; he created the universe out of pre-existing matter; all persons can be saved and many will become divine. Most other beliefs are traditionally Christian.	Mormons regard mainline churches as apostate, corrupt. Reorganized Church (founded 1860) rejects most Mormon doctrine and practice except Book of Mormon.	**Mormons**
Elaborate liturgy, usually in the vernacular, though extremely traditional. The liturgy is the essence of Orthodoxy. Veneration of icons.	Tolerant; very little social action; divorce, remarriage permitted in some cases. Priests need not be celibate; bishops are.	Emphasis on Christ's resurrection, rather than crucifixion; the Holy Spirit proceeds from God the Father only.	Orthodox Church in America, originally under Patriarch of Moscow, was granted autonomy in 1970. Greek Orthodox do not recognize this autonomy.	**Orthodox**
Loosely structured service with rousing hymns and sermons, culminating in spirit baptism.	Usually, emphasis on perfectionism with varying degrees of tolerance.	Simple traditional beliefs, usually Protestant, with emphasis on the immediate presence of God in the Holy Spirit.	Once confined to lower-class "holy rollers," Pentecostalism now appears in mainline churches and has established middle-class congregations.	**Pentecostal**
A simple, sober service in which the sermon is central.	Traditionally, a tendency toward strictness with firm church- and self-discipline; otherwise tolerant.	Emphasizes the sovereignty and justice of God; no longer doctrinaire.	While traces of belief in predestination (that God has foreordained salvation for the "elect") remain, this idea is no longer a central element in Presbyterianism.	**Presbyterians**
Relatively elaborate ritual; wide variety of public and private rites, eg., mass, rosary recitation, processions, novenas.	Theoretically very strict; tolerant in practice on most issues. Divorce and remarriage not accepted. Celibate clergy, except in Eastern rite.	Highly elaborated. Salvation by merit gained through faith. Unusual development of doctrines surrounding Mary. Dogmatic.	Roman Catholicism went through a period of relatively rapid change as a result of Vatican Council II.	**Roman Catholics**
Usually simple services with emphasis on the sermon.	Tolerant; some social action emphasis.	Standard Protestant; *Statement of Faith* (1959) is not binding.	The 2 main churches in the 1957 union represented earlier unions with small groups of almost every Protestant denomination.	**United Church of Christ**

The Major World Religions

Buddhism

Founded: About 525 BC, reportedly near Benares, India.
Founder: Gautama Siddhartha (ca. 563-480), the Buddha, who achieved enlightenment through intense meditation.
Sacred Texts: The *Tripitaka*, a collection of the Buddha's teachings, rules of monastic life, and philosophical commentaries on the teachings; also a vast body of Buddhist teachings and commentaries, many of which are called *sutras*.
Organization: The basic institution is the *sangha* or monastic order through which the traditions are passed to each generation. Monastic life tends to be democratic and anti-authoritarian. Large lay organizations have developed in some sects.
Practice: Varies widely according to the sect and ranges from austere meditation to magical chanting and elaborate temple rites. Many practices, such as exorcism of devils, reflect pre-Buddhist beliefs.
Divisions: A wide variety of sects grouped into 3 primary branches: Therevada (sole survivor of the ancient Hinayana schools) which emphasizes the importance of pure thought and deed; Mahayana, which includes Zen and Soka-gakkai, ranges from philosophical schools to belief in the saving grace of higher beings or ritual practices, and to practical meditative disciplines; and Tantrism, an unusual combination of belief in ritual magic and sophisticated philosophy.
Location: Throughout Asia, from Ceylon to Japan. Zen and Soka-gakkai have several thousand adherents in the U.S.
Beliefs: Life is misery and decay, and there is no ultimate reality in it or behind it. The cycle of endless birth and rebirth continues because of desire and attachment to the unreal "self". Right meditation and deeds will end the cycle and achieve Nirvana, the Void, nothingness.

Hinduism

Founded: Ca. 1500 BC by Aryan invaders of India where their Vedic religion intermixed with the practices and beliefs of the natives.
Sacred texts: The *Veda*, including the *Upanishads*, a collection of rituals and mythological and philosophical commentaries; a vast number of epic stories about gods, heroes and saints, including the *Bhagavadgita*, a part of the *Mahabharata*, and the *Ramayana;* and a great variety of other literature.
Organization: None, strictly speaking. Generally, rituals should be performed or assisted by Brahmins, the priestly caste, but in practice simpler rituals can be performed by anyone. Brahmins are the final judges of ritual purity, the vital element in Hindu life. Temples and religious organizations are usually presided over by Brahmins.
Practice: A variety of private rituals, primarily passage rites (eg. initiation, marriage, death, etc.) and daily devotions, and a similar variety of public rites in temples. Of the latter, the *puja*, a ceremonial dinner for a god, is the most common.
Divisions: There is no concept of orthodoxy in Hinduism, which presents a bewildering variety of sects, most of them devoted to the worship of one of the many gods. The 3 major living traditions are those devoted to the gods Vishnu and Shiva and to the goddess Shakti; each of them divided into further sub-sects. Numerous folk beliefs and practices, often in amalgamation with the above groups, exist side-by-side with sophisticated philosophical schools and exotic cults.
Location: Mainly India, Nepal, Malaysia, Guyana, Suriname, Sri Lanka.
Beliefs: There is only one divine principle; the many gods are only aspects of that unity. Life in all its forms is an aspect of the divine, but it appears as a separation from the divine, a meaningless cycle of birth and rebirth (*samsara*) determined by the purity or impurity of past deeds (*karma*). To improve one's *karma* or escape *samsara* by pure acts, thought, and/or devotion is the aim of every Hindu.

Islam

Founded: 622 AD in Medina, Arabian peninsula.
Founder: Mohammed (ca. 570-632), the Prophet.
Sacred texts: *Koran*, the words of God. *Hadith*, collections of the sayings of the Prophet.
Organization: Theoretically the state and religious community are one, administered by a caliph. In practice, Islam is a loose collection of congregations united by a very conservative tradition. Islam is basically egalitarian and non-authoritarian.
Practice: Every Moslem has 5 duties: to make the profession of faith ("There is no god but Allah . . ."), pray 5 times a day, give a regular portion of his goods to charity, fast during the day in the month of Ramadan, and make at least one pilgrimage to Mecca if possible.
Divisions: The 2 major sects of Islam are the Sunni (orthodox) and the Shi'ah. The Shi'ah believe in 12 *imams*, perfect teachers, who still guide the faithful from Paradise. Shi'ah practice tends toward the ecstatic, while the Sunni is staid and simple. The Shi'ah sect affirms man's free will; the Sunni is deterministic. The mystic tradition in Islam is Sufism. A Sufi adept believes he has acquired a special inner knowledge direct from Allah.
Location: From the west coast of Africa to the Philippines across a broad band that includes Tanzania, southern USSR and western China, India, Malaysia and Indonesia. Islam claims several million adherents in the U.S.
Beliefs: Strictly monotheistic. God is creator of the universe, omnipotent, just, and merciful. Man is God's highest creation, but limited and commits sins. He is misled by Satan, an evil spirit. God revealed the *Koran* to Mohammed to guide men to the truth. Those who repent and sincerely submit to God return to a state of sinlessness. In the end, the sinless go to Paradise, a place of physical and spiritual pleasure, and the wicked burn in Hell.

Judaism

Founded: About 1300 BCE.

Founder: Abraham is regarded as the founding patriarch, but the Torah of Moses is the basic source of the teachings.

Sacred Texts: The five books of Moses constitute the written Torah. Special sanctity is also assigned other writings of the Hebrew Bible—the teachings of oral Torah are recorded in the Talmud, the Midrash, and various commentaries.

Organization: Originally theocratic, Judaism has evolved a congregational polity. The basic institution is the local synagogue, operated by the congregation and led by a rabbi of their choice. Chief Rabbis in France and Great Britain have authority only over those who accept it; in Israel, the 2 Chief Rabbis have civil authority in family law.

Practice: Among traditional practitioners, almost all areas of life are governed by strict religious discipline. Sabbath and holidays are marked by special observances, and attendance at public worship is regarded as especially important then. The chief annual observances are Passover, celebrating the liberation of the Israelites from Egypt and marked by the ritual Seder meal in the home, and the 10 days from Rosh Hashana (New Year) to Yom Kippur (Day of Atonement), a period of fasting and penitence.

Divisions: Judaism is an unbroken spectrum from ultra conservative to ultra liberal, largely reflecting different points of view regarding the binding character of the prohibitions and duties—particularly the dietary and Sabbath observations—prescribed in the daily life of the Jew.

Location: Almost worldwide, with concentrations in Israel and the U.S.

Beliefs: Strictly monotheistic. God is the creator and absolute ruler of the universe. Men are free to choose to rebel against God's rule. God established a particular relationship with the Hebrew people: by obeying a divine law God gave them they would be a special witness to God's mercy and justice. The emphasis in Judaism is on ethical behavior (and, among the traditional, careful ritual obedience) as the true worship of God.

NATIONS OF THE WORLD

As of mid-1992

The nations of the world are listed in alphabetical order. Initials in the following articles include UN (United Nations), OAS (Org. of American States), NATO (North Atlantic Treaty Org.), EC (European Communities or Common Market), OAU (Org. of African Unity), ILO (Intl. Labor Org.), FAO (Food & Agricultural Org.), WHO (World Health Org.), IMF (Intl. Monetary Fund), GATT (General Agreements on Tarriffs & Trade), CIS (Commonwealth of Independent States). **Sources:** U.S. Dept. of State; U.S. Census Bureau; The World Factbook; International Monetary Fund; UN Statistical Yearbook; UN Demographic Yearbook; International Iron and Steel Institute; The Statesman's Year-Book; Encyclopaedia Britannica. All embassy addresses are Wash., DC; area codes (202), unless otherwise noted. Literacy rates are usually based on the ability to read and write on a lower elementary school level. The concept of literacy is changing in the industrialized countries, where literacy is defined as the ability to read instructions necessary for a job or a license. By these standards, illiteracy may be more common than present rates suggest. Per person figures in communications and health sections are post-1987.

See special color section for maps and flags.

Afghanistan

Republic of Afghanistan

De Afghanistan Jamhuriat

People: Population (1991 est.): 16,450,000. **Pop. density:** 65 per sq. mi. **Urban** (1987): 18%. **Ethnic groups:** Pushtun 50%; Tajik 25%; Uzbek 9%; Hazara 9%. **Languages:** Pushtu, Dari Persian (spoken by Tajiks, Hazaras), Uzbek (Turkic). **Religions:** Sunni Moslem 84%, Shi'a Moslem 15%.

Geography: Area: 251,773 sq. mi., about the size of Texas. **Location:** Between Soviet Central Asia and the Indian subcontinent. **Neighbors:** Pakistan on E, S, Iran on W, Turkmenistan, Tajik, Uzbekistan on N; the NE tip touches China. **Topography:** The country is landlocked and mountainous, much of it over 4,000 ft. above sea level. The Hindu Kush Mts. tower 16,000 ft. above Kabul and reach a height of 25,000 ft. to the E. Trade with Pakistan flows through the 35-mile long Khyber Pass. The climate is dry, with extreme temperatures, and large desert regions, though mountain rivers produce intermittent fertile valleys. **Capital:** Kabul. **Cities** (1988 est.): Kabul 1.4 mln.

Government: Type: In transition. **Head of state:** Pres. Burhanuddin Rabbani; in office: June 28, 1992. **Local divisions:** 30 provinces. **Defense:** 15% of GDP (1990).

Economy: Industries: Textiles, furniture, cement. **Chief crops:** Nuts, wheat, fruits. **Minerals:** Copper, coal, zinc, iron. **Other resources:** Wool, hides, karacul pelts. **Arable land:** 13%. **Livestock** (1990): cattle: 1.6 mln.; sheep: 13 mln. **Electricity prod.** (1989): 1.4 bln. kWh. **Labor force:** agriculture supports about 80% of the population.

Finance: Monetary unit: Afghani (Mar. 1992: 50.60 = $1 US). **Gross national product** (1988): $3.1 bln. **Per capita GNP:** $220. **Imports** (1990): $900 mln.; partners: CIS 55%, Jap. 8%. **Exports** (1990): $433 mln.; partners: CIS 72%. **International reserves less gold** (Feb. 1992): $229 mln. **Gold:** 965,000 oz t. **Consumer prices** (change in 1991): 56%.

Transport: Motor vehicles: in use (1990): 31,000 passenger cars, 30,000 comm. vehicles. **Civil aviation** (1989): 194 mln. passenger-km.

Communications: Television sets: 1 per 156 persons; **Radios:** 1 per 11 persons. **Telephones in use:** 1 per 443 persons. **Daily newspaper circ.** (1988): 10 per 1,000 pop.

Health: Life expectancy at birth (1991): 44 male; 43 female. **Births** (per 1,000 pop. 1989): 44. **Deaths** (per 1,000 pop. 1991): 21. **Natural increase:** 2.4%. **Hospital beds:** 1 per 2,054 persons. **Physicians:** 1 per 4,797 persons. **Infant mortality** (per 1,000 live births 1991): 164.

Education (1990): **Literacy:** 29%. Over 88% of adults have no formal schooling.

Major International Organizations: UN (World Bank, IMF)

Embassy: 2341 Wyoming Ave. NW, 20008; 234-3770.

Afghanistan, occupying a favored invasion route since antiquity, has been variously known as Ariana or Bactria (in ancient times) and Khorasan (in the Middle Ages). Foreign empires alternated rule with local emirs and kings until the 18th century, when a unified kingdom was established. In 1973, a military coup ushered in a republic.

Pro-Soviet leftists took power in a bloody 1978 coup, and concluded an economic and military treaty with the USSR.

Late in Dec. 1979, the USSR began a massive military airlift into Kabul. The three-month old regime of Hafizullah Amin ended with a Soviet backed coup, Dec. 27th. He was replaced by Babrak Karmal, a more pro-Soviet leader. Soviet troops fanned out over Afghanistan fighting rebels. Fighting continued for 9 years as the Soviets found themselves engaged in a long, protracted guerrilla war.

An UN-mediated agreement was signed Apr. 14, 1988 providing for the withdrawal of Soviet troops from Afghanistan, creation of a neutral Afghan state, and repatriation of millions of Afghan refugees. The U.S. and USSR pledged to serve as guarantors of the agreement. Afghan rebels rejected the pact and vowed to continue fighting while the "Soviets and their puppets" remained in Afghanistan.

The Soviets disclosed that during the war some 15,000 soldiers were killed. They completed their troop withdrawal Feb. 15, 1989 as Afghan rebels and the government began a civil war.

Communist Pres. Najibullah resigned Apr. 16, 1992 as competing guerrilla forces advanced on Kabul. The rebels achieved power, Apr. 28, ending 14 years of Soviet-backed regimes. Over 2 million Afghans had been killed and 6 million had fled the country since 1979. There were immediate clashes between moderates and Islamac fundamentalist forces. The fundamentalist forces shelled Kabul May 4-6. Burhanuddin Rabbani, a guerrilla leader, became President June 28. Fierce fighting continued around Kabul. (*See Chronology and Index for details*)

Albania

Republic of Albania

Republika e Shqipërisë

People: Population (1991 est.): 3,335,000. **Pop. density:** 300 per sq. mi. **Urban** (1989): 35%. **Ethnic groups:** Albanians (Gegs in N, Tosks in S) 90%, Greeks 8%. **Languages:** Albanian, Greek. **Religions:** officially atheist; (historically) mostly Moslems. All public worship and religious institutions were outlawed in 1967. In 1990, the right to practice religion was restored.

Geography: Area: 11,100 sq. mi., slightly larger than Maryland. **Location:** On SE coast of Adriatic Sea. **Neighbors:** Greece on S, Yugoslavia on N, E. **Topography:** Apart from a narrow coastal plain, Albania consists of hills and mountains covered with scrub forest, cut by small E-W rivers. **Capital:** Tiranë. **Cities** (1989 est.): Tirane 238,000; Durres 82,000; Vlore 71,000.

Government: Type: Democracy. **Head of state:** Pres. Sali Berisha; in office: Apr. 4, 1992. **Head of government:** Premier Alexander Meksi; in office: Apr. 4, 1992. **Local divisions:** 26 districts. **Defense:** 5.3% of GNP (1988).

Economy: Industries: Cement, textiles. **Chief crops:** Corn, wheat, cotton, potatoes, tobacco, fruits. **Minerals:** Chromium, coal, oil. **Other resources:** Forests. **Arable land:** 21%. **Livestock** (1989): 700,000 cattle; 1.6 mln. sheep. **Electricity prod.** (1990): 5.0 bln. kWh. **Labor force:** 60% agric; 40% ind. & comm.

Finance: Monetary unit: Lek (Nov. 1991: 5.77 = $1 US). **Gross national product** (1991): $4.0 bln. **Per capita GNP** (1987): $1,300. **Imports** (1987): $255 mln.; partners: Czech., Yugoslavia, Rom. **Exports** (1987): $378 mln.; partners: Czech., Yugoslavia, Italy.

Chief ports: Durres, Vlone, Sarande.

Communications: Television sets: 1 per 13 persons. **Radios:** 1 per 6 persons. **Daily newspaper circ.** 48 per 1,000 pop.

Health: Life expectancy at birth (1991): 72.0 yrs. male; 79 yrs. female. **Births** (per 1,000 pop. 1991): 25. **Deaths** (per

1,000 pop. 1991): 6. **Natural increase:** 1.9%. **Hospital beds:** 1 per 176 persons. **Physicians:** 1 per 574 persons. **Infant mortality** (per 1,000 live births 1991): 50.

Major International Organizations: UN (FAO, WHO).

Education (1989): **Literacy:** 75%. Free and compulsory ages 7-15.

Ancient Illyria was conquered by Romans, Slavs, and Turks (15th century); the latter Islamized the population. Independent Albania was proclaimed in 1912, republic was formed in 1920. King Zog I ruled 1925-39, until Italy invaded.

Communist partisans took over in 1944, allied Albania with USSR, then broke with USSR in 1960 over de-Stalinization. Strong political alliance with China followed, leading to several billion dollars in aid, which was curtailed after 1974. China cut off aid in 1978 when Albania attacked its policies after the death of Chinese ruler Mao Tse-tung.

Large-scale purges of officials occurred during the 1970s. Enver Hoxha, the nation's ruler for 4 decades, died Apr. 11, 1985.

There was some liberization in 1990, including measures providing for freedom to travel abroad and restoration of the right to practice religion.

In 1991, a general strike and urban opposition forced the communist cabinet to resign; a non-communist caretaker was installed. By March, over 40,000 Albanians had left their country and sailed to Italy. James Baker became the first U.S. secy. of state to visit Albania, June 22.

Albania's former Communists were routed in elections Mar. 1992 amid economic collapse and social unrest. Inflation was about 150%, unemployment was estimated at 70% nationwide, and almost all food came from foreign aid.

Algeria

Democratic and Popular Republic of Algeria

al-Jumhuriya al-Jazāiriya ad-Dimuqratiya ash-Shabiya

People: Population (1991 est.); 26,022,000. **Age distrib.** (%): 0–14: 43.9; 15–59: 50.3; 60+: 5.8. **Pop. density:** 28 per sq. mi. **Urban** (1987): 49%. **Ethnic groups:** Arabs 75%, Berbers 25%. **Languages:** Arabic (official), Berber (indigenous language). **Religions:** Sunni Moslem (state religion).

Geography: Area: 918,497 sq. mi., more than 3 times the size of Texas. **Location:** In NW Africa, from Mediterranean Sea into Sahara Desert. **Neighbors:** Morocco on W, Mauritania, Mali, Niger on S, Libya, Tunisia on E. **Topography:** The Tell, located on the coast, comprises fertile plains 50-100 miles wide, with a moderate climate and adequate rain. Two major chains of the Atlas Mts., running roughly E-W, and reaching 7,000 ft., enclose a dry plateau region. Below lies the Sahara, mostly desert with major mineral resources. **Capital:** Algiers (El Djazair). **Cities** (1987 est.): El Djazair 1,483,000; Wahran 590,000; Qacentina 483,000.

Government: Type: Military. **Head of state:** Pres. Ali Kafi; in office: July 1, 1992. **Head of government:** Prime Min. Belaid Abdesalam; in office: July 8, 1992. **Local divisions:** 48 provinces. **Defense:** 2.0% of GDP (1991).

Economy: Industries: Oil, light industry, food processing. **Chief crops:** Grains, wine-grapes, potatoes, dates, olives, oranges. **Minerals:** Mercury, iron, zinc, lead. **Crude oil reserves** (1987): 4.8 bln. bbls. **Other resources:** Cork trees. **Arable land:** 3%; **Livestock** (1988): cattle: 1.7 mln.; sheep: 14 mln. **Electricity prod.** (1990): 14.9 bln. kWh. **Crude steel prod.** (1990): 1.4 mln. metric tons **Labor force:** 24% agric.; 40% ind. and commerce; 24% government, & services.

Finance: Monetary Unit: Dinar (Mar. 1992: 22.35 = $1 US). **Gross national product** (1989): $53.1 bln. **Per capita GNP** (1989): $2,170. **Imports** (1990): $9.2 bln.; partners: EEC 64%. **Exports** (1990): $10.2 bln.; partners: EEC 74%. **National budget** (1990): $17.3 bln. **International reserves less gold** (Mar. 1992): $1.0 bln. **Gold:** 5.5 mln. oz t. **Consumer prices** (change in 1990): 26%

Transport: Motor vehicles: in use (1986): 712,000 passenger cars, 471,000 comm. vehicles. **Chief ports:** El Djazair.

Communications: Television sets: 1 per 15 persons. **Radios:** 1 per 4 persons. **Telephones in use:** 1 per 23 persons. **Daily newspaper circ.** (1990): 53 per 1,000 pop.

Health: Life expectancy at birth (1991): 66 male; 68 female. **Births** (per 1,000 pop. 1991): 32 **Deaths** (per 1,000 pop. 1991): 7.0. **Natural increase:** 2.5%. **Hospital beds:** 1 per 393 persons. **Physicians:** 1 per 1,199 persons. **Infant mortality** (per 1,000 live births 1991): 57.

Education (1991): **Literacy:** 52%. **School:** Free and compulsory to age 16; Attendance: 94% primary, 47% secondary.

Major International Organizations: UN (FAO, IMF, WHO), OAU, Arab League, OPEC.

Embassy: 2118 Kalorama Rd. NW, 20008; 328-5300.

Earliest known inhabitants were ancestors of Berbers, followed by Phoenicians, Romans, Vandals, and, finally, Arabs. Turkey ruled 1518 to 1830, when France took control.

Large-scale European immigration and French cultural inroads did not prevent an Arab nationalist movement from launching guerilla war. Peace, and French withdrawal, was negotiated with French Pres. Charles de Gaulle. One million Europeans left. Independence came July 5, 1962.

Ahmed Ben Bella was the victor of infighting, and ruled 1962-65, when an army coup installed Col. Houari Boumedienne as leader.

In 1967, Algeria declared war with Israel, broke with U.S., and moved toward eventual military and political ties with the USSR. Some 500 died in riots protesting economic hardship in 1988. In 1989, voters approved a new constitution which cleared the way for a multiparty system and guaranteed "fundamental rights and freedoms" of Algerians.

The government banned all nonreligious activities at Algeria's 10,000 mosques, Jan. 22, 1992, after the fundamentalist Islamic Salvation Front (FIS) called for the overthrow of the government. Pres. Boudiaf was assassinated June 29.

Andorra

Principality of Andorra

Principat d'Andorra

People: Population (1991 est.): 53,000. **Age distrib.** (%): 0–14: 19.0; 14–59: 68.5; 60+: 12.5. **Pop. density:** 286 per sq. mi. **Ethnic groups:** Catalan 61%, Spanish 30%, Andorran 6%, French 3%. **Languages:** Catalan (official), Spanish, French. **Religion:** Roman Catholic.

Geography: Area: 185 sq. mi., half the size of New York City. **Location:** In Pyrenees Mtns. **Neighbors:** Spain on S, France on N. **Topography:** High mountains and narrow valleys over the country. **Capital:** Andorra la Vella.

Government: Type: Co-principality. **Head of state:** Co-princes are the president of France and the Roman Catholic bishop of Urgel in Spain. **Local divisions:** 7 parishes.

Economy: Industries: Tourism, tobacco products. **Labor force:** 20% agric.; 80% ind. and commerce; services; government.

Finance: Monetary unit: French franc, Spanish peseta.

Communications: Television sets: 1 per 8 persons. **Radios:** 1 per 4 persons. **Telephones in use:** 1 per 2 persons.

Health: Births (per 1,000 pop. 1991): 10. **Deaths** (per 1,000 pop. 1991): 4. **Natural increase:** 0.7%.

Education (1991): **Literacy:** 99%. School compulsory to age 16.

The present political status, with joint sovereignty by France and the bishop of Urgel, dates from 1278.

Tourism, especially skiing, is the economic mainstay. A free port, allowing for an active trading center, draws some 10 million tourists annually. The ensuing economic prosperity accompanied by Andorra's virtual law-free status, has given rise to calls for reform. In July 1991, a trade agreement with the EC went into effect.

Angola

People's Republic of Angola

República Popular de Angola

People: Population (1991 est.): 8,668,000. **Pop. density:** 18 per sq. mi. **Ethnic groups:** Ovimbundu 38%, Kimbundu 25%; Bakongo 13%. **Languages:** Portuguese (official), various Bantu languages. **Religions:** Roman Catholic 38%, Protestant 15%, indigenous beliefs 47%.

Geography: Area: 481,353 sq. mi., larger than Texas and California combined. **Location:** In SW Africa on Atlantic coast. **Neighbors:** Namibia on S, Zambia on E, Zaire on N; Cabinda, an enclave separated from rest of country by short Atlantic coast of Zaire, borders Congo Republic. **Topography:** Most of Angola consists of a plateau elevated 3,000 to 5,000 feet above sea level, rising from a narrow coastal strip. There is also a temperate highland area in the west-central region, a desert in the S, and a tropical rain forest covering Cabinda. **Capital:** Luanda (1988 est.): 1.1 mln.

Government: Type: Republic. **Head of state:** Pres. Jose Eduardo dos Santos b. Aug. 28, 1942; in office: Sept. 20, 1979. Prime Min. Fernando Jose de Franca Dias van Dunem; in office: July 19, 1991. **Local divisions:** 18 provinces. **Defense:** 14.3% of GNP (1984).

Economy: Industries: Food processing, textiles, mining, tires, petroleum. **Chief crops:** Coffee, bananas. **Minerals:** Iron, diamonds (over 2 mln. carats a year), copper, phosphates, oil. **Livestock** (1989): cattle: 3.1 mln.; goats: 1 mln. **Crude oil reserves** (1987): 1.9 bln. bbls. **Arable land:** 3%. **Fish catch** (1989): 103,000 metric tons. **Electricity prod.** (1989): 737 mln. kWh. **Labor force:** 85% agric., 15% industry.

Finance: Monetary unit: new Kwanza (Nov. 1991: 103 = $1 US). **Gross domestic product** (1990): $7.9 bln. **Per Capita GNP:** $620. **Imports** (1990): $1.5 bln.; partners: Portugal 9%, Fra. 12%; U.S. 9.2%. **Exports** (1990): $3.8 bln.; partners: U.S. 38%.

Transport: Motor vehicles: in use (1989): 122,000 passenger cars, 44,000 comm. vehicles. **Chief ports:** Cabinda, Lobito, Luanda.

Communications: Television sets: 1 per 200 persons. Radios: 1 per 22 persons. **Telephones in use:** 1 per 122 persons. **Daily newspaper circ.** (1984): 13 per 1,000 pop.

Health: Life expectancy at birth (1991): 42.0 male; 46.0 female. **Births** (per 1,000 pop. 1991): 47. **Deaths** (per 1,000 pop. 1991): 21. **Natural increase:** 2.6%. **Hospital beds:** 1 per 672 persons. **Physicians:** 1 per 13,489 persons. **Infant mortality** (per 1,000 live births 1991): 151.

Education (1991): **Literacy:** 40%.

Major International Organizations: UN (ILO, WHO), OAU.

From the early centuries AD to 1500, Bantu tribes penetrated most of the region. Portuguese came in 1583, allied with the Bakongo kingdom in the north, and developed the slave trade. Large-scale colonization did not begin until the 20th century, when 400,000 Portuguese immigrated.

A guerrilla war begun in 1961 lasted until 1974, when Portugal offered independence. Violence between the National Front, based in Zaire, the Soviet-backed Popular Movement, and the National Union, aided by the U.S. and S. Africa, killed thousands of blacks, drove most whites to emigrate, and completed economic ruin. Cuban troops and Soviet aid helped the Popular Movement win most of the country after independence, igniting a Civil War.

Jonas Savimbi, leader of the National Union for Total Independence of Angola (UNITA), a rebel group fighting to overthrow the government, visited the U.S. in 1986 and was favorably received by the Reagan administration.

An agreement was signed Dec. 1988 between Angola, Cuba, and S. Africa on a timetable for withdrawal of Cuban troops—Cuba completed its troop withdrawel May 25, 1991—and for the independence of Namibia. The 16-year war ended May 1, 1991, as the government and UNITA signed a peace agreement which would lead to democracy.

Antigua and Barbuda

People: Population (1991 est.) 64,000. **Urban:** (1990) 32%. **Ethnic groups:** Mostly African. **Language:** English (official). **Religion:** Predominantly Church of England.

Geography: Area: 171 sq. mi. **Location:** Eastern Caribbean. **Neighbors:** approx. 30 mi. north of Guadeloupe. **Capital:** St. John's, (1988 est.) 27,000.

Government: Type: Constitutional monarchy with British-style parliament. **Head of State:** Queen Elizabeth II; represented by Sir Wilfred E. Jacobs. **Head of Government:** Prime Min. Vere Cornwall Bird; b. Dec. 7, 1910; in office Nov. 1, 1981.

Economy: Industries: Manufacturing, tourists. **Arable Land:** 18%.

Finance: Monetary unit: East Caribbean dollar (June 1992): 2.70 = $1 U.S. **Gross domestic product** (1990): $350 mln.

Health: infant mortality (per 1,000 live births 1989): 11.

Education (1990): **Literacy:** 90%.

Major International Organizations: UN, Commonwealth of Nations.

Embassy: 2400 International Dr., NW 20008; 362-5122.

Antigua was discovered by Columbus in 1493. The British colonized it in 1632.

The British associated state of Antigua achieved independence as Antigua and Barbuda on Nov. 1, 1981. The government maintains close relations with the U.S., United Kingdom, and Venezuela.

Argentina

Argentine Republic

República Argentina

People: Population (1991 est.): 32,663,000. **Age distrib.** (%): 0–14: 30.3; 15–59: 56.8; 60+: 12.9. **Pop. density:** 30 per sq. mi. **Urban** (1991): 87%. **Ethnic groups:** Europeans 85% (Spanish, Italian), Indians, Mestizos, Arabs. **Languages:** Spanish (official), Italian. **Religions:** Roman Catholic 92%.

Geography: Area: 1,065,189 sq. mi., 4 times the size of Texas, second largest in S. America. **Location:** Occupies most of southern S. America. **Neighbors:** Chile on W, Bolivia, Paraguay on N, Brazil, Uruguay on NE. **Topography:** The mountains in W: the Andean, Central, Misiones, and Southern. Aconcagua is the highest peak in the Western hemisphere, alt. 22,834 ft. E of the Andes are heavily wooded plains, called the Gran Chaco in the N, and the fertile, treeless Pampas in the central region. Patagonia, in the S, is bleak and arid. Rio de la Plata, 170 by 140 mi., is mostly fresh water, from 2,485-mi. Parana and 1,000-mi. Uruguay rivers. **Capital:** Buenos Aires. (The Senate has approved the moving of the capital to the Patagonia Region). **Cities** (1990 est.): Buenos Aires 10,500,000 met.; Cordoba 969,000; Rosario 750,455; Mendoza 597,000; San Miguel de Tucuman 497,000.

Government: Type: Republic. **Head of state:** Pres. Carlos Saúl Menem; b. July 2, 1930; in office: July 8, 1989. **Local divisions:** 22 provinces, 1 natl. terr. and 1 federal dist., under military governors. **Defense:** 1.4% of GNP (1991).

Economy: Industries: Meat processing, flour milling, chemicals, textiles, machinery, autos. **Chief crops:** Grains, corn, grapes, linseed, sugar, tobacco, rice, soybeans, citrus fruits. **Minerals:** Oil, lead, zinc, iron, copper, tin, uranium. **Crude oil reserves** (1987): 2.1 bln. bbls. **Arable land:** 9%. **Livestock** (1988): cattle: 50 mln.; sheep: 29 mln. **Fish catch** (1989): 475,000 metric tons. **Electricity prod.** (1990): 46.0 bln. kWh. **Crude steel prod.** (1990): 3.6 mln. metric tons. **Labor force:** 12% agric.; 31% ind. and comm.; 50% services.

Finance: Monetary unit: Peso (June 1992: .99 = $1 US). **Gross national product** (1990): $70.1 bln. **Per capita GNP** (1990): $2,134. **Imports** (1990): $4.0 bln.; partners: U.S. 21%, W. Ger. 9%, Braz. 16%, Jap. 7%. **Exports** (1990): $12.3 bln.; partners: USSR 13%, Neth. 9%, U.S. 12%. **Tourists** (1988): receipts: $634 mln. **National budget** (1990): $17.3 bln. expenditures. **International reserves less gold** (Jan. 1992): $6.6 bln. **Gold:** 4.12 mln. oz t. **Consumer prices** (change in 1990): 102.4%.

Transport: Railroads (1988): **Length:** 21,198 mi. **Motor vehicles:** in use (1989): 4.0 mln. passenger cars, 1.5 mln. comm. vehicles. **Civil aviation:** (1989) 8.2 mln. passenger-km. **Chief ports:** Buenos Aires, Bahia Blanca, La Plata.

Communications: Television sets: 1 per 4 persons. **Radios:** 1 per 1 person. **Telephones in use:** 1 per 9 persons. **Daily newspaper circ.** (1986): 88 per 1,000 pop.

Health: Life expectancy at birth (1990): 67 male; 74 female. **Births** (per 1,000 pop. 1991): 20. **Deaths** (per 1,000 pop. 1991): 9. **Natural increase:** 1.2%. **Hospital beds:** 1 per 186 persons. **Physicians:** 1 per 370 persons. **Infant mortality** (per 1,000 live births 1991): 32.

Education (1991): **Literacy:** 92%. School attendance: 21.5% through secondary school.

Major International Organizations: UN (WHO, IMF, FAO), OAS.

Embassy: 1600 New Hampshire Ave. NW 20009; 939-6400.

Nomadic Indians roamed the Pampas when Spaniards arrived, 1515-1516, led by Juan Diaz de Solis. Nearly all the Indians were killed by the late 19th century. The colonists won independence, 1916, and a long period of disorders ended in a strong centralized government.

Large-scale Italian, German, and Spanish immigration in the decades after 1880 spurred modernization, making Argentina the most prosperous, educated, and industrialized of the major Latin American nations. Social reforms were enacted in the 1920s, but military coups prevailed 1930-46, until the election of Gen. Juan Peron as president.

Peron, with his wife Eva Duarte effected labor reforms, but also suppressed speech and press freedoms, closed religious schools, and ran the country into debt. A 1955 coup exiled Peron, who was followed by a series of military and civilian regimes. Peron returned in 1973, and was once more elected president. He died 10 months later, succeeded by his wife, Isabel, who had been elected vice president, and who became the first woman head of state in the Western hemisphere.

A military junta ousted Mrs. Peron in 1976 amid charges of corruption. Under a continuing state of siege, the army battled guerrillas and leftists, killed 5,000 people, and jailed and tortured others. On Dec. 9, 1985, after a trial of 5 months and nearly 1,000 witnesses, 5 former junta members, including ex-presidents Jorge Videla and Gen. Roberto Eduardo Viola, were found guilty of murder and human rights abuses.

A severe worsening in economic conditions placed extreme pressure on the military government.

Argentine troops seized control of the British-held Falkland Islands on Apr. 2, 1982. Both countries had claimed sovereignty over the islands, located 250 miles off the Argentine coast, since 1833. The British dispatched a task force and declared a total air and sea blockade around the Falklands. Fighting began May 1; several hundred lost their lives as the result of the destruction of a British destroyer and the sinking of an Argentine cruiser.

British troops landed in force on East Falkland Island May 21. By June 2, the British had surrounded Stanley, the capital city and Argentine stronghold. The Argentine troops surrendered, June 14; Argentine President Leopoldo Galtieri resigned June 17.

Democratic rule returned to Argentina in 1983 as Raul Alfonsin's Radical Civic Union gained an absolute majority in the presidential electoral college and Congress. In 1989 the nation was plagued by severe financial problems as inflation reached crisis levels; over 6,000%. The hyperinflation sparked a week of looting and rioting in several cities; the government declared a 30-day state of siege May 29.

The government unveiled harsh economic measures in an effort to combat spiraling inflation and control government spending Apr. 1991.

Republic of Armenia

Haikakan Hanrapetoutioun

People: Population (1989 cen.): 3,300,000. **Pop. density:** 291 per sq. mi. **Language:** Armenian. **Ethnic groups:** Armenian 88%, Azerbaijanian 6%. **Religion:** Mostly Christian.

Georgraphy: Area: 11,306 sq. mi. **Neighbors:** Georgia on N., Azerbaijan on E., Iran on S., Turkey on W. **Topography:** Mountainous with many peaks above 10,000 ft. **Capital:** Yerevan.

Government: Type: Republic. **Head of state:** Pres. Levon Ter-Petrosyan; in office: Oct. 16, 1991.

Economy: Industries: Mining, chemicals. **Chief crops:** Cotton, figs, grain. **Minerals:** Copper, zinc.

Finance: Monetary unit: Ruble.

Health: Doctors (1989): 14,200; **Hospital beds** (1989): 30,000.

Major International Organizations: UN (IMF), CIS.

Embassy: 122 C St. NW 20001; 628-5766.

Armenia is an ancient country, part of which is now in Turkey and Iran. Present day Armenia was set up as a Soviet Republic Apr. 2, 1921. It joined Georgian and Azerbaijan SSRs Mar. 12, 1922 to form the Transcaucasion SFSR, which became part of the USSR Dec. 30, 1922. Armenia became a constituent republic of the USSR Dec. 5, 1936. An earthquake struck Armenia Dec. 7, 1988; over 55,000 were killed and several cities and towns were left in ruins. Armenia declared independence Sept. 23, 1991, and became an independent state when the USSR disbanded Dec. 25, 1991.

Fighting between mostly Christian Armenia and mostly Moslem Azerbaijan escalated in 1992. Each country claimed Nagorno-Karabakh, an enclave in Azerbaijan that has a majority population of ethnic-Armenians.

Australia

Commonwealth of Australia

People: Population (1991 cen.): 16,849,496. **Age distrib.** (%): 0–14: 21.9; 15–59: 62.6; ; 59 +: 15.5. **dop. density:** 5.8 per sq. mi. **Urban** (1990): 85%. **Ethnic groups:** European 95%, Asian 4%, aborigines (including mixed) 1.5%. **Languages:** English, aboriginal languages. **Religions:** Anglican 26%, other Protestant 25%, Roman Catholic 25%.

Geography: Area: 2,966,200 sq. mi., almost as large as the continental U.S. **Location:** SE of Asia, Indian O. is W and S, Pacific O. (Coral, Tasman seas) is E; they meet N of Australia in Timor and Arafura seas: Tasmania lies 150 mi. S of Victoria state, across Bass Strait. **Neighbors:** Nearest are Indonesia, Papua New Guinea on N, Solomons, Fiji, and New Zealand on E. **Topography:** An island continent. The Great Dividing Range along the E coast has Mt. Kosciusko, 7,310 ft. The W plateau rises to 2,000 ft., with arid areas in the Great Sandy and Great Victoria deserts. The NW part of Western Australia and Northern Terr. are arid and hot. The NE has heavy rainfall and Cape York Peninsula has jungles. The Murray R. rises in New South Wales and flows 1,600 mi. to the Indian O. **Capital:** Canberra. **Cities** (1991 est.): Sydney 3,600,000; Melbourne 3,000,000; Brisbane 1,200,000; Adelaide 1,000,000; Perth 1,200,000.

Government: Type: Democratic, federal state system. **Head of state:** Queen Elizabeth II, represented by Gov.-Gen. William Hayden; in office: Feb. 16, 1989. **Head of government:** Prime Min. Paul Keating; in office: Dec. 20, 1991. **Local divisions:** 6 states, 2 territories. **Defense:** 2.3% of GDP (1991).

Economy: Industries: Iron, steel, textiles, electrical equip., chemicals, autos, aircraft, ships, machinery. **Chief crops:** Wheat (a leading export), barley, oats, corn, hay, sugar, wine, fruit, vegetables. **Minerals:** Coal, copper, iron, lead, tin, uranium, zinc. **Crude oil reserves** (1987): 1.6 bln. bbls. **Other resources:** Wool (30% of world output). **Arable land:** 9%. **Livestock** (1989): cattle: 22 mln.; sheep: 162 mln.; pigs: 2.5 mln. **Fish catch** (1990): 175,000 metric tons. **Electricity prod.** (1989): 147 bln. kWh. **Crude steel prod.** (1990): 6.6 mln. metric tons. **Labor force:** 6% agric.; 33% finance & services; 36% trade & manuf.

Finance: Monetary unit: Dollar (June 1992: 1.31 = $1.00 US). **Gross domestic product** (1990): $311 bln. **Per capita income** (1990): $18,054. **Imports** (1991): $42.0 bln; partners: U.S. 21%, Jap. 20%, UK 7%. **Exports** (1991): $41.0 bln.; partners: Jap. 27%, U.S. 11%, NZ 5%. **Tourists** (1990): $3.7 bln. receipts. **National budget** (1991): $93 bln. expenditures. **International reserves less gold** (Mar. 1992): $13.6 bln. **Gold:** 7.93 mln. oz t. **Consumer prices** (change in 1991): 3.2%.

Transport: Motor vehicles: in use (1990): 7.6 mln. passenger cars, 2.1 mln. comm. vehicles. **Civil aviation** (1989): 26.2 mln. passenger-km.; 441 airports with scheduled flights. **Chief ports:** Sydney, Melbourne, Newcastle, Port Kembla, Fremantle, Geelong.

Communications: Television sets: 1 per 2 persons. **Radios:** 1 per 2 persons. **Telephones in use:** 1 per 2 persons. **Daily newspaper circ.** (1988): 405 per 1,000 pop.

Health: Life expectancy at birth (1991): 73 male; 80 female. **Births** (per 1,000 pop. 1989): 15. **Deaths** (per 1,000 pop. 1989): 8. **Natural increase:** 8%. **Hospital beds:** 1 per 186 persons. **Physicians:** 1 per 438 persons. **Infant mortality** (per 1,000 live births 1991): 9.0.

Education (1991): **Literacy:** 89%. **School:** compulsory to age 15; attendance 94%.

Major International Organizations: UN and all its specialized agencies, OECD, Commonwealth of Nations.

Embassy: 1601 Massachusetts Ave NW 20036; 797-3000.

Capt. James Cook explored the E coast in 1770, when the continent was inhabited by a variety of different tribes. The first settlers, beginning in 1788, were mostly convicts, soldiers, and government officials. By 1830, Britain had claimed the entire continent, and the immigration of free settlers began to accelerate. The commonwealth was proclaimed Jan. 1, 1901. Northern Terr. was granted limited self-rule July 1, 1978.

States	Area (sq. mi.)	Population (1991 cen.)
New South Wales, Sydney	309,500	5,731,926
Victoria, Melbourne	87,900	4,243,719
Queensland, Brisbane	666,990	2,976,617
Western Aust., Perth	975,100	1,586,393
South Aust., Adelaide	379,900	1.400,656
Tasmania, Hobart	26,200	452,847
Aust. Capital Terr., Canberra	900	280,085
Northern Terr., Darwin	519,800	175,253

Australia's racially discriminatory immigration policies were abandoned in 1973, after 3 million Europeans (half British) had entered since 1945. The 50,000 aborigines and 150,000 part-aborigines are mostly detribalized, but there are several preserves in the Northern Territory. They remain economically disadvantaged.

Australia's agricultural success makes it among the top exporters of beef, lamb, wool, and wheat. Major mineral deposits have been developed as well, largely for exports. Industrialization has been completed.

Australia harbors many plant and animal species not found elsewhere, including the kangaroo, koalas, platypus, dingo (wild dog), Tasmanian devil (racoon-like marsupial), wombat (bear-like marsupial), and barking and frilled lizards.

The nation suffered through a deep recession 1990-92. Unemployment passed 10 percent in Sept. 1991.

Australian External Territories

Norfolk Is., area 13½ sq. mi., pop. (1985) 1,800, was taken over, 1914. The soil is very fertile, suitable for citrus fruits, bananas, and coffee. Many of the inhabitants are descendants of the Bounty mutineers, moved to Norfolk 1856 from Pitcairn Is. Australia offered the island limited home rule, 1978.

Coral Sea Is. Territory, 1 sq. mi., is administered from Norfolk Is.

Territory of Ashmore and Cartier Is., area 2 sq. mi., in the Indian O. came under Australian authority 1934 and are administered as part of Northern Territory. **Heard** and **McDonald Is.** are administered by the Dept. of Science.

Cocos (Keeling) Is., 27 small coral islands in the Indian O. 1,750 mi. NW of Australia. Pop. (1981) 569, area: 5½ sq. mi. The residents voted to become part of Australia, Apr. 1984.

Kiritimati (Christmas Is.) 52 sq. mi., pop. 3,000 (1983), 230 mi. S of Java, was transferred by Britain in 1958. It has phosphate deposits.

Australian Antarctic Territory was claimed by Australia in 1933, including 2,360,000 sq. mi. of territory S of 60th parallel S Lat. and between 160th-45th meridians E Long. It does not include Adelie Coast.

Austria

Republic of Austria

Republik Österreich

People: Population (1991 est.): 7,665,000. **Age distrib.** (%): 0–14: 17.4; 15–59: 62.1; 60+: 20.5. **Pop. density:** 236 per sq. mi. **Urban** (1989): 62.1%. **Ethnic groups:** German 99%, Slovene, Croatian. **Languages:** German. **Religions:** Roman Catholic 85%.

Geography: Area: 32,374 sq. mi., slightly smaller than Maine. **Location:** In S Central Europe. **Neighbors:** Switzerland, Liechtenstein on W, Germany, Czechoslovakia on N, Hungary on E, Slovena, Italy on S. **Topography:** Austria is primarily mountainous, with the Alps and foothills covering the western and southern provinces. The eastern provinces and Vienna are located in the Danube River Basin. **Capital:** Vienna. **Cities** (1988 cen.): Vienna 1,500,000.

Government: Type: Federal republic. **Head of state:** Pres. Thomas Klestil; in office: June 8, 1992. **Head of government:** Chancellor Franz Vranitzky; b. Oct. 4, 1937; in office: June 16, 1986. **Local divisions:** 9 lander (states), each with a legislature. **Defense:** 1.2% of GDP (1990).

Economy: Industries: Steel, machinery, autos, electrical and optical equip., glassware, sport goods, paper, textiles, chemicals, cement. **Chief crops:** Grains, potatoes, beets. **Minerals:** Iron ore, oil, magnesite. **Crude oil reserves** (1985): 116 mln. bbls. **Other resources:** Forests, hydro power. **Arable land:** 18.3%. **Livestock** (1989): Cattle: 2.5 mln.; pigs: 3.8 mln. **Electricity prod.** (1990): 50.1 bln. kWh. **Crude steel prod.** (1990): 7 mln. metric tons. **Labor force:** 8% agric.; 35% ind. & comm.; 56% service.

Finance: Monetary unit: Schilling (June 1992: 11.12 = $1 US). **Gross domestic product** (1990): $111 bln. **Per capita GNP** (1989): $17,360. **Imports** (1991): $50.8 bln.; partners: EC 70%. **Exports** (1991): $41.1 bln.; partners: EC 68%. **Tourists** (1987): receipts: $7.6 bln. **National budget** (1990): $49.6 bln. expenditures. **International reserves less gold** (Mar. 1992): $10.3 bln. **Gold:** 20.0 mln. oz t. **Consumer prices** (change in 1991): 3.3%.

Transport: Railroads (1990): **Length:** 4,041 mi. **Motor vehicles:** in use (1989): 2.9 mln. passenger cars, 256,000 comm. **Civil aviation** (1990): 2.9 bln. passenger-km; 6 airports with scheduled flights.

Communications: Television sets: 1 per 2.8 persons. **Radios:** 1 per 1.6 persons. **Telephones in use:** 1 per 1.8 persons. **Daily newspaper circ.** (1990): 389 per 1,000 pop.

Health: Life expectancy at birth (1991): 74 male; 81 female. **Births** (per 1,000 pop. 1991): 12. **Deaths** (per 1,000 pop. 1989): 11. **Natural increase:** –.1%. **Hospital beds:** 1 per 101 persons. **Physicians:** 1 per 356 persons. **Infant mortality** (per 1,000 live births 1991): 5.

Education (1991): **Literacy:** 99%. **School years compulsory:** 9; attendance 95%.

Major International Organizations: UN and all of its specialized agencies, EFTA, OECD.

Embassy: 2343 Massachusetts Ave. NW 20008; 483-4474.

Rome conquered Austrian lands from Celtic tribes around 15 BC. In 788 the territory was incorporated into Charlemagne's empire. By 1300, the House of Hapsburg had gained control; they added vast territories in all parts of Europe to their realm in the next few hundred years.

Austrian dominance of Germany was undermined in the 18th century and ended by Prussia by 1866. But the Congress of Vienna, 1815, confirmed Austrian control of a large empire in southeast Europe consisting of Germans, Hungarians, Slavs, Italians, and others.

The dual Austro-Hungarian monarchy was established in 1867, giving autonomy to Hungary and almost 50 years of peace.

World War I, started after the June 28, 1914 assassination of Archduke Franz Ferdinand, the Hapsburg heir, by a Serbian nationalist, destroyed the empire. By 1918 Austria was reduced to a small republic, with the borders it has today.

Nazi Germany invaded Austria Mar. 13, 1938. The republic was reestablished in 1945, under Allied occupation. Full independence and neutrality were restored in 1955.

Austria produces most of its food, as well as an array of industrial products. A large part of Austria's economy is controlled by state enterprises. Socialists have shared or alternated power with the conservative People's Party.

An international panel of historians issued a report in 1988 which concluded that Pres. Kurt Waldheim knew of war crimes in Greece and Yugoslavia while serving in the German army during WW 2, did nothing to stop them, and later covered up his war record. The panel found no evidence that Waldheim committed war crimes.

Republic of Azerbaijan

Azerbaijchan Respublikasy

People: Population (1989 cen.): 7,000,000; **Pop. density:** 209 per sq. mi. **Ethnic groups:** Azerbaijan 78%, Russian 8%. **Language:** Azeri, Turkish, Russian. **Religions:** mostly Moslem.

Geography: Area: 33,400 sq. mi. **Neighbors:** Russia, Georgia on N., Iran on S., Armenia on W., Caspian Sea on E. **Capital:** Baku.

Government: Type: Republic. **Head of state:** Pres. Abulfez Elchibey; in office: June 8, 1992.

Economy: Industries: Oil refining. **Chief crops:** Grain, cotton, rice, silk. **Minerals:** Iron, copper, lead, zinc. **Livestock** (1989): cattle: 2.1 mln., goats & sheep: 5.7 mln.

Finance: Monetary unit: Ruble.

Health: Doctors (1989): 28,000; **Hospital beds** (1989): 71,000.

Major International Organizations: UN, CIS.

Azerbaijan was the home of Scythian tribes and part of the Roman Empire. It was overrun by Turks in the 11th century, and conquered by Russia in 1806 and 1813. It joined the USSR Dec. 30, 1922, and became a constituent republic in 1936. Azerbaijan declared independence Aug. 30, 1991 and became an independent state when the Soviet Union disbanded Dec. 25, 1991.

Fighting between mostly Moslem Azerbaijan and mostly Christian Armenia escalated in 1992. Each country claimed Nagorno-Karabakh, an enclave in Azerbaijan with a majority population of ethnic-Armenians.

A National Council ousted communist Pres. Mutaibov and took power May 19, 1992.

The Bahamas

The Commonwealth of the Bahamas

People: Population (1991 est.): 251,000. **Age distrib.** (%): 0–14: 38.0; 15–59: 56.3; 60+: 5.7. **Pop. density:** 48 per sq. mi. **Urban** (1990): 60%. **Ethnic groups:** black 85%, white (British, Canadian, U.S.) 15%. **Languages:** English. **Religions:** Baptist 32%, Anglican 20%, Roman Catholic 19%.

Geography: Area: 5,380 sq. mi., about the size of Connecticut. **Location:** In Atlantic O., E of Florida. **Neighbors:** Nearest are U.S. on W, Cuba on S. **Topography:** Nearly 700 islands (30 inhabited) and over 2,000 islets in the western Atlantic extend 760 mi. NW to SE. **Capital:** Nassau. **Cities:** (1990 est.) New Providence 171,000; Freeport 25,000.

Government: Type: Independent commonwealth. **Head of state:** Queen Elizabeth II, represented by Gov.-Gen. Henry Taylor, in office: June 25, 1988. **Head of government:** Prime Min. Hubert Ingraham; b. 1947; in office: Aug. 20, 1992. **Local divisions:** 21 districts.

Economy: Industries: Tourism (50% of GNP), rum, banking, pharmaceuticals. **Chief crops:** Fruits, vegetables. **Minerals:** Salt. **Other resources:** Lobsters. **Arable land:** 2%. **Electricity prod.** (1990): 828 mln. kWh. **Labor force:** 5% agric.; 25% tourism, 30% government.

Finance: Monetary unit: Dollar (Apr. 1992: 1 = $1 US). **Gross domestic product** (1989): $2.4 bln. **Per capita income** (1988): $7,178. **Imports** (1989): $3.1 bln.; partners: U.S. 74%, EC 30%. **Exports** (1989): $2.7 bln. (not incl. oil); partners: U.S. 41%, U.K. 7%. **Tourists** (1988): $1.1 bln. **National budget** (1990): $557 mln. expenditures. **International reserves less gold** (Mar. 1992): $199 mln. **Consumer prices** (change in 1991): 7.1%.

Transport: Motor vehicles: in use (1989): 67,000 passenger cars, 14,000 comm. vehicles. **Chief ports:** Nassau, Freeport.

Communications: Radios: 1 per 2 persons. **Television sets:** 1 per 4.6 persons. **Telephones in use:** 1 per 2 persons. **Daily newspaper circ.** (1988): 143 per 1,000 pop.

Health: Life expectancy at birth (1991): 69 male; 76 female. **Births** (per 1,000 pop. 1991): 19. **Deaths** (per 1,000 pop. 1991): 5. **Natural increase:** 1.4%. **Infant mortality** (per 1,000 live births 1991): 17.

Education (1990): Literacy: 95%; School compulsory through age 14.

Major International Organizations: UN (World Bank, IMF, WHO), OAS.

Embassy: 600 New Hampshire Ave. NW 20037; 338-3940.

Christopher Columbus first set foot in the New World on San Salvador (Watling I.) in 1492, when Arawak Indians inhabited the islands. British settlement began in 1647; the islands became a British colony in 1783. Internal self-government was granted in 1964; full independence within the Commonwealth was attained July 10, 1973.

International banking and investment management has become a major industry alongside tourism, despite controversy over financial irregularities.

Bahrain

State of Bahrain

Dawlat al-Bahrayn

People: Population (1991 est.): 536,000. **Age distrib.** (%): 0-14: 34.7; 15-59: 61.5; 60+ 3.8. **Pop. density:** 2,000 per sq. mi. **Urban** (1990): 82%. **Ethnic groups:** Bahraini 63%, Asian 13%, other Arab 10%, Iranian 6%. **Languages:** Arabic (official), Farsi, Urdu. **Religions:** Sunni Moslem 30%, Shi'ah Moslem 70%.

Geography: Area: 268 sq. mi., smaller than New York City. **Location:** In Persian Gulf. **Neighbors:** Nearest are Saudi Arabia on W. Qatar on E. **Topography:** Bahrain Island, and several adjacent, smaller islands, are flat, hot and humid, with little rain. **Capital:** Manama. **Cities** (1988 est.): Manama 151,000.

Government: Type: Traditional monarchy. **Head of state:** Amir Isa bin Sulman al-Khalifa; b. July 3, 1933; in office: Nov. 2, 1961. **Head of government:** Prime Min. Kahlifa ibn Sulman al-Khalifa; b. 1935; in office: Jan. 19, 1970. **Local divisions:** 6 towns & cities. **Defense:** 6.0% of GDP (1990).

Economy: Industries: Oil products, aluminum smelting. **Chief crops:** Fruits, vegetables. **Minerals:** Oil, gas. **Crude oil reserves** (1985): 173 mln. bbls. **Arable land:** 5%. **Electricity prod.** (1988): 5.4 bln. kWh. **Labor force:** 5% agric.; 85% ind. and commerce; 5% services; 3% gov.

Finance: Monetary unit: Dinar (Mar. 1992: 1.00 = $2.66 US). **Gross domestic product** (1989): $3.4 bln. **Per capita income** (1989): $7,300. **Imports** (1989): $3.0 bln.; partners: Sau. Ar. 60%, UK 6%, U.S. 9%. **Exports** (1989): $2.7 bln.; partners: UAE 18%, Jap. 12%, Sing. 10%, U.S. 6%. **National Budget** (1989): $1.3 bln. expenditures. **International reserves less gold** (Mar. 1992): $1.3 bln. **Gold:** 150,000 oz t. **Consumer prices** (change in 1991): 1.0%.

Transport: Motor vehicles: in use (1989): 90,000 passenger cars, 8,000 comm. vehicles. **Chief ports:** Sitra.

Communications: Television sets: 1 per 2.3 persons. **Radios:** 1 per 1.7 persons. **Telephones in use:** 1 per 3.4 persons.

Health: Life Expectancy at Birth (1991): 71 male; 76 female. **Births** (per 1,000 pop. 1991): 27. **Deaths** (per 1,000 pop. 1991): 3. **Natural Increase:** 2.4. Medical services are free. **Infant Mortality** (per 1,000 live births 1991): 17.

Education (1990): **Literacy:** 77%.

Major International Organizations: UN (GATT, IMF, WHO), Arab League.

Embassy: 3502 International Dr. NW 20008; 342-0741.

Long ruled by the Khalifa family, Bahrain was a British protectorate from 1861 to Aug. 15, 1971, when it regained independence.

Pearls, shrimp, fruits, and vegetables were the mainstays of the economy until oil was discovered in 1932. By the 1970s, oil reserves were depleted; international banking thrived.

Bahrain took part in the 1973-74 Arab oil embargo against the U.S. and other nations. The government bought controlling interest in the oil industry in 1975.

Bangladesh

People's Republic of Bangladesh

Gama Prajātantrī Bangladesh

People: Population (1991 est.): 116,601,000. **Age distrib.** (%): 0-14: 44.3; 15-59: 50.4; 60+: 5.3. **Pop. density:** 2,028 per sq. mi. **Urban** (1990): 24%. **Ethnic groups:** Bengali 98%, Bihari, tribesmen. **Languages:** Bengali (official), Chakma, Magh. **Religions:** Moslem 85%, Hindu 14%.

Geography: Area: 55,813 sq. mi. slightly smaller than Wisconsin. **Location:** In S Asia, on N bend of Bay of Bengal. **Neighbors:** India nearly surrounds country on W, N, E; Myanmar on SE. **Topography:** The country is mostly a low plain cut by the Ganges and Brahmaputra rivers and their delta. The land is alluvial and marshy along the coast, with hills only in the extreme SE and NE. A tropical monsoon climate prevails, among the rainiest in the world. **Capital:** Dhaka. **Cities** (1990 est.): Dhaka (met.) 5.7 mln.; Chittagong (met.) 2.1 mln.; Khulna (met.) 1,000,000.

Government: Type: Parliamentary. **Head of state:** Pres. Abdur Rahman Biswas in office: Oct. 10, 1991. **Head of Government:** Prime Min. Khaleda Zia; b. Nov. 1944; in office: Mar. 20, 1991. **Local divisions:** 64 districts. **Defense:** 1.8% of GDP (1990).

Economy: Industries: Food processing, jute, textiles, fertilizers, petroleum products. **Chief crops:** Jute (most of world output), rice, tea. **Minerals:** Natural gas, offshore oil, coal. **Arable land:** 67%. **Livestock** (1989): cattle: 23 mln.; goats: 10.7 mln. **Fish catch** (1989): 832,000 metric tons. **Electricity prod.** (1990): 5.7 bln. kWh. **Labor force:** 59% agric; 11% ind.; 30% services.

Finance: Monetary unit: Taka (Mar. 1992: 39 = $1 US). **Gross domestic product** (1990): $20.2 bln. **Per capita GNP** (1989) $180. **Imports** (1990): $3.6 bln.; partners: Jap. 13%, U.S. 13%. **Exports** (1991): $1.6 bln.; partners: U.S. 31%, It. 9%; Pak 5%. **Tourists** (1989): $13.0 mln. receipts. **National budget** (1990): $3.9 bln. expenditures. **International reserves less gold** (Mar. 1992): $1.3 bln. **Gold:** 85,000 oz t. **Consumer prices** (change in 1991): 7.2%.

Transport: Railroads (1989): **Length:** 1,750 mi. **Motor vehicles:** in use (1989): 39,000 passenger cars, 51,000 comm. vehicles. **Chief ports:** Chittagong, Chalna.

Communications: Radios: 1 per 24 persons. **Television sets:** 1 per 315 persons. **Telephones in use:** 1 per 572 persons. **Daily newspaper circ.** (1988) 8 per 1,000 pop.

Health: Life expectancy at birth (1991): 54 male; 53 female. **Births** (per 1,000 pop. 1991): 36. **Deaths** (per 1,000 pop. 1991): 13. **Natural increase:** 2.3%. **Hospital beds:** 1 per 3,233 persons. **Physicians:** 1 per 6,166 persons. **Infant mortality** (per 1,000 live births 1991): 118.

Education (1991): **Literacy:** 35%. **Attendance:** 24% primary school; 4% secondary school.

Major International Organizations: UN (GATT, IMF, WHO).

Embassy: 2201 Wisconsin Ave. NW 20007; 342-8372.

Moslem invaders conquered the formerly Hindu area in the 12th century. British rule lasted from the 18th century to 1947, when East Bengal became part of Pakistan.

Charging West Pakistani domination, the Awami League, based in the East, won National Assembly control in 1971. Assembly sessions were postponed; riots broke out. Pakistani troops attacked Mar. 25; Bangladesh independence was proclaimed the next day. In the ensuing civil war, one million died and 10 million fled to India.

War between India and Pakistan broke out Dec. 3, 1971. Pakistan surrendered in the East Dec. 15. Sheik Mujibur Rahman became prime minister. The country moved into the Indian and Soviet orbits, in response to U.S. support of Pakistan, and much of the economy was nationalized. Bangladesh adapted a parliamentary system of government in 1991.

Chronic destitution among the densely crowded population has been worsened by the decline of jute as a major world commodity.

On May 30, 1981, Pres. Ziaur Rahman was shot and killed in an unsuccessful coup attempt by army rivals. Vice President Abdus Sattar assumed the presidency but was ousted in a coup led by army chief of staff Gen. H.M. Ershad, Mar. 1982. Ershad declared Bangladesh an Islamic Republic in 1988. Bangladesh remains one of the world's poorest countries.

In 1988 and 1989, natural disasters and, monsoon rains brought devastation to Bangladesh: over 4,000 died, 30 million were made homeless. A cyclone struck Apr. 1991, killing over 131,000 people and causing $2.7 billion in damages. Some 7,500 U.S. military aided in the relief effort.

Barbados

People: Population (1991 est.): 254,000 **Age distrib.** (%): 0–14: 24.8%; 15–59: 60.6; 60+: 14.6. **Pop. density:** 1,530 per sq. mi. **Urban** (1985): 42%. **Ethnic groups:** African 80%, mixed 16%, Caucasian 4%. **Languages:** English. **Religions:** Protestant 67%, Roman Catholic 4%.

Geography: Area: 166 sq. mi. **Location:** In Atlantic, farthest E of W. Indies. **Neighbors:** Nearest are Trinidad, Grenada on SW. **Topography:** The island lies alone in the Atlantic almost completely surrounded by coral reefs. Highest point is Mt. Hillaby, 1,115 ft. **Capital:** Bridgetown. **Cities** (1986): Bridgetown 7,400.

Government: Type: Independent sovereign state within the Commonwealth. **Head of state:** Queen Elizabeth II, represented by Gov.-Gen. Dame Nita Barrow; in office: June 6, 1990. **Head of government:** Prime Min. Erskine Sandiford; b. Mar. 24, 1937; in office: June 1, 1987. **Local divisions:** 11 parishes and Bridgetown.

Economy: Industries: Sugar, tourism. **Chief crops:** Sugar, cotton. **Minerals:** Lime. **Other resources:** Fish. **Arable land:** 76%. **Electricity prod.** (1990): 484 mln. kWh. **Labor force:** 5% agric.; 17% ind. and comm.; 37% services and government.

Finance: Monetary unit: Dollar (June 1992: 2.01 = $1 US). **Gross domestic product** (1989): $1.7 bln. **Per capita GNP** (1987): $5,330. **Imports** (1990): $700 mln.; partners: U.S. 35%, CARACOM 12%. **Exports** (1990): $209 mln.; partners: U.S. 21%, CARACOM 30%. **Tourists** (1990): $502 mln. receipts. **National budget** (1991): $484 mln. expenditures. **International reserves less gold** (Mar. 1992): $145 mln. **Consumer prices** (change in 1991): 6.3%.

Transport: Motor vehicles: in use (1989): 38,000 passenger cars; 9,000 comm. vehicles. **Chief ports:** Bridgetown.

Communications: Television sets: 1 per 3.9 persons. **Radios:** 1 per 1.1 persons. **Telephones in use:** 1 per 2.4 persons. **Daily newspaper circ.** (1990): 161 per 1,000 pop.

Health: Life expectancy at birth (1989): male: 73 female: 77. **Births** (per 1,000 pop. 1991): 16. **Deaths** (per 1,000 pop. 1991): 9. **Natural increase:** 0.7%. **Hospital beds:** 1 per 123 persons. **Physicians:** 1 per 1,042 persons. **Infant mortality** (per 1,000 live births 1991): 23.

Education (1991): **Literacy:** 99%. **Years compulsory:** to age 16.

Major International Organizations: UN (FAO, GATT, ILO, IMF, WHO), OAS.

Embassy: 2144 Wyoming Ave. NW 20008; 939-9200.

Barbados was probably named by Portuguese sailors in reference to bearded fig trees. An English ship visited in 1605, and British settlers arrived on the uninhabited island in 1627. Slaves worked the sugar plantations, but were freed in 1834.

Self-rule came gradually, with full independence proclaimed Nov. 30, 1966. British traditions have remained.

Republic of Belarus

Respublika Belarus

People: Population (1989 cen.): 10,200,000. **Pop. density:** 127 per sq. mi. **Ethnic groups:** Belarus 80%, Poles 12%. **Language:** Belorussian, Russian.

Geography: Area: 80,134 sq. mi. **Neighbors:** Poland on W, Latvia, Lithuania on N, Russia on E, Ukraine on S. **Capital:** Minsk.

Government: Republic. **Head of state:** Pres. Stanislav Shushkevich; in office: Sept. 1991. **Head of government:** Prime Min. Vyacheslav Kebich. **Local divisions:** 6 regions.

Economy: Industries: Food processing, chemicals, machine-tool & agricultural machinery. **Chief crops:** Grain, flax, potatoes, sugar beets.

Finance: Monetary unit: Ruble.

Health: Doctors (1989): 41,000; **Hospital beds** (1989): 138,000.

Major International Organizations: UN, CIS.

The region was subject to Lithuanians and Poles in medieval times, and was a prize of war between Russia and Poland beginning in 1503. It became part of the USSR in 1922 although the western part of the region was controlled by Poland. Belarus was overrun by German armies in 1941; recovered by Soviet troops in 1944. Following World War II, Belarus increased in area through Soviet annexation of part of NE Poland. Belarus declared independence Aug. 25, 1991. It became an independent state when the Soviet Union disbanded Dec. 25, 1991.

Belgium

Kingdom of Belgium

Koninkrijk België (Dutch)

Royaume de Belgique (French)

People: Population (1991 est.): 9,921,000. **Age distrib.** (%): 0–14: 18.2; 15–59: 61.7; 60+: 20.1 **Pop. density:** 842 per sq. mi. **Urban** (1990): 96%. **Ethnic groups:** Fleming 55%, Walloon 33%. **Languages:** Flemish (Dutch) 57%, French 33%, Italian, German. **Religions:** Roman Catholic 75%.

Geography: Area: 11,799 sq. mi., slightly larger than Maryland. **Location:** In NW Europe, on N. Sea. **Neighbors:** France on W, S, Luxembourg on SE, Germany on E, Netherlands on N. **Topography:** Mostly flat, the country is trisected by the Scheldt and Meuse, major commercial rivers. The land becomes hilly and forested in the SE (Ardennes) region. **Capital:** Brussels. **Cities** (1988 est.): Brussels (met.) 970,000; Antwerp (met.) 479,000; Ghent 233,000; Charleroi 209,000; Liege 200,000.

Government: Type: Parliamentary democracy under a constitutional monarch. **Head of state:** King Baudouin; b. Sept. 7, 1930; in office: July 17, 1951. **Head of government:** Premier Jean-Luc Dehaene; in office: Mar. 7, 1992. **Local divisions:** 9 provinces; 3 regions; 3 cultural communities. **Defense:** 2.5% of GDP (1990).

Economy: Industries: Steel, glassware, diamond cutting, textiles, chemicals. **Chief crops:** Wheat, potatoes, sugar beets. **Minerals:** Coal. **Other resources:** Forests. **Arable land** (incl. Lux.): 26.5%. **Livestock:** (1989): cattle: 3.1 mln; pigs: 6.4 mln. **Fish catch** (1988): 23.3 metric tons. **Electricity prod.** (1989): 60 bln. kWh. **Crude steel prod.** (1990): 11.3 mln. metric tons. **Labor force:** 2% agric.; 26% ind. & comm.; 37% services & transportation; 23% public service.

Finance: Monetary unit: Franc (June 1992: 32.70 = $1 US). **Gross domestic product** (1990): $144 bln. **Per capita GDP** $14,600. *Note:* the following trade and tourist data includes Luxembourg. **Imports** (1991): $119 bln.; partners: EC 73%. **Exports** (1991): $118 bln.; partners: EC 74%. **Tourists** (1989): receipts: $3.5 bln. **National budget** (1989): $51 bln. expenditures. **International reserves less gold** (Mar. 1992): $11.2 bln. **Gold:** 30.2 mln. oz t. **Consumer prices** (change in 1991): 3.2%.

Transport: Railroads (1989): **Length:** 2,217 mi. **Motor vehicles:** in use (1990): 3.8 mln. passenger cars, 358,000 comm. vehicles. **Civil aviation** (1989): 6.5 bln. passenger-km; 4 airports with scheduled flights. **Chief ports:** Antwerp, Zeebrugge, Ghent.

Communications: Television sets: 1 per 3.2 persons. **Radios:** 1 per 2.2 persons; **Telephones in use:** 1 per 2.1 persons. **Daily newspaper circ.** (1990): 213 per 1,000 pop.

Health: Life expectancy at birth (1991): 74 male; 81 female. **Births** (per 1,000 pop. 1991): 12. **Deaths** (per 1,000 pop. 1991): 11. **Natural increase** 0.1%. **Hospital beds:** 1 per 108 persons. **Physicians:** 1 per 317 persons. **Infant mortality** (per 1,000 live births 1991): 6.

Education (1991): Literacy: 98%. School compulsory to age 18.

Major International Organizations: UN and all of its specialized agencies, NATO, EC, OECD.

Embassy: 3330 Garfield St. NW 20008; 333-6900

Belgium derives its name from the Belgae, the first recorded inhabitants, probably Celts. The land was conquered by Julius Caesar, and was ruled for 1800 years by conquerors, including Rome, the Franks, Burgundy, Spain, Austria, and France. After 1815, Belgium was made a part of the Netherlands, but it became an independent constitutional monarchy in 1830.

Belgian neutrality was violated by Germany in both world wars. King Leopold III surrendered to Germany, May 28, 1940. After the war, he was forced by political pressure to abdicate in favor of his son, King Baudouin.

The Flemings of northern Belgium speak Dutch while French is the language of the Walloons in the south. The language difference has been a perennial source of controversy and led to antagonism between the 2 groups. Parliament has passed measures aimed at transferring power from the central government to 3 regions—Wallonia, Flanders, and Brussels.

Belgium lives by its foreign trade; about 50% of its entire production is sold abroad.

Belize

People: Population (1991 est.): 228,000. **Age distrib.** (%): 0–14: 44.5; 15–59: 47.8; 60+: 7.6. **Pop. density:** 25 per sq. mi. **Ethnic groups:** Mestizo 33%, Creole 40%, Maya 10%. **Languages:** English (official), Spanish, native Creole dialects. **Religions:** Roman Catholic 60%, Protestant 30%.

Geography: Area: 8,867 sq. mi. **Location:** eastern coast of Central America. **Neighbors:** Mexico on N., Guatemala on W. and S. **Capital:** Belmopan. **Cities:** (1990 est.): Belmopan 60,000.

Government: Type: Parliamentary democracy. **Head of State:** Gov. Gen. Minita Gordon. **Head of government:** Prime Min. George Cadle Price; in office: Nov. 7, 1989. **Local divisions:** 6 districts.

Economy: Sugar is the main export.

Finance: Monetary unit: Belize dollar (Mar. 1992) 2 = $1 U.S. **Gross domestic product** (1990): $290 mln. **Per capita GDP** (1988): $1,312. **Imports** (1990): $211 mln.; partners: U.S. 55%, UK 8%. **Exports:** (1990): $129 mln.; partners: U.S. 46%, UK 31%. **National Budget** (1990): $72 mln. expenditures.

Health: life expectancy (1991) male: 67; female: 72. **Births** (per 1,000 pop. 1991): 38. **Deaths** (per 1,000 pop. 1991): 5. **Hospital beds:** 1 per 366 persons. **Physicians:** 1 per 2,046 persons. **Infant mortality** (per 1,000 live births, 1991): 35.

Education: (1991) **Literacy:** 93%.; **Years compulsory:** 9; attendance 55%.

Major International Organizations: OAS, UN (IMF, World Bank), Commonwealth of Nations.

Embassy: 3400 International Dr., NW 20005; 363-4505.

Belize (formerly called British Honduras), was Great Britain's last colony on the American mainland, achieved independence on Sept. 21, 1981. British troops in Belize guarantee security.

Benin

Republic of Benin

République du Benin

People: Population (1991 est.): 4,831,000. **Age distrib.** (%): 0–14: 46.5; 15–59: 49.0; 60+: 4.5. **Pop. density:** 111 per sq. mi. **Urban** (1985): 20%. **Ethnic groups:** Fon, Adja, Bariba, Yoruba. **Languages:** French (official), Fon, Yoruba, Somba. **Religions:** Mainly animist with Christian, Moslem minorities.

Geography: Area: 43,483 sq. mi., slightly smaller than Pennsylvania. **Location:** In W Africa on Gulf of Guinea. **Neighbors:** Togo on W, Burkina Faso, Niger on N, Nigeria on E. **Topography:** most of Benin is flat and covered with dense vegetation. The coast is hot, humid, and rainy. **Capital:** Porto-Novo. **Cities** (1984 est.): Cotonou 330,000.

Government: Type: Democracy. **Head of state:** Nicephore Soglo; in office: Apr. 4, 1991. **Local divisions:** 6 provinces. **Defense:** 2.1% of GDP (1988).

Economy: Chief crops: Palm products, peanuts, cotton, coffee, tobacco. **Minerals:** Oil. **Arable land:** 12%. **Livestock** (1989): sheep: 890,000; goats: 1.1 mln. **Fish catch** (1990): 39,000 metric tons. **Electricity prod.** (1990): 24 mln. kWh. **Labor force:** 60% agric; 38% serv. & comm.

Finance: Monetary unit: CFA franc (Mar. 1992: 278 = $1 US). **Gross domestic product** (1991): $1.7 bln. **Per capita GDP** (1991): $400. **Imports** (1986): $314 mln.; partners: Ind. 24%, Fr. 16%. **Exports** (1986): $100 mln.; partners: Port. 15%, Itl. 10% Fr. 26%. **National Budget** (1989): $317 bln. expenditures. **International reserves less gold** (Feb. 1992): $181 mln.

Transport: Railroads (1989): **Length:** 395 mi. **Chief ports:** Cotonou.

Communications: Radios: 1 per 14 persons. **Televisions:** 1 per 281 persons. **Daily newspaper circ.** (1990): 3 per 1,000 pop.

Health: Life expectancy at birth (1991): 49 male; 52 female. **Births** (per 1,000 pop. 1991): 49. **Deaths** (per 1,000 pop. 1991): 16. **Natural increase:** 3.7%. **Hospital beds:** 1 per 749 persons. **Physicians:** 1 per 16,025 persons. **Infant mortality** (per 1,000 live births 1991): 119.

Education (1991): **Literacy:** 28%. Years compulsory 6; attendance 43%.

Major International Organizations: UN (GATT, IMF, WHO), OAU.

Embassy: 2737 Cathedral Ave. NW 20008; 232-6656.

The Kingdom of Abomey, rising to power in wars with neighboring kingdoms in the 17th century, came under French domination in the late 19th century, and was incorporated into French West Africa by 1904.

Under the name Dahomey, the country became independent Aug. 1, 1960. The name was changed to Benin in 1975. In the fifth coup since independence Col. Ahmed Kerekou took power in 1972; two years later he declared a socialist state with a "Marxist-Leninist" philosophy. In Dec. 1989, Kerekou announced that Marxism-Leninism would no longer be the state ideology. In 1991, Kerekou was defeated in Benin's first free presidential elections in 30 years by Nicephore Soglo.

The economy relies on the development of agriculturally-based industries.

Bhutan

Kingdom of Bhutan

Druk-Yul

People: Population (1991 est.): 1,598,000. **Age distrib.** (%): 0–14: 39.8; 15–59: 53.8; over 60: 6.4 **Pop. density:** 88 per sq. mi. **Ethnic groups:** Bhote 60%, Napalese 25%. **Languages:** Dzongkha (official), Gurung, Assamese. **Religions:** Buddhist (state religion) 75%, Hindu 25%.

Geography: Area: 18,147 sq. mi., the size of Vermont and New Hampshire combined. **Location:** In eastern Himalayan Mts. **Neighbors:** India on W (Sikkim) and S, China on N. **Topography:** Bhutan is comprised of very high mountains in the N, fertile valleys in the center, and thick forests in the Duar Plain in the S. **Capital:** Thimphu (Paro Dzong is administrative capital). **City** (1987 est.): Thimphu 20,000.

Government: Type: Monarchy. **Head of state:** King Jigme Singye Wangchuk; b. Nov. 11, 1955; in office: July 21, 1972. **Local divisions:** 18 districts.

Economy: Industries: Handicrafts, chemicals. **Chief crops:** Rice, corn, wheat. **Other resources:** Timber. **Arable land:** 2%. **Labor force:** 93% agric.

Finance: Monetary unit: Ngultrum (Mar. 1992: 25.89 = 1 US). (Indian Rupee also used). **Gross domestic product** (1989): $273 mln. **Per capita GDP** (1989): $199. **Tourism** (1989): 2.0 mln. **Imports** (1991): $138 mln.; partners: India 67%. **Exports** (1989): $70 mln.; partners: India 93%.

Communications: Radios: 1 per 64 persons. **Telephones in use:** 1 per 675 persons.

Health: Life expectancy at birth (1991): 50 male; 48 female. **Births** (per 1,000 pop. 1991): 37. **Deaths** (per 1,000 pop. 1991): 17. **Natural increase:** 2.0%. **Hospital beds:** 1 per 1,457 persons. **Physicians:** 1 per 9,736 persons. **Infant mortality** (per 1,000 live births 1991): 139.

Education (1989): **Literacy:** 15%. School attendance: 25%.

Major International Organizations: UN (IMF, World Bank).

The region came under Tibetan rule in the 16th century. British influence grew in the 19th century. A monarchy, set up in 1907, became a British protectorate by a 1910 treaty. The country became independent in 1949, with India guiding foreign relations and supplying aid.

Links to India have been strengthened by airline service and a road network. Most of the population engages in subsistence agriculture.

Bolivia

Republic of Bolivia

República de Bolivia

People: Population (1991 est.): 7,156,000. **Age distrib.** (%): 0–14: 41.1; 15–59: 52.4; 60+: 5.5. **Pop. density:** 16 per sq. mi. **Urban** (1988): 49%. **Ethnic groups:** Quechua 30%, Aymara 25%, mixed 30%, European 14%. **Languages:** Spanish, Quechua, Aymara (all official). **Religions:** Roman Catholic 95%.

Geography: Area: 424,165 sq. mi., the size of Texas and California combined. **Location:** In central Andes Mtns. **Neighbors:** Peru, Chile on W, Argentina, Paraguay on S, Brazil on E and N. **Topography:** The great central plateau, at an altitude of 12,000 ft., over 500 mi. long, lies between two great cordilleras having 3 of the highest peaks in S. America. Lake Titicaca, on Peruvian border, is highest lake in world on which steamboats ply (12,506 ft.). The E central region has semitropical forests; the llanos, or Amazon-Chaco lowlands are in E. **Capitals:** Sucre, (legal), La Paz (de facto). **Cities** (1989 est.): La Paz 1,669,000; Santa Cruz 529,000; Cochabamba 403,000.

Government: Type: Republic. **Head of state:** Pres. Jaime Paz Zamora, in office: Aug. 6, 1989. **Local divisions:** 9 departments. **Defence:** 3% of GNP (1987).

Economy: Industry: Textiles, food processing, mining, clothing. **Chief crops:** Potatoes, sugar, coffee, corn, coca (sold for cocaine processing). **Minerals:** Antimony, tin, tungsten, silver, zinc, oil, gas, iron. **Crude oil reserves** (1985): 157 mln. bbls. **Other resources:** rubber, cinchona bark. **Arable land:** 3%. **Livestock** (1989): cattle: 5.3 mln.; sheep: 12.3 mln.; pigs: 1.6 mln. **Electricity prod.** (1990): 1.6 bln. kWh. **Labor force:** 50% agric., 10% ind. & comm, 26% serv. & govt.

Finance: Monetary unit: Bolivianos (Mar. 1992: 3.80 = $1 US). **Gross domestic product** (1990): $4.8 bln. **Per capita GDP** (1990): $690. **Imports** (1990): $690 mln.; partners: U.S. 20%, Jap. 10%, Arg. 14%, Braz. 20%. **Exports** (1990): $805 mln.; partners: Arg. 35%, U.S. 19%. **National budget** (1990): $2.8 bln. expenditures. **International reserves less gold** (Mar. 1992): $145 mln. **Gold:** 894,000 oz t. **Consumer prices** (change in 1991): 21%.

Transport: Railroads (1989): **Length:** 2,269 mi. **Motor vehicles:** in use (1988): 83,000 passenger cars, 150,000 comm. vehicles. **Civil aviation** (1990): 1.2 bln. passenger-km.; 19 airports with scheduled flights.

Communications: Television sets: 1 per 16 persons. **Radios:** 1 per 1.8 persons. **Telephones in use:** 1 per 37 persons. **Daily newspaper circ.** (1986): 35 per 1,000 pop.

Health: Life expectancy at birth (1990): 59 male; 64 female. **Births** (per 1,000 pop. 1991): 34. **Deaths** (per 1,000 pop. 1991): 19. **Natural increase:** 2.5%. **Hospital beds:** 1 per 472 persons. **Physicians:** 1 per 1,595 persons. **Infant mortality** (per 1,000 live births 1991): 83.

Education (1991): **Literacy:** 78%. **Years compulsory:** ages 7-14; attendance 82%.

Major International Organizations: UN (IMF, FAO, WHO), OAS.

Embassy: 3014 Massachusetts Ave. NW 20008; 483-4410.

The Incas conquered the region from earlier Indian inhabitants in the 13th century. Spanish rule began in the 1530s, and lasted until Aug. 6, 1825. The country is named after Simon Bolivar, independence fighter.

In a series of wars, Bolivia lost its Pacific coast to Chile, the oilbearing Chaco to Paraguay, and rubber-growing areas to Brazil, 1879-1935.

Economic unrest, especially among the militant mine workers, has contributed to continuing political instability. A reformist government under Victor Paz Estenssoro, 1951-64, nationalized tin mines and attempted to improve conditions for the Indian majority, but was overthrown by a military junta. A series of coups and countercoups continued through 1981, until the military junta elected Gen. Villa as president.

In July 1982, the military junta assumed power amid a growing economic crisis and foreign debt difficulties. The junta resigned in October and allowed the Congress, elected democratically in 1980, to take power.

U.S. pressure on the government to reduce the country's output of coca, the raw material for cocaine, has led to clashes between police and coca growers and increased anti-U.S. feeling among Bolivians.

Bosnia and Herzegovina

People: Population (1991 est.): 4,365,000. **Pop. density:** 221 per sq. mi. **Ethnic groups:** Moslem Slav 43%, Serbian 31%, Croatian 17%. **Languages:** Serbo-Croatian (official). **Religions:** Eastern Orthodox, Catholic, Moslem.

Geography: Area: 19,741 sq. mi. **Location:** in SE Europe. **Neighbors:** Yugoslavia, Croatia, Adriatic Sea. **Topography:** Hilly with some mountains. About 50% of the land is forested. **Capital:** Sarajevo.

Government: Type: Republic. **Head of state:** Pres. Alija Izetbegovic.

Economy: Industries: Textiles, rugs, timber. **Chief crops:** Corn, wheat, oats, barley. **Minerals:** Bauxite, iron ore, coal.

Finance: Monetary unit: Dinar.

Health: Doctors (1988): 55,000; **Hospital beds** (1988): 143,000.

Education: Literacy (1991): 90%.

International Organizations: UN.

The area was ruled by Croatian kings c. 958 A.D., and by Hungary 1000-1200. It became organized c. 1200 and later took control of Herzegovina. The kingdom disintegrated from 1391, with the southern part becoming the independent duchy Herzegovina. It was conquered by Turks in 1463 and made a Turkish province. The area was placed under control of Austria-Hungary in 1878, and made part of the province of **Bosnia and Herzegovina,** which was formally annexed to Austria-Hungary 1908, and became a province of Yugoslavia in 1918. It was reunited with Herzegovina as a federated republic in the 1946 constitution.

The Bosnia-Herzegovina parliament adopted a declaration of sovereignty Oct. 15, 1991. A referendum for independence was passed Feb. 29, 1992. Ethnic Serbs' opposition to the referendum spurred violent clashes and bombings. The U.S. and EC recognized the republic as independent Apr. 7. Fierce fighting continued—interrupted by 2 cease-fires in June—as Serbs massacred many thousands of Bosnians, most of them civilians. Serb forces launched major offensives, July 13, marking the 100th day of the siege of Sarajevo, Bosnia's capital. U.S. President Bush backed limited use of UN force in Bosnia, Aug. 6. *(See Chronology and Index for details).*

Botswana

Republic of Botswana

People: Population (1991 est.): 1,300,000. **Age distrib.** (%): 0–14: 39.6; 15–64: 48.3; 65+: 3.1. **Pop. density:** 5 per sq. mi. **Urban** (1991): 25%. **Ethnic groups:** Tswana, Kalanga, others. **Languages:** English (official), Tswana, Shona. **Religions:** indigenous beliefs 50%, Christian 50%.

Geography: Area: 231,804 sq. mi., slightly smaller than Texas. **Location:** In southern Africa. **Neighbors:** Namibia (S.W. Africa) on N and W, S. Africa on S, Zimbabwe on NE; Botswana claims border with Zambia on N. **Topography:** The Kalahari Desert, supporting nomadic Bushmen and wildlife, spreads over SW; there are swamplands and farming areas in N, and rolling plains in E where livestock are grazed. **Capital:** Gaborone. **Cities** (1991): Gaborone 138,000.

Government: Type: Parliamentary republic. **Head of state:** Pres. Quett Masire; b. 1925; in office: July 13, 1980. **Local divisions:** 10 district councils and 4 town councils. **Defense:** 3.5% of national budget (1991).

Economy: Industries: Livestock processing, mining. **Chief crops:** Corn, sorghum, beans. **Minerals:** Copper, coal, nickel, diamonds. **Other resources:** Big game. **Arable land:** 2%. **Electricity prod.** (1989): 845 mln. kWh. **Labor force:** 70% agric.

Finance: Monetary unit: Pula (Mar. 1992: 1.00 = $.46 US). **Gross domestic product** (1990): $3.1 bln. **Imports** (1991): $2.2 bln.; partners: S. Africa 88%. **Exports** (1991): $2.7 bln.; partners: Europe 67%, U.S. 17%, S. Africa 7%. **National budget** (1992): $1.7 bln. expenditures. **International reserves less gold** (Mar. 1992): $3.7 bln. **Consumer prices** (change in 1991): 11.8%

Transport: Railroads (1991): **Length:** 443 mi. **Motor vehicles:** in use (1991): 26,000 passenger cars, 47,000 comm. vehicles.

Communications: Radios: 1 per 8 persons. **Daily newspaper circ.** (1989): 22 per 1,000 pop.

Health: Life expectancy at birth (1991): male: 59; female: 65. **Births** (1,000 pop. 1991): 36. **Deaths** (per 1,000 pop. 1991): 9. **Natural increase:** 2.7%. **Hospital beds** (1990): 5,022. **Physicians:** 1 per 7,185 persons. **Infant mortality** (per 1,000 live births 1991): 43.

Education (1989): **Literacy:** 80%; 93% attend primary school.

Major International Organizations: UN (GATT, IMF, WHO), OAU, Commonwealth of Nations.

Embassy: 3400 International Dr. NW 20008; 244-4990.

First inhabited by bushmen, then by Bantus, the region became the British protectorate of Bechuanaland in 1886, halting encroachment by Boers and Germans from the south and southwest. The country became fully independent Sept. 30, 1966, changing its name to Botswana.

Cattle-raising and mining (diamonds, copper, nickel) have contributed to the country's economic growth. The economy is closely tied to S. Africa.

Brazil

Federative Republic of Brazil

República Federativa do Brasil

People: Population (1991 cen.): 148,000,000. **Age distrib.** (%): 0–14: 35.2; 15–59: 57.7; 60+: 7.1. **Pop. density:** 45 per sq. mi. **Urban** (1989): 76%. **Ethnic groups:** Portuguese, Africans, and mulattoes make up the vast majority; Italians, Germans, Japanese, Indians, Jews, Arabs. **Languages:** Portuguese (official), English, German, Italian. **Religions:** Roman Catholic 89%.

Geography: Area: 3,286,470 sq. mi., larger than contiguous 48 U.S. states; largest country in S. America. **Location:** Occupies eastern half of S. America. **Neighbors:** French Guiana, Suriname, Guyana, Venezuela on N, Colombia, Peru, Bolivia, Paraguay, Argentina on W, Uruguay on S. **Topography:** Brazil's Atlantic coastline stretches 4,603 miles. In N is the heavily-wooded Amazon basin covering half the country. Its network of rivers navigable for 15,814 mi. The Amazon itself flows 2,093 miles in Brazil, all navigable. The NE region is semiarid scrubland, heavily settled and poor. The S central region, favored by climate and resources, has almost half of the population, produces 75% of farm goods and 80% of industrial output. The narrow coastal belt includes most of the major cities. Almost the entire country has a tropical or semitropical climate. **Capital:** Brasilia. **Cities** (1989 met. est.): Sao Paulo 16.8 mln.; Rio de Janeiro 11.1 mln.; Belo Horizonte 3.4 mln.; Recife 2.9 mln.; Salvador 2.3 mln.; Porto Alegre 2.9 mln.

Government: Type: Federal republic. **Head of state:** Pres. Fernando Collor de Mello; b. Aug. 12, 1949; in office: Mar. 15, 1990. **Local divisions:** 26 states, federal district (Brasilia). **Defense:** 2.6% of GDP (1990).

Economy: Industries: Steel, autos, ships, appliances, petrochemicals, machinery. **Chief crops:** Coffee (largest grower), cotton, soybeans, sugar, cocoa, rice, corn, fruits. **Minerals:** Chromium, iron, manganese, diamonds, gold, nickel, gem stones, tin, bauxite, oil. **Crude oil reserves** (1987): 2.3 bln. bbls. **Arable land:** 8%. **Livestock** (1989): cattle: 136 mln.; pigs: 33 mln.; sheep: 20 mln. **Fish catch** (1989): 850,000 metric tons. **Electricity prod.** (1990): 214 bln. kWh. **Crude steel prod.** (1990): 20.5 mln. metric tons. **Labor force:** 42% services, 31% agric.; 25% ind.

Finance: Monetary unit: Cruzeiro (June 1992: 3,059 = $1 US). **Gross domestic product** (1990): $388 bln. **Per capita GDP** (1990): $2,540. **Imports** (1990): $20 bln.; partners: U.S. 21%, EC 23%. **Exports** (1990): $31 bln.; partners: U.S. 26%, EC 27%. **Tourists** (1989): receipts: $1.2 bln. **National budget** (1989): $48.2 bln expenditures. **International reserves less gold** (Jan. 1992): $10.1 bln. **Gold:** 3.4 mln. oz t. **Consumer prices** (change in 1991): 440%.

Transport: Railroads (1989): **Length:** 18,537 mi. **Motor vehicles:** in use (1988): 14 mln. passenger cars, 1.6 mln. **Civil aviation** (1990): 17.8 bln. passenger-km.; 112 airports with scheduled flights. **Chief ports:** Santos, Rio de Janeiro, Vitoria, Salvador, Rio Grande, Recife.

Communications: Television sets: 1 per 4 persons. **Radios:** 1 per 2.5 persons. **Telephones in use:** 1 per 11 persons. **Daily newspaper circ.** (1988): 55 per 1,000 pop.

Health: Life expectancy at birth (1991): 62 male; 68 female. **Births** (per 1,000 pop. 1991): 26. **Deaths** (per 1,000 pop. 1991): 7. **Natural increase:** 1.9%. **Hospital beds:** 1 per 285 persons. **Physicians:** 1 per 684 persons. **Infant mortality** (per 1,000 live births 1991): 67.

Education (1991): **Literacy:** 81%.

Major International Organizations: UN and most of its specialized agencies, OAS.

Embassy: 3006 Massachusetts Ave. NW 20008; 745-2700.

Pedro Alvares Cabral, a Portuguese navigator, is generally credited as the first European to reach Brazil, in 1500. The country was thinly settled by various Indian tribes. Only a few have survived to the present, mostly in the Amazon basin.

In the next centuries, Portuguese colonists gradually pushed inland, bringing along large numbers of African slaves. Slavery was not abolished until 1888.

The King of Portugal, fleeing before Napoleon's army, moved the seat of government to Brazil in 1808. Brazil thereupon became a kingdom under Dom Joao VI. After his return to Portugal, his son Pedro proclaimed the independence of Brazil, Sept.

7, 1822, and was acclaimed emperor. The second emperor, Dom Pedro II, was deposed in 1889, and a republic proclaimed, called the United States of Brazil. In 1967 the country was renamed the Federative Republic of Brazil.

A military junta took control in 1930; dictatorial power was assumed by Getulio Vargas, until finally forced out by the military in 1945. A democratic regime prevailed 1945-64, during which time the capital was moved from Rio de Janeiro to Brasilia in the interior.

The next 5 presidents were all military leaders. Censorship was imposed, and much of the opposition was suppressed amid charges of torture. In 1974 elections, the official opposition party made gains in the chamber of deputies; some relaxation of censorship occurred.

Since 1930, successive governments have pursued industrial and agricultural growth and the development of interior areas. Exploiting vast mineral resources, fertile soil in several regions, and a huge labor force, Brazil became the leading industrial power of Latin America by the 1970s, while agricultural output soared. Democratic elections were held in 1985 as the nation returned to civilian rule.

However, income maldistribution and inflation have led to severe economic recession. Foreign debt is among the largest in the world. Brazil and it's principal commercial bank lenders agreed to restructure the nation's $44 billion commercial debts, July 1992. The 1991 census revealed that population growth dipped below 2 percent for the first time in half a century.

Brazil unveiled a comprehensive environmental program for the Amazon region in 1989, amid an international outcry by environmentalists and others concerned about the ongoing destruction of the Amazon ecosystem. The Amazon rain forest was considered a global resource because of its impact on world weather patterns. Brazil hosted delegates from 178 countries at the Earth Summit June 3-14, 1992.

Brunei Darussalam

State of Brunei Darussalam

Negara Brunei Darussalam

People: Population (1991 est.): 397,000. **Pop. Density:** 178 per sq. mi. **Ethnic groups:** Malay 65%, Chinese 20%. **Language:** Malay, English, (both official), Chinese. **Religion:** Moslem 60%, Buddhist 14%, Christian 10%.

Geography: Area: 2,226 sq. mi.; larger than Delaware. **Location:** on the north coast of the island of Borneo; it is surrounded on its landward side by the Malaysian state of Sarawak. **Capital:** Bandar Seri Begawan. **Cities** (1982 est.): Bandar Seri Begawan 51,000.

Government: Type: Independent sultanate. **Head of Government:** Sultan Sir Muda Hassanal Bolkiah Mu'izzadin Waddaulah; in office: Jan. 1, 1984.

Economy: Industries: petroleum (about 90% of revenue is derived from oil exports). **Chief crops:** rice, bananas, cassava.

Finance: Monetary unit: Brunei dollar (Dec. 1991: 1.69 = $1). **Gross domestic product** (1989): $3.1 bln. **Per capita GDP** (1989): $9,600.

Communications: Television sets: 1 per 4.7 persons. **Radios:** 1 per 3 persons. **Telephones:** 1 per 6 persons.

Education (1987): **Literacy:** 95% among young.

Health: Life expectancy at birth: (1991): 74 male; 77 female. **Infant Mortality** (per 1,000 live births 1991): 10.

Major International Organizations: UN and some of its specialized agencies.

The Sultanate of Brunei was a powerful state in the early 16th century with authority over all of the island of Borneo as well as parts of the Sulu Islands and the Philippines. In 1888, a treaty was signed which placed the state under the protection of Great Britain.

Brunei became a fully sovereign and independent state on Jan. 1, 1984.

The Sultan of Brunei donated $10 million to the Nicaraguan *contras* in 1987; the subsequent misplacement of the funds generated much media attention in the U.S.

Bulgaria

Republic of Bulgaria

Republika Bulgaria

People: Population (1991 est.): 8,910,000. **Age distrib.** (%): 0–14: 20.6; 15–59: 60.5; 60+: 18.9. **Pop. density:** 200 per sq. mi. **Urban** (1990): 67%. **Ethnic groups:** Bulgarian 85%, Turk 8.5%. **Languages:** Bulgarian (official), Turkish. **Religions:** Bulgarian Orthodox, 85%, Moslem 13%.

Geography: Area: 44,365 sq. mi., about the size of Ohio. **Location:** In eastern Balkan Peninsula on Black Sea. **Neighbors:** Romania on N, Yugoslavia on W, Greece, Turkey on S. **Topography:** The Stara Planina (Balkan) Mts. stretch E-W across the center of the country, with the Danubian plain on N, the Rhodope Mts. on SW, and Thracian Plain on SE. **Capital:** Sofia. **Cities** (1989 est.): Sofia 1,200,000; Plovdiv 364,000; Varna 306,000.

Government: Type: Republic. **Head of state:** Pres. Zhelyu Zhelev; b. Mar. 3, 1935; in office: Aug. 1, 1990. **Head of government:** Premier Filip Dimitrov; in office: Nov. 8, 1991. **Local divisions:** 9 provinces. **Defense:** 12.7% of GNP (1988).

Economy: Industries: Chemicals, machinery, metals, textiles, processed food. **Chief crops:** Grains, fruit, corn, potatoes, tobacco. **Minerals:** Lead, manganese, lignite, coal. **Arable land:** 34%. **Livestock** (1990): cattle: 1.5 mln.; pigs: 4.3 mln.; sheep: 7.9 mln. **Fish catch** (1989): 121,000 metric tons. **Electricity prod.** (1990): 45 bln. kWh. **Crude steel prod.** (1990): 2.4 mln. metric tons. **Labor force:** 20% agric.; 33% ind.

Finance: Monetary unit: Leva (Dec. 1991: 17 = $1 US). **Gross National Product** (1990): $47.3 bln. **Per capita GNP** (1990): $5,300. **Imports** (1989): $15.0 bln.; partners: CIS 56%. **Exports** (1989): $16.8 bln.; partners: CIS 61%. **Tourists** (1989): revenues: $362 mln. **National budget** (1988): $28 bln. expenditures.

Transport: Railroads (1990): **Length:** 4,300 km. **Motor vehicles:** in use (1989): 1.2 mln. passenger cars, 163,000 commercial. **Civil aviation** (1990): 3.7 bln. passenger km.; 3 airports. **Chief ports:** Burgas, Varna.

Communications: Television sets: 1 per 5.3 persons. **Radios:** 1 per 3.6 persons. **Telephones in use:** 1 per 3.6 persons. **Daily newspaper circ.** (1988): 316 per 1,000 pop.

Health: Life expectancy at birth (1991): 69 male; 76 female. **Births** (per 1,000 pop. 1991): 13. **Deaths** (per 1,000 pop. 1991): 12. **Hospital beds:** 1 per 103 persons. **Physicians:** 1 per 319 persons. **Infant mortality** (per 1,000 live births 1991): 13.

Education (1990): **Literacy:** 98%. **Years compulsory:** 8.

Major International Organizations: UN.

Embassy: 1621-22d St. NW 20008; 387-7969.

Bulgaria was settled by Slavs in the 6th century. Turkic Bulgars arrived in the 7th century, merged with the Slavs, became Christians by the 9th century, and set up powerful empires in the 10th and 12th centuries. The Ottomans prevailed in 1396 and remained for 500 years.

A revolt in 1876 led to an independent kingdom in 1908. Bulgaria expanded after the first Balkan War but lost its Aegean coastline in World War I, when it sided with Germany. Bulgaria joined the Axis in World War II, but withdrew in 1944. Communists took power with Soviet aid; the monarchy was abolished Sept. 8, 1946.

On Nov. 10, 1989, Todor Zhivkov, who had held power for 35 years, resigned. Zhivkov was imprisoned, Jan. 1990, pending the outcome of charges of corruption and abuse of power. In Jan. 1990, parliament voted to revoke the constitutionally guaranteed dominant role of the Communist Party.

Burkina Faso

People: Population (1991 est.): 9,359,000. **Pop. density:** 88 per sq. mi. **Urban** (1988): 8%. **Ethnic groups:** Voltaic groups (Mossi, Bobo), Mande. **Languages:** French (official), Sudanic tribal languages. **Religions:** animist 65%, Moslem 25%, Christian 10%.

Geography: Area: 105,869 sq. mi., the size of Colorado. **Location:** In W. Africa, S of the Sahara. **Neighbors:** Mali on NW, Niger on NE, Benin, Togo, Ghana, Côte d' Ivoire on S. **Topography:** Landlocked Burkina Faso is in the savannah region of W. Africa. The N is arid, hot, and thinly populated. **Capital:** Ouagadougou. **Cities** (1990): Ouagadougou 500,000; Bobo-Dioulasso 250,000.

Government: Type: Military. **Head of state:** Pres. Blaise Compaore; in office: Oct. 15, 1987. **Local divisions:** 30 provinces. **Defense:** 2.7% of GDP (1988).

Economy: Chief crops: Millet, sorghum, rice, peanuts, grain. **Minerals:** Manganese, gold, limestone. **Arable land:** 10%. **Electricity prod.** (1989): 144 mln. kWh. **Labor force:** 82% agric.

Finance: Monetary unit: CFA Franc (Mar. 1992: 278 = $1 US). **Gross domestic product** (1989): $1.7 bln. **Per capita GDP** (1989): $205. **Imports** (1989): $322 mln.; partners: EC, Côte d' Ivoire. **Exports** (1989): $95 mln.; partners: Côte d' Ivoire, EC, China. **International reserves less gold** (Jan. 1992): $345 mln. **Gold:** 11,000 oz t. **Consumer prices** (change in 1991): –.5%.

Transport: Motor vehicles: in use (1983): 21,000 passenger cars, 6,600 comm. vehicles.

Communications: Television sets: 1 per 210 persons. **Radios:** 1 per 44 persons. **Telephones in use:** 1 per 482 persons. **Daily newspaper circ.** (1989): 1 per 1,000 pop.

Health: Life expectancy at birth (1991): 52 male; 53 female. **Births** (per 1,000 pop. 1991): 50. **Deaths** (per 1,000 pop. 1991): 16. **Natural increase:** 3.4%. **Hospital beds:** 1 per 1,359 persons. **Physicians:** 1 per 29,914 persons. **Infant mortality** (per 1,000 live births 1991): 119.

Education (1991): **Literacy:** 18%. Only 8% attend school.

Major International Organizations: UN and many of its specialized agencies, OAU.

Embassy: 2340 Massachusetts Ave. NW 20008; 332-5577.

The Mossi tribe entered the area in the 11th to 13th centuries. Their kingdoms ruled until defeated by the Mali and Songhai empires.

French control came by 1896, but Upper Volta (name changed to Burkina Faso on Aug. 4, 1984), was not finally established as a separate territory until 1947. Full independence came Aug. 5, 1960, and a pro-French government was elected. A 1982 coup established the current regime.

Several hundred thousand farm workers migrate each year to Cote D'Ivoire and Ghana. Burkina Faso is heavily dependent on foreign aid.

Burma

(See Myanmar)

Burundi

Republic of Burundi

Republika y'Uburundi

People: Population (1991 est.): 5,831,000. **Age distrib.** (%): 0–14: 45.1; 15–59: 50.1; 60+: 4.8. **Pop. density:** 541 per sq. mi. **Urban** (1986): 8%. **Ethnic groups:** Hutu 85%, Tutsi 14%, Twa (pygmy) 1%. **Languages:** French, Rundi (both official). **Religions:** Roman Catholic 62%, traditional African 32%.

Geography: Area: 10,759 sq. mi., the size of Maryland. **Location:** In central Africa. **Neighbors:** Rwanda on N, Zaire on W, Tanzania on E. **Topography:** Much of the country is grassy highland, with mountains reaching 8,900 ft. The southernmost source of the White Nile is located in Burundi. Lake Tanganyika is the second deepest lake in the world. **Capital:** Bujumbura. **Cities** (1991 est.): Bujumbura 240,000.

Government: Type: Republic. **Head of state:** Pres. Maj. Pierre Buyoya; in office: Sept. 9, 1987. **Head of government:** Prime Min: Adrien Sibomana, in office: Oct. 19, 1988. **Local divisions:** 15 provinces. **Defense** (1990): 19% of govt. budget.

Economy: Chief crops: Coffee (87% of exports), cotton, tea. **Minerals:** Nickel. **Arable land:** 43%. **Electricity prod.** (1990): 98 mln. kWh. **Labor force:** 93% agric.

Finance: Monetary unit: Franc (Apr. 1992: 199 = $1 US). **Gross domestic product** (1989): $1.2 bln. **Per capita GDP** $220. **Imports** (1989): $187 mln.; partners: Belg.-Lux. 17%; Ger. 18%. **Exports** (1991): $203 mln; partners: Ger. 31%, Belg. 20%. **Tourism** (1989): $3 mln. receipts. **National budget** (1990): $203 mln. expenditures. **International reserves less gold** (Mar. 1992): $155 mln. **Gold:** 17,000 oz t. **Consumer prices** (change in 1991): 8.9%.

Transport: Motor vehicles: in use (1989): 11,000 passenger cars, 10,000 comm. vehicles.

Communications: Radios: 1 per 45 persons. **Telephones in use:** 1 per 551 persons.

Health: Life expectancy at birth (1991): 50 male; 54 female. **Births** (per 1,000 pop. 1991): 48. **Deaths** (per 1,000 pop. 1991): 15. **Natural increase:** 3.3%. **Hospital beds:** 1 per 724 persons. **Physicians:** 1 per 18,365 persons. **Infant mortality** (per 1,000 live births 1991): 114.

Education (1991): **Literacy:** 40%. **Years compulsory:** 6; **Attendance** 45%.

Major International Organizations: UN (GATT, IMF, WHO), OAU.

Embassy: 2233 Wisconsin Ave. NW 20007; 342-2574.

The pygmy Twa were the first inhabitants, followed by Bantu Hutus, who were conquered in the 16th century by the tall Tutsi (Watusi), probably from Ethiopia. Under German control in 1899, the area fell to Belgium in 1916, which exercised successively a League of Nations mandate and UN trusteeship over Ruanda-Urundi (now 2 countries).

Independence came in 1962.

An unsuccessful Hutu rebellion in 1972-73 left 10,000 Tutsi and 150,000 Hutu dead. Over 100,000 Hutu fled to Tanzania and Zaire. Burundi is pledged to ethnic reconciliation, but remains one of the poorest and most densely populated countries in Africa.

Cambodia

State of Cambodia

People: Population (1991 est.): 7,146,000. **Pop. density:** 101 per sq. mi. **Urban** (1989): 10%. **Ethnic groups:** Cambodian 90%, Vietnamese 4%, Chinese 5%. **Languages:** Khmer (official), French. **Religions:** Theravada Buddhism 95%.

Geography: Area: 70,238 sq. mi., the size of Missouri. **Location:** In Indochina Peninsula. **Neighbors:** Thailand on W, N, Laos on NE, Vietnam on E. **Topography:** The central area, formed by the Mekong R. basin and Tonle Sap lake, is level. Hills and mountains are in SE, a long escarpment separates the country from Thailand on NW. 75% of the area is forested. **Capital:** Phnom Penh. **Cities** (1990 est.): Phnom Penh 400,000.

Government: Type: No single authority controls the whole country. **Head of State:** Pres., Prince Norodom Sihanouk; in office: Nov. 20, 1991. **Head of Government:** Premier Hun Sen; in office: Jan. 14, 1985. **Local divisions:** 19 provinces and municipalities.

Economy: Industries: Rice milling, wood & rubber. **Chief crops:** Rice, corn. **Minerals:** Iron, copper, manganese. **Other resources:** Forests, rubber, kapok. **Arable land:** 16%. **Livestock** (1989): cattle: 2.0 mln. pigs: 1.5 mln. **Fish catch** (1990): 70,000 metric tons. **Electricity prod.** (1990): 150 mln. kWh. **Labor force:** 74% agri.

Finance: Monetary unit: Riel (Jan. 1992: 800 = $1 US). **Gross domestic product** (1989): $890 mln. **Per capita GDP** (1989): $130. **Imports** (1988): $147 mln. **Exports** (1988): $32 mln.

Transport: Railroads (1989): **Length:** 649 mi. **Motor vehicles:** in use (1988): 4,000 passenger cars, 7,000 trucks. **Chief ports:** Kompong Som.

Communications: Television sets: 1 per 177 persons. **Radios:** 1 per 10 persons. **Telephones in use:** 1 per 179 persons.

Health: Life expectancy at birth (1991): 48 male; 51 female. **Births** (per 1,000 pop. 1991): 39. **Deaths** (per 1,000 pop. 1991): 17. **Natural increase:** 2. **Hospital beds:** 1 per 632 persons. **Physicians:** 1 per 27,000 persons. **Infant Mortality** (per 1,000 live births 1991): 125.

Education (1990): **Literacy:** 50%.

Major International Organizations: UN.

Early kingdoms dating from that of Funan in the 1st century AD culminated in the great Khmer empire which flourished from the 9th century to the 13th, encompassing present-day Thailand, Cambodia, Laos, and southern Vietnam. The peripheral areas were lost to invading Siamese and Vietnamese, and France established a protectorate in 1863. Independence came in 1953.

Prince Norodom Sihanouk, king 1941-1955 and head of state from 1960, tried to maintain neutrality. Relations with the U.S. were broken in 1965, after South Vietnam planes attacked Vietcong forces within Cambodia. Relations were restored in

1969, after Sihanouk charged Viet communists with arming Cambodian insurgents.

In 1970, pro-U.S. premier Lon Nol seized power, demanding removal of 40,000 North Viet troops; the monarchy was abolished. Sihanouk formed a government-in-exile in Peking, and open war began between the government and Khmer Rouge. The U.S. provided heavy military and economic aid.

Khmer Rouge forces captured Phnom Penh April 17, 1975. The new government evacuated all cities and towns, and shuffled the rural population, sending virtually the entire population to clear jungle, forest, and scrub, which covered half the country. Over one million people were killed in executions and enforced hardships.

Severe border fighting broke out with Vietnam in 1978; developed into a full-fledged Vietnamese invasion. The Vietnamese-backed Kampuchean National United Front for National Salvation, a Cambodian rebel movement, announced, Jan. 8, 1979, the formation of a government one day after the Vietnamese capture of Phnom Pehn. Thousands of refugees flowed into Thailand and widespread starvation was reported.

On Jan. 10, 1983, Vietnam launched an offensive against rebel forces in the west. They overran a refugee camp, Jan. 31, driving 30,000 residents into Thailand. In March, Vietnam launched a major offensive against camps on the Cambodian-Thailand border, engaged Khmer Rouge guerrillas, and crossed the border instigating clashes with Thai troops. Vietnam announced that it would withdraw all its troops by Sept. 1989.

Efforts to create a new government have been hampered by the fear both in Cambodia and internationally that the Khmer Rouge would return to power.

Cameroon

Republic of Cameroon

People: Population (1991 est.): 11,390,000. **Age distrib.** (%): 0–14: 46.1; 15–59: 48.3; 60+: 5.6. **Pop. density:** 63 per sq. mi. **Urban** (1988): 40%. **Ethnic groups:** Some 200 tribes; largest are Bamileke 30%, Fulani 7%. **Languages:** English, French (both official), numerous African groups. **Religions:** Animist 51%, Moslem 16%, Christian 33%.

Geography: Area: 179,714 sq. mi., somewhat larger than California. **Location:** Between W and central Africa. **Neighbors:** Nigeria on NW, Chad, Central African Republic on E, Congo, Gabon, Equatorial Guinea on S. **Topography:** A low coastal plain with rain forests is in S; plateaus in center lead to forested mountains in W, including Mt. Cameroon, 13,000 ft.; grasslands in N lead to marshes around Lake Chad. **Capital:** Yaounde. **Cities** (1988 est.): Douala 852,000; Yaounde 700,000.

Government: Type: Republic, one party presidential regime. **Head of state:** Pres. Paul Biya; b. Feb. 13, 1933; in office: Nov. 6, 1982. Prime Min. Sadou Hayatou; in office: Apr. 26, 1991. **Local divisions:** 10 provinces. **Defense:** 1.7% of GDP (1990).

Economy: Industries: Aluminum processing, oil prod., palm products. **Chief crops:** Cocoa, coffee, cotton. **Crude oil reserves** (1985): 531 mln. bbls. **Other resources:** Timber. **Arable land:** 14%. **Livestock** (1989): cattle: 4.5 mln.; sheep: 3.1 mln.; pigs: 1.2 mln. **Fish catch** (1990): 77,000 metric tons. **Electricity prod.** (1988): 2.5 bln. kWh. **Labor force:** 74% agric., 11% ind. and commerce.

Finance: Monetary unit: CFA franc (Mar. 1992: 278 = $1 US). **Gross domestic product** (1991): $11.6 bln. **Per capita GDP** (1991): $1,010. **Imports** (1990): $2.1 bln.; partners: Fr. 42%. **Exports** (1990): $928 mln.; partners: EC 50%. **National budget** (1990): $2.1 bln. **International reserves less gold** (Jan. 1992): $21 mln. **Gold:** 30,000 oz t.

Transport: Railroads (1988): **Length:** 686 mi. **Motor vehicles:** in use (1987): 78,000 passenger cars, 43,000 comm. vehicles. **Chief ports:** Douala.

Communications: Radios: 1 per 6 persons. **Telephones in use:** 1 per 179 persons. **Daily newspaper circ.** (1990): 6 per 1,000 pop.

Health: Life expectancy at birth (1991): 49 male; 53 female. **Births** (per 1,000 pop. 1991): 41. **Deaths** (per 1,000 pop. 1991): 15. **Natural increase:** 2.6%. **Hospital beds:** 1 per 377 persons. **Physicians:** 1 per 12,540 persons. **Infant mortality** (per 1,000 live births 1991): 118.

Education (1991): **Literacy:** 65%. About 70% attend school.

Major International Organizations: UN, OAU, EC (Associate).

Embassy: 2349 Massachusetts Ave. NW 20008; 265-8790.

Portuguese sailors were the first Europeans to reach Cameroon, in the 15th century. The European and American slave trade was very active in the area. German control lasted from 1884 to 1916, when France and Britain divided the territory, later receiving League of Nations mandates and UN trusteeships. French Cameroon became independent Jan. 1, 1960; one part of British Cameroon joined Nigeria in 1961, the other part joined Cameroon. Stability has allowed for development of roads, railways, agriculture, and petroleum production. Some 3,000 died in 1986 as a result of clouds of toxic gas of volcanic origin emanating from Lake Nyos.

Canada

People: Population (1991 est.): 26,835,500. **Age distrib.** (%): 0–14: 21.4; 15–59: 63.6; 60+: 15.0. **Pop. density:** 7 per sq. mi. **Urban** (1990): 77%. **Ethnic groups:** British 25%; French 24%; other European 16%; mixed 28%. **Language:** English, French (both official). **Religion:** Roman Catholic 46%, Protestant 41%.

Geography: Area: 3,849,000 sq. mi., the largest country in land size in the Western Hemisphere. Canada stretches 3,223 miles from east to west and extends southward from the North Pole to the U.S. border. Its seacoast includes 36,356 miles of mainland and 115,133 miles of islands, including the Arctic islands almost from Greenland to near the Alaskan border. Climate, while generally temperate, varies from freezing winter cold to blistering summer heat. **Capitol:** Ottawa. **Cities** (met. 1990 est.): Montreal 3,068,000; Toronto 3,751,000; Vancouver 1,547,000; Ottawa-Hull 863,000; Winnipeg 647,000; Edmonton 823,000, Calgary 723,000, Quebec 622,000.

Government: Type: Confederation with parliamentary democracy. **Head of state:** Queen Elizabeth II, represented by Gov.-Gen. Ramon Hnatyshyn; in office: Jan. 29, 1990. **Head of government:** Prime Min. Brian Mulroney; born: Mar. 20, 1939; in office: Sept. 4, 1984. **Local divisions:** 10 provinces, 2 territories. **Defense:** 2% of GDP (1991).

Economy: Minerals: Nickel, zinc, copper, gold, lead, molybdenum, potash, silver. **Crude oil reserves** (1990): 6.8 bln. barrels. **Arable land:** 5%. **Livestock** (1990): cattle: 12.0 mln.; pigs: 10.8 mln.; sheep: 722,000. **Fish catch** (1989): 1.6 mln. metric tons. **Electricity prod.** (1990): 500 bln. kWh. **Crude steel prod.** (1990): 12.1 mln. metric tons. **Labor force:** 4% agric.; 52% ind. & comm., 28% services.

Finance: Monetary unit: Dollar (June 1992: 1.19 = $1 US). **Gross domestic product** (1990): $516 bln. **Per capita GDP** (1990) $19,500. **Imports** (1991): $124 bln.; partners: U.S. 69%, EC 8%, Jap. 5%. **Exports** (1991): $126 bln.; partners: U.S. 75%, EC 9%, Jap. 5%. **Tourists** (1989): receipts: $4.7 bln. **National budget** (1990-91): $127 bln. expenditures. **International reserves less gold** (Mar. 1992): $14.6 bln. **Gold:** 12.3 mln. oz t. **Consumer prices** (change in 1991): 5.6%.

Transport: Railroads (1988): **Length:** 56,771 mi. **Motor vehicles:** in use (1989): 12.0 mln. passenger cars, 3.7 mln. comm. **Civil aviation** (1990): 46 bln. passenger-km: 65 airports with scheduled flights.

Communications: Television sets: 1 per 1.7 persons. **Radios:** 1 per 1.2 persons. **Telephones in use:** 1 per 1.3 persons. **Daily newspaper circ.** (1989): 221 per 1,000 pop.

Health: Life expectancy at birth (1991): 73 male; 80 female. **Births** (per 1,000 pop. 1991): 14. **Deaths** (per 1,000 pop. 1991): 7. **Natural increase:** .7%. **Hospital beds:** 1 per 148 persons. **Physicians:** 1 per 449 persons. **Infant mortality** (per 1,000 live births 1991): 7.3.

Education (1991): **Literacy:** 99%.

Major International Organizations: UN and all of its specialized agencies, NATO, OECD, Commonwealth of Nations.

Embassy: 501 Pennsylvania Ave. NW 20001; 682-1740.

French explorer Jacques Cartier, who discovered the Gulf of St. Lawrence in 1534, is generally regarded as the founder of Canada. But English seaman John Cabot sighted Newfoundland 37 years earlier, in 1497, and Vikings are believed to have reached the Atlantic coast centuries before either explorer.

Canadian settlement was pioneered by the French who established Quebec City (1608) and Montreal (1642) and declared New France a colony in 1663.

Britain, as part of its American expansion, acquired Acadia (later Nova Scotia) in 1717 and, through military victory over French forces in Canada (an extension of a European conflict between the 2 powers), captured Quebec (1759) and obtained control of the rest of New France in 1763. The French, through the Quebec Act of 1774, retained the rights to their own language, religion, and civil law.

The British presence in Canada increased during the American Revolution when many colonials, proudly calling themselves United Empire Loyalists, moved north to Canada.

Fur traders and explorers led Canadians westward across the continent. Sir Alexander Mackenzie reached the Pacific in 1793 and scrawled on a rock by the ocean, "from Canada by land."

In Upper and Lower Canada (later called Ontario and Quebec) and in the Maritimes, legislative assemblies appeared in the 18th century and reformers called for responsible government. But the War of 1812 intervened. The war, a conflict between Great Britain and the United States fought mainly in Upper Canada, ended in a stalemate in 1814.

In 1837 political agitation for more democratic government culminated in rebellions in Upper and Lower Canada. Britain sent Lord Durham to investigate and, in a famous report (1839), he recommended union of the 2 parts into one colony called Canada. The union lasted until Confederation, July 1, 1867, when proclamation of the British North America (BNA) Act launched the Dominion of Canada, consisting of Ontario, Quebec, and the former colonies of Nova Scotia and New Brunswick.

Since 1840 the Canadian colonies had held the right to internal self-government. The BNA act, which became the country's written constitution, established a federal system of government on the model of a British parliament and cabinet structure under the crown. Canada was proclaimed a self-governing Dominion within the British Empire in 1931.

In 1982 Canada severed its last formal legislative link with Britain by obtaining the right to amend its constitution (the British North America Act of 1867).

The Meech Lake Agreement was signed June 3, 1987. The historic accord, subject to ratification by Parliament and the provincial legislatures, assured constitutional protection for Quebec's efforts to preserve its French language and culture. Critics of the accord charged that it did not make any provision for other minority groups, and that it gave Quebec too much power, which might enable it to pass laws that conflicted with the nation's 1982 Charter of Rights and Freedoms. In 1988, Quebec had overridden a Canadian Supreme Court decision striking down a provincial language law that had restricted the use of any language other than French on public signs. The accord died June 22, 1990, as Newfoundland and Manitoba failed to approve it. The defeat set the stage for a possible reconsideration of Quebec separatism.

Voters in the Northwest Territories approved the creation of a self-governing homeland for the 17,500 Invit living in the territories. The area—to be known as Nanavut, "Our Land"—would cover an area of 772,000 sq. mi. and will take effect by 1999.

Canadian Provinces

	Sq. mi.	Population, 1990 est.
Alberta	248,800	2,472,500
British Columbia	358,971	3,138,900
Manitoba	211,723	1,090,700
New Brunswick	27,834	724,300
Newfoundland	143,510	573,000
Nova Scotia	20,402	892,000
Ontario	344,090	9,747,600
Prince Edward Island	2,185	130,400
Quebec	523,859	6,770,800
Saskatchewan	220,348	1,000,300
Territories		
Northwest Territories	1,271,442	54,000
Yukon	184,931	26,000

Prime Ministers of Canada

Canada is a constitutional monarchy with a parliamentary system of government. It is also a federal state. Canada's official head of state is the King or Queen of England, represented by a resident Governor-General. However, in practice the nation is governed by the Prime Minister, leader of the party that commands the support of a majority of the House of Commons, dominant chamber of Canada's bicameral Parliament.

Name	Party	Term
Sir John A. MacDonald	Conservative	1867-1873 1878-1891
Alexander Mackenzie	Liberal	1873-1878
Sir John J. C. Abbott	Conservative	1891-1892
Sir John S. D. Thompson	Conservative	1892-1894
Sir Mackenzie Bowell	Conservative	1894-1896
Sir Charles Tupper	Conservative	1896
Sir Wilfrid Laurier	Liberal	1896-1911
Sir Robert L. Borden	Cons. Union.	1911-1920
Arthur Meighen	Cons. Union.	1920-1921
W.L. Mackenzie King	Liberal	1921-1926[1] 1926-1930 1935-1948
R. B. Bennett	Conservative	1930-1935
Louis St. Laurent	Liberal	1948-1957
John G. Diefenbaker	Prog. Cons.	1957-1963
Lester B. Pearson	Liberal	1963-1968
Pierre Elliott Trudeau	Liberal	1968-1979
Joe Clark	Prog. Cons.	1979-1980
Pierre Elliott Trudeau	Liberal	1980-1984
John Turner	Liberal	1984
Brian Mulroney	Prog. Cons.	1984-

(1) King's term was interrupted from June 26-Sept. 25, 1926, when Arthur Meighen again served as prime minister.

Cape Verde

Republic of Cape Verde

República de Cabo Verde

People: Population (1991 est.): 386,000. **Age distrib.** (%): 0–14: 45.6; 15–59: 47.7; 60+: 6.7. **Pop. density:** 247 per sq. mi. **Urban** (1987): 33%. **Ethnic groups:** Creole (mulatto) 71%, African 28%, European 1%. **Languages:** Portuguese (official), Crioulo. **Religions:** 80% Roman Catholic.

Geography: Area: 1,557 sq. mi., a bit larger than Rhode Island. **Location:** In Atlantic O., off western tip of Africa. **Neighbors:** Nearest are Mauritania, Senegal. **Topography:** Cape Verde Islands are 15 in number, volcanic in origin (active crater on Fogo). The landscape is eroded and stark, with vegetation mostly in interior valleys. **Capital:** Praia. **Cities** (1990 est.): Mindelo 47,000; Praia 61,000.

Government: Type: Republic. **Head of state:** Pres. Antonio Mascarenhas Monteiro; in office: Mar. 17, 1991. **Head of government:** Prime Min. Carlos Veiga; in office: Apr. 4, 1991. **Local divisions:** 14 administrative districts.

Economy: Chief crops: Bananas, coffee, beats, corn, beans. **Minerals:** Salt. **Other resources:** Fish. **Arable land:** 10%. **Electricity prod.** (1989): 18 mln. kWh.

Finance: Monetary unit: Escudo (Mar. 1992: 71 = $1 US). **Gross domestic product** (1989): $281 mln. **Per capita GDP** (1989): $760. **Imports** (1989): $108 mln.; partners: Port. 33%, Neth. 12%. **Exports** (1989): $10.9 mln.; partners: Port. 32%, Ang. 21%.

Transport: Motor vehicles: in use (1988): 13,000 passenger cars, 4,000 comm. vehicles. **Chief ports:** Mindelo, Praia.

Communications: Radios: 1 per 6.8 persons. **Telephones in use:** 1 per 76 persons.

Health: Life expectancy at birth (1989): 59 male; 63 female. **Births** (per 1,000 pop. 1991): 48. **Deaths** (per 1,000 pop. 1991): 11. **Natural increase:** 3.8%. **Hospital beds:** 1 per 550 persons. **Physicians:** 1 per 4,334 persons. **Infant mortality** (per 1,000 live births 1991): 66.

Education (1989): **Literacy:** 37%.

Major International Organizations: UN (GATT, IMF, WHO), OAU.

Embassy: 3415 Massachusetts Ave. NW 20007; 965-6820.

The uninhabited Cape Verdes were discovered by the Portuguese in 1456 or 1460. The first Portuguese colonists landed in 1462; African slaves were brought soon after, and most Cape Verdeans descend from both groups. Cape Verde independence came July 5, 1975. The islands have suffered from repeated extreme droughts and famines. Emphasis is placed on the development of agriculture and on fishing.

Antonio Mascarenhas Monteiro won the nation's first free presidential election Feb. 1991.

Central African Republic

República Centrafricaine

People: Population (1991 est.): 2,952,000. **Pop. density:** 12 per sq. mi. **Urban** (1988): 37%. **Ethnic groups:** Banda 27%, Baya 34%, Mandja 21%, Sara 10%. **Languages:** French (official), local dialects. **Religions:** Protestant 25%, Roman Catholic 25%, traditional 24%.

Geography: Area: 240,534 sq. mi., slightly smaller than Texas. **Location:** In central Africa. **Neighbors:** Chad on N, Cameroon on W, Congo, Zaire on S, Sudan on E. **Topography:** Mostly rolling plateau, average altitude 2,000 ft., with rivers draining S to the Congo and N to Lake Chad. Open, well-watered savanna covers most of the area, with an arid area in NE, and tropical rainforest in SW. **Capital:** Bangui. **Cities** (1988 est.): Bangui (met.) 596,000.

Government: Type: Republic. (under military rule). **Head of state:** Gen. Andre Kolingba; in office: Sept. 1, 1981. **Head of government:** Prime Min. Edouard Frank. In office: Mar. 15, 1991. **Local divisions:** 16 prefectures. **Defense:** 2% of GDP (1989).

Economy: Industries: Textiles, light manuf, mining. **Chief crops:** Cotton, coffee, peanuts, tobacco. **Minerals:** Diamonds (chief export), uranium. **Other resources:** Timber. **Arable land:** 3%. **Electricity prod.** (1989): 93 mln. kWh. **Labor force:** 72% agric.

Finance: Monetary unit: CFA Franc (Mar. 1992: 278 = $1 US). **Gross domestic product** (1990): $1.3 bln. **Per capita GDP** (1990): $440. **Imports** (1989): $150 mln.; partners: Fr. 44%. **Exports** (1989): $134 mln.; partners: Fr. 53%, Bel.-Lux. 23%. **National budget** (1989): $305 mln. **International reserves less gold** (Oct. 1991): $83 mln. **Gold:** 12,000 oz t.

Transport: Motor vehicles: in use (1989): 10,000 passenger cars, 8,000 comm. vehicles.

Communications: Radios: 1 per 5 persons. **Telephones:** 1 per 380 persons.

Health: Life expectancy at birth (1989): 45 male; 48 female. **Births** (per 1,000 pop. 1991): 44. **Deaths** 1 per 1,000 pop. 1991): 19. **Natural increase:** 2.5%. **Hospital beds** (1984): 3,774. **Physicians** (1984): 112. **Infant mortality** (per 1,000 live births 1991): 138.

Education (1989): **Literacy:** 40%. **Attendance:** primary school 79%; secondary school 18%.

Major International Organizations: UN (GATT, IMF, WHO), OAU.

Embassy: 1618 22d St. NW 20008; 483-7800.

Various Bantu tribes migrated through the region for centuries before French control was asserted in the late 19th century, when the region was named Ubangi-Shari. Complete independence was attained Aug. 13, 1960.

All political parties were dissolved in 1960, and the country became a center for Chinese political influence in Africa. Relations with China were severed after 1965. Elizabeth Domitien, premier 1975-76, was the first woman to hold that post in an African country. Pres. Jean-Bedel Bokassa, who seized power in a 1965 military coup, proclaimed himself constitutional emperor of the renamed Central African Empire Dec. 1976.

Bokassa's rule was characterized by ruthless and cruel authority, and human rights violations. Bokassa was ousted in a bloodless coup aided by the French government, Sept. 20, 1979, and replaced by his cousin David Dacko, former president from 1960 to 1965. In 1981, the political situation deteriorated amid strikes and economic crisis. Gen. Kolingba replaced Dacko as head of state in a bloodless coup.

Chad

Republic of Chad

République du Tchad

People: Population (1991 est.): 5,122,000. **Age distrib.** (%): 0–14: 42.5; 15–59: 51.7; 60+: 5.8. **Pop. density:** 11 per sq. mi. **Urban** (1986): 23%. **Ethnic groups:** 200 distinct groups. **Languages:** French, Arabic, (both official), some 100 other languages. **Religions:** Moslem 44%, animist 23%, Christian 33%.

Geography: Area: 495,755 sq. mi., four-fifths the size of Alaska. **Location:** In central N. Africa. **Neighbors:** Libya on N, Niger, Nigeria, Cameroon on W, Central African Republic on S, Sudan on E. **Topography:** Southern wooded savanna, steppe, and desert, part of the Sahara, in the N. Southern rivers flow N to Lake Chad, surrounded by marshland. **Capital:** N'Djamena. **Cities** (1988 est.): N'Djamena 500,000.

Government: Type: Republic. **Head of state:** Pres. Idriss Deby; in office: Dec. 4, 1990. **Head of government:** Prime Min. Jean Alingue Bawoyeu. In office: Mar. 4, 1991. **Local divisions:** 14 prefectures. **Defense:** 4.3% of GDP (1988).

Economy: Chief crops: Cotton. **Minerals:** Uranium, salt. **Arable land:** 2%. **Fish catch** (1989): 110,000 metric tons. **Electricity prod.** (1990): 69 mln. kWh. **Labor force:** 85% agric.

Finance: Monetary unit: CFA franc (Mar. 1992: 278 = $1 US). **Gross Domestic product** (1989): $1.0 bln. **Per capita GDP** (1989): $190. **Imports** (1988): $419 mln.; partners: Fr. 47%. **Exports** (1988): $141 mln.; partners Fra, EDEAC countries. **International reserves less gold** (Oct. 1991): $119 mln. **Gold:** 11,000 oz t.

Transport: Motor vehicles: in use (1989): 8,000 passenger cars, 6,000 comm. vehicles.

Communications: Radios: 1 per 4.3 persons. **Telephones in use:** 1 per 1,114 persons.

Health: Life expectancy at birth (1991): 39 male; 41 female. **Births** (per 1,000 pop. 1991): 42. **Deaths** (per 1,000 pop. 1991): 22. **Natural increase:** 2.0%. **Hospital beds** (1980): 3,500. **Physicians** (1980): 94. **Infant mortality** (per 1,000 live births 1991): 134.

Education (1989): **Literacy:** 17%.

Major International Organizations: UN, (GATT, IMF, WHO), OAU, EEC.

Embassy: 2002 R St. NW 20009; 462-4009.

Chad was the site of paleolithic and neolithic cultures before the Sahara Desert formed. A succession of kingdoms and Arab slave traders dominated Chad until France took control around 1900. Independence came Aug. 11, 1960.

Northern Moslem rebels, have fought animist and Christian southern government and French troops from 1966, despite numerous cease-fires and peace pacts.

Libyan troops entered the country at the request of the Chad government, December 1980. On Jan. 6, 1981 Libya and Chad announced their intention to unite. France together with several African nations condemned the agreement as a menace to African security. The Libyan troops were withdrawn from Chad in November 1981.

Rebel forces, led by Hissen Habre, captured the capital and forced Pres. Oueddei to flee the country in June 1982.

In 1983, France sent some 3,000 troops to Chad to assist Habre in opposing Libyan-backed rebels. France and Libya agreed to a simultaneous withdrawal of troops from Chad in September 1984 but Libyan forces remained in the north until Mar. 1987 when Chad forces drove them from their last major stronghold. Libyan troops abandoned almost $1 billion of military equipment during their retreat.

Chile

Republic of Chile

República de Chile

People: Population (1991 est.): 13,286,000. **Age distrib.** (%): 0–14: 30.9 15–59: 60.4; 60+: 7.7. **Pop. density:** 45 per sq. mi. **Urban** (1988): 83%. **Ethnic groups:** Mestizo 66%, Spanish 25%, Indian 5%. **Languages:** Spanish. **Religions:** Roman Catholic 89%, Protestant 11%.

Geography: Area: 292,257 sq. mi., larger than Texas. **Location:** Occupies western coast of southern S. America. **Neighbors:** Peru on N, Bolivia on NE, Argentina on E. **Topography:** Andes Mtns. are on E border including some of the world's highest peaks; on W is 2,650-mile Pacific Coast. Width varies between 100 and 250 miles. In N is Atacama Desert, in center are agricultural regions, in S are forests and grazing lands. **Capital:** Santiago. **Cities** (1990 metro est.) Santiago 5,236,000.

Government: Type: Republic. **Head of state:** Pres. Patricio Aylwin Ozocar; b. Nov. 26, 1918; in office: Mar. 11, 1990. **Local divisions:** 12 regions and Santiago region. **Defense:** 3.6% of GNP (1988).

Economy: Industries: Fish processing, wood products, iron, steel. **Chief crops:** Grain, onions, beans, potatoes, peas, fruits. **Minerals:** Copper (54% of export revenues in 1989), molybdenum, nitrates, iodine (half world output), iron, coal, oil, gas, gold, cobalt, zinc, manganese, borate, mica, mercury, salt, sulphur, marble, onyx. **Crude oil reserves** (1985): 224 mln. bbls. **Other resources:** Water, forests. **Arable land:** 7%. **Livestock** (1989): cattle: 3.3 mln.; sheep: 6.5 mln.; pigs: 1.1 mln. **Fish catch** (1989): 5.2 mln. metric tons. **Electricity prod.** (1990): 17.7 bln. kWh. **Labor force:** 15% agric., forestry, fishing; 31% ind & comm., 38% serv.

Finance: Monetary unit: Peso (June 1992: 341 = $1 US). **Gross Domestic product** (1990): $27.8 bln. **Per capita GDP** (1990): $2,130. **Imports** (1990): $7.2 bln.; partners: U.S. 19%, EC 23%. **Exports** (1990): $8.6 bln.; partners: EC 34%, U.S. 22%. **Tourists** (1989): $248 mln. receipts. **National budget** (1990): $7.1 bln. expenditures. **International reserves less gold** (Mar. 1992): $6.9 bln. **Gold:** 1.86 mln. oz. t. **Consumer prices** (change in 1991): 22%.

Transport: Railroads (1990): **Length:** 4,281 mi. **Motor vehicles:** in use (1989): 690,000 passenger cars, 300,000 comm. vehicles. **Civil aviation** (1990): 2.9 bln. passenger-km.; 17 airports with scheduled flights. **Chief ports:** Valparaiso, Arica, Antofagasta.

Communications: Television sets: 1 per 4.1 persons. **Radios:** 1 per 3.3 persons. **Telephones in use:** 1 per 16 persons.

Health: Life expectancy at birth (1991): 70 male; 77 female. **Births** (per 1,000 pop. 1991): 21. **Deaths** (per 1,000 pop. 1991): 6. **Natural increase:** 1.5%. **Hospital beds:** 1 per 385 persons. **Physicians:** 1 per 922 persons. **Infant mortality** (per 1,000 live births 1991): 18.

Education (1991): **Literacy:** 92%. Compulsory ages 6-14.

Major International Organizations: UN and all of its specialized agencies, OAS.

Embassy: 1732 Massachusetts Ave. NW 20036; 785-1746.

Northern Chile was under Inca rule before the Spanish conquest, 1536-40. The southern Araucanian Indians resisted until the late 19th century. Independence was gained 1810-18, under Jose de San Martin and Bernardo O'Higgins; the latter, as supreme director 1817-23, sought social and economic reforms until deposed. Chile defeated Peru and Bolivia in 1836-39 and 1879-84, gaining mineral-rich northern land.

Eduardo Frei Montalva came into office in 1964, instituting social programs and gradual nationalization of foreign-owned mining companies. In 1970, Salvador Allende Gossens, a Marxist, became president with a third of the national vote.

The Allende government furthered nationalizations, and improved conditions for the poor. But illegal and violent actions by extremist supporters of the government, the regime's failure to attain majority support, and poorly planned socialist economic programs led to political and financial chaos.

A military junta seized power Sept. 11, 1973, and said Allende killed himself. The junta named a mostly military cabinet, and announced plans to "exterminate Marxism."

Repression continued during the 1980s with little sign of any political liberalization. In a plebiscite held Oct. 5, 1988, voters rejected junta-candidate Gen. Pinochet who, if victorious, would have governed Chile until 1997. Pinochet accepted the rejection and called for presidential elections. In Dec. 1989 voters removed Pinochet from office and elected Patricio Aylwin as president.

Tierra del Fuego is the largest (18,800 sq. mi.) island in the archipelago of the same name at the southern tip of South America, an area of majestic mountains, tortuous channels, and high winds. It was discovered 1520 by Magellan and named the Land of Fire because of its many Indian bonfires. Part of the island is in Chile, part in Argentina. Punta Arenas, on a mainland peninsula, is a center of sheep-raising and the world's southernmost city (pop. 67,600); Puerto Williams, pop. 949, is the southernmost settlement.

China

People's Republic of China

Zhonghua Renmin Gonghe Guo

People: Population (1991 est.): 1,151,486,000. **Pop. density:** 409 per sq. mi. **Urban** (1990): 27%. **Ethnic groups:** Han Chinese 94%, Mongol, Korean, Manchu, others. **Languages:** Mandarin (official), Yue, Wu Hakka, Xiang, Gan, Min, Zhuang, Hui, Yi. **Religions:** officially atheist; Confucianism, Buddhism, Taoism are traditional.

Geography: Area: 3,696,100 sq. mi., slightly larger than the conterminous U.S. **Location:** Occupies most of the habitable mainland of E. Asia. **Neighbors:** Mongolia on N, Russia on NE and NW, Afghanistan, Pakistan on W, India, Nepal, Bhutan, Myanmar, Laos, Vietnam on S, N. Korea on NE. **Topography:** Two-thirds of the vast territory is mountainous or desert, and only one-tenth is cultivated. Rolling topography rises to high elevations in the N in the Daxinganlingshanmai separating Manchuria and Mongolia; the Tienshan in Xinjiang; the Himalayan and Kunlunshanmai in the SW and in Tibet. Length is 1,860 mi. from N to S, width E to W is more than 2,000 mi. The eastern half of China is one of the best-watered lands in the world. Three great river systems, the Changjiang, the Huanghe, and the Xijiang provide water for vast farmlands. **Capital:** Beijing. **Cities** (1989 est.): Shanghai 7.3 mln.; Beijing 6.8 mln.; Tianjin 5.6 mln.; Canton 3.4 mln.; Shenyang 4.4 mln.; Wuhan 3.6 mln.

Government: Type: Communist Party led state. **Head of state:** Pres. Yang Shangkun; in office: Apr. 8, 1989. **Head of government:** Premier Li Peng; in office: Apr. 9, 1989. **Local divisions:** 22 provinces, 5 autonomous regions, and 3 cities. **Defense:** 3.9% of GNP (1988).

Economy: Industries: Iron and steel, textiles, agriculture implements, trucks. **Chief crops:** Grain, rice, cotton, tea. **Minerals:** tungsten, antimony, coal, iron, lead, manganese, molybdenum, tin. **Crude oil reserves** (1990): 24.0 bln. barrels. **Other resources:** Silk. **Arable land:** 11%. **Livestock** (1989): cattle: 77 mln.; pigs: 348 mln.; sheep: 102 mln. **Fish catch** (1989): 11.2 mln. metric tons. **Electricity prod.** (1990): 585 bln. kWh. **Crude steel prod.** (1990): 51.2 mln. metric tons. **Labor force:** 60% agric.; 17% ind. & comm.

Finance: Monetary unit: Yuan (Mar. 1992): 5.46 = $1 US). **Gross national product** (1989): $393 bln. **Per capita GNP** (1989): $360. **Imports** (1991): $62.5 bln.; partners: Jap. 20%, U.S. 11%, Hong Kong 20%. **Exports** (1991): $70.4 bln.; partners: Hong Kong 38%, Jap. 16%, U.S. 7%. **Tourism** (1990): $2.2 bln. receipts. **National budget** (1987): $66.1 bln. expenditures. **International reserves less gold** (Feb. 1992): $42.8 bln. **Gold:** 12.7 mln. oz t. **Consumer prices** (change in 1989): 16.3%.

Transport: Railroads (1990): **Length:** 41,581 mi. **Motor vehicles:** in use (1989): 1.4 mln. passenger cars, 3.1 mln. comm. vehicles. **Civil aviation** (1990): 21.8 bln. passenger km, 84 airports with scheduled flights. **Chief ports:** Shanghai, Tianjin, Luda.

Communications: Television sets: 1 per 8 persons. **Radios:** 1 per 9.1 persons. **Telephones:** 1 per 101 persons. **Daily newspaper circ.** (1989): 37 per 1,000 pop.

Health: Life expectancy at birth (1991): 68 male; 72 female. **Births** (per 1,000 pop. 1991): 22. **Deaths** (per 1,000 pop. 1991): 7. **Natural increase:** 1.5%. **Infant Mortality** (per 1,000 live births 1991): 33. **Hospital beds:** 1 per 432 persons. **Physicians:** 1 per 643 persons.

Education (1987): **Literacy:** 70%. Years compulsory 9; first grade enrollment 93%.

Major International Organizations: UN (IMF, FAO, WHO).

Embassy: 2300 Conn. Ave. NW 20008; 328-2500.

History. Remains of various man-like creatures who lived as early as several hundred thousand years ago have been found in many parts of China. Neolithic agricultural settlements dotted the Huanghe basin from about 5,000 BC. Their language, religion, and art were the sources of later Chinese civilization.

Bronze metallurgy reached a peak and Chinese pictographic writing, similar to today's, was in use in the more developed culture of the Shang Dynasty (c. 1500 BC-c. 1000 BC) which ruled much of North China.

A succession of dynasties and interdynastic warring kingdoms ruled China for the next 3,000 years. They expanded Chinese political and cultural domination to the south and west, and developed a brilliant technologically and culturally advanced society. Rule by foreigners (Mongols in the Yuan Dynasty, 1271-1368, and Manchus in the Ch'ing Dynasty, 1644-1911) did not alter the underlying culture.

A period of relative stagnation left China vulnerable to internal and external pressures in the 19th century. Rebellions left tens of millions dead, and Russia, Japan, Britain, and other powers exercised political and economic control in large parts of the country. China became a republic Jan. 1, 1912, following the Wuchang Uprising inspired by Dr. Sun Yat-sen.

For a period of 50 years, 1894-1945, China was involved in conflicts with Japan. In 1895, China ceded Korea, Taiwan, and other areas. On Sept. 18, 1931, Japan seized the Northeastern Provinces (Manchuria) and set up a puppet state called Manchukuo. The border province of Jehol was cut off as a buffer state in 1933. Japan invaded China proper July 7, 1937. After its defeat in World War II, Japan gave up all seized land.

Following World War II, internal disturbances arose involving the Kuomintang, communists, and other factions. China came under domination of communist armies, 1949-1950. The Kuomintang government moved to Taiwan, 90 mi. off the mainland, Dec. 8, 1949.

The People's Republic of China was proclaimed in Peking Sept. 21, 1949, by the Chinese People's Political Consultative Conference under Mao Zedong.

China and the USSR signed a 30-year treaty of "friendship, alliance and mutual assistance," Feb. 15, 1950.

The U.S. refused recognition of the new regime. On Nov. 26, 1950, the People's Republic sent armies into Korea against U.S. troops and forced a stalemate.

By the 1960s, relations with the USSR deteriorated, with disagreements on borders, ideology and leadership of world communism. The USSR cancelled aid accords, and China, with Albania, launched anti-Soviet propaganda drives.

On Oct. 25, 1971, the UN General Assembly ousted the Taiwan government from the UN and seated the People's Republic in its place. The U.S. had supported the mainland's admission but opposed Taiwan's expulsion.

U.S. Pres. Nixon visited China Feb. 21-28, 1972, on invitation from Premier Zhou Enlai, ending years of antipathy between the 2 nations. China and the U.S. opened liaison offices in each other's capitals, May-June 1973. The U.S., Dec. 15, 1978, formally recognized the People's Republic of China as the sole legal government of China; diplomatic relations between the 2 nations were established, Jan. 1, 1979.

Internal developments. After an initial period of consolidation, 1949-52, industry, agriculture, and social and economic institutions were forcibly molded according to Maoist ideals. However, frequent drastic changes in policy and violent factionalism interfered with economic development.

In 1957, Mao Tse-tung admitted an estimated 800,000 people had been executed 1949-54; opponents claimed much higher figures.

The Great Leap Forward, 1958-60, tried to force the pace of economic development through intensive labor on huge new rural communes, and through emphasis on ideological purity and enthusiasm. The program caused resistance and was largely abandoned. Serious food shortages developed, and the government was forced to buy grain from the West.

The Great Proletarian Cultural Revolution, 1965, was an attempt to oppose pragmatism and bureaucratic power and instruct a new generation in revolutionary principles. Massive purges took place. A program of forcibly relocating millions of urban teenagers into the countryside was launched.

By 1968 the movement had run its course; many purged officials returned to office in subsequent years, and reforms in education and industry that had placed ideology above expertise were gradually weakened.

In a continuing "reassessment" of the policies of Mao Zedong, Mao's widow, Jiang Quing, and other Gang of Four members were convicted of "committing crimes during the 'Cultural Revolution,' " Jan. 25, 1981.

In the mid-1970s, factional and ideological fighting increased, and emerged into the open after the 1976 deaths of Mao and Premier Zhou Enlai. Mao's widow and 3 other leading leftists were purged and placed under arrest, after reportedly trying to seize power. The new ruling group modified Maoist policies in education, culture, and industry, and sought better ties with non-communist countries.

Relations with Vietnam deteriorated in 1978 as China charged persecution of ethnic Chinese. In retaliation for Vietnam's invasion of Cambodia, China attacked 4 Vietnamese border provinces Feb. 17, 1979; heavy border fighting ensued.

By the mid 1980's, China had enacted far-reaching economic reforms highlighed by the departure from rigid central planning and the stressing of market-oriented socialism.

Some 100,000 students and workers staged a march in Beijing to demand democratic reforms, May 4, 1989. The demonstrations continued during a visit to Beijing by Soviet leader Mikhail Gorbachev May 15-18. It was the first Sino-Soviet summit since 1959. A million people gathered in Beijing to demand democratic reforms and the removal of Deng and other leaders. There were protests in at least 20 other Chinese cities. Martial law was imposed, May 20, but was mostly ignored by the protesters.

Chinese army troops entered Beijing, June 3-4, and crushed the pro-democracy protests. Tanks and armored personnel carriers attacked Tiananmen Square, outside the Great Hall of the People, which was the main scene of the demonstrations and hunger strikes. It was estimated that 5,000 died, 10,000 were injured, and hundreds of students and workers arrested.

China's population, the world's largest, is still increasing, but with more couples following the government's one-child policy some experts predict that the nation's population will actually decline after peaking in the early 21st century.

Manchuria. Home of the Manchus, rulers of China 1644-1911, Manchuria has accommodated millions of Chinese settlers in the 20th century. Under Japanese rule 1931-45, the area became industrialized. China no longer uses the name Manchuria for the region, which is divided into the 3 NE provinces of Heilongjiang, Jilin, and Liaoning.

Guangxi is in SE China, bounded on N by Kweichow and Hunan provinces, E and S by Kwangtung, on SW by North Vietnam, and on W by Yunnan. It produces rice in the river valleys and has valuable forest products. Pop (1987 est.) 39,000.

Inner Mongolia was organized by the People's Republic in 1947. Its boundaries have undergone frequent changes, reaching its greatest extent (and restored in 1979) in 1956, with an area of 454,000 sq. mi., allegedly in order to dilute the minority Mongol population. Chinese settlers outnumber the Mongols more than 10 to 1. Pop. (1988 est.): 20.0 mln. Capital: Hohhot.

Xinjiang, in Central Asia, is 633,802 sq. mi., pop. (1988 est.): 13.8 mln. (75% Uygurs, a Turkic Moslem group, with a heavy Chinese increase in recent years). Capital: Urumqi. It is China's richest region in strategic minerals. Some Uygurs have fled to the USSR, claiming national oppression.

Tibet, 470,000 sq. mi., is a thinly populated region of high plateaus and massive mountains, the Himalayas on the S, the Kunluns on the N. High passes connect with India and Nepal; roads lead into China proper. Capital: Lhasa. Average altitude is 15,000 ft. Jiachan, 15,870 ft., is believed to be the highest inhabited town on earth. Agriculture is primitive. Pop. (1988 est.): 2 mln. (of whom 500,000 are Chinese). Another 4 million Tibetans form the majority of the population of vast adjacent areas that have long been incorporated into China.

China ruled all of Tibet from the 18th century, but independence came in 1911. China reasserted control in 1951, and a communist government was installed in 1953, revising the theocratic Lamaist Buddhist rule. Serfdom was abolished, but all land remained collectivized.

A Tibetan uprising within China in 1956 spread to Tibet in 1959. The rebellion was crushed with Chinese troops, and Buddhism was almost totally suppressed. The Dalai Lama and 100,000 Tibetans fled to India.

Colombia

Republic of Colombia

República de Colombia

People: Population (1991 est.): 33,777,000. **Age distrib.** (%): 0–14: 36.1; 15–59: 57.8; 60+: 6.1. **Pop. density:** 76 per sq. mi. **Urban** (1983): 65.4%. **Ethnic groups:** Mestizo 58%, Caucasian 20%, Mulatto 14%. **Languages:** Spanish. **Religions:** Roman Catholic 95%.

Geography: Area: 439,735 sq. mi., about the size of Texas, and New Mexico combined. **Location:** At the NW corner of S. America. **Neighbors:** Panama on NW, Ecuador, Peru on S, Brazil, Venezuela on E. **Topography:** Three ranges of Andes, the Western, Central, and Eastern Cordilleras, run through the country from N to S. The eastern range consists mostly of high table lands, densely populated. The Magdalena R. rises in Andes, flows N to Carribean, through a rich alluvial plain. Sparsely-settled plains in E are drained by Orinoco and Amazon systems. **Capital:** Bogota. **Cities** (1990 est.): Bogota 4,819,000; Medellin 1,664,000; Cali 1,637,000; Barranquilla 1,000,000.

Government: Type: Republic. **Head of state:** Pres. Cesar Gaviria Trujillo; b. Mar. 31, 1947; in office: Aug. 7, 1990. **Local divisions:** 23 departments, 8 national territories, and special district of Bogota. **Defense:** 2.1% of GDP (1990).

Economy: Industries: Textiles, processed goods, hides, steel, cement, chemicals. **Chief crops:** Coffee (50% of exports), rice, corn, cotton, sugar, bananas. **Minerals:** Oil, gas, emeralds (90% world output), gold, copper, lead, coal, iron, nickel, salt. **Crude oil reserves** (1987): 1.6 bln. bbls. **Other resources:** Rubber, balsam, dye-woods, copaiba, hydro power. **Arable land:** 5%. **Livestock** (1989): cattle: 24.6 mln.; pigs: 2.6 mln.; sheep: 2.6 mln. **Fish catch** (1989): 91,000 metric tons. **Electricity prod.** (1990): 36.0 bln. kWh. **Labor force:** 26% agric.; 21% ind.; 53% services.

Finance: Currency: Peso (June 1992: 577 = $1 US). **Gross domestic product** (1990): $43 bln. **Per capita GDP** (1990): $1,300. **Imports** (1990): $5.0 bln.; partners: U.S. 34%, EC 16%. **Exports** (1990): $6.9 bln.; partners: U.S. 36%, EC 21%. **Tourists** (1989): $383 mln. receipts. **National budget** (1989): $3.9 bln. expenditures. **International reserves less gold** (Mar. 1992): $6.1 bln. **Gold:** 928,000 oz t. **Consumer prices** (change in 1991): 30.4.

Transport: Railway traffic (1989): 151 mln. passenger-km. **Motor vehicles:** in use (1989): 936,000 passenger cars, 364,000. **Civil aviation** (1990): 3.9 bln. passenger-km; airports with scheduled flights: 65. **Chief ports:** Buena Ventura, Santa Marta, Barranquilla, Cartagena.

Communications: Television sets: 1 per 5.6 persons. **Radios:** 1 per 7.3 persons. **Telephones:** 1 per 13 persons. **Daily newspaper circ.** (1991): 40 per 1,000 pop.

Health: Life expectancy at birth (1991): 68 male; 74 female. **Births** (per 1,000 pop. 1991): 26. **Deaths** (per 1,000 pop. 1991): 5. **Natural increase:** 2.1%. **Hospital beds** (1982): 28,880. **Physicians** (1983): 21,778. **Infant mortality** (per 1,000 live births 1991): 37%.

Education (1990): **Literacy:** 80%. Only 28% finish primary school.

Major International Organizations: UN (World Bank, GATT), OAS.

Embassy: 2118 Leroy Pl. NW, 20008; 387-8338.

Spain subdued the local Indian kingdoms (Funza, Tunja) by the 1530s, and ruled Colombia and neighboring areas as New Granada for 300 years. Independence was won by 1819. Venezuela and Ecuador broke away in 1829-30, and Panama withdrew in 1903.

One of the Latin American democracies, Colombia is plagued by rural and urban violence, though scaled down from "La Violencia" of 1948-58, which claimed 200,000 lives. Attempts at land and social reform, and progress in industrialization have not succeeded in reducing massive social problems aggravated by a very high birth rate. In 1989, the government's increased activity against local drug traffickers sparked a series of retaliation killings. On Aug. 18, Luis Carlos Galán, the ruling party's presidential hopeful in the 1990 election, was assassinated. In 1990, 2 other presidential candidates were slain as the drug traffickers carried on a campaign of intimidation to stop the presidential election. Cesar Gaviria Trujillo, a strong advocate of maintaining the government's war against the nation's drug cartels, was elected president in May.

Comoros

Federal Islamic Republic of the Comoros

Jumhurīyat al-Qumur al-Itthādīyah al-Islāmīyah

People: Population (1991 est.): 476,000. **Pop. density:** 568 per sq. mi. **Ethnic groups:** Arabs, Africans, East Indians. **Languages:** Arabic, French (both official). **Religions:** Islam (official), Roman Catholic.

Geography: Area: 838 sq. mi., half the size of Delaware. **Location:** 3 islands (Grande Comore, Anjouan, and Moheli) in the Mozambique Channel between NW Madagascar and SE Africa. **Neighbors:** Nearest are Mozambique on W, Madagascar on E. **Topography:** The islands are of volcanic origin, with an active volcano on Grand Comoro. **Capital:** Moroni. **Cities** (1988 est.): Moroni (met.) 28,000.

Government: Type: Republic. **Head of state:** Pres. Said Mohammed Djohar; in office: Nov. 26, 1989. **Local divisions:** each of the 3 main islands is a prefecture.

Economy: Industries: Perfume. **Chief crops:** Vanilla, copra, perfume plants, fruits. **Arable land:** 35%. **Electricity prod.** (1990): 24 mln. kWh. **Labor force:** 80% agric.

Finance: Monetary unit: CFA franc (Mar. 1992: 278 = $1 US). **Gross domestic product** (1990): $245 mln. **Per capita GDP** (1990): $530. **Imports** (1988): $41 mln.; partners: Fr. 22%. **Exports** (1988): $16 mln.; partners: Fr. 41%, U.S. 53%.

Transport: Chief ports: Dzaoudzi.

Communications: Radios: 1 per 9 persons. **Telephones in use:** 1 per 740 persons.

Health: Life expectancy at birth (1991): 54 male; 58 female. **Births** (per 1,000 pop. 1991): 47. **Deaths** (per 1,000 pop. 1991): 13. **Natural increase:** 3.5%. **Infant mortality** (per 1,000 live births 1991): 91.

Education: (1989): **Literacy:** 15%; less than 20% attend secondary school.

Major International Organizations: UN (IMF, World Bank); OAU.

Embassy: 336 E. 45th St., New York, NY 10017; (212) 972-8010.

The islands were controlled by Moslem sultans until the French acquired them 1841-1909. A 1974 referendum favored independence, with only the Christian island of Mayotte preferring association with France. The French National Assembly decided to allow each of the islands to decide its own fate. The Comoro Chamber of Deputies declared independence July 6, 1975. In a referendum in 1976, Mayotte voted to remain French. A leftist regime that seized power in 1975 was deposed in a pro-French 1978 coup.

In Nov. 1989, Pres. Ahmed Abdallah was assassinated.

Congo

Republic of the Congo

République du Congo

People: Population (1991 est.): 2,411,000. **Pop. density:** 18 per sq. mi. **Urban** (1986): 51%. **Ethnic groups:** Bakongo 45%, Bateke 20%, others. **Languages:** French (official), Kongo, Teke. **Religions:** Christians 47% (two-thirds Roman Catholic), animists 47%, Moslem 2%.

Geography: Area: 132,046 sq. mi., slightly smaller than Montana. **Location:** In western central Africa. **Neighbors:** Gabon, Cameroon on W, Central African Republic on N, Zaire on E, Angola (Cabinda) on SW. **Topography:** Much of the Congo is covered by thick forests. A coastal plain leads to the fertile Niari Valley. The center is a plateau; the Congo R. basin consists of flood plains in the lower and savanna in the upper portion. **Capital:** Brazzaville. **Cities** (1990 est.): Brazzaville (met.) 760,000; Pointe-Noire 387,000; Loubomo 62,000.

Government: Type: Republic. **Head of state:** Pres. Denis Sassou-Nguesso; b. 1943; in office: Feb. 8, 1979. **Head of government:** Prime Min. Andre Milongo; in office: June 8, 1991. **Local divisions:** 9 regions and capital district. **Defense:** 4.6% of GNP (1987).

Economy: Chief crops: Palm oil and kernels, cocoa, coffee, tobacco. **Minerals:** Gold, lead, copper, zinc. **Crude oil reserves** (1988): 750 mln. bbls. **Arable land:** 2%. **Fish catch** (1989): 19,000 metric tons. **Electricity prod.** (1989): 397 mln. kWh. **Labor force:** 90% agric.

Finance: Monetary unit: CFA franc (Mar. 1992: 278 = $1 US). **Gross domestic product** (1989): $2.0 bln. **Per capita GDP** (1989): $930. **Imports** (1989): $524 mln.; partners: Fr. 52%. **Exports** (1989): $912 mln.; partners: U.S. 45%, Fr. 15%. **Tourist receipts** (1989): $8 mln. **International reserves less gold** (Jan. 1991): $14.6 mln. **Gold:** 11,000 oz t. **Consumer prices** (change in 1989): 3.7%.

Transport: Railroads (1988): **Length:** 716 mi. **Motor vehicles:** in use (1989): 26,000 passenger cars, 20,000 comm. vehicles. **Chief ports:** Pointe-Noire, Brazzaville.

Communications: Television sets: 1 per 402 persons. **Radios:** 1 per 9.4 persons. **Telephones in use:** 1 per 111 persons.

Health: Life expectancy at birth (1991): 52 male; 56 female. **Births** (per 1,000 pop. 1991): 43. **Deaths** (per 1,000 pop. 1991): 13. **Natural increase:** 3.0%. **Hospital beds:** 1 per 456 persons. **Physicians:** 1 per 3,873 persons. **Infant mortality** (per 1,000 live births 1991): 110.

Education (1991): **Literacy:** 57%. Years compulsory 10; attendance 80%.

Major International Organizations: UN (GATT, IMF, WHO), OAU.

Embassy: 4891 Colorado Ave. NW 20011; 726-5500.

The Loango Kingdom flourished in the 15th century, as did the Anzico Kingdom of the Batekes; by the late 17th century they had become weakened. France established control by 1885. Independence came Aug. 15, 1960.

After a 1963 coup sparked by trade unions, the country adopted a Marxist-Leninist stance, with the USSR and China vying for influence. Tribal divisions remain strong. France remains a dominant trade partner and source of technical assistance, and French-owned private enterprise retained a major economic role. However, the government of Pres. Sassou-Nguesso favored a strengthening of relations with the USSR, a socialist constitution was adopted, 1979.

In 1990, Marxism was renounced and opposition parties legalized; elections were scheduled for 1992.

Costa Rica

Republic of Costa Rica

República de Costa Rica

People: Population (1991 est.): 3,111,000. **Age distrib.** (%): 0–14: 36.2; 15–49: 57.4; 50+: 6.4. **Pop. density:** 158 per sq. mi. **Urban** (1989): 50%. **Ethnic groups:** Spanish (with Mestizo minority). **Language:** Spanish (official). **Religions:** Roman Catholic 88%.

Geography: Area: 19,575 sq. mi., smaller than W. Virginia. **Location:** In central America. **Neighbors:** Nicaragua on N, Panama on S. **Topography:** Lowlands by the Caribbean are tropical. The interior plateau, with an altitude of about 4,000 ft., is temperate. **Capital:** San Jose. **Cities** (1988 met. est.): San Jose 890,000.

Government: Type: Democratic republic. **Head of state:** Pres. Rafael Angel Calderon; b. 1949; in office May 8, 1990. **Local divisions:** 7 provinces.

Economy: Industries: Furniture, food processing, aluminum, textiles, fertilizers, roofing, cement. **Chief crops:** Coffee (chief export), bananas, sugar, cocoa, cotton, hemp. **Minerals:** Gold, salt, sulphur, iron. **Other resources:** Fish, forests. **Arable land:** 12%. **Livestock** (1989): cattle: 1.7. mln. **Fish catch** (1988): 20,000 metric tons. **Electricity prod.** (1990): 2.9 bln. kWh. **Labor force:** 27% agric.; 35% ind. & comm.; 33% service and government.

Finance: Monetary unit: Colone (Mar. 1992: 133 = $1 US). **Gross domestic product** (1990): $5.5 bln. **Per capita GDP** (1990): $1,810. **Imports** (1990): $2.0 bln.; partners: U.S. 38%, CACM 10%, Jap. 10%. **Exports** (1990): $1.4 bln.; partners: U.S. 45%, CACM 18%. **Tourists** (1989): receipts: $206 mln. **National budget** (1988): $917 mln. expenditures. **International reserves less gold** (Mar. 1992): $1.0 bln. **Gold:** 39,000 oz t. **Consumer prices** (change in 1991): 28.7%.

Transport: Motor vehicles: in use (1990): 168,000 passenger cars, 94,000 comm. vehicles. **Civil aviation** (1990): 987 mln. passenger-km; 8 airports with scheduled flights. **Chief ports:** Limon, Puntarenas, Golfito.

Communications: Television sets: 1 per 4.9 persons. **Radios:** 1 per 11 persons. **Telephones:** 1 per 6.9 persons. **Daily newspaper circ.** (1990): 110 per 1,000 pop.

Health: Life expectancy at birth (1989): 74 male; 78 female. **Births** (per 1,000 pop. 1991): 27. **Deaths** (per 1,000 pop. 1991): 4. **Natural increase:** 2.3%. **Hospital beds:** 1 per 454 persons. **Physicians:** 1 per 1,798 persons. **Infant mortality** (per 1,000 live births 1991): 15.

Education (1991): **Literacy:** 93%. Years compulsory 6; attendance 99%.

Major International Organizations: UN (FAO, ILO, IMF, WHO), OAS.

Embassy: 1825 Connecticut Ave. NW, 20009; 234-2945.

Guaymi Indians inhabited the area when Spaniards arrived, 1502. Independence came in 1821. Costa Rica seceded from the Central American Federation in 1838. Since the civil war of 1948-49, there has been little violent social conflict, and free political institutions have been preserved.

Costa Rica, though still a largely agricultural country, has achieved a relatively high standard of living and social services, and land ownership is widespread.

Côte d'Ivoire

Ivory Coast

République de la Côte d'Ivoire

People: Population (1991 est.): 12,977,000. **Age distrib.** (%): 0–14: 45.1; 15–59: 50.2; 60+: 4.7. **Pop. density:** 104 per sq. mi. **Urban** (1986): 47%. **Ethnic groups:** Baule 23%, Bete 18%, Senufo 15%, Malinke 11%, over 60 tribes. **Languages:** French (official), Akan, Kru, Voltaic, Malinke. **Religions:** Moslem 25%, Christian 12%, indigenous 63%.

Geography: Area: 124,503 sq. mi., slightly larger than New Mexico. **Location:** On S. coast of W. Africa. **Neighbors:** Liberia, Guinea on W, Mali, Burkina Faso on N, Ghana on E. **Topography:** Forests cover the W half of the country, and range from a coastal strip to halfway to the N on the E. A sparse inland plain leads to low mountains in NW. **Capital:** Abidjan. **Cities** (1990 est.): Abidjan 2.7 mln.

Government: Type: Republic. **Head of state:** Pres. Felix Houphouet-Boigny; b. Oct. 18, 1905; in office: Aug. 7, 1960. **Local divisions:** 49 departments.

Economy: Chief crops: Coffee, cocoa. **Minerals:** Diamonds, manganese. **Other resources:** Timber, rubber, petroleum. **Arable land:** 9%. **Livestock** (1989): goats: 1.5 mln.; sheep: 1.5 mln.; cattle: 991,000. **Fish catch** (1989): 100,000 metric tons. **Electricity prod.** (1990): 2.4 bln. kWh. **Labor force:** 85% agric., forestry.

Finance: Monetary unit: CFA franc (Mar. 1992: 278 = $1 US). **Gross domestic product** (1989): $9.3 bln. **Per capita GDP** (1989): $820. **Imports** (1989): $2.1 bln.; partners: Fr. 31%, Jap. 5%, U.S. 5%. **Exports** (1989): $2.8 bln.; partners: Fr. 14%, Neth. 19%, U.S. 11%, It. 8%. **Tourists** (1989): $53 mln receipts; **International reserves less gold** (Jan. 1992): $16.5 mln. **Gold:** 45,000 oz t. **Consumer prices** (changed in 1991): 2.0%.

Transport: Railroads (1990): **Length:** 600 km. **Motor vehicles:** in use (1989): 168,000 passenger cars, 90,000 comm. vehicles. **Chief ports:** Abidjan, Sassandra.

Communications: Television sets: 1 per 19 persons. **Radios:** 1 per 8.1 persons. **Telephones:** 1 per 97 persons. **Daily newspaper circ.** (1990): 12 per 1,000 pop.

Health: Life expectancy at birth (1990): 52 male; 55 female. **Births** (per 1,000 pop. 1991): 48. **Deaths** (per 1,000 pop. 1991): 12. **Natural increase:** 3.6%. **Hospital beds** (1982): 10,062. **Physicians** (1982): 502. **Infant mortality** (per 1,000 live births 1991): 97.

Education (1990): **Literacy:** 45%. **Years compulsory:** none; attendance 75%.

Major International Organizations: UN and all of its specialized agencies, OAU.

Embassy: 2424 Massachusetts Ave. NW 20008; 483-2400.

A French protectorate from 1842, Côte D'Ivoire became independent in 1960. It is the most prosperous of tropical African nations, due to diversification of agriculture for export, close ties to France, and encouragement of foreign investment. About 20% of the population are workers from neighboring countries. Côte D'Ivoire, which officially changed its name from Ivory Coast in Oct. 1985, is a leader of the pro-Western bloc in Africa.

Students and workers protested, Feb. 1990, demanding the ouster of Pres. Houphouet-Boigny and multiparty democracy.

Croatia

Hrvatska

People: Population (1991 est.): 4,763,000. **Pop. density:** 218 per sq. mi. **Ethnic groups:** Croatian 75%, Serbian 18%. **Language:** Serbo-Croatian. **Religion:** Mostly Roman Catholic.

Geography: Area: 21,829 sq. mi. **Location:** in SE Europe. **Neighbors:** Slovenia, Bosnia and Herzegovina, Hungary, Yugoslavia, and the Adriatic Sea. Over 33 percent is forested. **Capital:** Zagreb.

Government: Type: Republic. **Head of state:** Pres. Franjo Tudjman; b. 1922; in office: May, 1990. **Head of government:** Prime Min. Franjo Greguric.

Economy: Industries: Textiles, chemicals, aluminum prods., paper. **Chief crops:** Olives, wine. **Minerals:** Bauxite, copper, coal.

Finance: Monetary unit: Croatian Dinar (June 1992: 320 = $1 U.S.).

Transport: Motor vehicles: in use (1989): 827,000 passenger cars, 55,000 commercial vehicles.

Health: Doctors (1989): 12,000: **Hospital beds** (1989): 36,000. **Infant mortality** (per 1,000 live births 1989): 11.3.

Education (1991): **Literacy:** 90%.

International Organizations: UN.

From the 7th century the area was inhabited by Croats, a south Slavic people. It was formed into a kingdom under Tomislav in 924, and joined with Hungary in 1102. The Croats became westernized and separated from Slavs under Serbian influence. The Croats retained autonomy under the Hungarian crown. Slavonia was taken by Turks in the 16th century, the northern part was restored by the Treaty of Karlowitz in 1699. Croatia helped Austria put down the Hungarian revolution 1848-49 and as a result was set up with Slavonia as the separate Austrian crownland of Croatia and Slavonia, which was reunited to Hungary as part of *Ausgleich* in 1867. It united with other Yugoslav areas to proclaim the kingdom of Serbs, Croats, and Slovenes in 1918. At the reorganization of Yugoslavia in 1929, Croatia and Slavonia became Savska co., which in 1939 was united with Primorje co. to form the county of Croatia. A nominally independent state between 1941-45, it became a constituent republic in the 1946 constitution.

On June 25, 1991, Croatia declared independence from Yugoslavia. Fighting began between ethnic Serbs and Croats. There were clashes between Croats and Yugoslavian army units and their Serb supporters. Croatia was granted EC recognition Jan. 15, 1992. Fighting continued in 1992. *(See Index & Chronology for details).*

Cuba

Republic of Cuba

República de Cuba

People: Population (1991 est.): 10,732,000. **Age distrib.** (%): 0-under 15: 23.3; 15–59: 64.9; 60+: 11.8. **Pop. density:** 242 per sq. mi. **Urban** (1991): 72%. **Ethnic groups:** Spanish, African. **Languages:** Spanish. **Religions:** Roman Catholic 42%, none 49%.

Geography: Area: 44,218 sq. mi., nearly as large as Pennsylvania. **Location:** Westernmost of West Indies. **Neighbors:** Bahamas, U.S., on N, Mexico on W, Jamaica on S, Haiti on E. **Topography:** The coastline is about 2,500 miles. The N coast is steep and rocky, the S coast low and marshy. Low hills and fertile valleys cover more than half the country. Sierra Maestra, in the E is the highest of 3 mountain ranges. **Capital:** Havana. **Cities** (1989 est.): Havana 2,077,000; Santiago de Cuba 397,000; Camaguey 274,000.

Government: Type: Communist state. **Head of state:** Pres. Fidel Castro Ruz; b. Aug. 13, 1926; in office: Dec. 3, 1976 (formerly Prime Min. since Feb. 16, 1959). **Local divisions:** 14 provinces, Havana. **Defense:** 6.0% of GNP (1989).

Economy: Industries: Cement, food processing, sugar. **Chief crops:** Sugar (75% of exports), tobacco, rice, coffee, tropical fruit. **Minerals:** Cobalt, nickel, iron, copper, manganese, salt. **Other resources:** Forests. **Arable land:** 29%. **Livestock** (1989): cattle: 4.9 mln.; pigs: 2.5 mln. **Fish catch** (1989): 191,000 metric tons. **Electricity prod.** (1990): 16.2 bln. kWh. **Labor force:** 13% agric.; 29% ind. & comm.; 30% services & govt.

Finance: Monetary unit: Peso (Dec. 1991: 1 peso = $1.34 U.S.). **Gross social product:** economic measure not convertible to GNP. **Per capita income** (1990): $2,644. **Imports** (1987): $7.6 bln.; partners: USSR 72%. **Exports** (1987): $5.4 bln.; partners: USSR 72%. **Tourists** (1990): Revenues: $250 mln. **National budget** (1990): $14.4 bln. expenditures.

Transport: Railroads (1989): **Length:** 3,009 mi. **Motor vehicles:** in use (1985): 200,000 passenger cars, 164,000 comm. vehicles. **Civil aviation** (1989): 3.1 bln. passenger-km.; 12 airports with scheduled flights. **Chief ports:** Havana, Matanzas, Cienfuegos, Santiago de Cuba.

Communications: Television sets: 1 per 5 persons. **Radios:** 1 per 3 persons. **Telephones in use** 1 per 19 persons. **Daily newspaper circ.** (1988): 155 per 1,000 pop.

Health: Life expectancy at birth: (1991): 73 male; 78 female. **Births** (per 1,000 pop. 1991): 18. **Deaths** (per 1,000 pop. 1991): 7. **Natural increase:** 1.1%. **Hospital beds:** 1 per 174 persons. **Physicians:** 1 per 303 persons. **Infant mortality** (per 1,000 live births 1991): 12.

Education (1990): **Literacy:** 98%. 92% of those between ages 6–14 attend school.

Major International Organizations: UN (UNESCO, WHO).

Some 50,000 Indians lived in Cuba when it was discovered by Columbus in 1492. Its name derives from the Indian Cubanacan. Except for British occupation of Havana, 1762-63, Cuba remained Spanish until 1898. A slave-based sugar plantation economy developed from the 18th century, aided by early mechanization of milling. Sugar remains the chief product and chief export despite government attempts to diversify.

A ten-year uprising ended in 1878 with guarantees of rights by Spain, which Spain failed to carry out. A full-scale movement under Jose Marti began Feb. 24, 1895.

The U.S. declared war on Spain in April, 1898, after the sinking of the U.S.S. Maine in Havana harbor, and defeated it in the Spanish-American War. Spain gave up all claims to Cuba. U.S. troops withdrew in 1902, but under 1903 and 1934 agreements, the U.S. leases a site at Guantanamo Bay in the SE as a naval base. U.S. and other foreign investments acquired a dominant role in the economy. In 1952, former president Fulgencio Batista seized control and established a dictatorship, which grew increasingly harsh and corrupt. Fidel Castro assembled a rebel band in 1956; guerrilla fighting intensified in 1958. Batista fled Jan. 1, 1959, and in the resulting political vacuum Castro took power, becoming premier Feb. 16.

The government began a program of sweeping economic and social changes, without restoring promised liberties. Opponents were imprisoned and some were executed. Some 700,000 Cubans emigrated in the years after the Castro takeover, mostly to the U.S.

Cattle and tobacco lands were nationalized, while a system of cooperatives was instituted. By 1960 all banks and industrial companies had been nationalized, including over $1 billion worth of U.S.-owned properties, mostly without compensation.

Poor sugar crops resulted in collectivization of farms, stringent labor controls, and rationing, despite continued aid from the USSR and other communist countries.

The U.S. imposed an export embargo in 1962, severely damaging the economy. In 1961, some 1,400 Cubans, trained and backed by the U.S. Central Intelligence Agency, unsuccessfully tried to invade and overthrow the regime.

In the fall of 1962, the U.S. learned that the USSR had brought nuclear missiles to Cuba. After an Oct. 22 warning from Pres. Kennedy, the missiles were removed.

In 1977, Cuba and the U.S. signed agreements to exchange diplomats, without restoring full ties, and to regulate offshore fishing. In 1978, and again in 1980, the U.S. agreed to accept political prisoners released by Cuba some of whom, it was later discovered, were criminals and mental patients. A 1987 agreement provided for 20,000 Cubans to immigrate to the U.S. each year; Cuba agreed to take back some 2,500 jailed in the U.S. since the 1980 Mariel boat lift.

In 1975-78, Cuba sent troops to aid one faction in the Angola Civil War. All Cuban troops were withdrawn by May 1991. Cuba's involvement in Central America, Africa, and the Caribbean, contributed to poor relations with the U.S.

In 1983, 24 Cubans died and over 700 were captured, later repatriated, as a result of the U.S.-led invasion of Grenada.

Cuba has resisted the social and economic reforms that have taken place in the USSR and other eastern bloc countries. The nation was feeling economic difficulties in the 1990s as the Soviet-bloc curtailed financial aid.

Cyprus

Republic of Cyprus

Kypriaki Dimokratia (Greek)
Kibris Cumhuriyeti (Turkish)

People: Population (1991 est.): 708,000. **Age distrib.** (%): 0–14: 25.4; 15–59: 60.4; 60+: 14.2. **Pop. density:** 194 per sq. mi. **Urban** (1982): 53%. **Ethnic groups:** Greeks 78%, Turks 18.7%, Armenians, Maronites. **Languages:** Greek, Turkish (both official), English. **Religions:** Orthodox 77%, Moslems 18%.

Geography: Area: 3,572 sq. mi., smaller than Connecticut. **Location:** In eastern Mediterranean Sea, off Turkish coast. **Neighbors:** Nearest are Turkey on N, Syria, Lebanon on E. **Topography:** Two mountain ranges run E-W, separated by a wide, fertile plain. **Capital:** Nicosia. **Cities** (1989 est.): Nicosia 166,000.

Government: Type: Republic. **Head of state:** Pres. George Vassiliou; b. May 21, 1931; in office: Feb. 28, 1988. **Local divisions:** 6 districts. **Defense:** 5.0% of GDP (1990).

Economy: Industries: Light manuf. **Chief crops:** Grains, grapes, carobs, citrus fruits, potatoes, olives. **Minerals:** Copper, pyrites, asbetos. **Arable land:** 40%. **Electricity prod.** (1990): 1.6 mln. kWh. **Labor force:** 21% agric.; 20% ind., 18% comm., 19% serv.

Finance: Monetary unit: Pound (Mar. 1992: 1.00 = $2.12 US). **Gross domestic product** (1990): $5.3 bln. **Per capita GDP** (1990): $7,585. **Imports** (1990): $2.2 bln.; partners: UK 13%, Itl. 12%. **Exports** (1990): $957 mln.; partners: UK 21%, Libya 9%. **Tourists** (1989): receipts: $990 mln. **National budget** (1989): $1.4 bln. expenditures. **International reserves less gold** (Mar. 1992): $1.1 bln. **Gold:** 459,000 oz. t. **Consumer prices** (change in 1991): 4.5%.

Transport: Motor vehicles: in use (1989): 159,000 passenger cars, 54,000 comm. vehicles. **Civil aviation** (1988): 1.6 bln. passenger-km; one airport. **Chief ports:** Famagusta, Limassol.

Communications: Television sets: 1 per 3.4 persons. **Radios:** 1 per 2.7 persons. **Telephones:** 1 per 2.0 persons. **Daily newspaper circ.** (1987): 157 per 1,000 pop.

Health: Life expectancy at birth (1991): 74 male; 80 female. **Births** (per 1,000 pop. 1991): 18. **Deaths** (per 1,000 pop. 1991): 8. **Natural increase:** 1.0%. **Hospital beds:** 1 per 165 persons. **Physicians** : 1 per 516 persons. **Infant mortality** (per 1,000 live births 1991): 10.

Education (1991): **Literacy:** 95%. **Years compulsory:** 9; attendance 99%.

Major International Organizations: UN (GATT, IMF, WHO), Commonwealth of Nations, EC (Assoc.).

Embassy: 2211 R St. NW, 20008; 462-5772.

Agitation for enosis (union) with Greece increased after World War II, with the Turkish minority opposed, and broke into violence in 1955-56. In 1959, Britain, Greece, Turkey, and Cypriot leaders approved a plan for an independent republic, with constitutional guarantees for the Turkish minority and permanent division of offices on an ethnic basis. Greek and Turkish Communal Chambers dealt with religion, education, and other matters.

Archbishop Makarios, formerly the leader of the enosis movement, was elected president, and full independence became final Aug. 16, 1960. Makarios was re-elected in 1968 and 1973.

Further communal strife led the United Nations to send a peace-keeping force in 1964; its mandate has been repeatedly renewed.

The Cypriot National Guard, led by officers from the army of Greece, seized the government July 15, 1974. Makarios fled the country. On July 20, Turkey invaded the island; Greece mobilized its forces but did not intervene. A cease-fire was arranged July 22. A peace conference collapsed Aug. 14; fighting resumed. By Aug. 16 Turkish forces had occupied the NE 40% of the island, despite the presence of UN peace forces. Makarios resumed the presidency in Dec., until his death, 1977.

Turkish Cypriots voted overwhelmingly, June 8, 1975, to form a separate Turkish Cypriot federated state. A president and assembly were elected in 1976. Some 200,000 Greeks have been expelled from the Turkish-controlled area, replaced by thousands of Turks, some from the mainland.

Turkish Republic of Northern Cyprus

A declaration of independence was announced by Turkish-Cypriot leader Rauf Denktash, Nov. 15, 1983. The new state is not internationally recognized although it does have trade relations with some countries. TRNC contains 1,295 sq mi., pop. (1990 est.): 171,000, 99% Turkish.

Czechoslovakia

Czech and Slovak Federal Republic

People: Population (1991 est.): 15,724,000. **Age distrib.** (%): 0–14: 22.5; 15–59: 60.8; 60+: 16.7. **Pop. density:** 318 per sq. mi. **Urban** (1990): 73%. **Ethnic groups:** Czechs 54%, Slovaks 31%, Hungarian, German, Ukrainian, Polish. **Languages:** Czech, Slovak (both official), Hungarian, Romany. **Religions:** Roman Catholic 50%, Protestant 20%.

Geography: Area: 49,365 sq. mi., the size of New York. **Location:** In E central Europe. **Neighbors:** Poland, E. Germany on N, W. Germany on W. Austria, Hungary on S, USSR on E. **Topography:** Bohemia, in W, is a plateau surrounded by mountains; Moravia is hilly, Slovakia, in E, has mountains (Carpathians) in N, fertile Danube plain in S. Vltava (Moldau) and Labe (Elbe) rivers flow N from Bohemia to G. **Capital:** Prague. **Cities** (1991 est.): Prague 1.2 mln.; Brno 385,000; Bratislava 441,000; Ostrava 327,000.

Government: Type: Federal republic. **Head of state:** vacant. **Head of government:** Prime Min. Jan Strasky; in office: July 3, 1992. **Local divisions:** Czech and Slovak republics each have an assembly. **Defense:** 6.8% of GNP (1987).

Economy: Industries: Machinery, oil products, iron and steel, glass, chemicals, motor vehicles, cement. **Chief crops:** Wheat, sugar beets, potatoes, rye, corn, barley. **Minerals:** coke, coal, iron. **Arable land:** 40%. **Livestock:** (1989): cattle: 5 mln.; pigs: 7 mln.; sheep: 1 mln. **Electricity prod.** (1991): 89.0 bln. kWh. **Crude steel prod.** (1990): 14.8 mln. metric tons. **Labor force:** 12% agric.; 37% ind.; 22% service, govt.

Finance: Monetary unit: Koruna (Apr. 1992: 29.03 = $1 US). **Gross domestic product** (1990): $120 bln. **Per capita GDP** (1990): $7,700. **Imports** (1991): $10.4 bln.; partners: USSR 31%, Ger. 19%, Pol. 6%. **Exports** (1991): $10.8 bln.; partners: USSR 35%, Ger. 7%, Pol. 7%. **Tourism** (1989): $689 mln. receipts. **National budget** (1991): $16.8 bln. expenditures. **International reserves less gold** (Mar. 1992): $1.5 bln. **Gold:** 2.9 mln. oz t. **Consumer prices** (change in 1991): 58.4%.

Transport: Railroads (1990): **Length:** 8,142 mi. **Motor vehicles:** in use (1989): 3.1 mln. passenger cars, 327,000 comm. **Civil aviation** (1989): 2.2 bln. passenger-km.; 8 airports.

Communications: Television sets: 1 per 2.7 persons. **Radios:** 1 per 3.3 persons. **Telephones:** 1 per 3.9 persons. **Daily newspaper circ.** (1990): 327 per 1,000 pop.

Health: Life expectancy at birth (1991): 69 male; 77 female. **Births** (per 1,000 pop. 1991): 14. **Deaths** (per 1,000 pop. 1991): 12. **Natural increase:** .2%. **Hospital beds:** 1 per 99 persons; **Physicians:** 1 per 317 persons. **Infant mortality** (per 1,000 live births 1991): 11.

Education (1991): **Literacy:** 99%.

Major International Organizations: UN (GATT, WHO).

Embassy: 3900 Linnean Ave. NW 20008; 263-6315.

Bohemia, Moravia and Slovakia were part of the Great Moravian Empire in the 9th century. Later, Slovakia was overrun by Magyars, while Bohemia and Moravia became part of the Holy Roman Empire. Under the kings of Bohemia, Prague in the 14th century was the cultural center of Central Europe. Bohemia and Hungary became part of Austria-Hungary.

In 1914-1918 Thomas G. Masaryk and Eduard Benes formed a provisional government with the support of Slovak leaders including Milan Stefanik. They proclaimed the Republic of Czechoslovakia Oct. 28, 1918.

By 1938 Nazi Germany had worked up disaffection among German-speaking citizens in Sudetenland and demanded its cession. Prime Min. Neville Chamberlain of Britain, with the acquiescence of France, signed with Hitler at Munich, Sept. 30, 1938, an agreement to the cession, with a guarantee of peace by Hitler and Mussolini. Germany occupied Sudetenland Oct. 1-2.

Hitler on Mar. 15, 1939, dissolved Czechoslovakia, made protectorates of Bohemia and Moravia, and supported the autonomy of Slovakia, which was proclaimed independent Mar. 14, 1939.

Soviet troops with some Czechoslovak contingents entered eastern Czechoslovakia in 1944 and reached Prague in May 1945; Benes returned as president. In May 1946 elections, the Communist Party won 38% of the votes, and Benes accepted Klement Gottwald, a communist, as prime minister.

In February, 1948, the communists seized power in advance of scheduled elections. In May 1948 a new constitution was approved. Benes refused to sign it. On May 30 the voters were offered a one-slate ballot and the communists won full control. Benes resigned June 7 and Gottwald became president. A harsh Stalinist period followed, with complete and violent suppression of all opposition.

In Jan. 1968 a liberalization movement spread explosively through Czechoslovakia. Antonin Novotny, long the Stalinist boss of the nation, was deposed as party leader and succeeded by Alexander Dubcek, a Slovak, who declared he intended to make communism democratic. On Mar. 22 Novotny resigned as president and was succeeded by Gen. Ludvik Svoboda. On Apr. 6, Premier Joseph Lenart resigned and was succeeded by Oldrich Cernik, whose new cabinet was pledged to carry out democratization and economic reforms.

In July 1968 the USSR and 4 Warsaw Pact nations demanded an end to liberalization. On Aug. 20, the Russian, Polish, East German, Hungarian, and Bulgarian armies invaded Czechoslovakia.

Despite demonstrations and riots by students and workers, press censorship was imposed, liberal leaders were ousted from office and promises of loyalty to Soviet policies were made by some old-line Communist Party leaders.

On Apr. 17, 1969, Dubcek resigned as leader of the Communist Party and was succeeded by Gustav Husak. In Jan. 1970, Premier Cernik was ousted. Censorship was tightened and the Communist Party expelled a third of its members. In 1973, amnesty was offered to some of the 40,000 who fled the country after the 1968 invasion, but repressive policies remained in force.

More than 700 leading Czechoslovak intellectuals and former party leaders signed a human rights manifesto in 1977, called Charter 77, prompting a renewed crackdown by the regime.

The police crushed the largest anti-government protests since 1968, when tens of thousands of demonstrators took to the streets of Prague, Nov. 17, 1989. As protesters demanded free elections, the Communist Party leadership resigned Nov. 24; millions went on strike Nov. 27.

On Dec. 10, 1989 the first Cabinet in 41 years without a communist majority took power; Vaclav Havel, playwright and human rights campaigner, was chosen president, Dec. 29. Havel failed to win reelection July 3, 1992; his bid was blocked by a Slovak-led coalition.

Slovaka declared sovereignty, July 17. Czech and Slovak leaders agreed, July 23, on a basic plan for a peaceful division of Czechoslovakia into 2 independent states by Jan. 1, 1993. *(See Chronology and Index for details).*

Denmark

Kingdom of Denmark

Kongeriget Danmark

People: Population (1991 est.): 5,134,000. **Age distrib.** (%): 0–14: 17.1; 15–59: 62.5; 60+: 20.4. **Pop. density:** 308 per sq. mi. **Urban** (1990): 86%. **Ethnic groups:** Almost all Scandinavian. **Languages:** Danish. **Religions:** Evangelical Lutheran 90%.

Geography: Area: 16,633 sq. mi., the size of Massachusetts and New Hampshire combined. **Location:** In northern Europe, separating the North and Baltic seas. **Neighbors:** W. Germany on S., Norway on NW, Sweden on NE. **Topography:** Denmark consists of the Jutland Peninsula and about 500 islands, 100 inhabited. The land is flat or gently rolling, and is almost all in productive use. **Capital:** Copenhagen. **Cities** (1988, met.): Copenhagen 619,000.

Government: Type: Constitutional monarchy. **Head of state:** Queen Margrethe II; b. Apr. 16, 1940; in office: Jan. 14, 1972. **Head of government:** Prime Min. Poul Schluter; b. 1929; in office: Sept. 10, 1982. **Local divisions:** 14 counties and one city (Copenhagen). **Defense:** 2.3% of GNP (1990).

Economy: Industries: Machinery, textiles, furniture, electronics. **Chief crops:** Dairy products. **Arable land:** 62%. **Livestock** (1987): cattle: 2.3 mln.; pigs: 9.2 mln. **Fish catch** (1989): 1.9 mln. metric tons. **Electricity prod.** (1989): 30.9 bln. kWh. **Labor force:** 6% agric.; 50% ind. & comm.; 11% serv.; 27% govt.

Finance: Monetary unit: Krone (June 1991: 6.50 = $1 US). **Gross domestic product** (1990): $78 bln. **Per capita GDP** (1990): $15,200. **Imports** (1991): $32.3 bln.; partners: Ger. 24%, Swed. 12%, UK 9%, Neth. 5%. **Exports** (1991): $35.8 bln.; partners: Ger. 15%, EC 42%, U.S. 8%. **Tourists** (1989): $2.4 bln. receipts. **International reserves less gold** (Mar. 1992): $6.2 bln. **Gold:** 2.0 mln. oz t. **Consumer prices** (change in 1991): 2.6%.

Transport: Railroads (1989): **Length:** 2,837 km. **Motor vehicles:** in use (1989): 1.5 mln. passenger cars, 294,000 comm. vehicles. **Civil aviation** (1990): 4.2 bln. passenger-km; 13 airports with scheduled flights. **Chief ports:** Copenhagen, Alborg, Arhus, Odense.

Communications: Television sets: 1 per 2.7 persons. **Radios:** 1 per 2.4 persons. **Telephones:** 1 per 1.2 persons. **Daily newspaper circ.** (1990): 361 per 1,000 pop.

Health: Life expectancy at birth (1991): 73 male; 79 female. **Births** (per 1,000 pop. 1991): 12. **Deaths** (per 1,000 pop. 1991): 11. **Hospital beds:** 1 per 164 persons. **Physicians:** 1 per 375 persons. **Infant mortality** (per 1,000 live births 1991): 6.

Education (1991): **Literacy:** 99%. Years compulsory 9; attendance 100%.

Major International Organizations: UN and all of its specialized agencies, OECD, EC, NATO.

Embassy: 3200 Whitehaven St. NW 20008; 234-4300.

The origin of Copenhagen dates back to ancient times, when the fishing and trading place named Havn (port) grew up on a cluster of islets, but Bishop Absalon (1128-1201) is regarded as the actual founder of the city.

Danes formed a large component of the Viking raiders in the early Middle Ages. The Danish kingdom was a major north European power until the 17th century, when it lost its land in southern Sweden. Norway was separated in 1815, and Schleswig-Holstein in 1864. Northern Schleswig was returned in 1920.

Voters rejected the EC Treaty on European union June 1992.

The **Faeroe Islands** in the N. Atlantic, about 300 mi. NE of the Shetlands, and 850 mi. from Denmark proper, 18 inhabited, have an area of 540 sq. mi. and pop. (1987) of 46,000. They are self-governing in most matters.

Greenland

(Kalaallit Nunaat)

Greenland, a huge island between the N. Atlantic and the Polar Sea, is separated from the North American continent by Davis Strait and Baffin Bay. Its total area is 840,000 sq. mi., 84% of which is ice-capped. Most of the island is a lofty plateau 9,000 to 10,000 ft. in altitude. The average thickness of the cap is 1,000 ft. The population (1991) is 56,752. Under the 1953 Danish constitution the colony became an integral part of the realm with representatives in the Folketing. The Danish parliament, 1978, approved home rule for Greenland, effective May 1, 1979. Accepting home rule the islanders elected a socialist-dominated legislature, Apr. 4th. With home rule, Greenlandic place names came into official use. The technically-correct name for Greenland is now Kalaallit Nunaat; its capital is Nuuk, rather than Gothab. Fish is the principal export.

Djibouti

Republic of Djibouti

Jumhouriyya Djibouti

People: Population (1991 est.): 541,000. **Ethnic groups:** Issa (Somali) 47%; Afar 37%; European 8%. **Languages:** French, Arabic (both official); Afar, Issa. **Religions:** Sunni Moslem 94%.

Geography: Area: 8,950 sq. mi., about the size of New Hampshire. **Location:** On E coast of Africa, separated from Arabian Peninsula by the strategically vital strait of Bab el-Mandeb. **Neighbors:** Ethiopia on N (Eritrea) and W, Somalia on S. **To-**

pography: The territory, divided into a low coastal plain, mountains behind, and an interior plateau, is arid, sandy, and desolate. The climate is generally hot and dry. **Capital:** Djibouti. **Cities** (1988): Djibouti (met.) 290,000.

Government: Type: Republic. **Head of state:** Pres. Hassan Gouled Aptidon b. 1916; in office: June 24, 1977; **Head of government:** Prem. Barkat Gourad Hamadou; in office: Sept. 30, 1978. **Local divisions:** 5 cercles (districts).

Economy: Minerals: Salt. **Electricity prod.** (1990): 190 mln. kWh.

Finance: Monetary unit Franc (Mar. 1992: 177=$1 US). **Gross domestic product:** (1989): $344 mln. **Per capita GDP** (1989): $1,030. **Imports** (1990): $311 mln.; partners: EC 36%. **Exports** (1990): $190 mln.; partners: Middle East 50%.

Transport: Motor vehicles: in use (1989): 13,000 passenger cars, 13,000 commercial vehicles. **Chief ports:** Djibouti.

Communications: Television sets: 1 per 38 persons. **Radios:** 1 per 18 persons. **Telephones:** 1 per 55 persons.

Health: Life expectancy at birth (1989): 45 male; 49 female. **Births** (per 1,000 pop. 1991): 43. **Deaths** (per 1,000 pop. 1991): 17. **Natural increase:** 2.6%. **Infant mortality** (per 1,000 live births 1991): 121.

Education (1988): **Literacy:** 20%.

Major International Organizations: UN, OAU, Arab League.

Embassy: 866 United Nations Plaza, New York, NY 10017; (212) 753-3163.

France gained control of the territory in stages between 1862 and 1900.

Ethiopia and Somalia have renounced their claims to the area, but each has accused the other of trying to gain control. There were clashes between Afars (ethnically related to Ethiopians) and Issas (related to Somalis) in 1976. Immigrants from both countries continued to enter the country up to independence, which came June 27, 1977.

Unemployment is high and there are few natural resources. French aid is the mainstay of the economy and some 5,000 French troops are present.

Dominica

Commonwealth of Dominica

People: Population (1991 est.): 86,000. **Pop. density:** 296 per sq. mi. **Ethnic groups:** nearly all African or mulatto, Caribs. **Languages:** English (official), French creole. **Religions:** mainly Roman Catholic.

Geography: Area: 290 sq. mi., about one-fourth the size of Rhode Island. **Location:** In Eastern Caribbean, most northerly Windward Is. **Neighbors:** Guadeloupe to N, Martinique to S. **Topography:** Mountainous, a central ridge running from N to S, terminating in cliffs; volcanic in origin, with numerous thermal springs; rich deep topsoil on leeward side, red tropical clay on windward coast. **Capital** (1987 est.) Roseau 22,000.

Government: Type: Parliamentary democracy. **Head of state:** Pres. Clarence Augustus Seignoret; in office: 1984. **Head of government:** Prime Min. Mary Eugenia Charles; b. 1919; in office: July 21, 1980. **Local divisions:** 10 parishes.

Economy: Industries: Agriculture, tourism. **Chief crops:** Bananas, citrus fruits, coconuts. **Minerals:** Pumice. **Other resources:** Forests. **Arable land:** 23%. **Electricity prod.** (1990): 16 mln. kWh. **Labor force:** 37% agric.; 20% ind & comm.; 30% services.

Finance: Monetary unit: East Caribbean dollar (May 1992: 2.70 = $1 US). **Gross domestic product** (1989): $153 mln. **Imports** (1990): $115 mln.; partners: UK 17%, U.S. 23%. **Exports** (1990): $59 mln.; partners: UK 70%. **Tourists** (1989): $19 mln. receipts. **Consumer prices** (change in 1991): 6.0%.

Transport: Chief ports: Roseau.

Communications: Telephones: 1 per 11 persons.

Health: Life expectancy at birth (1991): 73 male; 79 female. **Births** (per 1,000 pop. 1991): 26. **Deaths** (per 1,000 pop. 1991): 5. **Natural increase:** 2.1%. **Hospital beds:** 1 per 331 persons. **Physicians:** 1 per 2,619 persons. **Infant mortality** (per 1,000 live births 1991): 13.

Education: Literacy: 90%.

Major International Organizations: UN, OAS.

A British colony since 1805, Dominica was granted self government in 1967. Independence was achieved Nov. 3, 1978.

Hurricane David struck, Aug. 30, 1979, devastating the island and destroying the banana plantations, Dominica's economic mainstay. Coups were attempted in 1980 and 1981.

Dominica took a leading role in the instigation of the 1983 invasion of Grenada.

Dominican Republic

República Dominicana

People: Population (1991 est.): 7,384,000. **Age distrib.** (%): 0–14: 37.9; 15–59: 56.6; 60+: 5.5. **Pop. density:** 394 per sq. mi. **Urban** (1986): 55%. **Ethnic groups:** Caucasian 16%, mixed 73%, black 11%. **Languages:** Spanish. **Religions:** Roman Catholic 95%.

Geography: Area: 18,704 sq. mi., the size of Vermont and New Hampshire combined. **Location:** In West Indies, sharing I. of Hispaniola with Haiti. **Neighbors:** Haiti on W. **Topography:** The Cordillera Central range crosses the center of the country, rising to over 10,000 ft., highest in the Caribbean. The Cibao valley to the N is major agricultural area. **Capital:** Santo Domingo. **Cities** (1991 est.): Santo Domingo 2,400,000; Santiago de Los Caballeros 490,000.

Government: Type: Representative democracy. **Head of state:** Pres. Joaquin Balaguer; in office: Aug. 16, 1986. **Local divisions:** 29 provinces and Santo Domingo. **Defense:** 5.0% of GDP. (1990).

Economy: Industries: Sugar refining, cement, pharmaceuticals. **Chief crops:** sugar, cocoa, coffee, tobacco, rice. **Minerals:** Nickel, gold, silver. **Other resources:** Timber. **Arable land:** 23%. **Livestock.** (1989): cattle: 2.0 mln.; pigs: 409,000. **Electricity prod.** (1990): 4.2 bln. kWh. **Labor force:** 35% agric.; 13% ind.; 23% serv. & govt.

Finance: Monetary unit: Peso (Mar. 1992: 12.95 = $1 US). **Gross domestic product** (1990): $7.1 bln. **Per capita GDP** (1991): $998. **Imports** (1990): $1.7 bln.; partners: U.S. 41%, Venez. 11%, Jap. 15%. **Exports** (1990): $734 mln.; partners: U.S. 59%, Neth. 18%. **Tourists** (1989): $675 mln. receipts. **National budget** (1990): $938 mln. expenditures. **International reserves less gold** (Mar. 1992): $390 mln. **Gold:** 18,000 oz t. **Consumer prices** (change in 1991): 53.9%

Transport: Motor vehicles: in use (1989): 114,000 passenger cars, 72,000 comm. vehicles. **Civil Aviation** (1988): 247 mln. passenger km.; 5 airports. **Chief ports:** Santo Domingo, San Pedro de Macoris, Puerto Plata.

Communications: Television sets: 1 per 10 persons. **Radios:** 1 per 6 persons. **Telephones:** 1 per 24 persons. **Daily newspaper circ.** (1990): 37 per 1,000 pop.

Health: Life expectancy at birth (1991): 65 male; 69 female. **Births** (per 1,000 pop. 1991): 27. **Deaths** (per 1,000 pop. 1991): 7. **Natural increase:** 2.0%. **Hospital beds:** 1 per 1,016 persons. **Physicians:** 1 per 2,147 persons. **Infant mortality** (per 1,000 live births 1991): 60.

Education (1991): **Literacy:** 83%. Years compulsory 6; attendance 70%.

Major International Organizations: UN (World Bank, IMF, GATT), OAS.

Embassy: 1715 22d St. NW 20008; 332-6280.

Carib and Arawak Indians inhabited the island of Hispaniola when Columbus landed in 1492. The city of Santo Domingo, founded 1496, is the oldest settlement by Europeans in the hemisphere and has the supposed ashes of Columbus in an elaborate tomb in its ancient cathedral.

The western third of the island was ceded to France in 1697. Santo Domingo itself was ceded to France in 1795. Haitian leader Toussaint L'Ouverture seized it, 1801. Spain returned intermittently 1803-21, as several native republics came and went. Haiti ruled again, 1822-44, and Spanish occupation occurred 1861-63.

The country was occupied by U.S. Marines from 1916 to 1924, when a constitutionally elected government was installed.

In 1930, Gen. Rafael Leonidas Trujillo Molina was elected president. Trujillo ruled brutally until his assassination in 1961. Pres. Joaquin Balaguer, appointed by Trujillo in 1960, resigned under pressure in 1962. Juan Bosch, elected president in the first free elections in 38 years, was overthrown in 1963.

On April 24, 1965, a revolt was launched by followers of Bosch and others, including a few communists. Four days later U.S. Marines intervened against the pro-Bosch forces. Token units were later sent by 5 So. American countries as a peacekeeping force.

A provisional government supervised a June 1966 election, in which Balaguer defeated Bosch by a 3-2 margin. The Inter-American Peace Force completed its departure Sept. 20, 1966.

Continued depressed world prices have affected the main export commodity, sugar. Unemployment reached 30% in 1991.

Ecuador

Republic of Ecuador

República del Ecuador

People: Population (1991 est.): 10,751,000. **Age distrib.** (%): 0–14: 41.3; 15–64: 55.0; 65+: 3.7. **Pop. density:** 98 per sq. mi. **Urban** (1990): 54% **Ethnic groups:** Indians 25%, Mestizo 55%, Spanish 10%, African 10%. **Languages:** Spanish (official), Quechuan, Jivaroan. **Religions:** Roman Catholic 95%.

Geography: Area: 109,483 sq. mi., the size of Colorado. **Location:** In NW S. America, on Pacific coast, astride Equator. **Neighbors:** Colombia to N, Peru to E and S. **Topography:** Two ranges of Andes run N and S, splitting the country into 3 zones: hot, humid lowlands on the coast; temperate highlands between the ranges, and rainy, tropical lowlands to the E. **Capital:** Quito. **Cities** (1991 est.): Guayaquil 2,000,000; Quito 1,500,000.

Government: Type: Republic. **Head of state:** Pres. Sixto Duran Bellen; in office: July 5, 1992. **Local divisions:** 21 provinces. **Defense:** 1.6% of GDP (1990).

Economy: Industries: Food processing, wood prods., textiles. **Chief crops:** Bananas (largest exporter), coffee, rice, sugar, corn. **Minerals:** Oil, copper, iron, lead, silver, sulphur. **Crude oil reserves** (1987): 1.2 bln. bbls. **Other resources:** Rubber, bark. **Arable land:** 6%. **Livestock** (1989): cattle: 3.8 mln.; pigs: 4.1 mln.; sheep: 2.1 mln. **Fish catch** (1989): 767,000 metric tons. **Electricity prod.** (1989): 5.7 bln. kWh. **Labor force:** 39% agric., 12% ind., 42% services.

Finance: Monetary unit: Sucre (June 1992: 1,404 = $1 US). **Gross domestic product** (1990): $10.9 bln. **Per capita income** (1989): $1,040. **Imports** (1991): $2.3 bln.; partners: U.S. 26%, EC 16%, Jap. 13%. **Exports** (1991): $2.8 bln.; partners: U.S. 54%. **Tourism** (1988): $173 mln. receipts. **National budget** (1990): $1.4 bln. expenditures. **International reserves less gold** (Mar. 1992): $748 mln. **Gold:** 443,000 oz t. **Consumer prices** (change in 1991): 48.7%.

Transport: Railroads (1987): **Length:** 965 km. **Motor vehicles:** in use (1987): 272,000 passenger cars, 41,000 comm. vehicles. **Civil aviation** (1989): 979 mln. passenger-km. **Chief ports:** Guayaquil, Manta, Esmeraldas, Puerto Bolivar.

Communications: Television sets: 1 per 17 persons. **Radios:** 1 per 3.4 persons. **Telephones:** 1 per 28 persons. **Daily newspaper circ.** (1989): 87 per 1,000 pop.

Health: Life expectancy at birth (1989): 64 male, 68 female. **Births** (per 1,000 pop. 1991): 30. **Deaths** (per 1,000 pop. 1991): 7. **Natural increase:** 2.3%. **Hospital beds:** 1 per 610 persons. **Physicians** (1984): 11,000. **Infant mortality** (per 1,000 live births 1991): 60.

Education (1991): Literacy: 88%. Attendance through 6th grade—76% urban, 33% rural.

Major International Organizations: UN (IMF, WHO), OAS, OPEC.

Embassy: 2535 15th St. NW 20009; 234-7200.

Spain conquered the region, which was the northern Inca empire, in 1633. Liberation forces defeated the Spanish May 24, 1822, near Quito. Ecuador became part of the Great Colombia Republic but seceded, May 13, 1830.

Ecuador had been ruled by civilian and military dictatorships since 1968. A peaceful transfer of power from the military junta to the democratic civilian government took place, 1979.

Since 1972, the economy has revolved around its petroleum exports, which have declined since 1982 causing severe economic problems. Ecuador suspended interest payments for 1987 on its estimated $8.2 billion foreign debt following a Mar. 5-6 earthquake which left 20,000 homeless, and destroyed a stretch of the country's main oil pipeline.

Ecuador and Peru have long disputed their Amazon Valley boundary.

The **Galapagos Islands,** 600 mi. to the W, are the home of huge tortoises and other unusual animals.

Egypt

Arab Republic of Egypt

Jumhūrīyah Misr al-Arabiya

People: Population (1991 est.): 54,451,000. **Age distrib** (%) 0-14: 41.8; 15-59: 52.7; 60+: 5.5. **Pop. density:** 140 per sq. mi. **Urban** (1986): 44%. **Ethnic groups:** Eastern Hamitic stock 90%, Bedouin, Nubian. **Languages:** Arabic (official), English. **Religions:** 90% Sunni Moslem.

Geography: Area: 386,650 sq. mi, about the size of Texas, Oklahoma, and Arkansas combined. **Location:** NE corner of Africa. **Neighbors:** Libya on W, Sudan on S, Israel on E. **Topography:** Almost entirely desolate and barren, with hills and mountains in E and along Nile. The Nile Valley, where most of the people live, stretches 550 miles. **Capital:** Cairo. **Cities** (1990 est.): Cairo 6,452,000; Alexandria 3,170,000; al-Jizah 2,156,000.

Government: Type: Republic. **Head of state:** Pres. Hosni Mubarak; b. 1929; in office: Oct. 14, 1981. **Head of Government:** Atef Sedki in office: Nov. 10, 1986. **Local divisions:** 26 governorates. **Defense:** 7.3% of GDP (1991).

Economy: Industries: Textiles, chemicals, petrochemicals, food processing, cement. **Chief crops:** Cotton (one of largest producers), rice, beans, fruits, grains, vegetables, sugar, corn. **Minerals:** Oil, phosphates, gypsum, iron, manganese, limestone. **Crude oil reserves** (1987): 4 bln. bbls. **Arable land:** 4%. **Livestock** (1990): cattle: 1.9 mln.; sheep: 1.3 mln. **Fish catch** (1989): 250,000 metric tons. **Electricity prod.** (1990): 42 bln. kWh. **Labor force:** 44% agric.; 22% services; 14% industry.

Finance: Monetary unit: Pound (June 1992: 3.32 = $1 US). **Gross domestic product** (1990): $37 bln. **Per capita GDP** (1990): $700. **Imports** (1990): $9.2 bln.; partners: U.S. 19%, Ger. 10%, It. 8%, France 8%. **Exports** (1990): $2.5 bln.; partners: It. 22%, Rom. 12%. **Tourists** (1989): $1.7 bln. receipts. **National budget** (1991): $16.7 bln. expenditures. **International reserves less gold** (Jan. 1992): $5.3 bln. **Gold:** 2.43 mln. oz t. **Consumer prices** (change in 1991): 19.8%.

Transport: Railroads (1989): **Length:** 3,327 mi. **Motor vehicles:** in use (1989): 826,000 passenger cars, 550,000 comm. vehicles. **Civil aviation** (1990): 5.9 bln. passenger-km.; 11 airports. **Chief ports:** Alexandria, Port Said, Suez.

Communications: Television sets: 1 per 15 persons. **Radios:** 1 per 3.9 persons. **Telephones:** 1 per 34 persons. **Daily newspaper circ.** (1989): 77 per 1,000 pop.

Health: Life expectancy at birth (1991): 60 male; 61 female. **Births** (per 1,000 pop. 1991): 33. **Deaths** (per 1,000 pop. 1991): 10. **Natural increase:** 2.3%. **Hospital beds:** 1 per 505 persons. **Physicians:** 1 per 616 persons. **Infant mortality** (per 1,000 live births 1991): 82.

Education (1990): **Literacy:** 44%. Compulsory ages 6-12.

Major International Organizations: UN (IMF, World Bank, GATT), OAU.

Embassy: 2310 Decatur Pl. NW 20008; 232-5400.

Archeological records of ancient Egyptian civilization date back to 4000 BC. A unified kingdom arose around 3200 BC, and extended its way south into Nubia and north as far as Syria. A high culture of rulers and priests was built on an economic base of serfdom, fertile soil, and annual flooding of the Nile banks.

Imperial decline facilitated conquest by Asian invaders (Hyksos, Assyrians). The last native dynasty fell in 341 BC to the Persians, who were in turn replaced by Greeks (Alexander and the Ptolemies), Romans, Byzantines, and Arabs, who introduced Islam and the Arabic language. The ancient Egyptian language is preserved only in the liturgy of the Coptic Christians.

Egypt was ruled as part of larger Islamic empires for several centuries. The Mamluks, a military caste of Caucasian origin, ruled Egypt from 1250 until defeat by the Ottoman Turks in 1517. Under Turkish sultans the khedive as hereditary viceroy had wide authority. Britain intervened in 1882 and took control of administration, though nominal allegiance to the Ottoman Empire continued until 1914.

The country was a British protectorate from 1914 to 1922. A 1936 treaty strengthened Egyptian autonomy, but Britain retained bases in Egypt and a condominium over the Sudan. Britain fought German and Italian armies from Egypt, 1940-42. In 1951 Egypt abrogated the 1936 treaty. The Sudan became independent in 1956.

The uprising of July 23, 1952, led by the Society of Free Officers, named Maj. Gen. Mohammed Naguib commander in chief and forced King Farouk to abdicate. When the republic was proclaimed June 18, 1953, Naguib became its first president and premier. Lt. Col. Gamal Abdel Nasser removed Naguib and became premier in 1954. In 1956, he was voted president. Nasser died in 1970 and was replaced by Vice Pres. Anwar Sadat.

The Aswan High Dam, completed 1971, provides irrigation for more than a million acres of land. Artesian wells, drilled in the Western Desert, reclaimed 43,000 acres, 1960-66.

When the state of Israel was proclaimed in 1948, Egypt joined other Arab nations invading Israel and was defeated.

After terrorist raids across its border, Israel invaded Egypt's Sinai Peninsula, Oct. 29, 1956. Egypt rejected a cease-fire demand by Britain and France; on Oct. 31 the 2 nations dropped bombs and on Nov. 5-6 landed forces. Egypt and Israel accepted a UN cease-fire; fighting ended Nov. 7.

A UN Emergency Force guarded the 117-mile long border between Egypt and Israel until May 19, 1967, when it was withdrawn at Nasser's demand. Egyptian troops entered the Gaza Strip and the heights of Sharm el Sheikh and 3 days later closed the Strait of Tiran to all Israeli shipping. Full-scale war broke out June 5 and before it ended under a UN cease-fire June 10, Israel had captured Gaza and the Sinai Peninsula, controlled the east bank of the Suez Canal and reopened the gulf.

Sporadic fighting with Israel continued almost daily, 1968-70. Israel and Egypt agreed, Aug. 7, 1970, to a cease-fire and peace negotiations proposed by the U.S. Negotiations failed to achieve results, but the cease-fire continued.

In a surprise attack Oct. 6, 1973, Egyptian forces crossed the Suez Canal into the Sinai. (At the same time, Syrian forces attacked Israelis on the Golan Heights.) Egypt was supplied by a USSR military airlift; the U.S. responded with an airlift to Israel. Israel counter-attacked, crossed the canal, surrounded Suez City. A UN cease-fire took effect Oct. 24.

A disengagement agreement was signed Jan. 18, 1974. Under it, Israeli forces withdrew from the canal's W bank; limited numbers of Egyptian forces occupied a strip along the E bank. A second accord was signed in 1975, with Israel yielding Sinai oil fields. Pres. Sadat's surprise visit to Jerusalem, Nov. 1977, opened the prospect of peace with Israel. On Mar. 26, 1979, Egypt and Israel signed a formal peace treaty, ending 30 years of war, and establishing diplomatic relations. Israel returned control of the Sinai to Egypt in April 1982.

Tension between Moslem fundamentalists and Christians in 1981 caused street riots and culminated in a nationwide security crackdown in Sept. Pres Sadat was assassinated on Oct. 6.

Egypt was a political and military supporter of the Allied forces in their defeat of Iraq in the Persian Gulf War, 1991.

The **Suez Canal,** 103 mi. long, links the Mediterranean and Red seas. It was built by a French corporation 1859-69, but Britain obtained controlling interest in 1875. The last British troops were removed June 13, 1956. On July 26, Egypt nationalized the canal.

El Salvador

Republic of El Salvador

República de El Salvador

People: Population (1991 est.): 5,418,000. **Age distrib.** (%): 0–14: 45.3; 15–59: 51; 60+: 4.7. **Pop. density:** 666 per sq. mi. **Urban** (1990): 45%. **Ethnic groups:** Mestizo 89%, Indian 10%. **Languages:** Spanish (official). **Religions:** Roman Catholic 75%.

Geography: Area: 8,124 sq. mi., the size of Massachusetts. **Location:** In Central America. **Neighbors:** Guatemala on W, Honduras on N. **Topography:** A hot Pacific coastal plain in the south rises to a cooler plateau and valley region, densely populated. The N is mountainous, including many volcanoes. **Capital:** San Salvador. **Cities** (1987 est.): San Salvador 1.4 mln.

Government: Type: Republic. **Head of state:** Pres., Alfredo Cristiani; b. Nov, 22, 1947; in office: June 1, 1989. **Local divisions:** 14 departments. **Defense:** 3.6% of GDP (1989).

Economy: Industries: Food and beverages, textiles, petroleum products. **Chief crops:** Coffee (21% of GNP), cotton, corn, sugar. **Other resources:** Rubber, forests. **Arable land:** 27%. **Livestock** (1990): cattle: 1.1 mln.; pigs: 440,000. **Electricity prod.** (1990): 1.7 bln. kWh. **Labor force:** 40% agric.; 16% ind.; 27% services.

Finance: Monetary unit: Colon (Mar. 1992: 8.17 = $1 US). **Gross domestic product** (1990): $5.1 bln. **Per capita GDP** (1990): $940. **Imports** (1991): $1.4 bln.; partners: U.S. 39%, CACM 22%. **Exports** (1991): $588 mln.; partners: U.S. 49%, CACM 23%. **National budget** (1990): $790 mln. expenditures. **International reserves less gold** (Mar. 1992): $390 mln. **Gold:** 469,000 oz t. **Consumer prices** (change in 1991): 16.0%.

Transport: Railroads (1989): **Length:** 374 mi. **Motor vehicles:** in use (1989): 75,000 passenger cars, 80,000 comm. vehicles. **Chief ports:** La Union, Acajutla.

Communications: Television sets: 1 per 12 persons. **Radios:** 1 per 2.6 persons. **Telephones:** 1 per 36 persons. **Daily newspaper circ.** (1990): 52 per 1,000 pop.

Health: Life expectancy at birth (1985): 62.6 male; 66.3 female. **Births** (per 1,000 pop. 1991): 34. **Deaths** (per 1,000 pop. 1991): 7. **Natural increase:** 2.7%. **Hospital beds:** 1 per 1,129 persons. **Physicians:** 1 per 2,830 persons. **Infant mortality** (per 1,000 live births 1991): 47.

Education (1991): **Literacy:** 75%. Years compulsory 6; attendance 82%.

Major International Organizations: UN (IMF, WHO, ILO), OAS, CACM.

Embassy: 2308 California St. NW 20008; 265-3480.

El Salvador became independent of Spain in 1821, and of the Central American Federation in 1839.

A fight with Honduras in 1969 over the presence of 300,000 Salvadorean workers left 2,000 dead. Clashes were renewed 1970 and 1974.

A military coup overthrew the Romero government, 1979, but the ruling military-civilian junta failed to quell the civil war which has resulted in some 50,000 deaths. Some 10,000 leftists insurgents, armed by Cuba and Nicaragua, control about 25% of the country, mostly in the east. Extreme right-wing death squads organized to eliminate suspected leftists were blamed for over 1,000 deaths in 1983. The Reagan administration has staunchly supported the government with military aid.

Voters turned out in large numbers in the May 1984 presidential election. Christian Democrat Jose Napoleon Duarte, a moderate, was victorious with 54% of the vote.

The 12-year civil war ended Jan. 16, 1992 as the government and leftist rebels signed a formal peace treaty. The civil war had taken the lives of some 75,000 people. The treaty provided for military and political reforms and is supervised by UN observers.

Nine soldiers, including 3 officers, were indicted Jan. 1990 in the Nov. 1989 slaying of 6 Jesuit priests at a university in San Salvador. Two of the officers received maximum 30-year jail sentences.

Equatorial Guinea

Republic of Equatorial Guinea

República de Guinea Ecuatorial

People: Population (1991 est.): 360,000. **Age distrib.** (%): 0–14: 38.1; 15–59: 55.2; 60+: 6.7. **Pop. density:** 33 per sq. mi. **Ethnic groups:** Fangs 80%, Bubi 15%. **Languages:** Spanish (official), Fang, Bubi. **Religions:** Mostly Roman Catholic.

Geography: Area: 10,832 sq. mi., the size of Maryland. **Location:** Bioko Is. off W. Africa coast in Gulf of Guinea, and Rio Muni, mainland enclave. **Neighbors:** Gabon on S, Cameroon on E, N. **Topography:** Bioko Is. consists of 2 volcanic mountains and a connecting valley. Rio Muni, with over 90% of the area, has a coastal plain and low hills beyond. **Capital:** Malabo. **Cities** (1989 est.): Malabo 38,000.

Government: Type: Unitary Republic. **Head of state:** Pres., Supreme Military Council Teodoro Obiang Nguema Mbasogo; b. June 5, 1942; in office: Oct. 10, 1979. **Head of government:** Prime Min. Cristino Seriche Bioko. **Local divisions:** 7 provinces.

Economy: Chief crops: Cocoa, coffee, bananas, sweet potatoes. **Other resources:** Timber. **Arable land:** 8%. **Electricity prod.** (1989): 17 mln. kWh. **Labor force:** agric. 50%; public sector 40%.

Finance: Monetary unit: Bipkwele (Mar. 1992: 278 = $1 US). **Gross domestic product** (1987): $149 mln. **Per capita GDP** (1989): $430. **Imports** (1989): $58 mln.; partners: Spain 54%, China 17%. **Exports** (1989): $36 mln.; partners: Sp. 31%, Neth. 37%.

Transport: Chief ports: Malabo, Bata.

Communications: Radios: 1 per 3.5 persons.

Health: Life expectancy at birth (1990): 48 male; 52 female. **Births** (per 1,000 pop. 1989): 38. **Deaths** (per 1,000 pop. 1989):

19. **Natural increase:** 1.9% **Hospital beds** (1982): 3,200. **Physicians:** 1 per 3,622 persons. **Infant mortality** (per 1,000 live births 1990): 127.
Education (1989): **Literacy:** 55%. About 65% attend primary school.
Major International Organizations: UN (IMF, World Bank), OAU.
Embassy: 801 2d Ave., New York, NY 10017; (212) 599-1523.

Fernando Po (now Bioko) Island was discovered by Portugal in the late 15th century and ceded to Spain in 1778. Independence came Oct. 12, 1968. Riots occurred in 1969 over disputes between the island and the more backward Rio Muni province on the mainland. Masie Nguema Biyogo, himself from the mainland, became president for life in 1972.

Masie's 11-year reign was one of the most brutal in Africa, resulting in a bankrupted nation. Most of the nation's 7,000 Europeans emigrated. In 1976, 45,000 Nigerian workers were evacuated amid charges of a reign of terror. Masie was ousted in a military coup, Aug., 1979.

The nation is heavily dependent on external aid.

Estonia

Republic of Estonia

Eesti Vabariik

People: Population (1991 est.): 1,581,000. **Pop. density:** 91 per sq. mi. **Urban** (1991): 72%. **Ethnic groups:** Estonian 65%, Russian 30%. **Languages:** Estonian (official), Russian. **Religion:** Mostly Evangelical Lutheran.
Geography: Area: 17,413 sq. mi. **Neighbors:** bounded on N., W. by the Baltic Sea, E. by Russia, S. by Latvia. **Capital:** Tallinn. **Cities** (1991 est.): Tallinn 502,000.
Government: Type: Republic. **Head of state:** Pres. Arnold Ruutel. **Head of government:** Prime Min. Vahi Tiit. **Local divisions:** 15 districts, 33 towns, 26 urban settlements.
Economy: Industries: Agricultural machinery, electric motors. **Chief crops:** grain, vegetables. **Livestock** (1989): cattle: 823,000, sheep: 138,000.
Finance: Monetary unit: Ruble (Jan. 1992: 1.76 = $1 US).
Transport: Railroads (1989): **Length:** 640 mi. **Motor vehicles:** in use (1989): 198,000 passenger cars. **Chief port:** Tallinn.
Communications: Television sets: 1 per 2.7 persons. **Radios:** 1 per 1.7 persons. **Telephones:** 1 per 5.1 persons.
Health: Life expectancy at birth (1989): 65 male, 75 female. **Hospital beds:** 1 per 83 persons. **Physicians:** 1 per 207 persons. **Infant mortality** (per 1,000 live births, 1989): 14.7.
Education: 11 year school curriculum.
Major International Organizations: UN, IMF.

Estonia was a province of imperial Russia before World War I, was independent between World Wars I and II, but was conquered by the USSR in 1940. Estonia declared itself an "occupied territory," and proclaimed itself a free nation Mar. 1990. During the Soviet coup, Estonia declared immediate full independence, Aug. 20, 1991.

Ethiopia

People's Democratic Republic of Ethiopia

Ye Etiyop'iya Hezbawi Dimokrasiyawi Republek

People: Population (1991 est.): 53,131,000. **Age distrib.** (%): 0–14: 46.5; 15–59: 47.3; 60+: 6.2. **Pop. density:** 112 per sq. mi. **Urban** (1989): 11%. **Ethnic groups:** Oromo 40%, Amhara 25%, Tigre 12%, Sidama 9%. **Languages:** Amharic (official), Tigre (Semitic languages); Galla (Hamitic). **Religions:** Orthodox Christian 40%, Moslem 40%.
Geography: Area: 471,776 sq. mi., four-fifths the size of Alaska. **Location:** In E. Africa. **Neighbors:** Sudan on W, Kenya on S. Somalia, Djibouti on E. **Topography:** A high central plateau, between 6,000 and 10,000 ft. high, rises to higher mountains near the Great Rift Valley, cutting in from the SW. The Blue Nile and other rivers cross the plateau, which descends to plains on both W and SE. **Capital:** Addis Ababa. **Cities** (1984 est.): Addis Ababa 1,412,000.
Government: Type: In transition. **Head of state:** Pres. Meles Zenawi; in office: May 28, 1991. **Head of Government:** Prime Min. Timirat Laynie; in office: June 6, 1991. **Local divisions:** 25 administrative zones, 5 autonomous regions. **Defense:** 8% of GDP (1989).
Economy: Industries: Food processing, cement, textiles. **Chief crops:** Coffee (61% export earnings), grains. **Minerals:** Platinum, gold, copper, potash. **Arable Land:** 13%. **Livestock** (1990): cattle: 30 mln.; sheep: 23 mln. **Electricity prod.** (1989): 700 mln. kWh. **Labor force:** 80% agric.
Finance: Monetary unit: Birr (Mar. 1992: 2.07 = $1 US). **Gross domestic product** (1991): $6.6 bln. **Per capita GDP** (1991): $130. **Imports** (1990): $1.0 bln.; partners: USSR 22%, U.S. 15%, Italy 10%, Jap. 6%, Ger. 10%. **Exports** (1990): $298 mln.; partners: U.S. 20%, Ger. 18%, Italy 7%. **National budget** (1989): $1.7 bln. expenditures. **International reserves less gold** (Mar. 1992): $49 mln. **Gold:** 147,000 oz t. **Consumer prices** (change in 1990): 5.2%.
Transport: Railroads (1989): **Length:** 486 mi. **Motor vehicles:** in use (1989): 43,000 passenger cars, 21,000 comm. vehicles. **Civil aviation** (1989): 1.6 bln. passenger-km; 29 airports with scheduled flights. **Chief ports:** Masewa, Aseb.
Communications: Television sets: 1 per 503 persons. **Radios:** 1 per 5.5 persons. **Telephones:** 1 per 320 persons. **Daily newspaper circ.** (1990): 1 per 1,000 pop.
Health: Life expectancy at birth (1991): 50 male; 53 female. **Births** (per 1,000 pop. 1991): 45. **Deaths** (per 1,000 pop. 1991): 15. **Natural increase:** 3.1%. **Hospital beds:** 1 per 3,873 persons. **Physicians:** 1 per 36,660 persons. **Infant mortality** (per 1,000 live births 1991): 113.
Education (1985): **Literacy:** 18%.
Major International Organizations: UN (IMF, WHO), OAU.
Embassy: 2134 Kalorama Rd. NW 20008; 234-2281.

Ethiopian culture was influenced by Egypt and Greece. The ancient monarchy was invaded by Italy in 1880, but maintained its independence until another Italian invasion in 1936. British forces freed the country in 1941.

The last emperor, Haile Selassie I, established a parliament and judiciary system in 1931, but barred all political parties.

A series of droughts since 1972 have killed hundreds of thousands. An army mutiny, strikes, and student demonstrations led to the dethronement of Selassie in 1974. The ruling junta pledged to form a one-party socialist state, and instituted a successful land reform; opposition was violently suppressed. The influence of the Coptic Church, embraced in 330 AD, was curbed, and the monarchy was abolished in 1975.

The regime, torn by bloody coups, faced uprisings by tribal and political groups in part aided by Sudan and Somalia. Ties with the U.S., once a major arms and aid source, deteriorated, while cooperation accords were signed with the USSR in 1977. In 1978, Soviet advisors and Cuban troops helped defeat Somalia forces. Ethiopia and Somalia signed a peace agreement in 1988.

A world-wide relief effort began in 1984, as an extended drought caused millions to face starvation and death. In 1988, victories by Eritrean guerrillas forced the government to curtail the work of foreign aid workers in drought-stricken regions. Foreign relief officials expressed the fear that suspension of their operations would lead to the starvation death of hundreds of thousands.

The Ethopia People's Revolutionary Democractic Front (EPRDF), an umbrella group of 6 rebel armies, launched a major push against government forces, Feb. 1991. In May, Pres Mengistu resigned and left the country. The EPRDF took posession of the capital and announced plans for a coalition government.

Fiji

Republic of Fiji

People: Population (1991 est.): 744,000. **Age distrib.** (%): 0–14: 38.2; 15–59: 56.9; 60+: 4.9. **Pop. density:** 105 per sq. mi. **Urban** (1986): 39%. **Ethnic groups:** Indian 48%, Fijian (Melanesian-Polynesian) 46%, Europeans 2%. **Languages:** English (official), Fijian, Hindi. **Religions:** Christian 52%, Hindu 38%, Moslem 8%.
Geography: Area: 7,056 sq. mi., the size of Massachusetts. **Location:** In western S. Pacific O. **Neighbors:** Nearest are Solomons on NW, Tonga on E. **Topography:** 322 islands (106 inhabited), many mountainous, with tropical forests and large fer-

tile areas. Viti Levu, the largest island, has over half the total land area. **Capital:** Suva. **Cities** (1986 est.): Suva 69,000.

Government: Type: Republic. **Head of state:** Pres. Penaia Ganilau; in office: Dec. 5, 1987. **Head of government:** Prime Min. Sitiveni Rabuka; in office: June 2, 1992. **Local divisions:** 4 divisions, 1 dependency.

Economy: Industries: Sugar refining, light industry, tourism. **Chief crops:** Sugar, bananas, ginger. **Minerals:** Gold. **Other resources:** Timber. **Arable land:** 8%. **Electricity prod.** (1990): 325 mln. kWh. **Labor force:** 44% agric.

Finance: Monetary unit: Dollar (Mar. 1992: 1.48 = $1.00 US). **Gross domestic product** (1990): $1.3 bln. **Per capita GDP** (1990): $1,840. **Imports** (1990): $738 mln.; partners: Austral. 29%, Jap. 12%, N.Z. 19%. **Exports** (1990): $435 mln.; partners: UK 32%, Aust. 25%. **Tourists** (1989): $180 mln. receipts. **National budget** (1990): $355 mln. expenditures. **International reserves less gold** (Mar. 1992): $248 mln. **Gold:** 10,000 oz t. **Consumer prices** (change in 1991): 6.5%.

Transport: Motor vehicles: in use (1990): 40,000 passenger cars, 28,000 comm. vehicles. **Civil aviation** (1990): 882 mln. passenger-km; 17 airports with scheduled flights. **Chief ports:** Suva, Lautoka.

Communications: Televisions: 1 per 73 persons. **Radios:** 1 per 1.7 persons. **Telephones:** 1 per 12 persons. **Daily newspaper circ.** (1988): 56 per 1,000 pop.

Health: Life expectancy at birth (1991): 62 male; 67 female. **Births** (per 1,000 pop. 1991): 26. **Deaths** (per 1,000 pop. 1991): 7. **Natural increase:** 1.9%. **Hospital beds:** 1 per 413 persons. **Physicians:** 1 per 2,229 persons. **Infant mortality** (per 1,000 live births 1991): 19.

Education (1990): **Literacy:** 85%. 95% attend school.

Major International Organizations: UN (IMF, WHO), Commonwealth of Nations.

Embassy: 2233 Wisconsin Ave. NW 20007; 337-8320.

A British colony since 1874, Fiji became an independent parliamentary democracy Oct. 10, 1970.

Cultural differences between the majority Indian community, descendants of contract laborers brought to the islands in the 19th century, and the less modernized native Fijians, who by law own 83% of the land in communal villages, have led to political polarization.

In 1987, a military coup ousted the government; order was restored May 21 when a compromise was reached granting Lt. Col. Sitiveni Rabuka, the coup's leader, increased power. Rabuka staged a second coup Sept. 25 and in Oct. declared Fiji a republic. A civilian government was restored to power in Dec.

Finland

Republic of Finland

Suomen Tasavalta

People: Population (1991 est.): 4,991,000. **Age distrib.** (%): 0–14: 19.3; 15–59: 62.9; 60+: 17.8. **Pop. density:** 38 per sq. mi. **Urban** (1990): 61%. **Ethnic groups:** Finns 94%, Swedes, Lapps. **Languages:** Finnish, Swedish (both official). **Religions:** Lutheran 97%.

Geography: Area: 130,119 sq. mi., slightly smaller than Montana. **Location:** In northern Europe. **Neighbors:** Norway on N, Sweden on W, Russia on E. **Topography:** South and central Finland are mostly flat areas with low hills and many lakes. The N has mountainous areas, 3,000-4,000 ft. **Capital:** Helsinki. **Cities** (1991 est.). Helsinki 490,000; Tampere 170,000; Turku 160,000.

Government: Type: Constitutional republic. Head of state: Pres. Mauno Koivisto; b. Nov. 25, 1923; in office: Jan. 27, 1982. **Head of government:** Primo Min. Esko Aho: b. 1954; in office: Apr. 26, 1991. **Local divisions:** 12 laanit (provinces). **Defense:** 1.4% of GDP (1989).

Economy: Industries: Machinery, metal, shipbuilding, textiles, clothing. **Chief crops:** Grains, potatoes, dairy prods. **Minerals:** Copper, iron, zinc. **Other resources:** Forests (40% of exports). **Arable land:** 8%. **Livestock** (1990): cattle; 1.3 mln. pigs: 1.3 mln. **Fish catch** (1989): 160,000 metric tons. **Electricity prod.** (1990): 49.3 bln. kWh. **Crude steel prod.** (1990): 2.8 mln. metric tons. **Labor force:** 9% agric.; 54% ind., comm. & finance; 25% services.

Finance: Monetary unit: Markka (June 1992: 4.33 = $1 US). **Gross domestic product** (1990): $77 bln. **Per capita GDP** (1990): $15,500. **Imports** (1991): $21.8 bln.; partners: USSR 11%, EC 45%. **Exports** (1991): $23.0 bln.; partners: USSR 15%, EC 45%. **Tourists** (1990): $1.2 bln. receipts. **National budget** (1990): $33.1 bln. expenditures. **International reserves less gold** (Mar. 1992): $6.9 bln. **Gold** 2.0 mln. oz t. **Consumer prices** (change in 1991): 4.1%.

Transport: Railroads (1990): **Length:** 3,656 mi. **Motor vehicles:** in use (1989): 1.7 mln. passenger cars, 238,000 comm. vehicles; **Civil aviation** (1990): 4.8 bln. passenger-km; 23 airports. **Chief ports:** Helsinki, Turku.

Communications: Television sets: 1 per 2.7 persons. **Radios:** 1 per person. **Telephones:** 1 per 2.1 persons. **Daily newspaper circ.** (1990): 521 per 1,000 pop.

Health: Life expectancy at birth (1991): 71 male; 80 female. **Births** (per 1,000 pop. 1991): 12. **Deaths** (per 1,000 pop. 1991): 10. **Natural increase:** .02%. **Hospital beds:** 1 per 74 persons. **Physicians:** 1 per 503 persons. **Infant mortality** (per 1,000 live births 1991): 6.

Education (1991): **Literacy:** 99%. Years compulsory 9; attendance 99%.

Major International Organizations: UN (IMF, GATT), EFTA, OECD.

Embassy: 3216 New Mexico Ave. NW 20016; 363-2430.

The early Finns probably migrated from the Ural area at about the beginning of the Christian era. Swedish settlers brought the country into Sweden, 1154 to 1809, when Finland became an autonomous grand duchy of the Russian Empire. Russian exactions created a strong national spirit; on Dec. 6, 1917, Finland declared its independence and in 1919 became a republic. On Nov. 30, 1939, the Soviet Union invaded, and the Finns were forced to cede 16,173 sq. mi., including the Karelian Isthmus, Viipuri, and an area on Lake Ladoga. After World War II, in which Finland tried to recover its lost territory, further cessions were exacted. In 1948, Finland signed a treaty of mutual assistance with the USSR. In 1956 Russia returned Porkkala, which had been ceded as a military base. In 1992 Finland's economy suffered because of changes in the former Soviet Union and Eastern Europe. In Mar., it formally applied to join the EC.

Aland, constituting an autonomous department, is a group of small islands, 590 sq. mi., in the Gulf of Bothnia, 25 mi. from Sweden, 15 mi. from Finland. Mariehamn is the principal port.

France

French Republic

République Francaise

People: Population (1991 est.): 56,595,000. **Age distrib.** (%): 0–14: 19.1; 15–60: 61.0; 60+: 19.9. **Pop. density:** 256 per sq. mi. **Urban** (1985): 77.2%. **Ethnic groups:** A mixture of various European and Mediterranean groups. **Languages:** French (official); minorities speak Breton, Alsatian German, Flemish, Italian, Basque, Catalan. **Religions:** Mostly Roman Catholic.

Geography: Area: 220,668 sq. mi., four-fifths the size of Texas. **Location:** In western Europe, between Atlantic O. and Mediterranean Sea. **Neighbors:** Spain on S, Italy, Switzerland, Germany on E, Luxembourg, Belgium on N. **Topography:** A wide plain covers more than half of the country, in N and W, drained to W by Seine, Loire, Garonne rivers. The Massif Central is a mountainous plateau in center. In E are Alps (Mt. Blanc is tallest in W. Europe, 15,771 ft.), the lower Jura range, and the forested Vosges. The Rhone flows from Lake Geneva to Mediterranean. Pyrenees are in SW, on border with Spain. **Capital:** Paris. **Cities** (1990 est.): Paris 2,152,000; Marseille 801,000; Lyon 415,000; Toulouse 359,000; Nice 342,000; Nantes 245,000; Strasbourg 252,000; Bordeaux 201,000.

Government: Type: Republic. **Head of state:** Pres. François Mitterrand; b. Oct. 26, 1916; in office: May 21, 1981. **Head of government:** Prime Min. Pierre Beregovoy; b. Dec. 23, 1925; in office: Apr. 2, 1992. **Local divisions:** 22 administrative regions containing 95 departments. **Defense:** 3.6% of GDP (1990).

Economy: Industries: Steel, chemicals, textiles, wine, perfume, aircraft, electronic equipment. **Chief crops:** Grains, corn, rice, fruits, vegetables. France is largest food producer, exporter, in W. Eur. **Minerals:** Bauxite, iron, coal. **Crude oil reserves** (1985): 221 mln. bbls. **Other resources:** Forests. **Arable land:** 32%. **Livestock** (1990): cattle: 21.1 mln.; pigs: 12.2 mln.; sheep: 10.3 mln. **Fish catch** (1988): 843,000 metric tons. **Electricity prod.** (1990): 403 bln. kWh. **Crude steel prod.**

(1990): 19.0 mln. metric tons. **Labor force:** 9% agric.; 45% ind. & comm.; 46% services.

Finance: Monetary unit: Franc (June 1992: 5.35 = $1 US). **Gross domestic product** (1990): $873 bln. **Per capita GDP** (1990): $15,500. **Imports** (1991): $231 bln.; partners: EC 51%. **Exports** (1991): $216 bln.; partners: EC 50%, U.S. 9%.**Tourists** (1989) receipts: $16.5 bln. **National budget** (1990): $224 bln. expenditures. **International reserves less gold** (Feb. 1992): $32.6 bln. **Gold:** 81.85 mln. oz t. **Consumer prices** (change in 1991): 3.1%.

Transport: Railroads (1990): **Length:** 21,388 mi. **Motor vehicles:** in use (1989): 23.0 mln. passenger cars, 5.1 mln. **Civil aviation** (1989): 49.0 bln. passenger-km; 60 airports with scheduled flights. **Chief ports:** Marseille, LeHavre, Nantes, Bordeaux, Rouen.

Communications: Television sets: 1 per 2.6 persons. **Radios:** 1 per 1.1 persons. **Telephones:** 1 per 1.7 persons. **Daily newspaper circ.** (1990): 176 per 1,000 pop.

Health: Life expectancy at birth (1991): 74 male; 82 female. **Births** (per 1,000 pop. 1991): 14. **Deaths** (per 1,000 pop. 1991): 10. **Natural increase:** .3%. **Hospital beds:** 1 per 80 persons. **Physicians:** 1 per 403 persons. **Infant mortality** (per 1,000 live births 1991): 6.

Education (1991): **Literacy:** 99%. Years compulsory 10.

Major International Organizations: UN and most of its specialized agencies, OECD, EC, NATO.

Embassy: 4101 Reservoir Rd. NW 20007; 944-6000.

Celtic Gaul was conquered by Julius Caesar 58-51 BC; Romans ruled for 500 years. Under Charlemagne, Frankish rule extended over much of Europe. After his death France emerged as one of the successor kingdoms.

The monarchy was overthrown by the French Revolution (1789-93) and succeeded by the First Republic; followed by the First Empire under Napoleon (1804-15), a monarchy (1814-48), the Second Republic (1848-52), the Second Empire (1852-70), the Third Republic (1871-1946), the Fourth Republic (1946-58), and the Fifth Republic (1958 to present).

France suffered severe losses in manpower and wealth in the first World War, 1914-18, when it was invaded by Germany. By the Treaty of Versailles, France exacted return of Alsace and Lorraine, French provinces seized by Germany in 1871. Germany invaded France again in May, 1940, and signed an armistice with a government based in Vichy. After France was liberated by the Allies Sept. 1944, Gen. Charles de Gaulle became head of the provisional government, serving until 1946.

De Gaulle again became premier in 1958, during a crisis over Algeria, and obtained voter approval for a new constitution, ushering in the Fifth Republic. Using strong executive powers, he promoted French economic and technological advances in the context of the European Economic Community, and guarded French foreign policy independence.

France had withdrawn from Indochina in 1954, and from Morocco and Tunisia in 1956. Most of its remaining African territories were freed 1958-62.

In 1966, France withdrew all its troops from the integrated military command of NATO, though 60,000 remained stationed in Germany. France continued to attend political meetings of NATO.

In May 1968 rebellious students in Paris and other centers rioted, battled police, and were joined by workers who launched nationwide strikes. The government awarded pay increases to the strikers May 26. In elections to the Assembly in June, de Gaulle's backers won a landslide victory. Nevertheless, he resigned from office in April, 1969, after losing a nationwide referendum on constitutional reform.

On May 10, 1981, France elected François Mitterrand, a Socialist candidate, president. In September, the government nationalized 5 major industries and most private banks. In 1986, France began a privatization program in which some 80 state-owned companies would be sold. Mitterrand was elected to a 2d 7-year term in 1988.

Agents of France's external security service were responsible for the July 10, 1985 sinking of the *Rainbow Warrior*, flagship of the Greenpeace environmental movement, in the port of Auckland, New Zealand.

The island of **Corsica,** in the Mediterranean W of Italy and N of Sardinia, is an official region of France comprising 2 departments. Area: 3,369 sq. mi.; pop. (1986 est.): 248,000. The capital is Ajaccio, birthplace of Napoleon.

Overseas Departments

French Guiana is on the NE coast of South America with Suriname on the W and Brazil on the E and S. Its area is 43,740 sq. mi.; pop. (1991): 101,000. Guiana sends one senator and one deputy to the French Parliament. Guiana is administered by a prefect and has a Council General of 16 elected members; capital is Cayenne.

The famous penal colony, Devil's Island, was phased out between 1938 and 1951.

Immense forests of rich timber cover 90% of the land. Placer gold mining is the most important industry. Exports are shrimp, timber, and machinery.

Guadeloupe, in the West Indies' Leeward Islands, consists of 2 large islands, Basse-Terre and Grande-Terre, separated by the Salt River, plus Marie Galante and the Saintes group to the S and, to the N, Desirade, St. Barthelemy, and over half of St. Martin (the Netherlands portion is St. Maarten). A French possession since 1635, the department is represented in the French Parliament by 2 senators and 3 deputies; administration consists of a prefect (governor) and an elected general and regional councils.

Area of the islands is 660 sq. mi.; pop. (1991 est.) 395,000, mainly descendants of slaves; capital is Basse-Terre on Basse-Terre Is. The land is fertile; sugar, rum, and bananas are exported; tourism is an important industry.

Martinique, the northernmost of the Windward Islands, in the West Indies, has been a possession since 1635, and a department since March, 1946. It is represented in the French Parliament by 2 senators and 3 deputies. The island was the birthplace of Napoleon's Empress Josephine.

It has an area of 425 sq. mi.; pop. (1991 est.) 365,000, mostly descendants of slaves. The capital is Fort-de-France (pop. 1991: 101,000). It is a popular tourist stop. The chief exports are rum, bananas, and petroleum products.

Mayotte, formerly part of Comoros, voted in 1976 to become an overseas department of France. An island NW of Madagascar, area is 144 sq. mi., pop. (1988 est.) 77,000.

Reunion is a volcanic island in the Indian O. about 420 mi. E of Madagascar, and has belonged to France since 1665. Area, 969 sq. mi.; pop. (1991 est.) 612,000, 30% of French extraction. Capital: Saint-Denis. The chief export is sugar. It elects 3 deputies, 2 senators to the French Parliament.

St. Pierre and Miquelon, formerly an Overseas Territory, made the transition to department status in 1976. It consists of 2 groups of rocky islands near the SW coast of Newfoundland, inhabited by fishermen. The exports are chiefly fish products. The St. Pierre group has an area of 10 sq. mi.; Miquelon, 83 sq. mi. Total pop. (1988 est.), 6,300. The capital is St. Pierre. A deputy and a senator are elected to the French Parliament.

Overseas Territories

French Polynesia Overseas Territory, comprises 130 islands widely scattered among 5 archipelagos in the South Pacific; administered by a governor. Territorial Assembly and a Council with headquarters at Papeete, Tahiti, one of the **Society Islands** (which include the **Windward** and **Leeward** islands). A deputy and a senator are elected to the French Parliament.

Other groups are the **Marquesas Islands,** the **Tuamotu Archipelago,** including the **Gambier Islands,** and the **Austral Islands.**

Total area of the islands administered from Tahiti is 1,544 sq. mi.; pop. (1991 est.), 195,000, more than half on Tahiti. Tahiti is picturesque and mountainous with a productive coastline bearing coconut, banana and orange trees, sugar cane and vanilla.

Tahiti was visited by Capt. James Cook in 1769 and by Capt. Bligh in the Bounty, 1788-89. Its beauty impressed Herman Melville, Paul Gauguin, and Charles Darwin.

French Southern and Antarctic Lands Overseas Territory, comprises **Adelie Land,** on Antarctica, and 4 island groups in the Indian O. Adelie, discovered 1840, has a research station, a coastline of 185 mi. and tapers 1,240 mi. inland to the South Pole. The U.S. does not recognize national claims in Antarctica. There are 2 huge glaciers, Ninnis, 22 mi. wide, 99 mi. long, and Mentz, 11 mi. wide, 140 mi. long. The Indian O. groups are:

Kerguelen Archipelago, discovered 1772, one large and 300 small islands. The chief is 87 mi. long, 74 mi. wide, and has Mt. Ross, 6,429 ft. tall. Principal research station is Port-aux-Francais. Seals often weigh 2 tons; there are blue whales, coal, peat, semi-precious stones. **Crozet Archipelago,** discovered 1772, covers 195 sq. mi. Eastern Island rises to 6,560 ft. **Saint Paul,** in southern Indian O., has warm springs with earth at places heating to 120° to 390° F. **Amsterdam** is nearby; both produce cod and rock lobster.

New Caledonia and its dependencies, an overseas territory, are a group of islands in the Pacific O. about 1,115 mi. E of Australia and approx. the same distance NW of New Zealand. Dependencies are the **Loyalty Islands,** the **Isle of Pines, Huon Islands** and the **Chesterfield Islands.**

New Caledonia, the largest, has 6,530 sq. mi. Total area of the territory is 8,548 sq. mi.; population (1991 est.) 172,000. The group was acquired by France in 1853.

The territory is administered by a governor and government council. There is a popularly elected Territorial Assembly. A deputy and a senator are elected to the French Parliament. Capital: Noumea.

Mining is the chief industry. New Caledonia is one of the world's largest nickel producers. Other minerals found are chrome, iron, cobalt, manganese, silver, gold, lead, and copper. Agricultural products include coffee, copra, cotton, manioc (cassava), corn, tobacco, bananas and pineapples.

In 1987, New Caledonian voters chose by referendum to remain within the French Republic. There were clashes between French and Melanesians (Kanaks) in 1988.

Wallis and Futuna Islands, 2 archipelagos raised to status of overseas territory July 29, 1961, are in the SW Pacific S of the Equator between Fiji and Samoa. The islands have a total area of 106 sq. mi. and population (1988 est.) of 15,400. **Alofi,** attached to Futuna, is uninhabited. Capital: Mata-Utu. Chief products are copra, yams, taro roots, bananas. A senator and a deputy are elected to the French Parliament.

Gabon

Gabonese Republic

République Gabonaise

People: Population (1991 est.): 1,079,000. **Pop. density:** 10 per sq. mi. **Urban** (1985): 40%. **Ethnic groups:** Fang 25%, Bapounon 10%, others. **Languages:** French (official), Bantu dialects. **Religions:** Tribal beliefs, Christian minority.

Geography: Area: 103,346 sq. mi., the size of Colorado. **Location:** On Atlantic coast of central Africa. **Neighbors:** Equatorial Guinea, Cameroon on N, Congo on E, S. **Topography:** Heavily forested, the country consists of coastal lowlands plateaus in N, E, and S, mountains in N, SE, and center. The Ogooue R. system covers most of Gabon. **Capital:** Libreville. **Cities** (1991 est.): Libreville 275,000.

Government: Type: Republic. **Head of state:** Pres. Omar Bongo; b. Dec. 30, 1935; in office: Dec. 2, 1967. **Head of government:** Prime Min. Casimir Oye Mba; in office: May 3, 1990. **Local divisions:** 9 provinces. **Defense:** 3.2% of GDP (1990).

Economy: Industries: Oil products. **Chief crops:** Cocoa, coffee, rice, peanuts, palm products, cassava, bananas. **Minerals:** Manganese, uranium, oil, iron, gas. **Crude oil reserves** (1985): 623 mln. bbls. **Other resources:** Timber. **Arable land:** 2%. **Electricity prod.** (1990): 980 mln. kWh. **Labor force:** 65% agric.; 30% ind. & comm.

Finance: Monetary unit: CFA franc (Mar. 1992: 278 = $1 US). **Gross domestic product** (1991) $5.3 bln. **Per capita income** (1991): $4,400. **Imports** (1989): $889 mln.; partners: Fr. 51%, U.S. 14%. **Exports** (1989): $1.8 bln.; partners: Fr. 26%, U.S. 25%. **Tourists receipts** (1989): $7 mln. **National budget** (1991): $1.8 bln. **International reserves less gold** (Jan. 1992): $432 mln. **Gold:** 13,000 oz t. **Consumer prices** (change in 1990): 8.0%.

Transport: Motor vehicles: in use (1989): 19,000 passenger cars, 15,000 comm. vehicles. **Civil aviation** (1990): 445 mln. passengers-km. **Chief ports:** Port-Gentil, Owendo, Mayumba.

Communications: Television sets: 1 per 29 persons. **Radios:** 1 per 5 persons. **Telephones:** 1 per 98 persons.

Health: Life expectancy at birth (1991): 51 male; 56 female. **Births** (per 1,000 pop. 1991): 28. **Deaths** (per 1,000 pop. 1991): 15. **Natural increase:** 1.4%. **Hospital beds** (1985): 4,617. **Physicians** (1985): 265. **Infant mortality** (per 1,000 live births 1991): 104.

Education (1991): **Literacy:** 70%. Compulsory to age 16; attendance: 100% primary, 14% secondary.

Major International Organizations: UN (World Bank), OAU, OPEC.

Embassy: 2034 20th St NW 20009; 797-1000.

France established control over the region in the second half of the 19th century. Gabon became independent Aug. 17, 1960. It is one of the most prosperous black African countries, thanks to abundant natural resources, foreign private investment, and government development programs.

The Gambia

Republic of The Gambia

People: Population (1991 est.): 874,000. **Age distrib.** (%): 0–14: 45.9; 15–59: 54.4; 60+: 3.8. **Pop. density:** 211 per sq. mi. **Urban** (1985): 21%. **Ethnic groups:** Mandinka 42%, Fula 16%, Wolof 16%, others. **Languages:** English (official), Malinke, Wolof. **Religions:** Moslem 90%.

Geography: Area: 4,127 sq. mi., smaller than Connecticut. **Location:** On Atlantic coast near western tip of Africa. **Neighbors:** Surrounded on 3 sides by Senegal. **Topography:** A narrow strip of land on each side of the lower Gambia. **Capital:** Banjul. **Cities** (1986 est.): Banjul 40,000.

Government: Type: Republic. **Head of state:** Pres. Dawda Kairaba Jawara; b. May 16, 1924; in office: Apr. 24, 1970 (prime min. from June 12, 1962). **Local divisions:** 5 divisions and Banjul.

Economy: Industries: Tourism. **Chief crops:** Peanuts (main export), rice. **Arable land:** 16%. **Fish catch** (1989): 17,000 metric tons. **Electricity prod.** (1990): 63 mln. kWh. **Labor force:** 75% agric.; 18% ind. & comm.

Finance: Monetary unit: Dalasi (Mar. 1992: 8.74 = $1.00 US). **Gross domestic product** (1990): $196 mln. **Per capita GDP** (1990): $230. **Imports** (1990): $155 mln.; partners: EC 53%. **Exports** (1990): $122 mln.; partners: EC 45%. **Tourists** (1988): $36 mln. receipts. **National budget** (1990): $95 mln. expenditures. **International reserves less gold** (Jan. 1992): $64 mln. **Consumer prices** (change in 1991): 8.6%.

Transport: Motor vehicles: in use (1989): 5,200 passenger cars, 1,000 comm. vehicles. **Chief ports:** Banjul.

Communications: Radios: 1 per 6.1 persons. **Telephones:** 1 per 114 persons.

Health: Life expectancy at birth (1991): 47 male; 51 female. **Births** (per 1,000 pop. 1991): 48. **Deaths** (per 1,000 pop. 1991): 23. **Natural increase:** 2.5%. **Hospital beds** (1980): 635. **Physicians** (1980): 65. **Infant mortality** (per 100,000 live births 1991): 138.

Education (1989): **Literacy:** 12%.

Major International Organizations: UN (GATT, IMF, WHO), OAU.

Embassy: 19 E. 42 St., New York, NY 10017.

The tribes of Gambia were at one time associated with the West African empires of Ghana, Mali, and Songhay. The area became Britain's first African possession in 1588.

Independence came Feb. 18, 1965; republic status within the Commonwealth was achieved in 1970. Gambia is one of the only functioning democracies in Africa. The country suffered from severe famine in 1977-78.

Republic of Georgia

Sakartvelos Respublica

People: Population (1989 cen.): 5,500,000. **Pop. density:** 204 per sq. mi. **Ethnic groups:** Georgian 70%, Armenian 7%, Russian 6%. **Languages:** Georgian, Russian.

Geography: Area: 26,911 sq. mi. **Neighbors:** Black Sea on W., Turkey, Armenia on S., Azerbaijan on SE. **Topography:** Separated from Russia on NE by main range of the Caucasus mts. **Capital:** Tbilisi.

Government: Type: In transition. **Head of state:** State Council, Eduard A. Shevardnadze, chmn.

Economy: Industries: Manganese mining. **Chief crops:** Citrus fruits, wheat, grapes. **Livestock** (1989): cattle: 1.5 mln., sheep: 1.9 mln.

Finance: Monetary unit: Ruble.

Health: Doctors (1989): 32,000; **Hospital beds** (1989): 60,000.

The region contained the ancient kingdoms of Colchis and Iberia. It was Christianized in the 4th century and conquered by

Arabs in the 8th century. The region expanded to include area from the Black Sea to Caspian and parts of Armenia and Persia before its disintegration under the impact of Mongol and Turkish invasions. The annexation to Russia in 1801 caused the Russian war with Persia, 1804-1813. Georgia entered the USSR in 1922 and became a constituent republic in 1936.

In 1989, strong nationalist feelings led the USSR to attempts at repression; Soviet troops attacked nationalist demonstrators in April, killing some 20 persons. Georgia declared independence Apr. 9, 1991. It became an independent state when the Soviet Union disbanded Dec. 25, 1991, although it did not join the Commonwealth of Independent States.

There was fighting during 1991 between rebel forces and loyalists of Pres. Gamsakhurdia whom the rebels accused of aspiring to establish a dictatorship. Gamsakhurdia fled the capital Jan. 6, 1992. The ruling Military Council picked former Soviet Foreign Minister Eduard A. Shevardnadze to chair a newly created State Council. An attempted coup by forces loyal to ousted Pres. Gamsakhurdia was crushed June 24.

Germany

Federal Republic of Germany

Bundesrepublik Deutschland

(Figures prior to 1990 for original 11 states)

People: Population (1991 est.): 79,548,000. **Age distrib.** (%): 0–14: 14.7; 15–59: 64.7; 60+: 20.6. **Pop. density:** 577 per sq. mi. **Urban** (1990): 86% **Ethnic groups:** German 93%. **Languages:** German. **Religions:** Protestant 44%, Roman Catholic 37%.

Geography: Area: 137,838 sq. mi. **Location:** In central Europe. **Neighbors:** Denmark on N, Netherlands, Belgium, Luxembourg, France on W, Switzerland, Austria on S, Czechoslovakia, Poland on E. **Topography:** Germany is flat in N, hilly in center and W, and mountainous in Bavaria. Chief rivers are Elbe, Weser, Ems, Rhine, and Main, all flowing toward North Sea, and Danube, flowing toward Black Sea. **Capital:** Berlin. **Cities** (1991 est.): Berlin 3.0 mln.; Hamburg 1.6 mln.; Munich 1.3 mln.; Cologne 946,000; Essen 622,000; Frankfurt 635,000; Dortmund 575,000; Dusseldorf 593,000; Stuttgart 561,000; Leipzig 549,000; Dresden 521,000.

Government: Type: Federal republic. **Head of state:** Pres. Richard von Weizsacker; b. Apr. 15, 1920; in office: May 23, 1984. **Head of government:** Chan. Helmut Kohl; b. Apr. 3, 1930; in office: Oct. 1, 1982. **Local divisions:** 16 laender (states) with substantial powers. **Defense:** 3.2% of GNP (1989).

Economy: Industries: Steel, ships, vechicles, machinery, coal, chemicals. **Chief crops:** Grains, potatoes, sugar beets. **Minerals:** Coal, potash, lignite, iron, uranium. **Arable land:** 35%. **Livestock** (1990): cattle: 15.3 mln.; pigs: 10.0 mln.; sheep: 1.2 mln. **Fish catch** (1989): 408,000 metric tons. **Electricity prod.** (1989): 555 bln. kWh. **Crude steel prod.** (1990): 40.0 mln. metric tons. **Labor force:** 5% agric.; 40% ind. & comm.; 54% services.

Finance: Monetary unit: Mark (July 1992: 1.59 = $1 US). **Gross domestic product** (1991): $1,157 bln. **Per capita GDP** (1991): $14,600. **Imports** (1991): $383 bln.; partners: EC 52%; other European 16%. **Exports** (1991): $391 bln.; partners: EC 55%; other European 19%. **Tourists** (1989): receipts $8.6 bln. **National budget** (1990): $245 bln. expenditures. **International reserves less gold** (Mar. 1992): $61 bln. **Gold:** 95.18 mln. oz t. **Consumer prices** (change in 1991): 3.5%.

Transport: Railway traffic (1989): 66 bln. passenger-km. **Motor vehicles:** in use (1988): 28.8 mln. passenger cars, 1.3 mln. comm. **Civil aviation** (1988): 34.0 bln. passenger-km; 27 airports with scheduled flights. **Chief ports:** Hamburg, Bremen, Lubeck.

Communications: Television sets: 1 per 2.6 persons. **Radios:** 1 per 2.3 persons. **Telephones:** 1 per 1.5 persons. **Daily newspaper circ.** (1987): 417 per 1,000 pop.

Health: Life expectancy at birth (1991): 73 male; 79 female. **Births** (per 1,000 pop. 1991): 11. **Deaths** (per 1,000 pop.): 11. **Hospital beds:** 1 per 91 persons. **Physicians:** 1 per 346 persons. **Infant mortality** (per 1,000 live births 1991): 7.

Education (1991): **Literacy:** 99%. **Years compulsory:** 10; attendance 100%.

Major International Organizations: UN and all of its specialized agencies, EC, OECD, NATO.

Embassy: 4645 Reservoir Rd. NW 20007; 298-4000.

Germany, prior to World War II, was a central European nation composed of numerous states which had a common language and traditions and which had been united in one country since 1871; since World War II until 1990, had been split in 2 parts.

History and government. Germanic tribes were defeated by Julius Caesar, 55 and 53 BC, but Roman expansion N of the Rhine was stopped in 9 AD. Charlemagne, ruler of the Franks, consolidated Saxon, Bavarian, Rhenish, Frankish, and other lands; after him the eastern part became the German Empire. The Thirty Years' War, 1618-1648, split Germany into small principalities and kingdoms. After Napoleon, Austria contended with Prussia for dominance, but lost the Seven Weeks' War to Prussia, 1866. Otto von Bismarck, Prussian chancellor, formed the North German Confederation, 1867.

In 1870 Bismarck maneuvered Napoleon III into declaring war. After the quick defeat of France, Bismarck formed the **German Empire** and on Jan. 18, 1871, in Versailles, proclaimed King Wilhelm I of Prussia German emperor (Deutscher kaiser).

The German Empire reached its peak before World War I in 1914, with 208,780 sq. mi., plus a colonial empire. After that war Germany ceded Alsace-Lorraine to France; West Prussia and Posen (Poznan) province to Poland; part of Schleswig to Denmark; lost all of its colonies and the ports of Memel and Danzig.

Republic of Germany, 1919-1933, adopted the Weimar constitution; met reparation payments and elected Friedrich Ebert and Gen. Paul von Hindenburg presidents.

Third Reich, 1933-1945, Adolf Hitler led the National Socialist German Workers' (Nazi) party after World War I. In 1923 he attempted to unseat the Bavarian government and was imprisoned. Pres. von Hindenburg named Hitler chancellor Jan. 30, 1933; on Aug. 3, 1934, the day after Hindenburg's death, the cabinet joined the offices of president and chancellor and made Hitler fuehrer (leader). Hitler abolished freedom of speech and assembly, and began a long series of persecutions climaxed by the murder of millions of Jews and opponents.

Hitler repudiated the Versailles treaty and reparations agreements. He remilitarized the Rhineland 1936 and annexed Austria (Anschluss, 1938). At Munich he made an agreement with Neville Chamberlain, British prime minister, which permitted Hitler to annex part of Czechoslovakia. He signed a non-aggression treaty with the USSR, 1939. He declared war on Poland Sept. 1, 1939, precipitating World War II.

With total defeat near, Hitler committed suicide in Berlin Apr. 1945. The victorious Allies voided all acts and annexations of Hitler's Reich.

Postwar changes. The zones of occupation administered by the Allied Powers and later relinquished gave the USSR Saxony, Saxony-Anhalt, Thuringia, and Mecklenburg, and the former Prussian provinces of Saxony and Brandenburg.

The territory E of the Oder-Neisse line within 1937 boundaries comprising the provinces of Silesia, Pomerania, and the southern part of East Prussia, totaling about 41,220 sq. mi., was taken by Poland. Northern East Prussia was taken by the USSR.

The Western Allies ended the state of war with Germany in 1951. The USSR did so in 1955.

There was also created the area of Greater Berlin, within but not part of the Soviet zone, administered by the 4 occupying powers under the Allied Command. In 1948 the USSR withdrew, established its single command in East Berlin, and cut off supplies. The Allies utilized a gigantic airlift to bring food to West Berlin, 1948-1949. In Aug. 1961 the East Germans built a wall dividing Berlin, after over 3 million E. Germans had emigrated.

On Nov. 9, 1989 the E. German government announced the decision to open the border with the West signaling the end of the infamous Berlin Wall.

A New Era: As communism was being rejected in E. Germany, talks began concerning German reunification. At a meeting in Ottawa, Feb. 1990, the foreign ministers of the World War II "Big Four" Allied nations—U.S., USSR, UK, and France—as well as the foreign ministers of E. Germany and W. Germany reached agreement on a format for high-level talks on German reunification.

In May, NATO ministers adopted a package of proposals on reunification including the inclusion of the united Germany as a full member of NATO, and the barring of the new Germany from having its own nuclear, chemical, or biological weapons. In July, the USSR agreed to conditions that would allow Germany to become a member of NATO.

The 2 nations agreed to monetary unification under the W. German mark beginning in July. The merger of the 2 Germanys took place on Oct. 3, 1990, and the first all-German elections since 1932 were held Dec. 2, 1990.

(East Germany)

The German Democratic Republic was proclaimed in the Soviet sector of Berlin Oct. 7, 1949. It was proclaimed fully sovereign in 1954, but Soviet troops remained on grounds of security and the 4-power Potsdam agreement.

Coincident with the entrance of W. Germany into the European Defense community in 1952, the East German government decreed a prohibited zone 3 miles deep along its 600-mile border with W. Germany and cut Berlin's telephone system in two. Berlin was further divided by erection of a fortified wall in 1961, but the exodus of refugees to the West continued, though on a smaller scale.

E. Germany suffered severe economic problems until the mid-1960s. A "new economic system" was introduced, easing the former central planning controls and allowing factories to make profits provided they were reinvested in operations or redistributed to workers as bonuses. By the early 1970s, the economy was highly industrialized. In May 1972 the few remaining private firms were ordered sold to the government. The nation was credited with the highest standard of living among Warsaw Pact countries. But growth slowed in the late 1970s, due to shortages of natural resources and labor, and a huge debt to lenders in the West. Comparison with the lifestyle in the West caused many of the young to leave the country.

The government firmly resisted following the USSR's policy of *glasnost*, but by Oct. 1989, was faced with nationwide demonstrations demanding reform. Pres. Erich Honecker, in office since 1976, was forced to resign, Oct. 18. On Nov. 4, the border with Czechoslovakia was opened and permission granted for refugees to travel on to the West, On Nov. 9, the decision was made to open the border with the West, signaling the end of the "Berlin Wall," which separated the 2 Germanys and was the supreme emblem of the cold war.

On Aug. 23, 1990, the E. German Parliament agreed to formal unification with W. Germany; this took place on Oct. 3.

(West Germany)

The Federal Republic of Germany was proclaimed May 23, 1949, in Bonn, after a constitution had been drawn up by a consultative assembly formed by representatives of the 11 laender (states) in the French, British, and American zones. Later reorganized into 9 units, the laender numbered 10 with the addition of the Saar, 1957. Berlin also was granted land (state) status, but the 1945 occupation agreements placed restrictions on it.

The occupying powers, the U.S., Britain, and France, restored the civil status, Sept. 21, 1949. The U. S. resumed diplomatic relations July 2, 1951. The powers lifted controls and the republic became fully independent May 5, 1955.

Dr. Konrad Adenauer, Christian Democrat, was made chancellor Sept. 15, 1949, re-elected 1953, 1957, 1961. Willy Brandt, heading a coalition of Social Democrats and Free Democrats, became chancellor Oct. 21, 1969.

In 1970 Brandt signed friendship treaties with the USSR and Poland. In 1971, the U.S., Britain, France, and the USSR signed an agreement on Western access to West Berlin. In 1972 the Bundestag approved the USSR and Polish treaties and East and West Germany signed their first formal treaty, implementing the agreement easing access to West Berlin. In 1973 a West Germany-Czechoslovakia pact normalized relations and nullified the 1938 "Munich Agreement."

In May 1974 Brandt resigned, saying he took full responsibility for "negligence" for allowing an East German spy to become a member of his staff.

West Germany experienced economic growth since the 1950s. The country led Europe in provisions for worker participation in the management of industry.

The NATO decision to deploy medium-range nuclear missiles in Western Europe sparked a demonstration by some 400,000 protesters in 1983. In 1989, Chanceller Kohl's call for early negotiations with the Soviets on reducing short-range missiles caused a rift with the NATO allies, especially the U.S. and Great Britain.

In 1989, the changes in the E. German government and the opening of the Berlin Wall sparked talk of reunification of the 2 Germanys. In 1990, under the leadership of Chanceller Kohl, W. Germany moved rapidly to reunite with E. Germany.

Helgoland, an island of 130 acres in the North Sea, was taken from Denmark by a British Naval Force in 1807 and later ceded to Germany to become a part of Schleswig-Holstein province in return for rights in East Africa. The heavily fortified island was surrendered to UK, May 23, 1945, demilitarized in 1947, and returned to W. Germany, Mar 1, 1952. It is a free port.

Ghana

Republic of Ghana

People: Population (1991 est.): 15,616,000. **Age distrib.** (%): 0–14: 46.6; 15-59: 48.9; 60+: 4.5. **Pop. density:** 169 per sq. mi. **Urban** (1984): 31%. **Ethnic groups:** Akan 44%, Moshi-Dagomba 16%, Ewe 13%, Ga 8%, others. **Languages:** English (official), Akan, Mossi, Ewe, Ga-Adangme. **Religions:** Christian 24%, traditional beliefs 38%, Moslem 30%.

Geography: Area: 92,098 sq. mi., slightly smaller than Oregon. **Location:** On southern coast of W. Africa. **Neighbors:** Ivory Coast on W, Burkina Faso on N, Togo on E. **Topography:** Most of Ghana consists of low fertile plains and scrubland, cut by rivers and by the artificial Lake Volta. **Capital:** Accra. **Cities** (1988 est.): Accra 949,000.

Government: Type: Military. **Head of government:** Pres. Jerry Rawlings; b. 1947; in office: Dec. 31, 1981. **Local divisions:** 10 regions.

Economy: Industries: Aluminum, light industry. **Chief crops:** Cocoa, coffee. **Minerals:** Gold, manganese, industrial diamonds, bauxite. **Crude oil reserves:** (1980): 7 mln. bbls. **Other resources:** Timber, rubber. **Arable land:** 12%. **Livestock** (1989): Cattle: 1.1 mln.; sheep: 2.2 mln. **Fish catch** (1990): 360,000 metric tons. **Electricity prod.** (1990): 4.1 bln. kWh. **Labor force:** 55% agric.; 19% ind.

Finance: Monetary unit: Cedi (Mar. 1992: 378 = $1.00 US). **Gross national product** (1990): $5.8 bln. **Per capita GNP** (1990): $380. **Imports** (1990): $1.2 bln.; partners: UK 18%, Ger. 12%, Nigeria 12%. **Exports** (1990): $826 mln.; partners: UK 16%, U.S. 23%, Neth. 9%, Ger. 9%. **International reserves less gold** (Mar. 1992): 444 mln. **Gold:** 256,000 oz t. **Consumer prices** (change in 1990): 36.0%.

Transport: Railroads (1989): **Length:** 592 mi. **Motor vehicles:** in use (1986): 26,000 passenger cars, 28,000 comm. vehicles. **Civil aviation** (1990): 407 mln. passenger-km; 3 airports with scheduled flights. **Chief ports:** Tema, Takoradi.

Communications: Television sets: 1 per 83 persons. **Radios:** 1 per 4.7 persons. **Telephones:** 1 per 191 persons.

Health: Life expectancy at birth (1991): 53 male; 56 female. **Births** (per 1,000 pop. 1991): 46. **Deaths** (per 1,000 pop. 1991): 13. **Natural increase:** 3.3%. **Physicians:** 1 per 22,127 persons. **Infant mortality** (per 1,000 live births 1991): 86.

Education (1991): **Literacy:** 60%.

Major International Organizations: UN and all of its specialized agencies, OAU.

Embassy: 3512 International Dr., 20008; 686-4500.

Named for an African empire along the Niger River, 400-1240 AD, Ghana was ruled by Britain for 113 years as the Gold Coast. The UN in 1956 approved merger with the British Togoland trust territory. Independence came March 6, 1957. Republic status within the Commonwealth was attained in 1960.

Pres. Kwame Nkrumah built hospitals and schools, promoted development projects like the Volta R. hydroelectric and aluminum plants, but ran the country into debt, jailed opponents, and was accused of corruption. A 1964 referendum gave Nkrumah dictatorial powers and set up a one-party socialist state.

Nkrumah was overthrown in 1966 by a police-army coup, which expelled Chinese and East German teachers and technicians. Elections were held in 1969, but 4 further coups occurred in 1972, 1978, 1979, and 1981. The 1979 and 1981 coups were led by Flight Lieut. Jerry Rawlings.

Greece

Hellenic Republic

Elliniki Dimokratia

People: Population (1991 est.): 10,042,000. **Age distrib.** (%): 0–14: 20.5; 15-59: 61.1; 60+: 20.4. **Pop. density:** 196 per sq. mi. **Urban** (1990): 63.0%. **Ethnic groups:** Greeks 98.5%. **Languages:** Greek. **Religions:** Greek Orthodox 97% (official).

Geography: Area: 51,146 sq. mi., the size of Alabama. **Location:** Occupies southern end of Balkan Peninsula in SE Europe. **Neighbors:** Albania, Yugoslavia, Bulgaria on N, Turkey on E. **Topography:** About 75% of Greece is non-arable, with mountains in all areas. Pindus Mts. run through the country N to S. The heavily indented coastline is 9,385 mi. long. Of over 2,000 islands, only 169 are inhabited, among them Crete, Rhodes, Milos, Kerkira (Corfu), Chios, Lesbos, Samos, Euboea, Delos, Mykonos. **Capital:** Athens. **Cities** (1981 est.): Athens (met.) 3,016,457; Thessaloniki (met.) 800,000; Patras 120,000.

Government: Type: Presidential parliamentary republic. **Head of state:** Pres. Konstantinos Karamanlis; in office: May, 1990. **Head of government:** Prime Min. Konstantinos Mitsotakis; b. Oct. 18, 1918, in office: Apr. 11, 1990. **Local divisions:** 51 prefectures. **Defense:** 5.5% of GDP (1990).

Economy: Industries: Textiles, chemicals, metals, wine, food processng, cement. **Chief crops:** Grains, corn, rice, cotton, tobacco, olives, citrus fruits, raisins, figs. **Minerals:** Bauxite, lignite, oil, manganese. **Crude oil reserves** (1985): 35 mln. bbls. **Arable land:** 23%. **Livestock** (1989): sheep: 11.0 mln.; goats: 5.6 mln. **Fish catch** (1989): 126,000 metric tons. **Electricity prod.** (1990): 36.4 bln. kWh. **Labor force:** 28% agric.; 29% ind., 42% service.

Finance: Monetary unit: Drachma (June 1992: 192.00 = $1 US). **Gross domestic product** (1990): $76 bln. **Per capita GDP** (1990): $7,650. **Imports** (1990): $19.7 bln.; partners: Ger. 19%, It. 12%, Fr. 7%. **Exports** (1990): $8.1 bln.; partners: Ger. 20%, It. 13%, U.S. 8%. **Tourists** (1989): $1.6 bln. receipts. **National budget** (1990): $34.1 bln. expenditures. **International reserves less gold** (Mar. 1992): $4.1 bln. **Gold:** 3.4 mln. oz t. **Consumer prices** (change in 1991): 19.5%.

Transport: Railroads (1989): **Length:** 1,540 mi. **Motor vehicles:** in use (1990): 1.6 mln. passenger cars, 781,000 comm. vehicles. **Civil aviation** (1989): 8.0 bln. passenger-km; 30 airports with scheduled flights. **Chief ports:** Piraeus, Thessaloniki, Patrai.

Communications: Television sets: 1 per 5.7 persons. **Radios:** 1 per 2.4 persons. **Telephones:** 1 per 2.4 persons. **Daily newspaper circ.** (1986): 88 per 1,000 pop.

Health: Life expectancy at birth (1991): 75 male; 80 female. **Births** (per 1,000 pop. 1991): 11. **Deaths** (per 1,000 pop. 1991): 9. **Natural increase:** .2%. **Hospital beds:** 1 per 193 persons. **Physicians:** 1 per 327 persons. **Infant mortality** (per 1,000 live birth 1991): 10.

Education (1991): **Literacy:** men 96%, women 89%. **Years compulsory:** 9.

Major International Organizations: UN (GATT, IMF, WHO, ILO), EC, NATO, OECD.

Embassy: 2221 Massachusetts Ave. NW 20008; 667-3168.

The achievements of ancient Greece in art, architecture, science, mathematics, philosophy, drama, literature, and democracy became legacies for succeeding ages. Greece reached the height of its glory and power, particularly in the Athenian city-state, in the 5th century BC.

Greece fell under Roman rule in the 2d and 1st centuries BC. In the 4th century AD it became part of the Byzantine Empire and, after the fall of Constantinople to the Turks in 1453, part of the Ottoman Empire.

Greece won its war of independence from Turkey 1821-1829, and became a kingdom. A republic was established 1924; the monarchy was restored, 1935, and George II, King of the Hellenes, resumed the throne. In Oct., 1940, Greece rejected an ultimatum from Italy. Nazi support resulted in its defeat and occupation by Germans, Italians, and Bulgarians. By the end of 1944 the invaders withdrew. Communist resistance forces were defeated by Royalist and British troops. A plebiscite recalled King George II. He died Apr. 1, 1947, was succeeded by his brother, Paul I.

Communists waged guerrilla war 1947-49 against the government but were defeated with the aid of the U.S.

A period of reconstruction and rapid development followed, mainly with conservative governments under Premier Constantine Karamanlis. The Center Union led by George Papandreou won elections in 1963 and 1964. King Constantine, who acceded in 1964, forced Papandreou to resign. A period of political maneuvers ended in the military takeover of April 21, 1967, by Col. George Papadopoulos. King Constantine tried to reverse the consolidation of the harsh dictatorship Dec. 13, 1967, but failed and fled to Italy. Papadopoulos was ousted Nov. 25, 1973.

Greek army officers serving in the National Guard of Cyprus staged a coup on the island July 15, 1974. Turkey invaded Cyprus a week later, precipitating the collapse of the Greek junta, which was implicated in the Cyprus coup.

The 1981 victory of the Panhellenic Socialist Movement (Pasok) of Andreas Papandreou has brought about substantial changes in the internal and external policies that Greece has pursued for the past 5 decades. Greece has been victimized in the 1980s by incidents of international terrorism.

A scandal centered on George Kostokas, a banker and publisher, led to the arrest or investigation of about a dozen leading Socialists, implicated Papandreou, and led to the defeat of the Socialists at the polls in 1989.

Grenada

People: Population (1991 est.): 84,000. **Pop. density:** 654 per sq. mi. **Ethnic groups:** Mostly African descent. **Languages:** English (official), French, patois. **Religions:** Roman Catholic 64%, Anglican 22%.

Geography: Area: 133 sq. mi., twice the size of Washington, D.C. **Location:** 90 mi. N. of Venezuela. **Topography:** Main island is mountainous; country includes Carriacon and Petit Martinique islands. **Capital:** St. George's. **Cities** (1990 est.): St. George's 30,000.

Government: Type: Independent state. **Head of state:** Queen Elizabeth II, represented by Gov.-Gen. Paul Scoon, b. July 4, 1935; in office: Sept. 30, 1978. **Head of government:** Prime Minister: Nicholas Braithwaite; in office: Mar. 13, 1990. **Local divisions:** 6 parishes and one dependency.

Economy: Industries: Rum. **Chief crops:** Nutmegs, bananas, cocoa, mace. **Arable land:** 41%. **Electricity prod.** (1990): 26 mln. kWh. **Labor force:** 33% agric.; 31% services.

Finance: Monetary unit: East Caribbean dollar (Apr. 1992: 2.70 = $1 US). **Gross national product** (1989): $179 mln. **Per capita GNP** (1989): $1,900. **Imports** (1989): $200 mln.; partners: UK 19%, Trin./Tob. 12%, U.S. 24%. **Exports** (1988): $32 mln.; partners: UK 23%, CARICOM countries 38%. **Tourists** (1990): $38 mln. receipts. **National budget** (1989): $92.1 mln. expenditures. **International reserves less gold** (Jan. 1992): $17 mln.

Transport: Motor vehicles: in use (1981): 4,700 passenger cars, 1,000 comm. vehicles. **Chief ports:** Saint George's.

Communications: Radios: 1 per 2.4 persons. **Telephones:** 1 per 9 persons.

Health: Life expectancy at birth (1991): 69 male; 74 female. **Births** (per 1,000 pop. 1991): 35. **Deaths** (per 1,000 pop. 1991): 7. **Natural increase:** 2.8%. **Infant mortality** (per 1,000 live births 1991): 30.

Education (1991): **Literacy:** 95%; **Years compulsory:** 6.

Major International Organizations: UN (IMF, WHO), OAS.

Embassy: 1701 New Hampshire Ave. NW 20009; 265-2561.

Columbus sighted the island 1498. First European settlers were French, 1650. The island was held alternately by France and England until final British occupation, 1784. Grenada became fully independent Feb. 7, 1974 during a general strike. It is the smallest independent nation in the Western Hemisphere.

On Oct. 14, 1983, a military coup ousted Prime Minister Maurice Bishop, who was put under house arrest, later freed by supporters, rearrested, and, finally, on Oct. 19, executed. U.S. forces, with a token force from 6 area nations, invaded Grenada, Oct. 25. Resistance from the Grenadian army and Cuban advisors was quickly overcome as most of the population welcomed the invading forces as liberators. U.S. troops left Grenada in June 1985.

Guatemala

Republic of Guatemala

República de Guatemala

People: Population (1991 est.): 9,266,000. **Age distrib.** (%): 0–14: 45.4; 15–59: 49.5; 60+: 5.1. **Pop. density:** 220 per sq. mi. **Urban** (1986): 33%. **Ethnic groups:** Maya 55%, Mestizos 44%. **Languages:** Spanish (official), Mayan languages. **Religions:** Mostly Roman Catholics.

Geography: Area: 42,042 sq. mi., the size of Tennessee. **Location:** In Central America. **Neighbors:** Mexico N, W; El Salvador on S, Honduras, Belize on E. **Topography:** The central highland and mountain areas are bordered by the narrow Pacific coast and the lowlands and fertile river valleys on the Caribbean. There are numerous volcanoes in S, more than half a dozen over 11,000 ft. **Capital:** Guatemala City. **Cities** (1991 est.): Guatemala City 1,095,000.

Government: Type: Republic. **Head of state:** Pres. Jorge Serrano Elias; in office: Jan. 14, 1991. **Local divisions:** Guatemala City and 22 departments. **Defense:** 1.0% of GDP (1990).

Economy: Industries: Prepared foods, tires, textiles. **Chief crops:** Coffee (one third of exports), sugar, bananas, cotton, corn. **Minerals:** Oil, nickel. **Crude oil reserves** (1985): 500 mln. bbls. **Other resources:** Rare woods, fish, chicle. **Arable land:** 16%. **Electricity prod.** (1990): 2.5 bln. kWh. **Labor force:** 60% agric.; 21% ind. & comm., 12% services.

Finance: Monetary unit: Quetzal (Apr. 1992: 5.08 = $1 US). **Gross domestic product** (1990): $11.1 bln. **Per capita GDP** (1990): $1,180. **Imports** (1990): $1.7 bln.; partners: U.S. 37%, CACM 8%. **Exports** (1990): $1.2 bln.; partners: U.S. 28%, CACM 20%. **Tourism** (1989): $108 mln. **National budget** (1989): $1.3 bln. expenditures. **International reserves less gold** (Mar. 1992): $845 mln. **Gold:** 208,000 oz t. **Consumer prices** (change in 1990): 41.2%.

Transport: Motor vehicles: in use (1989): 125,000 passenger cars, 100,000 comm. vehicles. **Civil aviation** (1989): 164 mln. passenger-km; 2 airports with scheduled flights. **Chief ports:** Puerto Barrios, San Jose.

Communications: Television sets: 1 per 18 persons. **Radios:** 1 per 22 persons. **Telephones:** 1 per 63 persons. **Daily newspaper circ.** (1989): 22 per 1,000 pop.

Health: Life expectancy at birth (1989): 59 male; 63 female. **Births** (per 1,000 pop. 1991): 36. **Deaths** (per 1,000 pop. 1991): 9. **Natural increase:** 2.7% **Health: Physicians:** 1 per 2,356 persons. **Infant mortality** (per 1,000 live births 1991): 58.

Education (1991): **Literacy:** 55%. **Years compulsory:** 6; **Attendance:** 35%.

Major International Organizations: UN (IMF, World Bank), OAS.

Embassy: 2220 R St. NW 20008; 745-4952.

The old Mayan Indian empire flourished in what is today Guatemala for over 1,000 years before the Spanish.

Guatemala was a Spanish colony 1524-1821; briefly a part of Mexico and then of the U.S. of Central America, the republic was established in 1839.

Since 1945 when a liberal government was elected to replace the long-term dictatorship of Jorge Ubico, the country has seen a swing toward socialism, an armed revolt, renewed attempts at social reform, a military coup, and, in 1986, civilian rule. The Guerrilla Army of the Poor, an insurgent group founded 1975, led a military offensive by attacking army posts and succeeded in incorporating segments of the large Indian population in its struggle against the government.

Dissident army officers seized power, Mar. 23, 1982, denouncing the Mar. 7 presidential election as fraudulent and pledging to restore "authentic democracy" to the nation. Political violence has caused some 200,000 Guatemalans to seek refuge in Mexico. A second military coup occurred Oct. 8, 1983. The nation returned to civilian rule in 1986.

Guinea

Republic of Guinea

République de Guinée

People: Population (1991 est.): 7,455,000. **Pop. density:** 78 per sq. mi. **Urban** (1989): 26%. **Ethnic groups:** Foulah 35%, Malinké 30%, Soussous 20%, 15 other tribes. **Languages:** French (official), Peul, Mande. **Religions:** Moslem 85%, Christian 10%.

Geography: Area: 94,964 sq. mi., slightly smaller than Oregon. **Location:** On Atlantic coast of W. Africa. **Neighbors:** Guinea-Bissau, Senegal, Mali on N, Côte d'Ivoire on E, Liberia on S. **Topography:** A narrow coastal belt leads to the mountainous middle region, the source of the Gambia, Senegal, and Niger rivers. Upper Guinea, farther inland, is a cooler upland. The SE is forested. **Capital:** Conakry. **Cities** (1989 est.): Conakry 705,000; Labe 273,000; N'Zerekore 250,000; Kankan 278,000.

Government: Type: Republic. **Head of state:** Pres. Brig. Gen. Lansana Conte; b. 1944; in office: Apr. 5, 1984. **Local divisions:** 29 administrative regions. **Defense:** 1.2% of GDP (1988).

Economy: Chief crops: Bananas, pineapples, rice, corn, palm nuts, coffee, honey. **Minerals:** Bauxite, iron, diamonds. **Arable land:** 6%. **Electricity prod.** (1990) 300 mln. kWh. **Labor force:** 82% agric.; 9% ind. & comm.

Finance: Monetary unit: Franc (Jan. 1992: 621 = $1 US). **Gross domestic product** (1989): $2.7 bln. **Per capita GDP** (1989): $380. **Imports** (1988): $509 mln.; partners: Fr. 31%, U.S. 10%, It. 6%. **Exports** (1988): $553 mln.; partners: U.S. 24%, Fr. 10%. **National budget** (1988): 417 mln.

Transport: Motor vehicles: in use (1989): 13,000 passenger cars, 13,000 comm. vehicles. **Chief ports:** Conakry.

Communications: Radios: 1 per 34 persons.

Health: Life expectancy at birth (1991): 41 male; 45 female. **Births** (per 1,000 pop. 1991): 48. **Deaths** (per 1,000 pop. 1991): 22. **Natural increase:** 2.5%. **Physicians:** 1 per 9,732 persons. **Infant mortality** (per 1,000 live births 1991): 144.

Education (1989): **Literacy:** 35% (in French). Years compulsory: 8; attendance: 36% primary, 15% secondary.

Major International Organizations: UN and most specialized agencies, OAU.

Embassy: 2112 Leroy Pl. NW 20008; 483-9420.

Part of the ancient West African empires, Guinea fell under French control 1849-98. Under Sekou Toure, it opted for full independence in 1958, and France withdrew all aid.

Toure turned to communist nations for support, and set up a militant one-party state.

Thousands of opponents were jailed in the 1970s, in the aftermath of an unsuccessful Portuguese invasion. Many were tortured and killed.

The military took control of the government in a bloodless coup after the March 1984 death of Toure. A new constitution was approved in 1991, which promised full democracy by 1996.

Guinea-Bissau

Republic of Guinea-Bissau

República da Guiné-Bissau

People: Population (1991 est.): 1,023,000. **Pop. density:** 73 per sq. mi. **Ethnic groups:** Balanta 27%, Fula 23%, Manjaca 11%, Mandinka 12%. **Languages:** Portuguese (official), Criould, tribal languages. **Religion:** Traditional 65%, Moslem 30%, Christian 4%.

Geography: Area: 13,948 sq. mi. about the size of Connecticut and New Hampshire combined. **Location:** On Atlantic coast of W. Africa. **Neighbors:** Senegal on N, Guinea on E, S. **Topography:** A swampy coastal plain covers most of the country; to the east is a low savanna region. **Capital:** Bissau. **Cities** (1979): Bissau 109,500.

Government: Type: Republic. **Head of government:** Gen. Joao Bernardo Vieira; b. 1939; in office: Nov. 14,1980. **Local divisions:** 9 regions. **Defense:** 3.3% of GDP (1987).

Economy: Chief crops: Peanuts, cotton, rice. **Minerals:** Bauxite. **Arable land:** 10%. **Electricity prod.** (1990): 28 mln. kWh. **Labor force:** 90% agric.

Finance: Monetary unit: Peso (Jan. 1992: 650 = $1 US). **Gross domestic product** (1989): $154 mln. **Per capita GDP** (1991): $160. **Imports** (1989): $69 mln.; partners: Port. 20%, It. 27%. **Exports** (1989): $14 mln.; partners: Port. 35%. **National Budget** (1989): $30 mln. expenditures.

Communications: Radios: 1 per 27 persons. **Daily newspaper circ.** (1988): 7 per 1,000 pop.

Health: Life expectancy at birth (1991): 45 male; 48 female. **Births** (per 1,000 pop. 1991): 42. **Deaths** (per 1,000 pop. 1991): 18. **Natural increase:** 2.4%. **Infant mortality** (per 1,000 live births 1991): 125.

Education (1991): Literacy 36%. **Years compulsory:** 4.

Major International Organizations: UN, OAU.

Embassy: 211 E 43d St., New York, NY 10017; (212) 611-3977.

Portuguese mariners explored the area in the mid-15th century; the slave trade flourished in the 17th and 18th centuries, and colonization began in the 19th.

Beginning in the 1960s, an independence movement waged a guerrilla war and formed a government in the interior that achieved international support. Full independence came Sept. 10, 1974, after the Portuguese regime was overthrown.

The November 1980 coup gave Joao Bernardo Vieira absolute power. Vieira has promised political liberalization.

Guyana

Co-operative Republic of Guyana

People: Population (1991 est.): 748,000. **Age distrib.** (%): 0–14: 37.5; 5–59: 56.5; 60+: 6.0. **Pop. density:** 9 per sq. mi. **Urban** (1988): 39%. **Ethnic groups:** East Indians 51%, African 30%; mixed 14%. **Languages:** English (official), Amerindian dialects. **Religions:** Christian 46%, Hindu 37%; Moslem 9%.

Geography: Area: 83,000 sq. mi., the size of Idaho. **Location:** On N coast of S. America. **Neighbors:** Venezuela on W, Brazil on S, Suriname on E. **Topography:** Dense tropical forests cover much of the land, although a flat coastal area up to 40 mi. wide, where 90% of the population lives, provides rich alluvial soil for agriculture. A grassy savanna divides the 2 zones. **Capital:** Georgetown. **Cities** (1985 est.): Georgetown 170,000.

Government: Type: Republic within the Commonwealth of Nations. **Head of state:** President Hugh Desmond Hoyte; b. Mar. 9, 1929; in office: Aug. 6, 1985. **Head of Government:** Prime Min. Hamilton Green; in office: Aug. 6, 1985. **Local divisions:** 10 regions. **Defense:** 6% of GDP (1989).

Economy: Industries: Mining, textiles. **Chief crops:** Sugar, rice, citrus and other fruits. **Minerals:** Bauxite, diamonds. **Other resources:** Timber, shrimp. **Arable land:** 2%. **Electricity prod.** (1990): 635 bln. kWh. **Labor force:** 33% agric.; 45% ind. & comm.; 22% services.

Finance: Monetary unit: Dollar (Mar. 1992: 126 = $1 US). **Gross domestic product** (1989): $248 mln. **Per capita GDP** (1987): $380. **Imports** (1989): $257 mln.; partners: U.S. 33%, CARICOM 10%. **Exports** (1989): $224 mln.; partners: UK 31%, U.S. 23%. **National budget** (1989): $129 mln. **International reserves less gold** (Feb. 1992): $12.1 mln. **Consumer prices** (change in 1989): 35%.

Transport: Motor vehicles: in use (1989): 22,000 passenger cars, 9,000 comm. vehicles. **Chief ports:** Georgetown.

Communications: Radios: 1 per 2.5 persons. **Telephones:** 1 per 25 persons. **Daily newspaper circ.** (1989): 77 per 1,000 pop.

Health: Life expectancy at birth (1991): 61 male; 68 female. **Births** (per 1,000 pop. 1991): 23. **Deaths** (per 1,000 pop. 1991): 7. **Natural increase:** 1.6% **Hospital beds:** 1 per 341 persons. **Physicians:** 1 per 5,307 persons. **Infant mortality** (per 1,000 live births 1991): 51.

Education (1991): **Literacy:** 95%. **Years compulsory:** ages 5-14.

Major International Organizations: UN (GATT, ILO, IMF, World Bank), Commonwealth of Nations, OAS.

Embassy: 2490 Tracy Pl. NW 20008; 276-6900.

Guyana became a Dutch possession in the 17th century, but sovereignty passed to Britain in 1815. Indentured servants from India soon outnumbered African slaves. Ethnic tension has affected political life.

Guyana became independent May 26, 1966. A Venezuelan claim to the western half of Guyana was suspended in 1970 but renewed in 1982. The Suriname border is also disputed. The government has nationalized most of the economy which has remained severely depressed.

The Port Kaituma ambush of U.S. Rep. Leo J. Ryan and others investigating mistreatment of American followers of the Rev. Jim Jones' People's Temple cult, triggered a mass suicide-execution of 911 cultists in the Guyana jungle, Nov. 18, 1978.

Haiti

Republic of Haiti

Républiqe d'Haiti

People: Population (1991 est.): 6,286,000. **Age distrib.** (%): 4–14: 39.2; 15–59: 52.5; 60+: 8.3. **Pop. density:** 594 per sq. mi. **Urban** (1986): 29%. **Ethnic groups:** African descent 95%. **Languages:** French, Creole (both official). **Religions:** Roman Catholic 80%, Protestant 10%; Voodoo widely practiced.

Geography: Area: 10,579 sq. mi., the size of Maryland. **Location:** In West Indies, occupies western third of I. of Hispaniola. **Neighbors:** Dominican Republic on E, Cuba on W. **Topography:** About two-thirds of Haiti is mountainous. Much of the rest is semiarid. Coastal areas are warm and moist. **Capital:** Port-au-Prince. **Cities** (1989 est.): Port-au-Prince 514,000.

Government: Type: Military. **Head of state:** Pres. Prime Min. Marc Bazin; in office, June 19, 1992. **Head of government:** Prime Min. Jean-Jacques Honorat; in office: Oct. 11, 1991. **Local divisions:** 9 departments. **Defense:** 1.5% of GDP (1990).

Economy: Industries: Sugar refining, textiles. **Chief crops:** Coffee, sugar, bananas, cocoa, tobacco, rice. **Minerals:** Bauxite. **Other resources:** Timber. **Arable land:** 20%. **Livestock** (1989): cattle: 1.5 mln.; goats: 1.2 mln. **Electricity prod.** (1990): 264 mln. kWh. **Labor force:** 66% agric.; 9% ind. & comm.; 25% services.

Finance: Monetary unit: Gourde (Apr. 1992: 5.00 = $1 US). **Gross domestic product** (1990): $2.7 bln. **Per capita GDP** (1991): $440. **Imports** (1990): $344 mln.; partners: U.S. 64%. **Exports** (1990): $169 mln.; partners: U.S. 84%. **Tourists** (1989): receipts $66 mln. **National budget** (1990): $416 mln. expenditures. **International reserves less gold** (Mar. 1992): $17.3 mln. **Gold:** 18,000 oz t. **Consumer prices** (change in 1991): 15.4%.

Transport: Motor vehicles: in use (1989): 32,000 passenger cars, 21,000 comm. vehicles. **Chief ports:** Port-au-Prince, Les Cayes.

Communications: Television sets: 1 per 234 persons. **Radios:** 1 per 41 persons. **Telephones in use:** 1 per 114 persons. **Daily newspaper circ.** (1990): 8 per 1,000 pop.

Health: Life expectancy at birth (1991): 52 male; 55 female. **Births** (per 1,000 pop. 1991): 43. **Deaths** (per 1,000 pop. 1991): 15. **Natural increase:** 2.8%. **Hospital beds:** 1 per 1,258 persons. **Physicians:** 1 per 6,039 persons. **Infant mortality rate** (per 1,000 live births, 1991): 106.

Education (1991): **Literacy:** 53%. **Years compulsory:** 6; attendance 20%.

Major International Organizations: UN and some of its specialized agencies, OAS.

Embassy: 2311 Massachusetts Ave. NW 20008; 332-4090.

Haiti, visited by Columbus, 1492, and a French colony from 1677, attained its independence, 1804, following the rebellion led by former slave Toussaint L'Ouverture. Following a period of political violence, the U.S. occupied the country 1915-34.

Dr. Francois Duvalier was voted president in 1957; in 1964 he was named president for life. Upon his death in 1971, he was succeeded by his son, Jean-Claude. Drought in 1975-77 brought famine, and Hurricane Allen in 1980 destroyed most of the rice, bean, and coffee crops.

Following several weeks of unrest, President Jean Claude Duvalier fled Haiti aboard a U.S. Air Force jet Feb. 7, 1986, ending the 28-year dictatorship by the Duvalier family. A military-civilian council headed by Gen. Henri Namphy assumed control. In 1987, voters approved a new constitution.

The Jan. 17, 1988 elections led to Leslie Manigat being named president; opposition leaders charged widespread fraud. Gen. Namphy seized control, June 20, and named himself president of a military government. Namphy was ousted by a military coup in Sept. By mid-1990, there had been 5 governments since Duvalier fled. Father Jean-Bertrand Aristide was elected President Dec. 1990.

A coup led by leaders of the Tonton Macoutes, the private militia of the Duvalier family, was crushed by loyalist army forces, Jan. 1991. The attempted coup sparked riots which left some 70 dead. In Sept. 1991, Aristide was arrested by the military and expelled from the country.

Some 35,000 Haitian refugees were intercepted by the U.S. Coast Guard as they tried to enter the U.S., 1991-92. Most were returned to Haiti despite protests by U.S. human rights and legal organizations.

Honduras

Republic of Honduras

República de Honduras

People: Population (1991 est.): 4,949,000. **Age distrib.** (%): 0–14: 44.6; 15–59: 50.5; 60+: 4.9. **Pop. density:** 114 per sq. mi. **Urban** (1990): 40.0%. **Ethnic groups:** Mestizo 90%, Indian 7%. **Languages:** Spanish (official). **Religions:** Roman Catholic 95%.

Geography: Area: 43,277 sq. mi., slightly larger than Tennessee. **Location:** In Central America. **Neighbors:** Guatemala on W, El Salvador, Nicaragua on S. **Topography:** The Caribbean coast is 500 mi. long. Pacific coast, on Gulf of Fonseca, is 40 mi. long. Honduras is mountainous, with wide fertile valleys and rich forests. **Capital:** Tegucigalpa. **Cities** (1989 est.) Tegucigalpa 550,000; San Pedro Sula 399,000.

Government: Type: Democratic constitutional republic. **Head of State:** Pres. Rafael Leonardo Callejas; in office: Jan. 27, 1990. **Local divisions:** 18 departments. **Defense:** 1.9% of GDP (1990).

Economy: Industries: Textiles, wood prods. **Chief crops:** Bananas (chief export), coffee, corn, beans. **Minerals:** Gold, silver, copper, lead, zinc, iron, antimony, coal. **Other resources:** Timber. **Arable land:** 16%. **Livestock** (1989): cattle: 2.8 mln. **Electricity prod.** (1990): 2.0 bln. kWh. **Labor force:** 62% agric.; 20% services; 9% manuf.

Finance: Monetary unit: Lempira (Apr. 1992): 5.40 = $1 US). **Gross domestic product** (1990): $4.9 bln. **Per capita GDP** (1989): $960. **Imports** (1989): $981 mln.; partners: U.S. 39%, Jap. 8%. **Exports** (1989): $940 mln.; partners: U.S. 54%, Europe 34%. **Tourists** (1989): $28 mln. receipts. **International reserves less gold** (Mar. 1992): $180 mln. **Gold:** 21,000 oz t. **Consumer prices** (change in 1991): 35.0%.

Transport: Motor vehicles: in use (1989) 77,000 passenger cars, 24,000 comm. vehicles. **Civil aviation** (1988): 446 mln. passenger-km; 9 airports with scheduled flights. **Chief ports:** Puerto Cortes, La Ceiba.

Communications: Television sets: 1 per 25 persons. **Radios:** 1 per 2.4 persons. **Telephones:** 1 per 58 persons. **Daily newspaper circ.** (1989): 51 per 1,000 pop.

Health: Life expectancy at birth (1991): 64 male; 68 female. **Births** (per 1,000 pop. 1991): 38. **Deaths** (per 1,000 pop. 1991): 7. **Natural increase:** 3.0%. **Hospital beds:** 1 per 821 persons. **Physicians:** 1 per 1,586 persons. **Infant mortality** (per 1,000 live births 1991): 56.

Education (1991): **Literacy:** 73%. **Years compulsory:** 6; attendance 70%.

Major International Organizations: UN, (IMF, WHO, ILO), OAS.

Embassy: 4301 Connecticut Ave. NW 20008; 966-7700.

Mayan civilization flourished in Honduras in the 1st millenium AD. Columbus arrived in 1502. Honduras became independent after freeing itself from Spain, 1821 and from the Fed. of Central America, 1838.

Gen. Oswaldo Lopez Arellano, president for most of the period 1963-75 by virtue of one election and 2 coups, was ousted by the army in 1975 over charges of pervasive bribery by United Brands Co. of the U.S.

The government has resumed land distribution, raised minimum wages, and started a literacy campaign. An elected civilian government took power in 1982.

Some 3,200 U.S. troops were sent to Honduras after the Honduran border was violated by Nicaraguan forces, Mar. 1988.

Honduras is one of the poorest countries in the Western Hemisphere.

Hungary

Republic of Hungary

Magyar Köztársaság

People: Population (1991 est.). 10,588,000. **Age distrib.** (%): 0–14: 20.8; 15–59: 60.5; 60+: 18.7. **Pop. density:** 294 per sq. mi. **Urban** (1990): 62%. **Ethnic groups:** Magyar 92%, German 2.5%, Gypsy 3%. **Languages:** Hungarian (Magyar). **Religions:** Roman Catholic 67%, Protestant 25%.

Geography: Area: 35,919 sq. mi., slightly smaller than Indiana. **Location:** In East Central Europe. **Neighbors:** Czechoslovakia on N, Austria on W, Croatia on S, Romania, Slovenia, Moldova on E. **Topography:** The Danube R. forms the Czech border in the NW, then swings S to bisect the country. The eastern half of Hungary is mainly a great fertile plain, the Alfold; the W and N are hilly. **Capital:** Budapest. **Cities** (1990 est.): Budapest 2,016,000; Miskolc 196,000; Debrecen 212,000.

Government: Type: Republic. **Head of state:** Pres. Arpad Goncz; in office: May 2, 1990. **Head of government:** Prime Min. Jozsef Antall; in office: May 3, 1990. **Local divisions:** 20 regions. **Defense:** 5.2% of GNP (1987).

Economy: Industries: Iron and steel, machinery, pharmaceuticals, vehicles, communications equip., milling, distilling. **Chief crops:** Grains, vegetables, fruits, grapes. **Minerals:** Bauxite, coal, natural gas. **Arable land:** 57%. **Livestock** (1989): cattle: 1.6 mln.; pigs: 7.6 mln.; sheep: 2.0 mln. **Electricity prod.** (1990): 30.4 bln. kWh. **Crude steel prod.** (1990): 2.8 mln. metric tons. **Labor force:** 19% agric.; 48% ind. & comm.; 27% services.

Finance: Monetary unit: Forint (Mar. 1992: 80 = $1 US). **Gross national product** (1990): $60.9 bln. **Per capita GNP** (1990): $5,800. **Imports** (1990): $8.6 bln.; partners: USSR 25%, W. Ger. 14%, E. Ger. 7%, Czech. 5%. **Exports** (1990): $9.5 bln.; partners: USSR 27%, E. Ger. 6%, W. Ger. 9%, Czech. 6%. **National budget** (1989): $18.3 bln. **Tourists** (1990): $1 bln. receipts. **Consumer prices** (change in 1990): 28.3%.

Transport: Railroads (1989): **Length:** 8,382 mi. **Motor vehicles:** in use (1989): 1.8 mln. passenger cars, 205,000 comm. vehicles. **Civil aviation** (1990): 1.5 bln. passenger-km; 1 airport with scheduled flights.

Communications: Television sets: 1 per 2.5 persons. **Radios:** 1 per 1.7 persons. **Telephones:** 1 per 6.3 persons. **Daily newspaper circ.** (1990): 237 per 1,000 pop.

Health: Life expectancy at birth (1991): 68 male; 76 female. **Births** (per 1,000 pop. 1991): 12. **Deaths** (per 1,000 pop. 1991): 14. **Natural increase:** −2%. **Hospital beds:** 1 per 104 persons. **Physicians:** 1 per 324 persons. **Infant mortality** (per 1,000 live births 1991): 14.

Education (1989): **Literacy:** 98%. **Years compulsory:** to age 16; attendance 96%.

Major International Organizations: UN (IMF, World Bank, GATT).

Embassy: 3910 Shoemaker St. NW 20008; 362-6737.

Earliest settlers, chiefly Slav and Germanic, were overrun by Magyars from the east. Stephen I (997-1038) was made king by Pope Sylvester II in 1000 AD. The country suffered repeated Turkish invasions in the 15th-17th centuries. After the defeats of the Turks, 1686-1697, Austria dominated, but Hungary obtained concessions until it regained internal independence in 1867, with the emperor of Austria as king of Hungary in a dual monarchy with a single diplomatic service. Defeated with the Central Powers in 1918, Hungary lost Transylvania to Romania, Croatia and Bacska to Yugoslavia, Slovakia and Carpatho-Ruthenia to Czechoslovakia, all of which had large Hungarian minorities. A republic under Michael Karolyi and a bolshevist revolt under Bela Kun were followed by a vote for a monarchy in 1920 with Admiral Nicholas Horthy as regent.

Hungary joined Germany in World War II, and was allowed to annex most of its lost territories. Russian troops captured the country, 1944-1945. By terms of an armistice with the Allied powers Hungary agreed to give up territory acquired by the 1938 dismemberment of Czechoslovakia and to return to its borders of 1937.

A republic was declared Feb. 1, 1946; Zoltan Tildy was elected president. In 1947 the communists forced Tildy out. Premier Imre Nagy, in office since mid-1953, was ousted for his moderate policy of favoring agriculture and consumer production, April 18, 1955.

In 1956, popular demands for the ousting of Erno Gero, Communist Party secretary, and for formation of a government by Nagy, resulted in the latter's appointment Oct. 23; demonstrations against communist rule developed into open revolt. On Nov. 4 Soviet forces launched a massive attack against Budapest with 200,000 troops, 2,500 tanks and armored cars.

About 200,000 persons fled the country. In the spring of 1963 the regime freed many anti-communists and captives from the revolution in a sweeping amnesty. Nagy was executed by the Russians. In Mar. 1987, some 2,000 marched in Budapest calling for democracy.

Hungarian troops participated in the 1968 Warsaw Pact invasion of Czechoslovakia. Major economic reforms were launched early in 1968, switching from a central planning system to one in which market forces and profit control much of production.

In 1989 parliament passed legislation legalizing freedom of assembly and association as Hungary shifted away from communism toward democracy. In Oct., the communist party was formally dissolved. The last Soviet troops left Hungary June 19, 1991.

Iceland

Republic of Iceland

Lýoveldio Island

People: Population (1991 est.): 259,000. **Age distrib. (%):** 0–14: 25.5; 15–59: 60.1; 60+: 14.4. **Pop. density:** 6 per sq. mi. **Urban** (1991): 90% **Ethnic groups:** Homogeneous, descendants of Norwegians, Celts. **Language:** Icelandic (Islenska). **Religion:** Evangelical Lutheran 95%.

Geography: Area: 39,769 sq. mi., the size of Virginia. **Location:** At N end of Atlantic O. **Neighbors:** Nearest is Greenland. **Topography:** Iceland is of recent volcanic origin. Three-quarters of the surface is wasteland: glaciers, lakes, a lava desert. There are geysers and hot springs, and the climate is moderated by the Gulf Stream. **Capital:** Reykjavik. **Cities** (1991 est.): Reykjavik 97,000.

Government: Type: Constitutional republic. **Head of state:** Pres. Vigdis Finnbogadottir; b. Apr. 15, 1930; in office: Aug. 1, 1980. **Head of government:** Prime Min. David Oddsson; in office: Apr. 30, 1991. **Local divisions:** 23 counties.

Economy: Industries: Fish products (some 80% of exports), aluminum. **Chief crops:** Potatoes, turnips, hay. **Arable land:** 0.5%. **Livestock** (1990): sheep: 549,000. **Fish catch** (1990): 1.5 mln. metric tons. **Electricity prod.** (1990): 5.1 bln. kWh. **Labor force:** 11% agric.; 55% comm. & services, 14% fisheries.

Finance: Monetary unit: Kronur (Mar. 1992: 59.19 = $1 US). **Gross domestic product** (1990): $4.2 bln. **Per capita GDP** (1990): $16,300. **Imports** (1990): $1.7 bln.; partners: EC 50%. **Exports** (1990): $1.6 bln.; partners: EC 67%. **Tourists** (1990): receipts: $125 mln. **National budget** (1987): $1.2 bln. expenditures. **International reserves less gold** (Mar. 1992): $507 mln. **Gold:** 49,000 oz t. **Consumer prices** (change in 1991): 6.8%.

Transport: Motor vehicles: in use (1990): 121,000 passenger cars, 14,000 comm. vehicles. **Civil aviation** (1989): 1.4 bln. passenger-km; 30 airports with scheduled flights. **Chief ports:** Reykjavik.

Communications: Television sets: 1 per 3.3 persons. **Radios:** 1 per 1.6 persons. **Telephones:** 1 per 2.2 persons. **Daily newspaper circ.** (1990): 518 per 1,000 pop.

Health: Life expectancy at birth (1991): 75 male; 81 female. **Births** (per 1,000 pop. 1991): 17. **Deaths** (per 1,000 pop. 1991): 7. **Natural increase:** 1.0%. **Hospital beds:** 1 per 73 persons. **Physicians:** 1 per 373 persons. **Infant mortality** per (1,000 live births 1991): 7.

Education (1991): **Literacy:** 99%. **Years compulsory:** 8; **Attendance:** 99%.

Major International Organizations: UN (GATT), NATO, OECD.

Embassy: 2022 Connecticut Ave. NW 20008; 265-6653.

Iceland was an independent republic from 930 to 1262, when it joined with Norway. Its language has maintained its purity for 1,000 years. Danish rule lasted from 1380-1918; the last ties with the Danish crown were severed in 1941. The Althing, or assembly, is the world's oldest surviving parliament.

India

Republic of India

Bharat

People: Population (1991 est.): 866,000,000. **Age distrib.** (%): 0–14: 36.8; 15–59: 56.4; 60+: 5.8. **Pop. density:** 683 per sq. mi. **Urban** (1991): 28%. **Ethnic groups:** Indo-Aryan groups 72%, Dravidians 25%, Mongoloids 3%. **Languages:** 16 languages, including Hindi (official) and English (associate official). **Religions:** Hindu 83%, Moslem 11%, Christian 3%, Sikh 2%.

Geography: Area: 1,266,595 sq. mi., one third the size of the U.S. **Location:** Occupies most of the Indian subcontinent in S. Asia. **Neighbors:** Pakistan on W, China, Nepal, Bhutan on N, Myanmar, Bangladesh on E. **Topography:** The Himalaya Mts., highest in world, stretch across India's northern borders. Below, the Ganges Plain is wide, fertile, and among the most densely populated regions of the world. The area below includes the Deccan Peninsula. Close to one quarter the area is forested. The climate varies from tropical heat in S to near-Arctic cold in N. Rajasthan Desert is in NW; NE Assam Hills get 400 in. of rain a year. **Capital:** New Delhi. **Cities** (1991 est.): Calcutta 10.8 mln.; Bombay 12.5 mln.; New Delhi 8.3 mln.; Madras 5.3 mln.; Bangalore 4.1 mln.; Hyderabad 4.2 mln.

Government: Type: Federal republic. **Head of state:** Pres. Ramaswamy Venkataraman; b. Dec. 4, 1910; in office: July 25, 1987. **Head of government:** Prime Min. P. V. Narasimha Rao; b. June 28, 1921; in office: June 21, 1991. **Local divisions:** 25 states, 7 union territories. **Defense:** 3.5% of GNP (1991).

Economy: Industries: Textiles, steel, processed foods, cement, machinery, chemicals, fertilizers, consumer appliances, autos. **Chief crops:** Rice, grains, coffee, sugar cane, spices, tea, cashews, cotton, copra, coir, juta, linseed. **Minerals:** Chromium, coal, iron, manganese, mica salt, bauxite, gypsum, oil. **Crude oil reserves** (1987): 4.3 bln. bbls. **Other resources:** Rubber, timber. **Arable land:** 57%. **Livestock** (1989): cattle: 195 mln.; sheep: 55 mln. **Fish catch** (1990): 3.6 mln. metric tons. **Electricity prod.** (1990): 245 bln. kWh. **Crude steel prod.** (1990): 14.8 mln. metric tons. **Labor force:** 70% agric.; 19% ind. & comm.

Finance: Monetary unit: Rupee (June 1992: 28.57 = $1 US). **Gross national product** (1989): $287 bln. **Per capita GNP** (1989): $350. **Imports** (1990): $23.6 bln.; partners: Jap. 12%, U.S. 12%, Ger. 10%, UK 8%. **Exports** (1990): $17.9 bln.; partners: U.S. 18%, USSR 15%, UK 6%, Jap. 9%. **Tourists** (1991): receipts: $1.4 bln. **National budget** (1988): $56 bln. expenditures. **International reserves less gold** (Mar. 1992): $5.7 bln. **Gold:** 11.8 mln. oz. t. **Consumer prices** (change in 1991): 13.9%.

Transport: Railroads (1990): **Length:** 38,509 mi. **Motor vehicles:** in use (1989): 2.2 mln. passenger cars, 1.4 mln. comm. vehicles. **Civil aviation:** (1990): 16.5 bln. passenger-km; 98 airports with scheduled flights. **Chief ports:** Calcutta, Bombay, Madras, Cochin, Vishakhapatnam.

Communications: Television sets: 1 per 44 persons. **Radios:** 1 per 15 persons. **Telephones:** 1 per 200 persons. **Daily newspaper circ.** (1988): 21 per. 1,000 pop.

Health: Life expectancy at birth (1991): 57 male; 58 female. **Births** (per 1,000 pop. 1991): 29. **Deaths** (per 1,000 pop. 1991): 10. **Natural increase:** 1.9%. **Hospital beds:** 1 per 1,130 persons. **Physicians:** 1 per 2,471 persons. **Infant mortality** (per 1,000 live births 1991): 87.

Education (1991): **Literacy:** 48%. **Years Compulsory:** to age 14.

Major International Organizations: UN (IMF, World Bank).

Embassy: 2107 Massachusetts Ave. NW 20008; 939-7000.

India has one of the oldest civilizations in the world. Excavations trace the Indus Valley civilization back for at least 5,000 years. Paintings in the mountain caves of Ajanta, richly carved temples, the Taj Mahal in Agra, and the Kutab Minar in Delhi are among relics of the past.

Aryan tribes, speaking Sanskrit, invaded from the NW around 1500 BC, and merged with the earlier inhabitants to create classical Indian civilization.

Asoka ruled most of the Indian subcontinent in the 3d century BC, and established Buddhism. But Hinduism revived and eventually predominated. During the Gupta kingdom, 4th-6th century AD, science, literature, and the arts enjoyed a "golden age."

Arab invaders established a Moslem foothold in the W in the 8th century, and Turkish Moslems gained control of North India by 1200. The Mogul emperors ruled 1526-1857.

Vasco de Gama established Portuguese trading posts 1498-1503. The Dutch followed. The British East India Co. sent Capt. William Hawkins, 1609, to get concessions from the Mogul emperor for spices and textiles. Operating as the East India Co. the British gained control of most of India. The British parliament assumed political direction; under Lord Bentinck, 1828-35, rule by rajahs was curbed. After the Sepoy troops mutinied, 1857-58, the British supported the native rulers.

Nationalism grew rapidly after World War I. The Indian National Congress and the Moslem League demanded constitutional reform. A leader emerged in Mohandas K. Gandhi (called Mahatma, or Great Soul), born Oct. 2, 1869, assassinated Jan. 30, 1948. He advocated self-rule, non-violence, removal of untouchability. In 1930 he launched "civil disobedience," including boycott of British goods and rejection of taxes without representation.

In 1935 Britain gave India a constitution providing a bicameral federal congress. Mohammed Ali Jinnah, head of the Moslem League, sought creation of a Moslem nation, Pakistan.

The British government partitioned British India into the dominions of India and Pakistan. India became a self-governing member of the Commonwealth and a member of the UN. It became a democratic republic, Jan. 26, 1950.

More than 12 million Hindu & Moslem refugees crossed the India-Pakistan borders in a mass transferral of some of the 2 peoples during 1947; about 200,000 were killed in communal fighting.

After Pakistan troops began attacks on Bengali separatists in East Pakistan, Mar. 25, 1971, some 10 million refugees fled into India. India and Pakistan went to war Dec. 3, 1971, on both the East and West fronts. Pakistan troops in the east surrendered Dec. 16; Pakistan agreed to a cease-fire in the west Dec. 17. In Aug. 1973 India released 93,000 Pakistanis held prisoner since 1971. The 2 countries resumed full relations in 1976.

In 2 days of carnage, the Bengali population of the village of Mandai, Tripura State, 700 people, were massacred in a raid by indigenous tribal residents of the area, June 8-9, 1980. A similar year-long campaign against Bengali immigrants had been going on in Assam State.

Mrs. Indira Gandhi, was named prime minister Jan. 19, 1966. Threatened with adverse court rulings in a voting law case, and opposition protest campaign and strikes, Gandhi invoked emergency provisions of the constitution June, 1975. Thousands of opponents were arrested and press censorship imposed. Measures to control prices, protect small farmers, and improve productivity were adopted.

The emergency, especially enforcement of coercive birth control measures in some areas, and the prominent extra-constitutional role of Indira Gandhi's son Sanjay, was widely resented. Opposition parties, united in the Janata coalition, scored massive victories in federal and state parliamentary elections in 1977, turning Gandhi's New Congress Party from power.

Gandhi became prime minister for the second time, Jan. 14, 1980. She was assassinated by 2 of her Sikh bodyguards Oct. 31, 1984. Widespread rioting followed. Thousands of Sikhs were killed and some 50,000 left homeless. The assassination was in response to the government supression of a Sikh uprising in Punjab in June 1984 which included an assault on the Golden Temple, the holiest Sikh shrine. Rajiv, her son, replaced her as prime minister. He was swept from office in 1989 amid charges of incompetence and corruption. He was assassinated May 21, 1991 during an election campaign to regain the prime ministership.

Sikhs ignited several violent clashes during the 1980s. The government's May 1987 decision to bring the state of Punjab under the rule of the central government led to violence. Many died during a government siege of the Golden Temple at Amritsar, May 1988.

As India's population passed 800 mln., government officials expressed alarm that the failure to control the birth rate would lead to disaster.

Sikkim, bordered by Tibet, Bhutan and Nepal, formerly British protected, became a protectorate of India in 1950. Area, 2,740 sq. mi.; pop. 1991 cen. 405,000; capital, Gangtok. In Sept. 1974 India's parliament voted to make Sikkim an associate Indian state, absorbing it into India.

Kashmir, a predominantly Moslem region in the NW, has been in dispute between India and Pakistan since 1947. A cease-fire was negotiated by the UN Jan. 1, 1949; it gave Pakistan control of one-third of the area, in the west and northwest, and India the remaining two-thirds, the Indian state of Jammu and Kashmir, which enjoys internal autonomy.

In 1990 and 1991, there were repeated clashes between Indian army troops and pro-independence demonstrators triggered by India's decision to impose central government rule. The clashes strained relations between India and Pakistan which India charged was aiding the Moslem separatists.

France, 1952-54, peacefully yielded to India its 5 colonies, former French India, comprising Pondicherry, Karikal, Mahe, Yanaon (which became Pondicherry Union Territory, area 185 sq. mi., pop. 1991, 807,000) and Chandernagor (which was incorporated into the state of West Bengal).

Indonesia

Republic of Indonesia

Republik Indonesia

People: Population (1991 est.): 193,000,000. **Age distrib.** (%): 0–14: 39.2; 15–59: 56.5; 60+: 5.3. **Pop. density:** 262 per sq. mi. **Urban** (1990): 30%. **Ethnic groups:** Malay, Chinese, Irianese. **Languages:** Bahasa Indonesian (Malay) (official), Javanese, other Austronesian languages. **Religions:** Moslem 88%.

Geography: Area: 735,268 sq. mi. **Location:** Archipelago SE of Asia along the Equator. **Neighbors:** Malaysia on N, Papua New Guinea on E. **Topography:** Indonesia comprises some 17,000 islands, including Java (one of the most densely populated areas in the world with 1,500 persons to the sq. mi.), Sumatra, Kalimantan (most of Borneo), Sulawesi (Celebes), and West Irian (Irian Jaya, the W. half of New Guinea). Also: Bangka, Billiton, Madura, Bali, Timor. The mountains and plateaus on the major islands have a cooler climate than the tropical lowlands. **Capital:** Jakarta. **Cities** (1988 est.): Jakarta 8,800,000; Surabaya 2,500,000; Bandung 1,400,000; Medan 1,700,000.

Government: Type: Independent republic. **Head of state:** Pres. Suharto; b. June 8, 1921; in office: Mar. 6, 1967. **Local divisions:** 24 provinces, 3 special regions. **Defense:** 1.8% of GNP (1988).

Economy: Industries: Food processing, textiles, light industry. **Chief crops:** Rice, coffee, sugar. **Minerals:** Nickel, tin, oil, bauxite, copper, natural gas. **Crude oil reserves** (1987): 8.4 bln. bbls. **Other resources:** Rubber. **Arable land:** 8%. **Livestock** (1989): cattle: 6.5 mln.; sheep: 5.4 mln. **Fish catch** (1990): 3.1 mln. metric tons. **Electricity prod.** (1990): 38 bln. kWh. **Labor force:** 56% agric.; 23% ind. & comm.; 16% services.

Finance: Monetary unit: Rupiah (June 1992: 2,027 = $1 US). **Gross domestic product** (1990): $94 bln. **Per capita GDP** (1990): $490. **Imports** (1990): $21.8 bln.; partners: Jap. 23%, U.S. 12%, Sing. 6%. **Exports** (1990): $25.6 bln.; partners: Jap. 41%, U.S. 16%, Sing. 10%. **Tourists** (1989): $1.6 bln. receipts. **National budget** (1990): $21.1 bln. **International reserves less gold** (Feb. 1992): $9.6 bln. **Gold:** 3.11 mln. oz t. **Consumer prices** (change in 1991): 9.2%.

Transport: Railway traffic (1989): 7.8 bln. passenger-km. **Motor vehicles:** in use (1990): 1.2 mln. passenger cars, 1.4 mln. comm. **Civil aviation** (1990): 13.3 bln. passenger-km; 124 airports. **Chief ports:** Jakarta, Surabaya, Medan, Palembang, Semarang.

Communications: Television sets: 1 per 24 persons. **Radios:** 1 per 8 persons. **Telephones:** 1 per 172 persons.

Health: Life expectancy at birth (1991): male: 59; female 63 years. **Births** (per 1,000 pop. 1991): 26. **Deaths** (per 1,000 pop. 1991): 8. **Natural increase:** 1.8%. **Hospital beds:** 1 per 1,485 persons. **Physicians:** 1 per 7,427 persons. **Infant mortality** (per 1,000 live births 1990): 73.0.

Education (1990): **Literacy:** 85%. 84% attend primary school.

Major International Organizations: UN and all of its specialized agencies, ASEAN, OPEC.

Embassy: 2020 Massachusetts Ave. NW 20036; 775-5200.

Hindu and Buddhist civilization from India reached the peoples of Indonesia nearly 2,000 years ago, taking root especially in Java. Islam spread along the maritime trade routes in the 15th century, and became predominant by the 16th century. The Dutch replaced the Portuguese as the most important European trade power in the area in the 17th century. They secured territorial control over Java by 1750. The outer islands were not finally subdued until the early 20th century, when the full area of present-day Indonesia was united under one rule for the first time.

Following Japanese occupation, 1942-45, nationalists led by Sukarno and Hatta proclaimed a republic. The Netherlands ceded sovereignty Dec. 27, 1949, after 4 years of fighting. West Irian, on New Guinea, remained under Dutch control.

After the Dutch in 1957 rejected proposals for new negotiations over West Irian, Indonesia stepped up the seizure of Dutch property. A U.S. mediator's plan was adopted in 1962. In 1963 the UN turned the area over to Indonesia, which promised a plebiscite. In 1969, voting by tribal chiefs favored staying with Indonesia, despite an uprising and widespread opposition.

Sukarno suspended Parliament in 1960, and was named president for life in 1963. Russian-armed Indonesian troops staged raids in 1964 and 1965 into Malaysia, whose formation Sukarno had opposed.

Indonesia's Communist Party tried to seize control in 1965; the army smashed the coup. In parts of Java, communists seized several districts before being defeated; over 300,000 communists were executed.

Gen. Suharto, head of the army, was named president in 1968, reelected 1973, 1978, and 1988. A coalition his supporters won a strong majority in House elections in 1971. Moslem opposition parties made gains in 1977 elections but lost ground in the 1982 elections. The military retains a predominant political role.

In 1966 Indonesia and Malaysia signed an agreement ending hostility.

Oil export earnings, and political stability have made Indonesia's economy stable.

Iran

Islamic Republic of Iran

Jomhori-e-Islami-e-Irân

People: Population (1991 est.): 59,051,000. **Age distrib.** (%): 0–14: 44.4; 15–59: 50.3; 60+: 5.2. **Pop. density:** 92 per sq. mi. **Urban** (1987): 55%. **Ethnic groups:** Persian 51%, Azerbaijani 25%, Kurd 9%. **Languages:** Farsi (official), Turk, Kurdish, Arabic. **Religions:** Shi'a Moslem 95%.

Geography: Area: 636,293 sq. mi. slightly larger than Alaska. **Location:** Between the Middle East and S. Asia. **Neighbors:** Turkey, Iraq on W, USSR of N (Armenia, Azerbaijan, Turkmenistan), Afghanistan, Pakistan on E. **Topography:** Interior highlands and plains are surrounded by high mountains, up to 18,000 ft. Large salt deserts cover much of the area, but there are many oases and forest areas. Most of the population inhabits the N and NW. **Capital:** Tehran. **Cities** (1986 cen.): Tehran 6,022,000; Esfahan 1,001,000; Mashhad 1,466,000; Tabriz 994,000; Shiraz 848,000.

Government: Type: Islamic republic. **Religious head:** Ayatollah Sayyed Ali Khamenei; b. 1939; in office: June 4, 1989. **Head of state:** Pres. Hashemi Rafsanjani; in office: Aug 3, 1989. **Local divisions:** 24 provinces. **Defense:** 13.3% of GNP (1991).

Economy: Industries: Cement, sugar refining, carpets. **Chief crops:** Grains, rice, fruits, sugar beets, cotton, grapes. **Minerals:** Chromium, oil, gas. **Crude oil reserves** (1990): 92.0 bln. barrels. **Other resources:** Gums, wool, silk, caviar. **Arable land:** 9%. **Livestock** (1990): cattle: 8.3 mln.; sheep: 34.0 mln. **Electricity prod.** (1990): 40.2 bln. kWh. **Labor force:** 33% agric.; 21% ind. & comm; 27% services.

Finance: Monetary unit: Rial (Mar. 1992: 67.36 = $1 US). **Gross national product** (1990): $80 bln. **Per capita GNP** (1990): $1,400. **Imports** (1989): $14.7 bln.; partners: W. Ger. 20%, Jap. 10%, UK 6%. **Exports** (1989): $13.6 bln.; partners: Jap. 13%, Neth. 12%. **National budget** (1990): $80 bln. expenditures.

Transport: Motor vehicles: in use (1987): 2.4 mln. passenger cars, 550,000 comm. vehicles. **Civil Aviation** (1990): 5.5 bln. passenger km.; 17 airports. **Chief ports:** Bandar Abbas.

Communications: Television sets: 1 per 23 persons. **Radios:** 1 per 4.7 persons. **Telephones:** 1 per 25 persons. **Daily newspaper circ.** (1988): 13 per 1,000 pop.

Health: Life expectancy at birth (1991): 64 male; 65 female. **Births** (per 1,000 pop. 1991): 44. **Deaths** (per 1,000 pop. 1991): 10. **Natural increase:** 3.4%. **Hospital beds:** 1 per 704 persons. **Physicians:** 1 per 2,992 persons. **Infant mortality** (per 1,000 live births 1991): 66.

Education (1990): **Literacy:** 54%.
Major International Organizations: UN (IMF, WHO), OPEC.

Iran was once called Persia. The Iranians, who supplanted an earlier agricultural civilization, came from the E during the 2d millenium BC; they were an Indo-European group related to the Aryans of India.

In 549 BC Cyrus the Great united the Medes and Persians in the Persian Empire, conquered Babylonia in 538 BC, restored Jerusalem to the Jews. Alexander the Great conquered Persia in 333 BC, but Persians regained their independence in the next century under the Parthians, themselves succeeded by Sassanian Persians in 226 AD. Arabs brought Islam to Persia in the 7th century, replacing the indigenous Zoroastrian faith. After Persian political and cultural autonomy was reasserted in the 9th century, the arts and sciences flourished for several centuries.

Turks and Mongols ruled Persia in turn from the 11th century to 1502, when a native dynasty reasserted full independence. The British and Russian empires vied for influence in the 19th century, and Afghanistan was severed from Iran by Britain in 1857.

Reza Khan abdicated as Shah, 1941, and was succeeded by his son, Mohammad Reza Pahlavi. Under his rule, Iran underwent economic and social change but political opposition was not tolerated.

Conservative Moslem protests led to 1978 violence. Martial law in 12 cities was declared Sept. 8. A military government was appointed Nov. 6 to deal with striking oil workers. Prime Min. Shahpur Bakhtiar was designated by the shah to head a regency council in his absence. The shah left Iran Jan. 16, 1979.

Exiled religious leader Ayatollah Ruhollah Khomeini named a provisional government council in preparation for his return to Iran, Jan. 31. Clashes between Khomeini's supporters and government troops culminated in a rout of Iran's elite Imperial Guard Feb. 11, leading to the fall of Bakhtiar's government.

The Iranian revolution was marked by revolts among the ethnic minorities and by a continuing struggle between the clerical forces and westernized intellectuals and liberals. The Islamic Constitution established final authority to be vested in a Faghi, the Ayatollah Khomeini.

Iranian militants seized the U.S. embassy, Nov. 4, 1979, and took hostages including 62 Americans. Despite international condemnations and U.S. efforts, including an abortive Apr., 1980, rescue attempt, the crisis continued. The U.S. broke diplomatic relations with Iran, Apr. 7th. The shah died in Egypt, July 27th. The hostage drama finally ended Jan. 21, 1981 when an accord, involving the release of frozen Iranian assets, was reached.

A dispute over the Shatt al-Arab waterway that divides the two countries brought Iran and Iraq, Sept. 22, 1980, into open warfare. Iraqi planes attacked Iranian air fields including Teheran airport. Iranian planes bombed Iraqi bases. Iraqi troops occupied Iranian territory including the port city of Khorramshahr in October. Iranian troops recaptured the city and drove Iraqi troops back across the border, May 1982. Iraq, and later Iran, attacked several oil tankers in the Persian Gulf during 1984. Saudi Arabian war planes shot down 2 Iranian jets, June 5, which they felt were threatening Saudi shipping. In Aug. 1988, Iran agreed to accept a UN resolution calling for a cease fire.

In Nov. 1986, senior U.S. officials secretly visited Iran and exchanged arms for Iran's help in obtaining the release of U.S. hostages held by terrorists in Lebanon. The exchange sparked a major scandal in the Reagan administration.

A U.S. Navy warship shot down an Iranian commercial airliner, July 3, 1988, after mistaking it for an F-14 fighter jet; all 290 aboard the plane died.

A major earthquake struck northern Iran June 21, 1990, killing over 45,000, injuring 100,000, and leaving 400,000 homeless. A U.S. offer of assistance was accepted by the Iranian government.

Some one million Kurdish refugees crossed Iran's border to escape Iraqi forces following the Persian Gulf War.

Iraq

Republic of Iraq

al Jumhouriya al 'Iraqia

People: Population (1991 est.): 19,524,000. **Age distrib.** (%): 0–14: 45.3; 15–59: 49.6; 60+: 5.1. **Pop. density:** 116 per sq. mi. **Urban** (1988): 72%. **Ethnic groups:** Arabs, 75% Kurds,

15% Turks. **Languages:** Arabic (official), Kurdish. **Religions:** Moslem 95% (Shiites 60%, Sunnis 35%), Christian 5%.

Geography: Area: 167,924 sq. mi., larger than California. **Location:** In the Middle East, occupying most of historic Mesopotamia. **Neighbors:** Jordan, Syria on W, Turkey on N, Iran on E, Kuwait, Saudi Arabia on S. **Topography:** Mostly an alluvial plain, including the Tigris and Euphrates rivers, descending from mountains in N to desert in SW. Persian Gulf region is marshland. **Capital:** Baghdad. **Cities** (1985 est.): Baghdad (met.) 3,400,000, Basra 616,000, Mosul 570,000.

Government: Type: Republic. **Head of state:** Pres. Saddam Hussein At-Takriti, b. Apr. 29, 1937; in office: July 16, 1979. **Local divisions:** 18 provinces. **Defense:** 32% of GNP (1986).

Economy: Industries: Textiles, petrochemicals, oil refining, cement. **Chief crops:** Grains, rice, dates, cotton. **Minerals:** Oil, gas. **Crude oil reserves** (1990): 100 bln. barrels. **Other resources:** Wool, hides. **Arable land:** 13%. **Livestock** (1990): cattle: 1.5 mln.; sheep: 9.6 mln.; goats: 1.4 mln. **Electricity prod.** (1990): 20 bln. kWh. **Labor force:** 33% agric.; 39% services; 28% ind.

Finance: Monetary unit: Dinar (Mar. 1992: 1.00 = $3.21 US). **Gross national product** (1989): $35 bln. **Per capita GNP** (1989): $1,950. **Imports** (1989): $10.2 bln.; partners: Tur. 10%, U.S. 11%. **Exports** (1989): $12.0 bln.; partners: U.S. 20%, Tur. 12%, Jap. 9%. **National budget** (1990): $35 bln. expenditures.

Transport: Railway traffic (1988): 1.5 bln. passenger-km. **Motor vehicles:** in use (1989): 672,000 passenger cars, 368,000 comm. vehicles. **Civil aviation** (1985): 1.2 bln. passenger-km; 3 airports. **Chief ports:** Basra.

Communications: Television sets: 1 per 18 persons. **Radios:** 1 per 5 persons. **Telephones:** 1 per 17 persons. **Daily newspaper circ.** (1989): 30 per 1,000 pop.

Health: Life expectancy at birth (1991): 66 male; 68 female. **Births** (per 1,000 pop. 1991): 45. **Deaths** (per 1,000 pop. 1991): 8. **Natural increase:** 3.8%. **Hospital beds:** 1 per 552 persons. **Physicians:** 1 per 3,324 persons. **Infant mortality** (per 1,000 live births 1991): 66.

Major International Organizations: UN (IMF, ILO), Arab League, OPEC.

Education (1991): **Literacy:** 60%. Compulsory age 6 to grade 6.

Embassy: 1801 P St. NW 20036; 483-7500.

The Tigris-Euphrates valley, formerly called Mesopotamia, was the site of one of the earliest civilizations in the world. The Sumerian city-states of 3,000 BC originated the culture later developed by the Semitic Akkadians, Babylonians, and Assyrians.

Mesopotamia ceased to be a separate entity after the conquests of the Persians, Greeks, and Arabs. The latter founded Baghdad, from where the caliph ruled a vast empire in the 8th and 9th centuries. Mongol and Turkish conquests led to a decline in population, the economy, cultural life, and the irrigation system.

Britain secured a League of Nations mandate over Iraq after World War I. Independence under a king came in 1932. A leftist, pan-Arab revolution established a republic in 1958, which oriented foreign policy toward the USSR. Most industry has been nationalized, and large land holdings broken up.

A local faction of the international Baath Arab Socialist party has ruled by decree since 1968. Russia and Iraq signed an aid pact in 1972, and arms were sent along with several thousand advisers. The 1978 execution of 21 communists and a shift of trade to the West signalled a more neutral policy, straining relations with the USSR. In the 1973 Arab-Israeli war Iraq sent forces to aid Syria. Within a month of assuming power, Saddam Hussein instituted a bloody purge in the wake of a reported coup attempt against the new regime.

Years of battling with the Kurdish minority resulted in total defeat for the Kurds in 1975, when Iran withdrew support. The fighting led to Iraqi bombing of Kurdish villages in Iran, causing relations with Iran to deteriorate.

After skirmishing intermittently for 10 months over the sovereignty of the disputed Shatt al-Arab waterway that divides the two countries, Iraq and Iran, Sept. 22, 1980, entered into open warfare when Iraqi fighter-bombers attacked 10 Iranian airfields, including Teheran airport, and Iranian planes retaliated with strikes on 2 Iraqi bases. In the following days, there was heavy ground fighting around Abadan and the adjacent port of Khorramshahr as Iraq pressed its attack on Iran's oil-rich province of Khuzistan. In May 1982, Iraqi troops were driven back across the border.

Israeli airplanes destroyed a nuclear reactor near Baghdad on June 7, 1981, claiming that it could be used to produce nuclear weapons.

Iraq and Iran expanded their war to the Persian Gulf in Apr. 1984. There were several attacks on oil tankers. An Iraqi warplane launched a missile attack on the U.S.S. *Stark*, a U.S. Navy frigate on patrol in the Persian Gulf, May 17, 1987; 37 U.S. sailors died. Iraq apologized for the attack, claiming it was inadvertent. The fierce war ended Aug. 1988, when Iraq accepted a UN resolution for a ceasefire.

Iraq attacked and overran Kuwait Aug. 2, 1990, sparking an international crisis. The United Nations, Aug. 6, imposed a ban on all trade with Iraq and called on member countries to protect the assets of the legitimate government of Kuwait. Iraq declared Kuwait its 19th province, Aug. 28. A campaign of looting, murder, and pillage was mounted against Kuwaiti civilians. Westerners caught in Iraq and Kuwait were initially held as hostages, but by the end of 1990, all were released.

A U.S.-led coalition launched air & missile attacks on Iraq, Jan. 16, 1991, after the expiration of a UN Security Council deadline for Iraq to withdraw from Kuwait. Iraq retaliated by firing scud missiles at Saudi Arabia and Israel. The coalition began a ground attack to retake Kuwait Feb. 27. Iraqi forces showed little resistance and were soundly defeated in 4 days. Some 175,000 Iraqis were taken prisoner, and casualties were estimated at over 85,000. As part of the cease-fire agreement, Iraq agreed to scrap all poison gas and germ weapons and allow UN observers to inspect the sites. UN trade sanctions would remain in effect until Iraq complied.

In the aftermath of the war, there were revolts against Pres. Saddam Hussein throughout Iraq. In Feb., Iraqi troops drove Kurdish insurgents and civilians to the Iran and Turkey borders, causing a refugee crisis. The U.S. and allies established havens inside Iraq for the Kurds.

Tensions heightened over the UN's efforts to dismantle Iraq's arms-production program, July 5, 1992, when a UN inspection team was denied entrance to a ministry building in Baghdad. Iraq allowed the inspection team access to the building July 26; the team found no arms-related evidence.

Republic of Ireland

Eire

People: Population (1991 est.): 3,489,000. **Age distrib. (%):** 0–14: 30.5; 15–59: 54.5; 60+:15.0. **Pop. density:** 128 per sq. mi. **Urban** (1990): 57%. **Ethnic groups:** Celtic, English minority. **Languages:** English predominates, Irish (Gaelic) spoken by minority. **Religions:** Roman Catholic 95%, Anglican 3%.

Geography: Area: 27,137 sq. mi. slightly larger than W. Va. **Location:** In the Atlantic O. just W of Great Britain. **Neighbors:** United Kingdom (Northern Ireland). **Topography:** Ireland consists of a central plateau surrounded by isolated groups of hills and mountains. The coastline is heavily indented by the Atlantic O. **Capital:** Dublin. **Cities** (1991 est.): Dublin 502,000; Cork (met.) 133,000.

Government: Type: Parliamentary republic. **Head of State:** Pres. Mary Robinson; in office: Dec. 3, 1990. **Head of government:** Prime Min. Albert Reynolds; b. 1935; in office: Feb. 6, 1992. **Local divisions:** 26 counties. **Defense:** 1.6% of GDP (1990).

Economy: Industries: Food processing, textiles, chemicals, brewing, machinery, tourism. **Chief crops:** Potatoes, grain, sugar beets, fruits, vegetables. **Minerals:** Zinc, lead, silver, gas. **Arable land:** 14%. **Livestock** (1989): cattle: 5.6 mln.; pigs: 961,000; sheep: 4.9 mln. **Fish catch** (1990): 247,000 metric tons. **Electricity prod.** (1990): 14.4 bln. kWh. **Crude steel prod.** (1988): 203,000 metric tons. **Labor force:** 15% agric.; 29% ind. 51% services.

Finance: Monetary unit: Pound (June 1992: 0.59 = $1 US). **Gross domestic product** (1990): $33.9 bln. **Per capita GDP** (1990): $9,690. **Imports** (1990): $20 bln.; partners: UK 38%, U.S. 12%, other EC 28%. **Exports** (1990): $23 bln.; partners: UK 28%, other EC 47%, U.S. 8%. **Tourists** (1989): receipts: $1 bln. **National budget** (1990): $11.7 bln. expenditures. **International reserves less gold** (Mar. 1992): $5.8 bln. **Gold:** 360,000 oz. t. **Consumer prices** (change in 1992): 3.2%.

Transport: Railroads (1989): **Length:** 2,814 km. **Motor vehicles:** in use (1989): 773,000 passenger cars, 133,000 comm.

vehicles. **Civil aviation:** (1989): 4.2 bln. passenger-km; 11 airports. **Chief ports:** Dublin, Cork.

Communications: Television sets: 1 per 3.8 persons. **Radios:** 1 per 1.7 persons. **Telephones:** 1 per 3.8 persons. **Daily newspaper circ.** (1989): 169 per 1,000 pop.

Health: Life expectancy at birth (1991): 73 male; 79 female. **Births** (per 1,000 pop. 1991): 15. **Deaths** (per 1,000 pop. 1991): 9. **Natural increase:** 6%. **Hospital beds:** 1 per 137 persons. **Physicians:** 1 per 681 persons. **Infant mortality** (per 1,000 live births 1991): 6.

Education (1991): **Literacy:** 99%. **Years compulsory:** 9; attendance 91%.

Major International Organizations: UN (GATT, IMF, World Bank), EC, OECD.

Embassy: 2234 Massachusetts Ave. NW 20008; 462-3939.

Celtic tribes invaded the islands about the 4th century BC; their Gaelic culture and literature flourished and spread to Scotland and elsewhere in the 5th century AD, the same century in which St. Patrick converted the Irish to Christianity. Invasions by Norsemen began in the 8th century, ended with defeat of the Danes by the Irish King Brian Boru in 1014. English invasions started in the 12th century; for over 700 years the Anglo-Irish struggle continued with bitter rebellions and savage repressions.

The Easter Monday Rebellion (1916) failed but was followed by guerrilla warfare and harsh reprisals by British troops, the "Black and Tans." The Dail Eireann, or Irish parliament, reaffirmed independence in Jan. 1919. The British offered dominion status to Ulster (6 counties) and southern Ireland (26 counties) Dec. 1921. The constitution of the Irish Free State, a British dominion, was adopted Dec. 11, 1922. Northern Ireland remained part of the United Kingdom.

A new constitution adopted by plebiscite came into operation Dec. 29, 1937. It declared the name of the state Eire in the Irish language (Ireland in the English) and declared it a sovereign democratic state.

On Dec. 21, 1948, an Irish law declared the country a republic rather than a dominion and withdrew it from the Commonwealth. The British Parliament recognized both actions, 1949, but reasserted its claim to incorporate the 6 northeastern counties in the United Kingdom. This claim has not been recognized by Ireland. *(See United Kingdom — Northern Ireland.)*

Irish governments have favored peaceful unification of all Ireland. Ireland cooperated with England against terrorist groups.

Ireland suffered economic hardship in the 1980's; unemployment was 17% in 1992.

Israel

State of Israel

Medinat Israel

People: Population (1991 est.): 4,477,000. **Age distrib.** (%): 0–14: 32.4; 15–59: 55.3; 60+: 13.3. **Pop. density:** 570 per sq. mi. **Urban** (1986): 89%. **Ethnic groups:** Jewish 83%, Arab 16%. **Languages:** Hebrew and Arabic (official). **Religions:** Jewish 83%, Moslem 13%.

Geography: Area: 7,847 sq. mi. about the size of New Jersey. **Location:** On eastern end of Mediterranean Sea. **Neighbors:** Lebanon on N, Syria, Jordan on E, Egypt on W. **Topography:** The Mediterranean coastal plain is fertile and well-watered. In the center is the Judean Plateau. A triangular-shaped semi-desert region, the Negev, extends from south of Beersheba to an apex at the head of the Gulf of Aqaba. The eastern border drops sharply into the Jordan Rift Valley, including Lake Tiberias (Sea of Galilee) and the Dead Sea, which is 1,312 ft. below sea level, lowest point on the earth's surface. **Capital:** Jerusalem. Most countries maintain their embassy in Tel Aviv. **Cities** (1988 est.): Jerusalem 493,000; Tel Aviv-Yafo 317,000; Haifa 222,000.

Government: Type: Republic. **Head of state:** Pres. Chaim Herzog; b. Sept. 17, 1918; in office: May 5, 1983. **Head of government:** Prime Min. Yitzhak Rabin; b. Mar. 1, 1922; in office: July 13, 1992. **Local divisions:** 6 districts. **Defense:** 13.9% of GNP (1991).

Economy: Industries: Diamond cutting, textiles, electronics, machinery, food processing. **Chief crops:** Citrus fruit, vegetables. **Minerals:** Potash, copper, phosphate, manganese, sulphur. **Arable land:** 17%. **Livestock** (1989): cattle: 325,000; sheep: 375,000. **Fish catch** (1989): 18,000 metric tons. **Electricity prod.** (1990): 17.3 bln. kWh. **Labor force:** 6% agric.; 23% ind., 30% public services.

Finance: Monetary unit: Shekel (May 1992: 2.40 = $1 US). **GNP** (1990): $46.5 bln. **Per capita GNP** (1990): $10,500. **Imports** (1990): $16.5 bln.; partners: U.S. 16%, W. Ger. 13%, UK 9%. **Exports** (1990): $11.7 bln.; partners: U.S. 30%, W. Ger. 5%, UK 7%. **Tourists** (1989): receipts $1.4 bln. **National budget** (1991): $33 bln. expenditures. **International reserves less gold** (Jan. 1992): $6.5 bln. **Gold:** 388,000 oz t. **Consumer prices** (change in 1991): 19.0%.

Transport: Railroads: (1990): **Length:** 323 mi. **Motor vehicles:** in use (1989): 778,000 passenger cars, 149,000 comm. vehicles. **Civil aviation** (1989): 7.7 mln. passenger-km; 7 airports with scheduled flights. **Chief ports:** Haifa, Ashdod, Eilat.

Communications: Television sets: 1 per 6.9 persons. **Radios:** 1 per 2.2 persons. **Telephones:** 1 per 2.1 persons. **Daily newspaper circ.** (1989): 357 per 1,000 pop.

Health: Life expectancy at birth (1991) Jewish pop. only: 76 male; 79 female. **Births** (per 1,000 pop. 1991): 21. **Deaths** (per 1,000 pop. 1991): 6%. **Natural increase:** 1.5%. **Hospital beds:** 1 per 161 persons. **Physicians:** 1 per 345 persons. **Infant mortality** (per 1,000 live births 1991): 9.

Education (1991): **Literacy:** 92% (Jewish), 70% (Arab).

Major International Organizations: UN (GATT).

Embassy: 3514 International Dr. NW 20008; 364-5500.

Occupying the SW corner of the ancient Fertile Crescent, Israel contains some of the oldest known evidence of agriculture and of primitive town life. A more advanced civilization emerged in the 3d millenium BC. The Hebrews probably arrived early in the 2d millenium BC. Under King David and his successors (c.1000 BC-597 BC), Judaism was developed and secured. After conquest by Babylonians, Persians, and Greeks, an independent Jewish kingdom was revived, 168 BC, but Rome took effective control in the next century, suppressed Jewish revolts in 70 AD and 135 AD, and renamed Judea Palestine, after the earlier coastal inhabitants, the Philistines.

Arab invaders conquered Palestine in 636. The Arabic language and Islam prevailed within a few centuries, but a Jewish minority remained. The land was ruled from the 11th century as a part of non-Arab empires by Seljuks, Mamluks, and Ottomans (with a crusader interval, 1098-1291).

After 4 centuries of Ottoman rule, during which the population declined to a low of 350,000 (1785), the land was taken in 1917 by Britain, which in the Balfour Declaration that year pledged to support a Jewish national homeland there, as foreseen by the Zionists. In 1920 a British Palestine Mandate was recognized; in 1922 the land east of the Jordan was detached.

Jewish immigration, begun in the late 19th century, swelled in the 1930s with refugees from the Nazis; heavy Arab immigration from Syria and Lebanon also occurred. Arab opposition to Jewish immigration turned violent in 1920, 1921, 1929, and 1936. The UN General Assembly voted in 1947 to partition Palestine into an Arab and a Jewish state. Britain withdrew in May 1948.

Israel was declared an independent state May 14, 1948; the Arabs rejected partition. Egypt, Jordan, Syria, Lebanon, Iraq, and Saudi Arabia invaded, but failed to destroy the Jewish state, which gained territory. Separate armistices with the Arab nations were signed in 1949; Jordan occupied the West Bank, Egypt occupied Gaza, but neither granted Palestinian autonomy.

After persistent terrorist raids, Israel invaded Egypt's Sinai, Oct. 29, 1956, aided briefly by British and French forces. A UN cease-fire was arranged Nov. 6.

An uneasy truce between Israel and the Arab countries, supervised by a UN Emergency Force, prevailed until May 19, 1967, when the UN force withdrew at the demand of Egypt's Pres. Nasser. Egyptian forces reoccupied the Gaza Strip and closed the Gulf of Aqaba to Israeli shipping. In a 6-day war that started June 5, the Israelis took the Gaza Strip, occupied the Sinai Peninsula to the Suez Canal, and captured Old Jerusalem, Syria's Golan Heights, and Jordan's West Bank. The fighting was halted June 10 by UN-arranged cease-fire agreements.

Egypt and Syria attacked Israel, Oct. 6, 1973 (Yom Kippur, most solemn day on the Jewish calendar). Israel counter-attacked, driving the Syrians back, and crossed the Suez Canal.

A cease fire took effect Oct. 24; a UN peace-keeping force went to the area. A disengagement agreement was signed Jan. 18, 1974. Israel withdrew from the canal's W bank. A second withdrawal was completed in 1976; Israel returned the Sinai to Egypt in 1982.

Israeli forces raided Entebbe, Uganda, July 3, 1976, and rescued 103 hostages seized by Arab and German terrorists.

In 1977, the conservative opposition, led by Menachem Begin, was voted into office for the first time. Egypt's Pres. Sadat visited Jerusalem Nov. 1977 and on Mar. 26, 1979. Egypt and Israel signed a formal peace treaty, ending 30 years of war, and establishing diplomatic relations.

Israel invaded S. Lebanon, March 1978, following a Lebanon-based terrorist attack in Israel. Israel withdrew in favor of a 6,000-man UN force, but continued to aid Christian militiamen. Violence on the Israeli-occupied West Bank rose in 1982 when Israel announced plans to build new Jewish settlements. Israel affirmed the entire city of Jerusalem as its capital, July, 1980, encompassing the annexed Arab East Jerusalem.

On June 7, 1981, Israeli jets destroyed an Iraqi atomic reactor near Baghdad that, Israel claimed, would have enabled Iraq to manufacture nuclear weapons.

Israeli jets bombed Palestine Liberation Organization (PLO) strongholds in Lebanon April, May 1982. In reaction to the wounding of the Israeli ambassador to Great Britain, Israeli forces in a coordinated land, sea, and air attack invaded Lebanon, June 6, to destroy PLO strongholds in that country. Israeli and Syrian forces engaged in the Bekka Valley, June 9, but quickly agreed to a truce. Israeli forces encircled Beirut June 14. Following massive Israeli bombing of West Beirut, the PLO agreed to evacuate the city.

Israeli troops entered West Beirut after newly-elected Lebanese president Bashir Gemayel was assassinated on Sept. 14. Israel received widespread condemnation when Lebenese Christian forces, Sept. 16, entered 2 West Beirut refugee camps and slaughtered hundreds of Palestinian refugees.

In 1989, violence continued over the Israeli military occupation of the West Bank and Gaza Strip; protesters and Israeli troops clashed frequently. Israeli police and stone-throwing Palestinians clashed, Oct. 8, 1990, around the al-Aqsa mosque on the Temple Mount in Jerusalem. Some 20 Palestinians died and 150 were injured.

The Knesset approved a new right-wing coalition government led by Prime Minister Yitzhak Shamir, June 11, 1990, following a 3-month political crisis that began with the fall of the previous "National Unity" government of Shamir and the Labor Party of Shimon Peres.

During the Persian Gulf War, Iraq fired a series of scud missiles at Israel; most were intercepted by U.S. Patriot missiles. Israel agreed in Aug. 1991 to take part in a U.S.-Soviet sponsored Middle East peace conference.

The Labor Party of Yitzhak Rabin won a clear victory in elections held June 23, 1992. Rabin called for peace and reconciliation with its Arab neighbors.

Italy

Italian Republic

Repubblica Italiana

People: Population (1991 est.): 57,772,000. **Age distrib.** (%): 0–14: 17.8; 15–59: 62.8; 60+: 19.4. **Pop. density:** 496 per sq. mi. **Urban** (1991): 67%. **Ethnic groups:** Italians, small minorities of Germans, Slovenes, Albanians. **Languages:** Italian. **Religions:** Predominantly Roman Catholic.

Geography: Area: 116,303 sq. mi., about the size of Florida and Georgia combined. **Location:** In S Europe, jutting into Mediterranean S. **Neighbors:** France on W, Switzerland, Austria on N, Slovenia on E. **Topography:** Occupies a long boot-shaped peninsula, extending SE from the Alps into the Mediterranean, with the islands of Sicily and Sardinia offshore. The alluvial Po Valley drains most of N. The rest of the country is rugged and mountainous, except for intermittent coastal plains, like the Campania, S of Rome. Apennine Mts. run down through center of peninsula. **Capital:** Rome. **Cities** (1989 est.): Rome 2.8 mln.; Milan 1.4 mln.; Naples 1.2 mln.; Turin 1.0 mln.

Government: Type: Republic. **Head of state:** Pres. Oscal Luigi Scalfaro; in office: May 25, 1992. **Head of government:** Prime Min. Guiliano Amato; in office: June 28, 1992. **Local divisions:** 20 regions with some autonomy, 94 provinces. **Defense:** 2.2% of GDP (1990).

Economy: Industries: Steel, machinery, autos, textiles, shoes, machine tools, chemicals. **Chief crops:** Grapes, olives, citrus fruits, vegetables, wheat, rice. **Minerals:** Mercury, potash, sulphur. **Crude oil reserves** (1987): 951 mln. bbls. **Arable land:** 32%. **Livestock** (1989): cattle: 8.7 mln.; pigs: 9.3 mln.; sheep: 11.6 mln. **Fish catch** (1989): 395,000 metric tons. **Electricity prod.** (1990): 225 bln. kWh. **Crude steel prod.** (1990): 25.4 mln. metric tons. **Labor force:** 10% agric.; 32% ind. and comm.; 58% services and govt.

Finance: Monetary unit: Lira (June 1992: 1,202 = $1 US). **Gross domestic product** (1990): $844 bln. **Per capita GDP** (1990): $14,600. **Imports** (1991): $181 bln.; partners: Ger. 20%, Fr. 15%, U.S. 7%. **Exports** (1991): $170 bln.; partners: Ger. 16%, Fr. 15%, U.S. 10%, UK 6%. **Tourists** (1989): receipts $11.4 bln. **National budget** (1989): $448 bln. expenditures. **International reserves less gold** (Apr. 1992): $42 bln. **Gold:** 66.67 mln. oz t. **Consumer prices** (change in 1991): 6.5%.

Transport: Railroads (1989): **Length:** 12,158 mi. **Motor vehicles:** in use (1989): 24.3 mln. passenger cars, 2.0 mln. comm. vehicles. **Civil aviation** (1990): 22.7 bln. passenger-km; 34 airports. **Chief ports:** Genoa, Venice, Trieste, Taranto, Naples, La Spezia.

Communications: Television sets: 1 per 3.8 persons. **Radios:** 1 per 3.9 persons. **Telephones:** 1 per 2.0 persons. **Daily newspaper circ.** (1989): 142 per 1,000 pop.

Health: Life expectancy at birth (1991): 75 male; 82 female. **Births** (per 1,000 pop. 1991): 11. **Deaths** (per 1,000 pop. 1991): 10. **Natural increase:** .1%. **Hospital beds:** 1 per 135 persons. **Physicians:** 1 per 233 persons. **Infant mortality** (per 1,000 live births 1991): 6.

Education (1991): **Literacy:** 98%. **Years compulsory:** 8.

Major International Organizations: UN and all of its specialized agencies, NATO, OECD, EC.

Embassy: 1601 Fuller St. NW 20009; 328-5500.

Rome emerged as the major power in Italy after 500 BC, dominating the more civilized Etruscans to the N and Greeks to the S. Under the Empire, which lasted until the 5th century AD, Rome ruled most of Western Europe, the Balkans, the Near East, and North Africa. In 1988, archeologists unearthed evidence showing Rome as a dynamic society in the 6th and 7th centuries B.C.

After the Germanic invasions, lasting several centuries, a high civilization arose in the city-states of the N, culminating in the Renaissance. But German, French, Spanish, and Austrian intervention prevented the unification of the country. In 1859 Lombardy came under the crown of King Victor Emmanuel II of Sardinia. By plebiscite in 1860, Parma, Modena, Romagna, and Tuscany joined, followed by Sicily and Naples, and by the Marches and Umbria. The first Italian parliament declared Victor Emmanuel king of Italy Mar. 17, 1861. Mantua and Venetia were added in 1866 as an outcome of the Austro-Prussian war. The Papal States were taken by Italian troops Sept. 20, 1870, on the withdrawal of the French garrison. The states were annexed to the kingdom by plebiscite. Italy recognized the State of Vatican City as independent Feb. 11, 1929.

Fascism appeared in Italy Mar. 23, 1919, led by Benito Mussolini, who took over the government at the invitation of the king Oct. 28, 1922. Mussolini acquired dictatorial powers. He made war on Ethiopia and proclaimed Victor Emmanuel III emperor, defied the sanctions of the League of Nations, sent troops to fight for Franco against the Republic of Spain and joined Germany in World War II.

After Fascism was overthrown in 1943, Italy declared war on Germany and Japan and contributed to the Allied victory. It surrendered conquered lands and lost its colonies. Mussolini was killed by partisans Apr. 28, 1945.

Victor Emmanuel III abdicated May 9, 1946; his son Humbert II was king until June 10, when Italy became a republic after a referendum, June 2-3.

Reorganization of the Fascist party is forbidden. The cabinet normally represents a coalition of the Christian Democrats, largest of Italy's many parties, and several other parties.

Italy has enjoyed growth in industry and living standards since World War II, in part due to membership in the Common Market. Italy joined the European Monetary System, 1980. A wave of left-wing political violence began in the late 1970s with kidnappings and assassinations and continued through the 1980s. Christian Dem. leader and former Prime Min. Moro was murdered May 1978 by Red Brigade terrorists.

The Cabinet of Prime Min. Arnaldo Forlani resigned, May 26, 1981, in the wake of revelations that numerous high-ranking officials were members of an illegally secret Masonic lodge. The June 1983 elections saw Bettino Craxi chosen the nation's first Socialist premier. Craxi ended the longest tenure of an Italian leader since World War II by resigning Mar. 1987.

By mid-1991, some 20,000 Albanian refugees had entered Italy as the result of political unrest in their homeland. In Aug. an additional wave of 18,000 Albanians reached Italy. They were rounded up and sent back to Albania.

Sicily, 9,926 sq. mi., pop. (1990) 5,172,000, is an island 180 by 120 mi., seat of a region that embraces the island of **Pantelleria,** 32 sq. mi., and the **Lipari** group, 44 sq. mi., 63 14,000, including 2 active volcanoes: **Vulcano,** 1,637 ft. and **Stromboli,** 3,038 ft. From prehistoric times Sicily has been settled by various peoples; a Greek state had its capital at Syracuse. Rome took Sicily from Carthage 215 BC. **Mt. Etna,** 11,053 ft. active volcano, is tallest peak.

Sardinia, 9,301 sq. mi., pop. (1990) 1,657,000, lies in the Mediterranean, 115 mi. W of Italy and 7-½ mi. S of Corsica. It is 160 mi. long, 68 mi. wide, and mountainous, with mining of coal, zinc, lead, copper. In 1720 Sardinia was added to the possessions of the Dukes of Savoy in Piedmont and Savoy to form the Kingdom of Sardinia. Giuseppe Garibaldi is buried on the nearby isle of Caprera. **Elba,** 86 sq. mi., lies 6 mi. W of Tuscany. Napoleon I lived in exile on Elba 1814-1815.

Trieste. An agreement, signed Oct. 5, 1954, by Italy and Yugoslavia, confirmed, Nov. 10, 1975, gave Italy provisional administration over the northern section and the seaport of Trieste, and Yugoslavia the part of Istrian peninsula it has occupied.

Jamaica

People: Population (1991 est.): 2,489,000. **Age distrib.** (%): 0–14: 33.7; 15–59: 56.4; 60+: 9.9. **Pop. density:** 556 per sq. mi. **Urban** (1989): 48%. **Ethnic groups:** African 76%, mixed 15%, Chinese, Caucasians, East Indians. **Languages:** English, (official), Jamaican Creole. **Religions:** Protestant 60%.

Geography: Area: 4,232 sq. mi., slightly smaller than Connecticut. **Location:** In West Indies. **Neighbors:** Nearest are Cuba on N, Haiti on E. **Topography:** The country is four-fifths covered by mountains. **Capital:** Kingston. **Cities** (1984 est.): St. Andrew 393,000, Kingston 100,000.

Government: Type: Parliamentary Democracy. **Head of state:** Queen Elizabeth II, represented by Gov.-Gen. Howard Cooke; in office: Aug. 1, 1991. **Head of government:** Prime Min. Percival J. Patterson; in office: Mar. 28, 1992. **Local divisions:** 14 parishes; Kingston and St. Andrew corporate area. **Defense:** 1.0% of GDP (1991).

Economy: Industries: Rum, molasses, mining, tourism. **Chief crops:** Sugar cane, coffee, bananas, coconuts, citrus fruits. **Minerals:** Bauxite, limestone, gypsum. **Arable land:** 19%. **Livestock** (1989): cattle: 250,000; goats: 440,000. **Electricity prod.** (1990): 2.4 bln. kWh. **Labor force:** 31% agric.; 27% services; 41% ind.

Finance: Monetary unit: Dollar (Apr. 1992: 27.26 = $1 US). **Gross domestic product** (1990): $3.9 bln. **Per capita GDP** (1990): $150. **Imports** (1990): $1.8 bln.; partners: U.S. 48%. **Exports** (1990): $1.0 bln.; partners: U.S. 36%. **Tourists** (1990): receipts: $740 mln. **National budget** (1990): $1.0 bln. **International reserves less gold** (Feb. 1992): $195 mln. **Consumer prices** (change in 1991): 51.1%.

Transport: Railroads (1989): **Length:** 211 mi. **Motor vehicles:** in use (1989): 93,000 passenger cars, 16,000 comm. vehicles. **Civil aviation** (1990): 1.4 bln. passenger km.; 6 airports with scheduled flights. **Chief ports:** Kingston, Montego Bay.

Communications: Television sets: 1 per 5.9 persons. **Radios:** 1 per 2.6 persons. **Telephones:** 1 per 13 persons. **Daily newspaper circ.** (1991): 51 per 1,000 pop.

Health: Life expectancy at birth (1991): 72 male; 76 female. **Births** (per 1,000 pop. 1991): 24. **Deaths:** (per 1,000 pop. 1991): 6. **Natural increase:** 1.8%. **Hospital beds:** 1 per 448 persons. **Physicians:** 1 per 2,095 persons. **Infant mortality** (per 1,000 live births 1991): 17.

Education (1990): **Literacy:** 98%. Compulsory to age 14.

Major International Organizations: UN (World Bank, GATT), OAS.

Embassy: 1850 K St. NW 20008; 452-0660.

Jamaica was visited by Columbus, 1494, and ruled by Spain (under whom Arawak Indians died out) until seized by Britain, 1655. Jamaica won independence Aug. 6, 1962.

In 1974 Jamaica sought an increase in taxes paid by U.S. and Canadian companies which mine bauxite on the island. The socialist government acquired 50% ownership of the companies' Jamaican interests in 1976, and was reelected that year. Rudimentary welfare state measures were passed. Relations with the U.S. improved greatly in the 1980s following the election of Edward Seaga.

Hurricane Gilbert struck Jamaica Sept. 12, 1988, killing some 45 and causing extensive damage including half the nation's houses.

Japan

Nippon

People: Population (1991 est.): 124,017,000. **Age distrib.** (%): 0–14: 18.0; 15–59: 64.3; 60+: 17.7. **Pop. density:** 850 per sq. mi. **Urban** (1990): 77%. **Language:** Japanese. **Ethnic groups:** Japanese 99.4%, Korean 0.5%. **Religions:** Buddhism, Shintoism shared by large majority.

Geography: Area: 145,856 sq. mi., slightly smaller than California. **Location:** Archipelago off E. coast of Asia. **Neighbors:** USSR on N, S. Korea on W. **Topography:** Japan consists of 4 main islands: Honshu ("mainland"), 87,805 sq. mi.; Hokkaido, 30,144 sq. mi.; Kyushu, 14,114 sq. mi.; and Shikoku, 7,049 sq. mi. The coast, deeply indented, measures 16,654 mi. The northern islands are a continuation of the Sakhalin Mts. The Kunlun range of China continues into southern islands, the ranges meeting in the Japanese Alps. In a vast transverse fissure crossing Honshu E-W rises a group of volcanoes, mostly extinct or inactive, including 12,388 ft. Fuji-San (Fujiyama) near Tokyo. **Capital:** Tokyo. **Cities** (1990 cen.): Tokyo 8.1 mln.; Osaka 2.6 mln.; Yokohama 3.2 mln.; Nagoya 2.1 mln.; Kyoto 1.4 mln.; Kobe 1.4 mln.; Sapporo 1.6 mln.; Kitakyushu 1 mln.; Kawasaki 1.1 mln; Fukuoka 1.2 mln.

Government: Type: Parliamentary democracy. **Head of state:** Emp. Akihito; b. Dec. 23, 1933; in office: Jan. 7, 1989. **Head of government:** Prime Min. Kiichi Miyazawa in office: Nov. 6, 1991. **Local divisions:** 47 prefectures. **Defense:** Less than 1% of GNP (1991).

Economy: Industries: Electrical & electronic equip., autos, machinery, chemicals. **Chief crops:** Rice, grains, vegetables, fruits. **Minerals:** negligible. **Crude oil reserves** (1985): 26 mln. bbls. **Arable land:** 13%. **Livestock** (1989): cattle: 4.6 mln.; pigs: 11.7 mln. **Fish catch** (1989): 12.7 mln. metric tons. **Electricity prod.** (1990): 790 bln. kWh. **Crude steel prod.** (1990): 110.3 mln. metric tons. **Labor force:** 8% agric.; 32% manuf. & mining; 43% services & trade.

Finance: Monetary unit: Yen (June 1992: 127 = $1 US). **Gross national product** (1990): $2.1 trl. **Per capita GNP** (1990): $17,100. **Imports** (1991): $236 bln.; partners: U.S. 22%, Middle East 26%, SE Asia 22%, EC 6%. **Exports** (1991): $314 bln.; partners: U.S. 33%, EC 20%, SE Asia 23%. **Tourists** (1989): $3.1 bln. receipts. **National budget** (1990): $532 bln. expenditures. **International reserves less gold** (Mar. 1992): $72 bln. **Gold:** 24.23 mln. oz. t. **Consumer prices** (change in 1991): 3.3%.

Transport: Railroads (1988): **Length:** 17,059 mi. **Motor vehicles:** in use (1990): 36.6 mln. passenger cars, 22.2 mln. comm. vehicles. **Civil aviation** (1990): 95.3 bln. passenger-km; 71 airports with scheduled flights. **Chief ports:** Yokohama, Tokyo, Kobe, Osaka, Nagoya, Chiba, Kawasaki, Hakodate.

Communications: Television sets: 1 per 1.8 persons. **Radios:** 1 per 1.3 persons. **Telephones:** 1 per 2.3 persons. **Daily newspaper circ.** (1990): 429 per 1,000 pop.

Health: Life expectancy at birth (1991): 76 male; 82 female. **Births** (per 1,000 pop. 1991): 10. **Deaths** (per 1,000 pop. 1991): 7. **Natural increase:** 0.3%. **Hospital beds:** 1 per 77 persons. **Physicians:** 1 per 609 persons. **Infant mortality** (per 1,000 live births 1991): 4.

Education (1991): **Literacy:** 99%. Most attend school for 12 years.

Major International Organizations: UN (IMF, GATT, ILO), OECD.

Embassy: 2520 Massachusetts Ave. NW 20008; 939-6700.

According to Japanese legend, the empire was founded by Emperor Jimmu, 660 BC, but earliest records of a unified Japan date from 1,000 years later. Chinese influence was strong in the formation of Japanese civilization. Buddhism was introduced before the 6th century.

A feudal system, with locally powerful noble families and their samurai warrior retainers, dominated from 1192. Central power was held by successive families of shoguns (military dictators),

1192-1867, until recovered by the Emperor Meiji, 1868. The Portuguese and Dutch had minor trade with Japan in the 16th and 17th centuries; U.S. Commodore Matthew C. Perry opened it to U.S. trade in a treaty ratified 1854. Japan fought China, 1894-95, gaining Taiwan. After war with Russia, 1904-05, Russia ceded S half of Sakhalin and gave concessions in China. Japan annexed Korea 1910. In World War I Japan ousted Germany from Shantung, took over German Pacific islands. Japan took Manchuria 1931, started war with China 1932. Japan launched war against the U.S. by attack on Pearl Harbor Dec. 7, 1941. Japan surrendered Aug. 14, 1945.

In a new constitution adopted May 3, 1947, Japan renounced the right to wage war; the emperor gave up claims to divinity; the Diet became the sole law-making authority.

The U.S. and 48 other non-communist nations signed a peace treaty and the U.S. a bilateral defense agreement with Japan, in San Francisco Sept. 8, 1951, restoring Japan's sovereignty as of April 28, 1952.

On June 26, 1968, the U.S. returned to Japanese control the Bonin Is., the Volcano Is. (including Iwo Jima) and Marcus Is. On May 15, 1972, Okinawa, the other Ryukyu Is. and the Daito Is. were returned to Japan by the U.S.; it was agreed the U.S. would continue to maintain military bases on Okinawa.

Industrialization was begun in the late 19th century. After World War II, Japan emerged as one of the most powerful economies in the world, and as a leader in technology.

The U.S. and EC member nations have criticized Japan for its restrictive policy on imports which has given Japan a substantial trade surplus.

In Apr. 1987, the U.S. imposed 100% tariffs on Japanese electronics imports in retaliation for what the U.S. considered various unfair trade practices.

Pres. Bush visted Japan, Jan. 1992; he won trade concessions in the areas of auto parts and sales, computers, paper, and glass.

The Recruit scandal, the nation's worst political scandal since World War II, which involved illegal political donations and stock trading, led to the resignation of Premier Noboru Takeshita in May 1989. A series of scandals rocked Japan's financial sector in 1991; one involved the largest bank, another the 4 largest securities firms.

Jordan

Hashemite Kingdom of Jordan

al Mamlaka al Urduniya al Hashemiyah

Population (1991 est.): 3,412,000. **Age distrib.** (%): 0–14: 48.1; 15–59: 46.9; 60+: 4.0. **Pop. density:** 90 per sq. mi. **Urban** (1986): 70%. **Ethnic groups:** Arab 98%. **Languages:** Arabic (official). **Religions:** Sunni Moslem 92%, Christian 8%.

Geography: Area: 37,737 sq. mi., slightly larger than Indiana. **Location:** In W Asia. **Neighbors:** Israel on W, Saudi Arabia on S, Iraq on E, Syria on N. **Topography:** About 88% of Jordan is arid. Fertile areas are in W. Only port is on short Aqaba Gulf coast. Country shares Dead Sea (1,296 ft. below sea level) with Israel. **Capital:** Amman. **Cities** (1989 est.): Amman 936,000; az-Zarqa 318,000; Irbid 161,000.

Government: Type: Constitutional monarchy. **Head of state:** King Hussein I; b. Nov. 14, 1935; in office: Aug. 11, 1952. **Head of government:** Prime Min. Sharif Zaid ibn Shaker; in office: Nov. 16, 1991. **Local divisions:** 8 governorates. **Defense:** 13% of GNP (1990).

Economy: Industries: Textiles, cement, food processing. **Chief crops:** Grains, olives, vegetables, fruits. **Minerals:** Phosphate, potash. **Arable land:** 5%. **Electricity prod.** (1990): 3.5 bln. kWh. **Labor force:** 20% agric. 20% manuf. & mining.

Finance: Monetary unit: Dinar (Mar. 1992: 1.00 = $1.45 US). **Gross national product** (1990): $4.6 bln. **Imports** (1990): $2.1 bln.; partners: Saudi Ar. 6%, U.S. 11%, Jap. 8%. **Exports** (1990): $1.1 bln.; partners: Saudi Ar. 12%, Ind. 13%, Iraq. 18%. **Tourists** (1989): receipts: $546 mln. **National budget** (1991): $1.6 bln. expenditures. **International reserves less gold** (Mar. 1992): $907 mln. **Gold:** 789,000 oz t. **Consumer prices** (change in 1991): 8.2%.

Transport: Motor vehicles: in use (1989): 136,000 passenger cars, 68,000 comm. vehicles. **Civil aviation** (1990): 2.7 bln. passenger-km; 2 airports with scheduled flights. **Chief ports:** Aqaba.

Communications: Television sets: 1 per 12 persons. **Radios:** 1 per 4.5 persons. **Telephones:** 1 per 10 persons. **Daily newspaper circ.** (1990): 73 per 1,000 pop.

Health: Life expectancy at birth (1991): 70 male; 73 female. **Births** (per 1,000 pop. 1991): 46.7. **Deaths** (per 1,000 pop. 1991): 5. **Natural increase:** 4.1%. **Hospital beds:** 1 per 502 persons. **Physicians:** 1 per 632 persons. **Infant mortality** (per 1,000 live births 1991): 38.

Education (1989): **Literacy:** 71%.

Major International Organizations: UN (WHO, IMF), Arab League.

Embassy: 3504 International Dr. NW 20008; 966-2664.

From ancient times to 1922 the lands to the E of the Jordan were culturally and politically united with the lands to the W. Arabs conquered the area in the 7th century; the Ottomans took control in the 16th. Britain's 1920 Palestine Mandate covered both sides of the Jordan. In 1921, Abdullah, son of the ruler of Hejaz in Arabia, was installed by Britain as emir of an autonomous Transjordan, covering two-thirds of Palestine. An independent kingdom was proclaimed, 1946.

During the 1948 Arab-Israeli war the West Bank and old city of Jerusalem were added to the kingdom, which changed its name to Jordan. All these territories were lost to Israel in the 1967 war, which swelled the number of Arab refugees on the East Bank. A 1974 Arab summit conference designated the Palestine Liberation Organization as the sole representative of Arabs on the West Bank. Jordan accepted the move, and was granted an annual subsidy by Arab oil states.

In 1988 Jordan cut legal and administrative ties with the Israeli-occupied West Bank. In Apr. 1989, riots broke out over price increases imposed under an agreement with the International Monetary Fund.

Some 700,000 refugees entered Jordan following Iraq's invasion of Kuwait, Aug. 1990. Jordan was viewed as supporting Iraq during the Gulf crisis.

Republic of Kazakhstan

Kazak Respublikasy

People: Population (1989 census): 16,500,000. **Pop. density:** 15 per sq. mi. **Ethnic groups:** Kazakh 40%, Russian 37%, German 6%, Ukrainian 5%. **Languages:** Kazakh, Russian, German.

Geography: Area: 1,049,200 sq. mi. **Neighbors:** Russia on N, China on E, Kyrgyzstan, Uzbekistan, Turkmenistan on S, Caspian Sea on W. **Topography:** Extends from the lower reaches of Volga in Europe to the Altai Mtns. on the Chinese border. **Capital:** Alma-Ata.

Government: Type: Republic. **Head of state:** Pres. Nursultan A. Nazarbayev. **Head of government:** Prime Min. Sergei Tereshchenko.

Economy: Industries: Steel, cement, footwear, textiles. **Chief crops:** Grain, cotton. **Minerals:** Coal, tungsten, copper, lead, zinc. **Livestock** (1989): cattle: 9.7 mln., sheep: 36.5 mln., pigs: 3.2 mln.

Finance: Monetary unit: Ruble.

Health: Doctors (1989): 68,000; **Hospital beds** (1989): 225,000.

Major International Organizations: UN, CIS.

The region came under the Mongols in the 13th century and gradually came under Russian rule, 1730-1853. It was admitted to the USSR as a constituent republic 1936. Kazakhstan declared independence Dec. 16, 1991. It became an independent state when the Soviet Union dissolved Dec. 25, 1991.

Kenya

Republic of Kenya

Jamhuri ya Kenya

People: Population (1991 est.): 25,241,000. **Age distrib.** (%): 0–14: 51.2; 15–59: 45.4; 60+: 3.4. **Pop. density:** 112 per sq. mi. **Urban** (1991): 26%. **Ethnic groups:** Kikuyu 21%, Luo 13%, Luhya 14%, Kelenjin 11%, Kamba 11%, others, including Asians, Arabs, Europeans. **Languages:** Swahili (official), Kikuyu,

Luhya, Luo, Meru. **Religions:** Protestant 38%, Roman Catholic 26%, Moslem 6%, others.

Geography: Area: 224,960 sq. mi., slightly smaller than Texas. **Location:** On Indian O. coast of E. Africa. **Neighbors:** Uganda on W, Tanzania on S, Somalia on E, Ethopia, Sudan on N. **Topography:** The northern three-fifths of Kenya is arid. To the S, a low coastal area and a plateau varying from 3,000 to 10,000 ft. The Great Rift Valley enters the country N-S, flanked by high mountains. **Capital:** Nairobi. **Cities** (1987 est.): Nairobi 959,000; Mombasa 401,000.

Government: Type: Republic. **Head of state:** Pres. Daniel arap Moi, b. Sept., 1924; in office: Aug. 22, 1978. **Local divisions:** Nairobi and 7 provinces. **Defense:** 1.0% of GDP (1989).

Economy: Industries: Tourism, light industry, petroleum prods. **Chief crops:** Coffee, corn, tea, cereals, cotton, sisal. **Minerals:** Gold, limestone, diatomite, salt, barytes, magnesite, felspar, sapphires, fluospar, garnets. **Other resources:** Timber, hides. **Arable land:** 4%. **Livestock** (1989): cattle: 13.4 mln. **Fish catch** (1989): 144,000 metric tons. **Electricity prod.** (1990): 2.8 bln. kWh. **Labor force:** 78% agric.

Finance: Monetary unit: Shilling (Mar. 1992: 29.31 = $1 US). **Gross domestic product** (1990): $8.5 bln. **Per capita GDP** (1990): $380. **Imports** (1990): $2.4 bln.; partners: EC 45%. **Exports** (1990): $1.1 bln.; partners: EC 44%. **Tourists** (1989): receipts: $420 mln. **National budget** (1989): $2.3 bln expenditures. **International reserves less gold** (Mar. 1992): $84 mln. **Gold:** 80,000 oz t. **Consumer prices** (change in 1991): 14.8%.

Transport: Motor vehicles: in use (1989): 133,000 passenger cars, 149,000 comm. vehicles. **Civil Aviation** (1990): 2.1 bln. passenger-km; 16 airports with scheduled flights. **Chief ports:** Mombasa.

Communications: Television sets: 1 per 96 persons. **Radios:** 1 per 6 persons. **Telephones:** 1 per 96 persons. **Daily newspaper circ.** (1990): 13 per 1,000 pop.

Health: Life expectancy at birth (1989): 59 male; 63 female. **Births** (per 1,000 pop. 1989): 51. **Deaths** (per 1,000 pop. 1989): 9. **Natural increase:** 4.2%. **Hospital beds:** 1 per 737 persons. **Physicians:** 1 per 7,615 persons. **Infant mortality** (per 1,000 live births 1989): 70.

Education (1989): **Literacy:** 50%. 86% attend primary school.

Major International Organizations: UN and all of its specialized agencies, OAU, Commonwealth of Nations.

Embassy: 2249 R St. NW 20008; 387-6101.

Arab colonies exported spices and slaves from the Kenya coast as early as the 8th century. Britain obtained control in the 19th century. Kenya won independence Dec. 12, 1963, 4 years after the end of the violent Mau Mau uprising.

Kenya has shown steady growth in industry and agriculture under a modified private enterprise system, and has had a relatively free political life. But stability was shaken in 1974-5, with opposition charges of corruption and oppression.

Tribal clashes in the western provinces claimed some 2,000 lives and left 50,000 homeless in 1992. The unrest was the worst since independence in 1963. Several western nations issued travel advisories for Kenya.

Kenya has close ties to the West.

Kiribati

Republic of Kiribati

People: Population (1991 est.): 71,000. **Pop. density:** 266 per sq. mi. **Ethnic groups:** nearly all Micronesian, some Polynesians. **Languages:** Gilbertese and English (official). **Religions:** evenly divided between Protestant and Roman Catholic.

Geography: Area: 266 sq. mi., slightly smaller than New York City. **Location:** 33 Micronesian islands (the Gilbert, Line, and Phoenix groups) in the mid-Pacific scattered in a 2-mln. sq. mi. chain around the point where the International Date Line cuts the Equator. **Neighbors:** Nearest are Nauru to SW, Tuvalu and Tokelau Is. to S. **Topography:** except Banaba (Ocean) I., all are low-lying, with soil of coral sand and rock fragments, subject to erratic rainfall. **Capital** (1988): Tarawa 22,000.

Government: Type: Republic. **Head of state and of government:** Pres. Teateo Teannaki; in office: July 3, 1991.

Economy: Industries: Copra. **Chief crops:** Coconuts, breadfruit, pandanus, bananas, paw paw. **Other resources:** Fish. **Electricity prod.** (1990): 13 mln. kWh.

Finance: Monetary unit: Australian dollar. **Gross domestic product** (1990): $36 mln.

Transport: Chief port: Tarawa.

Communications: Radios: 1 per 7 persons. **Telephones:** 1 per 53 persons.

Health: Hospital beds: 1 per 231 persons. **Physicians:** 1 per 4,104 persons.

Education: Literacy (1985): 90%.

A British protectorate since 1892, the Gilbert and Ellice Islands colony was completed with the inclusion of the Phoenix Islands, 1937. Self-rule was granted 1971; the Ellice Islands separated from the colony 1975 and became independent Tuvalu, 1978. Kiribati (pronounced *Kiribass)* independence was attained July 12, 1979. Under a Treaty of Friendship the U.S. relinquished its claims to several of the Line and Phoenix islands, including Christmas, Canton, and Enderbury.

Tarawa Atoll was the scene of some of the bloodiest fighting in the Pacific during WW II.

North Korea

Democratic People's Republic of Korea

Chosun Minchu-chui Inmin Konghwa-guk

People: Population (1991 est.): 21,814,000. **Pop. density:** 468 per sq. mi. **Urban** (1989): 62%. **Ethnic groups:** Korean. **Languages:** Korean. **Religions:** activities almost nonexistent; traditionally Buddhism, Confucianism, Chondokyo.

Geography: Area: 46,540 sq. mi., slightly smaller than Mississippi. **Location:** In northern E. Asia. **Neighbors:** China, USSR on N, S. Korea on S. **Topography:** Mountains and hills cover nearly all the country, with narrow valleys and small plains in between. The N and the E coast are the most rugged areas. **Capital:** Pyongyang. **Cities** (1987 est.): Pyongyang 2,355,000.

Government: Type: Communist state. **Head of state:** Pres. Kim Il-Sung; b. Apr. 15, 1912; in office: Dec. 28, 1972. **Head of government:** Premier Yon Hyong Muk; in office: Dec. 12, 1988. **Head of Communist Party:** Gen. Sec. Kim Il-Sung; in office: 1945. **Local divisions:** 9 provinces, 3 special cities. **Defense** (1991): 24% of GNP.

Economy: Industries: Textiles, petrochemicals, food processing. **Chief crops:** Corn, potatoes, fruits, vegetables, rice. **Minerals:** Coal, lead tungsten, graphite, magnesite, iron, copper, gold, phosphate, salt, fluorspar. **Arable land:** 19%. **Livestock** (1989): cattle: 1.2 mln; pigs: 3.1 mln. **Fish catch** (1990): 1.7 mln. metric tons. **Crude steel prod.** (1990) 7.0 mln. metric tons. **Electricity prod.** (1990): 33 bln. kWh. **Labor force:** 48% agric.

Finance: Monetary unit: Won (Mar. 1992): 0.97 = $1 US). **Gross national product** (1990): $29 bln. **Imports** (1989): $2.8 bln.; partners: China 17%, USSR 36%, Jap. 19%. **Exports** (1989): $1.9 bln.; partners: USSR 43% China 13%, Jap. 15%. **National budget** (1989): $15.6 bln. expenditures.

Communications: Television sets: 1 per 90 persons. **Radios:** 1 per 6 persons.

Transport: Chief ports: Chonglin, Hamhung, Nampo.

Health: Life expectancy at birth (1991): 67 male; 73 female. **Births** (per 1,000 pop. 1991): 24. **Deaths** (per 1,000 pop. 1991): 6. **Natural increase:** 1.8%. **Hospital beds:** 1 per 74 persons. **Physicians:** 1 per 370 persons. **Infant mortality** (per 1,000 live births, 1991): 32.

Education (1989): **Literacy:** 99%. **Years compulsory:** 11.

Major International Organizations: UN.

The Democratic People's Republic of Korea was founded May 1, 1948, in the zone occupied by Russian troops after World War II. Its armies tried to conquer the south, 1950. After 3 years of fighting with Chinese and U.S. intervention, a cease-fire was proclaimed.

Industry, begun by the Japanese during their 1910-45 occupation, and nationalized in the 1940s, had grown substantially, using N. Korea's abundant mineral and hydroelectric resources.

In Mar. 1992 the U.S. tried unsuccessfully to intercept the N. Korean freighter *Dae Hung Ho* in the Persian Gulf claiming that the ship contained missiles bound for Syria. N. Korea denied the charge.

South Korea

Republic of Korea

Taehan Min'guk

People: Population (1991 est.): 43,134,000. **Age distrib.** (%): 0–14: 27.3; 15–59: 65.5; 60+: 7.2. **Pop. density:** 1,134 per sq. mi. **Urban** (1990): 74%. **Ethnic groups:** Korean. **Languages:** Korean. **Religions:** Christian 43%, Buddhist 18%.

Geography: Area: 38,025 sq. mi., slightly larger than Indiana. **Location:** In Northern E. Asia. **Neighbors:** N. Korea on N. **Topography:** The country is mountainous, with a rugged east coast. The western and southern coasts are deeply indented, with many islands and harbors. **Capital:** Seoul. **Cities** (1990 est.): Seoul 10.7 mln.; Pusan 3,800,000; Taegu 2,200,000; Inchon 1,600,000; Kwangju 1,200,000; Taejon 1,000,000.

Government: Type: Republic, with power centralized in a strong executive. **Head of state:** Pres. Roh Tae Woo; b. 1932; in office: Feb. 25, 1988. **Head of government:** Prime Min. Chung Won Shik; in office: May 24, 1991. **Local divisions:** 9 provinces and Seoul, Pusan, Inchon, and Taegu. **Defense:** 4.5% of GNP (1991).

Economy: Industries: Electronics, ships, textiles, clothing, motor vehicles. **Chief crops:** Rice, barley, vegetables, wheat. **Minerals:** Tungsten, coal, graphite. **Arable land:** 22%. **Livestock** (1989): cattle: 2.0 mln.; pigs: 4.8 mln. **Fish catch:** (1989): 3.3 mln. metric tons. **Electricity prod.** (1990). 85.0 bln. kWh. **Crude steel prod.** (1990): 23.1 mln. metric tons. **Labor force:** 21% agric.; 27% manuf. & mining; 52% services.

Finance: Monetary unit: Won (Mar. 1992: 775 = $1 US). **Gross national product** (1990): $238 bln. **Per capita GNP** (1990): $5,600. **Imports** (1991): $81 bln.; partners: Jap. 33%, U.S. 21%. **Exports** (1991): $71 bln.; partners: U.S. 40%, Jap. 15%. **Tourists** (1988): receipts: $1.3 bln. **National budget** (1990): $38 bln. expenditures. **International reserves less gold** (Mar. 1992): $14 bln. **Gold:** 320,000 oz t. **Consumer prices** (change in 1991): 9.7%.

Transport: Railroads (1989): **Length:** 4,000 mi. **Motor vehicles:** in use (1989): 1.5 mln. passenger cars, 1 mln. comm. vehicles. **Civil aviation** (1989): 18.1 bln. passenger-km; 12 airlines with scheduled flights. **Chief ports:** Pusan, Inchon.

Communications: Television sets: 1 per 4.9 persons. **Radios:** 1 per 1.0 persons. **Telephones:** 1 per 3.3 persons. **Daily newspaper circ.** (1988): 248 per 1,000 pop.

Health: Life expectancy at birth (1991): 67 male; 73 female. **Births** (per 1,000 pop. 1991): 15. **Deaths** (per 1,000 pop. 1991): 6. **Natural increase:** 0.9%. **Hospital beds:** 1 per 458 persons. **Physicians:** 1 per 1,066 persons. **Infant mortality** (per 1,000 live births 1991): 23.

Education (1991): **Literacy:** 96%. **Attendance:** High school 90%, college 14%.

Embassy: 2320 Massachusetts Ave. NW 20008; 939-5600.

Major International Organizations: UN.

Korea, once called the Hermit Kingdom, has a recorded history since the 1st century BC. It was united in a kingdom under the Silla Dynasty, 668 AD. It was at times associated with the Chinese empire; the treaty that concluded the Sino-Japanese war of 1894-95 recognized Korea's complete independence. In 1910 Japan forcibly annexed Korea as Chosun.

At the Potsdam conference, July, 1945, the 38th parallel was designated as the line dividing the Soviet and the American occupation. Russian troops entered Korea Aug. 10, 1945, U.S. troops entered Sept. 8, 1945. The Soviet military organized socialists and communists and blocked efforts to let the Koreans unite their country. *(See Index for Korean War.)*

The South Koreans formed the Republic of Korea in May 1948 with Seoul as the capital. Dr. Syngman Rhee was chosen president but a movement spearheaded by college students forced his resignation Apr. 26, 1960.

In an army coup May 16, 1961, Gen. Park Chung Hee became chairman of the ruling junta. He was elected president, 1963; a 1972 referendum allowed him to be reelected for 6 year terms unlimited times. Park was assassinated by the chief of the Korean CIA, Oct. 26, 1979. The calm of the new government was halted by the rise of Gen. Chun Doo Hwan, head of the military intelligence, who reinstated martial law, and reverted South Korea to the police state it was under Park.

In July 1972 South and North Korea agreed on a common goal of reunifying the 2 nations by peaceful means. But there had been no sign of a thaw in relations between the two regimes until 1985 when they agreed to discuss economic issues. In 1988, radical students demanding reunification clashed with police.

On June 10, 1987, middle class office workers, shopkeepers, and business executives joined students in antigovernment protests in Seoul. They were protesting President Chun's decision to choose his successor and not allow the next president to be chosen by direct vote of the people. Following weeks of rioting and violence, Chun, July 1, agreed to permit election of the next president by direct popular vote and other constitutional reforms. In Dec., Roh Tae Woo was elected president. In 1990, the nation's 3 largest political parties merged; some 100,000 students demonstrated, charging that the merger was undemocratic.

Kuwait

State of Kuwait

Dowlat al-Kuwait

People: Population (1991 est.): 2,024,000. **Age distrib.** (%): 0–14: 40.2; 15–59: 57.6; 60+: 2.3. **Pop. density:** 294 per sq. mi. **Urban** (1990): 95%. **Ethnic groups:** Kuwaiti 28%, other Arab 39%, Iranians, Indians, Pakistanis. **Languages:** Arabic, (official). **Religions:** Moslem 85%.

Geography: Area: 6,880 sq. mi., slightly smaller than New Jersey. **Location:** In Middle East, at N end of Persian Gulf. **Neighbors:** Iraq on N, Saudi Arabia on S. **Topography:** The country is flat, very dry, and extremely hot. **Capital:** Kuwait. **Cities** (1985 est.): Hawalli 145,000; as-Salimiyah 153,000.

Government: Type: Constitutional monarchy. **Head of state:** Emir Shaikh Jabir al-Ahmad al-Jabir as-Sabah; b. 1928; in office: Jan. 1, 1978. **Head of government:** Prime Min. Shaikh Saad Abdulla as-Salim as-Sabah; in office: Feb. 8, 1978. **Local divisions:** 4 governorates. **Defense:** 4.8% of GDP (1990).

Economy: Industries: Oil products. **Minerals:** Oil, gas. **Crude oil reserves** (1990): 94 bln. barrels. **Cultivated land:** 1%. **Electricity prod.** (1989): 20.5 bln. kWh. **Labor force:** social services 45%; construction 20%.

Finance: Monetary unit: Dinar (Mar. 1992: 1.00 = $3.39 US). **Gross domestic product** (1989): $19.9 bln. **Per capita GDP** (1989): $19,700. **Imports** (1989): $6.1 bln.; partners: Jap. 21%, U.S. 9%. **Exports** (1989): $11.4 bln.; partners: Jap. 16%, It. 10%. **Tourists** (1989): $123 mln. receipts. **National budget** (1992): $21 bln. expenditures. **International reserves less gold** (Mar. 1992): $2.9 bln. **Gold:** 2.53 mln. oz t. **Consumer prices** (change in (1989): 3.3%.

Transport: Motor vehicles: in use (1990): 500,000 passenger cars, 114,000 comm. vehicles. **Civil aviation** (1990): 311 mln. passenger-km. 1 airport with scheduled flight. **Chief ports:** Mina al-Ahmadi.

Communications: Television sets: 1 per 2.6 persons. **Radios:** 1 per 1.8 persons. **Telephones:** 1 per 6.9 persons. **Daily newspaper circ.** (1988): 223 per 1,000 pop.

Health: Life expectancy at birth (1991): 72 male; 76 female. **Births** (per 1,000 pop. 1990): 29. **Deaths** (per 1,000 pop. 1990): 2. **Natural increase:** 2.7%. **Hospital beds:** 1 per 319 persons. **Physician:** 1 per 675 persons. **Infant mortality** (per 1,000 live births 1991): 15.

Education (1989): **Literacy:** 71%. **Years compulsory:** 8.

Major International Organizations: UN (World Bank, IMF, GATT), Arab League, OPEC.

Embassy: 2940 Tilden St. NW 20008; 966-0702.

Kuwait is ruled by the Al-Sabah dynasty, founded 1759. Britain ran foreign relations and defense from 1899 until independence in 1961. The majority of the population is non-Kuwaiti, with many Palestinians, and cannot vote.

Oil, first exported in 1946, is the fiscal mainstay, providing most of Kuwait's income. Oil pays for free medical care, education, and social security. There are no taxes, except customs duties.

Kuwaiti oil tankers have come under frequent attack by Iran because of Kuwait's support of Iraq in the Iran-Iraq War. In July 1987, U.S. Navy warships began escorting Kuwaiti tankers in the Persian Gulf.

In 1988, a Kuwaiti Airways jet was hijacked by pro-Iranian Shiite Moslem terrorists who demanded the release of 17 Shiite terrorists. The ordeal lasted 16 days as Kuwait refused to release the terrorists.

Kuwait was attacked and overrun by Iraqian forces Aug. 2, 1990. The Emir and senior members of the ruling family fled to Saudi Arabia to establish a government in exile. On Aug. 28, Iraq announced that Kuwait was its 19th province.

Following several weeks of aerial attacks on Iraq and Iraqi forces in Kuwait, a U.S.-led coalition began a ground attack Feb. 23, 1991. By Feb. 27, Iraqi forces were routed and Kuwait liberated.

Following liberation, there were reports of abuse of Palestinians and others suspected of collaborating with Iraqi occupiers.

Republic of Kyrgyzstan

Kyrgyz Respublikasy

People: Population (1989 cen.): 4,300,000. **Pop density:** 56 per sq. mi. **Ethnic groups:** Kyrghiz 52%, Russian 22%, Uzbec 13%.

Geography: Area: 76,642 sq. mi. **Neighbors:** Kazakhstan on N., China on E., Uzbekistan on W., Tajikistan on S. **Capital:** Bishkek.

Government: Type: Republic. **Head of state:** Pres. Askar Akayev.

Economy: Industries: Tanning, tobacco, textiles, mining. **Chief crops:** Wheat, sugar beets, tobacco. **Livestock** (1989): cattle: 1.2 mln., sheep: 10.4 mln.

Finance: Monetary unit: Ruble.

Health: Doctors (1989): 16,000; **Hospital beds** (1989): 52,000.

Major International Organizations: UN (IMF), CIS.

The region was inhabited around the 13th century by the Kirghiz. It was annexed to Russia 1864. After 1917, it was nominally a Kara-Kirghiz autonomous area, which was reorganized 1926, and made a constituent republic of the USSR in 1936. Kyrgyzstan declared independence Aug. 31, 1991. It became an independent state when the Soviet Union disbanded Dec. 25, 1991.

Laos

Lao People's Democratic Republic

Sathalanalat Paxathipatai Paxaxōn Lao

People: Population (1991 est.): 4,113,000. **Pop. density:** 44 per sq. mi. **Urban** (1987): 15%. **Ethnic groups:** Lao 48%, Mon-Khmer tribes 25%, Thai 14%, Meo and Yao 13%, others. **Languages:** Lao (official), Palaung-Wa, Tai. **Religions:** Buddhists 50%, tribal 50%.

Geography: Area: 91,428 sq. mi., slightly larger than Utah. **Location:** In Indochina Peninsula in SE Asia. **Neighbors:** Burma, China on N, Vietnam on E, Cambodia on S, Thailand on W. **Topography:** Landlocked, dominated by jungle. High mountains along the eastern border are the source of the E-W rivers slicing across the country to the Mekong R., which defines most of the western border. **Capital:** Vientiane. **Cities** (1985 cen.); Vientiane 377,000.

Government: Type: Communist. **Head of state:** Pres. Kaysone Phomvihan; b. Dec. 13, 1920; in office: Aug. 15, 1991. **Head of government:** Prime Min. Khamtai Siphandon; in office: Aug. 15 1991. **Local divisions:** 17 provinces. **Armed forces: Defense:** 3.8% of GDP (1988).

Economy: Industries: Wood products, mining. **Chief crops:** Rice, corn, tobacco, cotton, opium, citrus fruits, coffee. **Minerals:** Tin. **Other resources:** Forests. **Arable land:** 4%. **Livestock** (1990): pigs: 1.3 mln. **Fish catch** (1990): 20,000 metric tons. **Electricity prod.** (1990): 1.1 bln. kWh. **Labor force:** 85% agric.; 6% ind.

Finance: Monetary unit: New kip (Dec. 1991): 700 = $1 US). **Gross domestic product** (1990): $600 mln. **Per capita GDP** (1990 est.): $150. **Imports** (1990): $240 mln.; partners: Thai. 45%, Jap. 20%. **Exports** (1990): $72 mln.; partners: Thai, Viet, USSR.

Transport: Motor vehicles: in use (1989): 17,000 passenger cars, 3,500 comm. vehicles. **Civil Aviation** (1987): 18 mln. passenger km; 4 airports with scheduled flights.

Communications: Radios: 1 per 9 persons.

Health: Life expectancy at birth (1991): 49 male; 52 female. **Births** (per 1,000 pop. 1991): 37. **Deaths** (per 1,000 pop. 1991): 15. **Natural increase:** 2.2%. **Hospital beds:** 1 per 369 persons. **Physicians:** 1 per 6,495 persons. **Infant mortality** (per 1,000 live births, 1991): 124.

Education: (1991): **Literacy:** 45%.

Major International Organizations: UN (FAO, IMF, WHO).

Embassy: 2222 S St. NW 20008; 332-6416.

Laos became a French protectorate in 1893, but regained independence as a constitutional monarchy July 19, 1949.

Conflicts among neutralist, communist and conservative factions created a chaotic political situation. Armed conflict increased after 1960.

The 3 factions formed a coalition government in June 1962, with neutralist Prince Souvanna Phouma as premier. A 14-nation conference in Geneva signed agreements, 1962, guaranteeing neutrality and independence. By 1964 the Pathet Lao had withdrawn from the coalition, and, with aid from N. Vietnamese troops, renewed sporadic attacks. U.S. planes bombed the Ho Chi Minh trail, supply line from N. Vietnam to communist forces in Laos and S. Vietnam.

In 1970 the U.S. stepped up air support and military aid. After Pathet Lao military gains, Souvanna Phouma in May 1975 ordered government troops to cease fighting; the Pathet Lao took control. A Lao People's Democratic Republic was proclaimed Dec. 3, 1975.

Latvia

Republic of Latvia

Latvijas Republika

People: Population (1991 est.): 2,680,000. **Pop density:** 108 per sq. mi. **Urban** (1991): 71%. **Language:** Latvian. **Religion:** Mostly Evangelical Lutheran. **Ethnic groups:** Latvian 54%, Russian 33%.

Geography: Area: 24,900 sq. mi. **Neighbors:** Estonia & Baltic Sea on N., Baltic Sea on W., Lithuania & Belarus on S., Russia on E. **Capital:** Riga. **Cities:** Riga 910,000.

Government: Type: Republic. **Head of state:** Anatolijs Gorbunovs. **Head of government:** Prime Min. Ivars Godmanis. **Local divisions:** 26 districts, 56 towns, 37 urban settlements.

Economy: Industries: Electric railway passenger cars, paper. **Chief crops:** oats, barley, potatoes. **Livestock** (1989): cattle 1.5 mln.

Finance: Monetary unit: Ruble.

Health: Life expectancy at birth (1990): 64 male, 75 female. **Hospital beds:** 1 per 60 persons. **Physicians:** 1 per 200 persons. **Infant mortality rates** (per 1,000 live births 1989): 11.1.

Transport: Motor vehicles: in use (1988): 241,000 passenger cars.

Communications: Television sets (1990): 1.2 per household, **Radios:** 1.4 per household. **Telephones:** 1 per 4.3 persons.

Transport: Chief port: Riga.

Prior to 1918, Latvia was occupied by the Russians, and Germans. It was an independent republic, 1918-39. The Aug. 1939 Soviet-German agreement assigned it to the Soviet sphere of influence. It was officially accepted as part of the USSR on Aug. 5, 1940. It was overrun by the German army, but retaken in 1945. It attempted to establish independence 1990.

During the Soviet coup, Latvia declared independence, Aug. 21, 1991. Several nations extended diplomatic recognition including the U.S. on Sept. 2.

Lebanon

Republic of Lebanon

al-Jumhouriya al-Lubnaniya

People: Population (1991 est.): 3,384,000. **Age distrib.** (%): 0–14: 37.0; 15–59: 55.1; 60+: 7.9. **Pop. density:** 842 per sq. mi. **Urban** (1986): 81%. **Ethnic groups:** Arab 95%, Armenian 4%, Palestinian 9%. **Languages:** Arabic (official), French. **Religions:** Moslem 75%; Christian 25%.

Geography: Area: 4,015 sq. mi., smaller than Connecticut. **Location:** On Eastern end of Mediterranean Sea. **Neighbors:** Syria on E. Israel on S. **Topography:** There is a narrow coastal strip, and 2 mountain ranges running N-S enclosing the fertile

Beqaa Valley. The Litani R. runs S through the valley, turning W to empty into the Mediterranean. **Capital:** Beirut. **Cities** (1991 est.): Beirut 1,100,000; Tripoli 240,000.

Government: Type: Republic. **Head of state:** Pres. Elias Hrawi; in office: Nov. 24, 1989. **Head of government:** Prime Min. Rashid Al-Solh; in office: May 13, 1992. **Local divisions:** 5 governorates. **Defense:** 7.3% of GDP (1991).

Economy: Industries: Trade, food products, textiles, cement, oil products. **Chief crops:** Fruits, olives, tobacco, grapes, vegetables, grains. **Minerals:** Iron. **Arable land:** 21%. **Livestock** (1989): goats: 475,000; sheep: 145,000. **Electricity prod.** (1990): 3.8 bln. kWh. **Labor force:** 11% agric.; 79% ind., comm., services.

Finance: Monetary unit: Pound (June 1992: 1,710 = $1 US). **Gross domestic product** (1990): $3.3 bln. **Per capita GDP** (1990): $1,000. **Imports** (1989): $1.9 bln.; partners: It. 15%, Fr. 10%, U.S. 6%. **Exports** (1989): $1.0 bln.; partners: Saudi Ar. 16%, Jor. 6%, Kuw. 8%. **National budget** (1990): $1.0 bln. expenditures. **International reserves less gold** (Mar. 1992): $808 mln. **Gold:** 9.22 mln. oz t.

Transport: Motor vehicles: in use (1982): 460,000 passenger cars, 21,000 comm. vehicles. **Civil aviation** (1990): 1.5 bln. passenger-km. **Chief ports:** Beirut, Tripoli, Sidon.

Communications: Television sets: 1 per 3.4 persons. **Radios:** 1 per 1.3 persons. **Telephones:** 1 per 18.4 persons. **Daily newspaper circ.** (1986): 211 per 1,000 pop.

Health: Life expectancy at birth (1991): 66 male; 71 female. **Births** (per 1,000 pop. 1991): 28. **Deaths** (per 1,000 pop. 1991): 7. **Natural increase:** 2.1%. **Hospital beds:** 1 per 263 persons. **Physicians:** 1 per 771 persons. **Infant mortality** (per 1,000 live births 1991): 50.

Education: (1991): **Literacy:** 75%. **Years compulsory:** 5; attendance 93%.

Major International Organizations: UN (IMF, ILO, WHO).

Embassy: 2560 28th St. NW 20008; 939-6300.

Formed from 5 former Turkish Empire districts, Lebanon became an independent state Sept. 1, 1920, administered under French mandate 1920-41. French troops withdrew in 1946.

Under the 1943 National Covenant, all public positions were divided among the various religious communities, with Christians in the majority. By the 1970s, Moslems became the majority, and demanded a larger political and economic role.

U.S. Marines intervened, May-Oct. 1958, during a Syrian-aided revolt. Continued raids against Israeli civilians, 1970-75, brought Israeli attacks against guerrilla camps and villages. Israeli troops occupied S. Lebanon, March 1978, and again in Apr. 1980.

An estimated 60,000 were killed and billions of dollars in damage inflicted in a 1975-76 civil war. Palestinian units and leftist Moslems fought against the Maronite militia, the Phalange, and other Christians. Several Arab countries provided political and arms support to the various factions, while Israel aided Christian forces. Up to 15,000 Syrian troops intervened in 1976, and fought Palestinian groups. Arab League troops from several nations tried to impose a cease-fire.

Clashes between Syrian troops and Christian forces erupted, Apr. 1, 1981, bringing to an end the ceasefire. By Apr. 22, fighting had also broken out between two Moslem factions. In July, Israeli air raids on Beirut killed or wounded some 800 persons. A cease-fire between Israel and the Palestinians was concluded July 24, but hostilities continued.

Israeli forces invaded Lebanon June 6, 1982, in a coordinated land, sea, and air attack aimed at crushing strongholds of the Palestine Liberation Organization (PLO). Israeli and Syrian forces engaged in the Bekka Valley. By June 14, Israeli troops had encircled Beirut. On Aug. 21, the PLO evacuated west Beirut following massive Israeli bombings of the city. Israeli troops withdrew from Lebanon in June 1985.

Israeli troops entered west Beirut following the Sept. 14 assassination of newly-elected Lebanese Pres. Bashir Gemayel. On Sept. 16, Lebanese Christian troops entered 2 refugee camps and massacred hundreds of Palestinian refugees.

In 1983, terrorist bombings became a way of life in Beirut as some 50 people were killed in an explosion at the U.S. Embassy, Apr. 18; 241 U.S. servicemen and 58 French soldiers died in separate Moslem suicide attacks, Oct. 23.

On Apr. 26, 1984, pro-Syrian Rashid Karami was appointed premier. The appointment failed to end virtual civil war in Beirut between Christian forces, and Druse and Shiite Moslem militias. There was heavy fighting between Shiite militiamen and Palestinian guerrillas in May 1985. In June, Beirut Airport was the scene of a hostage crisis where Shiite terrorists held U.S. citizens for 17 days. Fierce artillery duels between Christian east Beirut and Moslem west Beirut, Mar.-Apr., 1989, left some 200 dead and 700 wounded.

Kidnapping of foreign nationals by Islamic militants has become common in the 1980s. U.S., British, French, and Soviet citizens have been victims. All were released by 1992.

A treaty signed May 22, 1991, between Lebanon and Syria recognized Lebanon as a separate and independent state for the first time since the 2 countries gained independence in 1943.

Lesotho

Kingdom of Lesotho

People: Population (1991 est.): 1,801,000. **Age distrib.** (%): 0–14: 42.3; 15–59: 52.2; 60+: 5.7. **Pop. density:** 153 per sq. mi. **Ethnic groups:** Sotho 99%. **Languages:** English, Sotho (both official). **Religions:** Roman Catholic 38%, Protestant 42%.

Geography: Area: 11,716 sq. mi., slightly larger than Maryland. **Location:** In Southern Africa. **Neighbors:** Completely surrounded by Republic of South Africa. **Topography:** Landlocked and mountainous, with altitudes ranging from 5,000 to 11,000 ft. **Capital:** Maseru. **Cities** (1990 est.): Maseru 109,000.

Government: Type: Military regime & constitutional monarchy. **Head of state:** King Letsie 3d; in office: Nov. 12, 1990. **Head of government:** Col. Elias P. Ramaema; in office: May 2, 1991. **Local divisions:** 10 districts. **Defense:** 8.6% of GDP (1990).

Economy: Industries: Food processing. **Chief crops:** Corn, grains, peas, beans. **Other resources:** Diamonds. **Arable land:** 13%. **Electricity prod.** (1988): 1 mln. kWh. **Labor force:** 40% agric.

Finance: Monetary unit: Maloti (Mar. 1992: 1.00 = $.34 US). **Gross domestic product** (1990): $420 mln. **Per capita GDP** (1990): $240. **Imports** (1989): $500 mln.; partners: Mostly So. Afr. **Exports** (1989): $60 mln.; partners: Mostly So. Afr. **National budget** (1991): $288 mln.

Transport: Motor vehicles: in use (1987): 6,000 passenger cars, 15,000 comm. vehicles.

Communications: Radios: 1 per 34 persons. **Daily newspaper circ.** (1988): 10 per 1,000 pop.

Health: Life expectancy at birth (1991): 59 male; 62 female. **Births** (per 1,000 pop. 1991): 37. **Deaths** (per 1,000 pop. 1991): 10. **Natural increase:** 2.7%. **Hospital beds:** 1 per 672 persons. **Physicians:** 1 per 15,728 persons. **Infant mortality** (per 1,000 live births 1991): 81.

Education (1990): **Literacy:** 59%.

Major International Organizations: UN (IMF, UNESCO, WHO), OAU.

Embassy: 2511 Massachusetts Ave. NW 20008; 797-5533.

Lesotho (once called Basutoland) became a British protectorate in 1868 when Chief Moshesh sought protection against the Boers. Independence came Oct. 4, 1966. Elections were suspended in 1970. Most of Lesotho's GNP is provided by citizens working in S. Africa. Livestock raising is the chief industry; diamonds are the chief export.

S. Africa imposed a blockade, Jan. 1, 1986, because of Lesotho's giving sanctuary to rebel groups fighting to overthrow the S. African Government. The blockade sparked a Jan. 20 military coup, and was lifted, Jan. 25, when the new leaders agreed to expel the rebels.

In 1990, King Moshoeshoe was sent into exile by the military government.

Liberia

Republic of Liberia

People: Population (1991 est.): 2,730,000. **Age distrib.** (%): 0–14: 46.8; 15–59: 48.3; 60+: 4.9. **Pop. density:** 71 per sq. mi. **Urban** (1990): 46%. **Ethnic groups:** Americo-Liberians 5%, indigenous tribes 95% **Languages:** English (official), tribal dialects. **Religions:** Moslem 20%, Christian 10%, traditional beliefs 70%.

Geography: Area: 38,250 sq. mi., slightly smaller than Pennsylvania. **Location:** On SW coast of W. Africa. **Neighbors:** Sierra Leone on W, Guinea on N, Côte d'Ivoire on E. **Topography:**

Marshy Atlantic coastline rises to low mountains and plateaus in the forested interior; 6 major rivers flow in parallel courses to the ocean. **Capital:** Monrovia. **Cities** (1987 est.): Monrovia 400,000.

Government: Type: Civilian republic. **Head of state:** Pres. Amos Sawyer, act.; in office: Nov. 22, 1990. **Local divisions:** 13 counties. **Defense:** 3.8% of GDP (1987).

Economy: Industries: Food processing, mining. **Chief crops:** Rice, cassava, coffee, cocoa, sugar. **Minerals:** Iron, diamonds, gold. **Other resources:** Rubber, timber. **Arable land:** 1%. **Fish catch** (1988): 18,000 metric tons. **Electricity prod.** (1990): 728 mln. kWh. **Labor force:** 82% agric.

Finance: Monetary unit: Dollar (May 1992: 1.00 = $1 US). **Gross national product** (1989): $1.0 bln. **Per capita GNP** (1989): $440. **Imports** (1989): $394 mln.; partners: U.S. 32%, W. Ger. 10%, Jap. 6%, Neth. 7%. **Exports** (1989): $505 mln.; partners: W. Ger. 31%, U.S. 20%, It. 14%, Fr. 9%. **National budget** (1989): $435 mln. **International reserves less gold** (Feb. 1991): $7,000. **Consumer prices** (change in 1990): 5.8%.

Transport: Motor vehicles: in use (1987): 7,000 passenger cars, 4,000 comm. vehicles. **Chief ports:** Monrovia, Buchanan, Greenville.

Communications: Television sets: 1 per 55 persons. **Radios:** 1 per 4.4 persons. **Telephones:** 1 per 278 persons. **Daily newspaper circ.** (1987): 9 per 1,000 pop.

Health: Life expectancy at birth (1991): 54 male; 59 female. **Births** (per 1,000 pop. 1991): 45. **Deaths** (per 1,000 pop. 1991): 13. **Natural increase:** 3%. **Hospital beds** (1981): 3,000. **Physicians** (1981): 236. **Infant mortality** (per 1,000 live births 1991): 124.

Education (1989): **Literacy:** 25%; 35% attend primary school.

Major International Organizations: UN and most specialized agencies, OAU.

Embassy: 5201 16th St. NW 20011; 723-0437.

Liberia was founded in 1822 by U.S. black freedmen who settled at Monrovia with the aid of colonization societies. It became a republic July 26, 1847, with a constitution modeled on that of the U.S. Descendants of freedmen dominated politics.

Charging rampant corruption, an Army Redemption Council of enlisted men staged a bloody predawn coup, April 12, 1980, in which Pres. Tolbert was killed and replaced as head of state by Sgt. Samuel Doe. Doe was chosen president in a disputed election, and survived a subsequent coup, in 1985.

A civil war began Dec. 1989. Rebel forces seeking to depose Pres. Doe made major territorial gains and advanced on the capital, June 1990. In Sept., Doe was captured and put to death. A cease fire was declared Feb. 13, 1991. More than half of the nation's population became refugees as a result of the civil war.

Libya

Socialist People's Libyan Arab Jamahiriya

al-Jamahiriyah al-Arabiya al-Libya al-Shabiya al-Ishtirakiya

People: Population: (1991 est.): 4,350,000. **Age distrib.** (%): 0–14: 45.0; 15–59: 51.2; 60+: 3.8. **Pop. density:** 6 per sq. mi. **Urban** (1985): 64%. **Ethnic groups:** Arab-Berber 97%. **Languages:** Arabic. **Religions:** Sunni Moslem 97%.

Geography: Area: 679,359 sq. mi., larger than Alaska. **Location:** On Mediterranean coast of N. Africa. **Neighbors:** Tunisia, Algeria on W, Niger, Chad on S, Sudan, Egypt on E. **Topography:** Desert and semidesert regions cover 92% of the land, with low mountains in N, higher mountains in S, and a narrow coastal zone. **Capital:** Tripoli. **Cities** (1988 est.): Tripoli 591,000.

Government: Type: Islamic Arabic Socialist "Mass-State." **Head of state:** Col. Muammar al-Qaddafi; b. Sept. 1942; in office: Sept. 1969. **Head of government:** Premier Abu Zaid Umar Dourda; in office: Oct. 7, 1990. **Local divisions:** 46 municipalities. **Defense:** 11.1% of GNP (1987).

Economy: Industries: Carpets, textiles, petroleum. **Chief crops:** Dates, olives, citrus and other fruits, grapes, wheat. **Minerals:** Gypsum, oil, gas. **Crude oil reserves** (1987): 22 bln. bbls. **Arable land:** 2%. **Livestock** (1989): sheep: 5.8 mln.; goats: 1.0 mln. **Electricity prod.** (1990): 13.6 bln. kWh. **Labor force:** 18% agric.; 31% ind.; 27% services; 24% govt.

Finance: Monetary unit: Dinar (Feb. 1992: 1.00 = $3.46 US). **Gross national product** (1989): $24 bln. **Per capita income** (1986): $5,500. **Imports** (1989): $6.2 bln.; partners: It. 21%, W. Ger. 11%, Fr. 6%. **Exports** (1989): $6.1 bln.; partners: It. 57%, W. Ger. 27%, Sp. 13%. **International reserves less gold** (Mar. 1992): $5.6 bln. **Gold:** 3.6 mln. oz t.

Transport: Motor vehicles: in use (1989): 448,000 passenger cars, 322,000 comm. vehicles. **Chief ports:** Tripoli, Benghazi.

Communications: Television sets: 1 per 8 persons. **Radios:** 1 per 4 persons. **Daily newspaper circ.** (1990): 10 per 1,000 pop.

Health: Life expectancy at birth (1991): 66 male; 71 female. **Births** (per 1,000 pop. 1991): 36. **Deaths** (per 1,000 pop. 1991): 6. **Natural increase:** 3.0%. **Hospital beds** (1982): 16,051. **Physicians** (1982): 5,200. **Infant mortality** (per 1,000 live births 1991): 62.

Education (1989): Literacy: 60%. **Years compulsory:** 7; **Attendance:** 90%.

Major International Organizations: UN, Arab League, OAU, OPEC.

First settled by Berbers, Libya was ruled by Carthage, Rome, and Vandals, the Ottomans, Italy from 1912, and Britain and France after WW II. It became an independent constitutional monarchy Jan. 2, 1952. In 1969 a junta lead by Col. Muammar al-Qaddafi seized power.

In the mid-1970s, Libya helped arm violent revolutionary groups in Egypt and Sudan, and had aided terrorists of various nationalities.

Libya and Egypt fought several air and land battles along their border in July, 1977. Chad charged Libya with military occupation of its uranium-rich northern region in 1977. Libyan forces withdrew from Chad, Nov. 1981 but returned. Libyan troops were driven from their last major stronghold by Chad forces in 1987, leaving over $1 billion in military equipment behind.

The U.S. has accused Libya of masterminding numerous international terrorist actions, including the Dec. 1985 attacks on the Rome and Vienna airports.

On Jan. 7, 1986, the U.S. imposed economic sanctions against Libya, ordered all Americans to leave that country and froze all Libyan assets in the U.S. The U.S. commenced flight operations over the Gulf of Sidra, Jan. 27, and a U.S. Navy task force began conducting exercises in the Gulf, Mar. 23. When Libya fired antiaircraft missiles at American warplanes, the U.S. responded by sinking 2 Libyan ships and bombing a missile installation in Libya. The U.S. withdrew from the Gulf, Mar. 27.

The U.S. accused Libyan leader Qaddafi of having ordered the April 5 bombing of a West Berlin discotheque which killed 2, including a U.S. serviceman. After failing to get their European allies to join them in imposing economic sanctions against Libya, the U.S. sent warplanes to attack terrorist-related targets in Tripoli and Benghazi, Libya, Apr. 14.

The UN imposed limited sanctions, Apr. 15, 1992, for Libya's failure to extradite 2 intelligence agents linked to the 1988 bombing of Pan American World Airways Flight 103 over Lockerbie, Scotland, and 4 others linked to an airplane bombing over Niger.

Liechtenstein

Principality of Liechtenstein

Fürstentum Liechtenstein

People: Population (1991 est.): 28,000. **Age distrib.** (%): 0–14: 20.1; 15–59: 66.3; 60+: 11.6. **Pop. density:** 451 per sq. mi. **Ethnic groups:** Alemannic 95%, Italian 5%. **Languages:** German (official), Alemannic dialect. **Religions:** Roman Catholic 87%, Protestant 8%.

Geography: Area: 62 sq. mi., the size of Washington, D.C. **Location:** In the Alps. **Neighbors:** Switzerland on W, Austria on E. **Topography:** The Rhine Valley occupies one-third of the country, the Alps cover the rest. **Capital:** Vaduz. **Cities** (1991 cen.): Vaduz 4,874, Schaan 4,930.

Government: Type: Hereditary constitutional monarchy. **Head of state:** Prince Hans Adam; in office: Nov. 13, 1989. **Head of government:** Hans Brunhart; b. Mar. 28, 1945; in office: Apr. 26, 1978. **Local divisions:** 2 districts, 11 communities.

Economy: Industries: Machines, instruments, chemicals, furniture, ceramics. **Arable land:** 25%. **Labor force:** 54% industry, trade and building; 41% services; 4% agric., fishing, forestry.

Finance: Monetary unit: Swiss Franc. **Gross Domestic Product** (1990): $630 mln. **Tourists** (1989): 77,000.

Communications: Radios: 1 per 2.9 persons. **Telephones:** 1 per 1.0 persons. **Daily newspaper circ.** (1989): 577 per 1,000 pop.

Health: Births (per 1,000 pop. 1991): 13. **Deaths** (per 1,000 pop. 1991): 7. **Natural increase:** .6%. **Infant mortality** (per 1,000 live births 1991): 5.

Education (1991): **Literacy:** 100%. **Years compulsory** 9; attendance 100%.

Liechtenstein became sovereign in 1866. Austria administered Liechtenstein's ports up to 1920; Switzerland has administered its postal services since 1921. Liechtenstein is united with Switzerland by a customs and monetary union. Taxes are low; many international corporations have headquarters there. Foreign workers comprise a third of the population.

The 1986 general elections were the first in which women were allowed to vote.

Lithuania

Republic of Lithuania

Lietuvos Respublika

People: Population (1991 est.): 3,754,000. **Pop. density:** 149 per sq. mi. **Urban** (1990): 68%. **Ethnic groups:** Lithuanian 80%, Russian 9%, Polish 7%. **Religion:** mostly Roman Catholic.

Geography: Area: 25,170 sq. mi. **Neighbors:** Latvia on N., Belarus on E., S., Poland, Russia, & Baltic Sea on W. **Capital:** Vilnius. **Cities:** Vilnius 592,000; Kaunas 430,000.

Government: Type: Republic. **Head of state:** Pres. Vytautas Landsbergis. **Head of government:** Prime Min. Gedimanas Vagnorius. **Local divisions:** 44 districts, 92 towns, 22 urban settlements.

Economy: Industries: Engineering, shipbuilding. **Chief crops:** grain, potatoes, vegetables. **Arable land:** 49%. **Livestock** (1991): cattle: 2.4 mln., pigs: 2.7 mln.

Finance: Monetary unit: Ruble.

Transport: Railroads (1989): **Length:** 1,951 mi. **Civil aviation:** (1989): 2.3 mln. passenger km.; 3 airports. **Chief Port:** Klaipeda.

Communications: Television sets: 1 per 2.9 persons. **Radios:** 1 per 1.2 persons. **Telephones:** 1 per 4.5 persons.

Health: Life expectancy at birth: (1989); 67 male, 76 female. **Hospital beds:** 1 per 81 persons. **Physicians:** 1 per 218 persons. **Infant mortality rate** (per 1,000 live births): 10.3.

Major international organizations: UN

Lithuania, was occupied by the German Army, 1914-18. It was annexed by the USSR but, the Soviets were overthrown, 1919. Lithuania was a democratic republic until 1926 when the regime was ousted by a coup. In 1939, the Soviet-German treaty assigned most of Lithuania to the Soviet sphere of influence. It became part of the USSR Aug. 3, 1940. Lithuania formally declared its independence from the Soviet Union Mar. 11, 1990. Soviet forces began large-scale maneuvers Mar. 18; border controls were tightened Mar. 21. Pres. Gorbachev warned Lithuania to annul its declaration of independence or face "grave consequences." The Soviets cut off oil and gas supplies Apr. 19.

Soviet troops killed 15 protesters in Vilnius, Jan. 13, 1991, in an attempted coup. During the Soviet coup in Aug., the Western nations recognized Lithuania's independence.

Luxembourg

Grand Duchy of Luxembourg

Grand-Duché de Luxembourg

People: Population: (1991 est.): 388,000. **Age distrib.** (%): 0–14: 17.3; 15–59: 64.5; 60+: 18.2. **Pop. density:** 388 per sq. mi. **Urban** (1985): 81%. **Ethnic groups:** Mixture of French and Germans predominate. **Languages:** French, German (both official), Luxembourgish. **Religions:** Roman Catholic 97%.

Geography: Area: 998 sq. mi., smaller than Rhode Island. **Location:** In W. Europe. **Neighbors:** Belgium on W, France on S, Germany on E. **Topography:** Heavy forests (Ardennes) cover N, S is a low, open plateau. **Capital:** Luxembourg. **Cities** (1990 est.): Luxembourg 86,000.

Government: Type: Constitutional monarchy. **Head of state:** Grand Duke Jean; b. Jan. 5, 1921; in office: Nov. 12, 1964. **Head of government:** Prime Min. Jacques Santer; in office: July 21, 1984. **Local divisions:** 3 districts. **Defense:** 1.2% of GDP (1990).

Economy: Industries: Steel, chemicals, beer, tires, tobacco, metal products, cement. **Chief crops:** Corn, wine. **Minerals:** Iron. **Arable land:** 25%. **Electricity prod.** (1989): 1.3 bln. kWh. **Labor force:** 1% agric.; 42% ind. & comm.; 45% services.

Finance: Monetary unit: Franc (Mar. 1992: 33.79 = $1 US). **Gross domestic product** (1990): $6.9 bln. **Per capita GDP** (1990): $18,000. **Note:** trade and tourist data included in Belgian statistics. **Tourists** (1989): $286 mln. receipts. **Consumer prices** (change in 1991): 3.7%.

Transport: Railroads (1989): **Length:** 169 mi. **Motor vehicles:** in use (1991): 192,000 passenger cars, 18,000 comm. vehicles.

Communications: Television sets: 1 per 4.0 persons. **Radios:** 1 per 1.6 persons. **Telephones:** 1 per 2.3 persons. **Daily newspaper circ.** (1989): 389 per 1,000 pop.

Health: Life expectancy at birth (1991): 73 male; 80 female. **Births** (per 1,000 pop. 1991): 12. **Deaths** (per 1,000 pop. 1991): 11. **Hospital beds:** 1 per 75 persons. **Physicians:** 1 per 358 persons. **Infant mortality** (per 1,000 live births 1991): 7.

Education (1989): **Literacy:** 100%. **Years compulsory** 9; attendance 100%.

Major International Organizations: UN, OECD, EC, NATO.

Embassy: 2200 Massachusetts Ave. NW 20008; 265-4171.

Luxembourg, founded about 963, was ruled by Burgundy, Spain, Austria, and France from 1448 to 1815. It left the Germanic Confederation in 1866. Overrun by Germany in 2 world wars, Luxembourg ended its neutrality in 1948, when a customs union with Belgium and Netherlands was adopted.

Madagascar

Democratic Republic of Madagascar

Repoblika Demokratika Malagasy

People: Population (1991 est.): 12,185,000. **Pop. density:** 53 per sq. mi. **Urban** (1985): 21.8%. **Ethnic groups:** 18 Malayan-Indonesian tribes (Merina 26%), with Arab and African presence. **Languages:** Malagasy, French (both official). **Religions:** animists 52%, Christian 41%, Moslem 7%.

Geography: Area: 226,657 sq. mi., slightly smaller than Texas. **Location:** In the Indian O., off the SE coast of Africa. **Neighbors:** Comoro Is., Mozambique (across Mozambique Channel). **Topography:** Humid coastal strip in the E, fertile valleys in the mountainous center plateau region, and a wider coastal strip on the W. **Capital:** Antananarivo. **Cities** (1990 est.): Antananarivo 802,000.

Government: Type: Republic, strong presidential authority. **Head of state:** Pres. Didier Ratsiraka; b. Nov. 4, 1936; in office: June 15, 1975. **Head of government:** Prime Min. Guy Willy Razanamasy; in office: Aug. 8, 1991. **Local divisions:** 6 provinces. **Defense:** 2.2% of GDP (1989).

Economy: Industries: Food processing, textiles. **Chief crops:** Coffee (over 50% of exports), cloves, vanilla, rice, sugar, sisal, tobacco, peanuts. **Minerals:** Chromium, graphite, coal, bauxite. **Arable land:** 5%. **Livestock** (1990): cattle: 10.4 mln.; pigs: 1.3 mln. **Fish catch** (1990): 99,000 metric tons. **Electricity prod.** (1990): 430 mln. kWh. **Labor force:** 90% agric.

Finance: Monetary unit: Franc (Mar. 1992: 1,929 = $1 US). **Gross domestic product** (1990): $2.5 bln. **Per capita GDP** (1990): $200. **Imports** (1990): $436 mln.; partners: Fr. 32%, U.S. 15%. **Exports** (1990): $290 mln.; partners: Fr. 34%, U.S. 14%. **Tourists** (1989): $28 mln. receipts. **National budget** (1990): $525 mln. **International reserves less gold** (Jan. 1992): $140 mln. **Consumer prices** (change in 1990): 10.8%.

Transport: Railroads (1989): **Length:** 549 mi. **Motor vehicles:** in use (1989): 27,000 passenger cars, 20,000 comm. vehicles. **Civil aviation:** (1990): 512 mln. passenger-km; 52 airports with scheduled flights. **Chief ports:** Tamatave, Diego-Suarez, Majunga, Tulear.

Communications: Television sets: 1 per 92 persons. **Radios:** 1 per 8 persons. **Telephones in use:** 1 per 239 persons.

Health: Life expectancy at birth (1991): 51 male; 54 female. **Births** (per 1,000 pop. 1991): 47. **Deaths** (per 1,000 pop. 1991): 15. **Natural increase:** 3.2%. **Hospital beds** (1982): 20,800.

Physicians (1982): 940. **Infant mortality** (per 1,000 live births 1991): 95.

Education (1987): **Literacy:** 53%. **Years compulsory:** 5; attendance 83%.

Major International Organizations: UN (GATT, WHO, IMF), OAU.

Embassy: 2374 Massachusetts Ave. NW 20008; 265-5525.

Madagascar was settled 2,000 years ago by Malayan-Indonesian people, whose descendants still predominate. A unified kingdom ruled the 18th and 19th centuries. The island became a French protectorate, 1885, and a colony 1896. Independence came June 26, 1960.

Discontent with inflation and French domination led to a coup in 1972. The new regime nationalized French-owned financial interests, closed French bases and a U.S. space tracking station, and obtained Chinese aid. The government conducted a program of arrests, expulsion of foreigners, and repression of strikes, 1979.

In 1990, Madagascar ended a ban on multiparty politics that had been in place since 1975.

Malawi

Republic of Malawi

People: Population (1991 est.): 9,438,000. **Age distrib.** (%): 0–14: 47.8; 15–59: 48.0; 60+: 4.2. **Pop. density:** 206 per sq. mi. **Urban** (1987): 12%. **Ethnic groups:** Chewa, 90%, Nyanja, Lomwe, other Bantu tribes. **Languages:** English, Chewa (both official), Lomwe, Yao. **Religions:** Christian 75%, Moslem 20%.

Geography: Area: 45,747 sq. mi., the size of Pennsylvania. **Location:** In SE Africa. **Neighbors:** Zambia on W, Mozambique on SE, Tanzania on N. **Topography:** Malawi stretches 560 mi. N-S along Lake Malawi (Lake Nyasa), most of which belongs to Malawi. High plateaus and mountains line the Rift Valley the length of the nation. **Capital:** Lilongwe. **Cities** (1987 est.): Blantyre 402,000; Lilongwe 220,000.

Government: Type: One-party state. **Head of state:** Pres. Hastings Kamuzu Banda, b. May 14, 1906; in office: July 6, 1966. **Local divisions:** 24 districts. **Defense:** 1.6% of GDP (1989).

Economy: Industries: Textiles, sugar, cement. **Chief crops:** Tea, tobacco, sugar, coffee. **Other resources:** Rubber. **Arable land:** 25%. **Fish catch** (1990): 68 metric tons. **Electricity prod.** (1990): 535 mln. kWh. **Labor force:** 43% agric.; 23% ind. and comm.; 17% services.

Finance: Monetary unit: Kwacha (Mar. 1992: 3.31 = $1 US). **Gross domestic product** (1990): $1.6 bln. **Per capita GDP** (1990): $175. **Imports** (1990): $581 mln.; partners: So. Afr. 29%, UK 24%, Jap. 6%. **Exports** (1991): $417 mln.; partners: UK 27%, S. Afr. 8%., Ger. 10%. **National budget** (1991): $510 mln. **International reserves less gold** (Mar. 1992): $47 mln. **Gold:** 13,000 oz t. **Consumer prices** (change in 1990): 11.8%.

Transport: Railroads (1987): **Length:** 495 mi. **Motor vehicles:** in use (1987): 15,000 passenger cars, 15,000 comm. vehicles. **Civil aviation** (1990) 86 mln. passenger-km; 5 airports with scheduled flights.

Communications: Radios: 1 per 4.3 persons. **Telephones:** 1 per 172 persons. **Daily newspaper circ.** (1985): 5 per 1,000 pop.

Health: Life expectancy at birth (1991): 48 male; 51 female. **Births** (per 1,000 pop. 1991): 52. **Deaths** (per 1,000 pop. 1991): 18. **Natural increase:** 3.4%. **Hospital beds:** 1 per 627 persons. **Physicians:** 1 per 27,094 persons. **Infant mortality** (per 1,000 live births 1991): 136.

Education (1989): **Literacy:** 25%. About 45% attend school.

Major International Organizations: UN (World Bank, IMF), OAU, Commonwealth of Nations.

Embassy: 2408 Massachusetts Ave. NW 20008; 797-1007.

Bantus came in the 16th century, Arab slavers in the 19th. The area became the British protectorate Nyasaland, in 1891. It became independent July 6, 1964, and a republic in 1966.

Malaysia

People: Population (1991 est.): 17,981,000. **Age distrib.** (%): 0–14: 37.8; 15–59: 56.5; 60+: 5.7. **Pop. density:** 141 per sq. mi. **Urban** (1985): 38%. **Ethnic groups:** Malays 59%, Chinese 32%, Indian 9%. **Languages:** Malay (official), English, Chinese, Indian languages. **Religions:** Moslem, Hindu, Buddhist, Confucian, Taoist, local religions.

Geography: Area: 127,316 sq. mi., slightly larger than New Mexico. **Location:** On the SE tip of Asia, plus the N. coast of the island of Borneo. **Neighbors:** Thailand on N, Indonesia on S. **Topography:** Most of W. Malaysia is covered by tropical jungle, including the central mountain range that runs N-S through the peninsula. The western coast is marshy, the eastern, sandy. E. Malaysia has a wide, swampy coastal plain, with interior jungles and mountains. **Capital:** Kuala Lumpur. **Cities** (1991 est.): Kuala Lumpur 1 mln.

Government: Type: Federal parliamentary democracy with a constitutional monarch. **Head of state:** Paramount Ruler Sultan Azlan Shah; in office: Apr. 26, 1989. **Head of government:** Prime Min. Datuk Seri Mahathir bin Mohamad; b. Dec. 20, 1925; in office: July 16, 1981. **Local divisions:** 13 states and capital. **Defense:** 3.9% of GDP (1990).

Economy: Industries: Rubber goods, steel, electronics. **Chief crops:** Palm oil, copra, rice, pepper. **Minerals:** Tin (35% world output), iron. **Crude oil reserves** (1987): 3.2 bln. bbls. **Other resources:** Rubber (35% world output). **Arable land:** 13%. **Livestock** (1989): pigs: 2.2 mln. **Fish catch** (1990): 604,000 metric tons. **Electricity prod.** (1990): 16.5 bln. kWh. **Labor force:** 18% agric.; 11% tourism & trade; 10% govt.

Finance: Monetary unit: Ringgit (June 1992: 2.58 = $1 US). **Gross domestic product** (1990): $43 bln. **Per capita GDP** (1990) $2,460. **Imports** (1990): $26.5 bln.; partners: Jap. 21%, U.S. 18%, Sing. 14%. **Exports** (1990): $28.9 bln.; partners: Jap. 20%, U.S. 17% Sing. 19%, Neth. 6%. **Tourists** (1989): $839 mln. receipts. **National budget** (1991): $11.8 bln. **International reserves less gold** (Mar. 1992): $10.2 bln. **Gold:** 2.22 mln. oz t. **Consumer prices** (change in 1991): 4.4%.

Transport: Railroads (incl. Singapore) (1989): **Length:** 1,304 mi. **Motor vehicles:** in use (1989): 1.6 mln. passenger cars, 374,000 comm. vehicles. **Civil aviation:** (1989): 10.1 bln. passenger-km; 39 airports with scheduled flights. **Chief ports:** George Town, Kelang, Melaka, Kuching.

Communications: Television sets: 1 per 7 persons. **Radios:** 1 per 2.4 persons. **Telephones:** 1 per 11 persons. **Daily newspaper circ.** (1989): 145 per 1,000 pop.

Health: Life expectancy at birth (1991): 65 male; 70 female. **Births** (per 1,000 pop. 1991): 30. **Deaths** (per 1,000 pop. 1991): 6. **Natural increase:** 2.4%. **Hospital beds:** 1 per 442 persons. **Physicians:** 1 per 2,700 persons. **Infant mortality** (per 1,000 live births 1991): 29.

Education (1989): **Literacy:** 80%; 96% attend primary school, 65% attend secondary.

Major International Organizations: UN (World Bank, IMF, GATT), ASEAN.

Embassy: 2401 Massachusetts Ave. NW 20008; 328-2700.

European traders appeared in the 16th century; Britain established control in 1867. Malaysia was created Sept. 16, 1963. It included Malaya (which had become independent in 1957 after the suppression of Communist rebels), plus the formerly-British Singapore, Sabah (N Borneo), and Sarawak (NW Borneo). Singapore was separated in 1965, in order to end tensions between Chinese, the majority in Singapore, and Malays in control of the Malaysian government.

A monarch is elected by a council of hereditary rulers of the Malayan states every 5 years.

Abundant natural resources have assured prosperity, and foreign investment has aided industrialization.

Maldives

Republic of Maldives

Divehi Jumhuriya

People: Population (1991 est.): 226,000. **Age distrib.** (%): 0–14: 44.4; 15–59: 51.7; 60+: 3.9. **Pop. density:** 1,965 per sq. mi. **Urban** (1985): 26%. **Ethnic groups:** Sinhalese, Dravidian, Arab mixture. **Languages:** Divehi (Sinhalese dialect). **Religions:** Sunni Moslem.

Geography: Area: 115 sq. mi., twice the size of Washington, D.C. **Location:** In the Indian O. SW of India. **Neighbors:** Nearest is India on N. **Topography:** 19 atolls with 1,087 islands, about 200 inhabited. None of the islands are over 5 sq. mi. in area, and all are nearly flat. **Capital:** Male. **Cities** (1985 est.): Male 46,334.

Government: Type: Republic. **Head of state:** Pres. Maumoon Abdul Gayoom; b. Dec. 29, 1939; in office: Nov. 11, 1978. **Local divisions:** 19 districts.

Economy: Industries: Fish processing, tourism. **Chief crops:** Coconuts, fruit, millet. **Other resources:** Shells. **Arable land:** 10%. **Fish catch** (1990): 76,000 metric tons. **Electricity prod.** (1989): 14.0 mln. kWh. **Labor force:** 80% fishing, agriculture, & manufacturing.

Finance: Monetary unit: Rufiyaa (Mar. 1992: 9.98 = $1 US). **Gross domestic product** (1989): $136 mln. **Per capita GDP** (1989): $670. **Imports** (1988): $106 mln.; partners: Sing., Jap., Sri Lan. **Exports** (1988): $45 mln.; partners: Jap., Europe. **Tourists** (1990): $142 mln. receipts.

Transport: Chief ports: Male Atoll.

Communications: Radios: 1 per 8 persons. **Telephones:** 1 per 60 persons.

Health: Life expectancy at birth (1991): 61 male; 65 female. **Births** (per 1,000 pop. 1991): 47. **Deaths** (per 1,000 pop. 1991): 10. **Natural increase:** 3.7%. **Infant morality** (per 1,000 live births 1991): 72.

Education (1989): **Literacy:** 93%. Only 6% of those aged 11-15 attend school.

Major International Organizations: UN.

The islands had been a British protectorate since 1887. The country became independent July 26, 1965. Long a sultanate, the Maldives became a republic in 1968. Natural resources and tourism are being developed; however, it remains one of the world's poorest countries.

Mali

Republic of Mali

République du Mali

People: Population (1991 est.): 8,338,000. **Age distrib.** (%): 0–14: 46.0; 15–59: 49.4; 60+: 4.6. **Pop. density:** 17 per sq. mi. **Urban** (1988): 22%. **Ethnic groups:** Mande (Bambara, Malinke, Sarakole) 50%, Peul 17%, Voltaic 12%, Songhai 6%, Tuareg and Moor, 5%. **Languages:** French (official), Bambara, Senufo. **Religions:** Moslem 90%.

Geography: Area: 478,764 sq. mi., about the size of Texas and California combined. **Location:** In the interior of W. Africa. **Neighbors:** Mauritania, Senegal on W, Guinea, Côte d'Ivoire, Burkina Faso on S, Niger on E, Algeria on N. **Topography:** A landlocked grassy plain in the upper basins of the Senegal and Niger rivers, extending N into the Sahara. **Capital:** Bamako. **Cities** (1989 est.): Bamako (met.) 800,000.

Government: Type: In transition. **Head of state:** Pres. Col. Amadou Toumani Toure; in office: Mar. 31, 1991. **Local divisions:** 7 regions and a capital district. **Defense:** 2.4% of GDP (1988).

Economy: Chief crops: Millet, rice, peanuts, cotton. **Other resources:** Bauxite, iron, gold. **Arable land:** 2%. **Livestock** (1989): sheep: 5.7 mln.; cattle: 4.8 mln. **Fish catch** (1990): 71,000 metric tons. **Electricity prod.** (1990): 730 mln. kWh. **Labor force:** 72% agric.; 12% ind. & comm.; 16% services.

Finance: Monetary unit: Franc (Mar. 1992: 278 = $1 US). **Gross domestic product** (1989): $2.0 bln. **Per capita GDP** (1989): $250. **Imports** (1989): $513 mln.; partners: Fr. 22%, Ivory Coast 25%. **Exports** (1989): $285 mln.; partners: Belg.-Lux. 25%, Fr. 15%. **Tourists** (1989): $28 mln. receipts. **National budget** (1989): $519 mln. expenditures. **International reserves less gold** (Feb. 1992): $299 mln. **Gold:** 19,000 oz t.

Transport: Railroads (1989): **Length:** 401 mi. **Motor vehicles:** in use (1987): 29,000 passenger cars, 7,500 comm. vehicles.

Communications: Radios: 1 per 53 persons. **Telephones:** 1 per 527 persons.

Health: Life expectancy at birth (1991): 45 male; 47 female. **Births** (per 1,000 pop. 1991): 51. **Deaths** (per 1,000 pop. 1991): 21. **Natural increase:** 3.0%. **Hospital beds** (1983): 4,215. **Physicians** (1983): 283. **Infant mortality** (per 1,000 live births 1991): 114.

Education (1991): **Literacy:** 25%. **Attendance:** 21% attend primary school.

Major International Organizations: UN and all of its specialized agencies, OAU, EC.

Embassy: 2130 R St. NW 20008; 332-2249.

Until the 15th century the area was part of the great Mali Empire. Timbuktu was a center of Islamic study. French rule was secured, 1898. The Sudanese Rep. and Senegal became independent as the Mali Federation June 20, 1960, but Senegal withdrew, and the Sudanese Rep. was renamed Mali.

Mali signed economic agreements with France and, in 1963, with Senegal. In 1968, a coup ended the socialist regime. Famine struck in 1973-74, killing as many as 100,000 people. Drought conditions returned in the 1980s.

The military, Mar. 26, 1991, overthrew the government of Pres. Traore, who had been in power since 1968. A mutiparty democracy was promised.

Malta

Repubblika Ta' Malta

People: Population (1991 est.): 354,000. **Age distrib.** (%): 0–14: 23.6; 15–59: 61.8; 60+: 14.6. **Pop. density:** 2,901 per sq. mi. **Ethnic groups:** Italian, Arab, French. **Languages:** Maltese, English (both official). **Religions:** Mainly Roman Catholic.

Geography: Area: 122 sq. mi., twice the size of Washington, D.C. **Location:** In center of Mediterranean Sea. **Neighbors:** Nearest is Italy on N. **Topography:** Island of Malta is 95 sq. mi.; other islands in the group: Gozo, 26 sq. mi., Comino, 1 sq. mi. The coastline is heavily indented. Low hills cover the interior. **Capital:** Valletta. **Cities** (1990 est.): Birkirkara 21,000, Qormi 19,000.

Government: Type: Parliamentary democracy. **Head of state:** Pres. Censu Tabone; in office: Apr. 4, 1989. **Head of government:** Prime Min. Edward Fenech-Adami; b. Feb. 7, 1934; in office: May 12, 1987. **Local Divisions:** 13 electoral districts. **Defense:** 1.3% of GNP (1990).

Economy: Industries: Textiles, machinery, food & beverages, tourism. **Chief crops:** Potatoes, tomatoes. **Arable land:** 41%. **Electricity prod.** (1989): $1.1 bln. kWh. **Labor force:** 2% agric.; 24% manuf.; 43% services; 29% gov.

Finance: Monetary unit: Maltese Lera (Mar. 1992: 1.00 = $3.23 US). **Gross national product** (1989): $2.3 bln. **Per capita GNP** (1989): $6,564. **Imports** (1990): $1.9 bln.; partners: UK 16%, It. 30%, Ger. 14%, U.S. 4%. **Exports** (1990): $1.1 bln.; partners: Ger. 23%, UK 11%, It. 30%. **Tourists** (1989): receipts: $475 mln. **National budget** (1991): $1.3 bln. expenditures. **International reserves less gold** (Mar. 1992): 1.1 bln. **Gold:** 126,000 oz t. **Consumer prices** (change in 1991): 2.4% .

Transport: Motor vehicles: in use (1989): 110,000 passenger cars, 19,000 comm. vehicles. **Civil aviation** (1989): 636 mln. passenger-km; 1 airport. **Chief ports:** Valletta.

Communications: Television sets: 1 per 2.6 persons. **Radios:** 1 per 3.3 persons. **Telephones in use:** 1 per 2.1 persons.

Health: Life expectancy at birth (1991): 74 male; 79 female. **Births** (per 1,000 pop. 1991): 14. **Deaths** (per 1,000 pop. 1991): 8. **Natural increase:** .6%. **Hospital beds:** 1 per 108 persons. **Physicians:** 1 per 489 persons. **Infant mortality** (per 1,000 live births 1991): 7.

Education (1988): **Literacy:** 90%. **Compulsory:** until age 16.

Major International Organizations: UN (GATT, WHO, IMF), Commonwealth of Nations.

Embassy: 2017 Connecticut Ave. NW 20008; 462-3611.

Malta was ruled by Phoenicians, Romans, Arabs, Normans, the Knights of Malta, France, and Britain (since 1814). It became independent Sept. 21, 1964. Malta became a republic in 1974. The withdrawal of the last of its sailors, Apr. 1, 1979, ended 179 years of British military presence on the island.

Marshall Islands

Republic of the Marshall Islands

People: Population (1991 est.): 49,000. **Pop. density:** 697 per sq. mi. **Ethnic groups:** Marshallese 97%. **Languages:** English (official), Marshallese, Japanese. **Religions:** Protestant 90%.

Geography: Area: 70 sq. mi. **Location:** In central Pacific Ocean; comprised of 2 800-mi-long parallel chains of coral atolls. **Capital:** Majuro.

Government: Type: Republic. **Head of state:** Pres. Amata Kabua.

Economy: Agriculture and tourism are mainstays of the economy. **Electricity prod.** (1990): 80 mln. kwh.

Finance: Monetary unit: U.S. dollar. **Gross domestic product** (1989): $63 mln. **Per capita GDP** (1989): $1,500. **Imports** (1988): 34 mln. **Exports** (1988): $2 mln.

Transport: 24 airports with scheduled flights. **Port:** Majuro.

Health: Life expectancy at birth (1991): 61 male; 64 female. **Births** (per 1,000 pop. 1991): 47. **Deaths** (per 1,000 pop. 1991): 8. **Infant mortality** (per 1,000 live births 1991): 53.

Education (1990): **Literacy:** 86%.

Major International Organizations: UN.

The Marshall Islands were a German possession until World War 1 and were administered by Japan between the World Wars. After WW2, they were administered as part of the UN Trust Territory of the Pacific Islands by the U.S.

The Marshall Islands secured international recognition as an independent nation on Sept. 17, 1991.

Mauritania

Islamic Republic of Mauritania

République Islamique de Mauritanie

People: Population (1991 est.): 1,995,000. **Age distrib.** (%): 0–14: 46.4; 15–59: 49.0; 60+: 4.6. **Pop. density:** 5 per sq. mi. **Urban** (1987): 34%. **Ethnic groups:** Arab-Berber 80%, Negroes 20%. **Languages:** Arabic, French (both official), Hassanya Arabic (national). **Religion:** Nearly 100% Moslem.

Geography: Area: 397,954 sq. mi., the size of Texas and California combined. **Location:** In W. Africa. **Neighbors:** Morocco on N, Algeria, Mali on E, Senegal on S. **Topography:** The fertile Senegal R. valley in the S gives way to a wide central region of sandy plains and scrub trees. The N is arid and extends into the Sahara. **Capital:** Nouakchott. **Cities** (1987 est.): Nouakchott 400,000; Nouadhibou 70,000; Kaedi 22,000.

Government: Type: In transition. **Head of Government:** President & Premier Maaouya Ould Sidi Ahmed Taya; in office: Apr. 25, 1981. **Local divisions:** 12 regions, one capital district. **Defense:** 4.2% of GDP (1987).

Economy: Chief crops: Dates, grain. **Industries:** iron mining. **Minerals:** Iron, ore, gypsum. **Livestock** (1988): sheep: 4.1 mln.; goats: 3.9 mln.; cattle: 1.2 mln. **Fish catch** (1989): 92,000 metric tons. **Electricity prod.** (1990): 136 mln. kWh. **Labor force:** 47% agric., 14% ind. & comm., 29% services.

Finance: Monetary unit: Ouguiya (Mar. 1992: 81 = $1 US). **Gross domestic product** (1989): $953 mln. **Per capita GDP** (1989): $490. **Imports** (1990): $639 mln.; partners: Fr. 29%, Sp. 9%. **Exports** (1990): $437 mln.; partners: Fr. 21%, It. 26%, Jap. 20%. **International reserves less gold** (Feb. 1992): $51 mln.

Transport: Motor vehicles: in use (1989): 8,000 passenger cars, 5,000 comm. vehicles. **Chief ports:** Nouakchott, Nouadhibou.

Communications: Radios: 1 per 7.8 persons.

Health: Life expectancy at birth (1991): 44 male; 50 female. **Births** (per 1,000 pop. 1991): 49. **Deaths** (per 1,000 pop. 1991): 19. **Natural increase:** 3.0%. **Hospital beds:** 1 per 1,217 persons. **Physicians:** 1 per 10,128 persons. **Infant mortality** (per 1,000 live births 1991): 94.

Education (1991): **Literacy:** 30%. **Attendance:** 41% in primary school, 10% in secondary school.

Major International Organizations: UN (GATT, IMF, WHO), OAU, Arab League.

Embassy: 2129 Leroy Pl. NW 20008; 232-5700.

Mauritania was a French protectorate from 1903. It became independent Nov. 28, 1960. It annexed the south of former Spanish Sahara in 1976. Saharan guerrillas stepped up attacks in 1977; 8,000 Moroccan troops and French bomber raids aided the government. Mauritania signed a peace treaty with the Polisario Front, 1980, resumed diplomatic relations with Algeria while breaking a defense treaty with Morocco, and renounced sovereignty over its share of former Spanish Sahara. Morocco annexed the territory.

Famine struck repeatedly during the 1980s.

Mauritius

People: Population (1991 est.): 1,081,900. **Age distrib.** (%): 0–14: 36.3; 15–59: 57.2; 60+: 6.4. **Pop. density:** 1,368 per sq. mi. **Urban** (1990): 41%. **Ethnic groups:** Indo-Mauritian 68%, Creole 27%, others. **Languages:** English (official), French Creole, Bhojpuri. **Religions:** Hindu 51%, Christian 30%, Moslem 16%.

Geography: Area: 790 sq. mi., about the size of Rhode Island. **Location:** In the Indian O., 500 mi. E of Madagascar. **Neighbors:** Nearest is Madagascar on W. **Topography:** A volcanic island nearly surrounded by coral reefs. A central plateau is encircled by mountain peaks. **Capital:** Port Louis. **Cities** (1990 est.): Port Louis 139,000.

Government: Type: Parliamentary democracy. **Head of state:** Queen Elizabeth II, represented by Gov.-Gen. Sir Veerasamy Ringadoo; in office: Jan. 17, 1986. **Head of government:** Prime Min. Aneerood Jugnauth; in office: June 12, 1982. **Local divisions:** 9 districts, 3 dependencies.

Economy: Industries: Tourism, food processing. **Chief crops:** Sugar cane, tea. **Arable land:** 54%. **Electricity prod.** (1990): 423 mln. kWh. **Labor force:** 20% agric. & fishing; 38% manuf.; 19% govt. services.

Finance: Monetary unit: Rupee (Mar. 1992: 15.76 = $1 US). **Gross domestic product** (1989): $2.0 bln. **Per capita GDP** (1989): $1,950. **Imports** (1990): $1.6 bln.; partners: UK 9%, Fr. 12%, So. Afr. 9%. **Exports** (1990): $1.1 bln.; partners: UK 50%, Fr. 22%, U.S. 8%. **Tourists** (1989): $172 mln. receipts. **National budget** (1989): $540 mln. **International reserves less gold** (Feb. 1992): $895 mln. **Gold:** 61,000 oz t. **Consumer prices** (change in 1991): 7.0%.

Transport: Motor vehicles: in use (1989): 27,000 passenger cars, 6,000 comm. vehicles. **Chief ports:** Port Louis.

Communications: Television sets: 1 per 8.2 persons. **Radios:** 1 per 4.2 persons. **Telephones:** 1 per 15 persons. **Daily newspaper circ.** (1989): 75 per 1,000 pop.

Health: Life expectancy at birth (1991): 66 male; 74 female. **Births** (per 1,000 pop. 1991): 19. **Deaths** (per 1,000 pop. 1991): 6. **Natural increase:** 1.3%. **Hospital beds:** 1 per 364 persons. **Physicians:** 1 per 1,183 persons. **Infant mortality** (per 1,000 live births 1991): 20.

Education (1989): **Literacy:** 94%. **Attendance:** almost all children attend school.

Major International Organizations: UN and all of its specialized agencies, OAU, Commonwealth of Nations.

Embassy: 4301 Connecticut Ave. NW 20008; 244-1491.

Mauritius was uninhabited when settled in 1638 by the Dutch, who introduced sugar cane. France took over in 1721, bringing African slaves. Britain ruled from 1810 to Mar. 12, 1968, bringing Indian workers for the sugar plantations.

The economy suffered in the 1980s because of low world sugar prices.

Mexico

United Mexican States

Estados Unidos Mexicanos

People: Population (1991 est.): 90,007,000. **Age distrib.** (%): 0–14: 36.5; 15–59: 57.8; 60+: 5.7. **Pop. density:** 118 per sq. mi. **Urban** (1990): 72%. **Ethnic groups:** Mestizo 60%, American Indian 29%, Caucasian 9%. **Languages:** Spanish (official), Ameridian languages. **Religions:** Roman Catholic 97%.

Geography: Area: 761,604 sq. mi., three times the size of Texas. **Location:** In southern N. America. **Neighbors:** U.S. on N, Guatemala, Belize on S. **Topography:** The Sierra Madre Occidental Mts. run NW-SE near the west coast; the Sierra Madre Oriental Mts., run near the Gulf of Mexico. They join S of Mexico City. Between the 2 ranges lies the dry central plateau, 5,000 to 8,000 ft. alt., rising toward the S, with temperate vegetation. Coastal lowlands are tropical. About 45% of land is arid. **Capital:** Mexico City. **Cities** (1988 est.): Mexico City (metro) 20 mln.; Guadalajara (metro) 3 mln.; Monterrey (metro) 2.7 mln.

Government: Type: Federal republic. **Head of state:** Pres. Carlos Salinas de Gortari; b. Apr. 3, 1948; in office: Dec. 1, 1988. **Local divisions:** Federal district and 31 states. **Defense:** 0.6% of GDP (1988).

Economy: Industries: Steel, chemicals, electric goods, textiles, rubber, petroleum, tourism. **Chief crops:** Cotton, coffee, wheat, rice, sugar cane, vegetables, corn. **Minerals:** Silver, lead, zinc, gold, oil, natural gas. **Crude oil reserves** (1990): 54 bln. barrels. **Arable land:** 13%. **Livestock** (1991): cattle: 31 mln.; pigs: 15 mln.; sheep: 6 mln. **Fish catch** (1989): 1.3 mln. metric tons. **Electricity prod.** (1990): 108 bln. kWh. **Crude steel prod.** (1990): 8.5 mln. metric tons. **Labor force:** 26% agric.; 13% manuf.; 31% services; 14% comm.

Finance: Monetary unit: Peso (June 1992: 3,113 = $1 US). **Gross domestic product** (1990): $236 bln. **Per capita GDP** (1990): $2,680. **Imports** (1990): $30 bln.; partners: U.S. 64%, EC 18%. **Exports** (1990): $27 bln.; partners: U.S. 64%, EC 16%. **Tourists** (1989): receipts: $4.9 bln. **National budget** (1989): $55.2 bln. expenditures. **International reserves less gold** (Jan. 1992): $17.7 bln. **Gold:** 923,000 oz t. **Consumer prices** (change in 1991): 22.7%.

Transport: Railroads (1991): **Length:** 16,380 mi. **Motor vehicles:** in use (1989): 6.9 mln. passenger cars, 2.8 mln. comm. **Civil aviation** (1990): 16.4 bln. passenger-km; 78 airports. **Chief ports:** Veracruz, Tampico, Mazatlan, Coatzacoalcos.

Communications: Television sets: 1 in 6.6 persons. **Radios:** 1 in 5.1 persons. **Telephones:** 1 in 7.6 persons. **Daily newspaper circ.** (1986): 142 per 1,000 pop.

Health: Life expectancy at birth (1991): 68 male; 76 female. **Births** (per 1,000 pop. 1991): 29. **Deaths** (per 1,000 pop. 1991): 5. **Natural increase:** 2.4%. **Hospital beds:** 1 per 1,298 persons. **Physicians:** 1 per 600 persons. **Infant mortality** (per 1,000 live births 1991): 29.

Education (1989): **Literacy:** 88%. **Years compulsory:** 10.

Major International Organizations: UN (IMF, GATT), OAS.

Embassy: 1911 Pennsylvania Ave. NW 20006; 728-1600.

Mexico was the site of advanced Indian civilizations. The Mayas, an agricultural people, moved up from Yucatan, built immense stone pyramids, invented a calendar. The Toltecs were overcome by the Aztecs, who founded Tenochtitlan 1325 AD, now Mexico City. Hernando Cortes, Spanish conquistador, destroyed the Aztec empire, 1519-1521.

After 3 centuries of Spanish rule the people rose, under Fr. Miguel Hidalgo y Costilla, 1810, Fr. Morelos y Payon, 1812, and Gen. Agustin Iturbide, who made himself emperor as Agustin I, 1821. A republic was declared in 1823.

Mexican territory extended into the present American Southwest and California until Texas revolted and established a republic in 1836; the Mexican legislature refused recognition but was unable to enforce its authority there. After numerous clashes, the U.S.-Mexican War, 1846-48, resulted in the loss by Mexico of the lands north of the Rio Grande.

French arms supported an Austrian archduke on the throne of Mexico as Maximilian I, 1864-67, but pressure from the U.S. forced France to withdraw. A dictatorial rule by Porfirio Diaz, president 1877-80, 1884-1911, led to fighting by rival forces until the new constitution of Feb. 5, 1917 provided social reform. Since then Mexico has developed large-scale programs of social security, labor protection, and school improvement. A constitutional provision requires management to share profits with labor.

The Institutional Revolutionary Party has been dominant in politics since 1929. Radical opposition, including some guerrilla activity, has been contained by strong measures.

The presidency of Luis Echeverria, 1970-76, was marked by a more leftist foreign policy and domestic rhetoric. Some land redistribution begun in 1976 was reversed under the succeeding administration.

Some gains in agriculture, industry, and social services have been achieved. The land is rich, but the rugged topography and lack of sufficient rainfall are major obstacles. Crops and farm prices are controlled, as are export and import. Economic prospects brightened with the discovery of vast oil reserves, perhaps the world's greatest. But much of the work force is jobless or underemployed.

Inflation and the drop in world oil prices caused economic problems in the 1980s. The peso was devalued and private banks were nationalized to restore financial stability.

Micronesia

Federated States of Micronesia

People: Population: (1991 est.) 111,000. **Ethnic groups:** Trukese 41%, Pohnpeian 26%. **Languages:** English (official). **Religions:** Mostly Christian.

Geography: Area: 270 sq. mi. The Federation consists of 607 islands in the W. Pacific Ocean. **Capital:** Pohnpei.

Government: Type: Republic. **Head of state:** Bailey Olter; in office: May 21, 1991. **Local divisions:** 4 states.

Economy: Chief crops: Tropical fruits, vegetables, coconuts.

Finance: Monetary unit: U.S. dollar. **Gross national product:** $150 million. **Imports** (1988): 67 mln. **Exports** (1988): 3 mln.

Transport: 4 airports with scheduled flights.

Communications: Television sets: 1 per 77 persons. **Radios:** 1 per 6 persons. **Telephones:** 1 per 61 persons.

Health: Life expectancy at birth (1991): 68 male; 73 female. **Births** (per 1,000 pop. 1991): 34. **Deaths** (per 1,000 pop. 1991): 5. **Hospital beds:** 1 per 280 persons. **Physicians:** 1 per 2,540 persons. **Infant mortality** (per 1,000 live births): 65.

Education (1991): **Literacy:** 90%.

Major International Organizations: UN.

The Federated States of Micronesia, formerly known as the Caroline Islands, was ruled successively by Spain, Germany, Japan, and the U.S. It was internationally recognized as an independent nation Sept. 17, 1991.

Republic of Moldova

Republica Moldoveneasca

People: Population (1989 census): 4,300,000. **Pop. density:** 330 per sq. mi. **Ethnic groups:** Moldovian 65%, Ukrainian 14%, Russian 13%. **Language:** Romanian, Ukrainian.

Geography: Area: 13,012 sq. mi. **Neighbors:** Romania on W, Ukraine on N, E, and S. **Capital:** Kishinev.

Government: Type: Republic. **Head of state:** Pres. Mircea Snegur. **Head of government:** Prime Min. Valeriu Muravsky.

Economy: Industries: Canning, wine making, taxtiles. **Chief crops:** Grain, grapes. **Minerals:** Lignite, gypsum. **Livestock** (1989): cattle: 1.1 mln., pigs: 1.9 mln., sheep: 1.3 mln.

Finance: Monetary unit: Ruble.

Health: Doctors (1989): 17,500; **Hospital beds** (1989): 55,300.

Major International Organizations: UN, CIS.

In 1918, Romania annexed all of Bessarabia which Russia had acquired from Turkey in 1812 by the Treaty of Bucharest. In 1924, the Soviet Union established the Moldavian Autonomous Soviet Socialist Republic on the eastern bank of the Dniester. It was merged with the Romanian-speaking districts of Bessarabia in 1940 to form the Moldavian SSR.

During World War II, Romania, allied with Germany, occupied the area. It was recaptured by the USSR in 1944. Moldova declared independence Aug. 27, 1991. It became an independent state when the Soviet Union disbanded Dec. 25, 1991. Fighting erupted between Moldovan security forces and Slavic separatists—ethnic Russians and ethnic Ukrainians—Mar. 1992. The slavs feared that Moldovans, who are Romanian in language and culture, would merge with neighboring Romania.

Monaco

Principality of Monaco

People: Population (1991 est.): 29,712. **Age distrib.** (%): 0–14: 12.7; 15–59: 56.3 60+: 30.7. **Pop. density:** 4,952 per sq. mi. **Ethnic groups:** French 47%, Italian 16%, Monegasque 16%. **Languages:** French (official). **Religions:** Predominantly Roman Catholic.

Geography: Area: 0.6 sq. mi. **Location:** On the NW Mediterranean coast. **Neighbors:** France to W, N, E. **Topography:** Monaco-Ville sits atop a high promontory, the rest of the principality rises from the port up the hillside. **Capital:** Monaco.

Government: Type: Constitutional monarchy. **Head of state:** Prince Rainier III; b. May 31, 1923; in office: May 9, 1949. **Head**

of government: Min. of State Jean Ausseil; in office: Sept. 1985.

Economy: Industries: Tourism, gambling, chemicals, precision instruments, plastics.

Finance: Monetary unit: French franc or Monégasque franc.

Transport: Chief ports: La Condamine.

Communications: Television sets: 17,000 in use (1984). **Telephones in use** (1984): 18,000.

Health: Births (per 1,000 pop. 1991): 7. **Deaths** (per 1,000 pop. 1991): 7. **Infant mortality** (per 1,000 live births 1991): 8.

Education: (1989): **Literacy:** 99%. **Years compulsory:** 10; attendance 99%.

An independent principality for over 300 years, Monaco has belonged to the House of Grimaldi since 1297 except during the French Revolution. It was placed under the protectorate of Sardinia in 1815, and under that of France, 1861. The Prince of Monaco was an absolute ruler until a 1911 constitution.

Monaco's fame as a tourist resort is widespread. It is noted for its mild climate and magnificent scenery. The area has been extended by land reclamation.

Mongolia

Mongolian People's Republic

Bügd Nayramdakh Mongol Ard Uls

People: Population (1991 est.): 2,247,000. **Pop. density:** 3 per sq. mi. **Urban** (1991): 58%. **Ethnic groups:** Mongol 90%. **Languages:** Mongolian (official). **Religion:** traditionally Lama Buddhism.

Geography: Area: 604,247 sq. mi., more than twice the size of Texas. **Location:** In E Central Asia. **Neighbors:** USSR on N, China on S. **Topography:** Mostly a high plateau with mountains, salt lakes, and vast grasslands. Arid lands in the S are part of the Gobi Desert. **Capital:** Ulaanbaatar. **Cities** (1989 est.): Ulaanbaatar 548,000, Darhan 85,000.

Government: Type: In transition. **Head of state:** Pres. Punsalmaagiyn Ochirbat; b. 1942; in office: Mar. 21, 1990. **Head of government:** Prime Min. Dashiyn Byambasüren; in office: Sept. 11, 1990. **Local divisions:** 18 provinces, 3 municipalities. **Defense:** 11.5% of GNP (1984).

Economy: Industries: Food processing, textiles, chemicals, cement. **Chief crops:** Grain. **Minerals:** Coal, tungsten, copper, molybdenum, gold, tin. **Arable land:** 1%. **Livestock** (1990): sheep: 14.8 mln.; cattle 2.2 mln. **Electricity prod.** (1990): 2.8 bln. kWh. **Labor force:** 52% agric.; 10% manuf.

Finance: Monetary unit: Tugrik (Jan. 1992: 42 = $1 US). **Gross domestic product** (1990): $2.2 bln. **Per capita GDP** (1990): $1,000. **Imports** (1988): $1.2 bln.; partners: USSR 91%. **Exports** (1988): $768 mln.; partners: USSR 80%.

Transport: Railroads (1988): **Length:** 1,128 mi.

Communications: Television sets: 1 per 18 persons. **Radios:** 1 per 7.5 persons. **Telephones:** 1 per 36 persons. **Daily newspaper circ.** (1988): 91 per 1,000 pop.

Health: Life expectancy at birth (1991): 63 male; 67 female. **Births** (per 1,000 pop. 1991): 34. **Deaths** (per 1,000 pop. 1991): 8. **Natural increase:** 2.6%. **Hospital beds:** 1 per 85 persons. **Physicians:** 1 per 367 persons. **Infant mortality** (per 1,000 live births 1991): 49.

Major International Organizations: UN (ILO, WHO).

Education (1985): **Literacy:** 89%. **Years compulsory:** 7 in major population centers.

One of the world's oldest countries, Mongolia reached the zenith of its power in the 13th century when Genghis Khan and his successors conquered all of China and extended their influence as far west as Hungary and Poland. In later centuries, the empire dissolved and Mongolia became a province of China.

With the advent of the 1911 Chinese revolution, Mongolia, with Russian backing, declared its independence. A Mongolian Communist regime was established July 11, 1921.

Mongolia has been changed from a nomadic culture to one of settled agriculture and growing industries with aid from the USSR and East European nations.

In 1990, the Mongolian Communist Party surrendered its monopoly on power. Free elections were held July 1990; the communists were victorious.

Morocco

Kingdom of Morocco

al-Mamlaka al-Maghrebia

People: Population (1991 est.): 26,181,000. **Age distrib.** (%): 0–14: 41.2; 15–59: 53.7; 60+: 5.1. **Pop. density:** 151 per sq. mi. **Urban** (1988): 44%. **Ethnic groups:** Arab-Berber 99%. **Languages:** Arabic (official), Berber. **Religions:** Sunni Moslems 99%.

Geography: Area: 172,413 sq. mi., larger than California. **Location:** on NW coast of Africa. **Neighbors:** W. Sahara on S, Algeria on E. **Topography:** Consists of 5 natural regions: mountain ranges (Riff in the N, Middle Atlas, Upper Atlas, and Anti-Atlas); rich plains in the W; alluvial plains in SW; well-cultivated plateaus in the center; a pre-Sahara arid zone extending from SE. **Capital:** Rabat. **Cities** (1984): Casablanca 2,600,000; Rabat 556,000, Fes 852,000.

Government: Type: Constitutional monarchy. **Head of state:** King Hassan II; b. July 9, 1929; in office: Mar. 3, 1961. **Head of government:** Prime Min. Azzedine Laraki; in office: Sept. 30, 1986. **Local divisions:** 37 provinces, 5 municipalities. **Defense:** 5.0% of GDP (1990).

Economy: Industries: Carpets, clothing, leather goods, mining, tourism. **Chief crops:** Grain, fruits, dates, grapes. **Minerals:** Copper, cobalt, manganese, phosphates, lead, oil. **Crude oil reserves** (1980): 100 mln. bbls. **Arable land:** 18%. **Livestock** (1989): cattle: 3.5 mln.; sheep; 17 mln.; goats: 5.9 mln. **Fish catch** (1989): 551,000 metric tons. **Electricity prod.** (1990): 8.1 bln. kWh. **Labor force:** 50% agric., 26% services; 15% ind.

Finance: Monetary unit: Dirham (Mar. 1992: 8.91 = $1 US). **Gross domestic product** (1990): $25.4 bln. **Per capita GDP** (1990): $990. **Imports** (1990): $5.9 bln.; partners: EC 53%, U.S. 11%. **Exports** (1990): $4.0 bln.; partners: EC 58%. **Tourists** (1989): $1.1 bln. receipts. **National budget** (1990): $7.3 bln. expenditures. **International reserves less gold** (Mar. 1992): $2.9 bln. **Gold:** 704,000 oz t. **Consumer prices** (change in 1990): 5.9%.

Transport: Railroads (1990): **Length:** 1,893 km. **Motor vehicles:** in use (1987): 554,000 passenger cars, 255,000 comm. vehicles. **Civil aviation** (1989): 2.7 bln. passenger-km; 15 airports. **Chief ports:** Tangier, Casablanca, Kenitra.

Communications: Television sets: 1 per 21 persons. **Radios:** 1 per 5.4 persons. **Telephones in use:** 1 per 68 persons. **Daily newspaper circ.** (1988): 12 per 1,000 pop.

Health: Life expectancy at birth (1991): 63 male; 66 female. **Births** (per 1,000 pop. 1991): 30. **Deaths** (per 1,000 pop. 1991): 8. **Natural increase:** 2.2%. **Hospital beds:** 1 per 918 persons. **Physicians:** 1 per 4,873 persons. **Infant mortality** (per 1,000 live births 1991): 76.

Education (1985): **Literacy:** 35%.

Major International Organizations: UN (ILO, IMF, WHO), OAU, Arab League.

Embassy: 1601 21st St. NW 20009; 462-7979.

Berbers were the original inhabitants, followed by Carthaginians and Romans. Arabs conquered in 683. In the 11th and 12th centuries, a Berber empire ruled all NW Africa and most of Spain from Morocco.

Part of Morocco came under Spanish rule in the 19th century; France controlled the rest in the early 20th. Tribal uprisings lasted from 1911 to 1933. The country became independent Mar. 2, 1956. Tangier, an internationalized seaport, was turned over to Morocco, 1956. Ifni, a Spanish enclave, was ceded in 1969.

Morocco annexed over 70,000 sq. mi. of phosphate-rich land Apr. 14, 1976, two-thirds of former Spanish Sahara, with the remainder annexed by Mauritania. Spain had withdrawn in February. Polisario, a guerrilla movement, proclaimed the region independent Feb. 27, and launched attacks with Algerian support. Morocco accepted U.S. military and economic aid. When Mauritania signed a treaty with the Polisario Front, and gave up its portion of the former Spanish Sahara, Morocco occupied the area, 1980. Morocco accused Algeria of instigating Polisario attacks.

After years of bitter fighting, Morocco controls the main urban areas, but the Polisario Front's guerrillas move freely in the vast, sparsely populated deserts. The 2 sides signed a cease-fire agreement in 1990. The UN will conduct a referendum in Western Sahara on whether the territory should become independent or remain part of Morocco.

Mozambique

Republic of Mozambique

República de Mocambique

People: Population (1991 est.): 15,113,000. **Age distrib.** (%): 0–14: 45.3; 15–59: 50.6; 60+: 4.1. **Pop. density:** 49 per sq. mi. **Ethnic groups:** Bantu tribes. **Languages:** Portuguese (official), Makua, Malawi, Shona, Tsonga. **Religions:** Traditional beliefs 60%, Christian 30%, Moslem 10%.

Geography: Area: 303,769 sq. mi., about the size of Texas. **Location:** On SE coast of Africa. **Neighbors:** Tanzania on N, Malawi, Zambia, Zimbabwe on W, South Africa, Swaziland on S. **Topography:** Coastal lowlands comprise nearly half the country with plateaus rising in steps to the mountains along the western border. **Capital:** Maputo. **Cities:** (1989 est.): Maputo 1.0 mln., Beira 291,604

Government: Type: Socialist one-party state. **Head of state:** Pres. Joaquim Chissano; b. Oct. 22, 1939; in office: Oct. 19, 1986. **Head of Government:** Mario de Graca Machungo; in office: July 17, 1986. **Local divisions:** 10 provinces. **Defense:** 8.4% of GNP (1987).

Economy: Industries: Cement, alcohol, textiles. **Chief crops:** Cashews, cotton, sugar, copra, tea. **Minerals:** Coal, titanium. **Arable land:** 4%. **Livestock** (1989): cattle: 1.3 mln. **Fish catch** (1989): 33,000 metric tons. **Electricity prod.** (1990): 1.7 bln. kWh. **Labor force:** 85% agric., 9% ind. & comm., 2% services.

Finance: Monetary unit: Metical (Jan. 1992: 1,170 = $1 US). **Gross domestic product** (1989): $1.6 bln. **Per capita GDP** (1989): $110. **Imports** (1989): $764 mln.; partners: So. Afr. 11%, U.S. 8%, USSR 12%, It. 10%. **Exports** (1989): $90 mln.; partners: Sp. 21%, U.S. 16%, Jap. 15%. **National budget** (1989): $208 mln.

Transport: Railroads (1990): **Length:** 2,033 mi. **Motor vehicles:** in use (1989): 84,000 passenger cars, 24,000 comm. vehicles. **Chief ports:** Maputo, Beira, Nacala, Quelimane.

Communications: Television sets: 1 per 437 persons. **Radios:** 1 per 31 persons. **Telephones:** 1 per 235 persons. **Daily newspaper circ.** (1990): 3 per 1,000 pop.

Health: Life expectancy at birth (1991): 46 male; 49 female. **Births** (per 1,000 pop. 1991): 46. **Deaths** (per 1,000 pop. 1991): 17. **Natural increase:** 2.9%. **Hospital beds:** 1 per 1,227 persons. **Physicians:** 1 per 43,536 persons. **Infant mortality** (per 1,000 live births 1991): 134.

Education (1989): **Literacy:** 14%.

Major International Organization: UN (IMF, World Bank), OAU.

The first Portuguese post on the Mozambique coast was established in 1505, on the trade route to the East. Mozambique became independent June 25, 1975, after a ten-year war against Portuguese colonial domination. The 1974 revolution in Portugal paved the way for the orderly transfer of power to Frelimo (Front for the Liberation of Mozambique). Frelimo took over local administration Sept. 20, 1974, over the opposition, in part violent, of some blacks and whites. The new government, led by Maoist Pres. Samora Machel, promised a gradual transition to a communist system. Private schools were closed, rural collective farms organized, and private homes nationalized. Economic problems included the emigration of most of the country's whites, a politically untenable economic dependence on white-ruled South Africa, and a large external debt.

In the 1980s, severe drought and civil war caused famine and heavy loss of life.

Myanmar (Formerly Burma)

Union of Myanmar

Pyeidaungzu Myanma Naingngandaw

People: Population (1991 est.): 42,112,000. **Age distrib.** (%): 0–14: 41.2; 15–59: 52.8; 60+: 6.0. **Pop. density:** 160 per sq. mi. **Urban (1986):** 24%. **Ethnic groups:** Burmans (related to Tibetans) 68%; Karen 4%, Shan 7%, Rakhine 3%. **Languages:** Burmese (official), Karen, Shan. **Religions:** Buddhist 85%; animist, Christian.

Geography: Area: 261,789 sq. mi., nearly as large as Texas. **Location:** Between S. and S.E. Asia, on Bay of Bengal. **Neighbors:** Bangladesh, India on W, China, Laos, Thailand on E. **Topography:** Mountains surround Myanmar on W, N, and E, and dense forests cover much of the nation. N-S rivers provide habitable valleys and communications, especially the Irrawaddy, navigable for 900 miles. The country has a tropical monsoon climate. **Capital:** Yangon. **Cities** (1983 est.): Yangon 2,458,712; Mandalay 458,000; Karbe ('73 cen.): 253,600; Moulmein 188,000.

Government: Type: Military. **Head of state and head of government:** Gen. Than Shwe; in office: Apr. 23, 1992. **Local divisions:** 7 states and 7 divisions. **Defense:** 3.0% of GDP (1989).

Economy: Chief crops: Rice, sugarcane, peanuts, beans. **Minerals:** Oil, lead, silver, tin, tungsten, precious stones. **Crude oil reserves** (1985): 733 mln. bbls. **Other resources:** Rubber, teakwood. **Arable land:** 15%. **Livestock.** (1989): cattle: 9.9 mln.; pigs: 3.1 mln. **Fish catch** (1989): 704,000 metric tons. **Electricity prod.** (1990): 2.9 bln. kWh. **Labor force:** 66% agric; 12% ind.

Finance: Monetary unit: Kyat (Mar. 1992: 6.27 = $1 US). **Gross domestic product** (1990): $16.8 bln. **Per capita GDP** (1990): $408. **Imports** (1990): $270 mln.; partners: Jap. 50%, EC 20%. **Exports** (1990): $325 mln.; partners: SE Asian countries 30%; EC 12%. **Tourism** (1989): $26 mln. receipts. **National budget** (1989): $5.0 bln. **International reserves less gold** (Mar. 1992): $258 mln. **Gold:** 251,000 oz t. **Consumer prices** (change in 1990): 17%.

Transport: Railroads (1990): **Length:** 1,949 mi. **Motor vehicles:** in use (1989): 27,000 passenger cars, 42,000 comm. vehicles. **Civil aviation** (1988): 214 mln. passenger-km.; 21 airports with scheduled flights. **Chief ports:** Yangon, Bassein, Moulmein.

Communications: Television sets: 1 per 592 persons. **Radios:** 1 per 13 persons. **Telephones:** 1 per 501 persons. **Daily newspaper circ.** (1989): 14 per 1,000 pop.

Health: Life expectancy at birth (1991): 53 male; 56 female. **Births** (per 1,000 pop. 1991): 32. **Deaths** (per 1,000 pop. 1991): 13. **Natural increase:** 1.9%. **Hospital beds:** 1 per 1,498 persons. **Physicians:** 1 per 3,485 persons. **Infant mortality** (per 1,000 live births 1991): 95.

Education (1989): **Literacy:** 66%. **Years compulsory:** 4; **Attendance:** 84%.

Major International Organizations: UN (World Bank, IMF, GATT).

Embassy: 2300 S St. NW 20008; 332-9044.

The Burmese arrived from Tibet before the 9th century, displacing earlier cultures, and a Buddhist monarchy was established by the 11th. Burma was conquered by the Mongol dynasty of China in 1272, then ruled by Shans as a Chinese tributary, until the 16th century.

Britain subjugated Burma in 3 wars, 1824-84, and ruled the country as part of India until 1937, when it became self-governing. Independence outside the Commonwealth was achieved Jan. 4, 1948.

Gen. Ne Win dominated politics from 1962 to 1988, when he abdicated power, following waves of anti-government demonstrations. He led a Revolutionary Council which drove Indians from the civil service and Chinese from commerce. Socialization of the economy was advanced, isolation from foreign countries enforced.

In 1987 Burma, once the richest nation in SE Asia, was granted less developed country status by the UN. Following Ne Win's resignation, Sein Lwin and later Maung Maung, a civilian, took power but rioting and street violence continued. In Sept., Gen. Saw Maung, a close associate of Ne Win, seized power.

In 1989 the country's name was changed to Myanmar.

The first free, multiparty elections in 30 years took place May 27, 1990, with the main opposition party winning a decisive victory, but the military rulers refused to hand over power.

Namibia

Republic of Namibia

People: Population (1991 est.): 1,520,000. **Pop density:** 4 per sq. mi. **Ethnic groups:** Ovambo 50%, Kavango 10%, Herero 7%, Damara 7%. **Languages:** Afrikaans, English, (official), several indigenous languages. **Religion:** Lutheran 50%, other Christian 30%.

Geography: Area: 317,818 sq. mi., slightly more than half the size of Alaska. **Location:** In S. Africa on the coast of the Atlantic Ocean. Angola on the N., Botswana on the E., and South Africa on the S. **Capital:** Windhoek. **Cities** (1990 est.): Windhoek, 114,000.

Government: Type: Republic. **Head of state:** Pres. Sam Nujoma; in office: Feb. 16, 1990. **Head of government:** Prime Min. Hage Geingob. **Local divisions:** 14 regions.

Economy: Mining accounts for over 40% of GNP. **Minerals:** Diamonds. **Fish catch** (1989): 383,000. **Electricity prod.** (1990): 1.2 mln. kWh.

Finance: Monetary unit: South African Rand. **Gross National Product** (1990): $1.8 bln. **Per capital GNP** (1990): $1,240. **Imports** (1989): $894 mln. **Exports** (1989): $1.0 bln. **National budget** (1991): $1.0 bln. expenditures.

Communications: Television sets: 1 per 42 persons. **Radios:** 1 per 5.8 persons. **Telephones:** 1 per 17 persons.

Health: Life Expectancy at Birth (1991): 58 male; 63 female. **Births** (per 1,000 pop. 1991): 45. **Deaths** (per 1,000 pop 1991): 10. **Natural increase:** 3.5. **Hospital beds:** 1 per 166 persons. **Physicians:** 1 per 4,450 persons. **Infant Mortality** (per 1,000 live births 1991): 72.

Education (1989): **Literacy:** 16% nonwhite.

Embassy: 1413 K St. NW 20005; 289-3871.

Namibia was declared a protectorate by Germany in 1890 and officially called South-West Africa. South Africa seized the territory from Germany in 1915 during World War 1; the League of Nations gave South Africa a mandate over the territory in 1920. In 1966, the Marxist South-West Africa People's Organization (SWAPO) launched a guerrilla war for independence.

In 1968 the UN General Assembly gave the area the name Namibia.

In a 1977 referendum, white voters backed a plan for a multiracial interim government to lead to independence. SWAPO rejected the plan. Both S. Africa and Namibian rebels agreed to a UN plan for independence by the end of 1978. S. Africa rejected the plan, Sept. 20, 1978, and held elections, without UN supervision, for Namibia's constituent assembly, Dec., that were ignored by the major black opposition parties.

In 1982, So. African and SWAPO agreed in principle on a cease-fire and the holding of UN-supervised elections. So. Africa, however, insisted on the withdrawal of Cuban forces from Angola as a precondition to Namibian independence. On Jan. 18, 1983, South Africa dissolved the Namibian National Assembly and resumed direct control of the territory.

In 1988, A U.S. mediated plan was agreed upon by So. Africa, Angola, and Cuba, which called for withdrawal of Cuban troops from Angola and black majority rule in Namibia.

Namibia became an independent nation March 21, 1990.

Walvis Bay, the only deepwater port in the country, was turned over to South African administration in 1922. S. Africa said in 1978 it would discuss sovereignty only after Namibian independence. Discussions were held in 1991.

Nauru

Republic of Nauru

Naoero

People: Population (1991): 9,333. **Pop density:** 1,166 per sq. mi. **Ethnic groups:** Nauruans 57%, Pacific Islanders 26%, Chinese 8%, European 8%. **Languages:** Nauruan (official). **Religions:** Predominately Christian.

Geography: Area: 8 sq. mi. **Location:** In Western Pacific O. just S of Equator. **Neighbors:** Nearest are Solomon Is. **Topography:** Mostly a plateau bearing high grade phosphate deposits, surrounded by a coral cliff and a sandy shore in concentric rings. **Capital:** Yaren.

Government: Type: Republic. **Head of state:** Pres. Bernard Dowiyogo; in office: Dec. 12, 1989. **Local divisions:** 14 districts.

Economy: Phosphate mining. **Electricity prod.** (1990): 48 mln. kWh.

Finance: Monetary unit: Australian dollar. **Gross national product** (1989): $60 mln.

Communications: Radios: 4,000 in use (1985). **Telephones in use** (1980): 1,500.

Health: Births (per 1,000 pop. 1991): 19. **Deaths** (per 1,000 pop. 1991): 5. **Natural increase:** 1.4%. **Infant mortality** (per 1,000 live births 1991): 41.

Education (1988): Literacy 99%; compulsory ages 6-16.

The island was discovered in 1798 by the British but was formally annexed to the German Empire in 1886. After World War I, Nauru became a League of Nations mandate administered by Australia. During World War II the Japanese occupied the island.

In 1947 Nauru was made a UN trust territory, administered by Australia. Nauru became an independent republic Jan. 31, 1968.

Phosphate exports provide one of the world's highest per capita revenues for the Nauru people.

Nepal

Kingdom of Nepal

Sri Nepala Sarkar

People: Population (1991 est.): 19,611,000. **Age distrib.** (%): 0–14: 42.2; 15–59: 52.9; 60+: 4.9. **Pop. density:** 349 per sq. mi. **Urban** (1987): 8%. **Ethnic groups:** The many tribes are descendants of Indian, Tibetan, and Central Asian migrants. **Languages:** Nepali (official) (an Indic language), many others. **Religions:** Hindu (official) 90%, Buddhist 7%.

Geography: Area: 56,136 sq. mi., the size of North Carolina. **Location:** Astride the Himalaya Mts. **Neighbors:** China on N, India on S. **Topography:** The Himalayas stretch across the N, the hill country with its fertile valleys extends across the center, while the southern border region is part of the flat, subtropical Ganges Plain. **Capital:** Kathmandu. **Cities** (1987 est.): Kathmandu 422,000, Pokhara, Biratnagar, Birganj.

Government: Type: Democracy. **Head of state:** King Birendra Bir Bikram Shah Dev; b. Dec. 28, 1945; in office: Jan. 31, 1972. **Head of government:** Prime Min. Giriga Prasad Koirala; in office: May 26, 1991. **Local divisions:** 14 zones. **Defense:** 2.0% of GDP (1991).

Economy: Industries: Sugar, jute mills, tourism. **Chief crops:** Jute, rice, grain. **Minerals:** Quartz. **Other resources:** Forests. **Arable land:** 17%. **Livestock** (1989): cattle: 6.3 mln. **Electricity prod.** (1990): 530 mln. kWh. **Labor force:** 91% agric.

Finance: Monetary unit: Rupee (Mar. 1992: 42 = $1 US). **Gross domestic product** (1990): $3.1 bln. **Per capita GDP** (1990): $160. **Imports** (1990): $686 mln.; partners: India 47%, Jap. 25%. **Exports** (1990): $210 mln.; partners: India 68%. **Tourists** (1988): receipts: $28 mln. **National budget** (1991): $618 mln. **International reserves less gold** (Mar. 1992): $428 mln. **Gold:** 152,000 oz t. **Consumer prices** (change in 1990): 8.2%.

Transport: Civil aviation (1989): 408 mln. passenger-km.

Communications: Radios: 1 per 32 persons. **Telephones:** 1 per 415 persons.

Health: Life expectancy at birth (1989): 50 male; 49 female. **Births** (per 1,000 pop. 1991): 40. **Deaths** (per 1,000 pop. 1991): 15. **Natural increase:** 2.4%. **Hospital beds:** 1 per 4,234 persons. **Physicians:** 1 per 20,737 persons. **Infant mortality** (per 1,000 live births 1991): 98.

Education (1989): **Literacy:** 29%. **Years compulsory:** 3; Attendance: 79% primary, 22% secondary.

Major International Organizations: UN (IMF).

Embassy: 2131 Leroy Pl. NW 20008; 667-4550.

Nepal was originally a group of petty principalities, the inhabitants of one of which, the Gurkhas, became dominant about 1769. In 1951 King Tribhubana Bir Bikram, member of the Shah family, ended the system of rule by hereditary premiers of the Ranas family, who had kept the kings virtual prisoners, and established a cabinet system of government.

Virtually closed to the outside world for centuries, Nepal is now linked to India and Pakistan by roads and air service and to Tibet by road. Polygamy, child marriage, and the caste system were officially abolished in 1963.

In response to numerous pro-democracy protests, the government, which had banned all political parties since 1960, announced the legalization of political parties in 1990. Multi-party elections were held in 1991.

Netherlands

Kingdom of the Netherlands

Koninkrijk der Nederlanden

People: Population (1991 est.) 15,022,000. **Age distrib.** (%): 0–14: 18.8; 15–60: 64.2; 60+: 17.0. **Pop. density:** 952 per sq. mi. **Urban** (1990): 88.3%. **Ethnic groups:** Dutch 97%. **Languages:** Dutch. **Religions:** Roman Catholic 40%, Dutch Reformed 19.3%.

Geography: Area: 15,770 sq. mi., the size of Mass., Conn., and R.I. combined. **Location:** In NW Europe on North Sea. **Topography:** The land is flat, an average alt. of 37 ft. above sea level, with much land below sea level reclaimed and protected by some 1,500 miles of dikes. Since 1920 the government has been draining the IJsselmeer, formerly the Zuider Zee. **Capital:** Amsterdam. **Cities** (1989): Amsterdam 694,000; Rotterdam 576,100; Hague 443,500.

Government: Type: Parliamentary democracy under a constitutional monarch. **Head of state:** Queen Beatrix; b. Jan. 31, 1938; in office: Apr. 30, 1980. **Head of government:** Prime Min. Ruud Lubbers; in office: Nov. 4, 1982. **Seat of govt.:** The Hague. **Local divisions:** 12 provinces. **Defense:** 2.7% of GDP (1991).

Economy: Industries: Metals, machinery, chemicals, oil refinery, diamond cutting, electronics, tourism. **Chief crops:** Grains, potatoes, sugar beets, vegetables, fruits, flowers. **Minerals:** Natural gas, oil. **Crude oil reserves** (1987): 195 mln. bbls. **Arable land:** 26%. **Livestock** (1990): cattle: 4.9 mln.; pigs: 13.9 mln. **Fish catch** (1989): 421,000 metric tons. **Electricity prod.** (1990): 63.0 bln. kWh. **Crude steel prod.** (1990): 5.4 mln. metric tons. **Labor force:** 1% agric.; 30% ind., 44% services, 23% govt.

Finance: Monetary unit: Guilder (June 1992: 1.84 = $1 US). **Gross domestic product** (1990): $218 bln. **Per capita GDP** (1990): $14,600. **Imports** (1991): $125 bln.; partners: Ger. 26%, Belg. 14%, U.S. 9%, U.K. 9%. **Exports** (1991): $133 bln.; partners: Ger. 26%, Belg. 14%, Fr. 10%, UK 9%. **Tourists** (1989): receipts: $3.0 bln. **National budget** (1990): $76 bln. expenditures. **International reserves less gold** (Mar. 1992): $16.8 bln. **Gold:** 43.94 mln. oz t. **Consumer prices** (change in 1991): 3.9%.

Transport: Railroads (1989): **Length:** 2,828 km. **Motor vehicles:** in use (1990): 5.5 mln. passenger cars, 555,000 comm. vehicles. **Civil aviation** (1989): 25.2 bln. passenger-km; 5 airports. **Chief ports:** Rotterdam, Amsterdam, IJmuiden.

Communications: Television sets: 1 per 3.2 persons. **Radios:** 1 per 1.2 persons. **Telephones:** 1 per 1.6 persons. **Daily newspaper circ.** (1987): 312 per 1,000 pop.

Health: Life expectancy at birth (1991): 74 male; 81 female. **Births** (per 1,000 pop. 1991): 13 **Deaths** (per 1,000 pop. 1991): 9. **Natural increase:** .4%. **Hospital beds:** 1 per 157 persons. **Physicians:** 1 per 414 persons. **Infant mortality** (per 1,000 live births 1991): 7

Education (1991): **Literacy:** 99%. **Years compulsory:** 10; attendance: 100%.

Major International Organizations: UN and all of its specialized agencies, NATO, EC, OECD.

Embassy: 4200 Linnean Ave. NW 20008; 244-5300.

Julius Caesar conquered the region in 55 BC, when it was inhabited by Celtic and Germanic tribes.

After the empire of Charlemagne fell apart, the Netherlands (Holland, Belgium, Flanders) split among counts, dukes and bishops, passed to Burgundy and thence to Charles V of Spain. His son, Philip II, tried to check the Dutch drive toward political freedom and Protestantism (1568-1573). William the Silent, prince of Orange, led a confederation of the northern provinces, called Estates, in the Union of Utrecht, 1579. The Estates retained individual sovereignty, but were represented jointly in the States-General, a body that had control of foreign affairs and defense. In 1581 they repudiated allegiance to Spain. The rise of the Dutch republic to naval, economic, and artistic eminence came in the 17th century.

The United Dutch Republic ended 1795 when the French formed the Batavian Republic. Napoleon made his brother Louis king of Holland, 1806; Louis abdicated 1810 when Napoleon annexed Holland. In 1813 the French were expelled. In 1815 the Congress of Vienna formed a kingdom of the Netherlands, including Belgium, under William I. In 1830, the Belgians seceded and formed a separate kingdom.

The constitution, promulgated 1814, and subsequently revised, assures a hereditary constitutional monarchy.

The Netherlands maintained its neutrality in World War I, but was invaded and brutally occupied by Germany, 1940-45.

In 1949, after several years of fighting, the Netherlands granted independence to Indonesia, where it had ruled since the 17th century. In 1963, West New Guinea was turned over to Indonesia, after five years of controversy and seizure of Dutch property in Indonesia.

The independence of former Dutch colonies has instigated mass emigrations to the Netherlands.

Though the Netherlands has been heavily industrialized, its productive small farms export large quantities of pork and dairy foods. Rotterdam, located along the principal mouth of the Rhine, handles the most cargo of any ocean port in the world. Canals, of which there are 3,478 miles, are important in transportation.

Netherlands Antilles

The **Netherlands Antilles,** constitutionally on a level of equality with the Netherlands homeland within the kingdom, consist of 2 groups of islands in the West Indies. **Curacao, Aruba,** and **Bonaire** are near the South American coast; **St. Eustatius, Saba,** and the southern part of **St. Maarten** are SE of Puerto Rico. Northern two-thirds of St. Maarten belong to French Guadeloupe; the French call the island St. Martin. Total area of the 2 groups is 385 sq. mi., including: Aruba 75, Bonaire 111, Curacao 171, St. Eustatius 11, Saba 5, St. Maarten (Dutch part) 13.

Aruba was separated from The Netherlands Antilles on Jan. 1, 1986; it is an autonomous member of The Netherlands, the same status as the Netherland Antilles.

Total pop. (est. 1989) was 187,000. Willemstad, on Curacao, is the capital. Principal industry is the refining of crude oil from Venezuela. Tourism is an important industry, as is shipbuilding.

New Zealand

People: Population: (1991 est.): 3,308,000. **Age distrib.** (%): 0–14: 23.1, 15–59: 61.9; 60+: 15.0 **Pop. density:** 31 per sq. mi. **Urban** (1988): 84.0%. **Ethnic groups:** European (mostly British) 87%, Polynesian (mostly Maori) 9%. **Languages:** English, Maori (both official). **Religions:** Anglican 29%, Presbyterian 18%, Roman Catholic 15%, others.

Geography: Area: 103,736 sq. mi., the size of Colorado. **Location:** In SW Pacific O. **Neighbors:** Nearest are Australia on W, Fiji, Tonga on N. **Topography:** Each of the 2 main islands (North and South Is.) is mainly hilly and mountainous. The east coasts consist of fertile plains, especially the broad Canterbury Plains on South Is. A volcanic plateau is in center of North Is. South Is. has glaciers and 15 peaks over 10,000 ft. **Capital:** Wellington. **Cities** (1990 est.): Auckland 310,000; Christchurch 290,000; Wellington 148,000; Manukau 224,000.

Government: Type: Parliamentary democracy. **Head of state:** Queen Elizabeth II, represented by Gov.-Gen. Dame Catherine Tizard. **Head of government:** Prime Min. Jim Bolger; b. 1935; in office: Oct. 27, 1990. **Local divisions:** 93 counties, 12 towns & districts. **Defense:** 1.5% of GDP (1991).

Economy: Industries: Food processing, textiles, machinery, fish, forest prods. **Chief crops:** Grain. **Minerals:** Oil, gas, iron, coal **Crude oil reserves** (1987): 182 mln. bbls. **Other resources:** Wool, timber. **Arable land:** 2%. **Livestock** (1989): cattle: 7.8 mln.; sheep: 60 mln. **Fish catch** (1989): 509,000 metric tons. **Electricity prod.** (1990): 28.0 bln. kWh. **Labor force:** 11% agric. & mining; 41% ind. and commerce, 47% services and gov.

Finance: Monetary unit: Dollar (June 1992: 1.85 = $1 US). **Gross domestic product** (1990): $40 bln. **Per capita GDP** (1990): $12,200. **Imports** (1991): $8.4 bln.; partners: Austral. 22%, U.S. 16%, Jap. 20%. **Exports** (1991): $9.4 bln.; partners: UK 9%, U.S. 15%, Jap. 15%, Austral. 16%. **Tourists** (1989): receipts $1.1 bln. **National budget** (1991): $18.3 bln. **International reserves less gold** (Feb. 1992): $3.0 bln. **Gold:** 1,000 oz t. **Consumer prices** (change in 1991): 2.6%.

Transport: Railroads (1990): **Length:** 2,627 mi. **Motor vehicles:** in use (1989): 1.4 mln. passenger cars; 297,000 comm. vehicles. **Civil aviation:** (1989): 10.5 bln. passenger-km, 36 airports. **Chief ports:** Auckland, Wellington, Lyttleton, Tauranga.

Communications: Television sets: 1 per 3.1 persons. **Radios:** 1 per 1.1 persons. **Telephones:** 1 per 1.4 persons. **Daily newspaper circ.** (1989): 306 per 1,000 pop.

Health: Life expectancy at birth (1991): 72 male; 78 female. **Births** (per 1,000 pop. 1991): 15. **Deaths** (per 1,000 pop. 1991): 8. **Natural increase:** .8%. **Hospital beds:** 1 per 111 persons. **Physicians:** 1 per 373 persons. **Infant mortality** (per 1,000 live births 1991): 10.

Education (1991): **Literacy:** 99%. Compulsory ages 6-15; attendance: 100%.

Major International Organizations: UN (GATT, World Bank, IMF), Commonwealth of Nations, OECD.

Embassy: 37 Observatory Cir. NW 20008; 328-4800.

The Maoris, a Polynesian group from the eastern Pacific, reached New Zealand before and during the 14th century. The first European to sight New Zealand was Dutch navigator Abel Janszoon Tasman, but Maoris refused to allow him to land. British Capt. James Cook explored the coasts, 1769-1770.

British sovereignty was proclaimed in 1840, with organized settlement beginning in the same year. Representative institutions were granted in 1853. Maori Wars ended in 1870 with British victory. The colony became a dominion in 1907, and is an independent member of the Commonwealth.

In July 1985, the *Rainbow Warrior*, flagship of the Greenpeace organization, was bombed and sunk in Auckland harbour by French secret service agents.

A labor tradition in politics dates back to the 19th century. Private ownership is basic to the economy, but state ownership or regulation affects many industries. Transportation, broadcasting, mining, and forestry are largely state-owned.

The native Maoris number about 250,000. Four of 92 members of the House of Representatives are elected directly by the Maori people.

New Zealand comprises **North Island,** 44,035 sq. mi.; **South Island,** 58,304 sq. mi.; **Stewart Island,** 674 sq. mi.; **Chatham Islands,** 372 sq. mi.

In 1965, the **Cook Islands** (pop. 1986 est., 17,185; area 93 sq. mi.) became self-governing although New Zealand retains responsibility for defense and foreign affairs. **Niue** attained the same status in 1974; it lies 400 mi. to W (pop. 1987 est., 2,500; area 100 sq. mi.). **Tokelau Is.,** (pop. 1987 est., 1,600; area 4 sq. mi.) are 300 mi. N of Samoa.

Ross Dependency, administered by New Zealand since 1923, comprises 160,000 sq. mi. of Antarctic territory.

Nicaragua

Republic of Nicaragua

República de Nicaragua

People: Population (1991 est.): 3,751,000. **Age distrib.** (%): 0–14: 45.8; 15–59: 49.9; 60+: 4.3. **Pop. density:** 73 per sq. mi. **Urban** (1990): 60%. **Ethnic groups:** Mestizo 69%, Caucasian 17%, black 9%, Indian 5%. **Languages:** Spanish, (official). **Religion:** Roman Catholic 88%.

Geography: Area: 50,193 sq. mi., about the size of Iowa. **Location:** In Central America. **Neighbors:** Honduras on N, Costa Rica on S. **Topography:** Both Atlantic and Pacific coasts are over 200 mi. long. The Cordillera Mtns., with many volcanic peaks, runs NW-SE through the middle of the country. Between this and a volcanic range to the E lie Lakes Managua and Nicaragua. **Capital:** Managua. **Cities** (1986): Managua 1 mln.

Government: Type: Republic. **Head of Government:** Violeta Barrios de Chamorro; b. 1929; in office Apr. 25, 1990. **Local divisions:** 16 departments. **Defense:** 3.8% of GDP (1991).

Economy: Industries: Oil refining, food processing, chemicals, textiles. **Chief crops:** Bananas, cotton, fruit, yucca, coffee, sugar, corn, beans, cocoa, rice, sesame, tobacco, wheat. **Minerals:** Gold, silver, copper, tungsten. **Other resources:** Forests, shrimp. **Arable land:** 10%. **Livestock** (1989): cattle: 1.6 mln.; pigs: 680,000. **Electricity prod.** (1990): 1.2 bln. kWh. **Labor force:** 44% agric.; 13% Ind.; 43% services.

Finance: Monetary unit: Cordoba (May 1992: 25 mln. = $1 US). **Gross domestic product** (1990): $1.7 bln. **Per capita GDP** (1990): $470. **Imports** (1989): $710 mln.; partners: U.S. 25%, Latin Amer. 30%, EC 20%. **Exports** (1989): $298 mln.; partners: OECD 75%. **National budget** (1988): $550 mln. expenditures. **Consumer prices** (change in 1990): 11,000%.

Transport: Railroads (1990): **Length:** 186 mi. **Motor vehicles:** in use (1989): 46,000 passenger cars, 32,000 comm. vehicles. **Chief ports:** Corinto, Puerto Somoza, San Juan del Sur.

Communications: Television sets: 1 per 18 persons. **Radios:** 1 per 4.3 persons. **Telephones:** 1 per 77 persons. **Daily newspaper circ.** (1989): 62 per 1,000 pop.

Health: Life expectancy at birth (1991): 61 male; 65 female. **Births** (per 1,000 pop. 1991): 37. **Deaths** (per 1,000 pop. 1991): 8. **Natural increase:** 2.9%. **Hospital beds:** 1 per 761 persons. **Physicians:** 1 per 1,678 persons. **Infant mortality** (per 1,000 live births 1991): 60.

Education (1991): **Literacy:** 57%. **Years compulsory:** 11 years or 16 years old.

Major International Organizations: UN and all of its specialized agencies, OAS.

Embassy: 1627 New Hampshire Ave. NW 20009; 387-4371.

Nicaragua, inhabited by various Indian tribes, was conquered by Spain in 1552. After gaining independence from Spain, 1821, Nicaragua was united for a short period with Mexico, then with the United Provinces of Central America, finally becoming an independent republic, 1838.

U.S. Marines occupied the country at times in the early 20th century, the last time from 1926 to 1933.

Gen. Anastasio Somoza Debayle was elected president 1967. He resigned 1972, but was elected president again in 1974. Martial law was imposed in Dec. 1974, after officials were kidnapped by the Marxist Sandinista guerrillas. Violent opposition spread to nearly all classes in 1978; nationwide strikes called against the government touched off a state of civil war. Months of simmering civil war ended when Somoza fled, July 19, 1979.

Relations with the U.S. were strained due to Nicaragua's aid to leftist guerrillas in El Salvador and the U.S. backing anti-Sandinista contra guerrilla groups.

In 1983, the contras launched their first major offensive; the Sandinistas imposed rule by decree. In 1985, the U.S. House rejected Pres. Reagan's request for military aid to the contras.

The diversion of funds to the contras from the proceeds of a secret arms sale to Iran caused a major scandal in the U.S. The plan, masterminded by the administration's national security advisor and his deputy, took place at a time when military aid to the contras was forbidden by law.

In a stunning upset, Violeta Barrios de Chamorro defeat Ortega in national elections, Feb. 25, 1990.

Niger

Republic of Niger

République du Niger

People: Population (1991 est.): 8,154,000. **Age distrib.** (%): 0–14: 46.7; 15–59: 48.5; 60+: 4.8. **Pop. density:** 16 per sq. mi. **Urban** (1988): 21%. **Ethnic groups:** Hausa 56%, Djerma 22%, Fulani 8%, Tuareg 8%. **Languages:** French (official), Hausa, Fulani. **Religions:** Sunni Moslem 80%.

Geography: Area: 489,189 sq. mi., almost 3 times the size of California. **Location:** In the interior of N. Africa. **Neighbors:** Libya, Algeria on N, Mali, Burkina Faso on W, Benin, Nigeria on S, Chad on E. **Topography:** Mostly arid desert and mountains. A narrow savanna in the S and the Niger R. basin in the SW contain most of the population. **Capital:** Niamey. **Cities** (1987 est.): Niamey 350,000.

Government: Type: Republic; military in power. **Head of government:** Pres. Ali Seibou; in office: Dec. 20, 1989. Prime Min. Amadou Cheiffou; in office: Oct. 27, 1991. **Local divisions:** 7 departments. **Defense:** 0.8% of GDP (1989).

Economy: Chief crops: Peanuts, cotton. **Minerals:** Uranium, coal, iron. **Arable land:** 3%. **Livestock** (1989): cattle: 3.5 mln.; sheep 3.5 mln. **Electricity prod.** (1990): 227 mln. kWh. **Labor force:** 90% agric.

Finance: Monetary unit: CFA franc (Mar. 1992: 278 = $1 US). **Gross domestic product** (1989): $2.1 bln. **Per capita GDP** (1989): $290. **Imports** (1989): $386 mln.; partners: Fr. 32%. **Exports** (1989): $308 mln.; partners: Fr. 65%, Nig. 11%. **National budget** (1989): $452 mln. expenditures. **International reserves less gold** (Jan. 1992): $190 mln. **Gold:** 11,000 oz t. **Consumer prices** (change in 1991): −7.8%.

Transport: Motor vehicles: in use (1988): 27,000 passenger cars, 25,000 comm. vehicles.

Communications: Television sets: 1 per 301 persons. **Radios:** 1 per 19 persons. **Telephones:** 1 per 563 persons. **Daily newspaper cir.** (1990): 1 per 1,000 pop.

Health: Life expectancy at birth (1991): 49 male; 53 female. **Births** (per 1,000 pop. 1991): 49. **Deaths** (per 1,000 pop. 1991): 17. **Natural increase:** 3.2%. **Infant mortality** (per 1,000 live births 1991): 129.

Education (1991): **Literacy:** 28%. **Years compulsory:** 6; attendance: 15%.

Major International Organizations: UN (GATT, IMF, WHO, FAO), OAU.

Embassy: 2204 R St. NW 20008; 483-4224.

Niger was part of ancient and medieval African empires. European explorers reached the area in the late 18th century. The French colony of Niger was established 1900-22, after the defeat of Tuareg fighters, who had invaded the area from the N a century before. The country became independent Aug. 3, 1960. The next year it signed a bilateral agreement with France retaining close economic and cultural ties.

Nigeria

Federal Republic of Nigeria

People: Population (1991 cen.): 88,500,000. **Pop. density:** 248 per sq. mi. **Urban** (1990): 35%. **Ethnic groups:** Hausa 21%, Yoruba 20%, Ibo 17%, Fulani 9%, others. **Languages:** English (official), Hausa, Yoruba, Ibo. **Religions:** Moslem 50% (in N), Christian 40% (in S), others.

Geography: Area: 356,667 sq. mi., more than twice the size of California. **Location:** On the S coast of W. Africa. **Neighbors:** Benin on W, Niger on N, Chad, Cameroon on E. **Topography:** 4 E-W regions divide Nigeria: a coastal mangrove swamp 10-60 mi. wide, a tropical rain forest 50-100 mi. wide, a plateau of savanna and open woodland, and semidesert in the N. **Capital:** Abuja. **Cities:** (1991): Lagos 1,300,000; Ibadan 1,263,000.

Government: Type: Military. **Head of state:** Pres. Ibrahim Babangida; b. Aug. 17, 1941; in office: Aug. 30, 1985. **Local divisions:** 21 states plus federal capital territory. **Defense:** 1.0% of GNP (1990).

Economy: Industries: Crude oil (95% of export), food processing, assembly of vehicles, textiles. **Chief crops:** Cocoa (main export crop), tobacco, palm products, peanuts, cotton, soybeans. **Minerals:** Oil, gas, coal, iron, limestone, columbium, tin. **Crude oil reserves** (1987): 16.8 bln. bbls. **Other resources:** Timber, rubber, hides. **Arable land:** 31%. **Livestock** (1989): cattle: 12.1 mln.; goats: 26.3 mln.; sheep: 13.1 mln. **Fish catch** (1989): 315,000 metric tons. **Electricity prod.** (1990): 11.2 bln. kWh. **Labor force:** 54% agric., 19% ind., comm. and serv.

Finance: Monetary unit: Naira (Feb. 1992: 10.56 = $1.00 US). **Gross domestic product** (1990): $28 bln. **Per capita GDP** (1990): $230. **Imports** (1990): $9.5 bln.; partners: U.S., EC. **Exports** (1990): $13.0 bln.; partners: U.S., EC. **Tourist receipts** (1988): $78 mln. **National budget** (1990): $8.0 bln. expenditures. **International reserves less gold** (Jan. 1992): $4.4 bln. **Gold:** 687,000 oz t. **Consumer prices** (change in 1991): 13.0%.

Transport: Motor vehicles: in use (1989): 773,000 passenger cars, 606,000 comm. vehicles. **Civil aviation** (1990): 256 mln. passenger-km; 13 airports. **Chief ports:** Port Harcourt, Lagos, Warri, Calabar.

Communications: Television sets: 1 per 12 persons. **Radios:** 1 per 12 persons. **Telephones:** 1 per 240 persons. **Daily newspaper circ.** (1990): 12 per 1,000 pop.

Health: Life expectancy at birth (1991): 48 male; 50 female. **Births** (per 1,000 pop. 1991): 46. **Deaths** (per 1,000 pop. 1991): 17. **Natural increase:** 2.9%. **Hospital beds:** 1 per 1,142 persons. **Physicians:** 1 per 6,900 persons. **Infant mortality** (per 1,000 live births 1991): 118.

Education (1991): **Literacy:** 51%. **Primary school attendance:** 42%.

Major International Organizations: UN (GATT, IMO, WHO), OPEC, OAU, Commonwealth of Nations.

Embassy: 2201 M St. NW 20037; 822-1500.

Early cultures in Nigeria date back to at least 700 BC. From the 12th to the 14th centuries, more advanced cultures developed in the Yoruba area, at Ife, and in the north, where Moslem influence prevailed.

Portuguese and British slavers appeared from the 15th-16th centuries. Britain seized Lagos, 1861, during an anti-slave trade campaign, and gradually extended control inland until 1900. Nigeria became independent Oct. 1, 1960, and a republic Oct. 1, 1963.

On May 30, 1967, the Eastern Region seceded, proclaiming itself the Republic of Biafra, plunging the country into civil war. Casualties in the war were est. at over 1 million, including many "Biafrans" (mostly Ibos) who died of starvation despite international efforts to provide relief. The secessionists, after steadily losing ground, capitulated Jan. 12, 1970. Within a few years, the Ibos were reintegrated into national life.

Oil revenues have made possible a massive economic development program, largely using private enterprise, but agriculture has lagged.

After 13 years of military rule, the nation experienced a peaceful return to civilian government, Oct., 1979.

Military rule returned to Nigeria, Dec. 31, 1983 as a coup ousted the democratically-elected government. The government had promised a return to civilian rule by the end of 1992.

Norway

Kingdom of Norway

Kongeriket Norge

People: Population (1991 est.): 4,273,000. **Age distrib.** (%): 0–14: 19.0; 15–59: 59.9; 60+: 21.1. **Pop. density:** 34 per sq. mi. **Urban** (1990): 75%. **Ethnic groups:** Germanic (Nordic, Alpine, Baltic), minority Lapps. **Languages:** Norwegian (official). **Religions:** Evangelical Lutheran 94%.

Geography: Area: 125,181 sq. mi., slightly larger than New Mexico. **Location:** Occupies the W part of Scandinavian peninsula in NW Europe (extends farther north than any European land). **Neighbors:** Sweden, Finland, USSR on E. **Topography:** A highly indented coast is lined with tens of thousands of islands. Mountains and plateaus cover most of the country, which is only 25% forested. **Capital:** Oslo. **Cities** (1991): Oslo 461,000; Bergen 213,000.

Government: Type: Hereditary constitutional monarchy. **Head of state:** King Harald V; b. Feb. 21, 1937; in office: Jan. 17, 1991. **Head of government:** Prime Min. Gro Harlem Brundtland; in office: Nov. 3, 1990. **Local divisions:** Oslo, Svalbard and 18 fylker (counties). **Defense:** 3.2% of GDP (1990).

Economy: Industries: Paper, shipbuilding, engineering, metals, chemicals, food processing oil, gas. **Chief crops:** Grains, potatoes, fruits. **Minerals:** Oil, copper, pyrites, nickel, iron, zinc, lead. **Crude oil reserves** (1987): 11.1 bln. bbls. **Other resources:** Timber. **Arable land:** 3%. **Livestock** (1989): sheep: 2.3 mln.; cattle: 932,000; pigs: 750,000. **Fish catch** (1989): 1.8 mln. metric tons. **Electricity prod.** (1990): 118 bln. kWh. **Crude steel prod.** (1988): 900,000 metric tons. **Labor force:** 7% agric.; 47% ind., banking, comm.; 18% services, 26% govt.

Finance: Monetary unit: Kroner (June 1992: 6.44 = $1 US). **Gross domestic product** (1990): $74 bln. **Per capita GDP** (1990): $17,400. **Imports** (1991): $25.2 bln.; partners: EC 47%. **Exports** (1991): $34.0 bln.; partners: EC 65%. **Tourists** (1989): receipts: $1.4 bln. **National budget** (1988): $40.6 bln. expenditures. **International reserves less gold** (Mar. 1992): $13.0 bln. **Gold:** 1.18 mln. oz t. **Consumer prices** (change in 1991): 3.4%.

Transport: Railroads (1990): **Length:** 2,600 mi. **Motor vehicles:** in use (1989): 1.6 mln. passenger cars, 320,000 comm. vehicles. **Civil aviation:** (1989): 5.9 bln. passenger-km; 48 airports. **Chief ports:** Bergen, Stavanger, Oslo, Tonsberg.

Communications: Television sets: 1 per 2.9 persons. **Radios:** 1 per 1.3 persons. **Telephones:** 1 per 1.6 persons. **Daily newspaper circ.** (1990): 510 per 1,000 pop.

Health: Life expectancy at birth (1991): 74 male; 81 female. **Births** (per 1,000 pop. 1991): 14. **Deaths** (per 1,000 pop. 1991): 11. **Natural increase:** .3%. **Hospital beds:** 1 per 184 persons. **Physicians:** 1 per 327 persons. **Infant mortality** (per 1,000 live births 1991): 7.1.

Education (1991): **Literacy:** 99%. **Years Compulsory:** 9.

Major International Organizations: UN and all of its specialized agencies, NATO, OECD.

Embassy: 2720 34th St. NW 20008; 333-6000.

The first supreme ruler of Norway was Harald the Fairhaired who came to power in 872 AD. Between 800 and 1000, Norway's Vikings raided and occupied widely dispersed parts of Europe.

The country was united with Denmark 1381-1814, and with Sweden, 1814-1905. In 1905, the country became independent with Prince Charles of Denmark as king.

Norway remained neutral during World War I. Germany attacked Norway Apr. 9, 1940, and held it until liberation May 8, 1945. The country abandoned its neutrality after the war, and joined the NATO alliance.

Abundant hydroelectric resources provided the base for Norway's industrialization, producing one of the highest living standards in the world.

Norway's merchant marine is one of the world's largest.

Petroleum output from oil and mineral deposits under the continental shelf has raised state revenues.

Svalbard is a group of mountainous islands in the Arctic O., c. 23,957 sq. mi., pop. varying seasonally from 1,500 to 3,600. The largest, Spitsbergen (formerly called West Spitsbergen), 15,060 sq. mi., seat of governor, is about 370 mi. N of Norway. By a treaty signed in Paris, 1920, major European powers recognized the sovereignty of Norway, which incorporated it in 1925. Both Norway and the USSR mine rich coal deposits.

Oman

Sultanate of Oman

Saltanat 'Uman

People: Population (1991 est.): 1,534,000. **Pop. density:** 18 per sq. mi. **Urban** (1986): 9%. **Ethnic groups:** Omani Arab 74%, Pakistani 21%. **Languages:** Arabic (official). **Religions:** Ibadhi Moslem 75%, Sunni Moslem.

Geography: Area: 82,030 sq. mi., about the size of New Mexico. **Location:** On SE coast of Arabian peninsula. **Neighbors:** United Arab Emirates, Saudi Arabia, Yemen on W. **Topography:** Oman has a narrow coastal plain up to 10 mi. wide, a range of barren mountains reaching 9,900 ft., and a wide, stony, mostly waterless plateau, avg. alt. 1,000 ft. Also the tip of the Ruus-al-Jebal peninsula controls access to the Persian Gulf. **Capital:** Muscat. **Cities** (1990 est.): Muscat 85,000.

Government: Type: Absolute monarchy. **Head of state:** Sultan Qabus bin Said; b. Nov. 18, 1942; in office: July 23, 1970. **Local divisions:** 1 province, numerous districts. **Defense:** 12% of GDP (1991).

Economy: Chief crops: Dates, fruits vegetables, wheat, bananas. **Minerals:** Oil (95% of exports). **Crude oil reserves** (1987): 4.5 bln. bbls. **Fish catch** (1990): 110,000 metric tons. **Electricity prod.** (1990): 3.5 bln. kWh. **Labor force:** 60% agric. & fishing.

Finance: Monetary unit: Rial Omani (Mar. 1992: .38 = $1 US). **Gross domestic product** (1989): $7.7 bln. **Imports** (1990): $2.6 bln.; partners: Jap. 21%, UAE 17%, UK 14%. **Exports** (1990): $2.6 bln.; partners: Jap. 58%, Europe 30%. **National budget** (1989): $4.2 bln. revenues; $5.4 bln. expenditures. **International reserves less gold** (Mar. 1992): $1.6 bln. **Gold:** 289,000 oz t.

Transport: Chief ports: Matrah, Muscat.

Communications: Television sets: 1 per 1.4 persons. **Radios:** 1 per 1.6 persons. **Telephones:** 1 per 17 persons.

Health: Life expectancy at birth (1991): 65 male; 68 female. **Hospital beds:** 1 per 331 persons. **Physicians:** 1 per 1,071 persons. **Infant Mortality** (per 1,000 live births 1991): 40.

Education (1989): **Literacy:** 20%. **Attendance:** 80% primary, 30% secondary.

Major International Organizations: UN (World Bank, IMF), Arab League.

Embassy: 2342 Massachusetts Ave. NW 20008; 387-1980.

A long history of rule by other lands, including Portugal in the 16th century, ended with the ouster of the Persians in 1744. By the early 19th century, Muscat and Oman was one of the most important countries in the region, controlling much of the Persian and Pakistan coasts, and ruling far-away Zanzibar, which was separated in 1861 under British mediation.

British influence was confirmed in a 1951 treaty, and Britain helped suppress an uprising by traditionally rebellious interior tribes against control by Muscat in the 1950s.

On July 23, 1970, Sultan Said bin Taimur was overthrown by his son who changed the nation's name to Sultanate of Oman.

Oil has been the major source of income.

Oman opened its air bases to Western forces following the Iraqi invasion of Kuwait on Aug. 2, 1990.

Pakistan

Islamic Republic of Pakistan

Islam-i Jamhuriya-e Pakistan

People: Population (1991 est.): 117,490,000. **Pop. density:** 378 per sq. mi. **Urban** (1988): 32%. **Ethnic groups:** Punjabi 66%, Sindhi 13%, Pushtun (Iranian) 8.5%, Urdu 7.6%, Baluchi 2.5%, others. **Languages:** Urdu, (official), Punjabi, Sindhi, Pushtu, Baluchi, Brahvi. **Religions:** Moslem 97%.

Geography: Area: 310,403 sq. mi., about the size of Texas. **Location:** In W part of South Asia. **Neighbors:** Iran on W, Afghanistan, China on N, India on E. **Topography:** The Indus R. rises in the Hindu Kush and Himalaya mtns. in the N (highest is K2, or Godwin Austen, 28,250 ft., 2d highest in world), then flows over 1,000 mi. through fertile valley and empties into Arabian Sea. Thar Desert, Eastern Plains flank Indus Valley. **Capital:** Islamabad. **Cities** (1981 cen.): Karachi 5.1 mln.; Lahore 2.9 mln.; Faisalabad 1 mln.; Hyderabad 795,000; Rawalpindi 928,000.

Government: Type: Parliamentary democracy in a federal setting. **Head of government:** Pres. Ghulam Ishaq Khan; in office: Dec. 12, 1988. **Head of state:** Prime Min. Nawaz Sharif; in office: Nov. 6, 1990. **Local divisions:** Federal capital, 4 provinces, tribal areas. **Defense:** 6.4% of GNP (1991).

Economy: Industries: Textiles, food processing, chemicals, petroleum prods. **Chief crops:** Rice, wheat. **Minerals:** Natural gas, iron ore. **Crude oil reserves** (1987): 116 mln. bbls. **Other resources:** Wool. **Arable land:** 26%. **Livestock** (1989): cattle: 17.2 mln.; sheep: 28.3 mln.; goats: 34.2 mln. **Fish catch** (1989): 428,000 metric tons. **Electricity prod.** (1990): 29 bln. kWh. **Labor force:** 53% agric.; 13% ind; 33% services.

Finance: Monetary unit: Rupee (June 1992: 24.97 = $1 US). **Gross domestic product** (1990): $43 bln. **Per capita GDP** (1990): $380. **Imports** (1990): $7.3 bln.; partners: EC 26%, Jap. 16%, U.S. 16%. **Exports** (1990): $5.5 bln.; partners: EC 31%, Jap. 10%, U.S. 10%. **Tourist** (1989): $153 mln. receipts. **National budget** (1991): $8.3 bln. expenditures. **International reserves less gold** (Mar. 1992): $560 mln. **Gold:** 1.94 mln. oz t. **Consumer prices** (change in 1991): 6.5%.

Transport: Railroads (1990): **Length:** 5,453 mi. **Motor vehicles:** in use (1989): 738,000 passenger cars, 171,000 comm. vehicles. **Civil aviation** (1989): 8.7 bln. passenger-km; 34 airports with scheduled flights. **Chief ports:** Karachi.

Communications: Television sets: 1 per 73 persons. **Radios:** 1 per 11 persons. **Telephones:** 1 per 131 persons. **Daily newspaper circ.** (1988): 12 per 1,000 pop.

Health: Life expectancy at birth (1991): 56 male; 57 female. **Births** (per 1,000 pop. 1991): 43 **Deaths** (per 1,000 pop. 1991): 14. **Natural increase:** 2.9%. **Hospital beds:** 1 per 1,706 persons. **Physicians:** 1 per 2,364 persons. **Infant mortality** (per 1,000 live births 1991): 109.

Education (1991): **Literacy:** 35%.

Major International Organizations: UN (GATT, ILO, IMF, WHO).

Embassy: 2315 Massachusetts Ave. NW 20008; 939-6200.

Present-day Pakistan shares the 5,000-year history of the India-Pakistan sub-continent. At present day Harappa and Mohenjo Daro, the Indus Valley Civilization, with large cities and elaborate irrigation systems, flourished c. 4,000-2,500 BC.

Aryan invaders from the NW conquered the region around 1,500 BC, forging a Hindu civilization that dominated Pakistan as well as India for 2,000 years.

Beginning with the Persians in the 6th century BC, and continuing with Alexander the Great and with the Sassanians, successive nations to the west ruled or influenced Pakistan, eventually separating the area from the Indian cultural sphere.

The first Arab invasion, 712 AD, introduced Islam. Under the Mogul empire (1526-1857), Moslems ruled most of India, yielding to British encroachment and resurgent Hindus.

After World War I the Moslems of British India began agitation for minority rights in elections. Mohammad Ali Jinnah (1876-1948) was the principal architect of Pakistan. A leader of the Moslem League from 1916, he worked for dominion status for India; from 1940 he advocated a separate Moslem state.

When the British withdrew Aug. 14, 1947, the Islamic majority areas of India acquired self-government as Pakistan, with dominion status in the Commonwealth. Pakistan was divided into 2 sections, West Pakistan and East Pakistan. The 2 areas were nearly 1,000 mi. apart on opposite sides of India.

Pakistan became a republic in 1956. Pakistan had a National Assembly (legislature) with equal membership from East and West Pakistan, and 2 Provincial Assemblies. In Oct. 1958, Gen. Mohammad Ayub Khan took power in a coup. He was elected president in 1960, reelected in 1965.

Ayub resigned Mar. 25, 1969, after several months of violent rioting and unrest, most of it in East Pakistan, which demanded autonomy. The government was turned over to Gen. Agha Mohammad Yahya Khan and martial law was declared.

The Awami League, which sought regional autonomy for East Pakistan, won a majority in Dec. 1970 elections to a National Assembly which was to write a new constitution. In March, 1971 Yahya postponed the Assembly. Rioting and strikes broke out in the East.

On Mar. 25, 1971, government troops launched attacks in the East. The Easterners, aided by India, proclaimed the independent nation of Bangladesh. In months of widespread fighting, countless thousands were killed. Some 10 million Easterners fled into India.

Full scale war between India and Pakistan had spread to both the East and West fronts by Dec. 3. Pakistan troops in the East surrendered Dec. 16; Pakistan agreed to a cease-fire in the West Dec. 17. On July 3, 1972, Pakistan and India signed a pact agreeing to withdraw troops from their borders and seek peaceful solutions to all problems.

Zulfikar Ali Bhutto, leader of the Pakistan People's Party, which had won the most West Pakistan votes in the Dec. 1970 elections, became president Dec. 20.

Bhutto was overthrown in a military coup July, 1977. Convicted of complicity in a 1974 political murder, Bhutto was executed Apr.4, 1979. Benazir Bhutto, his daughter, returned to Pakistan from exile in Europe in 1986. Her efforts to relaunch the Pakistan People's Party sparked violence and antigovernment riots.

Pres. Mohammad Zia ul-Haq was killed when his plane exploded in Aug. 1988. Following Nov. elections, Benazir Bhutto was named Prime Minister, the first woman leader of a Moslem nation. Her party was soundly defeated in the Oct. 1990 elections; there were charges of corruption against Bhutto.

There are some 6 million Afghan refugees now in Pakistan.

Legislation was submitted in 1991 to adopt Islamic law in place of the current secular code.

Panama

Republic of Panama

República de Panamá

People: Population (1991 est.): 2,426,000. **Age distrib.** (%): 0–14: 35.5; 15–59: 57.6; 60+: 6.9. **Pop. density:** 84 per sq. mi. **Urban** (1987): 53%. **Ethnic groups:** Mestizo 70%, West Indian 14%, Caucasian 10%, Indian 6%. **Languages:** Spanish (official), English. **Religions:** Roman Catholic 93%, Protestant 6%.

Geography: Area: 29,208 sq. mi., slightly larger than West Virginia. **Location:** In Central America. **Neighbors:** Costa Rica on W., Colombia on E. **Topography:** 2 mountain ranges run the length of the isthmus. Tropical rain forests cover the Caribbean coast and eastern Panama. **Capital:** Panama. **Cities** (1990 est.): Panama City 411,000.

Government: Type: Centralized republic. **Head of state and head of government:** Pres. Guillermo Endara; in office: Dec. 20, 1989. **Local divisions:** 9 provinces, 1 territory. **Defense:** 1.5% of GDP (1990).

Economy: Industries: Oil refining, international banking. **Chief crops:** Bananas, pineapples, cocoa, corn, coconuts, sugar. **Minerals:** Copper. **Other resources:** Forests (mahogany), shrimp. **Arable land:** 6%. **Livestock** (1989): cattle: 1.5 mln.; pigs: 240,000. **Electricity prod.** (1990): 3.3 mln. kWh. **Labor force:** 26% agric., 28%, govt. & community services.

Finance: Monetary unit: Balboa (Apr. 1992: 1.00 = $1 US). **Gross domestic product** (1990): $4.8 bln. **Per capita GDP** (1990): $1,980. **Imports** (1990): $1.2 bln.; partners: U.S. 37%. **Exports** (1990): $355 mln.; partners: U.S. 90%. **Tourists** (1989): $102 mln. receipts. **National budget** (1990): $1.8 mln. **International reserves less gold** (Jan. 1992): $498 mln. **Consumer prices** (change in 1991): 1.7%.

Transport: Motor vehicles: in use (1989): 129,000 passenger cars, 46,000 comm. vehicles. **Civil aviation** (1987): 332 mln. passenger-km; 8 airports with scheduled flights. **Chief ports:** Balboa, Cristobal.

Communications: Television sets: 1 per 4.9 persons. **Radios:** 1 per 2.5 persons. **Telephones:** 1 per 9.3 persons. **Daily newspaper circ.** (1990): 60 per 1,000 pop.

Health: Life expectancy at birth (1991): 72 male; 76 female. **Births** (per 1,000 pop. 1991): 26. **Deaths** (per 1,000 pop. 1991): 5. **Natural increase:** 2.1%. **Hospital beds:** 1 per 311 persons. **Physicians:** 1 per 841 persons. **Infant mortality** (per 1,000 live births 1991): 21.

Education (1991): **Literacy:** 87%. **Primary school attendance:** almost 100%.

Major International Organizations: UN (IMF, IMO, World Bank), OAS.

Embassy: 2862 McGill Terrace NW 20008; 483-1407.

The coast of Panama was sighted by Rodrigo de Bastidas, sailing with Columbus for Spain in 1501, and was visited by Columbus in 1502. Vasco Nunez de Balboa crossed the isthmus and "discovered" the Pacific O. Sept. 13, 1513. Spanish colonies were ravaged by Francis Drake, 1572-95, and Henry Morgan, 1668-71. Morgan destroyed the old city of Panama which had been founded in 1519. Freed from Spain, Panama joined Colombia in 1821.

Panama declared its independence from Colombia Nov. 3, 1903, with U.S. recognition. U.S. naval forces deterred action by Colombia. On Nov. 18, 1903, Panama granted use, occupation and control of the Canal Zone to the U.S. by treaty, ratified Feb. 26, 1904.

In 1978, a new treaty provided for a gradual takeover by Panama of the canal, and withdrawal of U.S. troops, to be completed by 1999. U.S. payments were substantially increased in the interim. The permanent neutrality of the canal was also guaranteed.

President Delvalle was ousted by the National Assembly, Feb. 26, 1988, after he tried to fire the head of the Panama Defense Forces, Gen. Manuel Antonio Noriega. Noreiga had been indicted by 2 U.S. federal grand juries on drug charges. A general strike followed. Despite U.S.-imposed economic sanctions Noriega remained in power. Voters went to the polls to elect a new president May 7, 1989. Noriega claimed victory but foreign observers said that the opposition had won overwhelmingly and that Noriega was trying to steal the election. The government voided the election May 10, charging foreign interference. There was an attempted coup against Noriega Oct. 3.

U.S. troops invaded Panama Dec. 20 following a series of incidents, including the killing of a U.S. Marine by Panamanian soldiers. The operation, called Operation Just Cause, had as its chief objective the capture of Noriega, who was wanted in the U.S. on drug trafficking charges. Noriega took refuge in the Vatican diplomatic mission, but surrendered after 10 days to U.S. officials Jan. 3, 1990. He was convicted on 8 counts of racketeering and drug trafficking in a U.S. District Court in Miami, Fla. Apr. 9, 1992.

Papua New Guinea

People: Population (1991 est.): 3,913,000. **Age distrib.** (%): 0–14: 41.6; 15–59: 52.8; 60+: 5.6. **Pop. density:** 21 per sq. mi. **Urban** (1985): 14.0%. **Ethnic groups:** Papuans (in S and interior), Melanesian (N,E), pygmies, minorities of Chinese, Australians, Polynesians. **Languages:** English (official), Melanesian languages, Papuan languages. **Religions:** Protestant 63%, Roman Catholic 31%, local religions.

Geography: Area: 178,260 sq. mi., slightly larger than California. **Location:** Occupies eastern half of island of New Guinea. **Neighbors:** Indonesia (West Irian) on W, Australia on S. **Topography:** Thickly forested mtns. cover much of the center of the country, with lowlands along the coasts. Included are some of the nearby islands of Bismarck and Solomon groups, including Admiralty Is., New Ireland, New Britain, and Bougainville. **Capital:** Port Moresby. **Cities** (1987): Port Moresby 152,000; Lae 79,000.

Government: Type: Parliamentary democracy. **Head of state:** Queen Elizabeth II, represented by Gov. Gen. Wiwa Korowi; in office: Oct. 4, 1991. **Head of government:** Prime Min. Rabbie Namaliu; in office: July 4, 1988. **Local divisions:** 20 provinces. **Defense:** approx. 1.5% of GDP (1989).

Economy: Chief crops: Coffee, coconuts, cocoa. **Minerals:** Gold, copper, silver. **Arable land:** 1%. **Livestock** (1989): pigs: 1.7 mln. **Electricity prod.** (1989): 1.7 bln. kWh. **Labor force:** 82% agric., 3% ind. and commerce, 8% services.

Finance: Monetary unit: Kina (Mar. 1992: 1.00 = $1.04 US). **Gross domestic product** (1989): $2.7 bln. **Per capita GDP** (1989): $725. **Imports** (1991): $1.6 bln.; partners: Austral. 40%, Jap. 17%; U.S. 9%. **Exports** (1991): $1.2 bln.; partners: Jap. 26%, W. Ger. 36%, Austral. 8%. **National budget** (1990): $873 mln. **International reserves less gold** (Mar. 1992): $387 mln. **Gold:** 63,000 oz t. **Consumer prices** (change in 1991): 7.0%.

Transport: Motor vehicles: in use (1987): 17,000 passenger cars, 26,000 comm. vehicles. **Chief ports:** Port Moresby, Lae.

Communications: Television sets: 1 per 14 persons. **Radios:** 1 per 15 persons. **Telephones:** 1 per 48 persons. **Daily newspaper circ.** (1988): 8 per 1,000 pop.

Health: Life expectancy at birth (1991): 55 male; 56 female. **Births** (per 1,000 pop. 1991): 34. **Deaths** (per 1,000 pop. 1991): 11. **Natural increase:** 2.3%. **Hospital beds:** 1 per 222 persons. **Physicians:** 1 per 11,904 persons. **Infant mortality** (per 1,000 live births 1991): 66.

Education (1991): **Literacy:** 52%. **Attendance:** 65% primary school; 13% secondary school.

Major International Organizations: UN (GATT), Commonwealth of Nations.

Embassy: 1330 Connecticut Ave., NW 20036; 659-0856

Human remains have been found in the interior of New Guinea dating back at least 10,000 years and possibly much earlier. Successive waves of peoples probably entered the country from Asia through Indonesia. Europeans visited in the 15th century, but land claims did not begin until the 19th century, when the Dutch took control of the western half of the island.

The southern half of eastern New Guinea was first claimed by Britain in 1884, and transferred to Australia in 1905. The northern half was claimed by Germany in 1884, but captured in World War I by Australia, which was granted a League of Nations mandate and then a UN trusteeship over the area. The 2 territories were administered jointly after 1949, given self-government Dec. 1, 1973, and became independent Sept. 16, 1975.

The indigenous population consists of a huge number of tribes, many living in almost complete isolation with mutually unintelligible languages.

Paraguay

Republic of Paraguay

República del Paraguay

People: Population (1991 est.): 4,798,000. **Age distrib.** (%): 0–14: 41.0; 15–59: 52.0; 60+: 7.0. **Pop. density:** 30 per sq. mi. **Urban** (1990): 46%. **Ethnic groups:** Mestizo 95%, small Caucasian, Indian, black minorities. **Languages:** Spanish (official), Guarani. **Religions:** Roman Catholic (official) 97%.

Geography: Area: 157,047 sq. mi., the size of California. **Location:** One of the 2 landlocked countries of S. America. **Neighbors:** Bolivia on N, Argentina on S, Brazil on E. **Topography:** Paraguay R. bisects the country. To E are fertile plains, wooded slopes, grasslands. To W is the Chaco plain, with marshes and scrub trees. Extreme W is arid. **Capital:** Asunción. **Cities** (1990 est.): Asunción 607,000.

Government: Type: Republic. **Head of state:** Pres. Gen. Andres Rodriguez; in office: Feb. 3, 1989. **Local divisions:** 19 departments. **Defense:** 1.0% of GDP (1988).

Economy: Industries: Food processing, wood products, textiles, cement. **Chief crops:** Corn, cotton, beans, sugarcane. **Minerals:** Iron, manganese, limestone. **Other resources:** Forests. **Arable land:** 20%. **Livestock** (1989): cattle: 8.0 mln.; pigs: 2.3 mln. **Electricity prod.** (1989): 2.7 bln. kWh. **Labor force:** 44% agric., 34% ind. and commerce, 18% services.

Finance: Monetary unit: Guarani (Mar. 1992: 1,446 = $1 US). **Gross domestic product** (1990): $4.7 bln. **Per capita GDP** (1990): $1,100. **Imports** (1990): $1.4 bln.; partners: Braz. 32%, EC 20%. **Exports** (1990): $970 mln.; partners: EC 37%, Braz. 25%. **Tourists** (1989): $113 mln. receipts. **National budget** (1991): $1.2 bln. expenditures. **International reserves less gold** (Mar. 1992): $571 mln. **Gold:** 35,000 oz t. **Consumer prices** (change in 1991): 27.3%.

Transport: Motor vehicles: in use (1988): 34,000 passenger cars, 5,000 comm. vehicles. **Civil aviation** (1990): 571 mln. passenger-km; 1 airport with scheduled flights. **Chief ports:** Asuncion.

Communications: Television sets: 1 per 12 persons. **Radios:** 1 per 5.4 persons. **Telephones:** 1 per 42 persons. **Daily newspaper circ.** (1990): 29 per 1,000 pop.

Health: Life expectancy at birth (1991): 67 male; 72 female. **Births** (per 1,000 pop. 1991): 36. **Deaths** (per 1,000 pop. 1991): 6. **Natural increase:** 3.0%. **Hospital beds:** 1 per 1,489 persons. **Physicians:** 1 per 1,458 persons. **Infant mortality** (per 1,000 live births 1991): 47.

Education (1989): **Literacy:** 81%. **Years compulsory:** 7. **Attendance:** 83%.

Major International Organizations: UN (IMF, WHO, ILO), OAS.

Embassy: 2400 Massachusetts Ave. NW 20008; 483-6960.

The Guarani Indians were settled farmers speaking a common language before the arrival of Europeans.

Visited by Sebastian Cabot in 1527 and settled as a Spanish possession in 1535, Paraguay gained its independence from Spain in 1811. It lost much of its territory to Brazil, Uruguay, and Argentina in the War of the Triple Alliance, 1865-1870. Large areas were won from Bolivia in the Chaco War, 1932-35.

Gen. Alfredo Stroessner, who ruled since 1954, was ousted in a military coup led by Gen. Andres Rodriguez on Feb. 3, 1989. Rodriguez was elected president May 1.

Peru

Republic of Peru

República del Peru

People: Population (1991 est.): 22,361,000. **Age distrib.** (%): 0–14: 40.5; 15–59: 46.0; 60+: 5.5. **Pop. density:** 45 per sq. mi. **Urban** (1989): 70%. **Ethnic groups:** Indians 45%, Mestizos 37%, Caucasians 15%, blacks, Asians. **Languages:** Spanish, Quechua (both official), Aymara. **Religions:** Roman Catholic 90%.

Geography: Area: 496,222 sq. mi., 3 times larger than California. **Location:** On the Pacific coast of S. America. **Neighbors:** Ecuador, Colombia on N, Brazil, Bolivia on E, Chile on S. **Topography:** An arid coastal strip, 10 to 100 mi. wide, supports much of the population thanks to widespread irrigation. The Andes cover 27% of land area. The uplands are well-watered, as are the eastern slopes reaching the Amazon basin, which covers half the country with its forests and jungles. **Capital:** Lima. **Cities** (1990 est.): Lima 5,826,000; Arequipa 634,000; Callao 589,000.

Government: Type: Constitutional republic. **Head of state:** Pres. Alberto Fujimori; b. July 28, 1938; in office: July 28, 1990. **Head of government:** Prime Min. Alfonso de los Heros; in office: Nov. 6, 1991. **Local divisions:** 24 departments, 1 province. **Defense:** 2.4% of GDP (1991).

Economy: Industries: Fish meal, mineral processing, light industry, textiles. **Chief crops:** Cotton, sugar, coffee, corn. **Minerals:** Copper, lead, molybdenum, silver, zinc, iron, oil. **Crude oil reserves** (1987): 535 mln. bbls. **Other resources:** Wool, sardines. **Arable land:** 3%. **Livestock** (1989): cattle: 4.4 mln.; pigs: 2.3 mln.; sheep: 13.5 mln. **Fish catch** (1990): 6.1 mln. metric tons. **Electricity prod.** (1990): 15.5 bln. kWh. **Labor force:** 38% agric.; 17% ind. and mining; 45% govt. and other services.

Finance: Monetary unit: Sole (Mar. 1992: 960 = $1 US). **Gross domestic product** (1989): $19.3 bln. **Per capita GDP** (1990): $898. **Imports** (1990): $2.7 bln.; partners: U.S. 23%, EC 12%. **Exports** (1990): $3.0 bln.; partners: U.S. 20%, EC 22%, Jap. 6%. **Tourists** (1989): $402 mln. receipts. **National budget** (1990): $2.1 bln. **International reserves less gold** (Mar. 1992): $2.4 bln. **Gold:** 1.8 mln. oz t. **Consumer prices** (change in 1991): 409%.

Transport: Railroads (1988): **Length:** 2,157 mi. **Motor vehicles:** in use (1989): 388,000 passenger cars, 226,000 comm. vehicles. **Civil aviation** (1989): 2.0 bln. passenger-km; 24 airports. **Chief ports:** Callao, Chimbate, Mollendo.

Communications: Television sets: 1 per 14 persons. **Radios:** 1 per 4.9 persons. **Telephones:** 1 per 30 persons. **Daily newspaper circ.** (1987): 57 per 1,000 pop.

Health: Life expectancy at birth (1991): 62 male; 67 female. **Births** (per 1,000 pop. 1991): 28. **Deaths** (per 1,000 pop. 1991): 8. **Natural increase:** 2.0%. **Hospital beds:** 1 per 648 persons.

Physicians: 1 per 1,016 persons. **Infant mortality** (per 1,000 live births 1991): 66

Education (1991): **Literacy:** 85%. **Years compulsory:** 10.

Major International Organizations: UN and all of its specialized agencies, OAS.

Embassy: 1700 Massachusetts Ave. NW 20036; 833-9860.

The powerful Inca empire had its seat at Cuzco in the Andes covering most of Peru, Bolivia, and Ecuador, as well as parts of Colombia, Chile, and Argentina. Building on the achievements of 800 years of Andean civilization, the Incas had a high level of skill in architecture, engineering, textiles, and social organization.

A civil war had weakened the empire when Francisco Pizarro, Spanish conquistador, began raiding Peru for its wealth, 1532. In 1533 he had the seized ruling Inca, Atahualpa, fill a room with gold as a ransom, then executed him and enslaved the natives.

Lima was the seat of Spanish viceroys until the Argentine liberator, Jose de San Martin, captured it in 1821; Spain was defeated by Simon Bolivar and Antonio J. de Sucre; recognized Peruvian independence, 1824.

On Oct. 3, 1968, a military coup ousted Pres. Fernando Belaunde Terry. In 1968-74, the military government put through sweeping agrarian changes, and nationalized oil, mining, fishmeal, and banking industries.

Food shortages, escalating foreign debt, and strikes led to another coup, Aug. 29, 1976, and to a slowdown of socialist programs.

After 12 years of military rule, Peru returned to democratic leadership under former Pres. Fernando Belaunde Terry, July 1980.

There were strikes by police, oil workers, and other labor unions in 1987 and 1988. Terrorist activity, mostly by Maoist groups, continued; the government said that guerrilla insurgency caused nearly 13,000 deaths in the 1980s.

A cholera epidemic which began in Peru in Jan. 1991, threatened to spread and could affect over 100 million people in Latin America according to the World Health Organization.

Pres. Fujimori dissolved the National Congress, suspended parts of the constitution, and instituted press censorship, Apr. 5, 1992.

Philippines

Republic of the Philippines

People: Population (1991 est.): 65,758,000. **Age distrib.** (%): 0–14: 39.0; 15–59: 56.2; 60+: 4.8. **Pop. density:** 567 per sq. mi. **Urban** (1990): 41%. **Ethnic groups:** Malays the large majority, Chinese, Americans, Spanish are minorities. **Languages:** Pilipino (based on Tagalog), English (both official), Cebuano, Bicol, Ilocano, Pampango, many others. **Religions:** Roman Catholics 83%, Protestants 9%, Moslems 5%.

Geography: Area: 115,831 sq. mi., slightly larger than Nevada. **Location:** An archipelago off the SE coast of Asia. **Neighbors:** Nearest are Malaysia, Indonesia on S, Taiwan on N. **Topography:** The country consists of some 7,100 islands stretching 1,100 mi. N-S. About 95% of area and population are on 11 largest islands, which are mountainous, except for the heavily indented coastlines and for the central plain on Luzon. **Capital:** Quezon City (Manila is de facto capital). **Cities** (1990 est.): Manila 1.8 mln.; Quezon City 1.5 mln.; Cebu 552,000.

Government: Type: Republic. **Head of state:** Pres. Fidel V. Ramos; b. 1928; in office: June 30, 1992. **Local divisions:** 73 provinces, 61 cities. **Defense:** 2.0% of GNP (1990).

Economy: Industries: Food processing, textiles, clothing, drugs, wood prods., appliances. **Chief crops:** Sugar, rice, corn, pineapple, coconut. **Minerals:** Cobalt, copper, gold, nickel, silver, iron, petroleum. **Other resources:** Forests (42% of area). **Arable land:** 26%. **Livestock** (1989): cattle: 1.4 mln.; pigs: 7.8 mln. **Fish catch** (1989): 2.2 mln. metric tons. **Electricity prod.** (1990): 28 bln. kWh. **Labor force:** 47% agric., 20% ind. and comm., 13% services.

Finance: Monetary unit: Peso (May 1992: 25.38 = $1 US). **Gross national product** (1990): $45.2 bln. **Per capita GNP** (1990): $700. **Imports** (1990): $12.1 bln.; partners: U.S. 25%, Jap. 16%. **Exports** (1990): $8.1 bln.; partners: U.S. 35%, Jap. 17%, EC 19%. **Tourists** (1989): $1.4 bln. receipts. **National budget** (1989): $8.1 bln. expenditures. **International reserves less gold** (Mar. 1992): $4.3 bln. **Gold:** 2.7 mln. oz t. **Consumer prices** (change in 1991): 18.7%.

Transport: Railroads (1989): **Length:** 658 mi. **Motor vehicles:** in use (1988): 834,000 passenger cars, 121,000 comm. vehicles. **Civil aviation** (1989): 8.6 bln. passenger-km; 16 airports with scheduled flights. **Chief ports:** Cebu, Manila, Iloilo, Davao.

Communications: Television sets: 1 per 8.8 persons. **Radios:** 1 per 7.5 persons. **Telephones:** 1 per 6.5 persons. **Daily newspaper circ.** (1985): 44 per 1,000 pop.

Health: Life expectancy at birth (1991): 62 male; 67 female. **Births** (per 1,000 pop. 1991): 29. **Deaths** (per 1,000 pop. 1991): 7. **Natural increase:** 2.2%. **Hospital beds:** 1 per 683 persons. **Physicians:** 1 per 1,062 persons. **Infant mortality** (per 1,000 live births 1991): 54.

Education (1989): **Literacy:** 88%. **Attendance:** 97% in elementary, 55% secondary.

Major International Organizations: UN (World Bank, IMF, GATT), ASEAN.

Embassy: 1617 Massachusetts Ave. NW 20036; 483-1414

The Malay peoples of the Philippine islands, whose ancestors probably migrated from Southeast Asia, were mostly hunters, fishers, and unsettled cultivators when first visited by Europeans.

The archipelago was visited by Magellan, 1521. The Spanish founded Manila, 1571. The islands, named for King Philip II of Spain, were ceded by Spain to the U.S. for $20 million, 1898, following the Spanish-American War. U.S. troops suppressed a guerrilla uprising in a brutal 6-year war, 1899-1905.

Japan attacked the Philippines Dec. 8, 1941 and occupied the islands during WW II.

On July 4, 1946, independence was proclaimed in accordance with an act passed by the U.S. Congress in 1934. A republic was established.

Riots by radical youth groups and terrorism by leftist guerrillas and outlaws, increased from 1970. On Sept. 21, 1972, President Marcos declared martial law. Ruling by decree, he ordered some land reform and stabilized prices. But opposition was suppressed, and a high population growth rate aggravated poverty and unemployment. Political corruption was widespread. On Jan. 17, 1973, Marcos proclaimed a new constitution with himself as president. His wife received wide powers in 1978 to supervise planning and development.

Government troops battled Moslem (Moro) secessionists, 1973-76, in southern Mindanao. Fighting resumed, 1977, after a Libyan-mediated agreement on autonomy was rejected by the region's mainly Christian voters.

Martial law was lifted Jan. 17, 1981. Marcos turned over legislative power to the National Assembly, released political prisoners, and said he would no longer rule by decree. He was reelected to a new 6-year term as president.

The assassination of prominent opposition leader Benigno S. Aquino Jr, Aug. 21, 1983, sparked demonstrations calling for the resignation of Marcos.

A bitter presidential election campaign ended Feb. 7, 1986 as elections were held amid allegations of widespread fraud. On Feb. 16, Marcos was declared the victor over Corazon Aquino, widow of slain opposition leader Benigno Aquino. Aquino declared herself president and announced a nonviolent "active resistance" to overthrow the Marcos government; the 2 held separate inaugurals on Feb. 25.

On Feb. 22, 2 leading military allies of Marcos quit their posts to protest the rigged elections. Marcos, Feb. 24, declared a state of emergency as his military and religious support continued to erode. That same day U.S. President Ronald Reagan urged Marcos to resign. Marcos ended his 20-year tenure as president Feb. 26 as he fled the country. Aquino was recognized immediately as president by the U.S. and other nations.

In 1987, Aquino announced the start of land reforms. Candidates endorsed by Aquino won large majorities in legislative elections held in May, attesting to her popularity. She is plagued, however, by a weak economy, widespread poverty, communist insurgents, and lukewarm support from the military.

Rebel troops seized military bases, TV stations, and bombed the presidential palace, Dec. 1, 1989. Government forces defeated the attempted coup with the aid of air cover provided by U.S. F-4s.

The June 1991 eruption of Mt. Pinatubo led to the evacuation of 20,000 U.S. military personnel from Clark A.F.B. and their dependents at nearby bases.

The U.S. will vacate the Subic Bay Naval Station by the end of 1992; the Philippine government served a notice of eviction following the collapse of talks on a gradual 3-year pull out.

The archipelago has a coastline of 10,850 mi. Manila Bay, with an area of 770 sq. mi., and a circumference of 120 mi., is the finest harbor in the Far East.

All natural resources of the Philippines belong to the state; their exploitation is limited to citizens of the Philippines or corporations of which 60% of the capital is owned by citizens.

Poland

Republic of Poland

People: Population (1991 est.): 37,799,000. **Age distrib.** (%): 0–14: 25.7; 15–59: 60.2; 60+: 14.1. **Pop. density:** 313 per sq. mi. **Urban** (1991): 60%. **Ethnic groups:** Polish 98%, Germans, Ukrainians, Byelorussians. **Language:** Polish. **Religion:** Roman Catholic 94%.

Geography: Area: 120,727 sq. mi. **Location:** On the Baltic Sea in E Central Europe. **Neighbors:** Germany on W, Czechoslovakia on S, Lithuania, Byelorussia, Ukraine on E. **Topography:** Mostly lowlands forming part of the Northern European Plain. The Carpathian Mts. along the southern border rise to 8,200 ft. **Capital:** Warsaw. **Cities** (1990 est.): Warsaw 1.6 mln., Lodz 851,000, Kracow 748,000, Wroclaw 631,000, Poznan 570,000.

Government: Type: Democratic state. **Head of state:** Pres. Lech Walesa; in office: Dec. 22, 1990. **Head of government: Prime Min.:** Hanna Suchocka; in office: July 8, 1992. **Local divisions:** 49 provinces. **Defense:** 6% of GNP (1987).

Economy: Industries: Shipbuilding, chemicals, metals, autos, food processing. **Chief crops:** Grains, potatoes, sugar beets, tobacco, flax. **Minerals:** Coal, copper, zinc, silver, zinc, sulphur, natural gas. **Arable land:** 49%. **Livestock** (1989): cattle: 10.9 mln.; pigs: 20.1 mln. **Fish catch** (1989): 636,000 metric tons. **Electricity prod.** (1990): 136 bln. kWh. **Crude steel prod.** (1990): 13.5 mln. metric tons. **Labor force:** 27% agric.; 36% ind. & comm.; 21% services.

Finance: Monetary unit: Zloty (Mar. 1992: 13,497 = $1 US). **Gross national product** (1990): $158 bln. **Per capita GNP** (1990): $4,200. **Imports** (1991): $15.7 bln.; partners: USSR 18%, Ger. 15%, Czech. 5%. **Exports** (1991): $14.9 bln.; partners: USSR 25%, E. Ger. 14%, Czech. 6%. **National budget** (1989): $24 bln. expenditures. **Tourists** (1989): $202 mln. receipts. **International Reserves Less Gold** (Mar. 1992): $3.6 bln. **Gold:** 472,000. **Consumer prices** (change in 1991): 70%.

Transport: Railroads (1990): **Length:** 26,228 km. **Motor vehicles:** in use (1990): 5.2 mln. passenger cars, 1.1 mln. comm. vehicles. **Civil aviation** (1990): 3.4 bln. passenger-km; 6 airports. **Chief ports:** Gdansk, Gdynia, Szczecin.

Communications: Television sets: 1 per 3.9 persons. **Radios:** 1 per 3.6 persons. **Telephones:** 1 per 7.5 persons. **Daily newspaper circ.** (1988): 217 per 1,000 pop.

Health: Life expectancy at birth (1991): 69 male; 77 female. **Births** (per 1,000 pop. 1991): 14. **Deaths** (per 1,000 pop. 1991): 9. **Natural increase:** .5%. **Hospital beds:** 1 per 144 persons. **Physicians:** 1 per 480 persons. **Infant mortality** (per 1,000 live births 1991): 12.

Education (1991): **Literacy:** 98%. **Years compulsory:** 8; attendance 97%.

Major International Organizations: UN (GATT, WHO).

Embassy: 2640 16th St. NW 20009; 234-3800.

Slavic tribes in the area were converted to Latin Christianity in the 10th century. Poland was a great power from the 14th to the 17th centuries. In 3 partitions (1772, 1793, 1795) it was apportioned among Prussia, Russia, and Austria. Overrun by the Austro-German armies in World War I, its independence, self-declared on Nov.11, 1918, was recognized by the Treaty of Versailles, June 28, 1919. Large territories to the east were taken in a war with Russia, 1921.

Germany and the USSR invaded Poland Sept. 1-27, 1939, and divided the country. During the war, some 6 million Polish citizens were killed by the Nazis, half of them Jews. With Germany's defeat, a Polish government-in-exile in London was recognized by the U.S., but the USSR pressed the claims of a rival group. The election of 1947 was completely dominated by the Communists.

In compensation for 69,860 sq. mi. ceded to the USSR, 1945, Poland received approx. 40,000 sq. mi. of German territory E of the Oder-Neisse line comprising Silesia, Pomerania, West Prussia, and part of East Prussia.

In 12 years of rule by Stalinists, large estates were abolished, industries nationalized, schools secularized, and Roman Catholic prelates jailed. Farm production fell off. Harsh working conditions caused a riot in Poznan June 28-29, 1956.

A new Politburo, committed to development of a more independent Polish Communism, was named Oct. 1956, with Wladyslaw Gomulka as first secretary of the Communist Party. Collectivization of farms was ended and many collectives were abolished.

In Dec. 1970 workers in port cities rioted because of price rises and new incentive wage rules. On Dec. 20 Gomulka resigned as party leader; he was succeeded by Edward Gierek; the incentive rules were dropped, price rises were revoked.

Poland was the first communist state to get most-favored nation trade terms from the U.S.

A law promulgated Feb. 13, 1953, required government consent to high Roman Catholic church appointments. In 1956 Gomulka agreed to permit religious liberty and religious publications, provided the church kept out of politics. In 1961 religious studies in public schools were halted. Government relations with the Church improved in the 1970s.

After 2 months of labor turmoil had crippled the country, the Polish government, Aug. 30, 1980, met the demands of striking workers at the Lenin Shipyard, Gdansk. Among the 21 concessions granted were the right to form independent trade unions and the right to strike — unprecedented political developments in the Soviet bloc. By 1981, 9.5 mln. workers had joined the independent trade union (Solidarity). Farmers won official recognition for their independent trade union in May. Solidarity leaders proposed, Dec. 12, a nationwide referendum on establishing a non-Communist government if the government failed to agree to a series of demands which included access to the mass media and free and democratic elections to local councils in the provinces.

Spurred by the fear of Soviet intervention, the government, Dec. 13, imposed martial law. Public gatherings, demonstrations, and strikes were banned and an internal and external blackout was imposed. Solidarity leaders called for a nationwide strike, but there were only scattered work stoppages. Lech Walesa and other Solidarity leaders were arrested. The U.S. imposed economic sanctions which were lifted when martial law was suspended December 1982.

On Apr. 5, 1989, an accord was reached between the government and opposition factions on a broad range of political and economic reforms incl. free elections. In the first free elections in over 40 years, candidates endorsed by Solidarity swept the parliamentary elections, June 4. On Aug. 19, Tadeusz Mazowiecki became the first non-Communist to head an Eastern bloc nation, when he became prime minister.

The radical economic program designed to transform the economy into a free-market system drew protests from unions, farmers, and miners. Steep price increases took effect Jan 1, 1990; wages were frozen. In 1991, the government announced the most ambitious privatization plan of any country; each adult citizen would become a shareholder in industry.

Portugal

Republic of Portugal

República Portuguesa

People: Population (1991 est.): 10,387,000. **Age distrib.** (%): 0–14: 22.7; 15–59: 59.9; 60+: 17.4. **Pop. density:** 285 per sq. mi. **Urban** (1990): 34%. **Ethnic groups:** Homogeneous Mediterranean stock with small African minority. **Languages:** Portuguese. **Religions:** Roman Catholics 97%.

Geography: Area: 36,390 sq. mi., incl. the Azores and Madeira Islands, slightly smaller than Indiana. **Location:** At SW extreme of Europe. **Neighbors:** Spain on N, E. **Topography:** Portugal N of Tajus R, which bisects the country NE-SW, is mountainous, cool and rainy. To the S there are drier, rolling plains, and a warm climate. **Capital:** Lisbon. **Cities** (1987 est.): Lisbon 2 mln. (met.), Oporto, 1.5 mln. (met.).

Government: Type: Parliamentary democracy. **Head of state:** Pres. Mario Soares; b. Dec. 7, 1924; in office: Mar. 9, 1986. **Head of government:** Prime Min. Anibal Cavaco Silva; in office: Nov. 6, 1985. **Local divisions:** 18 districts, 2 autonomous regions, one dependency. **Defense:** 3.0% of GDP (1990).

Economy: Industries: Textiles, footwear, cork, chemicals, fish canning, wine, paper. **Chief crops:** Grains, potatoes, rice, grapes, olives, fruits. **Minerals:** Tungsten, uranium, copper, iron. **Other resources:** Forests (world leader in cork production). **Arable land:** 32%. **Livestock** (1989): sheep: 5.3 mln.; pigs: 2.3 mln; cattle: 1.3 mln. **Fish catch** (1989): 346,000 metric tons. **Electricity prod.** (1989): 25.5 bln. kWh. **Labor force:** 19% agric.; 34% ind. and comm.; 46% services and govt.

Finance: Monetary unit: Escudo (June 1992: 132 = $1 US). **Gross domestic product** (1990): $57 bln. **Per capita GDP** (1990): $5,580. **Imports** (1991): $26.1 bln.; partners: Ger. 12%, UK 8%, Fr. 11%. **Exports** (1991): $16.2 bln.; partners: UK 15%, Ger. 13%, Fr. 13%. **Tourists** (1989): $3.0 bln. receipts. **National budget** (1990): $23.2 bln. expenditures. **International reserves less gold** (Mar. 1992): $20.8 bln. **Gold:** 15.9 mln. oz t. **Consumer prices** (change in 1991): 11.4%.

Transport: Railroads (1989): **Length:** 2,229 mi. **Motor vehicles:** in use (1989): 2.8 mln. passenger cars, 189,000 comm. vehicles. **Civil aviation** (1989): 6.3 bln. passenger-km; 17 airports. **Chief ports:** Lisbon, Setubal, Leixoes.

Communications: Television sets: 1 per 6.2 persons. **Radios:** 1 per 4.2 persons. **Telephones:** 1 per 4.2 persons. **Daily newspaper circ.** (1987): 76 per 1,000 pop.

Health: Life expectancy at birth (1991): 71 male; 78 female. **Births** (per 1,000 pop. 1991): 12. **Deaths** (per 1,000 pop. 1991): 10. **Natural increase:** .2%. **Hospital beds:** 1 per 209 persons. **Physicians:** 1 per 388 persons. **Infant mortality** (per 1,000 live births 1991): 13.

Education (1990): **Literacy:** 83%. **Years compulsory:** 6; attendance 60%.

Major International Organizations: UN (GATT, IMF, WHO), NATO, EC, OECD.

Embassy: 2125 Kalorama Rd. NW 20008; 328-8610.

Portugal, an independent state since the 12th century, was a kingdom until a revolution in 1910 drove out King Manoel II and a republic was proclaimed.

From 1932 a strong, repressive government was headed by Premier Antonio de Oliveira Salazar. Illness forced his retirement in Sept. 1968.

On Apr. 25, 1974, the government was seized by a military junta led by Gen. Antonio de Spinola, who was named president.

The new government reached agreements providing independence for Guinea-Bissau, Mozambique, Cape Verde Islands, Angola, and Sao Tome and Principe. Despite a 64% victory for democratic parties in April 1975, the Soviet-supported Communist party increased its influence. Banks, insurance companies, and other industries were nationalized.

Parliament approved, June 1, 1989, a package of reforms that did away with the socialist economy and created a "democratic" economy and the denationalization of industries.

Azores Islands, in the Atlantic, 740 mi. W. of Portugal, have an area of 888 sq. mi. and a pop. (1990) of 252,000. A 1951 agreement gave the U.S. rights to use defense facilities in the Azores. The **Madeira Islands,** 350 mi. off the NW coast of Africa, have an area of 307 sq. mi. and a pop. (1990) of 275,000. Both groups were offered partial autonomy in 1976.

Macau, area of 6 sq. mi., is an enclave, a peninsula and 2 small islands, at the mouth of the Canton R. in China. Portugal granted broad autonomy in 1976. In 1987, Portugal and China agreed that Macau would revert to China in 1999. Macao, like Hong Kong, was guaranteed 50 years of noninterference in its way of life and capitalist system. Pop. (1991 est.): 399,000.

Qatar

State of Qatar

Dawlet al-Qatar

People: Population (1991 est.): 518,000. **Pop. density:** 121 per sq. mi. **Ethnic groups:** Arab 40%, Pakistani 18%, Indian 10%, Iranian 14%, others. **Languages:** Arabic (official), English. **Religions:** Moslem 95%.

Geography: Area: 4,247 sq. mi., smaller than Connecticut and Rhode Island combined. **Location:** Occupies peninsula on W coast of Persian Gulf. **Neighbors:** Saudi Arabia on W, United Arab Emirates on S. **Topography:** Mostly a flat desert, with some limestone ridges, vegetation of any kind is scarce. **Capital:** Doha. **Cities** (1987 est.): Doha 250,000.

Government: Type: Traditional emirate. **Head of state and head of government:** Emir & Prime Min. Khalifah ibn Hamad ath-Thani; b. 1932; in office: Feb. 22, 1972 (amir), 1970 (prime min.) **Defense:** 8.0% of GDP (1989).

Economy: Arable land: 2.9%. **Electricity prod.** (1990): 4.5 bln. kWh. **Labor force:** 10% agric., 70% ind., services and commerce.

Finance: Monetary unit: Riyal (Mar. 1992: 3.64 = $1.00 US). **Gross domestic product** (1988): $6.6 bln. **Per capita GDP** (1990): $12,500. **Imports** (1989): $1.4 bln.; partners: Jap. 20%, UK 16%, U.S. 11%. **Exports** (1989): $2.6 bln.; partners: Jap. 38%, Sing. 13%. **National budget** (1990): $3.4 bln. expenditures.

Transport: Chief ports: Doha, Musayid.

Communications: Television sets: 1 per 2.5 persons. **Radios:** 1 per 2.5 persons. **Telephones:** 1 per 3.4 persons.

Health: Life expectancy at birth (1991): 69 male; 74 female. **Hospital beds:** 1 per 399 persons. **Physicians:** 1 per 568 persons. **Infant mortality** (per 1,000 live births 1990): 24.

Education (1991): **Literacy:** 76%. **Compulsory:** ages 6-16; attendance: 98%.

Major International Organizations: UN (FAO, GATT, IMF, World Bank), Arab League, OPEC.

Embassy: 600 New Hampshire Ave. NW 20037; 338-0111.

Qatar was under Bahrain's control until the Ottoman Turks took power, 1872 to 1915. In a treaty signed 1916, Qatar gave Great Britain responsibility for its defense and foreign relations. After Britain announced it would remove its military forces from the Persian Gulf area by the end of 1971, Qatar sought a federation with other British protected states in the area; this failed and Qatar declared itself independent, Sept. 1 1971.

Oil revenues give Qatar a per capita income among the highest in the world, but lack of skilled labor hampers development plans.

Romania

People: Population (1991 est.): 23,397,000. **Age distrib.** (%): 0–14: 24.7; 15–59; 60.9; 60+: 14.4. **Pop. density:** 255 per sq. mi. **Urban** (1990): 53%. **Ethnic groups:** Romanians 89%, Hungarians 7.9%, Germans 1.6%. **Languages:** Romanian (official), Hungarian, German. **Religions:** Orthodox 80%, Roman Catholic 6%.

Geography: Area: 91,699 sq. mi., slightly smaller than New York and Pennsylvania combined. **Location:** In SE Europe on the Black Sea. **Neighbors:** Moldova on E, Ukraine on N, Hungary, Yugoslavia on W, Bulgaria on S. **Topography:** The Carpathian Mts. encase the north-central Transylvanian plateau. There are wide plains S and E of the mountains, through which flow the lower reaches of the rivers of the Danube system. **Capital:** Bucharest. **Cities** (1989 est.): Bucharest 2,036,000, Brasov 353,000, Timisoara 333,000.

Government: Type: In transition. **Head of state:** Pres. Ion Iliescu; in office; Dec. 25, 1989. **Head of government:** Prime Min. Theodor Stolojan; in office; Oct. 1, 1991. **Local divisions:** Bucharest and 40 counties. **Defense:** 4.3% of GNP (1985).

Economy: Industries: Steel, metals, machinery, oil products, chemicals, textiles, shoes, tourism. **Chief crops:** Grains, sunflower, vegetables, potatoes. **Minerals:** Oil, gas, coal. **Other resources:** Timber. **Arable land:** 45%. **Livestock** (1990): cattle: 6.2 mln.; pigs: 11.6 mln.; sheep: 15.4 mln. **Fish catch** (1989): 216,000 metric tons. **Electricity prod.** (1990): 64 bln. kWh. **Crude steel prod.** (1990): 11 mln. metric tons. **Labor force:** 28% agric.; 34% ind. & comm.

Finance: Monetary unit: Lei (Mar. 1992: 198 = $1 US). **Gross domestic product** (1990): $69 bln. **Per Capita GDP** (1990): $3,000. **Imports** (1990): $10.9 bln.; partners: USSR 36%, Iran 8%. **Exports** (1990): $19.2 bln.; partners: USSR 30%. **Tourists** (1989): $178 mln. receipts. **National budget** (1989): $28 bln. expenditures.

Transport: Railroads (1990): **Length:** 6,887 mi. **Motor vehicles:** in use (1990): 1.2 mln. passenger cars; 236,000 comm. vehicles. **Civil aviation** (1991): 1.6 bln. passenger-km; 14 airports. **Chief ports:** Constanta, Galati, Braila.

Communications: Television sets: 1 per 6.0 persons. **Radios:** 1 per 7.3 persons. **Telephones:** 1 per 11 persons. **Daily newspaper circ.** (1989): 134 per 1,000 pop.

Health: Life expectancy at birth (1991): 69 male; 75 female. **Births** (per 1,000 pop. 1991): 16. **Deaths** (per 1,000 pop. 1991): 11. **Natural increase:** 0.5%. **Hospital beds:** 1 per 107 persons.

Physicians: 1 per 559 persons. **Infant mortality** (per 1,000 live births 1991): 18.

Education (1991): **Literacy:** 96%. **Years compulsory:** 10; attendance 98%.

Major International Organizations: UN (World Bank, IMF, GATT).

Embassy: 1607 23d St. NW 20008; 232-4747.

Romania's earliest known people merged with invading Proto-Thracians, preceding by centuries the Dacians. The Dacian kingdom was occupied by Rome, 106 AD-271 AD; people and language were Romanized. The principalities of Wallachia and Moldavia, dominated by Turkey, were united in 1859, became Romania in 1861. In 1877 Romania proclaimed independence from Turkey, became an independent state by the Treaty of Berlin, 1878, a kingdom, 1881, under Carol I. In 1886 Romania became a constitutional monarchy with a bicameral legislature.

Romania helped Russia in its war with Turkey, 1877-78. After World War I it acquired Bessarabia, Bukovina, Transylvania, and Banat. In 1940 it ceded Bessarabia and Northern Bukovina to the USSR, part of southern Dobrudja to Bulgaria, and northern Transylvania to Hungary.

In 1941, Romanian premier Marshal Ion Antonescu led his country in support of Germany against the USSR. In 1944 Antonescu was overthrown by King Michael and Romania joined the Allies.

With occupation by Soviet troops the communist-headed National Democratic Front displaced the National Peasant party. A People's Republic was proclaimed, Dec. 30, 1947; Michael was forced to abdicate. Land owners were dispossessed; most banks, factories and transportation units were nationalized.

On Aug. 22, 1965, a new constitution proclaimed Romania a Socialist, rather than a People's Republic.

Internal policies were oppressive. Ethnic Hungarians protested cultural and job discrimination, which has led to strained relations with Hungary.

Romania became industrialized, but lagged in consumer goods and in personal freedoms. All industry was state owned, and state farms and cooperatives owned almost all the arable land.

On Dec. 16, 1989, security forces opened fire on demonstrators in Timisoara; hundreds were buried in mass graves. President Nicolae Ceausescu declared a state of emergency as protests spread to other cities. By Dec. 21, the protests had spread to Bucharest where security forces fired on protestors. Army units joined the rebellion, Dec. 22, and a group known as the "Council of National Salvation" announced that it had overthrown the government. Fierce fighting took place between the army, which backed the new government, and forces loyal to Ceausescu.

Ceausescu was captured, Dec. 23 and, following a trial in which he and his wife were found guilty of genocide, was executed Dec. 25. The U.S. and USSR quickly recognized the new provisional government.

Following months of unrest, Bucharest was beset by violence, as anti-government protestors and pro-government coal miners clashed, June 13-15, 1990. Anti-government protests continued throughout 1991.

Russia and the Russian Federation

Figures prior to 1990 are for the former USSR

People: Population (1991 est.): 148,542,000. **Pop. density:** 22 per sq. mi. **Urban** (1990): 66%. **Ethnic groups:** Russians 82%, Tatars 3%. **Languages:** Russian (official), Ukrainian, Byelorussian, Uzbek, Armenian, Azerbaijani, Georgian, many others. **Religions:** Russian Orthodox 25%, non-religious 60%.

Geography: Area: 6,592,800 sq. mi., over 76% of the total area of the former USSR and is the largest country in the world. **Location:** Stretches from E. Europe across N Asia to the Pacific O. **Neighbors:** Finland, Poland, Norway, Estonia, Belarus, Ukraine on W, Georgia, Azerbaijan, Kazakhstan, China, Mongolia, N. Korea on S. **Topography:** Russia contains every type of climate except the distinctly tropical, and has a varied topography.

The European portion is a low plain, grassy in S, wooded in N with Ural Mtns. on the E. Caucasus Mts. on the S. Urals stretch N-S for 2,500 mi. The Asiatic portion is also a vast plain, with mountains on the S and in the E; tundra covers extreme N, with forest belt below; plains, marshes are in W, desert in SW. **Capital:** Moscow. **Cities** (1990 est.): Moscow 8.8 mln.; St. Petersburg 5.0 mln.; Samara 1.5 mln.; Nizhniy Novgorod 1.4 mln.

Government: Type: Republic. **Head of state:** Pres. & Prime Min. Boris Yeltsin; b. Feb. 1, 1931; in office: July 10, 1991. **Defense:** 15-17% of GNP (1988).

Economy: Industries: Steel, machinery, machine tools, vehicles, chemicals, cement, textiles, appliances, paper. **Chief crops:** Grain, cotton, sugar beets, potatoes, vegetables, sunflowers. **Minerals:** Manganese, mercury, potash, bauxite, cobalt, chromium, copper, coal, gold, lead, molybdenum, nickel, phosphates, silver, tin, tungsten, zinc, oil, potassium salts. **Other resources:** Forests. **Arable land:** 11%. **Livestock** (1989): cattle: 118 mln.; sheep: 142 mln.; pigs: 77 mln.; goats 142 mln. **Fish catch** (1989): 10.9 mln. metric tons. **Electricity prod.** (1988): 1,730 bln. kwh. **Crude steel prod.** (1988): 164 mln. metric tons. **Labor force:** 22% agric.; 29% industry, 26% services.

Finance: Monetary unit: Ruble. **Gross national product** (1988): $2.5 trl. **Per capita income** (1987): $3,000. **Imports** (1988): $107.3 bln.; partners: E. Ger. 10%, Pol. 7%, Czech. 8%, Bulg. 8%. **Exports** (1988): $110.7 bln.; partners: E. Ger. 10%, Pol. 8%, Bulg. 8%, Czech. 8%. **National budget** (1989): $310 bln. expenditures. **Tourists** (1988): receipts: $216 mln.

Transport: Railway (1990): **Length:** 87,090 km. **Motor vehicles:** in use (1980): 9.2 mln. passenger cars, 7.9 mln. comm. vehicles; manuf. (1982): 1.3 mln. passenger cars; 874,000 comm. vehicles. **Civil aviation** (1989): 228 bln. passenger-km; 52 airports with scheduled flights. **Chief ports:** St. Petersburg, Murmansk, Tver, Archangelsk.

Communications: Television sets: 1 per 3.2 persons. **Radios:** 1 per 1.5 persons. **Telephones:** 1 per 6.7 persons. **Daily newspaper circ.** (1989): 383 per 1,000 pop.

Health: Life expectancy at birth (1991): 64 male; 74 female. **Births** (per 1,000 pop. 1989): 18. **Deaths** (per 1,000 pop. 1989): 11. **Natural increase:** .8%. **Hospital beds:** 1 per 72 persons. **Physicians:** 1 per 259 persons. **Infant mortality** (per 1,000 live births 1989): 25.2.

Education (1991): **Literacy:** 99%. Most receive 11 years of schooling.

Major International Organizations: UN (ILO, IMF, UNESCO, WHO), CIS.

Embassy: 1125 16th St. NW 20036; 628-7551.

History. Slavic tribes began migrating into Russia from the W in the 5th century AD. The first Russian state, founded by Scandinavian chieftains, was established in the 9th century, centering in Novgorod and Kiev.

In the 13th century the Mongols overran the country. It recovered under the grand dukes and princes of Muscovy, or Moscow, and by 1480 freed itself from the Mongols. Ivan the Terrible was the first to be formally proclaimed Tsar (1547). Peter the Great (1682-1725), extended the domain and in 1721, founded the Russian Empire.

Western ideas and the beginnings of modernization spread through the huge Russian empire in the 19th and early 20th centuries. But political evolution failed to keep pace.

Military reverses in the 1905 war with Japan and in World War I led to the breakdown of the Tsarist regime. The 1917 Revolution began in March with a series of sporadic strikes for higher wages by factory workers. A provisional democratic government under Prince Georgi Lvov was established but was quickly followed in May by the second provisional government, led by Alexander Kerensky. The Kerensky government and the freely-elected Constituent Assembly were overthrown in a communist coup led by Vladimir Ilyich Lenin Nov. 7.

Soviet Union

Lenin's death Jan. 21, 1924, resulted in an internal power struggle from which Joseph Stalin eventually emerged the absolute ruler of Russia. Stalin secured his position at first by exiling opponents, but from the 1930s to 1953, he resorted to a series of "purge" trials, mass executions, and mass exiles to work camps. These measures resulted in millions of deaths, according to most estimates.

Germany and the Soviet Union signed a non-aggression pact Aug. 1939; Germany launched a massive invasion of the Soviet Union, June 1941. Notable heroic episode was the "900 days" siege of Leningrad, lasting to Jan. 1944, and causing a million deaths; the city was never taken. Russian winter counterthrusts, 1941 to '42 and 1942 to '43, stopped the German advance. Turning point was the failure of German troops to take and hold

Stalingrad, Sept. 1942 to Feb. 1943. With British and U.S. Lend-Lease aid and sustaining great casualties, the Russians drove the German forces from eastern Europe and the Balkans in the next 2 years.

After Stalin died, Mar. 5, 1953, Nikita Khrushchev was elected first secretary of the Central Committee. In 1956 he condemned Stalin. "De-Stalinization" of the country on all levels was effected after Stalin's body was removed from the Lenin-Stalin tomb in Moscow.

Under Khrushchev the open antagonism of Poles and Hungarians toward domination by Moscow was brutally suppressed in 1956. He advocated peaceful co-existence with the capitalist countries, but continued arming the Soviet Union with nuclear weapons. He aided the Cuban revolution under Fidel Castro but withdrew Soviet missiles from Cuba during confrontation by U.S. Pres. Kennedy, Sept.-Oct. 1962.

Khrushchev was suddenly deposed, Oct. 1964, and replaced as party first secretary by Leonid I. Brezhnev.

In Aug. 1968 Russian, Polish, East German, Hungarian, and Bulgarian military forces invaded Czechoslovakia to put a curb on liberalization policies of the Czech government.

Massive Soviet military aid to North Vietnam in the late 1960s and early 1970s helped assure communist victories throughout Indo-China. Soviet arms aid and advisers were sent to several African countries in the 1970s, including Algeria, Angola, Somalia, and Ethiopia.

In 1979, Soviet forces entered Afghanistan to support that government against rebels. In 1988, the Soviets announced withdrawal of their troops, ending a futile 8-year war.

Mikhail Gorbachev was chosen Gen. Secy. of the Communist Party, Mar. 1985. He was the youngest member of the Politburo and signaled a change in Soviet leadership from those whose attitudes were shaped by Stalinism and World War II.

He held 4 summit meetings with U.S. Pres. Reagan. In 1987, in Washington, an INF treaty was signed.

In 1987, Gorbachev initiated a program of reforms, including expanded freedoms and the democratization of the political process, through openness (*glasnost*) and restructuring (*perestroika*). The reforms were opposed by some Eastern bloc countries and many old-line communists in the USSR. In 1989, the first Soviet Parliament was held since 1918.

Gorbachev faced economic problems as well as ethnic and nationalist unrest in the republics in 1990; the economy was in its worst state since WWII.

On Aug. 19, 1991, it was announced that the vice president had taken over the country due to Gorbachev's ilness. A state of emergency was imposed for 6 months with all power resting with the State Committee on the State of Emergency. The Russian republic's pres. Boris Yeltsin denounced the coup and called for a general strike. Some 50,000 demonstrated at the Russian parliament in support of Yeltsin. By Aug. 21, the coup had failed and Gorbachev was restored as pres. On Aug. 24, Gorbachev resigned as leader of the Communist Party and recommended that its central committee be disbanded. Several republics declared their independence including Russia, Ukraine, and Kazakhstan. On Aug. 29, the Soviet parliament voted to suspend all activities of the Communist Party.

On Sept. 2, Gorbachev declared that the nation was "on the brink of catastrophe," and proposed to transfer all central authority to himself, the leaders of 10 republics, and an appointed legislative council in order to form a new kind of Soviet Union.

The Soviet Union broke up Dec. 25, 1991 as Gorbachev resigned. The Soviet hammer and sickle flying over the Kremlin was lowered and replaced by the flag of Russia ending the domination of the Communist Party over all areas of national life since 1917.

Russian Federation

In the first major step in radical economic reform, Russia eliminated state subsidies of most goods and services, Jan. 1992. The effect was to allow prices to soar far beyond the means of ordinary workers. Pres. Yeltsin met with Pres. Bush in Washington, D.C., June 16-17. The two leaders agreed to massive arms reductions. Yeltsin addressed a joint session of Congress and appealed for economic aid for the CIS.

Rwanda

Republic of Rwanda

Republika y'u Rwanda

People: Population (1991 est.): 7,902,000. **Age distrib.** (%): 0–14: 48.7; 15–59: 47.1; 60+: 4.2. **Pop. density:** 777 per sq. mi. **Urban** (1985): 5.1%. **Ethnic groups:** Hutu 90%, Tutsi 9%, Twa (pygmies) 1%. **Languages:** French, Rwanda (both official). **Religions:** Christian 74%, traditional 25%, Moslem 1%.

Geography: Area: 10,169 sq. mi., the size of Maryland. **Location:** In E central Africa. **Neighbors:** Uganda on N, Zaire on W, Burundi on S, Tanzania on E. **Topography:** Grassy uplands and hills cover most of the country, with a chain of volcanoes in the NW. The source of the Nile R. has been located in the headwaters of the Kagera (Akagera) R., SW of Kigali. **Capital:** Kigali. **Cities** (1989 est.): Kigali 300,000.

Government: Type: Republic. **Head of state:** Pres. Juvenal Habyarimana; b. Mar. 8, 1937; in office: July 5, 1973. **Head of government:** Prime Min. Sylvestre Nsanzimana; in office: Oct. 12, 1991. **Local divisions:** 10 prefectures. **Defense:** 1.6% of GDP (1989).

Economy: Chief crops: Coffee, tea. **Minerals:** Tin, gold, wolframite. **Arable land:** 29%. **Electricity prod.** (1990): 110 mln. kWh. **Labor force:** 91% agric.

Finance: Monetary unit: Franc (Apr. 1992: 122 = $1 US). **Gross domestic product** (1989): $2.1 bln. **Per capita GDP** (1989): $310. **Imports** (1989): $293 mln.; partners: Ken. 21%, Belg. 16%, Jap. 12%, W. Ger. 9%. **Exports** (1989): $117 mln.; partners: Belg.-Lux. 17%, Ugan. 12%. **National budget** (1989): $491 million expenditures. **International reserves less gold** (Mar. 1992): $96 mln. **Consumer prices** (change in 1991): 19.6%.

Transport: Motor vehicles: in use (1989): 8,000 passenger cars, 10,000 comm. vehicles.

Communications: Radios: 1 per 16 persons. **Telephones:** 1 per 555 persons.

Health: Life expectancy at birth (1991): 51 male; 54 female. **Births** (per 1,000 pop. 1991): 52. **Deaths** (per 1,000 pop. 1991): 15. **Natural increase:** 3.7%. **Hospital beds** (1984): 9,000. **Physicians** (1984): 177. **Infant mortality** (per 1,000 live births 1991): 110.

Education (1991): **Literacy:** 50%. **Years compulsory:** 8; **attendance:** 70%.

Major International Organizations: UN (GATT, IMF, WHO), OAU.

Embassy: 1714 New Hampshire Ave. NW 20009; 232-2882.

For centuries, the Tutsi (an extremely tall people) dominated the Hutus (90% of the population). A civil war broke out in 1959 and Tutsi power was ended. A referendum in 1961 abolished the monarchic system. Some 8,000 exiled Tutsi invaded Rwanda from Uganda, Sept. 1990. A new constitution was signed into effect in 1991 calling for multiparty politics, freedom of the press, and a limited presidential term.

Rwanda, which had been part of the Belgian UN trusteeship of Rwanda-Urundi, became independent July 1, 1962. The government was overthrown in a 1973 military coup. Rwanda is one of the most densely populated countries in Africa. All available arable land is being used, and is being subject to erosion. The government has carried out economic and social improvement programs, using foreign aid and volunteer labor on public works projects.

St. Kitts and Nevis

Federation of St. Kitts & Nevis

People: Population (1991 est.): 40,293. **Ethnic groups:** black African 95%. **Language:** English. **Religion:** Protestant 76%.

Geography: Area: 101 sq. mi. in the northern part of the Leeward group of the Lesser Antilles in the eastern Caribbean Sea. **Capitol:** Basseterre. (1989): 15,000.

Government: Constitutional monarchy. **Head of state:** Queen Elizabeth represented by Sir Clement Arrindell. **Head of government:** Prime Minister Kennedy A. Simmonds; b. Apr. 12, 1936; in office: Sept. 19, 1983.

Economy: Sugar is the principal industry.

Finance: Monetary unit: E. Caribbean Dollar (Mar. 1992): 2.70 = $1 U.S. **Gross domestic product** (1988): $97 mln. **Tourists** (1988): $54 mln. receipts.

Communications: Telephones: 1 per 6 persons.

Health: Infant mortality (per 1,000 live births, 1991): 39.

Education: Literacy (1991): 98%.

St. Kitts (known by the natives as Liamuiga) and Nevis were discovered and named by Columbus in 1493. They were settled by Britain in 1623, but ownership was disputed with France until 1713. They were part of the Leeward Islands Federation, 1871-1956, and the Federation of the W. Indies, 1958-62. The colony achieved self-government as an Associated State of the UK in 1967, and became fully independent Sept. 19, 1983. Nevis, the smaller of the islands, has announced its intention to secede from the Federation by the end of 1992.

Saint Lucia

People: Population (1991 est.): 153,075. **Age distrib.** (%): 0–20: 44.5; 21–64: 47.5; 65+: 8.0. **Pop. density:** 643 per sq. mi. **Ethnic groups:** Predominantly African descent. **Languages:** English (official), French patois. **Religions:** Roman Catholic 90%.

Geography: Area: 238 sq. mi., about one-fifth the size of Rhode Island. **Location:** In Eastern Caribbean, 2d largest of the Windward Is. **Neighbors:** Martinique to N, St. Vincent to SW. **Topography:** Mountainous, volcanic in origin; Soufriere, a volcanic crater, in the S. Wooded mountains run N-S to Mt. Gimie, 3,145 ft., with streams through fertile valleys. **Capital:** Castries. **City:** Castries (1989 est.): 55,000.

Government: Type: Parliamentary democracy. **Head of state:** Queen Elizabeth II, represented by Gov.-Gen. S.A. James; **Head of government:** Prime Min. John Compton; in office: May 3, 1982. **Local divisions:** 11 quarters

Economy: Industries: Agriculture, tourism, manufacturing. **Chief crops:** Bananas, coconuts, cocoa, citrus fruits. **Other resources:** Forests. **Arable land:** 8%. **Electricity prod.** (1990): 112 mln. kWh. **Labor force:** 36% agric., 20% ind. & commerce, 18% services.

Finance: Monetary unit: East Caribbean dollar (Mar. 1992: 2.70 = $1 US). **Gross domestic product** (1989): $267 mln. **Per capita GDP** (1989): $1,810. **Imports** (1989): $265 mln.; partners: U.S. 36%, UK 12%, Trin./Tob. 11%. **Exports** (1989): $111 mln.; partners: U.S. 19%, UK 51%. **Tourists** (1990): receipts: $155 mln.

Transport: Motor vehicles: in use (1988): 7,000 passenger cars, 2,000 comm. vehicles. **Chief ports:** Castries, Vieux Fort.

Communications: Television sets: 1 per 26 persons. **Radios:** 1 per 1.5 persons. **Telephones:** 1 per 10 persons.

Health: Life expectancy at birth (1991): 69 male; 74 female. **Births** (per 1,000 pop. 1991): 31. **Deaths** (per 1,000 pop. 1991): 5. **Natural increase:** 2.6%. **Hospital beds:** 1 per 267 persons. **Physicians:** 1 per 2,432 persons. **Infant mortality** (per 1,000 live births 1991): 18.

Education: Literacy (1989) 78%; **Years compulsory:** ages 5-15; **Attendance:** 80%.

Major International Organizations: UN (IMF, ILO), CARICOM, OAS.

St. Lucia was ceded to Britain by France at the Treaty of Paris, 1814. Self government was granted with the West Indies Act, 1967. Independence was attained Feb. 22, 1979.

Saint Vincent and the Grenadines

People: Population (1991 est.): 114,000. **Pop. density:** 760 per sq. mi. **Ethnic groups:** Mainly of African descent. **Languages:** English. **Religions:** Methodists, Anglicans, Roman Catholics.

Geography: Area: 150 sq. mi., about twice the size of Washington, D.C. **Location:** In the eastern Caribbean, St. Vincent (133 sq. mi.) and the northern islets of the Grenadines form a part of the Windward chain. **Neighbors:** St. Lucia to N, Barbados to E, Grenada to S. **Topography:** St. Vincent is volcanic, with a ridge of thickly-wooded mountains running its length; Soufriere, rising in the N, erupted in Apr. 1979. **Capital:** Kingstown. **Cities** (1985 est.): Kingstown 18,378.

Government: Head of state: Queen Elizabeth II, represented by Gov.-Gen. David Jack; in office: Sept. 20 1989. **Head of government:** James Mitchell; in office: July 30, 1984.

Economy: Industries: Agriculture, tourism. **Chief crops:** Bananas (62% of exports), arrowroot, coconuts. **Arable land:** 50%. **Electricity prod.** (1988): 63 mln. kWh. **Labor force:** 30% agric.

Finance: Monetary unit: East Caribbean dollar (Mar. 1992: 2.70 = $1 US). **Gross domestic product** (1989): $146 mln. **Per capita GDP** (1989): $1,315. **Tourists** (1988): $45 mln. receipts. **National budget** (1990): $67 mln. expenditures.

Transport: Motor vehicles: in use (1989): 5,000 passenger cars, 2,800 comm. vehicles. **Chief port:** Kingstown.

Communications: Telephones: 1 per 10 persons.

Health: Life expectancy at birth (1991): 69 male; 74 female. **Births** (per 1,000 pop. 1991): 27. **Deaths** (per 1,000 pop. 1991): 6. **Natural increase:** 2.2%. **Infant mortality** (per 1,000 live births 1991): 31.

Education (1989): **Literacy:** 85%.

Columbus landed on St. Vincent on Jan. 22, 1498 (St. Vincent's Day). Britain and France both laid claim to the island in the 17th and 18th centuries; the Treaty of Versailles, 1783, finally ceded it to Britain. Associated State status was granted 1969; independence was attained Oct. 27, 1979.

The entire economic life of St. Vincent is dependent upon agriculture and tourism.

San Marino

Most Serene Republic of San Marino

Serenissima Repubblica di San Marino

People: Population (1991 est.): 23,000. **Age distrib.** (%): 0–14: 19.0; 15–59: 63.7; 60+: 17.3. **Pop. density:** 958 per sq. mi. **Urban** (1990): 90.5%. **Ethnic groups:** Sanmarinese 84%, Italian 15%. **Languages:** Italian. **Religion:** mostly Roman Catholic.

Geography: Area: 24 sq. mi. **Location:** In N central Italy near Adriatic coast. **Neighbors:** Completely surrounded by Italy. **Topography:** The country lies on the slopes of Mt. Titano. **Capital:** San Marino. **City** (1991 est.): San Marino 4,643.

Government: Type: Independent republic. **Head of state:** Two co-regents appt. every 6 months. **Local divisions:** 11 districts, 9 sectors.

Economy: Industries: Postage stamps, tourism, woolen goods, paper, cement, ceramics. **Arable land:** 17%.

Finance: Monetary unit: Italian lira. **Gross domestic product** (1990): $393 mln. **Tourists** (1990): 2.8 mln.

Communications: Television sets: 1 per 3.4 persons. **Radios:** 1 per 1.8 persons. **Telephones:** 1 per 1.6 persons.

Births (per 1,000 pop. 1991): 8. **Deaths** (per 1,000 pop. 1991): 7. **Natural increase:** 0.1%. **Infant mortality** (per 1,000 live births 1991): 8.

Education (1991): **Literacy:** 97%. **Years compulsory:** 8. **Attendance:** 93%.

Major International Organizations: UN.

San Marino claims to be the oldest state in Europe and to have been founded in the 4th century. A communist-led coalition ruled 1947-57; a similar coalition ruled 1978-86. It has had a treaty of friendship with Italy since 1862.

Sao Tome and Principe

Democratic Republic of Sao Tome and Principe

República Democrática de Sao Tome e Principe

People: Population (1991 est.): 128,000. **Pop. density:** 344 per sq. mi. **Ethnic groups:** Portuguese-African mixture, African minority (Angola, Mozambique immigrants). **Languages:** Portuguese. **Religions:** Christian 80%.

Geography: Area: 372 sq. mi., slightly larger than New York City. **Location:** In the Gulf of Guinea about 125 miles off W Central Africa. **Neighbors:** Gabon, Equatorial Guinea on E. **Topography:** Sao Tome and Principe islands, part of an extinct volcano chain, are both covered by lush forests and croplands. **Capital:** Sao Tome. **Cities** (1988 est.): Sao Tome 40,000.

Government: Type: Republic. **Head of state:** Pres. Miguel Trovoada; in office: Apr. 3, 1991. **Head of government:** Prime Min. Daniel Lima dos Santos Daio; in office: Feb. 7, 1991. **Local divisions:** 2 districts.

Economy: Chief crops: Cocoa (82% of exports), coconut products. **Arable land:** 38%. **Electricity prod.** (1990): 12 mln. kWh.

Finance: Monetary unit: Dobra (Jan. 1992: 240 = $1 US). **Gross domestic product** (1989): $46 mln. **Per capita GDP:** $384. **Imports** (1989): $26.8 mln.; partners: Port. 61%, Angola 13%. **Exports** (1989): $5.9 mln.; partners: Neth. 52%, Port. 33%, Ger. 8%.

Transport: Chief ports: Sao Tome, Santo Antonio.

Communications: Radios: 1 per 3.9 persons.

Health: Births (per 1,000 pop. 1991): 38. **Deaths** (per 1,000 pop. 1991): 7. **Natural increase:** 3.0%. **Physicians:** 1 per 2,819 persons. **Infant mortality** (per 1,000 live births 1991): 60.

Education (1988): **Literacy:** 50%.

Major International Organizations: UN, OAU.

Embassy: 801 2d Ave., New York, NY 10017; 212-697-4211.

The islands were uninhabited when discovered in 1471 by the Portuguese, who brought the first settlers — convicts and exiled Jews. Sugar planting was replaced by the slave trade as the chief economic activity until coffee and cocoa were introduced in the 19th century.

Portugal agreed, 1974, to turn the colony over to the Gabon-based Movement for the Liberation of Sao Tome and Principe, which proclaimed as first president its East German-trained leader Manuel Pinto da Costa. Independence came July 12, 1975. Democratic reforms were instituted in 1987. In 1991 Miguel Trovoada won the first free presidential election following the withdrawal of Pres. Manuel Pinto da Costa. Da Costa had ruled the country since independence.

Agriculture and fishing are the mainstays of the economy.

Saudi Arabia

Kingdom of Saudi Arabia

al-Mamlaka al-'Arabiya as-Sa'udiya

People: Population (1991 est.): 17,869,000. **Pop. density:** 21 per sq. mi. **Urban** (1986): 73%. **Ethnic groups:** Arab tribes, immigrants from other Arab and Moslem countries. **Language:** Arabic. **Religion:** Moslem 99%.

Geography: Area: 839,996 sq. mi., one-third the size of the U.S. **Location:** Occupies most of Arabian Peninsula in Middle East. **Neighbors:** Kuwait, Iraq, Jordan on N, Yemen, South Yemen, Oman on S, United Arab Emirates, Qatar on E. **Topography:** The highlands on W, up to 9,000 ft., slope as an arid, barren desert to the Persian Gulf. **Capital:** Riyadh. **Cities** (1986 est.): Riyadh 1,380,000; Jidda 1,210,000; Mecca 463,000.

Government: Type: Monarchy with council of ministers. **Head of state and head of government:** King Fahd; b. 1922; in office: June 13, 1982. **Local divisions:** 14 emirates. **Defense:** 17% of GDP (1989).

Economy: Industries: Oil products. **Chief crops:** Dates, wheat, barley, fruit. **Minerals:** Oil, gas, gold, copper, iron. **Crude oil reserves** (1990): 255 bln. barrels. **Arable land:** 2%. **Livestock** (1989): sheep: 7.6 mln.; goats; 3.7 mln. **Electricity prod.** (1990): 50 bln. kWh. **Labor force:** 14% agric.; 11% ind; 53% serv., comm., & govt.; 20% construction.

Finance: Monetary unit: Riyal (June 1992: 3.74 = $1 US). **Gross domestic product** (1989): $79 bln. **Per capita GDP:** $4,800. **Imports** (1989): $19.2 bln.; partners: US 15%, Jap. 12%. **Exports** (1989): $28.3 bln.; partners: U.S. 22%, Jap. 20%. **National budget** (1990): $38 bln. expenditures. **International reserves less gold** (Mar. 1992): $11.6 bln. **Gold:** 4.59 mln. oz t. **Consumer prices** (change in 1991): 4.1%.

Transport: Railroads (1989): **Length:** 555 mi. **Motor vehicles:** in use (1989): 2.2 mln. passenger cars, 2.0 mln. comm. vehicles. **Civil aviation** (1990): 16.0 bln.; passenger-km.; 25 airports. **Chief ports:** Jidda, Ad-Dammam, Ras Tannurah.

Communications: Television sets: 1 per 3.5 persons. **Radios:** 1 per 3.3 persons. **Telephones:** 1 per 13 persons. **Daily newspaper circ.** (1989): 49 per 1,000 pop.

Health: Life expectancy at birth (1991): 65 male; 68 female. **Births** (per 1,000 pop. 1991): 38. **Deaths** (per 1,000 pop. 1991): 7. **Natural increase:** 3.1%. **Hospital beds:** 1 per 406 persons. **Physicians:** 1 per 852 persons. **Infant mortality** (per 1,000 live births 1991): 69.

Education (1990): **Literacy:** 62%.

Major International Organizations: UN (IMF, WHO, FAO), Arab League, OPEC.

Embassy: 601 New Hampshire Ave. NW 20037; 342-3800.

Arabia was united for the first time by Mohammed, in the early 7th century. His successors conquered the entire Near East and North Africa, bringing Islam and the Arabic language. But Arabia itself soon returned to its former status.

Nejd, long an independent state and center of the Wahhabi sect, fell under Turkish rule in the 18th century, but in 1913 Ibn Saud, founder of the Saudi dynasty, overthrew the Turks and captured the Turkish province of Hasa; took the Hejaz in 1925 and by 1926, most of Asir. The discovery of oil in the 1930s transformed the new country.

Crown Prince Khalid was proclaimed king on Mar. 25, 1975, after the assassination of King Faisal. Fahd became king on June 13, 1982 following Khalid's death. There is no constitution and no parliament. The king exercises authority together with a Council of Ministers. The Islamic religious code is the law of the land. Alcohol and public entertainments are restricted, and women have an inferior legal status.

Saudi units fought against Israel in the 1948 and 1973 Arab-Israeli wars. Many billions of dollars of advanced arms have been purchased from Britain, France, and the U.S., including jet fighters, missiles, and, in 1981, 5 airborne warning and control system (AWACS) aircraft from the U.S., despite strong opposition from Israel. Beginning with the 1967 Arab-Israeli war, Saudi Arabia provided large annual financial gifts to Egypt; aid was later extended to Syria, Jordan, and Palestinian guerrilla groups, as well as to other Moslem countries.

Faisal played a leading role in the 1973-74 Arab oil embargo against the U.S. and other nations in an attempt to force them to adopt an anti-Israel policy. Saudi Arabia joined most other Arab states, 1979, in condemning Egypt's peace treaty with Israel.

In the 1980s, Saudi Arabia's moderate position on crude oil prices often prevailed at OPEC meetings.

The Hejaz contains the holy cities of Islam — Medina where the Mosque of the Prophet enshrines the tomb of Mohammed, who died in the city June 7, 632, and Mecca, his birthplace. More than 600,000 Moslems from 60 nations pilgrimage to Mecca annually.

Two Saudi oil tankers were attacked May 1984, as Iran and Iraq began air attacks against shipping in the Persian Gulf. On May 29, the U.S., citing grave concern over the growing escalation of the Iran-Iraq war in the Persian Gulf, authorized the sale of 400 Stinger antiaircraft missiles.

In 1987, Iranians making a pilgrimage to Mecca clashed with anti-Iranian pilgrims and Saudi police; over 400 were killed. Saudi Arabia broke diplomatic relations with Iran in 1988. Some 1,426 Moslem pilgrims died July 2, 1990 when a stampede occurred in a pedestrian tunnel leading to Mecca.

Following Iraq's attack on Kuwait, Aug. 2, 1990, Saudi Arabia accepted the Kuwait royal family and over 400,000 Kuwaiti refugees. King Fahd invited Western and Arab troops to deploy on its soil in support of Saudi defense forces. During the Persian Gulf war, Iraq fired a series of Scud missiles at Saudi Arabia; most were intercepted by U.S. Patriot missiles, although 28 U.S. soldiers were killed when a scud hit their barracks in Dhahran, Feb. 25. The nation's northern Gulf coastline suffered severe pollution as a result of Iraqi sabotage of the Kuwaiti oil fields.

Senegal

Republic of Senegal

République du Sénégal

People: Population (1991 est.): 7,952,000. **Age distrib.** (%): 0–14: 47.5; 15–59: 47.5; 60+: 5.0. **Pop. density:** 104 per sq. mi. **Urban** (1986): 30%. **Ethnic groups:** Wolof 36%, Serer 17%, Fulani 17%, Diola 9%, Toucouleur 9%, Mandingo 6%. **Languages:** French (official), Wolof, Serer, Peul, Tukulor, others. **Religions:** Moslems 92%, Christians 2%.

Geography: Area: 75,750 sq. mi., the size of South Dakota. **Location:** At western extreme of Africa. **Neighbors:** Mauritania on N, Mali on E, Guinea, Guinea-Bissau on S, Gambia surrounded on three sides. **Topography:** Low rolling plains cover most of Senegal, rising somewhat in the SE. Swamp and jungles are in SW. **Capital:** Dakar. **Cities** (1989): Dakar 1.4 mln. Thies 184,000; Kaolack 152,000.

Government: Type: Republic. **Head of state:** Pres. Abdou Diouf; b. Sept. 7, 1935; in office: Jan. 1, 1981. **Head of government:** Habib Thiam; in office: Apr. 8, 1991. **Local divisions:** 10 regions. **Defense:** 2.0% of GDP (1989).

Economy: Industries: Food processing, fishing. **Chief crops:** Peanuts are chief export; millet, rice. **Minerals:** Phosphates. **Arable land:** 27%. **Livestock** (1989): cattle: 2.6 mln.; sheep: 3.8 mln.; goats: 1.2 mln. **Fish catch** (1989): 255,000 metric tons. **Electricity prod.** (1990): 758 mln. kWh. **Labor force:** 77% agric.

Finance: Monetary unit: CFA franc (Mar. 1992: 278 = $1 US). **Gross domestic product** (1989): $4.7 bln. **Per capita GDP:** $615. **Imports** (1989): $1.0 bln.; partners Fr. 37%, U.S. 6%. **Exports** (1989): $801 mln.; partners Fr. 25%, UK 6%. **Tourists** (1989): $138 mln. receipts. **National budget** (1989): $1.0 bln. expenditures. **International reserves less gold** (Jan. 1992): $20.8 mln. **Gold:** 29,000 oz t. **Consumer prices** (change in 1990): 2.0%.

Transport: Railroads (1989): **Length:** 713 mi. **Motor vehicles:** in use (1989): 90,000 passenger cars, 36,000 comm. vehicles. **Chief ports:** Dakar, Saint-Louis.

Communications: Television sets: 1 per 118 persons. **Radios:** 1 per 8.7 persons. **Telephones:** 1 per 246 persons. **Daily newspaper circ.** (1990): 7 per 1,000 pop.

Health: Life expectancy at birth (1991): 54 male, 56 female. **Births** (per 1,000 pop. 1991): 44. **Deaths** (per 1,000 pop. 1991): 13. **Natural increase:** 2.9%. **Hospital beds:** 1 per 1,134 persons. **Physicians:** 1 per 17,072 persons. **Infant mortality** (per 1,000 live births 1991): 86.

Education (1988): **Literacy:** 10%. **Attendance:** 48% primary, 11% secondary.

Major International Organizations: UN and all of its specialized agencies, OAU.

Embassy: 2112 Wyoming Ave. NW 20008; 234-0540.

Portuguese settlers arrived in the 15th century, but French control grew from the 17th century. The last independent Moslem state was subdued in 1893. Dakar became the capital of French West Africa.

Independence as part, along with the Sudanese Rep., of the Mali Federation, came June 20, 1960. Senegal withdrew Aug. 20. French political and economic influence is strong.

A long drought brought famine, 1972-73, and again in 1978.

Senegal, Dec. 17, 1981, signed an agreement with The Gambia for confederation of the 2 countries under the name of Senegambia. The confederation began Feb. 1, 1982. The 2 nations retained their individual sovereignty but adopted joint defense and monetary policies.

In 1989, a border incident sparked ethnic violence against Senegalese in Mauritania and, in retaliation, against Mauritanians in Senegal.

Seychelles

Republic of Seychelles

People: Population (1991 est.): 68,000. **Age distrib.** (%): 0–14: 36.3; 15–64: 57.3; 65+: 6.4. **Pop. density:** 397 per sq. mi. **Urban** (1986): 50% **Ethnic groups:** Creoles (mixture of Asians, Africans, and French) predominate. **Languages:** English, French, (both official). **Religions:** Roman Catholic 90%.

Geography: Area: 171 sq. mi. **Location:** In the Indian O. 700 miles NE of Madagascar. **Neighbors:** Nearest are Madagascar on SW, Somalia on NW. **Topography:** A group of 86 islands, about half of them composed of coral, the other half granite, the latter predominantly mountainous. **Capital:** Victoria. **Cities** (1986): Victoria 23,000.

Government: Type: Single party republic. **Head of state:** Pres. France-Albert Rene, b. Nov. 16, 1935; in office: June 5, 1977. **Local divisions:** 23 districts. **Defense:** 6.0% of GDP (1990).

Economy: Industries: Food processing. **Chief crops:** Coconut products, cinnamon, vanilla, patchouli. **Electricity prod.** (1990): 67 mln. kWh. **Labor force:** 12% agric.; 19.4% tourism, comm.; 32% serv.; 40% govt.

Finance: Monetary unit: Rupee (Mar. 1992: 5.28 = $1 US). **Gross domestic product** (1989): $285 mln. **Per capita GDP:** $4,170. **Imports** (1991): $172 mln.; partners: UK 20%, So. Afr. 13%. **Exports** (1991): $48 mln.; partners: Pak. 38%; Jap. 26%. **National Budget** (1989): $168 mln. **Tourists** (1990): $119 mln. receipts. **International reserves less gold** (Mar. 1992): $26.5 mln. **Consumer prices** (change in 1991): 1.9%.

Transport: Motor vehicles: in use (1989): 4,000 passenger cars, 1,300 comm. vehicles. **Port:** Victoria.

Communications: Radios: 1 per 3 persons. **Telephones:** 1 per 5 persons. **Daily newspaper circ.** (1990): 47 per 1,000 pop.

Health: Life expectancy at birth (1991): 65 male; 71 female. **Births** (per 1,000 pop. 1991): 23. **Deaths** (per 1,000 pop. 1991): 7. **Natural increase:** 1.6%. **Hospital beds:** 1 per 154 persons. **Physicians:** 1 per 1,397 persons. **Infant mortality** (per 1,000 live births 1991): 15.

Education (1989): **Literacy:** 80%. **Years compulsory** 9; attendance 98%.

Major International Organizations: UN, OAU, Commonwealth of Nations.

The islands were occupied by France in 1768, and seized by Britain in 1794. Ruled as part of Mauritius from 1814, the Seychelles became a separate colony in 1903. The ruling party had opposed independence as impractical, but pressure from the OAU and the UN became irresistible, and independence was declared June 29, 1976. The first president was ousted in a coup a year later by a socialist leader.

A new constitution, announced Mar. 1979, turned the country into a one-party state.

Sierra Leone

Republic of Sierra Leone

People: Population (1991 est.): 4,274,000. **Age distrib.** (%): 0–14: 41.4; 15–59: 53.5; 60+: 5.1. **Pop. density:** 153 per sq. mi. **Ethnic groups:** Temne 30%, Mende 29%, others. **Languages:** English (official), tribal languages. **Religions:** animist 30%, Moslem 30%, Christian 10%.

Geography: Area: 27,925 sq. mi., slightly smaller than South Carolina. **Location:** On W coast of W. Africa. **Neighbors:** Guinea on N, E, Liberia on S. **Topography:** The heavily-indented, 210-mi. coastline has mangrove swamps. Behind are wooded hills, rising to a plateau and mountains in the E. **Capital:** Freetown. **Cities** (1985 est.): Freetown 469,000; Bo, Kenema, Makeni.

Government: Type: Military. **Head of government:** Military council. **Local divisions:** 4 provinces.

Economy: Industries: Mining, tourism. **Chief crops:** Cocoa, coffee, palm kernels, rice, ginger. **Minerals:** Diamonds, bauxite. **Arable land:** 25%. **Fish catch** (1989): 52,000 metric tons. **Electricity prod.** (1990): 180 mln. kWh. **Labor force:** 75% agric.; 15% ind. & serv.

Finance: Monetary unit: Leone (Mar. 1992: 476 = $1.00 US). **Gross domestic product** (1989): $1.3 bln. **Per capita GDP:** $325. **Imports** (1990): $144 mln.; partners: UK 22%, Fr. 11%. **Exports** (1990): $138 mln.; partners: Neth. 31%; UK 15%, U.S. 9%. **National budget** (1991): $181 mln. expenditures. **International reserves less gold** (Mar. 1992): $8 mln. **Consumer prices** (change in 1991): 102%.

Transport: Motor Vehicles: in use (1989): 29,000 passenger cars, 10,000 comm. vehicles. **Chief ports:** Freetown, Bonthe.

Communications: Television sets: 1 per 114 persons. **Radios:** 1 per 4.2 persons. **Telephones:** 1 per 251 persons. **Daily newspaper circ.** (1987): 3 per 1,000 pop.

Health: Life expectancy at birth (1991): 42 male; 48 female. **Births** (per 1,000 pop. 1991): 46. **Deaths** (per 1,000 pop. 1991): 21. **Natural increase:** 2.5%. **Hospital beds:** 1 per 980 persons. **Physicians:** 1 per 13,150 persons. **Infant mortality** (per 1,000 live births 1991): 151.

Education (1991): **Literacy:** 21%.

Major International Organizations: UN (GATT, IMF, WHO), Commonwealth of Nations, OAU.

Embassy: 1701 19th St. NW 20009; 939-9261.

Freetown was founded in 1787 by the British government as a haven for freed slaves. Their descendants, known as Creoles, number more than 60,000.

Successive steps toward independence followed the 1951 constitution. Full independence arrived Apr. 27, 1961. Sierra Leone became a republic Apr. 19, 1971. A one-party state approved by referendum 1978, brought political stability, but the economy has been plagued by inflation, corruption, and dependence upon the International Monetary Fund and creditors.

Mutinous soldiers ousted Pres. Momoh Apr. 29, 1992.

Singapore

Republic of Singapore

People: Population (1991 est.): 2,756,000. **Age distrib.** (%): 0–14: 23.4; 15–59: 68.4; 60+: 8.2. **Pop. density:** 12,303 per sq. mi. **Ethnic groups:** Chinese 77%, Malays 15%, Indians 6%. **Languages:** Chinese, Malay, Tamil, English all official. **Religions:** Buddhism 29%, Taoism 13%, Moslem 16%, Christian 19%.

Geography: Area: 224 sq. mi., smaller than New York City. **Location:** Off tip of Malayan Peninsula in S.E. Asia. **Neighbors:** Nearest are Malaysia on N, Indonesia on S. **Topography:** Singapore is a flat, formerly swampy island. The nation includes 40 nearby islets. **Capital:** Singapore.

Government: Type: Republic. **Head of state:** Pres. Wee Kim Wee; in office: Sept. 3, 1985. **Head of government:** Prime Min. Goh Chok Tong; b. May 20, 1941; in office: Nov. 28, 1990. **Defense:** 4% of GDP (1990).

Economy: Industries: Shipbuilding, oil refining, electronics, banking, textiles, food, rubber, lumber processing, tourism. **Arable land:** 11%. **Livestock** (1989): pigs: 321,000. **Electricity prod.** (1990): 14.4 bln. kWh. **Labor force:** 1% agric.; 58% ind. & comm.; 35% services.

Finance: Monetary unit: Dollar (May 1992: 1.66 = $1 US). **Gross domestic product** (1990): $34.6 bln. **Per capita GDP:** $12,700. **Imports** (1991): $662 bln.; partners: Jap. 18%, Malay. 13%, U.S. 17%, Sau. Ar. 9%. **Exports** (1991): $59.0 bln., partners: U.S. 20%, Malay. 16%, Jap. 11%, HK 6%. **Tourists** (1989): $2.9 bln. receipts. **National budget** (1990): $7.2 bln. expenditures. **Consumer prices** (change in 1991): 3.4%.

Transport: Motor vehicles: in use (1990): 286,000 passenger cars, 122,000 comm. vehicles. **Civil aviation:** (1990) 31.5 bln. passenger-km; 1 airport.

Communications: Television sets: 1 per 4.9 persons. **Radios:** 1 per 4.2 persons. **Telephones:** 1 per 2.1 persons. **Daily newspaper circ.** (1990): 289 per 1,000 pop.

Health: Life expectancy at birth (1991): 72 male; 77 female. **Births** (per 1,000 pop. 1991): 18. **Deaths** (per 1,000 pop. 1991): 5. **Natural increase:** 1.3%. **Hospital beds:** 1 per 260 persons. **Physicians:** 1 per 837 persons. **Infant mortality** (per 1,000 live births 1991): 8.

Education (1990): **Literacy:** 87%. **Years compulsory:** none; attendance 94%.

Major International Organizations: UN (GATT, IMF, WHO), ASEAN.

Embassy: 1824 R St. NW 20009; 667-7555.

Founded in 1819 by Sir Thomas Stamford Raffles, Singapore was a British colony until 1959 when it became autonomous within the Commonwealth. On Sept. 16, 1963, it joined with Malaya, Sarawak and Sabah to form the Federation of Malaysia.

Tensions between Malayans, dominant in the federation, and ethnic Chinese, dominant in Singapore, led to an agreement under which Singapore became a separate nation, Aug. 9, 1965.

Singapore is one of the world's largest ports. Standards in health, education, and housing are high. International banking has grown.

Slovenia

Slovenija

People: Population (1991 est.): 1,974,000. **Pop. density:** 252 per sq. mi. **Ethnic groups:** Slovenes. **Language:** Slovenian, Yugoslavian. **Religions:** Mostly Roman Catholic.

Geography: Area: 7,819 sq. mi. **Location:** in SE Europe. **Neighbors:** Italy, Austria, Hungary, Croatia. **Topography:** mostly hilly; 42% of the land is forested.

Government: Type: Republic. **Head of state:** Pres. Milan Kucan. **Head of government:** Lojze Peterle. **Capital:** Ljubljana.

Economy: Industries: Steel, textiles. **Minerals:** Coal, mercury. **Chief crops:** Wheat, potatoes. **Livestock** (1989): cattle: 546,000; pigs: 576,000.

Finance: Monetary unit: Tolar.

Transport: Motor vehicles: in use (1989): 545,000 passenger cars.

Education: Literacy (1991): 90%.

Major International Organizations: UN.

The Slovenes settled in their current territory in the period from the 6th to the 8th century. They fell under German domination as early as the 9th century. Modern Slovenian political history began after 1848 when the Slovenes, who were divided among several Austrian provinces, began their struggle for political and national unification. With the establishment of Yugoslavia in 1918, this unification was largely achieved when the majority of the Slovenes entered the new state, which became the Kingdom of the Serbs, Croats, and Slovenes.

Slovenia declared independence June 25, 1991.

Solomon Islands

People: Population (1991 est.): 347,000. **Age distrib.** (%): 0–14: 49; 15–59: 45.5; 60+: 5.5. **Pop. density:** 32 per sq. mi. **Urban** (1986): 15%. **Ethnic groups:** Melanesian 93%, Polynesian 4%. **Languages:** English (official), Papuan, Melanesian, Polynesian languages. **Religions:** Anglican 34%, Roman Catholic 19%, Evangelical 24%, traditional religions.

Geography: Area: 10,640 sq. mi., slightly larger than Maryland. **Location:** Melanesian archipelago in the western Pacific O. **Neighbors:** Nearest is Papua New Guinea on W. **Topography:** 10 large volcanic and rugged islands and 4 groups of smaller ones. **Capital:** Honiara. **Cities:** (1988): Honiara 30,000.

Government: Type: Parliamentary democracy within the Commonwealth of Nations. **Head of state:** Queen Elizabeth II, represented by Gov.-Gen. George Lepping. **Head of government:** Prime Min. Solomon Mamaloni; in office: Mar. 28, 1989. **Local divisions:** 7 provinces and Honiara.

Economy: Industries: Fish canning. **Chief crops:** Coconuts, rice, bananas, yams. **Other resources:** Forests, marine shell. **Arable land:** 2%. **Fish catch** (1990): 25,000 metric tons. **Electricity prod.** (1990): 39 mln. kWh. **Labor force:** 32% agric., 32% services, 18% ind. & comm.

Finance: Monetary unit: Dollar (Mar. 1992: 2.87 = $1 US). **Gross domestic product** (1989): $156 mln. **Per capita GDP** (1989): $570. **Imports** (1990): $92 mln.; partners: Austral. 31%, Jap. 14%, Sing. 18%. **Exports** (1990): $70 mln.; partners: Jap. 37%, UK 11%.

Communications: Radios: 1 per 4.6 persons. **Telephones:** 1 per 58 persons.

Health: Life expectancy at birth (1991): 67 male; 72 female. **Births:** (per 1,000 pop. 1991): 41. **Deaths** (per 1,000 pop. 1991): 5. **Natural increase:** 3.6%. **Infant mortality** (per 1,000 live births 1991): 39.

Education (1989): **Literacy:** 60%. **Primary school** 78%. **Secondary school:** 21%.

Major International Organizations: UN, Commonwealth of Nations.

The Solomon Islands were sighted in 1568 by an expedition from Peru. Britain established a protectorate in the 1890s over most of the group, inhabited by Melanesians. The islands saw major World War II battles. Self-government came Jan. 2, 1976, and independence was formally attained July 7, 1978.

Somalia

Somali Democratic Republic

Jamhuriyadda Dimugradiga Somaliya

People: Population (1991 est.): 6,709,000. **Pop. density:** 27 per sq. mi. **Urban** (1988): 36%. **Ethnic groups:** mainly Hamitic, others. **Languages:** Somali, Arabic (both official). **Religions:** Sunni Moslems 99%.

Geography: Area: 246,300 sq. mi., slightly smaller than Texas. **Location:** Occupies the eastern horn of Africa. **Neighbors:** Djibouti, Ethiopia, Kenya on W. **Topography:** The coastline extends for 1,700 mi. Hills cover the N; the center and S are flat. **Capital:** Mogadishu. **Cities** (1986 est.): Mogadishu 700,000.

Government: Type: Independent republic. **Head of state:** Pres. Ali Mahdi Muhammad; in office: Jan. 29, 1991. **Head of government:** Prime Min. Umar Arteh Ghalib; in office: Jan. 24, 1991. **Local divisions:** 16 regions. **Defense:** 6.5% of GNP (1984).

Economy: Chief crops: Incense, sugar, bananas, sorghum, corn, gum. **Minerals:** Iron, tin, gypsum, bauxite, uranium. **Arable**

land: 2%. **Livestock** (1989): cattle: 5.2 mln.; goats: 20 mln.; sheep: 6 mln. **Fish catch** (1990): 18,000 metric tons. **Electricity prod.** (1988): 86 mln. kWh. **Labor force:** 82% agric.

Finance: Monetary unit: Shilling (Dec. 1991: 2,626 = $1 US). **Gross domestic product** (1989): $1.7 bln. **Per capita GDP** (1989): $170. **Imports** (1989): $170 mln.; partners: It. 29%, Fra. 18%. **Exports** (1987): $95 mln.; partners: It. 17%. **Consumer prices** (change in 1990): 102%.

Transport: Motor vehicles: in use (1989): 19,000 passenger cars, 11,000 comm. vehicles. **Chief ports:** Mogadishu, Berbera.

Communications: Radios: 1 per 20 persons.

Health: Life expectancy at birth (1991): 56 male; 56 female. **Births** (per 1,000 pop. 1991): 46. **Deaths** (per 1,000 pop. 1991): 13. **Natural increase:** 3.3%. **Hospital beds:** 1 per 1,053 persons. **Physicians:** 1 per 19,071 persons. **Infant mortality** (per 1,000 live births 1991): 116.

Education (1990): Literacy: 24%. 50% attend primary school, 7% attend secondary school.

Major International Organizations: UN, OAU, Arab League.

Embassy: 600 New Hampshire Ave. NW 20037; 342-1575.

The UN in 1949 approved eventual creation of Somalia as a sovereign state and in 1950 Italy took over the trusteeship held by Great Britain since World War II.

British Somaliland was formed in the 19th century in the NW. Britain gave it independence June 26, 1960; on July 1 it joined with the former Italian part to create the independent Somali Republic.

On Oct. 21, 1969, a Supreme Revolutionary Council seized power in a bloodless coup, named a Council of Secretaries of State, and abolished the Assembly. In May, 1970, several foreign companies were nationalized.

Somalia has laid claim to Ogaden, the huge eastern region of Ethiopia, peopled mostly by Somalis. Ethiopia battled Somali rebels in 1977. Some 11,000 Cuban troops with Soviet arms defeated Somali army troops and ethnic Somali rebels in Ethiopia, 1978. As many as 1.5 mln. refugees entered Somalia. Guerrilla fighting in Ogaden continued until 1988 when a peace agreement was reached with Ethiopia.

Twenty-one years of one-man rule ended in Jan. 1991 with the flight of Gen. Muhammad Siyad Barrah from the capital.

South Africa

Republic of South Africa

Republiek van Suid-Afrika

People: Population (1991 est.): 40,600,000. **Age distrib.** (%): 0–14: 41.0; 15–59: 52.8; 60+: 6.2. **Pop. density:** 85 per sq. mi. **Urban** (1985): 55%. **Ethnic groups:** black 75%, white 14%, coloured 8%, Asian 3%. **Religions:** Mainly Christian, Hindu, Moslem minorities, **Languages:** Afrikaans, English (both official), Nguni, Sotho languages.

Geography: Area: 472,359 sq. mi., about twice the size of Texas. **Location:** At the southern extreme of Africa. **Neighbors:** Namibia (SW Africa), Botswana, Zimbabwe on N, Mozambique, Swaziland on E; surrounds Lesotho. **Topography:** The large interior plateau reaches close to the country's 2,700-mi. coastline. There are few major rivers or lakes; rainfall is sparse in W, more plentiful in E. **Capitals:** Cape Town (legislative). Pretoria (administrative), and Bloemfontein (judicial). **Cities** (1990 met.): Durban 1 mln. Cape Town 1.9 mln. Johannesburg 1.7 mln. Pretoria 850,000.

Government: Type: Tricameral parliament with one chamber each for whites, coloureds, and Asians. **Head of State:** State Pres. Frederik W. De Klerk; b. Mar. 18, 1936; in office: Sept. 20, 1989. **Local divisions:** 4 provinces, 10 "homelands" for black Africans. **Defense:** 11% of GDP (1992).

Economy: Industries: Steel, tires, motors, textiles, plastics. **Chief crops:** Corn, wool, dairy products, grain, tobacco, sugar, fruit, peanuts, grapes. **Minerals:** Gold (largest producer), chromium, antimony, coal, iron, manganese, nickel, phosphates, tin, uranium, gem diamonds, platinum, copper, vanadium. **Other resources:** Wool. **Arable land:** 12%. **Livestock** (1989): cattle: 11.8 mln.; sheep: 30.3 mln. **Fish catch** (1989): 878,000 metric tons. **Electricity prod.** (1990): 155 bln. kWh. **Crude steel prod.** (1990): 8.7 mln. metric tons. **Labor force:** 25% agric.; 32% ind. and commerce; 34% serv.; 7% mining.

Finance: Monetary unit: Rand (June 1992: 2.81 = $1 US). **Gross domestic product** (1990): $101 bln. **Per capita GDP** $2,600. **Imports** (1991): $18.7 bln.; partners: Ger. 19%, U.S. 68%, UK. 12%. **Exports** (1991): $24.1 bln.; partners: U.S. 43%, Jap. 9%. **Tourism** (1989): $709 mln. receipts. **National budget** (1992): $32.8 bln. **International reserves less gold** (Mar. 1992): $1.0 bln. **Gold:** 6.7 mln. oz t. **Consumer prices** (change in 1991): 15.3%.

Transport: Railroads (1989): **Length:** 14,681 mi. **Motor vehicles:** in use (1989): 3.3 mln. passenger cars, 1.2 mln. comm. vehicles. **Civil aviation:** (1989): 9.2 bln. passenger-km: 40 airports. **Chief ports:** Durban, Cape Town, East London, Port Elizabeth.

Communications: Television sets: 1 per 11 persons. **Radios:** 1 per 3.0 persons. **Telephones:** 1 per 8.5 persons. **Daily newspaper circ.** (1988): 41 per 1,000 pop.

Health: Life expectancy at birth (1991): 61 Male; 67 Female. **Births** (per 1,000 pop. 1991): 35. **Deaths** (per 1,000 pop. 1991): 8. **Natural increase:** 2.7%. **Physicians:** 1 per 1,340 persons. **Infant mortality** (per 1,000 live births 1991) 51.

Education (1990): **Literacy:** 99% (whites), 69% (Asians), 62% (coloureds), 50% (Africans).

Major International Organizations: UN (GATT).

Embassy: 3051 Massachusetts Ave. NW 20008; 232-4400.

Bushmen and Hottentots were the original inhabitants. Bantus, including Zulu, Xhosa, Swazi, and Sotho, had occupied the area from Transvaal to south of Transkei before the 17th century.

The Cape of Good Hope area was settled by Dutch, beginning in the 17th century. Britain seized the Cape in 1806. Many Dutch trekked north and founded 2 republics, the Transvaal and the Orange Free State. Diamonds were discovered, 1867, and gold, 1886. The Dutch (Boers) resented encroachments by the British and others; the Anglo-Boer War followed, 1899-1902. Britain won and, effective May 31, 1910, created the Union of South Africa, incorporating the British colonies of the Cape and Natal, the Transvaal and the Orange Free State. After a referendum, the Union became the Republic of South Africa, May 31, 1961, and withdrew from the Commonwealth.

With the election victory of Daniel Malan's National party in 1948, the policy of separate development of the races, or apartheid, already existing unofficially, became official. This called for separate development, separate residential areas, and ultimate political independence for the whites, Bantus, Asians, and Coloreds. In 1959 the government passed acts providing the eventual creation of several Bantu nations or Bantustans on 13% of the country's land area, though most black leaders opposed the plan.

Under apartheid, blacks were severely restricted to certain occupations, and paid far lower wages than whites for similar work. Only whites could vote or run for public office. There is an advisory Indian Council, partly elected, partly appointed. In 1969, a Colored People's Representative Council was created.

At least 600 persons, mostly Bantus, were killed in 1976 riots protesting apartheid. Black protests continued through the 1980s as violence broke out in several black townships. A new constitution was approved by referendum, Nov. 1983, which extended the parliamentary franchise to the Coloured and Asian minorities. Laws banning interracial sex and marriage were repealed in 1985.

In 1963, the Transkei, an area in the SE, became the first of these partially self-governing territories or "Homelands." Transkei became independent on Oct. 26, 1976, Bophuthatswana on Dec. 6, 1977, and Venda on Sept. 13, 1979; none received international recognition.

In 1981, So. Africa launched military operations in Angola and Mozambique to combat terrorists groups; So. African troops attacked the South West African People's Organization (SWAPO) guerrillas in Angola, March, 1982. South Africa and Mozambique signed a non-agression pact in 1984.

In 1986, Nobel Peace Prize winner Bishop Desmond Tutu called for Western nations to apply sanctions against S. Africa to force an end to apartheid. President Botha announced in Apr. the end to the nation's system of racial pass laws and offered blacks an advisory role in government.

On May 19, S. Africa attacked 3 neighboring countries—Zimbabwe, Botswana, Zambia—to strike at guerrilla strongholds of the African National Congress.

A nationwide state of emergency was declared June 12, giving almost unlimited power to the security forces. On Apr. 22, 1987, a 6-week-old walkout by railway workers erupted into violence after the dismissal of 16,000 strikers. As confrontation between blacks and government increased, there was widespread support in Western nations for a complete trade embargo on S. Africa.

Some 2 million South African black workers staged a massive strike, June 6-8, 1988, to protest the government's new labor laws and the banning of political activity by trade unions and antiapartheid groups. P.W. Botha, head of the government since 1978, resigned Aug. 14, 1989 and was replaced by Frederik W. De Klerk.

In 1990, the government lifted its bar on the African National Congress, the primary black group fighting to end white minority rule. On Feb. 11, black nationalist leader Nelson Mandela was freed after more than 27 years in prison. Mandela went on a 6-week, 14-nation tour, June-July, highlighted by an 11-day, 8-city tour of the U.S. In Oct. the Separate Amenities Act was repealed, ending the legal basis of segragation in public places. In Feb. 1991 Pres De Klerk announced plans to end all apartheid racial separation laws. In June the race registration law was repealed. The government admitted, in July, making payments to the Zulu-based Inkatha Freedom Party, main rival of the African National Congress.

A band of marauders swept through the township of Boipatong, June 17, 1992, killing over 40 blacks and prompting the African National Congress to break off constitutional talks with the white-minority government.

Bophuthatswana: Population (1990 est.): 1,959,000. **Area:** 16,988 sq. mi., 6 discontinuous geographic units. **Capital:** Mmabatho. **Head of state:** Pres. Kgosi Lucas Manyane Mangope, b. Dec. 27, 1923; in office: Dec. 6, 1977.

Ciskei: Population (1990 est.): 844,000. **Area:** 2,996 sq. mi. **Capitol:** Bisho. **Head of State:** Military council.

Transkei: Population (1990 est.): 3,301,000. **Area:** 16,855 sq. mi., 3 discontinuous geographic units. **Capital:** Umtata. **Head of government:** Gen. Bantu Holomisa; in office: Dec. 30, 1987.

Venda: Population (1990 est.): 518,000. **Area:** 2,771 sq. mi., 2 discontinuous geographic units. **Capital:** Thohoyandou. **Head of state:** Gabriel Ramushwana; in office: Apr. 5, 1990.

Spain

España

People: Population (1991 est.): 39,384,000 **Age distrib.** (%): 0–14: 24.6; 15–59: 59.5; 60+: 15.9. **Pop. density:** 202 per sq. mi. **Urban** (1987): 75%. **Ethnic groups:** Spanish (Castilian, Valencian, Andalusian, Asturian) 72.8%, Catalan 16.4%, Galician 8.2%, Basque 2.3%. **Languages:** Spanish (official), Catalan, Galician, Basque. **Religions:** Roman Catholic 90%.

Geography: Area: 194,896 sq. mi., the size of Arizona and Utah combined. **Location:** In SW Europe. **Neighbors:** Portugal on W. France on N. **Topography:** The interior is a high, arid plateau broken by mountain ranges and river valleys. The NW is heavily watered, the south has lowlands and a Mediterranean climate. **Capital:** Madrid. **Cities** (1990 est.): Madrid 3,120,000; Barcelona 1,707,000; Valencia 758,000; Seville 678,000.

Government: Type: Constitutional monarchy. **Head of state:** King Juan Carlos I de Borbon y Borbon, b. Jan. 5, 1938; in office: Nov. 22, 1975. **Head of government:** Prime Min. Felipe Gonzalez Marquez; in office: Dec. 2, 1982. **Local divisions:** 17 autonomous communities. **Defense:** 2.0% of GDP (1990).

Economy: Industries: Machinery, steel, textiles, shoes, autos, processed foods. **Chief crops:** Grains, olives, grapes, citrus fruits, vegetables, olives. **Minerals:** Lignite, uranium, lead, iron, copper, zinc, coal. **Other resources:** Forests (cork). **Arable land:** 31%. **Livestock** (1989): cattle: 4.9 mln.; pigs: 16.9 mln.; sheep: 23.7 mln. **Fish catch** (1989): 974,000 tons. **Electricity prod.** (1990): 149 bln. kWh. **Crude steel prod.** (1990): 12.7 mln. metric tons. **Labor force:** 16% agric.; 24% ind. and comm.; 52% serv.

Finance: Monetary unit: Peseta (May 1992: 103.82 = $1 US). **Gross domestic product** (1990): $435 bln. **Per capita GDP:** $11,100. **Imports** (1991): $93.8 bln.; partners: U.S. 8%, EC 57%. **Exports** (1991): $59.3 bln.; partners: EC 67%, U.S. 6%. **Tourists** (1989): $16.1 bln. receipts. **National budget** (1990): $111 bln. expenditures. **International reserves less gold** (Mar. 1992): $65.7 bln. **Gold:** 15.6 mln. oz t. **Consumer prices** (change in 1991): 5.9%.

Transport: Railroads (1990): **Length:** 12,563 km. **Motor vehicles:** in use (1989): 10.7 mln. passenger cars, 2.0 mln. comm. **Civil aviation:** (1989): 22.8 bln. passenger-km; 31 airports with scheduled flights. **Chief ports:** Barcelona, Bilbao, Valencia, Cartagena, Gijon.

Communications: Television sets: 1 per 2.6 persons. **Radios:** 1 per 3.4 persons. **Telephones:** 1 per 2.5 persons. **Daily newspaper circ.** (1990): 76 per 1,000 pop.

Health: Life expectancy at birth (1991): 75 male; 82 female. **Births** (per 1,000 pop. 1991): 11. **Deaths** (per 1,000 pop. 1991): 8. **Natural increase:** .3%. **Hospital beds:** 1 per 198 persons. **Physicians:** 1 per 275 persons. **Infant mortality** (per 1,000 live births 1991): 6.

Education (1991): Literacy: 97%. **School compulsory:** to age 16.

Major International Organizations: UN and all of its specialized agencies, NATO, OECD, EC.

Embassy: 2700 15th St. NW 20009; 265-0190.

Spain was settled by Iberians, Basques, and Celts, partly overrun by Carthaginians, conquered by Rome c.200 BC. The Visigoths, in power by the 5th century AD, adopted Christianity but by 711 AD lost to the Islamic invasion from Africa. Christian reconquest from the N led to a Spanish nationalism. In 1469 the kingdoms of Aragon and Castile were united by the marriage of Ferdinand II and Isabella I, and the last Moorish power was broken by the fall of the kingdom of Granada, 1492. Spain became a bulwark of Roman Catholicism.

Spain obtained a colonial empire with the discovery of America by Columbus, 1492, the conquest of Mexico by Cortes, and Peru by Pizarro. It also controlled the Netherlands and parts of Italy and Germany. Spain lost its American colonies in the early 19th century. It lost Cuba, the Philippines, and Puerto Rico during the Spanish-American War, 1898.

Primo de Rivera became dictator in 1923. King Alfonso XIII revoked the dictatorship, 1930, but was forced to leave the country 1931. A republic was proclaimed which disestablished the church, curtailed its privileges, and secularized education. A conservative reaction occurred 1933 but was followed by a Popular Front (1936-1939) composed of socialists, communists, republicans, and anarchists.

Army officers under Francisco Franco revolted against the government, 1936. In a destructive 3-year war, in which some one million died, Franco received massive help and troops from Italy and Germany, while the USSR, France, and Mexico supported the republic. War ended Mar. 28, 1939. Franco was named caudillo, leader of the nation. Spain was neutral in World War II but its relations with fascist countries caused its exclusion from the UN until 1955.

In July 1969, Franco and the Cortes designated Prince Juan Carlos as the future king and chief of state. After Franco's death, Nov. 20, 1975, Juan Carlos was sworn in as king. He presided over the formal dissolution of the institutions of the Franco regime. In free elections June 1977, moderates and democratic socialists emerged as the largest parties.

Catalonia and the Basque country were granted autonomy, Jan. 1980, following overwhelming approval in home-rule referendums. Basque extremists, however, have continued their campaign for independence.

The **Balearic Islands** in the western Mediterranean, 1,935 sq. mi., are a province of Spain; they include **Majorca** (Mallorca), with the capital, Palma; **Minorca, Cabrera, Ibiza** and **Formentera.** The **Canary Islands,** 2,807 sq. mi., in the Atlantic W of Morocco, form 2 provinces, including the islands of **Tenerife, Palma, Gomera, Hierro, Grand Canary, Fuerteventura,** and **Lanzarote** with Las Palmas and Santa Cruz thriving ports. **Ceuta** and **Melilla,** small enclaves on Morocco's Mediterranean coast, are part of Metropolitan Spain.

Spain has sought the return of Gibraltar, in British hands since 1704.

Sri Lanka

Democratic Socialist Republic of Sri Lanka

Sri Lanka Prajathanthrika Samajavadi Janarajaya

People: Population (1991 est.): 17,423,000. **Age distrib.** (%): 0–14: 35.3; 15–59: 58.1; 60+: 6.6. **Pop. density:** 687 per sq. mi. **Urban** (1985): 21.5%. **Ethnic groups:** Sinhalese 74%, Tamils 17%, Moors 7%. **Languages:** Sinhalese, and Tamil, (both official). **Religions:** Buddhist 69%, Hindu 15%, Christian 8%, Moslem 7%.

Geography: Area: 25,332 sq. mi. about the size of W. Va. **Location:** In Indian O. off SE coast of India. **Neighbors:** India on NW. **Topography:** The coastal area and the northern half are flat; the S-central area is hilly and mountainous. **Capital:** Colombo. **Cities** (1989): Colombo 1.2 mln.; Jaffna, 270,000; Galle, 168,000; Kandy, 147,000.

Government: Type: Republic. **Head of state:** Pres. Ranasinghe Premadasa; b. June 24, 1924; in office: Jan. 2, 1989. **Head of government:** Prime Minister Dingiri Banda Wijetunge, b. 1923, in office: Mar. 3, 1989. **Local divisions:** 8 provinces, 24 districts. **Defense:** 5% of GDP (1991).

Economy: Industries: Plywood, paper, milling, chemicals, textiles. **Chief crops:** Tea, coconuts, rice. **Minerals:** Graphite, limestone, gems, phosphate. **Other resources:** Forests, rubber. **Arable land:** 16%. **Livestock** (1989): cattle: 1.0 mln. **Fish catch** (1989): 197,000 metric tons. **Electricity prod.** (1990): 4.2 bln. kWh. **Labor force:** 46% agric.; 27% ind. and comm.; 26% serv.

Finance: Monetary unit: Rupee (Mar. 1992: 43 = $1 US). **Gross domestic product** (1990): $6.6 bln. **Per capita GDP:** $380. **Imports** (1990): $2.6 bln.; partners: Jap. 15%, UK 7%. **Exports** (1990): $1.9 bln.; partners: U.S. 22%, UK 7%. **Tourists** (1989): $79 mln. receipts. **National budget** (1990): $2.2 bln. expenditures. **International reserves less gold** (Mar. 1992): $698 mln. **Gold:** 175,000 oz t. **Consumer prices** (change in 1991): 12.2%.

Transport: Railroads (1990): **Length:** 1,453 km. **Motor vehicles:** in use (1988): 155,000 passenger cars, 139,000 comm. vehicles. **Civil aviation** (1990): 3.4 bln. passenger-km; 1 airport. **Chief ports:** Colombo, Trincomalee, Galle.

Communications: Television sets: 1 per 28 persons. **Radios:** 1 per 6 persons. **Telephones:** 1 per 102 persons.

Health: Life expectancy at birth (1991): 69 male; 74 female. **Births** (per 1,000 pop. 1991): 21. **Deaths** (per 1,000 pop. 1991): 6. **Natural increase:** 1.5%. **Hospital beds:** 1 per 373 persons. **Physicians:** 1 per 7,161 persons. **Infant mortality** (per 1,000 live births 1991): 21.

Education (1990): **Literacy:** 90%. **Years compulsory:** To age 12; attendance 98%.

Major International Organizations: UN (World Bank, IMF), Commonwealth of Nations.

Embassy: 2148 Wyoming Ave. NW 20008; 483-4025.

The island was known to the ancient world as Taprobane (Greek for copper-colored) and later as Serendip (from Arabic). Colonists from northern India subdued the indigenous Veddahs about 543 BC; their descendants, the Buddhist Sinhalese, still form most of the population. Hindu descendants of Tamil immigrants from southern India account for one-fifth of the population. Parts were occupied by the Portuguese in 1505 and by the Dutch in 1658. The British seized the island in 1796. As Ceylon it became an independent member of the Commonwealth in 1948. On May 22, 1972, Ceylon became the Republic of Sri Lanka.

Prime Min. W. R. D. Bandaranaike was assassinated Sept. 25, 1959. In new elections, the Freedom Party was victorious under Mrs. Sirimavo Bandaranaike, widow of the former prime minister.

After May 1970 elections, Mrs. Bandaranaike became prime minister again. In 1971 the nation suffered economic problems and terrorist activities by ultra-leftists, thousands of whom were executed. Massive land reform and nationalization of foreign-owned plantations was undertaken in the mid-1970s. Mrs. Bandaranaike was ousted in 1977 elections. A presidential form of government was installed in 1978 to restore stability.

Tension between the Sinhalese and Tamil separatists erupted into violence repeatedly in the 1980s. In 1987, hundreds died in an attack by Tamil rebels Apr. 17. Sri Lanka forces retaliated in June with attacks on the rebel-held Jaffna peninsula. Over 20,000 have died in the civil war since 1983.

Sudan

Republic of the Sudan

Jamhuryat as-Sudan

People: Population (1991 est.): 27,220,000. **Pop. density:** 28 per sq. mi. **Urban** (1983): 35%. **Ethnic groups:** black 52%, Arab 39%, Beja 6%. **Languages:** Arabic (official), Dinka, Nubian, Nuer, Beja, others. **Religions:** Sunni Moslem 70%, animist 18%, Christians 5%.

Geography: Area: 966,757 sq. mi., the largest country in Africa, over one-fourth the size of the U.S. **Location:** At the E end of Sahara desert zone. **Neighbors:** Egypt on N, Libya, Chad, Central African Republic on W, Zaire, Uganda, Kenya on S, Ethiopia on E. **Topography:** The N consists of the Libyan Desert in the W, and the mountainous Nubia desert in E, with narrow Nile valley between. The center contains large, fertile, rainy areas with fields, pasture, and forest. The S has rich soil, heavy rain. **Capital:** Khartoum. **Cities** (1983 est.): Khartoum 476,000; Omdurman 526,000; North Khartoum 341,000; Port Sudan 206,000.

Government: Type: Military. **Head of government:** Prime Min. Gen. Omar Al-Bashir; in office: June 30, 1989. **Local divisions:** 9 states. **Defense:** 7% of GDP (1990).

Economy: Industries: Textiles, food processing. **Chief crops:** Gum arabic (principal world source), durra (sorghum), cotton (main export), sesame, peanuts, rice, coffee, sugar cane, wheat, dates. **Minerals:** Chrome, copper, **Other resources:** Mahogany. **Arable land:** 5%. **Livestock** (1989): cattle: 22 mln.; sheep: 19 mln.; goats: 15 mln. **Electricity prod.** (1990): 900 mln. kWh. **Labor force:** 78% agric.; 9% ind., comm.

Finance: Monetary unit: Dinar (Mar. 1992: 1.00 = $2.20 US). **Gross domestic product** (1990): $8.5 bln. **Per capita GDP** (1990): $330. **Imports** (1990): $1.0 bln.; partners: EC 32%, U.S. 13%. **Exports** (1990): $465 mln.; partners: EC 46%. **National budget** (1990): $1.5 bln. expenditures. **International reserves less gold** (Mar. 1992): $3.7 mln. **Consumer Prices** (change in 1990): 66.3%.

Transport: Railroads (1988): **Length:** 5,503 km. **Motor vehicles:** in use (1985): 99,000 passenger cars, 17,000 comm. vehicles. **Civil aviation:** (1990): 588 mln. passenger-km; 13 airports with scheduled flights. **Chief ports:** Port Sudan.

Communications: Television sets: 1 per 23 persons. **Radios:** 1 per 4.6 persons. **Telephones:** 1 per 338 persons. **Daily newspaper circ.** (1989): 5 per 1,000 pop.

Health: Life expectancy at birth (1991): 52 male; 54 female. **Births** (per 1,000 pop. 1991): 44. **Deaths** (per 1,000 pop. 1991): 14. **Natural increase:** 3.0%. **Hospital beds:** 1 per 1,110 persons. **Physicians** (1983): 2,169. **Infant mortality** (per 1,000 live births 1991): 85.

Education (1991): **Literacy:** 27%. **Years compulsory:** 9; attendance 50%.

Major International Organizations: UN (IMF, WHO, FAO), Arab League, OAU.

Northern Sudan, ancient Nubia, was settled by Egyptians in antiquity, and was converted to Coptic Christianity in the 6th century. Arab conquests brought Islam in the 15th century.

In the 1820s Egypt took over the Sudan, defeating the last of earlier empires, including the Fung. In the 1880s a revolution was led by Mohammed Ahmed who called himself the Mahdi (leader of the faithful) and his followers, the dervishes.

In 1898 an Anglo-Egyptian force crushed the Mahdi's successors. In 1951 the Egyptian Parliament abrogated its 1899 and 1936 treaties with Great Britain, and amended its constitution, to provide for a separate Sudanese constitution.

Sudan voted for complete independence as a parliamentary government effective Jan. 1, 1956.

In 1969, a Revolutionary Council took power, but a civilian premier and cabinet were appointed; the government announced it would create a socialist state. The northern 12 provinces are predominantly Arab-Moslem and have been dominant in the central government. The 3 southern provinces are black Christians and animists. A 1972 peace agreement gave the South regional autonomy. The 2 halves of the nation began a civil war in 1988. Some 50,000 government soldiers launched a massive offensive against the southern rebels in 1992.

Economic problems plagued the nation in the 1980s, aggravated by a huge influx of refugees from neighboring countries. After 16 years in power, Pres. Nimeiry was overthrown in a bloodless military coup, Apr. 6, 1985. The Sudan held its first democratic parliamentary elections in 18 years in 1986. The elected government was overthrown in a bloodless coup June 30, 1989.

Sudan agreed to allow large-scale UN relief efforts in 1991, as some 7 million people were threatened with famine. The UN suspended aid to southern Sudan in 1992 because of the fighting.

Suriname

Republic of Suriname

People: Population (1991 est.): 402,000. **Pop. density:** 6 per sq. mi. **Ethnic groups** Hindustanis 37%, Creole 31%, Javanese 15%. **Languages:** Dutch (official), Sranantonga, English. **Religions:** Moslem 19%, Hindu 27%, Christian 47%.

Geography: Area: 63,037 sq. mi., slightly larger than Georgia. **Location:** On N shore of S. America. **Neighbors:** Guyana on W, Brazil on S, French Guiana on E. **Topography:** A flat Atlantic coast, where dikes permit agriculture. Inland is a forest belt; to the S, largely unexplored hills cover 75% of the country. **Capital:** Paramaribo. **Cities** (1989): Paramaribo 192,000.

Government: Type: Republic. **Head of State:** Pres. Roland Venetiaan; in office: Sept. 16, 1991. **Head of government:** Prime Min. Jules Adjodhia; in office: Sept. 16, 1991. **Local divisions:** 10 districts.

Economy: Industries: Aluminum. **Chief crops:** Rice, sugar, fruits. **Minerals:** Bauxite. **Other resources:** Forests, shrimp. **Arable land:** 1%. **Electricity prod.** (1990): 1.9 bln. kWh. **Labor force:** 29% agric.; 15% ind. and commerce; 42% govt.

Finance: Monetary unit: Guilder (Mar. 1992: 1.78 = $1 US). **Gross domestic product** (1989): $1.3 bln. **Per capita GDP:** $3,400. **Imports** (1988): $370 mln.; partners: U.S. 37%, Neth. 15%, Trin./Tob. 9%. **Exports** (1988): $425 mln.; partners: Nor. 33%, U.S. 13%, Neth. 26%. **Tourists** (1988): receipts: $6 mln. **National budget** (1990): $716 mln. expenditures. **International reserves less gold** (Mar. 1992): $12.9 mln. **Gold:** 54,000 oz t.

Transport: Motor vehicles: in use (1987): 33,000 passenger cars, 12,000 comm. vehicles. **Chief ports:** Paramaribo, Nieuw-Nickerie.

Communications: Television sets: 1 per 8 persons. **Radios:** 1 per 1.6 persons. **Telephones:** 1 per 10 persons. **Daily newspaper circ.** (1991): 43 per 1,000 pop.

Health: Life expectancy at birth (1991): 66 male; 71 female. **Births** (per 1,000 pop. 1991): 27. **Deaths** (per 1,000 pop. 1991): 5. **Natural increase:** 2.1%. **Infant mortality** (per 1,000 live births 1991): 40.

Education (1989): Literacy: 65%; compulsory ages 6–12.

Major International Organizations: UN (WHO, ILO, FAO, World Bank, IMF), OAS.

Embassy: 2600 Virginia Ave. NW 20037; 338-6980.

The Netherlands acquired Suriname in 1667 from Britain, in exchange for New Netherlands (New York). The 1954 Dutch constitution raised the colony to a level of equality with the Netherlands and the Netherlands Antilles. In the 1970s the Dutch government pressured for Suriname independence, which came Nov. 25, 1975, despite objections from East Indians. Some 40% of the population (mostly East Indians) emigrated to the Netherlands in the months before independence.

The National Military Council took over control of the government, Feb. 1982. The government came under democratic leadership in 1988.

Swaziland

Kingdom of Swaziland

People: Population (1991 est.): 859,000. **Age distrib.** (%): 0–14: 47.3; 15–59: 47.4; 60+: 5.3. **Pop. density:** 126 per sq. mi. **Urban** (1990): 30%. **Ethnic groups:** Swazi 90%, Zulu 2.3%, European 2.1%, other African, non-African groups. **Languages:** Swazi, English, (both official). **Religions:** Christians 60%, indigenous beliefs 40%.

Geography: Area: 6,704 sq. mi., slightly smaller than New Jersey. **Location:** In southern Africa, near Indian O. coast. **Neighbors:** South Africa on N, W, S, Mozambique on E. **Topography:** The country descends from W-E in broad belts, becoming more arid in the lowveld region, then rising to a plateau in the E. **Capital:** Mbabane. **Cities** (1990 est.): Mbabane 46,000; Manzini 53,000.

Government: Type: Monarchy. **Head of state:** King Mswati 3d; as of: Apr. 25, 1986. **Head of government:** Prime Min. Obed Dlamini; in office: July 12, 1989. **Local divisions:** 4 districts, 2 municipalities, 40 regions.

Economy: Industries: Wood pulp. **Chief crops:** Sugar, corn, cotton, rice, pineapples, sugar, citrus fruits. **Minerals:** Asbestos, iron, coal. **Other resources:** Forests. **Arable land:** 8%. **Electricity prod.** (1990): 130 mln. kWh. **Labor force:** 53% agric.; 9% ind. and commerce; 9% serv.

Finance: Monetary unit: Lilangeni (Mar. 1992: 1.00 = $.34 US). **Gross national product** (1990): $563 mln. **Per capita GNP** (1989): $900. **Imports** (1990): $651 mln.; partners: So. Afr., 92%. **Exports** (1990): $543 mln.; partners: So. Afr. 40%. **National budget** (1992): $325 mln. expenditures. **International reserves less gold** (Feb. 1992): $180 mln. **Consumer prices** (change in 1990): 11.7%.

Transport: Motor vehicles: in use (1991): 25,000 passenger cars, 28,000 comm. vehicles.

Communications: Radios: 1 per 6.3 persons. **Telephones:** 1 per 34 persons. **Daily newspaper circ.** (1990): 24 per 1,000 pop.

Health: Life expectancy at birth (1991): 51 male; 59 female. **Births** (per 1,000 pop. 1991): 44. **Deaths** (per 1,000 pop. 1991): 12. **Natural increase:** 3.2%. **Hospital beds** (1984): 1,608. **Physicians** (1984): 80. **Infant mortality rate** (per 1,000 live births 1991): 101.

Education (1990): **Literacy:** 65%. 82% attend primary school.

Major International Organizations: UN (IMF, WHO, FAO), OAU, Commonwealth of Nations.

Embassy: 3400 International Dr. NW 20008; 362-6683.

The royal house of Swaziland traces back 400 years, and is one of Africa's last ruling dynasties. The Swazis, a Bantu people, were driven to Swaziland from lands to the N by the Zulus in 1820. Their autonomy was later guaranteed by Britain and Transvaal, with Britain assuming control after 1903. Independence came Sept. 6, 1968. In 1973 the king repealed the constitution and assumed full powers.

Under the constitution political parties are forbidden; parliament's role in government is limited to debate and advice.

Sweden

Kingdom of Sweden

Konungariket Sverige

People: Population (1991 est.): 8,564,000. **Age distrib.** (%): 0–14: 17.9; 15–59: 59.0; 60+: 23.1. **Pop. density:** 49 per sq. mi. **Urban** (1985): 85%. **Ethnic groups:** Swedish 91%, Finnish 3%, Lapps, European immigrants. **Languages:** Swedish. **Religion:** Lutheran (official) 95%.

Geography: Area: 173,731 sq. mi., larger than California. **Location:** On Scandinavian Peninsula in N. Europe. **Neighbors:** Norway on W, Denmark on S (across Kattegat), Finland on E. **Topography:** Mountains along NW border cover 25% of Sweden, flat or rolling terrain covers the central and southern areas, which includes several large lakes. **Capital:** Stockholm. **Cities** (1991): Stockholm 672,000; Goteborg 433,000; Malmo 230,000.

Government: Type: Constitutional monarchy. **Head of state:** King Carl XVI Gustaf; b. Apr. 30, 1946; in office: Sept. 19, 1973. **Head of government:** Prime Min. Carl Bildt; b. July 15, 1949; in office: Oct. 3, 1991. **Local divisions:** 24 lan (counties), 278 municipalities. **Defense:** 2.5% of GDP (1990).

Economy: Industries: Steel, machinery, instruments, autos, shipbuilding, shipping, paper. **Chief crops:** Grains, potatoes, sugar beets. **Minerals:** Zinc, iron, lead, copper, gold, silver. **Other resources:** Forests (half the country); yield one fourth exports. **Arable land:** 7%. **Livestock** (1989): cattle: 1.7 mln.; pigs: 2.2 mln. **Fish catch** (1989): 240,000 metric tons. **Electricity prod.** (1990): 142 bln. kWh. **Crude steel prod.** (1990): 4.4 mln. metric tons. **Labor force:** 5% agric.; 24% manuf. & mining; 37% social services.

Finance: Monetary unit: Krona (June 1992: 5.70 = $1 US). **Gross domestic product** (1990): $137 bln. **Per capita GDP:** $16,200. **Imports** (1990): $54.7 bln.; partners: EC 56%. **Exports** (1990): $57.5 bln.; partners: EC 55%. **Tourists** (1989): $2.5 bln. receipts. **National budget** (1989): $60.5 bln. expenditures. **International reserves less gold** (Mar. 1992): $22.4 bln. **Gold:** 6.06 mln. oz t. **Consumer prices** (change in 1991): 9.3%.

Transport: Railroads (1989): **Length:** 7,140 mi. **Motor vehicles:** in use (1990): 3.6 mln. passenger cars, 324,000 comm. vehicles. **Civil aviation** (1989): 7.8 bln. passenger-km; 41 airports. **Chief ports:** Goteborg, Stockholm, Malmo.

Communications: Television sets: 1 per 2.4 persons. **Radios:** 1 per 1.2 persons. **Telephones:** 1 per 1.1 persons. **Daily newspaper circ.** (1988): 572 per 1,000 pop.

Health: Life expectancy at birth (1991): 75 male; 81 female. **Births** (per 1,000 pop. 1991): 12. **Deaths** (per 1,000 pop. 1991): 12. **Natural increase:** .0%. **Hospital beds:** 1 per 148 persons. **Physicians:** 1 per 320 persons. **Infant mortality** (per 1,000 live births (1991): 6.

Education (1991): **Literacy:** 99%. **Years compulsory:** 12; attendance 100%.

Major International Organizations: UN and all of its specialized agencies, EFTA, OECD.

Embassy: 600 New Hampshire Ave. NW 20037; 944-5600.

The Swedes have lived in present-day Sweden for at least 5,000 years, longer than nearly any other European people. Gothic tribes from Sweden played a major role in the disintegration of the Roman Empire. Other Swedes helped create the first Russian state in the 9th century.

The Swedes were Christianized from the 11th century, and a strong centralized monarchy developed. A parliament, the Riksdag, was first called in 1435, the earliest parliament on the European continent, with all classes of society represented.

Swedish independence from rule by Danish kings (dating from 1397) was secured by Gustavus I in a revolt, 1521-23; he built up the government and military and established the Lutheran Church. In the 17th century Sweden was a major European power, gaining most of the Baltic seacoast, but its international position subsequently declined.

The Napoleonic wars, in which Sweden acquired Norway (it became independent 1905), were the last in which Sweden participated. Armed neutrality was maintained in both world wars.

Over 4 decades of Social Democratic rule was ended in 1976 parliamentary elections but the party was returned to power in the 1982 elections. Although 90% of the economy is in private hands, the government holds a large interest in water power production and the railroads are operated by a public agency.

Carl Bildt, a non-Socialist, became prime minister Oct. 1991. His coalition government promised to turn the nation away from long-established economic and social programs.

Switzerland

Swiss Confederation

People: Population (1991 est.): 6,783,000. **Age distrib.** (%): 0–14: 17.0; 15–59: 63.7; 60+: 19.3. **Pop. density:** 425 per sq. mi. **Urban** (1990): 60%. **Ethnic groups:** Mixed European stock. **Languages:** German, French, Italian (all official). **Religions:** Roman Catholic 49%, Protestant 48%.

Geography: Area: 15,941 sq. mi., as large as Mass., Conn., and R.I., combined. **Location:** In the Alps Mts. in Central Europe. **Neighbors:** France on W, Italy on S, Austria on E, Germany on N. **Topography:** The Alps cover 60% of the land area, the Jura, near France, 10%. Running between, from NE to SW, are midlands, 30%. **Capital:** Bern. **Cities** (1990): Zurich 342,000; Basel 171,200; Geneva 161,000; Bern 135,000.

Government: Type: Federal republic. **Head of government:** Pres. Flavio Cotti; in office: Jan. 1, 1991. **Local divisions:** 20 full cantons, 6 half cantons. **Defense:** 2.2% of GDP (1990).

Economy: Industries: Machinery, machine tools, steel, instruments, watches, textiles, foodstuffs (cheese, chocolate), banking, tourism. **Chief crops:** Grains, potatoes, sugar beets, vegetables, tobacco. **Minerals:** Salt. **Other resources:** Hydro power potential. **Arable land:** 10%. **Livestock** (1989): cattle: 1.8 mln.; pigs: 1.9 mln. **Electricity prod.** (1990): 59 bln. kWh. **Crude steel prod.** (1988): 825,000 metric tons. **Labor force:** 39% ind. and commerce, 7% agric., 50% serv.

Finance: Monetary unit: Franc (May 1992: 1.49 = $1 US). **Gross domestic product** (1990): $126 bln. **Per capita GDP:** $18,700. **Imports** (1991): $66.4 bln.; partners: EC 71%. **Exports** (1991): $61.5 bln.; partners: EC 56%. **Tourists** (1989); receipts: $5.9 bln. **National budget** (1990): $23.8 bln. **International reserves less gold** (Mar. 1992): $27.1 bln. **Gold:** 83.28 mln. oz t. **Consumer prices** (change in 1991): 5.4%.

Transport: Railroads (1989): **Length:** 3,119 mi. **Motor vehicles:** in use (1989): 2.7 mln. passenger cars, 239,000 comm. vehicles. **Civil aviation:** (1990): 15.8 bln. passenger-km; 6 airports with scheduled flights.

Communications: Television sets: 1 per 2.9 persons. **Radios:** 1 per 2.6 persons. **Telephones:** 1 per 1.2 persons. **Daily newspaper circ.** (1990): 471 per 1,000 pop.

Health: Life expectancy at birth (1991): 75 male; 83 female. **Births** (per 1,000 pop. 1991): 12 **Deaths** (per 1,000 pop. 1991): 10 **Natural increase:** .2%. **Physicians:** 1 per 357 persons. **Infant mortality** (per 1,000 live births 1991): 5.

Education (1991): **Literacy:** 99%. **Years compulsory:** 9; attendance 100%.

Major International Organizations: Many UN specialized agencies (though not a member).

Embassy: 2900 Cathedral Ave. NW 20008; 745-7900.

Switzerland, the Roman province of Helvetia, is a federation of 23 cantons (20 full cantons and 6 half cantons), 3 of which in 1291 created a defensive league and later were joined by other districts. Voters in the French-speaking part of Canton Bern voted for self-government, 1978; Canton Jura was created Jan. 1, 1979.

In 1648 the Swiss Confederation obtained its independence from the Holy Roman Empire. The cantons were joined under a federal constitution in 1848, with large powers of local control retained by each canton.

Switzerland has maintained an armed neutrality since 1815, and has not been involved in a foreign war since 1515. It is the seat of many UN and other international agencies.

Switzerland is a leading world banking center; stability of the currency brings funds from many quarters. The nation's famed secret bank accounts were due to be phased out by Sept. 1992.

Syria

Syrian Arab Republic

al-jamhouriya al Arabia as-Souriya

People: Population (1991 est.): 12,965,000. **Age distrib.** (%): 0–14: 49.3; 15–59: 44.2; 60+: 6.5. **Pop. density:** 181 per sq. mi. **Urban** (1990): 50%. **Ethnic groups:** Arab 90%, Kurd, Armenian, others. **Languages:** Arabic (official), Kurdish, Armenian. **Religions:** Sunni Moslem 74%, other Moslem 16%, Christian 10%.

Geography: Area: 71,498 sq. mi., the size of North Dakota. **Location:** At eastern end of Mediterranean Sea. **Neighbors:** Lebanon, Israel on W, Jordan on S, Iraq on E, Turkey on N. **Topography:** Syria has a short Mediterranean coastline, then stretches E and S with fertile lowlands and plains, alternating with mountains and large desert areas. **Capital:** Damascus. **Cities** (1989 est.): Damascus 1,361,000; Aleppo 1,308,000; Homs 464,000.

Government: Type: Republic (under military regime). **Head of state:** Pres. Hafez al-Assad; b. Mar. 1930; in office: Feb. 22, 1971. **Head of government:** Prime Min. Mahmoud Zuabi; in office: Nov. 1, 1987. **Local divisions:** Damascus and 13 provinces. **Defense:** 10.9% of GDP (1989).

Economy: Industries: Oil products, textiles, tobacco, glassware, brassware. **Chief crops:** Cotton, grain, olives, fruits, vegetables. **Minerals:** Oil, phosphate, gypsum. **Crude oil reserves** (1987): 1.4 bln. bbls. **Other resources:** Wool. **Arable land:** 28%. **Livestock** (1989): sheep: 13 mln., goats: 1 mln. **Electricity prod.** (1990): 6 bln. kWh. **Labor force:** 32% agric.; 29% ind. & comm.; 39% services.

Finance: Monetary unit: Pound (Mar. 1992: 11.22 = $1 US). **Gross domestic product** (1990): $20.0 bln. **Per capita GDP:** $1,600.1. **Imports** (1990): $2.5 bln.; partners: EC 42%. **Exports** (1990): $2.3 bln.; partners: E. Europe 42%, EC 31%. **Tourists** (1989): receipts: $290 mln. **National budget** (1990): $5.5 bln. expenditures. **Consumer prices** (change in 1990): 15.0%.

Transport: Railroads (1989): **Length:** 1,100 mi. **Motor vehicles:** in use (1988): 112,000 passenger cars, 135,000 comm. vehicles **Civil aviation** (1989): 833 mln. passenger-km; 5 airports with scheduled flights. **Chief ports:** Latakia, Tartus.

Communications: Television sets: 1 per 17 persons. **Radios:** 1 per 4.1 persons. **Telephones:** 1 per 17 persons. **Daily newspaper circ.** (1989): 21 per 1,000 pop.

Health: Life expectancy at birth (1991): 68 male; 71 female. **Births** (per 1,000 pop. 1991): 43. **Deaths** (per 1,000 1991): 5. **Natural increase:** 3.8%. **Hospital beds:** 1 per 840 persons. **Physicians:** 1 per 1,347 persons. **Infant mortality** (per 1,000 live births 1991): 37.

Education (1990): **Literacy:** 64%. **Years compulsory:** 6; attendance: 94%.

Major International Organizations: UN (IMF, WHO, FAO), Arab League.

Embassy: 2215 Wyoming Ave. NW 20008; 232-6313.

Syria contains some of the most ancient remains of civilization. It was the center of the Seleucid empire, but later became absorbed in the Roman and Arab empires. Ottoman rule prevailed for 4 centuries, until the end of World War I.

The state of Syria was formed from former Turkish districts, made a separate entity by the Treaty of Sevres 1920 and divided into the states of Syria and Greater Lebanon. Both were administered under a French League of Nations mandate 1920-1941.

Syria was proclaimed a republic by the occupying French Sept. 16, 1941, and exercised full independence effective Apr. 17, 1946. Syria joined in the Arab invasion of Israel in 1948.

Syria joined with Egypt in Feb. 1958 in the United Arab Republic but seceded Sept. 30, 1961. The Socialist Baath party and military leaders seized power in Mar. 1963. The Baath, a pan-Arab organization, became the only legal party. The government has been dominated by members of the minority Alawite sect.

In the Arab-Israeli war of June 1967, Israel seized and occupied the Golan Heights area inside Syria, from which Israeli settlements had for years been shelled by Syria.

On Oct. 6, 1973, Syria joined Egypt in an attack on Israel. Arab oil states agreed in 1974 to give Syria $1 billion a year to aid anti-Israel moves. Some 30,000 Syrian troops entered Lebanon in 1976 to mediate in a civil war. They fought Palestinian guerrillas and, later, Christian militiamen. Syrian troops again battled Christian forces in Lebanon, Apr. 1981, ending a cease-fire that had been in place.

Following the June 6, 1982 Israeli invasion of Lebanon, Israeli planes destroyed 17 Syrian antiaircraft missile batteries in the Bekka Valley, June 9. Some 25 Syrian planes were downed during the engagement. Israel and Syria agreed to a cease fire June 11. In 1983, Syria backed the PLO rebels who ousted Yasir Arafat's forces from Tripoli.

Syria's role in promoting acts of international terrorism led to the breaking of diplomatic relations with Great Britain and the implementation of limited sanctions by the European Communities in 1986.

Syria condemned the Aug. 1990 Iraqi invasion on Kuwait and sent troops to help Allied Forces in the Gulf War.

In 1991, Syria accepted U.S. proposals for the terms of an Arab-Israeli peace conference.

Taiwan

Republic of China

Chung-hua Min-kuo

People: Population (1991 est.): 20,658,000. **Age distrib.** (%): 0-14: 29.6; 15-59: 53.2; 60+: 8.1. **Pop. density:** 1,478 per sq. mi. **Urban** (1989): 72%. **Ethnic groups:** Taiwanese 85%, Chinese 14%. Languages: Mandarin Chinese (official), Taiwan, Hakka dialects. **Religions:** Buddhism, Taoism, Confucianism prevail.

Geography: Area: 13,885 sq. mi., about the size of Connecticut & New Hampshire combined. **Location:** Off SE coast of China, between E. and S. China Seas. **Neighbors:** Nearest is China. **Topography:** A mountain range forms the backbone of the island; the eastern half is very steep and craggy, the western slope is flat, fertile, and well-cultivated. **Capital:** Taipei. **Cities** (1991): Taipei (met.) 2,724,000; Kaohsiung 1,398,000; Taichung 765,000; Tainan 685,000.

Government: Type: One-party system. **Head of state and Nationalist Party chmn.:** Pres. Lee Teng-hui; b. Jan. 15, 1923; in office: Jan. 13, 1988. **Head of government:** Prime Min. Hau Pei-tsum; in office: May 30, 1990. **Local divisions:** 16 counties, 5 cities, Taipei & Kao-Hsiung. **Defense:** 4.6% of GNP (1991).

Economy: Industries: Textiles, clothing, electronics, processed foods, chemicals, plastics. **Chief crops:** Rice, bananas, pineapples, sugarcane, sweet potatoes, peanuts. **Minerals:** Coal, limestone, marble. **Crude oil reserves** (1987): 10 mln. bbls. **Arable land:** 25%. **Livestock** (1989): pigs: 6.9 mln. **Fish catch** (1989): 1.2 mln. metric tons. **Electricity prod.** (1990): 68 bln. kWh. **Crude steel prod.** (1990): 9.5 mln. metric tons. **Labor force:** 15% agric.; 53% ind. & comm.; 22% services.

Finance: Monetary unit: New Taiwan dollar (June 1992: 24.64 = $1 US). **Gross national product** (1990): $150.2 bln. **Per capita GNP:** $7,380. **Imports** (1990): $54.7 bln.; partners: U.S. 23%, Jap. 30%. **Exports** (1990): $66.1 bln.; partners: U.S. 39%, Jap. 13%, Hong Kong 8%. **Tourists** (1989): $2.6 bln. receipts. **National budget** (1991): $30.1 bln.

Transport: Motor vehicles: in use (1989): 1.9 mln. passenger cars, 595,000 commercial vehicles. **Civil Aviation** (1989): 20.7 bln. passenger-km; 12 airports. **Chief ports:** Kaohsiung, Keelung, Hualien, Taichung.

Communications: Television sets: 1 per 3.2 persons. **Radios:** 1 per 1.5 persons. **Telephones:** 1 per 3.0 persons. **Daily newspaper circ.** (1989): 202 per 1,000 pop.

Health: Life expectancy at birth (1991): 72 male; 78 female. **Births** (per 1,000 pop. 1991): 16. **Deaths** (per 1,000 pop. 1991): 5. **Natural increase:** 1.1%. **Physicians:** 1 per 965 persons. **Hospital beds:** 1 per 232 persons. **Infant mortality** (per 1,000 live births 1991): 6.

Education (1991): **Literacy:** 90%. **Years compulsory:** 9; attendance 99%.

Large-scale Chinese immigration began in the 17th century. The island came under mainland control after an interval of Dutch rule, 1620-62. Taiwan (also called Formosa) was ruled by Japan 1895-1945. Two million Kuomintang supporters fled to Taiwan in 1949. Both the Taipei and Peking governments consider Taiwan an integral part of China. Taiwan has rejected Pekings efforts at reunification, but unofficial dealings with the mainland have grown more flexible in the 1980s.

The U.S. upon its recognition of the People's Republic of China, Dec. 15, 1978, severed diplomatic ties with Taiwan. It maintains the unofficial American Institute in Taiwan, while Taiwan has established the Coordination Council for North American Affairs in Washington, D.C.

Land reform, government planning, U.S. aid and investment, and free universal education have brought huge advances in industry, agriculture, and mass living standards. In 1987, martial law was lifted after 38 years and in 1991, the 43-year period of emergency rule ended.

The Penghu (Pescadores), 50 sq. mi., pop. 120,000, lie between Taiwan and the mainland. **Quemoy** and **Matsu,** pop. (1980) 61,000 lie just off the mainland.

Republic of Tajikistan

Respubliki i Tojikiston

People: Population (1989 cen.): 5,100,000. **Pop. density:** 94 per sq. mi. **Ethnic groups:** Tajik 55%, Uzbek 23%, Russian 13%. **Languages:** Tadzhik, Russian. **Religion:** Mostly Sunni Moslem.

Geography: Area: 54,019 sq. mi. **Neighbors:** Uzbekistan and Kyrgyzstan on N and W, China on E, Afghanistan on S and E. **Topography:** Mountainous region which contains the Pamirs, Trans Alai mountain system. **Capital:** Dushanbe.

Government: Type: Republic. **Head of state:** vacant. **Head of government:** Akbar Miroyev.

Economy: Industries: Cement, knitwear, footwear. **Chief crops:** Barley, cotton, wheat, vegetables. **Minerals:** Coal, lead, zinc. **Livestock** (1989): cattle: 1.3 mln., sheep: 3.3 mln.

Finance: Monetary Unit: Ruble.

Health: Doctors (1989): 15,000; **Hospital beds** (1989): 55,000.

Major International Organizations: UN, CIS.

There were settled societies in the region from about 3000 B.C. Throughout history, the region has undergone invasions by Iranians (Arabs who converted the population to Islam), Mongols, Uzbeks, Afghans, and Russians. In 1924, the Tadzhik ASSR was created within the Uzbek SSR. The Tadzhik SSR was proclaimed in 1929. Tajikistan declared independence Sept. 9, 1991. It became an independent state when the Soviet Union disbanded Dec. 25, 1991. The ruling Communist Party has retained power in Tajikistan. There were demonstrations by opposition forces—anti-communists and Islamic fundamentalists—in 1992.

Tanzania

United Republic of Tanzania

Jamhuri ya Mwungano wa Tanzania

People: Population (1991 est.) 26,869,000. **Pop. density:** 73 per sq. mi. **Urban** (1988): 18%. **Ethnic groups:** African. **Languages:** Swahili, English (both official), many others. **Religions:** Moslems 33%, Christians 33%, traditional beliefs 33%.

Geography: Area: 364,886 sq. mi., more than twice the size of California. **Location:** On coast of E. Africa. **Neighbors:** Kenya, Uganda on N, Rwanda, Burundi, Zaire on W, Zambia, Malawi, Mozambique on S. **Topography:** Hot, arid central plateau, surrounded by the lake region in the W, temperate highlands in N and S, the coastal plains. Mt. Kilimanjaro, 19,340 ft., is highest in Africa. **Capital:** Dar-es-Salaam. **Cities** (1989): Dar-es-Salaam 1.3 mln.

Government: Type: Republic. **Head of state:** Pres. Ali Hassan Mwinyi; b. May 8, 1925; in office: Nov. 5, 1985. **Head of government:** Prime Min. John Malecela; in office: Nov. 9, 1990. **Local divisions:** 35 regions. **Defense:** 3.9% of GDP (1988).

Economy: Industries: Food processing, clothing. **Chief crops:** Sisal, cotton, coffee, tea, tobacco. **Minerals:** Diamonds, gold, nickel. **Other resources:** Hides. **Arable land:** 6%. **Livestock** (1989): cattle: 14 mln.; goats: 6.4 mln.; sheep: 5.0 mln. **Fish catch** (1989): 340,000 metric tons. **Electricity prod.** (1990): 895 mln. kWh. **Labor force:** 90% agric., 10% ind., comm. & govt.

Finance: Monetary unit: Shilling (Mar. 1992: 247 = $1 US). **Gross domestic product** (1989): $5.9 bln. **Per capita GDP:** $240. **Imports** (1989): $1.2 bln.; partners: UK 14%, Jap. 12%, Ger. 10%. **Exports** (1989): $380 mln.; partners: Ger. 15%, UK 13%. **Tourists** (1989): $63 mln. receipts. **National budget** (1990): $631 mln. expenditures. **International reserves less gold** (Jan. 1992): $204 mln. **Consumer prices** (change in 1990): 24.5%.

Transport: Motor vehicles: in use (1989): 44,000 passenger cars; 52,000 comm. vehicles. **Civil aviation** (1990): $209 mln. passenger-km; 19 airports. **Chief ports:** Dar-es-Salaam, Mtwara, Tanga.

Communications: Radios: 1 per 6 persons. **Telephones:** 1 per 179 persons. **Daily newspaper circ.** (1989): 8 per 1,000 pop.

Health: Life expectancy at birth (1991): 50 male; 55 female. **Births** (per 1,000 pop. 1991): 50. **Deaths** (per 1,000 pop. 1991): 16. **Natural increase:** 3.4%. **Hospital beds** (1984): 22,800. **Physicians** (1984): 1,065. **Infant mortality** (per 1,000 live births 1991): 105.

Education (1987): **Literacy:** 85%. **Attendance:** 87% attend primary school.

Major International Organizations: UN and all of its specialized agencies, OAU, Commonwealth of Nations.

Embassy: 2139 R. St. NW 20008; 939-6125.

The Republic of Tanganyika in E. Africa and the island Republic of Zanzibar, off the coast of Tanganyika, joined into a single nation, the United Republic of Tanzania, Apr. 26, 1964. Zanzibar retains internal self-government.

Tanganyika. Arab colonization and slaving began in the 8th century AD; Portuguese sailors explored the coast by about 1500. Other Europeans followed.

In 1885 Germany established German East Africa of which Tanganyika formed the bulk. It became a League of Nations mandate and, after 1946, a UN trust territory, both under Britain. It became independent Dec. 9, 1961, and a republic within the Commonwealth a year later.

In 1967 the government set on a socialist course; it nationalized all banks and many industries. The government also ordered that Swahili, not English, be used in all official business.

Tanzanian forces drove Idi Amin from Uganda, Mar., 1979.

Zanzibar, the Isle of Cloves, lies 23 mi. off the coast of Tanganyika; its area is 621 sq. mi. The island of **Pemba,** 25 mi. to the NE, area 380 sq. mi., is included in the administration. The total population (1990 est.) is 375,000.

Chief industry is the production of cloves and clove oil of which Zanzibar and Pemba produce the bulk of the world's supply.

Zanzibar was for centuries the center for Arab slave-traders. Portugal ruled for 2 centuries until ousted by Arabs around 1700. Zanzibar became a British Protectorate in 1890; independence came Dec. 10, 1963. Revolutionary forces overthrew the Sultan Jan. 12, 1964. The new government ousted Western diplomats and newsmen, slaughtered thousands of Arabs, and nationalized farms. Union with Tanganyika followed, 1964. The ruling parties of Tanganyika and Zanzibar were united in 1977, as political tension eased.

Thailand

Kingdom of Thailand

Muang Thai or Prathet Thai

People: Population (1991 est.): 56,814,000. **Age distrib.** (%): 0–14: 45.0; 15–59: 49.0; 60+: 6.0. **Pop. density:** 286 per sq. mi. **Urban** (1990): 20%. **Ethnic groups:** Thais 75%, Chinese 14%, others 11%. **Languages:** Thai, (official), Chinese, Malay, regional dialects. **Religions:** Buddhist 95%, Moslem 4%.

Geography: Area: 198,456 sq. mi., about the size of Texas. **Location:** On Indochinese and Malayan Peninsulas in S.E. Asia. **Neighbors:** Myanmar on W. Laos on N, Cambodia on E, Malaysia on S. **Topography:** A plateau dominates the NE third of Thailand, dropping to the fertile alluvial valley of the Chao Phraya R. in the center. Forested mountains are in N, with narrow fertile valleys. The southern peninsula region is covered by rain forests. **Capital:** Bangkok. **Cities** (1991 est.): Bangkok (met.): 6.0 mln.

Government: Type: Military. **Head of state:** King Bhumibol Adulyadej; b. Dec. 5, 1927; in office: June 9, 1946. **Head of government:** Gen. Suchinda Kraprayoon; in office: Apr. 5, 1992. **Local divisions:** 73 provinces. **Defense:** 3.0% of GNP (1990).

Economy: Industries: Textiles, mining, wood prods., tourism. **Chief crops:** Rice (a major export), corn tapioca, sugarcane. **Minerals:** Antimony, tin (among largest producers), tungsten, iron, gas. **Other resources:** Forests (teak is exported), rubber. **Arable land:** 34%. **Livestock** (1989): cattle: 4.9 mln.; pigs: 4.2 mln. **Fish catch** (1989): 2.3 mln. metric tons. **Electricity prod.** (1990): 29.0 bln. kWh. **Labor force:** 59% agric.; 26% ind. & comm.; 10% serv.; 8% govt.

Finance: Monetary unit: Baht (Mar. 1992: 25.65 = $1 US). **Gross national product** (1989): $64.4 bln. **Per capita GNP** (1989): $1,170. **Imports** (1990): $32.7 bln.; partners: Jap. 30%, U.S. 11%. **Exports** (1990): $20.0 bln.; partners: Jap. 17%, U.S. 22%. **Tourists** (1989): $3.7 mln. receipts. **National budget** (1991): $15.2 bln. **International reserves less gold** (Mar. 1992): $17.9 bln. **Gold:** 2.47 mln. oz t. **Consumer prices** (change in 1990): 8.0%.

Transport: Railroads (1989): **Length:** 2,438 mi. **Motor vehicles:** in use (1988): 816,000 passenger cars, 1.1 mln. comm. vehicles. **Civil aviation** (1989): 18.8 bln. passenger-km; 24 airports with scheduled flights. **Chief ports:** Bangkok, Sattahip.

Communication: Television sets: 1 per 11 persons. **Radios:** 1 per 5.7 persons. **Telephones:** 1 per 48 persons. **Daily newspaper circ.** (1989): 50 per 1,000 pop.

Health: Life expectancy at birth (1991): 66 male; 71 female. **Births** (per 1,000 pop. 1991): 20 **Deaths** (per 1,000 pop. 1991): 7. **Natural increase:** 1.3%. **Hospital beds:** 1 per 515 persons. **Physicians:** 1 per 4,883 persons. **Infant mortality** (per 1,000 live births 1991): 37.

Education (1991): **Literacy:** 89%. **Years compulsory:** 6; attendance 96%.

Major International Organizations: UN (GATT, World Bank).

Embassy: 2300 Kalorama Rd. NW 20008; 483-7200.

Thais began migrating from southern China in the 11th century. Thailand is the only country in SE Asia never taken over by a European power, thanks to King Mongkut and his son King Chulalongkorn who ruled from 1851 to 1910, modernized the country, and signed trade treaties with both Britain and France. A bloodless revolution in 1932 limited the monarchy.

Japan occupied the country in 1941.

The military took over the government in a bloody 1976 coup. Kriangsak Chomanan, prime minister resigned, Feb. 1980, under opposition over soaring inflation, oil price increases, labor unrest and growing crime. Chatichai Choonhavan was chosen prime minister in a democratic election, Aug. 1988. In Feb. 1991, the military ousted Choonhavan in a bloodless coup.

Vietnamese troops had crossed the border and been repulsed by Thai forces in the 1980s.

Togo

Republic of Togo

République Togolaise

People: Population (1991 est.): 3,810,000. **Age distrib.** (%): 0-14: 49.8; 15-59: 44.6; 60+:5.6.**Pop. density:** 176 per sq. mi. **Urban** (1989): 25%. **Ethnic groups:** Ewe 35%, Mina 6%, Kabye 22%. **Languages:** French (official), Gur & Kwa languages. **Religions:** Traditional 50%, Christian 30%, Moslem 20%.

Geography: Area: 21,622 sq. mi., slightly smaller than West Virginia. **Location:** On S coast of W. Africa. **Neighbors:** Ghana on W, Burkina Faso on N, Benin on E. **Topography:** A range of hills running SW-NE splits Togo into 2 savanna plains regions. **Capital:** Lomé. **Cities** (1989 est.): Lomé 600,000.

Government: Type: Republic. **Head of state:** Pres. Kokou Koffigoh; in office: Aug. 28, 1991. **Head of government:** Prime Min. Joseph Kokou Koffgoh. In office: Aug. 27, 1991. **Local divisions:** 21 prefectures.

Economy: Industries: Textiles, shoes. **Chief crops:** Coffee, cocoa, yams, manioc, millet, rice. **Minerals:** Phosphates. **Arable land:** 26%. **Electricity prod.** (1990): 209 mln. kWh. **Labor force:** 75% agric.; 20% industry.

Finance: Monetary unit: CFA franc (Mar. 1992: 278 = $1 US). **Gross domestic product** (1989): $1.3 bln. **Per capita GDP:** $390. **Imports** (1988): $335 mln.; partners: EC 61%. **Exports** (1989): $331 mln.; partners: EC 70%. **Tourists** (1989): $41 mln. receipts. **International reserves less gold** (Jan. 1992): $324 mln. **Gold:** 13,000 oz t. **Consumer prices** (change in 1990): 1.0%.

Transport: Railroads (1990): **Length:** 334 mi. **Motor vehicles:** in use (1988): 47,000 passenger cars, 22,000 comm. vehicles. **Chief ports:** Lome.

Communications: Television sets: 1 per 152 persons. **Radios:** 1 per 5.0 persons. **Telephones:** 1 per 229 persons. **Daily newspaper circ.** (1989): 3 per 1,000 pop.

Health: Life expectancy at birth (1991): 54 male; 58 female. **Births** (per 1,000 pop. 1991): 49. **Deaths** (per 1,000 pop. 1991): 13. **Natural increase:** 3.6%. **Hospital beds:** 1 per 752 persons. **Physicians:** 1 per 12,992 persons. **Infant mortality** (per 1,000 live births 1991): 110.

Education (1990): **Literacy:** 45% (males).

Major International Organizations: UN (GATT, IMF), OAU.

Embassy: 2208 Massachusetts Ave. NW 20008; 234-4212.

The Ewe arrived in southern Togo several centuries ago. The country later became a major source of slaves. Germany took control in 1884. France and Britain administered Togoland as UN trusteeships. The French sector became the republic of Togo Apr. 27, 1960.

The population is divided between Bantus in the S and Hamitic tribes in the N. Togo has actively promoted regional integration, as a means of stimulating the economy.

Tonga

Kingdom of Tonga

Pule ‘anga Tonga

People: Population (1991 est.): 102,000. **Age distrib.** (%): 0–14: 44.4; 15–59: 50.5; 60+:5.1. **Pop. density:** 377 per sq. mi. **Ethnic groups:** Tongans 98%, other Polynesian, European. **Languages:** Tongan, English (both official). **Religions:** Free Wesleyan 47%, Roman Catholics 14%, Free Church of Tonga 14%, Mormons 9%, Church of Tonga 9%.

Geography: Area: 270 sq. mi., smaller than New York City. **Location:** In western S. Pacific O. **Neighbors:** Nearest is Fiji, on W, New Zealand, on S. **Topography:** Tonga comprises 169 volcanic and coral islands, 45 inhabited. **Capital:** Nuku'alofa. **Cities** (1986): Nuku'alofa (met.) 29,000.

Government: Type: Constitutional monarchy. **Head of state:** King Taufa'ahau Tupou IV; b. July 4, 1918; in office: Dec. 16, 1965. **Head of government:** Prime Min. Baron Vaea; in office: Aug. 21, 1991. **Local divisions:** 3 main island groups.

Economy: Industries: Tourism. **Chief crops:** Coconut products, bananas are exported. **Other resources:** Fish. **Arable land:** 25%. **Electricity prod.** (1990): 8 mln. kWh. **Labor force:** 45% agric, 27% services.

Finance: Monetary unit: Pa'anga (Apr. 1992: 1.26 = $1 US). **Gross domestic product** (1989): $89 mln. **Imports** (1990): $59 mln.; partners: N Z 39%, Aust. 25%. **Exports** (1990): $9.6 mln.; partners: Aust. 29%, N Z 56%. **Tourism** (1989): $7.4 mln. receipts.

Transport: Motor vehicles: in use (1989): 1,400 passenger cars, 2,700 comm. vehicles. **Chief ports:** Nuku'alofa.

Communications: Radios: 1 per 1.2 persons. **Telephones:** 1 per 24 persons.

Health: Life expectancy at birth (1991): 65 male; 70 female. **Births** (per 1,000 pop. 1991): 27. **Deaths** (per 1,000 pop. 1991): 5. **Natural increase:** 2.2%. **Infant mortality** (per 1,000 live births 1991): 23.

Education (1988): **Literacy:** 99%. **Years compulsory:** 8. **Attendance:** 77%.

The islands were first visited by the Dutch in the early 17th century. A series of civil wars ended in 1845 with establishment of the Tupou dynasty. In 1900 Tonga became a British protectorate. On June 4, 1970, Tonga became independent and a member of the Commonwealth.

Trinidad and Tobago

Republic of Trinidad and Tobago

People: Population (1991 est.): 1,285,000. **Age distrib.** (%): 0–14: 32.9; 15–59: 58.7; 60+: 8.4. **Pop. density:** 648 per sq. mi. **Ethnic groups:** Africans 43%, East Indians 40%, mixed 14%. **Languages:** English (official). **Religions:** Roman Catholic 32%, Protestant 29%, Hindu 25%, Moslem 6%.

Geography: Area: 1,980 sq. mi., the size of Delaware. **Location:** Off eastern coast of Venezuela. **Neighbors:** Nearest is Venezuela on SW. **Topography:** Three low mountain ranges cross Trinidad E-W, with a well-watered plain between N and Central Ranges. Parts of E and W coasts are swamps. Tobago, 116 sq. mi., lies 20 mi. NE. **Capital:** Port-of-Spain. **Cities** (1990 met. est.): Port-of-Spain 300,000; San Fernando 50,000.

Government: Type: Parliamentary democracy. **Head of state:** Pres. Noor Hassanali; in office: Mar. 19, 1987. **Head of government:** Prime Min. Patrick Manning; in office: Dec. 17, 1991. **Local divisions:** 8 counties, 3 municipilities.

Economy: Industries: Oil products, rum, cement, tourism. **Chief crops:** Sugar, cocoa, coffee, citrus fruits, bananas. **Minerals:** Asphalt, oil, **Crude oil reserves** (1987): 567 mln. bbls. **Arable land:** 14%. **Electricity prod.** (1990): 3.3 bln. kWh. **Labor force:** 18% construction-utilities, 14% manuf., mining, commerce, 47% services.

Finance: Monetary unit: Dollar (Mar. 1992: 4.25 = $1 US). **Gross domestic product** (1989): $4.0 bln. **Per capita GDP:** $3,363. **Imports** (1990): $1.3 bln.; partners: U.S. 51%, UK 8%. **Exports** (1990): $1.7 bln.; partners: U.S. 53%. **Tourists** (1989): $89 mln. receipts. **National budget** (1991): $1.7 bln. expenditures. **International reserves less gold** (Mar. 1992): $338 mln. **Gold:** 54,000 oz t. **Consumer prices** (change in 1991): 3.9%.

Transport: Motor vehicles: in use (1989): 269,000 passenger cars, 68,000 comm. vehicles. **Civil aviation:** (1989): 2.6 bln. passenger-km; 2 airports. **Chief ports:** Port-of-Spain.

Communications: Television sets: 1 per 3.6 persons. **Radios:** 1 per 3.1 persons. **Telephones:** 1 per 6.2 persons. **Daily newspaper circ.** (1990): 140 per 1,000 pop.

Health: Life expectancy at birth (1991): 68 male; 72 female. **Births** (per 1,000 pop. 1991): 21. **Deaths** (per 1,000 pop. 1991): 6. **Natural increase:** 1.5%. **Hospital beds:** 1 per 270 persons. **Physicians:** 1 per 1,213 persons. **Infant mortality** (per 1,000 pop. 1991): 18.

Education (1988): **Literacy:** 97%. **Years compulsory:** 8.

Major International Organizations: UN (GATT, IMF, WHO), Commonwealth of Nations, OAS.

Embassy: 1708 Massachusetts Ave. NW 20036; 467-6490.

Columbus sighted Trinidad in 1498. A British possession since 1802, Trinidad and Tobago won independence Aug. 31, 1962. It became a republic in 1976. The People's National Movement party has held control of the government since 1956.

The nation is one of the most prosperous in the Caribbean. Oil production has increased with offshore finds. Middle Eastern oil is refined and exported, mostly to the U.S.

In July 1990, some 120 Moslem extremists captured the parliament building and TV station and took about 50 hostages including Prime Minister Arthur Robinson, who was beaten, shot in the legs, and tied to explosives. After a 6-day siege, the rebels surrendered.

Tunisia

Republic of Tunisia

al Jumhuriyah at-Tunisiyah

People: Population (1991 est.): 8,276,000. **Age distrib.** (%) 0–14: 39.0; 15–59: 54.2; 60+: 6.8. **Pop. density:** 131 per sq. mi. **Ethnic groups:** Arab 98%. **Languages:** Arabic (official), French. **Religions:** Moslem 99%.

Geography: Area: 63,170 sq. mi., about the size of Missouri. **Location:** On N coast of Africa. **Neighbors:** Algeria on W, Libya on E. **Topography:** The N is wooded and fertile. The central coastal plains are given to grazing and orchards. The S is arid, approaching Sahara Desert. **Capital:** Tunis. **Cities** (1984 est.) Tunis 1,000,000, Sfax 475,000.

Government: Type: Republic. **Head of state:** Pres. Gen. Zine al-Abidine Ben Ali; b. Sept 3, 1936; in office: Nov. 7, 1987. **Head of government:** Prime Min. Hamed Karoui; in office: Sept. 27, 1989. **Local divisions:** 23 governorates. **Defense:** 2.6% of GDP (1990).

Economy: Industries: Food processing, textiles, oil products, mining, construction materials. **Chief crops:** Grains, dates, olives, citrus fruits, figs, vegetables, grapes. **Minerals:** Phosphates, iron, oil, lead, zinc. **Crude oil reserves** (1987): 1.7 bln. bbls. **Arable land:** 20%. **Livestock** (1989): sheep: 5.0 mln.; goats: 1 mln. **Fish catch** (1988): 99,000 metric tons. **Electricity prod.** (1990): 4.2 bln. kWh. **Labor force:** 25% agric.; 34% industry; 40% serv.

Finance: Monetary unit: Dinar (Mar. 1992: .91 = $1 US). **Gross domestic product** (1990): $10.0 bln. **Per capita GDP:** $1,253. **Imports** (1991): $5.1 bln.; partners: EC 68%. **Exports** (1991): $3.3 bln.; partners: EC 73%. **Tourists** (1989): $933 mln. receipts. **National budget** (1990): $3.2 bln. expenditures. **International reserves less gold** (Mar. 1992): $759 mln. **Gold:** 187,000 oz t. **Consumer prices** (change in 1991): 8.2%.

Transport: Railroads (1989): **Length:** 1,393 mi. **Motor vehicles:** in use (1989): 321,000 passenger cars, 208,000 comm. vehicles; **Civil aviation:** (1990): 1.5 bln. passenger-km; 5 airports. **Chief ports:** Tunis, Sfax, Bizerte.

Communications: Television sets: 1 per 15 persons. **Radios:** 1 per 4.7 persons. **Telephones:** 1 per 24 persons. **Daily newspaper circ.** (1989): 33 per 1,000 pop.

Health: Life expectancy at birth (1991): 70 male; 74 female. **Births** (per 1,000 pop. 1991): 26. **Deaths** (per 1,000 pop. 1991): 5. **Natural increase:** 2.1%. **Hospital beds:** 1 per 506 persons. **Physicians:** 1 per 1,834 persons. **Infant mortality** (per 1,000 pop. live births 1991): 38.

Education (1990): **Literacy:** 62%. **Years compulsory:** 8; attendance 85%.

Major International Organizations: UN, Arab League, OAU.

Embassy: 1515 Massachusetts Ave. NW 20005; 862-1850.

Site of ancient Carthage, and a former Barbary state under the suzerainty of Turkey, Tunisia became a protectorate of France under a treaty signed May 12, 1881. The nation became independent Mar. 20, 1956, and ended the monarchy the following year.

Tunisia has actively repressed Islamic fundamentalism.

Turkey

Republic of Turkey

Turkiye Cumhuriyeti

People: Population (1991 est.): 58,580,000. **Age distrib.** (%): 0–14: 38.5; 15–59: 54.9; 60+: 6.6. **Pop. density:** 194 per sq. mi. **Urban** (1990): 61%. **Ethnic groups:** Turks 80%, Kurds 17%. **Languages:** Turkish (official), Kurdish, Arabic. **Religions:** Moslem 98%.

Geography: Area: 301,381 sq. mi., twice the size of California. **Location:** Occupies Asia Minor, between Mediterranean and Black Seas. **Neighbors:** Bulgaria, Greece on W, Georgia, Armenia on N, Iran on E, Iraq, Syria on S. **Topography:** Central Turkey has wide plateaus, with hot, dry summers and cold winters. High mountains ring the interior on all but W, with more than 20 peaks over 10,000 ft. Rolling plains are in W; mild, fertile coastal plains are in S, W. **Capital:** Ankara. **Cities** (1990 est.): Istanbul 6,700,000; Ankara 2,553,000; Izmir 1,700,000; Adana 931,000.

Government: Type: Republic. **Head of state:** Pres. Turgut Ozal; b. 1927; in office: Nov. 9, 1989. **Head of government:** Prime Min. Suleyman Demirel; in office: Nov. 20, 1991. **Local divisions:** 73 provinces. **Defense:** 3.5% of GDP (1990).

Economy: Industries: Iron, steel, machinery, metal prods., cars, processed foods. **Chief crops:** Tobacco, cereals, cotton, barley, corn, fruits, potatoes, sugar beets. **Minerals:** Chromium, mercury, boron, copper, coal. **Crude oil reserves** (1987): 139 mln. bbls. **Other resources:** Wool, silk, forests. **Arable land:** 30%. **Livestock** (1989): cattle: 12.0 mln.; sheep: 40.4 mln. **Fish catch** (1989): 457,000 metric tons. **Electricity prod.** (1990): 41 bln. kWh. **Crude steel prod.** (1990): 9.2 mln. metric tons. **Labor force:** 56% agric.; 14% ind. and comm.; 29% serv.

Finance: Monetary unit: Lira (Mar. 1992: 6,247 = $1 US). **Gross domestic product** (1990): $178 bln. **Per capita GDP:** $3,100. **Imports** (1990): $22.3 bln.; partners: Ger. 16%, U.S. 13%. **Exports** (1990): $12.9 bln.; partners: Ger. 19%. **Tourists** (1989): $2.5 bln. receipts. **National budget** (1991): $34.4 bln. expenditures. **International reserves less gold** (Feb. 1992): $4.2 bln. **Gold:** 4.2 mln. oz t. **Consumer prices** (change in 1990): 60%.

Transport: Railroads (1989): **Length:** 5,238 mi. **Motor vehicles:** in use (1990): 1.6 mln. passenger cars, 584,000 comm. vehicles. **Civil aviation** (1990): 4.8 bln. passenger-km; 15 airports with scheduled flights. **Chief ports:** Istanbul, Izmir, Mersin, Samsun.

Communications: Television sets: 1 per 5 persons. **Radios:** 1 per 7.8 persons. **Telephones:** 1 per 8 persons.

Health: Life expectancy at birth (1991): 68 male; 72 female. **Births** (per 1,000 pop. 1991): 28. **Deaths** (per 1,000 pop. 1991): 6. **Natural increase:** 2.2%. **Hospital beds:** 1 per 476 persons. **Physicians:** 1 per 1,189 persons. **Infant mortality** (per 1,000 live births 1990): 54.

Education (1990): **Literacy:** 81%. **Years compulsory:** 6; attendance 95%.

Major International Organizations: UN (GATT, WHO, IMF), NATO, OECD, EC.

Embassy: 1714 Massachusetts Ave. NW 20036.

Ancient inhabitants of Turkey were among the worlds first agriculturalists. Such civilizations as the Hittite, Phrygian, and Lydian flourished in Asiatic Turkey (Asia Minor), as did much of Greek civilization. After the fall of Rome in the 5th century, Constantinople was the capital of the Byzantine Empire for 1,000 years. It fell in 1453 to Ottoman Turks, who ruled a vast empire for over 400 years.

Just before World War I, Turkey, or the Ottoman Empire, ruled what is now Syria, Lebanon, Iraq, Jordan, Israel, Saudi Arabia, Yemen, and islands in the Aegean Sea.

Turkey joined Germany and Austria in World War I and its defeat resulted in loss of much territory and fall of the sultanate. A republic was declared Oct. 29, 1923. The Caliphate (spiritual leadership of Islam) was renounced 1924.

Long embroiled with Greece over Cyprus, off Turkey's south coast, Turkey invaded the island July 20, 1974, after Greek officers seized the Cypriot government as a step toward unification with Greece. Turkey sought a new government for Cyprus, with Greek Cypriot and Turkish Cypriot zones. In reaction to Turkey's moves, the U.S. cut off military aid in 1975. Turkey, in turn, suspended the use of most U.S. bases. Aid was restored in 1978. There was a military takeover, Sept. 12, 1980.

Religious and ethnic tensions and active left and right extremists have caused endemic violence. Martial law, imposed in 1978, was lifted in 1984. The military formally transferred power to an elected parliament in 1983.

Turkey was a member of the Allied forces which ousted Iraq from Kuwait, 1991. In the aftermath of the war, millions of Kurdish refugees fled to Turkey's border to escape Iraqi forces.

Turkmenistan

People: Population (1989 cen.): 3,500,000. **Pop. density:** 18 per sq. mi. **Ethnic groups:** Turkmen 68%, Russian 13%, Uzbek 9%. **Language:** Turkmen, Russian.

Geography: Area: 188,417 sq. mi. **Neighbors:** Uzbekistan, Kazakhstan on N, NE, Afghanistan and Iran on S. The Kara Kum desert occupies 80% of the area. **Capital:** Ashkhabad.

Government: Type: Republic. **Head of state:** Pres. Saparmurad Niyazov. **Local divisions:** 5 regions.

Economy: Industries: Mining, textiles. **Chief crops:** Grain, cotton, grapes. **Minerals:** Coal, sulfur, salt. **Livestock** (1989): sheep: 5.0 mln.

Finance: Monetary unit: Ruble.

Health: Doctors (1989): 13,000; **Hospital beds** (1989): 40,000.

Major International Organizations: UN, CIS.

The region has been inhabited by Turki tribes since the 10th century. It became part of Russian Turkistan 1881, and a constituent republic of the USSR 1925. Turkmenistan declared independence Oct. 27, 1991, and became an independent state when the Soviet Union disbanded Dec. 25, 1991.

Tuvalu

People: Population (1991 est.): 9,317. **Pop. density:** 931 per sq. mi. **Ethnic group:** Polynesian. **Languages:** Tuvaluan, English. **Religions:** mainly Protestant.

Geography: Area: 10 sq. mi., less than one-half the size of Manhattan. **Location:** 9 islands forming a NW-SE chain 360 mi. long in the SW Pacific O. **Neighbors:** Nearest are Samoa on SE, Fiji on S. **Topography:** The islands are all low-lying atolls, nowhere rising more than 15 ft. above sea level, composed of coral reefs. **Capital:** Funafuti (pop. 1985): 2,800.

Government: Head of state: Queen Elizabeth II, represented by Gov.-Gen. Toaripi Lauti; in office: Oct. 1, 1990. **Head of government:** Prime Min. Bikenibeu Paeniu; in office: Oct. 16, 1989. **Local divisions:** 8 island councils on the permanently inhabited islands.

Economy: Industries: Copra. **Chief crops:** Coconuts. **Labor force:** Approx. 1,500 Tuvaluans work overseas in the Gilberts' phosphate industry, or as overseas seamen.

Finance: Monetary unit: Australian dollar.

Transport: Chief port: Funafuti.

Health: (including former Gilbert Is.) **Life expectancy at birth** (1991): 60 male; 63 female. **Births** (per 1,000 pop. 1991): 29. **Deaths** (per 1,000 pop. 1991): 10. **Natural increase:** 1.9%. **Infant mortality** (per 1,000 live births 1991) : 33.

Education: Literacy (1990): 96%.

The Ellice Islands separated from the British Gilbert and Ellice Islands colony, 1975, and became independent Tuvalu Oct. 1, 1978.

Uganda

Republic of Uganda

People: Population (1991 est.): 18,690,000. **Age distrib.** (%): 0–14: 48.5; 15–59: 47.3; 60+: 4.2. **Pop. density:** 200 per sq. mi. **Urban** (1988): 10%. **Ethnic groups:** Bantu, Nilotic, Nilo-Hamitic, Sudanic tribes. **Languages:** English (official), Luganda, Swahili. **Religions:** Christian 63%, Moslem 6%, traditional beliefs.

Geography: Area: 93,354 sq. mi., slightly smaller than Oregon. **Location:** In E. Central Africa. **Neighbors:** Sudan on N, Zaire on W, Rwanda, Tanzania on S, Kenya on E. **Topography:** Most of Uganda is a high plateau 3,000-6,000 ft. high, with high Ruwenzori range in W (Mt. Margherita 16,750 ft.), volcanoes in SW, NE is arid, W and SW rainy. Lakes Victoria, Edward, Albert form much of borders. **Capital:** Kampala. **Cities** (1991): Kampala 773,000.

Government: Type: Military. **Head of state:** Pres. Yoweri Kaguta Museveni; b. 1944; in office: Jan. 29, 1986. **Head of government:** Prime Min. George Cosmas Adyebo; in office: Jan. 22, 1991. **Local divisions:** 10 provinces. **Defense:** 1.5% of GDP (1989).

Economy: Chief Crops: Coffee, cotton, tea, corn, bananas, sugar. **Minerals:** Copper, cobalt. **Arable land:** 23%. **Livestock** (1987): cattle: 5.2 mln.; goats: 3.3 mln.; sheep: 1.3 mln. **Fish catch** (1986): 212,000 metric tons. **Electricity prod.** (1990): 312 mln. kWh. **Labor force:** 90% agric.

Finance: Monetary unit: Shilling (Mar. 1992: 1,160 = $1 US). **Gross domestic product** (1989): $4.9 bln. **Per capita GDP:** $290. **Imports** (1990): $209 mln.; partners: Kenya 24%, U.K. 17%. **Exports** (1990): $148 mln.; partners: U.S. 14%, U.K. 12%, Neth. 15%. **National budget** (1989): $790 mln. expenditures. **International reserves less gold** (Jan. 1992): $57.2 mln. **Consumer prices** (change in 1990): 32%.

Transport: Motor vehicles: in use (1990): 35,000 passenger cars, 6,000 comm. vehicles.

Communications: Television sets: 1 per 191 persons. **Radios:** 1 per 46 persons. **Telephones:** 1 per 272 persons. **Daily newspaper circ.** (1989): 2 per 1,000 pop.

Health: Life expectancy at birth (1991): 50 male; 52 female. **Births** (per 1,000 pop. 1991): 51. **Deaths** (per 1,000 pop. 1991): 15. **Natural increase:** 3.6%. **Hospital beds:** 1 per 817 persons. **Physicians:** 1 per 20,000 persons. **Infant mortality** (per 1,000 live births 1991): 94.

Education (1989): **Literacy:** 52%. About 50% attend primary school.

Major International Organizations: UN (GATT, WHO, IMF), OAU, Commonwealth of Nations.

Embassy: 5909 16th St. NW 20011; 726-7100.

Britain obtained a protectorate over Uganda in 1894. The country became independent Oct. 9, 1962, and a republic within the Commonwealth a year later. In 1967, the traditional kingdoms, including the powerful Buganda state, were abolished and the central government strengthened.

Gen. Idi Amin seized power from Prime Min. Milton Obote in 1971. As many as 300,000 of his opponents were reported killed in subsequent years. Amin was named president for life in 1976.

In 1972 Amin expelled nearly all of Uganda's 45,000 Asians. In 1973 the U.S. withdrew all diplomatic personnel.

Amid worsening economic and domestic crises, Uganda's troops exchanged invasion attacks with long-standing foe Tanzania, 1978 to 1979. Tanzanian forces, coupled with Ugandan exiles and rebels, ended the dictatorial rule of Amin, Apr. 11, 1979.

Ukraine

Ukrayina

People: Population (1991 est.): 51,994,000. **Age distrib.** (%): 0-19: 24.8; 20-59: 62.1; 60+: 13.0. **Pop. density:** 223 per sq. mi. **Urban** (1991): 68%. **Official language:** Ukrainian. **Ethnic groups:** Ukrainian 73%, Russian. **Religion:** Orthodox 76%, Ukrainian Catholic 13.5%, Moslem 8.2%.

Geography: Area: 233,100 sq. mi. **Location:** In SE Europe. **Neighbors:** Belarus on N, Russia on NE and E, Moldova and Romania on SW, Hungary, Czechoslovakia, and Poland on W. **Topography:** Part of the E. European plain. Mountainous areas include the Carpathians in the SW and the Crimean chain in the S. Arable black soil constitutes a large part of the country. **Climate:** Average temperature range from 21F in Jan. to 66F in July. Annual precipitation averages 27.5 in. in the W. part of the country and less than 11 in. in the East. **Capital:** Kiev. **Cities** (1991 est.): Kiev 2,637,000; Kharkiv 1,622,000; Donetske 1,121,000; Odessa 1,104,000; Lviv 803,000.

Government: Type: Constitutional republic. **Head of State:** Pres. Leonid M. Kravchuk; b. 1934; in office: December 5, 1991. **Head of Government:** Prime Min. Vitold Fokin: b. 1932; in office: November 14, 1990. **Local divisions:** 24 provinces (oblasts), 1 autonomous province.

Economy: Industries: Steel, chemicals, machinery, vehicles, cement. **Chief crops:** Grains, sugar beets, potatoes. **Minerals:** Iron, manganese, chromium, copper, coal, lead, gold, nickel, potassium salts. **Other resources:** Forests. **Fish catch** (1990): 550,000 metric tons. **Electricity prod.** (1990): 76.2 bln. kWh. **Crude steel prod.** (1990): 43.1 mln. metric tons. **Labor force:** 20.1% agric.; 40.2% ind. & comm.; 28.1% services.

Finance: Currency: Hryvnia. **Gross national product** (1990): $47.6 bln. **Per capita income** (1987): $2,500. **National budget** (1990): $8 bln. expenditures.

Transport: Railway traffic (1990): 75.8 bln. passenger-km.; 484.1 bln. net ton-km. **Civil aviation** (1990): 16.1 bln. passenger-km.; 1 bln. ton-km. **Chief ports:** Odessa, Kherson, Zhdanov, Sevastopil, Berdiansk.

Communications: Television sets (1990): 328 per 1,000 pop. **Radios** (1990): 280 per 1,000 pop. **Daily newspaper circ.** (1990): 202 per 1,000 pop.

Health: Life expectancy at birth (1989): 66 male; 75 female. **Births** (per 1,000 pop. 1990): 12.7. **Deaths** (per 1,000 pop. 1990): 12.1. **Natural Increase** (1990): .6%. **Hospital beds**

(1990): 696,800. **Physicians** (1990): 229,800. **Infant mortality** (per 1,000 live births 1990): 12.8.

Education (1990): **Literacy:** 99%.

Major International Organizations: UN, CIS.

The ancient ancestors of Ukrainians, the Trypilians, flourished along the Dnipro River, Ukraine's main artery, from 6000-1000 BC. The Slavic ancestors of the Ukrainians inhabited modern Ukrainian territory well before the first century AD.

The princes of Kyyiv established a strong state called Kyyivan Rus in the 9th century. A strong dynasty was established, with ties to virtually all major European royal families. St. Volodymyr the Great, ruler of Kyyivan Ukraine, accepted Christianity as the national faith in 988. At the crossroads of major European trade routes, Kyyivan Rus reached its zenith during the reign of Iaroslav the Wise (1019-1054). While directly absorbing most of the Asian invasion of Europe in the 13th century, the Ukrainian state slowly disintegrated and was divided mainly between Russia and Poland.

The Ukrainian Cossack State, founded in the late 16th century, waged numerous wars of liberation against the occupiers of Ukraine: Russia, Poland, and Turkey. By the late 18th century, Ukrainian independence was lost. Ukraine's neighbors once again divided its territory. At the turn of the last century, Ukraine was occupied by 2 colonial powers, Russia and Austria-Hungary.

An independent Ukrainian National Republic was proclaimed on January 22, 1918. In 1921, Ukraine's neighbors occupied and divided Ukrainian territory. In 1932-33, Russia engineered a man-made famine in eastern Ukraine, resulting in the deaths of 7-10 million Ukrainians.

In March 1939, independent Carpatho-Ukraine was the first European state to wage war against Nazi-led aggression in the region. During WW2 the Ukrainian nationalist underground and its Ukrainian Insurgent Army (UPA) fought both Nazi German and Soviet forces. The restoration of Ukrainian independence was declared on June 30, 1941. Over 5 million Ukrainians lost their lives during the War. With the reoccupation of Ukraine by Soviet Russia in 1944 came a renewed wave of mass arrests, executions, and deportations of Ukrainians.

The world's worst nuclear disaster occurred in Chernobyl, Ukraine, in April 1986. Radioactive contamination continue to effect the area.

Ukrainian independence was restored on Aug. 24, 1991. In a landslide national referendum, over 90% of Ukraine's population voted for independence on Dec. 1, 1991.

United Arab Emirates

Ittihād al-Imarat al-Arabiyah

People: Population (1991 est.): 2,389,000. **Pop. density:** 74 per sq. mi. **Ethnic groups:** Arab, Iranian, Pakistani, Indian. **Languages:** Arabic (official), several others. **Religions:** Moslem 96%, Christian, Hindu.

Geography: Area: 32,000 sq. mi., the size of Maine. **Location:** On the S shore of the Persian Gulf. **Neighbors:** Qatar on N, Saudi Ar. on W, S, Oman on E. **Topography:** A barren, flat coastal plain gives way to uninhabited sand dunes on the S. Hajar Mtns. are on E. **Capital:** Abu Dhabi. **Cities** (1990 est.): Abu Dhabi 722,000; Dubavy 266,000.

Government: Type: Federation of emirates. **Head of state:** Pres. Zaid ibn Sultan an-Nahayan b. 1923; in office: Dec. 2, 1971. **Head of government:** Prime Min. Sheikh Maktum ibn Rashid al-Maktum; in office: Nov. 20, 1990. **Local divisions:** 7 autonomous emirates: Abu Dhabi, Ajman, Dubai, Fujaira, Ras al-Khaimah, Sharjah, Umm al-Qaiwain. **Defense:** 6.8% of GDP (1989).

Economy: Chief crops: Vegetables, dates, limes. **Minerals:** Oil. **Crude oil reserves** (1990): 98 bln. barrels. **Arable land:** 1%. **Electricity prod.** (1990): 15.3 bln. kWh. **Labor force:** 5% agric.; 85% ind. and commerce; 5% serv.; 5% gvt.

Finance: Monetary unit: Dirham (June 1992: 3.67 = $1 US). **Gross domestic product** (1989): $28.4 bln. **Per capita GDP:** $12,100. **Imports** (1990): $11.1 bln.; partners: Jap. 18%, UK 11%, Ger. 6%. **Exports** (1987): $15.0 bln.; partners: Jap. 36%, U.S. 7%, Fr. 10%. **International reserves less gold** (Feb. 1992): $5.5 bln. **Gold:** 797,000 oz t.

Transport: Motor Vehicles (1985): 62,000 passenger cars; 17,000 commercial vehicles. **Chief ports:** Dubavy, Abu Dhabi.

Communications: Television sets: 1 per 12 persons. **Radios:** 1 per 4.7 persons. **Telephones:** 1 per 4.3 persons.

Health: Life Expectancy at Birth (1991): 69 male, 74 female. **Hospital beds:** 1 per 267 persons. **Physicians:** 1 per 659 persons. **Infant mortality** (per 1,000 live births 1991): 23%.

Education (1989): **Literacy:** 68%. **Years Compulsory:** ages 6-12.

Major International Organizations: UN (World Bank, IMF, ILO), Arab League, OPEC.

Embassy: 600 New Hampshire Ave. NW 20037; 338-6500.

The 7 "Trucial Sheikdoms" gave Britain control of defense and foreign relations in the 19th century. They merged to become an independent state Dec. 2, 1971.

The Abu Dhabi Petroleum Co. was fully nationalized in 1975. Oil revenues have given the UAE one of the highest per capita GNPs in the world. International banking has grown in recent years.

United Kingdom of Great Britain and Northern Ireland

People: Population (1991 cen.): 55,486,800. **Age distrib.** (%): 0–14: 19.2; 15–59: 60.1; 60+: 20.7. **Pop. density:** 588 per sq. mi. **Urban** (1990): 90%. **Ethnic groups:** English 81.5%, Scottish 9.6%, Irish 2.4%, Welsh 1.9%, Ulster 1.8%; West Indian, Indian, Pakistani over 2%; others. **Languages:** English, Welsh spoken in western Wales. **Religions:** Church of England, Roman Catholic.

Geography: Area: 94,226 sq. mi., slightly smaller than Oregon. **Location:** Off the NW coast of Europe, across English Channel, Strait of Dover, and North Sea. **Neighbors:** Ireland to W, France to SE. **Topography:** England is mostly rolling land, rising to Uplands of southern Scotland; Lowlands are in center of Scotland, granite Highlands are in N. Coast is heavily indented, especially on W. British Isles have milder climate than N Europe, due to the Gulf Stream, and ample rainfall. Severn, 220 mi., and Thames, 215 mi., are longest rivers. **Capital:** London. **Cities** (1988 est.): London 6,735,000; Birmingham 993,000; Glasgow 703,000; Leeds 710,000; Sheffield 532,000; Liverpool 469,000; Manchester 445,000; Edinburgh 433,000; Bradford 463,000; Bristol 377,000.

Government: Type: Constitutional monarchy. **Head of state:** Queen Elizabeth II; b. Apr. 21, 1926; in office: Feb. 6, 1952. **Head of government:** Prime Min. John Major; b. Mar. 29, 1943; in office: Nov. 28, 1990. **Local divisions:** England and Wales: 47 non-metro counties, 6 metro counties, Greater London; Scotland: 9 regions, 3 island areas; N. Ireland: 26 districts. **Defense:** 4.3% of GDP (1990).

Economy: Industries: Steel, metals, vehicles, shipbuilding, banking, textiles, chemicals, electronics, aircraft, machinery, distilling. **Chief crops:** Grains, sugar beets, fruits, vegetables. **Minerals:** Coal, tin, oil, gas, limestone, iron, salt, clay. **Crude oil reserves** (1987): 5.8 bln. bbls. **Arable land:** 30%. **Livestock** (1989): cattle: 12.6 mln.; pigs: 7.9 mln.; sheep: 29.0 mln. **Fish catch** (1989): 938,000 metric tons. **Electricity prod.** (1990): 316 bln. kWh. **Crude steel prod.** (1990): 17.9 mln. metric tons. **Labor force:** 2% agric.; 26% manuf. & eng., 60% services.

Finance: Monetary unit: Pound (June 1992: .54 = $1 US). **Gross domestic product** (1990): $858 bln. **Per capita GDP:** $15,000. **Imports** (1991): $222 bln.; partners: EC 52%, U.S. 10%. **Exports** (1991): $185 bln.; partners: EC 50%, U.S. 13%. **Tourists** (1990): receipts: $14.8 bln. **National budget** (1991): $385 bln. expenditures. **International reserves less gold** (Mar. 1992): $40 bln. **Gold:** 19.0 mln. oz t. **Consumer prices** (change in 1991): 5.9%.

Transport: Railroads (1990): **Length:** 23,518 mi. **Motor vehicles:** in use (1989): 19.2 mln. passenger cars, 2.7 mln. comm. vehicles. **Civil aviation** (1989): 68.9 bln. passenger-km: 56 airports with scheduled flights. **Chief ports:** London, Liverpool, Glasgow, Southampton, Cardiff, Belfast.

Communications: Television sets: 1 per 3 persons. **Radios:** 1 per 1 person. **Telephones:** 1 per 1.9 persons. **Daily newspaper circ.** (1990): 388 per 1,000 pop.

Health: Life expectancy at birth: (1991): 73 male; 79 female. **Births:** (per 1,000 pop. 1991): 14. **Deaths:** (per 1,000 pop. 1991): 11. **Natural increase:** 0.3%. **Hospital beds:** 1 per 138 persons. **Physicians:** 1 per 611 persons. **Infant mortality:** (per 1,000 live births 1991): 7.

Education (1991): **Literacy:** 99%. **Years compulsory:** 12; attendance 99%.

Major International Organizations: UN all of and its specialized agencies, NATO, EC, OECD.

Embassy: 3100 Massachusetts Ave. NW 20008; 462-1340.

The United Kingdom of Great Britain and Northern Ireland comprises England, Wales, Scotland, and Northern Ireland.

Queen and Royal Family. The ruling sovereign is Elizabeth II of the House of Windsor, born Apr. 21, 1926, elder daughter of King George VI. She succeeded to the throne Feb. 6, 1952, and was crowned June 2, 1953. She was married Nov. 20, 1947, to Lt. Philip Mountbatten, born June 10, 1921, former Prince of Greece. He was created Duke of Edinburgh, Earl of Merioneth, and Baron Greenwich, and given the style H.R.H., Nov. 19, 1947; he was given the title Prince of the United Kingdom and Northern Ireland Feb. 22, 1957. Prince Charles Philip Arthur George, born Nov. 14, 1948, is the Prince of Wales and heir apparent. His son, William Philip Arthur Louis, born June 21, 1982, is second in line to the throne.

Parliament is the legislative governing body for the United Kingdom, with certain powers over dependent units. It consists of 2 houses: The **House of Lords** includes 763 hereditary and 314 life peers and peeresses, certain judges, 2 archbishops and 24 bishops of the Church of England. Total membership is over 1,000. The **House of Commons** has 650 members, who are elected by direct ballot and divided as follows: England 516; Wales 36; Scotland 71; Northern Ireland 12.

Resources and Industries. Great Britain's major occupations are manufacturing and trade. Metals and metal-using industries contribute more than 50% of the exports. Of about 60 million acres of land in England, Wales and Scotland, 46 million are farmed, of which 17 million are arable, the rest pastures.

Large oil and gas fields have been found in the North Sea. Commercial oil production began in 1975. There are large deposits of coal.

Britain imports all of its cotton, rubber, sulphur, 80% of its wool, half of its food and iron ore, also certain amounts of paper, tobacco, chemicals. Manufactured goods made from these basic materials have been exported since the industrial age began. Main exports are machinery, chemicals, woolen and synthetic textiles, clothing, autos and trucks, iron and steel, locomotives, ships, jet aircraft, farm machinery, drugs, radio, TV, radar and navigation equipment, scientific instruments, arms, whisky.

Religion and Education. The Church of England is Protestant Episcopal. The queen is its temporal head, with rights of appointments to archbishoprics, bishoprics, and other offices. There are 2 provinces, Canterbury and York, each headed by an archbishop. The most famous church is Westminster Abbey (1050-1760), site of coronations, tombs of Elizabeth I, Mary of Scots, kings, poets, and of the Unknown Warrior.

The most celebrated British universities are Oxford and Cambridge, each dating to the 13th century. There are about 40 other universities.

History. Britain was part of the continent of Europe until about 6,000 BC, but migration of peoples across the English Channel continued long afterward. Celts arrived 2,500 to 3,000 years ago. Their language survives in Welsh, and Gaelic enclaves.

England was added to the Roman Empire in 43 AD. After the withdrawal of Roman legions in 410, waves of Jutes, Angles, and Saxons arrived from German lands. They contended with Danish raiders for control from the 8th through 11th centuries.

The last successful invasion was by French speaking Normans in 1066, who united the country with their dominions in France.

Opposition by nobles to royal authority forced King John to sign the Magna Carta in 1215, a guarantee of rights and the rule of law. In the ensuing decades, the foundations of the parliamentary system were laid.

English dynastic claims to large parts of France led to the Hundred Years War, 1338-1453, and the defeat of England. A long civil war, the War of the Roses, lasted 1455-85, and ended with the establishment of the powerful Tudor monarchy. A distinct English civilization flourished. The economy prospered over long periods of domestic peace unmatched in continental Europe. Religious independence was secured when the Church of England was separated from the authority of the Pope in 1534.

Under Queen Elizabeth I, England became a major naval power, leading to the founding of colonies in the new world and the expansion of trade with Europe and the Orient. Scotland was united with England when James VI of Scotland was crowned James I of England in 1603.

A struggle between Parliament and the Stuart kings led to a bloody civil war, 1642-49, and the establishment of a republic under the Puritan Oliver Cromwell. The monarchy was restored in 1660, but the "Glorious Revolution" of 1688 confirmed the sovereignty of Parliament: a Bill of Rights was granted 1689.

In the 18th century, parliamentary rule was strengthened. Technological and entrepreneurial innovations led to the Industrial Revolution. The 13 North American colonies were lost, but replaced by growing empires in Canada and India. Britain's role in the defeat of Napoleon, 1815, strengthened its position as the leading world power.

The extension of the franchise in 1832 and 1867, the formation of trade unions, and the development of universal public education were among the drastic social changes which accompanied the spread of industrialization and urbanization in the 19th century. Large parts of Africa and Asia were added to the empire during the reign of Queen Victoria, 1837-1901.

Though victorious in World War I, Britain suffered huge casualties and economic dislocation. Ireland became independent in 1921, and independence movements became active in India and other colonies.

The country suffered major bombing damage in World War II, but held out against Germany singlehandedly for a year after the fall of France in 1940.

Industrial growth continued in the postwar period, but Britain lost its leadership position to other powers. Labor governments passed socialist programs nationalizing some basic industries and expanding social security. The Thatcher government has however, tried to increase the role of private enterprise. In 1987, Margaret Thatcher became the first British leader in 160 years to be elected to a 3d consecutive term as prime minister. She resigned as prime minister in Nov. 1990.

The UK supported the UN resolutions against Iraq and sent military forces to the Persian Gulf war.

Wales

The Principality of Wales in western Britain has an area of 8,019 sq. mi. and a population (1991 cen.) of 2,798,000. Cardiff is the capital, pop. (1981 est.) 273,856.

England and Wales are administered as a unit. Less than 20% of the population of Wales speak both English and Welsh; about 32,000 speak Welsh solely. A 1979 referendum rejected, 4-1, the creation of an elected Welsh Assembly.

Early Anglo-Saxon invaders drove Celtic peoples into the mountains of Wales, terming them Waelise (Welsh, or foreign). There they developed a distinct nationality. Members of the ruling house of Gwynedd in the 13th century fought England but were crushed, 1283. Edward of Caernarvon, son of Edward I of England, was created Prince of Wales, 1301.

Scotland

Scotland, a kingdom now united with England and Wales in Great Britain, occupies the northern 37% of the main British island, and the Hebrides, Orkney, Shetland and smaller islands. Length, 275 mi., breadth approx. 150 mi., area, 30,405 sq. mi., population (1991 cen.) 4,957,000.

The Lowlands, a belt of land approximately 60 mi. wide from the Firth of Clyde to the Firth of Forth, divide the farming region of the Southern Uplands from the granite Highlands of the North, contain 75% of the population and most of the industry. The Highlands, famous for hunting and fishing, have been opened to industry by many hydroelectric power stations.

Edinburgh, pop. (1986 est.) 439,000, is the capital. Glasgow, pop. (1986 est.) 733,000, is Britain's greatest industrial center. It is a shipbuilding complex on the Clyde and an ocean port. Aberdeen, pop. (1986 est.) 215,000, NE of Edinburgh, is a major port, center of granite industry, fish processing, and North Sea oil exploitation. Dundee, pop. (1986 est.) 177,000, NE of Edinburgh, is an industrial and fish processing center. About 90,000 persons speak Gaelic as well as English.

History. Scotland was called Caledonia by the Romans who battled early Celtic tribes and occupied southern areas from the 1st to the 4th centuries. Missionaries from Britain introduced Christianity in the 4th century; St. Columba, an Irish monk, converted most of Scotland in the 6th century.

The Kingdom of Scotland was founded in 1018. William Wallace and Robert Bruce both defeated English armies 1297 and 1314, respectively.

In 1603 James VI of Scotland, son of Mary, Queen of Scots, succeeded to the throne of England as James I, and effected the Union of the Crowns. In 1707 Scotland received representation in the British Parliament, resulting from the union of former separate Parliaments. Its executive in the British cabinet is the Secretary of State for Scotland. The growing Scottish National Party urges independence. A 1979 referendum on the creation of an elected Scotland Assembly was defeated.

Memorials of Robert Burns, Sir Walter Scott, John Knox, Mary, Queen of Scots draw many tourists, as do the beauties of the Trossachs, Loch Katrine, Loch Lomond and abbey ruins.

Industries. Engineering products are the most important industry, with growing emphasis on office machinery, autos, electronics and other consumer goods. Oil has been discovered offshore in the North Sea, stimulating on-shore support industries.

Scotland produces fine woolens, worsteds, tweeds, silks, fine linens and jute. It is known for its special breeds of cattle and sheep. Fisheries have large hauls of herring, cod, whiting. Whisky is the biggest export.

The Hebrides are a group of c. 500 islands, 100 inhabited, off the W coast. The Inner Hebrides include **Skye, Mull,** and **Iona,** the last famous for the arrival of St. Columba, 563 AD. The Outer Hebrides include **Lewis** and **Harris.** Industries include sheep raising and weaving. The **Orkney Islands,** c. 90, are to the NE. The capital is Kirkwall, on Pomona Is. Fish curing, sheep raising and weaving are occupations. NE of the Orkneys are the 200 **Shetland Islands,** 24 inhabited, home of Shetland pony. The Orkneys and Shetlands have become centers for the North Sea oil industry.

Northern Ireland

Six of the 9 counties of Ulster, the NE corner of Ireland, constitute Northern Ireland, with the parliamentary boroughs of Belfast and Londonderry. Area 5,463 sq. mi., 1991 cen. pop. 1,570,000, capital and chief industrial center, Belfast, (1987 cen.) 303,000.

Industries. Shipbuilding, including large tankers, has long been an important industry, centered in Belfast, the largest port. Linen manufacture is also important, along with apparel, rope, and twine. Growing diversification has added engineering products, synthetic fibers, and electronics. They are large numbers of cattle, hogs, and sheep, potatoes, poultry, and dairy foods are also produced.

Government. An act of the British Parliament, 1920, divided Northern from Southern Ireland, each with a parliament and government. When Ireland became a dominion, 1921, and later a republic, Northern Ireland chose to remain a part of the United Kingdom. It elects 12 members to the British House of Commons.

During 1968-69, large demonstrations were conducted by Roman Catholics who charged they were discriminated against in voting rights, housing, and employment. The Catholics, a minority comprising about a third of the population, demanded abolition of property qualifications for voting in local elections. Violence and terrorism intensified, involving branches of the Irish Republican Army (outlawed in the Irish Republic), Protestant groups, police, and British troops.

A succession of Northern Ireland prime ministers pressed reform programs but failed to satisfy extremists on both sides. Over 2,000 were killed in over 15 years of bombings and shootings through 1990, many in England itself. Britain suspended the Northern Ireland parliament Mar. 30, 1972, and imposed direct British rule. A coalition government was formed in 1973 when moderates won election to a new one-house Assembly. But a Protestant general strike overthrew the government in 1974 and direct rule was resumed.

The turmoil and agony of Northern Ireland was dramatized in 1981 by the deaths of 10 imprisoned Irish nationalist hunger strikers in Maze Prison near Belfast. The inmates had starved themselves to death in an attempt to achieve status as political prisoners, but the British government refused to yield to their demands. In 1985, the Hillsborough agreement gave the Rep. of Ireland a voice in the governing of Northern Ireland; the accord was strongly opposed by Ulster loyalists.

Education and Religion. Northern Ireland is 2/3 Protestant, 1/3 Roman Catholic. Education is compulsory through age 15.

Channel Islands

The Channel Islands, area 75 sq. mi., est. pop. 1986 145,000, off the NW coast of France, the only parts of the one-time Dukedom of Normandy belonging to England, are **Jersey, Guernsey** and the dependencies of Guernsey — **Alderney, Brechou, Great Sark, Little Sark, Herm, Jethou and Lihou.** Jersey and Guernsey have separate legal existences and lieutenant governors named by the Crown. The islands were the only British soil occupied by German troops in World War II.

Isle of Man

The Isle of Man, area 227 sq. mi., 1986 est. pop. 64,000, is in the Irish Sea, 20 mi. from Scotland, 30 mi. from Cumberland. It is rich in lead and iron. The island has its own laws and a lieutenant governor appointed by the Crown. The Tynwald (legislature) consists of the Legislative Council, partly elected, and House of Keys, elected. Capital: Douglas. Farming, tourism, fishing (kippers, scallops) are chief occupations. Man is famous for the Manx tailless cat.

Gibraltar

Gibraltar, a dependency on the southern coast of Spain, guards the entrance to the Mediterranean. The Rock has been in British possession since 1704. The Rock is 2.75 mi. long, 3/4 of a mi. wide and 1,396 ft. in height; a narrow isthmus connects it with the mainland. Est. pop. 1987, 29,048.

In 1966 Spain called on Britain to give "substantial sovereignty" of Gibraltar to Spain and imposed a partial blockade. In 1967, residents voted for remaining under Britain. A new constitution, May 30, 1996, gave an elected House of Assembly more control in domestic affairs. A UN General Assembly resolution requested Britain to end Gibraltar's colonial status by Oct. 1, 1996. No settlement has been reached.

British West Indies

Swinging in a vast arc from the coast of Venezuela NE, then N and NW toward Puerto Rico are the Leeward Islands, forming a coral and volcanic barrier sheltering the Caribbean from the open Atlantic. Many of the islands are self-governing British possessions. Universal suffrage was instituted 1951-54; ministerial systems were set up 1956-1960.

The **Leeward Islands,** still associated with the UK are **Montserrat** (1987 pop. 11,600, area 32 sq. mi., capital Plymouth), the small **British Virgin Islands** (pop. 1987: 12,000), and **Anguilla** (pop. 1985: 7,000), the most northerly of the Leeward Islands.

The three **Cayman Islands,** a dependency, lie S of Cuba, NW of Jamaica. Pop. 23,000 (1987), most of it on Grand Cayman. It is a free port; in the 1970s Grand Cayman became a tax-free refuge for foreign funds and branches of many Western banks were opened there. Total area 102 sq. mi., capital Georgetown.

The **Turks and Caicos Islands,** at the SE end of the Bahama Islands, are a separate possession. There are about 30 islands, only 6 inhabited, 1987 pop. est. 9,000, area 193 sq. mi., capital Grand Turk. Salt, crayfish and conch shells are the main exports.

Bermuda

Bermuda is a British dependency governed by a royal governor and an assembly, dating from 1620, the oldest legislative body among British dependencies. Capital is Hamilton.

It is a group of 360 small islands of coral formation, 20 inhabited, comprising 20.6 sq. mi. in the western Atlantic, 580 mi. E of North Carolina. Pop., 1991 est., was 59,800 (about 61% of African descent). Density is high.

The U.S. has air and naval bases under long-term lease, and a NASA tracking facility.

Bermuda boasts many resort hotels. The government raises most revenue from import duties. Exports: petroleum products, medicine.

South Atlantic

Falkland Islands and Dependencies, a British dependency, lies 300 mi. E of the Strait of Magellan at the southern end of South America.

The Falklands or Islas Malvinas include about 200 islands, area 4,700 sq. mi., pop. (1980 est.) 1,800. Sheep-grazing is the main industry; wool is the principal export. There are indications of large oil and gas deposits. The islands are also claimed by Argentina though 97% of inhabitants are of British origin. Argentina invaded the islands Apr. 2, 1982. The British responded by sending a task force to the area, landing their main force on the Falklands, May 21, and forcing an Argentine surrender at Port Stanley, June 14. **South Georgia,** area 1,450 sq. mi., and the uninhabited **South Sandwich Is.** are dependencies of the Falklands.

British Antarctic Territory, south of 60° S lat., was made a separate colony in 1962 and comprises mainly the **South Shet-**

land Islands, the **South Orkneys** and **Graham's Land.** A chain of meteorological stations is maintained.

St. Helena, an island 1,200 mi. off the W coast of Africa and 1,800 E of South America, has 47 sq. mi. and est. pop., 1985 of 5,400. Flax, lace and rope making are the chief industries. After Napoleon Bonaparte was defeated at Waterloo the Allies exiled him to St. Helena, where he lived from Oct. 16, 1815, to his death, May 5, 1821. Capital is Jamestown.

Tristan da Cunha is the principal of a group of islands of volcanic origin, total area 40 sq. mi., half way between the Cape of Good Hope and South America. A volcanic peak 6,760 ft. high erupted in 1961. The 262 inhabitants were removed to England, but most returned in 1963. The islands are dependencies of St. Helena.

Ascension is an island of volcanic origin, 34 sq. mi. in area, 700 mi. NW of St. Helena, through which it is administered. It is a communications relay center for Britain, and has a U.S. satellite tracking center. Est. pop., 1985, was 1,500, half of them communications workers. The island is noted for sea turtles.

Hong Kong

A Crown Colony at the mouth of the Canton R. in China, 90 mi. S of Canton. Its nucleus is Hong Kong Is., 35½ sq. mi., acquired from China 1841, on which is located Victoria, the capital. Opposite is Kowloon Peninsula, 3 sq. mi. and Stonecutters Is., ¼ sq. mi., added, 1860. An additional 355 sq. mi. known as the New Territories, a mainland area and islands, were leased from China, 1898, for 99 years. Britain and China, Dec. 19, 1984, signed an agreement under which Hong Kong would be allowed to keep its capitalist system for 50 years after 1997, the year that the 99-year lease will expire. Total area of the colony is 409 sq. mi., with a population, 1989 est., of 5.7 million including fewer than 20,000 British. From 1949 to 1962 Hong Kong absorbed more than a million refugees from China.

Hong Kong harbor was long an important British naval station and one of the world's great trans-shipment ports.

Principal industries are textiles and apparel; also tourism, $4.2 bln. expenditures (1988), shipbuilding, iron and steel, fishing, cement, and small manufactures.

Spinning mills, among the best in the world, and low wages compete with textiles elsewhere and have resulted in the protective measures in some countries. Hong Kong also has a booming electronics industry.

British Indian Ocean Territory

Formed Nov. 1965, embracing islands formerly dependencies of Mauritius or Seychelles: the Chagos Archipelago (including Diego Garcia), Aldabra, Farquhar and Des Roches. The latter 3 were transferred to Seychelles, which became independent in 1976. Area 22 sq mi. No civilian population remains.

Pacific Ocean

Pitcairn Island is in the Pacific, halfway between South America and Australia. The island was discovered in 1767 by Carteret but was not inhabited until 23 years later when the mutineers of the Bounty landed there. The area is 1.7 sq. mi. and pop. 1983, was 61. It is a British colony and is administered by a British Representative in New Zealand and a local Council. The uninhabited islands of **Henderson, Ducie** and **Oeno** are in the Pitcairn group.

United States of America

People: Population (1990 cen.): 248,709,873. **Age distrib.(%):** 0–14: 21.7; 15–59: 61.4; 60+: 16.9. **Pop. density:** 68 per sq. mi. **Urban** (1987): 76%.

Geography: 3,618,770 sq. mi. (incl. 50 states and D. of C.) about four-tenths the size of USSR. Vast central plain, mountains in west, hills and low mountains in east. **Government:** Federal republic, strong democratic tradition. **Head of state:** George Bush; b. June 12, 1924; in office: Jan. 20, 1989. **Administrative divisions:** 50 states and Dist. of Columbia. **Defense:** 5.7% of GNP (1990).

Economy: Minerals: Coal, copper, lead, molybdenum, phosphates, uranium, bauxite, gold, iron, mercury, nickel, potash, silver, tungsten, zinc. **Crude oil reserves** (1990): 25 bln. barrels. **Arable land:** 21%. **Livestock** (1990): cattle: 98 mln.; pigs: 53 mln.; sheep: 11.3 mln. **Fish catch** (1990): 4.4 mln. metric tons. **Electricity prod.** (1990): 3,020 bln. kWh. **Crude steel prod.** (1990): 88.6 mln. metric tons.

Finance: Gross domestic product (1990): 5.4 trl. **Per capita GNP:** $21,800. **Imports** (1991): $508 bln.; partners: Can. 17%, Jap. 20%, Mex. 6%. **Exports** (1991): $422 bln.; partners: Can. 22%, Jap. 12%, Mex. 6%, UK 5%. **Tourists** (1990): receipts $40.5 bln. **International reserves less gold** (Mar. 1992): $63.6 bln. **Gold:** 261.0 mln. oz t. **Consumer prices** (change in 1991): 4.2%.

Transport: Railroads (1988): **Length:** 173,903 mi. **Motor vehicles:** in use (1989): 143 mln. passenger cars, 44 mln. comm. vehicles. **Civil aviation** (1990): 751 bln. passenger-km; 834 airports with scheduled flights.

Communications: Television sets: 1 per 1.3 persons. **Radios:** 1 per 0.5 persons. **Telephones:** 1 per 1.9 persons. **Daily newspaper circ.** (1990): 255 per 1,000 pop.

Health: Life expectancy at birth (1991): 72 male; 79 female. **Births** (per 1,000 pop. 1991): 15. **Deaths** (per 1,000 pop. 1991): 9. **Natural increase:** .6%. **Hospital beds:** 1 per 198 persons. **Physicians:** 1 per 404 persons. **Infant mortality** (per 1,000 live births 1991): 8.9.

Major International Organizations: UN (GATT, IMF, WHO, FAO), OAS, NATO, OECD.

Education (1991): **Literacy:** 97%.

Uruguay

Republic of Uruguay

República del Uruguay

People: Population (1991 est.): 3,121,000. **Age distrib.** (%): 0–14: 26.9; 15–59: 57.7; 60+: 15.4. **Pop. density:** 45 per sq. mi. **Urban** (1990): 86.0%. **Ethnic groups:** Caucasians (Iberians, Italians) 89%, mestizos 10%, mulatto and black. **Languages:** Spanish. **Religions:** 66% Roman Catholic.

Geography: Area: 68,037 sq. mi., the size of Washington State. **Location:** In southern S. America, on the Atlantic O. **Neighbors:** Argentina on W, Brazil on N. **Topography:** Uruguay is composed of rolling, grassy plains and hills, well-watered by rivers flowing W to Uruguay R. **Capital:** Montevideo. **Cities** (1990 est.): Montevideo 1,310,000.

Government: Type: Republic. **Head of state:** Pres. Luis Alberto Lacalle; in office: Nov. 26, 1989. **Local divisions:** 19 departments. **Defense:** 1.4% of GDP (1989).

Economy: Industries: Meat-packing, textiles, wine, cement, oil products. **Chief crops:** Corn, wheat, citrus fruits, rice, oats, linseed. **Arable land:** 8%. **Livestock** (1987): cattle: 9.9 mln.; sheep: 20.6 mln. **Fish catch** (1987): 134,000 metric tons. **Electricity prod.** (1990): 5.2 bln. kWh. **Labor force** 13% agric.; 22% manuf.; 16% serv.; 20% govt.

Finance: Monetary unit: New Peso (May 1992: 2,774 = $1 US). **Gross domestic product** (1990): $9.2 bln. **Per capita GDP:** $2,970. **Imports** (1990): $1.2 bln.; partners: EC 19%, Braz. 24%, Arg. 14%, U.S. 8%. **Exports** (1990): $1.4 bln.; partners: Braz. 28%, U.S. 11%, EC 23%. **Tourists** (1989): $228 mln. receipts. **National budget** (1989): $1.5 bln. expeditures. **International reserves less gold** (Jan. 1992): $274 mln. **Gold:** 2.26 mln. oz t. **Consumer prices** (change in 1991): 102%.

Transport: Railroads (1989): **Length:** 3,002 km. **Motor vehicles:** in use (1989): 190,000 passenger cars, 100,000 comm. vehicles. **Civil aviation** (1987): 459 mln. passenger-km; 7 airports. **Chief ports:** Montevideo.

Communications: Television sets: 1 per 4.8 persons. **Radios:** 1 per 1.0 persons. **Telephones:** 1 per 5.8 persons. **Daily newspaper circ.** (1989): 227 per 1,000 pop.

Health: Life expectancy at birth (1991): 69 male; 76 female. **Births** (per 1,000 pop. 1991): 17. **Deaths** (per 1,000 pop. 1991): 10. **Natural increase:** .7%. **Hospital beds:** 1 per 127 persons. **Physicians:** 1 per 344 persons. **Infant mortality** (per 1,000 live births 1991): 22.

Education (1990): **Literacy:** 96%.

Major International Organizations: UN (GATT, IMF, WHO), OAS.

Embassy: 1919 F St. NW 20006; 331-1313.

Spanish settlers did not begin replacing the indigenous Charrua Indians until 1624. Portuguese from Brazil arrived later, but Uruguay was attached to the Spanish Viceroyalty of Rio de la Plata in the 18th century. Rebels fought against Spain beginning in 1810. An independent republic was declared Aug. 25, 1825.

Socialist measures were adopted as far back as 1911. The state owns the power, telephone, railroad, cement, oil-refining and other industries.

Uruguay's standard of living was one of the highest in South America, and political and labor conditions among the freest. Economic stagnation, inflation, floods and drought, and a general strike in the late 1960s brought government attempts to strengthen the economy through devaluation of the peso and wage and price controls. But inflation continued in the 80's and the country asked international creditors to restructure $2.7 bln. in debt in 1983.

Terrorist activities led to Pres. Juan Maria Bordaberry agreeing to military control of his administration Feb. 1973. In June he abolished Congress and set up a Council of State in its place. Bordaberry was removed by the military in a 1976 coup. Civilian government was restored to the country in 1985.

Republic of Uzbekistan

Ozbekiston Republikasy

People: Population (1989 cen.): 19,900,000. **Pop. density:** 115 per sq. mi. **Urban** (1991): 40%. **Ethnic groups:** Uzbek 70%, Russian 11%. **Religions:** Mostly Sunni Moslem.

Geography: Area: 172,700 sq. mi. **Neighbors:** Kazakhstan on N. and W., Kyrgyzstan and Tajikistan on E., Afghanistan and Turkmenistan on S. **Topography:** mostly plains and desert. **Capital:** Tashkent.

Government: Type: Republic. **Head of state:** Pres. Islam A. Karimov. **Head of government:** Prime Min. Abdulkhashim Mutalov.

Economy: Industries: Steel, tractors, cars, textiles. **Chief crops:** Cotton, rice. **Minerals:** Coal, copper. **Livestock** (1989): cattle: 4.1 mln., sheep: 8.7 mln.

Finance: Monetary unit: Ruble.

Health: Doctors (1989): 72,000; **Hospital beds** (1989): 250,000.

Major International Organizations: UN, CIS.

The region was overrun by the Mongols under Genghis Khan in 1220. In the 14th century, Uzbekistan became the center of a native empire—that of the Timurids. In later centuries Moslem feudal states emerged. Russian military conquest began in the 19th century.

The Uzbek SSR became a Soviet Union republic in 1925. Uzbekistan declared independence Aug. 29, 1991. It became an independent republic when the Soviet Union disbanded Dec. 25, 1991.

Vanuatu

Republic of Vanuatu

Ripablik Blong Vanuatu

People: Population (1991 est.): 170,000. **Population density:** 29 per sq. mi. **Ethnic groups:** Mainly Melanesian, some European, Polynesian, Micronesian. **Languages:** Bislama, French and English all official. **Religions:** Presbyterian 40%, Anglican 14%, Roman Catholic 16%, animist 15%.

Geography: Area: 5,700 sq. mi. **Location:** SW Pacific, 1,200 mi NE of Brisbane, Australia. **Topography:** dense forest with narrow coastal strips of cultivated land. **Capital:** Port-Vila. **Cities:** Vila (1990): 19,000.

Government: Type: Republic. **Head of state:** Pres. Fred Timakata; in office: Jan. 12, 1989. **Head of gov't:** Prime Min. Maxime Carlot; in office: Dec. 16, 1991.

Economy: Industries: Fish-freezing, meat canneries, tourism. **Chief crops:** Copra (38% of export), cocoa, coffee. **Minerals:** Manganese. **Other resources:** Forests, cattle. **Fish catch** (1987): 2.9 metric tons.

Finance: Monetary unit: Vatu (Mar. 1992: 111 vatu = $1 US). **Gross domestic product** (1989): $131 mln. **Imports** (1989): $58 mln.; partners: Aus. 36%, Fr. 8%, Japan 13%. **Exports** (1989): $15 mln.; partners: Neth. 34%, Jap. 17%, Fr. 27%.

Health: Life expectancy at birth (1991): 67 male, 72 female. **Infant mortality** (per 1,000 live births 1991): 37.

Education: Literacy (1990): 90%. Education not compulsory, but 85-90% of children of primary school age attend primary schools.

The Anglo-French condominium of the New Hebrides, administered jointly by France and Great Britain since 1906, became the independent Republic of Vanuatu on July 30, 1980.

Vatican City

The Holy See

People: Population (1991 est.): 778. **Ethnic groups:** Italians, Swiss. **Languages:** Italian, Latin.

Geography: Area: 108.7 acres. **Location:** In Rome, Italy. **Neighbors:** Completely surrounded by Italy.

Monetary unit: Lira.

Apostolic Nunciature in U.S.: 3339 Massachusetts Ave. NW 20008; 333-7121.

The popes for many centuries, with brief interruptions, held temporal sovereignty over mid-Italy (the so-called Papal States), comprising an area of some 16,000 sq. mi., with a population in the 19th century of more than 3 million. This territory was incorporated in the new Kingdom of Italy, the sovereignty of the pope being confined to the palaces of the Vatican and the Lateran in Rome and the villa of Castel Gandolfo, by an Italian law, May 13, 1871. This law also guaranteed to the pope and his successors a yearly indemnity of over $620,000. The allowance, however, remained unclaimed.

A Treaty of Conciliation, a concordat and a financial convention were signed Feb. 11, 1929, by Cardinal Gasparri and Premier Mussolini. The documents established the independent state of Vatican City, and gave the Catholic religion special status in Italy. The treaty (Lateran Agreement) was made part of the Constitution of Italy (Article 7) in 1947. Italy and the Vatican reached preliminary agreement in 1976 on revisions of the concordat, that would eliminate Roman Catholicism as the state religion and end required religious education in Italian schools.

Vatican City includes St. Peter's, the Vatican Palace and Museum covering over 13 acres, the Vatican gardens, and neighboring buildings between Viale Vaticano and the Church. Thirteen buildings in Rome, outside the boundaries, enjoy extraterritorial rights; these buildings house congregations or officers necessary for the administration of the Holy See.

The legal system is based on the code of canon law, the apostolic constitutions and the laws especially promulgated for the Vatican City by the pope. The Secretariat of State represents the Holy See in its diplomatic relations. By the Treaty of Conciliation the pope is pledged to a perpetual neutrality unless his mediation is specifically requested. This, however, does not prevent the defense of the Church whenever it is persecuted.

The present sovereign of the State of Vatican City is the Supreme Pontiff John Paul II, Karol Wojtyla, born in Wadowice, Poland, May 18, 1920, elected Oct. 16, 1978 (the first non-Italian to be elected Pope in 456 years).

The U.S. restored formal relations in 1984 after the U.S. Congress repealed an 1867 ban on diplomatic relations with the Vatican.

Venezuela

Republic of Venezuela

Republica de Venezuela

People: Population (1991 est.): 20,189,000. **Age distrib.** (%): 0–14: 38.3; 15–59: 56.0; 60+: 5.7. **Pop. density:** 57 per sq. mi. **Urban** (1990): 83%. **Ethnic groups:** Mestizo 69%, white (Spanish, Portuguese, Italian) 20%, black 9%, Indian 2%. **Languages:** Spanish (official). **Religions:** Roman Catholic 92%.

Geography: Area: 352,143 sq. mi., more than twice the size of California. **Location:** On the Caribbean coast of S. America. **Neighbors:** Colombia on W, Brazil on S, Guyana on E. **Topography:** Flat coastal plain and Orinoco Delta are bordered by Andes Mtns. and hills. Plains, called llanos, extend between mountains and Orinoco. Guyana Highlands and plains are S of Orinoco, which stretches 1,600 mi. and drains 80% of Venezuela. **Capital:** Caracas. **Cities** (1990 est.): Caracas 1,290,000; Maracaibo 1,206,000; Barquisimeto 723,000; Valencia 955,000.

Government: Type: Federal republic. **Head of state:** Pres. Carlos Andres Perez; b. Oct. 27, 1922; in office: Feb. 2, 1989. **Local divisions:** 20 states, 2 federal territories, federal district, federal dependency. **Defense:** 4.3% of GDP (1991).

Economy: Industries: Steel, oil products, textiles, containers, paper. **Chief crops:** Coffee, rice, fruits, sugar. **Minerals:** Oil, iron (extensive reserves and production), gold. **Crude oil reserves** (1990): 58 bln. barrels. **Arable land:** 4%. **Livestock** (1989): cattle: 12.8 mln. **Fish catch** (1990): 327,000 metric tons. **Electricity prod.** (1990): 54.6 bln. kWh. **Crude steel prod.** (1990): 3.2 mln. metric tons. **Labor force:** 6% agric.; 35% ind.; 26% services.

Finance: Monetary unit: Bolivar (Apr. 1992: 65 = $1 US). **Gross domestic product** (1990): $42.4 bln. **Per capita GDP:** $2,150. **Imports** (1990): $7.3 bln.; partners: U.S. 41%, W. Ger. 6%, Jap. 8%. **Exports** (1990): $17.5 bln.; partners: U.S. 35%. Jap. 15%. **Tourists** (1989): $389 mln. receipts. **National budget** (1989): $8.6 bln. expenditures. **International reserves less gold** (Mar. 1992): $9.9 bln. **Gold:** 11.46 mln. oz t. **Consumer prices** (change in 1991): 34.2%.

Transport: Railroads (1989): **Length:** 226 mi. **Motor vehicles:** in use (1989): 1.6 mln. passenger cars, 459 mln. mm. vehicles. **Civil aviation** (1989): 6.4 mln. passenger-km; 33 airports with scheduled flights. **Chief ports:** Maracaibo, La Guaira, Puerto Cabello.

Communications: Television sets: 1 per 5.6 persons. **Radios:** 1 per 2.4 persons. **Telephones:** 1 per 11 persons. **Daily newspaper circ.** (1989): 111 per 1,000 pop.

Health: Life expectancy at birth (1991): 71 male; 78 female. **Births** (per 1,000 pop. 1991): 28. **Deaths** (per 1,000 pop. 1991): 4. **Natural increase:** 2.4%. **Hospital beds:** 1 per 395 persons. **Physicians:** 1 per 576 persons. **Infant mortality** (per 1,000 live births 1991): 26.

Education (1991): **Literacy:** 88%. **Years compulsory:** 8; attendance 82%.

Major International Organizations: UN (IMF, WHO, FAO), OAS, OPEC.

Embassy: 1099 30th St. NW 20007; 342-2214.

Columbus first set foot on the South American continent on the peninsula of Paria, Aug. 1498. Alonso de Ojeda, 1499, found Lake Maracaibo, called the land Venezuela, or Little Venice, because natives had houses on stilts. Venezuela was under Spanish domination until 1821. The republic was formed after secession from the Colombian Federation in 1830.

Military strongmen ruled Venezuela for most of the 20th century. They promoted the oil industry; some social reforms were implemented. Since 1959, the country has had democratically-elected governments.

Venezuela helped found the Organization of Petroleum Exporting States (OPEC). The government, Jan. 1, 1976, nationalized the oil industry with compensation. Oil accounts for much of total export earnings and the economy suffered a severe cash crisis in the 1980s as the result of falling oil revenues.

The government has attempted to reduce dependence on oil.

A coup attempt, led by mid-level military officers, was thwarted by loyalist troops Feb. 4, 1992. Pres. Perez announced a series of economic and political reforms Mar. 5.

Vietnam

Socialist Republic of Vietnam

Cong Hoa Xa Hoi Chu Nghia Viet Nam

People: Population (1991 est.): 67,568,000. **Age distrib.** (%): 0-14: 40.8; 15-59: 53.6; 60+: 5.6 **Pop. density:** 530 per sq. mi. **Urban** (1989): 20%. **Ethnic groups:** Vietnamese 84%, Chinese 2%, remainder Muong, Thai, Meo, Khmer, Man, Cham. **Languages:** Vietnamese (official), Chinese. **Religions:** Buddhists, Confucians, and Taoists most numerous, Roman Catholics, animists, Muslims, Protestants.

Geography: Area: 127,330 sq. mi., the size of New Mexico. **Location:** On the E coast of the Indochinese Peninsula in SE Asia. **Neighbors:** China on N, Laos, Cambodia on W. **Topography:** Vietnam is long and narrow, with a 1,400-mi. coast. About 24% of country is readily arable, including the densely settled Red R. valley in the N, narrow coastal plains in center, and the wide, often marshy Mekong R. Delta in the S. The rest consists of semi-arid plateaus and barren mountains, with some stretches of tropical rain forest. **Capital:** Hanoi. **Cities** (1989): Ho Chi Minh City 3.9 mln.; Hanoi 3.1 mln.

Government: Type: Communist. **Head of state:** Pres. Vo Chi Cong; in office: June 18, 1987. **Head of government:** Prime Min. Vo Van Kiet; in office: Aug. 8, 1991. **Head of Communist Party:** Do Muoi; b. 1917; in office: June 27, 1991. **Local divisions:** 40 provinces, 3 municipalities, one special zone. **Defense:** 19.4% of GNP (1986).

Economy: Industries: Food processing, textiles, cement, chemical fertilizers. **Chief crops:** Rice, rubber, fruits and vegetables, corn, manioc, sugarcane. **Minerals:** Phosphates, coal, iron, manganese, bauxite, apatite, chromate. **Other resources:** Forests. **Arable land:** 23%. **Livestock** (1989): cattle: 5.9 mln.; pigs: 11.7 mln. **Fish catch** (1988): 871,000 metric tons. **Electricity prod.** (1990): 7.5 bln. kWh. **Labor force:** 65% agric.; 35% ind. and service.

Finance: Monetary unit: Dong (Jan. 1992: 10,780 = $1 US). **Gross national product** (1990): $15.2 bln. **Per capita GNP:** $230. **Imports** (1990): $2.6 bln.; partners: USSR 73%, Jap. 8%. **Exports** (1990): $2.3 bln.; partners: USSR 57%. **National budget** (1990): $1.3 bln. expenditures.

Transport: Motor vehicles: in use (1976): 100,000 passenger cars, 200,000 comm. vehicles. **Civil Aviation** (1988): 10.3 bln. passenger km; 3 airports with scheduled flights. **Chief ports:** Ho Chi Minh City, Haiphong, Da Nang.

Communications: Television sets: 1 per 29 persons. **Radios:** 1 per 10 persons. **Telephones:** 1 per 544 persons. **Daily newspaper circ.** (1989): 38 per 1,000 pop.

Health: Life expectancy at birth (1991): 63 male; 67 female. **Births** (per 1,000 pop. 1991): 29. **Deaths** (per 1,000 pop. 1991): 8. **Natural increase:** 2.1%. **Hospital beds:** 1 per 292 persons. **Physicians:** 1 per 3,096 persons. **Infant mortality** (per 1,000 live births 1991): 48.

Education (1989): **Literacy:** 88%.

Major International Organizations: UN (IMF, WHO).

Vietnam's recorded history began in Tonkin before the Christian era. Settled by Viets from central China, Vietnam was held by China, 111 BC-939 AD, and was a vassal state during subsequent periods. Vietnam defeated the armies of Kublai Khan, 1288. Conquest by France began in 1858 and ended in 1884 with the protectorates of Tonkin and Annam in the N. and the colony of Cochin-China in the S.

In 1940 Vietnam was occupied by Japan; nationalist aims gathered force. A number of groups formed the Vietminh (Independence) League, headed by Ho Chi Minh, communist guerrilla leader. In Aug. 1945 the Vietminh forced out Bao Dai, former emperor of Annam, head of a Japan-sponsored regime. France, seeking to reestablish colonial control, battled communist and nationalist forces, 1946-1954, and was finally defeated at Dienbienphu, May 8, 1954. Meanwhile, on July 1, 1949, Bao Dai had formed a State of Vietnam, with himself as chief of state, with French approval. China backed Ho Chi Minh.

A cease-fire accord signed in Geneva July 21, 1954, divided Vietnam along the Ben Hai R. It provided for a buffer zone, withdrawal of French troops from the North and elections to determine the country's future. Under the agreement the communists gained control of territory north of the 17th parallel, with its capital at Hanoi and Ho Chi Minh as president. South Vietnam came to comprise the 39 southern provinces. Some 900,000 North Vietnamese fled to South Vietnam.

On Oct. 26, 1955, Ngo Dinh Diem, premier of the interim government of South Vietnam, proclaimed the Republic of Vietnam and became its first president.

The North, adopted a constitution Dec. 31, 1959, based on communist principles and calling for reunification of all Vietnam. North Vietnam sought to take over South Vietnam beginning in 1954. Fighting persisted from 1956, with the communist Vietcong, aided by North Vietnam, pressing war in the South. Northern aid to Vietcong guerrillas was intensified in 1959, and large-scale troop infiltration began in 1964, with Soviet and Chinese arms assistance. Large Northern forces were stationed in border areas of Laos and Cambodia.

A serious political conflict arose in the South in 1963 when Buddhists denounced authoritarianism and brutality. This paved the way for a military coup Nov. 1-2, 1963, which overthrew Diem. Several military coups followed.

In 1964, the U.S. began air strikes against North Vietnam. Beginning in 1965, the raids were stepped up and U.S. troops became combatants. U.S. troop strength in Vietnam, which reached a high of 543,400 in Apr. 1969, was ordered reduced by

President Nixon in a series of withdrawals, beginning in June 1969. U.S. bombings were resumed in 1972-73.

A ceasefire agreement was signed in Paris Jan. 27, 1973 by the U.S., North and South Vietnam, and the Vietcong. It was never implemented.

North Vietnamese forces launched attacks against remaining government outposts in the Central Highlands in the first months of 1975. Government retreats turned into a rout, and the Saigon regime surrendered April 30. North Vietnam assumed control, and began transforming society along communist lines. All businesses and farms were collectivized.

The U.S. accepted over 165,000 Vietnamese refugees, while scores of thousands more sought refuge in other countries.

The war's toll included — Combat deaths: U.S. 47,752; South Vietnam over 200,000; other allied forces 5,225. Civilian casualties were over a million. Displaced war refugees in South Vietnam totaled over 6.5 million.

The first National Assembly of both parts of the country met and the country was officially reunited July 2, 1976. The Northern capital, flag, anthem, emblem, and currency were applied to the new state. Nearly all major government posts went to officials of the former Northern government.

Heavy fighting with Cambodia took place, 1977-80, amid mutual charges of aggression and atrocities against civilians. Increasing numbers of Vietnamese civilians, ethnic Chinese, escaped the country, via the sea, or the overland route across Cambodia. Vietnam launched an offensive against Cambodian refugee strongholds along the Thai-Cambodian border in 1985; they also engaged Thai troops. Vietnam declared that it had removed all its troops from Cambodia, Sept. 1989.

Relations with China soured as 140,000 ethnic Chinese left Vietnam charging discrimination; China cut off economic aid. Reacting to Vietnam's invasion of Cambodia, China attacked 4 Vietnamese border provinces, Feb., 1979, instigating heavy fighting.

Vietnam announced a package of reforms aimed at reducing central control of the economy in 1987, as many of the old revolutionary followers of Ho Chi Minh were removed from office. By 1990, the economy was in a dire state with inflation estimated at 1,000% a year.

Progress has been made with the U.S. over the repatriating of "Amerasians," the children fathered by U.S. servicemen.

Western Samoa

Independent State of Western Samoa

Malotuto'atasi o Samoa i Sisifo

People: Population (1991 est.): 190,000. **Age distrib.** (%): 0–14: 50.4; 15–59: 45.4; 60+: 4.3. **Pop. density:** 167 per sq. mi. **Urban** (1981): 21.2%. **Ethnic groups:** Samoan (Polynesian) 88%, Euronesian (mixed) 10%, European, other Pacific Islanders. **Languages:** Samoan, English both official. **Religions:** Protestant 70%, Roman Catholic 20%.

Geography: Area: 1,133 sq. mi., the size of Rhode Island. **Location:** In the S. Pacific O. **Neighbors:** Nearest are Fiji on W, Tonga on S. **Topography:** Main islands, Savai'i (670 sq. mi.) and Upolu (429 sq. mi.), both ruggedly mountainous, and small islands Manono and Apolima. **Capital:** Apia. **Cities** (1983 est.): Apia 35,000.

Government: Type: Constitutional monarchy. **Head of state:** King Malietoa Tanumafili II; b. Jan. 4, 1913; in office: Jan. 1, 1962. **Head of government:** Prime Min. Toflau Eti Alesana; in office: Apr. 11, 1988. **Local divisions:** 11 districts.

Economy: Chief crops: Cocoa, copra, bananas. **Other resources:** Hardwoods, fish. **Arable land:** 43%. **Electricity prod.** (1990): 45 mln. kWh. **Labor force:** 67% agric.

Finance: Monetary unit: Tala (Mar. 1992: 1.00 = $.42 US). **Gross domestic product** (1989): $114 mln. **Per capita GNP** (1990): $115. **Imports** (1990): $87 mln.; partners: NZ 28% Austral. 20%, Jap. 13%, U.S. 5%. **Exports** (1990): $9.4 mln.; partners: EC 28%. **International reserves less gold** (Mar. 1992): $74.8 mln. **Consumer prices** (change in 1991): −1.4%.

Transport: Motor vehicles: in use (1985): 1,700 passenger cars, 2,400 comm. vehicles. **Chief ports:** Apia, Asau.

Communications: Radios: 1 per 2.3 persons. **Telephones:** 1 per 23 persons.

Health: Life expectancy at birth (1991): 64 male; 69 female. **Births** (per 1,000 pop. 1991): 34. **Deaths** (per 1,000 pop. 1991): 7. **Natural increase:** 2.8%. **Hospital beds:** 1 per 255 persons. **Physicians:** 1 per 4,103 persons. **Infant mortality** (per 1,000 live births 1991): 48.

Education (1989): **Literacy:** 90%. 95% attend elementary school.

Major International Organizations: UN (IMF, World Bank), Commonwealth of Nations.

Western Samoa was a German colony, 1899 to 1914, when New Zealand landed troops and took over. It became a New Zealand mandate under the League of Nations and, in 1945, a New Zealand UN Trusteeship.

An elected local government took office in Oct. 1959 and the country became fully independent Jan. 1, 1962.

Yemen

Republic of Yemen

al-Jumhūrīyah al-Yamanīyah

People: Population (1991 est.): 10,062,000. **Pop. density:** 48 per sq. mi. **Ethnic groups:** Arabs, Indians, some Negroids. **Languages:** Arabic. **Religions:** Sunni Moslem 53%; Shute Moslem 46%.

Geography: Area: 205,356 sq. mi., slightly smaller than France. **Location:** On the southern coast of the Arabian Peninsula. **Neighbors:** Saudi Arabia on NE, Oman on the E. **Topography:** A sandy coastal strip leads to well-watered fertile mountains in interior. **Capital:** Sanaa. **Cities** (1986 est.): Sanaa 427,000; Aden 250,000.

Government: Type: Republic. **Head of state:** Pres. Ali Abdullah Saleh, b. 1942; in office: July 17, 1978. **Head of government:** Prime Min. Haydar Abu Bakr-al Attas; in office: May 22, 1990. **Local divisions:** 17 provinces. **Defense:** 20% of GDP (1990).

Economy: Industries: Food processing, mining, petroleum refining. **Chief crops:** Wheat, sorghum, fruits, coffee, cotton. **Minerals:** Salt. **Crude oil reserves** (1984): 600 mln. bbls. **Arable land:** 14%. **Livestock** (1989): goats: 3.1 mln.; sheep: 3.6 mln. **Fish catch** (1989): 73,000 metric tons. **Electricity prod.** (1990): 1 bln. kWh. **Labor force:** 64% agric.; 22% ind. and commerce; 14% serv.

Finance: Monetary unit: Rial (Jan. 1992: 12.01 = $1 US). **Gross domestic product** (1990): $5.3 bln. **Per capita GDP:** $545. **Imports** (1987): $7.1 bln.; partners: Saudi Ar. 20%, Fr. 8%, Jap. 16%. **Exports** (1987): $3.8 mln.; partners: S. Yemen 23%, Saudi Ar. 8%, Pak. 19%.

Transport: Motor vehicles in use (1987): 150,000 passenger cars, 220,000 commercial vehicles. **Civil Aviation** (1990): 1.0 bln. passenger-km.; 13 airports with scheduled flights. **Chief ports:** Al-Hudaydah, Al-Mukha, Aden.

Communications: Television sets: 1 per 38 persons. **Radios:** 1 per 35 persons. **Telephones:** 1 per 157 persons.

Health: (N. Yemen only) Life expectancy at birth (1991): 49 male; 51 female. **Births** (per 1,000 pop. 1991): 51. **Deaths** (per 1,000 pop. 1991): 16. **Natural increase:** 3.5%. **Hospital beds:** 1 per 995 persons. **Physicians:** 1 per 5,531 persons. **Infant mortality** (per 1,000 live births 1991): 121.

Education (1990): **Literacy:** 38%. **Primary school attendance:** 59%.

Major International Organizations: UN (IMF, WHO), Arab League.

Embassy: 600 New Hampshire Ave. NW 20037; 965-4760.

Yemen's territory once was part of the ancient kindgom of Sheba, or Saba, a prosperous link in trade between Africa and India. A Biblical reference speaks of its gold, spices and precious stones as gifts borne by the Queen of Sheba to King Solomon.

Yemen became independent in 1918, after years of Ottoman Turkish rule, but remained politically and economically backward. Imam Ahmed ruled 1948-1962. Army officers headed by Brig. Gen. Abdullah al-Salal declared the country to be the Yemen Arab Republic.

The Imam Ahmed's heir, the Imam Mohamad al-Badr, fled to the mountains where tribesmen joined royalist forces; internal warfare between them and the republican forces continued. About 150,000 people died in the fighting.

There was a bloodless coup Nov. 5, 1967. In April 1970 hostilities ended with an agreement between Yemen and Saudi Arabia.

On June 13, 1974, an army group, led by Col. Ibrahim al-Hamidi, seized the government. He was assassinated in 1977.

Meanwhile, South Yemen won independence from Britain in 1967, formed out of the British colony of Aden and the British protectorate of South Arabia. It became the Arab world's only Marxist state, taking the name People's Democratic Republic of Yemen in 1970 and signing a 20-year friendship treaty with the USSR in 1979 that allowed for the stationing of Soviet troops in the south.

More than 300,000 Yemenis fled from the south to the north after independence, contributing to 2 decades of hostility between the 2 states that flared into warfare twice in the 1970's.

An Arab League-sponsored agreement between North and South Yemen on unification of the 2 countries was signed Mar. 29, 1979. An agreement providing for widespread political and economic cooperation was signed in 1988.

The 2 countries were formally united on May 22, 1990.

Yugoslavia

Federal Republic of Yugoslavia

Federativna Republika Jugoslavija

(Data prior to 1992 include former republics of Croatia, Slovenia, Bosnia and Herzegovina, and Macedonia)

People: Population (1992 est.): 10,337,000. **Age distrib.** (%): 0–14: 23.5; 15-59: 63.7; 60+: 12.8. **Pop. density:** 265 per sq. mi. **Urban** (1990): 50%. **Ethnic groups** (1990): Serbs 36%, Croats 20%, Bosnian Moslems 9%, Slovenes 8%, Macedonians 6%, Albanians 8%. **Languages:** Serbo-Croatian, Macedonian, Slovenian, Albanian. **Religions:** Eastern Orthodox 50%, Roman Catholic 30%, Moslem 9%.

Geography: Area: 39,000 sq. mi. **Location:** On the Balkan Peninsula in SE Europe. Present-day Yugoslavia consists of the former republics of Serbia and Montenegro, and the autonomous regions of Kosovo and Vojvodina. **Neighbors:** Croatia, Bosnia and Herzegovina on W., Hungary on N, Romania, Bulgaria on E, Greece, Albania, Macedonia on S. **Capital:** Belgrade. **Cities** (1991 est.): Belgrade 1,553,000.

Government: Type: Republic. **Head of government:** Prime Min. Milan Panic; in office: July 14, 1992. **Local divisions:** 2 republics, 2 autonomous provinces. **Defense:** 4.6% of GDP (1991).

Economy: Industries: Steel, wood products, cement, textiles, tourism. **Chief crops:** Corn, grains, tobacco, sugar beets. **Minerals:** Antimony, bauxite, lead, mercury, coal, iron, copper, chrome, zinc, salt. **Arable land:** 28%. **Livestock** (1989): cattle: 4.7 mln.; pigs: 7.3 mln.; sheep: 7.6 mln. **Fish catch:** (1989): 71,000 metric tons. **Electricity prod.** (1990): 83.4 bln. kWh. **Crude steel prod.** (1990): 3.6 mln. metric tons. **Labor force:** 22% agric.; 70% ind.

Finance: Monetary unit: Dinar (June 1992: 320 = $1 US). **Gross national product** (1990): $120.1 bln. **Per capita GNP:** $5,040. **Imports** (1990): $19.1 bln.; partners: EC 54%, USSR 15%. **Exports** (1990): $14.6 bln.; partners: EC 54%, USSR 17%. **Tourists** (1990): $2.7 bln. receipts. **National budget** (1990): $6.4 bln. expenditures. **International reserves less gold** (Mar. 1991): $4.7 bln. **Gold:** 1.90 mln. oz t. **Consumer prices** (change in 1990): 587%.

Transport: Railroads (1990): **Length:** 5,945 mi. **Motor vehicles:** in use (1989): 3.0 mln. passenger cars, 290,000 comm. vehicles. **Civil aviation** (1989): 7.9 bln. passenger-km; 20 airports.

Communications: Television sets: 1 per 3.6 persons. **Radios:** 1 per 6 persons. **Telephones:** 1 per 4.9 persons. **Daily newspaper circ.** (1990): 88 per 1,000 pop.

Health: Life expectancy at birth (1991): 70 male; 76 female. **Births** (per 1,000 pop. 1991): 14. **Deaths** (per 1,000 pop. 1991): 9. **Natural increase:** .5%. **Hospital beds:** 1 per 163 persons. **Physicians:** 1 per 511 persons. **Infant mortality** (per 1,000 live births 1991): 21.

Education (1991): **Literacy:** 90%. Almost all attend primary school.

Major International Organizations: UN (IMF, World Bank).

Embassy: 2410 California St. NW 20008; 462-6566.

Serbia, which had since 1389 been a vassal principality of Turkey, was established as an independent kingdom by the Treaty of Berlin, 1878. Montenegro, independent since 1389, also obtained international recognition in 1878. After the Balkan wars Serbia's boundaries were enlarged by the annexation of Old Serbia and Macedonia, 1913.

When the Austro-Hungarian empire collapsed after World War I, the Kingdom of the Serbs, Croats, and Slovenes was formed from the former provinces of Croatia, Dalmatia, Bosnia, Herzegovina, Slovenia, Voyvodina and the independent state of Montenegro. The name was later changed to Yugoslavia.

Nazi Germany invaded in 1941. Many Yugoslav partisan troops continued to operate. Among these were the Chetniks led by Draja Mikhailovich, who fought other partisans led by Josip Broz, known as Marshal Tito. Tito, backed by the USSR and Britain from 1943, was in control by the time the Germans had been driven from Yugoslavia in 1945. Mikhailovich was executed July 17, 1946, by the Tito regime.

A constituent assembly proclaimed Yugoslavia a republic Nov. 29, 1945. It became a federated republic Jan. 31, 1946, and Marshal Tito, a communist, became head of the government.

The Stalin policy of dictating to all communist nations was rejected by Tito. He accepted economic aid and military equipment from the U.S. and received aid in foreign trade also from France and Great Britain. Tito also supported the liberal government of Czechoslovakia in 1968 before the Soviet invasion.

A separatist movement among Croatians brought arrests and a change of leaders in the Croatian Republic in Jan. 1972. Violence by Croatian nationalists and fears of Soviet political intervention led to restrictions on political and intellectual dissent.

Beginning in 1965, reforms designed to decentralize the administration of economic development and to force industries to produce more efficiently in competition with foreign producers were introduced, and considerable trade with the West was developed.

Pres. Tito died May 4, 1980; with his death, the post as head of the Collective Presidency and also that as head of the League of Communists became a rotating system of succession among the members representing each republic and autonomous province.

On Jan. 22, 1990, a Communist Party conference renounced its constitutionally guaranteed leading role in society and called on parliament to enact "Political Pluralism, including a multiparty system."

Croatia and Slovenia formally declared independence June 25, 1991. In Croatia, fighting began between Croats and ethnic Serbs. Serbia sent arms and medical supplies to the Serb rebels in Croatia. In Aug., there were numerous clashes between Croatian forces and Yugoslavian army units and their Serb supporters.

The republics of Serbia and Montenegro proclaimed a new "Federal Republic of Yugoslavia" Apr. 17, 1992. Serbia was the main supplier of arms to the ethnic Serb guerrillas in Bosnia. The UN imposed sweeping international sanctions on Yugoslavia as a means of ending the bloodshed in Bosnia, May 30. Some 100,000 protesters in Belgrade called for the ouster of Serbian President Milosevic, June 28.

Milan Panic, a Serbian-born naturalized U.S. citizen, became prime Minister of Yugoslavia, July 14. He promised to end the bloodshed in Bosnia. *(See Index & Chronology for details.)*

Kosovo: An area in southern Serbia (4,203 sq. mi.), with a population of about 2,000,000, mostly Albanians. The capital is Pristina. The Albanian majority has declared its independence, which Serbia has not recognized.

Vojvodina: An area in northern Serbia (3,304 sq. mi.), with a population of about 2,000,000, mostly Serbian. The capital is Novi Sad.

Macedonia

A former republic of Yugoslavia (9,928 sq. mi.) is bounded by Bulgaria on the east, Greece on the south, Albania on the west, and Yugoslavia on the north. There are slightly over 2 million people, mostly Macedonians. The capital is Skopje.

Macedonians, in a referendum Sept. 8, 1991, voted to declare independence from Yugoslavia. At the request of Greece, the EC has not recognized Macedonia as an independent country until it changes its name. Macedonia has adamantly opposed a name change.

Zaire

Republic of Zaire

République du Zaïre

People: Population (1991 est.): 37,832,000. **Pop. density:** 41 per sq. mi. **Urban** (1988): 44.2%. **Ethnic groups:** Bantu tribes 80%, over 200 other tribes. **Languages:** French (official), Kongo, Luba, Mongo, Rwanda, others. **Religions:** Christian 70%, Moslem 10%.

Geography: Area: 905,563 sq. mi., one-fourth the size of the U.S. **Location:** In central Africa. **Neighbors:** Congo on W, Central African Republic, Sudan on N, Uganda, Rwanda, Burundi, Tanzania on E, Zambia, Angola on S. **Topography:** Zaire includes the bulk of the Zaire (Congo) R. Basin. The vast central region is a low-lying plateau covered by rain forest. Mountainous terraces in the W, savannas in the S and SE, grasslands toward the N, and the high Ruwenzori Mtns. on the E surround the central region. A short strip of territory borders the Atlantic O. The Zaire R. is 2,718 mi. long. **Capital:** Kinshasa. **Cities** (1991 est.): Kinshasa 3,741,000; Lubumbashi 709,000.

Government: Type: Republic with strong presidential authority (in transition). **Head of state:** Pres. Mobutu Sese Seko; b. Oct. 14, 1930; in office: Nov. 25, 1965. **Head of government:** Prime Min. Nguzi Karl-I-Bond; in office: Nov. 25, 1991. **Local divisions:** 10 regions, Kinshasa. **Defense:** 1% of GDP (1988).

Economy: Chief crops: Coffee, rice, sugar cane, bananas, plantains, manioc, mangoes, tea, cocoa, palm oil. **Minerals:** Cobalt (60% of world reserves), copper, cadmium, gold, silver, tin, germanium, zinc, iron, manganese, uranium, radium. **Crude oil reserves** (1987): 111 mln. bbls. **Other resources:** Forests, rubber, ivory. **Arable land:** 3%. **Livestock** (1989): cattle: 1.4 mln.; goats: 2.9 mln. **Fish catch** (1989): 166,000 metric tons. **Electricity prod.** (1990): 5.5 bln. kWh. **Labor force:** 75% agric.

Finance: Monetary unit: Zaire (Mar. 1992: 3,288 = $1 US). **Gross domestic product** (1990): $6.6 bln. **Per capita GDP:** $180. **Imports** (1989): $2.1 bln.; partners: Chi. 38%, Belg. 16%, W. Ger. 7%, Fra. 7%. **Exports** (1989): $2.2 bln.; partners: Belg.-Lux. 36%, U.S. 19%. **International reserves less gold** (Mar. 1992): $114 mln. **Gold:** 27,000 oz t. **Consumer prices** (change in 1991): 2,154.

Transport: Railroads (1989): **Length:** 3,193 mi. **Motor vehicles:** in use (1985): 24,000 passenger cars, 60,000 comm. vehicles. **Civil aviation** (1990): 487 mln. passenger-km; 26 airports with scheduled flights. **Chief ports:** Matadi, Boma.

Communications: Television sets: 1 per 1,707 persons. **Radios:** 1 per 9.7 persons. **Telephones:** 1 per 1,026 persons. **Daily newspaper circ.** (1988): 1 per 1,000 pop.

Health: Life expectancy at birth (1991): 52 male; 56 female. **Births** (per 1,000 pop. 1991): 45. **Deaths** (per 1,000 pop. 1991): 14. **Natural increase:** 3.1%. **Hospital beds:** 1 per 476 persons. **Physicians:** 1 per 23,193 persons. **Infant mortality** (per 1,000 live births 1991): 99.

Education (1990): **Literacy:** 72%.

Major International Organizations: UN and all of its specialized agencies, OAU.

Embassy: 1800 New Hampshire Ave. NW 20008; 234-7690.

The earliest inhabitants of Zaire may have been the pygmies, followed by Bantus from the E and Nilotic tribes from the N. The large Bantu Bakongo kingdom ruled much of Zaire and Angola when Portuguese explorers visited in the 15th century.

Leopold II, king of the Belgians, formed an international group to exploit the Congo in 1876. In 1877 Henry M. Stanley explored the Congo and in 1878 the king's group sent him back to organize the region and win over the native chiefs. The Conference of Berlin, 1884-85, organized the Congo Free State with Leopold as king and chief owner. Exploitation of native laborers on the rubber plantations caused international criticism and led to granting of a colonial charter, 1908.

Belgian and Congolese leaders agreed Jan. 27, 1960, that the Congo would become independent June 30. In the first general elections, May 31, the National Congolese movement of Patrice Lumumba won 35 of 137 seats in the National Assembly. He was appointed premier June 21, and formed a coalition cabinet.

Widespread violence caused Europeans and others to flee. The UN Security Council Aug. 9, 1960, called on Belgium to withdraw its troops and sent a UN contingent. President Kasavubu removed Lumumba as premier; he was murdered in 1961.

The last UN troops left the Congo June 30, 1964, and Moise Tshombe became president.

On Sept. 7, 1964, leftist rebels set up a "People's Republic" in Stanleyville. Tshombe hired foreign mercenaries and sought to rebuild the Congolese Army. In Nov. and Dec. 1964 rebels slew scores of white hostages and thousands of Congolese; Belgian paratroops, dropped from U.S. transport planes, rescued hundreds. By July 1965 the rebels had lost their effectiveness.

In 1965 Gen. Joseph D. Mobutu was named president. He later changed his name to Mobutu Sese Seko. The country changed its name to Republic of Zaire on Oct. 27, 1971; in 1972 Zairians with Christian names were ordered to change them to African names.

Serious economic difficulties, amid charges of corruption by government officials, have plagued Zaire in the 1980s. In 1990, Pres. Mobutu announced an end to a 20-year ban on multiparty politics.

Zambia

Republic of Zambia

People: Population (1991 est.): 8,445,000. **Age distrib.** (%): 0–14: 48.2; 15–59: 47.8; 60+: 4.0. **Pop. density:** 29 per sq. mi. **Urban** (1990): 49%. **Ethnic groups:** Mostly Bantu tribes. **Languages:** English (official), Bantu dialects. **Religions:** Predominantly animist, Roman Catholic 21%, Protestant, Hindu, Moslem minorities.

Geography: Area: 290,586 sq. mi., larger than Texas. **Location:** In southern central Africa. **Neighbors:** Zaire on N, Tanzania, Malawi, Mozambique on E, Zimbabwe, Namibia on S, Angola on W. **Topography:** Zambia is mostly high plateau country covered with thick forests, and drained by several important rivers, including the Zambezi. **Capital:** Lusaka. **Cities** (1991): Lusaka 982,000; Kitwe 348,000; Ndola 376,000.

Government: Type: Republic. **Head of state:** Pres. Frederick Chiluba; in office: Nov. 2, 1991. **Local divisions:** 9 provinces. **Defense:** 6.8% of GDP (1985).

Economy: Chief crops: Corn, tobacco, peanuts, cotton, sugar. **Minerals:** Cobalt, copper, zinc, gold, lead, vanadium, manganese, coal. **Other resources:** Rubber, ivory. **Arable land:** 7%. **Livestock** (1989): cattle: 2.8 mln. **Fish catch** (1989): 68,000 metric tons. **Electricity prod.** (1989): 6.7 bln. kWh. **Labor force:** 75% agric.; 40% ind. and commerce.

Finance: Monetary unit: Kwacha (Mar. 1992: 1.00 = $.01 US). **Gross domestic product** (1990): $4.7 bln. **Per capita GDP:** $580. **Imports** (1990): $1 bln.; S.Af. 13%, W. Ger. 6%, U.S. 7%. **Exports** (1990): $1.3 bln.; partners: Jap. 4%, UK 3%, U.S. 10%, W. Ger. 9%. **National budget** (1991): $1.5 bln. expenditures. **International reserves less gold** (Jan. 1992): $184 mln. **Gold:** 15,000 oz t. **Consumer prices** (change in 1991): 92%.

Transport: Motor vehicles: in use (1982): 105,000 passenger cars, 97,000 comm. vehicles. **Civil aviation** (1990): 232 mln. passenger-km; 8 airports with scheduled flights.

Communications: Television sets: 1 per 41 persons. **Radios:** 1 per 14 persons. **Telephones:** 1 per 87 persons. **Daily newspaper circ.** (1989): 15 per 1,000 pop.

Health: Life expectancy at birth (1991): 55 male; 58 female. **Births** (per 1,000 pop. 1991): 50. **Deaths** (per 1,000 pop. 1991): 12. **Natural increase:** 3.7%. **Hospital beds:** 1 per 311 persons. **Physicians:** 1 per 8,437 persons. **Infant mortality** (per 1,000 live births 1991): 79.

Education (1991): **Literacy:** 54%. **Attendance:** less than 50% in grades 1–7.

Major International Organizations: UN (GATT, IMF, WHO), OAU, Commonwealth of Nations.

Embassy: 2419 Massachusetts Ave. NW 20008; 265-9717.

As Northern Rhodesia, the country was under the administration of the South Africa Company, 1889 until 1924, when the office of governor was established, and, subsequently, a legislature. The country became an independent republic within the Commonwealth Oct. 24, 1964.

After the white government of Rhodesia declared its independence from Britain Nov. 11, 1965, relations between Zambia and Rhodesia became strained.

As part of a program of government participation in major industries, a government corporation in 1970 took over 51% of the ownership of 2 foreign-owned copper mining companies. Privately-held land and other enterprises were nationalized in 1975, as were all newspapers. In the 1980s, decline in copper prices has hurt the economy and severe drought caused famine.

Food riots erupted in June 1990, as the nation suffered its worst violence since independence.

Elections held Oct. 1991, resulted in an end to one-party rule.

Zimbabwe

Republic of Zimbabwe

People: Population (1991 est.): 10,720,000. **Age distrib.** (%): 0–14: 44.9; 15–59: 51.1; 60+: 4.0. **Pop. density:** 71 per sq. mi. **Urban** (1990): 25%. **Ethnic groups:** Shona 80%, Ndebele 19%. **Languages:** English (official), Shona, Sinde bele. **Religions:** Predominantly traditional tribal beliefs, Christian minority.

Geography: Area: 150,803 sq. mi., slightly larger than Montana. **Location:** In southern Africa. **Neighbors:** Zambia on N, Botswana on W, S. Africa on S, Mozambique on E. **Topography:** Zimbabwe is high plateau country, rising to mountains on eastern border, sloping down on the other borders. **Capital:** Harare. **Cities** (1988 est.): Harare 730,000; Bulawayo (met.) 415,000.

Government: Type: Parliamentary democracy. **Head of state:** Pres. Robert Mugabe; b. Feb. 21, 1924; in office: Jan. 1, 1988. **Local divisions:** 8 provinces. **Defense:** 5.0% of GNP (1987).

Economy: Industries: Clothing, chemicals, light industries. **Chief crops:** Tobacco, sugar, cotton, corn, wheat. **Minerals:** Chromium, gold, nickel, asbestos, copper, iron, coal. **Arable land:** 7%. **Livestock** (1989): cattle: 5.7 mln.; goats: 1.6 mln. **Electricity prod.** (1990): 5.4 bln. kWh. **Labor force:** 74% agric.; 16% serv.

Finance: Monetary unit: Dollar (Mar. 1992: 1.00 = $.19 US). **Gross domestic product** (1990): $5.5 bln. **Per capita GDP:** $540. **Imports** (1989): $1.4 bln. partners: EC 31%, So. Afr. 21%. **Exports** (1989): $1.7 bln.; partners: EC 40%. **National budget** (1991): $3.3 bln. expenditures. **Total reserves less gold** (Mar. 1992): $278 mln. **Consumer prices** (change in 1991): 24.3%.

Transport: Motor vehicles: in use (1989): 173,000 passenger cars, 80,000 comm. vehicles. **Civil aviation** (1989): 709 mln. passenger-km. 8 airports with scheduled flights.

Communications: Television sets: 1 per 67 persons. **Radios:** 1 per 20 persons. **Telephones:** 1 per 31 persons. **Daily newspaper circ.** (1990): 23 per 1,000 pop.

Health: Life expectancy at birth (1991): 60 male; 64 female. **Births** (per 1,000 pop. 1991): 41. **Deaths** (per 1,000 pop. 1991): 8. **Natural increase:** 3.3%. **Physicians:** 1 per 6,951 persons. **Infant mortality** (per 1,000 live births 1991): 61.

Education (1990): **Literacy:** 67%. **Attendance:** 90% primary, 15% secondary for Africans; higher for whites, Asians.

Major International Organizations: UN (IMF, World Bank), OAU, Commonwealth of Nations.

Embassy: 2852 McGill Terrace NW 20008; 332-7100.

Britain took over the area as Southern Rhodesia in 1923 from the British South Africa Co. (which, under Cecil Rhodes, had conquered the area by 1897) and granted internal self-government. Under a 1961 constitution, voting was restricted to maintain whites in power. On Nov. 11, 1965, Prime Min. Ian D. Smith announced his country's unilateral declaration of independence. Britain termed the act illegal, and demanded Zimbabwe (known as Rhodesia until 1980) broaden voting rights to provide for eventual rule by the majority Africans.

Urged by Britain, the UN imposed sanctions, including embargoes on oil shipments to Zimbabwe. Some oil and gasoline reached Zimbabwe, however, from South Africa and Mozambique, before the latter became independent in 1975. In May 1968, the UN Security Council ordered a trade embargo.

A new constitution came into effect, Mar. 2, 1970. The election law effectively prevented full black representation through income tax requirements.

Intermittent negotiations between the government and various black nationalist groups failed to prevent increasing skirmishes. By mid-1978, over 6,000 soldiers and civilians had been killed. An "internal settlement" signed Mar. 1978 in which Smith and 3 popular black leaders share control until transfer of power to the black majority was rejected by guerrilla leaders.

In the country's first universal-franchise election, Apr. 21, 1979, Bishop Abel Muzorewa's United African National Council gained a bare majority control of the black-dominated parliament. Britain, 1979, began efforts to normalize its relationship with Zimbabwe. A British cease-fire was accepted by all parties, Dec. 5th. Independence was finally achieved Apr. 18, 1980.

Pres. Mugabe declared Zimbabwe's drought a national disaster and appealed to foreign donors for food, money, and medicine, Mar. 6, 1992.

Area and Population of the World

Source: Bureau of the Census, U.S. Dept. of Commerce; prior to 1950, Rand McNally & Co.

Continent	Area (1,000 sq. mi.)	% of Earth	Population (est., thousands) 1650	1750	1850	1900	1950	1980	1991	% World Total, 1991
North America	9,400	16.2	5,000	5,000	39,000	106,000	166,000	252,000	279,000	5.1
South America	6,900	11.9	8,000	7,000	20,000	38,000	—	—	—	—
Latin America, Caribbean	—	—	—	—	—	—	166,000	364,000	458,000	8.4
Europe	3,800	6.6	100,000	140,000	265,000	400,000	392,000	484,000	502,000	9.2
Asia	17,400	30.1	335,000	476,000	754,000	932,000	1,368,000	2,494,000	3,046,000	56.2
Africa	11,700	20.2	100,000	95,000	95,000	118,000	281,000	594,000	817,000	15.0
Former USSR	—	—	—	—	—	—	180,000	266,000	293,000	5.4
Oceania, incl. Australia	3,300	5.7	2,000	2,000	2,000	6,000	12,000	23,000	27,000	0.4
Antarctica	5,400	9.3	Uninhabited							
World	**57,900**	—	**550,000**	**725,000**	**1,175,000**	**1,600,000**	**2,564,000**	**4,478,000**	**5,423,000**	—

Leading Countries in Population and Area

China has the highest population in the world with over 1.1 billion inhabitants, which is 21 percent of the world's population. India has almost 900 million people and is expected to reach 1 billion by the end of the decade. The United States has the third largest population with over 250 million, followed by Indonesia, Brazil, and Russia. Russia is the largest country in area with over 6.5 million square miles, followed by Canada, China, the United States, and Brazil.

Worldwide Illiteracy Shows a Decline

For the first time ever, the number of illiterate people in the world declined slightly in recent years. A report by the United Nations Educational, Scientific and Cultural Organization estimated the number of illiterate people to be 948 million in 1990, a slight drop from the 1985 estimate of 950 million.

The 948 million people represent 26.6 percent of the world's population. The report projects that the number of illiterate will decrease to 935 million, or 21.8 percent of the population by the year 2000. While the report shows a significant decrease in the proportion of illiterate people—the number in 1970 was 890 million, or 38.5 percent of the adult population—it refers to the progress of eradicating illiteracy as being "painfully slow."

Population of World's Largest Cities

Source: Bureau of the Census, U.S. Dept. of Commerce

The table below represents one attempt at comparing the world's largest cities. The cities are defined as population clusters of continuous built-up areas with a population density of a least 5,000 persons per square mile. The boundary of the city was determined by examining detailed maps of each city in conjunction with the most recent official population statistics. Exclaves of areas exceeding the minimum population density were added to the city if the intervening gap was less than one mile. To the extent practical, nonresidential areas such as parks, airports, industrial complexes and water were excluded from the area reported for each city, thus making the population density reflective of the concentrations in the residential portions of the city. By using a consistent definition for the city, it is possible to make comparisons of the cities on the basis of total population, area, and population density.

The population of each city was projected based on projected country populations and the proportion of each city population to the total population of the country at the time of the last 2 censuses. Figures in the table below may differ from city population figures elsewhere in The World Almanac because of different methods of determining population.

City, Country	1991 (thousands)	2000 (thousands projected)	Area (sq. mi.)	Density 1991 (pop per sq. mi.)
Tokyo-Yokohama, Japan	27,245	29,971	1,089	25,019
Mexico City, Mexico	20,899	27,872	522	40,037
Sao Paulo, Brazil	18,701	25,354	451	41,466
Seoul, South Korea	16,792	21,976	342	49,101
New York, U.S.	14,625	14,648	1,274	11,480
Osaka-Kobe-Kyoto, Japan	13,872	14,287	495	28,025
Bombay, India	12.101	15,357	95	127,461
Calcutta, India	11,898	14,088	209	56,927
Rio de Janeiro, Brazil	11,688	14,169	260	44,952
Buenos Aires, Argentina	11,657	12,911	535	21,790
Moscow, Russia	10,446	11,121	379	27,562
Manila, Philippines	10,156	12,846	188	54,024
Los Angeles, U.S.	10,130	10,714	1,110	9,126
Cairo, Egypt	10,099	12,512	104	97,106
Jakarta, Indonesia	9,882	12,804	76	130,026
Teheran, Iran	9,779	14,251	112	87,312
London, U.K.	9,115	8,574	874	10,429
Delhi, India	8,778	11,849	138	63,612
Paris, France	8,720	8,803	432	20,185
Karachi, Pakistan	8,014	11,299	190	42,179
Lagos, Nigeria	7,998	12,528	56	142,821
Essen, Germany	7,452	7,239	704	10,585
Shanghai, China	6,936	7,540	78	88,924
Lima, Peru	6,815	9,241	120	56,794
Taipei, Taiwan	6,695	8,516	138	48,517
Istanbul, Turkey	6,678	8,875	165	40,476
Chicago, U.S.	6,529	6,568	762	8,568
Bangkok, Thailand	5,955	7,587	102	58,379
Bogota, Colombia	5,913	7,935	79	74,851
Madras, India	5,896	7,384	115	51,270
Beijing, China	5,762	5,993	151	38,156
Hong Kong	5,693	5,956	23	247,501
Santiago, Chile	5,378	6,294	128	40,018
Pusan, S. Korea	5,008	6,700	54	92,735
Tianjin, China	4,850	5,298	49	98,990
Bangalore, India	4,802	6,764	50	96,041
Nagoya, Japan	4,791	5,303	307	15,606
Milan, Italy	4,749	4,839	344	13,806
St. Petersburg, Russia	4,672	4,738	139	33,614
Madrid, Spain	4,513	5,104	66	68,385
Dhaka, Bangladesh	4,419	6,492	32	138,108
Lahore, Pakistan	4,376	5,864	57	76,779
Shenyang, China	4,289	4,684	39	109,974
Barcelona, Spain	4,227	4,834	87	48,584
Baghdad, Iraq	4,059	5,239	97	41,843
Manchester, U.K.	4,030	3,827	357	11,287
Philadelphia, U.S.	4,003	3,979	471	8,499
San Francisco, U.S.	3,986	4,214	428	9,315
Belo Horizonte, Brazil	3,812	5,125	79	48,249
Kinshasa, Zaire	3,747	5,646	57	65,732
Ho Chi Minh City, Vietnam	3,725	4,481	31	120,168
Ahmadabad, India	3,709	4,837	32	115,893
Hyderabad, India	3,673	4,765	88	41,741
Sydney, Australia	3,536	3,708	338	10,460
Athens, Greece	3,507	3,866	116	30,237
Miami, U.S.	3,471	3,894	448	7,748
Guadalajara, Mexico	3,370	4,451	78	43,205
Guangzhou, China	3,360	3,652	79	42,537
Surabaya, Indonesia	3,248	3,632	43	75,544
Caracas, Venezuela	3,217	3,435	54	59,582
Wuhan, China	3,200	3,495	65	49,225
Toronto, Canada	3,145	3,296	154	20,420
Porto Alegre, Brazil	3,114	4,109	231	13,479
Rome, Italy	3,033	3,129	69	43,949
Greater Berlin, Germany	3,021	3,006	274	11,026
Naples, Italy	2,978	3,134	62	48,032
Casablanca, Morocco	2,973	3,795	35	84,953
Detroit, U.S.	2,969	2,735	468	6,343
Alexandria, Egypt	2,941	3,304	35	84,022
Monterrey, Mexico	2,939	3,974	77	38,169
Montreal, Canada	2,916	3,071	164	17,779
Melbourne, Australia	2,915	2,968	327	8,914
Ankara, Turkey	2,872	3,777	55	52,221
Rangoon, Myanmar	2,864	3,332	47	60,927
Kiev, Ukraine	2,796	3,237	62	45,095
Dallas, U.S.	2,787	3,257	419	6,652
Singapore, Singapore	2,719	2,913	78	34,856
Taegu, South Korea	2,651	4,051	NA	NA
Harbin, China	2,643	2,887	30	88,110
Washington, U.S.	2,565	2,707	357	7,184
Poona, India	2,547	3,647	NA	NA
Boston, U.S.	2,476	2,485	303	8,172
Lisbon, Portugal	2,426	2,717	NA	NA
Tashkent, Uzbekistan	2,418	2,947	NA	NA
Chongqing, China	2,395	2,961	NA	NA
Chengdu, China	2,372	2,591	25	94,870
Vienna, Austria	2,344	2,647	NA	NA
Houston, U.S.	2,329	2,651	310	7,512
Budapest, Hungary	2,303	2,335	138	16,691
Salvador, Brazil	2,298	3,286	NA	NA

Population Projections, by Region and for Selected Countries: 2000 and 2020

Source: Bureau of the Census, U.S. Dept. of Commerce

(in thousands)

Region and Country	2000	2020
Sub-Saharan Africa[1]	**736,325**	**1,279,014**
Angola	11,424	19,153
Benin	6,509	11,901
Botswana	1,554	2,181
Burkina Faso	12,464	23,016
Burundi	7,731	13,725
Cameroon	14,453	23,487
Central African Republic	3,702	5,944
Chad	6,204	9,361
Congo	2,995	4,955
Côte d'Ivoire	18,144	33,581
Ethiopia	69,374	123,584
Ghana	20,527	35,579
Guinea	9,232	14,419
Guinea-Bissau	1,265	1,926
Kenya	34,259	57,265
Liberia	3,674	6,534
Madagascar	16,185	29,183
Malawi	11,892	22,235
Mali	10,667	19,169
Mauritania	2,652	4,849
Mozambique	20,936	35,443
Namibia	2,081	3,925
Niger	11,056	20,606
Nigeria	160,751	273,197
Rwanda	11,047	21,948
Senegal	10,482	18,466
Sierra Leone	5,399	8,919
Somalia	9,409	17,190

(continued)

Region and Country	2000	2020
South Africa	51,375	82,882
Sudan	35,870	59,307
Tanzania	36,489	68,772
Togo	5,248	9,900
Uganda	25,802	48,393
Zaire	50,043	89,164
Zambia	11,572	21,973
Zimbabwe	13,806	21,338
Near East and North Africa[1]	**327,119**	**506,134**
Algeria	32,024	46,007
Cyprus	768	889
Egypt	66,498	97,505
Iraq	27,205	50,943
Israel	5,321	6,850
Jordan	4,880	8,987
Kuwait	2,879	4,564
Lebanon	4,058	5,755
Libya	5,599	8,549
Morocco	31,392	43,324
Oman	2,099	4,163
Saudi Arabia	25,003	45,836
Syria	18,212	35,761
Tunisia	9,713	12,597
Turkey	70,368	96,514
United Arab Emirates	3,598	6,182
Yemen	13,603	25,907
Asia[1]	**3,528,307**	**4,500,233**
Afghanistan	24,935	39,915
Bangladesh	143,226	209,898
Cambodia	8,498	11,947
China	1,303,342	1,541,143
India	1,018,092	1,316,989
Indonesia	223,820	287,289
Iran	78,246	143,230
Japan	128,144	127,716
Korea, North	25,491	30,969
Korea, South	45,962	48,649
Laos	4,964	6,923
Malaysia	21,950	31,598
Mongolia	2,836	4,390
Nepal	24,340	37,488
Myanmar (Burma)	49,787	67,689
Pakistan	149,147	251,305
Philippines	77,734	101,387
Singapore	3,021	3,401
Sri Lanka	19,296	23,283
Taiwan	22,441	25,059
Thailand	63,832	76,108
Vietnam	79,801	102,948

(1) Includes countries not shown separately.

Region and Country	2000	2020
Latin America and the Caribbean[1]	**537,168**	**704,930**
Argentina	36,036	43,462
Belize	301	451
Bolivia	8,721	12,435
Brazil	180,536	231,672
Chile	15,025	18,484
Colombia	39,745	51,443
Costa Rica	3,803	5,294
Cuba	11,613	12,795
Dominican Republic	8,676	11,439
Ecuador	12,997	18,029
El Salvador	6,471	8,811
Guatemala	11,315	15,632
Haiti	7,649	11,374
Honduras	6,243	9,064
Jamaica	2,762	3,533
Mexico	108,754	147,911
Nicaragua	4,729	7,013
Panama	2,937	3,908
Paraguay	6,023	8,812
Peru	26,435	35,055
Trinidad and Tobago	1,425	1,761
Uruguay	3,289	3,620
Venezuela	24,596	34,357
North America, Europe, and the former USSR[1]	**1,125,095**	**1,204,719**
Albania	3,824	4,677
Austria	7,762	7,488
Belgium	9,989	9,692
Bulgaria	9,004	9,071
Canada	29,301	33,128
Czechoslovakia	16,303	16,995
Denmark	5,147	4,980
Finland	5,075	5,024
France	58,548	60,149
Germany	81,532	81,883
Greece	10,166	9,902
Hungary	10,604	10,393
Ireland	3,509	3,837
Italy	58,592	56,068
Netherlands	15,642	15,698
Norway	4,411	4,497
Poland	38,889	41,698
Portugal	10,652	10,671
Romania	24,534	25,981
Spain	40,456	40,428
Sweden	8,761	8,645
Switzerland	7,018	6,843
USSR (Former)	311,637	355,092
United Kingdom	58,719	59,431
United States	268,266	294,364
Yugoslavia (Former)	25,112	26,349

Customs Exemptions and Advice to Travelers

Source: U.S. Customs Service

U.S. residents returning after a stay abroad of at least 48 hours are usually granted customs exemptions of $400 each. The duty-free articles must accompany the traveler at the time of his return, be for personal or household use, have been acquired as an incident of his trip, and be properly declared to Customs. Not more than one liter of alcoholic beverages may be included in the $400 exemption.

If a U.S. resident arrives directly or indirectly from the U.S. Virgin Islands, or a contiguous country which maintains a free zone or a free port, the purchase may be valued up to $800 fair retail value, but not more than $400 of the exemption may be applied to the value of articles acquired elsewhere than in such insular possessions, and 5 liters of alcoholic beverages may be included in the exemption, but not more than one liter of such beverages may have been acquired elsewhere than in the designated islands.

The exemption for alcoholic beverages is accorded only when the returning resident has attained 21 years of age at the time of his arrival. One hundred cigars and 200 cigarettes may be included in either exemption. Cuban cigars may be included if obtained in Cuba and all articles acquired there do not exceed $100 in retail value.

The $400 or $800 exemption may be granted only if the exemption, or any part of it, has not been used within the preceding 30-day period and the stay abroad was for at least 48 hours. The 48-hour absence requirement does not apply if you return from Mexico or the U.S. Virgin Islands.

Gifts costing no more than $50 fair retail value or $100 from American Samoa, Guam, or the Virgin Islands, may be mailed duty-free.

Most items—including alcoholic beverages, cigars, cigarettes and perfume—made in designated Caribbean and Central American countries may enter the U.S. duty-free under the Caribbean Basin Economic Recovery Act. Countries currently designated for such duty-free treatment are: Aruba, Antigua and Barbuda, Bahamas, Barbados, Belize, British Virgin Islands, Costa Rica, Dominica, Dominican Republic, El Salvador, Grenada, Guatemala, Guyana, Haiti, Honduras, Jamaica, Montserrat, Netherlands Antilles, Nicaragua, Panama, Saint Christopher-Nevis, Saint Lucia, Saint Vincent and the Grenadines, and Trinidad and Tobago. Exceptions are: most textiles (incl. clothing), footwear, handbags, luggage, flat goods, work gloves and leather wearing apparel, and certain watches and watch parts. Alcoholic beverages and perfumes, remain subject to IRS tax.

The World's Refugees

(as of Dec. 31, 1991)

Source: *World Refugee Survey 1992*, U.S. Committee for Refugees, a nonprofit corp. The refugees in this table include only those who are in need of protection and/or assistance, and do not include refugees who have resettled.

Country of Asylum	From	Number
Total Africa		**5,340,800**
Algeria	Mostly Western Sahara	240,000[1]
Angola	Zaire, S. Africa	10,400
Benin	Togo	15,100
Botswana	S. Africa	1,400
Burkina Faso	Chad	400
Burundi	Rwanda, Zaire	107,000[1]
Cameroon	Chad	6,900
Central African Rep.	Chad, Sudan	9,000
Congo	Chad, Zaire	3,400
Côte d'Ivoire	Liberia	240,400
Djibouti	Ethiopia, Somalia	120,000
Egypt	Palestinians, Somalia	7,750
Ethiopia	Sudan, Somalia	534,000[1]
Gabon	various	800
Gambia	Senegal, Liberia	1,500
Ghana	Liberia	6,150
Guinea	Liberia, Sierra Leone	566,000[1]
Guinea Bissau	Senegal	4,600
Kenya	Ethiopia, Rwanda, Somalia	107,150
Lesotho	South Africa	300
Liberia	Sierra Leone	12,000
Malawi	Mozambique	950,000
Mali	Mauritania	13,500
Mauritania	Senegal, Mali	40,000
Morocco	various	800
Mozambique	S. Africa	700
Namibia	Angola	30,200
Niger	Chad	1,400
Nigeria	Chad, Liberia	4,600
Rwanda	Burundi	32,500
Senegal	Mauritania	53,100
Sierra Leone	Liberia	17,200
Somalia	Ethiopia	35,000
S. Africa	Mozambique	201,000[1]
Sudan	Ethiopia, Chad, Zaire	717,200[1]
Swaziland	South Africa, Mozambique	47,200[1]
Tanzania	Burundi, Mozambique	351,100
Togo	various	450
Tunisia	various	50
Uganda	Zaire, Sudan	165,450[1]
Zaire	Angola, Burundi, Sudan	482,300
Zambia	Angola, Mozambique, Zaire	140,500
Zimbabwe	Mozambique	198,500[1]
Total East Asia/Pacific		**688,500**
Australia	various	23,000
China	Myanmar	14,200
Hong Kong	Vietnam	60,000
Indonesia	Vietnam, Cambodia	18,700
Japan	Vietnam	900
Korea	Vietnam	200
Macau	Vietnam	100
Malaysia	Vietnam	12,700
Papua New Guinea	Indonesia	6,700
Philippines	Vietnam	18,000
Singapore	Vietnam	150
Taiwan	Vietnam	150
Thailand	Myanmar, Laos, Cambodia	512,700
Vietnam	Cambodia	21,000

(1) Significant variance among sources in number reported.

Country of Asylum	From	Number
Total Europe & No. America		**677,700**
Austria	various	27,300
Belgium	various	15,200
Canada	various	30,500
Czechoslovakia	various	2,800
Denmark	various	4,600
Finland	various	2,100
France	various	46,800
Germany	various	256,100
Greece	various	2,700
Hungary	various	5,200
Italy	various	31,400
Netherlands	various	21,600
Norway	various	4,600
Poland	various	2,500
Portugal	various	200
Romania	various	500
Spain	various	8,100
Sweden	various	27,300
Switzerland	various	41,600
Turkey	Iran, Iraq	31,500
United Kingdom	various	44,700
United States	various	68,800
Yugoslavia	various	1,600
Total Latin America/Caribbean		**119,600**
Argentina	various	1,800
Belize	El Salvador, Guatemala	12,000
Bolivia	various	100
Brazil	various	200
Colombia	various	700
Costa Rica	El Salvador, Nicaragua	24,300
Cuba	various	1,100
Ecuador	Colombia	4,200[1]
El Salvador	various	250
French Guiana	Suriname	9,600
Guatemala	El Salvador, Nicaragua	8,300
Honduras	El Salvador	2,050
Mexico	Guatemala	48,500
Nicaragua	El Salvador	2,800
Panama	various	1,300
Peru	various	600
Uruguay	various	100
Venezuela	Cuba, Chile	1,700
Total Middle East/South Asia		**9,820,950**
Bangladesh	Myanmar	30,150
India	Bangladesh, Tibet, Sri Lanka	402,600[1]
Iran	Afghanistan, Iraq	3,150,000[1]
Iraq	Iran	48,000
Nepal	Tibet, Bhutan	24,000
Pakistan	Afghanistan	3,594,000
Saudi Arabia	Iraq	34,000
United Arab Emirates	Kuwait	40,000
Yemen	various	11,100
Palestinians		
Gaza Strip		528,700
Jordan		960,200
Lebanon		314,200
Syria		293,900
West Bank		430,100
Total Refugees		**16,647,550**

Principal Sources of Refugees

Afghanistan	6,600,800[1]	Cambodia	392,700	Sierra Leone	181,000[1]
Palestinians	2,525,000	Iraq	217,500[1]	Western Sahara	165,000[1]
Mozambique	1,483,500[1]	Sri Lanka	210,000	Vietnam	122,650
Ethiopia/Eritrea	752,400[1]	Burundi	208,500	Yugoslavia	120,000
Somalia	717,600[1]	Rwanda	203,900[1]	China (Tibet)	114,000
Liberia	661,700[1]	Sudan	202,500	Myanmar	112,000
Angola	443,200				

(1) Significant variance among sources in number reported.

U.S. Immigration Law

Source: Immigration and Naturalization Service, U.S. Dept. of Justice

The Immigration Act of 1990 became law when it was signed by President Bush on Nov. 29, 1990. Bush called the bill the "most comprehensive reform of U.S. immigration laws in 66 years." Most of its provisions amend the Immigration and Nationality Act which remains the basic law. The new law raised the total number of numerically limited immigrants entering the U.S. annually in FY 1992-94 to 700,000 (excluding refugees whose admission numbers are announced annually and some others not subject to limitation). The visas would be distributed as follows:

- 465,000 for family immigrants;
- 55,000 for the spouses and children of aliens legalized under IRCA;
- 140,000 for employment-based immigrants;
- 40,000 for nationals from "adversely affected" countries.

Beginning in FY 1995 the number drops to a minimum of 675,000. These visas would be distributed as follows:

- 480,000 for family immigrants;
- 140,000 for employment based immigrants;
- 55,000 for "diversity immigrants."

Family Immigrants

Fiscal year 1992-94: 465,000 minus the number of "immediate relatives" admitted the previous fiscal year, *plus* any numbers unused by the employment-based preference system. During this period, the number of family-sponsored visas cannot fall below 226,000 (10,000 visas higher than the current allocation). If visa availability dips below this new floor, the shortfall will be made up from the category below.

During this period, 55,000 additional visas will be made available to the spouses and children of aliens legalized under the Immigration Reform and Control Act (IRCA) of 1986.

Fiscal year 1995 and beyond: 480,000 minus the number of "immediate relatives" admitted during the previous fiscal year, plus any unused numbers under the employment-based preference system. That number may not drop below a floor of 226,000. If it does (*as it is certain to*), the "cap" simply gets pierced.

New Family Preference System

First preference—unmarried sons and daughters of U.S. citizens: 23,400 visas plus unused visas from the 4th preference.

Second preference—spouses and unmarried children of Lawful Permanent Residents (LPRs): 114,200 visas, plus any visas available above the floor of 226,000 family preference visas, plus any unused visas from the previous preference.

The category is subdivided as follows: A minimum of 77 percent of the visas allocated to the category goes to the spouses and minor children of LPRs; 75 percent of the visas are issued without regard to per country ceilings; these visas will be distributed in the order in which the petitions were filed; a maximum of 23 percent of the category visa allocation goes to the unmarried sons and daughters of LPRs. This group of visas will continue to be subject to per country ceilings.

Third preference—married sons and daughters of U.S. citizens; 23,400 visas plus unused visas from all earlier preferences.

Fourth preference—brothers and sisters of U.S. citizens: 65,000 plus unused visas from all earlier preferences.

Employment-Based Immigrants

A total of 140,000 plus, beginning in 1994, any unused numbers under the family-sponsored system. These visas would be distributed as follows:

First preference—Priority Workers—28.6 percent of the employment-based limit; 40,040 visas in 1992 plus visas unused by the fourth and fifth employment-based preferences "investors" and "special immigrants". The category is subdivided as follows: extraordinary ability, demonstrated by sustained national or international acclaim, in the sciences, arts, education, business, and athletics. No U.S. employer required;

Outstanding, internationally recognized and with at least 3 years of experience, professors and researchers seeking to enter in senior positions. U.S. employer required; executives and managers of multinationals—requires one year of prior service with the firm during the preceding 3 years. The terms are extensively defined. U.S. employer required.

Second preference—Professionals with advanced degrees and aliens of exceptional ability—28.6 percent of the employment-based limit; 40,040 visas in 1992 plus any unused "priority worker" visas. A U.S. employer and labor certification are required—although the Attorney General can waive both requirements. Members of the professions with advanced degrees or exceptional ability in the sciences, arts, or business. The possession of a degree, certificate, or license is not by itself considered sufficient evidence of exceptional ability.

Third preference—Skilled workers, professionals, and "Other" Workers—40,000 visas plus any visas unused by the 2 previous categories. Requires a U.S. employer and labor certification. Skilled workers must be in an occupation that requires at least 2 years training or experience. Professionals need a Bachelor's degree. "Other" workers refers to unskilled workers. Their numbers are limited to no more than 10,000 visas per year.

Fourth preference—Special immigrants—7.1 percent of the employment-based limit; 9,040 visas in 1992. This category includes ministers of religion and persons working for religious organizations for at least 2 years, foreign medical graduates, employees of the U.S. government abroad including certain employees of the U.S. mission in Hong Kong who file for admission as special immigrants before Jan. 1, 2002, retired employees of international organizations, etc.

Fifth preference—7.1 percent of the employment-based limit; 9,040 employment creation (investor) visas in 1992—7,000 for investors of $1 million in urban areas and 3,000 for investors of no less than $500,000 in rural or high-unemployment areas. The Attorney General may increase the required investment amount up to $3 million for high employment areas. Investment must create employment for at least 10 U.S. workers.

Labor Certification

A pilot program is created for FY 1992-94 giving Dept. of Labor the authority to identify up to 10 "shortage" or "surplus" occupations and make certifications for these occupations. If the occupation is in "shortage," automatic certification would be offered; if the occupation is in "surplus," the employer may still petition for the immigrant but will be required to demonstrate that he/she has undertaken extensive recruitment.

Student Visas

A 3-year program (FY 1992-94) allows foreign students to be employed off-campus for up to 20 hours per week during the school year, and without restrictions when school is out of session. The employment can only come after their first year of school but may be unrelated to their studies.

The employer must attest that he has recruited for U.S. workers for at least 60 days and that he offers both foreign and U.S. workers the actual wage level for the occupation at the place of employment or, if greater, the prevailing wage level for the occupation in the area of employment. If the Secretary of Labor finds the attestation to be a misrepresentation, the employer can be disqualified from employing a foreign student.

Major International Organizations

As of mid-1992

Association of Southeast Asian Nations (ASEAN), was formed in 1967 to promote economic, social, and cultural cooperation and development among the non-communist states of the region. Members in 1992 are Brunei Darussalam, Indonesia, Malaysia, Philippines, Singapore, Thailand. Annual ministerial meetings set policy; a central Secretariat in Jakarta and specialized intergovernmental committees work in trade, transportation, communications, agriculture, science, finance, and culture.

Caribbean Community & Common Market, (Caricom) was established July 4, 1973. Its function is to further co-operation in economics, health, education, culture, science and technology, and tax administration, as well as the co-ordination of foreign policy. Members in 1992 are Antigua, Bahamas, Barbados, Belize, Dominica, Grenada, Guyana, Jamaica, Montserrat, St. Kitts, St. Lucia, St. Vincent, Trinidad & Tobago. Observers are Dominican Republic, Haiti, and Suriname.

Commonwealth of Nations originally called the British Commonwealth of Nations, is an association of nations and dependencies loosely joined by a common interest based on having been parts of the old British Empire. The British monarch is the symbolic head of the Commonwealth.

There are 50 self-governing independent nations in the Commonwealth, plus various colonies and protectorates. As of May 1992, the members were the United Kingdom of Great Britain and Northern Ireland and 16 other nations recognizing the British monarch, represented by a governor-general, as their head of state: Antigua and Barbuda, Australia, Bahamas, Barbados, Belize, Canada, Grenada, Jamaica, Mauritius, New Zealand, Papua New Guinea, St. Kitts-Nevis, St. Lucia, St. Vincent and the Grenadines, Solomon Islands, and Tuvalu (a special member); and 32 countries with their own heads of state: Bangladesh, Botswana, Brunei, Cyprus, Dominica, The Gambia, Ghana, Guyana, India, Kenya, Kiribati, Lesotho, Malawi, Malaysia, The Maldives, Malta, Namibia, Nauru (a special member), Nigeria, Pakistan, Samoa, Seychelles, Sierra Leone, Singapore, Sri Lanka, Swaziland, Tanzania, Tonga, Trinidad and Tobago, Uganda, Vanuatu, Zambia, and Zimbabwe. In addition various Caribbean dependencies take part in certain Commonwealth activities.

The Commonwealth facilitates consultation among member states through meetings of prime ministers and finance ministers, and through a permanent Secretariat. Members consult on economic, scientific, educational, financial, legal, and military matters, and try to coordinate policies.

European Free Trade Association (EFTA), consisting of Austria, Finland, Iceland, Norway, Sweden, and Switzerland. Created Jan. 4, 1960, to gradually reduce customs duties and quantitative restrictions between members on industrial products. By Dec. 31, 1966, all tariffs and quotas had been eliminated. The association entered into free trade agreements with the EC, Jan. 1, 1973. Trade barriers were removed July 1, 1976.

Group of Seven (G-7), organization of the major industrial democracies who meet periodically to discuss world economic issues. Members are Canada, France, Germany, Italy, Japan, UK, and U.S.

International Criminal Police Organization (Interpol), created in 1923 to ensure and promote the widest possible mutual assistance between all police authorities within the limits of the law existing in the different countries and in the spirit of the Universal Declaration of Human Rights. There are 146 members in 1992.

League of Arab States (The Arab League) was created Mar. 22, 1945. Members in 1992 are Algeria, Bahrain, Djibouti, Egypt, Iraq, Jordan, Kuwait, Lebanon, Libya, Mauritania, Morocco, Oman, The Palestine Liberation Org., Qatar, Saudi Arabia, Somalia, Sudan, Syria, Tunisia, United Arab Emirates, Yemen. The League fosters cultural, economic, and communication ties and mediates disputes among the Arab states; it represents Arab states in certain international negotiations, and coordinates a military, economic, and diplomatic offensive against Israel. As a result of Egypt signing a peace treaty with Israel, the League, Mar. 1979, suspended Egypt's membership and transferred the League's headquarters from Cairo to Tunis. Egypt was readmitted to the organization in 1989.

North Atlantic Treaty Org. (NATO) was created by treaty (signed Apr. 4, 1949; in effect Aug. 24, 1949). Members in 1992 include Belgium, Canada, Denmark, France, Germany, Greece, Iceland, Italy, Luxembourg, Netherlands, Norway, Portugal, Spain, Turkey, United Kingdom, and the U.S. The members agreed to settle disputes by peaceful means; to develop their individual and collective capacity to resist armed attack; to regard an attack on one as an attack on all, and to take necessary action to repel an attack under Article 51 of the United Nations Charter.

The NATO structure consists of a Council and a Military Committee of 3 commands (Allied Command Europe, Allied Command Atlantic, Allied Command Channel) and the Canada-U.S. Regional Planning Group.

Following announcement in 1966 of nearly total French withdrawal from the military affairs of NATO, organization hq. moved, 1967, from Paris to Brussels.

At their summit conference in July 1990, members called for a reshaping of the alliance to assure the Soviet Union of their peaceful intentions. The U.S. is planning at least a 50% reduction of its forces in Europe beginning in 1994.

Organization of African Unity (OAU), formed May 25, 1963, by 32 African countries (50 in 1992) to coordinate cultural, political, scientific and economic policies; to end colonialism in Africa; and to promote a common defense of members' independence. It holds annual conferences of heads of state. Hq. is in Addis Ababa, Ethiopia.

Organization of American States (OAS) was formed in Bogota, Colombia, in 1948. Hq. is in Washington, D.C. It has a Permanent Council, Inter-American Economic and Social Council, and Inter-American Council for Education, Science and Culture, a Juridical Committee and a Commission on Human Rights. The Permanent Council can call meetings of foreign ministers to deal with urgent security matters. A General Assembly meets annually. A secretary general and assistant are elected for 5-year terms. There are 35 members, each with one vote in the various organizations: Antigua, Argentina, Bahamas, Barbados, Belize, Bolivia, Brazil, Canada, Chile, Colombia, Costa Rica, Cuba, Dominica, Dominican Republic, Ecuador, El Salvador, Grenada, Guatemala, Guyana, Haiti, Honduras, Jamaica, Mexico, Nicaragua, Panama, Paraguay, Peru, St. Kitts-Nevis, St. Lucia, St. Vincent, Suriname, Trinidad & Tobago, U.S., Uruguay, Venezuela. In 1962, the OAS excluded Cuba from OAS activities but not from membership.

Organization for Economic Cooperation and Development (OECD) was established Sept. 30, 1961 to promote economic and social welfare in member countries, and to stimulate and harmonize efforts on behalf of developing nations. Nearly all the industrialized "free market" countries belong, with Yugoslavia as an associate member. OECD collects and disseminates economic and environmental information. Members in 1992 are: Australia, Austria, Belgium, Canada, Denmark, Finland, France, Germany, Greece, Iceland, Ireland, Italy, Japan, Luxembourg, Netherlands, New Zealand, Norway, Portugal, Spain, Sweden, Switzerland, Turkey, United Kingdom, United States, Yugoslavia (special member). Hq. is in Paris.

Organization of Petroleum Exporting Countries (OPEC) was created Nov. 14, 1960 at Venezuelan initiative. The group attempts to set world oil prices by controlling oil production. It is also involved in advancing members' interests in trade and development dealings with industrialized oil-

(*continued*)

consuming nations. Members in 1992 are Algeria, Ecuador, Gabon, Indonesia, Iran, Iraq, Kuwait, Libya, Nigeria, Qatar, Saudi Arabia, United Arab Emirates, Venezuela.

Commonwealth of Independent States

The Commonwealth of Independent States (CIS) was created Dec. 25, 1991 upon the disbanding of the Soviet Union. It is made up of 11 of the 12 former Soviet Constituent republics (Georgia declined to join). Members are Armenia, Azerbaijan, Belarus, Kazakh, Kirgizstan, Moldova, Russia, Tajikistan, Turkmenistan, Ukraine, and Uzbek. The commonwealth is not in itself a state, but an alliance of fully independent states. Commonwealth policy is set through coordinating bodies such as a Council of Heads of State and Council of Heads of Government. The capital of the commonwealth is Minsk, Belarus.

The European Community

The European Community (EC) is the collective designation of three organizations with common membership: the European Economic Community (Common Market), the European Coal and Steel Community, and the European Atomic Energy Community (Euratom). The 12 full members are: Belgium, Denmark, France, Germany, Greece, Ireland, Italy, Luxembourg, Netherlands, Portugal, Spain, United Kingdom. Some 60 nations in Africa, the Caribbean, and the Pacific are affiliated under the Lomé Convention.

A merger of the 3 communities executives went into effect July 1, 1967, though the component organizations date back to 1951 and 1958. The Council of Ministers, the Commission of the European Communities, the European Parliament, and the European Court of Justice comprise the permanent structure. The communities aim to integrate their economies, coordinate social developments, and bring about political union of the democratic states of Europe. There is a single passport for EC citizens and no restrictions on the movement of tourists or workers within the Community. There are also common agricultural, fisheries, and nuclear research policies.

The members have agreed that a single European market which will remove all barriers to free trade and free movement of capital and people will take effect beginning in 1993.

Leaders of the 12 European Community nations met Dec. 9–11, 1991 in Maastricht, the Netherlands. The treaties on monetary union and political union and accompanying protocols agreed by the leaders:

- Committed the EC to launching a common currency for at least some nations by 1999. Britain and Denmark were allowed to "opt out" of joining.
- Sought to establish common foreign policies for the 12 members.
- Laid the groundwork for a common defense policy under the Western European Union.
- Expanded the policy issues in which the EC would have a voice.
- Gave the EC a leading role in social policy. Britain was not included in this plan.
- Pledged increased aid for the community's four poorest nations, Ireland, Greece, Spain and Portugal.
- Slightly increased the powers of the 518-member European Parliament.

Danish voters, June 2, 1992, rejected the European Community's Treaty on European Union agreed at the 1991 EC summit in Maastricht. The result of the Danish referendum was a serious blow for the Maastricht pact because the treaty required ratification by all 12 EC member nations before it could go into effect. During 1992, there was growing opposition to the pact in Great Britain and Germany.

United Nations

The 47th regular session of the United Nations General Assembly opened in September, 1992.

UN headquarters are in New York, N.Y., between First Ave. and Roosevelt Drive and E. 42d St. and E. 48th St. The General Assembly Bldg., Secretariat, Conference and Library bldgs. are interconnected.

A European office at Geneva includes Secretariat and agency staff members. Other offices of UN bodies and related organizations with a staff of some 23,000 from some 150 countries are scattered throughout the world.

The UN has a post office originating its own stamps.

Proposals to establish an organization of nations for maintenance of world peace led to the United Nations Conference on International Organization at San Francisco, Apr. 25-June 26, 1945, where the charter of the United Nations was drawn up. It was signed June 26 by 50 nations, and by Poland, one of the original 51, on Oct. 15, 1945. The charter came into effect Oct. 24, 1945, upon ratification by the permanent members of the Security Council and a majority of other signatories.

Purposes: To maintain international peace and security; to develop friendly relations among nations; to achieve international cooperation in solving economic, social, cultural, and humanitarian problems and in promoting respect for human rights and fundamental freedoms; to be a center for harmonizing the actions of nations in attaining these common ends.

Roster of the United Nations

(As of Sept. 1992)

The 178 members of the United Nations, with the years in which they became members.

Member	Year	Member	Year	Member	Year	Member	Year
Afghanistan	1946	Bahamas	1973	Bosnia and Herzegovina	1992	Canada	1945
Albania	1955	Bahrain	1971	Botswana	1966	Cape Verde	1975
Algeria	1962	Bangladesh	1974	Brazil	1945	Central Afr. Rep.	1960
Angola	1976	Barbados	1966	Brunei	1984	Chad	1960
Antigua and Barbuda	1981	Belarus	1945	Bulgaria	1955	Chile	1945
Argentina	1945	Belgium	1945	Burkina Faso	1960	China[4]	1945
Armenia	1992	Belize	1981	Burundi	1962	Colombia	1945
Australia	1945	Benin	1960	Cambodia	1955	Comoros	1975
Austria	1955	Bhutan	1971	Cameroon	1960	Congo	1960
Azerbaijan	1992	Bolivia	1945			Costa Rica	1945

(continued)

Member	Year
Côte d'Ivoire	1960
Croatia	1992
Cuba	1945
Cyprus	1960
Czechoslovakia	1945
Denmark	1945
Djibouti	1977
Dominica	1978
Dominican Rep.	1945
Ecuador	1945
Egypt[2]	1945
El Salvador	1945
Equatorial Guinea	1968
Ethiopia	1945
Estonia	1991
Fiji	1970
Finland	1955
France	1945
Gabon	1960
Gambia	1965
Germany	1973
Ghana	1957
Greece	1945
Grenada	1974
Guatemala	1945
Guinea	1958
Guinea-Bissau	1974
Guyana	1966
Haiti	1945
Honduras	1945
Hungary	1955
Iceland	1946
India	1945
Indonesia[6]	1950
Iran	1945
Iraq	1945

Member	Year
Ireland	1955
Israel	1949
Italy	1955
Jamaica	1962
Japan	1956
Jordan	1955
Kazakhstan	1992
Kenya	1963
Korea, N.	1991
Korea, S.	1991
Kuwait	1963
Kyrgyzstan	1992
Laos	1955
Latvia	1991
Lebanon	1945
Lesotho	1966
Liberia	1945
Libya	1955
Liechtenstein	1990
Lithuania	1991
Luxembourg	1945
Madagascar (Malagasy)	1960
Malawi	1964
Malaysia[1]	1957
Maldives	1965
Mali	1960
Malta	1964
Marshall Islands	1991
Mauritania	1961
Mauritius	1968
Mexico	1945
Micronesia	1991
Moldova	1992
Mongolia	1961
Morocco	1956
Mozambique	1975

Member	Year
Myanmar (Burma)	1948
Namibia	1990
Nepal	1955
Netherlands	1945
New Zealand	1945
Nicaragua	1945
Niger	1960
Nigeria	1960
Norway	1945
Oman	1971
Pakistan	1947
Panama	1945
Papua New Guinea	1975
Paraguay	1945
Peru	1945
Philippines	1945
Poland	1945
Portugal	1955
Qatar	1971
Romania	1955
Russia	1945
Rwanda	1962
Saint Christopher & Nevis	1983
Saint Lucia	1979
Saint Vincent and the Grenadines	1980
Samoa (Western)	1976
San Marino	1992
Sao Tome e Principe	1975
Saudi Arabia	1945
Senegal	1960
Seychelles	1976
Sierra Leone	1961
Singapore[1]	1965

Member	Year
Slovenia	1992
Solomon Islands	1978
Somalia	1960
South Africa[5]	1945
Spain	1955
Sri Lanka	1955
Sudan	1956
Suriname	1975
Swaziland	1968
Sweden	1946
Syria[2]	1945
Tajikistan	1992
Tanzania[3]	1961
Thailand	1946
Togo	1960
Trinidad & Tobago	1962
Tunisia	1956
Turkey	1945
Turkmenistan	1992
Uganda	1962
Ukraine	1945
United Arab Emirates	1971
United Kingdom	1945
United States	1945
Uruguay	1945
Uzbekistan	1992
Vanuatu	1981
Venezuela	1945
Vietnam	1977
Yemen	1947
Yugoslavia	1945
Zaire	1960
Zambia	1964
Zimbabwe	1980

(1) Malaya joined the UN in 1957. In 1963, its name was changed to Malaysia following the accession of Singapore, Sabah, and Sarawak. Singapore became an independent UN member in 1965. (2) Egypt and Syria were original members of the UN. In 1958, the United Arab Republic was established by a union of Egypt and Syria and continued as a single member of the UN. In 1961, Syria resumed its separate membership. (3) Tanganyika was a member of the United Nations from 1961 and Zanzibar was a member from 1963. Following the ratification in 1964 of Articles of Union between Tanganyika and Zanzibar, the United Republic of Tanganyika and Zanzibar continued as a single member of the United Nations, later changing its name to United Republic of Tanzania. (4) The General Assembly voted in 1971 to expel the Chinese government on Taiwan and admit the Peking government in its place. (5) The General Assembly rejected the credentials of the South African delegates in 1974, and suspended the country from the Assembly. (6) Indonesia withdrew from the UN in 1965 and rejoined in 1966.

United Nations Secretaries General

Year	Secretary, Nation
1946	Trygve Lie, Norway
1953	Dag Hammarskjold, Sweden
1961	U Thant, Burma
1972	Kurt Waldheim, Austria
1982	Javier Perez de Cuellar, Peru
1992	Boutros Boutros-Ghali, Egypt

U.S. Representatives to the United Nations

The U.S. Representative to the United Nations is the Chief of the U.S. Mission to the United Nations in New York and holds the rank and status of Ambassador Extraordinary and Plenipotentiary.

Year	Representative
1946	Edward R. Stettinius Jr.
1946	Herschel V. Johnson (act.)
1947	Warren R. Austin
1953	Henry Cabot Lodge Jr.
1960	James J. Wadsworth
1961	Adlai E. Stevenson
1965	Arthur J. Goldberg
1968	George W. Ball
1968	James Russell Wiggins
1969	Charles W. Yost
1971	George Bush
1973	John A. Scali
1975	Daniel P. Moynihan
1976	William W. Scranton
1977	Andrew Young
1979	Donald McHenry
1981	Jeane J. Kirkpatrick
1985	Vernon A. Walters
1989	Thomas R. Pickering

Visitors to the United Nations

United Nations headquarters is open to the public every day of the year except Christmas and New Year's Day. The public entrance is at 46th Street and First Avenue and opens at 9 a.m.

Guided tours begin from the main lobby of the General Assembly building and are given approximately every half hour from 9:15 a.m. to 4:45 p.m. daily. The tours last about one hour. Tours in languages other than English may be arranged.

Groups of 15 or more persons should make arrangements as far in advance as possible by writing to the Group Program Unit, Visitors' Service, Room GA-56, United Nations, New York, NY 10017, or telephone (212) 963-7713. Children under 5 are not permitted on tours.

Organization of the United Nations

The text of the UN Charter, and further information, may be obtained from the Office of Public Information, United Nations, New York, NY 10017.

General Assembly. The General Assembly is composed of representatives of all the member nations. Each nation is entitled to one vote.

The General Assembly meets in regular annual sessions and in special session when necessary. Special sessions are convoked by the Secretary General at the request of the Security Council or of a majority of the members of the UN.

On important questions a two-thirds majority of members present and voting is required; on other questions a simple majority is sufficient.

The General Assembly must approve the budget and apportion expenses among members. A member in arrears will have no vote if the amount of arrears equals or exceeds the amount of the contributions due for the preceeding two full years.

Security Council. The Security Council consists of 15 members, 5 with permanent seats. The remaining 10 are elected for 2-year terms by the General Assembly; they are not eligible for immediate reelection.

Permanent members of the Council: China, France, Russia, United Kingdom, United States.

Non-permanent members are Austria, Belgium, Ecuador, India, and Zimbabwe (until Dec. 31, 1992). Cape Verde, Hungary, Japan, Morocco, Venezuela (until Dec. 31, 1993).

The Security Council has the primary responsibility within the UN for maintaining international peace and security. The Council may investigate any dispute that threatens international peace and security.

Any member of the UN at UN headquarters may participate in its discussions and a nation not a member of UN may appear if it is a party to a dispute.

Decisions on procedural questions are made by an affirmative vote of 9 members. On all other matters the affirmative vote of 9 members must include the concurring votes of all permanent members; it is this clause which gives rise to the so-called "veto." A party to a dispute must refrain from voting.

The Security Council directs the various truce supervisory forces deployed throughout the world.

Economic and Social Council. The Economic and Social Council consists of 54 members elected by the General Assembly for 3-year terms of office. The council is responsible under the General Assembly for carrying out the functions of the United Nations with regard to international economic, social, cultural, educational, health and related matters. The council meets usually twice a year.

Trusteeship Council. The administration of trust territories is under UN supervision. The only remaining trust territory is Palau, administered by the U.S.

Secretariat. The Secretary General is the chief administrative officer of the UN. He may bring to the attention of the Security Council any matter that threatens international peace. He reports to the General Assembly.

Budget: The General Assembly approved a total budget for 1992-93 of $2.36 billion.

International Court of Justice (World Court). The International Court of Justice is the principal judicial organ of the United Nations. All members are *ipso facto* parties to the statute of the Court. Other states may become parties to the Court's statute.

The jurisdiction of the Court comprises cases which the parties submit to it and matters especially provided for in the charter or in treaties. The Court gives advisory opinions and renders judgments. Its decisions are only binding between the parties concerned and in respect to a particular dispute. If any party to a case fails to heed a judgment, the other party may have recourse to the Security Council.

The 15 judges are elected for 9-year terms by the General Assembly and the Security Council. Retiring judges are eligible for re-election. The Court remains permanently in session, except during vacations. All questions are decided by majority. The Court sits in The Hague, Netherlands.

Specialized and Related Agencies

These agencies are autonomous, with their own memberships and organs which have a functional relationship or working agreement with the UN (headquarters.)

Food & Agriculture Org. (FAO) aims to increase production from farms, forests, and fisheries; improve distribution, marketing, and nutrition; better conditions for rural people. (Viale delle Terme di Caracalla, 00100 Rome, Italy.)

General Agreement on Tariffs and Trade (GATT) is the only treaty setting rules for world trade. Provides a forum for settling trade disputes and negotiating trade liberalization. (Centre William Rappard, 154 rue de Lausanne, 1211 Geneva 21, Switzerland.)

International Atomic Energy Agency (IAEA) aims to promote the safe, peaceful uses of atomic energy. (Vienna International Centre, PO Box 100, A-1400, Vienna, Austria.)

International Bank for Reconstruction and Development (IBRD) (World Bank) provides loans and technical assistance for economic development projects in developing member countries; encourages cofinancing for projects from other public and private sources. **International Development Association (IDA),** an affiliate of the Bank, provides funds for development projects on concessionary terms to the poorer developing member countries. (both 1818 H St., NW, Washington, DC 20433.) **International Finance Corporation (IFC)** an affiliate of the Bank, promotes the growth of the private sector in developing member countries; encourages the development of local capital markets; stimulates the international flow of private capital. (1818 H St., NW, Washington, DC 20433.)

International Civil Aviation Org. (ICAO) promotes international civil aviation standards and regulations. (1000 Sherbrooke St. W., Montreal, Quebec, Canada H3A 2R2.)

International Fund for Agricultural Development (IFAD) aims to mobilize funds for agricultural and rural projects in developing countries. (107 Via del Serafico, Rome, Italy.)

International Labor Org. (ILO) aims to promote employment; improve labor conditions and living standards. (4 route de Morillons, CH-1211, Geneva 22, Switzerland.)

International Maritime Org. (IMO) aims to promote cooperation on technical matters affecting international shipping. (4 Albert Embankment, London, SE1 7SR, England.)

International Monetary Fund (IMF) aims to promote international monetary co-operation and currency stabilization; expansion of international trade. (700 19th St., NW, Washington, DC, 20431.)

International Telecommunication Union (ITU) sets up international regulations of radio, telegraph, telephone and space radio-communications. Allocates radio frequencies. (Place des Nations, 1211 Geneva 20, Switzerland.)

United Nations Educational, Scientific, & Cultural Org. (UNESCO) aims to promote collaboration among nations through education, science, and culture. The U.S. withdrew from this organization in 1985 because of UNESCO's anti-Western bias. (9 Place de Fontenoy, 75700 Paris, France.)

United Nations Children's Fund (UNICEF) provides aid and development assistance to children and mothers in developing countries. (1 UN Plaza, New York, NY 10017.)

United Nations High Commissioner for Refugees (UNHCR) provides essential assistance for refugees. (Place des Nations, 1211 Geneva 10, Switzerland.)

(continued)

Universal Postal Union (UPU) aims to perfect postal services and promote international collaboration. (Weltpoststrasse 4, 3000 Berne, 15 Switzerland.)

World Health Org. (WHO) aims to aid the attainment of the highest possible level of health. (1211 Geneva 27, Switzerland.)

World Intellectual Property Organization (WIPO) seeks to protect, through international cooperation, literary, industrial, scientific, and artistic works. (34, Chemin des Colom Bettes, 1211 Geneva, Switzerland.)

World Meteorological Org. (WMO) aims to co-ordinate and improve world meteorological work. (Case Postale 5, CH-1211, Geneva 20, Switzerland.)

Ambassadors and Envoys

As of mid-1992

The address of U.S. embassies abroad is the appropriate foreign capital. The U.S. does not have diplomatic relations with the following countries: Angola,[1] Cambodia,[2] Taiwan,[3] Cuba,[4] Iran,[5] Libya,[6] Vietnam,[2] N. Korea, Iraq,[7] Somalia.[8] There are informal relations with Bhutan and Vanuatu. Ambassadors to former Yugoslavia Republics not named at press time.

Countries	Envoys from United States	Envoys to United States
Afghanistan	Vacancy	Abdul Ghafoor Jawshan, Chargé
Albania	William E. Ryerson, Amb.	Arben Sotir Teta, Chargé
Algeria	Mary Ann Casey, Amb.	Nourredine Y. Zerhouni, Amb.
Antigua & Barbuda	Bryant J. Salter, Amb.	Patrick A. Lewis
Argentina	Terence A. Todman, Amb.	Carlos Ortiz de Rosas, Amb.
Armenia	Thomas L. Price, Chargé	Vacancy
Australia	Melvin F. Sembler, Amb.	Michael J. Cook, Amb.
Austria	Roy Michael Huffington, Amb.	Friedrich Hoess, Amb.
Azerbaijan	Richard Miles, Chargé	Vacancy
Bahamas	Chic Hecht, Amb.	Margaret E. McDonald, Amb.
Bahrain	Charles W. Hostler, Amb.	Abdul Al-Khalifa, Amb.
Bangladesh	William B. Milam, Amb.	Abdul Ahsan, Amb.
Barbados	C. Philip Hughes, Amb.	Rudi V. Webster, Amb.
Belarus	David Swartz, Chargé	Serguei Martynov, Chargé
Belgium	Bruce S. Gelb, Amb.	Jean Cassiers, Amb.
Belize	Eugene L. Scassa, Amb.	James V. Hyde, Amb.
Benin	Harriet W. Isom, Amb.	Candide Pierre Ahouansou, Amb.
Bolivia	Charles R. Bowers, Amb.	Jose Crespo-Velasco, Amb.
Botswana	David Passage, Amb.	Botsweletse K. Sebele, Amb.
Brazil	Richard H. Melton, Amb.	Rubens Ricupero, Amb.
Brunei	Vacancy	D.H. Mohammad Kassim, Amb.
Bulgaria	H. Kenneth Hill, Amb.	Ognian R. Pishev, Amb.
Burkina Faso	Edward P. Byrnn, Amb.	Paul-Désiré Kabore, Amb.
Burundi	Cynthia S. Perry, Amb.	Julien Kavakure, Amb.
Cameroon	Frances D. Cook, Amb.	Paul Pondi, Amb.
Canada	Peter B. Teeley, Amb.	Derek H. Burney, Amb.
Cape Verde	Francis T. McNamara, Amb.	Carlos Silva, Amb.
Central African Rep.	Daniel H. Simpson, Amb.	Jean-Pierre Sohahong-Kombet, Amb.
Chad	William W. Bogosian, Amb.	E. Acheikh ibn Oumar, Amb.
Chile	Curtis W. Kamman, Amb.	Patricio Silva, Amb.
China	J. Stapleton Roy, Amb.	Zhu Qizhen, Amb.
Colombia	Morris D. Busby, Amb.	Jamie Garcia-Parra, Amb.
Comoros	Kenneth N. Peltier, Amb.	Amini Ali Moumin, Amb.
Congo	James D. Phillips, Amb.	Roger Issombo, Amb.
Costa Rica	Luis Guinot Jr., Amb.	Gonzalo Facio, Amb.
Côte d'Ivoire	Kenneth L. Brown, Amb.	Charles Gomis, Amb.
Cyprus	Robert E. Lamb, Amb.	Michael E. Sherifis, Amb.
Czechoslovakia	Shirley Temple Black, Amb.	Rita Klimova, Amb.
Denmark	Richard B. Stone, Amb.	Peter P. Dyvig, Amb.
Djibouti	Charles Baquet, 3d, Amb.	Roble Olhale, Amb.
Dominica	C. Philip Hughes, Amb.	Edward I. Watty, Amb.
Dominican Republic	Robert S. Pastorino, Amb.	Jose del Carmen Ariza, Amb.
Ecuador	Vacancy	Jaime Moncayo, Amb.
Egypt	Robert H. Pelletreau Jr., Amb.	El Sayed A. R. El Reedy, Amb.
El Salvador	William Dieterich, Chargé	Miguel A. Salaverria, Amb.
Equatorial Guinea	John E. Bennett, Amb.	Damaso Obiang Ndong, Amb.
Estonia	Robert C. Frasure, Amb.	Ernst Jaakson, Amb.
Ethiopia	Marc Baas, Chargé	Berhane Gebre-Chirstos, Amb.
Fiji	Evelyn I.H. Teegen, Amb.	Pita Kewa Nacuva, Amb.
Finland	John H. Kelly, Amb.	Jukka Valtasaari, Amb.
France	Walter J. P. Curley, Amb.	Jacques Andreani, Amb.
Gabon	Keith L. Wauchope, Amb.	Alexandre Sambat, Amb.
Gambia, The	Arlene Render, Amb.	Ousman A. Sallah, Amb.
Georgia	Carey Cavanaugh, Chargé	Vacancy
Germany	Robert M. Kimmitt, Amb.	Juergen Ruhfus, Amb.
Ghana	Raymond C. Ewing, Amb.	Joseph Abbey, Amb.
Greece	Michael G. Sotirhos, Amb.	Christos Zacharakis, Amb.
Grenada	C. Philip Hughes, Amb.	Denneth Modeste, Amb.
Guatemala	Thomas F. Stroock, Amb.	Juan Jose Caso-Fanjul, Amb.
Guinea	Dane F. Smith, Amb.	Vacancy
Guinea-Bissau	William L. Jacobsen Jr., Amb.	Alfredo Lopes Cabral, Amb.
Guyana	George F. Jones, Amb.	Cedric H. Grant, Amb.
Haiti	Alvin P. Adams Jr., Amb.	Jean Casimir, Amb.
Honduras	Cresencio S. Arcos, Amb.	Jorge Hernandez-Alcerro, Amb.
Hungary	Charles H. Thomas, Amb.	Pal Tar, Amb.
Iceland	Janet Andres, Chargé	Tomas Tomasson, Amb.
India	William Clark Jr., Amb.	Abid Hussain, Amb.
Indonesia	John C. Monjo, Amb.	Abdul Rachman Ramly, Amb.

Countries	Envoys from United States	Envoys to United States
Ireland	William FitzGerald, Amb.	Dermot A. Gallagher, Amb.
Israel	William C. Harrop, Amb.	Zalman Shoval, Amb.
Italy	Peter F. Secchia, Amb.	Boris Biancheri, Amb.
Jamaica	Glen A. Holden, Amb.	Richard L. Bernal, Amb.
Japan	Michael H. Armacost, Amb.	Takakazu Kuriyama, Amb.
Jordan	Roger G. Harrison, Amb.	Hussein A. Hammami, Amb.
Kazakh	William Courtney, Chargé	Vacancy
Kenya	Smith Hempstone Jr., Amb.	Denis D. Afande, Amb.
Kirgizstan	Edward Hurwitz, Chargé	Vacancy
Kiribati	Evelyn I.H. Teegen, Amb.	Vacancy
Korea, South	Donald P. Gregg, Amb.	Hong-Choo Hyun, Amb.
Kuwait	Edward Gnehm, Amb.	Shaikh S. N. Al-Sabah, Amb.
Laos	Charles B. Salmon Jr., Amb.	Linthong Phetsavan, Chargé
Latvia	Ints M. Silins, Amb.	Anatol Dinbergs, Amb.
Lebanon	Ryan C. Crocker, Amb.	Vacancy
Lesotho	Leonard H.O. Spearman, Amb.	Tseliso Thamae, Amb.
Liberia	Peter J. de Vos, Amb.	Eugenia A. Wordsworth-Stevenson, Amb.
Lithuania	Darryl N. Johnson, Amb.	Stasys Lozoraitis Jr., Amb.
Luxembourg	Edward M. Rowell, Amb.	Alphonse Berns, Amb.
Madagascar	Howard K. Walker, Amb.	Pierrot J. Rajaonarivelo, Amb.
Malawi	Michael T. F. Pistor, Amb.	Robert Mbaya, Amb.
Malaysia	Paul M. Cleveland, Amb.	Dato Abdul Majid, Amb.
Mali	Herbert D. Gelber, Amb.	Mohamed A. Toure, Amb.
Malta	Sally J. Novetzke, Amb.	Borg Olivier de Puget, Amb.
Marshall Islands	William Bodde Jr., Amb.	Wilfred Kendall, Amb.
Mauritania	Gordon S. Brown, Amb.	Mohammed Fall Ainini, Amb.
Mauritius	Penne Percy Korth, Amb.	Chitmansing Jesseramsing, Amb.
Mexico	John Negroponte, Amb.	Gustavo Petricioli, Amb.
Micronesia	Aurelia E. Brazeal, Amb.	Jesse B. Marehalau, Amb.
Moldova	Howard Steers, Chargé	Vacancy
Mongolia	Joesph E. Lake, Amb.	Luvsandort Dawagiv, Amb.
Morocco	Frederick Vreeland, Amb.	Mohamed Belkhayat, Amb.
Mozambique	Townsend B. Friedman Jr., Amb.	Hipolito Patricio, Amb.
Myanmar	Vacancy	U Thaung, Amb.
Namibia	Genta Hawkins Holmes, Amb.	Tuliameni Kalomoh, Amb.
Nauru	Melvin F. Sembler, Amb.	Vacancy
Nepal	Julia Chang Bloch, Amb.	Yog Prasad Upadhyay, Amb.
Netherlands	C. Howard Wilkins Jr., Amb.	Johan H. Meesman, Amb.
New Zealand	Della M. Newman, Amb.	Denis B.G. McLean, Amb.
Nicaragua	Ronald D. Godard, Chargé	Ernesto Palizio, Amb.
Niger	Jennifer C. Ward, Amb.	Adam Illo, Chargé
Nigeria	Lannon Walker, Amb.	Zubair Kazaure, Amb.
Norway	Loret Miller Ruppe, Amb.	Kjeld Vibe, Amb.
Oman	Richard W. Boehm, Amb.	Awadh Bader Al-Shanfari, Amb.
Pakistan	Nicholas Platt, Amb.	Syeda A. Hussain, Amb.
Panama	Deane R. Hinton, Amb.	Jaime F. Boyd, Amb.
Papua New Guinea	Robert W. Farrand, Amb.	Margaret Taylor, Amb.
Paraguay	Jon David Glassman, Amb.	Juan E. Aguirre, Amb.
Peru	Anthony C.E. Quainton, Amb.	Ricardo Mac Lean, Amb.
Philippines	Frank C. Wisner, 3d, Amb.	Emmanuel Pelaez, Amb.
Poland	Thomas W. Simons Jr., Amb.	Kazimierz Dziewanowski, Amb.
Portugal	Edward Ellis Briggs, Amb.	Francisco Knopfli, Amb.
Qatar	Mark G. Hambley, Amb.	Hamad A. Al-Kawari, Amb.
Romania	John R. Davis Jr., Amb.	Aurel-Dragos Munteanu, Amb.
Russia	Robert S. Strauss, Amb.	Vladimir P. Lukin
Rwanda	Robert A. Flaten, Amb.	Aloys Uwimana, Amb.
St. Kitts & Nevis	C. Philip Hughes, Amb.	Aubrey Hart, Chargé
St. Lucia	C. Philip Hughes, Amb.	Joseph E. Edmunds, Amb.
St. Vincent and The Grenadines	C. Philip Hughes, Amb.	Kingsley C.A. Layne, Amb.
Sao Tome and Principe	Keith L. Wauchope, Amb.	Joaquim R. Branco, Amb.
Saudi Arabia	Charles W. Freeman Jr., Amb.	Bandar Bin Sultan, Amb.
Senegal	Katherine Shirley, Amb.	Ibra Deguene Ka, Amb.
Seychelles	Richard W. Carlson, Amb.	Marc Marengo, Chargé
Sierra Leone	Johnny Young, Amb.	William Wright, Chargé
Singapore	Robert D. Orr, Amb.	S.R. Nathan, Amb.
Solomon Islands	Robert W. Farrand, Amb.	Francis Bugotu, Amb.
South Africa	William L. Swing, Amb.	Harry H. Schwarz, Amb.
Spain	Joseph Zappala, Amb.	Jaime de Ojeda, Amb.
Sri Lanka	Marion V. Creekmore Jr., Amb.	W. Susanta de Alwis, Amb.
Sudan	James R. Cheek, Amb.	Abdalla Ahmed Abdalla, Amb.
Suriname	John P. Leonard, Amb.	Willem A. Udenhout, Amb.
Swaziland	Stephen H. Rogers, Amb.	Absalom V. Mamba, Amb.
Sweden	Charles E. Redman, Amb.	Anders I. Thunborg, Amb.
Switzerland	Joseph B. Gildenhorn, Amb.	Edouard Brunner, Amb.
Syria	Christopher W. S. Ross, Amb.	Walid Al-Moualem, Amb.
Tajikistan	Stanley Escudero, Chargé	Vacancy
Tanzania	Edward DeJarnette Jr., Amb.	Charles M. Nyirabu, Amb.
Thailand	David F. Lambertson, Amb.	M. L. B. Kasemeri, Amb.
Togo	Harmon E. Kirby, Amb.	Ellom-Kodjo Schupplus, Amb.
Tonga	Evelyn I.H. Teegen, Amb.	Siosaia Ma'Ulupekotova, Tuita, Amb.
Trinidad and Tobago	Sally G. Cowal, Amb.	Shastri Ali, Chargé
Tunisia	John T. McCarthy, Amb.	Ismail Khelil, Amb.
Turkey	Richard C. Barkley, Amb.	Nuzhet Kandemir, Amb.
Turkmenistan	Jeff White, Chargé	Vacancy
Tuvalu	Evelyn I.H. Teegen, Amb.	Vacancy
Uganda	Johnnie Carson, Amb.	Stephen K. Katenta-Apuli, Amb.

(continued)

Countries	Envoys from United States	Envoys to United States
Ukraine	Jon Gunderson, Chargé	Oleh H. Bilorus, Amb.
United Arab Emirates	Edward S. Walker, Amb.	Mohammad ben Hussein Al-Shaali, Amb.
United Kingdom	Raymond G.H. Seitz, Amb.	Robin R. Renwick, Amb.
Uruguay	Richard C. Brown, Amb.	Eduardo MacGillycuddy
Uzbek	Michael Mozur, Chargé	Vacancy
Vatican	Thomas P. Melady, Amb.	Agostino Cacciavillan, Pro-Nuncio
Venezuela	Michael M. Skol	Simon A. Consalvi, Amb.
Western Samoa	Della Newman, Amb.	Tuaopepe F. Wendt, Amb.
Yemen	Arthur H. Hughes, Amb.	Mohsin A. Alaini, Amb.
Yugoslavia[8]	Warren Zimmerman, Amb.	Dzevad Mujezinovic, Amb.
Zaire	Melissa F. Wells, Amb.	Tatanee Manata, Amb.
Zambia	Gordon L. Streeb, Amb.	Vacancy
Zimbabwe	Edward G. Lanpher	Stanislaus G. Chigwedere, Amb.

Special Missions

U.S. Mission to North Atlantic Treaty Organization, Brussels—William H. Taft 4th
U.S. Mission to the European Communities, Brussels—Vacancy
U.S. Mission to the United Nations, New York—Thomas P. Pickering, Amb.
U.S. Mission to the European Office of the UN, Geneva—Morris B. Abram, Amb.
U.S. Mission to the Organization for Economic Cooperation and Development, Paris—Alan P. Larson, Amb.
U.S. Mission to the Organization of American States, Washington—Luigi R. Einaudi, Amb.

(1) Post closed in 1975. (2) U.S. embassy closed in 1975. (3) U.S. severed relations in 1978; unofficial relations are maintained. (4) Relations severed in 1961; limited ties restored in 1977. (5) U.S. severed relations on Apr. 7, 1980. (6) Embassy closed, May 2, 1980. U.S. closed the Libyan mission, May 6, 1981. (7) Operations temporarily suspended. (8) Embassy evacuated Jan. 5, 1991.

Country Codes for Direct Dial Calling From the U.S.

Country	Code	Country	Code	Country	Code
Algeria	213	Greenland	299	Oman	968
American Samoa	684	Grenada	809*	Pakistan	92
Andorra	33	Guadeloupe	590	Panama	507
Anguilla	809*	Guam	671	Papua/New Guinea	675
Antigua	809*	Guantanamo	53	Paraguay	595
Argentina	54	Guatemala	502	Peru	51
Aruba	297	Guinea	224	Philippines	63
Ascension Island	247	Guyana	592	Poland	48
Australia	61	Haiti	509	Portugal	351
Austria	43	Honduras	504	Qatar	974
Bahamas	809*	Hong Kong	852	Reunion Island	262
Bahrain	973	Hungary	36	Romania	40
Bangladesh	880	Iceland	354	Russia (Moscow)	7
Barbados	809*	India	91	Rwanda	250
Belgium	32	Indonesia	62	Saipan	670
Belize	501	Iran	98	San Marino	39
Benin	229	Iraq	964	Saudi Arabia	966
Bermuda	809*	Ireland	353	Senegal	221
Bolivia	591	Israel	972	Seychelles Islands	248
Botswana	267	Italy	39	Sierra Leone	232
Brazil	55	Jamaica	809*	Singapore	65
British Virgin Islands	809*	Japan	81	Solomon Island	677
Brunei	673	Jordan	962	South Africa	27
Bulgaria	359	Kenya	254	Spain	34
Burkina Faso	226	Kiribati	686	Sri Lanka	94
Cameroon	237	Korea	82	St. Kitts	809*
Canada	Use Area Codes	Kuwait	965	St. Lucia	809*
Cape Verde Islands	238	Lesotho	266	St. Pierre & Miquelon	508
Cayman Islands	809*	Liberia	231	St. Vincent	809*
Chile	56	Libya	218	Suriname	597
China	86	Liechtenstein	41	Swaziland	268
Colombia	57	Luxembourg	352	Sweden	46
Congo	242	Macao	853	Switzerland	41
Costa Rica	506	Malawi	265	Syria	963
Cote d'Ivoire	225	Malaysia	60	Taiwan	886
Cyprus	357	Maldives	960	Tanzania	255
Czechoslovakia	42	Mali Republic	223	Thailand	66
Denmark	45	Malta	356	Togo	228
Djibouti	253	Marshall Islands	692	Tonga	676
Dominica	809*	Mauritius	230	Trinidad & Tobago	809*
Dominican Republic	809*	Mexico	52	Tunisia	216
Ecuador	593	Micronesia	691	Turkey	90
Egypt	20	Monaco	33	Turks & Caicos Islands	809*
El Salvador	503	Montserrat	809*	Uganda	256
Ethiopia	251	Morocco	212	United Arab Emirates	971
Faeroe Islands	298	Namibia	264	United Kingdom	44
Fiji Islands	679	Nauru	674	Uruguay	598
Finland	358	Nepal	977	Vatican City	39
France	33	Netherlands	31	Venezuela	58
French Antilles	596	Netherlands Antilles	599	Western Samoa	685
French Guiana	594	Nevis	809*	Yemen Arab Republic	967
French Polynesia	689	New Caledonia	687	Yugoslavia	38
Gabon	241	New Zealand	64	Zaire	243
Gambia	220	Nicaragua	505	Zambia	260
Germany	49	Niger	227	Zimbabwe	263
Ghana	233	Nigeria	234		
Gibraltar	350	Norway	47		
Greece	30				

* Follow Domestic Dialing instructions: dial "1" + 809 + number you're calling.

U.S. Aid to Foreign Nations in 1991

Source: Bureau of Economic Analysis, U.S. Dept. of Commerce

Figures are in millions of dollars. (*Less than $500,000.) Data include military supplies and services furnished under the Foreign Assistance Act and direct Defense Department appropriations, and include credits extended to private entities.

Net grants and credits take into account all known returns to the U.S., including reverse grants, returns of grants, and payments of principal. Also incl. are contributions received from coalition partners for Persian Gulf operations. A minus sign (–) indicates that the total of these returns is greater than the total of grants or credits. Nations with net grant or credit under $2 mln. are included with "Other and Unspecified."

Other assistance represents the transfer of U.S. farm products in exchange for foreign currencies, less the government's disbursements of such currencies as grants, credits, or for purchases.

Amounts do not include investments in the following: Asian Development Bank, $146 mln.; Inter-American Development Bank, $74 mln.; International Development Assn., $1.0 bln.; International Bank for Reconstruction and Development, $72 mln.; African Development Fund, $78 mln.; International Finance Corp., $40 mln.

	Total	Net grants	Net credits	Net other
Total	**–34,322**	**–28,451**	**–5,894**	**24**
Western Europe	**–5,862**	**–5,505**	**–357**	**1**
Austria	–19	(*)	–19	—
Belgium	–3	–3	—	—
Finland	–5	(*)	–6	(*)
France	–8	(*)	–8	—
Germany	–6,117	–6,117	—	—
Ireland	–6	(*)	–6	—
Italy	–14	(*)	–14	—
Portugal	44	100	–55	—
Spain	–76	1	–78	1
United Kingdom	–113	—	–113	—
Yugoslavia	–58	(*)	–58	(*)
Other & unspecified	513	513	—	—
Eastern Europe	**279**	**1,648**	**–1,365**	**–4**
Hungary	3	3	—	—
Poland	249	1,618	–1,366	–4
Romania	22	22	—	—
USSR	3	3	—	—
Other & unspecified	2	2	—	—
Near East & South Asia	**–24,790**	**–22,811**	**–2,002**	**22**
Afghanistan	59	63	–4	—
Bangladesh	136	443	–307	—
Cyprus	18	18	(*)	(*)
Egypt	2,478	3,339	–861	—
Greece	–181	75	–257	1
India	59	149	–90	(*)
Iran	312	336	–47	23
Israel	2,028	2,271	–243	(*)
Jordan	37	38	–1	(*)
Kuwait	–13,550	–13,550	—	—
Lebanon	2	18	–16	—
Nepal	15	15	(*)	(*)
Oman	5	5	1	—
Pakistan	333	442	–109	–1
Saudi Arabia	–13,913	–13,913	—	—
Sri Lanka	79	73	7	–1
Turkey	865	944	–79	(*)
United Arab Emirates	–3,709	–3,709	—	—
Yemen	19	16	4	(*)
UNRWA	76	76	—	—
Other & unspecified	43	42	(*)	—
East Asia & Pacific	**–9,187**	**–9,069**	**–121**	**3**
Australia	–26	—	–26	—
Cambodia	6	6	(*)	—
China	55	(*)	54	—
Indonesia	20	62	–42	(*)
Japan	–9,393	–9,393	—	—
Korea, South	–331	–188	–143	—
Marshall Islands	5	5	—	—
Micronesia	11	11	—	—
Myanmar	–3	(*)	–3	—
New Zealand	–2	—	–2	—
Philippines	380	347	33	(*)
Singapore	3	3	—	—
Taiwan	–8	—	–11	4
Thailand	49	29	20	—
Other & unspecified	35	35	–1	—
Africa	**1,363**	**1,983**	**–620**	**–1**
Algeria	–42	(*)	–42	—
Angola	–8	10	–18	—
Benin	3	3	(*)	—
Botswana	11	15	–4	—
Burkina Faso	27	26	—	(*)
Burundi	6	6	—	(*)
Cameroon	64	78	–14	(*)
Cape Verde	5	5	—	—

	Total	Net grants	Net credits	Net other
Cen. African Rep.	4	4	–1	—
Chad	22	22	—	—
Congo	3	1	1	—
Cote d'Ivoire	44	11	33	—
Djibouti	3	3	—	—
Equatorial Guinea	2	2	—	—
Ethiopia	89	89	—	(*)
Gabon	10	2	8	—
Gambia	8	7	1	—
Ghana	26	121	–95	(*)
Guinea	15	17	–1	(*)
Guinea-Bissau	4	4	—	—
Kenya	98	218	–120	—
Lesotho	11	11	—	—
Liberia	43	43	(*)	—
Madagascar	20	74	–54	—
Malawi	52	69	–16	—
Mali	40	40	(*)	(*)
Mauritania	3	3	—	—
Morocco	60	63	–1	–2
Mozambique	76	115	–39	—
Namibia	14	14	—	—
Niger	40	38	1	—
Nigeria	43	53	–11	—
Rwanda	27	27	—	—
Senegal	31	65	–35	1
Seychelles	2	2	—	—
Sierra Leone	9	5	4	—
Somalia	9	9	—	—
South Africa	28	28	—	—
Sudan	88	87	1	(*)
Swaziland	13	13	(*)	—
Tanzania	42	94	–52	—
Togo	11	11	(*)	—
Tunisia	5	19	–14	(*)
Uganda	35	51	–16	(*)
Zaire	43	38	5	(*)
Zambia	–79	26	–106	—
Zimbabwe	210	210	—	—
Other & unspecified	94	128	–35	—
Western Hemisphere	**1,781**	**3,209**	**–1,429**	**1**
Argentina	86	4	82	—
Belize	11	10	1	—
Bolivia	175	524	–349	—
Brazil	–22	4	–26	—
Canada	–50	—	–50	—
Chile	–40	26	–67	(*)
Colombia	–20	112	92	—
Costa Rica	61	48	11	2
Dominican Republic	22	25	–1	–2
Ecuador	22	25	–3	—
El Salvador	289	248	40	—
Grenada	2	1	—	—
Guatemala	75	57	18	—
Guyana	11	115	–103	(*)
Haiti	67	152	–85	–1
Honduras	182	566	–384	(*)
Jamaica	105	264	–159	(*)
Mexico	8	33	–25	—
Nicaragua	384	603	–219	—
Panama	127	96	32	—
Paraguay	1	3	–1	(*)
Peru	86	102	–16	—
Trinidad-Tobago	5	1	4	—
Uruguay	–5	2	–7	—
Venezuela	–14	(*)	–14	—
Other & unspecified	167	184	–18	—
Intl. orgs. & unspecified	**2,096**	**2,096**	—	—

SPORTS IN 1992

Winter Olympic Games Champions, 1924-1992

Sites of Games

1924 Chamonix, France	1956 Cortina d'Ampezzo, Italy	1980 Lake Placid, N.Y.
1928 St. Moritz, Switzerland	1960 Squaw Valley, Cal.	1984 Sarajevo, Yugoslavia
1932 Lake Placid, N.Y.	1964 Innsbruck, Austria	1988 Calgary, Alberta
1936 Garmisch-Partenkirchen, Germany	1968 Grenoble, France	1992 Albertville, France
1948 St. Moritz, Switzerland	1972 Sapporo, Japan	1994 Lillehammer, Norway
1952 Oslo, Norway	1976 Innsbruck, Austria	

In 1992, the Unified Team represented the former soviet republics of Russia, Ukraine, Belarus, Kazakhstan, and Uzbekistan.

Bobsledding

4-Man Bob

(Driver in parentheses)	Time
1924 Switzerland (Eduard Scherrer)	5:45.54
1928 United States (William Fiske) (5-man)	3:20.50
1932 United States (William Fiske)	7:53.68
1936 Switzerland (Pierre Musy)	5:19.85
1948 United States (Francis Tyler)	5:20.10
1952 Germany (Andreas Ostler)	5:07.84
1956 Switzerland (Franz Kapus)	5:10.44
1964 Canada (Victor Emery)	4:14.46
1968 Italy (Eugenio Monti) (2 races)	2:17.39
1972 Switzerland (Jean Wicki)	4:43.07
1976 E. Germany (Meinhard Nehmer)	3:40.43
1980 E. Germany (Meinhard Nehmer)	3:59.92
1984 E. Germany (Wolfgang Hoppe)	3:20.22
1988 Switzerland (Ekkehard Fasser)	3:47.51
1992 Austria (Ingo Appelt)	3:53.90

2-Man Bob	Time
1932 United States (Hubert Stevens)	8:14.74
1936 United States (Ivan Brown)	5:29.29
1948 Switzerland (F. Endrich)	5:29.20
1952 Germany (Andreas Ostler)	5:24.54
1956 Italy (Dalla Costa)	5:30.14
1964 Great Britain (Anthony Nash)	4:21.90
1968 Italy (Eugenio Monti)	4:41.54
1972 W. Germany (Wolfgang Zimmerer)	4:57.07
1976 E. Germany (Meinhard Nehmer)	3:44.42
1980 Switzerland (Erich Schaerer)	4:09.36
1984 E.Germany (Wolfgang Hoppe)	3:25.56
1988 USSR (Janis Kipours)	3:54.19
1992 Switzerland (Gustav Weber)	4:03.26

Luge

Men's Singles	Time
1964 Thomas Keohler, Germany	3:26.77
1968 Manfred Schmid, Austria	2:52.48
1972 Wolfgang Scheidel, E. Germany	3:27.58
1976 Detlef Guenther, E. Germany	3:27.688
1980 Bernhard Glass, E. Germany	2:54.796
1984 Paul Hildgartner, Italy	3:04.258
1988 Jens Mueller, E. Germany	3:05.548
1992 Georg Hackl, Germany	3:02.363

Men's Pairs	Time
1964 Austria	1:41.62
1968 E. Germany	1:35.85
1972 Italy, E. Germany (tie)	1:28.35
1976 E. Germany	1:25.604
1980 E. Germany	1:19.331
1984 W. Germany	1:23.620
1988 E. Germany	1:31.940
1992 Germany	1:32.053

Women's Singles	Time
1964 Ortun Enderlein, Germany	3:24.67
1968 Erica Lechner, Italy	2:28.66
1972 Anna M. Muller, E. Germany	2:59.18
1976 Margit Schumann, E. Germany	2:50.621
1980 Vera Zozulya, USSR	2:36.537
1984 Steffi Martin, E. Germany	2:46.570
1988 Steffi Walter, E. Germany	3:03.973
1992 Doris Neuner, Austria	3:06.696

Biathlon

Men's 10 Kilometers	Time
1980 Frank Ullrich, E. Germany	32:10.69
1984 Eirik Kvalfoss, Norway	30:53.80
1988 Frank-Peter Roetsch, E. Germany	25:08.10
1992 Mark Kirchner, Germany	26:02.30

Men's 20 Kilometers	Time
1960 Klas Lestander,Sweden	1:33:21.6
1964 Vladimir Melanin, USSR	1:20:26.8
1968 Magnar Solberg, Norway	1:13:45.9
1972 Magnar Solberg, Norway	1:15:55.50
1976 Nikolai Kruglov, USSR	1:14:12.26
1980 Anatoly Aljabiev, USSR	1:08:16.31
1984 Peter Angerer, W. Germany	1:11:52.7
1988 Frank-Peter Roetsch, E. Germany	0:56:33.33
1992 Yevgeny Redkine, Unified Team	0:57:34.4

Men's 30-Kilometer Relay	Time
1968 USSR, Norway, Sweden	2:13:02.4
1972 USSR, Finland, E. Germany	1:51:44.92
1976 USSR, Finland, E. Germany	1:57:55.64
1980 USSR, E. Germany, W. Germany (30 km.)	1:34:03.27
1984 USSR, Norway, W. Germany	1:38:51.70
1988 USSR, W. Germany, Italy	1:22:30.00
1992 Germany, Unified Team, Sweden	1:24:43.50

Biathlon

Women's 7.5 Kilometers	Time
1992 Anfissa Restsova, Unified Team	24:29.20

Women's 22.5 Kilometer Relay	Time
1992 France, Germany, Unified Team	1:15:55.6

Women's 15 Kilometers	Time
1992 Antje Misersky, Germany	51:47.2

Figure Skating

Men's Singles

1908 Ulrich Salchow, Sweden
1920 Gillis Grafstrom, Sweden
1924 Gillis Grafstrom, Sweden
1928 Gillis Grafstrom, Sweden
1932 Karl Schaefer, Austria
1936 Karl Schaefer, Austria
1948 Richard Button, U.S.
1952 Richard Button, U.S.
1956 Hayes Alan Jenkins, U.S.
1960 David W. Jenkins, U.S.
1964 Manfred Schnelldorfer, Germany
1968 Wolfgang Schwartz, Austria
1972 Ondrej Nepela, Czechoslovakia
1976 John Curry, Great Britain
1980 Robin Cousins, Great Britain
1984 Scott Hamilton, U.S.
1988 Brian Boitano, U.S.
1992 Viktor Petrenko, Unified Team

Women's Singles

1908 Madge Syers, Great Britain
1920 Magda Julin-Mauroy, Sweden
1924 Herma von Szabo-Planck, Austria
1928 Sonja Henie, Norway
1932 Sonja Henie, Norway
1936 Sonja Henie, Norway
1948 Barbara Ann Scott, Canada
1952 Jeanette Altwegg, Great Britain
1956 Tenley Albright, U.S.
1960 Carol Heiss, U.S.
1964 Sjoukje Dijkstra, Netherlands
1968 Peggy Fleming, U.S.
1972 Beatrix Schuba, Austria
1976 Dorothy Hamill, U.S.
1980 Anett Poetzsch, E. Germany
1984 Katarina Witt, E. Germany
1988 Katarina Witt, E. Germany
1992 Kristi Yamaguchi, U.S.

Pairs

1908 Anna Hubler & Heinrich Burger, Germany
1920 Ludovika & Walter Jakobsson, Finland
1924 Helene Engelman & Alfred Berger, Austria
1928 Andree Joly & Pierre Brunet, France
1932 Andree Joly & Pierre Brunet, France
1936 Maxi Herber & Ernst Baier, Germany
1948 Micheline Lannoy & Pierre Baugniet, Belgium
1952 Ria and Paul Falk, Germany
1956 Elisabeth Schwartz & Kurt Oppelt, Austria
1960 Barbara Wagner & Robert Paul, Canada
1964 Ludmila Beloussova & Oleg Protopopov, USSR
1968 Ludmila Beloussova & Oleg Protopopov, USSR
1972 Irina Rodnina & Alexei Ulanov, USSR
1976 Irina Rodnina & Aleksandr Zaitzev, USSR
1980 Irina Rodnina & Aleksandr Zaitzev, USSR
1984 Elena Valova & Oleg Vassiliev, USSR
1988 Ekaterina Gordeeva & Sergei Grinkov, USSR
1992 Natalia Mishkutienok & Artur Dimitriev, Unified Team

Ice Dancing

1976 Ludmila Pakhomova & Aleksandr Gorschkov, USSR
1980 Natalya Linichuk & Gennadi Karponosov, USSR
1984 Jayne Torvill & Christopher Dean, Great Britain
1988 Natalia Bestemianova & Andrei Bukin, USSR
1992 Marina Klimova & Sergei Ponomarenko, Unified Team

Ice Hockey

1920 Canada, U.S., Czechoslovakia
1924 Canada, U.S., Great Britain
1928 Canada, Sweden, Switzerland
1932 Canada, U.S., Germany
1936 Great Britain, Canada, U.S.
1948 Canada, Czechoslovakia, Switzerland
1952 Canada, U.S., Sweden
1956 USSR, U.S., Canada
1960 U.S., Canada, USSR
1964 USSR, Sweden, Czechoslovakia
1968 USSR, Czechoslovakia, Canada
1972 USSR, U.S., Czechoslovakia,
1976 USSR, Czechoslovakia, W. Germany
1980 U.S., USSR, Sweden
1984 USSR, Czechoslovakia, Sweden
1988 USSR, Finland, Sweden
1992 Unified Team, Canada, Czechlosovakia

Alpine Skiing

Men's Downhill	Time
1948 Henri Oreiller, France	2:55.0
1952 Zeno Colo, Italy	2:30.8
1956 Anton Sailer, Austria	2:52.2
1960 Jean Vuarnet, France	2:06.0
1964 Egon Zimmermann, Austria	2:18.16
1968 Jean-Claude Killy, France	1:59.85
1972 Bernhard Russi, Switzerland	1:51.43
1976 Franz Klammer, Austria	1:45.73
1980 Leonhard Stock, Austria	1:45.50
1984 Bill Johnson, U.S.	1:45:59
1988 Pirmin Zurbriggen, Switzerland	1:59.63
1992 Patrick Ortlieb, Austria	1:50.37

Men's Super Giant Slalom	Time
1988 Franck Piccard, France	1:39.66
1992 Kjetil-Andre Aamodt, Norway	1:13.04

Men's Giant Slalom	Time
1952 Stein Eriksen, Norway	2:25.0
1956 Anton Sailer, Austria	3:00.1
1960 Roger Staub, Switzerland	1:48.3
1964 Francois Bonlieu, France	1:46.71
1968 Jean-Claude Killy, France	3:29.28
1972 Gustavo Thoeni, Italy	3:09.62
1976 Heini Hemmi, Switzerland	3:26.97
1980 Ingemar Stenmark, Sweden	2:40.74
1984 Max Julen, Switzerland	2:41.18
1988 Alberto Tomba, Italy	2:06:37
1992 Alberto Tomba, Italy	2:06.98

Men's Slalom	Time
1948 Edi Reinalter, Switzerland	2:10.3
1952 Othmar Schneider, Austria	2:00.0
1956 Anton Sailer, Austria	194.7 pts.
1960 Ernst Hinterseer, Austria	2:08.9
1964 Josef Stiegler, Austria	2:11.13
1968 Jean-Claude Killy, France	1:39.73
1972 Francisco Fernandez Ochoa, Spain	1:49.27
1976 Piero Gros, Italy	2:03.29
1980 Ingemar Stenmark, Sweden	1:44.26
1984 Phil Mahre, U.S.	1:39.41
1988 Alberto Tomba, Italy	1:39.47
1992 Finn Christian Jagge, Norway	1:44.39

Men's Combined	Points
1988 Hubert Strolz, Austria	36.55
1992 Josef Polig, Italy	14.58

Women's Downhill	Time
1948 Hedi Schlunegger, Switzerland	2:28.3
1952 Trude Jochum-Beiser, Austria	1:47.1
1956 Madeleine Berthod, Switzerland	1:40.7
1960 Heidi Biebl, Germany	1:37.6
1964 Christl Haas, Austria	1:55.39
1968 Olga Pall, Austria	1:40.87
1972 Marie Therese Nadig, Switzerland	1:36.68
1976 Rosi Mittermaier, W. Germany	1:46.16
1980 Annemarie Proell Moser, Austria	1:37.52
1984 Michela Figini, Switzerland	1:13.36
1988 Marina Kiehl, W. Germany	1:25.86
1992 Kerrin Lee-Gartner, Canada	1:52.55

Women's Super Giant Slalom	Time
1988 Sigrid Wolf, Austria	1:19.03
1992 Deborah Compagnoni, Italy	1:21.22

Women's Giant Slalom	Time
1952 Andrea Mead Lawrence, U.S.	2:06.8
1956 Ossi Reichert, Germany	1:56.5
1960 Yvonne Ruegg, Switzerland	1:39.9
1964 Marielle Goitschel, France	1:52.24
1968 Nancy Greene, Canada	1:51.97
1972 Marie Therese Nadig, Switzerland	1:29.90
1976 Kathy Kreiner, Canada	1:29.13
1980 Hanni Wenzel, Liechtenstein (2 runs)	2:41.66
1984 Debbie Armstrong, U.S.	2:20.98
1988 Vreni Schneider, Switzerland	2:06.49
1992 Pernilla Wiberg, Sweden	2:12.74

Women's Slalom	Time
1948 Gretchen Fraser, U.S.	1:57.2
1952 Andrea Mead Lawrence, U.S.	2:10.6
1956 Renee Colliard, Switzerland	112.3 pts.
1960 Anne Heggtveigt, Canada	1:49.6
1964 Christine Goitschel, France	1:29.86
1968 Marielle Goitschel, France	1:25.86
1972 Barbara Cochran, U.S.	1:31.24
1976 Rosi Mittermaier, W. Germany	1:30.54
1980 Hanni Wenzel, Liechtenstein	1:25.09
1984 Paoletta Magoni, Italy	1:36.47
1988 Vreni Schneider, Switzerland	1:36.69
1992 Petra Kronberger, Austria	1:32.68

Women's Combined	Points
1988 Anita Wachter, Austria	29.25
1992 Petra Kronberger, Austria	2.55

Freestyle Skiing

Men's Moguls	Points
1992 Edgar Grospiron, France	25.81

Women's Moguls	Points
1992 Donna Weinbrecht, U.S.	23.69

Cross-Country Skiing

Men's 10 kilometers (6.2 miles)	Time
1992 Vegard Ulvang, Norway	27:36.0

Men's 15 kilometers (9.3 miles)	Time
1924 Thorleif Haug, Norway	1:14:31
1928 Johan Grottumsbraaten, Norway	1:37:01
1932 Sven Utterstrom, Sweden	1:23:07
1936 Erik-August Larsson, Sweden	1:14:38
1948 Martin Lundstrom, Sweden	1:13:50
1952 Hallgeir Brenden, Norway	1:01:34
1956 Hallgeir Brenden, Norway	49:39.0
1960 Haakon Brusveen, Norway	51:55.5
1964 Eero Maentyranta, Finland	50:54.1
1968 Harald Groenningen, Norway	47:54.2
1972 Sven-Ake Lundback, Sweden	45:28.24

(*continued*)

1976	Nikolai Balukov, USSR	43:58.47
1980	Thomas Wassberg, Sweden	41:57.63
1984	Gunde Svan, Sweden	41:25.6
1988	Mikhail Deviatiarov, USSR	41:18.9
1992	Bjorn Dahlie, Norway	38:01.9

(Note: approx. 18-km. course 1924-1952)

	30 kilometers (18.6 miles)	Time
1956	Veikko Hakulinen, Finland	1:44:06.0
1960	Sixten Jernberg, Sweden	1:51:03.9
1964	Eero Maentyranta, Finland	1:30:50.7
1968	Franco Nones, Italy	1:35:39.2
1972	Vyacheslav Vedenine, USSR	1:36:31.15
1976	Sergei Saveliev, USSR	1:30:29.38
1980	Nikolai Zimyatov, USSR	1:27:02.80
1984	Nikolai Zimyatov, USSR	1:28:56.3
1988	Aleksei Prokourorov, USSR	1:24:26.3
1992	Vegard Ulvang, Norway	1:22:27.8

	50 kilometers (31.2 miles)	Time
1924	Thorleif Haug, Norway	3:44:32.0
1928	Per Erik Hedlund, Sweden	4:52:03.0
1932	Veli Saarinen, Finland	4:28:00.0
1936	Elis Wiklund, Sweden	3:30:11.0
1948	Nils Karlsson, Sweden	3:47:48.0
1952	Veikko Hakulinen, Finland	3:33:33.0
1956	Sixten Jernberg, Sweden	2:50:27.0
1960	Kalevi Hamalainen, Finland	2:59:06.3
1964	Sixten Jernberg, Sweden	2:43:52.6
1968	Ole Ellefsaeter, Norway	2:28:45.8
1972	Paal Tyldum, Norway	2:43:14.75
1976	Ivar Formo, Norway	2:37:30.05
1980	Nikolai Zimyatov, USSR	2:27:24.60
1984	Thomas Wassberg, Sweden	2:15:55.8
1988	Gunde Svan, Sweden	2:04:30.9
1992	Bjorn Dahlie, Norway	2:03:41.5

	40-km. Relay	Time
1936	Finland, Norway, Sweden	2:41:33.0
1948	Sweden, Finland, Norway	2:32:08.0
1952	Finland, Norway, Sweden	2:20:16.0
1956	USSR, Finland, Sweden	2:15:30.0
1960	Finland, Norway, USSR	2:18:45.6
1964	Sweden, Finland, USSR	2:18:34.6
1968	Norway, Sweden, Finland	2:08:33.5
1972	USSR, Norway, Switzerland	2:04:47.94
1976	Finland, Norway, USSR	2:07:59.72
1980	USSR, Norway, Finland	1:57:03.46
1984	Sweden, USSR, Finland	1:55:06.30
1988	Sweden, USSR, Czechoslovakia	1:43:58.60
1992	Norway Italy, Finland	1:39:26.00

	Combined Cross-Country & Jumping	Points
1924	Thorleif Haug, Norway	453.800
1928	Johan Grottumsbraaten, Norway	427.800
1932	Johan Grottumsbraaten, Norway	446.000
1936	Oddbjorn Hagen, Norway	430.300
1948	Heikki Hasu, Finland	448.800
1952	Simon Slattvik, Norway	451.621
1956	Sverre Stenersen, Norway	455.000
1960	Georg Thoma, Germany	457.952
1964	Tormod Knutsen, Norway	469.280
1968	Franz Keller, W. Germany	449.040
1972	Ulrich Wehling, E. Germany	413.340
1976	Ulrich Wehling, E. Germany	423.390
1980	Ulrich Wehling, E. Germany	432.200
1984	Tom Sandberg, Norway	422.595
1988	Hippolyt Kempf, Switzerland	235.8
1992	Fabrice Guy, France	426.470

	Men's Team Ski Jumping (90 meters)	Points
1988	Finland, Yugoslavia, Norway	634.4
1992	Finland, Austria, Czechoslovakia	644.4

	Ski Jumping (90 meters)	Points
1924	Jacob Thams, Norway	227.5
1928	Alfred Andersen, Norway	230.5
1932	Birger Ruud, Norway	228.1
1936	Birger Ruud, Norway	232.0
1948	Petter Hugsted, Norway	228.1
1952	Arnfinn Bergmann, Norway	226.0
1956	Antti Hyvarinen, Finland	227.0
1960	Helmut Recknagel, Germany	227.2
1964	Toralf Engan, Norway	230.7
1968	Vladimir Beloussov, USSR	231.3
1972	Wojiech Fortuna, Poland	219.9
1976	Karl Schnabl, Austria	234.8
1980	Jouko Tormanen, Finland	271.0
1984	Matti Nykaenen, Finland	231.2
1988	Matti Nykaenen, Finland	224.0
1992	Ernst Vettori, Austria	222.8

	Ski Jumping (120 meters)	Points
1992	Toni Nicminen, Finland	239.5

	Men's Nordic Team Combined	Time
1988	W. Germany, Switzerland, Austria	1:20:46.0
1992	Japan, Norway, Austria	1:23:36.5

Women's Events

	5 kilometers (approx. 3.1 miles)	Time
1964	Claudia Boyarskikh, USSR	17:50.5
1968	Toini Gustafsson, Sweden	16:45.2
1972	Galina Koulacova, USSR	17:00.50
1976	Helena Takalo, Finland	15:48.69
1980	Raisa Smetanina, USSR	15:06.92
1984	Marja-Liisa Haemaelainen, Finland	17:04.0
1988	Marjo Matikainen, Finland	15:04.0
1992	Marjut Lukkarinen, Finland	14:13.8

	10 kilometers (6.2 miles)	Time
1952	Lydia Wideman, Finland	41:40.0
1956	Lyubov Kosyreva, USSR	38:11.0
1960	Maria Gusakova, USSR	39:46.6
1964	Claudia Boyarskikh, USSR	40:24.3
1968	Toini Gustafsson, Sweden	36:46.5
1972	Galina Koulacova, USSR	34:17.82
1976	Raisa Smetanina, USSR	30:13.41
1980	Barbara Petzold, E. Germany	30:31.54
1984	Marja-Liisa Haemaelainen, Finland	31:44.2
1988	Vida Ventsene, USSR	30:08.3
1992	Lyubov Yegorova, Unified Team	25:53.7

	15 kilometers (9.3 miles)	Time
1992	Lyubov Yegorova, Unified Team	42:20.8

	30 kilometers (18.6 miles)	Time
1992	Stefania Belmondo, Italy	1:22:30.1

	20-km. Relay	Time
1956	Finland, USSR, Sweden (15 km.)	1:09:01.0
1960	Sweden, USSR, Finland (15 km.)	1:04:21.4
1964	USSR, Sweden, Finland (15 km.)	59:20.2
1968	Norway, Sweden, USSR (15 km.)	57:30.0
1972	USSR, Finland, Norway (15 km.)	48:46.15
1976	USSR, Finland, E. Germany	1:07:49.75
1980	E. Germany, USSR, Norway	1:02:11.10
1984	Norway, Czechoslovakia, Finland	1:06:49.70
1988	USSR, Norway, Finland	59:51.1
1992	United Team, Norway, Italy	59:34.8

Speed Skating

	Men's 500 meters	Time
1924	Charles Jewtraw, U.S.	0:44.0
1928	Thunberg, Finland & Evensen, Norway (tie)	0:43.4
1932	John A. Shea, U.S.	0:43.4
1936	Ivar Ballangrud, Norway	0:43.4
1948	Finn Helgesen, Norway	0:43.1
1952	Kenneth Henry, U.S.	0:43.2
1956	Evgeniy Grishin, USSR	0:40.2
1960	Evgeniy Grishin, USSR	0:40.2
1964	Terry McDermott, U.S.	0:40.1
1968	Erhard Keller, W. Germany	0:40.3
1972	Erhard Keller, W. Germany	0:39.44
1976	Evgeny Kulikov, USSR	0:39.17
1980	Eric Heiden, U.S.	0:38.03
1984	Sergei Fokichev, USSR	0:38.19
1988	Uwe-Jens Mey, E. Germany	0:36.45
1992	Uwe-Jens Mey, Germany	0:37.14

	Men's 1,000 meters	Time
1976	Peter Mueller, U.S.	1:19.32
1980	Eric Heiden, U.S.	1:15.18
1984	Gaetan Boucher, Canada	1:15.80
1988	Nikolai Guiliaev, USSR	1:13.03
1992	Olaf Zinke, Germany	1:14.85

	Men's 1,500 meters	Time
1924	Clas Thunberg, Finland	2:20.8
1928	Clas Thunberg, Finland	2:21.1
1932	John A. Shea, U.S.	2:57.5
1936	Charles Mathiesen, Norway	2:19.2

1948	Sverre Farstad, Norway	2:17.6
1952	Hjalmar Andersen, Norway	2:20.4
1956	Grishin, & Mikhailov, both USSR (tie)	2:08.6
1960	Aas, Norway & Grishin, USSR (tie)	2:10.4
1964	Ants Anston, USSR	2:10.3
1968	Cornetis Verkerk, Netherlands	2:03.4
1972	Ard Schenk, Netherlands	2:02.96
1976	Jan Egil Storholt, Norway	1:59.38
1980	Eric Heiden, U.S.	1:55.44
1984	Gaetan Boucher, Canada	1:58.36
1988	Andre Hoffmann, E. Germany	1:52.06
1992	Johann Koss, Norway	1:54.81

	Men's 5,000 meters	Time
1924	Clas Thunberg, Finland	8:39.0
1928	Ivar Ballangrud, Norway	8:50.5
1932	Irving Jaffee, U.S.	9:40.8
1936	Ivar Ballangrud, Norway	8:19.6
1948	Reidar Liaklev, Norway	8:29.4
1952	Hjalmar Andersen, Norway	8:10.6
1956	Boris Shilkov, USSR	7:48.7
1960	Viktor Kosichkin, USSR	7:51.3
1964	Knut Johannesen, Norway	7:38.4
1968	F. Anton Maier, Norway	7:22.4
1972	Ard Schenk, Netherlands	7:23.61
1976	Sten Stensen, Norway	7:24.48
1980	Eric Heiden, U.S.	7:02.29
1984	Sven Tomas Gustafson, Sweden	7:12.28
1988	Tomas Gustafson, Sweden	6:44.63
1992	Geir Karlstad, Norway	6:59.97

	Men's 10,000 meters	Time
1924	Julius Skutnabb, Finland	18:04.8
1928	Event not held, thawing of ice	
1932	Irving Jaffee, U.S.	19:13.6
1936	Ivar Ballangrud, Norway	17:24.3
1948	Ake Seyffarth, Sweden	17:26.3
1952	Hjalmar Andersen, Norway	16:45.8
1956	Sigvard Ericsson, Sweden	16:35.9
1960	Knut Johannesen, Norway	15:46.6
1964	Jonny Nilsson, Sweden	15:50.1
1968	Jonny Hoeglin, Sweden	15:23.6
1972	Ard Schenk, Netherlands	15:01.35
1976	Piet Kleine, Netherlands	14:50.59
1980	Eric Heiden, U.S.	14:28.13
1984	Igor Malkov, USSR	14:39.90
1988	Tomas Gustafson, Sweden	13:48.20
1992	Bart Veldkamp, Netherlands	14:12.12

	Women's 500 meters	Time
1960	Helga Haase, Germany	0:45.9
1964	Lydia Skoblikova, USSR	0:45.0
1968	Ludmila Titova, USSR	0:46.1
1972	Anne Henning, U.S.	0:43.33
1976	Sheila Young, U.S.	0:42.76
1980	Karin Enke, E. Germany	0:41.78
1984	Christa Rothenburger, E. Germany	0:41.02
1988	Bonnie Blair, U.S.	0:39.10
1992	Bonnie Blair, U.S.	0:40.33

	Women's 1,000 meters	Time
1960	Klara Guseva, USSR	1:34.1
1964	Lydia Skoblikova, USSR	1:33.2
1968	Carolina Geijssen, Netherlands	1:32.6
1972	Monika Pflug, W. Germany	1:31.40
1976	Tatiana Averina, USSR	1:28.43
1980	Natalya Petruseva, USSR	1:24.10
1984	Karin Enke, E. Germany	1:21.61
1988	Christa Rothenburger, E. Germany	1:17.65
1992	Bonnie Blair, U.S.	1:21.90

	Women's 1,500 meters	Time
1960	Lydia Skoblikova, USSR	2:52.2
1964	Lydia Skoblikova, USSR	2:22.6
1968	Kaija Mustonen, Finland	2:22.4
1972	Dianne Holum, U.S.	2:20.85
1976	Galina Stepanskaya, USSR	2:16.58
1980	Anne Borckink, Netherlands	2:10.95
1984	Karin Enke, E. Germany	2:03.42
1988	Yvonne van Gennip, Netherlands	2:00.68
1992	Jacqueline Boerner, Germany	2:05.87

	Women's 3,000 meters	Time
1960	Lydia Skoblikova, USSR	5:14.3
1964	Lydia Skoblikova, USSR	5:14.9
1968	Johanna Schut, Netherlands	4:56.2
1972	Christina Baas-Kaiser, Netherlands	4:52.14
1976	Tatiana Averina, USSR	4:45.19
1980	Bjoerg Eva Jensen, Norway	4:32.13
1984	Andrea Schoene, E. Germany	4:24.79
1988	Yvonne van Gennip, Netherlands	4:11.94
1992	Gunda Niemann, Germany	4:19.90

	Women's 5,000 meters	Time
1988	Yvonne van Gennip, Netherlands	7:14:13
1992	Gunda Niemann, Germany	7:31.57

Short Track Speed Skating

	Men's 1,000 meters	Time
1992	Kim Ki-Hoon, S. Korea	1:30.76

	Men's 5,000-meter relay	Time
1992	S. Korea, Canada, Japan	7:14.02

	Women's 500 meters	Time
1992	Cathy Turner, U.S.	47:04

	Women's 3,000-meter relay	Time
1992	Canada, U.S., Unified Team	4:36.62

Winter Olympic Games in 1992

Albertville, France, Feb. 8-23, 1992

The 16th Olympics winter games in Albertville, France featured a record 2,174 athletes from 63 countries competing for medals. Germany, whose athletes won a games-high 26 medals, competed as a single team for the first time since 1964. The Unified Team, made up of some former Soviet republics, finished second with 23 medals.

Medal Winners

	Gold	Silver	Bronze	Total
Germany	10	10	6	26
Unified Team	9	6	8	23
Austria	6	7	8	21
Norway	9	6	5	20
Italy	4	6	4	14
United States	5	4	2	11
France	3	5	1	9
Canada	2	3	2	7
Finland	3	1	3	7
Japan	1	2	4	7
Netherlands	1	1	2	4
South Korea	2	1	1	4
Sweden	1	0	3	4
China	0	3	0	3
Czechoslovakia	0	0	3	3
Switzerland	1	0	2	3
Luxembourg	0	2	0	2
New Zealand	0	1	0	1
North Korea	0	0	1	1
Spain	0	0	1	1

Individual Medal Winners

(Gold, Silver, Bronze)

Alpine Skiing

Women's Combined—Petra Kronberger, Austria; Anita Wachter, Austria; Florence Masnada, France.
Women's Downhill—Kerrin Lee-Gartner, Canada; Hilary Lindh, U.S.; Veronika Wallinger, Austria.
Women's Giant Slalom—Pernilla Wiberg, Sweden; Diann Roffe, U.S.; Anita Wachter, Austria.
Women's Slalom—Petra Kronberger, Austria; Annelise Coberger, New Zealand; Bianca Fernández-Ochoa, Spain.
Women's Super Giant Slalom—Deborah Compagnoni, Italy; Carole Merle, France; Katja Seizinger, Germany.
Men's Combined—Josef Polig, Italy; Gianfranco Martin, Italy; Steve Locher, Switzerland.
Men's Downhill—Patrick Ortlieb, Austria; Franck Piccard, France; Günther Mader, Austria.
Men's Giant Slalom—Alberto Tomba, Italy; Marc Girardelli, Luxembourg; Kjetil-Andre Aamodt, Norway.
Men's Super Giant Slalom—Kjetil-Andre Aamodt, Norway; Marc Girardelli, Luxembourg; Jan Einar Thorsen, Norway.
Men's Slalom—Finn Christian Jagge, Norway; Alberto Tomba, Italy; Michael Tritscher, Austria.

Biathlon

Women's 15k—Antje Misersky, Germany; Svetlana Pecherskaia, Unified Team; Myriam Bedard, Canada.
Women's 7.5k—Anfissa Restsova, Unified Team; Antje Misersky, Germany; Yelena Belova, Unified Team.
Men's 10k—Mark Kirchner, Germany; Ricco Gross, Germany; Harri Eloranta, Finland.
Men's 20k—Yevgeny Redkine, Unified Team; Mark Kirchner, Germany; Mikael Lofgren, Sweden.

Cross-Country Skiing

Women's 5k—Marjut Lukkarinen, Finland; Lyubov Yegorova, Unified Team; Yelena Valbe, Unified Team.
Women's 10k—Lyubov Yegorova, Unified Team; Stefania Belmondo, Italy; Yelena Valbe, Unified Team.
Women's 15k—Lyubov Yegorova, Unified Team; Marjut Lukkarinen, Finland; Yelena Valbe, Unified Team.
Women's 30k—Stefania Belmondo, Italy; Lyubov Yegorova, Unified Team; Yelena Valbe, Unified Team.
Men's 10k—Vegard Ulvang, Norway; Marco Alvarello, Italy; Christer Majback, Sweden.
Men's 15k—Bjorn Dahlie, Norway; Vegard Ulvang, Norway; Giorgio Vanzetta, Italy.
Men's 30k—Vegard Ulvang, Norway; Bjorn Dahlie, Norway; Terje Langli, Norway.
Men's 50k—Bjorn Dahlie, Norway; Maurillo De Zolt, Italy; Giorgio Vanzetta, Italy.

Figure Skating

Men—Viktor Petrenko, Unified Team; Paul Wylie, U.S.; Petr Barna, Czechoslovakia.
Ice Dancing—Klimova/Ponomarenko, Unified Team; Duchesnay/Duchesnay, France; Usova/Zhulin, Unified Team.
Pairs—Mishkutienok/Dmitriev, Unified Team; Bechke/Petrov, Unified Team; Brasseur/Eisler, Canada.
Women—Kristi Yamaguchi, U.S.; Midori Ito, Japan; Nancy Kerrigán, U.S.

Freestyle Skiing

Women's Moguls—Donna Weinbrecht, U.S.; Elizaveta Kojevnikova, Unified Team; Stine Hattestad, Norway.
Men's Moguls—Edgar Grospiron, France; Oliver Allamand, France; Nelson Carmichael, U.S.

Luge

Women's Singles—Doris Neuner, Austria; Angelica Neuner, Austria; Susi Erdmann, Germany.
Men's Singles—Georg Hackl, Germany; Markus Prock, Austria; Markus Schmidt, Austria.
Men's Doubles—Stefan Krausse/Jan Behrendt, Germany; Yves Mankel/Thomas Rudolph, Germany; Hansjorg Raffl/Norbert Huber, Italy.

Nordic Combined

Individual—Fabrice Guy, France; Sylvain Guillaume, France; Klaus Sulzenbacher, Austria.

Ski Jump

Individual, 120m—Toni Nieminen, Finland; Martin Höllwarth, Austria; Heinz Kuttin, Austria.
Individual, Normal Hill—Ernst Vettori, Austria; Martin Höllwarth, Austria; Toni Nieminen, Finland.

Speed Skating

(Long Track)

Women's 500m—Bonnie Blair, U.S.; Ye Qiaobo, China; Christa Luding, Germany.
Women's 1,000m—Bonnie Blair, U.S.; Ye Qiaobo, China; Monique Gatbrecht, Germany.
Women's 1,500m—Jacqueline Börner, Germany; Gunda Niemann, Germany; Seiko Hashimoto, Japan.
Women's 3,000m—Gunda Niemann, Germany; Heike Warnicke, Germany; Emese Hunyady, Austria.
Women's 5,000m—Gunda Niemann, Germany; Heike Warnicke, Germany; Claudia Pechstein, Germany.
Men's 500m—Uwe-Jens Mey, Germany; Toshiyuki Kuroiwa, Japan; Junichi Inoue, Japan.
Men's 1,000m—Olaf Zinke, Germany; Kim Yoon Man, South Korea; Yukinori Miyabe, Japan.
Men's 1,500m—Johann Koss, Norway; Adne Sondral, Norway; Leo Visser, Netherlands.
Men's 5,000m—Geir Karlstad, Norway; Falco Zandstra, Netherlands; Leo Visser, Netherlands.
Men's 10,000m—Bart Veldkamp, Netherlands; Johann Koss, Norway; Geir Karlstad, Norway.

(Short Track)

Women's 500m—Cathy Turner, U.S.; Li Yan, China; Hwang Ok Sil, North Korea.
Men's 1,000m—Kim Ki Hoon, South Korea; Frederic Blackburn, Canada; Lee Yoon Ho, South Korea.

Most NHL Goals in a Season

Player	Team	Season	Goals
Wayne Gretzky	Edmonton	1981-82	92
Wayne Gretzky	Edmonton	1983-84	87
Brett Hull	St. Louis	1990-91	86
Mario Lemieux	Pittsburgh	1988-89	85
Phil Esposito	Boston	1970-71	76
Wayne Gretzky	Edmonton	1984-85	73
Brett Hull	St. Louis	1989-90	72
Wayne Gretzky	Edmonton	1982-83	71
Jari Kurri	Edmonton	1984-85	71
Mario Lemieux	Pittsburgh	1987-88	70
Bernie Nicholls	Los Angeles	1988-89	70
Bret Hull	St. Louis	1991-92	70
Mike Bossy	N.Y. Islanders	1978-79	69
Phil Esposito	Boston	1973-74	68
Mike Bossy	N.Y. Islanders	1980-81	68
Jari Kurri	Edmonton	1985-86	68
Phil Esposito	Boston	1971-72	66
Lanny McDonald	Calgary	1982-83	66
Steve Yzerman	Detroit	1988-89	65
Mike Bossy	N.Y. Islanders	1981-82	64
Wayne Gretzky	Edmonton	1986-87	62
Steve Yzerman	Detroit	1989-90	62
Mike Bossy	N.Y. Islanders	1985-86	61
Phil Esposito	Boston	1974-75	61
Reggie Leach	Philadelphia	1975-76	61
Mike Bossy	N.Y. Islanders	1982-83	60
Guy Lafleur	Montreal	1977-78	60
Steve Shutt	Montreal	1976-77	60
Dennis Maruk	Washington	1981-82	60

National Hockey League, 1991-92

Final Standings

Wales Conference

Adams Division

	W	L	T	GF	GA	PTS
Montreal	41	28	11	267	207	93
Boston	36	32	12	270	275	84
Buffalo	31	37	12	289	299	74
Hartford	26	41	13	247	283	65
Quebec	20	48	12	255	318	52

Patrick Division

	W	L	T	GF	GA	PTS
N.Y. Rangers	50	25	5	321	246	105
Washington	45	27	8	330	275	98
Pittsburgh	39	32	9	343	308	87
New Jersey	38	31	11	289	259	87
N.Y. Islanders	34	35	11	291	299	79
Philadelphia	32	37	11	252	273	75

Campbell Conference

Norris Division

	W	L	T	GF	GA	PTS
Detroit	43	25	12	320	256	98
Chicago	36	29	15	257	236	87
St. Louis	36	33	11	279	266	83
Minnesota	32	42	6	246	278	70
Toronto	30	43	7	234	294	67

Smythe Division

	W	L	T	GF	GA	PTS
Vancouver	42	26	12	285	250	96
Los Angeles	35	31	14	287	296	84
Edmonton	36	34	10	295	297	82
Winnipeg	33	32	15	251	244	81
Calgary	31	37	12	296	305	74
San Jose	17	58	5	219	359	39

Penguins Repeat as Stanley Cup Champions

The Pittsburgh Penguins repeated as Stanley Cup champions by defeating the Chicago Black Hawks in 4 straight games. Mario Lemieux of the Penguins was chosen the most valuable player in the playoffs for the second consecutive year.

Stanley Cup Playoff Results

Wales Conference

Pittsburgh defeated Washington 4-3
N.Y. Rangers defeated New Jersey 4-3
Montreal defeated Hartford 4-3
Boston defeated Buffalo 4-3
Boston defeated Montreal 4-0
Pittsburgh defeated N.Y. Rangers 4-2
Pittsburgh defeated Boston 4-0

Campbell Conference

Chicago defeated St. Louis 4-2
Edmonton defeated Los Angeles 4-2
Vancouver defeated Winnipeg 4-3
Detroit defeated Minnesota 4-3
Chicago defeated Detroit 4-0
Edmonton defeated Vancouver 4-2
Chicago defeated Edmonton 4-0

Finals

Pittsburgh defeated Chicago 4-0

Stanley Cup Champions Since 1927

Year	Champion	Coach	Final opponent
1927	Ottawa	Dave Gill	Boston
1928	N.Y. Rangers	Lester Patrick	Montreal
1929	Boston	Cy Denneny	N.Y. Rangers
1930	Montreal	Cecil Hart	Boston
1931	Montreal	Cecil Hart	Chicago
1932	Toronto	Dick Irvin	N.Y. Rangers
1933	New York	Lester Patrick	Toronto
1934	Chicago	Tommy Gorman	Detroit
1935	Montreal Maroons	Tommy Gorman	Toronto
1936	Detroit	Jack Adams	Toronto
1937	Detroit	Jack Adams	N.Y. Rangers
1938	Chicago	Bill Stewart	Toronto
1939	Boston	Art Ross	Toronto
1940	N.Y. Rangers	Frank Boucher	Toronto
1941	Boston	Cooney Weiland	Detroit
1942	Toronto	Hap Day	Detroit
1943	Detroit	Jack Adams	Boston
1944	Montreal	Dick Irvin	Chicago
1945	Toronto	Hap Day	Detroit
1946	Montreal	Dick Irvin	Boston
1947	Toronto	Hap Day	Montreal
1948	Toronto	Hap Day	Detroit
1949	Toronto	Hap Day	Detroit
1950	Detroit	Tommy Ivan	N.Y. Rangers
1951	Toronto	Joe Primeau	Montreal
1952	Detroit	Tommy Ivan	Montreal
1953	Montreal	Dick Irvin	Boston
1954	Detroit	Tommy Ivan	Montreal
1955	Detroit	Jimmy Skinner	Montreal
1956	Montreal	Toe Blake	Detroit
1957	Montreal	Toe Blake	Boston
1958	Montreal	Toe Blake	Boston
1959	Montreal	Toe Blake	Toronto
1960	Montreal	Toe Blake	Toronto
1961	Chicago	Rudy Pilous	Detroit
1962	Toronto	Punch Imlach	Chicago
1963	Toronto	Punch Imlach	Detroit
1964	Toronto	Punch Imlach	Detroit
1965	Montreal	Toe Blake	Chicago
1966	Montreal	Toe Blake	Detroit
1967	Toronto	Punch Imlach	Montreal
1968	Montreal	Toe Blake	St. Louis
1969	Montreal	Claude Ruel	St. Louis
1970	Boston	Harry Sinden	St. Louis
1971	Montreal	Al MacNeil	Chicago
1972	Boston	Tom Johnson	N.Y. Rangers
1973	Montreal	Scotty Bowman	Chicago
1974	Philadelphia	Fred Shero	Boston
1975	Philadelphia	Fred Shero	Buffalo
1976	Montreal	Scotty Bowman	Philadelphia
1977	Montreal	Scotty Bowman	Boston
1978	Montreal	Scotty Bowman	Boston
1979	Montreal	Scotty Bowman	N.Y. Rangers
1980	N.Y. Islanders	Al Arbour	Philadelphia
1981	N.Y. Islanders	Al Arbour	Minnesota
1982	N.Y. Islanders	Al Arbour	Vancouver
1983	N.Y. Islanders	Al Arbour	Edmonton
1984	Edmonton	Glen Sather	N.Y. Islanders
1985	Edmonton	Glen Sather	Philadelphia
1986	Montreal	Jean Perron	Calgary
1987	Edmonton	Glen Sather	Philadelphia
1988	Edmonton	Glen Sather	Boston
1989	Calgary	Terry Crisp	Montreal
1990	Edmonton	John Muckler	Boston
1991	Pittsburgh	Bob Johnson	Minnesota
1992	Pittsburgh	Scotty Bowman	Chicago

Individual Leaders

Points

Mario Lemieux, Pittsburgh, 131; Kevin Stevens, Pittsburgh, 123; Wayne Gretzky, Los Angeles, 121; Brett Hull, St. Louis, 109; Luc Robitaille, Los Angeles, 107.

Goals

Brett Hull, St. Louis, 70; Kevin Stevens, Pittsburgh, 54; Gary Roberts, Calgary, 53; Jeremy Roenick, Chicago, 53; Pat Lafontaine, Buffalo, 46.

Assists

Wayne Gretzky, Los Angeles, 90; Mario Lemieux, Pittsburgh, 87; Brian Leetch, N.Y. Rangers, 80; Adam Oates, St. Louis-Boston, 79; Dale Hawerchuk, Buffalo, 75.

Power-play goals

Dave Andreychuk, Buffalo, 28; Luc Robitaille, Los Angeles, 26; Pat Lafontaine, Buffalo, 23; Jeremy Roenick, Chicago, 22; Derek King, N.Y. Islanders, 21.

Short hand goals

Steve Yzerman, Detroit, 8; Brett Hull, St. Louis, 5; Mike Ridley, Washington, 5; Mario Lemieux, Pittsburgh, 4; Ron Sutter, St. Louis, 4.

Shooting percentage

(minimum 80 shots)

Gary Roberts, Calgary, 27.0; Sergei Makarov, Calgary, 26.5; Ray Ferraro, N.Y. Islanders, 26.0; Dale Hunter, Washington, 25.5; Sergei Nemchinov, N.Y. Rangers, 24.2.

Penalty Minutes

Mike Peluso, Chicago, 408; Rob Ray, Buffalo, 354; Gino Odjick, Vancouver, 348; Ronnie Stern, Calgary, 338; Link Gaetz, San Jose, 324.

Plus/Minus

Paul Ysebaert, Detroit, 44; Brad McCrimmon, Detroit, 39; Nicklas Lidstrom, Detroit, 36; James Patrick, N.Y. Rangers, 34; Mark Hardy, N.Y. Rangers, 33; Larry Murphy, Pittsburgh, 33.

Goaltending Leaders

(minimum 25 games)

Goals against average

Patrick Roy, Montreal, 2.36; Ed Belfour, Chicago, 2.70; Kirk McLean, Vancouver, 2.74; John Vanbiesbrouck, N.Y. Rangers, 2.85; Bob Essensa, Winnipeg, 2.88.

Wins

Kirk McLean, Vancouver, 38; Tim Cheveldae, Detroit, 38; Patrick Roy, Montreal, 36; Don Beaupre, Washington, 29; Andy Moog, Boston, 28.

Save percentage

Patrick Roy, Montreal, .914; Curtis Joseph, St. Louis, .910; Bob Essensa, Winnipeg, .910; John Vanbiesbrouck, N.Y. Rangers, .910; Kirk McLean, Vancouver, .901; Mike Richter, N.Y. Rangers, .901; Mark Fitzpatrick, N.Y. Islanders, .901.

Shutouts

Bob Essensa, Winnipeg; Ed Belfour, Chicago; Kirk McLean, Vancouver; Patrick Roy, Montreal, 5 each.

Individual Scoring

(40 or more games played)

Boston Bruins

	GP	G	A	Pts	+/–	PIM
Adam Oates	80	20	79	99	9–	22
Ray Bourque	80	21	60	81	11	56
Vladimir Ruzicka	77	39	36	75	10–	48
Stephen Leach	78	31	29	60	8–	147
Bob Carpenter	60	25	23	48	3–	46
Glen Wesley	78	9	37	46	9–	54
Brent Ashton	68	18	22	40	7–	51
Peter Douris	54	10	13	23	9	10
Bob Sweeney	63	6	14	20	9–	103
Gord Murphy	73	5	14	19	2–	84
Ken Hodge	42	6	11	17	8–	10
Dave Reid	43	7	7	14	5	27
Don Sweeney	75	3	11	14	9–	74
Jim Wiemer	47	1	8	9	10	84
Andy Moog	62	0	3	3	0	52

Coach—Rick Bowness

Buffalo Sabers

	GP	G	A	Pts	+/–	PIM
Dale Hawerchuk	77	23	75	98	22–	27
Pat Lafontaine	57	46	47	93	10	98
Dave Andreychuk	80	41	50	91	9–	71
Alexander Mogilny	67	39	45	84	7	73
Donald Audette	63	31	17	48	1–	75
Doug Bodger	73	11	35	46	1	108
Randy Wood	78	22	18	40	12–	86
Tony Tanti	70	15	16	31	4–	100
Petr Svoboda	71	6	22	28	1	146
Wayne Presley	59	10	16	26	27–	133
Christian Ruuttu	70	4	21	25	7–	76
Grant Ledyard	50	5	16	21	4–	45
Ken Sutton	64	2	18	20	5	71
Brad May	69	11	6	17	12–	309
Mike Ramsey	66	3	14	17	8	67
Colin Patterson	52	4	8	12	4–	30
Randy Moller	56	3	9	12	14–	137
Dave Hannan	47	4	6	10	9–	64
Rob Ray	63	5	3	8	9–	354
Gord Donnelly	71	2	3	5	12–	316
Brad Miller	42	1	4	5	5–	192

Coach—Rick Dudley; John Muckler

Calgary Flames

	GP	G	A	Pts	+/–	PIM
Gary Roberts	76	53	37	90	32	219
Al Macinnis	72	20	57	77	13	83
Theoren Fleury	80	33	40	73	0	133
Sergei Makarov	68	22	48	70	14	60
Joe Nieuwendyk	69	22	34	56	1–	55
Gary Suter	70	12	43	55	1	126
Robert Reichel	77	20	34	54	1	34
Paul Ranheim	80	23	20	43	16	32
Joel Otto	78	13	21	34	10–	163
Gary Leeman	63	9	19	28	12–	81
Michel Petit	70	4	23	27	15–	164
Carey Wilson	42	11	12	23	6–	37
Ronnie Stern	72	13	9	22	0	338
Marc Habscheid	46	7	11	18	11–	42
Craig Berube	76	6	11	17	5–	264
Trent Yawney	47	4	9	13	5–	45
Frank Musil	78	4	8	12	12	103
Mark Osiecki	50	2	7	9	4–	24
Mike Vernon	63	0	7	7	0	8

Coach—Doug Risebrough

Chicago Black Hawks

	GP	G	A	Pts	+/–	PIM
Jeremy Roenick	80	53	50	103	23	98
Steve Larmer	80	29	45	74	10	65
Michel Goulet	75	22	41	63	20	69
Brent Sutter	69	22	38	60	10–	36
Chris Chelios	80	9	47	56	24	245
Rob Brown	67	21	26	47	15–	71
Dirk Graham	80	17	30	47	5–	89
Brian Noonan	65	19	12	31	9	81
Steve Smith	76	9	21	30	23	304
Mike Hudson	76	14	15	29	11–	92
Keith Brown	57	6	10	16	7	69
Jocelyn Lemieux	78	6	10	16	2–	80
Bryan Marchment	58	5	10	15	4–	168
Tony Hrkac	40	3	12	15	2	10
Frantisek Kucera	61	3	10	13	3	36
Greg Gilbert	50	7	5	12	4–	35
Mike Peluso	63	6	3	9	1	408
Tony Horacek	46	2	7	9	7–	72
Stu Grimson	54	2	2	4	2–	234
Rod Buskas	47	0	4	4	13–	91
Ed Belfour	52	0	2	2	0	40

Coach—Mike Keenan

Detroit Red Wings

	GP	G	A	Pts	+/–	PIM
Steve Yzerman	79	45	58	103	26	64
Sergei Fedorov	80	32	54	86	26	72
Paul Ysebaert	79	35	40	75	44	55
Jimmy Carson	80	34	35	69	17	30
Ray Sheppard	74	36	26	62	7	27

	GP	G	A	Pts	+/–	PIM
Nicklas Lidstrom	80	11	49	60	36	22
Shawn Burr	79	19	32	51	26	118
Kevin Miller	80	20	26	46	6	53
Bob Probert	63	20	24	44	16	276
Gerard Gallant	69	14	22	36	16	187
Steve Chiasson	62	10	24	34	22	136
Vlad. Konstantinov	79	8	25	33	25	172
Brad McCrimmon	79	7	22	29	39	118
Yves Racine	61	2	22	24	6–	94
Brent Fedyk	61	5	8	13	5–	42
Alan Kerr	58	3	8	11	1	133
Brad Marsh	55	3	5	8	8	53
Bob McGill	74	3	1	4	37–	91
Tim Cheveldae	72	0	4	4	0	6

Coach—Bryan Murray

Edmonton Oilers

	GP	G	A	Pts	+/–	PIM
Vincent Damphousse	80	38	51	89	10	53
Joe Murphy	80	35	47	82	17	52
Craig Simpson	79	24	37	61	8	80
Scott Mellanby	80	23	27	50	5	197
Bernie Nicholls	50	20	29	49	4	40
Dave Manson	79	15	32	47	9	220
Kelly Buchberger	79	20	24	44	9	157
Anatoli Semenov	59	20	22	42	12	16
Norm Maciver	57	6	34	40	20	38
Petr Klima	57	21	13	34	18–	52
Craig MacTavish	80	12	18	30	1–	98
Martin Gelinas	68	11	18	29	14	62
Esa Tikkanen	40	12	16	28	8–	44
Josef Beranek	58	12	16	28	2–	18
Mark Lamb	59	6	22	28	4	46
David Maley	60	10	17	27	8	104
Brian Glynn	62	4	18	22	5–	30
Luke Richardson	75	2	19	21	9–	118
Geoff Smith	74	2	16	18	5–	43
Kevin Lowe	55	2	7	9	4–	107
Craig Muni	54	2	5	7	11	34
Bill Ranford	67	0	3	3	0	4

Coach—Ted Green

Hartford Whalers

	GP	G	A	Pts	+/–	PIM
John Cullen	77	26	51	77	28–	141
Murray Craven	73	27	33	60	2–	46
Pat Verbeek	76	22	35	57	16–	243
Zarley Zalapski	79	20	37	57	7–	116
Mikael Andersson	74	18	29	47	18	14
Bobby Holik	76	21	24	45	4	44
Andrew Cassels	67	11	30	41	3	18
Geoff Sanderson	64	13	18	31	5	18
Steve Konroyd	82	4	24	28	1–	97
Brad Shaw	62	3	22	25	1	44
Adam Burt	66	9	15	24	16–	93
Marc Bergevin	75	7	17	24	13–	64
Mark Hunter	63	10	13	23	8–	159
Randy Ladouceur	74	1	9	10	1–	127
Doug Houda	56	3	6	9	2–	125
Jim McKenzie	67	5	1	6	6–	87
Kay Whitmore	45	0	1	1	0	16

Coach—Jim Roberts

Los Angeles Kings

	GP	G	A	Pts	+/–	PIM
Wayne Gretzky	74	31	90	121	12–	34
Luc Robitaille	80	44	63	107	4–	95
Paul Coffey	64	11	58	69	1	87
Tony Granato	80	39	29	68	4	187
Jari Kurri	73	23	37	60	24–	24
Corey Millen	57	21	25	46	2	66
Mike Donnelly	80	29	16	45	5	20
Bob Kudelski	80	22	21	43	15–	42
Tomas Sandstrom	49	17	22	39	2–	70
Dave Taylor	77	10	19	29	10	63
Marty McSorley	71	7	22	29	13–	268
John McIntyre	73	5	19	24	0	100
Charlie Huddy	56	4	19	23	10–	43
Rob Blake	57	7	13	20	5–	102
Peter Ahola	71	7	12	19	12	101
Larry Robinson	56	3	10	13	1	37
Jay Miller	67	4	7	11	8–	237
Jim Thomson	45	1	2	3	1–	162
Kelly Hrudey	60	0	1	1	0	12

Coach—Tom Webster

Minnesota North Stars

	GP	G	A	Pts	+/–	PIM
Mike Modano	76	33	44	77	9–	46
Brian Bellows	80	30	45	75	20–	41
Dave Gagner	78	31	40	71	4–	107
Ulf Dahlen	79	36	30	66	5–	10
Todd Elik	62	15	31	46	0	125
Bobby Smith	68	9	37	46	24–	111
Brian Propp	51	12	23	35	3–	49
Neal Broten	76	8	26	34	15–	16
Mike Craig	67	15	16	31	12–	155
Mark Tinordi	63	4	24	28	13–	177
Gaetan Duchesne	73	8	15	23	6	102
Jim Johnson	71	4	10	14	11	102
Chris Dahlquist	74	1	13	14	10–	68
Basil McRae	59	5	8	13	14–	245
Derian Hatcher	43	7	5	12	7	88
Craig Ludwig	73	2	9	11	0	54
Marc Bureau	46	6	4	10	5–	50
David Shaw	59	1	9	10	12–	72
Shane Churla	57	4	1	5	12–	278
Jon Casey	52	0	2	2	0	26

Coach—Bob Gainey

Montreal Canadiens

	GP	G	A	Pts	+/–	PIM
Kirk Muller	78	36	41	77	15	86
Denis Savard	77	28	42	70	6	73
Stephan Lebeau	77	27	31	58	18	14
Shayne Corson	64	17	36	53	15	118
Brent Gilchrist	79	23	27	50	29	57
Mike Keane	67	11	30	41	16	64
Guy Carbonneau	72	18	21	39	2	39
Eric Desjardins	77	6	32	38	17	50
Matt Schneider	78	8	24	32	10	72
Mike McPhee	78	16	15	31	6	63
Kevin Haller	66	8	17	25	9–	92
Sylvain Turgeon	56	9	11	20	4–	39
John Leclair	59	8	11	19	5	14
J J. Daigneault	79	4	14	18	16	36
Sylvain Lefebvre	69	3	14	17	9	91
Chris Nilan	56	6	8	14	6–	260
Lyle Odelein	71	1	7	8	15	212
Brian Skrudland	42	3	3	6	4–	36
Patrick Roy	67	0	5	5	0	4
Todd Ewen	46	1	2	3	3	130

Coach—Pat Burns

New Jersey Devils

	GP	G	A	Pts	+/–	PIM
Claude Lemieux	74	41	27	68	9	109
Stephane Richer	74	29	35	64	1–	25
Kevin Todd	80	21	42	63	8	69
Peter Stastny	66	24	38	62	6	42
Scott Stevens	68	17	42	59	24	124
Claude Vilgrain	71	19	27	46	27	74
Bruce Driver	78	7	35	42	5	66
Alexei Kasatonov	76	12	28	40	14	70
Tom Chorske	76	19	17	36	8	32
Randy McKay	80	17	16	33	6	246
Eric Weinrich	76	7	25	32	10	55
Valeri Zelepukin	44	13	18	31	11	28
Doug Brown	71	11	17	28	17	27
Laurie Boschman	75	8	20	28	9	121
Viacheslav Fetisov	70	3	23	26	11	108
Dave Barr	41	6	12	18	9	32
Pat Conacher	44	7	3	10	0	16
Ken Daneyko	80	1	7	8	7	170
Chris Terreri	54	0	1	1	0	13

Coach—Tom McVie

New York Islanders

	GP	G	A	Pts	+/–	PIM
Pierre Turgeon	77	40	55	95	7	20
Ray Ferraro	80	40	40	80	25	92
Derek King	80	40	38	78	10–	46
Steve Thomas	82	30	48	78	8	97
Benoit Hogue	75	30	46	76	30	67
Dave Volek	74	18	42	60	0	35
Tom Kurvers	74	9	47	56	18–	30
Uwe Krupp	67	8	29	37	13	49
Adam Creighton	77	21	15	36	5–	118
Dan Marois	75	17	16	33	34–	94
Claude Loiselle	75	7	10	17	24–	115
Tom Fitzgerald	45	6	11	17	3–	28
Joe Reekie	54	4	12	16	15	85

(continued)

Bill Berg	47	5	9	14	18–	28
Jeff Finley	51	1	10	11	6–	26
Rob Dimaio	50	5	2	7	23–	43
Richard Pilon	65	1	6	7	1–	183
Mick Vukota	74	0	6	6	6–	293

Coach—Al Arbour

New York Rangers

	GP	G	A	Pts	+/–	PIM
Mark Messier	79	35	72	107	31	76
Brian Leetch	80	22	80	102	25	26
Mike Gartner	76	40	41	81	11	55
James Patrick	80	14	57	71	34	54
Tony Amonte	79	35	34	69	12	55
Adam Graves	80	26	33	59	19	139
Sergei Nemchinov	73	30	28	58	19	15
Darren Turcotte	71	30	23	53	11	57
John Ogrodnick	55	17	13	30	6	22
Doug Weight	53	8	22	30	3–	23
Paul Broten	74	13	15	28	14	102
Randy Gilhen	73	10	13	23	2	28
Kris King	79	10	9	19	13	224
Per Djoos	50	1	18	19	7	40
Jan Erixon	46	8	9	17	13	4
Jeff Beukeboom	74	1	15	16	23	200
Joe Cirella	67	3	12	15	11	121
Joey Kocur	51	7	4	11	4–	121
Jay Wells	52	2	9	11	1–	181
Mark Hardy	52	1	8	9	33	65
Tie Domi	42	2	4	6	4–	246
John Vanbiesbrouck	45	0	3	3	0	23
Mike Richter	41	0	0	0	0	6

Coach—Roger Neilson

Philadelphia Flyers

	GP	G	A	Pts	+/–	PIM
Mark Recchi	80	43	54	97	21–	96
Rod Brind'Amour	80	33	44	77	3–	100
Kevin Dineen	80	30	32	62	5–	143
Mike Ricci	78	20	36	56	10–	93
Steve Duchesne	78	18	38	56	7–	86
Brian Benning	75	4	42	46	5–	134
Mark Pederson	58	15	25	40	14	22
Dan Quinn	67	11	26	37	13–	26
Kerry Huffman	60	14	18	32	1	41
Garry Galley	77	5	27	32	2–	117
Andrei Lomakin	57	14	16	30	6–	26
Mark Howe	42	7	18	25	18	18
Per-Erik Eklund	51	7	16	23	0	4
Claude Boivin	58	5	13	18	2–	187
Brad Jones	48	7	10	17	2–	44
Keith Acton	50	7	9	16	4–	98
Terry Carkner	73	4	12	16	14–	195
Mark Freer	50	6	7	13	1–	18
Dave Brown	70	4	2	6	11–	81
Dan Kordic	46	1	3	4	1	126
Ron Hextall	45	0	4	4	0	35

Coach—Paul Holmgren; Bill Dineen

Pittsburgh Penguins

	GP	G	A	Pts	+/–	PIM
Mario Lemieux	64	44	87	131	27	94
Kevin Stevens	80	54	69	123	8	252
Joe Mullen	77	42	45	87	12	30
Larry Murphy	77	21	56	77	33	50
Jaromir Jagr	70	32	37	69	12	34
Rick Tocchet	61	27	32	59	15	151
Ron Francis	70	21	33	54	7–	30
Bob Errey	78	19	16	35	1	119
Bryan Trottier	63	11	18	29	11–	54
Phil Bourque	58	10	16	26	6–	58
Troy Loney	76	10	16	26	5–	127
Gordie Roberts	73	2	22	24	19	87
Kjell Samuelsson	74	5	11	16	1	110
Jiri Hrdina	56	3	13	16	4	16
Ulf Samuelsson	62	1	14	15	2	206
Ken Priestlay	50	2	8	10	5	4
Paul Stanton	54	2	8	10	8–	62
Grant Jennings	53	4	5	9	1–	104
Jim Paek	50	1	7	8	0	36
Peter Taglianetti	44	1	3	4	7	57
Jeff Chychrun	43	0	4	4	12–	103
Tom Barrasso	57	0	4	4	0	30
Jay Caufield	52	0	0	0	6–	183

Coach—Bob Johnson; Scotty Bowman

Quebec Nordiques

	GP	G	A	Pts	+/–	PIM
Joe Sakic	69	29	65	94	5	20
Mats Sundin	80	33	43	76	19–	105
Owen Nolan	75	42	31	73	9–	181
Greg Paslawski	80	28	17	45	12–	18
Mike Hough	61	16	22	38	1–	77
Mikhail Tatarinov	66	11	27	38	8	72
Claude Lapointe	78	13	20	33	8–	86
Doug Smail	46	10	18	28	11–	47
Gino Cavallini	66	10	14	24	9–	44
Alexei Gusarov	68	5	18	23	9–	22
Herb Raglan	62	6	14	20	5–	120
Jamie Baker	52	7	10	17	5–	32
Curtis Leschyshyn	42	5	12	17	28–	42
John Tonelli	52	3	11	14	5–	51
Craig Wolanin	69	2	11	13	12–	80
Steven Finn	65	4	7	11	9–	192
Adam Foote	46	2	5	7	4–	44
Tony Twist	46	0	1	1	3–	164

Coach—Dave Chambers; Pierre Page

St. Louis Blues

	GP	G	A	Pts	+/–	PIM
Brett Hull	73	70	39	109	2–	48
Craig Janney	78	18	69	87	6	22
Brendan Shanahan	80	33	36	69	3–	171
Nelson Emerson	79	23	36	59	5–	66
Jeff Brown	80	20	38	58	8	38
Ron Sutter	68	19	27	46	9	91
Dave Christian	78	20	24	44	2	41
Paul Cavallini	66	10	25	35	7	95
Bob Bassen	79	7	25	32	12	167
Ron Wilson	64	12	17	29	10	46
Rich Sutter	77	9	16	25	7	107
Dave Lowry	75	7	13	20	11–	77
Garth Butcher	68	5	15	20	5	189
Stephane Quintal	75	4	16	20	11–	109
Rick Zombo	67	3	15	18	1	61
Lee Norwood	50	3	11	14	14	110
Murray Baron	67	3	8	11	3–	94
Curtis Joseph	60	0	9	9	0	12
Darin Zimble	46	1	3	4	3–	166
Kelly Chase	46	1	2	3	6–	264

Coach—Brian Sutter

San Jose Sharks

	GP	G	A	Pts	+/–	PIM
Pat Falloon	79	25	34	59	32–	16
Brian Mullen	72	18	28	46	14–	66
David Bruce	60	22	16	38	20–	46
Brian Lawton	59	15	22	37	25–	42
Kelly Kisio	48	11	26	37	7–	54
Doug Wilson	44	9	19	28	38–	26
David Williams	56	3	25	28	13–	40
Dean Evason	74	11	15	26	22–	94
Perry Berezan	66	12	7	19	26–	30
Mike Sullivan	64	8	11	19	18–	15
Neil Wilkinson	60	4	15	19	11–	97
Dave Snuggerud	66	3	16	19	15–	45
Jay More	46	4	13	17	32–	85
Steve Bozek	58	8	8	16	30–	27
Paul Fenton	60	11	4	15	39–	33
Ken Hammond	46	5	10	15	17–	82
Link Gaetz	48	6	6	12	27–	324
Perry Anderson	48	4	8	12	17–	141
Jeff Odgers	61	7	4	11	21–	217
Rob Zettler	74	1	8	9	23–	103
Jeff Hackett	42	0	2	2	0	8

Coach—George Kingston

Toronto Maple Leafs

	GP	G	A	Pts	+/–	PIM
Doug Gilmour	78	26	61	87	25	78
Glenn Anderson	72	24	33	57	13–	100
Dave Ellett	79	18	33	51	13–	95
Peter Zezel	64	16	33	49	22–	26
Wendel Clark	43	19	21	40	14–	123
Brian Bradley	59	10	21	31	3–	48
Jamie Macoun	76	5	25	30	10	71
Mike Bullard	65	14	14	28	19–	42
Dave McIlwain	73	10	18	28	9–	36
Rob Pearson	47	14	10	24	16–	58
Mike Krushelnyski	72	9	15	24	5–	72
Bob Rouse	79	3	19	22	20–	97
Ric Nattress	54	2	19	21	1–	63

	GP	G	A	Pts	+/–	PIM
Mark Osborne	54	7	13	20	10–	73
Todd Gill	74	2	15	17	22–	91
Darryl Shannon	48	2	8	10	17–	23
Bob Halkidis	46	3	3	6	9–	145
Ken Baumgartner	55	0	1	1	9–	225
Grant Fuhr	65	0	1	1	0	4

Coach—Tom Watt

Vancouver Canucks

	GP	G	A	Pts	+/–	PIM
Trevor Linden	80	31	44	75	3	99
Cliff Ronning	80	24	47	71	18	42
Igor Larionov	72	21	44	65	7	56
Pavel Bure	65	34	26	60	0	30
Greg Adams	76	30	27	57	8	26
Geoff Courtnall	70	23	34	57	6–	118
Jyrki Lumme	75	12	32	44	25	65
Sergio Momesso	58	20	23	43	16	198
Jim Sandlak	66	16	24	40	22	176
Tom Fergus	55	15	23	38	10–	21
Petr Nedved	77	15	22	37	3–	36
Doug Lidster	66	6	23	29	9	39
Dave Babych	75	5	24	29	2–	63
Gerald Diduck	77	6	21	27	3–	224
Garry Valk	65	8	17	25	3	56
Ryan Walter	67	6	11	17	6	49
Dana Murzyn	70	3	12	15	15	145
Gino Odjick	65	4	6	10	1–	348
Robert Dirk	72	2	7	9	6	126
Kirk McLean	65	0	4	4	0	0

Coach—Pat Quinn

Washington Capitals

	GP	G	A	Pts	+/–	PIM
Michal Pivonka	80	23	57	80	10	47
Dale Hunter	80	28	50	78	2–	205
Dino Ciccarelli	78	38	38	76	10–	78
Dimitri Khristich	80	36	37	73	24	35
Mike Ridley	80	29	40	69	3	38
Randy Burridge	66	23	44	67	4–	50
Peter Bondra	71	28	28	56	16	42
Calle Johansson	80	14	42	56	2	49
Kevin Hatcher	79	17	37	54	18	105
Kelly Miller	78	14	38	52	20	49
Al Iafrate	78	17	34	51	1	180
Sylvain Cote	78	11	29	40	7	31
John Druce	67	19	18	37	14	39
Todd Krygier	67	13	17	30	1–	107
Paul MacDermid	74	12	16	28	6–	194
Alan May	75	6	9	15	7–	221
Rod Langway	64	0	13	13	11	22
Nick Kypreos	65	4	6	10	3–	206
Don Beaupre	54	0	0	0	0	30

Coach—Terry Murray

Winnipeg Jets

	GP	G	A	Pts	+/–	PIM
Phil Housley	74	23	63	86	5–	92
Ed Olczyk	64	32	33	65	11	67
Fredrik Olausson	77	20	42	62	31–	34
Pat Elynuik	60	25	25	50	2–	65
Troy Murray	74	17	30	47	13–	69
Darrin Shannon	69	13	27	40	6	41
Teppo Numminen	80	5	34	39	15	32
Luciano Borsato	56	15	21	36	6–	45
Lucien Deblois	65	9	13	22	2–	41
Stu Barnes	46	8	9	17	2–	26
Mike Eagles	65	7	10	17	17–	118
Mike Lalor	79	7	10	17	25	78
Danton Cole	52	7	5	12	15–	32
Randy Carlyle	66	1	9	10	4	54
Mike Hartman	75	4	4	8	10–	264
Phil Sykes	52	4	2	6	12–	72
Mario Marois	51	1	4	5	11–	72
Shawn Cronin	65	0	4	4	11–	271
Bob Essensa	47	0	2	2	0	2

Coach—John Paddock

Ross Trophy (Leading Scorer)

1927 Bill Cook, N.Y. Rangers
1928 Howie Morenz, Montreal
1929 Ace Bailey, Toronto
1930 Cooney Weiland, Boston
1931 Howie Morenz, Montreal
1932 Harvey Jackson, Toronto
1933 Bill Cook, N.Y. Rangers
1934 Charlie Conacher, Toronto
1935 Charlie Conacher, Toronto
1936 Dave Schriner, N.Y. Americans
1937 Dave Schriner, N.Y. Americans
1938 Gordie Drillon, Toronto
1939 Toe Blake, Montreal
1940 Milt Schmidt, Boston
1941 Bill Cowley, Boston
1942 Bryan Hextall, N.Y. Rangers
1943 Doug Bentley, Chicago
1944 Herbie Cain, Boston
1945 Elmer Lach, Montreal
1946 Max Bentley, Chicago
1947 Max Bentley, Chicago
1948 Elmer Lach, Montreal
1949 Roy Conacher, Chicago
1950 Ted Lindsay, Detroit
1951 Gordie Howe, Detroit
1952 Gordie Howe, Detroit
1953 Gordie Howe, Detroit
1954 Gordie Howe, Detroit
1955 Bernie Geoffrion, Montreal
1956 Jean Beliveau, Montreal
1957 Gordie Howe, Detroit
1958 Dickie Moore, Montreal
1959 Dickie Moore, Montreal
1960 Bobby Hull, Chicago
1961 Bernie Geoffrion, Montreal
1962 Bobby Hull, Chicago
1963 Gordie Howe, Detroit
1964 Stan Mikita, Chicago
1965 Stan Mikita, Chicago
1966 Bobby Hull, Chicago
1967 Stan Mikita, Chicago
1968 Stan Mikita, Chicago
1969 Phil Esposito, Boston
1970 Bobby Orr, Boston
1971 Phil Esposito, Boston
1972 Phil Esposito, Boston
1973 Phil Esposito, Boston
1974 Phil Esposito, Boston
1975 Bobby Orr, Boston
1976 Guy Lafleur, Montreal
1977 Guy Lafleur, Montreal
1978 Guy Lafleur, Montreal
1979 Bryan Trottier, N.Y. Islanders
1980 Marcel Dionne, Los Angeles
1981 Wayne Gretzky, Edmonton
1982 Wayne Gretzky, Edmonton
1983 Wayne Gretzky, Edmonton
1984 Wayne Gretzky, Edmonton
1985 Wayne Gretzky, Edmonton
1986 Wayne Gretzky, Edmonton
1987 Wayne Gretzky, Edmonton
1988 Mario Lemieux, Pittsburgh
1989 Mario Lemieux, Pittsburgh
1990 Wayne Gretzky, Los Angeles
1991 Wayne Gretzky, Los Angeles
1992 Mario Lemieux, Pittsburgh

James Norris Memorial Trophy (Outstanding Defenseman)

1954 Red Kelly, Detroit
1955 Doug Harvey, Montreal
1956 Doug Harvey, Montreal
1957 Doug Harvey, Montreal
1958 Doug Harvey, Montreal
1959 Tom Johnson, Montreal
1960 Doug Harvey, Montreal
1961 Doug Harvey, Montreal
1962 Doug Harvey, N.Y. Rangers
1963 Pierre Pilote, Chicago
1964 Pierre Pilote, Chicago
1965 Pierre Pilote, Chicago
1966 Jacques Laperriere, Montreal
1967 Harry Howell, N.Y. Rangers
1968 Bobby Orr, Boston
1969 Bobby Orr, Boston
1970 Bobby Orr, Boston
1971 Bobby Orr, Boston
1972 Bobby Orr, Boston
1973 Bobby Orr, Boston
1974 Bobby Orr, Boston
1975 Bobby Orr, Boston
1976 Denis Potvin, N.Y. Islanders
1977 Larry Robinson, Montreal
1978 Denis Potvin, N.Y. Islanders
1979 Denis Potvin, N.Y. Islanders
1980 Larry Robinson, Montreal
1981 Randy Carlyle, Pittsburgh
1982 Doug Wilson, Chicago
1983 Rod Langway, Washington
1984 Rod Langway, Washington
1985 Paul Coffey, Edmonton
1986 Paul Coffey, Edmonton
1987 Ray Bourque, Boston
1988 Ray Bourque, Boston
1989 Chris Chelios, Montreal
1990 Ray Bourque, Boston
1991 Ray Bourque, Boston
1992 Brian Leetch, N.Y. Rangers

*Vezina Trophy (Leading Goalie)

1927	George Hainsworth, Montreal
1928	George Hainsworth, Montreal
1929	George Hainsworth, Montreal
1930	Tiny Thompson, Boston
1931	Roy Worters, N.Y. Americans
1932	Charlie Gardiner, Chicago
1933	Tiny Thompson, Boston
1934	Charlie Gardiner, Chicago
1935	Lorne Chabot, Chicago
1936	Tiny Thompson, Boston
1937	Normie Smith, Detroit
1938	Tiny Thompson, Boston
1939	Frank Brimsek, Boston
1940	Dave Kerr, N.Y. Rangers
1941	Turk Broda, Toronto
1942	Frank Brimsek, Boston
1943	Johnny Mowers, Detroit
1944	Bill Durnan, Montreal
1945	Bill Durnan, Montreal
1946	Bill Durnan, Montreal
1947	Bill Durnan, Montreal
1948	Turk Broda, Toronto
1949	Bill Durnan, Montreal
1950	Bill Durnan, Montreal
1951	Al Rollins, Toronto
1952	Terry Sawchuk, Detroit
1953	Terry Sawchuk, Detroit
1954	Harry Lumley, Toronto
1955	Terry Sawchuk, Detroit
1956	Jacques Plante, Montreal
1957	Jacques Plante, Montreal
1958	Jacques Plante, Montreal
1959	Jacques Plante, Montreal
1960	Jacques Plante, Montreal
1961	John Bower, Toronto
1962	Jacques Plante, Montreal
1963	Glenn Hall, Chicago
1964	Charlie Hodge, Montreal
1965	Sawchuk, Bower, Toronto
1966	Worsley, Hodge, Montreal
1967	Hall, DeJordy, Chicago
1968	Worsley, Vachon, Montreal
1969	Hall, Plante, St. Louis
1970	Tony Esposito, Chicago
1971	Giacomin, Villemure, N.Y. Rangers
1972	Esposito, Smith, Chicago
1973	Ken Dryden, Montreal
1974	Bernie Parent, Philadelphia; Tony Esposito, Chicago
1975	Bernie Parent, Philadelphia
1976	Ken Dryden, Montreal
1977	Dryden, Larocque, Montreal
1978	Dryden, Larocque, Montreal
1979	Dryden, Larocque, Montreal
1980	Sauve, Edwards, Buffalo
1981	Sevigny, Larocque, Herron, Montreal
1982	Bill Smith, N.Y. Islanders
1983	Pete Peeters, Boston
1984	Tom Barrasso, Buffalo
1985	Pelle Lindbergh, Philadelphia
1986	John Vanbiesbrouck, N.Y. Rangers
1987	Ron Hextall, Philadelphia
1988	Grant Fuhr, Edmonton
1989	Patrick Roy, Montreal
1990	Patrick Roy, Montreal
1991	Ed Belfour, Chicago
1992	Patrick Roy, Montreal

* Awarded to goalie who played a minimum 25 games for the team which allowed the fewest goals; since 1982, awarded to outstanding goalie.

Calder Memorial Trophy (Rookie of the Year)

1933	Carl Voss, Detroit
1934	Russ Blinco, Montreal Maroons
1935	Dave Schriner, N.Y. Americans
1936	Mike Karakas, Chicago
1937	Syl Apps, Toronto
1938	Cully Dahlstrom, Chicago
1939	Frank Brimsek, Boston
1940	Kilby Macdonald, N.Y. Rangers
1941	John Quilty, Montreal
1942	Grant Warwick, N.Y. Rangers
1943	Gaye Stewart, Toronto
1944	Gus Bodnar, Toronto
1945	Frank McCool, Toronto
1946	Edgar Laprade, N.Y. Rangers
1947	Howie Meeker, Toronto
1948	Jim McFadden, Detroit
1949	Pentti Lund, N.Y. Rangers
1950	Jack Gelineau, Boston
1951	Terry Sawchuk, Detroit
1952	Bernie Geoffrion, Montreal
1953	Gump Worsley, N.Y. Rangers
1954	Camille Henry, N.Y. Rangers
1955	Ed Litzenberger, Chicago
1956	Glenn Hall, Detroit
1957	Larry Regan, Boston
1958	Frank Mahovlich, Toronto
1959	Ralph Backstrom, Montreal
1960	Bill Hay, Chicago
1961	Dave Keon, Toronto
1962	Bobby Rousseau, Montreal
1963	Kent Douglas, Toronto
1964	Jacques Laperriere, Montreal
1965	Roger Crozier, Detroit
1966	Brit Selby, Toronto
1967	Bobby Orr, Boston
1968	Derek Sanderson, Boston
1969	Danny Grant, Minnesota
1970	Tony Esposito, Chicago
1971	Gilbert Perreault, Buffalo
1972	Ken Dryden, Montreal
1973	Steve Vickers, N.Y. Rangers
1974	Denis Potvin, N.Y. Islanders
1975	Eric Vail, Atlanta
1976	Bryan Trottier, N.Y. Islanders
1977	Willi Plett, Atlanta
1978	Mike Bossy, N.Y. Islanders
1979	Bobby Smith, Minnesota
1980	Ray Bourque, Boston
1981	Peter Stastny, Quebec
1982	Dale Hawerchuk, Winnipeg
1983	Steve Larmer, Chicago
1984	Tom Barrasso, Buffalo
1985	Mario Lemieux, Pittsburgh
1986	Gary Suter, Calgary
1987	Luc Robitaille, Los Angeles
1988	Joe Nieuwendyk, Calgary
1989	Brian Leetch, N.Y. Rangers
1990	Sergei Makarov, Calgary
1991	Ed Belfour, Chicago
1992	Pavel Bure, Vancouver

Lady Byng Memorial Trophy (Most Gentlemanly Player)

1925	Frank Nighbor, Ottawa
1926	Frank Nighbor, Ottawa
1927	Billy Burch, N.Y. Americans
1928	Frank Boucher, N.Y. Rangers
1929	Frank Boucher, N.Y. Rangers
1930	Frank Boucher, N.Y. Rangers
1931	Frank Boucher, N.Y. Rangers
1932	Joe Primeau, Toronto
1933	Frank Boucher, N.Y. Rangers
1934	Frank Boucher, N.Y. Rangers
1935	Frank Boucher, N.Y. Rangers
1936	Doc Romnes, Chicago
1937	Marty Barry, Detroit
1938	Gordie Drillon, Toronto
1939	Clint Smith, N.Y. Rangers
1940	Bobby Bauer, Boston
1941	Bobby Bauer, Boston
1942	Syl Apps, Toronto
1943	Max Bentley, Chicago
1944	Clint Smith, Chicago
1945	Bill Mosienko, Chicago
1946	Toe Blake, Montreal
1947	Bobby Bauer, Boston
1948	Buddy O'Connor, N.Y. Rangers
1949	Bill Quackenbush, Detroit
1950	Edgar Laprade, N.Y. Rangers
1951	Red Kelly, Detroit
1952	Sid Smith, Toronto
1953	Red Kelly, Detroit
1954	Red Kelly, Detroit
1955	Sid Smith, Toronto
1956	Earl Reibel, Detroit
1957	Andy Hebenton, N.Y. Rangers
1958	Camille Henry, N.Y. Rangers
1959	Alex Delvecchio, Detroit
1960	Don McKenney, Boston
1961	Red Kelly, Toronto
1962	Dave Keon, Toronto
1963	Dave Keon, Toronto
1964	Ken Wharram, Chicago
1965	Bobby Hull, Chicago
1966	Alex Delvecchio, Detroit
1967	Stan Mikita, Chicago
1968	Stan Mikita, Chicago
1969	Alex Delvecchio, Detroit
1970	Phil Goyette, St. Louis
1971	John Bucyk, Boston
1972	Jean Ratelle, N.Y. Rangers
1973	Gil Perreault, Buffalo
1974	John Bucyk, Boston
1975	Marcel Dionne, Detroit
1976	Jean Ratelle, N.Y. R.-Boston
1977	Marcel Dionne, Los Angeles
1978	Butch Goring, Los Angeles
1979	Bob MacMillan, Atlanta
1980	Wayne Gretzky, Edmonton
1981	Rick Kehoe, Pittsburgh
1982	Rick Middleton, Boston
1983	Mike Bossy, N.Y. Islanders
1984	Mike Bossy, N.Y. Islanders
1985	Jari Kurri, Edmonton
1986	Mike Bossy, N.Y. Islanders
1987	Joe Mullen, Calgary
1988	Mats Naslund, Montreal
1989	Joe Mullen, Calgary
1990	Brett Hull, St. Louis
1991	Wayne Gretzky, Los Angeles
1992	Wayne Gretzky, Los Angeles

Frank J. Selke Trophy (Best Defensive Forward)

1978	Bob Gainey, Montreal
1979	Bob Gainey, Montreal
1980	Bob Gainey, Montreal
1981	Bob Gainey, Montreal
1982	Steve Kasper, Boston
1983	Bobby Clarke, Philadelphia
1984	Doug Jarvis, Washington
1985	Craig Ramsay, Buffalo
1986	Troy Murray, Chicago
1987	Dave Poulin, Philadelphia
1988	Guy Carbonneau, Montreal
1989	Guy Carbonneau, Montreal
1990	Rick Meagher, St. Louis
1991	Dirk Graham, Chicago
1992	Guy Carbonneau, Montreal

Hart Memorial Trophy (MVP)

1927 Herb Gardiner, Montreal
1928 Howie Morenz, Montreal
1929 Roy Worters, N.Y. Americans
1930 Nels Stewart, Montreal Maroons
1931 Howie Morenz, Montreal
1932 Howie Morenz, Montreal
1933 Eddie Shore, Boston
1934 Aurel Joliat, Montreal
1935 Eddie Shore, Boston
1936 Eddie Shore, Boston
1937 Babe Siebert, Montreal
1938 Eddie Shore, Boston
1939 Toe Blake, Montreal
1940 Ebbie Goodfellow, Detroit
1941 Bill Cowley, Boston
1942 Tom Anderson, N.Y. Americans
1943 Bill Cowley, Boston
1944 Babe Pratt, Toronto
1945 Elmer Lach, Montreal
1946 Max Bentley, Chicago
1947 Maurice Richard, Montreal
1948 Buddy O'Connor, N.Y. Rangers
1949 Sid Abel, Detroit
1950 Chuck Rayner, N.Y. Rangers
1951 Milt Schmidt, Boston
1952 Gordie Howe, Detroit
1953 Gordie Howe, Detroit
1954 Al Rollins, Chicago
1955 Ted Kennedy, Toronto
1956 Jean Beliveau, Montreal
1957 Gordie Howe, Detroit
1958 Gordie Howe, Detroit
1959 Andy Bathgate, N.Y. Rangers
1960 Gordie Howe, Detroit
1961 Bernie Geoffrion, Montreal
1962 Jacques Plante, Montreal
1963 Gordie Howe, Detroit
1964 Jean Beliveau, Montreal
1965 Bobby Hull, Chicago
1966 Bobby Hull, Chicago
1967 Stan Mikita, Chicago
1968 Stan Mikita, Chicago
1969 Phil Esposito, Boston
1970 Bobby Orr, Boston
1971 Bobby Orr, Boston
1972 Bobby Orr, Boston
1973 Bobby Clarke, Philadelphia
1974 Phil Esposito, Boston
1975 Bobby Clarke, Philadelphia
1976 Bobby Clarke, Philadelphia
1977 Guy Lafleur, Montreal
1978 Guy Lafleur, Montreal
1979 Bryan Trottier, N.Y. Islanders
1980 Wayne Gretzky, Edmonton
1981 Wayne Gretzky, Edmonton
1982 Wayne Gretzky, Edmonton
1983 Wayne Gretzky, Edmonton
1984 Wayne Gretzky, Edmonton
1985 Wayne Gretzky, Edmonton
1986 Wayne Gretzky, Edmonton
1987 Wayne Gretzky, Edmonton
1988 Mario Lemieux, Pittsburgh
1989 Wayne Gretzky, Los Angeles
1990 Mark Messier, Edmonton
1991 Brett Hull, St. Louis
1992 Mark Messier, N.Y. Rangers

Conn Smythe Trophy (MVP in Playoffs)

1965 Jean Beliveau, Montreal
1966 Roger Crozier, Detroit
1967 Dave Keon, Toronto
1968 Glenn Hall, St. Louis
1969 Serge Savard, Montreal
1970 Bobby Orr, Boston
1971 Ken Dryden, Montreal
1972 Bobby Orr, Boston
1973 Yvan Cournoyer, Montreal
1974 Bernie Parent, Philadelphia
1975 Bernie Parent, Philadelphia
1976 Reg Leach, Philadelphia
1977 Guy Lafleur, Montreal
1978 Larry Robinson, Montreal
1979 Bob Gainey, Montreal
1980 Bryan Trottier, N.Y. Islanders
1981 Butch Goring, N.Y. Islanders
1982 Mike Bossy, N.Y. Islanders
1983 Billy Smith, N.Y. Islanders
1984 Mark Messier, Edmonton
1985 Wayne Gretzky, Edmonton
1986 Patrick Roy, Montreal
1987 Ron Hextall, Philadelphia
1988 Wayne Gretzky, Edmonton
1989 Al MacInnis, Calgary
1990 Bill Ranford, Edmonton
1991 Mario Lemieux, Pittsburgh
1992 Mario Lemieux, Pittsburgh

NHL All Star Team, 1992

First team	Position	Second team
Patrick Roy, Montreal	Goalie	Kirk McLean, Vancouver
Ray Bourque, Boston	Defense	Phil Housley, Winnipeg
Brian Leetch, N.Y. Rangers	Defense	Scott Stevens, New Jersey
Mark Messier, N.Y. Rangers	Center	Mario Lemieux, Pittsburgh
Brett Hull, St. Louis	Right Wing	Mark Recchi, Philadelphia
Kevin Stevens, Pittsburgh	Left Wing	Luc Robitalle, Los Angeles

All-Time NHL Scoring Leaders

At end of 1991-92 season. *Active player.

	Games	G	A	Pts
Wayne Gretzky*	999	749	1,514	2,263
Gordie Howe	1,767	801	1,049	1,850
Marcel Dionne	1,348	731	1,040	1,771
Phil Esposito	1,282	717	873	1,590
Stan Mikita	1,394	541	926	1,467
Bryan Trottier*	1,438	520	890	1,410
John Bucyk	1,540	556	813	1,369
Guy Lafleur	1,126	560	793	1,353
Gil Perreault	1,191	512	814	1,326
Alex Delvecchio	1,549	456	825	1,281
Jean Ratelle	1,281	491	776	1,267
Norm Ullman	1,410	490	739	1,229
Jean Beliveau	1,215	507	712	1,219
Bobby Clarke	1,144	358	852	1,210
Peter Stastny*	892	427	754	1,181
Bobby Hull	1,063	610	560	1,170

NCAA Hockey Champions

1948 Michigan
1949 Boston College
1950 Colorado College
1951 Michigan
1952 Michigan
1953 Michigan
1954 RPI
1955 Michigan
1956 Michigan
1957 Colorado College
1958 Denver
1959 North Dakota
1960 Denver
1961 Denver
1962 Michigan Tech
1963 North Dakota
1964 Michigan
1965 Michigan Tech
1966 Michigan State
1967 Cornell
1968 Denver
1969 Denver
1970 Cornell
1971 Boston Univ.
1972 Boston Univ.
1973 Wisconsin
1974 Minnesota
1975 Michigan Tech
1976 Minnesota
1977 Wisconsin
1978 Boston Univ.
1979 Minnesota
1980 North Dakota
1981 Wisconsin
1982 North Dakota
1983 Wisconsin
1984 Bowling Green
1985 RPI
1986 Michigan State
1987 North Dakota
1988 Lake Superior St.
1989 Harvard
1990 Wisconsin
1991 N. Michigan
1992 Lake Superior St.

IGFA Freshwater & Saltwater All-Tackle World Records

Source: International Game Fish Association. Records confirmed to May, 1992

Saltwater Fish

Species	Weight	Where caught	Date	Angler
Albacore	88 lbs. 2 oz.	Pt. Mogan, Canary Islands	Nov. 19, 1977	Siegfried Dickemann
Amberjack, greater	155 lbs. 10 oz.	Bermuda	June 24, 1981	Joseph Dawson
Amberjack, Pacific	104 lbs.	Baja, Mexico	July 4, 1984	Richard Cresswell
Barracuda, great	83 lbs.	Lagos, Nigeria	Jan. 13, 1952	K.J.W. Hackett
Barracuda, Mexican	21 lbs.	Costa Rica	Mar. 27, 1987	E. Greg Kent
Barracuda, slender	17 lbs. 4 oz.	Sitra Channel, Bahrain	Nov. 21, 1985	Roger Cranswick
Bass, barred sand	13 lbs. 3 oz.	Huntington Beach, Cal.	Aug. 29, 1988	Robert Halal
Bass, black sea	9 lbs. 8 oz.	Virginia Beach, Va.	Jan. 9, 1987	Joe Mizelle Jr.
		Virginia Beach, Va.	Dec. 22, 1990	Jack Stallings, Jr.
Bass, European	20 lbs. 11 oz.	Stes Maries de la Mer, France	May 6, 1986	Jean Baptiste Bayle
Bass, giant sea	563 lbs. 8 oz.	Anacaba Island, Cal.	Aug. 20, 1968	James D. McAdam Jr.
Bass, striped	78 lbs. 8 oz.	Atlantic City, N.J.	Sept. 21, 1982	Albert McReynolds
Bluefish	31 lbs. 12 oz.	Hatteras Inlet, N.C.	Jan. 30, 1972	James M. Hussey
Bonefish	19 lbs.	Zululand, S. Africa	May 26, 1962	Brian W. Batchelor
Bonito, Atlantic	18 lbs. 14 oz.	Fayal I., Azores	July 8, 1953	D. G. Higgs
Bonito, Pacific	23 lbs. 8 oz.	Victoria, Mahe Seychelles	Feb. 19, 1975	Anne Cochain
Cabezon	23 lbs.	Juan De Fuca Strait, Wash.	Aug. 4, 1990	Wesley Hunter
Cobia	135 lbs. 9 oz.	Shark Bay, Australia	July 9, 1985	Peter W. Goulding
Cod, Atlantic	98 lbs. 12 oz.	Isle of Shoals, N.H.	June 8, 1969	Alphonse Bielevich
Cod, Pacific	30 lbs.	Andrew Bay, Alaska	June 7, 1984	Donald Vaughn
Conger	110 lbs. 8 oz.	Plymouth, England	Aug. 20, 1990	Hans Clausen
Dolphin	87 lbs.	Papagallo Gulf, Costa Rica	Sept. 25, 1976	Manual Salazar
Drum, black	113 lbs. 1 oz.	Lewes, Del.	Sept. 15, 1975	Gerald Townsend
Drum, red	94 lbs. 2 oz.	Avon, N.C.	Nov. 7, 1984	David Deuel
Eel, African mottled	36 lbs. 1 oz.	Durban, So. Africa	June 10, 1984	Ferdie van Nooten
Eel, American	7 lb. 8 oz.	Mashpee, Mass.	May 8, 1990	Paul Peitavino
Flounder, southern	20 lb. 9 oz.	Nassau Sound, Fla.	Dec. 23, 1983	Larenza Mungin
Flounder, summer	22 lbs. 7 oz.	Montauk, N.Y.	Sept. 15, 1975	Charles Nappi
Grouper, Warsaw	436 lbs. 12 oz.	Gulf of Mexico, Destin, Fla.	Dec. 22, 1985	Steve Haeusler
Halibut, Atlantic	255 lbs. 4 oz.	Gloucester, Mass.	July 28, 1989	Sonny Manley
Halibut, California	53 lbs. 4 oz.	Santa Rosa Is., Cal.	July 7, 1988	Russell Harmon
Halibut, Pacific	368 lbs.	Gustavus, Alaska	July 5, 1991	Celia Deuitt
Jack, crevalle	54 lbs. 7oz.	Pt. Michel, Gabon	Jan. 15, 1982	Thomas Gibson Jr.
Jack, horse-eye	24 lbs. 8 oz.	Miami, Fla.	Dec. 20, 1982	Tito Schnau
Jack, Pacific crevalle	24 lbs.	Baja, Cal., Mex.	Apr. 30, 1987	Sharon Swanson
Jewfish	680 lbs.	Fernandina Beach, Fla.	May 20, 1961	Lynn Joyner
Kawakawa	29 lbs.	Clarion Is., Mexico	Dec. 17, 1986	Ronald Nakamura
Lingcod	66 lbs.	Harris Bay, Alaska	July 31, 1990	James McKenzie
Mackerel, cero	17 lbs. 2 oz.	Islamorada, Fla.	Apr. 5, 1986	G. Michael Mills
Mackerel, king	90 lbs.	Key West, Fla.	Feb. 16, 1976	Norton Thornton
Mackeral, Spanish	13 lbs.	Ocracoke Inlet, N.C.	Nov. 4, 1987	Robert Cranton
Marlin, Atlantic blue	1,282 lbs.	St. Thomas, Virgin Islands	Aug. 6, 1977	Larry Martin
Marlin, black	1,560 lbs.	Cabo Blanco, Peru	Aug. 4, 1953	A. C. Glassell Jr.
Marlin, Pacific blue	1,376 lbs.	Kaaiwa Pt., Hawaii	May. 31, 1982	J.W. deBeaubien
Marlin, striped	494 lbs.	Tutukaka, New Zealand	Jan. 16, 1986	Bill Boniface
Marlin, white	181 lbs. 14 oz.	Vitoria, Brazil	Dec. 8, 1979	Evandro Luiz Caser
Permit	51 lbs. 8 oz.	Lake Worth, Fla.	Apr. 28, 1978	William M. Kenney
Pollack	27 lbs. 6 oz.	Devon, England	Jan. 16, 1986	Robert Milkins
Pollock	46 lbs. 10 oz.	Perkins Cove, Me.	Oct. 24, 1990	Linda Paul
Pompano, African	50 lbs. 8 oz.	Daytona Beach, Fla.	Apr. 21, 1990	Tom Sargent
Roosterfish	114 lbs.	La Paz, Mexico	June 1, 1960	Abe Sackheim
Runner, blue	8 lbs. 4 oz.	Bimini, Bahamas	Sept. 9, 1990	Brent Rowland
Runner, rainbow	37 lbs. 9 oz.	Clarion Is., Mexico	Nov. 21, 1991	Tom Pfleger
Sailfish, Atlantic	128 lbs. 1 oz.	Luanda, Angola	Mar. 27, 1974	Harm Steyn
Sailfish, Pacific	221 lbs.	Santa Cruz Is., Ecuador	Feb. 12, 1947	C. W. Stewart
Seabass, white	83 lbs. 12 oz.	San Felipe, Mexico	Mar. 31, 1953	L.C. Baumgardner
Seatrout, spotted	16 lbs.	Mason's Beach, Va.	May 28, 1977	William Katko
Shark, blue	437 lbs.	Catherine Bay, N.S.W. Australia	Oct. 2, 1976	Peter Hyde
Shark, Greenland	1,708 lbs. 9 oz.	Trondheim, Norway	Oct. 18, 1987	Terje Nordtvedt
Shark, hammerhead	991 lbs.	Sarasota, Fla.	May 30, 1982	Allen Ogle
Shark, man-eater or white	2,664 lbs.	Ceduna, Australia	Apr. 21, 1959	Alfred Dean
Shark, mako	1,115 lbs.	Black R., Mauritius	Nov. 16, 1988	Patrick Guillanton
Shark, porbeagle	465 lbs.	Cornwall, England	July 23, 1976	Jorge Potier
Shark, thresher	802 lbs.	Tutukaka, New Zealand	Feb. 8, 1981	Dianne North
Shark, tiger	1,780 lbs.	Cherry Grove, S.C.	June 14, 1964	Walter Maxwell
Skipjack, black	26 lbs.	Baja, Mexico	Oct. 23, 1991	Clifford Hamishi
Snapper, cubera	121 lbs. 8 oz.	Cameron, La.	July 5, 1982	Mike Hebert
Snook	53 lbs. 10 oz.	Costa Rica	Oct. 18, 1978	Gilbert Ponzi
Spearfish	90 lbs. 13 oz.	Madeira Island, Portugal	June 2, 1980	Joseph Larkin
Swordfish	1,182 lbs.	Iquique, Chile	May 7, 1953	L. Marron
Tanguigue	99 lbs.	Natal, So. Africa	Mar. 14, 1982	Michael J. Wilkinson
Tarpon	283 lbs. 4 oz.	Sierra Leone	Apr. 16, 1991	Yvon Sebag
Tautog	24 lbs.	Wachapreagee, Va.	Aug. 25, 1987	Gregory Bell
Tope	72 lbs. 12 oz.	Parengarenga Harbor, New Zealand	Dec. 19, 1986	Melanie Feldman
Trevally, bigeye	15 lbs.	Isla Coiba, Panama	Jan. 18, 1984	Sally Timms
Trevally, giant	145 lbs. 8 oz.	Makena, Hawaii	Mar. 28, 1991	Russell Mori
Tuna, Atlantic bigeye	375 lbs. 8 oz.	Ocean City, Md.	Aug. 26, 1977	Cecil Browne
Tuna, blackfin	42 lbs.	Bermuda	June 2, 1978	Alan J. Card
		Bermuda	July 18, 1989	Gilbert Pearman
Tuna, bluefin	1,496 lbs.	Aulds Cove, Nova Scotia	Oct. 26, 1979	Ken Fraser

Species	Weight	Where caught	Date	Angler
Tuna, longtail	79 lbs. 2 oz.	Montague Is., N.S.W., Australia	Apr. 12, 1982	Tim Simpson
Tuna, Pacific bigeye	435 lbs.	Cabo Blanco, Peru	Apr. 17, 1957	Dr. Russel Lee
Tuna, skipjack	41 lbs. 14 oz.	Mauritius	Nov. 12, 1985	Edmund Heinzen
Tuna, southern bluefin	348 lbs. 5 oz.	Whakatane, New Zealand	Jan. 16, 1981	Rex Wood
Tuna, yellowfin	388 lbs. 12 oz.	San Benedicto Island, Mexico	Apr. 1, 1977	Curt Wiesenhutter
Tunny, little	35 lbs. 2 oz.	Cap de Garde, Algeria	Dec. 14, 1988	Jean Yves Chatard
Wahoo	155 lbs. 8 oz.	Bahamas	Apr. 3, 1990	William Bourne
Weakfish	19 lbs. 2 oz.	Jones Beach Inlet, N.Y.	Oct. 11, 1984	Dennis Rooney
		Delaware Bay, Delaware	May 20, 1989	William Thomas
Yellowtail, California	79 lbs. 4 oz.	Alijos Rocks, Mexico	July 2, 1991	Robert Walker
Yellowtail, southern	114 lbs. 10 oz.	Tauranga, New Zealand	Feb. 5, 1984	Mike Godfrey

Freshwater Fish

Barramundi	63 lbs. 2 oz.	Normah R., Australia	Apr. 28, 1991	Scott Barnsley
Bass, largemouth	22 lbs. 4 oz.	Montgomery Lake, Ga.	June 2, 1932	George W. Perry
Bass, peacock	26 lbs. 8 oz.	Matevini R., Colombia	Jan. 26, 1982	Rod Neubert
Bass, redeye	8 lbs. 3 oz.	Flint River, Ga.	Oct. 23, 1977	David A. Hubbard
Bass rock	3 lbs.	York River, Ont.	Aug. 1, 1974	Peter Gulgin
Bass, smallmouth	11 lbs. 15 oz.	Dale Hollow Lake, Ky.	July 9, 1955	David L. Hayes
Bass, Suwannee	3 lbs. 14 oz.	Suwannee River, Fla.	Mar. 2, 1985	Ronnie Everett
Bass, white	6 lbs. 13 oz.	L. Orange, Va.	July 31, 1989	Ronald Sprouse
Bass, whiterock	24 lbs. 3 oz.	Leesville L., Va.	May 12, 1989	David Lambert
Bass, yellow	2 lbs. 4 oz.	Lake Monroe, Ind.	Mar. 27, 1977	Donald L. Stalker
Bluegill	4 lbs. 12 oz.	Ketona Lake, Ala.	Apr. 9, 1950	T.S. Hudson
Bowfin	21 lbs. 8 oz.	Florence, S.C.	Jan. 29, 1980	Robert Harmon
Buffalo, bigmouth	70 lbs. 5 oz.	Bastrop, La.	Apr. 21, 1980	Delbert Sisk
Buffalo, black	55 lbs. 8 oz.	Cherokee L., Tenn.	May 3, 1984	Edward McLain
Buffalo, smallmouth	68 lbs. 8 oz.	L. Hamilton, Ark.	May 16, 1984	Jerry Dolezal
Bullhead, brown	5 lbs. 8 oz.	Veal Pond, Ga.	May 22, 1975	Jimmy Andrews
Bullhead, yellow	4 lbs. 4 oz.	Mormon Lake, Ariz.	May 11, 1984	Emily Williams
Burbot	18 lbs. 4 oz.	Pickford, Mich.	Jan. 31, 1980	Thomas Courtemanche
Carp	75 lbs. 11 oz.	Lac de St. Cassien, France	May 21, 1987	Leo van der Gugten
Catfish, blue	109 lbs. 4 oz.	Cooper R., S.C.	Mar. 14, 1991	George Lijewski
Catfish, channel	58 lbs.	Santee-Cooper Res., S.C.	July 7, 1964	W.B. Whaley
Catfish, flathead	91 lbs. 4 oz.	L. Lewisville, Tex.	Mar. 28, 1982	Mike Rogers
Catfish, white	18 lbs. 14 oz.	Withlacoochee R., Fla.	Sept. 21, 1991	Jim Miller
Char, Arctic	32 lbs. 9 oz.	Tree River, Canada	July 30, 1981	Jeffrey Ward
Crappie, white	5 lbs. 3 oz.	Enid Dam, Miss.	July 31, 1957	Fred L. Bright
Dolly Varden	12 lbs. 5 oz.	Kenai R., Alaska	Sept. 19, 1990	Richard Seebold
Dorado	51 lbs. 5 oz.	Corrientes, Argentina	Sept. 27, 1984	Armando Giudice
Drum, freshwater	54 lbs. 8 oz.	Nickajack Lake, Tenn.	Apr. 20, 1972	Benny E. Hull
Gar, alligator	279 lbs.	Rio Grande River, Tex.	Dec. 2, 1951	Bill Valverde
Gar, Florida	21 lbs. 3 oz.	Boca Raton, Fla.	June 3, 1981	Jeff Sabol
Gar, longnose	50 lbs. 5 oz.	Trinity River, Tex.	July 30, 1954	Townsend Miller
Gar, shortnose	5 lbs.	Sally Jones L., Oklahoma	Apr. 26, 1985	Buddy Croslin
Gar, spotted	8 lbs. 12 oz.	Tennessee R., Ala.	Aug. 26, 1987	Winston Baker
Grayling, Arctic	5 lbs. 15 oz.	Katseyedie River, N.W.T.	Aug. 16, 1967	Jeanne P. Branson
Inconnu	53 lbs.	Pah R., Alaska	Aug. 20, 1986	Lawrence Hudnall
Kokanee	9 lbs. 6 oz.	Okanagan Lake, Vernon, B.C.	June 18, 1988	Norm Kuhn
Muskellunge	69 lbs. 15 oz.	St. Lawrence River, N.Y.	Sept. 22, 1957	Arthur Lawton
Muskellunge, tiger	51 lbs. 3 oz.	Lac Vieux-Desert, Wis., Mich.	July 16, 1919	John Knobla
Perch, Nile	191 lbs. 8 oz.	L. Victoria, Kenya	Sept. 5, 1991	Andy Davison
Perch, white	4 lbs. 12 oz.	Messalonskee Lake, Me.	June 4, 1949	Mrs. Earl Small
Perch, yellow	4 lbs. 3 oz.	Bordentown, N.J.	May, 1865	Dr. C.C. Abbot
Pickerel, chain	9 lbs. 6 oz.	Homerville, Ga.	Feb. 17, 1961	Baxley McQuaig Jr.
Pike, northern	55 lbs. 1 oz.	Lake of Grefeern, W., Germany	Oct. 16, 1986	Lothar Louis
Redhorse, greater	9 lbs. 3 oz.	Salmon R., Pulaski, N.Y.	May 11, 1985	Jason Wilson
Redhorse, silver	11 lbs. 7 oz.	Plum Creek, Wis.	May 29, 1985	Neal Long
Salmon, Atlantic	79 lbs. 2 oz.	Tana River, Norway	1928	Henrik Henriksen
Salmon, chinook	97 lbs. 4 oz.	Kenai R., Alas.	May 17, 1985	Les Anderson
Salmon, chum	32 lbs.	Behm Canal, Alas.	June 7, 1985	Fredrick Thynes
Salmon, coho	33 lbs. 4 oz.	Salmon R., Pulaski, N.Y.	Sept. 27, 1989	Jerry Lifton
Salmon, pink	12 lbs. 9 oz.	Morse, Kenai rivers, Alas.	Aug. 17, 1974	Steven A. Lee
Salmon, sockeye	15 lbs. 3 oz.	Kenai R., Alaska	Aug. 9, 1987	Stan Roach
Sauger	8 lbs. 12 oz.	Lake Sakakawea, N.D.	Oct. 6, 1971	Mike Fischer
Shad, American	11 lbs. 4 oz.	Connecticut R., Mass.	May 19, 1986	Bob Thibodo
Sturgeon, white	468 lbs.	Benicia, Cal.	July 9, 1983	Joey Pallotta 3d
Sunfish, green	2 lbs. 2 oz.	Stockton Lake, Mo.	June 18, 1971	Paul M. Dilley
Sunfish, redbreast	1 lb. 12 oz.	Suwannee R., Fla.	May 29, 1984	Alvin Buchanan
Sunfish, redear	4 lbs. 13 oz.	Marianna, Fla.	Mar. 13, 1986	Joey Floyd
Tigerfish	97 lbs.	Zaire R., Kinshasa, Zaire	July 9, 1988	Raymond Houtmans
Tilapia	6 lbs.	L. Okeechobee, Fla.	June 24, 1989	Joseph M. Tucker
Trout, Apache	5 lb. 3 oz.	Apache Res., Ariz.	May 29, 1991	John Baldwin
Trout, brook	14 lbs. 8 oz.	Nipigon River, Ont.	July 1916	Dr. W.J. Cook
Trout, brown	35 lbs. 15 oz.	Nahuel Huapi, Argentina	Dec. 16, 1952	Eugenio Cavaglia
Trout, bull	32 lbs.	L. Pend Oreille, Ida.	Oct. 27, 1949	N.L. Higgins
Trout, cutthroat	41 lbs.	Pyramid Lake, Nev.	Dec. 1925	J. Skimmerhorn
Trout, golden	11 lbs.	Cook's Lake, Wyo.	Aug. 5, 1948	Charles S. Reed
Trout, lake	66 lbs. 8 oz.	Great Bear Lake, N.W.T.	July 19, 1991	Rodney Harback
Trout, rainbow	42 lbs. 2 oz.	Bell Island, Alas.	June 22, 1970	David Robert White
Trout, tiger	20 lbs. 13 oz.	Lake Michigan, Wis.	Aug. 12, 1978	Pete Friedland
Walleye	25 lbs.	Old Hickory Lake, Tenn.	Aug. 1, 1960	Mabry Harper
Warmouth	2 lbs. 7 oz.	Yellow R., Holt, Fla.	Oct. 19, 1985	Tony D. Dempsey
Whitefish, lake	14 lbs. 6 oz.	Meaford, Ont.	May 21, 1984	Dennis Laycock
Whitefish, mountain	5 lbs. 6 oz.	Rioh R., Sask.	June 15, 1988	John Bell
Whitefish, river	11 lbs. 2 oz.	Nymoua, Sweden	Dec. 9, 1984	Jorgen Larsson
Whitefish, round	6 lbs.	Putahow R., Manitoba	June 14, 1984	Allen Ristori
Zander	22 lbs. 2 oz.	Trosa, Sweden	June 12, 1986	Harry Lee Tennison

COLLEGE BASKETBALL

Final Regular Season Conference Standings, 1991–92

(Column headings: Conference W L; Overall* Record W L)

Atlantic Coast

Team	Conf. W	Conf. L	Overall W	Overall L
Duke	14	2	29	2
Florida St.	11	5	20	9
North Carolina	9	7	21	10
Georgia Tech	8	8	21	11
Virginia	8	8	15	13
Wake Forest	7	9	17	11
North Carolina St.	6	10	12	18
Maryland	5	11	14	15
Clemson	4	12	14	14

Tournament Champion—Duke.

Atlantic 10

Team	Conf. W	Conf. L	Overall W	Overall L
Massachusetts	13	3	28	4
Temple	11	5	17	12
West Virginia	10	6	20	11
Rhode Island	9	7	20	9
George Washington	8	8	16	12
Rutgers	6	10	15	14
Duquesne	6	10	13	15
St. Joseph's (Pa.)	6	10	13	15
St. Bonaventure	3	13	9	19

Tournament Champion—Massachusetts.

Big East

Team	Conf. W	Conf. L	Overall W	Overall L
Seton Hall	12	6	21	8
Georgetown	12	6	21	10
St. John's (N.Y.)	12	6	19	10
Villanova	11	7	14	14
Syracuse	10	8	22	9
Connecticut	10	8	19	9
Pittsburgh	9	9	17	15
Boston College	7	11	16	13
Providence	6	12	14	17
Miami (Fla.)	1	17	8	24

Tournament Champion—Syracuse.

Big Eight

Team	Conf. W	Conf. L	Overall W	Overall L
Kansas	11	3	27	4
Oklahoma St.	8	6	26	7
Missouri	8	6	20	8
Oklahoma	8	6	21	9
Nebraska	7	7	19	9
Iowa St.	5	9	20	12
Kansas St.	5	9	15	13
Colorado	4	10	13	15

Tournament Champion—Kansas.

Big Sky

Team	Conf. W	Conf. L	Overall W	Overall L
Montana	14	2	27	3
Nevada	13	3	19	10
Idaho	10	6	18	14
Weber St.	10	6	16	13
Boise St.	7	9	16	13
Montana St.	6	10	14	14
Idaho St.	6	10	9	21
Northern Arizona	3	13	7	20
Eastern Washington	3	13	6	21

Tournament Champion—Montana.

Big South

Team	Conf. W	Conf. L	Overall W	Overall L
Radford	12	2	20	9
Liberty	10	4	22	7
Campbell	7	7	19	11
Charleston Southern	7	7	16	14
Coastal Carolina	6	8	12	19
Davidson	6	8	11	17
N.C.-Asheville	6	8	9	19
Winthrop	2	12	6	22

Tournament Champion—Campbell.

Big Ten

Team	Conf. W	Conf. L	Overall W	Overall L
Ohio St.	15	3	23	5
Indiana	14	4	23	6
Michigan St.	11	7	21	7
Michigan	11	7	20	8
Iowa	10	8	18	10
Minnesota	8	10	16	15
Purdue	8	10	16	14
Illinois	7	11	13	15
Wisconsin	4	14	13	18
Northwestern	2	16	9	19

Big West

Team	Conf. W	Conf. L	Overall W	Overall L
UNLV	18	0	26	2
UC Santa Barbara	13	5	20	8
New Mexico St.	12	6	24	7
Long Beach St.	11	7	18	11
Utah St.	10	8	16	12
Pacific	8	10	14	17
Cal St. Fullerton	8	10	12	16
Fresno St.	6	12	15	16
UC Irvine	3	15	7	22
San Jose St.	1	17	2	24

Tournament Champion—New Mexico St.

Colonial

Team	Conf. W	Conf. L	Overall W	Overall L
Richmond	12	2	22	7
James Madison	12	2	21	10
Old Dominion	8	6	15	14
American	8	6	11	18
N.C.-Wilmington	6	8	13	15
East Carolina	4	10	10	18
William & Mary	3	11	10	19
George Mason	3	11	7	21

Tournament Champion—Old Dominion.

East Coast

Team	Conf. W	Conf. L	Overall W	Overall L
Hofstra	10	2	20	9
Rider	9	3	16	13
Towson St.	9	3	17	13
Md.-Baltimore County	8	4	10	19
Central Connecticut St.	3	9	7	21
Brooklyn	3	9	5	23
Buffalo	0	12	2	26

Tournament Champion—Towson St.

Great Midwest

Team	Conf. W	Conf. L	Overall W	Overall L
DePaul	8	2	20	8
Cincinnati	8	2	25	4
Memphis St.	5	5	20	10
Marquette	5	5	16	13
Alabama Birmingham	4	6	20	8
St. Louis	0	10	5	23

Tournament Champion—Cincinnati.

Ivy League

Team	Conf. W	Conf. L	Overall W	Overall L
Princeton	12	2	22	5
Pennsylvania	9	5	16	10
Columbia	8	6	10	16
Yale	7	7	17	9
Brown	5	9	11	15
Dartmouth	5	9	10	16
Cornell	5	9	7	19
Harvard	5	9	6	20

Metropolitan

Team	Conf. W	Conf. L	Overall W	Overall L
Tulane	8	4	21	9
N.C.-Charlotte	7	5	24	8
South Florida	7	5	19	9
Louisville	7	5	18	10
Virginia Commonwealth	5	7	14	15
Southern Mississippi	5	7	13	16
Virginia Tech	3	9	10	18

Tournament Champion—N.C.-Charlotte.

Metro Atlantic

Team	Conf. W	Conf. L	Overall W	Overall L
Manhattan	13	3	23	8
La Salle	12	4	20	10
Siena	11	5	19	10
Loyola (Md.)	10	6	14	14
Iona	8	8	14	15
Niagara	8	8	14	14
Fairfield	4	12	8	20
St. Peter's	3	13	8	21
Canisius	3	13	8	22

Tournament Champion—La Salle.

Mid-American

Team	Conf. W	Conf. L	Overall W	Overall L
Miami (Ohio)	13	3	23	7
Ball St.	11	5	24	8
Western Michigan	11	5	21	8
Ohio	10	6	18	10
Bowling Green	8	8	14	15
Central Michigan	6	10	12	16
Kent	6	10	9	19
Eastern Michigan	4	12	9	22
Toledo	3	13	7	20

Tournament Champion—Miami (Oh.)

Mid-Continent

Team	Conf. W	Conf. L	Overall W	Overall L
Wisconsin-Green Bay	14	2	25	4
Akron	10	6	16	12
Illinois-Chicago	10	6	16	14
Eastern Illinois	9	7	17	13
Wright St.	9	7	15	13
Cleveland St.	7	9	16	13
Northern Illinois	7	9	11	17
Western Illinois	4	12	10	18
Valparaiso	2	14	5	22

Tournament Champion—Eastern Illinois.

Mid-Eastern

Team	Conf. W	Conf. L	Overall W	Overall L
North Carolina A&T	12	4	18	9
Howard	12	4	17	13
Florida A&M	11	5	16	14
Coppin St.	9	7	15	13
South Carolina St.	9	7	14	15
Delaware St.	9	7	12	16
Morgan St.	5	11	6	23
Bethune-Cookman	3	13	4	25
Maryland-East. Shore	2	14	3	25

Tournament Champion—Howard.

Midwestern

Team	Conf. W	Conf. L	Overall W	Overall L
Evansville	8	2	24	5
Butler	7	3	21	9
Xavier (Ohio)	7	3	15	12
Dayton	5	5	15	15
Loyola (Ill.)	2	8	13	16
Detroit Mercy	1	9	12	17

Tournament Champion—Evansville.

Missouri Valley

Team	Conf. W	Conf. L	Overall W	Overall L
Southern Illinois	14	4	22	7
Illinois St.	14	4	18	11
Southwest Missouri St.	13	5	23	7
Tulsa	12	6	17	13
Indiana St.	12	6	13	15
Creighton	7	11	9	19
Northern Iowa	6	12	10	18
Wichita St.	6	12	8	20
Bradley	3	15	7	23
Drake	3	15	6	21

Tournament Champion—SW Missouri St.

North Atlantic

Team	Conf. W	Conf. L	Overall W	Overall L
Delaware	14	0	27	3
Drexel	9	5	16	14
Maine	8	6	17	15
Vermont	7	7	16	13
Boston Univ.	5	9	10	18
Northeastern	5	9	9	19
New Hampshire	5	9	7	21
Hartford	3	11	6	21

Tournament Champion—Delaware.

Northeast

Team	Conf. W	Conf. L	Overall W	Overall L
Robert Morris	12	4	19	11
Monmouth (N.J.)	11	5	20	9
FDU-Teaneck	11	5	14	14
Wagner	9	7	16	12
St. Francis (N.Y.)	8	8	15	14
LIU-Brooklyn	7	9	11	18
Marist	6	10	10	20
St. Francis (Pa.)	5	11	13	16
Mt. St. Mary's (Md.)	3	13	6	22

Tournament Champion—Robert Morris.

Ohio Valley

Team	Conference W	Conference L	Overall* Record W	Overall* Record L
Murray St.	11	3	17	12
Eastern Kentucky	9	5	19	14
Middle Tennessee St.	9	5	16	11
Tennessee Tech	8	6	14	15
Morehead St.	6	8	14	15
Austin Peay	6	8	11	17
Southeast Missouri St.	5	9	12	16
Tennessee St.	2	12	4	24

Tournament Champion—Murray St.

Pacific-10

Team	Conference W	Conference L	Overall* Record W	Overall* Record L
UCLA	16	2	25	4
USC	15	3	23	5
Arizona	13	5	24	6
Stanford	10	8	18	10
Washington St.	9	9	21	10
Arizona St.	9	9	18	13
Oregon St.	7	11	15	16
Washington	5	13	12	17
California	4	14	10	18
Oregon	2	16	6	21

Patriot

Team	Conference W	Conference L	Overall* Record W	Overall* Record L
Bucknell	11	3	21	9
Fordham	11	3	18	12
Holy Cross	10	4	18	11
Lehigh	8	6	14	15
Colgate	7	7	14	14
Lafayette	6	8	8	20
Army	2	12	4	24
Navy	1	13	6	22

Tournament Champion—Fordham.

Southeastern
Eastern Division

Team	Conference W	Conference L	Overall* Record W	Overall* Record L
Kentucky	12	4	27	6
Florida	9	7	16	12
Tennessee	8	8	18	14
Georgia	7	9	15	14
Vanderbilt	6	10	15	14
South Carolina	3	13	11	17

Western Division

Team	Conference W	Conference L	Overall* Record W	Overall* Record L
Arkansas	13	3	25	7
Louisiana St.	12	4	20	9
Alabama	10	6	25	9
Mississippi St.	7	9	15	13
Auburn	5	11	12	15
Mississippi	4	12	11	17

Tournament Champion—Kentucky.

Southern

Team	Conference W	Conference L	Overall* Record W	Overall* Record L
East Tennessee St.	12	2	23	6
Tennessee-Chat.	12	2	23	7
Furman	9	5	17	11
Appalachian St.	9	5	15	14
Western Carolina	5	9	11	17
Citadel	3	11	10	18
Virginia Military	3	11	10	18
Marshall	3	11	7	22

Tournament Champion—E. Tenn. St.

Southland

Team	Conference W	Conference L	Overall* Record W	Overall* Record L
Texas-San Antonio	15	3	21	8
Northeast Louisiana	12	6	19	9
North Texas	12	6	15	14
Nicholls St.	12	6	15	13
Texas-Arlington	11	7	16	13
Stephen F. Austin	10	8	15	13
Northwestern Louisiana	9	9	15	13
Southwest Texas St.	4	14	7	20
McNeese St.	4	14	7	22
Sam Houston St.	1	17	2	25

Tournament Champion—NE Louisiana.

Southwest

Team	Conference W	Conference L	Overall* Record W	Overall* Record L
Houston	11	3	26	5
Texas	11	3	23	12
Texas Christian	9	5	22	10
Rice	8	6	20	11
Texas Tech	6	8	15	14
Baylor	5	9	13	15
Southern Methodist	4	10	10	18
Texas A&M	2	12	6	22

Tournament Champion—Houston.

Southwestern

Team	Conference W	Conference L	Overall* Record W	Overall* Record L
Mississippi Valley St.	11	3	16	13
Texas Southern	11	3	15	14
Southern-B.R.	9	5	18	12
Alcorn St.	8	6	15	14
Alabama St.	8	6	14	14
Jackson St.	7	7	12	16
Grambling	2	12	4	24
Prairie View	0	14	0	28

Tournament Champion—Mississippi Valley St.

Sun Belt

Team	Conference W	Conference L	Overall* Record W	Overall* Record L
Louisiana Tech	12	4	22	8
Southwestern Louisiana	12	4	20	10
Arkansas St.	11	5	17	11
Western Kentucky	10	6	21	10
New Orleans	9	7	18	14
South Alabama	9	7	14	14
Arkansas-Little Rock	8	8	17	13
Lamar	7	9	12	19
Jacksonville	6	10	12	17
Central Florida	3	13	10	18
Texas-Pan American	1	15	3	26

Tournament Champion—SW Louisiana.

Trans America

Team	Conference W	Conference L	Overall* Record W	Overall* Record L
Georgia Southern	13	1	25	5
Georgia St.	8	6	16	14
Florida International	7	7	11	17
Samford	7	7	11	18
Stetson	6	8	11	17
Mercer	6	8	11	18
Centenary	5	9	10	18
Southeastern Louisiana	4	10	6	22

Tournament Champion—Georgia So.

West Coast

Team	Conference W	Conference L	Overall* Record W	Overall* Record L
Pepperdine	14	0	24	6
Santa Clara	9	5	14	15
Gonzaga	8	6	20	10
Loyola (Cal.)	8	6	15	13
San Diego	6	8	14	14
San Francisco	4	10	13	16
St. Mary's (Cal.)	4	10	13	17
Portland	3	11	10	18

Tournament Champion—Pepperdine.

Western Athletic

Team	Conference W	Conference L	Overall* Record W	Overall* Record L
UTEP	12	4	25	6
Brigham Young	12	4	25	6
New Mexico	11	5	18	12
Utah	9	7	20	10
Hawaii	9	7	16	12
Wyoming	8	8	16	13
Colorado St.	8	8	14	17
Air Force	3	13	9	20
San Diego St.	0	16	2	26

Tournament Champion—Brigham Young.

* Incl. Conference Tournament Games.

Independents

Team	W	L
Penn St.	21	7
Southern Utah	20	8
Missouri-Kansas City	20	8
Wisconsin-Milwaukee	20	8
Charleston	19	8
Notre Dame	14	14
Cal St. Northridge	11	17
Northeastern Ill.	8	20
Chicago St.	7	21
N.C.-Greensboro	7	21
Youngstown St.	6	22
Cal St. Sacramento	4	24

National Invitation Tournament Champions

Year	Champion	Year	Champion	Year	Champion	Year	Champion
1938	Temple	1952	LaSalle	1966	Brigham Young	1980	Virginia
1939	Long Island Univ.	1953	Seton Hall	1967	Southern Illinois	1981	Tulsa
1940	Colorado	1954	Holy Cross	1968	Dayton	1982	Bradley
1941	Long Island Univ.	1955	Duquesne	1969	Temple	1983	Fresno State
1942	West Virginia	1956	Louisville	1970	Marquette	1984	Michigan
1943	St. John's	1957	Bradley	1971	North Carolina	1985	UCLA
1944	St. John's	1958	Xavior (Ohio)	1972	Maryland	1986	Ohio State
1945	De Paul	1959	St. John's	1973	Virginia Tech	1987	Southern Mississippi
1946	Kentucky	1960	Bradley	1974	Purdue	1988	Connecticut
1947	Utah	1961	Providence	1975	Princeton	1989	St. John's
1948	St. Louis	1962	Dayton	1976	Kentucky	1990	Vanderbilt
1949	San Francisco	1963	Providence	1977	St. Bonaventure	1991	Stanford
1950	CCNY	1964	Bradley	1978	Texas	1992	Virginia
1951	Brigham Young	1965	St. John's	1979	Indiana		

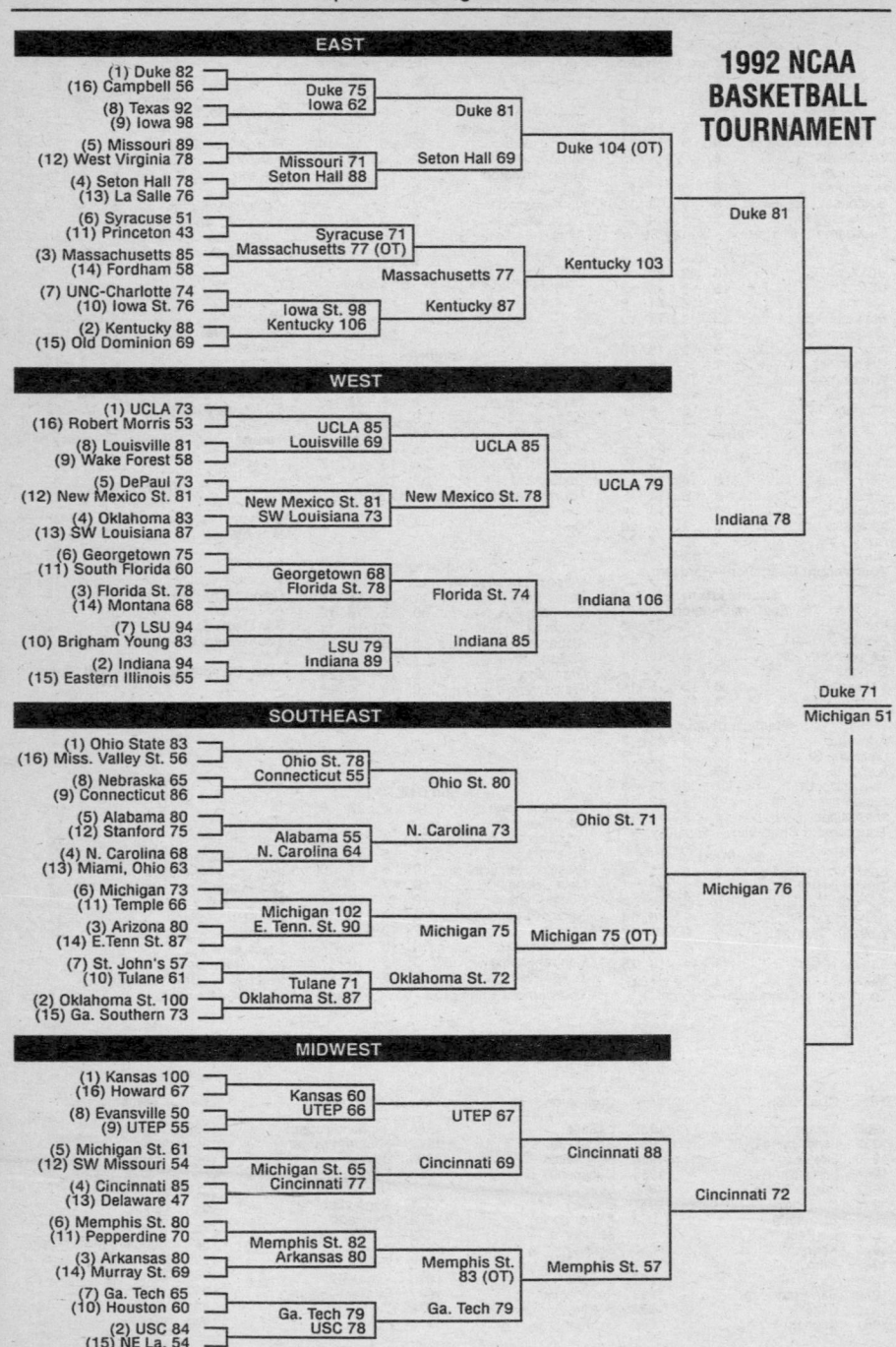

1992 NCAA BASKETBALL TOURNAMENT

EAST

(1) Duke 82
(16) Campbell 56
(8) Texas 92
(9) Iowa 98
(5) Missouri 89
(12) West Virginia 78
(4) Seton Hall 78
(13) La Salle 76
(6) Syracuse 51
(11) Princeton 43
(3) Massachusetts 85
(14) Fordham 58
(7) UNC-Charlotte 74
(10) Iowa St. 76
(2) Kentucky 88
(15) Old Dominion 69

Duke 75
Iowa 62
Missouri 71
Seton Hall 88
Syracuse 71
Massachusetts 77 (OT)
Iowa St. 98
Kentucky 106

Duke 81
Seton Hall 69
Massachusetts 77
Kentucky 87

Duke 104 (OT)
Kentucky 103

WEST

(1) UCLA 73
(16) Robert Morris 53
(8) Louisville 81
(9) Wake Forest 58
(5) DePaul 73
(12) New Mexico St. 81
(4) Oklahoma 83
(13) SW Louisiana 87
(6) Georgetown 75
(11) South Florida 60
(3) Florida St. 78
(14) Montana 68
(7) LSU 94
(10) Brigham Young 83
(2) Indiana 94
(15) Eastern Illinois 55

UCLA 85
Louisville 69
New Mexico St. 81
SW Louisiana 73
Georgetown 68
Florida St. 78
LSU 79
Indiana 89

UCLA 85
New Mexico St. 78
Florida St. 74
Indiana 85

UCLA 79
Indiana 106

SOUTHEAST

(1) Ohio State 83
(16) Miss. Valley St. 56
(8) Nebraska 65
(9) Connecticut 86
(5) Alabama 80
(12) Stanford 75
(4) N. Carolina 68
(13) Miami, Ohio 63
(6) Michigan 73
(11) Temple 66
(3) Arizona 80
(14) E.Tenn St. 87
(7) St. John's 57
(10) Tulane 61
(2) Oklahoma St. 100
(15) Ga. Southern 73

Ohio St. 78
Connecticut 55
Alabama 55
N. Carolina 64
Michigan 102
E. Tenn. St. 90
Tulane 71
Oklahoma St. 87

Ohio St. 80
N. Carolina 73
Michigan 75
Oklahoma St. 72

Ohio St. 71
Michigan 75 (OT)

MIDWEST

(1) Kansas 100
(16) Howard 67
(8) Evansville 50
(9) UTEP 55
(5) Michigan St. 61
(12) SW Missouri 54
(4) Cincinnati 85
(13) Delaware 47
(6) Memphis St. 80
(11) Pepperdine 70
(3) Arkansas 80
(14) Murray St. 69
(7) Ga. Tech 65
(10) Houston 60
(2) USC 84
(15) NE La. 54

Kansas 60
UTEP 66
Michigan St. 65
Cincinnati 77
Memphis St. 82
Arkansas 80
Ga. Tech 79
USC 78

UTEP 67
Cincinnati 69
Memphis St. 83 (OT)
Ga. Tech 79

Cincinnati 88
Memphis St. 57

FINAL FOUR

Duke 81
Indiana 78

Michigan 76
Cincinnati 72

CHAMPIONSHIP

Duke 71
Michigan 51

NCAA Division I Champions

Year	Champion	Coach	Final opponent	Score	Outstanding player	Site
1939	Oregon	Howard Hobson	Ohio St.	46-33	None	Evanston, Ill.
1940	Indiana	Branch McCracken	Kansas	60-42	Marvin Huffman, Indiana	Kansas City, Mo.
1941	Wisconsin	Harold Foster	Washington St.	39-34	John Kotz, Wisconsin	Kansas City, Mo.
1942	Stanford	Everett Dean	Dartmouth	53-38	Howard Dallmar, Stanford	Kansas City, Mo.
1943	Wyoming	Everett Shelton	Georgetown	46-34	Ken Sailors, Wyoming	New York, N.Y.
1944	Utah	Vadal Peterson	Dartmouth	42-40(1)	Arnold Ferrin, Utah	New York, N.Y.
1945	Oklahoma St.(2)	Henry Iba	NYU	49-45	Bob Kurland, Oklahoma St.	New York, N.Y.
1946	Oklahoma St.(2)	Henry Iba	North Carolina	43-40	Bob Kurland, Oklahoma St.	New York, N.Y.
1947	Holy Cross	Alvin Julian	Oklahoma	58-47	George Kaftan, Holy Cross	New York, N.Y.
1948	Kentucky	Adolph Rupp	Baylor	58-42	Alex Groza, Kentucky	New York, N.Y.
1949	Kentucky	Adolph Rupp	Oklahoma St.	46-36	Alex Groza, Kentucky	Seattle, Wash.
1950	CCNY	Nat Holman	Bradley	71-68	Irwin Dambrot, CCNY	New York, N.Y.
1951	Kentucky	Adolph Rupp	Kansas St.	68-58	None	Minneapolis, Minn.
1952	Kansas	Forrest Allen	St. John's	80-63	Clyde Lovellette, Kansas	Seattle, Wash.
1953	Indiana	Branch McCracken	Kansas	69-68	B.H. Born, Kansas	Kansas City, Mo.
1954	La Salle	Kenneth Loeffler	Bradley	92-76	Tom Gola, La Salle	Kansas City, Mo.
1955	San Francisco	Phil Woolpert	LaSalle	77-63	Bill Russell, San Francisco	Kansas City, Mo.
1956	San Francisco	Phil Woolpert	Iowa	83-71	Hal Lear, Temple	Evanston, Ill.
1957	N. Carolina	Frank McGuire	Kansas	54-53(1)	Wilt Chamberlain, Kansas	Kansas City, Mo.
1958	Kentucky	Adolph Rupp	Seattle	84-72	Elgin Baylor, Seattle	Louisville, Ky.
1959	California	Pete Newell	W. Virginia	71-70	Jerry West, W. Virginia	Louisville, Ky.
1960	Ohio St.	Fred Taylor	California	75-55	Jerry Lucas, Ohio St.	San Francisco, Cal.
1961	Cincinnati	Edwin Jucker	Ohio St.	70-65(1)	Jerry Lucas, Ohio St.	Kansas City, Mo.
1962	Cincinnati	Edwin Jucker	Ohio St.	71-59	Paul Hogue, Cincinnati	Louisville, Ky.
1963	Loyola (Ill.)	George Ireland	Cincinnati	60-58(1)	Art Heyman, Duke	Louisville, Ky.
1964	UCLA	John Wooden	Duke	98-83	Walt Hazzard, UCLA	Kansas City, Mo.
1965	UCLA	John Wooden	Michigan	91-80	Bill Bradley, Princeton	Portland, Ore.
1966	Texas-El Paso(3)	Don Haskins	Kentucky	72-65	Jerry Chambers, Utah	College Park, Md.
1967	UCLA	John Wooden	Dayton	79-64	Lew Alcindor, UCLA	Louisville, Ky.
1968	UCLA	John Wooden	N. Carolina	78-55	Lew Alcindor, UCLA	Los Angeles, Cal.
1969	UCLA	John Wooden	Purdue	92-72	Lew Alcindor, UCLA	Louisville, Ky.
1970	UCLA	John Wooden	Jacksonville	80-69	Sidney Wicks, UCLA	College Park, Md.
1971	UCLA	John Wooden	Villanova*	68-62	Howard Porter, Villanova*	Houston, Tex.
1972	UCLA	John Wooden	Florida St.	81-76	Bill Walton, UCLA	Los Angeles, Cal.
1973	UCLA	John Wooden	Memphis St.	87-66	Bill Walton, UCLA	St. Louis, Mo.
1974	N. Carolina St.	Norm Sloan	Marquette	76-64	David Thompson, N.C. St.	Greensboro, N.C.
1975	UCLA	John Wooden	Kentucky	92-85	Richard Washington, UCLA	San Diego, Cal.
1976	Indiana	Bob Knight	Michigan	86-68	Kent Benson, Indiana	Philadelphia, Pa.
1977	Marquette	Al McGuire	N. Carolina	67-59	Butch Lee, Marquette	Atlanta, Ga.
1978	Kentucky	Joe Hall	Duke	94-88	Jack Givens, Kentucky	St. Louis, Mo.
1979	Michigan St.	Jud Heathcote	Indiana St.	75-64	Magic Johnson, Michigan St.	Salt Lake City, Ut.
1980	Louisville	Denny Crum	UCLA*	59-54	Darrell Griffith, Louisville	Indianapolis, Ind.
1981	Indiana	Bob Knight	N. Carolina	63-50	Isiah Thomas, Indiana	Philadelphia, Pa.
1982	N. Carolina	Dean Smith	Georgetown	63-62	James Worthy, No. Carolina	New Orleans, La.
1983	N. Carolina St.	Jim Valvano	Houston	54-52	Hakeem Olajuwon, Houston	Albuquerque, N.M.
1984	Georgetown	John Thompson	Houston	84-75	Patrick Ewing, Georgetown	Seattle, Wash.
1985	Villanova	Rollie Massimino	Georgetown	66-64	Ed Pinckney, Villanova	Lexington, Ky.
1986	Louisville	Denny Crum	Duke	72-69	Pervis Ellison, Louisville	Dallas, Tex.
1987	Indiana	Bob Knight	Syracuse	74-73	Keith Smart, Indiana	New Orleans, La.
1988	Kansas	Larry Brown	Oklahoma	83-79	Danny Manning, Kansas	Kansas City, Mo.
1989	Michigan	Steve Fisher	Seton Hall	80-79(1)	Glen Rice, Michigan	Seattle, Wash.
1990	UNLV	Jerry Tarkanian	Duke	103-73	Anderson Hunt, UNLV	Denver, Col.
1991	Duke	Mike Krzyzewski	Kansas	72-65	Christian Laettner, Duke	Indianapolis, Ind.
1992	Duke	Mike Krzyzewski	Michigan	71-51	Bobby Hurley, Duke	Minneapolis, Minn.

* Declared ineligible subsequent to the tournament. (1) Overtime. (2) Known as Oklahoma A&M at that time. (3) Known as Texas Western at that time.

John R. Wooden Award

Awarded annually to the nation's outstanding college basketball playing student-athlete by a poll of sports writers and broadcasters.

1977 Marques Johnson, UCLA
1978 Phil Ford, North Carolina
1979 Larry Bird, Indiana State
1980 Darrell Griffith, Louisville
1981 Danny Ainge, Brigham Young
1982 Ralph Sampson, Virginia
1983 Ralph Sampson, Virginia
1984 Michael Jordan, North Carolina
1985 Chris Mullin, St. John's
1986 Walter Berry, St. John's
1987 David Robinson, Navy
1988 Danny Manning, Kansas
1989 Sean Elliott, Arizona
1990 Lionel Simmons, La Salle
1991 Larry Johnson, UNLV
1992 Christian Laettner, Duke

NCAA Division I Women's Champions

Year	Champion	Coach	Final opponent
1982	Louisiana Tech	Sonja Hogg	Cheyney
1983	USC	Linda Sharp	Louisiana Tech
1984	USC	Linda Sharp	Tennessee
1985	Old Dominion	Marianne Stanley	Georgia
1986	Texas	Jody Conradt	USC
1987	Tennessee	Pat Summitt	Louisiana Tech
1988	Louisiana Tech	Leon Barmore	Auburn
1989	Tennessee	Pat Summitt	Auburn
1990	Stanford	Tara VanDerveer	Auburn
1991	Tennessee	Pat Summitt	Virginia
1992	Stanford	Tara VanDerveer	W. Kentucky

NCAA Division I Basketball Statistical Trends

Averages and percentages are for both teams, per game.

Year	Games	FG Made	FG Att.	Pct.	FT Made	FT Att.	Pct.	PF	Pts.
1948	3945	40.6	138.7	29.3	25.3	42.2	59.8	36.9	106.5
1950	3659	43.2	136.8	31.6	28.7	46.5	61.8	39.0	115.1
1952	4009	47.5	140.6*	33.7	31.6	50.5	62.6	44.9*	126.6
1953	3754	48.0	138.1	34.7	42.1	65.8*	64.0	42.5	138.1
1955	3829	51.1	138.6	36.9	43.1*	64.7	66.5	37.9	145.3
1958	4153	51.6	134.2	38.4	33.6	50.5	66.4	36.4	136.8
1960	4295	52.6	132.3	39.8	34.7	51.5	67.4	36.7	139.9
1963	4180	53.2	127.6	41.7	32.6	47.8	68.2	36.4	139.0
1965	4520	58.3	135.4	43.1	34.7	50.3	69.0	38.5	151.4
1967	4602	57.7	131.9	43.8	34.4	49.8	69.0	38.3	149.8
1971	5232	60.2	135.6	44.4	35.0	51.3	68.1	38.5	155.4*
1973	5582	62.3*	139.2	44.8	26.2	38.3	68.4	38.4	150.9
1975	6147	62.9	136.7	46.0	27.4	39.7	69.0	40.3	153.1
1979	7131	59.2	124.1	47.7	29.5	42.2	69.7*	41.1	147.9
1983	7957	54.3	114.0	47.7	29.0	42.3	68.5	39.7	138.7
1985	8269	54.5	113.9	47.9	29.3	42.5	68.9	39.3	138.3
1986	8360	54.7	114.6	47.7	29.4	42.5	69.1	39.1	138.7
1987	8580	54.4	117.3	46.6	29.7	43.0	69.1	39.3	145.5
1988	8587	54.8	116.6	47.0	30.2	43.8	68.9	39.4	147.8
1989	8677	55.7	118.5	47.0	31.1	45.0	69.1	40.2	151.4
1990	8646	54.7	118.9	46.0	31.1	45.1	68.9	39.6	149.8
1991	8720*	55.6	121.3	45.8	31.7	46.3	68.5	39.2	152.9

*All-time high.

World Almanac All-America Team in 1992

First team	Position	Second team
Christian Laettner, Duke	Center	Shaquille O'Neal, LSU
Jimmy Jackson, Ohio St.	Forward	Malik Sealy, St. John's
Byron Houston, Oklahoma St.	Forward	Calbert Cheaney, Indiana
Walt Williams, Maryland	Guard	Bobby Hurley, Duke
Harold Miner, USC	Guard	Anthony Peeler, Missouri

Coach of the Year — Perry Clark, Tulane **Player of the Year** — Christian Laettner, Duke

World Almanac All-America Women's Team in 1992

First team	Position	Second team
Lisa Leslie, USC	Center	Cinietra Henderson, Texas
Susan Robinson, Penn St.	Forward	Shannon Cate, Montana
Val Whiting, Stanford	Forward	Michele Savage, Northwestern
Dena Head, Tennessee	Guard	Lady Hardmon, Georgia
Dawn Staley, Virginia	Guard	MaChelle Joseph, Purdue

Coach of the Year — Van Chancellor, Mississippi **Player of the Year** — Dawn Staley, Virginia

NATIONAL BASKETBALL ASSOCIATION, 1991-92

Final Standings

Eastern Conference

Atlantic Division

	W	L	Pct	GB
Boston	51	31	.622	...
New York	51	31	.622	...
New Jersey	40	42	.488	11
Miami	38	44	.463	13
Philadelphia	35	47	.427	16
Washington	25	57	.305	26
Orlando	21	61	.256	30

Central Division

	W	L	Pct	GB
Chicago	67	15	.817	...
Cleveland	57	25	.695	10
Detroit	48	34	.585	19
Indiana	40	42	.488	27
Atlanta	38	44	.463	29
Charlotte	31	51	.378	36
Milwaukee	31	51	.378	36

Western Conference

Midwest Division

	W	L	Pct	GB
Utah	55	27	.671	...
San Antonio	47	35	.573	8
Houston	42	40	.512	13
Denver	24	58	.293	31
Dallas	22	60	.268	33
Minnesota	15	67	.183	40

Pacific Division

	W	L	Pct	GB
Portland	57	25	.695	...
Golden State	55	27	.671	2
Phoenix	53	29	.646	4
Seattle	47	35	.573	10
Los Angeles Clippers	45	37	.549	12
Los Angeles Lakers	43	39	.524	14
Sacramento	29	53	.347	28

NBA Playoff Results

Eastern Division

Chicago defeated Miami 3 games to 0
Boston defeated Indiana 3 games to 0
Cleveland defeated New Jersey 3 games to 1
New York defeated Detroit 3 games to 2
Cleveland defeated Boston 4 games to 3
Chicago defeated New York 4 games to 3
Chicago defeated Cleveland 4 games to 2

Western Division

Phoenix defeated San Antonio 3 games to 0
Seattle defeated Golden State 3 games to 1
Portland defeated L.A. Lakers 3 games to 0
Utah defeated L.A. Clippers 3 games to 2
Portland defeated Phoenix 4 games to 1
Utah defeated Seattle 4 games to 1
Portland defeated Utah 4 games to 2

Championship

Chicago defeated Portland 4 games to 2

Bulls Repeat As Champions by Beating Trail Blazers in Six Games

The Chicago Bulls won their second consecutive National Basketball Championship by defeating the Portland Trail Blazers 4 games to 2. Michael Jordan was chosen the most valuable player in the finals for the second consecutive year.

Portland Trail Blazers

	FG M-A	FT M-A	Reb	Ast	Avg
Drexler . . .	48-118	50-56	47	32	24.8
Porter	33-70	28-34	26	28	16.1
Kersey. . . .	39-81	11-15	52	20	14.8
Robinson . .	23-52	16-27	18	13	10.3
Ainge	23-53	10-14	12	15	10.0
Bryant	5-8	0-0	5	0	10.0
Duckworth .	22-51	12-17	41	9	9.3
B. Williams .	16-32	15-16	44	6	7.8
Pack.	1-6	3-4	2	1	2.5
Whatley . . .	2-7	0-0	1	1	0.8
Cooper . . .	0-0	0-0	0	0	0.0
Abdelnaby .	0-1	1-2	0	0	0.0
Totals. . . .	**212-479**	**146-185**	**293**	**125**	**97.4**

Chicago Bulls

	FG M-A	FT M-A	Reb	Ast	Avg
Jordan. . . .	81-154	41-46	29	39	35.8
Pippen. . . .	45-93	33-42	50	46	20.8
Paxson . . .	26-50	3-4	5	16	10.3
Grant	23-41	9-17	47	24	9.1
Cartwright. .	16-32	6-12	24	9	6.3
Armstrong. .	15-35	4-7	5	14	5.8
S. Williams .	13-24	7-9	37	6	5.5
King	5-15	8-12	10	0	4.5
Levingston .	9-20	5-10	13	4	3.8
Hansen . . .	6-10	1-2	2	3	3.2
Hodges . . .	1-1	0-0	0	0	1.0
Perdue . . .	1-3	0-2	3	0	0.7
Totals. . . .	**241-478**	**117-163**	**281**	**161**	**104.0**

MVP in Playoffs

1969	Jerry West, Los Angeles
1970	Willis Reed, New York
1971	Lew Alcindor, Milwaukee
1972	Wilt Chamberlain, Los Angeles
1973	Willis Reed, New York
1974	John Havlicek, Boston
1975	Rick Barry, Golden State
1976	Jo Jo White, Boston
1977	Bill Walton, Portland
1978	Wes Unseld, Washington
1979	Dennis Johnson, Seattle
1980	Magic Johnson, Los Angeles
1981	Cedric Maxwell, Boston
1982	Magic Johnson, Los Angeles
1983	Moses Malone, Philadelphia
1984	Larry Bird, Boston
1985	Kareem Abdul-Jabbar, L.A. Lakers
1986	Larry Bird, Boston
1987	Magic Johnson, L.A. Lakers
1988	James Worthy, L.A. Lakers
1989	Joe Dumars, Detroit
1990	Isiah Thomas, Detroit
1991	Michael Jordan, Chicago
1992	Michael Jordan, Chicago

NBA Scoring Leaders

Year	Scoring champion	Pts	Avg
1947	Joe Fulks, Philadelphia.	1,389	23.2
1948	Max Zaslofsky, Chicago	1,007	21.0
1949	George Mikan, Minneapolis	1,698	28.3
1950	George Mikan, Minneapolis	1,865	27.4
1951	George Mikan, Minneapolis	1,932	28.4
1952	Paul Arizin, Philadelphia	1,674	25.4
1953	Neil Johnston, Philadelphia	1,564	22.3
1954	Neil Johnston, Philadelphia	1,759	24.4
1955	Neil Johnston, Philadelphia	1,631	22.7
1956	Bob Pettit, St. Louis.	1,849	25.7
1957	Paul Arizin, Philadelphia	1,817	25.6
1958	George Yardley, Detroit	2,001	27.8
1959	Bob Pettit, St. Louis.	2,105	29.2
1960	Wilt Chamberlain, Philadelphia	2,707	37.9
1961	Wilt Chamberlain, Philadelphia	3,033	38.4
1962	Wilt Chamberlain, Philadelphia	4,029	50.4
1963	Wilt Chamberlain, San Francisco	3,586	44.8
1964	Wilt Chamberlain, San Francisco	2,948	36.5
1965	Wilt Chamberlain, San Fran., Phila. . . .	2,534	34.7
1966	Wilt Chamberlain, Philadelphia	2,649	33.5
1967	Rick Barry, San Francisco	2,775	35.6
1968	Dave Bing, Detroit	2,142	27.1
1969	Elvin Hayes, San Diego	2,327	28.4
1970	Jerry West, Los Angeles.	2,309	31.2
1971	Lew Alcindor, Milwaukee.	2,596	31.7
1972	Kareem Abdul-Jabbar (Alcindor), Milwaukee	2,822	34.8
1973	Nate Archibald, Kansas City-Omaha . . .	2,719	34.0
1974	Bob McAdoo, Buffalo.	2,261	30.6
1975	Bob McAdoo, Buffalo.	2,831	34.5
1976	Bob McAdoo, Buffalo.	2,427	31.1
1977	Pete Maravich, New Orleans	2,273	31.1
1978	George Gervin, San Antonio.	2,232	27.2
1979	George Gervin, San Antonio.	2,365	29.6
1980	George Gervin, San Antonio.	2,585	33.1
1981	Adrian Dantley, Utah	2,452	30.7
1982	George Gervin, San Antonio.	2,551	32.3
1983	Alex English, Denver	2,326	28.4
1984	Adrian Dantley, Utah	2,418	30.6
1985	Bernard King, New York	1,809	32.9
1986	Dominique Wilkins, Atlanta.	2,366	30.3
1987	Michael Jordan, Chicago.	3,041	37.1
1988	Michael Jordan, Chicago.	2,868	35.0
1989	Michael Jordan, Chicago.	2,633	32.5
1990	Michael Jordan, Chicago.	2,753	33.6
1991	Michael Jordan, Chicago.	2,580	31.5
1992	Michael Jordan, Chicago.	2,404	30.1

NBA Champions 1947-1992

	Regular season		Playoffs		
Year	Eastern Conference	Western Conference	Winner	Coach	Runner-up
1947	Washington	Chicago	Philadelphia	Ed Gottlieb	Chicago
1948	Philadelphia	St. Louis	Baltimore	Buddy Jeannette	Philadelphia
1949	Washington	Rochester	Minneapolis	John Kundla	Washington
1950	Syracuse	Minneapolis	Minneapolis	John Kundla	Syracuse
1951	Philadelphia	Minneapolis	Rochester	Lester Harrison	New York
1952	Syracuse	Rochester	Minneapolis	John Kundla	New York
1953	New York	Minneapolis	Minneapolis	John Kundla	New York
1954	New York	Minneapolis	Minneapolis	John Kundla	Syracuse
1955	Syracuse	Ft. Wayne	Syracuse	Al Cervi	Ft. Wayne
1956	Philadelphia	Ft. Wayne	Philadelphia	George Senesky	Ft. Wayne
1957	Boston	St. Louis	Boston	Red Auerbach	St. Louis
1958	Boston	St. Louis	St. Louis	Alex Hannum	Boston
1959	Boston	St. Louis	Boston	Red Auerbach	Minneapolis
1960	Boston	St. Louis	Boston	Red Auerbach	St. Louis
1961	Boston	St. Louis	Boston	Red Auerbach	St. Louis
1962	Boston	Los Angeles	Boston	Red Auerbach	Los Angeles
1963	Boston	Los Angeles	Boston	Red Auerbach	Los Angeles
1964	Boston	San Francisco	Boston	Red Auerbach	San Francisco
1965	Boston	Los Angeles	Boston	Red Auerbach	Los Angeles
1966	Philadelphia	Los Angeles	Boston	Red Auerbach	Los Angeles
1967	Philadelphia	San Francisco	Philadelphia	Alex Hannum	San Francisco
1968	Philadelphia	St. Louis	Boston	Bill Russell	Los Angeles
1969	Baltimore	Los Angeles	Boston	Bill Russell	Los Angeles
1970	New York	Atlanta	New York	Red Holzman	Los Angeles

	Atlantic	Central	Midwest	Pacific	Winner	Coach	Runner-up
1971	New York	Baltimore	Milwaukee	Los Angeles	Milwaukee	Larry Costello	Baltimore
1972	Boston	Baltimore	Milwaukee	Los Angeles	Los Angeles	Bill Sharman	New York
1973	Boston	Baltimore	Milwaukee	Los Angeles	New York	Red Holzman	Los Angeles
1974	Boston	Capital	Milwaukee	Los Angeles	Boston	Tom Heinsohn	Milwaukee
1975	Boston	Washington	Chicago	Golden State	Golden State	Al Attles	Washington
1976	Boston	Cleveland	Milwaukee	Golden State	Boston	Tom Heinsohn	Phoenix
1977	Philadelphia	Houston	Denver	Los Angeles	Portland	Jack Ramsay	Philadelphia
1978	Philadelphia	San Antonio	Denver	Portland	Washington	Dick Motta	Seattle
1979	Washington	San Antonio	Kansas City	Seattle	Seattle	Len Wilkens	Washington
1980	Boston	Atlanta	Milwaukee	Los Angeles	Los Angeles	Paul Westhead	Philadelphia
1981	Boston	Milwaukee	San Antonio	Phoenix	Boston	Bill Fitch	Houston
1982	Boston	Milwaukee	San Antonio	Los Angeles	Los Angeles	Pat Riley	Philadelphia
1983	Philadelphia	Milwaukee	San Antonio	Los Angeles	Philadelphia	Billy Cunningham	Los Angeles
1984	Boston	Milwaukee	Utah	Los Angeles	Boston	K.C. Jones	Los Angeles
1985	Boston	Milwaukee	Denver	L.A. Lakers	L.A. Lakers	Pat Riley	Boston
1986	Boston	Milwaukee	Houston	L.A. Lakers	Boston	K.C. Jones	Houston
1987	Boston	Atlanta	Dallas	L.A. Lakers	L.A. Lakers	Pat Riley	Boston
1988	Boston	Detroit	Denver	L.A. Lakers	L.A. Lakers	Pat Riley	Detroit
1989	New York	Detroit	Utah	L.A. Lakers	Detroit	Chuck Daly	L.A. Lakers
1990	Philadelphia	Detroit	San Antonio	L.A. Lakers	Detroit	Chuck Daly	Portland
1991	Boston	Chicago	San Antonio	Portland	Chicago	Phil Jackson	L.A. Lakers
1992	Boston	Chicago	Utah	Portland	Chicago	Phil Jackson	Portland

NBA Most Valuable Player

1956 Bob Pettit, St. Louis
1957 Bob Cousy, Boston
1958 Bill Russell, Boston
1959 Bob Pettit, St. Louis
1960 Wilt Chamberlain, Philadelphia
1961 Bill Russell, Boston
1962 Bill Russell, Boston
1963 Bill Russell, Boston
1964 Oscar Robertson, Cincinnati
1965 Bill Russell, Boston
1966 Wilt Chamberlain, Philadelphia
1967 Wilt Chamberlain, Philadelphia
1968 Wilt Chamberlain, Philadelphia
1969 Wes Unseld, Baltimore
1970 Willis Reed, New York
1971 Lew Alcindor, Milwaukee
1972 Kareem Abdul-Jabbar (Alcindor), Milwaukee
1973 Dave Cowens, Boston
1974 Kareem Abdul-Jabbar, Milwaukee
1975 Bob McAdoo, Buffalo
1976 Kareem Abdul-Jabbar, Los Angeles
1977 Kareem Abdul-Jabbar, Los Angeles
1978 Bill Walton, Portland
1979 Moses Malone, Houston
1980 Kareem Abdul-Jabbar, Los Angeles
1981 Julius Erving, Philadelphia
1982 Moses Malone, Houston
1983 Moses Malone, Philadelphia
1984 Larry Bird, Boston
1985 Larry Bird, Boston
1986 Larry Bird, Boston
1987 Magic Johnson, L.A. Lakers
1988 Michael Jordan, Chicago
1989 Magic Johnson, L.A. Lakers
1990 Magic Johnson, L.A. Lakers
1991 Michael Jordan, Chicago
1992 Michael Jordan, Chicago

NBA All-League Team in 1992

First team	Position	Second team
Karl Malone, Utah	Forward	Charles Barkley, Philadelphia
Chris Mullin, Golden State	Forward	Scottie Pippen, Chicago
David Robinson, San Antonio	Center	Patrick Ewing, New York
Clyde Drexler, Portland	Guard	Tim Hardaway, Golden State
Michael Jordan, Chicago	Guard	John Stockton, Utah

Statistical Leaders, 1991-1992

Scoring

	G	FG	Pts	Avg
Jordan, Chicago	80	943	2404	30.1
K. Malone, Utah	81	798	2272	28.0
Mullin, Golden State	81	830	2074	25.6
Drexler, Portland	76	694	1903	25.0
Ewing, New York	82	796	1970	24.0
Hardaway, Golden State	81	734	1893	23.4
Robinson, San Antonio	68	592	1578	23.2
Barkley, Philadelphia	75	622	1730	23.1
Richmond, Sacramento	80	685	1803	22.5
Rice, Miami	79	672	1765	22.3
Pierce, Seattle	78	620	1690	21.7
Olajuwon, Houston	70	591	1510	21.6
Daugherty, Cleveland	73	576	1566	21.5
Pippen, Chicago	82	687	1720	21.0
Lewis, Boston	82	703	1703	20.8
Miller, Indiana	82	562	1695	20.7
Petrovic, New Jersey	82	668	1691	20.6
Gill, Charlotte	79	666	1622	20.5
J. Malone, Utah	81	691	1639	20.2
Hornacek, Phoenix	81	635	1632	20.1

Rebounds Per Game

	G	Def	Tot	Avg
Rodman, Detroit	82	1007	1530	18.7
Willis, Atlanta	81	840	1258	15.5
Mutombo, Denver	71	554	870	12.3
Robinson, San Antonio	68	568	829	12.2
Olajuwon, Houston	70	599	845	12.1
Seikaly, Miami	79	627	934	11.8
Anderson, Denver	82	604	941	11.5
Ewing, New York	82	693	921	11.2
K. Malone, Utah	81	684	909	11.2
Barkley, Philadelphia	75	559	830	11.1

Field Goal Percentage

	FG	FGA	Pct
Williams, Portland	340	563	.604
Thorpe, Houston	558	943	.592
Grant, Chicago	457	790	.578
Daugherty, Cleveland	576	1010	.570
Cage, Seattle	307	542	.566
Barkley, Philadelphia	622	1126	.552
Robinson, San Antonio	592	1074	.551
Manning, L.A. Clippers	650	1199	.542
Ellison, Washington	547	1014	.539
Nance, Cleveland	556	1032	.539
Rodman, Detroit	342	635	.539

Free Throw Percentage

	FT	FTA	Pct
Price, Cleveland	270	285	.947
Bird, Boston	150	162	.926
Pierce, Seattle	417	455	.916
Blackman, Dallas	239	266	.898
J. Malone, Utah	256	285	.898
Skiles, Orlando	248	277	.895
Hornacek, Phoenix	279	315	.886
Gamble, Boston	139	157	.885
Dawkins, Philadelphia	164	186	.882
Anderson, Philadelphia	143	163	.877

Assists Per Game

	G	Ast	Avg
Stockton, Utah	82	1126	13.7
Johnson, Phoenix	78	836	10.7
Hardaway, Golden State	81	807	10.0
Bogues, Charlotte	82	743	9.1
Strickland, San Antonio	57	491	8.6
Jackson, New York	81	694	8.6
Richardson, Minnesota	82	685	8.4
M. Williams, Indiana	79	647	8.2
Adams, Washington	78	594	7.6
Price, Cleveland	72	535	7.4

3-Point Field Goal Percentage

	FG	FGA	Pct
Barros, Seattle	83	186	.446
Petrovic, New Jersey	123	277	.444
Hornacek, Phoenix	83	189	.439
Iuzzolino, Dallas	59	136	.434
Ellis, Milwaukee	138	329	.419
Ehlo, Cleveland	69	167	.413
Stockton, Utah	83	204	.407
Bird, Boston	52	128	.406
Curry, Charlotte	74	183	.404
Hawkins, Philadelphia	91	229	.397

Steals Per Game

	G	Stl	Avg
Stockton, Utah	82	244	2.98
M. Williams, Indiana	79	233	2.95
Robertson, Milwaukee	82	210	2.56
Blaylock, New Jersey	72	170	2.36
Robinson, San Antonio	68	158	2.32
Jordan, Chicago	80	182	2.28
Mullin, Golden State	81	173	2.14
Bogues, Charlotte	82	170	2.07
Threatt, L.A. Lakers	82	168	2.05

Blocked Shots Per Game

	G	Blk	Avg
Robinson, San Antonio	68	305	4.49
Olajuwon, Houston	70	304	4.34
Nance, Cleveland	81	243	3.00
Ewing, New York	82	245	2.99
Mutombo, Denver	71	210	2.96
Bol, Philadelphia	71	205	2.89
Causwell, Sacramento	80	215	2.69
Ellison, Washington	66	177	2.68
Eaton, Utah	81	205	2.53
Lang, Phoenix	81	201	2.48

NBA Rookie of the Year

Year	Player
1953	Don Meineke, Ft. Wayne
1954	Ray Felix, Baltimore
1955	Bob Pettit, Milwaukee
1956	Maurice Stokes, Rochester
1957	Tom Heinsohn, Boston
1958	Woody Sauldsberry, Philadelphia
1959	Elgin Baylor, Minneapolis
1960	Wilt Chamberlain, Philadelphia
1961	Oscar Robertson, Cincinnati
1962	Walt Bellamy, Chicago
1963	Terry Dischinger, Chicago
1964	Jerry Lucas, Cincinnati
1965	Willis Reed, New York
1966	Rick Barry, San Francisco
1967	Dave Bing, Detroit
1968	Earl Monroe, Baltimore
1969	Wes Unseld, Baltimore
1970	Lew Alcindor, Milwaukee
1971	Dave Cowens, Boston; Geoff Petrie, Portland (tie)
1972	Sidney Wicks, Portland
1973	Bob McAdoo, Buffalo
1974	Ernie DiGregorio, Buffalo
1975	Keith Wilkes, Golden State
1976	Alvan Adams, Phoenix
1977	Adrian Dantley, Buffalo
1978	Walter Davis, Phoenix
1979	Phil Ford, Kansas City
1980	Larry Bird, Boston
1981	Darrell Griffith, Utah
1982	Buck Williams, New Jersey
1983	Terry Cummings, San Diego
1984	Ralph Sampson, Houston
1985	Michael Jordan, Chicago
1986	Patrick Ewing, New York
1987	Chuck Person, Indiana
1988	Mark Jackson, New York
1989	Mitch Richmond, Golden State
1990	David Robinson, San Antonio
1991	Derrick Coleman, New Jersey
1992	Larry Johnson, Charlotte

Individual Statistics, 1991-1992
(Over 600 Minutes Played)

Atlanta Hawks

	Min per game	Reb avg	Ast avg	FG%	3-pt FG%	FT%	Pts avg
Wilkins.	38.1	7.0	3.8	.464	.289	.835	28.1
Willis.	36.6	15.5	2.1	.483	.162	.804	18.3
Augmon.	30.5	5.1	2.5	.489	.167	.666	13.3
Robinson	27.4	2.7	5.5	.456	.327	.636	13.0
Ferrell.	24.2	3.2	1.4	.524	.333	.761	12.7
Graham	22.0	3.0	2.2	.447	.390	.741	10.1
Rasmussen. . . .	24.3	4.9	1.3	.478	.217	.750	9.0
Volkov.	19.7	3.4	3.2	.441	.318	.631	8.6
Cheeks	19.4	1.7	3.3	.462	.500	.605	4.6
Wiley	16.4	1.5	3.4	.430	.333	.686	3.8
Koncak	19.3	3.4	1.7	.391	.000	.655	3.1
Bennett	16.0	3.1	0.7	.378	.000	.700	3.7

Coach—Lenny Wilkens

Boston Celtics

	Min per game	Reb avg	Ast avg	FG%	3-pt FG%	FT%	Pts avg
Lewis	37.4	4.8	2.3	.503	.238	.851	20.8
Bird	36.9	9.6	6.8	.466	.406	.926	20.2
Parish	28.9	8.9	0.9	.535	—	.772	14.1
McHale	25.0	5.9	1.5	.509	.000	.822	13.9
Gamble	30.4	3.5	2.7	.529	.290	.885	13.5
Brown	28.5	2.5	5.3	.426	.227	.769	11.7
Fox	19.0	2.7	1.6	.459	.329	.755	8.0
Pinckney	23.7	7.0	0.8	.537	.000	.812	7.6
Douglas	17.9	1.5	4.1	.462	.100	.682	7.3
Bagley.	23.9	2.2	6.6	.441	.238	.716	7.2
Kleine	14.2	4.2	0.5	.491	.500	.708	4.7

Coach—Chris Ford

Charlotte Hornets

	Min per game	Reb avg	Ast avg	FG%	3-pt FG%	FT%	Pts avg
Gill.	36.8	5.1	4.2	.467	.240	.745	20.5
Johnson.	37.2	11.0	3.6	.490	.227	.829	19.2
Curry	26.2	3.4	2.3	.486	.404	.836	15.7
Newman	30.0	3.3	2.7	.477	.283	.766	15.3
Gattison.	27.1	7.1	1.6	.529	.000	.688	12.7
Hammonds	26.6	5.0	1.0	.488	.000	.610	11.9
Reid	24.6	6.2	1.[illegible]	.490	.000	.705	11.0
Bogues	34.0	2.9	9.1	.472	.074	.783	8.9
Frederick	12.9	2.2	1.1	.435	.235	.685	5.9
Lynch	14.9	1.5	1.5	.417	.375	.761	4.1
Leckner	12.1	3.5	0.5	.513	.000	.745	3.3

Coach—Allan Bristow

Chicago Bulls

	Min per game	Reb avg	Ast avg	FG%	3-pt FG%	FT%	Pts avg
Jordan.	38.8	6.4	6.1	.519	.270	.832	30.1
Pippen.	38.6	7.7	7.0	.506	.200	.760	21.0
Grant	35.3	10.0	2.7	.578	.000	.741	14.2
Armstrong	22.9	1.8	3.2	.481	.402	.806	9.9
Cartwright.	23.0	5.1	1.4	.467	—	.604	8.0
Paxson	24.6	1.2	3.1	.528	.273	.784	7.0
King	16.1	2.6	1.0	.506	.400	.753	7.0
Perdue	13.1	4.1	1.0	.547	.500	.495	4.5
Levingston	12.9	2.9	0.8	.498	.167	.625	3.9
Williams.	11.0	3.9	0.8	.483	.000	.649	3.4
Hansen	11.9	1.1	1.0	.444	.259	.364	2.5

Coach—Phil Jackson

Cleveland Cavaliers

	Min per game	Reb avg	Ast avg	FG%	3-pt FG%	FT%	Pts avg
Daugherty.	36.2	10.4	3.6	.570	.000	.777	21.5
Price.	29.7	2.4	7.4	.488	.387	.947	17.3
Nance	35.6	8.3	2.9	.539	.000	.822	17.0
Ehlo	32.0	4.9	3.8	.453	.413	.707	12.3
Williams.	30.4	7.6	2.5	.503	.000	.752	11.9
Battle	21.5	1.5	2.1	.480	.118	.848	10.3
Brandon.	19.6	2.0	3.9	.419	.043	.806	7.4
Sanders.	20.4	3.1	1.7	.571	.333	.766	7.1
Kerr	17.6	1.6	2.3	.511	.432	.833	6.6
James.	13.3	1.7	0.4	.407	.322	.803	6.4
Ferry	13.8	3.1	1.1	.409	.354	.836	5.1

Coach—Bob Weiss

Dallas Mavericks

	Min per game	Reb avg	Ast avg	FG%	3-pt FG%	FT%	Pts avg
Blackman.	33.7	3.2	2.7	.461	.385	.898	18.3
Harper.	34.6	2.6	5.7	.443	.312	.759	17.7
Williams.	27.2	6.1	1.3	.431	.167	.725	11.5
Lever	28.5	5.2	3.5	.387	.327	.750	11.2
T. Davis	31.6	9.9	0.8	.482	.000	.635	10.2
Iuzzolino.	24.6	1.9	3.7	.451	.434	.836	9.3
McCray	28.1	6.2	2.9	.436	.294	.719	9.0
Smith	22.5	5.1	1.7	.415	.000	.736	8.8
Moore	18.6	2.0	1.1	.400	.357	.833	8.5
Hodge.	20.7	5.4	0.8	.497	—	.667	8.4
White	15.7	3.6	0.5	.380	.148	.765	6.4

Coach—Richie Adabato

Denver Nuggets

	Min per game	Reb avg	Ast avg	FG%	3-pt FG%	FT%	Pts avg
Williams.	32.4	5.0	2.9	.471	.359	.803	18.2
Mutombo	38.3	12.3	2.2	.493	—	.642	16.6
Anderson	34.1	11.5	1.0	.456	.000	.623	11.5
Garland	28.3	2.4	5.3	.444	.321	.859	10.8
Macon.	30.3	2.9	2.2	.375	.133	.730	10.6
Jackson.	19.0	1.4	2.4	.421	.330	.870	10.3
Davis	16.1	1.5	1.5	.459	.313	.872	9.9
Liberty.	20.4	4.1	0.8	.443	.340	.728	9.3
Lichti.	17.3	1.7	1.1	.460	.111	.839	6.6
Wolf	17.3	3.6	0.9	.361	.091	.803	3.8

Coach—Paul Westhead

Detroit Pistons

	Min per game	Reb avg	Ast avg	FG%	3-pt FG%	FT%	Pts avg
Dumars	38.9	2.3	4.6	.448	.408	.867	19.9
I. Thomas	37.4	3.2	7.2	.446	.291	.772	18.5
Woolridge.	25.8	3.2	1.1	.498	.111	.683	14.0
Aguirre	21.1	3.1	1.7	.431	.211	.687	11.3
Rodman.	40.3	18.7	2.3	.539	.317	.600	9.8
Laimbeer	27.6	5.6	2.0	.470	.376	.893	9.7
Salley	24.6	4.1	1.6	.512	.000	.715	9.5
Walker	20.8	3.2	2.8	.423	.000	.619	5.2

Coach—Chuck Daly

Golden State Warriors

	Min per game	Reb avg	Ast avg	FG%	3-pt FG%	FT%	Pts avg
Mullin	41.3	5.6	3.5	.524	.366	.833	25.6
Hardaway.	41.1	3.8	10.0	.461	.338	.766	23.4
Marciulionis. . . .	29.4	2.9	3.4	.538	.300	.788	18.9
Owens	31.4	8.0	2.4	.525	.111	.654	14.3
Hill.	23.0	7.2	0.6	.522	.000	.694	8.2
Elie	21.2	2.9	2.2	.521	.329	.852	7.8
Alexander.	16.9	4.2	0.4	.529	.000	.691	7.4
Askew.	18.7	2.9	2.4	.509	.100	.694	6.2
Gatling	11.3	3.4	0.3	.568	.000	.661	5.7

Coach—Don Nelson

Houston Rockets

	Min per game	Reb avg	Ast avg	FG%	3-pt FG%	FT%	Pts avg
Olajuwon	37.7	12.1	2.2	.502	.000	.766	21.6
Thorpe	37.3	10.5	3.0	.592	.000	.657	17.3
Maxwell.	33.8	3.0	4.1	.413	.342	.772	17.2
K. Smith.	33.8	2.2	6.9	.475	.394	.866	14.0
Floyd	20.3	1.8	2.9	.406	.301	.794	9.1
B. Johnson	27.5	3.9	2.0	.458	.111	.727	8.6
Bullard	16.0	2.8	0.9	.459	.386	.760	6.4
A. Johnson	17.9	1.2	3.9	.479	.267	.653	5.6
L. Smith.	17.8	5.7	0.7	.543	.000	.364	2.3
Rollins.	11.8	2.9	0.3	.535	—	.867	2.0

Coach—Don Chaney; Rudy Tomjanovich

Indiana Pacers

	Min per game	Reb avg	Ast avg	FG%	3-pt FG%	FT%	Pts avg
Miller	38.0	3.9	3.8	.501	.378	.858	20.7
Person	36.1	5.3	4.7	.480	.373	.675	18.5
Schrempf	32.6	9.6	3.9	.536	.324	.828	17.3
M. Williams	34.8	3.6	8.2	.490	.242	.871	15.0
Smits	23.9	5.6	1.6	.510	.000	.788	13.8
Fleming	21.2	2.5	3.2	.482	.222	.737	8.9
McCloud	17.5	2.6	2.3	.409	.340	.781	6.6
Davis	20.3	6.4	0.5	.552	.000	.572	6.2
Thompson	16.2	4.8	1.3	.468	.000	.817	4.9

Coach—Bob Hill

Los Angeles Clippers

	Min per game	Reb avg	Ast avg	FG%	3-pt FG%	FT%	Pts avg
Manning	35.4	6.9	3.5	.542	.000	.725	19.3
Harper	38.3	5.5	5.1	.440	.303	.736	18.2
Smith	26.7	6.1	1.1	.466	.000	.785	14.6
Norman	26.1	5.8	1.6	.490	.143	.535	12.1
Rivers	28.1	2.5	3.9	.424	.283	.832	10.9
Edwards	20.0	2.8	0.7	.465	.000	.731	9.7
Polynice	24.1	7.1	0.6	.519	.000	.622	8.1
Grant	26.3	2.4	6.9	.462	.294	.815	7.8
Vaught	21.4	6.5	0.9	.492	.800	.797	7.6
Young	16.5	1.2	2.8	.392	.329	.851	4.5

Coach—Mike Schuler; Larry Brown

Los Angeles Lakers

	Min per game	Reb avg	Ast avg	FG%	3-pt FG%	FT%	Pts avg
Worthy	39.0	5.6	4.7	.447	.209	.814	19.9
Perkins	37.0	8.8	2.2	.450	.217	.817	16.5
Threatt	37.4	3.1	7.2	.489	.323	.831	15.1
Scott	32.7	3.8	2.8	.458	.344	.838	14.9
Green	35.4	9.3	1.4	.476	.214	.744	13.6
Divac	27.2	6.9	1.7	.495	.263	.768	11.3
Teagle	19.5	2.2	1.4	.452	.250	.766	10.7
Campbell	23.2	5.2	0.7	.448	.000	.619	7.1
Smith	13.0	1.2	1.7	.399	.000	.653	4.4

Coach—Mike Dunleavy

Miami Heat

	Min per game	Reb avg	Ast avg	FG%	3-pt FG%	FT%	Pts avg
Rice	38.1	5.0	2.3	.469	.391	.836	22.3
Seikaly	35.4	11.8	1.4	.489	.000	.733	16.4
Long	37.4	8.4	2.7	.494	.273	.807	14.8
Smith	29.6	3.1	4.6	.454	.320	.748	12.0
Burton	23.3	3.6	1.8	.450	.400	.800	11.2
Edwards	22.7	2.6	2.1	.454	.219	.848	10.1
Coles	24.4	2.3	4.5	.455	.192	.824	10.1
Shaw	22.6	3.2	4.0	.407	.217	.791	7.9
Kessler	15.5	4.1	0.4	.413	—	.817	5.3
Askins	14.3	2.4	0.6	.410	.342	.703	3.7
Bennett	15.4	3.0	0.7	.379	.000	.700	3.6

Coach—Kevin Loughery

Milwaukee Bucks

	Min per game	Reb avg	Ast avg	FG%	3-pt FG%	FT%	Pts avg
Ellis	27.0	3.1	1.3	.469	.419	.774	15.7
Malone	30.6	9.1	1.1	.474	.375	.786	15.6
Humphries	31.8	2.6	6.6	.469	.292	.783	14.0
Robertson	30.0	4.3	4.4	.430	.319	.763	12.3
Brickowski	23.9	5.3	1.9	.524	.500	.767	11.4
Roberts	21.8	3.2	1.5	.482	.514	.749	9.6
Krystkowiak	23.4	5.4	1.4	.444	.000	.757	9.0
Grayer	20.2	3.1	1.8	.448	.288	.667	9.0
Lohaus	15.4	3.6	1.1	.450	.396	.659	5.8
Schayes	16.9	3.9	0.8	.417	—	.771	5.6
Conner	17.5	2.3	3.6	.431	.000	.704	3.5

Coach—Del Harris; Frank Hamblen

Minnesota Timberwolves

	Min per game	Reb avg	Ast avg	FG%	3-pt FG%	FT%	Pts avg
Campbell	31.3	3.7	2.9	.464	.351	.803	16.8
Richardson	35.6	3.7	8.4	.466	.342	.691	16.5
West	31.8	3.2	3.5	.518	.174	.805	14.0
Glass	24.3	3.5	2.3	.440	.296	.616	11.5
Bailey	25.0	5.8	0.9	.440	.000	.796	11.3
Mitchell	26.2	5.8	1.1	.423	.182	.786	10.1
Spencer	24.3	7.1	0.9	.426	—	.691	6.6
Breuer	17.6	4.2	1.3	.468	.000	.532	5.4
Brooks	13.2	1.2	2.5	.447	.356	.810	5.1
Longley	15.0	3.9	0.8	.458	—	.663	4.3

Coach—Jimmy Rodgers

New Jersey Nets

	Min per game	Reb avg	Ast avg	FG%	3-pt FG%	FT%	Pts avg
Petrovic	36.9	3.1	3.1	.508	.444	.808	20.6
Coleman	34.0	9.5	3.2	.504	.303	.763	19.8
Bowie	30.7	8.1	2.6	.445	.320	.757	15.0
Blaylock	35.4	3.7	6.8	.432	.222	.712	13.8
Morris	31.1	6.4	2.6	.477	.200	.714	11.4
Mills	20.9	5.5	1.0	.463	.348	.750	9.0
Anderson	17.0	2.0	3.2	.390	.231	.745	7.0
George	14.8	1.5	2.3	.427	.167	.821	6.0
Addison	15.5	2.2	0.9	.433	.286	.737	5.8
Dudley	23.2	9.0	0.7	.403	—	.468	5.6

Coach—Bill Fitch

New York Knickerbockers

	Min per game	Reb avg	Ast avg	FG%	3-pt FG%	FT%	Pts avg
Ewing	38.4	11.2	1.9	.522	.167	.738	24.0
Starks	25.8	2.3	3.4	.449	.348	.778	13.9
McDaniel	28.6	5.6	1.8	.478	.308	.714	13.7
Wilkins	28.6	2.5	2.7	.447	.352	.730	12.4
Jackson	30.4	3.8	8.6	.491	.256	.770	11.3
Mason	26.8	7.0	1.3	.509	.000	.642	7.0
Vandeweghe	14.3	1.3	0.9	.491	.394	.802	7.0
Oakley	28.2	8.5	1.6	.522	.000	.735	6.2
Anthony	18.4	1.7	3.8	.370	.145	.741	5.5
Donaldson	18.5	5.0	0.6	.457	—	.709	4.9

Coach—Pat Riley

Orlando Magic

	Min per game	Reb avg	Ast avg	FG%	3-pt FG%	FT%	Pts avg
Scott	33.8	3.7	1.9	.402	.326	.901	19.9
Anderson	36.7	6.4	2.7	.463	.353	.667	19.9
Catledge	31.2	7.0	1.4	.496	.000	.694	14.8
Bowie	33.1	4.7	3.1	.493	.386	.860	14.6
Skiles	31.7	2.7	7.3	.414	.364	.895	14.1
Reynolds	25.2	3.2	3.3	.380	.125	.836	12.1
Vincent	22.7	2.6	3.8	.430	.077	.846	10.5
Roberts	20.3	6.1	0.7	.529	.000	.515	10.4
Williams	18.9	5.7	0.7	.528	—	.669	9.1
Higgins	16.2	2.7	1.1	.458	.240	.861	7.7
Turner	21.2	3.3	1.2	.451	.125	.693	7.1
Smith	15.9	2.1	1.0	.365	.381	.769	5.6
Corchiani	14.5	1.5	2.8	.399	.270	.875	5.0
Kite	20.5	5.6	0.6	.437	.000	.588	3.2
Acres	13.6	3.7	0.3	.517	.333	.761	3.1

Coach—Matt Guokas

Philadelphia 76ers

	Min per game	Reb avg	Ast avg	FG%	3-pt FG%	FT%	Pts avg
Barkley	38.4	11.1	4.1	.552	.234	.695	23.1
Hawkins	37.2	3.3	3.1	.462	.397	.874	19.0
Gilliam	34.2	8.1	1.5	.511	.000	.807	16.9
Anderson	29.7	3.4	1.6	.465	.331	.877	13.7
Dawkins	34.3	2.8	6.9	.437	.356	.882	12.0
Shackleford	19.4	5.8	0.6	.486	.000	.663	6.6
Williams	12.9	2.9	0.2	.364	—	.636	4.1
Grant	13.1	1.0	3.2	.440	.389	.833	3.3
Bol	17.8	3.1	0.3	.383	.000	.462	1.5

Coach—Jim Lynam

Phoenix Suns

	Min per game	Reb avg	Ast avg	FG%	3-pt FG%	FT%	Pts avg
Hornacek	38.0	5.0	5.1	.512	.439	.886	20.1
Johnson	37.2	3.7	10.7	.479	.217	.807	19.7
Majerle	34.8	5.9	3.3	.478	.382	.756	17.3
Chambers	28.2	5.8	2.1	.431	.367	.830	16.3
Perry	31.0	6.9	1.7	.523	.375	.712	12.3
Lang	24.3	6.7	0.5	.522	.000	.768	7.7
Ceballos	11.3	2.4	0.8	.482	.167	.736	7.2
West	17.5	4.5	0.3	.632	—	.637	6.1
Knight	15.0	1.1	2.7	.475	.308	.688	5.8

Coach—Cotton Fitzsimmons

Portland Trail Blazers

	Min per game	Reb avg	Ast avg	FG%	3-pt FG%	FT%	Pts avg
Drexler	36.2	6.6	6.7	.470	.337	.794	25.0
Porter	34.0	3.1	5.8	.461	.395	.856	18.1
Kersey	33.2	8.2	3.2	.467	.125	.664	12.6
Robinson	25.9	5.1	1.7	.466	.091	.664	12.4
Williams	31.5	8.8	1.4	.604	.000	.754	11.3
Duckworth	27.1	6.1	1.2	.461	.000	.690	10.7
Ainge	19.7	1.8	2.5	.442	.339	.824	9.7
Abdelnaby	13.2	3.7	0.4	.493	—	.752	6.1
Pack	12.4	1.3	1.9	.423	.000	.803	4.6
Bryant	14.3	3.6	0.7	.480	.000	.667	4.1

Coach—Rick Adelman

Sacramento Kings

	Min per game	Reb avg	Ast avg	FG%	3-pt FG%	FT%	Pts avg
Richmond	38.7	4.0	5.1	.468	.384	.813	22.5
Simmons	37.1	8.1	4.3	.454	.200	.770	17.1
Tisdale	35.0	6.5	1.5	.500	.000	.763	16.6
Webb	35.4	2.9	7.1	.445	.367	.859	16.0
Hopson	18.5	2.9	1.4	.465	.255	.708	10.5
Bonner	28.9	6.1	1.6	.447	.250	.627	9.4
Causwell	28.6	7.3	0.7	.549	.000	.613	8.0
Les	11.5	1.9	2.3	.385	.344	.809	3.7
Chilcutt	11.8	2.7	0.6	.452	1.000	.821	3.6

Coach—Dick Motta; Rex Hughes

San Antonio Spurs

	Min per game	Reb avg	Ast avg	FG%	3-pt FG%	FT%	Pts avg
Robinson	37.7	12.2	2.7	.551	.125	.701	23.2
Cummings	30.7	9.0	1.5	.488	.385	.711	17.3
Elliott	38.0	5.4	2.6	.494	.305	.861	16.3
Strickland	36.0	4.6	8.6	.455	.333	.687	13.8
Anderson	38.1	5.3	5.3	.455	.232	.775	13.1
Carr	23.0	4.3	0.8	.490	.200	.764	10.9
V. Johnson	22.5	3.0	2.4	.405	.317	.647	8.0
Green	14.1	4.3	0.5	.427	—	.820	4.6
Royal	12.0	2.1	0.6	.449	—	.692	4.2
Sutton	9.0	0.7	1.4	.388	.292	.756	3.7
Pressey	13.6	1.7	2.5	.373	.143	.683	2.7

Coach—Larry Brown; Bob Bass

Seattle SuperSonics

	Min per game	Reb avg	Ast avg	FG%	3-pt FG%	FT%	Pts avg
Pierce	34.1	3.0	3.1	.475	.268	.916	21.7
Johnson	29.2	3.6	2.0	.459	.252	.861	17.1
Kemp	28.3	10.4	1.3	.504	.000	.748	15.5
McKay	33.8	5.2	2.3	.472	.380	.847	14.9
Benjamin	30.8	8.1	1.2	.478	.000	.687	14.0
Payton	31.5	3.6	6.2	.451	.130	.669	9.4
Cage	30.0	8.9	1.1	.566	.000	.620	8.8
Barros	17.7	1.1	1.7	.483	.446	.759	8.3
McMillan	22.9	3.5	5.0	.437	.276	.643	6.0
Brown	11.5	1.5	0.8	.410	.302	.727	4.8

Coach—K.C. Jones; George Karl

Utah Jazz

	Min per game	Reb avg	Ast avg	FG%	3-pt FG%	FT%	Pts avg
K. Malone	37.7	11.2	3.0	.526	.176	.778	28.0
J. Malone	36.1	2.9	2.2	.511	.083	.898	20.2
Stockton	36.6	3.3	13.7	.482	.407	.842	15.8
Edwards	28.2	3.7	1.7	.522	.379	.774	12.6
Corbin	27.6	5.9	1.8	.481	.000	.866	9.8
M. Brown	21.7	5.8	1.0	.453	.000	.667	7.7
Benoit	15.1	3.8	0.4	.467	.214	.810	5.6
Eaton	25.0	6.1	0.5	.446	—	.598	3.3

Coach—Jerry Sloan

Washington Bullets

	Min per game	Reb avg	Ast avg	FG%	3-pt FG%	FT%	Pts avg
Ellison	38.0	11.2	2.9	.539	.333	.728	20.0
Adams	35.8	4.0	7.6	.393	.324	.869	18.1
Grant	37.3	6.8	2.7	.478	.125	.800	18.0
Eackles	22.5	2.7	1.9	.468	.200	.743	13.2
Hammonds	26.6	5.0	1.0	.488	.000	.610	11.9
English	20.6	2.1	1.8	.433	.176	.841	10.9
Stewart	29.3	5.9	1.6	.514	.000	.807	10.4
Wingate	26.3	3.3	3.0	.465	.056	.719	7.9
Smith	14.8	1.7	2.1	.407	.095	.804	5.1
Turner	12.4	1.3	2.5	.425	.063	.792	4.1
Jones	18.2	4.2	0.8	.367	-	.500	1.1

Coach—Wes Unseld

NBA Regular Season Individual Highs in 1992

Most minutes played, season — 3,346: Chris Mullin, Golden State.

Most points, game — 52: Dominique Wilkins, Altanta vs. N.Y., Nov. 7 (2OT); **Non-overtime** — 51: Michael Jordan, Chicago at Washington, March 19.

Most field goals made, game — 21: Michael Jordan (twice), Chicago vs. Cleveland, Feb. 17 and March 28.

Most field goal attempts, game — 39: Michael Jordan, Chicago at Portland, Nov. 29 (2OT); **Non-overtime** — 34: Hakeem Olajuwon, Houston vs. Phoenix, April 19.

Most 3-point field goals made, game — 8: John Starks, N.Y. vs. Chicago, March 31.

Most free throws made, game — 20: Karl Malone, Utah vs. Golden State, April 13.

Most rebounds, game — 34: Dennis Rodman, Detroit vs. Indiana, March 4 (OT). **Non-overtime** — 31: Kevin Willis, Atlanta at Dallas, Dec. 3; Dennis Rodman, Detroit at Sacramento, March 14.

Most offensive rebounds, season — 523: Dennis Rodman, Detroit.

Most defensive rebounds, season — 1,007: Dennis Rodman, Detroit.

Most assists, game — 23: John Stockton (twice), Utah vs. Golden State, Nov. 29; Utah vs. Minnesota, April 17.

Most blocked shots, game — 11: David Robinson, San Antonio vs. Portland, Feb. 4.

Most steals, game — 9: Michael Adams, Washington at Indiana, Nov. 1; Doc Rivers, L.A. Clippers vs. Phoenix, Nov. 6.

NBA All-Defensive Team in 1992

First team	Position	Second team
Dennis Rodman, Detroit	Forward	Larry Nance, Cleveland
Scottie Pippen, Chicago	Forward	Buck Williams, Portland
David Robinson, San Antonio	Center	Patrick Ewing, New York
Michael Jordan, Chicago	Guard	Michael Williams, Indiana
Joe Dumars, Detroit	Guard	John Stockton, Utah

All-Time NBA Statistical Leaders

(At the start of the 1991-92 season. *Includes 1991-92 season)

Scoring Average
(400 games or 10,000 Points Minimum)

	G	Pts.	Avg
*Michael Jordan	589	19,000	32.2
Wilt Chamberlain	1,045	31,419	30.1
Elgin Baylor	846	23,149	27.4
Jerry West	932	25,192	27.0
Bob Pettit	792	20,880	26.4
George Gervin	791	20,708	26.2
*Dominique Wilkins	762	19,975	26.2
*Karl Malone	570	14,770	25.9
Oscar Robertson	1,040	26,710	25.7
*Larry Bird	897	22,586	25.1

Field Goal Percentage
(2,000 FGM Minimum)

	FGA	FGM	Pct.
Artis Gilmore	9,570	5,732	.599
James Donaldson	5,109	2,941	.576
Charles Barkley	7,596	4,403	.580
Steve Johnson	4,965	2,841	.572
Darryl Dawkins	6,060	3,468	.572
Jeff Ruland	3,685	2,080	.564
Kevin McHale	11,051	6,209	.562
Kareem Abdul-Jabbar	28,307	15,837	.559
Buck Williams	8,583	4,752	.554
Bobby Jones	6,199	3,412	.550

Free Throw Percentage
(1,200 FTM Minimum)

	FTA	FTM	Pct.
Rick Barry	4,243	3,818	.900
Calvin Murphy	3,864	3,445	.892
Larry Bird	4,126	3,647	.884
Bill Sharman	3,357	3,143	.884
Chris Mullen	1,928	1,695	.879
Kiki Vandeweghe	2,562	3,102	.871
Mike Newlin	3,456	3,005	.870
Jeff Malone	2,231	1,939	.869
John Long	2,051	1,765	.861
Fred Brown	2,211	1,896	.858

Points

	Pts.
Kareem Abdul-Jabbar	38,387
Wilt Chamberlain	31,419
Elvin Hayes	27,313
*Moses Malone	27,016
Oscar Robertson	26,710
John Havlicek	26,395
Alex English	25,643
Jerry West	25,192
Adrian Dantley	23,177

Games Played

Kareem Abdul-Jabbar	1,560
Elvin Hayes	1,303
John Havlicek	1,270
Paul Silas	1,254
Alex English	1,193
*Robert Parish	1,260
*Moses Malone	1,246
Hal Greer	1,122
Dennis Johnson	1,100

Assists

*Magic Johnson	9,921
Oscar Robertson	9,887
*Isiah Thomas	7,991
*Maurice Cheeks	7,285
Len Wilkens	7,211
Bob Cousy	6,955
Guy Rodgers	6,917
Nate Archibald	6,476
John Lucas	6,454

Field Goals Made

Kareem Abdul-Jabbar	15,837
Wilt Chamberlain	12,681
Elvin Hayes	10,976
Alex English	10,659
John Havlicek	10,513
Oscar Robertson	9,508
*Moses Malone	9,307
Jerry West	9,016
Elgin Baylor	8,693

Rebounds

Wilt Chamberlain	23,924
Bill Russell	21,620
Kareem Addul-Jabbar	17,440
Elvin Hayes	16,279
*Moses Malone	15,894
Nate Thurmond	14,464
Walt Bellamy	14,241
Wes Unseld	13,769
Jerry Lucas	12,942

Individuals in The Basketball Hall of Fame

Springfield, Mass.

Players
Archibald, Nate
Arizin, Paul
Barlow, Thomas
Barry, Rick
Baylor, Elgin
Beckman, John
Belov, Sergei
Bing, Dave
Borgmann, Bennie
Bradley, Bill
Brennan, Joseph
Cervi, Al
Chamberlain, Wilt
Cooper, Charles
Cousy, Bob
Cowens, Dave
Cunningham, Billy
Davies, Bob
DeBernardi, Forrest
DeBusschere, Dave
Dehnert, Dutch
Endacott, Paul
Foster, Bud
Frazier, Walt
Friedman, Max
Fulks, Joe
Gale, Lauren
Gallatin, Harry
Gates, Pop
Gola, Tom
Greer, Hal
Gruenig, Ace
Hagan, Cliff
Hanson, Victor
Harris, Luisa
Havlicek, John
Hawkins, Connie
Hayes, Elvin
Heinsohn, Tom
Holman, Nat
Houbregs, Bob
Hyatt, Chuck
Johnson, William
Johnston, Neil
Jones, K.C.
Jones, Sam
Krause, Moose
Kurland, Bob
Lanier, Bob
Lapchick, Joe
Lovellette, Clyde
Lucas, Jerry
Luisetti, Hank
Macauley, Ed
Maravich, Pete
Martin, Slater
McCracken, Branch
McCracken, Jack
McDermott, Bobby
Mikan, George
Monroe, Earl
Murphy, Stretch
Page, Pat
Pettit, Bob
Phillip, Andy
Pollard, Jim
Ramsey, Frank
Reed, Willis
Robertson, Oscar
Roosma, John S.
Russell, Honey
Russell, Bill
Schayes, Adolph
Schmidt, Ernest
Schommer, John
Sedran, Barney
Sharman, Bill
Steinmetz, Christian
Thompson, Cat
Thurmond, Nate
Twyman, Jack
Unseld, Wes
Vandivier, Fuzzy
Wachter, Edward
Wanzer, Bobby
West, Jerry
White, Nera
Wilkins, Lenny
Wooden, John

Coaches
Auerbach, Red
Barry, Sam
Blood, Ernest
Cann, Howard
Carlson, Dr. H. C.
Carnesecca, Lou
Carnevale, Ben
Case, Everett
Dean, Everett
Diddle, Edgar
Drake, Bruce
Gaines, Clarence
Gardner, Jack
Gill, Slats
Hickey, Edgar
Hobson, Howard
Holzman, Red
Iba, Hank
Julian, Alvin
Keaney, Frank
Keogan, George
Knight, Bob
Lambert, Ward
Litwack, Harry
Loeffler, Kenneth
Lonborg, Dutch
McCutchan, Arad
McGuire, Al
McGuire, Frank
McLendon, John
Meyer, Ray
Meanwell, Dr. W.E.
Miller, Ralph
Newell, Pete
Ramsay, Jack
Rupp, Adolph
Sachs, Leonard
Shelton, Everett
Smith, Dean
Taylor, Fred
Teague, Bertha
Wade, Margaret
Watts, Stan
Wooden, John
Woolpert, Phil

Referees
Enright, James
Hepburn, George
Hoyt, George
Kennedy, Matthew
Leith, Lloyd
Mihalik, Red
Nucatola, John
Quigley, Ernest
Shirley, J. Dallas
Tobey, David
Walsh, David

Contributors
Abbott, Sendra B.
Allen, Phog
Bee, Clair
Brown, Walter
Bunn, John
Douglas, Bob
Duer, Al O.
Fagan, Cliff
Fisher, Harry
Fleisher, Larry
Gottlieb, Edward
Gulick, Dr. L. H.
Harrison, Lester
Hepp, Dr. Ferenc
Hickox, Edward
Hinkle, Tony
Irish, Ned
Jones, R. W.
Kennedy, Walter
Liston, Emil
Mokray, Bill
Morgan, Ralph
Morgenweck, Frank
Naismith, Dr. James
O'Brien, John
O'Brien, Larry
Olsen, Harold
Podoloff, Maurice
Porter, H. V.
Reis, William
Ripley, Elmer
St. John, Lynn
Saperstein, Abe
Schabinger, Arthur
Stagg, Amos Alonzo
Steitz, Edward
Taylor, Chuck
Tower, Oswald
Trester, Arthur
Wells, Clifford
Wilke, Lou

1992 NBA Player Draft

The following are the first round picks of the National Basketball Association.

Orlando—Shaquille O'Neal, LSU
Charlotte—Alonzo Mourning, Georgetown
Minnesota—Christian Laettner, Duke
Dallas—Jim Jackson, Ohio State
Denver—LaPhonso Ellis, Notre Dame
Washington—Tom Gugliotta, North Carolina St.
Sacramento—Walt Williams, Maryland
Milwaukee—Todd Day, Arkansas
Philadelphia—Clarence Weatherspoon, Southern Miss.
Atlanta—Adam Keefe, Stamford
Houston—Robert Horry, Alabama
Miami—Harold Miner, USC
Denver—Bryant Stith, Virginia
Indiana—Malik Sealy, St. John's
L.A. Lakers—Anthony Peeler, Missouri
L.A. Clippers—Randy Woods, La Salle
Seattle—Doug Christie, Pepperdine
San Antonio—Tracy Murray,[1] UCLA
Detroit—Don MacLean,[2] UCLA
New York—Hubert Davis, North Carolina
Boston—Jon Barry, Georgia Tech
Phoenix—Oliver Miller, Arkansas
Milwaukee—Lee Mayberry, Arkansas
Golden State—Latrell Sprewell, Alabama
L.A. Clippers—Elmore Spencer, UNLV
Portland—Dave Johnson, Syracuse
Chicago—Byron Houston, Oklahoma State

(1) Traded to Portland. (2) Traded to L.A. Clippers.

First Round NBA Draft Picks, 1966-92

Year	Team	Player, college
1966	New York	Cazzie Russell, Michigan
1967	Detroit	Jimmy Walker, Providence
1968	Houston	Elvin Hayes, Houston
1969	Milwaukee	Lew Alcindor, UCLA*
1970	Detroit	Bob Lanier, St. Bonaventure
1971	Cleveland	Austin Carr, Notre Dame
1972	Portland	LaRue Martin, Loyola-Chicago
1973	Philadelphia	Doug Collins, Illinois St.
1974	Portland	Bill Walton, UCLA
1975	Atlanta	David Thompson, [1] N.C. State
1976	Houston	John Lucas, Maryland
1977	Milwaukee	Kent Benson, Indiana
1978	Portland	Mychal Thompson, Minnesota
1979	L.A. Lakers	Magic Johnson, Michigan St.
1980	Golden State	Joe Barry Carroll, Purdue
1981	Dallas	Mark Aguirre, DePaul
1982	L.A. Lakers	James Worthy, N. Carolina
1983	Houston	Ralph Sampson, Virginia
1984	Houston	Akeem Olajuwon, Houston
1985	New York	Patrick Ewing, Georgetown
1986	Cleveland	Brad Daugherty, N. Carolina
1987	San Antonio	David Robinson, Navy
1988	L.A. Clippers	Danny Manning, Kansas
1989	Sacramento	Pervis Ellison, Louisville
1990	New Jersey	Derrick Coleman, Syracuse
1991	Charlotte	Larry Johnson, UNLV
1992	Orlando	Shaquille O'Neal, LSU

* Later Kareem Abdul-Jabbar. (1) Signed with Denver of ABA.

Figure Skating Champions

U.S. Champions			World Champions	
Men	Women	Year	Men	Women
Dick Button	Tenley Albright	1952	Dick Button, U.S.	Jacqueline du Bief, France
Hayes Jenkins	Tenley Albright	1953	Hayes Jenkins, U.S.	Tenley Albright, U.S.
Hayes Jenkins	Tenley Albright	1954	Hayes Jenkins, U.S.	Gundi Busch, W. Germany
Hayes Jenkins	Tenley Albright	1955	Hayes Jenkins, U.S.	Tenley Albright, U.S.
Hayes Jenkins	Tenley Albright	1956	Hayes Jenkins, U.S.	Carol Heiss, U.S.
Dave Jenkins	Carol Heiss	1957	Dave Jenkins, U.S.	Carol Heiss, U.S.
Dave Jenkins	Carol Heiss	1958	Dave Jenkins, U.S.	Carol Heiss, U.S.
Dave Jenkins	Carol Heiss	1959	Dave Jenkins, U.S.	Carol Heiss, U.S.
Dave Jenkins	Carol Heiss	1960	Alain Giletti, France	Carol Heiss, U.S.
Bradley Lord	Laurence Owen	1961	none	none
Monty Hoyt	Barbara Roles Pursley	1962	Don Jackson, Canada	Sjoukje Dijkstra, Neth.
Tommy Litz	Lorraine Hanlon	1963	Don McPherson, Canada	Sjoukje Dijkstra, Neth.
Scott Allen	Peggy Fleming	1964	Manfred Schnelldorfer, W. Germany	Sjoukje Dijkstra, Neth.
Gary Visconti	Peggy Fleming	1965	Alain Calmat, France	Petra Burka, Canada
Scott Allen	Peggy Fleming	1966	Emmerich Danzer, Austria	Peggy Fleming, U.S.
Gary Visconti	Peggy Fleming	1967	Emmerich Danzer, Austria	Peggy Fleming, U.S.
Tim Wood	Peggy Fleming	1968	Emmerich Danzer, Austria	Peggy Fleming, U.S.
Tim Wood	Janet Lynn	1969	Tim Wood, U.S.	Gabriele Seyfert, E. Germany
Tim Wood	Janet Lynn	1970	Tim Wood, U.S.	Gabriele Seyfert, E. Germany
John Misha Petkevich	Janet Lynn	1971	Ondrej Nepela, Czech.	Beatrix Schuba, Austria
Ken Shelley	Janet Lynn	1972	Ondrej Nepela, Czech.	Beatrix Schuba, Austria
Gordon McKellen Jr.	Janet Lynn	1973	Ondrej Nepela, Czech.	Karen Magnussen, Canada
Gordon McKellen Jr.	Dorothy Hamill	1974	Jan Hoffmann, E. Germany	Christine Errath, E. Germany
Gordon McKellen Jr.	Dorothy Hamill	1975	Sergei Volkov, USSR	Dianne de Leeuw, Neth.-U.S.
Terry Kubicka	Dorothy Hamill	1976	John Curry, Gt. Britain	Dorothy Hamill, U.S.
Charles Tickner	Linda Fratianne	1977	Vladimir Kovalev, USSR	Linda Fratianne, U.S.
Charles Tickner	Linda Fratianne	1978	Charles Tickner, U.S.	Anett Potzsch, E. Germany
Charles Tickner	Linda Fratianne	1979	Vladimir Kovalev, USSR	Linda Fratianne, U.S.
Charles Tickner	Linda Fratianne	1980	Jan Hoffmann, E. Germany	Anett Potzsch, E. Germany
Scott Hamilton	Elaine Zayak	1981	Scott Hamilton, U.S.	Denise Biellmann, Switzerland
Scott Hamilton	Rosalynn Sumners	1982	Scott Hamilton, U.S.	Elaine Zayak, U.S.
Scott Hamilton	Rosalynn Sumners	1983	Scott Hamilton, U.S.	Rosalynn Sumners, U.S.
Scott Hamilton	Rosalynn Sumners	1984	Scott Hamilton, U.S.	Katarina Witt, E. Germany
Brian Boitano	Tiffany Chin	1985	Aleksandr Fadeev, USSR	Katarina Witt, E. Germany
Brian Boitano	Debi Thomas	1986	Brian Boitano, U.S.	Debi Thomas, U.S.
Brian Boitano	Jill Trenary	1987	Brian Orser, Canada	Katarina Witt, E. Germany
Brian Boitano	Debi Thomas	1988	Brian Boitano, U.S.	Katarina Witt, E. Germany
Christopher Bowman	Jill Trenary	1989	Kurt Browning, Canada	Midori Ito, Japan
Todd Eldredge	Jill Trenary	1990	Kurt Browning, Canada	Jill Trenary, U.S.
Todd Eldredge	Tonya Harding	1991	Kurt Browning, Canada	Kristi Yamaguchi, U.S.
Christopher Bowman	Kristi Yamaguchi	1992	Viktor Petrenko, Ukraine	Kristi Yamaguchi, U.S.

Summer Olympic Games Records

The modern Olympic Games, first held in Athens, Greece in 1896, were the result of efforts by Baron Pierre de Coubertin, a French educator, to promote interest in education and culture, also to foster better international understanding through the universal medium of youth's love of athletics.

His source of inspiration for the Olympic Games was the ancient Greek Olympic Games, most notable of the four Panhellenic celebrations. The games were combined patriotic, religious, and athletic festivals held every four years. The first such recorded festival was held in 776 B.C., the date from which the Greeks began to keep their calendar by "Olympiads," or four-year spans between the games.

The first Olympiad is said to have consisted merely of a 200-yard foot race near the small city of Olympia, but the games gained in scope and became demonstrations of national pride. Only Greek citizens — amateurs — were permitted to participate. Winners received laurel, wild olive, and palm wreaths and were accorded many special privileges. Under the Roman emperors, the games deteriorated into professional carnivals and circuses. Emperor Theodosius banned them in 394 A.D.

Baron de Coubertin enlisted 9 nations to send athletes to the first modern Olympics in 1896; now more than 100 nations compete. Winter Olympic Games were started in 1924.

Sites of Olympic Games

1896	Athens, Greece
1900	Paris, France
1904	St. Louis, U.S.
1906	Athens*, Greece
1908	London, England
1912	Stockholm, Sweden
1920	Antwerp, Belgium
1924	Paris, France
1928	Amsterdam, Netherlands
1932	Los Angeles, U.S.
1936	Berlin, Germany
1948	London, England
1952	Helsinki, Finland
1956	Melbourne, Australia
1960	Rome, Italy
1964	Tokyo, Japan
1968	Mexico City, Mexico
1972	Munich, W. Germany
1976	Montreal, Canada
1980	Moscow, USSR
1984	Los Angeles, U.S.
1988	Seoul, S. Korea
1992	Barcelona, Spain
1996	Atlanta, U.S.

* Games not recognized by International Olympic Committee. Games 6 (1916), 12 (1940), and 13 (1944) were not celebrated. The 1980 games were boycotted by 62 nations, including the U.S. The 1984 games were boycotted by the USSR and most eastern bloc nations. East and West Germany competed separately 1968-88. The 1992 Unified Team consisted of 12 former Soviet republics. The 1992 Independent Olympic Participants (I.O.C.) were athletes from Serbia, Montenegro, and Macedonia.

Olympic Games Champions, 1896—1992

(*Indicates Gold Medal-Winning Record)

Track and Field — Men

100-Meter Run

1896	Thomas Burke, United States	12s
1900	Francis W. Jarvis, United States	11.0s
1904	Archie Hahn, United States	11s
1908	Reginald Walker, South Africa	10.8s
1912	Ralph Craig, United States	10.8s
1920	Charles Paddock, United States	10.8s
1924	Harold Abrahams, Great Britain	10.6s
1928	Percy Williams, Canada	10.8s
1932	Eddie Tolan, United States	10.3s
1936	Jesse Owens, United States	10.3s
1948	Harrison Dillard, United States	10.3s
1952	Lindy Remigino, United States	10.4s
1956	Bobby Morrow, United States	10.5s
1960	Armin Hary, Germany	10.2s
1964	Bob Hayes, United States	10.0s
1968	Jim Hines, United States	9.95s
1972	Valery Borzov, USSR	10.14s
1976	Hasely Crawford, Trinidad	10.06s
1980	Allan Wells, Great Britain	10.25s
1984	Carl Lewis, United States	9.99s
1988	Carl Lewis, United States	9.92s*
1992	Linford Christie, Great Britain	9.96

200-Meter Run

1900	Walter Tewksbury, United States	22.2s
1904	Archie Hahn, United States	21.6s
1908	Robert Kerr, Canada	22.6s
1912	Ralph Craig, United States	21.7s
1920	Allan Woodring, United States	22s
1924	Jackson Scholz, United States	21.6s
1928	Percy Williams, Canada	21.8s
1932	Eddie Tolan, United States	21.2s
1936	Jesse Owens, United States	20.7s
1948	Mel Patton, United States	21.1s
1952	Andrew Stanfield, United States	20.7s
1956	Bobby Morrow, United States	20.6s
1960	Livio Berruti, Italy	20.5s
1964	Henry Carr, United States	20.3s
1968	Tommie Smith, United States	19.83s
1972	Valeri Borzov, USSR	20.00s
1976	Donald Quarrie, Jamaica	20.23s
1980	Pietro Mennea, Italy	20.19s
1984	Carl Lewis, United States	19.80s
1988	Joe DeLoach, United States	19.75s*
1992	Mike Marsh, United States	20.01s

400-Meter Run

1896	Thomas Burke, United States	54.2s
1900	Maxey Long, United States	49.4s
1904	Harry Hillman, United States	49.2s
1908	Wyndham Halswelle, Great Britain, walkover	50s
1912	Charles Reidpath, United States	48.2s
1920	Bevil Rudd, South Africa	49.6s
1924	Eric Liddell, Great Britain	47.6s
1928	Ray Barbuti, United States	47.8s
1932	William Carr, United States	46.2s
1936	Archie Williams, United States	46.5s
1948	Arthur Wint, Jamaica	46.2s
1952	George Rhoden, Jamaica	45.9s
1956	Charles Jenkins, United States	46.7s
1960	Otis Davis, United States	44.9s
1964	Michael Larrabee, United States	45.1s
1968	Lee Evans, United States	43.8s
1972	Vincent Matthews, United States	44.66s
1976	Alberto Juantorena, Cuba	44.26s
1980	Viktor Markin, USSR	44.60s
1984	Alonzo Babers, United States	44.27s
1988	Steven Lewis, United States	43.87s
1992	Quincy Watts, United States	43.50s*

800-Meter Run

1896	Edwin Flack, Australia	2m. 11s
1900	Alfred Tysoe, Great Britain	2m. 1.2s
1904	James Lightbody, United States	1m. 56s
1908	Mel Sheppard, United States	1m. 52.8s
1912	James Meredith, United States	1m. 51.9s
1920	Albert Hill, Great Britain	1m. 53.4s
1924	Douglas Lowe, Great Britain	1m. 52.4s
1928	Douglas Lowe, Great Britain	1m. 51.8s
1932	Thomas Hampson, Great Britain	1m. 49.8s
1936	John Woodruff, United States	1m. 52.9s
1948	Mal Whitfield, United States	1m. 49.2s
1952	Mal Whitfield, United States	1m. 49.2s
1956	Thomas Courtney, United States	1m. 47.7s
1960	Peter Snell, New Zealand	1m. 46.3s
1964	Peter Snell, New Zealand	1m. 45.1s
1968	Ralph Doubell, Australia	1m. 44.3s
1972	Dave Wottle, United States	1m. 45.9s
1976	Alberto Juantorena, Cuba	1m. 43.50s
1980	Steve Ovett, Great Britain	1m. 45.40s
1984	Joaquim Cruz, Brazil	1m. 43.00s*

1988	Paul Ereng, Kenya	1m. 43.45s
1992	William Tanui, Kenya	1m. 43.66s

1,500-Meter Run

1896	Edwin Flack, Australia	4m. 33.2s
1900	Charles Bennett, Great Britain	4m. 6.2s
1904	James Lightbody, United States	4m. 5.4s
1908	Mel Sheppard, United States	4m. 3.4s
1912	Arnold Jackson, Great Britain	3m. 56.8s
1920	Albert Hill, Great Britain	4m. 1.8s
1924	Paavo Nurmi, Finland	3m. 53.6s
1928	Harry Larva, Finland	3m. 53.2s
1932	Luigi Beccali, Italy	3m. 51.2s
1936	Jack Lovelock, New Zealand	3m. 47.8s
1948	Henri Eriksson, Sweden	3m. 49.8s
1952	Joseph Barthel, Luxemburg	3m. 45.2s
1956	Ron Delany, Ireland	3m. 41.2s
1960	Herb Elliott, Australia	3m. 35.6s
1964	Peter Snell, New Zealand	3m. 38.1s
1968	Kipchoge Keino, Kenya	3m. 34.9s
1972	Pekka Vasala, Finland	3m. 36.3s
1976	John Walker, New Zealand	3m. 39.17s
1980	Sebastian Coe, Great Britain	3m. 38.4s
1984	Sebastian Coe, Great Britain	3m. 32.53s*
1988	Peter Rono, Kenya	3m. 35.96s
1992	Fermin Cacho Ruiz, Spain	3m. 40.12s

3,000-Meter Steeplechase

1920	Percy Hodge, Great Britain	10m. 0.4s
1924	Willie Ritola, Finland	9m. 33.6s
1928	Toivo Loukola, Finland	9m. 21.8s
1932	Volmari Iso-Hollo, Finland (About 3,450 mtrs. extra lap by error)	10m. 33.4s
1936	Volmari Iso-Hollo, Finland	9m. 3.8s
1948	Thore Sjoestrand, Sweden	9m. 4.6s
1952	Horace Ashenfelter, United States	8m. 45.4s
1956	Chris Brasher, Great Britain	8m. 41.2s
1960	Zdzislaw Krzyszkowiak, Poland	8m. 34.2s
1964	Gaston Roelants, Belgium	8m. 30.8s
1968	Amos Biwott, Kenya	8m. 51s
1972	Kipchoge Keino, Kenya	8m. 23.6s
1976	Anders Garderud, Sweden	8m. 08.2s
1980	Bronislaw Malinowski, Poland	8m. 09.7s
1984	Julius Korir, Kenya	8m. 11.8s
1988	Julius Kariuki, Kenya	8m. 05.51s*
1992	Matthew Birir, Kenya	8m. 08.84s

5,000-Meter Run

1912	Hannes Kolehmainen, Finland	14m. 36.6s
1920	Joseph Guillemot, France	14m. 55.6s
1924	Paavo Nurmi, Finland	14m. 31.2s
1928	Willie Ritola, Finland	14m. 38s
1932	Lauri Lehtinen, Finland	14m. 30s
1936	Gunnar Hockert, Finland	14m. 22.2s
1948	Gaston Reiff, Belgium	14m. 17.6s
1952	Emil Zatopek, Czechoslovakia	14m. 6.6s
1956	Vladimir Kuts, USSR	13m. 39.6s
1960	Murray Halberg, New Zealand	13m. 43.4s
1964	Bob Schul, United States	13m. 48.8s
1968	Mohamed Gammoudi, Tunisia	14m. 05.0s
1972	Lasse Viren, Finland	13m. 26.4s
1976	Lasse Viren, Finland	13m. 24.76s
1980	Miruts Yifter, Ethiopia	13m. 21.0s
1984	Said Aouita, Morocco	13m. 05.59s*
1988	John Ngugi, Kenya	13m. 11.70s
1992	Dieter Baumann, Germany	13m. 12.52s

10,000-Meter Run

1912	Hannes Kolehmainen, Finland	31m. 20.8s
1920	Paavo Nurmi, Finland	31m. 45.8s
1924	Willie Ritola, Finland	30m. 23.2s
1928	Paavo Nurmi, Finland	30m. 18.8s
1932	Janusz Kusocinski, Poland	30m. 11.4s
1936	Ilmari Salminen, Finland	30m. 15.4s
1948	Emil Zatopek, Czechoslovakia	29m. 59.6s
1952	Emil Zatopek, Czechoslovakia	29m. 17.0s
1956	Vladimir Kuts, USSR	28m. 45.6s
1960	Pyotr Bolotnikov, USSR	28m. 32.2s
1964	Billy Mills, United States	28m. 24.4s
1968	Naftali Temu, Kenya	29m. 27.4s
1972	Lasse Viren, Finland	27m. 38.4s
1976	Lasse Viren, Finland	27m. 40.38s
1980	Miruts Yifter, Ethiopia	27m. 42.7s
1984	Alberto Cova, Italy	27m. 47.54
1988	Brahim Boutaib, Morocco	27m. 21.46s*
1992	Khalid Skah, Morocco	27m. 46.70s

Marathon

1896	Spiridon Loues, Greece	2h. 58m. 50s
1900	Michel Theato, France	2h. 59m. 45s
1904	Thomas Hicks, United States	3h. 28m. 63s
1908	John J. Hayes, United States	2h. 55m. 18.4s
1912	Kenneth McArthur, South Africa	2h. 36m. 54.8s
1920	Hannes Kolehmainen, Finland	2h. 32m. 35.8s
1924	Albin Stenroos, Finland	2h. 41m. 22.6s
1928	A.B. El Ouafi, France	2h. 32m. 57s
1932	Juan Zabala, Argentina	2h. 31m. 36s
1936	Kijung Son, Japan (Korean)	2h. 29m. 19.2s
1948	Delfo Cabrera, Argentina	2h. 34m. 51.6s
1952	Emil Zatopek, Czechoslovakia	2h. 23m. 03.2s
1956	Alain Mimoun, France	2h. 25m.
1960	Abebe Bikila, Ethiopia	2h. 15m. 16.2s
1964	Abebe Bikila, Ethiopia	2h. 12m. 11.2s
1968	Mamo Wolde, Ethiopia	2h. 20m. 26.4s
1972	Frank Shorter, United States	2h. 12m. 19.8s
1976	Waldemar Cierpinski, E. Germany	2h. 09m. 55s
1980	Waldemar Cierpinski, E. Germany	2h. 11m. 03s
1984	Carlos Lopes, Portugal	2h. 09m. 21 s*
1988	Gelindo Bordin, Italy	2h. 10m. 32s
1992	Hwang Young-Cho, S. Korea	2h. 13m. 23s

20-Kilometer Walk

1956	Leonid Spirin, USSR	1h. 31m. 27.4s
1960	Vladimir Golubnichy, USSR	1h. 33m. 7.2s
1964	Kenneth Mathews, Great Britain	1h. 29m. 34.0s
1968	Vladimir Golubnichy, USSR	1h. 33m. 58.4s
1972	Peter Frenkel, E. Germany	1h. 26m. 42.4s
1976	Daniel Bautista, Mexico	1h. 24m. 40.6s
1980	Maurizio Damilano, Italy	1h. 23m. 35.5s
1984	Ernesto Canto, Mexico	1h. 23m. 13.0s
1988	Josef Pribilinec, Czech.	1h. 19m. 57.0s*
1992	Daniel Plaza Montero, Spain	1h. 21m. 45.0s

50-Kilometer Walk

1932	Thomas W. Green, Great Britain	4h. 50m. 10s
1936	Harold Whitlock, Great Britain	4h. 30m. 41.4s
1948	John Ljunggren, Sweden	4h. 41m. 52s
1952	Giuseppe Dordoni, Italy	4h. 28m. 07.8s
1956	Norman Read, New Zealand	4h. 30m. 42.8s
1960	Donald Thompson, Great Britain	4h. 25m. 30s
1964	Abdon Pamich, Italy	4h. 11m. 12.4s
1968	Christoph Hohne, E. Germany	4h. 20m. 13.6s
1972	Bern Kannenberg, W. Germany	3h. 56m. 11.6s
1980	Hartwig Gauter, E. Germany	3h. 49m. 24.0s
1984	Raul Gonzalez, Mexico	3h. 47m. 26.0
1988	Vayachselav Ivanenko, USSR	3h. 38m. 29.0s*
1992	Andrei Perlov, Unified Team	3h 50m. 13.0s

110-Meter Hurdles

1896	Thomas Curtis, United States	17.6s
1900	Alvin Kraenzlein, United States	15.4s
1904	Frederick Schule, United States	16s
1908	Forrest Smithson, United States	15s
1912	Frederick Kelly, United States	15.1s
1920	Earl Thomson, Canada	14.8s
1924	Daniel Kinsey, United States	15s
1928	Sydney Atkinson, South Africa	14.8s
1932	George Saling, United States	14.6s
1936	Forrest Towns, United States	14.2s
1948	William Porter, United States	13.9s
1952	Harrison Dillard, United States	13.7s
1956	Lee Calhoun, United States	13.5s
1960	Lee Calhoun, United States	13.8s
1964	Hayes Jones, United States	13.6s
1968	Willie Davenport, United States	13.3s
1972	Rod Milburn, United States	13.24s
1976	Guy Drut, France	13.30s
1980	Thomas Munkelt, E. Germany	13. 39s
1984	Roger Kingdom, United States	13.20s
1988	Roger Kingdom, United States	12.98s*
1992	Mark McCoy, Canada	13.12s

400-Meter Hurdles

1900	J.W.B. Tewksbury, United States	57.6s
1904	Harry Hillman, United States	53s

1908	Charles Bacon, United States	55s
1920	Frank Loomis, United States	54s
1924	F. Morgan Taylor, United States	52.6s
1928	Lord Burghley, Great Britain	53.4s
1932	Robert Tisdall, Ireland	51.7s
1936	Glenn Hardin, United States	52.4s
1948	Roy Cochran, United States	51.1s
1952	Charles Moore, United States	50.8s
1956	Glenn Davis, United States	50.1s
1960	Glenn Davis, United States	49.3s
1964	Rex Cawley, United States	49.6s
1968	Dave Hemery, Great Britain	48.12s
1972	John Akii-Bua, Uganda	47.82s
1976	Edwin Moses, United States	47.64s
1980	Volker Beck, E. Germany	48.70s
1984	Edwin Moses, United States	47.75s
1988	Andre Phillips, United States	47.19s
1992	Kevin Young, United States	46.78s*

High Jump

1896	Ellery Clark, United States	5ft. 11 1-4 in.
1900	Irving Baxter, United States	6ft. 2 4-5 in.
1904	Samuel Jones, United States	5ft. 11 in.
1908	Harry Porter, United States	6ft. 3 in.
1912	Alma Richards, United States	6ft. 4 in.
1920	Richmond Landon, United States	6ft. 4 in.
1924	Harold Osborn, United States	6ft. 6 in.
1928	Robert W. King, United States	6ft. 4 1-2 in.
1932	Duncan McNaughton, Canada	6ft. 5 5-8 in.
1936	Cornelius Johnson, United States	6ft. 8 in.
1948	John L. Winter, Australia	6ft. 6 in.
1952	Walter Davis, United States	6ft. 8.32 in.
1956	Charles Dumas, United States	6ft. 11 1-2 in.
1960	Robert Shavlakadze, USSR	7ft. 1 in.
1964	Valery Brumel, USSR	7ft. 1 3-4 in.
1968	Dick Fosbury, United States	7ft. 4 1-4 in.
1972	Yuri Tarmak, USSR	7ft. 3 3-4 in.
1976	Jacek Wszola, Poland	7ft. 4 1-2 in.
1980	Gerd Wessig, E. Germany	7ft. 8 3-4 in.
1984	Dietmar Mogenburg, W. Germany	7ft. 8 1-2 in.
1988	Guennadi Avdeenko, USSR	7ft. 9 1-2 in.*
1992	Javier Sotomayor, Cuba	7ft. 8 in.

Long Jump

1896	Ellery Clark, United States	20ft. 10 in.
1900	Alvin Kraenzlein, United States	23ft. 6 3-4 in.
1904	Myer Prinstein, United States	24ft. 1 in.
1908	Frank Irons, United States	24ft. 6 1-2 in.
1912	Albert Gutterson, United States	24ft. 11 1-4 in.
1920	William Petterssen, Sweden	23ft. 5 1-2 in.
1924	DeHart Hubbard, United States	24ft. 5 in.
1928	Edward B. Hamm, United States	25ft. 4 1-2 in.
1932	Edward Gordon, United States	25ft. 3-4 in.
1936	Jesse Owens, United States	26ft. 5 1-2 in.
1948	William Steele, United States	25ft. 8 in.
1952	Jerome Biffle, United States	24ft. 10 in.
1956	Gregory Bell, United States	25ft. 8 1-4 in.
1960	Ralph Boston, United States	26ft. 7 3-4 in.
1964	Lynn Davies, Great Britain	26ft. 5 3-4 in.
1968	Bob Beamon, United States	29ft. 2 1-2 in.*
1972	Randy Williams, United States	27ft. 1-2 in.
1976	Arnie Robinson, United States	27ft. 4 1-2 in.
1980	Lutz Dombrowski, E. Germany	28ft. 1-4 in.
1984	Carl Lewis, United States	28ft. 1-4 in.
1988	Carl Lewis, United States	28ft. 7 1-4 in.
1992	Carl Lewis, United States	28ft. 5 1-2 in.

400-Meter Relay

1912	Great Britain	42.4s
1920	United States	42.2s
1924	United States	41s
1928	United States	41s
1932	United States	40s
1936	United States	39.8s
1948	United States	40.6s
1952	United States	40.1s
1956	United States	39.5s
1960	Germany (U.S. disqualified)	39.5s
1964	United States	39.0s
1968	United States	38.2s
1972	United States	38.19s
1976	United States	38.33s
1980	USSR	38.26s
1984	United States	37.83s
1988	USSR (U.S. disqualified)	38.19s
1992	United States	37.40s*

1,600-Meter Relay

1908	United States	3m. 29.4s
1912	United States	3m. 16.6s
1920	Great Britain	3m. 22.2s
1924	United States	3m. 16s
1928	United States	3m. 14.2s
1932	United States	3m. 8.2s
1936	Great Britain	3m. 9s
1948	United States	3m. 10.4s
1952	Jamaica	3m. 03.9s
1956	United States	3m. 04.8s
1960	United States	3m. 02.2s
1964	United States	3m. 00.7s
1968	United States	2m. 56.16s
1972	Kenya	2m. 59.8s
1976	United States	2m. 58.65s
1980	USSR	3m. 01.1s
1984	United States	2m. 57.91s
1988	United States	2m. 56.16s
1992	United States	2m. 55.74s*

Pole Vault

1896	William Hoyt, United States	10ft. 10 in.
1900	Irving Baxter, United States	10ft. 10 in.
1904	Charles Dvorak, United States	11ft. 5 3-4 in.
1908	A. C. Gilbert, United States Edward Cook Jr., United States	12ft. 2 in.
1912	Harry Babcock, United States	12ft. 11 1-2 in.
1920	Frank Foss, United States	13ft. 5 in.
1924	Lee Barnes, United States	12ft. 11 1-2 in.
1928	Sabin W. Carr, United States	13ft. 9 1-4 in.
1932	William Miller, United States	14ft. 1 3-4 in.
1936	Earle Meadows, United States	14ft. 3 1-4 in.
1948	Guinn Smith, United States	14ft. 1 1-4 in.
1952	Robert Richards, United States	14ft. 11 in.
1956	Robert Richards, United States	14ft. 11 1-2 in.
1960	Don Bragg, United States	15ft. 5 in.
1964	Fred Hansen, United States	16ft. 8 3-4 in.
1968	Bob Seagren, United States	17ft. 8 1-2 in.
1972	Wolfgang Nordwig, E. Germany	18ft. 1-2 in.
1976	Tadeusz Slusarski, Poland	18ft. 1-2 in.
1980	Wladyslaw Kozakiewicz, Poland	18ft. 11 1-2 in.
1984	Pierre Quinon, France	18ft. 10 1-4 in.
1988	Sergei Bubka, USSR	19ft. 9 1-4 in.*
1992	Maksim Tarassov, Unified Team	19ft. 1-4 in.

Hammer Throw

1900	John Flanagan, United States	163ft. 1 in.
1904	John Flanagan, United States	168ft. 1 in.
1908	John Flanagan, United States	170ft. 4 1-4 in.
1912	Matt McGrath, United States	179ft. 7 1-8 in.
1920	Pat Ryan, United States	173ft. 5 5-8 in.
1924	Fred Tootell, United States	174ft. 10 1-8 in.
1928	Patrick O'Callaghan, Ireland	168ft. 7 1-2 in.
1932	Patrick O'Callaghan, Ireland	176ft. 11 1-8 in.
1936	Karl Hein, Germany	185ft. 4 in.
1948	Imre Nemeth, Hungary	183ft. 11 1-2 in.
1952	Jozsef Csermak, Hungary	197ft. 11 9-16 in.
1956	Harold Connolly, United States	207ft. 3 1-2 in.
1960	Vasily Rudenkov, USSR	220ft. 1 5-8 in.
1964	Romuald Klim, USSR	228ft. 9 1-2 in.
1968	Gyula Zsivotsky, Hungary	240ft. 8 in.
1972	Anatoli Bondarchuk, USSR	247ft. 8 in.
1976	Yuri Syedykh, USSR	254ft. 4 in.
1980	Yuri Syedykh, USSR	268ft. 4 1-2 in.
1984	Juha Tiainen, Finland	256ft. 2 in.
1988	Sergei Litinov, USSR	278ft. 2 1-2 in.*
1992	Andrey Abduvaliyev, Unified Team	270ft. 9 1-2 in.

Discus Throw

1896	Robert Garrett, United States	95ft. 7 1-2 in.
1900	Rudolf Bauer, Hungary	118ft. 3 in.
1904	Martin Sheridan, United States	128ft. 10 1-2 in.
1908	Martin Sheridan, United States	134ft. 2 in.
1912	Armas Taipale, Finland	148ft. 3 in.
	Both hands—Armas Taipale, Finland	271ft. 10 1-4 in.
1920	Elmer Niklander, Finland	146ft. 7 in.
1924	Clarence Houser, United States	151ft. 4 in.
1928	Clarence Houser, United States	155ft. 3 in.
1932	John Anderson, United States	162ft. 4 in.

1936	Ken Carpenter, United States	165ft. 7 in.
1948	Adolfo Consolini, Italy	173ft. 2 in.
1952	Sim Iness, United States	180ft. 6.85 in.
1956	Al Oerter, United States	184ft. 10 1-2 in.
1960	Al Oerter, United States	194ft. 2 in.
1964	Al Oerter, United States	200ft. 1 1-2 in.
1968	Al Oerter, United States	212ft. 6 1-2 in.
1972	Ludvik Danek, Czechoslovakia	211ft. 3 in.
1976	Mac Wilkins, United States	221ft. 5.4 in.
1980	Viktor Rashchupkin, USSR	218ft. 8 in.
1984	Rolf Dannenberg, W. Germany	218ft. 6 in.
1988	Jurgen Schult, E. Germany	225ft. 9 1-4 in.*
1992	Romas Ubartas, Lithuania	213ft. 7 3-4 in.

Triple Jump

1896	James Connolly, United States	44ft. 11 3-4 in.
1900	Myer Prinstein, United States	47ft. 5 3-4 in.
1904	Myer Prinstein, United States	47 ft.
1908	Timothy Ahearne, Great Britain, Ireland	48ft. 11 1-4 in.
1912	Gustaf Lindblom, Sweden	48ft. 5 1-4 in.
1920	Vilho Tuulos, Finland	47ft. 7 in.
1924	Anthony Winter, Australia	50ft. 11 1-4 in.
1928	Mikio Oda, Japan	49ft. 11 in.
1932	Chuhei Nambu, Japan	51ft. 7 in.
1936	Naoto Tajima, Japan	52ft. 6 in.
1948	Arne Ahman, Sweden	50ft. 6 1-4 in.
1952	Adhemar da Silva, Brazil	53ft. 2 3-4 in.
1956	Adhemar da Silva, Brazil	53ft. 7 3-4 in.
1960	Jozef Schmidt, Poland	55ft. 2 in.
1964	Jozef Schmidt, Poland	55ft. 3 1-2 in.
1968	Viktor Saneev, USSR	57ft. 3-4 in.
1972	Viktor Saneev, USSR	56ft. 11 in.
1976	Viktor Saneev, USSR	56ft. 8 3-4 in.
1980	Jaak Uudmae, USSR	56ft. 11 1-4 in.
1984	Al Joyner, United States	56ft. 7 1-2 in.
1988	Hristo Markov, Bulgaria	57ft. 9 1-4 in.
1992	Mike Conley, United States	59ft. 7 1-2 in.*

16-lb. Shot Put

1896	Robert Garrett, United States	36ft. 9 3-4 in.
1900	Richard Sheldon, United States	46ft. 3 1-4 in.
1904	Ralph Rose, United States	48ft. 7 in.
1908	Ralph Rose, United States	46ft. 7 1-2 in.
1912	Pat McDonald, United States	50ft. 4 in.
	Both hands—Ralph Rose, United States	90ft. 5 1-2 in.
1920	Ville Porhola, Finland	48ft. 7 1-4 in.
1924	Clarence Houser, United States	49ft. 2 1-4 in.
1928	John Kuck, United States	52ft. 3-4 in.
1932	Leo Sexton, United States	52ft. 6 in.
1936	Hans Woellke, Germany	53ft. 1 3-4 in.
1948	Wilbur Thompson, United States	56ft. 2 in.
1952	Parry O'Brien, United States	57ft. 1-2 in.
1956	Parry O'Brien, United States	60ft. 11 1-4 in.
1960	William Nieder, United States	64ft. 6 3-4 in.
1964	Dallas Long, United States	66ft. 8 1-2 in.
1968	Randy Matson, United States	67ft. 4 3-4 in.
1972	Wladyslaw Komar, Poland	69ft. 6 in.
1976	Udo Beyer, E. Germany	69ft. 3-4 in.
1980	Vladimir Kiselyov, USSR	70ft. 1-2 in.
1984	Alessandro Andrei, Italy	69ft. 9 in.
1988	Ulf Timmermann, E. Germany	73ft. 8 3-4 in.*
1992	Michael Stulce, United States	71ft. 2 1-4 in.

Javelin

1908	Erik Lemming, Sweden	178ft. 7 1-2 in.
	Held in middle—Erik Lemming, Sweden	179ft. 10 1-2 in.
1912	Erik Lemming, Sweden	198ft. 11 1-4 in.
	Both hands, Julius Saaristo, Finland	358ft. 11 7-8 in.
1920	Jonni Myyra, Finland	215ft. 9 3-4 in.
1924	Jonni Myyra, Finland	206ft. 6 3-4 in.
1928	Eric Lundkvist, Sweden	218ft. 6 1-8 in.
1932	Matti Jarvinen, Finland	238ft. 6 in.
1936	Gerhard Stoeck, Germany	235ft. 8 5-16 in.
1948	Tapio Rautavaara, Finland	228ft. 10 1-2 in.
1952	Cy Young, United States	242ft. 0.79 in.
1956	Egil Danielson, Norway	281ft. 2 1-4 in.
1960	Viktor Tsibulenko, USSR	277ft. 8 3-8 in.
1964	Pauli Nevala, Finland	271ft. 2 1-2 in.
1968	Janis Lusis, USSR	295ft. 7 1-4 in.
1972	Klaus Wolfermann, W. Germany	296ft. 10 in.
1976	Miklos Nemeth, Hungary	310ft. 4 in.*
1980	Dainis Kula, USSR	299ft. 2 3-8 in.
1984	Arto Haerkoenen, Finland	284ft. 8 in.
1988	Tapio Korjus, Finland	276ft. 6 in.
1992	Jan Zelezny, Czech.	294ft. 2 in.

Decathlon

1912	Hugo Wieslander, Sweden	7,724.49 pts.(a)
1920	Helge Lovland, Norway	6,804.35 pts.
1924	Harold Osborn, United States	7,710.77 pts.
1928	Paavo Yrjola, Finland	8,053.29 pts.
1932	James Bausch, United States	8,462.23 pts.
1936	Glenn Morris, United States	7,900 pts.
1948	Robert Mathias, United States	7,139 pts.
1952	Robert Mathias, United States	7,887 pts.
1956	Milton Campbell, United States	7,937 pts.
1960	Rafer Johnson, United States	8,392 pts.
1964	Willi Holdorf, Germany	7,887 pts.(c)
1968	Bill Toomey, United States	8,193 pts.
1972	Nikolai Avilov, USSR	8,454 pts.
1976	Bruce Jenner, United States	8,617 pts.
1980	Daley Thompson, Great Britain	8,495 pts.
1984	Daley Thompson, Great Britain	8,798 pts.*(b)
1988	Christian Schenk, E. Germany	8,488 pts.
1992	Robert Zmelik, Czech.	8,611 pts.

(a) Jim Thorpe of the U.S. won the 1912 Decathlon with 8,413 pts. but was disqualified and had to return his medals because he had played professional baseball prior to the Olympic games. The medals were restored posthumously in 1982. (b) Scoring change effective Apr., 1985. (c) Former point systems used prior to 1964.

Track and Field—Women

100-Meter Run

1928	Elizabeth Robinson, United States	12.2s
1932	Stella Walsh, Poland	11.9s
1936	Helen Stephens, United States	11.5s
1948	Francina Blankers-Koen, Netherlands	11.9s
1952	Marjorie Jackson, Australia	11.5s
1956	Betty Cuthbert, Australia	11.5s
1960	Wilma Rudolph, United States	11.0s
1964	Wyomia Tyus, United States	11.4s
1968	Wyomia Tyus, United States	11.0s
1972	Renate Stecher, E. Germany	11.07s
1976	Annegret Richter, W. Germany	11.08s
1980	Lyudmila Kondratyeva, USSR	11.6s
1984	Evelyn Ashford, United States	10.97s
1988	Florence Griffith-Joyner, United States	10.54s*
1992	Gail Devers, United States	10.82s

200-Meter Run

1948	Francina Blankers-Koen, Netherlands	24.4s
1952	Marjorie Jackson, Australia	23.7s
1956	Betty Cuthbert, Australia	23.4s
1960	Wilma Rudolph, United States	24.0s
1964	Edith McGuire, United States	23.0s
1968	Irena Szewinska, Poland	22.5s
1972	Renate Stecher, E. Germany	22.40s
1976	Barbel Eckert, E. Germany	22.37s
1980	Barbel Wockel, E. Germany	22.03
1984	Valerie Brisco-Hooks, United States	21.81s
1988	Florence Griffith-Joyner, United States	21.34s*
1992	Gwen Torrence, United States	21.81s

400-Meter Run

1964	Betty Cuthbert, Australia	52s
1968	Colette Besson, France	52s
1972	Monika Zehrt, E. Germany	51.08s
1976	Irena Szewinska, Poland	49.29s
1980	Marita Koch, E. Germany	48.88s
1984	Valerie Brisco-Hooks, United States	48.83s
1988	Olga Bryzgina, USSR	48.65s*
1992	Marie-Jose Perec, France	48.83s

800-Meter Run

1928	Lina Radke, Germany	2m. 16.8s

1960	Ludmila Shevtsova, USSR	2m. 4.3s
1964	Ann Packer, Great Britain	2m. 1.1s
1968	Madeline Manning, United States	2m. 0.9s
1972	Hildegard Falck, W. Germany	1m. 58.6s
1976	Tatyana Kazankina, USSR	1m. 54.94s
1980	Nadezhda Olizayrenko, USSR	1m. 53.5s*
1984	Doina Melinte, Romania	1m. 57.6s
1988	Sigrun Wodars, E. Germany	1m. 56.10s
1992	Ellen Van Langen, Netherlands	1m. 55.54s

1,500-Meter Run

1972	Lyudmila Bragina, USSR	4m. 01.4s
1976	Tatyana Kazankina, USSR	4m. 05.48s
1980	Tatyana Kazankina, USSR	3m. 56.6s
1984	Gabriella Dorio, Italy	4m. 03.25s
1988	Paula Ivan, Romania	3m. 53.96s*
1992	Hassiba Boulmerka, Algeria	3m. 55.30s

3,000-Meter Run

1984	Maricica Puica, Romania	8:35.96s
1988	Tatyana Samolenko, USSR	8:26.53s*
1992	Elena Romanova, Unified Team	8:46.04s

10,000-Meter Run

1988	Olga Boldarenko, USSR	31m. 44.69s
1992	Derartu Tulu, Ethiopia	31m. 06.02s*

400-Meter Relay

1928	Canada	48.4s
1932	United States	46.9s
1936	United States	46.9s
1948	Netherlands	47.5s
1952	United States	45.9s
1956	Australia	44.5s
1960	United States	44.5s
1964	Poland	43.6s
1968	United States	42.8s
1972	West Germany	42.81s
1976	East Germany	42.55s
1980	East Germany	41.60s*
1984	United States	41.65s
1988	United States	41.98s
1992	United States	42.11s

1,600-Meter Relay

1972	East Germany	3m. 23s
1976	East Germany	3m. 19.23s
1980	USSR	3m. 20.02s
1984	United States	3m. 18.29s
1988	USSR	3 m. 15.18s*
1992	Unified Team	3m. 20.20s

100-Meter Hurdles

1972	Annelie Ehrhardt, E. Germany	12.59s
1976	Johanna Schaller, E. Germany	12.77s
1980	Vera Komisova, USSR	12.56s
1984	Benita Brown-Fitzgerald, United States	12.84s
1988	Jordanka Donkova, Bulgaria	12.38s*
1992	Paraskevi Patoulidou, Greece	12.64s

400-Meter Hurdles

1984	Nawal el Moutawakii, Morocco	54.61s
1988	Debra Flintoff-King, Australia	53.17s*
1992	Sally Gunnell, Great Britain	53.23s

Heptathlon

1984	Glynis Nunn, Australia	6,390 pts.
1988	Jackie Joyner-Kersee, United States	7,215 pts.*
1992	Jackie Joyner-Kersee, United States	7,044 pts.

High Jump

1928	Ethel Catherwood, Canada	5ft. 2 1-2 in.
1932	Jean Shiley, United States	5ft. 5 1-4 in.
1936	Ibolya Csak, Hungary	5ft. 3 in.
1948	Alice Coachman, United States	5ft. 6 1-8 in.
1952	Esther Brand, South Africa	5ft. 5 3-4 in.
1956	Mildred L. McDaniel, United States	5ft. 9 1-4 in.
1960	Iolanda Balas, Romania	6ft. 3-4 in.
1964	Iolanda Balas, Romania	6ft. 2 3-4 in.
1968	Miloslava Reskova, Czechoslovakia	5ft. 11 1-2 in.
1972	Ulrike Meyfarth, W. Germany	6ft. 4 in.
1976	Rosemarie Ackermann, E. Germany	6ft. 3 3-4 in.
1980	Sara Simeoni, Italy	6ft. 5 1-2 in.
1984	Ulrike Meyfarth, W. Germany	6ft. 7 1-2 in.
1988	Louise Ritter, United States	6ft. 8 in.*
1992	Heike Henkel, Germany	6ft. 7 1-2 in.

Discus Throw

1928	Helena Konopacka, Poland	129ft. 11 3-4 in.
1932	Lillian Copeland, United States	133ft. 2 in.
1936	Gisela Mauermayer, Germany	156ft. 3 in.
1948	Micheline Ostermeyer, France	137ft. 6 1-2 in.
1952	Nina Romaschkova, USSR	168ft. 8 in.
1956	Olga Fikotova, Czechoslovakia	176ft. 1 in.
1960	Nina Ponomareva, USSR	180ft. 8 1-4 in.
1964	Tamara Press, USSR	187ft. 10 in.
1968	Lia Manoliu, Romania	191ft. 2 in.
1972	Faina Melnik, USSR	218ft. 7 in.
1976	Evelin Schlaak, E. Germany	226ft. 4 in.
1980	Evelin Jahl, E. Germany	229ft. 6 in.
1984	Ria Stalman, Netherlands	214ft. 5 in.
1988	Martina Hellmann, E. Germany	237ft. 2 1-4 in.*
1992	Maritza Marten Garcia, Cuba	222ft. 10 in.

Javelin Throw

1932	"Babe" Didrikson, United States	143ft. 4 in.
1936	Tilly Fleischer, Germany	148ft. 2 3-4 in.
1948	Herma Bauma, Austria	149ft. 6 in.
1952	Dana Zatopkova, Czechoslovakia	165ft. 7 in.
1956	Inese Jaunzeme, USSR	176ft. 8 in.
1960	Elvira Ozolina, USSR	183ft. 8 in.
1964	Mihaela Penes, Romania	198ft. 7 1-2 in.
1968	Angela Nemeth, Hungary	198ft. 1-2 in.
1972	Ruth Fuchs, E. Germany	209ft. 7 in.
1976	Ruth Fuchs, E. Germany	216ft. 4 in.
1980	Maria Colon, Cuba	224ft. 5 in.
1984	Tessa Sanderson, Great Britain	228ft. 2 in.
1988	Petra Felke, E. Germany	245ft.*
1992	Silke Renke, Germany	224ft. 2 1-2 in.

Shot Put (8lb., 13oz.)

1948	Micheline Ostermeyer, France	45ft. 1 1-2 in.
1952	Galina Zybina, USSR	50ft. 1 3-4 in.
1956	Tamara Tishkyevich, USSR	54ft. 5 in.
1960	Tamara Press, USSR	56ft. 10 in.
1964	Tamara Press, USSR	59ft. 6 1-4 in.
1968	Margitta Gummel, E. Germany	64ft. 4 in.
1972	Nadezhda Chizova, USSR	69ft.
1976	Ivanka Hristova, Bulgaria	69ft. 5 1-4 in.
1980	Ilona Slupianek, E. Germany	73ft. 6 1-4 in.*
1984	Claudia Losch, W. Germany	67ft. 2 1-4 in.
1988	Natalya Lisovskaya, USSR	72ft 11 1-2 in.
1992	Svetlana Kriveleva, Unified Team	69ft. 1 1-2in.

Long Jump

1948	Olga Gyarmati, Hungary	18ft. 8 1-4 in.
1952	Yvette Williams, New Zealand	20ft. 5 3-4 in.
1956	Elzbieta Krzeskinska, Poland	20ft. 9 3-4 in.
1960	Vyera Krepkina, USSR	20ft. 10 3-4 in.
1964	Mary Rand, Great Britain	22ft. 2 1-4 in.
1968	Viorica Viscopoleanu, Romania	22ft. 4 1-2 in.
1972	Heidemarie Rosendahl, W. Germany	22ft. 3 in.
1976	Angela Voigt, E. Germany	22ft. 3-4 in.
1980	Tatyana Kolpakova, USSR	23ft. 2 in.
1984	Anisoara Stanciu, Romania	22ft. 10 in.
1988	Jackie Joyner-Kersee, United States	24ft. 3 1-2 in.
1992	Heike Drechsler, Germany	23ft. 5 1-4 in.*

Marathon

1984	Joan Benoit, United States	2h. 24m. 52s*
1988	Rosa Mota, Portugal	2h. 25m. 40s
1992	Valentina Yegorova, Unified Team	2h. 32m. 41s

Swimming—Men

50-Meter Freestyle

1988	Matt Biondi, U.S.	22.14
1992	Alexandre Popov, Unified Team	21.91*

100-Meter Freestyle

1896	Alfred Hajos, Hungary	1:22.2
1904	Zoltan de Halmay, Hungary (100 yards)	1:02.8
1908	Charles Daniels, U.S.	1:05.6
1912	Duke P. Kahanamoku, U.S.	1:03.4
1920	Duke P. Kahanamoku, U.S.	1:01.4
1924	John Weissmuller, U.S.	59.0
1928	John Weissmuller, U.S.	58.6
1932	Yasuji Miyazaki, Japan	58.2
1936	Ferenc Csik, Hungary	57.6
1948	Wally Ris, U.S.	57.3
1952	Clark Scholes, U.S.	57.4
1956	Jon Henricks, Australia	55.4
1960	John Devitt, Australia	55.2
1964	Don Schollander, U.S.	53.4
1968	Mike Wenden, Australia	52.2
1972	Mark Spitz, U.S.	51.22
1976	Jim Montgomery, U.S.	49.99
1980	Jorg Woithe, E. Germany	50.40
1984	Rowdy Gaines, U.S.	49.80
1988	Matt Biondi, United States	48.63
1992	Alexandre Popov, Unified Team	49.02

200-Meter Freestyle

1968	Mike Wenden, Australia	1:55.2
1972	Mark Spitz, U.S.	1:52.78
1976	Bruce Furniss, U.S.	1:50.29
1980	Sergei Kopliakov, USSR	1:49.81
1984	Michael Gross, W. Germany	1:47.44
1988	Duncan Armstrong, Australia	1:47.25
1992	Evgueni Sadovyi, Unified Team	1:46.70*

400-Meter Freestyle

1904	C. M. Daniels, U.S. (440 yards)	6:16.2
1908	Henry Taylor, Great Britain	5:36.8
1912	George Hodgson, Canada	5:24.4
1920	Norman Ross, U.S.	5:26.8
1924	John Weissmuller, U.S.	5:04.2
1928	Albert Zorilla, Argentina	5:01.6
1932	Clarence Crabbe, U.S.	4:48.4
1936	Jack Medica, U.S.	4:44.5
1948	William Smith, U.S.	4:41.0
1952	Jean Boiteux, France	4:30.7
1956	Murray Rose, Australia	4:27.3
1960	Murray Rose, Australia	4:18.3
1964	Don Schollander, U.S.	4:12.2
1968	Mike Burton, U.S.	4:09.0
1972	Brad Cooper, Australia	4:00.27
1976	Brian Goodell, U.S.	3:51.93
1980	Vladimir Salnikov, USSR	3:51.31
1984	George DiCarlo, U.S.	3:51.23
1988	Ewe Dassler, E. Germany	3:46.95
1992	Evgeny Sodovyi, Unified Team	3:45.00*

1,500-Meter Freestyle

1908	Henry Taylor, Great Britain	22:48.4
1912	George Hodgson, Canada	22:00.0
1920	Norman Ross, U.S.	22:23.2
1924	Andrew Charlton, Australia	20:06.6
1928	Arne Borg, Sweden	19:51.8
1932	Kusuo Kitamura, Japan	19:12.4
1936	Noboru Terada, Japan	19:13.7
1948	James McLane, U.S.	19:18.5
1952	Ford Konno, U.S.	18:30.3
1956	Murray Rose, Australia	17:58.9
1960	Jon Konrads, Australia	17:19.6
1964	Robert Windle, Australia	17:01.7
1968	Mike Burton, U.S.	16:38.9
1972	Mike Burton, U.S.	15:52.58
1976	Brian Goodell, U.S.	15:02.40
1980	Vladimir Salnikov, USSR	14:58.27
1984	Michael O'Brien, U.S.	15:05.20
1988	Vladimir Salnikov, USSR	15:00.40
1992	Kieren Perkins, Australia	14:43.48*

400-Meter Medley Relay

1960	United States	4:05.4
1964	United States	3:58.4
1968	United States	3:54.9
1972	United States	3:48.16
1976	United States	3:42.22
1980	Australia	3:45.70
1984	United States	3:39.30
1988	United States	3:36.93*
1992	United States	3:36.93*

400-Meter Freestyle Relay

1964	United States	3:31.2
1968	United States	3:31.7
1972	United States	3:26.42
1984	United States	3:19.03
1988	United States	3:16.53*
1992	United States	3:16.74

800-Meter Freestyle Relay

1908	Great Britain	10:55.6
1912	Australia	10:11.6
1920	United States	10:04.4
1924	United States	9:53.4
1928	United States	9:36.2
1932	Japan	8:58.4
1936	Japan	8:51.5
1948	United States	8:46.0
1952	United States	8:31.1
1956	Australia	8:23.6
1960	United States	8:10.2
1964	United States	7:52.1
1968	United States	7:52.33
1972	United States	7:35.78
1976	United States	7:23.22
1980	USSR	7:23.50
1984	United States	7:15.69
1988	United States	7:12.51
1992	Unified Team	7:11.95*

100-Meter Backstroke

1904	Walter Brack, Germany (100 yds.)	1:16.8
1908	Arno Bieberstein, Germany	1:24.6
1912	Harry Hebner, U.S.	1:21.2
1920	Warren Kealoha, U.S.	1:15.2
1924	Warren Kealoha, U.S.	1:13.2
1928	George Kojac, U.S.	1:08.2
1932	Masaji Kiyokawa, Japan	1:08.6
1936	Adolph Kiefer, U.S.	1:05.9
1948	Allen Stack, U.S.	1:06.4
1952	Yoshi Oyakawa, U.S.	1:05.4
1956	David Thiele, Australia	1:02.2
1960	David Thiele, Australia	1:01.9
1968	Roland Matthes, E. Germany	58.7
1972	Roland Matthes, E. Germany	56.58
1976	John Naber, U.S.	55.49
1980	Bengt Baron, Sweden	56.33
1984	Rick Carey, U.S.	55.79
1988	Daichi Suzuki, Japan	55.05
1992	Mark Tewksbury, Canada	53.98*

200-Meter Backstroke

1964	Jed Graef, U.S.	2:10.3
1968	Roland Matthes, E. Germany	2:09.6
1972	Roland Matthes, E. Germany	2:02.82
1976	John Naber, U.S.	1:59.19
1980	Sandor Wladar, Hungary	2:01.93
1984	Rick Carey, U.S.	2:00.23
1988	Igor Polianski, USSR	1:59.37
1992	Martin Lopez-Zubero, Spain	1:58.47*

100-Meter Breaststroke

1968	Don McKenzie, U.S.	1:07.7
1972	Nobutaka Taguchi, Japan	1:04.94
1976	John Hencken, U.S.	1:03.11
1980	Duncan Goodhew, Great Britain	1:03.44
1984	Steve Lundquist, U.S.	1:01.65

1988	Adrian Moorhouse, Great Britain	1:02.04
1992	Nelson Diebel, U.S.	1:01.50*

200-Meter Breaststroke

1908	Frederick Holman, Great Britain	3:09.2
1912	Walter Bathe, Germany	3:01.8
1920	Haken Malmroth, Sweden	3:04.4
1924	Robert Skelton, U.S.	2:56.6
1928	Yoshiyuki Tsuruta, Japan	2:48.8
1932	Yoshiyuki Tsuruta, Japan	2:45.4
1936	Tetsuo Hamuro, Japan	2:41.5
1948	Joseph Verdeur, U.S.	2:39.3
1952	John Davies, Australia	2:34.4
1956	Masura Furukawa, Japan	2:34.7
1960	William Mulliken, U.S.	2:37.4
1964	Ian O'Brien, Australia	2:27.8
1968	Felipe Munoz, Mexico	2:28.7
1972	John Hencken, U.S.	2:21.55
1976	David Wilkie, Great Britain	2:15.11
1980	Robertas Zhulpa, USSR	2:15.85
1984	Victor Davis, Canada	2:13.34
1988	Jozsef Szabo, Hungary	2:13.52
1992	Mike Barrowman, U.S.	2:10.16*

100-Meter Butterfly

1968	Doug Russell, U.S.	55.9
1972	Mark Spitz, U.S.	54.27
1976	Matt Vogel, U.S.	54.35
1980	Par Arvidsson, Sweden	54.92
1984	Michael Gross, W. Germany	53.08
1988	Anthony Nesty, Suriname	53.00*
1992	Pablo Morales, U.S.	53.32

200-Meter Butterfly

1956	William Yorzyk, U.S.	2:19.3
1960	Michael Troy, U.S.	2:12.8
1964	Kevin J. Berry, Australia	2:06.6
1968	Carl Robie, U.S.	2:08.7
1972	Mark Spitz, U.S.	2:00.70
1976	Mike Bruner, U.S.	1:59.23
1980	Sergei Fesenko, USSR	1:59.76
1984	Jon Sieben, Australia	1:57.04
1988	Michael Gross, W. Germany	1:56.94
1992	Mel Stewart, U.S.	1:56.26*

200-Meter Individual Medley

1968	Charles Hickcox, U.S.	2:12.0
1972	Gunnar Larsson, Sweden	2:07.17
1984	Alex Baumann, Canada	2:01.42
1988	Tamas Darnyi, Hungary	2:00.17*
1992	Tamas Darnyi, Hungary	2:00.76

400-Meter Individual Medley

1964	Dick Roth, U.S.	4:45.4
1968	Charles Hickcox, U.S.	4:48.4
1972	Gunnar Larsson, Sweden	4:31.98
1976	Rod Strachan, U.S.	4:23.68
1980	Aleksandr Sidorenko, USSR	4:22.89
1984	Alex Baumann, Canada	4:17.41
1988	Tamas Darnyi, Hungary	4:14.75
1992	Tamas Darnyi, Hungary	4:14.23*

	Springboard Diving	Points
1908	Albert Zurner, Germany	85.5
1912	Paul Guenther, Germany	79.23
1920	Louis Kuehn, U.S.	675.40
1924	Albert White, U.S.	97.46
1928	Pete Desjardins, U.S.	185.04
1932	Michael Galitzen, U.S.	161.38
1936	Richard Degener, U.S.	163.57
1948	Bruce Harlan, U.S.	163.64
1952	David Browning, U.S.	205.29
1956	Robert Clotworthy, U.S.	159.56
1960	Gary Tobian, U.S.	170.00
1964	Kenneth Sitzberger, U.S.	159.90
1968	Bernie Wrightson, U.S.	170.15
1972	Vladimir Vasin, USSR	594.09
1976	Phil Boggs, U.S.	619.52
1980	Aleksandr Portnov, USSR	905.02
1984	Greg Louganis, U.S.	754.41
1988	Greg Louganis, U.S.	730.80
1992	Mark Lenzi, U.S.	676.530

	Platform Diving	Points
1904	Dr. G.E. Sheldon, U.S.	12.75
1908	Hjalmar Johansson, Sweden	83.75
1912	Erik Adlerz, Sweden	73.94
1920	Clarence Pinkston, U.S.	100.67
1924	Albert White, U.S.	97.46
1928	Pete Desjardins, U.S.	98.74
1932	Harold Smith, U.S.	124.80
1936	Marshall Wayne, U.S.	113.58
1948	Sammy Lee, U.S.	130.05
1952	Sammy Lee, U.S.	156.28
1956	Joaquin Capilla, Mexico	152.44
1960	Robert Webster, U.S.	165.56
1964	Robert Webster, U.S.	148.58
1968	Klaus Dibiasi, Italy	164.18
1972	Klaus Dibiasi, Italy	504.12
1976	Klaus Dibiasi, Italy	600.51
1980	Falk Hoffmann, E. Germany	835.65
1984	Greg Louganis, U.S.	710.91
1988	Greg Louganis, U.S.	638.61
1992	Sun Shuwei, China	677.310

Swimming—Women

50-Meter Freestyle

1988	Kristin Otto, E. Germany	25.49
1992	Yang Wenyi, China	24.76*

100-Meter Freestyle

1912	Fanny Durack, Australia	1:22.2
1920	Ethelda Bleibtrey, U.S.	1:13.6
1924	Ethel Lackie, U.S.	1:12.4
1928	Albina Osipowich, U.S.	1:11.0
1932	Helene Madison, U.S.	1:06.8
1936	Hendrika Mastenbroek, Holland	1:05.9
1948	Greta Andersen, Denmark	1:06.3
1952	Katalin Szoke, Hungary	1:06.8
1956	Dawn Fraser, Australia	1:02.0
1960	Dawn Fraser, Australia	1:01.2
1964	Dawn Fraser, Australia	59.5
1968	Jan Henne, U.S.	1:00.0
1972	Sandra Neilson, U.S.	58.59
1976	Kornelia Ender, E. Germany	55.65
1980	Barbara Krause, E. Germany	54.79
1984	(tie) Carrie Steinseifer, U.S.	55.92
	Nancy Hogshead, U.S.	55.92
1988	Kristin Otto, E. Germany	54.93
1992	Zhuang Yong, China	54.64*

200-Meter Freestyle

1968	Debbie Meyer, U.S.	2:10.5
1972	Shane Gould, Australia	2:03.56
1976	Kornelia Ender, E. Germany	1:59.26
1980	Barbara Krause, E. Germany	1:58.33
1984	Mary Wayte, U.S.	1:59.23
1988	Heike Friedrich, E. Germany	1:57.65*
1992	Nicole Haislett, U.S.	1:57.90

400-Meter Freestyle

1924	Martha Norelius, U.S.	6:02.2
1928	Martha Norelius, U.S.	5:42.8
1932	Helene Madison, U.S.	5:28.5
1936	Hendrika Mastenbroek, Netherlands	5:26.4
1948	Ann Curtis, U.S.	5:17.8
1952	Valerie Gyenge, Hungary	5:12.1
1956	Lorraine Crapp, Australia	4:54.6
1960	Susan Chris von Saltza, U.S.	4:50.6
1964	Virginia Duenkel, U.S.	4:43.3
1968	Debbie Meyer, U.S.	4:31.8
1972	Shane Gould, Australia	4:19.44
1976	Petra Thuemer E. Germany	4:09.89
1980	Ines Diers, E. Germany	4:08.76
1984	Tiffany Cohen, U.S.	4:07.10
1988	Janet Evans, U.S.	4:03.85*
1992	Dagmar Hase, Germany	4:07.18

800-Meter Freestyle

1968	Debbie Meyer, U.S.	9:24.0
1972	Keena Rothhammer, U.S.	8:53.68
1976	Petra Thuemer, E. Germany	8:37.14
1980	Michelle Ford, Australia	8:28.90
1984	Tiffany Cohen, U.S.	8:24.95
1988	Janet Evans, U.S.	8:20.20*
1992	Janet Evans, U.S.	8:25.52

100-Meter Backstroke

1924	Sybil Bauer, U.S.	1:23.2
1928	Marie Braun, Netherlands	1:22.0
1932	Eleanor Holm, U.S.	1:19.4
1936	Dina Senff, Netherlands	1:18.9
1948	Karen Harup, Denmark	1:14.4
1952	Joan Harrison, South Africa	1:14.3
1956	Judy Grinham, Great Britain	1:12.9
1960	Lynn Burke, U.S.	1:09.3
1964	Cathy Ferguson, U.S.	1:07.7
1968	Kaye Hall, U.S.	1:06.2
1972	Melissa Belote, U.S.	1:05.78
1976	Ulrike Richter, E. Germany	1:01.83
1980	Rica Reinisch, E. Germany	1:00.86
1984	Theresa Andrews, U.S.	1:02.55
1988	Kristin Otto, E. Germany	1:00.89
1992	Krisztina Egerszegi, Hungary	1:00.68*

200-Meter Backstroke

1968	Pokey Watson, U.S.	2:24.8
1972	Melissa Belote, U.S.	2:19.19
1976	Ulrike Richter, E. Germany	2:13.43
1980	Rica Reinisch, E. Germany	2:11.77
1984	Jolanda De Rover, Netherlands	2:12.38
1988	Krisztina Egerszegi, Hungary	2:09.29
1992	Krisztina Egerszegi, Hungary	2:07.06*

100-Meter Breaststroke

1968	Djurdjica Bjedov, Yugoslavia	1:15.8
1972	Cathy Carr, U.S.	1:13.58
1976	Hannelore Anke, E. Germany	1:11:16
1980	Ute Geweniger, E. Germany	1:10.22
1984	Petra Van Staveren, Netherlands	1:09.88
1988	Tania Dangalakova, Bulgaria	1:07.95*
1992	Elena Roudkovskaia, Unified Team	1:08.00

200-Meter Breaststroke

1924	Lucy Morton, Great Britain	3:33.2
1928	Hilde Schrader, Germany	3:12.6
1932	Clare Dennis, Australia	3:06.3
1936	Hideko Maehata, Japan	3:03.6
1948	Nelly Van Vliet, Netherlands	2:57.2
1952	Eva Szekely, Hungary	2:51.7
1956	Ursula Happe, Germany	2:53.1
1960	Anita Lonsbrough, Great Britain	2:49.5
1964	Galina Prozumenschikova, USSR	2:46.4
1968	Sharon Wichman, U.S.	2:44.4
1972	Beverly Whitfield, Australia	2:41.71
1976	Marina Koshevaia, USSR	2:33.35
1980	Lina Kachushite, USSR	2:29.54
1984	Anne Ottenbrite, Canada	2:30.38
1988	Silke Hoerner, E. Germany	2:26.71
1992	Kyoko Iwasaki, Japan	2:26.65*

200-Meter Individual Medley

1968	Claudia Kolb, U.S.	2:24.7
1972	Shane Gould, Australia	2:23.07
1984	Tracy Caulkins, U.S.	2:12.64
1988	Daniela Hunger, E. Germany	2:12.59
1992	Lin Li, China	2:11.65*

400-Meter Individual Medley

1964	Donna de Varona, U.S.	5:18.7
1968	Claudia Kolb, U.S.	5:08.5
1972	Gail Neall, Australia	5:02.97
1976	Ulrike Tauber, E. Germany	4:42.77
1980	Petra Schneider, E. Germany	4:36.29*
1984	Tracy Caulkins, U.S.	4:39.24
1988	Janet Evans, U.S.	4:37.76
1992	Krisztina Egerszegi, Hungary	4:36.54

100-Meter Butterfly

1956	Shelley Mann, U.S.	1:11.0
1960	Carolyn Schuler, U.S.	1:09.5
1964	Sharon Stouder, U.S.	1:04.7
1968	Lynn McClements, Australia	1:05.5
1972	Mayumi Aoki, Japan	1:03.34
1976	Kornelia Ender, E. Germany	1:00.13
1980	Caren Metschuck, E. Germany	1:00.42
1984	Mary T. Meagher, U.S.	59.26
1988	Kristin Otto, E. Germany	59.00
1992	Qian Hong, China	58.62*

200-Meter Butterfly

1968	Ada Kok, Netherlands	2:24.7
1972	Karen Moe, U.S.	2:15.57
1976	Andrea Pollack, E. Germany	2:11.41
1980	Ines Geissler, E. Germany	2:10.44
1984	Mary T. Meagher, U.S.	2:06.90*
1988	Kathleen Nord, E. Germany	2:09.51
1992	Summer Sanders, U.S.	2:08.67

400-Meter Medley Relay

1960	United States	4:41.1
1960	United States	4:33.9
1968	United States	4:28.3
1972	United States	4:20.75
1976	East Germany	4:07.95
1980	East Germany	4:06.67
1984	United States	4:08.34
1988	E. Germany	4:03.74
1992	United States	4:02.54*

400-Meter Freestyle Relay

1912	Great Britain	5:52.8
1920	United States	5:11.6
1924	United States	4:58.8
1928	United States	4:47.6
1932	United States	4:38.0
1936	Netherlands	4:36.0
1948	United States	4:29.2
1952	Hungary	4:24.4
1956	Australia	4:17.1
1960	United States	4:08.9
1964	United States	4:03.8
1968	United States	4:02.5
1972	United States	3:55.19
1976	United States	3:44.82
1980	East Germany	3:42.71
1984	United States	3:43.43
1988	E. Germany	3:40.63
1992	United States	3:39.46*

	Springboard Diving	Points
1920	Aileen Riggin, U.S.	539.90
1924	Elizabeth Becker, U.S.	474.50
1928	Helen Meany, U.S.	78.62
1932	Georgia Coleman U.S.	87.52
1936	Marjorie Gestring, U.S.	89.27
1948	Victoria M. Draves, U.S.	108.74
1952	Patricia McCormick, U.S.	147.30
1956	Patricia McCormick, U.S.	142.36
1960	Ingrid Kramer, Germany	155.81
1964	Ingrid Engel-Kramer, Germany	145.00
1968	Sue Gossick, U.S.	150.77
1972	Micki King, U.S.	450.03
1976	Jenni Chandler, U.S.	506.19
1980	Irina Kalinina, USSR	725.91
1984	Sylvie Bernier, Canada	530.70
1988	Gao Min, China	580.23
1992	Gao Min, China	572.400

	Platform Diving	Points
1912	Greta Johansson, Sweden	39.90
1920	Stefani Fryland-Clausen, Denmark	34.60
1924	Caroline Smith, U.S.	33.20
1928	Elizabeth B. Pinkston, U.S.	31.60
1932	Dorothy Poynton, U.S.	40.26
1936	Dorothy Poynton Hill, U.S.	33.93
1948	Victoria M. Draves, U.S.	68.87
1952	Patricia McCormick, U.S.	79.37
1956	Patricia McCormick, U.S.	84.85
1960	Ingrid Kramer, Germany	91.28

1964	Lesley Bush, U.S.	99.80	1980	Martina Jaschke, E. Germany	596.25
1968	Milena Duchkova, Czech	109.59	1984	Zhou Jihong, China	435.51
1972	Ulrika Knape, Sweden	390.00	1988	Xu Yanmei, China	445.20
1976	Elena Vaytsekhouskaya, USSR	406.59	1992	Fu Mingxia, China	461.430

Boxing

Light Flyweight (106 lbs)

1968 Francisco Rodriguez, Venezuela
1972 Gyorgy Gedo, Hungary
1976 Jorge Hernandez, Cuba
1980 Shamil Sabyrov, USSR
1984 Paul Gonzalez, U.S.
1988 Ivailo Hristov, Bulgaria
1992 Rogelio Marcelo, Cuba

Flyweight (112 lbs)

1904 George Finnegan, U.S.
1920 William Di Gennara, U.S.
1924 Fidel LaBarba, U.S.
1928 Antal Kocsis, Hungary
1932 Istvan Enekes, Hungary
1936 Willi Kaiser, Germany
1948 Pascual Perez, Argentina
1952 Nathan Brooks, U.S.
1956 Terence Spinks, Great Britain
1960 Gyula Torok, Hungary
1964 Fernando Atzori, Italy
1968 Ricardo Delgado, Mexico
1972 Georgi Kostadinov, Bulgaria
1976 Leo Randolph, U.S.
1980 Peter Lessov, Bulgaria
1984 Steve McCrory, U.S.
1988 Kim Kwang Sun, S. Korea
1992 Su Choi Choi, N. Korea

Bantamweight (119 lbs)

1904 Oliver Kirk, U.S.
1908 A Henry Thomas, Great Britain
1920 Clarence Walker, South Africa
1924 William Smith, South Africa
1928 Vittorio Tamagnini, Italy
1932 Horace Gwynne, Canada
1936 Ulderico Sergo, Italy
1948 Tibor Csik, Hungary
1952 Pentti Hamalainen, Finland
1956 Wolfgang Behrendt, E. Germany
1960 Oleg Grigoryev, USSR
1964 Takao Sakurai, Japan
1968 Valery Sokolov, USSR
1972 Orlando Martinez, Cuba
1976 Yong-Jo Gu, N. Korea
1980 Juan Hernandez, Cuba
1984 Maurizio Stecca, Italy
1988 Kennedy McKinney, U.S.
1992 Joel Casamayor, Cuba

Featherweight (126 lbs)

1904 Oliver Kirk, U.S.
1908 Richard Gunn, Great Britain
1920 Paul Fritsch, France
1924 John Fields, U.S.
1928 Lambertus van Klaveren, Netherlands
1932 Carmelo Robledo, Argentina
1936 Oscar Casanovas, Argentina
1948 Ernesto Formenti, Italy
1952 Jan Zachara, Czech.
1956 Vladimir Safronov, USSR
1960 Francesco Musso, Italy
1964 Stanislav Stephashkin, USSR
1968 Antonin Roldan, Mexico
1972 Boris Kousnetsov, USSR
1976 Angel Herrera, Cuba
1980 Rudi Fink, E. Germany
1984 Meldrick Taylor, U.S.
1988 Giovanni Parisi, Italy
1992 Andreas Tews, Germany

Lightweight (132 lbs)

1904 Harry Spanger, U.S.
1908 Frederick Grace, Great Britain
1920 Samuel Mosberg, U.S.
1924 Hans Nielsen, Denmark
1928 Carlo Orlandi, Italy
1932 Lawrence Stevens, South Africa
1936 Imre Harangi, Hungary
1948 Gerald Dreyer, South Africa
1952 Aureliano Bolognesi, Italy
1956 Richard McTaggart, Great Britain
1960 Kazimierz Pazdzior, Poland
1964 Jozef Grudzien, Poland
1968 Ronald Harris, U.S.
1972 Jan Szczepanski, Poland
1976 Howard Davis, U.S.
1980 Angel Herrera, Cuba
1984 Pernell Whitaker, U.S.
1988 Andreas Zuelow, E. Germany
1992 Oscar De La Hoya, U.S.

Light Welterweight (140 lbs)

1952 Charles Adkins, U.S.
1956 Vladimir Yengibaryan, USSR
1960 Bohumil Nemecek, Czech.
1964 Jerzy Kulej, Poland
1968 Jerzy Kulej, Poland
1972 Ray Seales, U.S.
1976 Ray Leonard, U.S.
1980 Patrizio Oliva, Italy
1984 Jerry Page, U.S.
1988 Viatcheslav Janovski, USSR
1992 Hector Vinent, Cuba

Welterweight (147 lbs)

1904 Albert Young, U.S.
1920 Albert Schneider, Canada
1924 Jean Delarge, Belgium
1928 Edward Morgan, New Zealand
1932 Edward Flynn, U.S.
1936 Sten Suvio, Finland
1948 Julius Torma, Czech.
1952 Zygmunt Chychia, Poland
1956 Nicolae Linca, Romania
1960 Giovanni Benvenuti, Italy
1964 Marian Kasprzyk, Poland
1968 Manfred Wolke, E. Germany
1972 Emilio Correa, Cuba
1976 Jochen Bachfeld, E. Germany
1980 Andres Aldama, Cuba
1984 Mark Breland, U.S.
1988 Robert Wangila, Kenya
1992 Michael Carruth, Ireland

Light Middleweight (157 lbs)

1952 Laszlo Papp, Hungary
1956 Laszlo Papp, Hungary
1960 Wilbert McClure, U.S.
1964 Boris Lagutin, USSR
1968 Boris Lagutin, USSR
1972 Dieter Kottysch, W. Germany
1976 Jerzy Rybicki, Poland
1980 Armando Martinez, Cuba
1984 Frank Tate, U.S.
1988 Park Si Hun, S. Korea
1992 Juan Lemus, Cuba

Middleweight (165 lbs)

1904 Charles Mayer, U.S.
1908 John Douglas, Great Britain
1920 Harry Mallin, Great Britain
1924 Harry Mallin, Great Britain
1928 Piero Toscani, Italy
1932 Carmen Barth, U.S.
1936 Jean Despeaux, France
1948 Laszio Papp, Hungary
1952 Floyd Patterson, U.S.
1956 Gennady Schatkov, USSR
1960 Edward Crook, U.S.
1964 Valery Popenchenko, USSR
1968 Christopher Finnegan, Great Britain
1972 Vyacheslav Lemechev, USSR
1976 Michael Spinks, U.S.
1980 Jose Gomez, Cuba
1984 Joon-Sup Shin, S. Korea
1988 Henry Maske, E. Germany
1992 Ariel Hernandez, Cuba

Light Heavyweight (179 lbs)

1920 Edward Eagan, U.S.
1924 Harry Mitchell, Great Britain
1928 Victor Avendano, Argentina
1932 David Carstens, South Africa
1936 Roger Michelot, France
1948 George Hunter, South Africa
1952 Norvel Lee, U.S.
1956 James Boyd, U.S.
1960 Cassius Clay, U.S.
1964 Cosimo Pinto, Italy
1968 Dan Poznyak, USSR
1972 Mate Parlov, Yugoslavia
1976 Leon Spinks, U.S.
1980 Slobodan Kacar, Yugoslavia
1984 Anton Josipovic, Yugoslavia
1988 Andrew Maynard, U.S.
1992 Torsten May, Germany

Heavyweight (201 lbs)

1984 Henry Tillman, U.S.
1988 Ray Mercer, U.S.
1992 Felix Savon, Cuba

Super Heavyweight (Unlimited)
(known as heavyweight from 1904-1980)

1904 Samuel Berger, U.S.
1908 Albert Oldham, Great Britain
1920 Ronald Rawson, Great Britain
1924 Otto von Porat, Norway
1928 Arturo Rodriguez Jurado, Argentina
1932 Santiago Lovell, Argentina
1936 Herbert Runge, Germany
1948 Rafael Inglesias, Argentina
1952 H. Edward Sanders, U.S.
1956 T. Peter Rademacher, U.S.
1960 Franco De Piccoli, Italy
1964 Joe Frazier, U.S.
1968 George Foreman, U.S.
1972 Teofilo Stevenson, Cuba
1976 Teofilo Stevenson, Cuba
1980 Teofilo Stevenson, Cuba
1984 Tyrell Biggs, U.S.
1988 Lennox Lewis, Canada
1992 Roberto Balado, Cuba

25th Summer Olympics

Barcelona, Spain, July 25–Aug. 9, 1992

Over 14,000 athletes gathered in Barcelona, Spain in July and August for 16 days to compete in the Games of the XXV Olympiad. The athletes represented a record 172 nations, 11 more than had participated in any previous Olympics, and competed for medals in 257 events.

The 1992 games will be remembered mostly for the appearance of the Dream Team—the United States basketball team—featuring, for the first time, the stars of the National Basketball Association. As expected, the team crushed all its opponents on the way to a gold medal. Other notable events at the games were the victory in the long jump for Carl Lewis, his third consecutive gold medal in the event; the successful defense in the heptathlon by Jackie Joyner-Kersee; and the domination in men's gymnastics by Vitaly Shcherbo of the Unified Team. Perhaps the biggest surprise was the failure of world-record holder Sergei Bubka (Ukraine) to win a medal in the pole vault. Also notable was the appearance of South African athletes after missing 7 consecutive Olympiads.

The Unified Team made up of athletes of 12 republics of the former Soviet Union won the most gold medals, 45, and the most medals, 112. The United States finished second with 37 gold medals and 108 medals overall.

Final Medal Standings

Medals Standing

	Gold	Silver	Bronze	Total		Gold	Silver	Bronze	Total
Unified Team[1]	45	38	29	**112**	Ethiopia	1	0	2	**3**
United States	37	34	37	**108**	Latvia	0	2	1	**3**
Germany	33	21	28	**82**	Croatia	0	1	2	**3**
China	16	22	16	**54**	Belgium	0	1	2	**3**
Cuba	14	6	11	**31**	Iran	0	1	2	**3**
Hungary	11	12	7	**30**	I.O.P.[2]	0	1	2	**3**
South Korea	12	5	12	**29**	Greece	2	0	0	**2**
France	8	5	16	**29**	Ireland	1	1	0	**2**
Australia	7	9	11	**27**	Algeria	1	0	1	**2**
Spain	13	7	2	**22**	Estonia	1	0	1	**2**
Japan	3	8	11	**22**	Lithuania	1	0	1	**2**
Britain	5	3	12	**20**	Austria	0	2	0	**2**
Italy	6	5	8	**19**	Namibia	0	2	0	**2**
Poland	3	6	10	**19**	South Africa	0	2	0	**2**
Canada	6	5	7	**18**	Israel	0	1	1	**2**
Romania	4	6	8	**18**	Mongolia	0	0	2	**2**
Bulgaria	3	7	6	**16**	Slovenia	0	0	2	**2**
Netherlands	2	6	7	**15**	Switzerland	1	0	0	**1**
Sweden	1	7	4	**12**	Mexico	0	1	0	**1**
New Zealand	1	4	5	**10**	Peru	0	1	0	**1**
North Korea	4	0	5	**9**	Taiwan	0	1	0	**1**
Kenya	2	4	2	**8**	Argentina	0	0	1	**1**
Czechoslovakia	4	2	1	**7**	Bahamas	0	0	1	**1**
Norway	2	4	1	**7**	Colombia	0	0	1	**1**
Turkey	2	2	2	**6**	Ghana	0	0	1	**1**
Denmark	1	1	4	**6**	Malaysia	0	0	1	**1**
Indonesia	2	2	1	**5**	Pakistan	0	0	1	**1**
Finland	1	2	2	**5**	Philippines	0	0	1	**1**
Jamaica	0	3	1	**4**	Puerto Rico	0	0	1	**1**
Nigeria	0	3	1	**4**	Qatar	0	0	1	**1**
Brazil	2	1	0	**3**	Suriname	0	0	1	**1**
Morocco	1	1	1	**3**	Thailand	0	0	1	**1**

(1) Athletes from 12 former Soviet republics. (2) Independent Olympic Participants (athletes from Serbia, Montenegro and Macedonia).

1992 Summer Olympics Medal Winners

(Gold, Silver, Bronze)

Archery

Men's 70-Meter Individual—G-Sebastien Flute, France; S-Chung Jae Hun, S. Korea; B-Simon Terry, Great Britain.

Men's Team—G-Spain; S-Finland; B-Great Britain.

Women's 70-Meter Individual—G-Cho Youn Jeong, S. Korea; S-Kim Soo Nyung, S. Korea; B-Natalia Valeeva, Unified Team.

Women's Team—G-S. Korea; S-China; B-Unified Team.

Badminton

Men's Singles—G-Alan Budi Kusuma, Indonesia; S-Ardy Wiranata, Indonesia; B-(tie) Thomas Stuer-Lauridsen, Denmark; Hermawan Susanto, Indonesia.

Men's Doubles—G-Kim Moon Soo and Park Joo Bong, S. Korea; S-Eddy Hartono and Rudy Gunawan, Indonesia; B-(tie) Li Yongbo and Tian Bingyi, China; Sidek Razif and Sidek Jalani, Malaysia.

Women's Singles—G-Susi Susanti, Indonesia; S-Bang Soo Hyun, S. Korea; B-(tie) Huang Hua, China and Tang Jiuhong, China.

Women's Doubles—G-Hwang Hye Young and Chung So-Young, S. Korea; S-Guan Weizhen and Nong Qunhua, China; B-(tie) Gil Young Ah and Shim Eun Jung, S. Korea; Lin Yanfen and Yao Fen, China.

Baseball

G-Cuba; S-Taiwan; B-Japan.

Basketball

Men—G-U.S.; S-Croatia; B-Lithuania.

Women—G-Cuba; S-China; B-U.S.

Boxing

106 Pounds—G-Rogelio Marcelo, Cuba; S-Daniel Bojinov, Bulgaria; B-(tie) Jan Quast, Germany; Roel Velasco, Philippines.

112 Pounds—G-Su Choi Chol, N. Korea; S-Raul Gonzalez, Cuba; B-(tie) Timothy Austin, U.S.; Istvan Kovacs, Hungary.

119 Pounds—G-Joel Casamayor, Cuba; S-Wayne McCollough, Ireland; B-Li Gwang Sik, N. Korea; Mohamed Achik, Morocco.

126 Pounds—G-Andreas Tews, Germany; S-Faustino Reyes, Spain; B-(tie) Hocine Soltani, Algeria; Ramazi Paliani, Unified Team.
132 Pounds—G-Oscar De La Hoya, U.S.; S-Marco Rudolph, Germany; B-Hong Sung Sik, N. Korea; Namjil Bayarsaikhan, Mongolia.
140 Pounds—G-Hector Vinent, Cuba; S-Mark Leduc, Canada; B-Jyri Kjall, Finland and Leonard Doroftei, Romania.
148 Pounds—G-Michael Carruth, Ireland; S-Juan Hernandez, Cuba; B-Aniibal Acevedo Santiago, Puerto Rico; Arkom Chenglai, Thailand.
157 Pounds—G-Juan Lemus, Cuba; S-Orhan Delibas, Netherlands; B-Gyorgy Mizsei, Hungary; Robin Reid, Great Britain.
165 Pounds—G-Ariel Hernandez, Cuba; S-Chris Byrd, U.S.; B-(tie) Chris Johnson, Canada; Lee Seung Bae, S. Korea.
179 Pounds—G-Torsten May, Germany; S-Rostislav Zaoulitchnyi, Unified Team; B-Zoltan Beres, Hungary; Wojciech Bartnik, Poland.
201 Pounds—G-Felix Savon, Cuba; S-David Izonritei, Nigeria; B-Arnold Van Der Lijde, Netherlands; David Tua, New Zealand.
Over 201 Pounds—G-Roberto Balado, Cuba; S-Richard Igbineghu, Nigeria; B-Brian Nielsen, Denmark; Svilen Roussinov, Bulgaria.

Canoe/Kayak

Men

Single Kayak Slalom—G-Pierpaolo Ferrazzi, Italy; S-Sylvain Curinier, France; B-Jochen Lettmann, Germany.
Kayak 500M Singles—G-Mikko Yrjoe Kolehmainen, Finland; S-Zsolt Gyulay, Hungary; B-Knut Holmann, Norway.
Kayak 500M Doubles—G-Germany; S-Poland; B-Italy.
Kayak 1,000M Singles—G-Clint Robinson, Australia; S-Knut Holmann, Norway; B-Greg Barton, U.S.
Kayak 1,000M Doubles—G-Germany; S-Sweden; B-Poland.
Kayak 1,000M Fours—G-Germany; S-Hungary; B-Australia.
Double Canoe Slalom—G-U.S.; S-Czechoslovakia; B-France.
Canoe Slalom—G-Lukas Pollert, Czechoslovakia; S-Gareth Marriott, Great Britain; B-Jacky Avril, France.
Canoe 500M Singles—G-Nikolai Boukhalov, Bulgaria; S-Mikhail Slivinski, Unified Team; B-Olaf Heukrodt, Germany.
Canoe 500M Doubles—G-Unified Team; S-Germany; B-Bulgaria.
Canoe 1,000M Singles—G-Nikolai Boukhalov, Bulgaria; S-Ivans Klementjevs, Latvia; B-Gyorgy Zala, Hungary.
Canoe 1,000M Doubles—G-Germany; S-Denmark; B-France.

Women

Kayak Slalom—G-Elisabeth Micheler, Germany; S-Danielle Anne Woodward, Australia; B-Dana Chladek, U.S.
Kayak 500M Singles—B-Birgit Schmidt, Germany; S-Rita Koban, Hungary; B-Izabella Dylewska, Poland.
Kayak 500M Doubles—G-Germany; S-Sweden; B-Hungary.
Kayak 500M Fours—G-Hungary; S-Germany; B-Sweden.

Cycling

Men

Individual Road Race—G-Fabio Casartelli, Italy; S-Erik Dekker, Netherlands; B-Dainis Ozols, Latvia.
Sprint—G-Jens Fiedler, Germany; S-Garry Neiwand, Australia; B-Curtis Harnett, Canada.
Individual Points Race—G-Giovanni Lombardi, Italy; S-Leon Van Bon, Netherlands; B-Cedric Mathy, Belgium.
4,000 Team Pursuit—G-Germany; S-Australia; B-Denmark.
4K Individual Pursuit—G-Chris Boardman, Great Britain; S-Jens Lehmann, Germany; B-Gary Anderson, New Zealand.
1 KM Time Trial—G-Jose Moreno, Spain; S-Shane Kelly, Australia; B-Erin Hartwell, U.S.
Road Race—G-Germany; S-Italy; B-France.

Women

Sprint—G-Erika Salumae, Estonia; S-Annett Neumann, Germany; B-Ingrid Haringa, Netherlands.
Individual Pursuit—G-Petra Rossner, Germany; S-Kathryn Watt, Australia; B-Rebecca Twigg, U.S.
Individual Road Race—G-Kathryn Watt, Australia; S-Jeannie Longo-Ciprelli, France; B-Monique Knol, Netherlands.

Diving

Men's Platform—G-Sun Shuwei, China; S-Scott Donie, U.S.; B-Xiong Ni, China.
Men's Springboard—G-Mark Lenzi, U.S.; S-Tan Liangde, China; B-Dmitri Saoutine, Unified Team.
Women's Platform—G-Fu Mingxia, China; S-Yelina Mirochina, Unified Team; B-Mary Ellen Clark, U.S.
Women's Springboard—G-Gao Min, China; S-Irina Lachko, Unified Team; B-Brita Pia Baldus, Germany.

Equestrian

Ind. Three-Day Event—G-Matthew Ryan, Australia; S-Herbert Blocker, Germany; B-Robert Tait, New Zealand.
Team Three-Day Event—G-Australia; S-New Zealand; B-Germany.
Individual Dressage—G-Nicole Uphoff, Germany; S-Isabelle Regina Werth, Germany; B-Klaus Balkenhol, Germany.
Team Dressage—G-Germany; S-Netherlands; B-U.S.
Individual Jumping—G-Ludger Beerbaum, Germany; S-Piet Raymakers, Netherlands; B-Norman Dello Joio, U.S.
Team Jumping—G-Netherlands; S-Austria; B-France.

Fencing

Men

Individual Foil—G-Philippe Omnes, France; S-Serguei Goloubitski, Unified Team; B-Elvis Gregory Gil, Cuba.
Team Foil—G-Germany; S-Cuba; B-Poland.
Individual Saber—G-Bence Szabo, Hungary; S-Marco Marin, Italy; B-Jean-Francois Lamour, France.
Team Saber—G-Unified Team; S-Hungary; B-France.
Individual Épée—G-Eric Srecki, France; S-Pavel Kolobkov, Unified Team; B-Jean-Michel Henry, France.
Team Épée—G-Germany; S-Hungary; B-Unified Team.

Women

Individual Foil—G-Giovanna Trillini, Italy; S-Wang Huifeng, China; B-Tatiana Sadovskaia, Unified Team.
Team Foil—G-Italy; S-Germany; B-Romania.

Field Hockey

Men—G-Germany; S-Australia; B-Pakistan.
Women—G-Spain; S-Germany; B-Great Britain.

Gymnastics

Men

Floor Exercise—G-Li Xiaosahuang, China; S-(tie) Grigori Misutin, Unified Team; Yukio Iketani, Japan.
Horizontal Bar—G-Trent Dimas, U.S.; S-(tie) Andreas Wecker, Germany; Grigori Misutin, Unified Team.
Parallel Bars—G-Vitaly Shcherbo, Unified Team; S-Li Jing, China; B-(tie) Igor Korobtchinski, Unified Team; Guo Linyao, China; Masayuki Matsunaga, Japan.
Pommel Horse—G-(tie) Vitaly Shcherbo, Unified Team; Pae Gil Su, N. Korea; B-Andreas Wecker, Germany.
Rings—G-Vitaly Shcherbo, Unified Team; S-Li Jing, China; B-(tie) Andreas Wecker, Germany; Li Xiaosahuang, China.
Vault—G-Vitaly Shcherbo, Unified Team; S-Grigori Misutin, Unified Team; B-Yoo Ok Ryul, S. Korea.
Individual All-Around—G-Vitaly Shcherbo, Unified Team; S-Grigori Misioutine, Unified Team; B-Valeri Belenki, Unified Team.
Team—G-Unified Team; S-China; B-Japan.

Women

Balance Beam—G-Tatiana Lisenko, Unified Team; S-(tie) Lu Li, China; Shannon Miller, U.S.
Floor Exercise—G-Lavinia Corina Milosovici, Romania; S-Henrietta Onodi, Hungary; B-(tie) Shannon Miller, U.S.; Cristina Bontas, Romania; Tatiana Gutsu, Unified Team.
Uneven Bars—G-Lu Li, China; S-Tatiana Gutsu, Unified Team; B-Shannon Miller, U.S.
Vault—G-(tie) Henrietta Onodi, Hungary; Lavinia Corina Milosovici, Romania; B-Tatiana Lisenko, Unified Team.
All-Around—G-Tatiana Gutsu, Unified Team; S-Shannon Miller, U.S.; B-Lavinia Corina Milosovici, Romania.
Team Artistic—G-Unified Team; S-Romania; B-U.S.

Rhythmic Gymnastics

G-Alexandra Timoshenko, Unified Team; S-Carolina Pascual Gracia, Spain; B-Oksana Skaldina, Unified Team.

(continued)

Judo

Men

132 Pounds—G-Nazim Gousseinov, Unified Team; S-Yoon Hyun, S. Korea; B-(tie) Tadanori Koshino, Japan; Richard Trautmann, Germany.
143 Pounds—G-Rogerio Sampaio Cardoso, Brazil; S-Josef Csak, Hungary; B-(tie) Udo Gunter Quellmalz, Germany; Israel Hernandez Planas, Cuba.
157 Pounds—G-Toshihiko Koga, Japan; S-Bertalan Hajtos, Hungary; B-(tie) Chung Hoon, S. Korea; Shay Oren Smadga, Israel.
172 Pounds—G-Hidehiko Yoshida, Japan; S-Jason Morris, U.S.; B-(tie) Bertrand Damaisin, France; Kim Byung Joo, S. Korea.
198 Pounds—G-Waldemar Legien, Poland; S-Pascal Tayot, France; B-(tie) Hirotaka Okada, Japan; Nicolas Gill, Canada.
209 Pounds—G-Antal Kovacs, Hungary; S-Raymond Stevens, Great Britain; B-(tie) Dmitri Sergeev, Unified Team; Theo Meijer, Netherlands.
Heavyweight—G-David Khakhaleichvili, Unified Team; S-Naoya Ogawa, Japan; B-(tie) David Douillet, France; Imre Csosz, Hungary.

Women

106 Pounds—G-Cecile Nowak, France; S-Ryoko Tamura, Japan; B-(tie) Hulya Senyurt, Turkey; Amarilis Savon, Cuba.
115 Pounds—G-Almudena Munoz Martinez, Spain; S-Moriko Mizoguchi, Japan; B-(tie) Li Zhongyun, China; Sharon Rendle, Great Britain.
123 Pounds—G-Miriam Blasco Soto, Spain; S-Nicola Fairbrother, Great Britain; B-(tie) Chiyori Tateno, Japan; Driulis Gonzalez, Cuba.
134 Pounds—G-Catherine Fleury, France; S-Yael Arad, Israel; B-(tie) Zhang Di, China; Yelina Petrova, Unified Team.
146 Pounds—G-Odalis Reve Jimenez, Cuba; S-Emanuela Pierantozzi, Italy; B-(tie) Kate Howey, Great Britain; Heidi Rakels, Belgium.
159 Pounds—G-Kim Mi Jung, S. Korea; S-Yoko Tanabe, Japan; B-(tie) Irene De Kok, Netherlands; Laetitia Meignan, France.
Over 159 Pounds—G-Zhuang Xiaoyan, China; S-Estela Rodriguez Villanueva, Cuba; B-(tie) Natalia Lupino, France; Yoko Sakaue, Japan.

Modern Pentathlon

Individual—G-Arkadiusz Skrzypaszek, Poland; S-Attila Mizser, Hungary; B-Eduard Zenovka, Unified Team.
Team—G-Poland; S-Unified Team; B-Italy.

Rowing

Men

Single Sculls—G-Thomas Lange, Germany; S-Vaclav Chalupa, Czechoslovakia; B-Kajetan Broniewski, Poland.
Double Sculls—G-Australia; S-Austria; B-Netherlands.
Coxless Pairs—G-Great Britain; S-Germany; B-Slovenia.
Coxed Pairs—G-Great Britain; S-Italy; B-Romania.
Coxed Fours—G-Romania; S-Germany; B-Poland.
Coxless Fours—G-Australia; S-U.S.; B-Slovenia.
Quadruple Sculls—G-Germany; S-Norway; B-Italy.
Coxed Eights—G-Canada; S-Romania; B-Germany.

Women

Single Sculls—G-Elisabeta Lipa, Romania; S-Annelies Bredael, Belgium; B-Silken Suzette Laumann, Canada.
Double Sculls—G-Germany; S-Romania; B-China.
Coxless Pairs—G-Canada; S-Germany; B-U.S.
Coxless Fours—G-Canada; S-U.S.; B-Germany.
Quadruple Sculls—G-Germany; S-Romania; B-Unified Team.
Coxed Eights—G-Canada; S-Romania; B-Germany.

Shooting

Men

Running Game Target—G-Michael Jakosits, Germany; S-Anatoly Asrabaev, Unified Team; B-Lubos Racansky, Czechoslovakia.
Rapid Fire Pistol—G-Ralf Schumann, Germany; S-Afanasijs Kuzmins, Latvia; B-Vladimir Vokhmianine, Unified Team.
Three-Position Rifle—G-Gratchia Petikiane, Unified Team; S-Bob Foth, U.S.; B-Ryohei Koba, Japan.
Free Rifle—G-Lee Eun Chul, S. Korea; S-Harald Stenvaag, Norway; B-Stevan Pletikosic, I.O.P.
Air Pistol—G-Wang Yifu, China; S-Serguei Pyjianov, Unified Team; B-Sorin Babii, Romania.
Air Rifle—G-Iouri Fedkine, Unified Team; S-Franck Badiou, France; B-Johann Riederer, Germany.
Free Pistol—G-Konstantine Loukachik, Unified Team; S-Wang Yifu, China; B-Ragnar Skanaker, Sweden.

Women

Air Pistol—G-Marina Logvinenko, Unified Team; S-Jasna Sekaric, I.O.P.; B-Maria Zdravkova Grousdeva, Bulgaria.
Three-Position Rifle—G-Launi Meili, U.S.; S-Nonka Detcheva Matova, Bulgaria; B-Malgorzata Ksiazkiewicz, Poland.
Sport Pistol—G-Marina Logvinenko, Unified Team; S-Li Duihong, China; B-Dorzhsuren Munkhbayar, Mongolia.
Air Rifle—G-Yeo Kab Soon, S. Korea; S-Vesela Letcheva, Bulgaria; B-Aranka Binder, I.O.P.

Mixed

Trap—G-Petr Hrdlicka, Czechoslovakia; S-Kazumi Watanabe, Japan; B-Marco Venturini, Italy.
Skeet—G-Zhang Shan, China; S-Juan Jorge Giha Yarur, Peru; B-Bruno Mario Rossetti, Italy.

Soccer

G-Spain; S-Poland; B-Ghana.

Swimming

Men

50M Freestyle—G-Aleksandr Popov, Unified Team; S-Matt Biondi, U.S.; B-Tom Jagar, U.S.
100M Freestyle—G-Aleksandr Popov, Unified Team; S-Gustavo Borges, Brazil; B-Stephan Caron, France.
200M Freestyle—G-Evgueni Sadovyi, Unified Team; S-Anders Holmertz, Sweden; B-Antti Alexander Kasvio, Finland.
400M Freestyle—G-Evgueni Sadovyi, Unified Team; S-Kieren Perkins, Australia; B-Anders Holmertz, Sweden.
1,500M Freestyle—G-Kieren Perkins, Australia; S-Glen Housman, Australia; B-Joerg Hoffmann, Germany.
100M Breast-Stroke—G-Nelson Diebel, U.S.; S-Norbert Rozsa, Hungary; B-Philip Rogers, Australia.
200M Breast-Stroke—G-Mike Barrowman, U.S.; S-Norbert Rozsa, Hungary; B-Nick Gillingham, Great Britain.
100M Butterfly—G-Pablo Morales, U.S.; S-Rafal Szukala, Poland; B-Anthony Conrad Nesty, Surinam.
200M Butterfly—G-Mel Stewart, U.S.; S-Danyon Loader, New Zealand; B-Franck Esposito, France.
100M Backstroke—G-Mark Tewksbury, Canada; S-Jeff Rouse, U.S.; B-David Berkoff, U.S.
200M Backstroke—G-Martin Lopez-Zubero, Spain; S-Vladimir Selkov, Unified Team; B-Stefano Battistelli, Italy.
200M Individual Medley—G-Tamas Darnyi, Hungary; S-Greg Burgess, U.S.; B-Attila Czene, Hungary.
400M Individual Medley—G-Tamas Darnyi, Hungary; S-Eric Namesnik, U.S.; B-Luca Sacchi, Italy.
400M Freestyle Relay—G-U.S.; S-Unified Team; B-Germany.
800M Freestyle Relay—G-Unified Team; S-Sweden; B-U.S.
400M Medley Relay—G-U.S.; S-Unified Team; B-Canada.

Women

50M Freestyle—G-Yang Wenyi, China; S-Zhuang Yong, China; B-Angel Martino, U.S.
100M Freestyle—G-Zhuang Yong, China; S-Jenny Thompson, U.S.; B-Franziska Van Almsick, Germany.
200M Freestyle—G-Nicole Haislett, U.S.; S-Franziska Van Almsick, Germany; B-Kerstin Kielgass, Germany.
400M Freestyle—G-Dagmar Hase, Germany; S-Janet Evans, U.S.; B-Hayley Lewis, Australia.
800M Freestyle—G-Janet Evans, U.S.; S-Hayley Lewis, Australia; B-Jana Henke, Germany.
100M Breast-Stroke—G-Yelina Roudkovskaia, Unified Team; S-Anita Nall, U.S.; B-Samantha Riley, Australia.
200M Breast-Stroke—G-Kyoko Iwasaki, Japan; S-Lin Li, China; B-Anita Nall, U.S.
100M Backstroke—G-Kristina Egerszegi, Hungary; S-Tunde Szabo, Hungary; B-Lea Loveless, U.S.
200M Backstroke—G-Kristina Egerszegi, Hungary; S-Dagmar Hase, Germany; B-Nicole Stevenson, Australia.
100M Butterfly—G-Qian Hong, China; S-Christine Ahmann-Leighton, U.S.; B-Catherine Plewinski, France.
200M Butterfly—G-Summer Sanders, U.S.; S-Wang Xiaohong, China; B-Susan O'Neill, Australia.
200M Individual Medley—G-Lin Li, China; S-Summer Sanders, U.S.; B-Daniela Hunger, Germany.

400M Individual Medley—G-Krisztina Egerszegi, Hungary; S-Lin Li, China; B-Summer Sanders, U.S.
400M Freestyle Relay—G-U.S.; S-China; B-Germany.
400M Medley Relay—G-U.S.; S-Germany; B-Unified Team.

Synchronized Swimming

Solo—G-Kristen Babb-Sprague, U.S.; S-Sylvie Frechette, Canada; B-Fumiko Okuno, Japan.
Duet—G-Karen Josephson, and Sarah Josephson, U.S.; S-Penny Vilagos and Vicky Vilagos, Canada; B-Fumiko Okuno and Aki Takayama, Japan.

Table Tennis

Men's Singles—G-Jan Waldner, Sweden; S-Jean Philippe Gatien, France; B-Kim Taek Soo, S. Korea.
Men's Doubles—G-Lu Lin and Wang Tao, China; S-Steffen Fetzner and Jorg Rosskopf, Germany; B-(tie) Kang Hee Chan and Lee Chul Seung, S. Korea; Kim Taek Soo and Yoo Nam Kyu, S. Korea.
Women's Singles—G-Deng Yaping, China; S-Qiao Hong, China; B-(tie) Hyun Jung Hwa, S. Korea; Li Bun Hui, N. Korea.
Women's Doubles—G-Deng Yaping and Qiao Hong, China; S-Chen Zihe and Gao Jun, China; B-(tie) Li Bun Hui and Yu Sun Bok, N. Korea; Hong Cha Ok and Hyun Jung Hwa, S. Korea.

Team Handball

Men—G-Unified Team; S-Sweden; B-France.
Women—G-S. Korea; S-Norway; B-Unified Team.

Tennis

Men's Singles—G-Marc Rosset, Switzerland; S-Jordi Arrese, Spain; B-Goran Ivanisevic, Croatia; Andrei Cherkasov, Unified Team.
Men's Doubles—G-Boris Becker and Michael Stich, Germany; S-Wayne Ferreira and Piet Norval, South Africa; B-(tie) Goran Ivanisevic and Goran Prpic, Croatia; Javier Frana and Christian Carlos Miniussi, Argentina.
Women's Singles—G-Jennifer Capriati, U.S.; S-Steffi Graf, Germany; B-Aranxta Sanchez Vicario, Spain; Mary Joe Fernandez, U.S.
Women's Doubles—G-Gigi Fernandez and Mary Joe Fernandez, U.S.; S-Conchita Martinez and Arantxa Sanchez Vicario, Spain; B-(tie) Natalya Zvereva and Leila Meskhi, Unified Team, and Rachel McQuillan and Nicole Provis, Austraila.

Track and Field

Men

100M—G-Linford Christie, Great Britain; S-Frankie Fredericks, Namibia; B-Dennis Mitchell, U.S.
200M—G-Mike Marsh, U.S.; S-Frankie Fredericks, Namibia; B-Michael Bates, U.S.
400M—G-Quincy Watts, U.S.; S-Steve Lewis, U.S.; B-Samson Kitur, Kenya.
800M—G-William Tanui, Kenya; S-Nixon Kiprotich, Kenya; B-Johnny Gray, U.S.
1,500M—G-Fermin Cacho Ruiz, Spain; S-Rachid El-Basir, Morocco; B-Mohamed Ahmed Sulaiman, Qatar.
5,000M—G-Dieter Baumann, Germany; S-Paul Bitok, Kenya; B-Fita Bayisa, Ethiopia.
10,000M—G-Khalid Skah, Morocco; S-Richard Chelimo, Kenya; B-Addis Abebe, Ethiopia.
110M Hurdles—G-Mark McKoy, Canada; S-Tony Dees, U.S.; B-Jack Pierce, U.S.
400M Hurdles—G-Kevin Young, U.S.; S-Winthrop Graham, Jamaica; B-Kriss Akabusi, Great Britain.
4x100M Relay—G-U.S.; S-Nigeria; B-Cuba.
4x400M Relay—G-U.S.; S-Cuba; B-Great Britain.
Shot-Put—G-Michael Stuice, U.S.; S-James Doehring, U.S.; B-Viacheslav Lykho, Unified Team.
Triple Jump—G-Mike Conley, U.S.; S-Charles Simpkins, U.S.; B-Frank Rutherford, Bahamas.
Javelin—G-Jan Zelezny, Czechoslovakia; S-Seppo Raty, Finland; B-Steve Backley, Great Britain.
High Jump—G-Javier Sotomayor, Cuba; S-Patrik Sjoeberg, Sweden; B-(tie) Artur Partyka, Poland; Timothy Forsythe, Australia; Hollis Conway, U.S.
Hammer Throw—G-Andrey Abduvaliyev, Unified Team; S-Igor Astapkovich, Unified Team; B-Igor Nikulin, Unified Team.
Long Jump—G-Carl Lewis, U.S.; S-Mike Powell, U.S.; B-Joe Greene, U.S.
Pole Vault—G-Maksim Tarassov, Unified Team; S-Igor Trandenkov, Unified Team; B-Javier Garcia Chico, Spain.
Decathlon—G-Robert Zmelik, Czechoslovakia; S-Antonio Penalver, Spain; B-Dave Johnson, U.S.
Discus—G-Romas Ubartas, Lithuania; S-Jurgen Schult, Germany; B-Roberto Moya, Cuba.
20KM Walk—G-Daniel Plaza Montero, Spain; S-Guillaume Leblanc, Canada; B-Giovanni de Benedictis, Italy.
50KM Walk—G-Andrei Perlov, Unified Team; S-Carlos Mercenario Carbajal, Mexico; B-Ronald Weigel, Germany.
3,000M Steeplechase—G-Mathew Birir, Kenya; S-Patrick Sang, Kenya; B-William Mutwol, Kenya.
Marathon—G-Hwang Young-Cho, S. Korea; S-Koitchi Morishita, Japan; B-Stephan Freigang, Germany.

Women

100M—G-Gail Devers, U.S.; S-Juliet Cuthbert, Jamaica; B-Irina Privalova, Unified Team.
200M—G-Gwen Torrence, U.S.; S-Juliet Cuthbert, Jamaica; B-Merlene Ottey, Jamaica.
400M—G-Marie-Jose Perec, France; S-Olga Bryzgina, Unified Team; B-Ximena Restrepo Gaviria, Colombia.
800M—G-Ellen Van Langen, Netherlands; S-Lilia Nurutdinova, Unified Team; B-Ana Quirot, Cuba.
1,500M—G-Hassiba Boulmerka, Algeria; S-Lyudmila Rogacheva, Unified Team; B-Qu Yunxia, China.
3,000M—G-Yelina Romanova, Unified Team; S-Tatyana Dorovskikh, Unified Team; B-Angela Frances Chalmers, Canada.
10,000M—G-Derartu Tulu, Ethiopia; S-Elana Meyer, South Africa; B-Lynn Jennings, U.S.
100M Hurdles—G-Paraskevi Patoulidou, Greece; S-LaVonna Martin, U.S.; B-Yordanka Donkova, Bulgaria.
400M Hurdles—G-Sally Gunnell, Great Britain; S-Sandra Farmer-Patrick, U.S.; B-Janeene Vickers, U.S.
4x100M Relay—G-U.S.; S-Unified Team; B-Nigeria.
4x400M Relay—G-Unified Team; S-U.S.; B-Great Britain.
Javelin—G-Silke Renke, Germany; S-Natalia Shikolenko, Unified Team; B-Karen Forkel, Germany.
Long Jump—G. Heike Drechsler, Germany; S-Inessa Kravets, Unified Team; B-Jackie Joyner-Kersee, U.S.
High Jump—G-Heike Henkel, Germany; S-Galina Astafei, Romania; B-Joanet Quintero, Cuba.
Shot-Put—G-Svetlana Kriveleva, Unified Team; S-Huang Zhihong, China; B-Kathrin Neimke, Germany.
Heptathlon—G-Jackie Joyner-Kersee, U.S.; S-Irina Belova, Unified Team; B-Sabine Braun, Germany.
10KM Walk—G-Chen Yueling, China; S-Yelina Nikolaeva, Unified Team; B-Li Chunxiu, China.
Discus—G-Maritza Marten Garcia, Cuba; S-Tzvetanka Mintcheva Khristova, Bulgaria; B-Daniela Costian, Australia.
Marathon—G-Valentina Yegorova, Unified Team; S-Yuko Arimori, Japan; B-Lorraine Moller, New Zealand.

Volleyball

Men—G-Brazil; S-Netherlands; B-U.S.
Women—G-Cuba; S-Unified Team; B-U.S.

Water Polo

G-Italy; S-Spain; B-Unified Team.

Weight Lifting

115 Pounds—G-Ivan Ivanov, Bulgaria; S-Lin Qisheng, China; B-Traian Ciharean, Romania.
123 Pounds—G-Chun Byung Kwan, S. Korea; S-Liu Shoubin, China; B-Luo Jianming, China.
132 Pounds—G-Naim Suleymanoglu, Turkey; S-Nikolai Peshalov, Bulgaria; B-He Yingqiang, China.
148 Pounds—G-Israel Militossian, Unified Team; S-Yoto Yotov, Bulgaria; B-Andreas Behm, Germany.
165 Pounds—G-Fedor Kassapu, Unified Team; S-Pablo Lara, Cuba; B-Kim Myong Nam, N. Korea.
180 Pounds—G-Pyrros Dimas, Greece; S-Krzysztof Siemion, Poland; B-None awarded, Ibragim Samadov of the Unified Team refused medal.
198 Pounds—G-Kakhi Kakhiachvili, Unified Team; S-Serguei Syrtsov, Unified Team; B-Sergiusz Wolczaniecki, Poland.
220 Pounds—G-Victor Tregoubov, Unified Team; S-Timour Taimazov, Unified Team; B-Waldemar Malak, Poland.
243 Pounds—G-Ronny Weller, Germany; S-Artour Akoev, Unified Team; B-Stefan Botev, Bulgaria.
Over 243 Pounds—G-Aleksandr Kourlovitch, Unified Team; S-Leonid Taranenko, Unified Team; B-Manfred Nerlinger, Germany.

(continued)

Wrestling

Freestyle

106 Pounds—G-Kim Il, N. Korea; S-Kim Jong Shin, S. Korea; B-Vougar Oroudjov, Unified Team.
115 Pounds—G-Li Hak Son, S. Korea; S-Zeke Jones, U.S.; B-Valentin Jordanov, Bulgaria.
126 Pounds—G-Alejandro Puerto Diaz, Cuba; S-Serguei Smal, Unified Team; B-Kim Young Sik, N. Korea.
137 Pounds—G-John Smith, U.S.; S-Asgari Mohammadian, Iran; B-Lazaro Reinoso Martinez, Cuba.
150 Pounds—G-Arsen Fadzaev, Unified Team; S-Valentin Dotchev Getzov, Bulgaria; B-Kosei Akaishi, Japan.
163 Pounds—G-Park Jang Soon, S. Korea; S-Kenny Monday, U.S.; B-Amir Reza Khadem Azghadi, Iran.
182 Pounds—G-Kevin Jackson, U.S.; S-Elmadi Jabraijlov, Unified Team; B-Rasul Khadem Azghadi, Iran.
198 Pounds—G-Makharbek Khadartsev, Unified Team; S-Kenan Simsek, Turkey; B-Chris Campbell, U.S.
220 Pounds—G-Leri Khabelov, Unified Team; S-Heiko Balz, Germany; B-Ali Kayali, Turkey.
286 Pounds—G-Bruce Baumgartner, U.S.; S-Jeff Thue, Canada; B-David Gobedjichvili, Unified Team.

Greco-Roman

106 Pounds—G-Oleg Koutherenko, Unified Team; S-Vincenzo Maenza, Italy; B-Wilber Sanchez, Cuba.
115 Pounds—G-Jon Ronningen, Norway; S-Alfred Ter-Mkrttchian, Unified Team; B-Min Kyung Kap, S. Korea.
126 Pounds—G-An Han Bong, S. Korea; S-Rifat Yildiz, Germany; B-Sheng Zetian, China.
137 Pounds—G-M. Akif Pirim, Turkey; S-Serguei Martynov, Unified Team; B-Juan Luis Maren Delis, Cuba.
150 Pounds—G-Attila Repka, Hungary; S-Islam Dougoutchiev, Unified Team; B-Rodney Smith, U.S.
163 Pounds—G-Mnatsakan Iskandarian, Unified Team; S-Jozef Tracz, Poland; B-Torbjorn Johansson, Sweden.
181 Pounds—G-Peter Farkas, Hungary; S-Piotr Stepien, Poland; B-Daoulet Tourlykhanov, Unified Team.
198 Pounds—G-Maik Bullmann, Germany; S-Hakki Basar, Turkey; B-Gogui Kogouachvili, Unified Team.
220 Pounds—G-Hector Milian Perez, Cuba; S-Dennis Marvin Koslowski, U.S.; B-Serguei Demiachkievitch, Unified Team.
286 Pounds—G-Aleksandr Karelin, Unified Team; S-Tomas Johansson, Sweden; B-Ioan Grigoras, Romania.

Yachting

Soling—G-Denmark; S-U.S.; B-Great Britain.
Finn—G-Jose Van Der Ploeg, Spain; S-Brian Ledbetter, U.S.; B-Craig Monk, New Zealand.
Tornado—G-France; S-U.S.; B-Australia.
Europe—G-Linda Anderson, Norway; S-Natalia Via Dufresne, Spain; B-Julia Trotman, U.S.
Flying Dutchman—G-Spain; S-U.S.; B-Denmark.
Star—G-U.S.; S-New Zealand; B-Canada.
Men's Sailboard—G-Franck David, France; S-Mike Gebhardt, U.S.; B-Lars Kleppich, Australia.
Women's Sailboard—G-Barbara Kendall, New Zealand; S-Zhang Xiaodong, China; B-Dorien De Vries, Netherlands.
Men's 470—G-Spain; S-U.S.; B-Estonia.
Women's 470—G-Spain; S-New Zealand; B-U.S.

Olympic Information

Symbol: Five rings or circles, linked together to represent the sporting friendship of all peoples. The rings also symbolize the 5 continents—Europe, Asia, Africa, Australia, and America. Each ring is a different color—blue, yellow, black, green, and red.

Flag: The symbol of the 5 rings on a plain white background.

Motto: "Citius, Altius, Fortius." Latin meaning "faster, higher, braver," or the modern interpretation "swifter, higher, stronger". The motto was coined by Father Didon, a French educator, in 1895.

Creed: "The most important thing in the Olympic Games is not to win but to take part, just as the most important thing in life is not the triumph but the struggle. The essential thing is not to have conquered but to have fought well."

Oath: An athlete of the host country recites the following at the opening ceremony. "In the name of all competitors I promise that we will take part in these Olympic Games, respecting and abiding by the rules which govern them, in the true spirit of sportsmanship for the glory of sport and the honor of our teams." Both the oath and the creed were composed by Pierre de Coubertin, the founder of the modern Games.

Flame: Symbolizes the continuity between the ancient and modern Games. The modern version of the flame was adopted in 1936. The torch used to kindle the flame is first lit by the sun's rays at Olympia, Greece, and then carried to the site of the Games by relays of runners. Ships and planes are used when necessary.

The America's Cup

The United States yacht *America* [3] defeated the Italian yacht *Il Moro di Venezia* 4-1 in the waters off San Diego, Cal. The *America* [3] was skippered by Bill Koch. The next America's Cup competition is scheduled for 1995 in San Diego.

Competition for the America's Cup grew out of the first contest to establish a world yachting championship, one of the carnival features of the London Exposition of 1851. The race, open to all classes of yachts from all over the world, covered a 60-mile course around the Isle of Wight; the prize was a cup worth about $500, donated by the Royal Yacht Squadron of England, known as the "America's Cup" because it was first won by the United States yacht *America*.

Winners of the America's Cup

1851	America
1870	Magic defeated Cambria, England, (1-0)
1871	Columbia (first three races) and Sappho (last two races) defeated Livonia, England, (4-1)
1876	Madeline defeated Countess of Dufferin, Canada, (2-0)
1881	Mischief defeated Atalanta, Canada, (2-0)
1885	Puritan defeated Genesta, England, (2-0)
1886	Mayflower defeated Galatea, England, (2-0)
1887	Volunteer defeated Thistle, Scotland, (2-0)
1893	Vigilant defeated Valkyrie II, England, (3-0)
1895	Defender defeated Valkyrie III, England, (3-0)
1899	Columbia defeated Shamrock, England, (3-0)
1901	Columbia defeated Shamrock II, England, (3-0)
1903	Reliance defeated Shamrock III, England, (3-0)
1920	Resolute defeated Shamrock IV, England, (3-2)
1930	Enterprise defeated Shamrock V, England, (4-0)
1934	Rainbow defeated Endeavour, England, (4-2)
1937	Ranger defeated Endeavour II, England, (4-0)
1958	Columbia defeated Sceptre, England, (4-0)
1962	Weatherly defeated Gretel, Australia, (4-1)
1964	Constellation defeated Sovereign, England, (4-0)
1967	Intrepid defeated Dame Pattie, Australia, (4-0)
1970	Intrepid defeated Gretel II, Australia, (4-1)
1974	Courageous defeated Southern Cross, Australia, (4-0)
1977	Courageous defeated Australia, Australia, (4-0)
1980	Freedom defeated Australia, Australia, (4-1)
1983	Australia II, Australia defeated Liberty, (4-3)
1987	Stars & Stripes defeated Kookaburra III, Australia, (4-0)
1988	Stars & Stripes defeated New Zealand, New Zealand, (2-0)
1992	America[3] defeated Il Moro di Venezia, Italy, (4-1)

Pro Rodeo Championship Standings in 1991

Event	Winner	Money won
All Around	Ty Murray, Stephenville, Tex.	$244,230
Saddle Bronc	Robert Etbauer, Goodwell, Okla.	129,408
Bareback	Clint Corey, Kennewick, Wash.	107,350
Bull Riding	Tuff Hedeman, Bowie, Tex.	111,071
Calf Roping	Fred Whitfield, Cypress, Tex.	115,040
Steer Wrestling	Scott Berry, Checotah, Okla.	$116,674
Steer Roping	Guy Allen, Vinita, Okla.	46,132
Women's Barrel Racing	Charmayne James Rodman, Galt, Cal.	92,404

Pro Rodeo Cowboy All Around Champions

Year	Winner	Money won
1969	Larry Mahan, Brooks, Ore.	$57,726
1970	Larry Mahan, Brooks, Ore.	41,493
1971	Phil Lyne, George West, Tex.	49,245
1972	Phil Lyne, George West, Tex.	60,852
1973	Larry Mahan, Dallas, Tex.	64,447
1974	Tom Ferguson, Miami, Okla.	66,929
1975	Leo Camarillo, Oakdale, Cal.	50,300
	Tom Ferguson, Miami, Okla.	50,300
1976	Tom Ferguson, Miami, Okla.	87,908
1977	Tom Ferguson, Miami, Okla.	76,730
1978	Tom Ferguson, Miami, Okla.	103,734
1979	Tom Ferguson, Miami, Okla.	96,272
1980	Paul Tierney, Rapid City, S.D.	$105,568
1981	Jimmie Cooper, Monument, N.M.	105,862
1982	Chris Lybbert, Coyote, Cal.	123,709
1983	Roy Cooper, Durant, Okla.	153,391
1984	Dee Pickett, Caldwell, Ida.	122,618
1985	Lewis Feild, Elk Ridge, Ut.	130,347
1986	Lewis Feild, Elk Ridge, Ut.	166,042
1988	Lewis Feild, Elk Ridge, Ut.	144,335
1988	Dave Appleton, Arlington, Tex.	121,546
1989	Ty Murray, Odessa, Tex.	134,806
1990	Ty Murray, Stephenville, Tex.	213,772
1991	Ty Murray, Stephenville, Tex.	244,230

Harness Racing

Harness Horse of the Year

(Chosen by the U.S. Trotting Assn. and the U.S. Harness Writers Assn.)

1951	Pronto Don	1962	Su Mac Lad	1972	Albatross	1982	Cam Fella
1952	Good Time	1963	Speedy Scot	1973	Sir Dalrae	1983	Cam Fella
1953	Hi Lo's Forbes	1964	Bret Hanover	1974	Delmonica Hanover	1984	Fancy Crown
1954	Stenographer	1965	Bret Hanover	1975	Savior	1985	Nihilator
1955	Scott Frost	1966	Bret Hanover	1976	Keystone Ore	1986	Forrest Skipper
1956	Scott Frost	1967	Nevele Pride	1977	Green Speed	1987	Mack Lobell
1957	Torpid	1968	Nevele Pride	1978	Abercrombie	1988	Mack Lobell
1958	Emily's Pride	1969	Nevele Pride	1979	Niatross	1989	Matt's Scooter
1959	Bye Bye Byrd	1970	Fresh Yankee	1980	Niatross	1990	Beach Towel
1960	Adios Butler	1971	Albatross	1981	Fan Hanover	1992	Precious Bunny
1961	Adios Butler						

The Hambletonian (3-year-old trotters)

Year	Winner	Driver
1965	Egyptian Candor	Del Cameron
1966	Kerry Way	Frank Ervin
1967	Speedy Streak	Del Cameron
1968	Nevele Pride	Stanley Dancer
1969	Lindy's Pride	Howard Beissinger
1970	Timothy T	John Simpson Sr.
1971	Speedy Crown	Howard Beissinger
1972	Super Bowl	Stanley Dancer
1973	Flirth	Ralph Baldwin
1974	Christopher T	Bill Haughton
1975	Bonefish	Stanley Dancer
1976	Steve Lobell	Bill Haughton
1977	Green Speed	Bill Haughton
1978	Speedy Somolli	Howard Beissinger
1979	Legend Hanover	George Sholty
1980	Burgomeister	Bill Haughton
1981	Shiaway St. Pat	Ray Remmen
1982	Speed Bowl	Tommy Haughton
1983	Duenna	Stanley Dancer
1984	Historic Freight	Ben Webster
1985	Prakas	Bill O'Donnell
1986	Nuclear Kosmos	Ulf Thoresen
1987	Mack Lobell	John Campbell
1988	Armbro Goal	John Campbell
1989	Park Avenue Joe	Ron Waples
1990	Harmonious	John Campbell
1991	Giant Victory	Jack Moiseyev
1992	Alf Palema	Mickey McNicholl

Leading Drivers

Races Won

Year	Driver	
1968	Herve Filion	407
1969	Herve Filion	394
1970	Herve Filion	486
1971	Herve Filion	543
1972	Herve Filion	605
1973	Herve Filion	445
1974	Herve Filion	637
1975	Daryl Buse	360
1976	Herve Filion	445
1977	Herve Filion	441
1978	Herve Filion	423
1979	Ron Waples	443
1980	Herve Filion	474
1981	Eddie Davis	404
	Herve Filion	404
1982	Herve Filion	495
1983	Eddie Davis	470
1984	Michel Lachance	466
1985	Michel Lachance	592
1986	Michel Lachance	770
1987	Michel Lachance	715
1988	Herve Filion	798
1989	Herve Filion	806
1990	Herve Filion	660
1991	Jack Moiseyev	769

Money Won

Year	Driver	Dollars
1968	Bill Haughton	1,654,172
1969	Del Insko	1,635,463
1970	Herve Filion	1,647,837
1971	Herve Filion	1,915,945
1972	Herve Filion	2,473,265
1973	Herve Filion	2,233,302
1974	Herve Filion	3,474,315
1975	Carmine Abbatiello	2,275,093
1976	Herve Filion	2,241,045
1977	Herve Filion	2,551,058
1978	Carmine Abbatiello	3,344,457
1979	John Campbell	3,308,984
1980	John Campbell	3,732,306
1981	Bill O'Donnell	4,065,608
1982	Bill O'Donnell	5,755,067
1983	John Campbell	6,104,082
1984	Bill O'Donnell	9,059,184
1985	Bill O'Donnell	10,207,372
1986	John Campbell	9,515,055
1987	John Campbell	10,186,495
1988	John Campbell	11,148,565
1989	John Campbell	9,738,450
1990	John Campbell	11,620,878
1991	Jack Moiseyev	9,568,468

THOROUGHBRED RACING

Triple Crown Winners

Since 1920, colts have carried 126 lbs. in triple crown events; fillies 121 lbs.

(Kentucky Derby, Preakness, and Belmont Stakes)

Year	Horse	Jockey	Trainer
1919	Sir Barton	J. Loftus	H. G. Bedwell
1930	Gallant Fox	E. Sande	J. Fitzsimmons
1935	Omaha	W. Sanders	J. Fitzsimmons
1937	War Admiral	C. Kurtsinger	G. Conway
1941	Whirlaway	E. Arcaro	B.A. Jones
1943	Count Fleet	J. Longden	G.D. Cameron
1946	Assault	Mehrtens	M. Hirsch
1948	Citation	E. Arcaro	H.A. Jones
1973	Secretariat	R. Turcotte	L. Laurin
1977	Seattle Slew	J. Cruguet	W.H. Turner Jr.
1978	Affirmed	S. Cauthen	L.S. Barrera

Kentucky Derby

Churchill Downs, Louisville, Ky.; inaugurated 1875; distance 1-1/4 miles; 1-1/2 miles until 1896. 3-year olds.
Best time: 1:59.2, Secretariat, 1973

Year	Winner	Jockey
1875	Aristides	O. Lewis
1876	Vagrant	R. Swim
1877	Baden Baden	W. Walker
1878	Day Star	J. Carter
1879	Lord Murphy	C. Schauer
1880	Fonso	G. Lewis
1881	Hindoo	J. McLaughlin
1882	Apollo	B. Hurd
1883	Leonatus	W. Donohue
1884	Buchanan	I. Murphy
1885	Joe Cotton	E. Henderson
1886	Ben Ali	P. Duffy
1887	Montrose	I. Lewis
1888	Macbeth II	G. Covington
1889	Spokane	T. Kiley
1890	Riley	I. Murphy
1891	Kingman	I. Murphy
1892	Azra	A. Clayton
1893	Lookout	E. Kunze
1894	Chant	F. Goodale
1895	Halma	J. Perkins
1896	Ben Brush	W. Simms
1897	Typhoon II	F. Garner
1898	Plaudit	W. Simms
1899	Manuel	F. Taral
1900	Lieut. Gibson	J. Boland
1901	His Eminence	J. Winkfield
1902	Alan-a-Dale	J. Winkfield
1903	Judge Himes	H. Booker
1904	Elwood	F. Prior
1905	Agile	J. Martin
1906	Sir Huon	R. Troxler
1907	Pink Star	A. Minder
1908	Stone Street	A. Pickens
1909	Wintergreen	V. Powers
1910	Donau	F. Herbert
1911	Meridian	G. Archibald
1912	Worth	C.H. Shilling
1913	Donerail	R. Goose
1914	Old Rosebud	J. McCabe
1915	Regret*	J. Notter
1916	George Smith	J. Loftus
1917	Omar Khayyam	C. Borel
1918	Exterminator	W. Knapp
1919	Sir Barton	J. Loftus
1920	Paul Jones	T. Rice
1921	Behave Yourself	C. Thompson
1922	Morvich	A. Johnson
1923	Zev	E. Sande
1924	Black Gold	J. D. Mooney
1925	Flying Ebony	E. Sande
1926	Bubbling Over	A. Johnson
1927	Whiskery	L. McAtee
1928	Reigh Count	C. Lang
1929	Clyde Van Dusen	L. McAtee
1930	Gallant Fox	E. Sande
1931	Twenty Grand	C. Kurtsinger
1932	Burgoo King	E. James
1933	Brokers Tip	D. Meade
1934	Cavalcade	M. Garner
1935	Omaha	W. Saunders
1936	Bold Venture	I. Hanford
1937	War Admiral	C. Kurtsinger
1938	Lawrin	E. Arcaro
1939	Johnstown	J. Stout
1940	Gallahadion	C. Bierman
1941	Whirlaway	E. Arcaro
1942	Shut Out	W. D. Wright
1943	Count Fleet	J. Longden
1944	Pensive	C. McCreary
1945	Hoop, Jr.	E. Arcaro
1946	Assault	W. Mehrtens
1947	Jet Pilot	E. Guerin
1948	Citation	E. Arcaro
1949	Ponder	S. Brooks
1950	Middleground	W. Boland
1951	Count Turf	C. McCreary
1952	Hill Gail	E. Arcaro
1953	Dark Star	H. Moreno
1954	Determine	R. York
1955	Swaps	W. Shoemaker
1956	Needles	D. Erb
1957	Iron Liege	W. Hartack
1958	Tim Tam	I. Valenzuela
1959	Tomy Lee	W. Shoemaker
1960	Venetian Way	W. Hartack
1961	Carry Back	J. Sellers
1962	Decidedly	W. Hartack
1963	Chateaugay	B. Baeza
1964	Northern Dancer	W. Hartack
1965	Lucky Debonair	W. Shoemaker
1966	Kauai King	D. Brumfield
1967	Proud Clarion	R. Ussery
1968	Dancer's Image (a)	R. Ussery
1969	Majestic Prince	W. Hartack
1970	Dust Commander	M. Manganello
1971	Canonero II	G. Avila
1972	Riva Ridge	R. Turcotte
1973	Secretariat	R. Turcotte
1974	Cannonade	A. Cordero
1975	Foolish Pleasure	J. Vasquez
1976	Bold Forbes	A. Cordero
1977	Seattle Slew	J. Cruguet
1978	Affirmed	S. Cauthen
1979	Spectacular Bid	R. Franklin
1980	Genuine Risk*	J. Vasquez
1981	Pleasant Colony	J. Velasquez
1982	Gato del Sol	E. Delahoussaye
1983	Sunny's Halo	E. Delahoussaye
1984	Swale	L. Pincay
1985	Spend a Buck	A. Cordero
1986	Ferdinand	W. Shoemaker
1987	Alysheba	C. McCarron
1988	Winning Colors*	G. Stevens
1989	Sunday Silence	P. Valenzuela
1990	Unbridled	C. Perret
1991	Strike The Gold	C. Antley
1992	Lil E. Tee	P. Day

(a) Dancer's Image was disqualified from purse money after tests disclosed that he had run with a pain-killing drug, phenylbutazone, in his system. All wagers were paid on Dancer's Image. Forward Pass was awarded first place money.

The Kentucky Derby has been won five times by two jockeys, Eddie Arcaro, 1938, 1941, 1945, 1948 and 1952; and Bill Hartack, 1957, 1960, 1962, 1964 and 1969; four times by Willie Shoemaker, 1955, 1959, 1965, and 1986; and three times by each of three jockeys, Isaac Murphy, 1884, 1890, and 1891; Earle Sande, 1923, 1925 and 1930, and Angel Cordero in 1974, 1976 and 1985. * Regret, Genuine Risk and Winning Colors are the only fillies to win the Derby.

Preakness

Pimlico, Baltimore, Md.; inaugurated 1873; 1 3-16 miles, 3 yr. olds. Best time: 1:53.2, Tank's Prospect, 1985

Year	Winner	Jockey
1873	Survivor	G. Barbee
1874	Culpepper	M. Donohue
1875	Tom Ochiltree	L. Hughes
1876	Shirley	G. Barbee
1877	Cloverbrook	C. Holloway
1878	Duke of Magenta	C. Holloway
1879	Harold	L. Hughes
1880	Grenada	L. Hughes
1881	Saunterer	W. Costello
1882	Vanguard	W. Costello
1883	Jacobus	G. Barbee
1884	Knight of Ellerslie	S. H. Fisher
1885	Tecumseh	J. McLaughlin
1886	The Bard	S. H. Fisher
1887	Dunboyne	W. Donohue
1888	Refund	F. Littlefield
1889	Buddhist	G. Anderson
1890	Montague	W. Martin
1894	Assignee	F. Taral
1895	Belmar	F. Taral
1896	Margrave	H. Griffin
1897	Paul Kauvar	C. Thorpe
1898	Sly Fox	W. Simms
1899	Half Time	R. Clawson
1900	Hindus	H. Spencer
1901	The Parader	F. Landry
1902	Old England	L. Jackson
1903	Flocarline	W. Gannon
1904	Bryn Mawr	E. Hildebrand
1905	Cairngorm	W. Davis
1906	Whimsical	W. Miller
1907	Don Enrique	G. Mountain
1908	Royal Tourist	E. Dugan

Year	Winner	Jockey
1909	Effendi	W. Doyle
1910	Layminster	R. Estep
1911	Watervale	E. Dugan
1912	Colonel Holloway	C. Turner
1913	Buskin	J. Butwell
1914	Holiday	A. Schuttinger
1915	Rhine Maiden	D. Hoffman
1916	Damrosch	L. McAtee
1917	Kalitan	E. Haynes
1918	War Cloud	J. Loftus
	Jack Hare Jr.	C. Peak
1919	Sir Barton	J. Loftus
1920	Man o' War	C. Kummer
1921	Broomspun	F. Coltiletti
1922	Pillory	L. Morris
1923	Vigil	B. Marinelli
1924	Nellie Morse	J. Merimee
1925	Coventry	C. Kummer
1926	Display	J. Malben
1927	Bostonian	A. Abel
1928	Victorian	R. Workman
1929	Dr. Freeland	L. Schaefer
1930	Gallant Fox	E. Sande
1931	Mate	G. Ellis
1932	Burgoo King	E. James
1933	Head Play	C. Kurtsinger
1934	High Quest	R. Jones
1935	Omaha	W. Saunders
1936	Bold Venture	G. Woolf
1937	War Admiral	C. Kurtsinger
1938	Dauber	M. Peters
1939	Challedon	G. Seabo
1940	Bimelech	F.A. Smith
1941	Whirlaway	E. Arcaro
1942	Alsab	B. James
1943	Count Fleet	J. Longden
1944	Pensive	C. McCreary
1945	Polynesian	W.D. Wright
1946	Assault	W. Mehrtens
1947	Faultless	D. Dodson
1948	Citation	E. Arcaro
1949	Capot	T. Atkinson
1950	Hill Prince	E. Arcaro
1951	Bold	E. Arcaro
1952	Blue Man	C. McCreary
1953	Native Dancer	E. Guerin
1954	Hasty Road	J. Adams
1955	Nashua	E. Arcaro
1956	Fabius	W. Hartack
1957	Bold Ruler	E. Arcaro
1958	Tim Tam	I. Valenzuela
1959	Royal Orbit	W. Harmatz
1960	Bally Ache	R. Ussery
1961	Carry Back	J. Sellers
1962	Greek Money	J.L. Rotz
1963	Candy Spots	W. Shoemaker
1964	Northern Dancer	W. Hartack
1965	Tom Rolfe	R. Turcotte
1966	Kauai King	D. Brumfield
1967	Damascus	W. Shoemaker
1968	Forward Pass	I. Valenzuela
1969	Majestic Prince	W. Hartack
1970	Personality	E. Belmonte
1971	Canonero II	G. Avila
1972	Bee Bee Bee	E. Nelson
1973	Secretariat	R. Turcotte
1974	Little Current	M. Rivera
1975	Master Derby	D. McHargue
1976	Elocutionist	J. Lively
1977	Seattle Slew	J. Cruguet
1978	Affirmed	S. Cauthen
1979	Spectacular Bid	R. Franklin
1980	Codex	A. Cordero
1981	Pleasant Colony	J. Velasquez
1982	Aloma's Ruler	J. Kaenel
1983	Deputed Testamony	D. Miller
1984	Gate Dancer	A. Cordero
1985	Tank's Prospect	P. Day
1986	Snow Chief	A. Solis
1987	Alysheba	C. McCarron
1988	Risen Star	E. Delahoussaye
1989	Sunday Silence	P. Valenzuela
1990	Summer Squall	P. Day
1991	Hansel	J. Bailey
1992	Pine Bluff	C. McCarren

Belmont Stakes

Elmont, N.Y.; inaugurated 1867; 1 1/2 miles, 3 year olds. Fastest time: 2:24, Secretariat

Year	Winner	Jockey
1867	Ruthless	J. Gilpatrick
1868	General Duke	R. Swim
1869	Fenian	C. Miller
1870	Kingfisher	W. Dick
1871	Harry Bassett	W. Miller
1872	Joe Daniels	J. Rowe
1873	Springbok	J. Rowe
1874	Saxon	G. Barbee
1875	Calvin	R. Swim
1876	Algerine	W. Donohue
1877	Cloverbrook	C. Holloway
1878	Duke of Magenta	L. Hughes
1879	Spendthrift	S. Evans
1880	Grenada	L. Hughes
1881	Saunterer	T. Costello
1882	Forester	J. McLaughlin
1883	George Kinney	J. McLaughlin
1884	Panique	J. McLaughlin
1885	Tyrant	P. Duffy
1886	Inspector B.	J. McLaughlin
1887	Hanover	J. McLaughlin
1888	Sir Dixon	J. McLaughlin
1889	Eric	W. Hayward
1890	Burlington	S. Barnes
1891	Foxford	E. Garrison
1892	Patron	W. Hayward
1893	Comanche	W. Simms
1894	Henry of Navarre	W. Simms
1895	Belmar	F. Taral
1896	Hastings	H. Griffin
1897	Scottish Chieftain	J. Scherrer
1898	Bowling Brook	F. Littlefield
1899	Jean Bereaud	R.R. Clawson
1900	Ildrim	N. Turner
1901	Commando	H. Spencer
1902	Masterman	J. Bullman
1903	Africander	J. Bullman
1904	Delhi	G. Odom
1905	Tanya	E. Hildebrand
1906	Burgomaster	L. Lyne
1907	Peter Pan	G. Mountain
1908	Colin	J. Notter
1909	Joe Madden	E. Dugan
1910	Sweep	J. Butwell
1913	Prince Eugene	R. Troxler
1914	Luke McLuke	M. Buxton
1915	The Finn	G. Byrne
1916	Friar Rock	E. Haynes
1917	Hourless	J. Butwell
1918	Johren	F. Robinson
1919	Sir Barton	J. Loftus
1920	Man o' War	C. Kummer
1921	Grey Lag	E. Sande
1922	Pillory	C.H. Miller
1923	Zev	E. Sande
1924	Mad Play	E. Sande
1925	American Flag	A. Johnson
1926	Crusader	A. Johnson
1927	Chance Shot	E. Sande
1928	Vito	C. Kummer
1929	Blue Larkspur	M. Garner
1930	Gallant Fox	E. Sande
1931	Twenty Grand	C. Kurtsinger
1932	Faireno	T. Malley
1933	Hurryoff	M. Garner
1934	Peace Chance	W.D. Wright
1935	Omaha	W. Saunders
1936	Granville	J. Stout
1937	War Admiral	C. Kurtsinger
1938	Pasteurized	J. Stout
1939	Johnstown	J. Stout
1940	Bimelech	F.A. Smith
1941	Whirlaway	E. Arcaro
1942	Shut Out	E. Arcaro
1943	Count Fleet	J. Longden
1944	Bounding Home	G.L. Smith
1945	Pavot	E. Arcaro
1946	Assault	W. Mehrtens
1947	Phalanx	R. Donoso
1948	Citation	E. Arcaro
1949	Capot	T. Atkinson
1950	Middleground	W. Boland
1951	Counterpoint	D. Gorman
1952	One Count	E. Arcaro
1953	Native Dancer	E. Guerin
1954	High Gun	E. Guerin
1955	Nashua	E. Arcaro
1956	Needles	D. Erb
1957	Gallant Man	W. Shoemaker
1958	Cavan	P. Anderson
1959	Sword Dancer	W. Shoemaker
1960	Celtic Ash	W. Hartack
1961	Sherluck	B. Baeza
1962	Jaipur	W. Shoemaker
1963	Chateaugay	B. Baeza
1964	Quadrangle	M. Ycaza
1965	Hail to All	J. Sellers
1966	Amberoid	W. Boland
1967	Damascus	W. Shoemaker
1968	Stage Door Johnny	H. Gustines
1969	Arts and Letters	B. Baeza
1970	High Echelon	J.L. Rotz
1971	Pass Catcher	W. Blum
1972	Riva Ridge	R. Turcotte
1973	Secretariat	R. Turcotte
1974	Little Current	M. Rivera
1975	Avatar	W. Shoemaker
1976	Bold Forbes	A. Cordero
1977	Seattle Slew	J. Cruguet
1978	Affirmed	S. Cauthen
1979	Coastal	R. Hernandez
1980	Temperence Hill	E. Maple
1981	Summing	G. Martens
1982	Conquistador Cielo	L. Pincay
1983	Caveat	L. Pincay
1984	Swale	L. Pincay
1985	Creme Fraiche	E. Maple
1986	Danzig Connection	C. McCarron
1987	Bet Twice	C. Perret
1988	Risen Star	E. Delahoussaye
1989	Easy Goer	P. Day
1990	Go and Go	M. Kinane
1991	Hansel	J. Bailey
1992	A.P. Indy	E. Delahoussaye

Eclipse Awards in 1991

Horse of the Year—Black Tie Affair
Best 2-year-old colt—Arazi
Best 2-year-old filly—Pleasant Stage
Best 3-year-old colt—Hansel
Best 3-year-old filly—Dance Smartly
Best colt, horse, or gelding (4-year-olds & up)—Black Tie Affair
Best filly or mare (4-year-olds & up)—Queena
Best male turf horse—Tight Spot
Best turf filly or mare—Miss Alleged
Best sprinter—Housebuster
Best steeplechase horse—Morley Street
Best trainer—Ron McNally
Best jockey—Pat Day
Best apprentice jockey—Mickey Walls
Best owner—Sam-son Farm
Best breeder—John & Betty Mabee

Eclipse Awards

The Eclipse Awards, honoring the Horse of the Year and other champions of the sport, began in 1971, and are sponsored by the *Daily Racing Form,* the Thoroughbred Racing Associations and the National Turf Writers Assn. Prior to 1971, the DRF (1936-70) and the TRA (1950-70) issued separate selections for horse of the year.

Horse of the Year

Year	Horse	Year	Horse	Year	Horse	Year	Horse
1936	Granville	1951	Counterpoint	1964	Kelso	1977	Seattle Slew
1937	War Admiral	1952	One Count (DRF)	1965	Roman Brother (DRF)	1978	Affirmed
1938	Seabiscuit		Native Dancer (TRA)		Moccasin (TRA)	1979	Affirmed
1939	Challedon	1953	Tom Fool	1966	Buckpasser	1980	Spectacular Bid
1940	Challedon	1954	Native Dancer	1967	Damascus	1981	John Henry
1941	Whirlaway	1955	Nashua	1968	Dr. Fager	1982	Conquistador Cielo
1942	Whirlaway	1956	Swaps	1969	Arts and Letters	1983	All Along
1943	Count Fleet	1957	Bold Ruler (DRF)	1970	Fort Marcy (DRF)	1984	John Henry
1944	Twilight Tear		Dedicate (TRA)		Personality (TRA)	1985	Spend A Buck
1945	Busher	1958	Round Table	1971	Ack Ack	1986	Lady's Secret
1946	Assault	1959	Sword Dancer	1972	Secretariat	1987	Ferdinand
1947	Armed	1960	Kelso	1973	Secretariat	1988	Alysheba
1948	Citation	1961	Kelso	1974	Forego	1989	Sunday Silence
1949	Capot	1962	Kelso	1975	Forego	1990	Criminal Type
1950	Hill Prince	1963	Kelso	1976	Forego	1991	Black Tie Affair

Annual Leading Jockey—Money Won

Year	Jockey	Dollars	Year	Jockey	Dollars	Year	Jockey	Dollars
1957	Bill Hartack	3,060,501	1969	Jorge Velasquez . .	2,542,315	1981	Chris McCarron . . .	8,397,604
1958	Willie Shoemaker . .	2,961,693	1970	Laffit Pincay Jr. . . .	2,626,526	1982	Angel Cordero Jr. .	9,483,590
1959	Willie Shoemaker . .	2,843,133	1971	Laffit Pincay Jr. . . .	3,784,377	1983	Angel Cordero Jr. .	10,116,697
1960	Willie Shoemaker . .	2,123,961	1972	Laffit Pincay Jr. . . .	3,225,827	1984	Chris McCarron . . .	12,045,813
1961	Willie Shoemaker . .	2,690,819	1973	Laffit Pincay Jr. . . .	4,093,492	1985	Laffit Pincay Jr. . . .	13,353,299
1962	Willie Shoemaker . .	2,916,844	1974	Laffit Pincay Jr. . . .	4,251,060	1986	Jose Santos	11,329,297
1963	Willie Shoemaker . .	2,526,925	1975	Braulio Baeza	3,695,198	1987	Jose Santos	12,375,433
1964	Willie Shoemaker . .	2,649,553	1976	Angel Cordero Jr. .	4,709,500	1988	Jose Santos	14,877,298
1965	Braulio Baeza	2,582,702	1977	Steve Cauthen . . .	6,151,750	1989	Jose Santos	13,838,389
1966	Braulio Baeza	2,951,022	1978	Darrel McHargue . .	6,029,885	1990	Gary Stevens	13,881,198
1967	Braulio Baeza	3,088,888	1979	Laffit Pincay Jr. . . .	8,193,535	1991	Chris McCarron . . .	14,441,083
1968	Braulio Baeza	2,835,108	1980	Chris McCarron . . .	7,663,300			

Lacrosse Champions in 1992

U.S. Club Lacrosse Association Championship—Hempstead, N.Y., June 13: Maryland L.C. 14, Brine L.C. 12.

NCAA Division I Championship—Philadelphia, Pa., May 25: Princeton 10, Syracuse 9 (Double O.T.).

NCAA Division III Championship—Philadelphia, Pa., May 24: Nazareth College 22, Roanoke College 11.

USILA Division I All-Star Game—Baltimore, Md., June 5: South 14, North 9.

USILA Division III All-Star Game—Baltimore, Md., June 5: North 15, South 14.

National Junior College Championship—Farmingdale, N.Y., May 9: Herkimer (N.Y.) C.C. 9, Nassau (N.Y.) C.C. 7.

NCAA Women's Division I Championship—Bethlehem, Pa., May 17: Maryland 11, Harvard 10 (Double O.T.).

NCAA Women's Division III Championship—Bethlehem, Pa., May 17: Trenton State 5, William Smith 3.

USILA Division I All America Team

Attack: Tom Marechek, Syracuse; Darrin Lowe, Brown; Mark Milton, Massachusetts.

Midfield: Adam Wright, Johns Hopkins; Charles Lockwood, Syracuse; Dom Fin, Syracuse; Jim Buczek, North Carolina.

Defense: David Morrow, Princeton; Alex Martin, North Carolina; Brian Burlace, Maryland.

Goal: Scott Bacigalupo, Princeton.

Coach of the Year: Bill Tierney, Princeton.

Note: 4 midfielders selected for the 3 midfield positions

NCAA Division I Champions

Year	Champion	Year	Champion	Year	Champion	Year	Champion
1972	Virginia	1978	Johns Hopkins	1983	Syracuse	1988	Syracuse
1973	Maryland	1979	Johns Hopkins	1984	Johns Hopkins	1989	Syracuse
1974	Johns Hopkins	1980	Johns Hopkins	1985	Johns Hopkins	1990	Syracuse
1975	Maryland	1981	North Carolina	1986	North Carolina	1991	North Carolina
1976	Cornell	1982	North Carolina	1987	Johns Hopkins	1992	Princeton
1977	Cornell						

NCAA Wrestling Champions

Year	Champion	Year	Champion	Year	Champion	Year	Champion	Year	Champion
1964	Oklahoma State	1970	Iowa State	1976	Iowa	1982	Iowa	1988	Arizona State
1965	Iowa State	1971	Oklahoma State	1977	Iowa State	1983	Iowa	1989	Oklahoma State
1966	Oklahoma State	1972	Iowa State	1978	Iowa	1984	Iowa	1990	Oklahoma State
1967	Michigan State	1973	Iowa State	1979	Iowa	1985	Iowa	1991	Iowa
1968	Oklahoma State	1974	Oklahoma	1980	Iowa	1986	Iowa	1992	Iowa
1969	Iowa State	1975	Iowa	1981	Iowa	1987	Iowa State		

NATIONAL FOOTBALL LEAGUE

Final 1991 Standings

National Conference

Eastern Division

	W	L	T	Pct	Pts	Opp
Washington	14	2	0	.875	485	224
Dallas	11	5	0	.688	342	310
Philadelphia	10	6	0	.625	285	244
N.Y. Giants	8	8	0	.500	281	297
Phoenix	4	12	0	.250	196	344

Central Division

	W	L	T	Pct	Pts	Opp
Detroit	12	4	0	.750	339	295
Chicago	11	5	0	.688	299	269
Minnesota	8	8	0	.500	301	306
Green Bay	4	12	0	.250	273	313
Tampa Bay	3	13	0	.188	199	365

Western Division

	W	L	T	Pct	Pts	Opp
New Orleans	11	5	0	.688	341	211
Atlanta	10	6	0	.625	361	338
San Francisco	10	6	0	.625	393	239
L.A. Rams	3	13	0	.188	234	390

American Conference

Eastern Division

	W	L	T	Pct	Pts	Opp
Buffalo	13	3	0	.813	458	318
N.Y. Jets	8	8	0	.500	314	293
Miami	8	8	0	.500	343	349
New England	6	10	0	.375	211	305
Indianapolis	1	15	0	.063	143	381

Central Division

	W	L	T	Pct	Pts	Opp
Houston	11	5	0	.688	386	251
Pittsburgh	7	9	0	.438	292	344
Cleveland	6	10	0	.375	293	298
Cincinnati	3	13	0	.188	263	435

Western Division

	W	L	T	Pct	Pts	Opp
Denver	12	4	0	.750	304	235
Kansas City	10	6	0	.625	322	252
L.A. Raiders	9	7	0	.563	298	297
Seattle	7	9	0	.438	276	261
San Diego	4	12	0	.250	274	342

NFC Playoffs—Atlanta 27, New Orleans 20; Dallas 17, Chicago 13; Detroit 38, Dallas 6; Washington 24, Atlanta 7; Washington 41, Detroit 10.

AFC Playoffs—Kansas City 10, L.A. Raiders 6; Houston 17, N.Y. Jets 10; Denver 26, Houston 24; Buffalo 37, Kansas City 14; Buffalo 10, Denver 7.

National Football League Champions

Year	East Winner (W-L-T)	West Winner (W-L-T)	Playoff
1933	New York Giants (11-3-0)	Chicago Bears (10-2-1)	Chicago Bears 23, New York 21
1934	New York Giants (8-5-0)	Chicago Bears (13-0-0)	New York 30, Chicago Bears 13
1935	New York Giants (9-3-0)	Detroit Lions (7-3-2)	Detroit 26, New York 7
1936	Boston Redskins (7-5-0)	Green Bay Packers (10-1-1)	Green Bay 21, Boston 6
1937	Washington Redskins (8-3-0)	Chicago Bears (9-1-1)	Washington 28, Chicago Bears 21
1938	New York Giants (8-2-1)	Green Bay Packers (8-3-0)	New York 23, Green Bay 17
1939	New York Giants (9-1-1)	Green Bay Packers (9-2-0)	Green Bay 27, New York 0
1940	Washington Redskins (9-2-0)	Chicago Bears (8-3-0)	Chicago Bears 73, Washington 0
1941	New York Giants (8-3-0)	Chicago Bears (10-1-1)(a)	Chicago Bears 37, New York 9
1942	Wash. Redskins (10-1-1)	Chicago Bears (11-0-0)	Washington 14, Chicago Bears 6
1943	Wash. Redskins (6-3-1)(a)	Chicago Bears (8-1-1)	Chicago Bears, 41, Washington 21
1944	New York Giants (8-1-1)	Green Bay Packers (8-2-0)	Green Bay 14, New York 7
1945	Wash. Redskins (8-2-0)	Cleveland Rams (9-1-0)	Cleveland 15, Washington 14
1946	New York Giants (7-3-1)	Chicago Bears (8-2-1)	Chicago Bears 24, New York 14
1947	Philadelphia Eagles (8-4-0)(a)	Chicago Cardinals (9-3-0)	Chicago Cardinals 28, Philadelphia 21
1948	Philadelphia Eagles (9-2-1)	Chicago Cardinals (11-1-0)	Philadelphia 7, Chicago Cardinals 0
1949	Philadelphia Eagles (11-1-0)	Los Angeles Rams (8-2-2)	Philadelphia 14, Los Angeles 0
1950	Cleveland Browns (10-2-0)(a)	Los Angeles Rams (9-3-0)(a)	Cleveland 30, Los Angeles 28
1951	Cleveland Browns (11-1-0)	Los Angeles Rams (8-4-0)	Los Angeles 24, Cleveland 17
1952	Cleveland Browns (8-4-0)	Detroit Lions (9-3-0)(a)	Detroit 17, Cleveland 7
1953	Cleveland Browns (11-1-0)	Detroit Lions (10-2-0)	Detroit 17, Cleveland 16
1954	Cleveland Browns (9-3-0)	Detroit Lions (9-2-1)	Cleveland 56, Detroit 10
1955	Cleveland Browns (9-2-1)	Los Angeles Rams (8-3-1)	Cleveland 38, Los Angeles 14
1956	New York Giants (8-3-1)	Chicago Bears (9-2-1)	New York 47, Chicago Bears 7
1957	Cleveland Browns (9-2-1)	Detroit Lions (8-4-0)(a)	Detroit 59, Cleveland 14
1958	New York Giants (9-3-0)(a)	Baltimore Colts (9-3-0)	Baltimore 23, New York 17(b)
1959	New York Giants (10-2-0)	Baltimore Colts (9-3-0)	Baltimore 31, New York 16
1960	Philadelphia Eagles (10-2-0)	Green Bay Packers (8-4-0)	Philadelphia 17, Green Bay 13
1961	New York Giants (10-3-1)	Green Bay Packers (11-3-0)	Green Bay 37, New York 0
1962	New York Giants (12-2-0)	Green Bay Packers (13-1-0)	Green Bay 16, New York 7
1963	New York Giants (11-3-0)	Chicago Bears (11-1-2)	Chicago 14, New York 10
1964	Cleveland Browns (10-3-1)	Baltimore Colts (12-2-0)	Cleveland 27, Baltimore 0
1965	Cleveland Browns (11-3-0)	Green Bay Packers (10-3-1)(a)	Green Bay 23, Cleveland 12
1966	Dallas Cowboys (10-3-1)	Green Bay Packers (12-2-0)	Green Bay 34, Dallas 27

(a) Won divisional playoff. (b) Won at 8:15 sudden death overtime period.

Year	Conference	Division	Winner (W-L-T)	Playoff
1967	East	Century	Cleveland (9-5-0)	Dallas 52, Cleveland 14
		Capitol	Dallas (9-5-0)	
	West	Central	Green Bay (9-4-1)	Green Bay 28, Los Angeles 7
		Coastal	Los Angeles (11-1-2)(a)	Green Bay 21, Dallas 17
1968	East	Century	Cleveland (10-4-0)	Cleveland 31, Dallas 20
		Capitol	Dallas (12-2-0)	
	West	Central	Minnesota (8-6-0)	Baltimore 24, Minnesota 14
		Coastal	Baltimore (13-1-0)	Baltimore 34, Cleveland 0

(continued)

Year	Conference	Division	Winner (W-L-T)	Playoff
1969	East	Century	Cleveland (10-3-1)	Cleveland 38, Dallas 14
		Capitol	Dallas (11-2-1)	
	West	Central	Minnesota (12-2-0)	Minnesota 23, Los Angeles 20
		Coastal	Los Angeles (11-3-0)	Minnesota 27, Cleveland 7
1970	American	Eastern	Baltimore (11-2-1)	Baltimore 17, Cincinnati 0
		Central	Cincinnati (8-6-0)	Oakland 21, Miami 14
		Western	Oakland (8-4-2)	Baltimore 27, Oakland 17
	National	Eastern	Dallas (10-4-0)	Dallas 5, Detroit 0
		Central	Minnesota (12-2-0)	San Francisco 17, Minnesota 14
		Western	San Francisco (10-3-1)	Dallas 17, San Francisco 10
1971	American	Eastern	Miami (10-3-1)	Miami 27, Kansas City 24
		Central	Cleveland (9-5-0)	Baltimore 20, Cleveland 3
		Western	Kansas City (10-3-1)	Miami 21, Baltimore 0
	National	Eastern	Dallas (11-3-0)	Dallas 20, Minnesota 12
		Central	Minnesota (11-3-0)	San Francisco 24, Washington 20
		Western	San Francisco (9-5-0)	Dallas 14, San Francisco 3
1972	American	Eastern	Miami (14-0-0)	Miami 20, Cleveland 14
		Central	Pittsburgh (11-3-0)	Pittsburgh 13, Oakland 7
		Western	Oakland (10-3-1)	Miami 21, Pittsburgh 17
	National	Eastern	Washington (11-3-0)	Washington 16, Green Bay 3
		Central	Green Bay (10-4-0)	Dallas 30, San Francisco 28
		Western	San Francisco (8-5-1)	Washington 26, Dallas 3
1973	American	Eastern	Miami (12-2-0)	Miami 34, Cincinnati 16
		Central	Cincinnati (10-4-0)	Oakland 33, Pittsburgh 14
		Western	Oakland (9-4-1)	Miami 27, Oakland 10
	National	Eastern	Dallas (10-4-0)	Dallas 27, Los Angeles 16
		Central	Minnesota (12-2-0)	Minnesota 27, Washington 20
		Western	Los Angeles (12-2-0)	Minnesota 27, Dallas 10
1974	American	Eastern	Miami (11-3-0)	Oakland 28, Miami 26
		Central	Pittsburgh (10-3-1)	Pittsburgh 32, Buffalo 14
		Western	Oakland (12-2-0)	Pittsburgh 24, Oakland 13
	National	Eastern	St. Louis (10-4-0)	Minnesota 30, St. Louis 14
		Central	Minnesota (10-4-0)	Los Angeles 19, Washington 10
		Western	Los Angeles (10-4-0)	Minnesota 14, Los Angeles 10
1975	American	Eastern	Baltimore (10-4-0)	Pittsburgh 28, Baltimore 10
		Central	Pittsburgh (12-2-0)	Oakland 31, Cincinnati 28
		Western	Oakland (11-3-0)	Pittsburgh 16, Oakland 10
	National	Eastern	St. Louis (11-3-0)	Dallas 17, Minnesota 14
		Central	Minnesota (12-2-0)	Los Angeles 35, St. Louis 23
		Western	Los Angeles (12-2-0)	Dallas 37, Los Angeles 7
1976	American	Eastern	Baltimore (11-3-0)	Pittsburgh 40, Baltimore 14
		Central	Pittsburgh (10-4-0)	Oakland 24, New England 21
		Western	Oakland (13-1-0)	Oakland 24, Pittsburgh 7
	National	Eastern	Dallas (11-3-0)	Minnesota 35, Washington 20
		Central	Minnesota (11-2-1)	Los Angeles 14, Dallas 12
		Western	Los Angeles (10-3-1)	Minnesota 24, Los Angeles 13
1977	American	Eastern	Baltimore (10-4-0)	Oakland 37, Baltimore 31
		Central	Pittsburgh (9-5-0)	Denver 34, Pittsburgh 21
		Western	Denver (12-2-0)	Dallas 37, Chicago 7
	National	Eastern	Dallas (12-2-0)	Minnesota 14, Los Angeles 7
		Central	Minnesota (9-5-0)	Denver 20, Oakland 17
		Western	Los Angeles (10-4-0)	Dallas 23, Minnesota 6
1978	American	Eastern	New England (11-5-0)	Pittsburgh 33, Denver 10
		Central	Pittsburgh (14-2-0)	Houston 31, New England 14
		Western	Denver (10-6-0)	Pittsburgh 34, Houston 5
	National	Eastern	Dallas (12-4-0)	Dallas 27, Atlanta 20
		Central	Minnesota (8-7-1)	Los Angeles 34, Minnesota 10
		Western	Los Angeles (12-4-0)	Dallas 28, Los Angeles 0
1979	American	Eastern	Miami (10-6-0)	Houston 17, San Diego 14
		Central	Pittsburgh (12-4-0)	Pittsburgh 34, Miami 14
		Western	San Diego (12-4-0)	Pittsburgh 27, Houston 13
	National	Eastern	Dallas (11-5-0)	Tampa Bay 24, Philadelphia 17
		Central	Tampa Bay (10-6-0)	Los Angeles 21, Dallas 19
		Western	Los Angeles (9-7-0)	Los Angeles 9, Tampa Bay 0
1980	American	Eastern	Buffalo (11-5-0)	San Diego 20, Buffalo 14
		Central	Cleveland (11-5-0)	Oakland 14, Cleveland 12
		Western	San Diego (11-5-0)	Oakland 34, San Diego 27
	National	Eastern	Philadelphia (12-4-0)	Philadelphia 31, Minnesota 16
		Central	Minnesota (9-7-0)	Dallas 30, Atlanta 27
		Western	Atlanta (12-4-0)	Philadelphia 20, Dallas 7
1981	American	Eastern	Miami (11-4-1)	San Diego 41, Miami 38
		Central	Cincinnati (12-4-0)	Cincinnati 28, Buffalo 21
		Western	San Diego (10-6-0)	Cincinnati 27, San Diego 7
	National	Eastern	Dallas (12-4-0)	Dallas 38, Tampa Bay 0
		Central	Tampa Bay (9-7-0)	San Francisco 38, N.Y. Giants 24
		Western	San Francisco (13-3-0)	San Francisco 28, Dallas 27
1982	American		L.A. Raiders (8-1-0)	
	National		Washington (8-1-0)	Strike-shortened season

AFC playoffs—Miami 28, New England 13; L.A. Raiders 27, Cleveland 10; N.Y. Jets 44, Cincinnati 17; San Diego 31, Pittsburgh 28; N.Y. Jets 17, L.A. Raiders 14; Miami 34, San Diego 13; Miami 14, N.Y. Jets 0. **NFC playoffs**—Washington 31, Detroit 7; Green Bay 41, St. Louis 16; Dallas 30, Tampa Bay 17; Minnesota 30, Atlanta 24; Washington 21, Minnesota 7; Dallas 37, Green Bay 26; Washington 31, Dallas 17.

Year	Conference	Division	Winner (W-L-T)	Playoff
1983	American	Eastern	Miami (12-4-0)	Seattle 27, Miami 20
		Central	Pittsburgh (10-6-0)	L.A. Raiders 38, Pittsburgh 10
		Western	L.A. Raiders (12-4-0)	L.A. Raiders 30, Seattle 14
	National	Eastern	Washington (14-2-0)	Washington 51, L.A. Rams 7
		Central	Detroit (9-7-0)	San Francisco 24, Detroit 23
		Western	San Francisico (10-6-0)	Washington 24, San Francisco 21

Year	Conference	Division	Winner (W-L-T)	Playoff
1984	American	Eastern	Miami (14-2-0)	Miami 31, Seattle 10
		Central	Pittsburgh (9-7-0)	Pittsburgh 24, Denver 17
		Western	Denver (13-3-0)	Miami 45, Pittsburgh 28
	National	Eastern	Washington (11-5-0)	Chicago 23, Washington 19
		Central	Chicago (10-6-0)	San Francisco 21, N.Y. Giants 10
		Western	San Francisco (15-1-0)	San Francisco 23, Chicago 0
1985	American	Eastern	Miami (12-4-0)	New England 27, L.A. Raiders 20
		Central	Cleveland (8-8-0)	Miami 24, Cleveland 21
		Western	L.A. Raiders (12-4-0)	New England 31, Miami 14
	National	Eastern	Dallas (10-6-0)	Chicago 21, N.Y. Giants 0
		Central	Chicago (15-1-0)	L.A. Rams 20, Dallas 0
		Western	L.A. Rams (11-5-0)	Chicago 24, L.A. Rams 0
1986	American	Eastern	New England (11-5-0)	Denver 22, New England 17
		Central	Cleveland (12-4-0)	Cleveland 23, N.Y. Jets 20
		Western	Denver (11-5-0)	Denver 23, Cleveland 20
	National	Eastern	N.Y. Giants (14-2-0)	N.Y. Giants 49, San Francisco 3
		Central	Chicago (14-2-0)	Washington 27, Chicago 13
		Western	San Francisco (10-5-1)	N.Y. Giants 17, Washington 0
1987	American	Eastern	Indianapolis (9-6-0)	Cleveland 38, Indianapolis 21
		Central	Cleveland (10-5-0)	Denver 34, Houston 10
		Western	Denver (10-4-1)	Denver 38, Cleveland 33
	National	Eastern	Washington (11-4-0)	Washington 21, Chicago 17
		Central	Chicago (11-4-0)	Minnesota 36, San Francisco 24
		Western	San Francisco (13-2-0)	Washington 17, Minnesota 10
1988	American	Eastern	Buffalo (12-4-0)	Buffalo 17, Houston 10
		Central	Cincinnati (12-4-0)	Cincinnati 21, Seattle 13
		Western	Seattle (9-7-0)	Cincinnati 21, Buffalo 10
	National	Eastern	Philadelphia (10-6-0)	Chicago 20, Philadelphia 12
		Central	Chicago (12-4-0)	San Francisco 34, Minnesota 9
		Western	San Francisco (10-6-0)	San Francisco 28, Chicago 3
1989	American	Eastern	Buffalo (9-7-0)	Cleveland 34, Buffalo 30
		Central	Cleveland (9-6-1)	Denver 24, Pittsburgh 23
		Western	Denver (11-5-0)	Denver 37, Cleveland 21
	National	Eastern	N.Y. Giants (12-4-0)	San Francisco 41, Minnesota 13
		Central	Minnesota (10-6-0)	L.A. Rams 19, N.Y. Giants 13
		Western	San Francisco (14-2-0)	San Francisco 30, L.A. Rams 3
1990	American	Eastern	Buffalo (13-3-0)	L.A. Raiders 20, Cincinnati 10
		Central	Cincinnati (9-7-0)	Buffalo 44, Miami 34
		Western	L.A. Raiders (12-4-0)	Buffalo 51, L.A. Raiders 3
	National	Eastern	N.Y. Giants (13-3-0)	San Francisco 28, Washington 10
		Central	Chicago (11-5-0)	N.Y. Giants 31, Chicago 3
		Western	San Francisco (14-2-0)	N.Y. Giants 15, San Francisco 13
1991	American	Eastern	Buffalo (13-3-0)	Denver 26, Houston 24
		Central	Houston (11-5-0)	Buffalo 37, Kansas City 14
		Western	Denver (12-4-0)	Buffalo 10, Denver 7
	National	Eastern	Washington (14-2-0)	Washington 24, Atlanta 7
		Central	Detroit (12-4-0)	Detroit 38, Dallas 6
		Western	New Orleans (11-5-0)	Washington 41, Detroit 10

World Almanac All-Pro Team in 1991

Chosen by a panel of sports experts representing the World Almanac, its co-sponsoring newspapers, and its publisher, Pharos Books.

First team	Offense	Second team
Gary Clark, Washington	Wide receiver	Andre Reed, Buffalo
Andre Rison, Atlanta	Wide receiver	Jerry Rice, San Francisco
Michael Irvin, Dallas	Wide receiver	Haywood Jeffires, Houston
Marv Cook, New England	Tight end	Jay Novacek, Dallas
Lomas Brown, Detroit	Tackle	Paul Gruber, Tampa Bay
Jim Lachey, Washington	Tackle	Mike Kenn, Atlanta
Steve Wisniewski, L.A. Raiders	Guard	Mike Munchak, Houston
Randall McDaniel, Minnesota	Guard	Jim Ritcher, Buffalo
Bruce Matthews, Houston	Center	Don Mosebar, L.A. Raiders
Jim Kelly, Buffalo	Quarterback	Mark Rypien, Washington
Barry Sanders, Detroit	Running back	Emmitt Smith, Dallas
Thurman Thomas, Buffalo	Running back	Christian Okoye, Kansas City
Pete Stoyanovich, Miami	Placekicker	Jeff Yeager, L.A. Raiders

First team	Defense	Second team
Reggie White, Philadelphia	End	Jeff Lageman, N.Y. Jets
Clyde Simmons, Philadelphia	End	Greg Townsend, L.A. Raiders
Jerry Ball, Detroit	Nose tackle	Michael Dean Perry, Cleveland
Ray Childress, Houston	Tackle	Cortez Kennedy, Seattle
Seth Joyner, Philadelphia	Inside linebacker	Sam Mills, New Orleans
Junior Seau, San Diego	Inside linebacker	Vincent Brown, New England
Cornelius Bennett, Buffalo	Outside Linebacker	Wilbur Marshall, Washington
Pat Swilling, New Orleans	Outside linebacker	Derrick Thomas, Kansas City
Deion Sanders, Atlanta	Cornerback	Rod Woodson, Pittsburgh
Darrell Green, Washington	Cornerback	Eric Allen, Philadelphia
Steve Atwater, Denver	Safety	Tim McDonald, Phoenix
Mark Carrier, Chicago	Safety	Bennie Blades, Detroit
Jeff Gossett, L.A. Raiders	Punter	Reggie Roby, Miami

Redskins Defeat Bills in Super Bowl

The Washington Redskins dominated throughout the game and defeated the Buffalo Bills 37-24 to win Super Bowl XXVI. It was the third Super Bowl victory for the Redskins, who were champions in 1983 and 1987. Mark Rypien, quarterback for the Redskins, was chosen the game's most valuable player.

Score by Quarters

Washington	0	17	14	6—37
Buffalo	0	0	10	14—24

Scoring

Washington—Lohmiller 34 yd. field goal
Washington—Byner 10 yd. pass from Rypien (Lohmiller kick)
Washington—Riggs 1 yd. run (Lohmiller kick)
Washington—Riggs 1 yd. run (Lohmiller kick)
Buffalo—Norwood 21 yd. field goal
Buffalo—Thomas 1 yd. run (Norwood kick)
Washington—Clark 30 yd. pass from Rypien (Lohmiller kick)
Washington—Lohmiller 25 yd. field goal
Washington—Lohmiller 25 yd. field goal
Buffalo—Metzelaars 2 yd. pass from Kelly (Norwood kick)
Buffalo—Beebe 4 yd. pass from Kelly (Norwood kick)

Individual Statistics

Rushing — Washington, Ervins 13-72, Byner 14-49, Riggs 5-7, Sanders 1-1, Rutledge 1-0, Rypien 6-(minus 4). Buffalo, Davis 4-17, Kelly 3-16, Thomas 10-13, Lofton 1-(minus 3).

Passing — Washington, Rypien 18-33-1-292. Buffalo, Kelly 28-58-4-275, Reich 1-1-0-11.

Receiving — Washington, Clark 7-114, Monk 7-113, Byner 3-24, Sanders 1-41. Buffalo, Lofton 7-92, Reed 5-34, Beebe 4-61, Davis 4-38, Thomas 4-27, McKeller 2-29, A. Edwards 1-11, Metzelaars 1-2, Kelly 1-(minus 8).

Team Statistics

	Washington	Buffalo
First downs	24	25
Total net yards	417	283
Total plays	73	82
Avg gain	5.7	3.5
Rushing yards	125	43
Passing yards	292	240
Yards per pass	8.8	3.8
Punts-average	4-37	6-35
Total return yards	95	90
Penalties yards	5-82	6-50
Fumbles-lost	1-0	6-1
Time of possession	33:43	26:17

Super Bowl

Year	Winner	Loser	Winning coach	Site
1967	Green Bay Packers, 35	Kansas City Chiefs, 10	Vince Lombardi	Los Angeles Coliseum
1968	Green Bay Packers, 33	Oakland Raiders, 14	Vince Lombardi	Orange Bowl, Miami
1969	New York Jets, 16	Baltimore Colts, 7	Weeb Ewbank	Orange Bowl, Miami
1970	Kansas City Chiefs, 23	Minnesota Vikings, 7	Hank Stram	Tulane Stadium, New Orleans
1971	Baltimore Colts, 16	Dallas Cowboys, 13	Don McCafferty	Orange Bowl, Miami
1972	Dallas Cowboys, 24	Miami Dolphins, 3	Tom Landry	Tulane Stadium, New Orleans
1973	Miami Dolphins, 14	Washington Redskins, 7	Don Shula	Los Angeles Coliseum
1974	Miami Dolphins, 24	Minnesota Vikings, 7	Don Shula	Rice Stadium, Houston
1975	Pittsburgh Steelers, 16	Minnesota Vikings, 6	Chuck Noll	Tulane Stadium, New Orleans
1976	Pittsburgh Steelers, 21	Dallas Cowboys, 17	Chuck Noll	Orange Bowl, Miami
1977	Oakland Raiders, 32	Minnesota Vikings, 14	John Madden	Rose Bowl, Pasadena
1978	Dallas Cowboys, 27	Denver Broncos, 10	Tom Landry	Superdome, New Orleans
1979	Pittsburgh Steelers, 35	Dallas Cowboys, 31	Chuck Noll	Orange Bowl, Miami
1980	Pittsburgh Steelers, 31	Los Angeles Rams, 19	Chuck Noll	Rose Bowl, Pasadena
1981	Oakland Raiders, 27	Philadelphia Eagles, 10	Tom Flores	Superdome, New Orleans
1982	San Francisco 49ers, 26	Cincinnati Bengals, 21	Bill Walsh	Silverdome, Pontiac, Mich.
1983	Washington Redskins, 27	Miami Dolphins, 17	Joe Gibbs	Rose Bowl, Pasadena
1984	Los Angeles Raiders, 38	Washington Redskins, 9	Tom Flores	Tampa Stadium
1985	San Francisco 49ers, 38	Miami Dolphins, 16	Bill Walsh	Stanford Stadium, Palo Alto, Cal.
1986	Chicago Bears, 46	New England Patriots, 10	Mike Ditka	Superdome, New Orleans
1987	New York Giants, 39	Denver Broncos, 20	Bill Parcells	Rose Bowl, Pasadena
1988	Washington Redskins, 42	Denver Broncos, 10	Joe Gibbs	San Diego Stadium
1989	San Francisco 49ers, 20	Cincinnati Bengals, 16	Bill Walsh	Joe Robbie Stadium, Miami
1990	San Francisco 49ers, 55	Denver Broncos, 10	George Seifert	Superdome, New Orleans
1991	New York Giants, 20	Buffalo Bills, 19	Bill Parcells	Tampa Stadium
1992	Washington Redskins, 37	Buffalo Bills, 24	Joe Gibbs	Metrodome, Minneapolis

Super Bowl MVPs

1967 Bart Starr, Green Bay
1968 Bart Starr, Green Bay
1969 Joe Namath, N.Y. Jets
1970 Len Dawson, Kansas City
1971 Chuck Howley, Dallas
1972 Roger Staubach, Dallas
1973 Jake Scott, Miami
1974 Larry Csonka, Miami
1975 Franco Harris, Pittsburgh
1976 Lynn Swann, Pittsburgh
1977 Fred Biletnikoff, Oakland
1978 Randy White, Harvey Martin, Dallas
1979 Terry Bradshaw, Pittsburgh
1980 Terry Bradshaw, Pittsburgh
1981 Jim Plunkett, Oakland
1982 Joe Montana, San Francisco
1983 John Riggins, Washington
1984 Marcus Allen, L.A. Raiders
1985 Joe Montana, San Francisco
1986 Richard Dent, Chicago
1987 Phil Simms, N.Y. Giants
1988 Doug Williams, Washington
1989 Jerry Rice, San Francisco
1990 Joe Montana, San Francisco
1991 Ottis Anderson, N.Y. Giants
1992 Mark Rypien, Washington

NFL Head Coaches in 1992

AFC

Buffalo—Marv Levy
Cincinnati—David Shula
Cleveland—Bill Belichick
Denver—Dan Reeves
Houston—Jack Pardee
Indianapolis—Ted Marchibroda
Kansas City—Marty Schottenheimer
L.A. Raiders—Art Shell
Miami—Don Shula
New England—Dick McPherson
N.Y. Jets—Bruce Coslet
Pittsburgh—Bill Cowher
San Diego—Bobby Ross
Seattle—Tom Flores

NFC

Atlanta—Jerry Glanville
Chicago—Mike Ditka
Dallas—Jimmy Johnson
Detroit—Wayne Fontes
Green Bay—Mike Holmgren
L.A. Rams—Chuck Knox
Minnesota—Dennis Green
New Orleans—Jim Mora
N.Y. Giants—Ray Handley
Philadelphia—Rich Kotite
Phoenix—Joe Bugel
San Francisco—George Seifert
Tampa Bay—Sam Wyche
Washington—Joe Gibbs

Number One NFL Draft Choices, 1936-92

Year	Team	Player, Pos., College
1936	Philadelphia	Jay Berwanger, HB, Chicago
1937	Philadelphia	Sam Francis, FB, Nebraska
1938	Cleve.Rams	Corbett Davis, FB, Indiana
1939	Chi.Cards	Ki Aldrich, C, TCU
1940	Chi.Cards	George Cafego, HB, Tennessee
1941	Chi.Bears	Tom Harmon, HB, Michigan
1942	Pittsburgh	Bill Dudley, HB, Virginia
1943	Detroit	Frank Sinkwich, HB, Georgia
1944	Boston Yanks	Angelo Bertelli, QB, Notre Dame
1945	Chi.Cards	Charley Trippi, HB, Georgia
1946	Boston Yanks	Frank Dancewicz, QB, Notre Dame
1947	Chi.Bears	Bob Fenimore, HB, Okla. A&M
1948	Washington	Harry Gilmer, QB, Alabama
1949	Philadelphia	Chuck Bednarik, C, Penn
1950	Detroit	Leon Hart, E, Notre Dame
1951	N.Y. Giants	Kyle Rote, HB, SMU
1952	L.A. Rams	Bill Wade, QB, Vanderbilt
1953	San Francisco	Harry Babcock, E, Georgia
1954	Cleveland	Bobby Garrett, QB, Stanford
1955	Baltimore	George Shaw, QB, Oregon
1956	Pittsburgh	Gary Glick, DB, Col. A&M
1957	Green Bay	Paul Hornung, QB, Notre Dame
1958	Chi.Cards	King Hill, QB, Rice
1959	Green Bay	Randy Duncan, QB, Iowa
1960	L.A. Rams	Billy Cannon, HB, LSU
1961	Minnesota	Tommy Mason, HB, Tulane
1962	Washington	Ernie Davis, HB, Syracuse
1963	L.A. Rams	Terry Baker, QB, Oregon St.
1964	San Francisco	Dave Parks, E, Texas Tech
1965	N.Y. Giants	Tucker Frederickson, HB, Auburn
1966	Atlanta	Tommy Nobis, LB, Texas
1967	Baltimore	Bubba Smith, DT, Michigan St.
1968	Minnesota	Ron Yary, T, USC
1969	Buffalo	O.J. Simpson, RB, USC
1970	Pittsburgh	Terry Bradshaw, QB, La.Tech
1971	New England	Jim Plunkett, QB, Stanford
1972	Buffalo	Walt Patulski, DE, Notre Dame
1973	Houston	John Matuszak, DE, Tampa
1974	Dallas	Ed "Too Tall" Jones, Tenn.St.
1975	Atlanta	Steve Bartkowski, QB, Cal.
1976	Tampa Bay	Lee Roy Selmon, DE, Oklahoma
1977	Tampa Bay	Ricky Bell, RB, USC
1978	Houston	Earl Campbell, RB, Texas
1979	Buffalo	Tom Cousineau, LB, Ohio St.
1980	Detroit	Billy Sims, RB, Oklahoma
1981	New Orleans	George Rogers, RB, S.Carolina
1982	New England	Kenneth Sims, DT, Texas
1983	Baltimore	John Elway, QB, Stanford
1984	New England	Irving Fryar, WR, Nebraska
1985	Buffalo	Bruce Smith, DE, Va.Tech
1986	Tampa Bay	Bo Jackson, RB, Auburn
1987	Tampa Bay	Vinny Testaverde, QB, Miami, (Fla.)
1988	Atlanta	Aundray Bruce, LB, Auburn
1989	Dallas	Troy Aikman, QB, UCLA
1990	Indianapolis	Jeff George, QB, Illinois
1991	Dallas	Russell Maryland, DL, Miami
1992	Indianapolis	Steve Emtman, DL, Washington

First-Round Selections in the 1992 NFL Draft

Team	Player	Pos.	College
1—Indianapolis	Steve Emtman*	DT	Washington
2—Indianapolis	Quentin Coryatt	LB	Texas A&M
3—L.A. Rams	Sean Gilbert*	DL	Pittsburgh
4—Washington	Desmond Howard*	WR	Michigan
5—Green Bay	Terrell Buckley*	DB	Florida St.
6—Cincinnati	David Klinger	QB	Houston
7—Miami	Troy Vincent	DB	Wisconsin
8—Atlanta	Bob Whitfield*	OT	Stanford
9—Cleveland	Tommy Vardell	FB	Stanford
10—Seattle	Ray Roberts	OT	Virginia
11—Pittsburgh	Leon Searcy	OT	Miami
12—Miami	Marco Coleman*	LB	Georgia Tech
13—New England	Eugene Chung	OL	Virginia Tech
14—N.Y. Giants	Derek Brown	TE	Notre Dame
15—N.Y. Jets	Johnny Mitchell*	TE	Nebraska
16—L.A. Raiders	Chester McGlockton*	DT	Clemson
17—Dallas	Kevin Smith	DB	Texas A&M
18—San Francisco	Dana Hall	DB	Washington
19—Atlanta	Tony Smith	RB	Southern Miss.
20—Kansas City	Dale Carter	DB	Tennessee
21—New Orleans	Vaughn Dunbar	RB	Indiana
22—Chicago	Alonzo Spellman*	DE	Ohio State
23—San Diego	Chris Mims	DL	Tennessee
24—Dallas	Robert Jones	LB	East Carolina
25—Denver	Tommy Maddox*	QB	UCLA
26—Detroit	Robert Porcher	DL	S. Carolina St.
27—Buffalo	John Fina	OL	Arizona
28—Cincinnati	Darryl Williams*	DB	Miami

* Under classmen who chose to enter the NFL draft.

Pro Football Hall of Fame, Canton, Ohio

Herb Adderley
Lance Alworth
Doug Atkins
Morris (Red) Badgro
Lem Barney
Cliff Battles
Sammy Baugh
Chuck Bednarik
Bert Bell
Bobby Bell
Raymond Berry
Charles Bidwell
Fred Biletnikoff
George Blanda
Mel Blount
Terry Bradshaw
Jim Brown
Paul Brown
Roosevelt Brown
Willie Brown
Buck Buchanan
Dick Butkus
Earl Campbell
Tony Canadeo
Joe Carr
Guy Chamberlin
Jack Christiansen
Dutch Clark
George Connor
Jim Conzelman
Larry Csonka
Al Davis
Willie Davis
Len Dawson
Mike Ditka
Art Donovan
Paddy Driscoll
Bill Dudley
Turk Edwards
Weeb Ewbank
Tom Fears
Ray Flaherty
Len Ford
Dr. Daniel Fortmann
Frank Gatski
Bill George
Frank Gifford
Sid Gillman
Otto Graham
Red Grange
Joe Greene
Forrest Gregg
Bob Griese
Lou Groza
Joe Guyon
George Halas
Jack Ham
John Hannah
Franco Harris
Ed Healey
Mel Hein
Ted Hendricks
Pete Henry
Arnold Herber
Bill Hewitt
Clarke Hinkle
Elroy (Crazy Legs) Hirsch
Paul Hornung
Ken Houston
Cal Hubbard
Sam Huff
Lamar Hunt
Don Hutson
John Henry Johnson
Deacon Jones
Stan Jones
Sonny Jurgensen
Walt Kiesling
Frank (Bruiser) Kinard
Curly Lambeau
Jack Lambert
Tom Landry
Dick (Night Train) Lane
Jim Langer
Willie Lanier
Yale Lary
Dante Lavelli
Bobby Layne
Tuffy Leemans
Bob Lilly
Vince Lombardi
Sid Luckman
Link Lyman
John Mackey
Tim Mara
Gino Marchetti
George Marshall
Ollie Matson
Don Maynard
George McAfee
Mike McCormack
Hugh McElhenny
John (Blood) McNally
Mike Michalske
Wayne Millner
Bobby Mitchell
Ron Mix
Lenny Moore
Marion Motley
George Musso
Bronko Nagurski
Joe Namath
Greasy Neale
Ernie Nevers
Ray Nitschke
Leo Nomellini
Merlin Olsen
Jim Otto
Steve Owen
Alan Page
Clarence (Ace) Parker
Jim Parker
Joe Perry
Pete Pihos
Hugh (Shorty) Ray
Dan Reeves
John Riggins
Jim Ringo
Andy Robustelli
Art Rooney
Pete Rozelle
Bob St. Clair
Gale Sayers
Joe Schmidt
Tex Schramm
Art Shell
O.J. Simpson
Bart Starr
Roger Staubach
Ernie Stautner
Jan Stenerud
Ken Strong
Joe Stydahar
Fran Tarkenton
Charlie Taylor
Jim Taylor
Jim Thorpe
Y.A. Tittle
George Trafton
Charlie Trippi
Emlen Tunnell
Clyde (Bulldog) Turner
Johnny Unitas
Gene Upshaw
Norm Van Brocklin
Steve Van Buren
Doak Walker
Paul Warfield
Bob Waterfield
Arnie Weinmeister
Bill Willis
Larry Wilson
Alex Wojciechowicz
Willie Wood

National Football Conference Leaders

(National Football League, 1960-69)

Passing

Player, team	Atts	Com	YG	TD	Year
Milt Plum, Cleveland	250	151	2,297	21	**1960**
Milt Plum, Cleveland	302	177	2,416	18	**1961**
Bart Starr, Green Bay	285	178	2,438	12	**1962**
Y.A. Tittle, N.Y. Giants	367	221	3,145	36	**1963**
Bart Starr, Green Bay	272	163	2,144	15	**1964**
Rudy Bukich, Chicago	312	176	2,641	20	**1965**
Bart Starr, Green Bay	251	156	2,257	14	**1966**
Sonny Jurgensen, Washington	508	288	3,747	31	**1967**
Earl Morrall, Baltimore	317	182	2,909	26	**1968**
Sonny Jurgensen, Washington	442	274	3,102	22	**1969**
John Brodie, San Francisco	378	223	2,941	24	**1970**
Roger Staubach, Dallas	211	126	1,882	15	**1971**
Norm Snead, N.Y. Giants	325	196	2,307	17	**1972**
Roger Staubach, Dallas	286	179	2,428	23	**1973**
Sonny Jurgensen, Washington	167	107	1,185	11	**1974**
Fran Tarkenton, Minnesota	425	273	2,294	25	**1975**
James Harris, Los Angeles	158	91	1,460	8	**1976**
Roger Staubach, Dallas	361	210	2,620	18	**1977**
Roger Staubach, Dallas	413	231	3,190	25	**1978**
Roger Staubach, Dallas	461	267	3,586	27	**1979**
Ron Jaworski, Philadelphia	451	257	3,529	27	**1980**
Joe Montana, San Francisco	488	311	3,565	19	**1981**
Joe Thiesmann, Washington	252	161	2,033	13	**1982**
Steve Bartkowski, Atlanta	423	274	3,167	22	**1983**
Joe Montana, San Francisco	432	279	3,630	28	**1984**
Joe Montana, San Francisco	494	303	3,653	27	**1985**
Tommy Kramer, Minnesota	372	208	3,000	24	**1986**
Joe Montana, San Francisco	398	266	3,054	31	**1987**
Wade Wilson, Minnesota	332	204	2,746	15	**1988**
Joe Montana, San Francisco	386	271	3,521	26	**1989**
Phil Simms, N.Y. Giants	311	184	2,284	15	**1990**
Steve Young, San Francisco	279	180	2,517	17	**1991**

Pass-Receiving

Player, team	Ct	YG	TD
Raymond Berry, Baltimore	74	1,298	10
Jim Phillips, L.A. Rams	78	1,092	5
Bobby Mitchell, Washington	72	1,384	11
Bobby Joe Conrad, St. Louis	73	967	10
Johnny Morris, Chicago	93	1,200	10
Dave Parks, San Francisco	80	1,344	12
Charley Taylor, Washington	72	1,119	12
Charley Taylor, Washington	70	990	9
Clifton McNeil, San Francisco	71	994	7
Dan Abramowicz, New Orleans	73	1,015	7
Dick Gordon, Chicago	71	1,026	13
Bob Tucker, Giants	59	791	4
Harold Jackson, Philadelphia	62	1,048	4
Harold Carmichael, Philadelphia	67	1,116	9
Charles Young, Philadelphia	63	696	3
Chuck Foreman, Minnesota	73	691	9
Drew Pearson, Dallas	58	806	6
Ahmad Rashad, Minnesota	51	681	2
Rickey Young, Minnesota	88	704	5
Ahmad Rashad, Minnesota	80	1,156	9
Earl Cooper, San Francisco	83	567	4
Dwight Clark, San Francisco	85	1,105	4
Dwight Clark, San Francisco	60	913	5
Roy Green, St. Louis	78	1,227	14
Charlie Brown, Washington	78	1,225	8
Earnest Gray, N.Y. Giants	78	1,139	5
Art Monk, Washington	106	1,372	7
Roger Craig, San Francisco	92	1,016	6
Jerry Rice, San Francisco	86	1,570	15
J.T. Smith, St. Louis	91	1,117	8
Henry Ellard, L.A. Rams	86	1,414	10
Sterling Sharpe, Green Bay	90	1,423	12
Jerry Rice, San Francisco	100	1,502	13
Michael Irvin, Dallas	93	1,523	8

Scoring

Player, team	TD	PAT	FG	Pts	Year
Paul Hornung, Green Bay	15	41	15	176	**1960**
Paul Hornung, Green Bay	10	41	15	146	**1961**
Jim Taylor, Green Bay	19	0	0	114	**1962**
Don Chandler, N.Y. Giants	0	52	18	106	**1963**
Lenny Moore, Baltimore	20	0	0	120	**1964**
Gale Sayers, Chicago	22	0	0	132	**1965**
Bruce Gossett, L.A. Rams	0	29	28	113	**1966**
Jim Bakken, St. Louis	0	36	27	117	**1967**
Leroy Kelly, Cleveland	20	0	0	120	**1968**
Fred Cox, Minnesota	0	43	26	121	**1969**
Fred Cox, Minnesota	0	35	30	125	**1970**
Curt Knight, Washington	0	27	29	114	**1971**
Chester Marcol, Green Bay	0	29	33	128	**1972**
David Ray, Los Angeles	0	40	30	130	**1973**
Chester Marcol, Green Bay	0	19	25	94	**1974**
Chuck Foreman, Minnesota	22	0	0	132	**1975**
Mark Moseley, Washington	0	31	22	97	**1976**
Walter Payton, Chicago	16	0	0	96	**1977**
Frank Corrall, Los Angeles	0	31	29	118	**1978**
Mark Moseley, Washington	0	39	25	114	**1979**
Ed Murray, Detroit	0	35	27	116	**1980**
Ed Murray, Detroit	0	46	25	121	**1981**
Wendell Tyler, L.A. Rams	13	0	0	78	**1982**
Mark Moseley, Washington	0	62	33	161	**1983**
Ray Wersching, San Francisco	0	56	25	131	**1984**
Kevin Butler, Chicago	0	51	31	144	**1985**
Kevin Butler, Chicago	0	36	28	120	**1986**
Jerry Rice, San Francisco	23	0	0	138	**1987**
Mike Cofer, San Francisco	0	40	27	121	**1988**
Mike Cofer, San Francisco	0	49	29	136	**1989**
Chip Lohmiller, Washington	0	41	30	131	**1990**
Chip Lohmiller, Washington	0	56	31	149	**1991**

Rushing

Player, team	Yds	Atts	TD
Jim Brown, Cleveland	1,257	215	9
Jim Brown, Cleveland	1,408	305	8
Jim Taylor, Green Bay	1,474	272	19
Jim Brown, Cleveland	1,863	291	12
Jim Brown, Cleveland	1,446	280	7
Jim Brown, Cleveland	1,544	289	17
Gale Sayers, Chicago	1,231	229	8
Leroy Kelly, Cleveland	1,205	235	11
Leroy Kelly, Cleveland	1,239	248	16
Gale Sayers, Chicago	1,032	236	8
Larry Brown, Washington	1,125	237	5
John Brockington, Green Bay	1,105	216	4
Larry Brown, Washington	1,216	285	8
John Brockington, Green Bay	1,144	265	3
Lawrence McCutcheon, Los Angeles	1,109	236	3
Jim Otis, St. Louis	1,076	269	5
Walter Payton, Chicago	1,390	311	13
Walter Payton, Chicago	1,852	339	14
Walter Payton, Chicago	1,395	333	11
Walter Payton, Chicago	1,610	369	14
Walter Payton, Chicago	1,460	317	15
George Rogers, New Orleans	1,674	378	13
Tony Dorsett, Dallas	745	177	5
Eric Dickerson, L.A. Rams	1,808	390	18
Eric Dickerson, L.A. Rams	2,105	379	14
Gerald Riggs, Atlanta	1,719	397	10
Eric Dickerson, L.A. Rams	1,821	404	11
Charles White, L.A. Rams	1,374	324	11
Herschel Walker, Dallas	1,514	361	5
Barry Sanders, Detroit	1,470	280	14
Barry Sanders, Detroit	1,304	255	13
Emmitt Smith, Dallas	1,563	365	12

American Football Conference Leaders

(American Football League, 1960-1969)

Passing

Player, team	Atts	Com	YG	TD	Year
Jack Kemp, Los Angeles	406	211	3,018	20	**1960**
George Blanda, Houston	362	187	3,330	36	**1961**

Pass-Receiving

Player, team	Ct	YG	TD
Lionel Taylor, Denver	92	1,235	12
Lionel Taylor, Denver	100	1,176	4

Player, team	Atts	Com	YG	TD	Year	Player, team	Ct	YG	TD
Len Dawson, Dallas	310	189	2,759	29	**1962**	Lionel Taylor, Denver	77	908	4
Tobin Rote, Kansas City	286	170	2,510	20	**1963**	Lionel Taylor, Denver	78	1,101	10
Len Dawson, Kansas City	354	199	2,879	30	**1964**	Charley Hennigan, Houston	101	1,546	8
John Hadl, San Diego	348	174	2,798	20	**1965**	Lionel Taylor, Denver	85	1,131	6
Len Dawson, Kansas City	284	159	2,527	26	**1966**	Lance Alworth, San Diego	73	1,383	13
Daryle Lamonica, Oakland	425	220	3,228	30	**1967**	George Sauer, N.Y. Jets	75	1,189	6
Len Dawson, Kansas City	224	131	2,109	17	**1968**	Lance Alworth, San Diego	68	1,312	10
Greg Cook, Cincinnati	197	106	1,854	15	**1969**	Lance Alworth, San Diego	64	1,003	4
Daryle Lamonica, Oakland	356	179	2,516	22	**1970**	Marlin Briscoe, Buffalo	57	1,036	8
Bob Griese, Miami	263	145	2,089	19	**1971**	Fred Biletnikoff, Oakland	61	929	9
Earl Morrall, Miami	150	83	1,360	11	**1972**	Fred Biletnikoff, Oakland	58	802	7
Ken Stabler, Oakland	260	163	1,997	14	**1973**	Fred Willis, Houston	57	371	1
Ken Anderson, Cincinnati	328	213	2,667	18	**1974**	Lydell Mitchell, Baltimore	72	544	2
Ken Anderson, Cincinnati	377	228	3,169	21	**1975**	Reggie Rucker, Cleveland	60	770	3
						Lydell Mitchell, Baltimore	60	554	4
Ken Stabler, Oakland	291	194	2,737	27	**1976**	MacArthur Lane, Kansas City	66	686	1
Bob Griese, Miami	307	180	2,252	22	**1977**	Lydell Mitchell, Baltimore	71	620	4
Terry Bradshaw, Pittsburgh	368	207	2,915	28	**1978**	Steve Largent, Seattle	71	1,168	8
Dan Fouts, San Diego	530	332	4,082	24	**1979**	Joe Washington, Baltimore	82	750	3
Brian Sipe, Cleveland	554	337	4,132	30	**1980**	Kellen Winslow, San Diego	89	1,290	9
Ken Anderson, Cincinnati	479	300	3,754	29	**1981**	Kellen Winslow, San Diego	88	1,075	10
Ken Anderson, Cincinnati	309	218	2,495	12	**1982**	Kellen Winslow, San Diego	54	721	6
Dan Marino, Miami	296	173	2,210	20	**1983**	Todd Christensen, L.A. Raiders	92	1,247	12
Dan Marino, Miami	564	362	5,084	48	**1984**	Ozzie Newsome, Cleveland	89	1,001	5
Ken O'Brien, N.Y. Jets	488	297	3,888	25	**1985**	Lionel James, San Diego	86	1,027	6
Dan Marino, Miami	623	378	4,746	44	**1986**	Todd Christensen, L.A. Raiders	95	1,153	8
Bernie Kosar, Cleveland	389	241	3,033	22	**1987**	Al Toon, N.Y. Jets	68	976	5
Boomer Esiason, Cincinnati	388	223	3,572	28	**1988**	Al Toon, N.Y. Jets	93	1,067	5
Boomer Esiason, Cincinnati	455	258	3,525	28	**1989**	Andre Reed, Buffalo	88	1,312	9
Jim Kelly, Buffalo	346	219	2,829	24	**1990**	Haywood Jeffires, Houston	74	1,048	8
						Drew Hill, Houston	74	1,019	5
Jim Kelly, Buffalo	474	304	3,844	33	**1991**	Haywood Jeffires, Houston	100	1,181	7

Scoring / Rushing

Player, team	TD	PAT	FG	Pts	Year	Player, team	Yds	Atts	TD
Gene Mingo, Denver	6	33	18	123	**1960**	Abner Haynes, Dallas	875	156	9
Gino Cappelletti, Boston	8	48	17	147	**1961**	Billy Cannon, Houston	948	200	6
Gene Mingo, Denver	4	32	27	137	**1962**	Cookie Gilchrest, Buffalo	1,096	214	13
Gino Cappelletti, Boston	2	35	22	113	**1963**	Clem Daniels, Oakland	1,099	215	3
Gino Cappelletti, Boston	7	36	25	155	**1964**	Cookie Gilchrest, Buffalo	981	230	6
Gino Cappelletti, Boston	9	27	17	132	**1965**	Paul Lowe, San Diego	1,121	222	7
Gino Cappelletti, Boston	6	35	16	119	**1966**	Jim Nance, Boston	1,458	299	11
George Blanda, Oakland	0	56	20	116	**1967**	Jim Nance, Boston	1,216	269	7
Jim Turner, N.Y. Jets	0	43	34	145	**1968**	Paul Robinson, Cincinnati	1,023	238	8
Jim Turner, N.Y. Jets	0	33	32	129	**1969**	Dick Post, San Diego	873	182	6
Jan Stenerud, Kansas City	0	26	30	116	**1970**	Floyd Little, Denver	901	209	3
Garo Yepremian, Miami	0	33	28	117	**1971**	Floyd Little, Denver	1,133	284	6
Bobby Howfield, N.Y. Jets	0	40	27	121	**1972**	O.J. Simpson, Buffalo	1,251	292	6
Roy Gerela, Pittsburgh	0	36	29	123	**1973**	O.J. Simpson, Buffalo	2,003	332	12
Roy Gerela, Pittsburgh	0	33	20	93	**1974**	Otis Armstrong, Denver	1,407	263	9
O.J. Simpson, Buffalo	23	0	0	138	**1975**	O.J. Simpson, Buffalo	1,817	329	16
Toni Linhart, Baltimore	0	49	20	109	**1976**	O.J. Simpson, Buffalo	1,503	290	8
Errol Mann, Oakland	0	39	20	99	**1977**	Mark van Eeghen, Oakland	1,273	324	7
Pat Leahy, N.Y. Jets	0	41	22	107	**1978**	Earl Campbell, Houston	1,450	302	13
John Smith, New England	0	46	23	115	**1979**	Earl Campbell, Houston	1,697	368	19
John Smith, New England	0	51	26	129	**1980**	Earl Campbell, Houston	1,934	373	13
Jim Breech, Cincinnati	0	49	22	115	**1981**	Earl Campbell, Houston	1,376	361	10
Marcus Allen, L.A. Raiders	14	0	0	84	**1982**	Freeman McNeil, N.Y. Jets	786	151	6
Gary Anderson, Pittsburgh	0	38	27	119	**1983**	Curt Warner, Seattle	1,446	335	13
Gary Anderson, Pittsburgh	0	45	24	117	**1984**	Earnest Jackson, San Diego	1,179	296	8
Gary Anderson, Pittsburgh	0	40	33	139	**1985**	Marcus Allen, L.A. Raiders	1,759	380	11
Tony Franklin, New England	0	44	32	140	**1986**	Curt Warner, Seattle	1,481	319	13
Jim Breech, Cincinnati	0	25	24	97	**1987**	Eric Dickerson, L.A. Rams, Indianapolis	1,288*	283	6
Scott Norwood, Buffalo	0	33	32	129	**1988**	Eric Dickerson, Indianapolis	1,659	388	14
David Treadwell, Denver	0	39	27	120	**1989**	Christian Okoye, Kansas City	1,480	370	12
Nick Lowery, Kansas City	0	37	34	139	**1990**	Thurman Thomas, Buffalo	1,297	271	11
Pete Stoyanovich, Miami	0	28	31	121	**1991**	Thurman Thomas, Buffalo	1,407	288	7

* 1,011 AFC yards led conference.

World Almanac/George Halas Trophy Winners

The World Almanac's George Halas Trophy, named after football coach George Halas, is awarded annually to the outstanding defensive player in the NFL as chosen by a panel of sports experts on behalf of *The World Almanac*, its co-sponsoring newspapers, and its publisher, Pharos Books.

1966	Larry Wilson, St. Louis
1967	Deacon Jones, Los Angeles
1968	Deacon Jones, Los Angeles
1969	Dick Butkus, Chicago
1970	Dick Butkus, Chicago
1971	Carl Eller, Minnesota
1972	Joe Greene, Pittsburgh
1973	Alan Page, Minnesota
1974	Joe Greene, Pittsburgh
1975	Curley Culp, Houston
1976	Jerry Sherk, Cleveland
1977	Harvey Martin, Dallas
1978	Randy Gradishar, Denver
1979	Lee Roy Selmon, Tampa Bay
1980	Lester Hayes, Oakland
1981	Joe Klecko, N.Y. Jets
1982	Mark Gastineau, N.Y. Jets
1983	Jack Lambert, Pittsburgh
1984	Mike Haynes, L.A. Raiders
1985	Howie Long, L.A. Raiders
	Andre Tippett, New England
1986	Lawrence Taylor, N.Y. Giants
1987	Reggie White, Philadelphia
1988	Mike Singletary, Chicago
1989	Tim Harris, Green Bay
1990	Bruce Smith, Buffalo
1991	Pat Swilling, New Orleans

1991 NFL Individual Leaders

National Football Conference

Passing

	Att	Comp	Pct comp	Yds	Avg gain	TD	Pct TD	Long	Int	Rating points
Young, Steve, San Francisco. . .	279	180	64.5	2517	9.02	17	6.1	97	8	101.8
Rypien, Mark, Washington	421	249	59.1	3564	8.47	28	6.7	82	11	97.9
Bono, Steve, San Francisco	237	141	59.5	1617	6.82	11	4.6	78	4	88.5
Aikman, Troy, Dallas	363	237	65.3	2754	7.59	11	3.0	61	10	86.7
Hostetler, Jeff, N.Y. Giants	285	179	62.8	2032	7.13	5	1.8	55	4	84.1
Gannon, Rich, Minnesota	354	211	59.6	2166	6.12	12	3.4	50	6	81.5
Miller, Chris, Atlanta.	413	220	53.3	3103	7.51	26	6.3	80	18	80.6
McMahon, Jim, Philadelphia . . .	311	187	60.1	2239	7.20	12	3.9	75	11	80.3
Walsh, Steve, New Orleans . . .	255	141	55.3	1638	6.42	11	4.3	41	6	79.5
Hebert, Bobby, New Orleans. . .	248	149	60.1	1676	6.76	9	3.6	65	8	79.0

Rushing

	Att	Yds	Avg	TD
Smith, Emmitt, Dallas	365	1563	4.3	12
Sanders, Barry, Detroit	342	1548	4.5	16
Hampton, Rodney, N.Y. Giants . . .	256	1059	4.1	10
Byner, Earnest, Washington.	274	1048	3.8	5
Walker, Herschel, Minnesota	198	825	4.2	10
Cobb, Reggie, Tampa Bay	196	752	3.8	7
Anderson, Neal, Chicago	210	747	3.6	6
Delpino, Robert, L.A. Rams	214	688	3.2	9
Ervins, Ricky, Washington	145	680	4.7	3
Johnson, Johnny, Phoenix.	196	666	3.4	4

Pass Receiving

	No	Yds	Avg	TD
Irvin, Michael, Dallas	93	1523	16.4	8
Rison, Andre, Atlanta	81	976	12.0	12
Rice, Jerry, San Francisco	80	1206	15.1	14
Carter, Cris, Minnesota	72	962	13.4	5
Monk, Art, Washington.	71	1049	14.8	8
Clark, Gary, Washington.	70	1340	19.1	10
Sharpe, Sterling, Green Bay	69	961	13.9	4
Martin, Eric, New Orleans	66	803	12.2	4
Ellard, Henry, L.A. Rams	64	1052	16.4	3
Taylor, John, San Francisco	64	1011	15.8	9

Scoring-Touchdowns

	TD	Rush	Pass	Pts
Sanders, Barry, Detroit	17	16	1	102
Rice, Jerry, San Francisco	14	0	14	84
Smith, Emmitt, Dallas	13	12	1	78
Rison, Andre, Atlanta	12	0	12	72

Scoring-Kicking

	PAT	FG	Pts
Lohmiller, Chip, Washington . . .	56/56	31/43	149
Willis, Ken, Dallas.	37/37	27/39	118
Andersen, Morten, New Orleans	38/38	25/32	113
Ruzek, Roger, Philadelphia . . .	27/29	28/33	111
Murray, Eddie, Detroit	40/40	19/28	97

Interceptions

	No	Yds	Long	TD
Crockett, Ray, Detroit	6	141	96	1
Sanders, Deion, Atlanta	6	119	55	1
Williams, Aeneas, Phoenix	6	60	32	0
McKyer, Tim, Atlanta.	6	24	24	0

Kickoff Returns

	No	Yds	Avg	TD
Gray, Mel, Detroit	36	929	25.8	0
Wright, Alexander, Dallas	21	514	24.5	1
Wilson, Charles, Green Bay.	23	522	22.7	1
Carter, Dexter, San Francisco . . .	37	839	22.7	1
Sanders, Deion, Atlanta	26	576	22.2	1

Punt Returns

	No	Yds	Avg	TD
Gray, Mel, Detroit	25	385	15.4	1
Mitchell, Brian, Washington	45	600	13.3	2
Martin, Kelvin, Dallas.	21	244	11.6	1
Meggett, Dave, N.Y. Giants	28	287	10.3	1
Drewrey, Willie, Tampa Bay.	38	360	9.5	0

Punters

	No	Yds	Long	Avg
Newsome, Harry, Minnesota	68	3095	65	45.5
Camarillo, Rich, Phoenix.	76	3445	60	45.3
Barnhardt, Tommy, New Orleans. .	86	3743	61	43.5
Landeta, Sean, N.Y. Giants	64	2768	61	43.3
Fulhage, Scott, Atlanta	81	3470	60	42.8

Sacks

	No
Swilling, Pat, New Orleans	17.0
White, Reggie, Philadelphia. . . .	15.0
Bennett, Tony, Green Bay	13.0
Simmons, Clyde, Philadelphia . .	13.0
Jackson, Rickey, New Orleans. .	11.5

American Football Conference

Passing

	Att	Comp	Pct comp	Yds	Avg gain	TD	Pct TD	Long	Int	Rating points
Kelly, Jim, Buffalo	474	304	64.1	3844	8.11	33	7.0	t77	17	97.6
Kosar, Bernie, Cleveland	494	307	62.1	3487	7.06	18	3.6	t71	9	87.8
Marino, Dan, Miami	549	318	57.9	3970	7.23	25	4.6	54	13	85.8
Krieg, Dave, Seattle	285	187	65.6	2080	7.30	11	3.9	60	12	82.5
Moon, Warren, Houston.	655	404	61.7	4690	7.16	23	3.5	t61	21	81.7
DeBerg, Steve, Kansas City . . .	434	256	59.0	2965	6.83	17	3.9	63	14	79.3
O'Donnell, Neil, Pittsburgh	286	156	54.5	1963	6.86	11	3.8	t89	7	78.8
O'Brien, Ken, N.Y. Jets	489	287	58.7	3300	6.75	10	2.0	53	11	76.6
Elway, John, Denver	451	242	53.7	3253	7.21	13	2.9	71	12	75.4
George, Jeff, Indianapolis.	485	292	60.2	2910	6.00	10	2.1	t49	12	73.8

Rushing

	Att	Yds	Avg	TD
Thomas, Thurman, Buffalo	288	1407	4.9	7
Green, Gaston, Denver	261	1037	4.0	4
Okoye, Christian, Kansas City	225	1031	4.6	9
Russell, Leonard, New England	266	959	3.6	4
Higgs, Mark, Miami	231	905	3.9	4
Butts, Marion, San Diego	193	834	4.3	6
Bernstine, Rod, San Diego	159	766	4.8	8
Williams, John L., Seattle	188	741	3.9	4
Green, Harold, Cincinnati	158	731	4.6	2
Thomas, Blair, N.Y. Jets	189	728	3.9	3

Pass Receiving

	No	Yds	Avg	TD
Jeffires, Haywood, Houston	100	1181	11.8	7
Hill, Drew, Houston	90	1109	12.3	4
Cook, Marv, New England	82	808	9.9	3
Reed, Andre, Buffalo	81	1113	13.7	10
Toon, Al, N.Y. Jets	74	963	13.0	0
Brooks, Bill, Indianapolis	72	888	12.3	4
Duper, Mark, Miami	70	1085	15.5	5
Clayton, Mark, Miami	70	1053	15.0	12
Blades, Brian, Seattle	70	1003	14.3	2
Givins, Ernest, Houston	70	996	14.2	5
Moore, Rob, N.Y. Jets	70	987	14.1	5

Scoring-Touchdowns

	TD	Rush	Pass	Pts
Clayton, Mark, Miami	12	0	12	72
Thomas, Thurman, Buffalo	12	7	5	72
Baxter, Brad, N.Y. Jets	11	11	0	66
Hoard, Leroy, Cleveland	11	2	9	66

Scoring-Kicking

	PAT	FG	Pts
Stoyanovich, Pete, Miami	28/29	31/37	121
Jaeger, Jeff, L.A. Raiders	29/30	29/34	116
Treadwell, David, Denver	31/32	27/36	112
Lowery, Nick, Kansas City	35/35	25/30	110
Norwood, Scott, Buffalo	56/58	18/29	110

Interceptions

	No	Yds	Long	TD
Lott, Ronnie, L.A. Raiders	8	52	27	0
Dishman, Cris, Houston	6	61	43	0
Byrd, Gill, San Diego	6	48	22	0

Kickoff Returns

	No	Yds	Avg	TD
Lewis, Nate, San Diego	23	578	25.1	1
Martin, Sammy, N.E.-Ind.	20	483	24.2	0
Warren, Chris, Seattle	35	792	22.6	0
Williams, Harvey, Kansas City	24	524	21.8	0
Vaughn, Jon, New England	34	717	21.1	1

Punt Returns

	No	Yds	Avg	TD
Woodson, Rod, Pittsburgh	28	320	11.4	0
Brown, Tim, L.A. Raiders	29	330	11.4	1
Taylor, Kitrick, San Diego	28	269	9.6	0
Warren, Chris, Seattle	32	298	9.3	1
Miller, Scott, Miami	28	248	8.9	0

Punters

	No	Yds	Long	Avg
Roby, Reggie, Miami	54	2466	64	45.7
Gossett, Jeff, L.A. Raiders	67	2961	61	44.2
Montgomery, Greg, Houston	48	2105	60	43.9
Johnson, Lee, Cincinnati	64	2795	62	43.7
Tuten, Rick, Seattle	49	2106	60	43.0
Stark, Rohn, Indianapolis	82	3492	65	42.6

Sacks

	No
Fuller, William, Houston	15.0
Fletcher, Simon, Denver	13.5
Thomas, Derrick, Kansas City	13.5
Townsend, Greg, L.A. Raiders	13.0
Smith, Anthony, L.A. Raiders	10.5

NFL Stadiums

Name, location	Capacity
Anaheim Stadium, Anaheim, Cal.	69,007
Arrowhead Stadium, Kansas City, Mo.	78,067
Astrodome, Houston, Tex.	60,502
Candlestick Park, San Francisco, Cal.	66,455
Cleveland Stadium	80,098
Foxboro Stadium, Mass.	60,794
Georgia Dome, Atlanta	70,500
Giants Stadium, E. Rutherford, N.J.	76,891
Hoosier Dome, Indianapolis, Ind.	60,127
Robert F. Kennedy Stadium, Wash., D.C.	55,683
Kingdome, Seattle, Wash.	64,984
Lambeau Field, Green Bay, Wis.	59,543
Los Angeles Memorial Coliseum	92,488
Louisiana Superdome, New Orleans	69,065
Metrodome, Minneapolis	63,000
Mile High Stadium, Denver, Col.	76,273
Milwaukee County Stadium	56,051
Pontiac Silverdome, Mich.	80,500
Rich Stadium, Buffalo, N.Y.	80,290
Riverfront Stadium, Cincinnati, Oh.	60,389
Joe Robbie Stadium, Miami, Fla.	73,000
San Diego Jack Murphy Stadium, San Diego	60,835
Soldier Field, Chicago, Ill.	66,949
Sun Devil Stadium, Tempe, Ariz.	72,608
Tampa Stadium, Tampa, Fla.	74,314
Texas Stadium, Irving, Tex.	65,024
Three Rivers Stadium, Pittsburgh, Pa.	59,492
Veterans Stadium, Philadelphia, Pa.	65,356

American Football League

Year	Eastern Division	Western Division	Playoff
1960	Houston Oilers (10-4-0)	L. A. Chargers (10-4-0)	Houston 24, Los Angeles 16
1961	Houston Oilers (10-3-1)	San Diego Chargers (12-2-0)	Houston 10, San Diego 3
1962	Houston Oilers (11-3-0)	Dallas Texans (11-3-0)	Dallas 20, Houston 17(b)
1963	Boston Patriots (8-6-1)(a)	San Diego Chargers (11-3-0)	San Diego 51, Boston 10
1964	Buffalo Bills (12-2-0)	San Diego Chargers (8-5-1)	Buffalo 20, San Diego 7
1965	Buffalo Bills (10-3-1)	San Diego Chargers (9-2-3)	Buffalo 23, San Diego 0
1966	Buffalo Bills (9-4-1)	Kansas City Chiefs (11-2-1)	Kansas City 31, Buffalo 7
1967	Houston Oilers (9-4-1)	Oakland Raiders (13-1-0)	Oakland 40, Houston 7
1968	New York Jets (11-3-0)	Oakland Raiders (12-2-0)(a)	New York 27, Oakland 23
1969	New York Jets (10-4-0)	Oakland Raiders (12-1-1)	Kansas City 17, Oakland 7(c)

(a) won divisional playoff (b) won at 2:45 of second overtime. (c) Kansas City defeated Jets to make playoffs.

All-Time Professional Football Records

NFL and AFL

(at start of 1992 season)

Leading Lifetime Rushers

Player	League	Yrs	Att	Yards	Avg
Walter Payton	NFL	13	3,838	16,726	4.4
Tony Dorsett	NFL	12	2,936	12,739	4.3
Eric Dickerson	NFL	9	2,783	12,439	4.5
Jim Brown	NFL	9	2,359	12,312	5.2
Franco Harris	NFL	13	2,949	12,120	4.1
John Riggins	NFL	14	2,916	11,352	3.9
O.J. Simpson	AFL-NFL	11	2,404	11,236	4.7
Ottis Anderson	NFL	13	2,552	10,242	4.0
Earl Campbell	NFL	8	2,187	9,407	4.3
Jim Taylor	NFL	10	1,941	8,597	4.4
Joe Perry	NFL	14	1,737	8,378	4.8
Marcus Allen	NFL	10	2,023	8,244	4.1
Gerald Riggs	NFL	10	1,989	8,188	4.1
Larry Csonka	AFL-NFL	11	1,891	8,081	4.3
James Brooks	NFL	11	1,667	7,918	4.7
Freeman McNeil	NFL	11	1,755	7,904	4.5
Roger Craig	NFL	9	1,848	7,654	4.1
Mike Pruitt	NFL	11	1,844	7,378	4.0
Leroy Kelly	NFL	10	1,727	7,274	4.2
George Rogers	NFL	7	1,692	7,176	4.2

Most Yards Gained, Season — 2,105, Eric Dickerson, Los Angeles Rams, 1984.
Most Yards Gained, Game — 275, Walter Payton, Chicago Bears vs. Minnesota Vikings, Nov. 20, 1977.
Most Games, 100 Yards or more, Season — 12, Eric Dickerson, Los Angeles Rams, 1984.
Most Games, 100 Yards or more, Career — 77, Walter Payton, Chicago Bears, 1975-87.
Most Touchdowns Rushing, Career — 110, Walter Payton, Chicago Bears, 1975-1987.
Most Touchdowns Rushing, Season — 24, John Riggins, Washington Redskins, 1983.
Most Touchdowns Rushing, Game — 6, Ernie Nevers, Chicago Cardinals vs. Chicago Bears, Nov. 8, 1929.
Most Rushing Attempts, Season — 407, James Wilder, Tampa Bay Buccaneers, 1984.
Most Rushing Attempts, Game — 45, Jamie Morris, Washington Redskins vs. Cincinnati Bengals, Dec. 17, 1988.
Longest run from Scrimmage — 99 yds., Tony Dorsett, Dallas vs. Minnesota, Jan. 3, 1983 (scored touchdown).

Leading Lifetime Passers

(Minimum 1,500 attempts)

Player	League	Yrs	Att	Comp	Yds	Pts*
Joe Montana	NFL	12	4,579	2,914	34,998	93.4
Dan Marino	NFL	9	4,730	2,798	35,386	88.2
Jim Kelly	NFL	6	2,562	1,555	19,574	88.0
Boomer Esiason	NFL	8	3,100	1,753	24,264	84.0
Roger Staubach	NFL	11	2,958	1,685	22,700	83.4
Neil Lomax	NFL	8	3,153	1,817	22,771	82.7
Sonny Jurgensen	NFL	18	4,262	2,433	32,224	82.6
Len Dawson	NFL-AFL	19	3,741	2,136	28,711	82.6
Dave Krieg	NFL	12	3,576	2,096	26,132	82.3
Ken Anderson	NFL	16	4,475	2,654	32,838	81.9
Danny White	NFL	13	2,950	1,761	21,959	81.7
Bernie Kosar	NFL	7	2,857	1,671	19,937	81.6
Ken O'Brien	NFL	8	3,367	1,984	23,744	81.3
Bart Starr	NFL	16	3,149	1,808	24,718	80.5
Fran Tarkenton	NFL	18	6,467	3,686	47,003	80.4
Warren Moon	NFL	8	3,680	2,105	27,679	80.3
Dan Fouts	NFL	15	5,604	3,294	43,040	80.2
Tony Eason	NFL	8	1,564	911	11,142	79.7
Jim Everett	NFL	6	2,528	1,431	18,783	79.7

* Rating points based on performances in the following categories: Percentage of completions, percentage of touchdown passes, percentage of interceptions, and average gain per pass attempt.

Most Yards Gained, Season — 5,084, Dan Marino, Miami Dolphins, 1984.
Most Yards Gained, Game — 554, Norm Van Brocklin, Los Angeles Rams vs. New York Yankees, Sept. 18, 1951 (27 completions in 41 attempts).
Most Touchdowns Passing, Career — 342, Fran Tarkenton, Minnesota Vikings, 1961-66; N.Y. Giants, 1967-71; Vikings, 1972-78.
Most Touchdown Passing, Season — 48, Dan Marino, Miami Dolphins, 1984.
Most Touchdown Passing, Game — 7, Sid Luckman, Chicago Bears vs. New York Giants, Nov. 14, 1943; Adrian Burk, Philadelphia Eagles vs. Washington Redskins, Oct. 17, 1954; George Blanda, Houston Oilers vs. New York Titans, Nov. 19, 1961; Y.A. Tittle, New York Giants vs. Washington Redskins, Oct. 28, 1962; Joe Kapp, Minnesota Vikings vs. Baltimore Colts, Sept. 28, 1969.
Most Passing Attempts, Season — 655, Warren Moon, Houston Oilers, 1991.
Most Passing Attempts, Game — 68, George Blanda, Houston Oilers vs. Buffalo Bills, Nov. 1, 1964 (37 completions).
Most Passes Completed, Season — 404, Warren Moon, Houston Oilers, 1991.
Most Passes Completed, Game — 42, Richard Todd, N.Y. Jets vs. San Francisco 49ers, Sept. 21, 1980.
Most Consecutive Passes Completed — 22, Joe Montana, S. F. vs. Cleveland, (5), Nov. 29, & Green Bay (17), Dec. 6, 1987.
Most Consecutive Games, Touchdown Passes — 47, John Unitas, Baltimore Colts, 1956-1960.

Leading Lifetime Receivers

Player	League	Yrs	No	Yds	Avg
Steve Largent	NFL	14	819	13,089	16.0
Art Monk	NFL	12	801	10,984	13.7
Charlie Joiner	NFL	18	750	12,146	16.2
James Lofton	NFL	14	699	13,035	18.6
Ozzie Newsome	NFL	13	662	7,980	12.1
Charley Taylor	NFL	13	649	9,110	14.0
Don Maynard	AFL-NFL	15	633	11,834	18.7
Raymond Berry	NFL	13	631	9,275	14.7
Harold Carmichael	NFL	14	590	8,985	15.2
Fred Biletnikoff	AFL-NFL	14	589	8,974	15.2
Harold Jackson	NFL	16	579	10,372	17.9
Lionel Taylor	AFL	10	567	7,195	12.7
Wes Chandler	NFL	11	559	8,966	16.0
Stanley Morgan	NFL	14	557	10,716	19.2
Roy Green	NFL	13	551	8,860	16.1
J.T. Smith	NFL	13	544	6,974	12.8
Lance Alworth	AFL-NFL	11	542	10,266	18.9
Kellen Winslow	NFL	9	541	6,741	12.5
Drew Hill	NFL	12	540	8,824	16.3
John Stallworth	NFL	14	537	8,723	16.2

Most Yards Gained, Season — 1,746, Charley Hennigan, Houston Oilers, 1961.
Most Yards Gained, Game — 336, Willie Anderson, L.A. Rams vs. New Orleans, Nov. 26, 1989.
Most Pass Receptions, Season — 106, Art Monk, Washington Redskins, 1984.
Most Pass Receptions, Game — 18, Tom Fears, Los Angeles Rams vs. Green Bay Packers, Dec. 3, 1950 (189 yards).
Most Consecutive Games, Pass Receptions — 177, Steve Largent, Seattle Seahawks, 1976-1989.
Most Touchdown Passes, Career — 100, Steve Largent, Seattle Seahawks, 1976-1989.
Most Touchdown Passes, Season — 22, Jerry Rice, San Francisco 49ers, 1987.
Most Touchdown Passes, Game — 5, Bob Shaw, Chicago Cardinals vs. Baltimore Colts, Oct. 2, 1950; Kellen Winslow, San Diego vs. Oakland, Nov. 22, 1981; Jerry Rice, San Francisco vs. Atlanta, Oct. 14, 1990.

Leading Lifetime Scorers

Player	League	Yrs	TD	PAT	FG	Total	Player	League	Yrs	TD	PAT	FG	Total
George Blanda	NFL-AFL	26	9	943	335	2,002	Jim Breech	NFL	13	0	486	224	1,158
Jan Stenerud	AFL-NFL	19	0	580	373	1,699	Gino Cappelletti	AFL	11	42	350	176	1,130
Pat Leahy	NFL	18	0	558	304	1,470	Ray Wersching	NFL	15	0	456	222	1,122
Jim Turner	AFL-NFL	16	1	521	304	1,439	Eddie Murray	NFL	12	0	381	244	1,113
Mark Moseley	NFL	16	0	482	300	1,382	Don Cockroft	NFL	13	0	432	216	1,080
Jim Bakken	NFL	17	0	534	282	1,380	Garo Yepremian	AFL-NFL	14	0	444	210	1,074
Fred Cox	NFL	15	0	519	282	1,365	Matt Bahr	NFL	13	0	221	402	1,065
Lou Groza	NFL	17	1	641	234	1,349	Bruce Gossett	NFL	11	0	374	219	1,031
Nick Lowery	NFL	13	0	410	284	1,262	Gary Anderson	NFL	10	0	323	229	1,010
Chris Bahr	NFL	14	0	490	241	1,213	Sam Baker	NFL	15	2	428	179	977

Most Points, Season — 176, Paul Hornung, Green Bay Packers, 1960 (15 TD's, 41 PAT's, 15 FG's).
Most Points, Game — 40, Ernie Nevers, Chicago Cardinals vs. Chicago Bears, Nov. 28, 1929 (6 TD's, 4 PAT's).
Most Touchdowns, Season — 24, John Riggins, Washington Redskins, 1984 (24 rushing).
Most Touchdowns, Game — 6, Ernie Nevers, Chicago Cardinals vs. Chicago Bears, Nov. 28, 1929 (6 rushing); Dub Jones, Cleveland Browns vs. Chicago Bears, Nov. 25, 1951 (4 rushing, 2 pass receptions); Gale Sayers, Chicago Bears vs. San Francisco 49ers, Dec. 12, 1965 (4 rushing, 1 pass reception, 1 punt return).
Most Points After Touchdown, Season — 66, Uwe von Schamann, Miami Dolphins, 1984.
Most Consecutive Points After Touchdown — 234, Tommy Davis, San Francisco 49ers, 1959-1969.
Most Field Goals, Game — 7, Jim Bakken, St. Louis Cardinals vs. Pittsburgh Steelers, Sept. 24, 1967; Rich Karlis, Minn. Vikings vs. L.A. Rams, Nov. 5, 1989.
Most Field Goals, Season — 35, Ali Haji-Sheikh, N.Y. Giants, 1983.
Most Field Goals Attempted, Season — 49, Bruce Gossett, Los Angeles Rams, 1966; Curt Knight, Washington Redskins, 1971.
Most Field Goals Attempted, Game — 9, Jim Bakken, St. Louis Cardinals vs. Pittsburgh Steelers, Sept. 24, 1967 (7 successful).
Most Consecutive Field Goals — 24, Kevin Butler, Chicago Bears, 1988-1989.
Most Consecutive Games, Field Goal — 31, Fred Cox, Minnesota Vikings, 1968-1970.
Longest Field Goal — 63 yds., Tom Dempsey, New Orleans Saints vs. Detroit Lions, Nov. 8, 1970.
Highest Field Goal Completion Percentage, Season (20 attempts) — 95.24 Mark Moseley, Washington Redskins, 1982; Eddie Murray, Detroit Lions, 1988 & 1989 (20 FG's in 21 attempts).

Pass Interceptions

Most Passes Had Intercepted, Game — 8, Jim Hardy, Chicago Cardinals vs. Philadelphia Eagles, Sept. 24, 1950 (39 attempts)
Most Passes Had Intercepted, Season — 42, George Blanda, Houston Oilers, 1962 (418 attempts).
Most Passes Had Intercepted, Career — 277, George Blanda, Chicago Bears, 1949-1958; Houston Oilers, 1960-1966; Oakland Raiders, 1967-1975 (4,000 attempts).
Most Consecutive Passes Attempted Without Interception — 308, Bernie Kosar, Cleveland Browns, 1990-1991.
Most Interceptions By, Season — 14, Dick Lane, Los Angeles Rams, 1952.
Most Interceptions By, Career — 81, Paul Krause, Washington Redskins, 1964-67; Minnesota Vikings, 1968-79.
Most Consecutive Games, Passes Intercepted By — 8, Tom Morrow, Oakland Raiders, 1962 (4), 1963 (4).

Punting

Most Punts, Game — 15, John Teltschick, Philadelphia Eagles vs. N.Y. Giants, Dec. 6, 1987.
Most Punts, Career — 1,154, Dave Jennings, N.Y. Giants, 1974-1984; N.Y. Jets, 1985-1987.
Most Punts, Season — 114, Bob Parsons, Chicago Bears, 1981.
Highest Punting Average, Season (20 punts) — 51.40, Sam Baugh, Washington Redskins, 1940 (35 punts).
Longest Punt — 98 yds., Steve O'Neal, New York Jets vs. Denver Broncos, Sept. 21, 1969.

Kickoff Returns

Most Yardage Returning Kickoffs, Career — 6,922, Ron Smith, Chicago Bears, 1965; Atlanta Falcons, 1966-67; Los Angeles Rams, 1968-69; Chicago Bears, 1970-72; San Diego Chargers, 1973; Oakland Raiders, 1974.
Most Yardage Returning Kickoffs, Season — 1,345, Buster Rhymes, Minnesota Vikings, 1985.
Most Yardage Returning Kickoffs, Game — 294, Wally Triplett, Detroit Lions vs. Los Angeles Rams, Oct. 29, 1950 (4 returns).
Most Touchdowns Scored via Kickoff Returns, Career — 6, Ollie Matson, Chicago Cardinals, 1952 (2), 1954, 1956, 1958 (2); Gale Sayers, Chicago Bears, 1965, 1966 (2), 1967 (3); Travis Williams, Green Bay Packers, 1967 (4), 1969; Los Angeles Rams, 1971.
Most Touchdowns Scored via Kickoff Returns, Game — 2, Tim Brown, Philadelphia Eagles vs. Dallas Cowboys, Nov. 6, 1966; Travis Williams, Green Bay Packers vs. Cleveland Browns, Nov. 12, 1967; Ron Brown, Los Angeles Rams vs. Green Bay Packers, Nov. 24, 1985.
Most Kickoff Returns, Career — 275, Ron Smith, Chicago Bears, 1965; Atlanta Falcons, 1966-67; Los Angeles Rams, 1968-69; Chicago Bears, 1970-72; San Diego Chargers, 1973; Oakland Raiders, 1974.
Most Kickoff Returns, Season — 60, Drew Hill, Los Angeles Rams, 1981.
Longest Kickoff Return — 106 yds., Al Carmichael, Green Bay Packers vs. Chicago Bears, October 7, 1956; Noland Smith, Kansas City vs. Denver, Dec. 17, 1967; Roy Green, St. Louis Cardinals vs. Dallas Cowboys, Oct. 21, 1979 (all scored TD).

Punt Returns

Most Yardage Returning Punts, Career — 3,317, Billy Johnson, Houston, 1974-80, Atlanta, 1982-87, Washington, 1988.
Most Yardage Returning Punts, Season — 692, Fulton Walker, Miami-L.A. Raiders, 1985.
Most Yardage Returning Punts, Game — 207, Leroy Irvin, Los Angeles Rams vs. Atlanta Falcons, Oct. 11, 1981.
Most Touchdowns Scored via Punt Returns, Career — 8, Jack Christiansen, Detroit Lions, 1951-1958; Rick Upchurch, Denver Broncos, 1975-83.
Most Punt Returns, Career — 282, Billy Johnson, Houston Oilers, 1974-1980; Atlanta Falcons, 1982-1987, Washington, 1988.
Most Punt Returns, Season — 70, Danny Reece, Tampa Bay Buccaneers, 1979.

Miscellaneous Records

Most Fumbles, Season — 18, Dave Krieg, Seattle Seahawks, 1989; Warren Moon, Houston Oilers, 1990.
Most Fumbles, Game — 7, Len Dawson, Kansas City Chiefs vs. San Diego Chargers, Nov. 15, 1964.
Most Sacks, Career—121.5, Lawrence Taylor, N.Y. Giants, 1982-91.
Most Sacks, Season—22, Mark Gastineau, N.Y. Jets, 1984.
Most Seasons, Active Player — 26, George Blanda, Chicago Bears, 1949-1958; Houston Oilers, 1960-1966 and Oakland, 67-75.
Most Consecutive Games Played, Career — 282, Jim Marshall, Cleveland Browns, 1960; Minnesota Vikings, 1961-1979.

World Almanac/Bert Bell Memorial Trophy Winners

The World Almanac's Bert Bell Memorial Trophy, named after the former NFL commissioner, is awarded annually to the outstanding NFL rookie as chosen by a panel of sports experts on behalf of *The World Almanac*, its co-sponsoring newspapers, and its publisher, Pharos Books.

1964	Charlie Taylor, Washington, WR
1965	Gale Sayers, Chicago, RB
1966	Tommy Nobis, Atlanta, LB
1967	Mel Farr, Detroit, RB
1968	Earl McCullouch, Detroit, WR
1969	Calvin Hill, Dallas, RB
1970	Raymond Chester, Oakland, TE
1971	AFC: Jim Plunkett, New England, QB
	NFC: John Brockington, Green Bay, RB
1972	AFC: Franco Harris, Pittsburgh, RB
	NFC: Willie Buchanon, Green Bay, DB
1973	AFC: Boobie Clark, Cincinnati, RB
	NFC: Chuck Foreman, Minnesota, RB
1974	Don Woods, San Diego, RB
1975	AFC: Robert Brazile, Houston, LB
	NFC: Steve Bartkowski, Atlanta, QB
1976	AFC: Mike Haynes, New England, CB
	NFC: Sammy White, Minnesota, WR
1977	Tony Dorsett, Dallas, RB
1978	Earl Campbell, Houston, RB
1979	Ottis Anderson, St. Louis, RB
1980	Billy Sims, Detroit, RB
1981	Lawrence Taylor, N.Y. Giants, LB
1982	Marcus Allen, L.A. Raiders, RB
1983	Eric Dickerson, L.A. Rams, RB
1984	Louis Lipps, Pittsburgh, WR
1985	Eddie Brown, Cincinnati, WR
1986	Rueben Mayes, New Orleans, RB
1987	Bo Jackson, L.A. Raiders, RB
1988	John Stephens, New England, RB
1989	Barry Sanders, Detroit, RB
1990	Eric Green, Pittsburgh, TE
1991	Mike Croel, Denver, LB

World Almanac Jim Thorpe Trophy Winners

The World Almanac's Jim Thorpe Trophy goes to the most valuable player as chosen by the NFL Players Association in 1991 on behalf of *The World Almanac*, its co-sponsoring newspapers, and its publisher, Pharos Books.

1955	Harlon Hill, Chicago Bears
1956	Frank Gifford, N.Y. Giants
1957	John Unitas, Baltimore Colts
1958	Jim Brown, Cleveland Browns
1959	Charley Conerly, N.Y. Giants
1960	Norm Van Brocklin, Philadelphia Eagles
1961	Y.A. Tittle, N.Y. Giants
1962	Jim Taylor, Green Bay Packers
1963	Jim Brown, Cleveland Browns; Y.A. Tittle, N.Y. Giants
1964	Lenny Moore, Baltimore Colts
1965	Jim Brown, Cleveland Browns
1966	Bart Starr, Green Bay Packers
1967	John Unitas, Baltimore Colts
1968	Earl Morrall, Baltimore Colts
1969	Roman Gabriel, Los Angeles Rams
1970	John Brodie, San Francisco 49ers
1971	Bob Griese, Miami Dolphins
1972	Larry Brown, Washington Redskins
1973	O.J. Simpson, Buffalo Bills
1974	Ken Stabler, Oakland Raiders
1975	Fran Tarkenton, Minnesota Vikings
1976	Bert Jones, Baltimore Colts
1977	Walter Payton, Chicago Bears
1978	Earl Campbell, Houston Oilers
1979	Earl Campbell, Houston Oilers
1980	Earl Campbell, Houston Oilers
1981	Ken Anderson, Cincinnati Bengals
1982	Dan Fouts, San Diego Chargers
1983	Joe Theismann, Washington Redskins
1984	Dan Marino, Miami Dolphins
1985	Walter Payton, Chicago Bears
1986	Phil Simms, N.Y. Giants
1987	Jerry Rice, San Francisco
1988	Roger Craig, San Francisco
1989	Joe Montana, San Francisco
1990	Warren Moon, Houston
1991	Thurman Thomas, Buffalo

Canadian Football League Championships (Grey Cup)

1956	Edmonton Eskimos 50, Montreal Alouettes 27
1957	Hamilton Tiger-Cats 32, Winnipeg Blue Bombers 7
1958	Winnipeg Blue Bombers 35, Hamilton Tiger-Cats 28
1959	Winnipeg Blue Bombers 21, Hamilton Tiger-Cats 7
1960	Ottawa Rough Riders 16, Edmonton Eskimos 6
1961	Winnipeg Blue Bombers 21, Hamilton Tiger-Cats 14
1962	Winnipeg Blue Bombers 28, Hamilton Tiger-Cats 27
1963	Hamilton Tiger-Cats 21, British Columbia Lions 10
1964	British Columbia Lions 34, Hamilton Tiger-Cats 24
1965	Hamilton Tiger-Cats 22, Winnipeg Blue Bombers 16
1966	Saskatchewan Roughriders 29, Ottawa Rough Riders 14
1967	Hamilton Tiger-Cats 24, Saskatchewan Roughriders 1
1968	Ottawa Rough Riders 24, Calgary Stampeders 21
1969	Ottawa Rough Riders 29, Saskatchewan Roughriders 11
1970	Montreal Alouettes 23, Calgary Stampeders 10
1971	Calgary Stampeders 14, Toronto Argonauts 11
1972	Hamilton Tiger-Cats 13, Saskatchewan Roughriders 10
1973	Ottawa Rough Riders 22, Edmonton Eskimos 18
1974	Montreal Alouettes 20, Edmonton Eskimos 7
1975	Edmonton Eskimos 9, Montreal Alouettes 8
1976	Ottawa Rough Riders 23, Saskatchewan Roughriders 20
1977	Montreal Alouettes 41, Edmonton Eskimos 6
1978	Edmonton Eskimos 20, Montreal Alouettes 13
1979	Edmonton Eskimos 17, Montreal Alouettes 9
1980	Edmonton Eskimos 48, Hamilton Tiger-Cats 10
1981	Edmonton Eskimos 26, Ottawa Rough Riders 23
1982	Edmonton Eskimos 32, Toronto Argonauts 16
1983	Toronto Argonauts 18, B.C. Lions 17
1984	Winnipeg Blue Bombers 47, Hamilton Tiger-Cats 17
1985	B.C. Lions 37, Hamilton Tiger-Cats 24
1986	Hamilton Tiger-Cats 39, Edmonton Eskimos 15
1987	Edmonton Eskimos 38, Toronto Argonauts 36
1988	Winnipeg Blue Bombers 22, B.C. Lions 21
1989	Saskatchewan Roughriders 43, Hamilton Tiger-Cats 40
1990	Winnipeg Blue Bombers 50, Edmonton Eskimos 11
1991	Toronto Argonauts 36, Calgary Stampeders 21

World Bowl in 1992

The second World Bowl, the championship game of the World League was won by the Sacramento Surge, 21-17, over the Orlando Thunder in Olympia Stadium in Montreal on June 7. The second season of the World League (previously called the World League of American Football) continued to have problems attracting U.S. fans.

COLLEGE FOOTBALL

Annual Results of Major Bowl Games

(Note: Dates indicate the year that the game was played.)

Rose Bowl, Pasadena

1902 Michigan 49, Stanford 0
1916 Wash. State 14, Brown 0
1917 Oregon 14, Pennsylvania 0
1918-19 Service teams
1920 Harvard 7, Oregon 6
1921 California 28, Ohio State 0
1922 Wash. & Jeff. 0, California 0
1923 So. California 14, Penn State 3
1924 Navy 14, Washington 14
1925 Notre Dame 27, Stanford 10
1926 Alabama 20, Washington 19
1927 Alabama 7, Stanford 7
1928 Stanford 7, Pittsburgh 6
1929 Georgia Tech 8, California 7
1930 So. California 47, Pittsburgh 14
1931 Alabama 24, Wash. State 0
1932 So. California 21, Tulane 12
1933 So. California 35, Pittsburgh 0
1934 Columbia 7, Stanford 0
1935 Alabama 29, Stanford 13
1936 Stanford 7, So. Methodist 0
1937 Pittsburgh 21, Washington 0
1938 California 13, Alabama 0
1939 So. California 7, Duke 3
1940 So. California 14, Tennessee 0
1941 Stanford 21, Nebraska 13
1942 Oregon St. 20, Duke 16 (at Durham)
1943 Georgia 9, UCLA 0
1944 So. California 29, Washington 0
1945 So. California 25, Tennessee 0
1946 Alabama 34, So. California 14
1947 Illinois 45, UCLA 14
1948 Michigan 49, So. California 0
1949 Northwestern 20, California 14
1950 Ohio State 17, California 14
1951 Michigan 14, California 6
1952 Illinois 40, Stanford 7
1953 So. California 7, Wisconsin 0
1954 Mich. State 28, UCLA 20
1955 Ohio State 20, So. California 7
1956 Mich. State 17, UCLA 14
1957 Iowa 35, Oregon St. 19
1958 Ohio State 10, Oregon 7
1959 Iowa 38, California 12
1960 Washington 44, Wisconsin 8
1961 Washington 17, Minnesota 7
1962 Minnesota 21, UCLA 3
1963 So. California 42, Wisconsin 37
1964 Illinois 17, Washington 7
1965 Michigan 34, Oregon St. 7
1966 UCLA 14, Mich. State 12
1967 Purdue 14, So. California 13
1968 Southern Cal. 14, Indiana 3
1969 Ohio State 27, Southern Cal 16
1970 Southern Cal 10, Michigan 3
1971 Stanford 27, Ohio State 17
1972 Stanford 13, Michigan 12
1973 So. California 42, Ohio State 17
1974 Ohio State 42, So. California 21
1975 So. California 18, Ohio State 17
1976 UCLA 23, Ohio State 10
1977 So. California 14, Michigan 6
1978 Washington 27, Michigan 20
1979 So. California 17, Michigan 10
1980 So. California 17, Ohio State 16
1981 Michigan 23, Washington 6
1982 Washington 28, Iowa 0
1983 UCLA 24, Michigan 14
1984 UCLA 45, Illinois 9
1985 So. California 20, Ohio State 17
1986 UCLA 45, Iowa 28
1987 Arizona St. 22, Michigan 15
1988 Mich. State 20, Southern Cal. 17
1989 Michigan 22, Southern Cal. 14
1990 Southern Cal. 17, Michigan 10
1991 Washington 46, Iowa 34
1992 Washington 34, Michigan 14

Orange Bowl, Miami

1935 Bucknell 26, Miami (Fla.) 0
1936 Catholic U. 20, Mississippi 19
1937 Duquesne 13, Miss. State 12
1938 Auburn 6, Mich. State 0
1939 Tennessee 17, Oklahoma 0
1940 Georgia Tech 21, Missouri 7
1941 Miss. State 14, Georgetown 7
1942 Georgia 40, TCU 26
1943 Alabama 37, Boston Col. 21
1944 LSU 19, Texas A&M 14
1945 Tulsa 26, Georgia Tech 12
1946 Miami (Fla.) 13, Holy Cross 6
1947 Rice 8, Tennessee 0
1948 Georgia Tech 20, Kansas 14
1949 Texas 41, Georgia 28
1950 Santa Clara 21, Kentucky 13
1951 Clemson 15, Miami (Fla.) 14
1952 Georgia Tech 17, Baylor 14
1953 Alabama 61, Syracuse 6
1954 Oklahoma 7, Maryland 0
1955 Duke 34, Nebraska 7
1956 Oklahoma 20, Maryland 6
1957 Colorado 27, Clemson 21
1958 Oklahoma 48, Duke 21
1959 Oklahoma 21, Syracuse 6
1960 Georgia 14, Missouri 0
1961 Missouri 21, Navy 14
1962 LSU 25, Colorado 7
1963 Alabama 17, Oklahoma 0
1964 Nebraska 13, Auburn 7
1965 Texas 21, Alabama 17
1966 Alabama 39, Nebraska 28
1967 Florida 27, Georgia Tech 12
1968 Oklahoma 26, Tennessee 24
1969 Penn State 15, Kansas 14
1970 Penn State 10, Missouri 3
1971 Nebraska 17, Louisiana St. 12
1972 Nebraska 38, Alabama 6
1973 Nebraska 40, Notre Dame 6
1974 Penn State 16, Louisiana St. 9
1975 Notre Dame 13, Alabama 11
1976 Oklahoma 14, Michigan 6
1977 Ohio State 27, Colorado 10
1978 Arkansas 31, Oklahoma 6
1979 Oklahoma 31, Nebraska 24
1980 Oklahoma 24, Florida St. 7
1981 Oklahoma 18, Florida St. 17
1982 Clemson 22, Nebraska 15
1983 Nebraska 21, Louisiana St. 20
1984 Miami (Fla.) 31, Nebraska 30
1985 Washington 28, Oklahoma 17
1986 Oklahoma 25, Penn State 10
1987 Oklahoma 42, Arkansas 8
1988 Miami (Fla.) 20, Oklahoma 14
1989 Miami (Fla.) 23, Nebraska 3
1990 Notre Dame 21, Colorado 6
1991 Colorado 10, Notre Dame 9
1992 Miami (Fla.) 22, Nebraska 0

Sugar Bowl, New Orleans

1935 Tulane 20, Temple 14
1936 TCU 3, LSU 2
1937 Santa Clara 21, LSU 14
1938 Santa Clara 6, LSU 0
1939 TCU 15, Carnegie Tech 7
1940 Texas A&M 14, Tulane 13
1941 Boston Col. 19, Tennessee 13
1942 Fordham 2, Missouri 0
1943 Tennessee 14, Tulsa 7
1944 Georgia Tech 20, Tulsa 18
1945 Duke 29, Alabama 26
1946 Oklahoma A&M 33, St. Mary's 13
1947 Georgia 20, No. Carolina 10
1948 Texas 27, Alabama 7
1949 Oklahoma 14, No. Carolina 6
1950 Oklahoma 35, LSU 0
1951 Kentucky 13, Oklahoma 7
1952 Maryland 28, Tennessee 13
1953 Georgia Tech. 24, Mississippi 7
1954 Georgia Tech 42, West Virginia 19
1955 Navy 21, Mississippi 0
1956 Georgia Tech 7, Pittsburgh 0
1957 Baylor 13, Tennessee 7
1958 Mississippi 39, Texas 7
1959 LSU 7, Clemson 0
1960 Mississippi 21, LSU 0
1961 Mississippi 14, Rice 6
1962 Alabama 10, Arkansas 3
1963 Mississippi 17, Arkansas 13
1964 Alabama 12, Mississippi 7
1965 LSU 13, Syracuse 10
1966 Missouri 20, Florida 18
1967 Alabama 34, Nebraska 7
1968 LSU 20, Wyoming 13
1969 Arkansas 16, Georgia 2
1970 Mississippi 27, Arkansas 22
1971 Tennessee 34, Air Force 13
1972 Oklahoma 40, Auburn 22
*1972 (Dec.) Okla. 14, Penn State 0
1973 Notre Dame 24, Alabama 23
1974 Nebraska 13, Florida 10
1975 Alabama 13, Penn State 6
1977 (Jan.) Pittsburgh 27, Georgia 3
1978 Alabama 35, Ohio State 6
1979 Alabama 14, Penn State 7
1980 Alabama 24, Arkansas 9
1981 Georgia 17, Notre Dame 10
1982 Pittsburgh 24, Georgia 20
1983 Penn State 27, Georgia 23
1984 Auburn 9, Michigan 7
1985 Nebraska 28, Louisiana St. 10
1986 Tennessee 35, Miami (Fla.) 7
1987 Nebraska 30, Louisiana St. 15
1988 Syracuse 16, Auburn 16
1989 Florida St. 13, Auburn 7
1990 Miami 33, Alabama 25
1991 Tennessee 23, Virginia 22
1992 Notre Dame 39, Florida 28

* Penn St. awarded game by forfeit

Fiesta Bowl, Tempe

1971 Arizona St. 45, Florida St. 38
1972 Arizona St. 49, Missouri 35
1973 Arizona St. 28, Pittsburgh 7
1974 Okla. St. 16, Brigham Young 6
1975 Arizona St. 17, Nebraska 14
1976 Oklahoma 41, Wyoming 7
1977 Penn St. 42, Arizona St. 30
1978 UCLA 10, Arkansas 10
1979 Pittsburgh 16, Arizona 10
1980 Penn St. 31, Ohio St. 19
1982 (Jan.) Penn St. 26, USC 10
1983 Arizona St. 32, Oklahoma 21
1984 Ohio State 28, Pittsburgh 23
1985 UCLA 39, Miami 37
1986 Michigan 27, Nebraska 23
1987 Penn St. 14, Miami (Fla.) 10
1988 Florida St. 31, Nebraska 28
1989 Notre Dame 34, W. Virginia 21
1990 Florida St. 41, Nebraska 17
1991 Louisville 34, Alabama 7
1992 Penn St. 42, Tennessee 17

Hall of Fame Bowl, Tampa

1986 (Dec.) Boston Coll. 27, Georgia 24
1988 (Jan.) Michigan 28, Alabama 24
1989 Syracuse 23, LSU 10
1990 Auburn 31, Ohio St. 14
1991 Clemson 30, Illinois 0
1992 Syracuse 24, Ohio St. 17

Cotton Bowl, Dallas

1937 TCU 16, Marquette 6
1938 Rice 28, Colorado 14
1939 St. Mary's 20, Texas Tech 13
1940 Clemson 6, Boston Col. 3
1941 Texas A&M 13, Fordham 12
1942 Alabama 29, Texas A&M 21
1943 Texas 14, Georgia Tech 7
1944 Randolph Field 7, Texas 7
1945 Oklahoma A&M 34, TCU 0
1946 Texas 40, Missouri 27
1947 Arkansas 0, LSU 0
1948 So. Methodist 13, Penn State 13
1949 So. Methodist 21, Oregon 13
1950 Rice 27, No. Carolina 13
1951 Tennessee 20, Texas 14
1952 Kentucky 20, TCU 7
1953 Texas 16, Tennessee 0
1954 Rice 28, Alabama 6
1955 Georgia Tech 14, Arkansas 6
1956 Mississippi 14, TCU 13
1957 TCU 28, Syracuse 27
1958 Navy 20, Rice 7
1959 TCU 0, Air Force 0
1960 Syracuse 23, Texas 14
1961 Duke 7, Arkansas 6
1962 Texas 12, Mississippi 7
1963 LSU 13, Texas 0
1964 Texas 28, Navy 6
1965 Arkansas 10, Nebraska 7
1966 LSU 14, Arkansas 7
1967 Georgia 24, So. Methodist 9
1968 Texas A&M 20, Alabama 16
1969 Texas 36, Tennessee 13
1970 Texas 21, Notre Dame 17
1971 Notre Dame 24, Texas 11
1972 Penn State 30, Texas 6
1973 Texas 17, Alabama 13
1974 Nebraska 19, Texas 3
1975 Penn State 41, Baylor 20
1976 Arkansas 31, Georgia 10
1977 Houston 30, Maryland 21
1978 Notre Dame 38, Texas 10
1979 Notre Dame 35, Houston 34
1980 Houston 17, Nebraska 14
1981 Alabama 30, Baylor 2
1982 Texas 14, Alabama 12
1983 SMU 7, Pittsburgh 3
1984 Georgia 10, Texas 9
1985 Boston Coll. 45, Houston 28
1986 Texas A&M 36, Auburn 16
1987 Ohio St. 28, Texas A&M 12
1988 Texas A&M 35, Notre Dame 10
1989 UCLA 17, Arkansas 3
1990 Tennessee 31, Arkansas 27
1991 Miami (Fla.) 46, Texas 3
1992 Florida St. 10, Texas A&M 2

John Hancock Bowl, El Paso (Sun Bowl until 1989)

1936 Hardin Simmons 14, New Mex. St. 14
1937 Hardin-Simmons 34, Texas Mines 6
1938 West Virginia 7, Texas Tech 6
1939 Utah 26, New Mexico 0
1940 Catholic U. 0, Arizona St. 0
1941 Western Reserve 26, Arizona St. 13
1942 Tulsa 6, Texas Tech 0
1943 2d Air Force 13, Hardin-Simmons 7
1944 Southwestern (Tex.) 7, New Mexico 0
1945 Southwestern (Tex.) 35, U. of Mex. 0
1946 New Mexico 34, Denver 24
1947 Cincinnati 18, Virginia Tech 6
1948 Miami (O.) 13, Texas Tech 12
1949 West Virginia 21, Texas Mines 12
1950 Texas Western 33, Georgetown 20
1951 West Texas St. 14, Cincinnati 13
1952 Texas Tech 25, Col. Pacific 14
1953 Col. Pacific 26, Miss. Southern 7
1954 Texas Western 37, Miss. Southern 14
1955 Texas Western 47, Florida St. 20
1956 Wyoming 21, Texas Tech 14
1957 Geo. Washington 13, Tex. Western 0
1958 Louisville 34, Drake 20
1959 Wyoming 14, Hardin-Simmons 6
1960 New Mexico St. 28, No. Texas St. 8
1961 New Mexico St. 20, Utah State 13
1962 Villanova 17, Wichita 9
1963 West Texas St. 15, Ohio U. 14
1964 Oregon 21, So. Methodist 14
1965 Georgia 7, Texas Tech 0
1966 Texas Western 13, TCU 12
1967 Wyoming 28, Florida St. 20
1968 UTex El Paso 14, Mississippi 7
1969 Auburn 34, Arizona 10
1969 (Dec.) Nebraska 45, Georgia 6
1970 Georgia Tech. 17, Texas Tech. 9
1971 LSU 33, Iowa State 15
1972 North Carolina 32, Texas Tech 28
1973 Missouri 34, Auburn 17
1974 Mississippi St. 26, No. Carolina 24
1975 Pittsburgh 33, Kansas 19
1977 (Jan.) Texas A&M 37, Florida 14
1977 (Dec.) Stanford 24, Louisiana St. 14
1978 Texas 42, Maryland 0
1979 Washington 14, Texas 7
1980 Nebraska 31, Mississippi St. 17
1981 Oklahoma 40, Houston 14
1982 North Carolina 26, Texas 10
1983 Alabama 28, SMU 7
1984 Maryland 28, Tennessee 27
1985 Georgia 13, Arizona 13
1986 Alabama 28, Washington 6
1987 Oklahoma St. 35, West Virginia 33
1988 Alabama 29, Army 28
1989 Pittsburgh 31, Texas A&M 28
1990 Michigan St. 17, USC 16
1991 UCLA 6, Illinois 3

Gator Bowl, Jacksonville

1946 Wake Forest 26, So. Carolina 14
1947 Oklahoma 34, N.C. State 13
1948 Maryland 20, Georgia 20
1949 Clemson 24, Missouri 23
1950 Maryland 20, Missouri 7
1951 Wyoming 20, Wash. & Lee 7
1952 Miami (Fla.) 14, Clemson 0
1953 Florida 14, Tulsa 13
1954 Texas Tech 35, Auburn 13
1955 Auburn 33, Baylor 13
1956 Vanderbilt 25, Auburn 13
1957 Georgia Tech 21, Pittsburgh 14
1958 Tennessee 3, Texas A&M 0
1959 Mississippi 7, Florida 3
1960 Arkansas 14, Georgia Tech 7
1961 Florida 13, Baylor 12
1962 Penn State 30, Georgia Tech 15
1963 Florida 17, Penn State 7
1964 No. Carolina 35, Air Force 0
1965 Florida St. 36, Oklahoma 19
1966 Georgia Tech 31, Texas Tech 21
1967 Tennessee 18, Syracuse 12
1968 Penn State 17, Florida St. 17
1969 Missouri 35, Alabama 10
1969 (Dec.) Florida 14, Tenn. 13
1971 (Jan.) Auburn 35, Mississippi 28
1972 Georgia 7, N. Carolina 3
1973 Auburn 24, Colorado 3
1973 (Dec.) Tex. Tech. 28, Tenn. 19
1974 Auburn 27, Texas 3
1975 Maryland 13, Florida 0
1976 Notre Dame 20, Penn State 9
1977 Pittsburgh 34, Clemson 3
1978 Clemson 17, Ohio State 15
1979 No. Carolina 17, Michigan 15
1980 Pittsburgh 37, So. Carolina 9
1981 No. Carolina 31, Arkansas 27
1982 Florida St. 31, West Va. 12
1983 Florida 14, Iowa 6
1984 Oklahoma St. 21, So. Carolina 14
1985 Florida St. 34, Oklahoma St. 23
1986 Clemson 27, Stanford 21
1987 LSU 30, So. Carolina 13
1989 (Jan.) Georgia 34, Michigan St. 27
1989 (Dec.) Clemson 27, W. Va. 7
1991 (Jan.) Michigan 35, Mississippi 3
1991 (Dec.) Oklahoma 48, Virginia 14

Liberty Bowl, Memphis

1959 Penn State 7, Alabama 0
1960 Penn State 41, Oregon 12
1961 Syracuse 15, Miami 14
1962 Oregon State 6, Villanova 0
1963 Miss. State 16, N.C. State 12
1964 Utah 32, West Virginia 6
1965 Mississippi 13, Auburn 7
1966 Miami (Fla.) 14, Va. Tech 7
1967 N.C. State 14, Georgia 7
1968 Mississippi 34, Va. Tech 17
1969 Colorado 47, Alabama 33
1970 Tulane 17, Colorado 3
1971 Tennessee 14, Arkansas 13
1972 Georgia Tech 31, Iowa State 30
1973 No. Carolina St. 31, Kansas 18
1974 Tennessee 7, Maryland 3
1975 USC 20, Texas A&M 0
1976 Alabama 36, UCLA 6
1977 Nebraska 21, N. Carolina 17
1978 Missouri 20, Louisiana St. 15
1979 Penn St. 9, Tulane 6
1980 Purdue 28, Missouri 25
1981 Ohio State 31, Navy 28
1982 Alabama 21, Illinois 15
1983 Notre Dame 19, Boston Coll. 18
1984 Auburn 21, Arkansas 15
1985 Baylor 21, Louisiana St. 7
1986 Tennessee 21, Minnesota 14
1987 Georgia 20, Arkansas 17
1988 Indiana 34, S. Carolina 10
1989 Mississippi 42, Air Force 29
1990 Air Force 23, Ohio State 11
1991 Air Force 38, Mississippi St. 15

Freedom Bowl, Anaheim

1984 Iowa 55, Texas 17
1985 Washington 20, Colorado 17
1986 UCLA 31, Brigham Young 10
1987 Arizona St. 33, Air Force 28
1988 Brigham Young 20, Colorado 17
1989 Washington 34, Florida 7
1990 Colorado St. 32, Oregon 31
1991 Tulsa 28, San Diego St. 17

Copper Bowl, Tucson

1989 Arizona 17, N.C. St. 10
1990 California 17, Wyoming 15
1991 Indiana 24, Baylor 0

Independence Bowl, Shreveport

1976 McNeese St. 20, Tulsa 16
1977 Louisiana Tech 24, Louisville 14
1978 E. Carolina 35, La. Tech 13
1979 Syracuse 31, McNeese St. 7
1980 So. Miss. 16, McNeese St. 14
1981 Texas A&M 33, Oklahoma St. 16
1982 Wisconsin 14, Kansas St. 3
1983 Air Force 9, Mississippi 3
1984 Air Force 23, Virginia Tech 7
1985 Minnesota 20, Clemson 13
1986 Mississippi 20, Texas Tech 17
1987 Washington 24, Tulane 12
1988 S. Mississippi 38, UTEP 18
1989 Oregon 27, Tulsa 24
1990 Louisiana Tech 34, Maryland 34
1991 Georgia 24, Arkansas 15

Citrus Bowl, Orlando

1947 Catawba 31, Maryville 6
1948 Catawba 7, Marshall 0
1949 Murray State 21, Sul Ross St. 21
1950 St. Vincent 7, Emory & Henry 6
1951 Morris Harvey 35, Emory & Henry 14
1952 Stetson 35, Arkansas St. 20
1953 East Texas St. 33, Tenn. Tech 0
1954 East Texas St. 7, Arkansas St. 7
1955 Neb.-Omaha 7, Eastern Kentucky 6
1956 Juniata 6, Missouri Valley 6
1957 West Texas St. 20, So. Miss. 13
1958 East Texas St. 10, So. Miss. 9
1958 (Dec.) East Texas St. 26, Missouri Valley 7
1960 (Jan.) Middle Tenn. 21, Presbyterian 12
1960 (Dec.) Citadel 27, Tenn. Tech 0
1961 Lamar 21, Middle Tennessee 14
1962 Houston 49, Miami (O.) 21
1963 Western Ky. 27, Coast Guard 0
1964 E. Carolina 14, Massachusetts 13
1965 East Carolina 31, Maine 0
1966 Morgan State 14, West Chester 6
1967 Tenn.-Martin 25, West Chester 8
1968 Richmond 49, Ohio U. 42
1969 Toledo 56, Davidson 33
1970 Toledo 40, William & Mary 12
1971 Toledo 28, Richmond 3
1972 Tampa 21, Kent State 18
1973 Miami (O.) 16, Florida 7
1974 Miami (O.) 21, Georgia 10
1975 Miami (O.) 20, South Carolina 7
1976 Okla. St. 49, Brigham Young 21
1977 Florida St. 40, Texas Tech 17
1978 N.C. State 30, Pittsburgh 17
1979 LSU 34, Wake Forest 10
1980 Florida 35, Maryland 20
1981 Missouri 19, Southern Miss. 17
1982 Auburn 33, Boston College 26
1983 Tennessee 30, Maryland 23
1984 Georgia 17, Florida St. 17
1985 Ohio St. 10, Brigham Young 7
1987 (Jan.) Auburn 16, USC 7
1988 Clemson 35, Penn St. 10
1989 Clemson 13, Oklahoma 6
1990 Illinois 31, Virginia 21
1991 Georgia Tech 45, Nebraska 21
1992 California 37, Clemson 13

Peach Bowl, Atlanta

1968 LSU 31, Florida St. 27
1969 West Virginia 14, S. Carolina 3
1970 Arizona St. 48, N. Carolina 26
1971 Mississippi 41, Georgia Tech. 18
1972 N. Carolina St. 49, W. Va. 13
1973 Georgia 17, Maryland 16
1974 Vanderbilt 6, Texas Tech. 6
1975 W. Virginia 13, No. Carolina St. 10
1976 Kentucky 21, North Carolina 0
1977 N. Carolina St. 24, Iowa St. 14
1978 Purdue 41, Georgia Tech. 21
1979 Baylor 24, Clemson 18
1981 (Jan.) Miami 20, Virginia Tech. 10
1981 (Dec.) West Virginia 26, Florida 6
1982 Iowa 28, Tennessee 22
1983 Florida St. 28, North Carolina 3
1984 Virginia 27, Purdue 22
1985 Army 31, Illinois 29
1986 Va. Tech 25, N.C. State 24
1988 (Jan.) Tennessee 28, Indiana 22
1988 (Dec.) N.C. State 28, Iowa 23
1989 Syracuse 19, Georgia 18
1990 Auburn 27, Indiana 23
1992 (Jan.) E. Carolina 37, N.C. State 34

Holiday Bowl, San Diego

1978 Navy 23, Brigham Young 16
1979 Indiana 38, Brigham Young 37
1980 Brigham Young 46, SMU 45
1981 Brigham Young 38, Wash. St. 36
1982 Ohio State 47, Brigham Young 17
1983 Brigham Young 21, Missouri 17
1984 Brigham Young 24, Michigan 17
1985 Arkansas 18, Arizona St. 17
1986 Iowa 39, San Diego St. 38
1987 Iowa 20, Wyoming 19
1988 Oklahoma St. 62, Wyoming 14
1989 Penn St. 50, Brigham Young 39
1990 Texas A&M 65, Brigham Young 14
1991 Iowa 13, Brigham Young 13

Aloha Bowl, Honolulu

1982 Washington 21, Maryland 20
1983 Penn State 13, Washington 10
1984 SMU 27, Notre Dame 20
1985 Alabama 24, USC 3
1986 Arizona 30, North Carolina 21
1987 UCLA 20, Florida 16
1988 Washington St. 24, Houston 22
1989 Michigan St. 33, Hawaii 13
1990 Syracuse 28, Arizona 0
1991 Georgia Tech 18, Stanford 17

California Raisin Bowl, Fresno

1981 Toledo 27, San Jose St. 25
1982 Fresno St. 29, Bowling Green 28
1983 N. Illinois 20, Cal. State Fullerton 13
1984 Nevada-Las Vegas 30, Toledo 13
1985 Fresno St. 51, Bowling Green 7
1986 San Jose St. 37, Miami (Oh.) 7
1987 E. Michigan 30, San Jose St. 27
1988 Fresno St. 35, W. Michigan 30
1989 Fresno St. 27, Ball St. 6
1990 San Jose St. 48, Central Mich. 24
1991 Bowling Green 28, Fresno 21

Blockbuster Bowl, Miami

1990 Florida St. 24, Penn St. 17
1991 Alabama 30, Colorado 25

World Almanac All-America Team in 1991

The 1991 All-America football team was chosen by a sports panel on behalf of *The World Almanac* and its co-sponsoring newspapers.

Offense

Wide receiver—Desmond Howard, Michigan
Wide receiver—Mario Bailey, Washington
Tight end—Derek Brown, Notre Dame
Tackle—Bob Whitfield, Stanford
Tackle—Greg Skrepenak, Michigan
Guard—Jeb Flesch, Clemson
Guard—Mirko Jurkovic, Notre Dame
Center—Jay Leeuwenburg, Colorado
Quarterback—Ty Detmer, BYU
Running back—Russell White, California
Running back—Vaughn Dunbar, Indiana
Placekicker—Carlos Huerta, Miami (Fla.)

Defense

Lineman—Steve Emtman, Washington
Lineman—Brad Culpepper, Florida
Lineman—Robert Stewart, Alabama
Linebacker—Marco Coleman, Georgia Tech
Linebacker—Robert Jones, E. Carolina
Linebacker—Quentin Coryatt, Texas A&M
Linebacker—Marvin Jones, Florida St.
Back—Terrell Buckley, Florida St.
Back—Troy Vincent, Wisconsin
Back—Dale Carter, Tennessee
Back—Darren Perry, Penn St.
Punter—Mark Bounds, Texas Tech

College Division I Football Teams

Team	Nickname	Team colors	Conference	Coach	1991 record (W-L-T)
Air Force	Falcons	Blue & silver	Western Athletic	Fisher De Berry	10-3-0
Akron	Zips	Blue & Gold	Mid-American	Gerry Faust	5-6-0
Alabama	Crimson Tide	Crimson & white	Southeastern	Gene Stallings	11-1-0
Alabama State	Hornets	Black & gold	Southwestern	Houston Markham	11-0-1
Alcorn State	Braves	Purple & gold	Southwestern	Cardell Jones	7-2-1
Appalachian State	Mountaineers	Black & gold	Southern	Jerry Moore	8-4-0
Arizona	Wildcats	Red & blue	Pacific Ten	Dick Tomey	4-7-0
Arizona State	Sun Devils	Maroon & gold	Pacific Ten	Bruce Snyder	6-5-0
Arkansas	Razorbacks	Cardinal & white	Southeastern	Jack Crowe	6-6-0
Arkansas State	Indians	Scarlet & black	Independent	Ray Perkins	1-10-0
Army	Cadets	Black, gold, gray	Independent	Bob Sutton	4-7-0
Auburn	Tigers	Orange & blue	Southeastern	Pat Dye	5-6-0
Austin Peay State	Governors	Red & white	Ohio Valley	Roy Gregory	5-6-0
Ball State	Cardinals	Cardinal & white	Mid-American	Paul Schudel	6-5-0
Baylor	Bears	Green & gold	Southwest	Grant Teaff	8-4-0
Bethune-Cookman	Wildcats	Maroon & gold	Mid-Eastern	Sylvester Collins	5-5-0
Boise State	Broncos	Orange & Blue	Big Sky	Skip Hall	7-4-0
Boston College	Eagles	Maroon & gold	Big East	Tom Coughlin	4-7-0
Boston Univ.	Terriers	Scarlet & white	Yankee	Dan Allen	4-7-0
Bowling Green	Falcons	Orange & brown	Mid-American	Gary Blackney	11-1-0
Brigham Young	Cougars	Royal blue & white	Western Athletic	LaVell Edwards	8-3-2
Brown	Bears	Brown, cardinal, white	Ivy	Mickey Kwiatowski	1-9-0
Bucknell	Bisons	Orange & blue	Patriot	Lou Maranzana	1-9-0
California	Golden Bears	Blue & gold	Pacific Ten	Keith Gilbertson	10-2-0
Central Florida	Knights	Black & gold	Independent	Gene McDowell	6-5-0
Central Michigan	Chippewas	Maroon & gold	Mid-American	Herb Deromedi	6-1-4
Cincinnati	Bearcats	Red & black	Independent	Tim Murphy	4-7-0
Citadel	Bulldogs	Blue & white	Southern	Charles Taaffe	7-4-0
Clemson	Tigers	Purple & orange	Atlantic Coast	Ken Hatfield	9-2-1
Colgate	Red Raiders	Maroon	Patriot	Mike Foley	4-7-0
Colorado State	Rams	Green & gold	Western Athletic	Earle Bruce	3-8-0
Colorado	Buffaloes	Silver, gold & black	Big Eight	Bill McCartney	8-3-1
Columbia	Lions	Blue & white	Ivy	Ray Tellier	1-9-0
Connecticut	Huskies	Blue & white	Yankee	Tom Jackson	3-8-0
Cornell	Big Red	Carnelian & white	Ivy	Jim Hofher	5-5-0
Dartmouth	Big Green	Dartmouth green & white	Ivy	Jim Lyons	7-2-1
Delaware	Fightin' Blue Hens	Blue & gold	Yankee	Harold Raymond	10-2-0
Delaware State	Hornets	Red & blue	Mid-Eastern	William Collick	8-3-0
Duke	Blue Devils	Royal blue & white	Atlantic Coast	Barry Wilson	4-6-1
East Carolina	Pirates	Purple & gold	Independent	Steve Logan	11-1-0
East Tennessee St.	Buccaneers	Blue & gold	Southern	Mike Cavan	1-10-0
Eastern Illinois	Panthers	Blue & Gray	Gateway	Bob Spoo	4-7-0
Eastern Kentucky	Colonels	Maroon & white	Ohio Valley	Roy Kidd	12-2-0
Eastern Michigan	Hurons	Green & white	Mid-American	Jim Harkema	3-7-1
Eastern Washington	Eagles	Red & white	Big Sky	Dick Zornes	5-6-0
Florida	Gators	Orange & blue	Southeastern	Steve Spurrier	10-2-0
Florida A&M	Rattlers	Orange & green	Mid-Eastern	Ken Riley	6-5-0
Florida State	Seminoles	Garnet & gold	Atlantic Coast	Bobby Bowden	11-2-0
Fordham	Rams	Maroon & white	Patriot	Larry Glueck	2-8-0
Fresno State	Bulldogs	Cardinal & blue	Western Athletic	Jim Sweeney	10-2-0
Fullerton, Cal State	Titans	Blue, orange, white	Big West	Gene Murphy	2-9-0
Furman	Paladins	Purple & white	Southern	Jimmy Satterfield	7-4-0
Georgia	Bulldogs	Red & black	Southeastern	Ray Goff	9-3-0
Georgia Southern	Eagles	Blue & white	Southern	Tim Stowers	7-4-0
Georgia Tech	Yellow Jackets	Old gold & white	Atlantic Coast	Bill Lewis	8-5-0
Grambling	Tigers	Black & gold	Southwestern	Eddie Robinson	5-6-0
Harvard	Crimson	Crimson	Ivy	Joe Restic	4-5-1
Hawaii	Rainbow Warriors	Green & white	Western Athletic	Bob Wagner	4-7-1
Holy Cross	Crusaders	Royal purple	Patriot	Peter Vaas	11-0-0
Houston	Cougars	Scarlet & white	Southwest	John Jenkins	4-7-0
Howard	Bison	Blue & white	Mid-Eastern	Steve Wilson	2-9-0
Idaho	Vandals	Silver & gold	Big Sky	John L. Smith	6-5-0
Idaho State	Bengals	Orange & black	Big Sky	Brian McNeely	3-7-1
Illinois	Fighting Illini	Orange & blue	Big Ten	Lou Tepper	6-6-0
Illinois State	Redbirds	Red & white	Gateway	Jim Heacock	5-6-0
Indiana	Fightin' Hoosiers	Cream & crimson	Big Ten	Bill Mallory	7-4-1
Indiana State	Sycamores	Blue & white	Gateway	Dennis Raetz	5-6-0
Iowa	Hawkeyes	Old gold & black	Big Ten	Hayden Fry	10-1-1
Iowa State	Cyclones	Cardinal & gold	Big Eight	Jim Walden	3-7-1
Jackson State	Tigers	Blue & white	Southwestern	James Carson	5-5-0
James Madison	Dukes	Purple & gold	Independent	Rip Scherer	9-4-0
Kansas	Jayhawks	Crimson & blue	Big Eight	Glen Mason	6-5-0
Kansas State	Wildcats	Purple & white	Big Eight	Bill Snyder	7-4-0
Kent	Golden Flashes	Blue & gold	Mid-American	Pete Cordelli	1-10-0
Kentucky	Wildcats	Blue & white	Southeastern	Bill Curry	3-8-0
Lafayette	Leopards	Maroon & white	Patriot	Bill Russo	6-5-0
Lehigh	Engineers	Brown & white	Patriot	Hank Small	9-2-0
Liberty	Flames	Red, White, Blue	Independent	Sam Rutigliano	4-7-0
Louisiana State	Fighting Tigers	Purple & gold	Southeastern	Curley Hallman	5-6-0
Louisiana Tech	Bulldogs	Red & blue	Independent	Joe Raymond Peace	8-1-2
Louisville	Cardinals	Red, black, white	Independent	Howard Schnellenberger	2-9-0
Maine	Black Bears	Blue & white	Yankee	Kirk Ferentz	3-8-0
Marshall	Thundering Herd	Green & white	Southern	Jim Donnan	11-4-0

Team	Nickname	Team colors	Conference	Coach	1991 record (W-L-T)
Maryland	Terps	Red, white, black & gold	Atlantic Coast	Mark Duffner	2-9-0
Massachusetts	Minutemen	Maroon & white	Yankee	Mike Hodges	4-7-0
McNeese State	Cowboys	Blue & gold	Southland	Bobby Keasier	6-4-2
Memphis State	Tigers	Blue & gray	Independent	Chuck Stobart	5-6-0
Miami (Fla.)	Hurricanes	Orange, green, white	Big East	Dennis Erickson	12-0-0
Miami (Ohio)	Redskins	Red & white	Mid-American	Randy Walker	6-4-1
Michigan	Wolverines	Maize & blue	Big Ten	Gray Moeller	10-2-0
Michigan State	Spartans	Green & white	Big Ten	George Perles	3-8-0
Middle Tennessee St.	Blue Raiders	Blue & white	Ohio Valley	Boots Donnelly	9-4-0
Minnesota	Golden Gophers	Maroon & gold	Big Ten	Jim Wacker	2-9-0
Mississippi	Rebels	Red & blue	Southeastern	Billy Brewer	5-6-0
Mississippi State	Bulldogs	Maroon & white	Southeastern	Jackie Sherrill	7-5-0
Miss. Valley	Delta Devils	Green & white	Southwestern	Larry Dorsey	7-3-1
Missouri	Tigers	Old gold & black	Big Eight	Bob Stull	3-7-1
Montana	Grizzlies	Copper, silver, gold	Big Sky	Don Read	7-4-0
Montana State	Bobcats	Blue & gold	Big Sky	Cliff Hyself	2-9-0
Morehead State	Eagles	Blue & gold	Ohio Valley	Cole Proctor	4-7-0
Morgan State	Bears	Blue & orange	Mid-Eastern	Ricky Diggs	1-10-0
Murray State	Racers	Blue & gold	Ohio Valley	Mike Mahoney	3-8-0
Navy	Midshipmen	Navy blue & gold	Independent	George Chaump	1-10-0
Nebraska	Cornhuskers	Scarlet & cream	Big Eight	Tom Osborne	9-2-1
Nevada-Las Vegas	Rebels	Scarlet & gray	Big West	Jim Strong	4-7-0
Nevada-Reno	Wolf Pack	Silver & blue	Big Sky	Chris Ault	12-1-0
New Hampshire	Wildcats	Blue & white	Yankee	Bill Bowes	9-3-0
New Mexico	Lobos	Cherry & silver	Western Athletic	Dennis Franchione	3-9-0
New Mexico State	Aggies	Crimson & white	Big West	Jim Hess	2-9-0
Nicholls St.	Colonels	Red & grey	Southland	Phil Greco	4-7-0
North Carolina	Tar Heels	Blue & white	Atlantic Coast	Mack Brown	7-4-0
North Carolina A & T	Aggies	Blue & gold	Mid-Eastern	Bill Hayes	9-3-0
North Carolina State	Wolfpack	Red & white	Atlantic Coast	Dick Sheridan	9-3-0
North Texas	Mean Green, Eagles	Green & white	Southland	Dennis Parker	3-7-1
Northeast Louisiana	Indians	Maroon & gold	Southland	Dave Roberts	7-3-1
Northeastern	Huskies	Red & black	Independent	Barry Gallup	4-7-0
Northern Arizona	Lumberjacks	Blue & gold	Big Sky	Steve Axman	3-8-0
Northern Illinois	Huskies	Cardinal & black	Independent	Charlie Sadler	2-9-0
Northern Iowa	Panthers	Purple & Old Gold	Gateway	Terry Allen	11-2-0
Northwestern	Wildcats	Purple & white	Big Ten	Gary Barnett	3-8-0
Northwestern State	Demons	Purple & White	Southland	Sam Goodwin	6-5-0
Notre Dame	Fighting Irish	Gold & blue	Independent	Lou Holtz	10-3-0
Ohio State	Buckeyes	Scarlet & gray	Big Ten	John Cooper	8-4-0
Ohio Univ	Bobcats	Green & white	Mid-American	Tom Lichtenberg	2-8-1
Oklahoma	Sooners	Crimsom & cream	Big Eight	Gary Gibbs	9-3-0
Oklahoma State	Cowboys	Orange & black	Big Eight	Pat Jones	0-10-1
Oregon	Ducks	Green & Yellow	Pacific Ten	Rich Brooks	3-8-0
Oregon State	Beavers	Orange & black	Pacific Ten	Jerry Pettibone	1-10-0
Pacific	Tigers	Orange & black	Big West	Walt Harris	5-7-0
Penn State	Nittany Lions	Blue & white	Big Ten	Joe Paterno	11-2-0
Pennsylvania	Red & Blue, Quakers	Red & blue	Ivy	Al Bagnoli	2-8-0
Pittsburgh	Panthers	Gold & blue	Big East	Paul Hackett	6-5-0
Prairie View A&M	Panthers	Purple & gold	Southwestern	Ron Beard	0-11-0
Princeton	Tigers	Orange & black	Ivy	Steve Tosches	8-2-0
Purdue	Boilermakers	Old gold & black	Big Ten	Jim Colletto	4-7-0
Rhode Island	Rams	Blue & white	Yankee	Bob Griffin	6-5-0
Rice	Owls	Blue & gray	Southwest	Fred Goldsmith	4-7-0
Richmond	Spiders	Red & blue	Yankee	Jim Marshall	2-9-0
Rutgers	Scarlet Knights	Scarlet	Big East	Doug Graber	6-5-0
Sam Houston State	Bear Kats	Orange & white	Southland	Ron Randleman	8-3-1
Samford	Bulldogs	Crimson & Blue	Independent	Terry Bowden	12-2-0
San Diego State	Aztecs	Scarlet & black	Western Athletic	Al Luginbill	8-4-1
San Jose State	Spartans	Gold & white	Big West	Ron Turner	6-4-1
South Carolina	Fighting Gamecocks	Garnet & black	Southeastern	Sparky Woods	3-6-2
South Carolina State	Bulldogs	Garnet & blue	Mid-Eastern	Willie Jeffries	7-4-0
SE Missouri St.	Indians	Red & black	Ohio Valley	John Mumford	3-8-0
Southern-Baton Rouge	Jaguars	Blue & gold	Southwestern	Marino Casem	4-7-0
Southern California	Trojans	Cardinal & gold	Pacific Ten	Larry Smith	3-8-0
Southern Illinois	Salukis	Maroon & white	Gateway	Bob Smith	7-4-0
Southern Methodist	Mustangs	Red & blue	Southwest	Tom Rossley	1-10-0
Southern Mississippi	Golden Eagles	Black & gold	Independent	Jeff Bower	4-7-0
SW Missouri St.	Bears	Maroon & white	Gateway	Jesse Branch	6-4-1
SW Texas St.	Bobcats	Maroon & gold	Southland	Jim Bob Helduser	6-4-1
Southwestern La.	Ragin' Cajuns	Vermillion & white	Independent	Nelson Stokley	2-8-1
Stanford	Cardinal	Cardinal & white	Pacific Ten	Bill Walsh	8-4-0
Stephen F. Austin St.	Lumberjacks	Purple & white	Southland	John Pearce	2-8-1
Syracuse	Orangemen	Orange	Big East	Paul Pasqualoni	10-2-0
Temple	Owls	Cherry & white	Big East	Jerry Berndt	2-9-0
Tennessee	Volunteers	Orange & white	Southeastern	John Majors	9-3-0
Tenn.-Chattanooga	Moccasins	Navy blue & gold	Southern	Buddy Nix	7-4-0
Tenn.-Martin	Pacers	Orange, white, blue	Ohio Valley	Don McLeary	5-6-0
Tennessee State	Tigers	Blue & white	Ohio Valley	Joe Gilliam Sr.	3-8-0
Tennessee Tech	Golden Eagles	Purple & gold	Ohio Valley	Jim Ragland	2-9-0
Texas	Longhorns	Orange & white	Southwest	John Mackovic	5-6-0
Texas A & M	Aggies	Maroon & white	Southwest	R.C. Slocum	10-2-0
Texas Christian	Horned Frogs	Purple & white	Southwest	Pat Sullivan	7-4-0

Team	Nickname	Team colors	Conference	Coach	1991 record (W-L-T)
Texas Southern	Tigers	Maroon & gray	Southwestern	Walter Highsmith	5-5-1
Texas Tech	Red Raiders	Scarlet & black	Southwest	Spike Dykes	6-5-0
Toledo	Rockets	Blue & gold	Mid-American	Gary Pinkel	5-5-1
Towson St.	Tigers	Gold & white	Independent	Gordy Combs	1-10-0
Tulane	Green Wave	Olive green & sky blue	Independent	Buddy Teevens	1-10-0
Tulsa	Golden Hurricane	Blue & gold	Independent	Dave Rader	10-2-0
UCLA	Bruins	Navy blue & gold	Pacific Ten	Terry Donahue	9-3-0
Utah State	Aggies	Navy blue & white	Big West	Charlie Weatherbie	5-6-0
UTEP	Miners	Orange, blue, white	Western Athletic	David Lee	4-7-1
Utah	Utes	Crimson & white	Western Athletic	Ron McBride	7-5-0
Vanderbilt	Commodores	Black & gold	Southeastern	Gerry DiNardo	5-6-0
Villanova	Wildcats	Blue & white	Yankee	Andy Talley	10-2-0
Virginia	Cavaliers	Orange & blue	Atlantic Coast	George Welsh	8-3-1
VMI	Keydets	Red, white & yellow	Southern	Jim Shuck	4-7-0
Virginia Tech	Gobblers, Hokies	Orange & maroon	Big East	Frank Beamer	5-6-0
Wake Forest	Demon Deacons	Old gold & black	Atlantic Coast	Bill Dooley	3-8-0
Washington	Huskies	Purple & gold	Pacific Ten	Don James	12-0-0
Washington State	Cougars	Crimson & gray	Pacific Ten	Mike Price	4-7-0
Weber State	Wildcats	Purple & white	Big Sky	Dave Arslanian	8-4-0
West Virginia	Mountaineers	Old gold & blue	Big East	Don Nehlen	6-5-0
Western Carolina	Catamounts	Purple & gold	Southern	Steve Hodgin	2-9-0
Western Illinois	Leathernecks	Purple & Gold	Gateway	Randy Ball	7-4-1
Western Kentucky	Hilltoppers	Red & white	Independent	Jack Harbaugh	3-8-0
Western Michigan	Broncos	Brown & gold	Mid-American	Al Molde	6-5-0
William & Mary	Tribe	Green & gold	Independent	Jimmye Laycock	5-6-0
Wisconsin	Badgers	Cardinal & white	Big Ten	Barry Alvarez	5-6-0
Wyoming	Cowboys	Brown & yellow	Western Athletic	Joe Tiller	4-6-1
Yale	Bulldogs, Elis	Yale blue & white	Ivy	Carmen Cozza	6-4-0
Youngstown St.	Penguins	Scarlet & white	Independent	Jim Tressel	12-3-0

Heisman Trophy Winners

Awarded annually to the nation's outstanding college football player.

1935	Jay Berwanger, Chicago, HB	1954	Alan Ameche, Wisconsin, FB	1973	John Cappelletti, Penn State, RB
1936	Larry Kelley, Yale, E	1955	Howard Cassady, Ohio St., HB	1974	Archie Griffin, Ohio State, RB
1937	Clinton Frank, Yale, HB	1956	Paul Hornung, Notre Dame, QB	1975	Archie Griffin, Ohio State, RB
1938	David O'Brien, Tex. Christian, QB	1957	John Crow, Texas A & M, HB	1976	Tony Dorsett, Pittsburgh, RB
1939	Nile Kinnick, Iowa, HB	1958	Pete Dawkins, Army, HB	1977	Earl Campbell, Texas, RB
1940	Tom Harmon, Michigan, HB	1959	Billy Cannon, La. State, HB	1978	Billy Sims, Oklahoma, RB
1941	Bruce Smith, Minnesota, HB	1960	Joe Bellino, Navy, HB	1979	Charles White, USC, RB
1942	Frank Sinkwich, Georgia, HB	1961	Ernest Davis, Syracuse, HB	1980	George Rogers, So. Carolina, RB
1943	Angelo Bertelli, Notre Dame, QB	1962	Terry Baker, Oregon State, QB	1981	Marcus Allen, USC, RB
1944	Leslie Horvath, Ohio State, QB	1963	Roger Staubach, Navy, QB	1982	Herschel Walker, Georgia, RB
1945	Felix Blanchard, Army, FB	1964	John Huarte, Notre Dame, QB	1983	Mike Rozier, Nebraska, RB
1946	Glenn Davis, Army, HB	1965	Mike Garrett, USC, HB	1984	Doug Flutie, Boston College, QB
1947	John Lujack, Notre Dame, QB	1966	Steve Spurrier, Florida, QB	1985	Bo Jackson, Auburn, RB
1948	Doak Walker, SMU, HB	1967	Gary Beban, UCLA, QB	1986	Vinny Testaverde, Miami, QB
1949	Leon Hart, Notre Dame, E	1968	O. J. Simpson, USC, RB	1987	Tim Brown, Notre Dame, WR
1950	Vic Janowicz, Ohio State, HB	1969	Steve Owens, Oklahoma, RB	1988	Barry Sanders, Oklahoma St., RB
1951	Richard Kazmaier, Princeton, HB	1970	Jim Plunkett, Stanford, QB	1989	Andre Ware, Houston, QB
1952	Billy Vessels, Oklahoma, HB	1971	Pat Sullivan, Auburn, QB	1990	Ty Detmer, BYU, QB
1953	John Lattner, Notre Dame, HB	1972	Johnny Rodgers, Nebraska, RB-R	1991	Desmond Howard, Michigan, WR

All-Time Division I-A Percentage Leaders

(Classified as Division I-A for the last 10 years; record includes bowl games; ties computed as half won and half lost)

	Years	Won	Lost	Tied	Pct.	Bowl Games W	L	T
Notre Dame	103	702	209	40	.759	11	6	0
Michigan	112	722	238	33	.744	10	13	0
Alabama	97	669	234	43	.730	24	17	3
Oklahoma	97	645	233	50	.722	19	10	1
Texas	99	676	263	31	.713	16	16	2
USC	99	616	244	51	.704	22	12	0
Ohio St.	102	641	261	51	.699	12	12	0
Penn St.	105	657	284	41	.690	17	9	2
Nebraska	102	653	286	40	.687	14	16	0
Tennessee	95	618	271	52	.684	17	15	0
Central Michigan	91	470	243	36	.652	3	1	0
Louisiana St.	98	566	310	46	.639	11	16	1
Army	102	577	316	50	.638	2	1	0
Miami (Ohio)	103	536	297	41	.637	5	2	0
Washington	102	546	303	49	.635	12	7	1
Arizona St.	79	432	245	24	.633	9	5	1
Georgia	98	574	325	53	.631	14	13	3
Florida St.	45	293	174	16	.623	12	7	2
Auburn	99	542	330	45	.616	12	9	2
Michigan St.	95	510	316	43	.612	5	5	0
Minnesota	108	549	343	43	.610	2	3	0
Colorado	102	540	343	34	.607	5	11	0
UCLA	73	423	271	37	.604	10	7	1
Arkansas	98	542	349	38	.604	9	15	3
Pittsburgh	102	560	366	42	.600	8	10	0

College Football Conference Champions

	Atlantic Coast		Ivy League		Big Eight		Big Ten
1978	Clemson	1978	Dartmouth			1978	Michigan St., Michigan
1979	No. Carolina St.	1979	Yale	1978	Nebraska, Oklahoma	1979	Ohio State
1980	North Carolina	1980	Yale	1979	Oklahoma	1980	Michigan
1981	Clemson	1981	Yale, Dartmouth	1980	Oklahoma	1981	Iowa, Ohio State
1982	Clemson	1982	Harvard, Dartmouth, Penn	1981	Nebraska	1982	Michigan
1983	Maryland	1983	Harvard, Penn	1982	Nebraska	1983	Illinois
1984	Maryland	1984	Penn	1983	Nebraska	1984	Ohio State
1985	Maryland	1985	Penn	1984	Nebraska, Oklahoma	1985	Iowa
1986	Clemson	1986	Penn	1985	Oklahoma	1986	Michigan, Ohio State
1987	Clemson	1987	Harvard	1986	Oklahoma	1987	Michigan St.
1988	Clemson	1988	Penn, Cornell	1987	Oklahoma	1988	Michigan
1989	Virginia, Duke	1989	Yale, Princeton	1988	Nebraska	1989	Michigan
1990	Georgia Tech	1990	Dartmouth	1990	Colorado	1990	Iowa, Illinois, Michigan, Michigan St.
1991	Clemson	1991	Darmouth	1991	Nebraska, Colorado	1991	Michigan

	Mid-America		Southern		Southeastern		Southwest
1978	Ball State	1978	Tenn.-Chattanooga, Furman	1978	Alabama	1978	Houston
1979	Central Michigan	1979	Tenn.-Chattanooga	1979	Alabama	1979	Houston, Arkansas
1980	Central Michigan	1980	Furman	1980	Georgia	1980	Baylor
1981	Toledo	1981	Furman	1981	Georgia, Alabama	1981	SMU
1982	Bowling Green	1982	Furman	1982	Georgia	1982	SMU
1983	Northern Illinois	1983	Furman	1983	Auburn	1983	Texas
1984	Toledo	1984	Tenn.-Chattanooga	1984	Florida (title vacated)	1984	SMU, Houston
1985	Bowling Green	1985	Furman	1985	Tennessee	1985	Texas A&M
1986	Miami	1986	Appalachian St.	1986	LSU	1986	Texas A&M
1987	E. Michigan	1987	Appalachian St.	1987	Auburn	1987	Texas A&M
1988	W. Michigan	1988	Marshall, Furman	1988	Auburn, LSU	1988	Arkansas
1989	Ball State	1989	Furman	1989	Alabama, Tennessee, Auburn	1989	Arkansas
1990	Central Michigan	1990	Furman	1990	Tennessee	1990	Texas
1991	Bowling Green	1991	Appalachian St.	1991	Florida	1991	Texas A&M

	Pacific Ten		Western Athletic		Big West
1978	USC	1978	Brigham Young	1978	Utah St., San Jose St.
1979	USC	1979	Brigham Young	1979	San Jose St.
1980	Washington	1980	Brigham Young	1980	Long Beach State
1981	Washington	1981	Brigham Young	1981	San Jose State
1982	UCLA	1982	Brigham Young	1982	Fresno State
1983	UCLA	1983	Brigham Young	1983	Cal State-Fullerton
1984	USC	1984	Brigham Young	1984	Nevada-Las Vegas
1985	UCLA	1985	Brigham Young, Air Force	1985	Fresno State
1986	Arizona State	1986	San Diego State	1986	San Jose State
1987	UCLA, USC	1987	Wyoming	1987	San Jose State
1988	USC	1988	Wyoming	1988	Fresno State
1989	USC	1989	Brigham Young	1989	Fresno State
1990	Washington	1990	Brigham Young	1990	San Jose State
1991	Washington	1991	Brigham Young	1991	San Jose St., Fresno St.

Outland Award

Honoring the outstanding interior lineman selected by the Football Writers' Association of America.

1946	George Connor, Notre Dame, T	1962	Bobby Bell, Minnesota, T	1978	Greg Roberts, Oklahoma, G
1947	Joe Steffy, Army, G	1963	Scott Appleton, Texas, T	1979	Jim Ritcher, No. Carolina St., C
1948	Bill Fischer, Notre Dame, G	1964	Steve Delong, Tennessee, T	1980	Mark May, Pittsburgh, OT
1949	Ed Bagdon, Michigan St., G	1965	Tommy Nobis, Texas, G	1981	Dave Rimington, Nebraska, C
1950	Bob Gain, Kentucky, T	1966	Loyd Phillips, Arkansas, T	1982	Dave Rimington, Nebraska, C
1951	Jim Weatherall, Oklahoma, T	1967	Ron Yary, Southern Cal, T	1983	Dean Steinkuhler, Nebraska, G
1952	Dick Modzelewski, Maryland, T	1968	Bill Stanfill, Georgia, T	1984	Bruce Smith, Virginia Tech, DT
1953	J. D. Roberts, Oklahoma, G	1969	Mike Reid, Penn State, DT	1985	Mike Ruth, Boston College, DT
1954	Bill Brooks, Arkansas, G	1970	Jim Stillwagon, Ohio State, LB	1986	Jason Buck, BYU, DT
1955	Calvin Jones, Iowa, G	1971	Larry Jacobson, Nebraska, DT	1987	Chad Hennings, Air Force, DT
1956	Jim Parker, Ohio State, G	1972	Rich Glover, Nebraska, MG	1988	Tracy Rocker, Auburn, DT
1957	Alex Karras, Iowa, T	1973	John Hicks, Ohio State, G	1989	Mohammed Elewonibi, BYU, G
1958	Zeke Smith, Auburn, G	1974	Randy White, Maryland, DE	1990	Russell Maryland, Miami (Fla.), DT
1959	Mike McGee, Duke, T	1975	Lee Roy Selmon, Oklahoma, DT	1991	Steve Emtman, Washington, DL
1960	Tom Brown, Minnesota, G	1976	Ross Browner, Notre Dame, DE		
1961	Merlin Olsen, Utah State, T	1977	Brad Shearer, Texas, DT		

All-Time Division I-A Coaching Victories

Paul "Bear" Bryant	323	Eddie Anderson	201	John Heisman	185
Amos Alonzo Stagg	314	Vince Dooley	201	Darrell Royal	184
Glenn "Pop" Warner	313	Dana Bible	198	LaVell Edwards	183
Joe Paterno	240	Dan McGugin	197	Carl Snavely	180
Woody Hayes	238	Fielding Yost	196	Gil Dobie	180
Bo Schembechler	234	Howard Jones	194	Jerry Claiborne	179
Bobby Bowden	216	John Vaught	190	Ben Schwartzwalder	178
Jess Neely	207	Hayden Fry	189	Ralph Jordan	176
Warren Woodson	203	Tom Osborne	186	Frank Kush	176

Eddie Robinson of Grambling State Univ. holds the record for most college football victories with 371 at the start of the 1992 season.

National College Football Champions

The unofficial national champion as selected each year by the AP (poll of writers) and the UPI (poll of coaches). When the polls disagree both teams are listed. The AP poll originated in 1936 and the UPI poll in 1950.

1936 Minnesota
1937 Pittsburgh
1938 Texas Christian
1939 Texas A&M
1940 Minnesota
1941 Minnesota
1942 Ohio State
1943 Notre Dame
1944 Army
1945 Army
1946 Notre Dame
1947 Notre Dame
1948 Michigan
1949 Notre Dame
1950 Oklahoma
1951 Tennessee
1952 Michigan State
1953 Maryland
1954 Ohio State, UCLA
1955 Oklahoma
1956 Oklahoma
1957 Auburn, Ohio State
1958 Louisiana State
1959 Syracuse
1960 Minnesota
1961 Alabama
1962 Southern Cal.
1963 Texas
1964 Alabama
1965 Alabama, Mich. State
1966 Notre Dame
1967 Southern Cal.
1968 Ohio State
1969 Texas
1970 Nebraska, Texas
1971 Nebraska,
1972 Southern Cal.
1973 Notre Dame, Alabama
1974 Oklahoma, So. Cal.
1975 Oklahoma
1976 Pittsburgh
1977 Notre Dame
1978 Alabama, So. Cal.
1979 Alabama
1980 Georgia
1981 Clemson
1982 Penn State
1983 Miami (Fla.)
1984 Brigham Young
1985 Oklahoma
1986 Penn State
1987 Miami (Fla.)
1988 Notre Dame
1989 Miami (Fla.)
1990 Colorado, Georgia Tech
1991 Miami (Fla.), Washington

College Football Coach of the Year

(Selected by the American Football Coaches Assn. & the Football Writers Assn. of America)

AFCA

1935	Lynn Waldorf, Northwestern
1936	Dick Harlow, Harvard
1937	Edward Mylin, Lafayette
1938	Bill Kern, Carnegie Tech
1939	Eddie Anderson, Iowa
1940	Clark Shaughnessy, Stanford
1941	Frank Leahy, Notre Dame
1942	Bill Alexander, Georgia Tech
1943	Amos Alonzo Stagg, Pacific
1944	Carroll Widdoes, Ohio St.
1945	Bo McMillin, Indiana
1946	Earl "Red" Blaik, Army
1947	Fritz Crisler, Michigan
1948	Bennie Oosterbaan, Michigan
1949	Bud Wilkinson, Oklahoma
1950	Charlie Caldwell, Princeton
1951	Chuck Taylor, Stanford
1952	Biggie Munn, Michigan St.
1953	Jim Tatum, Maryland
1954	Henry "Red" Sanders, UCLA
1955	Duffy Daugherty, Michigan St.
1956	Bowden Wyatt, Tennessee

	FWAA	AFCA
1957	Woody Hayes, Ohio St.	Woody Hayes, Ohio St.
1958	Paul Dietzel, LSU	Paul Dietzel, LSU
1959	Ben Schwartzwalder, Syracuse	Ben Schwartzwalder, Syracuse
1960	Murray Warmath, Minnesota	Murray Warmath, Minnesota
1961	Darrell Royal, Texas	Paul "Bear" Bryant, Alabama
1962	John McKay, USC	John McKay, USC
1963	Darrell Royal, Texas	Darrell Royal, Texas
1964	Ara Parseghian, Notre Dame	Frank Broyles, Arkansas; Ara Paraseghian, Notre Dame
1965	Duffy Daugherty, Michigan St.	Tommy Prothro, UCLA
1966	Tom Cahill, Army	Tom Cahill, Army
1967	John Pont, Indiana	John Pont, Indiana
1968	Woody Hayes, Ohio St.	Joe Paterno, Penn St.
1969	Bo Schembechler, Michigan	Bo Schembechler, Michigan
1970	Alex Agase, Northwestern	Charles McClendon, LSU; Darrell Royal, Texas
1971	Bob Devaney, Nebraska	Paul "Bear" Bryant, Alabama
1972	John McKay, USC	John McKay, USC
1973	Johnny Majors, Pittsburgh	Paul "Bear" Bryant, Alabama
1974	Grant Teaff, Baylor	Grant Teaff, Baylor
1975	Woody Hayes, Ohio St.	Frank Kush, Arizona St.
1976	Johnny Majors, Pittsburgh	Johnny Majors, Pittsburgh
1977	Lou Holtz, Arkansas	Don James, Washington
1978	Joe Paterno, Penn St.	Joe Paterno, Penn St.
1979	Earle Bruce, Ohio St.	Earle Bruce, Ohio St.
1980	Vince Dooley, Georgia	Vince Dooley, Georgia
1981	Danny Ford, Clemson	Danny Ford, Clemson
1982	Joe Paterno, Penn St.	Joe Paterno, Penn St.
1983	Howard Schnellenberger, Miami (Fla.)	Ken Hatfield, Air Force
1984	LaVell Edwards, Brigham Young	LaVell Edwards, Brigham Young
1985	Fisher De Berry, Air Force	Fisher De Berry, Air Force
1986	Joe Paterno, Penn St.	Joe Paterno, Penn St.
1987	Dick MacPherson, Syracuse	Dick MacPherson, Syracuse
1988	Lou Holtz, Notre Dame	Don Nehlen, W. Virginia
1989	Bill McCartney, Colorado	Bill McCartney, Colorado
1990	Bobby Ross, Georgia Tech	Bobby Ross, Georgia Tech
1991	Don James, Washington	Don James, Washington

Longest Division I-A Winning Streaks

Wins	Team	Years	Ended by	Score
47	Oklahoma	1953-57	Notre Dame	7-0
39	Washington	1908-14	Oregon State	0-0
37	Yale	1890-93	Princeton	6-0
37	Yale	1887-89	Princeton	10-0
35	Toledo	1969-71	Tampa	21-0
34	Pennsylvania	1894-96	Lafayette	6-4
31	Oklahoma	1948-50	Kentucky	13-7
31	Pittsburgh	1914-18	Cleveland Naval Reserve	10-9
31	Pennsylvania	1896-98	Harvard	10-0
30	Texas	1968-70	Notre Dame	24-11
29	Michigan	1901-03	Minnesota	6-6
28	Alabama	1978-80	Mississippi State	6-3
28	Oklahoma	1973-75	Kansas	23-3
28	Michigan State	1950-53	Purdue	6-0
27	Nebraska	1901-04	Colorado	6-0
26	Cornell	1921-24	Williams	14-7
26	Michigan	1903-05	Chicago	2-0
25	Michigan	1946-49	Army	21-7
25	Army	1944-46	Notre Dame	0-0
25	Southern Cal	1931-33	Oregon State	0-0
25	Brigham Young	1983-85	UCLA	27-24

World Swimming Records

As of Aug., 1992

Men's Records

Freestyle

Distance	Time	Holder	Country	Where made	Date
50 Meters	0:21.81	Tom Jager	U.S.	Nashville, Tenn.	Mar. 24, 1990
100 Meters	0:48.42	Matt Biondi	U.S.	Austin, Tex.	Aug. 10, 1988
200 Meters	1:46.69	Giorgio Lamberti	Italy	Bonn	Aug. 15, 1989
400 Meters	3:45.00	Evgeny Sadovyi	Unified Team	Barcelona	July 29, 1992
800 Meters	7:47.85	Kieren Perkins	Australia	Edmonton	Aug. 25, 1991
1,500 Meters	14:43.48	Kieren Perkins	Australia	Barcelona	July 31, 1992

Breaststroke

Distance	Time	Holder	Country	Where made	Date
100 Meters	1:01.29	Norbert Rosza	Hungary	Athens	Aug. 20, 1991
200 Meters	2:10.16	Mike Barrowman	U.S.	Barcelona	July 25, 1992

Butterfly

Distance	Time	Holder	Country	Where made	Date
100 Meters	0:52.84	Pablo Morales	U.S.	Orlando, Fla.	June 23, 1986
200 Meters	1:55.69	Melvin Stewart	U.S.	Australia	Jan. 12, 1991

Backstroke

Distance	Time	Holder	Country	Where made	Date
100 Meters	0:53.86	Jeff Rouse	U.S.	Barcelona	July 29, 1992
200 Meters	1:57.30	Martin Lopez-Zubero	Spain	Ft. Lauderdale, Fla.	Aug. 13, 1991

Individual Medley

Distance	Time	Holder	Country	Where made	Date
200 Meters	1:59.36	Tamas Darnyi	Hungary	Australia	Jan. 14, 1991
400 Meters	4:14.75	Tamas Darnyi	Hungary	Seoul	Sept. 21, 1988

Freestyle Relays

Distance	Time	Holder	Country	Where made	Date
400 M. (4×100)	3:16.53	Jacobs, Dalbey, Jager, Biondi	U.S.	Seoul	Sept. 23, 1988
800 M. (4×200)	7:11.95	(Lepikov, Pychnenko, Taianovitch, Sadovyi)	Unified Team	Barcelona	July 27, 1992

Medley Relays

Distance	Time	Holder	Country	Where made	Date
400 M. (4×100)	3:36.93	Berkoff, Schroeder, Jacobs, Biondi	U.S.	Seoul	Sept. 25, 1988

Women's Records

Freestyle

Distance	Time	Holder	Country	Where made	Date
50 Meters	0:24.79	Yang Wenyi	China	Barcelona	Aug. 31, 1992
100 Meters	0:54.48	Jenny Thompson	U.S.	Indianapolis	Mar. 1, 1992
200 Meters	1:57.55	Heike Friedrich	E. Germany	Berlin	June 18, 1986
400 Meters	4:03.85	Janet Evans	U.S.	Seoul	Sept. 22, 1988
800 Meters	8:16.22	Janet Evans	U.S.	Tokyo	Aug. 20, 1989
1,500 Meters	15:52.10	Janet Evans	U.S.	Orlando, Fla.	Mar. 26, 1988

Breaststroke

Distance	Time	Holder	Country	Where made	Date
100 Meters	1:07.91	Silke Hoerner	E. Germany	Strasbourg, France	Aug. 21, 1987
200 Meters	2:25.92	Anita Nall	U.S.	Indianapolis	Mar. 1, 1992

Butterfly

Distance	Time	Holder	Country	Where made	Date
100 Meters	0:57.93	Mary T. Meagher	U.S.	Brown Deer, Wis.	Aug. 16, 1981
200 Meters	2:05.96	Mary T. Meagher	U.S.	Brown Deer, Wis.	Aug. 13, 1981

Backstroke

Distance	Time	Holder	Country	Where made	Date
100 Meters	1:00.31	Krisztina Egerszegi	Hungary	Athens	Aug. 22, 1991
200 Meters	2:06.62	Krisztina Egerszegi	Hungary	Edmonton	Aug. 26, 1991

Individual Medley

Distance	Time	Holder	Country	Where made	Date
200 Meters	2:11.65	Lin Li	China	Barcelona	July 30, 1992
400 Meters	4:36.10	Petra Schneider	E. Germany	Ecuador	Aug. 1, 1982

Freestyle Relays

Distance	Time	Holder	Country	Where made	Date
400 M. (4×100)	3:39.46	(Haislett, Torres, Martino, Thompson)	U.S.	Barcelona	July 28, 1992
800 M. (4×200)	7:55:47	(Stellmach, Strauss, Mohring, Friedrich)	E. Germany	Strasbourg, France	Aug. 18, 1987

Medley Relays

Distance	Time	Holder	Country	Where made	Date
400 M. (4×100)	4:02.54	(Loveless, Nall, Ahmann-Leighton, Thompson)	U.S.	Barcelona	July 30, 1992

TRACK AND FIELD

World Track and Field Indoor Records

As of Sept., 1992

The International Amateur Athletic Federation began recognizing world indoor track & field records as official on January 1, 1987. Prior to that, there were only unofficial world indoor bests. World indoor bests set prior to January 1, 1987 are subject to approval as world records providing they meet the prescribed IAAF world records criteria, including drug testing. To be accepted as a world indoor record, a performance must meet the same criteria as a world record outdoors except that a track performance can't be set on an indoor track larger than 200 meters. *Record pending.

Men

Event	Record	Holder	Country	Date	Where made
60 meters	*6.41	Andre Cason	U.S.	Feb. 14, 1992	Madrid
200 meters	20.36	Bruno Marie-Rose	France	Feb. 22, 1987	Lievin, France
400 meters	*45.02	Danny Everett	U.S.	Feb. 2, 1992	Germany
800 meters	1:44.84	Paul Ereng	Kenya	Mar. 4, 1989	Budapest
1,000 meters	*2:15.26	Noureddine Morceli	Algeria	Feb. 22, 1992	Birmingham, Eng.
1,500 meters	3:34.16	Noureddine Morceli	Algeria	Feb. 28, 1991	Seville, Spain
1 Mile	3:49.78	Eamonn Coghlan	Ireland	Feb. 27, 1983	E. Rutherford, N.J.
3,000 meters	*7:36.36	Said Aouita	Morocco	Mar. 12, 1992	Greece
5,000 meters	13:20.40	Suleiman Nyambui	Tanzania	Feb. 6, 1981	New York
50-meter hurdles	6.25	Mark McKoy	Canada	Jan. 27, 1985	Rosemont, Ill.
60-meter hurdles	7.36	Roger Kingdom	U.S.	Mar. 9, 1989	Athens
High Jump	7 ft. 11½ in.	Javier Sotomayor	Cuba	Mar. 4, 1989	Budapest
Pole Vault	*20 ft. 1½ in.	Sergei Bubka	Ukraine	Feb. 22, 1992	Berlin
Long Jump	28 ft. 10¼ in.	Carl Lewis	U.S.	Feb. 27, 1984	New York
Triple Jump	58 ft. 3¼ in.	Mike Conley	U.S.	Feb. 27, 1987	New York
Shot Put	74 ft. 4¼ in.	Randy Barnes	U.S.	Jan. 20, 1989	Los Angeles

Women

Event	Record	Holder	Country	Date	Where made
60 meters	*6.96	Merlene Ottey	Jamaica	Feb. 15, 1992	Madrid
200 meters	22.24	Merlene Ottey	Jamaica	Mar. 10, 1991	Seville, Spain
400 meters	49.59	Jarmila Kratochvilova	Czechoslovakia	Mar. 7, 1982	Milan
800 meters	1:56.40	Christine Wachtel	E. Germany	Feb. 13, 1988	Vienna
1,000 meters	2:34.8	Brigitte Kraus	W. Germany	Feb. 19, 1978	Dortmund, Germany
1,500 meters	4:00.27	Doina Melinte	Romania	Feb. 9, 1990	E. Rutherford, N.J.
1 Mile	4:17.13	Doina Melinte	Romania	Feb. 9, 1990	E. Rutherford, N.J.
3,000 meters	8:33.82	Elly Van Hulst	Netherlands	Feb. 8, 1986	England
5,000 meters	*15:03.17	Liz McColgan	Scotland	Feb. 22, 1992	Birmingham, England
50-meter hurdles	6:58	Cornelia Oschkenat	E. Germany	Feb. 20, 1988	Berlin
60-meter hurdles	7.69	Lyudmila Narozhi-Lenko	USSR	Feb. 4, 1990	USSR
High Jump	6 ft. 9 in.	Stefka Kostadinova	Bulgaria	Feb. 20, 1988	Athens, Greece
Long Jump	24 ft. 2¼ in.	Heike Dreschler	E. Germany	Feb. 13, 1988	Vienna
Triple Jump	47 ft. 4½ in.	Inessa Kravets	USSR	Mar. 9, 1991	Seville, Spain
Shot Put	73 ft. 10 in.	Helena Fibingerova	Czechoslovakia	Feb. 19, 1977	Czech.

National Track & Field Hall of Fame

Indianapolis, Ind.

Jesse Abramson
Dave Albritton
Roxanne Anderson
Horace Ashenfelter
Andy Bakjian
Weems Baskin
James Bausch
Bob Beamon
Percy Beard
Jim Beatty
Greg Bell
Dee Boeckman
Tom Botts
Ralph Boston
Bill Bowerman
Avery Brundage
Jim Bush
Lee Calhoun
Milt Campbell
Ellery Clark
Alice Coachman (Davis)
Harold Connolly
Tom Courtney
Dean Cromwell
Glenn Cunningham
William Curtis
Willie Davenport
Glenn Davis
Harold Davis
Mildred (Babe) Didrikson
Harrison Dillard
Ken Doherty
Charles Dumas
Bill Easton
James (Jumbo) Elliott
Lee Evans
Barney Ewell
Ray Ewry
Mae Faggs (Starr)
Barbara Ferrell
Dan Ferris
John Flanagan
Dick Fosbury
Bob Giegengack
Fortune Gordien
John Griffith
Archie Hahn
Evelyne Hall
Brutus Hamilton
Glenn Hardin
Ted Haydon
Billy Hayes
Bob Hayes
Ward Haylett
Bud Held
Doris Brown Heritage
Ralph Higgins
Harry Hillman
Jim Hines
Bud Houser
DeHart Hubbard
Edward Hurt
Wilbur Hutsell
Nell Jackson
Bruce Jenner
Rafer Johnson
Hayes Jones
Thomas Jones
Payton Jordan
John Kelley
Abel Kiviat
Alvin Kraenzlein
Ron Laird
Clyde Littlefield
Bob Mathias
Randy Matson
Mildred McDaniel
Edith McGuire (DuVall)
Ted Meredith
Ralph Metcalfe
Billy Mills
Madeline Manning-Mims
Jack Moakley
Tom Moore
Bobby Morrow
Michael Murphy
Lon Myers
Bert Nelson
Cordner Nelson
Parry O'Brien
Al Oerter
Harold Osborn
Jesse Owens
Charlie Paddock
Mel Patton
Eulace Peacock
Steve Prefontaine
Joie Ray
Greg Rice
Bob Richards
Betty Robinson (Schwartz)
Ralph Rose
Wilma Rudolph
Jim Ryun
Jackson Scholz
Bob Schul
Bob Seagren
Mel Sheppard
Martin Sheridan
Frank Shorter
Dave Sime
Robert Simpson
Tommie Smith
Larry Snyder
Andy Stanfield
Les Steers
Helen Stephens
James Sullivan
Ed Temple
Dink Templeton
John Thomas
Earl Thomson
Jim Thorpe
Eddie Tolan
Bill Toomey
Forrest Towns
Wyomia Tyus
LeRoy Walker
Stella Walsh
Cornelius Warmerdam
Martha Watson
Willye White
Mal Whitfield
Fred Wilt
Lloyd "Bud" Winter
Rick Wohlhuter
John Woodruff
Dave Wottle
Frank Wykoff
Joe Yancey
George Young

World Track and Field Records

As of Sept. 5, 1992

*Indicates pending record; some new records await confirmation. The International Amateur Atheletic Federation, the world body of track and field, recognizes only records in metric distances except for the mile.

Men's Records

Running

Event	Record	Holder	Country	Date	Where made
100 meters	**9.86 s.**	Carl Lewis	U.S.	Aug. 25, 1991	Tokyo
200 meters	**19.72 s.**	Pietro Mennea	Italy	Sept. 17, 1979	Mexico City
400 meters	**43.29 s.**	Butch Reynolds	U.S.	Aug. 16, 1988	Zurich
800 meters	**1 m., 41.73 s.**	Sebastian Coe	Gr. Britain	June 10, 1981	Florence, Italy
1,000 meters	**2 m., 12.18 s.**	Sebastian Coe	Gr. Britain	July 11, 1981	Oslo
1,500 meters	***3 m., 28.86 s.**	Noureddine Morceli	Algeria	Sept. 5, 1992	Rieti, Italy
1 mile	**3 m., 46.32 s.**	Steve Cram	Gr. Britain	July 27, 1985	Oslo
2,000 meters	**4 m., 50.81 s.**	Said Aouita	Morocco	July 16, 1987	Paris
3,000 meters	***7 m., 28.96 s.**	Moses Kiptanui	Kenya	Aug. 16, 1992	Cologne
5,000 meters	**12 m., 58.39 s.**	Said Aouita	Morocco	July 22, 1987	Rome
10,000 meters	**27 m., 08.23 s.**	Arturo Barrios	Mexico	Aug. 18, 1989	W. Berlin
20,000 meters	**56 m., 55.6 s.**	Arturo Barrios	Mexico	May 30, 1991	France
25,000 meters	**1 hr., 13 m., 55.8 s.**	Toshihiko Seko	Japan	Mar. 22, 1981	New Zealand
3,000 meter stpl	***8 m., 02.08 s.**	Moses Kiptanui	Kenya	Aug. 19, 1992	Zurich
Marathon	**2 hr., 6 m., 50 s.**	Belayneh Densimo	Ethiopia	Apr. 17, 1988	Rotterdam

Hurdles

Event	Record	Holder	Country	Date	Where made
110 meters	**12.92 s.**	Roger Kingdom	U.S.	Aug. 16, 1989	Zurich
400 meters	***46.78 s.**	Kevin Young	U.S.	Aug. 6, 1992	Barcelona

Relay Races

Event	Record	Holder	Country	Date	Where made
400 mtrs.	***37.40 s.**	(Marsh, Burrell, Mitchell, Lewis)	U.S.	Aug. 8, 1992	Barcelona
800 mtrs. (4×200)	***1m., 19.11 s.**	(Marsh, Burrell, Heard Lewis)	U.S.	Apr. 25, 1992	Philadelphia
1,600 mtrs. (4×400)	**2 m., 55.74 s.**	(Valmon, Watts, Johnson, Lewis)	U.S.	Aug. 8, 1992	Barcelona
		(Everett, Lewis, Robinzine, Reynolds)	U.S.	Oct. 1, 1988	Seoul
3,200 mtrs. (4×800)	**7 m., 03.89 s.**	(Elliott, Cook, Cram, Coe)	Gr. Britain	Aug. 30, 1982	London

Field Events

Event	Record	Holder	Country	Date	Where made
High jump	**8 ft.**	Javier Sotomayor	Cuba	July 29, 1989	Puerto Rico
Long jump	**29 ft., 4½ in.**	Mike Powell	U.S.	Aug. 30, 1992	Tokyo
Triple jump	**58 ft., 11½ in.**	Willie Banks	U.S.	June 16, 1985	Indianapolis
Pole vault	***20 ft., 1 in.**	Sergei Bubka	Ukraine	Aug. 30, 1992	Padua, Italy
16 lb. shot put	**75 ft., 10¼ in.**	Randy Barnes	U.S.	May 20, 1990	Los Angeles
Discus	**243 ft.**	Juergen Schult	E. Germany	June 6, 1986	E. Germany
Javelin	***318 ft. 1 in.**	Seppo Raty	Finland	June 2, 1991	Finland
16 lb. hammer	**284 ft., 7 in.**	Yuri Sedykh	USSR	Aug. 30, 1986	Stuttgart
Decathlon	**8,647 pts.**	Daley Thompson	Gr. Britain	Aug. 8-9, 1984	Los Angeles

Women's Records

Running

Event	Record	Holder	Country	Date	Where made
100 meters	**10.49 s.**	Florence Griffith Joyner	U.S.	July 16, 1988	Indianapolis
200 meters	**21.34 s.**	Florence Griffith Joyner	U.S.	Sept. 29, 1988	Seoul
400 meters	**47.60 s.**	Marita Koch	E. Germany	Oct. 6, 1985	Canberra
800 meters	**1 m., 53.28 s.**	Jarmila Kratochvilova	Czech.	July 26, 1983	Munich
1,500 meters	**3 m., 52.47 s.**	Tatyana Kazankina	USSR	Aug. 13, 1980	Zurich
1 mile	**4 m., 15.61 s.**	Paula Ivan	Romania	July 10, 1989	Nice
2,000 meters	**5 m., 28.69 s.**	Maricica Puica	Romania	July 11, 1986	London
3,000 meters	**8 m., 22.62 s.**	Tatyana Kazankina	USSR	Aug. 26, 1984	Leningrad
5,000 meters	**14 m., 37.33 s.**	Ingrid Kristiansen	Norway	Aug. 5, 1986	Stockholm
10,000 meters	**30 m., 13.74 s.**	Ingrid Kristiansen	Norway	July 5, 1986	Oslo
Marathon	**2 h., 21 m., 06 s.**	Ingrid Kristiansen	Norway	Apr. 21, 1985	London

Hurdles

Event	Record	Holder	Country	Date	Where made
100 meters	**12.21 s.**	Yordanka Donkova	Bulgaria	Aug. 21, 1988	Bulgaria
400 meters	**52.94 s.**	Marina Stepanova	USSR	Sept. 17, 1986	USSR

Field Events

Event	Record	Holder	Country	Date	Where made
High jump	**6 ft., 10¼ in.**	Stefka Kostadinova	Bulgaria	Aug. 30, 1987	Rome
Shot put	**74 ft., 3 in.**	Natalya Lisouskaya	USSR	June 7, 1987	Moscow
Long jump	**24 ft., 8¼ in.**	Galina Chistyakova	USSR	June 11, 1988	Leningrad
Triple Jump	**49 ft., ¾ in.**	Inessa Kravets	USSR	June 10, 1991	Moscow
Discus	**252 ft.**	Gabriele Reinsch	E. Germany	July 9, 1988	E. Germany
Javelin	**262 ft., 5 in.**	Petra Felke	E. Germany	Sept. 9, 1988	Potsdam
Heptathlon	**7,291 pts.**	Jackie Joyner-Kersee	U.S.	Sept. 23-24, 1988	Seoul

Relay Races

Event	Record	Holder	Country	Date	Where made
400 mtrs. (4×100)	**41.37 s.**	National team	E. Germany	Oct. 6, 1985	Canberra
800 mtrs. (4×200)	**1 m., 28.15 s.**	National team	E. Germany	Aug. 9, 1980	E. Germany
1,600 mtrs. (4×400)	**3 m., 15.18 s.**	National team	USSR	Oct. 1, 1988	Seoul
3,200 mtrs. (4×800)	**7 m., 50.17 s.**	National team	USSR	Aug. 5, 1984	Moscow

Professional Sports Directory

Baseball

Commissioner's Office
350 Park Ave.
New York, NY 10022

National League

National League Office
350 Park Ave.
New York, NY 10022

Atlanta Braves
PO Box 4064
Atlanta, GA 30302

Chicago Cubs
Wrigley Field
Chicago, IL 60613

Cincinnati Reds
100 Riverfront Stadium
Cincinnati, OH 45202

Colorado Rockies
1700 Lincoln St.
Denver, CO 80203

Florida Marlins
(not available)

Houston Astros
PO Box 288
Houston, TX 77001

Los Angeles Dodgers
Dodger Stadium
Los Angeles, CA 90012

Montreal Expos
PO Box 500, Station M
Montreal, Que. H1V 3P2

New York Mets
Shea Stadium
Flushing, NY 11368

Philadelphia Phillies
PO Box 7575
Philadelphia, PA 19101

Pittsburgh Pirates
Three Rivers Stadium
Pittsburgh, PA 15212

St. Louis Cardinals
Busch Stadium
St. Louis, MO 63102

San Diego Padres
PO Box 2000
San Diego, CA 92112

San Francisco Giants
Candlestick Park
San Francisco, CA 94124

American League

American League Office
350 Park Ave.
New York, NY 10022

Baltimore Orioles
401 W. Camden St.
Baltimore, MD 21202

Boston Red Sox
24 Yawkey Way
Boston, MA 02215

California Angels
Anaheim Stadium
Anaheim, CA 92803

Chicago White Sox
333 W. 35th St.
Chicago, IL 60616

Cleveland Indians
Cleveland Stadium
Cleveland, OH 44114

Detroit Tigers
Tiger Stadium
Detroit, MI 48216

Kansas City Royals
P.O. Box 419969
Kansas City, MO 64141

Milwaukee Brewers
Milwaukee County Stadium
Milwaukee, WI 53215

Minnesota Twins
501 Chicago Ave. South
Minneapolis, MN 55415

New York Yankees
Yankee Stadium
Bronx, NY 10451

Oakland A's
Oakland Coliseum
Oakland, CA 94621

Seattle Mariners
P.O. Box 4100
Seattle, WA 98104

Texas Rangers
PO Box 90111
Arlington, TX 76004

Toronto Blue Jays
300 Bremner Blvd.
Toronto, Ont. M5V 3B3

National Basketball Association

League Office
645 5th Ave.
New York, NY 10022

Atlanta Hawks
1 CNN Center
Atlanta, GA 30303

Boston Celtics
151 Merrimac St.
Boston, MA 02114

Charlotte Hornets
Hive Drive
Charlotte, NC 28217

Chicago Bulls
980 North Michigan Ave.
Chicago, IL 60611

Cleveland Cavaliers
2923 Statesboro Rd.
Richfield, OH 44286

Dallas Mavericks
777 Sports St.
Dallas, TX 75207

Denver Nuggets
1635 Clay St.
Denver, CO 80204

Detroit Pistons
2 Championship Dr.
Auburn Hills, MI 48057

Golden State Warriors
Oakland Coliseum
Oakland, CA 94621

Houston Rockets
The Summit
Houston, TX 77277

Indiana Pacers
300 E. Market St.
Indianapolis, IN 46204

Los Angeles Clippers
3939 S. Figueroa
Los Angeles, CA 90037

Los Angeles Lakers
Great Western Forum
Inglewood, CA 90306

Miami Heat
Miami Arena
Miami, FL 33136

Milwaukee Bucks
1001 N. 4th St.
Milwaukee, WI 53203

Minnesota Timberwolves
600 First Ave. N.
Minneapolis, MN 55403

New Jersey Nets
Meadowlands Arena
E. Rutherford, NJ 07073

New York Knickerbockers
4 Pennsylvania Plaza
New York, NY 10001

Orlando Magic
1 Magic Place
Orlando, FL 32801

Philadelphia 76ers
PO Box 25040
Philadelphia, PA 19147

Phoenix Suns
2910 N. Central Ave.
Phoenix, AZ 85012

Portland Trail Blazers
700 NE Multnomah St.
Portland, OR 97232

Sacramento Kings
One Sports Pkwy.
Sacramento, CA 95834

San Antonio Spurs
600 E. Market St.
San Antonio, TX 78205

Seattle SuperSonics
190 Queen Ann Ave. N.
Seattle, WA 98109

Utah Jazz
5 Triad Center
Salt Lake City, UT 84180

Washington Bullets
1 Harry S. Truman Dr.
Landover, MD 20785

National Hockey League

League Headquarters
Sun Life Bldg.
Montreal, Quebec H3B 2W2

Boston Bruins
150 Causeway St.
Boston, MA 02114

Buffalo Sabres
Memorial Auditorium
Buffalo, NY 14202

Calgary Flames
P.O. Box 1540
Calgary, Alta. T2P 3B9

Chicago Black Hawks
1800 W. Madison St.
Chicago, IL 60612

Detroit Red Wings
600 Civic Center Drive
Detroit, MI 48226

Edmonton Oilers
Northlands Coliseum
Edmonton, Alta. T5B 4M9

Hartford Whalers
One Civic Center Plaza
Hartford, CT 06103

Los Angeles Kings
3900 W. Manchester Blvd.
Inglewood, CA 90306

Minnesota North Stars
7901 Cedar Ave. S.
Bloomington, MN 55425

Montreal Canadiens
2313 St. Catherine St., West
Montreal, Quebec H3H 1N2

New Jersey Devils
Meadowlands Arena
E. Rutherford, NJ 07073

New York Islanders
Nassau Coliseum
Uniondale, NY 11553

New York Rangers
4 Pennsylvania Plaza
New York, NY 10001

Ottawa Senators
301 Moodie Dr.
Ottawa, Ont. K2H 9C4

Philadelphia Flyers
Pattison Place
Philadelphia, PA 19148

Pittsburgh Penguins
Civic Arena
Pittsburgh, PA 15219

Quebec Nordiques
2205 Ave. du Colisee
Quebec, Que. G1L 4W7

St. Louis Blues
5700 Oakland Ave.
St. Louis, MO 63110

San Jose Sharks
10 Almaden Blvd.
San Jose, CA 95113

Tampa Bay Lightning
501 E. Kennedy Blvd.
Tampa, FL 33602

Toronto Maple Leafs
60 Carlton St.
Toronto, Ont. M5B 1L1

Vancouver Canucks
100 North Renfrew St.
Vancouver, B.C. V5K 3N7

Washington Capitals
Capital Centre
Landover, MD 20785

Winnipeg Jets
15-1430 Maroons Road
Winnipeg, Man. R3G 0L5

National Football League

League Office
410 Park Avenue
New York, NY 10022

Atlanta Falcons
Suwanee Road
Suwanee, GA 30174

Buffalo Bills
1 Bills Drive
Orchard Park, NY 14127

Chicago Bears
250 N. Washington Rd.
Lake Forest, IL 60045

Cincinnati Bengals
200 Riverfront Stadium
Cincinnati, OH 45202

Cleveland Browns
Cleveland Stadium
Cleveland, OH 44114

Dallas Cowboys
One Cowboys Pkwy.
Irving, TX 75063

Denver Broncos
13655 E. Dove Valley Pkwy.
Englewood, CO 80112

Detroit Lions
1200 Featherstone Rd.
Pontiac, MI 48057

Green Bay Packers
1265 Lombardi Ave.
Green Bay, WI 54304

Houston Oilers
6910 Fannin St.
Houston, TX 77030

Indianapolis Colts
P.O. Box 53500
Indianapolis, IN 46253

Kansas City Chiefs
1 Arrowhead Drive
Kansas City, MO 64129

Los Angeles Raiders
332 Center St.
El Segundo, CA 90245

Los Angeles Rams
2327 W. Lincoln Ave.
Anaheim, CA 92801

Miami Dolphins
2269 NW 199 St.
Miami, FL 33056

Minnesota Vikings
9520 Viking Dr.
Eden Prairie, MN 55344

New England Patriots
Foxboro Stadium
Foxboro, MA 02035

New Orleans Saints
1500 Poydras St.
New Orleans, LA 70003

New York Giants
Giants Stadium
E. Rutherford, NJ 07073

New York Jets
1000 Fulton Ave.
Hempstead, NY 11550

Philadelphia Eagles
Veterans Stadium
Philadelphia, PA 19148

Phoenix Cardinals
PO Box 888
Phoenix, AZ 85001

Pittsburgh Steelers
Three Rivers Stadium
Pittsburgh, PA 15212

San Diego Chargers
P.O. Box 20666
San Diego, CA 92120

San Francisco 49ers
4949 Centennial Blvd.
Santa Clara, CA 95054

Seattle Seahawks
11220 NE 53d St.
Kirkland, WA 98033

Tampa Bay Buccaneers
1 Buccaneer Place
Tampa, FL 33607

Washington Redskins
PO Box 17247
Dulles Intl. Airport
Washington, DC 20041

Other Sports Organizations

Amateur Athletic Union
3400 W. 86th St.
Indianapolis, IN 46268

Amateur Softball Assn.
2801 NE 50th St.
Oklahoma City, OK 73111

American Horse Show Assn.
220 E. 42d St.
New York, NY 10017

American Kennel Club
51 Madison Ave.
New York, NY 10010

American Water Ski Assn.
799 Overlook Dr. SE
Winter Haven, FL 33884

Athletic Congress
One Hoosier Dome
Indianapolis, IN 46225

LPGA
2570 Volusra Ave.
Daytona Beach, FL 32114

Little League Baseball
PO Box 3485
S. Williamsport, PA 17701

National Archery Assn.
1750 E. Boulder St.
Colorado Springs, CO 80909

NASCAR
PO Box 2875
Daytona Beach, FL 32120

NCAA
6201 College Blvd.
Overland Park, KS 66211

National Rifle Assn.
1600 Rhode Island Ave. NW
Washington, DC 20036

Pro Bowlers Assn.
1720 Merriman Rd.
Akron, OH 44334

Pro Rodeo Cowboys Assn.
101 Pro Rodeo Dr.
Colorado Springs, CO 80919

Special Olympics
1350 New York Ave. NW
Washington, DC 20005

Thoroughbred Racing Assn.
420 Fair Hill Dr.
Elkton, MD 21921

U.S. Auto Club
4910 W. 16th St.
Speedway, IN 46224

U.S. Figure Skating Assn.
20 1st St.
Colorado Springs, CO 80906

U.S. Olympic Committee
1750 E. Boulder St.
Colorado Springs, CO 80909

U.S. Ski Team
1500 Kearns
Park City, UT 84060

U.S. Soccer
1750 Boulder St.
Colorado Springs, CO 80909

U.S. Tennis Assn.
1212 Ave. of the Americas
New York, NY 10036

U.S. Trotting Assn.
750 Michigan Ave.
Columbus, OH 43215

BOWLING

PBA Hall of Fame

Performance

Bill Allen
Glenn Allison
Earl Anthony
Barry Asher
Ray Bluth
Roy Buckley
Nelson Burton Jr.
Don Carter
Pat Colwell
Dave Davis
Gary Dickinson
Mike Durbin
Buzz Fazio
Skee Foremsky
Jim Godman
Johnny Guenther
Billy Hardwick
Tommy Hudson
Don Johnson
Joe Joseph
Larry Laub
Don McCune
Mike McGrath
George Pappas
Johnny Petraglia
Dick Ritger
Mark Roth
Jim St. John
Carmen Salvino
Bob Strampe
Harry Smith
Dave Soutar
Jim Stefanich
Dick Weber
Billy Welu
Wayne Zahn

Meritorious service

John Archibald
Eddie Elias
Frank Esposito
Dick Evans
Raymond Firestone
E.A. "Bud" Fisher
Lou Frantz
Harry Golden
Ted Hoffman Jr.
John Jowdy
Joe Kelley
Steve Nagy
Chuck Pezzano
Jack Reichert
Joe Richards
Chris Schenkel
Lorraine Stilzlein
Al Thompson

Firestone Tournament of Champions

Year	Winner	Year	Winner	Year	Winner	Year	Winner
1965	Billy Hardwick	1972	Mike Durbin	1979	George Pappas	1986	Marshall Holman
1966	Wayne Zahn	1973	Jim Godman	1980	Wayne Webb	1987	Pete Weber
1967	Jim Stefanich	1974	Earl Anthony	1981	Steve Cook	1988	Mark Williams
1968	Dave Davis	1975	Dave Davis	1982	Mike Durbin	1989	Del Ballard Jr.
1969	Jim Godman	1976	Marshall Holman	1983	Joe Berardi	1990	Dave Ferraro
1970	Don Johnson	1977	Mike Berlin	1984	Mike Durbin	1991	David Ozio
1971	Johnny Petraglia	1978	Earl Anthony	1985	Mark Williams	1992	Marc McDowell

PBA Leading Money Winners

Total winnings are from PBA, ABC Masters, and BPAA All-Star tournaments only, and do not include numerous other tournaments or earnings from special television shows and matches.

Year	Bowler	Amount	Year	Bowler	Amount	Year	Bowler	Amount
1962	Don Carter	$49,972	1972	Don Johnson	$56,648	1982	Earl Anthony	$134,760
1963	Dick Weber	46,333	1973	Don McCune	69,000	1983	Earl Anthony	135,605
1964	Bob Strampe	33,592	1974	Earl Anthony	99,585	1984	Mark Roth	158,712
1965	Dick Weber	47,674	1975	Earl Anthony	107,585	1985	Mike Aulby	201,200
1966	Wayne Zahn	54,720	1976	Earl Anthony	110,833	1986	Walter Ray Williams Jr.	145,550
1967	Dave Davis	54,165	1977	Mark Roth	105,583	1987	Pete Weber	175,491
1968	Jim Stefanich	67,377	1978	Mark Roth	134,500	1988	Brian Voss	225,485
1969	Billy Hardwick	64,160	1979	Mark Roth	124,517	1989	Mike Aulby	298,237
1970	Mike McGrath	52,049	1980	Wayne Webb	116,700	1990	Amieto Monacelli	204,775
1971	Johnny Petraglia	85,065	1981	Earl Anthony	164,735	1991	David Ozio	225,585

Leading PBA Averages by Year

Year	Bowler	Average	Year	Bowler	Average	Year	Bowler	Average
1962	Don Carter	212.844	1972	Don Johnson	215.290	1982	Marshall Holman	212.844
1963	Billy Hardwick	210.346	1973	Earl Anthony	215.799	1983	Earl Anthony	216.645
1964	Ray Bluth	210.512	1974	Earl Anthony	219.394	1984	Marshall Holman	213.911
1965	Dick Weber	211.895	1975	Earl Anthony	219.060	1985	Mark Baker	213.718
1966	Wayne Zahn	208.663	1976	Mark Roth	215.970	1986	John Gant	214.378
1967	Wayne Zahn	212.342	1977	Mark Roth	218.174	1987	Marshall Holman	216.801
1968	Jim Stefanich	211.895	1978	Mark Roth	219.834	1988	Mark Roth	218.036
1969	Bill Hardwick	212.957	1979	Mark Roth	221.662	1989	Pete Weber	215.432
1970	Nelson Burton Jr.	214.908	1980	Earl Anthony	218.535	1990	Amieto Monacelli	218.158
1971	Don Johnson	213.977	1981	Mark Roth	216.699	1991	Norm Duke	218.208

American Bowling Congress Masters Tournament Champions

Year	Winner	Year	Winner	Year	Winner
1980	Neil Burton, St. Louis, Mo.	1984	Earl Anthony, Dublin, Cal.	1989	Mike Aulby, Indianapolis, Ind.
1981	Randy Lightfoot, St. Charles, Mo.	1985	Steve Wunderlich, St. Louis, Mo.	1990	Chris Warren, Dallas, Tex.
1982	Joe Berardi, Brooklyn, N.Y.	1986	Mark Fahy, Chicago, Ill.	1991	Doug Kent, Canandaigua, N.Y.
1983	Mike Lastowski, Havre de Grace, Md.	1987	Rick Steelsmith, Wichita, Kan.	1992	Ken Johnson, N. Richmond Hills, Tex.
		1988	Del Ballard Jr., Richardson, Tex.		

Most Sanctioned 300 Games

Bowler	Games	Bowler	Games	Bowler	Games
Bob Learn Jr, Erie, Pa.	42	Tony Torrice, Wolcott, Conn.	24	Paul Cannon, Binghamton, N.Y.	19
Jim Johnson Jr., Wilmington, Del.	36	Teata Semiz, Fairfield, N.J.	23	Randy Choat, Granite City, Ill.	18
Mike Whalin, Cincinnati, Oh.	36	Don Anthony, Columbus, Oh.	22	Dick Weber, St. Louis, Mo.	18
Ron Woolet, Louisville, Ky.	33	Jerry Kessler, Dayton, Oh.	22	Steve Wilson, Ft. Lauderdale, Fla.	18
John Wilcox Jr., Shavertown, Pa.	32	Mitch Jabczenski, Detroit, Mich.	21	Frank May Jr., Reading, Pa.	18
Elvin Mesger, Sullivan, Mo.	27	Dave Heller, Highland Falls, N.Y.	21	George Billick, Old Forge, Pa.	17
Ralph Burley Jr., Dayton, Oh.	25	Steve Carson, Oklahoma City, Okla.	21	Dave Williams, Sebastopal, Cal.	17
Steve Gehringer, Reading, Pa.	25	Mark Stibora, Cleveland, Oh.	20	Joe Vito Buenrostro, San Antonio, Tex.	17
Alan Hulsizer, Reading, Pa.	24	Dave Soutar, Kansas City, Mo.	20		

Women's International Bowling Congress Champions in 1992

Queens Tournament—Cindy Coburn-Carroll, Tonawanda, N.Y.
Singles Event—Patty Ann, Puerto Rico
All Events—Mitsuko Tokimoto, Japan
Doubles—Nancy Fehr & Lisa Wagner, Cincinnati, Oh. & Palmetto, Fla.
Team—Hoinke Classic Inc., Cincinnati, Oh.

Most Sanctioned 300 Games

Jeanne Maiden, Tacoma, Wash. 20
Vicki Fischel, Wheat Ridge, Col. 14
Tish Johnson, Panorama City, Cal. 13
Aleta Sill, Dearborn, Mich. 13
Betty Morris, Stockton, Cal. 11
Donna Adamek, Apple Valley, Cal. 10
Cindy Coburn-Carroll, Tonawanda, N.Y. 10
Leanne Barrette, Oklahoma City, Okla. 9
Robin Romeo, Van Nuys, Cal. 9
Cheryl Daniels, Detroit, Mich. 9

Boxing Champions by Classes

As of Aug. 1992 the only generally accepted title holder was in the heavyweight division. There are numerous governing bodies in boxing including the World Boxing Council, the World Boxing Assn., the International Boxing Federation, the United States Boxing Assn., the North American Boxing Federation, and the European Boxing Union. Other organizations are recognized by TV networks and the print media. All the governing bodies have their own champions and assorted boxing divisions. The following are the recognized champions in the principal divisions of the World Boxing Association, the World Boxing Council, and the International Boxing Federation.

Class, Weight Limit	WBA	WBC	IBF
Heavyweight	Evander Holyfield, U.S.	Evander Holyfield, U.S.	Evander Holyfield, U.S.
Cruiserweight (195 lbs.)	Bobby Cruz, U.S.	Anaclet Wamba, France	Jamer Warring, U.S.
Light Heavyweight (175 lbs.)	Iran Barkley, U.S.	Jeff Harding, Australia	Charles Williams, U.S.
Super Middleweight (168 lbs.)	Victor Cordoba, N. Ireland	Mauro Galvano, Italy	vacant
Middleweight (160 lbs.)	Reggie Johnson, U.S.	Julian Jackson, Virgin Islands	James Toney, U.S.
Jr. Middleweight (154 lbs.)	Vinny Pazienza, U.S.	Terry Norris, U.S.	Gianfranco Rosi, Italy
Welterweight (147 lbs.)	Meldrick Taylor, U.S.	Buddy McGirt, U.S.	Maurice Blocker, U.S.
Jr. Welterweight (140 lbs.)	Akinobu Hiranaka, Japan	Julio Cesar Chavez, Mexico	Rafael Pineda, Colombia
Lightweight (135 lbs.)	Joey Gamache, U.S.	vacant	vacant
Jr. Lightweight (130 lbs.)	Genaro Hernandez, U.S.	Azumah Nelson, Ghana	John-John Molina, Puerto Rico
Featherweight (126 lbs.)	Yung Kyun Park, S. Korea	Paul Hodkinson, England	Manual Medina, Mexico
Jr. Featherweight (122 lbs.)	Wilfredo Vasquez, Puerto Rico	Tracy Patterson, U.S.	Welcome Ncita, S. Africa
Bantamweight (118 lbs.)	Eddie Cook, U.S.	Victor Rabanales, Mexico	Orlando Canizales, U.S.
Flyweight (112 lbs.)	Yong Kang Kim, S. Korea	Yuri Arbachakov, Japan	Rudolfo Blanco, Colombia

Ring Champions by Years

*Abandoned title

Heavyweights

1882-1892	John L. Sullivan (a)
1892-1897	James J. Corbett (b)
1897-1899	Robert Fitzsimmons
1899-1905	James J. Jeffries (c)
1905-1906	Marvin Hart
1906-1908	Tommy Burns
1908-1915	Jack Johnson
1915-1919	Jess Willard
1919-1926	Jack Dempsey
1926-1928	Gene Tunney*
1928-1930	vacant
1930-1932	Max Schmeling
1932-1933	Jack Sharkey
1933-1934	Primo Carnera
1934-1935	Max Baer
1935-1937	James J. Braddock
1937-1949	Joe Louis*
1949-1951	Ezzard Charles
1951-1952	Joe Walcott
1952-1956	Rocky Marciano*
1956-1959	Floyd Patterson
1959-1960	Ingemar Johansson
1960-1962	Floyd Patterson
1962-1964	Sonny Liston
1964-1967	Cassius Clay* (Muhammad Ali) (d)
1970-1973	Joe Frazier
1973-1974	George Foreman
1974-1978	Muhammad Ali
1978-1979	Leon Spinks (e), Muhammad Ali*
1978	Ken Norton (WBC), Larry Holmes (WBC) (f)
1979	John Tate (WBA)
1980	Mike Weaver (WBA)
1982	Michael Dokes (WBA)
1983	Gerrie Coetzee (WBA)
1984	Tim Witherspoon (WBC); Pinklon Thomas (WBC); Greg Page (WBA)
1985	Tony Tubbs (WBA); Michael Spinks (IBF)
1986	Tim Witherspoon (WBA); Trevor Berbick (WBC); Mike Tyson (WBC); James (Bonecrusher) Smith (WBA).
1987	Mike Tyson (WBA).
1990	James "Buster" Douglas (WBA, WBC, IBF)
1990	Evander Holyfield (WBA, WBC, IBF)

(a) London Prize Ring (bare knuckle champion).
(b) First Marquis of Queensberry champion.
(c) Jeffries abandoned the title (1905) and designated Marvin Hart and Jack Root as logical contenders. Hart defeated Root in 12 rounds (1905) and in turn was defeated by Tommy Burns (1906) who laid claim to the title. Jack Johnson defeated Burns (1908) and was recognized as champion. He clinched the title by defeating Jeffries in an attempted comeback (1910).
(d) Title declared vacant by the WBA and other groups in 1967 after Clay's refusal to fulfill his military obligation. Joe Frazier was recognized as champion by 6 states, Mexico, and So. America. Jimmy Ellis was declared champion by the WBA. Frazier KOd Ellis, Feb. 16, 1970.
(e) After Spinks defeated Ali, the WBC recognized Ken Norton as champion. Norton subsequently lost his title to Larry Holmes.
(f) Holmes was stripped of his WBC title in 1984. He was the IBF champion when he lost to Michael Spinks.

Light Heavyweights

1903	Jack Root, George Gardner
1903-1905	Bob Fitzsimmons
1905-1912	Philadelphia Jack O'Brien*
1912-1916	Jack Dillon
1916-1920	Battling Levinsky
1920-1922	George Carpentier
1922-1923	Battling Siki
1923-1925	Mike McTigue
1925-1926	Paul Berlenbach
1926-1927	Jack Delaney*
1927-1929	Tommy Loughran*
1930-1934	Maxey Rosenbloom
1934-1935	Bob Olin
1935-1939	John Henry Lewis*
1939	Melio Bettina
1939-1941	Billy Conn*
1941	Anton Christoforidis (won NBA title)
1941-1948	Gus Lesnevich, Freddie Mills
1948-1950	Freddie Mills
1950-1952	Joey Maxim
1952-1960	Archie Moore
1961-1962	vacant
1962-1963	Harold Johnson
1963-1965	Willie Pastrano
1965-1966	Jose Torres
1966-1968	Dick Tiger
1968-1974	Bob Foster*, John Conteh (WBA)
1975-1977	John Conteh (WBC), Miguel Cuello (WBC), Victor Galindez (WBA)
1978	Mike Rossman (WBA), Mate Parlov (WBC), Marvin Johnson (WBC)
1979	Victor Galindez (WBA), Matthew Saad Muhammad (WBC)
1980	Eddie Mustava Muhammad (WBA)
1981	Michael Spinks (WBA), Dwight Braxton (WBC)
1983	Michael Spinks
1986	Marvin Johnson (WBA); Dennis Andries (WBC)
1987	Thomas Hearns (WBC); Leslie Stewart (WBA); Virgil Hill (WBA); Don Lalonde (WBC).
1988	Ray Leonard* (WBC)
1989	Jeff Harding (WBC)
1990	Dennis Andries (WBC)
1991	Thomas Hearns (WBA); Jeff Harding (WBC)
1992	Iran Barkley (WBA)

Middleweights

1884-1891	Jack "Nonpareil" Dempsey
1891-1897	Bob Fitzsimmons*
1897-1907	Tommy Ryan*
1907-1908	Stanley Ketchel, Billy Papke
1908-1910	Stanley Ketchel
1911-1913	vacant
1913	Frank Klaus, George Chip
1914-1917	Al McCoy
1917-1920	Mike O'Dowd
1920-1923	Johnny Wilson
1923-1926	Harry Greb
1926-1931	Tiger Flowers, Mickey Walker
1931-1932	Gorilla Jones (NBA)
1932-1937	Marcel Thil
1938	Al Hostak (NBA), Solly Krieger (NBA)
1939-1940	Al Hostak (NBA)
1941-1947	Tony Zale
1947-1948	Rocky Graziano
1948	Tony Zale, Marcel Cerdan
1949-1951	Jake LaMotta
1951	Ray Robinson, Randy Turpin, Ray Robinson*
1953-1955	Carl (Bobo) Olson
1955-1957	Ray Robinson
1957	Gene Fullmer, Ray Robinson, Carmen Basilio
1958	Ray Robinson
1959	Gene Fullmer (NBA); Ray Robinson (N.Y.)
1960	Gene Fullmer (NBA); Paul Pender (New York and Mass.)
1961	Gene Fullmer (NBA); Terry Downes (New York, Mass., Europe)
1962	Gene Fullmer, Dick Tiger (NBA), Paul Pender (New York and Mass.)*
1963	Dick Tiger (universal).
1963-1965	Joey Giardello
1965-1966	Dick Tiger
1966-1967	Emile Griffith
1967	Nino Benvenuti
1967-1968	Emile Griffith
1968-1970	Nino Benvenuti
1970-1977	Carlos Monzon*
1977-1978	Rodrigo Valdez
1978-1979	Hugo Corro
1979-1980	Vito Antuofermo
1980	Alan Minter, Marvin Hagler
1987	Ray Leonard* (WBC); Thomas Hearns (WBC); Sumbu Kalambay (WBA).
1988	Iran Barkley (WBC)
1989	Mike McCallum (WBA); Roberto Duran (WBC)
1991	Julian Jackson (WBC)
1992	Reggie Johnson (WBA)

Welterweights

1892-1894	Mysterious Billy Smith
1894-1896	Tommy Ryan
1896	Kid McCoy*
1900	Rube Ferns, Matty Matthews
1901	Rube Ferns
1901-1904	Joe Walcott
1904-1906	Dixie Kid, Joe Walcott, Honey Mellody
1907-1911	Mike Sullivan
1911-1915	vacant
1915-1919	Ted Lewis
1919-1922	Jack Britton
1922-1926	Mickey Walker
1926	Pete Latzo
1927-1929	Joe Dundee
1929	Jackie Fields
1930	Jack Thompson, Tommy Freeman
1931	Freeman, Thompson, Lou Brouillard
1932	Jackie Fields
1933	Young Corbett, Jimmy McLarnin
1934	Barney Ross, Jimmy McLarnin
1935-1938	Barney Ross
1938-1940	Henry Armstrong
1940-1941	Fritzie Zivic
1941-1946	Fred Cochrane
1946-1946	Marty Servo*; Ray Robinson (a)
1946-1950	Ray Robinson*
1951	Johnny Bratton (NBA)
1951-1954	Kid Gavilan
1954-1955	Johnny Saxton
1955	Tony De Marco, Carmen Basilio
1956	Carmen Basilio, Johnny Saxton, Basilio
1957	Carmen Basilio*
1958-1960	Virgil Akins, Don Jordan
1960	Benny Paret
1961	Emile Griffith, Benny Paret
1962	Emile Griffith
1963	Luis Rodriguez, Emile Griffith
1964-1966	Emile Griffith*
1966-1969	Curtis Cokes
1969-1970	Jose Napoles, Billy Backus
1971-1975	Jose Napoles
1975-1976	John Stracey (WBC), Angel Espada (WBA)
1976-1979	Carlos Palomino (WBC), Jose Cuevas (WBA)
1979	Wilfredo Benitez (WBC), Sugar Ray Leonard (WBC)
1980	Roberto Duran (WBC), Thomas Hearns (WBA), Sugar Ray Leonard (WBC)
1981-1982	Sugar Ray Leonard*
1983	Donald Curry (WBA); Milton McCrory (WBC)
1985	Donald Curry
1986	Lloyd Honeyghan (WBC)
1987	Mark Breland (WBA); Marlon Starling (WBA); Jorge Vaca (WBC).
1988	Tomas Molinares (WBA); Lloyd Honeyghan (WBC).
1989	Marlon Starling (WBC); Mark Breland (WBA)
1990	Maurice Blocker (WBC); Aaron Davis (WBA)
1991	Meldrick Taylor (WBA); Simon Brown (WBC); Buddy McGirt (WBC)

(a) Robinson gained the title by defeating Tommy Bell in an elimination agreed to by the NY Commission and the NBA. Both claimed Robinson waived his title when he won the middleweight crown from LaMotta in 1951.

Lightweights

1896-1899	Kid Lavigne
1899-1902	Frank Erne
1902-1908	Joe Gans
1908-1910	Battling Nelson
1910-1912	Ad Wolgast
1912-1914	Willie Ritchie
1914-1917	Freddie Welsh
1917-1925	Benny Leonard*
1925	Jimmy Goodrich, Rocky Kansas
1926-1930	Sammy Mandell
1930	Al Singer, Tony Canzoneri
1930-1933	Tony Canzoneri
1933-1935	Barney Ross*
1935-1936	Tony Canzoneri
1936-1938	Lou Ambers
1938	Henry Armstrong
1939	Lou Ambers
1940	Lew Jenkins
1941-1943	Sammy Angott
1944	S. Angott (NBA), J. Zurita (NBA)
1945-1951	Ike Williams (NBA: later universal)
1951-1952	James Carter
1952	Lauro Salas, James Carter
1953-1954	James Carter
1954	Paddy De Marco; James Carter
1955	James Carter; Bud Smith
1956	Bud Smith, Joe Brown
1956-1962	Joe Brown
1962-1965	Carlos Ortiz
1965	Ismael Laguna
1965-1968	Carlos Ortiz
1968-1969	Teo Cruz
1969-1970	Mando Ramos
1970	Ismael Laguna, Ken Buchanan (WBA)
1971	Mando Ramos (WBC), Pedro Carrasco (WBC)
1972-1979	Roberto Duran* (WBA)
1972	Pedro Carrasco, Mando Ramos, Chango Carmona, Rodolfo Gonzalez (all WBC)
1974-1976	Guts Ishimatsu (WBC)
1976-1977	Esteban De Jesus (WBC)
1979	Jim Watt (WBC), Ernesto Espana (WBA)
1980	Hilmer Kenty (WBA)
1981	Alexis Arguello (WBC), Sean O'Grady (WBA), Arturo Frias (WBA)
1982-1984	Ray Mancini (WBA)
1983	Edwin Rosario (WBC)
1984	Livingstone Bramble (WBA); Jose Luis Ramirez (WBC)
1985	Hector (Macho) Camacho (WBC)
1986	Edwin Rosario (WBA); Jose Luis Ramirez (WBC).
1987	Julio Cesar Chavez (WBA).
1989	Edwin Rosario (WBA); Pernell Whitaker (WBC).
1990	Juan Nazario (WBA); Pernell Whitaker (WBA)
1992	Joey Gamache (WBA)

Featherweights

1892-1900	George Dixon (disputed)
1900-1901	Terry McGovern, Young Corbett*
1901-1912	Abe Attell
1912-1923	Johnny Kilbane
1923	Eugene Criqui, Johnny Dundee
1923-1925	Johnny Dundee*
1925-1927	Kid Kaplan*
1927-1928	Benny Bass, Tony Canzoneri
1928-1929	Andre Routis
1929-1932	Battling Battalino*
1932-1934	Tommy Paul (NBA)
1933-1936	Freddie Miller
1936-1937	Petey Sarron
1937-1938	Henry Armstrong*
1938-1940	Joey Archibald (b)
1940-41	Harry Jeffra
1942-1948	Willie Pep
1948-1949	Sandy Saddler
1949-1950	Willie Pep
1950-1957	Sandy Saddler*
1957-1959	Hogan (Kid) Bassey
1959-1963	Davey Moore
1963-1964	Sugar Ramos
1964-1967	Vicente Saldivar*
1968-1971	Paul Rojas (WBA), Sho Saijo (WBA)
1971	Antonio Gomez (WBA), Kuniaki Shibada (WBC)
1972	Ernesto Marcel* (WBA), Clemente Sanchez* (WBC), Jose Legra (WBC)
1973	Eder Jofre (WBC)
1974	Ruben Olivares (WBA), Alexis Arguello (WBA), Bobby Chacon (WBC)
1975	Ruben Olivares (WBC), David Kotey (WBC)
1976	Danny Lopez (WBC)
1977	Rafael Ortega (WBA)
1978	Cecilio Lastra (WBA), Eusebio Pedrosa (WBA)
1980	Salvador Sanchez (WBC)
1982	Juan LaPorte (WBC)
1984	Wilfredo Gomez (WBC); Azumah Nelson (WBC)
1985	Barry McGuigan (WBA)
1986	Steve Cruz (WBA)
1987	Antonio Esparragoza (WBA)
1988	Jeff Fenech (WBC)
1990	Marcos Villasana (WBC)
1991	Park Yung Kyun (WBA)
1991	Paul Hodkinson (WBC)

(b) After Petey Scalzo knocked out Archibald in an overweight match and was refused a title bout, the NBA named Scalzo champion. The NBA title succession: Scalzo, 1938-1941; Richard Lemos, 1941; Jackie Wilson, 1941-1943; Jackie Callura, 1943; Phil Terranova, 1943-1944; Sal Bartolo, 1944-1946.

History of Heavyweight Championship Bouts

*Title Changed Hands

1889—July 8—John L. Sullivan def. Jake Kilrain, 75, Richburg, Miss. Last championship bare knuckles bout.

***1892**—Sept. 7—James J. Corbett def. John L. Sullivan, 21, New Orleans. Big gloves used for first time.

1894—Jan. 25—James J. Corbett KOd Charley Mitchell, 3, Jacksonville, Fla.

***1897**—Bob Fitzsimmons def. James J. Corbett, 14, Carson City, Nev.

***1899**—June 9—James J. Jeffries def. Bob Fitzsimmons, 11, Coney Island, N.Y.

1899—Nov. 3—James J. Jeffries def. Tom Sharkey, 25, Coney Island, N.Y.

1900—May 11—James J. Jeffries KOd James J. Corbett, 23, Coney Island, N.Y.

1901—Nov. 15—James J. Jeffries KOd Gus Ruhlin, 5, San Francisco.

1902—July 25—James J. Jeffries KOd Bob Fitzsimmons, 8, San Francisco.

1903—Aug. 14—James J. Jeffries KOd James J. Corbett, 10, San Francisco.

1904—Aug. 26—James J. Jeffries KOd Jack Monroe, 2, San Francisco.

***1905**—James J. Jeffries retired, July 3—Marvin Hart KOd Jack Root, 12, Reno. Jeffries refereed and presented the title to the victor. Jack O'Brien also claimed the title.

***1906**—Feb. 23—Tommy Burns def. Marvin Hart, 20, Los Angeles.

1906—Nov. 28—Philadelphia Jack O'Brien and Tommy Burns, 20, draw, Los Angeles.

1907—May 8—Tommy Burns def. Jack O'Brien, 20, Los Angeles.

1907—July 4—Tommy Burns KOd Bill Squires, 1, Colma, Cal.

1907—Dec. 2—Tommy Burns KOd Gunner Moir, 10, London.

1908—Feb. 10—Tommy Burns KOd Jack Palmer, 4, London.

1908—March 17—Tommy Burns KOd Jem Roche, 1, Dublin.

1908—April 18—Tommy Burns KOd Jewey Smith, 5, Paris.

1908—June 13—Tommy Burns KOd Bill Squires, 8, Paris.

1908—Aug. 24—Tommy Burns KOd Bill Squires, 13, Sydney, New South Wales.

1908—Sept. 2—Tommy Burns KOd Bill Lang, 2, Melbourne, Australia.

***1908**—Dec. 26—Jack Johnson KOd Tommy Burns, 14, Sydney, Australia. Police halted contest.

1909—May 19—Jack Johnson and Jack O'Brien, 6, draw, Philadelphia.

1909—June 30—Jack Johnson and Tony Ross, 6, draw, Pittsburgh.

1909—Sept. 9—Jack Johnson and Al Kaufman, 10, draw, San Francisco.

1909—Oct. 16—Jack Johnson KOd Stanley Ketchel, 12, Colma, Cal.

1910—July 4—Jack Johnson KOd Jim Jeffries, 15, Reno, Nev. Jeffries came back from retirement.

1912—July 4—Jack Johnson def. Jim Flynn, 9, Las Vegas, N.M. Contest stopped by police.

1913—Nov. 28—Jack Johnson KOd Andre Spaul, 2, Paris.

1913—Dec. 9—Jack Johnson and Jim Johnson, 10, draw, Paris. Bout called a draw when Jack Johnson declared he had broken his arm.

1914—June 27—Jack Johnson def. Frank Moran, 20, Paris.

***1915**—April 5—Jess Willard KOd Jack Johnson, 26, Havana. Cuba.

1916—March 25—Jess Willard and Frank Moran, 10, draw, New York.

***1919**—July 4—Jack Dempsey KOd Jess Willard, Toledo, Oh. Willard failed to answer bell for 4th round.

1920—Sept. 6—Jack Dempsey KOd Billy Miske, 3, Benton Harbor, Mich.

1920—Dec. 14—Jack Dempsey KOd Bill Brennan, 12, New York.

1921—July 2—Jack Dempsey KOd George Carpentier, 4, Boyle's Thirty Acres, Jersey City, N.J. Carpentier had held the so-called white heavyweight title since July 16, 1914, in a series established in 1913, after Jack Johnson's exile in Europe late in 1912.

1923—July 4—Jack Dempsey def. Tom Gibbons, 15, Shelby, Mont.

1923—Sept. 14—Jack Dempsey KOd Luis Firpo, 2, New York.

***1926**—Sept. 23—Gene Tunney def. Jack Dempsey, 10, Philadelphia.

1927—Sept. 22—Gene Tunney def. Jack Dempsey, 10, Chicago.

1928—July 26—Gene Tunney KOd Tom Heeney, 11, New York; soon afterward he announced his retirement.

***1930**—June 12—Max Schmeling def. Jack Sharkey, 4, New York. Sharkey fouled Schmeling in a bout which was generally considered to have resulted in the election of a successor to Gene Tunney, New York.

1931—July 3—Max Schmeling KOd Young Stribling, 15, Cleveland.

***1932**—June 21—Jack Sharkey def. Max Schmeling, 15, New York.

***1933**—June 29—Primo Carnera KOd Jack Sharkey, 6, New York.

1933—Oct. 22—Primo Carnera def. Paulino Uzcudun, 15, Rome.

1934—March 1—Primo Carnera def. Tommy Loughran, 15, Miami.

***1934**—June 14—Max Baer KOd Primo Carnera, 11, New York.

***1935**—June 13—James J. Braddock def. Max Baer, 15, New York.

***1937**—June 22—Joe Louis KOd James J. Braddock, 8, Chicago.

1937—Aug. 30—Joe Louis def. Tommy Farr, 15, New York.

1938—Feb. 23—Joe Louis KOd Nathan Mann, 3, New York.

1938—April 1—Joe Louis KOd Harry Thomas, 5, New York.

1938—June 22—Joe Louis KOd Max Schmeling, 1, New York.

1939—Jan. 25—Joe Louis KOd John H. Lewis, 1, New York.

1939—April 17—Joe Louis KOd Jack Roper, 1, Los Angeles.

1939—June 28—Joe Louis KOd Tony Galento, 4, New York.
1939—Sept. 20—Joe Louis KOd Bob Pastor, 11, Detroit.
1940—February 9—Joe Louis def. Arturo Godoy, 15, New York.
1940—March 29—Joe Louis KOd Johnny Paycheck, 2, New York.
1940—June 20—Joe Louis KOd Arturo Godoy, 8, New York.
1940—Dec. 16—Joe Louis KOd Al McCoy, 6, Boston.
1941—Jan. 31—Joe Louis KOd Red Burman, 5, New York.
1941—Feb. 17—Joe Louis KOd Gus Dorzaio, 2, Philadelphia.
1941—March 21—Joe Louis KOd Abe Simon, 13, Detroit.
1941—April 8—Joe Louis KOd Tony Musto, 9, St. Louis.
1941—May 23—Joe Louis def. Buddy Baer, 7, Washington, D.C., on a disqualification.
1941—June 18—Joe Louis KOd Billy Conn, 13, New York.
1941—Sept. 29—Joe Louis KOd Lou Nova, 6, New York.
1942—Jan. 9—Joe Louis KOd Buddy Baer, 1, New York.
1942—March 27—Joe Louis KOd Abe Simon, 6, New York.
1946—June 19—Joe Louis KOd Billy Conn, 8, New York.
1946—Sept. 18—Joe Louis KOd Tami Mauriello, 1, New York.
1947—Dec. 5—Joe Louis def. Joe Walcott, 15, New York.
1948—June 25—Joe Louis KOd Joe Walcott, 11, New York.
*1949—June 22—Following Joe Louis' retirement Ezzard Charles def. Joe Walcott, 15, Chicago, NBA recognition only.
1949—Aug. 10—Ezzard Charles KOd Gus Lesnevich, 7, New York.
1949—Oct. 14—Ezzard Charles KOd Pat Valentino, 8, San Francisco; clinched American title.
1950—Aug. 15—Ezzard Charles KOd Freddy Beshore, 14, Buffalo.
1950—Sept. 27—Ezzard Charles def. Joe Louis in latter's attempted comeback, 15, New York; universal recognition.
1950—Dec. 5—Ezzard Charles KOd Nick Barone, 11, Cincinnati.
1951—Jan. 12—Ezzard Charles KOd Lee Oma, 10, New York.
1951—March 7—Ezzard Charles def. Joe Walcott, 15, Detroit.
1951—May 30—Ezzard Charles def. Joey Maxim, light heavyweight champion, 15, Chicago.
*1951—July 18—Joe Walcott KOd Ezzard Charles, 7, Pittsburgh.
1952—June 5—Joe Walcott def. Ezzard Charles, 15, Philadelphia.
*1952—Sept. 23—Rocky Marciano KOd Joe Walcott, 13, Philadelphia.
1953—May 15—Rocky Marciano KOd Joe Walcott, 1, Chicago.
1953—Sept. 24—Rocky Marciano KOd Roland LaStarza, 11, New York.
1954—June 17—Rocky Marciano def. Ezzard Charles, 15, New York.
1954—Sept. 17—Rocky Marciano KOd Ezzard Charles, 8, New York.
1955—May 16—Rocky Marciano KOd Don Cockell, 9, San Francisco.
1955—Sept. 21—Rocky Marciano KOd Archie Moore, 9, New York. Marciano retired undefeated, Apr. 27, 1956.
*1956—Nov. 30—Floyd Patterson KOd Archie Moore, 5, Chicago.
1957—July 29—Floyd Patterson KOd Hurricane Jackson, 10, New York.
1957—Aug. 22—Floyd Patterson KOd Pete Rademacher, 6, Seattle.
1958—Aug. 18—Floyd Patterson KOd Roy Harris, 12, Los Angeles.
1959—May 1—Floyd Patterson KOd Brian London, 11, Indianapolis.
*1959—June 26—Ingemar Johansson KOd Floyd Patterson, 3, New York.
*1960—June 20—Floyd Patterson KOd Ingemar Johansson, 5, New York. First heavyweight in boxing history to regain title.
1961—Mar. 13—Floyd Patterson KOd Ingemar Johansson, 6, Miami Beach.
1961—Dec. 4—Floyd Patterson KOd Tom McNeeley, 4, Toronto.
*1962—Sept. 25—Sonny Liston KOd Floyd Patterson, 1, Chicago.
1963—July 22—Sonny Liston KOd Floyd Patterson, 1, Las Vegas.
*1964—Feb. 25—Cassius Clay KOd Sonny Liston, 7, Miami Beach.
1965—May 25—Cassius Clay KOd Sonny Liston, 1, Lewiston, Maine.
1965—Nov. 11—Cassius Clay KOd Floyd Patterson, 12, Las Vegas.
1966—Mar. 29—Cassius Clay def. George Chuvalo, 15, Toronto.
1966—May 21—Cassius Clay KOd Henry Cooper, 6, London.
1966—Aug. 6—Cassius Clay KOd Brian London, 3, London.
1966—Sept. 10—Cassius Clay KOd Karl Mildenberger, 12, Frankfurt, Germany.
1966—Nov. 14—Cassius Clay KOd Cleveland Williams, 3, Houston.
1967—Feb. 6—Cassius Clay def. Ernie Terrell, 15, Houston.
1967—Mar. 22—Cassius Clay KOd Zora Folley, 7, New York. Clay was stripped of his title by the WBA and others for refusing military service.
*1970—Feb. 16—Joe Frazier KOd Jimmy Ellis, 5, New York.
1970—Nov. 18—Joe Frazier KOd Bob Foster, 2, Detroit.
1971—Mar. 8—Joe Frazier def. Cassius Clay (Muhammad Ali), 15, New York.
1972—Jan. 15—Joe Frazier KOd Terry Daniels, 4, New Orleans.
1972—May 25—Joe Frazier KOd Ron Stander, 5, Omaha.
*1973—Jan. 22—George Foreman KOd Joe Frazier, 2, Kingston, Jamaica.
1973—Sept. 1—George Foreman KOd Joe Roman, 1, Tokyo.
1974—Mar. 3—George Foreman KOd Ken Norton, 2, Caracas.
*1974—Oct. 30—Muhammad Ali KOd George Foreman, 8, Zaire.
1975—Mar. 24—Muhammad Ali KOd Chuck Wepner, 15, Cleveland.
1975—May 16—Muhammad Ali KOd Ron Lyle, 11, Las Vegas.
1975—June 30—Muhammad Ali def. Joe Bugner, 15, Malaysia.
1975—Oct. 1—Muhammad Ali KOd Joe Frazier, 14, Manila.
1976—Feb. 20—Muhammad Ali KOd Jean-Pierre Coopman, 5, San Juan.
1976—Apr. 30—Muhammad Ali def. Jimmy Young, 15, Landover, Md.
1976—May 25—Muhammad Ali KOd Richard Dunn, 5, Munich.
1976—Sept. 28—Muhammad Ali def. Ken Norton, 15, New York.
1977—May 16—Muhammad Ali def. Alfredo Evangelista, 15, Landover, Md.
1977—Sept. 29—Muhammad Ali def. Earnie Shavers, 15, New York.
*1978—Feb. 15—Leon Spinks def. Muhammad Ali, 15, Las Vegas.
*1978—Sept. 15—Muhammad Ali def. Leon Spinks, 15, New Orleans. Ali retired in 1979.

(Bouts when title changed hands only)

*1978—June 9—(WBC) Larry Holmes def. Ken Norton, 15, Las Vegas.
*1980—Mar. 31—(WBA) Mike Weaver KOd John Tate, 15, Knoxville.
*1982—Dec. 10—(WBA) Michael Dokes KOd Mike Weaver, 1, Las Vegas.
*1983—Sept. 23—(WBA) Gerrie Coetzee KOd Michael Dokes, 10, Richfield, Oh.
*1984—Mar. 10—(WBC) Tim Witherspoon def. Greg Page, 12, Las Vegas, Nev.
*1984—Aug. 31—(WBC) Pinklon Thomas def. Tim Witherspoon, 12, Las Vegas, Nev.
*1984—Dec. 2—(WBA) Greg Page KOd Gerrie Coetzee, 8, Sun City, Bophuthatswana
*1985—Apr. 29—(WBA) Tony Tubbs def. Greg Page, 15, Buffalo, N.Y.
*1985—Sept. 21—(IBF) Michael Spinks def. Larry Holmes, 15, Las Vegas, Nev.
*1986—Jan. 17—(WBA) Tim Witherspoon def. Tony Tubbs, 15, Atlanta, Ga.
*1986—Mar. 23—(WBC) Trevor Berbick def. Pinklon Thomas, 12, Miami, Fla.
*1986—Nov. 22—(WBC) Mike Tyson KOd Trevor Berbick, 2, Las Vegas.
*1986—Dec. 12—(WBA) James (Bonecrusher) Smith KOd Tim Witherspoon, 1, New York.
*(1987—Mar. 7—(WBA) Mike Tyson def. James (Bonecrusher) Smith, 12, Las Vegas.
*1988—June 27—(IBF) Mike Tyson KOd Michael Spinks, 1, Atlantic City.
*1990—Feb. 11—(WBA, WBC, IBF) James "Buster" Douglas KOd Mike Tyson, 10, Tokyo.
*1990—Oct. 25—(WBA, WBC, IBF) Evander Holyfield KOd James "Buster" Douglas, 3, Las Vegas.

Notable Sports Personalities

Henry Aaron, b. 1934: Milwaukee-Atlanta outfielder hit record 755 home runs; led NL 4 times.
Kareem Abdul-Jabbar, b. 1947: Milwaukee, L.A. Lakers center; MVP 6 times; leading scorer twice; playoff MVP, 1971, 1985; all-time leading NBA scorer.
Grover Cleveland Alexander, (1887-1950): pitcher won 374 NL games; pitched 16 shutouts, 1916.
Muhammad Ali, b. 1942: 3-time heavyweight champion.
Ken Anderson, b. 1949: Cinn. Bengals quarterback led AFC in passing 4 times.
Mario Andretti, b. 1940; won Indy 500, 1969; Grand Prix champ, 1978.
Eddie Arcaro, b. 1916: jockey rode 4,779 winners including the Kentucky Derby 5 times; the Preakness and Belmont Stakes 6 times each.
Henry Armstrong, (1912-1988): boxer held feather-, welter-, light-weight titles simultaneously, 1937-38.
Arthur Ashe, b. 1943: U.S. singles champ, 1968, Wimbledon champ, 1975.
Red Auerbach, b. 1917: coached Boston Celtics to 9 NBA championships.
Ernie Banks, b. 1931: Chicago Cubs slugger hit 512 NL homers: twice MVP.
Roger Bannister, b. 1929: Briton ran first sub 4-minute mile, May 6, 1954.
Rick Barry, b. 1944: NBA scoring leader, 1967; ABA, 1969.
Sammy Baugh, b. 1914: Washington Redskins quarterback held numerous records upon retirement after 16 pro seasons.
Elgin Baylor, b. 1934: L.A. Lakers forward; 1st team all-star 10 times.
Jean Beliveau, b. 1931: Montreal Canadiens center scored 507 goals; twice MVP.
Johnny Bench, b. 1947: Cincinnati Reds catcher; MVP twice; led league in home runs twice, RBIs 3 times.
Patty Berg, b. 1918: won over 80 golf tournaments: AP Woman Athlete-of-the-Year 3 times.
Yogi Berra, b. 1925: N.Y. Yankees catcher; MVP 3 times; played in 14 World Series.
Raymond Berry, b. 1933: Baltimore Colts receiver caught 631 passes.
Matt Biondi, b. 1965: swimmer won 5 gold medals at 1988 Olympics.
Larry Bird, b. 1956: Boston Celtics forward; chosen MVP 1984-86, playoff MVP, 1984, 1986.
George Blanda, b. 1927: quarterback, kicker; 26 years as active player, scoring record 2,002 points.
Wade Boggs, b. 1958: AL Batting champ, 1983, 1985-88.
Bjorn Borg, b. 1956: led Sweden to first Davis Cup, 1975; Wimbledon champion, 5 times.
Mike Bossy, b.1957; N.Y. Islanders right wing scored over 50 goals 8 times.
Ray Bourque, b. 1960: Boston Bruins defenseman won Norris Trophy 4 times.
Terry Bradshaw, b. 1948; Pittsburgh Steelers quarterback led team to 4 Super Bowl titles.
George Brett, b. 1953: Kansas City Royals 3d baseman led AL in batting, 1976, 1980, 1990; MVP, 1980.
Lou Brock, b. 1939: St. Louis Cardinals outfielder stole record 118 bases, 1974; led NL 8 times.
Jimmy Brown, b. 1936: Cleveland Browns fullback ran for 12,312 career yards; MVP 3 times.
Paul Brown, (1908-1991), football owner, coach; led Cleveland Browns to 3 NFL championships.
Paul "Bear" Bryant, (1913-1983), college football coach with 323 victories.
Maria Bueno, b. 1939: U.S. singles champ 4 times; Wimbledon champ 3 times.
Dick Butkus, b. 1942: Chicago Bears linebacker twice chosen best NFL defensive player.
Dick Button, b. 1929: figure skater won 1948, 1952 Olympic gold medals; world titlist, 1948-52.
Walter Camp, (1859-1925): Yale football player, coach, athletic director; established many rules; promoted All-America designations.
Roy Campanella, b. 1921: Brooklyn Dodgers catcher; MVP 3 times.
Earl Campbell, b. 1955: NFL running back; NFL MVP 1978-1980.
Jose Canseco, b. 1964: outfielder; AL MVP 1988.
Rod Carew, b. 1945: AL infielder won 7 batting titles; MVP, 1977.
Steve Carlton, b. 1944: NL pitcher won 20 games 5 times, Cy Young award 4 times.
Billy Casper, b. 1931: PGA Player-of-the-Year 3 times; U.S. Open champ twice.
Wilt Chamberlain, b. 1936: center was NBA leading scorer 7 times; MVP 4 times.
Bobby Clarke, b. 1949: Philadelphia Flyers center led team to 2 Stanley Cup championships: MVP 3 times.
Roger Clemens, b. 1962: Boston Red Sox pitcher; AL MVP 1986; Cy Young Award 1986, 1987, 1991.
Roberto Clemente, (1934-1972): Pittsburgh Pirates outfielder won 4 batting titles; MVP, 1966.
Ty Cobb, (1886-1961): Detroit Tigers outfielder had record .367 lifetime batting average, 12 batting titles.
Sebastian Coe, b. 1956: Briton won Olympic 1,500-meter run, 1980, 1984.
Nadia Comaneci, b. 1961: Romanian gymnast won 3 gold medals, achieved 7 perfect scores, 1976 Olympics.
Maureen Connolly, (1934-1969): won tennis "grand slam," 1953; AP Woman-Athlete-of-the-Year 3 times.
Jimmy Connors, b. 1952: U.S. singles champ 5 times; Wimbledon champ twice.
James J. Corbett, (1866-1933): heavyweight champion, 1892-97; credited with being the first "scientific" boxer.
Angel Cordero, b. 1942: leading money winner, 1976, 1982-83; rode 3 Kentucky Derby winners.
Margaret Smith Court, b. 1942: Australian won U.S. singles championship 5 times; Wimbledon champ 3 times.
Bob Cousy, b. 1928: Boston Celtics guard led team to 6 NBA championships: MVP, 1957.
Andre Dawson, b. 1954: slugger led NL in home runs, MVP, 1987.
Dizzy Dean, (1911-1974): colorful pitcher for St. Louis Cardinals "Gashouse Gang" in the 30s; MVP, 1934.
Jack Dempsey, (1895-1983); heavyweight champion, 1919-26.
Eric Dickerson, b. 1960: running back ran for NFL record 2,105 yds., 1984; led NFC 3 times, AFC twice.
Joe DiMaggio, b. 1914: N.Y. Yankees outfielder hit safely in record 56 consecutive games, 1941; MVP 3 times.
Leo Durocher, (1906-1991); manager won 3 NL pennants.
Stefan Edberg, b. 1966; U.S. singles champ 1991, 1992; Wimbleton champ 1988, 1990.
Gertrude Ederle, b. 1906: first woman to swim English Channel, broke existing men's record, 1926.
Julius Erving, b. 1950: MVP and leading scorer in ABA 3 times; NBA MVP, 1981.
Phil Esposito, b. 1942: NHL scoring leader 5 times.
Chris Evert, b. 1954: U.S. singles champ 6 times, Wimbledon champ 3 times.
Patrick Ewing, b. 1962: center led Georgetown Univ. to 1984 NCAA championship.
Ray Ewry, (1873-1937): track and field star won 8 gold medals, 1900, 1904, and 1908 Olympics.
Juan Fangio, b. 1911: World Grand Prix champion 5 times.
Bob Feller, b. 1918: Cleveland Indians pitcher won 266 games; pitched 3 no-hitters, 12 one-hitters.
Peggy Fleming, b. 1948: world figure skating champion, 1966-68; gold medalist 1968 Olympics.
Whitey Ford, b. 1928: N.Y. Yankees pitcher won record 10 World Series games.
Dick Fosbury, b. 1947: high jumper won 1968 Olympic gold medal; developed the "Fosbury Flop."
Jimmie Foxx, (1907-1967): Red Sox, Athletics slugger; MVP 3 times; triple crown, 1933.
A.J. Foyt, b. 1935: won Indy 500 4 times; U.S. Auto Club champ 7 times.
Joe Frazier, b. 1944: heavyweight champion, 1970-73.
Lou Gehrig, (1903-1941): N.Y. Yankees 1st baseman played record 2,130 consecutive games; MVP, 1936.
George Gervin, b. 1952: leading NBA scorer, 1978-80, 1982.
Althea Gibson, b. 1927: twice U.S. and Wimbledon singles champ.
Bob Gibson, b. 1935: St. Louis Cardinals pitcher won Cy Young award twice; struck out 3,117 batters.
Frank Gifford, b. 1930: N.Y. Giants back; MVP, 1956.
Dwight Gooden, b. 1964: N.Y. Mets pitcher was NL Rookie of Year, 1984; Cy Young award, 1985.
Steffi Graf, b. 1969: W. German won tennis "grand slam," 1988; U.S. champ 1988, 1989; Wimbleton champ 4 times.
Otto Graham, b. 1921: Cleveland Browns quarterback; all-pro 4 times.
Red Grange, b 1903: All-America at Univ. of Illinois 1923-25; played for Chicago Bears, 1925-35.
Joe Greene, b. 1946: Pittsburgh Steelers lineman; twice NFL outstanding defensive player.
Wayne Gretzky, b. 1961: Edmonton Oilers center scored record 92 goals, 212 pts., 1982; MVP, 1980-87, 1989.
Florence Griffith Joyner, b. 1959: sprinter won 3 gold medals at 1988 Olympics.

Lefty Grove, (1900-1975): pitcher won 300 AL games; 20-game winner 8 times.
Tony Gwynn, b. 1960: NL batting champ, 1984, 1987-1989.
Walter Hagen, (1892-1969): won PGA championship 5 times. British Open 4 times.
George Halas, (1895-1983); founder-coach of Chicago Bears; won 5 NFL championships.
Bill Hartack, b. 1932: jockey rode 5 Kentucky Derby winners.
John Havlicek, b. 1940: Boston Celtics forward scored over 26,000 NBA points.
Rickey Henderson, b. 1958; AL outfielder stole record 130 bases, 1982, record lifetime steals; AL MVP, 1990.
Sonja Henie, (1912-1969): world champion figure skater, 1927-36; Olympic gold medalist, 1928, 1932, 1936.
Ben Hogan, b. 1912: won 4 U.S. Open championships, 2 PGA, 2 Masters.
Evander Holyfield, b. 1962; world heavyweight champion since 1990.
Rogers Hornsby, (1896-1963): NL 2d baseman batted record .424 in 1924; twice won triple crown; batting leader, 1920-25.
Paul Hornung, b. 1935: Green Bay Packers runner-placekicker scored record 176 points, 1960.
Gordie Howe, b. 1928: hockey forward; NHL MVP 6 times.
Carl Hubbell, (1903-1988): N.Y. Giants pitcher; 20-game winner 5 consecutive years, 1933-37.
Bobby Hull, b. 1939: NHL all-star 10 times.
Brett Hull, b. 1964; St. Louis Blues forward led NHL in goals, 1990-92; MVP 1991.
Catfish Hunter, b 1946: pitched perfect game, 1968; 20-game winner 5 times.
Don Hutson, b. 1913: Green Bay Packers receiver caught 99 NFL touchdown passes.
Reggie Jackson, b. 1946: slugger led AL in home runs 4 times; MVP, 1973; hit 5 World Series home runs, 1977.
Jack Johnson, (1878-1946): heavyweight champion, 1910-15.
Magic Johnson, b. 1959: NBA MVP 1987, 1989, 1990. Playoff MVP 1980, 1982, 1987.
Walter Johnson, (1887-1946): Washington Senators pitcher won 413 games.
Bobby Jones, (1902-1971); won "grand slam of golf" 1930; U.S. Amateur champ 5 times, U.S. Open champ 4 times.
Deacon Jones, b. 1938: L.A. Rams lineman; twice NFL outstanding defensive player.
Michael Jordan, b. 1963: NBA leading scorer, 1987-92; MVP, 1988, 1991, 1992; Playoff MVP, 1991, 1992.
Jackie Joyner-Kersee, b. 1962; Olympic gold medalist in heptathlon, 1988, 1992.
Sonny Jurgensen, b. 1934: quarterback named all-pro 5 times.
Duke Kahanamoku, (1890-1968): swimmer won 1912, 1920 Olympic gold medals in 100-meter freestyle.
Harmon Killebrew, b. 1936: Minnesota Twins slugger led AL in home runs 6 times.
Jean Claude Killy, b. 1943: French skier won 3 1968 Olympic gold medals.
Ralph Kiner, b. 1922: Pittsburgh Pirates slugger led NL in home runs 7 consecutive years, 1946-52.
Billie Jean King, b. 1943: U.S. singles champ 4 times; Wimbledon champ 6 times.
Bob Knight, b. 1940: Indiana U. basketball coach lead team to NCAA championships, 1976, 1981, 1987.
Olga Korbut, b. 1955: Soviet gymnast won 3 1972 Olympic gold medals.
Sandy Koufax, b. 1935: Dodgers pitcher won Cy Young award 3 times; lowest ERA in NL, 1962-66; pitched 4 no-hitters, one a perfect game.
Guy Lafleur, b. 1951: forward led NHL in scoring 3 times; MVP, 1977, 1978.
Tom Landry, b. 1924: Dallas Cowboys head coach 1960-88.
Rod Laver, b. 1938: Australian won tennis "grand slam," 1962, 1969; Wimbledon champ 4 times.
Mario Lemieux, b. 1965: NHL leading scorer, 1988-1989, 1992; MVP, 1988; Playoff MVP, 1991, 1992.
Ivan Lendl, b. 1960: U.S. singles champ, 1985-87.
Sugar Ray Leonard, b. 1956: former world welterweight champ.
Carl Lewis, b. 1961: track and field star won 8 Olympic gold medals in sprinting and the long jump.
Vince Lombardi, (1913-1970): Green Bay Packers coach led, team to 5 NFL championships and 2 Super Bowl victories.
Joe Louis, (1914-1981): 1914: heavyweight champion, 1937-49.
Sid Luckman, b. 1916: Chicago Bears quarterback led team to 4 NFL championships; MVP, 1943.
Connie Mack, (1862-1956): Philadelphia Athletics manager, 1901-50; won 9 pennants, 5 championships.
Bill Madlock, b. 1951: NL batting leader 4 times.
Moses Malone, b. 1955: NBA center was MVP 1979, 1982, 1983.
Mickey Mantle, b. 1931: N.Y. Yankees outfielder; triple crown, 1956; 18 World Series home runs.
Pete Maravich (1948-1988): guard scored NCAA record 44.2 ppg during collegiate career; led NBA in scoring, 1977.
Rocky Marciano, (1923-1969): heavyweight champion, 1952-56; retired undefeated.
Dan Marino, b. 1961: Miami Dolphins quarterback passed for NFL record 5,084 yds, 1984.
Roger Maris, (1934-1985): N.Y. Yankees outfielder hit record 61 home runs, 1961; MVP, 1960 and 1961.
Eddie Mathews, b. 1931: Milwaukee-Atlanta 3d baseman hit 512 career home runs.
Christy Mathewson, (1880-1925): N.Y. Giants pitcher won 373 games.
Bob Mathias, b. 1930: decathlon gold medalist, 1948, 1952.
Don Mattingly, b. 1961: N.Y. Yankees 1st baseman won 1984 AL batting title; MVP, 1985.
Willie Mays, b. 1931: N.Y.-S.F. Giants center fielder hit 660 home runs; twice MVP.
Willie McCovey, b. 1938: S.F. Giants slugger hit 521 home runs; led NL 3 times.
John McEnroe, b. 1959: U.S. singles champ, 1979-81, 1984; Wimbledon champ, 1981, 1983-84.
John McGraw, (1873-1934): N.Y. Giants manager led team to 10 pennants, 3 championships.
Mark Messier, center chosen NHL MVP, 1990; Conn Smythe Trophy, 1984.
George Mikan, b. 1924: Minn. Lakers center considered the best basketball player of the first half of the century.
Stan Mikita, b. 1940: Chicago Black Hawks center led NHL in scoring 4 times; MVP twice.
Joe Montana, b. 1956: S.F. 49ers QB was Super Bowl MVP, 1982, 1985, 1990.
Archie Moore, b. 1913: world light-heavyweight champion, 1952-62.
Howie Morenz, (1902-1937): Montreal Canadiens forward considered the best hockey player of the first half of the century.
Joe Morgan, b. 1943: National League MVP, 1975, 1976.
Thurman Munson, (1947-1979): N.Y. Yankees catcher; MVP, 1976.
Dale Murphy, b. 1956: outfielder chosen NL MVP 1982, 1983.
Stan Musial, b. 1920: St. Louis Cardinals star won 7 NL batting titles; MVP 3 times.
Bronko Nagurski, (1908-1990): Chicago Bears fullback and tackle; gained over 4,000 yds. rushing.
Joe Namath, b. 1943: quarterback led N.Y. Jets to 1969 Super Bowl title.
Martina Navratilova, b. 1956: Wimbledon champ 8 times, U.S. champ 1983-1984; 1986-87.
Byron Nelson, b. 1912: won 11 consecutive golf tournaments in 1945; twice Masters and PGA titlist.
Ernie Nevers, (1903-1976): Stanford star selected the best college fullback to play between 1919-1969.
John Newcombe, b. 1943: Australian twice U.S. singles champ; Wimbledon titlist 3 times.
Jack Nicklaus, b. 1940: PGA Player-of-the-Year, 1967, 1972; leading money winner 8 times; won Masters 6 times.
Chuck Noll, b. 1931: Pittsburgh Steelers coach led team to 4 Super Bowl titles.
Paavo Nurmi, (1897-1973): Finnish distance runner won 6 Olympic gold medals, 1920, 1924, 1928.
Al Oerter, b. 1936: discus thrower won gold medal at 4 consecutive Olympics, 1956-68.
Bobby Orr, b. 1948: Boston Bruins defenseman; Norris Trophy 8 times; led NHL in scoring twice, assists 5 times.
Mel Ott, (1909-1958): N.Y. Giants outfielder hit 511 home runs; led NL 6 times.
Jesse Owens, (1913-1980): track and field star won 4 1936 Olympic gold medals.
Satchel Paige, (1906-1982): pitcher starred in Negro leagues, 1924-48; entered major leagues at age 42.
Arnold Palmer, b. 1929: golf's first $1 million winner; won 4 Masters, 2 British Opens.
Jim Palmer, b. 1945: Baltimore Orioles pitcher; Cy Young award 3 times; 20-game winner 7 times.
Floyd Patterson, b. 1935: twice heavyweight champion.
Walter Payton, b. 1954: Chicago Bears running back has most rushing yards in NFL history; leading NFC rusher, 1976-80.
Pele, b. 1940: Brazilian soccer star scored 1,281 goals during 22-year career.
Bob Pettit, b. 1932: first NBA player to score 20,000 points; twice NBA scoring leader.
Richard Petty, b. 1937: NASCAR national champ 7 times; 7-times Daytona 500 winner.
Laffit Pincay Jr., b. 1946: leading money-winning jockey, 1970-74, 1979.
Jacques Plante, (1929-1986): goalie, 7 Vezina trophies; first goalie to wear a mask in a game.
Kirby Puckett, b. 1961: Minn. Twins outfielder won AL Batting Title, 1989; led Al in hits, 1987-89.

Willis Reed, b. 1942: N.Y. Knicks center; MVP, 1970; playoff MVP, 1970, 1973.
Jerry Rice, b. 1962: S.F. 49ers receiver chosen 1989 Super Bowl MVP.
Jim Rice, b. 1953: Boston Red Sox outfielder led AL in home runs, 1977-78, 1983; MVP 1978.
Maurice Richard, b. 1921: Montreal Canadiens forward scored 544 regular season goals, 82 playoff goals.
Branch Rickey, (1881-1965): executive instrumental in breaking baseball's color barrier, 1947; initiated farm system, 1919.
Oscar Robertson, b. 1938: guard averaged career 25.7 points per game; record 9,887 career assists; MVP, 1964.
Brooks Robinson, b. 1937: Baltimore Orioles 3d baseman played in 4 World Series; MVP, 1964.
Frank Robinson, b. 1935: slugger MVP in both NL and AL; triple crown winner, 1966; first black manager in majors.
Jackie Robinson, (1919-1972): broke baseball's color barrier with Brooklyn Dodgers, 1947; MVP, 1949.
Larry Robinson, b. 1951: NHL defenseman won Norris trophy, 1977, 1980.
Sugar Ray Robinson, (1920-1989): middleweight champion 5 times, welterweight champion.
Knute Rockne, (1888-1931): Notre Dame football coach, 1918-31; revolutionized game by stressing forward pass.
Pete Rose, b. 1941: won 3 NL batting titles; hit safely in 44 consecutive games, 1978; has most major league hits.
Wilma Rudolph, b. 1940: sprinter won 3 1960 Olympic gold medals.
Bill Russell, b. 1934: Boston Celtics center led team to 11 NBA titles; MVP 5 times; first black coach of major pro sports team.
Babe Ruth, (1895-1948): N.Y. Yankees outfielder hit 60 home runs, 1927; 714 lifetime; led AL 11 times.
Johnny Rutherford, b. 1938: auto racer won Indy 500 3 times.
Nolan Ryan, b. 1947: pitcher struck out record 383 batters, 1973; first to strike out 5,000 batters; pitched record 7 no-hitters; won 300th game, 1990.
Bret Saberhagan, b. 1964: Pitcher won AL Cy Young award, 1985, 1989; WS MVP, 1985.
Gene Sarazen, b. 1902: won PGA championship 3 times, U.S. Open twice; developer of sand wedge.
Gale Sayers, b. 1943: Chicago Bears back twice led NFC in rushing.
Mike Schmidt, b. 1949: Phillies 3d baseman led NL in home runs, 1974-76, 1980-81, 1983-84, 1986; NL MVP, 1980, 1981, 1986.
Tom Seaver, b. 1944: pitcher won NL Cy Young award 3 times, won 311 major league games.
Monica Seles, b. 1973; U.S. Open champ 1991, 1992.
Bill Shoemaker, b. 1931: jockey rode 3 Kentucky Derby and 5 Belmont Stakes winners; leading career money winner.
Eddie Shore, (1902-1985): Boston Bruins defenseman; MVP 4 times, first-team all-star 7 times.
Al Simmons, (1902-1956): AL outfielder had lifetime .334 batting average.
O.J. Simpson, b. 1947: running back rushed for 2,003 yds., 1973; AFC leading rusher 4 times.
George Sisler, (1893-1973): St. Louis Browns 1st baseman had record 257 hits, 1920; batted .340 lifetime.
Billy Smith, b. 1950: N.Y. Islanders goalie led team to 4 Stanley Cup championships.
Sam Snead, b. 1912: PGA and Masters champ 3 times each.
Warren Spahn, b. 1921: pitcher won 363 NL games; 20-game winner 13 times; Cy Young award, 1957.
Tris Speaker, (1885-1958): AL outfielder batted .344 over 22 seasons; hit record 793 career doubles.
Mark Spitz, b. 1950: swimmer won 7 1972 Olympic gold medals.
Amos Alonzo Stagg, (1862-1965): coached Univ. of Chicago football team for 41 years, including 5 undefeated seasons; introduced huddle, man-in-motion, and end-around play.
Willie Stargell, b. 1941: Pittsburgh Pirate slugger chosen NL, World Series MVP, 1979.
Bart Starr, b. 1934: Green Bay Packers quarterback led team to 5 NFL titles and 2 Super Bowl victories.
Roger Staubach, b. 1942: Dallas Cowboys quarterback; leading NFC passer 5 times.
Casey Stengel, (1890-1975): managed Yankees to 10 pennants, 7 championships, 1949-60.
Jackie Stewart, b. 1939: Scot auto racer retired with 27 Grand Prix victories.
John L. Sullivan, (1858-1918): last bareknuckle heavyweight champion, 1882-1892.
Fran Tarkenton, b. 1940: quarterback holds career passing records for touchdowns, completions, yardage.
Gustavo Thoeni, b. 1951: Italian 4-time world alpine ski champ.
Jim Thorpe, (1888-1953): football All-America, 1911, 1912; won pentathlon and decathlon, 1912 Olympics.
Bill Tilden, (1893-1953): U.S. singles champ 7 times; played on 11 Davis Cup teams.
Y.A. Tittle, b. 1926: N.Y. Giants quarterback; MVP, 1961, 1963.
Lee Trevino, b. 1939: won the U.S. and British Open championships twice.
Bryan Trottier, b. 1956: center played on 6 Stanley Cup championship teams.
Wyomia Tyus, b. 1945: sprinter won 1964, 1968 Olympic 100-meter dash.
Johnny Unitas, b. 1933: Baltimore Colts quarterback passed for over 40,000 yds.; MVP, 1957, 1967.
Al Unser, b. 1939: Indy 500 winner, 4 times.
Bobby Unser, b. 1934: Indy 500 winner 3 times.
Norm Van Brocklin, (1926-1983); quarterback passed for game record 554 yds., 1951; MVP, 1960.
Honus Wagner, (1874-1955): Pittsburgh Pirates shortstop won 8 NL batting titles.
Tom Watson, b. 1949: golfer won British Open 5 times.
Johnny Weissmuller, (1903-1984); swimmer won 52 national championships, 5 Olympic gold medals; set 67 world records.
Jerry West, b. 1938: L.A. Lakers guard had career average 27 points per game; first team all-star 10 times.
Kathy Whitworth, b. 1939: women's golf leading money winner 8 times: first woman to earn over $300,000.
Ted Williams, b. 1918: Boston Red Sox outfielder won 6 batting titles; last major leaguer to hit over .400: .406 in 1941: .344 lifetime batting average.
John Wooden, b. 1910: coached UCLA basketball team to 10 national championships.
Mickey Wright, b. 1935: won LPGA championship 4 times, Vare Trophy 5 times; twice AP Woman-Athlete-of-the-Year.
Carl Yastrzemski, b. 1939: Boston Red Sox slugger won 3 batting titles, triple crown, 1967.
Cy Young, (1867-1955): pitcher won record 511 major league games.
Babe Didrikson Zaharias, (1914-1956): track star won 2 1932 Olympic gold medals; won numerous golf tournaments.

American Power Boat Assn. Gold Cup Champions

Year	Boat	Driver
1974	Pay'N Pak	George Henley
1975	Pay 'N Pak	George Henley
1976	Miss U.S.	Tom D'Eath
1977	Atlas Van Lines	Bill Muncey
1978	Atlas Van Lines	Bill Muncey
1979	Atlas Van Lines	Bill Muncey
1980	Miss Budweiser	Dean Chenoweth
1981	Miss Budweiser	Dean Chenoweth
1982	Atlas Van Lines	Chip Hanauer
1983	Atlas Van Lines	Chip Hanauer
1984	Atlas Van Lines	Chip Hanauer
1985	Miller American	Chip Hanauer
1986	Miller American	Chip Hanauer
1987	Miller American	Chip Hanauer
1988	Miller American	Chip Hanauer
1989	Miss Budweiser	Tom D'Eath
1990	Miss Budweiser	Tom D'Eath
1991	Winston Eagle	Mark Tate
1992	Miss Budweiser	Chip Hanauer

Tour de France in 1992

Miguel Indurain of Spain won the 79th Tour de France, the world's most prestigious bicycle race. His margin of victory was 4 minutes 35 seconds, and he completed the 21-day, 2,490 mile race in a total time of 100 hours 49 minutes 30 seconds. Claudio Chiappucci of Italy finished second.

Tennis

U.S. Open Champions

Men's Singles

Year	Champion	Final opponent
1910	William Larned	T. C. Bundy
1911	William Larned	Maurice McLoughlin
1912	Maurice McLoughlin	Wallace Johnson
1913	Maurice McLoughlin	Richard Williams
1914	Richard Williams	Maurice McLoughlin
1915	William Johnston	Maurice McLoughlin
1916	Richard Williams	William Johnston
1917	Richard Murray	N. W. Niles
1918	Richard Murray	Bill Tilden
1919	William Johnston	Bill Tilden
1920	Bill Tilden	William Johnston
1921	Bill Tilden	Wallace Johnson
1922	Bill Tilden	William Johnston
1923	Bill Tilden	William Johnston
1924	Bill Tilden	William Johnston
1925	Bill Tilden	William Johnston
1926	Rene Lacoste	Jean Borotra
1927	Rene Lacoste	Bill Tilden
1928	Henri Cochet	Francis Hunter
1929	Bill Tilden	Francis Hunter
1930	John Doeg	Francis Shields
1931	H. Ellsworth Vines	George Lott
1932	H. Ellsworth Vines	Henri Cochet
1933	Fred Perry	John Crawford
1934	Fred Perry	Wilmer Allison
1935	Wilmer Allison	Sidney Wood
1936	Fred Perry	Don Budge
1937	Don Budge	Baron G. von Cramm
1938	Don Budge	C. Gene Mako
1939	Robert Riggs	S. Welby Van Horn
1940	Don McNeill	Robert Riggs
1941	Robert Riggs	F. L. Kovacs
1942	F. R. Schroeder Jr.	Frank Parker
1943	Joseph Hunt	Jack Kramer
1944	Frank Parker	William Talbert
1945	Frank Parker	William Talbert
1946	Jack Kramer	Thomas Brown Jr.
1947	Jack Kramer	Frank Parker
1948	Pancho Gonzales	Eric Sturgess
1949	Pancho Gonzales	F. R. Schroeder Jr.
1950	Arthur Larsen	Herbert Flam
1951	Frank Sedgman	E. Victor Seixas Jr.
1952	Frank Sedgman	Gardnar Mulloy
1953	Tony Trabert	E. Victor Seixas Jr.
1954	E. Victor Seixas Jr.	Rex Hartwig
1955	Tony Trabert	Ken Rosewall
1956	Ken Rosewall	Lewis Hoad
1957	Malcolm Anderson	Ashley Cooper
1958	Ashley Cooper	Malcolm Anderson
1959	Neale A. Fraser	Alejandro Olmedo
1960	Neale A. Fraser	Rod Laver
1961	Roy Emerson	Rod Laver
1962	Rod Laver	Roy Emerson
1963	Rafael Osuna	F. A. Froehling 3d
1964	Roy Emerson	Fred Stolle
1965	Manuel Santana	Cliff Drysdale
1966	Fred Stolle	John Newcombe
1967	John Newcombe	Clark Graebner
1968	Arthur Ashe	Tom Okker
1969	Rod Laver	Tony Roche
1970	Ken Rosewall	Tony Roche
1971	Stan Smith	Jan Kodes
1972	Ilie Nastase	Arthur Ashe
1973	John Newcombe	Jan Kodes
1974	Jimmy Connors	Ken Rosewall
1975	Manuel Orantes	Jimmy Connors
1976	Jimmy Connors	Bjorn Borg
1977	Guillermo Vilas	Jimmy Connors
1978	Jimmy Connors	Bjorn Borg
1979	John McEnroe	Vitas Gerulaitis
1980	John McEnroe	Bjorn Borg
1981	John McEnroe	Bjorn Borg
1982	Jimmy Connors	Ivan Lendl
1983	Jimmy Connors	Ivan Lendl
1984	John McEnroe	Ivan Lendl
1985	Ivan Lendl	John McEnroe
1986	Ivan Lendl	Miloslav Mecir
1987	Ivan Lendl	Mats Wilander
1988	Mats Wilander	Ivan Lendl
1989	Boris Becker	Ivan Lendl
1990	Pete Sampras	Andre Agassi
1991	Stefan Edberg	Jim Courier
1992	Stefan Edberg	Pete Sampras

Women's Singles

Year	Champion	Final opponent
1926	Molla B. Mallory	Elizabeth Ryan
1927	Helen Wills	Betty Nuthall
1928	Helen Wills	Helen Jacobs
1929	Helen Wills	M. Watson
1930	Betty Nuthall	L. A. Harper
1931	Helen Wills Moody	E. B. Whittingstall
1932	Helen Jacobs	Carolin A. Babcock
1933	Helen Jacobs	Helen Wills Moody
1934	Helen Jacobs	Sarah H. Palfrey
1935	Helen Jacobs	Sarah P. Fabyan
1936	Alice Marble	Helen Jacobs
1937	Anita Lizana	Jadwiga Jedrzejowska
1938	Alice Marble	Nancye Wynne
1939	Alice Marble	Helen Jacobs
1940	Alice Marble	Helen Jacobs
1941	Sarah Palfrey Cooke	Pauline Betz
1942	Pauline Betz	Louise Brough
1943	Pauline Betz	Louise Brough
1944	Pauline Betz	Margaret Osborne
1945	Sarah P. Cooke	Pauline Betz
1946	Pauline Betz	Doris Hart
1947	Louise Brough	Margaret Osborne
1948	Margaret Osborne duPont	Louise Brough
1949	Margaret Osborne duPont	Doris Hart
1950	Margaret Osborne duPont	Doris Hart
1951	Maureen Connolly	Shirley Fry
1952	Maureen Connolly	Doris Hart
1953	Maureen Connolly	Doris Hart
1954	Doris Hart	Louise Brough
1955	Doris Hart	Patricia Ward
1956	Shirley Fry	Althea Gibson
1957	Althea Gibson	Louise Brough
1958	Althea Gibson	Darlene Hard
1959	Maria Bueno	Christine Truman
1960	Darlene Hard	Maria Bueno
1961	Darlene Hard	Ann Haydon
1962	Margaret Smith	Darlene Hard
1963	Maria Bueno	Margaret Smith
1964	Maria Bueno	Carole Graebner
1965	Margaret Smith	Billie Jean Moffitt
1966	Maria Bueno	Nancy Richey
1967	Billie Jean King	Ann Haydon Jones
1968	Virginia Wade	Billie Jean King
1969	Margaret Court	Nancy Richey
1970	Margaret Court	Rosemary Casals
1971	Billie Jean King	Rosemary Casals
1972	Billie Jean King	Kerry Melville
1973	Margaret Court	Evonne Goolagong
1974	Billie Jean King	Evonne Goolagong
1975	Chris Evert	Evonne Goolagong
1976	Chris Evert	Evonne Goolagong
1977	Chris Evert	Wendy Turnbull
1978	Chris Evert	Pam Shriver
1979	Tracy Austin	Chris Evert Lloyd
1980	Chris Evert Lloyd	Hana Mandlikova
1981	Tracy Austin	Martina Navratilova
1982	Chris Evert Lloyd	Hana Mandlikova
1983	Martina Navratilova	Chris Evert Lloyd
1984	Martina Navratilova	Chris Evert Lloyd
1985	Hana Mandlikova	Martina Navratilova
1986	Martina Navratilova	Helena Sukova
1987	Martina Navratilova	Steffi Graf
1988	Steffi Graf	Gabriela Sabatini
1989	Steffi Graf	Martina Navratilova
1990	Gabriela Sabatini	Steffi Graf
1991	Monica Seles	Martina Navratilova
1992	Monica Seles	Arantxa Sanchez Vicario

U.S. Open in 1992

Men

Fourth Round

Jim Courier def. John McEnroe 6-2, 6-2, 7-6
Andre Agassi def. Carlos Costa 6-4, 6-3, 6-2
Pete Sampras def. Guy Forget 6-3, 1-6, 1-6, 6-4, 6-3
Aleksandr Volkov def. Brad Gilbert 6-2, 6-4, 5-7, 7-6
Wayne Ferreira def. Emilio Sanchez 6-2, 6-4, 2-6, 6-4
Michael Chang def. MaliVai Washington 6-2, 2-6, 3-6, 6-3, 6-1
Ivan Lendl def. Boris Becker 6-7, 6-2, 6-7, 6-3, 6-4
Stefan Edberg def. Richard Krajicek 6-4, 6-7, 6-3, 3-6, 6-4

Quarterfinals

Jim Courier def. Andre Agassi 6-3, 6-7, 6-1, 6-4
Pete Sampras def. Aleksandr Volkov 6-4, 6-1, 6-0
Michael Chang def. Wayne Ferreira 7-5, 2-6, 6-3, 6-7, 6-1
Stefan Edberg def. Ivan Lendl 6-3, 6-3, 3-6, 5-7, 7-6

Semifinals

Pete Sampras def. Jim Courier 6-1, 3-6, 6-2, 6-2
Stefan Edberg def. Michael Chang 6-7, 7-5, 7-6, 5-7, 6-4

Finals

Stefan Edberg def. Pete Sampras 3-6, 6-4, 7-6, 6-2

Women

Fourth Round

Monica Seles def. Gigi Fernandez 6-1, 6-2
Patricia Hy def. Helena Sukova 6-1, 7-6
Gabriela Sabatini def. Sabine Appelmans 6-1, 6-3
Mary Joe Fernandez def. Mary Pierce 6-0, 6-4
Manuela Maleeva-Fragniere def. Carrie Cunningham 6-3, 7-5
Magdalena Maleeva def. Chanda Rubin 7-5, 5-7, 6-1
Arantxa Sanchez Vicario def. Zina Garrison 6-0, 6-1
Steffi Graf def. Florencia Labat 6-2, 6-2

Quarterfinals

Monica Seles def. Patricia Hy 6-1, 6-2
Mary Joe Fernandez def. Gabriela Sabatini 6-2, 1-6, 6-4
Manuela Maleeva-Fragniere def. Magdalena Maleeva 6-2, 5-3
Arantxa Sanchez Vicario def. Steffi Graf 7-6, 6-3

Semifinals

Monica Seles def. Mary Joe Fernandez 6-3, 6-2
Arantxa Sanchez Vicario def. Manuela Maleeva-Fragniere 6-2, 6-1

Finals

Monica Seles def. Arantxa Sanchez Vicario 6-3, 6-3

Men's Doubles — Jim Grabb & Richey Reneberg def. Kelly Jones & Rick Leach 3-6, 7-6, 6-3, 6-3

Women's Doubles — Gigi Fernandez & Natalia Zvereva def. Jana Novotna & Larisa Sauchenko-Neiland 7-6, 6-1

Mixed Doubles — Nicole Provis & Mark Woodforde def. Helena Sukova & Tom Nijssen 4-6, 6-3, 6-3

All-England Champions, Wimbledon

Men's Singles

Year	Champion	Final opponent	Year	Champion	Final opponent
1933	Jack Crawford	Ellsworth Vines	1966	Manuel Santana	Dennis Ralston
1934	Fred Perry	Jack Crawford	1967	John Newcombe	Wilhelm Bungert
1935	Fred Perry	Gottfried von Cramm	1968	Rod Laver	Tony Roche
1936	Fred Perry	Gottfried von Cramm	1969	Rod Laver	John Newcombe
1937	Donald Budge	Gottfried von Cramm	1970	John Newcombe	Ken Rosewall
1938	Donald Budge	Wilfred Austin	1971	John Newcombe	Stan Smith
1939	Bobby Riggs	Elwood Cooke	1972	Stan Smith	Ilie Nastase
1940-45	not held		1973	Jan Kodes	Alex Metreveli
1946	Yvon Petra	Geoff E. Brown	1974	Jimmy Connors	Ken Rosewall
1947	Jack Kramer	Tom P. Brown	1975	Arthur Ashe	Jimmy Connors
1948	Bob Falkenburg	John Bromwich	1976	Bjorn Borg	Ilie Nastase
1949	Ted Schroeder	Jaroslav Drobny	1977	Bjorn Borg	Jimmy Connors
1950	Budge Patty	Frank Sedgman	1978	Bjorn Borg	Jimmy Connors
1951	Dick Savitt	Ken McGregor	1979	Bjorn Borg	Roscoe Tanner
1952	Frank Sedgman	Jaroslav Drobny	1980	Bjorn Borg	John McEnroe
1953	Vic Seixas	Kurt Nielsen	1981	John McEnroe	Bjorn Borg
1954	Jaroslav Drobny	Ken Rosewall	1982	Jimmy Connors	John McEnroe
1955	Tony Trabert	Kurt Nielsen	1983	John McEnroe	Chris Lewis
1956	Lew Hoad	Ken Rosewall	1984	John McEnroe	Jimmy Connors
1957	Lew Hoad	Ashley Cooper	1985	Boris Becker	Kevin Curren
1958	Ashley Cooper	Neale Fraser	1986	Boris Becker	Ivan Lendl
1959	Alex Olmedo	Rod Laver	1987	Pat Cash	Ivan Lendl
1960	Neale Fraser	Rod Laver	1988	Stefan Edberg	Boris Becker
1961	Rod Laver	Chuck McKinley	1989	Boris Becker	Stefan Edberg
1962	Rod Laver	Martin Mulligan	1990	Stefan Edberg	Boris Becker
1963	Chuck McKinley	Fred Stolle	1991	Michael Stich	Boris Becker
1964	Roy Emerson	Fred Stolle	1992	Andre Agassi	Goran Ivanisevic
1965	Roy Emerson	Fred Stolle			

Women's Singles

Year	Champion	Year	Champion	Year	Champion	Year	Champion
1946	Pauline Betz	1958	Althea Gibson	1970	Margaret Court	1982	Martina Navratilova
1947	Margaret Osborne	1959	Maria Bueno	1971	Evonne Goolagong	1983	Martina Navratilova
1948	Louise Brough	1960	Maria Bueno	1972	Billie Jean King	1984	Martina Navratilova
1949	Louise Brough	1961	Angela Mortimer	1973	Billie Jean King	1985	Martina Navratilova
1950	Louise Brough	1962	Karen Hantze-Susman	1974	Chris Evert	1986	Martina Navratilova
1951	Doris Hart	1963	Margaret Smith	1975	Billie Jean King	1987	Martina Navratilova
1952	Maureen Connolly	1964	Maria Bueno	1976	Chris Evert	1988	Steffi Graf
1953	Maureen Connolly	1965	Margaret Smith	1977	Virginia Wade	1989	Steffi Graf
1954	Maureen Connolly	1966	Billie Jean King	1978	Martina Navratilova	1990	Martina Navratilova
1955	Louise Brough	1967	Billie Jean King	1979	Martina Navratilova	1991	Steffi Graf
1956	Shirley Fry	1968	Billie Jean King	1980	Evonne Goolagong	1992	Steffi Graf
1957	Althea Gibson	1969	Ann Haydon-Jones	1981	Chris Evert Lloyd		

French Open Champions

Year	Men	Women	Year	Men	Women
1969	Rod Laver	Margaret Smith Court	1981	Bjorn Borg	Hana Mandlikova
1970	Jan Kodes	Margaret Smith Court	1982	Mats Wilander	Martina Navratilova
1971	Jan Kodes	Evonne Goolagong	1983	Yannick Noah	Chris Evert Lloyd
1972	Andres Gimeno	Billie Jean King	1984	Ivan Lendl	Martina Navratilova
1973	Ilie Nastase	Margaret Court	1985	Mats Wilander	Chris Evert Lloyd
1974	Bjorn Borg	Chris Evert	1986	Ivan Lendl	Chris Evert Lloyd
1975	Bjorn Borg	Chris Evert	1987	Ivan Lendl	Steffi Graf
1976	Adriano Panatta	Sue Barker	1988	Mats Wilander	Steffi Graf
1977	Guillermo Vilas	Mima Jausovec	1989	Michael Chang	Arantxa Sanchez
1978	Bjorn Borg	Virginia Ruzici	1990	Andres Gomez	Monica Seles
1979	Bjorn Borg	Chris Evert Lloyd	1991	Jim Courier	Monica Seles
1980	Bjorn Borg	Chris Evert Lloyd	1992	Jim Courier	Monica Seles

Australian Open Champions

Year*	Men	Women	Year*	Men	Women
1969	Rod Laver	Margaret Court	1980	Brian Teacher	Hana Mandlikova
1970	Arthur Ashe	Margaret Court	1981	Johan Kriek	Martina Navratilova
1971	Ken Rosewall	Margaret Court	1982	Johan Kriek	Chris Evert Lloyd
1972	Ken Rosewall	Virginia Wade	1983	Mats Wilander	Martina Navratilova
1973	John Newcombe	Margaret Court	1984	Mats Wilander	Chris Evert Lloyd
1974	Jimmy Connors	Evonne Goolagong	1985	Stefan Edberg	Martina Navratilova
1975	John Newcombe	Evonne Goolagong	1986	Not held	Not held
1976	Mark Edmondson	Evonne Goolagong	1987	Stefan Edberg	Hana Mandlikova
1977	Roscoe Tanner	Kerry Reid	1988	Mats Wilander	Steffi Graf
	Vitas Gerulaitis	Evonne Goolagong	1989	Ivan Lendl	Steffi Graf
1978	Guillermo Vilas	Chris O'Neill	1990	Ivan Lendl	Steffi Graf
1979	Guillermo Vilas	Barbara Jordan	1991	Boris Becker	Monica Seles
			1992	Jim Courier	Monica Seles

* Two tournaments were held in 1977 (Jan. & Dec.). Tournament moved back to Jan. in 1987, so no championship was decided in 1986.

Davis Cup Challenge Round

Year	Result	Year	Result	Year	Result
1900	United States 5, British Isles 0	1931	France 3, Great Britain 2	1964	Australia 3, United States 2
1901	(not played)	1932	France 3, United States 2	1965	Australia 4, Spain 1
1902	United States 3, British Isles 2	1933	Great Britain 3, France 2	1966	Australia 4, India 1
1903	British Isles 4, United States 1	1934	Great Britain 4, United States 1	1967	Australia 4, Spain 1
1904	British Isles 5, Belgium 0	1935	Great Britain 5, United States 0	1968	United States 4, Australia 1
1905	British Isles 5, United States 0	1936	Great Britain 3, Australia 2	1969	United States 5, Romania 0
1906	British Isles 5, United States 0	1937	United States 4, Great Britain 1	1970	United States 5, W. Germany 0
1907	Australia 3, British Isles 2	1938	United States 3, Australia 2	1971	United States 3, Romania 2
1908	Australasia 3, United States 2	1939	Australia 3, United States 2	1972	United States 3, Romania 2
1909	Australasia 5, United States 0	1940-45	(not played)	1973	Australia 5, United States 0
1910	(not played)	1946	United States 5, Australia 0	1974	South Africa (default by India)
1911	Australasia 5, United States 0	1947	United States 4, Australia 1	1975	Sweden 3, Czech. 2
1912	British Isles 3, Australasia 2	1948	United States 5, Australia 0	1976	Italy 4, Chile 1
1913	United States 3, British Isles 2	1949	United States 4, Australia 1	1977	Australia 3, Italy 1
1914	Australasia 3, United States 2	1950	Australia 4, United States 1	1978	United States 4, Great Britain 1
1915-18	(not played)	1951	Australia 3, United States 2	1979	United States 5, Italy 0
1919	Australasia 4, British Isles 1	1952	Australia 4, United States 1	1980	Czechoslovakia 4, Italy 1
1920	United States 5, Australasia 0	1953	Australia 3, United States 2	1981	United States 3, Argentina 1
1921	United States 5, Japan 0	1954	United States 3, Australia 2	1982	United States 3, France, 0
1922	United States 4, Australasia 1	1955	Australia 5, United States 0	1983	Australia 3, Sweden 1
1923	United States 4, Australasia 1	1956	Australia 5, United States 0	1984	Sweden 3, United States 0
1924	United States 5, Australasia 0	1957	Australia 3, United States 2	1985	Sweden 3, W. Germany 2
1925	United States 5, France 0	1958	United States 3, Australia 2	1986	Australia 3, Sweden 2
1926	United States 4, France 1	1959	Australia 3, United States 2	1987	Sweden 5, India 0
1927	France 3, United States 2	1960	Australia 4, Italy 1	1988	W. Germany 4, Sweden 1
1928	France 4, United States 1	1961	Australia 5, Italy 0	1989	W. Germany 3, Sweden 2
1929	France 3, United States 2	1962	Australia 5, Mexico 0	1990	United States 3, Australia 2
1930	France 4, United States 1	1963	United States 3, Australia 2	1991	France 3, United States 1

The World Cup

The World Cup, emblematic of International soccer supremacy, was won by West Germany on July 8, 1990, with a 1-0 victory over defending champion Argentina on a penalty shot in the 84th minute. It was the lowest-scoring final in the 60 years of World Cup play. It was the 3d World Cup title for West Germany, equaling Brazil and Italy. Winners and sites of previous World Cup play follow:

Year	Winner	Final opponent	Site	Year	Winner	Final opponent	Site
1930	Uruguay	Argentina	Uruguay	1966	England	W. Germany	England
1934	Italy	Czechoslovakia	Italy	1970	Brazil	Italy	Mexico
1938	Italy	Hungary	France	1974	W. Germany	Netherlands	W. Germany
1950	Uruguay	Brazil	Brazil	1978	Argentina	Netherlands	Argentina
1954	W. Germany	Hungary	Switzerland	1982	Italy	W. Germany	Spain
1958	Brazil	Sweden	Sweden	1986	Argentina	W. Germany	Mexico
1962	Brazil	Czechoslovakia	Chile	1990	W. Germany	Argentina	Italy

GOLF

United States Open

Year	Winner	Year	Winner	Year	Winner	Year	Winner
1903	Willie Anderson	1926	Bobby Jones*	1951	Ben Hogan	1972	Jack Nicklaus
1904	Willie Anderson	1927	Tommy Armour	1952	Julius Boros	1973	Johnny Miller
1905	Willie Anderson	1928	John Farrell	1953	Ben Hogan	1974	Hale Irwin
1906	Alex Smith	1929	Bobby Jones*	1954	Ed Furgol	1975	Lou Graham
1907	Alex Ross	1930	Bobby Jones*	1955	Jack Fleck	1976	Jerry Pate
1908	Fred McLeod	1931	Wm. Burke	1956	Cary Middlecoff	1977	Hubert Green
1909	George Sargent	1932	Gene Sarazen	1957	Dick Mayer	1978	Andy North
1910	Alex Smith	1933	John Goodman*	1958	Tommy Bolt	1979	Hale Irwin
1911	John McDermott	1934	Olin Dutra	1959	Billy Casper	1980	Jack Nicklaus
1912	John McDermott	1935	Sam Parks Jr.	1960	Arnold Palmer	1981	David Graham
1913	Francis Ouimet*	1936	Tony Manero	1961	Gene Littler	1982	Tom Watson
1914	Walter Hagen	1937	Ralph Guldahl	1962	Jack Nicklaus	1983	Larry Nelson
1915	Jerome Travers*	1938	Ralph Guldahl	1963	Julius Boros	1984	Fuzzy Zoeller
1916	Chick Evans*	1939	Byron Nelson	1964	Ken Venturi	1985	Andy North
1917-18	(Not played)	1940	Lawson Little	1965	Gary Player	1986	Ray Floyd
1919	Walter Hagen	1941	Craig Wood	1966	Billy Casper	1987	Scott Simpson
1920	Edward Ray	1942-45	(Not played)	1967	Jack Nicklaus	1988	Curtis Strange
1921	Jim Barnes	1946	Lloyd Mangrum	1968	Lee Trevino	1989	Curtis Strange
1922	Gene Sarazen	1947	L. Worsham	1969	Orville Moody	1990	Hale Irwin
1923	Bobby Jones*	1948	Ben Hogan	1970	Tony Jacklin	1991	Payne Stewart
1924	Cyril Walker	1949	Cary Middlecoff	1971	Lee Trevino	1992	Tom Kite
1925	Willie MacFarlane	1950	Ben Hogan				

Professional Golfer's Association Championships

Year	Winner	Year	Winner	Year	Winner	Year	Winner
1922	Gene Sarazen	1940	Byron Nelson	1959	Bob Rosburg	1976	Dave Stockton
1923	Gene Sarazen	1941	Victor Ghezzi	1960	Jay Hebert	1977	Lanny Wadkins
1924	Walter Hagen	1942	Sam Snead	1961	Jerry Barber	1978	John Mahaffey
1925	Walter Hagen	1944	Bob Hamilton	1962	Gary Player	1979	David Graham
1926	Walter Hagen	1945	Byron Nelson	1963	Jack Nicklaus	1980	Jack Nicklaus
1927	Walter Hagen	1946	Ben Hogan	1964	Bob Nichols	1981	Larry Nelson
1928	Leo Diegel	1947	Jim Ferrier	1965	Dave Marr	1982	Ray Floyd
1929	Leo Diegel	1948	Ben Hogan	1966	Al Geiberger	1983	Hal Sutton
1930	Tommy Armour	1949	Sam Snead	1967	Don January	1984	Lee Trevino
1931	Tom Creavy	1950	Chandler Harper	1968	Julius Boros	1985	Hubert Green
1932	Olin Dutra	1951	Sam Snead	1969	Ray Floyd	1986	Bob Tway
1933	Gene Sarazen	1952	James Turnesa	1970	Dave Stockton	1987	Larry Nelson
1934	Paul Runyan	1953	Walter Burkemo	1971	Jack Nicklaus	1988	Jeff Sluman
1935	Johnny Revolta	1954	Melvin Harbert	1972	Gary Player	1989	Payne Stewart
1936	Denny Shute	1955	Doug Ford	1973	Jack Nicklaus	1990	Wayne Grady
1937	Denny Shute	1956	Jack Burke	1974	Lee Trevino	1991	John Daly
1938	Paul Runyan	1957	Lionel Hebert	1975	Jack Nicklaus	1992	Nick Price
1939	Henry Picard	1958	Dow Finsterwald				

Masters Golf Tournament Champions

Year	Winner	Year	Winner	Year	Winner	Year	Winner
1934	Horton Smith	1951	Ben Hogan	1965	Jack Nicklaus	1979	Fuzzy Zoeller
1935	Gene Sarazen	1952	Sam Snead	1966	Jack Nicklaus	1980	Severiano Ballesteros
1936	Horton Smith	1953	Ben Hogan	1967	Gay Brewer Jr.	1981	Tom Watson
1937	Byron Nelson	1954	Sam Snead	1968	Bob Goalby	1982	Craig Stadler
1938	Henry Picard	1955	Cary Middlecoff	1969	George Archer	1983	Severiano Ballesteros
1939	Ralph Guldahl	1956	Jack Burke	1970	Billy Casper	1984	Ben Crenshaw
1940	Jimmy Demaret	1957	Doug Ford	1971	Charles Coody	1985	Bernhard Langer
1941	Craig Wood	1958	Arnold Palmer	1972	Jack Nicklaus	1986	Jack Nicklaus
1942	Byron Nelson	1959	Art Wall Jr.	1973	Tommy Aaron	1987	Larry Mize
1943-1945	(Not played)	1960	Arnold Palmer	1974	Gary Player	1988	Sandy Lyle
1946	Herman Keiser	1961	Gary Player	1975	Jack Nicklaus	1989	Nick Faldo
1947	Jimmy Demaret	1962	Arnold Palmer	1976	Ray Floyd	1990	Nick Faldo
1948	Claude Harmon	1963	Jack Nicklaus	1977	Tom Watson	1991	Ian Woosnam
1949	Sam Snead	1964	Arnold Palmer	1978	Gary Player	1992	Fred Couples
1950	Jimmy Demaret						

British Open Golf Champions

Year	Winner	Year	Winner	Year	Winner	Year	Winner
1931	Tommy Armour	1951	Max Faulkner	1965	Peter Thomson	1979	Seve Ballesteros
1932	Gene Sarazen	1952	Bobby Locke	1966	Jack Nicklaus	1980	Tom Watson
1933	Denny Shute	1953	Ben Hogan	1967	Roberto de Vicenzo	1981	Bill Rogers
1934	Henry Cotton	1954	Peter Thomson	1968	Gary Player	1982	Tom Watson
1935	Alf Perry	1955	Peter Thomson	1969	Tony Jacklin	1983	Tom Watson
1936	Alf Padgham	1956	Peter Thomson	1970	Jack Nicklaus	1984	Seve Ballesteros
1937	T.H. Cotton	1957	Bobby Locke	1971	Lee Trevino	1985	Sandy Lyle
1938	R.A. Whitcombe	1958	Peter Thomson	1972	Lee Trevino	1986	Greg Norman
1939	Richard Burton	1959	Gary Player	1973	Tom Weiskopf	1987	Nick Faldo
1940-45	(Not played)	1960	Kel Nagle	1974	Gary Player	1988	Seve Ballesteros
1946	Sam Snead	1961	Arnold Palmer	1975	Tom Watson	1989	Mark Calcavecchia
1947	Fred Daly	1962	Arnold Palmer	1976	Johnny Miller	1990	Nick Faldo
1948	Henry Cotton	1963	Bob Charles	1977	Tom Watson	1991	Ian Baker-Finch
1949	Bobby Locke	1964	Tony Lema	1978	Jack Nicklaus	1992	Nick Faldo
1950	Bobby Locke						

Professional Golf Tournaments in 1992

Date	Event	Winner	Score	Prize
Jan. 12	Tournament of Champions, Carlsbad, Cal.	Steve Elkington	279	$144,000
Jan. 19	Bob Hope Chrysler Classic, Bermuda Dunes, Cal.	John Cook	*336	198,000
Jan. 26	Phoenix Open, Ariz.	Mark Cascavecchia	264	180,000
Feb. 2	A.T.&T. National Pro-Am, Pebble Beach, Cal.	Mark O'Meara	*275	198,000
Feb. 9	Hawaiian Open, Honolulu	John Cook	265	216,000
Feb. 16	Northern Telecom Open, Tucson	Lee Janzen	270	198,000
Feb. 23	Buick Invitational, San Diego	Steve Pate	200	180,000
Mar. 1	Los Angeles Open	Fred Couples	*269	180,000
Mar. 8	Doral Ryder Open, Miami, Fla.	Ray Floyd	271	252,000
Mar. 15	Honda Classic, Ft. Lauderdale, Fla.	Corey Pavin	273	198,000
Mar. 22	Nestle Invitational, Orlando, Fla.	Fred Couples	269	180,000
Mar. 29	Tournament Players Championship, Ponte Vedra, Fla.	Davis Love 3d	273	324,000
Apr. 12	Masters Tournament, Augusta, Ga.	Fred Couples	275	270,000
Apr. 19	Heritage Classic, Hilton Head, S.C.	Davis Love 3d	269	180,000
Apr. 26	Greater Greensboro Open, N.C.	Davis Love 3d	272	225,000
May 3	Houston Open	Fred Funk	272	216,000
May 10	Atlanta Classic	Tom Kite	272	180,000
May 17	Byron Nelson Classic, Irving, Tex.	Billy Ray Brown	199	198,000
May 31	Kemper Open, Potomac, Md.	Bill Glasson	276	198,000
June 14	St. Jude Classic, Memphis, Tenn.	Jay Haas	263	198,000
June 21	U.S. Open, Pebble Beach, Cal.	Tom Kite	285	275,000
June 28	Buick Classic, Harrison, N.Y.	David Frost	268	180,000
July 5	Centel Western Open, Lemont, Ill.	Ben Crenshaw	276	198,000
July 12	Anheuser-Busch Classic, Williamsburg, Va.	David Peoples	271	198,000
July 26	New England Classic, Sutton, Mass.	Brad Faxon	268	180,000
Aug. 3	Greater Hartford Open, Cromwell, Conn.	Lanny Wadkins	274	180,000
Aug. 9	Buick Open, Grand Blanc, Mich.	Dan Forsman	276	180,000
Aug. 16	PGA Championship, St. Louis	Nick Price	278	280,000
Aug. 23	The International, Castle Rock, Col.	Brad Faxon	+14 pts.	216,000
Aug. 30	World Series of Golf, Akron, Oh.	Craig Stadler	273	252,000
Sept. 6	Greater Milwaukee Open	Richard Zokol	269	180,000
Sept. 14	Canadian Open, Oakville, Ont.	Greg Norman	280	198,000
Sept. 20	Hardee's Classic, Coal Valley, Ill.	David Frost	266	180,000
Sept. 27	B.C. Open, Endicott, N.Y.	John Daly	266	144,000

Women

Date	Event	Winner	Score	Prize
Feb. 15	Phar-Mor Classic, Lauderhill, Fla.	Shelley Hamlin	206	$75,000
Feb. 23	Hawaiian Open, Honolulu	Lisa Walters	208	60,000
Mar. 8	Inamori Classic, Poway, Cal.	Judy Dickinson	277	63,000
Mar. 22	Standard Register Classic, Phoenix, Ariz.	Danielle Ammaccapane	279	105,000
Mar. 29	Dinah Shore Invitational, Rancho Mirage, Cal.	Dottie Mochrie	279	105,000
Apr. 19	SEGA Championship, Stockbridge, Ga.	Dottie Mochrie	277	90,000
Apr. 26	Sara Lee Classic, Nashville, Tenn.	Maggie Will	*207	78,000
May 3	Centel Classic, Tallahassee, Fla.	Danielle Ammaccapane	275	180,000
May 17	Mazda Championship, Bethesda, Md.	Betsy King	267	150,000
May 24	Corning Classic, Corning, N.Y.	Colleen Walker	276	67,000
May 31	Oldsmobile Classic, E. Lansing, Mich.	Barb Mucha	276	75,000
June 7	McDonald's Championship, Wilmington, Del.	Ayako Okamoto	205	112,000
June 14	ShopRite Classic, Somers Pt., N.J.	Anne Marie Palli	*207	60,000
June 28	Rochester International, Pittsford, N.Y.	Patty Sheehan	269	60,000
July 5	Jamie Farr Toledo Classic, Oh.	Patty Sheehan	209	60,000
July 19	Big Apple Classic, New Rochelle, N.Y.	Juli Inkster	273	75,000
July 27	U.S. Women's Open, Oakmont, Pa.	Patty Sheehan	*280	130,000
Aug 3	Bay State Classic, Canton, Mass.	Dottie Mochrie	278	63,000
Aug. 9	McCall's Classic, Vt.	Florence Descampe	278	75,000
Aug. 23	Northgate Classic, Brooklyn Park, Minn.	Kris Tschetter	211	63,000
Sept. 7	Rail Charity Classic, Springfield, Ill.	Nancy Lopez	*199	67,000
Sept. 13	Ping Championship, Portland, Ore.	Nancy Lopez	*209	67,000
Sept. 27	LPGA Classic, Buena Park, Cal.	Nancy Scranton	279	75,000

* Won playoff.

U.S. Women's Open Golf Champions

Year	Winner	Year	Winner	Year	Winner	Year	Winner
1948	"Babe" Zaharias	1960	Betsy Rawls	1971	JoAnne Carner	1982	Janet Alex
1949	Louise Suggs	1961	Mickey Wright	1972	Susie Maxwell Berning	1983	Jan Stephenson
1950	"Babe" Zaharias	1962	Murle Lindstrom	1973	Susie Maxwell Berning	1984	Hollis Stacy
1951	Betsy Rawls	1963	Mary Mills	1974	Sandra Haynie	1985	Kathy Baker
1952	Louise Suggs	1964	Mickey Wright	1975	Sandra Palmer	1986	Jane Geddes
1953	Betsy Rawls	1965	Carol Mann	1976	JoAnne Carner	1987	Laura Davies
1954	"Babe" Zaharias	1966	Sandra Spuzich	1977	Hollis Stacy	1988	Liselotte Neumann
1955	Fay Crocker	1967	Catherine Lacoste*	1978	Hollis Stacy	1989	Betsy King
1956	Mrs. K. Cornelius	1968	Susie Maxwell Berning	1979	Jerilyn Britz	1990	Betsy King
1957	Betsy Rawls	1969	Donna Caponi	1980	Amy Alcott	1991	Meg Mallon
1958	Mickey Wright	1970	Donna Caponi	1981	Pat Bradley	1992	Patty Sheehan
1959	Mickey Wright						

* Amateur

PGA Leading Money Winners

Year	Player	Dollars	Year	Player	Dollars	Year	Player	Dollars
1946	Ben Hogan	$42,556	1962	Arnold Palmer	$81,448	1977	Tom Watson	$310,653
1947	Jimmy Demaret	27,936	1963	Arnold Palmer	128,230	1978	Tom Watson	362,429
1948	Ben Hogan	36,812	1964	Jack Nicklaus	113,284	1979	Tom Watson	462,636
1949	Sam Snead	31,593	1965	Jack Nicklaus	140,752	1980	Tom Watson	530,808
1950	Sam Snead	35,758	1966	Billy Casper	121,944	1981	Tom Kite	375,699
1951	Lloyd Mangrum	26,088	1967	Jack Nicklaus	188,988	1982	Craig Stadler	446,462
1952	Julius Boros	37,032	1968	Billy Casper	205,168	1983	Hal Sutton	426,668
1953	Lew Worsham	34,002	1969	Frank Beard	175,223	1984	Tom Watson	476,260
1954	Bob Toski	65,819	1970	Lee Trevino	157,037	1985	Curtis Strange	542,321
1955	Julius Boros	65,121	1971	Jack Nicklaus	244,490	1986	Greg Norman	653,296
1956	Ted Kroll	72,835	1972	Jack Nicklaus	320,542	1987	Curtis Strange	925,941
1957	Dick Mayer	65,835	1973	Jack Nicklaus	308,362	1988	Curtis Strange	1,147,644
1958	Arnold Palmer	42,407	1974	Johnny Miller	353,201	1989	Tom Kite	1,395,278
1959	Art Wall Jr.	53,167	1975	Jack Nicklaus	323,149	1990	Greg Norman	1,165,477
1960	Arnold Palmer	75,262	1976	Jack Nicklaus	266,438	1991	Corey Pavin	979,430
1961	Gary Player	64,540						

LPGA Leading Money Winners

Year	Player	Dollars	Year	Player	Dollars	Year	Player	Dollars
1954	Patty Berg	$16,011	1967	Kathy Whitworth	$32,937	1980	Beth Daniel	$231,000
1955	Patty Berg	16,492	1968	Kathy Whitworth	48,379	1981	Beth Daniel	206,977
1956	Marlene Hagge	20,235	1969	Carol Mann	49,152	1982	JoAnne Carner	310,399
1957	Patty Berg	16,272	1970	Kathy Whitworth	30,235	1983	JoAnne Carner	291,404
1958	Beverly Hanson	12,629	1971	Kathy Whitworth	41,181	1984	Betsy King	266,771
1959	Betsy Rawls	26,774	1972	Kathy Whitworth	65,063	1985	Nancy Lopez	416,472
1960	Louise Suggs	16,892	1973	Kathy Whitworth	82,854	1986	Pat Bradley	492,021
1961	Mickey Wright	22,236	1974	JoAnne Carner	87,094	1987	Ayako Okamoto	466,034
1962	Mickey Wright	21,641	1975	Sandra Palmer	94,805	1988	Sherri Turner	347,255
1963	Mickey Wright	31,269	1976	Judy Rankin	150,734	1989	Betsy King	654,132
1964	Mickey Wright	29,800	1977	Judy Rankin	122,890	1990	Beth Daniel	863,578
1965	Kathy Whitworth	28,658	1978	Nancy Lopez	189,813	1991	Pat Bradley	763,118
1966	Kathy Whitworth	33,517	1979	Nancy Lopez	215,987			

Rifle and Pistol Individual Championships in 1992

Source: National Rifle Association

National Outdoor Rifle and Pistol Championships

Pistol — Mario A. Lozoya, Triangle, Va., 2657-147X.
Civilian Pistol — Richard Rodriquez, Stafford, Va., 2644-108X.
Woman Pistol — Ruby Fox, Parker, Ariz., 2580-88X.
Smallbore Rifle Prone — David E. Chesser, Columbus, Ga., 5996-474X.
Civilian Smallbore Rifle Prone — William H. Dodd, Queentown, Md., 5991-442X.
Woman Smallbore Rifle Prone — Mary E. Sparling, Tucson, Ariz., 5990-478X.
Smallbore Rifle NRA 3-Position — Lones W. Wigger Jr., Colorado Springs, Col., 2281-83X.
Civilian Smallbore Rifle NRA 3-Position — Lones W. Wigger Jr., 2281-83X.
Woman Smallbore Rifle NRA 3-Position — Karen E. Monez, Colorado Springs, Col., 2247X.
Highpower Rifle — Carl R. Bernosky, Ashland, Pa., 2385-101X.
Civilian Highpower Rifle — Carl R. Bernosky, 2385-101X.
Woman Highpower Rifle — Nancy H. Tompkins-Gallagher, Prescott, Ariz., 2372-125X.

U.S. NRA International Shooting Championships

Smallbore Free Rifle Prone — William Beard, Danville, Ind., 1293.7.
Smallbore Free Rifle Position — Robert Foth, Colorado Springs, Col., 2439.1.
Men's Air Rifle — Robert Foth, 1283.2.
Women's Standard Rifle Prone — Beth Herzman, North Haven, Conn., 1180.
Women's Standard Rifle 3-Position — Launi Meili, Cheney, Wash., 1253.8.
Free Pistol — Richard Gardner, Vallejo, Cal., 1205.
Rapid Fire Pistol — John McNally, Columbus, Ga., 1472.
Center Fire Pistol — Eduardo Suarez, Ft. Benning, Ga., 1176.
Standard Pistol — Jerry L. Wilder, Remington, Ind., 1139.
Men's Air Pistol — Ben Amonettee, Radford, Va., 1260.1.
Women's Air Pistol — Constance Petracek, Nashville, Tenn., 864.6
Women's Sport Pistol — Elizabe Callahan, Upper Marlboro, Md., 1249.
International Trap — Bret Erickson, Buena Vista, Ga., 402.
Women's International Trap — Deena Julin, Omaha, Neb., 341.
International Skeet — Matt Dryke, Sequim, Wash., 420.
Women's International Skeet —Connie Fluker, Colorado Springs, Col., 308.

National Indoor Rifle & Pistol Championships

Smallbore Rifle 4-Position — Glenn Dubis, Ft. Benning, Ga., 799.
Woman Smallbore Rifle 4-Position — Deborah W. Lyman, Meriden, Conn., 798.
Smallbore Rifle NRA 3-Position — Steve Goff, Columbus, Ga., 1185.
Woman Smallbore Rifle NRA 3-Position — Karen E. Monez, Colorado Springs, Col., 1180.
Smallbore Rifle International — Michael Eric Anti, Columbus, Ga., 1183.
Woman Smallbore Rifle International — Kristin Ann Peterson, Columbus, Ga., 1179.
Air Rifle — Debra L. Sinclair, Colorado Springs, Col., 595.
Woman Air Rifle — Debra L. Sinclair, 595.
Conventional Pistol — Jim-Bob McCarty, Bolling AFB, DC, 891.
Woman Conventional Pistol — Roxane C. Thompson, Falmouth, Va., 862.
International Free Pistol — Frank Woolard, Point Richmond, Cal., 548.
Woman International Free Pistol — Joyce R. Scott, Portland, Or., 508.
International Standard Pistol — Scott Lorenz, Lynnwood, Wash., 566.
Woman International Standard Pistol — Frances DeLong, Salt Lake City, Ut., 528.
Air Pistol — Frank Woolard, Point Richmond, Cal., 577.
Woman Air Pistol — Rosemary Lyman, Whitefish, Mont., 543.

Auto Racing

Indianapolis 500 Winners

Year	Winner, Car	MPH	Year	Winner, Car	MPH
1911	Ray Harroun, Marmon Wasp	74.59	1954	Bill Vukovich, Fuel Injection	130.840
1912	Joe Dawson, National	78.72	1955	Bob Sweikert, John Zink Special	128.209
1913	Jules Goux, Peugeot	75.933	1956	Pat Flaherty, John Zink Special	128.490
1914	Rene Thomas, Delage	82.47	1957	Sam Hanks, Belond Exhaust	135.601
1915	Ralph DePalma, Mercedes	89.84	1958	Jimmy Bryan, Belond A.P.	133.791
1916	Dario Resta, Peugeot	84.00	1959	Rodger Ward, Leader Card Special	135.857
1917-18	race not held		1960	Jim Rathmann, Ken Paul Special	138.767
1919	Howdy Wilcox, Peugeot	88.05	1961	A.J. Foyt, Bowes Seal Fast	139.130
1920	Gaston Chevrolet, Monroe	88.16	1962	Rodger Ward, Leader Card Special	140.293
1921	Tommy Milton, Frontenac	89.62	1963	Parnelli Jones, Agajanian Special	143.137
1922	Jimmy Murphy, Murphy Special	94.48	1964	A.J. Foyt, Sheraton-Thompson Special	147.350
1923	Tommy Milton, H.C.S.	90.95	1965	Jim Clark, Lotus-Ford	150.686
1924	L.L. Corum-Joe Boyer, Duesenberg	98.23	1966	Graham Hill, American Red Ball	144.317
1925	Pete DePaolo, Duesenberg	101.13	1967	A.J. Foyt, Sheraton-Thompson Special	151.207
1926	Frank Lockhart, Miller	95.904	1968	Bobby Unser, Rislone Special	152.882
1927	George Souders, Duesenberg	97.545	1969	Mario Andretti, STP Oil Treatment Special	156.867
1928	Louis Meyer, Miller	99.482			
1929	Ray Keech, Simplex	97.585	1970	Al Unser, Johnny Lightning Special	155.749
1930	Billy Arnold, Miller-Hartz	100.448	1971	Al Unser, Johnny Lightning Special	157.735
1931	Louis Schneider, Bowes Seal Fast	96.629	1972	Mark Donohue, Sunoco McLaren	162.962
1932	Fred Frame, Miller-Hartz	104.144	1973	Gordon Johncock, STP Double Oil Filter	159.036
1933	Louis Meyer, Tydol	104.162	1974	Johnny Rutherford, McLaren	158.589
1934	Bill Cummings, Boyle Products	104.863	1975	Bobby Unser, Jorgenson Eagle	149.213
1935	Kelly Petillo, Gilmore Speedway	106.240	1976	Johnny Rutherford, Hygain McLaren	148.725
1936	Louis Meyer, Ring Free	109.069	1977	A.J. Foyt, Gilmore Coyote-Ford	161.331
1937	Wilbur Shaw, Shaw-Gilmore	113.580	1978	Al Unser, Lola Cosworth	161.363
1938	Floyd Roberts, Burd Piston Ring	117.200	1979	Rick Mears, Penske-Cosworth	158.899
1939	Wilbur Shaw, Boyle	115.035	1980	Johnny Rutherford, Chaparral-Cosworth	142.862
1940	Wilbur Shaw, Boyle	114.277	1981	Bobby Unser, Penske-Cosworth	139.085
1941	Floyd Davis-Mauri Rose, Knock-Out-Hose Clip	115.117	1982	Gordon Johncock, Wildcat-Cosworth	162.026
			1983	Tom Sneva, March-Cosworth	162.117
1942-45	race not held		1984	Rick Mears, March-Cosworth	163.621
1946	George Robson, Thorne Engineering	114.820	1985	Danny Sullivan, March-Cosworth	152.982
1947	Mauri Rose, Blue Crown Special	116.338	1986	Bobby Rahal, March-Cosworth	170.722
1948	Mauri Rose, Blue Crown Special	119.814	1987	Al Unser, March-Cosworth	162.175
1949	Bill Holland, Blue Crown Special	121.327	1988	Rick Mears, Penske-Chevy V8	144.809
1950	Johnny Parsons, Wynn Kurtis Kraft	124.002	1989	Emerson Fittipaldi, Penske PC 18-Chevy	167.581
1951	Lee Wallard, Belanger	126.224	1990	Arie Luyendyk, Lola-Chevy	185.984
1952	Troy Ruttman, Agajanian	128.922	1991	Rick Mears, Penske-Chevy	176.457
1953	Bill Vukovich, Fuel Injection	128.740	1992	Al Unser Jr., Galmer-Chevy A	134.477

The race was less than 500 miles in the following years: 1916 (300 mi.), 1926 (400 mi.), 1950 (345 mi.), 1973 (332.5 mi.), 1975 (435 mi.), 1976 (255 mi.). Race record—185.984 MPH, Arie Luyendyk, 1990.

Notable One-Mile Speed Records

Date	Driver	Car	MPH	Date	Driver	Car	MPH
1/26/06	Marriott	Stanley (Steam)	127.659	9/ 3/35	Campbell	Bluebird Special	301.13
3/16/10	Oldfield	Benz	131.724	11/19/37	Eyston	Thunderbolt 1	311.42
4/23/11	Burman	Benz	141.732	9/16/38	Eyston	Thunderbolt 1	357.5
2/12/19	DePalma	Packard	149.875	8/23/39	Cobb	Railton	368.9
4/27/20	Milton	Dusenberg	155.046	9/16/47	Cobb	Railton-Mobil	394.2
4/28/26	Parry-Thomas	Thomas Spl.	170.624	8/ 5/63	Breedlove	Spirit of America	407.45
3/29/27	Seagrave	Sunbeam	203.790	10/27/64	Arfons	Green Monster	536.71
4/22/28	Keech	White Triplex	207.552	11/15/65	Breedlove	Spirit of America	600.601
3/11/29	Seagrave	Irving-Napier	231.446	10/23/70	Gabelich	Blue Flame	622.407
2/ 5/31	Campbell	Napier-Campbell	246.086	10/9/79	Barrett	Budweiser Rocket	638.637*
2/24/32	Campbell	Napier-Campbell	253.96	10/4/83	Noble	Thrust 2	633.6
2/22/33	Campbell	Napier-Campbell	272.109				

*not recognized as official by sanctioning bodies.

IndyCar Champions

(U.S. Auto Club Champions prior to 1979; Cart Champions, 1979-91)

Year	Driver	Year	Driver	Year	Driver	Year	Driver
1960	A. J. Foyt	1968	Bobby Unser	1976	Gordon Johncock	1984	Mario Andretti
1961	A. J. Foyt	1969	Mario Andretti	1977	Tom Sneva	1985	Al Unser
1962	Rodger Ward	1970	Al Unser	1978	Tom Sneva	1986	Bobby Rahal
1963	A. J. Foyt	1971	Joe Leonard	1979	Rick Mears	1987	Bobby Rahal
1964	A. J. Foyt	1972	Joe Leonard	1980	Johnny Rutherford	1988	Danny Sullivan
1965	Mario Andretti	1973	Roger McCluskey	1981	Rick Mears	1989	Emerson Fittipaldi
1966	Mario Andretti	1974	Bobby Unser	1982	Rick Mears	1990	Al Unser Jr.
1967	A. J. Foyt	1975	A. J. Foyt	1983	Al Unser	1991	Michael Andretti

Le Mans 24-Hour Race in 1992

Derek Warwick and Mark Blundell of the U.K., and Yannick Dalmas of France, drove their Peugeot to victory in the 1992 Le Mans 24-hour race. They traveled the 2,974.40 miles at an average of 123.89 mph.

NASCAR Racing in 1992

Winston Cup Races

Date	Race, site	Winner	Car
Feb. 16	Daytona 500, Daytona Beach, Fla.	Davey Allison	Ford
Mar. 1	Goodwrench 500, Rocking Ham, N.C.	Bill Elliott	Ford
Mar. 8	Pontiac Excitement 400, Richmond, Va.	Bill Elliott	Ford
Mar. 15	Motorcraft 500, Atlanta, Ga.	Bill Elliott	Ford
Mar. 29	Transouth 500, Darlington, S.C.	Bill Elliott	Ford
Apr. 5	Food City 500, Bristol, Tenn.	Alan Kulwicki	Ford
Apr. 12	First Union 400, N. Wilkesboro, N.C.	Davey Allison	Ford
Apr. 19	Mountain Dew 500, Hickory, N.C.	Tommy Houston	Buick
Apr. 26	Hanes 500, Martinsville, Va.	Mark Martin	Ford
May 3	Winston 500, Talladega, Ala.	Davey Allison	Ford
May 24	Coca Cola 600, Concord, N.C.	Dale Earnhardt	Chevrolet
May 31	Budweiser 500, Dover, Del.	Harry Gant	Oldsmobile
June 14	Champion Spark Plug 500, Pocono, Pa.	Alan Kulwicki	Ford
June 21	Miller Genuine Draft 400, Brooklyn, Mich.	Davey Allison	Ford
July 4	Pepsi 400, Daytona Beach, Fla.	Ernie Irvan	Chevrolet
July 19	Miller Genuine Draft 500, Pocono, Pa.	Darrell Waltrip	Chevrolet
July 26	Die-Hard 500, Talladega, Ala.	Ernie Irvan	Chevrolet
Aug. 9	Budweiser at The Glen, Watkins Glen, N.Y.	Kyle Petty	Pontiac
Aug. 16	Champion Spark Plug 400, Brooklyn, Mich.	Harry Gant	Oldsmobile
Aug. 29	Bud 500, Bristol, Tenn.	Darrell Waltrip	Chevrolet
Sept. 6	Southern 500, Darlington, S.C.	Darrell Waltrip	Chevrolet
Sept. 20	Peak 500, Dover, Del.	Ricky Rudd	Chevrolet
Sept. 28	Goody's 500, Martinsville, Va.	Geoff Bodine	Ford

Winston Cup Champions (NASCAR)

Year	Driver	Year	Driver	Year	Driver	Year	Driver
1949	Red Byron	1960	Rex White	1971	Richard Petty	1982	Darrell Waltrip
1950	Bill Rexford	1961	Ned Jarrett	1972	Richard Petty	1983	Bobby Allison
1951	Herb Thomas	1962	Joe Weatherly	1973	Benny Parsons	1984	Terry Labonte
1952	Tim Flock	1963	Joe Weatherly	1974	Richard Petty	1985	Darrell Waltrip
1953	Herb Thomas	1964	Richard Petty	1975	Richard Petty	1986	Dale Earnhardt
1954	Lee Petty	1965	Ned Jarrett	1976	Cale Yarborough	1987	Dale Earnhardt
1955	Tim Flock	1966	David Pearson	1977	Cale Yarborough	1988	Bill Elliott
1956	Buck Baker	1967	Richard Petty	1978	Cale Yarborough	1989	Rusty Wallace
1957	Buck Baker	1968	David Pearson	1979	Richard Petty	1990	Dale Earnhardt
1958	Lee Petty	1969	David Pearson	1980	Dale Earnhardt	1991	Dale Earnhardt
1959	Lee Petty	1970	Bobby Isaac	1981	Darrell Waltrip		

Daytona 500 Winners

Year	Driver, car	Avg. MPH	Year	Driver, car	Avg. MPH
1959	Lee Petty, Oldsmobile	135.521	1976	David Pearson, Mercury	152.181
1960	Junior Johnson, Chevrolet	124.740	1977	Cale Yarborough, Chevrolet	153.218
1961	Marvin Panch, Pontiac	149.601	1978	Bobby Allison, Ford	159.730
1962	Fireball Roberts, Pontiac	152.529	1979	Richard Petty, Oldsmobile	143.977
1963	Tiny Lund, Ford	151.566	1980	Buddy Baker, Oldsmobile	177.602
1964	Richard Petty, Plymouth	154.334	1981	Richard Petty, Buick	169.651
1965	Fred Lorenzen, Ford (a)	141.539	1982	Bobby Allison, Buick	153.991
1966	Richard Petty, Plymouth (b)	160.627	1983	Cale Yarborough, Pontiac	155.979
1967	Mario Andretti, Ford	146.926	1984	Cale Yarborough, Chevrolet	150.994
1968	Cale Yarborough, Mercury	143.251	1985	Bill Elliott, Ford	172.265
1969	Lee Roy Yarborough, Ford	160.875	1986	Geoff Bodine, Chevrolet	148.124
1970	Pete Hamilton, Plymouth	149.601	1987	Bill Elliott, Ford	176,263
1971	Richard Petty, Plymouth	144.456	1988	Bobby Allison, Buick	137,531
1972	A. J. Foyt, Mercury	161.550	1989	Darrell Waltrip, Chevrolet	148.466
1973	Richard Petty, Dodge	157.205	1990	Derrike Cope, Chevrolet	165.761
1974	Richard Petty, Dodge (c)	140.894	1991	Ernie Irvin, Chevrolet	148.148
1975	Benny Parsons, Chevrolet	153.649	1992	Davey Allison, Ford	160.256

(a) 322.5 miles. (b) 495 miles. (c) 450 miles.

World Grand Prix Champions

Year	Driver	Year	Driver	Year	Driver
1951	Jan Fangio, Argentina	1965	Jim Clark, Scotland	1979	Jody Scheckter, So. Africa
1952	Alberto Ascari, Italy	1966	Jack Brabham, Australia	1980	Alan Jones, Australia
1953	Alberto Ascari, Italy	1967	Denis Hulme, New Zealand	1981	Nelson Piquet, Brazil
1954	Juan Fangio, Argentina	1968	Graham Hill, England	1982	Keke Rosberg, Finland
1955	Juan Fangio, Argentina	1969	Jackie Stewart, Scotland	1983	Nelson Piquet, Brazil
1956	Juan Fangio, Argentina	1970	Jochen Rindt, Austria	1984	Niki Lauda, Austria
1957	Juan Fangio, Argentina	1971	Jackie Stewart, Scotland	1985	Alain Prost, France
1958	Mike Hawthorne, England	1972	Emerson Fittipaldi, Brazil	1986	Alain Prost, France
1959	Jack Brabham, Australia	1973	Jackie Stewart, Scotland	1987	Nelson Piquet, Brazil
1960	Jack Brabham, Australia	1974	Emerson Fittipaldi, Brazil	1988	Ayrton Senna, Brazil
1961	Phil Hill, United States	1975	Niki Lauda, Austria	1989	Alain Prost, France
1962	Graham Hill, England	1976	James Hunt, England	1990	Ayrton Senna, Brazil
1963	Jim Clark, Scotland	1977	Niki Lauda, Austria	1991	Ayrton Senna, Brazil
1964	John Surtees, England	1978	Mario Andretti, U.S.	1992	Nigel Mansell, Britain

Grand Prix for Formula 1 Cars in 1992

Grand Prix	Winner, car
Belgian	Michael Schmacher, Benetton-Ford
Brazilian	Nigel Mansell, Williams-Renault
British	Nigel Mansell, Williams-Renault
Canadian	Gerhard Berger, McLaren-Honda
French	Nigel Mansell, Williams-Renault
German	Nigel Mansell, Williams-Renault
Hungarian	Ayrton Senna, McLaren-Honda
Italian	Ayrton Senna, McLaren-Honda
Mexico	Nigel Mansell, Williams-Renault
Monaco	Ayrton Senna, McLaren-Honda
Portuguese	Nigel Mansell, Williams-Renault
San Marino	Nigel Mansell, Williams-Renault
South Africa	Nigel Mansell, Williams-Renault
Spanish	Nigel Mansell, Williams-Renault

Skiing

World Cup Alpine Champions

Men

1967	Jean Claude Killy, France
1968	Jean Claude Killy, France
1969	Karl Schranz, Austria
1970	Karl Schranz, Austria
1971	Gustavo Thoeni, Italy
1972	Gustavo Thoeni, Italy
1973	Gustavo Thoeni, Italy
1974	Piero Gros, Italy
1975	Gustavo Thoeni, Italy
1976	Ingemar Stenmark, Sweden
1977	Ingemar Stenmark, Sweden
1978	Ingemar Stenmark, Sweden
1979	Peter Luescher, Switzerland
1980	Andreas Wenzel, Liechtenstein
1981	Phil Mahre, U.S.
1982	Phil Mahre, U.S.
1983	Phil Mahre, U.S.
1984	Pirmin Zurbriggen, Switzerland
1985	Marc Girardelli, Luxembourg
1986	Marc Girardelli, Luxembourg
1987	Pirmin Zurbriggen, Switzerland
1988	Pirmin Zurbriggen, Switzerland
1989	Marc Girardelli, Luxembourg
1990	Pirmin Zurbriggen, Switzerland
1991	Marc Girardelli, Luxembourg
1992	Paul Accola, Switzerland

Women

1967	Nancy Greene, Canada
1968	Nancy Greene, Canada
1969	Gertrud Gabl, Austria
1970	Michele Jacot, France
1971	Annemarie Proell, Austria
1972	Annemarie Proell, Austria
1973	Annemarie Proell, Austria
1974	Annemarie Proell, Austria
1975	Annemarie Proell, Austria
1976	Rose Mittermaier, W. Germany
1977	Lise-Marie Morerod, Switzerland
1978	Hanni Wenzel, Liechtenstein
1979	Annemarie Proell Moser, Austria
1980	Hanni Wenzel, Liechtenstein
1981	Marie-Theres Nadig, Switzerland
1982	Erika Hess, Switzerland
1983	Tamara McKinney, U.S.
1984	Erika Hess, Switzerland
1985	Michela Figini, Switzerland
1986	Maria Walliser, Switzerland
1987	Maria Walliser, Switzerland
1988	Michela Figini, Switzerland
1989	Vreni Schneider, Switzerland
1990	Petra Kronberger, Austria
1991	Petra Kronberger, Austria
1992	Petra Kronberger, Austria

Curling Champions

Source: U.S. Curling News

World Champions

Year	Country, skip
1978	United States, Bob Nichols
1979	Norway, Kristian Soerum
1980	Canada, Rich Folk
1981	Switzerland, Jurg Tanner
1982	Canada, Al Hackner
1983	Canada, Ed Werenich
1984	Norway, Eigil Ramsfjell
1985	Canada, Al Hackner
1986	Canada, Ed Luckowich
1987	Canada, Russ Howard
1988	Norway, Eigil Ramsfjell
1989	Canada, Pat Ryan
1990	Canada, Ed Werenich
1991	Scotland, David Smith
1992	Switzerland, Marcus Eggler

U.S. Men's Champions

Year	State, skip
1978	Wisconsin, Bob Nichols
1979	Minnesota, Scotty Baird
1980	Minnesota, Paul Pustover
1981	Wisconsin, Somerville-Nichols
1982	Wisconsin, Steve Brown
1983	Colorado, Don Cooper
1984	Minnesota, Bruce Roberts
1985	Illinois, Tim Wright
1986	Wisconsin, Steve Brown
1987	Washington, Jim Vukich
1988	Washington, Doug Jones
1989	Washington, Jim Vukich
1990	Washington, Doug Jones
1991	Wisconsin, Steve Brown
1992	Washington, Doug Jones

U.S. Women's Champions

Year	State, skip
1981	Washington, Nancy Langley
1982	Illinois, Ruth Schwenker
1983	Washington, Nancy Langley
1984	Minnesota, Amy Hatten
1985	Alaska, Bev Birklid
1986	Minnesota, Gerri Tilden
1987	Washington, Sharon Good
1988	Washington, Nancy Langey
1989	North Dakota, Jan Lagasse
1990	Colorado, Bev Behnke
1991	Texas, Maymar Gemmell
1992	Wisconsin, Lisa Schoeneberg

Westminster Kennel Club

Year	Best-in-show	Breed	Owner
1983	Ch. Kabik's The Challenger	Afghan	Chris & Marguerite Terrell
1984	Ch. Seaward's Blackbeard	Newfoundland	Elinor Ayers
1985	Ch. Braeburn's Close Encounter	Scottish terrier	Sonnie Novick
1986	Ch. Marjetta National Acclaim	Pointer	Mrs. Alan Robson & Michael Zollo
1987	Ch. Covy Tucker Hill's Manhattan	German shepherd	Shirley Braunstein & Jane Firestone
1988	Ch. Great Elms Prince Charming II	Pomeranian	Skip Piazza & Olga Baker
1989	Ch. Royal Tudor's Wild As The Wind	Doberman	Sue & Art Kemp, Richard & Carolyn Vida, Beth Wilhite
1990	Ch. Wendessa Crown Prince	Pekingese	Ed Jenner
1991	Ch. Whisperwind on a Carousel	Poodle	Joan & Frederick Hartsock
1992	Ch. Registry's Lonesome Dove	Fox terrier	Marion & Sam Lawrence

James E. Sullivan Memorial Trophy Winners

The James E. Sullivan Memorial Trophy, named after the former president of the AAU and inaugurated in 1930, is awarded annually by the AAU to the athlete who "by his or her performance, example and influence as an amateur, has done the most during the year to advance the cause of sportsmanship."

Year	Winner	Sport
1930	Bobby Jones	Golf
1931	Barney Berlinger	Track
1932	Jim Bausch	Track
1933	Glenn Cunningham	Track
1934	Bill Bonthron	Track
1935	Lawson Little	Golf
1936	Glenn Morris	Track
1937	Don Budge	Tennis
1938	Don Lash	Track
1939	Joe Burk	Rowing
1940	Greg Rice	Track
1941	Leslie MacMitchell	Track
1942	Cornelius Warmerdam	Track
1943	Gilbert Dodds	Track
1944	Ann Curtis	Swimming
1945	Doc Blanchard	Football
1946	Arnold Tucker	Football
1947	John Kelly Jr.	Rowing
1948	Robert Mathias	Track
1949	Dick Button	Skating
1950	Fred Wilt	Track
1951	Rev. Robert Richards	Track

Year	Winner	Sport
1952	Horace Ashenfelter	Track
1953	Dr. Sammy Lee	Diving
1954	Mal Whitfield	Track
1955	Harrison Dillard	Track
1956	Patricia McCormick	Diving
1957	Bobby Joe Morrow	Track
1958	Glenn Davis	Track
1959	Parry O'Brien	Track
1960	Rafer Johnson	Track
1961	Wilma Rudolph Ward	Track
1962	James Beatty	Track
1963	John Pennel	Track
1964	Don Schollander	Swimming
1965	Bill Bradley	Basketball
1966	Jim Ryun	Track
1967	Randy Matson	Track
1968	Debbie Meyer	Swimming
1969	Bill Toomey	Track
1970	John Kinsella	Swimming
1971	Mark Spitz	Swimming
1972	Frank Shorter	Track

Year	Winner	Sport
1973	Bill Walton	Basketball
1974	Rick Wohlhutter	Track
1975	Tim Shaw	Swimming
1976	Bruce Jenner	Track
1977	John Naber	Swimming
1978	Tracy Caulkins	Swimming
1979	Kurt Thomas	Gymnastics
1980	Eric Heiden	Speed Skating
1981	Carl Lewis	Track
1982	Mary Decker	Track
1983	Edwin Moses	Track
1984	Greg Louganis	Diving
1985	Joan Benoit Samuelson	Marathon
1986	Jackie Joyner-Kersee	Track
1987	Jim Abbott	Baseball
1988	Florence Griffith Joyner	Track
1989	Janet Evans	Swimming
1990	John Smith	Wrestling
1991	Mike Powell	Track

Chess

Source: U.S. Chess Federation

Chess dates back to antiquity, its exact origin unknown. The best players of their time, regarded by later generations as world champions, were Francois Philidor, Alexandre Deschappelles, Louis de la Bourdonnais, all France; Howard Staunton, England; Adolph Anderssen, Germany and Paul Morphy, U.S. In 1866 Wilhelm Steinitz defeated Adolph Anderssen and claimed the world champion title. Official world champions since the title was first used follow:

1866-1894 Wilhelm Steinitz, Austria
1894-1921 Emanuel Lasker, Germany
1921-1927 Jose R. Capablanca, Cuba
1927-1935 Alexander A. Alekhine, France
1935-1937 Max Euwe, Netherlands
1937-1946 Alexander A. Alekhine, France
1948-1957 Mikhail Botvinnik, USSR
1957-1958 Vassily Smyslov, USSR
1958-1959 Mikhail Botvinnik, USSR
1960-1961 Mikhail Tal, USSR
1961-1963 Mikhail Botvinnik, USSR
1963-1969 Tigran Petrosian, USSR
1969-1972 Boris Spassky, USSR
1972-1975 Bobby Fischer, U.S. (a)
1975-1985 Anatoly Karpov, USSR
1985 Gary Kasparov, USSR

(a) Defaulted championship after refusal to accept International Chess Federation rules for a championship match, April 1975.

United States Champions

Unofficial champions
1857-1871 Paul Morphy
1871-1876 George Mackenzie
1876-1880 James Mason
1880-1889 George Mackenzie
1889-1890 S. Lipschutz
1890 Jackson Showalter
1890-1891 Max Judd
Official champions
1891-1892 Jackson Showalter
1892-1894 S. Lipschutz
1894 Jackson Showalter
1894-1895 Albert Hodges
1895-1897 Jackson Showalter
1897-1906 Harry Pillsbury
1906-1909 vacant
1909-1936 Frank Marshall
1936-1944 Samuel Reshevsky
1944-1946 Arnold Denker
1946-1948 Samuel Reshevsky
1948-1951 Herman Steiner
1951-1954 Larry Evans
1954-1957 Arthur Bisguier
1957-1961 Bobby Fischer
1961-1962 Larry Evans
1962-1968 Bobby Fischer
1968-1969 Larry Evans
1969-1972 Samuel Reshevsky
1972-1973 Robert Byrne
1973-1974 Lubomir Kavalek, John Grefe
1974-1977 Walter Browne
1978-1980 Lubomir Kavalek
1980-1981 (tie) Larry Evans, Larry Christiansen, Walter Browne
1981-1983 (tie) Walter Browne, Yasser Seirawan
1983 (tie) Walter Browne, Larry Christiansen, Roman Dzindzichashvili
1984-1985 Lev Alburt
1986 Yasser Seirawan
1987 (tie) Joel Benjamin, Nick DeFirmian
1988 Michael Wilder
1989 (tie) Stuart Rachels, Yasser Seirawan, Roman Dzindzichashvili
1990 Lev Alburt
1991 Gata Kamsky

Iditarod Trail Sled Dog Race in 1992

Martin Buser won the 1992 Iditarod Trail Sled Dog Race in a record time of 10 days 19 hours and 17 minutes. By winning the 1,159-mile race from Anchorage to Nome, Buser received $50,000 in prize money and a pickup truck valued at about $25,000. Susan Butcher finished second and earned $39,500, while Tim Osmar finished third and earned $32,000.

GTE Academic All-America Team

The 1992 GTE Academic All-America Team boasted 4 athletes with perfect 4.0's. They were David Honea, North Carolina cross-country runner; Greg Lopez, track star at Northern Arizona; Sigall Kassutto, gymnast at California; and Claire Lavers, cross-country runner at Arkansas. Also on the team were lacrosse players Cathy Sharkey, Yale; and Oliver Marti, Brown.

BASEBALL

Major League Pennant Winners, 1901–1992

National League

Year	Winner	Won	Lost	Pct	Manager
1901	Pittsburgh	90	49	.647	Clarke
1902	Pittsburgh	103	36	.741	Clarke
1903	Pittsburgh	91	49	.650	Clarke
1904	New York	106	47	.693	McGraw
1905	New York	105	48	.686	McGraw
1906	Chicago	116	36	.763	Chance
1907	Chicago	107	45	.704	Chance
1908	Chicago	99	55	.643	Chance
1909	Pittsburgh	110	42	.724	Clarke
1910	Chicago	104	50	.675	Chance
1911	New York	99	54	.647	McGraw
1912	New York	103	48	.682	McGraw
1913	New York	101	51	.664	McGraw
1914	Boston	94	59	.614	Stallings
1915	Philadelphia	90	62	.592	Moran
1916	Brooklyn	94	60	.610	Robinson
1917	New York	98	56	.636	McGraw
1918	Chicago	84	45	.651	Mitchell
1919	Cincinnati	96	44	.686	Moran
1920	Brooklyn	93	60	.604	Robinson
1921	New York	94	56	.614	McGraw
1922	New York	93	61	.604	McGraw
1923	New York	95	58	.621	McGraw
1924	New York	93	60	.608	McGraw
1925	Pittsburgh	95	58	.621	McKechnie
1926	St. Louis	89	65	.578	Hornsby
1927	Pittsburgh	94	60	.610	Bush
1928	St. Louis	95	59	.617	McKechnie
1929	Chicago	98	54	.645	McCarthy
1930	St. Louis	92	62	.597	Street
1931	St. Louis	101	53	.656	Street
1932	Chicago	90	64	.584	Grimm
1933	New York	91	61	.599	Terry
1934	St. Louis	95	58	.621	Frisch
1935	Chicago	100	54	.649	Grimm
1936	New York	91	62	.597	Terry
1937	New York	95	57	.625	Terry
1938	Chicago	89	63	.586	Hartnett
1939	Cincinnati	97	57	.630	McKechnie
1940	Cincinnati	100	53	.654	McKechnie
1941	Brooklyn	100	54	.649	Durocher
1942	St. Louis	106	48	.688	Southworth
1943	St. Louis	105	49	.682	Southworth
1944	St. Louis	105	49	.682	Southworth
1945	Chicago	98	56	.636	Grimm
1946	St. Louis	98	58	.628	Dyer
1947	Brooklyn	94	60	.610	Shotton
1948	Boston	91	62	.595	Southworth
1949	Brooklyn	97	57	.630	Shotton
1950	Philadelphia	91	63	.591	Sawyer
1951	New York	98	59	.624	Durocher
1952	Brooklyn	96	57	.627	Dressen
1953	Brooklyn	105	49	.682	Dressen
1954	New York	97	57	.630	Durocher
1955	Brooklyn	98	55	.641	Alston
1956	Brooklyn	93	61	.604	Alston
1957	Milwaukee	95	59	.617	Haney
1958	Milwaukee	92	62	.597	Haney
1959	Los Angeles	88	68	.564	Alston
1960	Pittsburgh	95	59	.617	Murtaugh
1961	Cincinnati	93	61	.604	Hutchinson
1962	San Francisco	103	62	.624	Dark
1963	Los Angeles	99	63	.611	Alston
1964	St. Louis	93	69	.574	Keane
1965	Los Angeles	97	65	.599	Alston
1966	Los Angeles	95	67	.586	Alston
1967	St. Louis	101	60	.627	Schoendienst
1968	St. Louis	97	65	.599	Schoendienst

American League

Year	Winner	Won	Lost	Pct	Manager
1901	Chicago	83	53	.610	Griffith
1902	Philadelphia	83	53	.610	Mack
1903	Boston	91	47	.659	Collins
1904	Boston	95	59	.617	Collins
1905	Philadelphia	92	56	.622	Mack
1906	Chicago	93	58	.616	Jones
1907	Detroit	92	58	.613	Jennings
1908	Detroit	90	63	.588	Jennings
1909	Detroit	98	54	.645	Jennings
1910	Philadelphia	102	48	.680	Mack
1911	Philadelphia	101	50	.669	Mack
1912	Boston	105	47	.691	Stahl
1913	Philadelphia	96	57	.627	Mack
1914	Philadelphia	99	53	.651	Mack
1915	Boston	101	50	.669	Carrigan
1916	Boston	91	63	.591	Carrigan
1917	Chicago	100	54	.649	Rowland
1918	Boston	75	51	.595	Barrow
1919	Chicago	88	52	.629	Gleason
1920	Cleveland	98	56	.636	Speaker
1921	New York	98	55	.641	Huggins
1922	New York	94	60	.610	Huggins
1923	New York	98	54	.645	Huggins
1924	Washington	92	62	.597	Harris
1925	Washington	96	55	.636	Harris
1926	New York	91	63	.591	Huggins
1927	New York	110	44	.714	Huggins
1928	New York	101	53	.656	Huggins
1929	Philadelphia	104	46	.693	Mack
1930	Philadelphia	102	52	.662	Mack
1931	Philadelphia	107	45	.704	Mack
1932	New York	107	47	.695	McCarthy
1933	Washington	99	53	.651	Cronin
1934	Detroit	101	53	.656	Cochrane
1935	Detroit	93	58	.616	Cochrane
1936	New York	102	51	.667	McCarthy
1937	New York	102	52	.662	McCarthy
1938	New York	99	53	.651	McCarthy
1939	New York	106	45	.702	McCarthy
1940	Detroit	90	64	.584	Baker
1941	New York	101	53	.656	McCarthy
1942	New York	103	51	.669	McCarthy
1943	New York	98	56	.636	McCarthy
1944	St. Louis	89	65	.578	Sewell
1945	Detroit	88	65	.575	O'Neill
1946	Boston	104	50	.675	Cronin
1947	New York	97	57	.630	Harris
1948	Cleveland	97	58	.626	Boudreau
1949	New York	97	57	.630	Stengel
1950	New York	98	56	.636	Stengel
1951	New York	98	56	.636	Stengel
1952	New York	95	59	.617	Stengel
1953	New York	99	52	.656	Stengel
1954	Cleveland	111	43	.721	Lopez
1955	New York	96	58	.623	Stengel
1956	New York	97	57	.630	Stengel
1957	New York	98	56	.636	Stengel
1958	New York	92	62	.597	Stengel
1959	Chicago	94	60	.610	Lopez
1960	New York	97	57	.630	Stengel
1961	New York	109	53	.673	Houk
1962	New York	96	66	.593	Houk
1963	New York	104	57	.646	Houk
1964	New York	99	63	.611	Berra
1965	Minnesota	102	60	.630	Mele
1966	Baltimore	97	63	.606	Bauer
1967	Boston	92	70	.568	Williams
1968	Detroit	103	59	.636	Smith

National League

	East					West					
Year	Winner	W	L	Pct	Manager	Winner	W	L	Pct	Manager	Playoff winner
1969	N.Y. Mets	100	62	.617	Hodges	Atlanta	93	69	.574	Harris	New York
1970	Pittsburgh	89	73	.549	Murtaugh	Cincinnati	102	60	.630	Anderson	Cincinnati
1971	Pittsburgh	97	65	.599	Murtaugh	San Francisco	90	72	.556	Fox	Pittsburgh
1972	Pittsburgh	96	59	.619	Virdon	Cincinnati	95	59	.617	Anderson	Cincinnati
1973	N.Y. Mets	82	79	.509	Berra	Cincinnati	99	63	.611	Anderson	New York
1974	Pittsburgh	88	74	.543	Murtaugh	Los Angeles	102	60	.630	Alston	Los Angeles
1975	Pittsburgh	92	69	.571	Murtaugh	Cincinnati	108	54	.667	Anderson	Cincinnati
1976	Philadelphia	101	61	.623	Ozark	Cincinnati	102	60	.630	Anderson	Cincinnati

	East					West					
Year	Winner	W	L	Pct	Manager	Winner	W	L	Pct	Manager	Playoff winner
1977	Philadelphia .	101	61	.623	Ozark	Los Angeles . . .	98	64	.605	Lasorda	Los Angeles
1978	Philadelphia .	90	72	.556	Ozark	Los Angeles . . .	95	67	.586	Lasorda	Los Angeles
1979	Pittsburgh. . .	98	64	.605	Tanner	Cincinnati	90	71	.559	McNamara	Pittsburgh
1980	Philadelphia .	91	71	.562	Green	Houston.	93	70	.571	Virdon	Philadelphia
1981(a)	Philadelphia .	34	21	.618	Green	Los Angeles . . .	36	21	.632	Lasorda	(c)
1981(b)	Montreal . . .	30	23	.566	Williams, Fanning	Houston.	33	20	.623	Virdon	Los Angeles
1982	St. Louis . . .	92	70	.568	Herzog	Atlanta	89	73	.549	Torre	St. Louis
1983	Philadelphia .	90	72	.556	Corrales, Owens	Los Angeles . . .	91	71	.562	Lasorda	Philadelphia
1984	Chicago. . . .	96	65	.596	Frey	San Diego	92	70	.568	Williams	San Diego
1985	St. Louis . . .	101	61	.623	Herzog	Los Angeles . . .	95	67	.586	Lasorda	St. Louis
1986	N.Y. Mets. . .	108	54	.667	Johnson	Houston.	96	66	.593	Lanier	New York
1987	St. Louis . . .	95	67	.586	Herzog	San Francisco . .	90	72	.556	Craig	St. Louis
1988	N.Y. Mets. . .	100	60	.625	Johnson	Los Angeles . . .	94	67	.584	Lasorda	Los Angeles
1989	Chicago. . . .	93	69	.571	Zimmer	San Francisco . .	92	70	.568	Craig	San Francisco
1990	Pittsburgh. . .	95	67	.586	Leyland	Cincinnati	91	71	.562	Piniella	Cincinnati
1991	Pittsburgh. . .	98	64	.605	Leyland	Atlanta	94	68	.580	Cox	Atlanta
1992	Pittsburgh. . .	96	66	.593	Leyland	Atlanta	98	64	.605	Cox	Atlanta

American League

	East					West					
Year	Winner	W	L	Pct	Manager	Winner	W	L	Pct	Manager	Playoff winner
1969	Baltimore . . .	109	53	.673	Weaver	Minnesota	97	65	.599	Martin	Baltimore
1970	Baltimore . . .	108	54	.667	Weaver	Minnesota	98	64	.605	Rigney	Baltimore
1971	Baltimore . . .	101	57	.639	Weaver	Oakland	101	60	.627	Williams	Baltimore
1972	Detroit	86	70	.551	Martin	Oakland	93	62	.600	Williams	Oakland
1973	Baltimore . . .	97	65	.599	Weaver	Oakland	94	68	.580	Williams	Oakland
1974	Baltimore . . .	91	71	.562	Weaver	Oakland	90	72	.556	Dark	Oakland
1975	Boston.	95	65	.594	Johnson	Oakland	98	64	.605	Dark	Boston
1976	New York . . .	97	62	.610	Martin	Kansas City	90	72	.556	Herzog	New York
1977	New York . . .	100	62	.617	Martin	Kansas City	102	60	.630	Herzog	New York
1978	New York . . .	100	63	.613	Martin,	Lemon Kansas City	92	70	.568	Herzog	New York
1979	Baltimore . . .	102	57	.642	Weaver	California.	88	74	.543	Fregosi	Baltimore
1980	New York . . .	103	59	.636	Howser	Kansas City	97	65	.599	Frey	Kansas City
1981(a)	New York . . .	34	22	.607	Michael	Oakland	37	23	.617	Martin	(d)
1981(b)	Milwaukee . .	31	22	.585	Rodgers	Kansas City	30	23	.566	Frey, Howser	New York
1982	Milwaukee . .	95	67	.586	Rodgers,	Kuenn California .	93	69	.574	Mauch	Milwaukee
1983	Baltimore . . .	98	64	.605	Altobelli	Chicago	99	63	.611	LaRussa	Baltimore
1984	Detroit	104	58	.642	Anderson	Kansas City	84	78	.519	Howser	Detroit
1985	Toronto	99	62	.615	Cox	Kansas City	91	71	.562	Howser	Kansas City
1986	Boston.	95	66	.590	McNamara	California.	92	70	.568	Mauch	Boston
1987	Detroit	98	64	.605	Anderson	Minnesota	85	77	.525	Kelly	Minnesota
1988	Boston.	89	73	.549	McNamara, Morgan	Oakland	104	58	.642	LaRussa	Oakland
1989	Toronto	89	73	.549	Williams, Gaston	Oakland	99	63	.611	LaRussa	Oakland
1990	Boston.	88	74	.543	Morgan	Oakland	103	59	.636	LaRussa	Oakland
1991	Toronto	91	71	.562	Gaston	Minnesota	95	67	.586	Kelly	Minnesota
1992	Toronto	96	66	.593	Gaston	Oakland	96	66	.593	LaRussa	Toronto

(a) First half; (b) Second half; (c) Montreal and L.A. won the divisional playoffs; (d) N.Y. and Oakland won the divisional playoffs.

Cy Young Award Winners

Year	Player, club
1956	Don Newcombe, Dodgers
1957	Warren Spahn, Braves
1958	Bob Turley, Yankees
1959	Early Wynn, White Sox
1960	Vernon Law, Pirates
1961	Whitey Ford, Yankees
1962	Don Drysdale, Dodgers
1963	Sandy Koufax, Dodgers
1964	Dean Chance, Angels
1965	Sandy Koufax, Dodgers
1966	Sandy Koufax, Dodgers
1967	(NL) Mike McCormick, Giants
	(AL) Jim Lonborg, Red Sox
1968	(NL) Bob Gibson, Cardinals
	(AL) Dennis McLain, Tigers
1969	(NL) Tom Seaver, Mets
	(AL) (tie) Dennis McLain, Tigers
	Mike Cuellar, Orioles
1970	(NL) Bob Gibson, Cardinals
	(AL) Jim Perry, Twins
1971	(NL) Ferguson Jenkins, Cubs
	(AL) Vida Blue, A's
	(NL) Steve Carlton, Phillies
1972	(AL) Gaylord Perry, Indians
	(NL) Tom Seaver, Mets
1973	(AL) Jim Palmer, Orioles
	(NL) Mike Marshall, Dodgers
1974	(AL) Jim (Catfish) Hunter, A's
	(NL) Tom Seaver, Mets
1975	(AL) Jim Palmer, Orioles
	(NL) Randy Jones, Padres
1976	(AL) Jim Palmer, Orioles
	(NL) Steve Carlton, Phillies
1977	(AL) Sparky Lyle, Yankees
	(NL) Gaylord Perry, Padres
1978	(AL) Ron Guidry, Yankees
	(NL) Bruce Sutter, Cubs
1979	(AL) Mike Flanagan, Orioles
	(NL) Steve Carlton, Phillies
1980	(AL) Steve Stone, Orioles
	(NL) Fernando Valenzuela,
1981	Dodgers
	(AL) Rollie Fingers, Brewers
1982	(NL) Steve Carlton, Phillies
	(AL) Pete Vuckovich, Brewers
1983	(NL) John Denny, Phillies
	(AL) LaMarr Hoyt, White Sox
1984	(NL) Rick Sutcliffe, Cubs
	(AL) Willie Hernandez, Tigers
1985	(NL) Dwight Gooden, Mets
	(AL) Bret Saberhagen, Royals
1986	(NL) Mike Scott, Astros
	(AL) Roger Clemens, Red Sox
1987	(NL) Steve Bedrosian, Phillies
	(AL) Roger Clemens, Red Sox
1988	(NL) Orel Hershiser, Dodgers
	(AL) Frank Viola, Twins
1989	(NL) Mark Davis, Padres
	(AL) Bret Saberhagen, Royals
1990	(NL) Doug Drabek, Pirates
	(AL) Bob Welch, A's
1991	(NL) Tom Glavine, Braves
	(AL) Roger Clemens, Red Sox

Pitchers with 300 Major League Wins

Cy Young	511	Warren Spahn	363	Steve Carlton	329	Nolan Ryan	319	Mickey Welch	311
Walter Johnson	416	Pud Galvin	361	Eddie Plank	327	Phil Niekro	318	Old Hoss Radbourn	308
Christy Mathewson	373	Kid Nichols	360	John Clarkson	326	Gaylord Perry	314	Lefty Grove	300
Grover Alexander	373	Tim Keefe	344	Don Sutton	324	Tom Seaver	311	Early Wynn	300

Home Run Leaders

National League

Year	Player, Club	HR
1901	Sam Crawford, Cincinnati	16
1902	Thomas Leach, Pittsburgh	6
1903	James Sheckard, Brooklyn	9
1904	Harry Lumley, Brooklyn	9
1905	Fred Odwell, Cincinnati	9
1906	Timothy Jordan, Brooklyn	12
1907	David Brain, Boston	10
1908	Timothy Jordan, Brooklyn	12
1909	Red Murray, New York	7
1910	Fred Beck, Bos., Frank Schulte, Chi.	10
1911	Frank Schulte, Chicago	21
1912	Henry Zimmerman, Chicago	14
1913	Gavvy Cravath, Philadelphia	19
1914	Gavvy Cravath, Philadelphia	19
1915	Gavvy Cravath, Philadelphia	24
1916	Dave Robertson, N.Y., Fred (Cy) Williams, Chi.	12
1917	Dave Robertson, N.Y., Gavvy Cravath, Phil.	12
1918	Gavvy Cravath, Philadelphia	8
1919	Gavvy Cravath, Philadelphia	12
1920	Cy Williams, Philadelphia	15
1921	George Kelly, New York	23
1922	Rogers Hornsby, St. Louis	42
1923	Cy Williams, Philadelphia	41
1924	Jacques Fournier, Brooklyn	27
1925	Rogers Hornsby, St. Louis	39
1926	Hack Wilson, Chicago	21
1927	Hack Wilson, Chicago; Cy Williams, Philadelphia	30
1928	Hack Wilson, Chicago; Jim Bottomley, St. Louis	31
1929	Chuck Klein, Philadelphia	43
1930	Hack Wilson, Chicago	56
1931	Chuck Klein, Philadelphia	31
1932	Chuck Klein, Philadelphia, Mel Ott, New York	38
1933	Chuck Klein, Philadelphia	28
1934	Rip Collins, St. Louis; Mel Ott, New York	35
1935	Walter Berger, Boston	34
1936	Mel Ott, New York	33
1937	Mel Ott, New York; Joe Medwick, St. Louis	31
1938	Mel Ott, New York	36
1939	John Mize, St. Louis	28
1940	John Mize, St. Louis	43
1941	Dolph Camilli, Brooklyn	34
1942	Mel Ott, New York	30
1943	Bill Nicholson, Chicago	29
1944	Bill Nicholson, Chicago	33
1945	Tommy Holmes, Boston	28
1946	Ralph Kiner, Pittsburgh	23
1947	Ralph Kiner, Pittsburgh; John Mize, New York	51
1948	Ralph Kiner, Pittsburgh; John Mize, New York	40
1949	Ralph Kiner, Pittsburgh	54
1950	Ralph Kiner, Pittsburgh	47
1951	Ralph Kiner, Pittsburgh	42
1952	Ralph Kiner, Pittsburgh; Hank Sauer, Chicago	37
1953	Ed Mathews, Milwaukee	47
1954	Ted Kluszewski, Cincinnati	49
1955	Willie Mays, New York	51
1956	Duke Snider, Brooklyn	43
1957	Hank Aaron, Milwaukee	44
1958	Ernie Banks, Chicago	47
1959	Ed Mathews, Milwaukee	46
1960	Ernie Banks, Chicago	41
1961	Orlando Cepeda, San Francisco	46
1962	Willie Mays, San Francisco	49
1963	Hank Aaron, Milwaukee, Willie McCovey, S.F.	44
1964	Willie Mays, San Francisco	47
1965	Willie Mays, San Francisco	52
1966	Hank Aaron, Atlanta	44
1967	Hank Aaron, Atlanta	39
1968	Willie McCovey, San Francisco	36
1969	Willie McCovey, San Francisco	45
1970	Johnny Bench, Cincinnati	45
1971	Willie Stargell, Pittsburgh	48
1972	Johnny Bench, Cincinnati	40
1973	Willie Stargell, Pittsburgh	44
1974	Mike Schmidt, Philadelphia	36
1975	Mike Schmidt, Philadelphia	38
1976	Mike Schmidt, Philadelphia	38
1977	George Foster, Cincinnati	52
1978	George Foster, Cincinnati	40
1979	Dave Kingman, Chicago	48
1980	Mike Schmidt, Philadelphia	48
1981	Mike Schmidt, Philadelphia	31
1982	Dave Kingman, New York	37
1983	Mike Schmidt, Philadelphia	40

American League

Year	Player, Club	HR
1901	Napoleon Lajoie, Philadelphia	14
1902	Socks Seybold, Philadelphia	16
1903	Buck Freeman, Boston	13
1904	Harry Davis, Philadelphia	10
1905	Harry Davis, Philadelphia	8
1906	Harry Davis, Philadelphia	12
1907	Harry Davis, Philadelphia	8
1908	Sam Crawford, Detroit	7
1909	Ty Cobb, Detroit	9
1910	Jake Stahl, Boston	10
1911	J. Franklin Baker, Philadelphia	11
1912	J. Franklin Baker, Philadelphia, Tris Speaker, Boston	10
1913	J. Franklin, Baker, Philadelphia	12
1914	J. Franklin, Baker, Philadelphia	9
1915	Robert Roth, Chicago-Cleveland	7
1916	Wally Pipp, New York	12
1917	Wally Pipp, New York	9
1918	Babe Ruth, Bos., Tilly Walker, Phil.	11
1919	Babe Ruth, Boston	29
1920	Babe Ruth, New York	54
1921	Babe Ruth, New York	59
1922	Ken Williams, St. Louis	39
1923	Babe Ruth, New York	41
1924	Babe Ruth, New York	46
1925	Bob Meusel, New York	33
1926	Babe Ruth, New York	47
1927	Babe Ruth, New York	60
1928	Babe Ruth, New York	54
1929	Babe Ruth, New York	46
1930	Babe Ruth, New York	49
1931	Babe Ruth, Lou Gehrig, New York	46
1932	Jimmie Foxx, Philadelphia	58
1933	Jimmie Foxx, Philadelphia	48
1934	Lou Gehrig, New York	49
1935	Jimmie Foxx, Philadelphia, Hank Greenberg, Detroit	36
1936	Lou Gehrig, New York	49
1937	Joe DiMaggio, New York	46
1938	Hank Greenberg, Detroit	58
1939	Jimmie Foxx, Boston	35
1940	Hank Greenberg, Detroit	41
1941	Ted Williams, Boston	37
1942	Ted Williams, Boston	36
1943	Rudy York, Detroit	34
1944	Nick Etten, New York	22
1945	Vern Stephens, St. Louis	24
1946	Hank Greenberg, Detroit	44
1947	Ted Williams, Boston	32
1948	Joe DiMaggio, New York	39
1949	Ted Williams, Boston	43
1950	Al Rosen, Cleveland	37
1951	Gus Zernial, Chicago-Philadelphia	33
1952	Larry Doby, Cleveland	32
1953	Al Rosen, Cleveland	43
1954	Larry Doby, Cleveland	32
1955	Mickey Mantle, New York	37
1956	Mickey Mantle, New York	52
1957	Roy Sievers, Washington	42
1958	Mickey Mantle, New York	42
1959	Rocky Colavito, Cleve., Harmon Killebrew, Wash.	42
1960	Mickey Mantle, New York	40
1961	Roger Maris, New York	61
1962	Harmon Killebrew, Minnesota	48
1963	Harmon Killebrew, Minnesota	45
1964	Harmon Killebrew, Minnesota	49
1965	Tony Conigliaro, Boston	32
1966	Frank Robinson, Baltimore	49
1967	Carl Yastrzemski, Boston, Harmon Killebrew, Minn.	44
1968	Frank Howard, Washington	44
1969	Harmon Killebrew, Minnesota	49
1970	Frank Howard, Washington	44
1971	Bill Melton, Chicago	33
1972	Dick Allen, Chicago	37
1973	Reggie Jackson, Oakland	32
1974	Dick Allen, Chicago	32
1975	George Scott, Milwaukee; Reggie Jackson, Oakland	36
1976	Graig Nettles, New York	32
1977	Jim Rice, Boston	39
1978	Jim Rice, Boston	46
1979	Gorman Thomas, Milwaukee	45
1980	Reggie Jackson, New York; Ben Oglivie, Milwaukee	41
1981	Bobby Grich, California; Tony Armas, Oakland; Dwight Evans, Boston; Eddie Murray, Baltimore	22
1982	Gorman Thomas, Milwaukee; Reggie Jackson, Cal.	39
1983	Jim Rice, Boston	39

Year	Player, Club	HR	Year	Player, Club	HR
1984	Mike Schmidt, Phil.; Dale Murphy, Atlanta	36	1984	Tony Armas, Boston	43
1985	Dale Murphy, Atlanta	37	1985	Darrell Evans, Detroit	40
1986	Mike Schmidt, Philadelphia	37	1986	Jesse Barfield, Toronto	40
1987	Andre Dawson, Chicago	49	1987	Mark McGwire, Oakland	49
1988	Darryl Strawberry, New York	39	1988	Jose Canseco, Oakland	42
1989	Kevin Mitchell, San Francisco	47	1989	Fred McGriff, Toronto	36
1990	Ryne Sandberg, Chicago	40	1990	Cecil Fielder, Detroit	51
1991	Howard Johnson, New York	38	1991	Cecil Fielder, Detroit; Jose Canseco, Oakland	44
1992	Fred McGriff, San Diego	35	1992	Juan Gonzalez, Texas	43

Runs Batted In Leaders

National League

Year	Player, Club	RBI
1907	Honus Wagner, Pittsburgh	91
1908	Honus Wager, Pittsburgh	106
1909	Honus Wager, Pittsburgh	102
1910	Sherwood Magee, Philadelphia	116
1911	Frank Schulte, Chicago	121
1912	Henry Zimmerman, Chicago	98
1913	Gavvy Cravath, Philadelphia	118
1914	Sherwood Magee, Philadelphia	101
1915	Gavvy Cravath, Philadelphia	118
1916	Hal Chase, Cincinnati	94
1917	Henry Zimmerman, New York	100
1918	Frederick Merkle, Chicago	71
1919	Hi Myers, Boston	72
1920	George Kelly, N.Y., Rogers Hornsby, St. Louis	94
1921	Rogers Hornsby, St. Louis	126
1922	Rogers Hornsby, St. Louis	152
1923	Emil Meusel, New York	125
1924	George Kelly, New York	136
1925	Rogers Hornsby, St. Louis	143
1926	Jim Bottomley, St. Louis	120
1927	Paul Waner, Pittsburgh	131
1928	Jim Bottomley, St. Louis	136
1929	Hack Wilson, Chicago	159
1930	Hack Wilson, Chicago	190
1931	Chuck Klein, Philadelphia	121
1932	Don Hurst, Philadelphia	143
1933	Chuck Klein, Philadelphia	120
1934	Mel Ott, New York	135
1935	Walter Berger, Boston	130
1936	Joe Medwick, St. Louis	138
1937	Joe Medwick, St. Louis	154
1938	Joe Medwick, St. Louis	122
1939	Frank McCormick, Cincinnati	128
1940	John Mize, St. Louis	137
1941	Adolph Camilli, Brooklyn	120
1942	John Mize, New York	110
1943	Bill Nicholson, Chicago	128
1944	Bill Nicholson, Chicago	122
1945	Dixie Walker, Brooklyn	124
1946	Enos Slaughter, St. Louis	130
1947	John Mize, New York	138
1948	Stan Musial, St. Louis	131
1949	Ralph Kiner, Pittsburgh	127
1950	Del Ennis, Philadelphia	126
1951	Monte Irvin, New York	121
1952	Hank Sauer, Chicago	121
1953	Roy Campanella, Brooklyn	142
1954	Ted Kluszewski, Cincinnati	141
1955	Duke Snider, Brooklyn	136
1956	Stan Musial, St. Louis	109
1957	Hank Aaron, Milwaukee	132
1958	Ernie Banks, Chicago	129
1959	Ernie Banks, Chicago	143
1960	Hank Aaron, Milwaukee	126
1961	Orlando Cepeda, San Francisco	142
1962	Tommy Davis, Los Angeles	153
1963	Hank Aaron, Milwaukee	130
1964	Ken Boyer, St. Louis	119
1965	Deron Johnson, Cincinnati	130
1966	Hank Aaron, Atlanta	127
1967	Orlando Cepeda, St. Louis	111
1968	Willie McCovey, San Francisco	105
1969	Willie McCovey, San Francisco	126
1970	Johnny Bench, Cincinnati	148
1971	Joe Torre, St. Louis	137
1972	Johnny Bench, Cincinnati	125
1973	Willie Stargell, Pittsburgh	119
1974	Johnny Bench, Cincinnati	129
1975	Greg Luzinski, Philadelphia	120
1976	George Foster, Cincinnati	121
1977	George Foster, Cincinnati	149
1978	George Foster, Cincinnati	120
1979	Dave Winfield, San Diego	118

American League

Year	Player, Club	RBI
1907	Ty Cobb, Detroit	116
1908	Ty Cobb, Detroit	101
1909	Ty Cobb, Detroit	115
1910	Sam Crawford, Detroit	115
1911	Ty Cobb, Detroit	144
1912	J. Franklin Baker, Philadelphia	133
1913	J. Franklin Baker, Philadelphia	126
1914	Sam Crawford, Detroit	112
1915	Sam Crawford, Detroit	116
1916	Wally Pipp, New York	99
1917	Robert Veach, Detroit	115
1918	George Burns, Phila., Robert Veach, Detroit	74
1919	Babe Ruth, Boston	112
1920	Babe Ruth, New York	137
1921	Babe Ruth, New York	171
1922	Ken Williams, St. Louis	155
1923	Babe Ruth, New York	131
1924	Goose Goslin, Washington	129
1925	Bob Meusel, New York	138
1926	Babe Ruth, New York	145
1927	Lou Gehrig, New York	175
1928	Babe Ruth, N.Y., Lou Gehrig, N.Y.	142
1929	Al Simmons, Philadelphia	157
1930	Lou Gehrig, New York	174
1931	Lou Gehrig, New York	184
1932	Jimmie Foxx, Philadelphia	169
1933	Jimmie Foxx, Philadelphia	163
1934	Lou Gehrig, New York	165
1935	Hank Greenberg, Detroit	170
1936	Hal Trosky, Cleveland	162
1937	Hank Greenberg, Detroit	183
1938	Jimmie Foxx, Boston	175
1939	Ted Williams, Boston	145
1940	Hank Greenberg, Detroit	150
1941	Joe DiMaggio, New York	125
1942	Ted Williams, Boston	137
1943	Rudy York, Detroit	118
1944	Vern Stephens, St. Louis	109
1945	Nick Etten, New York	111
1946	Hank Greenberg, Detroit	127
1947	Ted Williams, Boston	114
1948	Joe DiMaggio, New York	155
1949	Ted Williams, Bos., Vern Stephens, Bos.	159
1950	Walt Dropo, Bos., Vern Stephens, Bos.	144
1951	Gus Zernial, Chicago-Philadelphia	129
1952	Al Rosen, Cleveland	105
1953	Al Rosen, Cleveland	145
1954	Larry Doby, Cleveland	126
1955	Ray Boone, Detroit, Jackie Jensen, Boston	116
1956	Mickey Mantle, New York	130
1957	Roy Sievers, Washington	114
1958	Jackie Jensen, Boston	122
1959	Jackie Jensen, Boston	112
1960	Roger Maris, New York	112
1961	Roger Maris, New York	142
1962	Harmon Killebrew, Minnesota	126
1963	Dick Stuart, Boston	118
1964	Brooks Robinson, Baltimore	118
1965	Rocky Colavito, Cleveland	108
1966	Frank Robinson, Baltimore	122
1967	Carl Yastrzemski, Boston	121
1968	Ken Harrelson, Boston	109
1969	Harmon Killebrew, Minnesota	140
1970	Frank Howard, Washington	126
1971	Harmon Killebrew, Minnesota	119
1972	Dick Allen, Chicago	113
1973	Reggie Jackson, Oakland	117
1974	Jeff Burroughs, Texas	118
1975	George Scott, Milwaukee	109
1976	Lee May, Baltimore	109
1977	Larry Hisle, Minnesota	119
1978	Jim Rice, Boston	139
1979	Don Baylor, California	139

Year	Player, Club	RBI
1980	Mike Schmidt, Philadelphia	121
1981	Mike Schmidt, Philadelphia	91
1982	Dale Murphy, Atlanta; Al Oliver, Montreal	109
1983	Dale Murphy, Atlanta	121
1984	Mike Schmidt, Phil.; Gary Carter, Montreal	106
1985	Dave Parker, Cincinnati	125
1986	Mike Schmidt, Philadelphia	119
1987	Andre Dawson, Chicago	137
1988	Will Clark, San Francisco	109
1989	Kevin Mitchell, San Francisco	125
1990	Matt Williams, San Francisco	122
1991	Howard Johnson, New York	117
1992	Darren Daulton, Philadelphia	109

Year	Player, Club	RBI
1980	Cecil Cooper, Milwaukee	122
1981	Eddie Murray, Baltimore	78
1982	Hal McRae, Kansas City	133
1983	Cecil Cooper, Milwaukee; Jim Rice, Boston	126
1984	Tony Armas, Boston	123
1985	Don Mattingly, New York	145
1986	Joe Carter, Cleveland	121
1987	George Bell, Toronto	134
1988	Jose Canseco, Oakland	124
1989	Ruben Sierra, Texas	119
1990	Cecil Fielder, Detroit	132
1991	Cecil Fielder, Detroit	133
1991	Cecil Fielder, Detroit	124

Batting Champions

National League

Year	Player	Club	Pct.
1901	Jesse C. Burkett	St. Louis	.382
1902	Clarence Beaumont	Pittsburgh	.357
1903	Honus Wagner	Pittsburgh	.355
1904	Honus Wagner	Pittsburgh	.349
1905	James Seymour	Cincinnati	.377
1906	Honus Wagner	Pittsburgh	.339
1907	Honus Wagner	Pittsburgh	.350
1908	Honus Wagner	Pittsburgh	.354
1909	Honus Wagner	Pittsburgh	.339
1910	Sherwood Magee	Philadelphia	.331
1911	Honus Wagner	Pittsburgh	.334
1912	Henry Zimmerman	Chicago	.372
1913	Jacob Daubert	Brooklyn	.350
1914	Jacob Daubert	Brooklyn	.329
1915	Larry Doyle	New York	.320
1916	Hal Chase	Cincinnati	.339
1917	Edd Roush	Cleveland	.341
1918	Zach Wheat	Brooklyn	.335
1919	Edd Roush	Cincinnati	.321
1920	Rogers Hornsby	St. Louis	.370
1921	Rogers Hornsby	St. Louis	.397
1922	Rogers Hornsby	St. Louis	.401
1923	Rogers Hornsby	St. Louis	.384
1924	Rogers Hornsby	St. Louis	.424
1925	Rogers Hornsby	St. Louis	.403
1926	Eugene Hargrave	Cincinnati	.353
1927	Paul Waner	Pittsburgh	.380
1928	Rogers Hornsby	Boston	.387
1929	Lefty O'Doul	Philadelphia	.398
1930	Bill Terry	New York	.401
1931	Chick Hafey	St. Louis	.349
1932	Lefty O'Doul	Brooklyn	.368
1933	Chuck Klein	Philadelphia	.368
1934	Paul Waner	Pittsburgh	.362
1935	Arky Vaughan	Pittsburgh	.385
1936	Paul Waner	Pittsburgh	.373
1937	Joe Medwick	St. Louis	.374
1938	Ernie Lombardi	Cincinnati	.342
1939	John Mize	St. Louis	.349
1940	Debs Garms	Pittsburgh	.355
1941	Pete Reiser	Brooklyn	.343
1942	Ernie Lombardi	Boston	.330
1943	Stan Musial	St. Louis	.357
1944	Dixie Walker	Brooklyn	.357
1945	Phil Cavarretta	Chicago	.355
1946	Stan Musial	St. Louis	.365
1947	Harry Walker	Philadelphia	.363
1948	Stan Musial	St. Louis	.376
1949	Jackie Robinson	Brooklyn	.342
1950	Stan Musial	St. Louis	.346
1951	Stan Musial	St. Louis	.355
1952	Stan Musial	St. Louis	.336
1953	Carl Furillo	Brooklyn	.344
1954	Willie Mays	New York	.345
1955	Richie Ashburn	Philadelphia	.338
1956	Hank Aaron	Milwaukee	.328
1957	Stan Musial	St. Louis	.351
1958	Richie Ashburn	Philadelphia	.350
1959	Hank Aaron	Milwaukee	.355
1960	Dick Groat	Pittsburgh	.325
1961	Roberto Clemente	Pittsburgh	.351
1962	Tommy Davis	Los Angeles	.346
1963	Tommy Davis	Los Angeles	.326
1964	Roberto Clemente	Pittsburgh	.339
1965	Roberto Clemente	Pittsburgh	.329
1966	Matty Alou	Pittsburgh	.342
1967	Roberto Clemente	Pittsburgh	.357
1968	Pete Rose	Cincinnati	.335
1969	Pete Rose	Cincinnati	.348
1970	Rico Carty	Atlanta	.366

American League

Year	Player	Club	Pct.
1901	Napoleon Lajoie	Philadelphia	.422
1902	Ed Delahanty	Washington	.376
1902	Napoleon Lajoie	Cleveland	.355
1904	Napoleon Lajoie	Cleveland	.381
1905	Elmer Flick	Cleveland	.308
1906	George Stone	St. Louis	.358
1907	Ty Cobb	Detroit	.350
1908	Ty Cobb	Detroit	.324
1909	Ty Cobb	Detroit	.377
1910	Ty Cobb	Detroit	.385
1911	Ty Cobb	Detroit	.420
1912	Ty Cobb	Detroit	.410
1913	Ty Cobb	Detroit	.390
1914	Ty Cobb	Detroit	.368
1915	Ty Cobb	Detroit	.369
1916	Tris Speaker	Cleveland	.386
1917	Ty Cobb	Detroit	.383
1918	Ty Cobb	Detroit	.382
1919	Ty Cobb	Detroit	.384
1920	George Sisler	St. Louis	.407
1921	Harry Heilmann	Detroit	.394
1922	George Sisler	St. Louis	.420
1923	Harry Heilmann	Detroit	.403
1924	Babe Ruth	New York	.378
1925	Harry Heilmann	Detroit	.393
1926	Henry Manush	Detroit	.378
1927	Harry Heilmann	Detroit	.398
1928	Goose Goslin	Washington	.379
1929	Lew Fonseca	Cleveland	.369
1930	Al Simmons	Philadelphia	.381
1931	Al Simmons	Philadelphia	.390
1932	Dale Alexander	Detroit-Boston	.367
1933	Jimmie Foxx	Philadelphia	.356
1934	Lou Gehrig	New York	.363
1935	Buddy Myer	Washington	.349
1936	Luke Appling	Chicago	.388
1937	Charlie Gehringer	Detroit	.371
1938	Jimmie Foxx	Boston	.349
1939	Joe DiMaggio	New York	.381
1940	Joe DiMaggio	New York	.352
1941	Ted Williams	Boston	.406
1942	Ted Williams	Boston	.356
1943	Luke Appling	Chicago	.328
1944	Lou Boudreau	Cleveland	.327
1945	George Stirnweiss	New York	.309
1946	Mickey Vernon	Washington	.353
1947	Ted Williams	Boston	.343
1948	Ted Williams	Boston	.369
1949	George Kell	Detroit	.343
1950	Billy Goodman	Boston	.354
1951	Ferris Fain	Philadelphia	.344
1952	Ferris Fain	Philadelphia	.327
1953	Mickey Vernon	Washington	.337
1954	Roberto Avila	Cleveland	.341
1955	Al Kaline	Detroit	.340
1956	Mickey Mantle	New York	.353
1957	Ted Williams	Boston	.388
1958	Ted Williams	Boston	.328
1959	Harvey Kuenn	Detroit	.353
1960	Pete Runnels	Boston	.320
1961	Norm Cash	Detroit	.361
1962	Pete Runnels	Boston	.326
1963	Carl Yastrzemski	Boston	.321
1964	Tony Oliva	Minnesota	.323
1965	Tony Oliva	Minnesota	.321
1966	Frank Robinson	Baltimore	.316
1967	Carl Yastrzemski	Boston	.326
1968	Carl Yastrzemski	Boston	.301
1969	Rod Carew	Minnesota	.332
1970	Alex Johnson	California	.328

Year	Player	Club	Pct.	Year	Player	Club	Pct.
1971	Joe Torre	St. Louis	.363	1971	Tony Oliva	Minnesota	.337
1972	Billy Williams	Chicago	.333	1972	Rod Carew	Minnesota	.318
1973	Pete Rose	Cincinnati	.338	1973	Rod Carew	Minnesota	.350
1974	Ralph Garr	Atlanta	.353	1974	Rod Carew	Minnesota	.364
1975	Bill Madlock	Chicago	.354	1975	Rod Carew	Minnesota	.359
1976	Bill Madlock	Chicago	.339	1976	George Brett	Kansas City	.333
1977	Dave Parker	Pittsburgh	.338	1977	Rod Carew	Minnesota	.388
1978	Dave Parker	Pittsburgh	.334	1978	Rod Carew	Minnesota	.333
1979	Keith Hernandez	St. Louis	.344	1979	Fred Lynn	Boston	.333
1980	Bill Buckner	Chicago	.324	1980	George Brett	Kansas City	.390
1981	Bill Madlock	Pittsburgh	.341	1981	Carney Lansford	Boston	.336
1982	Al Oliver	Montreal	.331	1982	Willie Wilson	Kansas City	.332
1983	Bill Madlock	Pittsburgh	.323	1983	Wade Boggs	Boston	.361
1984	Tony Gwynn	San Diego	.351	1984	Don Mattingly	New York	.343
1985	Willie McGee	St. Louis	.353	1985	Wade Boggs	Boston	.368
1986	Tim Raines	Montreal	.334	1986	Wade Boggs	Boston	.357
1987	Tony Gwynn	San Diego	.369	1987	Wade Boggs	Boston	.363
1988	Tony Gwynn	San Diego	.313	1988	Wade Boggs	Boston	.366
1989	Tony Gwynn	San Diego	.336	1989	Kirby Puckett	Minnesota	.339
1990	Willie McGee	St. Louis	.335	1990	George Brett	Kansas City	.329
1991	Terry Pendleton	Atlanta	.319	1991	Julio Franco	Texas	.342
1992	Gary Sheffield	San Diego	.330	1991	Edgar Martinez	Seattle	.343

Earned-Run Average Leaders

National League					American League				
Year	Player, club	G	IP	ERA	Year	Player, club	G	IP	ERA
1972	Steve Carlton, Philadelphia	41	346	1.98	1972	Luis Tiant, Boston	43	179	1.91
1973	Tom Seaver, New York	36	290	2.07	1973	Jim Palmer, Baltimore	38	296	2.40
1974	Buzz Capra, Atlanta	39	217	2.28	1974	Catfish Hunter, Oakland	41	318	2.49
1975	Randy Jones, San Diego	37	285	2.24	1975	Jim Palmer, Baltimore	39	323	2.09
1976	John Denny, St. Louis	30	207	2.52	1976	Mark Fidrych, Detroit	31	250	2.34
1977	John Candelaria, Pittsburgh	33	231	2.34	1977	Frank Tanana, California	31	241	2.54
1978	Craig Swan, New York	29	207	2.43	1978	Ron Guidry, New York	35	274	1.74
1979	J. R. Richard, Houston	38	292	2.71	1979	Ron Guidry, New York	33	236	2.78
1980	Don Sutton, Los Angeles	32	212	2.21	1980	Rudy May, New York	41	175	2.47
1981	Nolan Ryan, Houston	21	149	1.69	1981	Steve McCatty, Oakland	22	186	2.32
1982	Steve Rogers, Montreal	35	277	2.40	1982	Rick Sutcliffe, Cleveland	34	216	2.96
1983	Atlee Hammaker, San Fran.	23	172	2.25	1983	Rick Honeycutt, Texas	25	174	2.42
1984	Alejandro Pena, Los Angeles	28	199	2.48	1984	Mike Boddicker, Baltimore	34	261	2.79
1985	Dwight Gooden, New York	35	276	1.53	1985	Dave Stieb, Toronto	36	265	2.48
1986	Mike Scott, Houston	37	275	2.22	1986	Roger Clemens, Boston	33	254	2.48
1987	Nolan Ryan, Houston	34	211	2.76	1987	Jimmy Key, Toronto	36	261	2.76
1988	Joe Magrane, St. Louis	24	165	2.18	1988	Allan Anderson, Minnesota	30	202	2.45
1989	Scott Garrelts, San Francisco	30	193	2.28	1989	Bret Saberhagen, Kansas City	36	262	2.16
1990	Danny Darwin, Houston	48	162	2.21	1990	Roger Clemens, Boston	31	228	1.93
1991	Dennis Martinez, Montreal	31	222	2.39	1991	Roger Clemens, Boston	35	271	2.62
1992	Bill Swift, San Francisco	30	164	2.08	1992	Roger Clemens, Boston	32	246	2.41

ERA is computed by multiplying earned runs allowed by 9, then dividing by innings pitched.

Baseball Stadiums

National League

Team	Stadium (built)	Surface	Home run distances (ft.) LF	Center	RF	Seating capacity
Atlanta Braves	Atlanta-Fulton County Stadium (1966)	Natural grass	330	402	330	52,003
Chicago Cubs	Wrigley Field (1914)	Natural grass	355	400	353	38,710
Cincinnati Reds	Riverfront Stadium (1970)	Artificial	330	404	330	52,952
Houston Astros	Astrodome (1965)	Artificial	325	400	325	54,816
Los Angeles Dodgers	Dodger Stadium (1962)	Natural grass	330	395	330	56,000
Montreal Expos	Olympic Stadium (1977)	Artificial	325	404	325	43,739
New York Mets	Shea Stadium (1964)	Natural grass	338	410	338	55,601
Philadelphia Phillies	Veterans Stadium (1971)	Artificial	330	408	330	62,382
Pittsburgh Pirates	Three Rivers Stadium (1970)	Artificial	335	400	335	58,727
St. Louis Cardinals	Busch Stadium (1966)	Artificial	330	402	330	56,227
San Diego Padres	Jack Murphy Stadium (1969)	Natural grass	327	405	327	59,022
San Francisco Giants	Candlestick Park (1960)	Natural grass	335	400	330	58,000

American League

Team	Stadium (built)	Surface	LF	Center	RF	Seating capacity
Baltimore Orioles	Camden Yards (1992)	Natural grass	334	400	319	47,000
Boston Red Sox	Fenway Park (1912)	Natural grass	315	420	302	34,142
California Angels	Anaheim Stadium (1966)	Natural grass	333	404	333	64,593
Chicago White Sox	Comiskey Park (1991)	Natural grass	347	400	347	44,702
Cleveland Indians	Cleveland Stadium (1932)	Natural grass	320	404	320	74,483
Detroit Tigers	Tiger Stadium (1912)	Natural grass	340	440	325	52,416
Kansas City Royals	Royals Stadium (1973)	Artificial	330	410	330	40,625
Milwaukee Brewers	Milwaukee County Stadium (1953)	Natural grass	315	402	315	53,192
Minnesota Twins	Hubert H. Humphrey Metrodome (1982)	Artificial	343	408	327	55,883
New York Yankees	Yankee Stadium (1923)	Natural grass	318	408	314	57,545
Oakland A's	Oakland Alameda County Coliseum (1968)	Natural grass	330	400	330	47,313
Seattle Mariners	Kingdome (1977)	Artificial	331	405	312	59,643
Texas Rangers	Arlington Stadium (1972)	Natural grass	330	400	330	43,521
Toronto Blue Jays	Sky-Dome (1989)	Artificial	328	400	328	50,516

National League Records, 1992

Final standings

Eastern Division

	W	L	Pct.	GB	Home	vs. RHP	Grass	Night
Pittsburgh	96	66	.593	—	53-28	70-34	19-23	70-45
Montreal	87	75	.537	9	43-38	54-52	24-18	55-53
St. Louis	83	79	.512	13	45-36	52-55	22-20	63-53
Chicago	78	84	.481	18	43-38	52-52	58-56	33-44
New York	72	90	.444	24	41-40	46-58	57-57	51-63
Philadelphia	70	92	.432	26	41-40	43-51	16-26	52-62

Western Division

	W	L	Pct.	GB	Home	vs. RHP	Grass	Night
Atlanta	98	64	.605	—	51-30	64-45	76-44	71-46
Cincinnati	90	72	.556	8	53-28	62-43	22-26	61-48
San Diego	82	80	.506	16	45-36	56-60	64-56	54-60
Houston	81	81	.500	17	47-34	51-51	20-28	61-53
San Francisco	72	90	.444	26	42-39	40-64	57-63	36-58
Los Angeles	63	99	.389	35	37-44	35-62	51-69	43-65

National League Championship Series

Atlanta 5, Pittsburgh 1
Atlanta 13, Pittsburgh 5
Pittsburgh 3, Atlanta 2
Atlanta 6, Pittsburgh 4
Pittsburgh 7, Atlanta 1
Pittsburgh 13, Atlanta 4
Atlanta 3, Pittsburgh 2

Team Batting

	Avg.	AB	R	H	HR	RBI
St. Louis	**.262**	5594	631	1464	94	599
Cincinnati	**.260**	5460	660	1418	99	606
San Diego	**.255**	5476	617	1396	135	576
Pittsburgh	**.255**	5527	693	1409	106	656
Chicago	**.254**	5590	593	1420	104	566
Atlanta	**.254**	5480	682	1391	138	641
Philadelphia	**.253**	5500	686	1392	118	638
Montreal	**.252**	5477	648	1381	102	601
Los Angeles	**.248**	5368	548	1333	72	499
Houston	**.246**	5480	608	1350	96	582
San Francisco	**.244**	5456	574	1330	105	532
New York	**.235**	5340	599	1254	93	564

Team Pitching

	ERA	IP	H	BB	SO	Sv
Atlanta	**3.14**	1460	1321	489	948	41
Montreal	**3.25**	1468	1296	525	1014	49
Pittsburgh	**3.35**	1479⅔	1410	455	844	43
St Louis	**3.38**	1480	1405	400	842	47
Chicago	**3.39**	1469	1337	575	901	37
Los Angeles	**3.41**	1438	1401	553	981	29
Cincinnati	**3.46**	1449⅔	1362	470	1060	55
San Diego	**3.56**	1461⅓	1444	439	971	46
San Francisco	**3.61**	1461	1385	502	927	30
New York	**3.66**	1446⅔	1404	482	1025	34
Houston	**3.72**	1459⅓	1386	539	978	45
Philadelphia	**4.11**	1428	1387	549	851	34

Individual Batting (at least 150 at-bats); Individual Pitching (at least 75 innings or 10 saves)

Atlanta Braves

Batting	Avg	AB	R	H	HR	RBI
Pendleton	**.311**	640	98	199	21	105
Sanders	**.304**	303	54	92	8	28
Nixon	**.294**	456	79	134	2	22
Blauser	**.262**	343	61	90	14	46
Bream	**.261**	372	30	97	10	61
Gant	**.259**	544	74	141	17	80
Justice	**.256**	484	78	124	21	72
L Smith	**.247**	158	23	39	6	33
Hunter	**.239**	238	34	57	14	41
Olson	**.238**	302	27	72	3	27
Berryhill	**.228**	307	21	70	10	43
Lemke	**.227**	427	38	97	6	26
Belliard	**.211**	285	20	60	0	14

Pitching	W	L	ERA	IP	BB	SO	Sv
P. Smith	7	0	**2.05**	79.0	28	43	0
Bielecki	2	4	**2.57**	80.2	27	62	0
Glavine	20	8	**2.76**	225.0	70	129	0
Smoltz	15	12	**2.85**	246.2	80	215	0
Avery	11	11	**3.20**	233.2	71	129	0
Freeman	7	5	**3.22**	64.1	29	41	3
Leibrandt	15	7	**3.36**	193.0	42	104	0

Manager—Bobby Cox

Chicago Cubs

Batting	Avg	AB	R	H	HR	RBI
Grace	**.307**	603	72	185	9	79
Sandberg	**.304**	612	100	186	26	87
Dawson	**.277**	542	60	150	22	90
Dw. Smith	**.276**	217	28	60	3	24
May	**.274**	351	33	96	8	45
Wilkins	**.270**	244	20	66	8	22
Girardi	**.270**	270	19	73	1	12
Buechele	**.261**	524	52	137	9	64
Sosa	**.260**	262	41	68	8	25
Dascenzo	**.255**	376	37	96	0	20
Sanchez	**.251**	255	24	64	1	19
Daniels	**.241**	212	21	51	6	25
Vizcaino	**.225**	285	25	64	1	17
Salazar	**.208**	255	20	53	5	25

Pitching	W	L	ERA	IP	BB	SO	Sv
Maddux	20	11	**2.18**	268.0	70	199	0
Morgan	16	8	**2.55**	240.0	79	123	0
Scanlan	3	6	**2.89**	87.1	30	42	14
Robinson	4	3	**3.00**	78.0	40	46	1
Castillo	10	11	**3.46**	205.1	63	135	0
McElroy	4	7	**3.55**	83.2	51	83	6
Bullinger	2	8	**4.66**	85.0	54	36	7
Boskie	5	11	**5.01**	91.2	36	39	0

Manager—Jim LeFebvre

Cincinnati Reds

Batting	Avg	AB	R	H	HR	RBI
Roberts	.323	532	92	172	45	45
Larkin	.304	533	76	162	12	78
Morris	.271	395	41	107	6	53
Sanders	.270	385	62	104	12	36
Oliver	.270	485	42	131	10	57
Martinez	.254	393	47	100	3	31
O'Neill	.246	496	59	122	14	66
Sabo	.244	344	42	84	12	43
Braggs	.237	266	40	63	8	38
Doran	.235	387	48	91	8	47
Benavides	.231	173	14	40	1	17

Pitching	W	L	ERA	IP	BB	SO	Sv
Rijo	15	10	2.56	211.0	44	171	0
Swindell	12	8	2.70	213.2	41	138	0
Charlton	4	2	2.99	81.1	26	90	26
Dibble	3	5	3.07	70.1	31	110	25
Henry	3	3	3.33	83.2	44	72	0
Belcher	15	14	3.91	227.2	80	149	0
Hammond	7	10	4.21	147.1	55	79	0
Browning	6	5	5.07	87.0	28	33	0

Manager—Lou Piniella

Houston Astros

Batting	Avg	AB	R	H	HR	RBI
Caminiti	.294	506	68	149	13	62
Finley	.292	607	84	177	5	55
Biggio	.277	613	96	170	6	39
Bagwell	.273	586	87	160	18	96
Incaviglia	.266	349	31	93	11	44
Ramirez	.250	176	17	44	1	13
Gonzalez	.243	387	40	94	10	55
Servais	.239	205	12	49	0	15
Anthony	.239	440	45	105	19	80
Taubensee	.222	297	23	66	5	28
Candaele	.213	320	19	68	1	18
Cedeno	.173	220	15	38	2	13

Pitching	W	L	ERA	IP	BB	SO	Sv
D. Jones	11	8	1.85	111.2	17	93	36
Hernandez	9	1	2.11	111.0	42	96	7
Boever	3	6	2.51	111.1	45	67	2
Portugal	6	3	2.66	101.1	41	62	0
Harnisch	9	10	3.70	206.2	64	164	0
Williams	7	6	3.92	96.1	42	54	0
Kile	5	10	3.95	125.1	63	90	0
Blair	5	7	4.00	78.2	25	48	0
Henry	6	9	4.02	165.2	41	96	0
J. Jones	10	6	4.07	139.1	39	69	0

Manager—Art Howe

Los Angeles Dodgers

Batting	Avg	AB	R	H	HR	RBI
Butler	.309	553	86	171	3	39
Sharperson	.300	317	48	95	3	36
Harris	.271	347	28	94	0	30
Webster	.267	262	33	70	6	35
Offerman	.260	534	67	139	1	30
Hernandez	.260	173	11	45	3	17
Karros	.257	545	63	140	20	88
Benzinger	.239	293	24	70	4	31
Strawberry	.237	156	20	37	5	25
Davis	.228	267	21	61	5	32
Scioscia	.221	348	19	77	3	24
Hansen	.214	341	30	73	6	22

Pitching	W	L	ERA	IP	BB	SO	Sv
Astacio	5	5	1.98	82.0	20	43	0
Gott	3	3	2.45	88.0	41	75	6
Candiotti	11	15	3.00	203.2	63	152	0
Ke Gross	8	13	3.17	204.2	77	158	0
Ojeda	6	9	3.63	166.1	81	94	0
Hershiser	10	15	3.67	210.2	69	130	0
R. Martinez	8	11	4.00	150.2	69	101	0
McDowell	6	10	4.09	83.2	42	50	14
Crews	0	3	5.19	78.0	20	43	0

Manager—Tommy LaSorda

Montreal Expos

Batting	Avg	AB	R	H	HR	RBI
Walker	.301	528	85	159	23	93
DeShields	.292	530	82	155	7	56
Alou	.282	341	53	96	9	56
Grissom	.276	653	99	180	14	66
Owen	.269	386	52	104	7	40
Colbrunn	.268	168	12	45	2	18
Calderon	.265	170	19	45	3	24
Fletcher	.243	222	13	54	2	26
Vanderwal	.239	213	21	51	4	20
Barberie	.232	285	26	66	1	24
Wallach	.223	537	53	120	9	59
Carter	.218	285	24	62	5	29

Pitching	W	L	ERA	IP	BB	SO	Sv
Rojas	7	1	1.43	100.2	34	70	10
Martinez	16	11	2.47	226.1	60	147	0
Hill	16	9	2.68	218.0	75	150	0
Fassero	8	7	2.84	85.2	34	63	1
Wetteland	4	4	2.92	83.1	36	99	37
Barnes	6	6	2.97	100.0	46	65	0
Nabholz	11	12	3.32	195.0	74	130	0
Gardner	12	10	4.36	179.2	60	132	0

Manager—Tom Runnells; Felipe Alou

New York Mets

Batting	Avg	AB	R	H	HR	RBI
Walker	.289	253	26	73	4	38
Magadan	.283	321	33	91	3	28
Coleman	.275	229	37	63	2	21
Bass	.269	402	40	108	9	39
Murray	.261	551	64	144	16	93
Randolph	.252	286	29	72	2	15
Boston	.249	289	37	72	11	35
Bonilla	.249	438	62	109	19	70
Gallagher	.240	175	20	42	1	21
Pecota	.227	269	28	61	2	26
Johnson	.223	350	48	78	7	43
O'Brien	.212	156	15	33	2	13
Hundley	.209	358	32	75	7	32
Schofield	.205	420	52	86	4	36

Pitching	W	L	ERA	IP	BB	SO	Sv
Franco	6	2	1.64	33.0	11	20	15
Fernandez	14	11	2.73	214.2	67	193	0
Innis	6	9	2.86	88.0	36	39	1
Saberhagen	3	5	3.50	97.2	27	81	0
Whitehurst	3	9	3.62	97.0	33	70	0
Schourek	6	8	3.64	136.0	44	60	0
Gooden	10	13	3.67	206.0	70	145	0
Young	2	14	4.17	121.0	31	64	15

Manager—Jeff Torborg

Philadelphia Phillies

Batting	Avg	AB	R	H	HR	RBI
Kruk	.323	507	86	164	10	70
Jordan	.304	276	33	84	4	34
Dykstra	.301	345	53	104	6	39
Daulton	.270	485	80	131	27	109
Hollins	.270	586	104	158	27	93
Duncan	.267	574	71	153	8	50
Morandini	.265	422	47	112	3	30
Chamberlain	.258	275	26	71	9	41
Javier	.249	334	42	83	1	29
Amaro	.219	374	43	82	7	34

Pitching	W	L	ERA	IP	BB	SO	Sv
Schilling	14	11	2.35	226.1	59	147	2
Rivera	7	4	3.07	117.1	45	77	0
M. Williams	5	8	3.78	81.0	64	74	29
Mulholland	13	11	3.81	229.0	46	125	0
DeLeon	2	8	4.37	117.1	48	79	0
Brantley	2	6	4.60	76.1	58	32	0
Abbott	1	14	5.13	133.1	45	88	0

Manager—Jim Fregosi

Pittsburgh Pirates

Batting	Avg	AB	R	H	HR	RBI
Slaught	**.345**	255	26	88	4	37
Van Slyke	**.324**	614	103	199	14	89
Bonds	**.311**	473	109	147	34	103
A. Cole	**.278**	205	33	57	0	10
Bell	**.264**	632	87	167	9	55
Espy	**.258**	194	21	50	1	20
LaValliere	**.256**	293	22	75	2	29
Redus	**.256**	176	26	45	3	12
McClendon	**.253**	190	26	48	3	20
Merced	**.247**	405	50	100	6	60
Lind	**.235**	468	38	110	0	39
King	**.231**	480	56	111	14	65
Varsho	**.222**	162	22	36	4	22

Pitching	W	L	ERA	IP	BB	SO	Sv
Wakefield	8	1	**2.15**	92.0	35	51	0
Drabek	15	11	**2.77**	256.2	54	177	0
Smith	8	8	**3.06**	141.0	19	56	0
Belinda	6	4	**3.15**	71.1	29	57	18
Walk	10	6	**3.20**	135.0	43	60	2
Tomlin	14	9	**3.41**	208.2	42	90	0
Jackson	8	13	**3.84**	201.1	77	97	0
Mason	5	7	**4.09**	88.0	33	56	8
Neagle	4	6	**4.48**	86.1	43	77	2

Manager—Jim Leyland

St. Louis Cardinals

Batting	Avg	AB	R	H	HR	RBI
Pena	**.305**	203	31	62	7	31
Gilkey	**.302**	384	56	116	7	43
O. Smith	**.295**	518	73	153	0	31
Jose	**.295**	509	62	150	14	75
Thompson	**.293**	208	31	61	4	17
Lankford	**.293**	598	87	175	20	86
Zeile	**.257**	439	51	113	7	48
Pagnozzi	**.249**	485	33	121	7	44
Alicea	**.245**	265	26	65	2	32
Galarraga	**.243**	325	38	79	10	39

Pitching	W	L	ERA	IP	BB	SO	Sv
Perez	9	3	**1.84**	93.0	32	46	0
Tewksbury	16	5	**2.16**	233.0	20	91	0
Carpenter	5	4	**2.97**	88.0	27	46	1
L. Smith	4	9	**3.12**	75.0	26	60	43
Cormier	10	10	**3.68**	186.0	33	117	0
Osborne	11	9	**3.77**	179.0	38	104	0
Olivares	9	9	**3.84**	197.0	63	124	0
Clark	3	10	**4.45**	113.1	36	44	0

Manager—Joe Torre

San Diego Padres

Batting	Avg	AB	R	H	HR	RBI
Sheffield	**.330**	557	87	184	33	100
Gwynn	**.317**	520	77	165	6	41
McGriff	**.286**	531	79	152	35	104
Fernandez	**.275**	622	84	171	4	37
Walters	**.251**	179	14	45	4	22
Santiago	**.251**	386	37	97	10	42
Jackson	**.249**	587	72	146	17	70
Clark	**.242**	496	45	120	12	58
Stillwell	**.227**	379	35	86	2	24
Teufel	**.224**	246	23	55	6	25
Azocar	.190	168	15	32	0	8

Pitching	W	L	ERA	IP	BB	SO	Sv
Maddux	2	2	**2.37**	79.2	24	60	5
Rodriguez	6	3	**2.37**	91.0	29	64	0
Melendez	6	7	**2.92**	89.1	20	82	0
Deshales	4	7	**3.28**	96.0	33	46	0
Benes	13	14	**3.35**	231.1	61	169	0
Seminara	9	4	**3.68**	100.1	46	61	0
Hurst	14	9	**3.85**	217.1	51	131	0
Gr. Harris	4	8	**4.12**	118.0	35	66	0
Myers	3	6	**4.29**	79.2	34	66	38

Manager—Greg Riddoch; Jim Riggleman

San Francisco Giants

Batting	Avg	AB	R	H	HR	RBI
Clark	**.300**	513	69	154	16	73
McGee	**.297**	474	56	141	1	36
Felder	**.286**	322	44	92	4	23
Snyder	**.269**	390	48	105	14	57
Thompson	**.260**	443	54	115	14	49
Manwaring	**.244**	349	24	85	4	26
James	**.242**	248	25	60	5	32
Uribe	**.241**	162	24	39	2	13
Lewis	**.231**	320	38	74	1	18
Williams	**.227**	529	58	120	20	66
Clayton	**.224**	321	31	72	4	24

Pitching	W	L	ERA	IP	BB	SO	Sv
Beck	3	3	**1.76**	92.0	15	87	17
Swift	10	4	**2.08**	164.2	43	77	1
Brantley	7	7	**2.95**	91.2	45	86	7
Hickerson	5	3	**3.09**	87.1	21	68	0
Jackson	6	6	**3.73**	82.0	33	80	2
Burkett	13	9	**3.84**	189.2	45	107	0
Black	10	12	**3.97**	177.0	59	82	0
Wilson	8	14	**4.21**	154.0	64	88	0
Burba	2	7	**4.97**	70.2	31	47	0
Righetti	2	7	**5.06**	78.1	36	47	3

Manager—Roger Craig

The Sporting News Gold Glove Awards in 1991

National League

Will Clark, San Francisco, first base
Ryne Sandberg, Chicago, second base
Matt Williams, San Francisco, third base
Ozzie Smith, St. Louis, shortstop
Tony Gwynn, San Diego, outfield
Andy Van Slyke, Pittsburgh, outfield
Barry Bonds, Pittsburgh, outfield
Tom Pagnozzi, St. Louis, catcher
Greg Maddux, Chicago, pitcher

American League

Don Mattingly, New York, first base
Roberto Alomar, Toronto, second base
Robin Ventura, Chicago, third base
Cal Ripken Jr., Baltimore, shortstop
Devon White, Toronto, outfield
Kirby Puckett, Minnesota, outfield
Ken Griffey Jr., Seattle, outfield
Tony Pena, Boston, catcher
Mark Langston, California, pitcher

The following are the players at each position who have won the most Gold Gloves since the award was instituted in 1957.

First base:	Keith Hernandez	11
	George Scott	8
Second base:	Ryne Sandberg	9
	Bill Mazeroski	8
	Frank White	8
Third base:	Brooks Robinson	16
	Mike Schmidt	10
Shortstop:	Ozzie Smith	12
	Luis Aparicio	9
Outfield:	Roberto Clemente	12
	Willie Mays	12
	Al Kaline	10
	Paul Blair	8
	Dwight Evans	8
	Garry Maddox	8
Catcher:	Johnny Bench	10
	Bob Boone	7
Pitcher:	Jim Kaat	16
	Bob Gibson	9

Most Valuable Player

Baseball Writers' Association

National League

Year	Player, team
1931	Frank Frisch, St. Louis
1932	Charles Klein, Philadelphia
1933	Carl Hubbell, New York
1934	Dizzy Dean, St. Louis
1935	Gabby Hartnett, Chicago
1936	Carl Hubbell, New York
1937	Joe Medwick, St. Louis
1938	Ernie Lombardi, Cincinnati
1939	Bucky Walters, Cincinnati
1940	Frank McCormick, Cincinnati
1941	Dolph Camilli, Brooklyn
1942	Mort Cooper, St. Louis
1943	Stan Musial, St. Louis
1944	Martin Marion, St. Louis
1945	Phil Cavarretta, Chicago
1946	Stan Musial, St. Louis
1947	Bob Elliott, Boston
1948	Stan Musial, St. Louis
1949	Jackie Robinson, Brooklyn
1950	Jim Konstanty, Philadelphia
1951	Roy Campanella, Brooklyn
1952	Hank Sauer, Chicago
1953	Roy Campanella, Brooklyn
1954	Willie Mays, New York
1955	Roy Campanella, Brooklyn
1956	Don Newcombe, Brooklyn
1957	Henry Aaron, Milwaukee
1958	Ernie Banks, Chicago
1959	Ernie Banks, Chicago
1960	Dick Groat, Pittsburgh
1961	Frank Robinson, Cincinnati
1962	Maury Wills, Los Angeles
1963	Sandy Koufax, Los Angeles
1964	Ken Boyer, St. Louis
1965	Willie Mays, San Francisco
1966	Roberto Clemente, Pittsburgh
1967	Orlando Cepeda, St. Louis
1968	Bob Gibson, St. Louis
1969	Willie McCovey, San Francisco
1970	Johnny Bench, Cincinnati
1971	Joe Torre, St. Louis
1972	Johnny Bench, Cincinnati
1973	Pete Rose, Cincinnati
1974	Steve Garvey, Los Angeles
1975	Joe Morgan, Cincinnati
1976	Joe Morgan, Cincinnati
1977	George Foster, Cincinnati
1978	Dave Parker, Pittsburgh
1979	(tie) Willie Stargell, Pittsburgh Keith Hernandez, St. Louis
1980	Mike Schmidt, Philadelphia
1981	Mike Schmidt, Philadelphia
1982	Dale Murphy, Atlanta
1983	Dale Murphy, Atlanta
1984	Ryne Sandberg, Chicago
1985	Willie McGee, St. Louis
1986	Mike Schmidt, Philadelphia
1987	Andre Dawson, Chicago
1988	Kirk Gibson, Los Angeles
1989	Kevin Mitchell, San Francisco
1990	Barry Bonds, Pittsburgh
1991	Terry Pendleton, Atlanta

American League

Year	Player, team
1931	Lefty Grove, Philadelphia
1932	Jimmie Foxx, Philadelphia
1933	Jimmie Foxx, Philadelphia
1934	Mickey Cochrane, Detroit
1935	Hank Greenberg, Detroit
1936	Lou Gehrig, New York
1937	Charley Gehringer, Detroit
1938	Jimmie Foxx, Boston
1939	Joe DiMaggio, New York
1940	Hank Greenberg, Detroit
1941	Joe DiMaggio, New York
1942	Joe Gordon, New York
1943	Spurgeon Chandler, New York
1944	Hal Newhouser, Detroit
1945	Hal Newhouser, Detroit
1946	Ted Williams, Boston
1947	Joe DiMaggio, New York
1948	Lou Boudreau, Cleveland
1949	Ted Williams, Boston
1950	Phil Rizzuto, New York
1951	Yogi Berra, New York
1952	Bobby Shantz, Philadelphia
1953	Al Rosen, Cleveland
1954	Yogi Berra, New York
1955	Yogi Berra, New York
1956	Mickey Mantle, New York
1957	Mickey Mantle, New York
1958	Jackie Jensen, Boston
1959	Nellie Fox, Chicago
1960	Roger Maris, New York
1961	Roger Maris, New York
1962	Mickey Mantle, New York
1963	Elston Howard, New York
1964	Brooks Robinson, Baltimore
1965	Zoilo Versalles, Minnesota
1966	Frank Robinson, Baltimore
1967	Carl Yastrzemski, Boston
1968	Denny McLain, Detroit
1969	Harmon Killebrew, Minnesota
1970	John (Boog) Powell, Baltimore
1971	Vida Blue, Oakland
1972	Dick Allen, Chicago
1973	Reggie Jackson, Oakland
1974	Jeff Burroughs, Texas
1975	Fred Lynn, Boston
1976	Thurman Munson, New York
1977	Rod Carew, Minnesota
1978	Jim Rice, Boston
1979	Don Baylor, California
1980	George Brett, Kansas City
1981	Rollie Fingers, Milwaukee
1982	Robin Yount, Milwaukee
1983	Cal Ripken Jr., Baltimore
1984	Willie Hernandez, Detroit
1985	Don Mattingly, New York
1986	Roger Clemens, Boston
1987	George Bell, Toronto
1988	Jose Canseco, Oakland
1989	Robin Yount, Milwaukee
1990	Rickey Henderson
1991	Cal Ripken Jr., Baltimore

Rookie of the Year

Baseball Writers' Association

1947—Combined selection—Jackie Robinson, Brooklyn, 1b

1948—Combined selection—Alvin Dark, Boston, N.L. ss

National League

Year	Player, team
1949	Don Newcombe, Brooklyn, p
1950	Sam Jethroe, Boston, of
1951	Willie Mays, New York, of
1952	Joe Black, Brooklyn, p
1953	Jim Gilliam, Brooklyn, 2b
1954	Wally Moon, St. Louis, of
1955	Bill Virdon, St. Louis, of
1956	Frank Robinson, Cincinnati, of
1957	Jack Sanford, Philadelphia, p
1958	Orlando Cepeda, S.F., 1b
1959	Willie McCovey, S.F., 1b
1960	Frank Howard, Los Angeles, of
1961	Billy Williams, Chicago, of
1962	Ken Hubbs, Chicago, 2b
1963	Pete Rose, Cincinnati, 2b
1964	Richie Allen, Philadelphia, 3b
1965	Jim Lefebvre, Los Angeles, 2b
1966	Tommy Helms, Cincinnati, 2b
1967	Tom Seaver, New York, p
1968	Johnny Bench, Cincinnati c
1969	Ted Sizemore, Los Angeles, 2b
1970	Carl Morton, Montreal, p
1971	Earl Williams, Atlanta, c
1972	Jon Matlack, New York, p
1973	Gary Matthews, S.F., of
1974	Bake McBride, St. Louis, of
1975	John Montefusco, S.F., p
1976	(tie) Butch Metzger, San Diego, p Pat Zachry, Cincinnati, p
1977	Andre Dawson, Montreal, of
1978	Bob Horner, Atlanta, 3b
1979	Rick Sutcliffe, Los Angeles, p
1980	Steve Howe, Los Angeles, p
1981	Fernando Valenzuela, Los Angeles, p
1982	Steve Sax, Los Angeles, 2b
1983	Darryl Strawberry, New York, of
1984	Dwight Gooden, New York, p
1985	Vince Coleman, St. Louis, of
1986	Todd Worrell, St. Louis, p
1987	Benito Santiago, San Diego, c
1988	Chris Sabo, Cincinnati, 3b
1989	Jerome Walton, Chicago, of
1990	Dave Justice, Atlanta, 1b
1991	Jeff Bagwell, Houston, 1b

American League

Year	Player, team
1949	Roy Sievers, St. Louis, of
1950	Walt Dropo, Boston, 1b
1951	Gil McDougald, New York, 3b
1952	Harry Byrd, Philadelphia, p
1953	Harvey Kuenn, Detroit, ss
1954	Bob Grim, New York, p
1955	Herb Score, Cleveland, p
1956	Luis Aparicio, Chicago, ss
1957	Tony Kubek, New York, if-of
1958	Albie Pearson, Washington, of
1959	Bob Allison, Washington, of
1960	Ron Hansen, Baltimore, ss
1961	Don Schwall, Boston, p
1962	Tom Tresh, New York, if-of
1963	Gary Peters, Chicago, p
1964	Tony Oliva, Minnesota, of
1965	Curt Blefary, Baltimore, of
1966	Tommie Agee, Chicago, of
1967	Rod Carew, Minnesota, 2b
1968	Stan Bahnsen, New York, p
1969	Lou Piniella, Kansas City, of
1970	Thurman Munson, New York, c
1971	Chris Chambliss, Cleveland, 1b
1972	Carlton Fisk, Boston, c
1973	Al Bumbry, Baltimore, of
1974	Mike Hargrove, Texas, 1b
1975	Fred Lynn, Boston, of
1976	Mark Fidrych, Detroit, p
1977	Eddie Murray, Baltimore, dh
1978	Lou Whitaker, Detroit, 2b
1979	(tie) John Castino, Minnesota, 3b Alfredo Griffin, Toronto, ss
1980	Joe Charboneau, Cleveland, of
1981	Dave Righetti, New York, p
1982	Cal Ripken Jr., Baltimore, ss
1983	Ron Kittle, Chicago, of
1984	Alvin Davis, Seattle, 1b
1985	Ozzie Guillen, Chicago, ss
1986	Jose Canseco, Oakland, of
1987	Mark McGwire, Oakland, 1b
1988	Walt Weiss, Oakland, ss
1989	Gregg Olson, Baltimore, p
1990	Sandy Alomar Jr., Cleveland, c
1991	Chuck Knoblaugh, Minnesota, 2b

American League Records in 1992

Final standings

Eastern Division

	W	L	Pct.	GB	Home	vs. RHP	Grass	Night
Toronto	96	66	.593	—	53-28	69-48	32-31	65-44
Milwaukee	92	70	.568	4	53-28	64-57	79-59	61-46
Baltimore	89	73	.549	7	43-38	62-55	77-60	69-43
Cleveland	76	86	.469	20	41-40	56-67	68-69	55-55
New York	76	86	.469	20	41-40	52-57	66-71	50-60
Detroit	75	87	.463	21	38-42	56-74	63-75	54-52
Boston	73	89	.451	23	44-37	58-66	64-74	46-60

Western Division

	W	L	Pct.	GB	Home	vs. RHP	Grass	Night
Oakland	96	66	.593	—	51-30	74-56	80-57	58-41
Minnesota	90	72	.556	6	48-33	69-60	34-28	52-57
Chicago	86	76	.531	10	50-32	63-55	78-57	63-58
Texas	77	85	.475	19	36-45	56-64	63-73	60-71
California	72	90	.444	24	41-40	60-69	63-75	49-66
Kansas City	72	90	.444	24	44-37	48-66	22-40	58-63
Seattle	64	98	.395	32	38-43	42-76	21-41	47-71

American League Championship Series

Oakland 4, Toronto 3
Toronto 3, Oakland 1
Toronto 7, Oakland 5
Toronto 7, Oakland 6
Oakland 6, Toronto 2
Toronto 9, Oakland 2

Team Batting

	Avg.	AB	R	H	HR	RBI
Minnesota	**.277**	5582	747	1544	104	701
Milwaukee	**.268**	5504	740	1477	82	683
Cleveland	**.266**	5620	674	1495	127	637
Seattle	**.263**	5564	679	1466	149	638
Toronto	**.263**	5536	780	1458	163	737
New York	**.261**	5593	733	1462	163	703
Chicago	**.261**	5498	738	1434	110	686
Baltimore	**.259**	5485	705	1423	148	680
Oakland	**.258**	5387	745	1389	142	693
Kansas City	**.256**	5501	610	1411	75	568
Detroit	**.256**	5515	791	1411	182	746
Texas	**.250**	5537	682	1387	159	646
Boston	**.246**	5461	599	1343	84	567
California	**.243**	5364	579	1306	88	537

Team Pitching

	ERA	IP	H	BB	SO	Sv
Milwaukee	**3.43**	1457	1344	435	793	39
Boston	**3.58**	1448	1403	535	943	39
Minnesota	**3.70**	1453	1391	479	923	50
Oakland	**3.73**	1447	1396	601	843	58
Baltimore	**3.79**	1464	1419	518	846	48
Kansas City	**3.81**	1447	1426	512	834	44
Chicago	**3.82**	1461	1400	550	810	52
California	**3.84**	1446	1449	532	888	42
Toronto	**3.91**	1440	1346	541	954	49
Texas	**4.09**	1460	1471	598	1034	42
Cleveland	**4.11**	1470	1507	566	890	46
New York	**4.21**	1452	1453	612	851	44
Seattle	**4.55**	1445	1467	661	894	30
Detroit	**4.60**	1435	1534	564	693	36

Individual Batting (at least 150 at-bats); Individual Pitching (at least 75 innings or 10 saves)

Baltimore Orioles

Batting	Avg	AB	R	H	HR	RBI
Orsulak	**.289**	391	45	113	4	39
G. Davis	**.276**	398	46	110	13	48
Devereaux	**.276**	653	76	180	24	107
Hoiles	**.274**	310	49	85	20	40
Anderson	**.271**	623	100	169	21	80
Martinez	**.268**	198	26	53	5	25
Gomez	**.265**	468	62	124	17	64
C. Ripken	**.251**	637	73	160	14	72
McLemore	**.246**	228	40	56	0	27
Milligan	**.240**	462	71	111	11	53
Tackett	**.240**	179	21	43	5	24
Horn	**.235**	162	13	38	5	19
Segui	**.233**	189	21	44	1	17
B. Ripken	**.230**	330	35	76	4	36

Pitching	W	L	ERA	IP	BB	SO	Sv
Olson	1	5	**2.05**	61.1	24	58	36
Frohwirth	4	3	**2.46**	106.0	41	58	4
Mussina	18	5	**2.54**	241.0	48	130	0
Mills	10	4	**2.61**	103.1	54	60	2
S. Davis	7	3	**3.43**	89.1	36	53	4
Rhodes	7	5	**3.63**	94.1	38	77	0
McDonald	13	13	**4.24**	227.0	74	158	0
Sutcliffe	16	15	**4.47**	237.1	74	109	0
Milacki	6	8	**5.84**	115.2	44	51	1

Manager—John Oates

Boston Red Sox

Batting	Avg	AB	R	H	HR	RBI
Cooper	**.276**	337	34	93	5	33
Valentin	**.276**	185	21	51	5	25
Zupcic	**.276**	392	46	108	3	43
Brunansky	**.266**	458	47	122	15	74
Boggs	**.259**	514	62	133	7	50
Burks	**.255**	235	35	60	8	30
Reed	**.247**	550	64	136	3	40
Plantier	**.246**	349	46	86	7	30
Pena	**.241**	410	39	99	1	38
Hatcher	**.238**	315	37	75	1	23
Winningham	**.235**	234	27	55	1	14
Vaughn	**.234**	355	42	83	13	57
Greenwell	**.233**	180	16	42	2	18
Naehring	**.231**	186	12	43	3	14
Rivera	**.215**	288	17	62	0	29
Clark	**.210**	257	32	54	5	33

Pitching	W	L	ERA	IP	BB	SO	Sv
Clemens	18	11	**2.41**	246.2	62	208	0
Harris	4	9	**2.51**	107.2	60	73	4
Viola	13	12	**3.44**	238.0	89	121	0
Darwin	9	9	**3.96**	161.1	53	124	3
Dopson	7	11	**4.08**	141.1	38	55	0
Hesketh	8	9	**4.36**	148.2	58	104	1
Gardiner	4	10	**4.75**	130.2	58	79	0

Manager—Butch Hobson

California Angels

Batting	Avg	AB	R	H	HR	RBI
Polonia	.286	577	83	165	0	35
Gonzales	.277	329	47	91	7	38
Sojo	.272	368	37	100	7	43
Curtis	.259	441	59	114	10	46
Easley	.258	151	14	39	1	12
DiSarcina	.247	518	48	128	3	42
Felix	.246	509	63	125	9	72
Gaetti	.226	456	41	103	12	48
Stevens	.221	312	25	69	7	37
Brooks	.216	306	28	66	8	36
Fitzgerald	.212	189	19	40	6	17

Pitching	W	L	ERA	IP	BB	SO	Sv
Abbott	7	15	2.77	211.0	68	130	0
Harvey	0	4	2.83	28.2	11	34	13
Grahe	5	6	3.52	94.2	39	39	21
Langston	13	14	3.66	229.0	74	174	0
Valera	8	11	3.73	188.0	64	113	0
Finley	7	12	3.96	204.1	98	124	0
Blyleven	8	12	4.74	133.0	29	70	0
Crim	7	6	5.17	87.0	29	30	1

Manager—Buck Rodgers

Chicago White Sox

Batting	Avg	AB	R	H	HR	RBI
Thomas	.323	573	108	185	24	115
Raines	.294	551	102	162	7	54
Ventura	.282	592	85	167	16	93
Abner	.279	208	21	58	1	16
Johnson	.279	567	67	158	3	47
Grebeck	.268	287	24	77	3	35
Bell	.255	627	74	160	25	112
Karkovice	.237	342	39	81	13	50
Sax	.236	567	74	134	4	47
Fisk	.229	188	12	43	3	21
Pasqua	.211	265	26	56	6	33

Pitching	W	L	ERA	IP	BB	SO	Sv
Hernandez	7	3	1.65	71.0	20	68	12
Radinsky	3	7	2.73	59.1	34	48	15
McDowell	20	10	3.18	260.2	75	178	0
Hough	7	12	3.93	176.1	66	76	0
McCaskill	12	13	4.18	209.0	95	109	0
Fernandez	8	11	4.27	187.2	50	95	0
Hibbard	10	7	4.40	176.0	57	69	1
Thigpen	1	3	4.75	55.0	33	45	22
Alvarez	5	3	5.20	100.1	65	66	1

Manager—Gene Lamont

Cleveland Indians

Batting	Avg	AB	R	H	HR	RBI
Baerga	.312	657	92	205	20	105
Lofton	.285	576	96	164	5	42
Howard	.277	358	36	99	2	32
Fermin	.270	215	27	58	0	13
Sorrento	.269	458	52	123	18	60
Lewis	.264	413	44	109	5	30
Martinez	.263	228	23	60	5	35
Jacoby	.261	291	30	76	4	36
Belle	.260	585	81	152	34	112
Whiten	.254	508	73	129	9	43
Alomar	.251	299	22	75	2	26
Ortiz	.250	244	20	61	0	24
Hill	.241	369	38	89	18	49

Pitching	W	L	ERA	IP	BB	SO	Sv
Olin	8	5	2.34	88.1	27	47	29
Power	3	3	2.54	99.1	35	51	6
Nagy	17	10	2.96	252.0	57	169	0
Cook	5	7	3.82	158.0	50	96	0
Nichols	4	3	4.53	105.1	31	56	0
Mesa	7	12	4.59	160.2	70	62	0
Armstrong	6	15	4.64	166.2	67	114	0
Scudder	6	10	5.28	109.0	55	66	0
Otto	5	9	7.06	80.1	33	32	0

Manager—Mike Hargrove

Detroit Tigers

Batting	Avg	AB	R	H	HR	RBI
Livingstone	.282	354	43	100	4	46
Whitaker	.278	453	77	126	19	71
Phillips	.276	606	114	167	10	64
Barnes	.273	165	27	45	3	25
Fryman	.266	659	87	175	20	96
Gladden	.254	417	57	106	7	42
Kreuter	.253	190	22	48	2	16
Deer	.247	393	66	97	32	64
Fielder	.244	594	80	145	35	124
Cuyler	.241	291	39	70	3	28
Tettleton	.238	525	82	125	32	83
Carreon	.232	336	34	78	10	41
Bergman	.232	181	17	42	1	10

Pitching	W	L	ERA	IP	BB	SO	Sv
Doherty	7	4	3.88	116.0	25	37	3
Henneman	2	6	3.96	77.1	20	58	24
Leiter	8	5	4.18	112.0	43	75	0
Gullickson	14	13	4.34	221.2	50	64	0
Tanana	13	11	4.39	186.2	90	91	0
Terrell	7	10	5.20	136.2	48	61	0
King	4	6	5.22	79.1	28	45	1
Ritz	2	5	5.60	80.1	44	57	0
Lancaster	3	4	6.33	86.2	51	35	0

Manager—Sparky Anderson

Kansas City Royals

Batting	Avg	AB	R	H	HR	RBI
Brett	.285	592	55	169	7	61
Jefferies	.285	604	66	172	10	75
Miller	.284	416	57	118	4	38
Joyner	.269	572	66	154	9	66
Eisenreich	.269	353	31	95	2	28
Wilkerson	.250	296	27	74	2	29
McReynolds	.247	373	45	92	13	49
Thurman	.245	200	25	49	0	20
Macfarlane	.234	402	51	94	17	48
Mayne	.225	213	16	48	0	18
Howard	.224	219	19	49	1	18
McRae	.223	533	63	119	4	52

Pitching	W	L	ERA	IP	BB	SO	Sv
Montgomery	1	6	2.18	82.2	27	69	39
Appier	15	8	2.46	208.1	68	150	0
Meacham	10	4	2.74	101.2	21	64	2
Reed	3	7	3.68	100.1	20	49	0
Gubicza	7	6	3.72	111.1	36	81	0
Pichardo	9	6	3.95	143.2	49	59	0
Gordon	6	10	4.59	117.2	55	98	0
Magnante	4	9	4.94	89.1	35	31	0
Boddicker	1	4	4.98	86.2	37	47	3

Manager—Hal McRae

Milwaukee Brewers

Batting	Avg	AB	R	H	HR	RBI
Molitor	.320	609	89	195	12	89
Hamilton	.298	470	67	140	5	62
Listach	.290	579	93	168	1	47
Bichette	.287	387	37	111	5	41
Fletcher	.275	386	53	106	3	51
Seitzer	.270	540	74	146	5	71
Yount	.264	557	71	147	8	77
Surhoff	.252	480	63	121	4	62
Gantner	.246	256	22	63	1	18
Nilsson	.232	164	15	38	4	25
Stubbs	.229	288	37	66	9	42
Vaughn	.228	501	77	114	23	78

Pitching	W	L	ERA	IP	BB	SO	Sv
Eldred	11	2	1.79	100.1	23	62	0
Plesac	5	4	2.96	79.0	35	54	1
Wegman	13	14	3.20	261.2	55	127	0
Navarro	17	11	3.33	246.0	64	100	0
Bosio	16	6	3.62	231.1	44	120	0
Henry	1	4	4.02	65.0	24	52	29
Bones	9	10	4.57	163.1	48	65	0

Manager—Phil Garner

Minnesota Twins

Batting	Avg	AB	R	H	HR	RBI
Puckett	.329	639	104	210	19	110
Mack	.315	600	101	189	16	75
Harper	.307	502	58	154	9	73
Knoblauch	.297	600	104	178	2	56
Davis	.288	444	63	128	12	66
Munoz	.270	418	44	113	12	71
Leius	.249	409	50	102	2	35
Larkin	.246	337	38	83	6	42
Gagne	.246	439	53	108	7	39
Hrbek	.244	394	52	96	15	58
Bush	.214	182	14	39	2	22

Pitching	W	L	ERA	IP	BB	SO	Sv
Willis	7	3	2.72	79.1	11	45	1
Edens	6	3	2.83	76.1	36	57	3
Aguilera	2	6	2.84	66.2	17	52	41
Guthrie	2	3	2.88	75.0	23	76	5
Smiley	16	9	3.21	241.0	65	163	0
Erickson	13	12	3.40	212.0	83	101	0
Tapani	16	11	3.97	220.0	48	138	0

Manager—Tom Kelly

New York Yankees

Batting	Avg	AB	R	H	HR	RBI
Mattingly	.288	640	89	184	14	86
B. Williams	.280	261	39	73	5	26
Hall	.280	583	67	163	15	81
R. Kelly	.272	580	81	158	10	66
Velarde	.272	412	57	112	7	46
Stankiewicz	.268	400	52	107	2	25
Tartabull	.266	421	72	112	25	85
Hayes	.257	509	52	131	18	66
Gallego	.254	173	24	44	3	14
Stanley	.249	173	24	43	8	27
Maas	.248	286	35	71	11	35
P. Kelly	.226	318	38	72	7	27
Nokes	.224	384	42	86	22	59

Pitching	W	L	ERA	IP	BB	SO	Sv
Farr	2	2	1.56	52.0	19	37	30
Perez	13	16	2.87	247.2	93	218	0
Monteleone	7	3	3.30	92.2	27	62	0
Cadaret	4	8	4.25	103.2	74	73	1
Kamieniecki	6	14	4.36	188.0	74	88	0
Sanderson	12	11	4.93	193.1	64	104	0

Manager—Buck Showalter

Oakland A's

Batting	Avg	AB	R	H	HR	RBI
Bordick	.300	504	62	151	3	48
Browne	.287	324	43	93	3	40
R. Henderson	.283	396	77	112	15	46
Steinbach	.279	438	48	122	12	53
Sierra	.278	601	83	167	17	87
Wilson	.270	396	38	107	0	37
McGwire	.268	467	87	125	42	104
Lansford	.262	496	65	130	7	75
Baines	.253	478	58	121	16	76
Blankenship	.241	349	59	84	3	34
Quirk	.200	177	13	39	2	11
Weiss	.212	316	36	67	0	21

Pitching	W	L	ERA	IP	BB	SO	Sv
Russell	4	3	1.63	66.1	25	48	30
Eckersley	7	1	1.91	80.0	11	93	51
Parrett	9	1	3.02	98.1	42	78	0
Welch	11	7	3.27	123.2	43	47	0
Downs	5	5	3.29	82.0	46	38	0
Stewart	12	10	3.66	199.1	79	130	0
Darling	15	10	3.66	206.1	72	99	0
Moore	17	12	4.12	223.0	103	117	0
Witt	10	14	4.29	193.0	114	125	0
Hillegas	1	8	5.23	86.0	37	49	0

Manager—Tony LaRussa

Seattle Mariners

Batting	Avg	AB	R	H	HR	RBI
E. Martinez	.343	528	100	181	18	73
Griffey	.308	565	83	174	27	103
Vizquel	.294	483	49	142	0	21
Mitchell	.286	360	48	103	9	67
Briley	.275	200	18	55	5	12
Cotto	.259	294	42	76	5	27
T. Martinez	.257	460	53	118	16	66
Cochrane	.250	152	10	38	2	12
Reynolds	.247	458	55	113	3	33
Buhner	.243	543	69	132	25	79
Valle	.240	367	39	88	9	30
Parrish	.233	275	26	64	12	32
O'Brien	.222	396	40	88	14	52

Pitching	W	L	ERA	IP	BB	SO	Sv
Fleming	17	10	3.39	228.1	60	112	0
Nelson	1	7	3.44	81.0	44	46	6
Johnson	12	14	3.77	210.1	144	241	0
Grant	2	4	3.89	81.0	22	42	0
Fisher	4	3	4.53	91.1	47	26	1
Swan	3	10	4.74	104.1	45	45	9
Hanson	8	17	4.82	186.2	57	112	0
Leary	8	10	5.36	141.0	87	46	0
DeLucia	3	6	5.49	83.2	35	66	1

Manager—Bill Plummer

Texas Rangers

Batting	Avg	AB	R	H	HR	RBI
Downing	.278	320	53	89	10	39
Palmeiro	.268	608	84	163	22	85
Reimer	.267	494	56	132	16	58
Huson	.261	318	49	83	4	24
Gonzalez	.260	584	77	152	43	109
Rodriguez	.260	420	39	109	8	37
Frye	.256	199	24	51	1	12
Thon	.247	275	30	68	4	37
Canseco	.244	439	74	107	26	87
Palmer	.229	541	74	124	26	72
Newman	.220	246	25	54	0	12
Fariss	.217	166	13	36	3	21
Petralli	.198	192	11	38	1	18

Pitching	W	L	ERA	IP	BB	SO	Sv
Rogers	3	6	3.09	78.2	26	70	6
Brown	21	11	3.32	265.2	76	173	0
Guzman	16	11	3.66	224.0	73	179	0
Ryan	5	9	3.72	157.1	69	157	0
Burns	3	5	3.84	103.0	32	55	1

Manager—Bobby Valentine; Toby Harrah

Toronto Blue Jays

Batting	Avg	AB	R	H	HR	RBI
Alomar	.310	571	105	177	8	76
Winfield	.290	583	92	169	26	108
Olerud	.284	458	68	130	16	66
Maldonado	.272	489	64	133	20	66
Carter	.264	622	97	164	34	119
Lee	.263	396	49	104	3	39
White	.248	641	98	159	17	60
Bell	.242	161	23	39	2	15
Borders	.242	480	47	116	13	53
Griffin	.233	150	21	35	0	10
Gruber	.229	446	42	102	11	43

Pitching	W	L	ERA	IP	BB	SO	Sv
D. Ward	7	4	1.95	101.1	39	103	12
Guzman	16	5	2.64	180.2	72	165	0
Eichhorn	4	4	3.08	87.2	25	61	2
Key	13	13	3.53	216.2	59	117	0
Morris	21	6	4.04	240.2	80	132	0
Stottlemyre	12	11	4.50	174.0	63	98	0
Stieb	4	6	5.04	96.1	43	45	0
Wells	7	9	5.40	120.0	36	62	2

Manager—Cito Gaston

National Baseball Hall of Fame and Museum

Cooperstown, N.Y.

Aaron, Hank
Alexander, Grover Cleveland
Alston, Walt
Anson, Cap
Aparicio, Luis
Appling, Luke
Averill, Earl
Baker, Home Run
Bancroft, Dave
Banks, Ernie
Barlick, Al
Barrow, Edward G.
Beckley, Jake
Bell, Cool Papa
Bench, Johnny
Bender, Chief
Berra, Yogi
Bottomley, Jim
Boudreau, Lou
Bresnahan, Roger
Brock, Lou
Brouthers, Dan
Brown, (Three Finger), Mordecai
Bulkeley, Morgan C.
Burkett, Jesse C.
Campanella, Roy
Carew, Rod
Carey, Max
Cartwright, Alexander
Chadwick, Henry
Chance, Frank
Chandler, Happy
Charleston, Oscar
Chesbro, John
Clarke, Fred
Clarkson, John
Clemente, Roberto
Cobb, Ty
Cochrane, Mickey
Collins, Eddie
Collins, James
Combs, Earle
Comiskey, Charles A.
Conlan, Jocko
Connolly, Thomas H.
Connor, Roger
Coveleski, Stan
Crawford, Sam
Cronin, Joe
Cummings, Candy
Cuyler, Kiki
Dandridge, Ray
Dean, Dizzy
Delahanty, Ed
Dickey, Bill
DiHigo, Martin
DiMaggio, Joe
Doerr, Bobby
Drysdale, Don
Duffy, Hugh
Evans, Billy
Evers, John
Ewing, Buck
Faber, Urban
Feller, Bob
Ferrell, Rick
Fingers, Rollie
Flick, Elmer H.
Ford, Whitey
Foster, Andrew
Foxx, Jimmie
Frick, Ford
Frisch, Frank
Galvin, Pud
Gehrig, Lou
Gehringer, Charles
Gibson, Bob
Gibson, Josh
Giles, Warren
Gomez, Lefty
Goslin, Goose
Greenberg, Hank
Griffith, Clark
Grimes, Burleigh
Grove, Lefty
Hafey, Chick
Haines, Jesee
Hamilton, Bill
Harridge, Will
Harris, Bucky
Hartnett, Gabby
Heilmann, Harry
Herman, Billy
Hooper, Harry
Hornsby, Rogers
Hoyt, Waite
Hubbard, Cal
Hubbell, Carl
Huggins, Miller
Hunter, Catfish
Irvin, Monte
Jackson, Travis
Jenkins, Ferguson
Jennings, Hugh
Johnson, Byron
Johnson, William (Judy)
Johnson, Walter
Joss, Addie
Kaline, Al
Keefe, Timothy
Keeler, William
Kell, George
Kelley, Joe
Kelly, George
Kelly, King
Killebrew, Harmon
Kiner, Ralph
Klein, Chuck
Klem, Bill
Koufax, Sandy
Lajoie, Napoleon
Landis, Kenesaw M.
Lazzeri, Tony
Lemon, Bob
Leonard, Buck
Lindstrom, Fred
Lloyd, Pop
Lombardi, Ernie
Lopez, Al
Lyons, Ted
Mack, Connie
MacPhail, Larry
Mantle, Mickey
Manush, Henry
Maranville, Rabbit
Marichal, Juan
Marquard, Rube
Mathews, Eddie
Mathewson, Christy
Mays, Willie
McCarthy, Joe
McCarthy, Thomas
McCovey, Willie
McGinnity, Joe
McGowan, Bill
McGraw, John
McKechnie, Bill
Medwick, Joe
Mize, Johnny
Morgan, Joe
Musial, Stan
Newhouser, Hal
Nichols, Kid
O'Rourke, James
Ott, Mel
Paige, Satchel
Palmer, Jim
Pennock, Herb
Perry, Gaylord
Plank, Ed
Radbourn, Charlie
Reese, Pee Wee
Rice, Sam
Rickey, Branch
Rixey, Eppa
Roberts, Robin
Robinson, Brooks
Robinson, Frank
Robinson, Jackie
Robinson, Wilbert
Roush, Edd
Ruffing, Red
Rusie, Amos
Ruth, Babe
Schalk, Ray
Schoendienst, Red
Seaver, Tom
Sewell, Joe
Simmons, Al
Sisler, George
Slaughter, Enos
Snider, Duke
Spahn, Warren
Spalding, Albert
Speaker, Tris
Stargell, Willie
Stengel, Casey
Terry, Bill
Thompson, Sam
Tinker, Joe
Traynor, Pie
Vance, Dazzy
Vaughan, Arky
Veeck, Bill
Waddell, Rube
Wagner, Honus
Wallace, Roderick
Walsh, Ed
Waner, Lloyd
Waner, Paul
Ward, John
Weiss, George
Welch, Mickey
Wheat, Zach
Wilhelm, Hoyt
Williams, Billy
Williams, Ted
Wilson, Hack
Wright, George
Wright, Harry
Wynn, Early
Yastrzemski, Carl
Yawkey, Tom
Young, Cy
Youngs, Ross

All-Star Baseball Games, 1933-1992

Year	Winner	Score	Location
1933	American	4-2	Chicago
1934	American	9-7	New York
1935	American	4-1	Cleveland
1936	National	4-3	Boston
1937	American	8-3	Washington
1938	National	4-1	Cincinnati
1939	American	3-1	New York
1940	National	4-0	St. Louis
1941	American	7-5	Detroit
1942	American	3-1	New York
1943*	American	5-3	Philadelphia
1944*	National	7-1	Pittsburgh
1945	(not played)		
1946	American	12-0	Boston
1947	American	2-1	Chicago
1948	American	5-2	St. Louis
1949	American	11-7	New York
1950	National (1)	4-3	Chicago
1951	National	8-3	Detroit
1952	National	3-2	Philadelphia
1953	National	5-1	Cincinnati
1954	American	11-9	Cleveland
1955	National (2)	6-5	Milwaukee
1956	National	7-3	Washington
1957	American	6-5	St. Louis
1958	American	4-3	Baltimore
1959	National	5-4	Pittsburgh
1959	American	5-3	Los Angeles
1960	National	5-3	Kansas City
1960	National	6-0	New York
1961	National (3)	5-4	San Francisco
1961	Called-rain	1-1	Boston
1962	National (3)	3-1	Washington
1962	American	9-4	Chicago
1963	National	5-3	Cleveland
1964	National	7-4	New York
1965	National	6-5	Minnesota
1966	National (3)	2-1	St. Louis
1967	National (4)	2-1	Anaheim
1968*	National	1-0	Houston
1969	National	9-3	Washington
1970*	National (2)	5-4	Cincinnati
1971*	American	6-4	Detroit
1972*	National	4-3	Atlanta
1973*	National	7-1	Kansas City
1974*	National	7-2	Pittsburgh
1975*	National	6-3	Milwaukee
1976*	National	7-1	Philadelphia
1977*	National	7-5	New York
1978*	National	7-3	San Diego
1979*	National	7-6	Seattle
1980*	National	4-2	Los Angeles
1981*	National	5-4	Cleveland
1982*	National	4-1	Montreal
1983*	American	13-3	Chicago
1984*	National	3-1	San Francisco
1985*	National	6-1	Minneapolis
1986*	American	3-2	Houston
1987*	National (5)	2-0	Oakland
1988*	American	2-1	Cincinnati
1989*	American	5-3	Anaheim
1990*	American	2-0	Chicago
1991*	American	4-2	Toronto
1992*	American	13-6	San Diego

(1) 14 innings, (2) 12 innings, (3) 10 innings, (4) 15 innings (5) 13 innings. * Night game.

Major League Leaders in 1992

American League

Batting

E. Martinez, Seattle .343; Puckett, Minnesota .329; Thomas, Chicago .323; Molitor, Milwaukee .320; Mack, Minnesota .315.

Runs

Phillips, Detroit, 114; Thomas, Chicago, 108; R. Alomar, Toronto, 105; Knoblauch, Minnesota, 104; Puckett, Minnesota, 104.

Runs Batted In

Fielder, Detroit, 124; Carter, Toronto, 119; Thomas, Chicago, 115; Belle, Cleveland, 112; G. Bell, Chicago, 112.

Hits

Puckett, Minnesota, 210; Baerga, Cleveland, 205; Molitor, Milwaukee, 195; Mack, Minnesota, 189; Thomas, Chicago, 185.

Doubles

Thomas, Chicago, 46; E. Martinez, Seattle, 46; Mattingly, New York, 40; Yount, Milwaukee, 40; Griffey, Seattle, 39.

Triples

L. Johnson, Chicago, 12; Devereaux, Baltimore, 11; Anderson, Baltimore, 10; Raines, Chicago, 9; Lofton, Cleveland, 8; R. Alomar, Toronto, 8.

Home Runs

J. Gonzalez, Texas, 43; McGwire, Oakland, 42; Fielder, Detroit, 35; Belle, Cleveland, 34; Carter, Toronto, 34.

Stolen Bases

Lofton, Cleveland, 66; Listach, Milwaukee, 54; Anderson, Baltimore, 53; Polonia, California, 51; R. Alomar, Toronto, 49.

Pitching (18 Decisions)

Mussina, Baltimore, 18-5, .783, 2.54; J. Morris, Toronto, 21-6, .778, 4.04; JuGuzman, Toronto, 16-5, .762, 2.64; Bosio, Milwaukee, 16-6, .727, 3.62; McDowell, Chicago, 20-10, .667, 3.18.

Strikeouts

R. Johnson, Seattle, 241; Perez, New York, 218; Clemens, Boston, 208; JsGuzman, Texas, 179; McDowell, Chicago, 178.

Saves

Eckersley, Oakland, 51; Aguilera, Minnesota, 41; Montgomery, Kansas City, 39; Olson, Baltimore, 36; Henke, Toronto, 34.

National League

Batting

Sheffield, San Diego .330; VanSlyke, Pittsburg .324; Roberts, Cincinnati .323; Kruk, Philadelphia .323; Gwynn, San Diego .317.

Runs

Bonds, Pittsburgh, 109; D. Hollins, Philadelphia, 104; VanSlyke, Pittsburgh, 103; Sandberg, Chicago, 100; Grissom, Montreal, 99.

Runs Batted In

Daulton, Philadelphia, 109; Pendleton, Atlanta, 105; McGriff, San Diego, 104; Bonds, Pittsburgh, 103; Sheffield, San Diego, 100.

Hits

Pendleton, Atlanta, 199; VanSlyke, Pittsburgh, 199; Sandberg, Chicago, 186; Grace, Chicago, 185; Sheffield, San Diego, 184.

Doubles

VanSlyke, Pittsburgh, 45; Lankford, St. Louis, 40; W. Clark, San Francisco, 40; Duncan, Philadelphia, 40; Grissom, Montreal, 39; Pendleton, Atlanta, 39.

Triples

D. Sanders, Atlanta, 14; Finley, Houston, 13; VanSlyke, Pittsburgh, 12; Alicea, St. Louis, 11; Butler, Los Angeles, 11.

Home Runs

McGriff, San Diego, 35; Bonds, Pittsburgh, 34; Sheffield, San Diego, 33; D. Hollins, Philadelphia, 27; Daulton, Philadelphia, 27.

Stolen Bases

Grissom, Montreal, 78; DeShields, Montreal, 46; Finley, Houston, 44; Roberts, Cincinnati, 44; O. Smith, St. Louis, 43.

Pitching (18 Decisions)

Tewksbury, St. Louis, 16-5, .762, 2.16; Glavine, Atlanta, 20-8, .714, 2.76; Leibrandt, Atlanta, 15-7, .682, 3.36; Morgan, Chicago, 16-8, .667, 2.55; Cone, New York, 13-7, .650, 2.88.

Strikeouts

Smoltz, Atlanta, 215; Cone, New York, 214; G. Maddux, Chicago, 199; S. Fernandez, New York, 193; Drabek, Pittsburgh, 177.

Saves

L. Smith, St. Louis, 43; Myers, San Diego, 38; Wetteland, Montreal, 37; D. Jones, Houston, 36; M. Williams, Philadelphia, 29.

World Almanac All-Major League Baseball Team in 1992

The team was chosen by a panel of sports experts on behalf of the World Almanac.

Position	Player, team
First base	Frank Thomas, Chicago White Sox
Second base	Ryne Sandberg, Chicago Cubs
Third base	Gary Sheffield, San Diego Padres
Shortstop	Barry Larkin, Cincinnati Reds
Outfield	Barry Bonds, Pittsburgh Pirates
Outfield	Kirby Puckett, Minnesota Twins
Outfield	Larry Walker, Montreal Expos
Catcher	Darren Daulton, Philadelphia Phillies
Right-hand pitcher	Greg Maddux, Chicago Cubs
Left-hand pitcher	Tom Glavine, Atlanta Braves
Relief pitcher	Dennis Eckersley, Oakland A's
Rookie of the Year	Pat Listach, Milwaukee Brewers
Player of the Year	Barry Bonds, Pittsburgh Pirates
Manager of the Year	Tony LaRussa, Oakland A's

Major League Perfect Games Since 1900

Year	Player	Clubs	Score
1904	Cy Young	Boston vs. Phil. (AL)	3-0
1908	Addie Joss	Cleveland vs. Chicago (AL)	1-0
1917	Ernie Shore (a)	Boston vs. Wash. (AL)	4-0
1922	Charles Robertson	Chicago vs. Detroit (AL)	2-0
1956	Don Larsen (b)	N.Y. Yankees vs. Brooklyn	2-0
1959	Harvey Haddix (c)	Pitts. vs. Milwaukee (NL)	0-1
1964	Jim Bunning	Phil. vs. N.Y. Mets (NL)	6-0
1965	Sandy Koufax	Los Angeles vs. Chic. (NL)	1-0
1968	Jim Hunter	Oakland vs. Minn. (AL)	4-0
1981	Len Barker	Cleveland vs. Toronto (AL)	3-0
1984	Mike Witt	California vs. Texas (AL)	1-0
1988	Tom Browning	Cincinnati vs. L.A. (NL)	1-0
1991	Dennis Martinez	Montreal vs. L.A. (NL)	2-0

(a) Babe Ruth, the starting pitcher, was ejected from the game after walking the first batter. Shore replaced him and the baserunner was out stealing. Shore retired the next 26 batters. (b) World Series. (c) Pitched 12 perfect innings, lost in 13th on an error, sacrifice bunt, walk, and double.

1992 World Series Composite Box Score

Blue Jays Batting

	g	ab	r	h	2b	3b	hr	rbi	so	bb	avg	po	a	e	pct
David Cone p	2	4	0	2	0	0	0	1	0	1	.500	0	0	0	.000
Ed Sprague ph-1b	3	2	1	1	0	0	1	2	0	1	.500	0	0	0	.000
Pat Borders c	6	20	2	9	3	0	1	3	1	2	.450	48	5	1	.978
John Olerud 1b	4	13	2	4	0	0	0	0	4	0	.308	25	3	0	1.000
Joe Carter 1b-lf-rf	6	22	2	6	2	0	2	3	2	3	.273	27	1	0	1.000
Devon White cf	6	26	2	6	1	0	0	2	6	0	.231	22	0	0	1.000
Dave Winfield rf-dh	6	22	0	5	1	0	0	3	3	2	.227	7	0	0	1.000
Roberto Alomar 2b	6	24	3	5	1	0	0	0	3	3	.208	6	12	0	1.000
Candy Maldonado lf-ph	6	19	1	3	0	0	1	2	5	2	.158	8	2	0	1.000
Kelly Gruber 3b	6	19	2	2	0	0	1	1	5	2	.105	5	5	1	.909
Manuel Lee ss	6	19	1	2	0	0	0	0	2	1	.105	13	10	1	.947
Jack Morris p	2	2	0	0	0	0	0	0	2	0	.000	0	1	0	1.000
Pat Tabler ph	2	2	0	0	0	0	0	0	0	0	.000	0	0	0	.000
Derek Bell ph	2	1	1	0	0	0	0	0	0	1	.000	0	0	0	.000
Jimmy Key p	2	1	0	0	0	0	0	0	0	0	.000	2	4	0	1.000
Mark Eichorn p	1	0	0	0	0	0	0	0	0	0	.000	0	0	0	.000
Alfredo Griffin ss	2	0	0	0	0	0	0	0	0	0	.000	0	1	1	.500
Juan Guzman p	1	0	0	0	0	0	0	0	0	0	.000	2	0	0	1.000
Tom Henke p	3	0	0	0	0	0	0	0	0	0	.000	0	2	0	1.000
Todd Stottlemyre p	4	0	0	0	0	0	0	0	0	0	.000	0	0	0	.000
Mike Timlin p	2	0	0	0	0	0	0	0	0	0	.000	0	1	0	1.000
Duane Ward p	4	0	0	0	0	0	0	0	0	0	.000	0	0	0	.000
David Wells p	4	0	0	0	0	0	0	0	0	0	.000	0	0	0	.000
Totals	**6**	**196**	**17**	**45**	**8**	**0**	**6**	**17**	**33**	**18**	**.230**	**165**	**47**	**4**	**.981**

Braves Batting

	g	ab	r	h	2b	3b	hr	rbi	so	bb	avg	po	a	e	pct
Deion Sanders lf	4	15	4	8	2	0	0	1	1	2	.533	5	1	0	1.000
Otis Nixon cf	6	27	3	8	1	0	0	1	3	1	.296	18	0	0	1.000
Jeff Blauser ss	6	24	2	6	0	0	0	0	9	1	.250	7	22	0	1.000
Terry Pendleton 3b	6	25	2	6	2	0	0	2	5	1	.240	4	19	0	1.000
Mark Lemke 2b	6	19	0	4	0	0	0	2	3	1	.211	18	12	0	1.000
Sid Bream 1b	5	15	1	3	0	0	0	0	0	4	.200	42	1	1	.977
Brian Hunter ph-1b-pr	4	5	0	1	0	0	0	2	1	0	.200	14	1	0	1.000
Lonnie Smith ph-dh	5	12	1	2	0	0	1	5	4	1	.167	0	0	0	.000
Ron Gant lf-pr-ph	4	8	2	1	1	0	0	0	2	1	.125	3	1	0	1.000
David Justice rf	6	19	4	3	0	0	1	3	5	6	.158	16	0	1	.941
Damon Berryhill c	6	22	1	2	0	0	1	3	11	1	.091	32	3	0	1.000
John Smoltz p-pr	3	3	0	0	0	0	0	0	2	0	.000	1	2	0	1.000
Tom Glavine p	2	2	0	0	0	0	0	0	0	1	.000	0	2	0	1.000
Steve Avery p	2	1	0	0	0	0	0	0	1	0	.000	0	2	0	1.000
Francisco Cabrera ph	1	1	0	0	0	0	0	0	0	0	.000	0	0	0	.000
Pete Smith p	1	1	0	0	0	0	0	0	1	0	.000	0	0	0	.000
Jeff Treadway ph	1	1	0	0	0	0	0	0	0	0	.000	0	0	0	.000
Rafael Belliard ss-2b	4	0	0	0	0	0	0	0	0	0	.000	2	2	0	1.000
Charlie Leibrandt p	1	0	0	0	0	0	0	0	0	0	.000	1	0	0	1.000
Jeff Reardon p	2	0	0	0	0	0	0	0	0	0	.000	0	0	0	.000
Mike Stanton p	4	0	0	0	0	0	0	0	0	0	.000	0	0	0	.000
Mark Wohlers p	2	0	0	0	0	0	0	0	0	0	.000	0	0	0	.000
Totals	**6**	**200**	**20**	**44**	**6**	**0**	**3**	**19**	**48**	**20**	**.220**	**163**	**68**	**2**	**.991**

Blue Jays Pitching

	g	cg	ip	h	r	bb	so	hb	wp	w	l	sv	pct	er	era
David Wells	4	0	4⅓	1	0	2	3	0	0	0	0	0	.000	0	0.00
Todd Stottlemyre	4	0	3⅔	4	0	0	4	0	0	0	0	0	.000	0	0.00
Duane Ward	4	0	3⅓	1	0	1	6	0	1	2	0	0	1.000	0	0.00
Mike Timlin	2	0	1⅓	0	0	0	0	0	0	0	0	1	.000	0	0.00
Mark Eichhorn	1	0	1	0	0	0	1	0	0	0	0	0	.000	0	0.00
Jimmy Key	2	0	9	6	2	0	6	0	0	2	0	0	1.000	1	1.00
Juan Guzman	1	0	8	8	2	1	7	0	0	0	0	0	.000	1	1.13
Tom Henke	3	0	3⅓	2	1	2	1	1	0	0	0	2	.000	1	2.70
David Cone	2	0	10⅓	9	5	8	8	0	1	0	0	0	.000	4	3.48
Jack Morris	2	0	10⅔	13	10	6	12	0	1	0	2	0	.000	10	8.44
Totals	**6**	**0**	**55**	**44**	**20**	**20**	**48**	**1**	**3**	**4**	**2**	**3**	**.667**	**17**	**2.78**

Braves Pitching

	g	cg	ip	h	r	bb	so	hb	wp	w	l	sv	pct	er	era
Mike Stanton	4	0	5	3	0	2	1	0	0	0	0	1	.000	0	0.00
Pete Smith	1	0	3	3	0	0	0	0	0	0	0	0	.000	0	0.00
Mark Wohlers	2	0	⅔	0	0	1	0	0	0	0	0	0	.000	0	0.00
Tom Glavine	2	2	17	10	3	4	8	0	0	1	1	0	.500	3	1.59
John Smoltz	2	0	13⅓	13	5	7	12	0	2	1	0	0	1.000	4	2.70
Steve Avery	2	0	12	11	5	3	11	0	0	0	1	0	.000	5	3.75
Charlie Leibrandt	1	0	2	3	2	0	0	1	0	0	1	0	.000	2	9.00
Jeff Reardon	2	0	1⅓	2	2	1	1	0	0	0	1	0	.000	2	13.50
Totals	**6**	**2**	**54⅓**	**45**	**17**	**18**	**33**	**1**	**2**	**2**	**4**	**1**	**.333**	**16**	**2.65**

Score By Innings

Toronto	1	1	1	4	2	0	1	2	3	0	2	— 17
Atlanta	1	1	1	2	7	4	0	2	1	0	1	— 20

1992 World Series

First Game

Toronto	ab	r	h	bi	Atlanta	ab	r	h	bi
White, cf	4	0	0	0	Nixon, cf	3	0	1	0
Alomar, 2b	4	0	0	0	Blauser, ss	4	0	0	0
Carter, 1b	4	1	1	1	Belliard, ss	0	0	0	0
Winfield, rf	3	0	1	0	Pendleton, 3b	4	0	0	0
Maldonado, lf	3	0	0	0	Justice, rf	2	1	0	0
Gruber, 3b	3	0	0	0	Bream, 1b	3	0	1	0
Borders, c	3	0	2	0	Gant, lf	3	1	0	0
Lee, ss	3	0	0	0	Berryhill, c	4	1	1	3
Morris, p	2	0	0	0	Lemke, 2b	3	0	1	0
Stottlemyre, p	0	0	0	0	Glavine, p	2	0	0	0
Tabler, ph	1	0	0	0	**Totals**	**28**	**3**	**4**	**3**
Wells, p	0	0	0	0					
Totals	**30**	**1**	**4**	**1**					

Toronto	0	0	0	1	0	0	0	0	0—1
Atlanta.	0	0	0	0	0	3	0	0	x—3

Toronto	ip	h	r	er	bb	so
Morris L, 0-1	6	4	3	3	5	7
Stottlemyre	1	0	0	0	0	2
Wells	1	0	0	0	1	1
Atlanta						
Glavine W, 1-0	9	4	1	1	0	6

LOB - Toronto 2, Atlanta 7. HR - Berryhill (1) off Morris, Carter (1) off Glavine. RBI - Carter (1), Berryhill 3 (3). SB - Nixon (1), Gant (1).

How runs were scored—One in Blue Jays fourth: Carter hit a home run.

Three in Braves sixth: Justice walked. Bream singled. Gant reached on a fielder's choice. Berryhill hit a home run scoring Justice and Gant.

Second Game

Toronto	ab	r	h	bi	Atlanta	ab	r	h	bi
White, cf	5	0	1	1	Nixon, cf	5	0	0	0
Alomar, 2b	4	1	1	0	Sanders, lf	3	1	1	0
Carter, lf	3	0	1	0	Pendleton, 3b	4	1	1	0
Winfield, rf	4	0	1	1	Justice, rf	3	1	1	1
Olerud, 1b	4	0	0	0	Bream, 1b	1	1	0	0
Gruber, 3b	4	0	0	0	Hunter, ph-1b	1	0	0	1
Borders, c	3	1	1	0	Blauser, ss	3	0	1	0
Lee, ss	3	1	1	0	Belliard, ss	0	0	0	0
Bell, ph	0	1	0	0	Berryhill, c	3	0	0	0
Griffin, ss	0	0	0	0	Lemke, 2b	4	0	1	1
Cone, p	2	0	2	1	Smoltz, p	3	0	0	0
Wells, p	0	0	0	0	Stanton, p	0	0	0	0
Maldonado, ph	1	0	0	0	Reardon, p	0	0	0	0
Stottlemyre, p	0	0	0	0	Smith, ph	0	0	0	0
Ward, p	0	0	0	0	Gant, pr	0	0	0	0
Sprague, ph	1	1	1	2	**Totals**	**30**	**4**	**5**	**3**
Henke, p	0	0	0	0					
Totals	**34**	**5**	**9**	**5**					

Toronto	0	0	0	0	2	0	0	1	2—5
Atlanta.	0	1	0	1	2	0	0	0	0—4

Toronto	ip	h	r	er	bb	so
Cone	4⅓	5	4	3	5	2
Wells	1⅔	0	0	0	1	2
Stottlemyer	1	0	0	0	0	0
Ward W, 1-0	1	0	0	0	0	2
Henke, S, 1	1	0	0	0	1	0
Atlanta						
Smoltz	7⅓	8	3	2	3	8
Stanton	⅓	0	0	0	0	0
Reardon L, 0-1	1⅓	1	2	2	1	1

E - Borders (1), Lee (1), Bream (1). LOB - Toronto 6, Atlanta 8. 2B - Alomar (1), Borders (1). HR - Sprague (1) off Reardon. RBI - White (1), Winfield (1), Cone (1), Sprague 2 (2), Justice (1), Hunter (1), Lemke (1). SB - Sanders 2 (2), Justice (1), Blauser (1), Gant (2). SF - Hunter.

How runs were scored—One in Braves second: Justice walked and stole second, and went to third on a groundout. Justice scored on a wild pitch.

One in Braves fourth: Bream walked. Blauser singled. Lemke singled scoring Bream.

Two in Blue Jays fifth: Borders walked. Lee singled. Cone singled scoring Borders. White singled scoring Lee.

Two in Braves fifth: Sanders singled. Pendleton walked. Justice singled scoring Sanders. Hunter hit a sacrifice fly scoring Pendleton.

One in Blue Jays eighth: Alomar doubled. Winfield singled scoring Alomar.

Two in Blue Jays ninth: Bell walked. Sprague hit a home run scoring Bell.

Third Game

Atlanta	ab	r	h	bi	Toronto	ab	r	h	bi
Nixon, cf	4	1	0	0	White, cf	4	0	0	0
Sanders, lf	4	1	3	0	Alomar, 2b	4	1	1	0
Pendleton, 3b	4	0	2	0	Carter, rf	3	1	1	1
Justice, rf	3	0	1	1	Winfield, dh	3	0	1	0
Smith, dh	4	0	1	1	Olerud, 1b	3	0	0	0
Bream, 1b	4	0	2	0	Sprague, ph	0	0	0	0
Hunter, pr-1b	0	0	0	0	Maldonado, lf	4	0	1	1
Blauser, ss	4	0	0	0	Gruber, 3b	2	1	1	1
Berryhill, c	4	0	0	0	Borders, c	3	0	1	0
Lemke, 2b	3	0	0	0	Lee, ss	3	0	0	0
Totals	**34**	**2**	**9**	**2**	**Totals**	**29**	**3**	**6**	**3**

Atlanta	0	0	0	0	0	1	0	1	0—2
Toronto	0	0	0	1	0	0	0	1	1—3

Atlanta	ip	h	r	er	bb	so
Avery L, 0-1	8	5	3	3	1	9
Wohlers	⅓	0	0	0	1	0
Stanton	0	0	0	0	1	0
Reardon	0	1	0	0	0	0
Toronto						
Guzman	8	8	2	1	1	7
Ward W, 2-0	1	1	0	0	0	2

E - Gruber, (1). LOB - Atlanta 6, Toronto 5. 2B - Sanders (1). HR - Carter (2) off Avery, Gruber (1) off Avery. RBI - Justice (2), Smith (1), Carter (2), Maldonado (1), Gruber (1). SB - Nixon (2), Sanders (3), Alomar (1), Gruber (1). CS - Hunter (1). S - Winfield.

How runs were scored—One in Blue Jays fourth: Carter hit a home run.

One in Braves sixth: Sanders doubled. Justice singled scoring Sanders.

One in Braves eighth: Nixon was safe on an error and stole second. Smith singled scoring Nixon.

One in Blue Jays eighth: Gruber hit a home run.

One in Blue Jays ninth: Alomar singled and stole second. Maldonado singled scoring Alomar.

Fourth Game

Atlanta	ab	r	h	bi	Toronto	ab	r	h	bi
Nixon, cf	4	0	2	0	White, cf	4	0	3	1
Blauser, ss	4	0	1	0	Alomar, 2b	3	0	0	0
Pendleton, 3b	4	0	0	0	Carter, rf	3	0	0	0
Smith, dh	4	0	0	0	Winfield, dh	3	0	0	0
Justice, rf	4	0	0	0	Olerud, 1b	3	0	2	0
Gant, lf	3	1	1	0	Maldonado, lf	3	0	0	0
Hunter, 1b	3	0	1	0	Gruber, 3b	2	1	0	0
Berryhill, c	3	0	0	0	Borders, c	3	1	1	1
Lemke, 2b	3	0	0	1	Lee, ss	3	0	0	0
Totals	**32**	**1**	**5**	**1**	**Totals**	**27**	**2**	**6**	**2**

Atlanta.	0	0	0	0	0	0	0	1	0—1
Toronto	0	0	1	0	0	0	1	0	x—2

Atlanta	ip	h	r	er	bb	so
Glavine L, 1-1	8	6	2	2	4	2
Toronto						
Key W, 1-0	7⅔	5	1	1	0	6
Ward	⅓	0	0	0	0	1
Henke S, 2	1	0	0	0	0	1

LOB - Atlanta 4, Toronto 5. 2B - Gant (1), White (1). HR - Borders (1) off Glavine. RBI - Lemke (2), White (2), Borders (1). SB - Nixon (3), Blauser (2), Alomar (2).

How runs were scored—One in Blue Jays third: Borders hit a home run.

One in Blue Jays seventh: Gruber walked and went to second on a groundout. White singled scoring Gruber.

One in Braves eighth: Gant doubled. Hunter singled. Lemke grounded out scoring Gant.

Fifth Game

Atlanta	ab	r	h	bi	Toronto	ab	r	h	bi
Nixon, cf	5	2	3	0	White, cf	4	0	0	0
Sanders, lf	5	1	2	1	Alomar, 2b	3	0	0	0
Pendleton, 3b	5	1	2	1	Carter, rf	4	0	1	0
Justice, rf	3	2	1	1	Winfield, dh	4	0	1	0
Smith, dh	4	1	1	4	Olerud, 1b	3	2	2	0
Bream, 1b	4	0	0	0	Sprague, ph-1b	1	0	0	0
Blauser, ss	4	0	1	0	Maldonado, lf	2	0	0	0
Belliard, ss	0	0	0	0	Gruber, 3b	4	0	0	0
Berryhill, c	4	0	1	0	Borders, c	4	0	2	2
Lemke, 2b	4	0	2	0	Lee, ss	3	0	0	0
Totals	**38**	**7**	**13**	**7**	**Totals**	**32**	**2**	**6**	**2**

Atlanta	1	0	0	1	5	0	0	0	0—7
Toronto.	0	1	0	1	0	0	0	0	0—2

Atlanta	ip	h	r	er	bb	so
Smoltz W, 1-0	6	5	2	2	4	4
Stanton S, 1	3	1	0	0	0	1
Toronto						
Morris L, 0-2	4⅔	9	7	7	1	5
Wells	1⅓	1	0	0	0	0
Timlin	1	0	0	0	0	0
Eichhorn	1	0	0	0	0	1
Stottlemyre	1	3	0	0	0	1

LOB - Atlanta 5, Toronto 7. 2B - Nixon (1), Pendleton 2 (2), Borders (2). HR - Justice (1) off Morris, Smith (1) off Morris. RBI - Sanders (1), Pendleton (1), Justice (3), Smith 4 (5), Borders 2 (3). SB - Nixon 2 (5). CS - Blauser (1).

How runs were scored—One in Braves first: Nixon doubled. Pendleton doubled scoring Nixon.

One in Blue Jays second: Olerud singled. Maldonado walked. Borders doubled scoring Olerud.

One in Braves fourth: Justice hit a home run.

One in Blue Jays fourth: Olerud singled. Maldonado walked. Borders singled scoring Olerud.

Five in Braves fifth: Nixon singled and stole second. Sanders singled scoring Nixon. Pendleton doubled. Justice walked. Smith hit a home run scoring Sanders, Pendleton, and Justice.

Sixth Game

Toronto	ab	r	h	bi	Atlanta	ab	r	h	bi
White, cf	5	2	2	0	Nixon, cf	6	0	2	1
Alomar 2b	6	1	3	0	Sanders lf	3	1	2	0
Carter 1b	5	0	2	1	Gant ph-lf	2	0	0	0
Winfield rf	5	0	1	2	Pendelton 3b	4	0	1	1
Maldonado lf	6	1	2	1	Justice rf	4	0	0	0
Gruber 3b	4	0	1	0	Bream lb	3	0	0	0
Borders c	4	0	2	0	Blauser ss	5	2	3	0
Lee ss	4	0	1	0	Berryhill c	4	0	0	0
Tabler ph	1	0	0	0	Smoltz pr	0	0	0	0
Griffin ss	0	0	0	0	Lemke 2b	2	0	0	0
Cone p	2	0	0	0	Smith ph	0	0	0	0
Stottlemyre p	0	0	0	0	Belliard 2b	0	0	0	0
Wells p	0	0	0	0	Avery p	1	0	0	0
D Bell ph	1	0	0	0	Smith p	1	0	0	0
Ward p	0	0	0	0	Treadway ph	1	0	0	0
Henke p	0	0	0	0	Stanton p	0	0	0	0
Key p	1	0	0	0	Wohlers p	0	0	0	0
Timlin p	0	0	0	0	Cabrera ph	1	0	0	0
Totals	**44**	**4**	**14**	**4**	Leibrandt p	0	0	0	0
					Hunter ph	1	0	0	1
					Totals	**38**	**3**	**8**	**3**

Toronto	1	0	0	1	0	0	0	0	0	0	2—4
Atlanta.	0	0	1	0	0	0	0	0	1	0	1—3

Toronto	ip	h	r	er	bb	so
Cone	6	4	1	1	3	6
Stottlemyre	⅔	1	0	0	0	1
Wells	⅓	0	0	0	0	0
Ward	1	0	0	0	1	1
Henke	1⅓	2	1	1	1	0
Key W, 2-0	1⅓	1	1	0	0	0
Timlin S, 1	⅓	0	0	0	0	0
Atlanta						
Avery	4	6	2	2	2	2
Smith	3	3	0	0	0	0
Stanton	1⅔	2	0	0	1	0
Wohlers	⅓	0	0	0	0	0
Leibrandt L, 0-1	2	3	2	2	0	0

E - Griffin (1), Justice (1). LOB - Toronto 13, Atlanta 10. 2B - Carter 2 (2), Winfield (1), Borders (3), Sanders (2). HR - Maldonado (1) off Avery. RBI - Carter (3), Winfield 2 (3), Maldonado (2), Nixon (1), Pendleton (2), Hunter (2). SB - White (1), Alomar (3), Sanders 2 (5). CS - Nixon (1). S - Gruber, Berryhill, Belliard. SF - Carter, Pendleton.

How runs were scored—One in Blue Jays first: White singled and stole second. White went to third on a ground out. Carter hit a sacrifice fly scoring White.

One in Braves third: Sanders doubled and stole third. Pendleton hit a sacrifice fly scoring Sanders.

One in Blue Jays fourth: Maldonado hit a home run.

One in Braves ninth: Blauser singled. Smith walked. Nixon singled scoring Blauser.

Two in Blue Jays eleventh: White was hit by a pitch. Alomar singled. Winfield doubled scoring White and Alomar.

One in Braves eleventh: Blauser singled. Berryhill reached first on an error. Hunter grounded out scoring Blauser.

World Series Results, 1903-1992

1903 Boston AL 5, Pittsburgh NL 3
1904 No series
1905 New York NL 4, Philadelphia AL 1
1906 Chicago AL 4, Chicago NL 2
1907 Chicago NL 4, Detroit AL 0, 1 tie
1908 Chicago NL 4, Detroit AL 1
1909 Pittsburgh NL 4, Detroit AL 3
1910 Philadelphia AL 4, Chicago NL 1
1911 Philadelphia AL 4, New York NL 2
1912 Boston AL 4, New York NL 3, 1 tie
1913 Philadelphia AL 4, New York NL 1
1914 Boston NL 4, Philadelphia AL 0
1915 Boston AL 4, Philadelphia NL 1
1916 Boston AL 4, Brooklyn NL 1
1917 Chicago AL 4, New York NL 2
1918 Boston AL 4, Chicago NL 2
1919 Cincinnati NL 5, Chicago AL 3
1920 Cleveland AL 5, Brooklyn NL 2
1921 New York NL 5, New York AL 3
1922 New York NL 4, New York AL 0, 1 tie
1923 New York AL 4, New York NL 2
1924 Washington AL 4, New York NL 3
1925 Pittsburgh NL 4, Washington AL 3
1926 St. Louis NL 4, New York AL 3
1927 New York AL 4, Pittsburgh NL 0
1928 New York AL 4, St. Louis NL 0
1929 Philadelphia AL 4, Chicago NL 1
1930 Philadelphia AL 4, St. Louis NL 2
1931 St. Louis NL 4, Philadelphia AL 3
1932 New York AL 4, Chicago NL 0
1933 New York NL 4, Washington AL 1
1934 St. Louis NL 4, Detroit AL 3
1935 Detroit AL 4, Chicago NL 2
1936 New York AL 4, New York NL 2
1937 New York AL 4, New York NL 1
1938 New York AL 4, Chicago NL 0
1939 New York AL 4, Cincinnati NL 0
1940 Cincinnati NL 4, Detroit AL 3
1941 New York AL 4, Brooklyn NL 1
1942 St. Louis NL 4, New York AL 1
1943 New York AL 4, St. Louis NL 1
1944 St. Louis NL 4, St. Louis AL 2
1945 Detroit AL 4, Chicago NL 3
1946 St. Louis NL 4, Boston AL 3
1947 New York AL 4, Brooklyn NL 3
1948 Cleveland AL 4, Boston NL 2
1949 New York AL 4, Brooklyn NL 1
1950 New York AL 4, Philadelphia NL 0
1951 New York AL 4, New York NL 2
1952 New York AL 4, Brooklyn NL 3
1953 New York AL 4, Brooklyn NL 2
1954 New York NL 4, Cleveland AL 0
1955 Brooklyn NL 4, New York AL 3
1956 New York AL 4, Brooklyn NL 3
1957 Milwaukee NL 4, New York AL 3
1958 New York AL 4, Milwaukee NL 3
1959 Los Angeles NL 4, Chicago AL 2
1960 Pittsburgh NL 4, New York AL 3
1961 New York AL 4, Cincinnati NL 1
1962 New York AL 4, San Francisco NL 3
1963 Los Angeles NL 4, New York AL 0
1964 St. Louis NL 4, New York AL 3
1965 Los Angeles NL 4, Minnesota AL 3
1966 Baltimore AL 4, Los Angeles NL 0
1967 St. Louis NL 4, Boston AL 3
1968 Detroit AL 4, St. Louis NL 3
1969 New York NL 4, Baltimore AL 1
1970 Baltimore AL 4, Cincinnati NL 1
1971 Pittsburgh NL 4, Baltimore AL 3
1972 Oakland AL 4, Cincinnati NL 3
1973 Oakland AL 4, New York NL 3
1974 Oakland AL 4, Los Angeles NL 1
1975 Cincinnati NL 4, Boston AL 3
1976 Cincinnati NL 4, New York AL 0
1977 New York AL 4, Los Angeles NL 2
1978 New York AL 4, Los Angeles NL 2
1979 Pittsburgh NL 4, Baltimore AL 3
1980 Philadelphia NL 4, Kansas City AL 2
1981 Los Angeles NL 4, New York AL 2
1982 St. Louis NL 4, Milwaukee AL 3
1983 Baltimore AL 4, Philadelphia NL 1
1984 Detroit AL 4, San Diego NL 1
1985 Kansas City AL 4, St. Louis NL 3
1986 New York NL 4, Boston AL 3
1987 Minnesota AL 4, St. Louis NL 3
1988 Los Angeles NL 4, Oakland AL 1
1989 Oakland AL 4, San Francisco NL 0
1990 Cincinnati NL 4, Oakland AL 0
1991 Minnesota AL 4, Atlanta NL 3
1992 Toronto AL 4, Atlanta NL 2

World Series MVPs

1955 Johnny Podres, Brooklyn (NL)
1956 Don Larsen, New York (AL)
1957 Lew Burdette, Milwaukee (NL)
1958 Bob Turley, New York (AL)
1959 Larry Sherry, Los Angeles (NL)
1960 Bobby Richardson, New York (AL)
1961 Whitey Ford, New York (AL)
1962 Ralph Terry, New York (AL)
1963 Sandy Koufax, Los Angeles (NL)
1964 Bob Gibson, St. Louis (NL)
1965 Sandy Koufax, Los Angeles (NL)
1966 Frank Robinson, Baltimore (AL)
1967 Bob Gibson, St. Louis (NL)
1968 Mickey Lolich, Detroit (AL)
1969 Donn Clendenon, New York (NL)
1970 Brooks Robinson, Baltimore (AL)
1971 Roberto Clemente, Pittsburgh (NL)
1972 Gene Tenace, Oakland (AL)
1973 Reggie Jackson, Oakland (AL)
1974 Rollie Fingers, Oakland (AL)
1975 Pete Rose, Cincinnati (NL)
1976 Johnny Bench, Cincinnati (NL)
1977 Reggie Jackson, New York (AL)
1978 Bucky Dent, New York (AL)
1979 Willie Stargell, Pittsburgh (NL)
1980 Mike Schmidt, Philadelphia (NL)
1981 Ron Cey, Pedro Guerrero, Steve Yeager, Los Angeles (NL)
1982 Darrell Porter, St. Louis (NL)
1983 Rick Dempsey, Baltimore (AL)
1984 Alan Trammell, Detroit (AL)
1985 Bret Saberhagen, Kansas City (AL)
1986 Ray Knight, New York (NL)
1987 Frank Viola, Minnesota (AL)
1988 Orel Hershiser, Los Angeles (NL)
1989 Dave Stewart, Oakland (AL)
1990 Jose Rijo, Cincinnati (NL)
1991 Jack Morris, Minnesota (AL)
1992 Pat Borders, Toronto (AL)

All-Time Major League Leaders

(Includes 1992 season)

Games		At Bats		Runs Batted In		Stolen Bases Since 1898	
Pete Rose	3562	Pete Rose	14,043	Hank Aaron	2297	Rickey Henderson	1042
Carl Yastrzemski	3308	Hank Aaron	12,364	Babe Ruth	2204	Lou Brock	938
Hank Aaron	3298	Carl Yastrzemski	11,988	Lou Gehrig	1990	Ty Cobb	892
Ty Cobb	3033	Ty Cobb	11,429	Ty Cobb	1961	Eddie Collins	742
Stan Musial	3026	Stan Musial	10,972	Stan Musial	1951	Max Carey	738
Willie Mays	2992	Willie Mays	10,881	Jimmie Foxx	1922	Tim Raines	730
Rusty Staub	2951	Brooks Robinson	10,654	Willie Mays	1903	Honus Wagner	703
Brooks Robinson	2896	Robin Yount	10,554	Mel Ott	1860	Joe Morgan	689
Al Kaline	2834	Honus Wagner	10,427	Carl Yastrzemski	1844	Willie Wilson	660
Eddie Collins	2826	Lou Brock	10,332	Ted Williams	1839	Bert Campaneris	649

Runs		Hits		Strikeouts		Shutouts	
Ty Cobb	2245	Pete Rose	4256	Nolan Ryan	5668	Walter Johnson	110
Hank Aaron	2174	Ty Cobb	4191	Steve Carlton	4136	Grover C. Alexander	90
Babe Ruth	2174	Hank Aaron	3771	Bert Blyleven	3701	Christy Mathewson	83
Pete Rose	2165	Stan Musial	3630	Tom Seaver	3640	Cy Young	77
Willie Mays	2062	Tris Speaker	3515	Don Sutton	3574	Eddie Plank	69
Stan Musial	1949	Honus Wagner	3430	Gaylord Perry	3534	Warren Spahn	63
Lou Gehrig	1888	Carl Yastrzemski	3419	Walter Johnson	3508	Mordecai Brown	63
Tris Speaker	1881	Eddie Collins	3309	Phil Niekro	3340	Tom Seaver	61
Mel Ott	1859	Willie Mays	3283	Ferguson Jenkins	3192	Nolan Ryan	61
Frank Robinson	1829	Nap Lejoie	3252	Bob Gibson	3117	Bert Blyleven	60

All-Time Home Run Leaders

Player	HR	Player	HR	Player	HR	Player	HR
Hank Aaron	755	Ted Williams	521	Dave Kingman	442	Dale Murphy	398
Babe Ruth	714	Willie McCovey	521	Dave Winfield	432	Graig Nettles	390
Willie Mays	660	Ed Mathews	512	Billy Williams	426	Johnny Bench	389
Frank Robinson	586	Ernie Banks	512	Eddie Murray	414	Dwight Evans	385
Harmon Killebrew	573	Mel Ott	511	Darrell Evans	414	Frank Howard	382
Reggie Jackson	563	Lou Gehrig	493	Duke Snider	407	Jim Rice	382
Mike Schmidt	548	Stan Musial	475	Al Kaline	399	Orlando Cepeda	379
Mickey Mantle	536	Willie Stargell	475	Andre Dawson	399	Tony Perez	379
Jimmy Foxx	534	Carl Yastrzemski	452				

Players With 3,000 Major League Hits

Robin Yount of the Milwaukee Brewers and George Brett of the Kansas City Royals became the 17th and 18th players to record 3,000 major league hits in 1992.

Player	Hits	Player	Hits	Player	Hits
Pete Rose	4,256	Carl Yastrzemski	3,419	Rod Carew	3,053
Ty Cobb	4,191	Eddie Collins	3,309	Robin Yount	3,025
Hank Aaron	3,771	Willie Mays	3,283	Lou Brock	3,023
Stan Musial	3,630	Nap Lajoie	3,252	Al Kaline	3,007
Tris Speaker	3,515	Paul Waner	3,152	George Brett	3,005
Honus Wagner	3,430	Cap Anson	3,081	Roberto Clemente	3,000

Hall of Famers Chosen in First Year of Eligibility

1962 Jackie Robinson, Bob Feller
1966 Ted Williams
1969 Stan Musial
1972 Sandy Koufax
1973 Warren Spahn
1974 Mickey Mantle
1977 Ernie Banks
1979 Willie Mays
1980 Al Kaline
1981 Bob Gibson
1982 Hank Aaron, Frank Robinson
1983 Brooks Robinson
1985 Lou Brock
1986 Willie McCovey
1988 Willie Stargell
1989 Johnny Bench, Carl Yastrzemski
1990 Jim Palmer, Joe Morgan
1992 Tom Seaver

Major League Franchise Shifts and Additions

1953—Boston Braves (N. L.) became Milwaukee Braves.
1954—St. Louis Browns (A. L.) became Baltimore Orioles.
1955—Philadelphia Athletics (A. L.) became Kansas City Athletics.
1958—New York Giants (N. L.) became San Francisco Giants.
1958—Brooklyn Dodgers (N. L.) became Los Angeles Dodgers.
1961—Washington Senators (A. L.) became Minnesota Twins.
1961—Los Angeles Angels (later renamed the California Angels) enfranchised by the American League.
1961—Washington Senators enfranchised by the American League (a new team, replacing the former Washington club, whose franchise was moved to Minneapolis-St. Paul).
1962—Houston Colt .45's (later renamed the Houston Astros) enfranchised by the National League.
1962—New York Mets enfranchised by the National League.
1966—Milwaukee Braves (N. L.) became Atlanta Braves.
1968—Kansas City Athletics (A. L.) became Oakland Athletics.
1969—Two major leagues each added two teams for totals of 12 and split into two divisions. American League additions: Kansas City Royals and Seattle Pilots; National League additions: Montreal Expos and San Diego Padres.
1970—Seattle franchise shifted to Milwaukee. Club was renamed Milwaukee Brewers.
1971—Washington franchise to Dallas-Fort Worth area. Club was renamed Texas Rangers.
1977—Toronto Blue Jays and Seattle Mariners enfranchised by the American League.
1993—Colorado Rockies and Miami Marlins enfranchised by the National League.

NCAA Baseball Champions

1960	Minnesota	1969	Arizona St.	1977	Arizona St.	1985	Miami, Fla.
1961	USC	1970	USC	1978	USC	1986	Arizona
1962	Michigan	1971	USC	1979	Cal. St.-Fullerton	1987	Stanford
1963	USC	1972	USC	1980	Arizona	1988	Stanford
1964	Minnesota	1973	USC	1981	Arizona St.	1989	Wichita St.
1965	Arizona St.	1974	USC	1982	Miami, Fla.	1990	Georgia
1966	Ohio St.	1975	Texas	1983	Texas	1991	LSU
1967	Arizona St.	1976	Arizona	1984	Cal. St.-Fullerton	1992	Pepperdine
1968	USC						

Little League World Series in 1992

The team from the Philippines won the 1992 Little League World Series by defeating the team from Long Beach, Cal., 15-4, at Williamsport, Pa. It was the first Little League World Series title for the Philippines team. Little League baseball stripped the Philippines of their title and awarded the championship to Long Beach, saying the Asian team had used ineligible players.

Ten Most Dramatic Sports Events, Nov. 1991—Oct. 1992

Selected by The World Almanac Sports Staff

—Francisco Cabrera singled with the bases loaded and 2 out in the bottom of the 9th inning of the 7th game of the National League Championship Series, to score 2 runs and give the Atlanta Braves a 3-2 victory over the Pittsburgh Pirates. The hit capped a dramatic comeback by the Braves, who entered the final inning trailing 2-0.

—Christian Laettner sank a 17-foot jumper at the buzzer to give Duke a 104-103 victory in overtime over Kentucky in the East Regional final of the NCAA basketball tournament. The Blue Devils went on to win their 2nd consecutive NCAA championship.

—Carl Lewis won his 3rd consecutive Olympic gold medal in the long jump by beating world record-holder Mike Powell.

—Al Unser Jr. won the Indianapolis 500 auto race in the closest margin in Indy 500 history. His margin of victory was .043 seconds over 2nd-place finisher Scott Goodyear.

—Dave Winfield doubled with 2 out in the eleventh inning of game 6 of the World Series to score 2 runs and give the Toronto Blue Jays a 4-3 victory over the Atlanta Braves. The win gave the Jays their first World Series championship, and the first by a Canadian team.

—Magic Johnson came out of retirement to lead the Western Conference to a 153-113 victory over the Eastern Conference at the National Basketball Association All-Star game. Johnson, who retired because he was infected with HIV, was named the game's most valuable player.

—Robin Yount of the Milwaukee Brewers and George Brett of the Kansas City Royals became the 17th and 18th players to get 3,000 major league hits.

—The Washington Redskins defeated the Buffalo Bills in Super Bowl XXVI, 37-24. It was the 3rd Super Bowl victory for the Redskins and their coach, Joe Gibbs.

—Art Monk set a new National Football League record when he made the 820th reception of his career. The Washington Redskins receiver broke the record held by Steve Largent.

—Martina Navratilova won her 158th pro tennis tournament by defeating Jana Novotna in the finals of the Virginia Slims of Chicago. The victory broke the record for both men and women.

VITAL STATISTICS

Source: National Center for Health Statistics, U.S. Department of Health and Human Services

Births

According to provisional statistics for the first quarter of 1992, there were 999,000 live births, 2 percent more than the estimated number reported for the same 3-month period in 1991 (982,000). The birth rate declined by 1 percent, from 15.8 in the first quarter of 1991 to 15.7 in the first quarter of 1992.

During the 12 months ending with March 1992, there were an estimated 4,127,000 live births, 1 percent less than reported for the comparable period ending a year earlier (4,173,000). The birth rate was 16.2, 2 percent below the rate for the 12 months ending with March 1991 (16.6).

Marriages

The total number of marriages for the first quarter of 1992 was 421,000, an increase of 2 percent from the number for the comparable period in 1991 (411,000). The marriage rate was 6.6 per 1,000 population, the same as in the first quarter of 1991.

During the 12 months ending with March 1992, an estimated 2,382,000 couples married, a decrease of 2 percent from the previous 12-month period. The 12-month marriage rate was 9.4, down 3 percent from the rate for the 12 months ending with March 1991.

Divorces

A total of 297,000 couples divorced during the first quarter of 1992, a 5-percent increase over the first quarter of 1991 (284,000). The divorce rate was 4.7 per 1,000 population, an increase of 2 percent over the first quarter of 1991 (4.6).

During the 12 months ending with March 1992, an estimated 1,200,000 couples divorced, up from 1,168,000 during the 12 months ending March 1991, and the rate rose from 4.6 to 4.7 per 1,000 population.

Deaths

According to provisional statistics, there were 586,000 deaths during the first quarter of 1992, 4 percent more than for the first quarter of 1991 (565,000). The death rate was 9.2 per 1,000 population, 1 percent higher than the Jan.-March 1991 rate. Among the deaths for the first quarter of 1992 were 9,400 deaths at ages under 1 year, yielding an infant mortality rate of 9.3 per 1,000 live births, 2 percent lower than the rate of 9.5 for the first quarter of 1991.

The death rate for the 12 months ending with March 1992 (8.6 deaths per 1,000 population) was 1 percent higher than the comparable 12-month period a year earlier. The infant mortality rate for this 12-month-period was 8.8 per 1,000 live births, 3 percent lower than the rate of 9.1 for the 12 months ending with March 1991.

Provisional Statistics
12 months ending with March

	Number		Rate*	
	1992	1991	1992	1991
Live births	4,127,000	4,173,000	16.2	16.6
Deaths	2,185,000	2,139,000	8.6	8.5
Natural increase.	1,942,000	2,034,000	7.6	8.1
Marriages	2,382,000	2,433,000	9.4	9.7
Divorces	1,200,000	1,168,000	4.7	4.6
Infant deaths. . .	36,000	37,800	8.8	9.1

* Per 1,000 population **Note:** Figures include revisions.

Annual Report for the Year 1991 (Provisional Statistics)

Highlights

Provisional data for 1991 show that both the birth rate and the death rate per 1,000 population were lower than the comparable rates for the previous year. Between 1990 and 1991 a decrease was also observed for the infant mortality rate per 1,000 live births. The marriage rate per 1,000 population decreased from the rate for 1990, and the divorce rate remained unchanged.

Births

An estimated 4,111,000 lives births occurred in 1991, a decline of 2 percent from the 4,179,000 live births in 1990. The birth rate of 16.2 was 3 percent lower than the rate of 16.7 for the preceding year. The fertility rate for 1991 was 69.8, 2 percent lower than the rate for 1990 (71.1).

Deaths

The provisional count of deaths during 1991 was 2,165,000, about 3,000 more than in the previous year. The death rate of 8.5 per 1,000 population was 1 percent lower than the rate of 8.6 for 1990. About 36,500 of these deaths were to infants under 1 year of age. The infant mortality rate was 8.9 per 1,000 live births, 2 percent lower than the rate of 9.1 for 1990.

Natural Increase

As a result of natural increase, the excess of births over deaths, an estimated 1,946,000 persons were added to the population in 1991. This rate was 7.7, 5 percent lower than the rate of 8.1 for 1990. The decline in the rate of natural increase is due to a larger decrease in the birth rate than in the death rate.

Marriages

An estimated 2,371,000 marriages were performed in 1991, a 3-percent decline from the number in 1990 (2,448,000). The marriage rate for the 12-month period was 4 percent lower in 1991 (9.4) than in 1990 (9.8).

Divorces

The number of divorces granted in 1991 (1,187,000) was 1 percent higher than in 1990 (1,175,000). Despite the slight increase, the divorce rate for the 12-month period was 4.7 in both 1990 and 1991.

Births and Deaths in the U.S.

Refers only to events occurring within the U.S., including Alaska and Hawaii beginning in 1960. Excludes fetal deaths. Rates per 1,000 population enumerated as of April 1 for 1960, and 1970; estimated as of July 1 for all other years. Beginning 1970 excludes births and deaths occurring to nonresidents of the U.S.

	Births		Deaths	
Year	Total number	Rate	Total number	Rate
1955.	4,097,000	25.0	1,528,717	9.3
1960.	4,257,850	23.7	1,711,982	9.5
1965.	3,760,358	19.4	1,828,136	9.4
1970.	3,731,386	18.4	1,921,031	9.5
1975.	3,144,198	14.6	1,892,879	8.8
1980.	3,612,258	15.9	1,986,000	8.7
1985.	3,749,000	15.7	2,084,000	8.7
1990.	4,179,000	16.7	2,162,000	8.6
1991.	4,111,000	16.2	2,165,000	8.5

Births and Deaths by States and Regions, 1990-1991

Source: National Center for Health Statistics

Area	Live births 1991	Live births 1990	Deaths 1991	Deaths 1990
New England	**172,966[1]**	**202,889**	**101,459[1]**	**115,615**
Maine	—	16,908	—	11,160
New Hampshire	16,060	17,199	8,513	8,447
Vermont	7,712	8,282	4,541	4,601
Massachusetts	86,321	93,222	51,366	55,092
Rhode Island	14,591	14,963	9,294	9,380
Connecticut	48,282	52,315	27,745	26,935
Middle Atlantic	**460,984[1]**	**596,179**	**360,314**	**361,378**
New York	292,400	301,209	166,795	168,004
New Jersey	—	124,082	69,983	70,446
Pennsylvania	168,584	170,888	123,536	122,928
East North Central	**468,440[1]**	**678,268**	**273,072[1]**	**374,190**
Ohio	158,638	164,619	99,104	99,049
Indiana	84,707	85,227	50,247	49,940
Illinois	—	196,107	—	103,478
Michigan	153,359	159,346	79,972	78,979
Wisconsin	71,736	72,969	43,749	42,744
West North Central	**262,368**	**273,175**	**164,055**	**163,764**
Minnesota	67,020	68,378	35,270	34,802
Iowa	36,011	39,127	25,906	28,220
Missouri	77,991	81,157	53,461	51,558
North Dakota	9,071	9,517	5,648	5,657
South Dakota	11,042	10,912	6,594	6,394
Nebraska	23,933	24,010	14,665	14,785
Kansas	37,300	40,074	22,511	22,348
South Atlantic	**689,008**	**704,348**	**396,237**	**394,868**
Delaware	11,175	11,282	5,880	5,803
Maryland	84,396	83,664	37,982	39,132
District of Columbia	9,967	10,928	6,543	7,518
Virginia	96,610	99,942	49,151	48,374
West Virginia	22,195	22,202	19,801	19,502
North Carolina	102,442	104,715	58,909	57,532
South Carolina	57,742	59,075	29,983	29,891
Georgia	110,024	112,899	52,708	52,617
Florida	194,457	199,641	135,280	134,499
East South Central	**232,052**	**242,587**	**144,284**	**147,315**
Kentucky	54,913	57,791	35,281	35,544
Tennessee	73,104	72,747	45,351	45,228
Alabama	60,513	68,200	38,027	41,289
Mississippi	43,522	43,849	25,625	25,254
West South Central	**482,024**	**480,815**	**221,795**	**218,824**
Arkansas	34,588	36,109	24,230	24,922
Louisiana	74,562	71,704	38,290	36,832
Oklahoma	47,312	47,250	30,349	30,314
Texas[2]	325,562	325,752	128,926	126,756
Mountain	**243,405**	**243,123**	**99,248**	**97,162**
Montana	11,544	11,758	7,071	6,964
Idaho	17,233	16,594	7,789	7,603
Wyoming	6,801	6,984	3,167	3,248
Colorado	53,968	52,913	22,334	21,545
New Mexico	28,160	28,654	11,116	10,934
Arizona	67,656	68,749	29,329	28,653
Utah	35,070	36,216	9,199	9,325
Nevada	22,973	21,255	9,243	8,890
Pacific	**755,480**	**772,563**	**290,482**	**285,881**
Washington	75,734	78,106	37,682	36,525
Oregon	42,793	44,408	25,205	25,725
California[3]	605,694	617,989	218,735	214,692
Alaska	11,245	11,647	2,145	2,198
Hawaii	20,014	20,413	6,715	6,741

(1) Excludes figures for State(s) shown below as not available. (2) Beginning with data for February 1991, figures include adjustments for varying length of reporting period. (3) Figures for all years include adjustments for varying length of reporting period. **Note:** Data for all years are provisional estimates by State of residence rather than by State of occurrence: therefore, figures for 1990 differ from those published previously.

Deaths Under 1 Year and Infant Mortality Rates, for 10 Selected Causes, 1990-91

Source: National Center for Health Statistics, U.S. Dept. of Health and Human Services

Age and cause of death	1991 Number	1991 Rate	1990 Number	1990 Rate
Total, under 1 year	**36,500**	**892.8**	**38,100**	**908.0**
Under 28 days	22,660	554.7	23,920	570.2
28 days to 11 months	13,810	338.1	14,240	339.5
Certain gastrointestinal diseases	320	7.8	200	4.8
Pneumonia and influenza	620	15.2	590	14.1
Congenital anomalies	7,580	185.6	8,510	202.9
Disorders relating to short gestation and unspecified low birthweight	4,480	109.7	3,930	93.7
Birth trauma	160	3.9	170	4.1
Intrauterine hypoxia and birth asphyxia	720	17.6	790	18.8
Respiratory distress syndrome	2,310	56.5	2,460	58.6
Other conditions originating in the prenatal period	8,670	212.2	9,620	229.3
Sudden infant death syndrome	4,420	108.2	4,980	118.7
All other causes	7,180	175.8	6,910	164.7

Notes: Data are provisional, estimated from a 10-percent sample of deaths. Rates on an annual basis per 100,000 live births. Due to rounding of estimates, figures may not add to totals.

Estimated Death Rates for Selected Causes, 1990-91

Source: Natl. Center for Health Statistics, U.S. Depart. of Health and Human Services

Cause of death	Rate* 1990	Rate*p 1991
All causes	**862.1**	**851.6**
Viral hepatitis	0.7	0.7
Tuberculosis, all forms	0.7	0.6
Septicemia	7.9	7.6
Syphilis	*	0.0
All other infectious and parasitic diseases	12.4	13.8
Malignant neoplasms, including neoplasms of lymphatic and hematopoietic tissues	202.5	204.0
Diabetes mellitus	18.9	19.5
Meningitis	0.5	0.3
Major cardiovascular diseases	365.7	357.3
Diseases of heart	288.1	281.1
Rheumatic fever and rheumatic heart disease	2.5	2.4
Hypertensive heart disease	8.4	8.4
Ischemic heart disease	194.7	187.8
Acute myocardial infarction	96.2	91.7
All other forms of heart disease	76.8	76.3
Hypertension	3.4	3.3
Cerebrovascular diseases	57.5	56.3
Artherosclerosis	7.0	6.7
Other diseases of arteries, arterioles, and capillaries	9.7	9.8
Acute bronchitis and bronchiolitis	0.2	0.2
Influenza and pneumonia	31.4	29.2
Influenza	0.8	0.3
Pneumonia	30.6	28.9
Chronic obstructive pulmonary diseases	35.6	34.7
Chronic and unspecified bronchitis	1.2	1.4
Emphysema	6.7	6.4
Asthma	1.8	1.7
Ulcer of stomach and duodenum	2.3	2.4
Hernia and intestinal obstruction	2.2	2.3
Cirrhosis and chronic liver disease	10.1	9.7
Cholelithiasis, cholecystitis, and cholangitis	1.2	1.2
Nephritis, nephrosis and nephrotic syn.	8.5	8.9
Infections of kidney	0.5	0.5
Hyperplasia of prostate	0.1	0.1
Congenital anomalies	5.3	4.7
Certain conditions in perinatal period	7.0	6.6
Symptoms, signs, ill-defined conditions	14.2	13.6
All other diseases	68.2	68.9
Accidents	36.7	35.3
Motor vehicle accidents	18.7	17.5
Suicide	12.1	11.6
Homicide	9.8	10.4
All other external causes	0.7	0.7

* Per 100,000 population; based on a 10-percent sample of deaths from Jan. through Nov. p = provisional.

Life Expectancy at Birth Among 15 Industrialized Nations

Source: Metropolitan Life Insurance Co.

Rank	Nation (Year)	Total population	Men	Women
1.	Japan (1990)	78.9	75.9	81.8
2.	Iceland (1989-90)	78.0	75.7	80.3
3.	Sweden (1990)	77.6	74.8	80.4
4.	Switzerland (1989-90)	77.4	74.0	80.8
5.	Netherlands (1990)	77.0	73.8	80.1
6.	Australia (1990)	77.0	73.9	80.0
7.	Norway (1990)	76.6	73.4	79.8
8.	Canada (1985-87)	76.4	73.0	79.7
9.	France (1987)	76.2	72.0	80.3
10.	Germany, F.R. (1986-88)	75.5	72.2	78.7
11.	United States (1990*)	75.4	72.0	78.8
12.	Finland (1989)	75.0	70.9	78.9
13.	Denmark (1989-90)	74.9	72.0	77.7
14.	United Kingdom (1985-87)	74.8	71.9	77.6
15.	New Zealand (1987-89)	74.6	71.6	77.6

* = provisional

Life Expectancy in U.S. at Selected Ages

Source: Metropolitan Life Insurance Co.; 1991 estimates.

Age	Total	Men	Women
0	75.4	72.0	78.8
15	61.4	58.0	64.7
25	52.0	48.8	55.0
35	42.6	39.7	45.4
45	33.5	30.8	36.0
55	24.9	22.4	27.0
65	17.3	15.2	19.0
75	10.9	9.3	12.0
85	6.1	5.2	6.5

Ownership of Life Insurance in the U.S. and Assets of U.S. Life Insurance Companies

Source: American Council of Life Insurance

Legal Reserve Life Insurance Companies (millions of dollars)

	Purchases of life insurance				Insurance in force					
Year	Ordinary	Group	Industrial	Total	Ordinary	Group	Industrial	Credit	Total	Assets
1940	6,689	691	3,350	10,730	79,346	14,938	20,866	380	115,530	30,802
1950	17,326	6,068	5,402	28,796	149,116	47,793	33,415	3,844	234,168	64,020
1960	52,883	14,645	6,880	74,408	341,881	175,903	39,563	29,101	586,448	119,576
1965	83,485	51,385*	7,296	142,166*	499,638	308,078	39,818	53,020	900,554	158,884
1970	122,820	63,690*	6,612	193,122*	734,730	551,357	38,644	77,392	1,402,123	207,254
1975	188,003	95,190*	6,729	289,922*	1,083,421	904,695	39,423	112,032	2,139,571	289,304
1980	385,575	183,418	3,609	572,602	1,760,474	1,579,355	35,994	165,215	3,541,038	479,210
1985	910,944	319,503	722	1,231,169	3,247,289	2,561,595	28,250	215,973	6,053,107	825,901
1986	933,592	374,741*	418	1,308,751*	3,658,203	2,801,049	27,168	233,859	6,720,279	937,551
1987	986,660	365,529	324	1,352,513	4,139,071	3,043,782	26,668	242,977	7,452,498	1,044,459
1988	995,686	410,848	320	1,406,854	4,511,608	3,232,080	25,456	251,015	8,020,159	1,166,870
1989	1,020,719	420,707	252	1,441,678	4,939,964	3,469,498	24,446	260,107	8,694,015	1,299,756
1990	1,069,660	459,271	220	1,529,151	5,366,982	3,753,506	24,071	248,038	9,392,597	1,408,402
1991	1,041,508	573,953*	198	1,615,659	5,677,777	4,057,606	22,475	228,478	9,986,336	1,551,201

* Includes Servicemen's Group Life Insurance $27.8 billion in 1965, $17.1 billion in 1970, $1.7 billion in 1975, $45.6 billion in 1981, $51.0 billion in 1986, and $166.7 billion in 1991, as well as $84.4 billion of Federal Employees' Group Life Insurance in 1981 and $10.8 billion in 1986.

Marriages, Divorces, and Rates in the U.S.

Source: National Center for Health Statistics

Data refer only to events occurring within the United States, including Alaska and Hawaii beginning with 1960. Rates per 1,000 population.

Year	Marriages[1] No.	Marriages[1] Rate	Divorces[2] No.	Divorces[2] Rate	Year	Marriages[1] No.	Marriages[1] Rate	Divorces[2] No.	Divorces[2] Rate
1895	620,000	8.9	40,387	0.6	1950	1,667,231	11.1	385,144	2.6
1900	709,000	9.3	55,751	0.7	1955	1,531,000	9.3	377,000	2.3
1905	842,000	10.0	67,976	0.8	1960	1,523,000	8.5	393,000	2.2
1910	948,166	10.3	83,045	0.9	1965	1,800,000	9.3	479,000	2.5
1915	1,007,595	10.0	104,298	1.0	1970	2,158,802	10.6	708,000	3.5
1920	1,274,476	12.0	170,505	1.6	1975	2,152,662	10.0	1,036,000	4.8
1925	1,188,334	10.3	175,449	1.5	1980	2,413,000	10.6	1,182,000	5.2
1930	1,126,856	9.2	195,961	1.6	1985	2,425,000	10.2	1,187,000	5.0
1935	1,327,000	10.4	218,000	1.7	1990	2,448,000	9.8	1,175,000	4.7
1940	1,595,879	12.1	264,000	2.0	1991	2,433,000	9.7	1,168,000	4.6
1945	1,612,992	12.2	485,000	3.5[3]					

(1) Includes estimates and marriage licenses for some states for all years. (2) Includes reported annulments. (3) Divorce rates for 1945 based on population including armed forces overseas.

Median Age at First Marriage, 1890-1991

Source: Bureau of the Census

In 1890, the estimated median age at first marriage was 26.1 years for men and 22.0 years for women. At that time, a decline in the median age at first marriage began that did not end until 1956, when the median reached a low of 20.1 years for women and 22.5 years for men. The 66-year decline was reversed between 1956 and 1990, as the median returned to the 1890 level of 26.1 years for men and an even higher 23.6 median for women. In 1991, both the men's and women's median continued to rise.

Year	Men	Women	Year	Men	Women
1890	26.1	22.0	1960	22.8	20.3
1900	25.9	21.9	1965	22.8	20.6
1910	25.1	21.6	1970	23.2	20.8
1920	24.6	21.2	1975	23.5	21.1
1930	24.3	21.3	1980	24.7	22.0
1940	24.3	21.5	1985	25.5	23.3
1950	22.8	20.3	1990	26.1	23.9
1955	22.6	20.2	1991	26.3	24.1

Percent of Population Never Married, 1970-1991

Source: Bureau of the Census, U.S. Dept. of Commerce; as of March; persons 18 yrs. old and over.

Age	Male 1970	Male 1980	Male 1990	Male 1991	Female 1970	Female 1980	Female 1990	Female 1991
Total	**18.9**	**23.8**	**25.8**	**26.1**	**13.7**	**17.1**	**18.9**	**19.3**
18 to 19 years old	92.8	94.3	96.8	98.8	75.8	82.8	90.3	90.4
20 to 24 years old	54.7	68.8	79.3	79.7	35.8	50.2	62.8	64.1
25 to 29 years old	19.1	33.1	45.2	46.7	10.5	20.9	31.1	32.3
30 to 34 years old	9.4	15.9	27.0	27.3	6.2	9.5	16.4	18.7
35 to 39 years old	7.2	7.8	14.7	17.6	5.4	6.2	10.4	11.7
40 to 44 years old	6.3	7.1	10.5	10.0	4.9	4.8	8.0	8.8
45 to 54 years old	7.5	6.1	6.3	7.4	4.9	4.7	5.0	5.6
55 to 64 years old	7.8	5.3	5.8	5.9	6.8	4.5	3.9	3.7
65 years old and over	7.5	4.9	4.2	4.3	7.7	5.9	4.9	5.1
65 to 74 years old	8.0	5.2	4.7	4.7	7.8	5.6	4.8	4.8
74 years old and over	6.6	4.2	3.4	3.7	7.5	6.3	5.4	5.5

Types of Households, 1970-1990

Source: Bureau of the Census; U.S. Dept. of Commerce

	1970	1990	1970-90
Dual-earner married couples with children			
Percent of all households	20%	19%	−1%
Average household income*	$38,700	$49,600	$10,900
Other married couples with children			
Percent of all households	21%	8%	−13%
Average household income*	$35,600	$40,000	$4,400
Childless married couples with householders under age 45			
Percent of all households	6%	7%	1%
Average household income*	$33,100	$48,300	$15,200
Childless married couples with householders aged 45 to 64			
Percent of all households	15%	13%	−2%
Average household income*	$39,500	$53,800	$14,300
Childless married couples with householders aged 65 or older			
Percent of all households	9%	9%	0%
Average household income*	$20,900	$32,300	$11,400
Single parents			
Percent of all households	6%	9%	3%
Average household income*	$17,500	$21,400	$3,900
Childless singles under age 45			
Percent of all households	3%	9%	6%
Average household income*	$20,300	$25,200	$4,900
Childless singles aged 45 or older			
Percent of all households	14%	16%	2%
Average household income*	$11,900	$17,500	$5,600
Other multiple-member (shared households)			
Percent of all households	6%	10%	4%
Average household income*	$27,200	$36,900	$9,700

* = Mean income for 1969 and 1989, in 1989 dollars.

Divorced Persons Per 1,000 Married Persons With Spouse Present, 1970-1991

Source: Bureau of the Census, U.S. Dept. of Commerce; as of March; 1970 and 1975, persons 14 yrs. old and over; from 1980, 15 yrs. old and over.

Year	Total	Male	Female
1970	47	35	60
1975	69	54	84
1980	100	79	120
1985	128	103	153
1988	133	110	156
1989	138	114	161
1990	142	118	166
1991	148	124	172

Sex and Year		Race		Age			
		White	Black	15 to 29 years	30 to 44 years	45 to 64 years	65 years old and over
Male:	1970	32	62	28[1]	33	40	32
	1980	74	149	78	104	70	48
	1990	112	208	88	146	124	67
	1991	117	239	94	155	134	61
Female:	1970	56	104	46[1]	61	66	69
	1980	110	258	108	147	112	89
	1990	153	358	112	192	180	127
	1991	159	370	116	189	198	133

(1) 14 to 29 years.

Single-Parent Families, 1970-1991

Source: Bureau of the Census; U.S. Dept. of Commerce

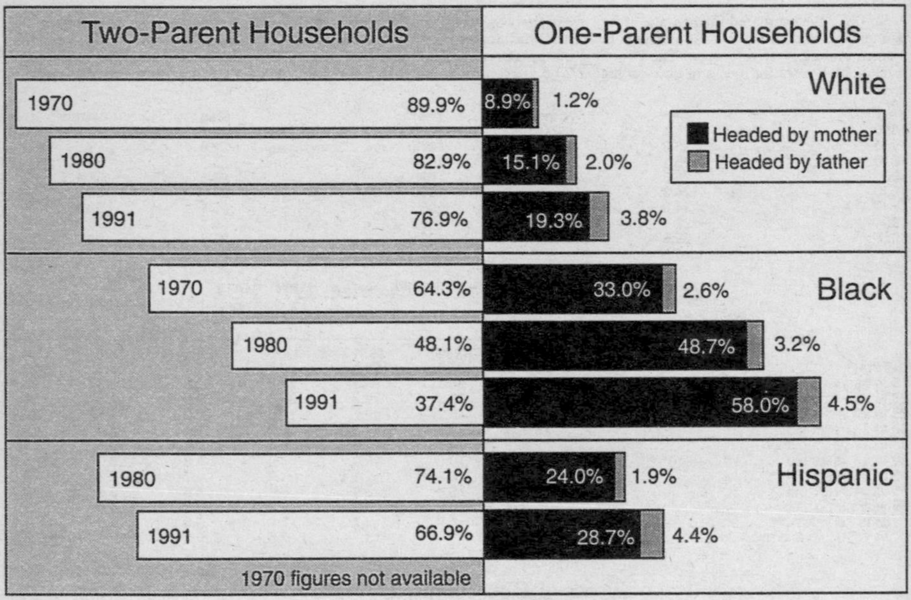

Unmarried Male-Female Couples Sharing a Household, 1991

Source: Bureau of the Census, U.S. Dept. of Commerce; as of March.

(thousands)

Presence of Children and Age of Householder	1980	1990	1991
Unmarried couples	1,589	2,856	3,039
No children under 15 yr.	1,159	1,966	2,077
Some children under 15 yr.	431	891	962
Under 25 yr. old	411	596	587
25-44 yr. old	837	1,775	1,858
45-64 yr. old	221	358	453
65 yr. old and over	119	127	141

Marital Status of Male	Total	Marital Status of Female			
		Never married	Divorced	Widowed	Married husband absent
Total, 1991	3,039	1,658	1,022	184	175
Never married	1,682	1,219	337	53	75
Divorced	1,075	357	593	73	53
Widowed	95	19	25	48	4
Married, wife absent	185	63	67	9	45

Note: "Unmarried couple" = unrelated male & female adult.

Persons Living Alone, 1970-1991

Source: Bureau of the Census, U.S. Dept. of Commerce

Sex and Age	Number of Persons (1,000) 1970	1980	1990	1991	Percent Distribution 1970	1980	1990	1991
Both sexes	**10,851**	**18,296**	**22,999**	**23,590**	**100**	**100**	**100**	**100**
15 to 24 years old[1]	558	1,726	1,210	1,140	5	9	5	5
25 to 34 years old	1,604[2]	4,729[2]	3,972	4,116	15[2]	26[2]	17	17
35 to 44 years old	(2)	(2)	3,138	3,402	(2)	(2)	14	14
45 to 64 years old	3,622	4,514	5,502	5,550	33	25	24	24
65 to 74 years old	2,815	3,851	4,350	4,494	26	21	19	19
75 years old and over	2,258	3,477	4,825	4,887	21	19	21	21
Male	**3,532**	**6,966**	**9,049**	**9,450**	**33**	**38**	**39**	**40**
15 to 24 years old[1]	274	947	674	622	3	5	3	3
25 to 34 years old	933[2]	2,920[2]	2,395	2,491	9[2]	16[2]	10	11
35 to 44 years old	(2)	(2)	1,836	2,008	(2)	(2)	8	9
45 to 64 years old	1,152	1,613	2,203	2,319	11	9	10	10
65 to 74 years old	611	775	1,042	1,096	6	4	5	5
75 years old and over	563	711	901	914	5	4	4	4
Female	**7,319**	**11,330**	**13,950**	**14,141**	**68**	**62**	**61**	**68**
15 to 24 years old[1]	282	779	538	518	3	4	2	2
25 to 34 years old	671[2]	1,809[2]	1,578	1,626	6[2]	10[2]	7	7
35 to 44 years old	(2)	(2)	1,303	1,394	(2)	(2)	6	6
45 to 64 years old	2,470	2,901	3,300	3,232	23	16	14	14
65 to 74 years old	2,204	3,076	3,309	3,397	20	17	14	14
75 years old and over	1,693	2,766	3,924	3,973	16	15	17	17

(1) 1970, persons 14 to 24 years old. (2) Data for persons 35 to 44 years old included with persons 25 to 34 years old.

Black-White Married Couples, 1980-1991

Source: Bureau of the Census, U.S. Dept. of Commerce; as of March; persons 15 yrs. old and over.

Item	Number (1,000) 1980	1990	1991	Percent 1980	1990	1991
Total married couples	**49,714**	**53,258**	**53,227**	**100.0**	**100.0**	**100.0**
Black-White married couples, total	**167**	**211**	**231**	**0.3**	**0.4**	**0.4**
Husband Black, wife White	122	150	156	0.2	0.3	0.3
Wife Black, husband White	45	61	75	0.1	0.1	0.1

Persons 65 Years and Over, 1970-1990

Source: Bureau of the Census, U.S. Dept. of Commerce; as of March, except as noted. Covers civilian noninstitutional population, except 1970 includes institutional population.

Characteristic	Total 1970	1980	1985	1990	Male 1970	1980	1985	1990	Female 1970	1980	1985	1990
Total[1] (million)	**19.9**	**24.2**	**26.8**	**29.6**	**8.3**	**9.9**	**11.0**	**12.3**	**11.5**	**14.2**	**15.8**	**17.2**
White (million)	18.2	21.9	24.2	26.5	7.6	9.0	9.9	11.0	10.6	12.9	14.3	15.4
Black (million)	1.5	2.0	2.2	2.5	0.7	0.8	0.9	1.0	0.9	1.2	1.3	1.5
Percent below poverty level[2]	25.3	15.2	12.4	11.4	20.2	11.1	8.7	7.8	29.2	17.9	15.0	13.9
Percent Distribution												
Marital status:												
Single	7.6	5.5	5.2	4.6	7.5	4.9	5.3	4.2	7.7	5.9	5.1	4.9
Married	51.3	55.4	55.2	56.1	73.1	78.0	77.2	76.5	35.6	39.5	39.9	41.4
Spouse present	49.0	53.6	53.4	54.1	69.9	76.1	75.0	74.2	33.9	37.9	38.3	39.7
Spouse absent	2.3	1.8	1.8	2.0	3.2	1.9	2.2	2.3	1.7	1.7	1.6	1.7
Widowed	38.8	35.7	35.6	34.2	17.1	13.5	13.8	14.2	54.4	51.2	50.7	48.6
Divorced	2.3	3.5	4.0	5.0	2.3	3.6	3.7	5.0	2.3	3.4	4.3	5.1
Family status:												
In families[3]	67.1	67.6	67.3	66.7	79.2	83.0	82.4	81.9	58.5	56.8	56.7	55.8
Nonfamily householders	26.6	31.2	31.1	31.9	14.9	15.7	15.4	16.6	35.2	42.0	42.1	42.8
Secondary individuals	2.1	1.2	1.6	1.4	2.4	1.3	2.2	1.5	1.9	1.1	1.1	1.4
Residents of institutions	4.1	NA	NA	NA	3.6	NA	NA	NA	4.4	NA	NA	NA
Living arrangements:												
Living in household	95.2	99.8	99.6	99.7	95.5	99.9	99.5	99.9	95.0	99.7	99.6	99.5
Living alone	25.5	30.3	30.2	31.0	14.1	14.9	14.7	15.7	33.8	41.0	41.1	42.0
Spouse present	49.0	53.6	53.4	54.1	69.9	76.1	75.0	74.3	33.9	37.9	38.3	39.7
Living with someone else	20.7	15.9	15.9	14.6	11.5	8.9	9.8	9.9	27.4	20.8	20.2	17.8
Not in household[4]	4.8	0.2	0.4	0.3	4.5	0.1	0.5	0.1	5.0	0.3	0.4	0.5
Years of school completed:												
8 years or less	58.3	43.1	35.4	28.5	61.5	45.3	37.2	30.0	56.1	41.6	34.1	27.5
1 to 3 years of high school	13.4	16.2	16.5	16.1	12.6	15.5	15.7	15.7	13.9	16.7	17.0	16.4
4 years of high school	15.7	24.0	29.0	32.9	12.5	21.4	26.4	29.0	18.1	25.8	30.7	35.6
1 to 3 years of college	6.2	8.2	9.8	10.9	5.6	7.5	9.1	10.8	6.7	8.6	10.3	11.0
4 years or more of college	6.3	8.6	9.4	11.6	7.9	10.3	11.5	14.5	5.2	7.4	8.0	9.5
Labor force participation:[5]												
Employed	16.4	12.2	10.4	11.5	25.9	18.4	15.3	15.9	9.4	7.8	7.0	8.4
Unemployed	0.5	0.4	0.3	0.4	0.9	0.6	0.5	0.5	0.3	0.3	0.2	0.3
Not in labor force	83.0	87.5	89.2	88.1	73.2	81.0	84.2	83.6	90.3	91.9	92.7	91.3

NA=Not available. (1) Includes other races, not shown separately. (2) Poverty status based on income in preceding year. (3) Beginning 1980, excludes those living in unrelated subfamilies. (4) In institutions (1970) and other group quarters. (5) Annual averages of monthly figures.

Marital Status of the Population, 1970-1991

Source: Bureau of the Census, U.S. Dept. of Commerce; in millions, except percent. As of March, except as noted. Persons 15 years old and over, except as noted. Excludes members of Armed Forces except those living off post or with their families on post.

Marital Status Race And Hispanic Origin	Total				Male				Female			
	1970	1980	1990	1991	1970	1980	1990	1991	1970	1980	1990	1991
Total[1]	**132.5**	**159.5**	**181.9**	**183.6**	**62.5**	**75.7**	**76.9**	**87.8**	**70.0**	**83.8**	**95.0**	**95.8**
Single	21.4	32.3	40.4	41.5	11.8	18.0	22.4	22.9	9.6	14.3	17.9	18.5
Married	95.0	104.6	112.6	112.7	47.1	51.8	55.8	55.9	47.9	52.8	56.7	56.8
Widowed	11.8	12.7	13.8	13.7	2.1	2.0	2.3	2.4	9.7	10.8	11.5	11.3
Divorced	4.3	9.9	15.1	15.8	1.6	3.9	6.3	6.6	2.7	6.0	8.8	9.2
Percent of total	100.0	100.0	100.0	100.0	100.0	100.0	100.0	100.0	100.0	100.0	100.0	100.0
Single	16.2	20.3	22.2	22.6	18.9	23.8	25.8	26.1	13.7	17.1	18.9	19.3
Married	71.7	65.5	61.9	61.3	75.3	68.4	64.3	63.6	68.5	63.0	59.7	59.3
Widowed	8.9	8.0	7.6	7.4	3.3	2.6	2.7	2.7	13.9	12.8	12.1	11.8
Divorced	3.2	6.2	8.3	8.6	2.5	5.2	7.2	7.5	3.9	7.1	9.3	9.6
Percent standardized for age:[2]												
Single	14.1	16.5	20.6	21.4	16.5	18.7	23.3	24.0	12.1	14.5	18.2	19.0
Married	74.2	69.3	63.7	63.0	77.6	72.9	66.5	65.5	70.8	65.9	61.2	60.6
Widowed	8.3	7.6	6.9	6.7	3.3	2.7	2.7	2.7	13.0	12.1	10.8	10.4
Divorced	3.4	6.6	8.7	9.0	2.6	5.6	7.6	7.8	4.1	7.6	9.8	10.0
White, total	**118.2**	**139.5**	**155.5**	**156.7**	**55.9**	**66.7**	**74.8**	**75.5**	**62.2**	**72.8**	**80.6**	**81.2**
Single	18.4	26.4	31.6	32.2	10.2	15.0	18.0	18.3	8.2	11.4	13.6	13.9
Married	85.8	93.8	99.5	99.8	42.7	46.7	49.5	49.7	43.1	47.1	49.9	50.1
Widowed	10.3	10.9	11.7	11.5	1.7	1.6	1.9	2.0	8.6	9.3	9.8	9.6
Divorced	3.7	8.3	12.6	13.2	1.3	3.4	5.4	5.6	2.3	5.0	7.3	7.6
Percent of total	100.0	100.0	100.0	100.0	100.0	100.0	100.0	100.0	100.0	100.0	100.0	100.0
Single	15.6	18.9	20.3	20.5	18.2	22.5	24.1	24.2	13.2	15.7	16.9	17.1
Married	72.6	67.2	64.0	63.7	76.3	70.0	66.2	65.8	69.3	64.7	61.9	61.8
Widowed	8.7	7.8	7.5	7.4	3.1	2.5	2.6	2.6	13.8	12.8	12.2	11.8
Divorced	3.1	6.0	8.1	8.4	2.4	5.0	7.2	7.4	3.8	6.8	9.0	9.3
Black, total	**13.0**	**16.6**	**20.3**	**20.6**	**5.9**	**7.4**	**9.1**	**9.3**	**7.1**	**9.2**	**11.2**	**11.4**
Single	2.7	5.1	7.1	7.7	1.4	2.5	3.5	3.7	1.2	2.5	3.6	3.9
Married	8.3	8.5	9.3	9.0	3.9	4.1	4.5	4.3	4.4	4.5	4.8	4.7
Widowed	1.4	1.6	1.7	1.8	0.3	0.3	0.3	0.3	1.1	1.3	1.4	1.4
Divorced	0.6	1.4	2.1	2.2	0.2	0.5	0.8	0.9	0.4	0.9	1.3	1.3
Percent of total	100.0	100.0	100.0	100.0	100.0	100.0	100.0	100.0	100.0	100.0	100.0	100.0
Single	20.6	30.5	35.1	37.1	24.3	34.3	38.4	40.2	17.4	27.4	32.5	34.5
Married	64.1	51.4	45.8	43.6	66.9	54.6	49.2	46.7	61.7	48.7	43.0	41.0
Widowed	11.0	9.8	8.5	8.6	5.2	4.2	3.7	3.6	15.8	14.3	12.4	12.7
Divorced	4.4	8.4	10.6	10.8	3.6	7.0	8.8	9.5	5.0	9.5	12.0	11.8
Hispanic,[3] total	**5.9**	**7.9**	**13.6**	**13.9**	**2.8**	**3.8**	**6.7**	**6.9**	**3.0**	**4.1**	**6.8**	**7.0**
Single	1.7	1.9	3.7	3.8	0.9	1.0	2.2	2.2	0.8	0.9	1.5	1.6
Married	3.7	5.2	8.4	8.5	1.8	2.5	4.1	4.2	1.9	2.6	4.3	4.3
Widowed	0.3	0.4	0.5	0.6	0.1	0.1	0.1	0.1	0.2	0.3	0.4	0.5
Divorced	0.2	0.5	1.0	1.0	0.1	0.2	0.4	0.4	0.1	0.3	0.6	0.6
Percent of total	100.0	100.0	100.0	100.0	100.0	100.0	100.0	100.0	100.0	100.0	100.0	100.0
Single	29.3	24.1	27.2	27.3	32.2	27.3	32.1	32.2	26.5	21.1	22.5	22.4
Married	62.4	65.6	61.7	61.1	63.5	67.1	60.9	60.2	61.5	64.3	62.4	61.9
Widowed	4.9	4.4	4.0	4.3	2.0	1.6	1.5	1.5	7.6	7.1	6.5	7.1
Divorced	3.4	5.8	7.0	7.3	2.3	4.0	5.5	6.0	4.4	7.6	8.5	8.6

(1) Includes persons of other races, not shown separately. (2) 1980 age distribution used as standard; standardization improves comparability over time by removing effects of changes in age distribution of population. (3) Hispanic persons may be of any race. **Note:** 1970 data as of April and covers persons 14 years old and over.

Living Arrangements of Young Adults, 1960-1990

Source: Bureau of the Census; U.S. Dept. of Commerce

(in thousands)

Living arrangement	1960	1970	1980	1990	Percent distribution			
					1960	1970	1980	1990
Adults 18-24 Years, Total	**14,718**	**22,357**	**29,122**	**25,310**	**100.0**	**100.0**	**100.0**	**100.0**
Male	**6,842**	**10,398**	**14,278**	**12,450**	**100.0**	**100.0**	**100.0**	**100.0**
Child of householder[1]	3,583	5,641	7,755	7,232	52.4	54.3	54.3	58.1
Family householder or spouse	2,160	3,119	3,041	1,838	31.6	30.0	21.3	14.8
Nonfamily householder	182	563	1,581	1,228	2.7	5.4	11.1	9.9
Other	917	1,075	1,902	2,152	13.4	10.3	13.3	17.3
Female	**7,876**	**11,959**	**14,844**	**12,860**	**100.0**	**100.0**	**100.0**	**100.0**
Child of householder[1]	2,750	4,941	6,336	6,135	34.9	41.3	42.7	47.7
Family householder or spouse	4,026	5,351	5,367	3,793	51.1	44.7	36.2	29.5
Nonfamily householder	172	503	1,195	1,024	2.2	4.2	8.1	8.0
Other	928	1,164	1,946	1,908	11.8	9.7	13.1	14.8
Adults 25-34 Years, Total	**22,483**	**24,556**	**36,796**	**43,240**	**100.0**	**100.0**	**100.0**	**100.0**
Male	**10,896**	**11,929**	**18,107**	**21,462**	**100.0**	**100.0**	**100.0**	**100.0**
Child of householder	1,185	1,129	1,894	3,213	10.9	9.5	10.5	15.0
Family householder or spouse	8,557	9,455	12,024	11,998	78.5	79.3	66.4	55.9
Nonfamily householder	398	775	2,765	3,467	3.7	6.5	15.3	16.2
Other	756	570	1,424	2,784	6.9	4.8	7.9	13.0
Female	**11,587**	**12,637**	**18,689**	**21,779**	**100.0**	**100.0**	**100.0**	**100.0**
Child of householder	853	829	1,300	1,774	7.4	6.6	7.0	8.1
Family householder or spouse	9,981	10,877	14,591	15,966	86.1	86.1	78.1	73.3
Nonfamily householder	244	440	1,646	2,151	2.1	3.5	8.8	9.9
Other	509	491	1,153	1,888	4.4	3.9	6.2	8.7

(1) Child of householder includes unmarried college students living in dormitories.

Living Arrangements of Children, 1970-1991

Source: Bureau of the Census, U.S. Dept. of Commerce; as of March; excludes persons under 18 yrs. who maintained households or family groups.

Race, Hispanic Origin and Year	Number (1,000)	Both parents	Percent Living With— Mother only: Total	Divorced	Married spouse absent	Single[1]	Widowed	Father only	Neither parent
All Races[2]									
1970	69,162	85	11	3	5	1	2	1	3
1980	63,427	77	18	8	6	3	2	2	4
1985	62,475	74	21	9	5	6	2	3	3
1990	64,137	73	22	8	5	7	2	3	3
1991	65,093	72	22	8	6	8	1	3	3
White									
1970	58,790	90	8	3	3	Z	2	1	2
1980	52,242	83	14	7	4	1	2	2	2
1985	50,836	80	16	8	4	2	1	2	2
1990	51,390	79	16	8	4	3	1	3	2
1991	51,918	79	17	8	5	3	1	3	2
Black									
1970	9,422	59	30	5	16	4	4	2	10
1980	9,375	42	44	11	16	13	4	2	12
1985	9,479	40	51	11	12	25	3	3	7
1990	10,018	38	51	10	12	27	2	4	8
1991	10,209	36	54	10	11	31	2	4	7
Hispanic[3]									
1970	4,006[4]	78	NA	NA	NA	NA	NA	NA	NA
1980	5,459	75	20	6	8	4	2	2	4
1985	6,057	68	27	7	11	7	2	2	3
1990	7,174	67	27	7	10	8	2	3	3
1991	7,462	66	27	7	10	9	2	3	4

NA=Not available. Z=Less than .5 percent. (1) Never married. (2) Includes other races not shown separately. (3) Hispanic persons may be of any race. (4) All persons under 18 years old.

Female Family Householders With No Spouse Present, 1980-1991

Source: Bureau of the Census, U.S. Dept. of Commerce; as of March. Persons 15 years old and over.

Characteristic	Unit	White 1980	White 1990	White 1991	Black 1980	Black 1990	Black 1991	Hispanic Origin[1] 1980	Hispanic Origin[1] 1990	Hispanic Origin[1] 1991
Female family householder	1,000	**6,052**	**7,306**	**7,512**	**2,495**	**3,275**	**3,430**	**610**	**1,116**	**1,186**
Percent of all families	Percent	12	13	13	40	44	46	20	23	24
Median age	Years	43.7	42.5	41.9	37.4	37.6	38.5	37.0	38.8	39.0
Marital status:										
Single (never married)	Percent	11	15	17	27	39	41	23	27	27
Married, spouse absent	Percent	17	16	18	29	21	19	32	29	31
Separated	Percent	14	14	14	27	19	16	29	23	24
Other	Percent	3	3	4	2	2	3	4	6	7
Widowed	Percent	33	26	24	22	17	17	15	16	16
Divorced	Percent	40	43	42	22	23	23	30	29	27
Presence of children under 18:										
No own children	Percent	41	43	42	28	32	33	25	33	33
With own children	Percent	59	58	58	72	68	67	75	67	67
1 child	Percent	28	30	30	26	30	28	28	25	26
2 children	Percent	20	19	19	23	22	21	23	22	23
3 children	Percent	7	7	7	11	9	11	15	13	11
4 or more children	Percent	3	2	2	11	7	7	9	6	7
Children per family	Number	1.03	0.95	0.95	1.51	1.26	1.27	1.56	1.37	1.37

(1) Person of Hispanic origin may be of any race.

Percent Changes in Juvenile Arrest Rates* for Crimes Related to Violence, 1990 over 1980

Source: 1991 *Uniform Crime Reports*, FBI

Offense	All Races	White	Black	Other
Violent Crime Total	**27.3**	**43.8**	**19.2**	**−53.4**
Murder	87.3	47.5	145.0	−45.4
Forcible Rape	36.7	85.9	8.5	−66.0
Robbery	−7.5	12.3	−15.6	−67.4
Aggravated Assault	63.7	59.2	88.9	−38.8
Weapon Law Violations	**62.6**	**57.6**	**102.9**	**−48.1**

Offense	All Races	White	Black	Other
Drug Abuse Total	**−20.1**	**−47.6**	**158.6**	**−77.0**
Heroin/Cocaine	713.4	251.1	2,372.9	126.8
Marijuana	−66.0	−66.7	−47.5	−80.1
Synthetic	−26.5	−34.1	144.7	−77.4
Nonnarcotic	−5.5	−34.6	223.3	−87.5

* Arrest rate per 100,000 for the age group 10-17.

Principal Types of Accidental Deaths

Source: National Safety Council

Year	Motor vehicle	Falls	Poison (solid, liquid)	Drowning	Fires, Burns	Injection of Food, Object	Firearms	Poison (gases)
1970	54,633	16,926	3,679	7,860	6,718	2,753	2,406	1,620
1975	45,853	14,896	4,694	8,000	6,071	3,106	2,380	1,577
1980	53,172	13,294	3,089	7,257	5,822	3,249	1,955	1,242
1985	45,901	12,001	4,091	5,316	4,938	3,551	1,649	1,079
1987	48,290	11,733	4,415	5,100	4,710	3,688	1,440	900
1988	48,900	12,200	5,100	4,600	4,700	4,000	1,500	900
1989	46,900	12,400	5,600	4,600	4,400	3,900	1,600	900
1990	46,300	12,400	5,700	5,200	4,300	3,200	1,400	800
1991	43,500	12,200	5,600	4,600	4,200	2,900	1,400	800
Death rates per 100,000 population								
1970	26.8	8.3	1.8	3.9	3.3	1.4	1.2	0.8
1975	21.3	6.9	2.2	3.7	2.8	1.4	1.1	0.7
1980	23.4	5.9	1.4	3.2	2.6	1.4	0.9	0.5
1985	19.2	5.0	1.7	2.2	2.1	1.5	0.7	0.5
1987	19.8	4.8	1.8	2.1	1.9	1.5	0.6	0.4
1988	19.9	5.0	2.1	1.9	1.9	1.6	0.6	0.4
1989	18.9	5.0	2.3	1.9	1.8	1.6	0.6	0.4
1990	8.6	5.0	2.3	2.1	1.7	1.3	0.6	0.3
1991	17.2	4.8	2.2	1.8	1.7	1.1	0.6	0.3

Note: There were 12,800 other accidental deaths in 1991; the most frequently occurring types were medical complications, machinery, air transport, excessive cold, and mechanical suffocation.

Types of Motor Vehicle Accidents, 1991

Source: National Safety Council

Motor-vehicle deaths decreased 7 percent from 1990 to 1991, while mileage increased 1 percent, the number of vehicles increased 1 percent, and the population increased 1 percent. Almost 2 out of 3 deaths in 1991 occurred in places classified as rural. In urban areas, about one fourth of the victims were pedestrians; in rural areas, the victims were mostly occupants of motor vehicles. More than one half of all deaths occurred in night accidents. About 50 percent of all traffic fatalities in 1990 involved an intoxicated or alcohol-impaired driver or non-occupant. Of these 22,083 alcohol-related traffic fatalities, an estimated 17,671 occurred in accidents in which a driver or non-occupant was intoxicated, and 4,412 involved a driver or non-occupant who had been drinking but was not legally intoxicated. Alcohol was also a factor in about 29 percent of serious injury accidents and 7 percent of property damage accidents. The estimated cost of all alcohol-related motor-vehicle accidents in 1991 was about $22.2 billion.

	Death Total	% Change from 1990	Death Rate[1]
All motor vehicle accidents	**43,500**	−7	**17.2**
Urban	15,400	−8	
Rural	28,100	−7	
Collision between motor vehicles	**18,500**	−7	**7.3**
Urban	7,900	−4	
Rural	10,600	−9	
Collision with fixed object	**12,100**	−8	**4.8**
Urban	2,000	−20	
Rural	10,100	−6	
Pedestrian accidents	**7,000**	−8	**2.8**
Urban	4,200	−13	
Rural	2,800	0	

	Death Total	% Change from 1990	Death Rate[1]
Noncollision accidents	**4,500**	−6	**1.8**
Urban	600	0	
Rural	3,900	−7	
Collision with pedalcycle	**800**	0	**0.3**
Urban	600	+20	
Rural	200	−33	
Collision with railroad train	**500**	0	**0.2**
Urban	100	0	
Rural	400	0	
Other collision (animal, animal-drawn vehicles, street cars)	**100**	0	**(2)**

(1) Deaths per 100,000 population. (2) Death rate was less than 0.05.

Types of Motor Vehicles Involved in Accidents, 1991

Source: National Safety Council

Type of Vehicle	In Fatal Accidents		In All Accidents		Percent of Total Vehicle Registrations[1]	No. of Occupant Fatalities
	Number	%	Number	%		
All Types	**57,800**	**100.0%**	**19,500,000**	**100.0%**	**100.0%**	**35,600[2]**
Passenger cars	34,000	58.8	13,720,000	70.3	74.4	23,100
Trucks	18,000	31.2	4,720,000	24.2	23.1	8,870
Light trucks	13,400	23.2	3,980,000	20.4	19.4	8,200
Medium/Heavy trucks	4,600	8.0	740,000	3.8	3.7	670
Farm tractors, equipment	100	0.2	7,000	(3)	(4)	60
Buses, commercial	200	0.3	54,000	0.3	0.1	10
Buses, school	100	0.2	40,000	0.2	0.3	30
Motorcycles	3,200	5.5	230,000	1.2		3,200
Motor scooters, motor bikes . . .	100	0.2	9,000	0.1	2.1	100
Other[4]	2,100	3.6	720,000	3.7	(3)	230

Note: Data were based on reports from 15 state traffic authorities. (1) Percentage figures were based on numbers of vehicles and do not reflect miles traveled or place of travel, both of which affect accident experience. (2) In addition to these occupant fatalities, there were 7,000 pedestrian, 800 pedalcyclist, and 100 other deaths. (3) Less than 0.05%. (4) Includes fire equipment, ambulances, special vehicles, other.

Accidental Deaths and Injuries by Severity of Injury

Source: National Safety Council

The estimated 88,000 accidental deaths in 1991 was the lowest accidental death toll in nearly 70 years. The last year a lower toll was recorded was 1924, when 85,600 lives were lost through accidents. This was especially notable in that the U.S. population was 252 million in 1991, compared with only 114 million in 1924. However, accidents continued to be the leading cause of death for persons aged 1 to 37 years.

1991 Severity of injury	Total*	Motor vehicle	Work	Home	Public
Deaths*	88,000	43,500	9,900	20,500	18,000
Disabling injuries*	8,600,000	1,600,000	1,700,000	3,100,000	2,300,000
Permanent impairments	310,000	130,000	60,000	80,000	50,000
Temporary total disabilities	8,200,000	1,500,000	1,600,000	3,000,000	2,200,000
Certain Costs of Accidental Deaths or Injuries, 1990 (billions)					
Total*	**$177.2**	**$96.1**	**$63.3**	**$22.0**	**$13.9**
Wage loss	45.8	24.5	10.0	7.4	6.3
Medical expense	29.6	6.7	8.7	9.3	5.6
Insurance administration	35.4	27.7	11.0	1.0	0.8

* Duplication between motor vehicle, work, and home are eliminated in the total column.

Home Accident Deaths

Source: National Safety Council

Year	Total home	Falls	Poison (solid, liquid)	Fires burns[2]	Suffo., ingesting object	Suffo., mechanical	Firearms	Poison (gases)	All Other[4]
1950	29,000	14,800	1,300	5,000	(1)	1,600	950	1,250	4,100
1960	28,000	12,300	1,350	6,350	1,850	1,500	1,200	900	2,550
1970	27,000	3,000	5,600	1,800	1,100*	1,400	1,100	3,300	—
1980	22,800	7,100	2,500	4,800	2,000	500	1,100	700	4,100[3]
1990	21,500	6,500	4,700	3,300	2,000	800	800	400	2,400
1991	20,500	6,100	4,400	3,500	1,800	600	800	500	2,200

* Data for this year and subsequent years not comparable with previous years due to classification changes. (1) Included in Other. (2) Includes deaths resulting from conflagration, regardless of nature of injury. (3) Includes about 1,000 excessive deaths due to summer heat wave. (4) Includes drowning in swimming pools and bathtubs.

Worldwide Airline Fatalities

Source: National Safety Council

Year	Aircraft Accidents[1]	Passenger Deaths	Death Rate[2]	Year	Aircraft Accidents[1]	Passenger Deaths	Death Rate[2]
1980	22	814	0.14	1986	17	331	0.04
1981	21	362	0.06	1987	24	890	0.10
1982	26	764	0.13	1988	25	699	0.08
1983	20	809	0.13	1989	27	817	0.08
1984	16	223	0.03	1990	22	440	0.04
1985	22	1,066	0.15	1991[3]	25	510	0.05

(1) Involving a passenger fatality. (2) Passenger deaths per 100 million passenger miles. (3) Preliminary.

U.S. Civil Aviation Accidents

Source: National Safety Council

1991	Accidents Total	Accidents Fatal	Deaths[1]	Accident Rates Per 100,000 Aircraft-Hours Total	Per 100,000 Aircraft-Hours Fatal	Per million Aircraft-Miles Total	Per million Aircraft-Miles Fatal
Large airlines	26	4	50	0.231	0.036	0.0058	0.0009
Commuter airlines	22	8	77	1.048	0.381	0.059	0.022
On-demand air taxis	84	26	69	2.57	0.80	—	—
General aviation	2,143	414	746	6.90	1.35	—	—

(1) Includes passengers, crew members and others.

Occupational Illnesses by Industry and Type of Illness, 1990

Source: National Safety Council

Occupational Illness	Private Sector[1]	Agriculture[1,2]	Mining[2]	Construction	Manufacturing	Trans. and Pub. Util.	Trade[2]	Finance[2]	Services
	Incidence Rate per 10,000 Full-Time Workers								
All Illnesses	**43.0**	**56.4**	**20.2**	**18.9**	**127.7**	**21.0**	**10.4**	**12.4**	**19.4**
Disorders associated with repeated trauma	24.1	6.7	7.5	2.9	86.7	7.8	4.4	5.6	3.1
Skin diseases, disorders	7.9	37.8	2.4	6.5	19.0	4.4	2.0	1.1	5.7
Respiratory conditions due to toxic agents	2.7	1.6	0.7	2.6	5.6	2.2	1.1	(4)	2.2
Disorders due to physical agents	2.4	2.7	1.6	1.9	6.8	1.4	0.6	(4)	1.1
Poisoning	0.8	0.8	1.6	1.0	1.7	0.6	0.3	(4)	0.6
Dust diseases of the lung	0.4	0.6	4.4	0.6	0.9	0.7	(4)	(5)	0.1
All other occupational diseases	4.8	6.3	2.0	3.4	7.1	3.9	1.9	4.0	6.5

Note: Components may not add to totals due to rounding. (1) Private sector includes all industries except government, but excludes farms with less than 11 employees. (2) Agriculture includes forestry and fishing; mining includes quarrying and oil and gas extraction; trade includes wholesale and retail; finance includes insurance and real estate. (3) Fewer than 50 cases. (4) Data not reported or do not meet publication guidelines. (5) Less than 0.05.

Crime in the U.S., 1982-1991

Source: 1991 *Uniform Crime Reports*, FBI

Population[1]	Crime Index total[2]	Violent crime[3]	Property crime[3]	Murder and non-negligent man-slaughter	Forcible rape	Robbery	Burglary	Larceny theft
			Number of offenses					
1982-231,534,000. . .	12,974,400	1,322,390	11,652,000	21,010	78,770	553,130	3,447,100	7,142,500
1983-233,981,000. . .	12,108,600	1,258,090	10,850,500	19,310	78,920	506,570	3,129,900	6,712,800
1985-238,740,000. . .	12,431,400	1,328,870	11,102,600	18,980	87,670	497,870	3,073,300	6,926,400
1986-241,077,000. . .	13,211,900	1,489,170	11,722,700	20,610	91,460	542,780	3,241,400	7,257,200
1987-243,400,000. . .	13,508,700	1,484,000	12,024,700	20,100	91,110	517,700	3,236,200	7,499,900
1988-245,807,000. . .	13,923,100	1,566,220	12,356,900	20,680	92,490	542,970	3,218,100	7,705,900
1989-248,239,000. . .	14,251,400	1,646,040	12,605,400	21,500	94,500	578,330	3,168,200	7,872,400
1990-248,709,873. . .	14,475,600	1,820,130	12,655,500	23,440	102,560	639,270	3,073,900	7,945,700
1991-252,177,000. . .	14,872,900	1,911,770	12,961,100	24,700	106,590	687,730	3,157,200	8,142,200
			Percent change; number of offenses:					
1991/1990.	+2.7	+5.0	+2.4	+5.4	+3.9	+7.6	+2.7	+2.5
1991/1987.	+10.1	+28.8	+7.8	+22.9	+17.0	+32.8	−2.4	+8.6
1991/1982.	+14.6	+44.6	+11.2	+17.6	+35.3	+24.3	−8.4	+14.0
1990/1989.	+1.6	+10.6	+0.4	+9.0	+8.5	+10.5	−3.0	+0.9
1990/1986.	+9.6	+22.2	+8.0	+13.7	+12.1	+17.8	−5.2	+9.5
1990/1981.	+7.8	+33.7	+4.9	+4.1	+24.3	+7.8	−11.7	+10.4
			Rate per 100,000 inhabitants:					
1982	5,603.6	571.1	5,032.5	9.1	34.0	238.9	1,488.8	3,084.8
1983	5,175.0	537.7	4,637.4	8.3	33.7	216.5	1,337.7	2,868.9
1985	5,207.1	556.6	4,650.5	7.9	37.1	208.5	1,287.3	2,901.2
1986	5,480.4	617.3	4,862.6	8.6	37.9	225.1	1,344.6	3,010.3
1987	5,550.0	609.7	4,904.3	8.3	37.4	212.7	1,329.6	3,081.3
1988	5,664.2	637.2	5,027.1	8.4	37.6	220.9	1,309.2	3,134.9
1989	5,741.0	663.1	5,077.9	8.7	38.1	233.0	1,276.3	3,171.3
1990	5,820.3	731.8	5,088.5	9.4	41.2	257.0	1,235.9	3,194.8
1991	5,897.8	758.1	5,139.7	9.8	42.3	272.7	1,252.0	3,228.8
			Percent change; rate per 100,000 inhabitants:					
1991/1990.	+1.3	+3.6	+1.0	+4.3	+2.7	+6.1	+1.3	+1.1
1991/1987.	+6.3	+24.3	+4.1	+18.6	+13.1	+28.2	−5.8	+4.8
1991/1982.	+5.3	+32.7	+2.1	+7.6	+24.4	+14.1	−15.9	+4.7
1990/1989.	+1.4	+10.4	+0.2	+8.0	+8.1	+10.3	−3.2	+0.7
1990/1986.	+6.2	+18.5	+4.6	+9.3	+8.7	+14.2	−8.1	+6.1
1990/1981.	−0.6	+23.1	−3.3	−4.1	+14.4	−0.7	−25.1	+1.8

(1) Populations are Bureau of the Census provisional estimates as of July 1, except 1990, which is the decennial census count. (2) Because of rounding, the offenses may not add to totals. (3) Violent crimes are offenses of murder, forcible rape, robbery, and aggravated assault. Property crimes are offenses of burglary, larceny-theft, and motor vehicle theft. Data are not included for the property crime of arson. **Note:** All rates were calculated on the offenses before rounding.

Law Enforcement Officers

Source: 1991 *Uniform Crime Reports*, FBI

The Nation's law enforcement community employed an average of 2.2 full-time officers for every 1,000 inhabitants as of October 31, 1991. Considering full-time civilians, the overall law enforcement employee rate was 3.1 per 1,000 inhabitants according to 12,805 city, county, and state police agencies. These agencies collectively offered law enforcement service to a population of nearly 238 million, employing 535,629 officers and 199,883 civilians.

The law enforcement employee average for all cities nationwide was 2.8 per 1,000 inhabitants. City law enforcement employee averages ranged from 3.3 per 1,000 inhabitants in those with populations of less than 10,000 to 3.6 for those with populations of 250,000 or more. Rural and suburban counties averaged full-time law enforcement employee rates of 3.8 and 3.6 per 1,000 population, respectively.

Regionally, the highest law enforcement employee rate was in the South, with 3.2. The Northeast averaged 3.0, the Midwest rate was 2.6 and the West 2.4.

Nationally, males comprised 91 percent of all sworn employees. Ninety-three percent of the officers in rural counties and 91 percent of those in cities were males, while in suburban counties they accounted for 88 percent.

Civilians made up 27 percent of the total U.S. law enforcement employee force. They represented 22 percent of the police employees in cities, 33 percent of those in rural counties, and 35 percent of suburban law enforcement.

Sixty-nine law enforcement officers were feloniously slain in the line of duty, four more than in 1990. Another 52 officers were killed due to accidents occurring while performing official duties.

Uniform Crime Reports and National Crime Victimization Survey Results, 1991

The U.S. Department of Justice administers 2 programs to measure the magnitude, nature, and impact of crime in the U.S.: the National Crime Victimization Survey (NCVS), and the Uniform Crime Reporting Program (UCR). The two programs examine the crime problem from somewhat different perspectives, and their results are not strictly comparable. The FBI's UCR Program, which began in 1929, collects information on homicide, rape, robbery, aggravated assault, burglary, larceny-theft, motor vehicle theft, and arson. The Bureau of Justice Statistics' NCVS, which began in 1973, collects information on crimes suffered by individuals and households, whether or not those crimes were reported to law enforcement, but it excludes homicide, arson, commercial crimes, and crimes against children under age 12.

According to the UCR, the crime rate rose 1.3 percent in 1991, with violent crime increasing by 3.6 percent, and property crime increasing by 1.0 percent. The rate of murders was up 4.3 percent; rape, up 2.7 percent; robbery, up 6.1 percent; aggravated assault, up 2.2 percent; burglary, up 1.3 percent; larceny, up 1.1 percent, and motor vehicle theft, up 0.2 percent.

According to the NCVS, nearly 23 million American households, or 24%, were victimized by crime in 1991, the same proportion as in 1990. The percentage continued to be the lowest recorded since 1975. Among the additional findings: 5 percent of U.S. households had at least one member age 12 or older who was the victim of a violent crime; black households were more likely to experience a crime than were white households; 30 percent of Hispanic households, but only 23 percent of non-Hispanic households, sustained at least 1 crime; the likelihood of a personal theft victimization increased as household income increased; households in urban areas were most likely, and households in rural areas least likely, to sustain a crime in 1991.

Prison Situation Among the States, 1991

Source: *Prisoners in 1991*, Bureau of Justice Statistics, U.S. Dept. of Justice; year-end 1991.

10 States with the Largest 1991 Prison Populations	Number of Inmates	10 States with the Highest Incarceration Rates, 1991*	Prisoners per 100,000 Residents	10 States with the Largest % Increases in Prison Population: 1990-91	% Increase	1985-91*	% Increase
California	101,808	Nevada	477	Rhode Island	15.9%	Colorado	129.9%
New York	57,862	South Carolina	473	Washington	14.5	New Hampshire	124.5
Texas	51,677	Louisiana	466	New Hampshire	14.2	Connecticut	112.3
Florida	46,533	Oklahoma	414	Arkansas	13.9	New Jersey	107.2
Michigan	36,423	Arizona	398	Idaho	12.7	Michigan	105.1
Ohio	35,750	Alabama	392	Ohio	12.3	California	104.0
Illinois	29,115	Michigan	387	New Jersey	11.1	Kentucky	96.7
Georgia	23,644	Maryland	366	Tennessee	10.7	Rhode Island	81.6
New Jersey	23,483	Florida	346	Nevada	10.5	Arizona	79.4
Pennsylvania	23,388	Alaska	344	Louisiana	10.0	Massachusetts	74.4

Note: The District of Columbia as a wholly urban jurisdiction is excluded. * Prisoners with sentences of more than 1 year.

State and Federal Prison Population; Death Penalty

Source: Prison population: Bureau of Justice Statistics, U.S. Dept. of Justice, Dec. 31, 1991; Death penalty: NAACP Legal Defense and Education Fund; Bureau of Justice Statistics; "Executions" and "Death penalty" as of Dec. 31, 1991; "Under sentence of death" as of Aug., 1991.

The number of prisoners under the jurisdiction of Federal or State correctional authorities at year-end 1991 reached a record high of 823,414. The States and the District of Columbia added 44,208 prisoners; the Federal system, 6,082. The increase for 1991 brought total growth in the prison population since 1980 to 493,593—an increase of about 150% in the 11-year period. However, the 1991 growth rate of 6.5 percent was less than the percentage increase recorded during 1990 (8.7 percent), and the number of new prisoners added during 1991 was 9,867 less than the number added during the preceding year (60,157). The 1991 increase translated into a nationwide need for approximately 967 prison bedspaces per week, compared to the 1,157 prison bedspaces per week needed in 1990. State prisons were estimated to be operating from 16 percent to 31 percent above their capacities at year end. The number of sentenced prisoners increased more in 1991 than in any year from 1985 to 1988 but less than in the peak years of 1989 and 1990.

	Sentenced to more than 1 yr.		% change	Death penalty		
	Final 1990	Advance 1991	1990-91	Under sentence of death	Executions	Death penalty
Total	**739,142**	**789,261**	**6.8%**	**2,632**	**0**	**—**
Federal institutions	**50,403**	**56,696**	**12.5**	**6**	**14**	**Yes**
State institutions	**688,739**	**732,565**	**6.4**	**2,626**	**0**	**36**
Northeast	**119,063**	**127,934**	**7.5**	**154**	**0**	**—**
Connecticut	7,771	8,585	10.5	4	0	Yes
Maine	1,480	1,600	8.1	0	0	No
Massachusetts	7,899	8,998	13.9	0	0	No
New Hampshire	1,342	1,533	14.2	0	0	Yes
New Jersey	21,128	23,483	11.1	7	0	Yes
New York	54,895	57,862	5.4	0	0	No
Pennsylvania	22,281	23,386	5.0	143	0	Yes
Rhode Island	1,586	1,749	10.3	0	0	No
Vermont	681	738	8.4	0	0	No
Midwest	**145,480**	**155,140**	**6.6**	**413**	**1**	**—**
Illinois	27,516	29,115	5.8	146	1	Yes
Indiana	12,615	12,876	2.1	55	0	Yes
Iowa	3,967	4,145	4.5	0	0	No
Kansas	5,777	5,903	2.2	0	0	No
Michigan	34,267	36,423	6.3	0	0	No
Minnesota	3,176	3,472	9.3	0	0	No
Missouri	14,943	15,411	3.1	82	4	Yes
Nebraska	2,286	2,389	4.5	12	0	Yes
North Dakota	435	441	1.4	0	0	No
Ohio	31,822	35,750	12.3	118	0	Yes
South Dakota	1,341	1,374	2.5	0	0	Yes
Wisconsin	7,335	7,841	6.9	0	0	No
South	**275,217**	**291,807**	**6.0**	**1,500**	**13**	**—**
Alabama	15,365	16,400	6.7	113	1	Yes
Arkansas	6,718	7,667	14.1	33	2	Yes
Delaware	2,241	2,406	7.4	6	0	Yes
District of Columbia	6,798	6,893	1.4	0	0	No
Florida	44,380	46,531	4.8	319	4	Yes
Georgia	21,605	22,859	5.8	110	0	Yes
Kentucky	9,023	9,799	8.6	26	0	Yes
Louisiana	18,599	20,307	9.2	39	1	Yes
Maryland	16,734	17,824	6.5	15	0	Yes
Mississippi	8,084	8,848	9.5	53	0	Yes
North Carolina	17,764	18,288	2.9	110	0	Yes
Oklahoma	12,285	13,376	8.9	120	1	Yes
South Carolina	16,208	17,173	6.0	45	1	Yes
Tennessee	10,388	11,502	10.7	104	0	Yes
Texas	50,042	51,677	3.3	356	4	Yes
Virginia	17,418	18,755	7.7	51	3	Yes
West Virginia	1,565	1,502	−4.0	0	0	No
West	**148,979**	**157,684**	**5.8**	**565**	**0**	**—**
Alaska	1,851	1,841	−.5	0	0	No
Arizona	13,781	14,843	7.7	102	0	Yes
California	94,122	98,515	4.7	331	0	Yes

(*continued*)

	Sentenced to more than 1 yr. Final 1990	Advance 1991	% change 1990-91	Death penalty: Under sentence of death	Executions	Death penalty
Colorado	7,671	8,347	8.8%	3	0	Yes
Hawaii	1,708	1,979	15.9	0	0	No
Idaho	1,961	2,211	12.7	23	0	Yes
Montana	1,425	1,478	3.7	8	0	Yes
Nevada	5,322	5,879	10.5	61	1	Yes
New Mexico	3,067	3,016	−1.7	1	0	Yes
Oregon	6,492	6,760	4.1	15	0	Yes
Utah	2,474	2,605	5.3	12	0	Yes
Washington	7,995	9,156	14.5	9	0	Yes
Wyoming	1,110	1,054	−5.0	0	0	Yes

Note: Prisoner counts for 1990 may differ from those reported previously. Counts for 1991 are subject to revision.

Court Commitments to State Prisons for Drug Offenses, 1960-1989

Source: *Prisoners in 1991*, Bureau of Justice Statistics, U.S. Dept. of Justice

Underlying the 116% growth in the State prison population during the 1980's was a change in the offense distribution: in 1989 an estimated 29.5% of persons admitted to State prison were drug offenders, up from 7.7 percent in 1981. The number of prison commitments for drug offenses grew 6-fold, from 11,487 in 1981 to 87,859 in 1989, while the total number of commitments doubled, from 149,186 to 297,827. The increase in prisoners admitted for drug offenses accounted for more than half the growth in the total admissions to State prisons. Growth in the number of persons arrested for drug law violations and an increase in the rate of incarceration for drug offenses accounted for the change in the prison offense distribution. Between 1981 and 1989, the estimated number of adult arrests for drug law violations increased by 166.6%, from 468,056 to 1,247,763. The impact of the increase in arrests was compounded by a rise in the rate of incarceration. In 1981 there were 24 drug offenders admitted to State prison for every 1,000 adult arrests for drug violations. By 1989, the rate increased to 70 admissions per 1,000 adult arrests.

Year	Number of court commitments: All offenses	Selected serious offenses	Drug offenses	Percent admitted for: Selected serious offense	Drug offenses
1960	74,952	40,924	3,148	54.6%	4.2%
1964	75,096	43,330	3,079	57.7	4.1
1970	67,304	39,777	6,596	59.1	9.8
1974	89,243	58,900	10,709	66.0	12.0
1978	112,874	72,578	9,481	64.3	8.4
1981	149,186	93,838	11,487	62.9	7.7
1982	164,648	105,539	13,336	64.1	8.1
1983	173,289	106,746	14,210	61.6	8.2
1984	166,927	87,971	18,529	52.7	11.1
1985	183,131	100,539	24,173	54.9	13.2
1986	203,315	106,740	33,140	52.5	16.3
1987	225,627	110,332	46,028	48.9	20.4
1988	245,310	112,843	61,573	46.0	25.1
1989	297,827	117,344	87,859	39.4	29.5

Index of Crime, by Type of Area, 1991

Source: *1991 Uniform Crime Reports*, FBI

Area	Population[1,2]	Crime Index total	Violent crime[3]	Property crime[3]	Murder	Forcible rape	Robbery	Aggravated assault	Burglary	Larceny theft	Motor vehicle theft
United States Total	**252,177,000**	**14,872,883**	**1,911,767**	**12,961,116**	**24,703**	**106,593**	**687,732**	**1,092,739**	**3,157,150**	**8,142,228**	**1,661,738**
Rate per 100,000 inhabitants		5,897.8	758.1	5,139.7	9.8	42.3	272.7	433.3	1,252.0	3,228.8	659.0
Metropolitan Statistical Area	**195,233,844**										
Area actually reporting[4]	96.9%	12,650,488	1,705,579	10,944,909	21,405	88,849	661,381	933,944	2,613,827	6,784,451	1,546,631
Estimated totals	100.0%	12,915,670	1,727,995	11,187,675	21,594	90,661	665,905	949,835	2,670,592	6,949,546	1,567,537
Rate per 100,000 inhabitants		6,615.5	885.1	5,730.4	11.1	46.4	341.1	486.5	1,367.9	3,559.6	802.9
Cities outside metropolitan areas	**22,775,569**										
Area actually reporting[4]	88.2%	1,095,800	96,980	998,820	1,031	6,964	14,170	74,815	215,353	736,546	46,921
Estimated totals	100.0%	1,238,034	109,575	1,128,459	1,155	7,839	15,923	84,658	244,616	830,686	53,157
Rate per 100,000 inhabitants		5,435.8	481.1	4,954.7	5.1	34.4	69.9	371.7	1,074.0	3,647.3	233.4
Rural Counties	**34,167,587**										
Area actually reporting[4]	85.5%	637,980	64,395	573,585	1,674	7,265	5,164	50,292	216,324	320,951	36,310
Estimated totals	100.0%	719,179	74,197	644,982	1,954	8,093	5,904	58,246	241,942	361,996	41,044
Rate per 100,000 inhabitants		2,104.9	217.2	1,887.7	5.7	23.7	17.3	170.5	708.1	1,059.5	120.1

(1) Populations are Bureau of the Census provisional estimates as of July 1, 1991, and are subject to change. (2) Although arson data are included in the trend and clearance tables, sufficient data are not available to estimate totals for this offense. (3) Violent crimes are offenses of murder, forcible rape, robbery, and aggravated assault. Property crimes are offenses of burglary, larceny-theft, and motor vehicle theft. Data are not included for the property crime of arson. (4) The percentage representing area actually reporting will not coincide with the ratio between reported and estimated crime totals, since these data represent the sum of the calculations for individual states which have varying populations, portions reporting, and crime rates. **Note:** Data for 1991 were not available for the state of Iowa; therefore, it was necessary that their crime counts be estimated.

School Crime

Source: Bureau of Justice Statistics, U.S. Dept. of Justice; Jan.-June 1989.

Student characteristic	Total number of students	% of students reporting victimization at school: Total	Violent	Property
Sex				
Male	11,166,316	9%	2%	7%
Female	10,387,776	9	2	8
Race				
White	17,306,626	9%	2%	7%
Black	3,449,488	8	2	7
Other	797,978	10	2*	8
Hispanic origin				
Hispanic	2,026,968	7%	3%	5%
Non-Hispanic	19,452,697	9	2	8
Not ascertained	74,428	3*	—	3*
Age				
12	3,220,891	9%	2%	7%
13	3,318,714	10	2	8
14	3,264,574	11	2	9
15	3,214,109	9	3	7
16	3,275,002	9	2	7
17	3,273,628	8	1	7
18	1,755,825	5	1*	4
19	231,348	2*	—	2*
Number of times family moved in last 5 years				
None	18,905,538	8%	2%	7%
Once	845,345	9	2*	7
Twice	610,312	13	3*	11
3 or more	1,141,555	15	6	9
Not ascertained	51,343	5*	5*	—
Family Income				
Less than $7,500	2,041,418	8%	2%	6%
$7,500-$9,999	791,086	4	1*	3
$10,000-$14,999	1,823,150	9	3	7
$15,000-$24,999	3,772,445	8	1	8
$25,000-$29,999	1,845,313	8	2	7
$30,000-$49,999	5,798,448	10	2	8
$50,000 and over	3,498,382	11	2	9
Not ascertained	1,983,849	7	3	5
Place of residence				
Central city	5,816,321	10%	2%	8%
Suburbs	10,089,207	9	2	7
Nonmetropolitan area	5,648,564	8	1	7

Notes: *Estimate is based on 10 or fewer sample cases; (—) Less than 0.5%.

U.S. Fires, 1990

Source: National Fire Protection Assn., Quincy, Mass.

Fires

- Public fire departments attended 2,019,000 fires in 1990, a 4.5 percent decrease from 1989.
- There were 624,000 structure fires in 1990, a significant 9.3 percent decrease from 1989.
- 75 percent of all structure fires—or 467,000 fires—occurred in residential properties.
- There were 436,500 vehicle fires in the past year, virtually no change from 1989.
- The number of outside property fires decreased by 3.3 percent to 958,500.
- The South experienced the highest fire incident rate in the nation, with 10.2 fires per 1,000 population.

Deaths

- There was a modest decrease in the number of civilian fire deaths, which dropped by 4.0 percent to 5,195.
- There were 4,050 home fire deaths in 1990, a decrease of 6.6 percent from 1989.
- The South had the highest regional death rate, with 26.2 civilian deaths per million population, followed by the North Central region, with 23.8 deaths per million, and the Northeast region, with 22.4 deaths per million.

Injuries

- There were 28,600 civilian fire injuries in 1990, virtually no change from the previous year. This estimate for civilian injuries is on the low side because of underreporting of civilian injuries to the fire service.
- 20,650 or 72.2 percent of all civilian injuries occurred in residential properties, while 12.0 percent, or 3,425 injuries, occurred in nonresidential structure fires.
- The South had the highest civilian injury rate—131.2 injuries per million population—followed closely by the North Central region, which had a rate of 128.1 per million.

Property damage

- Fires caused an estimated $7.818 billion in property damage in 1990, a decrease of 9.7 percent. It should be noted that this decrease reflects one large industrial fire with an estimated loss of $750 million that occurred in 1989.
- Structure fires accounted for $6.713 billion, or 86 percent, of all property damage.
- 63 percent of all structure property loss occurred in residential properties. The cost totaled $4.253 billion.
- The South and the Northeast had the highest property loss rates in the country, at $39.5 per person and $36.5 per person, respectively.

Incendiary and suspicious fires

- 15.5 percent of all structure fires, or an estimated 97,000 fires, were deliberately set or suspected of having been deliberately set.
- Incendiary or suspicious fires in structures resulted in the deaths of 715 people in 1990, a 16.3 percent increase from 1989. These fires cost $1.394 billion in property damage, a decrease of 10.5 percent, or 20.8 percent of all structure property loss.
- Vehicle fires of incendiary or suspicious origin jumped by 10.9 percent to 51,000 and caused $167 million in property damage, which rose 20.1 percent from 1989.

Physicians by Age, Sex, and Specialty

Source: American Medical Assn., Jan. 1, 1991

	Total Physicians*		Under 35 yrs.		35–44 yrs.		45–54 yrs.		55–64 yrs.	
	Male	Female	Male	Female	Male	Female	Male	Female	Male	Female
Specialty	**521,314**	**110,298**	**93,392**	**38,429**	**151,105**	**40,683**	**105,530**	**16,117**	**78,362**	**6,985**
Aerospace Medicine	655	38	142	14	191	16	145	6	112	2
Allergy & Immunology	2,880	536	211	101	942	237	749	110	560	47
Anesthesiology	22,022	4,830	5,269	1,318	7,519	1,807	4,483	1,071	3,322	442
Cardiovascular Disease	15,353	886	2,199	235	6,203	440	3,754	139	2,045	48
Child Psychiatry	2,912	1,553	256	243	1,028	660	855	369	545	179
Colon/Rectal Surgery	853	30	66	8	299	16	218	3	131	1
Dermatology	5,931	1,712	751	629	1,895	727	1,695	240	956	80
Diagnostic Radiology	13,746	2,682	3,570	1,108	5,229	1,187	3,410	289	1,109	75

(continued)

Specialty	Total Physicians* Male	Total Physicians* Female	Under 35 yrs. Male	Under 35 yrs. Female	35–44 yrs. Male	35–44 yrs. Female	45–54 yrs. Male	45–54 yrs. Female	55–64 yrs. Male	55–64 yrs. Female
Emergency Medicine	12,618	2,184	2,567	764	6,325	1,036	2,301	284	935	77
Family Practice	40,159	8,806	8,982	3,890	16,000	3,611	6,035	826	5,453	317
Forensic Pathology	320	92	22	13	99	38	82	25	78	13
Gastroenterology	7,285	493	1,128	166	3,258	254	1,864	58	719	10
General Practice	19,703	2,405	522	142	2,171	665	3,373	681	5,654	470
General Preventive Med.	807	278	97	73	233	115	188	47	158	22
General Surgery	36,001	2,552	8,884	1,458	8,902	847	7,704	154	6,254	54
Internal Medicine	81,200	20,546	22,101	9,464	27,928	7,823	14,633	2,157	9,724	728
Neurology	7,955	1,539	1,338	452	3,216	729	2,009	224	1,010	95
Neurological Surgery	4,278	143	772	62	1,170	63	1,147	15	805	3
Nuclear Medicine	1,185	202	88	31	372	91	355	56	271	18
Obstetrics/Gynecology	26,321	8,014	3,957	3,421	7,742	3,024	6,569	1,013	5,195	344
Occupational Medicine	2,493	315	128	45	505	140	415	54	691	48
Ophthalmology	14,567	1,628	2,293	616	4,271	679	3,975	202	2,517	72
Orthopedic Surgery	19,067	446	4,151	211	5,760	184	4,918	30	2,909	9
Otolaryngology	7,786	454	1,424	196	2,174	201	2,219	31	1,263	17
Pathology-Anat./Clin.	12,609	3,883	1,646	1,002	3,579	1,521	3,167	857	2,911	331
Pediatrics	25,662	16,521	5,409	6,342	8,569	6,227	5,746	2,572	3,752	894
Pediatric Cardiology	815	212	130	66	293	68	216	40	134	28
Physical Med./Rehab.	3,045	1,270	818	385	985	454	554	254	389	136
Plastic Surgery	4,307	308	439	65	1,535	168	1,397	49	690	18
Psychiatry	27,386	8,540	3,423	2,234	7,079	3,037	6,888	1,671	5,813	935
Public Health	1,513	479	44	29	334	124	343	97	358	108
Pulmonary Diseases	5,716	535	866	168	2,745	237	1,347	74	471	31
Radiology	7,264	756	264	104	1,046	265	2,529	232	2,242	115
Radiation Oncology	2,397	538	515	158	764	232	640	107	325	30
Thoracic Surgery	2,096	31	149	7	514	16	581	5	548	1
Urological Surgery	9,279	152	1,439	70	2,517	65	2,757	13	1,730	4
Other	6,316	973	433	117	1,562	347	1,323	205	1,489	158
Unspecified	7,540	2,718	5,222	2,057	1,142	452	386	113	333	50

* Includes physicians 65 years and over, those living in U.S. possessions, those "Inactive," "Not Classified," and with "Address Unknown."

Children Who Are Chronically Ill, with Special Needs

Source: National Center for Health Statistics, U.S. Dept. of Health and Human Services; 1988

Condition	Children with condition Number (thousands)	Children with condition Percent	Children with condition who have special needs Number (thousands)	Children with condition who have special needs Percent
Frequent or repeated ear infections . .	5,735	9.0	3,580	63.5
Digestive allergies . . .	1,593	2.5	512	32.3
Frequent diarrhea or bowel trouble	1,282	2.0	630	50.4
Diabetes . . .	64	0.1	32	50.6
Sickle cell anemia . . .	74	0.1	12	17.2
Anemia	703	1.1	179	25.5
Asthma	2,700	4.2	1,739	65.3
Hay fever or respiratory allergies . . .	5,830	9.2	2,300	40.4
Epilepsy or seizures . . .	422	0.7	269	65.5
Frequent or severe headaches .	1,796	2.8	1,280	76.3
Arthritis or other joint problems . .	290	0.5	178	62.1
Other musculo-skeletal impairments	630	1.0	358	59.0
Cerebral palsy	112	0.2	100	90.9
Heart disease	958	1.5	298	32.2
Other conditions . .	1,455	2.3	812	57.9

Selected Therapeutic Services Ordered or Provided in Visits to Physician's Office, 1990

Source: National Center for Health Statistics, U.S. Dept. of Health and Human Services.

Therapeutic services[1]	Number of visits (thousands)	% distribution
All visits	**704,604**	**100.0**
Medication therapy[2]		
Drug visits[3]	424,587	60.3
Number of medications ordered or provided by the physician		
None	280,017	39.7
1	230,716	32.7
2	110,865	15.7
3-5	83,007	11.8
Counseling and advice[1]		
None	442,833	62.8
Weight reduction	44,378	6.3
Cholesterol reduction	22,566	3.2
Breast self-exam	16,174	2.3
Smoking cessation	14,937	2.1
HIV transmission	1,740	0.2
Other	198,607	28.2
Other nonmedication therapy[1]		
None	566,077	80.3
Pschotherapy	26,922	3.8
Physiotherapy	16,572	2.4
Ambulatory surgery	14,203	2.0
Corrective lenses	9,580	1.4
Other	75,338	10.7

(1) Total may exceed total number of visits because more than one category may be reported per visit. (2) Medications include prescription drugs, over-the-counter preparations, immunizing agents, desensitizing agents, etc. (3) Drug visits are visits at which one or more medication is ordered or supplied by the physician.

20 Principal Reasons for Visits to Physician's Office, 1990

Source: National Center for Health Statistics, U.S. Dept. of Health and Human Services.

Rank	Reason for visit	Number of visits (thousands)	% of all visits	% of female visits	% of male visits
	All visits	**704,604**	**100.0**	**100.0**	**100.0**
1.	General medical examination	30,341	4.3	4.8	3.6
2.	Cough	25,740	3.7	3.2	4.3
3.	Routine prenatal examination	25,296	3.6	5.9	0.0
4.	Symptoms referable to throat	18,866	2.7	2.5	2.9
5.	Postoperative visit	17,523	2.5	2.6	2.4
6.	Earache or ear infection	14,633	2.1	1.8	2.5
7.	Well baby examination	14,534	2.1	1.6	2.8
8.	Back symptoms	12,497	1.8	1.6	2.0
9.	Stomach pain, cramps, spasms	12,054	1.7	1.8	1.5
10.	Skin rash	11,562	1.6	1.4	1.9
11.	Fever	11,500	1.6	1.3	2.1
12.	Vision dysfunctions	11,397	1.6	1.6	1.7
13.	Hypertension	10,391	1.5	1.5	1.4
14.	Headache, pain in head	10,203	1.4	1.6	1.2
15.	Knee symptoms	9,755	1.4	1.2	1.7
16.	Chest pain and related symptoms (not referable to body system)	9,684	1.4	1.2	1.6
17.	Head cold, upper respiratory infection (coryza)	8,557	1.2	1.2	1.3
18.	Nasal congestion	8,546	1.2	1.1	1.4
19.	Blood pressure test	7,922	1.1	1.1	1.1
20.	Neck symptoms	7,006	1.0	1.0	1.0
	All other reasons	426,597	60.5	60.0	61.6

20 Principal Diagnoses in Visits to Physician's Office, 1990

Source: National Center for Health Statistics, U.S. Dept. of Health and Human Services.

Rank	Principal diagnosis	Number of visits (thousands)	% of all visits	% of female visits	% of male visits
	All visits	**704,604**	**100.0**	**100.0**	**100.0**
1.	Essential hypertension	27,310	3.9	3.9	3.8
2.	Normal pregnancy	23,561	3.3	5.5	0.0
3.	Suppurative and unspecified otitis media	21,043	3.0	2.3	4.0
4.	General medical examination	20,555	2.9	2.9	3.0
5.	Acute upper respiratory infections of multiple or unspecified sites	18,676	2.7	2.4	3.0
6.	Health supervision of infant or child	15,676	2.2	1.7	3.0
7.	Diabetes mellitus	15,303	2.2	1.9	2.6
8.	Allergic rhinitis	12,123	1.7	1.7	1.8
9.	Bronchitis, not specified acute or chronic	12,098	1.7	1.6	1.9
10.	Acute pharyngitis	11,536	1.6	1.6	1.8
11.	Chronic sinusitis	11,141	1.6	1.6	1.5
12.	Neurotic disorders	9,531	1.4	1.5	1.1
13.	Diseases of sebaceous glands	8,346	1.2	1.1	1.3
14.	Disorders of refraction and accommodation	7,288	1.0	1.0	1.0
15.	Cataract	7,282	1.0	1.2	0.8
16.	Glaucoma	7,234	1.0	1.1	1.0
17.	Asthma	7,137	1.0	1.1	0.9
18.	Sprains and strains of other unspecified parts of back	6,951	1.0	0.9	1.1
19.	Other forms of chronic ischemic heart disease	6,429	0.9	0.5	1.5
20.	Osteoarthrosis and allied disorders	6,358	0.9	1.0	0.8

AIDS in the U.S.

Source: Federal Centers for Disease Control (cumulative as of June 30, 1992)

Cases		Race/Ethnicity[2]		Females	
Total reported:	230,179[1]	**Males**		White not Hispanic:	6,520
Adults/adolescents:	226,281	White not Hispanic:	115,242	Black not Hispanic:	13,873
Children:	3,898	Black not Hispanic:	54,099	Hispanic:	5,505
Deaths:	152,153	Hispanic:	32,608	Asian/Pacific Islander:	123
Adults/adolescents:	150,114	Asian/Pacific Islander:	1,303	Am. Indian/Alaska Native:	57
Children:	2,039	Am. Indian/Alaska Native:	331		

(1) Includes Guam, Puerto Rico, Virgin Islands, Pacific Islands. (2) Includes 518 persons whose race/ethnicity is unknown.

Mode of Transmission

Source: Federal Centers for Disease Control

(Adult and adolescent cases)

Male				Female	
Sex with men	65%	Heterosexual contact	3%	Injection drug use	50%
Injection drug use	19	Blood transfusion, blood components, or tissue	1	Heterosexual contact	35
Sex with men and inject drugs	7	Other/undetermined	4	Blood transfusion, blood components, or tissue	7
Hemophilia/coagulation disorder	1			Other/undetermined	8

AIDS

In the United States, the death rate for human immunodeficiency virus infection rose to 11.3 in 1991, up from 9.5 in 1990, per 100,000 estimated overall population, according to provisional figures from the National Center for Health Statistics. AIDS was in a virtual tie for sixth place among the leading causes of premature death for Americans, and was among the fastest-growing of such causes of death, according to 1990 figures from the Federal Centers for Disease Control.

Worldwide, women were becoming infected with the virus that causes AIDS about as often as men, and by the year 2000 most new cases would be women, according to the World Health Organization in July, 1992. The rising rates for women were accompanied by a corresponding rise in the number of children born to them infected with HIV. Homosexual men in urban areas accounted for about two-thirds of all AIDS cases in the U.S., Europe, and parts of South America during the first few years after the discovery of AIDS in 1981. But more recently, there was an increasing trend for heterosexual women to become infected through sexual intercourse with infected men, especially in third world countries. The W.H.O. estimated that from 10 million to 12 million adults and 1 million children were infected as of mid-1992, the overwhelming majority in Africa and Asia, and that by the year 2000 up to 40 million people would be infected. The Global AIDS Policy Coalition, based at Harvard University, estimated the possible infections at 110 million in the year 2000.

Health Insurance Coverage, 1990

Source: National Center for Health Statistics

(monthly average, first through fourth quarters)

	Quarter 1	Quarter 2	Quarter 3	Quarter 4
All persons.	**246,194**	**246,818**	**247,492**	**248,195**
% Covered by Private or Gvt. Health Insurance				
Total	**86.4**	**87.0**	**87.2**	**87.1**
Age				
Less than 16 years	85.4	86.0	86.4	86.2
16 to 24 years	78.2	78.7	78.7	78.1
25 to 34 years	81.3	82.8	83.1	83.0
35 to 44 years	86.9	87.4	88.1	87.9
45 to 54 years	88.3	88.6	88.5	88.6
55 to 64 years	89.9	89.9	89.9	89.5
65 years and over	99.6	99.7	99.7	99.7
Race and Hispanic Origin				
White	87.3	87.8	88.1	88.0
Black	81.4	82.2	82.2	82.0
Hispanic origin[1]	68.7	70.2	71.2	71.8
Covered by Private Health Insurance				
Total	**75.6**	**76.3**	**76.5**	**76.1**
Age				
Less than 16 years	70.8	71.2	71.1	70.7
16 to 24 years	69.8	70.1	70.6	70.0
25 to 34 years	73.4	74.8	75.0	74.9
35 to 44 years	81.4	82.1	82.9	82.7
45 to 54 years	83.2	83.8	83.9	83.8
55 to 64 years	80.8	80.9	80.8	80.2
65 years and over	77.1	78.4	77.8	77.4
Race and Hispanic Origin				
White	79.0	79.7	79.9	79.5
Black	56.0	56.9	56.2	55.9
Hispanic origin[1]	50.4	52.3	52.9	53.0

(1) Persons of Hispanic origin may be of any race.

	Quarter 1	Quarter 2	Quarter 3	Quarter 4
Covered by Private Health Insurance Related to Employment of Self or Other Family Member				
Total	**61.1**	**61.6**	**61.4**	**61.3**
Age				
Less than 16 years	59.6	59.5	59.1	59.0
16 to 24 years	54.8	54.3	54.0	53.4
25 to 34 years	66.3	67.6	67.3	67.1
35 to 44 years	74.1	75.0	75.7	75.3
45 to 54 years	72.9	73.7	73.4	73.5
55 to 64 years	65.0	65.4	64.8	64.7
65 years and over	34.2	34.6	34.6	35.1
Race and Hispanic Origin				
White	63.6	64.1	64.1	64.0
Black	47.0	46.9	46.4	46.2
Hispanic origin[1]	42.8	43.8	44.1	44.8
% Covered by Medicaid				
Total	**7.5**	**7.8**	**7.9**	**8.1**
Age				
Less than 16 years	13.8	14.5	14.9	15.5
16 to 24 years	7.4	7.8	7.7	8.0
25 to 34 years	6.2	6.6	6.6	6.8
35 to 44 years	3.7	3.6	3.7	3.8
45 to 54 years	3.2	3.3	3.2	3.4
55 to 64 years	4.6	4.6	4.9	5.1
65 years and over	7.6	7.5	7.6	7.4
Race and Hispanic Origin				
White	5.2	5.4	5.4	5.7
Black	21.7	22.6	22.8	23.0
Hispanic origin[1]	15.8	15.9	16.4	16.9

Insurance Coverage for Chronically Ill Children with Special Needs

Source: National Center for Health Statistics, U.S. Dept. of Health and Human Services; 1988

Characteristics	Number of children (thousands)	Insurance coverage: Private insurance	Medicaid	Neither
All children*	9,150	76.2	11.0	12.8
Age				
Under 5 years	2,713	75.3	11.9	12.8
5–17 years	6,437	76.5	10.6	12.9
Sex				
Male	4,895	75.2	11.3	13.5
Female	4,254	77.3	10.7	12.1
Race				
White	7,818	80.2	7.8	12.1
Black	1,114	51.5	34.1	14.4
Hispanic origin				
Hispanic	784	53.5	23.2	23.4
Non-Hispanic	8.198	78.2	9.8	12.0

Characteristics	Number of children (thousands)	Insurance coverage: Private insurance	Medicaid	Neither
Family Structure				
Biological mother and father	5,677	86.1	3.2	10.6
Biological mother only	2,834	58.9	24.9	16.2
All other	638	64.5	18.2	17.4
Family Income				
Less than $25,000	3,414	52.7	24.7	22.6
$25,000 or more	5,003	93.2	1.4	5.5
Place of Residence				
MSA				
Central city	2,557	67.5	16.7	15.8
Not central city	4,287	84.1	5.8	10.1
Not MSA	2,306	71.1	14.3	14.6

*Total number of cases is less than total number of children with special needs due to missing values on insurance coverage. Also, numbers for respective groups may not sum to total due to missing values.

U.S. Health Expenditures, 1960-1990

Source: Health Care Financing Administration, Office of the Actuary; data from Office of National Health Statistics

(in billions of dollars)

Type of expenditure	1960	1970	1980	1985	1986	1987	1988	1989	1990
National health expenditures	**$27.1**	**$74.4**	**$250.1**	**$422.6**	**$454.8**	**$494.1**	**$546.0**	**$602.8**	**$666.2**
Health services & supplies	**25.4**	**69.1**	**238.9**	**407.2**	**438.9**	**476.8**	**526.2**	**582.1**	**643.4**
Personal health care	23.9	64.9	219.4	369.7	400.8	439.3	482.8	529.9	585.3
Hospital care	9.3	27.9	102.4	168.3	179.8	194.2	212.0	232.6	256.0
Physician services	5.3	13.6	41.9	74.0	82.1	93.0	105.1	113.6	125.7
Dental services	2.0	4.7	14.4	23.3	24.7	27.1	29.4	31.6	34.0
Other professional services	0.6	1.5	8.7	16.6	18.6	21.1	23.8	27.1	31.6
Home health care	0.0	0.1	1.3	3.8	4.0	4.1	4.5	5.6	6.9
Drugs & other medical nondurables	4.2	8.8	21.6	36.2	39.7	43.2	46.3	50.6	54.6
Vision products & other medical durables	0.8	2.0	4.6	7.1	8.1	9.1	10.1	11.4	12.1
Nursing home care	1.0	4.9	20.0	34.1	36.7	39.7	42.8	47.7	53.1
Other personal health care	0.7	1.4	4.6	6.4	7.1	7.8	8.7	9.7	11.3
Program administration & net cost of private health insurance	1.2	2.8	12.2	25.2	24.6	22.9	26.8	33.9	38.7
Government public health activities	0.4	1.4	7.2	12.3	13.5	14.6	16.6	18.3	19.3
Research & construction	**1.7**	**5.3**	**11.3**	**15.4**	**16.0**	**17.3**	**19.8**	**20.7**	**22.8**
Research[1]	0.7	2.0	5.4	7.8	8.5	9.0	10.3	11.0	12.4
Construction	1.0	3.4	5.8	7.6	7.4	8.2	9.5	9.6	10.4
				Average annual % change from previous year shown					
National health expenditures	—	**10.6**	**12.9**	**11.1**	**7.6**	**8.6**	**10.5**	**10.4**	**10.5**
Health services & supplies	—	**10.5**	**13.2**	**11.3**	**7.8**	**8.7**	**10.3**	**10.6**	**10.5**
Personal health care	—	10.5	13.0	11.0	8.4	9.6	9.9	9.8	10.5
Hospital care	—	11.7	13.9	10.4	6.8	8.0	9.2	9.7	10.1
Physician services	—	9.9	11.9	12.1	10.9	13.3	13.1	8.0	10.7
Dental services	—	9.1	11.9	10.1	6.4	9.6	8.5	7.3	7.6
Other professional services	—	9.6	19.1	13.8	12.0	13.6	12.4	14.0	16.6
Home health care	—	14.5	25.2	23.3	3.6	3.6	9.6	24.9	22.5
Drugs & other medical nondurables	—	7.6	9.4	10.8	9.9	8.6	7.2	9.3	7.9
Vision products & other medical durables	—	9.6	8.5	9.4	13.0	12.3	11.8	12.9	6.1
Nursing home care	—	17.4	15.2	11.3	7.6	8.0	7.8	11.5	11.4
Other personal health care	—	7.1	12.8	6.9	11.1	10.0	12.1	11.2	16.4
Program administration & net cost of private health insurance	—	9.0	16.0	15.5	–2.5	–6.6	16.9	26.6	14.1
Government public health activities	—	13.9	18.0	11.3	9.6	8.3	13.5	10.4	5.6
Research & construction	—	**12.1**	**7.8**	**6.4**	**3.7**	**8.2**	**14.9**	**4.3**	**10.2**
Research[1]	—	10.9	10.8	7.4	9.5	5.7	14.5	6.8	11.9
Construction	—	12.8	5.6	5.4	–2.4	11.1	15.3	1.5	8.3

(1) Research and development expenditures of drug companies and other manufacturers and providers of medical equipment and supplies are excluded from "research expenditures," but included in the expenditure class in which the product falls. **Note:** Numbers may not add to totals because of rounding.

Cesarean Births

Source: Natl. Center for Health Statistics, U.S. Dept. of Health and Human Services (45 reporting States and District of Columbia, 1989)

Age and race of mother	All births	Cesarean				Cesarean delivery rate			Rate of vaginal birth after previous cesarean[4]
		Total	Primary	Repeat	Not stated	Total[1]	Primary[2]	Repeat[3]	
All races[5]	**3,798,734**	**826,955**	**521,873**	**305,082**	**178,316**	**22.8**	**16.1**	**36.9**	**18.9**
Under 20 years	484,420	77,801	66,844	10,957	24,291	16.9	15.0	14.1	24.0
20-24 years	1,009,739	198,722	134,697	64,025	48,800	20.7	15.3	32.2	20.0
25-29 years	1,187,826	265,121	161,382	103,739	55,011	23.4	16.1	39.1	18.9
30-34 years	795,041	195,305	107,529	87,776	35,961	25.7	16.5	44.9	18.4
35-39 years	278,117	76,714	43,108	33,606	12,283	28.9	19.1	43.8	16.8
40-49 years	43,591	13,292	8,313	4,979	1,970	31.9	23.2	37.5	14.0
White	**3,022,537**	**667,114**	**418,177**	**248,937**	**142,580**	**23.2**	**16.2**	**37.3**	**18.6**
Under 20 years	326,975	53,035	46,370	6,665	16,959	17.1	15.4	12.6	21.7
20-24 years	779,397	155,649	107,097	48,552	37,816	21.0	15.7	31.2	19.1
25-29 years	984,147	221,033	134,323	86,710	45,631	23.6	16.1	39.2	18.7
30-34 years	666,304	163,557	88,878	74,679	30,219	25.7	16.3	45.7	18.6
35-39 years	230,502	63,209	34,932	28,277	10,314	28.7	18.8	44.7	17.2
40-49 years	35,212	10,631	6,577	4,054	1,641	31.7	22.8	38.1	14.4
Black	**611,147**	**127,907**	**82,695**	**45,212**	**30,319**	**22.0**	**15.8**	**35.3**	**19.7**
Under 20 years	143,261	23,068	19,005	4,063	6,920	16.9	14.5	17.6	26.9
20-24 years	195,335	37,942	23,899	14,043	9,874	20.5	14.3	37.0	21.9
25-29 years	151,603	34,553	20,553	14,000	7,623	24.0	16.2	40.5	19.1
30-34 years	86,147	22,040	12,786	9,254	4,321	26.9	18.1	42.0	15.9
35-39 years	29,855	8,692	5,377	3,315	1,354	30.5	21.8	38.1	14.1
40-49 years	4,956	1,612	1,075	537	227	34.1	26.1	33.3	11.5

(1) Percent of all live births by cesarean delivery. (2) Number of primary cesareans per 100 live births to women who have not had a previous cesarean. (3) Percent of all cesareans that are repeat cesareans. (4) Number of vaginal births after previous cesarean delivery per 100 live births to women with a previous cesarean delivery. (5) Includes races other than white and black. **Note:** Excludes data for Louisiana, Maryland, Nebraska, Nevada, and Oklahoma, which did not require reporting of method of delivery.

Years of Life Expected at Birth

Source: National Center for Health Statistics

Year	Total Total	Total Male	Total Female	White Total	White Male	White Female	Black and Other Total	Black and Other Male	Black and Other Female
1920*	54.1	53.6	54.6	54.9	54.4	55.6	45.3	45.5	45.2
1930	59.7	58.1	61.6	61.4	59.7	63.5	48.1	47.3	49.2
1940	62.9	60.8	65.2	64.2	62.1	66.6	53.1	51.5	54.9
1950	68.2	65.6	71.1	69.1	66.5	72.2	60.8	59.1	62.9
1960	69.7	66.6	73.1	70.6	67.4	74.1	63.6	61.1	66.3
1965	70.2	66.8	73.7	71.0	67.6	74.7	64.1	61.1	67.4
1970	70.8	67.1	74.7	71.7	68.0	75.6	65.3	61.3	69.4
1971	71.1	67.4	75.0	72.0	68.3	75.8	65.6	61.6	69.8
1972	71.2	67.4	75.1	72.0	68.3	75.9	65.7	61.5	70.1
1973	71.4	67.6	75.3	72.2	68.5	76.1	66.1	62.0	70.3
1974	72.0	68.2	75.9	72.8	69.0	76.7	67.1	62.9	71.3
1975	72.6	68.8	76.6	73.4	69.5	77.3	68.0	63.7	72.4
1976	72.9	69.1	76.8	73.6	69.9	77.5	68.4	64.2	72.7
1977	73.3	69.5	77.2	74.0	70.2	77.9	68.9	64.7	73.2
1978	73.5	69.6	77.3	74.1	70.4	78.0	68.1	63.7	72.4
1979	73.9	70.0	77.8	74.6	70.8	78.4	69.8	65.4	74.1
1980	73.7	70.0	77.5	74.4	70.7	78.1	69.5	65.3	73.6
1981	74.2	70.4	77.8	74.8	71.1	78.4	70.3	66.1	74.4
1982	74.5	70.9	78.1	75.1	71.5	78.7	71.0	66.8	75.0
1983	74.6	71.0	78.1	75.2	71.7	78.7	71.1	67.2	74.3
1984	74.7	71.2	78.2	75.3	71.8	78.7	71.3	67.4	75.0
1985	74.7	71.2	78.2	75.3	71.9	78.7	71.2	67.2	75.0
1986	74.8	71.3	78.3	75.4	72.0	78.8	71.2	67.2	75.1
1987	75.0	71.5	78.4	75.6	72.2	78.9	71.3	67.3	75.2
1988	74.9	71.5	78.3	75.6	72.3	78.9	71.2	67.1	75.1
1989p	75.2	71.8	78.5	75.9	72.6	79.1	71.7	67.5	75.7
1990p	75.4	72.0	78.8	76.0	72.6	79.3	72.4	68.4	76.3

p= preliminary. * Data prior to 1940 for death-registration states only.

Average Height and Weight for Children

Source: *Physicians Handbook*, 1983.

Boys Age Years	Height ft	Height in	cm	Weight lb	Weight kg	Girls Age Years	Height ft	Height in	cm	Weight lb	Weight kg
(Birth)	1	8	50.8	7½	3.4	(Birth)	1	8	50.8	7½	3.4
½	2	2	66.0	17	7.7	½	2	2	66.0	16	7.2
1	2	5	73.6	21	9.5	1	2	5	73.6	20	9.1
2	2	9	83.8	26	11.8	2	2	9	83.8	25	11.3
3	3	0	91.4	31	14.0	3	3	0	91.4	30	13.6
4	3	3	99.0	34	15.4	4	3	3	99.0	33	15.0
5	3	6	106.6	39	17.7	5	3	5	104.1	38	17.2
6	3	9	114.2	46	20.9	6	3	8	111.7	45	20.4
7	3	11	119.3	51	23.1	7	3	11	119.3	49	22.2
8	4	2	127.0	57	25.9	8	4	2	127.0	56	25.4
9	4	4	132.0	63	28.6	9	4	4	132.0	62	28.1
10	4	6	137.1	69	31.3	10	4	6	137.1	69	31.3
11	4	8	142.2	77	34.9	11	4	8	142.2	77	34.9
12	4	10	147.3	83	37.7	12	4	10	147.3	86	39.0
13	5	0	152.4	92	41.7	13	5	0	152.4	98	45.5
14	5	2	157.5	107	48.5	14	5	2	157.5	107	48.5

This table gives a general picture of American children at specific ages. When used as a standard, the individual variation in children's growth should not be overlooked. In most cases the height-weight relationship is probably a more valid index of weight status than a weight-for-age assessment.

Average Weight of Americans by Height and Age

Source: Society of Actuaries; from the *1979 Build and Blood Pressure Study*

The figures represent weights in ordinary indoor clothing and shoes, and heights with shoes.

Men Height	20-24	25-29	30-39	40-49	50-59	60-69	Women Height	20-24	25-29	30-39	40-49	50-59	60-69
5'2"	130	134	138	140	141	140	4'10"	105	110	113	118	121	123
5'3"	136	140	143	144	145	144	4'11"	110	112	115	121	125	127
5'4"	139	143	147	149	150	149	5'0"	112	114	118	123	127	130
5'5"	143	147	151	154	155	153	5'1"	116	119	121	127	131	133
5'6"	148	152	156	158	159	158	5'2"	120	121	124	129	133	136
5'7"	153	156	160	163	164	163	5'3"	124	125	128	133	137	140
5'8"	157	161	165	167	168	167	5'4"	127	128	131	136	141	143
5'9"	163	166	170	172	173	172	5'5"	130	132	134	139	144	147
5'10"	167	171	174	176	177	176	5'6"	133	134	137	143	147	150
5'11"	171	175	179	181	182	181	5'7"	137	138	141	147	152	155
6'0"	176	181	184	186	187	186	5'8"	141	142	145	150	156	158
6'1"	182	186	190	192	193	191	5'9"	146	148	150	155	159	161
6'2"	187	191	195	197	198	196	5'10"	149	150	153	158	162	163
6'3"	193	197	201	203	204	200	5'11"	155	156	159	162	166	167
6'4"	198	202	206	208	209	207	6'0"	157	159	164	168	171	172

OBITUARIES

Deaths, Oct. 17, 1991-Oct. 25, 1992

A

Allen, Irwin, 75; film producer who made disaster epics, "The Towering Inferno"; Santa Monica, Cal., Nov. 2.

Allen, Peter, 48; Australian-born concert entertainer and songwriter; San Diego, June 18.

Almendros, Nestor, 61; Academy Award-winning cinematographer, "Days of Heaven"; New York, Mar. 4.

Alzado, Lyle, 43; football lineman, 1977 NFL defensive player of the year; Portland, Ore., May 14.

Anderson, Judith, 93; stage and film actress; Santa Barbara, Cal., Jan. 3.

Asimov, Isaac, 72; author of 468 books; famed for science fiction novels; New York, Apr. 6.

B

Bacon, Francis, 82; Irish-born abstract painter of macabre; Madrid, Apr. 28.

Baldwin, Hanson, 88; top U.S. military writer for over 50 years; Roxbury, Conn., Nov. 13.

Barber, Red, 84; baseball play-by-play announcer for Brooklyn Dodgers and N.Y. Yankees; Tallahassee, Fla., Oct. 22.

Bartholomew, Freddie, 67; child star in 1930s films; Sarasota, Fla., Jan. 23.

Begin, Menachem, 78; former Israeli prime minister; won 1978 Nobel Peace Prize; Jerusalem, Mar. 9.

Bellamy, Ralph, 87; actor in theater and over 100 films; Los Angeles, Nov. 29.

Bergalis, Kimberly, 23; woman who contacted AIDS from health care worker, sparked debate over risk of infection in health care settings; Ft. Pierce, Fla., Dec. 8.

Biasone, Danny, 83; basketball innovator, convinced NBA to adopt 24-second shot clock; Syracuse, N.Y., May 26.

Birnbaum, Stephen, 54; travel journalist, guidebook editor; New York, Dec. 20.

Blatnik, John, 80; U.S. representative from Minnesota, 1947-75; Forest Heights, Md., Dec. 17.

Bloom, Allan, 62; educator, author, "The Closing of the American Mind"; Chicago, Oct. 7.

Booth, Shirley, 94; actress in theater and "Hazel" 1960s TV series; N. Chatham, Mass., Oct. 16.

Boudiaf, Mohammed, 73; president of Algeria; Annaba, Algeria, June 29.

Brand, Neville, 72; actor in over 50 films, mostly as villain; Sacramento, Apr. 16.

Brandt, Willy, 78; chancellor of W. Germany, 1969-74; won 1971 Nobel Peace Prize; Unkel, Germany, Oct. 8.

Brooks, Richard, 79; screenwriter, director, and producer; Beverly Hills, Cal., Mar. 11.

Brown, Georgia, 58; British singer and actress; London, July 5.

Brown, Jerome, 27; Philadelphia Eagles defensive tackle; Brooksville, Fla., June 25.

Buchanan, Buck, 51; football hall of fame lineman, with Kansas City Chiefs, 1963-75; Kansas City, July 16.

Burdick, Quentin N., 84; U.S. senator from North Dakota since 1960; Fargo, N.D., Sept. 8.

C

Cage, John, 79; composer of experimental music; New York, Aug. 12.

Carnovsky, Morris, 94; character actor, career spanned 60 years; Easton, Conn., Sept. 1.

Carswell, G. Harrold, 72; judge, as Nixon nominee, rejected for the U.S. Supreme Court in 1970; Tallahassee, Fla., July 31.

Clarke, Mae, 84; actress famed for taking grapefruit in the face from James Cagney in 1931 film "Public Enemy"; Woodland Hills, Cal., Apr. 29.

Colby, Anita, 77; model, film actress, newspaper columnist, author; Oyster Bay, N.Y., Mar. 27.

D

Danton, Ray, 60; actor and director in 1960s films; Los Angeles, Feb. 11.

Dennis, Sandy, 54; actress starred in theater and films; Westport, Conn., Mar. 2.

Dietrich, Marlene, 90; actress, singer, and sex symbol starred in films from 1920s through 1950s; Paris, May 6.

Dixon, Willie, 76; singer and composer of blues; Burbank, Cal., Jan. 29.

Drake, Alfred, 78; singer and actor, the original Curly in "Oklahoma" in 1943; New York, July 25.

Dunne, Philip, 84; screenwriter and director; wrote "How Green Was My Valley"; Malibu, Cal., June 2.

E

Elliott, Denholm, 70; British character actor, career spanned 47 years in films, theater, and TV; Ibiza, Spain, Oct. 6.

Ephron, Henry, 81; screenwriter who, with wife, Phoebe, wrote numerous films in 30-year career; Los Angeles, Sept. 7.

F

Fenwick, Millicent, 82; retired U.S. representative from New Jersey who was model for "Doonesbury's" Lacey Davenport; Bernardsville, N.J., Sept. 16.

Ferrer, Jose, 80; actor and director in films and theater; won 1950 Oscar for "Cyrano de Bergerac"; Coral Gables, Fla., Jan. 26.

Fine Kaye, Sylvia, 78; lyricist and composer; New York, Oct. 28.

Fisher, M.F.K., 83; food writer, authored 15 books and hundreds of articles for *The New Yorker* magazine; Glen Ellen, Cal., June 22.

Ford, Tennessee Ernie, 72; country and western singer, *"Sixteen Tons"*; Reston, Va., Oct. 17, 1991.

France, William, 82; leading figure in establishment of NASCAR racing; founder of Daytona 500; Ormond Beach, Fla., June 8.

Furst, Anton, 47; production designer who created sets for 1989 film "Batman"; Los Angeles, Nov. 24.

G

Gaines, William, 70; founder and publisher of *Mad* magazine; New York, June 3.

Gann, Ernest K., 81; author of popular adventure novels; San Juan Island, Wash., Dec. 19.

Garber, Paul E., 93; founder and first curator of National Air and Space Museum; Arlington, Va., Sept. 23.

Garrison, Jim, 70; New Orleans district attorney; critic of Warren Commission report on JFK assassination; New Orleans, Oct. 21.

Graham, Bill, 60; rock impresario and developer of rock musicians; Cal., Oct. 25, 1991.

H

Habib, Philip C., 72; diplomat, a leading U.S. policymaker in Middle East and Asia; France, May 25.

Haley, Alex, 70; author, won Pulitzer Prize for "Roots"; later successful TV mini-series; Seattle, Feb. 10.

Hancock, John, 51; actor on TV series "Love and War"; Los Angeles, Oct. 13.

Hayakawa, S.I., 85; scholar, educator, and U.S. senator, 1977-83; Greenbrae, Cal., Feb. 27.

Hayek, Friedrich, 92; Austrian-born British economist, shared 1974 Nobel Prize; Freiberg, Germany, Mar. 23.

Hein, Mel, 82; football hall of fame center, played for N.Y. Giants in 1930s and 1940s; San Clemente, Cal., Jan. 31.

Henreid, Paul, 84; actor, producer, and director starred in films in 1940s; Santa Monica, Cal., Mar. 29.

Herman, Billy, 83; baseball hall of fame second baseman, manager; W. Palm Beach, Fla., Sept. 5.

Hill, Benny, 67; British TV comedian; London, Apr. 20.

Husak, Gustav, 78; president of Czechoslovakia, 1975-89; Bratislava, Czech., Nov. 18.

I

Ireland, John, 78; actor who appeared in films since 1940s; Santa Barbara, Cal., Mar. 21.

J

Jabara, Paul, 44; singer, actor and disco songwriter, *"Last Dance"*; Los Angeles, Sept. 29.

Johnson, Bob, 60; hockey coach who led the Pittsburgh Penguins to the 1991 Stanley Cup championship; Colorado Springs, Col., Nov. 26.

Jones, Allan, 84; actor and singer who starred in 1930s film musicals; New York, June 27.

Jones, Walter, 79; U.S. representative from North Carolina since 1966; Norfolk, Va., Sept. 15.

K

Kaufman, Irving R., 81; federal judge, served for over 30 years; famed for death sentence of Rosenbergs in 1950s; New York, Feb. 1.

Keltner, Ken, 75; major league third baseman mostly for Cleveland Indians; New Berlin, Wis., Dec. 12.

Kent, Clark; journalist who, as Superman, fought crime in America since 1938; 1992.

Kendricks, Eddie, 52; lead singer with Temptations; Princeton, Ala., Oct. 5.

Kinison, Sam, 38; comedian known for high-decibel routines; nr. Needles, Cal., Apr. 10.

Kinski, Klaus, 65; Polish-born character actor; Marin Co., Cal., Nov. 23.

L

Lantz, Gracie, 88; voice of Woody Woodpecker in some 200 cartoons; Burbank, Cal., Mar. 17.

Lerner, Max, 89; political columnist and author; New York, June 5.

Lewis, Robert Q., 71; comedian, TV host and panelist in 1950s; Los Angeles, Dec. 11.

Little, Cleavon, 53; actor in theater and films, "Blazing Saddles"; Sherman Oaks, Cal., Oct. 22.

Lopat, Eddie, 73; N.Y. Yankee pitcher, played on 5 World Series championship teams; Darien, Conn., June 15.

Lund, John, 81; film leading man in 1940s and 1950s; Los Angeles, May 10.
Luro, Horatio, 90; horseman who trained Kentucky Derby winners Decidely and Northern Dancer; Bal Harbour, Fla., Dec. 15.

M

MacMurray, Fred, 83; actor, starred in 84 films and "My Three Sons" TV series in 1960s; Santa Monica, Cal., Nov. 5.
Mann, Daniel, 79; theater, film, and TV director; Los Angeles, Nov. 21.
Marshall, James, 50; illustrator and author of children's books, "The Stupids"; New York, Oct. 13.
Maxwell, Robert, 68; British publisher who owned and ran newspapers throughout the world; at sea, Nov. 5.
McGee, Gale, 77; U.S. senator from Wyoming, 1959-77; Bethesda, Md., Apr. 9.
McClintock, Barbara, 90; gene research pioneer who won 1983 Nobel Prize in Physiology or Medicine; Huntington, N.Y., Sept. 2.
McGowan, William, 64; entrepreneur who led MCI in its challenge of phone monopoly; Washington, D.C., June 8.
McIntyre, Thomas J., 77; U.S. senator from New Hampshire, 1963-79; West Palm Beach, Fla., Aug. 9.
Mercury, Freddie, 45; lead singer and lyricist for British rock group "Queen"; London, Nov. 24.
Messiaen, Olivier, 83; French composer; Paris, Apr. 27.
Miller, Roger, 56; singer and songwriter, *King of the Road;* Los Angeles, Oct. 25.
Mills, Wilbur; 82; U.S. representative from Arkansas, 1938-76; headed House Ways and Means Committee for 17 years; Kensett, Ark., May 2.
Montand, Yves, 70; French actor and singer; Senlis, France, Nov. 9.
Morey, Walt, 84; children's book author, *"Gentle Ben";* Wilsonville, Ore., Jan. 12.
Morley, Robert, 84; British actor known for comically pompous and jovial roles; Reading, England, June 3.
Murphy, George, 89; actor, singer, and dancer in films in 1930s through 1950s; later, U.S. senator from Cal.; Palm Beach, Fla., May 3.

P

Page, Robert Morris, 88; physicist, helped pioneer development of radar; Edina, Minn., May 15.
Papp, Joseph, 70; theatrical producer whose plays won 3 Pulitzer Prizes; New York, Oct. 31, 1991.
Parks, Bert, 77; TV game show host, hosted 25 Miss America contests; La Jolla, Cal., Feb. 2.
Perkins, Anthony, 60; actor, starred in numerous films and plays; best known as Norman Bates in "Psycho" film series; Hollywood, Cal., Sept. 12.
Picon, Molly, 93; comedic actress and singer, starred in Yiddish theater; Lancaster, Pa., Apr. 5.
Poiret, Jean, 65; French actor and playwright, *"La Cage Aux Folles";* Paris, Mar. 14.

R

Ray, Satyajit, 70; Indian film maker; Calcutta, Apr. 23.
Reed, Robert, 59; actor, best known as father of TVs "The Brady Bunch"; Pasadena, Cal., May 12.
Reshevsky, Samuel, 80; Polish-born chess grandmaster, a dominant figure in chess in U.S. for 4 decades; Suffern, N.Y., Apr. 4.
Richardson, Tony, 63; film director, "Tom Jones"; Los Angeles, Nov. 14.
Roddenberry, Gene, 70; writer and producer, created "Star Trek" science-fiction TV series; Santa Monica, Cal., Oct. 24, 1991.
Rudd, Hughes, 71; TV correspondent for CBS News and ABC News; Toulouse, France, Oct. 13.
Russell, Andy, 72; singer popular in 1940s; Phoenix, Apr. 16.

S

Salk, Lee, 65; child psychologist and popular author; New York, May 2.
Scheib, Earl, 85; entrepreneur, owned some 200 car-painting shops; Beverly Hills, Cal., Feb. 29.
Sevareid, Eric, 79; CBS News correspondent and commentator; Washington, D.C., July 9.
Schuman, William, 81; composer, won 2 Pulitzer prizes; headed Juilliard School of Music, 1945-62; New York, Feb. 15.
Shuster, Joseph, 78; cartoonist, co-creater of "Superman"; Los Angeles, July 30.
Sirica, John J., 88; federal judge whose search for facts in Watergate break-in led to resignation of Pres. Nixon; Washington, DC., Aug. 14.
Stigler, George Joseph, 80; economist, won 1982 Nobel Prize; Chicago, Dec. 1.
Stotz, Carl, 82; founder of Little League baseball, Williamsport, Pa., June 4.
Sturges, John, 81; director of action films, "The Magnificent Seven"; San Luis Obispo, Cal., Aug. 18.
Swanberg, William A., 84; biographer, won 1973 Pulitzer prize for biography of Henry Luce; Southbury, Conn., Sept. 17.
Syms, Sylvia, 74; pop-jazz singer; New York, May 10.

T

Taylor, William, 53; chairman of Federal Deposit Insurance Corp.; Fairfax, Va., Aug. 20.
Thompson, Marshall, 66; actor, many films and TV series "Daktari" in 1960s; Royal Oak, Mich., May 25.
Tierney, Gene, 70; film leading lady in 1940s, "Laura"; Houston, Nov. 6.

V

Van Fleet, James, 100; U.S. Army general, led major campaigns in World War II and Korean War; Polk City, Fla., Sept. 23.
Ventura, Charlie, 75; tenor saxophonist, a star of big-band era; Pleasantville, N.Y., Jan. 17.

W

Walker, Nancy, 69; actress, starred in theater and TV sitcoms, "Rhoda," "True Colors"; Studio City, Cal., Mar. 25.
Walton, Sam, 74; founder of Wal-Mart stores; Little Rock, Ark., Apr. 5.
Webb, James, 85; administrator of NASA, 1961-1969; Washington, D.C., Mar. 27.
Weiss, Ted, 64; U.S. representative from New York City since 1977; New York, Sept. 14.
Welk, Lawrence, 89; band leader whose "Champagne Music" shaped one of longest-running shows in TV history; Santa Monica, Cal., May 17.
Wells, Mary, 49; pop and soul singer of 1960s, *"My Guy";* Los Angeles, July 26.
Werblin, Sonny, 81; entertainment and sports impresario, New York, Nov. 21.
Williams, Tony, 64; lead singer of "The Platters" rhythm-and-blues group; New York, Aug. 14.
Wojciechowicz, Alex, 76; lineman, in college and pro football halls of fame; South River, N.J., July 13.

Y

Yerby, Frank, 76; novelist, among most popular writers of 1940s and 1950s; Madrid, Nov. 29.
York, Dick, 63; actor, starred in "Bewitched" TV series in 1960s; Grand Rapids, Mich., Feb. 20.

Off-Beat News Stories of 1992

Democracy in action — It was election day in Dutton, Ala. and no one voted. There was a good reason: no one was running for Mayor or for any of the 5 seats on the Town Council, the only positions at stake. As a result, the town of 243 people will end up with no elected officials when the terms of the current officeholders expire.

Absolutely Nobody is a candidate for lieutenant governor in the State of Washington. David M. Powers had his name legally changed to capitalize on voter frustration. If elected, he promises to work to abolish the office which he calls a do-nothing job and a largely ceremonial drag on the taxpayer.

Family values — Sex, child abuse, incest, and prostitution were topics unfit for children said Gene Kasmar in his petition to the Brooklyn Center (Minn.) Independent School District to have the Bible taken out of the schools. "The lewd, indecent and violent content of that book are hardly suitable for young students," he wrote in his petition, "The Bible quickly reveals its unsuitability in a school and learning environment." Kasnar, an atheist, cited more than 20 pages of examples in the Good Book that frequently refer to concubines, explicit sex, child abuse, scatology, wine, nakedness, and mistreatment of women.

Unbalanced budget — The Budget of the United States Government for fiscal year 1993 with its facts, figures, projections, and Gross Domestic Product deflaters is not easy reading, especially when 32 pages are upside down. A few hundred copies of the 1,216-page, 6-pound volume were shipped before a worker in the Government Printing Office caught the mistake. Barbara Shaw, a spokeswoman for the agency, said of the defective copies, "We tried to catch as many as we could. Certainly nothing goes perfectly all the time."

How often do you water this? — Palm Beach County health inspectors were investigating a Loxahatchee, Fla. business after a woman complained that she had received a manure bouquet from a jilted boyfriend. The business, Poop-Poop We Do, delivers the bouquets from the vengeful. "You'd think they'd have something better to do," said Poop-Poop co-owner Lynda Black. A state health official downplayed any health hazard. "You can buy manure at any hardware store," he said.

Simply smashing — A study in the *British Medical Journal* recommends that beer mugs be made of tougher glass in order to prevent disfiguring injuries in bar fights. A team of Welsh doctors found that, when smashed deliberately, mugs made of specially tempered glass disintegrated into tiny glass cubes rather than forming jagged-edged weapons. British Home Office statistics record 3,400 to 5,400 fights a year in which mugs are used as a weapon in England and Wales.

A sting and a prayer — Dorothy Ries filed a $40 million lawsuit against Texas evangelist Robert Tilton, saying he continues to send solicitation letters to her dead husband promising that God will restore his health. Tilton had been under investigation by the Texas attorney general's office after a broadcast report alleged he promised to personally pray for people, but had a mail processing company cash mailed-in contributions and ignore accompanying prayer requests.

Order on the court — Stan Guffey, a high school basketball referee, was working a game in Oklahoma City when a policeman came onto the court and arrested him for not calling enough fouls during the game. During a timeout, Officer Eldredge Wyatt came onto the court to warn Guffey and Douglass High School coach Willie Kelley about physical play. Guffey told the intruder, "Sir, I don't know who you are, but you don't have any business on the floor." Wyatt told him he was under arrest and escorted him off the court.

It's a toss-up! — Like most politicians, Democratic presidential candidate Bill Clinton never saw a baby he didn't want to kiss. While campaigning in Rahway, N.J., he spotted 4-month-old Kerrin Garripoli and gave her a big kiss. Kerrin responded with a mighty upchuck, all over his blue pinstripe suit. Her dad, Ed, a Clinton campaign worker said, "She just threw up on the next president of the United States."

The game must go on — A 65-year-old man suffered a heart attack and died while playing golf on a course in Winter Haven, Fla. Officials at the golf course covered him with a sheet while attempting to locate a family member. The body remained on the 16th hole for 2 hours while other golfers played on. "We told them they had to skip from the 15 to 17," said Bob Sheffield, director of leisure services. "It was kind of obvious why. If they didn't understand it by the 16th tee, they understood it by time they got to the green."

Excuse moo — Scientists at Washington State Univ. announced that they would receive $210,000 grant from the Environmental Protection Agency to study the environmental effects of cow belches. The scientists noted that most researchers agreed that cows and other cud-chewing livestock produced about 15 percent of all methane gas released into the atmosphere. Some scientists believe that increased amounts of methane and carbon dioxide were causing a rise in global temperature, known as global warming.

Monkey Business — Monkeys made news during the year. Pro Primates, a Dutch animal rights group, claims to have founded the world's first trade union for monkeys. The group says it uses trade union techniques to negotiate better living conditions, such as early retirement for about 1,600 primates in Dutch laboratories and zoos.

NBC showed no respect for primates when they dissed J. Fred Muggs, the lovable chimp who starred as Dave Garroway's sidekick during the early years of the "Today" show. NBC officials didn't invite him to take part in the program's 40th birthday celebration, saying that the chimp was not included because the network had no knowledge of his condition, but that he was appropriately recognized on the show through clips. "They tell me that Muggs was snubbed because he's changed over the years and that he's fat and overweight," said the chimp's owner-trainer Bud Mennella. "Bryant Gumbel doesn't look the same; and neither does Willard Scott."

His way — Chicago teacher Bruce Janu deals with kids who are late to his class or talk out of turn by sentencing them to the Frank Sinatra Detention Club. Students are forced to listen to tapes of *My Way, Love and Marriage,* and other Sinatra classics. There is no talking and no homework. The students "just hate it," Janu says. "I get a grimace, like, 'I can't believe I'm listening to this, something my parents and grandparents listened to.' I get a lot of rolls of the eyes." Janu says the kids can sing along, but no one has. A senior got 2 "Franks" in a day—60 whole minutes of Sinatra. "It just got to where I couldn't stand it", he said. If it gets to the point where the threat of Sinatra wears off, Janu has other weapons in the wings: Tony Bennett or Mel Torme.

Bull — Coach Jackie Sherrill apologized for allowing the castration of a bull in front of his Mississippi State football team. He said, "If this incident was in any way not perceived as proper by those who love Mississippi State, then I apologize." The bull was castrated in front of the team on a practice field before Mississippi State defeated the Texas Longhorns 28-10. Sherrill said he allowed the procedure because it was educational and motivational.

Not so free market — Tens of thousands of would-be investors rampaged through Shenzhen, China after they were denied applications to buy stock on the fledgling Shenzhen stock exchange. Protesters kicked and beat plainclothes police, set a van on fire, and overturned several vehicles, including a police car. They chanted, "Down with corruption." The protesters were frustrated in their attempts to obtain applications to buy stock and charged that police allowed relatives into the best places in line. Some one million people descended on Shenzhen following official media reports of ordinary Chinese making fortunes in stocks.

Delecterble — A black thoroughbred has attracted a great deal of attention at Belmont Park race track because of his name—Hannibal Lecter. His trainer, Bob Klesaris, was not thrilled when he learned his young colt was named after the sociopath who liked to dine on his victims' flesh in *The Silence of the Lambs.* Nevertheless, a clocker from *The Daily Racing Form,* who watched the horse work out noted, "Hannibal Lecter was eating up the ground."

"I Shall Be Released" — Richard Dickinson, an Australian who trampled his mother to death to the strains of Bob Dylan's "One More Cup of Coffee for the Road" was released from prison to see Dylan in a concert performance. Dickinson, who was found not guilty because of insanity, was allowed to see the show because his doctors said he was responding well to treatment for schizophrenia. Dickinson killed his mother 5 years earlier when she complained that he was playing Dylan's *Desire* album at 4 a.m.

QUICK REFERENCE INDEX

For complete Index, see pp. 3-30

Readers' Survey

According to the 1992 Readers' Survey, the "favorite sections" of *The World Almanac* are: History, Population, Nations of the World, Elections, Chronology of the Year's Events, Sports, Noted Personalities, Astronomy, Government, and Maps and Flags.

In addition to receiving responses from all 50 states, replies came from many nations around the world, including: Mexico, Switzerland, Thailand, Japan, Finland, Brazil, Indonesia, Canada, Israel, Malaysia, Yugoslavia, Germany, India, Argentina, Lesotho, South Africa, Nigeria, Australia, and Trinidad and Tobago.

The editors would like to thank all of you who responded for your interest, concern, and many suggestions. We would especially like to thank you for your kind words and encouragement.